THE AUTHORITY SINCE 1868

THE WORLD ALMANAC®

AND BOOK OF FACTS

2006

WORLD ALMANAC BOOKS

THE WORLD ALMANAC®
AND BOOK OF FACTS
2006

Editorial Director: William A. McGeveran Jr.
Director of Desktop Publishing: Elizabeth J. Lazzara; **Managing Editor:** Zoë Kashner
Senior Editor: Erik C. Gopel; **Editor:** Vincent G. Spadafora
Associate Editors: Sarah Janssen, Elizabeth Sheedy
Desktop Publishing Associate: Michael Meyerhofer
Contributing Editors: Richard Hantula, Geoffrey M. Horn, Chris Larson, Cathy Millhauser, Tyler Roylance, Dr. Lee T. Shapiro, George W. Smith, Lori Wiesenfeld, Donald Young
Research: Maria Brock Schulman, Will Farrior, Emily Keyes, Sara Levin, Rachael Mason, Andrew Steinitz
Cover: Bill SMITH STUDIO

WORLD ALMANAC EDUCATION GROUP
General Manager/Publisher: Ken Park
Director–Purchasing and Production: Edward A. Thomas
Desktop Publishing Assistant: Sean Westmoreland
Director of Indexing Services: Marjorie B. Bank; **Index Editor:** Walter Kronenberg
Facts On File World News Digest: Marion Farrier, Editor in Chief; Jonathan Taylor, Managing Editor
World Almanac Reference Database@*FACTS.com*: Louise Bloomfield, Dennis La Beau

WORLD ALMANAC BOOKS
Director–Sales and Marketing: Charles Errig
Marketing Coordinator: Julia Suarez

We acknowledge with thanks the many helpful letters and e-mails from readers of THE WORLD ALMANAC. Because of the volume of mail, it is not possible to reply to each one. However, every communication is read by the editors, and all suggestions receive careful attention. THE WORLD ALMANAC's e-mail address is Walmanac@waegroup.com.

The first edition of THE WORLD ALMANAC, a 120-page volume with 12 pages of advertising, was published by the New York World in 1868. Annual publication was suspended in 1876. Joseph Pulitzer, publisher of the *New York World*, revived THE WORLD ALMANAC in 1886 with the goal of making it a "compendium of universal knowledge." It has been published annually since then. THE WORLD ALMANAC does not decide wagers.

Library of Congress Catalog Card Number 4-3781
International Standard Serial Number (ISSN) 0084-1382
Softcover ISBN-10: 0-88687-964-7; ISBN-13: 978-0-88687-964-8
Hardcover ISBN-10: 0-88687-965-5; ISBN-13: 978-0-88687-965-5
Otabind Library Edition ISBN-10: 0-88687-969-8; ISBN-13: 978-0-88687-969-3
The softcover and hardcover editions are distributed to the book trade by St. Martin's Press.
The Otabind Special Edition is distributed by World Almanac Education, (800) 321-1147.
Printed in the United States of America

WORLD ALMANAC BOOKS
A Division of World Almanac Education Group, Inc.
A WRC Media Company
512 Seventh Avenue
New York, NY 10018

CONTENTS

The World Almanac
and Book of Facts
2006

THE TOP TEN NEWS STORIES OF 2005

1. **The war in Iraq** continued as Sunni-led insurgents launched attacks on U.S. and Iraqi forces and civilians, amid progress toward formation of a democratic Iraqi government. **In elections**, Jan. 30, an estimated **57% of Iraqi voters turned out** despite threats of violence and attacks on polling stations by insurgents. Under the resulting government, dominated by Shiites and Kurds, a **constitution, opposed by many Sunni leaders**, was drafted and submitted to a nationwide vote Oct. 15. The voting proceeded with minimal disruptions. As of mid-October, some 138,000 U.S. troops remained in Iraq. As of Oct. 14, 1,531 U.S. soldiers had been killed in action in Iraq, and 15,000 had been wounded since the March 2003 U.S. invasion; 499 had been killed in action in 2005. According to Iraq Body Count, a group monitoring international press reports, at least 26,521 Iraqi civilians had been killed since the beginning of the war.

2. **Hurricane Katrina** Aug. 29 **devastated the Mississippi, Louisiana, and Alabama Gulf Coast** and caused massive flooding that forced the **evacuation of New Orleans**. More than 1,200 had died, according to estimates in mid-October, and hundreds of thousands were left homeless, with all levels of government blamed for lack of preparedness and bungled relief efforts. Federal Emergency Management Agency Director Michael Brown resigned Sept. 12 in the face of **widespread criticism**. By mid-October, the federal government had appropriated $62.4 bil in disaster-related funds.

3. **Pope John Paul II, 84, died** April 2, more than 26 years after he became the first non-Italian to be elected pope in 456 years. **Cardinal Joseph Ratzinger of Germany was elected** April 19 by the College of Cardinals to succeed him as head of the world's 1.1 bil Roman Catholics. Ratzinger, 78, who took the name Benedict XVI, had been head of the Vatican's Congregation for the Doctrine of the Faith and a close associate of John Paul.

4. **U.S. Chief Justice William H. Rehnquist died** Sept. 3, 9 weeks after Associate Justice Sandra Day O'Connor had announced her retirement from the Supreme Court. **Federal Appellate Court Judge John G. Roberts Jr.**, initially nominated by Pres. George W. Bush to succeed Justice O'Connor, was **confirmed by the Senate** as chief justice by a vote of 78-22, and sworn in, Sept. 29. Pres. George W. Bush Oct. 3 nominated **Harriet E. Miers**, his White House counsel and former personal attorney, to replace O'Connor.

5. In the first Islamic extremist **suicide bombings** in Western Europe, explosions **in the London mass transit system** July 7 killed 56 people (including the bombers, who were later identified as 1 Jamaican-born and 3 British-born Muslims) and injured 700. A similar round of attempted bombings in London July 21 was botched, leading to the arrests of 5 suspects. On Oct. 1, 3 suicide bombers killed 20 others on the Indonesian resort island of **Bali**.

6. Israel Sept. 12 completed its **evacuation of the Gaza Strip** and handed over control to the Palestinian Authority. The pullback from the territory, held by Israel since the 1967 Six-Day War, had been ordered by Israeli Prime Min. Ariel Sharon. **Mahmoud Abbas** had been elected **president of the PA** Jan. 9, succeeding the late Yasir Arafat.

7. After 2 years of unfruitful multination talks with S. Korea, Japan, Russia, the U.S., and host China, **N. Korea** issued a statement Sept. 19 **agreeing in principle to abandon its nuclear weapons programs**, in return for foreign economic and energy aid and future talks on providing a light-water nuclear reactor to generate power. Meanwhile, **Iran**, under newly elected Pres. Mahmoud Ahmadinejad, **continued to pursue its own controversial nuclear program**, which it claimed was peaceful. The IAEA, the UN nuclear watchdog group, Sept. 24 voted to bring Iran before the Security Council for possible sanctions. On Oct. 7 the agency and its head, Mohamed ElBaradei, were named winners of the **2005 Nobel Peace Prize**.

8. The **Kyoto Protocol** for the reduction of greenhouse gases took effect Feb.16 for the 141 nations that had ratified it. The treaty, initially drafted in Kyoto, Japan, in 1997, required industrialized nations to **collectively reduce emissions of heat-trapping gases**, believed to contribute to global warming, to levels 5.2% below their emissions in 1990, with a target date of 2012. The U.S. had not ratified the treaty.

9. **Theresa (Terri) Schiavo** died Mar. 31, 13 days after her **feeding tube was removed** amid a high-profile **legal battle**. Pres. Bush Mar. 21 had signed a law allowing her parents to bring their case in federal court seeking continued feeding. Schiavo had suffered massive brain damage in 1990; her guardian, husband Michael, had sought removal of the tube, maintaining she had told him she would not want to be kept alive in such a state.

10. An **earthquake** measured at magnitude 7.6 struck the northern reaches of **South Asia** Oct. 8. The epicenter was near Muzzafarabad, the capital of Pakistani-controlled territory in the disputed region of Kashmir. By Oct. 15, the death toll had reached 38,000 in Pakistan and Pakistani Kashmir and was expected to go higher. More than 1,000 were also dead on the Indian side of the border. Rescue efforts were hampered by the mountainous terrain and wintry weather conditions.

CONTENTS

The Katrina Disaster

By Geoffrey M. Horn

Geoffrey M. Horn, a freelance author and editor, writes frequently on political and economic affairs.

Catastrophe struck the U.S. Gulf Coast Aug. 29, when Hurricane Katrina carved a path of devastation across low-lying regions of S Louisiana, Mississippi, and Alabama. The storm, which hit S Florida 4 days earlier as a Category 1 hurricane, strengthened to Category 5 while crossing the warm waters of the Gulf of Mexico. By the time Katrina made landfall near Buras, SE Louisiana, it had weakened to Category 4. But the enormous storm still packed high storm surges and sustained winds of over 140 mph. (*See also* Chronology of the Year's Events, Disasters, Environment.)

Katrina was a Category 3 hurricane when its eye passed just E of New Orleans. Experts had long warned of the flood dangers faced by the nation's 35th-largest city, much of which lies below sea level. The storm caused breaches in the city's flood-protection levees, leaving about 80% of New Orleans under water and knocking out electric, water, sewage, transportation, and communications systems. Katrina also flattened much of Gulfport and Biloxi, MS; flooded Mobile, AL; and leveled or inundated smaller cities and towns across a 90,000-sq-mi area.

Up to 100,000 people were stranded in flooded New Orleans for days in squalid and dangerous conditions awaiting relief and evacuation.

Katrina was the deadliest hurricane to hit the U.S. in more than 75 years. By early October, the confirmed death toll exceeded 1,200, with more than 80% of the fatalities in Louisiana, predominantly in the New Orleans area. It was expected to rank among the costliest natural disasters in U.S. history. Nearly 3/4 of all houses in New Orleans were damaged or destroyed; from 25,000 to 50,000 homes were regarded as unsalvageable. In Mississippi, 2/3 of homes in the 6 southernmost counties were severely damaged or destroyed.

By Sept. 8, Pres. Bush had requested and Congress had approved more than $62 bil in emergency spending for hurricane relief. The Congressional Budget Office Oct. 7 estimated total minimum federal spending at $150 billion for cleanup, aid, and other projects. The cost to private insurers was expected to exceed $40 bil.

Katrina dealt a stiff blow to the U.S. petrochemical industry, which is concentrated in the Gulf region; to the New Orleans maritime industry, which handles about 15% of U.S. cargo tonnage; to Gulf Coast travel and tourism; and to Louisiana commercial fisheries and the state's sugarcane, rice, and cotton crops.

Poor coordination between local, state, and federal officials raised important questions about U.S. disaster preparedness. New Orleans Mayor Ray Nagin, Louisiana Gov. Kathleen Blanco, and Pres. George W. Bush all drew criticism for their response to Katrina. Many critics faulted the Federal Emergency Management Agency (FEMA) for its sluggish handling of Katrina rescue and relief efforts and for its reliance on no-bid or limited-bid contracts in the immediate aftermath of the disaster.

Americans reacted generously; by early Oct., donations to relief efforts totaled $1.7 bil, with 65% of the funds going to the American Red Cross. A Katrina relief fund headed by former Pres. George H. W. Bush and Bill Clinton soon raised more than $100 mil. According to the U.S. State Dept., more than 130 countries and a dozen international organizations offered help.

Hurricane Timeline

Tues., Aug 23: First advisory from NOAA for "Tropical Depression 12," at 5 PM; by 11 AM, Aug. 24, hurricane watch and tropical storm warning are issued for Florida.

Thurs., Aug. 25: Katrina reaches hurricane wind speeds, and hits SE Florida.

Sun., Aug. 28: Katrina strengthens in Gulf of Mexico. New Orleans Mayor Ray Nagin issues mandatory evacuation order.

Mon., Aug. 29: Katrina slams into SE Louisiana. Widespread destruction across Gulf Coast region. New Orleans levees fail.

Tues., Aug. 30: 80% of New Orleans under water. Rescuers save hundreds from rooftops. Thousands seek shelter in Superdome and Convention Center; conditions rapidly deteriorate.

Wed., Aug 31: Evacuation of Superdome begins.

Thurs., Sept. 1: Reports of lawlessness in New Orleans lead to suspension of Superdome evacuation.

Fri., Sept. 2: Pres. Bush calls results of federal relief efforts "not acceptable," but in his first visit to the disaster zone praises FEMA Director Michael Brown. Congress passes emergency $10.5 bil spending measure. Led by Army Lt. Gen. Russel Honoré, large numbers of National Guard troops begin arriving in New Orleans.

Sun., Sept. 4: Evacuation of Superdome and Convention Center is complete. When Katrina evacuees in Texas exceed 230,000, TX Gov. Rick Perry orders some airlifted to other states.

Thurs., Sept. 8: Congress approves and Pres. Bush signs additional $51.8 bil in Katrina relief funds.

Fri., Sept. 9: Coast Guard Vice Adm. Thad Allen replaces Brown as FEMA's hurricane relief coordinator.

Mon., Sept. 12: Brown resigns as FEMA director.

Thurs., Sept. 15: In TV speech broadcast from Jackson Square in New Orleans, Bush pledges massive Gulf Coast reconstruction effort.

Mon., Sept. 26: All residents of New Orleans' Algiers neighborhood, pop. 57,000, are allowed to return.

Mon., Oct. 3: Nearly all public schools in neighboring Jefferson Parish reopen, but New Orleans city schools remain closed.

Tues., Oct. 11: U.S. Army Corps of Engineers finishes pumping floodwaters from the New Orleans metropolitan area.

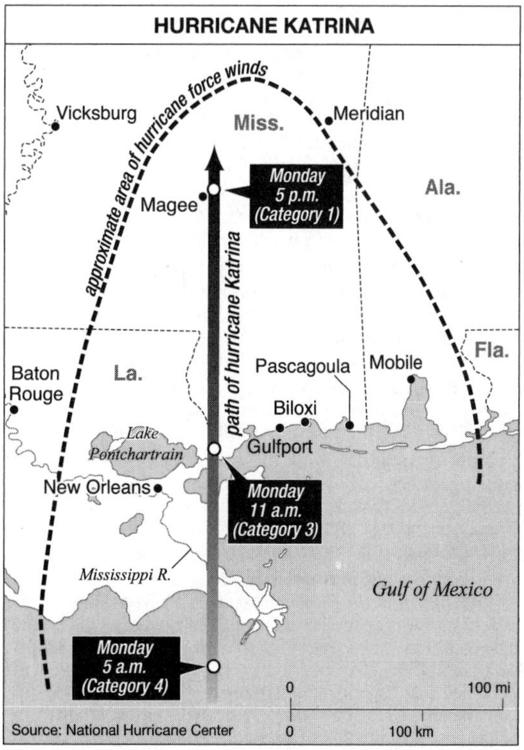

Dale Williams

Hurricane Facts

(All figures are latest available as of Oct. 15, unless otherwise indicated.)

• **Confirmed death toll from Katrina:** 1,277, including 1,035 in Louisiana, 224 in Mississippi, 14 in Florida, 2 in Alabama, and 2 in Georgia.

• **New Orleans city population before Katrina:** 462,000 (2004 est.). As of 2000, the African-American population of New Orleans totaled 325,947.

• **Number of survivors rescued or assisted by the U.S. Coast Guard:** 33,544 from Katrina.

• **People who stayed behind in New Orleans:** about 50,000-100,000. About 2/3 of those who stayed were African Americans. About 30% of African-American households and 15% of white households did not have cars.

• **Where the Katrina evacuees went:** FEMA records analyzed by *USA Today* show that evacuee families settled in all 50 states. About ¾ of evacuee households filed claims for aid from places within 250 mi of New Orleans; another 18% or more migrated to Houston and other communities within 500 mi.

• **Funds distributed by FEMA to hurricane survivors:** more than $3.1 bil to an estimated 1 mil households.

• **People remaining in shelters:** about 68,200, down from a high of 300,000.

• **Red Cross funds committed to hurricane relief:** $1.33 bil, of which $906 mil was emergency financial aid to some 963,000 families. The organization provided 3.2 mil overnight stays for hurricane survivors in 1,150 shelters in 27 states and Washington, DC. More than 483,000 people accounted for over 49 mil overnight stays at hotels and motels throughout the U.S., under a federal program funded by FEMA and operated by the Red Cross. In alliance with the Southern Baptist Convention, the Red Cross served survivors more than 20 mil hot meals.

• **New Orleans city population after Katrina:** estimated at 250,000 during the daytime, 60,000-70,000 at night.

• **Funds raised by the Salvation Army for hurricane relief:** more than $224 mil. The Salvation Army provided food, water, shelter, ice, and other essentials to more than 600,000 people.

• **Reduction in U.S. energy production caused by Katrina and Rita:** cumulative drop in output, Aug. 26-Oct. 13, 56.6 million barrels of oil (10.3% of annual U.S. production from the Gulf of Mexico) and 283 billion cu ft of gas (7.8% of yearly U.S. output from the Gulf of Mexico). The Gulf Coast region normally accounts for 47% of total U.S. oil refinery capacity.

• **Oil spills caused by Katrina:** 40 or more, releasing more than 193,000 barrels of oil and petrochemicals.

• **Losses to the Gulf Coast travel industry:** about $50 mil per day. According to the Travel Industry Association of America, travel spending annually accounts for $13.5 bil and 191,000 jobs in Louisiana, $2.8 bil and 38,000 jobs in Mississippi, and $2 bil and 30,000 jobs in Alabama.

• **Casino gambling:** The storm shut down 13 Gulf Coast and Mississippi River casinos in Biloxi, Gulfport, and Bay St. Louis, costing the state about $500,000 per day in taxes.

• **New Orleans maritime industry:** Ports in the New Orleans region normally service more than 6,000 ships a year. The Port of New Orleans is a leading U.S. entry point for imported steel, natural rubber, and coffee. Up to 80% of port operations remained closed more than a month after the storm.

• **Value of contracts awarded by FEMA with little or no bidding:** at least $1.5 bil. Acting FEMA Director R. David Paulison pledged at a Senate hearing Oct. 6 to review such contracts. These included a $236 mil deal with Carnival Cruise Lines for emergency housing on 3 ships with 7,116 beds. At full capacity the cost for housing and feeding each person would be $1,275 per week—more than twice the price of a ticket for a Carnival Caribbean cruise booked online.

• **Pets rescued from the Katrina disaster zone:** more than 8,000. In addition to cats and dogs, rescuers recovered exotic birds, snakes, goats, pot-bellied pigs, and other pets. As of Oct. 11, more than 10,000 animals from areas impacted by Katrina were listed in the online database maintained by Petfinder.com.

Living on the Edge: A Brief History of New Orleans

New Orleans has long had enormous military and commercial importance. The original town, known today as the French Quarter, or Vieux Carré ("Old Square"), was founded by French settlers in 1718 on a crescent-shaped strip of high ground at a bend in the river. Ruled by France and Spain before it became part of the U.S. through the Louisiana Purchase (1803), the city was both a center of the slave trade and a haven for free people of color. European, African, Caribbean, and Native American influences blended to produce a culture that was both Catholic and Creole. Unique among American cities, New Orleans is the home of the largest Mardi Gras celebration, and the birthplace of jazz. Blues, funk, and rock and roll have also contributed to the city's musical heritage.

Sometimes called the Big Easy, New Orleans has had a difficult history. Hurricanes in 1721 and 1722 knocked down much of what the early settlers built, and most of the city burned to the ground in the Good Friday fire of 1788. The British tried unsuccessfully to capture New Orleans in the War of 1812; 50 years later, Union troops occupied the city during the Civil War. Until the late 1850s, the threat of yellow fever epidemics, which had killed thousands in 1818, 1847, and 1853, dictated the evacuation of up to 1/3 of the population in the summer months.

The Crescent City is surrounded by water, which has been both a blessing and a curse. Waterborne trade, especially in cotton, made New Orleans the 3rd-biggest city in the U.S. at the 1840 Census, with a population of more than 100,000. The city grew to become a major U.S. port, with millions of tons of grains and other commodities passing through on the Mississippi.

To contain the river within bounds, the early French settlers began work a levee—an earthen embankment. Today, under the stewardship of the U.S. Army Corps of Engineers, the city is guarded by a complex system of levees, dikes, seawalls, canals, and pumps. This system was intended to channel the waters of the Mississippi and protect the region against powerful storm surges. But deprived of silt deposits from the natural river flow, the land has been eroding. Experts had warned that the combination of rising seas, sinking land, and natural wetland barriers vanishing at a rate of up to 25 sq mi per year was making New Orleans ever more vulnerable to a potent hurricane. Katrina confirmed their worst fears.

Other Major U.S. Natural Disasters

1889 Johnstown (PA) flood: the poorly maintained South Fork dam fails May 31, inundating the town with 20 mil tons of water; at least 2,200 dead, up to 30,000 homeless.

1900 Galveston (TX) hurricane: a Category 4 storm Sept. 8 lashes the island with 15 ft high waves and winds over 130 mph; at least 8,000 dead.

1906 San Francisco earthquake: about three-fourths of the city is devastated by a quake of at least 7.7 magnitude, Apr. 18, and ensuing fires; more than 3,000 dead, 225,000 homeless, 28,000 buildings destroyed.

1927 Great Mississippi flood: rising waters in April overwhelm levees from Cairo (IL) to Greenville (MS), inundating 165 mil acres and hundreds of towns; at least 246 dead, more than 700,000 homeless.

1992 Hurricane Andrew: the Category 4 storm makes landfall Aug. 24 and leaves a trail of destruction across S Florida 25 mi wide and 60 mi long; in S Florida alone, at least 40 dead, 250,000 homeless, $25 bil in property damage.

Transition at the Supreme Court

By Tyler Roylance

Tyler Roylance is a writer and editor for Facts On File World News Digest *who regularly covers the Supreme Court.*

Within 9 weeks in 2005, Pres. George W. Bush had the opportunity of appointing 2 justices to the Supreme Court. Associate Justice Sandra Day O'Connor announced her retirement on July 1, creating the first high court vacancy in 11 years. Bush on July 19 nominated Judge John G. Roberts Jr., a member of the U.S. Court of Appeals for the District of Columbia Circuit, to fill the seat. Before Roberts could be confirmed, however, Chief Justice William H. Rehnquist died of thyroid cancer on Sept. 3, and 2 days later, the president shifted Roberts's nomination to fill the chief justice's position. Roberts was confirmed by the Senate, 78-22, on Sept. 29. Bush nominated White House counsel Harriet Miers to replace O'Connor on Oct. 3. The court began its 2005-06 term that day. O'Connor had agreed to remain on the bench until her successor was confirmed.

The Rehnquist Court

Rehnquist was first appointed as an associate justice in 1971 by Pres. Nixon, and spent many years in the conservative minority. Pres. Richard Ronald Reagan elevated him to chief justice in 1986, and with the support of Republican appointees Antonin Scalia and Clarence Thomas, and to a lesser extent O'Connor and Anthony M. Kennedy, Rehnquist began to lead the court in a new direction. A dominant theme of his tenure was the balance of power between the states and the federal government. The Rehnquist court's decisions tended to push back federal authority and bolster state sovereignty. However, the court remained closely divided between liberals and conservatives, with O'Connor or Kennedy often contributing the deciding vote in 5-4 decisions. Key decisions under Rehnquist included:

Commerce Clause

Under the Constitution's Commerce Clause, Congress was granted the authority to regulate interstate commerce. It had used that authority to gradually expand its legal and regulatory reach into areas previously left to the states. The court under Rehnquist frequently took a narrower view, checking novel legislative forays by Congress. For example, in a seminal case, *U.S. v. Lopez* (1995), Rehnquist wrote a majority opinion, joined by O'Connor and 3 other justices, striking down the 1990 Gun-Free School Zones Act, which made it a federal crime to possess a firearm within 1,000 feet of a school. In defense of the law, the government had argued that gun-related violence harmed education, which in turn led to a less productive workforce and damaged the national economy.

Rehnquist's view of the Commerce Clause did not always prevail, however. In *Gonzales v. Raich* (2004), a 6-justice majority found that Congress had the authority to outlaw the local production and medicinal use of marijuana, even when state law permitted it and the drug was never sold across state lines. Rehnquist and O'Connor both dissented.

Death Penalty

In the 1987 decision *McCleskey v. Kemp*, Rehnquist and O'Connor joined a 5-justice majority that upheld Georgia's capital punishment system against charges of racism. A study of the system had shown that black defendants who killed white victims were far more likely to receive death sentences than whites who killed blacks. But the majority found that such general statistics were not sufficient to prove racism in a particular case. When the defendant, Warren McCleskey, filed another federal appeal, Rehnquist and O'Connor joined the 6-justice majority in the resulting 1991 case, *McCleskey v. Zant*, rejecting the prisoner's petition for a writ of *habeas corpus* and significantly raising the legal hurdles for such repeated federal appeals.

Although the Rehnquist court often voted to defend and streamline the capital punishment system, it also restricted the death penalty in some areas. Executions for the mentally retarded were upheld in the 1989 case *Penry v. Lynaugh*, with Rehnquist and O'Connor in the 5-justice majority, but the court, 6-3, reversed that decision in *Atkins v. Virginia* (2002), with the chief dissenting. On capital punishment for juveniles, a majority of 5 voted in *Thompson v. Oklahoma* (1988) to ban executions for those who committed crimes at age 16 or younger; O'Connor joined the majority and Rehnquist dissented. Both jurists found themselves in a 4-justice minority when the court in the 2005 case *Roper v. Simmons* (reversing a previous decision) banned executions for those who committed a capital crime while under 18.

Separation of Church and State

Rehnquist wrote, and O'Connor joined, the 5-4 majority opinion in a 2002 decision, *Zelman v. Simmons-Harris*, that upheld a local Ohio voucher program allowing parents to use public funds to send their children to religious schools. The chief justice revisited the issue in the 2004 case *Locke v. Davey*, finding with O'Connor and 5 other justices that Washington State's ban on scholarships for students training to become clergy did not violate the First Amendment's Free Exercise Clause. He reasoned that while the Constitution allowed government to support religion as in *Zelman*, it did not require such support, allowing room for variation among the states.

In the 1992 case *Lee v. Weisman*, O'Connor and 4 other justices forced Rehnquist into the minority, finding that nonsectarian prayers conducted at public high school graduation ceremonies violated the Establishment Clause.

Due Process

Rehnquist took a narrow view of the 14th Amendment's guarantee that states not deprive citizens of the due process of law, often opposing its invocation to assert various individual rights. In a 1989 case, *DeShaney v. Winnebago County*, he authored a 6-3 decision, joined by O'Connor and 4 others, finding that the government did not have a constitutional obligation to protect private individuals from one another. The case involved a woman who sued local child-welfare officials after they failed to protect her child from her abusive ex-husband.

In a pair of 1997 cases, *Washington v. Glucksberg* and *Vacco v. Quill*, Rehnquist wrote unanimous decisions rejecting attempts to use the due process clause to overturn state bans on physician-assisted suicide by terminally ill patients.

Affirmative Action

In 2003, the court found in *Grutter v. Bollinger* that race could be used as one of many factors in considering university admissions. However, in the related case *Gratz v. Bollinger*, the court rejected numerical systems that automatically favored members of underrepresented racial or ethnic minorities. O'Connor joined Rehnquist and 4 other justices in that case's majority, but she opposed the chief by handing a 5th vote to the majority in *Grutter*.

Privacy Rights and State Sovereignty

Rehnquist dissented from O'Connor's 5-justice majority when the court reaffirmed women's right to abort pregnancies in the 1992 case *Planned Parenthood of Southeastern Pennsylvania v. Casey*. It essentially upheld *Roe v. Wade*, the 1973 ruling that had protected abortion rights under what it found to be a constitutional right to privacy.

In the 1986 case *Bowers v. Hardwick*, Rehnquist and O'Connor joined 3 others to uphold Georgia's anti-sodomy law, declining to protect homosexual activity on constitutional privacy grounds. The chief dissented when that decision was overturned in 2003's *Lawrence v. Texas*, which struck down a Texas anti-sodomy statute. O'Connor added a 6th vote to part of the majority's decision, voting to overturn the Texas law, but not *Bowers*.

2000 Presidential Election

Rehnquist and O'Connor joined a conservative majority in 2000's *Bush v. Gore*, which settled that year's presidential election by blocking, 5-4, a recount of votes in the hotly contested state of Florida and effectively confirming victory for George W. Bush. The court found that differing recount procedures in various jurisdictions violated the Equal Protection Clause.

Chief Justice John G. Roberts Jr.

Full name: John Glover Roberts Jr.

Born: Jan. 27, 1955, Buffalo, N.Y.

Education: Harvard College, B.A., 1973; Harvard Law School, law degree, 1979

Religious Affiliation: Roman Catholic

Marriage: Jane Marie Sullivan 1996; 2 children: Josephine, John

Career: Law clerk for Judge Henry Friendly of U.S. 2nd Circuit Court of Appeals in New York City, 1979-80; clerk for Associate Justice William H. Rehnquist, 1980-81; special assistant to Attorney General William French Smith, 1981-82; associate counsel to Pres. Ronald Reagan, 1982-86; attorney for Washington, DC, law firm Hogan & Hartson LLP, 1986-89, 1993-2003; U.S. deputy solicitor general, 1989-93; judge, U.S. Court of Appeals for the DC Circuit, 2003-05; chief justice, U.S. Supreme Court, Oct. 3, 2005-present.

Issues and Record: Having served only 2 years on the bench, Roberts had not taken many judicial positions that would reveal his views on the major issues. A notable exception was his July 15 vote to uphold the constitutionality of special military tribunals being used to try terrorism suspects held at the U.S. military base in Guantánamo Bay, Cuba. Since only limited records of Roberts's work as deputy solicitor general were made available, members of the Senate Judiciary Committee, during Roberts's Sept. 12-15 confirmation hearings, focused on his writings as a lawyer for the Reagan administration.

In those documents and in certain 1989-93 writings that had been made public, Roberts often advocated conservative positions on issues including abortion, civil rights, and women's rights. However, he insisted that such positions represented his employers' views, not his own. He made a similar argument with respect to his work as a private lawyer. In one publicized incident in 1996, he had given free legal advice to a gay rights group that was preparing to argue a case before the Supreme Court, *Romer v. Evans*.

Roberts also gave advice to Florida Gov. Jeb Bush and to George W. Bush's election campaign during the 2000 Florida ballot dispute that left the latter man with the presidency. Despite Democratic senators' efforts to elicit a statement of personal opinion during the confirmation hearings, Roberts followed many of his predecessors in declining to answer questions on issues that might come before the Supreme Court. However, he showed an impressive command of the law in his detailed answers to some questions. Roberts supporters would also point to the assessment of the American Bar Association, which on Aug. 17 had given him its highest ranking, "well-qualified," with respect to his "integrity, professional competence and judicial temperament." Also of note was the fact that as a lawyer he had argued 39 cases before the Supreme Court, winning 25 of them.

Upcoming Cases

The Supreme Court's 2005-06 term began Oct. 3. Among the cases already on the docket:

Abortion

Ayotte v. Planned Parenthood hinged on the constitutionality of a New Hampshire law that required abortion providers to give 48 hours' notice to the parents of girls younger than 18 who were seeking an abortion, unless a judge waived the rule. The law was unusual in that it provided an exception only if the girl's life was at risk. Similar laws in other states allowed a broader exception, for the girl's health.

Scheidler v. National Organization for Women concerned a long-running attempt by abortion-rights groups to obtain triple damages under the Racketeer Influenced and Corrupt Organizations Act (RICO) for aggressive protest actions by anti-abortion groups.

Religion

The court accepted a case on whether the federal government could ban a hallucinogenic tea used in the rituals of a religious sect based in Brazil. The case, *Gonzales v. O Centro Espirita Beneficiente Uniao Do Vegetal*, represented a conflict between antidrug laws and the 1993 Religious Freedom Restoration Act, which protected religious practices from federal interference in most instances.

Capital Punishment

The court agreed to decide whether a capital defendant had a constitutional right to present evidence of his innocence during the sentencing phase of his trial, at which point a jury had already found him guilty beyond a reasonable doubt. The case was *Oregon v. Guzek*.

Kansas's death penalty statute, which required jurors to choose a death sentence over life imprisonment if they found aggravating and mitigating factors in a convicted defendant's case to be equally balanced, would be judged in *Kansas v. Marsh*.

In *House v. Bell*, a Tennessee inmate sought a fresh appeal of his death sentence based on new DNA evidence. At issue in the case was whether such evidence met the high standard for appeals that come after the normal appeals process is exhausted.

Assisted Suicide

Gonzales v. Oregon concerns federal authorities seeking to penalize doctors who prescribed lethal drugs to terminally ill patients under Oregon's Death With Dignity Act. The state law allowed physician-assisted suicide.

Rights for the Disabled

The court agreed to decide whether the burden of proof in lawsuits stemming from the Individuals with Disabilities Education Act should rest with defendants or plaintiffs. The case, *Schaffer v. Weast*, involved a student with learning disabilities whose parents disapproved of their public school's special accommodations and sought reimbursement for private school tuition instead.

Campaign Finance

The court accepted a case, *Wisconsin Right to Life Inc. v. Federal Election Commission*, in which "grassroots" political advocacy groups sought an exemption from the 2002 Bipartisan Campaign Reform Act. The law, also known as McCain-Feingold, barred corporations from paying for advertisements that named a political candidate in the final weeks before an election.

The court also agreed to rule on the constitutionality of a Vermont law that strictly limited candidates' campaign spending as well as the size of campaign contributions. Critics argued that the law violated First Amendment free speech rights. The case was *Randall v. Sorrell*.

Nominee: White House Counsel Harriet Miers

Full Name: Harriet Ellan Miers

Born: Aug. 10, 1945, Dallas, Texas

Education: Southern Methodist University (SMU), B.S., 1967; SMU, law degree, 1970

Religious Affiliation: Evangelical Christian

Marriage: Never married, no children

Career: Law clerk for Judge Joe Estes of U.S. District Court in Dallas, TX, 1970-72; first woman lawyer at Dallas law firm Locke Purnell Boren Laney & Neely, 1972; first woman president of Dallas Bar Association, 1985; member at large, Dallas City Council, 1989-91; first woman president of State Bar of Texas, 1992; general counsel, George W. Bush's Texas gubernatorial campaign, 1994; chaired Texas Lottery Commission, 1995-2000; co-managing partner at Locke Liddell & Sapp, 1999; White House staff secretary, 2001-03; White House deputy chief of staff for policy, 2003-05; White House counsel, 2005

Issues and Record: Miers had no experience as a judge when she was nominated and her lack of writings on key constitutional issues raised opposition among some conservatives that she would not be the persuasive conservative voice they had expected. She had worked mainly on corporate cases as a private attorney. Her writings as a White House lawyer were likely protected by executive privilege and attorney-client privilege, meaning senators would not have access to them during the confirmation process. Before her association with Bush, Miers had been a conservative Democrat. Her legal position on abortion rights remained unclear, but while head of the Texas bar, she sought to have the American Bar Association repudiate its position in support of abortion rights to a neutral stance. She is an evangelical Christian and member of the conservative Valley View Christian Church in Dallas.

PlayNation: Inside the Multibillion Dollar Fascination with Video Games

By David Kushner

David Kushner is the author of Masters of Doom, *a book about two computer-game creators. His latest book is* Jonny Magic and the Card Shark Kids: How a Gang of Geeks Beat the Odds and Stormed Las Vegas.

When I was turning 13 in 1981, a friend of my parents asked me, "if you could have anything for a present, what would it be?" I have no idea what he was expecting me to suggest—a baseball glove? encyclopedia? chemistry set?—but when I told him "video game tokens," his eyebrows raised.

"Video games, eh?" he replied cautiously, as if I had requested a barrel of nuclear waste, "Well, as long as your parents don't mind."

He returned a couple of weeks later with a crumpled brown paper bag of gold tokens. Each coin was embossed with a tiny sorcerer: the logo of my neighborhood arcade, Wizards. There were $20 worth of them, which came out to around 100 games. Score! I thanked him heartily, called my friends, and sped to the arcade on my green Schwinn. Maybe my parents' generation couldn't understand it, but for me and millions of other children of the 1970s and 80s, the video game revolution had begun. And it would get bigger, more controversial, and influential than anyone imagined.

Video games, and the accompanying culture and industry, have come a long way. In the 70s, there was Pong, a tennis-like game featuring white stick "paddles" and a bouncing blip ball. Today, games let players do everything from raising virtual humans (*The Sims*) and stealing cars (*Grand Theft Auto*) to playing professional football (*Madden NFL*) and adventuring through fantasy lands with thousands of players online (*EverQuest*).

In total, Americans spend more money on video games than on movie tickets. According to the Entertainment Software Association, game sales doubled from 1996 to 2004, hitting $7.3 bil. In total, nearly 250 mil games were sold. In 2004, sales of video games, consoles, and accessories topped $9.9 bil, compared to $9.4 bil reported as total movie ticket sales. In total, nearly 250 mil games were sold. In 3 out of 4 American homes, video or computer games are being played inside.

Compared to the time my contemporaries of "Generation Pong" were kids, we have many more ways to play games today. In addition to the trio of home consoles from Microsoft, Sony, and Nintendo, there are games for handhelds such as the Sony PSP and Nintendo DS, games for cell phones and personal digital assistants, computer games, Internet games, and, yes, arcade games still (though the virtual hang-gliders and jet-skis hardly resemble the *Pac-Man* and *Space Invaders* of yesterday).

Contrary to popular opinion, the players twitching at their controllers are not just teenage boys. In fact, 62% of gamers are over the age 18. That shouldn't be as surprising as it sounds. Older players, after all, have the discretionary income to spend $50 on the latest *Madden* football game. And with the boom in so-called "casual" games, such as bridge, backgammon, and billiards, on the Internet, baby-boomers and their parents clock millions of hours competing and chatting online. One of the most popular computer games comes bundled on nearly every machine: solitaire. Pres. George W. Bush, a fan of a solitaire computer game called *FreeCell*, is among the 19% of gamers over 50.

But even the president's passion for games hasn't rescued the medium from its sometimes bad reputation. Violent video games have become linked with controversy, despite the fact that relatively few of this type are released each year. The Entertainment Software Ratings Board (ESRB), the industry's voluntary ratings system, assigns ratings such as T for Teen and E for Everyone based on a game's violent or sexual content. So-called Mature titles, suitable for gamers over 17, account for only 16% of sales. For some, even the edgiest games are merely entertaining, and not to be confused with reality. But to many critics of the industry, the gory games go too far over the edge, and have a corrupting influence. They can inspire real-life acts of aggression—possibly, in the extreme, even murder.

This isn't the first time games have been blamed for spoiling the minds of youth. America has long had a love/hate relationship with the high-tech games young people play, from the banning of pinball machines, thought to breed delinquency, in New York in the 1930s to Sen. Joseph Lieberman's (D, CT) congressional hearings on *Mortal Kombat*'s spine-ripping gore in 1994. Much of the critics' concern centers on protecting children and adolescents from bad influences, though it is true that the audience—and buyers—of games is largely adult.

These days, the most notorious video game is *Grand Theft Auto*, a freeform action title that sets players loose in the middle of urban American gang warfare. Though the gamers advance farther by driving an ambulance than by shooting passersby, *Grand Theft Auto*'s cocktail of sex and violence has made it both a lightning rod and cottage industry. Controversy, as usual, sells; *Grand Theft Auto: San Andreas* was the best-selling Playstation 2 title of 2004.

In 2005, the creators of the *Grand Theft Auto* series, Rockstar Games, came under fire when a secret sex scene was unlocked by gamers playing *Grand Theft Auto: San Andreas*, the latest installment in the franchise. Spurred by Sen. Lieberman and Sen. Hillary Clinton (D, NY), *Grand Theft Auto* relabled existing copies of *San Andreas* with an Adults Only (AO) ESRB rating. Other critics are lobbying for laws which would ban the sale of M-rated games to children under 17. Many in the video game industry oppose such legislation.

An interesting point is that the U.S. military has for a long time used video games to help motivate real-life troops. In the 1980s, the military used a version of the tank warfare arcade game *Battlezone* for training. In the 1990s, the U.S. Marines modified the popular first-person shooter *Doom* for use in team-building exercises.

Today, *America's Army*, a free online game distributed by the military, is being used to recruit soldiers. In Los Angeles, CA, the Institute for Creative Technologies, a research and development facility funded by the U.S. Army, is employing Hollywood and video game talent, from the screenwriter of *Apocalypse Now* to the producers of *Star Trek: The Next Generation*, to create state-of-the-art training simulation games. These range from immersive virtual reality simulations of battle to real-time strategy games. One game, a team-based action title, *Full Spectrum Warrior*, was so compelling it ended up being sold in stores.

The military isn't the only organization tapping into the training and possibly therapeutic power of gaming. NASA has used the Playstation 2 game *Tony Hawk Pro Skater* to build concentration skills in pilots. In Finland, the Cognitive Brain Research Unit at the University of Helsinki developed a game to help victims overcome dyslexia. A pediatrician in Redlands, CA, now uses the dance-by-numbers Playstation 2 game *Dance Dance Revolution* to help kids lose weight. As games become more mainstream, universities from the University of North Texas to the Georgia Institute of Technology have even begun to offer courses studying them.

Not surprisingly, the exploding interest in video games has taken Hollywood by storm too. Titles from *Tomb Raider* to *Resident Evil* to *Doom* have made their way to the silver screen. TV shows like *Entourage* and *Law and Order* feature them in plot lines. There's an entire TV channel, G4TV, devoted to video games. And even the creators of video games are becoming icons too. My book *Masters of Doom*, which tells the story of *Doom*'s co-creators John Carmack and John Romero, is being developed into a biopic for Showtime.

For me and my peers, the mainstreaming of video games comes as no surprise. This stuff has always played an important role in our lives, and, as far as we're concerned, the rest of the world is finally catching up with it. The older we get, the less controversial, I believe, this medium will become. There was a time, after all, when Elvis Presley was shown on TV only from the waist up, because his dancing was considered too provocative. Today, Elvis is everywhere and no one cares how he shimmies. Video games are the new rock and roll. And they're here to stay.

Waking to China

By Ted C. Fishman

Ted C. Fishman is author of the best-seller China, Inc.: How the Rise of the Next Superpower Challenges America and the World *(2005). His articles have appeared in* The New York Times Magazine, The Times of London, *and other publications.*

Napoleon famously remarked that when China wakes the world will tremble. China, of course, was never really asleep. There are countries in this world that might be fairly described as sleepy. China is hardly one of them.

Over the last century China has had as much tumult as any country. It has been wracked by civil wars and colonial occupations. The Chinese Communist Revolution following World War II unleashed ideological policies that with enormous force repeatedly reordered public and private life, often to calamitous effect. During the economic program called the Great Leap Forward in 1959 and 1960, a period when China might have looked dormant to the outside world, 50 million people heeded government policies meant to move them off the farm into an industrial future. That disruption helped bring about the greatest man-made famine in the history of the world. Estimates of the deaths vary, but scholars often put the count above 30 million.

China's Industrial Revolution

Today no one would mistake China for a sleeping nation. China looks radically different from how it did when strict Communist ideologues ruled, and this is partly the result of the country's energy. Over the last two decades its economy has been one of the miracles of the world. The numbers are a bit foggy, but international agencies report the Chinese economy growing, on average, close to 9% a year over the 20-year period. That has been fast enough to send average incomes in China up four-fold and to create a middle class which may already include one quarter of a billion people.

Today, China's people are on the move more than ever, with 300 million farmers and residents of rural villages expected to move to big cities within a generation. This time famine will not be the result. China's farms remain productive and the new city dwellers are sending money home to their old villages. Since market reforms began and the people have been allowed to work outside of state-controlled industries, the Chinese have started 125 mil new businesses. The current count of going concerns is around 85 mil. By comparison, the United States, whose citizens have been living in a market economy for more than 3 centuries, has 26 mil businesses, or roughly the same number per capita as China.

China Opens Up

China's amazing progress has not been a matter of waking up, but of shifting gears toward a market economy and, above all, connecting to a world trading system.

China's new wealth owes some debt to the failure of its past social policies. The global manufacturers that increasingly make China their home, and the global buyers that import hundreds of billions of dollars worth of Chinese goods each year, find advantage in the vast poverty that sends low-wage workers into new factories to produce the world's lowest-cost goods. Ironically, China's success over the last 20 years owes a bitter debt to the harsh rule of the Maoists, who created the preconditions for the low-cost, well disciplined labor force that today serves China's and the world's capitalists.

Because of how China marshals its energies today, it is the country that presents the rest of the world with both the greatest opportunities and the greatest perils. No country has so swiftly and forcefully challenged the rest of the world on so many fronts since the rise of the United States during the Industrial Revolution of the 19th century.

China's Challenge

The U.S. relationship with China is a complicated one, and Americans need to consider from all angles any actions that affect the relations between the two countries. China, as the world has come to learn, can take manufacturing jobs away from nearly any country and any industry. In 2005, it also showed the growing financial might it can exercise in world markets. The country was acquiring nearly $2 bil in U.S. government bonds every single day. China's state-owned computer manufacturing giant, Lenovo, closed on a deal in May to acquire the personal computer division of IBM, thus making Lenovo the world's third-largest maker of PCs. And in June 2005, one of China's large, mostly government-owned oil companies, CNOOC, made a spectacular, though ultimately unsuccessful, $18.5 bil bid for the American oil giant UNOCAL.

These moves may not have made the whole world tremble. China had already become a welcome and aggressive buyer of industrial goods and natural resources in most of the world. Indeed, take the United States out of China's trade picture and the country runs a large trade deficit with the rest of the world, as it purchases the necessities to build up its urban, industrial infrastructure. But the UNOCAL bid did send tremors through American government, and the U.S. Congress threw up legislative roadblocks that ultimately killed the deal.

The current count of Chinese businesses is around 85 mil. By comparison, the United States, whose citizens have been living in a market economy for more than 3 centuries, has 26 mil businesses, or roughly the same number per capita as China.

The Yuan Factor

In July 2005, China made world headlines when the government adjusted how it calibrates the value of the yuan. China has come under attack for fixing the exchange rate of its currency too low against the dollar. The new move was a partial gesture toward what world finance officials had been long advocating.

The change was small, adjusting the Chinese currency up less than 3%. But it was big news in the U.S. and Europe, where China's currency regime has inflated the value of the dollar and the euro, making it tougher for manufacturers in those regions to compete against Chinese companies. The currency move demonstrated that the country, once characterized by ham-fisted diplomacy and command-and-control economic policies, is fully capable of diplomatic and financial finesse. With one fell swoop, China looked as though it was willing to show its international critics—such as the U.S. Treasury—that it can bend somewhat to the needs of its trading partners, while at the same time carefully serving its own needs as well.

By raising the value of its currency, China also gave itself more buying power in the world's resource markets. In the energy sector, the low value of China's currency had put the country at a marked disadvantage in world energy markets. That hardly served the goals of a nation strapped for energy for electricity and for fueling its cars and trucks. Power shortages have been chronic in China and often force plants or cities to go dim to enable the power infrastructure to catch up. China's car population is going straight up. By 2025, it is estimated, China will be using around 14 million barrels of oil a day—more than twice its consumption at present. Lifting China's currency from artificially low levels gives China's energy users more buying power and helps keep inflation down.

The currency reevaluation was also big news for the countries of Africa, Latin America, and Asia that supply China with raw materials and benefited when their Chinese clients gained that extra buying power. But their prosperity comes at a cost. As China builds its manufacturing base, it also takes low-end manufacturing away from developing countries and de-industrializes countries that themselves have been struggling for decades to diversify their economies. Indonesia, for example, has found that its once thriving shoemaking business has all but disappeared into China.

Champion of Rogue Regimes

The growing global influence of China, both politically and economically, raises difficult questions for other nations. The United States, for one, is unlikely to find a national strategy on how to counter China's growing political clout, which vexingly often comes at the expense of U.S. influence.

China has been willing to forge strong relationships with regimes that the U.S. and other Western powers have long been trying to isolate. Brutal regimes in Myanmar (formerly Burma), the Sudan, and Zimbabwe all benefited from support from Beijing and Chinese business interests. But in the long run, these ties may prove positive for the world. As the champion of rogue regimes, China could play a role that other countries cannot. For example, it hosted the 6-nation talks that in September resulted in a pledge by North Korea to give up its nuclear weapons program.

Human Rights

Over the near term, however, China's willingness to cozy up to the world's less savory regimes may serve to underscore the Chinese Communist Party's record of going its own way on human rights. China has long been less willing to accept international norms for human rights—an area where other big powers can claim to hold a higher ground. Democracy, self-expression, religious freedom, and the rule of law are all, at best, still distant goals in China. Instead, the government has moved aggressively to stifle protests and, while it seeks to emphasizes the economic progress and social stability of its people as a whole.

In 2005, according to Human Rights Watch, China took strong action against religious minorities, restricting the practices, publications, and habits of dress of the Muslim Uighur minority in the western province of Xinjiang. Tibetan Buddhists continued to fall under strict regulations that curtail public religious observance and prohibit many traditional ceremonies. Beijing announced in July that it would appoint the next Dalai Lama. Human Rights Watch also reports that some Protestant groups and Falungong, a spiritual group, have had their members jailed without fair trials, forced into reeducation camps, or committed to mental asylums. In early 2005, the U.S. State Department released its 2004 report on human rights in China. The report noted that the "government maintained tight restrictions on freedom of speech and of the press, and a wave of detentions late in the year signaled a new campaign targeting prominent writers and political commentators."

Uncertainties

With its continued strength, China spreads uncertainty, on both political and economic grounds. There are widespread doubts over whether China's growth is sustainable and whether the business environment is reliable.

Some concerns center around the mood of the Chinese people who, of course, have had more than their share of uncertainty and would be the first to suffer if the country's economy or social order collapsed. Despite migration and money sent home, hundreds of millions of people in China have been largely left out of its economic miracle, or worse yet, feel punished by it. According to UN statistics, the poorest 20% of China's 1.3 bil people account for only 4.7% of total income, while the richest 20% account for more than half.

Protests continue to grow in frequency and size in China. In July of 2005, Zhou Yongkang, China's public security minister, reported through Reuters that 74,000 "mass incidents" (demonstrations and riots) occurred in 2004, up from 58,000 in 2003 and 10,000 in 1995. But the incidents have mainly been localized; the Chinese Communist Party still has more than enough coercive power and ameliorative incentives to keep dissenters from linking across local borders and growing into a movement.

The Party does have its record of incredible economic growth. Yet again, after promising and enacting measures that were meant to pull the pace of China's economic growth back from dreamland, China's economy in the first half 2005 was up more than 9.4% from the first half of 2004. But economic and social reversals often result from factors the world little understands, and it is folly to predict with any certainty that China won't suffer a serious reversal sometime soon. The country's economy has over a billion "variables" with increasingly free wills, and nearly all of them have found their lives significantly disrupted by change.

Relationships With Other Countries

Aside from the unknowns within China itself, some of the uncertainty about China's future stems from uncertainty about how other countries, especially the United States, may act. For example, on the economic front, the U.S. Congress in 2005 vigorously debated tariffs and restrictions on Chinese goods, blocking Chinese companies from entering the U.S. mergers and acquisition games, and talked about answering a future military threat from China.

Japan, too, faces growing uncertainty in its relationship with China. In 2005, Chinese erupted in violence toward Japanese interests in their country and also held heated diplomatic exchanges over Japan's unwillingness to apologize for atrocities committed in China in the last century. Both China and Japan approach the issue with strong nationalistic impulses, and their mutual enmity seems destined to grow.

One possible bright spot is China's improving relationship with Taiwan, although this relationship is not without major problems. In 2005, the two countries continued their delicate dance, which so far has kept the island largely independent. On the negative side, China passed a law in March that authorized the use of force against Taiwan, should the region officially declare itself independent from the mainland. But there were signs that China and Taiwan may both be willing to consider a structured arrangement that would bring the two closer together. In a move laden with strong symbolism, China announced in May that it would allow mainland tourists to visit Taiwan.

Waking Up to the Challenge

In nearly every way that China challenges the U.S. and the world, strategies on how to stay competitive with the Chinese and how to prosper as that country grows will succeed far better if they do not depend on the Chinese deliberately taking action in the world's interest. Rather, China's competitors must find their own solutions. The world, and perhaps the United States in particular, do best to avoid vilifying the country. Behind everything economic that the world fears about China, there is something to admire. The country's strong economic run has lifted hundreds of millions of people out of the deepest depths of poverty. It has begun to create the world's largest middle class. And it is now home to some of the best manufacturing anywhere.

Some take objection to that view, pointing out that China is still a Communist country run by an elite that cares more for power than its own people. This need not be denied. However, a focus on the negative pays too little heed to China's amazing progress and does not provide the best strategies for dealing with it. The rest of the world will profit little by demonizing the Chinese. We would do better to study, and admire, perhaps grudgingly, the country's growing strengths—and, of course, its dynamic people. In other words, in many ways it is not China that needs waking, but the rest of us.

Recommended Reading

Peter Hays Gries, *China's New Nationalism: Pride, Politics, and Diplomacy*, University of California Press, 2004
Kellee S. Tsai, *Back-Alley Banking: Private Entrepreneurs in China*, Cornell University Press, 2002
Rachel DeWoskin, *Foreign Babes in Beijing: Behind the Scenes of the New China*, W.W. Norton and Co., 2005

Traveling by the Book

By Nancy Pearl

Nancy Pearl is the author of the best-selling Book Lust: Recommended Reading for Every Mood, Moment, and Reason *and* More Book Lust: 1,000 New Reading Recommendations for Every Mood, Moment, and Reason. *Her website: www.nancypearl.com*

I love to travel. There's nothing more exciting to me than picking a country, a city, a continent—anywhere in the world—and then embarking on a trip.

But I hate to leave home. I lack the patience to wait in long lines at airports, and don't want to swap my comfortable chair for the benches in a railroad waiting room, or be jostled by the crowd as we all wait to see that famous fresco, statue, palace, or church. I'm too old for the variations in temperature, unfamiliar food, missed connections, or risk of getting a toothache in a land far, far away from my much loved dentist.

My resolution to this dilemma? I've become an inveterate armchair traveler. I've discovered over the years that my favorite way to travel is by reading (and either fiction or nonfiction will do). From Alberta, Canada, to Zanzibar, with stops at every letter in between, I've been there and done that—all without ever leaving home.

Here are some of my favorite books set in places far and wide. Reading these, you can be transported to a new world, filled with interesting people, exotic tastes and smells, and new landscapes. Or maybe, unlike me, you would prefer to go there in person, and bring the book along for flavor.

Australia: All of Tim Winton's novels give you a good sense of his native country, but *Dirt Music*, a combination road novel and love story in which every character is haunted by the past, brings Western Australia to life. Ordinary life in Australia following World War II is described with humor and compassion in *Cloudstreet*, the story of the Pickles and the Lambs, two families who (frequently to their dismay) find their lives fatefully intertwined.

Brazil: The often gritty and noirish Inspector Espinosa mysteries, by Luiz Alfredo Garcia-Roza, take place in a Rio de Janeiro far from the glitz and glamour of Carnival and give readers a good sense of the city off the beaten tourist track. Try *A Window in Copacabana* or *Southwesterly Wind*.

China: If you're interested in the Cultural Revolution period, two of the best books to read are *Stones of the Wall* by Dai Houying and the somewhat lighter-in-tone *Balzac and the Little Chinese Seamstress* by Dai Sijie. There's also a wonderful series of mysteries set in contemporary China, by Qui Xiaolong, featuring Inspector Cao Chen, a poetry-loving intellectual on the Shanghai police force. His adventures begin in *Death of a Red Heroine*. If you're looking for a novel that will give you insight into the sweep of Chinese history, you'll want to read Cao Xuequin's 18th-century classic, *A Dream of Red Mansions*.

Egypt: Nobody portrays Egyptian society during the years of upheaval following World War I better than the Nobel Prize-winning Naguib Mahfouz. His Cairo trilogy, including *Palace Walk*, *Palace of Desire*, and *Sugar Street*, looks at the lives of the family of al-Sayyid Ahmad, a tyrannical middle-class merchant, whose adherence to the laws of the Koran applies only to his wife and children.

Haiti: To understand contemporary Haiti, it's really necessary to get a feel for its history, and you'll not find any better reading than Madison Smartt Bell's trilogy, starting with *All Souls' Rising*. Together these novels provide a fictionalized biography of Haitian freedom fighter Toussant L'Ouverture, who led the slave revolt from 1791 to 1804 that ultimately led to the making of modern Haiti. Several of Edwidge Danticat's stories and novels show the effects of living under a dictatorship, including *Krik? Krak!* and *The Dew Breaker*, in which the main character, now living in Brooklyn, looks back at his life as a prison guard in Haiti in the 1960s, and asks himself and others for forgiveness.

Ireland: Nearly everyone is familiar with Frank McCourt's memoir *Angela's Ashes*, which tells his story of growing up poor in Limerick. Among many wonderful novels set in Ireland, *A Star Called Henry* by Roddy Doyle chronicles the making and unmaking of an IRA assassin in the first two decades of the 20th century. Nuala O'Faolain's *My Dream of You* explores the place of passion and memory in the life of Kathleen de Burca, who returns home to Ireland after 30 years to try to make her peace with the past.

Italy: Donna Leon, an American who has lived in Italy for many years, has written a number of mysteries featuring Commissario Guido Brunetti, a member of the Venice police department, whose despair about the bureaucracy he labors under is balanced by his love of the city where he lives and, most especially, his country's food. Two particularly good choices are *Uniform Justice* and *Blood From a Stone*. Other great novels set in Italy include Ann Cornelisen's laugh-aloud-funny *Any Four Women Could Rob the Bank of Italy* and *The Sixteen Pleasures* by Robert Hellenga, set in Florence just after the flooding of the Arno River in 1966.

Kenya: Esmé, the main character in *Rules of the Wild* by Francesca Marciano, is one of a group of expatriates who now make Kenya their home, whether it is the ultra-chic world of Nairobi wealth or a remote jungle outpost.

Newfoundland, Canada: Probably the best known novel set here is E. Annie Proulx's *The Shipping News*. However, if you are intrigued by Canada's smallest province, you'll also want to check out Howard Norman's *The Bird Artist*, with its terrific opening paragraph. Or try *The Colony of Unrequited Dreams*, Wayne Johnston's tale of 20th-century Newfoundland, told through the lives of a boy determined to escape from poverty and make a name for himself, and the newspaperwoman who tracks his rise to power.

Tibet, China: Eliot Pattison, author of many articles on international affairs, sets his suspense thrillers in Tibet (and there aren't a lot of contemporary novels set in that mysterious locale). *The Skull Mantra* introduces his hero Shan, who has been sent from his job as Inspector General in the Ministry of Economy in Beijing to a forced labor camp in Tibet. As we follow Shan's attempts to survive and solve a complex mystery, we are introduced to a singular, and singularly beautiful, region, its people, and its customs.

Travelers' Tales

Besides fiction, another good way to get to know any country is by reading accounts of travelers who've been there. One of my favorite works of armchair travel is Tahir Shah's *In Search of King Solomon's Mines*, a delightful and fact-filled description of Shah's attempt to find the exact location of the biblical king's mines, a search that eventually took him all across Ethiopia.

Another favorite is Colin Thubron's *In Siberia*, an account of his journey from Mongolia to the Arctic Circle, via car, boat, train, bus, and on foot. He meets skinny-dipping grandmothers, sees the place where the tsar and his family were brutally murdered, and drops in on museums, private homes, and former prison camps of the Soviet Gulag.

Paul Theroux is a great lover of train travel. I reread his *The Great Railway Bazaar: By Train Through Asia* regularly, mostly because I love his evocative descriptions of the various trains he took on his journey, including the Orient Express (the setting for one of Agatha Christie's best-known mysteries, *Murder on the Orient Express*), the Khyber Mail, and the Trans-Siberian Express.

Another one of my favorite writers is inveterate traveler Jan Morris. A good introduction to her work is *The World: Travels 1950-2000*, a compendium of her journeys to destinations as diverse Addis Ababa, San Francisco, and Mount Everest. Other titles in which Morris's impressionistic travel writing shines include *Trieste and the Meaning of Nowhere*, *The World of Venice*, and *Sydney*.

One of the tests of a truly great work of travel literature (fiction or nonfiction) is whether it gets the reader to put down the book and make plans to go to the destinations described. That happened to me when I read these books; I had to take several deep breaths, make a cup of tea, and sit back down in my chair until the feeling passed, and I realized once again that, for me, at least, the best travel is done via literature!

Country Music

By Cathy Millhauser

Cathy Millhauser's crosswords appear in numerous publications, including the New York Times *and* Wall Street Journal, *and in an original collection,* Humorous Crosswords.

(For answers, see page 1007)

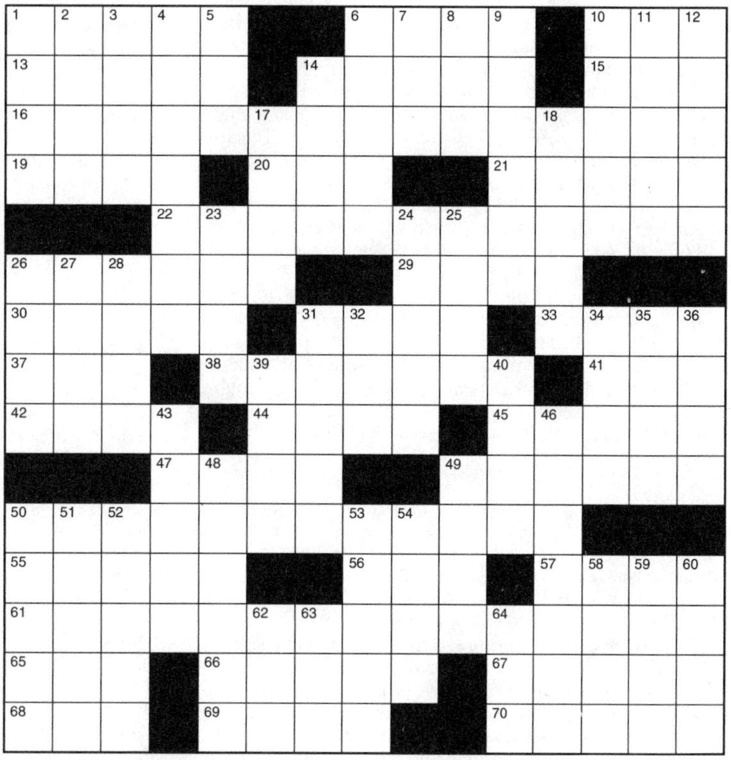

Across

1 *The Power of Positive Thinking* author
6 Unilever's "brisk" beverages
10 Dept. once headed by Butz
13 The "A" in CAT scan
14 South Africa's mountain __, endangered species
15 "Nothin' But a 'G' Thang" singer, Dr. _
16 Like a Manama vocalist? (Gene Kelly)
19 Football hall-of-famer Graham
20 Fair abbr. in job ads
21 "Save Me" singer Mann
22 Muscat Country: Mountain Formation (Trad. cowboy song)?
26 Like some Schoenberg music
29 "And colleagues," on invention lists
30 Taiwanese island
31 Shepard, the 1st American in space
33 _______-official (Like Romansch, in Switzerland)
37 Renamed 1960 light heavyweight gold medalist
38 My capital is Baghdad, therefore __? (Simon & Garfunkel)
41 Actress Tyler or Ullmann
42 Org. with far-out missions?
44 Sullivan took the title in a bare-knuckles one
45 NY birthplace of V.P. James Sherman
47 One-named Indian actor who died at age 39
49 Tuskegee historic site honorees
50 SOS to Kigali and country? (Beach Boys)
55 Three-time Pulitzer dramatist Edward
56 A treatment for depression (abbr.)
57 Like Notable New Book titles (abbr.)
61 Niamey nation's youth smitten? (Dion & The Belmonts)
65 Chicago's 45-story __ Plaza
66 University in Des Moines
67 1978 Peace Nobelist with Sadat
68 Chinese dynasty, 202 BC-AD 220
69 Virus that broke out in Hong Kong, 2003
70 1980 Grammy winner Christopher

Down

1 Sun Bowl site, El __
2 Word in a noted Sartre title
3 Broadway's long-running "__ Misbehavin'"
4 Features of St. Croix's topography
5 First name among pharmaceutical companies
6 Clinton CIA director George
7 "Cabaret" and "Chicago" lyricist
8 The Altar constellation
9 World's largest desert
10 Rhett's last words in an Am. film ranked 4th-best of all time
11 "Peer Gynt Suite" composer
12 Zellweger, Oscar-winning sup. actress for "Cold Mountain"
14 National park in Utah
17 Best actress for 1963's "Hud"
18 They're tender in Iran?
23 Hawaiian island, site of Haleakala National Park
24 Carson McCullers' "Lonely Hunter"
25 Active volcano of Italy
26 Percy Sledge's woman-lover of song
27 Samoan monetary unit
28 Elevator brake inventor
31 Westerns writer Louis L'__
32 Actress Lucy
34 __ Fellowship (Pentecostal sect)
35 Their average longevity is 3 years
36 First formally proclaimed tsar of Russia
39 Priest, á la manual alphabet developer Charles Michel de L'Epee
40 __ pro quo (something for something, literally)
43 Site of a Colorado sporting attraction
46 Preview for a top-grossing movie
48 Alters, as the Constitution
49 Prefix with coagulant or depressant
50 Utah senator Orrin
51 Cosmonaut Kondakova
52 Famous "Down Easter" L. __
53 Oklahoma's state fair is the last 2 in September
54 One equals 160 square rods
58 Its capital is Lomé
59 Company that lends getaway cars
60 Franklin invented a bifocal one
62 Roth, e.g.
63 Freshwater catch
64 "Cheers" network

Across: 1 p. 226, **6** p. 219, **10** p. 51 **13** p. 727, **14** p. 305, **15** p. p. 243, **16** p. 756, **19** p. 931, **20** p. 727, **21** p. 243, **22** p. 820, **26** p. 680, **29** p. 315, **30** p. 838, **31** p. 319, **33** p. 837, **37** p. 956, **38** p. 789, **41** p. 257, **42** p. 319, **44** p. 958, **45** p. 594, **47** p. 262, **49** p. 552, **50** p. 827, **55** p. 285, **56** p. 171, **57** p. 272, **61** p. 818, **65** p. 734, **66** p. 652, **67** p. 284, **68** p. 668, **69** p. 767, **70** p. 298.

Down: 1 p. 934, **2** p. 226, **3** p. 269, **4** p. 454, **5** p. 101, **6** p. 75, **7** p. 239, **8** p. 334, **9** p. 713, **10** p. 268, **11** p. 237, **12** p. 297, **14** p. 550, **17** p. 296, **18** p. 789, **23** p. 550, **24** p. 235, **25** p. 703, **26** p. 244, **27** p. 828, **28** p. 316, **31** p. 234, **32** p. 252, **34** p. 715, **35** p. 305, **36** p. 826, **39** p. 730, **40** p. 726, **43** p. 429, **46** p. 266, **48** p. 581; **49** p. 190, **50** p. 211, **51** p. 321, **52** p. 435, **53** p. 444, **54** p. 370, **58** p. 840, **59** p. 748, **60** p. 316, **62** p. 103, **63** p. 972, **64** p. 280.

CHRONOLOGY OF EVENTS

REPORTED MONTH BY MONTH, OCT. 16, 2004, TO OCT. 15, 2005

OCTOBER 16-31, 2004

National

Presidential Candidates Battle as Campaign Nears Its End—The major-party presidential candidates campaigned aggressively during the last weeks of the 2004 campaign, concentrating on a dozen so-called battleground states, where polls showed the contest was very close. Pres. George W. Bush said **Oct. 24** that he disagreed with the Republican Party platform's opposition to same-sex civil unions, though he was opposed to defining such unions as marriage. The apparent disappearance from an installation in Iraq of 380 tons of explosives, reported Oct. 25 in the *New York Times*, triggered heated debate, with Kerry charging the Bush administration with failure to secure sensitive sites. Former Pres. Bill Clinton, who was recovering from heart surgery, joined Sen. John Kerry for a rally in Philadelphia **Oct. 27**.

Air Crash Blamed on Pilot Error and Design Flaw—After conducting an investigation, the National Transportation Safety Board, Oct. 26, cited pilot error and poor rudder design as chief factors in the Nov. 2001 crash of an American Airlines Airbus A300, bound for the Dominican Republic, just after takeoff from Kennedy Internat. Airport in Queens, NY; 265 people were killed in the crash.

International

U.S. Sergeant Pleads Guilty to Prison Abuse—At a court-martial in Baghdad, Staff Sgt. Ivan L. Frederick II pleaded guilty **Oct. 20** to mistreating Iraqi captives in Abu-Ghraib prison. Frederick, who agreed to cooperate with investigators, was the 3rd soldier convicted in the scandal. On **Oct. 21** he was sentenced to 8 years in prison.

Iraqi Insurgents Continue Attacks and Atrocities—Forty-nine unarmed Iraqi National Guard trainees were taken from buses on a remote road near Iran, **Oct. 23**, and executed; 3 drivers were also killed. Their captors were disguised as police. On **Oct. 24,** a U.S. State Dept. security officer was killed in a rocket attack near the Baghdad airport. Insurgents executed 11 captured Iraqi soldiers **Oct. 28**.

Insurgents bombed 5 Christian churches in Baghdad **Oct. 16**. Peace talks between the Iraqi government and insurgents in Fallujah broke down **Oct. 18**. On **Oct. 27**, nearly 800 British troops left their base in southern Iraq for redeployment further north in order to free U.S. troops for planned assaults against insurgent strongholds.

Insurgents fired a rocket into a Tikrit hotel, **Oct. 31**, killing 15 Iraqis. The day before, 9 U.S. Marines were killed in insurgent attacks. On **Oct. 29** the Pentagon announced it was ordering about 6,500 U.S. soldiers in Iraq to extend their tours of duty by up to 2 months.

Bin Laden Appears in New Tape—In a tape believed to be authentic, obtained by Al-Jazeera and broadcast **Oct. 28,** al-Qaeda leader Osama bin Laden warned that al-Qaeda would wage new attacks against the U.S. so long as U.S. policies did not change. No specific threats were made.

Arafat's Failing Health Adds to Middle East Uncertainty—On **Oct. 29**, with Israeli permission, Yasir Arafat, the ailing chairman of the Palestinian Authority, left confienment at his headquarters in Ramallah, for medical treatment in Paris; no diagnosis of his illness was released.

On **Oct. 16**, Israel had completed a redeployment of troops and armored vehicles from the Gaza Strip, but other troops continued to guard refugee camps. On **Oct. 26**, the Israeli Parliament approved, 67-45, Prime Min. Ariel Sharon's controversial plan to remove all Israeli settlements in Gaza.

Heads of State Sign EU Constitution—25 European leaders signed EU's first constitution, **Oct. 29** in Rome. The constitution, which incorporates a number of earlier treaties and is subject to ratification by member states, would remove national vetoes from certain policy areas, provide for weighted votes favoring larger countries, and create a single presidency with a 2 ½-year term, in place of the existing 6-month rotating presidency.

General

Red Sox Win World Series—In an amazing comeback, the Boston Red Sox **Oct. 27** won the World Series. Their 4 straight victories over the St. Louis Cardinals, the last in St. Louis by 3-0, were almost an anti-climax. The Sox had won the league pennant after falling behind the New York Yankees, 3 games to 0. One highlight of the comeback was a 3-2 14-inning marathon Game 5, won by the Sox in Boston **Oct. 18**. On **Oct. 20**, the Sox romped in the Game 7 finale, 10-3, in New York. Johnny Damon drove in 6 runs with 2 home runs, one a grand slam. Derek Lowe was the winning pitcher in the final game against the Yankees and the final Series game. Boston pitcher Curt Schilling also excelled in the post-season, despite an injured ankle. The Sox had not won the World Series since 1918.

NOVEMBER 2004

National

Ailing Chief Justice Interrupts Duties—Chief Justice William Rehnquist announced **Nov. 1** that continuing treatment for thyroid cancer prevented his returning to the court that day as planned. Rehnquist's illness led to speculation that he might be resigning in the near future.

Pres. Bush Reelected—Pres. George W. Bush won reelection **Nov. 2**, capturing 31 states with 286 electoral votes, just 16 more than the 270 needed. His Democratic opponent, Sen. John Kerry, conceded defeat at midday Nov. 3, after concluding he could not win enough uncounted provisional ballots in Ohio to get that state's crucial 20 electoral votes. In the popular vote, Bush received about 60.6 mil votes (51%), compared to 57.2 mil (48%) for Kerry, with independent Ralph Nader and other candidates splitting the rest.

Bush thus preserved the tradition that no president who sought reelection in wartime lost. He became the first incumbent president since Calvin Coolidge to win reelection with majorities for his party in both houses of Congress.

Only one state, New Hampshire, that had gone to Bush in 2000 went to Kerry in 2004. Two states—Iowa and New Mexico—that had voted for Vice Pres. Al Gore (D) in 2000 switched to Bush. Kerry ran strong in the Northeast, Middle Atlantic, and West Coast states, while the Southern, Plains, and Rocky Mountain states were solid for Bush.

In exit polls, 86% of voters who listed terrorism as the issue that mattered most to them supported Bush, while 74% of those citing Iraq voted for Kerry. Of voters who cited moral values as the most important issue, 79% favored Bush. Voters who cited the economy as the issue that mattered most went strongly (80%) for Kerry. Blacks voted 89% for Kerry. But compared to 2000, Bush still did better among blacks, as well as among Hispanics, Catholics, Jews, and the elderly, according to exit polling, which was subsequently exposed as faulty.

In the Senate, Republicans gained 4 seats for a 55-44 majority. Tom Daschle (SD), the Senate minority leader, narrowly lost his bid for a 4th term to former U.S. Rep. John Thune. Five Democrats from southern states did not seek reelection, and all 5 seats fell to Republicans. Tom Coburn, an outspoken conservative, kept the open seat in Oklahoma for Republicans. Jim Bunning (R, KY) narrowly won despite erratic remarks, which included comparing his dark-complexioned opponent to one of Saddam Hussein's sons. Veteran Republicans reelected included Arlen Specter (PA), John McCain (AZ), and Chuck Grassley (IA).

The Democrats picked up 2 open Senate seats. In Illinois, State Sen. Barack Obama, keynote speaker at the Democratic National Convention, swamped another African American, conservative commentator Alan Keyes. In Colorado, State Atty. Gen. Ken Salazar, riding a wave of support from Hispanics, defeated Pete Coors, whose family owned the brewing company. Democrats reelected included Barbara Boxer (CA), Charles Schumer (NY), Evan Bayh (IN), Christopher Dodd (CT), and Harry Reid (NV), the assistant Senate Democratic leader.

Republicans won the House of Representatives for the 6th straight time. Not since the 1920s and early 1930s had the GOP controlled the House for so long. Gerrymandering, in which both parties were complicit, had ensured that most seats were safe for one party or the other. Republicans began the day with a 227-205 majority (with 1 independent and 2 vacancies) and emerged with at least 231 seats.

In Texas, House Majority Leader Tom DeLay had devised a redistricting plan that threw 5 Democratic incumbents into redrawn districts with majority Republican registration; 4 of them lost. In Louisiana Bobby Jindal (R) became the second person of East Indian descent elected to Congress.

Only 11 states elected governors. Four incumbent governors won reelection, but in Indiana Mitch Daniels (R), former White House budget director, turned out the incumbent, Joseph Kernan, who had succeeded to office upon the death in 2003 of Gov. Frank O'Bannon. An extremely tight contest in Washington, where Gov. Gary Locke (D) did not seek reelection, remained in doubt, pending recounts.

In all, 11 states proposed ballot measures for constitutional amendments banning gay marriage; all 11 passed. Californians approved a ballot initiative to support spending $3 bil in seed money for stem-cell research. Republicans came out of **Nov. 2** with control of 20 state legislatures, while Democrats held 19; 10 were divided and one (Nebraska) is nonpartisan.

Powell, Ashcroft, Ridge, Others Resign From Bush Cabinet—A flurry of resignations by cabinet members followed Pres. Bush's reelection. On **Nov. 8**, Atty. Gen. John Ashcroft and Commerce Sec. Donald Evans announced they would step down. On **Nov. 10**, Pres. Bush nominated White House counsel Alberto Gonzales, a former Texas supreme court judge and longtime supporter, to succeed Ashcroft.

Sec. of State Colin Powell announced **Nov. 15** that he would step down once a successor was confirmed. Bush announced the next day that he would nominate his national security adviser, Condoleezza Rice, to succeed him. Three other cabinet members announced resignations **Nov. 15**: Ann Veneman (Agriculture), Rod Paige (Education), and Spencer Abraham (Energy). Bush **Nov. 17** nominated Margaret Spellings, his chief adviser on domestic issues, to succeed Paige. On **Nov. 29** he nominated Kellogg CEO Carlos Gutierrez to succeed Evans. On **Nov. 30**, Homeland Security Sec. Tom Ridge announced he would resign.

New Director Shakes Up the CIA—Newly appointed CIA Director Porter Goss was reportedly stirring up the agency, and generating some antagonisms, as he brought in new personnel. Deputy Director John McLaughlin said **Nov. 12** that he would be leaving; 2 more top CIA officials resigned **Nov. 15**.

International

Boy Joins Ranks of Suicide Bombers—A 16-year-old boy killed himself and 3 Israelis in a bombing in Tel Aviv **Nov. 1**. An Israeli newspaper report said the same day that 165 Palestinians died in the intifada in October, the most for any month since April 2002.

Yasir Arafat Dies—Longtime Palestinian leader Yasir Arafat died **Nov. 10** in a Paris hospital where he was being treated for an undisclosed illness. He had been president of the Palestinian Authority, Palestine Liberation Organization head, and head of the PLO's largest movement, Fatah. His body was flown to Cairo **Nov. 11** to lie in state; foreign dignitaries attended a service there the next day. Later that day he was buried at his headquarters compound, at Ramallah in the West Bank, as some 20,000 Palestinians gave an emotional farewell. On **Nov. 11**, Palestinian leaders chose Mahmoud Abbas as PLO head. He had served briefly as the Palestinian Authority's prime minister in 2003, resigning because Arafat resisted giving him authority.

Karzai Elected First President of Afghanistan—On **Nov. 3**, a UN–Afghanistan electoral commission declared that interim president Hamid Karzai had won the October presidential election in Afghanistan, with 55% of the vote, enough to avoid a runoff. His nearest challenger got only 16%. Despite unsettled conditions, threats from insurgents, and a long history of internal strife, the election had proceeded without major disruption.

UN Warned About Lawlessness in Sudan—Jan Pronk, the UN envoy to Sudan, told the UN Security Council **Nov. 4** that the country might soon descend into lawlessness and rule by warlords. On **Nov. 16**, Amnesty International accused Russia, China, and other countries of selling weapons to Sudan that were being used against civilians. Despite a partial agreement between the Sudanese government and rebels, the latter, operating out of the Darfur region, attacked the town of Tawila in western Sudan **Nov. 22**. Some 15 to 20 police officers and 6 civilians were killed.

Côte d'Ivoire Government Kills 9 French Peacekeepers—An obscure civil war in the Côte d'Ivoire came to wide attention **Nov. 6** when an attack by 2 government planes near Bouake killed 9 French peacekeeping troops and an American civilian. The French shot down both jets.

A shaky year-long ceasefire in the West African country—the world's largest producer of cocoa—had ended **Nov. 4** when government planes bombed 2 rebel-held towns. France had about 4,500 troops in Côte d'Ivoire, and on **Nov. 7**, as government supporters attacked French homes and civilians, the French sent hundreds more to the country. A **Nov. 9** clash between French soldiers and protesters and Ivoirian security forces left 10 dead and 300 injured. French charter planes began evacuating foreigners **Nov. 10**.

U.S., Iraqi Troops Overrun Fallujah; Insurgents Strike Back Elsewhere—U.S. soldiers and Marines, supported by Iraqi troops, launched a ground offensive in Fallujah, Nov. 7, and secured most of the terrorist stronghold in house-to-house fighting. The offensive, involving some 10,000- 15,000 U.S. and Iraqi troops, was part of an effort to secure more of the country before January elections.

Before ground offensive, U.S. forces bombed the city for several days. The military said **Nov. 5** that 75%-80% of Fallujah's 250,000-300,000 residents had by then evacuated. As advancing forces sought to clear houses of terrorists, insurgents sometimes resisted and at other times faded away. By **Nov. 9** U.S. and Iraqi forces controlled one-third of the city. On **Nov. 13**, 2 days after a strong counterattack by insurgents, Army troops and tanks stormed their last major stronghold, overrunning it by the next day. U.S. commanders said **Nov. 14** that 38 Americans had been killed and 275 wounded in the Falluja assault; insurgent deaths were put at 1,200-1,600. Americans **Nov. 18** said they had found a house used as a headquarters for Jordanian terrorist Abu Musab al-Zarqawi; troops also uncovered sites where insurgents had tortured and executed captives.

Insurgents struck back elsewhere, with bombings, kidnappings, and executions. A suicide bomber killed 3 British soldiers **Nov. 4**. In Samarra, where coalition forces had routed insurgents in October, 4 car bombs exploded **Nov. 6** and 3 police stations were attacked.

Two Americans died in a mortar attack in Mosul, where rebels were deeply ensconced, **Nov. 9**. A car bomb killed 17 in Baghdad **Nov. 11**. On **Nov. 13**, Americans occupied the largest mosque in Ramadi; there and in other mosques large weapons caches were found. Iraqi troops raided a mosque in Baghdad **Nov. 19** and killed 3 Iraqis. A leading Sunni cleric was shot to death in Mosul **Nov. 22**.

On **Nov. 23**, U.S., British, and Iraqi troops invaded the so-called Triangle of Death south of Baghdad. The lawless area had attracted many insurgents. Kurd and Sunni Muslim political parties **Nov. 26** called for a postponement of the January elections, citing security concerns.

The November death toll for U.S. troops in Iraq came to 135, the most for any month since April 2004.

Iran Pledges to Suspend Uranian Enrichment—In a **Nov. 14** letter to 3 European governments, Iran promised to suspend its uranium enrichment program. Iran had been under pressure from the International Atomic Energy Agency to abandon the program, which Iran alleged was aimed at development of nuclear energy but which critics charged was part of a clandestine effort to develop nuclear weapons. Britain, France, and Germany announced a formal agreement with Iran **Nov. 15**, with economic benefits that would come to Iran still being negotiated.

Iraqi Debt Cancelled—In a boost for the Iraqi government, leading creditor nations **Nov. 21** voted to cancel 80% of Iraq's $39 bil debt.

Ukrainians Stage Massive Protests—Tens of thousands took to the streets in Ukraine's capital, and blockaded government offices over several days to protest alleged fraud in Ukraine's presidential runoff election, held **Nov. 21**. Protesters claimed government tabulations were being manipulated to show that incumbent Prime Min. Viktor Yanukovich was the winner, rather than opposition candidate Viktor Yushchenko. International observers agreed. In the first round of voting, **Oct. 31**, Yanukovich, with 40%, had run narrowly ahead of Yushchenko, while falling short of the needed majority. Yanukovich favored close ties with Russia; Yushchenko favored an independent foreign policy and closer relations with the European Union. Both candidates said they would pull the 1,600 Ukrainian troops out of Iraq.

The government of Ukraine **Nov. 24** declared Yanukovich the winner, but the Ukraine Supreme Court the next day temporarily blocked Yanukovich's victory until it could study allegations of abuse. Ukraine's parliament **Nov. 27** voted to declare the election result invalid, though it could not actually overturn the outcome.

Red Cross Charges Guantanamo Prisoner Abuse—According to a *New York Times* story, **Nov. 29**, the Internat. Committee of the Red Cross, in a confidential report to the U.S. government in July, charged that the U.S. military was using psychological and sometimes physical intimidation "tantamount to torture" on prisoners being held in Guantanamo Bay. A Pentagon spokesman disputed the charges.

Bush Visits Canada—Pres. Bush met with Canadian Prime Min. Paul Martin in Ottawa, **Nov. 30**, on his first official visit to Canada. The two leaders pledged to work cooperatively, despite strong policy differences over such issues as Iraq and trade.

General

Peterson Guilty in Murder of Wife, Unborn Son—Scott Peterson, a Modesto (CA) fertilizer salesman, was found guilty by a jury in Redwood City **Nov. 12** in the murder of his wife, Laci, and their unborn son, after a stormy trial that attracted nationwide coverage. He had reported his wife missing Dec. 24, 2002; her body washed ashore in April 2003, near where he said he had been on a fishing trip in San Francisco Bay. Shortly after her body was found, Peterson was arrested while allegedly seeking to flee to Mexico. He had been having an affair with Amber Frey, a massage therapist, who later allowed police to record their phone conversations and testified at the trial. The jury **Dec. 13** recommended the death penalty.

9 Players Suspended After "Basketbrawl"—A fight broke out between Indiana Pacers and Detroit Pistons at a game in Auburn Hills, MI, **Nov. 19**, after Detroit's Ben Wallace was fouled by Indiana's Ron Artest. Wallace shoved Artest, and both benches cleared. When a fan hit Artest with a cup of beer, fighting escalated. A subsequent melee involved Artest, Indiana's Jermain O'Neal, and a fan. The game was stopped and Indiana declared the winner, 97-82. In all, 9 fans were hurt. On **Nov. 21**, Artest was suspended without pay for the rest of the season. O'Neal and teammate Stephen Jackson were suspended for 25 and 30 games, respectively; 6 other players drew lesser suspensions.

Star *Jeopardy!* Contestant Ends Record Winning Streak—In a show taped in early September and broadcast **Nov. 30**, Ken Jennings, a software engineer from Salt Lake City, UT, was defeated by a rival contestant, California real estate agent Nancy Zerg, on the syndicated quiz show *Jeopardy!* and had to retire from the competition. He had won a record $2,520,700 in 75 games, the first of which was broadcast on June 2.

DECEMBER 2004

National

U.S. Raises Troop Levels—The Pentagon announced **Dec. 1** that the U.S. troop level in Iraq would rise from 138,000 to 150,000 in January, with tours of duty extended for many. Defense Sec. Donald Rumsfeld encountered some complaints in Kuwait **Dec. 8** from U.S. Army reservists bound for Iraq. Pres. George W. Bush conceded **Dec. 20** that training of Iraqi troops was having mixed results but defended Rumsfeld's performance as defense secretary.

Bush Names More to 2nd-Term Cabinet—Pres. Bush continued to make changes in his cabinet prior to the start of his 2nd term. On **Dec. 2** he nominated Gov. Michael Johanns (R, NE) to succeed Ann Veneman as secretary of agriculture. Bush said **Dec. 9** he would nominate Jim Nicholson, U.S. ambassador to the Vatican, to succeed Anthony Principi as secretary of veterans affairs. On **Dec. 10** he picked Samuel Bodman, deputy treasury secretary and a former chemical industry executive, to succeed Spencer Abraham as secretary of energy.

The White House said **Dec. 2** that John Danforth had submitted his resignation as U.S. ambassador to the UN. Health and Human Services Sec. Tommy Thompson announced his resignation **Dec. 3**; on **Dec. 13** Bush named EPA head and former Utah Gov. Michael Leavitt to succeed him.

Republicans Hold 30-Vote Margin in House—The **Dec. 4** runoff elections for 2 U.S. House seats in Louisiana resulted in the 2 major parties winning one seat each. The new House will have 232 Republicans and 202 Democrats, with 1 independent.

Congress Approves Intelligence Reform Bill—A bill to restructure the U.S. intelligence community got through Congress **Dec. 7** after 2 influential House committee chairmen came close to stopping it. The bill, signed into law by Pres. Bush on **Dec. 17**, incorporated key recommendations of the bipartisan commission that investigated the Sept. 11, 2001, terrorist attacks. It created the position of director of national intelligence (DNI), to oversee 15 intelligence agencies, with substantial budgetary control over them. A National Counterterrorism Center would plan intelligence and counterterrorism operations, and a Privacy and Civil Liberties Board would monitor conduct of federal agencies. The bill also created a minimum national standard for drivers' licenses. Rep. Duncan Hunter (R, CA), chair of the House Armed Services Committee, had opposed the restructuring, contending it could inhibit the flow of intelligence from the Pentagon to combat troops. Rep. James Sensenbrenner (R, WI), House Judiciary Committee chair, had sought tougher restrictions on immigration. After a wording change and assurances that immigration issues would be considered in 2005, the two agreed to support the bill. On **Dec. 7** the House, 336-75, and the Senate, 89-2, approved it.

Bush Choice for Homeland Security Secretary Withdraws—Bernard Kerik, nominated **Dec. 3** for homeland security secretary, withdrew his name 6 days later. Kerik said a nanny he had once employed was not clearly a legal immigrant and "required tax payments and related filings" had not been made. Kerik, the New York City police commissioner under Mayor Rudolph Giuliani, had played a major role in the city's response to the 2001 terror attacks. Later on, he spent 4 months training the new Iraqi police force. After he withdrew his name, media reports raised other potential issues, including huge profits he had made from companies doing business with the Dept. of Homeland Security.

Ex-Governor of Connecticut Pleads Guilty—John Rowland, who resigned as governor of Connecticut in July 2004 amid a growing scandal, pleaded guilty **Dec. 23** to a single charge of corruption in office. He acknowledged accepting $107,000 in gratuities and failing to pay taxes on them. The charge carries a prison sentence of up to 5 years.

Democrat Certified Winner in Washington—Christine Gregoire (D) was certified **Dec. 30** as the winner of the gubernatorial election in Washington state. Seven weeks after the election, the secretary of state declared that she had defeated her Republican opponent, Dino Rossi, by 129 votes, out of 2.9 mil cast. Rossi had previously been certified the winner by 261 votes, and the first recount showed him ahead by 42 votes. Another recount, completed **Dec. 22**, put Gregoire, the state attorney general, ahead by 10 votes. A count of some overlooked votes raised her lead on **Dec. 23**.

Stocks Post Gains During 2004—The stock market indices showed gains for 2004 after the closing bell rang **Dec. 31**. The Dow Jones industrial average rose 3.1% while the broader Standard & Poor's 500-stock index jumped 9.0% and the Nasdaq composite climbed 8.9%.

U.S. Economy at a Glance: Calendar Year 2004	
Unemployment rate	5.5%
Consumer prices (change over 2003)	+3.3%
Trade deficit	$617.6 bil
Dow Jones closing (year end)	10,783.01
Dow Jones highest close (Dec. 28)	10,854.54
Dow Jones lowest close (Oct. 25)	9,749.99
GDP (change over 2003)	+4.2%

International

Gunmen Kill 5 at U.S. Consulate in Saudi Arabia—Five gunmen attacked the U.S. consulate in Jidda, Saudi Arabia, **Dec. 6**, and engaged in a 3-hour shootout with Saudi security forces. Five U.S. employees (none of them American) were killed. Four of the attackers were killed and a 5th was wounded and captured. A group linked to al-Qaeda claimed responsibility.

Violence in Iraq Grows as Election Approaches—Iraqi officials prepared for January's nationwide parliamentary election, as insurgents seeking to prevent or disrupt the voting stepped up their terrorist campaign. Voters were to choose the 275 members of the National Assembly from among slates of candidates. The influential Shiite cleric Ayatollah Ali Sistani supported the United Iraqi Alliance, comprising mostly Shiite parties, which announced its slate **Dec. 9**. The Iraqi electoral commission **Dec. 15** announced that more than 230 political groups and 3,500 candidates had entered the race. Interim Iraqi Def. Min. Hazim al-Shalaan charged that the Shiite slate of candidates drawn up by allies of Sistani was an "Iranian list" designed to bring Iraq under that country's control.

In Baghdad **Dec. 3**, a bomb at a Shiite mosque killed 18 and a raid by gunmen killed 12 police officers. A bomb **Dec. 4** killed 18 Kurdish militiamen in Mosul. Gunmen killed 17 Iraqi contractors on a bus in Tikrit **Dec. 5**. On Dec. 13-14, car bombs at a Baghded checkpoint killed 20. On **Dec. 19**, car bombs in Najaf and Karbala killed about 70 and wounded at least 175, and 3 election officials were dragged from their car in Baghdad and shot to death.

An explosion **Dec. 21** in a mess tent during lunch at an American base in Mosul killed 22, including 14 U.S. troops and 4 American contractors; about 70 were wounded. Ansar al-Sunna, a Sunni group, claimed responsibility. The incident was blamed on a suicide bomber.

On **Dec. 28**, 23 Iraqi police and national guardsmen were killed in a series of attacks. In Baghdad **Dec. 28**, insurgents lured Iraqi police into a booby-trapped house, then set off a bomb that killed 7 police officers and 25 civilians.

On **Dec. 27**, Iraq's largest Sunni party, the Iraqi Islamic Party, announced it would not participate the upcoming Jan. 30 elections claiming that widespread violence made a fair election impossible. Voter registration in Sunni areas of Iraq had been low or nonexistent according to Iraq's top election official, Hussain Hindawi. Mohsen Abdul Hamid, head of the party, said that the election should be postponed until the security situation is resolved. From the beginning of hostilities in March 2003 through Dec. 31, 2004, 1,341 U.S. troops had died in Iraq, 1,041 of them through hostile causes.

Ukrainian Opposition Leader Wins Runoff—After a 2nd presidential runoff election in Ukraine on **Dec. 26**, Viktor Yushchenko came away as the apparent winner, defeating the Russian-backed incumbent, Prime Min. Viktor Yanukovich, who had been declared the winner of the previous runoff Nov. 21. International observers called the new election fair.

Parliament had passed a no-confidence vote in the government, **Dec. 1**, and the Supreme Court, **Dec. 3**, having found "systematic and massive violations" in the 1st runoff, had called a 2nd runoff. On Dec. 7 Parliament completed action on election-law reforms aimed at preventing abuses. On **Dec. 27**, the Central Election Commission said Yushchenko had received 52% of the vote and Yanukovich 44%; the latter said he would challenge the results in court. Demonstrators took to the street **Dec. 29** and blocked an attempt by Yanukovich to meet with his cabinet. On **Dec. 31**, he resigned as prime minister.

While campaigning earlier in 2004, Yushchenko had fallen seriously ill and been hospitalized twice in Vienna. On **Dec. 10** he entered the hospital again, this time with his face swollen, discolored, and covered with cysts. Dr. Michael Zimpfer, head of the Rudolfinerhaus hospital, said **Dec. 11** that Yushchenko had been poisoned by dioxin.

General

More Painkillers Linked to Health Risks—Pfizer announced **Dec. 17** that a study by the National Cancer Institute involving more than 2,000 patients linked its drug Celebrex to increased risk of heart attacks, strokes, and death. The FDA had approved Celebrex for relieving pain from osteoarthritis and rheumatoid arthritis, and in 2003, physicians wrote more than 21 mil prescriptions for it. Both Celebrex and Vioxx are classified as COX-2 inhibitors; Merck withdrew Vioxx in September after a study showed it carried an increased heart-attack risk.

The Celebrex trial, to test whether it could inhibit development of colorectal cancer, showed that a patient taking 800 milligrams a day had 3.4 times the ordinary risk of heart disease, while one taking 400 mg a day had 2.5 times the risk. Pfizer, noting that another study showed no increased heart problems, said it had no plan to withdraw the drug. A recent study of Bextra, another COX-2 drug made by Pfizer, showed that it increased the risk for heart-attack among patients undergoing heart surgery. The FDA **Dec. 23** advised doctors to show restraint in prescribing the 2 Pfizer drugs.

A National Institutes of Health study, reported **Dec. 20**, linked Aleve, an over-the-counter painkiller, to increased risk of heart disease.

Indian Ocean Tsunami Claims Vast Toll—One of history's worst calamities occurred **Dec. 26**, when a powerful earthquake in the Indian Ocean propelled towering waves, called tsunamis, toward the shores of a dozen Asian and African nations along the ocean's rim. By year's end, the death toll was estimated at more than 150,000.

A report issued in May 2005 by the International Federation of Red Cross and Red Crescent Societies, based on official reports from countries, put the death toll at 176,459 with 49,869 missing. Countries reported these deaths: Indonesia, 128,645; Sri Lanka, 31,147; India: 10,749; Thailand: 5,395; all others, 523, including over 300 as far away as East Africa. The number missing was to be added to the death toll one year after the disaster. As the dead were cremated or buried, often in mass graves, close to 2 mil people were left homeless. Although most victims were poor or of modest means, the tsunamis also struck resort hotels, notably in Phuket, Thailand, that attracted foreign tourists. On **Dec. 28**, reporters discovered a train in Sri Lanka that had been swept into a marsh, causing about 800 deaths.

The U.S. Geological Survey initially reported that the triggering earthquake had measured 8.5 on the Richter scale and had struck at 8 AM local time about 100 miles off the west coast of Sumatra. The magnitude was later put at 9.0, the 4th strongest in a century. Once the tsunamis were set in motion, they traveled as long as 6 hours to reach as far as the coast of Tanzania, in Africa. They moved at heights of up to 40 feet with speeds of up to 500 mph. The nations most severely affected lacked alert systems, leaving no advance warning as the waves struck, smashing well inland and destroying almost everything in their path.

Relief efforts appeared to move slowly at first but later gathered momentum. The Bush administration, criticized for a slow response, raised its aid package from an initial $15 mil to $35 mil and, on Dec. 31, $350 mil. The Pentagon also deployed ground forces, air surveillance and transport planes, an aircraft carrier, and ships with drinking water to the affected areas. The World Bank pledged $250 mil, and private citizens contributed millions of dollars; by **Dec. 31** the worldwide relief total was estimated at $1.2 bil. A ceasefire to the civil war in Sumatra's devastated Aceh Province was declared by rebels to facilitate relief efforts there.

Truce Reached in Africa's Longest Civil War—Delegates from the Sudanese government and the insurgent Sudan People's Liberation Movement (SPLM) signed protocols **Dec. 31** aimed at ending a 21-year-old north-south civil war during which an estimated 2 mil people were killed through fighting, famine, and disease. Under the accords, the south would have autonomy for 6 years, then vote in a referendum on succession. Also, oil revenue, a major reason for the conflict, would be split 50-50 between the region and the government. The war in the oil-rich, mostly Christian southern portion of the country began in 1983 when the central government tried to impose strict Islamic law.

JANUARY 2005

National

CBS Report on Bush's Guard Service Found Wanting—Results from an independent probe into a questionable CBS report presented 2 months before the 2004 presidential election were released **Jan. 10**, and led to the dismissal of Mary Mapes, the segment's producer, later that day. Three other employees were asked to resign. The segment, aired Sept. 8 on *60 Minutes,* was reported by news anchor Dan Rather, based on memos supposedly from George W. Bush's commanding officer; they described pressure to "sugarcoat" Bush's record in the National Guard and questioned whether he had discharged his duties. However, examination of the documents suggested they had been produced on a computer after the fact, and retired National Guard Lt. Col. Bill Burkett, a controversial figure who gave CBS the documents, later admitted he had lied about who had given them to him. Rather eventually apologized for the report, Sept. 20, 2004. On Nov. 23, he announced his retirement as anchor effective Mar. 9, 2005, but no linkage was made between the announcement and the controversy.

Louis Boccardi, a former Associated Press executive, and former U.S. Atty. Gen. Richard Thornburgh conducted the inquiry for CBS. They found that the documents had not been properly authenticated, though they did not find proof of forgery. They concluded that CBS had rushed the anti-Bush report on the air in a "myopic zeal" to scoop the competition, while failing to do routine fact checking.

Bush Picks a 2nd Nominee to Head Homeland Security—A month after his first nominee, Bernard Kerik, had withdrawn his name, Pres. Bush **Jan. 11** nominated U.S. Court of Appeals Judge Michael Chertoff to head the Dept. of Homeland Security. As head of the criminal division in the Justice Dept. in 2001, Chertoff had helped formulate the government's response to the 9/11 terror attacks.

Soldier Found Guilty of Abusing Iraqi Prisoners—A jury of 10 soldiers, at Ft. Hood, TX, found U.S. Army Reserve Spec. Charles Graner guilty **Jan. 14** of assault, dereliction of duties, and other charges in connection with abuses of prisoners at the Abu Ghraib prison in Iraq. Graner, said by investigators to be the "ringleader" of those abusing prisoners, was sentenced **Jan. 15** to 10 years in prison and given a dishonorable discharge. Graner contended he had been told by superiors to administer rough treatment.

Pres. Bush Inaugurated for a 2nd Term—George W. Bush took the presidential oath of office for the 2nd time, **Jan. 20** at the U.S. Capitol in Washington, DC, before a large crowd of dignitaries and members of the public. Chief Justice William Rehnquist, although suffering from thyroid cancer, was able to be present to administer the oath. The 43rd president then gave an inaugural address in which he spoke mostly of security issues. He said the U.S. goal would be to bring freedom to people around the world.

The president and First Lady Laura Bush then led the inaugural parade to the White House. All of the ceremonies were conducted under tight security. On the evening of **Jan. 20**, Pres. and Mrs. Bush attended 9 inaugural balls.

There were several anti-Bush demonstrations around the country. In Washington DC, there were scattered protests, including one where protesters carried cardboard coffins representing U.S. troops killed in Iraq.

Senate Approves Rice, Questions Gonzales—Condoleezza Rice, Pres. Bush's nominee for secretary of state, was approved by the Senate, 85-13, on **Jan. 26**; she took the oath of office later that day. Rice became the first African-American woman to serve as secretary of state. A close confidant of Pres. Bush and a strong supporter of the Iraq war, she had faced tough questioning from some Democrats during Senate confirmation hearings.

Alberto Gonzales, Bush's nominee for attorney general, was criticized by some senators at a hearing **Jan. 6**. They cited a draft memo he had written as White House counsel in 2002 concluding that captive members of al-Qaeda and the Taliban were not protected by the Geneva Convention. Gonzales told the senators that he stood by his legal reasoning, but said that the administration did not engage in or condone torture and that he would look into reports of prisoner abuse at the U.S. facility at Guantanamo Bay, Cuba. On **Jan. 26** the Senate Judiciary Committee recommended his confirmation, 10-8, voting along party lines.

International

Abbas Elected President of Palestinian Authority—Mahmoud Abbas was easily elected president of the Palestinian Authority (PA) **Jan. 9**, winning 62% of the vote in a field of 7 candidates. Sworn in **Jan. 12**, he succeeded Yasir Arafat, who died in Nov. Abbas had supported the Middle East peace process and opposed the suicide bombings and other violence by Palestinian.

By a narrow 58-56 margin, Israel's Knesset approved **Jan. 10** a new coalition government that would allow Prime Min. Ariel Sharon to remain in office and pursue his plan to dismantle all Israeli settlements in Gaza as well as 4 in the West Bank. Abbas said **Jan. 10** that he wanted to resume peace talks with Israel. On **Jan. 13**, Palestinian militants killed 6 Israelis, and the next day Sharon ordered all government authorities to end contacts with the PA. However, on orders of Abbas, Palestinian security forces were deployed in northern Gaza **Jan. 21** to prevent militant groups from firing mortars and rockets at Israeli settlements and towns, and Israel **Jan. 28** ordered its army to stop offensive operations in Gaza and reduce them in the West Bank.

Sudan Government and Rebel Group Sign Peace Accord—In a step toward peace in war-wracked Sudan, the Islamic government **Jan. 9** signed a peace accord with one of the country's principal rebel groups, composed mostly of Christians from the oil-rich south. During the 21-year civil war, there were an estimated 2 million deaths, mostly from starvation. Under the agreement, neither force would be required to disband, oil wealth would be shared, and a new constitution drafted. The agreement did not resolve fighting in the western Darfur region, involving another rebel group.

Ukraine Finally Gets a New President—After a first-round election and 2 bitterly contested runoffs, Ukraine got a new president **Jan. 23** when Viktor Yushchenko took the oath of office in Kiev. After the 2nd runoff, which showed a clear margin for Yushchenko, his opponent, Viktor Yanukovich, had briefly pursued, then dropped a court challenge. Yushchenko called his election "a victory of freedom over tyranny, of law over lawlessness, of future over past." He met with Pres. Vladimir Putin in Moscow **Jan. 24** and sought to reassure him that Ukraine would remain close to Russia while also seeking closer ties to western Europe.

Millions Vote in Iraq Election Despite Threats of Violence —Iraq's first democratic election in more than 50 years took place **Jan. 30**, despite threats of violence against Iraqi voters, election officials, and security forces.

There were over 100 political parties on the ballot. Voting was reported heavy in areas occupied by Shiite Muslims and Kurds, but in heavily Sunni Muslim areas turnout was low; the Sunnis, who constitute 20% of the population, had dominated the country during the Hussein regime, and the hostility of many of them had made it difficult to establish and open voting sites in Sunni areas. Later estimates put the average turnout at 57% of Iraqis eligible. Also participating in the election were hundreds of thousands of Iraqis living abroad.

Insurgents on election day initiated 38 attacks and suicide bombings that claimed 44 lives in Iraq. Additionally, 10 soldiers died when a British C-130 military plane crashed; it was not clear whether insurgents were involved. Despite a number of attacks by militants the widespread violence that had been predicted by some did not materialize.

Prior to the election, insurgents had sought to step up the level of violence and create a climate of fear. Supporters of the Jordanian militant Abu Musab al-Zarqawi **Jan. 1** posted a video on the Internet showing the execution of 5 members of the Iraqi security forces. North of Baghdad **Jan. 2**, a suicide car bomber killed 18 Iraqi National Guardsmen and a civilian. The governor of Baghdad province, Ali al-Haidari, was shot dead **Jan. 4**. Seven U.S. soldiers died **Jan. 6** in a roadside bombing in Baghdad. Insurgents killed Baghdad's deputy chief of police and his son **Jan. 10**. Several truck and car bombs exploded in Baghdad **Jan. 19**, killing 26 people. Fourteen died and 40 were injured **Jan. 21** when a car bomb exploded outside a Baghdad mosque.

On **Jan. 26** 30 Marines and a sailor were killed when their helicopter crashed near the border with Jordan during a sandstorm. Four Marines and 2 soldiers were killed the same day in other incidents. The number of American dead since the invasion of Iraq now exceeded 1,400.

Interim Prime Min. Iyad Allawi, **Jan. 31**, called the elections "a victory over terrorism" and urged the beginning of a new national dialogue.

General

Relief Supplies Rushed to Millions of Tsunami Survivors—A massive worldwide relief effort brought food, water, medicine, and supplies to millions who had survived the Dec. tsunamis in the Indian Ocean. By **Jan. 1**, 40 nations, led by Japan ($500 mil), had pledged help totaling $2 bil. On **Jan. 5** Australia and Germany raised their pledges to $1 bil and $663 mil, respectively.

The U.S. sent the aircraft carrier *Abraham Lincoln* and smaller American ships, which arrived **Jan. 1** offshore from Indonesia's devastated Aceh Province; helicopters began transporting supplies, and U.S. and other foreign troops on the ground assisted in relief efforts. Sec. of State Colin Powell and Gov. Jeb Bush (FL), the president's brother, arrived in Thailand **Jan. 3** and began a trip aimed at assuring hard-hit countries of American support. The State Dept. **Jan. 5** put the number of Americans presumed dead in the tsunami at 36.

California Diocese to Pay $100 Mil in Sex Abuse Case—The Roman Catholic diocese in Orange County, CA, agreed **Jan. 3** to a $100 mil settlement in a sexual abuse suit involving 90 plaintiffs. The sum was the highest so far in the scandal shaking the Catholic Church in the U.S. The Orange County plaintiffs alleged abuse between 1936 and 1996 by 44 individuals, including 31 priests and 2 nuns. Payments to individual plaintiffs ranged from about $500,000 to $4 mil.

Southern Cal Wins NCAA Football Title Game—The University of Southern California Trojans routed the Oklahoma Sooners, 55-19, in the NCAA national-championship football game in Miami, FL, **Jan. 4**. USC's quarterback, Matt Leinart, who had been awarded the Heisman Trophy as the nation's top college football player, tossed 5 touchdown passes, while running back LenDale White rushed for 118 yards. USC, coached by Pete Carroll, had now won 22 games in a row and 33 of its last 34. Both teams had been unbeaten in the season. Two other teams, Auburn and Utah, went unbeaten through the regular season and their respective bowl games. On **Jan. 5**, USC was voted the nation's best team in both AP and Coaches polls.

2 Train Wrecks Claim 20 Lives—A freight train transporting deadly chlorine gas crashed into a smaller train on a siding in Graniteville, SC, **Jan. 6**. Nine people died and about 50 were hospitalized, mostly with respiratory problems. Some 5,500 people within a mile of the accident were asked to evacuate. Authorities determined that crewmembers on the smaller train had failed to reset a crucial switch.

On **Jan. 26**, 11 people were killed and some 200 injured in a crash near Glendale, CA, involving 3 trains. According to authorities, a driver attempting suicide drove his sport utility vehicle onto a commuter rail track, then changed his mind and fled. His vehicle was struck by a southbound Metrolink train, which derailed and struck a parked Union Pacific locomotive and a northbound Metrolink train on adjacent tracks. The SUV driver, Juan Manuel Alvarez, was charged **Jan. 27** with 11 counts of murder.

Heavy Rains in California Bring Death, Devastation—By early Jan., more than a week of heavy rains had begun to create dangerous conditions in southern California. The 15 inches of rain in Los Angeles in the first 10 days of 2005 exceeded the normal total for an entire year. A mountainside saturated with rain crashed into the seaside town of La Conchita **Jan. 10**, killing 10 people.

FEBRUARY 2005

National

Bush Pushes for Social Security Reform—In his State of the Union address **Feb. 2**, Pres. George W. Bush called for an overhaul of the Social Security system, the first since the program was introduced in the 1930s. His key proposal was to allow workers born in 1950 or later the option of setting aside part of their wages subject to Social Security taxes into personal accounts invested in relatively conservative stock and bond funds that could grow in value. Warning that Social Security by 2018 would begin paying out more money than it took in through taxation, he said he would be open to various future benefit cuts for persons now under 55. Congressional Democrats and other critics argued that Social Security shortfalls did not call for immediate action and opposed the partial privatization plan as risky and expensive. The plan would create a large shortfall, at least short-term, in taxes paid into the system, although it would reduce the government's Social Security obligations down the road.

In his address, Pres. Bush said he would send Congress a pared down budget that eliminated or cut back more than 150 government programs. Citing the large turnout in Iraqi elections as a triumph for democracy, Bush said he would not set a time line for ending the U.S. mission in Iraq, as some of his critics sought, but would stress training of Iraqi security forces with the goal of enabling them to eventually control the continuing insurgency on their own. Noting an improved situation for Israeli-Palestinian negotiations, he pledged an additional $350 mil in U.S. aid to the Palestinians.

Gonzales Becomes Attorney General—Alberto Gonzales **Feb. 3** became the first Hispanic person to serve as U.S. attorney general. He was sworn in just after the Senate approved his nomination, 60-36.

Bush's Budget Aims to Slow Spending—Pres. Bush sent to Congress **Feb. 7** a $2.57 tril federal budget for the fiscal year beginning Oct. 1, 2005. The budget would slow the growth of government spending from 8.2% to 3.6% in one year, and, he said, put the country on the road to cutting the federal budget deficit in half by 2009 from the 2004 fiscal year amount of $445 bil. Pentagon spending would jump by 4.8%, or $19.2 bil, not including the cost of operations in Afghanistan and Iraq. The budget called for an end to subsidies for Amtrak and a cap on subsidy payments to farmers.

Democrats Elect Dean as Chairman—Former VT Gov. Howard Dean, an unsuccessful candidate for the 2004 Democratic presidential nomination, was chosen by his party **Feb. 12** to be its new national chairman. He was elected by voice vote after his rivals dropped out. During his failed presidential bid Dean had successfully utilized the Internet to raise funds for his campaign; he was popular among many of the Democratic rank and file for his opposition to the Iraq war. Dean succeeded Terry McAuliffe, also a prodigious fundraiser, but more closely allied to former Pres. Bill Clinton. Dean, **Feb. 13**, denounced the Republican Party for "fiscal recklessness" and said Democrats were the party more committed to national security.

Bush Names Intelligence Czar—Pres. Bush **Feb. 17** tapped John Negroponte to serve in the newly created post of director of national intelligence. Currently U.S. ambassador to Iraq, Negroponte had also been U.S. delegate to the UN in the current administration, and was a former deputy national security adviser.

International

Report Rebukes Ex-Head of UN Oil-for-Food Program—A UN commission investigating the organization's oil-for-food program in Iraq issued an interim report **Feb. 3**, finding that the former head of the program had violated the UN charter by helping a friend's company obtain contracts to sell Iraqi oil. The official, Benon Sevan, of Cyprus, had run the program from 1997 until the U.S. invasion in 2003. The commission, headed by Paul Volcker, former U.S. Federal Reserve chairman, also reported that other officials had violated UN rules on competitive bidding. On **Feb. 6**, the UN suspended Sevan, who had since become a UN adviser, and Joseph Stephanides, an official on the Security Council staff, who had helped choose the oil-for-food program contractors. A Senate subcommittee reported **Feb. 14** that Sevan may have made up to $1.5 mil from illegal oil shipments.

Rice and Bush Visit Europe—Sec. of State, Condoleezza Rice, and later Pres. Bush, visited Europe as part of a mission to mend U.S.-European relations damaged by the Iraq war. At the beginning of the trip, Rice in London **Feb. 3** strongly denounced Iran's human rights record, but said the U.S. backed negotiations to resolve the dispute over Iran's suspected nuclear-arms program. After meeting with Rice in Berlin **Feb. 4**, German Chancellor Gerhard Schroeder said he would do more to help the recovery of Iraq, but continued to rule out any military commitment. In Ankara, Turkey, **Feb. 5**, Rice said that Russia's punishment of political dissenters was complicating relations with the U.S. In Jerusalem **Feb. 6**, Rice told Prime Min. Ariel Sharon that Israel would need to make "hard decisions" if a democratic Palestinian state were to emerge. By meeting with Palestinian leader Mahmoud Abbas, **Feb. 7** in Ramallah, she signaled a resumption of direct U.S. involvement in the peace process.

Bush, speaking in Brussels **Feb. 21**, reproached Russian Pres. Vladimir Putin for his government's recent moves against dissenters and retrenching on democratic reforms. Responding to an appeal by Bush, the 16 members of NATO **Feb. 22** agreed to help equip and train Iraqi's security forces. In Wiesbaden, **Feb. 23**, Bush said that he and European leaders had discussed ways to persuade Iran to give up its nuclear program, but the administration opposed offering Iran incentives to disarm. At a meeting in Bratislava, Slovakia, **Feb. 24**, Bush and Putin agreed to step up dismantling of Russia's nuclear materials; later, during a tense press conference, Putin showed displeasure at Bush's continued call for more democracy in Russia.

Georgia's Prime Minister Dies in Accident—Prime Min. Zurab Zhvania of Georgia died in Tbilisi, **Feb. 3**, from carbon monoxide poisoning due to a malfunctioning space heater. He was visiting the apartment of an acquaintance, Raul Usupov, a deputy governor from the Kvemo Kartli region, who also died. Zhvania was a major figure in the reform government under Pres. Mikhail Saakashvili, which had come to power in 2003.

Israeli, Palestinian Leaders Come to Agreement—Prime Min. Ariel Sharon of Israel and the Palestinian leader, Mahmoud Abbas, met in Sharm el Sheik, Egypt, **Feb. 8** and agreed to halt acts of political violence in their respective territories. Sharon had refused to meet with Yasir Arafat, Abbas's predecessor. Israel reportedly would pull back its forces from 5 West Bank cities, including Jericho and Bethlehem. Spokesmen for the militant Palestinian group Hamas issued conflicting statements as to whether Hamas would honor the agreement. On **Feb. 17** Israel ended the practice of demolishing homes of suicide bombers. On **Feb. 20**, the Israeli cabinet, 17-5, approved Sharon's plan to withdraw Jewish settlers from the Gaza Strip. The cabinet also approved a revised route for the West Bank barrier being built to protect Israelis from terrorist attacks; an Israeli court had found that the present route imposed undue hardships on Palestinians. In another goodwill step, Israel **Feb. 21** freed 500 Palestinian prisoners of the 7,000 it held. The Palestinian parliament **Feb. 24** approved a cabinet that appeared to represent a break with the Arafat era. The sense of progress was set back **Feb. 25**, when a suicide bomber killed 4 and wounded dozens in an explosion at a Tel Aviv nightclub.

North Korea Acknowledges Nuclear Weapons—North Korea **Feb. 9** confirmed what had been widely suspected, that it possessed nuclear weapons. The reclusive Communist regime said that nuclear fuel had been placed in weapons, which were needed for self-defense. The government also said it would suspend participation in disarmament talks. China **Feb. 13** called for "denuclearization" of the Korean peninsula and urged North Korea to return to regional talks.

Religious Shiites Win Plurality in Iraq, Amid Heavy Turnout—An alliance of Shiite Muslims led by 2 religious parties, and backed by Grand Ayatollah Ali al-Sistani, won 48% of the vote in Iraq's national election, according to official results announced **Feb. 13**. An alliance of the 2 major Kurdish parties received 26%, and the secular Iraqi List, headed by interim Prime Min. Ayad Allawi, got 14%. With seats in the 275-member national assembly to be allocated according to the number of votes for each list, the religious Shiites would have 140 seats, the Kurds 75, and the secular Shiites 40. Nine other parties won a few seats each. The Sunni Muslims, who were in power under ex-Pres. Saddam Hussein, had largely boycotted the election. But defying threats by insurgents, 8.5 million Iraqis, or 58% of all eligible Iraqis, cast ballots. A two-thirds majority in the assembly was required to approve a new government. The winning alliance **Feb. 22** backed Ibrahim al-Jaafari, a Shiite with ties to religious elements, for prime minister.

Unable to disrupt the elections, insurgents resumed their deadly attacks soon after. In the week ending **Feb. 13**, more than 100 people were killed in bombings and by gunfire. On **Feb. 18-19**, during a Shiite holy day and its eve, bombs killed 70. Another wave of bombings **Feb. 24** killed 25. In the deadliest single bombing since the U.S. invasion, a suicide car bomber in the city of Hilla killed 127 and injured as many as 170 others **Feb. 28**. The blast took place in a crowded city square where many were waiting in line outside a police recruiting office.

Iraqi officials said **Feb. 27** that Syria had captured and handed over Saddam Hussein's half brother, reportedly a leader in the insurgency. Sabawi Ibrahim al-Hassan was seized with 29 other members of Hussein's Baath Party in northeastern Syria.

Bomb Kills Anti-Syrian Figure in Lebanon; Protests Ensue—A former prime minister of Lebanon, Rafik al-Hariri, was killed **Feb. 14** when a bomb exploded in his motorcade in Beirut. Thirteen others also died, and more than 100 were wounded. Hariri had resigned in Oct. 2004 in protest against Syria's domination of Lebanon, where it maintains about 15,000 troops.

While no hard evidence pointed to Hariri's assassins, U.S. officials hinted that Syria was to blame and were pursuing efforts to tighten economic sanctions against the Syrian regime. On **Feb. 15** the U.S. recalled its ambassador to Syria and demanded that Syria withdraw its troops from Lebanon. On **Feb. 21**, Syrian Pres. Bashar al-Assad pledged to do so.

After nearly 2 weeks of demonstrations by tens of thousands of protestors in Beirut, precipitated by the assassination of Harari, pro-Syria Lebanese Prime Min. Omar Karami announced **Feb. 28** that he was resigning. Demonstrators had blamed Karami and the Syrian government for the assassination, and called for the removal of Syrian troops. Both the U.S. and France voiced support for the protests and offered to help the country hold free elections.

General

New England Wins Super Bowl—The New England Patriots, **Feb. 6**, defeated the Philadelphia Eagles, 24-21, to win Super Bowl XXXIX in Jacksonville, FL. It was their 3rd NFL title in 4 years and 2nd in a row. Quarterback Tom Brady threw for 2 touchdowns, completing 23 of 33 passes for 236 yards. The Patriots' Deion Branch, named MVP, caught 11 passes, tying a Super Bowl record, for 133 yards. However, it was a 2-yard run by Corey Dillon, and a 22-yard field goal by kicker Adam Vinatieri in the 4th quarter that put the Pats ahead to stay. New England's overall record of 17-2 included 3 wins in the post-season.

Prince Charles and Camilla Parker-Bowles to Marry—Prince Charles, heir to the British throne, announced **Feb. 10** that he would marry Camilla Parker Bowles, his longtime companion, in a small civil ceremony at Windsor Castle; Parker-Bowles would be formally known as the Duchess of Cornwall and would not become queen in the event of Charles's succession.

Hockey Season Canceled—The National Hockey League season was canceled **Feb. 16**; no games had yet been played because of a lockout. Citing heavy losses over the last 2 seasons, the league had sought to reduce average players' salaries from $1.8 mil to $1.3 mil per year. After long debate, the players' union **Feb. 14** agreed to accept a salary cap. But on **Feb. 15** they said they would accept nothing less than a team cap of $49 mil per year, while the league would only go as high as $42.5 mil.

2 Ex-Presidents Visit Tsunami Areas—Former Pres. George H.W. Bush and Bill Clinton toured areas devastated by the December tsunami, as official representatives of the current Pres. Bush, beginning **Feb. 19** in Thailand. On **Feb. 20**, they visited Lampuuk, which had lost nearly 90% of its 6,500 residents; the delegation then flew to Sri Lanka. Previously, on **Feb. 9**, Pres. Bush raised the U.S. relief pledge to $950 mil. In all, it was estimated that public and private contributions to tsunami aid from around the world had reached nearly $6 bil.

Ray Charles Big Winner at Grammys—*Genius Loves Company*, the final, posthumous recording by Ray Charles, received 8 awards, including album of the year and best pop album, at the 47th annual Grammy Awards **Feb. 13**. Other winners included Alicia Keys, who collected 4 awards in the R&B category, and Usher and U2, who collected 3 each.

Pope Undergoes Tracheotomy—Pope John Paul II was rushed to a hospital in Rome **Feb. 24** and underwent an emergency tracheotomy to relieve difficulties in breathing. The 84-year-old pontiff, in poor health for several years, had been hospitalized earlier in Feb. The surgical procedure was described as a success, but the underlying condition remained a matter of concern as the pope recovered. He appeared at a hospital window **Feb. 27**, blessing the faithful.

***Million Dollar Baby* Named Best Movie**—*Million Dollar Baby*, the story of a young woman determined to succeed as a boxer, was named best motion picture of 2004 by the Academy of Motion Picture Arts and Sciences on **Feb. 27**. The film also won Oscars in 3 other major categories: directing (Clint Eastwood), best actress (Hilary Swank), and best supporting actor (Morgan Freeman). Other top awards went to Jamie Foxx, best actor, for his role as the late singer Ray Charles in *Ray*, and Cate Blanchett, best actress in a supporting role, for her role as the late actress Katherine Hepburn in *The Aviator*.

MARCH 2005

National

Supreme Court Ends Executions for Juveniles—The Supreme Court **Mar. 1** ruled, 5-4, that executing convicts who committed their crimes before age 18 was unconstitutional. Writing for the majority in *Roper* v. *Simmons*, Justice Anthony Kennedy argued that such executions could now be considered "cruel and unusual punishment," violating a developing national consensus. His opinion also included the observation that the U.S. was one of only 8 countries that had executed juveniles since 1990.

Pres. Bush Nominates Bolton, Wolfowitz—Pres. George W. Bush **Mar. 7** nominated Undersec. of State for Arms Control and frequent UN critic John Bolton to succeed John Danforth as U.S. ambassador to the UN. On **Mar. 16**, he nominated Deputy Defense Sec. Paul Wolfowitz to head the World Bank. Wolfowitz was a key advocate and architect of the war and postwar U.S. policies in Iraq.

WorldCom's Former CEO Convicted of Fraud—Bernard Ebbers, former CEO of WorldCom Inc., was convicted on 9 criminal counts of fraud and conspiracy **Mar. 15** in U.S. District Court in New York City. Ebbers had built WorldCom Inc. into a telecommunications giant before it collapsed into a $107 bil bankruptcy in 2002, the largest ever in U.S. history. Ebbers was subsequently charged with conspiracy, securities fraud, and filing false securities documents. His principal accuser, former CFO Scott Sullivan, testified that Ebbers had told him to meet profit projections by disguising fees paid out. Ebbers, who claimed that he had not paid attention to the details of the company's finances, appealed the verdict.

Schiavo Dies After Epic Legal Battle—Terri Schiavo, a Florida woman who had been in a persistent vegetative state since 1990, died **Mar. 31** at age 41 after an intense legal battle, 13 days after her feeding tube was removed. She had been the center of a legal dispute between her husband and legal guardian, Michael, who sought to have the tube removed, and her parents, Robert and Mary Schindler, who opposed its removal. Doctors had found Schiavo to be in a persistent vegetative state, able to breathe but unable to consciously react to stimuli. Michael Schiavo claimed that Terri had previously stated a wish not to be kept alive under such circumstances. Her parents insisted that her condition could improve and sought legal custody of her.

By March 2005, 19 judges had considered the case, and the U.S. Supreme Court had declined to hear it 5 times. The Florida District Court of Appeal **Mar. 16** refused to stay an order by Judge George Greer of Pinellas-Pasco (FL) Circuit Court that the tube be removed. It was removed **Mar. 18**.

U.S. Sen. Bill Frist (R, TN), the Senate majority leader and a heart surgeon, said **Mar. 18** that he had studied video footage of Schiavo and questioned the pessimistic diagnosis by Schiavo's doctors. The Senate by a voice vote and the House, 203-58, **Mar. 20**, approved a bill that allowed the Schindlers to challenge the removal of the tube in federal court. Pres. Bush, having flown back from Texas, signed the bill early on **Mar. 21**.

In Tampa, FL, **Mar. 22**, U.S. District Court Judge James Whittemore rejected a request by the Schindlers to restore the feeding tube. On **Mar. 23**, a federal appeals court panel (2-1) and the full 11th Circuit Court of Appeals (10-2) also ruled against the parents. The Florida Senate, 21-18, defeated a bill that would have barred removal of life support unless the patient left written instructions to do so. On **Mar. 24**, the U.S. Supreme Court again declined to hear the case.

Baseball Stars Testify on Steroids—The use of steroids by athletes reached wide public attention when former and current MLB stars testified before House Committee on Government Reform **Mar. 17**. Those who testified included, retired player Jose Canseco, Orioles outfielder Sammy Sosa, Orioles first baseman Rafael Palmeiro, and retired slugger Mark McGuire. In *Juiced*, a book published in Feb., Canseco admitted he had used steroids, and accused other players of the same, including McGuire, Palmeiro, and Sosa. Sosa and Palmeiro both denied Canseco's published allegations. McGuire declined to confirm or deny them.

Also testifying were parents of 2 young baseball players who had committed suicide after using steroids. MLB Commissioner Bud Selig testified, and promised zero tolerance for drugs, but denied that baseball had a "major problem." U.S. law forbids the use of anabolic steroids without a prescription.

Scathing Report on U.S. Intelligence—According to a report presented to Pres. Bush **Mar. 31** by the 9-member presidential Commission on the Intelligence Capabilities of the United States Regarding Weapons of Mass Destruction, the U.S. was "dead wrong" on almost all of its prewar assessments of Iraq's weapons of mass destruction. The findings were based on a year-long investigation into the U.S. intelligence community. The report also stated that the U.S. knows "disturbingly little" about the weapons programs of many of its adversaries and rivals, including N. Korea, Iran, China, and Russia. Bush praised the commission for its findings and said he would "correct what needs to be fixed."

U.S. Economy at a Glance: March 2005

Unemployment rate	5.2%
Consumer prices (change over 2004)	+3.1%
Trade deficit (12 mo. through Mar.)	$697 bil
Dow Jones closing (1st quarter)	10,503.76
Dow Jones highest close, 1st quarter (Mar. 4)	10,940.55
Dow Jones lowest close, 1st quarter (Jan. 24)	10,368.61
1st quarter GDP growth (annual rate)	3.8%

International

Syria Agrees to Pull Back Troops in Lebanon—Presidents Bashar al-Assad of Syria and Emile Lahoud of Lebanon agreed **Mar. 7** that Syria would move its 15,000 troops in Lebanon to the Bekaa Valley, still in Lebanon but near the Syrian border. The troops had been a focus of controversy since the February assassination of former Lebanese Premier Rafik al-Hariri, a critic of Syrian influence.

U.S. Sec. of State Condoleezza Rice and French Foreign Min. Michael Barnier jointly demanded **Mar. 1** that Syria immediately pull all of its troops and intelligence agents out of Lebanon. Pres. Bush made the same demand **Mar. 2**. On **Mar. 8**, 500,000 people, at a rally organized by Hezbollah, a militant Shiite organization, massed in Beirut, in support of Syria. Syrian troops began pulling back **Mar. 12**. In Beirut, **Mar. 14**, nearly one million demonstrators demanded Syria's withdrawal. By **Mar. 17**, the remaining Syrian troops had reportedly redeployed in the Bekaa Valley.

A UN report concluded **Mar. 24** that Syrian interference in Lebanon had caused the tensions that led to Hariri's assassination. Sec. Gen. Kofi Annan called for an international investigation.

Former Chechnyan Leader Killed in Raid—Aslan Maskhadov, a former president of Chechnya, was killed **Mar. 8** in a raid by Russian troops on a bunker 12 miles from Grozny, the Chechen capital. Russian Pres. Vladimir Putin had blamed several recent terrorist attacks in Russia on Maskhadov. In February Masckadov had ordered Chechen fighters to observe a cease-fire and had called for peace talks.

Death Toll in Sudan Rises—Jan Egeland, the UN undersec. for humanitarian affairs, estimated **Mar. 14** that 180,000 Sudanese had died from hunger or disease in the past 18 months. A recent UN report described atrocities committed by the government of Sudan and Arab militias against blacks in Darfur. Egeland deplored the failure of the international community to assist Darfur.

Italian Killed by U.S. Forces; Italian Troops to Pull Back—Prime Min. Silvio Berlusconi said **Mar. 15** that Italy would soon reduce its troop strength in Iraq, currently at 3,000. Italian opposition to the war, already significant, was further fueled by reports that on **Mar. 4** U.S. troops had shot and killed an Italian intelligence officer, Nicola Calipari, who was escorting a freed hostage, Italian journalist Giuliana Sgrena. The U.S. troops shot at their vehicle as it approached a checkpoint; Sgrena, a reporter for a Communist paper, was wounded as was the car's driver. U.S. and Italian officials disagreed on whether the car had ignored warning signals and on other details of the incident.

In another incident in Iraq, the defense minister of Bulgaria, Nikolai Svinarov, said **Mar. 7** that gunfire that killed a Bulgarian soldier **Mar. 4** apparently had come from U.S. troops. The incident was under investigation by a U.S. commission. Svinarov said **Mar. 17** that Bulgaria would pull its 460 personnel out of Iraq by the end of 2005.

Insurgent violence against Iraqis continued, as a suicide bomber killed 47 and wounded 100 at a Shiite mosque in Mosul, **Mar. 10**.

President of Kyrgyzstan Ousted—A popular uprising in Bishkek, the capital of Kyrgyzstan, forced the country's president since 1990, Askar Akayev, to flee from his presidential palace on **Mar. 24**. A ruling by the Kyrgyzstan Supreme Court had effectively annulled **Mar. 13** election results that had given Akayev another term. The police and army refused to aid Akayev, president since 1990.

Parliament **Mar. 25** appointed Kurmanbek Bakiyev, the senior leader of the political opposition, as acting president, and named other opposition leaders to top positions. Akayev, from an unknown location, claimed **Mar. 25** that he was still the legitimate head of government. Russia said **Mar. 26** that it had opened its doors to Akayev.

UN Leader Criticized in Oil-for-Food Report—UN Sec. Gen. Kofi Annan said **Mar. 29** that he would not resign after a UN commission issued its 2nd report on the oil-for-food scandal, which criticized him. The commission, chaired by Paul Volcker, sought to determine whether UN representatives were incompetent or corrupt in allowing the government of former Iraqi Pres. Saddam Hussein to gain billions of dollars from illegal oil exports. The report did not find evidence that Annan had used his influence to get a $10 mil contract awarded to a company that paid his son, Kojo, $450,000 in counsulting fees. But the commission said Annan should have been more aggressive in investigating the company, and it criticized 2 of his aides, one for shredding documents, another for paying a high-level apprentice for work not done.

General

BTK Murderer Charged—Dennis Rader, a municipal employee, was charged with 10 counts of first-degree murder **Mar. 1** in Wichita, KS. Authorities had arrested him Feb. 25, and on Feb. 26 said that he was the BTK murderer responsible for at least 10 deaths between 1974 and 1991. The initials, for "bind, torture, kill," were a nickname the killer had applied to himself in communications with police.

Ailing Pope Misses Easter Week Ceremonies—Pope John Paul II, hospitalized for influenza and respiratory problems, was released **Mar. 13**. On Palm Sunday, **Mar. 20** he appeared briefly at his window at the Vatican, but did not speak. On Sunday morning, **Mar. 27**, for the first time in his tenure, he was unable to conduct an Easter mass. The Vatican said **Mar. 30** that the pope was receiving nutrition from a tube in his nose.

Litigant Kills Himself, Confesses to Murdering Judge's Family—Bart Ross, an unsuccessful litigant in a medical malpractice case, shot himself to death in a Milwaukee suburb **Mar. 9** as police approached his vehicle. He left a suicide note saying that on Feb. 28 he had killed the husband and mother of U.S. District Judge Joan Humphrey Lefkow in Chicago, who had ruled against him.

Court Shooting in Atlanta, GA—In the Fulton County Courthouse **Mar. 11**, Brian Nichols, a defendant in a rape case, broke free from custody, took a deputy's gun, and shot and killed Superior Court Judge Roland Barnes, along with a court stenographer and a sheriff's deputy. While in flight he may have killed a customs agent. Nichols also held a woman, Ashley Smith, hostage for several hours. He was seized by police **Mar. 12**.

***Baretta* Actor Found Innocent**—Actor Robert Blake, star of the 1970s TV series *Baretta,* was found not guilty **Mar. 16** of murdering his wife, Bonny Lee Bakley. A Los Angeles County Superior Court jury also found him not guilty of soliciting a stunt man to kill her. Judge Darlene Schempp dismissed a 3rd charge on which the jury had deadlocked. Bakley was shot to death in 2001 in a car outside a restaurant where the couple had dined. Blake said she had been killed while he returned to the restaurant to retrieve a revolver, which was not the murder weapon.

Scott Peterson Sentenced to Death—Acting on the recommendation of the jury, Judge Alfred Delucchi, in Redwood City, CA, **Mar. 16**, sentenced Scott Peterson to death for the murder of his wife Laci and their unborn son. Laci Peterson was reported missing on Christmas Eve 2002. Her torso and the fetus washed up on shore in April 2003. Peterson was convicted Nov. 13, 2004.

School Shooting on Reservation—A student who had been treated for depression killed 9 people before committing suicide on the native American Red Lake Reservation in Minnesota **Mar. 21**. Jeff Weise, 16, a Chippewa (Ojibwa), first shot his grandfather and his companion, then went to his high school where he killed 7 more, and wounded 7, before killing himself. Authorities said **Mar. 29** that they had arrested Louis Jourdain, 16, the son of the tribal chairman, Floyd Jourdain, Jr., on charges of involvement in planning the shootings.

Oil Refinery Explosion Claims 15 Lives—An explosion at the BP oil refinery in Texas City, TX, **Mar. 23** killed 15 people and injured 100. Investigators believed a chemical leak was responsible.

Quake Near Site of 2004 Tsunami Disaster Kills Hundreds—An 8.7 magnitude earthquake off the coast of Indonesia **Mar. 28** claimed over 500 lives, mostly on the islands of Nias and Simeulue. The epicenter was 200 miles south of the Dec. 2004 earthquake that unleashed tsunamis that left 175,000 dead and 50,000 missing.

APRIL 2005

National

Former National Security Adviser Pleads Guilty—Samuel Berger, who served as national security adviser to Pres. Bill Clinton, under a plea agreement with the Justice Department, subject to approval by a judge, pleaded guilty **Apr. 1** to intentionally removing classified documents from the National Archives and destroying others. The agreement called for him to pay a fine of $10,000. He did not say why he had removed or destroyed documents.

Bush Nominee for UN Post Takes Heavy Criticism—John Bolton, undersec. of state for arms control and international security and Pres. George W. Bush's controversial choice as U.S. ambassador to the UN, began his confirmation hearings **Apr. 11** before the Senate Foreign Relations Committee. Responding to suggestions that he had displayed a pattern of abuse toward employees and others, he said he had lost confidence in intelligence officials with whom he disagreed, but denied that he had sought to have them dismissed.

Bolton's defenders, including Sec. of State Condoleezza Rice, declared that Bolton was just the person to shake up a UN that needed reform. With several Republicans not yet ready to endorse Bolton, Committee Chairman Richard Lugar (R, IN) agreed **Apr. 19** to postpone a vote on Bolton's confirmation.

Anti-Abortion Activist Admits Bombings—Eric Rudolf, as part of a deal to avoid the death penalty, pleaded guilty **Apr. 13** to 4 bombings between 1996 and 1998 that killed 2 people in all and injured more than 120. He admitted to 3 bombings in Atlanta, GA, including the blast at 1996 Olympic Games (where 1 person was killed), and to 2 in 1997, at a gay and lesbian nightclub and a family-planning clinic that performed abortions. He also pleaded guilty to the 1998 bombing of a clinic in Birmingham, AL, where abortions were performed (1 person was killed). Rudolph had eluded capture for over 5 years in the mountains of North Carolina. He was finally arrested in 2003.

Suspect Admits Role in Planning U.S. Terror Attack—Zacarias Moussaoui, the defendant in the plot to attack the U.S. with hijacked airplanes, pleaded guilty to 6 counts of conspiracy **Apr. 22** in federal district court in Alexandria, VA, and admitted that Osama bin Laden had instructed him to fly a plane into the White House; but denied that he was to be one of the Sept. 11 hijackers. Moussaoui, a French citizen with Moroccan roots, was the only person facing a U.S. trial in connection with the Sept. 11, 2001, terror strikes. He was arrested more than 3 weeks before the Sept. 11 attacks because of his suspicious behavior at a Minnesota flight school. In a written statement, he acknowledged that he knew of al-Qaeda's plot to fly planes into buildings and had agreed to come to the U.S. to help carry out the attacks.

Bush Meets Saudi Leader—Pres. Bush met with Crown Prince Abdullah of Saudi Arabia in Crawford, TX, **Apr. 25,** with oil prices foremost on the agenda. Oil prices had recently hit new highs on international markets, and the price of gas in the U.S. had risen well above $2 per gallon. Bush urged Abdullah to increase production to help reduce oil prices.

In a speech **Apr. 27**, Bush called for constructing more nuclear power plants and urged Congress to give tax breaks for fuel-efficient hybrid and clean-diesel cars. He acknowledged that these steps would not, however, serve in the short term to bring down gas prices.

House Votes on Ethics Rules—The House of Representatives voted **Apr. 27** to revert to previous ethics rules, first instituted in 1997, paving the way for an investigation into trips taken Majority Leader Tom DeLay which were allegedly paid for by lobbyists. The Republican majority in January had changed House rules for investigating members and staff, making it difficult for the Committee on Standards of Official Conduct (evenly divided between Republicans and Democrats) to look into ethics violations without a majority vote of the committee. Under the restored rules, if the committee reaches an impasse, complaints will be sent to a special investigatory committee.

Bush Pitches Social Security Reform—Pres. Bush, in a rare prime-time press conference **Apr. 28**, continued to press his controversial plan for optional private investment accounts as a component of social security, while also, for the first time, outlining benefit cuts for future high-income and middle-income retirees as a key ingredient in putting social security on a sound financial footing. Bush said these cuts would slow the annual growth in benefits for all but low-income recipients. He said he would work with Congress on other proposals, provided they did not raise the payroll tax or endanger the economy. Democrats responded that Bush's cuts would impact heavily on the middle class.

Also during the press conference Bush called for greater use of alternative energy resources and pledged to encourage oil-producing nations to increase production, and he called on Congress to enact an energy bill before the summer.

International

Kyrgyzstan Parliament Rejects, Then Accepts President's Resignation—The political leadership in Kyrgyzstan remained in turmoil as the month began. Pres. Askar Akayev, who had been in Moscow since a popular uprising in March, met with legislators **Apr. 3**, and on **Apr. 4** offered to resign. The Kyrgyz parliament did not initially accept the offer because Akayev would have been immune from prosecution for alleged wrongdoing in office. Finally, parliament did accept it **Apr. 11** and scheduled a presidential election for July.

Iraq Seeks to Complete Forming Government; Insurgent Attacks Continue—Three months after the Iraqi people chose the members of a National Assembly, political leaders were gradually making headway in forming a transitional government. The assembly **Apr. 6** chose a president, Kurdish leader Jalal Talabani. Two vice presidents, a Shiite Muslim and a Sunni Muslim, were also chosen **Apr. 6**. For the more powerful position of premier, the 3-member presidential council **Apr. 7** nominated Ibrahim al-Jaafari, a Shiite Muslim who had the support of the United Iraqi Alliance, which controlled a majority of the seats in the assembly.

On **Apr. 28**, Iraq's National Assembly approved a Shiite-led cabinet consisting primarily of Shiites, but also including some Kurds and Sunnis, and including some women. A number of positions were left vacant; Prime Min. al-Jaafari said these would be filled within a week.

In continuing violence, an **Apr. 2** assault on the Abu Ghraib prison wounded 23 U.S. soldiers and 13 prisoners. Bombs in Kirkuk **Apr. 13** killed 9 Iraqi policemen. Two bombs **Apr. 14** killed 19 Iraqis in Baghdad, and a bomb in a Baquba restaurant **Apr. 16** killed at least 13 Iraqis, mostly policemen. Police **Apr. 20** found 58 bodies in the Tigris River. That same day, 19 people were found shot to death in a stadium in Haditha. Insurgents shot down a civilian helicopter north of Baghdad **Apr. 21**; all 11 aboard, including 6 American contractors, were killed. Bombs in Baghdad and Tikrit **Apr. 24** killed 21 and wounded scores. A roadside bomb killed 4 American soldiers and wounded 4 others **Apr. 28** 150 mi. north of Baghdad.

Following installation of the new government, insurgents began a coordinated series of deadly car bomb and mortar attacks in Baghdad and nearby areas **Apr. 29** killing over 40 people, including 3 U.S. soldiers, and wounding at least 90 more. Five car bombings in the Baghdad area **Apr. 30** left at least 11 Iraqis dead and more than 40 wounded; that same day in Mosul, insurgent attacks left at least 3 Iraqis killed and 9 people wounded, including 1 American soldier.

Prince Rainier Dies—Prince Rainier III, ruler of the Mediterranean principality of Monaco since 1949, died **Apr. 6** at age 81. Long known as a gambling resort, Monaco had enjoyed a boom in tourism and development during his reign. Rainier in 1956 had married American actress Grace Kelly, who died in 1982. Prince Albert, their only son (they also had 2 daughters), succeeded his father.

Bush Meets Israeli Prime Minister in Texas—Prime Min. Ariel Sharon met with Pres. George W. Bush **Apr. 11**

at his ranch in Crawford, TX. Pres. Bush supported Sharon's decision to evacuate Jewish settlers living in the Gaza Strip. However, Sharon said that in any final settlement with the Palestinians "large Israeli population centers" would remain in the West Bank. Bush disapproved of the planned expansion of the largest Israeli West Bank settlement, which would eventually touch the eastern edge of Jerusalem.

Indictments Announced in UN Oil-for-Food Scandal—Several indictments were handed down **Apr. 14** as the UN oil-for-food scandal continued to unfold. U.S. Atty. David Kelley announced in New York that David Chalmers Jr. and his Houston-based company, Bayoil USA, had been charged with paying kickbacks to Iraqis to win contracts under the oil-for-food program. Chalmers and another of his companies, Bayoil Supply and Trading Ltd., faced additional charges. Also, South Korean businessman Tongsun Park was charged with trying to bribe a UN official.

President of Ecuador Flees His Palace—Pres. Lucio Gutierrez **Apr. 20** fled from his palace in Quito, Ecuador, after the Ecuadorian Congress voted to remove him, and sought refuge at the Brazilian embassy. Gutierrez, elected in 2002 as a leftist, had angered supporters by embracing free-market policies. Accusations of nepotism and corruption had been leveled against his administration, causing large crowds to demand his resignation. After his departure, Vice Pres. Alfredo Palacio was sworn in as president **Apr. 20**. A high-level delegation from the Organization of American States **Apr. 27** began an investigation into Gutierrez's ouster and the justification for the congress's action.

Syria Completes Troop Withdrawal from Lebanon—Syria **Apr. 26** fulfilled its pledge to withdraw its troops from Lebanon; the last group departed with a farewell ceremony at the international border. The Syrians had entered Lebanon in 1976, ostensibly as peacekeepers during a civil war, but remained and exercised great influence in Lebanon's politics. The impact of the Feb. 14 assassination of former Prime Min. Rafik al-Hariri continued to be felt in the Lebanese government. Prime Min. Omar Karami resigned **Apr. 13**. Pres. Emile Lahoud **Apr. 15** named Najib Mikati, a pro-Syria business man, as acting prime minister, pending parliamentary elections later in the spring.

U.S. Soldier Sentenced to Death—A military jury at Fort Bragg, NC, **Apr. 28** sentenced army Sgt. Hasan Akbar to death for killing 2 fellow soldiers at Camp Pennsylvania in Kuwait in March 2003. Using grenades and a rifle, Akbar, a Muslim, also wounded 14 other soldiers in the attack, attributed to religious extremism.

Taiwan Opposition Leader Meets With Chinese President—In the highest level meeting between the 2 sides in almost 60 years, the chairman of Taiwan's opposition Nationalist Party, Lien Chan, met with Chinese Pres. Hu Jintao **Apr. 29** to discuss a possible easing of hostilities between the People's Republic and Taiwan. The Taiwanese government, led by Pres. Chen Shui-bian, criticized the talks saying they did nothing to improve relations. Lien urged leaders from both governments to "maintain the status quo," meaning the unwritten arrangement under which China refrains from military action against Taiwan while Taiwan refrains from proclaiming independence.

General

Pope John Paul II Dies; Cardinal Ratzinger Elected to Succeed Him—Pope John Paul II, supreme pontiff of the Roman Catholic Church for more than a quarter century, died **April 2** in his apartment at the Vatican. Already afflicted with arthritis and Parkinson's disease, he suffered in his last weeks from a urinary tract infection and a bacterial infection that led to organ failure. Having chosen not to return to the hospital, he received last rites **Mar. 31.** The Vatican said **Apr. 1** that he remained lucid, but he lapsed into unconsciousness the next day.

The pope's body was carried to St. Peter's Basilica to lie in state on **Apr. 4**, and during the next 3 days some 2 million people passed by his bier. In Rome and throughout the world, the public mourned the passing of a widely admired, though to some extent controversial, figure who had been called the people's pope. (*See* Obituaries.)

Some 200 world leaders attended services for the pope. The U.S. contingent, which included Pres. George W. Bush and former presidents George H.W. Bush and Bill Clinton, arrived in Rome **Apr. 6**. The pope's body was taken outside the basilica for the funeral mass **Apr. 8**, with 300,000 in attendance, including a large Polish delegation, in St. Peter's Square. Many chanted for the pope to be proclaimed a saint. Cardinal Joseph Ratzinger, head of the Congregation for the Doctrine of the Faith, gave the homily. John Paul II was then buried in the church's crypt.

Cardinal Joseph Ratzinger of Germany, already one of the most powerful leaders of the Roman Catholic Church, was elected pope in voting by the Church's College of Cardinals in Rome on **Apr. 19**. Since 1981, he had headed the Congregation for the Doctrine of the Faith, which enforced doctrinal orthodoxy. He was also a close adviser to Pope John Paul II, and was seen as someone who would continue to implement the late pope's conservative policies. The new pope chose the name Benedict XVI; at 78, he was the oldest pope elected since 1730.

On **Apr. 18**, the cardinals had begun their conclave to choose the new pope. Voting was limited to the 115 cardinals who were present and under age 80. Meeting in the Sistine Chapel and pledged to secrecy, they reached a quick decision, giving Ratzinger the required two-thirds majority by the 4th ballot. The decision was signaled by the release of white smoke from a chimney above the stove in which the ballots were burned, and by a clanging of bells throughout Rome. Shortly thereafter, Benedict XVI appeared on a balcony above St. Peter's Square and greeted a huge crowd that had awaited the outcome.

In celebrating his first mass as pope, **Apr. 20**, he said he would continue John Paul's policies. On **Apr. 24** he was formally installed as the 265th pope.

North Carolina Wins Men's College Basketball Title—The University of North Carolina Tar Heels **Apr. 4** won the men's NCAA Division I basketball championship, defeating Fighting Illini of Illinois 75–70 in St. Louis, MO. The title was the 4th for the Tar Heels and the first for Coach Roy Williams, who had reached the Final Four four times while coaching at Kansas. Carolina's Sean May was named the outstanding player of the Final Four. North Carolina finished 33–4. Illinois ended its season at 37–2.

Baylor won the women's title in Indianapolis, IN, **Apr. 5**, over Michigan State, 84–62. Baylor was coached by Kim Mulkey-Robertson. Baylor's Sophia Young was named most outstanding palyer of the Final Four.

Prince Charles Marries His Longtime Companion—Prince Charles, heir to the British throne, married Camilla Parker-Bowles in a civil ceremony **Apr. 9** at the Guildhall in the town of Windsor. They had been romantically involved off and on since the 1970s. She was to be known as Her Royal Highness, the Duchess of Cornwall. After the ceremony, the archbishop of Canterbury, Rowan Williams, blessed the couple at Windsor Castle. Queen Elizabeth II, mother of the groom, attended only the latter event. The wedding had been postponed one day because of the pope's funeral, which Charles attended.

Tiger Woods Wins His 4th Masters Title—Tiger Woods, who had not won a major golf title since 2002, broke his slump **Apr. 10** by taking his 4th Masters tournament title. He beat Chris DiMarco by sinking a 15-foot birdie putt on the first playoff hole after the 2 had tied for the lead at 12 under par over 72 holes. In all, Woods had now won 9 major titles.

Extinct Woodpecker Rediscovered—The existence of at least one male ivory-billed woodpecker, a bird previously thought to be extinct, was confirmed **Apr. 28** by researchers after a careful study of video clips from 2004 and 2005. The last reliable sighting of the woodpecker, much of whose habitat was destroyed by human activity, was in 1944. Since then, there have been several possible sightings, but none could be confirmed. The bird was found in a protected forest area in eastern Arkansas, along the Louisiana border.

MAY 2005

National

Mistrial Declared in Iraq Prisoner Abuse Case—On **May 2** at Ft. Hood, TX, Pfc. Lynndie England pleaded guilty to 7 criminal counts related to her alleged mistreatment of prisoners at the Abu Ghraib prison in Iraq, shown in photos that came to symbolize the prisoner-abuse scandal. However, after her plea, on **May 4**, Pvt. Charles Graner, convicted in the same case, testified that England had obeyed his order in bringing a prisoner from his cell on a leash. Army Judge Col. James Pohl declared a mistrial the same day, and threw out England's guilty plea, saying it was not certain she understood she was acting illegally. Graner was the father of a child recently born to England.

The Army announced **May 5** that it had demoted Gen. Janis Karpinski, commander of the 800th Military Police Brigade, to colonel, for dereliction of duty and for failing to disclose an arrest for shoplifting; she had been responsible for the Abu Ghraib prison and other detention centers. The Army **May 5** confirmed reports that Lt. Gen. Ricardo Sanchez, former commander of U.S. troops in Iraq, had been cleared of responsibility for prison abuses. The Army said **May 11** it had reprimanded and fined Col. Thomas Pappas for dereliction of duty in mishandling interrogations. At Ft. Hood on **May 16**, Army Reserve Spec. Sabrina Harmon was convicted of abusing prisoners at Abu Ghraib; she was sentenced **May 17** to 6 months in prison and given a bad-conduct discharge. On **May 25**, Amnesty International released its 2004 Report, which accused the Bush administration of what it called "atrocious" human rights violations in Guantanamo Bay (Cuba), Afghanistan, and Iraq.

Bush Nominee to UN Post Stalled in Senate—Pres. George W. Bush's nominee for U.S. representative at the UN, John Bolton, narrowly survived a vote **May 12** in the Senate Foreign Relations Committee, which sent the nomination on to the full Senate but without a positive recommendation. One Republican, George Voinovich (OH), joined Democrats in refusing to recommend him. In the Senate some Democrats called for the White House to make available classified documents that they said might have bearing on Bolton's conduct. An attempt (requiring 60 votes) by Republicans on **May 26** to cut off debate failed, 56-42.

Pentagon Seeks to Close 33 Major Military Bases—The Defense Dept. revealed the names **May 13** of 33 major military bases that it wanted to close to save money—nearly $50 bil over 20 years. The realignment of personnel at 29 other bases was part of the plan. Members of Congress strongly objected to closings in their states, and the list was under review by an independent commission.

Hispanic Elected Mayor of Los Angeles—On **May 17**, Los Angeles got its first Hispanic mayor since 1872. Antonio Villaraigosa (D), a member of the City Council, defeated the incumbent mayor, James Hahn (D), 59% to 41%.

Compromise Averts "Nuclear Option"—Fourteen U.S. senators reached a compromise averting a deadlock over judicial nominees that could have stalled legislation for months. Democrats had indicated they would filibuster to prevent an up or down Senate vote on nominees they described as extreme. As the Senate began debate **May 18** on one nominee, Justice Priscilla Owen of the Texas Supreme Court, Majority Leader Bill Frist (R, TN) said he was prepared to invoke what others nicknamed the "nuclear option"—changing Senate rules to reduce from 60 to 51 the number of votes needed to cut off debate. Sen. Harry Reid (D, NV), the minority leader, warned that if the Republicans changed the rules Democrats would use parliamentary tactics to prevent transaction of regular business. On **May 23** a group of 7 senators from each party came up with a compromise; the Democrats would allow 3 of the 10 currently stalled judicial nominees to come to a vote, while Republicans would not support the rule change proposal. The Democrats said they would filibuster judicial nominees in the future only in "extraordinary circumstances." With that, the Senate, **May 24**, voted 81-18 to end the debate over Owen, and the next day she was confirmed, 55-43, to a seat on the U.S. 5th Circuit Court of Appeals.

Arthur Andersen Conviction Overturned—The U.S. Supreme Court, **May 3**, unanimously overturned the 2002 conviction of the accounting firm Arthur Andersen LLP for obstruction of justice in hindering an SEC investigation into Enron Corp., especially by destroying documents. The justices found that jury instructions did not make clear that the company had to be conscious that its actions were wrong. The conviction had resulted in the firm's going out of business.

International

Nuclear Nonproliferation Session Fails—Some 150 of the 187 nations that had signed the Nuclear Nonproliferation Treaty sent representatives to a treaty review conference, which opened at the UN in New York City **May 2**, but the conference ended in stalemate **May 27**. While the U.S. sought to focus attention on nuclear proliferation threats posed by Iran and North Korea, nonnuclear nations insisted on addressing reductions in nuclear armaments by the U.S. and other nuclear states. U.S. Asst. Sec. of State Stephen Rademaker, in a **May 2** speech, said that Iran's nuclear program should be curtailed because Iran had concealed it for almost 2 decades; Iran claimed its program was directed at producing energy for civilian use. Talks between Iran and the European Union had broken down, and an Iranian spokesman said **May 3** that Iran would restart some nuclear activities. On **May 25**, 3 European foreign ministers persuaded Iran to continue a temporary freeze.

Pakistan Captures Terrorist Leader—Pakistani forces **May 2** captured the man believed to be the 3rd-ranking leader in the al-Qaeda terrorist network, Abu Faraj al-Libbi. He was thought to have played a leading role in 2 attempts to assassinate Pres. Pervez Musharraf.

Iraqi Cabinet Sworn in; Violence Surges; Officials Visit—On **May 3**, over 3 months after the January elections, an Iraqi cabinet was sworn in. The new cabinet, headed by Prem. Ibrahim al-Jaafari, had 7 vacancies: 5 ministers and 2 deputy premiers. Some vacancies were filled **May 8**. Meanwhile violence continued. A car bomb **May 1** killed 25 at a funeral near the Syrian border. Prospective Kurdish police recruits were most of the 60 who died **May 4** when a bomb exploded in Erbil. A bombing in Baghdad **May 5** killed 22. In a U.S. offensive in northwestern Iraq, first reported **May 9**, some 125 insurgents were killed; 9 U.S. troops involved in the operation also died. On **May 11**, 79 Iraqis died in attacks in 3 cities. On **May 15**, the bodies of 46 Iraqi soldiers and civilians were found in and around Baghdad. An aide to the Grand Ayatollah Ali al-Sistani was killed **May 15.** U.S. officials said **May 18** that more than 450 Iraqis had been killed during the month to that point.

Sec. of State Condoleezza Rice, in Iraq **May 15**, urged the appointment of more Sunnis to the government. Two days later, Iranian Foreign Min. Kamal Kharrazi came to Baghdad, signaling the possibility of closer ties between Iran and Iraq. On **May 21** in Baghdad, 1,000 Sunnis agreed to form an alliance and join the political process. Beginning **May 24**, reports spread that Abu Musab al-Zarqawi, a top al-Qaeda leader, had been wounded. On **May 25**, U.S. Marines and Iraqi forces began a new offensive in Haditha, 180 miles west of Baghdad.

British Voters Return Blair to Power—The Labour Party, led by Prime Min. Tony Blair, retained control of Britain's Parliament in **May 5** elections. Labour won 356 seats in the 646-member House of Commons, the Conservatives 197, and the Liberal Democrats 62. The nationwide popular vote was closer among the 3 largest parties: Labour 35%, Conservative 32%, and Liberal Democrat 22%. Labour had never before won 3 straight elections; at the same time, no winning party had ever polled so small a portion of the popular vote. Labour's majority in Commons had shrunk to 67 seats over the combined total of all other parties, less than half its previous advantage. In Northern Ireland, the militant Democratic Unionist Party led by the Rev. Ian Paisley won 9 seats and became dominant there.

Blair's declining support was attributed in large part to his handling of the Iraq war. He campaigned with Chancellor of the Exchequer Gordon Brown, his rival within the Labour Party and expected successor. Michael Howard, the

Conservative leader, had called for controls on immigration and lower taxes. On **May 6**, Howard said he would step down as Conservative leader. David Trimble, winner of a Nobel Peace Prize and leader of the moderate Ulster Unionist Party, resigned **May 7**.

Leaders Commemorate End of World War II—Leaders of many nations came to Moscow **May 9** to observe the 60th anniversary of the end of World War II in Europe. Pres. George W. Bush was among those at a Victory Day parade in Red Square. While maintaining cordial relations with Russian Pres. Vladimir Putin, he spoke out against past Soviet and Russian policies. In a letter to Pres. Vaira Vike-Freiberga of Latvia, released **May 4**, Bush had recalled the suffering caused by the Soviet occupation and annexation of Baltic nations after the war. And in a speech in Riga, Latvia, **May 7**, he criticized the 1945 Yalta agreement between the U.S., Britain, and Soviet Union. On **May 8**, at Margraten, in the Netherlands, Bush visited a cemetery for U.S. troops. In Tbilisi, Georgia, **May 10**, he urged that all nations respect Georgia's "sovereignty and territorial integrity." Authorities then found a hand grenade lying 100 feet from the stage where Bush had stood; investigators **May 18** confirmed that the grenade had been live, perhaps failing to explode because of a soft landing.

Riots in Afghanistan Follow Magazine Report—Sixteen people were killed during riots that erupted in Afghanistan beginning **May 10**. The demonstrations came a week after a report in the **May 9** issue of *Newsweek* contending that interrogators at the U.S. detention center in Guantanamo Bay had flushed a copy of the Koran down a toilet. Most of the deaths occurred when Afghani police fired on demonstrators. Saying that its source could no longer confirm the Koran incident, *Newsweek* **May 15** apologized for the report, and on **May 16** issued a retraction. An Army investigation, reported **May 26**, found "no credible evidence" that the incident ever occurred, but five incidents involving some deliberate or unintentional mishandling of the Koran were found. The reported mishandling sparked anti-American protests in several Muslim countries, **May 27**. On **May 20** the *Sun*, a British newspaper, and the *New York Post* published photographs of imprisoned Iraqi dictator Saddam Hussein in his underwear; several groups criticized them as as inappropriate.

Canadian Prime Minister Survives Parliament Votes—Liberal Party Prime Min. Paul Martin of Canada barely held on to his job in May. Opponents in Parliament **May 10** prevailed, 153-150, in a vote that they said forced Martin to call a new election, but he discounted the vote as only procedural. On **May 19**, a confidence vote ended in a tie, but the presiding Speaker, a Liberal, then voted in Martin's favor. Martin had also been saved by a defection from Conservative Party ranks by Belinda Stronach, who was promised a cabinet seat.

Uzbek Troops Shoot Hundreds of Civilians—Government troops shot hundreds of civilians in Uzbekistan in May following an uprising. Protests had been building in Andijon in early May during the trial of 23 businessman accused of belonging to an Islamic movement. On the night of **May 12** 13 residents of Andijon seized arms from a garrison and freed 2,000 inmates from a prison. Troops moved into a square **May 13** and opened fire. Reports of the death toll, including those from refugees who had fled the city, ranged from 169 to 745. Pres. Islam Karimov said **May 14** that 10 troops had been killed.

First Lady Visits Middle East—First Lady Laura Bush traveled to the Middle East, beginning in Jordan, where on **May 20** she spoke to the World Economic Forum, emphasizing the importance of women's rights and education. She met with Palestinian women's leaders in the West Bank and with Jewish women in Jerusalem, **May 22**. Some Muslims objected to her presence at the Dome of the Rock, a Muslim shrine, and some Jewish protestors badgered her during her visit to the Western Wall, where she left a written prayer. In Egypt **May 23**, she congratulated Pres. Hosni Mubarak for scheduling an open presidential election. In Washington, **May 26**, Pres. Bush met with Palestinian Authority Pres. Mahmoud Abbas, the first visit by a Palestinian leader during Bush's presidency.

French Voters Reject European Constitution—In a nationwide referendum **May 29**, French voters refused to ratify the European Union constitution, which requires unanimous approval by member nations in order to go into force. The 55% vote against the constitution was a rebuff to Pres. Jacques Chirac, who had campaigned vigorously for its approval. Nine of 25 EU member countries had previously given approval; France was the first country to dissent. Opponents of the constitution contended that it would jeopardize French sovereignty and bring on an influx of cheap labor. On **May 31**, Jean-Pierre Raffarin was replaced as French premier by Interior Min. and former Foreign Min. Dominique de Villepin.

Blast Kills Muslim Pilgrims—A suicide bomb at a crowded Muslim shrine in Islamabad, Pakistan, exploded on **May 27**, the last day of a Shiite-Sunni religious festival, killing 19 people.

General

50-1 Long Shot Wins Kentucky Derby—A 50-1 dark horse, Giacomo, emerged from far back in a field of 20 horses to win the Kentucky Derby in Louisville **May 7**. He finished in 2 minutes, 2.75 seconds, a half-length ahead of Closing Argument, who was 71-1 to win. In the 2nd leg of horse racing's Triple Crown, the Preakness, held **May 21** in Baltimore, the favorite, Afleet Alex, prevailed in one minute, 55.04 seconds. Giacomo was third.

Koreans Score Breakthrough in Stem-Cell Research—*Science* magazine's web site reported **May 19** that scientists at Seoul National University in South Korea had achieved a major advance in stem-cell research. They had cloned embryos from patients with serious injuries and illnesses and then extracted stem cells matching the patients' cells, which the patients' immune systems would then accept. Pres. George W. Bush said **May 20** that he would veto a bill then in Congress that would fund research using new human embryonic stem cell lines. On **May 24**, the House, 238-194, approved the bill.

Wheldon Outduels Woman Driver to Win Indy 500—Dan Wheldon won the Indianapolis 500-mile auto race **May 29**, twice taking the lead from a female driver, Danica Patrick, during the last few dramatic laps. Patrick reduced her speed near the end to save gas. Wheldon, also low on fuel, ran out after crossing the finish line. Patrick, the only female contestant among the 33 starters, led 19 of the race's 200 laps, and became the first woman driver ever to head the pack.

Deep Throat Speaks Out—After a more than 30-year silence, W. Mark Felt, 91, revealed that he was "Deep Throat"—the source who guided and advised *Washington Post* reporters Bob Woodward and Carl Bernstein as they followed the story of the 1972 break-in at the Democratic National Committee headquarters at the Watergate complex in Washington all the way to the top of the Nixon administration. At the time, Felt was the No. 2 official at the FBI. Felt's identity was revealed **May 31** in a *Vanity Fair* article, and the story was confirmed by Woodward and Bernstein. His identity as Deep Throat had been suspected by many.

JUNE 2005

National

SEC Chairman Resigns—William Donaldson, chairman of the Securities and Exchange Commission, announced **June 1** that he would step down at the end of the month. A Republican, he had often sided with the 2 Democrats on the 5-member SEC, and some business leaders had accused him of going overboard in pursuing corporate abuses. Pres. George W. Bush announced **June 2** that he would nominate Rep. Christopher Cox (R, CA) as SEC head.

Washington Governor's Victory Upheld—The 2004 election of Washington state's Democratic governor, Christine Gregoire, was upheld **June 6** by a Washington court, effectively ending appeals by Dino Rossi, the defeated Republican candidate.

GM to Cut 25,000 Jobs—General Motors announced **June 7** that it would cut 25,000 jobs by 2008 and close some factories. At the time of the announcement, GM had 181,000 workers in North America. According to GM, the company was finding fewer buyers for its sport utility vehicles, largely because of soaring gas prices.

More Bush Federal Court Nominees Approved—A bipartisan May compromise in the Senate over judicial nominations resulted in the confirmation of 4 more nominees made by Pres. George W. Bush. Of these, 2 of had been strongly opposed by Democrats: Janice Rogers Brown, confirmed **June 8** for the U.S. Court of Appeals for the District of Columbia Circuit, 56-43; William Pryor, confirmed **June 9** for the 11th Circuit Court of Appeals in Atlanta, GA, 53-45.

Schiavo Autopsy Shows Irreversible Condition—Results of an autopsy of Terri Schiavo, a brain-damaged woman who died in March after her feeding tube was removed following a series of legal battles, was released **June 15**. Pinellas-Pasco County (FL) medical examiner Jon Thogmartin said that Schiavo had a brain only about half of its original size, and that the damage had been irreversible.

2 Ex-Tyco Executives Found Guilty—Two former executives of Tyco International Ltd. were found guilty **June 17** of conspiracy, grand larceny, securities fraud, and falsifying business records. A jury in New York State Supreme Court in Manhattan returned convictions on 22 of 23 counts against former CEO Dennis Kozlowski and former CFO Mark Swartz. They had allegedly sold artificially inflated stock for $430 mil, taken out $150 mil in unapproved loans and bonuses, and paid a former director an unapproved sum of $20 mil. Kozlowski testified that he had forgotten to include a $25 mil bonus on his 1999 tax return. Swartz said he did not realize until 2002 that a 1999 bonus of $12.5 mil had not been reported on his return.

Ex-Klansman Guilty in Deaths of 3 Civil Rights Workers—A former Ku Klux Klan member, Edgar Ray Killen, 80, was found guilty **June 21** of manslaughter in the deaths 3 civil rights workers, murdered in Mississippi 41 years earlier, to the day. The 3 victims were James Earl Chaney, Andrew Goodman, and Michael Schwerner. Killen had been one of 19 defendants charged in connection with the 1964 killings 3 years later. Seven were convicted of conspiracy and 8 acquitted, while 3, including Killen, went free when the all-white jury deadlocked. Killen, who was in poor health, did not take the stand at the new trial. On **June 23**, Judge Marcus Gordon sentenced him to 60 years in prison.

Supreme Court Term Ends With Flurry of Rulings—The U.S. Supreme Court ended its 2004-2005 term **June 27**, after several noteworthy rulings during the month.

On **June 6**, the court ruled 6-3 that Congress had the authority to forbid local, noncommercial production and use of marijuana for medicinal purposes. The case, *Gonzales v. Raich*, began in California as an attempt to block enforcement of federal anti-drug laws against uses of medicinal marijuana allowed by California state law. The lower court ruled that Congress had no authority to overrule the state law, but the Supreme Court reversed that opinion.

In a case involving municipal use of eminent domain for private development, *Kelo v. City of New London*, the court ruled 5-4, on **June 23**, that the city of New London, CT, could use the power of eminent domain to take, with compensation to the owners, private property along the Thames River so that private developers could build office space and a hotel. Usually, the power of eminent domain is used to obtain land for public works or transportation.

In the case *Van Orden v. Perry*, the court **June 27** ruled 5-4 that a monument on the grounds of the Texas state Capitol that displayed the Ten Commandments did not violate the First Amendment because it was part of a larger display commemorating state history and culture that had been built for a mostly secular purpose. However, in *McCreary County v. American Civil Liberties Union*, the court ruled, 5-4, that displays of the Ten Commandments on the walls of 2 Kentucky courthouses must come down, contending that they lacked a secular purpose.

In *MGM Studios v. Grokster, Ltd.*, the court **June 27** ruled that software companies producing internet file-sharing software can be sued if they intend for their customers to use the software to share songs, movies, and other software in violation of copyright laws.

Police cannot be sued for how they handle the enforcement of restraining orders, the court said **June 27** in a 7-2 ruling. The case, *Castle Rock v. Gonzalez*, involved a Colorado woman who sued police for not doing enough to prevent her estranged husband from killing her 3 daughters.

The court **June 27** declined to hear an appeal by 2 reporters who faced jail terms for refusing to reveal their sources of information pertaining to the leak of an undercover CIA agent's name. Matthew Cooper, reporter for *Time* magazine, and *New York Times* reporter Judith Miller, faced up to 18 months in jail for not naming their sources.

Bush Approves Spy Agency Changes—Pres. Bush **June 29** said he would create a national security service within the FBI to focus on intelligence as part of a reform of U.S. spy and investigation agencies. The shake-up came as part of the recommendations of a White House commission. Other actions taken by Bush included issuing an executive order to freeze the assets in the U.S. of those involved in the spread of weapons of mass destruction and forming a National Counter Proliferation Center to coordinate intelligence on foreign nuclear, chemical, and biological weapons.

Fed Boosts Interest Rates Again—The Federal Reserve Board boosted interest rates **June 30** by another quarter point, making the federal funds rate 3.25%, compared to 1% a year earlier.

U.S. Economy at a Glance: June 2005

Unemployment rate	5.0%
Consumer prices (change over 2004)	2.5%
Trade deficit (12 mo. through June)	$670.3 bil
Dow Jones closing, 2nd quarter	10,274.97
Dow Jones highest close, 2nd quarter (June 17)	10,623.07
Dow Jones lowest close, 2nd quarter (April 20)	10,012.36
2nd quarter GDP growth (annual rate)	3.3%

International

Netherlands Opposes European Constitution—Voters in the Netherlands **June 1** by a 62% majority rejected a draft constitution for the European Union that would have created a more politically and economically connected Europe. The vote came just 3 days after French voters as well had rejected the constitution. Some Dutch voters said they feared the Netherlands would be swallowed up in a European "superstate."

On **June 2**, Latvia became the 9th country to approve the constitution by parliamentary action. A 10th country, Spain, was the only country to have approved the constitution in a referendum. The charter can go into effect only when all 25 EU members ratify it. Government officials in Britain said **June 6** that Britain would suspend indefinitely its own planned referendum on the constitution. At a summit meeting in Brussels, **June 16**, EU leaders voted to drop the Nov. 2006 deadline for ratification. The EU's problems deepened **June 17** when a summit meeting in Brussels to adopt a budget for future years broke up amid acrimony.

Israel Releases More Palestinians—Continuing its promised prisoner-release program that began in February, Israel **June 2** released 398 Palestinians from a prison in the southern Negev desert.

Iraq Violence Continues, Stirring Debate—Insurgent activity in June continued to take a heavy toll. On **June 2**, the Iraqi interior ministry put the death toll among Iraqis at 12,000 during the past 18 months. On that day, at least 36 people were reported killed in insurgent attacks. Five U.S. marines were killed **June 9** in Haqlaniya when a bomb destroyed their vehicle. A bomb at a Baghdad restaurant **June 19** killed 23 Iraqis. A suicide car bombing in Falluja **June 23** killed 6 U.S. military personnel and wounded 13, mostly marines. Marines **June 17** opened an offensive near the Syrian border as part of an effort to stop the flow of insurgents and equipment across the border.

Rep. Walter Jones (R, NC), a supporter of the war, said **June 12** that he would introduce a bill asking the Bush administration to set a timetable for U.S. military withdrawal. The *New York Times* **June 22** quoted from a CIA report concluding that Iraq was now a training ground for Islamic fighters. Gen. John Abizaid told the Senate Armed Services Committee **June 23** that the Iraqi insurgency remained strong and that more foreign fighters were entering the country. During a CNN interview later the same day, however, Vice Pres. Richard Cheney, reiterated an earlier assertion that the insurgency was in its "last throes."

Pres. Bush **June 28** spoke to a military audience at Fort Bragg, NC, and to a prime-time television audience. He said that the Iraqi war was "vital" to U.S. national security, comparing insurgents there to the perpetrators of the Sept. 11, 2001, attacks. He said that setting a timetable for the withdrawal of U.S. forces would be helpful to insurgents and a "serious mistake."

In an advance for the political process, Iraqi political leaders agreed **June 16** to allow 15 Sunni Muslims to join the committee to write Iraq's new constitution.

Debate Over Guantanamo Continues—U.S. leaders continued to debate the future of the U.S. prison facility at Guantanamo, in Cuba. On **June 3**, the Defense Dept. released details of its investigation into incidents of desecration of the Koran at the prison, where 540 detainees were being held. Five incidents were noted. In one incident, an interrogator stood on the Koran during an interrogation. In another, a guard inadvertently splashed urine onto the holy book. The investigation came weeks after the retraction of a *Newsweek* article which erroneously accused guards of flushing copies of the Koran down the toilet.

Former Pres. Jimmy Carter **June 7** called for the closing of Guantanamo, while Pres. George W. Bush said **June 8** that his administration was exploring all options. Deputy Associate Atty. Gen. J. Michael Wiggins told a Senate committee **June 15** it was the Justice Department's position that legally Guantanamo detainees could be held indefinitely

North Korea Committed to Nuclear Talks—North Korean delegates to the UN told U.S. diplomats **June 6** that North Korea was committed to returning to the 6-nation talks on its nuclear weapons program. Getting the talks restarted was the focus of a meeting between Pres. Bush and South Korean Pres. Roh Moo Hyun in Washington, DC, **June 10**.

President of Bolivia Resigns—Pres. Carlos Mesa of Bolivia resigned **June 9** after several weeks of public protests. Demonstrators and police had clashed in the central plaza of La Paz, site of the presidential palace and Congress building. The crisis pits laborers and indigenous people from the poorer eastern highlands of Bolivia, against a wealthy population in the oil-rich south, who were calling for greater sectional autonomy. The former demanded nationalization of the country's energy resources and called for a new constitution that would give stronger representation to indigenous groups.

The president of the Supreme Court, Eduardo Rodriguez, was sworn in as president later on **June 9**; he promised early elections.

G-8 Countries Relieve Debt of Poorest Nations—Finance ministers of the Group of Eight (G-8) industrialized countries agreed at a meeting in London **June 11** to relieve 18 of the poorest countries of $40 bil in debt. The proposal was part of a British-led campaign to ease the debt burdens of poor nations while increasing development aid. Most G-8 nations would replace payments that the World Bank and the African Development Bank would have received. Payments due to the International Monetary Fund would be covered out of "existing sources."

Foes of Syria Win Election in Lebanon—Anti-Syrian candidates won a majority of seats in the Lebanese parliament in elections that ended **June 19**. The winning bloc was headed by Saad al-Hariri, a Sunni Muslim whose father, a critic of Syria and a former prime minister, had been assassinated in February, and by Walid Jumblatt, Druse leader of the Progressive Socialist Party. They would hold 72 of 128 seats.

Conservative Mayor of Tehran Elected President of Iran—In a **June 24** runoff presidential election, Iranian voters, in a landslide, elected religious conservative and mayor of Tehran Mahmoud Ahmadinejad. He defeated former Pres. Ali Akbar Hashemi Rafsanjani. Incumbent Pres. Mohammed Khatami, whose attempts at reform had mostly been thwarted by religious leaders, had served the maximum 2 terms allowed. The 2 finalists had survived the first round of voting **June 17,** in which none of the 7 presidential candidates got more than about 20% of the vote. The new president said **June 25** that he wanted to create a strong Islamic country, and on **June 26** that Iran would move forward with its nuclear program while continuing negotiations with Europeans.

U.S. Death Toll Reaches 19 in Afghan Mission—Nineteen U.S. military personnel died after a 4-man reconnaissance team was attacked on the ground in eastern Afghanistan and a helicopter transporting rescuers was shot down. The helicopter crash **June 28** killed all aboard, 8 Army crewmen and 8 Navy Seals. Other rescuers found the bodies of 2 members of the reconnaissance team **June 30**. A 3rd was found alive **July 3**, and the 4th was found dead **July 10**.

Bank of America to Buy MBNA—The Bank of America Corp **June 30** announced plan to acquire the credit card giant MBNA for $35 bil in cash and stock. The merger would make Bank of America the biggest U.S. credit card issuer, ahead of J.P. Morgan Chase and Citigroup.

General

Michael Jackson Acquitted of Molestation Charges—Pop star Michael Jackson was found not guilty of child molestation on **June 13** in Santa Barbara County Superior Court in Santa Maria, CA. He had been indicted on 10 counts of sexual misconduct, including charges that in 2003 he had molested a 13-year-old boy, a cancer patient, and had given the boy alcohol. The jury, having listened to more than 140 witnesses, including several celebrities, over 14 weeks, began deliberating **June 3**. Jurors later told the press that they didn't believe the accuser and his mother, apparently accepting the defense claim that the family was out to get money from Jackson.

New Zealand Golfer Wins U.S. Open—Michael Campbell of New Zealand won the U.S. Open golf tournament **June 19** in Pinehurst, NC. The defending champion, Retief Goosen of South Africa, faded from the lead in the final round. Campbell also outlasted Tiger Woods to win by 2 strokes. Campbell, ranked 80th in the world, joined Bob Charles as the only New Zealanders to win one of golf's 4 major tournaments.

San Antonio Takes NBA Title From Detroit—The San Antonio Spurs, playing at home in the 7th and final game of the NBA championship series **June 23**, defeated the defending champion Detroit Pistons 81-74 to claim the title. It was the Spurs' 3rd title in 7 years. During the game, Spurs center Tim Duncan led his team in scoring with 25 points and captured the Series MVP award for the 3rd time in his career.

Rev. Billy Graham Visits New York City—The Rev. Billy Graham, 86 years old and in weakening health, conducted a crusade in New York City **June 24-26**. The dominant American Christian evangelist of the last 60 years, Graham preached at the former World's Fair site in the borough of Queens. After acknowledging his advanced years, Graham admonished his audience, "Prepare to meet your God." His organizers said 230,000 people had attended the crusade.

Killer of 10 Pleads Guilty in Kansas—The notorious "B.T.K." killer, Dennis Rader, pleaded guilty **June 27** in Wichita, KS, to murdering 10 people during a killing spree that began in 1974. Rader, finally arrested in Feb. 2005, had given himself the nickname B.T.K. for "bind, torture, kill." Speaking in a matter-of-fact manner he recounted lurid details of his attacks on random targets aimed at fulfillment of sexual fantasies.

JULY 2005

National

Justice O'Connor To Retire—Sandra Day O'Connor, 75, the first woman to serve on the U.S. Supreme Court, announced **July 1** that she would retire, effective when her replacement was confirmed. O'Connor, who was nominated to the court in 1981 by Pres. Ronald Reagan and confirmed 99-0 by the Senate, was generally described as a moderate conservative. She often cast the deciding vote in 5-4 rulings. Her resignation created the first Supreme Court vacancy in 11 years, a near-record. A court spokesperson said **July 1** that she wanted to spend more time with her husband, who had Alzheimer's disease.

Chief Justice William Rehnquist, who was being treated for thyroid cancer, denied **July 14** that he had any plans to retire.

Reporter Jailed in CIA "Leak" Case—Judith Miller, a *New York Times* reporter, went to jail **July 6** for refusing to reveal information to a special prosecutor, citing an obligation to keep her source confidential. U.S. District Court Judge Thomas Hogan, in Washington, DC, had found her in civil contempt for refusing to cooperate with an investigation into the leaking of a CIA agent's name, Valerie Plame Wilson, to members of the press.

Time magazine reporter Matthew Cooper also faced contempt charges (both he and Miller had lost an appeal to the U.S. Supreme Court), but on **July 6** he stated that his source had released him from a pledge of confidentiality, allowing him to testify before a grand jury. *Time*, meanwhile, had agreed to hand over his notes and other documents.

By early July it became known that Karl Rove, deputy White House chief of staff, had spoken to reporters about the affair, but what he exactly said was unclear. Former Amb. Joseph Wilson claimed the Bush administration, by "outing" his wife, had sought revenge against him for disputing administration charges that Iraqi Pres. Saddam Hussein was seeking materials in Africa that could be used to build nuclear weapons. Pres. George W. Bush said **July 18** that he would fire any member of his staff who "committed a crime."

Bush Nominates Roberts for Court—Pres. Bush **July 19** nominated Judge John G. Roberts of the U.S. Court of Appeals for the District of Columbia Circuit for the Supreme Court seat being vacated by O'Connor. Bush had nominated Roberts for that the appeals court in 2003, and the Senate had approved him unanimously.

Roberts, 50, a graduate of Harvard College and Law School, had clerked for then-Assoc. Justice William Rehnquist. As deputy solicitor general during Pres. George H.W. Bush's tenure, he argued 39 cases before the U.S. Supreme Court. Confirmation hearings were expected in September.

Major Unions Pull Out of AFL-CIO—The U.S. labor movement split apart at the AFL-CIO national convention in Chicago on **July 25** when 2 major unions, the Teamsters and the Service Employees International Union (SEIU), declared they were pulling out of the federation. The latter union, with 1.8 mil members, had been the biggest component of the AFL-CIO. A 3rd union, the United Food and Commercial Workers, with 1.3 mil members, announced **July 29** that it was seceding. The seceding unions said they would form their own coalition and do more to reverse the long decline in union membership.

Congress Clears Transportation and Energy Bills, Trade Pact; Senate OKs Gun Bill—Before recessing for a month, the House (voting 402-8) and Senate (voting 91-4) gave final approval **July 29** to a $286.4 bil highway bill, criticized by some on both sides of the aisle for a high price tag and many giveaways. The Senate, the same day, also voted, 65-32, to approve a measure shielding gun manufacturers and dealers from liability in lawsuits brought by victims of shootings (the House had not acted on such a measure in the current Congress).

Earlier, the House (voting 275-156 **July 28**) and Senate (voting 74-26 **July 29**) gave final approval to a long pending energy bill. It provided incentives for development of new technologies, alternative fuels, and nuclear energy, many in the form of tax breaks, subsidies, and loan guarantees to the energy industry. The final measure did not include a controversial provision to open the Arctic Wildlife Refuge for oil drilling. The Bush administration hailed passage of the energy bill, though conceding that it would not have any short-term impact on rising gas prices. Critics said the energy bill was too timid in regard to curbing consumption and was a giveway to the energy industry.

On **July 29** the House, voting 217-215, narrowly passed the Central American Free Trade Agreement, eliminating most trade barriers between the U.S, and Central American countries. The Senate had approved it 54-45 on **June 30**. Most Democrats opposed the measure, partly because they contended it would cost American jobs; most Republicans supported it, arguing it would promote exports.

International

G-8 Nations Meet—Prime Min. Tony Blair was host **July 6-8** for a summit meeting of Group of 8 leaders, held in Gleneagles, Scotland. Those present represented the 7 major industrialized nations and Russia. Meanwhile, 200,000 demonstrators turned out in Edinburgh, Scotland, to support African aid and protest international trade and other policies.

Blair pushed for action on aid to impoverished African nations and on steps to alleviate global warming. He asked G-8 nations to triple their annual development aid to Africa, to $75 bil; the leaders agreed only to an increase to $50 bil by 2010. The global warming issue found the U.S. at odds with members who, unlike the U.S., had ratified the 1997 Kyoto Treaty, calling for specific sharp reductions in the emission of greenhouse gases. On **July 3**, G-8 negotiators found language that all 8 countries could accept when the U.S. agreed that humans were at least partly responsible for global warming. In return, the G-8 communiqué issued **July 8** omitted a call for specific targets.

Suicide Bombers Kill 52 Others in London; Second Attack Misfires—Coordinating their attacks, terrorists struck London's transportation system on the morning of **July 7**. While riding as passengers on 3 subway cars and a bus, 4 alleged suicide bombers ignited blasts that killed 52 other people and injured 700. The city had not experienced such violence since World War II. More attempted bombings occurred **July 21**, but no one was killed.

In a **July 7** claim on the Internet, a group saying it was affiliated with al-Qaeda took responsibility, but investigators remained unsure of a connection. Britain's Muslim Council condemned the attacks and promised to help with the investigation. Britain's population of 59 million includes about 1.6 mil Muslims.

Prime Min. Blair returned briefly from the G-8 summit in to oversee the investigation. Except for damaged sites, the London transportation system resumed service on **July 8**. Police determined that the bombs had weighed less than 10 pounds each and that the underground explosions occurred within 50 sec of each other at 8:50 AM. The bomb on the bus exploded at 9:47 AM. Police **July 12** said they had identified the 4 bombers, all Muslims. Three were of Pakistani descent but were born in Britain; the 4th was a native of Jamaica. Closed circuit TV images showed the 4 wearing backpacks at the King's Cross station 20 minutes before the first explosions.

During a botched bombing, 4 more bombs in backpacks—once again 3 on subway cars and 1 on a bus—were detonated **July 21**, but none exploded, and the would-be bombers fled. The next day, police released photos of the 4 suspects taken by security cameras. British police **July 22** shot dead a man on a subway car who reportedly failed to heed warnings to halt and was thought to be carrying explosives; the next day, British authorities admitted that the man, who in fact was unarmed, apparently had no link to the bombings. Over the following days, British authorities raided homes in London, Leeds, Birmingham, and Bristol in search of suspects and information. On **July 29** police arrested 3 men in London and 1 in Rome who were said to be the 4 suspects in the failed **July 21** bombing. By **July 31** about 20 people were in custody in connection with that bombing.

Al-Qaeda Kills Egyptian Envoy to Iraq; Bombings Continue—The terror organization al-Qaeda claimed **July 7** that it was responsible for the murder of Egypt's ambassador-designate to Iraq, Ihab al-Sharif, who was abducted in Baghdad **July 2**. On **July 5** a diplomat from Bahrain was shot in the hand, and shots were fired at the motorcade of the Pakistani ambassador.

Suicide bombers killed 40 people in Iraq **July 10,** including 25 at an army recruiting center in Baghdad, and on **July 13** a car bomber in Baghdad killed 28, including many children and a U.S. soldier. Eight suicide bombings in Baghdad **July 15** killed 22 and wounded scores, including 6 U.S. soldiers. In Musayyib, south of Baghdad, a bomber wearing explosives detonated them **July 16** next to a gasoline tanker, killing more than 70 and wounding 156. A truck bomber killed 22 outside a police station in Baghdad **July 24**. Insurgents launched coordinated attacks against Iraqi army checkpoints north of Baghdad **July 28** killing 6 Iraqi soldiers; 2 U.S. soldiers were killed the same day by roadside bombs. On **July 29** suicide bombers killed as many as 26 people at an army recruitment center in a N Iraqi town near the Syrian border.

The process of drafting a constitution continued. On **July 5**, the committee writing the document added 15 Sunni Arabs to create more balance. On **July 19** one of the Sunnis on the committee and a Sunni consultant to the committee were shot dead. Other Sunnis on the committee withdrew, fearing for their safety, but 12 returned to the committee **July 25**.

Rivals for Power in Sudan Sign Constitution—The crisis in Sudan eased **July 9** when Pres. Lt. Gen. Omar Hassan al-Bashir and his rival John Garang signed a constitution approved by parliament **July 6**. Garang, who had led the rebel Sudan People's Liberation Army, was then sworn in as vice president. Under the new constitution Garang would control an autonomous region in southern Sudan, and oil revenues were to be shared between the north and south. The southern region was to hold a referendum on independence in 2011. Although the civil war had basically ended in 2002, the death toll related to it, now put at 2 mil, continued to rise. Disease and famine were rampant. In separate negotiations in the western Darfur region, the government **July 5** reached agreement in principle with 2 rebel groups.

Sec. of State Condoleezza Rice came to Sudan **July 21** to meet with Bashir. The occasion was marred, however, when Sudanese security guards manhandled a U.S. reporter, NBC's Andrea Mitchell, and several members of the U.S. delegation.

John Garang, Sudanese Vice Pres. and former rebel leader was killed, along with 13 others, when his helicopter crashed into a mountain in southern Sudan **July 30**. Poor visibility was blamed for the crash. Garang was returning from a meeting with Pres. Yoweri Museveni of Uganda. His death was considered a blow to the fragile Jan. 2005 peace deal that ended Sudan's 21-year civil war.

Senate Gets Report on Guantanamo Prison—The Senate Armed Forces Committee **July 13** received a report from Air Force Lt. Gen. Randall Schmidt on interrogation methods at the Guantanamo Bay, Cuba, detention facility. The investigation concluded that methods were "safe, secure, and humane" and did not constitute torture, although they were abusive and degrading. The investigation also examined 26 complaints about mistreatment of detainees and determined that the methods used had been approved by the chain of command and were permissible.

China to Stop Tying Its Currency to Dollar—China announced **July 21** that it would no longer tie the value of its currency, the yuan, to the U.S. dollar, a move that some other countries regarded as long overdue. By pegging the value of the yuan to the dollar, China had given its exporters an advantage over those from other countries. China said that the yuan would be allowed to fluctuate in a narrow range against a group of other currencies.

Terrorist Bombs Strike Egyptian Resort—Three bombs, including 2 in cars, exploded within 5 minutes of each other in Sharm el-Sheik, an Egyptian resort, **July 23**, killing more than 80 people and wounding over 200. Many international tourists were present at the Ghazala Gardens Hotel, where a suicide bomber drove a truck through a glass window into the lobby. Other bombs exploded near a market and a café.

IRA Announces Disarmament—The Irish Republican Army, in a statement released **July 28**, renounced violence as a political tactic and said that all of its units were ordered to disarm and cease all terrorist activities, including armed robbery and money laundering Prime Min. Tony Blair praised the move, calling it "a step of unparalleled magnitude in the recent history of Northern. Ireland." Irish Prime Min. Bertie Ahern urged caution, saying IRAs deeds needed to match their words. The IRA's 36-year campaign of violence against Britain has claimed more than 3,600 lives.

General

Williams, Federer Each Win 3rd Wimbledon—On July 2, Venus Williams, the women's singles champion at Wimbledon in 2000 and 2001, reclaimed the title in 2005 by defeating Lindsay Davenport of the U.S., 4-6, 7-6, 9-7, in the longest (2 hours, 45 minutes) women's final ever at Wimbledon. The next day Roger Federer of Switzerland won his 3rd straight men's singles tennis championship at Wimbledon, defeating Andy Roddick of the U.S., 6-2, 7-6, 6-4.

U.S. Spacecraft Hits Comet, as Planned—An "impactor" module from the U.S. Deep Impact probe hit its target, Comet Tempel 1, on **July 4**. NASA had planned the collision in order to study the composition of the comet, whose inner core may hold material and compounds present in the early solar system. The probe was launched **Jan.12** and traveled 83 million miles to its rendezvous with Tempel 1.

London Chosen for 2012 Olympics—In a close vote July 6 in Singapore, the International Olympic Committee chose London as the site of the 2012 Olympic Summer Games. Three of the other contenders—Moscow, New York, and Madrid—were eliminated on the 1st, 2nd, and 3rd ballots, respectively. New York's chances were hurt when the city failed to get approval to spend $300 mil in public funds for a stadium on Manhattan's West Side. In the final round of Olympic voting, London edged Paris, 54-50.

Early Hurricanes Claim Lives—Hurricane Dennis hit Haiti and Jamaica July 7 and Cuba July 7-8, killing 57 people. After disrupting oil and natural gas production in the Gulf of Mexico, Dennis entered the U.S. east of Pensacola, FL, **July 10**. The storm killed at least 3 more people and causing widespread damage and power outages. The next hurricane, Emily, claimed 5 lives in Jamaica **July 17**, then hit Mexico's Yucatan Peninsula **July 18**, indirectly causing 3 deaths and leaving millions without water or power.

Tiger Woods Wins 10th Major—Tiger Woods won the British Open for the 2nd time **July 17**, posting a 14-under-par 274 on the historic St. Andrews golf course in Scotland. He finished 5 strokes ahead of Colin Montgomerie of Scotland. Jack Nicklaus, who had won a record 18 majors, had announced he would retire after competing in this tournament; his career ended when he failed to make the cut.

Armstrong Wins 7th Tour de France, Retires—Lance Armstrong, who had announced in advance that he would retire, won his 7th straight Tour de France on **July 24**. Armstrong had been diagnosed in 1996 with an aggressive form of testicular cancer. After aggressive chemotherapy he recovered, and went on to win a record 7 Tours de France.

***Discovery* Returns to Space**—The space shuttle *Discovery* and its 7-person crew blasted off from Cape Canaveral, FL, at 10:23 AM EST **July 26** ending a 2 ½–year shutdown of the shuttle program following the 2003 *Columbia* disaster. Its mission was to test safety improvements to the craft and bring supplies to the International Space Station. Though *Discovery* achieved successful orbit, analysis of footage taken from a camera on the giant liquid fuel tank showed that a piece of insulating foam had ripped off and barely missed hitting the orbiter craft. The *Columbia* disaster had been caused by a similar problem. On **July 27**, NASA announced it was suspending all future shuttle missions until the problem with the foam and heat shield could be resolved. On **July 28**, *Discovery* performed an in-space "backflip" as it approached the space station, so that crew members at the station could inspect the heat shield; the shuttle then successfully docked with the station.

Monsoon Floods Hit India—Heavy rains hit Mumbai (Bombay), India, and surrounding areas, reaching 37 inches in some areas, **July 26-27**, leading to severe flooding that by the end of the month had been found to cause close to 1,000 deaths according to authorities.

Astronomers Claim New Solar System Planet—Astronomers at the California Institute of Technology's Palomar Observatory reported **July 29** that an object they had discovered in 2003 that was 3 times as far away as Pluto, should be classified as the 10th solar system planet, based on recent determinations of its size and motion. The exact size of the object could not be determined, but it was now said to be larger than Pluto. Some astronomers have disputed whether Pluto itself, smallest of the known solar system planets, should be called a planet, but it remained classified as such by the International Astronomical Union.

AUGUST 2005

National

Bush Appoints Bolton as UN Ambassador—John Bolton was appointed U.S. ambassador to the UN by Pres. George W. Bush **Aug. 1**. As a recess appointment, the move did not require Senate confirmation. Senate Democrats had previously blocked the nomination of Bolton. Without a formal confirmation, Bolton would be able to serve only until the next Congress was convened in Jan. 2007.

Mother of Dead Soldier Protests Outside Bush Ranch—Pres. Bush began a 33-day working vacation at his ranch in Crawford, TX, **Aug. 2.** On **Aug. 6**, Cindy Sheehan, whose son Casey had been killed in Iraq, set up camp outside the Bush ranch and asked for a meeting with the president. Attracting media attention, she became a vehement critic of the war and was joined by about 50 supporters at "Camp Casey," set up along a road to the ranch. Bush, who had previously met with her and other parents of soldiers killed in Iraq, declined to meet with her. At an **Aug. 11** news conference he did respond, arguing that pulling out of Iraq now would endanger U.S. security. In a Salt Lake City (UT) speech **Aug. 22**, Bush argued that the nation owed it to the Americans killed in Iraq and Afghanistan to continue the fight. On **Aug. 27**, a contingent of military families and others who supported the war held a counter-rally in Crawford attended by 1,500.

Energy and Transportation Bills Signed as Oil Prices Soar—Pres. Bush signed a major energy bill **Aug. 8** at Sandia National Laboratories in Albuquerque, NM as the price of oil climbed toward $70 a barrel, and gas rose to near $3 a gallon, both all-time highs. The bill, passed with bipartisan support but regarded by many critics as too mild, sought to stimulate domestic production of both traditional and alternative energy sources by granting $14.6 bil in tax breaks for producers of energy and providing subsidies for deep-water drilling research. The bill also mandated greater use of gasoline additives, including ethanol, and extended daylight saving time by a month to encourage conservation. On **Aug. 10**, in a plant in Montgomery, IL, Bush signed the $286.4 bil surface transportation bill, which will fund construction of highways, bridges, and other public works. It was loaded with $24 bil in "pork barrel" projects.

Republicans Retain Ohio House Seat by Close Margin—In a special election **Aug. 2** to fill a U.S. House vacancy, the Republicans narrowly held onto a traditionally Republican seat. The winner, with 52%, was Jean Schmidt, a former state legislator and abortion opponent. She defeated Paul Hackett (D), a Marine Corps reserve major who was the first veteran of the Iraq war to run for Congress and a critic of Pres. Bush's Iraq policies.

More Ex-WorldCom Officials Sentenced—Between **Aug. 5** and **11**, 4 former WorldCom executives were given prison sentences in the $11 bil accounting fraud case that had wrecked that telecommunications company. A 5th received probation. Former CFO Scott Sullivan was sentenced, **Aug. 11**, to the longest term, 5 years. In July, former WorldCom CEO Bernard Ebbers had been sentenced to 25 years.

Katrina Strikes New Orleans and Gulf Coast—After striking the Atlantic coast of Florida **Aug. 26**, causing flooding that claimed 11 lives, Hurricane Katrina moved into the Gulf of Mexico, where it picked up strength, reaching Category 5 for a time. Heeding government advice, thousands of Gulf Coast residents fled, in one of the largest evacuations in U.S. history. Katrina finally struck the coast early on **Aug. 29,** causing devastation, particularly in Gulfport and Biloxi, MS, and Mobile, AL.

New Orleans, vulnerable because of being below sea level, initially escaped the brunt, but a major breech in a levee on Lake Pontchartrain the next day brought flooding to severe levels. With more than 10,000 refugees crowded into the Superdome and the city as a whole uninhabitable, Louisiana Gov. Kathleen Blanco ordered a total evacuation **Aug. 31,** as the Army Corps of Engineers sought to stem the flooding. But many were unable to evacuate.

There was no reliable estimate of the total damages and death toll as of **Aug. 31**. At least 1 mil people were left without power from Louisiana to the Florida Panhandle. The Bush administration **Aug. 31** announced the release of oil from the strategic petroleum reserve to compensate for a crippling of Gulf oil production, and the price of crude began to fall from an Aug. 30 high of $71 a barrel.

See also "The Katrina Disaster" feature, page 5.

International

U.S. Troop Deaths Rise as Iraqis Debate Constitution—As Iraqis debated a new constitution, a sharp increase in American casualties added to a growing sense of unrest. Between July 31 and Aug. 4, 30 U.S. service members were killed. U.S. and Iraqi troops looking to secure the international border, launched a new offensive **Aug. 5**. Defense Sec. Donald Rumsfeld said **Aug. 9** that insurgents were using explosives brought in from Iran. Car-bomb attacks killed 43 in Baghdad **Aug. 17**. A roadside bomb killed 4 U.S. soldiers in Samarra **Aug. 18**. In neighboring Jordan, 3 rockets were fired at 2 U.S. Navy ships in port at Aqaba; they missed, but one Jordanian soldier was killed.

After negotiators failed to meet an **Aug. 15** deadline for a draft constitution, the National Assembly granted a one-week extension. Kurdish and Shiite leaders were pushing for a loose regional federation; Sunnis opposed this, partly because they feared being shut out of oil proceeds. Kurds in particular wanted the right to be able to secede from the country. Secularists, especially supporters of equal rights for women, fought to prevent language establishing Islamic law as supreme.

The drafting body presented the text of a constitution to the National Assembly **Aug. 22**, while they continued to negotiate over disputed issues. Those talks ended **Aug. 26** when the Shiite and Kurd representatives gave up trying to find compromise language acceptable to the Sunni delegates. The draft text was formally presented to the assembly **Aug. 28**. Sunni leaders urged that the constitution be rejected in the October referendum.

King Fahd Dies—King Fahd, who had ruled Saudi Arabia since 1982, died in Riyadh **Aug. 1** after a long period of ill health. He was succeeded by his half-brother, Crown Prince Abdullah bin Abdul Aziz, who had been the country's de facto leader for a decade.

Violence Returns to Sudan After Vice President Dies—The government of Sudan confirmed **Aug. 1** that Vice Pres. John Garang, along with 13 others onboard, had been killed the night of July 30-31 when their helicopter crashed into the mountains in bad weather. On learning of Garang's death, his followers rioted in the capital and elsewhere for several days; 130 persons were killed. Salva Kiir Mayardit, who with Garang had co-founded a rebel army, was sworn in as vice president **Aug. 11**.

Bush Signs Central America Trade Agreement—Pres. Bush **Aug. 2** signed the Central America Free Trade Agreement (CAFTA), which the U.S. had negotiated with 6 other countries. The agreement would allow greater access for U.S. products in El Salvador, Guatemala, Honduras, Costa Rica, the Dominican Republic, and Nicaragua. The last 3 countries had not yet approved it. About half of U.S. farm products and 80% of U.S. manufactures would become tariff-free immediately; other tariffs would be dropped over time. The agreement, opposed by labor and environmental groups, narrowly made it through the House (217-215) and the Senate (55-45) on July 28.

Blair Gets Tough With Extremists; Bomb Suspects Arrested—Responding to the July bombings and attempted bombings in London, Prime Min. Tony Blair **Aug. 5** proposed steps to make it easier to deport those inciting terrorism and advocated shutting down extremist organizations, mosques, bookstores, and Internet sites.

On **Aug. 1**, Italian prosecutors charged an Ethiopian man with international terrorism; he had been seized in Rome in late July and reportedly admitted being part of the botched July 21 plot. In the following days in London, 4 other suspects were charged with conspiracy to commit murder or attempted murder. By **Aug. 8**, 5 others had been charged in Britain with assisting the would-be bombers.

Six Nations Discuss North Korea's Nuclear Plans—Six-nation talks focused on N. Korea's nuclear ambitions recessed in Beijing **Aug. 7** with no agreement. The 5 other participants—China, Japan, Russia, S. Korea, and the U.S.—all sought unsuccessfully to persuade N. Korea to abandon its nuclear-weapons program.

Third Report Issued on UN Oil-for-Food Scandal—New evidence and allegations relating to the oil-for-food scandal came to light **Aug. 8** with the 3rd report by the UN Independent Inquiry Committee. The report said that Efraim Nadler, a friend of Benon Sevan, former director of the oil-for-food program, had used a front company in Switzerland to hide almost $600,000 in profits from oil allocations to the Middle East Petroleum Co. Paul Volcker, head of the committee, said that Alexander Yakovlev, a UN procurement officer, had gotten $1 mil in improper payments from contractors. In a separate case resulting from a separate investigation into improper payments from contractors, Yakovlev pleaded guilty in U.S. District Court in New York **Aug. 8** to conspiracy, wire fraud, and money laundering. Sevan **Aug. 7** denied wrongdoing. A Danish company, Grundfos, admitted **Aug. 19** that it had paid kickbacks to Iraqi authorities to win 2 orders.

Israeli Evacuation of Gaza Settlements Completed—Prime Min. Ariel Sharon accomplished his goal of evacuating Israeli settlers from the Gaza Strip **Aug. 23**, after the army used force to remove many occupants and their supporters. In addition to 21 Gaza settlements, 4 West Bank settlements were part of the evacuation plan, which included 8,500 people altogether. Sharon saw the evacuation as a necessary step to show Israel's commitment to ongoing negotiations with the Palestinians. Former Prime Min. Benjamin Netanyahu had dissented, resigning from the cabinet **Aug. 7.**

General

First Cloning of a Dog Reported by Korean Scientists—South Korean scientists reported **Aug. 3** the first successful cloning of a dog. Dogs had presented difficulties for cloning. The research team had implanted 1,095 cloned eggs in female dogs, achieving only 3 pregnancies. One was a miscarriage, and one pup survived only 22 days. The 3rd, a male named "Snuppy" for "Seoul National University Puppy," was born Apr. 24 and thrived. The genetic donor was a male Afghan hound and the mother a Labrador retriever.

Shuttle Lands Safely After In-Space Repairs—The space shuttle *Discovery*, diverted by bad weather from its scheduled landing site in Florida, landed safely **Aug. 9** at Edwards Air Force Base, CA. *Discovery* had orbited earth 219 times in 14 days. In the first-ever in-flight repair of a shuttle, **Aug. 3,** Stephen Robinson, joined in a spacewalk by Soichi Noguchi, removed 2 strips of ceramic-coated cloth from the shuttle's nose that could have overheated on the shuttle's return to the Earth's atmosphere.

Hundreds Killed in Baghdad Stampede—A suicide-bomb scare during a Shiite religious procession attended by thousands **Aug. 31**, led to a stampede on a bridge spanning the Tigris River in Baghdad, leaving about 1,000 dead and hundreds injured. Most of those killed drowned in the river or were trampled to death. In the end there was no evidence of a suicide bomber.

SEPTEMBER 2005

National

Two More Airlines Declare Bankruptcy—Delta and Northwest airlines both filed for bankruptcy **Sept. 14**, joining United and US Airways, which were already operating under bankruptcy. Delta and Northwest cited a sharp increase in the cost of fuel.

2nd Hurricane Pounds Gulf Coast; Bush Acknowledges Slow Katrina Response—The Gulf Coast, devastated after Hurricane Katrina struck in late August, suffered a 2nd, lighter blow when Hurricane Rita hit land at the Louisiana-Texas state line **Sept. 24**.

After widespread criticism of the federal rescue and recovery effort, Pres. George W. Bush had visited Mobile (AL), Biloxi (MS), and New Orleans (LA) **Sept. 2**, and conceded that the government's efforts were "not acceptable." The same day he signed a $10.5 bil disaster-recovery bill approved by Congress. The president revisited the area **Sept. 5**, and signed a $51.8 bil relief measure on **Sept. 8**.

National Guard and active-duty troops had begun to arrive in New Orleans in force **Sept. 2**, and by **Sept. 3** the thousands who had jammed the convention center and the Superdome had largely been evacuated, mostly to Houston, TX. Gov. Rick Perry (TX) said **Sept. 3** that at least 230,000 evacuees had taken shelter in the state. In New Orleans **Sept. 4**, police shot and killed 4 people after allegedly being fired upon. It was reported **Sept. 5** that 500 of 1,500 New Orleans police officers were not reporting for duty.

On **Sept. 5**, Michael Chertoff, secretary of Homeland Security, announced that Coast Guard Vice Adm. Thad Allen would take over major responsibilities in the Gulf region; the much-criticized FEMA head Michael Brown returned to Washington, DC, and on **Sept. 12** resigned his post, saying that he did not want controversy over his performance to be a distraction.

Prosecutors **Sept. 13** charged the operators of St. Rita's Nursing Home in Violet, LA, with negligent homicide in the deaths of 34 people at the home, who had apparently been left to the mercy of the floods.

On **Sept. 15**, Pres. Bush, speaking from Jackson Square in the French Quarter of New Orleans acknowledged responsibility for an inadequate federal response, and outlined proposals for recovery. He called for a Gulf Opportunity Zone offering tax incentives and small-business loans and an Urban Homesteading Act that would provide land, job-training, and education to people seriously impacted by Hurricane Katrina.

As Hurricane Rita approached the Gulf Coast, Nagin **Sept. 19** ordered New Orleans evacuated once again. Rita passed 50 miles south of Key West, FL, on **Sept. 20**. On **Sept. 21**, Gov. Perry ordered residents along the Texas coast to evacuate. A mass exodus began from Houston, the nation's 4th-largest city, and nearby Galveston, a small island city that in 1900 was hit by the deadliest hurricane in U.S. history. On **Sept. 23**, a bus transporting elderly people from a senior center caught fire south of Dallas; exploding oxygen tanks added to the chaos, and 23 aboard died.

By the time Rita touched land **Sept. 24**, nearby areas had been largely evacuated, and the death toll was expected to be low. Immense rainfall created rising waters inland, and parts of New Orleans that had dried out were reflooded. On **Sept. 25**, even as some small coastal towns remained underwater, residents of Houston were streaming back home. With energy costs projected to remain high, Bush **Sept. 26** called upon citizens and federal agencies to cut back on nonessential driving.

Chief Justice Rehnquist Dies; Roberts Is Named and Confirmed to Replace Him—William H. Rehnquist, the 16th chief justice of the United States, died **Sept. 3**. He had been suffering from thyroid cancer. Pres. Bush announced **Sept. 5** that he would nominate U.S. Circuit Judge John G. Roberts Jr. to succeed him. He had already nominated Roberts to replace retiring Associate Justice Sandra Day O'Connor, with confirmation hearings for that position still pending.

(*See also* the feature "Transition at the Supreme Court," page 7.)

Pres. Richard Nixon had nominated Rehnquist to the Supreme Court as an associate justice in 1971, and Pres. Ronald Reagan had nominated him for chief justice in 1986. Highly regarded for his collegial approach to leading the court, Rehnquist generally voted with conservatives on issues ranging from states rights to abortion. He was part of a 5-4 majority in 2000 that left George W. Bush as the winner of the 2000 presidential election. After funeral services **Sept. 7**, Rehnquist was buried in Arlington National Cemetery.

From **Sept. 12** to **15**, Roberts testified before the Senate Judiciary Committee. Like many past nominees to the Court, he declined to answer specific questions on issues that the Supreme Court might take up in the future, but he did say he would respect precedents, which seemed to encourage supporters of *Roe* v. *Wade*, the controversial 1973 decision that upheld abortion rights.

The committee approved the Roberts nomination, **Sept. 22**, by a vote of 13-5, with 3 Democrats joining all 10 Republicans in support. On **Sept. 29**, Roberts easily won confirmation by the full Senate, 78-22, with half of the Democrats (22) and 1 independent joining all 55 Republicans to support him. Roberts was sworn in the same day as 17th chief justice of the Supreme Court; at 50 years of age he became the youngest chief justice since John Marshall (45) in 1801.

Female Private Convicted in Abu Ghraib Abuse Case—Pfc. Lynndie England was convicted **Sept. 26** of conspiracy and abuse of Iraqi prisoners. She had been photographed posing with prisoners at the Abu Ghraib prison in Iraq. A jury of 5 Army officers at Ft. Hood, TX, found her guilty of 6 of 7 counts. On **Sept. 28** she was sentenced to 3 years in prison.

U.S. Economy at a Glance: September 2005

Unemployment rate	5.1%
Dow Jones closing, 3rd quarter	10,568.70
Dow Jones highest close, 3rd quarter (July 28)	10,705.55
Dow Jones lowest close, 3rd quarter (July 6)	10,270.68

House Majority Leader Indicted—Rep. Tom DeLay (R, TX), majority leader of the House, was indicted in Texas **Sept. 28** for allegedly conspiring to violate a state fundraising law. Ronnie Earle, a prosecutor in Austin, TX, charged that DeLay had conspired with 2 associates to launder illegal corporate political campaign donations through the Republican National Committee, using the funds in support of GOP candidates for the Texas legislature. DeLay denounced the indictment as political and said he was innocent of the charges. Complying with a GOP House rule, he temporarily stepped down from his leadership post after being indicted. The GOP House caucus chose Majority Whip Rep. Roy Blunt (MO) as interim leader. DeLay was indicted Oct. 3 on additional charges related to money laundering.

Reporter Freed, Testifies in CIA Leak Case—*New York Times* reporter Judith Miller was freed **Sept. 29** after 12 weeks in jail, when she agreed to testify before a grand jury investigating the leak of a CIA agent's name to the media; she said she had been personally released from a pledge of confidentiality by a source.

International

U.S. Troops Take Iraq Border City; Insurgents Step Up Bombings of Civilians—On **Sept. 2**, 5,000 U.S. and Iraqi troops entered Tal Afar, a northern Iraqi city controlled by insurgents. Iraqi and U.S. officials said **Sept. 11** that most insurgents had fled from Tal Afar, and that about 150 had been killed. Elsewhere in northern Iraq, on **Sept. 3**, 17 Iraqi soldiers and 4 civilians were killed in insurgent attacks. Near the Syrian border, **Sept. 5**, insurgents seized the town of Qaim. In the south, 2 bombings in Basra **Sept. 7** killed 20 people. Twelve suicide bombings in Baghdad **Sept. 14**, aimed at Shiites and apparently carried out by Sunnis, claimed at least 167 lives and wounded nearly 600. A suicide car bombing was the most lethal attack, killing at least 112. A bomb in a Shiite suburb of Baghdad killed 30 people **Sept. 17**. Among other incidents a wave of bombings in late Sept. killed more than 150 people, including more than 60 Iraqis killed by car bombs **Sept. 29** in the Shiite city of Balad. As of Sept. 17, there had been 1,895 military deaths in Iraq since Mar. 19, 2003, 1,472 of them being battle deaths.

Mubarak Wins Contested Presidential Election—Pres. Hosni Mubarak of Egypt won election **Sept. 7** to his 5th 6-year term. Under internal and international pressure, he had agreed for the first time to allow a contested election for president. Official results announced **Sept. 9** gave him 88.6% of the vote. The turnout was low, with only 23% of registered voters going to the polls.

Report Cites Corruption in UN Oil-for-Food Program—An independent committee, headed by former U.S. Fed chairman Paul Volcker, issued a report to the United Nations **Sept. 7** on the oil-for-food scandal. The report described "corrosive corruption" in the UN administration of the program, which allowed Iraq under Saddam Hussein to sell limited amounts of oil supposedly to purchase humanitarian supplies such as food and medicine. The report found that the program had been laxly and corruptly administered, enriching the regime of Saddam Hussein as well as some UN personnel and others. UN Sec.-Gen. Kofi Annan was blamed for lax oversight and ineffective management, but not accused of intentional wrongdoing. Deputy Sec.-Gen. Louise Frechette was criticized for not mentioning in her reports a kickback scheme in which Saddam Hussein got billions of dollars from companies to which the regime awarded lucrative oil-for-food contracts.

On **Sept. 1**, Vladimir Kuznetsov, a Russian who was chairman of the UN General Assembly's budget oversight committee, was indicted in New York City on money-laundering charges.

Israel Completes Pullout from Gaza Strip—The last Israeli troops left the Gaza Strip **Sept. 12**, under a pullout plan adopted by the Israeli government. Palestinians immediately reclaimed the area, which Israel had controlled since the 1967 war. On **Sept. 15**, in his first-ever address to the UN General Assembly in New York, Prime Min. Ariel Sharon of Israel said the withdrawal showed Israel was serious about making peace with the Palestinians.

German Parliamentary Election Is Inconclusive—Germans voted in a national parliamentary election **Sept. 18**, but no clear winner emerged. Incumbent chancellor Gerhard Schroeder and his party, the Social Democrats, had been the underdogs, primarily because of a slack economy and an 11% unemployment rate. The leader in the polls had been Angela Merkel, leader of the more conservative Christian Democrats. Although the voting in Dresden was delayed for 2 weeks, a nearly complete tally did give a plurality to the Christian Democrats, but only a small one—225 seats over the Social Democrats' 222 seats in the 613-seat Bundestag. Neither side initially appeared able to form a government.

North Korea Agrees to Abandon Nuclear Weapons Programs—North Korea and 5 other nations **Sept. 19** signed a statement in which North Korea agreed in principle to forgo its nuclear-weapons development in return for economic assistance. The agreement, in Beijing, China, was hailed as a possible end to years of sporadic, often tense negotiations.

In 1994, North Korea and the United States had agreed that the former would dismantle its nuclear programs, but North Korea reneged on that agreement in 2002. Six-way talks, also including China, Japan, Russia, and South Korea, began in 2003. North Korea conceded in Feb. 2005 that it had nuclear weapons. The current round of talks began **Sept. 13**.

A breakthrough occurred **Sept. 16** when the parties agreed in principle to discuss giving North Korea a light-water nuclear reactor, designed to meet energy needs but not a likely component of an arms program. In its **Sept. 19** statement, North Korea agreed to give up all its existing nuclear weapons and ongoing programs and also to rejoin the Nuclear Nonproliferation Treaty and allow inspection of its facilities. In the statement, the United States said it had no nuclear weapons deployed in South Korea and did not intend to attack North Korea.

General

Federer Repeats as U.S. Open Tennis Champion—Roger Federer of Switzerland won his 2nd straight men's U.S. Open tennis title in New York **Sept. 11**, defeating Andre Agassi of the United States, 6-3, 2-6, 7-6, 6-1. On **Sept. 10**, Kim Clijsters of Belgium had won the women's title, defeating Mary Pierce of France, 6-3, 6-1.

OCTOBER 1-15

National

Bush Nominates Miers; New Court Session Opens— Pres. George W. Bush announced **Oct. 3** that he would nominate his White House counsel, Harriet E. Miers, to be an associate justice on the U.S. Supreme Court. If confirmed, she would succeed Justice Sandra Day O'Connor, who had agreed to continue on the court until her successor was confirmed. Miers, would be the 3rd woman ever to serve on the nation's highest court. Some conservative leaders expressed disapproval of Miers, saying she had no known position on abortion and other issues of concern. In an **Oct. 4** news conference, Bush defended his choice, saying that he understood "the type of person she is and the type of judge she will be."

The Supreme Court opened its new term **Oct. 3**, with John G. Roberts Jr. presiding for the first time as the 17th chief justice of the United States.

(See the feature article "Transition at the Supreme Court," page 7.)

Abuses by Priests Documented in Los Angeles—Documents released **Oct. 11** showed that the Roman Catholic archdiocese of Los Angeles had moved priests accused of sexual abuse from one parish to another and given them counseling in the belief that their behavior could be changed. Information concerning 126 priests dated as far back as the 1920s. Cardinal Roger Mahony, head of the archdiocese, came under harsh criticism **Oct. 12** for allegedly having shielded priests from the law.

Inflation Shows Strong Rise for September—The Commerce Dept. **Oct. 14** reported that the consumer price index, which had been rising steadily during 2005, jumped 1.2% in September, the biggest monthly rise since March 1980, putting it up 4.7% from Sept. 2004. Energy costs in the wake of Hurricane Katrina were a major factor, and the average retail price for a gallon of regular gas was $2.82 by Oct. 14, up from $1.99 a year earlier. However, the core inflation rate, excluding energy and food, a rate that had been steady for several months, rose just 0.1%, and was up just 2% from a year earlier.

International

Bombs Kill 22 in Indonesia—Bombs exploded in 3 restaurants in tourist areas on the Indonesian island of Bali, **Oct. 1**, killing 23 people, including the 3 bombers, and injuring more than 90. Photographs of the heads of the presumed bombers, severed in the explosions, were shown on television and in newspapers. The U.S. **Oct. 6** offered a $10 mil award for capture of a suspect known as Dulmatin, a senior figure in the Islamic militant group Jemaah Islamiah. He was believed to be behind this bombing and the bombing of nightclubs in Bali that killed over 200 people in 2004.

Elsewhere, authorities in the Netherlands **Oct. 14** arrested 7 Islamic radicals believed to have been planning attacks on government politicians and buildings.

Operation "Iron Fist" Launched in Iraq—In the latest effort to rout insurgents from Iraqi towns near the Syrian border, 1,000 U.S. troops attacked Sadah and neighboring towns **Oct. 1**. The U.S. military said that it had killed more than 50 insurgents in the operation, which ended **Oct. 7**.

Insurgents threatened to step up attacks during the Islamic holy month of Ramadan, which began **Oct. 5**. A bomb outside a Shiite mosque in Hilla, south of Baghdad, **Oct. 5** killed 25. An explosion on a bus in Baghdad on **Oct. 6** killed 10. The U.S. military said **Oct. 7** that 6 Marines had been killed in 2 bomb attacks. More than 40 people were killed in attacks **Oct. 11**, and 30 died in a bombing at an army recruitment center **Oct. 12**.

Atomic Energy Agency Wins Nobel Peace Prize—The Nobel Peace Prize was awarded **Oct. 7** to Egyptian diplomat Mohamed ElBaradei and the International Atomic Energy Agency (IAEA) that he headed. The Nobel committee honored him and the IAEA "for their efforts to prevent nuclear energy from being used for military purposes and to ensure that nuclear energy for peaceful purposes is used in the safest possible way."

Germany Gets First Woman Chancellor—Angela Merkel, leader of the Christian Democratic Union (CDU), became the first woman chancellor of Germany **Oct. 10**, succeeding Gerhard Schroeder of the Social Democratic Party (SDP), who had been chancellor for 7 years. The September voting for the Bundestag had been inconclusive with the CDU winning a few more seats than the SDP, but falling well short of a majority. Under an **Oct. 10** compromise, the SDP would lose the chancellorship but control 8 of the 14 ministries in the new government, including finance and foreign affairs. Merkel was the first person from the former East Germany to become chancellor.

Iraqis Vote on New Constitution—Millions of Iraqis went to the polls, **Oct. 15**, to vote on a new constitution. In contrast to the situation in the January election, violence was not widespread. However, in one major incident, 5 U.S. soldiers were killed by a roadside bomb west of Baghdad. Voting was reported as heavy in some Sunni areas. On **Oct. 12**, after the transitional assembly agreed it would consider changes in the constitution following a general election slated for Dec. 2005, the Iraqi Islamic Party, the largest Sunni party, had dropped its opposition to a yes vote. But it remained uncertain whether the constitution would achieve the minimal 1/3 vote in Sunni areas that was needed for passage.

At Least 128 Killed in Clashes in Southern Russian Town—On **Oct. 13**, an estimated 100 Islamic militants attacked several law enforcement offices and two gun shops in Nalchik, Russia. The fighting resulted in the deaths of 72 militants, 24 law enforcement officers, and at least 12 civilians, according to initial government figures. Chechen rebels claimed involvement, but officials said most of the militants were from local areas. At least 18 hostages were taken, but all survived and were released or freed. Order was restored by **Oct. 15**.

General

Avian Flu Responsible for 1918 Pandemic—Two teams of federal and university scientists announced **Oct. 5** that the highly infectious 1918 influenza virus that killed 50 mil people worldwide was a bird flu that jumped directly to humans. This was discovered from tests done on the preserved lung tissue of 2 soldiers and an Alaskan woman who died during the pandemic. Scientists say, however, that current strains of bird flu are not normally passed from one person to another as was the 1918 flu. British medical tests confirmed **Oct. 13** that H5N1, the current deadly strain of avian flu, was responsible for killing thousands of birds in Turkey in October. H5N1 was also confirmed in Romanian birds **Oct. 15**; the first appearance of the flu in Europe. Since 1997, 120 people have been infected by H5N1, with about 50% dying from it.

Experimental Vaccine Effective Against Cervical Cancer—A study involving more than 12,000 women showed that an experimental vaccine was effective in preventing cervical cancer. The experiment was conducted by scientists for Merck & Co., the manufacturer of the vaccine, Gardasil, which announced the findings **Oct. 6**. Merck said it would seek approval of the drug from the U.S. Food and Drug Administration. The vaccine makes people immune to 2 strains of a common sexually transmitted virus that cause cervical cancer.

Huge Numbers Killed in South Asia Earthquake—An earthquake hit South Asia **Oct. 8**, killing close to 40,000 people in Pakistan and Pakistan-administered territory, over 1,000 in India and Indian-administered territory. The quake's epicenter was in the Pakistan-administered section of Kashmir, with heavy casualties also in Pakistan's North-West Frontier Province and in Indian-administered Kashmir. The U.S. Geological Survey put the magnitude at 7.6, which made it the biggest temblor to hit the region in a century. Damage was widespread in the region, and some villages were completely wiped out. The United Nations estimated that 2.5 million people were left homeless in the mountainous region, where wintry conditions and impassable roads hampered relief operations.

OBITUARIES

Deaths, Oct. 16, 2004–Oct. 15, 2005

A

Adams, Don, 82, comedian best known as bumbling secret agent Maxwell Smart in the TV spy spoof *Get Smart* (1965-70); Los Angeles, CA, Sept. 25, 2005.

Albert, Eddie, 99, starred in the TV sitcom *Green Acres* (1965-71); won Oscar nominations for *Roman Holiday* (1953) and *The Heartbreak Kid* (1972); Los Angeles, CA, May 26, 2005.

Alexander, Shana, 79, pioneering woman columnist; liberal "point-counterpoint" commentator on CBS TV's *60 Minutes* in the 1970s; Hermosa Beach, CA, June 23, 2005.

Arafat, Yasir, 75, PLO chairman since 1969; president of the Palestinian Authority since 1996; shared the 1994 Nobel Peace Prize after signing a peace accord with Israel, but was seen by some as an obstacle to further peace; Paris, France, Nov. 11, 2004.

Axelrod, Julius, 92, neuroscientist who won a 1970 Nobel Prize for research into brain chemicals; Rockville, MD, Dec. 29, 2004.

B

Bancroft, Anne, 73, won a Tony for playing Helen Keller's teacher in *The Miracle Worker* (1959), and an Oscar for the 1962 film; played Mrs. Robinson in *The Graduate* (1967); New York, NY, June 6, 2005.

Bel Geddes, Barbara, 82, played the family matriarch on the nighttime TV soap opera *Dallas* and Maggie on Broadway in *Cat on a Hot Tin Roof* (1955); Northeast Harbor, ME, Aug. 8, 2005.

Bellow, Saul, 89, Nobel Prize-winning author of *The Adventures of Augie March* (1953) and other exuberant novels capturing modern urban life; Brookline, MA, April 5, 2005.

Benenson, Peter, 83, founded the human rights organization Amnesty International in 1961; Oxford, England, Feb. 25, 2005.

Benson, Obie, 69, charter member of the Four Tops, one of Motown's most successful groups; Detroit, MI, July 1, 2005.

Berman, Lazar, 74, Russian classical pianist esteemed for his mastery of the Romantic repertoire; Florence, Italy, Feb. 6, 2005.

Bernhard, Prince, 93, husband of the late Dutch Queen Juliana; Utrecht, the Netherlands, Dec. 1, 2004.

Bethe, Hans, 98, 1967 Nobel laureate and giant of 20th-century physics; played key role in A-bomb development, also an ardent advocate of nuclear arms control; Ithaca, NY, March 6, 2005.

Bronfenbrenner, Urie, 88, psychologist and child-development expert who helped create the Head Start program in the 1960s; Ithaca, NY, Sept. 25, 2005.

Bronfman, Edward, 77, leading Canadian businessman; Toronto, ON, April 4, 2004.

Brown, Clarence "Gatemouth," 81, Grammy-winning guitarist and singer who blended jazz, country, rhythm and blues, and Cajun elements; Orange, TX, Sept. 10, 2005.

Brown, Herbert C., 92, chemist whose research into boron compounds won him a Nobel Prize in 1979; Lafayette, IN, Dec. 19, 2004.

C

Callaghan, James (Lord Callaghan of Cardiff), 92, British Labour Party politician; held major cabinet posts before serving as prime minister (1976-79); Ringmer, England, March 26, 2005.

Carson, Johnny, 79, TV icon who hosted NBC's *Tonight* show from 1962 to 1992; a skilled comedian himself, he also jump-started the careers of Bill Cosby, Jerry Seinfeld, and others; Los Angeles, CA, Jan. 23, 2005.

Charles, Dame Eugenia, 86, prime minister of Dominica, 1980-95, and first woman leader of any Caribbean nation; Fort-de-France, Guadeloupe, Sept. 6, 2005.

Cherry, Bobby Frank, 74, ex-Klansman convicted in 2002 in the 1963 Birmingham, AL, church bombing that left 4 black girls dead; in prison near Montgomery, AL, Nov. 18, 2004.

Chisholm, Shirley, 80, first black woman elected to the U.S. House (1968); first woman or black person to campaign seriously for a major party presidential nomination (1972); Ormond Beach, FL, Jan. 1, 2005.

Clark, Kenneth B., 90, educational psychologist whose research into racial segregation was cited in *Brown v. Board of Education* (1954); Hastings-on-Hudson, NY, May 1, 2005.

Cochran, Johnnie, 67, famed attorney; led the "dream team" that defended O.J. Simpson in a 1995 murder trial; Los Angeles, CA, March 29, 2005.

Coleman, Cy, 75, composer known for *Sweet Charity* (1966) and other Broadway hits; New York, NY, Nov. 18, 2004.

Conroy, Frank, 69, author of the memoir *Stop-Time* (1967) and longtime director of the Iowa Writers' Workshop; Iowa City, IA, April 6, 2005.

Cook, Robin, 59, British foreign secretary, 1997-2001, then leader of the House of Commons; resigned in 2003 over Britain's intervention in Iraq; near Inverness, Scotland, Aug. 6, 2005.

Cutler, Lloyd, 87, Washington insider who was White House counsel to Pres. Carter and Clinton; Washington, DC, May 8, 2005.

D

Dancer, Stanley, 78, dominant figure in harness racing—as trainer, driver, owner, and breeder—for 5 decades; Pompano Beach, FL, Sept. 8, 2005.

Davis, Glenn, 80, halfback who teamed with fullback Doc Blanchard on the undefeated Army football teams of the mid-1940s; La Quinta, CA, March 9, 2005.

Davis, Ossie, 87, actor, playwright, film director, and civil rights and antiwar activist; Miami Beach, FL, Feb. 4, 2005.

Dee, Sandra, 62, actress who personified mild teenage rebelliousness in such films as *Gidget* (1959); Thousand Oaks, CA, Feb. 20, 2005.

DeLorean, John Z., 80, automobile designer; left GM to found his own company, which went bankrupt in 1982; Summit, NJ, March 19, 2005.

De los Angeles, Victoria, 81, renowned Spanish lyric soprano of the 1950s and 60s; Barcelona, Spain, Jan. 15, 2005.

Denver, Bob, 70, played the inept shipwrecked first mate in the classic TV sitcom *Gilligan's Island* (1963-67); Winston-Salem, NC, Sept. 2, 2005.

Doohan, James M., 85, played chief engineer Montgomery Scott in the original *Star Trek* TV series (1966-69) and in films; Redmond, WA, July 20, 2005.

Dos Santos, Sister Lucia, 97, Portuguese nun, last surviving of 3 cousins who reported childhood visions of the Virgin Mary near Fatima in 1917; Coimbra, Portugal, Feb. 13, 2005.

Dworkin, Andrea, 58, radical feminist and antipornography crusader; Washington, DC, April 9, 2005.

E

Eberhart, Richard, 101, prizewinning lyric poet and poetry consultant to the Library of Congress, 1959-61; Hanover, NH, June 9, 2005.

Eisner, Will, 87, comic-book artist who created "The Spirit" in 1940 and pioneered the graphic novel in the late 1970s; Ft. Lauderdale, FL, Jan. 3, 2005.

Eitan, Rafael, 75, Israeli army chief of staff (1978-83) who led Israel's invasion of Lebanon; drowned off Israel's coast, Nov. 22, 2004.

Exon, J. James, 83, Nebraska Democrat who was governor,1971-79, and a U.S. senator, 1979-97; Lincoln, NE, June 10, 2005.

Eyadema, Gnassingbe, 69, dictatorial ruler of the African nation of Togo since 1967; died en route to France for medical treatment, Feb. 5, 2005.

F

Fahd, King, 82?, Saudi Arabia's monarch since 1982; largely a figurehead since 1996, when, after suffering a stroke, he turned over responsibility to his brother; Riyadh, Saudi Arabia, Aug. 1, 2005.

Fairclough, Ellen L., 99, Canada's first female cabinet minister; held 3 cabinet posts between 1957 and 1963; Hamilton, ON, Nov. 13, 2004.

Ferrer, Ibrahim, 78, Cuban singer famous late in life for the album (1997) and film (1999) *Buena Vista Social Club*; Havana, Cuba, Aug. 6, 2005.

Fitzgerald, Geraldine, 91, distinguished Irish-born actress, director, and, late in life, cabaret singer; New York, NY, July 17, 2005.

Fletcher, Arthur A., 80, black civil rights leader who held high posts in several GOP administrations; Washington, DC, July 12, 2005.

Foote, Shelby, 88, novelist turned historian who wrote a 3-volume study of the Civil War and appeared in Ken Burns's 1990 TV documentary on the war; Memphis, TN, June 27, 2005.

Forman, James, 76, civil rights activist; as a leader of the Student Nonviolent Coordinating Committee (1961-66) organized voter-registration drives in the South; Wash. DC, Jan. 10, 2005.

G

Goodpaster, Andrew J., 90, U.S. general who was supreme allied commander of NATO (1969-74) and later headed West Point; Washington, DC, May 16, 2005.

Gorshin, Frank, 72, impressionist and character actor; played the Riddler in TV's *Batman* in the 1960s and George Burns in a 2002 one-man Broadway show; Burbank, CA, May 17, 2005.

Gray III, L. Patrick, 88, acting FBI director for 11 months after the death of J. Edgar Hoover; a casualty of the Watergate scandal, he resigned in April 1973; Atlantic Beach, FL, July 6, 2005.

Grunwald, Henry A., 82, top editor of *Time* magazine, 1968-79, and of all Time Inc. publications, 1979-87; later a U.S. ambassador; New York, NY, Feb. 26, 2005.

Giulini, Carlo Maria, 91, Italian conductor devoted to operas by Mozart and Verdi; principal conductor of the Los Angeles Philharmonic, 1978-85; Brescia, Italy, June 14, 2005.

H

Hackworth, David H., 74, military analysts; combat legend as a Vietnam War colonel; turned against the war in 1971 and turned in his medals; Tijuana, Mexico, May 4, 2005.

Hailey, Arthur, 84, British-born author of *Hotel* (1965), *Airport* (1968), and other best-sellers; Lyford Cay, the Bahamas, Nov. 24, 2004.

Hanson, Lord (James Edward), 82, British industrialist; Newbury, England, Nov. 1, 2004.

Hargis, Billy James, 79, evangelist whose anti-Communist Church of the Christian Crusade reached millions in the 1950s and 60s; Tulsa, OK, Nov. 27, 2004.

JOHN PAUL II

Pope John Paul II, 84, bishop of Rome and leader of the Roman Catholic Church for 26 years, the 3rd longest pontificate in history, died in his Vatican apartment April 2, 2005. Born Karol Jozef Wojtyla in Wadowice, Poland, on May 18, 1920, he lost his parents and only sibling by age 21. As a young man in German-occupied Poland during WWII, he joined a cultural resistance movement and began studying for the priesthood in secrecy. He was ordained in 1946, earned a doctorate in Rome in 1948, and returned to Poland to lead a small rural church. He earned a 2nd doctorate in 1953 and joined the faculty of the Catholic Univ. of Lublin. Named auxiliary bishop of Krakow in 1958, he became the archbishop in 1964 and was made a cardinal 3 years later. Elected pope on Oct. 16, 1978, at age 58, he was the youngest pope elected in the 20th century, the 1st non-Italian pontiff in 456 years, and the 1st pope from a Slavic country.

The most widely traveled pontiff in history, the charismatic John Paul drew huge crowds in his journeys to some 130 countries in all and is credited with a major role in in collapse of communism in Poland and Eastern Europe. He was conservative in matters of doctrine, morals, and church tradition and discipline; at the same time he encouraged Christian unity and greatly improved Jewish-Catholic relations. John Paul II was seriously wounded in an assassination attempt in St. Peter's Square, May 13, 1981, but recovered and later forgave his attacker. His health declined in recent years and he visibly suffered from Parkinson's disease. More than 1 mil people lined up in St. Peter's Square to view the pope's body, which lay in state Apr. 6-7; he was buried Apr. 8 in a crypt beneath St. Peter's Basilica in Vatican City.

Haver, June, 79, star of 1940s Hollywood musicals who made her last film in 1953; married to actor Fred MacMurray; Brentwood, CA, July 4, 2005.

Heath, Sir Edward, 89, British prime minister, 1970-74, and leading Tory advocate of European unity; Salisbury, England, July 17, 2005.

Heath, Percy, 81, bassist who anchored the Modern Jazz Quartet for 4 decades, up to the late 1990s; Southampton, NY, April 28, 2005.

Hecht, Anthony, 81, formalist poet whose experiences of World War II and the Holocaust were crucial to his work; Washington, DC, Oct. 20, 2004.

Heflin, Howell, 83, Democrat, was chief justice of his state's high court before serving three terms in the U.S. Senate (1979-97); Sheffield, AL, March 29, 2005.

Heilbroner, Robert L., 85, economic historian whose first book, *The Worldly Philosophers* (1953), became a classic; New York, NY, Jan. 4, 2005.

Herman, George, 85, CBS newsman; moderator (1969-83) of the Sunday morning TV show *Face the Nation*; Washington, DC, Feb. 8, 2005.

Hickey, Cardinal James A., 84, Roman Catholic archbishop of Washington, DC, from 1980 to 2000; Washington, DC, Oct. 24, 2004.

Hildegarde (Hildegarde Loretta Sell), 99, durable cabaret artist dubbed the "First Lady of the Supper Clubs"; New York, NY, July 29, 2005.

Horner, Red, rugged hockey Hall of Fame defenseman, 1928-40; Toronto, ON, April 27, 2005.

Hunter, Evan, 78, author of *The Blackboard Jungle* (1954) and, as Ed McBain, of pioneering police procedural novels; Weston, CT, July 6, 2005.

Hussey, Ruth, 93, actress nominated for a supporting Oscar in the *Philadelphia Story* (1940); Newbury Park, CA, April 19, 2005.

I

Iakovos, Archbishop, 93, primate of the Greek Orthodox Archdiocese of North and South America, 1959-96; Stamford, CT, April 10, 2005.

Irvine, Reed, 82, founder (1969) of the conservative media-watchdog group Accuracy in Media (AIM); Rockville, MD, Nov. 16, 2004.

J

Janeway, Elizabeth, 91, best-selling novelist and feminist who wrote *Man's World, Woman's Place* (1971); Rye, NY, Jan. 15, 2004.

Jennings, Peter, 67, Canadian-born TV reporter, foreign correspondent, co-anchor, and from 1983 sole anchor of *ABC World News Tonight*; effectively retired in April 2005 because of lung cancer; New York, NY, Aug. 7, 2005.

Johnson, John H., 87, builder of a U.S. publishing empire whose cornerstones were the black-oriented magazines *Ebony* and *Jet*; Chicago, IL, Aug. 8, 2005.

Johnson, Johnnie, 80, rollicking pianist who worked closely with rock-and-roll legend Chuck Berry; St. Louis, MO, April 13, 2005.

Johnson, Philip, 98, influential U.S. architect; promoted the austere, International Style before abandoning it in favor of an exuberant postmodernism; New Canaan, CT, Jan. 25, 2005.

K

Kennan, George F., 101, diplomat and historian; main architect of the U.S. cold-war "containment" strategy; Princeton, NJ, March 17, 2005.

Kennedy, Rosemary, 86, sister of Pres. John F. Kennedy; mildly retarded, she was institutionalized after a 1941 lobotomy; Fort Atkinson, WI, Jan. 7, 2005.

Keys, Ancel, 100, physiologist; invented the K rations fed to U.S. troops in WWII; implicated saturated fat in heart disease; Minneapolis, MN, Nov. 20, 2004.

Kilby, Jack St. Clair, 81, Nobel Prize-winning electrical engineer who in 1958 invented the integrated circuit, or microchip; Dallas, TX, June 20, 2005.

L

Lange, David, 63, New Zealand prime minister, 1983-89, who banned nuclear-armed and nuclear-powered ships from the country's territorial waters; Auckland, New Zealand, Aug. 13, 2005.

Langford, Frances, 92, singer and actress; she played herself in *The Glenn Miller Story* (1954); Jensen Beach, FL, July 11, 2005.

Linowitz, Sol M., 91, chairman of Xerox Corp. (1960-66); later a diplomat and presidential counselor; Washington, DC, March 18, 2005.

Luft, Sid, 89, film producer who was Judy Garland's 3rd husband; produced her "comeback" movie, *A Star Is Born* (1954); Santa Monica, CA, Sept. 15, 2005.

M

Markova, Dame Alicia, 94, British ballerina; known worldwide for her interpretation of the title role in *Giselle*; Bath, England, Dec. 2, 2004.

Martin, Agnes, 92, Canadian-born abstract painter who rose to prominence in New York City before moving to New Mexico in the 1970s; Taos, NM, Dec. 16, 2004.

Mayo, Virginia, 84, Hollywood film star of the 1940s and 1950s who played opposite leading men from James Cagney to Ronald Reagan; Thousand Oaks, CA, Jan. 17, 2005.

Meader, Vaughn, 68, stand-up comic whose best-selling *First Family* album spoofed the Kennedys; Auburn, ME, Oct. 29, 2004.

Melcher, Terry, 62, singer, songwriter, and record producer; son of actress Doris Day; Beverly Hills, CA, Nov. 19, 2004.

Merchant, Ismail, 68, Indian-born film producer whose partnership with director James Ivory produced sumptuous screen adaptations of such works as E.M. Forster's *A Room With a View* (1985); London, England, May 25, 2005.

Merrill, Robert, 87, leading baritone at the Metropolitan Opera from 1945 to 1975; New York, NY, Oct. 23, 2004.

Messick, Dale, 98, pioneering female comic-strip artist; in 1940 created intrepid reporter Brenda Starr; Penngrove, CA, April 5, 2005.

Mikan, George, 80, pro basketball's first "big man"—at 6'10"—and dominant player in the decade after World War II; Scottsdale, AZ, June 1, 2005.

Miller, Arthur, 89, stirring playwright deeply concerned with political and social issues; his tragedy *Death of a Salesman* (1949) was hailed as an American classic; other renowned plays include *All My Sons* (1947) and *The Crucible* (1953); also known for his troubled marriage (1956-61) to Marilyn Monroe; Roxbury, CT, Feb. 10, 2005.

Mills, Sir John, 97, veteran British stage and screen actor; won a 1971 supporting actor Oscar for *Ryan's Express*; Denham, England, April 23, 2005.

Moog, Robert, 71, inventor (1964) of the Moog synthesizer, the first commercially successful electronic music device; Asheville, NC, Aug. 21, 2005.

Morris, Howard, 85, comic actor who was a regular on Sid Caesar's 1950s TV classic *Your Show of Shows*; Los Angeles, CA, May 21, 2005.

Motley, Constance Baker, 84, first black woman to become a federal judge (in 1966); was on the NAACP legal team that won *Brown v. Board of Education* (1954); New York, NY, Sept. 28, 2005.

N

Nelson, Gaylord, 89, Wisconsin governor (1959-63) and senator (1963-81); a leading environmentalist, he conceived the idea of Earth Day; Kensington, MD, July 3, 2005.

Newfield, Jack, 66, muckraking New York City journalist; New York, NY, Dec. 20, 2004.

Nitze, Paul H., 97, diplomat who served under 8 presidents; a key figure in arms negotiations with the Soviet Union; Washington, DC, Oct. 19, 2004.

Nye, Louis, 92, popular comedian and actor who was a regular on *The Steve Allen Show* in the 1950s; Los Angeles, CA, Oct. 9, 2005.

O

Obote, Milton, 80, Ugandan dictator deposed in 1971 by Idi Amin; South Africa, Oct. 10, 2005.

ODB (Ol' Dirty Bastard) (Russell T. Jones), 35, rap artist who was a founding member of the Wu Tang Clan hip hop group of the 1990s; New York, NY, Nov. 13, 2004.

O'Herlihy, Dan, 85, Irish-born character actor; nominated for an Oscar for *The Adventures of Robinson Crusoe* (1954); Malibu, CA, Feb. 17, 2005.

Orbach, Jerry, 69, celebrated Broadway song-and-dance man; played Detective Lennie Briscoe on the TV series *Law & Order* (1992-2004); New York, NY, Dec. 28, 2004.

P

Peck, M. Scott, 69, psychiatrist who wrote the best-selling self-help book *The Road Less Traveled* (1978); Warren, CT, Sept. 25, 2005.

Perdue, Frank, 84, poultry prducer and a longtime pitchman for his company; Salisbury, MD, March 31, 2005.

Peters, Brock, 78, actor best known for his role as a black janitor wrongfully accused of rape in the film *To Kill a Mockingbird* (1962); Los Angeles, CA, Aug. 23, 2005.

Pickle, J. J. ("Jake"), 91, Democratic Texas U.S representative, 1963-95; Austin, TX, June 18, 2005.

R

Raitt, John, 88, singing actor who was the male lead on Broadway in *Carousel* (1945) and *The Pajama Game* (1954); Los Angeles, CA, Feb. 20, 2005.

Rainier III, Prince, 81, ruler of Monaco since 1949 and Europe's longest-reigning monarch; married to film star Grace Kelly from 1956 until her death in 1982; Monaco, April 6, 2005.

Rao, P.V. Narasimha, 83, prime minister of India in the early 1990s; oversaw the adoption of major economic reforms; New Delhi, India, Dec. 23, 2004.

Rehnquist, William H., 80, chief justice of the U.S. Supreme Court since 1986 and associate justice from 1971. Born Oct. 1, 1924, in Milwaukee, WI, Rehnquist graduated from Stanford Univ., where he also earned his law degree. He clerked for Supreme Court Justice Robert H. Jackson in 1952-53, went into private practice in Phoenix, AZ, and was active in GOP politics. From 1969 to 1971 he served as assistant attorney general under Pres. Nixon, who nominated him to the Court. Liberals groups found fault with his record, but he was easily confirmed. On the Court, he took conservative positions in most areas, including states' rights and abortion. Pres. Reagan nominated him to be chief justice in 1986, and he was confirmed, 65-33. As chief justice he sought with limited success to move the Court in a conservative direction; he also was known for his collegiality and lack of formality. In Oct. 2004 he was diagnosed with thyroid cancer, but served until his death; Arlington, VA, Sept. 3, 2005.

Rodino Jr., Peter W., 95, longtime congressman (D, NJ) who as House Judiciary Committee chairman led the 1974 impeachment inquiry into Pres. Nixon; West Orange, NJ, May 7, 2005.

Roger, Brother (Roger Schutz-Marsauche), 90, Swiss Protestant monk who in 1940 founded ecumenical religious community in Taizé, France; stabbed by a deranged woman during a service; Taizé, France, Aug. 16, 2005.

Rossner, Judith, 70, author of the novel *Looking for Mr. Goodbar* (1975), about a schoolteacher murdered by a man she picked up in a singles bar; New York, NY, Aug. 9, 2005.

Rothblat, Sir Joseph, 96, physicist who quit working on the A bomb and won the 1995 Nobel Peace Prize for his anti-nuclear activism; London, England; Aug. 31, 2005.

Russell, Nipsey, 80, rhyming comedian, actor; 1st African American comic to appear regularly on TV; New York, NY; Oct. 2, 2005.

S

Saunders, Dame Cicely, 87, British nurse, social worker, and physician who launched the modern system of hospice care in 1967 with St. Christopher's Hospice in London; London, England, July 14, 2005.

Salinger, Pierre, 79, White House press secretary under Pres. Kennedy and Johnson; later a foreign correspondent; Cavaillon, France, Oct. 16, 2004.

Schell, Maria, 79, Austrian-born actress who starred in U.S., British, and European films of the 1950s; Preitenegg, Austria, April 26, 2005.

Schenkel, Chris, 82 radio and TV sportscaster; longtime voice of the Professional Bowlers Association Tour; Fort Wayne, IN, Sept. 11, 2005.

Schiavo, Terri, 41, severely brain-damaged woman kept alive by a feeding tube since 1990; the legal battle over whether to remove it was a national controversy; Pinellas Park, FL, March 31, 2005.

Schmeling, Max, 99, German world heavyweight boxing champ who shockingly beat Joe Louis in 1936 but was crushed by him in a 1938 rematch; Hollenstedt, Germany, Feb. 2, 2005.

Shaw, Artie, 94, swing-era bandleader and jazz clarinetist; his 8 wives included Lana Turner and Ava Gardner; Thousand Oaks, CA, Dec. 30, 2004.

Short, Bobby, 80, cabaret singer and pianist, renowned for his interpretations of Cole Porter; a fixture at the elegant Café Carlyle from 1968 to 2004; New York NY, March 21, 2005.

Simon, Claude, 91, Nobel Prize-winning French author (1985); known as a pioneer of the unconventional "nouveau roman"; Paris, France, July 6, 2005.

Sin, Cardinal Jaime, 76, influential Roman Catholic prelate who was archbishop of Manila from 1974 to 2003; Manila, the Philippines, June 21, 2005.

Sisco, Joseph J., 85, diplomat who helped shape U.S. Mideast policy in the 1960s and 1970s; Chevy Chase MD, Nov. 23, 2004.

Smith, Jimmy, 78, "soul jazz" performer who turned the Hammond B-3 electric organ into an important jazz instrument; Scottsdale, AZ, Feb. 8, 2005.

Sontag, Susan, 71, critic, essayist, novelist, and political activist, perhaps the best known American intellectual of her time; New York, NY, Dec. 28, 2004.

Stockdale, James B., 81, former Vietnam POW and retired admiral who was Ross Perot's running mate in the 1992 presidential campaign; Coronado, CA, July 5, 2005.

Stram, Hank, 82, Hall of Fame coach of the Kansas City Chiefs; later a football analyst on radio and TV; Covington, LA, July 4, 2005.

T

Tange, Kenzo, 91, Pritzker Prize architect (1987) who designed the Hiroshima peace park and the twin stadiums for the 1964 Tokyo Olympics; Tokyo, Japan, March 22, 2005.

Tebaldi, Renata, 82, Italian opera singer regarded as one of the world's finest lyric-dramatic sopranos; San Marino, Dec. 19, 2004.

Thompson, Hunter S., 67, pioneer of "gonzo" journalism, the highly personal, often drug- or alcohol-fueled writing exemplified by his 1972 classic, *Fear and Loathing in Las Vegas*; Woody Creek, CO, Feb. 20, 2005.

Trotman, Alexander J. (Lord Trotman of Osmotherly), 71, Briton who in 1993 became Ford's first non-American chairman and CEO; Yorkshire, England, April 25, 2005.

V

Vandross, Luther, 54, rhythm-and-blues singer known for his mastery of romantic ballads; sold more than 25 mil records and won 8 Grammys; Edison, NJ, July 1, 2005,

Van Duyn, Mona, 83, poet of suburbia who in 1992 was named the first female U.S. poet laureate; University City, MO, Dec. 2, 2004.

Vane, Sir Robert, 77, British pharmacologist; won a 1982 Nobel Prize for research into painkillers; Farnborough, England, Nov. 19, 2004.

Vernon, John, 72, Canadian-born character actor who played Dean Wormer in *National Lampoon's Animal House* (1978); Los Angeles, CA, Feb. 1, 2005.

W

Walton, John T., 58, middle son of Wal-Mart founder Sam Walton and one of the world's richest men; died in crash of an experimental ultralight aircraft he had been piloting; Grand Teton National Park, WY, June 27, 2005.

Warrick, Ruth, 88, actress who debuted in *Citizen Kane* (1941) and for decades played matriarch Phoebe Tyler Wallingford on the TV soap opera *All My Children*; New York, NY, Jan. 15, 2005.

Weber, Dick, 75, professional bowler who was one of his sport's leading lights in the 1960s; Florissant, MO, Feb. 14, 2005.

Weizman, Ezer, 80, Israeli military leader and cabinet minister who from 1993 to 2000 served as his nation's 7th president; Caesarea, Israel, April 24, 2005.

Westmoreland, William C., 91, Army general who commanded U.S. forces in Vietnam, 1964-68; in 1985 agreed to a non-monetary settlement in a suit over a CBS documentary suggesting he had deceived the public about enemy troop strength; Charleston, SC, July 18, 2005.

White, Reggie, 43, defensive end and all-time NFL sack leader; nicknamed the "Minister of Defense"; Huntersville, NC, Dec. 26, 2004.

Wiesenthal, Simon, 96, Jewish survivor of World War II concentration camps who became the world's best-known hunter of Nazi fugitives; Vienna, Austria, Sept. 20, 2005.

Wilson, August, 60, Pulitzer-Prize-winning playwright whose 10-play cycle, including *The Piano Lesson* (1987) and *Fences* (1990), both of which won Pulitzers, chronicled the contemporary black experience in America; Seattle, WA, Oct. 2, 2005.

Winchell, Paul, 82, ventriloquist who brought dummy Jerry Mahoney to life on TV; voice of Tigger in "Winnie-the-Pooh" productions; patented a version of the artificial heart; Moorpark, CA, June 24, 2005.

Wise, Robert, 91, director of the Oscar-winning musicals *West Side Story* (1961) and *The Sound of Music* (1965); Los Angeles, CA, Sept. 14, 2005.

Woods, Rose Mary, 87, Pres. Nixon's long-serving private secretary, known for her testimony that she accidentally erased 18½ minutes of a crucial Watergate-related White House tape; Alliance, OH, Jan. 22, 2005.

Wright, Teresa, 86, leading actress in the 1940s; won an Oscar for best supporting actress for *Mrs. Miniver* (1942); New Haven, CT, March 6, 2005.

Wriston, Walter, 85, CEO (1967-84) of Citibank, which he helped transform into the world's largest bank; New York, NY, Jan. 19, 2005.

Y

Yard, Molly, 93, activist who took over the National Organization for Women in 1987, at age 75, and led it until 1991; Pittsburgh, PA, Sept. 21, 2005.

Z

Zayed bin Sultan al-Nuhayyan, Sheik, 86?, founding president (1971) of the United Arab Emirates (UAE) and ruler of Abu Dhabi since 1966; Abu Dhabi, UAE, Nov. 2, 2004.

Zhao Ziyang, 85, Chinese Communist Party general secretary; deposed during the 1989 Tiananmen Square uprising, after opposing the use of force; under house arrest ever since; Beijing, China, Jan. 17, 2005.

Offbeat News Stories, 2005

The Super Bowl of . . . Bowls

About 350 plumbing and hygiene experts met in Belfast, Northern Ireland, Sept. 27-29, 2005, to discuss a subject near and dear to them—toilets. The World Toilet Summit, sponsored by the World Toilet Organization (founder of the World Toilet College), brought together experts from around the world to discuss subjects ranging from antisocial bathroom behavior to portable toilets to facilities for the blind. The meeting's crowning achievement was agreement on a universal protocol for the provision and maintenance of public toilets. Most agreed that Singapore's public toilets were the plumbing equivalent of a gold standard.

Real Turkmen Don't Lip-Synch

Under the order of Saparmurad Niyazov, president of the former Soviet republic of Turkmenistan, even tone-deaf Turkmens are being held to a new decree: No Lip-Synching. Citing "a negative effect on the development of singing and musical art," Pres. Niyazov announced Aug. 23 a ban on lip-synching at cultural events, concerts, on TV, and even at private celebrations. Niyazov has been president of the central Asian nation since 1990, and is responsible for several other unusual regulations, including a ban on opera and ballet in 2001, and a 2004 proclamation against gold-capped teeth on young people, beards, and long hair for men.

Skiing on Thin Ice

A Swiss ski resort has wrapped a glacier in a reflective foil cover to minimize melting. The resort, in central Andermatt, obtained an $83,000 cover for its diminishing Gurschen glacier; about 4,000 square yards of the glacier are now covered in synthetic fibers in order to protect the ski runs on its surface. Urs Elmiger, a board member of the ski lift company that initiated the project, said that the threat of global warming meant that it might soon become "common practice" to cover parts of the glaciers.

Lingweenies' Ginormous Confuzzlements

Merriam-Webster dictionary editors loosened their strict linguistic standards for a few weeks in 2005 when they asked visitors to their website to submit favorite words that don't appear in the dictionary. The response was so enthusiastic—over 3,000 entries in only 2 weeks—that some words received multiple mentions, and editors came up with an unofficial list of top ten verbal concoctions. "Ginormous" (bigger than gigantic and enormous) landed in first place, followed by "confuzzled" (simultaneously confused and puzzled). "Lingweenie" (a person unable to make up new words) also managed to make the list. Another submission was "Supercalifragilisticexpialidocious"—which does appear in the Oxford English Dictionary, but not in Merriam-Webster (yet).

Jerk-O-Meter Is Listening

Are you inclined to talk only about yourself? Do you speak too loudly and constantly interrupt others? If so, the Jerk-O-Meter may be of assistance. The device, in development at MIT, can attach to your cell phone and use mathematical algorithms to analyze a speaker's tone of voice and speaking style and determine the degree of attentiveness and empathy shown. At first it will only monitor the user's voice, issuing messages displayed on screen, such as "Don't be a jerk!" or "Be a little nicer now." But developers also plan to program the Jerk-O-Meter to monitor the person on the other end and clue in the user with messages like "This person is acting like a jerk. Do you want to hang up?" Project leader Anmol Madan believes the device can pressure people to be more thoughtful conversationalists. After all, a sympathetic style doesn't go unrewarded on the Jerk-O-Meter—a high score prompts the message, "Wow, you're a smooth talker."

Dam-Filthy Lucre

Three bags of money stolen from the Lucky Dollar poker casino in Greensburg, LA, in late Nov. 2004 turned up a few days later in a creek frequented by beavers. Two of the bags were stuck in a beaver dam, and one had been broken into by the beavers, who had woven many of the bills into the dam with sticks and other materials. Officials in St. Helena Parish at first tried to dry out the cash by airing it in a bank vault. When that proved too smelly, they used an industrial dryer at the parish jail to "launder" the money properly, adding a pair of old tennis shoes to the mix when the money began clumping. In the end, the authorities were able to recover all but a few thousand of some $70,000 lifted from the casino.

Puff the Naughty Zoo Chimp

Chimpanzees are our closest relatives in the animal kingdom, and they can be almost as smart—or dumb—as we are. Zoo officials in South Africa reported in Apr. 2005 that Charlie, an adult chimp at Bloemfontein Zoo, had learned to smoke cigarettes thrown to him by visitors. Zoo spokesman Daryl Barnes said Charlie had probably started mimicking the actions of smoking visitors, inducing them to pass him real cigarettes. The zoo has tried to discourage Charlie from smoking, and pleads with visitors to stop feeding his habit. Meanwhile, Charlie "acts like a naughty schoolboy," according to Barnes, concealing his cigarette when a zoo staffer approaches.

Scent-sible Driving

If your car is a lemon, you've got problems. But if it actually *smells* like lemon, it may make you a better driver. Or so concludes the British RAC Foundation for Motoring, which in June 2005 released the results of a study on the effects of smells on drivers. Scents like coffee, peppermint, cinnamon, and salty sea air, the researchers claim, can increase alertness and concentration. But certain natural odors, like pine, cut grass, or wildflowers can be distracting. And fried food and baking smells can stir up road rage potential, because they make drivers hungry; hungry drivers tend to be irritable, and also may drive too fast. On the other hand, scents like chamomile, jasmine, and lavender can make drivers relax—possibly too much—and feel sleepy. Before throwing out the air freshener dangling from the rearview mirror, take note: even having no scents may make no sense, since a lack of aromas can also lead to irritability.

We'd Like to See the Infomercial

If you think you've got a weight problem, it's nothing compared to Maggie's. Zookeepers at the Alaska Zoo, in Anchorage, recently installed a specially designed treadmill for the 9,200-pound African elephant. In her natural habitat she would spend about 16 hours a day walking and foraging, but the frigid Alaska climate confines Maggie to her sedentary indoor habitat for months every year, making her hundreds of pounds too heavy. The world's first elephant exercise treadmill, based on heavy-duty conveyor technology used in mining operations, was installed in Sept. 2005. John Seawell, head of the elephant habitat, said her exercise regimen would eventually entail 2 or 3 hours a day on the treadmill.

Notable Quotes: The Lighter Side

"I'm so overexposed, I'm making Paris Hilton look like a recluse."
—*Barack Obama*, freshman senator (D, IL), and national figure since his keynote speech at the 2004 Democratic National Convention.

"You don't know the history of psychiatry. I do."
—*Tom Cruise*, actor and Scientologist, after *Today* show host Matt Lauer questioned his criticism of actress Brooke Shields for taking antidepressants.

"She said that she had taken to calling me son. . . I wish I could get them to adopt Hillary."
—*Bill Clinton*, former President, on his closeness with former First Lady Barbara Bush and her husband after the 2 ex-presidents' collaboration on tsunami-relief fund raising.

"I want to curse. Nine years. It's been nine years since I cursed on camera."
—*Ray Romano*, saying he'd like to do an edgier cable series after his hit sitcom *Everybody Loves Raymond* ended its 9-year run.

"That would be unlikely. Who would cook?"
—*Edie Falco*, on whether her *Sopranos* character Carmela would be killed off during the show's next season.

Notable Quotes in 2005

Hurricane Katrina

"This is mass chaos. To tell you the truth, I'd rather be in Iraq."
—*Jason Defess*, National Guard sergeant and Iraq War veteran, Aug. 31, on conditions at the New Orleans Superdome being used as a shelter for people displaced by Hurricane Katrina.

"Don't tell me 40,000 people are coming here. They're not here. It's too doggone late. Now get off your asses and do something, and let's fix the biggest . . . crisis in the history of this country."
—*C. Ray Nagin*, the mayor of New Orleans, Sept. 1.

"Brownie, you're doing a heck of a job."
—*Pres. George W. Bush*, to FEMA Director Michael Brown, Sept. 2, in Mobile, AL. Replaced as coordinator of the Katrina relief effort a week later, Brown resigned from FEMA Sept. 12.

"Katrina exposed serious problems in our response capability at all levels of government, and to the extent that the federal government didn't fully do its job right, I take responsibility."
—*Pres. George W. Bush,* on Sept. 13.

National News

"I'm the guy they used to call Deep Throat."
—*W. Mark Felt*, 91, former FBI deputy director, disclosing in *Vanity Fair*'s July issue that he was the secret source relied upon by Bob Woodward and Carl Bernstein in breaking the Watergate scandal.

"We know many of these recommendations are going to be implemented. The question is whether they're going to be implemented before the next attack or after it."
—*Thomas Kean*, 9/11 Commission co-chair, showing frustration Apr. 25 with the pace of action on its proposals to stregthen homeland security.

"That's my job. I'm a newsman. That's what I try to do, is make news. And you try to avoid news. That's your job."
—*CNN anchor Wolf Blitzer*, to former Pres. Bill Clinton Aug. 11, after Clinton accused Blitzer of trying to get him to make news by saying the Iraq War was a mistake.

"Everyone wants to get to heaven, but no one wants to die."
—*Rep. Jim Nussle* (R, IA), House budget committee chairman, referring Mar. 9 to opposition to his proposed budget, which included cuts to several social programs.

"We're all grown men and women and we're behaving like we're in the third grade."
—*Sen. Lindsey Graham* (R, SC), May 22, on the atmosphere around Capitol Hill during the bitter fight over judicial filibusters.

"Both sides ought to be properly taught . . . so people can understand what the debate is about. Part of education is to expose people to different schools of thought. . . . You're asking me whether people ought to be exposed to different ideas, and the answer is yes."
—*Pres. George W. Bush*, reluctantly commenting on including discussions of alternatives to evolution, such as intelligent design, in public school classrooms, Aug. 1.

"Intelligent design is not a scientific concept."
—*John H. Marburger III*, director of the Office of Science and Technology Policy and science advisor to Pres. Bush, Aug 2.

"The strong have a duty to protect the weak. In cases where there are serious doubts and questions, the presumption should be in favor of life."
—*Pres. George W. Bush* in response to news of brain-damaged Terri Schiavo's death, Mar. 31, 13 days after her feeding tube was removed.

"I kept my promise."
—*Michael Schiavo* on the grave marker for his wife Terri, installed June 20 after an epic legal battle over her end-of-life wishes, referring to a pledge he once made to her that he would not keep her alive artificially.

"*Never* is a bad word."
—*Rev. Billy Graham*, 86 years old, on whether his June 24-26 revival meeting in New York City would be his last.

"I will be open to the considered views of my colleagues on the bench. And I will decide every case based on the record, according to the rule of law."
—*Judge John G. Roberts,* at Senate confirmation hearings for Supreme Court chief justice, Sept. 12.

"He's good in every way, except he's not a woman."
—*Sandra Day O'Connor*, retiring Supreme Court justice, commenting July 20 on John Roberts, Pres. Bush's nominee initially to replace her on the high court.

"A pitbull in size six shoes."
—*Then-Texas Gov. George W. Bush* in 1996, describing Harriet Miers, then a prominent Texas lawyer, later his Supreme Court nominee.

International News

"One minute we're trying to catch a fly ball; the next minute, we're praying not to get blown into a million pieces."
—*Staff Sgt. Dawayne Harterson*, Aug. 17, on playing softball with his Army Reserve unit to relax on breaks from searching Iraqi highways for bombs.

"He's said that my son—and the other children we've lost—died for a noble cause. I want to find out what the noble cause is."
—*Cindy Sheehan,* whose son Casey died while serving in Iraq, demonstrating outside Pres. Bush's Crawford, TX, ranch and demanding an audience with him, Aug. 6.

"The truth is, the administration's mishandling of the war in Iraq has made us less safe, and Iraq risks becoming what it was not before the war: a training ground for terrorists."
—*Senator Harry Reid* (D, NV), Oct. 3

"The stakes in Iraq could not be higher. The brutal violence in Iraq today is a clear sign of the terrorists' determination to stop democracy from taking root in the Middle East. They know that the success of a free Iraq, who can be a key ally in the war on terror and a symbol of success for others, will be a crushing blow to their strategy to dominate the region, and threaten America and the free world."
—*Pres. Bush*, addressing National Guard families, Oct. 6 in Nampa, ID.

"I'm the one who presented it to the world, and [it] will always be a part of my record. . . . It was painful. It is painful now."
—*Former Sec. of State Colin Powell* to Barbara Walters referring to his Feb. 2003 speech to the UN on presenting evidence of Iraqi weapons of mass destruction, in an interview aired Sept. 9.

"I say to those who planned this dreadful attack, whether they are still here in hiding or somewhere abroad, watch next week as we bury our dead and mourn them, but see also in those same days new people coming to this city to make it their home, to call themselves Londoners, and doing it because of that freedom to be themselves."
—*London Mayor Ken Livingstone*, July 8, commenting on July 7 terrorist attacks on the London transit system.

"This evening or this night, Christ opens the door to the pope."
—*Bishop Angelo Comastri*, vicar of the Vatican, on Apr. 1, to tens of thousands keeping vigil in St. Peter's Square. Pope John Paul II died the next evening.

Historical Anniversaries, 2006

1906 – 100 Years Ago

In one of the worst **mining disasters** in history, an **explosion** at Courrieres near Lens, France, kills more than 1,060 coal miners Mar. 10.

An 7.7-magnitude **earthquake** and subsequent fires ravage **San Francisco** Apr. 18-19, leaving an estimated 3,000 dead, 225,000-300,000 homeless, and some $350 mil in damages.

The **Pure Food and Drug Act** and Meat Inspection Act, which together provided the first U.S. federal safety regulations and consumer protections, are passed by Congress June 30.

Alfred Dreyfus, a Jewish army officer hastily and wrongly convicted of treason in 1899, is exonerated July 12 and reinstated in the French Army July 21, ending the **"Dreyfus Affair"** that exposed anti-Semitism in French society.

Unable to control a rebellion in the newly-formed Cuban republic, Pres. Tomás Estrada Palma requests **U.S. intervention** Aug. 23.

Hong Kong is struck Sept. 18 by a massive **typhoon** and tsunami that kills more than 10,000 people.

Race riots sweep through **Atlanta** Sept. 22-25; at least 21 people are killed and the black-owned business district is severely damaged.

Pres. **Theodore Roosevelt** Nov. 9 travels to the **Panama Canal Zone** to inspect the progress of canal construction; he is the first sitting president to travel outside of the U.S.

Russian Prime Min. Peter Stolypin Nov. 22 introduces **agrarian reforms** aimed at creating a large class of land-owning peasants.

Pres. **Theodore Roosevelt** is awarded the **Nobel Peace Prize** Dec. 10, for his role in negotiating peace in the Russo-Japanese War (1905).

The **All-India Muslim League**, a political organization that represented the interests of Indian Muslims, is formed Dec. 30.

Art. Paul Cézanne's *The Gardener Vallier*; Henri Matisse's *The Young Sailor II*; Pablo Picasso's *Gertrude Stein* and *Self-Portrait with Palette*. Paul Cézanne dies Oct. 22.

Literature. O. Henry's *The Four Million*; Jack London's *White Fang*; Paul Valéry's *Monsieur Teste*.

Movies. *The Dream of a Rarebit Fiend, Humorous Phases of Funny Faces.*

Music. Charles Ives's *Central Park in the Dark*; Sergey Rachmaninoff's *Symphony No. 2 in E minor*; Arnold Schoenberg's *Chamber Symphony No. 1.*

Nonfiction. Albert Schweitzer's *The Quest of the Historical Jesus*, Upton Sinclair's *The Jungle*, Mark Twain's *What Is Man*?

Pop Music. "Grand Old Rag" (aka "You're a Grand Old Flag"); Jack Drislane & Theodore Morse's "Keep on the Sunny Side."

Science and Technology. Walther Nernst articulates the third law of thermodynamics; Clemens Peter von Pirquet, with Bela Schick, coins the term "allergy" to describe hypersensitive reactions.

Sports. Intercollegiate Athletic Association (later NCAA) forms and revises football rules to allow the forward pass; the Chicago White Sox beat the Chicago Cubs, 4 games to 2, in the World Series.

Theatre. J.M. Barrie's *Peter Pan* debuts in New York; *Brewster's Millions; The Man of the Hour*; *The Red Mill.* Playwright Henrik Ibsen dies May 23.

Miscellaneous. New York architect Stanford White is murdered on the roof of Madison Square Garden by Pittsburgh millionaire Harry K. Thaw. W.K. Kellogg Toasted Corn Flake Company launches one of the first prepared breakfast cereals.

1956 – 50 Years Ago

Sudan, Jan. 1, and **Morocco**, Mar. 2, officially gain **independence** from Britain and France, respectively.

Communist Party Sec. Nikita **Khrushchev** begins **"de-Stalinization"** in the USSR Feb. 25.

A new constitution makes Pakistan the **first Islamic republic** Mar. 23.

101 members of Congress representing 11 Southern states call for massive resistance to earlier Supreme Court **school desegregation** rulings Mar. 12.

Pres. Dwight Eisenhower signs the Federal-Aid **Highway Act** June 29, inaugurating the interstate highway system.

Two **jets collide** in mid-air over the **Grand Canyon**, leaving 128 people dead.

Egypt nationalizes the **Suez Canal** July 26.

Two oceanliners, the Italian liner *Andrea Doria* and Swedish ship *Stockholm*, **collide** in the waters off of Nantucket, killing 51 people.

The **Suez Canal crisis** heightens Oct. 29 as Israeli forces invade the Sinai Peninsula and Britain and France begin military action against Egypt. A UN-enforced **truce** is reached and British, French, and Israeli troops leave by the year's end.

A nationwide **uprising in Hungary** leads to the formation of an interim government that promises free elections and seeks Western support. No support comes. Soviet troops attack the capital, Nov. 4, and crush the revolt after several weeks of bloody fighting.

Pres. **Eisenhower** and Vice Pres. **Richard Nixon** are **reelected** Nov. 6 over Dem. nominees Adlai Stevenson and Estes Kefauver, in a landslide vote.

Art. Alberto Giacometti's *Femme de Venise* series; Richard Hamilton's *Just what is it that makes today's homes so different, so appealing?*; "This Is Tomorrow" exhibition at London's Whitechapel Gallery launches Pop Art.

Literature. James Baldwin's *Giovanni's Room*; Albert Camus's *The Fall*; Allen Ginsberg's *Howl and Other Poems*; Naguib Mahfouz's *The Cairo Trilogy*; Grace Metalious's *Peyton Place*; V.S. Pritchett's *Collected Stories*.

Movies. *Anastasia* starring Ingrid Bergman; *The Court Jester* starring Danny Kaye; *Giant* starring James Dean, Rock Hudson, & Elizabeth Taylor; *Invasion of the Body Snatchers*; *The King and I* starring Yul Brynner & Deborah Kerr; Alfred Hitchcock's *The Man Who Knew Too Much* starring Jimmy Stewart & Doris Day; *The Searchers* starring John Wayne; Cecil B. DeMille's *The Ten Commandments* starring Charlton Heston, Yul Brynner, & Edward G. Robinson. *Marty* wins Best Picture, Actor (Ernest Borgnine), and Director (Delbert Mann) at Oscar ceremonies Mar. 21.

Music. Leonard Bernstein's *Candide*; Karlheinz Stockhausen's *Gesang der Jünglinge*.

Nonfiction. Winston Churchill's *History of the English-Speaking Peoples*; George F. Kennan's *Russia Leaves the War*; John F. Kennedy's *Profiles in Courage*.

Pop Music. Johnny Cash's "Folsom Prison Blues" and "I Walk the Line"; Doris Day's "Que será, será"; Fats Domino's "Blueberry Hill." Elvis Presley has 5 Billboard No. 1s, including "Heartbreak Hotel," "Hound Dog," and "Love Me Tender."

Science and Technology. Calder Hall, the world's first large-scale nuclear power plant, opens Oct. 17 in England;

FORTRAN, the first widely-used computer programming language, is introduced; Peter Berg identifies transfer-RNA.

Sports. Boxer Rocky Marciano retires as undefeated world heavyweight champ; Yankee pitcher Don Larsen throws a perfect game in game 5 of the World Series, en route to victory over the Brooklyn Dodgers in 7 games; Olympic Games, held in Melbourne, Australia, are dampened by political boycotts.

Theatre. *My Fair Lady* starring Julie Andrews and Rex Harrison, Eugene O'Neill's *Long Day's Journey Into Night* open on Broadway.

Miscellaneous. The words "under God" are added to the U.S. Pledge of Allegiance, and "In God We Trust" becomes the U.S. motto. Playwright Arthur Miller and actress Marilyn Monroe marry, as do actress Grace Kelly and Prince Rainier of Monaco.

1981 – 25 Years Ago

Minutes after Ronald Reagan is inaugurated as the 39th U.S. president Jan. 20, 52 American **hostages are released** from the U.S. embassy in Iran, where they were held captive by Iranian militants for 444 days.

Pres. **Ronald Reagan is shot** and seriously wounded in an assassination attempt Mar. 30 in Washington, DC; Press Sec. James Brady, a police officer, and a Secret Service agent are also seriously wounded; John Hinckley Jr. is arrested for the crime.

France elects **Francois Mitterrand** as its **first Socialist president**, May 10.

Pope John Paul II is shot twice and seriously injured by a would-be assassin, May 13 in St. Peter's Square. Mehmet Ali Agca, a convicted murderer who had escaped from a Turkish prison, is arrested immediately following the shooting and sentenced to life in prison July 22.

A U.S. Marine **combat jet crashes** into the deck of the *Nimitz* aircraft carrier May 26, killing 14.

A **train crash kills more than 800** people June 6 in Bihar, India, following a bridge collapse brought on by flash floods.

Israeli warplanes destroy the Iraqi Osirak **nuclear reactor** under construction near Baghdad June 7.

Congress passes the **largest tax cut bill** in the nation's history, expected to save taxpayers $750 bil over 5 years, July 29.

Federal air traffic controllers begin an illegal nationwide **strike** Aug. 3; most defy Pres. Reagan's back-to-work order and are fired Aug. 5.

Sandra Day O'Connor is confirmed, 99-0, Sept. 21 as the **first woman justice** on the U.S. Supreme Court.

Egyptian Pres. **Anwar al-Sadat is assassinated** by Muslim extremists in the army while reviewing a military parade Oct. 6 in Cairo.

Under Soviet pressure, **Poland imposes martial law** Dec. 13 and arrests Lech Walesa and other Solidarity labor union leaders and sympathizers.

Prolonged **famine** confronts some 60 million **North Africans** throughout the year.

Art. David Salle's *An Illustrator Was There*; Julian Schnabel's *Voltaire*; Chuck Close's *Phil/Fingerprint*. Picasso's *Guernica* is moved from the Museum of Modern Art in New York to the Prado in Milan.

Literature. Raymond Carver's *What We Talk About When We Talk About Love*; Minoru Oda's *Hiroshima*; Salman Rushdie's *Midnight's Children*; John Updike's *Rabbit Is Rich*; Mario Vargas Llosa's *The War of the End of the World*.

Movies. *Arthur* starring Dudley Moore & Liza Minnelli; *Chariots of Fire*; *The French Lieutenant's Woman* starring Meryl Streep & Jeremy Irons; *On Golden Pond* starring Henry Fonda & Katharine Hepburn; *Raiders of the Lost Ark* starring Harrison Ford; *Reds* starring Warren Beatty & Diane Keaton. Robert Redford's *Ordinary People* wins Best Picture and Best Director at Oscar ceremonies Mar. 31.

Music. Giya Kancheli's *Symphony No. 6*; Alfred Schnittke's *Symphony No. 3*; Karlheinz Stockhausen's *Donnerstag aus Licht*.

Nonfiction. Tracy Kidder's *The Soul of a New Machine*; William S. McFeely's *Grant: A Biography*.

Popular Songs. Kim Carnes's "Bette Davis Eyes"; Olivia Newton John's "Physical"; Queen & David Bowie's "Under Pressure"; Diana Ross & Lionel Richie's "Endless Love"; Soft Cell's "Tainted Love"; John Lennon's "Starting Over"; Rolling Stones' "Start Me Up."

Science and Technology. The U.S. space shuttle *Columbia*, the world's first reusable spacecraft, completes its inaugural flight, April 14. The U.S. Center for Disease Control recognizes the first cases of the disease that would come to be known as AIDS.

Sports. A Major League Baseball players strike stops the season for 49 days, before ending with a settlement July 31. The Arlington Million, the first horse race with a million-dollar purse, is won by 6-year-old bay John Henry in Arlington Heights, IL.

TV. MTV debuts; new network TV shows include *Dynasty*, *Falcon Crest*, and *Hill Street Blues*; highest-rated programs are *60 Minutes*, *Dallas*, *Three's Company*, *M*A*S*H*.

Theatre. *Cats* debuts in London; *The Life and Adventures of Nicholas Nickelby*; *The Pirates of Penzance* revival starring Linda Ronstadt & Rex Smith; *The West Side Waltz* starring Katharine Hepburn & Dorothy Loudon.

Miscellaneous. Maya Ying Lin's design for a Vietnam Veteran's Memorial is selected from more than 1,000 entries. Prince Charles and Lady Diana Spencer marry at St. Paul's Cathedral in London, July 29, in ceremonies televised worldwide.

WORLD ALMANAC EDITORS' PICKS
2005 Time Capsule

The editors of *The World Almanac* have selected following items as representative of the year 2005.

1. The bible that Chief Justice William H. Rehnquist used to swear in President George W. Bush for his second term.
2. A flag from the coffin of a U.S. Marine who was killed in Iraq.
3. A piece of the broken levee along the 17th Street Canal in New Orleans.
4. An Apple iPod nano with 1,000 songs including "Here We Go Again," by Ray Charles and Norah Jones.
5. The dissolution papers ending the marriage of actors Brad Pitt and Jennifer Aniston.
6. A vial of stanozolol, the steroid that allegedly led to the suspension of baseball star Rafael Palmeiro.
7. J. K. Rowlings' *Harry Potter and the Half-Blood Prince*.
8. Security camera video of the 4 Islamic extremists who carried out the July 7 suicide bombings in London.
9. A sign reading "Save Terri's Life."
10. Ashes from the white smoke signaling that a new pope, German Cardinal Joseph Ratzinger, had been elected to succeed the late Pope John Paul II.
11. A copy of the Iraqi constitution put before voters Oct 15.
12. *The World Almanac and Book of Facts 2006*.

Notable Supreme Court Decisions, 2004-05

During the Supreme Court's 2004-05 term, which ended June 27, 80 decisions were announced; 17, or 21%, were decided by 5-4 votes, compared with 23% in 2003-04, 20% in 2002-03, and 28% in 2001-02. Chief Justice William H. Rehnquist and Associate Justices Antonin Scalia and Clarence Thomas tended to vote as a conservative bloc, often at odds with members of the court's liberal wing—Justices Ruth Bader Ginsburg, Stephen G. Breyer, John Paul Stevens, and David H. Souter. Justices Sandra Day O'Connor and Anthony M. Kennedy were less clearly aligned but often voted with the conservatives in close cases. Chief Justice William H. Rehnquist, under treatment for thyroid cancer, was absent from 11 rulings.

Associate Justice O'Connor announced her retirement July 1, 2005, pending confirmation of a successor, and Chief Justice Rehnquist died on Sept. 3. Federal appellate court judge John G. Roberts Jr. was confirmed by the Senate to replace Rehnquist as chief justice, and on Oct. 3, Pres. George W. Bush nominated White House Counsel Harriet E. Miers to fill O'Connor's seat, subject to Senate confirmation.

See also the feature article *Transition at the Supreme Court*, pages 7-8, and listings of justices on page 53.

Following are some of the major rulings of the 2004-2005 term.

Criminal Law: The Supreme Court Jan. 12 ruled, 5-4, that the existing system of federal criminal sentencing guidelines was unconstitutional, but another 5-justice bloc voted to maintain the guidelines by making them advisory only. The decision came in a pair of consolidated cases, *United States v. Booker* and *United States v. Fanfan*.

Church and State: The court June 27 produced divergent results in 2 cases involving display of the Ten Commandments on public property, both of which were decided by 5-4 votes. In one case, *Van Orden v. Perry*, the court found that a long-standing Ten Commandments monument on the Texas state capitol grounds in Austin, which was among a number of monuments on the grounds expressing mostly civic themes, did not violate the First Amendment's establishment clause. In the other case, *McCreary County v. ACLU of Kentucky,* the majority found the display of framed copies of the Ten Commandments in 2 Kentucky courthouses to be unconstitutional.

Capital Punishment: The court March 1 ruled, 5-4, that executions of convicts who committed their crimes before age 18 were prohibited under the Eighth Amendment ban on cruel and unusual punishment. The court in 1988 had abolished executions for offenders 15 and younger, but in 1989 had rejected a bid to raise the minimum age to 18. In the new decision, *Roper v. Simmons,* the majority concluded that a national consensus against executing juvenile offenders had developed since then.

Federalism: The court June 6 ruled, 6-3, that the Constitution's commerce clause gave Congress the power to outlaw the local, noncommercial production and use of marijuana for medicinal purposes, legalized in California and a number of other states. The case, *Gonzales v. Raich,* had begun as an attempt to block enforcement of federal antidrug laws against medicinal marijuana users in California.

The court May 16 ruled, 5-4, that states could not bar out-of-state wineries from shipping their product directly to consumers while allowing in-state wineries to do so. The decision was prompted by 3 consolidated cases—*Granholm v. Heald, Michigan Beer & Wine Wholesalers v. Heald,* and *Swedenburg v. Kelly*—concerning liquor laws in New York and Michigan. The high court relied on the Constitution's commerce clause, barring state-established trade barriers between states.

Civil Rights: The court March 30 ruled, 5-3, that the 1967 Age Discrimination in Employment Act (ADEA) permitted lawsuits in cases where an employer's policy had a disproportionate, even if unintentional, impact on workers aged 40 and older. The case was *Smith v. City of Jackson.*

The court March 29 ruled, 5-4, that individuals who claimed to have suffered retaliation for raising complaints of sexual discrimination in education could sue under the 1972 statute known as Title IX, which bans sexual discrimination by institutions receiving federal education funding, but does not specifically allow lawsuits. The case was *Jackson v. Birmingham Board of Education.*

Eminent Domain: The court June 23 ruled, 5-4, that local governments could force property owners to sell their land to facilitate private development projects deemed to be economically beneficial, even though the public would not directly own or use the land. The ruling endorsed a broad reading of the Fifth Amendment provision for the government to take over private property "for public use" when just compensation is provided. The case was *Kelo v. City of New London.*

Obstruction of Justice: The court May 31 ruled unanimously in *Arthur Andersen LLP v. United States* that flawed jury instructions invalidated a June 2002 obstruction of justice conviction against auditing firm Arthur Andersen LLP. The company, now defunct, had been convicted for destroying documents related to its auditing work for Enron Corp., which collapsed in a 2001 financial scandal.

Copyright Infringement: The court June 27 ruled unanimously that firms responsible for Internet file-sharing software could be held liable for copyright infringement if they purposefully induced or encouraged illegal activity by users. The case was *MGM Studios v. Grokster Ltd.*

The 2005 Nobel Prizes

The 2005 Nobel Prize winners were announced Oct. 3-13. Each prize is worth about $1.3 million.

Chemistry: Americans Robert H. Grubbs and Richard R. Schrock and France's Yves Chauvin shared the prize for developing a method of organic synthesis that allows industries to manufacture new drugs, stronger plastics, and better food preservatives more efficiently while reducing hazardous byproducts of chemical reactions.

Literature: The Nobel Prize Committee awarded the literature prize to British playwright Harold Pinter, "who in his plays uncovers the precipice under everyday prattle and forces entry into oppression's closed rooms." *The Caretaker* (1959) and *The Homecoming* (1964) were among major plays noted by the Academy.

Economics: Israeli-American Robert J. Aumann and American Thomas C. Schelling were recognized "for having enhanced our understanding of conflict and cooperation through game-theory analysis." Game theory is used to illuminate political and economic conflict and cooperation.

Peace: The International Atomic Energy Agency and its chief, Mohamed ElBaradei, were awarded the prize for efforts to prevent proliferation of nuclear weapons and to ensure that nuclear energy for peaceful purposes is used safely. The Nobel committee chairman said the prize was not intended as a rebuff to a particular nation or leader. In 2004, the Bush administration had opposed ElBaradei for a 3rd term as head of the UN watchdog agency.

Physics: Americans Roy J. Glauber and John L. Hall and German Theodor W. Hänsch shared the prize for applying quantum physics to the study of optics, which led to improved lasers and Global Positioning System technologies. Glauber received ½ of the award, while Hall and Hänsch were awarded ¼ each.

Physiology or Medicine: Australians Barry Marshall and Robin Warren shared the honor for their 1982 discovery of the bacterium *Helicobacter pylori* and its role in causing stomach and intestinal ulcers. Their findings were initially met with skepticism, since the long-prevailing medical view was that stomach acid and stress caused peptic ulcers. Discovery of the role *H. pylori* plays in gastrointestinal inflammation has led to antibiotic treatments for ulcers, as well as to research into microbial causes of other chronic inflammatory conditions.

UNITED STATES GOVERNMENT

EXECUTIVE BRANCH	LEGISLATIVE BRANCH	JUDICIAL BRANCH
PRESIDENT **Vice President** **Executive Office of the President** White House Office Office of the Vice President Council of Economic Advisers Council on Environmental Quality National Security Council Office of Administration Office of Management and Budget Office of National Drug Control Policy Office of Policy Development Office of Science and Technology Policy Office of the U.S. Trade Representative	**CONGRESS** **Senate** **House** Architect of the Capitol U.S. Botanic Garden General Accounting Office Government Printing Office Library of Congress Congressional Budget Office	**Supreme Court of the United States** Courts of Appeals District Courts Territorial Courts Court of International Trade Court of Federal Claims Tax Court Court of Appeals for Veterans Claims Administrative Office of the Courts Federal Judicial Center Sentencing Commission

The Bush Administration

As of Oct. 2005; mailing addresses are for Washington, DC, except for the Pentagon.

Terms of office of the president and vice president: Jan. 20, 2005 to Jan. 20, 2009.

President — By law, Pres. George W. Bush receives an annual salary of $400,000 (taxable) and an annual expense allowance of $50,000 (nontaxable) for costs resulting from official duties. In addition, up to $100,000 a year may be spent on travel expenses and $19,000 on official entertainment (both nontaxable). This does not include amounts available for expenditures within the Executive Office of the President, including $3,850,000 for necessary expenses for the White House and amounts for travel and entertainment.
Website: www.whitehouse.gov/president; **E-mail:** president@whitehouse.gov

Vice President — By law, Vice Pres. Dick Cheney receives an annual salary of $208,100 (taxable), plus $90,000 for official entertainment expenses (nontaxable).
Website: www.whitehouse.gov/vicepresident; **E-mail:** vice.president@whitehouse.gov

The Cabinet Department Heads

(Salary: $180,100 per year)

Secretary of State — Condoleezza Rice
Secretary of the Treasury — John W. Snow
Secretary of Defense — Donald H. Rumsfeld
Attorney General — Alberto Gonzales
Secretary of the Interior — Gale Norton
Secretary of Agriculture — Mike Johanns
Secretary of Commerce — Carlos M. Gutierrez
Secretary of Labor — Elaine L. Chao
Secretary of Health and Human Services — Michael O. Leavitt
Secretary of Housing and Urban Development — Alphonso Jackson
Secretary of Transportation — Norman Y. Mineta
Secretary of Energy — Samuel W. Bodman
Secretary of Education — Margaret Spellings
Secretary of Veterans Affairs — R. James Nicholson
Secretary of Homeland Security — Michael Chertoff

The White House Staff

1600 Pennsylvania Ave. NW 20500; www.whitehouse.gov

Counselor to the President — Dan Bartlett
Physician to the President — Richard Tubb
Assistants to the President:
- **Chief of Staff** — Andrew H. Card
- **Deputy Chief of Staff and Senior Advisor** — Karl Rove
- **Deputy Chief of Staff** — Joe Hagin
- **White House Press Secretary** — Scott McClellan
- **Deputy National Security Advisor** — Jack D. Crouch II
- **Director, Office of Faith-Based and Community Initiatives** — H. James Towey II
- **Staff Secretary** — Brett Kavanaugh
- **Communications** — Nicolle Devenish
- **Domestic Policy** — Claude A. Allen
- **Economic Policy and Director of the National Economic Council** — Allen B. Hubbard
- **Homeland Security and Counterterrorism** — Frances Fragos Townsend
- **Legislative Affairs** — Candida Wolff
- **National Security Affairs** — Steve Hadley
- **Policy and Strategic Planning** — Michael J. Gerson
- **Presidential Personnel** — Dina Powell
- **Speechwriting** — William McGurn

Chief of Staff to the Vice President — I. Lewis Libby
Special Assistants to the President:
- **Senior Director for Legislative Affairs** — Michael Allen
- **White House Social Secretary** —Janet Lea Berman

Deputy Assistant to the President and Chief of Staff to the First Lady — Anita McBride
Press Secretary, Office of the First Lady — Susan Whitson

Executive Agencies

Council of Economic Advisers — Ben Bernanke, chair; www.whitehouse.gov/cea
Office of Administration — Tim Campen, dir.; www.whitehouse.gov/oa
Office of Science & Technology Policy — John H. Marburger III; www.ostp.gov
Office of Natl. Drug Control Policy — John P. Walters, dir.; www.whitehousedrugpolicy.gov
Office of Management and Budget — Joshua B. Bolten, dir.; www.whitehouse.gov/omb
U.S. Trade Representative — Rob Portman; www.ustr.gov
Council on Environ. Quality — James L. Connaughton, chair; www.whitehouse.gov/ceq

IT'S A FACT: With his $400,000 salary Pres. George W. Bush earns twice as much for the job as did his father, former Pres. George H. W. Bush, and 16 times the salary Congress authorized for the father of the country, George Washington. Washington's salary of $25,000 would be worth a lot more in today's dollars—more than $500,000—but he never took it; only one other president declined a salary, John F. Kennedy.

Department of State

2201 C St. NW 20520; www.state.gov

Secretary of State — Condoleezza Rice
Deputy Secretary — Robert B. Zoellick
U.S. Permanent Rep. to the United Nations — John R. Bolton
U.S. Agency for Intl. Dev. — Andrew S. Natsios
Under Sec. for Political Affairs — R. Nicholas Burns
Under Sec. for Management — Henrietta H. Fore
Under Sec. for Global Affairs — Paula Dobriansky
Under Sec. for Economic, Business, & Agricultural Affairs — Josette S. Shiner
Under Sec. for Arms Control & International Security Affairs — Robert Joseph
Under Sec. for Public Diplomacy & Public Affairs — Karen Hughes
Policy Planning Director — Stephen Krasner
Chief of Protocol — Donald B. Ensenat
Inspector General — Howard J. Krongard
Legal Adviser — John B. Bellinger III
Counterterrorism — Henry A. Crumpton
Director General of the Foreign Service & Director of Human Resources — W. Robert Pearson
Assistant Secretaries for:
- **Administration** — Frank Coulter, act.
- **African Affairs** — Jendayi Frazer
- **Arms Control** — Stephen G. Rademaker
- **Consular Affairs** — Maura Harty
- **Democracy, Human Rights, & Labor** — Glyn T. Davies
- **Diplomatic Security** — Richard J. Griffin
- **East Asian & Pacific Affairs** — Christopher R. Hill
- **Education & Cultural Affairs** — Dina Powell
- **European & Eurasian Affairs** — Daniel Fried
- **Intelligence & Research** — Carol A. Rodley, act.
- **International Narcotics & Law Enforcement Affairs** — Nancy J. Powell, act.
- **International Organization Affairs** — Kristen Silverberg
- **Legislative Affairs** — Paul V. Kelly
- **Near Eastern Affairs** — C. David Welch
- **Nonproliferation** — Stephen Rademaker
- **Oceans, International Environmental, & Scientific Affairs** — Anthony F. Rock, act.
- **Political-Military Affairs** — John Hillen
- **Population, Refugees, & Migration** — Richard L. Greene, act.
- **Public Affairs** — Sean McCormack
- **Resource Management** — Jay N. Anania
- **South Asian Affairs** — Christina B. Rocca
- **Verification & Compliance** — Paula A. DeSutter
- **Western Hemisphere Affairs** — Roger F. Noriega

Department of the Treasury

1500 Pennsylvania Ave. NW 20220; www.ustreas.gov

Secretary of the Treasury — John W. Snow
Deputy Sec. of the Treasury — Robert M. Kimmitt
Chief of Staff — Christopher Smith
Executive Secretary — Paul W. Curry
White House Liaison — Kim Nickles
Under Sec. for Domestic Finance — Randal K. Quarles
Under Sec. for International Affairs — Timothy D. Adams
Under Sec. for Terrorism & Financial Crimes — Stuart Levey
General Counsel — Arnold I. Havens
Inspector General — Harold Damelin
Inspector General for Tax Administration — J. Russell George
Treasurer of the U.S. — Anna Escobedo Cabral
Assistant Secretaries for:
- **Economic Policy** — Mark Warshawsky
- **Financial Institutions** — vacant
- **Financial Markets**— Timothy Bitsberger
- **Fiscal Affairs** — Donald V. Hammond
- **International Affairs** — vacant
- **Legislative Affairs** — Kevin I. Fromer
- **Management** — Sandra Pack
- **Public Affairs** — Tony Fratto, act.
- **Tax Policy** — vacant
- **Terrorism & Financial Intelligence (Terrorist Financing)**— Daniel Glaser, act.

Bureaus:
- **Alcohol and Tobacco Tax and Trade** — John Manfreda, admin.
- **Comptroller of the Currency** — John Dugan, compt., act.
- **Engraving & Printing** — Thomas A. Ferguson, dir.
- **Financial Crimes Enforcement Network** — William J. Fox, dir.
- **Financial Management Service** — Richard Gregg, comm.
- **Internal Revenue Service** — Mark W. Everson, comm.
- **U.S. Mint** — David Lebryk, act. dir.
- **Office of Thrift Supervision** — John Reich, dir.
- **Public Debt** — Van Zeck, comm.

Department of Defense

The Pentagon, Arlington, VA 20301; www.dod.gov

Secretary of Defense — Donald H. Rumsfeld
Deputy Secretary — Gordan England, act.
Under Sec. Comptroller/CIO — Tina W. Jonas
Under Sec. for Acquis. and Tech. — Kenneth J. Krieg
Under Sec. for Intelligence — Stephen A. Cambone
Under Sec. for Personnel & Readiness — David S. C. Chu
Under Sec. for Policy — Eric S. Edelman
Principal Deputy Under Secretary (Personnel & Readiness)— Charles S. Abell
Assistant Secretaries for:
- **Network & Info Integration**— Linton Wells II, act.
- **Health Affairs** — William Winkenwerder Jr.
- **International Security Affairs** — Peter W. Rodman
- **Legislative Affairs** — Daniel Stanley
- **Public Affairs** — Lawrence Di Rita
- **Reserve Affairs** — Thomas F. Hall
- **Special Operations & Low-Intensity Conflict** — Thomas W. O'Connell

Inspector General — Joseph E. Schmitz
General Counsel — William J. Haynes II
Operational Test & Evaluation — Thomas P. Christie, dir.
Chairman, Joint Chiefs of Staff — Gen. Peter Pace
Secretary of the Army — Francis J. Harvey
Secretary of the Navy — Gordon R. England.
Commandant of the Marine Corps — Gen. Michael W. Hagee
Secretary of the Air Force — Michael L. Dominguez, act.

Department of Justice

Constitution Ave. & 10th St. NW 20530; www.usdoj.gov

Attorney General — Alberto Gonzales
Deputy Attorney General — Robert D. McCallum Jr., act.
Associate Attorney General — Robert D. McCallum Jr
Office of Dispute Resolution — Linda A. Cinciotta, dir.
Solicitor General — Paul D. Clement, act.
Office of Inspector General — Glenn A. Fine
Assistants:
- **Antitrust Division** — Thomas O. Barnett, act.
- **Civil Division** — Peter D. Keisler
- **Civil Rights Division** — Bradley J. Schlozman, act.
- **Criminal Division** — Alice S. Fisher
- **Environ. & Nat. Resources Division** — Kelly A. Johnson, act.
- **Justice Programs** — Regina B. Schofield
- **Legal Counsel** — Dan Levin, act.
- **Legislative Affairs** — William E. Moschella
- **Legal Policy** — Rachel Brand, act.
- **Tax Division** — Eileen O'Connor

Office of Public Affairs — Tasia Scolinos, dir.
Office of Information & Privacy — Richard L. Huff/Daniel J. Metcalfe
Community Oriented Policing Services — Carl R. Peed
Federal Bureau of Investigation — Robert S. Mueller III
Bureau of Alcohol, Tobacco, Firearms, and Explosives— Carl J. Truscott.
Exec. Off. for Immigration Review — Kevin D. Rooney, dir.
Bureau of Prisons — Harley G. Lappin
Community Relations Service — Sharee M. Freeman, dir.
Drug Enforcement Admin. — Karen P. Tandy
Office of Intelligence Policy & Review — James A. Baker
Office of Professional Responsibility — H. Marshall Jarrett
Exec. Off. for U.S. Trustees — Lawrence A. Friedman
Foreign Claims Settlement Comm. — Mauricio J. Tamargo
Exec. Office for U.S. Attorneys — Michael Battle, dir.
Pardon Attorney — Roger C. Adams
U.S. Parole Commission — Edward F. Reilly Jr.
U.S. Marshals Service — John Clark, act.
U.S. Natl. Central Bureau of INTERPOL — James M. Sullivan
Office of Intergovernmental and Public Liaison — Crystal Roberts, dir.
Violence Against Women Office — Diane Stewart
National Drug Intelligence Center — Martin W. Pracht

Department of the Interior

1849 C St. NW 20240; www.doi.gov

Secretary of the Interior — Gale Norton
Deputy Secretary — vacant
Assistant Secretaries for:
Fish, Wildlife, & Parks — Craig Manson
Indian Affairs — vacant
Land & Minerals Management — Rebecca W. Watson
Policy, Management, & Budget — P. Lynn Scarlett
Water & Science — Mark Limbaugh
Bureau of Land Management — Kathleen Clarke
Bureau of Reclamation — John W. Keys III
Fish & Wildlife Service — Matt Hogan, act.
Geological Survey — P. Patrick Leahy
Minerals Management Service — R.M. "Johnnie" Burton
National Park Service — Fran P. Mainella, dir.
Surf. Mining Reclam. & Enforcement — Jeffrey Jarrett
Communications — Tina Kreisher
Congressional & Legislative Affairs — Matt Eames, dir.
Solicitor — Sue Ellen Wooldridge
External Affairs — Kit Kimball
Exec. Secretariat & Regulatory Affairs — Fay S. Iudicello

Department of Agriculture

1400 Independence Ave. SW 20250; www.usda.gov

Secretary of Agriculture — Mike Johanns
Deputy Secretary — Chuck Conner
Under Secretaries for:
Farm & Foreign Agric. Services — J. B. Penn
Food, Nutrition, & Consumer Services — Eric M. Bost
Food Safety — Richard Raymond
Marketing & Regulatory Progs. — William T. Hawks
Natural Resources & Environment — Mark E. Rey
Research, Education, & Economics — Joseph Jen
Rural Development — Thomas C. Dorr
Assistant Secretaries for:
Administration — Michael Harrison
Civil Rights — Vernon Parker
Congressional Relations — Mary Waters
General Counsel — vacant
Inspector General — Phyllis Fong
Chief Financial Officer — Patricia Healy, act.
Chief Information Officer — Dave Combs
Chief Economist — Keith Collins
Communications — Terri Teuber, dir.

Department of Commerce

1401 Constitution Ave. NW 20230; www.commerce.gov

Secretary of Commerce — Carlos M. Gutierrez
Deputy Secretary — David A. Sampson
Chief of Staff — Claire Buchan
General Counsel — John J. Sullivan
Inspector General — Johnnie E. Frazier
Under Sec. for Industry and Security — Peter Lichtenbaum, act.
Under Sec. for Economic Affairs — Kathleen Cooper
Under Sec. for International Trade — Peter Lichtenbaum, act.
Under Sec. and Administrator for NOAA — Vice Admiral Conrad C. Lautenbacher Jr.
Under Sec. for Intellectual Property and Director USPTO — Jon W. Dudas
Under Sec. for Technology — Michelle O'Neill, act.
Assistant Secretaries:
Administration and Chief Financial Officer — Otto J. Wolff
Communications and Information — Michael Gallagher
Economic Development Administration — Sandy K. Baruah, act.
Export Administration — Peter Lichtenbaum
Export Enforcement — Wendy Wysong, act.
Import Administration — Joseph A. Spetrini, act.
Legislative and Intergovernmental Affairs — Nathaniel Wienecke, act.
Oceans and Atmosphere and Deputy Administrator — Dr. James Mahoney
Manufacturing and Services — Albert Frink
Market Access and Compliance — Peter Hale, act.
Technology Policy — Ben Wu
Business Liaison — Dan McCardell
Policy and Strategic Planning — David Bohigian
Public Affairs — Christine Gunderson
Bureau of the Census — Charles Louis Kincannon, dir.
Bureau of Economic Analysis — J. Steven Landefeld, dir.
Minority Business Development Agency — Ronald Langston, dir.
Natl. Institute of Standards and Technology — William A. Jeffrey

Department of Labor

200 Constitution Ave. NW 20210; www.dol.gov

Secretary of Labor — Elaine L. Chao
Deputy Secretary — Steven J. Law
Chief of Staff — Paul Conway
Assistant Secretaries for:
Admin. & Management — Patrick Pizzella
Congressional & Intergov. Affairs — Kristine Iverson
Employment & Training — Emily Stover DeRocco
Employment Standards — Victoria A. Lipnic
Occupational Safety & Health — vacant
Mine Safety & Health — vacant
Employee Benefits Security Admin. — Ann L. Combs
Policy — Veronica Vargas Stidvent
Public Affairs — Lisa Kruska
Veterans Employment & Training — Charles S. Ciccollela
Solicitor of Labor — Martha Newton, act.
Bureau of International Affairs — Martha Newton, act.
Women's Bureau — Shinae Chun
Inspector General — Gordon S. Heddell
Bureau of Labor Statistics — Kathleen P. Utgoff

Department of Health and Human Services

200 Independence Ave. SW 20201; www.hhs.gov

Secretary of Health & Human Services — Michael O. Leavitt
Deputy Secretary — Alex Azar II
Chief of Staff — Rich McKeown
Centers for Disease Control and Prevention— Julie Louise Gerberding, dir.
Health Care Research & Quality— Carolyn M. Clancy, dir.
National Institutes of Health— Elias Zerhouni, dir.
Assistant Secretaries for:
Aging — Josefina Carbonell
Children & Families — Wade F. Horn
Health — Cristina V. Beato, act.
Legislation — Jennifer Young
Administration & Management — Joe Ellis
Planning & Evaluation — Michael O'Grady
Public Affairs — Suzy DeFrancis
General Counsel — Alex Azar II
Inspector General — Daniel R. Levinson
Office for Civil Rights — Richard M. Campanelli, dir.
Surgeon General — Richard Carmona
Centers for Medicare and Medicaid Services — Mark McClellan
Faith-Based & Community Initiatives — Robert J. Polito, dir.

Department of Housing and Urban Development

451 7th St. SW 20410; www.hud.gov

Secretary of Housing & Urban Development — Alphonso Jackson
Deputy Secretary — Roy A. Bernardi
Chief of Staff — Camille T. Pierce
Assistant Secretaries for:
Community Planning & Development — Pamela Patenaude
Congressional & Intergov. Relations — Steven B. Nesmith
Fair Housing & Equal Opportunity — vacant
Administration — vacant
Housing/Federal Housing Comm. — Brian Montgomery
Policy Development & Research — vacant
Public & Indian Housing — vacant
Public Affairs — Cathy M. MacFarlane
General Counsel — vacant
Inspector General — Kevin M. Donohue Sr.
Chief Financial Officer — vacant
Chief Executive Officer — Marcella E. Belt
Government National Mortgage Assn. — vacant

Department of Transportation

400 7th St. SW 20590; www.dot.gov

Secretary of Transportation — Norman Y. Mineta
Deputy Secretary — Maria Cino
Under Secretary for Policy — Jeffrey N. Shane
General Counsel —Jeffrey A. Rosen
Assistant Secretaries for:
Administration — Linda J. Washington, act.
Aviation & International Affairs — Karan K. Bhatia
Budget & Programs — Phyllis F. Scheinberg
Governmental Affairs — Nicole Nason
Public Affairs — Robert Johnson
Transportation Policy — Tyler Duvall, act.
Bureau of Transportation Statistics — Mary Hutzler, act.
Federal Aviation Admin. — Marion C. Blakey
Federal Highway Admin. — Mary E. Peters
Federal Motor Carrier Safety Admin. — Annette M. Sandberg
Federal Railroad Admin. — Joseph H. Boardman
Maritime Admin. — John E. Jamian, act.
Natl. Highway Traffic Safety Admin. — Jeffrey W. Runge
Federal Transit Admin. — Jennifer L. Dorn
Inspector General — Kenneth M. Mead
St. Lawrence Seaway Devel. Corp. — Albert S. Jacquez

Department of Energy

1000 Independence Ave. SW 20585; www.energy.gov

Secretary of Energy — Samuel W. Bodman
Deputy Secretary — Clay Sell
Under Sec. for Energy, Science & Environment — David K. Garman
Under Sec. & Admin. for Nuclear Security — Linton Brooks
General Counsel — David R. Hill
Inspector General — Gregory Friedman
Assistant Secretaries for:
Congressional & Intergov. Affairs — Jill L. Sigal, act.
Energy Efficiency & Renewable Energy — David L. Faulkner
Environment, Safety, & Health — John Shaw
Environmental Management — James Rispoli
Fossil Energy — Mark R. Maddox, act.
International Affairs & Policy — Karen A. Harbert
Nuclear Energy, Science, and Technology — R. Shane Johnson, act. dir.
Energy Information Admin. — Guy F. Caruso
Economic Impact & Diversity — Theresa Alvillar-Speake
Hearings & Appeals — George Breznay
Civilian Radioactive Waste Management — vacant
Chief Financial Officer — Susan Grant
Energy Advisory Board — M. Peter McPherson
Office of Public Affairs — Anne Womack Kolton

Department of Education

400 Maryland Ave. SW 20202; www.ed.gov

Secretary of Education — Margaret Spellings
Deputy Secretary — Raymond J. Simon
Under Secretary — Edward R. McPherson
Chief of Staff — David Dunn
Assistant Secretaries for:
Special Education and Rehabilitative Services — John H. Hager
Vocational and Adult Education — vacant
Civil Rights — vacant
Elementary and Secondary Education — Henry Johnson
Postsecondary Education — Sally L. Stroup
Planning, Evaluation, and Policy Development — Tom Luce
Legislation and Congressional Affairs — Terrell Halaska
Intergovernmental and Interagency Affairs — Christina Culver, act.
Management and Chief Information Officer — Michell Clark, act.
Chief Financial Officer — Jack Martin
Office of Federal Student Aid — Theresa S. Shaw
Public Affairs — D.J. Nordquist, act.
Institute of Education Sciences — Grover J. Whitehurst, dir.
General Counsel — Kent D. Talbert, act.
Office of Educational Technology — vacant

Department of Veterans Affairs

810 Vermont Ave. NW 20420; www.va.gov

Secretary of Veterans Affairs — R. James Nicholson
Deputy Secretary — Gordon H. Mansfield
Chief of Staff — Claude M. Kicklighter
Under Sec. for Health — Jonathan B. Perlin
Under Sec. for Benefits — Daniel L. Cooper
Under Sec. for Memorial Affairs — Richard A. Wannemacher Jr., act.
Assistant Secretaries for:
Policy, Planning, Preparedness — Dennis M. Duffy
Human Resource Administration — R. Allen Pittman
Public and Intergovernmental Affairs — Thomas E. Harvey, act.
Information and Technology — Robert N. McFarland
Congressional and Legislative Affairs — Pamela M. Iovino
General Counsel — Tim S. McClain
Inspector General — Jon A. Wooditch, act.
Board of Veterans' Appeals — Ron H. Garvin, act. chair.
Board of Contract Appeals — Gary J. Krump, chair.

Department of Homeland Security

20528 (no street address used); www.dhs.gov/dhspublic

Secretary of Homeland Security — Michael Chertoff
Deputy Secretary — Michael P. Jackson
Chief of Staff — John Wood
Under Sec. for Border & Trans. Sec. — Randy Beardsworth, act.
Under Sec. for Emergency Preparedness & Response — R. David Paulison
Under Sec. for Info. Analysis & Infrastructure Protection — Robert B. Stephan, act.
Under Sec. for Management — Janet Hale
Under Sec. for Science & Tech. — Dr. Charles E. McQueary
Assistant Secretaries for:
Immigration & Customs Enforcement — John Clark, act.
Legislative Affairs — Pamela J. Turner
Public Affairs — Brian R. Besanceney
State and Local Gov. Coordination — Joshua D. Filler
Transportation Security Administration — Kip Hawley, act.
U.S. Coast Guard Commandant — Adm. Thomas H. Collins
U.S. Secret Service — W. Ralph Basham, dir.
Inspector General — Richard L. Skinner, act.
Bur. of Citizenship & Immigration Services — Prakash I. Khatri, ombudsman.
Office of Natl. Capital Region Coordination — Thomas J. Lockwood
Officer for Civil Rights & Civil Liberties — Daniel W. Sutherland
Chief Privacy Officer — Nuala O'Connor Kelly
Chief Security Officer — Dwight M. Williams
Chief Financial Officer — Andrew B. Maner
Chief Human Capital Officer — Ronald J. James
Customs & Border Protection — Robert C. Bonner, comm.
Federal Law Enforcement Training — Connie L. Patrick, dir.

Notable U.S. Government Agencies

Source: The U.S. Government Manual; National Archives and Records Administration; World Almanac research
All addresses are Washington, DC, unless otherwise noted; as of Oct. 2005
* = independent agency

Bureau of Alcohol, Tobacco, Firearms and Explosives — Carl J. Truscott, dir. (Dept. of Justice, 650 Mass. Ave NW, 20226; www.atf.gov

Bureau of the Census — Charles Louis Kincannon, dir. (Dept. of Commerce, 4700 Silver Hill Rd., 20233); www.census.gov

Bureau of Citizenship & Immigration Services — Prakash I. Khatri, ombudsman (Dept. of Homeland Security, 425 I St. NW, 20536); www.uscis.gov

Bureau of Economic Analysis — J. Steven Landefeld, dir. (Dept. of Commerce, 1441 L St. NW, 20230); www.bea.gov

Bureau of Indian Affairs — vacant, asst. sec. (Dept. of the Interior, 1849 C St. NW, 20240); www.doi.gov/bureau-indian-affairs.html

Bureau of Prisons — Harley G. Lappin, dir. (Dept. of Justice, 320 First St. NW, 20534); www.bop.gov

Centers for Disease Control & Prevention — Julie Louise Gerberding, dir. (Dept. of HHS, 1600 Clifton Rd., Atlanta, GA 30333); www.cdc.gov

***Central Intelligence Agency** — Porter Goss, dir. (Wash., DC 20505; www.cia.gov

*__Commission on Civil Rights__ — Gerald A. Reynolds, chair (624 9th St. NW, 20425); www.usccr.gov

*__Commodity Futures Trading Commission__ — Reuben Jeffery III, chair (3 Lafayette Centre, 1155 21st St. NW, 20581); www.cftc.gov

*__Consumer Product Safety Commission__ — Hal Stratton, chair (East-West Towers, 4330 East-West Hwy., Bethesda, MD 20814); www.cpsc.gov

*__Environmental Protection Agency__ — Stephen L. Johnson, adm. (Ariel Rios Bldg., 1200 Pennsylvania Ave. NW, 20460); www.epa.gov

*__Equal Employment Opportunity Commission__ — Cari M. Dominguez, chair (1801 L St. NW, 20507); www.eeoc.gov

*__Export-Import Bank of the United States__ — James H. Lambright, act. pres. and chair (811 Vermont Avenue NW, 20571); www.exim.gov

*__Farm Credit Administration__ — Nancy C. Pellett, chair (1501 Farm Credit Drive, McLean, VA 22102); www.fca.gov

Federal Aviation Administration — Marion C. Blakey, adm. (Dept. of Trans., 800 Independence Ave. SW, 20591); www.faa.gov

Federal Bureau of Investigation — Robert S. Mueller III, dir. (Dept. of Justice, 935 Pennsylvania Ave. NW, 20535); www.fbi.gov

*__Federal Communications Commission__ — Kevin J. Martin, chair (445 12th St. SW, 20554); www.fcc.gov

*__Federal Deposit Insurance Corporation__ — Donald E. Powell, chair (550 17th St. NW, 20429); www.fdic.gov

*__Federal Election Commission__ — Scott E. Thomas, chair (999 E St. NW, 20463); www.fec.gov

*__Federal Emergency Management Agency__ — R. David Paulison, act. under sec. (500 C St. SW, 20472); www.fema.gov

*__Federal Energy Regulatory Commission__ — Joseph T. Kelliher, chair (888 1st St. NE, 20426); www.ferc.gov

Federal Highway Administration — Mary E. Peters, adm. (Dept. of Trans., 400 7th St. SW, 20590); www.fhwa.dot.gov

*__Federal Maritime Commission__ — Steven R. Blust, chair (800 N. Capitol St. NW, 20573); www.fmc.gov

*__Federal Mine Safety & Health Review Commission__ — Michael F. Duffy, chair (601 New Jersey Ave. NW, 20001); www.fmshrc.gov

*__Federal Reserve System__ — Alan Greenspan, chair, Board of Governors (20th St. & Constitution Ave. NW, 20551); www.federalreserve.gov

*__Federal Trade Commission__ — Deborah Platt Majoras, chair (600 Pennsylvania Ave. NW, 20580); www.ftc.gov

Fish & Wildlife Service — Dale Hall, dir. (Dept. of the Interior, 1849 C St. NW, 20240); www.fws.gov

Food and Drug Administration — Andrew C. Eschenbach, act. comm. (Dept. of HHS, 5600 Fishers Lane, Rockville, MD 20857); www.fda.gov

Forest Service — Dale N. Bosworth, chief (Dept. of Agriculture, 1400 Independence Ave. SW, 20250); www.fs.fed.us

Government Accountability Office — (cong. agency) David M. Walker, comptroller gen. (441 G St. NW, 20548); www.gao.gov

*__General Services Administration__ — vacant (1800 F St. NW, 20405); www.gsa.gov

Government Printing Office — (cong. agency) Bruce R. James, public printer (732 N. Capitol St. NW, 20401); www.gpoaccess.gov

*__Inter-American Foundation__ — Roger W. Wallace, pres. (901 N Stuart St., 10th floor, Arlington, VA 22203); www.iaf.gov

Internal Revenue Service — Mark W. Everson, comm. (Dept. of Treas., 1111 Constitution Ave. NW, 20224); www.irs.gov

Library of Congress — (cong. agency) James H. Billington, Librarian of Congress (101 Indep. Ave. SE, 20540); www.loc.gov

*__National Aeronautics and Space Administration__ — Michael Griffin, adm. (300 E St. SW, 20546); www.nasa.gov

*__National Archives & Records Administration__ — Allen Weinstein, archivist (700 Pennsylvania Ave. NW, 20408).; www.archives.gov

*__National Endowment for the Arts__ — Dana Gioia, chair (1100 Pennsylvania Ave. NW, 20506); www.arts.gov

*__National Endowment for the Humanities__ — Bruce Cole, chair (1100 Pennsylvania Ave. NW, 20506); www.neh.fed.us

National Institutes of Health — Elias Zerhouni, dir. (Dept. of HHS, 9000 Rockville Pike, Bethesda, MD 20892); www.nih.gov

*__National Labor Relations Board__ — Robert J. Battista, chair (1099 14th St. NW, 20570); www.nlrb.gov

National Oceanic and Atmospheric Administration — Conrad C. Lautenbacher Jr., admin. (Dept. of Commerce, 14th & Constitution Ave. NW, 20230).; www.noaa.gov

National Park Service — Fran B. Mainella, dir. (Dept. of the Interior, 1849 C St. NW, 20240); www.nps.gov

*__National Railroad Passenger Corp. (Amtrak)__ — David Gunn, pres. and CEO (60 Mass. Ave. NE, 20002); www.amtrak.com

*__National Science Foundation__ — Arden L. Bement Jr., dir., National Science Foundation; Warren M. Washington, chair, National Science Board (4201 Wilson Blvd., Arlington, VA 22230); www.nsf.gov

*__National Transportation Safety Board__ — Mark V. Rosenker, act. chair (490 L'Enfant Plaza SW, 20594); www.ntsb.gov

*__Nuclear Regulatory Commission__ — Nils J. Diaz, chair (Office of Public Affairs, 20555); www.nrc.gov

Occupational Safety & Health Administration — vacant (Dept. of Labor, 200 Constitution Ave. NW, 20210); www.osha.gov

*__Occupational Safety & Health Review Commission__ — W. Scott Railton, chair (1120 20th St. NW, 9th Floor, 20036); www.oshrc.gov

*__Office of Government Ethics__ — vacant (1201 New York Ave. NW, Suite 500, 20005); www.usoge.gov

*__Office of Personnel Management__ — Linda M. Springer, dir. (1900 E St. NW, 20415-0001); www.opm.gov

*__Office of Special Counsel__ — Scott J. Bloch, spec. counsel (1730 M St. NW, Suite 300, 20036); www.osc.gov

*__Peace Corps__ — Gaddi H. Vasquez, dir. (1111 20th St., NW, 20526); www.peacecorps.gov

*__Postal Rate Commission__ — George A. Omas, chair (1333 H St. NW, Suite 300, 20268); www.prc.gov

*__Securities and Exchange Commission__ — Christopher Cox, chair (100 F Street NE, 20549); www.sec.gov

*__Selective Service System__ — William A. Chatfield, dir. (National Headquarters, 1515 Wilson Blvd., Arlington, VA 22209-2425); www.sss.gov

*__Small Business Administration__ — Hector V. Barreto, adm. (409 Third St. SW, 20416; www.sba.gov

Smithsonian Institution — (quasi-official agency) Lawrence M. Small, sec. (PO Box 37012, SI Building, Rm. 153, MRC 010, 20013); www.si.edu

*__Social Security Administration__ — Jo Anne B. Barnhart, comm. (6401 Security Blvd., Baltimore, MD 21235); www.ssa.gov

Surgeon General — Richard Carmona (Dept. of HHS, 200 Independence Ave SW, 20201); www.surgeongeneral.gov

*__Tennessee Valley Authority__ — Bill Baxter, chair, Board of Directors (400 W. Summit Hill Dr., Knoxville, TN 37902); www.tva.gov

*__Trade and Development Agency__ — Thelma J. Askey, dir. (1000 Wilson Blvd. Ste. 1600, Arlington, VA 22209); www.tda.gov

United States Coast Guard — Adm. Thomas H. Collins, commandant (Dept. of Homeland Security, 2100 2nd St. SW, 20593); www.uscg.mil

United States Customs and Border Protection — Robert C. Bonner, comm. (Dept. of Homeland Security, 1300 Pennsylvania Ave. NW, 20229); www.customs.gov

United States Geological Survey — P. Patrick Leahy, act. dir. (Dept. of the Interior, 12201 Sunrise Valley Dr., Reston, VA 20192); www.usgs.gov

*__United States International Trade Commission__ — Stephen Koplan, chair (500 E St. SW, 20436); www.usitc.gov

United States Mint — David Lebryk, dir. (Dept. of Treas., U.S. Mint Headquarters, 801 9th St., NW, 20002); www.usmint.gov

*__United States Postal Service__ — John E. Potter, Postmaster General (475 L'Enfant Plaza SW, 20260); www.usps.com

United States Secret Service — W. Ralph Basham, dir. (Dept. of Homeland Security, 245 Murray Dr., Bldg. 410, 20223); www.secretservice.gov

CABINETS OF THE U.S.

The U.S. Cabinet and Its Role

The heads of major executive departments of government constitute the Cabinet. This institution, not provided for in the U.S. Constitution, developed as an advisory body out of the desire of presidents to consult on policy matters. Aside from its advisory role, the Cabinet as a body has no formal function and wields no executive authority. Individual members exercise authority as heads of their departments, reporting to the president.

In addition to the heads of federal departments as listed below, the Cabinet commonly includes other officials designated by the president as of Cabinet rank.

The officials so designated by Pres. George W. Bush include: Vice Pres. Richard B. Cheney, Chief of Staff to the President Andrew H. Card Jr., Environmental Protection Agency Administrator Stephen Johnson, Office of Management and Budget Director Joshua B. Bolten, Office of National Drug Control Policy Director John P. Walters, and United States Trade Representative Rob Portman.

The Cabinet meets at times set by the president. Members of Pres. Bush's Cabinet listed in this chapter are as of Oct. 2005.

Secretaries of State

The Department of Foreign Affairs was created by act of Congress on July 27, 1789, and the name changed to Department of State on Sept. 15, 1789.

President	Secretary	Home	Sworn In
Washington	Thomas Jefferson	VA	1789
	Edmund Randolph	VA	1794
	Timothy Pickering	PA	1795
Adams, J.	Timothy Pickering	PA	1797
	John Marshall	VA	1800
Jefferson	James Madison	VA	1801
Madison	Robert Smith	MD	1809
	James Monroe	VA	1811
Monroe	John Quincy Adams	MA	1817
Adams, J.Q.	Henry Clay	KY	1825
Jackson	Martin Van Buren	NY	1829
	Edward Livingston	LA	1831
	Louis McLane	DE	1833
	John Forsyth	GA	1834
Van Buren	John Forsyth	GA	1837
Harrison, W.H.	Daniel Webster	MA	1841
Tyler	Daniel Webster	MA	1841
	Abel P. Upshur	VA	1843
	John C. Calhoun	SC	1844
Polk	John C. Calhoun	SC	1845
	James Buchanan	PA	1845
Taylor	James Buchanan	PA	1849
	John M. Clayton	DE	1849
Fillmore	John M. Clayton	DE	1850
	Daniel Webster	MA	1850
	Edward Everett	MA	1852
Pierce	William L. Marcy	NY	1853
Buchanan	William L. Marcy	NY	1857
	Lewis Cass	MI	1857
	Jeremiah S. Black	PA	1860
Lincoln	Jeremiah S. Black	PA	1861
	William H. Seward	NY	1861
Johnson, A.	William H. Seward	NY	1865
Grant	Elihu B. Washburne	IL	1869
	Hamilton Fish	NY	1869
Hayes	Hamilton Fish	NY	1877
	William M. Evarts	NY	1877
Garfield	William M. Evarts	NY	1881
	James G. Blaine	ME	1881
Arthur	James G. Blaine	ME	1881
	F.T. Frelinghuysen	NJ	1881
Cleveland	F.T. Frelinghuysen	NJ	1885
	Thomas F. Bayard	DE	1885
Harrison, B.	Thomas F. Bayard	DE	1889
Harrison, B.	James G. Blaine	ME	1889
	John W. Foster	IN	1892
Cleveland	Walter Q. Gresham	IN	1893
	Richard Olney	MA	1895
McKinley	Richard Olney	MA	1897
	John Sherman	OH	1897
	William R. Day	OH	1898
	John Hay	DC	1898
Roosevelt, T.	John Hay	DC	1901
	Elihu Root	NY	1905
	Robert Bacon	NY	1909
Taft	Robert Bacon	NY	1909
	Philander C. Knox	PA	1909
Wilson	Philander C. Knox	PA	1913
	William J. Bryan	NE	1913
	Robert Lansing	NY	1915
	Bainbridge Colby	NY	1920
Harding	Charles E. Hughes	NY	1921
Coolidge	Charles E. Hughes	NY	1923
	Frank B. Kellogg	MN	1925
Hoover	Frank B. Kellogg	MN	1929
	Henry L. Stimson	NY	1929
Roosevelt, F.D.	Cordell Hull	TN	1933
	E.R. Stettinius Jr.	VA	1944
Truman	E.R. Stettinius Jr.	VA	1945
	James F. Byrnes	SC	1945
	George C. Marshall	PA	1947
	Dean G. Acheson	CT	1949
Eisenhower	John Foster Dulles	NY	1953
	Christian A. Herter	MA	1959
Kennedy	Dean Rusk	NY	1961
Johnson, L.B.	Dean Rusk	NY	1963
Nixon	William P. Rogers	NY	1969
	Henry A. Kissinger	DC	1973
Ford	Henry A. Kissinger	DC	1974
Carter	Cyrus R. Vance	NY	1977
	Edmund S. Muskie	ME	1980
Reagan	Alexander M. Haig Jr.	CT	1981
	George P. Shultz	CA	1982
Bush, G.H.W.	James A. Baker III	TX	1989
	Lawrence S. Eagleburger	MI	1992
Clinton	Warren M. Christopher	CA	1993
	Madeleine K. Albright	DC	1997
Bush, G.W.	Colin L. Powell	NY	2001
	Condoleezza Rice	DC	2005

Secretaries of the Treasury

The Treasury Department was organized by act of Congress on Sept. 2, 1789.

President	Secretary	Home	Sworn In
Washington	Alexander Hamilton	NY	1789
	Oliver Wolcott	CT	1795
Adams, J.	Oliver Wolcott	CT	1797
	Samuel Dexter	MA	1801
Jefferson	Samuel Dexter	MA	1801
	Albert Gallatin	PA	1801
Madison	Albert Gallatin	PA	1809
	George W. Campbell	TN	1814
	Alexander J. Dallas	PA	1814
	William H. Crawford	GA	1816
Monroe	William H. Crawford	GA	1817
Adams, J.Q.	Richard Rush	PA	1825
Jackson	Samuel D. Ingham	PA	1829
	Louis McLane	DE	1831
	William J. Duane	PA	1833
	Roger B. Taney	MD	1833
	Levi Woodbury	NH	1834
Van Buren	Levi Woodbury	NH	1837
Harrison, W.H.	Thomas Ewing	OH	1841
Tyler	Thomas Ewing	OH	1841
	Walter Forward	PA	1841
	John C. Spencer	NY	1843
	George M. Bibb	KY	1844
Polk	Robert J. Walker	MS	1845
Taylor	William M. Meredith	PA	1849
Fillmore	Thomas Corwin	OH	1850
Pierce	James Guthrie	KY	1853
Buchanan	Howell Cobb	GA	1857
	Phillip F. Thomas	MD	1860
	John A. Dix	NY	1861
Lincoln	Salmon P. Chase	OH	1861
	William P. Fessenden	ME	1864
	Hugh McCulloch	IN	1865
Johnson, A.	Hugh McCulloch	IN	1865

President	Secretary	Home	Sworn In
Hayes	John Sherman	OH	1877
Garfield	William Windom	MN	1881
Arthur	Charles J. Folger	NY	1881
	Walter Q. Gresham	IN	1884
	Hugh McCulloch	IN	1884
Cleveland	Daniel Manning	NY	1885
	Charles S. Fairchild	NY	1887
Harrison, B.	William Windom	MN	1889
	Charles Foster	OH	1891
Cleveland	John G. Carlisle	KY	1893
McKinley	Lyman J. Gage	IL	1897
Roosevelt, T.	Lyman J. Gage	IL	1901
	Leslie M. Shaw	IA	1902
	George B. Cortelyou	NY	1907
Taft	Franklin MacVeagh	IL	1909
Wilson	William G. McAdoo	NY	1913
	Carter Glass	VA	1918
	David F. Houston	MO	1920
Harding	Andrew W. Mellon	PA	1921
Coolidge	Andrew W. Mellon	PA	1923
Hoover	Andrew W. Mellon	PA	1929
	Ogden L. Mills	NY	1932
Roosevelt, F.D.	William H. Woodin	NY	1933
	Henry Morgenthau, Jr.	NY	1934
Truman	Fred M. Vinson	KY	1945
	John W. Snyder	MO	1946
Eisenhower	George M. Humphrey	OH	1953
	Robert B. Anderson	CT	1957
Kennedy	C. Douglas Dillon	NJ	1961
Johnson, L.B.	C. Douglas Dillon	NJ	1963
	Henry H. Fowler	VA	1965
	Joseph W. Barr	IN	1968
Nixon	David M. Kennedy	IL	1969
	John B. Connally	TX	1971
	George P. Shultz	IL	1972
	William E. Simon	NJ	1974
Ford	William E. Simon	NJ	1974
Carter	W. Michael Blumenthal	MI	1977
	G. William Miller	RI	1979
Reagan	Donald T. Regan	NY	1981
	James A. Baker III	TX	1985
	Nicholas F. Brady	NJ	1988
Bush, G.H.W.	Nicholas F. Brady	NJ	1989
Clinton	Lloyd Bentsen	TX	1993
	Robert E. Rubin	NY	1995
	Lawrence H. Summers	CT	1999
Bush, G.W.	Paul H. O'Neill	PA	2001
	John W. Snow	PA	2003

Secretaries of Defense

The Department of Defense, originally designated the National Military Establishment, was created on Sept. 18, 1947. It is headed by the secretary of defense, who is a member of the president's Cabinet. The departments of the army, of the navy, and of the air force function within the Defense Department, and since 1947 the secretaries of these departments have not been members of the president's Cabinet.

President	Secretary	Home	Sworn In
Truman	James V. Forrestal	NY	1947
	Louis A. Johnson	WV	1949
	George C. Marshall	PA	1950
	Robert A. Lovett	NY	1951
Eisenhower	Charles E. Wilson	MI	1953
	Neil H. McElroy	OH	1957
	Thomas S. Gates Jr.	PA	1959
Kennedy	Robert S. McNamara	MI	1961
Johnson, L.B.	Robert S. McNamara	MI	1963
	Clark M. Clifford	MD	1968
Nixon	Melvin R. Laird	WI	1969
	Elliot L. Richardson	MA	1973
	James R. Schlesinger	VA	1973
Ford	James R. Schlesinger	VA	1974
	Donald H. Rumsfeld	IL	1975
Carter	Harold Brown	CA	1977
Reagan	Caspar W. Weinberger	CA	1981
	Frank C. Carlucci	PA	1987
Bush, G.H.W.	Richard B. Cheney	WY	1989
Clinton	Les Aspin	WI	1993
	William J. Perry	CA	1994
	William S. Cohen	ME	1997
Bush, G.W.	Donald H. Rumsfeld	IL	2001

Secretaries of War

The War Department (which included jurisdiction over the navy until 1798) was created by act of Congress on Aug. 7, 1789, and Gen. Henry Knox was commissioned secretary of war under that act on Sept. 12, 1789.

President	Secretary	Home	Sworn In
Washington	Henry Knox	MA	1789
	Timothy Pickering	PA	1795
	James McHenry	MD	1796
Adams, J.	James McHenry	MD	1797
	Samuel Dexter	MA	1800
Jefferson	Henry Dearborn	MA	1801
Madison	William Eustis	MA	1809
	John Armstrong	NY	1813
	James Monroe	VA	1814
	William H. Crawford	GA	1815
Monroe	John C. Calhoun	SC	1817
Adams, J.Q.	James Barbour	VA	1825
	Peter B. Porter	NY	1828
Jackson	John H. Eaton	TN	1829
	Lewis Cass	MI	1831
	Benjamin F. Butler	NY	1837
Van Buren	Joel R. Poinsett	SC	1837
Harrison, W.H.	John Bell	TN	1841
Tyler	John Bell	TN	1841
	John C. Spencer	NY	1841
	James M. Porter	PA	1843
	William Wilkins	PA	1844
Polk	William L. Marcy	NY	1845
Taylor	George W. Crawford	GA	1849
Fillmore	Charles M. Conrad	LA	1850
Pierce	Jefferson Davis	MS	1853
Buchanan	John B. Floyd	VA	1857
	Joseph Holt	KY	1861
Lincoln	Simon Cameron	PA	1861
	Edwin M. Stanton	PA	1862
Johnson, A.	Edwin M. Stanton	PA	1865
	John M. Schofield	IL	1868
Grant	John A. Rawlins	IL	1869
	William T. Sherman	OH	1869
	William W. Belknap	IA	1869
	Alphonso Taft	OH	1876
	James D. Cameron	PA	1876
Hayes	George W. McCrary	IA	1877
	Alexander Ramsey	MN	1879
Garfield	Robert T. Lincoln	IL	1881
Arthur	Robert T. Lincoln	IL	1881
Cleveland	William C. Endicott	MA	1885
Harrison, B.	Redfield Proctor	VT	1889
	Stephen B. Elkins	WV	1891
Cleveland	Daniel S. Lamont	NY	1893
McKinley	Russel A. Alger	MI	1897
	Elihu Root	NY	1899
Roosevelt, T.	Elihu Root	NY	1901
	William H. Taft	OH	1904
	Luke E. Wright	TN	1908
Taft	Jacob M. Dickinson	TN	1909
	Henry L. Stimson	NY	1911
Wilson	Lindley M. Garrison	NJ	1913
	Newton D. Baker	OH	1916
Harding	John W. Weeks	MA	1921
Coolidge	John W. Weeks	MA	1923
	Dwight F. Davis	MO	1925
Hoover	James W. Good	IL	1929
	Patrick J. Hurley	OK	1929
Roosevelt, F.D.	George H. Dern	UT	1933
	Harry H. Woodring	KS	1937
	Henry L. Stimson	NY	1940
Truman	Robert P. Patterson	NY	1945
	Kenneth C. Royall[1]	NC	1947

(1) Last member of the Cabinet with this title. The War Department became the Department of the Army and became a branch of the Department of Defense in 1947.

Secretaries of the Navy

The Navy Department was created by act of Congress on Apr. 30, 1798.

President	Secretary	Home	Sworn In
Adams, J.	Benjamin Stoddert	MD	1798
Jefferson	Benjamin Stoddert	MD	1801
	Robert Smith	MD	1801
Madison	Paul Hamilton	SC	1809
	William Jones	PA	1813
	Benjamin W. Crowninshield	MA	1814
Monroe	Benjamin W. Crowninshield	MA	1817
	Smith Thompson	NY	1818
	Samuel L. Southard	NJ	1823
Adams, J.Q.	Samuel L. Southard	NJ	1825
Jackson	John Branch	NC	1829
	Levi Woodbury	NH	1831
	Mahlon Dickerson	NJ	1834
Van Buren	Mahlon Dickerson	NJ	1837
	James K. Paulding	NY	1838
Harrison, W.H.	George E. Badger	NC	1841
Tyler	George E. Badger	NC	1841
	Abel P. Upshur	VA	1841
	David Henshaw	MA	1843
	Thomas W. Gilmer	VA	1844
	John Y. Mason	VA	1844
Polk	George Bancroft	MA	1845
	John Y. Mason	VA	1846
Taylor	William B. Preston	VA	1849
Fillmore	William A. Graham	NC	1850
	John P. Kennedy	MD	1852
Pierce	James C. Dobbin	NC	1853
Buchanan	Isaac Toucey	CT	1857
Lincoln	Gideon Welles	CT	1861
Johnson, A.	Gideon Welles	CT	1865
Grant	Adolph E. Borie	PA	1869
	George M. Robeson	NJ	1869
Hayes	Richard W. Thompson	IN	1877
	Nathan Goff Jr.	WV	1881
Garfield	William H. Hunt	LA	1881
Arthur	William E. Chandler	NH	1882
Cleveland	William C. Whitney	NY	1885
Harrison, B.	Benjamin F. Tracy	NY	1889
Cleveland	Hilary A. Herbert	AL	1893
McKinley	John D. Long	MA	1897
Roosevelt, T.	John D. Long	MA	1901
	William H. Moody	MA	1902
	Paul Morton	IL	1904
	Charles J. Bonaparte	MD	1905
	Victor H. Metcalf	CA	1906
	Truman H. Newberry	MI	1908
Taft	George von L. Meyer	MA	1909
Wilson	Josephus Daniels	NC	1913
Harding	Edwin Denby	MI	1921
Coolidge	Edwin Denby	MI	1923
	Curtis D. Wilbur	CA	1924
Hoover	Charles Francis Adams	MA	1929
Roosevelt, F.D.	Claude A. Swanson	VA	1933
	Charles Edison	NJ	1940
	Frank Knox	IL	1940
	James V. Forrestal	NY	1944
Truman	James V. Forrestal[1]	NY	1945

(1) Last member of Cabinet with this title. The Navy Department became a branch of the Department of Defense when the latter was created on Sept. 18, 1947.

Attorneys General

The Office of Attorney General was established by act of Congress on Sept. 24, 1789. It officially reached Cabinet rank in Mar. 1792, when the first attorney general, Edmund Randolph, attended his initial Cabinet meeting. The Department of Justice, headed by the attorney general, was created June 22, 1870.

President	Secretary	Home	Sworn In
Washington	Edmund Randolph	VA	1789
	William Bradford	PA	1794
	Charles Lee	VA	1795
Adams, J.	Charles Lee	VA	1797
Jefferson	Levi Lincoln	MA	1801
	John Breckenridge	KY	1805
	Caesar A. Rodney	DE	1807
Madison	Caesar A. Rodney	DE	1807
	William Pinkney	MD	1811
	Richard Rush	PA	1814
Monroe	Richard Rush	PA	1817
	William Wirt	VA	1817
Adams, J.Q.	William Wirt	VA	1825
Jackson	John M. Berrien	GA	1829
	Roger B. Taney	MD	1831
	Benjamin F. Butler	NY	1833
Van Buren	Benjamin F. Butler	NY	1837
	Felix Grundy	TN	1838
	Henry D. Gilpin	PA	1840
Harrison, W.H.	John J. Crittenden	KY	1841
Tyler	John J. Crittenden	KY	1841
	Hugh S. Legare	SC	1841
	John Nelson	MD	1843
Polk	John Y. Mason	VA	1845
	Nathan Clifford	ME	1846
	Isaac Toucey	CT	1848
Taylor	Reverdy Johnson	MD	1849
Fillmore	John J. Crittenden	KY	1850
Pierce	Caleb Cushing	MA	1853
Buchanan	Jeremiah S. Black	PA	1857
	Edwin M. Stanton	PA	1860
Lincoln	Edward Bates	MO	1861
	James Speed	KY	1864
Johnson, A.	James Speed	KY	1865
	Henry Stanbery	OH	1866
	William M. Evarts	NY	1868
Grant	Ebenezer R. Hoar	MA	1869
	Amos T. Akerman	GA	1870
	George H. Williams	OR	1871
	Edwards Pierrepont	NY	1875
	Alphonso Taft	OH	1876
Hayes	Charles Devens	MA	1877
Garfield	Wayne MacVeagh	PA	1881
Arthur	Benjamin H. Brewster	PA	1882
Cleveland	Augustus Garland	AR	1885
Harrison, B.	William H. H. Miller	IN	1889
Cleveland	Richard Olney	MA	1893
	Judson Harmon	OH	1895
McKinley	Joseph McKenna	CA	1897
	John W. Griggs	NJ	1898
	Philander C. Knox	PA	1901
Roosevelt, T.	Philander C. Knox	PA	1901
	William H. Moody	MA	1904
	Charles J. Bonaparte	MD	1906
Taft	George W. Wickersham	NY	1909
Wilson	J.C. McReynolds	TN	1913
	Thomas W. Gregory	TX	1914
	A. Mitchell Palmer	PA	1919
Harding	Harry M. Daugherty	OH	1921
Coolidge	Harry M. Daugherty	OH	1923
	Harlan F. Stone	NY	1924
	John G. Sargent	VT	1925
Hoover	William D. Mitchell	MN	1929
Roosevelt, F.D.	Homer S. Cummings	CT	1933
	Frank Murphy	MI	1939
	Robert H. Jackson	NY	1940
	Francis Biddle	PA	1941
Truman	Thomas C. Clark	TX	1945
	J. Howard McGrath	RI	1949
	J.P. McGranery	PA	1952
Eisenhower	Herbert Brownell Jr.	NY	1953
	William P. Rogers	MD	1957
Kennedy	Robert F. Kennedy	MA	1961
Johnson, L.B.	Robert F. Kennedy	MA	1963
	N. de B. Katzenbach	IL	1964
	Ramsey Clark	TX	1967
Nixon	John N. Mitchell	NY	1969
	Richard G. Kleindienst	AZ	1972
	Elliot L. Richardson	MA	1973
	William B. Saxbe	OH	1974
Ford	William B. Saxbe	OH	1974
	Edward H. Levi	IL	1975
Carter	Griffin B. Bell	GA	1977
	Benjamin R. Civiletti	MD	1979

President	Secretary	Home	Sworn In
Reagan	William French Smith	CA	1981
	Edwin Meese III	CA	1985
	Richard Thornburgh	PA	1988
Bush, G.H.W.	Richard Thornburgh	PA	1989
	William P. Barr	NY	1991
Clinton	Janet Reno	FL	1993
Bush, G.W.	John Ashcroft	MO	2001
	Alberto Gonzales	DC	2005

Secretaries of the Interior

The Department of the Interior was created by act of Congress on Mar. 3, 1849.

President	Secretary	Home	Sworn In
Taylor	Thomas Ewing	OH	1849
Fillmore	Thomas M. T. McKennan	PA	1850
	Alex H. H. Stuart	VA	1850
Pierce	Robert McClelland	MI	1853
Buchanan	Jacob Thompson	MS	1857
Lincoln	Caleb B. Smith	IN	1861
	John P. Usher	IN	1863
Johnson, A.	John P. Usher	IN	1865
	James Harlan	IA	1865
	Orville H. Browning	IL	1866
Grant	Jacob D. Cox	OH	1869
	Columbus Delano	OH	1870
	Zachariah Chandler	MI	1875
Hayes	Carl Schurz	MO	1877
Garfield	Samuel J. Kirkwood	IA	1881
Arthur	Henry M. Teller	CO	1882
Cleveland	Lucius Q.C. Lamar	MS	1885
	William F. Vilas	WI	1888
Harrison, B.	John W. Noble	MO	1889
Cleveland	Hoke Smith	GA	1893
	David R. Francis	MO	1896
McKinley	Cornelius N. Bliss	NY	1897
	Ethan A. Hitchcock	MO	1898
Roosevelt, T.	Ethan A. Hitchcock	MO	1901
	James R. Garfield	OH	1907
Taft	Richard A. Ballinger	WA	1909
	Walter L. Fisher	IL	1911
Wilson	Franklin K. Lane	CA	1913
	John B. Payne	IL	1920
Harding	Albert B. Fall	NM	1921
	Hubert Work	CO	1923
Coolidge	Hubert Work	CO	1923
	Roy O. West	IL	1929
Hoover	Ray Lyman Wilbur	CA	1929
Roosevelt, F.D.	Harold L. Ickes	IL	1933
Truman	Harold L. Ickes	IL	1945
	Julius A. Krug	WI	1946
	Oscar L. Chapman	CO	1949
Eisenhower	Douglas McKay	OR	1953
	Fred A. Seaton	NE	1956
Kennedy	Stewart L. Udall	AZ	1961
Johnson, L.B.	Stewart L. Udall	AZ	1963
Nixon	Walter J. Hickel	AK	1969
	Rogers C.B. Morton	MD	1971
Ford	Rogers C.B. Morton	MD	1971
	Stanley K. Hathaway	WY	1975
	Thomas S. Kleppe	ND	1975
Carter	Cecil D. Andrus	ID	1977
Reagan	James G. Watt	CO	1981
	William P. Clark	CA	1983
	Donald P. Hodel	OR	1985
Bush, G.H.W.	Manuel Lujan	NM	1989
Clinton	Bruce Babbitt	AZ	1993
Bush, G.W.	Gale Norton	CO	2001

Secretaries of Agriculture

The Department of Agriculture was created by act of Congress on May 15, 1862. On Feb. 8, 1889, its commissioner was renamed secretary of agriculture and became a member of the Cabinet.

President	Secretary	Home	Sworn In
Cleveland	Norman J. Colman	MO	1889
Harrison, B.	Jeremiah M. Rusk	WI	1889
Cleveland	J. Sterling Morton	NE	1893
McKinley	James Wilson	IA	1897
Roosevelt, T.	James Wilson	IA	1901
Taft	James Wilson	IA	1909
Wilson	David F. Houston	MO	1913
	Edwin T. Meredith	IA	1920
Harding	Henry C. Wallace	IA	1921
Coolidge	Henry C. Wallace	IA	1923
	Howard M. Gore	WV	1924
	William M. Jardine	KS	1925
Hoover	Arthur M. Hyde	MO	1929
Roosevelt, F.D.	Henry A. Wallace	IA	1933
	Claude R. Wickard	IN	1940
Truman	Clinton P. Anderson	NM	1945
Truman	Charles F. Brannan	CO	1948
Eisenhower	Ezra Taft Benson	UT	1953
Kennedy	Orville L. Freeman	MN	1961
Johnson, L.B.	Orville L. Freeman	MN	1963
Nixon	Clifford M. Hardin	IN	1969
	Earl L. Butz	IN	1971
Ford	Earl L. Butz	IN	1974
	John A. Knebel	VA	1976
Carter	Bob Bergland	MN	1977
Reagan	John R. Block	IL	1981
	Richard E. Lyng	CA	1986
Bush, G.H.W.	Clayton K. Yeutter	NE	1989
	Edward Madigan	IL	1991
Clinton	Mike Espy	MS	1993
	Dan Glickman	KS	1995
Bush, G.W.	Ann M. Veneman	CA	2001
	Mike Johanns	NE	2005

Secretaries of Commerce and Labor

The Department of Commerce and Labor, created by Congress on Feb. 14, 1903, was divided by Congress Mar. 4, 1913, into separate departments of Commerce and Labor. The secretary of each was made a Cabinet member.

Secretaries of Commerce and Labor

President	Secretary	Home	Sworn In
Roosevelt, T.	George B. Cortelyou	NY	1903
	Victor H. Metcalf	CA	1904
	Oscar S. Straus	NY	1906
Taft	Charles Nagel	MO	1909

Secretaries of Labor

President	Secretary	Home	Sworn In
Wilson	William B. Wilson	PA	1913
Harding	James J. Davis	PA	1921
Coolidge	James J. Davis	PA	1923
Hoover	James J. Davis	PA	1929
	William N. Doak	VA	1930
Roosevelt, F.D.	Frances Perkins	NY	1933
Truman	L.B. Schwellenbach	WA	1945
	Maurice J. Tobin	MA	1949
Eisenhower	Martin P. Durkin	IL	1953
	James P. Mitchell	NJ	1953
Kennedy	Arthur J. Goldberg	IL	1961
	W. Willard Wirtz	IL	1962
Johnson, L.B.	W. Willard Wirtz	IL	1963
Nixon	George P. Shultz	IL	1969
	James D. Hodgson	CA	1970
	Peter J. Brennan	NY	1973
Ford	Peter J. Brennan	NY	1974
	John T. Dunlop	CA	1975
	W.J. Usery Jr.	GA	1976
Carter	F. Ray Marshall	TX	1977
Reagan	Raymond J. Donovan	NJ	1981
	William E. Brock	TN	1985
	Ann D. McLaughlin	DC	1987
Bush, G.H.W.	Elizabeth Hanford Dole	NC	1989
	Lynn Martin	IL	1991
Clinton	Robert B. Reich	MA	1993
	Alexis M. Herman	AL	1997
Bush, G.W.	Elaine L. Chao	KY	2001

Secretaries of Commerce

President	Secretary	Home	Sworn In
Wilson	William C. Redfield	NY	1913
	Joshua W. Alexander	MO	1919
Harding	Herbert C. Hoover	CA	1921
Coolidge	Herbert C. Hoover	CA	1923
	William F. Whiting	MA	1928
Hoover	Robert P. Lamont	IL	1929
	Roy D. Chapin	MI	1932
Roosevelt, F.D.	Daniel C. Roper	SC	1933
	Harry L. Hopkins	NY	1939
	Jesse Jones	TX	1940
	Henry A. Wallace	IA	1945
Truman	Henry A. Wallace	IA	1945
	W. Averell Harriman	NY	1947
	Charles Sawyer	OH	1948
Eisenhower	Sinclair Weeks	MA	1953
	Lewis L. Strauss	NY	1958
	Frederick H. Mueller	MI	1959
Kennedy	Luther H. Hodges	NC	1961
Johnson, L.B.	Luther H. Hodges	NC	1963
	John T. Connor	NJ	1965
	Alex B. Trowbridge	NJ	1967
	Cyrus R. Smith	NY	1968
Nixon	Maurice H. Stans	MN	1969
	Peter G. Peterson	IL	1972
	Frederick B. Dent	SC	1973
Ford	Frederick B. Dent	SC	1974
	Rogers C.B. Morton	MD	1975
	Elliot L. Richardson	MA	1975
Carter	Juanita M. Kreps	NC	1977
	Philip M. Klutznick	IL	1979
Reagan	Malcolm Baldrige	CT	1981
	C. William Verity Jr.	OH	1987
Bush, G.H.W.	Robert A. Mosbacher	TX	1989
	Barbara H. Franklin	PA	1992
Clinton	Ronald H. Brown	DC	1993
	Mickey Kantor	CA	1996
	William M. Daley	IL	1997
	Norman Y. Mineta	CA	2000
Bush, G.W.	Donald L. Evans	TX	2001
	Carlos Gutierrez	MI	2005

Secretaries of Housing and Urban Development

The Department of Housing and Urban Development was created by act of Congress on Sept. 9, 1965.

President	Secretary	Home	Sworn In
Johnson, L.B.	Robert C. Weaver	WA	1966
	Robert C. Wood	MA	1969
Nixon	George W. Romney	MI	1969
	James T. Lynn	OH	1973
Ford	James T. Lynn	OH	1974
	Carla Anderson Hills	CA	1975
Carter	Patricia Roberts Harris	DC	1977
	Moon Landrieu	LA	1979
Reagan	Samuel R. Pierce Jr.	NY	1981
Bush, G.H.W.	Jack F. Kemp	NY	1989
Clinton	Henry G. Cisneros	TX	1993
	Andrew M. Cuomo	NY	1997
Bush, G.W.	Mel Martinez	FL	2001
	Alphonso Jackson	TX	2004

Secretaries of Transportation

The Department of Transportation was created by act of Congress on Oct. 15, 1966.

President	Secretary	Home	Sworn In
Johnson, L.B.	Alan S. Boyd	FL	1966
Nixon	John A. Volpe	MA	1969
	Claude S. Brinegar	CA	1973
Ford	Claude S. Brinegar	CA	1974
	William T. Coleman Jr.	PA	1975
Carter	Brock Adams	WA	1977
	Neil E. Goldschmidt	OR	1979
Reagan	Andrew L. Lewis Jr.	PA	1981
	Elizabeth Hanford Dole	NC	1983
	James H. Burnley	NC	1987
Bush, G.H.W.	Samuel K. Skinner	IL	1989
	Andrew H. Card Jr.	MA	1992
Clinton	Federico F. Peña	CO	1993
	Rodney E. Slater	AR	1997
Bush, G.W.	Norman Y. Mineta	CA	2001

Secretaries of Energy

The Department of Energy was created by federal law on Aug. 4, 1977.

President	Secretary	Home	Sworn In
Carter	James R. Schlesinger	VA	1977
	Charles Duncan Jr.	WY	1979
Reagan	James B. Edwards	SC	1981
	Donald P. Hodel	OR	1982
	John S. Herrington	CA	1985
Bush, G.H.W.	James D. Watkins	CA	1989
Clinton	Hazel R. O'Leary	MN	1993
	Federico F. Peña	CO	1997
	Bill Richardson	NM	1998
Bush, G.W.	Spencer Abraham	MI	2001
	Samuel W. Bodman	MA	2005

Secretaries of Health, Education, and Welfare

The Department of Health, Education, and Welfare was created by Congress on Apr. 11, 1953. On Sept. 27, 1979, it was divided by Congress into the departments of Education and of Health and Human Services, with the secretary of each being a Cabinet member.

President	Secretary	Home	Sworn In
Eisenhower	Oveta Culp Hobby	TX	1953
	Marion B. Folsom	NY	1955
	Arthur S. Flemming	OH	1958
Kennedy	Abraham A. Ribicoff	CT	1961
	Anthony J. Celebrezze	OH	1962
Johnson, L.B.	Anthony J. Celebrezze	OH	1963
	John W. Gardner	NY	1965
	Wilbur J. Cohen	MI	1968
Nixon	Robert H. Finch	CA	1969
	Elliot L. Richardson	MA	1970
	Caspar W. Weinberger	CA	1973
Ford	Caspar W. Weinberger	CA	1974
	Forrest D. Mathews	AL	1975
Carter	Joseph A. Califano Jr.	DC	1977
	Patricia Roberts Harris	DC	1979

Secretaries of Health and Human Services

President	Secretary	Home	Sworn In
Carter	Patricia Roberts Harris	DC	1979
Reagan	Richard S. Schweiker	PA	1981
	Margaret M. Heckler	MA	1983
Reagan	Otis R. Bowen	IN	1985
Bush, G.H.W.	Louis W. Sullivan	GA	1989
Clinton	Donna E. Shalala	WI	1993
Bush, G.W.	Tommy Thompson	WI	2001
	Michael O. Leavitt	UT	2005

Secretaries of Education

President	Secretary	Home	Sworn In
Carter	Shirley Hufstedler	CA	1979
Reagan	Terrel Bell	UT	1981
	William J. Bennett	NY	1985
	Lauro F. Cavazos	TX	1988
Bush, G.H.W.	Lauro F. Cavazos	TX	1989
	Lamar Alexander	TN	1991
Clinton	Richard W. Riley	SC	1993
Bush, G.W.	Roderick R. Paige	TX	2001
	Margaret Spellings	TX	2005

Secretaries of Veterans Affairs

The Department of Veterans Affairs was created on Oct. 25, 1988, when Pres. Ronald Reagan signed a bill that made the Veterans Administration into a Cabinet department, effective Mar. 15, 1989.

President	Secretary	Home	Sworn In
Bush, G.H.W.	Edward J. Derwinski	IL	1989
Clinton	Jesse Brown	IL	1993
Clinton	Togo D. West Jr.	NC	1998
	Hershel W. Gober (acting)	AR	2000
Bush, G.W.	Anthony Principi	CA	2001
	Jim Nicholson	CO	2005

Department of Homeland Security

The Department of Homeland Security was created by act of Congress on Nov. 25, 2002.

President	Secretary	Home	Sworn In
Bush, G.W.	Thomas Ridge	PA	2003
	Michael Chertoff	DC	2005

U.S. SUPREME COURT

(data as of Oct. 2005)

Justices of the U.S. Supreme Court

The Supreme Court comprises the chief justice of the U.S. and 8 associate justices, all appointed for life by the president with advice and consent of the Senate. Names of chief justices are in **boldface**. Salaries: chief justice, $208,100; associate justice, $199,200. The U.S. Supreme Court Bldg. is at 1 First St. NE, Washington, DC 20543. The Court website is www.supremecourtus.gov

Members at start of 2005-2006 term (Oct. 3, 2005): Chief justice: John G. Roberts, Jr.; assoc. justices: Stephen G. Breyer, Ruth Bader Ginsburg, Anthony M. Kennedy, Sandra Day O'Connor (to retire on confirmation of a successor), Antonin Scalia, David H. Souter, John Paul Stevens, Clarence Thomas. *See* the feature article *Transition at the Supreme Court.*

Name, apptd. from	Service Term	Service Yrs	Born	Died
John Jay, NY	1789-1795	5	1745	1829
John Rutledge, SC[1]	1789-1791	1	1739	1800
William Cushing, MA	1789-1810	20	1732	1810
James Wilson, PA	1789-1798	8	1742	1798
John Blair, VA	1789-1796	6	1732	1800
James Iredell, NC	1790-1799	9	1751	1799
Thomas Johnson, MD	1791-1793	1	1732	1819
William Paterson, NJ	1793-1806	13	1745	1806
John Rutledge, SC[2,3]	1795	—	1739	1800
Samuel Chase, MD	1796-1811	15	1741	1811
Oliver Ellsworth, CT	1796-1800	4	1745	1807
Bushrod Washington, VA	1798-1829	31	1762	1829
Alfred Moore, NC	1799-1804	4	1755	1810
John Marshall, VA	1801-1835	34	1755	1835
William Johnson, SC	1804-1834	30	1771	1834
Henry B. Livingston, NY	1806-1823	16	1757	1823
Thomas Todd, KY	1807-1826	18	1765	1826
Joseph Story, MA	1811-1845	33	1779	1845
Gabriel Duval, MD	1811-1835	22	1752	1844
Smith Thompson, NY	1823-1843	20	1768	1843
Robert Trimble, KY	1826-1828	2	1777	1828
John McLean, OH	1829-1861	32	1785	1861
Henry Baldwin, PA	1830-1844	14	1780	1844
James M. Wayne, GA	1835-1867	32	1790	1867
Roger B. Taney, MD	1836-1864	28	1777	1864
Philip P. Barbour, VA	1836-1841	4	1783	1841
John Catron, TN	1837-1865	28	1786	1865
John McKinley, AL	1837-1852	15	1780	1852
Peter V. Daniel, VA	1841-1860	19	1784	1860
Samuel Nelson, NY	1845-1872	27	1792	1873
Levi Woodbury, NH	1845-1851	5	1789	1851
Robert C. Grier, PA	1846-1870	23	1794	1870
Benjamin R. Curtis, MA	1851-1857	6	1809	1874
John A. Campbell, AL	1853-1861	8	1811	1889
Nathan Clifford, ME	1858-1881	23	1803	1881
Noah H. Swayne, OH	1862-1881	18	1804	1884
Samuel F. Miller, IA	1862-1890	28	1816	1890
David Davis, IL	1862-1877	14	1815	1886
Stephen J. Field, CA	1863-1897	34	1816	1899
Salmon P. Chase, OH	1864-1873	8	1808	1873
William Strong, PA	1870-1880	10	1808	1895
Joseph P. Bradley, NJ	1870-1892	21	1813	1892
Ward Hunt, NY	1872-1882	9	1810	1886
Morrison R. Waite, OH	1874-1888	14	1816	1888
John M. Harlan, KY	1877-1911	34	1833	1911
William B. Woods, GA	1880-1887	6	1824	1887
Stanley Matthews, OH	1881-1889	7	1824	1889
Horace Gray, MA	1881-1902	20	1828	1902
Samuel Blatchford, NY	1882-1893	11	1820	1893
Lucius Q.C. Lamar, MS	1888-1893	5	1825	1893
Melville W. Fuller, IL	1888-1910	21	1833	1910
David J. Brewer, KS	1889-1910	20	1837	1910
Henry B. Brown, MI	1890-1906	15	1836	1913
George Shiras Jr., PA	1892-1903	10	1832	1924
Howell E. Jackson, TN	1893-1895	2	1832	1895
Edward D. White, LA[1]	1894-1910	16	1845	1921
Rufus W. Peckham, NY	1895-1909	13	1838	1909
Joseph McKenna, CA	1898-1925	26	1843	1926
Oliver W. Holmes, MA	1902-1932	29	1841	1935
William R. Day, OH	1903-1922	19	1849	1923
William H. Moody, MA	1906-1910	3	1853	1917
Horace H. Lurton, TN	1909-1914	4	1844	1914
Charles E. Hughes, NY[1]	1910-1916	5	1862	1948
Willis Van Devanter, WY	1910-1937	26	1859	1941
Joseph R. Lamar, GA	1910-1916	5	1857	1916
Edward D. White, LA[2]	1910-1921	10	1845	1921
Mahlon Pitney, NJ	1912-1922	10	1858	1924
James C. McReynolds, TN	1914-1941	26	1862	1946
Louis D. Brandeis, MA	1916-1939	22	1856	1941
John H. Clarke, OH	1916-1922	5	1857	1945
William H. Taft, CT	1921-1930	8	1857	1930
George Sutherland, UT	1922-1938	15	1862	1942
Pierce Butler, MN	1922-1939	16	1866	1939
Edward T. Sanford, TN	1923-1930	7	1865	1930
Harlan F. Stone, NY[1]	1925-1941	16	1872	1946
Charles E. Hughes, NY[2]	1930-1941	11	1862	1948
Owen J. Roberts, PA	1930-1945	15	1875	1955
Benjamin N. Cardozo, NY	1932-1938	6	1870	1938
Hugo L. Black, AL	1937-1971	34	1886	1971
Stanley F. Reed, KY	1938-1957	19	1884	1980
Felix Frankfurter, MA	1939-1962	23	1882	1965
William O. Douglas, CT	1939-1975	36[4]	1898	1980
Frank Murphy, MI	1940-1949	9	1890	1949
Harlan F. Stone, NY[2]	1941-1946	5	1872	1946
James F. Byrnes, SC	1941-1942	1	1879	1972
Robert H. Jackson, NY	1941-1954	12	1892	1954
Wiley B. Rutledge, IA	1943-1949	6	1894	1949
Harold H. Burton, OH	1945-1958	13	1888	1964
Fred M. Vinson, KY	1946-1953	7	1890	1953
Tom C. Clark, TX	1949-1967	18	1899	1977
Sherman Minton, IN	1949-1956	7	1890	1965
Earl Warren, CA	1953-1969	16	1891	1974
John Marshall Harlan, NY	1955-1971	16	1899	1971
William J. Brennan Jr., NJ	1956-1990	33	1906	1997
Charles E. Whittaker, MO	1957-1962	5	1901	1973
Potter Stewart, OH	1958-1981	23	1915	1985
Byron R. White, CO	1962-1993	31	1917	2002
Arthur J. Goldberg, IL	1962-1965	3	1908	1990
Abe Fortas, TN	1965-1969	4	1910	1982
Thurgood Marshall, NY	1967-1991	24	1908	1993
Warren E. Burger, VA	1969-1986	17	1907	1995
Harry A. Blackmun, MN	1970-1994	24	1908	1999
Lewis F. Powell Jr., VA	1971-1987	16	1907	1998
William H. Rehnquist, AZ[1]	1971-1986	15	1924	2005
John Paul Stevens, IL	1975-		1920	
Sandra Day O'Connor, AZ	1981-		1930	
William H. Rehnquist, AZ[2]	1986-2005	19	1924	2005
Antonin Scalia, VA	1986-		1936	
Anthony M. Kennedy, CA	1988-		1936	
David H. Souter, NH	1990-		1939	
Clarence Thomas, VA	1991-		1948	
Ruth Bader Ginsburg, DC	1993-		1933	
Stephen G. Breyer, MA	1994-		1938	
John G. Roberts Jr., DC	2005-		1955	

(1) Later, chief justice, as listed. (2) Formerly assoc. justice. (3) Named as acting chief justice; confirmation rejected by the Senate. (4) Longest term of service.

IT'S A FACT: John Roberts, 50, is the youngest Supreme Court chief justice in 204 years since John Marshall (he was 45). The youngest-ever chief justice was John Jay, who also happened to be the first. Nominated by Pres. George Washington, Jay took the oath of office at the age of 44 years, 10 months, on Oct. 19, 1789.

CONGRESS

The One Hundred and Ninth Congress, With Official 2004 Election Results

The 109th Congress convened Jan. 3, 2005.

The Senate

Rep., 55; Dem., 44; Ind., 1; Total, 100. As of Oct. 2005.

Senate officials as of Oct. 2005 were: Pres. Pro Tempore, Ted Stevens (AK); Majority Leader, Bill Frist (TN); Majority Whip, Mitch McConnell (KY); Minority Leader, Harry Reid (NV); Minority Whip, Dick Durbin (IL). The Senate had 14 women (9 D, 5 R), same number as in the previous Senate; 2 Hispanics (Mel Martinez, R, FL, and Ken Salazar, D, CO) compared to none before; 1 African American (Barack Obama, D, IL), compared to none before; no Native Americans, compared to 1 before.

Terms are for 6 years and end Jan. 3 of the year preceding the senator's name in the following table. Annual salary, $162,100; President Pro Tempore, Majority Leader, and Minority Leader, $180,100. To be eligible for the Senate, one must be at least 30 years old, a U.S. citizen for at least 9 years, and a resident of the state from which chosen.

The address is U.S. Senate, Washington DC 20510; telephone, 202-224-3121; website, www.senate.gov

Boldface denotes the 2004 election winner. *Incumbent candidate. D–Democrat; R–Republican; Ind–Independent.

Term ends	Senator (Party); Service from[1]	2004 Election
	Alabama	
2009	Jeff Sessions (R); 1/7/97	
2011	**Richard Shelby* (R)**; 1/6/87	**1,242,200**
	Wayne Sowell (D)	595,018
	Alaska	
2009	Ted Stevens (R); 12/24/68	
2011	**Lisa Murkowski* (R)**; 12/20/02	**149,773**
	Tony Knowles (D)	140,424
	Arizona	
2007	Jon Kyl (R); 1/4/95	
2011	**John McCain* (R)**; 1/6/87	**1,505,372**
	Stuart Starky (D)	404,507
	Arkansas	
2009	Mark Pryor (D); 1/7/03	
2011	**Blanche L. Lincoln* (D)**; 1/6/99	**580,973**
	Jim Holt (R)	458,036
	California	
2007	Dianne Feinstein (D); 11/10/92	
2011	**Barbara Boxer* (D)**; 1993	**6,955,728**
	Bill Jones (R)	4,555,922
	Colorado	
2009	Wayne Allard (R); 1/7/97	
2011	**Ken Salazar (D)**	**1,081,188**
	Pete Coors (R)	980,668
	Connecticut	
2007	Joe Lieberman (D); 1989	
2011	**Christopher J. Dodd* (D)**; 1981	**945,347**
	Jack Orchulli (R)	457,749
	Delaware	
2007	Thomas R. Carper (D); 2001	
2007	Joseph Biden (D); 1973	
	Florida	
2007	Bill Nelson (D); 2001	
2011	**Mel Martinez (R)**	**3,672,864**
	Betty Castor (D)	3,590,201
	Georgia	
2009	Saxby Chambliss (R); 1/7/03	
2011	**Johnny Isakson (R)**	**1,864,202**
	Denise Majette (D)	1,287,690
	Hawaii	
2007	Daniel K. Akaka (D); 4/28/90	
2011	**Daniel K. Inouye* (D)**; 1963	**313,629**
	Cam Cavasso (R)	87,172
	Idaho	
2009	Larry E. Craig (R); 1991	
2011	**Mike Crapo* (R); 1/6/99**	**499,796**
	Scott F. McClure (D) (write in)	4,136
	Illinois	
2009	Richard J. Durbin (D); 1/7/97	
2011	**Barack Obama (D)**	**3,597,456**
	Alan Keyes (R)	1,390,690
	Indiana	
2007	Richard G. Lugar (R); 1977	
2011	**Evan Bayh* (D)**; 1/6/99	**1,496,976**
	Marvin Scott (R)	903,913
	Iowa	
2009	Tom Harkin (D); 1985	
2011	**Chuck Grassley* (R)**; 1981	**1,038,175**
	Arthur Small (D)	412,365
	Kansas	
2009	Pat Roberts (R); 1/7/97	
2011	**Sam Brownback* (R)**; 11/27/96	**780,863**
	Lee Jones (D)	310,337
	Kentucky	
2009	Mitch McConnell (R); 1985	
2011	**Jim Bunning* (R)**; 1/6/99	**873,507**
	Daniel Mongiardo (D)	850,855
	Louisiana	
2009	Mary L. Landrieu (D); 1/7/97	
2011	**David Vitter (R)**	**943,014**
	Christopher John (D)	542,150
	Maine	
2007	Olympia J. Snowe (R); 1/4/95	
2009	Susan M. Collins (R); 1/7/97	
	Maryland	
2007	Paul S. Sarbanes (D); 1977	
2011	**Barbara Ann Mikulski* (D)**; 1/6/87	**1,504,691**
	E.J. Pipkin (R)	783,055
	Massachusetts	
2007	Edward M. Kennedy (D); 11/7/62	
2009	John F. Kerry (D); 1/2/85	
	Michigan	
2007	Debbie Stabenow (D); 2001	
2009	Carl Levin (D); 1979	
	Minnesota	
2007	Mark Dayton (D); 2001	
2009	Norm Coleman (R); 1/7/03	
	Mississippi	
2007	Trent Lott (R); 1989	
2009	Thad Cochran (R); 12/27/78	
	Missouri	
2009	Jim Talent (R); 11/23/02	
2011	**Christopher (Kit) Bond* (R)**; 1/6/87	**1,518,089**
	Nancy Farmer (D)	1,158,261
	Montana	
2007	Conrad Burns (R); 1989	
2009	Max Baucus (D); 12/15/78	
	Nebraska	
2007	Ben Nelson (D); 2001	
2009	Chuck Hagel (R); 1/7/97	
	Nevada	
2007	John Ensign (R); 2001	
2011	**Harry Reid* (D)**; 1/6/87	**494,805**
	Richard Ziser (R)	284,640
	New Hampshire	
2009	John Sununu (R); 1/7/03	
2011	**Judd Gregg* (R)**; 1993	**434,847**
	Doris Haddock (D)	221,549
	New Jersey	
2007	Jon S. Corzine (D); 2001	
2009	Frank Lautenberg (D); 1/7/03	
	New Mexico	
2007	Jeff Bingaman (D); 1983	
2009	Pete V. Domenici (R); 1973	
	New York	
2007	Hillary Rodham Clinton (D); 2001	
2011	**Charles E. Schumer* (D)**; 1/6/99	**4,769,824**
	Howard Mills (R)	1,625,069
	North Carolina	
2009	Elizabeth H. Dole (R); 1/7/03	
2011	**Richard Burr (R)**	**1,791,450**
	Erskine B. Bowles (D)	1,632,527

Term ends	Senator (Party); Service from[1]	2004 Election
	North Dakota	
2007	Kent Conrad (D); 1/6/87	
2011	**Byron L. Dorgan* (D)**; 12/14/92	**212,143**
	Mike Liffrig (R)	98,553
	Ohio	
2007	Mike DeWine (R); 1/4/95	
2011	**George V. Voinovich* (R)**; 1/6/99	**3,464,356**
	Eric Fingerhut (D)	1,961,171
	Oklahoma	
2009	James M. Inhofe (R); 11/21/94	
2011	**Tom Coburn (R)**	**763,433**
	Brad Carson (D)	596,750
	Oregon	
2009	Gordon Smith (R); 1/7/97	
2011	**Ron Wyden* (D)**; 2/6/96	**1,128,728**
	Al King (R)	565,254
	Pennsylvania	
2007	Rick Santorum (R); 1/4/95	
2011	**Arlen Specter* (R)**; 1981	**2,925,080**
	Joe Hoeffel (D)	2,334,126
	Rhode Island	
2007	Lincoln D. Chafee (R); 11/2/99	
2009	John F. Reed (D); 1/7/97	
	South Carolina	
2009	Lindsey Graham (R); 1/7/03	
2011	**Jim DeMint (R)**	**857,167**
	Inez Tenenbaum (D)	704,384
	South Dakota	
2009	Tim Johnson (D); 1/7/97	
2011	**John Thune (R)**	**197,848**
	Tom Daschle* (D); 1/6/87	193,340
	Tennessee	
2007	Bill Frist (R); 1/4/95	
2009	Lamar Alexander (R); 1/7/03	
	Texas	
2007	Kay Bailey Hutchison (R); 6/5/93	
2009	John Cornyn (R); 12/2/02	
	Utah	
2007	Orrin G. Hatch (R); 1977	
2011	**Robert F. Bennett* (R)**; 1993	**626,640**
	R. Paul Van Dam (D)	258,955
	Vermont	
2007	James M. Jeffords (Ind.); 1989	
2011	**Patrick Leahy* (D)**; 1975	**216,972**
	Jack McMullen (R)	75,398
	Virginia	
2007	George F. Allen (R); 2001	
2009	John W. Warner (R); 1/2/79	
	Washington	
2007	Maria Cantwell (D); 2001	
2011	**Patty Murray* (D)**; 1993	**1,549,708**
	George Nethercutt, Jr. (R)	1,204,584
	West Virginia	
2007	Robert C. Byrd (D); 1959	
2009	John D. Rockefeller IV (D); 1/15/85	
	Wisconsin	
2007	Herbert H. Kohl (D); 1989	
2011	**Russ Feingold* (D)**; 1993	**1,632,697**
	Tim Michels (R)	1,301,183
	Wyoming	
2007	Craig Thomas (R); 1/4/95	
2009	Michael B. Enzi (R); 1/7/97	

(1) Jan. 3, unless otherwise noted.

The House of Representatives

Rep., 231; Dem., 202; Ind., 1; Vac., 1; Total, 435. As of Oct. 2005

House officials as of Oct. 2005 were: Speaker of the House, J. Dennis Hastert (IL); Majority Leader (interim) and Majority Whip, Roy Blunt (MO); Minority Leader, Nancy Pelosi (CA); Minority Whip, Steny Hoyer (MD). As of Oct. 7, 2005, there were 70 women in the House (46 D, 24 R), an increase of 7 from the 108th Congress. There were 42 African Americans (all D), up from 5 from before, and 24 Hispanics (19 D, 5 R), an increase of 2.

Terms are for 2 years ending Jan. 3, 2007. Annual salary, $162,100; Speaker of the House, $208,100; Majority Leader and Minority Leader, $180,100. To be eligible for membership, a person must be at least 25 years of age, a U.S. citizen for at least 7 years, and a resident of the state from which he or she is chosen.

The address is U.S. House of Representatives, Washington, DC 20515; telephone, 202-224-3121; website, www.house.gov

Boldface denotes the election winner. *Incumbent. D=Democrat; R=Republican; C=Conservative; GR=Green; Ind. =Independent; LB=Libertarian.

Dist.	Representative (Party)	2004 Election
	Alabama	
1	**Jo Bonner* (R)**	**161,067**
	Judy Belk (D)	93,938
2	**Terry Everett* (R)**	**177,086**
	Chuck James (D)	70,562
3	**Mike Rogers* (R)**	**150,411**
	Bill Fuller (D)	95,240
4	**Robert Aderholt* (R)**	**191,110**
	Carl Cole (D)	64,278
5	**Bud Cramer* (D)**	**200,999**
	Gerald Wallace (R)	74,145
6	**Spencer Bachus* (R)**	**unopposed**
7	**Artur Davis* (D)**	**183,408**
	Steve Cameron (R)	61,019
	Alaska	
	Don Young* (R)	**213,216**
	Thomas Higgins (D)	67,074
	Arizona	
1	**Rick Renzi* (R)**	**148,315**
	Paul Babbitt (D)	91,776
2	**Trent Franks* (R)**	**165,260**
	Randy Camacho (D)	107,406
3	**John Shadegg* (R)**	**181,012**
	Mark Yannone (LB)	44,962
4	**Ed Pastor* (D)**	**77,150**
	Don Karg (R)	28,238
5	**J.D. Hayworth* (R)**	**159,455**
	Elizabeth Rogers (D)	102,363
6	**Jeff Flake* (R)**	**202,882**
	Craig Stritar (LB)	52,695
7	**Raúl Grijalva* (D)**	**108,868**
	Joseph Sweeney (R)	59,066
8	**Jim Kolbe* (R)**	**183,363**
	Eva Bacal (D)	109,963
	Arkansas	
1	**Marion Berry* (D)**	**162,388**
	Vernon Humphrey (R)	81,556
2	**Vic Snyder* (D)**	**160,834**
	Marvin Parks (R)	115,655
3	**John Boozman* (R)**	**160,629**
	Jan Judy (D)	103,158
4	**Mike Ross (D)**	**unopposed**
	California	
1	**Mike Thompson* (D)**	**189,366**
	Lawrence Wiesner (R)	79,970
2	**Wally Herger* (R)**	**182,119**
	Mike Johnson (D)	90,310
3	**Daniel E. Lungren (R)**	**177,738**
	Gabe Castillo (D)	100,025
4	**John Doolittle* (R)**	**221,926**
	David Winters (D)	117,443
5	**Doris Matsui* (D)#**	**56,173**
	Julie Padilla (D)	7,156
6	**Lynn Woolsey* (D)**	**226,423**
	Paul Erickson (R)	85,244

Dist.	Representative (Party)	2004 Election
7	**George Miller* (D)**	**166,831**
	Charles Hargrave (R)	52,446
8	**Nancy Pelosi* (D)**	**224,017**
	Jennifer Depalma (R)	31,074
9	**Barbara Lee* (D)**	**215,630**
	Claudia Bermudez (R)	31,278
10	**Ellen Tauscher* (D)**	**182,750**
	Jeff Ketelson (R)	95,349
11	**Richard Pombo* (R)**	**163,582**
	Jerry McNerney (D)	103,587
12	**Tom Lantos* (D)**	**171,852**
	Mike Garza (R)	52,593
13	**Fortney Pete Stark* (D)**	**144,605**
	George Bruno (R)	48,439
14	**Anna Eshoo* (D)**	**182,712**
	Chris Haugen (R)	69,564
15	**Michael M. Honda* (D)**	**154,385**
	Raymond Chukwu (R)	59,953
16	**Zoe Lofgren* (D)**	**129,222**
	Douglas McNea (R)	47,992
17	**Sam Farr* (D)**	**148,958**
	Mark Risley (R)	65,117
18	**Dennis Cardoza* (D)**	**103,732**
	Charles Pringle (R)	49,973
19	**George Radanovich* (R)**	**155,354**
	James Bufford (D)	64,047
20	**Jim Costa (D)**	**61,005**
	Roy Ashburn (R)	53,231
21	**Devin Nunes* (R)**	**140,721**
	Fred Davis (D)	51,594
22	**William M. Thomas* (R)**	**unopposed**
23	**Lois Capps* (D)**	**153,980**
	Don Regan (R)	83,926
24	**Elton Gallegly* (R)**	**178,660**
	Brett Wagner (D)	96,397
25	**Howard "Buck" McKeon* (R)**	**145,575**
	Tim Willoughby (D)	80,395
26	**David Dreier* (R)**	**134,596**
	Cynthia Matthews (D)	107,522
27	**Brad Sherman* (D)**	**125,296**
	Robert Levy (R)	66,946
28	**Howard Berman* (D)**	**115,303**
	David Hernandez (R)	37,868
29	**Adam Schiff* (D)**	**133,670**
	Harry Scolinos (R)	62,871
30	**Henry Waxman* (D)**	**216,682**
	Victor Elizalde (R)	87,465
31	**Xavier Becerra* (D)**	**89,363**
	Luis Vega (R)	22,048
32	**Hilda Solis* (D)**	**119,144**
	Leland Faegre (LB)	21,002
33	**Diane Watson* (D)**	**166,801**
	Bob Weber (LB)	21,513
34	**Lucille Roybal-Allard* (D)**	**82,282**
	Wayne Miller (R)	28,175
35	**Maxine Waters* (D)**	**125,949**
	Ross Moen (R)	23,591
36	**Jane Harman* (D)**	**151,208**
	Paul Whitehead (R)	81,666
37	**Juanita Millender-McDonald* (D)**	**118,823**
	Vernon Van (R)	31,960
38	**Grace F. Napolitano* (D)**	**unopposed**
39	**Linda Sánchez* (D)**	**100,132**
	Tim Escobar (R)	64,832
40	**Ed Royce* (R)**	**147,617**
	Tilman Williams (D)	69,684
41	**Jerry Lewis* (R)**	**181,605**
	Peymon Mottahedeh (LB)	37,332
42	**Gary Miller* (R)**	**167,632**
	Lewis Myers (D)	78,393
43	**Joe Baca* (D)**	**86,830**
	Ed Laning (R)	44,004
44	**Ken Calvert* (R)**	**138,768**
	Louis Vandenberg (D)	78,796
45	**Mary Bono* (R)**	**153,523**
	Richard Meyer (D)	76,967
46	**Dana Rohrabacher* (R)**	**171,318**
	Jim Brandt (D)	90,129
47	**Loretta Sanchez* (D)**	**65,684**
	Alex Coronado (R)	43,099
48	**Christopher Cox* (R)##**	**189,004**
	John Graham (D)	93,525
49	**Darrell Issa* (R)**	**141,658**
	Mike Byron (D)	79,057
50	**Randy Cunningham* (R)**	**169,025**
	Francine Busby (D)	105,590
51	**Bob Filner* (D)**	**111,441**
	Michael Giorgino (R)	63,526
52	**Duncan Hunter* (R)**	**187,799**
	Brian Keliher (D)	74,857
53	**Susan Davis* (D)**	**146,449**
	Darin Hunzeker (R)	63,897

#Doris O. Matsui won a special election Mar. 8, 2005, to replace Robert T. Matsui (D), who died on Jan. 1, 2005. ##Christopher Cox resigned on Aug. 2, 2005 to become chairman of the Securities and Exchange Commission. A special election for his replacement was scheduled for Dec. 6, 2005.

Dist.	Representative (Party)	2004 Election
	Colorado	
1	**Diana DeGette* (D)**	**177,077**
	Roland Chicas (R)	58,659
2	**Mark Udall* (D)**	**207,900**
	Stephen Hackman (R)	94,160
3	**John Salazar (D)**	**153,500**
	Greg Walcher (R)	141,376
4	**Marilyn Musgrave* (R)**	**155,958**
	Stan Matsunaka (D)	136,812
5	**Joel Hefley* (R)**	**193,333**
	Fred Hardee (D)	74,098
6	**Tom Tancredo* (R)**	**212,778**
	Joanna Conti (D)	139,870
7	**Bob Beauprez* (R)**	**135,571**
	Dave Thomas (D)	106,026
	Connecticut	
1	**John Larson* (D)**	**198,802**
	John Halstead (R)	73,601
2	**Rob Simmons* (R)**	**166,412**
	Jim Sullivan (D)	140,536
3	**Rosa DeLauro* (D)**	**200,638**
	Richter Elser (R)	69,160
4	**Christopher Shays* (R)**	**152,493**
	Diane Farrell (D)	138,333
5	**Nancy Johnson* (R)**	**168,268**
	Theresa Gerratana (D)	107,438
	Delaware	
	Mike Castle* (R)	**245,978**
	Paul Donnelly (D)	105,716
	Florida	
1	**Jeff Miller* (R)**	**236,604**
	Mark Coutu (D)	72,506
2	**Allen Boyd* (D)**	**201,577**
	Bev Kilmer (R)	125,399
3	**Corrine Brown* (D)**	**unopposed**
4	**Ander Crenshaw* (R)**	**unopposed**
5	**Ginny Brown-Waite* (R)**	**240,315**
	Robert Whittel (D)	124,140
6	**Cliff Stearns* (R)**	**211,137**
	David Bruderly (D)	116,680
7	**John L. Mica* (R)**	**unopposed**
8	**Ric Keller* (R)**	**172,232**
	Stephen Murray (D)	112,343
9	**Michael Bilirakis* (R)**	**unopposed**

Dist.	Representative (Party)	2004 Election
10	**C. W. Bill Young* (R)**	**207,175**
	Bob Derry (D)	91,658
11	**Jim Davis* (D)**	**191,780**
	Robert Johnson (LB)	31,579
12	**Adam Putnam* (R)**	**179,204**
	Bob Hagenmaier (D)	96,965
13	**Katherine Harris* (R)**	**190,477**
	Jan Schneider (D)	153,961
14	**Connie Mack (R)**	**226,662**
	Robert Neeld (D)	108,672
15	**Dave Weldon* (R)**	**210,388**
	Simon Pristoop (D)	111,538
16	**Mark Foley* (R)**	**215,563**
	Jeff Fisher (D)	101,247
17	**Kendrick B. Meek (D)**	**unopposed**
18	**Ileana Ros-Lehtinen* (R)**	**143,647**
	Sam Sheldon (D)	78,281
19	**Robert Wexler* (D)**	**unopposed**
20	**Debbie Wasserman Schultz (D)**	**191,195**
	Margaret Hostetter (R)	81,213
21	**Lincoln Diaz-Balart* (R)**	**146,507**
	Frank Gonzalez (LB)	54,736
22	**E. Clay Shaw* (R)**	**192,581**
	Jim Stork (D)	108,258
23	**Alcee L. Hastings* (D)**	**unopposed**
24	**Tom Feeney* (R)**	**unopposed**
25	**Mario Diaz-Balart* (R)**	**unopposed**
	Georgia	
1	**Jack Kingston* (R)**	**unopposed**
2	**Sanford Bishop* (D)**	**129,984**
	Dave Eversman (R)	64,645
3	**Jim Marshall* (D)**	**136,273**
	Calder Clay (R)	80,435
4	**Cynthia McKinney (D)**	**157,461**
	Catherine Davis (R)	89,509
5	**John Lewis* (D)**	**unopposed**
6	**Tom Price (R)**	**unopposed**
7	**John Linder* (R)**	**unopposed**
8	**Lynn Westmoreland (R)**	**227,524**
	Silvia Delamar (D)	73,632
9	**Charlie Norwood* (R)**	**197,869**
	Bob Ellis (D)	68,462
10	**Nathan Deal* (R)**	**unopposed**
11	**Phil Gingrey* (R)**	**120,696**
	Rick Crawford (D)	89,591
12	**John Barrow (D)**	**113,036**
	Max Burns* (R)	105,132
13	**David Scott* (D)**	**unopposed**
	Hawaii	
1	**Neil Abercrombie* (D)**	**128,567**
	Dalton Tanonaka (R)	69,371
2	**Ed Case* (D)**	**133,317**
	Mike Gabbard (R)	79,072
	Idaho	
1	**C. L. "Butch" Otter* (R)**	**207,662**
	Naomi Preston (D)	90,927
2	**Mike Simpson* (R)**	**193,704**
	Lin Whitworth (D)	80,133
	Illinois	
1	**Bobby Rush* (D)**	**212,109**
	Ray Wardingley (R)	37,840
2	**Jesse Jackson Jr.* (D)**	**207,535**
	Stephanie Sailor (LB)	26,990
3	**Daniel Lipinski (D)**	**167,034**
	Ryan Chlada (R)	57,845
4	**Luis Gutierrez* (D)**	**104,761**
	Tony Cisneros (R)	15,536
5	**Rahm Emanuel* (D)**	**158,400**
	Bruce Best (R)	49,530
6	**Henry Hyde* (R)**	**139,627**
	Christine Cegelis (D)	110,470

Dist.	Representative (Party)	2004 Election
7	**Danny Davis* (D)**	**221,133**
	Antonio Davis-Fairman (R)	35,603
8	**Melissa Bean (D)**	**139,792**
	Philip Crane* (R)	130,601
9	**Janice Schakowsky* (D)**	**175,282**
	Kurt Eckhardt (R)	56,135
10	**Mark Kirk* (R)**	**177,493**
	Lee Goodman (D)	99,218
11	**Jerry Weller* (R)**	**173,057**
	Tari Renner (D)	121,903
12	**Jerry Costello* (D)**	**198,962**
	Erin Zweigart (R)	82,677
13	**Judy Biggert* (R)**	**200,472**
	Gloria Schor Andersen (D)	107,836
14	**J. Dennis Hastert* (R)**	**191,618**
	Ruben Zamora (D)	87,590
15	**Tim Johnson* (R)**	**178,114**
	David Gill (D)	113,625
16	**Donald Manzullo* (R)**	**204,350**
	John Kutsch (D)	91,452
17	**Lane Evans* (D)**	**172,320**
	Andrea Lane Zinga (R)	111,680
18	**Ray LaHood* (R)**	**216,047**
	Steve Waterworth (D)	91,548
19	**John Shimkus* (R)**	**213,451**
	Tim Bagwell (D)	94,303
	Indiana	
1	**Peter Visclosky* (D)**	**178,406**
	Mark Leyva (R)	82,858
2	**Chris Chocola* (R)**	**140,496**
	Joe Donnelly (D)	115,513
3	**Mark Souder* (R)**	**171,389**
	Maria Parra (D)	76,232
4	**Steve Buyer* (R)**	**190,445**
	David Sanders (D)	77,574
5	**Dan Burton* (R)**	**228,718**
	Katherine Carr (D)	82,637
6	**Mike Pence* (R)**	**182,529**
	Mel Fox (D)	85,123
7	**Julia Carson* (D)**	**121,303**
	Andy Horning (R)	97,491
8	**John Hostettler* (R)**	**145,576**
	Jon Jennings (D)	121,522
9	**Mike Sodrel (R)**	**142,197**
	Baron Hill* (D)	140,772
	Iowa	
1	**Jim Nussle* (R)**	**159,993**
	Bill Gluba (D)	125,490
2	**Jim Leach* (R)**	**176,684**
	Dave Franker (D)	117,405
3	**Leonard Boswell* (D)**	**168,007**
	Stan Thompson (R)	136,099
4	**Tom Latham* (R)**	**181,294**
	Paul Johnson (D)	116,121
5	**Steve King* (R)**	**168,583**
	Joyce Schulte (D)	97,597
	Kansas	
1	**Jerry Moran* (R)**	**239,776**
	Jack Warner (LB)	24,517
2	**Jim Ryun* (R)**	**165,325**
	Nancy Boyda (D)	121,532
3	**Dennis Moore* (D)**	**184,050**
	Kris Kobach (R)	145,542
4	**Todd Tiahrt* (R)**	**173,151**
	Michael Kinard (D)	81,388
	Kentucky	
1	**Ed Whitfield* (R)**	**175,972**
	Billy Cartwright (D)	85,229
2	**Ron Lewis* (R)**	**185,394**
	Adam Smith (D)	87,585

Dist.	Representative (Party)	2004 Election
3	**Anne Northup* (R)**	**197,736**
	Tony Miller (D)	124,040
4	**Geoff Davis (R)**	**160,982**
	Nick Clooney (D)	129,876
5	**Harold "Hal" Rogers* (R)**	**unopposed**
6	**Ben Chandler* (D)**	**175,355**
	Tom Buford (R)	119,716
	Louisiana	
1	**Bobby Jindal (R)**	**225,708**
	Roy Armstrong (D)	19,266
2	**William Jefferson* (D)**	**173,510**
	Art Schwertz (R)	46,097
#3	**Charlie Melancon (D)**	57,609
	Billy Tauzin III (R)	57,092
4	**Jim McCrery* (R)**	**unopposed**
5	**Rodney Alexander* (R)**	**141,495**
	Zelma Blakes (D)	58,591
6	**Richard H. Baker* (R)**	**189,106**
	Rufus Craig (D)	50,732
#7	**Charles Boustany (R)**	**75,035**
	Willie Mount (D)	61,483

In Louisiana, all candidates of all parties ran against one another on Nov. 2, 2004, in a non-partisan primary. Candidates who received more than 50% of the vote were declared elected. Because no candidate received a majority of the vote in Districts 3 or 7, runoffs were held in those districts, Dec. 4, 2004, between the top 2 vote-getters.

Dist.	Representative (Party)	2004 Election
	Maine	
1	**Tom Allen* (D)**	**219,077**
	Charles Summers (R)	147,663
2	**Michael Michaud* (D)**	**199,303**
	Brian Hamel (R)	135,547
	Maryland	
1	**Wayne Gilchrest* (R)**	**245,149**
	Kostas Alexakis (D)	77,872
2	**C. A. Dutch Ruppersberger* (D)**	**164,751**
	Jane Brooks (R)	75,812
3	**Ben Cardin* (D)**	**182,066**
	Bob Duckworth (R)	97,008
4	**Albert Russell Wynn* (D)**	**196,809**
	John McKinnis (R)	52,907
5	**Steny Hoyer* (D)**	**204,867**
	Brad Jewitt (R)	87,189
6	**Roscoe Bartlett* (R)**	**206,076**
	Kenneth Bosley (D)	90,108
7	**Elijah Cummings* (D)**	**179,189**
	Tony Salazar (R)	60,102
8	**Chris Van Hollen* (D)**	**215,129**
	Chuck Floyd (R)	71,989
	Massachusetts	
1	**John W. Olver* (D)**	**unopposed**
2	**Richard E. Neal* (D)**	**unopposed**
3	**Jim McGovern* (D)**	**192,036**
	Ron Crews (R)	80,197
4	**Barney Frank* (D)**	**219,260**
	Charles Morse (Ind.)	62,293
5	**Marty Meehan* (D)**	**179,652**
	Thomas Tierney (R)	88,232
6	**John Tierney* (D)**	**213,458**
	Stephen O'Malley (R)	91,597
7	**Ed Markey* (D)**	**202,399**
	Ken Chase (R)	60,334
8	**Michael E. Capuano* (D)**	**unopposed**
9	**Stephen F. Lynch* (D)**	**unopposed**
10	**Bill Delahunt* (D)**	**222,013**
	Michael Jones (R)	114,879
	Michigan	
1	**Bart Stupak* (D)**	**211,571**
	Don Hooper (R)	105,706
2	**Pete Hoekstra* (R)**	**225,343**
	Kimon Kotos (D)	94,040
3	**Vernon Ehlers* (R)**	**214,465**
	Peter Hickey (D)	101,395
4	**Dave Camp* (R)**	**205,274**
	Mike Huckleberry (D)	110,885
5	**Dale Kildee* (D)**	**208,163**
	Myrah Kirkwood (R)	96,934
6	**Fred Upton* (R)**	**197,425**
	Scott Elliott (D)	97,978
7	**John J. H. "Joe" Schwarz (R)**	**176,053**
	Sharon Renier (D)	109,527
8	**Mike Rogers* (R)**	**207,925**
	Robert Alexander (D)	125,619
9	**Joe Knollenberg* (R)**	**199,210**
	Steven Reifman (D)	134,764
10	**Candice Miller* (R)**	**227,720**
	Rob Casey (D)	98,029
11	**Thad McCotter* (R)**	**186,431**
	Phillip Truran (D)	134,301
12	**Sander Levin* (D)**	**210,827**
	Randell Shafer (R)	88,256
13	**Carolyn C. Kilpatrick* (D)**	**173,246**
	Cynthia Cassell (R)	40,935
14	**John Conyers* (D)**	**213,681**
	Veronica Pedraza (R)	35,089
15	**John Dingell* (D)**	**218,409**
	Dawn Reamer (R)	81,828
	Minnesota	
1	**Gil Gutknecht* (R)**	**193,132**
	Leigh Pomeroy (D)	115,088
2	**John Kline* (R)**	**206,313**
	Teresa Daly (D)	147,527
3	**Jim Ramstad* (R)**	**231,871**
	Deborah Watts (D)	126,665
4	**Betty McCollum* (D)**	**182,387**
	Patrice Bataglia (R)	105,467
5	**Martin Olav Sabo* (D)**	**218,434**
	Daniel Mathias (R)	76,600
6	**Mark Kennedy* (R)**	**203,669**
	Patty Wetterling (D)	173,309
7	**Collin Peterson* (D)**	**207,628**
	David Sturrock (R)	106,349
8	**James Oberstar* (D)**	**228,586**
	Mark Groettum (R)	112,693
	Mississippi	
1	**Roger Wicker* (R)**	**219,328**
	Barbara Washer (R)	58,256
2	**Bennie Thompson* (D)**	**154,626**
	Clinton LeSueur (R)	107,647
3	**Charles "Chip" Pickering* (R)**	**234,874**
	Jim Giles (Ind.)	40,426
4	**Gene Taylor* (D)**	**179,979**
	Michael Lott (R)	96,740
	Missouri	
1	**William Lacy Clay* (D)**	**213,658**
	Leslie Farr (R)	64,791
2	**Todd Akin* (R)**	**228,725**
	George Weber (D)	115,366
3	**Russ Carnahan (D)**	**146,894**
	Bill Federer (R)	125,422
4	**Ike Skelton* (D)**	**190,800**
	Jim Noland (R)	93,334
5	**Emanuel Cleaver (D)**	**161,727**
	Jeanne Patterson (R)	123,431
6	**Sam Graves* (R)**	**196,516**
	Charles Broomfield (D)	106,987
7	**Roy Blunt* (R)**	**210,080**
	Jim Newberry (D)	84,356
8	**Jo Ann Emerson* (R)**	**194,039**
	Dean Henderson (D)	71,543
9	**Kenny Hulshof* (R)**	**193,429**
	Linda Jacobsen (D)	101,343

Dist.	Representative (Party)	2004 Election
	Montana	
	Denny Rehberg* (R)	**286,076**
	Tracy Velazquez (D)	145,606
	Nebraska	
1	**Jeff Fortenberry (R)**	**143,756**
	Matt Connealy (D)	113,971
2	**Lee Terry* (R)**	**152,608**
	Nancy Thompson (D)	90,292
3	**Tom Osborne* (R)**	**218,751**
	Donna Anderson (D)	26,434
	Nevada	
1	**Shelley Berkley* (D)**	**133,569**
	Russ Mickelson (R)	63,005
2	**Jim Gibbons* (R)**	**195,466**
	Angie Cochran (D)	79,978
3	**Jon Porter* (R)**	**162,240**
	Tom Gallagher (D)	120,365
	New Hampshire	
1	**Jeb Bradley* (R)**	**204,836**
	Justin Nadeau (D)	118,226
2	**Charles Bass* (R)**	**191,188**
	Paul Hodes (D)	125,280
	New Jersey	
1	**Rob Andrews* (D)**	**201,163**
	Daniel Hutchison (R)	66,109
2	**Frank LoBiondo* (R)**	**172,779**
	Timothy Robb (D)	86,792
3	**Jim Saxton* (R)**	**195,938**
	Herb Conaway (D)	107,034
4	**Chris Smith* (R)**	**192,671**
	Amy Vasquez (D)	92,826
5	**Scott Garrett* (R)**	**171,220**
	Anne Wolfe (D)	122,259
6	**Frank Pallone* (D)**	**153,981**
	Sylvester Fernandez (R)	70,942
7	**Mike Ferguson* (R)**	**162,597**
	Steve Brozak (D)	119,081
8	**Bill Pascrell* (D)**	**152,001**
	George Ajjan (R)	62,747
9	**Steve Rothman* (D)**	**146,038**
	Edward Trawinski (R)	68,564
10	**Donald Payne* (D)**	**155,697**
	Sara Lobman (Ind.)	2,927
11	**Rodney Frelinghuysen* (R)**	**200,915**
	James Buell (D)	91,811
12	**Rush Holt* (D)**	**171,691**
	Bill Spadea (R)	115,014
13	**Bob Menendez* (D)**	**121,018**
	Richard Piatkowski (R)	35,288
	New Mexico	
1	**Heather Wilson* (R)**	**147,372**
	Richard Romero (D)	123,339
2	**Steve Pearce* (R)**	**130,498**
	Gary King (D)	86,292
3	**Tom Udall* (D)**	**175,269**
	Gregory Tucker (R)	79,935
	New York	
1	**Timothy Bishop* (D)**	**156,354**
	William Manger Jr. (R)	121,855
2	**Steve Israel (D)***	**161,593**
	Richard Hoffmann (R)	80,950
3	**Peter King* (R)**	**171,259**
	Blair Mathies Jr. (D)	100,737
4	**Carolyn McCarthy* (D)**	**159,969**
	James Garner (R)	94,141
5	**Gary Ackerman* (D)**	**119,726**
	Stephen Graves (R)	46,867
6	**Gregory W. Meeks* (D)**	**unopposed**
7	**Joseph Crowley* (D)**	**104,275**
	Joseph Cinquemani (R)	24,548

Dist.	Representative (Party)	2004 Election
8	**Jerrold Nadler* (D)**	**162,082**
	Peter Hort (R)	39,240
9	**Anthony Weiner* (D)**	**113,025**
	Gerard Cronin (R)	45,451
10	**Edolphus Towns* (D)**	**136,113**
	Harvey Clarke (R)	11,099
11	**Major Owens* (D)**	**144,999**
	Lorraine Stevens (C)	4,721
12	**Nydia Velázquez* (D)**	**107,796**
	Paul Rodriguez (R)	17,166
13	**Vito Fossella* (R)**	**112,934**
	Frank Barbaro (D)	78,500
14	**Carolyn Maloney* (D)**	**186,688**
	Anton Srdanovic (R)	43,623
15	**Charles Rangel* (D)**	**161,351**
	Kenneth Jefferson Jr. (R)	12,355
16	**José Serrano* (D)**	**111,638**
	Ali Mohamed (R)	5,610
17	**Eliot Engel* (D)**	**140,530**
	Matt Brennan (R)	40,524
18	**Nita Lowey* (D)**	**170,715**
	Richard Hoffman (R)	73,975
19	**Sue Kelly* (R)**	**175,401**
	Michael Jaliman (D)	87,429
20	**John Sweeney* (R)**	**188,753**
	Doris Kelly (D)	96,630
21	**Michael McNulty* (D)**	**194,033**
	Warren Redlich (R)	80,121
22	**Maurice Hinchey* (D)**	**167,489**
	William Brenner (R)	81,881
23	**John McHugh* (R)**	**160,079**
	Robert Johnson (D)	66,448
24	**Sherwood Boehlert* (R)**	**143,000**
	Jeffrey Miller (D)	85,140
25	**James Walsh* (R)**	**189,063**
	Howie Hawkins (Peace & Justice)	20,106
26	**Thomas Reynolds* (R)**	**157,466**
	Jack Davis Jr. (D)	125,613
27	**Brian Higgins (D)**	**143,332**
	Nancy Naples (R)	139,558
28	**Louise McIntosh Slaughter* (D)**	**159,655**
	Michael Laba (R)	54,543
29	**John "Randy" Kuhl Jr. (R)**	**136,883**
	Samara Barend (D)	110,241
	North Carolina	
1	**G.K. Butterfield* (D)**	**137,667**
	Greg Dority (R)	77,508
2	**Bob Etheridge* (D)**	**145,079**
	Billy Creech (R)	87,811
3	**Walter Jones* (R)**	**171,863**
	Roger Eaton (D)	71,227
4	**David Price* (D)**	**217,441**
	Todd Batchelor (R)	121,717
5	**Virginia Foxx (R)**	**167,546**
	Jim Harrell (D)	117,271
6	**Howard Coble* (R)**	**207,470**
	William Jordan (D)	76,153
7	**Mike McIntyre* (D)**	**180,382**
	Ken Plonk (R)	66,084
8	**Robin Hayes* (R)**	**125,070**
	Beth Troutman (D)	100,101
9	**Sue Myrick* (R)**	**210,783**
	Jack Flynn (D)	89,318
10	**Patrick McHenry (R)**	**157,884**
	Anne Fischer (D)	88,233
11	**Charles Taylor* (R)**	**159,709**
	Patsy Keever (D)	131,188
12	**Mel Watt* (D)**	**154,908**
	Ada Fisher (R)	76,898
13	**Brad Miller* (D)**	**160,896**
	Virginia Johnson (R)	112,788

Dist.	Representative (Party)	2004 Election
	North Dakota	
	Earl Pomeroy* (D)	**185,130**
	Duane Sand (R)	125,684
	Ohio	
1	**Steve Chabot* (R)**	**173,430**
	Greg Harris (D)	116,235
2	**Jean Schmidt (R)#**	**17,320**
	Paul Hackett (D)	12,439
3	**Mike Turner* (R)**	**197,290**
	Jane Mitakides (D)	119,448
4	**Michael Oxley* (R)**	**167,807**
	Ben Konop (D)	118,538
5	**Paul Gillmor* (R)**	**196,649**
	Robin Weirauch (D)	96,656
6	**Ted Strickland* (D)**	**unopposed**
7	**Dave Hobson* (R)**	**186,534**
	Kara Anastasio (D)	100,617
8	**John Boehner* (R)**	**201,675**
	Jeff Hardenbrook (D)	90,574
9	**Marcy Kaptur* (D)**	**205,149**
	Larry Kaczala (R)	95,983
10	**Dennis Kucinich* (D)**	**172,406**
	Edward Herman (R)	96,463
11	**Stephanie Tubbs Jones (D)**	**unopposed**
12	**Pat Tiberi* (R)**	**198,912**
	Edward Brown (D)	122,109
13	**Sherrod Brown* (D)**	**201,004**
	Robert Lucas (R)	97,090
14	**Steven LaTourette* (R)**	**201,652**
	Capri Cafaro (D)	119,714
15	**Deborah Pryce* (R)**	**166,520**
	Mark Brown (D)	110,915
16	**Ralph Regula* (R)**	**202,544**
	Jeff Seemann (D)	101,817
17	**Tim Ryan* (D)**	**212,800**
	Frank Cusimano (R)	62,871
18	**Bob Ney* (R)**	**177,600**
	Brian Thomas (D)	90,820

Rob Portman resigned effective April 29, 2005 to become U.S. trade representative. Jean Schmidt was elected Aug. 2 to replace him.

Dist.	Representative (Party)	2004 Election
	Oklahoma	
1	**John Sullivan* (R)**	**187,145**
	Doug Dodd (D)	116,731
2	**Dan Boren (D)**	**179,579**
	Wayland Smalley (R)	92,963
3	**Frank Lucas* (R)**	**215,510**
	Gregory Wilson (Ind.)	46,621
4	**Tom Cole* (R)**	**198,985**
	Charlene Bradshaw (Ind.)	56,869
5	**Ernest Istook* (R)**	**180,430**
	Bert Smith (D)	92,719
	Oregon	
1	**David Wu* (D)**	**203,771**
	Goli Ameri (R)	135,164
2	**Greg Walden* (R)**	**248,461**
	John McColgan (D)	88,914
3	**Earl Blumenauer* (D)**	**245,559**
	Tami Mars (R)	82,045
4	**Peter DeFazio* (D)**	**228,611**
	Jim Feldkamp (R)	140,882
5	**Darlene Hooley* (D)**	**184,833**
	Jim Zupancic (R)	154,993
	Pennsylvania	
1	**Robert Brady* (D)**	**214,462**
	Deborah Williams (R)	33,266
2	**Chaka Fattah* (D)**	**253,226**
	Stewart Bolno (R)	34,411
3	**Phil English* (R)**	**166,580**
	Steven Porter (D)	110,684
4	**Melissa Hart* (R)**	**204,329**
	Stevan Drobac (D)	116,303

Dist.	Representative (Party)	2004 Election
5	**John Peterson* (R)**	**192,852**
	Thomas Martin (LB)	26,239
6	**Jim Gerlach* (R)**	**160,348**
	Lois Murphy (D)	153,977
7	**Curt Weldon* (R)**	**196,556**
	Paul Scoles (D)	134,932
8	**Michael Fitzpatrick (R)**	**183,229**
	Virginia Schrader (D)	143,427
9	**Bill Shuster* (R)**	**184,320**
	Paul Politis (D)	80,787
10	**Don Sherwood* (R)**	**191,967**
	Veronica Hannevig (C)	14,805
11	**Paul Kanjorski* (D)**	**171,147**
	Kenneth Brenneman (C)	10,105
12	**John P. Murtha* (D)**	**unopposed**
13	**Allyson Schwartz (D)**	**171,763**
	Melissa Brown (R)	127,205
14	**Michael F. Doyle* (D)**	**unopposed**
15	**Charles Dent (R)**	**170,634**
	Joe Driscoll (D)	114,646
16	**Joseph Pitts* (R)**	**183,620**
	Lois Herr (D)	98,410
17	**Tim Holden* (D)**	**172,412**
	Scott Paterno (R)	113,592
18	**Tim Murphy* (R)**	**197,894**
	Mark Boles (D)	117,420
19	**Todd Platts* (R)**	**224,274**
	Charles Steel (GR)	8,890
	Rhode Island	
1	**Patrick Kennedy* (D)**	**124,923**
	Dave Rogers (R)	69,819
2	**Jim Langevin* (D)**	**154,392**
	Chuck Barton (R)	43,139
	South Carolina	
1	**Henry Brown* (R)**	**186,448**
	James Dunn (G)	25,674
2	**Joe Wilson* (R)**	**181,862**
	Michael Ray Ellisor (D)	93,249
3	**J. Gresham Barrett* (R)**	**unopposed**
4	**Bob Inglis (R)**	**188,795**
	Brandon Brown (D)	78,376
5	**John Spratt* (D)**	**152,867**
	Albert Spencer (R)	89,568
6	**Jim Clyburn* (D)**	**161,987**
	Gary McLeod (R)	75,443
	South Dakota	
	Stephanie Herseth* (D)	**207,837**
	Larry Diedrich (R)	178,823
	Tennessee	
1	**Bill Jenkins* (R)**	**172,543**
	Graham Leonard (D)	56,361
2	**John Duncan* (R)**	**215,795**
	John Greene (D)	52,155
3	**Zach Wamp* (R)**	**166,154**
	John Wolfe (D)	84,295
4	**Lincoln Davis* (D)**	**138,459**
	Janice Bowling (R)	109,993
5	**Jim Cooper* (D)**	**168,970**
	Scott Knapp (R)	74,978
6	**Bart Gordon* (D)**	**167,448**
	Nick Demas (R)	87,523
7	**Marsha Blackburn* (R)**	**unopposed**
8	**John Tanner* (D)**	**173,623**
	James Hart (R)	59,853
9	**Harold Ford* (D)**	**190,648**
	Ruben Fort (R)	41,578
	Texas	
1	**Louis Gohmert (R)**	**157,068**
	Max Sandlin* (D)	96,281
2	**Ted Poe (R)**	**139,951**
	Nick Lampson* (D)	108,156

Dist.	Representative (Party)	2004 Election
3	**Sam Johnson* (R)**	**180,099**
	Paul Jenkins (Ind.)	16,966
4	**Ralph Hall* (R)**	**182,866**
	Jim Nickerson (D)	81,585
5	**Jeb Hensarling* (R)**	**148,816**
	Bill Bernstein (D)	75,911
6	**Joe Barton* (R)**	**168,767**
	Morris Meyer (D)	83,609
7	**John Culberson* (R)**	**175,440**
	John Martinez (D)	91,126
8	**Kevin Brady* (R)**	**179,599**
	James Wright (D)	77,324
9	**Al Green (D)**	**114,462**
	Arlette Molina (R)	42,132
10	**Michael McCaul (R)**	**182,113**
	Robert Fritsche (LB)	35,569
11	**Mike Conaway (R)**	**177,291**
	Wayne Raasch (D)	50,339
12	**Kay Granger* (R)**	**173,222**
	Felix Alvarado (D)	66,316
13	**Mac Thornberry* (R)**	**189,448**
	M. J. Smith (LB)	15,793
14	**Ron Paul* (R)**	**unopposed**
15	**Rubén Hinojosa* (D)**	**96,089**
	Michael Thamm (R)	67,917
16	**Silvestre Reyes* (D)**	**108,577**
	David Brigham (R)	49,972
17	**Chet Edwards* (D)**	**125,309**
	Arlene Wohlgemuth (R)	116,049
18	**Sheila Jackson-Lee* (D)**	**136,018**
	Tom Bazan (Ind.)	9,787
19	**Randy Neugebauer* (R)**	**136,459**
	Charlie Stenholm* (D)	93,531
20	**Charlie Gonzalez* (D)**	**112,480**
	Roger Scott (R)	54,976
21	**Lamar Smith* (R)**	**209,774**
	Rhett Smith (D)	121,129
22	**Tom DeLay* (R)**	**150,386**
	Richard Morrison (D)	112,034
23	**Henry Bonilla* (R)**	**170,716**
	Joe Sullivan (D)	72,480
24	**Kenny Marchant (R)**	**154,435**
	Gary Page (D)	82,599
25	**Lloyd Doggett* (D)**	**108,309**
	Rebecca Klein (R)	49,252
26	**Michael Burgess* (R)**	**180,519**
	Lico Reyes (D)	89,809
27	**Solomon Ortiz* (D)**	**112,081**
	Willie Vaden (R)	61,955
28	**Henry Cuellar (D)**	**106,323**
	Jim Hopson (R)	69,538
29	**Gene Green* (D)**	**78,256**
	Clifford Messina (LB)	4,868
30	**Eddie Bernice Johnson* (D)**	**144,513**
	John Davis (LB)	10,821
31	**John Carter* (R)**	**160,247**
	Jon Porter (D)	80,292
32	**Pete Sessions* (R)**	**109,859**
	Martin Frost* (D)	89,030

Redistricting in effect for the 2004 election resulted in incumbents facing off in the 19th and 32nd districts.

Dist.	Representative (Party)	2004 Election
	Utah	
1	**Rob Bishop* (R)**	**199,615**
	Steve Thompson (D)	85,630
2	**Jim Matheson* (D)**	**187,250**
	John Swallow (R)	147,778
3	**Chris Cannon* (R)**	**173,010**
	Beau Babka (D)	88,748
	Vermont	
	Bernie Sanders* (Ind.)	**205,774**
	Greg Parke (R)	74,271
	Virginia	
1	**Jo Ann Davis* (R)**	**225,071**
	William Lee (I)	57,434
2	**Thelma Drake (R)**	**132,946**
	David Ashe (D)	108,180
3	**Bobby Scott* (D)**	**159,373**
	Winsome Sears (R)	70,194
4	**Randy Forbes* (R)**	**182,444**
	Jonathan Menefee (D)	100,413
5	**Virgil Goode* (R)**	**172,431**
	Al Weed (D)	98,237
6	**Bob Goodlatte* (R)**	**unopposed**
7	**Eric Cantor* (R)**	**230,765**
	W. Brad Blanton (Ind.)	74,325
8	**Jim Moran* (D)**	**171,986**
	Lisa Marie Cheney (R)	106,231
9	**Rick Boucher* (D)**	**150,039**
	Kevin Triplett (R)	98,499
10	**Frank Wolf* (R)**	**205,982**
	James Socas (D)	116,654
11	**Tom Davis* (R)**	**186,299**
	Ken Longmyer (D)	118,305
	Washington	
1	**Jay Inslee* (D)**	**204,121**
	Randy Eastwood (R)	117,850
2	**Rick Larsen* (D)**	**202,383**
	Suzanne Sinclair (R)	106,333
3	**Brian Baird* (D)**	**193,626**
	Thomas Crowson (R)	119,027
4	**Doc Hastings* (R)**	**154,627**
	Sandy Matheson (D)	92,486
5	**Cathy McMorris (R)**	**179,600**
	Don Barbieri (D)	121,333
6	**Norm Dicks* (D)**	**202,919**
	Doug Cloud (R)	91,228
7	**Jim McDermott* (D)**	**272,302**
	Carol Cassady (R)	65,226
8	**Dave Reichert (R)**	**173,298**
	Dave Ross (D)	157,148
9	**Adam Smith* (D)**	**162,433**
	Paul Lord (R)	88,304
	West Virginia	
1	**Alan Mollohan* (D)**	**166,583**
	Alan Parks (R)	79,196
2	**Shelley Moore Capito* (R)**	**147,676**
	Erik Wells (D)	106,131
3	**Nick Rahall* (D)**	**142,682**
	Rick Snuffer (R)	76,170
	Wisconsin	
1	**Paul Ryan* (R)**	**233,372**
	Jeff Thomas (D)	116,250
2	**Tammy Baldwin* (D)**	**251,637**
	Dave Magnum (R)	145,810
3	**Ron Kind* (D)**	**204,856**
	Dale Schultz (R)	157,866
4	**Gwen Moore (D)**	**212,382**
	Gerald Boyle (R)	85,928
5	**F. James Sensenbrenner* (R)**	**271,153**
	Bryan Kennedy (D)	129,384
6	**Tom Petri* (R)**	**238,620**
	Jef Hall (D)	107,209
7	**David Obey* (D)**	**241,306**
	Mike Miles (G)	26,518
8	**Mark Green* (R)**	**248,070**
	Dottie Le Clair (D)	105,513
	Wyoming	
	Barbara Cubin* (R)	**132,107**
	Ted Ladd (D)	99,989

The following members of Congress are nonvoting: Luis G. Fortuño (R) resident commissioner, Puerto Rico; Eleanor Holmes Norton (D), District of Columbia; Eni F. H. Faleomavaega (D) American Samoa; Donna M. Christian-Christensen (D), Virgin Islands; Madeleine Bordallo (D), Guam.

Congressional Committees

(as of Oct. 2005)

Rep. = Republican; Dem. = Democrat

Senate Standing Committees

Agriculture, Nutrition, and Forestry
Chairman: Saxby Chambliss, GA
Ranking Dem.: Tom Harkin, IA

Appropriations
Chairman: Thad Cochran, MS
Ranking Dem.: Robert C. Byrd, WV

Armed Services
Chairman: John W. Warner, VA
Ranking Dem.: Carl Levin, MI

Banking, Housing, and Urban Affairs
Chairman: Richard C. Shelby, AL
Ranking Dem.: Paul S. Sarbanes, MD

Budget
Chairman: Gregg Judd, NH
Ranking Dem.: Kent Conrad, ND

Commerce, Science, and Transportation
Chairman: Ted Stevens, AK
Co-Chair: Daniel Inouye, HI

Energy and Natural Resources
Chairman: Pete V. Domenici, NM
Ranking Dem.: Jeff Bingaman, NM

Environment and Public Works
Chairman: James M. Inhofe, OK
Ranking: James M. Jeffords, VT

Finance
Chairman: Charles Grassley, IA
Ranking Dem.: Max Baucus, MT

Foreign Relations
Chairman: Richard G. Lugar, IN
Ranking Dem.: Joseph R. Biden Jr., DE

Health, Education, Labor, and Pensions
Chairman: Michael Enzi, WY
Ranking Dem.: Edward Kennedy, MA

Homeland Security and Governmental Affairs
Chairman: Susan Collins, ME
Ranking Dem.: Joseph Lieberman, CT

Judiciary
Chairman: Arlen Specter, PA
Ranking Dem.: Patrick Leahy, VT

Rules and Administration
Chairman: Trent Lott, MS
Ranking Dem.: Joseph Lieberman, CT

Small Business and Entrepreneurship
Chairman: Olympia Snowe, ME
Ranking Dem.: John F. Kerry, MA

Veterans' Affairs
Chairman: Larry Craig, ID
Ranking Dem.: Daniel Akaka, HI

Senate Special, Select, and Other Committees

Special Committee on Aging
Chairman: Gordon Smith, OR
Ranking Dem.: Herb Kohl, WI

Select Committee on Ethics
Chairman: George V. Voinovich (Rep., OH)
Vice Chairman: Tim Johnson (Dem., SD)

Indian Affairs
Chairman: John McCain, AZ
Ranking Dem.: Byron Dorgan, ND

Select Committee on Intelligence
Chairman: Pat Roberts (Rep., KS)
Vice Chairman: John D. Rockefeller IV (Dem., WV)

Joint Committees of Congress

Economic
Chairman: Representative Jim Saxton (Rep., NJ)
Vice Chairman: Senator Robert Bennett (Rep., UT)

Library
Vice Chairman: Representative Vernon Ehlers (Rep., MI)
Vice Chairman: Senator Ted Stevens (Rep., AK)

Taxation
Chairman: Representative Bill Thomas (Rep., CA)
Vice Chairman: Senator Charles E. Grassley (Rep., IA)

Printing
Chairman: Senator Trent Lott, Chairman (Rep., MS)
Vice Chairman: Representative Robert W. Ney (Rep., OH)

House Standing Committees

Agriculture
Chairman: Bob Goodlatte, VA
Ranking Dem.: Collin C. Peterson, MN

Appropriations
Chairman: Jerry Lewis, CA
Ranking Dem.: David R. Obey, WI

Armed Services
Chairman: Duncan Hunter, CA
Ranking Dem.: Ike Skelton, MO

Budget
Chairman: Jim Nussle, IA
Ranking Dem.: John Spratt, SC

Education and the Workforce
Chairman: John A. Boehner, OH
Ranking Dem.: George Miller, CA

Energy and Commerce
Chairman: Joe Barton, TX
Ranking Dem.: John D. Dingell, MI

Financial Services
Chairman: Michael G. Oxley, OH
Vice Chairwoman: Sue W. Kelly, NY

Government Reform
Chairman: Tom Davis, VA
Vice Chairman: Christopher Shays, CT

Homeland Security
Chairman: Peter T. King, NY
Vice Chairman: Curt Weldon, PA

House Administration
Chairman: Robert W. Ney, OH
Ranking Dem.: Juanita Millender-McDonald, CA

Judiciary
Chairman: F. James Sensenbrenner Jr, WI
Ranking Dem.: John Conyers Jr, MI

International Relations
Chairman: Henry J. Hyde, IL
Ranking Dem.: Tom Lantos, CA

Resources
Chairman: Richard Pombo, CA
Ranking Dem.: Nick J. Rahall II, WV

Rules
Chairman: David Dreier, CA
Ranking Dem.: Louise Slaughter, NY

Science
Chairman: Sherwood L. Boehlert, NY
Ranking Dem.: Bart Gordon, TN

Small Business
Chairman: Donald A. Manzullo, IL
Ranking Dem.: Nydia M. Velazquez, NY

Standards of Official Conduct
Chairman: Doc Hastings, WA
Ranking Dem.: Alan B. Mollohan, WV

Transportation and Infrastructure
Chairman: Don E. Young, AK
Ranking Dem.: James L. Oberstar, MN

Veterans' Affairs
Chairman: Steve Buyer, IN
Ranking Dem.: Lane A. Evans, IL

Ways and Means
Chairman: Bill Thomas, CA
Ranking Dem.: Charles B. Rangel, NY

House Select Committee

Intelligence
Chairman: Peter Hoekstra, MI
Ranking Dem.: Jane Harman, CA

Congress divides its tasks among some 250 committees and subcommittees. Standing committees generally have legislative jurisdiction and operate with subcommittees that handle work in specific areas. Select and joint committees are chiefly for oversight or housekeeping. The chair of each House or Senate committee and a majority of its members come from the majority party, which, as of Oct. 2005, was the Republican Party in both the Senate and the House.

Floor Leaders in the U.S. Senate Since the 1920s

Majority Leaders

Name	Party	State	Tenure
Charles Curtis[1]	Rep.	KS	1925-1929
James E. Watson	Rep.	IN	1929-1933
Joseph T. Robinson	Dem.	AR	1933-1937
Alben W. Barkley	Dem.	KY	1937-1947
Wallace H. White	Rep.	ME	1947-1949
Scott W. Lucas	Dem.	IL	1949-1951
Ernest W. McFarland	Dem.	AZ	1951-1953
Robert A. Taft	Rep.	OH	1953
William F. Knowland	Rep.	CA	1953-1955
Lyndon B. Johnson	Dem.	TX	1955-1961
Mike Mansfield	Dem.	MT	1961-1977
Robert C. Byrd	Dem.	WV	1977-1981
Howard H. Baker Jr.	Rep.	TN	1981-1985
Robert J. Dole	Rep.	KS	1985-1987
Robert C. Byrd	Dem.	WV	1987-1989
George J. Mitchell	Dem.	ME	1989-1995
Robert J. Dole	Rep.	KS	1995-1996
Trent Lott	Rep.	MS	1996-2001[3]
Thomas A. Daschle	Dem.	SD	2001-2003[3]
Bill Frist	Rep.	TN	2003-

Minority Leaders

Name	Party	State	Tenure
Oscar W. Underwood[2]	Dem.	AL	1920-1923
Joseph T. Robinson	Dem.	AR	1923-1933
Charles L. McNary	Rep.	OR	1933-1944
Wallace H. White	Rep.	ME	1944-1947
Alben W. Barkley	Dem.	KY	1947-1949
Kenneth S. Wherry	Rep.	NE	1949-1951
Henry Styles Bridges	Rep.	NH	1951-1953
Lyndon B. Johnson	Dem.	TX	1953-1955
William F. Knowland	Rep.	CA	1955-1959
Everett M. Dirksen	Rep.	IL	1959-1969
Hugh D. Scott	Rep.	PA	1969-1977
Howard H. Baker Jr.	Rep.	TN	1977-1981
Robert C. Byrd	Dem.	WV	1981-1987
Robert J. Dole	Rep.	KS	1987-1995
Thomas A. Daschle	Dem.	SD	1995-2001[3]
Trent Lott	Rep.	MS	(3)
Bill Frist	Rep.	TN	2002-2003[3]
Thomas A. Daschle	Dem.	SD	2003-2005[4]
Harry M. Reid	Dem.	NV	2005-

Note: The offices of party (majority and minority) leaders in the Senate did not evolve until the 20th century. (1) First Republican to be designated floor leader. (2) First Democrat to be designated floor leader. (3) Starting Jan. 3, 2001, the Senate was split 50-50; with Al Gore (D) as outgoing vice pres. with the deciding vote, Thomas A. Daschle (D) briefly became majority leader and Trent Lott (R) was minority leader. From Jan. 20, 2001, with Dick Cheney (R) installed as vice pres., the positions were reversed. From June 6, 2001, the switch of Sen. James Jeffords (VT) from Republican to Independent meant the Democrats had a majority; Daschle resumed as majority leader, Lott as minority leader. Lott resigned as party leader Dec. 20, 2002, and Bill Frist was elected to replace him in the 108th Congress; since Republicans now had a majority, Frist became majority leader as of Jan. 7, 2003, with Daschle as minority leader. (4) Daschle was defeated in the 2004 election, and retired from the Senate Jan. 3, 2005; Democratic Whip Harry M. Reid was elected to the post for the 109th Congress.

Speakers of the House of Representatives

(as of Oct. 2005)

Name	Party	State	Tenure
Frederick Muhlenberg	Federalist	PA	1789-1791
Jonathan Trumbull	Federalist	CT	1791-1793
Frederick Muhlenberg	Federalist	PA	1793-1795
Jonathan Dayton	Federalist	NJ	1795-1799
Theodore Sedgwick	Federalist	MA	1799-1801
Nathaniel Macon	Dem.-Rep.	NC	1801-1807
Joseph B. Varnum	Dem.-Rep.	MA	1807-1811
Henry Clay	Dem.-Rep.	KY	1811-1814
Langdon Cheves	Dem.-Rep.	SC	1814-1815
Henry Clay	Dem.-Rep.	KY	1815-1820
John W. Taylor	Dem.-Rep.	NY	1820-1821
Philip P. Barbour	Dem.-Rep.	VA	1821-1823
Henry Clay	Dem.-Rep.	KY	1823-1825
John W. Taylor	Dem.	NY	1825-1827
Andrew Stevenson	Dem.	VA	1827-1834
John Bell	Dem.	TN	1834-1835
James K. Polk	Dem.	TN	1835-1839
Robert M. T. Hunter	Dem.	VA	1839-1841
John White	Whig	KY	1841-1843
John W. Jones	Dem.	VA	1843-1845
John W. Davis	Dem.	IN	1845-1847
Robert C. Winthrop	Whig	MA	1847-1849
Howell Cobb	Dem.	GA	1849-1851
Linn Boyd	Dem.	KY	1851-1855
Nathaniel P. Banks	American	MA	1856-1857
James L. Orr	Dem.	SC	1857-1859
William Pennington	Rep.	NJ	1860-1861
Galusha A. Grow	Rep.	PA	1861-1863
Schuyler Colfax	Rep.	IN	1863-1869
Theodore M. Pomeroy	Rep.	NY	1869
James G. Blaine	Rep.	ME	1869-1875
Michael C. Kerr	Dem.	IN	1875-1876
Samuel J. Randall	Dem.	PA	1876-1881
Joseph W. Keifer	Rep.	OH	1881-1883
John G. Carlisle	Dem.	KY	1883-1889
Thomas B. Reed	Rep.	ME	1889-1891
Charles F. Crisp	Dem.	GA	1891-1895
Thomas B. Reed	Rep.	ME	1895-1899
David B. Henderson	Rep.	IA	1899-1903
Joseph G. Cannon	Rep.	IL	1903-1911
Champ Clark	Dem.	MO	1911-1919
Frederick H. Gillett	Rep.	MA	1919-1925
Nicholas Longworth	Rep.	OH	1925-1931
John N. Garner	Dem.	TX	1931-1933
Henry T. Rainey	Dem.	IL	1933-1935
Joseph W. Byrns	Dem.	TN	1935-1936
William B. Bankhead	Dem.	AL	1936-1940
Sam Rayburn	Dem.	TX	1940-1947
Joseph W. Martin Jr.	Rep.	MA	1947-1949
Sam Rayburn	Dem.	TX	1949-1953
Joseph W. Martin Jr.	Rep.	MA	1953-1955
Sam Rayburn	Dem.	TX	1955-1961
John W. McCormack	Dem.	MA	1962-1971
Carl Albert	Dem.	OK	1971-1977
Thomas P. O'Neill Jr.	Dem.	MA	1977-1987
James Wright	Dem.	TX	1987-1989
Thomas S. Foley	Dem.	WA	1989-1995
Newt Gingrich	Rep.	GA	1995-1999
J. Dennis Hastert	Rep.	IL	1999-

Political Divisions of the U.S. Senate and House of Representatives, 1901-2005

Source: *Congressional Directory*; Senate Library

Note: all figures reflect immediate post-election party breakdown; **boldface** denotes party in majority immediately after election.

		SENATE					HOUSE OF REPRESENTATIVES				
Congress	Years	Total Sens.	Demo-crats	Repub-licans	Other parties	Vacant	Total Members	Demo-crats	Repub-licans	Other parties	Vacant
57th	1901-03	90	29	**56**	3	2	357	153	**198**	5	1
58th	1903-05	90	32	**58**			386	178	**207**		1
59th	1905-07	90	32	**58**			386	136	**250**		
60th	1907-09	92	29	**61**		2	386	164	**222**		
61st	1909-11	92	32	**59**		1	391	172	**219**		
62nd	1911-13	92	42	**49**		1	391	**228**	162	1	
63rd	1913-15	96	**51**	44	1		435	**290**	127	18	
64th	1915-17	96	**56**	39	1		435	**231**	193	8	3
65th	1917-19	96	**53**	42	1		435	210[1]	**216**	9	
66th	1919-21	96	47	**48**	1		435	191	**237**	7	
67th	1921-23	96	37	**59**			435	132	**300**	1	2
68th	1923-25	96	43	**51**	2		435	207	**225**	3	
69th	1925-27	96	40	**54**	1	1	435	183	**247**	5	
70th	1927-29	96	47	**48**	1		435	195	**237**	3	

Congress	Years	SENATE Total Sens.	Demo-crats	Repub-licans	Other parties	Vacant	HOUSE OF REPRESENTATIVES Total Members	Demo-crats	Repub-licans	Other parties	Vacant
71st	1929-31	96	39	**56**	1		435	163	**267**	1	4
72nd	1931-33	96	47	**48**	1		435	216[2]	**218**	1	
73rd	1933-35	96	**59**	36	1		435	**313**	117	5	
74th	1935-37	96	**69**	25	2		435	**322**	103	10	
75th	1937-39	96	**75**	17	4		435	**333**	89	13	
76th	1939-41	96	**69**	23	4		435	**262**	169	4	
77th	1941-43	96	**66**	28	2		435	**267**	162	6	
78th	1943-45	96	**57**	38	1		435	**222**	209	4	
79th	1945-47	96	**57**	38	1		435	**243**	190	2	
80th	1947-49	96	45	**51**			435	188	**246**	1	
81st	1949-51	96	**54**	42			435	**263**	171	1	
82nd	1951-53	96	**48**	47	1		435	**234**	199	2	
83rd	1953-55	96	46	**48**	2		435	213	**221**	1	
84th	1955-57	96	**48**	47	1		435	**232**	203		
85th	1957-59	96	**49**	47			435	**234**	201		
86th	1959-61	98	**64**	34			436[3]	**283**	153		
87th	1961-63	100	**64**	36			437[4]	**262**	175		
88th	1963-65	100	**67**	33			435	**258**	176		1
89th	1965-67	100	**68**	32			435	**295**	140		
90th	1967-69	100	**64**	36			435	**248**	187		
91st	1969-71	100	**58**	42			435	**243**	192		
92nd	1971-73	100	**54**	44	2		435	**255**	180		
93rd	1973-75	100	**56**	42	2		435	**242**	192	1	
94th	1975-77	100	**60**	37	2		435	**291**	144	1	
95th	1977-79	100	**61**	38	1		435	**292**	143		
96th	1979-81	100	**58**	41	1		435	**277**	158		
97th	1981-83	100	46	**53**	1		435	**242**	192	1	
98th	1983-85	100	46	**54**			435	**269**	166		
99th	1985-87	100	47	**53**			435	**253**	182		
100th	1987-89	100	**55**	45			435	**258**	177		
101st	1989-91	100	**55**	45			435	**260**	175		
102nd	1991-93	100	**56**	44			435	**267**	167	1	
103rd	1993-95	100	**57**	43			435	**258**	176	1	
104th	1995-97	100	48	**52**			435	204	**230**	1	
105th	1997-99	100	45	**55**			435	207	**227**	1	
106th	1999-2001	100	45	**55**			435	211	**223**	1	
107th	2001-03	100	50	50[5]			435	212	**221**	2	
108th	2003-05	100	48	**51**	1		435	205	**229**	1	
109th	2005-2007	100	44	**55**			435	202	**231**	1	1

(1) Democrats organized the House with help of other parties. (2) Democrats organized House because of Republican deaths. (3 Proclamation declaring Alaska a state issued Jan. 3, 1959. (4) Proclamation declaring Hawaii a state issued Aug. 21, 1959. (5) While the Senate was split 50-50, control was held by whichever party had an incumbent vice president. Republican Sen. James M. Jeffords (VT) changed his party designation to Independent on June 6, 2001, switching control of the Senate to Democrats from Republicans.

Congressional Bills Vetoed, 1789-2004

Source: Senate Library

President	Regular vetoes	Pocket vetoes	Total vetoes	Vetoes overridden
Washington	2	—	2	—
John Adams	—	—	—	—
Jefferson	—	—	—	—
Madison	5	2	7	—
Monroe	1	—	1	—
John Q. Adams	—	—	—	—
Jackson	5	7	12	—
Van Buren	—	1	1	—
William Harrison	—	—	—	—
Tyler	6	4	10	1
Polk	2	1	3	—
Taylor	—	—	—	—
Fillmore	—	—	—	—
Pierce	9	—	9	5
Buchanan	4	3	7	—
Lincoln	2	4	6	—
Andrew Johnson	21	8	29	15
Grant	45	48	93	4
Hayes	12	1	13	1
Garfield	—	—	—	—
Arthur	4	8	12	1
Cleveland[1]	304	110	414	2
Benjamin Harrison	19	25	44	1
Cleveland[2]	42	128	170	5
McKinley	6	36	42	—
Theodore Roosevelt	42	40	82	1
Taft	30	9	39	1
Wilson	33	11	44	6
Harding	5	1	6	—
Coolidge	20	30	50	4
Hoover	21	16	37	3
Franklin Roosevelt	372	263	635	9
Truman	180	70	250	12
Eisenhower	73	108	181	2
Kennedy	12	9	21	—
Lyndon Johnson	16	14	30	—
Nixon	26	17	43	7
Ford	48	18	66	12
Carter	13	18	31	2
Reagan	39	39	78	9
George H. W. Bush[3]	29	15	44	1
Clinton[4]	36	1	37	2
George W. Bush[5]	—	—	—	—
Total[3,4]	**1,484**	**1,065**	**2,549**	**106**

— = 0. (1) First term only. (2) Second term only. (3) Excluded from the figures are 2 additional bills, which Pres. George H. W. Bush claimed to be vetoed but Congress considered enacted into law because the president failed to return them to Congress during a recess period. (4) Does not include line-item vetoes, which were ruled unconstitutional by the Supreme Court on June 25, 1998. (5) As of Oct. 2005.

Librarians of Congress

Librarian	Served	Appointed by President
John J. Beckley	1802-1807	Jefferson
Patrick Magruder	1807-1815	Jefferson
George Watterston	1815-1829	Madison
John Silva Meehan	1829-1861	Jackson
John G. Stephenson	1861-1864	Lincoln
Ainsworth Rand Spofford	1864-1897	Lincoln
John Russell Young	1897-1899	McKinley
Herbert Putnam	1899-1939	McKinley
Archibald MacLeish	1939-1944	F. D. Roosevelt
Luther H. Evans	1945-1953	Truman
L. Quincy Mumford	1954-1974	Eisenhower
Daniel J. Boorstin	1975-1987	Ford
James H. Billington	1987-	Reagan

STATE GOVERNMENT

Governors of States and Puerto Rico

As of Oct. 2005. Of the 50 state governors, 29 are Republicans, 21 are Democrats.

State	Capital, ZIP Code	Governor	Party	Term years	Term expires	Annual salary
Alabama	Montgomery 36130	Bob Riley	Rep.	4	Jan. 2007	$96,361
Alaska	Juneau 99811	Frank Murkowski	Rep.	4	Dec. 2006	85,776
Arizona	Phoenix 85007	Janet Napolitano	Dem.	4	Jan. 2007	95,000
Arkansas	Little Rock 72201	Mike Huckabee	Rep.	4	Jan. 2007	77,028
California	Sacramento 95814	Arnold Schwarzenegger	Rep.	4	Jan. 2007	175,000
Colorado	Denver 80203	Bill Owens	Rep.	4	Jan. 2007	90,000
Connecticut	Hartford 06106	M. Jodi Rell	Rep.	4	Jan. 2007	150,000
Delaware	Dover 19901	Ruth Ann Minner	Dem.	4	Jan. 2007	114,000
Florida	Tallahassee 32399	Jeb Bush	Rep.	4	Jan. 2007	129,060
Georgia	Atlanta 30334	Sonny Perdue	Rep.	4	Jan. 2007	128,903
Hawaii	Honolulu 96813	Linda Lingle	Rep.	4	Dec. 2006	94,780
Idaho	Boise 83720	Dirk Kempthorne	Rep.	4	Jan. 2007	98,500
Illinois	Springfield 62706	Rod R. Blagojevich	Dem.	4	Jan. 2007	150,691
Indiana	Indianapolis 46204	Mitch E. Daniels Jr.[3]	Rep.	4	Jan. 2009	95,000
Iowa	Des Moines 50319	Tom Vilsack	Dem.	4	Jan. 2007	107,482
Kansas	Topeka 66612	Kathleen Sebelius	Dem.	4	Jan. 2007	103,813
Kentucky	Frankfort 40601	Ernie Fletcher	Rep.	4	Dec. 2007	112,705
Louisiana	Baton Rouge 70804	Kathleen Babineaux Blanco	Dem.	4	Jan. 2008	95,000
Maine	Augusta 04333	John E. Baldacci	Dem.	4	Jan. 2007	70,000
Maryland	Annapolis 21401	Robert L. Ehrlich Jr.	Rep.	4	Jan. 2007	145,000
Massachusetts	Boston 02133	Mitt Romney	Rep.	4	Jan. 2007	135,000
Michigan	Lansing 48909	Jennifer M. Granholm	Dem.	4	Jan. 2007	177,000
Minnesota	St. Paul 55155	Tim Pawlenty	Rep.	4	Jan. 2007	120,303
Mississippi	Jackson 39205	Haley Barbour	Rep.	4	Jan. 2008	122,160
Missouri	Jefferson City 65102	Matt Blunt[3]	Rep.	4	Jan. 2009	120,087
Montana	Helena 59620	Brian Schweitzer[3]	Dem.	4	Jan. 2009	96,462[1]
Nebraska	Lincoln 68509	David Heineman	Rep.	4	Jan. 2007	85,000
Nevada	Carson City 89710	Kenny C. Guinn	Rep.	4	Jan. 2007	117,000
New Hampshire	Concord 03301	John H. Lynch[3]	Dem.	2	Jan. 2007	104,758
New Jersey	Trenton 08625	Richard J. Codey	Dem.	4	Jan. 2006	175,000
New Mexico	Santa Fe 87503	Bill Richardson	Dem.	4	Jan. 2007	110,000
New York	Albany 12224	George E. Pataki	Rep.	4	Jan. 2007	179,000
North Carolina	Raleigh 27603	Mike Easley	Dem.	4	Jan. 2009	123,819
North Dakota	Bismarck 58505	John Hoeven	Rep.	4	Jan. 2007	88,926
Ohio	Columbus 43205	Bob Taft	Rep.	4	Jan. 2007	132,292
Oklahoma	Oklahoma City 73105	Brad Henry	Dem.	4	Jan. 2007	117,571
Oregon	Salem 97310	Ted Kulongoski	Dem.	4	Jan. 2007	93,600
Pennsylvania	Harrisburg 17120	Edward G. Rendell	Dem.	4	Jan. 2007	144,416
Rhode Island	Providence 02903	Donald L. Carcieri	Rep.	4	Jan. 2007	105,194
South Carolina	Columbia 29211	Mark Sanford	Rep.	4	Jan. 2007	106,078
South Dakota	Pierre 57501	Mike Rounds	Rep.	4	Jan. 2007	103,222
Tennessee	Nashville 37243	Phil Bredesen	Dem.	4	Jan. 2007	85,000
Texas	Austin 78711	Rick Perry	Rep.	4	Jan. 2007	115,345
Utah	Salt Lake City 84114	John M. Huntsman Jr.[3]	Rep.	4	Jan. 2009	104,600
Vermont	Montpelier 05609	James H. Douglas	Rep.	2	Jan. 2007	168,466
Virginia	Richmond 23219	Mark R. Warner	Dem.	4	Jan. 2006	175,000[1]
Washington	Olympia 98504	Christine Gregoire[3]	Dem.	4	Jan. 2009	148,035
West Virginia	Charleston 25305	Joe Manchin III[3]	Dem.	4	Jan. 2009	95,000
Wisconsin	Madison 53707	Jim Doyle	Dem.	4	Jan. 2007	131,768
Wyoming	Cheyenne 82002	Dave Freudenthal	Dem.	4	Jan. 2007	105,000
Puerto Rico	San Juan 00936	Anibal Acevedo-Vila[3]	PDP[2]	4	Jan. 2009	70,000

(1) Salary in effect in Nov. 2005. (2) Popular Democratic Party. (3) New governor, began term in 2005.

State Officials, Salaries, Party Membership

As of Oct. 2005, 19 legislatures were controlled by Democrats; 20 by Republicans; 10 were split; Nebraska is non-partisan.

Alabama

Governor — Bob Riley, R, $96,361
Lt. Gov. — Lucy Baxley, D, $12 per day, plus $50 per day expenses, plus $3,780 per mo expenses
Atty. Gen. — Troy King, R, $163,429
Sec. of State — Nancy L. Worley, D, $71,500
Treasurer — Kay Ivey, R, $71,500
Auditor — Beth Chapman, R, $71,500
Legislature: meets annually at Montgomery 1st Tues. in Mar., 1st year of term of office; 1st Tues. in Feb., 2nd and 3rd yr; 2nd Tues. in Jan., 4th yr. Members receive $10 per day salary, plus $50 per day and $2,280 per month for expenses.
Senate — Dem., 25; Rep., 10. Total, 35
House — Dem., 63; Rep., 42. Total, 105

Alaska

Governor — Frank Murkowski, R, $85,776
Lt. Gov — Loren D. Leman, R, $80,040
Atty. General — David W. Márquez (acting), R, $124,752
Legislature: meets annually in Jan. at Juneau for 120 days with a 10-day extension possible upon 2/3 vote. Members receive $24,012 annually, plus $204 per diem.
Senate — Dem., 8; Rep., 12. Total, 20
House — Dem., 14; Rep., 26. Total, 40

Arizona

Governor — Janet Napolitano, D, $95,000
Sec. of State — Jan Brewer, R, $70,000
Atty. Gen. — Terry Goddard, D, $90,000
Treasurer — David Petersen, R, $70,000
Legislature: meets annually in Jan. at Phoenix. Each member receives an annual salary of $24,000 plus a per diem.
Senate — Dem., 12; Rep., 18. Total, 30
House — Dem., 22; Rep., 38. Total, 60

Arkansas

Governor — Mike Huckabee, R, $77,028
Lt. Gov. — Winthrop P. Rockefeller, R, $37,229
Sec. of State — Charlie Daniels, D, $48,142
Atty. Gen. — Mike Beebe, D, $64,189
Treasurer — Gus Wingfield, D, $48,142
Auditor — Jim Wood, D, $48,142
General Assembly: meets odd years in Jan. at Little Rock. Members receive $14,067 annually.
Senate — Dem., 27; Rep., 8. Total, 35
House — Dem., 72; Rep., 28. Total, 100

California

Governor — Arnold Schwarzenegger, R, $175,000[1]
Lt. Gov. — Cruz Bustamante, D, $131,250
Sec. of State — Bruce McPherson, R, $131,250
Controller — Steve Westly, D, $140,000
Treasurer — Phil Angelides, D, $140,000
Atty. Gen. — Bill Lockyer, D, $148,750
Legislature: meets at Sacramento on the 1st Mon. in Dec. of even-numbered years; each session lasts 2 years. Members receive $110,880 annually, plus $121 per diem. High-ranking legislators earn an extra $7,425 or more, depending on post.
Senate — Dem., 25; Rep., 15. Total, 40
Assembly — Dem., 48; Rep., 32. Total, 80
(1) Does not accept salary.

Colorado
Governor — Bill Owens, R, $90,000
Lt. Gov. — Jane Norton, R, $68,500
Sec. of State — Gigi Dennis, R, $68,500
Atty. Gen. — John Suthers, D, $80,000
Treasurer — Mike Coffman, R, $68,500 (currently serving in Iraq); acting treasurer, Mark Hillman
General Assembly: meets annually in Jan. at Denver. Members receive $30,000 annually plus $99 per diem for attendance at interim committee meetings.
Senate — Dem., 18; Rep., 17. Total, 35
House — Dem., 35; Rep., 30. Total, 65

Connecticut
Governor — M. Jodi Rell, R, $150,000
Lt. Gov. — Keith B. Sullivan, D, $110,000
Sec. of State — Susan Bysiewicz, D, $110,000
Treasurer — Denise Nappier, D, $110,000
Comptroller — Nancy S. Wyman, D, $110,000
Atty. Gen. — Richard Blumenthal, D, $110,000
General Assembly: meets annually odd years in Jan. and even years in Feb., at Hartford. Members receive $28,000 annually, plus $5,500 (senator), $4,500 (representative) per year for expenses.
Senate — Dem., 24; Rep., 12. Total, 36
House — Dem., 99; Rep., 52. Total, 151

Delaware
Governor — Ruth Ann Minner, D, $114,000
Lt. Gov. — John C. Carney Jr., D, $64,900
Sec. of State — Harriet Smith Windsor, D, $109,800
Atty. Gen. — M. Jane Brady, R, $120,800
Treasurer — Jack A. Markell, D, $97,400
General Assembly: meets annually the 2nd Tues. in Jan. and continues each Tues., Wed., and Thurs. until June 30, at Dover. Members receive $36,400 annually.
Senate — Dem., 13; Rep., 8. Total, 21
House — Dem., 15; Rep., 26. Total, 41

Florida
Governor — Jeb Bush, R, $129,060
Lt. Gov. — Toni Jennings, R, $123,688
Chief Financial Officer — Tom Gallagher, R, $127,771
Atty. Gen. — Charlie Crist, R, $127,771
Comm. of Agriculture — Charles Bronson, R, $127,771
Legislature: meets annually at Tallahassee. Members receive $29,916 annually, plus expense allowance.
Senate — Dem., 14; Rep., 26. Total, 40
House — Dem., 36; Rep., 84. Total, 120

Georgia
Governor — Sonny Perdue, R, $128,903
Lt. Gov. — Mark Taylor, D, $84,748
Sec. of State — Cathy Cox, D, $114,376
Atty. Gen. — Thurbert Baker, D, $127,471
General Assembly: meets annually at Atlanta on 2nd Mon. in Jan. Members receive $16,524 annually ($128 per diem and $7,000 annual expense reimbursement).
Senate — Dem., 22; Rep., 34. Total, 56
House — Dem., 79; Rep., 100; 1 ind. Total, 180

Hawaii
Governor — Linda Lingle, R, $94,780
Lt. Gov. — James R. Aiona Jr., R, $90,041
Atty. Gen. — Mark J. Bennett, $107,100
Comptroller — Russ K. Saito, $102,000
Dir. of Budget & Finance — Georgina K. Kawamura, $102,000
Legislature: meets annually on 3rd Wed. in Jan. at Honolulu. Members receive $34,200 annually; presiding officers $41,700.
Senate — Dem., 20; Rep., 5. Total, 25
House — Dem., 41; Rep., 10. Total, 51

Idaho
Governor — Dirk Kempthorne, R, $98,500
Lt. Gov. — Jim Risch, R, $26,750
Sec. of State — Ben Ysursa, R, $82,500
Treasurer — Ron Crane, R, $82,500
Atty. Gen. — Lawrence Wasden, R, $91,500
Legislature: meets annually the Mon. on or nearest Jan. 9 at Boise. Members receive $15,646 annually, plus $99 per day during session if required to maintain a 2nd residence, $38 if no 2nd residence; plus $1,700 unvouchered constituent service allowance.
Senate — Dem., 7, Rep., 28. Total, 35
House — Dem., 13; Rep., 57. Total, 70

Illinois
Governor — Rod R. Blagojevich, D, $150,691
Lt. Gov. — Patrick Quinn, D, $115,235
Sec. of State — Jesse White, D, $132,963
Comptroller — Daniel Hynes, D, $115,235
Atty. Gen. — Lisa Madigan, D, $132,963
Treasurer — Judy Baar Topinka, R, $115,235
General Assembly: meets annually in Nov. and Jan. at Springfield. Members receive $57,619 annually.
Senate — Dem., 31; Rep., 27; 1 ind. Total, 59
House — Dem., 65; Rep., 53. Total, 118

Indiana
Governor — Mitch E. Daniels Jr., R, $95,000
Lt. Gov. — Becky Skillman, R, $76,000
Sec. of State — Todd Rokita, R, $66,000
Atty. Gen. — Steve Carter, R, $79,400
Treasurer — Tim Berry, R, $66,000
Auditor — Connie Kay Nass, R, $66,000
General Assembly: meets annually on the Tues. after 2nd Mon. in Jan. at Indianapolis. Members receive $11,600 annually, plus $112 per day in session, $25 per day while not in session.
Senate — Dem., 17; Rep., 33. Total, 50
House — Dem., 48; Rep., 52. Total, 100

Iowa
Governor — Tom Vilsack, D, $107,482
Lt. Gov. — Sally Pederson, D, $76,698
Sec. of State — Chester J. Culver, D, $87,990
Atty. Gen. — Tom Miller, D, $105,430
Treasurer — Michael L. Fitzgerald, D, $87,990
Auditor — David A. Vaudt, R, $87,990
Sec. of Agriculture — Patty Judge, D, $87,990
General Assembly: meets annually in Jan. at Des Moines. Members receive $21,381 annually, plus expense allowance.
Senate — Dem., 25; Rep., 25. Total, 50
House — Dem., 49; Rep., 51. Total, 100

Kansas
Governor — Kathleen Sebelius, D, $103,813
Lt. Gov. — John Moore, D, $29,363
Sec. of State — Ron Thornburgh, R, $80,647
Atty. Gen. — Phill Kline, R, $92,742
Treasurer — Lynn Jenkins, R, $80,647
Insurance Commissioner — Sandy Praeger, R, $80,647
Legislature: meets annually on the 2nd Mon. of Jan. at Topeka, for a maximum of 90 days. Members receive $83.14 per day salary, plus $91 per diem in session, plus $6,480 total allowance.
Senate — Dem., 10; Rep., 30. Total, 40
House — Dem., 45; Rep., 80. Total, 125

Kentucky
Governor — Ernie Fletcher, R, $112,705
Lt. Gov. — Stephen Pence, R, $95,815
Sec. of State — Trey Grayson, R, $95,815
Atty. Gen. — Gregory Stumbo, D, $95,815
Treasurer — Jonathan Miller, D, $95,815
Auditor — Crit (Eugenia) Luallen, D, $95,815
Sec. of Economic Dev. — Gene Strong, $225,000
General Assembly: meets annually on the 1st Tues. after the 1st Mon. in Jan. at Frankfort. Members receive $166 per day, plus $100 per day expenses during session and $1,581 per month for expenses for interim.
Senate — Dem., 15; Rep., 22; 1 ind. Total, 38
House — Dem., 57; Rep., 43. Total, 100

Louisiana
Governor — Kathleen Babineaux Blanco, D, $95,000
Lt. Gov. — Mitch Landrieux, D, $85,000
Sec. of State — Al Ater, D, $85,000
Atty. Gen. — Charles C. Foti Jr., D, $85,000
Treasurer — John Kennedy, D, $85,000
Legislature: meets in even-numbered years at Baton Rouge starting last Mon. in Mar., for 60 legislative days of 85 calendar days; meets in odd-numbered years on last Mon. in Apr. for 45 days of 60 calendar days. Members receive $16,800 annually, plus $121 per day expenses while in session and $500 per month as an unvouchered expense allowance.
Senate — Dem., 25; Rep., 14. Total, 39
House — Dem., 69; Rep., 36. Total, 105

Maine
Governor — John E. Baldacci, D, $70,000
Sec. of State — Matthew Dunlap, D, $65,978
Atty. Gen. — G. Steven Rowe, D, $92,186
Treasurer — David G. Lemoine, D, $65,978
State Auditor — Neria R. Douglass, D, $77,709
Legislature: meets in odd-numbered years at Augusta on first Wed. in Dec.; meets in even-numbered years on Wed. after first Tues. in Jan. Members receive $11,384 for first regular session, $8,722 (est.) for 2nd, plus a daily expense allowance.
Senate — Dem., 18; Rep., 17. Total, 35
House — Dem., 75; Rep., 73; unenrolled, 2; Green, 1; 1 vacancy. Total, 151

Maryland
Governor — Robert L. Ehrlich Jr., R, $150,000
Lt. Gov. — Michael S. Steele, R, $125,000
Comptroller — William Donald Schaefer, D, $125,000
Atty. Gen. — J. Joseph Curran Jr., D, $125,000
Sec. of State — Mary D. Kane, R, $87,500
Treasurer — Nancy Kopp, D, $125,000
General Assembly: meets 90 consecutive days annually beginning on 2nd Wed. in Jan. at Annapolis. Members receive $43,500 annually, plus expenses.
Senate — Dem., 33; Rep., 14. Total, 47
House — Dem., 98; Rep., 43. Total, 141

Massachusetts

Governor — Willard "Mitt" Romney[1], R, $135,000
Lt. Gov. — Kerry Healey[1], R, $120,000
Sec. of the Commonwealth — William F. Galvin, D, $120,000
Atty. Gen. — Thomas F. Reilly, D, $122,500
Treasurer — Timothy P. Cahill, D, $120,000
State Auditor — A. Joseph DeNucci, D, $120,000
General Court (legislature): meets Jan. annually in Boston. Members receive $53,380 annually.
Senate — Dem., 33; Rep., 7. Total, 40
House — Dem., 137; Rep., 23. Total, 160
(1) Does not accept salary.

Michigan

Governor — Jennifer M. Granholm, D, $177,000
Lt. Gov. — John Cherry, D, $123,900
Sec. of State — Terri Lynn Land, R, $124,900
Atty. Gen. — Michael Cox, R, $124,900
Treasurer — Jay B. Rising, $174,204
Legislature: meets annually in Jan. at Lansing. Members receive $79,650 annually.
Senate — Dem., 16; Rep., 22. Total, 38
House — Dem., 52; Rep., 58; Total, 110

Minnesota

(DFL=Democratic-Farmer-Labor Party)
Governor — Tim Pawlenty, R, $120,303
Lt. Gov. — Carol Molnau, R, $78,197
Sec. of State — Mary Kiffmeyer, R, $90,227
Atty. Gen. — Michael Hatch, DFL, $114,288
Auditor — Patricia Anderson, R, $102,258
Legislature: meets for a total of 120 days within every 2 years, at St. Paul. Members receive $31,141 annually, plus expense allowance during session.
Senate — DFL, 35; Rep., 31; 1 ind. Total, 67
House — DFL, 66; Rep., 68. Total, 134

Mississippi

Governor — Haley Barbour, R, $122,160
Lt. Gov. — Amy Tuck, R, $60,000
Sec. of State — Eric Clark, D, $90,000
Atty. Gen. — Jim Hood, D, $108,960
Treasurer — Tate Reeves, R, $90,000
Auditor — Phil Bryant, R, $90,000
Legislature: meets annually in Jan. at Jackson. Members receive $10,000 per regular session, plus travel allowance, and $1,500 per month when not in session.
Senate — Dem., 28; Rep., 24. Total, 52
House — Dem., 77; Rep., 45. Total, 122

Missouri

Governor — Matt Blunt, R, $120,087
Lt. Gov. — Peter Kinder, R, $77,184
Sec. of State — Robin Carnahan, D, $96,455
Atty. Gen. — Jeremiah W. Nixon, D, $104,332
Treasurer — Sarah Steelman, R, $96,455
State Auditor — Claire McCaskill, D, $96,455
General Assembly: meets annually at Jefferson City beginning 1st Wed. after 1st Mon. in Jan. Members receive $31,351 annually.
Senate — Dem., 11; Rep., 22; 1 vacancy. Total, 34
House — Dem., 64; Rep., 97; 2 vacancies. Total, 163

Montana

Governor — Brian Schweitzer, D, $96,462
Lt. Gov. — John Bohlinger, R, $66,724
Sec. of State — Brad Johnson, R, $76,539
Atty. Gen. — Mike McGrath, D, $85,762
Legislative Assembly: meets odd years in Jan. at Helena. Members receive $76.80 per legislative day, plus $90.31 per day for expenses while in session.
Senate — Dem., 27; Rep., 23. Total, 50
House — Dem., 50; Rep., 50. Total, 100

Nebraska

Governor — David Heineman, R, $85,000
Lt. Gov. — Rick Sheehy, R, $60,000
Sec. of State — John A. Gale, R, $65,000
Atty. Gen. — Jon Bruning, R, $75,000
Treasurer — Ron Ross, R, $60,000
State Auditor — Kate Witek, R, $60,000
Legislature: Unicameral body composed of 49 members who are elected on a nonpartisan ballot and are called senators; meets annually in Jan. at Lincoln. Members receive $12,000 annually, plus expenses.

Nevada

Governor — Kenny C. Guinn, R, $117,000
Lt. Gov. — Lorraine Hunt, R, $50,000
Sec. of State — Dean Heller, R, $80,000
Controller — Kathy Augustine, R, $80,000
Atty. Gen. — Brian Sandoval, R, $110,000
Treasurer — Brian Krolicki, R, $80,000
Legislature: meets at Carson City odd years starting on 1st Mon. in Feb. for 120 days. Members receive $130 per day salary, plus a total of $10,000 in expenses and $2,860 in communications costs, while in session. Each legislator is allowed $1,200 in expenses during a special session, plus a $130 per diem for the first 20 days.
Senate — Dem., 9; Rep., 12. Total, 21
Assembly — Dem., 26; Rep., 16. Total, 42

New Hampshire

Governor — John H. Lynch, D, $104,758
Sec. of State — William M. Gardner, D, $90,911
Atty. Gen. — Kelly A. Ayotte, R, $101,303
Treasurer — Michael A. Ablowich, R, $90,911
General Court (Legis.): meets every year in Jan. at Concord. Members receive $200, presiding officers $250, biannually.
Senate — Dem., 8; Rep., 16. Total, 24
House — Rep., 249; Dem., 147; 4 vacancies. Total, 400

New Jersey

Acting Governor — Richard J. Codey, D, $175,000
Sec. of State — Regena L. Thomas, D, $141,000
Atty. Gen. — Peter Harvey, D, $141,000
Treasurer — John E. McCormac, $141,000
Legislature: meets throughout the year at Trenton. Members receive $49,000 annually, except president of Senate and speaker of Assembly, who receive 1/3 more.
Senate — Dem., 22; Rep., 18. Total, 40
Assembly — Dem., 47; Rep., 33. Total, 80

New Mexico

Governor — Bill Richardson, D, $110,000
Lt. Gov. — Diane D. Denish, D, $85,000
Sec. of State — Rebecca Vigil-Giron, D, $85,000
Atty. Gen. — Patricia Madrid, D, $95,000
Treasurer — Robert E. Vigil, D, $85,000
Auditor — Domingo P. Martinez, D, $85,000
Commissioner of Public Lands — Patrick Lyons, R, $90,000
Legislature: meets starting on the 3rd Tues. in Jan. at Santa Fe; odd years for 60 days, even years for 30 days. Members receive $145 per day while in session.
Senate — Dem., 24; Rep., 18. Total, 42
House — Dem., 42; Rep., 28. Total, 70

New York

Governor — George E. Pataki, R, $179,000
Lt. Gov. — Mary O. Donohue, R, $151,500
Sec. of State — vacant, $120,800
Comptroller — Alan G. Hevesi, D, $151,500
Atty. Gen. — Eliot Spitzer, D, $151,500
Legislature: meets annually on the 1st Wed. after the 1st Mon. in Jan. at Albany. Members receive $79,500 annually, plus $138 per day expenses.
Senate — Dem., 27; Rep., 35. Total, 62
Assembly — Dem., 104; Rep., 45, 1 vacant. Total, 150

North Carolina

Governor — Mike Easley, D, $123,819
Lt. Gov. — Beverly Perdue, D, $109,279
Sec. of State — Elaine F. Marshall, D, $109,279
Atty. Gen. — Roy Cooper, D, $109,279
Treasurer — Richard H. Moore, D, $109,279
General Assembly: meets odd years starting on the 3rd Wed. following the 2nd Mon. in Jan. at Raleigh. Members receive $13,951 annually and a $559 monthly expense allowance, plus travel and other allowances in session. Also meets in even years for a short session (about 6-8 weeks), usually in May.
Senate — Dem., 29; Rep., 21. Total, 50
House — Dem., 63; Rep., 57. Total, 120

North Dakota

Governor — John Hoeven, R, $88,926
Lt. Gov. — John S. Dalrymple III, R, $69,035
Sec. of State — Alvin A. Jaeger, R, $70,739
Atty. Gen. — Wayne Stenehjem, R, $77,655
Treasurer — Kelly Schmidt, R, $66,474
Legislative Assembly: meets odd years in Jan. at Bismarck. Members receive $350 per month salary, plus $125 per calendar day salary during session and $50 per day expenses, plus any additional state or local taxes on lodging, with a limit of $900 per month.
Senate — Dem., 15; Rep., 32. Total, 47
House — Dem., 27; Rep., 67. Total, 94

Ohio

Governor — Bob Taft, R, $132,292
Lt. Gov. — Bruce Johnson, R, $68,295
Sec. of State — Jennette B. Bradley, R, $104,154
Atty. Gen. — Jim Petro, R, $104,154
Treasurer — Joseph T. Deters, R, $104,154
Auditor — Betty D. Montgomery, R, $104,154
General Assembly: begins odd years at Columbus starting on 1st Mon. in Jan. Members receive $55,917 annually.
Senate — Dem., 11; Rep., 22. Total, 33
House — Dem., 39; Rep., 60. Total, 99

Oklahoma

Governor — Brad Henry, D, $117,571
Lt. Gov. — Mary Fallin, R, $94,839
Sec. of State — M. Susan Savage, D, $90,000
Atty. Gen. — Drew Edmondson, D, $109,731
Treasurer — Scott Meacham, D, $94,839
Auditor — Jeff A. McMahan, D, $94,839
Legislature: meets annually the first Mon. in Feb. at Oklahoma City. In odd-numbered years, the session includes one day (1st Tues. after 1st Mon.) in Jan. Members receive $38,400 annually.
Senate — Dem., 26; Rep., 22; 1 vacancy. Total, 48
House — Dem., 44; Rep., 57. Total, 101

Oregon

Governor — Ted Kulongoski, D, $93,600
Sec. of State — Bill Bradbury, D, $72,000
Atty. Gen. — Hardy Myers, D, $77,200
Treasurer — Randall Edwards, D, $72,000
Legislative Assembly: meets odd years in Jan. at Salem. Members receive $1,437 monthly, $91 expenses per day during session and when attending meetings during the interim, plus between $450 and $750 expense account during interim.
Senate — Dem., 18; Rep., 12. Total, 30
House — Dem., 27; Rep., 33. Total, 60

Pennsylvania

Governor — Edward G. Rendell, D, $144,416
Lt. Gov. — Catherine Baker Knoll, D, $121,309
Sec. of the Commonwealth — Pedro A. Cortés, D, $103,890
Atty. Gen. — Tom Corbett, R, $120,154
Treasurer — Robert P. Casey, D, $120,154
General Assembly: convenes annually on the 1st Tues. in Jan. at Harrisburg. Members receive $64,638 annually, plus expenses.
Senate — Dem., 20; Rep., 30. Total, 50
House — Dem., 93; Rep., 110. Total, 203

Rhode Island

Governor — Donald L. Carcieri, R, $105,194
Lt. Gov. — Charles J. Fogarty, D, $88,584
Sec. of State — Matthew A. Brown, D, $88,584
Atty. Gen. — Patrick C. Lynch, D, $94,121
Treasurer — Paul J. Tavares, D, $88,584
General Assembly: meets annually in Jan. at Providence. Members receive $10,000 annually (plus mileage and cost-of-living increase).
Senate — Dem., 33; Rep., 5. Total, 38
House — Dem., 60; Rep., 15; 1 ind. Total, 75

South Carolina

Governor — Mark Sanford, R, $106,078
Lt. Gov. — R. André Bauer, R, $46,545
Sec. of State — Mark Hammond, R, $92,007
Comptroller — Richard A. Eckstrom, R, $92,007
Atty. Gen. — Henry McMaster, R, $92,007
Treasurer — Grady L. Patterson Jr., D, $92,007
General Assembly: meets annually on the 2nd Tues. in Jan. at Columbia. Members receive $10,400 annually, plus $130 per day for expenses.
Senate — Dem., 20; Rep., 26. Total, 46
House — Dem., 49; Rep., 73; 2 vacancies. Total, 124

South Dakota

Governor — Mike Rounds, R, $103,222
Lt. Gov. — Dennis M. Daugaard, R, $14,083
Sec. of State — Chris Nelson, R, $70,135
Treasurer — Vernon L. Larson, R, $70,135
Atty. Gen. — Larry Long, R, $87,646
Auditor — Rich Sattgast, R, $70,135
Legislature: meets annually beginning the 2nd Tues. in Jan. at Pierre, for 40-day session in odd-numbered years, and 35-day session in even-numbered years. Members receive $12,000 per 2-year term plus $110 per diem for days in session.
Senate — Dem., 10; Rep., 25. Total, 35
House — Dem., 19; Rep., 50; 1 vacancy. Total, 70

Tennessee

Governor — Phil Bredesen, D, $85,000
Lt. Gov. — John S. Wilder, D, $49,500
Sec. of State — Riley C. Darnell, D, $139,116
Treasurer — Dale Sims, D, $139,116
Comptroller — John Morgan, D, $139,116
Atty. Gen. — Paul Summers, D, $129,984
General Assembly: meets annually on the 2nd Tues. in Jan. at Nashville. Members receive $16,500 annual salary, plus $150 per day expenses while in session.
Senate — Dem., 16; Rep., 17. Total, 33
House — Dem., 53; Rep., 46. Total, 99

Texas

Governor — Rick Perry, R, $115,345
Lt. Gov. — David Dewhurst, R, $7,200 (plus $128 per day during legislative sessions)
Sec. of State — Roger Williams, R, $117,516
Comptroller — Carole Keeton Strayhorn, R, $125,000
Atty. Gen. — Greg W. Abbott, R, $125,000
Railroad Commissioners — Elizabeth Jones, R, Chair; Michael L. Williams, R; Victor G. Carrillo, R; $125,000
Legislature: meets odd years in Jan. at Austin. Members receive $7,200 annually, plus $125 per day expenses while in session.
Senate — Dem., 12; Rep., 19. Total, 31
House — Dem., 61; Rep., 88; 1 vacancy. Total, 150

Utah

Governor — Jon M. Huntsman Jr., R, $104,600
Lt. Gov. — Gary R. Herbert, R, $81,000
Atty. Gen. — Mark Shurtleff, R, $98,900
Auditor — Auston G. Johnson, R, $83,500
Treasurer — Edward T. Alter, R, $81,000
Legislature: convenes for 45 days on 3rd Mon. in Jan. each year at Salt Lake City. Members receive $120 per day, plus $38 a day expenses.
Senate — Dem., 8; Rep., 21. Total, 29
House — Dem., 19; Rep., 56. Total, 75

Vermont

Governor — Jim Douglas, R, $138,466
Lt. Gov. — Brian E. Dubie, R, $58,777
Sec. of State — Deborah L. Markowitz, D, $87,800
Atty. Gen. — William H. Sorrell, D, $105,109
Treasurer — Jeb (George B.) Spaulding, D, $87,800
Auditor — Randy Brock, R, $87,800
General Assembly: meets in Jan. at Montpelier (annual and biennial session). Members receive $536 per week while in session plus $105 per day for special session, plus expenses.
Senate — Dem., 21; Rep., 9. Total, 30
House — Dem., 83; Rep., 60; Progressive, 6; 1 ind. Total, 150

Virginia

Governor — Mark R. Warner, D, $175,000[1]
Lt. Gov. — Timothy M. Kaine, D, $36,321
Atty. Gen. — Judith W. Jagdmann, R, $150,000[1]
Sec. of the Commonwealth — Anita A. Rimler, D, $141,265[2]
Treasurer — Jody M. Wagner, D, $123,864[2]
General Assembly: meets annually in Jan. at Richmond. Members receive $18,000 (senate), $17,640 (assembly) annually, plus expense and mileage allowances.
Senate — Dem., 16; Rep., 24. Total, 40
House — Dem., 38; Rep., 59; 2 ind; 1 vacancy. Total, 100
(1) Salary increase, effective Nov. 2005. (2) Salary increase, effective Jan. 2006.

Washington

Governor — Christine Gregoire, D, $148,035
Lt. Gov. — Brad Owen, D, $77,382
Sec. of State — Sam Reed, R, $103,736
Atty. Gen. — Rob McKenna, R, 134,577
Treasurer — Mike Murphy, D, $103,736
Auditor — Brian Sonntag, D, $103,736
Legislature: meets annually in Jan. at Olympia. Members receive $35,254 annually, plus $101 per diem while in session, and $101 per diem for attending meetings during interim.
Senate — Dem., 26; Rep., 23. Total, 49
House — Dem., 55; Rep., 43. Total, 98

West Virginia

Governor — Joe Manchin III, D, $95,000
Sec. of State — Betty Ireland, R, $75,000
Atty. Gen. — Darrell McGraw, D, $80,000
Treasurer — John D. Perdue, D, $75,000
Comm. of Agric. — Gus R. Douglass, D, $75,000
Auditor — Glen B. Gainer III, D, $75,000
Legislature: meets annually in Jan. at Charleston, except after gubernatorial elections, when the legislature meets in Feb. Members receive $15,000 annually.
Senate — Dem., 21; Rep., 13. Total, 34
House — Dem., 68; Rep., 32. Total, 100

Wisconsin

Governor — Jim Doyle, D, $131,768
Lt. Gov. — Barbara Lawton, D, $65,579
Sec. of State — Douglas La Follette, D, $62,549
Treasurer — Jack Voight, R, $62,549
Atty. Gen. — Peggy A. Lautenschlager, D, $127,868
Legislature: meets in Jan. at Madison. Members receive $45,569 annually, plus $88 per day expenses.
Senate — Dem., 14; Rep., 19. Total, 33
Assembly — Dem., 39; Rep., 60. Total, 99

Wyoming

Governor — Dave Freudenthal, D, $105,000
Sec. of State — Joseph B. Meyer, R, $92,000
Atty. Gen. — Patrick J. Crank, R, $95,000
Treasurer — Cynthia Lummis, R, $92,000
State Auditor — Max Maxfield, R, $92,000
Legislature: meets odd years in Jan., even years in Feb., at Cheyenne. Members receive $125 per day while in session, plus $80 per day for expenses.
Senate — Dem., 7; Rep., 23. Total, 30
House — Dem., 14; Rep., 46. Total, 60

NATIONAL DEFENSE

Chief Commanding Officers of the U.S. Military

Chairman, Joint Chiefs of Staff
Gen. Peter Pace (USMC)
Vice Chairman
Adm. Edmund P. Giambastiani Jr. (USN)

The **Joint Chiefs of Staff** consists of the Chairman and Vice Chairman of the Joint Chiefs of Staff; the Chief of Staff, U.S. Army; the Chief of Naval Operations; the Chief of Staff, U.S. Air Force; and the Commandant of the Marine Corps. * = date nominated.

Army

Chief of Staff	Date of Rank
Gen. Peter J. Schoomaker	Oct. 31, 1997
Other Generals	
Abizaid, John	Aug. 1, 2003
Bell, Burwell B.	Dec. 3, 2002
Brown, Bryan D.	Nov. 1, 2003
Casey, George W., Jr.	Dec. 1, 2003
Cody, Richard	June 8, 2004
Craddock, Bantz J.	Jan. 1, 2005
Griffin, Benjamin S.	Jan. 1, 2005
LaPorte, Leon	May 1, 2002
McNeill, Dan K.	July 1, 2004

Air Force

Chief of Staff	Date of Rank
Moseley, T. Michael	Oct. 1, 2003
Other Generals	
Carlson, Bruce	Sept. 1, 2005
Corley, John D.W.	June 2005*
Foglesong, Robert H.	Nov. 5, 2001
Hester, Paul V.	Aug. 1, 2004
Keys, Ronald E.	May 27, 2005
Looney III, William R.	Aug. 1, 2005
Lord, Lance W.	Apr. 19, 2002
Schwartz, Norton	Oct. 1, 2005
Wald, Charles F.	Jan. 1, 2003

Navy

Chief of Naval Operations	Date of Rank
Mullen, Michael G. (surface warfare)	Aug. 28, 2003
Other Admirals	
Donald, Kirkland H. (submariner)	Jan. 1, 2005
Fallon, William J. (aviator)	Nov. 1, 2000
Giambastiani, Edmund P., Jr. (submariner)	Oct. 2, 2002
Keating, Timothy J. (aviator)	Jan. 1, 2005
Nathman, John B. (aviator)	Dec. 1, 2004
Roughead, Gary (surface warfare)	Sept. 1, 2005
Ulrich III, H.G. (surface warfare)	July 22, 2005
Willard, Robert F. (aviator)	Mar. 18, 2005

Marine Corps

Commandant of the Marine Corps (CMC)	Date of Rank
Gen. Michael W. Hagee	Jan. 13, 2003
Other Generals	
Cartwright, James E.	July 9, 2004
Jones, James L.	June 30, 1999
Magnus, Robert	Apr. 2005*
Nyland, William L.	Sept. 4, 2002
Pace, Peter	Sept. 8, 2000

Coast Guard

Commandant, with rank of Admiral	Date of Rank
Collins, Thomas H.	May 30, 2002
Vice Commandant, with rank of Vice Admiral	
Crass, Terry M.	July 2004

Unified Combatant Commands Commanders-in-Chief

U.S. European Command, Stuttgart-Vaihingen, Germany —Gen. James L. Jones (USMC)
U.S. Pacific Command, Honolulu, HI — Adm. William J. Fallon (USN)
U.S. Joint Forces Command, Norfolk, VA — Lt. Gen. Robert W. Wagner (U.S. Army) (Acting Commander)
U.S. Special Operations Command, MacDill AFB, Florida — Gen. Bryan D. Brown (U.S. Army)
U.S. Transportation Command, Scott AFB, Illinois — Gen. Norton Schwartz (USAF)
U.S. Central Command, MacDill AFB, Florida — Gen. John Abizaid (U.S. Army)
U.S. Southern Command, Miami, FL — Gen. Bantz J. Craddock (U.S. Army)
U.S. Northern Command, Peterson AFB, Colorado — Adm. Timothy J. Keating (USN)
U.S. Strategic Command, Offutt AFB, Nebraska — Gen. James E. Cartwright (USMC)

North Atlantic Treaty Organization (NATO) International Commands

NATO Headquarters: Chairman, NATO Military Committee — Gen. Raymond Henault (Canada)
Strategic Commands:
Allied Command Operations (ACO) — Gen. James L. Jones (USMC), Supreme Allied Commander, Europe
Allied Command Transformation (ACT) — Adm. Sir Mark Stanhope (UK Royal Navy), Supreme Allied Commander Transformation
Allied Command Operations (ACO) Subordinate Commands:
Joint Force Command Brunssum (JFC Brunnsum) — Gen. Gerhard W. Back (German Luftwaffe), Commander, Brunssum
Joint Force Command Naples (JFC Naples) — Adm. H.G. Ulrich III (USN), Commander, Naples
Joint Headquarters Lisbon (JHQ Lisbon) — Vice Adm. John Stufflebeem (USN), Commander, Lisbon

Chairmen of the Joint Chiefs of Staff, 1949-2005

Gen. of the Army Omar N. Bradley, USA	8/16/49 –8/14/53
Adm. Arthur W. Radford, USN	8/15/53 – 8/14/57
Gen. Nathan F. Twining, USAF	8/15/57 – 9/30/60
Gen. Lyman L. Lemnitzer, USA	10/1/60 – 10/30/62
Gen. Maxwell D. Taylor, USA	10/1/62 – 7/3/64
Gen. Earle G. Wheeler, USA	7/3/64 – 7/2/70
Adm. Thomas H. Moorer, USN	7/3/70 – 6/30/74
Gen. George S. Brown, USAF	7/1/74 – 6/20/78
Gen. David C. Jones, USAF	6/21/78 – 6/18/82
Gen. John W. Vessey Jr., USA	6/18/82 – 9/30/85
Adm. William J. Crowe, Jr., USN	10/1/85 – 9/30/89
Gen. Colin L. Powell, USA	10/1/89 – 9/30/93
Gen. John M. Shalikashvili, USA	10/1/93 – 9/30/97
Gen. Henry H. Shelton, USA	10/1/97 – 9/30/01
Gen. Richard B. Myers, USAF	10/1/01 – 9/30/05
Gen. Peter Pace, USMC	10/1/05 –

Military Units, U.S. Army and Air Force

ARMY UNITS. Squad: In infantry usually 4-10 enlisted personnel under a staff sergeant. **Platoon:** In infantry 3-4 squads under a lieutenant. **Company:** Headquarters section and 3-4 platoons under a captain. (Company-size unit in the artillery is a battery; in the cavalry, a troop.) **Battalion:** Hdqts. and 3-5 companies under a lieutenant colonel. (Battalion-size unit in the cavalry is a squadron.) **Brigade:** Hdqts. and 3 or more battalions under a colonel. **Division:** Hdqts. and 3 brigades with artillery, combat support, and combat service support units under a major general. **Army Corps:** Two or more divisions with corps troops under a lieutenant general. **Field Army:** Hdqts. and 2 or more corps with field Army troops under a general.

AIR FORCE UNITS. Flight: Numerically designated flights are the lowest level unit in the Air Force. They are used primarily where there is a need for small mission elements to be incorporated into an organized unit. **Squadron:** A squadron is the basic unit in the Air Force. It is used to designate the mission units in operational commands. **Group:** The group is a flexible unit composed of 2 or more squadrons whose functions may be operational, support, or administrative in nature. **Wing:** An operational wing normally has 2 or more assigned mission squadrons in an area such as combat, flying training, or airlift. **Numbered Air Forces:** Normally an operationally oriented agency, the numbered air force is designed for the control of 2 or more wings with the same mission and/or geographical location. **Major Command:** A major subdivision of the Air Force that is assigned a major segment of the USAF mission. Major Command is composed of 3 or more numbered air forces.

Principal U.S. Military Training Centers

Air Force

Name, PO address	ZIP	Nearest city
Columbus AFB, MS	39701	Tupelo
Goodfellow AFB, TX	76908	San Angelo
Keesler AFB, MS	39534	Biloxi
Lackland AFB, TX	78236	San Antonio
Maxwell AFB, AL	36112	Montgomery
Sheppard AFB, TX	76311	Wichita Falls

All are Air Education and Training Command Bases.

Army

Name, PO address	ZIP	Nearest city
Aberdeen Proving Ground, MD	21005	Aberdeen
Carlisle Barracks, PA	17013	Carlisle
Fort Benning, GA	31905	Columbus
Fort Bliss, TX	79916	El Paso
Fort Bragg, NC	28307	Fayetteville
Fort Gordon, GA	30905	Augusta
Fort Huachuca, AZ	85613	Sierra Vista
Fort Jackson, SC	29207	Columbia
Fort Knox, KY	40121	Radcliff
Fort Leavenworth, KS	66027	Leavenworth
Fort Lee, VA	23801	Petersburg
Fort Rucker, AL	36362	Dothan
Fort Sill, OK	73503	Lawton
Fort Leonard Wood, MO	65473	Waynesville
Joint Readiness Training Center, Ft. Polk, LA	71459	Leesville
National Training Center, Ft. Irwin, CA	92310	Barstow
The Judge Advocate General's Legal Center and School, VA	22903	Charlottesville

Marine Corps

Name, PO address	ZIP	Nearest city
MCB Camp Lejeune, NC	28547	Jacksonville
MCB Camp Pendleton, CA	92055	Oceanside
MCB Kaneohe Bay, HI	96863	Kailua
MCAGCC Twentynine Palms, CA	92278	Palm Springs
MCCDC Quantico, VA	22134	Quantico
MCRD Parris Island, SC	29905	Beaufort
MCRD San Diego, CA	92140	San Diego
MCAS Cherry Point, NC	28533	Havelock
MCAS Miramar, CA	92145	San Diego
MCAS New River, NC	28545	Jacksonville
MCAS Beaufort, SC	29904	Beaufort
MCAS Yuma, AZ	85369	Yuma
MCMWTC Bridgeport, CA	93517	Bridgeport

MCB = Marine Corps Base. MCAGCC = Marine Corps Air-Ground Combat Center. MCCDC = Marine Corps Combat Development Command. MCRD = Marine Corps Recruit Depot. MCAS = Marine Corps Air Station. MCMWTC = Marine Corps Mountain Warfare Training Center.

Navy

Name, PO address	ZIP	Nearest city
Naval Education & Training Ctr.	32508	Pensacola, FL
Naval Air Training Center	78419	Corpus Christi,TX
Training Command Fleet	92113	San Diego, CA
Naval Aviation Schools Command	32508	Pensacola, FL
Naval Education & Training Ctr.	02841	Newport, RI
Naval Post Graduate School	93943	Monterey, CA
Naval Submarine School	06349	Groton, CT
Naval Training Ctr., Great Lakes	60088	N. Chicago, IL
Naval War College	02841	Newport, RI
Naval Air Tech. Training Ctr.	32508	Pensacola, FL
Fleet Antisubmarine Warfare	92147	San Diego, CA

The Federal Service Academies

U.S. Military Academy, West Point, NY. Founded 1802. Awards BS degree and Army commission for a 5-year service obligation. For admissions information, write USMA Admissions, Bldg. 606, USMA, West Point, NY 10996. www.usma.edu

U.S. Naval Academy, Annapolis, MD. Founded 1845. Awards BS degree and Navy or Marine Corps commission for a 5-year service obligation. For admissions information, write Candidate Guidance Office, United States Naval Academy, 117 Decatur Rd., Annapolis, MD 21402-5018. www.usna.edu

U.S. Air Force Academy, Colorado Springs, CO. Founded 1954. Awards BS degree and Air Force commission for a 6-year service obligation. For admissions information, write Director of Admissions, 2304 Cadet Drive, U.S. Air Force Academy, CO 80840-5025. www.usafa.edu

U.S. Coast Guard Academy, New London, CT. Founded 1876. Awards BS degree and Coast Guard commission for a 5-year service obligation. For admissions information, write Director of Admissions, Coast Guard Academy, 31 Mohegan Ave., New London, CT 06320-8103. www.cga.edu

U.S. Merchant Marine Academy, Kings Point, NY. Founded 1943. Awards BS degree, a license as a deck, engineer, or dual officer, and a U.S. Naval Reserve commission. Service obligations vary according to options taken by the graduate. For admissions information, write Admission Office, U.S. Merchant Marine Academy, 300 Steamboat Rd., Kings Point, NY 11024. www.usmma.edu

Personal Salutes and Honors, U.S.

The U.S. **national salute,** 21 guns, is also the salute to a national flag. U.S. independence is commemorated by the salute to the Union—one gun for each state—fired at noon July 4, at all military posts provided with suitable artillery.

A 21-gun salute on arrival and departure, with 4 ruffles and flourishes, is rendered to the **president** of the United States, to a former president, and to a president-elect. The national anthem or "Hail to the Chief," as appropriate, is played for the president, and the national anthem for the others. A 21-gun salute on arrival and departure, with 4 ruffles and flourishes, also is rendered to the **sovereign or chief of state of a foreign country** or a member of a reigning royal family, and the national anthem of his or her country is played. The music is considered an inseparable part of the salute and immediately follows the ruffles and flourishes without pause. For the Honors March, generals receive the "General's March," admirals receive the "Admiral's March," and all others receive the 32-bar medley of "The Stars and Stripes Forever."

GRADE, TITLE, OR OFFICE	SALUTE (IN GUNS) Arriving	Leaving	Ruffles and flourishes	Music
Vice president of United States	19		4	Hail, Columbia
Speaker of the House	19		4	Honors March
U.S. or foreign ambassador	19		4	Nat. anthem of official
Premier or prime minister	19		4	Nat. anthem of official
Secretary of Defense, Army, Navy, or Air Force	19	19	4	Honors March
Other cabinet members, Senate president pro tempore, governor, or chief justice of U.S.	19		4	Honors March
Chairman, Joint Chiefs of Staff	19	19	4	
Army chief of staff, chief of naval operations, Air Force chief of staff, Marine commandant	19	19	4	Honors March
General of the Army, general of the Air Force, fleet admiral	19	19	4	
Generals, admirals	17	17	4	
Assistant secretaries of Defense, Army, Navy, or Air Force	17	17	4	Honors March
Chair of a committee of Congress	17		4	Honors March

OTHER SALUTES (on arrival only) include: 15 guns, with 3 ruffles and flourishes, for U.S. envoys or ministers and foreign envoys or ministers accredited to the U.S.; 15 guns, for a lieutenant general or vice admiral; 13 guns, with 2 ruffles and flourishes, for a major general or rear admiral (upper half) and for U.S. ministers resident and ministers resident accredited to the U.S.; 11 guns, with 1 ruffle and flourish, for a brigadier general or rear admiral (lower half) and for U.S. charges d'affaires and like officials accredited to the U.S.; 11 guns, no ruffles and flourishes, for consuls general accredited to the U.S.

U.S. Army, Navy, Air Force, Marine Corps, and Coast Guard Insignia

Source: Dept. of the Army, Dept. of the Navy, Dept. of the Air Force, U.S. Dept. of Defense

Army

General of the Armies — Gen. John J. Pershing (1860-1948), the only person to have held this rank in life, was authorized to prescribe his own insignia, but never wore in excess of four stars. The rank originally was established posthumously by Congress for George Washington in 1799, and he was promoted to the rank by joint resolution of Congress, approved by Pres. Gerald Ford, Oct. 19, 1976.

General of the Army — Five silver stars fastened together in a circle and the coat of arms of the United States in gold color metal with shield and crest enameled. Reserved for wartime use only.

General	Four silver stars
Lieutenant General	Three silver stars
Major General	Two silver stars
Brigadier General	One silver star
Colonel	Silver eagle
Lieutenant Colonel	Silver oak leaf
Major	Gold oak leaf
Captain	Two silver bars
First Lieutenant	One silver bar
Second Lieutenant	One gold bar

Warrant Officers

Grade Five — Silver bar with enamel black line
Grade Four — Silver bar with 4 enamel black squares
Grade Three — Silver bar with 3 enamel black squares
Grade Two — Silver bar with 2 enamel black squares
Grade One — Silver bar with 1 enamel black square

Noncommissioned Officers

Sergeant Major of the Army (E-9) — Three chevrons above 3 arcs, with an U.S. Coat of Arms centered on the chevrons, flanked by 2 stars—one star on each side of the eagle. Also wears distinctive red and white shield collar insignia.

Command Sergeant Major (E-9) — Three chevrons above 3 arcs with a 5-pointed star with a wreath around the star between the chevrons and arcs.

Sergeant Major (E-9) — Three chevrons above 3 arcs with a 5-pointed star between the chevrons and arcs.

First Sergeant (E-8) — Three chevrons above 3 arcs with a lozenge between the chevrons and arcs.

Master Sergeant (E-8) — Three chevrons above 3 arcs.

Sergeant First Class (E-7) — Three chevrons above 2 arcs.

Staff Sergeant (E-6) — Three chevrons above 1 arc.

Sergeant (E-5) — Three chevrons.

Corporal (E-4) — Two chevrons.

Specialists

Specialist (E-4) — Eagle device only.

Other enlisted

Private First Class (E-3) — One chevron above one arc.

Private (E-2) — One chevron.

Private (E-1) — None.

Air Force

Insignia for Air Force officers are identical to those of the Army. Insignia for enlisted personnel are worn on both sleeves and consist of a star and an appropriate number of rockers. Chevrons appear above 5 rockers for the top 3 noncommissioned officer ranks, as follows (in ascending order): Master Sergeant, 1 chevron; Senior Master Sergeant, 2 chevrons; and Chief Master Sergeant, 3 chevrons. The insignia of the Chief Master Sergeant of the Air Force has 3 chevrons and a wreath around the star design. General of the Air Force is reserved for wartime use only.

Navy

The following stripes are worn on the lower sleeves of the Service Dress Blue uniform. They are of gold embroidery.

Rank	Insignia
Fleet Admiral*	1 two inch with 4 one-half inch
Admiral	1 two inch with 3 one-half inch
Vice Admiral	1 two inch with 2 one-half inch
Rear Admiral (upper half)	1 two inchwith 1 one-half inch
Rear Admiral (lower half)	1 two inch
Captain	4 one-half inch
Commander	3 one-half inch
Lieutenant Commander	2 one-half inch with 1 one-quarter inch between
Lieutenant	2 one-half inch
Lieutenant (j.g.)	1 one-half inch with one-quarter inch above
Ensign	1 one-half inch
Warrant Officer-W-4	½″ stripe with 1 break
Warrant Officer W-3	½″ stripe with 2 breaks, 2″ apart
Warrant Officer W-2	½″ stripe with 3 breaks, 2″ apart

Enlisted personnel (noncommissioned petty officers)—A rating badge worn on the upper left sleeve, consisting of a spread eagle, appropriate number of chevrons, and centered specialty mark.

*The rank of Fleet Admiral is reserved for wartime use only.

Marine Corps

Marine Corps' distinctive cap and collar ornament is the Marine Corps Emblem—a combination of the American eagle, a globe, and an anchor. Marine Corps and Army officer insignia are similar. Marine Corps enlisted insignia, although basically similar to the Army's, feature crossed rifles beneath the chevrons. Marine Corps enlisted rank insignia are as follows:

Sergeant Major of the Marine Corps (E-9) — Same as Sergeant Major (below) but with Marine Corps emblem in the center with a 5-pointed star on both sides of the emblem.

Sergeant Major (E-9) — Three chevrons above 4 rockers with a 5-pointed star in the center.

Master Gunnery Sergeant (E-9) — Three chevrons above 4 rockers with a bursting bomb insignia in the center.

First Sergeant (E-8) — Three chevrons above 3 rockers with a diamond in the middle.

Master Sergeant (E-8) — Three chevrons above 3 rockers with crossed rifles in the middle.

Gunnery Sergeant (E-7) — Three chevrons above 2 rockers with crossed rifles in the middle.

Staff Sergeant (E-6) — Three chevrons above 1 rocker with crossed rifles in the middle.

Sergeant (E-5) — Three chevrons above crossed rifles.

Corporal (E-4) — Two chevrons above crossed rifles.

Lance Corporal (E-3) — One chevron above crossed rifles.

Private First Class (E-2) — One chevron.

Private (E-1) — None.

Coast Guard

Coast Guard insignia follow Navy custom, with certain minor changes such as the officer cap insignia. The Coast Guard shield is worn on both sleeves of officers and on the right sleeve of all enlisted personnel.

For Further Information on the U.S. Armed Forces

Army — Office of the Chief of Public Affairs, Attention: Media Relations Division—MRD, Army 1500, Washington, DC 20310-1500. **Website:** www.army.mil

Navy — Chief of Information, 1200 Navy Pentagon, Washington, DC 20350-1200. **Website:** www.navy.mil

Air Force — Office of Public Affairs, 1690 Air Force, Pentagon, Washington, DC 20330-1690. **Website:** www.af.mil

Marine Corps — Marine Corps Headquarters , Division of Public Affairs, U.S. Marine Corps, Washington, DC 20380-1775. **Website:** www.usmc.mil

Coast Guard — Commandant (G-IPA), U.S. Coast Guard, 2100 Second St. SW, Washington, DC 20593-0001. **Website:** www.uscg.mil

Additional information on all the U.S. Armed Forces branches, as well as many other related organizations, can be accessed through DefenseLINK, the official Internet site of the Dept. of Defense: www.defenselink.mil

U.S. Army Personnel on Active Duty[1]

Source: Dept. of the Army, U.S. Dept. of Defense
(As of midyear, except where noted)

Date	Total strength[2]	Commissioned officers Total	Commissioned officers Male	Commissioned officers Female[3]	Warrant officers Male[4]	Warrant officers Female	Enlisted personnel Total	Enlisted personnel Male	Enlisted personnel Female
1940	267,767	17,563	16,624	939	763	—	249,441	249,441	—
1942	3,074,184	203,137	190,662	12,475	3,285	—	2,867,762	2,867,762	—
1943	6,993,102	557,657	521,435	36,222	21,919	—	6,413,526	6,358,200	55,325
1944	7,992,868	740,077	692,351	47,726	36,893	10	7,215,888	7,144,601	71,287
1945	8,266,373	835,403	772,511	62,892	56,216	44	7,374,710	7,283,930	90,780
1946	1,889,690	257,300	240,643	16,657	9,826	18	1,622,546	1,605,847	16,699
1950	591,487	67,784	63,375	4,409	4,760	22	518,921	512,370	6,551
1955	1,107,606	111,347	106,173	5,174	10,552	48	985,659	977,943	7,716
1960	871,348	91,056	86,832	4,224	10,141	39	770,112	761,833	8,279
1965	967,049	101,812	98,029	3,783	10,285	23	854,929	846,409	8,520
1970	1,319,735	143,704	138,469	5,235	23,005	13	1,153,013	1,141,537	11,476
1975	781,316	89,756	85,184	4,572	13,214	22	678,324	640,621	37,703
1980 (Sept. 30)	772,661	85,339	77,843	7,496	13,265	113	673,944	612,593	61,351
1985 (Sept. 30)	776,244	94,103	83,563	10,540	15,296	288	666,557	598,639	67,918
1990 (Mar. 31)	746,220	91,330	79,520	11,810	15,177	470	639,713	567,015	72,698
1995	521,036	72,646	62,250	10,396	12,053	599	435,807	377,832	57,975
1996 (May 31)	493,330	68,850	58,875	9,975	11,456	660	408,511	351,669	56,842
1997 (May 31)	487,297	67,986	58,270	9,716	11,021	719	403,072	342,817	60,255
1998	491,707	67,048	56,650	10,398	10,989	661	402,000	345,149	56,851
1999	479,100	66,613	56,952	9,661	10,767	757	388,211	329,803	58,408
2000	471,633	66,344	56,391	9,953	10,608	781	393,900	333,947	59,953
2001	478,918	64,809	54,570	10,239	10,575	795	398,983	336,264	62,719
2002	485,536	66,446	55,715	10,731	10,900	812	404,363	341,794	62,569
2003 (Sept. 30)	499,301	68,198	56,980	11,218	11,273	854	414,769	351,921	62,848
2004 (Sept. 30)	499,543	68,640	57,245	11,395	11,414	914	414,438	354,043	60,395
2005	489,971	69,731	NA	NA	12,421[5]	NA	403,548	NA	NA

NA = Not available. (1) Represents strength of the active Army, including Philippine Scouts, retired Regular Army personnel on extended active duty, and National Guard and Reserve personnel on extended active duty; excludes U.S. Military Academy cadets, contract surgeons, and National Guard and Reserve personnel not on extended active duty. (2) Includes categories not listed, e.g. West Point Cadets. Data for 1940 to 1946 include personnel in the Army Air Forces and its predecessors (Air Service and Air Corps). (3) Includes women doctors, dentists, and Medical Service Corps officers for 1946 and subsequent years, women in the Army Nurse Corps for all years, and the Women's Army Corps and Women's Medical Specialists Corps (dietitians, physical therapists, and occupational specialists) for 1943 and subsequent years. (4) Act of Congress approved Apr. 27, 1926, directed the appointment as warrant officers of field clerks still in active service. Includes flight officers as follows: 1943, 5,700; 1944, 13,615; 1945, 31,117; 1946, 2,580. (5) Total male and female.

U.S. Navy Personnel on Active Duty

Source: Dept. of the Navy, U.S. Dept. of Defense
(As of midyear, except where noted)

Date	Officers	Nurses	Enlisted	Officer Candi-dates	Total[1]
1940	13,162	442	144,824	2,569	160,997
1945	320,293	11,086	2,988,207	61,231	3,380,817
1950	42,687	1,964	331,860	5,037	381,538
1960	67,456	2,103	544,040	4,385	617,984
1970	78,488	2,273	605,899	6,000	692,660
1980[2]	63,100	—	464,100	—	527,200
1990 (Sept.)	74,429	—	530,133	—	604,562
1993 (Mar.)	66,787	—	445,409	—	512,196
1994 (Apr.)	64,430	—	418,378	—	482,808
1995 (May)	61,075	—	402,626	—	463,701
1996	60,013	—	376,595	—	436,608
1997	57,341	—	340,616	—	397,957
1998 (Sept.)	55,007	—	326,196	—	381,203
1999	55,726	—	322,372	—	378,098
2000 (Oct.)	53,698	—	320,212	—	373,910
2001 (Aug.)	54,177	—	317,100	—	375,618
2002	55,506	—	324,712	—	384,576
2003	55,852	—	324,927	—	380,779
2004	55,592	—	319,929	—	375,521
2005	54,039	—	305,368	—	363,858

(1) May include categories not shown, e.g. midshipmen. (2) Starting in 1980, "Nurses" are included with "Officers," and "Officer Candidates" are included with "Enlisted."

U.S. Air Force Personnel on Active Duty

Source: Air Force Dept., U.S. Dept. of Defense
(As of midyear)

Year[1]	Strength
1918	195,023
1920	9,050
1930	13,531
1940	51,165
1941	152,125
1942	764,415
1943	2,197,114
1944	2,372,292
1945	2,282,259
1950	411,277
1960	814,213
1970	791,078
1980	557,969
1986	608,200
1990	535,233
1991	510,432
1992	470,315
1993	444,351
1994	426,327
1995	400,051
1996	389,400
1997	378,681
1998	363,479
1999	357,929
2000	357,777
2001	351,935
2002	369,721
2003	373,116
2004	379,887
2005	358,705

(1) Prior to 1947, data are for U.S. Army Air Corps and Air Service of the Signal Corps.

U.S. Marine Corps Personnel on Active Duty

Source: Dept. of the Marines, U.S. Dept. of Defense
(As of midyear)

Year	Officers	Enlisted	Total
1940	1,800	26,545	28,345
1945	37,067	437,613	474,680
1950	7,254	67,025	74,279
1960	16,203	154,418	170,621
1970	24,941	234,796	259,737
1980	18,198	170,271	188,469
1990	19,958	176,694	196,652
1991	19,753	174,287	194,040
1992	19,132	165,397	184,529
1993	18,878	161,205	180,083
1994	18,430	159,949	178,379
1995	18,017	153,929	171,946
1996	18,146	154,141	172,287
1997	18,089	154,240	172,329
1998	17,984	154,648	172,632
1999	17,892	155,250	173,142
2000	17,897	154,744	172,641
2001	18,072	152,559	170,631
2002	18,472	154,913	173,385
2003	18,908	160,814	179,722
2004	19,052	157,150	176,202
2005	19,118	159,113	178,231

IT'S A FACT: Arlington National Cemetery, in Arlington, VA, was originally part of the estate of Confederate Gen. Robert E. Lee. When Lee left home to join the Confederate Army in 1861, it was occupied by Union troops, who set up forts there and also used the area to bury Union and Confederate soldiers who died in nearby hospitals. After the war, Lee's son petitioned to have the land returned, and in 1882, the Supreme Court ruled in his favor. To avoid moving the 16,000 or more bodies buried there, the U.S. government bought the land in 1883 for $150,000.

U.S. Coast Guard Personnel on Active Duty

Source: U.S. Coast Guard, U.S. Dept. of Defense
(As of mid year)

Year	Total	Officers	Cadets	Enlisted
1970	37,689	5,512	653	31,524
1980	39,381	6,463	877	32,041
1985	38,595	6,775	733	31,087
1990	37,308	6,475	820	29,860
1992	39,185	7,348	919	30,918
1993	38,832	7,724	691	30,417
1994	37,284	7,401	881	29,002
1995	36,731	7,489	841	28,401
1996	35,229	7,270	830	27,129
1997	34,717	7,079	868	26,770
1998	34,890	7,140	805	26,945
1999	35,266	7,135	880	27,251
2000	35,712	7,154	863	27,695
2001	35,328	7,112	631	27,585
2002	37,166	7,267	694	29,205
2003	39,000	7,532	983	30,859
2004	40,151	7,835	1,030	31,286
2005	40,814	7,908	1,006	31,900

Women in the U.S. Armed Forces

Source: U.S. Dept. of Defense, U.S. Census Bureau

Women in the Army, Navy, Air Force, Marines, and Coast Guard are fully integrated with male personnel. Expansion of military women's programs began in the Dept. of Defense in fiscal year 1973. Admission of women to the service academies began in the fall of 1976. Under rules instituted in 1993, women were allowed to fly combat aircraft and serve aboard warships. Women remained restricted from service in ground combat units.

Between Apr. 1993 and July 1994, almost 260,000 positions in the armed forces were opened to women. By the mid-1990s, 80% of all jobs and more than 90% of all career fields in the military had been opened to women. In 1975, women made up 4.6% of the armed forces. This figure had grown to 15.2% by Sept. 2004, with about 217,000 women on active duty.

Women Active Duty Troops in 2004

Service	% Women
Army	14.7
Navy	14.5
Marines	6.1
Air Force	19.6
Coast Guard	11.0

Women on Active Duty, All Services: 1973-2004

Year	% Women
1973	2.5
1975	4.6
1981	8.9
1987	10.2
1993	11.6
1997	13.6
2000	14.4
2004	15.2

African American Service in U.S. Wars

American Revolution. About 5,000 African Americans served in the Continental Army, mostly in integrated units, some in all-black combat units.

Civil War. Some 200,000 African Americans served in the Union Army; about 38,000 died, mainly from disease; and 22 won the Medal of Honor (the nation's highest award).

World War I. About 367,000 African Americans served in the armed forces, 100,000 in France.

World War II. Over 1 mil African Americans served in the armed forces; all-black fighter and bomber AAF units and infantry divisions gave distinguished service. (By 1954, armed forces were completely desegregated.)

Korean War. Approximately 3,100 African Americans lost their lives in combat.

Vietnam War. 274,937 African Americans served in the armed forces (1965-74); 5,681 were killed in combat.

Persian Gulf War. About 104,000 African Americans served in the Kuwaiti theater—20% of all U.S. troops, compared with 8.7% of all troops for World War II and 9.8% for Vietnam.

Iraq War. More than 200 African-American military deaths (as of Sept. 2005).

Defense Contracts, 2004

Source: U.S. Dept. of Defense
(in thousands of dollars)

Listed are the 50 companies or organizations receiving the largest dollar volume of prime contract awards from the U.S. Department of Defense during fiscal year 2004.

Company	Total[1]
Lockheed Martin	$20,690,912
Boeing	17,066,413
Northrop Grumman	11,894,090
General Dynamics	9,563,280
Raytheon	8,472,814
Halliburton	7,996,794
United Technologies	5,056,938
Science Applications Intl.	2,450,781
Computer Sciences	2,390,806
Humana	2,372,078
L-3 Communications Holding	2,260,293
BAE Systems PLC	2,192,647
Health Net	1,899,825
General Electric	1,822,720
Bechtel Group, Inc.	1,742,470
Bell Boeing Joint Program	1,539,815
ITT Industries	1,539,742
Electronic Data Systems	1,538,272
Honeywell International	1,462,915
Carlyle Group	$1,442,680
Triwest Healthcare Alliance	1,279,718
Renco Group Inc.	1,107,715
N.V. Koninklijke Nederlandsche	1,070,123
Oshkosh Truck	1,024,394
Government of the United States	1,005,126
North American Airlines	961,601
FedEx Corp.	953,938
Textron	940,267
The Titan Corporation	933,554
Boeing Sikorsky Comanche Team	929,238
Booz Allen Hamilton	909,663
Veritas Capital Management LLC	863,011
GM GDLS Defense Group	811,807
Parsons Corp.	809,150
Public Warehousing Co.	$804,820
URS Corporation	803,827
Government of Canada	751,147
Anteon Intl. Corp.	700,777
Johnson Controls	696,616
Engineered Support Systems, Inc.	693,854
Dell Inc.	642,979
A P Moller Gruppen	638,728
McKesson Corp.	627,637
Massachusetts Institute of Technology	607,115
Harris	605,789
B P PLC	597,674
Alliant Techsystems	592,439
Rockwell Collins	588,368
American Body Armor and Equipment	579,264
Cardinal Health	575,550

(1) Totals include subsidiaries of each company.

Veterans Compensation and Pension Case Payments

Source: Office of Policy Planning and Preparedness, Dept. of Veterans Affairs

Fiscal year	Living veteran cases	Deceased veteran cases	Total cases	Total expenditures (dollars)
1900	752,510	241,019	993,529	$138,462
1910	602,622	318,461	921,083	159,974
1920	419,627	349,916	769,543	316,418
1930	542,610	298,223	840,833	418,433
1940	610,122	239,176	849,298	429,138
1950	2,368,238	658,123	3,026,361	2,009,462
1960	3,008,935	950,802	3,959,737	3,314,761
1970	3,127,338	1,487,176	4,614,514	5,251,902
1980	3,195,395	1,450,785	4,646,180	11,044,453
1990	2,746,329	837,596	3,583,925	14,674,411
1995	2,668,576	661,679	3,330,255	$17,765,044
1996	2,671,026	637,232	3,308,258	18,489,468
1997	2,666,785	613,976	3,280,761	19,307,852
1998	2,668,030	594,782	3,262,812	20,199,306
1999	2,673,167	578,508	3,251,675	21,069,431
2000	2,672,407	563,754	3,236,161	22,011,965
2001	2,669,156	548,589	3,217,745	23,275,902
2002	2,744,866	539,796	3,284,662	25,572,913
2003	2,831,784	537,513	3,369,297	27,995,345
2004	2,898,599	533,482	3,432,081	29,936,868

U.S. Veteran Population, 2005

Source: U.S. Dept. of Veterans Affairs; as of Sept. 2005

TOTAL VETERANS IN CIVILIAN LIFE[1]	**24,387,000**
Total wartime veterans[2]	**18,156,000**
Total Gulf War[3]	4,378,000
Gulf War with no prior wartime service	4,027,000
Gulf War with service in Vietnam era	344,000
Gulf War, with service in Vietnam and Korea	6,000
Gulf War with service in Vietnam, Korea and WWII	1,000
Total Vietnam era[3]	8,055,000
Vietnam era with no prior wartime service	7,364,000
Vietnam era with service in Korean conflict	231,000
Vietnam era with service in Korea and WWII	109,000
Total Korean conflict[3]	3,257,000
Korean conflict with no prior wartime service	2,658,000
Korean conflict with service in WWII	253,000
Total World War II[3]	3,526,000
WWII only[3]	3,163,000
Total peacetime veterans[4]	**6,231,000**
Service between Vietnam era and Gulf War only	3,458,000
Service between Korean conflict and Vietnam era only	2,606,000
Other peacetime	168,000

NOTE: Figures are for U.S. veterans worldwide. (1) Includes those who served on active duty in Army, Navy, Air Force, Marines, Coast Guard, uniformed Public Health Service and NOAA, and reservists called to federal active duty. Excludes those dishonorably discharged, those whose only active duty was training, and those currently on active duty. (2) Veterans serving in more than one period are counted only once in total. (3) Total includes Iraq War veterans and veterans who served in multiple periods. (4) Veterans with both wartime and peacetime service are counted only as "wartime veterans."

The Medal of Honor

The Medal of Honor is the highest military award for bravery that can be given to any individual in the United States. The first Army Medals were awarded on Mar. 25, 1863, and the first Navy Medals went to sailors and Marines on Apr. 3, 1863.

On Dec. 21, 1861, Pres. Abraham Lincoln signed into law a bill to create the Navy Medal of Honor. Lincoln later (July 14, 1862) approved a resolution providing for the presentation of Medals of Honor to enlisted men of the Army and Voluntary Forces, making it a law. The law was amended on March 3, 1863, to extend its provisions to include officers as well as enlisted men.

The Medal of Honor is awarded in the name of Congress to a person who, while a member of the armed forces, distinguishes himself or herself conspicuously by gallantry and intrepidity at the risk of life above and beyond the call of duty while engaged in an action against any enemy of the United States; while engaged in military operations involving conflict with an opposing foreign force; or while serving with friendly foreign forces engaged in an armed conflict against an opposing armed force in which the United States is not a belligerent party.

The deed performed must have been one of personal bravery or self-sacrifice so conspicuous as to clearly distinguish the individual above his or her comrades and must have involved risk of life. Incontestable proof of the performance of service is required, and each recommendation for award of this decoration is considered on the standard of extraordinary merit.

Prior to World War I, the 2,625 Army Medal of Honor awards up to that time were reviewed to determine which past awards met new stringent criteria. The Army removed 911 names from the list, most of them former members of a volunteer infantry group during the Civil War who had been induced to extend their enlistments when they were promised the medal. However, in 1977 a medal was restored to Dr. Mary Walker, and in 1989 medals were restored to Buffalo Bill Cody and 7 other Indian scouts.

Since then, Medals of Honor have been awarded for:

World War I	124	Korean War	132
Peacetime (1920-40)	18	Vietnam War	245
World War II	464	Somalia	2

The figure for World War II includes 7 African-American soldiers who were awarded Medals of Honor (6 of them posthumously) in Jan. 1997. Previously, no black soldier had received the medal for World War II service; an Army inquiry begun in 1993 concluded that the prevailing political climate and Army practices of the time had prevented proper recognition of heroism on the part of black soldiers in that war. In June 2002, 22 Asian Americans received the award for World War II service.

The most recent recipient was Corporal Tibor "Ted" Rubin, who was awarded the medal on Sept. 23, 2005. While serving in Korea, 1950-1953, Rubin distinguished himself in combat and by refusing release from a Chinese POW camp in order to secretly obtain food and medical care for his fellow prisoners, ultimately saving up to 40 lives.

Active Duty U.S. Military Personnel Strengths, Worldwide, 2005

Source: U.S. Dept. of Defense

(as of June 30, 2005)

TOTAL WORLDWIDE[1]	**1,390,765**
U.S. TERRITORIES & SPEC. LOCATIONS	
U.S., 48 contiguous states	900,088
Alaska	17,714
Hawaii	33,343
Guam	3,384
Puerto Rico	252
Transients	48,759
Afloat	109,119
Regional Total[2]	**1,112,684**
OTHER WESTERN HEMISPHERE	
Canada	145
Cuba (Guantánamo)	850
Honduras	475
Afloat	27
Regional Total[2]	**1,978**
FORMER SOVIET UNION TOTAL	**158**
EUROPE	
Belgium	1,415
Bosnia and Herzegovina	265
Germany	69,395
Greece	450
Iceland	1,289
Italy	12,258
Netherlands	648
Portugal	997
Serbia (incl. Kosovo)	1,749
Spain	1,715
Turkey	1,768
United Kingdom	11,093
Afloat	1,919
Regional Total[2]	**105,570**
SUB-SAHARAN AFRICA	
Djibouti	188
Regional Total[2]	**448**
EAST ASIA & PACIFIC	
Australia	183
Japan	35,307
Korea, South	32,744
Philippines	95
Singapore	165
Thailand	489
Afloat	11,618
Regional Total[2]	**80,755**
NORTH AFRICA, NEAR EAST, & SOUTH ASIA*	
Afghanistan	NA
Bahrain	1,664
Diego Garcia	986
Egypt	384
Iraq[3]	169,200
Qatar	417
Saudi Arabia	230
Afloat	2,298
Regional Total[2]	**175,463**

*Special Forces personnel involved in Operation Enduring Freedom in Afghanistan not reported by Dept. of Defense. (1) Total worldwide also includes undistributed personnel. (2) Most countries and areas with fewer than 100 assigned U.S. military members not listed; regional totals include personnel stationed in those countries and areas not shown. (3) Includes troops in surrounding areas.

Directors of the Central Intelligence Agency

In 1942, Pres. Franklin D. Roosevelt established the Office of Strategic Services (OSS); it was disbanded in 1945. In 1946, Pres. Harry Truman established the Central Intelligence Group (CIG) to operate under the National Intelligence Authority (NIA). A 1947 law replaced the NIA with the National Security Council and the CIG with the Central Intelligence Agency.

Director	Served	Appointed by President
Adm. Sidney W. Souers	1946	Truman
Gen. Hoyt S. Vandenberg	1946-1947	Truman
Adm. Roscoe H. Hillenkoetter	1947-1950	Truman
Gen. Walter Bedell Smith	1950-1953	Truman
Allen W. Dulles	1953-1961	Eisenhower
John A. McCone	1961-1965	Kennedy
Adm. William F. Raborn Jr.	1965-1966	Johnson
Richard Helms	1966-1973	Johnson
James R. Schlesinger	1973	Nixon
William E. Colby	1973-1976	Nixon
George H. W. Bush	1976-1977	Ford
Adm. Stansfield Turner	1977-1981	Carter
William J. Casey	1981-1987	Reagan
William H. Webster	1987-1991	Reagan
Robert M. Gates	1991-1993	Bush
R. James Woolsey	1993-1995	Clinton
John M. Deutch	1995-1997	Clinton
George J. Tenet	1997-2004	Clinton
Porter Goss*	2004-	Bush

*Took office Sept. 2004.

Nations with Largest Armed Forces, by Active-Duty Troop Strength

Source: *The Military Balance. 2004-2005* (International Institute for Strategic Studies, published by Oxford University Press, UK)

	Troop strength				Navy		Combat aircraft	
	Active troops (thousands)	Reserve troops (thousands)	Defense expend. ($ bil)	Tanks (MBT) (army only)	Cruisers/ Frigates/ Destroyers	Sub-marines	FGA (air force only)	Fighters (air force only)
1. China	2,255	800	55.9	7,580	42F/21D	69	700	1,000
2. United States	1,434	1,162	404.9	7,620	27C/30F/49D*	72	3,513 aircraft	
3. India	1,325	535	15.5	3,898	16F/8D*	16	472	127
4. Russia	1,213	2,400	65.2	22,800	6C/6F/14D*	51	606	908
5. N. Korea	1,106	4,700	5.5	3,500	3F	26	504 FGA/FTR	
6. S. Korea	688	4,500	14.6	1,000	9F/6D	20	468 FGA/FTR	
7. Pakistan	619	513	3.1	2,461	7F	11	109	207
8. Iran	540	350	3.1	1,613	3F	3	186	74
9. Turkey	515	379	11.6	4,205	19F	13	480 aircraft	
10. Myanmar	485	—	6.3	150	—	—	22	70
11. Vietnam	484	3,000	2.9	1,315	6F	2	71	124
12. Egypt	450	410	2.7	3,755	10F/1D	4	131	327
13. Thailand	306	200	1.9	333	12F*	—	133	—
14. Brazil	303	1,115	9.3	178	15F*	4	254+ aircraft	
15. Indonesia	302	400	6.4	—	16F	2	63	12
16. Syria	297	354	1.5	4,600	2F	—	130	289
17. Taiwan	290	1,657	6.6	926+	11D/21F	4	386	57
18. Germany	285	359	35.1	2,398	12F/1D	12	384 aircraft	
19. Ukraine	273	1,000	5.5	3,784	1C/2F	1	63	340
20. France	259	100	45.7	614	12D/20F*	10	478 aircraft	
21. Japan	240	44	42.8	980	45D/9F*	16	80	180
22. United Kingdom	208	273	42.8	543	11D/20F	15	426 aircraft	
23. Colombia	207	61	3.2	—	—	4	22	—
24. Eritrea	202	120	73 mil	150	—	—	18 aircraft	
25. Saudi Arabia	200	—	18.7	1,055	7F	—	171	106
26. Morocco	196	150	1.8	744	2F	—	53	15
27. Italy	194	63	27.8	1,293	4D/12F*	6	321 aircraft	
28. Mexico	193	300	2.9	—	3D/8F	—	107 aircraft	
29. Ethiopia	183	—	326 mil	250+	—	—	48	—
30. Greece	171	291	7.2	1,723	2D/12F	8	389 aircraft	

MBT = main battle tank. FGA = fighter, ground attack; rgt = regiment; sqn = squadron (12-24 aircraft); wg = wing (72 fighter aircraft). *Denotes navies with aircraft carriers, as follows: United States 12, United Kingdom 3, France 1, India 1, Italy 1, Russia 1, Brazil 1, Thailand 1. (1) All figures are for Aug. 2004, except Defense Expenditure, which is for 2003. — = not available.

Nuclear Arms Treaties and Negotiations: A Historical Overview

Aug. 5, 1963—Limited Test Ban Treaty signed in Moscow by U.S., USSR, and Britain; prohibited testing of nuclear weapons in space, above ground, and under water.

Jan. 27, 1967—Outer Space Treaty banned the introduction of other weapons of mass destruction in space.

July 1, 1968—Nuclear Nonproliferation Treaty, with U.S., USSR, and Great Britain as major signers, limited spread of nuclear material for military purposes by agreement not to help nonnuclear nations get or make nuclear weapons. In 1995, the treaty was extended indefinitely. As of Sept. 2005, 188 countries had signed the treaty; Israel, India, and Pakistan were not signatories. In Jan. 2003, N. Korea withdrew from the treaty.

May 26, 1972—Strategic Arms Limitation Treaty (SALT I) signed in Moscow by U.S. and USSR. This short-term agreement imposed a 5-year freeze on both testing and deployment of intercontinental ballistic missiles (ICBMs) as well as submarine-launched ballistic missiles (SLBMs). In the area of defensive nuclear weapons, the separate **ABM Treaty,** signed on the same occasion, limited antiballistic missiles to 2 sites of 100 antiballistic missile launchers in each country (amended in 1974 to 1 site in each country).

July 3, 1974—ABM Treaty Revision (protocol on antiballistic missile systems) and **Threshold Test Ban Treaty** on limiting underground testing of nuclear weapons to 150 kilotons were signed by U.S. and USSR in Moscow.

Sept. 1977—U.S. and USSR agreed to continue to abide by **SALT I**, despite its expiration date.

June 18, 1979—SALT II signed in Vienna by the U.S. and USSR, constrained offensive nuclear weapons, limiting each side to 2,400 missile launchers and heavy bombers; ceiling to apply until Jan. 1, 1985. Treaty also set a subceiling of 1,320 ICBMs and SLBMs with multiple warheads on each side. SALT II never reached the Senate floor for ratification because Pres. Jimmy Carter withdrew support following Dec. 1979 Soviet invasion of Afghanistan.

Dec. 8, 1987—Intermediate-Range Nuclear Forces (INF) Treaty signed in Washington, DC, by U.S. and USSR, eliminating all U.S. and Soviet intermediate- and shorter-range nuclear missiles from Europe and Asia. Ratified, with conditions, by U.S. Senate May 27, 1988; by USSR June 1, 1988. Entered into force June 1, 1988.

July 31, 1991—Strategic Arms Reduction Treaty (START I) signed in Moscow by USSR and U.S. to reduce strategic offensive arms by about 30% in 3 phases over 7 years. START I was the first treaty to mandate reductions by the superpowers. Treaty was approved by U.S. Senate Oct. 1, 1992.

With the Soviet Union breakup in Dec. 1991, 4 former Soviet republics became independent nations with strategic nuclear weapons—Russia, Ukraine, Kazakhstan, and Belarus. The last 3 agreed in principle in 1992 to transfer their nuclear weapons to Russia and ratify START I. The Russian Supreme Soviet voted to ratify, Nov. 4, 1992, but Russia decided not to provide instruments of ratification until the other 3 republics ratified START I and acceded to the Nuclear Nonproliferation Treaty (NPT) as nonnuclear nations. By late 1994, all 3 nations had done so, and NPT entered into force on Dec. 5, 1994.

Jan. 3, 1993—START II signed in Moscow by U.S. and Russia, called for both sides to reduce their long-range nuclear arsenals to about one-third of their then-current levels within a decade and disable and dismantle launching systems. The U.S. ratified START II Jan. 26, 1996; Russia ratified it Apr. 13, 2000. On Sept. 26, 1997, the U.S. and Russia signed an agreement that would delay the dismantling of launching systems under START II to the end of 2007.

Sept. 24, 1996—Comprehensive Test Ban Treaty (CTBT) signed by U.S. and Russia. The CTBT banned all nuclear weapon tests and other nuclear explosions. It was intended to help prevent the nuclear powers from developing more advanced weapons, while limiting the ability of other states to acquire such devices. As of July 2004, the CTBT had been signed by 172 nations, including China, Russia, the U.S., the U.K, and France; ratified by 117, including France, Russia, and the U.K., but not the U.S. or China. Enters into force after 44 nuclear-capable states ratify it. As of Sept. 25, 2004, 32 of the 44 had done so.

Sept. 1997—ABM Treaty amended to allow greater flexibility in development of shorter-range nuclear weapons.

May 24, 2002—Nuclear Arms Reduction Pact (Treaty of Moscow) signed by U.S. and Russia in Moscow, committed both countries to cutting nuclear arsenals to 1,700 to 2,200 warheads each, down from about 6,000, by 2012. No intermediate timetable established, but joint committee set up for monitoring implementation; either side allowed to back out with 90 days notice. Ratified by U.S. Senate, Mar. 6, 2003.

June 2002—U.S. formally withdrew from the **ABM Treaty**, effective June 13, with the intent of developing a defensive missile system. Russia, June 14, announced its withdrawal from **START II**, stating that U.S. withdrawal from the ABM Treaty effectively invalidated START II.

Monthly Military Pay Scale[1]

Source: U.S. Dept. of Defense; effective Jan. 1, 2005

Years of Service:	<2	2	3	4	6	8	10	12	14	16	18	20	22	24	26
Grade							**Commissioned officers**								
O-10 . . .	NA	NA	NA	NA	NA	NA	NA	NA	NA	NA	NA	$12,963	$13,027	$13,298	$13,769
O-9	NA	NA	NA	NA	NA	NA	NA	NA	NA	NA	NA	11,338	11,501	11,737	12,149
O-8	$8,022	$8,285	$8,459	$8,508	$8,726	$9,089	$9,174	$9,519	$9,618	$9,915	$10,346	10,742	11,008	11,008	11,008
O-7	6,666	6,976	7,119	7,233	7,439	7,643	7,878	8,114	8,349	9,089	9,715	9,715	9,715	9,715	9,764
O-6	4,941	5,428	5,784	5,784	5,806	6,055	6,088	6,088	6,434	7,046	7,405	7,763	7,968	8,174	8,576
O-5	4,119	4,640	4,961	5,021	5,222	5,342	5,606	5,799	6,049	6,431	6,613	6,793	6,998	6,998	6,998
O-4	3,554	4,114	4,388	4,450	4,704	4,978	5,318	5,583	5,767	5,872	5,934	5,934	5,934	5,934	5,934
O-3	3,125	3,542	3,823	4,168	4,368	4,587	4,729	4,962	5,083	5,083	5,083	5,083	5,083	5,083	5,083
O-2	2,699	3,075	3,541	3,661	3,736	3,736	3,736	3,736	3,736	3,736	3,736	3,736	3,736	3,736	3,736
O-1	2,344	2,439	2,948	2,948	2,948	2,948	2,948	2,948	2,948	2,948	2,948	2,948	2,948	2,948	2,948
Commissioned officers with over 4 years' active duty service as enlisted member or warrant officer															
O-3E . . .	NA	NA	NA	4,168	4,368	4,587	4,729	4,962	5,159	5,271	5,425	5,425	5,425	5,425	5,425
O-2E . . .	NA	NA	NA	3,661	3,736	3,855	4,056	4,211	4,327	4,327	4,327	4,327	4,327	4,327	4,327
O-1E . . .	NA	NA	NA	2,948	3,149	3,265	3,384	3,501	3,661	3,661	3,661	3,661	3,661	3,661	3,661
Warrant officers															
W-5. . . .	NA	NA	NA	NA	NA	NA	NA	NA	NA	NA	NA	5,548	5,738	5,929	6,121
W-4. . . .	3,229	3,473	3,573	3,671	3,840	4,007	4,176	4,341	4,512	4,779	4,950	5,117	5,291	5,462	5,636
W-3. . . .	2,948	3,072	3,197	3,239	3,371	3,522	3,722	3,919	4,128	4,286	4,442	4,509	4,579	4,730	4,881
W-2. . . .	2,594	2,742	2,871	2,966	3,046	3,268	3,438	3,564	3,687	3,771	3,842	3,977	4,112	4,247	4,247
W-1. . . .	2,290	2,478	2,603	2,684	2,900	3,031	3,146	3,275	3,361	3,438	3,564	3,660	3,660	3,660	3,660
Enlisted members															
E-9	NA	NA	NA	NA	NA	NA	3,901	3,990	4,101	4,232	4,364	4,576	4,755	4,944	5,232
E-8	NA	NA	NA	NA	NA	3,194	3,335	3,422	3,527	3,641	3,845	3,949	4,126	4,224	4,465
E-7	2,220	2,423	2,516	2,639	2,735	2,900	2,992	3,085	3,250	3,332	3,411	3,459	3,620	3,725	3,990
E-6	1,920	2,113	2,206	2,297	2,391	2,604	2,687	2,779	2,860	2,889	2,908	2,908	2,908	2,908	2,908
E-5	1,760	1,877	1,968	2,061	2,205	2,330	2,422	2,451	2,451	2,451	2,451	2,451	2,451	2,451	2,451
E-4	1,613	1,696	1,787	1,878	1,958	1,958	1,958	1,958	1,958	1,958	1,958	1,958	1,958	1,958	1,958
E-3	1,456	1,548	1,641	1,641	1,641	1,641	1,641	1,641	1,641	1,641	1,641	1,641	1,641	1,641	1,641
E-2	1,385	1,385	1,385	1,385	1,385	1,385	1,385	1,385	1,385	1,385	1,385	1,385	1,385	1,385	1,385
E-1>4 . .	1,235	1,235	1,235	1,235	1,235	1,235	1,235	1,235	1,235	1,235	1,235	1,235	1,235	1,235	1,235
E-1<4 . .	1,143	NA	NA	NA	NA	NA	NA	NA	NA	NA	NA	NA	NA	NA	NA

NA = Not applicable. (1) Basic pay is limited for O-7 to O-10 to $12,133 per month, and for O-6 and below to $10,683 per month. (2) E-1>4 = E-1 grade personnel with 4 or more months service. E-1<4 = E-1 grade personnel with less than 4 months service.

World Almanac Editors' Picks
Top Ten Military Geniuses

The World Almanac staff ranked the following leaders as the top ten military geniuses of all time.

1. Alexander the Great
2. Napoleon
3. Julius Caesar
4. Genghis Khan
5. Robert E. Lee
6. Dwight D. Eisenhower
7. Charlemagne
8. Douglas MacArthur
9. Saladin
10. Attila the Hun

Casualties in Principal Wars of the U.S.

Source: U.S. Dept. of Defense, U.S. Coast Guard

Data prior to World War I are based on incomplete records in many cases. Casualty data are confined to dead and wounded personnel and, therefore, exclude personnel captured or missing in action who were subsequently returned to military control. Dash (—) indicates information is not available. off. = officers.

WAR	Branch of service	Number serving	CASUALTIES Battle deaths	Other deaths	Wounds not mortal[7]	Total[13]
Revolutionary War	**Total**	**—**	**4,435**	**—**	**6,188**	**10,623**
1775-83	Army	184,000	4,044	—	6,004	10,048
	Navy	to	342	—	114	456
	Marines	250,000	49	—	70	119
War of 1812	**Total**	**286,730[8]**	**2,260**	**—**	**4,505**	**6,765**
1812-15	Army	—	1,950	—	4,000	5,950
	Navy	—	265	—	439	704
	Marines	—	45	—	66	111
Mexican War	**Total**	**78,789[8]**	**1,733**	**11,550**	**4,152**	**17,435**
1846-48	Army	—	1,721	11,550	4,102	17,373
	Navy	—	1	—	3	4
	Marines	—	11	—	47	58
	Coast Guard[12]	71 off.	—	—	—	—
Civil War						
Union forces	**Total**	**2,213,363[8]**	**140,415**	**224,097**	**281,881**	**646,392**
1861-65	Army	2,128,948	138,154	221,374	280,040	639,568
	Navy	—	2,112	2,411	1,710	6,233
	Marines	84,415	148	312	131	591
Confederate forces	**Total**	**—**	**74,524**	**59,297**	**—**	**133,821**
(estimate)[1]	Army	600,000	—	—	—	—
1863-66	Navy	to	—	—	—	—
	Marines	1,500,000	—	—	—	—
	Coast Guard[12]	219 off.	1	—	—	1
Spanish-American War	**Total**	**307,420**	**385**	**2,061**	**1,662**	**4,108**
1898	Army[3]	280,564	369	2,061	1,594	4,024
	Navy	22,875	10	0	47	57
	Marines	3,321	6	0	21	27
	Coast Guard[12]	660	0	—	—	—
World War I	**Total**	**4,743,826**	**53,513**	**63,195**	**204,002**	**320,710**
April 6, 1917 - Nov. 11, 1918	Army[4]	4,057,101	50,510	55,868	193,663	300,041
	Navy	599,051	431	6,856	819	8,106
	Marines	78,839	2,461	390	9,520	12,371
	Coast Guard	8,835	111	81	—	192
World War II	**Total**	**16,353,659**	**292,131**	**115,185**	**671,846**	**1,079,162**
Dec. 7, 1941 - Dec. 31, 1946[2]	Army[5]	11,260,000	234,874	83,400	565,861	884,135
	Navy[6]	4,183,466	36,950	25,664	37,778	100,392
	Marines	669,100	19,733	4,778	68,207	91,718
	Coast Guard	241,093	574	1,343	—	1,917
Korean War[9]	**Total**	**5,764,143**	**33,667**	**3,249**	**103,284**	**140,200**
June 25, 1950 - July 27, 1953	Army	2,834,000	27,709	2,452	77,596	107,757
	Navy	1,177,000	493	160	1,576	2,226
	Marines	424,000	4,267	339	23,744	28,353
	Air Force	1,285,000	1,198	298	368	1,864
	Coast Guard	44,143	—	—	—	—
Vietnam War[10]	**Total**	**8,752,000**	**47,393**	**10,800**	**153,363**	**211,556**
Aug. 4, 1964 - Jan. 27, 1973	Army	4,368,000	30,929	7,272	96,802	135,003
	Navy	1,842,000	1,631	931	4,178	6,740
	Marines	794,000	13,085	1,753	51,392	66,230
	Air Force	1,740,000	1,741	842	931	3,514
	Coast Guard	8,000	7	2	60	69
Persian Gulf War	**Total**	**467,939[11]**	**148**	**151**	**467**	**766**
1991	Army	246,682	98	105	—	203
	Navy	98,852	6	14	—	20
	Marines	71,254	24	26	—	50
	Air Force	50,751	20	6	—	26
	Coast Guard	400	—	—	—	—
Iraq War[14]	**Total**	**269,363**	**1,472**	**423**	**14,641**	**16,536**
Mar. 19, 2003-Sept. 17, 2005	Army	99,664	979	304	9,561	10,844
	Navy	61,018	23	13	307	343
	Marines	66,166	461	95	4,585	5,141
	Air Force	42,515	8	11	188	207
	Coast Guard	1,250	1	—	—	1

(1) Authoritative statistics for the Confederate forces are not available. An estimated 26,000-31,000 Confederate personnel died in Union prisons. (2) Data are for Dec. 1, 1941, through Dec. 31, 1946, when hostilities were officially terminated by presidential proclamation; few battle deaths or wounds not mortal were incurred after Japanese acceptance of Allied peace terms on Aug. 14, 1945. Numbers serving Dec. 1, 1941-Aug. 31, 1945, were: Total—14,903,213; Army—10,420,000; Navy—3,883,520; Marine Corps—599,693. (3) Number serving covers the period April 21-Aug. 13, 1898, while dead and wounded data are for the period May 1-Aug. 31, 1898. Active hostilities ceased on Aug. 13, 1898, but ratifications of the treaty of peace were not exchanged between the U.S. and Spain until April 11, 1899. (4) Includes Army Air Forces battle deaths and wounds not mortal, as well as casualties suffered by American forces in northern Russia to Aug. 25, 1919, and in Siberia to April 1, 1920. Other deaths covered the period April 1, 1917-Dec. 31, 1918. (5) Includes Army Air Forces. (6) Battle deaths and wounds not mortal include casualties incurred in Oct. 1941 due to hostile action. (7) Marine Corps data for Iraq War, World War II, the Spanish-American War, and prior wars represent the number of individuals wounded, whereas all other data in this column represent the total number (incidence) of wounds. (8) As reported by Commissioner of Pensions in his Annual Report for Fiscal Year 1903. (9) As a result of an ongoing Dept. of Defense review of available Korean War casualty record information, updates to previously reported figures for battle deaths and other deaths are reflected in this table. (10) Number serving covers the period Aug. 4, 1964-Jan. 27, 1973 (date of ceasefire). Includes casualties incurred in Mayaguez incident. Wounds not mortal exclude 150,332 persons not requiring hospital care. (11) Estimated. (12) Actually the U.S. Revenue Cutter Services, predecessor to the U.S. Coast Guard. (13) Totals do not include categories for which no data are listed. (14) Including deaths from May 1, 2003 (declared end of major combat) through Sept. 4, 2004. Military deaths through Apr. 30, 2003 only totaled 115 combat-related and 23 other. As of Sept. 17, 2005, there were 1,896 total military deaths. **NOTE:** As of Sept. 17, there have been 233 military deaths in Op. Enduring Freedom, mostly in Afghanistan and the Persian Gulf area.

Homeland Security

On Nov. 25, 2002, Pres. George W. Bush signed a measure creating a cabinet-level **Department of Homeland Security (DHS)**. It became operational on Jan. 24, 2003, headed by Sec. Tom Ridge, a former Pennsylvania governor (1995-2001). On Feb. 15, 2005, Michael Chertoff, a federal judge, replaced Ridge becoming the 2nd DHS secretary.

The main **objectives** of the DHS are to prevent terrorist attacks within the U.S., reduce the vulnerability to attacks, and minimize the effects of such attacks should they occur. The DHS is responsible for border and transportation security, protecting critical infrastructure, coordinating emergency response activities, and overseeing research and development for homeland security efforts. The new department also responds to natural disasters.

Following the attacks of Sept. 11, 2001, Pres. Bush created a small-scale advisory office known as the Office of Homeland Security. When a congressional inquiry in the summer of 2002 revealed extensive failures in intelligence gathering and communication, sentiment grew in favor of creating a large agency that could coordinate anti-terrorism efforts. The final plan passed by Congress in Nov. 2002 called for the integration of 22 federal agencies from many different departments.

The DHS is organized into 5 directorates: Border and Transportation Security, Emergency Preparedness, Science and Technology, Information Analysis and Infrastructure Protection, and Management, the administrative arm of the department. The U.S. Coast Guard, Secret Service, and Bureau of Citizenship and Immigration Services (formerly part of the INS) became part of DHS as discrete entities, separate from the directorates. The fiscal year 2006 budget for DHS was $41.1 billion.

Emergency Preparedness

In Feb. 2003, the DHS launched its public service "Ready" campaign in association with the Ad Council and the Sloan Foundation. People are advised to take 3 steps.

1. Make a Kit

Make a home emergency supply kit with at least 3 days' worth of essential provisions for "sheltering-in-place," and assemble a lightweight version in case evacuation is necessary. Kits should include 1 gallon of water per person per day. Provide enough easily prepared canned or dried foods. In colder climates, supply warm clothes and a sleeping bag for each member of the family.

Kits should contain a first-aid kit, flashlight, battery-powered radio, extra batteries, toiletries, and any needed medical prescriptions. They should include a filter mask (available in hardware stores) or other covering to use as a filter when breathing. Duct tape and heavy-duty garbage bags or plastic sheeting should be available in case it is necessary to seal windows and doors.

2. Make a Plan

Form a communication plan, with designated contacts for each family member. Provisions should be made both for staying in place and for evacuating.

Shelter-in-place. Designate in advance an interior room, or one with the fewest windows and doors, for shelter. In an emergency, if there is heavy debris in the air or authorities deem the air contaminated, close windows, doors, vents, and fireplace dampers, and turn off air conditioners, forced-air heating systems, exhaust fans, and clothes dryers. Take family members and emergency supplies to a selected room and seal doors and windows as needed. Follow TV or radio broadcasts, or the Internet, for further instructions.

Evacuation. Create an evacuation plan with a specific meeting place for family members. Keep at least half a tank of gas in the car at all times, and learn alternate driving routes, as well as alternate means of transportation in your area. If the air is contaminated, drive with the windows and vents closed and keep the air conditioning or heater off.

Work and School. Talk to schools and employers about emergency plans and how they will communicate with families in emergencies.

3. Be Informed

What to do depends partly on the nature of the threat.

Biological Threat. If a biological danger is reported, keep in contact with TV, radio, or the Internet for news and advice. If you become aware of a release of an unknown substance nearby, get away and cover your mouth and nose with layers of fabric that can filter the air but still allow breathing. Wash with soap and water, and seek medical attention.

Chemical Threat. In the event of a chemical attack, leave the contaminated area immediately, if you can safely do so. Signs of a chemical attack in the area may include people with symptoms such as watery eyes, twitching, choking, difficulty breathing, or loss of coordination. Listen to news reports. If you believe you may have been exposed to a chemical agent, remove clothes promptly and wash with soap and water. Do not scrub chemical into skin. Be sure to seek medical attention.

Explosions. If there is an explosion, take shelter from the blast under a desk or table. Leave the building or area when feasible; check for fire, and never use elevators.

Nuclear Blast. In case of a nuclear blast, take cover immediately, preferably below ground. Decide whether to shelter-in-place or evacuate; bear in mind that the more shielding and distance between you and the blast, and the less time of exposure, the more you reduce your risk.

For Further Information

FEMA publishes a handbook, *Are You Ready? A Guide to Citizen Preparedness*, which can be obtained electronically at www.fema.gov/areyouready, or in print by calling 1-800-480-2520. You can also visit www.ready.gov or call 1-800-BE-READY.

Security Advisories

The Homeland Security Advisory System, established on Mar. 12, 2002, indicates the estimated threat level for a terrorist attack in the U.S.; state and local authorities may have separate alert systems and criteria.

Low (Green)	Governments should refine and exercise pre-planned protective measures and train personnel, assess and update vulnerabilities, and take steps to reduce them.
Guarded (Blue)	In addition to the above, authorities should check communications with emergency response and command locations, review emergency response procedures, and provide public information as needed.
Elevated (Yellow)	Authorities should also increase surveillance of critical locations, coordinate emergency plans with nearby jurisdictions, implement response plans as appropriate.
High (Orange)	Authorities should coordinate with federal, state, and local law enforcement agencies, or National Guard or other armed service; take additional precautions at public events, including possible cancellation; prepare to execute contingency procedures and move to alternate locations; restrict access to threatened facilities.
Severe (Red)	Authorities should increase or redirect personnel to address critical emergency needs; assign or pre-position emergency response and specialty teams; monitor, redirect, or limit access to transportation systems; close public and government facilities.

As of Oct. 2005, the national threat level had reached "high" 6 times: Sept. 10–24, 2002, around the anniversary of Sept. 11; Feb. 7–27, 2003, based on threats of attacks during the Haj pilgrimage in Mecca; Mar. 17–Apr. 16, 2003, during the beginning of the Iraq War; and May 20–30, following bombings in Saudi Arabia and Morocco, and as a precaution for Memorial Day; Dec. 21, 2003–Jan. 15, 2004, based on threats specific to the holiday season; Aug. 1–Nov. 10, 2004, covering only specific financial targets in New York City, NY, northern NJ, and Washington, DC. As of Sept. 30, 2005, the nation was on "elevated" alert. New York City remained at "high" alert, as it had been since the system was established.

ECONOMICS

Consumer Price Index

The Consumer Price Index (CPI) is a measure of the change in prices over time of one or more kinds of basic consumer goods and services.

From Jan. 1978, the Bureau of Labor Statistics began publishing CPIs for 2 population groups: (1) a CPI for all urban consumers (CPI-U), which covers about 87% of the total population; and (2) a CPI for urban wage earners and clerical workers (CPI-W), which covers about 32% of the total population. The CPI-U includes, in addition to wage earners and clerical workers, groups such as professional, managerial, and technical workers, the self-employed, short-term workers, the unemployed, retirees, and others not in the labor force.

The CPI is based on prices of food, clothing, shelter, and fuels; transportation fares; charges for doctors' and dentists' services; drug prices; and prices of other goods and services bought for day-to-day living. The index currently measures price changes from a designated reference period, 1982-84, which equals 100.0. Use of this reference period began in Jan. 1988.

U.S. Consumer Price Indexes, 2004-2005

Source: Bureau of Labor Statistics, U.S. Dept. of Labor

(Data are semiannual averages of monthly figures. For all urban consumers; **1982-84 = 100**; unless otherwise noted; % change not annualized)

	1st half 2004	% change 2nd half 2003 to 1st half 2004	2nd half 2004	% change 1st half 2004 to 2nd half 2004	1st half 2005	% change 2nd half 2004 to 1st half 2005
ALL ITEMS	**187.6**	**1.6**	**190.2**	**1.4**	**193.2**	**1.6**
Food, beverages	185.3	1.8	187.9	1.4	190.2	1.2
Housing	188.1	1.3	190.9	1.5	193.8	1.5
Apparel	121.0	0.5	119.9	–0.9	120.5	0.5
Transportation	161.5	2.9	164.7	2.0	169.3	2.8
Medical care	307.4	2.6	312.9	1.8	320.6	2.5
Recreation[1]	108.6	0.8	108.6	0.0	109.1	0.5
Education and communication[1]	111.0	0.5	112.2	1.1	112.8	0.5
Other goods, services	303.1	1.1	306.4	1.1	311.3	1.6
Services	221.1	1.4	224.5	1.5	227.9	1.5
SPECIAL INDEXES						
All items less food	188.1	1.6	190.6	1.3	193.8	1.7
Commodities less food	138.1	1.9	139.5	1.0	142.2	1.9
Nondurables	170.7	3.0	173.6	1.7	176.9	1.9
Energy	146.8	6.9	156.0	6.3	163.3	4.7
All items less energy	193.5	1.2	195.4	1.0	198.0	1.3

(1) Dec. 1997 = 100.

U.S. Consumer Price Indexes (CPI-U),[1] Annual Percent Change, 1990-2004

Source: Bureau of Labor Statistics, U.S. Dept. of Labor

	1990	1991	1992	1993	1994	1995	1996	1997	1999	2000	2001	2002	2003	2004
ALL ITEMS	**5.4**	**4.2**	**3.0**	**3.0**	**2.6**	**2.8**	**3.0**	**2.3**	**2.2**	**3.4**	**2.8**	**1.6**	**2.3**	**2.7**
Food	5.8	2.9	1.2	2.2	2.4	2.8	3.3	2.6	2.1	2.3	3.2	1.8	2.2	3.4
Shelter	5.4	4.5	3.3	3.0	3.1	3.2	3.2	3.1	2.9	3.3	3.7	3.7	2.4	2.7
Rent, residential	5.6	6.1	2.5	2.3	2.5	2.5	2.7	2.9	3.1	3.6	4.5	4.0	2.9	2.7
Fuel and other utilities	3.5	3.3	2.2	3.0	1.0	0.7	3.1	2.6	0.2	7.1	8.9	–4.4	7.6	4.8
Apparel and upkeep	4.6	3.7	2.5	1.4	–0.2	–1.0	–0.2	0.9	–1.3	–1.3	–1.8	–2.6	–2.5	–0.4
Private transportation	5.2	2.6	2.2	2.3	3.1	3.7	2.7	0.7	1.9	6.1	0.6	–0.8	3.2	3.8
New cars	1.8	3.8	2.5	2.4	3.4	2.2	1.7	0.2	–0.3	–0.1	–0.5	–1.2	–1.5	–0.6
Gasoline	14.1	–1.8	–0.2	–1.3	0.5	1.6	6.1	–0.1	9.3	28.5	–3.6	–6.5	16.5	18.2
Public transportation	10.1	4.4	1.7	10.3	3.0	2.3	3.4	2.6	3.9	6.0	0.5	–1.5	0.9	–0.1
Medical care	9.0	8.7	7.4	5.9	4.8	4.5	3.5	2.8	3.5	4.1	4.6	4.7	4.0	4.4
Entertainment, Recreation[2,3]	4.7	4.5	2.8	2.5	2.9	2.5	3.4	2.1	0.9	1.3	1.5	1.2	1.2	1.0
Education[3]	—	—	—	—	6.3	5.6	5.3	5.0	4.8	5.1	5.3	6.3	1.8	6.9
Commodities	5.2	4.2	2.0	1.9	1.7	1.9	2.6	1.4	1.8	3.3	1.0	–0.7	1.0	2.3

(1) The Consumer Price Index CPI-U measures average change in prices of goods and services purchased by all urban consumers. 1982-1984 = 100 unless otherwise noted. (2) The Bureau of Labor Statistics reclassified Entertainment as Recreation in 1997. (3) Dec. 1997 = 100.

Consumer Price Index, 1915-2005

Source: Bureau of Labor Statistics, U.S. Dept. of Labor

(1967 = 100. Annual averages of monthly figures, specified for all urban consumers.)

Prices as measured by the U.S. Consumer Price Index have risen steadily since World War II. What cost $1.00 in 1967 cost about 30 cents in 1915, 54 cents in 1945, and $5.79 by the first half of 2005.

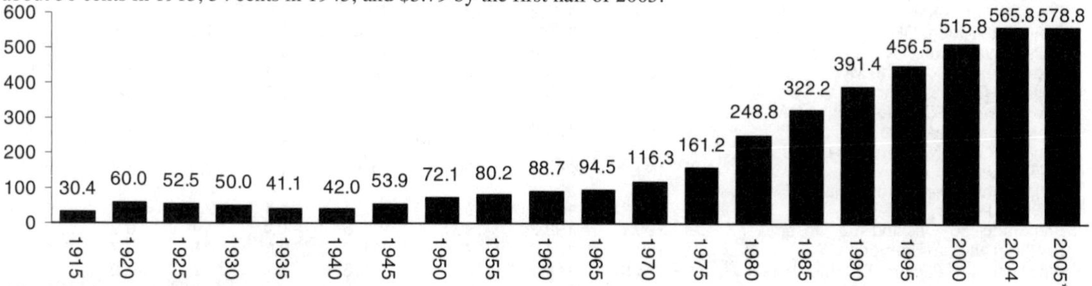

*Average for 1st half 2005.

U.S. Consumer Price Indexes for Selected Items and Groups, 1970-2004

Source: Bureau of Labor Statistics, U.S. Dept. of Labor

(**1982-84 = 100**, unless otherwise noted. Annual averages of monthly figures. For all urban consumers.)

	1970	1975	1980	1985	1990	1995	1999	2000	2001	2002	2003	2004
ALL ITEMS	**38.8**	**53.8**	**82.4**	**107.6**	**130.7**	**152.4**	**166.6**	**172.2**	**177.1**	**179.9**	**184.0**	**188.9**
Food and beverages	**40.1**	**60.2**	**86.7**	**105.6**	**132.1**	**148.9**	**164.6**	**168.4**	**173.6**	**176.8**	**180.5**	**186.6**
Food	39.2	59.8	86.8	105.6	132.4	148.4	164.1	167.8	173.1	176.2	180.0	186.2
Food at home	39.9	61.8	88.4	104.3	132.3	148.8	164.2	167.9	173.4	175.6	179.4	186.2
Cereals and bakery products	37.1	62.9	83.9	107.9	140.0	167.5	185.0	188.3	193.8	198.0	202.8	206.0
Meats, poultry, fish, and eggs	44.6	67.0	92.0	100.1	130.0	138.8	147.9	154.5	161.3	162.1	169.3	181.7
Dairy products	44.7	62.6	90.9	103.2	126.5	132.8	159.6	160.7	167.1	168.1	167.9	180.2
Fruits and vegetables	37.8	56.9	82.1	106.4	149.0	177.7	203.1	204.6	212.2	220.9	225.9	232.7
Sugar and sweets	30.5	65.3	90.5	105.8	124.7	137.5	152.3	154.0	155.7	159.0	162.0	163.2
Fats and oils	39.2	73.5	89.3	106.9	126.3	137.3	148.3	147.4	155.7	155.4	157.4	167.8
Nonalcoholic beverages	27.1	41.3	91.4	104.3	113.5	131.7	134.3	137.8	139.2	139.2	139.8	140.4
Other foods	39.6	58.9	83.6	106.4	131.2	151.1	168.9	172.2	176.0	177.1	178.8	179.7
Food away from home	37.5	54.5	83.4	108.3	133.4	149.0	165.1	169.0	173.9	178.3	182.1	187.5
Alcoholic beverages	52.1	65.9	86.4	106.4	129.3	153.9	169.7	174.7	179.3	183.6	187.2	192.1
Housing	**36.4**	**50.7**	**81.1**	**107.7**	**128.5**	**148.5**	**163.9**	**169.6**	**176.4**	**180.3**	**184.8**	**189.5**
Shelter	35.5	48.8	81.0	109.8	140.0	165.7	187.3	193.4	200.6	208.1	213.1	218.8
Rent of primary residence	46.5	58.0	80.9	111.8	138.4	157.8	177.5	183.9	192.1	199.7	205.5	211.0
Fuel and other utilities	29.1	45.4	75.4	106.5	111.6	123.7	128.8	137.9	150.2	143.6	154.5	161.9
Gas (piped) and electricity	25.4	40.1	71.4	107.1	109.3	119.2	120.9	128.0	142.4	134.4	145.0	150.6
Household furnishings & operations	46.8	63.4	86.3	103.8	113.3	123.0	126.7	128.2	129.1	128.3	126.1	125.5
Apparel	**59.2**	**72.5**	**90.9**	**105.0**	**124.1**	**132.0**	**131.3**	**129.6**	**127.3**	**124.0**	**120.9**	**120.4**
Men's and boys'	62.2	75.5	89.4	105.0	120.4	126.2	131.1	129.7	125.7	121.7	118.0	117.5
Women's and girls'	71.8	85.5	96.0	104.9	122.6	126.9	123.3	121.5	119.3	115.8	113.1	113.0
Footwear	56.8	69.6	91.8	102.3	117.4	125.4	125.7	123.8	123.0	121.4	119.6	119.3
Transportation	**37.5**	**50.1**	**83.1**	**106.4**	**120.5**	**139.1**	**144.4**	**153.3**	**154.3**	**152.9**	**157.6**	**163.1**
Private	37.5	50.6	84.2	106.2	118.8	136.3	140.5	149.1	150.0	148.8	153.6	159.4
New vehicles	53.0	62.9	88.4	106.1	121.4	139.0	142.9	142.8	142.1	140.0	137.9	137.1
Used cars and trucks	31.2	43.8	62.3	113.7	117.6	156.5	152.0	155.8	158.7	152.0	142.9	133.3
Gasoline	27.9	45.1	97.5	98.6	101.0	99.8	100.1	128.6	124.0	116.0	135.1	159.7
Public	35.2	43.5	69.0	110.5	142.6	175.9	197.7	209.6	210.6	207.4	209.3	209.1
Medical care	**34.0**	**47.5**	**74.9**	**113.5**	**162.8**	**220.5**	**250.6**	**260.8**	**272.8**	**285.6**	**297.1**	**310.1**
Entertainment/Recreation[1]	**47.5**	**62.0**	**83.6**	**107.9**	**132.4**	**153.9**	**102.0**	**103.3**	**104.9**	**106.2**	**107.5**	**108.6**
Other goods and services	**40.9**	**53.9**	**75.2**	**114.5**	**159.0**	**206.9**	**258.3**	**271.1**	**282.6**	**293.2**	**298.7**	**304.7**
Tobacco products	43.1	54.7	72.0	116.7	181.5	225.7	355.8	394.9	425.2	461.5	469.0	478.0
Personal care	43.5	57.9	81.9	106.3	130.4	147.1	161.1	165.6	170.5	154.7	153.5	181.7
Personal care products	42.7	58.0	79.6	107.6	128.2	143.1	151.8	153.7	155.1	174.7	178.0	153.9
Personal care services	44.2	57.7	83.7	108.9	132.8	151.5	171.4	178.1	184.3	188.4	193.2	197.6

(1) Dec. 1997 = 100; Entertainment was reclassified as Recreation in 1997.

Consumer Price Indexes by Region and Selected Cities, 2003-2005[1]

Source: Bureau of Labor Statistics, U.S. Dept. of Labor

(**1982-84 = 100**, unless otherwise noted; % change not annualized)

	Semiannual averages				Percent change from preceding semiannual average			
	2nd half 2003	1st half 2004	2nd half 2004	1st half 2005	2nd half 2003	1st half 2004	2nd half 2004	1st half 2005
U.S. CITY AVERAGE	**184.6**	**187.6**	**190.2**	**193.2**	**0.7**	**1.6**	**1.4**	**1.6**
Northeast urban	**194.7**	**198.6**	**201.7**	**205.3**	**1.3**	**2.0**	**1.6**	**1.8**
Size A—More than 1,500,000	196.9	200.7	203.8	207.7	1.5	1.9	1.5	1.9
Size B/C—50,000 to 1,500,000[2]	114.9	117.5	119.5	121.0	0.7	2.3	1.7	1.3
Midwest urban	**178.8**	**118.4**	**183.9**	**186.4**	**0.6**	**1.5**	**1.4**	**1.4**
Size A—More than 1,500,000	181.3	183.6	186.1	188.4	0.8	1.3	1.4	1.2
Size B/C—50,000 to 1,500,000[2]	113.5	115.5	117.0	118.8	0.4	1.8	1.3	1.5
Size D—Nonmetro. (less than 50,000)	171.8	174.3	177.0	180.5	–0.1	1.5	1.5	2.0
South urban	**177.8**	**180.5**	**183.1**	**186.1**	**0.6**	**1.5**	**1.4**	**1.6**
Size A—More than 1,500,000	179.6	182.1	184.4	188.0	0.7	1.4	1.3	2.0
Size B/C—50,000 to 1,500,000[2]	113.4	115.3	117.1	118.6	0.5	1.7	1.6	1.3
Size D—Nonmetro. (less than 50,000)	175.6	178.1	181.4	185.1	0.5	1.4	1.9	2.0
West urban	**188.9**	**191.9**	**194.0**	**197.1**	**0.4**	**1.6**	**1.1**	**1.6**
Size A—More than 1,500,000	191.4	194.3	196.5	199.7	0.2	1.5	1.1	1.6
Size B/C—50,000 to 1,500,000[2]	115.3	117.5	118.7	120.6	0.6	1.9	1.0	1.6
SELECTED AREAS								
Atlanta, GA	180.5	182.4	183.9	187.1	–0.3	1.1	0.8	1.7
Boston–Brockton–Nashua, MA–NH–ME–CT	205.9	208.6	210.3	213.9	2.0	1.3	0.8	1.7
Chicago–Gary–Kenosha, IL–IN–WI	185.3	187.2	190.1	192.0	0.8	1.0	1.5	1.0
Cleveland–Akron, OH	177.6	180.2	183.0	185.8	1.5	1.5	1.6	1.5
Dallas–Fort Worth, TX	176.4	177.8	179.6	182.0	0.2	0.8	1.0	1.3
Detroit–Ann Arbor–Flint, MI	182.9	184.2	186.6	188.7	0.4	0.7	1.3	1.1
Houston–Galveston–Brazoria, TX	164.6	168.7	170.2	174.3	1.1	2.5	0.9	2.4
L.A.–Riverside–Orange County, CA	187.2	191.5	194.9	199.2	0.3	2.3	1.8	2.2
Miami–Fort Lauderdale, FL	181.2	184.5	186.6	191.8	0.7	1.8	1.1	2.8
New York, NY–Northern NJ–Long Island, NY–NJ–CT–PA	199.2	203.1	206.4	210.7	1.4	2.0	1.6	2.1
Philadelphia–Wilmington–Atlantic City, PA–DE–NJ–MD	190.2	194.0	199.0	202.1	1.4	2.0	2.6	1.6
San Francisco–Oakland–San Jose, CA	196.1	198.2	199.5	201.5	–0.4	1.1	0.7	1.0
Seattle–Tacoma–Bremerton, WA	193.1	194.0	195.4	199.2	0.8	0.5	0.7	1.9
Washington–Baltimore, DC–MD–VA–WV[3]	116.9	118.3	120.7	122.8	1.1	1.2	2.0	1.7

(1) For all urban consumers. (2) Dec. 1996 = 100. (3) Nov. 1996 = 100.

Index of Leading Economic Indicators

Source: The Conference Board

The index of leading economic indicators is used to project the U.S. economy's performance. The index is made up of 10 measurements of economic activity that tend to change direction in advance of the overall economy. The index has predicted economic downturns from 8 to 20 months in advance and recoveries from 1 to 10 months in advance; however, it can be inconsistent, and has occasionally shown "false signals" of recessions.

Components

Average weekly hours of production workers in manufacturing
Average weekly initial claims for unemployment insurance, state programs
Manufacturers' new orders for consumer goods and materials, adjusted for inflation
Vendor performance (slower deliveries diffusion index)
Manufacturers' new orders, nondefense capital goods industries, adjusted for inflation
New private housing units authorized by local building permits
Stock prices, 500 common stocks
Money supply: M-2, adjusted for inflation
Interest rate spread, 10-yr Treasury bonds less federal funds
Consumer expectations (researched by Univ. of Michigan)

U.S. Gross Domestic Product, Gross National Product, Net National Product, National Income, and Personal Income

Source: Bureau of Economic Analysis, U.S. Dept. of Commerce

(billions of current dollars; revised)

	1960	1970	1980	1990	2000	2002	2003	2004
Gross domestic product	**526.4**	**1,038.5**	**2,789.5**	**5,803.1**	**9,817.0**	**10,487.0**	**10,971.2**	**11,734.3**
Gross national product	**529.5**	**1,044.9**	**2,823.7**	**5,837.9**	**9,855.9**	**10,514.1**	**11,039.3**	**11,788.0**
Less: Consumption of fixed capital	55.6	106.7	343.0	682.5	1,187.8	1,303.9	1,331.3	1,435.3
Net national product	**473.9**	**938.2**	**2,480.7**	**5,155.4**	**8,668.1**	**9,210.1**	**9,708.0**	**10,352.8**
Less: Statistical discrepancy	−0.9	7.3	41.4	66.2	−127.2	−15.3	47.0	76.8
Equals: National income	**474.9**	**930.9**	**2,439.3**	**5,089.1**	**8,795.2**	**9,225.4**	**9,660.1**	**10,275.9**
Less: Corporate profits with inventory valuation and capital consumption adjustments	53.8	83.6	201.1	437.8	817.9	874.6	1,031.8	1,161.5
Taxes on production and imports less subsidies	43.4	86.7	190.9	398.7	664.6	724.4	754.8	809.4
Contributions for government social insurance	16.4	46.4	166.2	410.1	702.7	748.3	776.6	822.2
Net interest and miscellaneous payments on assets	10.6	39.1	181.8	442.2	559.0	532.9	528.5	505.5
Business current transfer payments (net)	1.9	4.5	14.4	39.4	87.1	80.9	81.6	91.1
Current surplus of government enterprises	0.9	0.0	−4.8	1.6	5.3	2.8	1.3	−3.0
Wage accruals less disbursements	0.0	0.0	0.0	0.1	0.0	0.0	0.0	0.0
Plus: Personal income receipts on assets	37.9	93.5	338.7	924.0	1,387.0	1,334.6	1,338.7	1,396.5
Personal current transfer receipts	25.7	74.7	279.5	595.2	1,084.0	1,282.7	1,344.0	1,427.5
Equals: Personal income	**411.5**	**838.8**	**2,307.9**	**4,878.6**	**8,429.7**	**8,878.9**	**9,169.1**	**9,713.3**

U.S. Gross Domestic Product

Source: Bureau of Economic Analysis, U.S. Dept. of Commerce

(billions of current dollars)

	1994	2004	2nd quarter 2005[1]
Gross domestic product	**7,072.2**	**11,734.3**	**12,373.1**
Personal consumption expenditures	**4,743.3**	**8,214.3**	**8,667.7**
Durable goods	582.2	987.8	1,035.0
Nondurable goods	1,437.2	2,368.3	2,532.8
Services	2,723	4,858.2	5,099.9
Gross private domestic investment	**1,097.1**	**1,928.1**	**2,054.2**
Fixed investment	1,033.3	1,872.6	2,053.7
Nonresidential	731.4	1,198.8	1,312.9
Structures	186.8	298.4	325.7
Equipment and software	544.6	900.4	987.3
Residential	301.9	673.8	740.8
Change in private inventories	63.8	55.4	0.5

(1) Seasonally adjusted at annual rates.

	1994	2004	2nd quarter 2005[1]
Net exports of goods and services	**−93.6**	**−624.0**	**−687.0**
Exports	720.9	1,173.8	1,304.2
Goods	510.1	818.1	904.4
Services	210.8	355.7	399.8
Imports	814.5	1,797.8	1,991.2
Goods	676.8	1,495.9	1,661.8
Services	137.7	301.9	329.5
Government consumption expenditures and gross investment	**1,325.5**	**2,215.9**	**2,338.2**
Federal	519.1	827.6	868.2
National defense	353.7	552.7	580.7
Nondefense	165.5	274.9	287.4
State and local	806.3	1,388.3	1,470.1

U.S. Gross Domestic Product, 1930-2004

Source: Bureau of Economic Analysis, U.S. Dept. of Commerce

(billions of 2000 dollars)

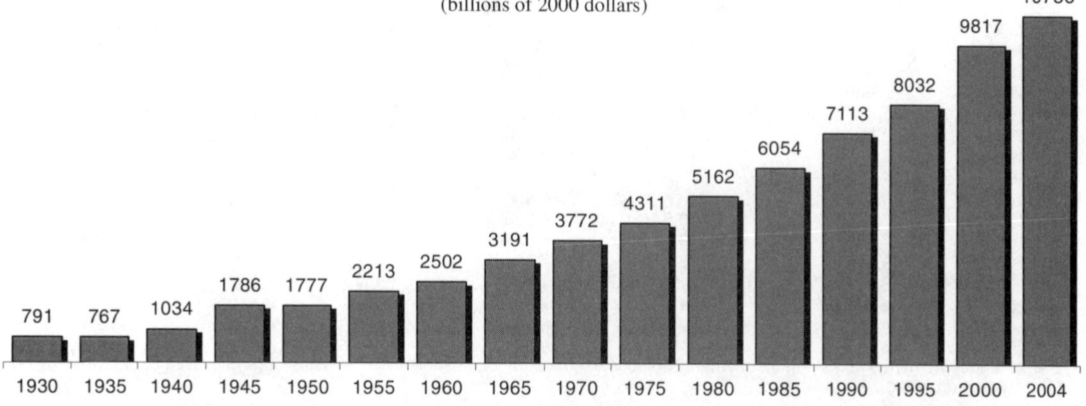

U.S. National Income by Industry[1]

Source: Bureau of Economic Analysis, U.S. Dept. of Commerce; in billions of current dollars; revised

	1998	1999	2000	2001	2002	2003	2004
National income without capital consumption adjustment	**7,661.4**	**8,122.9**	**8,687.4**	**8,854.9**	**9,011.8**	**9,444.8**	**10,020.7**
Domestic industries	**7,640.1**	**8,089.2**	**8,648.5**	**8,811.2**	**8,984.7**	**9,376.7**	**9,966.9**
Private industries	**6,724.6**	**7,134.9**	**7,642.8**	**7,758.4**	**7,861.6**	**8,179.7**	**8,711.5**
Agriculture, forestry, fishing, and hunting	78.5	73.6	70.1	69.3	66.9	80.0	96.9
Mining	72.6	69.3	93.8	101	79.1	103.1	124.1
Utilities	138.6	142.6	144.3	149.2	146	151.1	157.0
Construction	366.6	408.7	440.6	463.3	460.8	483.4	529.8
Manufacturing	1,112.1	1,150.3	1,228.5	1,094.1	1,074.8	1,113.4	1,190.2
Durable goods	672.5	695	744	617.8	615	642.7	690.2
Nondurable goods	439.5	455.3	484.5	476.2	459.8	490.7	500.0
Wholesale trade	505.4	537.1	563.8	557.7	554.2	577.6	618.4
Retail trade	591.1	626.8	665.3	689	708.2	738.9	772.5
Transportation and warehousing	235.3	247.4	261.2	251.9	248.5	261.6	279.8
Information	273.7	302.8	308.3	305.6	306.6	310.2	338.6
Finance, insurance, real estate, rental, leasing	1,328.5	1,396.3	1,529.3	1,643.7	1,672.3	1,674.6	1,766.7
Professional and business services	975.1	1072.2	1,151.6	1,171.3	1,205.2	1,249.4	1,334.8
Educ. services, health care, social assistance	582.7	,615.8	664.6	719.2	774.9	824.4	877.7
Arts, entert., recreation, accommodation, food service	267.9	289.1	310.5	316.8	328.7	344.6	365.5
Other services, except government	196.6	202.9	215.8	226.2	235.4	247.3	259.6
Government	**915.5**	**954.3**	**1,005.7**	**1,052.8**	**1,123.2**	**1,197.0**	**1,255.4**
Rest of the world	**21.3**	**33.8**	**38.9**	**43.6**	**27.0**	**68.1**	**53.8**

(1) Figures may not add because of rounding. Total national income also includes income from outside the U.S.

U.S. National Income by Type of Income[1]

Source: Bureau of Economic Analysis, U.S. Dept. of Commerce; in billions of current dollars; revised

	1960	1970	1980	1990	2000	2002	2003	2004
National income[2]	**474.9**	**930.9**	**2,439.3**	**5,089.1**	**8,795.2**	**9,225.4**	**9,679.6**	**10,275.9**
Compensation of employees	**296.4**	**617.2**	**1,651.8**	**3,338.2**	**5,782.7**	**6,069.5**	**6289.0**	**6,687.6**
Wage and salary accruals	272.9	551.6	1,377.6	2754	4,829.2	4,976.3	5,103.6	5,389.4
Government	49.2	117.2	261.5	517.7	774.7	862.6	897.9	939.5
Supplements to wages and salaries	23.6	65.7	274.2	584.2	953.4	1,093.2	1,185.5	1,298.1
Employer contributions for employee pension and insurance funds	14.3	41.8	185.2	377.8	609.9	729.6	808.9	895.5
Employer contributions for government social insurance	9.3	23.8	88.9	206.5	343.5	363.6	376.6	402.7
Proprietors' income with inventory valuation and capital consumption adjustments	**50.8**	**78.4**	**174.1**	**380.6**	**728.4**	**769.6**	**834.1**	**889.6**
Farm	10.5	12.7	11.3	31.9	22.7	9.7	21.8	35.8
Nonfarm	40.3	65.7	162.8	348.7	705.7	759.9	812.3	853.8
Rental income of persons with capital consumption adjustments	17.1	21.4	30.0	50.7	150.3	170.9	153.8	134.2
Corporate profits with inventory valuation and capital consumption adjustment	**53.8**	**83.6**	**201.1**	**437.8**	**817.9**	**874.6**	**1,021.1**	**1,161.5**
Taxes on corporate income	22.8	34.8	87.2	145.4	265.2	183.8	234.9	271.1
Profits after tax with inventory valuation and capital consumption adjustments	31.0	48.9	113.9	292.4	552.7	690.7	786.2	890.3
Net dividends	13.4	24.3	64.1	169.1	377.9	390.0	395.3	493.0
Undistributed profits with inventory valuation and capital consumption adjustments	17.6	24.6	49.9	123.3	174.8	300.7	390.9	397.3
Net interest and miscellaneous payments	**10.6**	**39.1**	**181.8**	**442.2**	**559**	**532.9**	**543.0**	**505.5**

(1) Figures do not add, because of rounding and incomplete enumeration. (2) National income is the aggregate of labor and property earnings that arises in the production of goods and services. It is the sum of employee compensation, proprietors' income, rental income, adjusted corporate profits, and net interest. It measures the total factor costs of goods and services produced by the economy. Income is measured before deduction of taxes. Total national income figures include adjustments not itemized.

Distribution of U.S. Total Personal Income[1]

Source: Bureau of Economic Analysis, U.S. Dept. of Commerce; in billions of current dollars

Year	Personal income	Personal taxes and nontax payments	Disposable personal income	Personal outlays	Personal Savings: Amount	Personal Savings: As pct. of disposable income
1960	$411.5	$46.1	$365.4	$338.8	$26.7	7.3%
1965	555.7	57.7	498.1	455.1	43.0	8.6
1970	838.8	103.1	735.7	666.2	69.5	9.4
1975	1,335.0	147.6	1,187.4	1,061.9	125.6	10.6
1980	2,307.9	298.9	2,009.0	1,807.5	201.4	10.0
1985	3,526.7	417.4	3,109.3	2,829.3	280.0	9.0
1990	4,878.6	592.8	4,285.8	3,986.4	299.4	7.0
1995	6,152.3	744.1	5,408.2	5,157.3	250.9	4.6
1998	7,391.0	1,070.9	6,320.0	6,054.7	265.4	4.2
1999	7,773.3	1,159.2	6,618.0	6,457.2	160.9	2.4
2000	8,429.7	1,235.7	7,194.0	7,025.6	168.5	2.3
2001	8,724.1	1,237.3	7,486.8	7,354.5	132.3	1.8
2002	8,878.9	1,051.2	7,827.7	7,668.5	159.2	2.0
2003	9,169.1	999.9	8,169.2	7,996.3	172.8	2.1
2004	9,713.3	1,049.1	8,664.2	8,512.5	151.8	1.8

(1) Personal income minus taxes/nontax payments=disposable income; disposable income minus outlays=savings. Figures may not add because of rounding.

Selected Personal Consumption Expenditures in the U.S., 1998-2004[1]

Source: Bureau of Economic Analysis, U.S. Dept. of Commerce
(billions of dollars)

	1998	1999	2000	2001	2002	2003	2004
Personal consumption expenditures	**5,879.5**	**6,282.5**	**6,739.4**	**7,055.0**	**7,376.1**	**7,709.9**	**8,214.3**
Durable goods	**750.2**	**817.6**	**863.3**	**883.7**	**916.2**	**950.1**	**987.8**
Motor vehicles and parts	336.1	370.8	386.5	407.9	426.1	439.1	441.8
New autos	87.7	97.5	103.6	103.2	101.6	98.0	97.5
Tires, tubes, accessories, and other parts	43.9	47.0	49.0	49.1	50.7	51.8	54.3
Furniture and household equipment	273.1	293.9	312.9	312.1	319.9	330.3	354.1
Furniture, including mattresses and bedsprings	59.6	63.5	67.6	67.2	68.3	70.0	75.5
Kitchen and other household appliances	27.5	29.2	30.4	30.8	31.5	32.8	35.3
China, glassware, tableware, and utensils	27.2	29.3	31.0	31.0	31.8	33.2	35.3
Video and audio goods, including musical instruments	62.7	67.8	72.8	73.6	74.9	75.8	79.8
Computers, peripherals, and software	37.0	40.4	43.8	42.0	44.2	46.5	51.0
Ophthalmic products and orthopedic appliances	20.0	20.8	22.1	20.8	21.6	22.1	22.9
Wheel goods, sports and photographic equipment, boats, and pleasure aircraft	48.3	52.6	57.6	59.2	60.6	65.7	70.4
Jewelry and watches	43.9	48.1	50.6	49.2	51.0	53.9	57.2
Books and maps	28.8	31.5	33.7	34.6	36.9	39.0	41.4
Nondurable goods	**1,683.6**	**1,804.8**	**1,947.2**	**2,017.1**	**2,080.1**	**2,189.0**	**2,368.3**
Food	829.8	873.1	925.2	967.9	1,005.8	1048.5	1134.7
Food purchased for off-premise consumption	509.0	536.9	566.7	595.2	615.6	638.4	688.4
Purchased meals and beverages	311.9	326.9	348.8	362.8	380.0	399.1	434.9
Food furnished to employees (including military) and food produced and consumed on farms	9.0	9.3	9.7	9.9	10.2	11.0	11.4
Alcoholic beverages purchased for off-premise consumption	63.2	66.1	71.2	73.7	75.5	78.1	85.0
Clothing and shoes	270.9	286.3	297.7	297.7	302.1	310.8	329.0
Shoes	43.0	45.4	47.0	47.8	49.3	51.3	54.2
Women's and children's clothing and accessories except shoes	141.2	149.9	156.7	156.5	158.3	162.6	172.2
Men's and boys' clothing and accessories except shoes	86.6	91.0	94.0	93.4	94.6	97.0	102.5
Gasoline, fuel oil, and other energy goods	133.9	149.8	191.5	187.1	177.5	209.7	249.9
Gasoline and oil	122.4	137.9	175.7	171.6	163.4	192.6	230.4
Fuel oil and coal	11.5	11.9	15.8	15.4	14.1	17.0	19.5
Tobacco products	58.9	71.6	78.5	84.0	89.1	87.9	87.6
Toilet articles and preparations	52.6	53.9	55.0	54.4	54.2	54.1	55.8
Semidurable house furnishings	32.8	35.1	36.5	36.5	37.4	38.6	40.3
Cleaning and polishing preparations, misc. household supplies and paper products	55.9	59.2	61.6	64.5	66.6	68.7	73.4
Drug preparations and sundries	128.0	148.9	169.4	192.7	213.0	234.1	253.3
Nondurable toys and sport supplies	51.3	54.7	56.6	57.6	59.0	60.1	64.0
Stationery and writing supplies	17.7	18.5	19.0	18.3	18.1	18.1	18.3
Magazines, newspapers, and sheet music	32.1	33.5	35.0	35.0	35.3	35.9	38.7
Flowers, seeds, and potted plants	16.4	17.1	18.0	18.0	18.0	17.8	18.2
Services	**3,445.7**	**3,660.0**	**3,928.8**	**4,154.3**	**4,379.8**	**4570.8**	**4858.2**
Housing	894.6	948.4	1,006.5	1,073.7	1,144.8	1,158.0	1,221.1
Owner-occupied nonfarm dwellings—space rent	627.5	668.4	712.2	768.7	820.7	842.9	897.0
Tenant-occupied nonfarm dwellings—rent	209.0	219.0	227.5	240.7	258.7	245.3	248.2
Rental value of farm dwellings	9.9	10.2	10.7	11.4	11.8	12.2	12.9
Household operation	350.5	364.8	390.1	409.0	409.0	428.8	446.2
Electricity	97.1	97.2	102.3	108.0	111.7	115.4	120.5
Gas	32.7	33.4	41.0	48.6	40.8	51.1	55.4
Water and other sanitary services	46.2	48.8	50.8	52.8	55.2	57.8	60.6
Telephone and telegraph	110.3	118.4	125.1	128.4	128.3	129.9	132.1
Domestic service	17.1	16.1	17.4	16.9	16.8	18.5	19.5
Transportation	259.5	276.4	291.3	292.8	288.0	296.8	306.9
User-operated transportation	205.9	220.6	231.6	238.8	237.7	241.5	248.2
Purchased local transportation	11.8	11.9	12.2	12.5	12.4	13.1	14.1
Mass transit systems	8.3	8.6	9.1	9.2	9.0	9.5	10.3
Taxicab	3.5	3.3	3.1	3.2	3.4	3.6	3.8
Purchased intercity transportation	41.8	43.9	47.4	41.6	37.9	42.2	44.6
Railway	0.4	0.5	0.5	0.6	0.6	0.6	0.6
Bus	2.2	2.2	2.4	2.4	2.3	2.3	2.1
Airline	31.8	33.3	36.7	31.4	28.1	31.2	33.1
Medical care	921.4	961.1	1,026.8	1,113.8	1,210.3	1,299.4	1,401.1
Physicians	210.3	220.8	236.8	256.8	278.3	301.1	323.3
Dentists	54.1	57.4	61.8	66.8	72.2	74.6	80.0
Other professional services	149.4	153.3	161.6	175.5	189.7	203.4	219.9
Hospitals and nursing homes	435.9	453.6	482.6	525.3	574.0	612.6	657.4
Health insurance	71.6	76.1	84.0	89.4	96.1	107.7	120.5
Recreation	229.3	248.6	268.3	284.1	299.6	318.0	338.8
Admissions to specified spectator amusements	26.2	28.4	30.4	32.2	34.6	36.1	37.4
Personal care	75.0	80.7	87.0	90.4	92.9	99.5	106.7
Cleaning, storage, and repair of clothing and shoes	14.3	15.1	15.7	15.8	15.8	15.2	15.5
Barbershops, beauty parlors, and health clubs	33.6	35.6	38.4	40.1	41.6	44.4	47.3
Personal business	446.1	491.6	539.1	536.5	552.1	568.5	612.2
Brokerage charges and investment counseling	69.1	84.4	100.6	77.8	75.7	77.4	85.7
Bank service charges, trust services, and safe deposit box rental	50.2	58.3	64.2	69.1	75.5	82.9	90.6
Expense of handling life insurance and pension plans	82.7	85.2	96.1	91.9	84.8	92.6	98.4
Legal services	57.5	61.0	63.9	68.0	71.3	78.1	81.0
Funeral and burial expenses	13.8	14.0	14.0	14.6	14.6	15.9	16.4
Education and research	140.0	150.5	163.8	178.1	190.7	200.4	211.3
Higher education	75.0	80.0	86.4	95.1	103.9	110.0	117.7
Nursery, elementary, and secondary schools	31.0	32.7	34.6	36.5	38.3	40.4	42.1
Religious and welfare activities	146.0	154.5	172.3	186.5	202.9	206.7	219.0
Net foreign travel	–16.6	–16.6	–16.2	–10.8	–10.4	–5.3	–5.0
Foreign travel by U.S. residents	71.1	75.5	84.4	80.7	77.4	80.5	91.6
Less: Expenditures in the United States by nonresidents	87.7	92.1	100.7	91.5	87.9	85.8	96.6

NA = Not available. (1) Subtotals may not add to total, due to rounding or incomplete enumeration.

Median Income by Race, Hispanic Origin, and Sex, 1947-2003[1]

Source: U.S. Census Bureau

		Male			Female		
			Median income			Median income	
	Year	No. with income (thous.)	Current dollars	2003 dollars	No. with income	Current dollars	2003 dollars
All Races	2003	100,769	$29,931	$29,931	102,713	$17,259	$17,259
	2002	99,788	29,238	29,908	102,487	16,812	17,197
	2001	98,873	29,101	30,241	101,941	16,614	17,265
	2000	98,504	28,343	30,275	101,704	16,063	17,158
	1995	92,066	22,562	27,044	96,007	12,130	14,540
	1990	88,220	20,293	27,695	92,245	10,070	13,743
	1985	83,631	16,311	26,596	86,531	7,217	11,768
	1980	78,661	12,530	26,494	80,826	4,920	10,403
	1975	71,234	8,853	26,679	60,807	3,385	10,201
	1970	65,008	6,670	27,364	51,647	2,237	9,178
	1965	59,157	5,023	24,828	42,160	1,521	7,518
	1960	55,172	4,080	21,474	36,526	1,261	6,637
	1955	51,446	3,358	19,514	29,791	1,120	6,509
	1950	47,585	2,570	16,631	24,651	953	6,167
	1947	46,813	2,230	15,598	21,479	1,017	7,114
White	2003	84,405	30,732	30,732	83,852	17,422	17,422
	2002	83,899	30,383	31,079	84,014	16,838	17,224
	2001	83,750	30,240	31,425	84,207	16,652	17,304
	2000	83,372	29,797	31,829	84,123	16,079	17,175
	1995	79,022	23,895	28,642	80,608	12,316	14,763
	1990	76,480	21,170	28,892	78,566	10,317	14,080
	1985	73,222	17,111	27,900	74,640	7,357	11,996
	1980	69,420	13,328	28,181	70,573	4,947	10,460
	1975	63,629	9,300	28,026	52,936	3,420	10,306
	1970	58,447	7,011	28,763	45,288	2,266	9,296
	1965	53,276	5,290	26,147	36,996	1,613	7,973
	1960	49,788	4,296	22,611	32,001	1,352	7,116
	1955	46,586	3,544	20,595	25,985	1,252	7,276
	1950	(NA)	2,709	17,530	(NA)	1,060	6,859
Black	2003	10,291	21,935	21,935	12,924	16,540	16,540
	2002	10,096	21,509	22,002	12,665	16,671	17,053
	2001	9,944	21,466	22,307	12,414	16,282	16,920
	2000	9,905	21,343	22,798	12,461	15,881	16,964
	1995	9,339	16,006	19,186	11,607	10,961	13,138
	1990	8,820	12,868	17,562	10,687	8,328	11,366
	1985	8,127	10,768	17,558	9,611	6,277	10,235
	1980	7,387	8,009	16,935	8,596	4,580	9,684
	1975	6,485	5,560	16,755	6,969	3,107	9,363
	1970	5,844	4,157	17,055	5,844	2,063	8,464
	1965	5,881	2,847	14,072	5,165	1,174	5,803
	1960	5,384	2,260	11,895	4,525	837	4,405
	1955	4,860	1,865	10,838	3,806	653	3,795
	1950	(NA)	1,471	9,519	(NA)	474	3,067
White not Hispanic	2003	72,535	32,331	32,331	74,486	18,301	18,301
	2002	72,146	32,034	32,768	74,814	17,389	17,787
	2001	72,649	31,791	33,036	75,117	17,229	17,904
	2000	72,530	31,508	33,656	75,206	16,665	17,801
	1995	70,754	25,481	30,543	73,506	12,807	15,351
	1990	69,987	21,958	29,967	72,939	10,581	14,440
	1985	67,859	17,692	28,848	69,972	7,438	12,128
	1980	65,564	13,681	28,928	67,084	4,980	10,530
	1975	60,755	9,514	28,670	50,628	3,616	10,897
Asian	2003	4,266	31,737	31,737	4,252	17,879	17,879
	2002	4,139	30,839	31,546	4,137	17,898	18,308
	2001	4,165	31,096	32,314	4,164	18,525	19,251
	2000	4,303	30,833	32,935	4,192	17,356	18,539
	1995	3,095	22,162	26,565	3,025	12,862	15,417
	1990	2,235	19,394	26,468	2,333	11,086	15,130
	1988	2,123	18,422	27,525	2,093	9,244	13,812
Hispanic	2003	12,753	21,053	21,053	10,175	13,642	13,642
	2002	12,624	20,702	21,176	10,018	13,364	13,670
	2001	11,766	20,189	20,980	9,691	12,583	13,076
	2000	11,343	19,498	20,827	9,431	12,248	13,083
	1995	8,577	14,840	17,788	7,478	8,928	10,702
	1990	6,767	13,470	18,383	5,903	7,532	10,279
	1985	5,523	11,434	18,644	4,843	6,020	9,816
	1980	3,996	9,659	20,423	3,617	4,405	9,314
	1975	2,945	6,777	20,422	2,380	3,202	9,649

(1) People 15 years old and over beginning with March 1980, and people 14 years old and over as of March of the following year for previous years.

World's 50 Largest Banking Companies[1]

Source: *American Banker* (as of Dec. 31, 2004)

Assets[2]	(millions)	Assets[2]	(millions)
UBS AG Zurich	$1,533,036	Fortis Bank Brussels	$659,437
Citigroup Inc. New York	1,484,101	Rabobank Group Utrecht, Netherlands	648,211
Allianz AG Munich	1,357,166	Merrill Lynch New York	648,059
NG Group NV Amsterdam	1,357,166	HVB Group Munich	636,622
Mizuho Financial Group Tokyo	1,295,942	Commerzbank Frankfurt	579,705
HSBC Holdings PLC London	1,276,778	Norinchukin Bank Tokyo	553,720
Credit Agricole Paris	1,243,047	Lloyds TSB Group PLC London	539,146
BNP Paribas Paris	1,233,912	Dexia Brussels	530,039
JPMorgan Chase & Co. New York	1,157,248	Credit Mutuel Paris	527,611
Deutsche Bank AG Frankfurt	1,144,195	Wachovia Corp. Charlotte	493,324
Royal Bank of Scotland Group PLC Edinburgh	1,119,480	Axa Paris	449,223
Bank of America Corp. Charlotte	1,110,457	Wells Fargo & Co. San Francisco	427,849
Barclays PLC London	992,103	Banco Bilbao Vizcaua Argentaria Spain	423,689
Mitsubishi Tokyo Financial Group	980,285	Almanik NV Antwerp, Belgium	384,781
Credit Suisse Group Zurich	962,953	Danske Bank SA Copenhagen	380,120
Sumitomo Mitsui Financial Group Tokyo	896,909	Nordea Bank AB Stockholm	375,974
ABN Amro Amsterdam	828,961	Banca Intesa Milan	374,010
Societe Generale Paris	818,699	Resona Holdings Inc. Osaka	368,542
Santander Central Hispano SA Spain	783,707	UniCredit Milan	362,102
Morgan Stanley New York	775,410	MetLife New York	356,808
Hbos PLC Edinburgh	759,594	Royal Bank of Canada Toronto	346,532
Bayerische Hypo-und-Vereinsbanken AG Munich	753,700	West LB Dusseldorf	344,955
Groupe Caisse d'Epargne Paris	740,821	Group Banques Populaires Paris	341,057
UFJ Holdings Osaka	730,394	KBC Bank Brussels	339,463
Dresdner Bank Frankfurt	713,688	Eurohypo AG Frankfurt	309,082

(1) Includes bank holding companies and commercial and savings banks. (2) Currency conversion based on Exchange rates on Dec. 31, 2004 or at end of latest fiscal year.

50 Largest U.S. Bank Holding Companies, 2004[1]

Source: *American Banker* (as of Dec. 31, 2004)

Company Name	Total Assets (in thousands)	Company Name	Total Assets (in thousands)
Citigroup Inc. New York	$1,484,101,000	Mitsubishi Tokyo Financial Group	$53,808,367
JPMorgan Chase & Co. New York	1,157,248,000	Capital One Financial Corp. Mc Lean, Va.	53,747,255
Bank of America Corp. Charlotte	1,112,035,486	M&T Bank Corp. Buffalo	52,780,722
Wachovia Corp. Charlotte	493,324,000	Comerica Inc. Detroit	52,375,773
Wells Fargo & Co. San Francisco	427,849,000	AmSouth Bancorp. Birmingham, Ala.	49,757,521
MetLife Inc. New York	356,807,967	BNP Paribas Paris	49,375,674
Washington Mutual Inc. Seattle	301,956,039	Charles Schwab Corp. San Francisco	47,132,922
U.S. Bancorp Minneapolis	195,104,000	Northern Trust Corp. Chicago	45,276,690
SunTrust Banks Inc. Atlanta	158,869,784	Popular Inc. San Juan, Puerto Rico	44,402,000
HSBC Holdings PLC London	140,210,571	Marshall & Ilsley Corp. Milwaukee	40,479,185
National City Corp. Cleveland	139,280,377	Mellon Financial Corp. Pittsburgh	37,315,548
Royal Bank of Scotland Group Edinburgh	137,159,399	ING USA Holding Corp. Wilmington, Del.[2]	36,023,828
Countrywide Financial Corp. Calabasas, Calif.	128,495,705	Bank of Montreal	35,222,928
Golden West Financial Corp. Oakland, Calif.	106,816,527	Deutsche Bank Frankfurt	34,038,701
ABN Amro Amsterdam	102,863,282	Huntington Bancshares Inc. Columbus, Ohio	32,566,899
BB&T Corp. Winston-Salem, N.C.	100,508,641	Zions Bancorp. Salt Lake City	31,472,754
Bank of New York Co. Inc.	94,572,074	Commerce Bancorp Inc. Cherry Hill, N.J.	30,509,365
Fifth Third Bancorp Cincinnati	94,455,731	First Horizon National Corp. Memphis	29,773,975
State Street Corp. Boston	94,047,042	Banknorth Group Inc. Portland, Maine	28,702,887
KeyCorp Cleveland	90,653,059	Compass Bancshares Birmingham, Ala.	28,287,984
Regions Financial Corp. Birmingham, Ala.	84,366,269	E-Trade Financial Corp. New York	25,548,964
PNC Financial Services Group Pittsburgh	79,742,776	Synovus Financial Corp. Columbus, Ga.	25,061,114
MBNA Corp. Wilmington, Del.	61,714,140	New York Community Bancorp Inc. Westbury	24,051,636
North Fork Bancorp. Melville, N.Y.	60,667,055	Astoria Financial Corp. Lake Success, N.Y.	23,170,238
Sovereign Bancorp Inc. Philadelphia	54,454,684	Hibernia Corp. New Orleans	22,308,088

(1) Includes foreign-owned banks with a strong presence in the U.S. (2) U.S. assets for this unit of ING.

U.S. Bank Failures, 1934-2004

Source: Federal Deposit Insurance Corp.

Covers all FDIC-insured commercial and savings banks, including savings and loan institutions (S&Ls) 1980 and after.

Year	Closed or assisted	Year	Closed or assisted	Year	Closed or assisted	Year	Closed or assisted	Year	Closed or assisted
1934	9	1961	5	1973	6	1985	180	1995	8
1935	26	1963	2	1975	13	1986	204	1996	6
1936	69	1964	7	1976	17	1987	262	1997	1
1937	77	1965	5	1978	7	1988	465	1998	3
1938	74	1966	7	1979	10	1989	534	1999	8
1939	60	1967	4	1980	22	1990	382	2000	7
1940	43	1969	9	1981	40	1991	271	2001	4
1955	5	1970	7	1982	119	1992	181	2002	11
1959	3	1971	7	1983	99	1993	50	2003	3
1960	1	1972	2	1984	106	1994	15	2004	4

Banks in the U.S.–Number, Deposits

Source: Federal Deposit Insurance Corp. (as of Dec. 31, 2004)

Comprises all FDIC-insured commercial and savings banks, including savings and loan institutions (S&Ls).

	TOTAL NUMBER OF BANKS					TOTAL DEPOSITS (millions of dollars)				
		Commercial banks[1]					Commercial banks[1]			
Year	ALL BANKS	Natl.	State	Non-members	All savings	ALL DEPOSITS	Natl.	State	Non-members	All savings
1935	**15,295**	5,386	1,001	7,735	1,173	**$45,102**[2]	$24,802	$13,653	$5,669	$978[2]
1940	**15,772**	5,144	1,342	6,956	2,330	**67,494**	35,787	20,642	7,040	4,025
1945	**15,969**	5,017	1,864	6,421	2,667	**151,524**	77,778	41,865	16,307	15,574
1950	**16,500**	4,958	1,912	6,576	3,054	**171,963**	84,941	41,602	19,726	25,694
1955	**17,001**	4,692	1,847	6,698	3,764	**235,211**	102,796	55,739	26,198	50,478
1960	**17,549**	4,530	1,641	6,955	4,423	**310,262**	120,242	65,487	34,369	90,164
1965	**18,384**	4,815	1,405	7,327	4,837	**467,633**	185,334	78,327	51,982	151,990
1970	**18,205**	4,621	1,147	7,743	4,694	**686,901**	285,436	101,512	95,566	204,367
1975	**18,792**	4,744	1,046	8,595	4,407	**1,157,648**	450,308	143,409	187,031	376,900
1980	**18,763**	4,425	997	9,013	4,328	**1,832,716**	656,752	191,183	344,311	640,470
1985	**18,033**	4,959	1,070	8,378	3,626	**3,140,827**	1,241,875	354,585	521,628	1,022,739
1990	**15,158**	3,979	1,009	7,355	2,815	**3,637,292**	1,558,915	397,797	693,438	987,142
1995	**11,970**	2,858	1,042	6,040	2,030	**3,769,477**	1,695,817	614,924	716,829	741,907
2000	**9,905**	2,230	991	5,094	1,590	**4,914,808**	2,250,464	1,032,110	894,000	738,234
2001	**9,631**	2,137	972	4,971	1,533	**5,189,444**	2,384,462	1,079,388	927,772	797,822
2002	**9,354**	2,077	950	4,861	1,439	**5,568,508**	2,565,771	1,152,380	971,730	878,627
2003	**9,182**	2,001	935	4,833	1,413	**5,954,288**	2,786,756	1,195,914	1,046,195	925,423
2004	**8,975**	1,906	919	4,805	1,345	**6,584,200**	3,581,416	872,228	1,139,168	991,388

(1) "Nonmembers" are banks that are not members of the Federal Reserve System; "National" and "State" institutions are members. (2) Figures for 1935 do not include data for S&Ls (not available).

Federal Deposit Insurance Corporation (FDIC)

The Federal Deposit Insurance Corporation (FDIC) is the independent deposit insurance agency created by Congress to maintain stability and public confidence in the nation's banking system. In its unique role as deposit insurer of banks and savings associations, and in cooperation with other federal and state regulatory agencies, the FDIC seeks to promote the safety and soundness of insured depository institutions in the U.S. financial system by identifying, monitoring, and addressing risks to the deposit insurance funds. The FDIC aims at promoting public understanding and sound public policies by providing financial and economic information and analyses. It seeks to minimize disruptive effects from the failure of banks and savings associations, and to ensure fairness in the sale of financial products and the provision of financial services.

To maintain its insurance funds, the FDIC assesses depository institutions insurance premiums twice a year. The amount of the premium is based on the institution's balance of insured deposits for the preceding two quarters and the institution's risk to the insurance fund. The Corporation may borrow from the U.S. Treasury, not to exceed $30 billion outstanding, but the agency has made no such borrowings since it was organized in 1933. The FDIC's Bank Insurance Fund was $34.8 billion (unaudited) and the Savings Association Insurance Fund stood at $12.8 bil (unaudited), as of June 30, 2005.

Federal Reserve System

The Federal Reserve System is the central bank for the U.S. The system was established on Dec. 23, 1913, originally to give the country an elastic currency, provide facilities for discounting commercial paper, and improve the supervision of banking. Since then, the system's responsibilities have been broadened. Over the years, stability and growth of the economy, a high level of employment, stability in the purchasing power of the dollar, and reasonable balance in transactions with other countries have come to be recognized as primary objectives of governmental economic policy.

The Federal Reserve System consists of the Board of Governors, the 12 District Reserve Banks and their branch offices, and the Federal Open Market Committee. Several advisory councils help the board meet its varied responsibilities.

The hub of the system is the 7-member **Board of Governors** in Washington, DC. The members of the board are appointed by the president and confirmed by the Senate, to serve 14-year terms. The president also appoints the chairman and vice chairman of the board from among the board members for 4-year terms that may be renewed. As of Oct. 2005 the board members were: Alan Greenspan, chair; Roger W. Ferguson Jr., vice chair; Susan Schmidt Bies; Mark W. Olson; and Donald L. Kohn.

The 12 **District Reserve Banks** and their branch offices serve as the decentralized portion of the system, carrying out day-to-day operations such as circulating currency and coin and providing fiscal agency functions and payments mechanism services. The 12 are in Boston, New York, Philadelphia, Cleveland, Richmond, Atlanta, Chicago, St. Louis, Minneapolis, Kansas City, Dallas, and San Francisco.

The system's principal function is monetary policy, which it controls using 3 tools: reserve requirements, the discount rate, and open market operations.

Uniform **reserve requirements**, set by the board, are applied to the transaction accounts and nonpersonal time deposits of all depository institutions. Responsibility for setting the **discount rate** (the interest rate at which depository institutions can borrow money from the Reserve Banks) is shared by the Board of Governors and the Reserve Banks. Changes in the discount rate are recommended by the individual boards of directors of the Reserve Banks and are subject to approval by the Board of Governors.

The most important tool of monetary policy is **open market operations** (the purchase and sale of government securities). Responsibility for influencing the cost and availability of money and credit through the purchase and sale of government securities lies with the **Federal Open Market Committee** (FOMC), which is composed of the 7 members of the Board of Governors, the president of the Federal Reserve Bank of New York, and 4 other Federal Reserve Bank presidents, who each serve 1-year terms on a rotating basis. The committee bases its decisions on economic and financial developments and outlook, setting yearly growth objectives for key measures of money supply and credit. The decisions of the committee are carried out by the Domestic Trading Desk of the Federal Reserve Bank of New York.

A Federal Advisory Council meets with the Federal Reserve Board 4 times a year to discuss business and financial conditions, as well as to make recommendations.

Website: www.federalreserve.gov

Federal Reserve Board Primary and Secondary Credit Rate

Prior to Jan. 9, 2003, the federal reserve set a single "discount rate," the interest rate that member banks were charged when borrowing money through the Federal Reserve System. The discount rate was replaced with two rates, the *primary credit rate* and *secondary credit rate*. The primary credit rate (listed first) is available to banks in generally sound financial condition. The secondary credit (listed second) rate is given to banks that do not qualify for the primary credit rate. Both are extended for very short terms, usually overnight. Under the new system, financially sound institutions are not required to exhaust all funds before borrowing from the Fed.

Effective date	Rates
1980:	
Feb. 15	13%
May 30	12
June 13	11
July 28	10
Sept. 26	11
Nov. 17	12
Dec. 5	13
1981:	
May 5	14
Nov. 2	13
Dec. 4	12
1982:	
July 20	11½
Aug. 2	11
Aug. 16	10
Aug. 27	10
Oct. 12	9½
Dec. 15	8½

Effective date	Rates
1984:	
April 9	9%
Nov. 21	8½
Dec. 24	8
1985:	
May 20	7½
1986:	
March 7	7
April 21	6½
July 11	6
Aug. 21	5½
1987:	
Sept. 4	6
1988:	
Aug. 9	6½
1989:	
Feb. 24	7
1990:	
Dec. 18	6½

Effective date	Rates
1991:	
Apr. 30	5½%
Sept. 13	5
Nov. 6	4½
Dec. 20	3½
1992:	
July 2	3
1994:	
May 17	½
Aug. 16	4
Nov. 15	4¾
1995:	
Feb. 1	5
1996:	
Jan. 31	5
1998:	
Oct. 15	4¾
Nov. 17	4½

Effective date	Rates
1999:	
Aug. 24	4¾%
Nov. 16	5
2000:	
Feb. 2	5¼
Mar. 21	5½
May 16	6
2001:	
Jan. 3	5¾
Jan. 31	5
Mar. 20	4½
Apr. 18	4
May 15	3½
June 27	3¼
Aug. 21	3
Sept. 17	2½
Oct. 2	2
Dec. 11	1¼

Effective date	Rates
2002:	
Nov. 6	¾%
2003:	
Jan. 9[1]	2¼, 2¾
June 25[1]	2, 2½
2004:	
Jun. 30	2¼, 2¾
Aug. 10	2½, 3
Sept. 21	2¾, 3¼
Nov. 10	3, 3½
Dec. 14	3¼, 3¾
2005[1]:	
Feb. 2	3½, 4
Mar. 22	3¾, 4¼
May 3	4, 4½
June 30	4¼, 4¾
Aug. 9	4½, 5
Sept. 20	4¾, 5¼

(1)Through Oct. 1, 2005.

United States Mint

Source: United States Mint, U.S. Dept. of the Treasury

The United States Mint was created on Apr. 2, 1792, by an act of Congress, which established the U.S. national coinage system. In 1799 the mint became an independent agency reporting directly to the president. It was made a statutory bureau of the Treasury Department in 1873, with a director appointed by the president. The mint manufactures and ships all U.S. coins for circulation to Federal Reserve banks and branches, which in turn issue coins to the public and business community through depository institutions. The mint also safeguards the Treasury Department's stored gold and silver, as well as other monetary assets.

The composition of dimes, quarters, and half dollars, traditionally produced from silver, was changed by the Coinage Act of 1965, which mandated that these coins from then on be minted from a cupronickel-clad alloy and reduced the silver content of the half dollar to 40%. In 1970, legislative action mandated that the half dollar and a dollar coin be minted from the same alloy.

The Eisenhower dollar was minted from 1971 through 1978, when legislation called for the minting of the smaller Susan B. Anthony dollar coin. The Anthony dollar, which was minted through 1981, marked the first time that a woman other than a mythical figure, appeared on a U.S. coin produced for general circulation. This coin was replaced in 2000 by the Golden Dollar Coin. Golden in color, with a smooth edge and wide border, the obverse side depicts Sacagawea (a Shoshone woman who helped guide Lewis and Clark) and her infant son. The reverse shows an American eagle and 17 stars, one for each of the states at the time of the Lewis and Clark expedition.

Mint headquarters are in Washington, DC. Mint production facilities are in Philadelphia, Denver, San Francisco, and West Point, NY. In addition, the mint is responsible for the U.S. Bullion Depository at Fort Knox, KY.

Proof coin sets, silver proof coin sets, and uncirculated coin sets are available from the mint, which also produces medals in honor of significant persons, events, and sites.

Among recent congressionally authorized commemorative coins are: the 2001 American Buffalo Proof Silver Dollar; the 2001 U.S. Capitol Visitor Center Commemorative Coin Program, featuring the Half Dollar Clad Proof coin, the Proof Silver Dollar, and the Proof Gold $5 coin; the 2002 Olympic Winter Games Silver Dollar and Gold $5 coins, and 2002 West Point Bicentennial Commemorative Silver Dollar; the 2003 First Flight Centennial Commemorative coins (Gold, Silver, and Clad); the 2004 Lewis and Clark Bicentennial Silver Dollar; the 2004 Thomas A. Edison Commemorative Silver Dollar; the 2005 Marine Corps 230th Anniversary Silver Dollar; the 2005 Chief Justice John Marshall Silver Dollar.

The congressionally authorized American Eagle gold, platinum, and silver bullion coins are available through dealers worldwide. The gold and platinum eagles are sold in one-ounce, half-ounce, quarter-ounce, and one-tenth-ounce sizes. The American eagle silver bullion coin contains one troy ounce of .999 fine silver and is priced according to the daily market value of silver. These coins also are available directly from the mint in proof condition, separately priced.

The mint offers free public tours and operates sales centers at the U.S. mints in Denver and Philadelphia. Further information is available from the U.S. Mint, Customer Care Center, 801 9th St., NW, Washington, DC 20220; (800) USA-MINT.

Website: www.usmint.gov

New Commemorative State Quarters, 2006-08

Source: United States Mint, U.S. Dept. of the Treasury

Beginning in Jan. 1999, a series of 5 quarter dollars with new reverses are being issued each year through 2008, celebrating each of the 50 states. To make room on the reverse of the commemorative quarters for each state's design, certain design elements have been moved, thereby creating a new obverse design as well. The coins are being issued in the sequence the states became part of the Union (date each state entered the union is shown); listed below are the quarters being issued in 2006-08.

2006	Nevada Oct. 31, 1864	Nebraska Mar. 1, 1867	Colorado Aug. 1, 1876	North Dakota Nov. 2, 1889	South Dakota Nov. 2, 1889
2007	Montana Nov. 8, 1889	Washington Nov. 11, 1889	Idaho July 3, 1890	Wyoming July 10, 1890	Utah Jan. 4, 1896
2008	Oklahoma Nov. 16, 1907	New Mexico Jan. 6, 1912	Arizona Feb. 14, 191	Alaska Jan. 3, 1959	Hawaii Aug. 21, 195

The Bureau of Engraving and Printing

Source: Bureau of Engraving and Printing, U.S. Dept. of the Treasury

The Bureau of Engraving and Printing manufactures the financial and other securities of the United States. It designs and prints a variety of products, including Federal Reserve notes (bills in various denominations), Treasury securities, identification cards, naturalization certificates, and other special security documents. Denominations of the various types of printings produced by the bureau range from a 1/5-cent wine stamp to a $100,000,000 International Monetary Fund special note. Among its products are all hand-engraved invitations issued by the White House.

The first general circulation of paper money by the federal government dates back to 1861, prior to the establishment of the bureau, when, to finance the Civil War, Congress authorized the U.S. Treasury to issue non-interest-bearing demand notes, nicknamed "greenbacks" because of their color. A portrait of Pres. Abraham Lincoln appeared on the face of the first $10 notes. By 1862, the design of U.S. currency incorporated fine-line engraving, intricate geometric lathework patterns, a Treasury seal, and engraved signatures, to aid in counterfeit deterrence. All U.S. currency issued since 1861 remains valid and redeemable at full face value.

The Bureau of Engraving and Printing began operations by 1862, originally separating and sealing bank notes that were printed by private companies. In 1877, the bureau became the sole producer of U.S. currency. In 1894, it also began producing Postage Stamps. On June 10, 2005, the bureau printed its last stamps, a roll of 37-cent flag stamps; stamps are now produced by private printers.

The Federal Reserve Act of 1913 created the Federal Reserve as the nation's central bank, and provided for currency called Federal Reserve notes. The first notes, issued the following year, were $10 notes bearing a portrait of Pres. Andrew Jackson. In 1929, the look of U.S. currency was standardized.The national motto, "In God We Trust," began appearing on paper money in 1957.

The Bureau of Engraving and Printing currently operates 2 facilities, one in Washington, DC, opened in 1914, and one in Forth Worth, TX, which began operations in 1991.

The bureau has its own lore and legends. The youngest employee ever to be hired there was an 11-year-old girl, Emma S. Brown, whose mother was disabled and whose brother, the family's sole support, was killed in action in the Civil War. Emma Brown's U.S. representative gave her a political appointment in the bureau. She retired in 1924 after 59 years of service.

More information on the Bureau of Engraving and Printing can be found at www.moneyfactory.com

New U.S. Currency Designs

On Mar. 25, 1996, the U.S. Treasury issued a redesigned $100 note incorporating many new and modified anti-counterfeiting features. It was the first of the U.S. currency series to be redesigned. A new $50 note was issued Oct. 27, 1997, a new $20 bill was released into circulation Sept. 24, 1998, and new $10 and $5 notes were issued May 24, 2000. Old notes are being removed from circulation as they are returned to the Federal Reserve.

The new $100 bill has a larger portrait, moved off-center; a watermark (seen only when held up to the light) to the right of the portrait, depicting the same person (Benjamin Franklin); a security thread that glows red when exposed to ultraviolet light in a dark environment; color-shifting ink that changes from green to black when viewed at different angles, to appear in the numeral on the lower, front right-hand corner of the bill; microprinting in the numeral in the note's lower, front left-hand corner and on the portrait; and other features for security, machine authentication, and processing of the currency. The redesigned $5, $10, $20, and $50 bills incorporate the same features as the $100 bill, with the notable addition of a low-vision feature, a large (14-mm high, as compared to 7.8-mm on the old design), dark numeral on a light background on the back of the note. (The security thread glows yellow in the $50, green in the $20, orange in the $10, and blue in the $5. There is no color-shifting ink on the $5 note.)

On Oct. 9, 2003, the U.S. Treasury introduced a new $20 note, using background colors for the first time since 1905. The notes have a security thread running vertically up one side, with "USA TWENTY" and a small U.S. flag; the thread glows green under UV light. Other security features include color-shifting ink in the number "20" in the lower right corner on the note's face. A new $50 note with similar security features was released Sept. 28, 2004, and a new $10 note will enter circulation in early 2006.

More new currency information is available on the U.S. Treasury's website: www.ustreas.gov/topics/currency/

Denominations of U.S. Currency

Since 1969 the largest denomination of U.S. currency that has been issued is the $100 bill. As larger-denomination bills reach the Federal Reserve Bank, they are removed from circulation. Because some discontinued currency is expected to be in the hands of holders for many years, the description of the various denominations below is continued.

Amt.	Portait	Embellishment on Back
$1	Washington	Great Seal of U.S.
2	Jefferson	Signers of Declaration
5	Lincoln	Lincoln Memorial
10	Hamilton	U.S. Treasury
20	Jackson	White House
50	Grant	U.S. Capitol
$100	Franklin	Independence Hall
500	McKinley	Ornate denominational marking
1,000	Cleveland	Ornate denominational marking
5,000	Madison	Ornate denominational marking
10,000	Salmon Chase	Ornate denominational marking
100,000*	Wilson	Ornate denominational marking

*For use only in transactions between Federal Reserve System and Treasury Department.

Portraits on U.S. Treasury Bills, Bonds, Notes, and Savings Bonds

Denomination	Savings bonds	Treasury bills*	Treasury bonds*	Treasury notes*
$50	Washington		Jefferson	
75	Adams			
100	Jefferson		Jackson	
200	Madison			
500	Hamilton		Washington	
1,000	B. Franklin	H. McCulloch	Lincoln	Lincoln
5,000	P. Revere	J. G. Carlisle	Monroe	Monroe
10,000	J. Wilson	J. Sherman	Cleveland	Cleveland
50,000	C. Glass			
100,000		A. Gallatin	Grant	Grant
1,000,000		O. Wolcott	T. Roosevelt	T. Roosevelt
100,000,000				Madison
500,000,000				McKinley

*The U.S. Treasury discontinued issuing treasury bill, bond, and note certificates in 1986. Since then, all issues of marketable treasury securities have been available only in book-entry form, although some certificates remain in circulation.

The U.S. $1 Bill

Plate position: Shows where on the 32-note plate this bill was printed.

Serial number Each bill has its own.

Federal Reserve District Number: Shows which district issued the bill.

Federal Reserve District Seal: The name of the Federal Reserve Bank that issued the bill is printed in the seal. The letter tells you quickly where the bill is from. Here are the letter codes for the 12 Federal Reserve Districts:

- **A:** Boston
- **B:** New York
- **C:** Philadelphia
- **D:** Cleveland
- **E:** Richmond
- **F:** Atlanta
- **G:** Chicago
- **H:** St. Louis
- **I:** Minneapolis
- **J:** Kansas City
- **K:** Dallas
- **L:** San Francisco

The Treasury Department seal: The balancing scales represent justice. The pointed stripe across the middle has 13 stars for the original 13 colonies. The key represents authority.

Plate serial number Shows which printing plate was used for the face of the bill.

Treasurer of the U.S. signature

Series indicator (year note's design was first used)

Secretary of the Treasury signature

Plate serial number Shows which plate was used for the back.

Front of the Great Seal of the United States: The bald eagle is the national bird. The shield has 13 stripes for the 13 original colonies. The eagle holds 13 arrows (symbol of war) and an olive branch (symbol of peace). Above the eagle is the motto "E Pluribus Unum," Latin for "out of many, one," and a constellation of 13 stars.

Reverse of the Great Seal of the United States: The pyramid symbolizes something that endures for ages. The eye, known as the "Eye of Providence," probably comes from an ancient Egyptian symbol. The pyramid has 13 levels; at its base are the Roman numerals for 1776, the year of American independence. "Annuit Coeptis" is Latin for "God has favored our undertaking." "Novus Ordo Seclorum" is Latin for "a new order of the ages." Both phrases are from the works of the Roman poet Virgil.

U.S. Currency and Coin

Source: Financial Management Service, U.S. Dept. of the Treasury (June 30, 2005)

Amounts Outstanding and in Circulation

Currency	Total currency and coin	Total currency	Federal Reserve notes[1]	U.S. notes	Currency no longer issued
Amounts outstanding	$904,155,948,126	$868,115,816,268	$867,611,541,861	$255,672,566	$248,601,841
Less amounts held by:					
Treasury	246,956,268	24,949,724	24,758,860	7,505	183,359
Federal Reserve banks	139,280,783,663	138,650,421,779	138,650,416,148	—	5,631
Amounts in circulation	$764,628,208,195	$729,440,444,765	$728,936,366,853	$255,665,061	$248,412,851

Coins[2]	Total	Dollars[3]	Fractional coins
Amounts outstanding	$36,040,131,858	$3,505,529,008	$32,534,602,850
Less amounts held by:			
Treasury	222,006,544	186,132,544	35,874,000
Federal Reserve banks	630,361,884	94,252,595	536,109,289
Amounts in circulation	$35,187,763,430	$3,225,143,869	$31,962,619,561

(1) Issued on or after July 1, 1929. (2) Excludes coins sold to collectors at premium prices. (3) Includes $481,781,898 in standard silver dollars.

Currency in Circulation by Denominations

(June 30, 2005)

Denomination	Total currency in circulation	Federal Reserve notes[1]	U.S. notes	Currency no longer issued
$1	$8,397,526,319	$8,252,965,986	$143,503	$144,416,830
$2	1,428,842,156	1,296,590,962	132,238,618	12,576
$5	9,715,702,340	9,578,010,665	109,266,110	28,425,565
$10	14,810,410,070	14,788,984,360	6,300	21,419,410
$20	110,116,823,780	110,096,716,880	3,840	20,103,060
$50	60,189,902,300	60,178,405,000	500	11,496,800
$100	524,467,735,200	524,431,753,000	13,995,600	21,986,600
$500	142,500,000	142,306,000	5,500	188,500
$1,000	165,777,000	165,564,000	5,000	208,000
$5,000	1,765,000	1,710,000	—	55,000
$10,000	3,460,000	3,360,000	—	100,000
Fractional notes[2]	600	—	90	510
TOTAL CURRENCY	**$729,440,444,765**	**$728,936,366,853**	**$255,665,061**	**$248,412,851**

(1) Issued on or after July 1, 1929. (2) Represents the value of certain partial denominations not presented for redemption.

Comparative Totals of Money in Circulation — Selected Dates

Date	Dollars (in millions)	Per capita[1]	Date	Dollars (in millions)	Per capita[1]	Date	Dollars (in millions)	Per capita[1]
June 30, 2005	$764,628.2	$2,579.00	Mar. 31, 1995	$401,610.0	$1,531.39	June 30, 1950	$27,156.3	$179.03
June 30, 2004	733,171.0	2,497.00	Mar. 31, 1990	257,664.4	1,028.71	June 30, 1940	7,847.5	59.40
April 30, 2003	688.772.0	2,368.17	June 30, 1985	185,890.7	778.58	June 30, 1930	4,522.0	36.74
Mar. 31, 2002	641,909.0	2,238.45	June 30, 1980	127,097.2	558.28	June 30, 1920	5,467.6	51.36
Mar. 30, 2001	585,916.0	2,121.82	June 30, 1970	54,351.0	265.39	June 30, 1910	3,148.7	34.07
Mar. 31, 2000	562,949.0	2,050.00	June 30, 1960	32,064.6	177.47			

(1) Based on Bureau of the Census estimates of population. The requirement for a gold reserve against U.S. notes was repealed by Public Law 90-269, approved Mar. 18, 1968. Silver certificates issued on and after July 1, 1929, became redeemable from the general fund on June 24, 1968. The amount of security after those dates has been reduced accordingly.

U.S. Budget Receipts and Outlays, 2000-2005

Source: Financial Management Service, U.S. Dept. of the Treasury; Congressional Budget Office

As of Oct. 2005, the estimate from the Congressional Budget Office of the total U.S. budget deficit for the fiscal year 2005 was $318.6 billion, or 2.6% of GDP, an $93.7 bil decrease from the $412.3 billion deficit in 2004.

(in millions of current dollars; many figures do not add to totals because of independent rounding or omitted subcategories, including some subcategories with negative values.)

NET RECEIPTS — FISCAL YEAR[1]:	2000	2001	2002	2003	2004	2005[2]
Individual income taxes	$1,004,461	$994,339	$858,345	$793,699	$808,958	$927,222
Corporation income taxes	207,288	151,075	148,044	131,778	189,370	278,281
Social insurance taxes and contributions:						
Federal old-age and survivors insurance	411,676	434,057	440,541	447,806	457,120	493,646
Federal disability insurance	68,907	73,463	74,780	76,036	77,624	83,829
Federal hospital insurance	135,528	149,650	149,049	147,186	150,589	166,068
Railroad retirement fund	4,336	4,272	4,177	3,954	—	
Total employment taxes and contributions	620,447	661,442	668,548	674,982	689,359	747,663
Other insurance and retirement:						
Unemployment	27,641	27,812	27,620	33,366	39,453	42,999
Federal employees retirement	4,693	4,647	4,533	4,578	4,545	4,409
Non-federal employees	70	66	61	53	51	50
Total social insurance taxes and contributions	**652,851**	**693,967**	**700,761**	**712,979**	**733,408**	**795,121**
Excise taxes	68,866	66,232	66,989	67,522	69,851	73,093
Estate and gift taxes	29,010	28,400	26,507	21,959	24,831	24,764
Customs duties	19,913	19,616	18,602	19,862	21,083	23,378
Miscellaneous Receipts	42,669	37,664	33,803	34,317	32,277	32,445
Deposits of earnings by Federal Reserve Banks	32,293	26,124	23,683	21,878	19,652	19,297
Net Budget Receipts	**2,025,038**	**1,990,930**	**1,853,296**	**1,782,115**	**1,879,777**	**2,154,305**
NET OUTLAYS						
Legislative Branch	**2,913**	**3,029**	**3,230**	**3,428**	**3,880**	**3,989**
The Judiciary	**4,087**	**4,409**	**4,824**	**5,123**	**5,396**	**5,562**
Executive Office of the President:						
The White House Office	53	52	58	60	56	56
Office of Management and Budget	64	64	71	62	61	68
Total Executive Office	**284**	**280**	**496**	**388**	**3,309**	**7,725**
International Assistance Program:						
International security assistance	6,534	6,783	7,982	8,640	8,411	7,942
Multilateral assistance	1,759	2,166	2,187	2,115	2,640	2,395
Agency for International Development	2,622	2,764	3,682	4,024	4,327	4,068
International Development Assistance	2,953	2,895	3,752	4,284	4,623	3,922
Total International Assistance Program	**12,083**	**11,767**	**13,309**	**13,466**	**13,793**	**14,787**
Agriculture Department:						
Food stamp program	18,295	19,097	22,069	24,537	27,720	32,613
Farm Service Agency	33,353	22,974	17,519	18,344	11,348	21,247
Forest Service	3,978	4,225	5,438	5,147	5,481	5,036
Total Agriculture Department	**75,728**	**68,156**	**68,989**	**72,467**	**71,714**	**85,129**
Commerce Department:						
Bureau of the Census	4,214	1,025	628	612	681	694
Total Commerce Department	**7,931**	**5,017**	**5,322**	**5,680**	**5,849**	**6,165**
Defense Department—Military:						
Military personnel	75,950	73,977	86,802	106,746	113,576	127,463
Operation and maintenance	105,871	112,019	130,167	42,458	174,048	188,120
Procurement	51,616	54,991	62,511	67,925	76,217	82,294
Research, development, test, evaluation	37,608	40,462	44,388	53,102	60,756	65,691
Military construction	5,111	4,978	5,055	5,850	6,310	5,330
Total Defense Department—Military	**281,233**	**290,980**	**332,116**	**408,578**	**437,111**	**474,436**
Defense Department—Civil	**32,019**	**34,161**	**35,159**	**39,881**	**41,732**	**43,484**
Education Department	**33,308**	**35,959**	**46,285**	**57,399**	**62,814**	**72,944**
Energy Department	**15,010**	**16,420**	**17,772**	**19,385**	**19,974**	**21,635**
Health and Human Services Department:						
Public Health Service	28,281	32,667	36,597	41,239	44,419	46,035
Centers for Medicare and Medicaid Services[3]	413,124	450,751	243,001	532,746	586,515	651,685
Food and Drug Administration	1,023	1,075	1,127	1,397	1,380	1,320
National Institutes of Health	15,415	17,254	20,450	22,834	25,292	27,123
Total Health and Human Services Dept.	**382,627**	**426,444**	**466,104**	**508,405**	**543,215**	**581,492**
Homeland Security Department:						
Citizenship and Immigration Services	—	—	—	1,297	1,541	1,623
U.S. Secret Service	—	—	—	1,152	1,320	1,406
Border and Transportation Security	—	—	—	17,208	13,936	13,931
U.S. Coast Guard	—	—	—	6,093	6,843	7,317
Total Homeland Security Department	—	—	—	**31,843**	**26,665**	**39,307**
Housing and Urban Development Department	**30,830**	**33,937**	**31,880**	**37,470**	**45,024**	**42,514**
Interior Department	**8,036**	**8,024**	**9,641**	**9,204**	**8,916**	**9,093**
Justice Department:						
Federal Bureau of Investigation	3,088	20,810	3,556	4,216	4,927	5,111
Drug Enforcement Administration	1,339	3,208	1,602	1,590	1,725	1,759
Immigration and Naturalization Service[4]	4,163	4,558	5,340	—	—	—

NET RECEIPTS FISCAL YEAR[1]:	2000	2001	2002	2003	2004	2005[2]
Federal Prison System	$3,708	$4,205	$4,746	$4,580	$4,751	$4,844
Total Justice Department	**19,561**	**20,810**	**24,197**	**21,529**	**28,953**	**22,740**
Labor Department:						
Unemployment Trust Fund	24,149	31,530	62,211	66,640	46,321	37,059
Total Labor Department	**31,354**	**39,280**	**64,252**	**69,171**	**56,708**	**47,946**
State Department	**6,849**	**7,446**	**9,453**	**9,257**	**10,942**	**12,838**
Transportation Department:						
Federal Aviation Administration	9,561	10,731	13,096	12,561	12,835	13,839
Total Transportation Department	**46,030**	**54,075**	**61,282**	**50,808**	**54,539**	**56,934**
Treasury Department:						
Internal Revenue Service	37,986	38,695	46,996	51,508	57,393	65,410
Interest on the public debt	362,118	359,508	332,537	318,149	321,689	352,350
Total Treasury Department	**390,813**	**389,944**	**374,516**	**366,756**	**374,737**	**409,114**
Veterans Affairs Department	**47,087**	**45,043**	**50,881**	**56,892**	**59,556**	**69,995**
Environmental Protection Agency	7,236	7,390	7,451	8,065	8,335	7,918
General Services Administration	25	–8	–271	336	–403	53
National Aeronautics and Space Administration	13,442	14,094	14,429	14,552	15,186	15,611
Office of Personnel Management	48,660	50,915	52,512	54,135	56,533	59,510
Small Business Administration	–422	–569	492	1,559	4,077	2,503
Social Security Administration	**441,810**	**461,748**	**488,694**	**508,160**	**530,206**	**561,324**
Other independent agencies:						
Corporation for Natl. and Community Service	684	757	793	839	765	793
Corporation for Public Broadcasting	316	360	375	411	437	466
District of Columbia	312	539	927	781	805	659
Equal Employment Opportunity Commission	290	289	324	315	324	320
Export-Import Bank of the U.S.	–743	–1,749	–140	–3,428	–1,902	–814
Federal Communications Commission	4,073	4,011	5,253	6,398	3,848	7,549
Federal Deposit Insurance Corporation	–2,837	–1,220	–353	–732	–1,554	–874
National Archives & Records Adm.	201	217	268	301	307	338
National Foundation on the Arts and Humanities	218	223	227	230	247	260
National Labor Relations Board	198	220	230	231	242	246
National Science Foundation	3,487	3,691	4,187	4,735	5,118	5,432
Nuclear Regulatory Commission	33	31	40	48	71	111
Railroad Retirement Board	4,992	5,541	5,425	3,056	2,792	2,123
Securities and Exchange Commission	–506	–330	–536	–532	–685	–799
Smithsonian Institution	517	561	616	614	782	757
Tennessee Valley Authority	–307	–662	124	227	–413	–205
Total other independent agencies	**10,526**	**12,581**	**15,874**	**11,634**	**5,801**	**14,182**
Undistributed offsetting receipts	–172,844	–190,946	–201,149	–211,901	–212,522	–226,210
NET BUDGET OUTLAYS	**$1,788,045**	**$1,863,909**	**$2,010,962**	**$2,156,906**	**$2,292,061**	**2,472,920**
Less net receipts	2,025,038	1,990,930	1,853,296	1,782,115	1,879,777	2,154,305
DEFICIT (-) OR SURPLUS (+)	**$+236,993**	**$+127,021**	**$–157,666**	**$–374,791**	**$–412,300**	**–318,615**

— = Not available. (1) Fiscal year ends Sept. 30. (2) Figures for some agencies are preliminary. (3) Formerly the Health Care Financing Adm. (4) As of Jan. 2003, transferred to Homeland Security Dept.

Summary of Receipts, Outlays, and Surpluses or Deficits, 1936-2004

Source: Financial Management Service, U.S. Dept. of the Treasury; Congressional Budget Office

(millions of current dollars)

Fiscal Year[1]	Receipts	Outlays	Surplus or Deficit (–)[2]	Fiscal Year[1]	Receipts	Outlays	Surplus or Deficit (–)[2]
1936	$3,923	$8,228	$–4,304	1971	$187,139	$210,172	$–23,033
1937	5,387	7,580	–2,193	1972	207,309	230,681	–23,373
1938	6,751	6,840	–89	1973	230,799	245,707	–14,908
1939	6,295	9,141	–2,846	1974	263,224	269,359	–6,135
1940	6,548	9,468	–2,920	1975	279,090	332,332	–53,242
1941	8,712	13,653	–4,941	1976	298,060	371,779	–73,719
1942	14,634	35,137	–20,503	Transition quarter[3]	81,232	95,973	–14,741
1943	24,001	78,555	–54,554	1977	355,559	409,203	–53,644
1944	43,747	91,304	–47,557	1978	399,561	458,729	–59,168
1945	45,159	92,712	–47,553	1979	463,302	503,464	–40,162
1946	39,296	55,232	–15,936	1980	517,112	590,920	–73,808
1947	38,514	34,496	4,018	1981	599,272	678,209	–78,936
1948	41,560	29,764	11,796	1982	617,766	745,706	–127,940
1949	39,415	38,835	580	1983	600,562	808,327	–207,764
1950	39,443	42,562	–3,119	1984	666,457	851,781	–185,324
1951	51,616	45,514	6,102	1985	734,057	946,316	–212,260
1952	66,167	67,686	–1,519	1986	769,091	990,231	–221,140
1953	69,608	76,101	–6,493	1987	854,143	1,003,804	–149,661
1954	69,701	70,855	–1,154	1988	908,166	1,063,318	–155,151
1955	65,451	68,444	–2,993	1989	990,701	1,144,020	–153,319
1956	74,587	70,640	3,947	1990	1,031,308	1,251,776	–220,469
1957	79,990	76,578	3,412	1991	1,054,265	1,323,757	–269,492
1958	79,636	82,405	–2,769	1992	1,090,453	1,380,794	–290,340
1959	79,249	92,098	–12,849	1993	1,153,226	1,408,532	–255,306
1960	92,492	92,191	301	1994	1,257,451	1,460,553	–203,102
1961	94,388	97,723	–3,335	1995	1,351,495	1,515,412	–163,917
1962	99,676	106,821	–7,146	1996	1,452,763	1,560,094	–107,331
1963	106,560	111,316	–4,756	1997	1,578,955	1,600,911	–21,957
1964	112,613	118,528	–5,915	1998	1,721,421	1,652,224	+70,039
1965	116,817	118,228	–1,411	1999	1,827,302	1,704,942	+124,360
1966	130,835	134,532	–3,698	2000	2,025,060	1,788,143	+236,917
1967	148,822	157,464	–8,643	2001	1,991,044	1,863,769	+127,021
1968	152,973	178,134	–25,161	2002R	1,853,051	2,010,871	–157,820
1969	186,882	183,640	3,242	2003R	1,782,115	2,156,906	–374,791
1970	192,807	195,649	–2,842	2004E	1,879,799	2,292,352	–412,553

R = Revised. E = Estimated. (1) Fiscal years 1936 to 1976 end June 30; after 1976, fiscal years end Sept. 30. (2) May not equal difference between figures shown, because of rounding. (3) Transition quarter covers July 1, 1976-Sept. 30, 1976.

Budget Receipts and Outlays, 1789-1935

Source: U.S. Dept. of the Treasury; annual statements for years ending June 30 unless otherwise noted

(thousands of dollars)

Yearly Average	Receipts	Outlays	Yearly Average	Receipts	Outlays	Yearly Average	Receipts	Outlays
1789-1800[1]	$5,717	$5,776	1866-1870	$447,301	$377,642	1901-1905	$559,481	$535,559
1801-1810[2]	13,056	9,086	1871-1875	336,830	287,460	1906-1910	628,507	639,178
1811-1820[2]	21,032	23,943	1876-1880	288,124	255,598	1911-1915	710,227	720,252
1821-1830[2]	21,928	16,162	1881-1885	366,961	257,691	1916-1920	3,483,652	8,065,333
1831-1840[2]	30,461	24,495	1886-1890	375,448	279,134	1921-1925	4,306,673	3,578,989
1841-1850[2]	28,545	34,097	1891-1895	352,891	363,599	1926-1930	4,069,138	3,182,807
1851-1860	60,237	60,163	1896-1900	434,877	457,451	1931-1935	2,770,973	5,214,874
1861-1865	160,907	683,785						

(1) Average for period March 4, 1789, to Dec. 31, 1800. (2) Years from 1801 to 1842 end Dec. 31; average for 1841-1850 is for the period Jan. 1, 1841, to June 30, 1850.

Public Debt of the U.S.

Source: Bureau of Public Debt, U.S. Dept. of the Treasury; World Almanac research

Fiscal year	Debt (billions)	Debt per cap. (dollars)	Interest paid (billions)	% of federal outlays	Fiscal year	Debt (billions)	Debt per cap. (dollars)	Interest paid (billions)	% of federal outlays
1870	$2.4	$61.06	—	—	1984	$1,572.3	$6,640	$153.8	$18.1
1880	2.0	41.60	—	—	1985	1,823.1	7,598	178.9	18.9
1890	1.1	17.80	—	—	1986	2,125.3	8,774	190.2	19.2
1900	1.2	16.60	—	—	1987	2,350.3	9,615	195.4	19.5
1910	1.1	12.41	—	—	1988	2,602.3	10,534	214.1	20.1
1920	24.2	228	—	—	1989	2,857.4	11,545	240.9	21.0
1930	16.1	131	—	—	1990	3,233.3	13,000	264.8	21.1
1940	43.0	325	$1.0	10.5	1991	3,665.3	14,436	285.5	21.6
1950	256.1	1,688	5.7	13.4	1992	4,064.6	15,846	292.3	21.2
1955	272.8	1,651	6.4	9.4	1993	4,411.5	17,105	292.5	20.8
1960	284.1	1,572	9.2	10.0	1994	4,692.8	18,025	296.3	20.3
1965	313.8	1,613	11.3	9.6	1995	4,974.0	18,930	332.4	22.0
1970	370.1	1,814	19.3	9.9	1996	5,224.8	19,805	344.0	22.0
1975	533.2	2,475	32.7	9.8	1997	5,413.1	20,026	355.8	22.2
1976	620.4	2,852	37.1	10.0	1998	5,526.2	20,443	363.8	22.0
1977	698.8	3,170	41.9	10.2	1999	5,656.3	20,746	353.5	20.7
1978	771.5	3,463	48.7	10.6	2000	5,674.2	20,108	362.0	20.3
1979	826.5	3,669	59.8	11.9	2001	5,807.5	20,370	359.5	19.3
1980	907.7	3,985	74.9	12.7	2002	6,228.2	21,598	332.5	16.5
1981	997.9	4,338	95.6	14.1	2003	6,783.2	23,325	318.1	14.7
1982	1,142.0	4,913	117.4	15.7	2004	7,379.1	25,182	321.6	14.0
1983	1,377.2	5,870	128.8	15.9	2005[1]	7,392.7	26,832	352.4	14.3

Note: As of end of fiscal year. Through 1976, the fiscal year ended June 30. From 1977 on, the fiscal year ends Sept. 30. (1) Estimated.

Budget Deficits as Percent of GDP, Selected Countries[1]

Source: Organization of Economi c Cooperation and Development

	1990	1995	1998	2000	2005	2006		1990	1995	1998	2000	2005	2006
Australia	-1.7	-3.9	0.7	0.9	0.9	0.8	Korea	3.2	3.8	1.7	5.4	2.8	2.9
Austria	-2.4	-5.7	-2.5	-1.6	-2.0	-1.9	Luxembourg	4.8	2.5	3.2	6.2	-1.5	-1.5
Belgium	-6.8	-4.4	-0.7	0.2	-0.5	-1.2	Netherlands	-5.3	-4.2	-0.8	2.2	-2.2	-1.7
Canada	-5.8	-5.3	0.1	2.9	1.2	0.8	New Zealand	-4.3	3.0	-0.8	3.1	3.2	2.8
Czech Republic	–	-13.4	-5.0	-3.7	-4.5	-4.2	Norway	2.2	3.4	3.6	15.6	14.4	14.6
Denmark	-1.2	-2.3	1.1	2.5	1.8	1.5	Poland	–	-3.9	-4.0	-2.4	-4.3	-4.0
Finland	5.5	-3.9	1.6	7.1	1.3	1.1	Portugal	-6.6	-5.5	-3.2	-2.9	-5.3	-4.8
France	-2.1	-5.5	-2.7	-1.4	-3.0	-3.0	Slovak Republic	–	-0.9	-3.8	-12.3	-3.4	-3.2
Germany	-2.0	-3.3	-2.2	1.3	-3.5	-3.2	Spain	-3.9	-6.6	-3.0	-0.9	0.5	0.6
Greece[1]	-15.7	-10.2	-2.5	-4.2	-3.8	-3.5	Sweden	3.4	-6.9	1.9	5.0	0.8	0.8
Hungary	–	-7.6	-8.0	-3.0	-4.2	-4.1	Switzerland	0.6	-1.2	-1.5	2.3	-1.0	-0.8
Iceland	-3.3	-3.0	0.5	2.5	1.1	1.1	United Kingdom	-1.6	-5.8	0.1	3.8	-2.9	-3.0
Ireland	-2.8	-2.1	2.3	4.4	-0.7	-0.7	United States	-4.2	-3.1	0.4	1.6	-4.1	-3.9
Italy	-11.8	-7.6	-3.1	-0.7	-4.4	-5.0	Euro area	-4.6	-5.1	-2.3	0.1	-2.8	-2.7
Japan	2.1	-4.7	-5.5	-7.5	-6.1	-5.3	Total OECD	-3.0	-4.0	-1.2	0.3	-3.2	-3.0

(1) Financial balances include revenues from the sale of mobile telephone licenses.

State Finances: Revenue, Expenditures, Debt, and Taxes

Source: Census Bureau, U.S. Dept. of Commerce

(fiscal year 2003)

STATE	Revenue (millions)	Expenditures (millions)	Debt (millions)	Per capita debt	Per capita taxes	Per capita expenditures
Alabama	$19,099	$18,471	$6,285	$1,395	$1,425	$4,101
Alaska	6,924	8,122	5,830	8,997	1,729	12,533
Arizona	17,927	19,606	5,554	996	1,558	3,514
Arkansas	11,805	12,085	3,295	1,208	1,886	4,430
California	195,545	204,438	95,210	2,685	2,233	5,765
Colorado	13,806	17,691	8,921	1,962	1,459	3,890
Connecticut	18,241	20,721	22,490	6,450	2,727	5,942
Delaware	5,041	4,858	4,358	5,328	2,587	5,939
Florida	55,213	56,317	21,993	1,294	1,588	3,313
Georgia	29,874	32,527	8,890	1,025	1,546	3,749
Hawaii	6,808	7,611	5,653	4,526	2,858	6,094
Idaho	5,493	5,415	2,603	1,904	1,715	3,961
Illinois	44,423	51,291	46,689	3,691	1,756	4,055
Indiana	24,553	23,090	11,854	1,912	1,809	3,724

STATE	Revenue (millions)	Expenditures (millions)	Debt (millions)	Per capita debt	Per capita taxes	Per capita expenditures
Iowa	12,973	13,088	4,279	1,455	1,673	4,449
Kansas	10,402	10,954	2,472	907	1,838	4,020
Kentucky	18,377	19,117	7,109	1,726	2,020	4,642
Louisiana	19,438	18,681	9,773	2,175	1,658	4,157
Maine	6,801	6,706	4,417	3,375	2,061	5,123
Maryland	21,801	24,592	12,951	2,350	1,992	4,462
Massachusetts	30,371	32,710	48,479	7,551	2,431	5,095
Michigan	50,077	51,016	22,479	2,230	2,256	5,060
Minnesota	25,596	28,899	7,150	1,412	2,761	5,707
Mississippi	13,393	13,503	4,167	1,445	1,734	4,684
Missouri	22,024	21,566	13,855	2,423	1,509	3,771
Montana	4,608	4,437	2,879	3,137	1,620	4,833
Nebraska	7,285	6,824	2,136	1,229	1,927	3,929
Nevada	8,351	7,816	3,604	1,608	1,842	3,486
New Hampshire	5,207	5,276	5,594	4,340	1,520	4,093
New Jersey	46,078	44,948	33,609	3,889	2,307	5,201
New Mexico	9,848	10,673	4,601	2,449	1,920	5,680
New York	118,275	127,475	91,635	4,770	2,199	6,635
North Carolina	30,043	34,361	12,142	1,442	1,882	4,080
North Dakota	3,359	3,121	1,599	2,526	1,861	4,931
Ohio	49,905	56,392	21,054	1,841	1,806	4,930
Oklahoma	14,919	15,125	6,747	1,924	1,685	4,314
Oregon	19,252	18,006	7,464	2,094	1,600	5,052
Pennsylvania	49,459	57,428	24,330	1,967	1,874	4,642
Rhode Island	5,856	5,977	6,189	5,752	2,097	5,554
South Carolina	19,669	21,040	10,990	2,649	1,531	5,071
South Dakota	3,000	2,898	2,567	3,355	1,324	3,788
Tennessee	20,564	21,022	3,496	598	1,508	3,597
Texas	82,621	76,386	14,616	661	1,317	3,456
Utah	11,534	10,252	5,064	2,153	1,681	4,359
Vermont	3,639	3,859	2,532	4,091	2,518	6,234
Virginia	28,185	29,129	13,530	1,837	1,761	3,955
Washington	29,661	32,600	14,621	2,385	2,114	5,317
West Virginia	9,766	10,004	4,260	2,353	1,985	5,524
Wisconsin	25,165	27,658	14,801	2,704	2,209	5,053
Wyoming	3,403	3,264	1,111	2,214	2,425	6,503
ALL STATES[1]	**$1,295,659**	**$1,359,048**	**$697,929**	**$2,405**	**$1,892**	**$4,683**

(1) Totals may not add because of rounding.

State and Local Government Receipts and Current Expenditures

Source: Bureau of Economic Analysis, U.S. Dept. of Commerce

(billions of current dollars; revised)

	1999	2000	2001	2002	2003	2004
RECEIPTS	**$1,236.7**	**$1,319.5**	**$1,373.0**	**$1,411.9**	**$1,494.9**	**$1,581.7**
Current tax receipts	840.4	893.2	915.8	926.5	969.2	1,047.6
Personal current taxes	214.5	236.6	242.7	220.1	226.1	247.2
Income taxes	195.5	217.3	223.1	199.6	204.6	224.0
Other	19.0	19.4	19.6	20.5	21.6	23.2
Taxes on production and imports	590.2	621.1	642.8	675.3	708.7	758.8
Sales taxes	301.6	316.6	321.1	329.1	343.9	370.4
Property taxes	242.8	254.6	269.3	291.5	305.0	322.8
Other	45.8	49.9	52.4	54.7	59.7	65.5
Taxes on corporate income	35.8	35.5	30.2	31.2	34.4	41.5
Contributions for government social insurance	9.8	11.0	13.6	14.5	15.0	19.7
Income receipts on assets	85.3	92.2	88.8	81.6	81.0	77.1
Interest receipts	78.4	84.0	80.3	73.2	71.3	67.0
Dividends	1.8	1.9	2.0	2.1	2.5	2.4
Rents and royalties	5.1	6.3	6.5	6.2	7.1	7.7
Current transfer receipts	290.8	315.4	350.8	385.9	425.9	439.8
Federal grants-in-aid	232.9	247.3	276.1	304.4	339.9	348.3
From business (net)	23.0	28.8	31.4	32.8	32.2	35.5
From persons	34.9	39.2	43.3	48.7	53.8	56.0
Current surplus of government enterprises	10.4	7.7	4.0	3.3	3.7	-2.5
CURRENT EXPENDITURES	**1,186.3**	**1,269.5**	**1,368.2**	**1,436.9**	**1,498.1**	**1,587.5**
Consumption expenditures	858.9	917.8	969.8	1,016.5	1,058.5	1,117.7
Government social benefit payments to persons	252.4	271.7	305.2	331.9	350.3	380.5
Interest payments	74.6	79.5	85.5	87.4	88.9	88.9
Subsidies	0.4	0.5	7.7	1.0	0.3	0.5
Less: Wage accruals less disbursements	0.0	0.0	0.0	0.0	0.0	0.0
Net state and local government saving	50.4	50.0	4.8	–25.0	–3.2	-5.9
Social insurance funds	1.7	2.0	2.6	1.6	1.1	1.8
Other	48.7	47.9	2.2	–26.6	–4.3	-7.7
Addenda:						
Total receipts	1,276.6	1,363.2	1,421.6	1,463.7	1,546.4	1,633.6
Current receipts	1,236.7	1,319.5	1,373.0	1,411.9	1,494.9	1,581.7
Capital transfer receipts	39.9	43.7	48.6	51.8	51.5	51.9
Total expenditures	1,298.8	1,393.5	1,502.7	1,583.9	1,645.0	1,734.6
Current expenditures	1,186.3	1,269.5	1,368.2	1,436.9	1,498.1	1,587.5
Gross government investment	206.0	225.0	243.0	259.3	264.9	270.6
Net purchases of nonproduced assets	8.6	8.8	9.2	9.8	10.0	11.7
Less: Consumption of fixed capital	102.1	109.8	117.8	122.1	127.9	135.3
NET LENDING OR NET BORROWING (–)	**–22.3**	**–30.4**	**–81.1**	**–120.2**	**–98.7**	**–101.0**

Top U.S. Charities by Donations[1]

Source: The Chronicle of Philanthropy, 2005
(ranked by private support; in millions of dollars)

Rank/Organization	Private Support[2]	Total Income[3]
1. Salvation Army (Alexandria, VA)	$1,324	$3,040
2. American Cancer Society (Atlanta, GA)	794	836
3. Gifts In Kind International (Alexandria, VA)	787	791
4. YMCA (Chicago, IL)	757	4,657
5. Lutheran Services in America (Baltimore, MD)	723	8,031
6. AmeriCares Foundation (Stamford, CT)	696	698
7. Fidelity Charitable Gift Fund (Boston, MA)	619	530
8. American National Red Cross (Washington, DC)	587	3,019
9. Feed the Children (Oklahoma City, OK)	565	568
10. Harvard University (Cambridge, MA)	558	3,319
11. Catholic Charities USA (Alexandria, VA)	532	2,859
12. Boys & Girls Clubs of America (Atlanta, GA)	501	1,151
13. Stanford University (Palo Alto, CA)	$486	$2,507
14. World Vision (Federal Way, WA)	482	679
15. Nature Conservancy (Arlington, VA)	480	762
16. America's Second Harvest (Chicago, IL)	465	468
17. King Benevolent Fund (Bristol, VA)	433	432
18. Habitat for Humanity International (Americus, GA)	418	760
19. Food for the Poor (Deerfield Beach, FL)	405	465
20. University of Pennsylvania (Philadelphia, PA)	400	NA
21. American Heart Association (Dallas, TX)	384	503
22. University of Arkansas at Fayetteville	365	440
23. Campus Crusade for Christ International (Orlando, FL)	365	405
24. Goodwill Industries International (Bethesda, MD)	360	2,215
25. United Jewish Communities (New York, NY)	345	423

(1) Fiscal year 2003 data used, except: 2004 data used for organizations with fiscal years ending in Jan.–March; 2002 data used for organizations with incomplete 2003 data. (2) Private support consists of donations from individuals, foundations, and corporations. Total income also includes government funding and fees charged. (3) Total income includes private support as well as revenue or losses from investments made by the charity. NA = not available.

Consumer Credit Outstanding, 2002-2004

Source: Federal Reserve System
(in billions of dollars)
Estimated amounts of credit outstanding as of end of year. Not seasonally adjusted.

	2002	2003	2004
TOTAL	**1,942.6**	**2,025.5**	**2,139.9**
Major Holders			
Commercial banks	587.2	636.4	711.4
Finance companies	237.8	295.4	368.2
Credit unions	195.7	205.9	215.4
Fed. govt. and Sallie Mae	129.6	114.6	98.4
Savings institutions	68.7	77.9	91.3
Nonfinancial business	86.5	70.3	64.8
Pools of securitized assets[1]	637.1	625.0	590.5
Major Types of Credit			
Revolving[2]	**747.5**	**763.1**	**817.8**
Commercial banks	231.0	260.1	321.8
Finance companies	38.9	37.6	43.3
Credit unions	22.2	22.4	23.2
Savings institutions	16.3	23.8	27.9
Nonfinancial business	48.8	26.5	17.9
Pools of securitized assets[1]	390.3	392.7	383.7
Nonrevolving[2]	**1,195.0**	**1,262.5**	**1,322.1**
Commercial banks	356.2	376.4	389.6
Finance companies	198.8	257.8	324.8
Credit unions	173.5	183.5	192.1
Fed. government and Sallie Mae	129.6	114.6	98.4
Savings institutions	52.4	54.0	63.4
Nonfinancial business	37.7	43.8	46.9
Pools of securitized assets[1]	246.8	232.3	206.8

(1) Outstanding balances of pools upon which securities have been issued; these balances are no longer carried on the balance sheets of the loan originators. (2) Includes estimates for holders that do not separately report consumer credit holding by type.

Global Stock Markets

Source: The Conference Board; not seasonally adjusted

Stock price indexes (1990[1]=100):	June 1, 1960	June 1, 1970	June 1, 1980	June 1, 1990	June 1, 2000	June 1, 2001	June 1, 2002	June 1, 2003	June 1, 2004	Jan. 1 2005	June 1 2005
United States	17.1	21.9	34.3	107.6	437.2	368.0	297.5	292.9	342.9	355.1	358.1
Japan	4.4	7.3	23.8	110.8	60.4	45.0	36.8	31.5	41.1	39.5	40.2
Germany	36.1	27.5	30.5	111.1	407.9	358.2	259.1	190.4	239.6	251.6	271.2
France	16.3	15.6	23.8	112.0	354.7	287.5	214.5	169.7	205.4	215.3	232.7
United Kingdom	8.2	11.6	24.9	108.2	279.9	252.0	209.1	182.1	205.9	255.5	236.5
Italy	28.9	20.6	15.9	117.3	309.0	254.1	196.7	181.1	206.5	234.9	241.1
Canada	14.8	25.0	60.3	103.6	298.0	226.1	208.9	204.1	249.8	269.0	289.5

(1) 12-month average.

U.S. Holdings of Foreign Stocks[1]

Source: Bureau of Economic Analysis, U.S. Dept. of Commerce
(billions of dollars)

	2002	2003	2004
Europe	**$789.4**	**$1,135.3**	**$1,382.7**
United Kingdom	289.5	426.2	540.3
France	94.3	130.8	156.1
Switzerland	75.6	117.9	136.3
Netherlands	88.1	115.8	134.2
Germany	66.5	103.2	122.6
Spain	29.9	43.8	53
Italy	28.2	39	47.4
Finland	34.3	35.2	40.8
Sweden	19.2	27.5	39.9
Canada	**88.2**	**149.3**	**188.5**
Latin America and Caribbean	**191.6**	**260.4**	**302.8**
Bermuda	88.6	107.5	124.1
Cayman Islands	$32.9	$45.3	$53.8
Brazil	19.7	31.8	39.4
Mexico	22	28.5	31.7
Asia	**258.7**	**454.4**	**575.3**
Japan	148.1	255.5	333.3
Korea, Republic of	27.8	49.1	60.9
Hong Kong	22	36.2	39.5
Taiwan	8.5	27	35.5
Africa	**9.6**	**18.7**	**22.5**
South Africa	7.9	15.1	18.3
Other countries	**37.2**	**61.3**	**48.3**
Australia	34.6	56.5	42.5
TOTAL HOLDINGS	**1,374.7**	**2,079.4**	**2,520.1**

(1) As of year end.

Standard & Poor's 500 Index, 1993-2005

Source: *Facts On File World News Digest;* monthly closing levels; record high daily closing was 1527.46, Mar. 24, 2000.

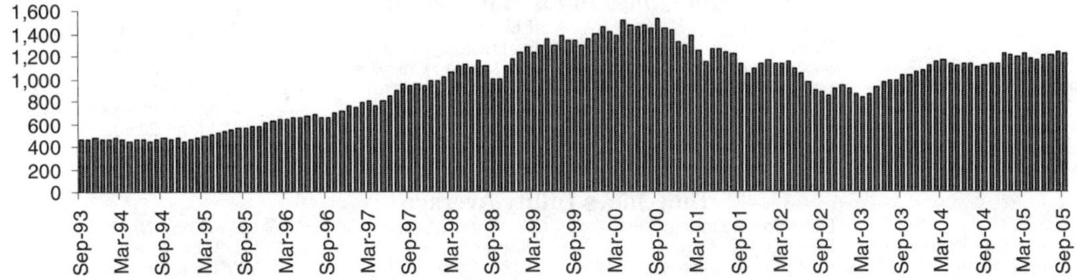

Record One-Day Gains and Losses on the Dow Jones Industrial Average

Source: Dow Jones & Co., Inc.; as of Sept. 30, 2005

GREATEST POINT GAINS

Rank	Date	Close	Net Chg	% Chg
1.	3/16/2000	10630.60	499.19	4.93
2.	7/24/2002	8191.29	488.95	6.35
3.	7/29/2002	8711.88	447.49	5.41
4.	4/5/2001	9918.05	402.63	4.23
5.	4/18/2001	10615.83	399.10	3.91
6.	9/8/1998	8020.78	380.53	4.98
7.	10/15/2002	8255.68	378.28	4.80
8.	9/24/2001	8603.86	368.05	4.47
9.	10/1/2002	7938.79	346.86	4.57
10.	5/16/2001	11215.92	342.95	3.15

GREATEST POINT LOSSES

Rank	Date	Close	Net Chg	% Chg
1.	9/17/2001	8920.70	–684.81	–7.13
2.	4/14/2000	10305.77	–617.78	–5.66
3.	10/27/1997	7161.15	–554.26	–7.18
4.	8/31/1998	7539.07	–512.61	–6.37
5.	10/19/1987	1738.74	–508.00	–22.61
6.	3/12/2001	10208.25	–436.37	–4.10
7.	7/19/2002	8019.26	–390.23	–4.64
8.	9/20/2001	8376.21	–382.92	–4.37
9.	10/12/2000	10034.58	–379.21	–3.64
10.	3/7/2000	9796.03	–374.47	–3.68

GREATEST % GAINS

Rank	Date	Close	Net Chg	% Chg
1.	3/15/1933	62.10	8.26	15.34
2.	10/6/1931	99.34	12.86	14.87
3.	10/30/1929	258.47	28.40	12.34
4.	9/21/1932	75.16	7.67	11.36
5.	10/21/1987	2027.85	186.84	10.15
6.	8/3/1932	58.22	5.06	9.52
7.	2/11/1932	78.60	6.80	9.47
8.	11/14/1929	217.28	18.59	9.36
9.	12/18/1931	80.69	6.90	9.35
10.	2/13/1932	85.82	7.22	9.19

GREATEST % LOSSES

Rank	Date	Close	Net Chg	% Chg
1.	12/12/1914	54.00	–17.42	–24.39
2.	10/19/1987	1738.74	–508.00	–22.61
3.	10/28/1929	260.64	–38.33	–12.82
4.	10/29/1929	230.07	–30.57	–11.73
5.	11/6/1929	232.13	–25.55	–9.92
6.	12/18/1899	58.27	–5.57	–8.72
7.	8/12/1932	63.11	–5.79	–8.40
8.	3/14/1907	76.23	–6.89	–8.29
9.	10/26/1987	1793.93	–156.83	–8.04
10.	7/21/1933	88.71	–7.55	–7.84

Dow Jones Industrial Average, 1963-2005

High		YEAR	Low	
Dec. 18	767.21	**1963**	Jan. 2	646.79
Nov. 18	891.71	**1964**	Jan. 2	766.08
Dec. 31	969.26	**1965**	June 28	840.59
Feb. 9	995.15	**1966**	Oct. 7	744.32
Sept. 25	943.08	**1967**	Jan. 3	786.41
Dec. 3	985.21	**1968**	Mar. 21	825.13
May 14	968.85	**1969**	Dec. 17	769.93
Dec. 29	842.00	**1970**	May 6	631.16
Apr. 28	950.82	**1971**	Nov. 23	797.97
Dec. 11	1036.27	**1972**	Jan. 26	889.15
Jan. 11	1051.70	**1973**	Dec. 5	788.31
Mar. 13	891.66	**1974**	Dec. 6	577.60
July 15	881.81	**1975**	Jan. 2	632.04
Sept. 21	1014.79	**1976**	Jan. 2	858.71
Jan. 3	999.75	**1977**	Nov. 2	800.85
Sept. 8	907.74	**1978**	Feb. 28	742.12
Oct. 5	897.61	**1979**	Nov. 7	796.67
Nov. 20	1000.17	**1980**	Apr. 21	759.13
Apr. 27	1024.05	**1981**	Sept. 25	824.01
Dec. 27	1070.55	**1982**	Aug. 12	776.92
Nov. 29	1287.20	**1983**	Jan. 3	1027.04
Jan. 6	1286.64	**1984**	July 24	1086.57
Dec. 16	1553.10	**1985**	Jan. 4	1184.96
Dec. 2	1955.57	**1986**	Jan. 22	1502.29
Aug. 25	2722.42	**1987**	Oct. 19	1738.74
Oct. 21	2183.50	**1988**	Jan. 20	1879.14
Oct. 9	2791.41	**1989**	Jan. 3	2144.64
July 16	2999.75	**1990**	Oct. 11	2365.10
Dec. 31	3168.83	**1991**	Jan. 9	2470.30
June 1	3413.21	**1992**	Oct. 9	3136.58
Dec. 29	3794.33	**1993**	Jan. 20	3241.95
Jan. 31	3978.36	**1994**	Apr. 4	3593.35
Dec. 13	5216.47	**1995**	Jan. 30	3832.08
Dec. 27	6560.91	**1996**	Jan. 10	5032.94
Aug. 6	8259.31	**1997**	Apr. 11	6391.69
Nov. 23	9374.27	**1998**	Aug. 31	7539.07
Dec. 31	11497.12	**1999**	Jan. 22	9120.67
Jan. 14	11722.98*	**2000**	Mar. 7	9796.03
May 21	11337.92	**2001**	Sept. 21	8235.81
Mar. 19	10635.25	**2002**	Oct. 9	7286.27
Dec. 31	10453.90	**2003**	Mar. 11	7524.06
Dec. 28	10854.54	**2004**	Oct. 25	9749.99

Sept. 30, 2005 close: 10,459.63

* Record high closing.

Milestones of the Dow Jones Industrial Average

(as of Sept. 30, 2005)

First close over...		First close over...		First close over...		First close over...		First close over...	
100	Jan. 12, 1906	5500	Feb. 8, 1996	8400	Feb. 18, 1998	9300	July 16, 1998	10500	Apr. 21, 1999
500	Mar. 12, 1956	6000	Oct. 14, 1996	8300	Feb. 12, 1998	9500	Jan. 6, 1999*	10700	Apr. 22, 1999*
1000	Nov. 14, 1972	6500	Nov. 25, 1996	8400	Feb. 18, 1998	9600	Jan. 8, 1999	10800	Apr. 27, 1999
1500	Dec. 11, 1985	7000	Feb. 13, 1997	8500	Feb. 27, 1998	9700	Mar. 5, 1999	11000	May 3, 1999*
2000	Jan. 8, 1987	7500	June 10, 1997	8600	Mar. 10, 1998	9800	Mar. 11, 1999	11100	May 13, 1999
2500	July 17, 1987	8000	July 16, 1997	8700	Mar. 16, 1998	9900	Mar. 15, 1999	11200	July 12, 1999
3000	April 17, 1991	8100	July 24, 1997	8800	Mar. 19, 1998	10000	Mar. 29, 1999	11300	Aug. 25, 1999
3500	May 19, 1993	8200	July 30, 1997	8900	Mar. 20, 1998	10100	Apr. 8, 1999	11400	Dec. 23, 1999
4000	Feb. 23, 1995	8100	July 24, 1997	9000	Apr. 6, 1998	10300	Apr. 12, 1999*	11500	Jan. 7, 2000
4500	June 16, 1995	8200	July 30, 1997	9100	Apr. 14, 1998	10400	Apr. 14, 1999	11700	Jan. 14, 2000*
5000	Nov. 21, 1995	8300	Feb. 12, 1998	9200	May 13, 1998				

*9400, 10200, 10600, 10900, and 11600 are not listed because the Dow had risen another 100 points or more by the time the market closed for the day. The all-time record closing was 11722.98 on Jan. 14, 2000.

Components of the Dow Jones Averages

(as of Sept. 30, 2005)

Dow Jones Industrial Average

Alcoa
Altria Group
American Express Co.
American International Group (AIG)
Boeing Co.
Caterpillar
Citigroup
Coca-Cola
DuPont
Exxon Mobil Corp.
General Electric Co.
General Motors Corp.
Hewlett-Packard Co.
Home Depot
Honeywell International
IBM
Intel Corp.
J.P. Morgan Chase & Co.
Johnson & Johnson
McDonald's Corp.
Merck & Co.
Microsoft Corp.
Pfizer
Procter & Gamble Co.
SBC Communications
3M Company
United Technologies Corp.
Verizon Communications
Wal-Mart Stores
Walt Disney Co.

Dow Jones Utility Average

AES Corp.
American Electric Power Co.
CenterPoint Energy
Consolidated Edison
Dominion Resources
Duke Energy Corp.
Edison International
Exelon Corp.
FirstEnergy Corp.
NiSource
PG&E Corp.
Public Service Enterprise Group
Southern Co.
TXU Corp.
Williams Cos.

Dow Jones Transportation Average

Alexander & Baldwin
AMR (American Airlines) Corp.
Burlington Northern Santa Fe Corp.
C.H. Robinson Worldwide
CNF Inc.
Continental Airlines
CSX Corp.
Expeditors International of Washington, Inc.
FedEx Corp.
GATX Corp.
J.B. Hunt Transportation Services
JetBlue Airways
Landstar System Inc.
Norfolk Southern
Overseas Shipholding Group
Ryder System
Southwest Airlines Co.
Union Pacific Corp.
United Parcel Service
Yellow Roadway Corp.

Record One-Day Gains and Losses on the Nasdaq Stock Market

Source: Nasdaq Stock Market; as of Sept. 30, 2005

GREATEST POINT GAINS

Rank	Date	Change
1.	1/3/2001	324.83
2.	12/5/2000	274.05
3.	4/18/2000	254.41
4.	5/30/2000	254.37
5.	10/19/2000	247.04
6.	10/13/2000	242.09
7.	6/2/2000	230.88
8.	4/25/2000	228.75
9.	4/17/2000	217.87
10.	6/1/2000	181.59

GREATEST % GAINS

Rank	Date	% Change
1.	1/3/2001	14.17%
2.	12/5/2000	10.48%
3.	4/5/2001	8.92%
4.	4/18/2001	8.12%
5.	5/30/2000	7.94%
6.	10/13/2000	7.87%
7.	10/19/2000	7.79%
8.	5/8/2002	7.78%
9.	12/22/2000	7.56%
10.	10/21/1987	7.34%

GREATEST POINT LOSSES

Rank	Date	Change
1.	4/14/2000	–355.49
2.	4/3/2000	–349.15
3.	4/12/2000	–286.27
4.	4/10/2000	–258.25
5.	1/4/2000	–229.46
6.	3/14/2000	–200.61
7.	5/10/2000	–200.28
8.	5/23/2000	–199.66
9.	10/25/2000	–190.22
10.	3/29/2000	–189.22

GREATEST % LOSSES

Rank	Date	% Change
1.	10/19/1987	–11.35%
2.	4/14/2000	–9.67%
3.	10/20/1987	–9.00%
4.	10/26/1987	–9.00%
5.	8/31/1998	–8.56%
6.	4/3/2000	–7.64%
7.	1/2/2001	–7.23%
8.	12/20/2000	–7.12%
9.	4/12/2000	–7.06%
10.	10/27/1997	–7.02%

Nasdaq Stock Market, 1971-2005

High	YEAR	Low
114.12	**1971**	99.68
135.15	**1972**	113.65
136.84	**1973**	88.67
96.53	**1974**	54.87
88.00	**1975**	60.70
97.88	**1976**	78.06
105.05	**1977**	93.66
139.25	**1978**	99.09
152.29	**1979**	117.84
208.29	**1980**	124.09
223.96	**1981**	170.80
241.63	**1982**	158.92
329.11	**1983**	229.88
288.41	**1984**	223.91
325.53	**1985**	245.82
411.21	**1986**	322.14
456.27	**1987**	288.49
397.54	**1988**	329.00
487.60	**1989**	376.87
470.30	**1990**	322.93
586.35	**1991**	352.85
676.95	**1992**	545.85
790.56	**1993**	645.02
803.93	**1994**	691.23
1072.82	**1995**	740.53
1328.45	**1996**	978.17
1748.62	**1997**	1194.39
2200.63	**1998**	1357.09
4090.61	**1999**	2193.13
5048.62*	**2000**	2332.78
2892.36	**2001**	1387.06
2059.38	**2002**	1114.11
2009.88	**2003**	1271.47
2178.00	**2004**	1752.00
Sept. 30, 2005 close: 2147.90		

* Record high closing, Mar. 10, 2000.

Milestones of the Nasdaq Stock Market

Source: Nasdaq Stock Market; as of Sept. 30, 2005

First close over...	
100	Feb. 8, 1971
200	Nov. 13, 1980
300	May 6, 1986
400	May 30, 1986
500	Apr. 12, 1991
1,000	July 17, 1995
1,500	July 11, 1997
2,000	July 16, 1998
2,500	Jan. 29, 1999
3,000	Nov. 3, 1999
3,500	Dec. 3, 1999
4,000	Dec. 29, 1999
4,500	Feb. 17, 2000
5,000	Mar. 9, 2000

Most Active Common Stocks in 2004

New York Exchange Volume (millions of shares)

Lucent Technologies, Inc.	5,811.0
Nortel Networks Corporation	4,805.5
Pfizer, Inc.	4,430.4
General Electric Company	4,118.5
Motorola, Inc.	2,862.5
Time Warner, Inc.	2,712.8
Citigroup, Inc.	2,649.8
Texas Instruments, Inc.	2,559.7
EMC Corporation	2,506.7
AT&T Wireless Services, Inc.	2,350.0

American Exchange Volume (millions of shares)

Bema Gold Corporation	9,403.6
Eagle Broadband, Inc.	8,138.5
Devon Energy Corporation	5,972.6
Harken Energy Corporation	5,348.7
Golden Star Resources Ltd.	5,306.7
Avitar, Inc.	4,929.1
Internap Network Services Corp	4,866.2
ISCO International, Inc.	4,563.5
IVAX Corporation	4,527.1
Nabors Industries Limited	4,123.7

NASDAQ Volume (millions of shares)

Microsoft Corporation	17,333,799
Sirius Satellite Radio Inc.	17,020,339
Intel Corporation	16,698,223
Cisco Systems, Inc.	13,951,370
Oracle Corporation	11,479,446
Sun Microsystems, Inc.	10,367,515
JDS Uniphase Corporation	8,297,736
Applied Materials, Inc.	8,249,963
TASER International, Inc	5,434,110
Yahoo! Inc.	5,134,065

The Wealthiest Americans

On Sept. 22, 2005, *Forbes* magazine released its 24th annual roster of the 400 wealthiest Americans. Here are the top ten (with Forbes's estimate of their net worth):

1. Bill Gates, $51 bil. (Microsoft)
2. Warren Buffett, $40 bil. (Berkshire Hathaway)
3. Paul Allen, $23 bil. (Microsoft)
4. Michael Dell, $18 bil. (Dell)
5. Larry Ellison, $17 bil. (Oracle)
6. Christy Walton, $15.7 bil. (Wal-Mart heir)
   Jim C. Walton, $15.7 bil. (Wal-Mart heir)
8. Robson Walton, $15.6 bil. (Wal-Mart heir)
9. Alice Walton, $15.5 bil. (Wal-Mart heir)
10. Helen Walton, $15.4 bil. (Wal-Mart heir)

The total estimated net worth of all 400 came to $1.13 tril., $125 bil. more than 2004.

Average Yields of Long-Term Treasury, Corporate, and Municipal Bonds

Source: Office of Market Finance, U.S. Dept. of the Treasury; Federal Reserve System

Period	Treasury 30-year bonds[1]	New Aa corporate bonds[2]	New Aa municipal bonds[3]
1986			
June	7.57	9.39	7.87
Dec.	7.37	8.87	6.87
1987			
June	8.57	9.64	7.79
Dec.	9.12	10.22	7.96
1988			
June	9.00	10.08	7.78
Dec.	9.01	10.05	7.61
1989			
June	8.27	9.24	7.02
Dec.	7.90	9.23	6.98
1990			
June	8.46	9.69	7.24
Dec.	8.24	9.55	7.09
1991			
June	8.47	9.37	7.13
Dec.	7.70	8.55	6.69
1992			
June	7.84	8.45	6.49
Dec.	7.44	8.12	6.22
1993			
June	6.81	7.48	5.63
Dec.	6.25	7.22	5.35
1994			
June	7.40	8.16	6.11
Dec.	7.87	8.66	6.80
1995			
June	6.57	7.42	5.84
Dec.	6.06	7.02	5.45
1996			
June	7.06	8.00	6.02
Dec.	6.55	7.45	5.64
1997			
June	6.77	7.71	5.53
Dec.	5.99	6.68	5.19
1998			
Jun	5.70	6.43	5.12
Dec	5.06	6.13	4.98
1999			
Jun.	6.04	7.21	5.37
Dec.	6.35	7.55	5.95
2000			
June	5.93	7.75	5.80
Dec.	5.49	7.21	5.22
2001			
June	5.67	7.11	5.20
Dec.	5.48	6.80	5.25
2002			
June	5.65	6.57	5.09
Dec.	5.01	5.93	4.85
2003			
June	4.34	4.97	4.33
Dec.	5.11	5.62	4.65
2004			
June	5.45	6.01	5.05
Dec.	4.88	5.47	4.49
2005			
June	4.35	4.96	4.24

NA = Not available. (1) On Feb. 18, 2002, the U.S. treasury discontinued the 30-year constant maturity yield; rates thereafter are for 20-year yields. (2) Treasury series based on 3-week moving average of reoffering yields of new corporate bonds rated Aa by Moody's Investors Service with an original maturity of at least 20 years. Treasury discontinued yield index after Jan. 31, 2003. Rates thereafter are for Moody's seasoned Aaa corporate bonds as listed by Federal Reserve. (3) Index of new reoffering yields on 20-year general obligations rated Aa by Moody's Investors Service; discontinued by Treasury Jan. 31, 2003; rates thereafter are from Bond Buyer Index of general obligation, 20-year-to-maturity, mixed quality state and local bonds.

Performance of Mutual Funds by Type, 2005

Source: Thomson Financial, Rockville, MD, 800-232-2285

(data for periods ending Sept. 30; all figures are percents)

Fund Type/Fund Objective	AVERAGE ANNUAL RETURN 1–year	3–year	5–year
Diversified Stock			
Aggressive Growth	15.41	16.56	-8.06
Equity Income	13.30	16.34	3.60
Growth–Domestic	13.99	16.19	-2.80
Growth & Income	12.74	15.90	1.58
Mid Cap	19.84	20.95	1.61
S&P 500 Index	11.14	14.83	-1.80
Small Cap	18.67	22.10	5.10
Specialty Stock			
Sector–Energy/Natural Res	47.43	36.98	17.36
Sector–Financial Services	8.77	16.50	6.88
Sector–Precious Metals	14.56	23.40	28.11
Sector–Health/Biotechnology	15.82	16.40	-0.37
Sector–Other	0.82	-2.70	0.76
Sector–Real Estate	25.95	25.74	18.49
Sector–Tech/Communications	17.69	23.89	-15.65
Sector–Utilities	32.91	25.28	1.08
World Stock			
Emerging Market Equity	43.79	37.54	13.75
Global Equity	22.43	21.65	1.93
Non–US Equity	26.94	24.42	3.43
Emerging Market Income	16.47	22.04	15.70
Hybrid			
Asset Allocation–Domestic	10.72	12.27	1.75
Asset Allocation–Global	12.83	14.08	4.65
Balanced–Domestic	9.28	11.58	2.35
Balanced–Global	16.85	15.49	3.54
Bond			
Corporate–High Yield	5.72	13.39	5.80
Corporate–Investment Grade	2.72	4.67	6.14
Convertible	9.26	14.50	2.22
General Bd–Investment Grade	2.38	4.03	5.77
General Bd–Long	3.52	5.25	6.64
General Bd–Short & Interm.	3.59	5.94	5.91
General Mortgage	2.26	2.66	4.97
Global Income	5.04	8.86	7.73
Loan Participation	3.84	5.65	4.76
Multi–Sector Bond	3.39	NA	NA
US Government/Agency	2.46	2.72	5.45
US Government–Long	3.27	3.08	6.21
US Government–Short & Interm	1.61	2.00	4.71
US Treasury	3.11	3.00	6.70
Municipal Bond			
Municipal–High Yield	5.89	5.23	6.03
Municipal–Insured	2.64	2.87	5.19
Municipal–National	2.68	2.98	4.98
Municipal–Single State	3.10	3.14	5.23

Chicago Board of Trade, Contracts Traded 1994, 2004

Source: Chicago Board of Trade

	1994	2004	% change 1994-2004
FUTURES GROUP			
Agricultural	36,091,553	68,067,223	88.6
Financial	139,483,486	397,119,229	184.7
Stock index	—	23,276,014	NA
Metals	122,637	726,796	492.6
Total futures	**175,697,680**	**489,230,144**	**178.4**
OPTIONS GROUP			
Agricultural	6,256,931	17,082,347	173.0
Financial	37,534,091	92,919,888	147.6
Stock index	—	762,007	NA
Metals	5,952	0	−100.0
Total options	**43,806,394**	**110,764,242**	**152.8**
COMBINED FUTURES AND OPTIONS			
Agricultural	42,348,484	85,149,570	101.0
Financial	177,017,577	490,039,117	176.8
Stock index[1]	—	24,038,021	NA
Metals	128,589	726,796	465.2
GRAND TOTAL	**219,504,074**	**599,994,386**	**173.34**

(1) Now called the Equity Index, and composed of 6 Dow Jones Indexes; not comparable to Stock Index shown for 1994. A dash indicates item delisted from Board of Trade. NA = not applicable.

U.S. Mutual Fund Shareholders[1]

Source: The Investment Company Institute

Shareholder Characteristics, 2004

Median age[2]	48
Median annual household income	$68,700
Median household financial assets[4]	$125,000
Median mutual fund assets	$48,000
Median number of funds owned	4
Employed[2]	77%
Married or living with a partner[2]	71%
Spouse or partner employed	75%
Four-year college degree or more[2]	57%

Owning:

Equity funds	80%
Bond funds	44%
Hybrid funds	34%
Money market funds	49%

Households owning mutual funds

Year	(in mil)[3]	Year	(in mil)[3]
1980	4.6	1999	48.4
1984	10.2	2000	51.7
1988	22.2	2001	56.3
1992	25.8	2002	54.2
1994	30.2	2003	53.3
1996	36.8	2004	53.7
1998	44.4		

(1) Except where noted, data include mutual funds both inside and outside employer-sponsored retirement plans. (2) Of persons responding to survey. (3) Data from 1980-88 exclude households owning mutual funds solely through employer-sponsored retirement plans. (4) Excluding primary residence.

Distribution of Financial Assets of U.S. Families[1]

Source: Federal Reserve System (by type of asset, in percent of family financial assets)

Type of financial asset	1989	1992	1995	1998	2001
Transaction accounts	19.0	17.5	13.9	11.4	11.5
Certificates of deposit	10.2	8.0	5.6	4.3	3.1
Savings bonds	1.5	1.1	1.3	0.7	0.7
Bonds	10.2	8.4	6.3	4.3	4.6
Stocks	15.0	16.5	15.6	22.7	21.6
Mutual funds (excluding money market funds)	5.3	7.6	12.7	12.4	12.2
Retirement accounts	21.5	25.7	28.1	27.6	28.4
Cash value of life insurance	6.0	5.9	7.2	6.4	5.3
Other managed assets	6.6	5.4	5.9	8.6	10.6
Other	4.8	3.8	3.3	1.7	1.9
Financial assets as a percentage of total assets	30.5	31.6	36.7	40.7	42.0

(1) Data from the triennial *Survey of Consumer Finances.* Results of 2004 survey will be released in 2006.

Stock Ownership of U.S. Families, by Income & Age, 1989, 1995, 1998, & 2001[1]

Source: Federal Reserve System

(in percent, except as noted)

		Families having direct or indirect stock holdings[2]				Median value of portfolios (thousands of 2001 dollars)				Stock holdings as share of financial assets[3]			
		1989	1995	1998	2001	1989	1995	1998	2001	1989	1995	1998	2001
All families		**31.7%**	**40.4%**	**48.9%**	**51.9%**	**$11.7**	**$16.9**	**$27.2**	**$34.3**	**27.8%**	**39.9%**	**53.9%**	**56.0%**
Annual Income (in thousands of dollars):	Under $20	3.3	6.5	10.0	12.4	NA	4.3	5.4	7.0	13.6	14.2	20.4	36.9
	$20-40	15.2	24.7	30.8	33.5	8.3	7.3	10.9	7.5	10.0	26.7	29.7	34.9
	$40-60	28.6	41.5	50.2	52.1	6.3	7.2	13.1	15.0	16.7	28.4	37.9	46.4
	$60-80	44.0	54.3	69.3	75.7	8.0	14.6	20.4	28.5	21.7	35.6	45.7	51.7
	$80-90	57.6	69.7	77.9	82.0	13.1	28.9	49.0	64.6	26.1	41.3	50.4	57.4
	$90-100	76.9	80.0	90.4	89.6	53.7	69.3	146.5	247.7	34.3	45.4	62.5	60.4
By age of family head (years):	Under 35	22.4	36.6	40.8	48.9	4.1	5.9	7.6	7.0	20.2	27.2	44.8	52.6
	35-44	39.0	46.4	56.7	59.5	7.1	11.6	21.8	27.5	29.3	39.5	54.6	57.3
	45-54	41.8	48.9	58.6	59.2	18.1	30.0	41.4	50.0	33.5	42.6	55.7	59.1
	55-64	36.2	40.0	55.9	57.1	25.3	35.8	51.2	81.2	27.6	44.2	58.4	56.1
	65-74	26.7	34.4	42.7	39.2	27.9	39.3	61.0	150.0	26.0	35.8	51.3	55.1
	75 +	25.9	27.9	29.4	34.2	34.4	23.1	65.3	120.0	25.0	39.8	48.7	51.4

NA = Not available. (1) Data from the triennial *Survey of Consumer Finances.* Results of 2004 survey will be released in 2006. (2) Indirect holdings are those in mutual funds, retirement accounts, and other managed assets. (3) Among stock-holding families.

Poverty Rate

Source: Bureau of the Census, U.S. Dept. of Commerce

The poverty rate is the proportion of the population whose income falls below the government's official poverty level,and is adjusted each year for inflation. The national poverty rate was 12.7% in 2004, up from the 2003 rate of 12.5%, but below the 1990 rate of 13.5%. About 37.0 million people in the U.S. were in poverty in 2004, 1.1 million more than in 2003. In 2004 17.8% of children and 9.8% of people aged 65 and older were defined as poor.

Poverty Thresholds by Family Size, 1980-2004[1]

Source: Bureau of the Census, U.S. Dept. of Commerce

	2004	2000	1990	1980
1 person	$9,645	$8,794	$6,652	$4,186
Under 65 years	9,827	8,959	6,800	4,284
65 years and over	9,060	8,259	6,268	3,950
2 persons	12,334	11,239	8,509	5,361
Householder under 65	12,714	11,590	8,794	5,537
Householder 65 and over	11,430	10,419	7,905	4,982
3 persons	$15,067	$13,783	$10,419	$6,570
4 persons	19,307	17,603	13,359	8,415
5 persons	22,831	20,819	15,792	9,967
6 persons	25,788	23,528	17,839	11,272
7 persons	29,236	26,754	20,241	12,761
8 persons	32,641	29,701	22,582	14,199
9 persons or more	39,048	35,060	26,848	16,896

(1) Weighted average; not used for computing poverty data.

Persons Below Poverty Level, 1960-2004

Source: Bureau of the Census, U.S. Dept. of Commerce

	Number below poverty level (in millions)				Percentage below poverty level				Avg. income cutoffs for family of 4 at poverty level[3]
YEAR	All races[1]	White	Black	Hispanic origin[2]	All races[1]	White	Black	Hispanic origin[2]	
1960	39.9	28.3	NA	NA	22.2	17.8	NA	NA	$3,022
1970	25.4	17.5	7.5	NA	12.6	9.9	33.5	NA	3,968
1980	29.3	19.7	8.6	3.5	13.0	10.2	32.5	25.7	8,414
1990	33.6	22.3	9.8	6.0	13.5	10.7	31.9	28.1	13,359
1991	35.7	23.7	10.2	6.3	14.2	11.3	32.7	28.7	13,924
1992	38.0	25.3	10.8	7.6	14.8	11.9	33.4	29.6	14,335
1993	39.3	26.2	10.9	8.1	15.1	12.2	33.1	30.6	14,763
1994	38.1	25.4	10.2	8.4	14.5	11.7	30.6	30.7	15,141
1995	36.4	24.4	9.9	8.6	13.8	11.2	29.3	30.3	15,569
1996	36.5	24.7	9.7	8.7	13.7	11.2	28.4	29.4	16,036
1997	35.6	24.4	9.1	8.3	13.3	11.0	26.5	27.1	16,400
1998	34.5	23.5	9.1	8.1	12.7	10.5	26.1	25.6	16,660
1999	32.3	21.9	8.4	7.4	11.8	9.8	23.6	22.8	17,029
2000	31.1	21.2	7.9	7.2	11.3	9.4	22.2	21.2	17,063
2002	34.6	23.5	8.6	8.6	12.1	10.2	24.1	21.8	18,556
2003	35.9	24.3	8.8	9.1	12.5	10.5	24.4	22.5	18,979
2004	37.0	25.3	9.0	9.1	12.7	10.8	24.7	21.9	19,307

NA = Not available. **NOTE:** Because of a change in the definition of poverty, data prior to 1980 are not directly comparable to data since 1980. (1) Includes other races not shown separately. (2) Persons of Hispanic origin may be of any race. (3) Figures for 1960-80 represent only nonfarm families.

Poverty by Family Status, Sex, and Race, 1986-2004

Source: Bureau of the Census, U.S. Dept. of Commerce

(No. in thousands)

	2004		2000		1995		1990		1986	
	No.	%[1]	No.	%[1]	No.	%[1]	No.	%[1]	No.	%[1]
TOTAL POOR	**36,997**	**12.7**	**31,054**	**11.3**	**36,425**	**13.8**	**33,585**	**13.5**	**32,370**	**13.6**
In families	**26,564**	**11.0**	**22,015**	**9.6**	**27,501**	**12.3**	**25,232**	**12.0**	**24,754**	**12.0**
Head of household	7,854	10.2	6,222	8.6	7,532	10.8	7,098	10.7	7,023	10.9
Related children	12,460	17.3	11,018	15.6	13,999	20.2	12,715	19.9	12,257	19.8
Unrelated individuals	**9,864**	**20.5**	**8,503**	**18.9**	**8,247**	**20.9**	**7,446**	**20.7**	**6,846**	**21.6**
Families, female householder, no husband present	**12,823**	**30.5**	**10,425**	**27.9**	**14,205**	**36.5**	**12,578**	**37.2**	**11,944**	**38.3**
Head of household	3,973	28.4	3,096	24.7	4,057	32.4	3,768	33.4	3,613	34.6
Related children	7,140	41.8	6,116	39.8	8,364	50.3	7,363	53.4	6,943	54.4
Unrelated female individuals	**5,580**	**22.5**	**5,071**	**21.6**	**4,865**	**23.5**	**4,589**	**24.0**	**4,311**	**25.1**
All other families	**NA**	**NA**	**NA**	**NA**	**13,296**	**7.2**	**12,654**	**7.1**	**12,811**	**7.3**
Head of household	NA	NA	NA	NA	3,475	6.1	3,330	6.0	3,410	6.3
Related children	NA	NA	NA	NA	5,635	10.7	5,352	10.7	5,313	10.8
Unrelated male individuals	**4,284**	**18.3**	**3,548**	**16.0**	**3,382**	**18.0**	**2,857**	**16.9**	**2,536**	**17.5**
TOTAL WHITE POOR[2]	**25,301**	**10.8**	**21,242**	**9.4**	**24,423**	**11.2**	**22,326**	**10.7**	**22,183**	**11.0**
In families	**17,477**	**9.0**	**14,392**	**7.7**	**17,593**	**9.6**	**15,916**	**9.0**	**16,393**	**9.4**
Head of household	5,315	8.4	4,151	6.9	4,994	8.5	4,622	8.1	4,811	8.6
Related children	7,868	14.2	6,838	12.3	8,474	15.5	7,696	15.1	7,714	15.3
Families with female householder, no husband present	**6,905**	**26.4**	**1,655**	**20**	**2,200**	**26.6**	**2,010**	**26.8**	**2,041**	**28.2**
Unrelated individuals	**7,356**	**18.7**	**6,402**	**17.2**	**6,336**	**19.0**	**5,739**	**18.6**	**5,198**	**19.2**
TOTAL BLACK POOR[2]	**9,000**	**24.7**	**7,862**	**22.0**	**9,872**	**29.3**	**9,837**	**31.9**	**8,983**	**31.1**
In families	**7,142**	**23.7**	**6,108**	**20.7**	**8,189**	28.5	**8,160**	**31.0**	**7,410**	**29.7**
Head of household	2,034	22.8	1,685	19.1	2,127	26.4	2,193	29.3	1,987	28.0
Related children	3,694	33.3	3,417	30.4	4,644	41.5	4,412	44.2	4,039	42.7
Families with female householder, no husband present	**5,228**	**39.5**	**1,301**	**34.6**	**1,701**	**45.1**	**1,648**	**48.1**	**1,488**	**50.1**
Unrelated individuals	**1,790**	**28.9**	**1,708**	**28.0**	**1,551**	**32.6**	**1,491**	**35.1**	**1,431**	**38.5**

NA = Not available. (1) Percentage of total U.S. population in each category who fell below poverty level and are enumerated here. For example, of all persons in families in 2004, 11.0%, or 26,564,000, were poor. (2) Data are for one race only. The Census Bureau revised race categories in 2002; 2004 figures are not directly comparable with previous years.

Persons in Poverty, by State, 2002-2004

Source: Bureau of the Census, U.S. Dept. of Commerce

	2003-04[1]	2002-03[1]
Alabama	16.0%	14.7%
Alaska	9.4	9.2
Arizona	13.9	13.5
Arkansas	16.4	18.8
California	13.2	13.1
Colorado	9.9	9.7
Connecticut	9.1	8.2
Delaware	8.2	8.2
District of Columbia	16.7	16.9
Florida	12.2	12.6
Georgia	12.5	11.5
Hawaii	8.9	10.3
Idaho	10.0	10.8
Illinois	12.4	12.7
Indiana	10.8	9.5
Iowa	9.9	9.1
Kansas	11.1	10.4
Kentucky	16.0%	14.3%
Louisiana	16.8	17.2
Maine	11.6	12.5
Maryland	9.2	8.0
Massachusetts	9.7	10.1
Michigan	12.3	11.5
Minnesota	7.2	6.9
Mississippi	17.3	17.2
Missouri	11.5	10.3
Montana	14.6	14.3
Nebraska	9.6	10.2
Nevada	10.9	9.9
New Hampshire	5.6	5.8
New Jersey	8.3	8.3
New Mexico	17.3	18.0
New York	14.6	14.2
North Carolina	15.1	15.0
North Dakota	9.7	10.6
Ohio	11.3%	10.3%
Oklahoma	11.8	13.5
Oregon	12.1	11.7
Pennsylvania	10.9	10.0
Rhode Island	11.5	11.3
South Carolina	13.8	13.5
South Dakota	13.0	12.1
Tennessee	15.0	14.4
Texas	16.7	16.3
Utah	9.5	9.5
Vermont	8.2	9.2
Virginia	9.7	10.0
Washington	12.0	11.8
West Virginia	15.8	17.1
Wisconsin	11.0	9.2
Wyoming	9.9	9.4
U.S. Total	**12.6**	**12.3**

(1) 2-year average.

U.S. Capital Gains Tax, 1960-2005

Source: George W. Smith IV, CPA, Partner, George W. Smith & Company, P.C.

The following shows changes in the maximum tax rate on net long-term capital gains for individuals since 1960.

Year	Max %	Year	Max %	Year	Max %	Year	Max %	Year	Max %
1960	25.0	1972	35.0[1]	1987	28.0	1997	20.0[4]	2001	20/18[6]
1970	29.5	1978	28.0	1988	33.0[2]	1999	20.0[5]	2003	20/15[7]
1971	32.5	1981	20.0	1990	28.0[3]				

(1) From 1972 to 1976, the interplay of minimum tax and maximum tax resulted in a marginal rate of 49.125%. (2) Statutory maximum of 28%, but "phase-out" notch increased marginal rate to 33%; interplay of all "phase-outs" could produce an effective marginal rate to 49.5%. (3) The Budget Act of 1990 increased the statutory rate to 31% and capped the marginal rate at 28%; effective marginal rates could exceed 34% because of the phase-out of personal exemptions and itemized deductions. (4) New rate was for those who, after July 28, 1997, sell capital assets held for more than 18 mos (12 mos for sales after Dec. 31, 1997). A 10% capital gains rate applied to individuals in the 15% income tax bracket. (Those who, after July 28, 1997, but before Jan. 1, 1998, sold capital assets held between 12 and 18 mos to be taxed at the old top rate of 28%. Those who sold capital assets after May 6, 1997, but before July 29, 1997, to be taxed at the 20% rate, so long as such assets were held for at least a year.) (5) The IRS Restructuring and Reform Act of 1998 repealed the more-than-18-month holding period for sales after Dec. 31, 1997. Beginning Jan. 1, 1998, capital assets needed only be held 12 months to have the 20%/10% capital gains rates apply. (6) For capital assets bought after Dec. 31, 2000, and held for more than 5 years, the 20% minimum capital gains rate was lowered to 18%. The 10% rate was lowered to 8%, regardless of when the assets were bought. This provision was repealed in 2003. (7) The maximum capital gains rate for capital assets held more than one year and sold on or after May 6, 2003, was decreased to 15%. The 10% bracket was reduced to 5%. The capital gains rate for the sale of collectibles such as antiques remained at 28%, and the sale of certain depreciable real estate was to be taxed at a maximum of 25%.

2005 Federal Corporate Tax Rates

Taxable Income Amount	Tax Rate
Not more than $50,000	15%
$50,001 to $75,000	25%
$75,001 to $100,000	34%
$100,001 to $335,000	39%
$335,001 to $10,000,000	34%
$10,000,001 to $15,000,000	35%
$15,000,001 to $18,333,333	38%
More than $18,333,333	35%

Personal service corporations (used by incorporated professionals such as attorneys and doctors) pay a flat rate of 35%.

Leading U.S. Businesses in 2004

Source: FORTUNE Magazine

(millions of dollars in revenues)

Advertising, Marketing	
Omnicom	$9,747
Interpublic Group	6,077
Vertis	1,645
Aerospace	
Boeing	$52,553
United Technologies	37,445
Lockheed Martin	35,526
Northrop Grumman	29,868
Honeywell Intl.	25,601
Raytheon	20,245
General Dynamics	19,552
Textron	10,312
L-3 Communications	6,897
Goodrich	4,725
Airlines	
AMR	$18,645
UAL	16,391
Delta Air Lines	15,002
Northwest Airlines	11,279
Continental Airlines	9,744
US Airways Group	7,117
Southwest Airlines	6,530
Alaska Air Group	2,724
America West Holdings	2,339
Apparel	
Nike	$12,253
VF	6,055
Jones Apparel Group	4,650
Liz Claiborne	4,633
Levi Strauss	4,073
Reebok International	3,785
Polo Ralph Lauren	2,650
Kellwood	2,556
Phillips-Van Heusen	1,641
Timberland	1,501
Automotive Retailing, Services	
AutoNation	$19,734
United Auto Group	10,011
Sonic Automotive	7,886
Asbury Automotive Group	5,468
Group 1 Automotive	5,435
CarMax	4,598
Banks (commercial and savings)	
Citigroup	$108,276
Bank of America Corp.	63,324
J.P. Morgan Chase & Co.	56,931
Wells Fargo	33,876
Wachovia Corp.	28,067
Washington Mutual	15,962
U.S. Bancorp	14,706
MBNA	12,327
Capital One Financial	$10,695
National City Corp.	10,560
Beverages	
Coca-Cola	$21,962
Coca-Cola Enterprises	18,158
Anheuser-Busch	14,934
Pepsi Bottling	10,906
Molson Coors Brewing	4,306
Constellation Brands	3,552
PepsiAmericas	3,345
Brown-Forman	2,213
Building Materials, Glass	
Owens Corning	$5,675
USG	4,509
Armstrong Holdings	3,448
Vulcan Materials	3,121
Martin Marietta Materials	1,775
Texas Industries	1,673
Chemicals	
Dow Chemical	$40,161
DuPont	27,995
PPG Industries	9,513
Ashland	8,781
Air Products & Chem.	7,411
Computer & Data Services	
Electronic Data Systems	$21,033
Computer Sciences	14,768
First Data	10,101
Science Applications Intl.	7,761
Automatic Data Proc.	7,755
Unisys	5,821
Computers, Office Equipment	
Intl. Business Machines	$96,293
Hewlett-Packard	79,905
Dell	49,205
Xerox	15,722
Sun Microsystems	11,185
Apple Computer	8,279
NCR	5,984
Computer Peripherals	
EMC	$8,230
Lexmark International	5,314
Maxtor	3,796
Western Digital	3,047
Storage Technology	2,224
Symbol Technologies	1,732
Computer Software	
Microsoft	$36,835
Oracle	10,156
Computer Assoc. Intl.	3,354
Electronic Arts	2,957
Veritas Software	2,042
Diversified Financials	
General Electric	$152,363
American Express	29,115
Countrywide Financial	14,051
Marsh & McLennan	12,159
Aon	10,205
SLM	5,218
CIT Group	4,676
Electronics, Electrical Equipment	
Emerson Electric	$15,615
Whirlpool	13,220
SPX	5,796
Maytag	4,722
Rockwell Automation	4,517
Energy	
Duke Energy	$22,779
American Electric Power	14,357
Williams	12,815
Constellation Energy	12,550
TXU	11,161
Engineering, Construction	
Fluor	$9,380
Emcor Group	4,748
Jacobs Engineering Grp.	4,594
URS	3,382
Peter Kiewit Sons'	3,352
Entertainment	
Time Warner	$42,869
Walt Disney	30,752
Viacom	27,055
News Corp.	20,802
Clear Channel Communic.	9,419
Food	
PepsiCo	$29,261
Sara Lee	19,566
ConAgra Foods	18,179
General Mills	11,070
Dean Foods	10,822
Smithfield Foods	10,107
Kellogg	9,614
H.J. Heinz	8,415
Land O'Lakes	7,742
Campbell Soup	7,109
Dole Food	5,316
Hormel Foods	4,780
Hershey Foods	4,429
Food & Drug Stores	
Kroger	$56,434
Albertson's	40,052
Walgreen	37,508
Safeway	35,823
CVS	30,594

Publix Super Markets	$18,686
Rite Aid	16,600
Winn-Dixie Stores	11,733

Food Production	
Archer Daniels Midland	$36,151
Tyson Foods	26,441
Pilgrim's Pride	5,364
Chiquita Brands Intl.	3,072
Seaboard	2,684
Corn Products Intl.	2,284

Food Services	
McDonald's	$19,065
Yum Brands	9,011
Starbucks	5,294
Darden Restaurants	5,003
Brinker International	3,708
Wendy's Intl.	3,630

Forest & Paper Products	
International Paper	$26,722
Weyerhaeuser	22,665
Georgia-Pacific	18,876
MeadWestvaco	8,227
Bonwater	3,190

Furniture	
Leggett & Platt	$5,086
Furniture Brands Intl.	2,447
Steelcase	2,377
HNI	2,093
La-Z-Boy	1,999

General Merchandisers	
Wal-Mart Stores	$288,189
Target	49,934
Sears Roebuck	36,099
J.C. Penney	25,678
Kmart Holding	19,701
Federated Dept. Stores	15,630
May Dept. Stores	14,441

Health Care: Wholesalers	
McKesson	$69,509
Cardinal Health	65,131
AmerisourceBergen	53,179

Health Care: Insurance	
UnitedHealth Group	$37,218
Wellpoint	20,815
Aetna	19,904
Cigna	18,176
Humana	13,104
PacifiCare Health Sys.	12,277
Health Net	11,646

Health Care: Medical Facilities	
HCA	$23,502
Tenet Healthcare	12,496
Triad Hospitals	4,534
Universal Health Svcs.	4,158
Kindred Healthcare	3,617
Community Health Sys.	3,360
Manor Care	3,209
Health Management Associates	3,206
DaVita	2,299
Beverly Enterprises	2,167

Healthcare: Pharmacy and Other Services	
Medco Health Solutions	$35,352
Caremark Rx	25,801
Express Scripts	15,115
Quest Diagnostics	5,127
Omnicare	4,120
Laboratory Corp. of America	3,085

Hotels, Casinos, Resorts	
Marriott International	$10,099
Harrah's Entertainment	4,928
Caesars Entertainment	4,805
Starwood Hotels & Rsrts.	4,385
MGM Mirage	4,283
Hilton Hotels	3,020

Household & Personal Products	
Procter & Gamble	$51,407
Kimberly-Clark	15,401
Colgate-Palmolive	10,584
Gillette	10,477
Avon Products	7,748
Estée Lauder	5,790
Clorox	4,324

Industrial & Farm Equipment	
Caterpillar	$30,251
Deere	19,986
Illinois Tool Works	11,731
Eaton	9,817
American Standard	9,509

Insurance: Life, Health (Mutual)	
New York Life Insurance	$27,176
TIAA-CREF	23,411
Mass. Mutual Life Ins.	23,159
Northwestern Mutual	17,806
Guardian Life of America	8,893

Insurance: Life, Health (Stock)	
MetLife	$39,535
Prudential Financial	28,348
AFLAC	13,281
UnumProvident	10,611

Insurance: P & C (Mutual)	
State Farm Insurance Cos.	$58,819
Auto-Owners Insurance	4,737
Country Insurance & Financial Services	2,608

Insurance: P & C (Stock)	
American Intl. Group	$98,610
Berkshire Hathaway	74,382
Allstate	33,936
St. Paul Travelers Cos.	22,934
Hartford Financial Services	22,693

Metals	
Alcoa	$23,960
United States Steel	14,108
Nucor	11,377
International Steel Group	9,016
Phelps Dodge	7,089
AK Steel Holding	5,243

Mining, Crude-Oil Production	
Occidental Petroleum	$11,611
Devon Energy	9,189
Unocal	8,217
Anadarko Petroleum	6,067
Burlington Resources	5,618

Motor Vehicles & Parts	
General Motors	$193,517
Ford Motor	172,233
Delphi	28,700
Johnson Controls	26,553
Visteon	18,657

Network & Other Communications Equipment	
Motorola	$35,349
Cisco Systems	22,045
Lucent Technologies	9,045
Qualcomm	4,916
Avaya	4,245

Oil and Gas Equipment Services	
Halliburton	$20,466
Baker Hughes	6,135
Smith Intl.	4,419

Package, Mail, Freight Delivery	
United Parcel Service	$36,582
FedEX	24,710
Brink's	4,724

Petroleum Refining	
Exxon Mobil	$270,772
ChevronTexaco	147,967
ConocoPhillips	121,663
Valero Energy	53,919
Marathon Oil	45,444

Pharmaceuticals	
Pfizer	$52,921
Johnson & Johnson	47,348
Merck	22,939
Bristol-Myers Squibb	21,886
Abbott Laboratories	20,473
Wyeth	17,358
Eli Lilly	13,858
Amgen	10,550
Schering-Plough	8,272
Forest Laboratories	2,680

Pipelines	
Plains All Amer. Pipeline	$20,976
TransMontaigne	11,215
Enterprise Products	8,321
Kinder Morgan Energy	7,933
El Paso	6,640

Publishing & Printing	
R.R. Donnelley & Sons	$7,791
Gannett	7,381
Tribune	5,726
McGraw-Hill	5,254
New York Times	3,304
Washington Post	3,300
Knight-Ridder	3,014
Reader's Digest Assn.	2,389
Scholastic	$2,234
E.W. Scripps	2,168

Railroads	
Union Pacific	$12,215
Burlington No. Santa Fe	10,946
CSX	8,187
Norfolk Southern	7,312

Scientific, Photo, Control Equipment	
Eastman Kodak	$13,829
Agilent Technologies	7,181
Danaher	6,889
Thermo Electron	2,325

Securities	
Morgan Stanley	$39,549
Merrill Lynch	32,467
Goldman Sachs Group	29,839
Lehman Brothers Hldgs.	21,250
Bear Stearns	8,422
Charles Schwab	4,705

Semiconductors and Other Electronic Components	
Intel	$34,209
Solectron	12,903
Texas Instruments	12,580
Sanmina-SCI	12,205
Applied Materials	8,013

Specialty Retailers	
Home Depot	$73,094
Costco Wholesale	48,107
Lowe's	36,464
Best Buy	24,901
Gap	16,267
TJX	14,914
Staples	14,448
Office Depot	13,565
OfficeMax	13,270
Toys 'R' Us	11,231
Circuit City Stores	9,745

Telecommunications	
Verizon Communications	$71,563
SBC Communications	41,098
AT&T	30,537
Sprint	27,428
BellSouth	22,729
MCI	22,615
Comcast	20,307
Qwest Communications	13,809
Nextel Communications	13,368
DIRECTV Group	11,905

Temporary Help	
Manpower	$14,930
Kelly Services	4,984
Robert Half Intl.	2,676
Spherion	2,259
Volt Info. Sciences	1,925
MPS Group	1,427

Textiles	
Mohawk Industries	$5,880
WestPoint Stevens	1,655

Tobacco	
Altria Group	$64,440
Reynolds American	6,437
Universal	3,008

Toys, Sporting Goods	
Mattel	$5,103
Hasbro	2,998

Transportation Equipment	
Harley-Davidson	$5,321
Brunswick	5,229

Utilities: Gas & Electric	
Exelon	$14,515
Dominion Resources	13,980
FirstEnergy	12,949
Southern	11,902
Edison International	11,499
PG&E Corp.	11,080
Public Service Enterprise Group	11,034
CenterPoint Energy	10,610
FPL Group	10,522
Entergy	10,124

Waste Management	
Waste Management	$12,516
Allied Waste Industries	5,375
Republic Services	2,708

Miscellaneous	
3M	$20,011
H&R Block	4,206

25 U.S. Corporations with Largest Revenues in 2004

Source: FORTUNE Magazine
(millions of dollars)

Rank	Company	Revenues
1.	Wal-Mart Stores, Bentonville, AR	$288,189
2.	Exxon Mobil, Irving, TX	270,772
3.	General Motors, Detroit, MI	193,517
4.	Ford Motor, Dearborn, MI	172,233
5.	General Electric, Fairfield, CT	152,363
6.	ChevronTexaco, San Ramon, CA	147,967
7.	ConocoPhillips, Houston, TX	121,663
8.	Citigroup, New York, NY	108,276
9.	American Intl. Group, New York, NY	98,610
10.	IBM, Armonk, NY	96,293
11.	Hewlett-Packard, Palo Alto, CA	79,905
12.	Berkshire Hathaway, Omaha, NE	74,382
13.	Home Depot, Atlanta, GA	73,094
14.	Verizon Communications, New York, NY	$71,563
15.	McKesson, San Francisco, CA	69,506
16.	Cardinal Health, Dublin, OH	65,131
17.	Altria Group, New York, NY	64,440
18.	Bank of America, Charlotte, NC	63,324
19.	State Farm Insurance, Bloomington, IL	58,819
20.	J.P. Morgan Case & Co., New York, NY	56,931
21.	Kroger, Cincinnati, OH	56,434
22.	Valero Energy, San Antonio, TX	53,919
23.	AmerisourceBergen, Chesterbrook, PA	53,179
24.	Pfizer, New York, NY	52,921
25.	Boeing, Chicago, IL	52,553

Fastest-Growing U.S. Franchises in 2004[1]

Source: *Entrepreneur* Magazine

Company	Type of Business	Minimum start-up cost[2]
Subway	Submarine sandwiches & salads	$70,000
Curves	Women's fitness & weight-loss centers	36,400
7-Eleven Inc.	Convenience store	Varies
Kumon Math & Reading Centers	Supplemental education	10,000
Jan-Pro Franchising Int'l. Inc.	Commercial cleaning	5,000
Quizno's Franchise Co., The	Submarine sandwiches, soups, salads	208,400
Jani-King	Commercial cleaning	11,300
Coverall Cleaning Concepts	Commercial cleaning	6,300
Liberty Tax Service	Income-tax preparation services	40,500
Jazzercise Inc.	Dance/exercise classes	3,000
RE/MAX Int'l. Inc.	Real estate	20,000
Jackson Hewitt Tax Service	Tax preparation services	51,700
Choice Hotels Int'l.	Hotels, inns, suites, resorts	4,000,000
WSI Internet	Internet services	49,700
Dunkin' Donuts	Donuts & baked goods	255,700
Action Int'l. Business Coaching	Business coaching, consulting & training	75,000
Baskin-Robbins USA Co.	Ice cream & yogurt	145,700
Great Clips Inc.	Family hair salons	98,800
Rezcity.com Plus	Online local city guides, travel store, eBay auction store	6,700
UPS Store, The	Postal, business & communications services	138,700
Results Travel	Travel services	25,000
Sonic Drive In Restaurants	Drive-in restaurant	710,000
Cartridge World	Printer/fax cartridge replacements & sales	104,1000
Maids Home Service, The	Residential cleaning	74,000

(1) Ranked by number of new franchise units added. (2) Not including franchise fee, which varies.

Largest Corporate Mergers or Acquisitions in U.S.

Source: Securities Data Co.
(as of Sept. 2005; * denotes an announced merger or acquisition not yet complete; year = year effective or announced)

Company	Acquirer	Dollars (in billions)	Year
Time Warner	America Online, Inc.	$181.6	2001
Warner-Lambert	Pfizer Inc.	88.8	2000
Mobil Corp.	Exxon Corp.	86.4	1999
Citicorp	Travelers Group Inc.	72.6	1998
Ameritech Corp	SBC Communic. Inc.	72.4	1999
GTE Corp.	Bell Atlantic Corp.	71.3	2000
Tele-Communications	AT&T	69.9	1999
AirTouch Communic.	Vodafone Group PLC	65.8	1999
BankAmerica Corp.	NationsBank Corp.	61.6	1998
Pharmacia Corp.	Pfizer, Inc	61.3	2003
Bank One Corp.	JP Morgan Chase	58.8	2004
US West	Qwest Communication	56.3	2000
Amoco Corp.	British Petroleum Co. PLC	55.0	1998
*Gillette	Procter & Gamble	54.9	2005
MediaOne Group	AT&T	51.9	2000
FleetBoston Fin. Corp.	Bank of America	47.0	2004
Liberty Media Group (AT&T)	shareholders	46.0	2001
Texaco	Chevron	43.3	2001
MCI Communications	WorldCom Inc.	41.4	1998
AT&T Wireless Service	Cingular Wireless	41.0	2004
SDL Inc.	JDS Uniphase Corp.	41.0	2001
CBS Corp.	Viacom	40.9	2000
Chrysler Corp	Daimler-Benz AG	40.5	1998
*MBNA	Bank of America	35.8	2005
Wells Fargo & Co.	Norwest Corp.	34.4	1998
VoiceStream Wireless Corp.	Deutsche Telekom AG	34.1	2001
ARCO	BP Amoco PLC	33.7	2000
J.P. Morgan & Co.	Chase Manhattan	33.6	2000
US West Media Group	shareholders	31.7	1998
Agilent Technologies	shareholders	31.2	2000
Associates First Capital	Citigroup	31.0	2000
NYNEX	Bell Atlantic	30.8	1997
AT&T Broadband & Internet Services	Comcast Corp.	$30.0	2001
Electronic Data Syst.	shareholders	29.7	1996
First Chicago NBD	BANC ONE Corp.	29.6	1998
RJR Nabisco	Kohlberg Kravis Roberts	29.4	1989
Pharmacia & Upjohn	Monsanto Co.	26.9	2000
Associates First Capital	shareholders	26.6	1998
Conoco	Phillips Petroleum	24.8	2002
Lucent Technologies (AT&T)	shareholders	24.1	1996
Bestfoods	Unilever PLC	23.7	2000
Compaq Computer	Hewlett-Packard	23.5	2002
Amer. General Corp.	American Int'l. Group	23.4	2001
AMFM, Inc.	Clear Channel Communications	22.7	2000
Pacific Telesis Group	SBC Communications, Inc.	22.4	1997
General Re Corp.	Berkshire Hathaway Inc.	22.3	1998
US Bancorp, MN	Firstar Corp.	21.1	2001
Ascend Communic.	Lucent Technologies	21.1	1999
Network Solutions, Inc.	VeriSign, Inc.	20.8	2000
Waste Management	USA Waste Services	20.0	1998
Nabisco Holdings	Philip Morris	19.4	2000
AT&T Wireless Serv.	shareholders	18.8	2001
Unocal Corp	Chevron Corp.	18.7	2005
Capital Cities/ABC Inc	Walt Disney	18.3	1996
SunAmerica Inc.	American Int'l. Group	18.1	1999
May Dept. Stores	Federated Dept. Stores	16.5	2005
*AT&T	SBC Comm.	14.7	2005
Vivendi Universal	General Electric	14.0	2003
Travelers Life & Annuity Co	MetLife Inc	11.7	2005
John Hancock Financial Services	Manulife Financial	11.0	2003

Economic and Financial Glossary

Source: Reviewed by William M. Gentry, Graduate School of Business, Columbia University

Annuity contract: An investment vehicle sold by insurance companies. Annuity buyers can elect to receive periodic payments for the rest of their lives. Annuities provide insurance against outliving one's wealth.

Arbitrage: A form of hedged investment meant to capture slight differences in the prices of 2 related securities—for example, buying gold in London and selling it at a higher price in New York.

Balanced budget: A budget is balanced when receipts equal expenditures. When receipts exceed expenditures, there is a **surplus;** when they fall short of expenditures, there is a **deficit.**

Balance of payments: The difference between all payments, for some categories of transactions, made to and from foreign countries over a set period of time. A *favorable* balance of payments exists when more payments are coming in than going out; an *unfavorable* balance of payments obtains when the reverse is true. Payments may include gold, the cost of merchandise and services, interest and dividend payments, money spent by travelers, and repayment of principal on loans.

Balance of trade (trade gap): The difference between exports and imports, in both actual funds and credit. A nation's balance of trade is *favorable* when exports exceed imports and *unfavorable* when the reverse is true.

Bear market: A market in which prices are falling.

Bearer bond: A bond issued in bearer form rather than being registered in a specific owner's name. Ownership is determined by possession.

Bond: A written promise, or IOU, by the issuer to repay a fixed amount of borrowed money on a specified date and generally to pay interest at regular intervals in the interim.

Bull market: A market in which prices are on the rise.

Capital gain (loss): An increase (decrease) in the market value of an asset over some period of time. For tax purposes, capital gains are typically calculated from when an asset is bought to when it is sold.

Commercial paper: An extremely short-term corporate IOU, generally due in 270 days or less.

Consumer price index (CPI): A statistical measure of the change in the price of consumer goods.

Convertible bond: A corporate bond (see below) that may be converted into a stated number of shares of common stock. Its price tends to fluctuate along with fluctuations in the price of the stock and with changes in interest rates.

Corporate bond: A bond issued by a corporation. The bond normally has a stated life and pays a fixed rate of interest. Considered safer than the common or preferred stock of the same company.

Cost of living: The cost of maintaining a standard of living measured in terms of purchased goods and services. Inflation typically measures changes in the cost of living.

Cost-of-living adjustments: Changes in promised payments, such as retirement benefits, to account for changes in the cost of living.

Credit crunch (liquidity crisis): A situation in which cash for lending is in short supply.

Debenture: An unsecured bond backed only by the general credit of the issuing corporation.

Deficit spending: Government spending in excess of revenues, generally financed with the sale of bonds. A deficit increases the government debt.

Deflation: A decrease in the level of prices.

Depression: A long period of economic decline marked by low prices, high unemployment, and many business failures.

Derivatives: Financial contracts, such as options, whose values are based on, or *derived* from, the price of an underlying financial asset or indicator such as a stock or an interest rate.

Devaluation: The official lowering of a nation's currency, decreasing its value in relation to foreign currencies.

Discount rate: The rate of interest set by the Federal Reserve that member banks are charged when borrowing money through the Federal Reserve System.

Disposable income: Income after taxes that is available to persons for spending and saving.

Diversification: Investing in more than one asset in order to reduce the riskiness of the overall asset portfolio. By holding more than one asset, losses on some assets may be offset by gains realized on other assets.

Dividend: Discretionary payment by a corporation to its shareholders, usually in the form of cash or stock shares.

Dow Jones Industrial Average: An index of stock market prices, based on the prices of 30 companies, 28 of which are on the New York Stock Exchange.

Econometrics: The use of statistical methods to study economic and financial data.

Federal Deposit Insurance Corp. (FDIC): A U.S. government-sponsored corporation that insures accounts in national banks and other qualified institutions against bank failures.

Federal Reserve System: The entire banking system of the U.S., incorporating 12 Federal Reserve banks (one in each of 12 Federal Reserve districts), 25 Federal Reserve branch banks, all national banks, and state-chartered commercial banks and trust companies that have been admitted to its membership. The governors of the system greatly influence the nation's monetary and credit policies.

Full employment: The economy is said to be at full employment when everyone who wishes to work at the going wage-rate for his or her type of labor is employed, save only for the small amount of unemployment due to the time it takes to switch from one job to another.

Futures: A futures contract is an agreement to buy or sell a specific amount of a commodity or financial instrument at a particular price at a set date in the future. For example, futures based on a stock index (such as the Dow Jones Industrial Average) are bets on the future price of that group of stocks.

Golden parachute: Provisions in contracts of some high-level executives guaranteeing substantial severance benefits if they lose their position in a corporate takeover.

Government bond: A bond issued by the U.S. Treasury, considered a safe investment. These are divided into 2 categories—marketable and not marketable. *Savings bonds* cannot be bought and sold once the original purchase is made. Marketable bonds fall into several categories. *Treasury bills* are short-term U.S. obligations, maturing in 3, 6, or 12 months. *Treasury notes* mature in up to 10 years. *Treasury bonds* mature in 10 to 30 years. *Indexed bonds* are adjusted for inflation.

Greenmail: A company buying back its own shares for more than the going market price to avoid a threatened hostile takeover.

Gross domestic product (GDP): The market value of all goods and services that have been bought for final use during a period of time. It became the official measure of the size of the U.S. economy in 1991, replacing *gross national product (GNP),* in use since 1941. GDP covers workers and capital employed within the nation's borders. GNP covers production by U.S. residents regardless of where it takes place. The switch aligned U.S. terminology with that of most other industrialized countries.

Hedge fund: A flexible investment fund for a limited number of large investors (the minimum investment is typically $1 million). Hedge funds use a variety of investment techniques, including those forbidden to mutual funds, such as short-selling and heavy leveraging.

Hedging: Taking 2 positions whose gains and losses will offset each other if prices change, in order to limit risk.

Individual retirement account (IRA): A self-funded tax-advantaged retirement plan that allows employed individuals to contribute up to a maximum yearly sum. With a *traditional* IRA, individuals contribute pre-tax earnings and defer income taxes until retirement. With a *Roth* IRA, individuals contribute after-tax earnings but do not pay taxes on future withdrawals (the interest is never taxed). *401(k) plans* are employer-sponsored plans similar to traditional IRAs, but having higher contribution limits.

Inflation: An increase in the level of prices.

Insider information: Important facts about the condition or plans of a corporation that have not been released to the general public.

Interest: The cost of borrowing money.

Investment bank: A financial institution that arranges the initial issuance of stocks and bonds and offers companies advice about acquisitions and divestitures.

Junk bonds: Bonds issued by companies with low credit ratings. They typically pay relatively high interest rates because of the fear of default.

Leading indicators: A series of 11 indicators from different segments of the economy used by the U.S. Commerce Department to predict when changes in the level of economic activity will occur.

Leverage: The extent to which a purchase was paid for with borrowed money. Amplifies the potential gain or loss for the purchaser.

Leveraged buyout (LBO): An acquisition of a company in which much of the purchase price is borrowed, with the debt to be repaid from future profits or by subsequently selling off company assets. A leveraged buyout is typically carried out by a small group of investors, often including incumbent management.

Liquid assets: Assets consisting of cash and/or items that are easily converted into cash.

Margin account: A brokerage account that allows a person to trade securities on credit. A **margin call** is a demand for more collateral on the account.

Money supply: The currency held by the public, plus checking accounts in commercial banks and savings institutions.

Mortgage-backed securities: Created when a bank, builder, or government agency gathers together a group of mortgages and then sells bonds to other institutions and the public. The investors receive their proportionate share of the interest payments on the loans as well as the principal payments. Usually, the mortgages in question are guaranteed by the government.

Municipal bond: Issued by governmental units such as states, cities, local taxing authorities, and other agencies. Interest is exempt from U.S.—and sometimes state and local—income tax. *Municipal bond unit investment trusts* offer a portfolio of many different municipal bonds chosen by professionals. The income is exempt from federal income taxes.

Mutual fund: A portfolio of professionally bought and managed financial assets in which you pool your money along with that of many other people. A share price is based on net asset value, or the value of all the investments owned by the funds, less any debt, and divided by the total number of shares. The major advantage, relative to investing individually in only a small number of stocks, is less risk—the holdings are spread out over many assets and if one or two do badly the remainder may shield you from the losses. *Bond funds* are mutual funds that deal in the bond market exclusively. *Money market mutual funds* buy in the so-called money market—institutions that need to borrow large sums of money for short terms. These funds often offer special checking account advantages.

National debt: The debt of the national government, as distinguished from the debts of political subdivisions of the nation and of private business and individuals.

National debt ceiling: Total borrowing limit set by Congress beyond which the U.S. national debt cannot rise. This limit is periodically raised by congressional vote.

Option: A type of contractual agreement between a buyer and a seller to buy or sell shares of a security. A **call** option contract gives the right to purchase shares of a specific stock at a stated price within a given period of time. A **put** option contract gives the buyer the right to sell shares of a specific stock at a stated price within a given period of time.

Per capita income: The total income of a group divided by the number of people in the group.

Prime interest rate: The rate charged by banks on short-term loans to large commercial customers with the highest credit rating.

Producer price index: A statistical measure of the change in the price of wholesale goods. It is reported for 3 different stages of the production chain: crude, intermediate, and finished goods.

Program trading: Trading techniques involving large numbers and large blocks of stocks, usually used in conjunction with computer programs. Techniques include *index arbitrage,* in which traders profit from price differences between stocks and futures contracts on stock indexes, and *portfolio insurance,* which is the use of stock-index futures to protect stock investors from potentially large losses when the market drops.

Public debt: The total of a nation's debts owed by state, local, and national government. Increases in this sum, reflected in public-sector deficits, indicate how much of the nation's spending is being financed by borrowing rather than by taxation.

Recession: A mild decrease in economic activity marked by a decline in real (inflation-adjusted) GDP, employment, and trade, usually lasting from 6 months to a year, and marked by widespread decline in many sectors of the economy.

Savings Association Insurance Fund (SAIF): Created in 1989 to insure accounts in savings and loan associations up to $100,000.

Seasonal adjustment: Statistical changes made to compensate for regular fluctuations in data that are so great they tend to distort the statistics and make comparisons meaningless. For instance, seasonal adjustments are made for a slowdown in housing construction in midwinter and for the rise in farm income in the fall after summer crops are harvested.

Short-selling: Borrowing shares of stock from a brokerage firm and selling them, hoping to buy the shares back at a lower price, return them, and realize a profit from the decline in prices.

Stagnation: Economic slowdown in which there is little growth in the GDP, capital investment, and real income.

Stock: *Common stocks* are shares of ownership in a corporation. For publicly held firms, the stock typically trades on an exchange, such as the New York Stock Exchange; for closely held firms, the founders and managers own most of the stock. There can be wide swings in the prices of this kind of stock. *Preferred stock* is a type of stock on which a fixed dividend must be paid before holders of common stock are issued their share of the issuing corporation's earnings. Preferred stock is less risky than common stock. *Convertible preferred stock* can be converted into the common stock of the company that issued the preferred. *Over-the-counter stock* is not traded on the major or regional exchanges, but rather through dealers from whom you buy directly. *Blue chip* stocks are so called because they have been leading stocks for a long time. *Growth* stocks are from companies that reinvest their earnings, rather than pay dividends, with the expectation of future stock price appreciation.

Supply-side economics: A school of thinking about economic policy holding that lowering income tax rates will inevitably lead to enhanced economic growth and general revitalization of the economy.

Takeover: Acquisition of one company by another company or group by sale or merger. A *friendly takeover* occurs when the acquired company's management is agreeable to the merger; when management is opposed to the merger, it is a *hostile* takeover.

Tender offer: A public offer to buy a company's stock; usually priced at a premium above the market.

Zero coupon bond: A corporate or government bond that is issued at a deep discount from the maturity value and pays no interest during the life of the bond. It is redeemable at face value.

Minerals

Source: U.S. Geological Survey, U.S. Dept. of the Interior, as of mid-2005; minerals.usgs.gov/minerals

Aluminum: the 2nd most abundant metallic element in the earth's crust. Bauxite is the main source of aluminum. Guinea, Australia, and Jamaica have about 60% of the world's reserves. Main uses in the U.S. are for transportation (37%), packaging (22%), and construction (16%).

Chromium: produced mostly in India, Kazakhstan, and South Africa. The metallurgical industry uses about 91% of the chromite consumed in the world; the chemical industry, 6%; and the refractory and foundry industry, 3%.

Cobalt: used in superalloys for jet engines; cemented carbides for cutting tools; batteries, catalysts, ceramics, and other chemical applications; permanent magnets, tool steels, and other alloys. Australia, Canada, Dem. Rep. of the Congo (Congo-Kinshasa), Cuba, Russia, and Zambia account for most of the world cobalt mine production.

Construction aggregates: construction sand and gravel and crushed stone are two of the most accessible natural resources in the world. Construction sand and gravel is produced in every U.S. state, and crushed stone is mined in every State except Delaware. They are used in construction, agriculture, chemicals, and metallurgy and are produced worldwide.

Copper: main uses of copper and copper alloy products in the U.S. are in building construction (48%), electrical and electronic products (21%), consumer and general products (11%), industrial machinery and equipment (10%), and transportation (10%). The leading mine producers are Chile, the U.S. (mostly in Arizona, Utah, and New Mexico), Indonesia, Peru, Australia, Russia, China, and Canada.

Gold: used in the U.S. in jewelry and the arts (92%), electrical and electronics (4%), dentistry (3%), and other industrial (1%). South Africa has about half of the world's resources; significant quantities are also present in the U.S. (mined in most western states and Alaska), Australia, Russia, Uzbekistan, Canada, and Brazil.

Gypsum: used in wallboard and plaster products, cement production, and agriculture. Leading producers are the U.S., Iran, Canada, Spain, China, and Mexico.

Iron ore: the source of primary iron for the world's iron and steel industries. Major iron ore producers include Brazil, Australia, China, India, Russia, Ukraine, and the U.S.

Lead: Australia, China, the U.S. (mostly in Alaska and Missouri), Peru, Canada, and Mexico are the world's largest producers of lead. The major end use in the U.S. is in lead acid storage batteries (87%). The U.S. produces and consumes about 20% of the world's lead metal. Most U.S. lead production (88%) is recycled material, and 97% of lead acid batteries (mostly automotive) are recycled.

Manganese: essential to iron and steel production. South Africa and Ukraine have over 80% and 10%, respectively, of the world's identified resources.

Nickel: vital to the stainless steel industry, and used to make superalloys. Leading producers are Russia, Canada, Australia, the French overseas territory of New Caledonia, and Indonesia.

Phosphate rock: used in fertilizers, animal feed supplements, chemicals, and food. Phosphorus is an essential element for plant and animal nutrition. The U.S., Morocco, China, Russia, and Tunisia are the world's leading producers.

Platinum-group metals: this group consists of 6 metals: platinum, palladium, rhodium, ruthenium, iridium, and osmium. They commonly occur together in nature and are among the scarcest of the metallic elements. In the U.S., the automotive and chemical industries use PGMs mainly as catalysts. They also are consumed in electrical and electronics, glass, dental, and medical industries. Russia and South Africa have most of the world's reserves.

Salt: used in chemicals, highway deicing, industry, agriculture, food, and water treatment. Leading producers are the U.S., China, Germany, India, and Canada.

Silver: used in industrial and decorative applications, coins, jewelry and silverware, and photography. Silver is mined in more than 60 countries. Alaska and Nevada produce more than 70% of U.S. silver.

Soda ash: a raw material for glass, chemicals, and detergents, it can be mined or produced synthetically. The U.S. is now the world's second leading producer of natural soda ash, having been displaced in 2004 by China.

Sulfur: used in agricultural chemicals production, oil refining, metal mining, and many other industries. It is produced as a byproduct of oil refining, natural gas processing, and nonferrous metal smelting. Leading producers are the U.S., Canada, Russia, China, and Japan.

Titanium: ilmenite and rutile are the major mineral sources of titanium. Titanium minerals are used to produce TiO_2 pigments (95%) and other uses (5%) including alloys, ceramics, chemicals, titanium metal, and welding rod coatings. Major mining operations are in Australia, Canada, China, Norway, and South Africa. U.S. mine production is in Florida, Georgia, and Virginia.

Zinc: used as a protective coating on steel, as diecastings, as an alloying metal with copper to make brass, and as a component of chemical compounds in rubber and paints. Leading producers are China, Australia, Peru, Canada, the U.S. (in Alaska, Missouri, and Tennessee), and Mexico.

U.S. Reliance on Foreign Supplies of Minerals

Source: U.S. Geological Survey, U.S. Dept. of the Interior

Mineral	% Imported in 2004	Major sources (2000-2003)	Major Uses
Arsenic (trioxide)	100%	China, Chile, Morocco, Mexico	Wood preservatives, nonferrous alloys
Asbestos	100	Canada	Roofing products, gaskets, friction products
Bauxite & alumina	100	Australia, Jamaica, Guinea, Suriname	Aluminum production, refractories, abrasives, chemicals
Columbium (niobium)	100	Brazil, Canada, Estonia, Germany	Steelmaking, superalloys
Fluorspar	100	China, South Africa, Mexico	Hydrofluoric acid, aluminum fluoride, steelmaking
Graphite (natural)	100	China, Mexico, Canada, Brazil	Refractories, brake linings, pencils, electrodes, motor brushes, high-modulus fibers
Indium	100	China, Canada, Japan, France	Coatings, solders, alloys, electrical components
Manganese	100	South Africa, Gabon, Australia, France	Iron & steelmaking, batteries, agricultural chemicals
Mica, sheet (natural)	100	India, Belgium, China, Germany	Electronic & electrical equipment
Quartz crystal (industrial)	100	Brazil, Germany, Madagascar	Electronics, optical applications
Rare earths	100	China, France, Japan, Estonia	Catalysts, glass polishing, ceramics, magnets, metallurgy, phosphors
Rubidium	100	Canada	Inorganic chemicals, DNA separation, night vision devices
Strontium	100	Mexico, Germany	Television picture tubes, ferrite magnets, pyrotechnics
Thallium	100	Belgium, France, Russia, United Kingdom	Electronics, alloys, glass
Thorium	100	France	High-temperature ceramics, catalysts, welding electrodes
Vanadium	100	Czech Republic, South Africa, Canada, China	Steelmaking, catalysts
Yttrium	100	China, Japan, Austria, Netherlands	Television phosphors, fluorescent lights, oxygen sensors, ceramics
Gallium	99	France, China, Russia, Kazakhstan	Electronic components
Gemstones	99	Israel, India, Belgium	Jewelry, carvings, gem & mineral collections
Platinum	91	South Africa, United Kingdom, Germany, Canada, Russia	Catalysts, jewelry, dental & medical alloys
Bismuth	90	Belgium, Mexico, China, United Kingdom	Pharmaceuticals, chemicals, alloys, metallurgical additives, solders, ammunition
Tin	88	Peru, China, Bolivia, Brazil	Solder, tin chemicals, tinplate, alloys
Antimony	85	China, Mexico, South Africa, Belgium	Flame retardants, transportation, chemicals, ceramics & glass
Diamond (natural industrial)	85	Ireland, Switzerland, United Kingdom, Russia	Abrasives, stone cutting, highway repair & construction
Stone (dimension)	85	Italy, Canada, India, Spain	Construction, monuments
Titanium (sponge)	85	Kazakhstan, Japan, Russia	Aerospace, armor, chemical processing, power generation, medical devices
Palladium	81	Russia, South Africa, United Kingdom, Belgium, Germany	Catalysts, dental, electronics, electrical
Tantalum	80	Australia, Kazakhstan, Canada, China	Capacitors, superalloys, cemented carbide cutting tools
Barite	79	China, India	Oil & gas well drilling fluids, chemicals
Rhenium	79	Chile, Kazakhstan, Mexico	Superalloys, petroleum-reforming catalysts
Cobalt	76	Finland, Norway, Russia, Canada	Chemicals, superalloys, cemented carbides, magnetic alloys
Iodine	74	Chile, Japan, Russia	Animal feed, catalysts, heat stabilizers, pharmaceuticals, sanitation
Tungsten	73	China, Canada	Cemented carbides, electrical & electronic components, tool steels, alloys
Chromium	72	South Africa, Kazakhstan, Zimbabwe, Russia	Steel, chemicals, refractories
Potash	70	Canada, Belarus, Russia, Germany	Fertilizers, chemicals
Magnesium metal	68	Canada, Russia, China, Israel	Aluminum alloys, castings & wrought products, desulfurization of iron & steel
Titanium mineral concentrates	65	South Africa, Australia, Canada, Ukraine	Pigment, metal, welding rod coatings, chemicals, ceramics
Peat	56	Canada	Horticulture, agriculture
Silicon	56	South Africa, Norway, Brazil, Russia	Iron & steel alloys, aluminum & aluminum alloys, specialty chemicals
Zinc	56	Canada, Mexico, Peru	Galvanizing, zinc-base alloys, brass & bronze
Beryllium	55	Kazakhstan, Japan, Brazil, Spain	Electronic &electrical components, aerospace & defense applications
Silver	54	Mexico, Canada, United Kingdom, Peru	Photography, electrical & electronic products, catalysts, brazing alloys, jewelry

World Mineral Reserve Base, 2004

Source: U.S. Geological Survey, U.S. Dept. of the Interior; as of year-end 2004

Mineral	Reserve Base[1]
Aluminum	33,000 mil metric tons[2]
Chromium	1,800 mil metric tons[3]
Cobalt	13 mil metric tons
Copper	940 mil metric tons
Gold	90,000 metric tons
Iron Ore	370,000 mil metric tons
Lead	140 mil metric tons
Manganese	5,000 mil metric tons
Nickel	140 mil metric tons
Phosphate Rock	50,000 mil metric tons
Platinum-Group Metals	80,000 metric tons
Silver	570,000 metric tons
Soda Ash (Natural)	40,000 mil metric tons
Titanium (ilmenite/rutile)	1,400 mil metric tons[4]
Zinc	460 mil metric tons

(1) Includes demonstrated resources that are currently economic or marginally economic, plus some that are currently subeconomic. (2) Bauxite. (3) Chromite ore, gross weight, marketable product. (4) Titanium dioxide (TiO_2) content of ilmenite and rutile.

World Gold Production, 1980-2004[1]

Source: U.S. Geological Survey, U.S. Dept. of the Interior

(thousands of troy ounces)

		Africa			North and South America				Other			
Year	World prod.	South Africa	Ghana	Congo Dem. Rep.	United States	Canada	Mexico	Colombia	Australia	China	Philip-pines	Russia[2]
1980	39,197	21,669	353	96	970	1,627	196	510	548	NA	753	8,425
1985	49,284	21,565	299	257	2,427	2,815	266	1,142	1,881	1,950	1,063	8,700
1990	70,207	19,454	541	299	9,458	5,447	311	944	7,849	3,215	791	9,710
1991	70,423	19,326	846	283	9,454	5,676	326	1,120	7,530	3,858	833	8,359
1992	73,530	19,743	998	225	10,617	5,189	318	1,033	7,825	4,501	730	8,232
1993	73,300	19,908	1,250	280	10,642	4,917	357	883	7,948	5,144	509	8,228
1994	72,500	16,650	1,400	357	10,500	4,710	447	668	8,237	4,240	870	8,173
1995	71,800	16,800	1,710	322	10,200	4,890	652	680	8,150	4,500	873	4,250
1996	73,600	16,000	1,580	264	10,500	5,350	787	710	9,310	4,660	970	3,960
1997	78,900	15,800	1,760	13	11,600	5,510	836	605	10,100	5,630	1,050	3,990
1998	80,300	15,000	2,330	5	11,800	5,320	817	605	10,000	5,720	1,090	3,690
1999	82,600	14,500	2,570	7	11,000	5,070	764	1,410	9,680	5,560	1,000	4,050
2000	83,300	13,900	2,320	2	11,300	5,020	848	1,190	9,530	5,790	1,170	4,600
2001	83,600	12,700	2,200	2	10,800	5,110	846	701	9,160	5,950	1,090	4,890
2002	82,900	12,800	2,230	2	9,580	4,870	663	669	8,780	6,170	1,290	5,410
2003	83,300	12,100	2,240	3	8,910	4,520	643	1,500	9,070	6,490	1,220	5,470
2004E	79,000	11,000	1,900	10	8,290	4,130	720	720	8,300	6,990	926	5,440

(1) Figures are rounded. (2) Figures for 1980-94 are for USSR as constituted prior to Dec. 1991; after 1994, Russia only. E = Estimated. NA = Not available.

U.S. Nonfuel Minerals Production, 1998-2004

Source: U.S. Geological Survey, U.S. Dept. of the Interior

Production as measured by mine shipments, sales, or marketable production (including consumption by producers).

		1998	1999	2000	2001	2002	2003	2004
Beryllium (metal equivalent)	metric tons	243	200	180	100	80	85	90
Copper (recoverable content of ores, etc.)	thousand metric tons	1,860	1,600	1,450	1,340	1,140	1,120	1,160
Gold (recoverable content of ores, etc.)	metric tons	366	341	353	335	298	277	258P
Iron ore, usable (includes byproduct material)	million metric tons	62.9	57.7	63.1	46.2	51.6	48.6	54.7E
Lead (recoverable content of ores, etc.)	thousand metric tons	481	503	449	454	440	449	430
Magnesium metal (primary)	thousand metric tons	106	W	W	W	W	W	W
Molybdenum (content of ore and concentrates)	metric tons	53,300	42,400	40,900	37,600	32,300	33,500	41,500
Silver (recoverable content of ores, etc.)	metric tons	2,060	1,950	1,860	1,740	1,420	1,240	1,250
Zinc (recoverable content of ores, etc.)	thousand metric tons	722	808	805	799	754	738	715
Asbestos	thousand metric tons	6	7	5	5	3	—	—
Barite (sold or used)	thousand metric tons	476	434	392	400	420	468	532
Boron minerals (B_2O_3 equivalent)	thousand metric tons	587	618	546	536	543	605	637
Bromine	million kilograms	230	239	228	212	222	216	222
Cement (portland, masonry)	thousand metric tons	83,931	85,952	87,846	88,900	89,732	92,843	97,434
Clays	thousand metric tons	41,900	42,200	40,800	39,600	39,300	40,000	41,300E
Diatomite	thousand metric tons	725	747	677	644	599	625	620
Feldspar	thousand metric tons	820E	875E	790E	800E	790E	800E	770E
Garnet (industrial)	metric tons	74,000	60,700	60,200	52,700	38,500	29,200	28,400
Gemstones (natural)	million dollars	14.3	16.1	17.2	14.9	12.6	12.5	14.5
Gypsum	thousand metric tons	19,000	22,400	19,500	16,300	15,700	16,600	17,200
Helium (extracted from natural gas)	million cubic meters	114	114	98	87	87E	87E	86
Helium (Grade A sold)	million cubic meters	114	117	127	132	127	122E	130
Iodine	thousand kilograms	1,490	1,620	1,470	1,290	1,420	1,090	1,130
Lime	thousand metric tons	20,100	19,700	19,500	18,900	17,900	19,200	20,000
Mica (scrap & flake)	thousand metric tons	87	95	101	98	81	79	99
Peat	thousand metric tons	685	731	792	736	642	634	696
Perlite (sold and used by producers)	thousand metric tons	685	711	672	588	521	493	508
Phosphate rock (marketable product)	thousand metric tons	44,200	40,600	38,600	31,900	36,100	35,000	35,800
Potash (K2O equivalent)	thousand metric tons	1,300	1,200	1,300	1,200	1,200	1,100	1,300
Pumice and pumicite	thousand metric tons	872	1,000	1,050	920	956	870	1,490
Salt	thousand metric tons	40,800	44,400	43,300	42,200	37,700	41,100	45,000
Sand and gravel (construction)	million metric tons	1,070	1,110	1,120	1,130	1,130	1,160	1,240
Sand and gravel (industrial)	thousand metric tons	28,200	28,900	28,400	27,900	27,300	27,500	29,700
Soda ash (sodium carbonate)	thousand metric tons	10,100	10,200	10,200	10,300	10,500	10,600	11,000
Sodium sulfate (natural)	thousand metric tons	290	NA	NA	NA	NA	NA	NA
Stone (crushed)	million metric tons	1,510	1,530	1,550	1,590	1,510	1,530	1,590
Stone (dimension)	thousand metric tons	1,140	1,250	1,320	1,220	1,260	1,340	1,510
Sulfur (in all forms)	thousand metric tons	11,700	11,500	10,500	9,470	9,270	9,600	10,100
Talc	thousand metric tons	971	925	851	863	828	840	857
Titanium mineral concentrates	thousand metric tons	400	300	300	300	300	300	300
Vermiculite concentrate	thousand metric tons	W	175E	150E	NA	NA	NA	NA

W = Withheld to avoid disclosing company proprietary data. — = No production. E = Estimated. NA = Not available. P = Preliminary.

TRADE AND TRANSPORTATION

U.S. Trade With Selected Countries and Major Areas, 2004

Source: Office of Trade and Economic Analysis, U.S. Dept. of Commerce
(in millions of dollars; top 25 countries ranked by amount of total trade with U.S.)

COUNTRY	Total Trade with U.S.	U.S. Exports to	Rank[1]	U.S. Imports from	Rank[1]	U.S. Trade Balance with	Rank[2]
Canada	$446,239.7	$189,879.9	1	$256,359.8	1	$–66,480.0	3
Mexico	266,736.5	110,835.0	2	155,901.5	3	–45,066.5	5
China	231,426.1	34,744.1	5	196,682.0	2	–161,938.0	1
Japan	184,048.3	54,243.1	3	129,805.2	4	–75,562.1	2
Federal Republic of Germany	108,681.5	31,415.9	6	77,265.6	5	–45,849.7	4
United Kingdom	82,274.0	36,000.2	4	46,273.8	6	–10,273.6	16
South Korea	72,580.4	26,412.5	7	46,167.9	7	–19,755.5	7
Taiwan	56,368.0	21,744.4	9	34,623.6	8	–12,879.2	13
France	52,869.0	21,263.3	10	31,605.7	9	–10,342.5	15
Malaysia	39,100.1	10,921.2	16	28,178.9	10	–17,257.6	10
Italy	38,782.0	10,684.7	17	28,097.3	11	–17,412.5	9
Netherlands	36,739.5	24,289.1	8	12,450.5	22	11,838.6	230
Ireland	35,615.1	8,167.2	20	27,447.9	12	–19,280.7	8
Brazil	35,057.2	13,897.3	15	21,159.9	14	–7,262.7	22
Singapore	34,978.9	19,608.5	11	15,370.4	19	4,238.1	226
Venezuela	29,688.0	4,767.4	26	24,920.6	13	–20,153.1	6
Belgium	29,317.3	16,871.1	12	12,446.2	23	4,424.9	227
Saudi Arabia	26,215.4	5,256.7	25	20,958.7	15	–15,701.9	11
Hong Kong	25,141.3	15,827.4	13	9,313.9	27	6,513.5	228
Thailand	23,947.3	6,368.4	23	17,578.9	16	–11,210.5	14
Israel	23,720.6	9,169.1	19	14,551.5	20	–5,382.4	24
Australia	21,770.8	14,225.3	14	7,545.5	30	6,679.8	229
India	21,681.4	6,109.4	24	15,572.0	18	–9,462.7	17
Switzerland	20,907.6	9,279.9	18	11,627.7	25	–2,347.8	34
Nigeria	17,802.8	1,554.3	52	16,248.5	17	–14,694.2	12
MAJOR AREA/GROUP							
North America	712,976.3	300,714.9	NA	412,261.4	NA	–111,546.5	NA
Western Europe	481,610.3	184,115.8	NA	297,494.5	NA	–113,378.8	NA
Euro Area	336,764.0	127,158.2	NA	209,605.8	NA	–82,447.5	NA
European Union (EU)	441,011.2	168,572.3	NA	272,438.9	NA	–103,866.6	NA
European Free Trade Association	29,900.2	11,203.6	NA	18,696.6	NA	–7,492.9	NA
Eastern Europe	33,073.1	9,136.7	NA	23,936.4	NA	–14,799.7	NA
Former Soviet Republics	20,592.6	5,389.3	NA	15,203.3	NA	–9,814.0	NA
OECD	479,255.3	183,161.3	NA	296,094.0	NA	–112,932.7	NA
Pacific Rim Countries	702,282.9	209,733.6	NA	492,549.3	NA	–282,815.7	NA
Asia/Near East	74,776.7	23,520.0	NA	51,256.7	NA	–27,736.7	NA
Asia/NICS	189,068.5	83,592.7	NA	105,475.8	NA	–21,883.1	NA
Asia/South	31,425.5	8,551.7	NA	22,873.8	NA	–14,322.1	NA
ASEAN	136,202.5	47,945.2	NA	88,257.3	NA	–40,312.1	NA
APEC	1,473,067.1	526,563.7	NA	946,503.4	NA	–419,939.7	NA
South/Central America	160,112.3	61,464.5	NA	98,647.8	NA	–37,183.3	NA
Twenty Latin American Republics	409,561.0	164,577.6	NA	244,983.4	NA	–80,405.8	NA
Central American Common Market	24,565.5	11,395.7	NA	13,169.8	NA	–1,774.1	NA
LAFTA	272,511.0	145,911.1	NA	226,599.9	NA	–80,688.7	NA
NATO	911,795.0	369,026.5	NA	542,768.5	NA	–173,742.0	NA
OPEC	116,367.5	22,262.1	NA	94,105.4	NA	–71,843.3	NA
WORLD TOTAL	**2,288,479.3**	**818,774.9**	**NA**	**1,469,704.4**	**NA**	**–650,929.5**	**NA**

(1) Rank shown is for column to the left. (2) Ranking includes the territories as well as nations. Rank is by size of U.S. trade deficit. NA = Not applicable. **Note:** Details may not equal totals because of rounding or incomplete enumeration.

Definitions of areas/groups used in the table, as provided by the source: **North America**—Canada, Mexico. **Western Europe**—Andorra, Austria, Belgium, Bosnia and Herzegovina, Croatia, Cyprus, Denmark, Faroe Islands, Finland, France, Germany, Gibraltar, Greece, Iceland, Ireland, Italy, Liechtenstein, Luxembourg, Macedonia, Malta and Gozo, Monaco, Netherlands, Norway, Portugal, San Marino, Serbia & Montenegro, Slovenia, Spain, Svalbard/Jan Mayen Island, Sweden, Switzerland, Turkey, United Kingdom, Vatican City. **Euro Area**—Austria, Belgium, Finland, France, Germany, Greece, Ireland, Italy, Luxembourg, Netherlands, Portugal, Spain. **EU**—(European Union) Euro Area plus Denmark, Sweden, United Kingdom. *Not including 10 states that joined 5/1/04.* **EFTA**—(European Free Trade Assoc.) Iceland, Liechtenstein, Norway, Switzerland. **Eastern Europe**—Albania, Armenia, Azerbaijan, Belarus, Bulgaria, Czech Republic, Estonia, Georgia, Hungary, Kazakhstan, Kyrgyzstan, Latvia, Lithuania, Moldova, Poland, Romania, Russia, Slovakia, Tajikistan, Turkmenistan, Ukraine, Uzbekistan. **Former Soviet Republics**—Armenia, Azerbaijan, Belarus, Estonia, Georgia, Kazakhstan, Kyrgyzstan, Latvia, Lithuania, Moldova, Russia, Tajikistan, Turkmenistan, Ukraine, Uzbekistan. **OECD**—(Org. for Econ. Cooperation & Development in Europe) Austria, Belgium, Denmark, Finland, France, Germany, Greece, Iceland, Ireland, Italy, Liechtenstein, Luxembourg, Monaco, Netherlands, Norway, Portugal, San Marino, Spain, Svalbard/Jan Mayen Island, Sweden, Switzerland, Turkey, United Kingdom. **Pacific Rim Countries/Territories**—Australia, Brunei, China, Indonesia, Japan, Macao, Malaysia, New Zealand, Papua New Guinea, Philippines, Singapore, South Korea, Taiwan. **Asia/Near East**—Bahrain, Iran, Iraq, Israel, Jordan, Kuwait, Lebanon, Oman, Qatar, Saudi Arabia, Syria, U.A.E., Yemen. **Asia/NICS**—(Newly Industrialized Countries) Hong Kong (spec. admin. region of China), Singapore, South Korea, Taiwan. **Asia/South**—Afghanistan, Bangladesh, India, Nepal, Pakistan, Sri Lanka. **ASEAN**—(Association of Southeast Asian Nations) Brunei, Cambodia, Indonesia, Malaysia, Philippines, Singapore, Thailand. **APEC**—(Asia-Pacific Economic Cooperation) Australia, Brunei, Canada, Chile, China, Indonesia, Japan, Malaysia, Mexico, New Zealand, Papua New Guinea, Peru, Philippines, Russia, Singapore, South Korea, Taiwan, Thailand, Vietnam. **South/Central America**—Anguilla, Antigua and Barbuda, Argentina, Aruba, Bahamas, Barbados, Belize, Bermuda, Bolivia, Brazil, British Virgin Islands, Cayman Islands, Chile, Colombia, Costa Rica, Cuba, Dominica, Dominican Republic, Ecuador, El Salvador, Falkland Islands, French Guiana, Grenada, Guadeloupe, Guatemala, Guyana, Haiti, Honduras, Jamaica, Martinique, Montserrat, Netherland Antilles, Nicaragua, Panama, Paraguay, Peru, St. Kitts and Nevis, St. Lucia, St. Vincent and the Grenadines, Suriname, Trinidad and Tobago, Turks and Caicos Islands, Uruguay, Venezuela. Guatemala, Haiti, Honduras, Mexico, Nicaragua, Panama, Paraguay, Peru, Uruguay, Venezuela. **Central American Common Market**—Costa Rica, El Salvador, Guatemala, Honduras, Nicaragua. **LAFTA**—(Latin American Free Trade Assoc.) Argentina, Bolivia, Brazil, Chile, Colombia, Ecuador, Mexico, Paraguay, Peru, Uruguay, Venezuela. **NATO**—Belgium, Canada, Denmark, France, Germany, Greece, Iceland, Ireland, Italy, Liechtenstein, Luxembourg, Monaco, Netherlands, Norway, Portugal, San Marino, Spain, Svalbard/Jan Mayan Island, Sweden, Switzerland, Turkey, United Kingdom. **OPEC**—Algeria, Indonesia, Iran, Iraq, Kuwait, Libya, Nigeria, Qatar, Saudi Arabia, United Arab Emirates, Venezuela.

U.S. Exports and Imports by Principal Commodity Groupings, 2004

Source: Office of Trade and Economic Analysis, U.S. Dept. of Commerce

(millions of dollars)

Items	Exports	Imports
TOTAL	**$818,775**	**$1,469,704**
Agricultural commodities	**61,383**	**54,222**
Animal feeds	3,808	778
Cereal flour	1,802	2,730
Coffee	7	1,868
Corn	6,132	127
Cotton, raw and linters	4,251	18
Hides and skins	1,581	80
Live animals	504	1,438
Meat and preparations	5,203	5,707
Oils/fats, vegetable	1,043	1,981
Rice	1,161	237
Soybeans	6,680	53
Sugar	4	516
Tobacco, unmanufactured	1,044	690
Vegetables and fruits	8,890	12,787
Wheat	5,148	162
Manufactured goods	**623,961**	**1,174,788**
ADP equipment; office machines	28,241	93,762
Airplane parts	15,295	4,824
Airplanes	24,493	11,389
Aluminum	3,807	9,547
Artwork/antiques	1,322	5,307
Basketware, etc.	5,084	8,435
Chemicals - cosmetics	7,441	6,948
Chemicals - dyeing	4,569	2,667
Chemicals - fertilizers	2,595	2,536
Chemicals - inorganic	6,196	8,726
Chemicals - medicinal	23,433	34,937
Chemicals - organic	25,852	35,447
Chemicals - plastics	25,202	14,222
Chemicals[1]	14,563	7,982
Clothing	4,423	72,316
Copper	1,918	4,754
Electrical machinery	73,320	93,290
Footwear	453	16,506
Furniture and bedding	4,084	27,737
Gem diamonds	939	14,661
General industrial machinery	34,824	45,632
Glass	2,651	2,711
Glassware	811	2,067
Gold, nonmonetary	4,430	3,996
Iron and steel mill products	8,022	22,400
Jewelry	$2,566	$8,557
Lighting, plumbing	1,476	6,811
Metal manufactures[1]	12,121	21,777
Metalworking machinery	5,983	6,262
Nickel	511	1,897
Optical goods	2,556	3,534
Paper and paperboard	10,689	16,581
Photographic equipment	3,534	4,905
Plastic articles[1]	7,390	11,776
Platinum	548	3,508
Pottery	107	1,681
Power generating mach.	36,177	35,981
Printed materials	4,910	4,508
Records/magnetic media	4,757	6,799
Rubber articles[1]	1,520	2,733
Rubber tires and tubes	2,532	6,305
Scientific instruments	33,049	28,449
Ships, boats	1,649	2,084
Silver and bullion	275	1,013
Spacecraft	467	39
Specialized industrial machinery	28,842	26,417
Television, VCR, etc.	20,072	87,885
Textile yarn, fabric	11,516	19,505
Toys/games/sporting goods	3,403	22,479
Travel goods	312	5,655
Vehicles	65,217	187,723
Watches/clocks/parts	272	3,790
Wood manufactures	1,796	12,309
Mineral fuels	**18,642**	**206,660**
Coal	2,758	2,416
Crude oil	277	136,030
Liquified propane/butane	426	2,899
Mineral fuels[1]	2,701	2,349
Natural gas	2,125	23,908
Petroleum preparations	9,726	37,988
Other commodities		
Alcoholic bev.,distilled	684	4,022
Cigarettes	1,294	257
Cork, wood, lumber	3,857	10,605
Crude fertilizers	1,724	1,471
Fish and preparations	3,517	11,177
Metal ores; scrap	7,766	4,583
Pulp and waste paper	4,488	2,949

(1) Those not specified elsewhere. **NOTE:** Not all products are listed in each commodity group, but they are included in totals.

Trends in U.S. Foreign Trade, 1790-2004

Source: Office of Trade and Economic Analysis, U.S. Dept. of Commerce

In 1790, U.S. exports and imports combined came to $43 million and there was a $3 million trade deficit. In 2004, U.S. exports and imports combined amounted to $2.3 trillion, and the trade deficit, which has steadily been climbing since the last recorded surplus in 1975, reached more than $650 billion, the highest dollar total in history.

(in millions of dollars)

Year	Exports	Imports	Trade Balance
1790	$20	$23	$–3
1795	48	70	–22
1800	71	91	–20
1805	96	121	–25
1810	67	85	–19
1815	53	113	–60
1820	70	74	–5
1825	91	90	1
1830	72	63	9
1835	115	137	–22
1840	124	98	25
1845	106	113	–7
1850	144	174	–29
1855	219	258	–39
1860	334	354	–20
1865	166	239	–73
1870	393	436	–43
1875	513	533	–20
1880	836	668	168
1885	$742	$578	$165
1890	858	789	69
1895	808	732	76
1900	1,394	850	545
1905	1,519	1,118	401
1910	1,745	1,557	188
1915	2,769	1,674	1,094
1920	8,228	5,278	2,950
1925	4,910	4,227	683
1930	3,843	3,061	782
1935	2,283	2,047	235
1940	4,021	2,625	1,396
1945	9,806	4,159	5,646
1950	9,997	8,954	1,043
1955	14,298	11,566	2,732
1960	19,659	15,073	4,586
1965	26,742	21,520	5,222
1970	42,681	40,356	2,325
1975	$107,652	$98,503	$9,149
1980	220,626	244,871	–24,245
1985	213,133	345,276	–132,143
1990	394,030	495,042	–101,012
1991	421,730	485,453	–63,723
1992	448,164	532,665	–84,501
1993	465,091	580,659	–115,568
1994	512,626	683,256	–170,630
1995	584,742	743,445	–158,703
1996	625,075	795,289	–170,214
1997	689,182	870,671	–181,489
1998	682,138	911,896	–229,758
1999	695,797	1,024,618	–328,821
2000	781,918	1,218,022	–436,104
2001	729,100	1,140,999	–411,899
2002	693,103	1,161,366	–468,263
2003	724,771	1,257,121	–532,350
2004	818,775	1,469,704	–650,930

World Trade Organization (WTO)

Following World War II, the major world economic powers negotiated a set of rules for reducing and limiting trade barriers and settling trade disputes. These rules were called the General Agreement on Tariffs and Trade (GATT). Headquarters to oversee administration of the GATT were established in Geneva, Switzerland. Rounds of multilateral trade negotiations under the GATT were carried out periodically. The 8th round, begun in 1986 in Punta del Este, Uruguay, and dubbed the Uruguay Round, ended Dec. 15, 1993, when 117 countries completed a new trade-liberalization agreement. The name for the GATT was changed to the World Trade Organization (WTO), which officially came into being Jan. 1, 1995.

Foreign Exchange Rates, 1970-2004

Source: International Monetary Fund, Federal Reserve Board; Federal Reserve Board

(National currency units per dollar except as indicated; data are annual averages)

Note: As of 2002, the euro, the European Union's single currency, replaced the national currencies in the EU nations shown (Austria, Belgium, France, Germany, Greece, Ireland, Italy, Netherlands, Portugal, and Spain), as well as in Finland and Luxembourg.

Year	Australia[1] (dollar)	Austria[1] (schilling)	Belgium[1] (franc)	Canada (dollar)	China (yuan)	Denmark (krone)	France[1] (franc)	Germany[1,2] (deutsche mark)	Greece[1] (drachma)
1970	1.1136	25.880	49.680	1.0103	NA	7.489	5.5200	3.6480	30.00
1975	1.3077	17.443	36.799	1.0175	NA	5.748	4.2876	2.4613	32.29
1980	1.1400	12.945	29.237	1.1693	NA	5.634	4.2250	1.8175	42.62
1985	0.7003	20.690	59.378	1.3655	NA	10.596	8.9852	2.9440	138.12
1990	0.7813	11.370	33.418	1.1668	NA	6.189	5.4453	1.6157	158.51
1995	0.7415	10.081	29.480	1.3724	8.3700	5.602	4.9915	1.4331	231.66
2000	0.5815	0.9232[3]	0.9232[3]	1.4855	8.2784	8.095	0.9232[3]	0.9232[3]	365.92
2003	0.6524	1.1321[3]	1.1321[3]	1.4008	8.2772	6.5774	1.1321[3]	1.1321[3]	1.1321[3]
2004	0.7365	1.2438[3]	1.2438[3]	1.3017	8.2768	5.9891	1.2438[3]	1.2438[3]	1.2438[3]

Year	Hong Kong (dollar)	India (rupee)	Ireland[1] (pound)	Italy[1] (lira)	Japan (yen)	Malaysia (ringgit)	Mexico (new peso)	Netherlands[1] (guilder)	Norway (krone)
1970	NA	7.576	2.3959	623	357.60	3.0900	—	3.5970	7.1400
1975	NA	8.409	2.2216	653	296.78	2.4030	—	2.5293	5.2282
1980	NA	7.887	2.0577	856	226.63	2.1767	—	1.9875	4.9381
1985	NA	12.369	1.0656	1,909	238.54	2.4830	—	3.3214	8.5972
1990	NA	17.504	1.6585	1,198	144.79	2.7049	2.8126	1.8209	6.2597
1995	7.7357	32.427	1.6038	1,628.9	94.06	2.5044	6.4194	1.6057	6.3352
2000	7.7925	45.000	0.9232[3]	0.9232[3]	107.80	3.8000	9.4590	0.9232[3]	8.8131
2003	7.7875	46.59	1.1321[3]	1.1321[3]	115.94	3.8000	10.793	1.1321[3]	7.0803
2004	7.7891	45.26	1.2438[3]	1.2438[3]	108.15	3.8000	11.290	1.2438[3]	6.7399

Year	Portugal[1] (escudo)	Singapore (dollar)	South Korea (won)	Spain[1] (peseta)	Sweden (krona)	Switzerland (franc)	Taiwan (dollar)	Thailand (baht)	UK[1] (pound)
1970	28.75	3.0800	310.57	69.72	5.1700	4.3160	NA	21.000	2.3959
1975	25.51	2.3713	484.00	57.43	4.1530	2.5839	NA	20.379	2.2216
1980	50.08	2.1412	607.43	71.76	4.2309	1.6772	NA	20.476	2.3243
1985	170.39	2.2002	870.02	170.04	8.6039	2.4571	NA	27.159	1.2963
1990	142.55	1.8125	707.76	101.93	5.9188	1.3892	NA	25.585	1.7847
1995	151.11	1.4174	771.27	124.69	7.1333	1.1825	26.495	24.915	1.5785
2000	0.9232[3]	1.7250	1,130.90	0.9232[3]	9.1735	1.6904	31.260	40.210	1.5156
2003	1.1321[3]	1.7429	1,192.08	1.1321[3]	8.0787	1.3450	34.405	41.556	1.6347
2004	1.2438[3]	1.6902	1,145.24	1.2438[3]	7.3480	1.2428	33.372	40.271	1.8330

NA= Not Available. (1) U.S. dollars per unit of national currency. (2) West Germany before 1991. (3) Euro Area member, figures in euros per dollar.

The North American Free Trade Agreement (NAFTA)

NAFTA, a free trade pact between the U.S., Canada, and Mexico, took effect Jan. 1, 1994. Major provisions are:

Agriculture—Tariffs on all farm products to be eliminated over 15 years. Domestic price-support systems may continue provided they do not distort trade.

Automobiles—At least 62.5% of an automobile's value must have been produced in North America for it to qualify for duty-free status. Tariffs were phased out over 10 years.

Disputes—Special judges have jurisdiction to resolve disagreements within strict timetables.

Energy—Mexico continues to bar foreign ownership of its oil fields but, as of 2004, U.S. and Canadian companies could bid on contracts offered by Mexican oil and electricity monopolies.

Environment—The trade agreement cannot be used to overrule national and state environmental, health, or safety laws.

Finance—Limits on ownersip of banks, insurance companies, and brokerages eliminated by Jan. 1, 2000.

Immigration—All 3 countries eased restrictions on the movement of business executives and professionals.

Jobs—Barriers to limit Mexican migration to U.S. remain unaffected by NAFTA.

Patent and copyright protection—Mexico strengthened its laws providing protection to intellectual property and agreed to honor pharmaceutical patents for 20 years.

Tariffs—Tariffs on 10,000 customs goods are to be eliminated over 15 years. One-half of U.S. exports to Mexico were considered duty-free by 1999.

Textiles—A "rule of origin" provision requires most garments to be made from yarn and fabric that have been produced in North America. Most tariffs phased out by 1999.

Trucking—Trucks were to have free access on crossborder routes and throughout the 3 countries by 1999, but the U.S. continued to impose restrictions on Mexican trucks. In 2001, an arbitration panel ruled that the U.S. restrictions were in violation of NAFTA. Pres. Bush in Nov. 2002 eased restrictions on Mexican trucks entering the U.S.

U.S. Trade With Mexico and Canada, 1993-2004

Source: Office of Trade and Economic Analysis, U.S. Dept. of Commerce

(U.S. exports to, imports from, Mexico and Canada in millions of dollars)

	With MEXICO		
Year	Exports	Imports	U.S. Trade Balance[1]
1993	$41,581	$39,917	$1,664
1994[2]	50,844	49,494	1,350
1995	46,292	61,685	–15,393
1996	56,792	74,297	–17,506
1997	71,388	85,938	–14,549
1998	78,773	94,629	–15,857
1999	86,909	109,721	–22,812
2000	111,349	135,926	–24,577
2001	101,297	131,338	–30,041
2002	97,470	134,616	–37,146
2003	97,412	138,060	–40,648
2004	110,835	155,902	–45,067

	With CANADA		
Year	Exports	Imports	U.S. Trade Balance[1]
1993	$100,444	$111,216	$–10,772
1994[2]	114,439	128,406	–13,968
1995	127,226	145,349	–18,123
1996	134,210	155,893	–21,682
1997	151,767	167,234	–15,467
1998	156,603	173,256	–16,653
1999	166,600	198,711	–32,111
2000	178,941	230,838	–51,897
2001	163,424	216,268	–52,844
2002	160,923	209,088	–48,165
2003	169,924	221,595	–51,671
2004	189,880	256,360	–66,480

(1) Totals may not add due to rounding. (2) NAFTA provisions began to take effect Jan. 1, 1994.

The Central American Free Trade Agreement (CAFTA)

CAFTA (also known as CAFTA-DR), a free trade agreement between the U.S. and Costa Rica, Dominican Republic, El Salvador, Guatemala, Honduras, and Nicaragua, was signed into law Aug. 2, 2005, by Pres. George W. Bush, following approval by Congress July 28. Ratification was pending in Costa Rica and the Dominican Republic as of Sept. 2005.

Some highlights are:

Agriculture: Tariffs on 50% of U.S. farm goods eliminated; other goods deemed "sensitive"—including corn, milk, and potatoes—to have tariffs reduced to zero over 20 years. Sugar imports to the U.S. allowed to rise to 1.2% of annual U.S. production, and to 1.7% over 15 years.

Automobiles: Tariffs to be phased out over 5 years.

Environment and Labor: Party nations agree to enforce local labor and environmental protections (no mechanisms in place to monitor enforcement).

Manufacturing: Tariffs eliminated on 80% of U.S. goods.

Market Barriers: Barriers for services such as telecommunications, insurance, and financial services eliminated or reduced.

Pharmaceuticals: U.S. pharmaceuticals given 5-year patent protection from their date of introduction to CAFTA markets, regardless of date introduced in U.S.

Textiles and Clothing: Open access of CAFTA-nation textiles and clothing to U.S. markets instituted, retroactive to Jan. 1, 2004.

50 Busiest U.S. Ports, 2003

Source: Corps of Engineers, Dept. of the Army, U.S. Dept. of Defense
(ports ranked by tonnage handled; all figures in tons)

Rank	Port	Total	Domestic	Foreign	Imports	Exports
1.	South Louisiana, LA, Port of	198,825,125	118,392,253	80,432,872	30,857,319	49,575,553
2.	Houston, TX	190,923,145	64,029,740	126,893,405	90,335,647	36,557,758
3.	New York, NY and NJ	145,889,166	66,204,392	79,684,774	70,251,263	9,433,511
4.	Beaumont, TX	87,540,979	18,753,708	68,787,271	63,336,752	5,450,519
5.	New Orleans, LA	83,846,626	34,970,176	48,876,450	20,889,868	27,986,582
6.	Huntington, WV-KY-OH	77,641,149	77,641,149	0	0	0
7.	Corpus Christi, TX	77,224,732	23,830,641	53,394,091	44,758,661	8,635,430
8.	Long Beach, CA	69,195,350	16,824,018	52,371,332	37,969,522	14,401,810
9.	Texas City, TX	61,337,525	17,945,721	43,391,804	40,184,521	3,207,283
10.	Baton Rouge, LA	61,264,412	38,112,248	23,152,164	18,701,796	4,450,368
11.	Plaquemines, LA	55,916,880	36,915,174	19,001,706	8,519,740	10,481,966
12.	Lake Charles, LA	53,363,966	21,558,472	31,805,494	27,825,176	3,980,318
13.	Los Angeles, CA	51,327,289	8,535,853	42,791,436	29,962,253	12,829,183
14.	Mobile, AL	50,214,435	25,186,458	25,027,977	17,553,389	7,474,588
15.	Valdez, AK	49,856,714	49,851,043	5,671	0	5,671
16.	Tampa, FL	48,251,710	30,882,969	17,368,741	9,230,682	8,138,059
17.	Pittsburgh, PA	41,675,421	41,675,421	0	0	0
18.	Baltimore, MD	40,183,371	16,087,194	24,096,177	18,984,957	5,111,220
19.	Duluth-Superior, MN and WI	38,295,106	25,212,530	13,082,576	529,060	12,553,516
20.	Philadelphia, PA	33,248,697	14,455,774	18,792,923	18,615,848	177,075
21.	St. Louis, MO and IL	32,431,145	32,431,145	0	0	0
22.	Pascagoula, MS	31,291,735	10,508,707	20,783,028	17,513,754	3,269,274
23.	Norfolk Harbor, VA	31,190,698	6,886,237	24,304,461	9,219,073	15,085,388
24.	Freeport, TX	30,536,657	5,435,996	25,100,661	22,665,591	2,435,070
25.	Portland, ME	29,160,899	1,854,036	27,306,863	27,133,777	173,086
26.	Paulsboro, NJ	27,283,400	9,064,893	18,218,507	17,908,339	310,168
27.	Port Arthur, TX	27,169,763	8,702,968	18,466,795	14,259,432	4,207,363
28.	Portland, OR	26,795,881	11,043,016	15,752,865	4,398,499	11,354,366
29.	Marcus Hook, PA	26,163,571	10,076,190	16,087,381	16,077,374	10,007
30.	Charleston, SC	25,198,899	6,420,173	18,778,726	13,041,525	5,737,201
31.	Boston, MA	24,832,103	8,390,508	16,441,595	15,634,152	807,443
32.	Savannah, GA	23,368,591	1,866,457	21,502,134	13,174,550	8,327,584
33.	Port Everglades, FL	23,040,269	12,632,616	10,407,653	8,426,945	1,980,708
34.	Richmond, CA	23,000,661	12,125,481	10,875,180	10,017,014	858,166
35.	Tacoma, WA	22,965,750	7,556,415	15,409,335	5,702,602	9,706,733
36.	Chicago, IL	22,609,742	20,875,735	1,734,007	1,057,337	676,670
37.	Jacksonville, FL	21,731,239	10,900,053	10,831,186	9,878,816	952,370
38.	Seattle, WA	19,448,157	5,874,775	13,573,382	6,748,803	6,824,579
39.	Memphis, TN	18,191,319	18,191,319	0	0	0
40.	Honolulu, HI	17,835,850	12,427,773	5,408,077	4,918,596	489,481
41.	Anacortes, WA	15,820,495	13,222,168	2,598,327	1,492,029	1,106,298
42.	San Juan, PR	14,555,649	9,111,163	5,444,486	5,008,816	435,670
43.	Detroit, MI	14,308,032	10,425,379	3,882,653	3,493,535	389,118
44.	Indiana Harbor, IN	14,132,553	13,772,711	359,842	314,107	45,735
45.	Two Harbors, MN	13,032,598	13,032,598	0	0	0
46.	Oakland, CA	12,627,486	2,564,070	10,063,416	4,203,403	5,860,013
47.	Cleveland, OH	12,620,794	9,508,542	3,112,252	2,708,093	404,159
48.	Cincinnati, OH	11,828,259	11,828,259	0	0	0
49.	Matagorda Ship Channel, TX	11,672,706	3,648,665	8,024,041	6,451,220	1,572,821
50.	Ashtabula, OH	10,426,942	4,588,798	5,838,144	960,441	4,877,703

Impact of Hurricane Katrina

The ports of Louisiana, Mississippi, and Alabama are vital outlets for U.S. agricultural products; oil is the chief import. All told these ports handle almost 25% of all U.S. imports and exports, and Hurricane Katrina had a serious impact on some ports. The Port of South Louisiana, which handles the most cargo tonnage of any U.S. port, sustained only minor structural damage and was soon 85% operational. But the Port of New Orleans (5th in tonnage handled) was moderately damaged; it anticipated operating at 80% capacity after 3 months, and full capacity after 6 months. The Ports of Plaquemines and St. Bernard, LA, as well as Pascagoula and Gulfport, MS, suffered heavy damage, with substantially reduced capacity expected. Louisiana's Lake Charles port (12th in tonnage handled) sustained minor damage, and was soon operational, with some draft restrictions; the Port of Baton Rouge was undamaged, and Louisiana's 21 inland and river ports also remained fully operational. Hurricane Rita caused minor damage to Gulf ports in Texas.

Merchant Fleets of the World, 2004

Source: Maritime Administration, U.S. Dept. of Commerce

Self-propelled oceangoing vessels of 1,000 gross deadweight tons and over, as of July 1, 2004 (tonnage in thousands)

		All Vessels		Tanker		Dry Bulk Carrier		Container		Other[1]	
		No.	Tons	No.	Tons	No.	Tons	No.	Tons	No.	Tons
By flag of registry	Panama	4,822	187,164	1,134	58,382	1,503	94,482	587	20,803	1,598	13,497
	Liberia	1,477	81,821	572	46,084	311	18,876	398	13,818	196	3,043
	Greece	730	54,442	301	32,032	295	19,781	43	2,116	91	513
	Bahamas	979	43,513	249	26,362	183	10,085	70	2,042	477	5,024
	Hong Kong	733	38,844	124	9,864	402	23,775	91	3,086	116	2,119
	Malta	1,172	38,798	243	14,841	445	19,011	57	1,296	427	3,651
	Singapore	886	36,843	445	19,834	134	10,187	177	4,616	130	2,206
	Cyprus	975	34,285	142	7,070	396	20,684	120	3,286	317	3,245
	Marshall Islands	456	33,269	231	24,606	80	5,480	78	1,734	67	1,449
	China[2]	1,557	26,490	300	5,088	351	12,499	130	2,683	776	6,220
	Norway (NIS)[3]	575	23,207	285	13,000	77	6,963	4	80	209	3,165
	United States	412	13,035	104	5,618	20	837	84	3,257	204	3,322
	Japan	555	11,871	233	5,940	140	4,628	13	469	169	833
	India	286	11,363	118	7,549	88	3,401	7	131	73	282
	Isle of Man	246	10,604	136	7,623	23	2,175	14	238	73	568
	United Kingdom	378	10,369	87	2,078	16	1,527	135	5,580	140	1,185
	Italy	438	10,197	235	5,300	36	2,613	19	640	148	1,644
	Korea (South)	530	9,861	160	1,783	105	6,139	58	892	207	1,048
	Denmark (DIS)[4]	244	9,034	76	3,648	2	76	81	4,984	85	325
	Iran	123	8,827	34	6,096	40	1,773	10	285	39	673
	All Other	11,461	154,749	2,295	50,402	1,212	45,094	921	21,170	6,973	38,084
By Country[5]	Greece	2,923	160,450	857	71,079	1,334	77,711	157	5,498	575	6,162
	Japan	2,713	111,163	797	40,469	869	54,937	218	8,002	829	7,756
	Germany	2,258	51,351	249	10,295	171	7,709	945	26,750	893	6,596
	China	2,169	48,900	327	9,216	630	26,756	223	4,871	989	8,057
	Norway	1,061	41,844	393	25,658	166	8,636	14	487	488	7,063
	United States	931	39,574	371	28,390	76	3,242	89	3,105	395	4,837
	Hong Kong	542	37,354	154	14,505	233	19,358	41	1,770	114	1,721
	Korea (South)	801	26,093	238	8,566	188	13,524	106	2,361	269	1,642
	United Kingdom	621	24,174	173	8,876	95	8,115	115	4,790	238	2,393
	Singapore	697	23,757	324	14,487	123	5,130	134	3,076	116	1,064
	Taiwan	532	23,730	41	3,741	186	12,351	184	6,654	121	983
	Denmark	492	15,997	154	6,388	29	1,770	130	6,817	179	1,022
	Russia	1,673	15,762	422	9,083	120	1,926	24	329	1,107	4,422
	India	282	12,824	125	8,335	101	4,128	3	87	53	274
	Italy	466	11,971	244	5,925	49	3,499	11	227	162	2,320
	Saudi Arabia	97	11,891	78	11,584	1	2	—	—	18	305
	Malaysia	289	9,524	128	6,373	40	1,946	34	695	87	511
	Iran	127	9,316	36	6,321	45	2,051	10	285	36	659
	Turkey	548	8,769	88	1,406	133	5,277	30	336	297	1,749
	Switzerland	266	8,258	36	1,016	30	1,335	126	5,001	74	906
	All Other	9,547	155,883	2,269	61,486	1,240	50,684	503	12,063	5,535	31,651
TOTAL ALL SHIPS		**29,035**	**848,586**	**7,504**	**353,200**	**5,859**	**310,088**	**3,097**	**93,204**	**12,575**	**92,094**

(1) Includes roll-on/roll-off, passenger, breakbulk ships, partial container ships, refrigerated cargo ships, barge carriers, and specialized cargo ships. (2) Excluding Hong Kong. (3) NIS = Norwegian International Ship Registry. (4) DIS = Denmark International Shipping Registry. (5) Based on parent company nationality.

U.S. International Transactions, 1970-2004

Source: Bureau of Economic Analysis, U.S. Dept. of Commerce; revised as of June 2005

(millions of dollars)

	1970	1975	1980	1985	1990	1995	2000	2004
Exports of goods, services, and income[1]	$68,387	$157,936	$344,440	$387,612	$706,975	$1,004,631	$1,422,402	$1,530,975
Merchandise, bal. of payments basis[2]	42,469	107,088	224,250	215,915	387,401	575,204	771,994	807,536
Services	14,171	25,497	47,584	73,155	147,832	219,183	299,490	343,912
Income receipts on U.S.-owned assets abroad	11,748	25,351	72,606	98,542	170,570	208,065	348,083	376,489
Imports of goods and services and income payments	–59,901	–132,745	–333,774	–483,769	–759,290	–1,080,124	–1,779,620	–2,118,119
Merchandise, balance of payments basis[2]	–39,866	–98,185	–249,750	–338,088	–498,438	–749,374	–1,224,408	–1,472,926
Services	–14,520	–21,996	–41,491	–72,862	–117,659	–141,397	–225,348	–296,105
Income payments on foreign-owned assets in the U.S.	–5,515	–12,564	–42,532	–72,819	–139,728	–183,090	–322,345	–340,255
Unilateral transfers, net	–6,156	–7,075	–8,349	–21,998	–26,654	–38,177	–58,781	–80,930
Capital acct. transactions, net	NA	NA	NA	315	–6,579	–927	–929	–1,648
U.S.-owned assets abroad, net (increase)/financial outflow [–])	–8,470	–39,703	–85,815	–44,752	–81,234	–352,264	–560,523	–855,509
U.S. official reserve assets, net	3,348	–849	–7,003	–3,858	–2,158	–9,742	–290	2,805
U.S. government assets, other than official reserve assets, net	–1,589	–3,474	–5,162	–2,821	2,317	–984	–941	1,215
U.S. private assets, net	–10,229	–35,380	–73,651	–38,074	–81,393	–341,538	–559,292	–859,529
Foreign-owned assets in the U.S., net (increase/financial inflow [+])	6,359	17,170	62,612	146,115	141,571	438,562	1,046,896	1,440,105
Stat. discrepancy (sum of above items with sign reversed)	–219	4,417	20,886	16,478	25,211	28,299	–69,445	85,126
Memorandum: Balance on current account	2,331	18,116	2,317	–118,155	–78,968	113,670	–415,999	–668,074

NA = Not available. (1) Excludes transfers of goods and services under U.S. military grant programs. (2) Excludes exports of goods under U.S. military agency sales contracts identified in Census export documents, excludes imports of goods under direct defense expenditures identified in Census import documents, and reflects various other adjustments.

Foreign Direct Investment[1] in the U.S. by Selected Countries and Territories, 1995, 2000, 2004

Source: Bureau of Economic Analysis; U.S. Dept. of Commerce

(millions of dollars)

	1995	2000	2004
ALL COUNTRIES[2]	**$560,850**	**$1,214,254**	**$1,526,306**
Canada	**48,258**	**114,599**	**133,761**
Europe[3]	**357,193**	**835,137**	**1,078,287**
Austria	1,555	3,174	3,720
Belgium	3,676	14,585	11,285
Denmark	2,990	4,428	5,450
Finland	2,752	9,107	5,509
France	38,480	131,484	148,242
Germany	49,269	124,839	163,372
Ireland	7,418	23,528	21,153
Italy	2,750	5,994	7,421
Liechtenstein	135	202	310
Luxembourg	5,957	53,794	107,842
Netherlands	65,806	146,493	167,280
Norway	2,089	2,241	3,136
Spain	2,452	5,459	5,669
Sweden	9,581	22,427	23,853
Switzerland	35,593	69,240	122,944
United Kingdom	126,177	213,820	251,562
South and Central America[3]	**7,878**	**13,682**	**26,295**
Brazil	751	886	1,286
Mexico	1,980	7,832	7,880
Panama	4,721	3,726	10,707
Venezuela	–259	802	5,548

	1995	2000	2004
Other Western Hemisphere[3]	**$17,362**	**$40,782**	**$59,569**
Bahamas	–1,780	1,268	1,179
Bermuda	1,592	18,502	8,442
Netherlands Antilles	8,481	3,940	4,749
UK islands, Caribbean	8,417	15,353	24,243
Africa[3]	**1,164**	**2,756**	**1,611**
South Africa	–3	1,218	356
Middle East[3]	**6,008**	**6,189**	**8,200**
Israel	1,995	2,690	4,107
Kuwait	2,527	908	1,238
Lebanon	–9	1	1
Saudi Arabia	1,310	NA	NA
United Arab Emirates	98	64	24
Asia and Pacific[3]	**122,986**	**201,110**	**218,583**
Australia	7,833	20,701	28,083
Hong Kong	1,557	1,544	1,709
Japan	107,933	163,577	176,906
Korea, South	626	3,287	4,212
Malaysia	402	92	335
New Zealand	149	385	814
Philippines	75	50	25
Singapore	1,548	7,751	1,801
Taiwan	2,139	3,131	3,227
European Union[4]	**318,995**	**760,017**	**941,679**
OPEC[5]	**3,740**	**4,363**	**9,007**

(1) The book value of foreign direct investors' equity in, and net outstanding loans to, their U.S. affiliates. A U.S. affiliate is a U.S. business enterprise in which a single foreign direct investor owns at least 10% of the voting securities or the equivalent. (2) Totals includes sources not reflected in regional subtotals. (3) Totals include countries or territories not shown. (4) Total for the European Union in 2004 includes Austria, Belgium, Denmark, Finland, France, Germany, Greece, Ireland, Italy, Luxembourg, the Netherlands, Portugal, Spain, Sweden, the United Kingdom and 10 additional countries (Cyprus, Czech Republic, Estonia, Hungary, Latvia, Lithuania, Malta, Poland, Slovakia, and Slovenia) in May 2004. (5) Organization of Petroleum Exporting Countries: Algeria, Indonesia, Iran, Iraq, Kuwait, Libya, Nigeria, Qatar, Saudi Arabia, United Arab Emirates, and Venezuela. NA = Not available.

U.S. Direct Investment[1] Abroad in Selected Countries and Territories

Source: Bureau of Economic Analysis, U.S. Dept. of Commerce

(millions of dollars)

	1995	2000	2004
ALL COUNTRIES[2]	**$717,554**	**$1,293,431**	**$2,063,998**
Canada	**85,441**	**128,814**	**216,571**
Europe	**360,994**	**679,457**	**1,089,941**
Austria	2,777	2,686	5,278
Belgium	17,969	19,527	27,761
Czech Republic	NA		2,188
Denmark	2,123	5,363	6,618
Finland	825	1,110	2,071
France	32,950	38,752	58,927
Germany	44,226	50,963	79,579
Greece	424	637	1,255
Hungary	NA	NA	3,285
Ireland	8,400	33,816	73,153
Italy	17,587	22,392	33,378
Luxembourg	5,857	25,571	74,902
Netherlands	39,344	117,557	201,918
Norway	5,133	5,833	9,104
Poland	NA	NA	6,059
Portugal	1,755	1,888	3,151
Russia	NA	NA	2,231
Spain	10,770	19,846	45,251
Sweden	7,339	22,676	36,399
Switzerland	33,532	55,854	100,727
Turkey	948	1,356	2,225
United Kingdom	122,767	241,663	302,523
South America[3]	**46,914**	**84,012**	**72,584**
Argentina	7,496	15,646	11,629
Brazil	23,706	39,033	33,267
Chile	5,878	9,451	10,196
Colombia	3,352	4,606	2,987
Ecuador	833	763	814
Peru	1,279	3,485	3,934
Venezuela	3,220	9,530	8,493
Central America[3]	**33,688**	**70,474**	**75,433**
Costa Rica	870	1,655	1,098

	1995	2000	2004
Honduras	$191	$257	$339
Mexico	15,980	37,332	66,554
Panama	16,216	29,316	5,868
Other Western Hemisphere[3]	**47,650**	**97,377**	**177,873**
Bahamas	1,806	2,317	NA
Barbados	755	1,170	1,369
Bermuda	29,980	56,594	91,265
Dominican Republic	394	813	1,041
UK islands, Caribbean	8,941	28,514	63,066
Africa[3]	**6,383**	**14,417**	**22,259**
Egypt	1,388	2,344	4,240
Nigeria	706	1,237	955
South Africa	1,275	3,245	4,966
Middle East[3]	**7,669**	**11,087**	**19,235**
Israel	1,662	3,386	6,790
Saudi Arabia	3,245	4,225	3,835
United Arab Emirates	660	737	2,368
Asia and Pacific[3]	**125,834**	**205,317**	**390,101**
Australia	25,003	35,364	NA
China	2,127	9,861	15,430
Hong Kong	14,206	26,621	43,743
India	838	1,431	6,203
Indonesia	6,607	8,514	NA
Japan	38,406	59,441	80,246
Korea, South	5,169	8,914	17,332
Malaysia	4,200	7,400	8,690
New Zealand	4,845	3,854	4,481
Philippines	2,531	2,735	6,338
Singapore	12,689	25,634	56,900
Taiwan	4,210	7,821	NA
Thailand	4,315	6,635	7,747
European Union[4]	**315,112**	**604,445**	**965,379**
Eastern Europe[5]	**4,739**	**11,149**	**NA**
OPEC[6]	**16,036**	**28,736**	**34,482**

(1) The book value of U.S. direct investors' equity in, and net outstanding loans to, their foreign affiliates. A foreign affiliate is a foreign business enterprise in which a single U.S. investor owns at least 10% of the voting securities or the equivalent. (2) Totals include countries not reflected in regional totals. (3) Total includes countries not shown. (4) The members of the European Union in 2004 were Austria, Belgium, Denmark, Finland, France, Germany, Greece, Ireland, Italy, Luxembourg, the Netherlands, Portugal, Spain, Sweden, the United Kingdom, and 10 additional countries (Cyprus, Czech Republic, Esotnia, Hungary, Latvia, Lithuania, Malta, Poland, Slovakia, and Slovenia after May 2004. (5) Eastern Europe is defined to include Albania, Armenia, Azerbaijan, Belarus, Bulgaria, Czech Republic, Estonia, Georgia, Hungary, Kazakhstan, Kyrgyzstan, Latvia, Lithuania, Moldova, Poland, Romania, Russia, Slovakia, Tajikistan, Turkmenistan, Ukraine, and Uzbekistan. (6) Organization of Petroleum Exporting Countries: Algeria, Indonesia, Iran, Iraq, Kuwait, Libya, Nigeria, Qatar, Saudi Arabia, the United Arab Emirates, and Venezuela. NA = not available.

U.S. Railroad Miles, 1830-2003

Source: Association of American Railroads

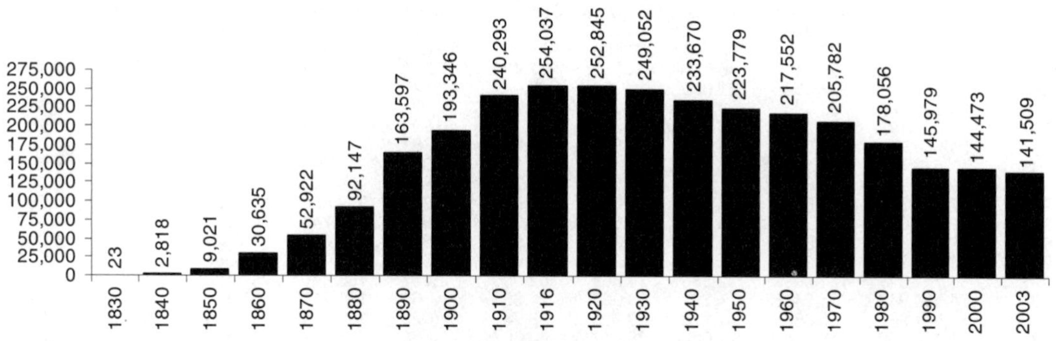

Note: Figures show aggregate length of U.S.-owned operating roadway, excluding yard tracks, sidings, and parallel tracks.

U.S. Railroad Freight, 1890-2003

Source: Association of American Railroads
(in bil ton-miles)

Year	Class I[1]	All	Year	Class I[1]	All	Year	Class I[1]	All	Year	Class I[1]	All	Year	Class I[1]	All
1890	NA	76	1940	373	375	1990	1,034	1,091	1995	1,306	1,375	2000	1,466	1,534
1900	NA	142	1950	589	592	1991	1,039	1,100	1996	1,356	1,426	2001	1,495	1,558
1910	NA	255	1960	572	575	1992	1,067	1,138	1997	1,349	1,421	2002	1,507	1,564
1920	410	414	1970	765	771	1993	1,109	1,183	1998	1,377	1,442	2003	1,551	1,610
1930	383	386	1980	919	932	1994	1,201	1,275	1999	1,433	1,499			

Note: A ton-mile equals 1 ton of freight transported 1 statute mile. (1) Class One, the largest class of freight railroads, determined by an annual operating revenue cut-off ($266.7 mil in 2003).

Leading Motor Vehicle Producing Nations, 2004

Source: Automotive News Data Center and R.L. Polk Marketing Systems GmbH

	Total	Passenger Cars	Trucks
United States	12,021,216	4,236,736	7,784,480
Japan	10,511,518	8,720,385	1,791,133
Germany	5,402,061	5,033,555	368,506
China	5,208,013	2,485,213	2,722,800
France	3,576,701	3,155,681	421,020
S. Korea	3,469,464	3,122,600	346,864
Spain	3,012,148	2,402,501	609,647
Canada	2,698,460	1,400,129	1,298,331
Brazil	2,169,601	1,716,889	452,712
United Kingdom	1,856,430	1,647,156	209,274
Mexico	1,567,584	903,774	663,810
Russia	1,297,528	1,016,650	280,878
India	1,176,810	902,281	274,529
Italy	1,142,362	833,000	309,362
Belgium	904,756	864,888	39,868
Thailand	856,128	232,396	623,732
Turkey	783,786	407,530	376,256
Iran	769,623	682,800	86,823
Poland	582,207	510,000	72,207
Indonesia	519,310	50,600	468,710
Malaysia	469,452	364,852	104,600
Czech Republic	448,354	443,049	5,305
South Africa	432,470	287,350	145,120
Taiwan	425,274	299,639	125,635
Australia	413,985	340,000	73,985
Sweden	412,319	290,358	121,961
Argentina	261,282	171,400	89,882
Netherlands	234,281	187,597	46,684
Austria	221,434	200,052	21,382
Portugal	208,145	132,393	75,752
World Total[1]	**64,388,215**	**44,065,363**	**20,322,852**

(1) Total includes countries or territories not shown.

World Motor Vehicle Production, 1950-2004

Source: For 1950-97, American Automobile Manufacturers Assn.; for 1998-2003, Automotive News Data Center and R.L. Polk Marketing Systems GmbH
(in thousands)

Year	United States	Canada	W. Europe	Japan	Other	World total	U.S. % of world total
1950	8,006	388	1,991	32	160	10,577	75.7
1960	7,905	398	6,837	482	866	16,488	47.9
1970	8,284	1,160	13,049	5,289	1,637	29,419	28.2
1980	8,010	1,324	15,496	11,043	2,692	38,565	20.8
1985	11,653	1,933	16,113	12,271	2,939	44,909	25.9
1990	9,783	1,928	18,866	13,487	4,496	48,554	20.1
1991	8,811	1,888	17,804	13,245	5,180	46,928	18.8
1992	9,729	1,961	17,628	12,499	6,269	48,088	20.2
1993	10,898	2,246	15,208	11,228	7,205	46,785	23.3
1994	12,263	2,321	16,195	10,554	8,167	49,500	24.8
1995	11,985	2,408	17,045	10,196	8,349	49,983	24.0
1996	11,799	2,397	17,550	10,346	9,241	51,332	23.0
1997	12,119	2,571	17,773	10,975	10,024	53,463	22.7
1998	12,047	2,568	16,332	10,050	12,844	53,841	22.4
1999	13,107	3,042	17,603	9,985	14,050	57,787	22.7
2000	12,832	2,952	17,678	10,145	16,098	59,704	21.5
2001	11,518	2,535	17,825	9,777	16,170	57,705	19.7
2002	12,328	2,624	17,419	10,240	16,975	59,587	20.7
2003	12,147	2,568	16,943	10,286	20,619	61,562	19.7
2004	12,021	2,698	16,982	10,512	22,175	64,388	18.7

Note: Data for 1998-2001 not fully comparable with earlier years because derived from different source.

New Passenger Cars Imported Into the U.S., by Country of Origin,[1] 1970-2004

Source: Bureau of the Census, Foreign Trade Division

	Japan	Germany[2]	Italy	United Kingdom	Sweden	France	South Korea	Mexico	Canada	Total[3]
1970	381,338	674,945	42,523	76,257	57,844	37,114	NA	NA	692,783	2,013,420
1975	695,573	370,012	102,344	67,106	51,993	15,647	NA	0	733,766	2,074,653
1980	1,991,502	338,711	46,899	32,517	61,496	47,386	NA	1	594,770	3,116,448
1981	1,911,525	234,052	21,635	12,728	68,042	42,477	NA	1	563,943	2,856,286
1982	1,801,185	259,385	9,402	13,023	89,231	50,032	NA	27	702,495	2,926,407
1983	1,871,192	239,807	5,442	17,261	114,726	40,823	NA	2	835,665	3,133,836
1984	1,948,714	335,032	8,582	19,833	114,854	37,788	NA	NA	1,073,425	3,559,427
1985	2,527,467	473,110	8,689	24,474	142,640	42,882	NA	13,647	1,144,805	4,397,679
1986	2,618,711	451,699	11,829	27,506	148,700	10,869	169,309	41,983	1,162,226	4,691,297
1987	2,417,509	377,542	8,648	50,059	138,565	26,707	399,856	126,266	926,927	4,589,010
1988	2,123,051	264,249	6,053	31,636	108,006	15,990	455,741	148,065	1,191,357	4,450,213
1989	2,051,525	216,881	9,319	29,378	101,571	4,885	270,609	133,049	1,151,122	4,042,728
1990	1,867,794	245,286	11,045	27,271	93,084	1,976	201,475	215,986	1,220,221	3,944,602
1991	1,762,347	171,097	2,886	14,862	62,905	1,727	186,740	249,498	1,109,248	3,612,665
1992	1,598,919	205,248	1,791	10,997	76,832	65	130,110	266,111	1,119,223	3,447,200
1993	1,501,953	180,383	1,178	20,029	58,742	23	122,943	299,634	1,371,856	3,604,361
1994	1,488,159	178,774	1,010	28,217	63,867	58	213,962	360,367	1,525,746	3,909,079
1995	1,114,360	204,932	1,031	42,450	82,593	14	131,718	462,800	1,552,691	3,624,428
1996	1,190,896	234,909	1,365	44,373	86,619	27	225,623	550,867	1,690,733	4,069,113
1997	1,387,812	300,489	1,912	43,691	79,780	67	222,568	544,075	1,731,209	4,378,295
1998	1,456,081	373,330	2,104	49,891	84,543	56	211,650	584,795	1,837,615	4,673,418
1999	1,707,277	461,061	1,697	68,394	83,399	186	372,965	639,878	2,170,427	5,639,616
2000	1,839,093	488,323	3,125	81,196	86,707	134	568,121	934,000	2,138,811	6,324,284
2001	1,790,346	494,131	2,580	82,487	92,439	92	633,769	861,853	1,855,789	6,065,138
2002	2,046,902	574,455	3,504	157,633	87,709	150	627,881	845,181	1,882,660	6,477,659
2003	1,770,355	561,482	2,943	207,158	119,773	298	692,863	680,214	1,811,892	6,127,485
2004	1,727,065	547,008	3,373	185,621	98,131	2,417	860,424	652,509	2,035,345	6,521,248

(1) Excludes cars assembled in U.S. foreign trade zones. (2) Figures prior to 1991 are for West Germany. (3) Includes countries not shown separately.

Passenger Car Production, U.S. Plants, 2003, 2004

Source: Ward's AutoInfoBank

	2004	2003
TOTAL CARS	**4,229,625**	**4,510,469**
Ford Mustang	41,925	—
Mazda6	91,339	83,422
AUTOALLIANCE TOTAL[1]	**133,264**	**83,422**
BMW Z4	35,136	56,589
BMW TOTAL	**35,136**	**56,589**
Neon	1,844	1,859
Sebring Convertible	39,388	46,158
Sebring Sedan	77,269	64,308
Chrysler Total	**118,501**	**112,325**
Neon	139,004	150,957
Stratus Sedan	90,792	97,261
Viper	2,469	2,484
Dodge Total	**232,265**	**250,702**
CHRYSLER GROUP TOTAL	**350,766**	**363,027**
Five Hundred	42,782	—
Focus	184,805	204,328
Ford GT	500	—
Mustang	69,704	154,937
Taurus	254,842	294,326
Thunderbird	10,716	18,837
Ford Total	**563,349**	**672,428**
Lincoln LS	27,146	39,579
Town Car	53,958	54,458
Lincoln Total	**81,104**	**94,037**
Montego	7,448	—
Sable	44,216	55,215
Mercury Total	**51,664**	**55,215**
FORD TOTAL	**696,117**	**821,680**
LeSabre	103,311	131,962
Park Ave.	12,601	26,616
Buick Total	**115,912**	**158,578**
CTS	71,518	59,250
Deville	63,459	82,965
Seville	5	15,619
STS	20,496	—
XLR	5,314	1,731
Cadillac Total	**160,792**	**159,565**
Cavalier	180,175	282,424
Cobalt	25,994	—
Corvette	28,723	36,026
Malibu	315,171	184,155
Chevrolet Total	**550,063**	**502,605**
Alero	18,906	111,680
Aurora	—	1,786
Oldsmobile Total	**18,906**	**113,466**
Bonneville	31,693	22,649
G6	42,186	—
Grand Am	116,877	174,324
Grand Prix	—	18,687
Pursuit	2,575	—
Sunfire	21,298	52,393
Pontiac Total	**214,629**	**268,053**
Ion	110,902	138,008
Saturn L	11,729	45,440
Saturn Total	**122,631**	**183,448**
GM TOTAL	**1,182,933**	**1,385,715**
Acura CL	—	4,201
Acura TL	82,635	60,397
Acura Total	**82,635**	**64,598**
Accord	350,337	380,946
Civic	133,995	147,564
Honda Total	**484,332**	**528,510**
HONDA GROUP TOTAL	**566,967**	**593,108**
Stratus Coupe	23,035	18,056
Dodge Total	**23,035**	**18,056**
Eclipse	11,210	39,287
Galant	45,188	59,572
Mitsubishi Total	**56,398**	**98,859**
Chrysler Sebring Coupe	12,103	9,332
MITSUBISHI TOTAL	**91,536**	**126,247**
Altima	279,642	240,666
Maxima	87,129	81,402
NISSAN TOTAL	**366,771**	**322,068**
Pontiac Vibe	69,226	74,223
Toyota Corolla	167,970	157,561
Toyota Voltz*	201	1,733
NUMMI TOTAL[2]	**237,397**	**233,517**
Subaru Legacy	98,298	89,243
SUBARU TOTAL	**98,298**	**89,243**
Avalon	33,074	49,250
Camry	388,119	356,829
Solara	49,247	29,774
TOYOTA TOTAL	**470,440**	**435,853**

* For export only. (1) Company is a joint venture between Ford and Mazda. (2) NUMMI (New United Motor Manufacturing, Inc.) is a joint venture between GM and Toyota.

Domestic and Imported Retail Cars Sales in the U.S., 1980-2004

Source: Ward's Communications

Year	Domestic[1]	Imports				Total U.S. Sales	Import Percent		
		Japan	Germany	Other Countries	Total		Total	Japan	Germany
1980	6,581,307	1,905,968	305,219	186,700	2,397,887	8,979,194	26.7	21.2	3.3
1981	6,208,760	1,858,896	282,881	185,502	2,327,279	8,536,039	27.3	21.8	3.3
1982	5,758,586	1,801,969	247,080	174,508	2,223,557	7,982,143	27.9	22.6	3.0
1983	6,795,295	1,915,621	279,748	191,403	2,386,772	9,182,067	26.0	20.9	3.0
1984	7,951,523	1,906,206	344,416	188,220	2,438,842	10,390,365	23.5	18.3	3.8
1985	8,204,542	2,217,837	423,983	195,925	2,837,745	11,042,287	25.7	20.1	3.8
1986	8,214,897	2,382,614	443,721	418,286	3,244,621	11,459,518	28.3	20.8	3.9
1987	7,080,858	2,190,405	347,881	657,465	3,195,751	10,276,609	31.1	21.3	3.4
1988	7,526,038	2,022,602	280,099	700,991	3,003,692	10,529,730	28.5	19.2	2.7
1989	7,072,902	1,897,143	248,561	553,660	2,699,364	9,772,266	27.6	19.4	2.5
1990	6,896,888	1,719,384	265,116	418,823	2,403,323	9,300,211	25.8	18.5	2.9
1991	6,136,757	1,500,309	192,776	344,814	2,037,899	8,174,656	24.9	18.4	2.4
1992	6,276,557	1,451,766	200,851	283,938	1,936,555	8,213,112	23.6	17.7	2.4
1993	6,741,667	1,328,445	186,177	261,570	1,776,192	8,517,859	20.9	15.6	2.2
1994	7,255,303	1,239,450	192,275	303,489	1,735,214	8,990,517	19.3	13.8	2.1
1995	7,128,707	981,506	207,482	317,269	1,506,257	8,634,964	17.4	11.4	2.4
1996	7,253,582	726,940	237,984	308,247	1,273,171	8,526,753	14.9	8.5	2.8
1997	6,916,769	726,104	297,028	332,173	1,355,305	8,272,074	16.4	8.8	3.6
1998	6,761,940	691,162	366,724	321,895	1,379,781	8,141,721	16.9	8.5	4.5
1999	6,979,357	757,568	466,870	494,489	1,718,927	8,698,284	19.8	8.7	5.4
2000	6,830,505	862,780	516,614	636,726	2,016,120	8,846,625	22.8	9.8	5.8
2001	6,324,996	836,685	522,659	738,285	2,097,629	8,422,625	24.9	9.9	6.2
2002	5,877,645	923,182	546,654	755,748	2,225,584	8,103,229	27.5	11.4	6.7
2003	5,527,430	817,038	543,823	722,190	2,083,051	7,610,481	27.4	10.7	7.1
2004	5,356,873	798,222	541,940	808,897	2,149,059	7,505,932	28.6	10.6	7.2

(1) Includes cars manufactured in Canada and Mexico.

U.S. Car Sales by Vehicle Size and Type, 1985-2004

Source: Ward's Communications; percent of total U.S. sales

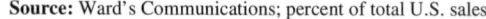

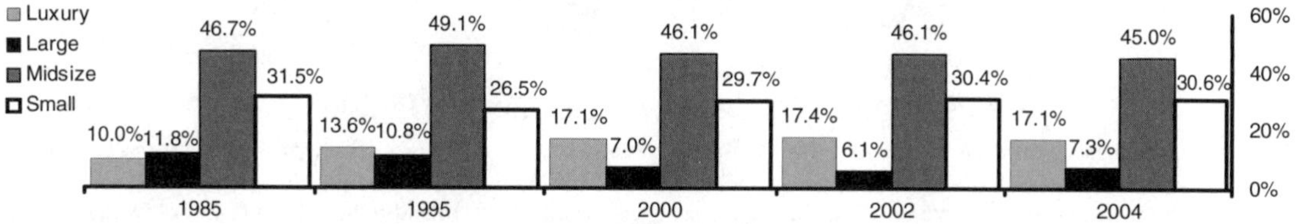

Top-Selling Passenger Cars in the U.S. by Calendar Year, 2001-04

Source: Ward's Communications

2004

1. Toyota Camry 426,990
2. Honda Accord 386,770
3. Toyota Corolla/Matrix 333,161
4. Honda Civic 309,196
5. Chevrolet Impala 290,259
6. Chevrolet Malibu 268,017
7. Ford Taurus 248,148
8. Nissan Altima 235,889
9. Ford Focus 208,339
10. Chevrolet Cavalier 195,275
11. Pontiac Grand Am 133,707
12. Pontiac Grand Prix 131,551
13. Ford Mustang 129,858
14. Buick Lesabre 114,157
15. Dodge Neon 113,476
16. Hyundai Elantra 112,892
17. Chrysler 300 Series 107,820
18. Hyundai Sonata 107,189
19. Nissan Sentra 106,934
20. BMW 3- Series 106,549

2003

1. Toyota Camry 413,296
2. Honda Accord 397,750
3. Toyota Corolla/Matrix 325,477
4. Ford Taurus 300,496
5. Honda Civic 299,672
6. Chevrolet Impala 267,882
7. Chevrolet Cavalier 256,550
8. Ford Focus 229,353
9. Nissan Altima 201,240
10. Chevrolet Malibu 173,263

2002

1. Toyota Camry 434,145
2. Honda Accord 398,980
3. Ford Taurus 332,690
4. Honda Civic 313,159
5. Toyota Corolla/Matrix 254,360
6. Ford Focus 243,199
7. Chevrolet Cavalier 238,225
8. Nissan Altima 201,822
9. Chevrolet Impala 198,918
10. Chevrolet Malibu 169,377

2001

1. Honda Accord 414,718
2. Toyota Camry 390,449
3. Ford Taurus 353,560
4. Honda Civic 331,780
5. Ford Focus 264,414
6. Toyota Corolla 245,023
7. Chevrolet Cavalier 233,298
8. Chevrolet Impala 208,395
9. Pontiac Grand Am 182,046
10. Chevrolet Malibu 176,583

Top-Selling Light Trucks in the U.S. by Calendar Year, 2002-04

2004

1. Ford F Series 891,482
2. Chevrolet Silverado 680,663
3. Dodge Ram Pickup 426,289
4. Ford Explorer 339,333
5. Chevrolet TrailBlazer 283,484
6. Dodge Caravan 242,307
7. GMC Sierra 213,736
8. Chevrolet Tahoe 186,161
9. Ford Escape 183,430
10. Jeep Grand Cherokee 182,313

2003

1. Ford F Series 806,887
2. ChevroletSilverado 683,889
3. Dodge Ram Pickup 449,371
4. Ford Explorer 373,118
5. Chevrolet TrailBlazer 261,334
6. Dodge Caravan 233,394
7. Ford Ranger 209,117
8. Jeep Grand Cherokee 207,479
9. Chevy Tahoe 199,065
10. GMC Sierra 196,429

2002

1. Ford F Series 774,037
2. Chevrolet Silverado 648,040
3. Ford Explorer 433,847
4. Dodge Ram Pickup 396,934
5. Chevrolet TrailBlazer 249,568
6. Dodge Caravan 244,911
7. Ford Ranger 226,094
8. Jeep Grand Cherokee 224,233
9. Chevy Tahoe 209,767
10. GMC Sierra 200,146

Sport Utility Vehicle Sales in the U.S., 1988-2004

Source: Ward's Communications

In 1988, 960,852 sport utility vehicles (SUVs) were sold in the United States, accounting for almost 19% of all light trucks and just over 6% of all sales of light vehicles (cars, SUVs, minivans, vans, pickup trucks, and trucks under 14,000 lbs.). In 2004, SUV sales increased 4.3% over the previous year to 4,728,627, or 28.0% of all light vehicles sold (50.5% of light trucks).

Sales shown here include those for SUVs and lighter SUV models known as crossover or cross utility vehicles, which are generally smaller and get better mileage. If separated, SUV sales declined 6.5% since 2002, from 2,974,466 to 2,781,457 in 2004. But crossover vehicle sales increased dramatically, to 1,946,170 in 2004, up 57.3% from 1,237,620 in 2002.

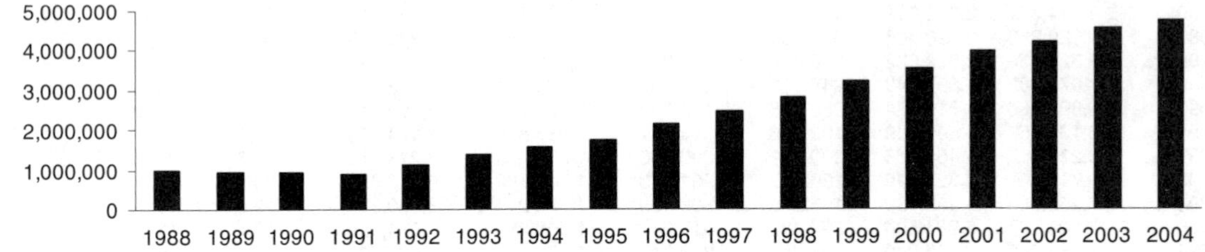

Most Popular Colors, by Type of Vehicle, 2004 Model Year

Source: Ward's Communications; Du Pont Automotive Products

Luxury Cars		Full Size/Intermediate Cars		Compact/Sports Cars		Light Trucks	
Color	**Percent**	**Color**	**Percent**	**Color**	**Percent**	**Color**	**Percent**
Silver/Gray	26	Silver	24	Silver	20	White/White Pearl	20
White Pearl	17	Light Brown	17	Red	17	Silver	16
White	12	White	13	Black	13	Red	14
Black	12	Red	12	Blue	13	Black	12
Light Brown	11	Medium/Dark Gray	11	White	9	Blue	12
Red	9	Black	9	Light Brown	9	Medium/Dark Gray	10
Blue	9	Blue	6	Medium/Dark Gray	8	Light Brown	9
Yellow/Gold	4	Green	5	Green	4	Green	5
Other	1	Yellow/Gold	1	Yellow	4	Yellow/Gold	1
		Other	2	Other	3	Other	1

U.S. Light-Vehicle Fuel Efficiency, 1975-2005

Source: Environmental Protection Agency, Office of Transportation and Air Quality, National Vehicle and Fuel Emissions Laboratory

After showing significant fuel-efficiency improvements from 1974 through 1985, both light-duty trucks (SUVs, minivans, vans, and light trucks) and cars have failed to show consistent gains since then. In addition, light-duty trucks, which are less fuel-efficient than cars, have captured an increasing proportion of the total light vehicle market, rising from only 19% in 1975 to an estimated 50% by 2005. This increase has been a major factor in the leveling off in the fuel efficiency of the average light vehicle sold.

YEAR	Cars (MPG*)	Light-duty Trucks (MPG*)	All Light Vehicles (MPG*)
1975	13.5	11.6	13.1
1980	20.0	15.8	19.2
1985	23.0	17.5	21.3
1990	23.7	17.7	21.5
1995	24.2	17.5	21.1
1996	24.2	17.8	21.2
1997	24.3	17.6	20.9
1998	24.4	17.8	20.9
1999	24.1	17.5	20.6
2000	24.1	17.7	20.7
2001	24.3	17.6	20.7
2002	24.5	17.6	20.6
2003	24.7	17.8	20.8
2004	24.7	17.9	20.8
2005	24.7	18.2	21.0

*MPG value represents laboratory city and highway fuel efficiency combined in a 55%/45% ratio.

Cars Registered in the U.S., 1900-2003[1]

Source: U.S. Dept. of Transportation, Federal Highway Administration
(includes automobiles for public and private use)

Year	Cars Reg.
1900	8,000
1905	77,400
1910	458,377
1915	2,332,426
1920	8,131,522
1925	17,481,001
1930	23,034,753
1935	22,567,827
1940	27,465,826
1945	25,796,985
1950	40,339,077
1955	52,144,739
1960	61,671,390
1965	75,257,588
1970	89,243,557
1975	106,705,934
1980	121,600,843
1985	127,885,193
1990	133,700,497
1991	128,299,601
1992	126,581,148
1993	127,327,189
1994	127,883,469
1995	128,386,775
1996	129,728,311
1997	129,748,704
1998	131,838,538
1999	132,432,044
2000	133,621,420
2001	137,633,467
2002	135,920,677
2003	135,669,897

(1) There were no publicly owned vehicles before 1925; statistics also exclude military vehicles for all years. Alaska and Hawaii data included since 1960.

IT'S A FACT: In 2004, U.S. registrations of hybrid vehicles—motor vehicles powered by internal combustion engines in combination with an automatically recharged battery and electric motor—increased by 81%, to 83,153, over the previous year. Gas-electric hybrids—such as the Toyota Prius, Ford Escape Hybrid, and Honda Insight, Accord, and Civic hybrid models—reduce tailpipe emissions and are more fuel efficient than vehicles with standard internal combustion engines. The Honda Insight is the most fuel efficient vehicle available in the U.S., able to drive an estimated 60 city/66 highway miles per gallon of gasoline, and has the Environmental Protection Agency's best greenhouse gas rating, reflecting its low emissions of carbon dioxide.

Licensed Drivers, by Age, 1980-2003

Source: Federal Highway Administration, U.S. Dept. of Transportation
(in thousands)

AGE	1980 Male	1980 Female	1980 Total[1]	1990 Male	1990 Female	1990 Total[1]	2003 Male	2003 Female	2003 Total[1]
(under 16)	52	41	93	23	20	43	19	18	37
16	1,001	822	1,823	769	674	1,443	643	620	1,263
17	1,530	1,260	2,790	1,136	996	2,132	1,112	1,066	2,178
18	1,763	1,484	3,247	1,378	1,217	2,595	1,424	1,342	2,766
19	1,900	1,643	3,542	1,608	1,429	3,037	1,549	1,470	3,019
(19 and under)	6,246	5,249	11,496	4,913	4,336	9,249	4,746	4,517	9,263
20	1,930	1,706	3,636	1,691	1,538	3,229	1,625	1,553	3,178
21	1,961	1,772	3,733	1,694	1,555	3,249	1,679	1,627	3,306
22	1,998	1,813	3,811	1,701	1,561	3,262	1,706	1,664	3,370
23	2,062	1,876	3,938	1,767	1,631	3,398	1,741	1,700	3,441
24	2,047	1,868	3,915	1,951	1,807	3,758	1,742	1,700	3,442
(20-24)	9,998	9,034	19,032	8,804	8,093	16,897	8,494	8,243	16,737
25-29	9,865	9,060	18,925	10.239	9,656	19,895	8,670	8,394	17,064
30-34	9,010	8,359	17,369	10,507	10,071	20,578	9,623	9,303	18,925
35-39	7,113	6,583	13,696	9,684	9,371	19,055	9,960	9,724	19,684
40-44	5,828	5,306	11,134	8,610	8,295	16,905	10,654	10,606	21,260
45-49	5,311	4,765	10,076	6,642	6,378	13,020	10,136	10,206	20,342
50-54	5,351	4,739	10,090	5,376	5,108	10,484	8,917	9,002	17,918
55-59	5,198	4,572	9,770	4,855	4,583	9,438	7,483	7,502	14,985
60-64	4,439	3,793	8,232	4,738	4,497	9,235	5,680	5,702	11,382
65-69	3,631	2,949	6,580	4,266	4,109	8,375	4,370	4,407	8,777
(70 and over)	5,195	3,699	8,894	7,159	6,726	13,885	9,497	10,329	19,828
70-74	NA	NA	NA	NA	NA	NA	3,613	3,749	7,363
75-79	NA	NA	NA	NA	NA	NA	2,894	3,173	6,068
80-84	NA	NA	NA	NA	NA	NA	1,857	2,103	3,960
85 and over	NA	NA	NA	NA	NA	NA	1,133	1,304	2,437
TOTAL	**77,187**	**68,108**	**145,295**	**85,792**	**81,223**	**167,015**	**98,228**	**97,937**	**196,166**

(1) These totals may not add due to rounding. NA = not available.

Highway Speed Limits, by State

Source: Insurance Institute for Highway Safety

Under the National Highway System Designation Act, signed Nov. 28, 1995, by Pres. Bill Clinton, states were allowed to set their own highway speed limits, as of Dec. 8, 1995. Under federal legislation enacted in 1974 during the energy crisis, states had been, in effect, restricted to a National Maximum Speed Limit (NMSL) of 55 miles per hour (raised in 1987 to 65 mph on rural interstates).

Maximum posted speed limits, in miles per hour, are given by state in the table below. (Speeds shown in parentheses are for commercial trucks.) Most data current as of Sept. 2005. For more information visit the Insurance Institute for Highway Safety website at www.hwysafety.org

STATE	Rural Interstate	Urban[1] Interstate	Limited[2] Access Roads	Other Roads
AL	70	65	65	65
AK	65	55	65	55
AZ	75	55	55	55
AR	70 (65)	55	60	55
CA	70 (55)	65	70	65
CO	75	65	65	65
CT	65	55	65	55
DE	65	55	65	55
FL	70	65	70	65
GA	70	65	65	65
HI	60	50	45	45
ID	75 (65)	75	65	65
IL	65 (55)	55	65	55
IN	70 (65)	55	55	55
IA	70	55	65	55
KS	70	70	70	65
KY	65	65	65	55
LA	70	70	70	65
ME	65	65	65	60
MD	65	65	65	55
MA	65	65	65	55
MI	70 (55)	65	70	55
MN	70	65	65	55
MS	70	70	70	65
MO	70	60	70	65
MT	75 (65)	65	70[3]	70[3]
NE	75	65	65	60
NV	75	65	70	70
NH	65	65	55	55
NJ	65	55	65	55
NM	75	75	65	55
NY	65	65	65	55
NC	70	70	70	55
ND	75	75	70	65
OH	65 (55)	65	55	55
OK	75	70	70	70
OR	65 (55)	55	55	55
PA	65	55	65	55
RI	65	55	55	55
SC	70	70	60	55
SD	75	75	65	65
TN	70	70	70	65
TX	75 (65)[3]	70[3]	75 (65)[3]	60[4]
UT	75	65	75	65
VT	65	55	50	50
VA	65	65	65	55
WA	70 (60)	60	60	60
WV	70	55	65	55
WI	65	65	65	55
WY	75	60	65	65

(1) Urban interstates are determined from U.S. Census Bureau criteria, which may be adjusted by state and local governments to reflect planning and other issues. (2) Limited access roads are multiple-lane highways with restricted access via exit and entrance ramps rather than intersections. (3) Speed limit is 65 mph at night (½ hour after sunset to ½ hour before sunrise). (4) Speed limit is 55 mph at night (½ hour after sunset to ½ hour before sunrise).

Selected Motor Vehicle Statistics

Source: Federal Highway Admin.; U.S. Dept. of Transportation; Insurance Institute for Highway Safety; American Petroleum Institute

Driver's license age requirements, state gas tax, and safety belt laws (incl. laws passed, but not in effect) as of 2005; other figures for 2003.

STATE	Driver's license age requirements: Regular[1]	Driver's license age requirements: Learner's Permit	State gas tax cents/ gal.	Safety belt use law[10]	Licensed drivers per 1,000 resident pop.	Licensed drivers per motor vehicle	Regist. motor vehicles per 1,000 pop.	Gals. of fuel used per vehicle	Miles per gal.	Annual miles driven per vehicle	Vehicle miles per licensed driver
Alabama	17	15	18	P	799	0.84	962	744	18.21	13,544	16,297
Alaska	16y, 6m	14	8	S	742	0.77	981	611	12.71	7,761	10,264
Arizona	16	15y, 7m	18	S	684	1.08	640	945	15.95	15,080	14,111
Arkansas	16	14	21.5	S	733	1.07	693	1,082	14.99	16,224	15,334
California	17[2]	15y, 6m	18	P	639	0.84	852	594	18.01	10,698	14,282
Colorado	17	15[3]	22	S	654	1.50	446	1,285	16.65	21,396	14,580
Connecticut	18[2]	16[3]	25	P	764	0.91	851	630	16.84	10,606	11,817
Delaware	16y, 10m[2]	15y, 10m[3]	23	P	716	0.87	840	706	18.66	13,168	15,456
Dist. of Col.	18[4]	16	20	P	556	1.44	405	765	23.75	18,174	13,258
Florida	18	15	14.5	S	758	0.91	854	662	19.30	12,771	14,374
Georgia	18	15	7.5	P	663	0.76	890	838	16.86	14,132	18,973
Hawaii	17[2,4]*	15y, 6m	16	P	663	0.94	718	536	19.23	10,313	11,163
Idaho	16[5]	14y, 6m	25	S	674	0.72	952	656	16.75	10,983	15,511
Illinois	17[2]	15[3]	19	P	637	0.88	731	710	16.22	11,517	13,227
Indiana	18	15	18	P	732	0.80	926	834	15.15	12,634	15,985
Iowa	17[2]	14	20.7	P	672	0.60	1144	637	14.50	9,234	15,728
Kansas	16	14	24	S	730	0.87	850	772	16.04	12,388	14,428
Kentucky	16y, 6m[6]	16	18.5	S	680	0.84	823	894	15.43	13,795	16,698
Louisiana	17[5,7]	15	20	P	694	0.86	826	832	14.29	11,890	14,153
Maine	16y, 6m[2]	15[3]	25.9	S	714	0.90	805	932	15.22	14,180	15,992
Maryland	17y, 9m[2]	15y, 9m[3]	23.5	P	645	0.93	704	811	17.39	14,111	15,399
Massachusetts	17[2]	16	23.5	S	722	0.86	852	596	16.45	9,802	11,561
Michigan	17[2]	14y, 9m	19	P	701	0.84	847	709	16.64	11,798	14,260
Minnesota	16[2]	15[3]*	20	S	600	0.68	894	746	16.38	12,220	18,216
Mississippi	16	15	18	S(a)	655	0.98	677	1,142	16.82	19,204	19,866
Missouri	18	15	17	S(a)	695	0.90	782	938	16.29	15,284	17,189
Montana	16**	14y, 6m	27.75	S	768	0.71	1101	697	15.45	10,761	15,435
Nebraska	17	15	25.3	S	754	0.80	964	753	15.05	11,338	14,501
Nevada	18	15y, 6m[2]	23	S	664	1.24	545	1,117	14.14	15,796	12,972
New Hampshire	17y, 1m	15y, 6m	18	none	752	0.86	889	719	16.00	11,511	13,619
New Jersey	18	16[3]	14.5	P	663	0.87	777	800	13.00	10,397	12,180
New Mexico	16y, 6m[2]	15	17	P	660	0.84	805	935	16.19	15,135	18,475
New York	18	16	27.4	P	592	1.59	563	661	18.91	12,502	11,891
North Carolina	16y, 6m[2]	15	27.1	P	715	1.00	728	878	17.45	15,323	15,588
North Dakota	16	14	23	S	725	0.68	1095	766	14.04	10,757	16,242
Ohio	17[2]	15y, 6m	28	S	670	0.74	921	642	16.10	10,339	14,228
Oklahoma	16y, 6m	15y, 6m	16	P	669	0.78	875	878	16.95	14,876	19,470
Oregon	17[2]	15	24	P	728	0.86	860	671	17.08	11,467	13,553
Pennsylvania	18	16	31.1	S	677	0.87	786	670	16.32	10,936	12,706
Rhode Island	17y, 6m[2]	16	30	S(a)	680	0.92	749	566	18.34	10,382	11,438
South Carolina	16y, 6m	15	16	P	704	0.94	762	954	15.95	15,219	16,485
South Dakota	16	14	22	S	726	0.69	1082	729	14.14	10,311	15,376
Tennessee	17	15[3]	20	P	720	0.89	821	841	17.15	14,420	16,449
Texas	16y, 6m	15[3]	20	P	610	0.93	673	987	15.20	15,006	16,552
Utah	17[9]	15y, 6m	24.5	S(a)	659	0.78	853	688	17.40	11,976	15,518
Vermont	16y, 6m[2]	15	20	S	878	1.08	834	816	19.73	16,100	15,290
Virginia	18[2]	15y, 6m	17.5	S	683	0.81	859	786	15.42	12,113	15,234
Washington	17[2]	15	31	P	719	0.83	877	621	16.47	10,228	12,483
West Virginia	17	15	20.5	S	703	0.93	778	785	18.15	14,255	15,786
Wisconsin	16y, 9m[2]	15y, 6m	32.9	S	688	0.82	849	699	18.36	12,828	15,831
Wyoming	16y, 6m	15	14	S	754	0.63	1237	1,040	14.28	14,860	24,367
AVERAGE			21.1		675	0.89	796	753	16.60	12,494	14,737

NOTE: Many states are moving toward graduated licensing systems that phase in full driving privileges. During the learner's phase, driving generally is not permitted unless there is an adult supervisor. In an intermediate phase, young licensees not yet having unrestricted licenses may be allowed to drive unsupervised under certain conditions but not others.

*As of Jan. 2006; **As of July 2006. (1) Unrestricted operation of private passenger car. (2) Applicants under age 18 (19 in VA) must have completed an approved driver education course (or home training in CT). (3) May not use cell phones during learner's phase (may also extend to intermediate states). (4) Learner's phase mandatory for all ages. Applicants under age 21 must complete a 6-month intermediate phase. (5) Applicants under age 17 must have completed an approved driver education course. (6) License holders under age 18 must complete a 4-hour course on safe driving within 1 yr. of receiving license (7) Applicants age 17 and older must have completed an educational program, but doesn't require behind-the-wheel training. (8) Driving in New York City is prohibited for all licensees under 18, or under 17 if driver has completed an approved driver education course. (9) Regardless of age, applicants must enroll in an approved driver education course. (10) P = officer may stop vehicle for a violation (primary); S = an officer may issue seat belt citation only when vehicle is stopped for another moving violation (secondary).

(a) Primary enforcement for children under a specified age: MS-8; MO-16; RI-18; UT-19.

Road Mileage Between Selected U.S. Cities

	Atlanta	Boston	Chicago	Cincin-nati	Cleve-land	Dallas	Denver	Des Moines	Detroit	Houston
Atlanta, GA	...	1,037	674	440	672	795	1,398	870	699	789
Boston, MA	1,037	...	963	840	628	1,748	1,949	1,280	695	1,804
Chicago, IL	674	963	...	287	335	917	996	327	266	1,067
Cincinnati, OH	440	840	287	...	244	920	1,164	571	259	1,029
Cleveland, OH	672	628	335	244	...	1,159	1,321	652	170	1,273
Dallas TX.	795	1,748	917	920	1,159	...	781	684	1,143	243
Denver, CO	1,398	1,949	996	1,164	1,321	781	...	669	1,253	1,019
Detroit, MI	699	695	266	259	170	1,143	1,253	584	...	1,265
Houston, TX	789	1,804	1,067	1,029	1,273	243	1,019	905	1,265	...
Indianapolis, IN	493	906	181	106	294	865	1,058	465	278	987
Kansas City, MO	798	1,391	499	591	779	489	600	195	743	710
Los Angeles, CA	2,182	2,979	2,054	2,179	2,367	1,387	1,059	1,727	2,311	1,538
Memphis, TN	371	1,296	530	468	712	452	1,040	599	713	561
Milwaukee, WI	761	1,050	87	374	422	991	1,029	361	353	1,142
Minneapolis, MN	1,068	1,368	405	692	740	936	841	252	671	1,157
New Orleans, LA	479	1,507	912	786	1,030	496	1,273	978	1,045	356
New York, NY	841	206	802	647	473	1,552	1,771	1,119	637	1,608
Omaha, NB	986	1,412	459	693	784	644	537	132	716	865
Philadelphia, PA	741	296	738	567	413	1,452	1,691	1,051	573	1,508
Pittsburgh, PA	687	561	452	287	129	1,204	1,411	763	287	1,313
Portland OR	2,601	3,046	2,083	2,333	2,418	2,009	1,238	1,786	2,349	2,205
St. Louis, MO	541	1,141	289	340	529	630	857	333	513	779
San Francisco, SC	2,496	3,095	2,142	2,362	2,467	1,753	1,235	1,815	2,399	1,912
Seattle, WA	2,618	2,976	2,013	2,300	2,348	2,078	1,307	1,749	2,279	2,274
Tulsa, OK	772	1,537	683	736	925	257	681	443	909	478
Washington, DC	608	429	671	481	346	1,319	1,616	984	506	1,375

	India-napolis	Kansas City	Los Angeles	Louis-ville	Memphis	Mil-waukee	Minne-apolis	New Orleans	New York	Omaha
Atlanta, GA	493	798	2,182	382	371	761	1,068	479	841	986
Boston, MA	906	1,391	2,979	941	1,296	1,050	1,368	1,507	206	1,412
Chicago, IL	181	499	2,054	292	530	87	405	912	802	459
Cincinnati, OH	106	591	2,179	101	468	374	692	786	647	693
Cleveland, OH	294	779	2,367	345	712	422	740	1,030	473	784
Dallas TX.	865	489	1,387	819	452	991	936	496	1,552	644
Denver, CO	1,058	600	1,059	1,120	1,040	1,029	841	1,273	1,771	537
Detroit, MI	278	743	2,311	360	713	353	671	1,045	637	716
Houston, TX	987	710	1,538	928	561	1,142	1,157	356	1,608	865
Indianapolis, IN	...	485	2,073	111	435	268	586	796	713	587
Kansas City, MO	485	...	1,589	520	451	537	447	806	1,198	201
Los Angeles, CA	2,073	1,589	...	2,108	1,817	2,087	1,889	1,883	2,786	1,595
Memphis, TN	435	451	1,817	367	...	612	826	390	1,100	652
Milwaukee, WI	268	537	2,087	379	612	...	332	994	889	493
Minneapolis, MN	586	447	1,889	697	826	332	...	1,214	1,207	357
New Orleans, LA	796	806	1,883	685	390	994	1,214	...	1,311	1,007
New York, NY	713	1,198	2,786	748	1,100	889	1,207	1,311	...	1,251
Omaha, NB	587	201	1,595	687	652	493	357	1,007	1,251	...
Philadelphia, PA	633	1,118	2,706	668	1,000	825	1,143	1,211	100	1,183
Pittsburgh, PA	353	838	2,426	388	752	539	857	1,070	368	895
Portland OR	2,272	1,809	959	2,320	2,259	2,010	1,678	2,505	2,885	1,654
St. Louis, MO	235	257	1,845	263	285	363	552	673	948	449
San Francisco, SC	2,293	1,835	379	2,349	2,125	2,175	1,940	2,249	2,934	1,683
Seattle, WA	2,194	1,839	1,131	2,305	2,290	1,940	1,608	2,574	2,815	1,638
Tulsa, OK	631	248	1,452	659	401	757	695	647	1,344	387
Washington, DC	558	1,043	2,631	582	867	758	1,076	1,078	233	1,116

	Phila-delphia	Pitts-burgh	Portland	St. Louis	Salt Lake City	San Francisco	Seattle	Toledo	Tulsa	Wash., DC
Atlanta, GA	741	687	2,601	541	1,878	2,496	2,618	640	772	608
Boston, MA	296	561	3,046	1,141	2,343	3,095	2,976	739	1,537	429
Chicago, IL	738	452	2,083	289	1,390	2,142	2,013	232	683	671
Cincinnati, OH	567	287	2,333	340	1,610	2,362	2,300	200	736	481
Cleveland, OH	413	129	2,418	529	1,715	2,467	2,348	111	925	346
Dallas TX.	1,452	1,204	2,009	630	1,242	1,753	2,078	1,084	257	1,319
Denver, CO	1,691	1,411	1,238	857	504	1,235	1,307	1,218	681	1,616
Detroit, MI	576	287	2,349	513	1,647	2,399	2,279	59	909	506
Houston, TX	1,508	1,313	2,205	779	1,438	1,912	2,274	1,206	478	1,375
Indianapolis, IN	633	353	2,272	235	1,504	2,293	2,194	219	631	558
Kansas City, MO	1,118	838	1,809	257	1,086	1,835	1,839	687	248	1,043
Los Angeles, CA	2,706	2,426	959	1,845	715	379	1,131	2,276	1,452	2,631
Memphis, TN	1,000	752	2,259	285	1,535	2,125	2,290	654	401	867
Milwaukee, WI	825	539	2,010	363	1,423	2,175	1,940	319	757	758
Minneapolis, MN	1,143	857	1,678	552	1,186	1,940	1,608	637	695	1,076
New Orleans, LA	1,211	1,070	2,505	673	1,738	2,249	2,574	986	647	1,078
New York, NY	100	368	2,885	948	2,182	2,934	2,815	578	1,344	233
Omaha, NB	1,183	895	1,654	449	931	1,683	1,638	681	387	1,116
Philadelphia, PA	...	288	2,821	868	2,114	2,866	2,751	514	1,264	133
Pittsburgh, PA	288	...	2,535	588	1,826	2,578	2,465	228	984	221
Portland OR	2,821	2,535	...	2,060	767	636	172	2,315	1,913	2,754
St. Louis, MO	868	588	2,060	...	1,337	2,089	2,081	454	396	793
San Francisco, SC	2,866	2,578	636	2,089	752	...	808	2,364	1,760	2,799
Seattle, WA	2,751	2,465	172	2,081	836	808	...	2,245	1,982	2,684
Tulsa, OK	1,264	984	1,913	396	1,172	1,760	1,982	850	...	1,189
Washington, DC	133	221	2,754	793	2,047	2,799	2,684	447	1,189	...

Air Distances Between Selected World Cities in Statute Miles

Point-to-point measurements are usually from City Hall.

	Bangkok	Beijing	Berlin	Cairo	Cape Town	Caracas	Chicago	Hong Kong	Honolulu	Lima
Bangkok	...	2,046	5,352	4,523	6,300	10,555	8,570	1,077	6,609	12,244
Beijing	2,046	...	4,584	4,698	8,044	8,950	6,604	1,217	5,077	10,349
Berlin	5,352	4,584	...	1,797	5,961	5,238	4,414	5,443	7,320	6,896
Cairo	4,523	4,698	1,797	...	4,480	6,342	6,141	5,066	8,848	7,726
Cape Town	6,300	8,044	5,961	4,480	...	6,366	8,491	7,376	11,535	6,072
Caracas	10,555	8,950	5,238	6,342	6,366	...	2,495	10,165	6,021	1,707
Chicago	8,570	6,604	4,414	6,141	8,491	2,495	...	7,797	4,256	3,775
Hong Kong	1,077	1,217	5,443	5,066	7,376	10,165	7,797	...	5,556	11,418
Honolulu	6,609	5,077	7,320	8,848	11,535	6,021	4,256	5,556	...	5,947
London	5,944	5,074	583	2,185	5,989	4,655	3,958	5,990	7,240	6,316
Los Angeles	7,637	6,250	5,782	7,520	9,969	3,632	1,745	7,240	2,557	4,171
Madrid	6,337	5,745	1,165	2,087	5,308	4,346	4,189	6,558	7,872	5,907
Melbourne	4,568	5,643	9,918	8,675	6,425	9,717	9,673	4,595	5,505	8,059
Mexico City	9,793	7,753	6,056	7,700	8,519	2,234	1,690	8,788	3,789	2,639
Montreal	8,338	6,519	3,740	5,427	7,922	2,438	745	7,736	4,918	3,970
Moscow	4,389	3,607	1,006	1,803	6,279	6,177	4,987	4,437	7,047	7,862
New York	8,669	6,844	3,979	5,619	7,803	2,120	714	8,060	4,969	3,639
Paris	5,877	5,120	548	1,998	5,786	4,732	4,143	5,990	7,449	6,370
Rio de Janeiro	9,994	10,768	6,209	6,143	3,781	2,804	5,282	11,009	8,288	2,342
Rome	5,494	5,063	737	1,326	5,231	5,195	4,824	5,774	8,040	6,750
San Francisco	7,931	5,918	5,672	7,466	10,248	3,902	1,859	6,905	2,398	4,518
Singapore	883	2,771	6,164	5,137	6,008	11,402	9,372	1,605	6,726	11,689
Stockholm	5,089	4,133	528	2,096	6,423	5,471	4,331	5,063	6,875	7,166
Tokyo	2,865	1,307	5,557	5,958	9,154	8,808	6,314	1,791	3,859	9,631
Warsaw	5,033	4,325	322	1,619	5,935	5,559	4,679	5,147	7,366	7,215
Washington, DC	8,807	6,942	4,181	5,822	7,895	2,047	596	8,155	4,838	3,509

	London	Los Angeles	Madrid	Melbourne	Mexico City	Montreal	Moscow	New Delhi	New York	Paris
Bangkok	5,944	7,637	6,337	4,568	9,793	8,338	4,389	1,813	8,669	5,877
Beijing	5,074	6,250	5,745	5,643	7,753	6,519	3,607	2,353	6,844	5,120
Berlin	583	5,782	1,165	9,918	6,056	3,740	1,006	3,598	3,979	548
Cairo	2,185	7,520	2,087	8,675	7,700	5,427	1,803	2,758	5,619	1,998
Cape Town	5,989	9,969	5,308	6,425	8,519	7,922	6,279	5,769	7,803	5,786
Caracas	4,655	3,632	4,346	9,717	2,234	2,438	6,177	8,833	2,120	4,732
Chicago	3,958	1,745	4,189	9,673	1,690	745	4,987	7,486	714	4,143
Hong Kong	5,990	7,240	6,558	4,595	8,788	7,736	4,437	2,339	8,060	5,990
Honolulu	7,240	2,557	7,872	5,505	3,789	4,918	7,047	7,412	4,969	7,449
London	...	5,439	785	10,500	5,558	3,254	1,564	4,181	3,469	214
Los Angeles	5,439	...	5,848	7,931	1,542	2,427	6,068	7,011	2,451	5,601
Madrid	785	5,848	...	10,758	5,643	3,448	2,147	4,530	3,593	655
Melbourne	10,500	7,931	10,758	...	8,426	10,395	8,950	6,329	10,359	10,430
Mexico City	5,558	1,542	5,643	8,426	...	2,317	6,676	9,120	2,090	5,725
Montreal	3,254	2,427	3,448	10,395	2,317	...	4,401	7,012	331	3,432
Moscow	1,564	6,068	2,147	8,950	6,676	4,401	...	2,698	4,683	1,554
New York	3,469	2,451	3,593	10,359	2,090	331	4,683	7,318	...	3,636
Paris	214	5,601	655	10,430	5,725	3,432	1,554	4,102	3,636	...
Rio de Janeiro	5,750	6,330	5,045	8,226	4,764	5,078	7,170	8,753	4,801	5,684
Rome	895	6,326	851	9,929	6,377	4,104	1,483	3,684	4,293	690
San Francisco	5,367	347	5,803	7,856	1,887	2,543	5,885	7,691	2,572	5,577
Singapore	6,747	8,767	7,080	3,759	10,327	9,203	5,228	2,571	9,534	6,673
Stockholm	942	5,454	1,653	9,630	6,012	3,714	716	3,414	3,986	1,003
Tokyo	5,959	5,470	6,706	5,062	7,035	6,471	4,660	3,638	6,757	6,053
Warsaw	905	5,922	1,427	9,598	6,337	4,022	721	3,277	4,270	852
Washington, DC	3,674	2,300	3,792	10,180	1,885	489	4,876	7,500	205	3,840

	Rio de Janeiro	Rome	San Francisco	Singapore	Stockholm	Tehran	Tokyo	Vienna	Warsaw	Wash., DC
Bangkok	9,994	5,494	7,931	883	5,089	3,391	2,865	5,252	5,033	8,807
Beijing	10,768	5,063	5,918	2,771	4,133	3,490	1,307	4,648	4,325	6,942
Berlin	6,209	737	5,672	6,164	528	2,185	5,557	326	322	4,181
Cairo	6,143	1,326	7,466	5,137	2,096	1,234	5,958	1,481	1,619	5,822
Cape Town	3,781	5,231	10,248	6,008	6,423	5,241	9,154	5,656	5,935	7,895
Caracas	2,804	5,195	3,902	11,402	5,471	7,320	8,808	5,372	5,559	2,047
Chicago	5,282	4,824	1,859	9,372	4,331	6,502	6,314	4,698	4,679	596
Hong Kong	11,009	5,774	6,905	1,605	5,063	3,843	1,791	5,431	5,147	8,155
Honolulu	8,288	8,040	2,398	6,726	6,875	8,070	3,859	7,632	7,366	4,838
London	5,750	895	5,367	6,747	942	2,743	5,959	771	905	3,674
Los Angeles	6,330	6,326	347	8,767	5,454	7,682	5,470	6,108	5,922	2,300
Madrid	5,045	851	5,803	7,080	1,653	2,978	6,706	1,128	1,427	3,792
Melbourne	8,226	9,929	7,856	3,759	9,630	7,826	5,062	9,790	9,598	10,180
Mexico City	4,764	6,377	1,887	10,327	6,012	8,184	7,035	6,320	6,337	1,885
Montreal	5,078	4,104	2,543	9,203	3,714	5,880	6,471	4,009	4,022	489
Moscow	7,170	1,483	5,885	5,228	716	1,532	4,660	1,043	721	4,876
New York	4,801	4,293	2,572	9,534	3,986	6,141	6,757	4,234	4,270	205
Paris	5,684	690	5,577	6,673	1,003	2,625	6,053	645	852	3,840
Rio de Janeiro	...	5,707	6,613	9,785	6,683	7,374	11,532	6,127	6,455	4,779
Rome	5,707	...	6,259	6,229	1,245	2,127	6,142	477	820	4,497
San Francisco	6,613	6,259	...	8,448	5,399	7,362	5,150	5,994	5,854	2,441
Singapore	9,785	6,229	8,448	...	5,936	4,103	3,300	6,035	5,843	9,662
Stockholm	6,683	1,245	5,399	5,936	...	2,173	5,053	780	494	4,183
Tokyo	11,532	6,142	5,150	3,300	5,053	4,775	...	5,689	5,347	6,791
Warsaw	6,455	820	5,854	5,843	494	1,879	5,689	347	...	4,472
Washington, DC	4,779	4,497	2,441	9,662	4,183	6,341	6,791	4,438	4,472	...

U.S. Farms—Number and Acreage by State, 2000, 2004

Source: National Agricultural Statistics Service, U.S. Dept. of Agriculture

	No. of farms (1,000)		Acreage in farms (mil.)		Acreage per farm	
STATE	2004	2000[1]	2004	2000	2004	2000
AL	44	47	8.7	9	198	191
AK	0.62	0.58	0.9	0.91	1,452	1,569
AZ	10.2	10.7	26.4	26.9	2,588	2,518
AR	47.5	48	14.4	14.6	303	304
CA	77	83.1	26.7	28	347	337
CO	30.9	30	30.9	31.6	1,000	1,060
CT	4.2	4.2	0.36	0.36	86	86
DE	2.3	2.6	0.53	0.56	230	215
FL	43	44	10.1	10.4	235	239
GA	49	49.1	10.7	10.9	218	223
HI	5.5	5.5	1.3	1.38	236	251
ID	25	24.5	11.8	11.9	472	486
IL	73	77	27.5	27.5	377	357
IN	59.3	63.4	15	15.2	253	240
IA	89.7	94	31.7	32.5	353	346
KS	64.5	64.5	47.2	47.5	732	736
KY	85	90	13.8	13.7	162	152
LA	27.2	29	7.85	8.03	289	277
ME	7.2	7.1	1.37	1.35	190	190
MD	12.1	12.4	2.05	2.13	169	172
MA	6.1	6.1	0.52	0.54	85	89
MI	53.2	53	10.1	10.15	190	192
MN	79.8	81	27.6	27.9	346	344
MS	42.2	42	11.05	11.16	262	266
MO	106	109	30.1	30.2	284	277
MT	28	27.8	60.1	59.3	2,146	2,133
NE	48.3	46.1	45.9	46.1	950	887
NV	3	3.1	6.3	6.4	2,100	2,065
NH	3.4	3.3	0.45	0.44	132	133
NJ	9.9	9.7	0.82	0.83	83	86
NM	17.5	18	44.7	44.9	2,554	2,494
NY	36	37.5	7.6	7.67	211	205
NC	52	55.5	9	9.21	173	166
ND	30.3	30.8	39.4	39.4	1,300	1,279
OH	77.3	79	14.6	14.77	189	187
OK	83.5	84.5	33.7	33.8	404	401
OR	40	40	17.2	17.3	430	433
PA	58.2	59	7.7	7.69	132	130
PR[2]	13.4	NA	0.59	NA	44	NA
RI	0.85	0.8	0.06	0.06	71	75
SC	24.4	24.2	4.85	4.91	199	203
SD	31.6	32.4	43.8	44	1,386	1,358
TN	85	88	11.6	11.8	136	134
TX	229	228.3	130	130.9	568	573
UT	15.3	15.5	11.6	11.6	758	747
VT	6.4	6.6	1.25	1.27	195	192
VA	47.5	48.5	8.6	8.71	181	180
WA	35	37	15.2	15.55	434	420
WV	20.8	20.8	3.6	3.6	173	173
WI	76.5	77.5	15.5	16	203	206
WY	9.2	9.2	34.4	34.5	3,743	3,750
U.S.	**2,113.0**	**2,166.78**	**936.6**	**945.08**	**443**	**436**

(1) Figs. for 2000 are revised. (2) Puerto Rico. Not included in U.S. total.

U.S. Farms, Number and Average Size, 1940-2004

Source: National Agricultural Statistics Service, U.S. Dept. of Agriculture

The number of farms in the United States in 2004 was estimated at 2.11 million, 0.6% fewer than in 2003. Total land in farms decreased 2.25 million acres from 2003, to 936.6 mil acres. The average farm size during 2004 was 443 acres, an increase of 2 acres from the previous year. The continuing decline in the number of farms and land in farms reflects consolidation in farming operations and use of agricultural land for other purposes.

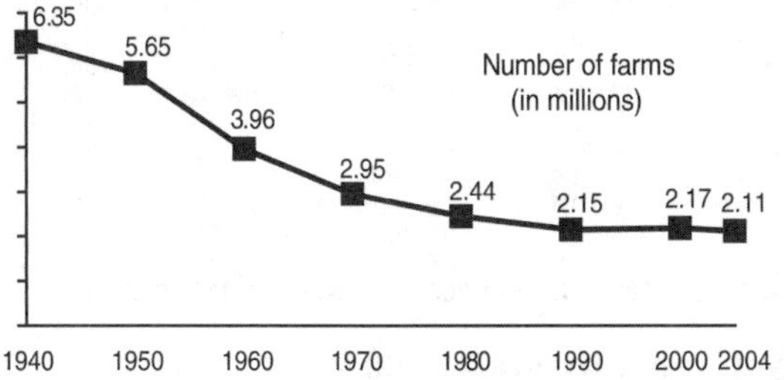

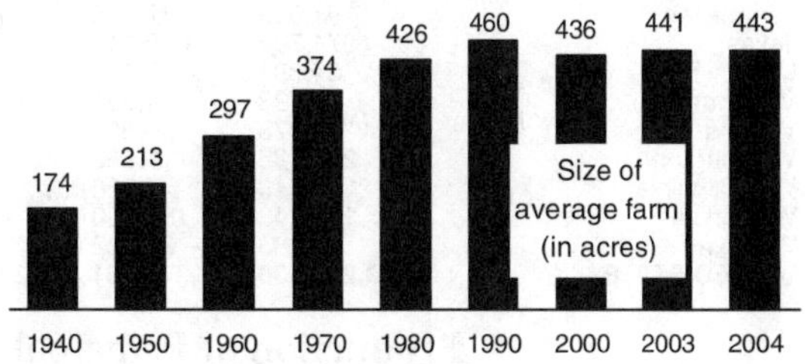

U.S. Federal Food Assistance Programs, 1990-2004[1]

Source: Food and Nutrition Service, U.S. Dept. of Agriculture

(in millions of dollars)

	1990	1995	1998	2000	2001	2002	2003	2004
Food stamps[2]	$15,491	$24,620	$18,893	$17,054	$17,789	$20,644	$23,872	$27,159
Puerto Rico nutrition asst.[3]	937	1,131	1,204	1,268	1,296	1,351	1,395	1,413
Natl. school lunch[4]	3,834	5,160	5,830	6,149	6,475	6,854	7,189	7,628
School breakfast[4,5]	596	1,048	1,272	1,393	1,450	1,567	1,651	1,774
WIC[6]	2,122	3,440	3,890	3,982	4,150	4,341	4,525	4,890
Summer food service[7]	164	237	263	267	271	263	257	263
Child/adult care[8]	813	1,464	1,553	1,683	1,737	1,853	1,926	2,020
Special milk[9]	19	17	17	15	16	16	14	14
Nutrition for the elderly[10]	142	148	141	137	152	150	3	4
Food distrib. to Indian reserv.[11]	66	65	72	76	72	76	75	78
Commodity supp. food prog.[11]	85	99	94	98	106	115	122	146
Food dist. to charitable inst.[12]	104	64	9	2	7	16	6	10
Emergency food assistance[13]	334	135	234	225	377	435	456	417
TOTAL[14]	**$24,707**	**$37,628**	**$33,472**	**$32,317**	**$33,905**	**$37,719**	**$41,476**	**$45,816**

(1) Data are for fiscal years, ending Sept. 30. All 2004 data are preliminary; all data subject to revision by the FNS. (2) Includes benefits and admin. expenses. (3) Puerto Rico does not participate in the Food Stamp Program. (4) Data are 9-month averages (summer months excluded). (5) Costs are cash payments (federal reimbursements to states). (6) Includes food benefits, nutrition services and admin. funds, Farmers' Market Nutrition Program, infrastructure, program evaluation, and technical assistance. (7) Includes cash payments, commodity costs, and admin. expenditures. Similar services provided by Natl. School Lunch & Breakfast Program. (8) Includes cash payments, entitlement and bonus commodities, cash-in-lieu of commodities, sponsor admin. costs, start-up costs and audits. (9) Costs are cash payments. (10) Cash grants administered by the Agency on Aging; Food and Nutrition Service costs limited to value of commodities distributed. (11) FY 2003 costs are preliminary. Includes commodity distribution costs and admin. expenses. (12) Includes summer camps. (13) Food made available to hunger relief orgs. such as food banks and soup kitchens. (14) Totals may not add because of rounding.

Total U.S. Government Agricultural Payments, by State, 1990-2004

Source: Economic Research Service, U.S. Dept. of Agriculture; in thousands of dollars

STATE	1990	1995	2000	2001	2002	2003	2004
Alabama	$82,226	$54,140	$170,852	$230,126	$263,127	$219,214	$128,668
Alaska	1,117	1,735	1,672	2,173	1,762	1,830	5,434
Arizona	43,349	9,456	107,066	99,254	70,241	135,261	82,256
Arkansas	312,696	383,783	900,648	832,135	450,038	819,994	404,890
California	252,333	239,809	667,466	586,699	461,041	645,272	381,353
Colorado	236,723	167,661	351,116	319,271	210,367	316,893	216,185
Connecticut	2,123	2,382	18,143	7,540	4,940	7,237	4,312
Delaware	3,213	3,150	25,028	24,963	11,944	17,096	13,067
Florida	37,155	55,778	56,741	107,311	82,651	109,824	206,157
Georgia	130,593	67,332	380,057	426,534	656,717	549,155	278,131
Hawaii	519	947	11,927	3,860	1,911	1,294	1,706
Idaho	133,431	89,482	261,297	207,636	165,391	151,620	150,504
Illinois	506,603	543,753	1,943,916	1,849,734	614,734	854,099	1,154,266
Indiana	244,170	246,026	938,464	925,249	334,330	438,053	521,365
Iowa	753,733	786,652	2,302,094	1,971,615	739,864	1,045,632	1,251,809
Kansas	834,746	422,226	1,231,923	1,068,601	456,622	807,415	640,189
Kentucky	81,610	67,382	448,473	293,367	138,254	145,219	140,215
Louisiana	154,631	164,251	451,831	434,012	253,108	422,076	230,532
Maine	6,982	14,114	13,851	7,794	13,740	11,494	9,485
Maryland	17,386	15,241	88,470	86,543	48,848	66,299	48,307
Massachusetts	3,023	2,490	10,973	10,129	6,064	11,439	4,099
Michigan	168,831	151,055	381,056	352,730	190,536	251,608	208,631
Minnesota	511,759	467,807	1,502,230	1,242,073	466,801	781,677	694,197
Mississippi	185,969	133,544	463,901	516,314	251,315	470,694	297,698
Missouri	299,065	256,629	869,390	817,027	398,355	506,049	426,638
Montana	299,599	189,809	490,002	475,972	261,998	353,350	276,013
Nebraska	624,646	507,302	1,406,971	1,297,564	537,903	722,620	720,919
Nevada	5,347	4,264	3,918	5,860	11,288	11,953	6,379
New Hampshire	1,856	1,216	4,768	2,774	3,642	4,762	2,619
New Jersey	15,744	5,491	22,481	16,399	6,446	12,041	8,371
New Mexico	63,840	55,134	79,495	93,560	73,726	92,390	76,908
New York	59,304	43,563	159,876	114,009	159,105	160,276	79,775
North Carolina	73,255	41,476	447,096	330,312	277,739	357,543	176,422
North Dakota	545,378	296,215	1,170,234	944,546	383,452	651,484	464,508
Ohio	197,006	167,351	678,104	681,519	280,826	395,322	326,313
Oklahoma	319,040	164,662	439,851	391,712	317,124	355,332	209,142
Oregon	89,137	52,145	137,401	104,725	80,081	106,595	73,414
Pennsylvania	41,414	41,096	147,848	103,435	129,275	182,426	87,143
Rhode Island	191	317	1,218	292	651	611	877
South Carolina	62,637	34,586	144,499	129,742	65,264	126,461	63,907
South Dakota	332,851	245,016	789,895	714,936	333,439	547,920	395,774
Tennessee	91,029	47,405	298,873	247,454	108,144	175,199	124,594
Texas	974,702	643,119	1,647,066	1,702,477	998,215	1,661,141	998,199
Utah	34,897	25,045	36,181	39,689	54,278	55,479	34,473
Vermont	5,793	4,334	26,093	7,863	36,294	28,479	14,991
Virginia	32,378	25,967	152,452	116,801	181,891	175,585	63,744
Washington	205,425	116,062	352,503	298,547	215,689	263,950	192,665
West Virginia	6,049	5,268	23,509	9,807	5,640	12,962	6,206
Wisconsin	181,243	184,350	603,213	414,981	332,068	475,696	291,465
Wyoming	31,283	31,432	34,302	50,171	65,792	51,042	33,867
UNITED STATES	**$9,298,030**	**$7,279,451**	**$22,896,433**	**$20,990,842**	**$11,365,194**	**$16,177,044**	**$12,581,287**

Production of Principal U.S. Crops, by State, 2004

Source: National Agricultural Statistics Service, U.S. Dept. of Agriculture

STATE	Barley (1,000 bu)	Corn, grain (1,000 bu)	Upland Cotton (1,000 b)	All hay (1,000 t)	Oats (1,000 bu)	Potatoes (1,000 cwt)	Soybeans (1,000 bu)	Tobacco (1,000 lb)	All wheat (1,000 bu)
Alabama	—	23,985	820	2,295	—	228	6,650	—	2,880
Alaska	145	—	—	28	41	177	—	—	—
Arizona	4,180	4,860	680	2,119	—	1,767	—	—	9,963
Arkansas	—	42,700	2,085	3,570	—	—	124,425	—	32,860
California	4,050	26,250	1,770	9,000	2,125	18,099	—	—	36,200
Colorado	9,086	140,400	—	3,666	1,100	25,484	—	—	46,880
Connecticut	—	NE	—	143	—	—	—	3,889	—
Delaware	2,080	23,256	—	41	—	806	8,736	—	2,726
Florida	—	2,880	95	650	—	9,246	578	9,800	675
Georgia	—	36,400	1,800	1,620	1,250	—	8,370	46,690	8,550
Hawaii	—	—	—	—	—	—	—	—	—
Idaho	59,800	12,750	—	5,350	1,440	131,970	—	—	101,710
Illinois	—	2,088,000	—	2,560	2,450	1,992	499,950	—	53,100
Indiana	—	929,040	—	2,303	900	1,120	287,040	8,610	27,280
Iowa	—	2,244,400	—	6,240	10,080	—	497,350	—	1,320
Kansas	336	432,000	130	7,880	1,720	1,360	111,110	—	314,500
Kentucky	616	173,280	—	5,928	—	—	57,200	234,500	20,520
Louisiana	—	55,350	885	1,110	—	—	32,670	—	8,250
Maine	1,430	NE	—	296	2,400	19,220	—	—	—
Maryland	2,847	65,025	—	570	—	1,196	21,285	1,870	8,555
Massachusetts	—	NE	—	181	—	800	—	1,989	—
Michigan	612	257,280	—	3,270	4,420	13,650	75,240	—	40,960
Minnesota	7,820	1,120,950	—	5,895	13,300	18,920	236,175	—	89,605
Mississippi	—	59,840	2,370	1,656	—	—	62,320	—	7,155
Missouri	—	466,560	820	9,420	650	1,922	223,200	3,335	48,360
Montana	48,970	2,145	—	4,760	2,400	3,551	—	—	173,165
Nebraska	162	1,319,700	—	6,143	3,740	9,228	220,875	—	61,050
Nevada	210	NE	—	1,481	—	2,881	—	—	960

STATE	Barley (1,000 bu)	Corn, grain (1,000 bu)	Upland Cotton (1,000 b)	All hay (1,000 t)	Oats (1,000 bu)	Potatoes (1,000 cwt)	Soybeans (1,000 bu)	Tobacco (1,000 lb)	All wheat (1,000 bu)
New Hamp.	—	NE	—	105	—	—	—	—	—
New Jersey	126	10,296	—	282	—	594	4,326	—	1,128
New Mexico	—	10,440	125	1,365	—	2,060	—	—	7,800
New York	530	61,000	—	2,916	3,250	5,184	6,708	—	5,300
North Carolina	960	86,580	1,350	1,776	1,750	2,700	51,000	351,630	23,000
North Dakota	91,760	120,750	—	3,666	14,080	26,765	82,110	—	306,650
Ohio	200	491,380	—	3,232	3,150	1,080	207,740	10,976	55,180
Oklahoma	—	30,000	310	6,030	555	—	8,700	—	164,500
Oregon	4,818	4,760	—	3,624	2,000	19,775	—	—	55,980
Pennsylvania	3,410	137,200	—	4,296	6,050	2,640	19,550	8,100	6,615
Rhode Island	—	NE	—	20	—	175	—	—	—
South Carolina	—	29,500	390	792	1,100	—	14,840	60,750	7,920
South Dakota	3,150	539,500	—	6,870	13,940	NE	140,080	—	128,610
Tennessee	—	86,100	990	4,883		—	48,380	67,970	13,720
Texas	—	233,520	7,500	12,295	6,400	6,429	8,640	—	108,500
Utah	3,440	86,100	—	2,469	624	NE	—	—	5,856
Vermont	—	NE	—	384	—	—	—	—	—
Virginia	2,960	52,200	150	3,272	—	1,200	20,670	67,787	9,900
Washington	17,150	21,000	—	3,392	616	93,810	—	—	143,500
West Virginia	—	3,799	—	1,062	—	—	828	1,690	260
Wisconsin	1,650	353,600	—	4,880	13,650	30,450	54,520	3,585	12,852
Wyoming	6,900	6,681	—	2,016	795	—	—	—	3,750
UNITED STATES	**279,253**	**11,807,217**	**22,270**	**157,774**	**115,935**	**456,362**	**3,140,996**	**883,171**	**2,158,245**

NE = Not estimated; bu = bushels; b = bales (480-lbs); t = tons; cwt = hundredweight.

Production of Principal U.S. Crops, 1990-2004

Source: National Agricultural Statistics Service, U.S. Dept. of Agriculture

Year	Corn for grain (1,000 bu)	Oats (1,000 bu)	Barley (1,000 bu)	Sorghum for grain (1,000 bu)	All wheat (1,000 bu)	Rye (1,000 bu)	Flaxseed (1,000 bu)	Upland Cotton (1,000 b)	Cottonseed (1,000 t)
1990	7,934,028	357,654	422,196	573,303	2,729,778	10,176	3,812	15,505.4	5,968.5
1991	7,474,765	243,851	464,326	584,860	1,980,139	9,734	6,200	17,614.3	6,925.5
1992	9,476,698	294,229	455,090	875,022	2,466,798	11,440	3,288	16,219.5	6,230.1
1993	6,336,470	206,770	398,041	534,172	2,396,440	10,340	3,480	16,134.6	6,343.2
1994	10,102,735	229,008	374,862	649,206	2,320,981	11,341	2,922	19,662.0	7,603.9
1995	7,373,876	162,027	359,562	460,373	2,182,591	10,064	2,211	17,532.2	6,848.7
1996	9,293,435	155,273	395,751	802,974	2,285,133	9,016	1,602	18,413.5	7,143.5
1997	9,206,832	167,246	359,878	633,545	2,481,466	8,132	2,420	18,245.0	6,934.6
1998	9,758,685	165,981	352,125	519,933	2,547,321	12,161	6,708	13,475.9	5,365.4
1999	9,430,612	146,193	280,292	595,166	2,299,010	11,038	7,864	16,293.7	6,354.0
2000	9,915,051	149,545	318,728	470,526	2,232,460	8,386	10,730	16,799.2	6,435.6
2001	9,506,840	117,024	249,420	514,524	1,957,043	6,971	11,455	19,602.4	7,452.2
2002[1]	8,966,787	116,002	226,906	360,713	1,605,878	6,488	11,863	16,530.3	6,183.9
2003[1]	10,089,222	144,383	278,283	411,237	2,344,760	8,634	10,516	17,822.9	6,664.6
2004	11,807,217	115,935	279,253	454,899	2,158,245	8,615	10,471	22,270.0	8,411.0

Year	Tobacco (1,000 lb)	All hay (1,000 t)	Beans, dry edible (1,000 cwt)	Peas, dry edible (1,000 cwt)	Peanuts[2] (1,000 lb)	Soybeans[3] (1,000 bu)	Potatoes (1,000 cwt)	Sweet potatoes (1,000 cwt)
1990	1,626,380	146,212	32,379	2,372	3,602,770	1,925,947	402,110	12,594
1991	1,664,372	152,073	33,765	3,715	4,926,570	1,986,539	417,622	11,203
1992	1,721,671	146,903	22,615	2,535	4,284,416	2,190,354	425,367	12,005
1993	1,613,319	146,799	21,913	3,292	3,392,415	1,870,958	428,693	11,053
1994	1,582,896	150,060	29,028	2,255	4,247,455	2,516,694	467,054	13,395
1995	1,268,538	154,166	30,812	4,765	4,247,455	2,176,814	443,606	12,906
1996	1,517,334	149,457	27,960	2,671	3,661,205	2,382,364	498,633	13,456
1997	1,787,399	152,536	29,370	5,752	3,539,380	2,688,750	467,091	13,327
1998	1,479,867	151,780	30,418	5,934	3,963,440	2,741,014	475,771	12,382
1999	1,292,692	159,707	33,085	4,773	3,829,490	2,653,758	478,216	12,234
2000	1,052,999	151,921	26,409	3,474	3,265,505	2,757,810	513,621	13,794
2001	991,223	156,764	19,583	3,763	4,276,704	2,890,682	437,888	14,637
2002[1]	871,122	149,467	30,312	4,727	3,321,040	2,756,147	458,171	12,799
2003[1]	802,654	157,585	22,492	5,202	4,144,150	2,453,665	457,814	15,891
2004	883,171	157,774	17,799	11,419	4,261,700	3,140,996	456,362	16,399

Year	Rice (1,000 cwt)	Sugarcane (1,000 t)	Sugar beets (1,000 t)	Pecans[4] (1,000 lb)	Apples (1,000 t)	Grapes (1,000 t)	Peaches (1,000 t)	Oranges[5] (1,000 bx)	Grapefruit[5] (1,000 bx)
1990	156,088	28,136	27,513	205,000	4,828.4	5,659.9	1,121.1	184,415	49,300
1991	159,367	30,252	28,203	299,000	4,853.4	5,555.9	1,347.8	178,950	55,500
1992	179,658	30,363	29,143	166,000	5,284.3	6,052.1	1,336.0	209,610	55,265
1993	156,110	31,101	26,249	365,000	5,342.4	6,023.2	1,330.1	255,760	68,375
1994	197,779	30,929	31,853	199,000	5,667.8	5,870.6	1,253.3	240,450	65,100
1995	173,871	30,944	27,954	268,000	5,292.5	5,922.3	1,150.8	263,605	71,050
1996	171,321	29,462	26,680	221,500	5,196.0	5,554.3	1,058.2	263,890	66,200
1997	182,992	31,709	29,886	335,000	5,161.9	7,290.9	1,312.3	292,620	70,200
1998	184,443	32,743	32,499	73,200	5,381.3	5,816.4	1,162.8	315,525	63,150
1999	206,027	35,299	33,420	203,100	5,223.3	6,234.8	1,216.7	224,580	61,200
2000	190,872	36,114	32,541	209,800	5,291.9	7,688.0	1,289.9	299,760	66,980
2001	215,270	34,587	25,764	388,500	4,711.5	6,569.3	1,203.9	280,935	59,750
2002[1]	210,960	35,553	27,707	172,900	4,262.0	7,338.9	1,267.5	283,760	58,660
2003[1]	199,897	33,858	30,710	282,100	4,306.6	6,552.5	1,259.5	267,040	50,080
2004	230,818	29,295	29,932	185,800	4,728.9	5,972.5	1,279.1	294,620	52,540

(1) Some totals revised. (2) Harvested for nuts. (3) Harvested for beans. (4) Utilized production only. (5) Crop year ending in year cited.

IT'S A FACT: U.S. per capita consumption of ice cream peaked in 1946, with an average 23.12 lbs consumed annually by each American. In 2003, per capita consumption of ice cream had fallen to 16.74 lbs per year.

Eggs: U.S. Production, Price, and Value, 2003-2004[1]

Source: National Agricultural Statistics Service, U.S. Dept. of Agriculture

STATE	Eggs, Produced 2003 (mil)	2004	Price[2] per Dozen 2003 (dollars)	2004	Value of Production 2003 (1,000 dollars)	2004	STATE	Eggs, Produced 2003 (mil)	2004	Price[2] per Dozen 2003 (dollars)	2004	Value of Production 2003 (1,000 dollars)	2004
AL	2,190	2,099	1.620	1.650	295,101	287,956	NE	3,126	3,174	0.535	0.525	139,368	138,863
AR	3,590	3,565	1.200	1.220	359,000	362,442	NH	43	43	0.910	0.935	3,261	3,350
CA	5,439	5,380	0.623	0.643	282,458	288,412	NJ	556	558	0.630	0.622	29,208	28,912
CO	1,073	1,105	0.670	0.653	59,915	60,103	NY	1,048	1,163	0.645	0.617	56,330	59,798
CT	795	818	0.667	0.674	44,189	45,944	NC	2,523	2,522	1.150	1.140	241,788	239,590
FL	2,804	3,068	0.621	0.625	145,027	159,878	OH	7,642	7,355	0.588	0.545	374,458	334,040
GA	5,047	5,038	0.941	0.939	395,769	394,223	OK	933	937	0.927	0.956	72,074	74,648
HI	117	119	0.962	1.080	9,396	10,665	OR	783	818	0.667	0.714	43,549	48,693
ID	243	238	0.717	0.730	14,525	14,479	PA	6,754	6,585	0.659	0.619	371,170	339,676
IL	973	1,044	0.629	0.592	51,001	51,504	PR	227	230	0.943	0.838	17,811	16,067
IN	6,035	6,256	0.612	0.560	307,785	291,947	SC	1,373	1,351	0.762	0.735	87,186	82,749
IA	10,446	11,613	0.529	0.508	460,648	491,586	SD	761	933	0.500	0.517	31,708	40,197
KY	1,122	1,231	0.889	0.858	83,153	88,067	TN	290	319	1.320	1.340	31,922	35,511
LA	487	465	0.886	0.902	35,967	34,966	TX	4,745	4,825	0.784	0.762	310,007	306,388
ME	1,121	957	0.755	0.770	70,530	61,408	UT	866	831	0.520	0.520	37,556	36,012
MD	811	843	0.682	0.651	46,104	45,737	VT	54	55	0.815	0.746	3,667	3,419
MA	77	74	0.802	0.810	5,149	4,995	VA	744	761	1.180	1.100	73,160	69,758
MI	1,888	2,009	0.595	0.563	93,613	94,256	WA	1,307	1,332	0.646	0.697	70,323	77,348
MN	3,028	2,930	0.592	0.583	149,381	142,349	WV	271	273	1.510	1.420	34,128	32,325
MS	1,599	1,606	1.270	1.290	168,636	172,166	WI	1,137	1,206	0.587	0.564	55,579	56,679
MO	1,861	1,865	0.645	0.652	99,989	101,395	WY	4	4	0.620	0.607	186	182
MT	107	107	0.650	0.657	5,796	5,862	**U.S.[3]**	**87,473**	**89,131**	**0.732**	**0.714**	**5,333,014**	**5,303,244**

(1) Estimates cover the 12-month period from Dec. 1 of the previous year through Nov. 30. (2) Average of all eggs sold by producers, including hatching eggs. (4) Total states includes other states not listed. Puerto Rico (PR) not included.

Livestock on Farms in the U.S., 1900-2005

Source: National Agricultural Statistics Service, U.S. Dept. of Agriculture
(in thousands)

Year (On Jan. 1)	All cattle[1]	Milk cows	Sheep and lambs	Hogs and pigs[2]	Year (On Jan. 1)	All cattle[1]	Milk cows	Sheep and lambs	Hogs and pigs[2]
1900	59,739	16,544	48,105	51,055	1980	111,242	10,758	12,699	67,318
1910	58,993	19,450	50,239	48,072	1985	109,582	10,777	10,716	54,073
1920	70,400	21,455	40,743	60,159	1990	95,816	10,015	11,358	53,788
1930	61,003	23,032	51,565	55,705	1995	102,755	9,487	8,886	57,150
1940	68,309	24,940	52,107	61,165	2000	98,198	9,190	7,032	59,117
1950	77,963	23,853	29,826	58,937	2001	97,277	9,183	6,965	58,603
1955	96,592	23,462	31,582	50,474	2002	96,704	9,112	6,685	60,288
1960	96,236	19,527	33,170	59,026	2003	96,100	9,142	6,300	59,602
1965	109,000	16,981	25,127	56,106	2004	94,888	8,990	6,105	60,698
1970	112,369	12,091	20,423	57,046	2005[3]	95,848	9,005	6,135	60,812
1975	132,028	11,220	14,515	54,693					

(1) From 1970, includes milk cows and heifers that have calved. (2) 1900-95, as of Dec. 1 of preceding year; 1996-2004 as of June 1 of same year. (3) Preliminary.

U.S. Meat Production and Consumption, 1940-2004

Source: Economic Research Service, U.S. Dept. of Agriculture
(in millions of pounds)

Year	Beef Prod.	Beef Cons.	Veal Prod.	Veal Cons.	Lamb and mutton Prod.	Lamb and mutton Cons.	Pork Prod.	Pork Cons.	All red meats[1] Prod.	All red meats[1] Cons.	All Poultry Prod.	All Poultry Cons.
1940	7,175	7,257	981	981	876	873	10,044	9,701	19,076	18,812	NA	NA
1950	9,534	9,529	1,230	1,206	597	596	10,714	10,390	22,075	21,721	3,174	3,097
1960	14,728	15,465	1,109	1,118	769	857	13,905	14,057	30,511	31,497	6,310	6,168
1970	21,684	23,451	588	613	551	669	14,699	14,957	37,522	39,689	10,193	9,981
1980	21,643	23,560	400	420	318	351	16,617	16,838	38,978	41,170	14,173	13,525
1990	22,743	24,030	327	325	363	397	15,354	16,025	38,787	40,778	23,468	22,152
1995	25,222	25,534	319	319	285	346	17,849	17,768	43,675	43,967	30,393	25,944
2000	26,888	27,338	225	225	234	354	18,952	18,643	46,299	46,560	36,073	30,508
2001	26,212	27,026	205	204	227	368	19,160	18,492	45,804	46,089	38,942	30,823
2002	27,192	27,878	205	204	223	383	19,685	19,147	47,305	47,612	38,079	32,575
2003	26,339	26,999	202	204	203	367	19,966	19,435	46,710	47,005	38,477	33,129
2004*	24,650	27,750	176	177	200	273	20,529	19,439	45,555	47,739	39,585	34,157

* Preliminary. (1) Meats may not add to total because of rounding. (2) Consumption (also called total disappearance) is estimated as: production plus beginning stocks, plus imports, minus exports, minus ending stocks. NA = Not available.

U.S. Annual Per Capita Consumption of Selected Foods, 1910-2003

Source: USDA/Economic Research Service

Year	Whole milk[1]	Low-fat & skim milk[1]	Butter[2]	Margarine[2]	Total fat[2,3]	Red meat[2,4]	Poultry[2,5]
1910	25.2	7.1	18.4	1.6	37.7	NA	11.8
1940	29.2	4.7	17.0	2.4	50.1	92.4	12.3
1970	25.5	5.8	5.4	10.8	55.7	131.9	33.8
2000	8.1	14.4	4.5	7.5	84.5	113.7	67.9
2003	7.6	13.9	4.2	6.2	87.9	111.9	71.2

(1) Gallons. (2) Pounds. (3) Includes edible rapeseed (canola) oil beginning in 1985. Includes specialty fats used mainly in confectionary products and non-dairy creamers. (4) Figures are calculated on the basis of raw and edible meat. Excludes edible offals, bones, and viscera. Excludes game consumption. (5) Figures are calculated on the basis of raw and edible meat. Includes skin, neck, and giblets. Excludes chicken for commercially prepared pet food.

U.S. Farm Business Real Estate Debt Outstanding, by Lender Groups,[1] 1960-2004

Source: Economic Research Service, U.S. Dept. of Agriculture
(in millions of dollars)

		AMOUNTS HELD BY PRINCIPAL LENDER GROUPS				
Dec. 31	Total farm real estate debt[2]	Farm Credit System[2]	Farm Service Agency[3]	Life insurance companies[4]	All operating banks	Other[5]
1960	$11,310	$2,222	$624	$2,652	$1,356	$4,456
1970	27,506	6,420	2,180	5,123	3,329	10,455
1980	89,692	33,225	7,435	11,998	7,765	27,813
1985	100,076	42,169	9,821	11,273	10,732	25,775
1990	74,732	25,924	7,639	9,704	16,288	15,169
1991	74,944	25,305	7,041	9,546	17,417	15,632
1992	75,421	25,408	6,394	8,765	18,757	16,095
1993	76,036	24,900	5,837	8,985	19,595	16,719
1994	77,680	24,597	5,465	9,025	21,079	17,514
1995	79,287	24,851	5,055	9,092	22,277	18,012
1996	81,657	25,730	4,702	9,468	23,276	18,481
1997	85,359	27,098	4,373	9,699	25,240	18,950
1998	89,615	28,888	4,073	10,723	27,168	18,763
1999	94,226	30,302	3,872	11,490	29,799	18,763
2000	91,109	29,692	3,418	11,053	29,757	17,188
2001	96,008	32,855	3,347	11,205	31,082	17,519
2002	103,356	37,815	3,181	11,421	33,060	17,880
2003	107,981	40,095	2,848	11,597	35,126	18,316
2004[6]	113,600	42,400	2,600	11,800	37,900	18,900

(1) Excludes operator households. (2) Includes data for joint stock land banks and real estate loans by Agricultural Credit Association. (3) Includes loans made directly by Farm Services Agency for farm ownership, soil, and water loans to individuals, Native American tribe land acquisition, grazing associations, and half of economic emergency loans. Also includes loans for rural housing on farm tracts and labor housing. (4) American Council of Life Insurance members. (5) Estimated by ERS, USDA. Includes Commodity Credit Corporation storage and drying facility loans. (6) Preliminary.

U.S. Farm Marketings by State, 2003-04

Source: Economic Research Service, U.S. Dept. of Agriculture; in thousands of dollars

		2004 FARM MARKETINGS			2003 FARM MARKETINGS		
STATE	2004 RANK	Total	Crops	Livestock and products	Total	Crops	Livestock and products
Alabama	(25)	$4,009,729	$768,246	$3,241,483	$3,415,299	$676,130	$2,739,169
Alaska	(50)	50,896	23,316	27,580	50,896	23,316	27,580
Arizona	(29)	3,146,134	1,524,170	1,621,964	2,586,022	1,327,419	1,258,603
Arkansas	(11)	6,393,597	2,495,606	3,897,991	5,298,210	2,083,103	3,215,107
California	(1)	30,435,319	21,850,265	8,585,054	27,804,796	20,811,838	6,992,958
Colorado	(17)	5,328,052	1,296,640	4,031,412	4,964,312	1,288,643	3,675,669
Connecticut	(44)	470,463	307,229	163,234	484,832	320,175	164,657
Delaware	(38)	961,523	187,069	774,453	760,221	167,559	592,662
Florida	(9)	7,066,400	5,670,913	1,395,487	6,449,582	5,243,766	1,205,816
Georgia	(12)	6,169,500	2,148,357	4,021,143	5,246,327	2,024,455	3,221,872
Hawaii	(42)	553,236	467,890	85,346	549,353	463,539	85,814
Idaho	(21)	4,390,035	1,807,816	2,582,219	3,953,243	1,775,893	2,177,350
Illinois	(6)	9,754,066	7,761,576	1,992,490	8,289,956	6,490,105	1,799,851
Indiana	(13)	6,113,530	3,957,964	2,155,566	5,161,610	3,362,656	1,798,954
Iowa	(3)	14,801,321	7,373,725	7,427,595	12,633,201	6,560,187	6,073,014
Kansas	(7)	9,585,311	3,088,849	6,496,462	9,046,097	2,867,497	6,178,600
Kentucky	(26)	3,640,659	1,394,741	2,245,918	3,469,003	1,243,300	2,225,703
Louisiana	(33)	2,187,990	1,438,760	749,230	1,993,366	1,296,021	697,345
Maine	(45)	466,578	210,449	256,129	498,764	226,886	271,878
Maryland	(35)	1,709,511	693,214	1,016,298	1,466,500	619,888	846,612
Massachusetts	(47)	372,452	286,494	85,958	384,746	297,624	87,122
Michigan	(22)	4,181,910	2,496,487	1,685,423	3,820,824	2,421,523	1,399,301
Minnesota	(5)	9,807,390	4,869,507	4,937,884	8,587,960	4,515,789	4,072,171
Mississippi	(24)	4,145,938	1,490,000	2,655,939	3,411,002	1,246,444	2,164,558
Missouri	(14)	5,774,400	2,769,443	3,004,958	4,972,762	2,344,433	2,628,329
Montana	(34)	2,161,802	962,909	1,198,893	1,892,145	786,879	1,105,266
Nebraska	(4)	11,815,140	4,447,225	7,367,915	10,621,276	3,753,907	6,867,369
Nevada	(46)	403,105	147,120	255,985	395,801	141,474	254,327
New Hampshire	(48)	150,807	88,666	62,141	149,848	87,642	62,206
New Jersey	(40)	851,438	668,984	182,454	845,886	658,034	187,852
New Mexico	(31)	2,488,745	540,800	1,947,945	2,139,590	542,790	1,596,800
New York	(27)	3,569,513	1,282,731	2,286,783	3,139,377	1,224,759	1,914,618
North Carolina	(8)	8,046,671	2,842,747	5,203,924	6,916,349	2,758,504	4,157,845
North Dakota	(23)	4,167,439	3,205,391	962,048	3,777,519	2,907,322	870,197
Ohio	(16)	5,398,458	3,345,133	2,053,325	4,662,233	2,852,781	1,809,452
Oklahoma	(18)	5,003,720	1,092,836	3,910,884	4,526,113	1,022,107	3,504,006
Oregon	(28)	3,391,785	2,513,460	878,324	3,283,732	2,478,876	804,856
Pennsylvania	(19)	4,761,965	1,498,202	3,263,763	4,266,265	1,407,088	2,859,177
Rhode Island	(49)	58,681	49,897	8,783	57,225	48,556	8,669
South Carolina	(36)	1,662,807	847,071	815,736	1,644,456	754,455	890,001
South Dakota	(20)	4,748,409	2,446,264	2,302,145	4,017,915	1,898,701	2,119,214
Tennessee	(32)	2,435,346	1,320,758	1,114,588	2,338,653	1,267,803	1,070,850
Texas	(2)	16,027,226	4,995,626	11,031,600	15,341,961	5,030,520	10,311,441
Utah	(37)	1,169,198	272,810	896,388	1,138,153	258,420	879,733
Vermont	(41)	567,934	79,145	488,789	481,650	78,928	402,722
Virginia	(30)	2,582,645	821,207	1,761,438	2,227,292	695,131	1,532,161
Washington	(15)	5,751,960	4,043,045	1,708,915	5,345,293	3,818,221	1,527,072
West Virginia	(43)	538,968	241,564	297,405	389,541	72,551	316,990
Wisconsin	(10)	6,630,420	1,655,107	4,975,313	5,876,052	1,782,346	4,093,706
Wyoming	(39)	933,749	150,880	782,869	873,645	149,919	723,726
UNITED STATES		**$236,833,871**	**$115,938,304**	**$120,895,569**	**$211,646,854**	**$106,175,903**	**$105,470,951**

Average Prices Received by U.S. Farmers, 1940-2004

Source: National Agricultural Statistics Service, U.S. Dept. of Agriculture

Figures below represent dollars per 100 lb for hogs, beef cattle, veal calves, sheep, lamb, and milk (wholesale); dollars per head for milk cows; cents per lb for chickens, broilers, turkeys, and wool; cents per dozen for eggs; weighted calendar year prices for livestock and livestock products other than wool. For 1943-63, wool prices are weighted on marketing year basis. The marketing year was changed in 1964 from a calendar year to a Dec.-Nov. basis for hogs, chickens, broilers, and eggs.

Year	Hogs	Cattle (beef)	Calves (veal)	Sheep	Lambs	Milk cows	Milk	Chickens (excl. broilers)	Broilers	Turkeys	Eggs	Wool
1940...	5.39	7.56	8.83	3.95	8.10	61	1.82	13.0	17.3	15.2	18.0	28.4
1950...	18.00	23.30	26.30	11.60	25.10	198	3.89	22.2	27.4	32.8	36.3	62.1
1960...	15.30	20.40	22.90	5.61	17.90	223	4.21	12.2	16.9	25.4	36.1	42.0
1970...	22.70	27.10	34.50	7.51	26.40	332	5.71	9.1	13.6	22.6	39.1	35.4
1975...	46.10	32.20	27.20	11.30	42.10	412	8.75	9.9	26.3	34.8	54.5	44.8
1980...	38.00	62.40	76.80	21.30	63.60	1,190	13.05	11.0	27.7	41.3	56.3	88.1
1985...	44.00	53.70	62.10	23.90	67.70	860	12.76	14.8	30.1	49.1	57.1	63.3
1990...	53.70	74.60	95.60	23.20	55.50	1,160	13.74	9.3	32.6	39.4	70.9	80.0
1991...	49.10	72.70	98.00	19.70	52.20	1,100	12.27	7.1	30.8	38.4	67.8	55.0
1992...	41.60	71.30	89.00	25.80	59.50	1,130	13.15	8.6	31.8	37.7	57.6	74.0
1993...	45.20	72.60	91.20	28.60	64.40	1,160	12.84	10.0	34.0	39.0	63.4	51.0
1994...	39.90	66.70	87.20	30.90	65.60	1,170	13.01	7.6	35.0	40.4	61.4	78.0
1995...	40.50	61.80	73.10	28.00	78.20	1,130	12.78	6.5	34.4	41.6	62.4	104.0
1996...	51.90	58.70	58.40	29.90	82.20	1,090	14.75	6.6	38.1	43.3	74.9	70.0
1997...	52.90	63.10	78.90	37.90	90.30	1,100	13.36	7.7	37.7	39.9	70.3	84.0
1998...	34.40	59.60	78.80	30.60	72.30	1,120	15.41	8.0	39.3	38.0	65.5	60.0
1999...	30.30	63.40	87.70	31.10	74.50	1,280	14.38	7.1	37.1	40.8	62.2	38.0
2000...	42.30	68.60	104.00	34.30	79.80	1,340	12.40	5.7	33.6	40.7	61.8	33.0
2001...	44.30	71.30	106.00	34.60	66.90	1,500	15.04	4.5	39.3	39.0	62.2	36.0
2002...	33.40	66.50	96.40	27.90	73.80	1,600	12.18	4.8	30.5	36.5	58.9	53.0
2003...	37.20	79.70	102.00	34.90	94.40	1,340	12.55	4.9	34.6	36.1	73.2	73.0
2004...	49.30	85.90	119.00	38.80	101.00	1,580	16.13	5.8	44.6	42.0	71.4	80.0

Figures below represent cents per lb for cotton, apples, and peanuts; dollars per bushel for oats, wheat, corn, barley, and soybeans; dollars per 100 lb for rice, sorghum, and potatoes; dollars per ton for cottonseed and baled hay; weighted crop year prices. The marketing year is described as follows: apples, June-May; wheat, oats, barley, hay, and potatoes, July-June; cotton, rice, peanuts, and cottonseed, Aug.-July; soybeans, Sept.-Aug.; and corn and sorghum grain, Oct.-Sept.

Year	Corn	Wheat	Upland cotton*	Oats	Barley	Rice	Soybeans	Sorghum	Peanuts	Cottonseed	Hay	Potatoes	Apples
1940...	0.62	0.67	9.8	0.30	0.39	1.80	0.89	0.87	3.7	21.70	9.78	0.85	NA
1950...	1.52	2.00	39.9	0.79	1.19	5.09	2.47	1.88	10.9	86.60	21.10	1.50	NA
1960...	1.00	1.74	30.1	0.60	0.84	4.55	2.13	1.49	10.0	42.50	21.70	2.00	2.7
1970...	1.33	1.33	21.9	0.62	0.97	5.17	2.85	2.04	12.8	56.40	26.10	2.21	6.5
1975...	2.54	3.55	51.1	1.45	2.42	8.35	4.92	4.21	19.0	97.00	52.10	4.48	8.8
1980...	3.11	3.91	74.4	1.79	2.86	12.80	7.57	5.25	25.1	129.00	71.00	6.55	12.1
1985...	2.23	3.08	56.8	1.23	1.98	6.53	5.05	3.45	24.4	66.00	67.60	3.92	17.3
1990...	2.28	2.61	67.1	1.14	2.14	6.68	5.74	3.79	34.7	121.00	80.60	6.08	20.9
1991...	2.37	3.00	56.8	1.21	2.10	7.58	5.58	4.01	28.3	71.00	71.20	4.96	25.1
1992...	2.07	3.24	53.7	1.32	2.04	5.89	5.56	3.38	30.0	97.50	74.30	5.52	19.5
1993...	2.50	3.26	58.1	1.36	1.99	7.98	6.40	4.13	30.4	113.00	84.70	6.18	18.4
1994...	2.26	3.45	72.0	1.22	2.03	6.78	5.48	3.80	28.9	101.00	86.70	5.58	18.6
1995...	3.24	4.55	75.4	1.67	2.89	9.15	6.72	5.69	29.3	106.00	82.20	6.77	24.0
1996...	2.71	4.30	69.3	1.96	2.74	9.96	7.35	4.17	28.1	126.00	95.80	4.93	20.8
1997...	2.43	3.38	65.2	1.60	2.38	9.70	6.47	3.95	28.3	121.00	100.00	5.62	22.1
1998...	1.90	2.65	64.2	1.10	1.98	8.50	5.35	3.10	25.7	129.00	84.60	5.24	17.1
1999...	1.82	2.48	45.0	1.12	2.13	5.93	4.63	2.80	25.4	89.00	76.90	5.77	21.3
2000...	1.85	2.62	49.8	1.10	2.11	5.61	4.54	3.37	27.4	105.00	84.60	5.08	17.8
2001...	1.97	2.78	29.8	1.59	2.22	4.25	4.38	4.25	23.4	90.50	96.50	6.99	22.9
2002...	2.32	3.56	44.5	1.81	2.72	4.49	5.53	4.14	18.2	101.00	92.40	6.69	25.6
2003[1]..	2.42	3.40	61.8	1.48	2.83	8.08	7.34	4.26	19.3	117.00	85.50	5.89	29.4
2004...	1.95	3.40	46.0	1.48	2.48	7.40	5.10	3.05	19.6	105.00	89.70	5.62	21.7

*Beginning in 1964, 480-lb net weight bales. NA = Not available. (1) Revised.

Value of U.S. Agricultural Exports and Imports, 1978-2004

Source: Economic Research Service, U.S. Dept. of Agriculture

(in billions of dollars, except percent)

Year[1]	Agric. Trade surplus	Agric. exports	% of all exports	Agric. imports	% of all imports
1978.....	13.4	27.3	21	13.9	8
1979.....	15.8	32.0	19	16.2	8
1980.....	23.2	40.5	19	17.3	7
1981.....	26.4	43.8	19	17.3	7
1982.....	23.6	39.1	18	15.5	6
1983.....	18.5	34.8	18	16.3	7
1984.....	19.1	38.0	18	18.9	6
1985.....	11.5	31.2	15	19.7	6
1986.....	5.4	26.3	13	20.9	6
1987.....	7.2	27.9	12	20.7	5
1988.....	14.3	35.3	12	21.0	5
1989.....	18.1	39.7	12	21.6	5
1990.....	16.6	39.5	11	22.9	5
1991.....	16.4	39.3	10	22.9	5
1992.....	18.3	43.1	10	24.8	5
1993.....	17.7	42.9	10	25.1	4
1994.....	19.2	46.2	10	27.0	4
1995.....	26.0	56.3	10	30.3	4
1996.....	26.8	60.3	10	33.5	4
1997.....	21.0	57.2	9	36.1	4
1998.....	14.9	51.8	8	36.9	4
1999.....	10.7	48.4	8	37.7	4
2000.....	12.2	51.2	7	39.0	3
2001.....	14.3	53.7	8	39.4	4
2002.....	11.2	53.1	8	41.9	4
2003[2].....	10.3	56.0	9	45.7	4
2004[3].....	9.6	62.3	9	52.7	4

(1) Fiscal year (Oct.-Sept.). (2) Revised. (3) Preliminary.

World Wheat, Rice, and Corn Production, 2004

Source: UN Food and Agriculture Organization; in metric tons

Country	Wheat	Rice[1]	Corn
Algeria	2,600,000	300	1,000
Argentina	14,560,000	1,060,000	15,000,000
Australia	20,376,000	535,000	392,000
Austria	1,718,820	—	1,653,750
Azerbaijan	1,600,000	20,000	150,000
Bangladesh	1,253,000	37,910,000	10,000
Belarus	1,025,000	—	65,000
Belgium	1,913,177	—	637,807
Brazil	5,962,604	13,251,200	41,863,756
Bulgaria	3,961,178	28,116	2,123,022
Cambodia	—	4,170,000	256,000
Cameroon	400	62,000	750,000
Canada	25,860,400	—	8,835,700
Chile	1,921,652	119,265	1,320,606
China	91,330,265	177,434,000	132,160,000
Colombia	36,548	2,663,239	1,458,434
Congo, Dem. Rep.	8,540	315,130	1,155,030
Côte d'Ivoire	—	1,150,000	910,000
Croatia	840,000	—	2,200,000
Cuba	—	610,000	300,000
Czech Rep.	5,042,523	—	551,628
Denmark	4,758,500	—	—
Ecuador	12,000	1,100,000	651,000
Egypt	7,177,855	6,150,000	5,800,000
Ethiopia	1,618,093	15,500	2,743,881
France	39,704,764	115,110	16,391,359
Germany	25,427,000	—	4,200,000
Ghana	—	241,807	1,157,621
Greece	1,800,000	175,000	2,300,000
Guatemala	11,339	34,926	1,072,310
Hungary	6,020,000	12,000	8,317,000
India	72,060,000	129,000,000	14,000,000
Indonesia	—	54,060,816	11,354,900
Iran	14,000,000	3,400,000	1,500,000
Ireland	849,000	—	—
Israel	165,635	—	80,000
Italy	8,628,758	1,496,000	10,983,080
Japan	860,000	10,912,000	160
Kazakhstan	9,942,300	276,661	300,000
Kenya	300,000	50,000	2,138,425
Korea, North	175,000	2,370,000	1,727,000
Korea, South	12,000	6,800,000	70,000
Laos	—	2,529,000	203,500
Lithuania	1,315,000	—	—
Madagascar	10,000	3,030,000	349,646
Malaysia	—	2,183,664	75,000
Mali	7,000	877,000	365,174
Mexico	2,500,000	191,540	20,000,000
Moldova	690,000	—	1,840,000
Morocco	5,539,840	16,900	224,130
Mozambique	2,100	201,000	1,248,000
Myanmar	130,000	22,000,000	600,000
Nepal	1,387,191	4,300,000	1,590,097
Netherlands	1,224,000	—	196,000
Nigeria	71,000	3,542,000	4,779,000
Pakistan	19,767,000	7,486,500	2,775,000
Paraguay	715,000	125,000	1,120,000
Peru	168,744	1,816,621	1,180,769
Philippines	—	14,496,800	5,413,390
Poland	9,450,486	—	2,201,956
Portugal	251,000	148,000	798,000
Romania	7,734,980	4,963	14,541,564
Russia	45,412,712	471,060	3,515,690
Saudi Arabia	2,358,000	—	43,697
Serbia and Montenegro	2,746,000	—	6,287,000
Slovakia	1,764,846	—	862,435
South Africa	1,761,000	3,200	9,737,000
Spain	7,107,900	900,400	4,748,400
Sri Lanka	—	2,509,800	26,000
Sudan	332,000	15,748	60,000
Sweden	2,412,300	—	—
Syria	4,537,459	—	180,000
Tanzania	71,000	647,000	2,800,000
Thailand	800	26,948,000	4,094,000
Tunisia	1,722,000	—	—
Turkey	21,000,000	400,000	3,000,000
Turkmenistan	2,600,000	110,000	13,000
Uganda	15,000	140,000	1,350,000
Ukraine	17,517,700	170,000	8,793,100
United Kingdom	15,706,000	—	—
U.S.	58,737,800	10,469,730	299,917,120
Uruguay	532,600	1,262,600	223,000
Uzbekistan	4,476,000	279,000	135,000
Venezuela	150	989,478	2,068,465
Vietnam	—	36,117,800	3,453,600
Zambia	135,000	12,000	1,161,000
Zimbabwe	80,000	600	1,000,000
World[2]	**627,130,584**	**605,758,530**	**721,379,361**

— Production is small or nonexistent. (1) Paddy rice only. (2) Includes countries not listed.

Wheat, Rice, and Corn—Exports/Imports of 10 Leading Countries, 2003, 1995

Source: UN Food and Agriculture Organization; in metric tons

TOP EXPORTERS

Wheat

2003		1995	
U.S.	25,429,428	U.S.	32,420,000
France	16,366,886	Canada	16,960,000
Canada	11,719,888	France	16,310,000
Australia	9,503,389	Australia	7,818,000
Russia	7,587,902	Argentina	6,913,286
Argentina	6,169,213	Germany	3,681,597
Kazakhstan	5,194,873	Hungary	2,764,541
Germany	4,473,168	U.K.	2,669,090
India	4,093,081	Kazakhstan	2,485,588
U.K.	3,657,581	Denmark	1,540,179

Rice

2003		1995	
Thailand	8,394,979	Thailand	6,197,990
Vietnam	3,813,000	India	4,913,156
U.S.	3,784,544	U.S.	3,083,609
India	3,401,931	Vietnam	1,988,000
China	2,597,176	Pakistan	1,852,267
Pakistan	1,819,982	Australia	541,848
Uruguay	625,001	Italy	523,898
Egypt	585,759	Uruguay	462,471
Italy	570,519	Argentina	390,091
Spain	381,904	Myanmar	353,800

Corn

2003		1995	
U.S.	43,411,753	U.S.	60,240,000
China	16,399,462	France	6,474,138
Argentina	11,912,789	Argentina	6,000,873
France	7,079,809	South Africa	1,508,450
Hungary	1,310,644	Hungary	600,950
Ukraine	943,109	Canada	443,612
Germany	856,604	Belgium-Lux.	442,645
Paraguay	805,424	Zimbabwe	287,818
South Africa	785,141	Germany	244,000
India	543,271	Paraguay	203,430

TOP IMPORTERS

Wheat

2003		1995	
Italy	6,986,068	China	12,601,814
Brazil	6,611,943	Brazil	6,135,235
Japan	5,246,121	Japan	5,965,296
Algeria	4,080,955	Italy	5,078,844
Egypt	4,057,234	Egypt	5,069,599
Spain	3,860,967	Indonesia	4,054,203
South Korea	3,763,634	Algeria	3,504,679
Belgium	3,510,144	Iran	3,100,000
Indonesia	3,502,373	Spain	2,757,498
Mexico	3,499,911	Belgium-Lux.	2,719,024

Rice

2003		1995	
Indonesia	1,625,753	Indonesia	3,157,700
Bangladesh	1,250,712	China	1,645,837
Brazil	1,066,208	Iran	1,633,000
Iran	945,729	Bangladesh	995,946
Senegal	890,044	Brazil	870,506
Saudi Arabia	844,182	North Korea	587,000
Philippines	842,159	U. Arab Em.	540,888
North Korea	802,700	Saudi Arabia	522,942
South Africa	790,842	Côte d'Ivoire	483,688
Nigeria	761,879	South Africa	466,154

Corn

2003		1995	
Japan	17,064,246	Japan	16,580,000
South Korea	17,064,246	China	11,702,350
Mexico	8,782,362	South Korea	9,035,169
China	5,076,318	Spain	2,912,371
Egypt	4,052,619	Mexico	2,686,921
Spain	3,886,300	Egypt	2,425,162
Canada	3,478,100	Malaysia	2,383,267
Iran	3,089,731	Belgium-Lux.	1,815,945
Malaysia	2,666,460	Netherlands	1,589,800
Colombia	2,031,673	U.K.	1,501,563

World Commercial Catch of Fish, Crustaceans, and Mollusks, by Major Fishing Areas, 1996-2003

Source: Food and Agriculture Organization of the United Nations (FAO)

(in thousands of metric tons; live weight)

AREA	1996	1997	1998	1999	2000	2001	2002	2003
Marine								
Pacific Ocean	63,452	62,657	57,047	63,631	65,524	63,298	64,561	63,020
Atlantic Ocean	25,237	26,385	25,606	25,648	26,049	26,386	25,972	25,191
Indian Ocean	8,432	8,777	8,940	9,100	9,284	9,204	9,886	10,137
Total Marine	**97,121**	**97,820**	**91,593**	**98,378**	**100,857**	**98,888**	**100,418**	**98,348**
Inland Waters								
Asia	19,501	21,104	22,431	24,397	25,577	26,861	27,958	29,407
Africa	1,950	2,018	2,134	2,245	2,406	2,414	2,500	2,618
Europe	838	821	856	901	886	821	823	832
N. America[1]	564	600	597	627	618	618	615	627
S. America	448	465	477	524	556	579	657	673
Former USSR	412	388	432	507	498	412	426	419
Oceania	22	24	25	26	26	27	22	19
Total Inland	**23,323**	**25,032**	**26,520**	**28,720**	**30,070**	**31,320**	**32,574**	**34,176**
GRAND TOTAL	**120,444**	**122,852**	**118,113**	**127,098**	**130,927**	**130,207**	**132,993**	**132,524**

(1) N. America includes figures for Central America. **Note:** Data for marine mammals and aquatic plants are excluded. Totals include areas or territories not shown. Includes weight of clam, oyster, scallop and other mollusk shells.

Commercial Catch of Fish, Crustaceans, and Mollusks, for 20 Leading Countries, 1998-2003[1]

Source: Food and Agriculture Organization of the United Nations (FAO)

(in thousands of metric tons; live weight; ranked for 2003)

COUNTRY	2003	2002	2001	2000	1999	1998	COUNTRY	2003	2002	2001	2000	1999	1998
China	47,298	45,869	44,063	43,069	41,513	39,545	Philippines	2,629	2,474	2,384	2,291	2,225	2,146
Peru	6,103	8,775	7,990	10,665	8,437	4,345	Vietnam	2,604	2,210	2,078	1,949	1,785	1,633
India	5,905	5,924	5,897	5,609	5,607	5,282	S. Korea	2,035	1,968	2,285	2,118	2,423	1,355
Indonesia	5,672	5,258	5,138	4,909	4,794	4,591	Bangladesh	1,998	1,890	1,781	1,661	1,552	1,414
U.S.	5,483	5,435	5,424	5,174	5,228	5,154	Iceland	1,984	2,133	1,985	1,986	1,740	1,686
Japan	5,456	5,191	5,513	5,751	5,947	6,071	Myanmar	1,606	1,434	1,288	1,169	1,011	912
Chile	4,185	4,817	4,363	4,692	5,324	3,558	Mexico	1,524	1,524	1,475	1,369	1,254	1,221
Thailand	3,590	3,464	3,548	3,736	3,646	3,525	Malaysia	1,454	1,441	1,393	1,441	1,407	1,287
Russia	3,390	3,334	3,718	4,048	4,210	4,518	Canada	1,230	1,234	1,195	1,125	1,130	1,095
Norway	3,132	3,292	3,198	3,191	3,103	3,274	Spain	1,210	1,216	1,406	1,358	1,494	1,558

(1) Includes aquaculture. Includes weight of clam, oyster, scallop, and other mollusk shells, this weight is not included in U.S. landings statistics shown elsewhere.

U.S. Commercial Landings of Fish and Shellfish, 1986-2003[1]

Source: U.S. Dept. of Commerce, Natl. Oceanic and Atmospheric Admin., Natl. Marine Fisheries Service

YEAR	Landings for human food		Landings for industrial purposes[2]		TOTAL	
	mil lbs	mil dollars	mil lbs	mil dollars	mil lbs	mil dollars
1986	3,393	$2,641	2,638	$122	6,031	$2,763
1987	3,946	2,979	2,950	136	6,896	3,115
1988	4,588	3,362	2,604	158	7,192	3,520
1989	6,204	3,111	2,259	127	8,463	3,238
1990	7,041	3,366	2,363	156	9,404	3,522
1991	7,031	3,169	2,453	139	9,484	3,308
1992	7,618	3,531	2,019	147	9,637	3,678
1993	8,214	3,317	2,253	154	10,467	3,471
1994	7,936	3,751	2,525	95	10,461	3,846
1995	7,667	3,625	2,121	145	9,788	3,770
1996	7,474	3,355	2,091	132	9,565	3,487
1997	7,244	3,285	2,598	163	9,842	3,448
1998	7,173	3,009	2,021	119	9,194	3,128
1999	6,832	3,265	2,507	202	9,339	3,467
2000	6,912	3,398	2,157	152	9,069	3,550
2001	7,314	3,074	2,178	154	9,492	3,228
2002	7,205	2,940	2,192	152	9,397	3,092
2003	7,519	3,185	1,986	157	9,505	3,342

Note: Data do not include products of aquaculture, except oysters and clams. (1) Statistics on landings are shown in round (live) weight for all items except univalve and bivalve mollusks such as clams, oysters, and scallops, which are shown in weight of meats (excluding the shell). (2) Processed into meal, oil, solubles, and shell products or used as bait or animal food.

U.S. Domestic Landings, by Regions, 2002-2003[1]

Source: U.S. Dept. of Commerce, Natl. Oceanic and Atmospheric Admin., Natl. Marine Fisheries Service

REGION	2002		2003	
	Weight (1,000 lbs)	Value ($1,000)	Weight (1,000 lbs)	Value ($1,000)
New England	583,915	$685,428	666,179	$683,395
Middle Atlantic	206,697	170,134	214,454	177,404
Chesapeake	495,675	172,320	496,178	179,701
South Atlantic	214,799	173,429	203,566	161,445
Gulf	1,716,140	692,717	1,600,481	683,276
Pacific Coast incl. Alaska	6,138,249	1,130,633	6,277,566	1,375,763
Great Lakes	17,848	15,544	17,471	13,174
Hawaii	23,841	52,113	23,556	52,433
TOTAL	**9,397,164**	**$3,092,318**	**9,505,448**	**$3,342,184**

(1) Landings reported in round (live) weight items except for univalve and bivalve mollusks (e.g., clams, oysters, scallops), which are reported in weight of meats (excluding shell). Landings for Mississippi River Drainage Area states not included (not available).

EMPLOYMENT

Employment and Unemployment in the U.S., 1900-2004

Source: Bureau of Labor Statistics, U.S. Dept. of Labor
(civilian labor force, persons 16 years of age and older; annual averages; in thousands)

Year[1]	Employed	Unemployed	Unemployment rate
1900[2]	26,956	1,420	5.0%
1910[2]	34,599	2,150	5.9
1920[2]	39,208	2,132	5.2
1930[2]	44,183	4,340	8.9
1940[2]	47,520	8,120	14.6
1950	58,918	3,288	5.0
1955	62,170	2,852	4.4
1960	65,778	3,852	5.5
1965	71,088	3,366	4.5
1970	78,678	4,093	4.9
1975	85,846	7,929	8.5
1980	99,303	7,637	7.1
1985	107,150	8,312	7.2
1986	109,597	8,237	7.0
1987	112,440	7,425	6.2
1988	114,968	6,701	5.5
1989	117,342	6,528	5.3%
1990[3]	118,793	7,047	5.6
1991	117,718	8,628	6.8
1992	118,492	9,613	7.5
1993	120,259	8,940	6.9
1994[4]	123,060	7,996	6.1
1995	124,900	7,404	5.6
1996	126,708	7,236	5.4
1997[5]	129,558	6,739	4.9
1998[5]	131,463	6,210	4.5
1999[6]	133,488	5,880	4.2
2000[7]	136,891	5,692	4.0
2001[7]	136,933	6,801	4.7
2002[7]	136,485	8,378	5.8
2003[7]	137,736	8,774	6.0
2004[7]	139,252	8,149	5.5

(1) **Other unemployment rates (1905-1945): 1905**, 4.3; **1915**, 8.5; **1925**, 3.2; **1935**, 20.3; **1936**, 16.9; **1937**, 14.3; **1938**, 19.0; **1939**, 17.2; **1945**, 1.9; all for 14 years of age and older. (2) Persons 14 years of age and older. (3) Beginning in 1990, data incorporate 1990 census-based population controls, adjusted for estimated undercount. (4) Beginning in 1994, not strictly comparable with prior years, because of major redesign of the survey used. (5) From 1997 not strictly comparable with 1994-96 because of revisions in population controls used in household survey. (6) From 1999 not strictly comparable with 1998 and earlier years because of further revisions in population controls used in household survey. (7) From 2000, not strictly comparable with earlier years because of revisions to the controls used in the survey.

Unemployment Insurance Data, by State, 2004

Source: Employment and Training Admin., U.S. Dept. of Labor; state programs only

STATE	Monetarily eligible claimants	First payments	Final payments	Initial claims	Benefits paid	Average weekly benefit	Employers subject to state law
AL	144,216	118,550	36,144	271,006	$228,206,498	$176.64	86,031
AK	50,750	46,224	20,192	91,135	113,863,043	193.71	16,996
AZ	130,155	96,132	43,435	218,122	276,171,263	176.95	110,203
AR	113,731	84,827	34,365	187,286	229,338,651	228.16	61,417
CA	1,436,213	1,111,416	565,799	2,463,943	4,699,124,028	260.27	1,057,681
CO	117,525	87,518	46,300	143,594	388,820,279	298.04	144,262
CT	148,002	127,875	47,731	221,032	549,714,700	284.04	96,696
DE	33,250	27,595	9,307	55,083	100,413,811	246.63	25,805
FL	423,423	299,915	149,910	653,067	968,696,395	223.15	440,125
GA	314,304	208,293	92,853	468,744	559,429,015	242.02	201,966
HI	32,632	23,921	7,103	66,707	104,632,152	323.32	29,658
ID	60,825	50,019	17,661	112,389	137,869,579	229.00	42,832
IL	455,492	392,265	174,155	766,032	1,954,285,086	279.12	283,071
IN	240,974	186,543	78,182	395,003	584,441,176	266.88	125,731
IA	115,180	88,976	26,896	167,879	305,409,532	261.08	69,129
KS	84,736	68,335	31,135	143,275	222,918,958	271.76	68,847
KY	168,565	120,721	32,093	274,296	400,490,320	257.38	82,550
LA	123,405	89,576	37,901	193,119	274,695,789	194.78	95,783
ME	45,380	32,712	11,475	70,783	110,325,813	235.33	40,031
MD	149,393	109,204	40,753	222,961	405,028,342	253.70	137,024
MA	286,238	238,902	96,787	412,109	1,372,965,878	351.35	177,586
MI	559,085	461,928	165,081	862,333	1,790,964,992	289.15	213,329
MN	181,124	147,127	52,722	284,948	628,584,044	317.67	133,477
MS	90,149	60,410	22,104	152,580	151,114,123	171.87	53,986
MO	229,791	166,435	68,495	407,449	497,995,400	205.05	132,984
MT	32,101	22,291	8,837	50,940	66,347,405	197.32	34,532
NE	57,977	42,705	18,638	78,419	118,968,158	219.51	45,916
NV	84,403	66,419	26,154	146,041	248,766,597	244.83	50,491
NH	30,886	20,891	5,329	49,685	79,394,670	250.69	39,594
NJ	380,835	331,928	168,412	563,555	1,840,551,585	330.90	255,235
NM	43,147	32,446	15,284	64,470	117,575,788	220.41	42,054
NY	662,675	513,350	257,891	1,100,923	2,373,928,153	270.53	480,786
NC	357,701	273,015	115,456	705,052	825,978,491	255.66	182,087
ND	17,333	13,184	4,622	26,049	38,334,535	226.39	19,023
OH	350,390	305,935	102,796	687,782	1,171,045,517	251.97	230,892
OK	83,879	59,770	30,506	142,956	195,361,437	218.55	76,402
OR	185,447	147,548	61,814	376,470	601,183,352	251.61	103,315
PA	604,631	486,975	165,590	1,115,201	2,132,370,670	293.61	274,226
RI	49,507	40,610	16,151	81,157	202,266,575	324.34	33,006
SC	170,547	122,814	50,680	317,551	336,315,180	210.66	92,182
SD	13,719	10,261	1,666	21,456	28,128,512	205.31	23,477
TN	199,424	167,849	63,368	365,971	452,395,421	209.26	110,129
TX	666,723	422,421	215,479	904,949	1,574,485,606	259.34	402,733
UT	68,523	44,858	17,077	78,009	149,197,967	265.71	59,871
VT	26,509	22,650	4,764	39,271	73,362,592	256.36	21,158
VA	182,613	125,529	47,806	303,136	371,373,223	240.28	171,571
WA	287,672	208,210	68,768	524,961	985,813,682	309.76	196,035
WV	57,451	44,493	12,304	77,013	141,362,248	219.07	36,864
WI	315,026	269,306	76,573	628,428	801,604,288	250.67	124,829
WY	28,522	13,954	4,507	22,795	39,814,378	238.36	19,904
DC	17,535	16,815	10,302	17,358	84,537,641	257.35	27,234
PR	92,962	95,608	51,552	161,334	198,048,905	106.50	54,945
VI	1,767	1,369	630	2,112	4,076,166	242.25	3,038
U.S.	**10,804,443**	**8,368,623**	**3,531,535**	**17,957,919**	**32,308,087,611**	**262.50**	**7,138,722**

U.S. Unemployment Rates by Selected Characteristics, 1995-2005[1]

Source: Bureau of Labor Statistics, U.S. Dept. of Labor

	1995	2000	2001	2002	2003	2004 Jan.	2004 June	2004 Annual	2005 Jan.	2005 June
Total (all civilian workers)	**5.6**	**4.0**	**4.7**	**5.8**	**6.0**	**6.3**	**5.8**	**5.5**	**5.7**	**5.2**
Men, 20 years and older	4.8	3.3	4.2	5.3	5.6	6.1	4.8	5.0	5.6	4.1
Women, 20 years and older	4.9	3.6	4.1	5.1	5.1	5.3	5.2	4.9	4.8	4.8
Both sexes, 16 to 19 years	17.3	13.1	14.7	16.5	17.5	17.5	19.9	17.0	16.6	19.1
White	4.9	3.5	4.2	5.1	5.2	5.6	5.1	4.8	5.0	4.4
Black	10.4	7.6	8.6	10.2	10.8	10.7	10.7	10.4	11.0	10.8
Hispanic origin	9.3	5.7	6.6	7.5	7.7	8.3	6.5	7.0	6.9	5.6
Asian	—	3.6	4.5	5.9	6.0	5.2	5.0	4.4	4.2	4.0
Married men, spouse present	3.3	—	—	—	—	3.3	3.2	—	3.1	2.6
Married women, spouse present	3.9	—	—	—	—	3.7	3.7	—	3.2	3.3
Women who maintain families	8.0	5.9	6.6	8.0	8.5	8.3	8.2	8.0	8.2	8.2
OCCUPATION										
Management, professional, and related occupations	2.4	1.8	2.3	3.0	3.1	3.0	2.9	2.7	2.4	2.6
Service occupations	7.5	5.2	5.8	6.6	7.1	8.0	6.8	6.6	7.3	6.3
Sales and office occupations	5.0	3.8	4.4	5.6	5.5	5.8	5.5	5.2	5.3	4.9
Nat. resources, constr., maint. occupations	—	5.3	6.4	7.8	8.1	9.0	6.4	7.3	9.4	5.5
Prod., trans., material moving occupations	—	5.1	6.4	7.6	7.9	8.3	7.4	7.2	7.3	6.3
INDUSTRY										
Nonagricultural, private wage, and salary workers	5.8	4.1	5.0	6.2	6.3	6.7	5.8	5.7	6.0	5.1
Mining	5.2	4.4	4.2	6.3	6.7	5.8	5.0	3.9	4.9	4.0
Construction	11.5	6.2	7.1	9.2	9.3	11.3	7.0	8.4	11.8	5.7
Manufacturing	4.9	3.5	5.2	6.7	6.6	6.4	5.6	5.7	5.3	4.4
Durable goods	4.4	3.2	5.2	6.9	6.9	6.4	5.1	5.5	5.1	4.3
Non durable goods	5.7	4.0	5.2	6.2	6.1	6.3	6.3	5.9	5.7	4.6
Wholesale and retail trade	6.5	4.3	4.9	6.1	6.0	6.5	5.8	5.8	6.2	5.7
Transportation and utilities	4.5	3.4	4.3	4.9	5.3	4.6	4.3	4.4	5.0	4.5
Information	—	3.2	4.9	6.9	6.8	7.0	5.0	5.7	5.4	5.0
Financial activities	3.3	2.4	2.9	3.5	3.5	4.3	3.6	3.6	2.7	3.3
Professional and business services	—	4.8	6.1	7.9	8.2	8.7	6.5	6.8	7.6	5.8
Education and health services	—	2.5	2.8	3.4	3.6	3.7	4.2	3.4	3.4	3.6
Leisure and hospitality	—	6.6	7.5	8.4	8.7	10.0	9.6	8.3	8.7	7.6
Other services	8.4	3.9	4.0	5.1	5.7	5.3	5.4	5.3	4.7	4.6
Agriculture and related	11.1	9.0	11.2	10.1	10.2	15.1	7.6	9.9	13.2	5.2
Government	2.9	2.1	2.2	2.5	2.8	2.5	2.8	2.7	2.6	3.2
Self-employed and unpaid family workers	—	2.1	2.1	2.6	2.7	2.8	2.8	2.8	3.2	2.4

(1) All monthly rates unadjusted, except for married men and women, which are seasonally adjusted. — = Not available.

Employed Persons in the U.S., by Occupation and Sex, 2003 and 2004

Source: Bureau of Labor Statistics, U.S. Dept. of Labor

(in thousands)

	Total 16 years and older 2003	Total 16 years and older 2004	Men 16 years and older 2003	Men 16 years and older 2004	Women 16 years and older 2003	Women 16 years and older 2004
Total	**137,736**	**139,252**	**73,332**	**74,524**	**64,404**	**64,728**
Management, professional, and related occupations	47,929	48,532	23,735	24,136	24,194	24,396
Management, business, and financial operations occupations	19,934	20,235	11,534	11,718	8,400	8,517
Management occupations	14,468	14,555	9,094	9,210	5,374	5,344
Business and financial operations occupations	5,465	5,680	2,440	2,508	3,026	3,172
Professional and related occupations	27,995	28,297	12,201	12,418	15,794	15,879
Computer and mathematical occupations	3,122	3,140	2,223	2,292	900	848
Architecture and engineering occupations	2,727	2,760	2,343	2,380	384	380
Life, physical, and social science occupations	1,375	1,365	783	777	592	588
Community and social services occupations	2,184	2,170	862	845	1,323	1,325
Legal occupations	1,508	1,554	811	795	697	759
Education, training, and library occupations	7,768	7,900	2,038	2,104	5,730	5,796
Arts, design, entertainment, sports, and media occupations	2,663	2,687	1,395	1,425	1,267	1,262
Healthcare practitioner and technical occupations	6,648	6,721	1,746	1,799	4,902	4,922
Service occupations	22,086	22,720	9,460	9,826	12,626	12,894
Healthcare support occupations	2,926	2,921	311	311	2,616	2,609
Protective service occupations	2,727	2,847	2,164	2,230	563	616
Food preparation and serving related occupations	7,254	7,279	3,151	3,196	4,104	4,084
Building and grounds cleaning and maintenance occupations	4,947	5,185	2,920	3,085	2,027	2,100
Personal care and service occupations	4,232	4,488	915	1,004	3,316	3,484
Sales and office occupations	35,496	35,464	12,851	12,805	22,645	22,660
Sales and related occupations	15,960	15,983	8,137	8,105	7,823	7,878
Office and administrative support occupations	19,536	19,481	4,714	4,700	14,823	14,781
Natural resources, construction, and maintenance occupations	14,205	14,582	13,541	13,930	665	652
Farming, fishing, and forestry occupations	1,050	991	819	786	231	204
Construction and extraction occupations	8,114	8,522	7,891	8,306	223	216
Installation, maintenance, and repair occupations	5,041	5,069	4,830	4,838	211	231
Production, transportation, and material moving occupations	18,020	17,954	13,745	13,827	4,274	4,126
Production occupations	9,700	9,462	6,696	6,587	3,004	2,875
Transportation and material moving occupations	8,320	8,491	7,049	7,240	1,270	1,251

NOTE: Beginning in Jan. 2000, data reflect revised population controls used in the household survey. Totals may not add because of independent rounding.

IT'S A FACT: On an average weekday in 2004, people employed full-time spent 9.2 hours working, 7.5 hours sleeping, 3 hours doing leisure and sports activities, and 0.9 hour doing household activities, according to the U.S. Dept. of Labor's annual American Time Use Survey. Household activities include housework, cooking, lawn care, and financial or other household management. Full-time workers watch 1.79 hours of TV on weekdays, but 2.78 hours on each weekend day.

Elderly in U.S. Labor Force, 1890-2004

Source: Bureau of the Census, U.S. Dept. of Commerce

The percentage of men 65 years of age and older in the U.S. labor force steadily declined between 1890 and 1990, dropping 76% in 100 years, but more recently has increased slightly. The percentage of women 65 or older in the work force has always been much lower than that of men; after ranging from around 6% to 10% from 1890 to 1950, it has increased slightly to 8%-11% in recent decades.

(labor force participation rate; figs. for 1910 not available)

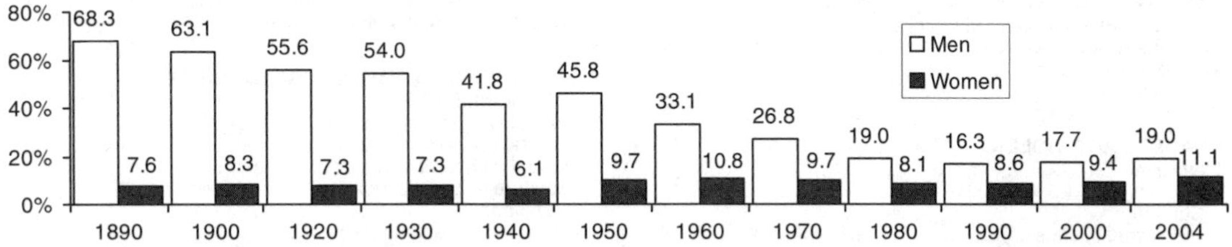

Projected Openings for Selected High-Paying Occupations, 2002-2012

Source: Bureau of Labor Statistics, U.S. Dept. of Labor

Job openings shown below represent the average number expected each year for workers in the U.S. who are entering these occupations for the first time.

Occupation	Annual avg. job openings[1]	Median annual earnings[2]
Registered nurses	110,119	$48,090
Postsecondary teachers	95,980	49,090
Gen. & operations mgrs.	76,245	68,210
Sales representatives[3]	66,239	42,730
Truck drivers, heavy & tractor trailer	62,517	33,210
Elementary school teachers	54,701	41,780
First-line retail superv. or mgrs.	48,645	29,700
Secondary school teachers[4]	45,761	43,950
Gen. maintenance & repair wkrs	44,978	29,370
Exec. secretaries, admin. assists.	42,444	33,410
First-line office superv. or mgrs.	40,909	$38,820
Accountants and auditors	40,465	47,000
Carpenters	31,917	34,190
Auto mechanics/technicians	31,887	30,590
Police & Sheriff's patrol officers	31,290	42,270
Lic. practical and voc. nurses	29,480	31,440
Electricians	28,485	41,390
Management analysts	25,470	60,340
Computer systems analysts	23,735	62,890
Special education teachers	23,297	43,450

(1) As a result of growth and net replacement needs. (2) Median earnings are for 2002. (3) Wholesale and manufacturing, except technical and scientific products. (4) Except special and vocational education.

Top-Paying U.S. Metropolitan Areas, by Average Annual Salary, 2002

Source: Bureau of Labor Statistics, U.S. Dept. of Labor

Rank	Metropolitan area	Average annual salary[1]
1.	San Jose, CA	$63,056
2.	New York, NY	57,708
3.	San Francisco, CA	56,602
4.	New Haven–Bridgeport–Stamford–Waterbury–Danbury, CT	51,170
5.	Middlesex–Somerset–Hunterdon, NJ	50,457
6.	Jersey City, NJ	49,562
7.	Newark, NJ	48,781
8.	Washington, DC–MD–VA–WV	48,430
9.	Trenton, NJ	$47,969
10.	Oakland, CA	46,877
11.	Seattle–Bellevue–Everett, WA	46,093
12.	Boston–Worcester–Lawrence–Lowell–Brockton, MA–NH	45,685
13.	Bergen–Passaic, NJ	45,185
14.	Hartford, CT	44,387
15.	Boulder–Longmont, CO	44,037

NOTE: Jacksonville, NC, recorded the **lowest average annual pay** among U.S. metropolitan areas in 2002—$22,269—followed by Brownsville–Harlingen–San Benito, TX ($22,892), McAllen–Edinburg–Mission, TX ($23,179), Yuma, AZ ($23,429), and Myrtle Beach, SC ($24,672). The nationwide metropolitan average was $38,423. (1) Data include workers covered by Unemployment Insurance and Unemployment Compensation for Federal Employees programs.

Federal Minimum Hourly Wage Rates Since 1950

Source: Bureau of Labor Statistics, U.S. Dept. of Labor

The Fair Labor Standards Act of 1938 and subsequent amendments provide for minimum wage-coverage applicable to nonprofessional workers in specified nonsupervisory employment categories.

EFFECTIVE DATE	NONFARM WORKERS			FARM WORKERS[4]
	Under laws prior to 1966[1]	Percent of avg. earnings[2]	Under 1966 and later provis.[3]	
Jan. 25, 1950	$0.75	54	NA	NA
Mar. 1, 1956	1.00	52	NA	NA
Sept. 3, 1961	1.15	50	NA	NA
Sept. 3, 1963	1.25	51	NA	NA
Feb. 1, 1967	1.40	50	$1.00	$1.00
Feb. 1, 1968	1.60	54	1.15	1.15
Feb. 1, 1969	(5)	(5)	1.30	1.30
Feb. 1, 1970	(5)	(5)	1.45	(5)
Feb. 1, 1971	(5)	(5)	1.60	(5)
May 1, 1974	2.00	46	1.90	1.60
Jan. 1, 1975	2.10	45	2.00	1.80
Jan. 1, 1976	$2.30	46	$2.20	$2.00
Jan. 1, 1977	(5)	(5)	2.30	2.20
Jan. 1, 1978	2.65	44	2.65	2.65
Jan. 1, 1979	2.90	45	2.90	2.90
Jan. 1, 1980	3.10	43	3.10	3.10
Jan. 1, 1981	3.35	42	3.35	3.35
Apr. 1, 1990	3.80[6]	35	3.80	3.80[6]
Apr. 1, 1991	4.25[6]	38	4.25	4.25[6]
Oct. 1, 1996	4.75[7]	37	4.75	4.75[7]
Sept. 1, 1997	5.15[7]	39[8]	5.15	5.15[7]

NA = not applicable. (1) Applies to workers covered prior to 1961 Amendments and, after Sept. 1965, to workers covered by 1961 Amendments. Rates set by 1961 Amendments were: Sept. 1961, $1.00; Sept. 1964, $1.15; and Sept. 1965, $1.25. (2) Percent of gross average hourly earnings of production workers in manufacturing. (3) Applies to workers newly covered by Amendments of 1966, 1974, and 1977, and Title IX of Education Amendments of 1972. (4) Included in coverage as of 1966, 1974, and 1977 Amendments. (5) No change in rate. (6) Training wage for workers age 16-19 in first 6 months of first job: Apr. 1, 1990, $3.35; Apr. 1, 1991, $3.62. The training wage expired Mar. 31, 1993. (7) Under 1996 legislation, a subminimum training wage of $4.25 an hour was established for employees under 20 years of age during their first 90 consecutive calendar days of employment with an employer. For workers receiving gratuities, the minimum wage remained $2.13 per hour.
(8) Minimum wage was 32-7% by this measure in 2003.

Fatal Occupational Injuries, 2004

Source: Bureau of Labor Statistics, U.S. Dept. of Labor

	FATALITIES Number	FATALITIES Percent
TRANSPORTATION INCIDENTS	**2,460**	**43**
Highway	1,374	24
Collision between vehicles, mobile equipment	687	12
Vehicle struck stationary object or equipment	27	(1)
Worker struck by a vehicle	377	7
Rail vehicle	50	1
Water vehicle	90	2
Aircraft	230	4
ASSAULTS AND VIOLENT ACTS	**795**	**14**
Homicides	551	10
Shooting	416	7
Stabbing	66	1
Self-inflicted injuries	200	4
CONTACT WITH OBJECTS & EQUIPMENT	**1,004**	**18**
Struck by object	596	10
Struck by falling object	370	6
Struck by flying object	42	1
Caught in or compressed by equipment or objects	270	5
Caught in running equipment or machinery	142	2
Caught in or crushed in collapsing materials	117	2
FALLS	**815**	**14**
EXPOSURE TO HARMFUL SUBSTANCE OR ENVIRONMENTS	**459**	**8**
Contact with electric current	253	4
Contact with overhead power lines	123	2
Contact with temperature extremes	27	(1)
Exposure to caustic, noxious, or allergenic substances	114	2
Inhalation of substance	52	1
Oxygen deficiency	63	1
Drowning, submersion	49	1
FIRES AND EXPLOSIONS	**159**	**3**
TOTAL	**5,703**	**100**

NOTE: Totals for categories may include subcategories not shown separately. Percentages based on incidence rate per total fatalities. (1) Less than or equal to 0.5%.

U.S. Occupational Illnesses, by Industry and Type of Illness, 2003

Source: Bureau of Labor Statistics, U.S. Dept. of Labor
(percent distribution)

	All private sector[1]	Goods Producing: Agri-culture & Mining[2, 3]	Goods Producing: Con-struc-tion	Goods Producing: Manu-facturing	Service Providing: Trans. pub. utilities[4]	Service Providing: Info.	Service Providing: Financial	Service Providing: Profes. & Business	Service Providing: Edu. & Health	Service Providing: Leisure & Hos-pitality
Total [1,315,920 cases]	**100.0**	**100.0**	**100.0**	**100.0**	**100.0**	**100.0**	**100.0**	**100.0**	**100.0**	**100.0**
Nature of injury or illness:										
Sprains, strains	42.9	36.0	35.8	37.3	46.2	43.5	40.0	41.9	53.9	36.8
Bruises, contusions	9.0	10.0	6.5	8.0	9.8	10.6	8.1	9.7	9.0	11.5
Cuts, lacerations	7.3	6.1	11.4	8.3	6.6	3.8	5.8	7.7	2.5	11.8
Fractures	7.2	10.2	11.7	7.3	6.6	7.5	6.5	7.0	5.3	6.0
Heat burns	1.5	1.9	1.0	1.7	0.7	0.3	0.7	0.6	0.9	6.9
Carpal tunnel syndrome	1.7	0.4	0.5	3.5	1.1	2.7	5.4	2.3	1.0	0.8
Tendinitis	0.6	0.4	0.3	1.1	0.5	0.7	0.9	0.5	0.4	0.4
Chemical burns	0.6	1.3	0.5	0.9	0.5	0.3	0.8	0.4	0.3	0.7
Amputations	0.6	1.3	0.7	1.7	0.4	0.2	0.2	0.6	0.1	0.3
Multiple traumatic injuries	3.6	4.2	4.0	3.3	3.5	3.6	5.0	4.0	3.6	3.5
Part of body affected by the injury or illness:										
Head	6.4	7.7	7.6	7.2	6.3	5.0	6.2	6.9	4.6	5.9
Eye	2.8	3.9	4.1	4.5	2.3	1.9	2.7	2.3	1.3	2.1
Neck	1.6	1.2	1.2	1.2	1.8	1.3	1.4	2.2	2.1	1.1
Trunk	35.9	32.4	31.9	34.0	38.3	30.3	31.9	31.8	43.7	31.0
Shoulder	6.4	6.6	5.0	7.1	7.2	6.1	6.1	5.2	7.0	4.9
Back	23.1	18.5	20.3	19.6	24.2	19.1	21.3	21.8	31.1	19.9
Upper extremities	22.7	20.9	23.7	31.5	19.7	21.1	22.0	21.9	15.5	28.4
Wrist	5.0	3.1	3.9	7.0	4.3	6.8	8.4	4.8	4.3	4.7
Hand, except finger	3.9	4.4	4.8	4.6	3.3	3.2	3.1	3.7	2.4	6.4
Finger	8.1	7.4	9.4	12.9	6.7	5.4	5.1	8.4	3.9	10.6
Lower extremities	21.2	26.6	24.8	17.3	22.7	27.7	21.0	22.9	18.1	21.2
Knee	8.0	9.0	8.6	6.6	8.5	12.9	7.3	8.5	7.7	8.0
Foot, except toe	3.3	3.1	4.6	3.1	3.7	4.9	2.3	3.1	2.4	2.6
Toe	0.9	1.1	1.2	0.8	1.2	0.7	0.6	1.0	0.6	0.7
Body systems	1.4	1.0	1.1	1.0	1.2	1.1	2.5	2.2	1.9	1.5
Multiple parts	9.9	9.4	8.8	6.9	9.3	12.8	13.8	11.0	13.6	9.8
Source of injury or illness:										
Chemicals and chemical products	1.5	3.4	0.9	2.1	1.1	1.0	1.5	2.0	1.3	1.6
Containers	13.1	7.8	4.9	12.3	21.5	9.3	7.4	11.4	5.3	15.9
Furniture and fixtures	3.6	.6	1.7	2.5	4.0	2.2	6.3	3.4	4.7	5.3
Machinery	6.2	8.4	6.3	11.9	5.3	4.0	6.2	5.8	2.3	5.1
Parts and materials	9.6	11.0	21.8	16.9	8.1	5.8	6.1	6.7	0.9	1.8
Worker motion or position	15.4	11.9	11.7	19.8	14.8	25.2	19.3	16.4	13.3	15.0
Floors, walkways, ground surfaces	18.8	19.0	20.9	12.1	17.0	24.9	25.1	22.3	20.0	27.3
Tools, instruments, and equipment	6.3	5.6	11.7	6.5	4.8	5.8	4.3	6.3	4.8	7.1
Vehicles	8.3	6.8	5.2	5.0	13.3	9.6	10.3	9.5	5.2	3.9
Health care patient	4.8	–	–	–	(5)	–	0.5	1.0	30.8	0.1
Event or exposure leading to injury or illness:										
Contact with objects and equipment	26.0	33.3	34.9	33.1	25.6	17.8	19.3	25.1	13.2	25.0
Struck by object	12.6	16.3	18.6	13.1	13.2	6.9	9.3	12.1	6.5	13.6
Struck against object	6.9	7.9	8.7	7.5	6.7	6.5	6.6	8.0	4.4	7.9
Caught in equipment or	4.3	7.0	3.6	9.6	4.0	3.5	1.6	3.4	1.6	2.1
Fall to lower level	6.3	9.2	13.0	3.8	6.1	7.9	10.4	7.5	3.4	3.9

	All private sector[1]	Goods Producing: Agri-culture & Mining[2, 3]	Goods Producing: Con-struc-tion	Goods Producing: Manu-facturing	Service Providing: Trans. pub. utilities[4]	Service Providing: Info.	Service Providing: Financial	Service Providing: Profes. & Business	Service Providing: Edu. & Health	Service Providing: Leisure & Hos-pitality
Fall on same level	13.3	9.6	9.0	9.1	11.9	17.6	15.0	15.2	17.1	24.1
Slip, trip, loss of balance—without fall	3.2	2.2	3.0	2.7	3.4	3.9	2.8	3.2	3.3	3.9
Overexertion	25.8	19.5	19.6	24.3	28.7	17.3	20.8	19.8	37.6	17.1
Overexertion in lifting	14.1	8.4	11.2	12.4	16.7	8.5	12.0	11.3	18.3	10.5
Repetitive motion	4.4	1.8	1.7	9.3	3.2	9.1	9.2	4.8	2.6	2.9
Exposure to harmful substances	4.2	6.7	3.6	4.9	2.7	4.3	3.4	4.1	4.3	9.4
Transportation accidents	4.4	3.9	3.8	2.1	6.3	5.8	6.2	6.5	3.3	1.8
Fires and explosions	0.2	0.3	0.2	0.3	0.2	–	0.1	0.1	(5)	0.2
Assaults and violent acts by person	1.3	0.2	0.1	0.1	0.6	0.3	1.0	0.8	5.4	1.3

NOTE: Dashes (—) indicate data are not available. Because of rounding and classifications not shown, percentages may not add to 100. All injuries and illnesses reported involved days away from work. (1) Excludes farms with fewer than 11 employees. (2) Agriculture includes forestry and fishing, but excludes farms with fewer than 11 employees. (3) Data conforming to OSHA definitions for mining operators in coal, metal, and nonmetal mining are provided by the Mine Safety and Health Administration, U.S. Dept. of Labor. Independent mining contractors are excluded from the coal, metal, and nonmetal industries. Data for mining include establishments not governed by Mine Safety and Health Administration rules, such as those in oil and gas extraction. (4) Data for employers in railroad transportation are provided by the Federal Railroad Administration, U.S. Department of Transportation. (5) Less than 0.1%.

Civilian Employment of the Federal Government, November 2004

Source: Statistical Analysis and Services Division, U.S. Office of Personnel Management

(monthly payroll in thousands of dollars)

	ALL AREAS Employ-ment*	ALL AREAS Payroll*	UNITED STATES Employ-ment	UNITED STATES Payroll	WASH., D.C., MSA[2] Employ-ment	WASH., D.C., MSA[2] Payroll	OVERSEAS Employ-ment	OVERSEAS Payroll
TOTAL, all agencies[1]	**2,692,098**	**$11,975,266**	**2,599,027**	**$11,621,537**	**327,056**	**$1,870,301**	**93,071**	**$353,729**
Legislative Branch[1]	**30,071**	**167,227**	**30,063**	**167,152**	**29,044**	**160,876**	**8**	**75**
Congress	17,169	96,078	17,169	96,078	17,169	96,078	—	—
U.S. Senate	6,727	33,298	6,727	33,298	6,727	33,298	—	—
House of Representatives	10,442	62,780	10,442	62,780	10,442	62,780	—	—
Architect of the Capitol	2,183	9,227	2,183	9,227	2,183	9,227	—	—
Congressional Budget Ofc	236	1,712	236	1,712	236	1,712	—	—
Govt. Accountability Ofc	3,253	22,612	3,252	22,601	2,432	17,204	1	11
Govt. Printing Ofc	2,399	11,583	2,399	11,583	2,236	10,873	—	—
Library of Congress	4,334	22,960	4,327	22,896	4,301	22,792	7	64
U.S. Tax Court	243	1,585	243	1,585	243	1,585	—	—
Judicial Branch	**33,569**	**154,142**	**33,142**	**152,388**	**1,919**	**10,448**	**427**	**1,754**
Supreme Court	449	1,550	449	1,550	449	1,550	—	—
U.S. Courts	33,120	152,592	32,693	150,838	1,470	8,898	427	1,754
Executive Branch	**2,628,462**	**11,653,939**	**2,535,826**	**11,302,039**	**296,095**	**1,698,992**	**92,636**	**351,900**
Exec Ofc of the President	1,791	11,745	1,780	11,675	1,780	11,675	11	70
White House Office	412	2,076	412	2,076	412	2,076	—	—
Ofc of Vice President	28	176	28	176	28	176	—	—
Ofc of Mgmt & Budget	511	3,642	511	3,642	511	3,642	—	—
Ofc of Administration	217	1,289	217	1,289	217	1,289	—	—
Council Economic Advisors	29	178	29	178	29	178	—	—
Council Environmental Quality	21	152	21	152	21	152	—	—
Ofc of Policy Development	31	173	31	173	31	173	—	—
National Security Council	60	378	60	378	60	378	—	—
Ofc of Natl Drug Control Policy	113	770	113	770	113	770	—	—
Ofc of U.S. Trade Rep.	217	1,878	206	1,808	206	1,808	11	70
Executive Departments	1,667,544	7,567,238	1,581,620	7,250,068	227,003	1,290,071	85,924	317,170
State	33,483	193,702	13,068	76,152	11,311	63,656	20,415	117,550
Treasury	95,153	433,435	94,557	431,288	8,624	58,579	596	2,147
Defense, Total	668,244	2,425,086	615,968	2,282,570	64,221	247,067	52,276	142,516
Defense, Mil Function	644,531	2,360,978	592,312	2,218,537	63,408	245,000	52,219	142,441
Defense, Civ Function	23,713	64,108	23,656	64,033	813	2,067	57	75
Dept of the Army	233,887	646,788	211,349	581,613	19,075	41,076	22,538	65,175
Army, Mil Function	210,175	582,681	187,694	517,581	18,262	39,009	22,481	65,100
Army, Civil Function	23,712	64,107	23,655	64,032	813	2,067	57	75
Corps of Engineers	23,615	63,860	23,558	63,785	716	1,820	57	75
Dept of the Navy	178,600	723,066	171,286	693,300	24,430	98,943	7,314	29,766
Dept of the Air Force	156,581	633,175	150,289	607,745	5,730	23,166	6,292	25,430
Defense Logist. Agency	21,601	98,086	20,847	94,524	1,637	10,402	754	3,562
Other Defense Activities	77,575	323,971	62,197	305,388	13,349	73,480	15,378	18,583
Justice	104,770	609,759	102,979	599,014	22,574	157,131	1,791	10,745
Interior	71,124	305,817	70,785	304,735	7,896	42,992	339	1,082
Agriculture	103,140	432,592	101,890	428,220	11,724	68,474	1,250	4,372
Commerce	37,200	211,457	36,435	206,299	20,243	132,324	765	5,158
Labor	15,787	95,375	15,749	95,147	5,361	35,848	38	228
Health & Human Services	60,903	340,462	60,650	338,872	27,920	174,522	253	1,590
Housing & Urban Dev.	10,214	62,355	10,131	61,875	3,311	21,745	83	480
Transportation	56,858	469,925	56,514	467,301	9,313	68,771	344	2,624
Energy	15,163	104,331	15,152	104,241	5,087	39,978	11	90
Education	4,452	28,252	4,443	28,209	3,162	20,659	9	43
Veterans Affairs	237,620	1,132,660	233,939	1,123,653	7,169	42,657	3,681	9,007
Homeland Security	153,433	722,030	149,360	702,492	19,087	115,668	4,073	19,538
Independent Agencies	**959,127**	**4,074,956**	**952,426**	**4,040,296**	**67,312**	**397,246**	**6,701**	**34,660**
Bd of Govt, Fed Rsrv Sys	1,831	13,241	1,831	13,241	1,831	13,241	—	—
Environmtl Protect Agcy	18,551	114,212	18,496	113,862	6,750	41,143	55	350
Equal Employ Opp Comm	2,466	13,943	2,456	13,901	602	3,881	10	42

	ALL AREAS		UNITED STATES		WASH., D.C., MSA[2]		OVERSEAS	
	Employ-ment*	Payroll*	Employ-ment	Payroll	Employ-ment	Payroll	Employ-ment	Payroll
Federal Communic Comm.	1,966	13,808	1,964	13,792	1,644	11,816	2	16
Federal Deposit Ins Corp	5,299	38,857	5,290	38,799	1,855	15,193	9	58
Federal Trade Comm.	1,053	7,440	1,053	7,440	899	6,298	—	—
General Svcs Admin	12,715	75,466	12,644	75,075	4,573	30,162	71	391
Natl Aero & Space Admin	19,555	130,166	19,536	130,004	4,402	30,534	19	162
Natl Fnd Arts & Humanities.	374	2,346	374	2,346	374	2,346	—	—
Nuclear Regulatory Comm	3,219	23,417	3,218	23,405	2,245	16,803	1	12
Peace Corps	1,057	5,751	656	3,486	531	2,978	401	2,265
Securities & Exch. Comm	3,870	32,036	3,870	32,036	2,290	18,719	—	—
Small Business Adm.	5,056	28,871	4,973	28,483	836	5,511	83	388
Smithsonian Inst.	5,021	22,846	4,996	22,678	4,611	20,732	25	168
Social Security Admin	65,362	300,391	64,903	298,578	1,724	8,725	459	1,813
Tennessee Valley Authority	12,796	133,853	12,796	133,853	7	48	—	—
U.S. Postal Service	772,980	2,970,178	769,198	2,954,204	17,119	76,348	3,782	15,974

NOTE: *Denotes figures that are preliminary or are based in whole or part on figures for the previous month. (1) Totals include agencies not listed. (2) Metropolitan Statistical Area.

U.S Median Weekly Earnings, 2nd Quarter 2005*

Source: Bureau of Labor Statistics, U.S. Dept. of Labor

	Total		Men		Women	
Age, Race, Hispanic or Latino ethnicity	**Number of workers (in thousands)**	**Median weekly earnings**	**Number of workers (in thousands)**	**Median weekly earnings**	**Number of workers (in thousands)**	**Median weekly earning**
ALL WORKERS, BY AGE						
16 years and over	103,332	$643	58,242	$713	45,090	$580
16 to 24 years	11,219	393	6,511	407	4,708	374
16 to 19 years	1,718	311	995	319	723	300
20 to 24 years	9,501	408	5,516	421	3,985	389
25 years and over	92,113	688	51,730	762	40,382	608
25 to 54 years	77,459	685	43,812	756	33,647	608
25 to 34 years	24,861	604	14,471	628	10,390	574
35 to 44 years	27,101	728	15,537	804	11,564	620
45 to 54 years	25,497	743	13,803	848	11,694	636
55 years and over	14,654	707	7,919	806	6,735	605
55 to 64 years	12,761	732	6,904	841	5,857	624
65 years and over	1,893	534	1,015	593	878	499
WHITE[1]						
16 years and over	83,903	663	48,487	732	35,416	590
16 to 24 years	9,124	403	5,398	418	3,726	383
25 years and over	74,779	710	43,089	785	31,690	619
25 to 54 years	62,515	706	36,320	776	26,195	619
55 years and over	12,264	729	6,769	849	5,495	615
BLACK OR AFRICAN AMERICAN[1]						
16 years and over	12,293	518	5,882	565	6,411	487
16 to 24 years	1,406	327	744	331	662	323
25 years and over	10,887	565	5,138	602	5,749	511
25 to 54 years	9,458	564	4,468	599	4,990	512
55 years and over	1,429	575	670	621	759	498
ASIAN[1]						
16 years and over	4,697	743	2,580	810	2,118	664
16 to 24 years	274	437	161	459	113	384
25 years and over	4,423	765	2,418	841	2,005	677
25 to 54 years	3,742	779	2,086	856	1,656	687
55 years and over	681	687	332	742	349	627
HISPANIC AND LATINO[2]						
16 years and over	14,817	473	9,575	487	5,242	437
16 to 24 years	2,261	360	1,555	361	706	359
25 years and over	12,556	496	8,020	511	4,536	459
25 to 54 years	11,402	494	7,333	509	4,069	456
55 years and over	1,154	522	687	543	467	492
Occupation						
Managerial, professional, and related occupations	36,148	926	17,936	1,089	18,211	805
Management, business, and financial operations occupations	14,664	979	8,131	1,144	6,533	838
Professional and related occupations	21,484	894	9,805	1,054	11,679	785
Service occupations	14,217	406	6,937	473	7,281	371
Sales and office occupations	25,379	577	9,623	684	15,755	523
Sales and related occupations	10,460	624	5,806	744	4,655	495
Office and administrative support occupations	14,918	550	3,817	608	11,101	531
Natural resources, construction, and maintenance occupations	12,337	616	11,793	621	545	438
Farming, fishing, and forestry occupations	735	374	575	402	160	333
Construction and extraction occupations	7,061	595	6,873	599	188	406
Installation, maintenance, and repair occupations	4,542	692	4,344	693	197	659
Production, transportation, and material moving occupations	15,250	546	11,952	593	3,298	409
Production occupations	8,373	552	6,026	607	2,347	417
Transportation and material moving occupations	6,878	536	5,926	580	951	391

*Not seasonally adjusted; figures are for median usual weekly earnings of full-time wage and salary workers. (1) Persons who selected this race group only; persons who selected more than one race group are not included. (2) May be of any race.

Average Hours and Earnings of U.S. Production Workers, 1969-2004[1]

Source: Bureau of Labor Statistics, U.S. Dept. of Labor
(annual averages)

	Weekly hours	Hourly earnings	Weekly earnings		Weekly hours	Hourly earnings	Weekly earnings		Weekly hours	Hourly earnings	Weekly earnings
1969	37.5	$3.22	$120.75	1981	35.2	$7.43	$261.54	1993	34.3	$11.03	$378.40
1970	37.0	3.40	125.80	1982	34.7	7.86	272.74	1994	34.5	11.32	390.73
1971	36.8	3.63	133.58	1983	34.9	8.19	285.83	1995	34.3	11.64	399.53
1972	36.9	3.90	143.91	1984	35.1	8.48	297.65	1996	34.3	12.03	412.74
1973	36.9	4.14	152.77	1985	34.9	8.73	304.68	1997	34.5	12.49	431.25
1974	36.4	4.43	161.25	1986	34.7	8.92	309.52	1998	34.5	13.00	448.04
1975	36.0	4.73	170.28	1987	34.7	9.13	316.81	1999	34.3	13.47	462.49
1976	36.1	5.06	182.67	1988	34.6	9.43	326.28	2000	34.3	14.00	480.41
1977	35.9	5.44	195.30	1989	34.5	9.80	338.10	2001	34.0	14.53	493.20
1978	35.8	5.87	210.15	1990	34.3	10.19	349.29	2002	33.9	14.95	506.07
1979	35.6	6.33	225.35	1991	34.1	10.50	358.06	2003	33.7	15.35	517.30
1980	35.2	6.84	240.77	1992	34.2	10.76	367.83	2004	33.7	15.67	528.56

(1) Data refer to production workers in natural resources, mining and manufacturing, construction workers, and non-supervisory workers in the service industries. Figures may be revised.

Union Affiliation and Median Weekly Earnings of Wage and Salary Workers in the U.S., 1996, 2004

Source: Bureau of Labor Statistics, U.S. Dept. of Labor

	1996				2004			
SEX AND AGE	TOTAL	Members of unions[1]	Represented by unions[2]	Non-union	TOTAL	Members of unions[1]	Represented by unions[2]	Non-union
Total, 16 years and older	$490	$615	$610	$462	$638	$781	$776	$612
16 to 24 years	298	371	362	294	390	498	494	385
25 years and older	520	625	621	498	683	798	793	656
25 to 34 years	463	554	548	447	604	724	717	590
35 to 44 years	559	636	632	530	713	813	808	690
45 to 54 years	594	687	686	552	743	834	831	718
55 to 64 years	535	620	616	505	725	835	835	693
65 years and older	384	510	510	367	560	728	744	520
Men, 16 years and older	557	653	651	520	713	829	828	685
16 to 24 years	307	375	369	303	400	504	496	395
25 years and older	599	669	668	580	762	846	846	743
25 to 34 years	499	591	587	485	639	751	748	620
35 to 44 years	632	683	683	617	804	868	865	787
45 to 54 years	698	718	721	682	857	878	881	847
55 to 64 years	643	667	664	633	843	870	877	829
65 years and older	477	589	593	424	641	753	776	620
Women, 16 years and older	418	549	543	398	573	723	719	541
16 to 24 years	284	358	339	280	375	487	491	370
25 years and older	444	560	555	420	599	733	730	580
25 to 34 years	415	497	495	405	561	678	665	541
35 to 44 years	463	561	556	439	608	735	733	590
45 to 54 years	481	620	616	445	625	758	755	604
55 to 64 years	420	524	523	395	615	767	767	592
65 years and older	334	417	413	321	478	687	733	455

Note: Data refer to the sole or principal job of full-time workers. Excluded are self-employed workers regardless of whether or not their businesses are incorporated. (1) Including members of an employee association similar to a union. (2) Including members of a labor union or employee association similar to a union, and others whose jobs are covered by a union or an employee-association contract.

Work Stoppages (Strikes and Lockouts) in the U.S., 1950-2004[1]

Source: Bureau of Labor Statistics, U.S. Dept. of Labor; involving 1,000 workers or more

Year	Number[1]	Workers (thous.)	Days idle (thous.)	Year	Number[1]	Workers (thous.)	Days idle (thous.)	Year	Number[1]	Workers (thous.)	Days idle (thous.)
1950	424	1,698	30,390	1979	235	1,021	20,409	1992	35	364	3,989
1955	363	2,055	21,180	1980	187	795	20,844	1993	35	182	3,981
1960	222	896	13,260	1981	145	729	16,908	1994	45	322	5,020
1965	268	999	15,140	1982	96	656	9,061	1995	31	192	5,771
1970	381	2,468	52,761	1983	81	909	17,461	1996	37	273	4,889
1971	298	2,516	35,538	1984	62	376	8,499	1997	29	339	4,497
1972	250	975	16,764	1985	54	324	7,079	1998	34	387	5,116
1973	317	1,400	16,260	1986	69	533	11,861	1999	17	73	1,996
1974	424	1,796	31,809	1987	46	174	4,481	2000	39	394	20,419
1975	235	965	17,563	1988	40	118	4,381	2001	29	99	1,151
1976	231	1,519	23,962	1989	51	452	16,996	2002	19	46	660
1977	298	1,212	21,258	1990	44	185	5,926	2003	14	129	4,091
1978	219	1,006	23,774	1991	40	392	4,584	2004	17	171	3,344

(1) Numbers cover stoppages that began in the year indicated. Workers are counted more than once if they are involved in more than 1 stoppage during the year. For work stoppages still open at the end of a calendar year, days idle include only the days for the calendar year.

Work Stoppages Involving 5,000 Workers or More Beginning in 2004

The number of work stoppages, and of workers idled because of strikes and lockouts in the U.S. rose in 2004, but was still low by historical standards. The number of days of idleness declined. There were 17 major work stoppages beginning in 2004, idling 170,000 workers and resulting in 3.3 million workdays lost. There were 6 stoppages in which more than 5,000 workers participated. The largest by far involved the Communications Workers of America (CWA) and SBC Communications, Inc, which lasted from May 21-24. That stoppage involved more than 102,000 workers and accounted for 204,000 workdays lost.

IT'S A FACT: In 2004, two groups—education, training, and library occupations; and protective service occupations (firefighters and police officers)—had the highest union membership rates, with 37% each.

U.S. Union Membership, 1930-2004

Source: Bureau of Labor Statistics, U.S. Dept. of Labor; figures in thousands

Year	Total employed[1]	% in unions	Union members[2]	Year	Total employed[1]	% in unions	Union members[2]	Year	Total employed[1]	% in unions	Union members[2]
1930....	29,424	11.6	3,401	1975....	76,945	25.5	19,611	1996...	111,960	14.5	16,269
1935....	27,053	13.2	3,584	1980....	90,564	21.9	19,843	1997...	114,533	14.1	16,110
1940....	32,376	26.9	8,717	1985....	94,521	18.0	16,996	1998...	116,730	13.9	16,211
1945....	40,394	35.5	14,322	1990....	103,905	16.1	16,740	1999...	118,963	13.9	16,477
1950....	45,222	31.5	14,267	1991....	102,786	16.1	16,568	2000...	120,786	13.5	16,258
1955....	50,675	33.2	16,802	1992....	103,688	15.8	16,390	2001...	122,482	13.4	16,387
1960....	54,234	31.4	17,049	1993....	105,067	15.8	16,598	2002[3]...	121,826	13.3	16,145
1965....	60,815	28.4	17,299	1994....	107,989	15.5	16,748	2003[4]...	122,358	12.9	15,776
1970....	70,920	27.3	19,381	1995....	110,038	14.9	16,360	2004[4]...	123,554	12.5	15,472

(1) Does not include agricultural employment; from 1985, does not include self-employed or unemployed persons. (2) From 1930 to 1980, includes dues-paying members of traditional trade unions, regardless of employment status; after that includes employed only. From 1985, includes members of employee associations that engage in collective bargaining with employers. (3) Revised to incorporate changes to the class of worker status associated with the introduction of the 2002 Census industry and occupational classification systems into the Current Population Survey. (4) Data reflect revised population controls used in the household survey.

Labor Union Directory

Source: Bureau of Labor Statistics, U.S. Dept. of Labor; AFL-CIO; World Almanac research.

(#) Member of Change to Win Coalition formed in 2005 by unions disaffiliated from AFL-CIO. (*) Independent union. All others are affiliated with AFL-CIO. Year established in parenthesis.

Air Line Pilots Association, (1931); 64,000+ members, 42 airlines; www.alpa.org

American Federation of Labor & Congress of Industrial Organizations (AFL-CIO), (1955); 9 mil. members; www.aflcio.org

Automobile, Aerospace & Agricultural Implement Workers of America, International Union, United (UAW), (1935); 710,000 active (500,000 ret.) members, 950+ locals; www.uaw.org

Bakery, Confectionery, Tobacco Workers and Grain Millers International Union (BCTGM), (1886); 120,000 members; www.bctgm.org

Boilermakers, Iron Ship Builders, Blacksmiths, Forgers and Helpers, International Brotherhood of (IBBISB/BF&H), (1880); 100,000+ members, 420 locals; www.boilermakers.org

Bricklayers and Allied Craftworkers, International Union of (BAC), (1865); 100,000 members, 200 locals; www.bacweb.org

#Carpenters and Joiners of America, United Brotherhood of, (1881); 520,000 members, 1,000 locals; www.carpenters.org

#Change to Win Coalition, (2005); 7 unions, 6 ex-affiliates unions of AFL-CIO, 1 independent; www.changetowin.org

***Communications Workers of America (IUE-CWA),** (1938); 700,000+ members, 1,200 locals; www.cwaunion.org

***Education Association, National,** (1857); 2.7 mil. members, 14,000+ affiliates; www.nea.org

Electrical Workers, International Brotherhood of (IBEW), (1891); 750,000 members, 1,019 locals; www.ibew.org

Engineers, International Union of Operating (IUOE), (1896); 400,000 members, 170 locals; www.iuoe.org

#Farm Workers of America, United (UFW), (1962); 27,000+ members; www.ufw.org

***Federal Employees, Federal District 1, National Federation of (NFFE FD1, IAMAW, AFL-CIO),** (1917); 70,000 members, 200 locals; www.nffe.org

Fire Fighters, International Association of, (1918); 263,000 members, 2,900 locals; www.iaff.org

Flight Attendants, Association of, (1945); 46,000 members, 22 carriers; www.afanet.org

#Food and Commercial Workers International Union, United (UFCW), (1979); 1.4 mil. members, 997 locals; www.ufcw.org

Glass, Molders, Pottery, Plastics & Allied Workers Intl. Union (GMP), (1842); 51,000 members, 290+ locals; www.gmpiu.org

Government Employees, American Federation of (AFGE), (1932); 600,000 members, 1,100 locals; www.afge.org

Graphic Communications International Union (GCIU), (1983); 150,000 members, 321 locals; www.gciu.org

Iron Workers, International Association of Bridge, Structural, Ornamental and Reinforcing, (1896); 127,000 members, 225 locals; www.ironworkers.org

#Laborers' International Union of North America (LIUNA), (1903); 800,000 members, 500 locals; www.liuna.org

Letter Carriers, National Association of (NALC), (1889); 300,000+ members, 2,500+ locals; www.nalc.org

Locomotive Engineers and Trainmen, Brotherhood of (BLET), (1863); 59,000 members, 600+ divisions; www.ble.org

Longshoremen's Association, International (ILA), (1892); 65,000 members; www.ilaunion.org

Machinists and Aerospace Workers, International Association of (IAMAW), (1888); 614,000 members, 1,174 locals; www.iamaw.org

Maintenance of Way Employees, Brotherhood of (BMWE), (1887); 45,000 members, 770 locals; www.bmwe.org

Mine Workers of America, United (UMWA), (1890); 110,000 members, 600 locals; www.umwa.org

Musicians of the United States and Canada, American Federation of (AFM), (1896); 125,000 members, 250+ locals; www.afm.org

Newspaper Guild-Communications Workers of America (CWA), The, (1933); 34,000 members, 90 locals; www.newsguild.org

***Nurses Association, American (ANA),** (1897); 2.6 mil. members, 54 constituent state & territorial assns; www.nursingworld.org

Office and Professional Employees International Union (OPEIU), (1945); 145,000 members, 200 locals; www.opeiu.org

PACE International Union, AFL-CIO, CLC (PACE), (1884); 320,000 members, 1,500 locals; www.paceunion.org

Painters and Allied Trades, International Union of (IUPAT), (1887); 140,000 members, 425 locals; www.ibpat.org

Plumbing and Pipe Fitting Industry of the United States and Canada, United Association of Journeymen and Apprentices of the, (1889); 326,000 members, 321 locals; www.ua.org

***Police, National Fraternal Order of,** 321,000 members, 2,100+ affiliates; www.grandlodgefop.org

Police Associations, International Union of, (1979); 80,000 members, 500 locals; www.iupa.org

Postal Workers Union, American (APWU), (1971); 333,000+ members, 1,600+ locals; www.apwu.org

Roofers, Waterproofers & Allied Workers, United Union of, (1906); 22,000 members; www.unionroofers.com

***Rural Letter Carriers' Association, National,** (1903); 100,000+ members; 50 state org; www.nrlca.org

Seafarers International Union of North America (SIU), (1938); 80,000 members, 18 affiliates; www.seafarers.org

***Security, Police, and Fire Professionals of America (SPFPA),** (1948); 12,000 members, 200 locals; www.spfpa.org

#Service Employees International Union (SEIU), (1921); 1.6 million members, 350 locals; www.seiu.org

Sheet Metal Workers' International Association (SMWIA), (1888); 150,000 members, 194 locals; www.smwia.org

State, County, and Municipal Employees, American Federation of (AFSCME), 1.4 mil. members, 3,617 locals; www.afscme.org

Steelworkers of America, United (USWA), (1936); 1.2 mil. members, 1,800 locals; www.uswa.org

Teachers, American Federation of (AFT), (1916); 1.3 mil. members, 3,000 locals; www.aft.org

#Teamsters, International Brotherhood of (IBT), (1903); 1.4 mil. members, 521 locals; www.teamsters.org

Television and Radio Artists, American Federation of, (AFTRA) (1937); 80,000 members, 33 locals; www.aftra.org

Theatrical Stage Employees, Moving Picture Technicians, Artists and Allied Crafts of the United States, Its Territories, and Canada, International Alliance of (IATSE), (1893); 105,000+ members, 555+ locals; www.iatse-intl.org

Transit Union, Amalgamated (ATU), (1892); 180,000+ members, 273 locals; www.atu.org

Transportation-Communications International Union (TCU), (1899); 100,000 members; www.tcunion.org

Transportation Union, United (UTU), (1969); 125,000 members, 680 locals; www.utu.org

Transport Workers Union of America, (1934); 110,000 members, 92 locals; www.twu.org

***Treasury Employees Union, National (NTEU),** (1938); 150,000+ represented, 270+ chapters; www.nteu.org

#UNITE HERE, UNITE, (1900), HERE, (1891); unions merged 2004; 440,000+ members, www.unitehere.org

ENERGY

U.S. Energy Overview, 1960-2004

Source: Energy Information Administration, U.S. Dept. of Energy, *Annual Energy Review 2004;* in quadrillion Btu

	1960	1965	1970	1975	1980	1985	1990	1995	2000	2003	2004[P]
Production	**42.80**	**50.68**	**63.50**	**61.36**	**67.24**	**67.65**	**70.77**	**71.18**	**71.27**	**70.01**	**70.37**
Fossil fuels	39.87	47.23	59.19	54.73	59.01	57.54	58.53	57.44	57.25	55.97	56.02
Coal	10.82	13.06	14.61	14.99	18.60	19.33	22.46	22.03	22.62	21.97	22.69
Natural gas (dry)	12.66	15.78	21.67	19.64	19.91	16.98	18.33	19.08	19.66	19.63	19.34
Crude oil[1]	14.93	16.52	20.40	17.73	18.25	18.99	15.57	13.89	12.36	12.03	11.53
Natural gas plant liquids (NGPL)	1.46	1.88	2.51	2.37	2.25	2.24	2.18	2.44	2.61	2.35	2.47
Nuclear electric power	0.01	0.04	0.24	1.90	2.74	4.08	6.10	7.08	7.86	7.96	8.23
Hydroelectric pumped storage[2]	(3)	(3)	(3)	(3)	(3)	(3)	–0.04	–0.03	–0.06	–0.09	(3)
Renewable energy	2.93	3.40	4.08	4.72	5.49	6.03	6.13	6.67	6.16	6.08	6.12
Conventional hydroelectric power[4]	1.61	2.06	2.63	3.15	2.90	2.97	3.05	3.21	2.81	2.82	2.73
Wood, waste, alcohol[5]	1.32	1.33	1.43	1.50	2.48	2.86	2.66	3.07	2.91	2.74	2.85
Geothermal energy	(*)	(*)	0.01	0.07	0.11	0.20	0.34	0.29	0.32	0.34	0.34
Solar	NA	NA	NA	NA	NA	(*)	0.06	0.07	0.07	0.06	0.06
Wind	NA	NA	NA	NA	NA	(*)	0.03	0.03	0.06	0.11	0.14
Imports	**4.19**	**5.89**	**8.34**	**14.03**	**15.80**	**11.78**	**18.82**	**22.26**	**28.97**	**31.11**	**33.00**
Coal	0.01	(*)	(*)	0.02	0.03	0.05	0.07	0.24	0.31	0.63	0.68
Natural gas	0.16	0.47	0.85	0.98	1.01	0.95	1.55	2.90	3.87	4.10	4.36
All crude oil and petroleum prods.[6]	4.00	5.40	7.47	12.95	14.66	10.61	17.12	18.88	24.53	26.22	27.68
Other[7]	0.02	0.01	0.02	0.08	0.10	0.17	0.08	0.24	0.26	0.17	0.29
Exports	**1.48**	**1.83**	**2.63**	**2.32**	**3.69**	**4.20**	**4.75**	**4.51**	**4.01**	**4.07**	**4.43**
Coal	1.02	1.38	1.94	1.76	2.42	2.44	2.77	2.32	1.53	1.12	1.25
Natural gas	0.01	0.03	0.07	0.07	0.05	0.06	0.09	0.16	0.25	0.70	0.86
All crude oil and petroleum prods.[6]	0.43	0.39	0.55	0.44	1.16	1.66	1.82	1.99	2.15	2.15	2.21
Other[7]	0.01	0.03	0.08	0.05	0.07	0.04	0.07	0.05	0.08	0.10	0.11
Consumption	**45.09**	**54.02**	**67.84**	**72.00**	**78.29**	**76.47**	**84.70**	**91.25**	**98.96**	**98.31**	**99.74**
Fossil fuels	42.14	50.58	63.52	65.35	69.98	66.22	72.46	77.49	84.96	84.49	85.65
Coal	9.84	11.58	12.26	12.66	15.42	17.48	19.17	20.09	22.58	22.32	22.39
Coal coke net imports	–0.01	–0.02	–0.06	0.01	–0.04	–0.01	0.00	0.06	0.07	0.05	0.14
Natural gas[8]	12.39	15.77	21.80	19.95	20.39	17.83	19.73	22.78	23.92	23.07	22.99
Petroleum[9]	19.92	23.25	29.52	32.73	34.20	30.92	33.55	34.55	38.40	39.05	40.13
Nuclear electric power	0.01	0.04	0.24	1.90	2.74	4.08	6.10	7.08	7.86	7.96	8.23
Hydroelectric pumped storage[2]	(3)	(3)	(3)	(3)	(3)	(3)	–0.04	–0.03	–0.06	–0.09	(3)
Renewable energy	2.93	3.40	4.08	4.72	5.49	6.03	6.13	6.67	6.16	6.08	6.12
Conventional hydroelectric power[4]	1.61	2.06	2.63	3.15	2.90	2.97	3.05	3.21	2.81	2.82	2.73
Geothermal energy	(*)	(*)	0.01	0.07	0.11	0.20	0.34	0.29	0.32	0.34	0.34
Wood, waste, alcohol[5]	1.32	1.33	1.43	1.50	2.48	2.86	2.66	3.07	2.91	2.74	2.85
Solar energy	NA	NA	NA	NA	NA	(*)	0.06	0.07	0.07	0.06	0.06
Wind energy	NA	NA	NA	NA	NA	(*)	0.03	0.03	0.06	0.11	0.14

(1) Incl. lease condensate. (2) Total pumped storage facility production minus energy used for pumping. (3) Included in conventional hydroelectric power. (4) Starting in 1990, pumped storage is removed and expanded coverage of industrial use of hydroelectric power is included. (5) Substituted in 2000 for former "Biofuels" category; figures for 1960-99 were recalculated. Alcohol is ethanol blended into motor gasoline. Ethanol is included in both "Petroleum" and "Wood, Waste, Alcohol" categories, but is only counted once in totals. (6) Incl. imports of crude oil for the Strategic Petroleum Reserve, which began in 1977. (7) Coal coke and small amts. of electricity transmitted across borders with Canada and Mexico. (8) Incl. supplemental gaseous fuels. (9) Petroleum products supplied, incl. natural gas plant liquids and crude oil burned as fuel. NA = Not available. P = preliminary. (*) = Less than 0.005 quadrillion Btu. **Note:** Some figures here have been revised. Some totals may not add because of rounding.

U.S. Energy Flow, 2004[1]

Source: Energy Information Administration, U.S. Dept. of Energy, *Annual Energy Review 2004*; in quadrillion Btu

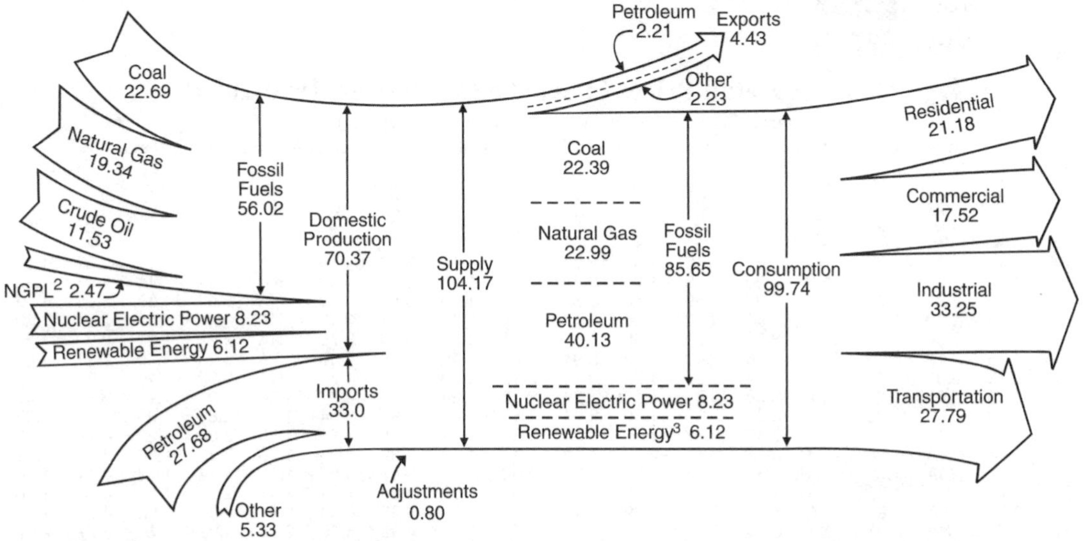

(1) Preliminary figures. (2) Natural Gas Plant Liquids. (3) Conventional hydroelectric power; wood, waste, and ethanol blended into gasoline; geothermal; solar; and wind power. **Note:** Some totals may not add because of rounding.

World Energy Consumption and Production Trends, 2003

Source: Energy Information Administration, U.S. Dept. of Energy, International Energy Database, Sept. 2005

The world's **consumption** of primary energy—petroleum, natural gas, coal, net hydroelectric, nuclear, geothermal, solar, wind, and wood and waste electric power, and other wood and waste increased from 397 quadrillion Btu in 2000, 404 in 2001, 412 in 2002, and 422 in 2003.

The 30 countries of the Organization for Economic Cooperation and Development (OECD), which include some of the world's largest economies (United States, Japan, and Germany), continued to dominate global energy use. OECD nations accounted for 60% of the world's primary energy consumption in 2003.

World **production** of primary energy increased from 405 quadrillion Btu in 2002 to 418 in 2003. World production of petroleum in 2003 was about 76.7 million barrels per day, or 159 quadrillion Btu; petroleum remained the most heavily used source of energy.

In 2003, 3 countries—U.S., Russia, and China—were the world's leading producers (39%) and consumers (41%) of energy. Russia and the U.S. together supplied 29% of the world total. The U.S. alone accounted for 23% of the world's energy consumption. The U.S. consumed 40% more energy than it produced—an imbalance of 28 quadrillion Btu. Energy consumption in China has increased rapidly in recent years, from 38.8 quadrillion Btu in 2000 to 45.5 in 2003, a 17% increase, and up 70% from 27.0 quadrillion Btu in 1990.

World's Major Consumers of Primary Energy, 2003

Source: Energy Information Administration, Dept. of Energy, *International Energy Annual 2003,* July 2005; quadrillion Btu

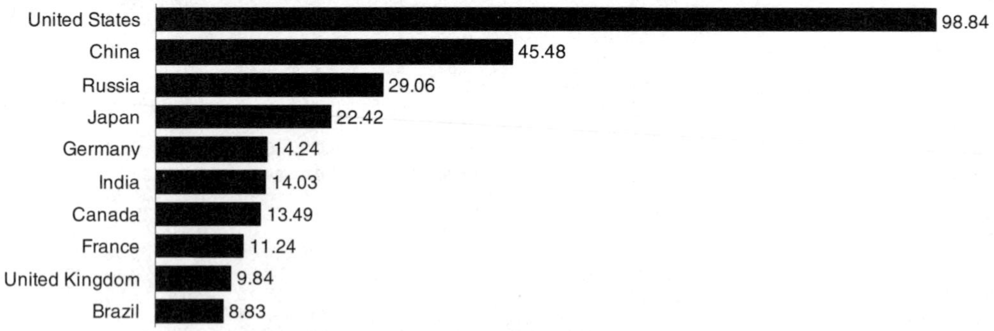

World's Major Producers of Primary Energy, 2003

Source: Energy Information Administration, Dept. of Energy, *International Energy Annual 2003,* July 2005; quadrillion Btu

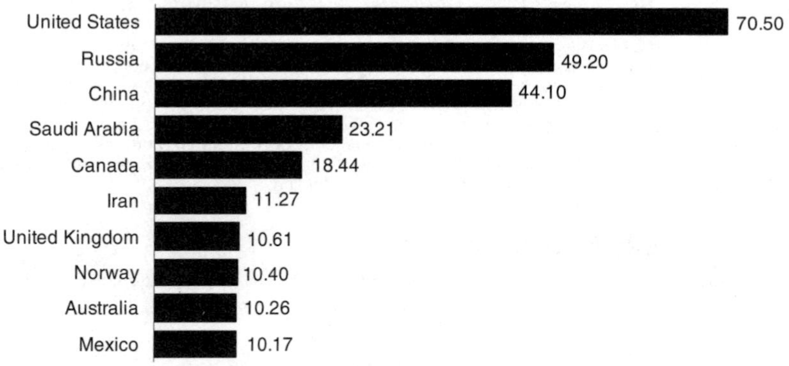

Gasoline Retail Prices in Selected Countries, 1990-2004

Source: Energy Information Administration, U.S. Dept. of Energy

(average price of unleaded regular gas unless otherwise noted; in dollars per gallon, including taxes)

Year	Australia	Brazil	Canada	China	Germany	Japan	Mexico	S. Korea	Taiwan	U.S.	France*	Italy*	S. Africa*	Spain*	Thailand*	UK*	U.S.*
1990	NA	$3.82	$1.87	NA	$2.65	$3.16	$1.00	$2.05	$2.49	$1.16	$3.63	$4.59	NA	NA	NA	$2.82	$1.35
1991	$1.96	2.91	1.92	NA	2.90	3.46	1.30	2.49	2.39	1.14	3.45	4.50	NA	NA	NA	3.01	1.32
1992	1.89	2.92	1.73	NA	3.27	3.59	1.50	2.65	2.42	1.13	3.57	4.53	NA	$3.50	$1.35	3.06	1.32
1993	1.73	2.40	1.57	NA	3.07	4.02	1.56	2.88	2.27	1.11	3.41	3.68	NA	3.01	1.26	2.84	1.30
1994	1.84	2.80	1.45	$0.96	3.52	4.39	1.48	2.87	2.14	1.11	3.59	3.70	NA	2.99	1.21	2.99	1.31
1995	1.95	2.16	1.53	1.03	3.96	4.43	1.12	2.94	2.23	1.15	4.26	4.00	NA	3.24	1.26	3.21	1.34
1996	2.12	2.31	1.61	1.03	3.94	3.65	1.26	3.18	2.15	1.23	4.41	4.39	NA	3.32	1.49	3.34	1.41
1997	2.05	2.61	1.62	1.07	3.53	3.27	1.47	3.34	2.23	1.23	4.00	4.07	$1.72	3.01	1.27	3.83	1.42
1998	1.63	2.80	1.38	0.95	3.34	2.83	1.50	3.04	1.86	1.06	3.87	3.84	1.51	2.80	1.09	4.06	1.25
1999	1.72	NA	1.52	0.95	3.42	3.27	1.80	3.80	1.86	1.17	3.85	3.87	1.55	2.82	1.22	4.29	1.36
2000	1.94	NA	1.86	1.06	3.45	3.65	2.02	4.18	2.15	1.51	3.80	3.77	1.78	2.86	1.38	4.58	1.69
2001	1.71	NA	1.72	NA	3.40	3.27	2.21	3.76	2.02	1.46	3.51	3.57	1.59	2.74	1.33	4.14	1.66
2002	1.76	NA	1.70	NA	3.67	3.15	2.25	3.84	1.93	1.36	3.62	3.74	1.41	2.90	1.35	4.16	1.56
2003	2.20	NA	1.99	NA	4.59	3.47	2.09	4.12	2.16	1.59	4.35	4.53	1.91	3.50	1.52	4.70	1.78
2004	2.72	NA	2.37	NA	5.24	3.93	NA	4.51	2.46	1.88	4.99	5.30	2.58	4.09	NA	5.57	2.07

NA = Not available. *Premium unleaded gasoline. **Note:** Some countries report only premium averages and some do not sell unleaded regular gasoline.

Gasoline Retail Prices, U.S. City Average, 1974-2005

Source: Energy Information Administration, U.S. Dept. of Energy, *Monthly Energy Review,* Aug. 2005
(cents per gallon, including taxes)

AVERAGE	Leaded regular	Unleaded regular	Unleaded premium	All types[1]	AVERAGE	Leaded regular	Unleaded regular	Unleaded premium	All types[1]
1974	53.2	NA	NA	NA	1990	114.9	116.4	134.9	121.7
1975	56.7	NA	NA	NA	1991	NA	114.0	132.1	119.6
1976	59.0	61.4	NA	NA	1992	NA	112.7	131.6	119.0
1977	62.2	65.6	NA	NA	1993	NA	110.8	130.2	117.3
1978	62.6	67.0	NA	65.2	1994	NA	111.2	130.5	117.4
1979	85.7	90.3	NA	88.2	1995	NA	114.7	133.6	120.5
1980	119.1	124.5	NA	122.1	1996	NA	123.1	141.3	128.8
1981[2]	131.1	137.8	147.0[3]	135.3	1997	NA	123.4	141.6	129.1
1982	122.2	129.6	141.5	128.1	1998	NA	105.9	125.0	111.5
1983	115.7	124.1	138.3	122.5	1999	NA	116.5	135.7	122.1
1984	112.9	121.2	136.6	119.8	2000	NA	151.0	169.3	156.3
1985	111.5	120.2	134.0	119.6	2001	NA	146.1	165.7	153.1
1986	85.7	92.7	108.5	93.1	2002	NA	135.8	157.8	144.1
1987	89.7	94.8	109.3	95.7	2003	NA	159.1	177.7	163.8
1988	89.9	94.6	110.7	96.3	2004	NA	188.0	206.8	192.3
1989	99.8	102.1	119.7	106.0	2005 (Jan.-June)	NA	208.0	226.8	212.2

Until unleaded gas became available in 1976, leaded was the only type used in automobiles. Average retail prices (in cents per gallon) for selected years preceding those in the table above were as follows: 1950: .27; 1955: .29; 1960: .31; 1965: .31; 1970: .36. (1) Also includes types of motor gasoline not shown separately. (2) In Sept. 1981, the Bureau of Labor Statistics changed the weights in the calculation of average motor gasoline prices. Starting in Sept. 1981, gasohol is included in average for all types, and unleaded premium is weighted more heavily. (3) Based on Sept. through Dec. data only. **NOTE:** Geographic coverage for 1974-77 is 56 urban areas; for 1978 and later, 85 urban areas. NA = Not applicable.

U.S. Petroleum Trade, 1976-2005

Source: Energy Information Administration, U.S. Dept. of Energy, *Monthly Energy Review,* Aug. 2005
(in thousands of barrels per day; average for the year)

Year	Imports from Persian Gulf[1]	Total imports	Total exports	Net imports[2]	Petroleum products supplied[3]	Year	Imports from Persian Gulf[1]	Total imports	Total exports	Net imports[2]	Petroleum products supplied[3]
1976	1,840	7,313	223	7,090	17,461	1991	1,845	7,627	1,001	6,626	16,714
1977	2,448	8,807	243	8,565	18,431	1992	1,778	7,888	950	6,938	17,033
1978	2,219	8,363	362	8,002	18,847	1993	1,782	8,620	1,003	7,618	17,237
1979	2,069	8,456	471	7,985	18,513	1994	1,728	8,996	942	8,054	17,718
1980	1,519	6,909	544	6,365	17,056	1995	1,573	8,835	949	7,886	17,725
1981	1,219	5,996	595	5,401	16,058	1996	1,604	9,478	981	8,498	18,309
1982	696	5,113	815	4,298	15,296	1997	1,755	10,162	1,003	9,158	18,620
1983	442	5,051	739	4,312	15,231	1998	2,136	10,708	945	9,764	18,917
1984	506	5,437	722	4,715	15,726	1999	2,464	10,852	940	9,912	19,519
1985	311	5,067	781	4,286	15,726	2000	2,488	11,459	1,040	10,419	19,701
1986	912	6,224	785	5,439	16,281	2001	2,761	11,871	971	10,900	19,649
1987	1,077	6,678	764	5,914	16,665	2002	2,269	11,530	984	10,546	19,761
1988	1,541	7,402	815	6,587	17,283	2003	2,501	12,264	1,027	11,238	20,034
1989	1,861	8,061	859	7,202	17,325	2004	2,493	13,145	1,048	12,097	20,731
1990	1,966	8,018	857	7,161	16,988	2005[4]	2,335	13,367	1,290	12,078	20,573

(1) Bahrain, Iran, Iraq, Kuwait, Qatar, Saudi Arabia, and United Arab Emirates. (2) Net imports are total imports minus total exports. (3) Includes domestic production and imports minus change in stocks, refinery imports, and exports. (4) Annualized 6-month average, for Jan.-June 2005. **Notes:** Beginning in Oct. 1977, imports for the Strategic Petroleum Reserves are included. U.S. exports include shipments to U.S. territories; imports include receipts from U.S. territories. Totals may not add because of rounding. Some figures are revised.

Energy Consumption, Total and Per Capita, by State, 2001

Source: Energy Information Administration, U.S. Dept. of Energy, State Energy Data Report 2001; latest available

Total Consumption				Consumption Per Capita			
Rank/State	Trillion Btu	Rank/State	Trillion Btu	Rank/State	Million Btu	Rank/State	Million Btu
1. Texas	12,028.8	27. Colorado	1,270.0	1. Alaska	1,164.3	27. Washington	339.4
2. California	7,853.4	28. Mississippi	1,172.6	2. Wyoming	889.5	28. South Dakota	327.1
3. Florida	4,134.8	29. Iowa	1,150.7	3. Louisiana	783.6	29. Missouri	322.0
4. New York	4,134.6	30. Arkansas	1,106.3	4. North Dakota	639.5	30. Virginia	321.8
5. Ohio	3,982.3	31. Oregon	1,064.3	5. Texas	563.7	31. Pennsylvania	318.9
6. Pennsylvania	3,922.5	32. Kansas	1,043.7	6. Kentucky	462.1	32. Utah	318.2
7. Illinois	3,870.2	33. Connecticut	853.1	7. Indiana	457.3	33. North Carolina	316.1
8. Louisiana	3,499.5	34. West Virginia	761.7	8. Oklahoma	444.0	34. Michigan	311.8
9. Michigan	3,120.0	35. Alaska	736.6	9. Alabama	434.9	35. Illinois	309.2
10. Georgia	2,880.6	36. Utah	725.4	10. West Virginia	422.8	36. Oregon	306.5
11. Indiana	2,801.7	37. New Mexico	679.2	11. Arkansas	411.0	37. Nevada	300.5
12. North Carolina	2,590.5	38. Nevada	629.4	12. Mississippi	410.3	38. New Jersey	294.0
13. New Jersey	2,500.4	39. Nebraska	627.1	13. Montana	403.5	39. Dist. of Columbia	293.7
14. Virginia	2,314.6	40. Idaho	501.0	14. Iowa	392.4	40. Colorado	286.8
15. Tennessee	2,195.4	41. Maine	490.7	15. Kansas	386.5	41. Vermont	266.9
16. Washington	2,033.9	42. Wyoming	439.1	16. Tennessee	382.1	42. Maryland	263.8
17. Alabama	1,942.6	43. North Dakota	406.9	17. Maine	381.9	43. New Hampshire	255.9
18. Kentucky	1,879.5	44. Montana	365.6	18. South Carolina	381.5	44. Arizona	255.4
19. Wisconsin	1,863.4	45. New Hampshire	322.2	19. Idaho	379.2	45. Florida	252.8
20. Missouri	1,815.0	46. Delaware	292.5	20. New Mexico	371.3	46. Connecticut	248.5
21. Minnesota	1,744.5	47. Hawaii	282.2	21. Delaware	367.6	47. Massachusetts	242.0
22. South Carolina	1,548.8	48. South Dakota	248.0	22. Nebraska	364.8	48. Hawaii	230.3
23. Massachusetts	1,548.8	49. Rhode Island	227.3	23. Minnesota	349.9	49. California	227.4
24. Oklahoma	1,539.5	50. Dist. of Columbia	168.2	24. Ohio	349.8	50. NewYork	216.8
25. Maryland	1,420.4	51. Vermont	163.6	25. Wisconsin	344.7	51. Rhode Island	214.7
26. Arizona	1,353.0	**U.S.**	**96,275.3**	26. Georgia	343.1	**U.S.**	**337.7**

World Crude Oil and Natural Gas Reserves, Jan. 1, 2004

Sources: Energy Information Administration, U.S. Dept. of Energy, *U.S. Crude Oil, Natural Gas, and Natural Gas Liquids Reserves, Nov. 2004; Oil and Gas Journal (OGJ),* Dec. 2003; *World Oil (WO),* Sept. 2004

Region/Country	Crude oil (billion barrels)		Natural gas (trillion cubic feet)	
	OGJ	*WO*	*OGJ*	*WO*
North America	**216.5**	**41.5**	**263.1**	**268.9**
Canada	178.9[1]	5.0	59.1	59.1
Mexico	15.7	14.6	15.0	20.7
United States	21.9	21.9	189.0	189.0
Central & South America	**98.8**	**75.2**	**249.4**	**240.9**
Argentina	2.8	2.7	23.4	21.6
Barbados	(2)	NA	(2)	NA
Bolivia	0.4	0.5	24.0	27.6
Brazil	8.5	10.6	8.5	8.7
Chile	0.2	(2)	3.5	0.9
Colombia	1.8	1.5	4.5	4.0
Cuba	0.8	0.5	2.5	0.5
Ecuador	4.6	5.0	0.3	0.4
Guatemala	0.5	NA	0.1	NA
Peru	0.3	0.9	8.7	8.8
Suriname	0.1	NA	(2)	NA
Trinidad and Tobago	1.0	0.8	25.9	19.1
Venezuela	77.8	52.5	148.0	149.2
Western Europe	**18.4**	**16.4**	**185.1**	**170.1**
Austria	0.1	0.1	0.5	0.7
Croatia	0.1	0.1	0.9	0.9
Denmark	1.3	1.3	2.6	2.8
France	0.1	0.2	0.5	0.5
Germany	0.4	0.3	10.8	7.7
Greece	(2)	NA	(2)	NA
Ireland	(2)	NA	0.7	NA
Italy	0.6	0.5	8.0	4.8
Netherlands	0.1	0.1	62.0	55.1
Norway	10.4	9.4	74.8	74.7
Spain	0.2	NA	0.1	NA
Turkey	0.3	0.3	0.3	0.3
United Kingdom	4.7	4.3	22.2	21.8
Yugoslavia	0.1	NA	1.7	NA
Eastern Europe & Former U.S.S.R.	**79.2**	**89.0**	**1,964.2**	**2,693.2**
Albania	0.2	0.2	0.1	0.1
Azerbaijan	7.0	NA	30.0	NA
Belarus	0.2	NA	0.1	NA
Bulgaria	(2)	(2)	0.2	0.1
Czech Republic	(2)	(2)	0.1	0.1
Georgia	(2)	NA	0.3	NA
Hungary	0.1	0.1	1.2	2.4
Kazakhstan	9.0	NA	65.0	NA
Kyrgyzstan	(2)	NA	0.2	NA
Poland	0.1	0.3	5.8	6.2
Romania	1.0	0.5	3.6	5.0
Russia	60.0	65.4	1,680.0	2,340.5
Slovakia	(2)	NA	0.5	NA
Tajikistan	(2)	NA	0.2	NA
Turkmenistan	0.5	NA	71.0	NA
Ukraine	0.4	NA	39.6	NA
Uzbekistan	0.6	NA	66.2	NA
Middle East	**726.8**	**686.3**	**2,518.2**	**2,539.7**
Bahrain	0.1	NA	3.3	NA
Iran	125.8	105.0	940.0	935.0
Iraq	115.0	115.0	110.0	112.6
Israel	(2)	NA	1.4	NA
Jordan	(2)	NA	0.2	NA
Kuwait	99.0	99.4	55.5	56.6
Oman	5.5	5.7	29.3	31.0
Qatar	15.2	27.4	910.0	913.4
Saudi Arabia	261.9	261.8	231.1	238.5
Syria	2.5	2.4	8.5	18.0
United Arab Emirates	97.8	66.2	212.1	204.1
Yemen	4.0	2.9	16.9	17.0
Africa	**87.0**	**104.6**	**453.5**	**443.2**
Algeria	11.3	14.0	160.0	171.5
Angola	5.4	8.8	1.6	4.0
Cameroon	0.4	NA	3.9	NA
Congo, Rep. of	1.5	1.4	3.2	4.2
Congo, Dem. Rep. of.	0.2	NA	(2)	NA
Côte d'Ivoire	0.1	NA	1.1	NA
Egypt	3.7	3.6	58.5	7.1
Equatorial Guinea	(2)	1.3	1.3	3.4
Ethiopia	(2)	NA	0.9	NA
Gabon	2.5	2.3	1.2	3.4
Ghana	(2)	NA	0.8	NA
Libya	36.0	30.5	46.4	46.0
Mozambique	(2)	(2)	4.5	(2)
Namibia	(2)	(2)	2.2	(2)
Nigeria	25.0	33.0	159.0	180.0
Rwanda	(2)	NA	2.0	NA
Somalia	(2)	NA	0.2	NA
Sudan	0.6	6.3	3.0	4.0
Tanzania	(2)	NA	0.8	NA
Tunisia	0.3	0.5	2.8	2.6
Asia & Oceania	**38.3**	**37.7**	**445.1**	**449.9**
Afghanistan	(2)	NA	3.5	NA
Australia	3.5	4.0	90.0	142.9
Bangladesh	0.1	NA	10.6	NA
Brunei	1.4	1.1	13.8	8.3
China	18.3	15.5	53.3	47.9
India	5.4	4.0	30.1	14.6
Indonesia	4.7	5.5	90.3	67.7
Japan	0.1	NA	1.4	NA
Malaysia	3.0	3.1	75.0	57.6
Myanmar	0.1	0.2	10.0	10.9
New Zealand	0.1	0.1	1.3	1.5
Pakistan	0.3	0.3	26.8	28.2
Papua New Guinea	0.2	0.3	12.2	13.3
Philippines	0.2	0.1	3.8	2.2
Taiwan	(2)	NA	2.7	NA
Thailand	0.6	0.5	13.3	12.8
Vietnam	0.6	2.3	6.8	7.2
World Total	**1,265.0**	**1,050.7**	**6,078.6**	**6,805.8**

NOTE: NA=Not reported seperately, amounts included in totals. Totals may not add because of rounding. Data for Kuwait and Saudi Arabia include one-half of the reserves in the Neutral Zone between Kuwait and Saudi Arabia. All reserve figures except those for the former USSR and natural gas reserves in Canada are *proved reserves*. Former USSR and Canadian natural gas figures include amounts understood as *proved*, and some *probable reserves*. Totals may include small amounts not listed. (1) Figure includes 4.1 bil barrels of conventional crude oil and 174.4 bil barrels contained in Alberta's oil sands. (2) Less than 50 mil barrels of crude oil or less than 50 mil cubic feet of natural gas.

U.S. Production of Crude Oil by State, 2004

Source: Energy Information Administration, *Petroleum Supply Annual 2004*

(thousand barrels)

State	Total	State	Total	State	Total	State	Total
1. Texas[1]	392,867	9. North Dakota	31,154	17. Michigan	6,409	25. West Virginia	1,339
2. Alaska[1]	332,465	10. Montana	24,724	18. Ohio	5,785	26. Nevada	463
3. California[1]	240,206	11. Colorado	22,097	19. Florida	2,875	27. Tennessee	361
4. Louisiana[1]	83,411	12. Mississippi	17,153	20. Kentucky	2,548	28. New York	170
5. New Mexico	64,236	13. Utah	14,629	21. Pennsylvania	2,538	29. Missouri	88
6. Oklahoma	62,502	14. Illinois	10,984	22. Nebraska	2,507	30. Arizona	52
7. Wyoming	51,619	15. Alabama	7,443	23. Indiana	1,755	31. Virginia	19
8. Kansas	33,858	16. Arkansas	6,732	24. South Dakota	1,357	**US TOTAL**	**1,983,302**

(1) Includes the following offshore production (thous. bbls.): Alaska (104,205), California (15,654), Louisiana (9,681), Texas (638).

IT'S A FACT: Nationwide gasoline prices reached record-highs—over $3 per gallon according to American Automobile Association estimates—in the aftermath of Hurricane Katrina. The price of gas had never climbed that high before, but if historical gas prices were converted to 2005 dollars, the price of a gallon would have topped out at about $3.03 in 1981.

U.S. Crude Oil Imports by Selected Country, 1988-2005

Source: Energy Information Administration, *Petroleum Supply Monthly*, Aug. 2005; ranked by 2005 totals

(thousand barrels per day)

The United States has become increasingly dependent on foreign oil. From 1990 to 2005 (based on annualized Jan-June data for the latter year), total U.S. oil imports went up 73%. Over the same period, oil imports from OPEC countries increased 39%. The proportion of U.S. oil imports from OPEC nations has been declining, however; in 1998 they accounted for 60% of U.S. oil imports, while in 2005 they accounted for 48%. Although OPEC countries, especially in the Persian Gulf region, have a significant production advantage because of the relatively low cost of developing their oil resources, non-OPEC oil production has been rising year by year; North American dominated this growth in the early 1970s, the North Sea and Mexico became major producers in the 1980s, and more recent production increases have come from oil supplies in Latin America, West Africa, and the former Soviet Union.

	1988	1990	1995	1998	2000	2001	2002	2003	2004	2005[1]
Mexico	674	689	1,027	1,305	1,301	1,379	1,490	1,589	1,597	1,568
Canada	681	643	1,040	1,208	1,267	1,297	1,418	1,535	1,587	1,557
Saudi Arabia#	911	1,195	1,260	1,386	1,521	1,610	1,521	1,724	1,494	1,526
Venezuela#	439	666	1,151	1,357	1,223	1,281	1,195	1,193	1,294	1,329
Nigeria#	607	784	621	679	865	813	567	838	1,062	1,040
Iraq#	343	514	0	334	613	778	442	470	651	548
Angola	203	236	360	445	289	314	315	361	306	430
Ecuador[4]	33	38	96	96	126	108	99	138	228	289
Russia[2]	0	1	14	9	7	0	86	149	150	253
United Kingdom	254	155	341	155	272	226	406	347	235	227
Algeria#	58	63	27	17	1	11	30	113	214	195
Kuwait#	80	79	213	280	261	233	212	205	241	186
Colombia	106	140	207	327	308	245	233	163	138	142
Norway	62	96	258	221	292	267	335	164	146	139
Gabon[3]	15	64	229	204	142	138	143	131	142	120
Brazil	0	0	0	0	5	13	57	48	51	80
Trinidad and Tobago	NA	NA	NA	71	53	55	68	54	59	63
Argentina	71	76	62	53	56	51	68	67	49	66
China	82	77	53	25	34	13	21	13	12	23
Indonesia#	186	98	64	48	36	40	50	26	34	16
Malaysia	19	40	6	17	29	15	9	21	18	13
Australia	59	47	16	31	42	36	51	26	21	9
United Arab Emirates#	23	9	5	3	1	21	16	10	5	4
Non-OPEC	**2,411**	**2,381**	**3,889**	**4,335**	**4,361**	**4,336**	**4,996**	**5,055**	**4,994**	**5,297**
OPEC	**2,696**	**3,514**	**3,341**	**4,105**	**4,520**	**4,787**	**4,042**	**4,579**	**5,018**	**4,882**
Arab-OPEC[5]	**1,415**	**1,864**	**1,505**	**2,021**	**2,396**	**2,653**	**2,230**	**2,522**	**2,628**	**2,497**
TOTAL	**5,107**	**5,894**	**7,230**	**8,440**	**8,882**	**9,123**	**9,038**	**9,633**	**10,012**	**10,179**

#Denotes OPEC members. NA=Not available. (1) Jan.-June average. (2) May include oil from USSR states before 1992. (3) Gabon withdrew from OPEC Dec. 31, 1994. Imports after Jan. 1, 1995, appear in Non-OPEC totals. (4) Ecuador withdrew from OPEC Dec. 31, 1992. Imports after Jan. 1, 1993, appear in Non-OPEC totals. (5) Includes Algeria, Iraq, Kuwait, Libya, Qatar, Saudi Arabia, and United Arab Emirates.

World Nuclear Power Summary, 2004

Source: International Atomic Energy Agency, Power Reactor Information System, Dec. 31, 2004

Country	Reactors in operation: No. of units	Reactors in operation: Total MW(e)	Reactors under construction: No. of units	Reactors under construction: Total MW(e)	Nuclear electricity supplied in 2004: TW(e).h[1]	Nuclear electricity supplied in 2004: % of nation's total	Total operating experience[2]: Years	Total operating experience[2]: Months
Argentina	2	935	1	692	7.31	8.24	52	7
Armenia	1	376	—	—	2.21	38.83	37	3
Belgium	7	5,801	—	—	44.86	55.13	198	7
Brazil	2	1,901	—	—	11.54	3.00	27	3
Bulgaria	4	2,722	—	—	15.60	41.58	133	3
Canada	17	12,113	—	—	85.27	15.02	509	7
China	9	6,602	2	2,000	47.80	2.19	47	11
Czech Republic	6	3,548	—	—	26.32	31.22	80	10
Finland	4	2,656	—	—	21.78	26.59	103	4
France	59	63,363	—	—	426.80	78.08	1,405	2
Germany	18	20,679	—	—	158.39	32.11	666	0
Hungary	4	1,755	—	—	11.21	33.83	78	2
India	14	2,550	9	4,092	15.04	2.82	237	5
Iran	—	—	1	915	—	—	0	0
Japan	54	45,468	3	3,237	273.81	29.31	1,176	4
Korea, South	19	15,850	1	960	123.97	37.95	239	8
Lithuania	1	1,185	—	—	13.92	72.11	38	6
Mexico	2	1,310	—	—	10.58	5.20	25	11
Netherlands	1	449	—	—	3.61	3.79	59	0
Pakistan	2	425	—	—	1.93	2.37	37	10
Romania	1	655	1	655	5.14	10.08	8	6
Russia	31	21,743	4	3,775	133.02	15.61	791	5
Slovakia	6	2,442			15.62	55.18	106	6
Slovenia	1	656	—	—	5.20	38.85	23	3
South Africa	2	1,800	—	—	14.28	6.61	40	3
Spain	9	7,585	—	—	60.89	22.86	228	2
Sweden	11	9,451	—	—	75.04	51.82	322	1
Switzerland	5	3,220	—	—	25.43	40.04	148	10
Taiwan	6	4,884	2	2,600	37.94	20.93	140	1
Ukraine	15	13,107	2	1,900	81.81	51.11	293	6
United Kingdom	23	11,852	—	—	73.68	19.43	1,354	8
United States	104	99,210	—	—	788.56	19.95	2,975	8
TOTAL	**440**	**366,293**	**26**	**20,826**	**2,618.56**	**—**	**11,588**	**6**

(1) 1 terawatt-hour [TW(e).h] = 10^6 megawatt-hour [MW(e).h]. For an average power plant, 1 TW(e).h = 0.39 megatons of coal equivalent (input) and 0.23 megatons of oil equivalent (input). (2) Through Dec. 31, 2004.

Nations Most Reliant on Nuclear Energy, 2004

Source: International Atomic Energy Agency

(Nuclear electricity generation as % of total electricity generated)

Country	%	Country	%	Country	%	Country	%	Country	%
1. France	78.1	6. Ukraine	51.1	11. South Korea	37.9	16. Finland	26.6	21. Canada	15.0
2. Lithuania	72.1	7. Bulgaria	41.6	12. Hungary	33.8	17. Spain	22.9	22. Romania	10.1
3. Slovakia	55.2	8. Switzerland	40.0	13. Germany	32.1	18. **United States**	**19.9**	23. Argentina	8.2
4. Belgium	55.1	9. Armenia	38.8	14. Czech Republic	31.2	19. United Kingdom	19.4	24. South Africa	6.6
5. Sweden	51.8	Slovenia	38.8	15. Japan	29.3	20. Russia	15.6	25. Mexico	5.2

U.S. Nuclear Reactor Units and Power Plant Operations, 1980-2004

Source: Energy Information Administration, U.S. Dept. of Energy, Annual Energy Review 2004

	Number of reactor units									
	Licensed for operation		Construction permits							
	Operable	In startup	Granted	Pending	On order	Shutdowns	Total	Total design capacity (million KWs)	Nuclear-based electricity generation (million net KW-hrs)	Nuclear portion of domestic electricity generation (percent)
1980	71	1	82	12	3	0	168	162	251,116	11.0
1981	75	0	76	11	2	0	163	157	272,674	11.9
1982	78	2	60	3	2	1	144	134	282,773	12.6
1983	81	3	53	0	2	0	138	129	293,677	12.7
1984	87	6	38	0	2	0	132	123	327,634	13.5
1985	96	3	30	0	2	0	130	121	383,691	15.5
1986	101	7	19	0	2	0	128	119	414,038	16.6
1987	107	4	14	0	2	2	127	119	455,270	17.7
1988	109	3	12	0	0	0	123	115	526,973	19.5
1989	111	1	10	0	0	2	121	113	529,355	17.8
1990	112	0	8	0	0	1	119	111	576,862	19.0
1991	111	0	8	0	0	1	119	111	612,565	19.9
1992	109	0	8	0	0	2	117	111	618,776	20.1
1993	110	0	7	0	0	0	116	110	610,291	19.1
1994	109	0	7	0	0	1	116	110	640,440	19.7
1995	109	1	6	0	0	0	116	110	673,402	20.1
1996	109	0	6	0	0	1	116	110	674,729	19.6
1997	107	0	3	0	0	2	110	102	628,644	18.0
1998	104	0	3	0	0	3	107	99	673,702	18.6

From 1999 through 2004 the number of reactor units remained unchanged at 104, with no new permits and no shutdowns. Nuclear-based electricity generation increased from 728,254 mil net KW-hrs in 1999 to (prelim. figures) 788,556 mil net KW-hrs in 2004, representing 19.9% of domestic electricity generation.

Major U.S. Coal Producers[1]

Source: Energy Information Administration, U.S. Dept. of Energy, 2003

Rank	Company Name	Production (thousand short tons)	Percent of total production
1.	Peabody Coal Co.	156,845	14.6
2.	Kennecott Energy & Coal Co.	115,001	10.7
3.	Arch Coal, Inc.	107,731	10.1
4.	RAG American Coal Holding, Inc.	63,306	5.9
5.	CONSOL Energy Inc	58,499	5.5
6.	Vulcan Partners, L.P.	41,480	3.9
7.	A.T. Massey Coal Co., Inc.	39,719	3.7
8.	Horizon Natural Resources Inc.	32,742	3.1
9.	North American Coal Corp.	31,778	3.0
10.	Westmoreland Mining LLC	27,635	2.6
11.	TXU Corp.	24,386	2.3
12.	Black Beauty Coal Co.	19,895	1.9
13.	Robert Murray	19,407	1.8
14.	Alliance Coal, LLC	19,068	1.8
15.	Alpha Natural Resources., LLC	16,117	1.5
16.	BHP Minerals Group	14,326	1.3
17.	Pittsburg & Midway Coal Mining Co.	12,190	1.1
18.	PacifiCorp	9,543	0.9
19.	James River Coal Co.	9,357	0.9
20.	Wexford Capital LLC	8,880	0.8
	All Other Coal Producers	**243,849**	**22.9**
U.S. TOTAL		**1,071,753**	**100.0**

Note: The company is the firm controlling the coal, particularly the sale of the coal. (1) Preliminary.

Major U.S. Coal Mines[1]

Source: Energy Information Administration, U.S. Dept. of Energy, 2003

Rank	Mine Name/Company	Mine Type	State	Production (short tons)
1.	North Antelope Rochelle Complex/Powder River Coal Company	Surface	Wyoming	80,083,444
2.	Black Thunder/Thunder Basin Coal Company LLC	Surface	Wyoming	62,620,417
3.	Cordero Mine/Cordero Mining Co.	Surface	Wyoming	36,083,743
4.	Jacobs Ranch Mine/Jacobs Ranch Coal Company	Surface	Wyoming	35,491,218
5.	Antelope Coal Mine/Antelope Coal Company	Surface	Wyoming	29,533,072
6.	Eagle Butte Mine/RAG Coal West, Inc.	Surface	Wyoming	24,728,392
7.	North Rochelle/Triton Coal Company LLC	Surface	Wyoming	23,923,145
8.	Caballo Mine/Caballo Coal Company	Surface	Wyoming	22,743,284
9.	Belle Ayr Mine/RAG Coal West Inc.	Surface	Wyoming	17,844,826
10.	Buckskin Mine/Triton Coal Company	Surface	Wyoming	17,539,156
	All Other Mines			**578,552,030**
	U.S. TOTAL			**1,071,752,573**

Note: The company is the firm operating the mine. (1) Preliminary.

WORLD ALMANAC QUICK QUIZ

Texas was the largest crude oil producer among the 50 states as of 2004. Can you put these other states in order, from highest to lowest, by the amount of crude oil produced there in 2004?

(a) California (b) New Mexico (c) Alaska (d) Louisiana

For the answer look in this chapter, or see page 1008.

METEOROLOGY

National Weather Service Watches and Warnings

Source: National Weather Service, NOAA, U.S. Dept. of Commerce; *Glossary of Meteorology,* American Meteorological Society

The **National Weather Service** issues watches, warnings, and advisories for specific geographic areas to alert people to the possibility or imminent arrival of various forms of **severe weather**. A *Severe Thunderstorm* or *Tornado Watch* is issued for a specific area when a severe convective storm that usually covers a relatively small geographic area or moves in a narrow path is sufficiently intense to threaten life and/or property. Examples include thunderstorms with large hail, damaging winds, and/or tornadoes. Excessive *localized convective rains* are not classified as severe storms but are often the product of severe local storms. Such rainfall may result in phenomena that threaten life and property, such as *flash floods. Lightning* occurs with all thunderstorms and, along with flash floods, is a leading cause of storm deaths and injuries.

Severe Thunderstorm—a thunderstorm that produces a tornado, winds of at least 50 knots (58 mph), and/or hail at least ¾ inch in diameter. A *Severe Thunderstorm Watch* is issued for an area where such storms are most likely to develop. A *Severe Thunderstorm Warning* indicates that a severe thunderstorm has been sighted or indicated by radar.

Tornado—a violent rotating column of air, usually pendant to a cumulonimbus cloud, with circulation reaching the ground. A tornado nearly always starts as a funnel cloud and may be accompanied by a loud roaring noise. On a local scale, it is the most destructive of all atmospheric phenomena. Tornado paths range from a few feet to more than 100 miles long (avg. 5 mi) and from a few feet to more than 1 mile in diameter (avg. 220 yd); the average forward speed is 30 mph. Tornado watches and warnings follow the same criteria as those for thunderstorms.

Cyclone—an atmospheric circulation of winds rotating counterclockwise in the northern hemisphere and clockwise in the southern hemisphere. Tornadoes, hurricanes, and the lows shown on weather maps are all examples of cyclones of various size and intensity. Cyclones are usually accompanied by precipitation or stormy weather.

Subtropical Storm— a cyclone that develops over subtropical waters (N of 20° lat.) with one-minute sustained surface winds of 34 knots (39 mph) or more. It may form over warm or cold water, and can develop into a tropical storm or a hurricane.

Tropical Storm—a cyclone that develops over tropical waters (23.5° N-23.5° S lat.), with one-minute sustained surface winds within a range of 34 to 63 knots (39 to 73 mph). A *Tropical Storm Watch* is issued when tropical storm conditions pose a threat to specified coastal areas within 36 hours. A *Tropical Storm Warning* is issued when tropical storm conditions are expected in a specified coastal area in 24 hours or less.

Hurricane—a severe cyclone originating over tropical ocean waters and having one-minute sustained surface winds of 64 knots (74 mph) or higher. (West of the international date line, in the western Pacific, such storms are known as *typhoons*.) The area of hurricane-force winds forms a circle or an oval, sometimes as wide as 300 mi in diameter. In the lower latitudes, hurricanes usually move west or northwest at 10 to 15 mph. When the center approaches 25° to 30° N Lat., the direction of motion often changes to northeast, with increased forward speed. In the W Atlantic and E Pacific, hurricane season is June 1-Nov. 30. Hurricane watches and warnings follow the same criteria as those for tropical storms.

Winter Storm and Blizzard—A *Winter Storm Watch* is issued when conditions are favorable for hazardous winter weather, such as heavy snow, sleet, or freezing rain. A *Winter Storm Warning* is issued when hazardous winter weather conditions are imminent. A *Blizzard Warning* is issued for winter storm conditions with winds of 35 mph or higher and sufficient falling and/or blowing snow to frequently reduce visibility to less than ¼ mi. for at least 3 hours.

Flood—Flooding takes many forms. *River Flooding:* This occurs when rains, sometimes coupled with melting snow, fill river basins with too much water too quickly; torrential rains from decaying hurricanes or tropical systems can also be a major cause of river flooding. *Coastal Flooding:* Winds from tropical storms and hurricanes or intense offshore low pressure systems can drive ocean water inland and cause significant flooding. Coastal floods can also be produced by sea waves called *tsunamis,* sometimes referred to as tidal waves; these waves are produced by earthquakes or volcanic activity. *Flash Flooding:* Usually due to copious amounts of rain falling in a short time, flash flooding typically occurs within 6 hours of the rain event. Flash floods account for the majority of flood deaths in the U.S, and are the leading cause of deaths associated with thunderstorms. *Urban Flooding:* Urbanization significantly increases runoff over what would occur on natural terrain, making flash flooding in these areas extremely dangerous. Streets can become swift-moving rivers, and basements can fill with water. *Ice Jam Flooding:* Ice can accumulate at natural or artificial obstructions and stop the flow of water. As the water flow is stopped, water builds up and flooding can occur upstream. If the jam suddenly gives way, the gush of ice and water can cause downstream flash flooding.

A *Flash Flood or Flood Watch* means that flash flooding or flooding is possible within a designated area. A *Flash Flood or Flood Warning* means that flash flooding or flooding has been reported or is imminent; all necessary precautions should be taken immediately.

National Weather Service Marine Warnings and Advisories

Small Craft Advisory—alerts mariners to sustained (exceeding 2 hours) weather and/or sea conditions, present or forecast, potentially hazardous to small boats, including winds of 18 to 33 knots and/or dangerous wave conditions. The advisory is also issued for lower wind speeds that may affect small craft. Criteria vary depending on region and type of marine environment. Upon receiving a Small Craft Advisory, the mariner should immediately obtain the latest marine forecast for details.

Gale Warning—indicates that winds within the range 34 to 47 knots, not directly associated with a tropical storm, are forecast for the area.

Tropical Storm Warning—indicates that winds within the range of 34 to 63 knots associated with a tropical storm are forecast to occur within 24 hours or less.

Storm Warning—indicates that winds 48 knots or above, not directly associated with a tropical storm, are forecast for the area.

Hurricane Warning—indicates that winds 64 knots or greater associated with a hurricane are forecast for the area within 24 hours.

Special Marine Warning—indicates potentially hazardous weather conditions, usually of short duration (2 hours or less) and producing wind speeds of 34 knots or more, not adequately covered by existing marine warnings.

Primary sources of dissemination are commercial radio, TV, U.S. Coast Guard radio stations, and NOAA VHF-FM broadcasts. These NOAA broadcasts on 162.40 to 162.55 MHz can usually be received 20-40 mi from the transmitting antenna site.

IT'S A FACT: Storm surges, abnormal rising of sea levels due to high winds, are one of the deadliest and most destructive aspects of tropical storms and hurricanes. The highest storm surge ever recorded due to a tropical storm was the 42-foot surge that hit Bathurst Bay, Australia, in 1899. Storm surges from Hurricane Katrina reached 20-30+ feet near Biloxi and Gulfport, MS. The last storm surge to reach those heights was Hurricane Camille in 1969, which a brought 24.2-foot surge to the MS coast.

Monthly Normal Mean Temperatures, Normal Precipitation, U.S. Cities

Source: National Climatic Data Center, NESDIS, NOAA, U.S. Dept. of Commerce

Normals are averages covering a 30-year period. The temperature and precipitation normals given here are based on records for 1971-2000. Temperatures listed below represent means of the normal daily maximum and normal daily minimum temperatures for each month. For stations that did not have continuous records from the same site for the entire 30 years, the means have been adjusted to the record at the present site. (*) = city station. Other figures are for airport stations. T = temp. in Fahrenheit; P = precipitation in inches.

Station	Jan. T	Jan. P	Feb. T	Feb. P	Mar. T	Mar. P	Apr. T	Apr. P	May T	May P	June T	June P	July T	July P	Aug. T	Aug. P	Sept. T	Sept. P	Oct. T	Oct. P	Nov. T	Nov. P	Dec. T	Dec. P
Albany, NY	22	2.7	25	2.3	35	3.2	47	3.3	58	3.7	66	3.7	71	3.5	69	3.7	61	3.3	49	3.2	39	3.3	28	2.8
Albuquerque, NM	36	0.5	41	0.4	48	0.6	56	0.5	65	0.6	75	0.7	79	1.3	76	1.7	69	1.1	57	1.0	44	0.6	36	0.5
Anchorage, AK	16	0.7	19	0.7	26	0.7	36	0.5	47	0.7	55	1.1	58	1.7	56	2.9	48	2.9	34	2.1	22	1.1	18	1.1
Asheville, NC	36	3.1	39	3.2	46	3.9	54	3.2	62	3.5	69	3.2	73	3.0	72	3.3	66	3.0	55	2.4	46	2.9	39	2.6
Atlanta, GA	43	5.0	47	4.7	54	5.4	62	3.6	70	4.0	77	3.6	80	5.1	79	3.7	73	4.1	63	3.1	53	4.1	45	3.8
Atlantic City, NJ	32	3.6	34	2.9	42	4.1	51	3.5	61	3.4	70	2.7	75	3.9	74	4.3	66	3.1	55	2.9	46	3.3	37	3.2
Baltimore, MD	32	3.5	36	3.0	44	3.9	53	3.0	63	3.9	72	3.4	77	3.9	75	3.7	67	4.0	55	3.2	46	3.1	37	3.4
Barrow, AK	–14	0.1	–16	0.1	–14	0.1	–1	0.1	20	0.1	35	0.3	40	0.9	39	1.0	31	0.7	15	0.4	–1	0.2	–11	0.1
Birmingham, AL	43	5.5	47	4.2	55	6.1	61	4.7	69	4.8	76	3.8	80	5.1	80	3.5	74	4.1	63	3.2	53	4.6	46	4.5
Bismarck, ND	10	0.5	18	0.5	30	0.9	43	1.5	56	2.2	65	2.6	70	2.6	69	2.2	58	1.6	45	1.3	28	0.7	15	0.4
Boise, ID	30	1.4	37	1.1	44	1.4	51	1.3	59	1.3	67	0.7	75	0.4	74	0.3	64	0.8	53	0.8	40	1.4	31	1.4
Boston, MA	29	3.9	32	3.3	39	3.9	48	3.6	59	3.2	68	3.2	74	3.1	72	3.4	65	3.5	54	3.8	45	4.0	35	3.7
Buffalo, NY	25	3.2	26	2.4	34	3.0	45	3.0	57	3.4	66	3.8	71	3.1	69	3.9	62	3.8	51	3.2	40	3.9	30	3.8
Burlington, VT	18	2.2	20	1.7	31	2.3	44	2.9	57	3.3	66	3.4	71	4.0	68	4.0	59	3.8	48	3.1	37	3.1	25	2.2
Caribou, ME	10	3.0	13	2.1	25	2.6	38	2.6	52	3.3	61	3.3	66	3.9	63	4.2	54	3.3	43	3.0	31	3.1	16	3.2
Charleston, SC	48	4.1	51	3.1	58	4.0	64	2.8	72	3.7	78	5.9	82	6.1	81	6.9	76	6.0	66	3.1	58	2.7	51	3.2
Charleston, WV	33	3.3	37	3.2	45	3.9	54	3.3	62	4.3	70	4.1	74	4.9	73	4.1	66	3.5	55	2.7	46	3.7	38	3.3
Chicago, IL	22	1.8	27	1.6	37	2.7	48	3.7	59	3.4	68	3.6	73	3.5	72	4.6	64	3.3	52	2.7	39	3.0	27	2.4
Cleveland, OH	26	2.5	28	2.3	38	2.9	48	3.4	59	3.5	68	3.9	72	3.5	70	3.7	63	3.8	52	2.7	42	3.4	31	3.1
Columbus, OH	28	2.5	32	2.2	42	2.9	52	3.3	63	3.9	71	4.1	75	4.6	74	3.7	67	2.9	55	2.3	44	3.2	34	2.9
Dallas–Ft. Worth, TX	44	1.9	49	2.4	57	3.1	65	3.2	73	5.2	81	3.2	85	2.1	84	2.0	78	2.4	67	4.1	55	2.6	47	2.6
Denver, CO	29	0.5	33	0.5	40	1.3	48	1.9	57	2.3	68	1.6	73	2.2	72	1.8	62	1.1	51	1.0	38	1.0	30	0.6
Des Moines, IA	20	1.0	27	1.2	38	2.2	51	3.6	62	4.3	71	4.6	76	4.2	74	4.5	65	3.2	53	2.6	38	2.1	25	1.3
Detroit, MI	25	1.9	27	1.9	37	2.5	48	3.1	60	3.1	69	3.6	74	3.2	72	3.1	64	3.3	52	2.2	41	2.7	30	2.5
Dodge City, KS	30	0.6	36	0.7	44	1.8	54	2.3	64	3.0	74	3.2	80	3.2	78	2.7	69	1.7	57	1.5	42	1.0	33	0.8
Duluth, MN	8	1.1	15	0.8	25	1.7	39	2.1	52	3.0	60	4.3	66	4.2	64	4.2	55	4.1	44	2.5	28	2.1	14	0.9
Fairbanks, AK	–10	0.6	–4	0.4	11	0.3	32	0.2	49	0.6	60	1.4	62	1.7	56	1.7	45	1.1	24	1.0	2	0.7	–6	0.7
Fresno, CA	46	2.2	51	2.1	56	2.2	61	0.8	69	0.4	76	0.2	81	0.0	80	0.0	75	0.3	65	0.7	53	1.1	45	1.3
Galveston, TX*	56	4.1	58	2.6	64	2.8	70	2.6	77	3.7	82	4.0	84	3.5	84	4.2	81	5.8	74	3.5	65	3.6	58	3.5
Grand Rapids, MI	22	2.0	25	1.5	35	2.6	46	3.5	58	3.4	67	3.7	71	3.6	69	3.8	61	4.3	50	2.8	38	3.4	28	2.7
Hartford, CT	26	3.8	29	3.0	38	3.9	49	3.9	60	4.4	69	3.9	74	3.7	72	4.0	63	4.1	52	3.9	42	4.1	31	3.6
Helena, MT	20	0.5	26	0.4	35	0.6	44	0.9	53	1.8	61	1.8	68	1.3	67	1.3	56	1.1	45	0.7	31	0.5	21	0.5
Honolulu, HI	73	2.7	73	2.4	74	1.9	76	1.1	77	0.8	80	0.4	81	0.5	82	0.5	82	0.7	80	2.2	78	2.3	75	2.9
Houston, TX	52	3.7	55	3.0	62	3.4	69	3.6	76	5.2	81	5.4	84	3.2	83	3.8	79	4.3	70	4.5	61	4.2	54	3.7
Huron, SD	14	0.5	21	0.6	33	1.7	46	2.3	58	3.0	68	3.3	73	2.9	72	2.1	61	1.8	48	1.6	31	0.9	19	0.4
Indianapolis, IN	27	2.5	31	2.4	42	3.4	52	3.6	63	4.4	72	4.1	75	4.4	74	3.8	66	2.9	55	2.8	43	3.6	32	3.0
Jackson, MS	45	5.7	49	4.5	57	5.7	63	6.0	72	4.9	79	3.8	81	4.7	81	3.7	76	3.2	64	3.4	55	5.0	48	5.3
Jacksonville, FL	53	3.7	56	3.2	62	3.9	67	3.1	73	3.5	79	5.4	82	6.0	81	6.9	78	7.9	69	3.9	62	2.3	55	2.6
Juneau, AK	26	4.8	29	4.0	34	3.5	41	3.0	48	3.5	54	3.4	57	4.1	56	5.4	50	7.6	42	8.3	33	5.4	29	5.4
Kansas City, MO	27	1.2	33	1.3	44	2.4	54	3.4	64	5.4	74	4.4	79	4.4	77	3.5	68	4.6	57	3.3	43	2.3	31	1.6
Knoxville, TN	38	4.6	42	4.0	50	5.2	58	4.0	66	4.7	74	4.0	78	4.7	77	2.9	71	3.0	59	2.7	49	4.0	41	4.5
Lander, WY	20	0.5	26	0.5	36	1.2	44	2.1	53	2.4	64	1.2	71	0.8	69	0.6	59	1.1	46	1.4	30	1.0	21	0.6
Lexington, KY	32	3.3	36	3.3	46	4.4	55	3.7	64	4.8	72	4.6	76	4.8	75	3.8	68	3.1	57	2.7	46	3.4	36	4.0
Little Rock, AR	40	3.6	45	3.3	53	4.9	61	5.5	70	5.1	78	4.0	82	3.3	81	2.9	74	3.7	63	4.3	52	5.7	43	4.7
Los Angeles, CA*	57	3.0	58	3.1	58	2.4	61	0.6	63	0.2	66	0.1	69	0.0	71	0.1	70	0.3	67	0.4	62	1.1	58	1.8
Louisville, KY	33	3.3	38	3.3	47	4.4	56	3.9	66	4.9	74	3.8	78	4.3	77	3.4	70	3.1	59	2.8	48	3.8	38	3.7
Marquette, MI*	12	2.6	15	1.9	24	3.1	36	2.8	50	3.1	59	3.2	64	3.0	62	3.6	54	3.7	43	3.7	29	3.3	17	2.4
Memphis, TN	40	4.2	45	4.3	54	5.6	62	5.8	71	5.2	79	4.3	83	4.2	81	3.0	75	3.3	64	3.3	52	5.8	43	5.7
Miami, FL	68	1.9	69	2.1	72	2.6	76	3.4	80	5.5	82	8.5	84	5.8	84	8.6	82	8.4	79	6.2	74	3.4	70	2.2
Milwaukee, WI	21	1.9	25	1.7	35	2.6	45	3.8	56	3.1	66	3.6	72	3.6	71	4.0	63	3.3	51	2.5	38	2.7	26	2.2
Minneapolis, MN	13	1.0	20	0.8	32	1.9	47	2.3	59	3.2	68	4.3	73	4.0	71	4.1	61	2.7	49	2.1	33	1.9	19	1.0
Mobile, AL	61	5.8	65	5.1	71	7.2	77	5.1	84	6.1	89	5.0	91	6.5	91	6.2	87	6.0	79	3.3	70	5.4	63	4.7
Moline, IL	21	1.6	27	1.5	39	2.9	51	3.8	62	4.3	71	4.6	75	4.0	73	4.4	65	3.2	53	2.8	39	2.7	26	2.2
Nashua, NH	23	3.9	26	3.1	35	4.1	46	3.9	57	3.7	66	3.9	71	3.7	69	3.8	61	3.6	49	3.9	39	4.2	28	3.7
Nashville, TN	37	4.0	41	3.7	50	4.9	59	3.9	67	5.1	75	4.1	79	3.8	78	3.3	71	3.6	60	2.9	49	4.5	41	4.5
Newark, NJ	31	4.0	34	3.0	42	4.2	52	3.9	63	4.5	72	3.4	77	4.7	76	4.0	68	4.0	56	3.2	46	3.9	36	3.6
New Orleans, LA	53	5.9	56	5.5	62	5.2	68	5.0	76	4.6	81	6.8	83	6.2	83	6.2	79	5.6	70	3.1	61	5.1	55	5.1
New York, NY*	33	3.6	35	2.8	42	3.9	52	3.7	62	4.2	72	3.6	77	4.4	76	4.1	69	3.8	58	3.3	48	3.7	38	3.5
Norfolk, VA	40	3.9	42	3.3	49	4.1	57	3.4	66	3.7	75	3.8	79	5.2	77	4.8	72	4.1	61	3.5	52	3.0	44	3.0
Oklahoma City, OK	37	1.3	42	1.6	51	2.9	60	3.0	68	5.4	77	4.6	82	2.9	81	2.5	73	4.0	62	3.6	49	2.1	40	1.9
Omaha, NE	22	0.8	28	0.8	39	2.1	51	2.9	62	4.4	72	4.0	77	3.9	75	3.2	65	3.2	53	2.2	38	1.8	26	0.9
Philadelphia, PA	32	3.5	35	2.7	43	3.8	53	3.5	64	3.9	72	3.3	78	4.4	76	3.8	69	3.9	57	2.8	47	3.2	37	3.3
Phoenix, AZ	54	0.8	58	0.8	63	1.1	70	0.3	79	0.2	89	0.1	93	1.0	91	0.9	86	0.8	75	0.8	62	0.7	54	0.9
Pittsburgh, PA	28	2.7	31	2.4	40	3.2	50	3.0	60	3.8	68	4.1	73	4.0	71	3.4	64	3.2	53	2.3	42	3.0	33	2.9
Portland, ME	22	4.1	25	3.1	34	4.1	44	4.3	54	3.8	63	3.3	69	3.3	67	3.1	59	3.4	48	4.4	38	4.7	28	4.2
Portland, OR	40	5.1	43	4.2	47	3.7	51	2.6	57	2.4	63	1.6	68	0.7	69	0.9	64	1.7	54	2.9	46	5.6	40	5.7
Providence, RI	29	4.4	31	3.5	39	4.4	49	4.2	59	3.7	68	3.4	73	3.2	72	3.9	64	3.7	53	3.7	44	4.4	34	4.1
Raleigh, NC	40	4.0	43	3.5	51	4.0	59	2.8	67	3.8	75	3.4	79	4.3	77	3.8	71	4.3	60	3.2	51	3.0	43	3.0
Rapid City, SD	22	0.4	27	0.5	35	1.0	45	1.9	55	3.0	65	2.8	72	2.0	71	1.6	61	1.1	48	1.4	33	0.6	25	0.4
Reno, NV	34	1.1	39	1.1	43	0.9	49	0.4	56	0.6	65	0.5	71	0.2	70	0.3	62	0.5	52	0.4	41	0.8	34	0.9
Richmond, VA	36	3.6	40	3.0	48	4.1	57	3.2	65	4.0	74	3.5	78	4.7	76	4.2	70	4.0	58	3.6	49	3.1	40	3.1
St. Louis, MO	30	2.1	35	2.3	46	3.6	57	3.7	67	4.1	77	3.8	80	3.9	78	3.0	70	3.0	58	2.8	45	3.7	34	2.9
Salt Lake City, UT	29	1.4	35	1.3	43	1.9	50	2.0	59	2.1	69	0.8	77	0.7	76	0.8	65	1.3	53	1.6	40	1.4	30	1.2
San Antonio, TX	51	1.7	55	1.8	63	1.9	69	2.6	76	4.7	81	4.3	84	2.0	84	2.6	79	3.0	71	3.9	60	2.6	53	2.0
San Diego, CA	58	2.3	59	2.0	60	2.3	63	0.8	65	0.2	67	0.1	71	0.0	73	0.1	72	0.2	68	0.4	62	1.1	58	1.3
San Francisco, CA	49	4.5	52	4.0	54	3.3	56	1.2	59	0.4	61	0.1	63	0.0	64	0.1	64	0.2	61	1.0	55	2.5	50	2.9
San Juan, PR	77	3.0	77	2.3	78	2.1	79	3.7	81	5.3	82	3.5	82	4.2	82	5.2	82	5.6	82	5.1	80	6.2	78	4.6
Santa Fe, NM	29	0.6	35	0.5	41	0.8	48	0.7	57	1.3	66	1.2	70	2.3	68	2.1	62	1.7	51	1.3	38	1.1	30	0.7
Savannah, GA	49	4.0	53	2.9	59	3.6	65	3.3	73	3.6	79	5.5	82	6.0	81	7.2	77	5.1	67	3.1	59	2.4	51	2.8
Seattle, WA	41	5.1	43	4.2	46	3.8	50	2.6	56	1.8	61	1.5	65	0.8	66	1.0	61	1.6	53	3.2	45	5.9	41	5.6
Spokane, WA	27	1.8	33	1.5	40	1.5	47	1.3	54	1.6	62	1.2	69	0.8	69	0.7	59	0.8	47	1.1	35	2.2	27	2.3
Springfield, MO	32	2.1	37	2.3	46	3.8	56	4.3	65	4.6	73	5.0	79	3.6	78	3.4	69	4.8	58	3.5	46	4.5	36	3.2
Tampa, FL	61	2.3	63	2.7	67	2.9	72	1.8	78	2.9	82	5.5	83	6.5	83	7.6	82	6.5	76	2.3	69	1.6	63	2.3
Washington, DC	34	3.6	36	2.8	44	3.9	54	3.3	64	4.3	73	3.6	78	4.2	76	3.9	69	4.1	57	3.4	47	3.3	38	3.2
Wilmington, DE	32	3.4	34	2.8	43	4.0	52	3.4	63	4.1	72	4.0	77	4.3	75	3.5	68	4.0	56	3.0	46	3.2	36	3.4

Normal High and Low Temperatures, Precipitation, U.S. Cities

Source: National Climatic Data Center, NESDIS, NOAA, U.S. Dept. of Commerce

The **normal** temperatures and precipitation data given here are based on records for the period 1971-2000. The **extreme** temperatures are based on records from time of each station's installation. (*) = city station. Other figures are for airport stations. Temperatures are Fahrenheit.

		NORMAL TEMPERATURE				EXTREME TEMPERATURE		AVG. ANNUAL PRECIPITATION
		January		July				
State	Station	Max.	Min.	Max.	Min.	Highest	Lowest	(inches)
Alabama	Mobile	61	40	91	72	105	3	66.29
Alaska	Anchorage	22	9	65	52	85	–34	16.08
Alaska	Barrow	–8	–20	47	34	79	–56	4.16
Alaska	Juneau	31	21	64	49	90	–22	58.33
Arizona	Phoenix	65	43	104	81	122	17	8.29
Arkansas	North Little Rock	49	31	94	73	111	–6	49.19
California	Los Angeles*	66	49	75	63	110	23	13.15
California	San Francisco	56	43	71	55	106	20	20.11
Colorado	Denver	43	15	88	59	101	–19	15.81
Connecticut	Hartford	34	17	85	62	102	–26	46.16
Delaware	Wilmington	39	24	86	67	102	–14	42.81
District of Columbia	Washington–National	43	27	89	67	105	–5	39.35
Florida	Jacksonville	64	42	91	72	105	7	52.34
Florida	Miami	77	60	91	77	98	30	58.53
Georgia	Atlanta	52	34	89	71	105	–8	50.20
Georgia	Savannah	60	38	92	72	105	3	49.58
Hawaii	Honolulu	80	66	88	74	95	53	18.29
Idaho	Boise	37	24	89	60	111	–25	12.19
Illinois	Chicago	30	14	84	63	104	–27	36.27
Indiana	Indianapolis	35	19	86	65	104	–27	40.95
Iowa	Des Moines	29	12	86	66	108	–26	34.72
Kansas	Dodge City	41	19	93	67	110	–21	22.35
Kentucky	Lexington	40	24	86	66	103	–21	45.91
Kentucky	Louisville	41	25	87	70	106	–22	44.54
Louisiana	New Orleans	62	43	91	74	102	11	64.16
Maine	Caribou	19	0	76	55	96	–41	37.44
Maine	Portland	31	13	79	59	103	–39	45.83
Maryland	Baltimore	41	24	87	66	105	–7	41.94
Massachusetts	Boston	37	22	82	66	102	–12	42.53
Michigan	Detroit	31	18	83	64	104	–21	32.89
Michigan	Grand Rapids	29	16	82	61	100	–22	37.13
Michigan	Sault Ste. Marie*	22	5	76	52	98	–36	34.67
Minnesota	Duluth	18	–1	76	55	97	–39	31.00
Minnesota	Minneapolis-St. Paul	22	4	83	63	105	–34	29.41
Mississippi	Jackson	55	35	91	71	107	2	55.95
Missouri	Kansas City	36	18	89	68	109	–23	37.98
Missouri	St. Louis	38	21	90	71	107	–18	38.75
Montana	Helena	31	10	83	52	105	–42	11.32
Nebraska	Omaha	32	12	87	66	114	–23	30.22
Nevada	Reno	46	22	91	51	108	–16	7.48
New Hampshire	Concord	31	10	83	57	102	–37	37.60
New Jersey	Atlantic City	41	23	85	65	106	–11	40.59
New Mexico	Albuquerque	48	24	92	65	107	–17	9.47
New York	Albany	31	13	82	60	100	–28	38.60
New York	Buffalo	31	18	80	62	99	–20	40.54
New York	New York–Central Park*	38	26	84	69	106	–15	49.69
North Carolina	Raleigh	50	30	89	69	105	–9	43.05
North Dakota	Bismarck	21	–1	85	56	111	–44	16.84
Ohio	Cleveland	33	19	81	62	104	–20	38.71
Ohio	Columbus	36	20	85	65	102	–22	38.52
Oklahoma	Oklahoma City	47	26	93	71	110	–8	35.85
Oregon	Portland	46	34	79	57	107	–3	37.07
Pennsylvania	Philadelphia	39	26	86	70	104	–7	42.05
Pennsylvania	Pittsburgh	35	20	83	62	103	–22	37.85
Puerto Rico	San Juan	82	71	87	77	98	46	50.76
Rhode Island	Providence	37	20	83	64	104	–13	46.45
South Carolina	Charleston	59	37	91	73	105	6	51.53
South Dakota	Huron	25	4	86	61	112	–41	20.90
South Dakota	Rapid City	34	11	86	58	110	–31	16.64
Tennessee	Memphis	49	31	92	73	108	–13	54.65
Tennessee	Nashville	46	28	89	70	107	–17	48.11
Texas	Dallas-Fort Worth	54	34	95	75	109	17	34.73
Texas	Houston	62	41	94	74	109	17	47.84
Utah	Salt Lake City	37	21	91	63	107	–30	16.50
Vermont	Burlington	27	9	81	60	101	–30	36.05
Virginia	Norfolk	48	32	87	71	104	–3	45.74
Virginia	Richmond	45	28	88	68	105	–12	43.91
Washington	Seattle-Tacoma	46	36	75	55	100	0	37.07
Washington	Spokane	33	22	83	55	108	–25	16.67
West Virginia	Charleston	43	24	85	63	104	–16	44.05
Wisconsin	Milwaukee	28	13	81	63	103	–26	34.81
Wyoming	Lander	32	9	86	55	101	–37	13.42

Mean Annual Snowfall (inches) based on climate normals 1971-2000: Boston, MA, 41.8; Sault Ste. Marie, MI, 132.6; Albany, NY, 62.7; Burlington, VT, 83.1; Lander, WY, 102.9; Anchorage, AK, 69.5.

Wettest Spot: Mount Waialeale, HI, on the island of Kauai, is the rainiest place in the world and in the U.S., according to the National Geographic Society; it has an average annual rainfall of 460 inches.

Temperature Extremes: A temperature of 136° F observed at El Azizia (Al Aziziyah), near Tripoli, Libya, on Sept. 13, 1922, is generally accepted as the world's highest temperature recorded under standard conditions. The record high in the U.S. was 134° F in Death Valley, CA, July 10, 1913. A record low of –129° F was recorded at the Soviet Antarctica station of Vostok on July 21, 1983. The record low in the U.S. was –80° F at Prospect Creek, AK, Jan. 23, 1971.

Annual Climatological Data for U.S. Cities, 2004

Source: National Climatic Data Center, NESDIS, NOAA, U.S. Dept. of Commerce

Station	Elev. (ft.)	Temperature °F				Precipitation[1]						Fastest[2] wind		No. of Days	
									Sleet or snow						
		Highest	Date	Lowest	Date	Total (in.)	Greatest in 24 hours	Date	Total (in.)	Greatest in 24 hours	Date	MPH	Date	Prec. .01 in. or more	Snow, sleet 1" or more
Albany, NY	278	93	6/9	–13	1/14	39.99	2.79	8/15-8/16	47.5	7.0	3/16	40	4/19	146	15
Albuquerque, NM	5,305	97	7/21	10	12/24	11.80	1.70	4/2-4/3	5.6	1.7	11/29	53	6/2	59	2
Anchorage, AK	130	81	8/16	–18	1/17	19.53	1.71	9/29-9/30	94.7	8.6	11/3	35	3/18	111	28
Asheville, NC	2,171	88	7/14	7	12/20	52.36	4.23	9/16-9/17	11.4	5.5	2/26	38	3/7	141	3
Atlanta, GA	971	95	7/24	16	12/20	53.60	5.02	9/16-9/17	—	—	—	41	9/16	111	—
Atlantic City, NJ	114	93	7/5	3	1/11	39.07	3.35	7/12	12.5	3.5	1/26	40	12/1	124	5
Baltimore, MD	193	92	7/5	6	1/10	45.67	4.45	7/27	8.7	3.3	1/25	45	12/1	127	3
Barrow, AK	35	70	7/23	–42	3/19	6.01	0.40	7/10-7/11	34.8	2.8	9/27	46	11/15	107	8
Birmingham, AL	636	95	7/24	15	1/7	61.32	9.75	9/16	T	T	10/14	39	9/16	131	0
Bismarck, ND	1,651	103	7/18	–30	2/3	16.10	1.52	6/10	28.9	3.7	1/31	47	12/20	106	10
Boise, ID	2,858	104	7/17	1	1/5	11.56	0.92	5/27-5/28	18.2	2.6	1/24	44	8/31	85	7
Boston, MA	19	93	6/9	–7	1/16	44.57	4.29	4/1	29.0	6.5	3/16	45	11/5	122	10
Buffalo, NY	714	88	7/4	–7	1/10	41.73	3.93	9/8-9/9	98.1	15.1	3/16-3/17	45	12/7	175	28
Burlington, VT	345	88	6/9	–20	1/15	38.14	2.54	8/30-8/31	63.5	5.1	1/28	36	11/28	151	21
Caribou, ME	627	85	7/30	–23	2/17	34.18	1.62	9/9-9/10	82.7	12.8	1/19	43	1/17	147	21
Charleston, SC	45	97	7/14	22	12/16	39.23	4.11	8/28-8/29	T	T	12/26	43	8/29	119	0
Chicago, IL	655	91	6/8	–9	1/30	31.58	1.58	5/20-5/21	29.0	5.6	1/4	43	5/21	107	9
Cleveland, OH	802	91	6/9	–7	1/25	39.39	1.82	12/22-12/23	95.8	9.4	12/22	53	12/7	174	26
Columbus, OH	846	90	7/6	–6	1/31	49.27	2.96	6/10-6/11	27.8	5.2	12/22	44	12/1	164	8
Dallas-Ft. Worth, TX	559	100	7/16	18	12/23	47.57	4.01	7/28-7/29	—	—	—	46	3/4	97	0
Denver, CO	5,379	99	7/13	–11	1/5	14.66	1.71	8/18-8/19	—	—	—	48	7/7	82	—
Des Moines, IA	968	91	8/3	–8	1/31	37.67	3.21	5/22	49.2	15.6	3/15	46	10/30	112	10
Detroit, MI	628	91	7/22	–7	1/25	33.57	2.12	5/20-5/21	32.6	8.4	12/23	61	5/23	143	8
Duluth, MN	1,426	90	7/21	–30	1/29	29.83	1.77	7/11	96.3	23.2	1/25-1/26	37	8/18	147	22
Fairbanks, AK	461	88	6/20	–46	1/19	8.59	0.74	5/6-5/7	67.4	4.0	10/19	30	5/31	111	26
Fresno, CA	372	106	8/11	29	12/4	10.63	1.15	3/1-3/2	—	—	—	28	2/2	40	—
Grand Rapids, MI	785	90	7/21	–4	2/16	39.28	2.46	5/21	84.7	9.7	11/24	45	4/19	161	21
Hartford, CT	162	94	7/9	–7	1/15	42.27	2.91	9/17-9/18	33.2	5.0	4/16	38	11/5	141	14
Helena, MT	3,864	99	7/17	–32	1/6	12.05	1.14	8/22-8/23	—	—	—	45	3/6	88	—
Honolulu, HI	15	92	10/10	60	1/5	39.01	5.63	2/27-2/28	—	—	—	40	1/22	122	—
Houston, TX	118	100	8/3	28	12/26	65.06	3.58	6/13	T	T	12/24	45	6/13	123	0
Huron, SD	1,281	96	7/21	–23	1/27	29.71	2.18	7/10-7/11	19.2	2.3	1/25	70	8/1	104	10
Indianapolis, IN	794	89	7/22	–11	1/31	48.88	3.80	5/30	28.9	5.2	12/22	44	10/30	123	9
Jackson, MS	293	97	7/15	19	1/28	62.78	3.58	5/31	—	—	—	31	9/16	111	—
Jacksonville, FL	31	97	5/31	23	1/29	69.47	6.15	6/13-6/14	—	—	—	46	9/26	124	—
Kansas City, MO	1,005	95	8/03	–4	12/24	37.59	2.03	5/18-5/19	19.9	7.5	2/5	41	7/5	105	6
Knoxville, TN	979	91	9/6	12	12/20	56.19	3.40	7/26-7/27	1.1	1.0	1/9	37	12/1	131	1
Lander, WY	5,557	95	7/12	–18	1/6	13.87	2.25	8/17-8/18	93.4	13.0	11/28	44	1/1	82	20
Lexington, KY	977	89	8/19	–6	1/31	62.44	3.73	7/30-7/31	5.0	2.2	1/9	37	5/27	144	2
Los Angeles, CA	323	101	9/5	41	12/6	16.32	4.72	12/28-12/29	—	—	—	32	9/19	33	—
Louisville, KY	481	93	7/22	–1	1/31	52.28	4.33	10/18-10/19	13.6	7.5	12/22	55	7/13	122	4
Marquette, MI	1,415	90	6/8	–24	12/25	39.33	1.89	5/31	233.1	16.8	12/13	—	—	185	51
Memphis, TN	283	97	7/14	15	12/25	53.71	2.84	11/01-11/02	—	—	—	43	3/20	126	—
Miami, FL	26	95	7/7	46	12/15	54.44	3.43	8/1-8/2	—	—	—	36	9/4	126	—
Milwaukee, WI	677	91	6/8	–10	1/30	32.94	1.78	8/3	39.3	5.2	1/9	38	5/17	134	14
Minn.-St. Paul, MN	871	95	7/21	–24	1/30	27.39	2.24	9/14-9/15	—	—	—	41	4/18	111	—
Mobile, AL	209	97	7/25	25	12/20	76.16	5.55	9/15–9/16	T	T	12/25	59	9/16	122	0
Moline, IL	604	94	7/13	–12	1/31	36.56	2.57	5/30-5/31	31.0	6.0	1/4	43	8/17	110	8
Nashville, TN	571	94	7/13	11	1/31	59.18	4.13	2/5-2/6	—	—	—	58	7/13	138	—
Newark, NJ	25	97	6/9	0	1/16	48.37	3.61	9/28-9/29	28.4	5.8	1/15	46	12/1	130	10
New Orleans, LA	4	95	8/1	25	12/26	79.28	7.68	4/25-4/26	—	—	—	45	4/11	125	—
New York, NY	158	91	6/9	1	1/16	51.93	4.54	9/28-9/29	25.8	6.0	1/27	31	3/16	128	6
Norfolk, VA	66	93	6/18	15	12/20	50.09	3.73	8/14-8/15	11.7	5.0	12/26	38	8/14	124	4
North Little Rock, AR	563	100	7/14	13	12/24	57.79	2.92	10/7-10/8	6.4	3.8	2/14	—	—	121	2
Oklahoma City, OK	1,281	98	8/4	7	1/6	36.78	2.62	6/21-6/22	0.6	0.3	2/4	49	6/2	99	0
Philadelphia, PA	10	93	7/5	4	1/10	49.18	4.68	7/12	12.4	2.6	1/26	43	12/1	136	5
Phoenix, AZ	1,103	112	8/8	35	12/25	7.98	1.16	3/4-3/5	—	—	—	45	8/13	41	—
Pittsburgh, PA	1,172	87	6/9	–1	2/1	57.41	5.95	9/17	39.0	3.9	1/25	41	5/21	166	16
Portland, ME	69	92	6/9	–11	1/16	41.22	3.06	4/1-4/2	31.5	4.6	3/16-3/17	39	11/5	121	14
Portland, OR	220	103	7/23	18	1/6	27.65	1.41	8/21-8/22	—	—	—	41	12/12	158	—
Providence, RI	50	92	6/9	–6	1/16	45.33	3.20	9/28-9/29	32.3	5.1	12/26	38	11/5	122	13
Raleigh, NC	427	96	7/10	11	1/11	47.03	2.82	7/29	14.9	4.5	2/27	48	9/17	114	5
Rapid City, SD	3,150	103	7/19	–16	1/6	13.16	1.72	7/4-7/5	—	—	—	49	3/1	81	—
Reno, NV	4,404	101	8/11	4	11/29	9.41	1.38	12/30-12/31	—	—	—	51	2/17	41	—
Richmond, VA	164	93	7/8	11	1/11	58.50	6.68	8/30	7.6	4.0	1/25	38	8/30	128	3
St. Louis, MO	707	97	7/21	3	1/30	42.27	2.32	7/29-7/30	5.9	1.4	11/24	43	7/5	117	2
Salt Lake City, UT	4,221	98	8/13	–5	2/13	14.89	1.50	6/9-6/10	41.7	5.2	2/28	47	5/10	95	16
San Antonio, TX	818	104	5/31	24	12/25	45.32	3.90	11/21-11/22	0.7	0.6	2/14	39	7/23	101	0
San Diego, CA	78	96	9/5	41	11/30	13.29	2.79	12/28-12/29	—	—	—	46	12/29	39	—
San Francisco, CA	86	94	9/6	35	1/04	19.30	2.34	12/27-12/28	—	—	—	48	2/17	57	—
San Juan, PR	7	94	9/24	67	2/23	64.35	4.89	9/15-9/16	0.0	0.0	—	49	9/15	223	0
Sault Ste. Marie, MI	724	83	7/28	–22	1/16	31.92	1.31	10/23-10/24	—	—	—	33	10/9	149	—
Savannah, GA	48	98	6/12	24	12/21	37.18	3.38	4/11-4/12	T	T	12/16	35	5/2	112	0
Scottsbluff, NE	3,946	102	6/6	–29	1/6	12.04	1.86	9/4-9/5	32.4	8.6	11/28	51	3/6	83	8
Seattle, WA	447	96	7/23	20	1/5	31.10	1.72	1/29-1/30	—	—	—	35	12/12	146	—
Spokane, WA	2,381	97	8/14	–22	1/5	15.02	2.19	5/21	40.1	5.5	1/1	46	8/2	109	17
Springfield, MO	1,277	92	7/13	–14	1/31	34.32	2.76	7/9-7/10	16.7	5.7	11/24	41	6/10	119	6
Tampa, FL	8	95	7/10	34	12/15	59.31	5.03	9/5-9/6	0.0	0.0	—	45	9/5	103	0
Washington, DC[3]	10	92	7/5	8	1/10	42.49	2.46	9/28	6.3	3.5	1/25	40	12/1	130	3
Wilmington, DE	92	91	6/9	4	1/25	56.73	5.73	9/28-9/29	12.6	3.6	1/26	41	12/1	137	6

In some cases the value for the extreme also occurred on an earlier date in 2004. (T) Trace. (—) Data not available or incomplete. (1) Where one date is shown, it is the starting date of the storm. (2) Sustained for at least 2 minutes, not peak gust. (3) As measured at Reagan Nat'l. Airport.

Record Temperatures by State

Source: National Climatic Data Center, NESDIS, NOAA; U.S. Dept. of Commerce, through Dec. 2003

	LOWEST TEMPERATURE				HIGHEST TEMPERATURE			
State	°F	Latest date	Station	Approx. elevation in feet	°F	Latest date	Station	Approx. elevation in feet
Alabama	–27	Jan. 30, 1966	New Market	760	112	Sept. 5, 1925	Centerville	345
Alaska	–80	Jan. 23, 1971	Prospect Creek Camp	1,100	100	June 27, 1915	Fort Yukon	c. 420
Arizona	–40	Jan. 7, 1971	Hawley Lake	8,180	128	June 29, 1994	Lake Havasu City	505
Arkansas	–29	Feb. 13, 1905	Pond	1,250	120	Aug. 10, 1936	Ozark	396
California	–45	Jan. 20, 1937	Boca	5,532	134	July 10, 1913	Greenland Ranch	–178
Colorado	–61	Feb. 1, 1985	Maybell	5,920	118	July 11, 1888	Bennett	5,484
Connecticut	–32	Jan. 22, 1961	Coventry	480	106	July 15, 1995	Danbury	450
Delaware	–17	Jan. 17, 1893	Millsboro	20	110	July 21, 1930	Millsboro	20
Florida	–2	Feb. 13, 1899	Tallahassee	193	109	June 29, 1931	Monticello	207
Georgia	–17	Jan. 27, 1940	CCC Camp F-16	1,000	112	Aug. 20, 1983	Greenville	860
Hawaii	12	May 17, 1979	Mauna Kea Obs. 111.2	13,770	100	Apr. 27, 1931	Pahala	850
Idaho	–60	Jan. 18, 1943	Island Park Dam	6,285	118	July 28, 1934	Orofino	1,027
Illinois	–36	Jan. 5, 1999	Congerville	635	117	July 14, 1954	East St. Louis	410
Indiana	–36	Jan. 19, 1994	New Whiteland	785	116	July 14, 1936	Collegeville	672
Iowa	–47	Feb. 3, 1996[1]	Elkader	770	118	July 20, 1934	Keokuk	614
Kansas	–40	Feb. 13, 1905	Lebanon	1,812	121	July 24, 1936[1]	Alton (near)	1,651
Kentucky	–37	Jan. 19, 1994	Shelbyville	730	114	July 28, 1930	Greensburg	581
Louisiana	–16	Feb. 13, 1899	Minden	194	114	Aug. 10, 1936	Plain Dealing	268
Maine	–48	Jan. 19, 1925	Van Buren	510	105	July 10, 1911[1]	North Bridgton	450
Maryland	–40	Jan. 13, 1912	Oakland	2,461	109	July 10, 1936[1]	Cumberland Frederick	623 325
Massachusetts	–35	Jan. 12, 1981	Chester	640	107	Aug. 2, 1975	Chester New Bedford	640 120
Michigan	–51	Feb. 9, 1934	Vanderbilt	785	112	July 13, 1936	Mio	963
Minnesota	–60	Feb. 2, 1996	Tower	1,460	114	July 6, 1936[1]	Moorhead	904
Mississippi	–19	Jan. 30, 1966	Corinth	420	115	July 29, 1930	Holly Springs	600
Missouri	–40	Feb. 13, 1905	Warsaw	700	118	July 14, 1954[1]	Warsaw Union	705 560
Montana	–70	Jan. 20, 1954	Rogers Pass	5,470	117	July 5, 1937	Medicine Lake	1,950
Nebraska	–47	Dec. 22, 1989	Oshkosh	3,379	118	July 24, 1936[1]	Minden	2,169
Nevada	–50	Jan. 8, 1937	San Jacinto	5,200	125	June 29, 1994[1]	Laughlin	605
New Hampshire	–47	Jan. 29, 1934	Mt. Washington	6,262	106	July 4, 1911	Nashua	125
New Jersey	–34	Jan. 5, 1904	River Vale	70	110	July 10, 1936	Runyon	18
New Mexico	–50	Feb. 1, 1951	Gavilan	7,350	122	June 27, 1994	Waste Isolat. Pilot Plt.	3,418
New York	–52	Feb. 18, 1979[1]	Old Forge	1,720	108	July 22, 1926	Troy	35
North Carolina	–34	Jan. 21, 1985	Mt. Mitchell	6,525	110	Aug. 21, 1983	Fayetteville	213
North Dakota	–60	Feb. 15, 1936	Parshall	1,929	121	July 6, 1936	Steele	1,857
Ohio	–39	Feb. 10, 1899	Milligan	800	113	July 21, 1934[1]	Gallipolis (near)	673
Oklahoma	–27	Jan. 18, 1930	Watts	958	120	June 27, 1994[1]	Tipton	1,350
Oregon	–54	Feb. 10, 1933[1]	Seneca	4,700	119	Aug. 10, 1898[1]	Pendleton	1,074
Pennsylvania	–42	Jan. 5, 1904	Smethport	c. 1,500	111	July 10, 1936[1]	Phoenixville	100
Rhode Island	–25	Feb. 5, 1996	Greene	425	104	Aug. 2, 1975	Providence	51
South Carolina	–19	Jan. 21, 1985	Caesars Head	3,115	111	June 28, 1954[1]	Camden	170
South Dakota	–58	Feb. 17, 1936	McIntosh	2,277	120	July 5, 1936	Gannvalley	1,750
Tennessee	–32	Dec. 30, 1917	Mountain City	2,471	113	Aug. 9, 1930[1]	Perryville	377
Texas	–23	Feb. 8, 1933[1]	Seminole	3,275	120	June 28 1994	Monahans	2,660
Utah	–69	Feb. 1, 1985	Peter's Sink	8,092	117	Jul. 5, 1985	Saint George	2,880
Vermont	–50	Dec. 30, 1933	Bloomfield	915	105	July 4, 1911	Vernon	310
Virginia	–30	Jan. 22, 1985	Mountain Lake Bio. Station	3,870	110	July 15, 1954	Balcony Falls	725
Washington	–48	Dec. 30, 1968	Mazama Winthrop	2,120 1,755	118	Aug. 5, 1961[1]	Ice Harbor Dam	475
West Virginia	–37	Dec. 30, 1917	Lewisburg	2,200	112	July 10, 1936[1]	Martinsburg	435
Wisconsin	–55	Feb. 4, 1996	Couderay	1,300	114	July 13, 1936	Wisconsin Dells	900
Wyoming	–66	Feb. 9, 1933	Riverside R.S.	6,500	115	Aug. 8, 1983	Basin	3,500

(1) Also on earlier dates at the same or other places.

Hurricane and Tornado Classifications

Source: National Weather Service, NOAA, U.S. Dept. of Commerce

The Saffir-Simpson Hurricane Scale is a 1-5 rating based on a hurricane's intensity. The scale is used to give an estimate of the potential property damage and flooding expected along the coast from a hurricane landfall. Wind speed is the determining factor in the scale. The Fujita (or F) Scale, created by T. Theodore Fujita, is used to classify tornadoes. The F Scale uses rating numbers from 0 to 5, based on the amount and type of wind damage.

Saffir-Simpson Scale (Hurricanes)

Category	Wind Speed	Severity	Storm Surge[1]
1	74-95 MPH	Weak	4-5 feet
2	96-110 MPH	Moderate	6-8 feet
3	111-130 MPH	Strong	9-12 feet
4	131-155 MPH	Very Strong	13-18 feet
5	above 155 MPH	Devastating	above 18 feet

(1) Above normal tides.

Fujita Scale (Tornadoes)

Rank	Wind Speed	Damage	Strength
F-0	40-72 MPH	Light	Weak
F-1	73-112 MPH	Moderate	Weak
F-2	113-157 MPH	Considerable	Strong
F-3	158-206 MPH	Severe	Strong
F-4	207-260 MPH	Devastating	Violent
F-5	above 261 MPH	Incredible	Violent

Atlantic Hurricane Names in 2006

Source: National Weather Service, NOAA, U.S. Dept. of Commerce

Names for Atlantic hurricanes in 2006 are: Alberto, Beryl, Chris, Debby, Ernesto, Florence, Gordon, Helene, Isaac, Joyce, Kirk, Leslie, Michael, Nadine, Oscar, Patty, Rafael, Sandy, Tony, Valerie, William. If all letters are used up (except Q, U, X, Y, and Z, which are not used), remaining storms are called by Greek letters, starting with alpha.

World Temperature and Precipitation

Source: World Meteorological Organization

Average daily maximum and minimum temperatures and annual precipitation based on records for the period 1961-90. Records of extreme temperatures include all available years of data for a given location and are usually for a longer period. Surface elevations are supplied by the WMO and may differ from figures in other sections of *The World Almanac*. NA = Not available.

Station	Surface elevation (feet)	Temperature °F						Average annual precipitation (inches)
		AVERAGE DAILY				EXTREME		
		January		July				
		Max.	Min.	Max.	Min.	Max.	Min.	
Algiers, Algeria	82	61.7	42.6	87.1	65.3	NA	NA	27.0
Athens, Greece	49	56.1	44.6	88.9	73.0	NA	NA	14.6
Auckland, New Zealand	20	74.8	61.2	58.5	46.4	NA	NA	49.4
Bangkok, Thailand	66	89.6	69.8	90.9	77.0	104	51	59.0
Berlin, Germany	190	35.2	26.8	73.6	55.2	107	–4	23.3
Bogotá, Colombia	8,357	67.3	41.7	64.6	45.5	75	21	32.4
Bombay (Mumbai), India	36	85.3	66.7	86.2	77.5	110	46	85.4
Bucharest, Romania	298	34.7	22.1	83.8	60.1	105	–18	23.4
Budapest, Hungary	456	34.2	24.8	79.7	59.7	103	–10	20.3
Buenos Aires, Argentina	82	85.8	67.3	59.7	45.7	104	22	45.2
Cairo, Egypt	243	65.8	48.2	93.9	71.1	118	34	1.0
Cape Town, South Africa	138	79.0	60.3	63.3	44.6	105	28	20.5
Caracas, Venezuela	2,739	79.9	60.8	81.3	66.0	96	45	36.1
Casablanca, Morocco	203	62.8	47.1	77.7	66.7	NA	NA	16.8
Copenhagen, Denmark	16	35.6	28.4	68.9	55.0	NA	NA	NA
Damascus, Syria	2,004	54.3	32.9	97.2	61.9	NA	NA	5.6
Dublin, Ireland	279	45.7	36.5	66.0	52.5	86	8	28.8
Geneva, Switzerland	1,364	38.3	27.9	76.3	53.2	101	–3	35.6
Havana, Cuba	164	78.4	65.5	88.3	74.8	NA	NA	46.9
Hong Kong, China	203	65.5	56.5	88.7	79.9	97	32	87.2
Istanbul, Turkey	108	47.8	37.2	82.8	65.3	105	7	27.4
Jerusalem, Israel	2,483	53.4	39.4	83.8	63.0	107	26	23.2
Lagos, Nigeria	125	90.0	72.3	82.8	72.1	NA	NA	59.3
Lima, Peru	43	79.0	66.9	66.4	59.4	NA	NA	0.2
London, England	203	44.1	32.7	71.1	52.3	99	2	29.7
Manila, Philippines	79	85.8	74.8	89.1	76.8	NA	NA	49.6
Mexico City, Mexico	7,570	70.3	43.7	73.8	53.2	NA	NA	33.4
Montreal, Canada	118	21.6	5.2	79.2	59.7	100	–36	37.0
Nairobi, Kenya	5,897	77.9	50.9	71.6	48.6	NA	NA	41.9
Paris, France	213	42.8	33.6	75.2	55.2	105	–1	25.6
Prague, Czech Republic	1,197	32.7	22.5	73.9	53.2	98	–16	20.7
Reykjavik, Iceland	200	35.4	26.6	55.9	46.9	76	–3	31.5
Rome, Italy	79	53.8	35.4	88.2	62.1	NA	NA	33.0
San Salvador, El Salvador	2,037	86.5	61.3	86.2	66.4	105	45	68.3
São Paulo, Brazil	2,598	81.1	65.7	71.2	53.1	NA	NA	57.4
Shanghai, China	23	45.9	32.9	88.9	76.6	104	10	43.8
Singapore	52	85.8	73.6	87.4	75.6	NA	NA	84.6
Stockholm, Sweden	171	30.7	23.0	71.4	56.1	97	–26	21.2
Sydney, Australia	10	79.5	65.5	62.4	43.9	114	32	46.4
Tehran, Iran	3,906	45.0	30.0	98.2	75.2	109	–5	9.1
Tokyo, Japan	118	49.1	34.2	83.8	72.1	NA	NA	55.4
Toronto, Canada	567	27.5	12.0	80.2	57.6	105	–26	30.8

Speed of Winds in the U.S.

Source: National Climatic Data Center, NESDIS, NOAA, U.S. Dept. of Commerce

In miles per hour; based on available records through 2004. Max. values for highest one-minute average, except where noted.

Station	Avg.	Max.	Station	Avg.	Max.	Station	Avg.	Max.
Albuquerque, NM	8.9	53	Helena, MT[2]	7.7	73	Mt. Washington, NH[1]	35.1	231
Anchorage, AK[1]	7.1	75	Honolulu, HI	11.3	46	New Orleans, LA	8.2	69
Atlanta, GA	9.1	60	Houston, TX	7.6	51	New York, NY[4]	9.3	40
Baltimore, MD	8.8	80	Indianapolis, IN	9.6	49	Omaha, NE	10.5	58
Bismarck, ND	10.2	64	Jacksonville, FL	7.8	57	Philadelphia, PA[2]	9.5	73
Boston, MA[2]	12.4	54	Kansas City, MO	10.6	58	Phoenix, AZ	6.2	51
Buffalo, NY	11.8	91	Las Vegas, NV	9.2	56	Pittsburgh, PA	9.0	58
Cape Hatteras, NC	10.9	60	Lexington, KY	9.1	47	Portland, OR	7.9	88
Casper, WY	12.7	81	Little Rock, AR[2]	7.8	65	Rochester, NY	9.6	68
Chicago, IL	10.3	58	Los Angeles, CA[2]	5.5	49	St. Louis, MO	9.6	52
Cleveland, OH	10.5	53	Louisville, KY	8.3	56	Salt Lake City, UT[2]	8.8	71
Dallas-Fort Worth, TX	10.7	73	Memphis, TN	8.8	51	San Diego, CA[2]	7.0	56
Denver, CO	8.6	47	Miami, FL[3]	9.2	86	San Francisco, CA[2]	8.7	47
Des Moines, IA[2]	10.7	76	Milwaukee, WI	11.5	54	Seattle, WA[2]	8.8	66
Detroit, MI	10.2	61	Minn.-St. Paul, MN	10.5	51	Spokane, WA[2]	8.9	59
Hartford, CT	8.4	46	Mobile, AL	8.8	63	Washington, DC[5]	9.4	49

(1) Short gust. (2) Calculated from minimum time during which one mile of wind passed station. (3) Highest velocity ever recorded in Miami area was 132 mph, at former station in Miami Beach in Sept. 1926. (4) Data for Central Park; Battery Place data through 1960, avg. 14.5, high 113. (5) Data from Ronald Reagan National Airport.

IT'S A FACT: Although many hurricanes have reached Category 5 status on the Saffir-Simpson scale, most make landfall with diminished intensity. Since official records have been kept, only 3 hurricanes (as of Oct. 1, 2005) have been Category 5 storms when they hit the U.S. mainland: the "Labor Day Hurricane" in 1935, Hurricane Camille in 1969, and Hurricane Andrew in 1992.

Tides and Their Causes

Source: U.S. Dept. of Commerce, Natl. Oceanic & Atmospheric Admin. (NOAA), Natl. Ocean Service (NOS)

The tides are a natural phenomenon involving the alternating rise and fall in the large fluid bodies of the earth caused by the combined gravitational attraction of the sun and moon. The combination of these 2 variable influences produces the complex recurrent cycle of the tides. Tides may occur in both oceans and seas, to a limited extent in large lakes, in the atmosphere, and, to a very minute degree, in the earth itself. The length of time between succeeding tides varies as the result of many factors.

The tide-generating force represents the difference between (1) the centrifugal force produced by the revolution of the earth around the common center-of-gravity of the earth-moon system and (2) the gravitational attraction of the moon acting upon the earth's overlying waters. The moon is about 400 times closer than the sun; so despite its smaller mass, the moon's tide-raising force is 2.5 times greater.

The tide-generating forces of the moon and sun acting tangentially to the earth's surface tend to cause a maximum accumulation of waters at 2 diametrically opposite positions on the surface of the earth and to withdraw compensating amounts of water from all points 90° removed from these tidal bulges. As the earth rotates beneath the maxima and minima of these tide-generating forces, a sequence of 2 high tides, separated by 2 low tides, ideally is produced each day (semidiurnal tide). Each ocean basin reacts differently to this tidal forcing.

Twice in each month, when the sun, moon, and earth are directly aligned, with the moon between the earth and sun (at new moon) or on the opposite side of the earth from the sun (at full moon), the sun and moon exert gravitational force in a mutual or additive fashion. The highest high tides and lowest low tides are produced at these times. These are called *spring* tides. At 2 positions 90° in between, the gravitational forces of the moon and sun—imposed at right angles—counteract each other to the greatest extent, and the range between high and low tides is reduced. These are called *neap* tides.

The inclination to the equator of the moon's monthly orbit and the inclination of the sun to the equator during the earth's yearly orbit produce a difference in the height of succeeding high tides and in the extent of depression of succeeding low tides that is known as the *diurnal inequality*. In most cases, this produces a so-called *mixed tide*. In extreme cases, these phenomena may result in only one high tide and one low tide each (*diurnal tide*). There are other monthly and yearly variations in the tide because of the elliptical shape of the orbits themselves.

U.S. convention distinguishes between Mean Higher High Water (MHHW), Mean High Water (MHW), Mean Tide Level (MTL), Mean Sea Level (MSL), Mean Low Water (MLW), and Mean Lower Low Water (MLLW). Diurnal range of tide is the difference in height between MHHW and MLLW. Mean range of tide is the difference between MHW and MLW.

The range of tide in the open ocean is generally less than the coastal regions, as the range of the incoming tide can be augmented by the continental shelves, as well as by bays and estuaries. In some shallow inlets and bays, the range may be diminished. In the Bay of Fundy in Nova Scotia, the range of tide, or difference between high and low waters, may reach 43½ feet or more (under spring tide conditions).

In every case, actual high or low tide can vary considerably from the average, as a result of weather conditions such as strong winds, abrupt barometric pressure changes, or prolonged periods of extreme high or low pressure.

Average Rise and Fall of Tides[1]

Place	Ft.	In.	Place	Ft.	In.	Place	Ft.	In.
Baltimore, MD	1	8	Hampton Roads, VA	2	10	St. John's, Nfld.	2	7
Boston, MA	10	4	Key West, FL	1	10	St. Petersburg, FL	2	3[2]
Charleston, SC	5	10	Mobile, AL	1	6[2]	San Diego, CA	5	9
Cristobal, Panama	1	1	New London, CT	3	1	Sandy Hook, NJ	5	2
Eastport, ME	19	4	Newport, RI	3	11	San Francisco, CA	5	10
Ft. Pulaski, GA	7	6	New York, NY	5	1	Seattle, WA	11	4
Galveston, TX	1	5[2]	Philadelphia, PA	6	9	Vancouver, B.C.	10	6
Halifax, N.S.	4	5[2]	Portland, ME	9	11	Washington, DC	3	2

(1) Mean ranges, except where noted. (2) Diurnal range.

El Niño and La Niña

Source: National Weather Service, NOAA, U.S. Dept. of Commerce

El Niño is a climatically significant disruption of the ocean-atmosphere system characterized by large-scale weakening of trade winds and warming of the surface layers in the central and E equatorial Pacific. The term *El Niño*, Spanish for "the Christ Child," was originally used by fishermen to refer to a warm ocean current appearing around Christmas off the W coasts of Ecuador and Peru and lasting several months. The term has come to be reserved for exceptionally strong, warm currents that bring heavy rains.

El Niño events generally occur at irregular intervals of 2 to 7 years, at an average of once every 3 to 4 years. They typically last 12 to 18 months. The intensity of El Niño events varies; some are strong, such as the 1982-83 and 1997-98 events; others are considerably weaker, such as the 2004-05 event, all depending on the intensity of and area encompassed by the abnormally warm ocean temperatures. The eastward extent of warmer than normal water varies from episode to episode.

El Niño influences weather around the globe, and its impacts are most clearly seen in the winter. During El Niño years, winter temperatures in the continental U.S. tend to be warmer than normal in the N and W coast states and cooler than normal in the SE. Conditions tend to be wetter than normal over central and southern California, the SW states and across much of the South, and drier than normal over the N portions of the Rocky Mountains and in the Ohio valley. Globally, El Niño brings wetter than normal conditions to Peru and Chile and dry conditions to Australia and Indonesia. It should be noted that El Niño is only one of a number of factors influencing seasonal variations of climate.

The opposite of El Niño is La Niña, characterized by colder than normal sea surface temperatures in the equatorial Pacific. La Niña typically brings wetter, cooler conditions to the Pacific NW and drier, warmer conditions to much of the southern U.S. El Niño and La Niña are opposite phases of the El Niño-Southern Oscillation (ENSO) cycle, a shift in tropical sea-level pressure between the E and W hemispheres.

The events are monitored by the National Weather Service's Climate Prediction Center, using satellites and buoys in the Pacific Ocean. Highly sophisticated numerical computer models of the ocean and atmosphere use these data to predict the onset and evolution of El Niño and La Niña. As of Sept. 2005, prospects for the next El Niño were uncertain, but conditions were expected to remain neutral for 3-6 months.

Wind Chill Table

Source: National Weather Service, NOAA, U.S. Dept. of Commerce

Temperature and wind combine to cause heat loss from body surfaces. The following table shows that, for example, a temperature of 5° Fahrenheit, plus a wind of 10 miles per hour, causes a body heat loss equal to that in minus 10° F with no wind. In other words, a 10-mph wind makes 5° feel like minus 10°.

The National Weather Service issued new wind chill calculations in 2002. The top line of figures shows temperatures in degrees Fahrenheit. The column at far left shows wind speeds up to 45 mph. (Wind speeds greater than 45 mph have little additional chilling effect.) At wind chills in the shaded area, frostbite occurs in 15 minutes or less.

Calm	40	35	30	25	20	15	10	5	0	–5	–10	–15	–20	–25	–30	–35	–40	–45
5	36	31	25	19	13	7	1	– 5	–11	–16	–22	–28	–34	–40	–46	–52	–57	–63
10	34	27	21	15	9	3	–4	–10	–16	–22	–28	–35	–41	–47	–53	–59	–66	–72
15	32	25	19	13	6	0	–7	–13	–19	–26	–32	–39	–45	–51	–58	–64	–71	–77
20	30	24	17	11	4	–2	–9	–15	–22	–29	–35	–42	–48	–55	–61	–68	–74	–81
25	29	23	16	9	3	–4	–11	–17	–24	–31	–37	–44	–51	–58	–64	–71	–78	–84
30	28	22	15	8	1	–5	–12	–19	–26	–33	–39	–46	–53	–60	–67	–73	–80	–87
35	28	21	14	7	0	–7	–14	–21	–27	–34	–41	–48	–55	–62	–69	–76	–82	–89
40	27	20	13	6	–1	–8	–15	–22	–29	–36	–43	–50	–57	–64	–71	–78	–84	–91

Heat Index

The heat index is a measure of the contribution high humidity makes, in combination with abnormally high temperatures, to reducing the body's ability to cool itself. For example, the index shows that an air temperature of 100°Fahrenheit with a relative humidity of 50% has the same effect on the human body as a temperature of 120°F. Sunstroke and heat exhaustion are likely when the heat index reaches 105. This index is a measure of what hot weather "feels like" to the average person.

					Air Temperature (°F)						
Relative Humidity	70	75	80	85	90	95	100	105	110	115	120
					Apparent Temperature (°F)						
0%	64	69	73	78	83	87	91	95	99	103	107
10%	65	70	75	80	85	90	95	100	105	111	116
20%	66	72	77	82	87	93	99	105	112	120	130
30%	67	73	78	84	90	96	104	113	123	135	148
40%	68	74	79	86	93	101	110	123	137	151	
50%	69	75	81	88	96	107	120	135	150		
60%	70	76	82	90	100	114	132	149			
70%	70	77	85	93	106	124	144				
80%	71	78	86	97	113	136					
90%	71	79	88	102	122						
100%	72	80	91	108							

Ultraviolet (UV) Index Forecast

Source: National Weather Service, NOAA, U.S. Dept. of Commerce

The National Weather Service (NWS), Environmental Protection Agency (EPA), and Centers for Disease Control and Prevention (CDC) developed and began offering a UV index on June 28, 1994, in response to increasing incidence of skin cancer, cataracts, and other effects from exposure to the sun's harmful rays. The UV Index is now a regular element of NWS atmospheric forecasts.

UV Index number and forecast. The UV Index number, ranging from 0 to 10+, is an indication of the expected intensity of UV radiation reaching the earth's surface during the solar noon hour (11:30 AM-12:30 PM standard time). The lower the number, the less the radiation. The UV Index forecast is produced daily for 58 cities by the NWS Climate Prediction Center, and uses the following scale.

UV Index	Exposure	Minimum Precautions
0-2	Minimal	SPF 15 sun screen
3-4	Low	Sun screen and hat
5-6	Moderate	Sun screen, hat, UV sunglasses
7-9	High	Above; and avoid sun 10am - 4pm
10+	Very High	Same

The index number is based on several factors: latitude, day of year, time of day, total atmospheric ozone, elevation, and predicted cloud conditions. The index is valid for a radius of about 30 miles around a listed city; however, adjustments should be made for a number of factors.

Ozone. Ozone, a form of oxygen, the molecules of which consist of three atoms rather than two, blocks UV radiation. The more ozone, the lower the UV radiation at the surface.

Cloudiness. Cloud conditions affect the Index number. Clear skies allow 100% UV transmission to the surface, broken clouds allow about 73%, and overcast conditions allow 32%.

Reflectivity. Reflective surfaces intensify UV exposure. As an example, grass reflects 2.5% to 3% of UV radiation reaching the surface; sand, 20% to 30%; snow and ice, 80% to 90%; water, up to 100% (depending on reflection angle).

Elevation. At higher elevations, UV radiation travels a shorter distance to reach the surface so there is less atmosphere to absorb the rays. For every 4,000 ft. one travels above sea level, the UV Index increases by 1 unit. Snow and lack of pollutants intensify UV exposure at higher altitudes.

Latitude. The closer to the equator, the higher the UV radiation level.

SPF number. The UV Index is not linked in any way to the SPF number on suntan lotions and sunscreens. For an explanation of the SPF factor, contact the product's manufacturer or the Food and Drug Administration.

Further information. For precautions to take after learning the UV Index number, call the U.S. EPA hotline (800-296-1996) or your doctor. For questions on scientific aspects, call the NWS at 301-713-0622.

Lightning

Source: National Weather Service

There are an estimated 25 million cloud-to-ground lightning bolts in the U.S. each year, killing an annual average of 67 people. This is a small number compared to U.S. deaths from fire (about 4,000 a year) and motor vehicle accidents (about 40,000), but still significant. In comparison, tornadoes cause an average of 65 deaths a year, and hurricanes an average of 16. Documented injuries from lightning number about 300 a year; there are probably many more.

Lightning is a result of ice in storm clouds. As ice particles rise and sink in the cloud, numerous collisions between them cause a separation of electrical charge. Positively charged crystals rise to the top, while negatively charged crystals drop to lower parts. As the storm travels, a pool of positive charges gathers in the ground below and follows along, traveling up objects like trees and telephone poles. In a common form of lightning, the negatively charged area in the storm sends charges downward; these are attracted to positively charged objects, and a channel develops, with an electrical transfer that you see as lightning. Lightning can travel as far as miles away from the area of a storm.

The transfer of charges in lightning generates a huge amount of heat, sending the temperature in the channel to 30,000 degrees Fahrenheit and causing the air within it to expand rapidly; the sound of that expansion is thunder. Sound travels more slowly than light, so you usually see lightning before you hear thunder.

To (very roughly) gauge one's danger, use the 30-30 rule. In good visibility, count the time between a lightning flash and the crack of thunder. If it's less than 30 seconds the storm is within 6 miles and dangerous. Find shelter immediately. The threat of more lightning does not stop right away; you need to wait about 30 minutes after the last flash of the storm to be sure.

Most lightning deaths and injuries occur in the summer months when people are outdoors; when a storm threatens people need to move to a safe place promptly. Even while indoors, people are advised to stay away from windows and avoid contact with anything conducting electricity.

For more information about lightning, try the website www.lightningsafety.noaa.gov/overview.htm

Global Measured Extremes of Temperature and Precipitation Records

Source: National Climatic Data Center; based on latest available records data

Highest Temperature Extremes

Continent	Highest Temp. (deg F)	Place	Elevation (feet)	Date
Africa	136	El Azizia, Libya	367	Sept. 13, 1922
North America	134	Death Valley, CA (Greenland Ranch)	–178	July 10, 1913
Asia	129	Tirat Tsvi, Israel	–722	June 22, 1942
Australia	128	Cloncurry, Queensland	622	Jan. 16, 1889
Europe	122	Seville, Spain	26	Aug. 4, 1881
South America	120	Rivadavia, Argentina	676	Dec. 11, 1905
Oceania	108	Tuguegarao, Philippines	72	Apr. 29, 1912
Antarctica	59	Vanda Station, Scott Coast	49	Jan. 5, 1974

Lowest Temperature Extremes

Continent	Lowest Temp. (deg F)	Place	Elevation (feet)	Date
Antarctica	–129.0	Vostok	11,220	July 21, 1983
Asia	–90.0	Oimekon, Russia	2,625	Feb. 6, 1933
Asia	–90.0	Verkhoyansk, Russia	350	Feb. 7, 1892
Greenland	–87.0	Northice	7,687	Jan. 9, 1954
North America	–81.4	Snag, Yukon, Canada	2,120	Feb. 3, 1947
Europe	–67.0	Ust'Shchugor, Russia	279	Jan.*
South America	–27.0	Sarmiento, Argentina	879	June 1, 1907
Africa	–11.0	Ifrane, Morocco	5,364	Feb. 11, 1935
Australia	–9.4	Charlotte Pass, NSW	5,758	June 29, 1994
Oceania	12.0	Mauna Kea Observatory, HI	13,773	May 17,1979

* Exact day and year unknown.

Greatest Measured Average Annual Precipitation Extremes

Continent	Highest Avg. (inches)	Place	Elevation (feet)	Years of Data
South America	523.6[1,2]	Lloro, Colombia	520[3]	29
Asia	467.4[1]	Mawsynram, India	4,597	38
Oceania	460.0[1]	Mt. Waialeale, Kauai, HI	5,148	30
Africa	405.0	Debundscha, Cameroon	30	32
South America	354.0[2]	Quibdo, Colombia	120	16
Australia	340.0	Bellenden Ker, Queensland	5,102	9
North America	256.0	Henderson Lake, British Columbia	12	14
Europe	183.0	Crkvica, Bosnia-Herzegovina	3,337	22

(1) The value given is continent's highest and possibly the world's, depending on measurement practices, procedures, and period of record variations. (2) The official greatest average annual precipitation for South America is 354 inches at Quibdo, Colombia. The 523.6 inch average at Lloro, Colombia (14 mi SE and at a higher elevation than Quibdo) is an estimate. (3) Approximate elevation.

Lowest Measured Average Annual Precipitation Extremes

Continent	Lowest Avg. (inches)	Place	Elevation (feet)	Years of Data
South America	0.03	Arica, Chile	95	59
Africa	<0.1	Wadi Halfa, Sudan	410	39
Antarctica	0.8[1]	Amundsen-Scott South Pole Station	9,186	10
North America	1.2	Batagues, Mexico	16	14
Asia	1.8	Aden, Yemen	22	50
Australia	4.05	Mulka (Troudaninna), South Australia	160[2]	42
Europe	6.4	Astrakhan, Russia	45	25
Oceania	8.93	Puako, Hawaii	5	13

(1) The value given is the average amount of solid snow accumulating in one year as indicated by snow markers. The amount of liquid content of the snow is undetermined. (2) Approximate elevation.

DISASTERS

Some Notable Aircraft Disasters Since 1937

Date	Aircraft	Site of accident	Deaths
1937, May 6	**German zeppelin Hindenburg**	**Burned at mooring, Lakehurst, NJ**	**36***
1944, Aug. 23	U.S. Air Force B-24 Liberator bomber	Hit school, Freckleton, England	61*
1945, July 28	U.S. Army B-25	Hit Empire State Building, New York, NY	14*
1952, Dec. 20	U.S. Air Force C-124	Fell, burned, Moses Lake, WA	87
1953, Mar. 3	**Canadian Pacific Comet Jet**	**Karachi, Pakistan**	**11**[1]
1953, June 18	U.S. Air Force C-124	Crashed, burned near Tokyo	129
1955, Oct. 6	United Airlines DC-4	Crashed in Medicine Bow Peak, WY	66
1955, Nov. 1	United Airlines DC-6B	Exploded, crashed near Longmont, CO	44[2]
1956, June 20	Venezuelan Super-Constellation	Crashed in Atlantic off Asbury Park, NJ	74
1956, June 30	TWA Super-Const., United DC-7	Collided over Grand Canyon, AZ	128
1960, Dec. 16	United DC-8 jet, TWA Super-Const.	Collided over New York City	134[3]
1962, Mar. 16	Flying Tiger Super-Constellation	Vanished in W Pacific	107
1962, June 3	Air France Boeing 707 jet	Crashed on takeoff from Paris	130
1962, June 22	Air France Boeing 707 jet	Crashed in storm, Guadeloupe, W.I.	113
1963, Feb. 1	Lebanese Middle East Airlines Vickers Viscount 754, Turkish Mil. Douglas C-47	Planes collided in mid-air over Ankara, Turkey, killing all 17 on planes, 87 on ground	104
1963, June 3	Chartered Northwest Airlines DC-7	Crashed in Pacific off British Columbia	101
1963, Nov. 29	Trans-Canada Airlines DC-8F	Crashed after takeoff from Montreal	118
1964, Mar. 1	Paradise Airlines Constellation	Crashed on approach in heavy weather	85
1965, May 20	Pakistani Boeing 720-B	Crashed at Cairo, Egypt, airport	121
1965, Sept. 17	Pan Am Boeing 707-121B	Crashed into mountains on approach to Montserrat, France	30
1966, Jan. 24	Air India Boeing 707 jetliner	Crashed on Mont Blanc, France-Italy	117
1966, Feb. 4	All-Nippon Boeing 727	Plunged into Tokyo Bay	133
1966, Mar. 5	BOAC Boeing 707 jetliner	Crashed on Mount Fuji, Japan	124
1966, Dec. 24	U.S. military-chartered CL-44	Crashed into village in South Vietnam	129*
1967, Apr. 20	Swiss Britannia turboprop	Crashed at Nicosia, Cyprus	126
1967, July 19	Piedmont Boeing 727, Cessna 310	Collided in air, Hendersonville, NC	82
1968, Apr. 20	S. African Airways Boeing 707	Crashed on takeoff, Windhoek, South-West Africa	122
1968, May 3	Braniff International Electra	Crashed in storm near Dawson, TX	85
1969, Mar. 16	Venezuelan DC-9	Crashed after takeoff from Maracaibo, Venezuela	155[4]
1969, Dec. 8	Olympic Airways DC-6B	Crashed near Athens in storm	93
1970, Feb. 15	Dominican DC-9	Crashed into sea on takeoff from Santo Domingo	102
1970, July 3	British chartered jetliner	Crashed near Barcelona, Spain	112
1970, July 5	Air Canada DC-8	Crashed near Toronto International Airport	108
1970, Aug. 9	Peruvian turbojet	Crashed after takeoff from Cuzco, Peru	101*
1970, Nov. 14	Southern Airways DC-9	Crashed in mountains near Huntington, WV	75[5]
1971, July 30	All-Nippon Boeing 727, Jap. AF F-86	Collided over Morioka, Japan	162[6]
1971, Sept. 4	Alaska Airlines Boeing 727	Crashed into mountain near Juneau, AK	111
1972, Aug. 14	East German Ilyushin-62	Crashed on takeoff, East Berlin	156
1972, Oct. 13	Aeroflot Ilyushin-62	Crashed near Moscow	176
1972, Dec. 3	Chartered Spanish airliner	Crashed on takeoff, Canary Islands	155
1972, Dec. 29	Eastern Airlines Lockheed Tristar	Crashed on approach to Miami Intl. Airport	101
1973, Jan. 22	Chartered Boeing 707	Burst into flames during landing, Kano Airport, Nigeria	176
1973, Feb. 21	**Libyan jetliner**	**Shot down by Israeli fighter planes over Sinai**	**108**
1973, Apr. 10	British Vanguard turboprop	Crashed during snowstorm at Basel, Switzerland	104
1973, June 3	Soviet Supersonic TU-144	Crashed near Goussainville, France	14[7]
1973, July 11	Brazilian Boeing 707	Crashed on approach to Orly Airport, Paris	122
1973, July 31	Delta Airlines jetliner	Crashed, landing in fog at Logan Airport, Boston	89
1973, Dec. 23	French Caravelle jet	Crashed in Morocco	106
1974, Mar. 3	Turkish DC-10 jet	Crashed at Ermenonville near Paris	346
1974, Apr. 23	Pan American 707 jet	Crashed in Bali, Indonesia	107
1974, Dec. 1	TWA-727	Crashed in storm, Upperville, VA	92
1974, Dec. 4	Dutch-chartered DC-8	Crashed in storm near Colombo, Sri Lanka	191
1975, Apr. 4	Air Force Galaxy C-5A	Crashed near Saigon, S Viet., after takeoff (carrying orphans)	172
1975, June 24	Eastern Airlines 727 jet	Crashed in storm, JFK Airport, NY	113
1975, Aug. 3	Chartered 707	Hit mountainside, Agadir, Morocco	188
1976, Sept. 10	Brit. Airways Trident, Yug. DC-9	Collided near Zagreb, Yugoslavia	176
1976, Sept. 19	Turkish 727	Hit mountain, S Turkey	155
1976, Oct. 13	Bolivian 707 cargo jet	Crashed in Santa Cruz, Bolivia	100[8]
1977, Mar. 27	**KLM 747, Pan American 747**	**Collided on runway, Tenerife, Canary Islands**	**583**[9]
1977, Nov. 19	TAP Boeing 727	Crashed on Madeira	130
1977, Dec. 4	Malaysian Boeing 737	Hijacked, then exploded in mid-air over Straits of Johore	100
1977, Dec. 13	U.S. DC-3	Crashed after takeoff at Evansville, IN	29[10]
1978, Jan. 1	Air India 747	Exploded, crashed into sea off Bombay	213
1978, Sept. 25	Boeing 727, Cessna 172	Collided in air, San Diego, CA	150
1978, Nov. 15	Chartered DC-8	Crashed near Colombo, Sri Lanka	183
1979, May 25	**American Airlines DC-10**	**Crashed after takeoff at O'Hare Intl. Airport, Chicago**	**275**[11]
1979, Aug. 17	Two Soviet Aeroflot jetliners	Collided over Ukraine	173
1979, Nov. 26	Pakistani Boeing 707	Crashed near Jidda, Saudi Arabia	156
1979, Nov. 28	New Zealand DC-10	Crashed into mountain in Antarctica	257
1980, Mar. 14	Polish Ilyushin 62	Crashed making emergency landing, Warsaw	87[12]
1980, Aug. 19	Saudi Arabian Tristar	Burned after emergency landing, Riyadh	301
1981, Dec. 1	Yugoslavian DC-9	Crashed into mountain in Corsica	178
1982, Jan. 13	Air Florida Boeing 737	Crashed into Potomac R. after takeoff	78
1982, July 9	Pan Am Boeing 727	Crashed after takeoff in Kenner, LA	153[13]
1983, Sept. 1	**S. Korean Boeing 747**	**Shot down after violating Soviet airspace**	**269**
1983, Nov. 27	Colombian Boeing 747	Crashed near Barajas Airport, Madrid	183
1985, Feb. 19	Spanish Boeing 727	Crashed into Mt. Oiz, Spain	148
1985, June 23	Air-India Boeing 747	Crashed into Atlantic Ocean S of Ireland	329
1985, Aug. 2	Delta Air Lines L-1011	Crashed at Dallas-Ft. Worth Intl. Airport	137
1985, Aug. 12	**Japan Air Lines Boeing 747**	**Crashed into Mt. Ogura, Japan**	**520**[14]
1985, Dec. 12	Arrow Air DC-8	Crashed after takeoff in Gander, Newfoundland	256[15]
1986, Mar. 31	Mexican Boeing 727	Crashed NW of Mexico City	166
1986, Aug. 31	Aeromexico DC-9	Collided with Piper PA-28 over Cerritos, CA	82[16]

Date	Aircraft	Site of accident	Deaths
1987, May 9	Polish Ilyushin 62M	Crashed after takeoff in Warsaw, Poland	183
1987, Aug. 16	Northwest Airlines MD-82	Crashed after takeoff in Romulus, MI	156
1987, Nov. 28	S. African Boeing 747	Crashed into Indian Ocean near Mauritius	159
1987, Nov. 29	S. Korean Boeing 707	Exploded over Thai-Burmese border	155
1988, Mar. 17	Colombian Boeing 707	Crashed into mountainside near Venezuela border	137
1988, July 3	**Iranian A300 Airbus**	**Shot down by U.S. Navy warship *Vincennes* over Pers. Gulf**	**290**
1988, Dec. 21	**Pan Am Boeing 747**	**Bomb on board; exploded over Lockerbie, Scot.**	**270**[17]
1989, Feb. 8	U.S. Boeing 707	Crashed into mountain in Azores Islands off Portugal	144
1989, June 7	Suriname DC-8	Crashed near Paramaribo Airport, Suriname	168
1989, July 19	United Airlines DC-10	Crashed while landing in Sioux City, IA	111
1989, Sept. 19	**French DC-10**	**Bomb on board; exploded in air over Niger**	**171**
1990, Jan. 25	Avianca Air Boeing 707	Crashed on landing, JFK Airport, NY	73
1990, Feb. 14	Indian Airlines Airbus 320	Crashed and burned landing in Bangalore, India	91
1990, Oct. 2	Chinese airline Boeing 737, 707	Hijacked; 737 jet landing in Guangzhou, crashed into 707	132
1991, May 26	Lauda-Air Boeing 767-300	Exploded over rural Thailand	223
1991, July 11	Nigerian DC-8	Crashed while landing at Jidda, Saudi Arabia	261
1991, Oct. 5	Indonesian military transport	Crashed after takeoff from Jakarta	137*
1992, July 31	Thai Airbus A-300-310	Crashed into mountain S. of Kathmandu, Nepal	113
1992, Oct. 4	**El Al Boeing 747-200F**	**Crashed into 2 apartment bldgs., Amsterdam, Netherlands**	**120***
1993, Feb. 8	Iran Air TU-154	Collided in air with military plane	132
1993, Mar. 5	Macedonian Pal Air Fokker 100	Crashed after takeoff in snowstorm in Skopje, Macedonia	83
1994, Jan. 3	Aeroflot TU-154	Crashed and exploded after takeoff in Irkhutsk, Russia	125[18]
1994, Apr. 26	China Airlines Airbus A-300-600R	Crashed at Japan's Nagoya Airport	264
1994, June 16	China Northwest Airlines TU-154	Crashed 10 min. after takeoff	160
1994, Sept. 8	USAir Boeing 737-300	Crashed in Aliquippa, PA, near Pittsburgh Intl. Airport	132
1994, Oct. 31	American Eagle ATR-72-210	Crashed in field near Roselawn, IN	68
1995, Aug. 11	Aviateca Boeing 737	Crashed into Chichontepec volcano, El Salvador	65
1995, Dec. 18	Zairian passenger jet	Crashed in Angola, location disputed	136
1995, Dec. 20	American Airlines Boeing 757	Crashed into mountain 50 mi N of Cali, Colombia	160
1996, Jan. 8	Antonova 32 cargo jet	Crashed into central market, Kinshasa, Zaire	350+*
1996, Feb. 6	Turkish Boeing 757	Crashed into Atlantic Ocean, off Dominican Republic	189
1996, Apr. 25	T-43, a military version of a Boeing 737	Crashed into mountain near Dubrovnik, Croatia	35[19]
1996, May 11	ValuJet DC-9	Crashed into the Florida Everglades after takeoff	110
1996, July 17	Trans World Airlines Boeing 747	Exploded and crashed in Atlantic Ocean, off Long Isl., NY	230
1996, Aug. 29	Vnukovo TU-154	Crashed into mountain on Arctic island of Spitsbergen	141
1996, Oct. 2	Aeroperu Boeing 757	Crashed in Pacific after takeoff from Lima, Peru	70
1996, Oct. 31	Brazilian TAM Fokker-100	Crashed into houses in São Paulo, Brazil	98[20]
1996, Nov. 7	Nigerian Boeing 727	Crashed into a lagoon 40 mi SE of Lagos, Nigeria	143
1996, Nov. 12	**Saudi Arabian Boeing 747, Kazakh Ilyushin-76 cargo plane**	**Collided in midair near New Delhi, India**	**349**[21]
1996, Nov. 23	Ethiopian Boeing 767	Hijacked, then crashed in Indian Ocean off the Comoros	127
1997, Jan. 9	Comair Embraer 120	Crashed on approach into Detroit Metro. Airport	29
1997, Feb. 4	2 Sikorsky CH-53 transport helicopters	Collided in midair over northern Galilee, Israel	73
1997, May 8	China Southern Airlines Boeing 737	Crashed on approach into Shenzhen's Huangtian Airport	35
1997, July 11	Cubana de Aviación Antonov-24	Crashed into the Caribbean off SE Cuba	44
1997, Aug. 6	Korean Air Boeing 747-300	Crashed into jungle on Guam on approach into airport	228
1997, Sept. 3	Vietnamese Airlines TU-134	Crashed on approach into Phnom Penh airport	64
1997, Sept. 14	U.S. C-141 cargo plane, Ger. TU-154	Collided in midair off SW Africa	33
1997, Sept. 26	Indonesian Airbus A-300	Crashed near Medan, Indonesia, airport	234
1997, Oct. 10	Austral Airlines DC-9-32	Crashed and exploded near Neuvo Berlin, Uruguay	74
1997, Dec. 6	Russian AN-124 transport cargo plane	Crashed into apartment complex near Irkutsk, Siberia	67*
1997, Dec. 15	Chartered TU-154 from Tajikistan	Crashed in desert near Sharja, U.A.E., airport	85
1997, Dec. 17	Chartered Yakovlev-42 from Ukraine	Crashed in mountains near Katerini, Greece	70
1997, Dec. 19	SilkAir Boeing 737-300	Crashed in Musi River, Sumatra, Indonesia	104
1998, Jan. 14	Afghan cargo plane	Crashed into mountain, SW Pakistan	50+
1998, Feb. 2	Cebu Pacific Air DC-9-32	Crashed into mountain near Cagayan de Oro, Philippines	104
1998, Feb. 16	China Airlines Airbus 300-622R	Crashed on approach to airport, Taipei, Taiwan	203[22]
1998, Apr. 20	Air France Boeing 727-200	Crashed into mountain after takeoff from Bogotá, Colombia	53
1998, Sept. 2	Swissair MD-11	Crashed into Atlantic Ocean off Halifax, Nova Scotia	229
1998, Sept. 25	Pauknair BAE146	Crashed into hillside in Morocco	38
1998, Oct. 11	Congo Air Lines Boeing 727	Shot down by rebels in Kindu, Congo	40
1998, Dec. 11	Thai Airways Airbus A310-200	Crashed short of runway at Surat Thani airport, S Thailand	101
1999, Feb. 24	China Southwest Airlines TU-154	Crashed on approach to Wenzhou airport, eastern China	61
1999, Sept. 1	LAPA Boeing 737-200	Crashed on takeoff from Jorge Newbery Airport, Buenos Aires	74[23]
1999, Oct. 31	EgyptAir Boeing 767-300	Crashed off Nantucket, MA	217
2000, Jan. 31	Alaska Airlines MD-83	Crashed into Pacific Ocean NW of Malibu, CA	88
2000, Apr. 19	Air Philippines Boeing 737-200	Crashed by Davao airport	131
2000, May 21	Chartered Jetstream 31	Crashed near Wilkes-Barre, PA	19
2000, July 25	Air France Concorde	Crashed into hotel after takeoff from Paris	113[24]
2000, Aug. 23	Gulf Air Airbus A320	Crashed into Persian Gulf near Manama, Bahrain	143
2000, Oct. 31	Singapore Airlines 747-400	Crashed immediately after takeoff, Taipei, Taiwan	81
2000, Oct. 31	Chartered Antonov 26	Exploded after takeoff in northern Angola	50
2000, Nov. 15	Chartered Antonov 24	Crashed after takeoff from Luanda, Angola	40+
2001, Jan. 27	Chartered Beechcraft King Air 200	Crashed after takeoff from Boulder, CO	10[25]
2001, Mar. 3	C23 Sherpa mil. transp.	Crashed in storm, central GA	21
2001, Apr. 7	M-17 helicopter	Crashed into mountain S. of Hanoi, Vietnam	16[26]
2001, July 3	Vladivostokavia Tu-154	Crashed on approach to landing at Irkutsk, Russia	145
2001, Sept. 11	**2 Boeing 767s, 2 Boeing 757s**	**See below**[27]	**265**[27]
2001, Oct. 4	Sibir Airlines Tupelov Tu-154	Crashed into Black Sea, struck by errant Ukrainian missile	78
2001, Oct. 8	Twin-engine Cessna, Scandinavian Airlines System (SAS) jetliner	Collided in heavy fog during takeoff from Milan, Italy	118*
2001, Nov. 12	**American Airlines Airbus A-300**	**Crashed after takeoff from JFK Airport, New York, NY**	**265***
2002, Jan. 28	Ecuadoran airline Boeing 727-100	Crashed in Andes mountains in southern Colombia	92
2002, Feb. 12	Iran Air Tours Tu-154	Crashed before landing in Khorramabad, Iran	119
2002, Apr. 15	Air China Boeing 767-200	Crashed into hillside amid rain and fog near Pusan, South Korea	122
2002, Apr. 18	4-seat Rockwell Commander	Crashed into Pirelli building, tallest skyscraper in Milan, Italy	3*
2002, May 4	EAS Airlines BAC 1-11-500	Crashed in suburb of Kano, Nigeria, shortly after takeoff	148+*
2002, May 7	China Northern MD-82	Plunged into Yellow Sea near Dalian, China, after fire in cabin	112
2002, May 25	China Airlines Boeing 747-200	Broke apart in mid-air and plunged into Taiwan Strait	225

Date	Aircraft	Site of accident	Deaths
2002, July 1	Bashkirian Airlines Tu-154, DHL (Ger. cargo) Boeing 757	Collided over S Germany	71
2002, July 4	Prestige Airlines Cargo Boeing B-707	Crashed short of runway in Bangui, Central African Rep.	25
2002, July 27	Ukraine Air Force Sukhoi SU-27	Crashed into spectators at airshow in Lviv, Ukraine	85
2002, Aug. 19	Russian Mi-26 helicopter	Troop-carrier hit by Chechen missile near Grozny	127
2002, Dec. 23	Aeromist Kharkiv Antonov AN-140	Crashed into mountain in fog approaching Isfahan, Iran	46
2003, Jan. 8	Air Midwest, Beechcraft 1900D	Crashed after takeoff at Charlotte, N.C.	21
2003, Jan. 8	Turkish Airlines Avro RJ-100	Crashed on landing in Diyarbakir, Turkey	75
2003, Jan. 9	TANS Airlines Fokker 28 Fellowship	Crashed into mountain near Chachopoyas, Peru	46
2003, Feb. 19	Iranian Guard Ilyushin IL-76	Troop-carrying plane crashed into mountain near Kerman, Iran	275
2003, Mar. 6	Air Algerie Boeing 737	Crashed on takeoff at Tamanrasset, Algeria	102
2003, May 8	**Congolese Army IL-76**	**On flight from Kinshasa door opened, people sucked out**	60-170(?)
2003, May 26	Ukrain.-Medit. Airlines Yak. 42D	Crashed into mountain in fog approaching Trabzon, Turkey	75
2003, July 8	Sudan Airways, Boeing 737-2J8C	Crashed into hillside after takeoff from Port Sudan Airport	116
2003, Aug. 24	Tropical Airways Let 410UVP-E	Crashed after takeoff in Haiti, because of overloading	21
2003, Nov. 29	Congolese Air Force Antonov 26	Crashed on takeoff attempt from Boendo, Dem. Rep. of Congo.	33
2003, Dec. 25	Union Transp. Africaines Boeing B-727	Crashed after takeoff from Cotonou, Benin	140
2004, Jan. 3	Flash Airlines Boeing B-737	Crashed after takeoff from Sharm el-Sheik, Egypt	148
2004, Jan. 13	Uzbekistan Airways Yakovlev YAK-40	Crashed on landing attempt in fog at Tashkent, Uzbekistan	37
2004, Jan. 17	Cessna 208B Grand Caravan	Crashed into L. Erie after takeoff from island nr. Can	10
2004, Feb. 10	Iranian Kish Airline Fokker-50	Crashed on approach to Sharjah, UAE	43
2004, Mar. 21	Med-Trans Corp. Bell 407 helicopter	Crashed in Pyote, TX, enroute to Lubbock, TX	4
2004, May 15	Rico Linhas Aereas Embraer 120ER Brasilia	Crashed in Amazon jungle near Manaus, Brazil	33
2004, June 8	Gabon Express Hawker Siddeley HS-748	Crashed into sea after takeoff from Libreville, Gabon	19
2004, June 29	UN Mi-8 helicopter	Crashed in forest in Sierra Leone	24 (28)
2004, Aug. 24	Volga-Aviaexpress TU-134A-3, Sibir Airlines TU-154B2	2 planes crashed after takeoff from Moscow, Russia; brought down by Chechen terrorists	90
2005, Jan. 13	Colombian Black Hawk helicopter	Crashed in Narino prov. in bad weather	20
2005, Jan. 26	CH-53-Super Stallion Marine helicopter	Crashed in Iraq's western desert	31
2005, Feb. 3	Kam Air Boeing 737	Crashed after attempting to land at Kabul airport, Afghan.	104
2005, Mar. 16	Russian Antonov-24	Crashed in Varandei, Russia, near Barents Sea	29
2005, Apr. 7	Russian AN-24 turboprop	Crashed into hill near Barents Sea port	28+
2005, July 14	Ugandan mil. helicopter	Crashed in mountains; among the killed was former Sudan rebel leader John Garang	14
2005, Aug. 6	Tunisian ATR-72 turboprop	Crashed off Sicilia Coast after engine fail	13+
2005, Aug. 14	Helios Airways Boeing 737	Crashed near Athens, Greece	121
2005, Aug. 16	West Caribbean Airways MD82	Crashed in western Venezuela	160
2005, Aug. 23	TANS Peru Boeing 737	Crashed near Pucallpa, Peru, during emergency landing	41
2005, Sept. 4	Mandala Airlines Boeing 737-200	Crashed after takeoff from Medan, Sumatra, Indon.	140+

*Including those on ground and in buildings. (1) First fatal crash of commercial jet. (2) Caused by bomb planted by John G. Graham in insurance plot to kill his mother, a passenger. (3) Incl. all 128 aboard planes and 6 on ground. (4) Killed 84 on plane and 71 on ground. (5) Incl. 43 Marshall Univ. football players and coaches. (6) Airliner-fighter crash; pilot of fighter parachuted to safety, was arrested for negligence. (7) First supersonic plane crash; killed 8 on ground. (8) Crew of 3 killed; 97 killed on the ground. (9) World's worst airline disaster. (10) Incl. Univ. of Evansville basketball team. (11) Incl. 2 on ground. Highest death toll in U.S. aviation history. (12) Incl. 22 members of U.S. boxing team. (13) Incl. 8 on ground. (14) Worst single-plane disaster. (15) Incl. 248 members of U.S. 101st Airborne Division. (16) Incl. 15 on ground. (17) Incl. 11 on ground. (18) Incl. 1 on ground. (19) Incl. U.S. Sec. of Commerce Ron Brown. (20) Incl. 2 on ground. (21) World's worst midair collision. (22) Incl. 6 on ground. (23) Incl. 10 on ground. (24) World's first Concorde crash; deaths incl. 5 on ground. (25) Incl. 7 players and staff of Oklahoma State Univ. men's basketball team. (26) Carried U.S. mil. personnel, searching for MIAs from Vietnam War. (27) 4 planes were hijacked and crashed, with all on board (265, incl. 19 hijackers) killed: American Airlines Flight 11, a Boeing 767-200, with 81 passengers,11 crew, crashed into Tower 1 of the World Trade Center in NYC; United Airlines Flight 175, a Boeing 767-200, with 56 passengers, 9 crew, crashed into Tower 2 of the World Trade Center; American Airlines Flight 77, a Boeing 757-200, with 58 passengers, 6 crew, crashed into the Pentagon outside Washington, DC; United Air Lines Flight 93, a Boeing 757-200, with 37 passengers, 7 crew, crashed near Shanksville, PA. About 2,600 people on ground died at the 2 World Trade Center towers, and 125 in the Pentagon. (28) Incl. 14 Pakistani UN Peacekeepers.

Some Notable Shipwrecks Since 1854

(Figures indicate estimated lives lost. Does not include most wartime disasters.)

1854, Mar.—City of Glasgow; Brit. steamer missing in N Atlantic; 480.

1854, Sept. 27—Arctic; U.S. (Collins Line) steamer sunk in collision with French steamer *Vesta* near Cape Race; 285-351.

1856, Jan. 23—Pacific; U.S. (Collins Line) steamer missing in N Atlantic; 186-286.

1858, Sept. 23—Austria; German steamer destroyed by fire in N Atlantic; 471.

1863, Apr. 27—Anglo-Saxon; Brit. steamer wrecked at Cape Race; 238.

1865, Apr. 27—Sultana; Mississippi River steamer blew up near Memphis, TN; 1,450.

1869, Oct. 27—Stonewall; steamer burned on Mississippi River below Cairo, IL; 200.

1870, Jan. 25—City of Boston; Brit. (Inman Line) steamer vanished between New York and Liverpool; 177.

1870, Oct. 19—Cambria; Brit. steamer off N Ireland; 196.

1872, Nov. 7—Mary Celeste; U.S. half-brig sailed from New York for Genoa; found abandoned; loss of life unknown.

1873, Jan. 22—Northfleet; Brit. steamer foundered off Dungeness, England; 300.

1873, Apr. 1—Atlantic; Brit. (White Star) steamer off Nova Scotia; 585.

1873, Nov. 23—Ville du Havre; French steamer sank after collision with Brit. sailing ship *Loch Earn*; 226.

1875, May 7—Schiller; German steamer off Scilly Isles; 312.

1875, Nov. 4—Pacific; U.S. steamer sank after collision off Cape Flattery; 236.

1878, Sept. 3—Princess Alice; Brit. steamer sank after collision in Thames River; 700.

1878, Dec. 18—Byzantin; French steamer sank after collision in Dardanelles; 210.

1881, May 24—Victoria; steamer capsized in Thames River, Canada; 200.

1883, Jan. 19—Cimbria; German steamer sank in collision with Brit. steamer *Sultan* in North Sea; 389.

1887, Nov. 15—Wah Yeung; Brit. steamer burned at sea; 400.

1890, Feb. 17—Duburg; Brit. steamer wrecked, China Sea; 400.

1890, Sept. 19—Ertogrul; Turkish frigate off Japan; 540.

1891, Mar. 17—Utopia; Brit. steamer sank in collision with Brit. ironclad *Anson* off Gibraltar; 562.

1895, Jan. 30—Elbe; German steamer sank in collision with Brit. steamer *Craithie* in North Sea; 332.

1895, Mar. 11—Reina Regenta; Spanish cruiser foundered near Gibraltar; 400.

1898, Feb. 15—Maine; U.S. battleship blown up in Havana Harbor; 260.

1898, July 4—La Bourgogne; French steamer sank in collision with Brit. sailing ship *Cromartyshire* off Nova Scotia; 549.

1898, Nov. 26—Portland; U.S. steamer off Cape Cod; 157.

1904, June 15—General Slocum; excursion steamer burned in East River, New York City; 1,030.

1904, June 28—Norge; Danish steamer wrecked on Rockall Island, Scotland; 620.

1906, Aug. 4—Sirio; Italian steamer wrecked off Cape Palos, Spain; 350.

1908, Mar. 23—Matsu Maru; Japanese steamer sank in collision near Hakodate, Japan; 300.

1909, Aug. 1—Waratah; Brit. steamer, Sydney to London, vanished; 300.

1910, Feb. 9—General Chanzy; French steamer wrecked off Minorca, Spain; 200.
1911, Sept. 25—Liberté; French battleship exploded at Toulon; 285.
1912, Mar. 5—Principe de Asturias; Spanish steamer wrecked off Spain; 500.
1912, Apr. 14-15—Titanic; Brit. (White Star) steamer hit iceberg in N Atlantic; 1,503.
1912, Sept. 28—Kichemaru; Japanese steamer sank off Japanese coast; 1,000.
1914, May 29—Empress of Ireland; Brit. (Canadian Pacific) steamer collided with Norw. collier in St. Lawrence River; 1,014.
1915, May 7—Lusitania; Brit. (Cunard Line) steamer torpedoed and sunk by German submarine off Ireland; 1,198.
1915, July 24—Eastland; steamer capsized in Chicago River; 844.
1916, Feb. 26—Provence; French cruiser sank in Medit.; 3,100.
1916, Mar. 3—Principe de Asturias; Spanish steamer wrecked near Santos, Brazil; 558.
1916, Aug. 29—Hsin Yu; Chinese steamer sank off Chinese coast; 1,000.
1917, Dec. 6—Mont Blanc, Imo; French ammunition ship and Belgian steamer collided in Halifax Harbor; 1,600.
1918, Apr. 25—Kiang-Kwan; Chinese steamer sank in collision off Hankow; 500.
1918, July 12—Kawachi; Japanese battleship blew up in Tokayama Bay; 500.
1918, Oct. 25—Princess Sophia; Canadian steamer sank off Alaskan coast; 398.
1919, Jan. 17—Chaonia; French steamer lost in Straits of Messina, Italy; 460.
1919, Sept. 9—Valbanera; Spanish steamer lost off Florida coast; 500.
1921, Mar. 18—Hong Kong; steamer wrecked in South China Sea; 1,000.
1922, Aug. 26—Niitaka; Japanese cruiser sank in storm off Kamchatka, USSR; 300.
1924, June 12—USS Mississippi; U.S. battleship; explosions in gun turret, off San Pedro, CA; 48.
1927, Oct. 25—Principessa Mafalda; Italian steamer blew up, sank off Porto Seguro, Brazil; 314.
1928, Nov. 12—Vestris; Brit. steamer sank off Virginia; 113.
1934, Sept. 8—Morro Castle; U.S. steamer, Havana to New York, burned off Asbury Park, NJ; 134.
1939, May 23—Squalus; U.S. submarine sank off Portsmouth, NH; 26.
1939, June 1—Thetis; submarine sank, Liverpool Bay; 99.
1942, Feb. 18—Truxtun and **Pollux;** U.S. destroyer and cargo ship ran aground, sank off Newfoundland; 204.
1942, Oct. 2—Curacao; Brit. cruiser sank after collision with liner *Queen Mary;* 338.
1944, Dec. 17-18—3 U.S. Third Fleet destroyers sank during typhoon in Philippine Sea; 790.
1945, Jan. 30—Wilhelm Gustloff; Liner with German refugees, soldiers sunk by Soviet submarine in Baltic; 5,000-9,000.
1945, Apr. 16—Goya; Cargo ship carrying German refugees, soldiers sunk by Soviet submarine in Baltic; 6,000-7,000.
1945, May 3—Cap Arcona, Thielbek; German liners carrying concentration camp inmates sunk by British warplanes in Lubeck Bay; 7,000-8,000.
1947, Jan. 19—Himera; Greek steamer hit a mine off Athens; 392.
1947, Apr. 16—Grandcamp; French freighter exploded in Texas City, TX, harbor, starting fires; 576+.
1948, Nov.—Chinese army evacuation ship exploded and sank off S Manchuria; 6,000.
1948, Dec. 3—Kiangya; Chinese refugee ship wrecked in explosion S of Shanghai; 1,100+.
1949, Sept. 17—Noronic; Canadian Great Lakes Cruiser burned at Toronto dock; 130.
1952, Apr. 26—Hobson and **Wasp;** U.S. destroyer and aircraft carrier collided in Atlantic; 176.
1954, May 26—Bennington; U.S. carrier damaged by explosions off Rhode Island; 103.
1954, Sept. 26—Toya Maru; Japanese ferry sank in Tsugaru Strait, Japan; 1,172.
1956, July 26—Andrea Doria and **Stockholm;** Italian liner and Swedish liner collided off Nantucket; 51.
1957, July 14—Eshghabad; Soviet ship ran aground in Caspian Sea; 270.
1960, Dec. 19—Constellation; U.S. aircraft carrier caught fire in Brooklyn Navy Yard, NY; 49.
1961, Apr. 8—Dara of British liner exploded in Persian Gulf; 236.
1961, July 8—Save; Portuguese ship ran aground off Mozambique; 259.
1963, Apr. 10—Thresher; U.S. Navy atomic submarine sank in N Atlantic; 129.
1964, Feb. 10—Voyager; Australian destroyer sank after collision with aircraft carrier *Melbourne* off New South Wales; 82.
1965, Nov. 13—Yarmouth Castle; Panamanian registered cruise ship burned and sank off Nassau; 89.
1967, July 29—Forrestal; U.S. aircraft carrier caught fire off N Vietnam; 134.
1968, Jan. 25—Dakar; Israeli submarine vanished in Medit.; 69.
1968, late May—Scorpion; U.S. nuclear submarine sank in Atlantic near Azores; 99 (located Oct. 31).
1969, June 2—Evans; U.S. destroyer cut in half by Australian carrier *Melbourne*, S China Sea; 74.
1970, Mar. 4—Eurydice; French submarine sank in Mediterranean near Toulon; 57.
1970, Dec. 15—Namyong-Ho; South Korean ferry sank in Korea Strait; 308.
1974, May 1—Motor launch capsized off Bangladesh; 250.
1974, Sept. 26—Soviet destroyer sank in Black Sea; 200+.
1975, Nov. 10—Edmund Fitzgerald; U.S. cargo ship sank during storm on Lake Superior; 29.
1976, Oct. 20—George Prince and **Frosta;** ferryboat and Norwegian tanker collided on Mississippi R. at Luling, LA; 77.
1976, Dec. 25—Patria; Egyptian liner caught fire and sank in the Red Sea; 100.
1979, Aug. 14—23 yachts competing in Fastnet yacht race sank or abandoned during storm in S Irish Sea; 18.
1981, Jan. 27—Tamponas II; Indonesian passenger ship caught fire and sank in Java Sea; 580.
1981, May 26—Nimitz; U.S. Marine combat jet crashed on deck of U.S. aircraft carrier; 14.
1983, Feb. 12—Marine Electric; coal freighter sank during storm off Chincoteague, VA; 33.
1983, May 25—10th of Ramadan; Nile steamer caught fire and sank in Lake Nasser; 357.
1986, Apr. 20—ferry sank near Barisal, Bangladesh; 262.
1986, Aug. 31—Soviet passenger ship *Admiral Nakhimov* and Soviet freighter *Pyotr Vasev* collided in Black Sea; 398.
1987, Mar. 6—British ferry capsized off Zeebrugge, Belgium; 189.
1987, Dec. 20—Philippine ferry *Dona Paz* and oil tanker *Victor* collided in Tablas Strait; 4,341.
1988, Aug. 6—Indian ferry capsized on Ganges R.; 400+.
1989, Apr. 19—USS Iowa; explosion in gun turret; 47.
1989, Apr. 7—Komsolets; Soviet submarine; sank after fire off Norwegian coast; 42.
1989, Aug. 20—Brit. barge *Bowbelle* struck Brit. pleasure cruiser *Marchioness* on Thames R. in central London; 56.
1989, Sept. 10—Romanian pleasure boat and Bulgarian barge collided on Danube R.; 161.
1991, Apr. 10—Auto ferry and oil tanker collided outside Livorno Harbor, Italy; 140.
1991, Dec. 14—Salem Express; ferry rammed coral reef near Safaga, Egypt; 462.
1993, Feb. 17—Neptune; ferry capsized off Port-au-Prince, Haiti; 500+.
1993, Oct. 10—West Sea Ferry; capsized in Yellow Sea near W South Korea during storm; 285.
1994, Sept. 28—Estonia; ferry sank in Baltic Sea; 1,049.
1996, May 21—Bukoba; ferry sank in Lake Victoria (Africa); 500.
1997, Feb. 20—Tamil refugee boat sank off Sri Lanka; 165.
1997, Mar. 28—Albanian refugee boat sank in Adriatic Sea after being rammed by Italian navy warship *Sibilla*; 83.
1997, Sept. 8—Pride of la Gonâve; Haitian ferry sank off Montrouis, Haiti; 200+.
1998, Apr. 4—passenger boat capsized off coast near Ibaka beach, Nigeria; 280.
1998, Sept. 2—2 passenger boats capsized on Lake Kivu, near Bukavu, Congo; 200+.
1998, Sept. 18—ferry sank S of Manila; 97.
1999, Feb. 6—Harta Rimba; cargo ship sank off Indonesia; 280+.
1999, Mar. 26—passenger boat overturned off coast, Sierra Leone; 150+.
1999, Apr. 2—passenger ferry sank off coast of Nigeria; 100+.
1999, May 1—excursion boat sank in Lake Hamilton, AR; 13.
1999, May 8—passenger ferry capsized off Bangladesh; 200+.
1999, Nov. 24—Dashun; passenger ferry capsized near Yantai, China; 280.
2000, May 3—2 ferries capsized, Meghna R., Bangladesh; 72+.
2000, June 29—overloaded ferry capsized in storm off Sulawesi Island, Indonesia; 500+.
2000, Aug. 12—Kursk; Russian sub sank in Barents Sea; 118.
2000, Sept. 26—Express Samina; Greek ferry sank off Paros, Greece; 81+.
2001, Feb. 9—Ehime Maru; Japanese trawler sunk by surfacing U.S. submarine *Greeneville*, near Hawaii; 9.
2001, Dec. 22—North Korean spy ship sank after exchanging fire with Japanese coast guard; 15.
2001, Oct. 19—Indonesian fishing boat overloaded with asylum-seekers sank off Java's south coast; 350+.
2002, May 4—Bangladesh ferry sank, Meghna R.; 370+.
2002, May 26—barge struck Interstate highway bridge over Arkansas R. in Oklahoma; 13+.
2002, Sept. 26—overloaded Senegalese ferry capsized in ocean off The Gambia; 1,863.
2003, Mar. 23—overloaded ferry capsized in Lake Tanganyika off Burundi; 111+.

2003, Apr. 21—2 ferries capsized in storms in Bangladesh on Meghna and Buriganga rivers; 180+.
2003, Apr. 4—ferry sank near Chhatak in Bangladesh; 80+.
2003, July 8—overcrowded ferry sank near Chandpur in the Bangladesh River; c. 400.
2003, Oct. 15—Andrew J. Barberi; NYC ferry crashed into dock on approaching Staten Is.; 11.
2003, Nov. 25—Overloaded ferry sank on Lake Mayi Ndombe, Dem. Rep. of Congo; 130-200.
2004, Jan. 26—Convoi Lengi; ferry caught fire on Congo R. in Dem. Rep. of Congo; 200.
2004, Feb. 28—Bow Mariner; tanker carrying ethanol caught fire and exploded off Virginia coast; 21.
2004, Mar 6—Water taxi capsized in storm in Baltimore's Inner Harbor; 5.
2004, Mar. 11—Ferry sank off Madagascar during cyclone; 113.
2004, May 24—Lightning Sun; ferry sank in Meghna river in Bangladesh; 60+.
2004, Dec. 8—Selendang Ayu; Malaysian freighter ran aground, Aleutian Islands; 6
2005, Oct. 2.—Ethan Allen; glass boat carrying senior citizens, cruising Lake George, in NY, capsized; 20.

Some Notable Railroad Disasters Since 1925

Date	Location	Deaths
1925, June 16	Hackettstown, NJ	50
1925, Oct. 27	Victoria, MS	21
1926, Sept. 5	Waco, CO	30
1937, July 16	Nr. Patna, India	107
1938, June 19	Saugus, MT	47
1939, Aug. 12	Harney, NV	24
1939, Dec. 22	Near Magdeburg, Germany	132
1939, Dec. 22	Near Friedrichshafen, Germany	99
1940, Apr. 19	Little Falls, NY	31
1940, July 31	Cuyahoga Falls, OH	43
1943, Aug. 29	Wayland, NY	27
1943, Sept. 6	Frankford Junction, Philad. PA	79
1943, Dec. 16	Between Rennert and Buie, NC	72
1944, Jan. 16	León Prov., Spain	500
1944, Mar. 2	Salerno, Italy	521
1944, July 6	High Bluff, TN	35
1944, Aug. 4	Near Stockton, GA	47
1944, Sept. 14	Dewey, IN	29
1944, Dec. 31	Bagley, UT	50
1945, Aug. 9	Michigan, ND	34
1946, Mar. 20	Aracaju, Mexico	185
1946, Apr. 25	Naperville, IL	45
1947, Feb. 18	Gallitzin, PA	24
1949, Oct. 22	Nr. Dwor, Poland	200+
1950, Feb. 17	Rockville Centre, NY	31
1950, Sept. 11	Coshocton, OH	33
1950, Nov. 22	Richmond Hill, NY	79
1951, Feb. 6	Woodbridge, NJ	84
1952, Mar. 4	Nr. Rio de Janeiro, Brazil	119
1952, July 9	Rzepin, Poland	160
1952, Oct. 8	Harrow, England	112
1953, Mar. 27	Conneaut, OH	21
1955, Apr. 3	Guadalajara, Mexico	300
1956, Jan. 22	Los Angeles, CA	30
1957, Sept. 1	Kendal, Jamaica	178
1957, Sept. 29	Montgomery, W Pakistan	250
1957, Dec. 4	London, England	90
1958, May 8	Rio de Janeiro, Brazil	128
1958, Sept. 15	Elizabethport, NJ	48
1960, Nov. 14	Pardubice, Czech	110
1962, Jan. 8	Woerden, Netherlands	91
1962, May 3	Tokyo, Japan	163
1963, Nov. 9	Yokohama, Japan	120+
1964, July 26	Porto, Portugal	94
1967, July 6	Madgeburg, Germany	94
1970, Feb. 1	Buenos Aires, Argentina	236
1972, June 16	Vierzy, France	107
1972, July 21	Seville, Spain	76
1972, Oct. 6	Saltillo, Mexico	208
1972, Oct. 30	Chicago, IL	45
1974, Aug. 30	Zagreb, Yugoslavia	153
1975, Feb. 28	London subway train	41
1977, Jan. 18	Granville, Australia	83
1981, June 6	Bihar, India	800+
1982, Jan. 27	El Asnam, Algeria	130
1982, July 11	Tepic, Mexico	120
1983, Feb. 19	Empalme, Mexico	100
1985, Feb. 23	Madhya Pradesh, India	50
1985, Aug. 3	southern France	35
1987, July 2	Kasumbalesha Shaba, Zaire	125
1988, June 27	Paris train station, Gare de Lyon	57
1988, Dec. 12	London, England	35
1989, Jan. 15	Maizdi Khan, Bangladesh	110+
1989, June 9	train collided with bus in S Russia	31
1990, Jan. 4	Sindh Prov., Pakistan	210+
1991, May 14	Shigaraki, Japan	42
1993, Sept. 22	Big Bayou Conot, AL	47
1994, Mar. 8	Nr. Durban, South Africa	63
1994, Sept. 22	Tolunda, Angola	300
1995, Aug. 20	Firozabad, India	358
1996, Feb. 16	Silver Spring, MD	11
1997, Mar. 3	Punjab State, Pakistan	125
1997, Mar. 31	Huarte Arakil, Spain	21
1997, Apr. 29	Hunan, China	58
1997, May 4	Rwanda	100+
1997, Sept. 14	Central India	77
1998, June 3	Eschede, Germany	102
1998, Feb. 19	Yaounde, Cameroon	100+
1999, Mar. 15	Bourbonnais, IL	11
1999, Mar. 24	Nairobi, Kenya	32+
1999, Aug. 2	Gauhati, India	285+
1999, Oct. 5	London, England	31
2000, Jan. 4	Rena, Norway	35
2000, July 28	São Paulo, Brazil	12
2000, Nov. 11	Kaprun, Austria	155
2001, Feb. 28	Great Heck, England	13
2001, June 22	Cochin, India	64
2001, Sept. 1	Indonesia	40
2002, Feb. 20	South of Cairo, Egypt	373
2002, Apr. 18	Seville, FL	4
2002, Apr. 23	Placentia, CA	2
2002, May 25	Muamba, Mozambique	196+
2002, June 24	Igandu, Tanzania	281+
2002, Sept. 10	Bihar, India	118
2002, Nov. 6	Nancy, France	12
2003, Jan. 3	Maharashtra, India	18
2003, Feb. 1	NW Zimbabwe	46
2003, May 8	near Lake Balaton in Hungary	33
2003, May 15	Ludhiana, India	36
2003, June 3	Spain, Albacete province	19
2003, June 22	Rajapur, India	33
2003, July 2	Andhra Pradesh, India	22
2004, Feb. 18	Neyshabur, NE Iran	300+
2004, Apr. 22	Ryongchon, North Korea	161
2004, July 22	Mekece, NW Turkey	36
2005, Jan. 6	Graniteville, SC	9
2005, Jan. 26	Glendale, CA	11
2005, Apr. 25	near Amagasaki, Japan	106
2005, July 13	Ghotki, Pakistan	133

Some Notable U.S. Tornadoes Since 1925

Date	Location	Deaths
1925, Mar. 18	MO, IL, IN	689
1927, Apr. 12	Rock Springs, TX	74
1927, May 9	AR, Poplar Bluff, MO	92
1927, Sept. 29	St. Louis, MO	90
1930, May 6	Hill, Navarro, Ellis Co., TX	41
1932, Mar. 21	AL (series of tornadoes)	268
1936, Apr. 5	MS, GA	455
1936, Apr. 6	Gainesville, GA	203
1938, Sept. 29	Charleston, SC	32
1942, Mar. 16	Central to NE Mississippi	75
1942, Apr. 27	Rogers and Mayes Co., OK	52
1944, June 23	OH, PA, WV, MD	150
1945, Apr. 12	OK-AR	102
1947, Apr. 9	TX, OK, KS	169
1948, Mar. 19	Bunker Hill and Gillespie, IL	33
1949, Jan. 3	LA and AR	58
1952, Mar. 21	AR, MO, TN (series)	208
1953, May 11	Waco, TX	114
1953, June 8	MI, OH	142
1953, June 9	Worcester and vicinity, MA	90
1953, Dec. 5	Vicksburg, MS	38
1955, May 25	KS, MO, OK, TX	115
1957, May 20	KS, MO	48
1958, June, 4	NW Wisconsin	30
1959, Feb. 10	St. Louis, MO	21
1960, May 5, 6	Southeastern OK, AR	30
1962, Mar. 31	Milton, FL	17
1965, Apr. 11	IN, IL, OH, MI, WI	271
1966, Mar. 3	Jackson, MS	57
1966, Mar. 3	MS, AL	61
1967, Apr. 21	IL, MI	33
1968, May 15	Midwest	71

Date	Location	Deaths
1969, Jan. 23	MS	32
1971, Feb. 21	Mississippi delta	110
1973, May 26-27	South, Midwest (series)	47
1974, Apr. 3-4	AL, GA, IN, KY, OH, TN, et al.	315
1977, Apr. 4	AL, MS, GA	22
1979, Apr. 10	TX, OK	60
1984, Mar. 28	NC, SC	57
1985, May 31	NY, PA, OH, Ont. (series)	75
1987, May 22	Saragosa, TX	29
1989, Nov. 15	Huntsville, AL	18
1990, Aug. 28	Northern IL	25
1991, Apr. 26	KS, OK	23
1992, Nov. 21-23	South, Midwest	26
1994, Mar. 27-28	AL, TN, GA, NC, SC (series)	52
1995, May 6-7	Southern OK, northern TX	23
1997, Mar. 1	Central AR	26
1997, May 27	Jarrell, TX	27
1998, Feb. 22-23	Central FL	42
1998, Mar. 20	Northeast GA	12
1998, Mar. 24	Eastern India	145
1998, Apr. 8	AL, GA, MS	39
1999, May 3-4	OK, KS	42
2000, Feb. 14	Southwest GA	22+
2000, July 14	Alberta	11
2000, Dec. 16	AL	12
2001, Nov. 23-24	AL, AR, MS (series)	13
2002, Nov. 9-11	AL, MS, OH, PA, TN	36
2003, Mar. 20	GA	6
2003, May 4-11	TN, MO, KS, IL, OK, WV, AL	48
2004, Apr. 20-21	IL, IN	8

Principal U.S. Mine Disasters Since 1900

Source: Bureau of Mines, U.S. Dept. of the Interior; Mine Safety and Health Admin., U.S. Dept. of Labor

(All are bituminous-coal mines unless otherwise noted.)

Date	Location	Deaths
1900, May 1	Scofield, UT	200
1902, May 19	Coal Creek, TN	184
1902, July 10	Johnstown, PA	112
1903, June 30	Hanna, WY	169
1904, Jan. 25	Cheswick, PA	179
1905, Feb. 26	Virginia City, AL	112
1907, Jan. 29	Stuart, WV	84
1907, Dec. 6	Monongah, WV	361
1907, Dec. 19	Jacobs Creek, PA	239
1908, Nov. 28	Marianna, PA	154
1909, Nov. 13	Cherry, IL	259
1910, Jan. 31	Primero, CO	75
1910, May 5	Palos, AL	90
1910, Nov.8	Delagua, CO	79
1911, Apr. 8	Littleton, AL	128
1911, Dec. 9	Briceville, TN	84
1912, Mar. 26	Jed, WV	83
1913, Apr. 23	Finleyville, PA	96
1913, Oct. 22	Dawson, NM	263
1914, Apr. 28	Eccles, WV	181
1915, Mar. 2	Layland, WV	112
1917, Apr. 27	Hastings, CO	121
1917, June 8	Butte, MT[1]	163
1919, June 5	Wilkes-Barre, PA[2]	92
1922, Nov. 6	Spangler, PA	77
1922, Nov. 22	Dolomite, AL	90
1923, Feb. 8	Dawson, NM	120
1923, Aug. 14	Kemmerer, WY	99
1924, Mar. 8	Castle Gate, UT	171
1924, Apr. 28	Benwood, WV	119
1926, Jan. 13	Wilburton, OK	91
1927, Apr. 30	Everettville, WV	97
1928, May 19	Mather, PA	195
1930, Nov. 5	Millfield, OH	82
1940, Jan. 10	Bartley, WV	91
1947, Mar. 25	Centralia, IL	111
1951, Dec. 21	West Frankfort, IL	119
1959, Jan. 22	Port Griffith, PA	12
1968, Nov. 20	Farmington, WV	78
1970, Dec. 30	Hyden, KY	38
1972, May 2	Kellogg, ID[1]	91
1976, Mar. 9	Oven Fork, KY	15
1981, Apr. 15	Redstone, CO	15
1981, Dec. 8	Whitwell, TN	13
1984, Dec. 19	Huntington, UT	27
1989, Sept. 13	Sturgis, KY	10
2001, Sept. 23	Brookwood, AL	13

Note: World's worst mine disaster killed 1,549 workers in Manchuria, Apr. 25, 1942. (1) Metal mine. (2) Anthracite mine.

Some Notable Hurricanes, Typhoons, Blizzards, Other Storms

As of Oct. 1, 2005. See also the feature article on Hurricane Katrina and consult the Index for other coverage of 2005 storms.

H.—hurricane; T.—typhoon

Date	Location	Deaths
1881, Aug. 24-29	H., GA, SC	700
1888, Mar. 11-14	Blizzard, eastern U.S.	400
1893, Aug. 15-Sept. 2	H., GA, SC	1,000+
1893, Oct. 1	H., LA	1,100+
1900, Sept. 8	H., Galveston, TX	8,000+
1906, Sept. 19-24	H., LA, MS	350
1906, Sept. 18	T., Hong Kong	10,000+
1909, Sept. 20	H., LA	350+
1915, Aug. 16	H., Galveston, TX	275
1915, Sept. 29	H., LA	275
1919, Sept. 6-14	Carib., Florida Keys, Gulf, TX	600+[1]
1926, Sept. 11-22	H., FL, AL, MS	370+
1926, Oct. 20	H., Cuba	600
1928, Sept. 6-20	H., southern FL	2,500+
1930, Sept. 3	H., Dominican Republic	2,000
1935, Aug. 29-Sept. 10	H., Caribbean, southeastern U.S.	400+
1937, Sept. 2	T., "The Great Typhoon," Hong Kong	10,000+
1938, Sept. 21	H., Long Island, NY; New England	287[2]
1940, Nov. 11-12	Blizzard, NE, Midwest U.S.	144
1942, Oct. 15-16	H., Bengal, India	40,000
1947, Dec. 26	Blizzard, NYC, N Atlant. states	55
1952, Oct. 22	T., Philippines	440
1954, Aug. 30	H. *Carol,* northeastern U.S.	68
1954, Oct. 5-18	H. *Hazel,* E Canada, U.S.; Haiti	347
1955, Aug. 12-13	H. *Connie,* NC, SC, VA, MD	43
1955, Aug. 7-21	H. *Diane,* eastern U.S.	400
1955, Sept. 19	H. *Hilda,* Mexico	200
1956, Feb. 1-29	Blizzard, W Europe	1,000
1957, June 25-30	H. *Audrey,* TX to AL	390
1958, Feb. 15-16	Blizzard, NE U.S.	171
1959, Sept. 17-19	T. *Sarah,* Japan, South Korea	2,000
1959, Sept. 26-27	T. *Vera,* Honshu, Japan	4,466
1960, Sept. 4-12	H. *Donna,* Caribbean, E U.S.	148
1961, Oct. 31	H. *Hattie,* Br. Honduras	400
1962, Sept. 1	T. Wanda, Hong Kong	130-200
1963, May 28-29	Windstorm, Bangladesh	22,000
1963, Oct. 4-8	H. *Flora,* Caribbean	6,000
1964, June 30	T. *Winnie,* N Philippines	107
1964, Sept. 5	T. *Ruby,* Hong Kong and China	735
1965, May 11-12	Windstorm, Bangladesh	17,000
1965, June 1-2	Windstorm, Bangladesh	30,000
1965, Sept. 7-12	H. *Betsy,* FL, MS, LA	74
1965, Dec. 15	Windstorm, Bangladesh	10,000
1966, June 4-10	H. *Alma,* Honduras, SE U.S.	51

IT'S A FACT: With over 1,000 deaths along the Gulf Coast and the city of New Orleans left in chaos, Hurricane Katrina may be considered the worst U.S. natural disaster in living memory. However, on the evening of Sept. 8, 1900, an unnamed hurricane struck the low-lying Gulf Coast island city of Galveston, TX, in what is still considered the most deadly U.S. natural disaster. Although they had some warning that a storm was approaching, residents were not prepared for what happened. Many reportedly had gone to the seaside to watch the rising surf, when a Category 4 hurricane, with a storm surge 15 feet or higher and wind howling at 130 mph or more, barreled into Galveston. The storm destroyed about half the homes in the city and killed 8,000 people or more, about one-fifth of the population, in just a few hours.

Date	Location	Deaths
1966, Sept. 24-30	H. *Inez,* Carib., FL, Mexico	293
1967, July 9	T. *Billie,* SW Japan	347
1967, Sept. 5-23	H. *Beulah,* Carib., Mex., TX	54
1967, Dec. 12-20	Blizzard, SW U.S.	51
1968, Nov. 18-28	T. *Nina,* Philippines	63
1969, Aug. 17-18	H. *Camille,* MS, LA	256
1970, Sept. 15	T. *Georgia,* Philippines	300
1970, Oct. 14	T. *Sening,* Philippines	583
1970, Oct. 15	T. *Titang,* Philippines	526
1970, Nov. 13	Cyclone, Bangladesh	300,000
1971, Aug. 1	T. *Rose,* Hong Kong	130
1972, June 19-29	H. *Agnes,* FL to NY	118
1972, Dec. 3	T. *Theresa,* Philippines	169
1973, June-Aug.	Monsoon rains, India	1,217
1974, June 11	Storm Dinah, Luzon Isl., Phil.	71
1974, July 11	T. *Gilda,* Japan, S. Korea	108
1974, Sept. 19-20	H. *Fifi,* Honduras	2,000
1974, Dec. 25	Cyclone leveled Darwin, Austral.	50
1975, Sept. 13-27	H. *Eloise,* Caribbean, NE U.S.	71
1976, May 20	T. *Olga,* floods, Philippines	215
1978, Oct. 27	T. *Rita,* Philippines	c. 400
1979, Aug. 30 - Sept. 7	H. *David,* Caribbean, E U.S.	1,100
1980, Aug. 4-11	H. *Allen,* Caribbean, TX	272
1981, Nov. 25	T. *Irma,* Luzon Isl., Philippines	176
1983, June	Monsoon, India	900
1984, Sept. 2	T. *Ike,* S Philippines	1,363
1985, May 25	Cyclone, Bangladesh	10,000
1985, Oct. 26-Nov. 6	H. *Juan,* SE U.S.	97
1987, Nov. 25	T. *Nina,* Philippines	650
1988, Sept. 10-17	H. *Gilbert,* Carib., Gulf of Mex.	260
1989, Sept. 16-22	H. *Hugo,* Caribbean, SE U.S.	504
1990, May 6-11	Cyclones, SE India	450
1991, Apr. 30	Cyclone, Bangladesh	139,000
1991, Nov. 5	Tropical storm, Philippines	7,000+
1992, Aug. 24-26	H. *Andrew,* southern FL, LA	58
1993, Mar. 13-14	Blizzard, E U.S.	200
1993, June	Monsoon, Bangladesh	2,000
1994, Nov. 8-18	Storm Gordon, Caribbean, FL	830
1995, Oct. 2-4	H. *Opal,* S Mexico, FL, AL	59
1995, Nov. 2-3	T. *Angela,* Philippines	600+
1996, Jan. 7-8	Blizzard, NE U.S.	100
1996, Aug. 22	Blizzard, Himalayas, N India.	239
1996, Aug. 29- Sept. 6	H. *Fran,* Carib., NC, VA, WV.	30
1996, Sept. 9-10	H. *Hortense,* Caribbean.	24
1996, Sept. 9	T. *Sally,* S China.	114
1996, Nov. 6	Cyclone, Andhra Pradesh, India	1,000+
1996, Nov. 24-25	Ice storms, TX to MO	26
1996, Dec. 25	Tropical storm, E Malaysia	100+
1997, May 19	Cyclone, Bangladesh	108
1997, Aug. 18	Typhoon, Taiwan.	24
1997, Oct. 8-10	H. *Pauline,* SW Mexico	230
1998, Feb. 4-6	Blizzard, KY, WV	10+
1998, June 9	Cyclone, Gujarat, India	1,320
1998, Aug.	Monsoon, Bangladesh.	326
1998, Sept. 21-23	H. *Georges,* Caribbean, FL Keys, U.S. Gulf Coast	600+
1998, Oct. 27-29	H. *Mitch,* Honduras, Nicaragua, Guatemala, El Salvador	10,866+
1999, Sept. 4-17	H. *Floyd,* Baha., E seaboard, U.S	69+
1999, Oct. 29	Cyclone, E India	9,392
1999, Dec. 26-29	Gales, France, Switz., Germany	120
2000, Dec. 27	Winter storm, TX, OK, AR	40+
2001, June 6-17	Tropical storm *Allison,* SE U.S.	47
2001, July 30	T. *Toraji,* Taiwan	200
2001, Oct. 8-9	H. *Iris,* Belize	22
2001, Nov. 2-5	H. *Michelle,* Cuba, Jamaica.	17
2001, Nov. 6-12	T. *Lingling,* S Philip., Vietnam	220+
2002, July 1-11	T. *Chata'an,* Micron., Philip., Jap.	70+
2002, Aug.-Sept.	T. *Rusa,* North & South Korea.	115+
2003, Feb. 16-17	Blizzard, E seaboard U.S.	59
2003, Sept. 2	T. Dujuan, S China	32
2003, Sept. 12	T. *Maemi,* South Korea	130
2003, Sept. 7-19	H. *Isabel,* NC, VA, MD E seaboard, U.S.	40+
2003, Dec. 17	Cyclone, southern India.	50
2004, Jan. 26-Feb. 4	Cyclone *Elita,* Madagascar	29
2004, Mar. 7-19	Cyclone *Gafilo,* Madagascar	198
2004, Apr. 8	Cyclone 22P, Fiji	22
2004, May 18	T. *Nida,* Philippines	19+
2004, May 19	Cyclone, Myanmar	220
2004, Aug. 12-15	T. *Rananim,* E China.	164
2004, Aug. 13-14	H. *Charley,* Fl, SC	36
2004, Aug. 24-Sept. 10	T. *Aere,* China, Taiwan, Philip.	67
2004, Sept. 5-6	H. *Frances,* Bahamas, Florida.	35
2004, Sept. 7-16	H. *Ivan,* Barbados, Grenada, Jamaica, Cuba, U.S. Gulf Coast.	115
2004, Sept. 16-26	H. *Jeanne,* Dom. Rep., Haiti, FL	1,500+
2005, July 7-11	H. *Dennis,* Jamaica, Haiti, Cuba, FL	60+
2005, Aug. 25-29	H. *Katrina,* LA, MS, FL, AL, GA	1,200+[3]
2005, Aug. 31-Sept. 1	T. *Talim,* Taiwan; E China	97
2005, Sept. 21-24	H. *Rita,* TX, LA	100[4]
2005, Sept. 21-28	T. *Damrey,* SE Asia, Philippines, Hainan (China)	120+
2005, Oct. 4	H. *Stan,* Central Amer., Mex.	650+[5]

(1) Incl. c. 500 lost on ships at sea. (2) 600 incl. offshore deaths and deaths from flooding that started Sept. 12. (3) Official toll as of 10/05 was 972 in LA, 221 in MS, 14 in FL, 2 in AL, 2 in GA. (4) Prelim. estimate, incl. about 60 who died in the evacuation, among them 24 nursing home residents whose bus exploded and caught fire outside Dallas, Sept. 23. (5) Including floods.

Some Notable Floods, Tidal Waves

Date	Location	Deaths
1889, May 31	Johnstown, PA	2,200+
1903, June 15	Heppner, OR	325
1911	Chang Jiang River, China	100,000
1913, Mar. 25-27	OH, IN	732
1915, Aug. 17	Galveston, TX.	275
1927, Jan.-July	Mississippi Valley	246+
1928, Mar. 13	Dam collapse, Saugus, CA	450
1928, Sept. 16	Lake Okeechobee, FL	1,770+
1931, Aug.	Huang He River, China	3,700,000
1937, Jan. 22	OH, MS Valleys	250
1939	N China	200,000
1946, Apr. 1	HI, AK.	159
1947, Sept. 20	Honshu Island, Japan.	1,900
1951, Aug.	Manchuria.	1,800
1953, Jan. 31	W Europe	2,000
1954, Aug. 17	Farahzad, Iran	2,000
1955, Oct. 7-12	India, Pakistan	1,700
1959, Nov. 1	W Mexico	2,000
1959, Dec. 2	Frejus, France	412
1960, Oct. 10	Bangladesh	6,000
1960, Oct. 31	Bangladesh	4,000
1962, Feb. 17	North Sea coast, Germany.	343
1962, Sept. 27	Barcelona, Spain	445
1963, Oct. 9	Dam collapse, Vaiont, Italy.	1,800
1966, Nov. 3-4	Florence, Venice, Italy	113
1967, Jan. 18-24	E Brazil.	894
1967, Mar. 19	Rio de Janeiro, Brazil	436
1967, Nov. 26	Lisbon, Portugal	464
1968, Aug. 7-14	Gujarat State, India	1,000
1968, Oct. 7	NE India	780
1969, Jan. 18-26	Southern CA.	100
1969, Mar. 17	Mundau Valley, Alagoas, Brazil.	218
1969, Aug. 20-22	Western VA	189
1969, Sept. 15	South Korea	250
1969, Oct. 1-8	Tunisia	500
1970, May 20	Central Romania	160
1970, July 22	Himalayas, India.	500
1971, Feb. 26	Rio de Janeiro, Brazil	130
1972, Feb. 26	Buffalo Creek, WV	118
1972, June 9	Rapid City, SD	238
1972, Aug. 7	Luzon Isl., Philippines.	454
1972, Aug. 19-31	Pakistan	1,500
1974, Mar. 29	Tubaro, Brazil.	1,000
1974, Aug. 12	Monty-Long, Bangladesh	2,500
1976, June 5	Teton Dam collapse, ID	11
1976, July 31	Big Thompson Canyon, CO	140
1976, Nov. 17	East Java, Indonesia	136
1977, July 19-20	Johnstown, PA	68
1977, Nov. 6	Toccoa, GA	39
1978, June-Sept.	N India	1,200
1979, Jan.-Feb.	Brazil	204
1979, July 17	Lomblem Isl., Indonesia	539
1979, Aug. 11	Morvi, India.	15,000
1980, Feb. 13-22	Southern CA, AZ	26
1981, Apr.	N China	550
1981, July	Sichuan, Hubei Prov., China	1,300
1982, Jan. 23	Nr. Lima, Peru	600

IT'S A FACT: From 1851 to 2004, the greatest number of hurricanes to form in the Atlantic Basin in one season was 12, in 1969. The highest number of *major* hurricanes—Category 3 or higher—was 8, in 1950, and the average number is 2.5. For the 2005 season as of Oct. 1, there were 9 hurricanes in all—including 5 that reached Category 3 or higher.

Date	Location	Deaths
1982, May 12	Guangdong, China	430
1982, Sept. 17-21	El Salvador, Guatemala	1,300+
1984, Aug-Sept.	South Korea	200+
1985, July 19	Dam collapse, N Italy	361
1987, Aug.-Sept.	N Bangladesh	1,000+
1988, Sept.	N India	1,000+
1990, June 14	Shadyside, OH	26
1993, July-Aug.	Midwest	48
1994, July	GA, AL	32
1995, Jan. 30- Feb. 9	NW Europe	40
1995, July	NE China	1,200
1995, Aug. 19	SW Morocco	136
1995, Dec. 25	KwaZulu Natal, South Africa	166
1996, Feb. 17	Biak Isl., Indonesia	105
1996, April	Afghanistan	100+
1996, June-July	S China	950+
1996, Aug. 7	Pyrenees Mts., Spain	71
1996, Dec.-1997, Jan.	NW U.S.	29
1997, Mar.	Ohio R. Valley	35
1997, July	Poland, Czech Republic	98
1997, Nov.	Spanish-Portuguese border	31+
1997, Nov.	Bardera, Somalia	1,300+
1998, Jan.	Kenya	86
1998, Feb.	California to Tijuana, Mexico	30+
1998, Mar.	SW Pakistan	300+
1998, July-Aug.	China	4,150
1998, July-Sept.	Bangladesh	1,441
1998, July 17	Papua New Guinea	3,000
1999, Aug. 1-4	Philippines, SE Asia	188+
1999, Sept.-Oct.	NE Mexico	350+
1999, Oct.-Dec.	Central Vietnam	700+
1999, Feb. 6-11	Botswana	70+
1999, Dec.	Venezuela	9,000+
2000, Feb.-Mar.	Madagascar	150+
2000, Feb.-Mar.	Mozambique	700
2000, May 17	Timor Island	50+
2000, Aug. 2	Himachal Pradesh, India	120+
2000, Aug. 2	Bhutan	200+
2000, Sept. 19-30	India, Bangladesh	1,000+
2000, Oct. 12-17	France, Brit., Italy, Switz.	35
2001, Jan.-Feb.	Mozambique	84+
2001, Aug.-Nov.	S Vietnam and Cambodia	360+
2001, Aug. 1-6	Taiwan	100+
2001, Aug. 10-12	NE Iran	247
2001, Aug.	Northern Thailand	170
2001, Nov. 9-10	Northern Algeria	711+
2001, Dec. 23-31	Rio de Janeiro	66
2002, Jan. 30-Feb. 15	Java Isl., Indonesia	147
2002, Feb. 19	La Paz, Bolivia	65
2002, Apr.-May	E Africa	150+
2002, early May	MO, IL, IN, WV, VA KY	20
2002, Apr.-Aug.	China	800+
2002, July-Aug.	India, Nepal, Bangladesh	1,100+
2002, Aug.	Russia	110
2002, Aug.	Germany, Hungary, Austria, Czech Rep.	100+
2003, May 17-27	Sri Lanka	250
2003, Aug.-mid-Sept.	E India	200+
2003, early Nov.	Sumatra, Indonesia	65+
2003, Dec. 10-Jan. 23, 2004	Sumatra, Indonesia	148
2003, Dec. 19-Jan. 7, 2004	Central Philippines	200
2004, Jan. 10-Mar. 8	Brazil	161
2004, Apr. 4-6	Coahuila, N Mexico	37
2004, Apr. 9-May 11	W Kenya	50
2004, Apr. 12-16	Djibouti City, Djibouti	53
2004, May 23-25	Dom. Repubiic and Haiti	2,000
2004, June-Sept.	Banglad., India, Myan., Nepal	2,000+
2004, June-Sept.	China	500
2004, Aug. 8-12	NE Nigeria	65
2004, Nov-Dec.	Philippines	1,060+
2004, Dec. 26	12 Indian Ocean nations, espec. Indonesia, Sri Lanka, India, Thailand	226,328[1]
2005, July 26-Aug. 2	India	1,040+
2005, Aug. 21-23	Central Europe, espec. Romania	43

(1) Based on official estimates assembled by the Internat. Fed of Red Cross and Red Crescent Societies, including 49,869 missing; as reported 5/20/2005; 1 year after the disaster, those listed as missing will be declared officially dead. The 176,459 listed as dead include 128,645 from Indonesia, 31,147 from Sri Lanka, 10,749 from India, 5,385 from Thailand.

Some Major Earthquakes

Source: Global Volcanism Network, Smithsonian Institution; U.S. Geological Survey, Dept. of the Interior; World Almanac research

Magnitude of earthquakes (Mag.) is measured on the Richter scale; an increase of one whole point represents a release of about 30 times more energy. Adopted in 1935, the scale is applied to earthquakes as far back as reliable seismograms are available, but those earlier figures should be considered estimates.

Date	Location	Deaths	Mag.
526, May 20	Antioch, Syria	250,000	NA
856	Corinth, Greece	45,000	NA
1057	Chihli, China	25,000	NA
1169, Feb. 11	Near Mt. Etna, Sicily	15,000[1]	NA
1268	Cilicia, Asia Minor	60,000	NA
1290, Sept. 27	Chihli, China	100,000	NA
1293, May 20	Kamakura, Japan	30,000	NA
1531, Jan. 26	Lisbon, Portugal	30,000	NA
1556, Jan. 24	Shaanxi, China	830,000	NA
1667, Nov.	Shemaka, Caucasia	80,000	NA
1693, Jan. 11	Catania, Italy	60,000	NA
1730, Dec. 30	Hokkaido, Japan	137,000	NA
1737, Oct. 11	India, Calcutta	300,000	NA
1755, June 7	N Persia	40,000	NA
1755, Nov. 1	Lisbon, Portugal	60,000	8.75*
1783, Feb. 4	Calabria, Italy	30,000	NA
1797, Feb. 4	Quito, Ecuador	41,000	NA
1822, Sept. 5	Asia Minor, Aleppo	22,000	NA
1828, Dec. 28	Echigo, Japan	30,000	NA
1868, Aug. 13-15	Peru, Ecuador	40,000	NA
1875, May 16	Venezuela, Colombia	16,000	NA
1886, Aug. 31	Charleston, SC	60	6.6
1896, June 15	Japan, sea wave	27,120	NA
1905, Apr. 4	Kangra, India	19,000	8.6
1906, Apr. 18-19	San Francisco, CA	3,000[2]	7.7[2]
1906, Aug. 17	Valparaiso, Chile	20,000	8.6
1907, Oct. 21	Central Asia	12,000	8.1
1908, Dec. 28	Messina, Italy	83,000	7.5
1915, Jan. 13	Avezzano, Italy	29,980	7.5
1918, Oct. 11	Mona Passage, P.R.	116	7.5
1920, Dec. 16	Gansu, China	200,000	8.6
1923, Sept. 1	Yokohama, Japan	143,000	8.3
1925, Mar. 16	Yunnan, China	5,000	7.1
1927, May 22	Nan-Shan, China	200,000	8.3
1932, Dec. 25	Gansu, China	70,000	7.6
1933, Mar. 2	Japan	2,990	8.9
1933, Mar. 10	Long Beach, CA	115	6.2
1934, Jan. 15	India, Bihar-Nepal	10,700	8.4
1935, Apr. 21	Taiwan (Formosa)	3,276	7.4
1935, May 30	Quetta, India	50,000	7.5
1939, Jan. 25	Chillan, Chile	28,000	8.3
1939, Dec. 26	Erzincan, Turkey	30,000	8.0
1946, Dec. 20	Honshu, Japan	1,330	8.4
1948, June 28	Fukui, Japan	5,390	7.3
1949, Aug. 5	Pelileo, Ecuador	6,000	6.8
1950, Aug. 15	Assam, India	1,530	8.7
1953, Mar. 18	NW Turkey	1,200	7.2
1956, June 10-17	N Afghanistan	2,000	7.7
1957, July 2	N Iran	1,200	7.4
1957, Dec. 13	W Iran	1,130	7.3
1960, Feb. 29	Agadir, Morocco	12,000	5.9
1960, May 21-30	S Chile	5,000	9.5
1962, Sept. 1	NW Iran	12,230	7.3
1963, July 26	Skopje, Yugoslavia	1,100	6.0
1964, Mar. 27	Alaska	131	9.2
1966, Aug. 19	E Turkey	2,520	7.1
1968, Aug. 31	NE Iran	12,000	7.3
1970, Jan. 5	Yunnan Prov., China	15,621	7.7
1970, Mar. 28	W Turkey	1,100	7.3
1970, May 31	N Peru	66,000	7.8
1971, Feb. 9	San Fernando Val., CA	65	6.6
1972, Apr. 10	S Iran	5,054	7.1
1972, Dec. 23	Managua, Nicaragua	5,000	6.2
1974, Dec. 28	Pakistan (9 towns)	5,200	6.3
1975, Sept. 6	Turkey (Lice, etc.)	2,300	6.7
1976, Feb. 4	Guatemala	23,000	7.5
1976, May 6	NE Italy	1,000	6.5
1976, June 25	Irian Jaya, New Guinea	422	7.1
1976, July 27	Tangshan, China	255,000	8.0
1976, Aug. 16	Mindanao, Philippines	8,000	7.8
1976, Nov. 24	NW Iran-USSR border	5,000	7.3
1977, Mar. 4	Romania	1,500	7.2
1977, Aug. 19	Indonesia	200	8.0

Date	Location	Deaths	Mag.
1978, Sept. 16	NE Iran	15,000	7.8
1979, Sept. 12	Indonesia	100	8.1
1979, Dec. 12	Colombia, Ecuador	800	7.9
1980, Oct. 10	NW Algeria	3,500	7.7
1980, Nov. 23	S Italy	3,000	7.2
1981, June 11	S Iran	3,000	6.9
1981, July 28	S Iran	1,500	7.3
1982, Dec. 13	W Arabian Peninsula	2,800	6.0
1983, Oct. 30	E Turkey	1,342	6.9
1985, Mar. 3	Chile	146	7.8
1985, Sept. 19	Michoacan, Mexico	9,500	8.1
1986, Oct. 10	El Salvador	1,000+	5.5
1987, Mar. 6	Colombia-Ecuador	4,000+	7.0
1988, Aug. 20	India-Nepal border	1,450	6.6
1988, Nov. 6	China-Burma border	1,000	7.3
1988, Dec. 7	Soviet Armenia	55,000	7.0
1989, Oct. 17	San Francisco Bay area	63	6.9
1990, May 30	N Peru	115	6.3
1990, June 20	W Iran	40,000+	7.7
1990, July 16	Luzon, Philippines	1,621	7.8
1991, Feb. 1	Pakistan, Afgh. border	1,200	6.8
1991, Oct. 19	N India	2,000	7.0
1992, Mar. 13, 15	E Turkey	4,000	6.2/6.0
1992, June 28	S California	1	7.5/6.6
1992, Dec. 12	Flores Isl., Indonesia	2,500	7.5
1993, July 12	off Hokkaido, Japan	200+	7.7
1992, Sept. 1	SW Nicaragua	116	7.0
1992, Oct. 12	Cairo, Egypt	450	5.9
1993, Sept. 30	Maharashtra, S India	9,748[3]	6.3
1994, Jan. 17	Northridge, CA	61	6.8
1994, Feb. 15	S Sumatra, Indon.	215	7.0
1994, June 6	Cauca, SW Colombia	1,000	6.8
1994, Aug. 19	N Algeria	164	6.0
1995, Jan. 16	Kobe, Japan	5,502	6.9
1995, May 27	Sakhalin Isl., Russia	1,989	7.5
1996, Feb. 3	SW China	200+	7.0
1997, Feb. 27	W Pakistan	100+	7.3
1997, Feb. 28	NW Iran	1,000+	6.1
1997, May 10	N Iran	1,560	7.5
1998, Feb. 4, 8	Takhar province, NE Afghanistan	2,323	6.1
1998, May 22	Central Bolivia	105	6.5
1998, May 30	NE Afghanistan	4,700+	6.9
1998, June 27	Adana, Turkey	144	6.3
1999, Jan. 25	Armenia, Colombia	1,185+	6.0
1999, Aug. 17	Western Turkey	17,200+	7.4
1999, Sept. 7	Athens, Greece	143	5.9
1999, Sept. 21	Taichung, Taiwan	2,474	7.6
1999, Nov. 12	Duzce, Turkey	675+	7.2
2000, June 4	Sumatra, Indonesia	103	7.9
2001, Jan. 13	San Vicente, El Salv.	800+	7.6
2001, Jan. 26	Gujarat, India	20,000+	7.9
2001, Feb. 13	San Vicente, El Salv.	255	6.6
2001, June 23	Arequipa, Peru	102	8.1
2002, Feb. 3	Central Turkey	44+	6.5
2002, Mar. 3	N Afghanistan	166	7.4
2002, Mar. 25-26	Nahrin, N Afghanistan.	1,000+	6.1
2002, Apr. 1	E New Guinea	36	5.0
2002, Apr. 12	Hindu Kush, Afghanistan	50+	5.9
2002, June 22	W Iran	261+	6.5
2002, Oct. 31	S Italy	29	5.9
2003, Jan. 22	Colima, Mexico	29	7.6
2003, Feb. 24	S Xinjiang prov., China	261	6.4
2003, May 1	E Turkey	177	6.4
2003, May 21	N Algeria	2,200+	6.8
2003, Dec. 26	Bam, SE Iran	26,271	6.6
2004, Feb. 4	Papua, Indonesia	37	7.0
2004, Feb. 14	NW Pakistan	24	5.5
2004, Feb. 24	Al Hoceima, NE Morocco	629	6.4
2004, May 28	N Iran	35	6.3
2004, Dec. 26	Nr. Sumatra, Indon.	(4)	9.3
2005, Feb. 21	central Iran	549	6.4
2005, Mar. 28	islands off Sumatra, Indonesia	1,000+	8.7
2005, June 14	N Chile	12	7.9

*Estimated from earthquake intensity. NA = Not available. (1) Once thought to have been a volcanic eruption; evidence indicates a destructive earthquake and tsunami occurred on this date. (2) Total estimate includes deaths from resulting fires; revised estimates of magnitude range from 7.7 to 7.9. (3) Official death toll from Indian government. Other sources reported estimates of about 30,000 deaths. (4) This undersea earthquake triggered devastating tsunamis that hit 12 Indian Ocean nations. See listing above under Floods; see also Chronology of the Year's Events; Nations of the World.

Some Notable Fires Since 1930

(See also Some Notable Explosions Since 1920.)

Date	Location	Deaths
1930, Apr. 21	Columbus, OH, penitentiary	320
1931, July 24	Pittsburgh, PA, home for aged	48
1934, Dec. 11	Hotel Kerns, Lansing, MI	34
1938, May 16	Atlanta, GA, Terminal Hotel	35
1940, Apr. 23	Natchez, MS, dance hall	198
1942, Nov. 28	Cocoanut Grove, Boston	491
1942, Dec. 12	St. John's, Nfld., hostel	100
1943, Sept. 7	Gulf Hotel, Houston, TX	55
1944, July 6	Ringling Circus, Hartford, CT	168
1946, June 5	LaSalle Hotel, Chicago	61
1946, Dec. 7	Winecoff Hotel, Atlanta	119
1946, Dec. 12	NY, NY, ice plant, tenement	37
1949, Apr. 5	Effingham, IL, hospital	77
1950, Jan. 7	Davenport, IA, Mercy Hospital	41
1953, Mar. 29	Largo, FL, nursing home	35
1953, Apr. 16	Chicago, metalworking plant	35
1957, Feb. 17	Warrenton, MO, home for aged	72
1958, Mar. 19	New York, NY, loft building	24
1958, Dec. 1	Chicago, parochial school	95
1958, Dec. 16	Bogotá, Colombia, store	83
1959, June 23	Stalheim, Norway, resort hotel	34
1960, Mar. 12	Pusan, Korea, chemical plant	68
1960, July 14	Guatemala City, mental hospital	225
1960, Nov. 13	Amude, Syria, movie theater	152
1961, Jan. 6	Thomas Hotel, San Francisco	20
1961, Dec. 8	Hartford, CT, hospital	16
1961, Dec. 17	Niteroi, Brazil, circus	323
1963, May 4	Diourbel, Senegal, theater	64
1963, Nov. 18	Surfside Hotel, Atlantic City, NJ	25
1963, Nov. 23	Fitchville, OH, rest home	63
1963, Dec. 29	Roosevelt Hotel, Jacksonville, FL	22
1964, May 8	Manila, apartment bldg.	30
1964, Dec. 18	Fountaintown, IN, nursing home	20
1965, Mar. 1	LaSalle, Quebec, apartment	28
1965, Aug. 11-16	Watts riot fires, CA	30+
1966, Mar. 11	Numata, Japan, 2 ski resorts	31
1966, Oct. 17	New York, NY, bldg. (firefighters)	12
1966, Dec. 7	Erzurum, Turkey, barracks	68
1967, Feb. 7	Montgomery, AL, restaurant	25
1967, May 22	Brussels, Belgium, store	322
1967, July 16	Jay, FL, state prison	37
1968, May 11	Vijayawada, India, wedding hall	58
1969, Dec. 2	Notre Dame, Can., nursing home	54
1970, Jan. 9	Marietta, OH, nursing home	27
1970, Nov. 1	Grenoble, France, dance hall	145
1970, Dec. 20	Tucson, AZ, hotel	28
1971, Dec., 25	Seoul, South Korea, hotel	162
1972, May 13	Osaka, Japan, nightclub	116
1972, July 5	Sherborne, England, hospital	30
1973, June 24	New Orleans, LA, bar	32
1973, Aug. 3	Isle of Man, Eng., amusement park	51
1973, Sept. 1	Copenhagen, Denmark, hotel	35
1973, Nov. 29	Kumamoto, Japan, dept. store	107
1973, Dec. 2	Seoul, South Korea, theater	50
1974, Feb. 1	São Paulo, Brazil, bank building	189
1974, June 30	Port Chester, NY, discotheque	24
1974, Nov. 3	Seoul, S. Korea, hotel, disco	88
1975, Dec. 12	Mina, Saudi Arabia, tent city	138
1976, Oct. 24	Bronx, NY, social club	25
1977, Feb. 25	Moscow, Russia, Rossiya hotel	45
1977, May 28	Southgate, KY, nightclub	164
1977, June 9	Abidjan, Ivory Coast, nightclub	41
1977, June 26	Columbia, TN, jail	42
1977, Nov. 14	Manila, Philippines, hotel	47
1978, Jan. 28	Kansas City, Coates House Hotel	16
1978, Aug. 19	Abadan, Iran, movie theater	425+
1979, July 14	Saragossa, Spain, hotel	80
1979, Dec. 31	Chapais, Quebec, social club	42
1980, May 20	Kingston, Jamaica, nursing home	157
1980, Nov. 21	MGM Grand Hotel, Las Vegas	84
1980, Dec. 4	Stouffer Inn, Harrison, NY	26
1981, Jan. 9	Keansburg, NJ, boarding home	30
1981, Feb. 10	Las Vegas Hilton	8
1981, Feb. 14	Dublin, Ireland, discotheque	44
1982, Sept. 4	Los Angeles, apartment house	24
1982, Nov. 8	Biloxi, MS, county jail	29
1983, Feb. 13	Turin, Italy, movie theater	64
1983, Dec. 17	Madrid, Spain, discotheque	83
1984, May 11	Great Adventure Amusement Pk., NJ	8
1985, Apr. 21	Tabaco, Phil., movie theater	44
1985, Apr. 26	Buenos Aires, Argentina, hospital	79
1985, May 11	Bradford, England, soccer stadium	53

Date	Location	Deaths
1985, May 13	Philadelphia, MOVE hdqrtrs, row houses	11
1986, Dec. 31	Puerto Rico, Dupont Plaza Hotel	96
1987, May 6-June 2	N China, forest fire	193
1987, Nov. 17	London, England, subway	30
1988, Mar. 20	Lashio, Burma, 2,000 buildings	134
1990, Mar. 25	Bronx, NY, social club	87
1991, Mar. 3	Addis Ababa, Ethiopia, munitions dump	260+
1991, Sept. 3	Hamlet, NC, processing plant	25
1991, Oct. 20-21	Oakland, Berkeley, CA, wildfire	24
1993, Apr. 19	Waco, TX, cult compound	72
1994, May 10	Bangkok, Thailand, toy factory	213
1994, July 4-10	Glenwood Springs, CO (firefighters)	14
1994, Dec. 10	Karamay, China, theater	300
1994, Nov. 2	Durunka, Egypt, burning fuel flood	500
1995, Oct. 28	Baku, Azerbaijan, subway train	300
1995, Dec. 23	Mandi Dabwali, India, school	500+
1996, Mar. 19	Quezon City, Philippines, nightclub	150+
1996, Mar. 28	Bogor, Indonesia, shopping mall	78
1996, Oct. 22	Caracas, Venezuela, jail	25
1996, Nov. 20	Hong Kong, building	39
1997, Feb. 23	Baripada, India, worship site	164
1997, Apr. 15	Mina, Saudi Arabia, encampment	343
1997, June 7	Thanjavur, India, temple	60+
1997, June 13	New Delhi, India, movie theater	60
1997, July 11	Pattaya, Thailand, hotel	90
1997, Sept. 29	Children's home, near Colina, Chile	30
1998, Dec. 3	Manila, Philippines, orphanage	28
1999, Mar. 24	France and Italy, Mont Blanc tunnel	40
1999, Oct. 30	Inchon, S. Korea, karaoke salon	55+
2000, Mar. 17	Kanungu, Uganda, church	530
2000, Oct. 20	Mexico City, Mexico, nightclub	20
2000, Dec. 25	Luoyang, China, shopping center	309
2001, Jan. 1	Volendam, Netherlands, cafe	10
2001, Mar. 6	Central China, school	41
2001, Mar. 26	Machakos, Kenya, school	64
2001, Aug. 6	Madras, India, home for mentally ill.	27
2001, Aug. 18	Quezon City, Philippines, hotel	73
2001, Sept. 1	Tokyo, Japan, nightclub	44
2001, Oct. 24	Swiss Alps, St. Gotthard Tunnel	11
2001, Dec. 29	Lima, Peru, fireworks accident	291
2002, Mar. 11	Mecca, Saudi Arabia, girls' school	15
2002, June 16	Beijing, China, internet cafe	24
2002, July 7	Donetsk region, Ukraine, coal mine.	34+
2002, July 20	Lima, Peru, disco	25+
2002, July 31	Donetsk region, Ukraine, coal mine	20
2003, Feb. 20	Warwick, RI, nightclub (pyrotechnics)	100
2003, Sept. 15	Riyadh, Saudi Arabia, prison	94
2003, Nov. 24	Moscow, Russ., students' hostel	36
2004, May 17	Honduras, prison in San Pedro Sula	104
2004, July 16	Kumbakonam, India, pvt. school	80+
2004, Aug. 1	Asunción, Paraguay, market	400+
2004, Dec. 30	Buenos Aires, Argentina, club	194
2005, Feb. 14	Tehran, Iran, mosque	59
2005, Mar. 7	Higuey, Dom. Republic, prison	136
2005, May 5	Paris, France, hotel	22
2005, Sept. 5	Beni Suet, Egypt, theater fire	30+

Some Notable Explosions Since 1920

(See also Principal U.S. Mine Disasters Since 1900.) **Note**: Some bombings related to political conflicts and terrorism are not included.

Date	Location	Deaths
1920, Sept. 16	Wall Street, NY, NY, bomb	30
1921, Sept. 21	Chem. storage facility, Oppau, Ger.	561
1924, Jan. 3	Food plant, Pekin, IL	42
1927, May 18	Bath school, Lansing, MI	38
1928, April 13	Dance hall, West Plains, MO	40
1937, Mar. 18	New London, TX, school	311
1940, Sept. 12	Hercules Powder, Kenvil, NJ	55
1942, June 5	Ordnance plant, Elwood, IL	49
1944, Apr. 14	Bombay, India, harbor	700
1944, July 17	Port Chicago, CA, pier	322
1944, Oct. 21	Liquid gas tank, Cleveland	135
1947, Apr. 16	Texas City, TX, pier	576
1948, July 28	Farben works, Ludwigshafen, Ger.	184
1950, May 19	Munitions barges, S. Amboy, NJ	30
1956, Aug. 7	Dynamite trucks, Cali, Colombia	1,100
1958, Apr. 18	Sunken munitions ship, Okinawa, Japan	40
1958, May 22	Nike missiles, Leonardo, NJ	10
1959, Apr. 10	World War II bomb, Philippines	38
1959, June 28	Rail tank cars, Meldrim, GA	25
1959, Aug. 7	Dynamite truck, Roseburg, OR	13
1959, Nov. 2	Jamuri Bazar, India, explosives	46
1959, Dec. 13	2 apt. bldgs., Dortmund, Ger.	26
1960, Mar. 4	Belgian munitions ship, Havana, Cuba	100
1962, Oct. 3	Telephone Co. office, NY, NY	23
1963, Jan. 2	Packing plant, Terre Haute, IN	17
1963, Mar. 9	Dynamite plant, S. Africa	45
1963, Aug. 13	Explosives dump, Gauhaiti, India	32
1963, Oct. 31	State Fair Coliseum, Indianapolis, IN	73
1964, July 23	Bone, Algeria, harbor munitions	100
1965, Mar. 4	Gas pipeline, Natchitoches, LA	17
1965, Aug. 9	Missile silo, Searcy, AR	53
1965, Oct. 21	Bridge, Tila Bund, Pakistan	80
1965, Oct. 30	Cartagena, Colombia	48
1965, Nov. 24	Armory, Keokuk, IA	20
1967, Dec. 25	Apartment bldg., Moscow, USSR	20
1968, Apr. 6	Sports store, Richmond, IN	43
1970, Apr. 8	Subway construction, Osaka, Japan	73
1971, June 24	Tunnel, Sylmar, CA	17
1973, Feb., 10	Liquid gas tank, Staten Island, NY	40
1975, Dec. 27	Coal mine, Chasnala, India	431
1976, Apr. 13	Lapua, Finland, munitions works	40
1977, Nov. 11	Freight train, Iri, South Korea	57
1977, Dec. 22	Grain elevator, Westwego, LA	35
1978, Feb. 24	Derailed tank car, Waverly, TN	12
1978, July 11	Propylene tank truck, Spanish campsite	150
1980, Oct. 23	School, Ortuella, Spain	64
1982, Apr. 25	Antiques exhibition, Todi, Italy	33
1982, Nov. 2	Salang Tunnel, Afghanistan	1,000+
1984, Feb. 25	Oil pipeline, Cubatao, Brazil	508
1984, June 21	Naval supply depot, Severomorsk, USSR	200+
1984, Nov. 19	Gas storage area, NE Mexico City	334
1984, Dec. 3	Chemical plant, Bhopal, India	3,849
1984, Dec. 5	Coal mine, Taipei, Taiwan	94
1985, June 25	Fireworks factory, Hallett, OK	21
1988, Apr. 10	Pakistani army ammunitions dump near Rawalpindi and Islamabad	100
1988, July 6	Oil rig, North Sea	167
1989, June 3	Gas pipeline, between Ufa, Asha, USSR	650+
1992, Mar. 3	Coal mine, Kozlu, Turkey	270+
1992, Apr. 22	Sewer, Guadalajara, Mexico	190
1992, May 9	Coal mine, Plymouth, Nova Scotia	26
1993, Feb. 26	World Trade Center, NY, NY	6
1994, July 18	Jewish com. center, Buenos Aires, Arg.	100
1995, Apr. 19	Fed'l. office building, Oklahoma City	168
1995, Apr. 29	Subway construction, South Korea	110
1995, Nov. 13	Military facility, Riyadh, Saudi Arabia	7
1996, Jan. 31	Bank, Colombo, Sri Lanka	53
1996, Feb. 25	Jerusalem and Ashkelon, Israel	27
1996, Mar. 3-4	Jerusalem and Tel Aviv, Israel	33
1996, June 25	U.S. military housing complex, near Dhahran, Saudi Arabia	19 19
1996, July 24	Train, Colombo, Sri Lanka	86
1996, Nov. 16	Russian military apartment, Dagestan region, Russia	68
1996, Nov. 21	Building, San Juan, Puerto Rico	29
1996, Nov. 27	Coal mine, Shanxi province, China	91+
1996, Dec. 30	Train, Assam, India	59+
1997, Jan. 18	Near courthouse, Lahore, Pakistan	25
1997, Mar. 19	Ammunition depot, Jalalabad, Afgh.	16
1997, July 8	Train, Punjab, India	36
1997, Nov. 19	Car, Hyderabad, India	23
1997, Dec. 2	Coal mine, Novokuznetsk, Siberia	68
1998, Jan. 17	Coal mine, Sokobanja, Serbia	29
1998, Feb. 14	Oil tankers (2), Yaounde, Cameroon	120
1998, Feb. 14	17 bombs, Coimbatore, India	50
1998, Mar. 5	Bus, Colombo, Sri Lanka	32
1998, Apr. 4	Coal mine, Donetsk, Ukraine	63
1998, Aug. 7	Bomb, U.S. emb., Nairobi, Kenya	213
	Bomb, U.S. emb., Dar-es-Salaam, Tanz	11
1998, Aug. 15	Car bomb, Omagh, Ireland	29
1998, Sept. 8	Two buses, Sao Paulo, Brazil	59
1998, Oct. 17	Oil pipeline, Jesse, Nigeria	700+
1999, May 16	Fuel truck, Punjab province, Pakistan	75
1999, July 29	Gold mine, Carletonville, S. Africa	17
1999, Sept. 10	Apartment building, Moscow	94
1999, Sept. 13	Apartment building, Moscow	118
1999, Sept. 16	Apartment building, Moscow	18
1999, Sept. 26	Fireworks factory, Celaya, Mexico	56
2000, Feb. 25	Bombs on 2 buses, Ozamis, Philip.	41
2000, Mar. 11	Coal mine, Krasnodon, Ukraine	80
2000, Apr. 16	Airport hangar, Congo, Dem. Rep. of.	100+
2000, July 16	Oil pipeline, Warri, Nigeria	30
2000, Aug. 19	Train derailed in Nairobi, Kenya	25
2000, Aug. 20	Natural gas pipeline, Carlsbad, NM	10
2000, Sept. 9	Truck explodes in Urumqi, China	60
2000, Sept. 13	Bomb, Jakarta, Indonesia	15
2000, Sept. 19	Bomb, Islamabad, Pakistan	16
2000, Oct. 12	U.S. destroyer, Yemen	17
2001, Mar. 6	School, Wanzai County China	41

Date	Location	Deaths
2001, Apr. 21	Coal mine, Shaanxi, China	51
2001, June 1	Dance club, Tel Aviv, Israel	21
2001, July 17	Coal mine, Guanxi, China	76+
2001, Aug. 19	Coal mine, Donetsk region, Ukraine	52
2001, Sept. 21	Chem. plant, Toulouse, France	29
2002, Jan. 21	Volcanic lava causes gas station blast in Goma, Dem. Rep. of the Congo	50+
2002, Jan. 27	Munitions dump, Lagos, Nigeria	1,000+
2002, Mar. 21	Car bomb near U.S. embassy, Lima, Peru	9
2002, Apr. 11	Truck nr. synagogue, Djerba, Tunisia	17
2002, Apr. 21	Bomb, dept. store, Mindanao, Philip.	14
2002, Apr. 26	Bomb at mosque, central Pakistan	12
2002, May 8	Bomb on bus outside hotel, Karachi, Pak.	14
2002, May 9	Land mine at parade, Kaspiisk, Russia	34+
2002, June 14	Car bomb outside U.S. consulate, Karachi, Pak.	12
2002, June 18	Bomb on bus, Jerusalem, Israel	20
2002, July 5	Bomb in market, Larba, Algeria	35+
2002, Aug. 9	Explosion, Jalalabad, Afghanistan	25+
2002, Sept. 5	Car bomb, Kabul, Afghanistan	30
2002, Oct. 12	Bombings of nightclubs in Bali, Indon.	202
2003, Aug. 5	Car bomb at hotel in Jakarta, Indon.	12
2003, Aug. 19	Truck bomb, UN headquarters, Baghdad	22
2003, Aug. 25	Bombs in 2 taxis, Mumbai, India	52
2003, Dec. 5	Bomb on train in Yessentuki, Russia	45
2003, Dec. 23	Gas well explosion in Chongqing, China	233
2004, Jan. 19	Natural gas facility in Skikda, Algeria	27
2004, Feb. 6	Bomb on subway car in Moscow, Russia	39
2004, Mar. 11	Madrid commuter trains bombed, Spain	191
2004, Apr. 17	Chemical factory in China	9+
2004, May 6-7	Ammunition dump in Ukraine	5
2004, May 11	Plastics factory in Glasgow, Scotland	4+
2004, July 19	Coal mine, Ukraine	31
2005, Mar. 23	Oil refinery, Texas City, Texas	15
2005, May 2	Arms cache in Baghlan prov. Afghan.	34+
2005, May 3	Accidental detonation of hand grenade, Mogadishu, Somalia	15+
2005, July, 7	Bombs in London mass transit	56
2005, Oct. 1	Bombings of restaurants in Bali, Indon.	22

Notable Nuclear Accidents

Oct. 7, 1957 — A fire in the Windscale plutonium production reactor N of Liverpool, England, released radioactive material; later blamed for 39 cancer deaths.

Jan. 3, 1961 — A reactor at a federal installation near Idaho Falls, ID, killed 3 workers. Radiation contained.

Oct. 5, 1966 — A sodium cooling system malfunction caused a partial core meltdown at the Enrico Fermi demonstration breeder reactor, near Detroit, MI. Radiation contained.

Jan. 21, 1969 — A coolant malfunction from an experimental underground reactor at Lucens Vad, Switzerland, released radiation into a cavern, which was then sealed.

Mar. 22, 1975 — Fire at the Brown's Ferry reactor in Decatur, AL, caused dangerous lowering of cooling water levels.

Mar. 28, 1979 — The worst commercial nuclear accident in the U.S. occurred as equipment failures and human mistakes led to a loss of coolant and a partial core meltdown at the Three Mile Island reactor in Middletown, PA.

Feb. 11, 1981 — 8 workers were contaminated when 100,000 gallons of radioactive coolant fluid leaked into containment building of TVA's Sequoyah 1 plant in Tennessee.

Apr. 25, 1981 — Some 100 workers were exposed to radiation during repairs of a nuclear plant at Tsuruga, Japan.

Jan. 6, 1986 — A cylinder of nuclear material burst after being improperly heated at a Kerr-McGee plant at Gore, OK. One worker died; 100 were hospitalized.

Apr. 26, 1986 — In the worst nuclear accident in the history of nuclear power, fires and explosions resulting from an unauthorized experiment at the Chernobyl nuclear power plant near Kiev, USSR (now in Ukraine), left at least 31 dead in the immediate aftermath and spread radioactive material over much of Europe. An estimated 135,000 people were evacuated from the region, some of which was uninhabitable for years. As a result of the radiation released, tens of thousands of excess cancer deaths (as well as increased birth defects) were expected.

Sept. 30, 1999 — Japan's worst nuclear accident ever occurred at a uranium-reprocessing facility in Tokaimura, NE of Tokyo, when workers accidentally overloaded a container with uranium, thereby exposing workers and area residents to extremely high radiation levels.

Record Oil Spills

The number of tons can be multiplied by 7 to estimate roughly the number of barrels spilled; the exact number of barrels in a ton varies with the type of oil. Each barrel contains 42 gallons.

Name, place	Date	Cause	Tons
Ixtoc I oil well, S Gulf of Mexico	June 3, 1979	Blowout	600,000
Nowruz oil field, Persian Gulf	Feb. 1983	Blowout	600,000 (est.)
Atlantic Empress & *Aegean Captain*, off Trinidad and Tobago	July 19, 1979	Collision	300,000
Castillo de Bellver, off Cape Town, South Africa	Aug. 6, 1983	Fire	250,000
Amoco Cadiz, near Portsall, France	Mar. 16, 1978	Grounding	223,000
Torrey Canyon, off Land's End, England	Mar. 18, 1967	Grounding	119,000
Sea Star, Gulf of Oman	Dec. 19, 1972	Collision	115,000
Urquiola, La Coruna, Spain	May 12, 1976	Grounding	100,000

Other Notable Oil Spills

Name, place	Date	Cause	Gallons
Persian Gulf	began Jan. 23, 1991	Spillage by Iraq	130,000,000[1]
Braer, off Shetland Islands	Jan. 5, 1993	Grounding	26,000,000
Prestige, off N Spain	Nov. 13-19, 2002	Ship broke in half	22,600,000
Aegean Sea, off N Spain	Dec. 3, 1992	Unknown	21,500,000
Sea Empress, off SW Wales	Feb. 15, 1996	Grounding	18,000,000
World Glory, off South Africa	June 13, 1968	Hull failure	13,524,000
Exxon Valdez, Prince William Sound, AK	Mar. 24, 1989	Grounding	10,080,000

(1) Est. by Saudi Arabia. Some estimates as low as 25 mil gal.

Some Notable Miscellaneous Disasters, 1950-2005

Date	Event	Location	Details	Est. Deaths
1952, Dec.	Pollution	London, England	Heavy smog blanketed city; caused difficulty breathing	4,000
1973-74	Drought and famine	Ethiopia	Caused by a 6-year drought	200,000
1974	Famine	Bangladesh	Caused by flooding	26,000+
1974-75	Famine	Sub-Saharan Africa	Drought in some regions, torrential rains in others, compounded by government mismanagement	40,000+
1980, summer	heat wave	United States	June through Sept.	1,265
1984, Dec. 3	Industrial accident	Bhopal, India	Toxic gas leaked from a Union Carbide factory	3,000+
1984	Famine	Africa, chiefly Ethiopia	Several years of drought compounded by government mismanagement	800,000-1 mil
1986, Aug. 21	Gas	Near Lake Nyos, Cameroon	Volcanic lake released toxic gas	1,700
1990, July 2	Stampede	Mecca, Saudi Arabia	Pilgrims panicked in tunnel leading to the holy city	1,426
2003, summer	heat wave	Europe	Abnormally high temperatures from Russia to Britain; France suffered most, with 14,800 dead	35,000
2005, Aug. 31	Stampede	Baghdad, Iraq	Fear of suicide bomber caused bridge stampede	1,000

HEALTH

Health News

• Newer, more **expensive antipsychotic drugs that treat schizophrenia are no better** for treating the disease than older, much less expensive drugs according to research published in *The New England Journal of Medicine* on Sept. 22, 2005. The study, the biggest ever conducted without significant funding from private drug companies, compared four newer "atypical" antipsychotic drugs to one old-line antipsychotic. Researchers selected 1,493 patients and randomly treated them over 18 months with the new drugs—ziprasidone, olanzapine, quetiapine, or risperidone—or with perhenazine, an older drug. Though all of the drugs reduced the symptoms of the disease, 74% of the patients abandoned their regime before the end of the study period because of side effects.

• The Food and Drug Administration (FDA) for the first time **approved a race-specific drug** on June 23, 2005. The drug, BiDil, has been proven effective in treating heart failure in black people. In a study of 1,050 black people, BiDil when combined with traditional medications was shown to reduce heart failure death by 43% compared to a placebo. The study was launched after two previous studies suggested the drug helped black people but not other races. Researches believe this may be a step toward "personalized medicine." However, critics contend that racially-based medicine is risky, since some races are social constructs rather than genetic ones. NitroMed, the manufacturer, suggests that socio-economic factors could also explain the difference between results for black and white patients.

• A stronger version of the **chickenpox vaccine** may be able to **prevent cases of shingles** and reduce severity of symptoms in patients over 60, according to a study conducted by the Department of Veterans Affairs and published June 2 in the *New England Journal of Medicine*. Over a course of 5 ½ years, researchers randomly gave 38,546 participants over the age of 60 either the vaccine or placebo. In the 3 years of follow-up, results showed that the vaccine reduced the incidence of shingles by 51%. In addition, pain and discomfort caused by the disease was measured by incidence, severity, and duration. Among those vaccinated who developed the disease, the total burden of pain associated with shingles was reported as 61% lower than for the placebo group. This is the first time a vaccine has been shown to have effect on shingles, which is caused by the reactivation of the dormant chickenpox virus.

• **Statins**, a type of cholesterol-lowering drug (such as Zocor, Pravachol, or Lipitor), **may help lower the risk of colon cancer** according to a study published in the May 26 *New England Journal of Medicine*. Research was based on data from the Molecular Epidemiology Colorectal Cancer study, during which researchers analyzed 3,968 people in Northern Israel, 1,953 of whom had colon cancer, and 2,015 of whom did not. After an analysis of the types of drugs taken by both groups, researchers found that those without colon cancer were twice as likely to have taken statins for at least 5 years compared to those who had the disease. Researchers looked into other possible risk factors including demographic background, diet, and family history, but found that statins were still associated with a 47% reduced risk for colon cancer. Other recent research has suggested similar links between statins and lessened risk for other types of cancer; however, more research will be needed before statins can be used for cancer prevention.

• A promising new **vaccine may help improve survival** in men with **advanced prostate cancer**, according to researchers who reported their findings at the 2005 Multidisciplinary Prostate Cancer Symposium in Orlando, FL, Feb. 19. Researchers tested Provenge, which is called a vaccine though it does not prevent cancer, but instead treats it. Either the vaccine or placebo was randomly given to 127 patients with advanced prostate cancer. To make the vaccine, doctors extracted proteins found in the cancer from the patient's blood, and combined them with Provenge. This helps immune system cells recognize the cancer as a threat. The mixture was injected back into the patients selected to get the treatment. Results showed that 34% of patients who received the vaccine survived at least 3 years, compared to only 11% of those receiving placebos. Similar vaccines are being tested.

• Doctors commonly remove the ovaries during hysterectomy for benign conditions such as fibroids, so as to eliminate the possibility of ovarian cancer. But according to a study published in the Aug. 2005 issue of *Obstetrics and Gynecology*, **women** aged 65 years and younger **who undergo hysterectomies** for non-cancerous diseases **may** derive an important **benefit from keeping their ovaries**. Using 20 years of published data, doctors analyzed 4 post-hysterectomy treatment strategies for women in 5-year age groups from age 40 to 80 years at average risk of ovarian cancer: conservation of ovaries with estrogen therapy, removal of ovaries without estrogen therapy, removal of ovaries with estrogen therapy, and conservation of ovaries without estrogen therapy. Results showed that women who undergo ovary removal before age 55 were 9% more likely to die before age 80 and those before the age of 59 are at a 4% increased risk of death before age 80. The benefit of conservation of ovaries is that until about age 65, the estrogen that ovaries produce protects the heart and bones, possibly reducing the incidence or severity of heart disease and osteoporosis.

• For those at particular risk of a first heart attack, whether women or men, doctors often recommend **low doses of aspirin**. Studies in the past have shown this therapy to be effective, but those studies mostly included men. For patients aged 45-64 the therapy **does not prevent heart attacks for women**, according to a long-term study published Mar. 31 in the *New England Journal of Medicine*. The study did find that aspirin therapy was beneficial in **protecting women from stroke.** As part of the Women's Health Study, nearly 40,000 women age 45 years and over were randomly given either one baby aspirin (100mg) or a placebo every other day over 10 years. Results showed that the aspirin takers had a 17% reduced risk for stroke compared to the placebo group, but there was no benefit in reducing heart attack risk. However, women over 64 had a 34% reduced risk of heart attack and 30% reduced risk for ischemic stroke. The results did not apply to people taking aspirin who had already had a heart attack.

• **A drug that boosts white blood cell production** may help relieve symptoms of patients with **Crohn's disease**, according to a study published in the May 26 *New England Journal of Medicine*. Crohn's disease, an incurable, often debilitating form of inflammatory bowel disease that can cause pain and bouts of diarrhea, affects about half a million people in the U.S. The study involved 124 patients with moderate to severe Crohn's who were randomly given either sargramostim (trade name, Leukine), a white-blood-cell-enhancing drug usually given to cancer patients, or a placebo. After 8 weeks, 48% of those given the drug saw significant relief—a result similar to that obtained from traditional treatment—as opposed to 26% of those given a placebo. It has been widely believed that Crohn's is caused by an overactive immune response, possibly to some organism in the intestine, and doctors typically treat patients with immunosuppressant drugs (which makes the patient less able to fight infections). But there is another theory that Crohn's may actually be associated with insufficient stimulation of the immune system. The new study was preliminary, but pointed to a need for further research in this area.

• Bacteria in **household dust** produce chemicals called endotoxins when they die. These **endotoxins** may trigger **asthma symptoms**, according to a study published online Sept. 7 in the *American Journal of Respiratory and Critical Care Medicine*. Researchers collected 2,552 dust samples from rooms in 831 homes across the U.S., and measured the concentration within each sample. The data suggest that endotoxins worsen asthma symptoms even in people without allergies. Regular cleaning, especially washing sheets in hot soapy water, can remove endotoxins.

Basic First Aid

Source: American Red Cross

NOTE: This information is not intended to be a substitute for formal training. It is recommended that you contact your local American Red Cross chapter to sign up for a First Aid/CPR/AED course.

It is important to get medical assistance as soon as possible, but knowing what to do until a doctor or other trained person gets to the scene can save a life, especially in cases of severe bleeding, stoppage of breathing, poisoning, and shock.

People with special medical problems, such as diabetes, cardiovascular disease, epilepsy, or allergies, are urged to wear some sort of emblem identifying the problem, as a safeguard against receiving medication that might be harmful or even fatal. Emblems may be obtained from Medic Alert Foundation, 2323 Colorado Ave., Turlock, CA 95382; 888-633-4298.

Animal bite — Wash wound with soap under running water and apply antibiotic ointment and dressing. When possible, the animal should be caught alive for rabies testing.

Asphyxiation — Call 9-1-1, or the local emergency number, then start rescue breathing.

Bleeding — Elevate the wound above the heart if possible. Apply direct pressure to the wound with sterile compress until bleeding stops. Call 9-1-1, or the local emergency number if bleeding is severe.

Burn — If mild, with skin unbroken and no blisters, flush with cool water until pain subsides. Apply a loose sterile dry dressing if necessary. If severe, call 9-1-1 or the local emergency number. Apply sterile compresses and keep patient comfortably warm until advanced medical assistance arrives. Do not try to clean burn or break blisters.

Chemical in eye — Call or have someone call 9-1-1 or the local emergency number. With the victim's head turned to the side, continuously flush the injured eye with water, letting the water run away from the other eye.

Choking — See **Abdominal Thrust**, below.

Convulsions — Place person on back on bed or rug. Loosen clothing. Turn head to side. Do not place a blunt object between the patient's teeth. If convulsions do not stop, get medical attention immediately.

Cut (minor) — Apply mild antiseptic and sterile compress after washing with soap under warm running water.

Fainting — If victim feels faint, lower him or her to the ground. Lay the victim down on his or her back. If there are no signs of a spinal injury or nausea, elevate the victim's legs approximately 12 inches. Loosen any restrictive clothing and check for any other signs of injury. Call 9-1-1 or the local emergency number if the victim remains unconscious for more than a few minutes.

Foreign object in eye — Try to remove the object by having the victim blink several times. If the object doesn't come out, try gently flushing the eye with water. Do not rub the eye. If the object still doesn't come out, the victim should receive professional medical attention.

Frostbite — Handle frostbitten area gently. Do not rub. Soak affected area in warm water (100–105°F). Do not allow frostbitten area to touch the container. Soak until frostbitten part looks red and feels warm. Loosely bandage with dry, sterile dressings. If fingers or toes are frostbitten, put sterile gauze between them.

Heat Stroke and Heat Exhaustion — Remove the victim from the heat. Loosen any tight clothing and apply cool, wet cloths to the skin. If the victim is conscious, give him or her cool water, to drink slowly. Call 9-1-1 or the local emergency number if the victim becomes unconscious.

Hypothermia — Call 9-1-1 or the local emergency number. Move victim to a warm place. Remove wet clothing and dry victim, if necessary. Warm victim gradually by wrapping the person in warm blankets or clothing. Apply heat pads or other heat sources if available, but not directly to the body. Give the victim warm, non-alcoholic and decaffeinated liquids to drink.

Loss of Limb — If a limb is severed, it is important to properly protect the limb so that it can possibly be reattached. After the victim is cared for, the limb should be wrapped in a sterile gauze or clean material and placed in a clean plastic bag, garbage can or other suitable container. Pack ice around the limb on the OUTSIDE of the bag to keep the limb cold. Call ahead to the hospital to alert staff there.

Poisoning — Call 9-1-1 or the local emergency number and Poison Control Center (800-222-1222) and follow their directions. Do not give the victim any food or drink or induce vomiting, unless specified by the Poison Control Center.

Shock (injury-related) — Monitor breathing and consciousness. Help the victim rest as comfortably as possible. If uncertain as to his or her injuries, keep the victim flat on the back. Otherwise elevate feet and legs 12 inches. Maintain normal body temperature; if the weather is cold or damp, place blankets or extra clothing over and under the victim; if weather is hot, provide shade. Do not attempt to move victim if spinal injury is suspected.

Snakebite — Call 9-1-1 or the local emergency number. Wash the injury. Keep the area still and at a lower level than the heart. Keep the victim calm. If the victim cannot get professional medical help within 30 minute, consider using a snakebite kit if available.

Sprains and fractures — Apply ice to reduce swelling and pain. Do not try to straighten or move broken limbs. Apply a splint to immobilize the injured area if the victim must be transported. If you suspect a serious injury, call 9-1-1 or the local emergency number.

Sting from insect — If possible, remove stinger by scraping it away or using tweezers. Wash the area with soap and water; cover it to keep it clean. Apply a cold pack to reduce pain and swelling. Call 9-1-1 or the local emergency number immediately if body swells, patient collapses, or you know that the victim is allergic to the sting.

Unconsciousness — Call 9-1-1 or the local emergency number immediately. If the person has signs of circulation, place him or her in the recovery position (i.e., lying on a side, with head supported, so that the airway is open). Do not move the person if a spinal injury is suspected.

Abdominal Thrust (Heimlich Maneuver)

The recommended first aid for conscious choking victims is the abdominal thrust, commonly known as the Heimlich maneuver, after its creator, Dr. Henry Heimlich.

- Get behind the victim and wrap your arms around him or her about 1-2 inches above the navel.
- Make a fist with one hand and place it, with the thumb knuckle pressing inward at the abdomen.
- Grasp the fist with the other hand and give upward thrusts until object is removed or help arrives.

Rescue Breathing

- Determine consciousness by tapping the victim on the shoulder and asking loudly, "Are you okay?"
- If victim is unconscious, tilt the victim's head back so that the chin is pointing upward. Do not press on the soft tissue under the chin, as this might obstruct the airway. If you suspect that an accident victim might have neck or back injuries, open the airway by placing the tips of your index and middle fingers on the corners of the person's jaw, and your thumbs on the victim's cheekbones, to lift the jaw forward without tilting the head.
- Place your cheek and ear close to the victim's mouth and nose. Look at the chest to see if it rises and falls. Listen and feel for air to be exhaled for about 5 seconds.
- If there is no breathing, pinch the victim's nostrils shut with the thumb and index finger of your hand that is pressing on the victim's forehead. Another way to prevent leakage of air when the lungs are inflated is to press your cheek against the victim's nose.
- Blow air into the mouth by taking a deep breath and then sealing your mouth tightly around the victim's mouth. Initially, give 2 rescue (approx. 2 seconds each) breaths.
- Watch to see whether the victim's chest rises.
- Stop when the chest is expanded. Raise your mouth; turn your head to the side and listen for exhalation.
- Watch the chest to see if it falls. Check for signs of circulation, including movement or coughing in response to the rescue breaths. If there are signs of circulation, but no breathing, continue rescue breathing. If there are no signs of circulation, begin CPR.
- Repeat giving 1 breath every 5 seconds until the victim starts breathing or advanced medical help arrives and takes over. Recheck for breathing and movement about every minute.

Note: Infants (up to 1 year) and children (1 to 8 years) should be treated as described above, except for the following:

- Do not tilt the head as far back as an adult's head.
- Both the mouth and nose of an infant should be sealed by the mouth.
- Blow into the infant's mouth and nose once every 3 seconds with less pressure and volume than for a child.

Heart and Blood Vessel Disease

Sources: American Heart Association, 7272 Greenville Ave., Dallas, TX 75231-4596; phone: (800) 242-8721; Centers for Disease Control and Prevention; National Institutes of Health

Warning Signs

Of Heart Attack

- Chest discomfort. Most heart attacks involve discomfort in the center of the chest that lasts more than a few minutes, or that goes aways and comes back. It can feel like uncomfortable pressure, squeezing, fullness, or pain.
- Discomfort in other areas of the upper body. Symptoms can include pain or discomfort in one or both arms, the back, neck, jaw, or stomach.
- Shortness of breath. This feeling may occur with or without chest discomfort.
- Other signs: These may include breaking out in a cold sweat, nausea, or lightheadedness.

The American Heart Assoc. advises immediate action at onset of symptoms, as more than half of heart attack victims die witin an hour of symptoms.

Of Stroke

- Sudden numbness or weakness of face, arm or leg, especially on one side of the body
- Sudden confusion, trouble speaking or understanding
- Sudden trouble seeing in one or both eyes
- Sudden trouble walking, dizziness, loss of balance or coordination
- Sudden severe headache with no known cause

Prompt treatment of stroke can be a major factor in controlling the effects.

Some Major Risk Factors

Blood pressure—High blood pressure, or hypertension, increases the risk of stroke, heart attack, kidney failure, and heart failure. It affects people of all races, sexes, ethnic origins, and ages. Obesity, physical inactivity, and an unhealthy diet can contribute to this **often symptomless** disease, and it is recommended that individuals have a blood pressure reading at least once every 2 years (more often if advised by a physician).

A blood pressure reading is really two measurements in one, with one written over the other, such as 122/78. The **upper number (systolic pressure)** represents the amount of pressure in the blood vessels when the heart contracts (beats) and pushes blood through the circulatory system. The **lower number (diastolic pressure)** represents the pressure in the blood vessels between beats, when the heart is resting. According to recent National Institutes of Health guidelines, a blood pressure reading below 120/80 is considered normal, while readings from 120/80 to 139/89 are considered "prehypertension."

High blood pressure is divided into 2 stages:
Stage 1 is 140-159 (systolic) over 90-99 (diastolic);
Stage 2 is 160+ (systolic) over 100+ (diastolic).

Individuals with diabetes or chronic kidney disease are considered to have high blood pressure if they have a reading of 130/80 or higher. The diagnosis can be based on either the systolic or the diastolic reading.

High blood pressure usually cannot be cured, but it can be controlled in a variety of ways, including lifestyle modifications and medication. Treatment always should be at the direction and under the supervision of a physician.

Cholesterol—Cholesterol is a waxy fat-like substance found in all cells of the body. It is produced by the body and also comes in some foods. The body needs some cholesterol, but excess levels increase the risk of heart disease. High cholesterol itself **does not cause symptoms**, so many people are unaware that they have a problem.

There are 2 kinds of cholesterol: **LDL (low-density lipoprotein)**, often called "bad" cholesterol, leads to narrowing of the arteries; **HDL (high-density lipoprotein)**, known as "good" cholesterol, helps reduce this risk.

National Institutes of Health guidelines classify total cholesterol levels (determined by a blood test) of less than 200 mg/dl as desirable, 200-239 as borderline high, and 240 and above as high. About 37 mil. Americans have a cholesterol level of 240 mg/dl or higher. LDL levels of less than 100 are considered optimal, 130-159 as borderline high, 160-189 as high, and 190 and over as very high. For HDL, levels of 60 mg/dl and above are considered protective against heart disease, while levels under 40 mg/dl are considered a risk factor for heart disease.

Like high-blood pressure, high cholestrol can be controlled by life-style modification and medication, and should be treated under supervision of a physician.

Triglycerides, another form of fat in the blood, can also raise the risk of heart disease. Levels that are borderline high (150-199) or high (200 or more) may need treatment.

Diabetes—Diabetes is a major risk factor for heart disease; 2/3 to 3/4 of people with diabetes mellitus die of some form of heart or blood vessel disease. See also "Diabetes" on page 169.

Smoking—Cigarette smokers have more than twice the risk of heart attack and 2-4 times the risk of sudden cardiac death as nonsmokers. Young smokers also have a higher risk for early death from stroke. See also "Some Benefits of Quitting Smoking" on page 166.

Obesity—Using a body mass index (BMI) of 25 and higher for overweight and 30 and higher for obesity, an estimated 131 mil Americans age 20 and over are overweight and 62 mil are obese. See also "Weight Guidelines for Adults" on page 175.

Women and Cardiovascular Disease

The American Heart Association reports that heart disease and stroke, respectively, are the No. 1 and No. 3 killers of women over the age of 25 (cancer is the 2nd); one in 2.5 women eventually dies of some form of cardiovascular disease. Because heart disease was long viewed as a "man's" disease, many of the major cardiovascular studies were conducted only on men. Much recent attention has been directed toward understanding the influence of gender on cardiovascular disease risk and prevention, but important gaps in knowledge remain.

Women often present some of the same "classic" symptoms of heart attack that men feel, such as chest pain that spreads to the shoulders and arms, but they may more often report atypical chest pain or complain of abdominal pain, difficulty breathing (dyspnea), and nausea. Another problem in diagnosis is that women tend to have heart attacks later in life than men, so symptoms may more often be masked by other age-related diseases such as arthritis or osteoporosis. Even certain diagnostic tests and procedures such as the exercise stress test may not be as accurate in women, with the result that the disease process that leads to heart attack or stroke may not be detected early on, with potentially serious consequences.

Avian Flu

Avian influenzas (also known as bird flu) are a group of viruses carried by birds. They are usually harmless in wild birds, but can be fatal to domesticated birds. The H5N1 subtype of the virus is the most deadly to humans, killing almost 50% of those infected. Symptoms include common flu ailments such as fever, cough, sore throat, or muscle aches, and can progress to pneumonia or acute respiratory distress. The human form of the disease was first reported in Hong Kong in 1997, where 18 people were hospitalized, 6 of whom died. According to the World Health Organization, between 2003 and 2005, out of a total of 115 people infected, about half died: 41 in Vietnam, 12 in Thailand, 4 in Cambodia, and 2 in Indonesia. Poultry workers in the U.S. and Canada have come down with other avian flu strains, but not H5N1.

The only known way to catch avian flu is by coming into contact with an infected chicken or bird, or a contaminated surface (although there is a possibility that some cases may have been transferred between people in close contact). But because viruses like the H5N1 are constantly mutating, scientists worry the bird flu may merge with a common human influenza virus and spread rapidly. The WHO predicted that such an outbreak could cause between 7 mil and 360 mil deaths. Risks are highest in affected agricultural areas or open-air markets where contact with sick chickens or their eggs is likely.

Public health officials around the world, in an effort to prevent the spread of H5N1, have exterminated millions of birds, including small flocks in the U.S, that may have been exposed. In Feb. 2004, the U.S. Dept. of Agriculture issued a ban on poultry imports from affected Asian countries. The virus is resistant to some antiviral medications. However, neuraminidase inhibitors such as oseltamavir and zanamavir may be effective in fighting the flu. In Aug. 2005, the U.S. government announced plans to acquire 20 mil doses of an experimental vaccine that has shown some promise.

Finding Your Target Heart Rate

Source: Carole Casten, EdD, *Aerobics Today;* Peg Jordan, RN, Aerobics and Fitness Assoc. of America

The target heart rate is the heartbeat rate a person should have during aerobic exercise (such as running, fast walking, cycling, or cross-country skiing) to get the full benefit of the exercise for cardiovascular conditioning.

First, determine the intensity level at which one would like to exercise. A sedentary person may want to begin an exercise regimen at the 60% level and work up gradually to the 70% level. Athletes and highly fit individuals must work at an 85% or higher level to receive benefits.

Second, calculate the target heart rate. One common way is by using the American College of Sports Medicine Method.

To obtain cardiovascular fitness benefits from aerobic exercise, it is recommended that an individual participate in an aerobic activity at least 3-5 times a week for 20-30 minutes per session, although cardiac patients and very sedentary individuals can obtain benefits with shorter periods (15-20 minutes). Generally, training changes occur in 4-6 weeks, but they can occur in as little as 2 weeks.

Using the American College of Sports Medicine Method to calculate one's target heart rate, an individual should subtract his or her age from 220, then multiply by the desired intensity level of the workout. Then divide the answer by 6 for a 10-second pulse count. (The 10-second pulse count is useful for checking whether the target heart rate is being achieved during the workout. One can easily check one's pulse—at the wrist or side of the neck—counting the number of beats in 10 seconds.)

For example, a 20-year-old wishing to exercise at 70% intensity would employ the following steps:

Maximum Heart Rate	220 – 20 = 200
Target Heart Rate	200 × .70 = 140
10-second Pulse Count	140/6 = 23

To work at the desired level of intensity, this 20-year-old would strive for a target heart rate of 140 beats per minute, or a 10-second pulse count of 23.

Calories Used During Physical Activity

Source: U.S. Dept. of Agriculture

Amounts of calories burned during physical activities are estimates for a 154-pound person. The more an individual weighs the more calories he or she will burn up with the same degree of exercise.

Moderate physical activities:	In 1 hour	In 30 min.
Hiking	370	185
Light gardening/yard work	330	165
Dancing	330	165
Golf (walking and carrying clubs)	330	165
Bicycling (less than 10 miles per hour)	290	145
Walking (3 ½ miles per hour)	280	140
Weight training (general light workout)	220	110
Stretching	180	90

Vigorous physical activities	In 1 hour	In 30 min.
Running/jogging (5 miles per hour)	590	295
Bicycling (more than 10 miles per hour)	590	295
Swimming (slow freestyle laps)	510	255
Aerobics	480	240
Walking (4 ½ miles per hour)	460	230
Heavy yard work (e.g., chopping wood)	440	220
Weight lifting (vigorous effort)	440	220
Basketball (vigorous)	440	220

Trends in Daily Use of Cigarettes, for U.S. 8th, 10th, and 12th Graders

Source: *Monitoring the Future,* Univ. of Michigan Inst. for Social Research and National Inst. on Drug Abuse

(percent who smoked daily in last 30 days; change 2002-2003 in percentage points)

	8th grade					
	1995	2001	2002	2003	2004	'03-'04 change
TOTAL	9.3	5.5	5.1	4.5	4.4	–0.2
Sex						
Male	9.2	5.9	5.4	4.4	4.3	–0.1
Female	9.2	4.9	4.9	4.5	4.3	–0.3
College plans						
None or under 4 yrs.	22.5	17.7	17.1	16.1	15.4	–0.7
Complete 4 yrs.	7.5	3.9	3.9	3.2	3.1	–0.1
Region						
Northeast	9.2	6.1	3.7	2.9	3.3	+0.4
North central	11.0	6.4	5.7	5.5	5.7	+0.2
South	9.4	6.1	6.6	5.7	4.7	–1.0
West	7.0	2.6	2.9	2.4	3.3	+0.9
Race/Ethnicity[1]						
White	10.5	7.5	6.0	5.3	4.7	–0.6
Black	2.8	2.8	2.8	2.9	2.7	–0.2
Hispanic	9.2	5.0	4.4	3.7	3.5	–0.2

	10th grade					
	1995	2001	2002	2003	2004	'03-'04 change
TOTAL	16.3	12.2	10.1	8.9	8.3	–0.6
Sex						
Male	16.3	12.4	9.4	8.6	8.2	–0.4
Female	16.1	11.9	10.8	9.0	8.2	–0.8
College plans						
None or under 4 yrs.	32.7	27.3	22.9	22.1	21.4	–0.7
Complete 4 yrs.	13.3	9.6	7.9	6.7	6.4	–0.3
Region						
Northeast	15.8	11.0	8.3	8.6	8.5	0.0
North central	17.6	13.2	11.5	10.2	7.4	–2.8
South	19.3	14.3	11.3	10.1	11.0	+0.9
West	9.4	7.0	7.8	6.0	5.2	–0.9
Race/Ethnicity[1]						
White	17.6	15.5	13.3	11.4	10.0	–1.4
Black	4.7	5.2	5.0	4.3	4.4	+0.1
Hispanic	9.9	7.4	6.4	6.0	6.0	0.0

	12th grade					
	1995	2001	2002	2003	2004	'03-'04 change
TOTAL	21.6	19.0	16.9	15.8	15.6	–0.3
Sex						
Male	21.7	18.4	17.2	17.0	15.4	–1.5
Female	20.8	18.9	16.1	14.0	15.0	+1.0
College plans						
None or under 4 yrs.	33.7	30.1	27.6	27.9	26.9	–1.0
Complete 4 yrs.	17.4	15.5	13.8	12.1	12.2	+0.1
Region						
Northeast	22.5	21.9	18.4	16.4	16.2	–0.3
North central	25.7	25.2	22.5	18.2	18.5	+0.4
South	21.7	15.5	16.6	16.3	15.8	–0.4
West	14.5	13.4	9.5	11.8	10.1	–1.6
Race/Ethnicity[1]						
White	23.9	23.8	21.8	19.5	18.3	–1.2
Black	6.1	7.5	6.4	5.4	5.2	–0.2
Hispanic	11.6	12.0	9.2	8.0	8.2	+0.2

(1) For each of these groups, data for the specified year and previous year have been combined to increase sample size and thus provide a more reliable estimate.

Some Benefits of Quitting Smoking

Source: American Cancer Society, Inc., 1599 Clifton Road NE, Atlanta, GA 30329-4251; phone: (800) 227-2345

Within 20 Minutes
- Blood pressure drops to a level close to that before the last cigarette
- Temperature of hands and feet increases to normal

Within 8 Hours
- Carbon monoxide level in the blood drops to normal

Within 24 Hours
- Chance of heart attack decreases

Within 2 Weeks to 3 Months
- Circulation improves
- Lung function increases up to 30%

Within 1 to 9 Months
- Coughing, sinus congestion, fatigue, and shortness of breath decrease
- Cilia regain normal function in the lungs, increasing the ability to handle mucus, clean the lungs, and reduce infection

Within 1 Year
- Excess risk of coronary heart disease is half that of a smoker's

Within 5 Years
- Stroke risk is reduced to that of a nonsmoker 5-15 years after quitting

Within 10 Years
- Lung cancer death rate about half that of a continuing smoker's
- Risk of cancer of the mouth, throat, esophagus, bladder, kidney, and pancreas decreases

Within 15 Years
- Risk of coronary heart disease is that of a nonsmoker's

Vioxx

Merck & Co., manufacturer of the pain reliever Vioxx, recalled that drug in Sept. 2004, after tests showed that long-term use (18 months and over) may double the risk of heart attack or stroke. By Sept. 2005 more than 4,000 Vioxx-related lawsuits had been filed against the pharmaceutical giant. In the first verdict rendered, in Aug. 2005, a Texas jury found the company liable in the 2001 death of Robert Ernst, and awarded his widow $253.4 mil in damages (Merck was appealing the verdict). Ernst, who had been taking Vioxx for 8 months prior to his death, died of an arrhythmia alleged to have been caused by a heart attack triggered by the drug.

Vioxx is in a family of pain-relieving anti-inflammatory drugs known as Cox-2 inhibitors, which have been shown to be associated with an increased risk of heart attack. The FDA in Feb. 2005 concluded that despite the risk the drugs should still be available to consumers. However, after further research on the risks connected with the Cox-2 drug Bextra, that drug was taken off the market in April by its manufacturer, Pfizer, at the FDA's request. A third major Cox-2 drug, Celebrex, also made by Pfizer, remained available, with a warning label. The FDA also said that all prescription nonsteroidal anti-inflammatory drugs should carry a warning about possible cardiovascular risk.

Arthritis

Source: Arthritis Foundation, 1330 West Peachtree Street, Atlanta, GA 30309; phone: (800) 283-7800; www.arthritis.org

The term "arthritis" refers to more than 100 different diseases that cause pain, stiffness, swelling, and restricted movement in joints. The condition is usually chronic. The Centers for Disease Control and Prevention (CDC) estimates that nearly 70 million adults suffer from arthritis and/or chronic joint symptoms. The cause for most types of arthritis is unknown; scientists are studying the roles played by genetics, lifestyle, and the environment.

Symptoms of arthritis may develop either slowly or suddenly. A visit to the doctor is indicated when pain, stiffness, or swelling in a joint or difficulty in moving a joint persists for more than two weeks. To make a diagnosis of arthritis, the doctor records the patient's symptoms and examines joints, looking for any swelling or limited movement. In addition, the doctor checks for other signs often seen with arthritis, such as rashes, mouth sores, or eye involvement. Finally, the doctor may test the blood, urine, or joint fluid, or take X-rays of the joints.

Of the 3 most prevalent forms of arthritis, **osteoarthritis** is the most common, affecting more than 20 million Americans; it usually occurs after age 45. In this type, which is also called degenerative arthritis, the protective cartilage of joints is lost and changes occur in the bone, leading to pain and stiffness. It usually occurs in the fingers, knees, feet, hips, and back.

Fibromyalgia, another common arthritis condition, affects more than 2 million Americans and affects more women than men. In this form, widespread pain and tenderness occur in muscles and their attachments to the bone. Common symptoms include fatigue, disturbed sleep, stiffness, and psychological distress.

Rheumatoid arthritis, which also affects more than 2 million people in the U.S., is one of the most serious and disabling forms of the disease. In this type, which is also more common in women, inflammation of the joints leads to damage of the cartilage and bone. The areas of the body that can be affected are the hands, wrists, feet, knees, ankles, shoulders, neck, jaw, and elbows.

Other forms of arthritis and related conditions include lupus, gout, ankylosing spondylitis, and scleroderma; also related are bursitis and tendinitis, which may result from injuring or overusing a joint.

Medications to treat arthritis include drugs that relieve pain and swelling such as analgesics, anti-inflammatory drugs, biologic response modifiers, glucocorticoids and antirheumatic drugs that also tend to slow the disease process. Most treatment programs call for exercise, use of heat or cold, and joint-protection techniques, such as avoiding excess stress on joints, using assistive devices, and controlling weight. In some cases, surgery can help.

Alzheimer's Disease

Source: Alzheimer's Association, 225 N Michigan Ave., 17th Fl., Chicago, IL 60601-7633; phone: (800) 272-3900; www.alz.org

Alzheimer's disease, the most common form of dementia, is a progressive, degenerative disease of the brain in which nerve cells deteriorate and die for unknown reasons. Its first symptoms usually involve impaired memory and confusion about recent events. As the disease advances, it results in greater impairment of memory, thinking, behavior, and physical health.

The **rate of progression** of Alzheimer's varies, ranging from 3 to 20 years; the average length of time from onset of symptoms until death is 8 years. Eventually, affected individuals lose their ability to care for themselves and become susceptible to infections of the lungs, urinary tract, or other organs as they grow progressively debilitated.

Alzheimer's disease affects an estimated 4.5 million Americans, striking men and women of all ethnic groups. Although most people diagnosed with Alzheimer's are older than age 60, some cases occur in people in their 40s and 50s. An estimated 10% of the population over age 65 have Alzheimer's, and the disease affects almost half of those over 85. In the United States, annual costs of diagnosis, treatment, and long-term care are estimated at $100 billion.

Diagnosis involves a comprehensive evaluation that may include a complete health history, a physical examination, neurological and mental status assessments, and other testing as needed. Skilled health care professionals can generally diagnose Alzheimer's with about 90% accuracy. Other conditions that can cause similar symptoms include depression, drug interactions, nutritional imbalances, infections such as AIDS, meningitis, and syphilis, and other forms of dementia, such as those associated with stroke, Huntington's disease, Parkinson's disease, frontotemporal dementia, and vascular disease. Absolute confirmation of diagnosis requires a brain biopsy or autopsy.

Treatments for cognitive and behavioral symptoms are available, but no intervention has yet been developed that prevents Alzheimer's or reverses its course. Some research suggests that risk factors for heart disease, such as high blood pressure, elevated cholesterol, and excess body weight may also increase risk of developing Alzheimer's. Studies also suggest that staying physically and mentally active and socially connected may be associated with a lower risk for the disease.

Providing care for people with Alzheimer's is physically and psychologically demanding. Nearly 70% of affected individuals live at home, where family or friends care for them. In advanced stages of the disease, many individuals require care in a nursing home. Nearly half of all nursing home residents in the U.S. have Alzheimer's.

People with Alzheimer's need a safe, stable environment and a regular daily schedule offering appropriate stimulation. Physical exercise and social interaction are important, as is proper nutrition. Security is also a consideration, because many people with Alzheimer's tend to wander. An identification bracelet listing the person's name, address, and condition may help ensure the safe return of an individual who wanders.

Warning Signs of Alzheimer's Disease

- Forgetting recently learned information or inability to learn new information
- Difficulty with everyday tasks such as cooking or dressing
- Inability to remember simple words
- Use of inappropriate words when communicating
- Disorientation of time and place
- Poor or decreased judgment
- Problems with abstract thinking
- Putting objects in inappropriate places
- Rapid changes in mood or behavior
- Increased irritability, anxiety, depression, confusion, and restlessness
- Prolonged loss of initiative

Cancer Prevention

Source: American Cancer Society, 1599 Clifton Road NE, Atlanta, GA 30329-4251; phone: (800) 227-2345

PRIMARY PREVENTION: Modifiable determinants of cancer risk.

Smoking	Lung cancer mortality rates are about 22 times higher for current male smokers, and 12 times higher for current female smokers, than for those who have never smoked. Smoking accounts for about 30% of all cancer deaths in the U.S. Tobacco use is responsible for nearly 1 in 5 deaths in the U.S. Smoking is associated with cancer of the lung, mouth, nasal cavities, pharynx, larynx, esophagus, stomach, pancreas, liver, uterine cervix, kidney, bladder, and myeloid leukemia.
Nutrition and Diet	Risk for colon, rectum, breast (among postmenopausal women), kidney, prostate, and endometrial cancers increases in obese people. While a diet high in fat may be a factor in the development of certain cancers, particularly cancer of the colon and rectum, prostate, and endometrium, the link between obesity and cancer is more the result of an imbalance between caloric intake and energy expenditure than fat per se. Eating 5 or more servings of fruits and vegetables each day, and eating other foods from plant sources (especially grains and beans), may reduce risk for many cancers. Physical activity can help protect against some cancers .
Sunlight	Many of the 1 million skin cancers that are diagnosed annually in the U.S. could have been prevented by protection from the sun's rays. Epidemiological evidence shows that sun exposure is a major factor in the development of melanoma and that the incidence rates are increasing around the world.
Alcohol	Heavy drinking, especially when accompanied by cigarette smoking or smokeless tobacco use, increases risk of cancers of the mouth, larynx, pharynx, esophagus, and liver. Studies have also noted an association between regular alcohol consumption and an increased risk of breast cancer.
Smokeless Tobacco	Use of chewing tobacco or snuff increases risk of cancers of the mouth and pharynx. The excess risk of cancer of the cheek and gum may reach nearly 50-fold among long-term snuff users.
Estrogen	Estrogen replacement therapy (ERT) to control menopausal symptoms can increase the risk of endometrial cancer. However, adding progesterone to estrogen (hormone replacement therapy, or HRT) helps to minimize this risk. Most studies suggest that long-term use (5 years or more) of HRT after menopause increases the risk of breast cancer, and recent studies suggest that risks from taking HRT exceed benefits. The benefits and risks of the use of HRT or ERT by menopausal women should be discussed carefully by the woman and her doctor.
Radiation	Excessive exposure to ionizing radiation can increase cancer risk. Medical and dental X rays are adjusted to deliver the lowest dose possible without sacrificing image quality. Excessive radon exposure in the home may increase lung cancer risk, especially in cigarette smokers.
Environmental Hazards	Exposure to various chemicals (including benzene, asbestos, vinyl chloride, arsenic, and aflatoxin) increases risk of various cancers. Risk of lung cancer from asbestos is greatly increased when combined with smoking.

Cancer-Detection Guidelines

SECONDARY PREVENTION: Steps to diagnose a cancer or precursor as early as possible after it has developed.

For people having periodic health examinations, a cancer-related checkup should include health counseling and, depending on a person's age, might include examinations for cancers of the thyroid, oral cavity, skin, lymph nodes, testes, and ovaries, as well as for some nonmalignant diseases. Special tests for certain cancer sites for individuals at average risk are recommended as outlined below:

Breast Cancer	Yearly mammograms starting at age 40 and continuing for as long as a woman is in good health. Breast clinical physical exams should be part of a periodic health exam, about every three years for women in their 20s and 30s and every year for women 40 and over. Women should report any breast change promptly to their healthcare providers. Breast self-exam is an option for women starting in their 20s. Women at increased risk (e.g., family history, genetic tendency, past breast cancer) should speak with their doctors about the benefits and limitations of starting mammography screening earlier, having additional tests (e.g., breast ultrasound or MRI), or having more frequent exams.
Cervical Cancer	Women should begin cervical cancer screening about 3 years after they begin having vaginal intercourse, but no later than when they are 21 years old. Screening should be done every year with the regular Pap test or every 2 years using the newer liquid-based Pap test. Beginning at age 30, women who have had 3 normal Pap test results in a row may get screened every 2 to 3 years. Women who have certain risk factors such as diethylstilbestrol (DES) exposure before birth, HIV infection, or a weakened immune system due to organ transplant, chemotherapy, or chronic steroid use should continue to be screened annually. Another reasonable option for women over 30 is to get screened every 3 years (but no more frequently) with either the conventional or liquid-based Pap test, *plus* the HPV DNA test. Women 70 years of age or older who have had 3 or more normal Pap tests in a row and no abnormal Pap test results in the last 10 years may choose to stop having cervical cancer screening. Women with a history of cervical cancer, DES exposure before birth, HIV infection or a weakened immune system should continue to have screening as long as they are in good health. Women who have had a total hysterectomy (removal of the uterus and cervix) may also choose to stop having cervical cancer screening, unless the surgery was done as a treatment for cervical cancer or precancer. Women who have had a hysterectomy without removal of the cervix should continue to follow the guidelines above.
Colorectal Cancer	Beginning at age 50, both men and women should follow one of these testing schedules: Yearly fecal occult blood test; or flexible sigmoidoscopy every five years; or yearly fecal occult blood test plus flexible sigmoidoscopy every 5 years; or colonoscopy every 10 years; or double-contrast barium enema every 5-10 years. **Note:** Persons known to be at increased risk for colorectal cancer (due to inflammatory bowel disease, personal or family history, etc.) need to begin screening at an early age and may need more frequent screening.
Endometrial Cancer	For women with or at high risk of hereditary nonpolyposis colon cancer (HNPCC), annual screening including endometrial biopsy should be obtained beginning at age 35.
Prostate Cancer	Both Prostate-Specific Antigen (PSA) and Digital Rectal Examination (DRE) should be offered annually, beginning at age 50, to men who have at least a 10-year life expectancy. Men at high risk, such as African-Americans and men who have a first-degree relative (father, brother, or son) diagnosed with prostate cancer at an early age, should begin testing at age 45. Health care professionals should give men the opportunity to openly discuss the benefits and risks of testing at annual checkups. Men should actively participate in the decision by learning about prostate cancer and the pros and cons of early detection and treatment of prostate cancer, so that they can make an informed decision about testing.
Skin Cancer	Adults should practice skin self-exam regularly. Suspicious lesions and moles should be evaluated promptly by a physician.

Breast Cancer

Source: American Cancer Society, Inc., 1599 Clifton Road NE, Atlanta, GA 30329-4251; phone: (800) 227-2345

In 2005, an estimated 211,240 women and 1,690 men in the U.S. will have been diagnosed with breast cancer, and about 40,870 women and 460 men will have died from it. Currently, an estimated 2 mil women are living with breast cancer, the 2nd biggest cause of cancer death for women in the U.S. (lung cancer ranks first). But mortality rates have been declining, especially among younger women, probably because of earlier detection and improved treatment.

The **risk** for breast cancer increases with age. It is higher for women with a personal or family history, a long menstrual history (menstrual periods that started early and ended late in life), recent use of birth control pills, long-term use of postmenopausal hormone replacement therapy, and no children or no live birth until age 30 or older. Other risk factors include alcohol consumption and obesity. Inherited mutations such as in the BRCA1 and BRCA2 genes greatly increase risk, but these probably account for less than 10% of all breast cancers. By far the majority of women who develop breast cancer have no family history of it.

Breast cancer is often **manifested** first as an abnormality on a mammogram, a type of X-ray. Physical symptoms that show up later, which may be detectable by a woman or her doctor, include a breast lump and, less commonly, breast thickening, swelling, distortion, or tenderness; skin irritation or dimpling; or pain, scaliness, or retraction of the nipple. Breast pain is more commonly associated with benign (noncancerous) conditions.

Studies show that **early detection** increases survival and treatment options (See "Cancer Prevention" above). Although most breast lumps that are detected are noncancerous, any suspicious lump needs to be biopsied.

Treatment for breast cancer may involve lumpectomy (local removal of a tumor), mastectomy (surgical removal of the breast), radiation therapy, chemotherapy, hormone therapy, immunotherapy, or some combination. For early-stage breast cancer, long-term survival rates following lumpectomy plus radiation therapy are similar to survival rates after modified radical mastectomy.

Prostate Cancer

Source: Prostate Cancer Foundation, 1250 Fourth Street Santa Monica, CA 90401

The **prostate** is a male gland located between the bladder and scrotum that secretes seminal fluid. Prostate cancer is the most common form of cancer among American men after skin cancer, and the most common cause of cancer death among American men after lung cancer. The American Cancer Society estimates that 232,000 men will be diagnosed with the disease in 2005, and over 30,000 will die from it. Over the course of a lifetime, 1 in 6 men will develop prostate cancer, but only 1 in 34 will die from it.

The exact **cause** of prostate cancer is unknown. The most identifiable risk factors are age, family history, and race. About 80% of all prostate cancers are diagnosed in men over the age of 65, and the chances of developing the disease rise dramatically with age. Men with a single relative with a history of prostate cancer are twice as likely to develop the disease, and those with two or more relatives are more than four times as likely to get it. African-American men are 65% more likely to get the disease than white men and are twice as likely to die from it. The cause for this disparity remains unknown; it is likely that both socioeconomic and biologic differences are involved.

Usually, the disease has no **symptoms** in its early stages. If symptoms arise, they may include: a need to urinate frequently; difficulty starting urination; weak or interrupted flow; pain during urination; difficulty having an erection; painful ejaculation; blood in urine or semen; frequent pain or stiffness in lower back, hips or upper thighs.

White men over 50 with no family history of prostate cancer are typically encouraged to be screened annually for the disease with both a prostate specific antigen **(PSA) blood test** and a **digital rectal exam** (DRE). African-American men or those with a family history of the disease may be encouraged to undergo screening beginning at age 40 or 45. Men under 40 seldom get prostate cancer.

Treatment may include surgery, radiation, hormone deprivation therapy, chemotherapy, or a combination. If caught early, while tumor cells are localized within the prostate, the cure rate is over 90%.

Diabetes

Source: American Diabetes Association, 1701 N Beauregard St., Alexandria, VA 22311; phone: (800) 342-2383

Diabetes is a chronic disease in which the body does not produce or properly use **insulin**, a hormone needed to convert sugar, starches, and other foods into energy necessary for daily life. Both genetics and environment appear to play roles in the onset of diabetes. This disease, which has no cure, is the 5th-leading cause of death by disease in the U.S. According to death certificate data, diabetes contributed to 213,000 deaths in 2000.

It is estimated that there are 18.2 mil Americans with diabetes, 5.2 mil of whom are undiagnosed.

In 1997, the American Diabetes Association issued **new guidelines for diagnosing diabetes**. The recommendations include: lowering the acceptable level of blood sugar in a fasting glucose test from 140 mg of glucose/deciliter of blood to 126 mg/deciliter; testing all adults 45 years and older, and then every 3 years if normal; and testing at a younger age, or more frequently, in high-risk individuals. The American Diabetes Association supports studies that have proven that detection at an earlier stage and modest lifestyle changes, such as eating better and exercising more, will help prevent or delay complications.

There are 2 major types of diabetes:

Type 1 (formerly known as insulin dependent, or juvenile diabetes). The body produces very little or no insulin; disease most often begins in childhood or early adulthood. People with type 1 diabetes must take daily insulin injections to stay alive.

Type 2 (formerly known as non-insulin dependent, or adult-onset diabetes). The body does not produce enough or cannot properly use insulin. It is the most common form of the disease (90-95% of cases in people over age 20) and often begins later in life.

Warning Signs of Diabetes

Type 1 Diabetes (usually occurs suddenly):

frequent urination	unusual weight loss
unusual thirst	extreme fatigue
extreme hunger	irritability

Type 2 Diabetes (occurs less suddenly):

any type 1 symptoms	cuts/bruises slow to heal
frequent infections	tingling/numbness in hands or feet
blurred vision	recurring skin, gum, or bladder infections

Pre-Diabetes

Among U.S. adults 40-74 years of age, 41 mil (40.1% of the population) have **pre-diabetes**, the state that occurs when a person's blood glucose levels are higher than normal but not high enough for a diagnosis of diabetes.

In a recent study, about 11% of people with pre-diabetes developed type 2 diabetes during each year of the study. Other studies show that most people with pre-diabetes develop type 2 diabetes in 10 years.

Complications of Diabetes

People often have diabetes many years before it is diagnosed. During that time, serious complications have a chance to develop. Potential complications include:

Blindness. Diabetes is the leading cause of blindness in people ages 20-74. Each year, from 12,000 to 24,000 people lose their sight because of diabetes.

Kidney disease. 10% to 21% of all people with diabetes develop kidney disease. In 2000, more than 41,046 people initiated treatment for end-stage renal disease (kidney failure) because of diabetes.

Amputations. Diabetes is the most frequent cause of non-traumatic lower limb amputations. The risk of a leg amputation is 15 to 40 times greater for a person with diabetes than for the average American. Each year, an estimated 80,000 people lose a foot or leg as a result of complications brought on by diabetes.

Heart disease and stroke. People with diabetes are 2 to 4 times more likely to have heart disease. And they are 2 to 4 times more likely to suffer a stroke. (About 65% of deaths among people with diabetes are due to heart disease and stroke.)

Acquired Immune Deficiency Syndrome

Source: Centers for Disease Control and Prevention; www.cdc.gov

AIDS (Acquired Immune Deficiency Syndrome) is caused by the human immunodeficiency virus (**HIV**). HIV kills or disables crucial cells of the immune system, progressively destroying the body's ability to fight disease.

HIV is commonly spread through unprotected sexual contact with an infected partner. It is also spread through contact with infected blood. Where modern screening techniques are used it is rare to contract HIV from transfusion, but it can be contracted when intravenous drug users share syringes with others. Though HIV can be spread through semen, vaginal fluids, and breast milk, there is no evidence it can be spread through saliva. The rate of transmission from a pregnant woman to her infant is about 25% without treatment, but can be reduced to less than 2% with treatment. Studies have indicated no evidence of HIV transmission through casual contact such as the sharing of food utensils, towels and bedding, telephones, or toilet seats.

Some people experience flu-like symptoms a short time after infection with HIV, and scientists estimate that about half of those infected with HIV develop more serious, often chronic symptoms within ten years. Even when symptoms are not present, HIV is active in the body, multiplying, infecting, and killing CD4+ T cells, or "T-helper cells," the crucial immune cells that signal other cells in the immune system to perform their functions.

The term **AIDS** applies to the most advanced stages of HIV infection. According to the official definition set by the Centers for Disease Control and Prevention (CDC), an HIV–infected person with fewer than 200 CD4+ T cells can be said to have AIDS. (Healthy adults usually have 1,000 or more). An HIV-infected person, regardless of T cell count, is diagnosed with AIDS if he or she develops one of 26 conditions that typically affect people with advanced HIV. Most of these conditions are "opportunistic infections" that occur when the immune system is so ravaged by HIV that the body cannot fight off certain bacteria, viruses and microbes.

Months or years prior to the onset of AIDS, many people experience such symptoms as swollen glands, lack of energy, fevers and sweats, and skin rashes. People with full-blown AIDS may develop infections of the intestinal tract, lungs, brain, eyes, and other organs, with a variety of symptoms, and may become severely debilitated. They also are prone to developing certain cancers, especially those caused by viruses, such as Kaposi's sarcoma, cervical cancer, and lymphoma. Children with AIDS may have delayed development or failure to thrive.

HIV is primarily **detected** by testing a person's blood for the presence of antibodies (disease-fighting proteins) to HIV. In about 5% of infected individuals, HIV antibodies may take more than 6 months after exposure to reach detectable levels, but in most cases the antibodies are detectable in about 6 weeks. HIV testing may also be performed on oral fluid and urine samples. New rapid HIV tests can provide preliminary results in about 20 minutes.

The **U.S. Food and Drug Administration** has approved a number of **drugs** that may slow down the growth of HIV in the body and treat the infections and cancers associated with AIDS. The first group of drugs used to treat HIV, called nucleoside analog reverse transcriptase inhibitors (NRTIs), include the drug zidovudine (commonly known as AZT). Non-nucleoside reverse transcriptase inhibitors (NNRTIs) have also been approved to treat HIV. A third class of drugs, called protease inhibitors, are also approved for HIV. In 2003 the FDA granted accelerated approval of Fuzeon for use with other anti-HIV drugs to treat advanced cases of infection. Fuzeon was the first among a new class of medications called fusion inhibitors; drugs in this class interfered with HIV's entry into cells by hindering the fusion of viral and cellular membranes.

Patients are typically given a combination of different drugs, because HIV can much more easily become resistant to a single drug. While these drugs extend the period between HIV infection and serious illness, they do not prevent the spread of the disease to others, and can have severe side effects.

Since there is no vaccine or cure for AIDS, the only **protection** is to avoid activities that carry a risk. When it cannot be known with certainty whether a sexual partner has HIV, the CDC recommends abstinence (the only certain protection), mutual monogamy with an uninfected partner, or correct and consistent use of male latex condoms.

Organ and Tissue Donation

Source: U.S. Dept of Health and Human Services

Each year, over 20,000 Americans receive organ transplants that save or enhance their lives, but about 6,000 others die while waiting for a transplant. Over 80,000 people are on the waiting list for transplants, and there is an acute shortage of available organs to transplant. A similar situation exists with regard to tissue.

In Apr. 2001, the U.S. Dept of Health and Human Services announced a **Gift of Life Donation Initiative** aimed at encouraging organ donation. The HHS plan included enlisting the cooperation of major corporations, issuing a model donor card (which would identify its carrier as someone wishing to donate organs and/or tissue), and investigating donor registries as a way of ensuring that an individual's intent to donate is communicated.

Officials stress that individuals wishing to donate organs/tissues should inform their families, so that they know this when the issue is brought up by medical personnel. Prospective donors should also carry a signed organ donor card, and indicate their intentions on their driver's license. The organs that can be donated are the heart, kidneys, pancreas, lungs, liver, and intestines. The tissues are bone marrow, corneas, skin, heart valves, and connective tissue.

Officials stress that an agreement to donate one's organs after death will not affect the quality of medical care and that the process does not disfigure the body or prevent an open-casket funeral. There is no cost to the donor's family; all costs are borne by the recipient.

A number of factors determine each patient's priority in receiving an organ, such as blood and tissue type, medical urgency, location, and time elapsed on the waiting list. Organs and tissues cannot be bought or sold; this is illegal.

For more information, go to www.organdonor.gov/faq.html or call UNOS at 1-888-894-6361.

Allergies and Asthma

Source: Asthma and Allergy Foundation of America, 1233 20th St., NW, Suite 402, Wash., DC 20036; phone: (800) 7-ASTHMA; www.aafa.org

One out of five Americans suffers from **allergies** of some kind. People with allergies have extra-sensitive immune systems that react to normally harmless substances. Common allergens that may produce this reaction include plant pollens, dust mites, or animal dander; plants such as poison ivy; certain drugs, such as penicillin; and certain foods such as eggs, milk, nuts, or seafood.

The **tendency to develop allergies** is usually inherited, and allergies usually begin to appear in childhood, but they can show up at any age. **Common allergies** for infants include food allergies and eczema (patches of dry skin). Older children and adults may often develop allergic rhinitis (hay fever), a reaction to an inhaled allergen; common symptoms include nasal congestion, runny nose, and sneezing.

It is best to avoid contact with the allergen, if feasible. In some cases, **medications** such as antihistamines are used to decrease the reaction, and there are treatments aimed at gradually desensitizing the patient to the allergen. Other effective allergy treatments include decongestants, eye drops, and ointments.

Some people with allergies also have **asthma**, and allergens are a common asthma trigger. Asthma is a disease of chronic inflammation affecting the passages that carry air into and out of the lungs. It can develop at any age.

People with asthma have inflamed, supersensitive airways that tighten and become filled with mucus during an asthma episode. Wheezing, difficulty in breathing, tightening of the chest, and coughing are common symptoms. Asthma can progress through stages to become life-threatening if not controlled. **Emergency symptoms** include: no improvement minutes after initial treatment; struggling to breathe, with patient hunched over and/or chest and neck pulled in; trouble walking or talking; stopping activity and not starting activity again; gray or blue lips or fingernails.

Besides common allergens, tobacco smoke, cold air, and pollution can trigger an asthma attack, as can viral infections or physical exercise. An accurate diagnosis by a physician is important. Although there is no cure for asthma or allergies, they can be controlled with medications and lifestyle changes.

Depression

Source: National Institute of Mental Health

Depression is a serious illness that affects thoughts, feelings, and the ability to function in everyday life. It strikes across all age groups, and often goes unrecognized or inadequately treated. A study released in 2003 by the National Institutes of Health estimated that 13-14 million Americans suffer from depression in any given year and that over 16% have depression at some point in life. Young people are among those at risk; the study found that in a one-year period, 3 times as many persons with depression were 18 to 29 years old as were 60 or older.

Nearly twice as many women as men suffer from a depressive illness in a given year. Although conventional wisdom holds that depression is most closely associated with menopause, in fact, the childbearing years are marked by the highest rates of depression, followed by the years prior to menopause. The influence of hormones on depression in women has been an active area of NIMH research.

In a given year, 1-2% of people over age 65 living in the community (outside of institutions) suffer from major depression. Depression frequently occurs with other physical illnesses, including heart disease, stroke, cancer, and diabetes. It is not a normal part of aging.

The **treatments** that are now available can alleviate symptoms, and with awareness growing, more people with depression are seeking the help they need. But many depressed people—and those around them—still fail to realize that they have an illness or could benefit from medical help. The 2003 NIH study also concluded that more than half of those seeking help do not get adequate treatment, often because they consult family practioners who do not deal aggressively enough with the problem.

Symptoms and Types of Depression

- persistent sad mood
- loss of interest or pleasure in activities once enjoyed, including sex
- significant change in appetite or body weight
- difficulty sleeping or oversleeping
- physical slowing down or agitation
- loss of energy
- feelings of worthlessness or inappropriate guilt
- difficulty thinking or concentrating
- recurrent thoughts of death or suicide

A diagnosis of **major depressive disorder** (or **unipolar major depression**) is made if an individual has 5 or more of these symptoms during the same two-week period. Unipolar major depression typically comes to the fore in episodes that recur during a person's lifetime.

Bipolar disorder (or **manic-depressive illness**) is characterized by episodes of major depression as well as episodes of mania—abnormally and persistently elevated mood or irritability, accompanied by such symptoms as inflated self-esteem, less need for sleep, increased talkativeness, racing thoughts, distractibility, agitation, and excessive involvement in pleasurable activities that have a high potential for painful consequences. While sharing some of the features of major depression, bipolar disorder is a distinct illness.

Dysthymic disorder (or **dysthymia**), a less severe yet typically more chronic form of depression, is diagnosed when a depressed mood persists for at least two years in adults (one year in children or adolescents) and is accompanied by at least 2 other depressive symptoms. Many people with dysthymic disorder also experience major depressive episodes.

In contrast to the normal experiences of sadness, or passing moods, depression is extreme and persistent and can interfere significantly with an individual's ability to function. A recent study sponsored by the World Health Organization and the World Bank found unipolar major depression to be the leading cause of disability in the U.S. and worldwide.

Treatments for Depression

A variety of **medicines** are used to treat depression. These drugs influence the functioning of certain neurotransmitters in the brain, primarily serotonin and norepinephrine, known as monoamines. Older drugs—so-called tricyclic antidepressants (TCAs) and monoamine oxidase inhibitors (MAOIs)—affect the functioning of both of these neurotransmitters. But they can have strong side effects or, in the case of MAOIs, require dietary restrictions. Newer medications, such as the selective serotonin reuptake inhibitors (SSRIs), have fewer side effects. All of these medications can be effective, but some people respond to one type and not another.

NIMH research has shown that certain types of **psychotherapy**, particularly cognitive-behavioral therapy (CBT) and interpersonal therapy (IPT), can help relieve depression. CBT helps patients change the negative styles of thinking and behaving often associated with depression. IPT focuses on working through disturbed personal relationships that may contribute to depression. Studies of adults have shown that a combination of psychotherapy and antidepressant medication is most effective in treating moderate-to-severe depression.

Electroconvulsive therapy (ECT) has been found effective in treating 80-90% of cases of severe depression, particularly those that have not responded to other forms of treatment. ECT involves producing a seizure in the brain of a patient under general anesthesia by applying electrical stimulation through electrodes placed on the scalp. Memory loss and other cognitive problems are common, but typically short-lived, side effects.

For more information, start with the website www.nimh.nih.gov/publicat/depressionmenu.cfm

IT'S A FACT: According to research published in *Nature* Aug. 31, scientists found that freshly-pressed extra virgin olive oil contains a pain-relieving compound called oleocanthal that works like ibuprofen. By the researchers' calculations, a 50-gram daily dose of fresh extra-virgin olive oil is equal to about 10% of an adult dose of ibuprofen.

Eating Disorders

Source: National Institute of Mental Health

Eating disorders involve serious disturbances in eating behavior, usually in the form of extreme and unhealthy reduction of food intake or severe overeating. They are not due to a failure of will; rather, they are real and treatable medical illnesses in which certain patterns of behavior get out of control. The **main types** are anorexia nervosa, bulimia nervosa, and binge-eating disorder. These disorders usually develop in adolescence or early adulthood and often occur with other illnesses such as depression, substance abuse, and anxiety disorders. They are much more common among females; only about 5% to 15% of anorexia or bulimia patients and 35% of binge eaters are male.

If not treated, eating disorders can lead serious complications, including heart conditions and kidney failure, which may lead to death.

Anorexia nervosa affects an estimated 0.5% to 3.7% of females during their lifetime. Symptoms include resistance to maintaining weight at even minimally normal levels, intense fear of gaining weight, exaggerated importance of body weight or shape in one's self image, and infrequent or absent menstrual periods. Anorexics see themselves as overweight even though they are dangerously thin. In response, they avoid food, and often takes other extreme measures to lose weight, such as compulsive exercise or purging by means of vomiting or laxatives and enemas. While some anorexics fully recover after a single episode, others may relapse frequently or experience chronic deterioration.

Bulimia nervosa affects an estimated 1.1% to 4.2% of females. It is characterized by recurrent uncontrolled binge-eating episodes followed by a compensatory behavior to prevent weight gain, such as self-induced vomiting, excessive exercise, or fasting. Persons with bulimia usually end up weighing within a normal range for their age and height, but they may fear gaining weight and feel intensely dissatisfied with their bodies. They often perform their behaviors in secret, feeling ashamed when they binge and relieved when they purge.

Binge-eating disorder (not officially approved as a psychiatric diagnosis) affects an estimated 2% to 5% of Americans in any given 6-month period. Like bulimia, a binge-eating disorder involves episodes of excessive eating during which the sufferer may lose all control, but individuals with this disorder do not compensate by purging, exercising, or fasting. Many are thus overweight, and the shame associated with the illness can lead to further bingeing.

Eating disorder sufferers may not admit they are ill and may resist treatment. Early diagnosis and a comprehensive treatment program are essential to recovery. Some patients may need immediate hospitalization. For anorexia, treatment usually follows 3 established steps: weight restoration (usually in an inpatient hospital setting), treatment of any accompanying psychological disturbances, and achieving long-term remission or recovery. Medications may be helpful in treating underlying depression or anxiety. Families are sometimes involved in the therapeutic process.

Food Guide Pyramid

MyPyramid.gov
STEPS TO A HEALTHIER YOU

In 2005 the U.S. Dept. of Agriculture issued a revised food guide pyramid called MyPyramid, along with new dietary guidelines for Americans. The new pyramid represents the latest findings in health and nutrition, with a focus on reducing calorie consumption and increasing physical activity. More specifically, the new system factors in weight, age, gender, physical activity in putting together a nutrition plan and distinguishes between necessary and unnecessary types of fats and sugars. In addition, the new pyramid allows for variation and personalization according to an individual's caloric needs. The guidelines below are general guidelines for better health and nutrition. To get a personalized nutrition and exercise assessment and for dietary recommendations visit MyPyramid.gov

2005 Dietary Guidelines for Americans—Some Key Recommendations:

- Choose nutrient-dense foods and beverages among the basic food groups, while limiting the intake of foods with saturated and trans fats, cholesterol, added sugars, salt, and alcohol.
- To maintain a healthy body weight, balance calories consumed with calories expended.
- To prevent gradual weight gain over time, make small decreases in calories and increase physical activity.
- Engage in regular physical activity and cut down on sedentary activities.
- Keep fit through cardiovascular conditioning, stretching exercises for flexibility, and resistance exercises or calisthenics for muscle strength and endurance.
- Eat a sufficient amount of fruits and vegetables each day.
- Choose from all 5 vegetable subgroups, dark greens, orange, legumes, starchy vegetables, and other vegetables.
- Consume 3 cups per day of fat-free or low-fat milk or equivalent milk products.
- Consume less than 10% of calories from saturated fatty acids and less than 300 mg/day of cholesterol, and keep trans fatty acid consumption as low as possible.
- Keep total fat intake between 20%-35% of calories, with most fats coming from sources of polyunsaturated and monounsaturated fatty acids, such as fish, nuts, and vegetable oils.
- Choose lean, low-fat, or fat-free meat, poultry, dry beans, and milk or milk products.
- Eat fiber-rich fruits, vegetables, and whole grains often.
- Consume less than 2,300 mg (approx. 1 teaspoon of salt) of sodium per day. Eat potassium-rich foods, such as fruits and vegetables.
- If you drink alcoholic beverages, do so in moderation: up to 1 drink per day for women and up to 2 drinks per day for men.

Estimated Calorie Requirements[1]

Estimated amounts of calories, rounded to the nearest 200, needed to maintain energy balance for various gender, age groups, and levels of physical activity.

	Age (years)	Sedentary[2]	Moderately[3] Active	Active[4]
Child	2–3	1,000	1,000–1,400	1,000–1,400
Female	4–8	1,200	1,400–1,600	1,400–1,800
	9–13	1,600	1,600–2,000	1,800–2,200
	14–18	1,800	2,000	2,400
	19–30	2,000	2,000–2,200	2,400
	31–50	1,800	2,000	2,200
	51+	1,600	1,800	2,000–2,200
Male	4–8	1,400	1,400–1,600	1,600–2,000
	9–13	1,800	1,800–2,200	2,000–2,600
	14–18	2,200	2,400–2,800	2,800–3,200
	19–30	2,400	2,600–2,800	3,000
	31–50	2,200	2,400–2,600	2,800–3,000
	51+	2,000	2,200–2,400	2,400–2,800

(1) Based on median height and weight for ages up to age 18 years and Body Mass Index (BMI) of 21.5 for adult females and 22.5 for adult males. (2) Engaging only in minimal activities associated with ordinary day-to-day life. (3) Includes physical activity equivalent to walking 1.5 to 3 miles per day at 3-4 mph. (4) Includes physical activity equivalent to walking more than 3 miles per day at 3-4 mph.

Food Ingredients

PROTEIN

Proteins, composed of amino acids, are essential to good nutrition. They build, maintain, and repair the body. Best sources: eggs, milk, fish, meat, poultry, soybeans, nuts. High-quality proteins such as eggs, meat, or fish supply all 8 amino acids needed in the diet. Plant foods can be combined to meet protein needs as well: whole grain breads and cereals, rice, oats, soybeans, other beans, split peas, and nuts.

FATS

Fats provide energy by furnishing calories to the body, and they also carry vitamins A, D, E, and K. They are the most concentrated source of energy in the diet. Best sources of polyunsaturated and monounsaturated fats: margarine, vegetable/plant oils, nuts. Meats, cheeses, butter, cream, egg yolks, lard are concentrated sources of saturated fats.

CARBOHYDRATES

Carbohydrates provide energy for body function and activity by supplying immediate calories. The carbohydrate group includes sugars, starches, fiber, and starchy vegetables. Best sources: grains, legumes, potatoes, vegetables, fruits.

FIBER

The portion of plant foods that our bodies cannot digest is known as fiber. There are 2 basic types: *insoluble* ("roughage") and *soluble*. Insoluble fibers help move food materials through the digestive tract; soluble fibers tend to slow them down. Both types absorb water, thus prevent and treat constipation by softening and increasing the bulk of the undigested food components passing through the digestive tract. Soluble fibers have also been reported to be helpful in reducing blood cholesterol levels. Best sources: beans, bran, fruits, whole grains, vegetables.

WATER

Water dissolves and transports other nutrients throughout the body, aiding the processes of digestion, absorption, circulation, and excretion. It helps regulate body temperature.

VITAMINS

Vitamin A—promotes good eyesight and helps keep the skin and mucous membranes resistant to infection. Best sources: liver, sweet potatoes, carrots, kale, cantaloupe, turnip greens, collard greens, broccoli, fortified milk.

Vitamin B_1 (thiamine)—prevents beriberi. Essential to carbohydrate metabolism and health of nervous system. Best sources: pork, enriched cereals, grains, soybeans, nuts.

Vitamin B_2 (riboflavin)—protects the skin, mouth, eyes, eyelids, and mucous membranes. Essential to protein and energy metabolism. Best sources: milk, meat, poultry, cheese, broccoli, spinach.

Vitamin B_6 (pyridoxine)—important in the regulation of the central nervous system and in protein metabolism. Best sources: whole grains, meats, fish, poultry, nuts, brewers' yeast.

Vitamin B_{12} (cobalamin)—needed to form red blood cells. Best sources: meat, fish, poultry, eggs, dairy products.

Niacin—maintains health of skin, tongue, digestive system. Best sources: poultry, peanuts, fish, enriched flour and bread.

Folic acid (folacin)—required for normal blood cell formation, growth, and reproduction and for important chemical reactions in body cells. Best sources: yeast, orange juice, green leafy vegetables, wheat germ, asparagus, broccoli, nuts.

Other B vitamins—biotin, pantothenic acid.

Vitamin C (ascorbic acid)—maintains collagen, a protein necessary for the formation of skin, ligaments, and bones. It helps heal wounds and mend fractures and aids in resisting some types of viral and bacterial infections. Best sources: citrus fruits and juices, cantaloupe, broccoli, brussels sprouts, potatoes and sweet potatoes, tomatoes, cabbage.

Vitamin D—important for bone development. Best sources: sunlight, fortified milk and milk products, fish-liver oils, egg yolks.

Vitamin E (tocopherol)—helps protect red blood cells. Best sources: vegetable oils, wheat germ, whole grains, eggs, peanuts, margarine, green leafy vegetables.

Vitamin K—necessary for formation of prothrombin, which helps blood to clot. Also made by intestinal bacteria. Best dietary sources: green leafy vegetables, tomatoes.

MINERALS

Calcium—works with phosphorus in building and maintaining bones and teeth. Best sources: milk and milk products, cheese, blackstrap molasses, some types of tofu.

Phosphorus—performs more functions than any other mineral, and plays a part in nearly every chemical reaction in the body. Best sources: cheese, milk, meats, poultry, fish, tofu.

Iron—Necessary for the formation of myoglobin, which is a reservoir of oxygen for muscle tissue, and hemoglobin, which transports oxygen in the blood. Best sources: lean meats, beans, green leafy vegetables, shellfish, enriched breads and cereals, whole grains.

Other minerals—chromium, cobalt, copper, fluorine, iodine, magnesium, manganese, molybdenum, potassium, selenium, sodium, sulfur, and zinc.

Understanding Food Label Claims

Source: U.S. Food and Drug Admin., Center for Food Safety and Applied Nutrition

The federal Nutrition Labeling and Education Act of 1990 provides that manufacturers can make certain claims on processed food labels only if they meet the definitions specified here:

SUGAR

Sugar free: less than 0.5g per serving

No added sugar; Without added sugar; No sugar added:

- No sugars added during processing or packing, including ingredients that contain sugars (for example, fruit juices, applesauce, or dried fruit).
- Processing does not increase sugar content above the amount naturally in the ingredients. (A functionally insignificant increase in sugars is acceptable from processes used for purposes other than increasing sugar content.)
- Food for which it substitutes normally contains added sugars.

Reduced sugar: at least 25% less sugar than reference food

FAT

Fat free: less than 0.5g of fat per serving

Saturated fat free: less than 0.5g of saturated fat per serving, and the level of trans fatty acids does not exceed 1% of total fat

Low fat: 3g or less per serving and, if the serving is 30g or less or 2 tbs or less, per 50g of the food

Low saturated fat: 1g or less per serving and not more than 15% of calories from saturated fatty acids

Reduced or Less fat: at least 25% less per serving than reference food

FIBER

High fiber: 5g or more per serving. (Also, must meet low-fat definition, or must state level of total fat.)

Good source of fiber: 2.5g to 4.9g per serving

More or Added fiber: at least 2.5g more per serving than reference food

SODIUM

Sodium free: less than 5mg per serving

Low sodium: 140 mg or less per serving and, if the serving is 30g or less or 2 tbs or less, per 50g of the food

Very low sodium: 35 mg or less per serving and, if the serving is 30g or less or 2 tbs or less, per 50g of the food

Reduced or Less sodium: at least 25% less per serving than reference food

CALORIES

Low calorie: 40 calories or less per serving; if the serving is 30g or less or 2 tablespoons or less, 40 calories or less per 50g of food

Calorie free: under 5 calories per serving

Reduced or Fewer calories: at least 25% fewer calories than reference food

CHOLESTEROL

Cholesterol free: less than 2mg of cholesterol and 2g or less of saturated fat per serving

Low cholesterol: 20mg or less and 2g or less of saturated fat per serving and, if the serving is 30g or less or 2 tbs or less, per 50g of the food

Reduced or Less cholesterol: at least 25% less than reference food

Dietary Requirements

Recommended Levels for Vitamins

Source: Food and Nutrition Board, National Academy of Sciences—Institute of Medicine, 2005

in milligrams per day (mg/d) or in micrograms per day (µg/d); asterisks denote levels defined as "adequate intake" (AI). *See* page 175.

		Vitamin A (µg/d)[1]	Vitamin C (mg/d)	Vitamin D (µg/d)[2]	Vitamin E (mg/d)	Vitamin K (µg/d)	Thiamin (mg/d)	Riboflavin (mg/d)	Niacin (mg/d)[3]	Vitamin B6 (mg/d)	Folate (µg/d)[4]	Vitamin B12 (µg/d)	Pantothenic Acid (mg/d)	Biotin (µg/d)	Choline (mg/d)[5]
Infants	0-6 mos	400*	40*	5*	4*	2.0*	0.2*	0.3*	2*	0.1*	65*	0.4*	1.7*	5*	125*
	7-12 mos	500*	50*	5*	5*	2.5*	0.3*	0.4*	4*	0.3*	80*	0.5*	1.8*	6*	150*
Children	1-3 yrs	300	15	5*	6	30*	0.5	0.5	6	0.5	150	0.9	2*	8*	200*
	4-8 yrs	400	25	5*	7	55*	0.6	0.6	8	0.6	200	1.2	3*	12*	250*
Males	9-13 yrs	600	45	5*	11	60*	0.9	0.9	12	1.0	300	1.8	4*	20*	375*
	14-18 yrs	900	75	5*	15	75*	1.2	1.3	16	1.3	400	2.4	5*	25*	550*
	19-30 yrs	900	90	5*	15	120*	1.2	1.3	16	1.3	400	2.4	5*	30*	550*
	31-50 yrs	900	90	5*	15	120*	1.2	1.3	16	1.3	400	2.4	5*	30*	550*
	51-70 yrs	900	90	10*	15	120*	1.2	1.3	16	1.7	400	2.4[6]	5*	30*	550*
	over 70 yrs . . .	900	90	15*	15	120*	1.2	1.3	16	1.7	400	2.4[6]	5*	30*	550*
Females	9-13 yrs	600	45	5*	11	60*	0.9	0.9	12	1.0	300	1.8	4*	20*	375*
	14-18 yrs	700	65	5*	15	75*	1.0	1.0	14	1.2	400[7]	2.4	5*	25*	400*
	19-30 yrs	700	75	5*	15	90*	1.1	1.1	14	1.3	400[7]	2.4	5*	30*	425*
	31-50 yrs	700	75	5*	15	90*	1.1	1.1	14	1.3	400[7]	2.4	5*	30*	425*
	51-70 yrs	700	75	10*	15	90*	1.1	1.1	14	1.5	400	2.4[6]	5*	30*	425*
	over 70 yrs . . .	700	75	15*	15	90*	1.1	1.1	14	1.5	400	2.4[6]	5*	30*	425*
Pregnancy	18 yrs. or less.	750	80	5*	15	75*	1.4	1.4	18	1.9	600[8]	2.6	6*	30*	450*
	19-30 yrs.	770	85	5*	15	90*	1.4	1.4	18	1.9	600[8]	2.6	6*	30*	450*
	31-50 yrs.	770	85	5*	15	90*	1.4	1.4	18	1.9	600[8]	2.6	6*	30*	450*
Lactation	18 yrs. or less.	1,200	115	5*	19	75*	1.4	1.6	17	2.0	500	2.8	7*	35*	550*
	19-30 yrs.	1,300	120	5*	19	90*	1.4	1.6	17	2.0	500	2.8	7*	35*	550*
	31-50 yrs.	1,300	120	5*	19	90*	1.4	1.6	17	2.0	500	2.8	7*	35*	550*

NOTE: For healthy breastfed infants, the AI is the mean intake. The AI for other life stage and gender groups is believed to cover needs of all individuals in the group, but lack of data or uncertainty in the data prevent being able to specify with confidence the percentage of individuals covered by this intake. (1) As retinol activity equivalents. (2) In the absence of adequate exposure to sunlight. (3) As niacin equivalents (NE). 1 mg of niacin = 60 mg of tryptophan; 0-6 months = preformed niacin (not NE). (4) As dietary folate equivalents (DFE). 1 DFE = 1 µg food folate = 0.6 µg of folic acid from fortified food or as a supplement consumed with food = 0.5 µg of a supplement taken on an empty stomach. (5) Although AIs have been set for choline, there are few data to assess whether a dietary supply of choline is needed at all stages of the life cycle, and it may be that the choline requirement can be met by endogenous synthesis at some of these stages. (6) Because 10-30% of older people may malabsorb food-bound B_{12}, it is advisable for those older than 50 years to meet their RDA mainly by consuming foods fortified with B_{12} or a supplement containing B_{12}. (7) In view of evidence linking folate intake with neural tube defects in the fetus, it is recommended that all women capable of becoming pregnant consume 400 µg from supplements or fortified foods in addition to intake of food folate from a varied diet. (8) It is assumed that women will continue consuming 400 µg from supplements or fortified food until their pregnancy is confirmed and they enter prenatal care, which ordinarily occurs after the end of the periconceptional period—the critical time for formation of the neural tube.

Recommended Levels for Elements (Minerals)

Source: Food and Nutrition Board, National Academy of Sciences—Institute of Medicine, 2005

in milligrams per day (mg/d) or in micrograms per day (µg/d); asterisks denote levels defined as "adequate intake" (AI).

		Calcium (mg/d)	Chromium (µg/d)	Copper (µg/d)	Fluoride (mg/d)	Iodine (µg/d)	Iron (mg/d)	Magnesium (mg/d)	Manganese (mg/d)	Molybdenum (µg/d)	Phosphorus (mg/d)	Selenium (µg/d)	Zinc (mg/d)
Infants	0-6 mos.	210*	0.2*	200*	0.01*	110*	0.27*	30*	0.003*	2*	100*	15*	2*
	7-12 mos.	270*	5.5*	220*	0.5*	130*	11	75*	0.6*	3*	275*	20*	3
	1-3 yrs.	500*	11*	340	0.7*	90	7	80	1.2*	17	460	20	3
	4-8 yrs.	800*	15*	440	1*	90	10	130	1.5*	22	500	30	5
Males	9-13 yrs.	1,300*	25*	700	2*	120	8	240	1.9*	34	1,250	40	8
	14-18 yrs.	1,300*	35*	890	3*	150	11	410	2.2*	43	1,250	55	11
	19-30 yrs.	1,000*	35*	900	4*	150	8	400	2.3*	45	700	55	11
	31-50 yrs.	1,000*	35*	900	4*	150	8	420	2.3*	45	700	55	11
	51-70 yrs.	1,200*	30*	900	4*	150	8	420	2.3*	45	700	55	11
	over 70 yrs . . .	1,200*	30*	900	4*	150	8	420	2.3*	45	700	55	11
Females	9-13 yrs.	1,300*	21*	700	2*	120	8	240	1.6*	34	1,250	40	8
	14-18 yrs.	1,300*	24*	890	3*	150	15	360	1.6*	43	1,250	55	9
	19-30 yrs.	1,000*	25*	900	3*	150	18	310	1.8*	45	700	55	8
	31-50 yrs.	1,000*	25*	900	3*	150	18	320	1.8*	45	700	55	8
	51-70 yrs.	1,200*	20*	900	3*	150	8	320	1.8*	45	700	55	8
	over 70 yrs . . .	1,200*	20*	900	3*	150	8	320	1.8*	45	700	55	8
Pregnancy	18 yrs. or less.	1,300*	29*	1,000	3*	220	27	400	2.0*	50	1,250	60	12
	19-30 yrs.	1,000*	30*	1,000	3*	220	27	350	2.0*	50	700	60	11
	31-50 yrs.	1,000*	30*	1,000	3*	220	27	360	2.0*	50	700	60	11
Lactation	18 yrs. or less.	1,300*	44*	1,300	3*	290	10	360	2.6*	50	1,250	70	13
	19-30 yrs.	1,000*	45*	1,300	3*	290	9	310	2.6*	50	700	70	12
	31-50 yrs.	1,000*	45*	1,300	3*	290	9	320	2.6*	50	700	70	12

The Food and Nutrition Board of the National Academy of Sciences' Institute of Medicine, in reports published from 1997 to 2005, set **Dietary Reference Intakes (DRIs)** for vitamins and elements (often called minerals). The DRIs, based on recent scientific research, establish daily consumption values that aim to optimize health at all stages of life, not just to guard against nutritional deficiencies.

The DRIs include 4 categories of values. The **Recommended Dietary Allowance (RDA)** gives an intake that meets the nutrient requirements of almost all (97-98%) healthy individuals in a specified group. The **Estimated Average Requirement (EAR)** is the intake that meets the estimated nutrient need of half the individuals in a specified group, while the **Adequate Intake (AI)** is the value given when adequate scientific evidence is not available to calculate an EAR. For healthy breastfed infants, the AI is the mean intake; for other life stage groups the AI is thought to cover the needs of all individuals in the group, but lack of data or uncertainty in the data prevents the percentage of individuals covered from being specified with confidence. The **Tolerable Upper Intake Level (UL)** designates the maximum intake that is unlikely to pose risks of adverse health effects in almost all healthy individuals in a specified group; taking the nutrient above that level could be bad for one's health. RDAs and AIs may both be used as goals for individual intake.

The tables give the RDA or, where not available, the AI, followed by an asterisk(*).

Weight Guidelines for Adults

Source: *Dietary Guidelines for Americans, 2005,* U.S. Dept. of Agriculture.

Guidelines on identification, evaluation, and treatment of overweight and obesity in adults were released in June 1998 by the National Heart, Lung, and Blood Institute (NHLBI), in cooperation with the National Institute of Diabetes and Digestive and Kidney Diseases. The guidelines, based on research into risk factors in heart disease, stroke, and other conditions, define degrees of overweight and obesity in terms of **body mass index (BMI)**, which is based on weight and height and is strongly correlated with total body fat content. A BMI of 25-29 is said to indicate **overweight**; a BMI of 30 or above is said to indicate **obesity**. Weight reduction is advised for persons with a BMI of 25 or higher. (Previous guidelines have been less stringent.) Factors such as large waist circumference, high blood pressure or cholesterol, and a family history of obesity-related disease may increase risk.

Despite growing awareness of the health problems associated, nearly 1/3 of Americans adults are obese (have a BMI of 30 or greater) and the number is growing, according to the National Center for Health Statistics. A high prevalence of overweight and obesity is a huge public health concern because excess body fat has been associated with type 2 diabetes, hypertension, dyslipidemia, cardiovascular disease, stroke, gall bladder disease, respiratory dysfunction, gout, osteoarthritis, and certain kinds of cancers. Over the last 2 decades, the prevalence of overweight children has doubled, and among adolescents it has tripled. It is estimated that, in 2005, as many as 16% of children and adolescents were overweight.

The table below shows the BMI for certain heights and weights. For weight reduction tips, contact the Weight-control Information Network, 1 WIN Way, Bethesda, MD 20892-3665. Phone: 1-877-946-4627. Website: win.niddk.nih.gov

	Weight (lbs)																			
Height	HEALTHY						OVERWEIGHT					OBESE								
4'10"	91	96	100	105	110	115	119	124	129	134	138	143	148	153	158	162	167	172	177	181
4'11"	94	99	104	109	114	119	124	128	133	138	143	148	153	158	163	168	173	178	183	188
5'0"	97	102	107	112	118	123	128	133	138	143	148	153	158	163	168	174	179	184	189	194
5'1"	100	106	111	116	122	127	132	137	143	148	153	158	164	169	174	180	185	190	195	201
5'2"	104	109	115	120	126	131	136	142	147	153	158	164	169	175	180	186	191	196	202	207
5'3"	107	113	118	124	130	135	141	146	152	158	163	169	175	180	186	191	197	203	208	214
5'4"	110	116	122	128	134	140	145	151	157	163	169	174	180	186	192	197	204	209	215	221
5'5"	114	120	126	132	138	144	150	156	162	168	174	180	186	192	198	204	210	216	222	228
5'6"	118	124	130	136	142	148	155	161	167	173	179	186	192	198	204	210	216	223	229	235
5'7"	121	127	134	140	146	153	159	166	172	178	185	191	198	204	211	217	223	230	236	242
5'8"	125	131	138	144	151	158	164	171	177	184	190	197	203	210	216	223	230	236	243	249
5'9"	128	135	142	149	155	162	169	176	182	189	195	203	209	216	223	230	236	243	250	257
5'10"	132	139	146	153	160	167	174	181	188	195	202	209	216	222	229	236	243	250	257	264
5'11"	136	143	150	157	165	172	179	186	193	200	208	215	222	229	236	243	250	257	265	272
6'0"	140	147	154	162	169	177	184	191	199	206	213	221	228	235	242	250	258	265	272	279
6'1"	144	151	159	166	174	182	189	197	204	212	219	227	235	242	250	257	265	272	280	288
6'2"	148	155	163	171	179	186	194	202	210	218	225	233	241	249	256	264	272	280	287	295
6'3"	152	160	168	176	184	192	200	208	216	224	232	240	248	256	264	272	279	287	295	303
6'4"	156	164	172	180	189	197	205	213	221	230	238	246	254	263	271	279	287	295	304	312
BMI[1]	**19**	**20**	**21**	**22**	**23**	**24**	**25**	**26**	**27**	**28**	**29**	**30**	**31**	**32**	**33**	**34**	**35**	**36**	**37**	**38**

(1) The BMI numbers apply to both men and women. Some very muscular people may have a high BMI without health risks.

Spending on Health in the 50 Most Populous Countries

Source: *The World Health Report 2005*, The World Health Organization

Country	As % of GDP	Per capita[1]
Afghanistan	8.0	$14
Algeria	4.3	77
Argentina	8.9	238
Bangladesh	3.1	11
Brazil	7.9	206
Canada	9.6	2,222
China	5.8	63
Colombia	8.1	151
Congo, Dem. Rep. of the	2.2	18
Egypt	4.9	59
Ethiopia	5.7	5
France	9.7	2,348
Germany	10.9	2,631
Ghana	5.6	17
India	6.1	30
Indonesia	3.2	26

Country	As % of GDP	Per capita[1]
Iran	6.0	$104
Iraq	1.5	11
Italy	8.5	1,737
Japan	7.9	2,476
Kenya	4.9	19
Malaysia	3.8	149
Mexico	6.1	379
Morocco	4.6	55
Myanmar	2.2	315
Nepal	5.2	12
Nigeria	4.7	19
North Korea	4.6	0.3
Pakistan	3.2	13
Peru	4.4	93
Philippines	2.9	28
Poland	6.1	303
Romania	6.3	128

Country	As % of GDP	Per capita[1]
Russia	6.2	$150
Saudi Arabia	4.3	345
South Africa	8.7	206
South Korea	5.0	532
Spain	7.6	1,192
Sudan	4.9	19
Tanzania	4.9	13
Thailand	4.4	90
Turkey	6.5	172
Uganda	7.4	18
Ukraine	4.7	40
United Kingdom	7.7	2,031
United States	**14.6**	**5,274**
Uzbekistan	5.5	21
Venezuela	4.9	184
Vietnam	5.2	23
Yemen	3.7	23

(1) At average exchange rates.

Where to Get Help

Source: Based on *Health & Medical Year Book.* © by Collier Newfield, Inc.; additional data, World Almanac research

Listed here are some of the major U.S. and Canadian organizations providing information about good health practices generally, or about specific conditions and how to deal with them. (Canadian sources are identified as such.) Where a toll-free number is not available, an address is given when possible.

Some entries conclude with an e-mail address for the organization and/or an address for its Internet site, where you can also obtain useful information. In addition to these selected sites, there is a vast array of medical information on the Internet; however, it is very important to be certain that the source of information is reliable and accurate. Always check with a physician before embarking on any new health-related undertaking.

General Sources

Centers for Disease Control and Prevention Voice Information System
800-311-3435
Recorded information about public health topics, such as AIDS and Lyme disease. Also, you can request to talk with a CDC expert or have information faxed to you.
Website: www.cdc.gov

National Health Information Center
800-336-4797; in Maryland, 301-565-4167
Phone numbers for more than 1,000 health-related organizations in the United States. Printed materials offered.
E-mail: info@nhic.org
Website: www.health.gov/NHIC

National Institutes of Health
301-496-4000
Free information, including the latest research findings, on many diseases.
E-mail: NIHinfo@OD.NIH.GOV
Website: www.nih.gov

Aging

Administration on Aging's Eldercare Locator Line
800-677-1116
Information and assistance on a wide range of services and programs including adult day-care and respite services, consumer fraud, hospital and nursing home information, legal services, elder abuse/protective services, Medicaid/Medigap information, tax assistance, and transportation.
E-mail: eldercarelocator@apherix.gov
Website: www.eldercare.gov

National Institute on Aging
800-222-2225
Information and publications about disabling conditions, support groups, and community resources.
Website: www.nia.nih.gov

AIDS

AIDSinfo
800-HIV-0440
Information on federally and privately sponsored clinical trials for patients with AIDS or HIV; treatment information for people with AIDS, their families and health care providers
E-mail: ContactUs@aidsinfo.nih.gov
Website: www.aidsinfo.nih.gov

Canadian AIDS Society
613-230-3580
Written materials and referrals.
Website: www.cdnaids.ca
E-mail: CASinfo@cdnaids.ca

CDC-INFO
1-800 CDC-INFO (232-4636);
TTY: 1-818-232-6348
Information on the prevention and spread of AIDS, along with referrals.
E-mail: cdcinfo@cdc.gov
Website: www.cdc.gov/hiv/hivinfo/nah.htm

Alcoholism and Drug Abuse

Alcoholics Anonymous
212-870-3400
Worldwide support groups for alcoholics. Check phone book for local chapters.
Websites: www.alcoholics-anonymous.org or www.AA.org

American Council on Alcoholism
800-527-5344
Treatment referrals and counseling for recovering alcoholics.
E-mail: info@aca-usa.org
Website: www.aca-usa.org

DrugHelp
Answers questions on substance abuse and provides referrals to treatment centers.
Website: www.drughelp.org

National Clearinghouse for Alcohol and Drug Information
800-729-6686
Provides written materials on alcohol and drug-related subjects.
Website: www.health.org

National Council on Alcoholism and Drug Dependence Hopeline
800-622-2255
Advisory and referral service.
E-mail: national@ncadd.org
Website: www.ncadd.org

Wellplace
800-821-4357, 24 hours
Referrals to local facilities
Website: www.wellplace.com

Alzheimer's Disease

Alzheimer's Association
800-272-3900
Gives referrals to local chapters and support groups; offers information on publications available from the association.
E-mail: info@alz.org
Website: www.alz.org

Alzheimer's Society of Canada
416-488-8772
Gives phone numbers for local support chapters. Publishes support materials.
E-mail: info@alzheimer.ca
Website: www.alzheimer.ca

Amyotrophic Lateral Sclerosis (ALS)

ALS Association 818-880-9007
Information about ALS (Lou Gehrig's Disease) and referrals to ALS specialists, local chapters and support groups.
Website: www.alsa.org

Arthritis

Arthritis Foundation
800-283-7800
Information, publications, and referrals to local groups.
Website: www.arthritis.org

Arthritis Society (Canada)
393 University Ave., Suite 1700
Toronto, ON M5G 1E6
416-979-7228; in Ontario only, 800-321-1433
Phone numbers for local chapters.
E-mail: info@arthritis.ca
Website: www.arthritis.ca

National Institute of Arthritis and Musculoskeletal and Skin Diseases
877-226-4267 or 301-495-4484
Subject searches and resource referrals.
E-mail: niamsweb–l@mail.nih.gov
Website: www.niams.nih.gov

Asthma and Allergies

See also Lung Diseases

Asthma and Allergy Foundation of America
800-7-ASTHMA
Information; education; links to support groups.
E-mail: info@aafa.org
Website: www.aafa.org

American Academy of Allergy, Asthma, and Immunology Referral Line
800-822-ASMA, 24 hours; 414-272-6071
Patient information and referrals for asthma and allergies.
E-mail: info@aaaai.org
Website: www.aaaai.org

Autism

Autism Society of America
301-657-0881 or 800-3AUTISM
Information about autism, referral to local chapters.
E-mail: chapters@autism-society.org
Website: www.autism-society.org

Blindness and Eye Care

Canadian National Institute for the Blind
416-486-2500
National office offers training and library with braille books and audiotapes. Local chapters provide core services: orientation in mobility, sight enhancement, counseling, referrals, career aid, technology services.
Website: www.cnib.ca

Foundation Fighting Blindness
888-394-3937; TDD 800-683-5555
Answers questions about retinal degenerative diseases; has written materials.
E-mail: info@blindness.org
Website: www.blindness.org

Library of Congress National Library Service for the Blind and Physically Handicapped
800-424-8567; in Washington, DC, 202-707-5100; for the hearing impaired, TDD 202-707-0744
Information on libraries that offer talking books and books in **braille**.
E-mail: nls@loc.gov
Website: www.loc.gov/nls

National Association for Parents of Children with Visual Impairments
800-562-6265 or 617-972-7441
Support and information for parents of individuals who are visually impaired.
E-mail: napvi@perkins.org
Website: www.napvi.org

Blood Disorders

Cooley's Anemia Foundation
800-522-7222
Information on patient care and support groups; makes referrals to local chapters.
E-mail: info@cooleysanemia.org
Website: www.thalassemia.org

Sickle Cell Disease Association of America
800-421-8453; 310-216-6363
Referrals for genetic counseling and information packet.
E-mail: scdaa@sicklecelldisease.org
Website: www.sicklecelldisease.org

Burns

Phoenix Society
800-888-2876; 616-458-2773
Counseling network for burn survivors and information on self-help services for burn survivors and their families.
E-mail: info@phoenix-society.org
Website: www.phoenix-society.org

Cancer

American Cancer Society
800-ACS-2345
Publications and information about cancer and coping with cancer; makes referrals to local chapters for support services.
Website: www.cancer.org

Canadian Cancer Information Service
888-939-3333 or 416-961-7223
Information on prevention, treatment, drugs, clinical trails, local services.
E-mail: info@cis.cancer.ca
Website: www.cancer.ca

National Cancer Institute's Cancer Information Service
800-4-CANCER
Information about clinical trials, treatments, symptoms, prevention, referrals to support groups, and screening. Includes chat online information inquiries.
Website: cis.nci.nih.gov

Y-Me Breast Cancer Support Program
800-221-2141, 24 hours;
800-986-9505, Spanish, 24-hours
Information and literature on breast cancer, counseling, and referrals.
Website: www.y-me.org

Cerebral Palsy

Ontario Federation for Cerebral Palsy
Ontario only: 877-244-9686; 416-244-9686
Canada does not have a national cerebral palsy organization, but the provincial organizations offer information on housing, services, and coping with life, and each one will provide contact numbers for the others.
E-mail: info@ofcp.on.ca
Website: www.ofcp.on.ca

United Cerebral Palsy Associations
800-872-5827, (TTY) 202-973-7197; in Washington, DC, 202-776-0406
Written materials.
Website: www.ucpa.org

Child Abuse

See Domestic Violence

Children

American Academy of Pediatrics
847-434-4000
Child-care publications and materials; referrals to pediatricians.
E-mail: kidsdocs@aap.org
Website: www.aap.org

National Center for Missing and Exploited Children
800-843-5678; 703-274-3900. Operates 24 hours.
Hotline for reporting missing children and sightings of missing children.
Website: www.missingkids.com

National Runaway Switchboard
800-786-2929 (Runaway)
Crisis intervention and referrals for runaways. Runaways can leave messages for parents, and vice versa. Operates 24 hours.
E-mail: info@nrscrisisline.org
Website: www.nrscrisisline.org

Chronic Fatigue Syndrome

CFIDS Association of America
704-365-2343
Literature and a list of support groups.
E-mail: cfids@cfids.org
Website: www.cfids.org

Cystic Fibrosis

Canadian Cystic Fibrosis Foundation
416-485-9149;
800-378-2233 in Canada only,
Information and brochures; makes referrals to local chapters.
E-mail: info@cysticfibrosis.ca
Website: www.cysticfibrosis.ca

Cystic Fibrosis Foundation
800-FIGHT-CF or 301-951-4422
Answers questions and offers literature and referrals to local clinics.
E-mail: info@cff.org
Website: www.cff.org

Diabetes

American Diabetes Association
800-342-2383
Information about diabetes, nutrition, exercise, and treatment; offers referrals.
E-mail: askADA@diabetes.org
Website: www.diabetes.org

Canadian Diabetes Association
416-363-0177;
800-226-8464 in Canada only.
Information about diabetes and its management.
E-mail: info@diabetes.ca
Website: www.diabetes.ca

Juvenile Diabetes Research Foundation Hotline
800-533-2873
Answers questions, provides literature (some in Spanish). Offers referrals to local chapters, physicians, and clinics.
E-mail: info@jdf.org
Website: www.jdf.org

Digestive Diseases

Crohn's and Colitis Foundation of America
800-932-2423
Educational materials; offers referrals to local chapters, which can provide referrals to support groups and physicians.
E-mail: info@ccfa.org
Website: www.ccfa.org

Crohn's and Colitis Foundation of Canada
416-920-5035;
in Canada only, 800-387-1479
Will send out educational materials upon request.
E-mail: ccfc@ccfc.ca
Website: www.ccfc.ca

Domestic Violence

Childhelp's USA National Child Abuse Hotline
800-4-A-CHILD
Crisis intervention, professional counseling, referrals to local groups and shelters for runaways, and literature. Operates 24 hours.
Website: www.childhelpusa.org

National Council on Child Abuse and Family Violence
800-422-4453, (TTY) 800-787-3244
Information and referrals.
Website: www.nccafv.org

National Domestic Violence Hotline
800-799-7233; (TTY) 800-787-3224

Down Syndrome

National Down Syndrome Congress
800-232-6372; in Georgia, 770-604-9500
Answers questions on all aspects of Down syndrome. Provides referrals.
E-mail: info@ndsccenter.org
Website: www.ndsccenter.org

National Down Syndrome Society
800-221-4602; 212-460-9330 (NYC)
E-mail: info@ndss.org
Website: www.ndss.org

Drug Abuse

See *Alcoholism and Drug Abuse*

Dyslexia

International Dyslexia Association
800-ABCD-123; in Maryland, 410-296-0232
Information on testing, tutoring, and computers used to aid people with dyslexia and related disorders.
E-mail: info@interdys.org
Website: www.interdys.org

Eating Disorders

National Association of Anorexia Nervosa and Associated Disorders
847-831-3438
Written materials, referrals to health professionals treating eating disorders, telephone counseling, offers self-help groups and information on how to set up a self-help group.
E-mail: anad20@aol.com
Website: www.anad.org

Endometriosis

Endometriosis Association
800-992-ENDO, an answering machine for callers to request information; 414-355-2200
Website: www.endometriosisassn.org

Epilepsy

Epilepsy Foundation's Answer Place
800-332-1000, Mon. through Thurs.
Information and referrals to local chapters.
Website: www.epilepsyfoundation.org

Erectile Dysfunction

American Urological Association
866-746-4282.
Information on various urological disorders and referrals.
E-mail: aua@auanet.org
Website: www.auanet.org

Food Safety and Nutrition

Meat and Poultry Hotline of the U.S. Department of Agriculture's Food, Safety, and Inspection Service
888-674-6854; TTY 800-256-7072
Information on prevention of food-borne illness and the proper handling, preparation, storage, labeling, and cooking of meat, poultry, and eggs.
E-mail: MPHotline.fsis@usda.gov
Website: www.foodsafety.gov

FDA Center for Food Safety and Applied Nutrition Outreach & Information Center
888-SAFE-FOOD
Information on how to buy and use food products and on their proper handling and storage, women's health, and cosmetics & colors. Callers may speak to food specialists, Mon. through Fri., 10 am to 4 PM (EST).
Website: www.cfsan.fda.gov

Headaches

National Headache Foundation
888-NHF-5552
Literature on headaches and treatment.
E-mail: info@headaches.org
Website: www.headaches.org

Heart Disease and Stroke

American Heart Association
800-242-8721
Information, publications, and referrals to organizations.
Website: www.americanheart.org

National Institute of Neurological Disorders and Stroke
800-352-9424, 301-496-5751;
TTY 301-468-5981
Literature and information.
Website: www.ninds.nih.gov

National Stroke Association
800-787-6537; in Colorado, 303-649-9299
Information on support networks for stroke victims and their families; referrals to local support groups.
Website: www.stroke.org

Hospices

Children's Hospice International
800-242-4453, in Virginia, 703-684-0330
Information, referrals to children's hospices.
E-mail: info@chionline.org
Website: www.chionline.org

Hospice Education Institute Hospicelink
800-331-1620; in Maine, 207-255-8800
Information, referrals to local programs.
E-mail: info@hospiceworld.org
Website: www.hospiceworld.org

Huntington's Disease

Huntington's Disease Society of America
800-345-4372; in New York, 212-242-1968
Information and referrals to physicians and support groups.
E-mail: hdsainfo@hdsa.org
Website: www.hdsa.org

Kidney Diseases

Kidney Foundation of Canada
514-369-4806;
in Canada only, 800-361-7494
Educational materials and general information.
Website: www.kidney.ca

National Kidney and Urologic Diseases Information Clearinghouse
800-891-5390
Information, referrals to organizations.
Website: www.kidney.niddk.nih.gov

National Kidney Foundation
800-622-9010, 212-889-2210
Information and referrals.
E-mail: info@kidney.org
Website: www.kidney.org

Lead Exposure

National Lead Information Center
800-424-LEAD
Recommendations (in English and Spanish) for reducing a child's exposure to lead. Referrals to state and local agencies.
Website: www.epa.gov/lead

Liver Diseases

American Liver Foundation
800-465-4837; 800-443-7872
Information on hepatitis, liver, and gallbladder diseases.
E-mail: info@liverfoundation.org
Website: www.liverfoundation.org

Lung Diseases

See also *Asthma and Allergies*

American Lung Association
Check the phone book for local listings or call the national office at 800-LUNG-USA for automatic connection to the office nearest you. Answers questions about asthma and lung diseases; publications and referrals.
Website: www.lungusa.org

Lung Line Information Service at the National Jewish Medical and Research Center
800-222-LUNG; outside the U.S.: 303-388-4461
Answers questions on asthma, emphysema, allergies, smoking, and other respiratory and immune system disorders.
E-mail: lungline@njc.org
Website: www.njc.org

Lupus

Lupus Foundation of America
800-558-0121; 202-349-1155
Sends information to those who leave name and address on answering machine.
E-mail: info@lupus.org
Website: www.lupus.org

Lyme Disease

Lyme Disease Foundation
860-870-0070
Written information; doctor referrals.
E-mail: lymefnd@aol.com
Website: www.lyme.org

Mental Health

Depression and Bipolar Support Alliance
800-826-3632
Support for patients and families, provides publications, and makes referrals to affiliated organizations.
E-mail: questions@dbsalliance.org
Website: www.dbsalliance.org

National Institute of Mental Health
301-443-4513, toll free 866-615-6464; TTY 301-443-8431
Information on a range of topics, from children's mental disorders to schizophrenia, depression, eating disorders, and others.
E-mail: nimhinfo@nih.gov
Website: www.nimh.nih.gov

National Mental Health Association
800-969-6642
Referrals to mental health groups.
Website: www.nmha.org

Multiple Sclerosis

Multiple Sclerosis Society of Canada
416-922-6065, 800-268-7582 in Canada only.
Counseling, literature, and referrals to local chapters.
E-mail: info@mssociety.ca
Website: www.mssociety.ca

National Multiple Sclerosis Society
800-344-4867
Information about local chapters.
Website: www.nationalmssociety.org

Muscular Dystrophy

Muscular Dystrophy Association
800-572-1717
Written materials on 40 neuromuscular diseases, including muscular dystrophy. Will give information over the phone about such matters as MDA clinics, support groups, summer camps, and wheelchair purchase assistance.
E-mail: mda@mdausa.org
Website: www.mdausa.org

Nutrition

See ***Food Safety and Nutrition***

Organ Donation

Living Bank
800-528-2971, 24 hours
A registry and referral service for people wanting to commit organs to transplantation or research.
E-mail: info@livingbank.org
Website: www.livingbank.org

Osteoporosis

National Osteoporosis Foundation
800-223-9994; in Washington, DC, 202-223-2226
Inforvmation packet available on request.
Website: www.nof.org

Pain

National Chronic Pain Outreach Association
540-862-9437
Information packet available on request.
Website: www.chronicpain.org

Parkinson's Disease

National Parkinson Foundation
800-327-4545; in Miami, 305-547-6666
Answers questions, makes physician referrals, and provides written information in English and Spanish.
E-mail: contact@parkinson.org
Website: www.parkinson.org

Parkinson Society Canada
800-565-3000, Canada only; 416-227-9700
Information; referrals to support groups.
E-mail: General.info@parkinson.ca
Website: www.parkinson.ca

Plastic Surgery

Plastic Surgery Refferal Service
888-475-2784
Referrals to board-certified plastic surgeons in the U.S. and Canada; general information.
Website: www.plasticsurgery.org

Polio

Post-Polio Health International
314-534-0475
Information on coping with the late effects of polio; referrals to other organizations.
E-mail: info@post-polio.org
Website: www.post-polio.org

Prostate Problems

American Urological Association Foundation
800-828-7866, 410-689-3990
Information and publications.
Website: www.urologyhealth.org

Rare Disorders

National Organization for Rare Disorders
800-999-6673, 203-744-0100
Information on diseases and networking programs; referrals to organizations for specific disorders.
E-mail: orphan@rarediseases.org
Website: www.rarediseases.org

Rehabilitation

National Rehabilitation Information Center
800-34-NARIC; in Maryland, 301-459-5900; TTY 301-459-5984
Research referrals and information on rehabilitation issues.
E-mail: naricinfo@heitechservices.com
Website: www.naric.com

Scleroderma

United Scleroderma Foundation
800-722-4673
Referrals to local support groups and treatment centers, as well as information on scleroderma and related skin disorders.
E-mail: sfinfo@scleroderma.org
Website: www.scleroderma.org

Sexually Transmitted Diseases

See also ***AIDS***

National STD Hotline
800-227-8922; Spanish 800-344-7432
Information; confidential referrals.
E-mail: std-hivnet@ashastd.org
Website: www.ashastd.org

Sjogren's Syndrome

Sjogren's Syndrome Foundation
800-475-6473;
Provides an answering machine for callers to request treatment literature.
Website: www.sjogrens.org

Skin Problems

National Psoriasis Foundation
800-723-9166
Information and referrals.
E-mail: getinfo@psoriasis.org
Website: www.psoriasis.org

Speech and Hearing

American Speech-Language-Hearing Association Action Center
800-638-8255 (also TTY)
Materials on speech and language disorders and hearing impairment; referrals.
E-mail: actioncenter@asha.org
Website: www.asha.org

Canadian Hard of Hearing Association
800-263-8068, Canada only; TTY 613-526-2692; 613-526-1584
Publications; answers general questions.
E-mail: chhanational@chha.ca
Website: www.chha.ca

Dial a Hearing Screening Test
800-222-EARS
Answers questions on hearing problems. Makes referrals to local telephone numbers for a two-minute hearing test. Also to ear, nose, and throat specialists and to organizations that can provide specialized ear and hearing aid information. 9 AM-5 PM EST

Hearing Aid Helpline
800-521-5247, ext. 333
Information and distributes a directory of hearing aid specialists certified by the International Hearing Society.
Website: www.ihsinfo.org

National Center for Stuttering
800-221-2483; 212-532-1460
Information on stuttering in all age groups.
E-mail: martin.schwartz@nyu.edu
Website: www.stuttering.com

Stuttering Foundation of America
800-992-9392
Referrals to speech pathologists; resource lists, publications.
E-mail: info@stutteringhelp.org
Website: www.stutteringhelp.org

Spinal Injuries

National Spinal Cord Injury Association
800-962-9629; 301-214-4006
Peer counseling; referrals to local chapters and other organizations.
E-mail: info@spinalcord.org
Website: www.spinalcord.org

Stroke

See ***Heart Disease and Stroke***

Sudden Infant Death Syndrome

American Sudden Infant Death Syndrome Institute
800-232-SIDS; in Georgia, 770-426-8746
Answers questions; literature; referrals to other organizations.
E-mail: prevent@sids.org
Website: www.sids.org

Tourette Syndrome

Tourette Syndrome Association
718-224-2999
Printed information.
E-mail: ts@tsa-usa.org
Website: tsa-usa.org

Urinary Incontinence

National Association for Continence
800-BLADDER, 843-377-0900
Information on bladder control, services available for incontinence, and assistive devices.
E-mail: memberservices@nafc.org
Website: www.nafc.org

Simon Foundation for Continence
800-23-SIMON
Support and literature on incontinence.
E-mail: Simoninfo@simonfoundation.org; jasmineschmidt@simonfoundation.org
Website: www.simonfoundation.org

Women's Health

National Women's Health Network
202-347-1140; 202-628-7814
Information and referrals on more than 70 women's health concerns.
E-mail: nwhn@nwhn.org
Website: www.nwhn.org

National Women's Health Resource Center
877-986-9472
A national clearinghouse for women's health information.
E-mail: snelson@healthywomen.org
Website: www.healthywomen.org

VITAL STATISTICS

Recent Trends in Vital Statistics

Source: National Center for Health Statistics, U.S. Dept. of Health and Human Services; latest years available

Highlights

Final U.S. data for 2003 reported by the National Center for Health Statistics show that birth rates went up slightly from 2002, which had shown the lowest rate of any year since national data were first collected in 1909.

The teen birth rate declined in 2003 for the 12th straight year, dropping to 41.6 births per 1,000 women aged 15-19 years; this was a 33% reduction since 1991.

According to provisional 2003 data, marriage rates and divorce rates both declined slightly from 2002, continuing the trend for the past 2 decades. Life expectancy for all Americans at birth was 77.3 years in 2002, an all-time high and an increase of nearly 2 years since 1990.

Births

An estimated 4,089,950 babies were born in the U.S. in 2003, a rise from 4,021,726 births in 2002. The birth rate increased to 14.1 per 1,000 total population, up from 13.9 in 2002.

The fertility rate (number of live births per 1,000 women aged 15-44 years) rose to an estimated 66.3 for 2003, up from the 2002 rate of 64.8; the highest rate since 1993, but low by historical standards.

Deaths

The number of deaths during 2003 was estimated at 2,443,908 according to provisional data, up from 2,443,387 in 2002. The 2003 data showed a death rate of 8.4 per 1,000 population, slightly lower than the previous year. The infant mortality rate was 6.9 infant deaths per 1,000 live births in 2003, down from 7.0 in 2002.

Natural Increase

As a result of natural increase (the excess of births over deaths), an estimated 1,646,000 persons were added to the population in 2003. The rate of increase (5.7 per 1,000 population) was up slightly from the revised figure of 5.4 for 2002.

Marriages

An estimated 2,187,700 marriages were performed in 2003, compared to 2,254,000 in 2002. The provisional marriage rate for 2003 (7.5 per 1,000 population) was down from the 2002 rate of 7.8.

Divorces

The provisional 2003 data give a divorce rate of 3.8 per 1,000 population, down from 4.0 in 2002. Data are incomplete, however. The NCHS no longer includes divorce data for California, Hawaii, Indiana, Louisiana, and Oklahoma.

Births and Deaths in the U.S.

Source: National Center for Health Statistics, U.S. Dept. of Health and Human Services

Year	BIRTHS Total number	BIRTHS Rate	DEATHS Total number	DEATHS Rate
1960	4,257,850	23.7	1,711,982	9.5
1970	3,731,386	18.4	1,921,031	9.5
1980	3,612,258	15.9	1,989,841	8.8
1990	4,092,994	16.7	2,148,463	8.6
1991	4,094,566	16.2	2,169,518	8.6
1992	4,049,024	15.8	2,175,613	8.5
1993	4,000,240	15.4	2,268,553	8.7
1994	3,952,767	15.0	2,278,994	8.7
1995	3,899,589	14.6	2,312,132	8.7
1996	3,891,494	14.4	2,314,690	8.6
1997	3,880,894	14.2	2,314,245	8.5
1998	3,941,553	14.3	2,337,256	8.5
1999	3,959,417	14.2	2,391,399	8.6
2000	4,058,814	14.4	2,403,351	8.5
2001	4,025,933	14.1	2,416,425	8.5
2002	4,021,726	13.9	2,443,387	8.5
2003	4,089,950	14.1	2,443,908(P)	8.4(P)

(P) = provisional data. **NOTE:** Statistics cover only events occurring within the U.S. and exclude fetal deaths. Rates per 1,000 population; enumerated as of Apr. 1 for 1960 and 1970; estimated as of July 1 for all other years. Beginning 1970 statistics exclude births and deaths occurring among nonresidents of the U.S. Data include revisions. Birth and death rates for years in the 1990s revised on basis of the 2000 Census.

U.S. Median Age at First Marriage, 1890-2003

Source: Bureau of the Census, U.S. Dept. of Commerce

Year[1]	Men	Women	Year[1]	Men	Women	Year[1]	Men	Women	Year[1]	Men	Women	Year[1]	Men	Women
2003	27.1	25.3	1997	26.8	25.0	1991	26.3	24.1	1970	23.2	20.8	1930	24.3	21.3
2002	26.9	25.3	1996	27.1	24.8	1990	26.1	23.9	1965	22.8	20.6	1920	24.6	21.2
2001	26.9	25.1	1995	26.9	24.5	1985	25.5	23.3	1960	22.8	20.3	1910	25.1	21.6
2000	26.8	25.1	1994	26.7	24.5	1980	24.7	22.0	1950	22.8	20.3	1900	25.9	21.9
1999	26.9	25.1	1993	26.5	24.5	1975	23.5	21.1	1940	24.3	21.5	1890	26.1	22.0
1998	26.7	25.0	1992	26.5	24.4									

(1) Figures after 1940 based on Current Population Survey data; earlier figures based on decennial censuses.

Marriage and Divorce Rates, 1920-2003

Source: National Center for Health Statistics, U.S. Dept. of Health and Human Services

The U.S. marriage rate dipped during the Depression and peaked sharply just after World War II; the trend after that has been more gradual. The divorce rate generally rose from the 1920s through 1981, when it peaked at 5.3 per 1,000 population, before declining somewhat. The graph below shows marriage and divorce rates since 1920. (Recent divorce rates are calculated excluding data and populations from the non-reporting states California, Indiana, Louisiana, and Oklahoma; incomplete reporting from Oklahoma may lead to slight underestimation of marriage rate. Some data are provisional.)

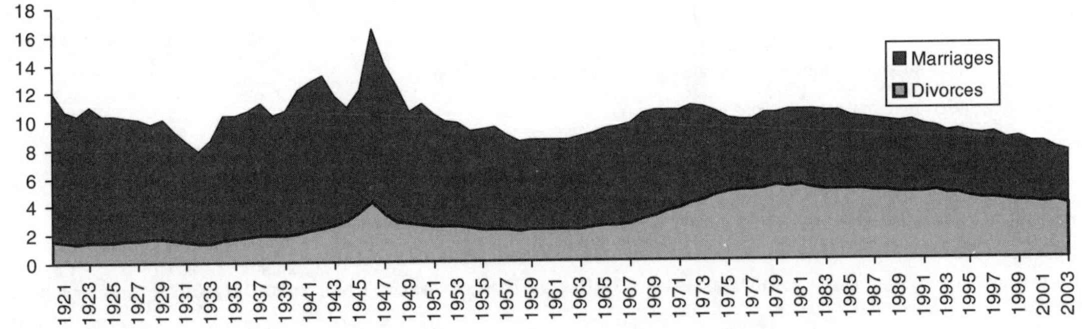

Birth Rates; Fertility Rates by Age of Mother, 1950-2003

Source: National Center for Health Statistics, U.S. Dept. of Health and Human Services

	Birth rate[1]	Fertility rate[2]	10-14 years	15-19 years Total	15-17	18-19	20-24 years	25-29 years	30-34 years	35-39 years	40-44 years	45-49 years
			AGE OF MOTHER — Live births per 1,000 women by age group									
1950	24.1	106.2	1.0	81.6	40.7	132.7	196.6	166.1	103.7	52.9	15.1	1.2
1960	23.7	118.0	0.8	89.1	43.9	166.7	258.1	197.4	112.7	56.2	15.5	0.9
1970	18.4	87.9	1.2	68.3	38.8	114.7	167.8	145.1	73.3	31.7	8.1	0.5
1980	15.9	68.4	1.1	53.0	32.5	82.1	115.1	112.9	61.9	19.8	3.9	0.2
1990	16.7	70.9	1.4	59.9	37.5	88.6	116.5	120.2	80.8	31.7	5.5	0.2
1991	16.2	69.3	1.4	61.8	38.6	94.0	115.3	117.2	79.2	31.9	5.5	0.2
1992	15.8	68.4	1.4	60.3	37.6	93.6	113.7	115.7	79.6	32.3	5.9	0.3
1993	15.4	67.0	1.4	59.0	37.5	91.1	111.3	113.2	79.9	32.7	6.1	0.3
1994	15.0	65.9	1.4	58.2	37.2	90.2	109.2	111.0	80.4	33.4	6.4	0.3
1995	14.6	64.6	1.3	56.0	35.5	87.7	107.5	108.8	81.1	34.0	6.6	0.3
1996	14.4	64.1	1.2	53.5	33.3	84.7	107.8	108.6	82.1	34.9	6.8	0.3
1997	14.2	63.6	1.1	51.3	31.4	82.1	107.3	108.3	83.0	35.7	7.1	0.4
1998	14.3	64.3	1.0	50.3	29.9	80.9	108.4	110.2	85.2	36.9	7.4	0.4
1999	14.2	64.4	0.9	48.8	28.2	79.1	107.9	111.2	87.1	37.8	7.4	0.4
2000	14.4	65.9	0.9	47.7	26.9	78.1	109.7	113.5	91.2	39.7	8.0	0.5
2001	14.1	65.3	0.8	45.3	24.7	76.1	106.2	113.4	91.9	40.6	8.1	0.5
2002	13.9	64.8	0.7	43.0	23.2	72.8	103.6	113.6	91.5	41.4	8.3	0.5
2003	14.1	66.3	0.6	41.6	22.4	70.7	102.6	115.6	95.1	43.8	8.7	0.5

(1) Live births per 1,000 population. (2) Live births per 1,000 women 15-44 years of age.

Numbers of Multiple Births in the U.S., 1990-2003

Source: National Center for Health Statistics, U.S. Dept. of Health and Human Services

The general upward trend in multiple births reflects greater numbers of births to older women and increased use of fertility drugs.

Year	Twins	Triplets	Quadruplets	Quintuplets and higher
1990	93,865	2,830	185	13
1992	95,372	3,547	310	26
1993	96,445	3,834	277	57
1994	97,064	4,233	315	46
1995	96,736	4,551	365	57
1996	100,750	5,298	560	81
1997	104,137	6,148	510	79
1998	110,670	6,919	627	79
1999	114,307	6,742	512	67
2000	118,916	6,742	506	77
2001	121,246	6,885	501	85
2002	125,134	6,898	434	69
2003	128,665	7,110	468	85

Top 20 Countries for U.S. Foreign Adoptions, 1998-2004[1]

Source: Dept. of Homeland Security, Office of Immigration Statistics.

Country	2004	2003	2002	2001	2000	1999	1998
China	7,033	6,638	6,062	4,629	4,943	4,009	3,988
Russia	5,878	5,134	4,904	4,210	4,210	4,250	4,320
Guatemala	3,252	2,327	2,361	1,601	1,504	987	938
South Korea	1,708	1,793	1,713	1,863	1,711	1,956	1,705
Kazakhstan	824	819	801	664	392	108	54
Ukraine	772	691	1,093	1,227	645	307	168
India	394	466	459	540	491	486	462
Haiti	355	246	192	187	136	93	113
Colombia	279	275	329	261	246	226	221
Ethiopia	277	166	102	160	103	100	88
Belarus	200	187	163	129	41	23	2
Philippines	188	218	208	220	176	185	189
Bulgaria	112	196	261	288	207	213	147
Poland	102	92	102	89	81	97	70
Mexico	98	67	71	105	115	145	170
Taiwan	89	104	41	44	24	26	18
Liberia	88	22	23	50	20	20	9
Brazil	72	30	26	33	26	67	86
Nepal	72	42	12	4	11	9	16
Thailand	67	67	65	75	85	77	78
Total[2]	**22,911**	**21,320**	**21,100**	**19,087**	**18,120**	**16,037**	**14,867**

Note: Totals are for U.S. government fiscal years. (1) Ranked by 2004 totals. (2) Total includes countries not shown.

10 Leading Causes of Infant Death in the U.S., 2002

Source: National Center for Health Statistics, U.S. Dept. of Health and Human Services

Cause	Number	Rate[1]	% change 2001-2002[2]
Congenital malformations, deformations, and chromosomal abnormalities	5,623	139.8	2.1
Disorders relating to short gestation and low birthweight, not elsewhere classified	4,637	115.3	5.3
Sudden infant death syndrome	2,295	57.1	2.9
Newborn affected by maternal complications of pregnancy	1,708	42.5	14.2
Newborn affected by complications of placenta, cord, and membranes	1,028	25.6	1.2
Accidents (unintentional injuries)	946	23.5	–2.9
Respiratory distress of newborn	943	23.4	–6.8
Bacterial sepsis[3] of newborn	749	18.6	7.5
Diseases of the circulatory system	667	16.6	7.8
Intrauterine hypoxia and birth asphyxia	583	14.5	9.0
All other causes	8,855	220.2	NA
All causes	**28,034**	**697.1**	**1.8**

NA = Not available. (1) Infant deaths per 100,000 live births. (2) Refers to change in mortality rates from 2000 to 2001. (3) Toxic condition resulting from the spread of bacteria.

Nonmarital Childbearing in the U.S., 1970-2002

Source: National Center for Health Statistics, U.S. Dept. of Health and Human Services

	1970	1975	1980	1985	1990	1995	1996	1997	1998	1999	2000	2001	2002
Race of Mother	**Percent of live births to unmarried mothers**												
All races	10.7	14.3	18.4	22.0	28.0	32.2	32.4	32.4	32.8	33.0	33.2	33.5	34.0
White	5.5	7.1	11.2	14.7	20.4	25.3	25.7	25.8	26.3	26.8	27.1	27.7	28.5
Black	37.5	49.5	56.1	61.2	66.5	69.9	69.8	69.2	69.1	68.9	68.5	68.4	68.2
American Indian or Alaska Native	22.4	32.7	39.2	46.8	53.6	57.2	58.0	58.7	59.3	58.9	58.4	59.7	59.7
Asian or Pacific Islander	—	—	7.3	9.5	13.2	16.3	16.7	15.6	15.6	15.4	14.8	14.9	14.9
Hispanic origin (selected states)[1,2]	—	—	23.6	29.5	36.7	40.8	40.7	40.9	41.6	42.2	42.7	42.5	43.5
White, non-Hispanic (selected states)[1]	—	—	9.6	12.4	16.9	21.2	21.5	21.5	21.9	22.1	22.1	22.5	23.0
Black, non-Hispanic (selected states)[1]	—	—	57.3	62.1	66.7	70.0	70.0	69.4	69.3	69.1	68.7	68.6	68.4
Births to unmarried mothers (1,000s)	399	448	666	828	1,165	1,254	1,260	1,257	1,294	1,309	1,347	1,349	1,366
Maternal age	**Percent distribution of live births to unmarried mothers**												
Under 20 years	50.1	52.1	40.8	33.8	30.9	30.9	30.4	30.7	30.1	29.3	28.0	26.6	25.4
20–24 years	31.8	29.9	35.6	36.3	34.7	34.5	34.2	34.9	35.6	36.4	37.4	38.2	38.6
25 years and over	18.1	18.0	23.5	29.9	34.4	34.7	35.3	34.4	34.3	34.3	34.6	35.2	34.7
	Live births per 1,000 unmarried women 15–44 years of age[3]												
All races and origins	26.4	24.5	29.4	32.8	43.8	45.1	44.8	44.0	44.3	44.4	45.2	45.0	43.7
White[4]	13.9	12.4	18.1	22.5	32.9	37.5	37.6	37.0	37.5	38.1	38.9	39.2	38.9
Black[4]	95.5	84.2	81.1	77.0	90.5	75.9	74.4	73.4	73.3	71.5	72.5	70.1	66.2
Hispanic origin (selected states)[1,2]	—	—	—	—	89.6	95.0	93.2	91.4	90.1	93.4	97.3	98.0	87.9
White, non-Hispanic	—	—	—	—	—	28.2	28.3	27.0	27.4	27.9	27.9	27.7	27.8

— Data not available. (1) Data for Hispanics and non-Hispanics are affected by expansion of the reporting area for an Hispanic-origin item on the birth certificate and by immigration. The states in the reporting area increased from 22 in 1980, to 23 and the District of Columbia in 1983, 48 and DC by 1990, and 50 and DC by 1993. (2) Includes mothers of all races. (3) Rates computed by relating births to unmarried mothers, regardless of mother's age, to unmarried women 15–44 years of age. (4) For 1970 and 1975, birth rates are by race of child.

U.S. Infant Mortality Rates, by Race and Sex, 1960-2003[1]

Source: National Center for Health Statistics, U.S. Dept. of Health and Human Services

	ALL RACES			WHITE			BLACK		
Year	Total	Male	Female	Total	Male	Female	Total	Male	Female
1960	26.0	29.3	22.6	22.9	26.0	19.6	44.3	49.1	39.4
1970	20.0	22.4	17.5	17.8	20.0	15.4	32.6	36.2	29.0
1980	12.6	13.9	11.2	11.0	12.3	9.6	21.4	23.3	19.4
1985	10.6	11.9	9.3	9.3	10.6	8.0	18.2	19.9	16.5
1988	10.0	11.0	8.9	8.5	9.5	7.4	17.6	19.0	16.1
1989	9.8	10.8	8.8	8.1	9.0	7.1	18.6	20.0	17.2
1990	9.2	10.3	8.1	7.6	8.5	6.6	18.0	19.6	16.2
1991	8.9	10.0	7.8	7.3	8.3	6.3	17.6	19.4	15.7
1992	8.5	9.4	7.6	6.9	7.7	6.1	16.8	18.4	15.3
1993	8.4	9.3	7.4	6.8	7.6	6.0	16.5	18.3	14.7
1994	8.0	8.8	7.2	6.6	7.2	5.9	15.8	17.5	14.1
1995	7.6	8.3	6.8	6.3	7.0	5.6	15.1	16.3	13.9
1996	7.3	8.0	6.6	6.1	6.7	5.4	14.7	16.0	13.3
1997	7.2	8.0	6.5	6.0	6.7	5.4	14.2	15.5	12.8
1998	7.2	7.8	6.5	6.0	6.5	5.4	14.3	15.7	12.8
1999	7.1	7.7	6.4	5.8	6.4	5.2	14.6	15.9	13.2
2000	6.9	7.6	6.2	5.7	6.2	5.1	14.1	15.5	12.6
2001	6.8	7.5	6.1	5.7	6.2	5.1	14.0	15.5	12.5
2002	7.0	7.6	6.3	5.8	6.4	5.1	14.4	15.4	13.3
2003[2]	6.9	NA	NA	5.8	NA	NA	14.1	NA	NA

NA = Not available. (1) Rates per 1,000 live births. (2) Preliminary .

Years of Life Expected at Birth in U.S., 1900-2002

Source: National Center for Health Statistics, U.S. Dept. of Health and Human Services

	ALL RACES			WHITE			BLACK		
Year[1]	Total	Male	Female	Total	Male	Female	Total	Male	Female
1900	47.3	46.3	48.3	47.6	46.6	48.7	NA	NA	NA
1910	50.0	48.4	51.8	50.3	48.6	52.0	NA	NA	NA
1920	54.1	53.6	54.6	54.9	54.4	55.6	NA	NA	NA
1930	59.7	58.1	61.6	61.4	59.7	63.5	NA	NA	NA
1940	62.9	60.8	65.2	64.2	62.1	66.6	NA	NA	NA
1950	68.2	65.6	71.1	69.1	66.5	72.2	NA	NA	NA
1960	69.7	66.6	73.1	70.6	67.4	74.1	NA	NA	NA
1970	70.8	67.1	74.7	71.7	68.0	75.6	64.1	60.0	68.3
1975	72.6	68.8	76.6	73.4	69.5	77.3	68.8	62.4	71.3
1980	73.7	70.0	77.5	74.4	70.7	78.1	68.1	63.8	72.5
1985	74.7	71.2	78.2	75.3	71.9	78.7	69.3	65.0	73.4
1987	75.0	71.5	78.4	75.6	72.2	78.9	69.1	64.7	73.4
1988	74.9	71.5	78.3	75.6	72.3	78.9	68.9	64.4	73.2
1989	75.1	71.7	78.5	75.9	72.5	79.2	68.8	64.3	73.3
1990	75.4	71.8	78.8	76.1	72.9	79.4	69.1	64.5	73.6
1991	75.5	72.0	78.9	76.3	72.9	79.2	69.3	64.6	73.8
1992	75.5	72.1	78.9	76.4	73.0	79.5	69.6	65.0	73.9
1993	75.5	72.1	78.9	76.3	73.0	79.5	69.2	64.6	73.7
1994	75.7	72.4	79.0	76.5	73.3	79.6	69.5	64.9	73.9
1995	75.8	72.5	78.9	76.5	73.4	79.6	69.6	65.2	73.9
1996	76.1	73.1	79.1	76.8	73.9	79.7	70.2	66.1	74.2
1997	76.5	73.6	79.4	77.1	74.3	79.9	71.1	67.2	74.7
1998	76.7	73.8	79.5	77.3	74.5	80.0	71.3	67.6	74.8
1999	76.7	73.9	79.4	77.3	74.6	79.9	71.4	67.8	74.7
2000	76.9	74.1	79.5	77.4	74.8	80.0	71.7	68.2	74.9
2001	77.2	74.4	79.8	77.7	75.0	80.2	72.2	68.6	75.5
2002	77.3	74.5	79.9	77.7	75.1	80.3	72.3	68.8	75.6

NA = Not available. (1) Data prior to 1940 for death-registration states only.

U.S. Life Expectancy at Selected Ages, 2002

Source: National Center for Health Statistics, U.S. Dept. of Health and Human Services

Exact age in years	ALL RACES[1] Both sexes	Male	Female	WHITE Both sexes	Male	Female	BLACK Both sexes	Male	Female
0	77.3	74.5	79.9	77.7	75.1	80.3	72.3	68.8	75.6
1	76.8	74.1	79.4	77.2	74.6	79.7	72.4	68.8	75.6
5	72.9	70.2	75.4	73.3	70.7	75.8	68.5	65.0	71.7
10	67.9	65.3	70.5	68.3	65.7	70.8	63.6	60.1	66.8
15	63.0	60.3	65.5	63.4	60.8	65.9	58.7	55.2	61.8
20	58.2	55.6	60.7	58.6	56.1	61.0	53.9	50.5	57.0
25	53.5	51.0	55.8	53.8	51.4	56.1	49.3	46.0	52.1
30	48.7	46.3	51.0	49.0	46.7	51.2	44.7	41.6	47.4
35	44.0	41.6	46.1	44.3	42.0	46.4	40.1	37.1	42.7
40	39.3	37.0	41.4	39.6	37.4	41.6	35.6	32.8	38.1
45	34.8	32.6	36.7	35.0	32.9	36.9	31.3	28.5	33.7
50	30.3	28.3	32.2	30.5	28.5	32.4	27.3	24.6	29.5
55	26.1	24.1	27.7	26.2	24.3	27.9	23.4	21.0	25.4
60	22.0	20.2	23.5	22.1	20.3	23.6	19.9	17.6	21.6
65	18.2	16.6	19.5	18.2	16.6	19.5	16.6	14.6	18.0
70	14.7	13.2	15.8	14.7	13.3	15.8	13.5	11.8	14.7
75	11.5	10.3	12.4	11.5	10.3	12.3	10.9	9.5	11.7
80	8.8	7.8	9.4	8.7	7.7	9.3	8.6	7.5	9.2
85	6.5	5.7	6.9	6.4	5.7	6.8	6.6	5.8	7.0
90	4.8	4.2	5.0	4.7	4.1	4.9	5.1	4.5	5.3
95	3.6	3.2	3.7	3.4	3.0	3.5	3.9	3.6	4.0
100	2.7	2.5	2.8	2.4	2.3	2.5	3.0	2.9	3.0

(1) Includes races other than white and black.

U.S. Abortions, by State, 1992-2000

Source: Alan Guttmacher Institute, New York, NY

	Reported abortions[1]			Rate per 1,000 women[2]			% change
	1992	1996	2000	1992	1996	2000	1996-2000[3]
U.S. TOTAL	**1,528,930**	**1,360,160**	**1,312,990**	**25.7**	**22.4**	**21.3**	**–5**
Alabama	17,450	15,150	13,830	18.1	15.5	14.3	–8
Alaska	2,370	2,040	1,660	16.6	14.2	11.7	–18
Arizona	20,600	19,310	17,940	23.4	19.2	16.5	–14
Arkansas	7,130	6,200	5,540	13.5	11.2	9.8	–12
California	304,230	237,830	236,060	41.8	32.8	31.2	–5
Colorado	19,880	18,310	15,530	23.6	19.9	15.9	–20
Connecticut	19,720	16,230	15,240	25.9	21.9	21.1	–4
Delaware	5,730	4,090	5,440	34.9	24.0	31.3	31
District of Columbia	21,320	15,220	9,800	134.6	104.5	68.1	–39
Florida	84,680	94,050	103,050	29.3	30.7	31.9	4
Georgia	39,680	37,320	32,140	23.7	20.8	16.9	–19
Hawaii	12,190	6,930	5,630	46.4	26.8	22.2	–17
Idaho	1,710	1,600	1,950	7.3	6.1	7.0	15
Illinois	68,420	69,390	63,690	25.2	25.3	23.2	–8
Indiana	15,840	14,850	12,490	12.0	11.1	9.4	–15
Iowa	6,970	5,780	5,970	11.3	9.3	9.8	5
Kansas	12,570	10,630	12,270	22.4	18.6	21.4	15
Kentucky	10,000	8,470	4,700	11.4	9.5	5.3	–44
Louisiana	13,600	14,740	13,100	13.5	14.5	13.0	–10
Maine	4,200	2,700	2,650	14.8	9.8	9.9	1
Maryland	31,260	31,310	34,560	26.2	26.2	29.0	11
Massachusetts	40,660	41,160	30,410	28.1	28.8	21.4	–26
Michigan	55,580	48,780	46,470	25.1	22.1	21.6	–2
Minnesota	16,180	14,660	14,610	15.6	13.7	13.5	–2
Mississippi	7,550	4,490	3,780	12.4	7.1	6.0	–17
Missouri	13,510	10,810	7,920	11.5	9.0	6.6	–27
Montana	3,300	2,900	2,510	18.5	15.4	13.5	–12
Nebraska	5,580	4,460	4,250	15.6	12.2	11.6	–4
Nevada	13,300	15,450	13,740	43.0	41.7	32.2	–23
New Hampshire	3,890	3,470	3,010	14.6	12.9	11.2	–13
New Jersey	55,320	63,100	65,780	30.5	34.9	36.3	4
New Mexico	6,410	5,470	5,760	17.7	14.1	14.7	4
New York	195,390	167,600	164,630	45.7	39.7	39.1	–2
North Carolina	36,180	33,550	37,610	22.2	19.5	21.0	8
North Dakota	1,490	1,290	1,340	10.7	9.2	9.9	7
Ohio	49,520	42,870	40,230	19.5	17.1	16.5	–3
Oklahoma	8,940	8,400	7,390	12.5	11.6	10.1	–13
Oregon	16,060	15,050	17,010	23.9	21.2	23.5	11
Pennsylvania	49,740	39,520	36,570	18.6	15.0	14.3	–5
Rhode Island	6,990	5,420	5,600	29.5	23.3	24.1	3
South Carolina	12,190	9,940	8,210	14.2	11.4	9.3	–18
South Dakota	1,040	1,030	870	6.9	6.5	5.5	–15
Tennessee	19,060	17,990	19,010	16.2	14.6	15.2	4
Texas	97,400	91,270	89,160	23.0	20.2	18.8	–7
Utah	3,940	3,700	3,510	9.2	7.5	6.6	–11
Vermont	2,900	2,300	-1,660	21.5	17.3	12.7	–27
Virginia	35,020	29,940	28,780	22.6	19.0	18.1	–5
Washington	33,190	26,340	26,200	27.7	20.9	20.2	–3
West Virginia	3,140	2,610	2,540	7.8	6.6	6.8	3
Wisconsin	15,450	14,160	11,130	13.5	12.2	9.6	–21
Wyoming	460	280	100	4.4	2.6	1.0	–64

(1) Rounded to the nearest 10. (2) Aged 15-44 years old. (3) Percentage change in the rate.

Contraceptive Use in the U.S.

Source: National Center for Health Statistics, U.S. Dept. of Health and Human Services; as of 2002; latest data available.

	Percent of women in each age group						
	15-44	15-19	20-24	25-29	30-34	35-39	40-44
Using any method	61.9	31.5	60.7	68.0	69.2	70.8	69.1
Female sterilization	16.7	—	2.2	10.3	19.0	29.2	34.7
Male sterilization	5.7	—	0.5	2.8	6.4	10.0	12.7
Pill	18.9	16.7	31.9	25.6	21.8	13.2	7.6
Implant	0.8	0.4	0.9	1.7	0.9	0.5	0.2
Injectable	3.3	4.4	6.1	4.4	2.9	1.5	1.1

	Percent of women in each age group						
	15-44	15-19	20-24	25-29	30-34	35-39	40-44
Intrauterine device (IUD)	1.3	0.1	1.1	2.5	2.2	1.0	0.8
Diaphragm	0.2	–	0.1	0.3	0.1	–	0.4
Condom	11.1	8.5	14.0	14.0	11.8	11.1	8.0
Periodic abstinence	0.7	—	0.8	0.3	0.9	1.1	1.2
Natural family planning	0.2	—	—	0.4	0.2	0.3	0.4
Withdrawal	2.5	0.8	3.1	5.3	2.6	2.4	1.0
Other methods[1]	0.6	0.6	0.2	0.4	0.4	0.5	1.1

(1) These include morning-after pill, foam, cervical cap, Today sponge, suppository, jelly or cream (without diaphragm), and other methods not shown separately.

Alcohol Use by 8th and 12th Graders, 1980-2004

Source: *Monitoring the Future,* Univ. of Michigan Inst. for Social Research and National Inst. on Drug Abuse

	1980	1990	1993	1994	1995	1996	1997	1998	1999	2000	2001	2002	2003	2004
ALCOHOL[1]	Percent using alcohol in the month before the survey													
All 12th graders	72.0	57.1	51.0	50.1	51.3	50.8	52.7	52.0	51.0	50.0	49.8	48.6	47.5	48.0
Male	77.4	61.3	54.9	55.5	55.7	54.8	56.2	57.3	55.3	54.0	54.7	52.3	51.7	51.1
Female	66.8	52.3	46.7	45.2	47.0	46.9	48.9	46.9	46.8	46.1	45.1	45.1	43.8	45.1
White	75.4	63.8	55.6	54.0	54.5	54.8	56.4	57.7	56.3	55.1	55.3	54.0	52.3	52.2
Black	47.6	35.8	32.4	33.8	35.2	36.5	34.3	33.3	32.2	30.0	29.4	30.1	29.9	29.2
Hispanic	63.6	49.1	50.5	45.9	48.7	47.5	48.2	49.8	50.2	51.2	48.9	47.5	46.4	45.4
All 8th graders	—	—	26.2	25.5	24.6	26.2	24.5	23.0	24.0	22.4	21.5	19.6	19.7	18.6
Male	—	—	26.7	26.5	25.0	26.6	25.2	24.0	24.8	22.5	22.3	19.1	19.4	17.9
Female	—	—	26.1	24.7	24.0	25.8	23.9	21.9	23.3	22.0	20.6	20.0	19.8	19.0
White	—	—	27.1	25.3	25.4	26.6	26.7	24.8	24.7	24.7	23.2	21.5	20.1	19.2
Black	—	—	19.7	19.4	18.7	18.1	17.9	16.1	16.0	16.0	15.0	14.8	15.5	16.2
Hispanic	—	—	32.3	33.5	32.4	29.7	29.8	29.5	29.0	26.7	25.7	26.5	25.3	23.5
HEAVY ALCOHOL[2]	Percent heavily using the 2 weeks before the survey													
All 12th graders	41.2	32.2	27.5	28.2	29.8	30.2	31.3	31.5	30.8	30.0	29.7	28.6	27.9	29.2
Male	52.1	39.1	34.6	37.0	36.9	37.0	37.9	39.2	38.1	36.7	36.0	34.2	34.2	34.3
Female	30.5	24.4	20.7	20.2	23.0	23.5	24.4	24.0	23.6	23.5	23.7	23.0	22.1	24.2
White	44.3	36.6	31.3	31.5	32.3	33.4	35.1	36.4	35.7	34.6	34.5	33.7	32.4	32.5
Black	17.7	14.4	12.6	14.4	14.9	15.3	13.4	12.3	12.3	11.5	11.8	11.5	10.8	11.4
Hispanic	33.1	25.6	27.2	24.3	26.6	27.1	27.6	28.1	29.3	31.0	28.4	26.4	25.9	26.0
All 8th graders	—	—	13.5	14.5	14.5	15.6	14.5	13.7	15.2	14.1	13.2	12.4	11.9	11.4
Male	—	—	14.8	16.0	15.1	16.5	15.3	14.4	16.4	14.4	13.7	12.5	12.2	10.8
Female	—	—	12.3	13.0	13.9	14.5	13.5	12.7	13.9	13.6	12.4	12.1	11.6	11.8
White	—	—	12.6	12.9	13.9	15.1	15.1	14.1	14.3	14.9	13.8	12.7	11.8	11.3
Black	—	—	10.7	11.8	10.8	10.4	9.8	9.0	9.9	10.0	9.0	9.4	10.4	9.8
Hispanic	—	—	21.4	22.3	22.0	21.0	20.7	20.4	20.9	19.1	17.6	17.8	16.6	16.1

— Data not available. **Note**: *Monitoring the Future* study excludes high school dropouts (about 3-6% of the class group, according to a 1996 report) and absentees (about 16-17% of 12th graders and about 9-10% of 8th graders). High school dropouts and absentees have higher alcohol usage than those included in the survey. (1) In 1993 the alcohol question was changed to indicate that a "drink" meant "more than a few sips." (2) Five or more drinks in a row at least once in the prior 2-week period.

Cigarette Use in the U.S., 1985-2004

4**Source:** Substance Abuse and Mental Health Services Administration (SAMHSA), U.S. Dept. of Health and Human Services

(percentage reporting use in the month prior to the survey; figures exclude persons under age 12)

	1985	2000	2002	2003	2004
TOTAL	**38.7**	**24.9**	**26.0**	**25.4**	**24.9**
Sex					
Male	43.4	26.9	28.7	28.1	27.7
Female	34.5	23.1	23.4	23.0	22.3
Age group					
12-17	29.4	13.4	13.0	12.2	11.9
18-25	47.4	38.3	40.8	40.2	39.5
26 and older	45.7[1]	24.2	25.2	24.7	24.1

	1985	2000	2002	2003	2004
Race/Ethnicity					
White	38.9	25.9	26.9	26.6	26.4
Black	38.0	23.3	25.3	25.9	23.5
Hispanic	40.0	20.7	23.0	21.4	21.3
Education[2]					
Non-high school graduate	37.3	32.4	35.2	35.3	34.8
High school graduate	37.0	31.1	32.3	31.5	30.4
Some college	32.6	27.7	29.0	28.9	29.0
College graduate	23.0	13.9	14.5	14.0	13.6

(1) Figures are for all persons aged 26 to 34 only. (2) Estimates for Education are for persons aged 18 and older.

Drug Use in the General U.S. Population, 2003

Source: Substance Abuse and Mental Health Services Administration (SAMHSA), U.S. Dept. of Health and Human Services

According to the Substance Abuse and Mental Health Services Administration's 2004 National Survey on Drug Use and Health, an estimated 110 million Americans 12 years of age and older (45.8%) had used an illicit drug at least once during their lifetimes, 14.5% had used one during the previous year, and 7.9% had used one in the most recent month.

The rate of current illicit drug use (in the past month) in 2004 was 9.9% for men; for women it was 6.1%. An estimated 29.4% of Americans 12 or older (70.7 million) had used an illicit drug other than marijuana at least once in their life. There was a slight 0.2% decrease in the overall rate of illicit drug use between 2003 and 2004.

The Substance Abuse and Mental Health Services Administration's Drug Abuse Warning Network (DAWN) reported 627,923 drug-related episodes in hospital emergency departments in the coterminous U.S in 2003, or 217 episodes per 100,000 population—down from 266 in 2002. Cocaine was a factor in 20% of these. Alcohol in combination with illegal drug use was a factor in 19%.

Drug Use: America's High School Seniors, 1980-2004

Source: *Monitoring the Future,* Univ. of Michigan Inst. for Social Research and National Inst. on Drug Abuse

Class of:	1980	1985	1990	1995	1998	1999	2000	2001	2002	2003	2004	'03-'04 change[7]
Marijuana/hashish	60.3%	54.2%	40.7%	41.7%	49.1%	49.7%	48.8%	49.0%	47.8%	46.1%	45.7%	-0.4
Inhalants[1]	17.3	18.1	18.5	17.8	16.5	16.0	14.2	13.0	11.7	11.2	11.4	–0.8
Amyl & butyl nitrites	11.1	7.9	2.1	1.5	2.7	1.7	0.8	1.9	1.5	1.6	1.3	–0.3
Hallucinogens[2]	15.6	12.1	9.7	12.7	14.1	13.7	13.0	14.7	12.0	10.6	9.9	–1.0
LSD	9.3	7.5	8.7	11.7	12.6	12.2	11.1	10.9	8.4	5.9	4.6	–1.3
PCP	9.6	4.9	2.8	2.7	3.9	3.4	3.4	3.5	3.1	2.5	1.6	–0.9
Ecstasy	NA	NA	NA	NA	5.8	8.0	11.0	11.7	10.5	8.3	7.5	–0.8
Cocaine	15.7	17.3	9.4	6.0	9.3	9.8	8.6	8.2	7.8	7.7	8.1	+0.5
Crack	NA	NA	3.5	3.0	4.4	4.6	3.9	3.7	3.8	3.6	3.9	+0.3
Heroin[3]	1.1	1.2	1.3	1.6	2.0	2.0	2.4	1.8	1.7	1.5	1.5	–0.1
Other opiates[4]	9.8	10.2	8.3	7.2	9.8	10.2	10.6	9.9	13.5	13.2	13.5	+0.3
Amphetamines[4,5]	26.4	26.2	17.5	15.3	16.4	16.3	15.6	16.2	16.8	14.4	15.0	+0.6
Methamphetamine	—	—	—	—	—	8.2	7.9	6.9	6.7	6.2	6.2	0.0
Crystal Meth.	—	—	2.7	3.9	5.3	4.8	4.0	4.0	4.7	3.9	4.0	+0.2
Barbiturates[4]	11.0	9.2	6.8	7.4	8.7	8.9	9.2	8.7	9.5	8.8	9.9	+1.0
Methaqualone[4]	9.5	6.7	2.3	1.2	1.6	1.8	0.8	1.1	1.5	1.0	1.3	+0.3
Tranquilizers[4]	15.2	11.9	7.2	7.1	8.5	9.3	8.9	10.3	11.4	10.2	10.6	+0.4
Alcohol[6]	93.2	92.2	89.5	80.7	81.4	80.0	80.3	79.7	78.4	76.6	76.8	+0.2
Cigarettes	71.0	68.8	64.4	64.2	65.3	64.6	62.5	61.0	57.2	53.7	52.8	–0.9
Steroids	NA	NA	2.9	2.3	2.7	2.9	2.5	3.7	4.0	3.5	3.4	–0.2

NA = Not available. (1) Adjusted for underreporting of amyl and butyl nitrites. (2) Adjusted for underreporting of PCP. (3) Reflects use with or without injection. (4) Includes only drug use that was not under a doctor's orders. (5) Data for 1990-2002 are not directly comparable to prior years. (6) Data for 1994-2003 are not directly comparable to prior years. (7) In percentage points.

U.S. Motor Vehicle Accidents

Source: National Safety Council

A total of 44,800 people in the U.S. were killed in motor vehicle accidents in 2003, according to preliminary figures, up 700 from the revised total for 2003. The number of drivers and vehicle miles driven also increased slightly, and the fatality rate per motor vehicle declined, as has happened most years since the introduction of the automobile. Motor-vehicle deaths per 10,000 registered vehicles went from 2.43 in 1990 to 1.87 (preliminary figure) in 2003, a decrease of 23% over 13 years, and the rate in 2003 was a decline of 0.5% from 1.88 the year before. The rate of fatalities per 100,000 population has declined 18% from 1990 to 2003, but it showed an increase from 2002 to 2003 (see table below).

Among the estimated 196.7 mil licensed drivers in 2003, there were slightly more male drivers than female (98.6 mil male vs. 98.1 mil female; 50.1% male), but males accounted for 62% of all miles driven. About 11.6 mil male drivers and 8.4 mil female drivers were involved in an accident in 2003. Male drivers were also involved in many more fatal accidents than female drivers; about 40,000 male drivers compared to 14,000 females. The rate was also substantially higher for males (22 fatal accidents per bil miles) than for females (13).

In 2003, 34% of all traffic fatalities involved an intoxicated (blood alcohol concentration of 0.08 or greater) driver or nonoccupant (pedestrian, bicyclist, etc.) and 40% involved a driver or nonoccupant who had been drinking. Alcohol was a factor in about 7% of all traffic accidents.

	Deaths 2003	% change from 2002	Rate 2003[1]
All motor vehicle accidents	44,800	+2	15.4
Collision between motor vehicles	19,900	+6	6.8
Collision with fixed object	13,000	–3	4.5
Pedestrian accidents	5,600	–2	1.9
Noncollision accidents	5,200	0	1.8
Collision with pedal cycle	700	0	0.2
Collision with railroad train	300	0	0.1
Other collision (animal, animal-drawn vehicles)	100	0	(2)

(1) Deaths per 100,000 population. (2) Less than 0.05.

Improper Driving Reported in Accidents, 2000, 2002, 2003

Source: National Safety Council

Type	Percentage of fatal accidents 2003	2002	2000	Percentage of injury accidents 2003	2002	2000	Percentage of all accidents 2003	2002	2000
Improper driving	**57.0**	**59.5**	**61.6**	50.3	**54.7**	**60.3**	**49.9**	**50.3**	**57.8**
Speed too fast or unsafe	24.9	21.9	18.6	17.2	12.6	16.3	13.1	10.1	13.6
Right of way	16.3	17.4	10.1	16.5	18.9	19.9	18.1	16.4	20.1
Failed to yield	8.0	10.1	4.6	12.8	14.3	15.0	10.6	11.4	12.7
Disregarded signal	5.3	4.0	8.2	2.9	3.3	1.3	5.7	3.4	2.2
Passed stop sign	3.0	3.3	3.8	0.8	1.3	3.6	1.8	1.6	5.3
Drove left of center	5.9	5.7	0.7	0.8	0.9	1.1	0.8	0.7	1.0
Improper overtaking	0.5	1.0	0.9	1.2	0.5	2.0	1.7	0.8	2.4
Made improper turn	1.3	0.5	0.7	1.1	1.2	0.6	1.7	1.7	0.9
Followed too closely	0.4	0.4	0.9	3.4	2.8	4.3	6.3	3.8	5.7
Other improper driving	7.7	12.5	9.0	10.1	17.9	16.1	8.2	16.8	14.1
No improper driving stated	**43.0**	**40.5**	**38.4**	**49.7**	**45.3**	**39.7**	**50.1**	**49.7**	**42.2**

Note: Based on reports from state traffic authorities. When a driver was under the influence of alcohol or drugs, the accident was considered a result of the driver's physical condition—not a driving error. For this reason, accidents in which the driver was reported to be under the influence are included under "no improper driving stated."

Death Rates[1] for Suicide at Selected Ages, 1960, 1980, 2000, 2002

Source: *Health, United States, 2004,* National Center for Health Statistics, U.S. Dept. of Health and Human Services

AGE	2002 Both sexes	Male	Female	2000 Both sexes	Male	Female	1980 Both sexes	Male	Female	1960 Both sexes	Male	Female
15-24	9.9	16.5	2.9	10.2	17.1	3.0	12.3	20.2	4.3	5.2	8.2	2.2
25-44	14.0	22.2	5.8	13.4	21.3	5.4	15.6	24.0	7.7	12.2	17.9	6.6
45-64	14.9	23.5	6.7	13.5	21.3	6.2	15.9	23.7	8.9	22.0	34.4	10.2
65 and older	15.6	31.8	4.1	15.2	31.1	4.0	17.6	35.0	6.1	24.5	44.0	8.4
All ages	**10.9**	**18.4**	**4.2**	**10.4**	**17.7**	**4.0**	**12.2**	**19.9**	**5.7**	**12.5**	**20.0**	**5.6**

(1) Per 100,000 population.

The 10 Leading Causes of Death in the U.S., 2002

Source: National Center for Health Statistics, U.S. Dept. of Health and Human Services

	Number	Death rate[1]	% of deaths
ALL CAUSES	**2,443,387**	**847.3**	**100.0**
1. Heart disease	696,947	241.7	28.5
2. Cancer	557,271	193.2	22.8
3. Stroke	162,672	56.4	6.7
4. Chronic lower respiratory diseases	124,816	43.3	5.1
5. Accidents	106,742	37.0	4.4
6. Diabetes mellitus	73,249	25.4	3.0
7. Influenza and pneumonia	65,681	22.8	2.7
8. Alzheimer's disease	58,866	20.4	2.4
9. Kidney disease	40,974	14.2	1.7
10. Blood poisoning	33,865	11.7	1.4

(1) Per 100,000 population.

Principal Types of Accidental Deaths in the U.S., 1970-2003

Source: National Safety Council

Year	Motor vehicle	Falls	Poisoning	Drowning	Fires, flames, smoke	Suffocation: Ingestion of food, object	Firearms	Mechanical Suffocation
1970	54,633	16,926	5,299	7,860	6,718	2,753	2,406	NA
1980	53,172	13,294	4,331	7,257	5,822	3,249	1,955	NA
1985	45,901	12,001	5,170	5,316	4,938	3,551	1,649	NA
1990	46,814	12,313	5,803	4,685	4,175	3,303	1,416	NA
1991	43,536	12,662	6,434	4,818	4,120	3,240	1,441	NA
1992	40,982	12,646	7,082	3,542	3,958	3,182	1,409	NA
1993	41,893	13,141	8,537	3,807	3,900	3,160	1,521	NA
1994	42,524	13,450	8,994	3,942	3,986	3,065	1,356	NA
1995	43,363	13,986	9,072	4,350	3,761	3,185	1,225	NA
1996	43,649	14,986	9,510	3,959	3,741	3,206	1,134	NA
1997	43,458	15,447	10,163	4,051	3,490	3,275	981	NA
1998	43,501	16,274	10,801	4,406	3,255	3,515	866	NA
1999[1]	42,401	13,162	12,186	3,529	3,348	3,885	824	1,618
2000	43,354	13,322	12,757	3,482	3,377	4,313	776	1,335
2001[2]	43,788	15,019	14,078	3,281	3,309	4,185	802	1,370
2002[2]	44,100	15,300	16,100	3,000	2,800	4,400	800	1,500
2003[3]	44,800	16,200	13,900	2,900	2,600	4,300	700	1,200
Death rates per 100,000 population								
1970	26.8	8.3	2.6	3.9	3.3	1.4	1.2	NA
1980	23.4	5.9	1.9	3.2	2.6	1.4	0.9	NA
1985	19.3	5.0	2.2	2.2	2.1	1.5	0.7	NA
1990	18.8	4.9	2.3	1.9	1.7	1.3	0.6	NA
1991	17.3	5.0	2.6	1.8	1.6	1.3	0.6	NA
1992	16.1	5.0	2.7	1.4	1.6	1.2	0.6	NA
1993	16.3	5.1	3.4	1.5	1.5	1.2	0.6	NA
1994	16.3	5.2	3.5	1.5	1.5	1.2	0.5	NA
1995	16.5	5.3	3.4	1.7	1.4	1.2	0.5	NA
1996	16.5	5.6	3.5	1.5	1.4	1.2	0.4	NA
1997	16.2	5.8	3.8	1.5	1.3	1.2	0.4	NA
1998	16.1	6.0	4.0	1.6	1.2	1.3	0.3	NA
1999[1]	15.5	4.8	4.5	1.3	1.2	1.4	0.3	0.6
2000	15.7	4.8	4.6	1.3	1.2	1.6	0.3	0.5
2001[2]	15.4	5.3	4.9	1.2	1.2	1.5	0.3	0.5
2002[2]	15.3	5.3	5.6	1.0	1.0	1.5	0.3	0.5
2003[3]	15.4	5.6	4.8	1.0	0.9	1.5	0.2	0.4

NA = Not available. **Note:** There were 14,900 other accidental deaths in 2003. All figures include on-the-job deaths. (1) Data for 1999 and later not comparable with earlier data because of classification changes. (2) Revised data. (3) Preliminary data.

Risk Behaviors in High School Students, 2003

Source: CDC, *Youth Risk Behavior Surveillance—United States, 2003*

		Percent rarely or never wear seatbelts[1]			Percent rarely or never wear bicycle helmets[2]			Percent who rode with a driver who had been drinking alcohol[3]		
		Female	Male	Total	Female	Male	Total	Female	Male	Total
Race	Non-Hispanic White	14.1	19.4	16.9	82.0	85.2	83.8	29.8	27.3	28.5
	Non-Hispanic Black	15.6	25.6	20.6	94.3	95.0	94.6	29.8	31.8	30.9
	Hispanic	15.8	24.2	20.2	87.9	91.4	90.1	40.0	32.8	36.4
Grade	9	17.6	22.9	20.4	80.3	86.4	83.9	30.2	26.4	28.2
	10	13.3	20.4	16.9	85.9	88.1	87.1	31.0	27.6	29.3
	11	15.5	21.4	18.5	86.8	87.6	87.3	30.7	30.3	30.5
	12	10.9	21.1	16.2	86.1	87.5	86.9	32.6	34.0	33.3
Total		**14.6**	**21.5**	**18.2**	**84.2**	**87.2**	**85.9**	**31.1**	**29.2**	**30.2**

(1) When riding in a car or truck driven by someone else. (2) Among the 62.3% of students who rode bicycles during the 12 months preceding the survey. (3) In a car or truck one or more times during the 30 days preceding the survey.

Sexual Activity of High School Students, 2003

Source: CDC, *Youth Risk Behavior Surveillance—United States, 2003*

		Ever had sexual intercourse			First sexual intercourse before age 13			Currently sexually active[1]			Responsible sexual behavior[2]		
		Female	Male	Total	Female	Male	Total	Female	Male	Total	Female	Male	Total
Race/Ethnicity	White[3]	43.0	40.5	41.8	3.4	5.0	4.2	33.1	28.5	30.8	56.5	69.0	62.5
	Black[3]	60.9	73.8	67.3	6.9	31.8	19.0	44.2	54.0	49.0	63.6	81.2	72.8
	Hispanic	46.4	56.8	51.4	5.2	11.6	8.3	35.8	38.5	37.1	52.3	62.5	57.4
Grade	9	27.9	37.3	32.8	5.3	13.2	9.3	18.3	24.0	21.2	66.1	71.2	69.0
	10	43.1	45.1	44.1	5.7	11.2	8.5	31.2	30.0	30.6	66.4	71.8	69.0
	11	53.1	53.4	53.2	3.2	7.5	5.4	42.9	39.2	41.1	55.5	66.7	60.8
	12	62.3	60.7	61.6	1.9	8.8	5.5	51.0	46.5	48.9	48.5	67.0	57.4
Total		**45.3**	**48.0**	**46.7**	**4.2**	**10.4**	**7.4**	**34.6**	**33.8**	**34.3**	**57.4**	**68.8**	**63.0**

(1) Sexual intercourse during the 3 months preceding the survey. (2) Used condom during last sexual intercourse. (3) Non-Hispanic.

Deaths in the U.S. Involving Firearms, by Age, 2002

Source: National Safety Council

	All ages	Under 5	5-14	15-19	20-24	25-44	45-64	65-74	75 & over
Total firearms deaths	**30,242**	**71**	**348**	**2,474**	**4,306**	**11,586**	**7,040**	**1,993**	**2,424**
Male	26,098	42	242	2,209	3,887	9,850	5,875	1,768	2,225
Female	4,144	29	106	265	419	1,736	1,165	225	199
Unintentional	762	12	48	107	103	266	151	36	39
Male	667	8	39	101	94	227	134	32	32
Female	95	4	9	6	9	39	17	4	7
Suicide	17,108	—	86	742	1,346	5,556	5,370	1,776	2,232
Male	15,045	—	68	668	1,229	4,750	4,607	1,620	2,103
Female	2,063	—	18	74	117	806	763	156	129
Homicide	11,829	58	205	1,567	2,750	5,507	1,434	161	147
Male	9,899	33	127	1,384	2,467	4,640	1,062	101	85
Female	1,930	25	78	183	283	867	372	60	62
Legal Intervention	300	0	3	23	63	161	44	5	1
Male	288	0	3	22	60	155	42	5	1
Female	12	0	0	1	3	6	2	0	0
Undetermined[1]	243	1	6	35	44	96	41	15	5
Male	199	1	5	34	37	78	30	10	4
Female	44	0	1	1	7	18	11	5	1

Note: There were 28,663 firearms deaths in 2000. (1) "Undetermined" means that the intention involved (whether accident, suicide, or homicide) could not be determined.

Worldwide Airline Fatalities, 1986-2004

Source: National Safety Council

Year	Aircraft accidents[1]	Passenger deaths	Death rate[2]	Year	Aircraft accidents[1]	Passenger deaths	Death rate[2]	Year	Aircraft accidents[1]	Passenger deaths	Death rate[2]
1986	24	641	0.04	1993	33	864	0.04	1999	21	499	0.02
1987	25	900	0.06	1994	27	1,170	0.05	2000	18	757	0.03
1988	29	742	0.04	1995	25	711	0.03	2001[3]	13	577	0.02
1989	29	879	0.05	1996	24	1,146	0.05	2002[4]	13	791	0.03
1990	27	544	0.03	1997	25	921	0.04	2003	7	466	0.02
1991	29	638	0.03	1998	20	904	0.03	2004[5]	9	203	0.01
1992	28	1,070	0.06								

(1) Involving 1 or more passenger fatalities and an aircraft with a maximum take-off mass greater than 2,250 kg. (2) Passenger deaths per 100 mil passenger kilometers. (3) Excluding accidents caused by terrorism or sabotage. (4) Revised data. (5) Preliminary.

U.S. Fires, 2004

Source: National Fire Protection Assn.

Fires

- Public fire departments responded to 1,550,500 fires in 2004, a decrease of 2.2% from 2003.
- There were 526,000 structure fires in 2004, an increase of 1.3% from the 2003 figure.
- 78% of all structure fires, or 410,500 fires, occurred in residential properties.
- Fires in vehicles dropped 4.8% from the previous year, totaling 297,000 in 2004.
- There were 727,500 fires in outside properties, a decline of 3.4% from 2003.

Civilian deaths

- There were 3,900 civilian fire deaths in 2004. This was a slight decrease of 0.6% from the year before.
- The number of civilian fire deaths in the home increased by 1.4%, to 3,190.
- 82% (3,190) of all fire deaths were caused by fires in the home.
- Home fires caused an average of one civilian death every 3 hours.

Civilian injuries

- There were an estimated 17,785 civilian fire injuries reported in 2004, a decrease of 1.4% from 2003.
- Residential properties were the site of 14,175 civilian fire injuries in 2004, and nonresidential structure fires accounted for 1,350 civilian injuries.
- Nationwide, a civilian was injured in a fire every half hour.

Property damage

- Direct property damage from fires amounted to an estimated $9,794,000,000 in 2004, a significant decrease of 20.2% from 2003. This decrease reflects the impact of the 2003 Southern California wildfires (Cedar and Old wildfires), which caused an estimated property loss of $2,040,000,000.
- Structure fires accounted for $8,314,000,000 of property damage.
- Property loss in residential properties came to $5,948,000,000 for 2003.

Intentionally set fires

- There were an estimated 36,500 intentionally set structure fires in 2004, a slight decrease of 2.7% from the 2003 number.
- Intentionally set structure fires resulted in 320 civilian deaths in 2004, an increase of 4.9% from the year before. Property damage from intentionally set structure fires totaled $714,000,000, an increase of 3.2% from the 2003 figure.
- The number of intentionally set vehicle fires in 2004 was 36,000, an increase of 18% from 2003. The 2004 intentionally set vehicle fires caused an estimated $161,000,000 in property damage, an increase of 25% from 2003.

Physicians by Age, Sex, and Specialty, 2002

Source: American Medical Assn., as of Dec. 31, 2002

	Male	Female
All Specialties[1]	638,182	215,005
Aerospace Medicine	461	32
Allergy & Immunology	9,120	981
Anaesthesiology	28,756	7,855
Cardiovascular Disease	20,088	1,882
Child Psychiatry	3,759	2,758
Colon/Rectal Surgery	1,084	113
Dermatology	6,506	3,482
Diagnostic Radiology	18,086	4,698
Emergency Medicine	20,429	5,098
Family Practice	63,194	23,317
Forensic Pathology	399	181
Gastroenterology	10,220	1,109
General Practice	11,297	2,249
General Preventive Med.	1,203	626
General Surgery	32,678	4,525
Internal Medicine	101,633	41,658
Medical Genetics	230	203
Neurological Surgery	4,770	238
Neurology	10,088	2,895
Nuclear Medicine	1,200	255
Obstetrics/Gynecology	25,606	15,432
Occupational Medicine	2,346	494
Ophthalmology	15,670	2,914
Orthopedic Surgery	22,329	882
Otolaryngology	8,839	987
Pathology-Anat./Clin.	12,575	5,604
Pediatric Cardiology	1,241	459
Pediatrics	33,020	33,351
Physical Med./Rehab.	4,619	2,302

	Male	Female
Plastic Surgery	5,822	713
Psychiatry	27,803	12,292
Public Health	1,231	600
Pulmonary Diseases	8,148	1,290
Radiation Oncology	3,215	968
Radiology	7,574	1,218
Thoracic Surgery	4,904	152
Transplantation Surgery	75	8
Urology	10,048	383
Other Speciality	4,732	907
Unspecified	3,300	1,413

(1) Includes "Inactive," "Address Unknown," and certain specialties with very few practitioners.

U.S. Health Expenditures, 1960-2002

Source: *Health, United States, 2004,* National Center for Health Statistics, U.S. Dept. of Health and Human Services

	1960	1970	1980	1990	1995	1999	2000	2001	2002
	Amount in billions								
National health expenditures	**$26.7**	**$73.1**	**$245.8**	**$696.0**	**$990.2**	**$1,222.6**	**$1,309.4**	**$1,420.7**	**$1,553.0**
	Percent distribution								
Health services and supplies	**93.6**	**92.2**	**95.0**	**96.2**	**96.7**	**96.7**	**96.3**	**96.4**	**96.4**
Personal health care	87.6	86.5	87.3	87.6	87.4	87.1	86.7	86.7	86.3
Hospital care	34.4	37.8	41.3	36.5	34.7	32.2	31.6	31.3	31.3
Professional services	31.3	28.3	27.4	31.2	32.0	32.5	32.6	32.7	32.3
Physician and clinical services	20.1	19.1	19.2	22.6	22.3	22.2	22.2	22.2	21.9
Other professional services	1.5	1.0	1.5	2.6	2.9	3.0	3.0	3.0	3.0
Dental services	7.4	6.4	5.4	4.5	4.5	4.6	4.6	4.6	4.5
Other personal health care	2.4	1.7	1.3	1.4	2.3	2.8	2.8	2.9	2.9
Nursing home and home health	3.4	6.1	8.2	9.4	10.6	10.0	9.6	9.3	9.0
Home health care	0.2	0.3	1.0	1.8	3.1	2.6	2.4	2.4	2.3
Nursing home care	3.2	5.8	7.2	7.6	7.5	7.3	7.2	7.0	6.6
Retail outlet sales of medical products	18.6	14.3	10.5	10.5	10.2	12.4	13.0	13.4	13.7
Prescription drugs	10.0	7.5	4.9	5.8	6.1	8.5	9.3	9.9	10.5
Other medical products	8.5	6.8	5.6	4.7	4.0	3.9	3.7	3.5	3.3
Government administration and net cost of private health insurance	4.5	3.8	4.9	5.7	6.1	6.0	6.1	6.4	6.8
Government public health activities[1]	1.5	1.9	2.7	2.9	3.2	3.6	3.5	3.4	3.3
Investment	**6.4**	**7.8**	**5.0**	**3.8**	**3.3**	**3.3**	**3.7**	**3.6**	**3.6**
Research	2.6	2.7	2.2	1.8	1.7	1.9	2.2	2.2	2.2
Construction	3.8	5.2	2.8	2.0	1.6	1.4	1.5	1.3	1.4
	Average annual percent change from previous year shown								
National health expenditures	—	**10.6**	**12.9**	**11.0**	**7.3**	**5.4**	**7.1**	**8.5**	**9.3**
Health services and supplies	—	**10.4**	**13.2**	**11.1**	**7.4**	**5.4**	**6.8**	**8.6**	**9.2**
Personal health care	—	10.5	13.0	11.0	7.3	5.3	6.6	8.5	8.8
Hospital care	—	11.7	13.9	9.6	6.2	3.4	5.0	7.5	9.5
Professional services	—	9.5	12.5	12.4	7.9	5.9	7.3	8.8	8.0
Physician and clinical services	—	10.1	12.9	12.8	7.0	5.3	7.2	8.6	7.7
Other professional services	—	6.6	17.1	17.5	9.5	6.4	5.8	9.9	7.6
Dental services	—	9.1	11.1	9.0	7.1	6.1	7.7	8.0	7.2
Other personal health care	—	7.2	10.0	11.4	18.9	10.1	9.0	11.3	12.1
Nursing home and home health	—	17.2	16.3	12.5	10.0	3.8	3.0	5.8	4.9
Home health care	—	14.5	26.9	18.1	19.4	1.4	-1.8	6.2	7.2
Nursing home care	—	17.4	15.4	11.5	7.2	4.7	4.7	5.7	4.1
Retail outlet sales of medical products	—	7.8	9.4	11.1	6.5	10.9	11.9	11.7	12.0
Prescription drugs	—	7.5	8.2	12.8	8.6	14.5	16.4	15.9	15.3
Other medical products	—	8.1	10.6	9.2	3.8	4.6	2.1	1.3	2.6
Government administration and net cost of private health insurance	—	8.6	15.9	12.7	8.6	4.8	10.0	12.5	16.2
Government public health activities[1]	—	13.2	17.4	11.6	9.2	8.6	4.8	5.5	5.9
Investment	—	**12.9**	**7.9**	**8.0**	**4.3**	**5.9**	**17.3**	**5.5**	**11.9**
Research	—	10.9	10.8	8.8	6.2	8.1	23.1	9.4	8.9
Construction	—	14.1	6.1	7.3	2.4	3.2	9.5	–0.3	16.8

Note: Numbers may not add to totals because of rounding. (1) Includes personal care services delivered by government public health agencies.

Persons Not Covered by Health Insurance, by Selected Characteristics, 2004

Source: Bureau of the Census, U.S. Dept. of Commerce

	Number[1]	% of specified population
Sex		
Male	24,528	17.2
Female	21,293	14.3
Race and Ethnicity		
White	34,788	14.9
Non-Hispanic	21,958	11.3
Black	7,186	19.7
Asian and Pacific Islander	2,070	16.8
Hispanic[2]	13,678	32.7
Education (18 years and older)		
No high school diploma	10,072	29.5
High school graduate only	13,832	20.0
Some college, no degree	6,846	16.4
Associate degree	2,118	12.0
Bachelor's degree or higher	4,683	8.6
Nativity		
Native	33,962	13.3
Foreign born	11,858	33.7
Naturalized citizen	2,317	17.2
Not a citizen	9,542	44.1
Age		
Under 18 years	8,269	11.2
18 to 24 years	8,772	31.4
25 to 34 years	10,177	25.9
35 to 44 years	8,110	18.7
45 to 54 years	6,260	14.9
55 to 64 years	3,936	13.3
65 years and over	297	0.8
Region		
Northeast	7,106	13.2
Midwest	7,737	11.9
South	19,262	18.3
West	11,715	17.4
Household Income		
Less than $25,000	15,102	24.3
$25,000 to $49,999	14,784	20.0
$50,000 to $74,999	7,842	13.3
$75,000 or more	8,092	8.4
TOTAL	**45,820**	**15.7**

(1) In thousands. (2) Persons of Hispanic origin may be of any race.

Health Coverage for Persons Under 65, by Characteristics, 1984, 2000-2002

Source: *Health, United States, 2004,* National Center for Health Statistics, U.S. Dept. of Health and Human Services

	PRIVATE INSURANCE				MEDICAID[1]				NOT COVERED[2]			
	1984	2000[3]	2001	2002	1984	2000[3]	2001	2002	1984	2000[3]	2001	2002
Age					Percent of each population group							
Under 18 years	72.6	67.0	66.7	63.9	11.9	19.4	21.2	24.5	13.9	12.4	11.0	10.7
18-44 years	76.5	70.9	70.6	69.2	5.1	5.6	6.3	7.1	17.1	22.0	21.7	22.5
45-64 years	83.3	78.7	78.6	77.2	3.4	4.5	4.7	5.4	9.6	12.7	12.3	13.1
Race and Hispanic origin[4,5]												
White, non-Hispanic	82.4	79.3	79.2	77.6	3.7	6.3	7.0	8.0	11.8	12.5	11.9	12.6
Black, non-Hispanic	59.4	57.0	57.6	56.2	19.1	19.3	20.3	21.5	19.7	20.0	19.2	19.2
All Hispanic	57.1	49.0	47.6	46.1	12.2	14.2	16.0	18.9	29.1	35.4	34.8	33.8
Percent of poverty level[4]												
Below 100%	33.0	26.6	26.8	26.7	30.5	35.2	36.7	39.4	34.7	35.2	34.0	31.4
100-149%	61.8	42.2	42.1	39.2	7.5	19.1	21.7	25.2	27.0	35.2	32.0	32.8
150-199%	77.2	58.8	57.3	56.6	3.1	10.7	13.1	14.9	17.4	27.2	26.5	25.6
200% or more	91.6	85.7	85.6	83.9	0.6	2.5	2.7	3.3	5.8	10.0	9.9	10.9
Geographic region[4]												
Northeast	80.7	76.5	76.5	73.9	8.5	10.5	10.8	12.6	10.1	12.1	11.6	12.7
Midwest	80.9	78.9	78.1	76.5	7.2	7.9	9.0	10.3	11.1	12.3	11.7	12.4
South	74.5	67.0	66.3	64.8	5.0	9.4	10.7	12.0	17.4	20.4	20.0	20.2
West	72.3	67.1	68.6	66.7	6.9	10.2	10.6	12.5	17.8	20.2	18.6	18.8

Note: Data based on household interviews of a sample of the civilian noninstitutionalized population. Percents do not add to 100 because other types of health insurance (e.g., Medicare, military) are not shown and persons with both private insurance and Medicaid appear in both sections. (1) Includes Medicaid or other public assistance. In 2002, the age-adjusted percent of the population under 65 covered by Medicaid was 9.2%; 1.2% were covered by state-sponsored health plans and 1.4% were covered by State Children's Health Insurance Program (SCHIP). (2) Includes persons not covered by private insurance, Medicaid or other public assistance, Medicare, or military plans. (3) In 1997 the questionnaire changed compared with previous years. (4) Age adjusted. (5) Changed reporting methods make percentages for race before 1999 not strictly comparable with those from 1999 on.

Health Insurance Coverage,[1] by State, 1990, 2000, 2004

Source: Bureau of the Census, U.S. Dept. of Commerce

	2004		2000		1990			2004		2000		1990	
	Not covered[2]	% not covered	Not covered[2]	% not covered	Not covered[2]	% not covered		Not covered[2]	% not covered	Not covered[2]	% not covered	Not covered[2]	% not covered
AL	609	13.5	582	13.3	710	17.4	MT	174	19.1	150	16.8	115	14.0
AK	110	17.0	117	18.7	77	15.4	NE	197	11.4	154	9.1	138	8.5
AZ	989	17.1	869	16.7	547	15.5	NV	443	18.5	344	16.8	201	16.5
AR	448	16.4	379	14.3	421	17.4	NH	152	11.7	103	8.4	107	9.9
CA	6,710	18.7	6,299	18.5	5,683	19.1	NJ	1,322	15.3	1,021	12.2	773	10.0
CO	767	17.0	620	14.3	495	14.7	NM	399	21.0	435	24.2	339	22.2
CT	407	11.6	330	9.8	226	6.9	NY	2,705	14.2	3,056	16.3	2,176	12.1
DE	120	14.5	72	9.3	96	13.9	NC	1,322	15.7	1,084	13.6	883	13.8
DC	73	13.3	78	14.0	109	19.2	ND	70	11.2	71	11.3	40	6.3
FL	3,479	19.9	2,829	17.7	2,376	18.0	OH	1,282	11.4	1,248	11.2	1,123	10.3
GA	1,513	17.4	1,166	14.3	971	15.3	OK	685	19.9	641	18.9	574	18.6
HI	120	9.6	113	9.4	81	7.3	OR	591	16.5	433	12.7	360	12.4
ID	212	15.4	199	15.4	159	15.2	PA	1,454	11.9	1,047	8.7	1,218	10.1
IL	1,764	14.0	1,704	13.9	1,272	10.9	RI	120	11.4	77	7.4	105	11.1
IN	872	14.2	674	11.2	587	10.7	SC	605	14.7	480	12.1	550	16.2
IA	277	9.5	253	8.8	225	8.1	SD	90	12.0	81	11.0	81	11.6
KS	297	11.1	289	10.9	272	10.8	TN	828	14.1	615	10.9	673	13.7
KY	582	14.3	545	13.6	480	13.2	TX	5,583	25.0	4,748	22.9	3,569	21.1
LA	761	17.2	789	18.1	797	19.7	UT	337	14.1	281	12.5	156	9.0
ME	130	10.0	138	10.9	139	11.2	VT	69	11.2	52	8.6	54	9.5
MD	810	14.6	547	10.4	601	12.7	VA	1,061	14.4	814	11.6	996	15.7
MA	748	11.7	549	8.7	530	9.1	WA	793	13.0	792	13.5	557	11.4
MI	1,156	11.6	901	9.2	865	9.4	WV	294	16.4	250	14.1	249	13.8
MN	458	8.9	399	8.1	389	8.9	WI	566	10.4	406	7.6	321	6.7
MS	489	17.1	380	13.6	531	19.9	WY	70	14.0	76	15.7	58	12.5
MO	707	12.6	524	9.5	665	12.7	**U.S.**	**45,820**	**15.7**	**39,804**	**14.2**	**34,719**	**13.9**

(1) For population, all ages, including those 65 or over, an age group largely covered by Medicare. (2) In thousands.

Enrollment in Health Maintenance Organizations (HMOs), 1976-2003

Source: *Health, United States, 2004,* National Center for Health Statistics, U.S. Dept. of Health and Human Services

	1976	1980	1990	1995	1997	1998	1999	2000	2001	2002	2003
					Number of enrolled in millions						
TOTAL	**6.0**	**9.1**	**33.0**	**50.9**	**66.8**	**76.6**	**81.3**	**80.9**	**79.5**	**76.1**	**71.8**
Model type[1]											
Individual practice assoc.[2]	0.4	1.7	13.7	20.1	26.7	32.6	32.8	33.4	33.1	31.6	28.0
Group[3]	5.6	7.4	19.3	13.3	11.0	13.8	15.9	15.2	15.6	15.0	16.1
Mixed	—	—	—	17.6	29.0	30.1	32.6	32.3	30.9	29.6	27.7
Federal program[4]											
Medicaid[5]	—	0.3	1.2	3.5	5.6	7.8	10.4	10.8	11.4	12.8	14.5
Medicare	—	0.4	1.8	2.9	4.8	5.7	6.5	6.6	6.1	5.4	4.9

	1976	1980	1990	1995	1997	1998	1999	2000	2001	2002	2003
				Percent of population enrolled in HMOs							
TOTAL	**2.8**	**4.0**	**13.4**	**19.4**	**25.2**	**28.6**	**30.1**	**30.0**	**28.3**	**26.4**	**24.6**
Geographic region											
Northeast	2.0	3.1	14.6	24.4	32.4	37.8	36.7	36.5	35.1	33.4	31.8
Midwest	1.5	2.8	12.6	16.4	19.5	22.7	23.3	23.2	21.7	20.6	19.7
South	0.4	0.8	7.1	12.4	17.9	21.0	23.9	22.6	21.0	19.8	17.1
West	9.7	12.2	23.2	28.6	36.4	39.1	41.4	41.7	40.7	38.2	35.8

— = Not available. **Note:** Data as of June 30 in 1976-80, Jan. 1 from 1990 onwards. HMOs in Guam included starting in 1994; Puerto Rico, 1998; Guam HMO enrollment was 32,000 in 2003 and Puerto Rico enrollment was 1,726,000 in 2003. Open-ended enrollment in HMO plans, amounting to 7.6 million on Jan. 1, 2003, included from 1994 onwards. (1) Enrollment may not equal total because some plans did not report these characteristics. (2) This type of HMO contracts with an association of physicians from various settings (a mixture of solo and group practices) to provide health services. (3) Group includes staff, group, and network model types. (4) Enrollment by Medicaid or Medicare beneficiaries, where the Medicaid or Medicare program contracts directly with the HMO to pay the premium. (5) Data for 1990 and later include enrollment in managed-care health insuring organizations.

Hospitals and Nursing Homes in the U.S., 2002

Source: *Hospital Statistics™ 2003* ed., Health Forum, LLC, An American Hospital Assoc. Company, © 2003; *Health, United States, 2004*

For information on choosing a nursing home, go to the website www.medicare.gov/nursing/overview.asp

STATE	Hospitals[1]	% of beds occupied[1]	Nursing homes	% of beds occupied	STATE	Hospitals[1]	% of beds occupied[1]	Nursing homes	% of beds occupied
AL	107	56	230	90.3	MT	53	69	102	77.3
AK	19	60	15	79.4	NE	84	58	230	82.7
AZ	61	64	134	79.4	NV	24	68	44	79.9
AR	83	58	247	72.1	NH	28	62	83	90.3
CA	384	69	1,347	81.6	NJ	78	70	360	86.7
CO	66	62	224	80.3	NM	35	65	82	84.1
CT	35	80	252	91.9	NY	212	77	674	93.0
DE	5	74	42	83.7	NC	111	69	415	88.0
DC	10	77	21	90.5	ND	40	60	84	94.1
FL	202	66	704	85.6	OH	166	62	994	76.6
GA	147	65	362	91.2	OK	108	58	373	68.4
HI	23	74	45	93.6	OR	60	61	145	70.2
ID	40	53	82	75.5	PA	205	70	757	88.0
IL	192	63	848	74.7	RI	11	73	97	87.9
IN	110	59	545	76.1	SC	62	72	176	89.2
IA	116	60	463	77.8	SD	50	59	112	92.1
KS	133	55	376	79.0	TN	123	60	339	89.5
KY	103	62	303	88.7	TX	411	64	1,139	70.3
LA	125	59	321	77.3	UT	42	55	90	72.1
ME	37	66	121	90.7	VT	14	61	44	90.5
MD	49	73	245	86.8	VA	87	68	277	84.5
MA	80	74	499	89.4	WA	84	60	267	82.5
MI	145	66	431	84.3	WV	57	62	137	90.2
MN	133	68	425	92.2	WI	121	64	407	84.6
MS	96	57	204	88.2	WY	24	54	39	82.3
MO	117	61	538	69.2	**U.S.**	**4,908**	**66**	**16,491**	**82.4**

(1) Community hospitals (excludes federal hospitals, hospital units of institutions, facilities for the mentally retarded, and alcoholism and chemical dependency hospitals).

Health Care Visits, by Selected Characteristics, 1997, 2001, 2002

Source: Centers for Disease Control and Prevention, National Center for Health Statistics. National Health Interview Survey, family core and sample adult questionnaires.

	No visits			1-3 visits			4-9 visits			10 or more visits		
	1997	2001	2002	1997	2001	2002	1997	2001	2002	1997	2001	2002
						Percent distribution						
All persons	**16.5**	**16.5**	**15.9**	**46.2**	**45.8**	**45.5**	**23.6**	**24.4**	**25.2**	**13.7**	**13.3**	**13.4**
Age												
Under 6 years	5.0	5.5	5.6	44.9	45.8	47.0	37.0	37.9	37.1	13.0	10.8	10.4
6–17 years	15.3	14.6	13.0	58.7	58.9	59.0	19.3	20.5	22.3	6.8	6.1	5.7
18–24 years	22.0	25.4	24.8	46.8	44.7	45.6	20.0	19.5	18.7	11.2	10.5	10.8
25–44 years	21.6	22.6	21.8	46.7	46.5	45.7	18.7	18.7	19.6	13.0	12.2	12.9
45–54 years	17.9	17.1	17.0	43.9	44.9	43.3	23.4	23.6	25.4	14.8	14.4	14.3
55–64 years	15.3	13.3	11.5	41.3	39.6	39.7	26.7	28.9	29.0	16.7	18.2	19.7
65–74 years	9.8	8.1	9.1	36.9	35.8	33.7	31.6	33.5	36.8	21.6	22.6	20.5
75 years and over	7.7	5.8	7.3	31.8	28.2	28.6	33.8	38.1	35.8	26.6	27.9	28.3
Sex												
Male	21.3	21.3	20.6	47.1	46.5	46.5	20.6	21.6	22.2	11.0	10.7	10.7
Female	11.8	11.9	11.4	45.4	45.1	44.5	26.5	27.1	28.0	16.3	15.9	16.1
Race and Hispanic origin												
White, non-Hispanic	14.7	14.3	15.6	46.6	46.4	45.1	24.4	25.4	25.4	14.3	13.9	13.8
Black, non-Hispanic	16.9	16.4	15.3	46.1	46.4	45.8	23.1	24.0	26.0	13.8	13.1	13.0
Hispanic[1]	24.9	27.0	25.7	42.3	40.2	41.5	20.3	20.7	21.1	12.5	12.0	11.7
Geographic region												
Northeast	13.2	11.8	11.0	45.9	47.2	45.5	26.0	26.6	27.7	14.9	14.3	15.7
Midwest	15.9	14.9	14.4	47.7	47.2	47.7	22.8	24.0	25.0	13.6	13.9	13.0
South	17.2	17.7	17.4	46.1	45.2	44.7	23.3	24.4	25.2	13.5	12.8	12.8
West	19.1	20.5	19.9	44.8	44.1	44.2	22.8	22.8	23.0	13.3	12.7	12.9

NOTE: Covers visits to doctor's offices, emergency departments, and home visits. (1) Persons of Hispanic origin may be of any race.

Top 20 Reasons Given by Patients for Emergency Room Visits, 2003

Source: National Center for Health Statistics, U.S. Dept. of Health and Human Services

Rank	Principal reason for visit	Number (thous.)	%
	ALL VISITS	**113,903**	**100.0**
1.	Stomach pain, cramps, and spasms	7,583	6.7
2.	Chest pain and related symptoms (not referable to body system)	5,838	5.1
3.	Fever	5,732	5.0
4.	Cough	3,597	3.2
5.	Headache, pain in head	3,140	2.8
6.	Shortness of breath	2,984	2.6
7.	Back symptoms	2,696	2.4
8.	Vomiting	2,369	2.1
9.	Symptoms referable to throat	2,698	2.1
10.	Accident, not otherwise specified	2,239	2.0
11.	Pain, site not referrable to a specific body system	2,234	2.0
12.	Lacerations and cuts-upper extremity	2,143	1.9
13.	Earache or ear infection	1,867	1.6
14.	Motor vehicle accident, type of injury unspecified	1,760	1.5
15.	Skin rash	1,688	1.5
16.	Leg symptoms	1,615	1.4
17.	Labored or difficult breathing (dyspnea)	1,584	1.4
18.	Vertigo-dizziness	1,503	1.3
19.	Injury, other and unspecified type-head, neck, and face	1,501	1.3
20.	Nausea	1,408	1.2

Top 20 Reasons Given by Patients for Physicians' Office Visits, 2002

Source: National Center for Health Statistics, U.S. Dept. of Health and Human Services

Rank		Number of visits (1,000)	PERCENT DISTRIBUTION Total	Female	Male
	ALL VISITS	**889,980[1]**	**100.0**	**100.0**	**100.0**
1.	General medical examination	64,726	7.3	6.8	7.9
2.	Progress visit, not otherwise specified	40,983	4.6	3.9	5.6
3.	Cough	28,469	3.2	3.1	3.4
4.	Postoperative visit	22,083	2.5	2.4	2.6
5.	Prenatal examination, routine	19,582	2.2	3.7	–
6.	Symptoms referable to throat	18,515	2.1	2.2	2.0
7.	Hypertension	17,195	1.9	2.0	1.8
8.	Knee symptoms	14,803	1.7	1.7	1.7
9.	Well-baby examination	14,293	1.6	1.4	1.9
10.	Medication, other and unspecified kinds	14,076	1.6	1.6	1.6
11.	Stomach pain, cramps, and spasms	13,547	1.5	1.7	1.2
12.	Earache, or ear infection	13,160	1.5	1.4	1.5
13.	Back symptoms	12,902	1.4	1.4	1.6
14.	Vision dysfunctions	12,897	1.4	1.4	1.5
15.	Blood pressure test	12,630	1.4	1.5	1.3
16.	Fever	12,258	1.4	1.2	1.7
17.	Nasal congestion	12,149	1.4	1.2	1.5
18.	Skin rash	11,887	1.3	1.2	1.6
19.	Chest pain and related symptoms	11,189	1.3	1.4	1.1
20.	Diabetes mellitus	11,189	1.3	1.0	1.6

(1) Based on 529,075,000 visits by women and 360,905,000 by men.

Drugs Most Frequently Prescribed in Physicians' Offices, 2002

Source: National Center for Health Statistics, U.S. Dept. of Health and Human Services; *Physicians' Desk Reference*; in thousands

Rank	Name of drug (principal generic substance)[1]	Times prescribed	% distrib.	Therapeutic use
1.	Lipitor (atorvastatin calcium)	18,842	1.4	Lowers cholesterol
2.	Albuterol sulfate	15,442	1.1	Anti-inflammatory agent
3.	Amoxicillin	14,690	1.1	Antibiotic
4.	Synthroid	14,525	1.1	Thyroid hormone therapy
5.	Lasix (furosemide)	14,004	1.0	Diuretic, antihypertensive
6.	Celebrex (celecoxib)	13,763	1.0	Anti-inflammatory agent
7.	Tylenol (acetaminophen)	12,919	1.0	Analgesic (for pain relief)
8.	Vioxx (rofecoxib)[2]	12,650	0.9	Anti-inflammatory agent
9.	Augmentin	11,995	0.9	Antibiotic
10.	Norvasc (amlodipine besylate)	11,853	0.9	Lowers blood pressure
11.	Zyrtec	11,573	0.9	Antihistamine
12.	Zocor (simvastatin)	11,429	0.8	Lowers cholesterol
13.	A.S.A. (acetylsalicylic acid, aspirin)	10,670	0.8	Analgesic (for pain relief)
14.	Prednisone	10,422	0.8	Steroid, anti-inflammatory agent
15.	Allegra	10,420	0.8	Antihistamine
16.	Coumadin	10,090	0.7	Anticoagulant
17.	Atenolol	9,694	0.7	Beta blocker
18.	Claritin (loratadine)	9,208	0.7	Antihistamine
19.	Paxil	9,118	0.7	Antidepressant
20.	Prevacid	8,981	0.7	Acid/peptic disorders
	All Other	**1,105,025**	**82.0**	

(1) The trade or generic name used by the physician on the prescription or other medical records. The use of trade names is for identification only and does not imply endorsement by the Public Health Service or the U.S. Dept. of Health and Human Services. (2) Recalled by manufacturer 9/30/04 after new research showed that people taking the drug for 18 months or more were at an increased risk for heart attack and stroke.

Expected New Cancer Cases and Deaths, by Sex, for Leading Sites, 2005

Source: American Cancer Society

The estimates of expected new cases are offered as a rough guide only. They exclude basal and squamous cell skin cancers and in situ carcinomas, except urinary bladder. Carcinoma in situ of the breast accounts for about 54,890 new cases annually, melanoma carcinoma in situ for about 46,170. More than 1 million cases of basal cell and squamous cell cancer, which are highly curable forms of skin cancer, occur annually.

EXPECTED NEW CASES

Both sexes		Women		Men	
Lung	172,570	Breast	211,240	Prostate	232,090
Colorectal	145,290	Lung	79,560	Lung	93,010
Urinary bladder	60,210	Colorectal	73,470	Colorectal	71,820
Non-Hodgkin lymphoma	56,390	Uterine corpus (endometrium)	40,880	Urinary bladder	47,010
Pancreas	32,180	Ovary	22,220	Non-Hodgkin lymphoma	29,070
ALL SITES	**1,372,910**	**ALL SITES**	**662,870**	**ALL SITES**	**710,040**

EXPECTED DEATHS

Both sexes		Women		Men	
Lung	163,510	Lung	73,020	Lung	90,490
Colorectal	56,290	Breast	40,410	Prostate	30,350
Non-Hodgkin's lymphoma	19,200	Colorectal	27,750	Colorectal	28,540
Pancreas	31,800	Ovary	16,210	Pancreas	15,820
Urinary bladder	13,180	Pancreas	15,980	Non-Hodgkin's lymphoma	10,150
ALL SITES	**570,280**	**ALL SITES**	**275,000**	**ALL SITES**	**295,280**

U.S. Cancer Incidence for Top 15 Sites, 1992-2002

Source: Surveillance, Epidemiology, and End Results (SEER) Program, National Cancer Institute

	Rate[1]	Average yearly % change[2]		Rate[1]	Average yearly % change[2]		Rate[1]	Average yearly % change[2]
ALL SITES	475.4	−0.6	Urinary bladder	20.3	−0.2	Pancreas	11.1	−0.3
Prostate	180.1	−2.0	Non-Hodgkin's lymphoma	19.2	0.1	Kidney and renal pelvis	11.1	1.5
Breast (female only)	132.4	0.4	Melanoma of the skin	16.2	2.4	Oral cavity and pharynx	11.0	−1.5
Lung	63.2	−1.3	Ovary	14.2	−0.9	Cervix Uteri	9.7	−2.8
Colon and rectum	53.9	−0.8	Leukemia	12.5	−0.9	Stomach	9.1	−1.5
Corpus and uterus	24.4	−0.2						

(1) Per 100,000 population; rates for prostate, breast, corpus and uterus, and ovary are sex-specific; rates age-adjusted to the 2000 population, and so not comparable with previously published rates. (2) For 1992-2002.

U.S. Cancer Mortality for Top 15 Sites, 1992-2002

Source: Surveillance, Epidemiology, and End Results (SEER) Program, National Cancer Institute

	Rate[1]	Average yearly % change[2]		Rate[1]	Average yearly % change[2]		Rate[1]	Average yearly % change[2]
ALL SITES	204.0	−1.0	Non-Hodgkin's lymphoma	8.4	−0.8	Liver and intrahepatic bile duct	4.4	1.9
Lung	57.1	−0.8	Leukemia	7.7	−0.6	Urinary bladder	4.4	−0.3
Prostate	33.9	−3.6	Stomach	4.9	−3.0	Esophagus	4.3	0.6
Breast (female only)	28.5	−2.4	Brain and other nervous system	4.7	−0.9	Kidney and renal pelvis	4.2	−0.1
Colon and rectum	21.6	−1.8				Corpus and uterus	4.1	−0.1
Pancreas	10.6	−0.1						
Ovary	9.0	−0.5						

(1) Per 100,000 population; rates age-adjusted to the 2000 population, and so not comparable with previously published rates; annual average for 8-year period; rates for prostate, breast, and ovary are sex-specific. (2) For 1992-2002.

Cardiovascular Diseases Statistical Summary, 2003

Source: American Heart Association

Prevalence — An estimated 71,300,000 Americans had one or more forms of heart and blood vessel disease in 2003.
- hypertension (high blood pressure)—65,000,000
- coronary heart disease—13,200,000
- stroke—500,000
- heart failure—5,000,000

Mortality — 910,614* in 2003 (37.3% of all deaths).
- Someone in the U.S. dies from cardiovascular disease every 35 seconds.

Congenital or inborn heart defects — Mortality from such heart defects was 4,178 in 2002.

* Preliminary data

Coronary heart disease (heart attack and angina pectoris) — caused 479,305* deaths in 2003.
- 13,200,000 Americans had a history of heart attack and/or angina pectoris.
- As many as 1,200,000 Americans have coronary attacks every year.

Heart failure — killed 57,218* in 2003.
Stroke — killed 157,804* Americans in 2003.
Rheumatic fever/rheumatic heart disease — killed 3,554* in 2003.
High blood pressure — killed 52,602* in 2003

Transplant Waiting List, Sept. 2005*

Transplants Performed, 2004

Source: United Network for Organ Sharing

Type of transplant	Patients waiting
Kidney	65,275
Liver	17,922
Lung	3,381
Heart	3,109
Kidney-pancreas	2,533
Pancreas	1,704
Intestine	187
Heart-lung	157
Total[1]	**92,268**

Type of transplant	Number
Kidney	16,004
Liver	6,169
Heart	2,016
Lung	1,173
Kidney-pancreas	881
Pancreas	604
Intestine	152
Heart-lung	39
Total	**27,038**

* As of Sept. 23, 2005. (1) This table shows the totals of patients waiting for each organ; some patients are waiting for more than one organ, so the total number waiting for organs is less than 92,268.

AIDS Deaths and New AIDS Cases in the U.S., 1985-2003

Source: *Health, United States, 2003;* National Center for Health Statistics, U.S. Dept. of Health and Human Services

		Percent Distribution	All Years[1]	1985	1990	1995	2000	2001	2002	2003	2003 rate[2]
TOTAL DEATHS		—	**524,060**	**6,981**	**31,988**	**52,254**	**17,741**	**18,524**	**17,557**	**18,017**	**4.7**
						NEW AIDS CASES					
All races		—	874,230	8,131	41,449	70,373	40,165	41,312	42,478	44,232	14.7
All males, 13 years and over		100.0	708,452	7,484	36,180	56,650	30,047	30,570	31,425	32,781	27.4
Race	White, non-Hispanic	47.1	333,873	4,743	20,818	25,972	11,224	10,971	11,069	11,831	13.6
	Black, non-Hispanic	35.7	253,078	1,695	10,244	20,812	13,041	13,720	14,214	13,820	109.2
	Hispanic[3]	15.8	112,101	989	4,746	9,128	5,295	5,329	5,550	6,344	37.2
	American Indian or Alaska Native[4]	0.3	2,353	9	81	196	135	145	146	169	16.0
	Asian or Pacific Islander[4]	0.8	5,875	47	254	463	275	325	351	458	7.2
Age	13-19 years	0.4	2,861	27	106	223	142	179	197	249	1.3
	20-29 years	15.2	107,651	1,497	6,917	8,387	3,327	3,280	3,418	3,570	17.1
	30-39 years	44.4	314,224	3,575	16,670	25,680	12,510	12,041	12,011	12,214	55.8
	40-49 years	28.1	199,248	1,632	8,832	16,120	9,614	10,234	10,593	11,257	48.4
	50-59 years	8.9	62,905	596	2,645	4,691	3,372	3,629	3,926	4,239	23.9
	60 years and over	3.0	21,563	157	1,010	1,549	1,082	1,207	1,280	1,252	6.3
All females, 13 years and over		100.0	156,837	519	4,544	12,978	9,932	10,572	10,914	11,297	9.0
Race	White, non-Hispanic	21.5	33,766	143	1,230	3,031	1,841	1,977	1,893	1,923	2.2
	Black, non-Hispanic	61.4	96,338	275	2,557	7,581	6,455	6,927	7,304	7,373	49.0
	Hispanic[4]	15.9	24,997	98	724	2,244	1,476	1,547	1,579	1,776	11.3
	American Indian or Alaska Native[4]	0.4	562	2	9	38	68	41	41	61	4.3
	Asian or Pacific Islander[4]	0.6	905	1	20	69	71	64	67	105	1.3
Age	13-19 years	1.4	2,177	5	67	157	168	167	195	209	1.4
	20-29 years	20.2	31,748	175	1,117	2,676	1,749	1,720	1,815	1,774	9.5
	30-39 years	43.1	67,523	230	2,088	5,937	3,965	4,125	3,977	4,075	18.6
	40-49 years	24.7	38,685	45	780	3,055	2,851	3,123	3,375	3,547	15.1
	50-59 years	7.3	11,483	26	273	818	859	998	1,147	1,253	6.6
	60 years and over	3.3	5,221	38	219	335	340	439	405	439	1.5
All children, under 13 years		100.0	8,939	128	725	745	186	170	139	153	0.7
Race	White, non-Hispanic	18.0	1,613	26	156	117	30	29	21	23	0.2
	Black, non-Hispanic	61.6	5,504	84	390	483	121	111	92	93	3.0
	Hispanic[4]	19.2	1,714	18	169	135	30	27	22	34	0.6
	American Indian or Alaska Native[4]	0.3	31	—	5	2	1	—	—	—	0.0
	Asian or Pacific Islander[4]	0.6	57	—	4	5	3	3	4	1	0.5
Age	Under 5 years	76.2	6,812	108	586	553	116	105	87	85	0.4
	5-12 years	23.8	2,127	20	139	192	70	65	52	68	0.2

Note: The definition of AIDS cases for reporting purposes was expanded in 1985, 1987, and 1993, as more was learned about the spectrum of human immunodeficiency virus-associated diseases. Data exclude residents of U.S. territories. Figures were updated Dec. 31, 2002 to include delayed case reports and may differ from previous reports of *Health, United States.* (1) Revised figures; includes cases and deaths prior to 1985 and for years not shown. Through 2003. (2) Rate is per 100,000 pop. (3) Persons of Hispanic origin may be of any race. (4) Excludes persons of Hispanic origin.

New AIDS Cases in the U.S., 1985-2003, by Transmission Category

Source: *HIV/AIDS Surveillance Report, 2003*, CDC, National Center for HIV, STD, and TB Prevention, Div. of HIV/AIDS Prevention

TRANSMISSION CATEGORY	Percent distribution	All years[1]	1985	1990	2000	2001	2002	2003
All males 13 years and older	**100**	**729,478**	**7,504**	**36,193**	**30,251**	**31,901**	**32,513**	**33,250**
Men who have sex with men	55	401,392	5,348	23,658	13,648	13,265	14,545	15,859
Injecting drug use	21	156,575	1,103	6,923	5,554	5,261	5,121	4,866
Men who have sex with men and injecting drug use	8	57,998	661	2,943	1,587	1,502	1,510	1,695
Hemophilia/coagulation disorder	1	5,130	68	332	93	97	79	74
Heterosexual contact[2]	6	40,947	32	715	2,537	2,762	3,213	3,371
Sex with injecting drug user	1	10,930	25	454	514	549	519	477
Transfusion[3]	1	5,219	102	440	146	105	147	111
Undetermined[4]	9	62,217	190	1,182	6,686	8,909	7,898	7,274
All females 13 years and older	**100**	**163,396**	**524**	**4,547**	**9,979**	**11,082**	**11,279**	**11,561**
Injecting drug use	38	61,621	287	2,347	2,545	2,212	2,381	2,262
Hemophilia/coagulation disorder	<1	318	3	15	5	9	11	11
Heterosexual contact[2]	43	70,200	119	1,538	4,025	4,142	4,740	5,234
Sex with injecting drug user	15	24,148	82	1,030	976	937	985	985
Transfusion[3]	2	4,076	63	330	151	113	118	108
Undetermined[4]	17	27,181	52	317	3,253	4,606	4,029	3,946

Note: The definition of AIDS cases for reporting purposes was expanded in 1985, 1987, and 1993, as more was learned about the spectrum of human immunodeficiency virus-associated diseases. Data exclude residents of U.S. territories. (1) Includes cases prior to 1985 and for years not shown. (2) Includes persons who have had heterosexual contact with a person with human immunodeficiency virus (HIV) infection or at risk of HIV infection. (3) Receipt of blood transfusion, blood components, or tissue. (4) Includes persons for whom risk information is incomplete, persons still under investigation, men reported only to have had heterosexual contact with prostitutes, and interviewed persons for whom no specific risk is identified.

Year in Pictures

AP/WIDE WORLD PHOTOS

AP/WIDE WORLD PHOTOS

AP/WIDE WORLD PHOTOS

AP/WIDE WORLD PHOTOS

AP/WIDE WORLD PHOTOS

AP/WIDE WORLD PHOTOS

1 FOUR MORE YEARS
Pres. George W. Bush being sworn in Jan. 20, 2005, for a second term by Chief Justice William Rehnquist, as Laura, Barbara, and Jenna Bush look on.

2 BUSH & SOCIAL SECURITY
Pres. Bush, pictured in Milwaukee May 19, traveled widely in support of his plan to introduce personal accounts into the Social Security system, but his initiative made little headway.

3 MADAM SECRETARY
Sec. of State Condoleezza Rice hosts Afghan Pres. Hamid Karzai May 23 in Washington, DC. Rice became the first African American woman to assume the nation's top diplomatic role when she succeeded Colin Powell in January.

4 EL ALCALDE DE LOS ANGELES
Antonio Villaraigosa defeated incumbent Los Angeles Mayor James Hahn in a non-partisan election May 1. He became the city's first Hispanic mayor in 133 years.

ROGER D.WALLENBERG/UPI/LANDOV

1 ATTORNEY GENERAL GONZALES

Alberto Gonzales became the nation's first Hispanic attorney general, succeeding John Ashcroft. He was sworn in Feb. 14 by Justice Sandra Day O'Connor, with his wife, Rebecca, at his side.

2 3 SUPREME COURT CHANGES

After Justice O'Connor announced her retirement in July, Pres. Bush nominated federal appeals court judge John G. Roberts Jr., 50, to replace her. When Chief Justice William C. Rehnquist (below left) died on Sept. 3, Bush made Roberts his nominee for Chief Justice.

AP/WIDE WORLD PHOTOS

AP/WIDE WORLD PHOTOS

National

1 2 KATRINA DEVASTATES GULF COAST; NEW ORLEANS SWAMPED
In one of the worst natural disasters in U.S. history, Hurricane Katrina struck Florida and, on Aug. 29, hit the Gulf coast with greater force, causing hundreds of deaths and heavy devastation. New Orleans was flooded and rendered virtually uninhabitable when levees burst Aug. 31; amid chaotic relief efforts, thousands who had not left the city were stranded on rooftops or crowded into the Superdome in squalid conditions.

3 4 LIFE AND DEATH STRUGGLE
Terri Schiavo (pictured before she suffered massive brain damage in 1990) died Mar. 31, 13 days after her feeding tube was removed following a high-profile legal battle. A law signed by Pres. Bush Mar. 21 had specifically allowed Schiavo's parents to press in federal court their case against the removal of the tube. The legislative effort was spear-headed by (left to right) Rep. James Sensenbrenner (R, WI) and House Majority Leader Tom Delay (R, TX), shown with Schiavo's brother Bobby Schindler.

1 "DEEP THROAT" UNSCARVED

Former FBI Acting Assoc. Director W. Mark Felt, 91, came forward in May as "Deep Throat," the secret source who helped *Washington Post* journalists Carl Bernstein (left) and Bob Woodward (right) unravel the Watergate scandal that led to the resignation of Pres. Richard Nixon in 1974.

2 GLORIOUS UNEXTINCTION

Ornithologists in April announced evidence that ivory-billed woodpeckers (illustrated here), believed to have been extinct since the 1940s, had been located in Arkansas.

3 RETURN TO SPACE

The space shuttle *Discovery* flew into space July 26, in the first shuttle flight since the fatal *Columbia* disaster of Feb. 2003. *Discovery* returned safely 14 days later, but problems at liftoff with foam coming off the shuttle's fuel tank had already caused NASA to suspend future flights.

1

AP/WIDE WORLD PHOTOS

AP/WIDE WORLD PHOTOS

2

AP/WIDE WORLD PHOTOS

3

NASA

Arts & Entertainment

1 EVERYBODY HATES GOODBYES

Ray Romano in the final episode of the hit sitcom *Everybody Loves Raymond*, broadcast May 16. The hit sitcom ran for 9 seasons on CBS.

2 LET THE GOOD TIMES ROLL

Jamie Foxx earned the Best Actor Oscar in 2005 for his portrayal of the late Ray Charles in *Ray*.

3 BEST PICTURE

Million Dollar Baby director Clint Eastwood and leading actress Hilary Swank both earned Academy Awards in 2005 for their work on the film.

4 A SAGA CONCLUDES

R2D2 and his Jedi knight comrades on a rescue mission in *Star Wars Episode III: Revenge of the Sith*, the last of George Lucas's six Star Wars movies. The films, the first of which came out in 1977, have generated more than $4 bil worldwide in box office revenues since then.

1

CBS/LANDOV

2

3

AP/WIDE WORLD PHOTOS

4

Arts & Entertainment

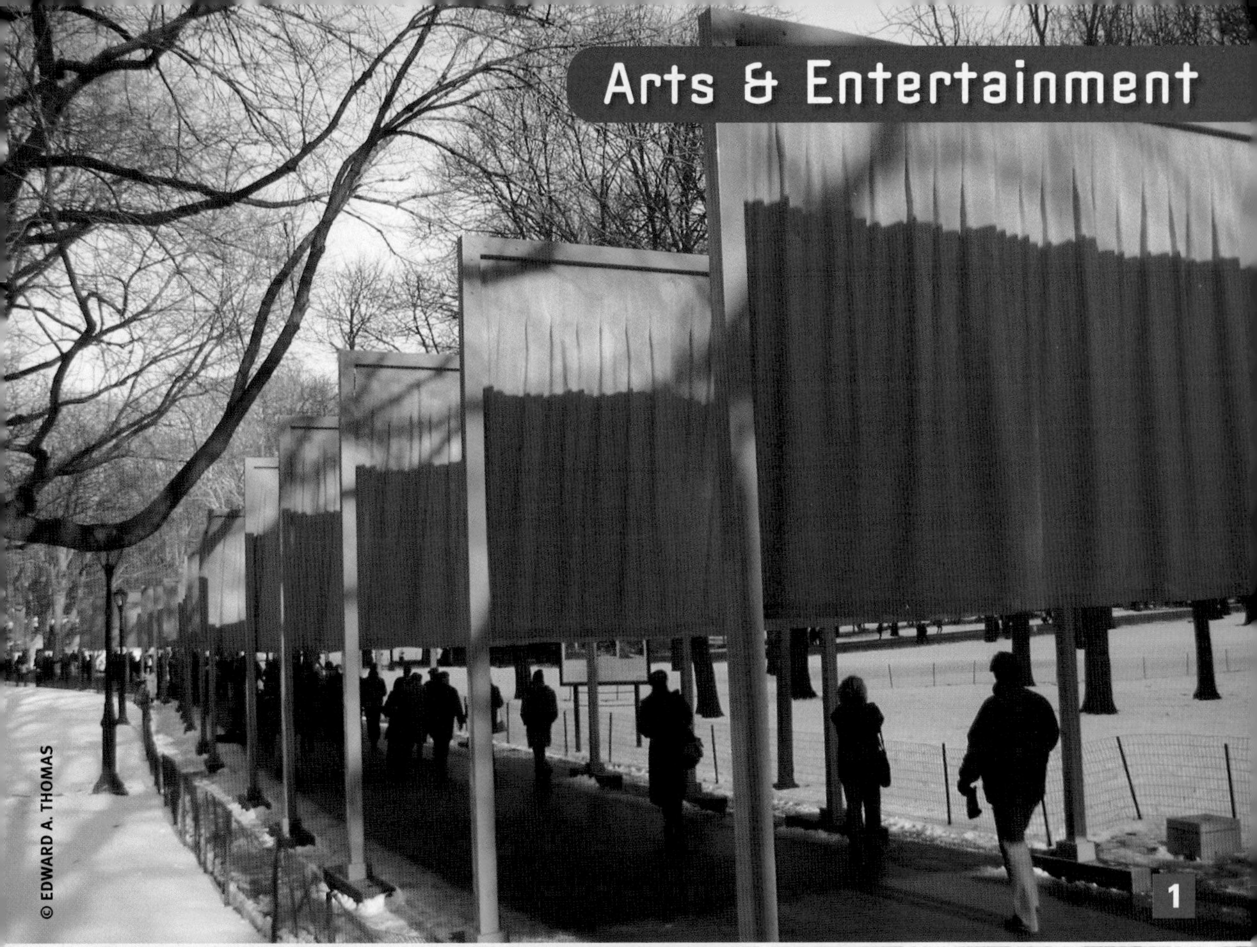

1 SAFFRON IN WINTER
The Gates, by husband-and-wife Christo and Jeanne-Claude, bloomed in New York's Central Park in February.

2 RETURN OF THE PHARAOH
The exhibit "Tutankhamun and the Golden Age of the Pharaohs," which debuted in June at the Los Angeles County Museum of Art, returned Egypt's 3,300-year-old boy pharaoh to the public eye. Here visitors view the coffin of Tjuya, Tut's great-grandmother.

3 BRING OUT YOUR TONYS
Monty Python's Spamalot, an adaptation of the 1975 cult classic film comedy *Monty Python and the Holy Grail*, earned the 2005 Tony for Best Musical.

4 HARRY POTTER
Boys in New Delhi, India, July 16 with their new copies of *Harry Potter and the Half-Blood Prince*, by J.K. Rowling. The sixth book in the series sold a record 6.9 mil copies in the U.S. alone (estimated) just in its first day on sale.

Farewell

1 SHIRLEY CHISHOLM

2 PETER JENNINGS

3 HUNTER S. THOMPSON

4 JOHNNY CARSON

5 JOHNNIE COCHRAN

6 ANNE BANCROFT

7 JERRY ORBACH

8 SAUL BELLOW

9 ARTHUR MILLER

10 JOHN H. JOHNSON

11 PHILIP JOHNSON

12 OSSIE DAVIS

CRIME

Measuring Crime

The U.S. Dept. of Justice administers 2 statistical programs to measure the magnitude, nature, and impact of crime in the U.S. Because of a difference in focus and methodology, their results are not strictly comparable.

The **Uniform Crime Report (UCR)** program, conducted through the Federal Bureau of Investigation, provides statistics for law enforcement administration, operation, and management. It collects information on the crimes of homicide, forcible rape, robbery, aggravated assault, burglary, larceny-theft, motor vehicle theft, and arson, as they are reported to law enforcement authorities. A preliminary annual report is released by the Justice Dept. each spring, and a more final report is released in the following year.

The **National Crime Victimization Survey (NCVS)** is conducted annually by the Bureau of Justice Statistics through interviews with members of a nationally representative sample of households, who report on their experience of crime. It complements the UCR by providing alternative information about crimes, including those not reported to police. In contrast to the UCR, it does not cover murder, arson, commercial crimes, or crimes against children under age 12.

Further explanation of the NCVS and UCR is available at: www.ojp.usdoj.gov/bjs/abstract/ntmc.htm

Uniform Crime Reports for 2004

Source: FBI, *Uniform Crime Reports*, 2004, preliminary

From 2003 to 2004, based on preliminary statistics, the number of violent crimes in the U.S. decreased by 1.7% to about 1.36 mil reported crimes, and property crime fell by 1.8%. In the violent crime category, murder and robbery each fell by 3.6%. Forcible rape decreased by 0.3% and aggravated assault by 0.8%. The drop in violent crime continued a general long-term trend. Final statistics showed a total decline of 25.6% between 1994 and 2003.

Among property crimes reported in 2004 (preliminary), burglary decreased by 1.4% from 2003, larceny-theft by 1.8%, and motor vehicle theft by 2.6%. Reports of arson, which is considered a property crime but not counted in the property crime total, declined 6.8%.

Violent crime decreased from 2003 in all regions, falling by 2.6% in the Northeast, 1.5% in the Midwest, 1.2% in the South, and 2.0% in the West. Property crime remained at about the same level as 2003 in the West, but fell by 3.5% in the Midwest, 2.5% in the Northeast, and 2.0% in the South.

Cities with populations of 1 million and over had the greatest decline in violent crime, 5.4%, followed by cities of 500,000 to 999,999 people, where it decreased by 3.4%. Violent crime rose slightly—0.3%—in cities of 9,999 residents or fewer and cities with 50,000 to 99,999 residents, but the murder rate (murders per 100,000 pop.) dropped in both categories, by 12.2% and 4.9%, respectively. In other urban population groups overall, the rate of violent crimes stayed about the same.

In metropolitan areas, violent crime dropped by 2.1%, while in nonmetropolitan areas, it rose by 0.7%.

In cities in all population categories, property crime decreased by 1.5%. The steepest decline was in cities with populations of 250,000 to 499,999, where it dropped by 4.2%.

In 2003, the UCR program temporarily suspended publication of the Crime Index, an aggregate total of offenses that include murder, forcible rape, aggravated assault, robbery, burglary, larceny theft, and motor-vehicle theft. Because the index had included both violent and property crimes and because property crimes predominate, the UCR program was developing an index that would differentiate between violent and property crimes.

National Crime Victimization Survey for 2004

Source: Bureau of Justice Statistics, U.S. Dept. of Justice

The NCVS estimated that there were about 24.2 mil victimizations of Americans age 12 and up in 2004 (including unreported crimes), about the same as in 2003. Crime rates—calculated per 1,000 persons over age 12 for violent crime or per 1,000 households for property crimes—remained at their lowest level since the NCVS began in 1973, when there were about 44 mil victimizations.

Based on NCVS, the rate for violent crimes decreased 57% from 1993 to 2004. During that same period, the percentage of crimes actually reported to the police increased significantly—from 42% to 50% for violent crimes, and from 34% to 39% for property crimes according to the NCVS.

There were significant drops in violent crime when aggregated two-year rates from 2001-02 to 2003-04 are compared. Rates of violent crimes against women dropped 15.3% (to 18.6 per 1,000), while violent crime against men dropped by only 2.6% (to 25.7 per 1,000). In urban areas violent crime dropped by 13.7%, more than in rural areas (down by 0.1%) and suburban areas (down by 7.4%).

Criminal Victimization, 2003-2004

Source: National Crime Victimization Survey, U.S. Dept. of Justice

Type of Crime	Number of victimizations 2003	Number of victimizations 2004	Victimization rates[1] 2003	Victimization rates[1] 2004
All crimes	**24,212,800**	**24,061,140**	**NA**	**NA**
Violent crimes[2]	5,401,720	**5,182,670**	**22.6**	**21.4**
Rape/sexual assault	198,850	209,880	0.8	0.9
Robbery	596,130	501,820	2.5	2.1
Assault	4,606,740	4,470,960	19.3	18.5
Aggravated[3]	1,101,110	1,030,080	4.6	4.3
Simple[4]	3,505,630	3,440,880	14.6	14.2
Property crimes	**18,626,380**	**18,654,400**	**163.2**	**161.1**
Household burglary	3,395,620	3,427,690	29.8	29.6
Motor vehicle theft	1,032,470	1,014,770	9.0	8.8
Theft[5]	14,198,290	14,211,940	124.4	122.8

NA = Not applicable (1) Per 1,000 persons age 12 or older or per 1,000 households. (2) The survey does not measure murder. (3) Attack with a weapon or including serious injury. (4) Attack without a weapon resulting in no injury, minor injury, or undetermined injury requiring less than 2 days' hospitalization. (5) Purse snatching and pocket picking.

WORLD ALMANAC EDITORS' PICKS
Favorite TV Cop Shows of All-Time

The editors of *The World Almanac* have ranked the following as their favorite police shows in TV history.

1. *Law and Order* (1990-)
2. *NYPD Blue* (1993-2005)
3. *Hill Street Blues* (1981-87)
4. *Columbo* (1971-78, 1989-2003)
5. *CSI: Crime Scene Investigation* (2000-)
6. *Dragnet* (1951-59, 1967-70)
7. *Miami Vice* (1984-89)
8. *Cagney and Lacey* (1982-88)
9. *The Mod Squad* (1968-73)
10. *21 Jump Street* (1987-91)

Crime in the U.S., 1982-2003[1]

Source: FBI, *Uniform Crime Reports*, 2003, final statistics; additional data may be available at www.fbi.gov/ucr/ucr.htm

Year	Population[2]	Crime Index (total)	Violent crime[3]	Property crime[3]	Murder and non-negligent manslaughter[1]	Forcible rape	Robbery	Aggravated assault	Burglary	Larceny-theft
				NUMBER OF REPORTED OFFENSES						
1982	231,664,458	12,974,400	1,322,390	11,652,000	21,010	78,770	553,130	669,480	3,447,100	7,142,500
1983	233,791,994	12,108,630	1,258,087	10,850,543	19,308	78,918	506,567	653,294	3,129,851	6,712,759
1984	235,824,902	11,881,755	1,273,282	10,608,476	18,692	84,233	485,008	685,349	2,984,434	6,591,874
1985	237,923,795	12,430,357	1,327,767	11,102,590	18,976	87,671	497,874	723,246	3,073,348	6,926,380
1986	240,132,887	13,211,869	1,489,169	11,722,700	20,613	91,459	542,775	834,322	3,241,410	7,257,153
1987	242,288,918	13,508,708	1,483,999	12,024,709	20,096	91,111	517,704	855,088	3,236,184	7,499,851
1988	244,498,982	13,923,086	1,566,221	12,356,865	20,675	92,486	542,968	910,092	3,218,077	7,705,872
1989	246,819,230	14,251,449	1,646,037	12,605,412	21,500	94,504	578,326	951,707	3,168,170	7,872,442
1990	249,464,396	14,475,613	1,820,127	12,655,486	23,438	102,555	639,271	1,054,863	3,073,909	7,945,670
1991	252,153,092	14,872,883	1,911,767	12,961,116	24,703	106,593	687,732	1,092,739	3,157,150	8,142,228
1992	255,029,699	14,438,191	1,932,274	12,505,917	23,760	109,062	672,478	1,126,974	2,979,884	7,915,199
1993	257,782,608	14,144,794	1,926,017	12,218,777	24,526	106,014	659,870	1,135,607	2,834,808	7,820,909
1994	260,327,021	13,989,543	1,857,670	12,131,873	23,326	102,216	618,949	1,113,179	2,712,774	7,879,812
1995	262,803,276	13,862,727	1,798,792	12,063,935	21,606	97,470	580,509	1,099,207	2,593,784	7,997,710
1996	265,228,572	13,493,863	1,688,540	11,805,323	19,645	96,252	535,594	1,037,049	2,506,400	7,904,685
1997	267,783,607	13,194,571	1,636,096	11,558,475	18,208	96,153	498,534	1,023,201	2,460,526	7,743,760
1998	270,248,003	12,485,714	1,533,887	10,951,827	16,974	93,144	447,186	976,583	2,332,735	7,376,311
1999	272,690,813	11,634,378	1,426,044	10,208,334	15,522	89,411	409,371	911,740	2,100,739	6,955,520
2000	281,421,906	11,608,070	1,425,486	10,182,584	15,586	90,178	408,016	911,706	2,050,992	6,971,590
2001	285,317,559	11,876,669	1,439,480	10,437,189	16,037	90,863	423,557	909,023	2,116,531	7,092,267
2002	288,368,698	11,877,218	1,426,325	10,450,893	16,204	95,136	420,637	894,348	2,151,875	7,052,922
2003	290,809,777	(4)	1,381,259	10,435,523	16,503	93,433	413,402	857,921	2,153,464	7,021,588
				PERCENT CHANGE: NUMBER OF OFFENSES						
2003/2002		(4)	−3.0	−0.2	1.7	−1.9	−1.8	−3.8	0.1	−0.5
2003/1999		(4)	−3.1	2.2	6.3	4.5	1.0	−5.9	2.5	0.9
2003/1994		(4)	−25.6	−14.0	−29.3	−8.6	−33.2	−22.9	−20.6	−10.9
				RATE PER 100,000 INHABITANTS						
1982		5,600.5	570.8	5,029.7	9.1	34.0	238.8	289.0	1,488.0	3,083.1
1983		5,179.2	538.1	4,641.1	8.3	33.8	216.7	279.4	1,338.7	2,871.3
1984		5,038.4	539.9	4,498.5	7.9	35.7	205.7	290.6	1,265.5	2,795.2
1985		5,224.5	558.1	4,666.4	8.0	36.8	209.3	304.0	1,291.7	2,911.2
1986		5,501.9	620.1	4,881.8	8.6	38.1	226.0	347.4	1,349.8	3,022.1
1987		5,575.5	612.5	4,963.0	8.3	37.6	213.7	352.9	1,335.7	3,095.4
1988		5,694.5	640.6	5,054.0	8.5	37.8	222.1	372.2	1,316.2	3,151.7
1989		5,774.0	666.9	5,107.1	8.7	38.3	234.3	385.6	1,283.6	3,189.6
1990		5,802.7	729.6	5,073.1	9.4	41.1	256.3	422.9	1,232.2	3,185.1
1991		5,898.4	758.2	5,140.2	9.8	42.3	272.7	433.4	1,252.1	3,229.1
1992		5,661.4	757.7	4,903.7	9.3	42.8	263.7	441.9	1,168.4	3,103.6
1993		5,487.1	747.1	4,740.0	9.5	41.1	256.0	440.5	1,099.7	3,033.9
1994		5,373.8	713.6	4,660.2	9.0	39.3	237.8	427.6	1,042.1	3,026.9
1995		5,274.9	684.5	4,590.5	8.2	37.1	220.9	418.3	987.0	3,043.2
1996		5,087.6	636.6	4,451.0	7.4	36.3	201.9	391.0	945.0	2,980.3
1997		4,927.3	611.0	4,316.3	6.8	35.9	186.2	382.1	918.8	2,891.8
1998		4,620.1	567.6	4,052.5	6.3	34.5	165.5	361.4	863.2	2,729.5
1999		4,266.5	523.0	3,743.6	5.7	32.8	150.1	334.3	770.4	2,550.7
2000		4,124.8	506.5	3,618.3	5.5	32.0	145.0	324.0	728.8	2,477.3
2001		4,162.6	504.5	3,658.1	5.6	31.8	148.5	318.6	714.8	2,485.7
2002		4,118.8	494.6	3,624.1	5.6	33.0	145.9	310.1	746.2	2,445.8
2003		(4)	475.0	3,588.4	5.7	32.1	142.2	295.0	740.5	2,414.5
				PERCENT CHANGE: RATE PER 100,000 INHABITANTS						
2003/2002		(4)	−3.9	−1.2	0.7	−2.8	−2.7	−4.7	−0.9	−1.5
2003/1999		(4)	−9.2	−4.1	−0.3	−2.0	−5.3	−11.8	−3.9	−5.3
2003/1994		(4)	−33.4	−23.0	−36.7	−18.2	−40.2	−31.0	−28.9	−20.2

(1) The murder and nonnegligent homicides that occurred as a result of the attacks of Sept. 11, 2001, are not included in this table. (2) Populations are Bureau of the Census provisional estimates as of July 1 for each year except 1990 and 2000, which are decennial census counts. (3) Violent crimes are offenses of murder, forcible rape, robbery, and aggravated assault. Property crimes are offenses of burglary, larceny-theft, and motor vehicle theft. (4) The publication of the Crime Index in Uniform Crime Reports ended in 2003.

Law Enforcement Officers, 2003

Source: FBI, *Uniform Crime Reports*, 2003;
Later data may be available at www.fbi.gov/ucr/ucr.htm

The U.S. law enforcement community employed an average of 2.3 sworn law enforcement officers for every 1,000 inhabitants as of Oct. 31, 2003.

Including full-time civilian employees, the overall law enforcement employee rate was 3.5 per 1,000 inhabitants. Nationally, 14,072 city, county, and state police agencies collectively employed 663,796 officers and 285,146 civilians, who provided service to more than 274 mil people.

The law enforcement employee average for all cities nationwide was 3.0 per 1,000 inhabitants. The highest rate, 4.2 per 1,000 inhabitants, was in cities with populations of less than 10,000 people. Cities with populations of 25,000 to 99,999 had the lowest rate, 2.3. Metropolitan counties had 4.4 law enforcement employees per 1,000 people, and nonmetropolitan counties had 4.6. Regionally, the law enforcement employee rate in cities was highest in the South, with 3.5 employees per 1,000 inhabitants. Northeastern cities had a rate of 3.2, and in cities in the Midwest and West, the rate was 2.8 and 2.4, respectively.

Nationally, males constituted 88.6% of sworn law enforcement officers; in metropolitan counties, they accounted for 86.7% of sworn officers, and in nonmetropolitan counties, the figure was 92.2%.

Civilians made up 30.0% of the nation's law enforcement employees. Females accounted for 62.5% of all civilian employees.

Fifty-two law enforcement officers in the U.S. were slain in the line of duty in 2003, 4 fewer than in 2002 and 18 fewer than in 2001. Another 80 were accidentally killed while on duty, 4 more than in 2002. In 2003, 57,841 officers were assaulted while on duty, 225 fewer than in 2002.[1]

(1) Number for 2003 assaults on officers does not include data for Illinois, Vermont, and West Virginia, which were not available.

Federal Bureau of Investigation

The Federal Bureau of Investigation was created July 26, 1908, and was referred to as Office of Chief Examiner. It later became the Bureau of Investigation (Mar. 16, 1909), United States Bureau of Investigation (July 1, 1932), Division of Investigation (Aug. 10, 1933), and finally, Federal Bureau of Investigation (July 1, 1935).

Director	Assumed office	Director	Assumed office	Director	Assumed office
Stanley W. Finch	July 26, 1908	J. Edgar Hoover	Dec. 10, 1924	John E. Otto, act.	May 26, 1987
A(lexander) Bruce Bielaski	Apr. 30, 1912	L. Patrick Gray, act.	May 3, 1972	William S. Sessions	Nov. 2, 1987
William E. Allen, act.	Feb. 10, 1919	William D. Ruckelshaus, act.	Apr. 27, 1973	Floyd I. Clarke, act.	July 19, 1993
William J. Flynn	July 1, 1919	Clarence M. Kelley	July 9, 1973	Louis J. Freeh	Sept. 1, 1993
William J. Burns	Aug. 22, 1921	William H. Webster	Feb. 23, 1978	Thomas J. Pickard, act.	June 25, 2001
J. Edgar Hoover, act.	May 10, 1924			Robert S. Mueller III	Sept. 4, 2001

U.S. Crime Rates by Region, Geographic Division, and State, 2003

Source: FBI, *Uniform Crime Reports*, 2003; final statistics
(rate per 100,000 population)

	Violent crime[1]	Murder	Rape	Robbery	Aggravated assault	Property crime[2]	Burglary	Larceny-theft	Motor vehicle theft
U.S. TOTAL	**475.0**	**5.7**	**32.1**	**142.2**	**295.0**	**3,588.4**	**740.5**	**2,414.5**	**433.4**
Northeast	**400.9**	**4.2**	**23.0**	**148.7**	**225.0**	**2,410.1**	**446.3**	**1,673.0**	**290.7**
New England	**338.1**	**2.2**	**27.2**	**97.1**	**211.6**	**2,528.6**	**492.4**	**1,719.9**	**316.3**
Connecticut	308.2	3.0	18.7	119.0	167.5	2,606.7	448.1	1,842.1	316.5
Maine	108.9	1.2	27.1	22.1	58.4	2,456.7	503.9	1,841.3	111.5
Massachusetts	469.4	2.2	27.9	124.1	315.1	2,549.5	539.7	1,613.3	396.5
New Hampshire	148.8	1.4	33.2	37.1	77.1	2,053.9	353.5	1,551.5	148.9
Rhode Island	285.6	2.3	46.9	77.1	159.3	2,995.0	513.3	2,074.0	407.7
Vermont	110.2	2.3	19.5	9.7	78.7	2,200.1	477.8	1,618.0	104.3
Middle Atlantic	**423.1**	**5.0**	**21.5**	**167.0**	**229.7**	**2,368.2**	**430.1**	**1,656.5**	**281.7**
New Jersey	365.8	4.7	15.3	154.7	191.0	2,544.4	503.0	1,641.3	400.2
New York	465.2	4.9	19.7	186.3	254.3	2,248.3	393.4	1,619.3	235.6
Pennsylvania	398.0	5.3	28.8	145.4	218.6	2,431.3	436.0	1,724.8	270.4
Midwest	**397.4**	**4.9**	**35.8**	**118.5**	**238.1**	**3,369.5**	**661.3**	**2,351.2**	**359.6**
East North Central	**423.3**	**5.6**	**37.4**	**136.9**	**243.5**	**3,333.6**	**675.5**	**2,288.2**	**370.0**
Illinois	556.8	7.1	32.9	188.2	328.6	3,284.4	618.7	2,335.6	330.1
Indiana	352.8	5.5	27.8	103.3	216.2	3,357.7	671.1	2,351.4	335.2
Michigan	511.2	6.1	54.1	111.7	339.3	3,277.3	677.2	2,067.1	533.1
Ohio	333.2	4.6	40.1	147.7	140.8	3,640.5	830.1	2,451.9	358.5
Wisconsin	221.0	3.3	21.9	80.1	115.7	2,882.6	485.4	2,172.1	225.1
West North Central	**336.7**	**3.4**	**32.1**	**75.6**	**225.6**	**3,453.4**	**628.2**	**2,498.8**	**326.4**
Iowa	272.4	1.6	25.9	38.1	206.8	2,961.1	596.0	2,174.9	190.2
Kansas	395.5	4.5	38.3	82.5	270.2	3,994.0	803.6	2,904.8	285.6
Minnesota	262.6	2.5	41.2	77.2	141.8	3,116.8	547.4	2,297.4	272.0
Missouri	472.8	5.0	24.4	108.7	334.5	4,014.5	717.1	2,794.9	502.4
Nebraska	289.0	3.2	28.5	66.8	190.5	3,711.4	579.1	2,780.2	352.1
North Dakota	77.8	1.9	23.8	8.0	44.0	2,096.1	306.2	1,619.8	170.1
South Dakota	173.4	1.3	46.3	13.6	112.1	2,001.7	375.9	1,511.4	114.4
South	**549.3**	**6.9**	**33.6**	**153.7**	**355.1**	**4,115.6**	**928.5**	**2,771.0**	**416.1**
South Atlantic	**576.2**	**6.7**	**31.3**	**164.7**	**373.4**	**4,020.1**	**887.4**	**2,694.4**	**438.3**
Delaware	658.0	2.9	43.2	169.9	442.0	3,384.4	729.8	2,302.3	352.3
District of Columbia	1,608.1	44.2	48.6	699.5	815.8	5,800.3	829.1	3,213.4	1,757.8
Florida	730.2	5.4	39.5	185.2	500.1	4,452.0	1,002.7	2,970.1	479.2
Georgia	453.9	7.6	25.7	161.8	258.8	4,254.6	909.2	2,846.0	499.4
Maryland	703.9	9.5	24.7	241.5	428.3	3,801.4	701.4	2,439.2	660.8
North Carolina	454.9	6.1	25.4	145.5	278.0	4,278.0	1,197.6	2,760.5	319.9
South Carolina	793.5	7.2	44.4	136.7	605.1	4,477.1	1,050.9	3,046.1	380.1
Virginia	275.8	5.6	24.0	90.3	155.9	2,704.1	391.5	2,070.0	242.5
West Virginia	257.5	3.5	16.4	40.3	197.3	2,359.4	562.2	1,602.6	194.7
East South Central	**459.4**	**6.6**	**33.9**	**124.7**	**294.2**	**3,781.0**	**945.4**	**2,419.5**	**334.2**
Alabama	429.5	6.6	36.8	134.2	251.9	4,049.1	960.8	2,756.0	332.3
Kentucky	261.7	4.6	25.6	77.6	153.9	2,681.5	671.6	1,782.4	227.5
Mississippi	325.5	9.3	37.4	104.8	174.1	3,720.4	1,035.6	2,374.2	310.6
Tennessee	687.8	6.8	35.7	160.4	484.9	4,379.4	1,082.0	2,845.3	452.1
West South Central	**552.3**	**7.3**	**37.3**	**150.8**	**359.9**	**4,450.0**	**987.5**	**3,045.3**	**417.2**
Arkansas	456.1	6.4	33.1	81.7	334.8	3,621.4	913.6	2,487.3	220.5
Louisiana	646.3	13.0	41.1	157.2	435.0	4,349.5	998.1	2,909.3	442.2
Oklahoma	505.7	5.9	42.7	91.8	365.3	4,306.0	992.3	2,944.7	369.0
Texas	552.5	6.4	36.2	167.4	342.5	4,595.3	993.7	3,157.7	444.0
West	**495.0**	**5.7**	**33.7**	**141.9**	**313.8**	**3,939.3**	**763.6**	**2,522.9**	**652.8**
Mountain	**435.4**	**5.4**	**37.9**	**105.0**	**287.2**	**4,391.6**	**841.3**	**2,926.8**	**623.5**
Arizona	513.2	7.9	33.3	136.5	335.5	5,632.4	1,050.3	3,560.9	1,021.3
Colorado	345.1	3.9	41.6	82.1	217.6	3,940.9	711.3	2,730.8	498.8
Idaho	242.7	1.8	37.2	17.9	185.8	2,908.7	570.2	2,147.5	190.9
Montana	365.2	3.3	26.8	32.5	302.6	3,098.0	405.6	2,484.7	207.7
Nevada	614.2	8.8	39.0	230.3	336.1	4,288.4	980.6	2,378.0	929.8
New Mexico	665.2	6.0	50.0	104.0	505.2	4,123.6	1,025.2	2,711.3	387.1
Utah	248.6	2.5	37.9	53.4	154.8	4,225.5	713.1	3,182.2	330.2
Wyoming	262.1	2.8	27.1	16.8	215.5	3,321.3	520.9	2,641.2	159.2
Pacific	**519.5**	**5.8**	**32.0**	**157.1**	**324.7**	**3,753.0**	**731.6**	**2,356.6**	**664.9**
Alaska	593.4	6.0	92.5	68.4	426.5	3,742.2	594.2	2,770.7	377.3
California	579.3	6.8	28.2	179.7	364.6	3,424.3	682.8	2,061.4	680.1
Hawaii	270.4	1.7	29.2	92.9	146.5	5,237.5	907.2	3,562.9	767.4
Oregon	295.5	1.9	34.2	80.1	179.3	4,782.3	804.2	3,444.6	533.5
Washington	347.0	3.0	46.7	93.3	204.0	4,754.9	950.3	3,142.1	662.5
Puerto Rico	**306.4**	**20.1**	**5.3**	**199.5**	**81.6**	**1,802.1**	**537.8**	**949.5**	**314.8**

Note: Offense totals are based on all reporting agencies and estimates for unreported areas. Totals may not add because of rounding. (1) Violent crimes are murder, forcible rape, robbery, and aggravated assault. (2) Property crimes are burglary, larceny-theft, and motor vehicle theft. Data not included for property crime of arson.

State and Federal Prison Population, Death Penalty, 2003-2004[1]

Source: Bureau of Justice Statistics, U.S. Dept. of Justice

As of June 30, 2004, there were 1,494,216 prisoners under the jurisdiction of federal or state adult correctional authorities. The total prison population grew 2.3%, which was less than the average annual growth of 3.5% since 1995. As of mid-2004, these two systems housed 2/3 of the incarcerated population. Jails, which are locally operated and typically hold persons awaiting trial and those with sentences of a year or less, held most of the remainder (713,990); not including those held in community-based programs.

As of June 30, 2004, the rate of incarceration in state and federal prisons for sentences of more than one year was 486 per 100,000 U.S. residents, up from 411 at year-end 1995. Sentenced prisoners numbered 63 out of every 100,000 women and 923 out of every 100,000 men. The number of persons under sentence of death at the end of 2003 was 3,374, down from 3,562 the year before. In 2003, 65 prisoners were executed—6 fewer than in the previous year. Also in 2003, 267 death sentences were overturned or removed, including 155 death sentences commuted and 4 pardons issued by outgoing Illinois Gov. George Ryan in Jan. 2003.

	SENTENCED PRISONERS[1]			DEATH PENALTY, 2003		
	mid-2004	mid-2003	% change 2003-2004	Under sentence of death	Executions	Death penalty
U.S. TOTAL	**1,494,216**	**1,464,197**	**2.1**	**3,374**	**65**	—
Federal institutions	**179,210**	**170,461**	**5.1**	**23**	**1**	**Yes**
State institutions	**1,315,006**	**1,293,736**	**1.6**	**3,351**	**64**	**38**
Northeast	**173,967**	**175,753**	**–1**	256	**0**	—
Connecticut[2]	20,018	20,525	–2.5	7	0	Yes
Maine	2,014	2,009	0.2	—	—	No
Massachusetts[3]	10,365	10,511	–1.4	—	—	No
New Hampshire	2,441	2,483	–1.7	0	0	Yes
New Jersey[4]	28,107	28,213	–0.4	14	0	Yes
New York	64,596	65,914	–2	5	0	(6)
Pennsylvania	40,692	40,545	0.4	230	0	Yes
Rhode Island[2]	3,701	3,569	3.7	—	—	No
Vermont	2,033	1,984	2.5	—	—	No
Midwest	**249,965**	**247,464**	**1.0**	**315**	**7**	—
Illinois[4]	44,379	43,186	2.8	2	0	Yes
Indiana	23,760	22,576	5.2	35	2	Yes
Iowa	8,611	8,395	2.6	—	—	No
Kansas[4]	9,152	9,009	1.6	6	0	(6)
Michigan	48,591	49,524	–1.9	—	—	No
Minnesota	8,613	7,612	13.2	—	—	No
Missouri	30,775	30,649	0.4	52	2	Yes
Nebraska	4,042	4,103	–1.5	7	0	Yes
North Dakota	1,266	1,168	8.4	—	—	No
Ohio[4]	44,770	45,831	–2.3	209	3	Yes
South Dakota	3,101	3,059	1.4	4	0	Yes
Wisconsin	22,905	22,352	2.5	—	—	No
South	**598,246**	**585,211**	**2.2**	**1,866**	**57**	—
Alabama	26,521	28,440	-6.7	192	3	Yes
Arkansas	13,477	12,378	8.9	—	1	Yes
Delaware[2]	6,973	6,879	1.4	16	0	Yes
Florida	84,733	80,352	5.5	364	3	Yes
Georgia[5]	48,625	47,004	3.4	111	3	Yes
Kentucky	17,763	16,377	8.5	35	0	Yes
Louisiana	36,745	36,091	1.8	87	0	Yes
Maryland	23,727	24,186	-1.9	11	0	Yes
Mississippi	20,429	20,542	-0.6	66	0	Yes
North Carolina	34,917	33,334	4.7	195	7	Yes
Oklahoma[2]	24,767	23,004	7.7	102	14	Yes
South Carolina	24,173	24,247	-0.3	71	0	Yes
Tennessee	25,834	25,409	1.7	96	0	Yes
Texas	169,110	167,532	0.9	453	24	Yes
Virginia	35,472	34,733	2.1	27	2	Yes
West Virginia	4,980	4,703	5.9	—	—	No
West	**292,828**	**285,308**	**2.6**	**914**	0	—
Alaska[2]	4,515	4,431	1.9	—	—	No
Arizona[5]	31,631	30,741	2.9	123	0	Yes
California	166,053	163,361	1.6	629	0	Yes
Colorado[4]	19,756	19,085	3.5	3	0	Yes
Hawaii[2]	5,946	5,635	5.5	—	—	No
Idaho	6,312	5,825	8.4	19	0	Yes
Montana	3,800	3,440	10.5	5	0	Yes
Nevada	10,971	10,527	4.2	84	0	Yes
New Mexico	6,341	6,145	3.2	2	0	Yes
Oregon	13,219	12,422	6.4	28	0	Yes
Utah	5,802	5,603	3.6	10	0	Yes
Washington	16,559	16,284	1.7	10	0	Yes
Wyoming	1,923	1,809	6.3	1	0	Yes

Note: District of Columbia inmates sentenced to more than 1 year are now under the jurisdiction of the Federal Bureau of Prisons. Numbers excludes persons held under Armed Forces jurisdiction with a military death sentence for murder. (1) The number of prisoners with a sentence of more than 1 year per 100,000 residents. (2) Prisons and jails form one integrated system. Data include total jail and prison population. (3) The incarceration rate includes an estimated 6,200 inmates sentenced to more than 1 year but held in local jails or houses of corrections. (4) Includes some inmates sentenced to 1 year or less. (5) Population figures are based on custody counts. (6) The New York (6/24) and Kansas (12/17) death penalty statutes were declared unconstitutional in 2004.

IT'S A FACT: The FBI's National DNA Index System (NDIS) database has about 2.5 million DNA profiles for convicted offenders. The NDIS is part of the FBI Laboratory's Combined DNA Index System (CODIS). Since the system began operations in 1990, it has aided in some 26,000 investigations.

Prison Situation Among the States and in the Federal System, Mid-2004

Source: *Prison and Jail Inmates at Midyear 2004,* Bureau of Justice Statistics, U.S. Dept. of Justice

10 largest prison populations, 2004	Number of inmates	10 highest incarceration rates, 2004	Prisoners per 100,000 residents[1]
1. Federal	179,210	1. Louisiana	814
2. Texas	169,110	2. Texas	704
3. California	166,053	3. Oklahoma	684
4. Florida	84,733	4. Mississippi	682
5. New York	64,625	5. South Carolina	555
6. Georgia	48,625	6. Alabama	554
7. Michigan	48,591	7. Georgia	551
8. Ohio	44,770	8. Missouri	536
9. Illinois	44,379	9. Arizona	506
10. Pennsylvania	40,692	10. Florida	489

10 largest % increases in prison population			
Growth 2003-2004	% annual increase	Growth since 1995	% increase
1. Minnesota	13.2	1. Wisconsin	115.4
2. Montanta	10.5	2. North Dakota	107.5
3. Arkansas	8.9	3. West Virginia	104.3
4. Kentucky	8.5	4. Montana	100.6
5. Idaho	8.4	5. Idaho	94.8
North Dakota	8.4	6. Vermont	92.2
7. Oklahoma	7.7	7. Colorado	83.7
8. Oregon	6.4	8. Minnesota	80.8
9. Wyoming	6.3	9. Utah	77.3
10. West Virginia	5.9	10. Oregon	76.1

(1) Prisoners with sentences of more than 1 year. As of Dec. 31, 2002, the District of Columbia had transferred all sentenced felons to federal prison system.

Executions, by State and Method, 1977-2004

Source: Bureau of Justice Statistics, *Capital Punishment 2003,* Nov. 2004; Death Penalty Information Center, NAACP Legal Defense and Education Fund, *Death Row, U.S.A.*

		Lethal injection	Electro-cution	Lethal gas	Firing squad	Hang-ing
TOTAL U.S.	**944**	**776**	**152**	**11**	**2**	**3**
Federal govt.	3	3	0	0	0	0
Alabama	30	6	24	0	0	0
Arizona	22	20	0	2	0	0
Arkansas	26	25	1	0	0	0
California	10	8	0	2	0	0
Colorado	1	1	0	0	0	0
Delaware	13	12	0	0	0	1
Florida	59	15	44	0	0	0
Georgia	36	13	23	0	0	0
Idaho	1	1	0	0	0	0
Illinois	12	12	0	0	0	0
Indiana	11	8	3	0	0	0
Kentucky	2	1	1	0	0	0
Louisiana	27	7	20	0	0	0
Maryland	4	4	0	0	0	0
Mississippi	6	2	0	4	0	0
Missouri	61	61	0	0	0	0
Montana	2	2	0	0	0	0
Nebraska	3	0	3	0	0	0
Nevada	11	10	0	1	0	0
New Mexico	1	1	0	0	0	0
North Carolina	34	32	0	2	0	0
Ohio	15	15	0	0	0	0
Oklahoma	74	74	0	0	0	0
Oregon	2	2	0	0	0	0
Pennsylvania	3	3	0	0	0	0
South Carolina	32	26	6	0	0	0
Tennessee	1	1	0	0	0	0
Texas	336	336	0	0	0	0
Utah	6	4	0	0	2	0
Virginia	94	67	27	0	0	0
Washington	4	2	0	0	0	2
Wyoming	1	1	0	0	0	0

Note: Table shows methods used since the 1976 reinstatement of the death penalty by the Supreme Court. Lethal injection was used in 82% of total executions. 17 states—Alabama, Arizona, Arkansas, California, Delaware, Florida, Georgia, Indiana, Kentucky, Louisiana, Mississippi, Nevada, North Carolina, South Carolina, Utah, Virginia, and Washington—have used 2 methods. 18 states had no executions during the period.

Total Estimated Arrests, 2003

Source: FBI, *Uniform Crime Reports*, 2003

Total, all arrests[1,2]	**13,639,479**
Murder and non-negligent manslaughter	13,190
Forcible rape	26,350
Robbery	107,553
Aggravated assault	449,933
Violent crime[3]	**597,026**
Burglary	290,956
Larceny-theft	1,145,074
Motor vehicle theft	152,934
Arson	16,163
Property crime[4]	**1,605,127**
Other assaults	1,246,698
Forgery and counterfeiting	111,823
Fraud	299,138
Embezzlement	16,826
Stolen property; buying, receiving, possessing	126,775
Vandalism	273,431
Weapons; carrying, possessing, etc.	167,972
Prostitution and commercialized vice	75,190
Sex offenses (except forcible rape and prostitution)	91,546
Drug abuse violations	1,678,192
Gambling	10,954
Offenses against the family and children	136,034
Driving under the influence	1,448,148
Liquor laws	612,079
Drunkenness	548,616
Disorderly conduct	639,371
Vagrancy	28,948
All other offenses	3,665,543
Suspicion	7,163
Curfew and loitering law violations	136,461
Runaways	123,581

(1) Does not include suspicion. (2) Because of rounding, the figures may not add to total. (3) Violent crimes are offenses of murder, forcible rape, robbery, and aggravated assault. (4) Property crimes are offenses of burglary, larceny-theft, motor vehicle theft, and arson.

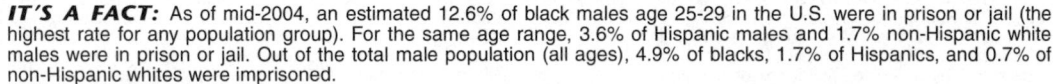

IT'S A FACT: As of mid-2004, an estimated 12.6% of black males age 25-29 in the U.S. were in prison or jail (the highest rate for any population group). For the same age range, 3.6% of Hispanic males and 1.7% non-Hispanic white males were in prison or jail. Out of the total male population (all ages), 4.9% of blacks, 1.7% of Hispanics, and 0.7% of non-Hispanic whites were imprisoned.

Notable Assassinations Since 1865

1865—Apr. 14: U.S. Pres. Abraham Lincoln shot by John Wilkes Booth, a well-known actor with Confederate sympathies, at Ford's Theater in Washington, DC; died Apr. 15.

1881—Mar. 13: Alexander II, of Russia. **July 2:** U.S. Pres. James A. Garfield shot by Charles J. Guiteau, a disappointed office seeker, in Washington, DC; died Sept. 19.

1894—June 24: Pres. Sadi Carnot of France, by Italian anarchist, Sante Caserio, in Lyon.

1898—Sept. 10: Empress Elizabeth of Austria, stabbed by Italian anarchist Luigi Luccheni.

1900—July 29: Umberto I, king of Italy.

1901—Sept. 6: U.S. Pres. William McKinley in Buffalo, NY; died Sept. 14; Leon Czolgosz executed for the crime.

1908—Feb. 1: King Carlos I of Portugal and his son Luis Felipe, in Lisbon.

1913—Feb. 23: Mexican Pres. Francisco I. Madero and Vice Pres. Jose Pino Suarez. **Mar. 18:** George, king of Greece.

1914—June 28: Archduke Francis Ferdinand of Austria-Hungary and his wife in Sarajevo, Bosnia, by Gavrilo Princip.

1916—Dec. 30: Grigori Rasputin, powerful Russian monk.

1918—July 12: Grand Duke Michael of Russia, at Perm. **July 16:** Nicholas II, former (abdicated) czar of Russia; his wife, the Czarina Alexandra; their son, Czarevitch Alexis; their daughters, Grand Duchesses Olga, Tatiana, Marie, Anastasia; and 4 members of their household, executed by Bolsheviks at Ekaterinburg.

1920—May 20: Mexican Pres. Gen. Venustiano Carranza in Tlaxcalantongo.

1922—Aug. 22: Michael Collins, Irish revolutionary. **Dec. 16:** Polish Pres.Gabriel Narutowicz in Warsaw.

1923—July 20: Gen. Francisco "Pancho" Villa, ex-rebel leader, in Parral, Mexico.

1928—July 17: Gen. Alvaro Obregon, president-elect of Mexico, in San Angel, Mexico.

1932—May 6: Pres. Paul Doumer of France shot by Russian émigré, Pavel Gorgulov, in Paris.

1934—July 25: In Vienna, Austrian Chancellor Engelbert Dollfuss by Nazis.

1935—Sept. 8: U.S. Sen. Huey P. Long shot in Baton Rouge, LA, by Dr. Carl Austin Weiss; died Sept. 10.

1940—Aug. 20: Leon Trotsky (Lev Bronstein), 63, exiled Soviet war minister, near Mexico City.

1948—Jan. 30: Mohandas K. Gandhi, 78, shot in New Delhi, India, by Nathuram Vinayak Godse. **Sept. 17:** Count Folke Bernadotte, UN mediator for Palestine, by Jewish extremists in Jerusalem.

1951—July 20: King Abdullah ibn Hussein of Jordan. **Oct. 16:** Prime Min. Liaquat Ali Khan of Pakistan shot in Rawalpindi.

1956—Sept. 21: Pres. Anastasio Somoza of Nicaragua, shot in Leon; died Sept. 29.

1957—July 26: Pres. Carlos Castillo Armas of Guatemala, in Guatemala City by one of his own guards.

1958—July 14: King Faisal of Iraq, Crown Prince Abdullah, and July 15, Prem. Nuri as-Said, by rebels in Baghdad.

1959—Sept. 25: Prime Min. Solomon Bandaranaike of Ceylon, by Buddhist monk in Colombo.

1961—Jan. 17: Ex-Prem. Patrice Lumumba of the Congo, in Katanga Province. **May 30:** Dominican dictator Rafael Leonidas Trujillo Molina, near Ciudad Trujillo.

1963—June 12: Medgar W. Evers, NAACP's Mississippi field secretary, shot dead by Byron De La Beckwith in Jackson, MS. **Nov. 2:** Pres. Ngo Dinh Diem of South Vietnam and his brother, Ngo Dinh Nhu, in a military coup. **Nov. 22:** U.S. Pres. John F. Kennedy shot while riding in motorcade in Dallas, TX; accused gunman Lee Harvey Oswald murdered by Jack Ruby while awaiting trial.

1965—Jan. 21: Iranian Prem. Hassan Ali Mansour in Tehran; 4 executed. **Feb. 21**. Malcolm X, black nationalist, shot in New York City.

1966—Sept. 6: Prime Min. Hendrik F. Verwoerd of South Africa stabbed to death in parliament at Cape Town.

1968—Apr. 4: Rev. Dr. Martin Luther King Jr. fatally shot in Memphis, TN; James Earl Ray convicted of crime. **June 5:** Sen. Robert F. Kennedy (D, NY) shot in Los Angeles; Sirhan Sirhan convicted of crime.

1971—Nov. 28: Prime Min. Wasfi Tal of Jordan, in Cairo, by Palestinian guerrillas.

1973—Mar. 2: U.S. Amb. Cleo A. Noel Jr., U.S. Charge d'Affaires George C. Moore, and Belgian Charge d'Affaires Guy Eid killed by Palestinian guerrillas in Khartoum, Sudan.

1974—Aug. 19: U.S. Amb. to Cyprus, Rodger P. Davies, killed by sniper's bullet in Nicosia.

1975—Feb. 11: Pres. Richard Ratsimandrava, of Madagascar, shot in Tananarive. **Mar. 25:** Saudi Arabian King Faisal shot by nephew Prince Musad Abdel Aziz, in Riyadh. **Aug. 15:** Bangladesh Pres. Sheik Mujibur Rahman killed in coup.

1976—Feb. 13: Nigerian head of state, Gen. Murtala Ramat Mohammed, by self-styled "young revolutionaries."

1977—Mar. 16: Kamal Jumblat, Lebanese Druse chieftain, shot near Beirut. **Mar. 18:** Congo Pres. Marien Ngouabi shot in Brazzaville.

1978—May 9: Former Italian Prem. Aldo Moro killed by Red Brigades terrorists who abducted him Mar. 16 in Rome and killed 5 bodyguards. **July 9**. Former Iraqi Prem. Abdul Razak Al-Naif shot in London.

1979—Feb. 14: U.S. Amb. Adolph Dubs shot by Afghan Muslim extremists in Kabul. **Aug. 27:** Lord Mountbatten, World War II hero, and 2 others killed when a bomb exploded on his fishing boat off the coast of Co. Sligo, Ire. IRA claimed responsibility. **Oct. 26:** South Korean Pres. Park Chung Hee and 6 bodyguards fatally shot by Kim Jae Kyu, head of South Korean CIA, and 5 aides in Seoul.

1980—Apr. 12: Liberian Pres. William R. Tolbert slain in military coup. **Sept. 17:** Former Nicaraguan Pres. Anastasio Somoza Debayle shot in Paraguay.

1981—Oct. 6: Egyptian Pres. Anwar al-Sadat shot by commandos while reviewing a military parade in Cairo; 7 others killed, 28 wounded; 4 convicted as assassins and executed.

1982—Sept. 14: Lebanese Pres.-elect Bashir Gemayel killed by bomb in east Beirut.

1983—Aug. 21: Philippine opposition leader Benigno Aquino Jr. shot by gunman at Manila International Airport.

1984—Oct. 31: Indian Prime Min. Indira Gandhi shot and killed by 2 Sikh bodyguards, in New Delhi.

1986—Feb. 28: Swedish Prem. Olof Palme shot by gunman on Stockholm street.

1987—June 1: Lebanese Prem. Rashid Karami killed when bomb exploded aboard a helicopter.

1988—Apr. 16: PLO military chief Khalil Wazir (Abu Jihad) gunned down by Israeli commandos in Tunisia.

1989—Aug. 18: Colombian pres. candidate Luis Carlos Galan killed by Medellín cartel drug traffickers at campaign rally in Bogotá. **Nov. 22:** Lebanese Pres. Rene Moawad killed when bomb exploded next to his motorcade.

1990—Mar. 22: Pres. candidate Bernando Jamamillo Ossa shot by gunman at an airport in Bogotá.

1991—May 21: Rajiv Gandhi, former prime min. of India, killed by bomb during election rally in Madras.

1992—June 29: Mohammed Boudiaf, pres. of Algeria, shot by gunman in Annaba.

1993—May 1: Ranasinghe Premadasa, pres. of Sri Lanka, killed by bomb in Colombo.

1994—Mar. 23: Luis Donaldo Colosio Murrieta, Mexican pres. candidate, shot by gunman Mario Aburto Martinez. **Apr. 6:** Burundian Pres. Cyprien Ntaryamira and Rwandan Pres. Juvenal Habyarimana killed, with 8 others, when their plane was apparently shot down.

1995—Nov. 4: Yitzhak Rabin, prime min. of Israel, shot by gunman Yigal Amir at peace rally in Tel Aviv.

1996—Oct. 2: Andrei Lukanov, former Bulgarian prime min., shot outside his home by an unidentified gunman.

1998—Feb. 6: Claude Erigmac, prefect of Corsica, shot in the back while walking to a concert, by 2 unidentified gunmen. **Apr. 26:** Guatemalan Rom. Catholic Bishop Juan Gerardi Conedera, human rights champion, found beaten to death in Guatemala City; 4 persons convicted, June 8, 2001.

1999—Mar. 23: Paraguayan Vice-Pres. Luis Maria Argaña, ambushed and shot to death, along with his driver, by 4 unidentified assailants. **Apr. 9:** Niger's Pres. Ibrahim Bare Mainassara, ambushed and killed by dissident soldiers. **Oct. 27:** Armenia's Prime Min. Vazgen Sarkissian, along with 7 others, was shot to death during a session of Parliament.

2000—Jan. 15: Serbian paramilitary leader Zeljko Raznjatovic (alias Arkan), with 2 others, shot and killed by unidentified gunman in Belgrade hotel lobby; 4 suspects later charged with the killing. **June 8:** Brig. Gen. Stephen Saunders, Britain's senior military representative in Greece, shot and killed by 2 men on motorcycle, while driving a car in an Athens suburb.

2001—Jan. 16: Congolese Pres. Laurent Kabila, shot to death by bodyguard at pres. palace in Kinshasa. **June 1:** Nepal's King Birendra, Queen Aiswarya, and 7 other royals fatally shot by Crown Prince Dipendra, who also fatally wounded himself. **Sept. 9:** Afghan Northern Alliance (anti-Taliban) guerrilla leader Ahmed Shah Massoud, injured in suicide-attack bombing in N. Afghanistan by 2 Arabs posing as journalists; died Sept. 15. **Oct. 14:** Abdel Rahman Hamad, a leader of Palestinian militant group Hamas, shot dead by Israeli military snipers. **Oct. 17:** Israeli tourism min. Rehavam Zeevi, fatally shot; Popular Front for the Liberation of Palestine (PFLP) claimed responsibility.

2002—May 6: Dutch right-wing politician Pim Fortuyn shot dead outside a radio station in Hilversum, Netherlands. **July 6:** Afghan Vice Pres. Haji Abdul Qadir, shot dead outside his office in Kabul. **July 23:** Salah Sherhada, a founder of the armed wing of Hamas, killed with 14 others in an assassination air strike on Gaza City by an Israeli fighter jet.

2003—Mar. 12: Serbian Prime Min. Zoran Djindjic, shot dead by snipers outside government headquarters in Belgrade. **Apr. 10:** Shiite Muslim cleric Abdul Majid al-Khoei attacked by crowd, hacked to death at Imam Ali mosque, Najaf, Iraq. **Apr. 17:** Sergei Yushenkov, former Russian legislator and Liberal Party head, shot dead outside apartment in Moscow. **Aug. 29:** Prominent Shiite Muslim cleric Bakir al-Hakim killed in car bombing at Imam Ali mosque in Najaf, Iraq. **Sept. 10:** Swedish Foreign Min. Anna Lindh stabbed in dept. store in Stockholm; died Sept. 11.

2004—Feb. 13: Former Chechen Pres. Zelimkhan Yandarbiyev killed after car exploded in Qatar. **Mar. 22:** Sheik Ahmed Yassin, spiritual leader of Hamas, killed by Israeli missile attack in Gaza City. **Apr. 17:** Hamas leader Abdel Aziz Rantisi killed by Israeli missile strike in Gaza City. **May 9:** Bomb exploded at WWII memorial service in Grozny, Chechnya, killing republic's pres., Akhmad Kadyrov. **May 17:** Car bomb exploded at Green Zone checkpoint in Baghdad, killing Iraqi Gov. Council Pres. Ezzedine Salim. **June 12:** Iraqi Dep. Foreign Min. Bassam Salih Kubba gunned down outside home in Baghdad.

2005—Jan. 4: Baghdad Gov. Ali al-Haidari gunned down by insurgents in Baghdad, Iraq. **Feb. 14:** Former Lebanese P.M.. Rafik al-Hariri killed when motorcade bombed in Beirut, Lebanon. **June 21:** Lebanese Communist Party leader George Hawi killed after car bombed in Beirut. **July 1:** Sheik Kamaledding al-Ghuraifi, senior aide to Grand Ayatollah Ali Sistani, in Iraq, shot and killed on his way to Friday prayers. **July 7:** Egyptian Amb.-designate Ihab al-Sherif was killed in Iraq, by kidnappers who had abducted him July 2. **Aug. 12:** Sri Lanka Foreign Minister Lakshman Kadirgamar, an ethnic Tamil, shot to death at his home in Colombo. Liberation Tigers of Tamil Eelam suspected.

Assassination Attempts

1912—Oct. 14: Former U.S. Pres. Theodore Roosevelt shot and wounded by demented man in Milwaukee, WI.

1933—Feb. 15: In Miami, FL, Joseph Zangara, anarchist, shot at Pres.-elect Franklin D. Roosevelt, but a woman seized his arm; bullet fatally wounded Mayor Anton J. Cermak, of Chicago, who died Mar. 6.

1944—July 20: Adolf Hitler injured when a bomb, planted by a German officer, exploded in his headquarters. One aide killed and 12 injured.

1950—Nov. 1: In an attempt to assassinate Pres. Harry Truman, 2 members of a Puerto Rican nationalist movement—Griselio Torresola and Oscar Collazo—tried to shoot their way into Blair House. Torresola killed, a White House policeman, Pvt. Leslie Coffelt, was fatally shot.

1970—Nov. 27: Pope Paul VI unharmed by knife-wielding assailant who attempted to attack him in Manila airport.

1972—May 15: Alabama Gov. George Wallace shot in Laurel, MD, by Arthur Bremer; seriously crippled.

1975—Sept. 5: Pres. Gerald R. Ford unharmed when a Secret Service agent grabbed a pistol aimed at him by Lynette (Squeaky) Fromme, a Charles Manson follower, in Sacramento, CA. **Sept. 22:** Pres. Ford again unharmed when Sara Jane Moore fired a revolver at him in San Francisco; a bystander helped deflect the shot.

1980—May 29: Civil rights leader Vernon E. Jordan Jr. shot and wounded in Ft. Wayne, IN.

1981—Jan. 16: Irish political activist Bernadette Devlin McAliskey and her husband shot and seriously wounded by 3 members of a Protestant paramilitary group in Co. Tyrone, Ire. **Mar. 30:** Pres. Ronald Reagan, along with Press Sec. James Brady, Secret Service agent Timothy J. McCarthy, and Washington, DC, policeman Thomas Delahanty shot and seriously wounded by John W. Hinckley Jr. in Washington, DC. **May 13:** Pope John Paul II and 2 bystanders shot and wounded by Mehmet Ali Agca, an escaped Turkish murderer, in St. Peter's Square, Rome.

1982—May 12: Pope John Paul II unharmed after guards overpowered a man with a knife, in Fatima, Portugal.

1984—Oct. 12: British Prime Min. Margaret Thatcher unharmed when a bomb, said to have been planted by the IRA, exploded at the Grand Hotel in Brighton, England, during a Party conference. Four died, including a member of Parliament.

1986—Sept. 7: Chilean Pres. Gen. Augusto Pinochet Ugarte unharmed after motorcade was attacked by rebels.

1995—June 26: Egyptian Pres. Hosni Mubarak unharmed when gunmen fired on his motorcade in Addis Ababa, Ethiopia. Four died, including 2 Ethiopian police officers.

1997—Feb. 12: Colombian Pres. Ernesto Samper Pizano unharmed when a bomb exploded on a runway in Barranquilla as his plane was preparing to land. **Apr. 30:** Tajik Pres. Imamali Rakhmanov injured when a grenade was thrown at him.

1998—Feb. 9: Georgian Pres. Eduard A. Shevardnadze unharmed when gunmen fired on his motorcade in Tbilisi, Georgia. Three died, including 2 bodyguards and 1 assailant.

2000—Sept. 18: Armed men attempted to assassinate Côte d'Ivoire military leader Gen. Robert Guei in a predawn raid.

2002—Apr. 14: Leading Colombian pres. candidate Alvaro Uribe Velez unharmed after bomb exploded under parked bus as his motorcade passed in Barranquilla; 3 bystanders killed. **July 14:** French Pres. Jacques Chirac, unharmed after Maxime Brunerie, a gunman with ties to neo-Nazi groups, fired at his open-top jeep during a Bastille Day parade in Paris. **Sept. 5:** Afghan Pres. Hamid Karzai, unharmed after militant shot at car in Kandahar. **Nov. 25:** Turkmenistan Pres. Saparmurat Niyazov unharmed after gunmen open fire on his motorcade in Ashgabat.

2003—Dec. 14: Pakistani Pres. Pervez Musharraf unharmed after bomb detonates on bridge in Rawalpindi seconds after his motorcade crosses over.

2004—Mar. 19: Taiwanese Pres. Chen Shui-bian shot while campaigning in motorcade; minor injuries. **July 13:** Separatists bombed motorcade of Sergei Abramov, Chenchya's acting pres. **Sept. 16:** Rocket fired at helicopter carrying Afghan Pres. Hamid Karzai, nr. Gardez, Afghanistan.

2005—Mar. 15: Kosovo Pres. Ibrahim Rugova survived after a bomb damaged the vehicle he was in, as his motorcade traveled through Pristina. **July 12:** Lebanon's pro-Syrian defense min. Elias Murr, wounded by a car explosion in Beirut suburb.

Notable U.S. Kidnappings Since 1924

Robert Franks, 13, in Chicago, **May 22, 1924,** by 2 youths, Richard Loeb and Nathan Leopold, who killed boy. Demand for $10,000 ignored. Loeb died in prison; Leopold paroled 1958.

Charles A. Lindbergh Jr., 20 mos. old, in Hopewell, NJ, **Mar. 1, 1932;** found dead **May 12.** Ransom of $50,000 paid to man identified as Bruno Richard Hauptmann, 35, paroled German convict who entered U.S. illegally. Hauptmann convicted after spectacular trial at Flemington; electrocuted in Trenton, NJ, prison, **Apr. 3, 1936.**

William A. Hamm Jr., 39, in St. Paul, **June 15, 1933.** $100,000 paid. Alvin Karpis given life, paroled in 1969.

Charles F. Urschel, in Oklahoma City, **July 22, 1933.** Released **July 31** after $200,000 paid. George "Machine Gun" Kelly and 5 others sentenced to life.

Brooke L. Hart, 22, in San Jose, CA. Thomas Thurmond and John Holmes arrested after demanding $40,000 ransom. When Hart's body was found in San Francisco Bay, **Nov. 26, 1933,** a mob attacked the jail and lynched the 2 kidnappers.

June Robles, 6, abducted in Tucson, AZ, **Apr. 25, 1934.** Missing for 19 days after ransom note sent to parents. Found alive in iron cage buried in the desert. No arrests made.

George Weyerhaeuser, 9, in Tacoma, WA, **May 24, 1935.** Returned home **June 1** after $200,000 paid. Kidnappers given 20 to 60 years.

Charles Mattson, 10, in Tacoma, WA, **Dec. 27, 1936.** Found dead **Jan. 11, 1937.** Kidnapper asked $28,000, but failed to contact for delivery.

Arthur Fried, in White Plains, NY, **Dec. 4, 1937.** Body not found. Two kidnappers executed.

Robert C. Greenlease, 6, taken from Kansas City, MO, school **Sept. 28, 1953,** held for $600,000. Body was found Oct. 7. Bonnie Brown Heady and Carl A. Hall pleaded guilty and were executed.

Peter Weinberger, 32 days old, Westbury, NY, **July 4, 1956,** for $2,000 ransom, not paid. Child found dead. Angelo John LaMarca, 31, convicted, executed.

Lee Crary, 8, in Everett, WA, **Sept. 22, 1957;** $10,000 ransom, not paid. Escaped after 3 days, led police to George E. Collins, who was convicted.

Frank Sinatra Jr., 19, from hotel room in Lake Tahoe, CA, **Dec. 8, 1963.** Released **Dec. 11** after his father paid $240,000 ransom. Three men sentenced to prison.

Barbara Jane Mackle, 20, abducted **Dec. 17, 1968,** from Atlanta, GA, motel; found unharmed 3 days later, buried in a coffin-like box 18 inches underground, after her father had paid $500,000 ransom; Gary Steven Krist sentenced to life, Ruth Eisenmann-Schier to 7 years.

Mrs. Roy Fuchs, 35, and 3 children held hostage 2 hours, **May 14, 1969,** in Long Island, NY, released after her husband, a bank manager, paid kidnappers $129,000 in bank funds; 4 men arrested, ransom recovered.

Virginia Piper, 49, abducted **July 27, 1972,** from her home in suburban Minneapolis; found unharmed near Duluth 2 days later after husband paid $1 million ransom.

Patricia "Patty" Hearst, 19, taken from her Berkeley, CA, apartment **Feb. 4, 1974.** "Symbionese Liberation Army" captors demanded her father, publisher Randolph Hearst, give millions to the area's poor. Implicated in a San Francisco bank holdup, **Apr. 15.** The FBI, **Sept. 18, 1975,** captured her and others; they were indicted on various charges. Patricia Hearst convicted of bank robbery, **Mar. 20, 1976;** released from prison under executive clemency, **Feb. 1, 1979.** In 1978, William and Emily Harris were sentenced to 10 years to life for the kidnapping; both were paroled in 1983.

J. Reginald Murphy, 40, an editor of *Atlanta* (GA) *Constitution,* kidnapped **Feb. 20, 1974;** freed **Feb. 22** after newspaper paid $700,000 ransom. William A. H. Williams arrested; most of the money recovered.

E. B. Reville, Hepzibah, GA, banker, and wife, Jean, kidnapped **Sept. 30, 1974.** Ransom of $30,000 paid. He was found alive; Jean Reville was found dead **Oct. 2.**

Jack Teich, Kings Point, NY, steel executive, seized **Nov. 12, 1974;** released **Nov. 19** after payment of $750,000.

Adam Walsh, 6, abducted from a Hollywood, FL, department store, **July 27, 1981.** Severed head found 2 weeks later. John Walsh, Adam's father, became active in raising awareness about missing children.

Sidney J. Reso, oil company executive, seized **Apr. 29, 1992;** died **May 3;** Arthur D. Seale and wife, Irene, arrested **June 19.** Arthur Seale pleaded guilty, sentenced to life in prison; Irene Seale sentenced to 20-year prison term.

Polly Klaas, 12, Petaluma, CA, abducted at knife point, **Oct. 1, 1993,** during a slumber party at her home. Police arrested Richard Allen Davis on **Nov. 30;** he led them to her body, found **Dec. 4** in wooded area of Cloverdale, CA. Davis found guilty **June 18, 1996**, and sentenced to death **Sept. 26.**

Marshall I. Wais, 79, owner of 2 San Francisco steel companies, kidnapped **Nov. 19, 1996,** from his San Francisco home. Released unharmed the same day after $500,000 ransom paid; Thomas William Taylor and Michael K. Robinson arrested the same day.

Daniel Pearl, 38, reporter for *Wall Street Journal*, disappeared **Jan. 23, 2002,** while researching story in Karachi, Pakistan. British-born militant Ahmad Omar Saeed Sheikh **Feb. 14** admitted to organizing the kidnapping and said Pearl was dead. Sheikh and 3 others convicted **July 15** of kidnapping and murder by a judge in Hyderabad.

Elizabeth Smart, 14, abducted from her home in Salt Lake City, UT, **June 5, 2002,** allegedly by Brian D. Mitchell, and forced to live with Mitchell and wife Wanda for 9 months in various U.S. cities; found walking down street with captors in Sandy, UT, 15 miles from Smart family home, **Mar. 12, 2003.** Mitchell was found incompetent to stand trial, **July 26, 2005**, with review to be held after 90 days' treatment.

Natalee Holloway, 18, of Birmingham, AL, vanished **May 24, 2005,** on high school graduation trip to Aruba. Officials believed she was kidnapped and murdered, and detained several suspects; as of Sept. 2005, all had been released.

Notable Terrorist Incidents Worldwide, 1971-Sept. 2005

Note: Selected noteworthy incidents, excluding most assassinations, kidnappings, and military targets. Not including 2005 incidents in Iraq; see Chronology of the Year's Events.

Source: U.S. Dept. of State; *Facts On File World News Digest @ Facts.com*; World Almanac research

1971—Mar. 1: Senate wing of U.S. Capitol Building in Wash., DC, bombed by Weather Underground; no deaths.

1972—July 21: "Bloody Friday." Provisional IRA exploded 20+ bombs across Belfast, N. Ireland; 9 killed, hundreds injured. **Sept. 5:** Members of Palestinian group Black September killed 2 Israeli athletes and seized 9 others at Olympic Village in Munich, W. Germany, during Summer Olympics. 9 hostages, 5 militants, 1 Ger. officer died in botched rescue.

1973—Dec. 17: Palestinian gunmen attacked Rome airport and bombed plane on tarmac; hijacked Lufthansa plane with 5 Italian hostages to Athens, then to Kuwait; 31 killed in all.

1974—June 17: Houses of Parliament in London, England, bombed by Provisional IRA; 11 injured.

1975—Jan. 27: Puerto Rican FALN nationalists bombed Fraunces Tavern in lower Manhattan; 4 killed, 53 injured. **Jan. 29:** U.S. State Dept. building in Wash., DC, bombed by Weather Underground; no deaths.

1976—June 27: Palestinian and Baader-Meinhof militants forced Air France jet to land at Entebbe, Uganda. Israeli army rescued 103 hostages from airport terminal in battle with terrorists and Ugandan troops, July 3-4; 32 killed in all.

1978—Mar. 11: Palestinian militants landed on beach nr. Haifa, Israel; shot civilians and hijacked bus with hostages to Tel Aviv; exploded at roadblock; 43 killed.

1979—Nov. 4: Iranian radicals seized U.S. embassy in Tehran, taking 66 Americans hostage. 52 were held until Jan. 20, 1981. **Nov. 20:** 200 Islamic terrorists seized Grand Mosque in Mecca, Saudi Arabia, and held hundreds of pilgrims hostage. Saudi forces retook mosque Dec. 4; about 250 died.

1983—April 18: Hezbollah suicide truck bomb at the U.S. embassy in Beirut, Lebanon, killed 63 people. **Oct. 9:** N. Korean agents ambushed a S. Korean govt. delegation in Rangoon, Burma, killing 21. **Oct. 23:** Hezbollah suicide truck bombings of U.S. and French military bases, Beirut, Lebanon; 242 Americans, 58 French killed.

1984——Sept. 20: U.S. embassy annex near Beirut, Lebanon, bombed, killing approx. 20.

1985—June 14: Hezbollah members hijacked TWA Flight 847 with 153 passengers and crew to Beirut; 39 held for 17 days; 1 U.S. Navy sailor killed. **June 23:** Air India Flight 182 destroyed by bomb off coast of Ireland; 329 killed. Blamed on Sikh terrorists. **Apr. 12:** 18 killed in bomb blast at restaurant near Air Force base in Torrejon, Spain. **Oct. 7:** 4 Palestinians hijacked Italian cruise ship *Achille Lauro*; 1 passenger killed. **Nov. 23:** EgyptAir Flight 648 from Athens to Cairo hijacked to Malta by Palestinian group Abu Nidal; 60 killed in rescue. **Dec. 27:** Palestinian militants opened fire at El-Al airline counters at Rome and Vienna airports; 19 killed.

1986—Apr. 5: Nightclub in Berlin, W. Germany, bombed, 3 killed, incl. 2 U.S. servicemen; 200+ hurt. 3 Libyan embassy workers in Germany convicted in bombing.

1987—Apr. 17: 21. Bomb in Sri Lanka capital killed 100+; blamed on Tamil rebels who, 4 days later, attacked Sinhalese travelers on highway, killing 127. **June 19:** Basque group ETA bombed supermarket garage in Barcelona, Spain; 21 killed, 45 injured. **Nov. 29:** Bomb planted by N. Korean agents exploded on Korean Air Lines Flight 858 over Indian Ocean; 115 killed.

1988—Dec. 21: Pan Am Flight 103 exploded over Lockerbie, Scotland, killing all 259 aboard and 11 on the ground; Libya took responsibility for bombing in Aug. 2003.

1989—Sept. 19: French UTA Flight 722 from Congo to Paris destroyed by bomb in midair over Niger; 171 killed. Several Libyan officials convicted in absentia; no official admission.

1992—Mar. 17: Israeli embassy in Buenos Aires, Argentina, bombed; 28 killed, 200+ injured. Hezbollah suspected.

1993—Feb. 2: Truck bomb exploded in World Trade Center garage in New York City; 6 killed. Blast later linked to al-Qaeda. **Mar. 12-19:** At least 11 bombs ripped through Bombay and Calcutta, India; 300+ killed.

1994—Feb. 25: U.S.-born Israeli settler Baruch Goldstein opened fire in mosque in Hebron, West Bank; about 30 Muslim worshippers killed. **July 18:** Buenos Aires Jewish center bombed; 87 killed; blamed on Hezbollah.

1995—Mar. 20: 12 killed and over 5,000 injured when Japanese Aum Shinri-kyu cult members released Sarin nerve gas in several Tokyo subway cars. **Apr. 19:** Murrah Federal Building in Oklahoma City bombed, killing 168 and injuring 500+. Timothy McVeigh and Terry Nichols convicted in bombing. McVeigh executed, June 11, 2001; Nichols sentenced to life in prison, 1998, 2004. **Nov. 13:** U.S. miltary compound in Riyadh, Saudi Arabia, bombed by Islamic Movement of Change; 7 killed. **Nov. 19:** Suicide bomber drove into Egyptian embassy in Islamabad, Pakistan; at least 16 killed, 60 injured.

1996—Jan. 31: Tamil Tigers drove explosive-laden truck into Central Bank in Colombo, Sri Lanka; 90 killed. **Feb. 25:** Hamas suicide bombers hit 2 buses in Jerusalem; 26 killed. **Mar. 4:** Bomb outside Tel Aviv shopping mall killed 14, injured 130. **June 25:** Bomb-laden fuel truck exploded outside Khobar Towers, a U.S. military complex in Dhahran, Saudi Arabia; killed 19. **June 27:** Bomb exploded at Centennial Olympic Park in Atlanta, GA, during Summer Games; killed 2, injured 100+; suspect Eric Robert Rudolph arrested in 2003, pleaded guilty; sentenced ot life in prison Aug. 22, 2005. **Dec. 3:** Bomb exploded on subway train in Paris; 4 killed, 86 injured; blamed on Algerian extremists.

IT'S A FACT: A reporter's request in late 1949 for the names of the "toughest guys" the FBI was seeking led to the founding of the Ten Most Wanted Fugitives program in March 1950. Criminals on the list have long records of serious crimes and/or are considered a menace to society. As of March 2005, there have been 480 fugitives on the list, 7 of them women. Over the years, 147 captures of Most-Wanted Fugitives have come about because of citizens' recognition of fugitives through the publicity program. In the 1950s, those listed were primarily bank robbers, burglars, and car thieves. As of Sept. 2005, the list included terrorist leaders Osama bin Laden, as well as several fugitives charged with bank robbery, murder, or child pornography.

1997—Nov. 17: Gamaa al-Islamiya gunmen killed 58 tourists and 4 Egyptians in Valley of the Kings near Luxor, Egypt.
1998—Aug. 7: U.S. embassies in Nairobi, Kenya, and Dar-es-Salaam, Tanzania, bombed; 257 people killed; al-Qaeda blamed. **Aug. 15:** IRA car bomb exploded outside courthouse in Omagh, N. Ireland; killed 29, injured 300+. **Oct. 18:** National Liberation Army of Colombia blew up Ocensa oil pipeline; about 71 killed, 100+ injured.
1999—Sept. 9-16: 3 apt. buildings bombed in Moscow and Volgodansk, S. Russia; about 300 killed. Chechen rebels blamed.
2000—Oct. 12: U.S.S. *Cole* rammed by dinghy full of explosives while docking in Aden, Yemen; 17 U.S. sailors killed, 39 injured. Blamed on al-Qaeda.
2001—Sept. 11: 19 al-Qaeda terrorists hijacked 4 U.S. domestic flights, including planes that crashed into World Trade Center towers and Pentagon. Total dead minus hijackers: 2,973, deadliest attack of terrorism yet on U.S. soil. **Sept.-Nov. 7:** letters tainted with deadly anthrax bacteria mailed through U.S. postal system killed 5; unsolved.
2002—Mar. 27: Suicide bombing at hotel in Netanya, Israel, during Passover celebration; 27 killed. **Oct 12:** Resort in Bali, Indonesia, bombed; 202 dead; Jemaah Islamiah blamed. **Oct. 23:** Chechen guerrillas seized theater in Moscow, held 700+ hostages; Russian authorities gassed theater; most guerrillas and about 128 hostages were killed. **Nov. 28:** Suicide bombers destroyed Israeli-owned hotel near Mombasa, Kenya; 13 killed. At the same time, 2 missiles narrowly missed Israeli plane taking off from Mombasa airport; blamed on al-Qaeda. **Dec. 27:** Chechen rebels plowed truck bomb into pro-Russian gov. headquarters in Grozny, Chechnya; 80 killed, 152 injured.
2003—May 12.: Truck bombing near gov. buildings hits Znamenskoye, Chechnya; 59 killed. **May 12-13:** Al-Qaeda militants detonated car bombs at 3 residential complexes used by westerners in Riyadh, Saudi Arabia; 34 killed. **May 16:** 5 explosions in Casablanca, Morocco; 44 killed, 100+ wounded. Blamed on al-Qaeda. **May 17-19:** 5 suicide bombings in Israel; 17 killed; Hamas and al-Aqsa Martyrs brigade blamed. **Aug. 1:** Truck bomb hit military hospital in Mozdok, Russia, near Chechnya; 50 killed; blamed on Chechen rebels. **Aug. 5:** Car bomb hit Marriott hotel in Jakarta, Indonesia; 12 killed, 150 injured, blamed on Jemaah Islamiah. **Aug. 19:** UN headquarters in Baghdad bombed by truck, 22 killed, including UN envoy to Iraq. **Aug. 25:** 2 bombs exploded in taxis in Mumbai (Bombay), India; 46 killed, 100+ injured; Islamic militants suspected. **Oct. 27:** Suicide bombings at Intl. Red Cross and police stations; 40 killed. **Nov. 15:** 2 synagogues in Istanbul, Turkey, bombed; 25 killed. **Nov. 20:** British consulate and offices of HSBC, a British bank, bombed in Istanbul, Turkey; 27 killed incl. Br. cons. gen. Blamed on al-Qaeda. **Dec. 5:** Suicide bombing on commuter train in Yessentuki, S Russia; 44 killed, 150 injured; blamed on Chechen rebels. **Dec. 9:** Chechen suicide bombing outside National Hotel in Red Square, Moscow; 5 killed.
2004—Feb. 6: Bomb exploded on Moscow subway; 39 killed, 130 injured; Chechen rebels blamed. **Mar. 11:** Al-Qaeda cell bombed 4 commuter trains during morning rush hour in Madrid, Spain; 191 killed, about 1,200 injured. **Mar. 28-29:** Suicide bombings by Muslim militants hit Tashkent, Uzbekistan; 19 killed. **Apr. 21:** Car bomb destroyed Saudi govt. security building in Riyadh; 4 killed, 148 injured. **May 29:** Al-Qaeda militants stormed foreigner compound in Khobar, Saudi Arabia, taking hostages; 22 killed. **July 30:** U.S. and Israeli embassies in Tashkent, Uzbekistan, bombed simultaneously; 2 killed. **Aug. 24:** 2 Russian passenger planes crashed nearly simultaneously in diff. parts of Russia; 90 killed; blamed on Chechen rebels. **Sept. 1:** Militants seized school in Beslan, in N Ossetia, Russia; held 1,000+ hostage for 3 days before Russian troops stormed school. About 330 killed, incl. 27 hostage-takers. Blamed on Chechen militants. **Sept. 9:** Australian embassy in Jakarta, Indonesia, bombed; 9 killed; blamed on Jemaah Islamiah.
2005—July 7: Four bombs exploded on 3 separate subways and a bus in central London, UK; 52 killed, incl. bombers; about 700 injured. **July 21:** Four bombs placed on 3 subways and a bus in London malfunction. **July 23:** 3 car bombs explode near resorts at Sharm el Sheik, Egypt; about 90 killed. **Aug. 17:** More than 400 small bombs exploded in cities and towns across Bangladesh, killing 2 and injuring at least 125; Jamaat ul-Mujahedeen Bangladesh claimed responsility. **Aug. 19:** Three rockets fired from Jordan hit cities of Eilat, Israel, and Aqaba, Jordan. One missile flies over a docked U.S. naval ship; 1 death.

Genocide

by Aram A. Schvey, Crowley Fellow and Adjunct Professor at Fordham University School of Law

Sources include: Convention on the Prevention and Punishment of the Crime of Genocide, United Nations Treaty Series 277; Rome Statute of the International Criminal Court.

The term "genocide" (literally "murder of a race") was coined by Professor Raphael Lemkin (1900-1959) in 1944 and refers to the intentional destruction or attempted destruction of a national, ethnic, racial, or religious group, whether in wartime or peacetime. Genocide is defined as killing members of the group, causing serious bodily harm to members of the group, or otherwise attempting to bring about its destruction, including preventing births or transferring children away from the group. Although the legal definition of genocide does not extend to political groups, the term is often used colloquially to refer to large-scale political violence.

The prohibition against genocide is part of customary international law and is codified in the Convention on the Prevention and Punishment of the Crime of Genocide ("Genocide Convention"), entered into force in 1951. Today, more than 130 nations, including the United States, are parties to it. Genocide is also prohibited by the domestic laws of many nations.

The first modern trials for genocide were conducted by the victorious Allies after World War II. Although the charter of the Nuremberg Tribunal (the international court set up to try Nazi war criminals) did not use the term "genocide," its definition of "crimes against humanity" included persecution on racial or religious grounds. More recently, the UN Security Council created ad hoc tribunals to try those responsible for genocide and other serious crimes in the former Yugoslavia and in Rwanda. The International Criminal Court (ICC), which began functioning on July 1, 2002, also has jurisdiction to try perpetrators of genocide. In Mar. 2005, the UN Security Council referred the situation in Darfur, Sudan, to the ICC prosecutor.

Examples of Genocides Since 1900

Year	Event	Location	Estimated Deaths
1915	Extermination of Armenians by the Young Turks	Turkey/Ottoman Empire	1,000,000+
1930s	Intentional infliction of famine on Ukraine	Soviet Union (Ukraine)	6,000,000–7,000,000
1933–1945	Attempted destruction of European Jewry (Holocaust)	Europe	6,000,000
1975–1979	Khmer Rouge campaign of extermination under Pol Pot	Cambodia	1,500,000–2,000,000
1988	Anfal Campaign (named by the Iraqi government) against Iraqi Kurds	Iraq	100,000–200,000
1992–1995	Ethnic killings during the breakup of Yugoslavia, chiefly Serbs against Bosnian Muslims	Bosnia-Herzegovina, Serbia, Croatia	200,000
1994	Hutu massacre of Tutsis	Rwanda	800,000
2003–Present	Military and militia attacks on non-Arab southern tribes	Darfur region, Sudan	100,000–400,000

Note: Estimates based on historical evidence.

The legal definition of "genocide" does not include politically motivated mass killings. Therefore, instances of mass violence against political or class enemies, such as Josef Stalin's purges in the 1930s, which killed some 20 million Soviets, and Mao Zedong's Cultural Revolution, which killed several million Chinese, are not included. The mass killings of an estimated 1.7 milion during the Khmer Rouge regime in Cambodia are often spoken of as a genocide, despite the fact that many of the murders were politically or class motivated.

NOTED PERSONALITIES

This chapter contains the following sections:

Widely Known Americans of the Present

Political leaders, journalists, other prominent living persons. As of Sept. 2005. Excludes most who fall in categories listed elsewhere in Noted Personalities, such as Writers of the Present and Entertainment Personalities of the Present, or in Sports Personalities. Includes some figures active in American life but not U.S. citizens.

Roger Ailes, b 5/15/40 (Warren, OH), TV exec.
Madeleine K. Albright, b 5/15/37 (Prague, Czech.), former sec. of state.
Edwin "Buzz" Aldrin, b 1/20/30 (Montclair, NJ), former astronaut; 2nd person on the Moon.
Paul Allen, b 121/53 (Mercer Is., WA), co-founder of Microsoft.
Christiane Amanpour, b 1/12/58 (London, Eng.), TV journalist.
Richard K. Armey, b 7/7/40 (Cando, ND), former U.S. rep., House majority leader.
Neil Armstrong, b 8/5/30 (Wapakoneta, OH), former astronaut, 1st person on Moon.
John Ashcroft, b 5/9/42 (Chicago, IL), former MO gov., attorney gen.
Kathleen Babineaux Blanco, b 12/15/42 (Coteau, LA), LA governor.
F. Lee Bailey, b 6/10/33 (Waltham, MA), attorney.
Russell Baker, b 8/14/25 (Loudoun Co., VA), columnist.
Haley Barbour, b 10/22/47 (Yazoo City, MS), MS governor.
Dave Barry, b 7/3/47 (Armonk, NY), humorist.
Marion Barry, b 3/6/36 (Itta Bena, MS), former Wash., DC, mayor; D.C. city council member.
Gary Bauer, b 5/4/46 (Covington, KY), political activist.
William Bennett, b 7/31/43 (Brooklyn, NY), author, former education secretary.
Lloyd Bentsen, b 2/11/21 (Mission, TX), former senator, treasury sec., vice-presid. nominee.
Samuel "Sandy" Berger, b 10/28/45 (Sharon, CT), former national security adviser.
Chris Berman, b 5/10/55 (Greenwich, CT), sportscaster.
Carl Bernstein, b 2/14/44 (Washington, DC), journalist; with Woodward cracked Watergate scandal.
Jeff Bezos, b 1/12/64 (Albuquerque, NM), founder and CEO of Amazon.com.
Joseph R. Biden Jr., b 11/20/42 (Scranton, PA), senator (DE).
James H. Billington, b 6/1/29 (Bryn Mawr, PA), librarian of Congress.
Wolf Blitzer, b 3/22/48 (Buffalo, NY), TV journalist.
Harold Bloom, b 7/11/30 (NYC), literary critic.
Michael R. Bloomberg, b 2/14/42 (Medford, MA), NYC mayor; financial information/media entrepreneur.
Roy Blunt, b 1/10/50 (Niangua, MO), U.S. House majority whip, interim Houe majority leader.
Samuel W. Bodman, b 11/26/38 (Chicago, IL), sec. of energy.
John Bolton, b 11/20/48 (Baltimore), U.S. amb. to UN.
Julian Bond, b 1/14/40 (Nashville), civil rights leader; NAACP chairman
Barbara Boxer, b 11/11/40 (Brooklyn, NY), senator (CA).
Bill Bradley, b 7/28/43 (Crystal City, MO), former senator (NJ), basketball player, presid. candidate.
Ed Bradley, b 6/22/41 (Philadelphia), TV journalist.
James Brady, b 8/29/40 (Centralia, IL), former presid. press sec.; gun control advocate.
L. Paul Bremer III, b 9/30/41 (Hartford, CT), diplomat, former top U.S. civilian administrator in Iraq.
Jimmy Breslin, b 10/17/30 (Queens, NY), columnist, author.
Stephen Breyer, b 8/15/38 (San Francisco), Sup. Ct. justice.
Sergey Brin, b 3/26/73 (Moscow, Russia), co-founder of Google.
David Broder, b 9/11/29 (Chicago Heights, IL), journalist.
Tom Brokaw, b 2/6/40 (Webster, SD), TV journalist, retired NBC anchor.
David Brooks, b 1961 (NYC), columnist, political commentator.
Joyce Brothers, b 10/20/28 (NYC), psychologist.
Aaron Brown, b 11/10/48 (Hopkins, MN), CNN anchor.
Michael Brown, b 11/11/54 (Guymon, OK), former FEMA head, resigned under fire after Hurricane Katrina.
Jerry (Edmund G.) Brown Jr., b 4/7/38 (San Francisco), Oakland mayor; former CA gov., pres. candidate.
Pat Buchanan, b 11/2/38 (Washington, DC), journalist, former presid. candidate.
Art Buchwald, b 10/20/25 (Mt. Vernon, NY), humorist.
William F. Buckley Jr., b 11/24/25 (NYC), columnist, author.
Warren Buffett, b 8/30/30 (Omaha), investor.
Barbara Bush, b 6/8/25 (Rye, NY), former first lady.
Barbara Bush, b 11/25/81 (Dallas, TX), daughter of Pres. George W. Bush.
George H. W. Bush, b 6/12/24 (Milton, MA), former president.
George W. Bush, b 7/6/46 (New Haven, CT), U.S. president.
Jeb Bush, b 2/11/53 (Midland, TX), FL governor.
Jenna Bush, b 11/25/81(Dallas, TX), daughter of Pres. George W. Bush.
Laura Bush, b 11/4/46 (Midland, TX), first lady.
Robert Byrd, b 11/20/17 (N. Wilkesboro, NC), senator (WV), former majority leader.
Andrew Card, b 5/10/47 (Brockton, MA), White House chief of staff.
Tucker Carlson, b 5/16/69 (San Francisco), journalist, TV commentator.
Richard Carmona, b 11/22/49 (NYC), surgeon general.
Jimmy Carter, b 10/1/24 (Plains, GA), former president; won 2002 Nobel Peace Prize.
James Carville Jr., b 10/25/44 (Fort Benning, GA), TV political commentator.
Steve Case, b 8/21/58 (Honolulu, HI), former AOL Time Warner chairman.
Oleg Cassini, b 4/11/13 (Paris, France), fashion designer.
Elaine Chao, b 3/26/53 (Taipei, Taiwan), labor sec.
Dick Cheney, b 1/30/41 (Lincoln, NE), U.S. vice president.
Lynne Cheney, b 8/14/41 (Casper, WY), political commentator, wife of Dick Cheney.
Michael Chertoff, b 11/28/53 (Elizabeth, NJ), sec. of homeland security.
Noam Chomsky, b 12/7/28 (Philadelphia), linguist; activist.
Connie Chung, b 8/20/46 (Washington, DC), TV journalist.
Liz Claiborne, b 3/31/29 (Brussels, Belg.), fashion designer.
Wesley Clark, b 12/23/44 (Chicago), retired general, former NATO commander in Europe; 2004 presid. contender.
Bill Clinton, b 8/19/46 (Hope, AR), former U.S. president.
Chelsea Clinton, b 2/27/80 (Little Rock, AR), daughter of Pres. Clinton and Hillary Rodham Clinton.
Hillary Rodham Clinton, b 10/26/47 (Chicago), senator (NY), former first lady.
Anderson Cooper, b 6/3/67 (NYC), CNN anchor.
Bob Costas, b 3/22/52 (Queens, NY), TV sports journalist.
Ann Coulter, b 12/8/61 (New Canaan, CT), political commentator, author.
Katie Couric, b 1/7/57 (Arlington, VA), TV journalist; NBC morning anchor.
Walter Cronkite, b 11/4/16 (St. Joseph, MO), former NBC news anchor.
Mario Cuomo, b 6/15/32 (Queens, NY), former NY gov.
Richard M. Daley, b 4/24/42 (Chicago), Chicago mayor.
John Danforth, b 9/5/36 (St, Louis, MO), former senator.
Thomas Daschle, b 12/9/47 (Aberdeen, SD), former senator and Senate minority leader.
Patti Davis, b 10/21/52 (LA county), daughter of Pres. Reagan.
Howard Dean, b 11/17/48 (NYC), former VT gov., 2004 pres. contender; Democratic National Committee chair.
Oscar de la Renta, b 7/22/36 (Santo Domingo, Dominican Rep.), fashion designer.
Tom DeLay, b 4/8/47 (Laredo, TX), U.S. rep. temp. stepped down as House majority leader after 2005 indictment.

Michael Dell, b 2/23/65 (Houston, TX), founder, chairman, and CEO of Dell computers.
Alan Dershowitz, b 9/1/38 (Brooklyn, NY), attorney.
Barry Diller, b 2/2/42 (San Francisco), TV exec.
Lou Dobbs, b 9/24/45 (Childress, TX), TV journalist.
Christopher Dodd, b 5/27/44 (Willimantic, CT), senator.
Elizabeth Hanford Dole, b 7/29/36 (Salisbury, NC), senator; former Red Cross pres., cabinet member, presid. contender.
Robert Dole, b 7/22/23 (Russell, KS), former Senate majority leader, presid. nominee.
Sam Donaldson, b 3/11/34 (El Paso, TX), TV journalist.
Elizabeth Drew, b 11/16/35 (Cincinnati), journalist.
Matt Drudge, b 10/27/67 (Tacoma Park, MD), internet journalist.
Michael S. Dukakis, b 11/3/33 (Brookline, MA), former MA gov., presid. nominee.
Dick Durbin, b 11/21/44 (East. St. Louis, IL), Senate minority whip.
Bernard Ebbers, b 8/27/41 (Edmonton, Alberta, Can.), former WorldCom CEO, jailed for fraud.
Roger Ebert, b 6/18/42 (Urbana, IL), film critic.
Marian Wright Edelman, b 6/6/39 (Bennettsville, SC), children's rights advocate.
John Edwards, b 6/10/53 (Seneca, SC), former senator; 2004 vice-presid. candidate.
Edward Egan, b 4/2/32 (Oak Park, IL), Rom. Cath. cardinal, archbishop of New York.
Michael Eisner, b 3/7/42 (Mt. Kisco, NY), Disney Co. CEO.
Lawrence J. Ellison, b 8/17/44 (NYC), Oracle Corp. founder, CEO.
Rev. Jerry Falwell, b 8/11/33 (Lynchburg, VA), TV evangelist, religious commentator.
Louis Farrakhan, b 5/11/33 (Roxbury, MA), Nation of Islam leader.
Russell Feingold, b 3/2/53 (Janesville, WI), senator.
Dianne Feinstein, b 6/22/33 (San Francisco), senator.
W. Mark Felt, b 8/17/13 (Twin Falls, ID), former No. 2 person at FBI, revealed (2005) as "Deep Throat" Watergate informant.
Geraldine Ferraro, b 8/26/35 (Newburgh, NY), former U.S. rep., vice-presid. nominee.
Bobby Fischer, b 3/9/43 (Chicago, IL), former chess champion.
Larry Flynt, b 11/1/42 (Salyersville, KY), publisher.
Steve (Malcolm) Forbes Jr., b 7/18/47 (Morristown, NJ), publisher, former presid. contender.
Betty Ford, b 4/8/18 (Chicago), former first lady.
Gerald R. Ford, b 7/14/13 (Omaha), former president.
Steve Fossett, b 4/22/1944 (Jackson, TN), adventurer, balloonist.
Al Franken, b 5/21/51 (NYC), humorist, political writer.
Tommy R. Franks, b 6/17/45 (Wynnewood, OK), gen., former commander in chief U.S. Central Command.
Betty Friedan, b 2/4/21 (Peoria, IL), author, feminist.
Milton Friedman, b 7/31/12 (Brooklyn, NY), economist.
Thomas Friedman, b 7/20/53 (Minneapolis), columnist, author.
Bill Frist, b 8/19/42 (Nashville, TN), Senate majority leader; physician.
John Kenneth Galbraith, b 10/15/08 (Iona Station, Ont., Canada), economist, author, former amb. to India.
Bill Gates, b 10/28/55 (Seattle), software pioneer; Microsoft exec.
Henry Louis Gates Jr., b 9/16/50 (Keyser, WV), Afro-American studies scholar.
David Geffen, b 2/21/43 (Brooklyn, NY), entertainment exec.
Richard Gephardt, b 1/31/41 (St. Louis, MO), former House party leader; 2004 presid. contender.
Louis Gerstner, b 3/1/42 (Mineola, NY), retired IBM exec.
Charles Gibson, b 3/4/43 (Evanston, IL), TV journalist; ABC morning anchor.
Newt Gingrich, b 6/17/43 (Harrisburg, PA), former House Speaker.
Ruth Bader Ginsburg, b 3/15/33 (Brooklyn, NY), Sup. Ct. justice.
Rudolph Giuliani, b 5/28/44 (Brooklyn, NY), former NYC mayor.
John Glenn, b 7/18/21 (Cambridge, OH), former senator, astronaut.
Alberto Gonzales, b 8/4/55 (San Antonio, TX), attorney gen.
Ellen Goodman, b 4/11/41 (Newton, MA), columnist.
Doris Kearns Goodwin, b 1/4/43 (Rockville Centre, NY), historian, TV commentator.
Berry Gordy, b 11/28/29 (Detroit), Motown founder.
Al Gore Jr., b 3/31/48 (Washington, DC), former senator, U.S. vice president, presid. candidate.
Tipper Gore, b 8/19/48 (Washington, DC), wife of Al Gore.
Porter Goss, b 11/26/38 (Waterbury, CT), CIA director; former CIA operative, U.S. rep. (FL).
Rev. Billy Graham, b 11/7/18 (Charlotte, NC), evangelist.
Bob Graham, b 4/9/36 (Coral Gables, FL), former U.S. senator, FL gov; 2004 pres. contender.
(William) Franklin Graham III, b 7/14/52 (Asheville, NC), evangelist, son of Billy Graham.
Andrew Greeley, b 2/5/28 (Oak Park, IL), Rom. Cath. priest, sociologist, writer.
Jeff Greenfield, b 6/10/43 (NYC), TV journalist.
Alan Greenspan, b 3/6/26 (NYC), Fed chairman.
Michael Griffin, b 1949 (Aberdeen, MD), NASA head.
Andrew Grove, b 9/2/36 (Budapest, Hungary), Intel chairman.
Bryant Gumbel, b 9/29/48 (New Orleans), TV journalist.
Greg Gumbel, b 5/3/46 (New Orleans), sportscaster.
Carlos Gutierrez, b 11/4/52 (Havana, Cuba), sec. of commerce.
Chuck Hagel, b 10/4/46 (North Platte, NE), U.S. senator.
David Halberstam, b 4/10/34 (NYC), journalist, author.
Pete Hamill, b 6/24/35 (Brooklyn, NY), journalist, author.
Lee Hamilton, b 4/20/31 (Daytona Beach, FL), 9-11 commission vice-chair; former U.S. rep. from Indiana.
Paul Harvey, b 9/4/18 (Tulsa, OK), radio journalist.
J. Dennis Hastert, b 1/2/42 (Aurora, IL), House Speaker.
Orrin Hatch, b 3/22/34 (Homestead Park, PA), senator (UT).
Hugh Hefner, b 4/9/26 (Chicago), publisher.
Jesse Helms, b 10/18/21 (Monroe, NC), former senator.
Leona Helmsley, b 7/4/20 (NYC), real estate exec.
Heloise, b 4/15/51 (Waco, TX), advice columnist.
Tommy Hilfiger, b 3/24/51 (Elmira, NY), fashion designer.
Anita Hill, b 7/30/56 (Morris, OK), legal scholar, complainant against Clarence Thomas.
Christopher Hitchens, b 4/13/49 (Portsmouth, England), journalist, author.
James P. Hoffa, b 5/19/41, (Detroit), Teamsters Union head.
Richard Holbrooke, b 4/24/41 (Scarsdale, NY), former U.S. rep. to UN.
Russel Honoré, b 1948 (Lakeland, LA), lt. gen. commander U.S. 1st Army, in charge of Army Hurricane Katrina relief.
David Horowitz, b 1/10/39 (NYC), consumer advocate, columnist, author.
Steny H. Hoyer, b 6/14/39 (NYC), U.S. House minority whip.
Arianna Huffington, b 7/15/50 (Athens, Greece), political commentator.
H. Wayne Huizenga, b 12/29/39 (Evergreen Park, IL), entrepreneur, sports exec.
Brit Hume, b 6/22/43 (Washington DC), TV journalist (FOX).
Kay Bailey Hutchison, b 7/22/43 (Galveston, TX), senator.
Henry J. Hyde, b 4/18/24 (Chicago), U.S. rep.
Lee Iacocca, b 10/15/24 (Allentown, PA), former auto exec.
Carl Icahn, b 1936 (Queens, NY), financier.
Gwen Ifil, b 9/29/55 (Queens, NY), TV journalist, moderator (PBS).
Jeffrey Immelt, b 2/19/56 (Cincinnati, OH), General Electric CEO.
Don Imus, b 7/23/40 (Riverside, CA), talk-show host.
Patricia Ireland, b 10/19/45 (Oak Park, IL), feminist leader.
Molly Ivins, b 8/30/44 (Monterey, CA), author, columnist.
Alphonso Jackson, b 1947 (Marshall, TX), sec. of housing and urban development.
Rev. Jesse Jackson, b 10/8/41 (Greenville, SC), civil rights leader, former presid. contender.
Steve Jobs, b 2/24/55 (San Francisco), Apple Computer exec.; Pixar exec.
Mike Johanns, b 6/18/50 (Osage, IA), sec. of agriculture.
Jasper Johns, b 5/15/30 (Augusta, GA), artist.
Lady Bird Johnson, b 12/22/12 (Karnack, TX), former first lady.
Vernon E. Jordan Jr., b 8/15/35 (Atlanta), attorney, former presid. adviser, civil rights leader.
Donna Karan, b 10/2/48 (Queens, NY), fashion designer.
Jeffrey Katzenberg, b 12/21/50 (NYC), entertainment exec.
Thomas Kean, b 4/21/35 (NYC), 9-11 commission chair, Drew Univ. pres., former NJ gov.
Garrison Keillor, b 8/7/42 (Anoka, MN), author, broadcaster.
Jack Kemp, b 7/13/35 (Los Angeles), former vice-presid. nominee, HUD sec., pro football quarterback.
Anthony M. Kennedy, b 7/23/36 (Sacramento, CA), Sup. Ct. justice.
Edward M. Kennedy, b 2/22/32 (Brookline, MA), senator.
Robert ("Bob") Kerrey, b 8/27/43 (Lincoln, NE), former senator.
Teresa Heinz Kerry, b 10/5/38 (Mozambique), heiress, philanthropist; wife of John Kerry.
John Kerry, b 12/11/43 (Aurora, CO), senator (MA), 2004 presid. candidate.
Jack Kevorkian, b 5/26/28 (Pontiac, MI), physican, assisted-suicide activist; imprisoned on murder charges.
Coretta Scott King, b 4/27/27 (Marion, AL), civil rights leader, widow of Martin Luther King Jr.
Larry King, b 11/19/33 (Brooklyn, NY), TV talk show host.
Michael Kinsley, b 3/9/51 (Detroit), editor, pol. commenator.
Jeane J. Kirkpatrick, b 11/19/26 (Duncan, OK), political scientist, former ambassador to UN.
Henry Kissinger, b 5/27/23 (Fuerth, Germany), former sec. of state, nat. security adviser; won 1973 Nobel Peace Prize.
Calvin Klein, b 11/19/42 (Bronx, NY), fashion designer.
Philip H. Knight, b 2/24/38 (Portland, OR), founder and CEO of Nike.
Edward I. Koch, b 12/12/24 (NYC), former NYC mayor.
Ted Koppel, b 2/8/40 (Lancashire, England), TV journalist.

Larry Kramer, b 6/25/35 (Bridgeport, CT), AIDS activist, writer.
William Kristol, b 12/23/52 (NYC), editor, columnist.
Steve Kroft, b 8/22/45 (Kokomo, IN), TV journalist.
Dennis Kucinich, b 10/8/46 (Cleveland, OH), U.S. repr., 2004 pres. contender.
Brian Lamb, b 10/9/41 (Lafayette, IN), cable TV exec., journalist.
Matt Lauer, b 12/30/57 (NYC), TV journalist; ABC morning anchor.
Ralph Lauren, b 10/14/39 (Bronx, NY), fashion designer.
Bernard F. Law, b 11/4/31 (Torreon, Mexico), cardinal, former Rom. Cath. archbishop of Boston, figure in church scandal.
Kenneth L. Lay, b 4/15/42 (Tyrone, MO), former CEO of Enron, indicted on fraud charges.
Patrick Leahy, b 3/31/40 (Montpelier, VT), senator.
Norman Lear, b 7/27/22 (New Haven, CT), TV producer, political activist.
Michael O. Leavitt, b 2/11/51 (Cedar City, UT), sec. of health and human services.
Jim Lehrer, b 5/19/34 (Wichita, KS), TV journalist, author.
Carl Levin, b 6/28/34 (Detroit), senator.
Monica Lewinsky, b 7/23/73 (San Francisco), former White House intern, key figure in Clinton White House scandal.
Joseph Lieberman, b 2/24/42 (Stamford, CT), senator, former vice presid. candidate; 2004 presid. contender.
Rush Limbaugh, b 1/12/51 (Cape Girardeau, MO), radio talk-show host.
Trent Lott, b 10/9/41 (Grenada, MS), senator, former Senate party leader.
Shannon Lucid, b 1/14/43 (Shanghai, China), NASA scientist, astronaut.
Richard Lugar, b 4/4/32 (Indianapolis), senator.
Roger Mahony, b 2/27/36 (Hollywood, CA), Rom. Cath. cardinal, archbishop of Los Angeles.
Mary Matalin, b 8/19/53 (Chicago), political commentator.
Chris Matthews, b 12/18/45 (Philadelphia), TV journalist.
John McCain, b 8/29/36 (Panama Canal Zone), senator (AZ); former presid. contender.
Scott McClellan, b 1968(?) (Austin, TX), White House press sec.
Mitch McConnell, b 2/20/42 (Tuscumbia, AL), senator (KY), majority whip.
David McCullough, b 7/7/33 (Pittsburgh, PA), historian, biographer.
John McLaughlin, b 3/29/27 (Providence, RI), TV journalist.
George McGovern, b 7/19/22 (Avon, SD), former senator, presid. nominee.
Dr. Phil McGraw, b 9/1/50 (Vinita, OK), talk-show host, motivational speaker, author.
Robert S. McNamara, b 6/9/16 (San Francisco), former defense sec., World Bank head.
Russell Means, b 11/10/39 (Pine Ridge Indian Reserv., SD), Native American activist.
Kate Michelman, b 8/4/42 (NJ), abortion-rights activist.
Ken Mehlman, b. 1967 (Baltimore, MD), Republican National Committee chair.
Zell Miller, b 2/24/32 (Young Harris, GA), former GA gov., senator.
Kate Millett, b 9/14/34 (St. Paul, MN), author, feminist.
Norman Mineta, b 11/12/31 (San Jose, CA), transportation sec.
George Mitchell, b 8/20/33, (Waterville, ME), former Senate majority leader; diplomat, Disney Co. chairman.
Walter Mondale, b 1/5/28 (Ceylon, MN), former vice pres., senator, presid. nominee.
Michael Moore, b 4/23/54 (Davison, MI), activist, documentary filmmaker; author.
Bill Moyers, b 6/5/34 (Hugo, OK), TV journalist, author.
Robert S. Mueller III, b 8/7/44 (NYC), FBI director.
Rupert Murdoch, b 3/11/31 (Melbourne, Aust.), media exec.
Richard B. Myers, b 3/1/42 (Kansas City, MO), chairman of Joint Chiefs of Staff.
Ralph Nader, b 2/27/34 (Winsted, CT), consumer advocate, . 2000, 2004 independent presid. cand.
(Clarence) Ray Nagin, b 6/11/56 (New Orleans, LA), New Orleans mayor.
John Negroponte, b 7/21/39 (London, Eng.), U.S. amb. to Iraq, former U.S. rep. to UN.
Peggy Noonan, b 9/7/50 (Brooklyn, NY), columnist, speechwriter.
Oliver North, b 10/7/43 (San Antonio, TX), talk-show host, former Nat. Sec. Council aide, fig. in Iran-contra scandal.
Eleanor Holmes Norton, b 6/13/37 (Washington, DC), U.S. House delegate.
Gale Norton, b 3/11/54 (Wichita, KS), interior sec.
Robert Novak, b 2/26/31 (Joliet, IL), journalist.
Sam Nunn, b 9/8/38 (Perry, GA), former senator.
Barack Obama, b 8/4/61 (Hawaii), senator (IL); 2004 Dem. convention keynote speaker.
Sandra Day O'Connor, b 3/26/30 (El Paso, TX), retiring Sup. Ct. justice.
Paul O'Neill, b 12/4/35 (St. Louis, MO), former treasury sec.
Bill O'Reilly, b 9/10/49 (NYC), TV commentator, host.
Michael Ovitz, b 12/14/46 (Encino, CA), entertainment exec.
Clarence Page, b 6/2/47 (Dayton, OH), journalist, TV commentator.
Lawrence Page, b 8/21/73 (Ann Arbor, MI), co-founder of Google.
Camille Paglia, b 4/2/47 (Endicott, NY), scholar, author.
Leon F. Panetta, b 6/28/38 (Monterey, CA), former White House chief of staff, U.S. rep.
Rosa Parks, b 2/4/13 (Tuskegee, AL), civil rights activist; her actions sparked 1955 Montgomery bus boycott.
Richard Parsons, b 4/4/48 (NYC), Time Warner CEO.
George Pataki, b 6/24/45 (Peekskill, NY), NY gov.
Jane Pauley, b 10/31/50 (Indianapolis), TV journalist.
Nancy Pelosi, b 3/26/40 (Baltimore, MD), U.S. rep. (CA); House minority leader.
Ross Perot, b 6/27/30 (Texarkana, TX), entrepreneur, former presid. nominee.
Rob Portman, b 12/19/55 (Cincinnati), U.S. trade rep.
Colin Powell, b 4/5/37 (NYC), former sec. of state, nat. security adviser, Joint Chiefs of Staff chairman.
Dan Quayle, b 2/4/47 (Indianapolis), former U.S. vice pres., senator, presid. contender.
Anna Quindlen, b 7/8/53 (Philadelphia), author, columnist.
Dan Rather, b 10/31/31 (Wharton, TX), TV journalist, retired CBS anchor.
Nancy Reagan, b 7/6/21 (NYC), former first lady.
Michael Reagan, b 3/18/45, talk-show host, adopted son of Pres. Reagan and his 1st wife.
Ron Reagan, b 5/20/58 (Los Angeles), journalist, TV talk show host, son of Pres. Reagan.
Sumner Redstone, b 5/27/23 (Boston), Viacom chairman, CEO.
Ralph Reed, b 6/24/61 (Portsmouth, VA), political adviser.
Robert B. Reich, b 6/24/46 (Scranton, PA), economist, author, former labor sec.
Harry Reid, b 12/2/39 (Searchlight, NV), Senate minority leader.
Janet Reno, b 7/21/38 (Miami, FL), former attorney gen.
Condoleezza Rice, b 11/14/54 (Birmingham, AL), sec. of state, former nat. security advisor.
Ann Richards, b 9/1/33 (Lakeview, TX), former TX gov.
Bill Richardson, b 11/15/47 (Pasadena, CA), NM gov.; former energy sec., UN ambassador, U.S. rep.
Sally K. Ride, b 5/26/51 (Encino, CA), former astronaut, 1st U.S. woman in space.
Tom (Thomas Joseph) Ridge, b 8/26/45 (Munhall, PA) former sec. of homeland security; former PA gov.
Geraldo Rivera, b 7/4/43 (NYC), TV journalist.
Cokie Roberts, b 12/27/43 (New Orleans), TV journalist.
John G. Roberts, b 1/27/55 (Buffalo, NY), Sup. Ct. chief justice.
Rev. Oral Roberts, b 1/24/18 (nr. Ada, OK), TV evangelist, educator.
Rev. Pat Robertson, b 3/22/30 (Lexington, VA), religious broadcasting exec, former presid. contender.
V. Gene Robinson, b 5/29/47 (Lexington, KY), first openly gay Episcopal bishop.
David Rockefeller, b 6/12/15 (NYC), banker.
John D. "Jay" Rockefeller 4th, b 6/18/37 (NYC), senator (WV), former WV gov.
Al Roker, b 8/20/54 (Queens, NY), TV weather person.
Mitt Romney, b 3/12/47 (Detroit), MA gov, former Olympics organizer.
Andy Rooney, b 1/14/19 (Albany, NY), TV commentator.
Charlie Rose, b 1/5/42 (Henderson, NC), TV journalist.
Karl Rove, b 12/25/50 (Denver, CO) White House senior domestic policy advisor.
Louis Rukeyser, b 1/30/33 (NYC), TV journalist, financial analyst.
Donald Rumsfeld, b 7/9/32 (Chicago), defense sec.
Tim Russert, b 5/7/50 (Buffalo, NY), TV journalist, moderator *Meet the Press* (NBC).
Morley Safer, b 11/8/31 (Toronto, Can.), TV journalist.
Diane Sawyer, b 12/22/45 (Glasgow, KY), TV journalist; ABC morning anchor.
Antonin Scalia, b 3/11/36 (Trenton, NJ), Sup. Ct. justice.
Bob Schieffer, b 2/25/37 (Austin, TX), CBS TV news anchor.
Phyllis Schlafly, b 8/15/24 (St. Louis, MO), political activist.
Arthur Schlesinger Jr., b 10/15/17 (Columbus, OH), historian.
Caroline Kennedy Schlossberg, b 11/27/57 (NYC), author, daughter of Pres. Kennedy.
Patricia Schroeder, b 7/30/40 (Portland, OR), former U.S. rep.
Rev. Robert Schuller, b 9/16/26 (Alton, IA), TV evangelist.
Charles Schumer, b 11/23/50 (Brooklyn, NY), senator.
Arnold Schwarzenegger, b 7/30/47 (Thal, Styria, Austria), CA governor; former actor.
H. Norman Schwarzkopf, b 8/22/34 (Trenton, NJ), former military leader.
Willard Scott, b 3/7/34 (Alexandria, VA), TV weather person.
Allan H. ("Bud") Selig, b 7/30/34 (Milwaukee), MLB comm.
Richard Serra, b 11/2/39 (San Francisco), sculptor.

Rev. Al Sharpton, b 10/3/54 (Brooklyn, NYC), activist, civil rights leader; 2004 presid. contender.
Cindy Sheehan, b 7/140/57 (Bellflower, CA), anti-Iraq-War activist.
Maria Shriver, b 11/6/55 (Chicago), TV journalist
George P. Shultz, b 12/13/20 (NYC), former sec. of state; other cabinet posts.
Russell Simmons, b 10/4/57 (Queens, NY), music producer.
O. J. Simpson, b 7/9/47 (San Francisco), former football star, murder defendant.
Harry Smith, b 8/21/51 (Lansing, IL), TV journalist; CBS morning anchor.
Liz Smith, b 2/2/23 (Ft. Worth, TX), gossip columnist.
John Snow, b 8/2/39 (Toledo, OH), treasury sec, former CSX CEO.
George Soros, b 8/12/30 (Budapest, Hungary), financier, philanthropist.
David H. Souter, b 9/17/39 (Melrose, MA), Sup. Ct. justice.
Arlen Specter, b 2/12/30 (Wichita, KS), senator (PA), Judiciary Committee chair.
Margaret Spellings, b 11/30/57 (Michigan), sec of education.
Steven Spielberg, b 12/18/46 (Cincinnati, OH), movie director, producer.
Lesley Stahl, b 12/16/41 (Swampscott, MA), TV journalist.
Kenneth Starr, b 7/21/46 (Vernon, TX), former Whitewater indep. counsel.
Shelby Steele, b 1/1/46 (Chicago), scholar, critic.
George Steinbrenner, b 7/4/30 (Rocky River, OH), NY Yankees owner.
Gloria Steinem, b 3/25/34 (Toledo, OH), author, feminist.
Frank Stella, b 5/12/36 (Malden, MA), painter.
George Stephanopoulos, b 2/10/61 (Fall River, MA), TV journalist, former presid. adviser.
David J. Stern, b 9/22/42 (NYC), NBA comm.
Howard Stern, b 1/12/54 (Roosevelt, NY), radio talk show host.
John Paul Stevens, b 4/20/20 (Chicago), Sup. Ct. justice.
Ted Stevens, b 11/18/23 (Indianapolis, IN), senator (AK), Senate pres. pro tempore.
Martha Stewart, b 8/3/41 (Nutley, NJ), homemaking adviser, entrepreneur; TV personality.
Arthur Ochs Sulzberger Jr., b 9/22/51 (Mt. Kisco, NY), newspaper publisher.
Lawrence H. Summers, b 11/30/54 (New Haven, CT), Harvard Univ. pres.
John J. Sweeney, b 5/5/34 (NYC), AFL-CIO pres.
Paul Tagliabue, b 11/24/40 (Jersey City, NJ), NFL comm.
George Tenet, b 1/5/53 (Queens, NY), former CIA director.
Clarence Thomas, b 6/23/48 (Savannah, GA), Sup. Ct. justice.
Helen Thomas, b 8/4/20 (Winchester, KY), journalist.
Fred Thompson, b 8/19/42 (Sheffield, AL), former senator; actor.
Tommy G. Thompson, b 11/19/41 (Elroy, WI), former sec. of health and human services, former WI gov.
Margaret Truman (Daniel), b 2/17/24 (Independence, MO), author, daughter of Pres. Truman.
Donald Trump, b 6/14/1946 (NYC), real estate exec.; TV personality.
Ted Turner, b 11/19/38 (Cincinnati), TV exec, philanthropist.
Peter Ueberroth, b 9/2/37 (Chicago), sports & travel exec.
Jack Valenti, b 9/5/21 (Houston), former White House aide, movie industry exec.
Abigail Van Buren, b 7/4/18 (Sioux City, IA), retired advice columnist.
Gloria Vanderbilt, 2/20/24 (NYC), fashion designer, heiress.
Jesse Ventura, b 7/15/51 (Minneapolis), former wrestler, MN governor.
Antonio Villaraigosa, b 1/23/53 (East LA), 1st Hispanic mayor of LA since 1870s.
Paul Volcker, b 9/5/27 (Cape May, NJ), economist, former Fed chairman; chair of inquiry into UN Oil for Food scandal.
Mike Wallace, b 5/9/18 (Brookline, MA), TV journalist.
Barbara Walters, b 9/25/31 (Boston), TV journalist.
James Watson, b 4/6/28 (Chicago), biochemist, DNA pioneer, co-winner 1962 Nobel Prize.
Dr. Andrew Weil, b 6/8/42 (Philadelphia), health adviser.
Sanford I. Weill, b 3/16/33 (Brooklyn, NY), CEO of Citigroup.
Caspar Weinberger, b 8/18/17 (San Francisco), business exec, former defense sec., other cabinet posts.
Harvey Weinstein, b 3/19/52 (NYC), movie exec.
Jack Welch, b 11/19/35 (Peabody, MA), former General Electric CEO.
Jann Wenner, b 1/7/46 (NYC), publisher, founder *Rolling Stone*.
Cornel West, b 6/23/53 (Tulsa, OK), African American scholar, critic.
Ruth Westheimer, b 6/4/28 (Frankfurt am Main, Germany), human sexuality expert.
Christine Todd Whitman, b 9/26/46 (NYC), former EPA head, NJ gov.
Meg Whitman, b 8/4/56 (Cold Spring Harbor, NY), eBay pres. and CEO.
Elie Wiesel, b 9/30/28 (Sighet, Romania), scholar, author, 1986 Nobel Peace Prize winner.
George Will, b 5/4/41 (Champaign, IL), journalist, author.
Brian Williams, b 1959 (Elmira, NY), NBC TV news anchor.
Oprah Winfrey, b 1/29/54 (Kosciusko, MS), TV and media personality, businesswoman, actress.
Paul Wolfowitz, b 12/22/43 (NYC), World Bank head.
Bob Woodward, b 3/26/43 (Geneva, IL), journalist; with Bernstein cracked Watergate scandal.
Paula Zahn, b 2/24/56 (Omaha, NE), TV journalist.
Mortimer Zuckerman, b 6/4/37 (Montreal, Quebec, Can.), publisher, columnist.

Widely Known World Personalities of the Present

Living Non-Americans only. Generally excludes current heads of state or government (see Nations chapter) and excludes most others covered elsewhere, such as in Widely Known Americans, Entertainers and Writers lists, or Sports Personalities.

Mahmoud Abbas (Abu Mazen), b 3/35 Safed, Palestine (now Israel), chairman of the Palestinian Liberation Organization (PLO).
Gerry Adams, b 10/6/48 (Belfast, N. Ireland), Sinn Fein leader.
Theo Albrecht, b 3/28/22 (Schonebeck, Ger.), German billionaire, CEO of Aldi.
Giulio Andreotti, b 1/14/19 (Rome, Italy), former Italian premier.
Prince Andrew, b 2/19/60 (London, Eng.), Duke of York (2nd son of Queen Elizabeth II).
Kofi Annan, b 4/8/38 (Kumasi, Ghana), UN sec.-gen.; 2001 Nobel laureate.
Princess Anne, b 8/15/50 (London, Eng.), Princess Royal (daughter of Queen Elizabeth II).
Corazon Aquino, b 1/25/33 (Manila, Philip.), former pres. of Philippines.
Oscar Arias Sánchez, b 9/13/41 (Heredia, Costa Rica), former Costa Rican pres., peace negotiator, 1987 Nobel laureate.
Giorgio Armani, b 7/11/34 (Piacenza, Italy), fashion designer.
Ehud Barak, b 2/12/42 (Mishmar Ha-Sharon Kibbutz, Israel), former Israeli prime min.
Ahmed Ben Bella, b 12/25/18 (Marnia, Algeria), 1st Algerian prime min.; revolutionary leader.
Benedict XVI (Joseph Ratzinger), b 4/16/27 (Marktl am Inn, Germany), pope of Rom. Cath. Church, elected 2005.
Boris Berezovsky, b 1/23/46 (Moscow, USSR), businessman, politician.
Tim Berners-Lee, b 6/8/55 (London, Eng.), World Wide Web inventor.
Benazir Bhutto, b 6/21/53 (Karachi, Pak.), former prime min. of Pakistan.
Osama bin Laden, b 1957(?) (Riyadh, Saudi Ar.), leader of al-Qaeda terrorist organization.
Hans Blix, b 6/28/28 (Uppsala, Sweden), former UN weapons inspector.
Fernando Botero, b 1932 (Medellín, Col.), Colombian artist.
Boutros Boutros-Ghali, b 11/14/22 (Cairo, Egypt), former UN sec.-gen.
Richard Branson, b 7/18/50 (S. London, Eng.), British Virgin Records and Airways founder.
Gordon Brown, b 2/20/51 (Glasgow, Scot.), Brit. chancellor of the exchequer.
Kim Campbell, b 3/10/47 (Port Alberni, British Columbia, Can.), former Canadian prime min.
Pierre Cardin, b 7/7/22 (Venice, Italy), fashion designer.
Princess Caroline, b 1/23/57 (Monte Carlo, Monaco), Monaco royal (eldest daughter of Prince Rainier and Princess Grace).
Prince Charles, b 11/14/48 (London, Eng.), Prince of Wales (eldest son of Queen Elizabeth II); heir to British throne.
Jean Chrétien, b 1/11/34 (Shawinigan, Que., Can.), former Canadian prime min.
Christo (Javacheff), b 6/13/35 (Gabrovo, Bulg.), artist.
Joe (Charles Joseph) Clark, b 6/5/39 (High River, Alberta, Can.), former Canadian prime min.
King Constantine II, b 6/2/40 (Psychiko, Greece), former king of Greece.
Dalai Lama (Tenzin Gyatso), b 7/6/35 (Taktser, Amdo, Tibet), Buddhist leader; 1989 Nobel laureate.
Jean Claude Duvalier ("Baby Doc"), b 7/3/51 (Port-au-Prince, Haiti), former Haitian dictator.
Shirin Ebadi, b 1947 (Hamadan, Iran), human rights activist, 2003 Nobel laureate.
Prince Edward, b 3/10/64 (London, Eng.), Earl of Essex (3rd son of Queen Elizabeth II).
Prince Felipe, b 1/30/68 (Madrid, Spain), heir to Spanish throne.
Sarah Ferguson, b 10/15/58 (London, Eng.), Duchess of York; ex-wife of Prince Andrew.
John Galliano, b 1960 (Gibraltar), fashion designer.

Valery Giscard d'Estaing, b 2/2/26 (Koblenz, Ger.), former French pres.
Jane Goodall, b 4/3/34 (London, Eng.), British anthropologist.
Mikhail Gorbachev, b 3/2/31 (Privolnoye, USSR), former Soviet pres.; 1990 Nobel laureate.
Jurgen Habermas, b 6/18/29 (Dusseldorf, Ger.), philosopher.
Prince Henry ("Harry") of Wales, b 9/15/84 (London, Eng.), son of Prince Charles; 3rd in line to British throne.
Vaclav Havel, b 10/5/36 (Prague, Czech.), former Czech pres.; playwright.
Stephen Hawking, b 1/8/42 (Oxford, Eng.), physicist; author.
Sir Edmund Hillary, b 7/20/19 (Auckland, New Zeal.), 1st to reach summit of Mt. Everest, with Tenzing Norgay, 1953.
David Hockney, b 7/9/37 (Bradford, Eng.), artist.
Saddam Hussein, b 4/28/37 (Tikrit, Iraq), captured former Iraqi ruler.
Jiang Zemin, b 8/17/26 (Yangzhou, Jiangsu Prov., China), former pres. of China.
Kim Dae Jung, b 12/3/25 (near Mokpo, S. Korea), former S. Korean dissident, opposition leader, pres.; 2000 Nobelist.
Garry Kasparov, b 4/13/63 (Baku, Azerbaijan, USSR), former world chess champion.
Mikhail Khodorkovsky, b 6/26/63 (Moscow, Russia), oil oligarch, jailed for tax evasion (2005).
F.W. (Frederik Willem) de Klerk, b 3/18/36 (Johannesburg, S. Africa), former S. African pres.; 1993 Nobel laureate.
Helmut Kohl, b 4/3/30 (Ludwigshafen, Ger.), former German chancellor.
Vladimir Kramnik, b 7/25/75 (Tuapse, Russia, USSR), world chess champion.
Hans Kung, b 3/19/28 (Sursee, Switz.), Rom. Cath. theologian.
Richard Leakey, b 12/19/44 (Nairobi, Kenya), Kenyan anthropologist.
Claude Lévi-Strauss, b 11/28/08 (Brussels, Belg.), French anthropologist, structuralist.
John Major, b 3/29/43 (Wimbledon, Eng.), former British prime min.
Nelson Mandela, b 7/18/18 (Transkei, S. Africa), former pres. of S. Africa; 1993 Nobel laureate.
Imelda Marcos, b 7/2/29 (Manila, Philip.), former first lady of Philippines.
Peter Max, b 10/19/37 (Berlin, Ger.), artist, designer.
Angela Merkel, b 7/17/54 (Hamburg, Ger.), German Christian Dem. leader, chancellor candidate.
Jean-Marie Messier, b 12/13/56 (Grenoble, Fr.), former CEO of Vivendi Universal.
Empress Michiko, b 10/20/34 (Tokyo, Jap.), empress of Japan.
Slobodan Milosevic, b 8/20/41 (Pozarevac, Serbia, Yugoslavia), former Yugoslav pres.; on trial for war crimes.
Rev. Sun Myung Moon, b 1/6/20 (Kwangju Sangsa Ri, N. Korea), Unification Church founder.
Brian Mulroney, b 3/20/39 (Baie-Corneau, Quebec, Can.), former Canadian prime min.
Prince Naruhito, b 2/23/60 (Tokyo, Jap.), crown prince of Japan.
Benjamin Netanyahu, b 10/21/49 (Tel-Aviv, Israel), former Israeli prime min.
Queen Noor (Lisa Halaby), 8/23/51 (Washington, DC), American-born widow of Jordan's King Hussein.
Manuel Noriega, 2/11/34 (Panama City, Pan.), ousted Panamanian pres., jailed in Miami.
Daniel Ortega Saavedra, b 11/11/45 (La Libertad, Nicar.), former Nicaraguan pres., Sandinista leader.
Camilla Parker-Bowles, Duchess of Cornwall, b 7/17/47 (London, Eng.) wife of Prince Charles.
Jean-Marie le Pen, b 6/20/28 (La Trinite-sur-Mer, Fr.), French right-wing politician
Shimon Peres, b 8/21/23 (Wolozyn, Pol.), former Israeli prime min.; 1994 Nobel laureate.
Javier Perez de Cuellar, b 1/19/20 (Lima, Peru), former UN sec. gen.
Prince Philip, b 6/10/21 (Corfu, Greece), Duke of Edinburgh (husband of Queen Elizabeth II).
Augusto Pinochet Ugarte, b 11/25/15 (Valparaiso, Chile), former Chilean ruler; indicted for crimes in office.
Gerhard Richter, b 2/9/32 (Dresden, Ger.), artist.
Mary Robinson, b 5/21/44 (Ballina, Co. Mayo, Ireland), former Irish pres., UN High Commissioner for Human Rights.
Moqtada al-Sadr, b 1974 (Iraq), extremist Shiite cleric.
Yves Saint Laurent, b 8/1/36 (Oran, Algeria), fashion designer.
Carlos Salinas de Gortari, b 4/3/48 (Mexico City, Mex.), former Mexican pres.
Eduard Shevardnadze, b 1/25/28 (Mamati, Georgia, USSR), former Georgian pres.
Ayatollah Ali al-Sistani, b 8/4/30 (?) (Mashhad, Iran), major Iraqi Shiite religious leader.
Princess Stephanie, b 2/1/65 (Monte Carlo, Monaco), youngest daughter and child of Prince Rainier and Princess Grace.
Jack Straw, b 8/3/46 (Buckhurst Hill, Essex, Eng.), British foreign sec.
Suharto, b 6/8/21 (Kemusa Argamulja, Java), former longtime Indonesian ruler.
Aung San Suu Kyi, b 6/19/45 (Rangoon, Burma), political activist, 1991 Nobel laureate, under effective house arrest.
Valentina Tereshkova, b 3/6/37 (Maslennikovo, Russia, USSR), 1st woman in space.
Margaret Thatcher, b 10/13/25 (Grantham, Eng.), former British prime min.
John Napier Turner, b 6/7/29 (Richmond, Surrey, Eng.), former Canadian prime min.
Desmond Tutu, b 10/7/31 (Klerksdorp, Transvaal, S. Africa), former S. African archbishop; 1984 Nobel laureate.
Kurt Waldheim, b 12/21/18 (St. Andra-Wordern, Austria), former UN sec.-gen. and Austrian pres.
Lech Walesa, b 9/29/43 (Popowo, Pol.), Solidarity leader; 1983 Nobel laureate.
Prince William (of Wales), b 6/21/82 (London, Eng.), son of Prince Charles; 2nd in line to British throne.
Rowan Williams, b 6/14/50 (Ystradgynlais, Wales), Archbishop of Canterbury.
Boris Yeltsin b 2/1/31 (Butka, USSR), former Russian pres.
Abu Musab al-Zarqawi, b 10/20/66 (Al-Zarqaa, Jordan), Al-Qaeda terrorist leader in Iraq.
Ayman al-Zawahri, b 6/19/51 (Cairo, Egypt), reputed No. 2 al-Qaeda leader.

African-Americans of the Past

See also other categories.

Ralph David Abernathy, 1926-90, organizer, 1957, pres., 1968, Southern Christian Leadership Conf.
Crispus Attucks, c1723-70, killed by British soldiers in 1770 Boston Massacre.
Benjamin Banneker, 1731-1806, inventor, astronomer, mathematician, gazetteer.
Daisy Bates, 1920?-99, Arkansas, civil rights leader who fought for school integration.
James P. Beckwourth, 1798-c1867, western fur trader, scout; Beckwourth Pass in California named for him.
Mary McCleod Bethune, 1875-1955, adviser to FDR and Truman; founder, pres., Bethune-Cookman College.
Henry Blair, 19th cent., pioneer inventor; obtained patents for a corn-planter, 1834, and cotton-planter, 1836.
Tom Bradley, 1917-98, first African-American mayor of LA.
Sterling A. Brown, 1901-89, poet, literature professor; helped establish African-American literary criticism.
William Wells Brown, 1815-84, memoirist, ex-slave; first African American to publish a novel, 1853.
Ralph Bunche, 1904-71, first black to win the Nobel Peace Prize, 1950; undersecretary of the UN, 1950.
Stokely Carmichael (Kwame Toure), 1941-98, black power activist.
George Washington Carver, 1864-1943, botanist, chemist, and educator; transformed the economy of the South.
Charles Waddell Chesnutt, 1858-1932, author known for his short stories, such as in *The Conjure Woman (1899).*
Shirley Chisholm, 1924-2005, first black woman elected to U.S. House (1968); pres. contender, 1972.
Eldridge Cleaver, 1935-98, revolutionary social critic; former "minister of information" for Black Panthers; *Soul on Ice.*
James Cleveland, 1931-91, composer, musician, singer; first black gospel artist to appear at Carnegie Hall.
Johnnie L. Cochran Jr., 1937-2005, attorney.
Countee Cullen, 1903-46, poet, prominent in the Harlem Renaissance of the 1920s; *The Black Christ.*
Benjamin O. Davis Jr., 1912-2002, leader of World War II black aviators, first African-American general in U.S. Air Force.
Benjamin O. Davis Sr., 1877-1970, first African-American general, 1940, in U.S. Army.
Ossie Davis, 1917-2005, civil rights activist, actor, director.
William L. Dawson, 1886-1970, Illinois congressman, first black chairman of a major U.S. House committee.
Aaron Douglas, 1900-79, "father of black American art."
Frederick Douglass, 1817-95, author, editor, orator, diplomat; edited abolitionist weekly *The North Star.*
St. Clair Drake, 1911-90, black studies pioneer, *Black Metropolis* (1945), with Horace R. Cayton.
William Edward Burghardt (W.E.B.) Du Bois, 1868-1963, historian, sociologist; an NAACP founder, 1909.
Paul Laurence Dunbar, 1872-1906, poet, novelist; won fame with *Lyrics of Lowly Life,* 1896.
Jean Baptiste Point du Sable, c1750-1818, pioneer trader and first settler of Chicago, 1779.

Medgar Evers, 1925-63, Mississippi civil rights leader; campaigned to register black voters; assassinated.
James Farmer, 1920-99, civil rights leader; founded Congress of Racial Equality (CORE).
Henry O. Flipper, 1856-1940, first African-American to graduate, 1877, from West Point.
Marcus Garvey, 1887-1940, founded Universal Negro Improvement Assn., 1911.
Ewart Guinier, 1911-90, trade unionist; first chairman of Harvard Univ.'s Dept. of African American Studies.
Prince Hall, 1735-1807, activist; founded black Freemasonry; served in American Revolutionary war.
Jupiter Hammon, c1720-1800, poet; first African-American to have his works published, 1761.
Lorraine Hansberry, 1930-65, playwright; won New York Drama Critics Circle Award, 1959; *A Raisin in the Sun.*
William H. Hastie, 1904-76, first black federal judge, appointed 1937; governor of Virgin Islands, 1946-49.
Matthew A. Henson, 1866-1955, member of Peary's 1909 expedition to the North Pole; placed U.S. flag at the pole.
Chester Himes, 1909-84, novelist; *Cotton Comes to Harlem.*
William A. Hinton, 1883-1959, physician, developed tests for syphilis; first black prof., 1949, at Harvard Med. School.
Charles Hamilton Houston, 1895-1950, lawyer, Howard University instructor, champion of minority rights,
Langston Hughes, 1902-67, poet, lyric writer, author; a major influence in 1920s Harlem Renaissance.
Daniel James Jr., 1920-78, first black 4-star general, 1975; commander, North American Air Defense Command.
James Weldon Johnson, 1871-1938, poet, novelist, diplomat; lyricist for *Lift Every Voice and Sing.*
John H. Johnson, 1918-2005; built publishing empire based on *Ebony* and *Jet.*
Barbara Jordan, 1936-96, congresswoman, orator, educator.; first black woman to win a seat in the Texas senate, 1966.
Ernest Everett Just, 1883-1941, marine biologist; studied egg development; author, *Biology of Cell Surfaces,* 1941.
Rev. Martin Luther King Jr., 1929-68, civil rights leader; led 1956 Montgomery, AL, boycott; founder, pres., Southern Christian Leadership Conference, 1957; Nobel laureate (1964); assassinated.
Lewis H. Latimer, 1848-1928, associate of Edison; supervised installation of first electric street lighting in NYC.
Henry Lewis, 1932-1996, (U.S.) conductor; first black conductor and musical director of major American orchestra.
Malcolm X (Little), 1925-65, Black Muslim, black nationalist leader; promoted black pride; assassinated.
Thurgood Marshall, 1908-93, first black U.S. solicitor general, 1965; first black justice of U.S. Sup. Ct., 1967-91.
Benjamin Mays, 1895-1984, educator, civil rights leader; headed Morehouse College, 1940-67.
Ronald McNair, 1950-86, physicist, astronaut; killed in *Challenger* explosion.
Dorie Miller, 1919-43, Navy hero of Pearl Harbor attack.
Elijah Muhammad, 1897-1975, founded Nation of Islam, 1931.
Huey P. Newton, 1942-89, co-founded Black Panther Party, 1966.
Frederick D. Patterson, 1901-88, founder of United Negro College Fund, 1944.
Harold R. Perry, 1916-91, first black American Roman Catholic bishop in the 20th cent.
Adam Clayton Powell Jr., 1908-72, early civil rights leader, congressman, 1945-69.
Joseph H. Rainey, 1832-87, first black person elected to U.S. House, 1869, from South Carolina.
A. Philip Randolph, 1889-1979, organized Brotherhood of Sleeping Car Porters, 1925; an organizer of 1941 and 1963 March on Washington movements.
Hiram R. Revels, 1822-1901, first African-American U.S. senator, elected in Mississippi, served 1870-71.
Norbert Rillieux, 1806-94; invented a vacuum pan evaporator, 1846, revolutionized sugar-refining industry.
Paul Robeson, 1898-1976, actor, singer, civil rights activist.
Jackie Robinson, 1919-72, first African-American in major league baseball, 1947, and the Baseball Hall of Fame, 1962.
Carl T. Rowan, 1925-2000, reporter, columnist, author.
Bayard Rustin, 1910-87, an organizer of the 1963 March on Washington; exec. director, A. Philip Randolph Institute.
Carl Stokes, 1927-1996, first black mayor of a major American city (Cleveland), 1967-72.
Willard Townsend, 1895-1957, organized the United Transport Service Employees (redcaps), 1935.
Sojourner Truth, 1797-1883, born Isabella Baumfree; preacher, abolitionist; worked for black educ. opportunity.
Harriet Tubman, 1823-1913, Underground Railroad conductor, nurse and spy for Union Army in the Civil War.
Nat Turner, 1800-31, led most significant of more than 200 slave revolts in U.S., in Southampton, VA; hanged.
Booker T. Washington, 1856-1915, founder, 1881, and first pres. of Tuskegee Institute; *Up From Slavery.*
Harold Washington, 1922-87, first black mayor of Chicago.
Robert C. Weaver, 1907-97, first African-American appointed to cabinet; secretary of HUD.
Phillis Wheatley, c1753-84, poet; 2d American woman and first black woman to be published, 1770.
Walter White, 1893-1955, exec. sec., NAACP, 1931-55.
Roy Wilkins, 1901-81, exec. director, NAACP, 1955-77.
Daniel Hale Williams, 1858-1931, surgeon; performed one of first two open-heart operations, 1893.
Carter G. Woodson, 1875-1950, historian; founded Assn. for the Study of Negro Life and History.
Frank Yerby, 1916-91, first best-selling African-American novelist; *The Foxes of Harrow.*
Coleman A. Young, 1918-97, first Afr.-Amer. mayor of Detroit, 1974-93.

Architects and Some of Their Projects

Max Abramovitz, 1908-2004, Avery Fisher Hall, NYC; U.S. Steel Bldg. (now USX Towers), Pittsburgh, PA.
Henry Bacon, 1866-1924, Lincoln Memorial, Washington, DC.
Pietro Belluschi, 1899-1994, Juilliard School, Lincoln Center, Pan Am, now MetLife, Bldg. (with Walter Gropius), NYC.
Marcel Breuer, 1902-81, Whitney Museum of American Art (with Hamilton Smith), NYC.
Charles Bulfinch, 1763-1844, State House, Boston; Capitol (part), Washington, DC.
Gordon Bunshaft, 1909-90, Lever House, Park Ave, NYC; Hirshhorn Museum, Washington, DC.
Daniel H. Burnham, 1846-1912, Union Station, Washington DC; Flatiron Bldg., NYC.
Irwin Chanin, 1892-1988, theaters, skyscrapers, NYC.
David Childs, b 1941, Washington Mall Master Plan/Constitution Gardens, Washington, DC; WTC Freedom Tower, NYC.
Lucio Costa, 1902-98, master plan for city of Brasilia, with Oscar Niemeyer.
Ralph Adams Cram, 1863-1942, Cath. of St. John the Divine, NYC; U.S. Military Acad. (part), West Point, NY.
Norman Foster, b 1935, Commerzbank Headquarters, Frankfurt-am-Main, Ger.; London Millennium Bridge, London.
R. Buckminster Fuller, 1895-1983, U.S. Pavilion (geodesic domes), Expo 67, Montreal.
Frank O. Gehry, b 1929, Guggenheim Museum, Bilbao, Spain; Experience Music Project, Seattle, WA.
Cass Gilbert, 1859-1934, Custom House, Woolworth Bldg., NYC; Supreme Court Bldg., Washington, DC.
Bertram G. Goodhue, 1869-1924, Capitol, Lincoln, NE; St. Thomas's Church, St. Bartholomew's Church, NYC.
Michael Graves, b 1934, Portland Bldg., Portland, OR; Humana Bldg., Louisville, KY.
Walter Gropius, 1883-1969, Pan Am Bldg. (now MetLife Bldg.) (with Pietro Belluschi), NYC.
Lawrence Halprin, b 1916, Ghirardelli Sq., San Francisco; Nicollet Mall, Minneapolis; FDR Memorial, Washington, DC.
Peter Harrison, 1716-75, Touro Synagogue, Redwood Library, Newport, RI.
Wallace K. Harrison, 1895-1981, Metropolitan Opera House, Lincoln Center, NYC.
Thomas Hastings, 1860-1929, NY Public Library (with John Carrère), Frick Mansion, NYC.
James Hoban, 1762-1831, White House, Washington, DC.
Raymond Hood, 1881-1934, Rockefeller Center (part), Daily News, NYC; Tribune, Chicago, IL.
Richard M. Hunt, 1827-95, Metropolitan Museum (part), NYC; National Observatory, Washington, DC.
Helmut Jahn, b 1940, United Airlines Terminal, O'Hare Airport, Chicago.
William Le Baron Jenney, 1832-1907, Home Insurance (demolished 1931), Chicago, IL.
Philip C. Johnson, 1906-2005, AT&T headquarters (now 550 Madison Ave.), NYC; Transco Tower, Houston, TX.
Albert Kahn, 1869-1942, General Motors Bldg., Detroit, MI.
Louis Kahn, 1901-74, Salk Laboratory, La Jolla, CA; Yale Art Gallery, New Haven, CT.
Christopher Grant LaFarge, 1862-1938, Roman Catholic Chapel, West Point, NY.
Benjamin H. Latrobe, 1764-1820, Capitol (part), Washington, DC; State Capitol Bldg., Richmond, VA.
Le Corbusier, (Charles-Edouard Jeanneret), 1887-1965, Salvation Army Hostel and Swiss Dormitory, both Paris; master plan for cities of Algiers and Buenos Aires.
William Lescaze, 1896-1969, Philadelphia Savings Fund Society; Borg-Warner Bldg., Chicago.
Maya Lin, b 1959, Vietnam Veterans Mem., Washington, DC.
Charles Rennie Mackintosh, 1868-1928, Glasgow School of Art; Hill House, Helensburgh.

Bernard R. Maybeck, 1862-1957, Hearst Hall, Univ. of CA, Berkeley; First Church of Christ Scientist, Berkeley, CA.
Charles F. McKim, 1847-1909, Public Library, Boston; Columbia Univ. (part), NYC.
Charles M. McKim, b 1920, KUHT-TV Transmitter Bldg., Lutheran Church of the Redeemer, Houston, TX.
Richard Meier, b 1934, Getty Center Museum, Los Angeles, CA; High Museum of Art, Atlanta, GA.
Ludwig Mies van der Rohe, 1886-1969, Seagram Bldg. (with Philip C. Johnson), NYC; National Gallery, Berlin.
Robert Mills, 1781-1855, Washington Monument, Wash., DC.
Charles Moore, 1925-93, Sea Ranch, near San Francisco; Piazza d'Italia, New Orleans, LA.
Richard J. Neutra, 1892-1970, Mathematics Park, Princeton, NJ; Orange Co. Courthouse, Santa Ana, CA.
Oscar Niemeyer, b 1907, government buildings, Brasilia Palace Hotel, all Brasilia.
Gyo Obata, b 1923, Natl. Air & Space Museum, Smithsonian Inst., Washington, DC; Dallas-Ft. Worth Airport.
Frederick L. Olmsted, 1822-1903, Central Park, NYC; Fairmount Park, Philadelphia, PA.
I(eoh) M(ing) Pei, b 1917, East Wing, Natl. Gallery of Art, Washington, DC; Pyramid, The Louvre, Paris; Rock & Roll Hall of Fame and Museum, Cleveland, OH.
Cesar Pelli, b 1926, World Financial Center, Carnegie Hall Tower, NYC; Petronas Twin Towers, Malaysia.
William Pereira, 1909-85, Cape Canaveral; Transamerica Bldg., San Francisco, CA.
John Russell Pope, 1874-1937, National Gallery, Wash., DC.
John Portman, b 1924, Peachtree Center, Atlanta, GA.
George Browne Post, 1837-1913, NY Stock Exchange; Capitol, Madison, WI.
James Renwick Jr., 1818-95, Grace Church, St. Patrick's Cath., NYC.; Corcoran (Renwick) Gallery, Washington, DC.
Henry H. Richardson, 1838-86, Trinity Church, Boston, MA.
Kevin Roche, b 1922, Oakland Museum, Oakland, CA; Fine Arts Center, University of Massachusetts, Amherst.
James Gamble Rogers, 1867-1947, Columbia-Presbyterian Medical Center, NYC; Northwestern Univ., Evanston, IL.
John Wellborn Root, 1887-1963, Palmolive Bldg., Chicago; Hotel Statler, Washington, DC.
Paul Rudolph, 1918-97, Jewitt Art Center, Wellesley Colllege, MA; Art & Architecture Bldg., Yale Univ., New Haven, CT.
Eero Saarinen, 1910-61, Gateway to the West Arch, St. Louis, MO; Trans World Airlines Flight Center, NYC.
Louis Skidmore, 1897-1962, Atomic Energy Commission town site, Oak Ridge, TN; Terrace Plaza Hotel, Cincinnati, OH.
Clarence S. Stein, 1882-1975, Temple Emanu-El, NYC.
Edward Durell Stone, 1902-78, U.S. Embassy, New Delhi, India; (H. Hartford) Gallery of Modern Art, NYC.
Louis H. Sullivan, 1856-1924, Auditorium Bldg., Chicago, IL.
Kenzo Tange, 1913-2005, Hiroshima Peace Park, 1964 Tokyo Olympics twin stadiums.
Richard Upjohn, 1802-78, Trinity Church, NYC.
Max O. Urbahn, 1912-95, Vehicle Assembly Bldg., Cape Canaveral, FL.
Robert Venturi, b 1925, Gordon Wu Hall, Princeton, NJ; Mielparque Nikko Kirifuri Resort, Japan.
Ralph T. Walker, 1889-1973, NY Telephone Bldg. (now NYNEX); IBM Research Lab, Poughkeepsie, NY.
Roland A. Wank, 1898-1970, Cincinnati Union Terminal, OH; head architect (1933-44), Tennessee Valley Authority.
Stanford White, 1853-1906, Washington Arch in Washington Square Park, first Madison Square Garden, NYC.
Frank Lloyd Wright, 1867-1959, Imperial Hotel, Tokyo; Guggenheim Museum, NYC; Marin County Civic Center, San Rafael; Kaufmann "Fallingwater" house, Bear Run, PA.; Taliesin West, Scottsdale, AZ.
William Wurster, 1895-1973, Ghirardelli Sq., San Francisco.
Minoru Yamasaki, 1912-86, World Trade Center, NYC.

Artists, Photographers, and Sculptors of the Past

Artists are painters unless otherwise indicated.

Berenice Abbott, 1898-1991, (U.S.) photographer. Documentary of New York City, *Changing New York* (1939).
Ansel Easton Adams, 1902-84, (U.S.) photographer. Landscapes of the American Southwest.
Washington Allston, 1779-1843, (U.S.) landscapist. *Belshazzar's Feast.*
Albrecht Altdorfer, 1480-1538, (Ger.) landscapist.
Andrea del Sarto, 1486-1530, (It.) frescoes. *Madonna of the Harpies.*
Fra Angelico, c1400-55, (It.) Renaissance muralist. *Madonna of the Linen Drapers' Guild.*
Diane Arbus, 1923-71, (U.S.) photographer. Disturbing images.
Alexsandr Archipenko, 1887-1964, (U.S.) sculptor. *Boxing Match, Medranos.*
Eugène Atget, 1856-1927, (Fr.) photographer. Paris life.
John James Audubon, 1785-1851, (U.S.) *Birds of America.*
Hans Baldung-Grien, 1484-1545, (Ger.) *Todentanz.*
Ernst Barlach, 1870-1938, (Ger.) Expressionist sculptor. *Man Drawing a Sword.*
Frederic-Auguste Bartholdi, 1834-1904, (Fr.) *Liberty Enlightening the World, Lion of Belfort.*
Fra Bartolommeo, 1472-1517, (It.) *Vision of St. Bernard.*
Romare Bearden, 1911-88, (U.S.) collage and other media. *The Visitation.*
Aubrey Beardsley, 1872-98, (Br.) illustrator. *Salome, Lysistrata, Morte d'Arthur, Volpone.*
Max Beckmann, 1884-1950, (Ger.) Expressionist. *The Descent From the Cross.*
Gentile Bellini, 1426-1507, (It.) Renaissance. *Procession in St. Mark's Square.*
Giovanni Bellini, 1428-1516, (It.) *St. Francis in Ecstasy.*
Jacopo Bellini, 1400-70, (It.) *Crucifixion.*
George Wesley Bellows, 1882-1925, (U.S.) sports artist, portraitist, landscapist. *Stag at Sharkey's, Edith Clavell.*
Thomas Hart Benton, 1889-1975, (U.S.) American regionalist. *Threshing Wheat, Arts of the West.*
Gianlorenzo Bernini, 1598-1680, (It.) Baroque sculpture. *The Assumption.*
Albert Bierstadt, 1830-1902, (U.S.) landscapist. *The Rocky Mountains, Mount Corcoran.*
George Caleb Bingham, 1811-79, (U.S.) *Fur Traders Descending the Missouri.*
William Blake, 1752-1827, (Br.) engraver. *Book of Job, Songs of Innocence, Songs of Experience.*
Rosa Bonheur, 1822-99, (Fr.) *The Horse Fair.*
Pierre Bonnard, 1867-1947, (Fr.) Intimist. *The Breakfast Room, Girl in a Straw Hat.*
Gutzon Borglum, 1871-1941, (U.S.) sculptor. Mt. Rushmore Memorial.
Hieronymus Bosch, 1450-1516, (Flem.) religious allegories. *The Crowning With Thorns.*
Sandro Botticelli, 1444-1510, (It.) Renaissance. *Birth of Venus, Adoration of the Magi, Guiliano de'Medici.*
Margaret Bourke-White, 1906-71, (U.S.) photographer, photojournalist. WW2, USSR, rural South during the Depression.
Mathew Brady, c1823-96, (U.S.) photographer. Official photographer of the Civil War.
Constantin Brancusi, 1876-1957, (Romanian-Fr.) Nonobjective sculptor. *Flying Turtle, The Kiss.*
Georges Braque, 1882-1963, (Fr.) Cubist. *Violin and Palette.*
Pieter Bruegel the Elder, c1525-69, (Flem.) *The Peasant Dance, Hunters in the Snow, Magpie on the Gallows.*
Pieter Bruegel the Younger, 1564-1638, (Flem.) *Village Fair, The Crucifixion.*
Edward Burne-Jones, 1833-98, (Br.) Pre-Raphaelite artist-craftsman. *The Mirror of Venus.*
Alexander Calder, 1898-1976, (U.S.) sculptor. *Lobster Trap and Fish Tail.*
Julia Cameron, 1815-79, (Br.) photographer. Considered one of the most important portraitists of the 19th cent.
Robert Capa (Andrei Friedmann), 1913-54, (Hung.-U.S.) photographer. War photojournalist; invasion of Normandy.
Michelangelo Merisi da Caravaggio, 1573-1610, (It.) Baroque. *The Supper at Emmaus.*
Emily Carr, 1871-1945, (Can.) landscapist. *Blunden Harbour, Big Raven, Rushing Sea of Undergrowth.*
Carlo Carrà, 1881-1966, (It.) Metaphysical school. *Lot's Daughters, The Enchanted Room.*
Henri Cartier-Bresson, 1908-2004, (Fr.) photographer. *Imagenes à la sauvette.*
Mary Cassatt, 1844-1926, (U.S.) Impressionist. *The Cup of Tea, Woman Bathing, The Boating Party.*
George Catlin, 1796-1872, (U.S.) American Indian life. *Gallery of Indians, Buffalo Dance.*
Benvenuto Cellini, 1500-71, (It.) Mannerist sculptor, goldsmith. *Perseus and Medusa.*
Paul Cézanne, 1839-1906, (Fr.) *Card Players, Mont-Sainte-Victoire With Large Pine Trees.*
Marc Chagall, 1887-1985, (Russ.) Jewish life and folklore. *I and the Village, The Praying Jew.*
Jean Simeon Chardin, 1699-1779, (Fr.) still lifes. *The Kiss, The Grace.*
Giorgio de Chirico, 1888-1978, (It.) painter, founded the metaphysical school. *Enigma of an Autumn Night.*
Frederick Church, 1826-1900, (U.S.) Hudson River school. *Niagara, Andes of Ecuador.*
Giovanni Cimabue, 1240-1302, (It.) Byzantine mosaicist. *Madonna Enthroned With St. Francis.*
Claude Lorrain (Claude Gellée), 1600-82, (Fr.) ideal-landscapist. *The Enchanted Castle.*
Thomas Cole, 1801-48, (U.S.) Hudson River school. *The Ox-Bow, In the Catskills.*

John Constable, 1776-1837, (Br.) landscapist. *Salisbury Cathedral From the Bishop's Grounds.*
John Singleton Copley, 1738-1815, (U.S.) portraitist. *Samuel Adams, Watson and the Shark.*
Lovis Corinth, 1858-1925, (Ger.) Expressionist. *Apocalypse.*
Jean-Baptiste-Camille Corot, 1796-1875, (Fr.) landscapist. *Souvenir de Mortefontaine, Pastorale.*
Correggio, 1494-1534, (It.) Renaissance muralist. *Mystic Marriages of St. Catherine.*
Gustave Courbet, 1819-77, (Fr.) Realist. *The Artist's Studio.*
Lucas Cranach the Elder, 1472-1553, (Ger.) Protestant Reformation portraitist. *Luther.*
Imogen Cunningham, 1883-1976, (U.S.) photographer, portraitist. Plant photography.
Nathaniel Currier, 1813-88, and **James M. Ives,** 1824-95, (both U.S.) lithographers. *A Midnight Race on the Mississippi, American Forest Scene—Maple Sugaring.*
John Steuart Curry, 1897-1946, (U.S.) Americana, murals. *Baptism in Kansas.*
Salvador Dalí, 1904-89, (Sp.) Surrealist. *Persistence of Memory, The Crucifixion.*
Honoré Daumier, 1808-79, (Fr.) caricaturist. *The Third-Class Carriage.*
Jacques-Louis David, 1748-1825, (Fr.) Neoclassicist. *The Oath of the Horatii.*
Arthur Davies, 1862-1928, (U.S.) Romantic landscapist. *Unicorns, Leda and the Dioscuri.*
Willem de Kooning, 1904-1997, (Dutch-U.S.) abstract expressionist. *Excavation, Woman I, Door to the River.*
Edgar Degas, 1834-1917, (Fr.) *The Ballet Class.*
Eugène Delacroix, 1798-1863, (Fr.) Romantic. *Massacre at Chios, Liberty Leading the People.*
Paul Delaroche, 1797-1856, (Fr.) historical themes. *Children of Edward IV.*
Luca Della Robbia, 1400-82, (It.) Renaissance terracotta artist. *Cantoria* (singing gallery), Florence cathedral.
Donatello, 1386-1466, (It.) Renaissance sculptor. *David, Gattamelata.*
Jean Dubuffet, 1902-85, (Fr.) painter, sculptor, printmaker. *Group of Four Trees.*
Marcel Duchamp, 1887-1968, (Fr.) Dada artist. *Nude Descending a Staircase, No. 2.*
Raoul Dufy, 1877-1953, (Fr.) Fauvist. *Chateau and Horses.*
Asher Brown Durand, 1796-1886, (U.S.) Hudson River school. *Kindred Spirits.*
Albrecht Dürer, 1471-1528, (Ger.) Renaissance painter, engraver, woodcuts. *St. Jerome in His Study, Melencolia I.*
Anthony van Dyck, 1599-1641, (Flem.) Baroque portraitist. *Portrait of Charles I Hunting.*
Thomas Eakins, 1844-1916, (U.S.) Realist. *The Gross Clinic.*
Alfred Eisenstaedt, 1898-1995, (Ger.-U.S.) photographer, photojournalist. Famous photo, V-J Day, Aug. 14, 1945.
Peter Henry Emerson, 1856-1936, (Br.) photographer. Promoted photography as an independent art form.
Jacob Epstein, 1880-1959, (Br.) religious and allegorical sculptor. *Genesis, Ecce Homo.*
Erté, 1892-1990, (Fr.) b. Romain de Tiertoff; painter, fashion and stage designer.
Jan van Eyck, c1390-1441, (Flem.) naturalistic panels. *Adoration of the Lamb.*
Roger Fenton, 1819-68, (Br.) photographer. Crimean War.
Anselm Feuerbach, 1829-80, (Ger.) Romantic Classicist. *Judgment of Paris, Iphigenia.*
John Bernard Flannagan, 1895-1942, (U.S.) animal sculptor. *Triumph of the Egg.*
Jean-Honoré Fragonard, 1732-1806, (Fr.) Rococo. *The Swing.*
Daniel Chester French, 1850-1931, (U.S.) *The Minute Man of Concord;* seated *Lincoln,* Lincoln Memorial, Washington, DC.
Caspar David Friedrich, 1774-1840, (Ger.) Romantic landscapes. *Man and Woman Gazing at the Moon.*
Thomas Gainsborough, 1727-88, (Br.) portraitist. *The Blue Boy, The Watering Place, Orpin the Parish Clerk.*
Alexander Gardner, 1821-82, (U.S.) photographer. Civil War; railroad construction; Great Plains Indians.
Paul Gauguin, 1848-1903, (Fr.) Post-impressionist. *The Tahitians, Spirit of the Dead Watching.*
Lorenzo Ghiberti, 1378-1455, (It.) Renaissance sculptor. Gates of Paradise baptistery doors, Florence.
Alberto Giacometti, 1901-66, (Swiss) attenuated sculptures of solitary figures. *Man Pointing.*
Giorgione, c1477-1510, (It.) Renaissance. *The Tempest.*
Giotto di Bondone, 1267-1337, (It.) Renaissance. *Presentation of Christ in the Temple.*
François Girardon, 1628-1715, (Fr.) Baroque sculptor of classical themes. *Apollo Tended by the Nymphs.*
Vincent van Gogh, 1853-90, (Dutch) *The Starry Night, L'Arlesienne, Bedroom at Arles, Self-Portrait.*
Edward Gorey, 1925-2000, (U.S.) artist, illustrator. *The Doubtful Guest.*
Arshile Gorky, 1905-48, (U.S.) Surrealist. *The Liver Is the Cock's Comb.*
Francisco de Goya y Lucientes, 1746-1828, (Sp.) *The Naked Maja, The Disasters of War* (etchings).
El Greco, 1541-1614, (Sp.) *View of Toledo, Assumption of the Virgin.*
Horatio Greenough, 1805-52, (U.S.) Neo-classical sculptor.
Matthias Grünewald, 1480-1528, (Ger.) mystical religious themes. *The Resurrection.*
Frans Hals, c1580-1666, (Dutch) portraitist. *Laughing Cavalier, Gypsy Girl.*
Austin Hansen, 1910-96, (U.S.) photographer. Harlem, NY, life.
Childe Hassam, 1859-1935, (U.S.) Impressionist. *Southwest Wind, July 14 Rue Daunon.*
Edward Hicks, 1780-1849, (U.S.) folk painter. *The Peaceable Kingdom.*
Lewis Wickes Hine, 1874-1940, (U.S.) photographer. Studies of immigrants, children in industry.
Hans Hofmann, 1880-1966, (U.S.) early abstract Expressionist. *Spring, The Gate.*
William Hogarth, 1697-1764, (Br.) caricaturist. *The Rake's Progress.*
Katsushika Hokusai, 1760-1849, (Jpn.) printmaker. *Crabs.*
Hans Holbein the Elder, 1460-1524, (Ger.) late Gothic. *Presentation of Christ in the Temple.*
Hans Holbein the Younger, 1497-1543, (Ger.) portraitist. *Henry VIII, The French Ambassadors.*
Winslow Homer, 1836-1910, (U.S.) naturalist painter, marine themes. *Marine Coast, High Cliff.*
Edward Hopper, 1882-1967, (U.S.) realistic urban scenes. *Nighthawks, House by the Railroad.*
Horst P. Horst, 1906-99, (Ger.) fashion, celebrity photographer.
Jean-Auguste-Dominique Ingres, 1780-1867, (Fr.) Classicist. *Valpincon Bather.*
George Inness, 1825-94, (U.S.) luminous landscapist. *Delaware Water Gap.*
William Henry Jackson, 1843-1942, (U.S.) photographer. American West, building of Union Pacific Railroad.
Donald Judd, 1928-94, (U.S.) sculptor, major Minimalist.
Frida Kahlo, 1907-54, (Mex.) painter; *Self-Portrait With Monkey.*
Vasily Kandinsky, 1866-1944, (Russ.) Abstractionist. *Capricious Forms, Improvisation 38 (second version).*
Paul Klee, 1879-1940, (Swiss) Abstractionist. *Twittering Machine, Pastoral, Death and Fire.*
Gustav Klimt, 1862-1918, (Austrian) cofounder of Vienna Secession Movement, *The Kiss.*
Oscar Kokoschka, 1886-1980, (Austrian) Expressionist. *View of Prague, Harbor of Marseilles.*
Kathe Kollwitz, 1867-1945, (Ger.) printmaker, social justice themes. *The Peasant War.*
Gaston Lachaise, 1882-1935, (U.S.) figurative sculptor. *Standing Woman.*
John La Farge, 1835-1910, (U.S.) muralist. *Red and White Peonies, The Ascension.*
Sir Edwin (Henry) Landseer, 1802-73, (Br.) painter, sculptor. *Shoeing, Rout of Comus.*
Dorothea Lange, 1895-1965, (U.S.) photographer. Depression photographs, migrant farm workers.
Fernand Léger, 1881-1955, (Fr.) machine art. *The Cyclists.*
Leonardo da Vinci, 1452-1519, (It.) *Mona Lisa, Last Supper, The Annunciation.*
Emanuel Leutze, 1816-68, (U.S.) historical themes. *Washington Crossing the Delaware.*
Roy Lichtenstein, 1923-97, (U.S.) pop artist.
Jacques Lipchitz, 1891-1973, (Fr.) Cubist sculptor. *Harpist.*
Filippino Lippi, 1457-1504, (It.) Renaissance.
Fra Filippo Lippi, 1406-69, (It.) Renaissance. *Coronation of the Virgin, Madonna and Child With Angels.*
Morris Louis, 1912-62, (U.S.) abstract Expressionist. *Signa, Stripes, Alpha-Phi.*
René Magritte, 1898-1967, (Belgian) Surrealist. *The Descent of Man, The Betrayal of Images.*
Aristide Maillol, 1861-1944, (Fr.) sculptor. *L'Harmonie.*
Édouard Manet, 1832-83, (Fr.) forerunner of Impressionism. *Luncheon on the Grass, Olympia.*
Andrea Mantegna, 1431-1506, (It.) Renaissance frescoes. *Triumph of Caesar.*
Franz Marc, 1880-1916, (Ger.) Expressionist. *Blue Horses.*
John Marin, 1870-1953, (U.S.) Expressionist seascapes. *Maine Island.*
Reginald Marsh, 1898-1954, (U.S.) satirical artist. *Tattoo and Haircut.*
Agnes Martin, 1912-2004, (U.S.) abstract artist. *Night Sea.*
Masaccio, 1401-28, (It.) Renaissance. *The Tribute Money.*
Henri Matisse, 1869-1954, (Fr.) Fauvist. *Woman With the Hat.*
Michelangelo Buonarroti, 1475-1564, (It.) *Pietà, David, Moses, The Last Judgment,* Sistine Chapel ceiling.
Jean-Francois Millet, 1814-75, (Fr.) painter of peasant subjects. *The Gleaners, The Man With a Hoe.*

Joan Miró, 1893-1983, (Sp.) Exuberant colors, playful images. Catalan landscape, *Dutch Interior.*
Amedeo Modigliani, 1884-1920, (It.) *Reclining Nude.*
Piet Mondrian, 1872-1944, (Dutch) Abstractionist. *Composition With Red, Yellow and Blue.*
Claude Monet, 1840-1926, (Fr.) Impressionist. *The Bridge at Argenteuil, Haystacks.*
Henry Moore, 1898-1986, (Br.) sculptor of large-scale, abstract works. *Reclining Figure* (several).
Gustave Moreau, 1826-98, (Fr.) Symbolist. *The Apparition, Dance of Salome.*
James Wilson Morrice, 1865-1924, (Can.) landscapist. *The Ferry, Quebec, Venice, Looking Over the Lagoon.*
William Morris, 1834-1896, (Br.) decorative artist, leader of the Arts and Crafts movement.
Grandma Moses, 1860-1961, (U.S.) folk painter. *Out for the Christmas Trees, Thanksgiving Turkey.*
Edvard Munch, 1863-1944, (Nor.) Expressionist. *The Cry.*
Bartolome Murillo, 1618-82, (Sp.) Baroque religious artist. *Vision of St. Anthony, The Two Trinities.*
Eadweard Muybridge, 1830-1904, (Br.-U.S.) photographer. Studies of motion, *Animal Locomotion.*
Nadar (Gaspar-Félix Tournachon), 1820-1910, (Fr.) photographer, caricaturist, portraitist. Invented photo-essay.
Barnett Newman, 1905-70, (U.S.) abstract Expressionist. *Stations of the Cross.*
Isamu Noguchi, 1904-88, (U.S.) abstract sculptor, designer. *Kouros, BirdC(MU),* sculptural gardens.
Georgia O'Keeffe, 1887-1986, (U.S.) Southwest motifs. *Cow's Skull: Red, White, and Blue, The Shelton With Sunspots.*
José Clemente Orozco, 1883-1949, (Mex.) frescoes. *House of Tears, Pre-Columbian Golden Age.*
Timothy H. O'Sullivan, 1840-82, (U.S.) Civil War photographer.
Charles Willson Peale, 1741-1827, (U.S.) Amer. Revolutionary portraitist. *The Staircase Group,* U.S. presidents.
Rembrandt Peale, 1778-1860, (U.S.) portraitist. Thomas Jefferson.
Pietro Perugino, 1446-1523, (It.) Renaissance. *Delivery of the Keys to St. Peter.*
Pablo Picasso, 1881-1973, (Sp.) painter, sculptor. *Guernica; Dove; Head of a Woman; Head of a Bull, Metamorphosis.*
Piero della Francesca, c1415-92, (It.) Renaissance. *Duke of Urbino, Flagellation of Christ.*
Camille Pissarro, 1830-1903, (Fr.) Impressionist. *Boulevard des Italiens, Morning, Sunlight; Bather in the Woods.*
Jackson Pollock, 1912-56, (U.S.) abstract Expressionist. *Autumn Rhythm.*
Nicolas Poussin, 1594-1665, (Fr.) Baroque pictorial classicism. *St. John on Patmos.*
Maurice B. Prendergast, c1860-1924, (U.S.) Post-impressionist water colorist. *Umbrellas in the Rain.*
Pierre-Paul Prud'hon, 1758-1823, (Fr.) Romanticist. *Crime Pursued by Vengeance and Justice.*
Pierre Cecile Puvis de Chavannes, 1824-98, (Fr.) muralist. *The Poor Fisherman.*
Raphael Sanzio, 1483-1520, (It.) Renaissance. *Disputa, School of Athens, Sistine Madonna.*
Man Ray, 1890-1976, (U.S.) Dada artist. *Observing Time, The Lovers, Marquis de Sade.*
Odilon Redon, 1840-1916, (Fr.) Symbolist painter, lithographer. *In the Dream, Vase of Flowers.*
Rembrandt van Rijn, 1606-69, (Dutch) *The Bridal Couple, The Night Watch.*
Frederic Remington, 1861-1909, (U.S.) painter, sculptor. Portrayer of the American West, *Bronco Buster.*
Pierre-Auguste Renoir, 1841-1919, (Fr.) Impressionist. *The Luncheon of the Boating Party, Dance in the Country.*
Joshua Reynolds, 1723-92, (Br.) portraitist. *Mrs. Siddons as the Tragic Muse.*
Herb Ritts, 1952-2002, (U.S.) photographer. Nudes, celebrities.
Diego Rivera, 1886-1957, (Mex.) frescoes. *The Fecund Earth.*
Larry Rivers, 1923-2002, (U.S.) painter, sculptor, often realistic; Dutch Masters series.
Henry Peach Robinson, 1830-1901 (Br.) photographer. A leader of "high art" photography.
Norman Rockwell, 1894-1978, (U.S.) painter, illustrator. *Saturday Evening Post* covers.
Auguste Rodin, 1840-1917, (Fr.) sculptor. *The Thinker.*
Mark Rothko, 1903-70, (U.S.) abstract Expressionist. *Light, Earth and Blue.*
Georges Rouault, 1871-1958, (Fr.) Expressionist. *Three Judges.*
Henri Rousseau, 1844-1910, (Fr.) primitive exotic themes. *The Snake Charmer.*
Theodore Rousseau, 1812-67, (Swiss-Fr.) landscapist. *Under the Birches, Evening.*
Peter Paul Rubens, 1577-1640, (Flem.) Baroque. *Mystic Marriage of St. Catherine.*
Jacob van Ruisdael, c1628-82, (Dutch) landscapist. *Jewish Cemetery.*
Charles M. Russell, 1866-1926, (U.S.) Western life.
Salomon van Ruysdael, c1600-70, (Dutch) landscapist. *River With Ferry-Boat.*
Albert Pinkham Ryder, 1847-1917, (U.S.) seascapes and allegories. *Toilers of the Sea.*
Augustus Saint-Gaudens, 1848-1907, (U.S.) memorial statues. *Farragut, Mrs. Henry Adams (Grief).*
Andrea Sansovino, 1460-1529, (It.) Renaissance sculptor. *Baptism of Christ.*
Jacopo Sansovino, 1486-1570, (It.) Renaissance sculptor. *St. John the Baptist.*
John Singer Sargent, 1856-1925, (U.S.) Edwardian society portraitist. The Wyndham Sisters, Madam X.
George Segal, 1924-2000, (U.S.) sculptor of life-sized figures realistically depicting daily life.
Georges Seurat, 1859-91, (Fr.) Pointillist. *Sunday Afternoon on the Island of La Grande Jatte.*
Gino Severini, 1883-1966, (It.) Futurist and Cubist. *Dynamic Hieroglyph of the Bal Tabarin.*
Ben Shahn, 1898-1969, (U.S.) social and political themes. Sacco and Vanzetti series, *Seurat's Lunch, Handball.*
Charles Sheeler, 1883-1965, (U.S.) abstractionist.
David Alfaro Siqueiros, 1896-1974, (Mex.) political muralist. *March of Humanity.*
David Smith, 1906-65, (U.S.) welded metal sculpture. *Hudson River Landscape, Zig, Cubi* series.
Edward Steichen, 1879-1973, (U.S.) photographer. Credited with transforming photography into an art form.
Alfred Stieglitz, 1864-1946, (U.S.) photographer, editor; helped create acceptance of photography as art.
Paul Strand, 1890-1976, (U.S.) photographer. People, nature, landscapes.
Gilbert Stuart, 1755-1828, (U.S.) portraitist. George Washington, Thomas Jefferson, James Madison.
Thomas Sully, 1783-1872, (U.S.) portraitist. *Col. Thomas Handasyd Perkins, The Passage of the Delaware.*
William Henry Fox Talbot, 1800-77, (Br.) photographer. *Pencil of Nature,* early photographically illustrated book.
George Tames, 1919-94, (U.S.) photographer. Chronicled presidents, political leaders.
Yves Tanguy, 1900-55, (Fr.) Surrealist. *Rose of the Four Winds, Mama, Papa Is Wounded!*
Giovanni Battista Tiepolo, 1696-1770, (It.) Rococo frescoes. *The Crucifixion.*
Jacopo Tintoretto, 1518-94, (It.) Mannerist. *The Last Supper.*
Titian, c1485-1576, (It.) Renaissance. *Venus and the Lute Player, The Bacchanal.*
Jose Rey Toledo, 1916-94, (U.S.) Native American artist. Captured the essence of tribal dances on canvas.
Henri de Toulouse-Lautrec, 1864-1901, (Fr.) *At the Moulin Rouge.*
John Trumbull, 1756-1843, (U.S.) historical themes. *The Declaration of Independence.*
J(oseph) M(allord) W(illiam) Turner, 1775-1851, (Br.) Romantic landscapist. *Snow Storm.*
Paolo Uccello, 1397-1475, (It.) Gothic-Renaissance. *The Rout of San Romano.*
Maurice Utrillo, 1883-1955, (Fr.) Impressionist. *Sacre-Coeur de Montmartre.*
John Vanderlyn, 1775-1852, (U.S.) Neo-classicist. *Ariadne Asleep on the Island of Naxos.*
Diego Velázquez, 1599-1660, (Sp.) Baroque. *Las Meninas, Portrait of Juan de Pareja.*
Jan Vermeer, 1632-75, (Dutch) interior genre subjects. *Young Woman With a Water Jug.*
Paolo Veronese, 1528-88, (It.) devotional themes, vastly peopled canvases. *The Temptation of St. Anthony.*
Andrea del Verrocchio, 1435-88, (It.) Floren. sculptor. *Colleoni.*
Maurice de Vlaminck, 1876-1958, (Fr.) Fauvist landscapist. *Red Trees.*
Andy Warhol, 1928-87, (U.S.) Pop Art. *Campbell's Soup Cans, Marilyn Diptych.*
Antoine Watteau, 1684-1721, (Fr.) Rococo painter of "scenes of gallantry." *The Embarkation for Cythera.*
George Frederic Watts, 1817-1904, (Br.) painter and sculptor of grandiose allegorical themes. *Hope.*
Benjamin West, 1738-1820, (U.S.) realistic historical themes. *Death of General Wolfe.*
Edward Weston, 1886-1958, (U.S.) photographer. Landscapes of American West.
James Abbott McNeill Whistler, 1834-1903, (U.S.) *Arrangement in Grey and Black, No. 1: The Artist's Mother.*
Archibald M. Willard, 1836-1918, (U.S.) *The Spirit of '76.*
Grant Wood, 1891-1942, (U.S.) Midwestern regionalist. *American Gothic, Daughters of Revolution.*
Ossip Zadkine, 1890-1967, (Russ.) School of Paris sculptor. *The Destroyed City, Musicians, Christ.*

Business Leaders and Philanthropists of the Past

Giovanni Agnelli, 1921-2003, (It.) industrialist, principal shareholder of Fiat.
Walter Annenberg, 1908-2002, (U.S.) publisher, founder *TV Guide*, philanthropist.
Elizabeth Arden (F. N. Graham), 1884-1966, (U.S.) Canadian-born founder of cosmetics empire.
Philip D. Armour, 1832-1901, (U.S.) industrialist; streamlined meatpacking.
John Jacob Astor, 1763-1848, (U.S.) German-born fur trader, banker, real estate magnate; at death, richest in U.S.
Francis W. Ayer, 1848-1923, (U.S.) ad industry pioneer.
August Belmont, 1816-90, (U.S.) German-born financier.
James B. (Diamond Jim) Brady, 1856-1917, (U.S.) financier, philanthropist, legendary bon vivant.
Adolphus Busch, 1839-1913, (U.S.) German-born businessman; established brewery empire.
Asa Candler, 1851-1929, (U.S.) founded Coca-Cola Co.
Andrew Carnegie, 1835-1919, (U.S.) Scottish-born industrialist; philanthropist; founded Carnegie Steel Co.
Tom Carvel, 1908-89, (Gr.-U.S.) founded ice cream chain.
William Colgate, 1783-1857, (Br.-U.S.) Br.-born businessman, philanthropist; founded soap-making empire.
Jay Cooke, 1821-1905, (U.S.) financier; sold $1 billion in Union bonds during Civil War.
Peter Cooper, 1791-1883, (U.S.) industrialist, inventor, philanthropist; founded Cooper Union (1859).
Ezra Cornell, 1807-74, (U.S.) businessman, philanthropist; headed Western Union, established university.
Erastus Corning, 1794-1872, (U.S.) financier; headed N.Y. Central.
Charles Crocker, 1822-88, (U.S.) railroad builder, financier.
Samuel Cunard, 1787-1865, (Can.) pioneered trans-Atlantic steam navigation.
Marcus Daly, 1841-1900, (U.S.) Irish-born copper magnate.
W. Edwards Deming, 1900-93, (U.S.) quality-control expert who revolutionized Japanese manufacturing.
Walt Disney, 1901-66, (U.S.) pioneer in cinema animation; built entertainment empire.
Herbert H. Dow, 1866-1930, (U.S.) founder of chemical co.
James Duke, 1856-1925, (U.S.) founded American Tobacco, Duke Univ.
Eleuthere I. du Pont, 1771-1834, (Fr.-U.S.) gunpowder manufacturer; founded one of the largest business empires.
Thomas C. Durant, 1820-85, (U.S.) railroad official, financier.
William C. Durant, 1861-1947, (U.S.) industrialist; formed General Motors.
George Eastman, 1854-1932, (U.S.) inventor; manufacturer of photographic equipment.
Marshall Field, 1834-1906, (U.S.) merchant; founded Chicago's largest department store.
Harvey Firestone, 1868-1938, (U.S.) founded tire company.
Avery Fisher, 1906-94, (U.S.) industrialist, philanthropist, founded Fisher electronics.
Henry M. Flagler, 1830-1913, (U.S.) financier; helped form Standard Oil; developed Florida as resort state.
Malcolm Forbes, 1919-90, (U.S.) magazine publisher.
Henry Ford, 1863-1947, (U.S.) auto maker; developed first popular low-priced car.
Henry Ford 2nd, 1917-87, (U.S.) headed auto company founded by grandfather.
Henry C. Frick, 1849-1919, (U.S.) steel and coke magnate; had prominent role in development of U.S. Steel.
Jakob Fugger (Jakob the Rich), 1459-1525, (Ger.) headed leading banking, trading house, in 16th-cent. Europe.
Alfred C. Fuller, 1885-1973, (U.S.) Canadian-born businessman; founded brush company.
Elbert H. Gary, 1846-1927, (U.S.) one of the organizers of U.S. Steel; chaired board of directors, 1903-27.
Jean Paul Getty, 1892-1976, (U.S.) founded oil empire.
Amadeo Giannini, 1870-1949, (U.S.) founded Bank of America.
Stephen Girard, 1750-1831, (U.S.) French-born financier, philanthropist; richest man in U.S. at his death.
Leonard H. Goldenson, 1905-99, (U.S.) turned ABC into major TV network.
Jay Gould, 1836-92, (U.S.) railroad magnate, financier.
Hetty Green, 1834-1916, (U.S.) financier, the "witch of Wall St."; richest woman in U.S. in her day.
William Gregg, 1800-67, (U.S.) launched textile industry in S.
Meyer Guggenheim, 1828-1905, (U.S.) Swiss-born merchant, philanthropist; built merchandising, mining empires.
Armand Hammer, 1898-1990, (U.S.) headed Occidental Petroleum; promoted U.S.-Soviet ties.
Edward H. Harriman, 1848-1909, (U.S.) railroad financier, administrator; headed Union Pacific.
Henry J. Heinz, 1844-1919, (U.S.) founded food empire.
Milton Snavely Hershey, 1857-1945, (U.S.) chocolate co. founder, philanthropist.
James J. Hill, 1838-1916, (U.S.) Canadian-born railroad magnate, financier; founded Great Northern Railway.
Conrad N. Hilton, 1888-1979, (U.S.) hotel chain founder.
Howard Hughes, 1905-76, (U.S.) industrialist, aviator, movie maker.
H. L. Hunt, 1889-1974, (U.S.) oil magnate.
Collis P. Huntington, 1821-1900, (U.S.) railroad magnate.
Henry E. Huntington, 1850-1927, (U.S.) railroad builder, philanthropist.
Walter L. Jacobs, 1898-1985, (U.S.) founder of the first rental car agency, which later became Hertz.
Howard Johnson, 1896-1972, (U.S.) founded restaurants.
Samuel Curtis Johnson, 1928-2004, (U.S.) headed S.C. Johnson & Sons.
Henry J. Kaiser, 1882-1967, (U.S.) industrialist; built empire in steel, aluminum.
Minor C. Keith, 1848-1929, (U.S.) railroad magnate; founded United Fruit Co.
Will K. Kellogg, 1860-1951, (U.S.) businessman, philanthropist; founded breakfast food co.
Richard King, 1825-85, (U.S.) cattleman; founded half-million-acre King Ranch in Texas.
William S. Knudsen, 1879-1948, (U.S.) Danish-born auto industry executive.
Samuel H. Kress, 1863-1955, (U.S.) businessman, art collector, philanthropist; founded "dime store" chain.
Ray A. Kroc, 1902-84, (U.S.) original CEO of McDonald's Corp.; oversaw company's vast expansion.
Alfred Krupp, 1812-87, (Ger.) armaments magnate.
William Levitt, 1907-94, (U.S.) industrialist, "suburb maker".
Thomas Lipton, 1850-1931, (Scot.) merchant, tea empire.
James McGill, 1744-1813, (Scot.-Can.) founded university.
Andrew W. Mellon, 1855-1937, (U.S.) financier, industrialist; benefactor of National Gallery of Art.
Charles E. Merrill, 1885-1956, (U.S.) financier; developed firm of Merrill Lynch.
John Pierpont Morgan, 1837-1913, (U.S.) most powerful figure in finance and industry at the turn of the cent.
Akio Morita, 1921-99, (Japan) co-founded Sony Corp.
Malcolm Muir, 1885-1979, (U.S.) created *Business Week* magazine; headed *Newsweek,* 1937-61.
Samuel Newhouse, 1895-1979, (U.S.) publishing and broadcasting magnate; built communications empire.
Aristotle Onassis, 1906-75, (Gr.) shipping magnate.
William S. Paley, 1901-90, (U.S.) built CBS communic. empire.
George Peabody, 1795-1869, (U.S.) merchant, financier, philanthropist.
James C. Penney, 1875-1971, (U.S.) businessman; developed department store chain.
William C. Procter, 1862-1934, (U.S.) headed soap co.
Frank Perdue, 1920-2005, (U.S.) founder of Perdue Farms, chicken-processing company.
John D. Rockefeller, 1839-1937, (U.S.) industrialist; established Standard Oil.
John D. Rockefeller Jr., 1874-1960, (U.S.) philanthropist; established foundation; provided land for UN.
Laurance S. Rockefeller, 1910-2004, (U.S.) philanthropist, conservationist.
Meyer A. Rothschild, 1743-1812, (Ger.) founded international banking house.
Thomas Fortune Ryan, 1851-1928, (U.S.) financier; a founder of American Tobacco.
Edmond J. Safra, 1932-99, (U.S.), banker.
David Sarnoff, 1891-1971, (U.S.) broadcasting pioneer; established first radio network, NBC.
Richard Sears, 1863-1914, (U.S.) founded mail-order co.
Werner von Siemens, 1816-92, (Ger.) industrialist; inventor.
Alfred P. Sloan, 1875-1966, (U.S.) industrialist, philanthropist; headed General Motors.
A. Leland Stanford, 1824-93, (U.S.) railroad official, philanthropist; founded university.
Nathan Straus, 1848-1931, (U.S.) German-born merchant, philanthropist; headed Macy's.
Levi Strauss, c1829-1902, (U.S.) pants manufacturer.
Clement Studebaker, 1831-1901, (U.S.) wagon, carriage maker.
Gustavus Swift, 1839-1903, (U.S.) pioneer meatpacker.
Gerard Swope, 1872-1957, (U.S.) industrialist, economist; headed General Electric.
Dave Thomas, 1932-2002, (U.S.) Wendy's founder.
James Walter Thompson, 1847-1928, (U.S.) ad executive.
Alice Tully, 1902-93, (U.S.) philanthropist, arts patron.
Theodore N. Vail, 1845-1920, (U.S.) organized Bell Telephone system; headed AT&T.
Cornelius Vanderbilt, 1794-1877, (U.S.) financier; established steamship, railroad empires.
Henry Villard, 1835-1900, (U.S.) German-born railroad executive, financier.

George Westinghouse, 1846-1914, (U.S) inventor, manufacturer; organized Westinghouse Electric Co., 1886.
Charles R. Walgreen, 1873-1939, (U.S.) founded drugstore chain.
DeWitt Wallace, 1889-1981, (U.S.) and **Lila Wallace,** 1889-1984, (U.S.) cofounders of *Reader's Digest* magazine.
Sam Walton, 1918-92, (U.S.) founder of Wal-Mart stores.
John Wanamaker, 1838-1922, (U.S.) pioneered department-store merchandising.
Aaron Montgomery Ward, 1843-1913, (U.S.) established first mail-order firm.
Thomas J. Watson, 1874-1956, (U.S.) IBM head, 1914-56.
John Hay Whitney, 1905-82, (U.S.) publisher, sportsman, philanthropist.
Charles E. Wilson, 1890-1961, (U.S.) auto exec., public official.
Frank W. Woolworth, 1852-1919, (U.S.) created 5 & 10 chain.
William Wrigley Jr., 1861-1932, (U.S.) founded Wrigley chewing gum company.

American Cartoonists

Reviewed by Lucy Shelton Caswell, Professor and Curator, Cartoon Research Library, Ohio State University

Scott Adams, b 1957, Dilbert.
Charles Addams, 1912-88, macabre cartoons.
Brad Anderson, b 1924, Marmaduke.
Sergio Aragones, b 1937, *MAD Magazine.*
Peter Arno, 1904-68, *The New Yorker.*
Tex Avery, 1908-80, animator, Bugs Bunny, Porky Pig.
George Baker, 1915-75, The Sad Sack.
Carl Barks, 1901-2000, Donald Duck comic books.
C. C. Beck, 1910-89, Captain Marvel.
Dave Berg, 1920-2002, *Mad Magazine.*
Jim Berry, b 1932, Berry's World.
Herb Block (Herblock), 1909-2001, political cartoonist.
George Booth, b 1926, *The New Yorker.*
Berkeley Breathed, b 1957, Bloom County.
Dik Browne, 1917-89, Hi & Lois, Hagar the Horrible.
Marjorie Buell, 1904-93, Little Lulu.
Ernie Bushmiller, 1905-82, Nancy.
Milton Caniff, 1907-88, Terry & the Pirates, Steve Canyon.
Al Capp, 1909-79, Li'l Abner.
Roz Chast, b 1954, *The New Yorker.*
Paul Conrad, 1924, political cartoonist.
Roy Crane, 1901-77, Captain Easy, Buz Sawyer.
Robert Crumb, b 1943, underground cartoonist.
Shamus Culhane, 1908-96, animator.
Jay N. Darling (Ding), 1876-1962, political cartoonist.
Jack Davis, b 1926, *MAD Magazine.*
Jim Davis, b 1945, Garfield.
Billy DeBeck, 1890-1942, Barney Google.
Rudolph Dirks, 1877-1968, The Katzenjammer Kids.
Walt Disney, 1901-66, produced animated cartoons, created Mickey Mouse, Donald Duck.
Steve Ditko, b 1927, Spider-Man.
Mort Drucker, b 1929, *MAD Magazine.*
Will Eisner, 1917-2005, The Spirit.
Jules Feiffer, b 1929, political cartoonist.
Bud Fisher, 1884-1954, Mutt & Jeff.
Ham Fisher, 1900-55, Joe Palooka.
Max Fleischer, 1883-1972, Betty Boop.
Hal Foster, 1892-1982, Tarzan, Prince Valiant.
Fontaine Fox, 1884-1964, Toonerville Folks.
Isadore "Friz" Freleng, 1905-95, animator, Yosemite Sam, Porky Pig, Sylvester and Tweety Bird.
Rube Goldberg, 1883-1970, Boob McNutt.
Chester Gould, 1900-85, Dick Tracy.
Harold Gray, 1894-1968, Little Orphan Annie.
Matt Groening, b 1954, Life in Hell, The Simpsons.
Cathy Guisewite, b 1950, Cathy.
Bill Hanna, 1910-2001, & **Joe Barbera,** b 1911, animators, Tom & Jerry, Yogi Bear, Flintstones.
Johnny Hart, b 1931, BC, Wizard of Id.
Oliver Harrington, 1912-95, Bootsie.
Alfred Harvey, 1913-94, created Casper the Friendly Ghost.
Jimmy Hatlo, 1898-1963, Little Iodine.
John Held Jr., 1889-1958, Jazz Age.
George Herriman, 1881-1944, Krazy Kat.
Harry Hershfield, 1885-1974, Abie the Agent.
Al Hirschfeld, 1903-2003, *N.Y. Times* theater caricaturist.
Burne Hogarth, 1911-96, Tarzan.
Helen Hokinson, 1900-49, *The New Yorker.*
Nicole Hollander, b 1939, Sylvia.
Chuck Jones, 1912-2002, animator, Bugs Bunny, Porky Pig.
Mike Judge, b. 1962, Beavis and Butt-head, King of the Hill.
Bob Kane, b 1916-98, Batman.
Bil Keane, b 1922, The Family Circus.
Walt Kelly, 1913-73, Pogo.
Hank Ketcham, 1920-2001, Dennis the Menace.
Ted Key, b 1912, Hazel.
Frank King, 1883-1969, Gasoline Alley.
Jack Kirby, 1917-94, Fantastic Four, The Incredible Hulk.
Rollin Kirby, 1875-1952, political cartoonist.
B(ernard) Kliban, 1935-91, cat books.
Edward Koren, b 1935, *The New Yorker.*
Harvey Kurtzman, 1921-93, *MAD Magazine.*
Walter Lantz, 1900-94, Woody Woodpecker.
Gary Larson, b 1950, The Far Side.
Mell Lazarus, b 1929, Momma, Miss Peach.
Stan Lee, b 1922, Marvel Comics.
David Levine, b 1926, *N.Y. Review of Books* caricatures.
Doug Marlette, b 1949, political cartoonist, Kudzu.
Don Martin, 1931-2000, *MAD Magazine.*
Bill Mauldin, 1921-2003, political cartoonist.
Jeff MacNelly, 1947-2000, political cartoonist, Shoe.
Winsor McCay, 1872-1934, Little Nemo.
John T. McCutcheon, 1870-1949, political cartoonist.
Aaron McGruder, b 1974, The Boondocks.
George McManus, 1884-1954, Bringing Up Father.
Dale Messick, 1906-2005, Brenda Starr.
Norman Mingo, 1896-1980, Alfred E. Neuman.
Bob Montana, 1920-75, Archie.
Dick Moores, 1909-86, Gasoline Alley.
Willard Mullin, 1902-78, sports cartoonist; Dodgers "Bum," Mets "Kid."
Russell Myers, b 1938, Broom Hilda.
Thomas Nast, 1840-1902, political cartoonist; Republican elephant and Democratic donkey.
Pat Oliphant, b 1935, political cartoonist.
Frederick Burr Opper, 1857-1937, Happy Hooligan.
Richard Outcault, 1863-1928, Yellow Kid, Buster Brown.
Brant Parker, b 1920, Wizard of Id.
Trey Parker, b 1969, animator, co-creator of *South Park.*
Mike Peters, b 1943, cartoonist, Mother Goose & Grimm.
George Price, 1901-95, *The New Yorker.*
Antonio Prohias, 1921-98, Spy vs. Spy.
Alex Raymond, 1909-56, Flash Gordon, Jungle Jim.
Forrest (Bud) Sagendorf, 1915-94, Popeye.
Art Sansom, 1920-91, The Born Loser.
Charles Schulz, 1922-2000, Peanuts.
Elzie C. Segar, 1894-1938, Popeye.
Joe Shuster, 1914-92, & **Jerry Siegel,** 1914-96, Superman.
Sidney Smith, 1887-1935, The Gumps.
Otto Soglow, 1900-75, Little King.
Art Spiegelman, b 1948, Raw, Maus.
William Steig, b 1907, *The New Yorker.*
Matt Stone, b 1971, animator, co-creator of South Park.
Paul Szep, b 1941, political cartoonist.
James Swinnerton, 1875-1974, Little Jimmy, Canyon Kiddies.
Paul Terry, 1887-1971, animator of Mighty Mouse.
Bob Thaves, b 1924, Frank and Ernest.
James Thurber, 1894-61, *The New Yorker.*
Garry Trudeau, b 1948, Doonesbury.
Mort Walker, b 1923, Beetle Bailey.
Bill Watterson, b 1958, Calvin and Hobbes.
Russ Westover, 1887-1966, Tillie the Toiler.
Signe Wilkinson, b 1950, political cartoonist.
Frank Willard, 1893-1958, Moon Mullins.
J. R. Williams, 1888-1957, The Willets Family, Out Our Way.
Gahan Wilson, b 1930, *The New Yorker.*
Tom Wilson, b 1931, Ziggy.
Art Young, 1866-1943, political cartoonist.
Chic Young, 1901-73, Blondie.

WORLD ALMANAC QUICK QUIZ

O'Shea Jackson is better known under which of these names below?

(a) Ice Cube (b) Ice-T (c) Meat Loaf (d) Slim Pickens

For the answer look in this chapter, or see page 1008.

Economists, Educators, Historians, and Social Scientists of the Past

For Psychologists see Scientists of the Past.

Brooks Adams, 1848-1927, (U.S.) historian, political theoretician; *The Law of Civilization and Decay.*
Henry Adams, 1838-1918, (U.S.) historian, autobiographer; *The Education of Henry Adams.*
Francis Bacon, 1561-1626, (Eng.) philosopher, essayist, and statesman; championed observation and induction.
George Bancroft, 1800-91, (U.S.) historian; wrote 10-volume *History of the United States.*
Jack Barbash, 1911-94, (U.S.) labor economist who helped create the AFL-CIO.
Henry Barnard, 1811-1900, (U.S.) public school reformer.
Charles A. Beard, 1874-1948, (U.S.) historian; *The Economic Basis of Politics.*
(St.) Bede (the Venerable), c673-735, (Br.) scholar, historian; *Ecclesiastical History of the English People.*
Ruth Benedict, 1887-1948, (U.S.) anthropologist; studied Indian tribes of the Southwest.
Sir Isaiah Berlin, 1909-97, (Br.) philosopher, historian; *The Age of Enlightenment.*
Leonard Bloomfield, 1887-1949, (U.S.) linguist; *Language.*
Franz Boas, 1858-1942, (U.S.) German-born anthropologist; studied American Indians.
Van Wyck Brooks, 1886-1963, (U.S.) historian; critic of New England culture, especially literature.
Edmund Burke, 1729-97, (Ir.) British parliamentarian and political philosopher; *Reflections on the Revolution in France.*
Nicholas Murray Butler, 1862-1947, (U.S.) educator; headed Columbia Univ., 1902-45; Nobel Peace Prize, 1931.
Joseph Campbell, 1904-87, (U.S.) author, editor, teacher; wrote books on mythology, folklore.
Thomas Carlyle, 1795-1881, (Sc.) historian, critic; *Sartor Resartus, Past and Present, The French Revolution.*
Edward Channing, 1856-1931, (U.S.) historian; wrote 6-volume *History of the United States.*
Henry Steele Commager, 1902-98, (U.S.) historian, educator; wrote *The Growth of the American Republic.*
John R. Commons, 1862-1945, (U.S.) economist, labor historian; *Legal Foundations of Capitalism.*
James B. Conant, 1893-1978, (U.S.) educator, diplomat; *The American High School Today.*
Benedetto Croce, 1866-1952, (It.) philosopher, statesman, and historian; *Philosophy of the Spirit.*
Bernard A. De Voto, 1897-1955, (U.S.) historian; wrote trilogy on American West; edited Mark Twain manuscripts.
Melvil Dewey, 1851-1931, (U.S.) devised decimal system of library-book classification.
Emile Durkheim, 1858-1917, (Fr.) a founder of modern sociology; *The Rules of Sociological Method.*
Charles Eliot, 1834-1926, (U.S.) educator, Harvard president.
Friedrich Engels, 1820-95, (Ger.) political writer; with Marx wrote the *Communist Manifesto.*
Irving Fisher, 1867-1947, (U.S.) economist; contributed to the development of modern monetary theory.
John Fiske, 1842-1901, (U.S.) historian and lecturer; popularized Darwinian theory of evolution.
Charles Fourier, 1772-1837, (Fr.) utopian socialist.
Giovanni Gentile, 1875-1944, (It.) philosopher, educator; reformed Italian educational system.
Sir James George Frazer, 1854-1941, (Br.) anthropologist; studied myth in religion; *The Golden Bough.*
Henry George, 1839-97, (U.S.) economist, reformer; led single-tax movement.
Edward Gibbon, 1737-94, (Br.) historian; *The History of the Decline and Fall of the Roman Empire.*
Francesco Guicciardini, 1483-1540, (It.) historian; *Storia d'Italia,* principal historical work of the 16th cent.
Thomas Hobbes, 1588-1679, (Eng.) philosopher, political theorist; *Leviathan.*
Richard Hofstadter, 1916-70, (U.S.) historian; *The Age of Reform.*
George F. Kennan, 1904-2005, (U.S.) diplomat, historian; main architect of the U.S. Cold War "containment" strategy.
John Maynard Keynes, 1883-1946, (Br.) economist; principal advocate of deficit spending.
Russell Kirk, 1918-94, (U.S.), social philosopher; *The Conservative Mind.*
Alfred L. Kroeber, 1876-1960, (U.S.) cultural anthropologist; studied Indians of North and South America.
Elisabeth Kubler-Ross, 1926-2004, (Swiss) psychiatrist, author. *On Death and Dying.*
Christopher Lasch, 1932-94, (U.S.) social critic, historian; *The Culture of Narcissism.*
James L. Laughlin, 1850-1933, (U.S.) economist; helped establish Federal Reserve System.
Lucien Lévy-Bruhl, 1857-1939, (Fr.) philosopher; studied the psychology of primitive societies; *Primitive Mentality.*
John Locke, 1632-1704, (Eng.) philosopher and political theorist; *Two Treatises of Government.*
Thomas B. Macaulay, 1800-59, (Br.) historian, statesman.
Niccolò Machiavelli, 1469-1527, (It.) writer, statesman. *The Prince.*
Bronislaw Malinowski, 1884-1942, (Pol.) considered the father of social anthropology.
Thomas R. Malthus, 1766-1834, (Br.) economist; famed for *Essay on the Principle of Population.*
Horace Mann, 1796-1859, (U.S.) pioneered modern public school system.
Karl Mannheim, 1893-1947, (Hung.) sociologist, historian; *Ideology and Utopia.*
Harriet Martineau, 1802-76, (Eng.) writer, feminist; *Society in America*
Karl Marx, 1818-83, (Ger.) political theorist, proponent of Communism; *Communist Manifesto, Das Kapital.*
Giuseppe Mazzini, 1805-72, (It.) political philosopher.
William H. McGuffey, 1800-73, (U.S.) whose *Reader* was a mainstay of 19th-cent. U.S. public education.
George H. Mead, 1863-1931, (U.S.) philosopher, social psychologist.
Margaret Mead, 1901-78, (U.S.) cultural anthropologist; popularized field; *Coming of Age in Samoa.*
Alexander Meiklejohn, 1872-1964, (U.S.) Br.-born educator; championed academic freedom and experimental curricula.
James Mill, 1773-1836, (Sc.) philosopher, historian, economist; a proponent of utilitarianism.
John Stuart Mill, 1806-73, (Eng.) philosopher, economist, *Utilitarianism*; eldest son of James Mill.
Perry G. Miller, 1905-63, (U.S.) historian; interpreted 17th-cent. New England.
Theodor Mommsen, 1817-1903, (Ger.) historian; *The History of Rome.*
Ashley Montagu, 1905-99, (Eng.) anthropologist; *The Natural Superiority of Women.*
Charles-Louis Montesquieu, 1689-1755, (Fr.) social philosopher; *The Spirit of Laws.*
Maria Montessori, 1870-1952, (It.) educator, physician; started Montessori method of student self-motivation.
Samuel Eliot Morison, 1887-1976, (U.S.) historian; chronicled voyages of early explorers.
Lewis Mumford, 1895-1990, (U.S.) sociologist, critic; *The Culture of Cities.*
Gunnar Myrdal, 1898-1987, (Swed.) economist, social scientist; *Asian Drama: An Inquiry Into the Poverty of Nations.*
Allan Nevins, 1890-1971, (U.S.) historian, biographer; *The Ordeal of the Union.*
José Ortega y Gasset, 1883-1955, (Sp.) philosopher; advocated control by elite, *The Revolt of the Masses.*
Robert Owen, 1771-1858, (Br.) political philosopher, reformer; pioneer in cooperative movement.
Thomas (Tom) Paine, 1737-1809, (U.S.) political theorist, writer. *Common Sense.*
Vilfredo Pareto, 1848-1923, (It.) economist, sociologist.
Francis Parkman, 1823-93, (U.S.) historian; *France and England in North America.*
Elizabeth P. Peabody, 1804-94, (U.S.) education pioneer; founded 1st kindergarten in U.S., 1860.
William Prescott, 1796-1859, (U.S.) early American historian; *The Conquest of Peru.*
Pierre Joseph Proudhon, 1809-65, (Fr.) social theorist; father of anarchism; *The Philosophy of Property.*
François Quesnay, 1694-1774, (Fr.) economic theorist.
David Ricardo, 1772-1823, (Br.) economic theorist; advocated free international trade.
David Riesman, 1909-2002, (U.S.) sociologist, coauthor *The Lonely Crowd.*
Jean-Jacques Rousseau, 1712-78, (Fr.) social philosopher; the father of romantic sensibility; *Confessions.*
Edward Sapir, 1884-1939, (Ger.-U.S.) anthropologist; studied ethnology and linguistics of U.S. Indian groups.
Ferdinand de Saussure, 1857-1913, (Swiss) a founder of modern linguistics.
Joseph Schumpeter, 1883-1950, (Czech.-U.S.) economist, sociologist.
Elizabeth Seton, 1774-1821, (U.S.) nun; est. parochial school education in U.S.; first native-born American saint.
George Simmel, 1858-1918, (Ger.) sociologist, philosopher; helped establish German sociology.
Adam Smith, 1723-90, (Br.) economist; advocated laissez-faire economy, free trade; *The Wealth of Nations.*
Jared Sparks, 1789-1866, (U.S.) historian, educator, editor; *The Library of American Biography.*
Oswald Spengler, 1880-1936, (Ger.) philosopher and historian; *The Decline of the West.*

William G. Sumner, 1840-1910, (U.S.) social scientist, economist; laissez-faire economy, Social Darwinism.
Hippolyte Taine, 1828-93, (Fr.) historian; basis of naturalistic school; *The Origins of Contemporary France.*
A(lan) J(ohn) P(ercivale) Taylor, 1906-89, (Br.) historian; *The Origins of the Second World War.*
Nikolaas Tinbergen, 1907-88, (Dutch-Br.) ethologist; pioneer in study of animal behavior.
Alexis de Tocqueville, 1805-59, (Fr.) political scientist, historian; *Democracy in America.*
Francis E. Townsend, 1867-1960, (U.S.) led old-age pension movement, 1933.
Arnold Toynbee, 1889-1975, (Br.) historian; *A Study of History,* sweeping analysis of hist. of civilizations.
George Trevelyan, 1838-1928, (Br.) historian, statesman; favored "literary" over "scientific" history; *History of England.*
Frederick J. Turner, 1861-1932, (U.S.) historian, educator; *The Frontier in American History.*
Thorstein B. Veblen, 1857-1929, (U.S.) economist, social philosopher; *The Theory of the Leisure Class.*
Giovanni Vico, 1668-1744, (It.) historian, philosopher; regarded by many as first modern historian; *New Science.*
Izaak Walton, 1593-1683, (Eng.) wrote biographies; political-philosophical study of fishing, *The Compleat Angler.*
Sidney J., 1859-1947, and **Beatrice,** 1858-1943, **Webb,** (Br.) leading figures in Fabian Society and Labor Party.
Max Weber, 1864-1920, (Ger.) sociologist; *The Protestant Ethic and the Spirit of Capitalism.*
Emma Hart Willard, 1787-1870, (U.S.) pioneered higher education for women.
C. Vann Woodward, 1908-99, (U.S.) historian; *The Strange Career of Jim Crow.*

American Journalists of the Past

Reviewed by Dean Mills, Dean, Missouri School of Journalism

See also African-Americans, Business Leaders, Cartoonists, Writers of the Past.

Franklin P. Adams (F.P.A.), 1881-1960, humorist; wrote column "The Conning Tower."
Joseph W. Alsop, 1910-89, and **Stewart Alsop,** 1914-74, Washington-based political analysts, columnists.
Brooks Atkinson, 1894-1984, theater critic.
Bartley, Robert L., 1937-2003, editorial-page editor for *Wall Street Journal.*
James Gordon Bennett, 1795-1872, editor and publisher; founded *NY Herald.*
James Gordon Bennett, 1841-1918, succeeded father, financed expeditions, founded afternoon paper.
Elias Boudinot, d 1839, founding editor of first Native American newspaper in U.S., *Cherokee Phoenix* (1828-34).
David Brinkley, 1920-2003, co-anchor of NBC's *Huntley-Brinkley Report,* host of ABC's *This Week With David Brinkley.*
Margaret Bourke-White, 1904-71, photojournalist.
Arthur Brisbane, 1864-1936, editor; helped introduce "yellow jounalism" with sensational, simply written articles.
Heywood Broun, 1888-1939, author, columnist; founded American Newspaper Guild.
Herb Caen, 1916-97, longtime columnist for *San Francisco Chronicle* and *Examiner.*
John Campbell, 1653-1728, published *Boston News-Letter,* first continuing newspaper in the American colonies.
Jimmy Cannon, 1909-73, syndicated sports columnist.
John Chancellor, 1927-96, NBC TV reporter, anchor.
Harry Chandler, 1864-1944, *Los Angeles Times* publisher, 1917-41; made it a dominant force.
Marquis Childs, 1903-90, reporter and columnist for *St. Louis Post-Dispatch* and United Feature syndicate.
Craig Claiborne, 1920-2000, *NY Times* food editor and critic; key in internationalizing American taste.
Elizabeth Cochrane (Nellie Bly), pioneer woman journalist, investig. reporter, noted for series on trip around the world.
Charles Collingwood, 1917-85, CBS news correspondent.
Alistair Cooke, 1908-2004, journalist, TV narrator, naturalized American citizen, "Letter from America" series.
Howard Cosell, 1920-95, TV and radio sportscaster.
Gardner Cowles, 1861-1946, founded newspaper chain.
Cyrus Curtis, 1850-1933, publisher of *Saturday Evening Post, Ladies' Home Journal, Country Gentleman.*
John Charles Daly, 1914-91, war correspondent; TV journalist; Voice of America head.
Charles Anderson Dana, 1819-97, editor, publisher; made *NY Sun* famous for its news reporting.
Elmer (Holmes) Davis, 1890-1958, *NY Times* editorial writer; radio commentator.
Richard Harding Davis, 1864-1916, war correspondent, travel writer, fiction writer.
Benjamin Day, 1810-89, published *NY Sun* beginning in 1833, introducing penny press to the U.S.
Finley Peter Dunne, 1867-1936, humorist, social critic, wrote "Mr. Dooley" columns.
Mary Baker Eddy, 1821-1910, founded Christian Science movement and *Christian Science Monitor.*
Rowland Evans Jr., 1921-2001, Washington columnist.
Fanny Fern (Sarah Willis Parton), 1811-1872, newspaper columnist, author.
Marshall Field III, 1893-1956, retail magnate, *Chicago Sun* founder.
Doris Fleeson, 1901-70, war correspondent, columnist.
James Franklin, 1697-1735, printer, pioneer journalist, publisher of *New England Courant* and *Rhode Island Gazette.*
Fred W. Friendly, 1915-98, radio, TV reporter, producer, executive, collaborator with Edward R. Murrow.
Margaret Fuller, 1810-50, social reformer, transcendentalist, critic and foreign correspondent for *NY Tribune.*
Frank E. Gannett, 1876-1957, founded newspaper chain.
William Lloyd Garrison, 1805-79, abolitionist; publisher of *The Liberator.*
Elizabeth Meriwether Gilmer (Dorothy Dix), 1861-1951, reporter, pioneer of the advice column genre.
Edwin Lawrence Godkin, 1831-1902, founder of *The Nation,* editor of *N.Y. Evening Post.*
Katharine Graham,1917-2001, *Washington Post* publisher.
Sheilah Graham, 1904-89, Hollywood gossip columnist.
Horace Greeley, 1811-72, editor and politician; founded *NY Tribune.*
Meg Greenfield, 1930-1999, *Newsweek* columnist, editorial page editor *Washington Post.*
Gilbert Hovey Grosvenor, 1875-1966, longtime editor of *National Geographic* magazine.
John Gunther, 1901-70, *Chicago Daily News* foreign correspondent, author.
Sarah Josepha Buell Hale, 1788-1879, first female magazine editor, (Ladies' Magazine, later Godey's Lady's Book)
William Randolph Hearst, 1863-1951, founder of Hearst newspaper chain and one of the pioneer yellow journalists.
Gabriel Heatter, 1890-1972, radio commentator.
John Hersey, 1914-98, foreign correspondent for *Time, Life,* and *The New Yorker,* author.
Marguerite Higgins, 1920-66, reporter, war correspondent.
Hedda Hopper, 1885-1966, Hollywood gossip columnist.
Roy Howard, 1883-1964, editor, executive, Scripps-Howard papers and United Press (later United Press International).
Chet (Chester Robert) Huntley, 1911-74, co-anchor of NBC's *Huntley-Brinkley Report.*
Ralph Ingersoll, 1900-85, editor, *Fortune, Time, Life* exec.
Peter Jennings, 1938-2005, ABC TV correspondent, anchor.
H. V. (Hans von) Kaltenborn, 1878-1965, radio commentator, reporter.
Murray Kempton, 1917-97, reporter, columnist for magazines and newspapers, including *NY Post.*
Dorothy Kilgallen, 1913-65, crime reporter; columnist.
John S. Knight, 1894-1981, editor, publisher; founded Knight newspaper group, which merged into Knight-Ridder.
Joseph Kraft, 1942-86, foreign policy columnist.
Arthur Krock, 1886-1974, *NY Times* political writer, Washington bureau chief.
Charles Kuralt, 1934-97, TV anchor and host of CBS "On the Road" featuring stories about life in the U.S.
Ann Landers (Eppie Lederer), 1918-2002, advice columnist.
David Lawrence, 1888-1973, reporter, columnist, publisher; founded *U.S. News & World Report.*
Frank Leslie, 1821-80, engraver and publisher of newspapers and magazines, notably *Leslie's Illustrated Newspaper.*
Alexander Liberman, 1912-99, editorial director for Conde Nast magazines.
A(bbott) J(oseph) Liebling, 1904-63, foreign correspondent, critic, principally with *The New Yorker.*
Walter Lippmann, 1889-1974, political analyst, social critic, columnist, author.
Peter Lisagor, 1915-76, Washington bureau chief, *Chicago Daily News;* broadcast commentator.
David Ross Locke, 1833-88, humorist, satirist under pseudonym P.V. Nasby; owned *Toledo (Ohio) Blade.*
Elijah Parish Lovejoy, 1802-37, abolitionist editor in St. Louis and in Alton, IL; killed by proslavery mob.
Clare Booth Luce, 1903-87, war correspondent for *Life;* diplomat, playwright.
Henry R. Luce, 1898-1967, founded *Time, Fortune, Life, Sports Illustrated.*
C(harles) K(enny) McClatchy, 1858-1936 founder of McClatchy newspaper chain.
Sarah McClendon, 1910-2003, (U.S.) veteran White House correspondent.

Samuel McClure, 1857-1949, founder (1893) of *McClure's Magazine*, famous for its investigative reporting.
Anne O'Hare McCormick, 1889-1954, foreign correspondent, first woman on *NY Times* editorial board.
Robert R. McCormick, 1880-1955, editor, publisher, executive of *Chicago Tribune* and *NY Daily News.*
Dwight Macdonald, 1906-1982, reporter, social critic.
Ralph McGill, 1893-1969, crusading editor and publisher of *Atlanta Constitution.*
Mary McGrory, 1918-2004, Washington, DC, columnist.
O(scar) O(dd) McIntyre, 1884-1938, feature writer, syndicated columnist on everyday life in New York City.
Don Marquis, 1878-1937, humor columnist for *NY Sun* and *N.Y. Tribune;* wrote "archy and mehitabel" stories.
Robert Maynard, 1937-97, first African-American editor and then owner of major U.S. paper, the *Oakland Tribune.*
Joseph Medill, 1823-99, longtime *editor of Chicago Tribune.*
H(enry) L(ouis) Mencken, 1880-1956, reporter, editor, columnist with *Baltimore Sun* papers; anti-establishment viewpoint.
Edwin Meredith, 1876-1928, founder of magazine company.
Frank A. Munsey, 1854-1925, owner, editor, and publisher of newspapers and magazines, including *Munsey's Magazine.*
Edward R. Murrow, 1908-65, broadcast reporter, executive; reported from Britain in WW2; hosted *See It Now, Person to Person.*
Louella Parsons, 1881-1972, Hollywood gossip columnist.
Drew (Andrew Russell) Pearson, 1897-1969, investigative reporter and columnist.
(James) Westbrook Pegler, 1894-1969, reporter, columnist.
Shirley Povich, 1905-98, sports columnist.
Joseph Pulitzer, 1847-1911, *NY World* publisher; founded Columbia Journalism School, Pulitzer Prizes.
Joseph Pulitzer II, 1885-1955, longtime *St. Louis Post-Dispatch* editor, publisher; built it into major paper.
Ernie (Ernest Taylor) Pyle, 1900-45, reporter, war correspondent; killed in WW2.
Henry Raymond, 1820-69, cofounder, editor, *NY Times.*
Harry Reasoner, 1923-91, ABC and CBS news reporter, anchor.
John Reed, 1887-1920, reporter, foreign correspondent famous for coverage of Bolshevik Revolution.
Whitelaw Reid, 1837-1912, longtime editor, *NY Tribune.*
James Reston, 1909-95 *NY Times* political reporter, columnist.
Frank Reynolds, 1923-83, ABC reporter, anchor.
(Henry) Grantland Rice, 1880-1954, sportswriter.
Jacob Riis, 1849-1914, reporter, photographer; exposed slum conditions in *How the Other Half Lives.*
Max Robinson, 1939-88, first African-American to anchor network news (ABC), 1978.
Harold Ross, 1892-1951, founder, editor, The *New Yorker.*
Mike Royko, 1932-97, Chicago newspaper columnist; wrote *Boss*, biography of Mayor Richard Daley.
(Alfred) Damon Runyon, 1884-1946, sportswriter, columnist; stories collected in *Guys and Dolls.*
John B. Russwurm, 1799-1851, cofounded (1827) nation's first black newspaper, *Freedom's Journal,* in NYC.
Adela Rogers St. Johns, 1894-1988, reporter, sportswriter for Hearst newspapers.
Pierre Salinger, 1925-2004, press secretary under Pres. Kennedy and Johnson; foreign correspondent.
Harrison Salisbury, 1908-93, reporter, foreign correspondent; a Soviet specialist.
E(dward) W(yllis) Scripps, 1854-1926, founded first large U.S. newspaper chain, pioneered syndication.
Eric Sevareid, 1912-92, war correspondent, radio newscaster, CBS commentator.
William L. Shirer, 1904-93, broadcaster, foreign correspondent; wrote *The Rise and Fall of the Third Reich.*
Howard K. Smith, 1914-2002, ABC TV reporter, anchor.
Red (Walter) Smith, 1905-82, sportswriter.
Edgar P. Snow, 1905-71, correspondent, expert on Chinese Communist movement.
Lawrence Spivak, 1900-94, co-creator, moderator, producer of *Meet the Press.*
(Joseph) Lincoln Steffens, 1866-1936, muckraking journalist.
I(sidor) F(einstein) Stone, 1907-89, one-man editor of *I.F. Stone's Weekly.*
Arthur Hays Sulzberger, 1891-1968, longtime publisher of *N.Y. Times.*
C(yrus) L(eo) Sulzberger, 1912-93, *N.Y. Times* foreign correspondent and columnist.
David Susskind, 1920-87, TV producer, public affairs talk-show host (*Open End*).
John Cameron Swayze, 1906-95, early TV newscaster (NBC).
Herbert Bayard Swope, 1882-1958, war correspondent and editor of *N.Y. World.*
Ida Tarbell, 1857-1944, muckraking journalist.
Isaiah Thomas, 1750-1831, printer, publisher, cofounder of revolutionary journal, *Massachusetts Spy.*
Lowell Thomas, 1892-1981, radio newscaster, world traveler.
Dorothy Thompson, 1894-1961, foreign correspondent, columnist, radio commentator.
Hunter S. Thompson, 1937-20058, political journalist, author *Fear and Loathing* on the Campaign Trail (1972).
Ida Bell Wells-Barnett, 1862-1931, African-American reporter, editor, anti-lynching crusader.
William Allen White, 1868-1944, newspaper editor, publisher.
Walter Winchell, 1897-1972, reporter, columnist, broadcaster of celebrity news.
John Peter Zenger, 1697-1746, printer and journalist; acquitted in precedent-setting libel suit (1735).

Military and Naval Leaders of the Past

Reviewed by Alan C. Aimone, USMA Library

Alexander the Great, 356-323 B.C., (Maced.) conquered Persia and much of the world known to Europeans.
Harold Alexander, 1891-1969, (Br.) led Allied invasion of Italy, 1943, WW2.
Ethan Allen, 1738-89, (U.S.) headed Green Mountain Boys; captured Ft. Ticonderoga, 1775, Amer. Rev.
Edmund Allenby, 1861-1936, (Br.) in Boer War, WW1; led Egyptian expeditionary force, 1917-18.
Benedict Arnold, 1741-1801, (U.S.) victorious at Saratoga; tried to betray West Point to British, Amer. Rev.
Henry "Hap" Arnold, 1886-1950, (U.S.) commanded Army Air Force in WW2.
Ashurnasirpal II, 884-859 B.C., (Assyria) king, began Assyrian conquest of Middle East.
John Barry, 1745-1803, (U.S.) won numerous sea battles during Amer. Rev.
Belisarius, c505-565, (Byzant.) won remarkable victories for Byzantine Emperor Justinian I.
Pierre Beauregard, 1818-93, (U.S.) Confed. general, ordered bombardment of Ft. Sumter that began Civil War.
Gebhard von Blücher, 1742-1819, (Ger.) helped defeat Napoleon at Waterloo.
Simón Bolívar, 1783-1830, (Venez.) S. Amer. Revolutionary who liberated much of the continent from Spanish rule.
Napoleon Bonaparte, 1769-1821, (Fr.) defeated Russia and Austria at Austerlitz, 1805; invaded Russia, 1812; defeated at Waterloo, 1815.
Edward Braddock, 1695-1755, (Br.) commanded forces in French and Indian War.
Omar N. Bradley, 1893-1981, (U.S.) headed U.S. ground troops in Normandy invasion, 1944, WW2.
John Burgoyne, 1722-92, (Br.) general, defeated at Saratoga, Amer. Rev.
Julius Caesar, 100-44 B.C., (Rom.) general and politician; conquered N Gaul; overthrew Roman Republic.
Charlemagne, 742-814, (Fr.) king of the Franks, Holy Roman Emperor, conquered most of Western Europe.
El Cid (Rodrigo Diaz de Vivar), 1040-99, (Sp.) renowned knight, captured Valencia (1094); hero of Song of Cid epic.
Claire Lee Chennault, 1893-1958, (U.S.) headed Flying Tigers in WW2.
Mark W. Clark, 1896-1984, (U.S.) helped plan N. African invasion in WW2; commander of UN forces, Korean War.
Karl von Clausewitz, 1780-1831, (Pruss.) military theorist.
Lucius D. Clay, 1897-1978, (U.S.) led Berlin airlift, 1948-49.
Henry Clinton, 1738-95, (Br.) commander of forces in Amer. Rev., 1778-81.
Cochise, c1815-74, (Nat. Am.) chief of Chiricahua band of Apache Indians in Southwest.
Charles Cornwallis, 1738-1805, (Br.) victorious at Brandywine, 1777; surrendered at Yorktown, Amer. Rev.
Hernán Cortés, 1485-1547, (Sp.) led Spanish conquistadors in the defeat of the Aztec empire, 1519-28.
Crazy Horse, 1849-77, (Nat. Am.) Sioux war chief victorious at battle of Little Bighorn.
George Armstrong Custer, 1839-76, (U.S.) U.S. army officer defeated and killed at battle of Little Bighorn.
Moshe Dayan, 1915-81, (Isr.) directed campaigns in the 1967, 1973 Arab-Israeli wars.
Stephen Decatur, 1779-1820, (U.S.) naval hero of Barbary wars, War of 1812.
Anton Denikin, 1872-1947, (Russ.) led White forces in Russian civil war.
George Dewey, 1837-1917, (U.S.) destroyed Spanish fleet at Manila, 1898, Span.-Amer. War.
Karl Doenitz, 1891-1980, (Ger.) submarine com. in chief and naval commander, WW2.

Jimmy Doolittle, 1896-1993, (U.S.) led 1942 air raid on Tokyo and other Japanese cities in WW2.
Hugh C. Dowding, 1883-1970, (Br.) headed RAF, 1936-40, WW2.
Jubal Early, 1816-94, (U.S.) Confed. general, led raid on Washington, 1864, Civil War.
Dwight D. Eisenhower, 1890-1969, (U.S.) commanded Allied forces in Europe, WW2.
Erich von Falkenhayn, 1861-1922, (Ger.) minister of war, general, commander at Verdun in WW1.
David Farragut, 1801-70, (U.S.) Union admiral, captured New Orleans, Mobile Bay, Civil War.
John Arbuthnot Fisher, 1841-1920, (Br.) WW1 admiral, naval reformer.
Ferdinand Foch, 1851-1929, (Fr.) headed victorious Allied armies, 1918, WW1.
Nathan Bedford Forrest, 1821-77, (U.S.) Confed. general, led raids against Union supply lines, Civil War.
Frederick the Great, 1712-86, (Pruss.) led Prussia in Seven Years War.
Horatio Gates, 1728-1806, (U.S.) commanded army at Saratoga, Amer. Rev.
Genghis Khan, 1162-1227, (Mongol) unified Mongol tribes and subjugated much of Asia, 1206-21.
Geronimo, 1829-1909, (Nat. Am.) leader of Chiricahua band of Apache Indians.
Charles G. Gordon, 1833-85, (Br.) led forces in China, Crimean War; killed at Khartoum.
Ulysses S. Grant, 1822-85, (U.S.) headed Union army, Civil War, 1864-65; forced Lee's surrender, 1865.
Nathanael Greene, 1742-86, (U.S.) defeated British in Southern campaign, 1780-81, Amer. Rev.
Heinz Guderian, 1888-1953, (Ger.) tank theorist, led panzer forces in Poland, France, Russia, WW2.
Gustavus Adolphus, 1594-1632, (Swed.) King; military tactician; reformer; led forces in Thirty Years' War.
Douglas Haig, 1861-1928, (Br.) led British armies in France, 1915-18, WW1.
William F. Halsey, 1882-1959, (U.S.) defeated Japanese fleet at Leyte Gulf, 1944, WW2.
Hannibal, 247-183 B.C., (Carthag.) invaded Rome, crossing Alps, in Second Punic War, 218-201 B.C.
Sir Arthur Travers Harris, 1895-1984, (Br.) led Britain's WW2 bomber command.
Paul von Hindenburg, 1847-1934, (Ger.) chief of general staff, WW1; 2nd pres. of Weimar Republic.
Richard Howe, 1726-99, (Br.) commanded navy in Amer. Rev., 1776-78; June 1 victory against French, 1794.
William Howe, 1729-1814, (Br.) commanded forces in Amer. Rev., 1776-78.
Isaac Hull, 1773-1843, (U.S.) sunk British frigate Guerriere, War of 1812.
Thomas (Stonewall) Jackson, 1824-63, (U.S.) Confed. general, led Shenandoah Valley campaign, Civil War.
Joseph Joffre, 1852-1931, (Fr.) headed Allied armies, won Battle of the Marne, 1914, WW1.
Chief Joseph, c1840-1904, (Nat. Am.) chief of the Nez Percé, forced by army to retreat and surrender.
John Paul Jones, 1747-92, (U.S.) commanded Bonhomme Richard in victory over Serapis, Amer. Rev., 1779.
Stephen Kearny, 1794-1848, (U.S.) headed Army of the West in Mexican War.
Albert Kesselring, 1885-1960 (Ger.) field marshal who led the defense of Italy in WW2.
Ernest J. King, 1878-1956, (U.S.) key WW2 naval strategist.
Horatio H. Kitchener, 1850-1916, (Br.) led forces in Boer War; victorious at Khartoum; organized army in WW1.
Henry Knox, 1750-1806, (U.S.) general in Amer. Rev.; first sec. of war under U.S. Constitution.
Lavrenti Kornilov, 1870-1918, (Russ.) commander-in-chief, 1917; led counter-revolutionary march on Petrograd.
Thaddeus Kosciusko, 1746-1817, (Pol.) aided Amer. Rev.
Walter Krueger, 1881-1967, (U.S.) led Sixth Army in WW2 in Southwest Pacific.
Mikhail Kutuzov, 1745-1813, (Russ.) fought at Borodino, Napol. Wars, 1812; abandoned Moscow; forced French retreat.
Marquis de Lafayette, 1757-1834, (Fr.) fought in, secured French aid for Amer. Rev.
T(homas) E. Lawrence (of Arabia), 1888-1935, (Br.) organized revolt of Arabs against Turks in WW1.
William Daniel Leahy, 1875-1959, (U.S.) chief of staff to Pres. Roosevelt in WWII, Fleet Admiral.
Henry (Light-Horse Harry) Lee, 1756-1818, (U.S.) cavalry officer in Amer. Rev.
Robert E. Lee, 1807-70, (U.S.) Confed. general defeated at Gettysburg, Civil War; surrendered to Grant, 1865.
Curtis LeMay, 1906-90, (U.S.) Air Force commander in WW2, Korean War, and Vietnam War.
Lyman Lemnitzer, 1899-1988, (U.S.) WW2 hero, later general, chairman of Joint Chiefs of Staff.
James Longstreet, 1821-1904, (U.S.) aided Lee at Gettysburg, Civil War.
Erich Ludendorff, 1865-1937, (Ger.) general, victor at Tannenberg, WW1.
Maurice, Count of Nassau, 1567-1625, (Dutch) military innovator; led forces in Thirty Years' War.
Douglas MacArthur, 1880-1964, (U.S.) commanded forces in SW Pacific in WW2; headed occupation forces in Japan, 1945-51; UN commander in Korean War.
Erich von Manstein, 1887-1973, (Ger.) served WW1–2, planned inv. of France (1940), convicted of war crimes.
Carl Gustaf Mannerheim, 1867-1951, (Finn.) army officer and pres. of Finland 1944-46.
Francis Marion, 1733-95, (U.S.) led guerrilla actions in South Carolina during Amer. Rev.
Duke of Marlborough, 1650-1722, (Br.) led forces against Louis XIV in War of the Spanish Succession.
George C. Marshall, 1880-1959, (U.S.) chief of staff in WW2; authored Marshall Plan.
George B. McClellan, 1826-85, (U.S.) Union general, commanded Army of the Potomac, 1861-62, Civil War.
George Meade, 1815-72, (U.S.) commanded Union forces at Gettysburg, Civil War.
Billy Mitchell, 1879-1936, (U.S.) WW1 air-power advocate; court-martialed for insubordination, later vindicated.
Helmuth von Moltke, 1800-91, (Ger.) victorious in Austro-Prussian, Franco-Prussian wars.
Louis de Montcalm, 1712-59, (Fr.) headed troops in Canada, French and Indian War; defeated at Quebec, 1759.
Bernard Law Montgomery, 1887-1976, (Br.) stopped German offensive at Alamein, 1942, WW2; helped plan Normandy.
Daniel Morgan, 1736-1802, (U.S.) victorious at Cowpens, 1781, Amer. Rev.
Louis Mountbatten, 1900-79, (Br.) Supreme Allied Commander of SE Asia, 1943-46, WW2.
Joachim Murat, 1767-1815, (Fr.) led cavalry at Marengo, Austerlitz, and Jena, Napoleonic Wars.
Horatio Nelson, 1758-1805, (Br.) naval commander, destroyed French fleet at Trafalgar.
Michel Ney, 1769-1815, (Fr.) commanded forces in Switz., Aust., Russ., Napoleonic Wars; defeated at Waterloo.
Chester Nimitz, 1885-1966, (U.S.) commander of naval forces in Pacific in WW2.
George S. Patton, 1885-1945, (U.S.) led assault on Sicily, 1943, Third Army invasion of Europe, WW2.
Oliver Perry, 1785-1819, (U.S.) won Battle of Lake Erie in War of 1812.
John Pershing, 1860-1948, (U.S.) commanded Mexican border campaign, 1916, Amer. Expeditionary Force, WW1.
Henri Philippe Pétain, 1856-1951, (Fr.) defended Verdun, 1916; headed Vichy government in WW2.
George E. Pickett, 1825-75, (U.S.) Confed. general famed for "charge" at Gettysburg, Civil War.
Charles Portal, 1893-1971, (Br.) chief of staff, Royal Air Force, 1940-45, led in Battle of Britain.
Manfred Frieherr von Richthofen (Red Baron), 1892-1918, (Ger.) WW1 flying ace, led elite fighter squadron.
Hyman Rickover, 1900-86, (U.S.) father of nuclear navy.
Matthew Bunker Ridgway, 1895-1993, (U.S.) commanded Allied ground forces in Korean War.
Erwin Rommel, 1891-1944, (Ger.) headed Afrika Korps, WW2.
Gerd von Rundstedt, 1875-1953, (Ger.) supreme commander in West, 1942-45, WW2.
Saladin, 1138-93, (Kurdish Muslim) recaptured Jerusalem from Crusaders.
Aleksandr Samsonov, 1859-1914, (Russ.) led invasion of E Prussia, WW1, defeated at Tannenberg, 1914.
Antonio Lopez de Santa Anna, 1794-1876, (Mex.) defeated Texans at the Alamo; defeated in Mexican War.
Maurice, Count of Saxe, 1696-1750, (Fr.) general, War of Aust. Succession, War of Pol. Succession; noted tactician.
Scipio Africanus the Elder, 234?-183, (Rom.) hero of 2nd Punic War, defeated Hannibal, invaded N. Africa.
Winfield Scott, 1786-1866, (U.S.) hero of War of 1812; headed forces in Mexican War, took Mexico City.
Philip Sheridan, 1831-88, (U.S.) Union cavalry officer, headed Army of the Shenandoah, 1864-65, Civil War.
William T. Sherman, 1820-91, (U.S.) Union general, sacked Atlanta during "march to the sea," 1864, Civil War.
Carl Spaatz, 1891-1974, (U.S.) directed strategic bombing against Germany, later Japan, in WW2.
Raymond Spruance, 1886-1969, (U.S.) victorious at Midway Island, 1942, WW2.
Joseph W. Stilwell, 1883-1946, (U.S.) headed forces in the China, Burma, India theater in WW2.
J.E.B. Stuart, 1833-64, (U.S.) Confed. cavalry commander, Civil War.
Sun Tzu, 6th? cent. B.C., (Chin.) general, author of *The Art of War.*
Aleksandr Suvorov, 1729-1800, (Rus.) commanded Allied Russian and Austrian armies, Russo-Turkish War.

Tamerlane, 1336-1405, (Turkoman Mongol) conqueror, established empire from India to Mediterranean Sea.
George H. Thomas, 1816-70, (U.S.) saved Union army at Chattanooga, 1863; won at Nashville, 1864, Civil War.
Semyon Timoshenko, 1895-1970, (USSR) defended Moscow, Stalingrad, WW2; led winter offensive, 1942-43.
Alfred von Tirpitz, 1849-1930, (Ger.) responsible for submarine blockade in WW1.
Henri de la Tour d'Auvergne, Viscount of Turenne, 1611-75, (Fr.) marshal, Thirty Years' War, Fronde, War of Devolution.
Sebastien Le Prestre de Vauban, 1633-1707, (Fr.) innovative military engineer and theorist.
Jonathan M. Wainwright, 1883-1953, (U.S.) forced to surrender on Corregidor, 1942, WW2.
George Washington, 1732-99, (U.S.) led Continental army, 1775-83, Amer. Rev.
Archibald Wavell, 1883-1950, (Br.) commanded forces in N and E Africa, and SE Asia in WW2.
Anthony Wayne, 1745-96, (U.S.) captured Stony Point, 1779, Amer. Rev.
Duke of Wellington, 1769-1852, (Br.) defeated Napoleon at Waterloo, 1815.
William Westmoreland, 1914-2005, (U.S.) commanded forces in Vietnam 1964-68.
William I (The Conqueror), 1027-87, (Br.) victor Battle of Hastings 1066, became first Norman king of England.
James Wolfe, 1727-59, (Br.) captured Quebec from French, 1759, French and Indian War.
Isoroku Yamamoto, 1884-1943, (Jpn.) com. in chief of Japanese fleet and naval planner before and during WW2.
Georgi Zhukov, 1895-1974, (Russ.) defended Moscow, 1941, led assault on Berlin, 1945, WW2.

Philosophers and Religious Figures of the Past

Excludes most biblical figures and popes (see Religion chapter). For Greeks and Romans, see also Historical Figures chapter.

Lyman Abbott, 1835-1922, (U.S.) clergyman, reformer; advocate of Christian Socialism.
Pierre Abelard, 1079-1142, (Fr.) philosopher, theologian, teacher; used dialectic method to support Christian beliefs.
Mortimer Adler, 1902-2001, (U.S.) philosopher, helped create "Great Books" program.
Felix Adler, 1851-1933, (U.S.) German-born founder of the Ethical Culture Society.
(St.) Anselm, c1033-1109, (It.) philosopher-theologian, church leader; "ontological argument" for God's existence.
(St.) Thomas Aquinas, 1225-74, (It.) preeminent medieval philosopher-theologian; *Summa Theologica.*
Aristotle, 384-322 BC, (Gr.) pioneering wide-ranging philosopher, logician, ethician, naturalist.
(St.) Augustine, 354-430, (N Africa) philosopher, theologian, bishop; *Confessions, City of God, On the Trinity.*
J. L. Austin, 1911-60, (Br.) ordinary-language philosopher.
Averroes (Ibn Rushd), 1126-98, (Sp.) Islamic philosopher, physician.
Avicenna (Ibn Sina), 980-1037, (Iran.) Islamic philosopher, scientist.
A(lfred) J(ules) Ayer, 1910-89, (Br.) philosopher; logical positivist; *Language, Truth, and Logic.*
Roger Bacon, c1214-94, (Eng.) philosopher and scientist.
Bahaullah (Mirza Husayn Ali), 1817-92, (Pers.) founder of Bahá'í faith.
Karl Barth, 1886-1968, (Swiss) theologian; a leading force in 20th-cent. Protestantism.
Thomas à Becket, 1118-70, (Eng.) archbishop of Canterbury; opposed Henry II; murdered by King's men.
(St.) Benedict, c480-547, (It.) founded the Benedictines.
Jeremy Bentham, 1748-1832, (Br.) philosopher, reformer; enunciated utilitarianism.
Henri Bergson, 1859-1941, (Fr.) philosopher of evolution.
George Berkeley, 1685-1753, (Ir.) idealist philosopher, bishop.
John Biddle, 1615-62, (Eng.) founder of English Unitarianism.
Jakob Boehme, 1575-1624, (Ger.) theosophist and mystic.
Dietrich Bonhoeffer, 1906-1945 (Ger.) Lutheran theologian, pastor; executed as opponent of Nazis.
William Brewster, 1567-1644, (Eng.) headed Pilgrims.
Emil Brunner, 1889-1966, (Swiss) Protestant theologian.
Giordano Bruno, 1548-1600, (It.) philosopher, pantheist.
Martin Buber, 1878-1965, (Ger.) Jewish philosopher, theologian; *I and Thou.*
Buddha (Siddhartha Gautama**),** c563-c483 BC, (Indian) philosopher; founded Buddhism.
John Calvin, 1509-64, (Fr.) theologian; a key figure in the Protestant Reformation.
Rudolph Carnap, 1891-1970, (U.S.) German-born analytic philosopher; a founder of logical positivism.
William Ellery Channing, 1780-1842, (U.S.) clergyman; early spokesman for Unitarianism.
Auguste Comte, 1798-1857, (Fr.) philosopher; originated positivism.
Confucius, 551-479 BC, (Chin.) founder of Confucianism.
John Cotton, 1584-1652, (Eng.) Puritan theologian.
Thomas Cranmer, 1489-1556, (Eng.) Anglican churchman; wrote much of *Book of Common Prayer.*
Jacques Derrida, 1930-2004 (Fr.), deconstructionist philosopher.
René Descartes, 1596-1650, (Fr.) philosopher, mathematician; "father of modern philosophy." *Discourse on Method, Meditations on First Philosophy.*
John Dewey, 1859-1952, (U.S.) philosopher, educator; instrumentalist theory of knowledge; progressive education.
Denis Diderot, 1713-84, (Fr.) philosopher, encyclopedist.
John Duns Scotus, c1266-1308, (Sc.) Franciscan philosopher and theologian.
Mary Baker Eddy, 1821-1910, (U.S.) founder of Christian Science; *Science and Health.*
Jonathan Edwards, 1703-58, (U.S.) preacher, theologian; "Sinners in the Hands of an Angry God."
(Desiderius) Erasmus, c1466-1536, (Dutch) Renaissance humanist; *On the Freedom of the Will.*
Johann Fichte, 1762-1814, (Ger.) idealist philosopher.
Michel Foucault, 1926-84, (Fr.) structuralist philosopher, historian.
George Fox, 1624-91, (Br.) founder of Society of Friends.
(St.) Francis of Assisi, 1182-1226, (It.) espoused voluntary poverty; founded Franciscans.
al-Ghazali, 1058-1111, Islamic philosopher.
Billy James Hargis, 1925-2004, (U.S.) anti-Communist televangelist; founder of the Church of the Christian Crusade.
Georg W. F. Hegel, 1770-1831, (Ger.) idealist philosopher; *Phenomenology of Mind.*
Martin Heidegger, 1889-1976, (Ger.) existentialist philosopher; affected many fields; *Being and Time.*
Johann G. Herder, 1744-1803, (Ger.) philosopher, cultural historian; a founder of German Romanticism.
Thomas Hobbes, 1588-1679, (Eng.) philosopher, political theorist; *Leviathan.*
David Hume, 1711-76, (Sc.) empiricist philosopher; *Enquiry Concerning Human Understanding.*
Jan Hus, 1369-1415, (Czech.) religious reformer.
Edmund Husserl, 1859-1938, (Ger.) philosopher; founded the phenomenological movement.
Thomas Huxley, 1825-95, (Br.) philosopher, educator.
William Inge, 1860-1954, (Br.) theologian; explored mystic aspects of Christianity.
William James, 1842-1910, (U.S.) philosopher, psychologist; pragmatist; studied religious experience.
Karl Jaspers, 1883-1969, (Ger.) existentialist philosopher.
Joan of Arc, 1412-1431, (Fr.) national heroine and a patron saint of France; key figure in the Hundred Years' War.
Immanuel Kant, 1724-1804, (Ger.) philosopher; founder of modern critical philosophy; *Critique of Pure Reason.*
Thomas à Kempis, c1380-1471, (Ger.) monk, devotional writer; *Imitation of Christ* attributed to him.
Soren Kierkegaard, 1813-55, (Dan.) religious philosopher; pre-existentialist; *Either/Or, The Sickness Unto Death.*
John Knox, 1505-72, (Sc.) leader of the Protestant Reformation in Scotland.
Lao-Tzu, 604-531 BC, (Chin.) philosopher; considered the founder of the Taoist religion.
Gottfried von Leibniz, 1646-1716, (Ger.) rationalistic philosopher, logician, mathematician.
John Locke, 1632-1704, (Eng.) political theorist, empiricist philosopher; *Essay Concerning Human Understanding.*
(St.) Ignatius Loyola, 1491-1556, (Sp.) founder of the Jesuits; *Spiritual Exercises.*
Martin Luther, 1483-1546, (Ger.) leader of the Protestant Reformation, founded Lutheran church.
Jean-Francois Lyotard, 1924-98, (Fr.) postmodern philosopher, lecturer; *The Post-Modern Condition.*
Maimonides, 1135-1204, (Sp.) major Jewish philosopher.
Gabriel Marcel, 1889-1973, (Fr.) Rom. Cath. existentialist philosopher, dramatist,
Jacques Maritain, 1882-1973, (Fr.) Neo-Thomist philosopher.
Cotton Mather, 1663-1728, (U.S.) defender of orthodox Puritanism; founded Yale, 1701.
Philipp Melanchthon, 1497-1560, (Ger.) theologian, humanist; an important voice in the Reformation.
Maurice Merleau-Ponty, 1908-61, (Fr.) existentialist philosopher; *Phenomenology of Perception.*
Thomas Merton, 1915-68, (U.S.) Trappist monk, spiritual writer; *The Seven Storey Mountain.*
Dwight Moody, 1837-99, (U.S.) evangelist.

G(eorge) E(dward) Moore, 1873-1958, (Br.) philosopher; *Principia Ethica,* "A Defense of Common Sense."
Muhammad, c570-632, (Arab) the prophet of Islam.
Elijah Muhammad, 1897-1975, (U.S.) Black Muslim sect leader.
Heinrich Muhlenberg, 1711-87, (Ger.) organized the Lutheran Church in America.
John H. Newman, 1801-90, (Br.) Rom. Cath. convert, cardinal; led Oxford Movement; *Apologia pro Vita Sua.*
Reinhold Niebuhr, 1892-1971, (U.S.) Protestant theologian.
Richard Niebuhr, 1894-1962 (U.S.) Protestant theologian.
Friedrich Nietzsche, 1844-1900, (Ger.) philosopher; *The Birth of Tragedy, Beyond Good and Evil, Thus Spake Zarathustra.*
Robert Nozick, 1938-2002, (U.S.) political philosopher; *Anarchy, State, and Utopia.*
Blaise Pascal, 1623-62, (Fr.) philosopher, mathematician; *Pensées.*
(St.) Patrick, c389-c461, (Br.) brought Christianity to Ireland.
Norman Vincent Peale, 1898-1993, (U.S.) minister, author; *The Power of Positive Thinking.*
C(harles) S. Peirce, 1839-1914, (U.S.) philosopher, logician; originated concept of pragmatism, 1878.
Plato, c428-347 BC, (Gr.) philosopher; wrote Socratic dialogues; argued for immortality of soul, indep. reality of ideas or forms; *Republic, Meno, Phaedo, Apology.*
Plotinus, 205-70, (Rom.) a founder of neo-Platonism; *Enneads.*
W(illard) V(an) O(rman) Quine, 1908-2001, (U.S.) philosopher, logician; "On What There Is."
John Rawls, 1922-2002, (U.S.) political philosopher; *A Theory of Justice* (1971).
Josiah Royce, 1855-1916, (U.S.) idealist philosopher
Bertrand Russell, 1872-1970, (Br.) philosopher, logician; one of the founders of modern logic; a prolific popular writer.
Charles T. Russell, 1852-1916, (U.S.) founder of Jehovah's Witnesses.
Gilbert Ryle, 1900-76, (Br.) analytic philosopher; *The Concept of Mind.*
George Santayana, 1863-1952, (U.S.) philosopher, writer, critic; *The Sense of Beauty, The Realms of Being.*
Jean-Paul Sartre, 1905-80, (Fr.) philosopher, novelist, playwright. *Nausea, No Exit, Being and Nothingness.*
Friedrich von Schelling, 1775-1854, (Ger.) philosopher of romantic movement.
Friedrich Schleiermacher, 1768-1834, (Ger.) theologian; a founder of modern Protestant theology.
Arthur Schopenhauer, 1788-1860, (Ger.) philosopher; *The World as Will and Idea.*
Albert Schweitzer, 1875-1965, (Ger.) theologian, social philosopher, medical missionary.
Joseph Smith, 1805-44, (U.S.) founded Latter-Day Saints (Mormon) movement, 1830.
Socrates, 469-399 BC, (Gr.) philosopher immortalized by Plato.
Herbert Spencer, 1820-1903, (Br.) philosopher of evolution.
Baruch de Spinoza, 1632-77, (Dutch) rationalist philosopher; *Ethics.*
Billy Sunday, 1862-1935, (U.S.) evangelist.
Emanuel Swedenborg, 1688-1772, (Swed.) philosopher, mystic; *Principia.*
Pierre Teilhard de Chardin, 1881-1955, (Fr.) Jesuit priest, paleontologist, philosopher-theologian; *The Divine Milieu.*
Daisetz Teitaro Suzuki, 1870-1966, (Jpn.) Buddhist scholar.
(St.) Therese of Lisieux, 1873-97, (Fr.) Carmelite nun ("Little Flower"), revered for everyday sanctity; *The Story of a Soul.*
Paul Tillich, 1886-1965, (U.S.) German-born philosopher and theologian; brought depth psychology to Protestantism.
John Wesley, 1703-91, (Br.) theologian, evangelist; founded Methodism.
Alfred North Whitehead, 1861-1947, (Br.) philosopher, mathematician; *Process and Reality.*
William of Occam, c1285-c1349 (Eng.) medieval scholastic philosopher; nominalist.
Roger Williams, c1603-83, (U.S.) clergyman; championed religious freedom and separation of church and state.
Ludwig Wittgenstein, 1889-1951, (Austrian) philosopher; major influence on contemporary language philosophy; *Tractatus Logico-Philosophicus, Philosophical Investigations.*
John Woolman, 1720-72, (U.S.) Quaker social reformer, abolitionist, writer; *The Journal.*
John Wycliffe, 1320-84, (Eng.) theologian, reformer.
(St.) Francis Xavier, 1506-52, (Sp.) Jesuit missionary, "Apostle of the Indies."
Brigham Young, 1801-77, (U.S.) Mormon leader after Smith's assassination; colonized Utah.
Huldrych Zwingli, 1484-1531, (Swiss) theologian; led Swiss Protestant Reformation.

Political Leaders of the Past

(U.S. presidents, vice presidents, Supreme Ct. justices, signers of Decl. of Indep. listed elsewhere.)

Abu Bakr, 573-634, Muslim leader, first caliph, chosen successor to Muhammad.
Dean Acheson, 1893-1971, (U.S.) sec. of state; architect of cold war foreign policy.
Samuel Adams, 1722-1803, (U.S.) patriot, Boston Tea Party firebrand.
Konrad Adenauer, 1876-1967, (Ger.) first West German chancellor.
Emilio Aguinaldo, 1869-1964, (Philip.) revolutionary; fought against Spain and the U.S.
Akbar, 1542-1605, greatest Mogul emperor of India.
Carl Albert, 1908-2000 (U.S.) House rep. from OK, Speaker, 1971-76.
Salvador Allende Gossens, 1908-1973, (Chilean) Marxist pres. 1970-73; ousted and died in coup.
Idi Amin, 1925-2003 (Uganda), Ugandan ruler from 1971 to 1979, blamed for hundreds of thousands of deaths.
Hafez al Assad, 1930-2000 (Syr.), Syrian ruler from 1970.
Herbert H. Asquith, 1852-1928, (Br.) liberal prime min.; instituted major social reform.
Atahualpa, ?-1533, Inca (ruling chief) of Peru.
Kemal Ataturk, 1881-1938, (Turk.) founded modern Turkey.
Clement Attlee, 1883-1967, (Br.) Labour party leader, prime min.; enacted natl. health, nationalized many industries.
Stephen F. Austin, 1793-1836, (U.S.) led Texas colonization.
Mikhail Bakunin, 1814-76, (Rus.) revolutionary; leading exponent of anarchism.
Arthur J. Balfour, 1848-1930, (Br.) foreign sec. under Lloyd George; issued Balfour Declaration backing Zionism.
Bernard M. Baruch, 1870-1965, (U.S.) financier, govt. adviser.
Fulgencio Batista y Zaldívar, 1901-73, (Cub.) Cuban pres. (1940-44, 1952-59), overthrown by Castro.
Lord Beaverbrook, 1879-1964, (Br.) financier, statesman, newspaper owner.
Menachem Begin, 1913-92, (Isr.) Israeli prime min., shared 1978 Nobel Peace Prize.
Eduard Benes, 1884-1948, (Czech.) pres. during interwar and post-WW2 eras.
David Ben-Gurion, 1886-1973, (Isr.) first prime min. of Israel, 1948-53, 1955-63.
Thomas Hart Benton, 1782-1858, (U.S.) Missouri senator; championed agrarian interests and westward expansion.
Aneurin Bevan, 1897-1960, (Br.) Labour party leader.
Ernest Bevin, 1881-1951, (Br.) Labour party leader, foreign minister; helped lay foundation for NATO.
Otto von Bismarck, 1815-98, (Ger.) statesman known as the Iron Chancellor; uniter of Germany, 1870.
James G. Blaine, 1830-93, (U.S.) Republican politician, diplomat; influential in Pan-American movement.
Léon Blum, 1872-1950, (Fr.) socialist leader, writer; headed first Popular Front government.
William E. Borah, 1865-1940, (U.S.) isolationist senator; helped block U.S. membership in League of Nations.
Cesare Borgia, 1476-1507, (It.) soldier, politician; an outstanding figure of the Italian Renaissance.
Willy Brandt, 1913-92, (Ger.) statesman, chancellor of West Germany, 1969-74; promoted East/West peace, *Ostpolitik.*
Leonid Brezhnev, 1906-82, (USSR) Soviet leader, 1964-82.
Aristide Briand, 1862-1932, (Fr.) foreign min.; chief architect of Locarno Pact and anti-war Kellogg-Briand Pact.
William Jennings Bryan, 1860-1925, (U.S.) Democratic, populist leader, orator; 3 times lost race for presidency.
Ralph Bunche, 1904-71, (U.S.) a founder and key diplomat of United Nations for more than 20 years.
John C. Calhoun, 1782-1850, (U.S.) political leader; champion of states' rights and a symbol of the Old South.
James Callaghan (Baron Callaghan), 1912-2005 (Br.) Labour Party politican, prime min. 1976-79.
Robert Castlereagh, 1769-1822, (Br.) foreign sec.; guided Grand Alliance against Napoleon.
Camillo Benso Cavour, 1810-61, (It.) statesman; largely responsible for uniting Italy under the House of Savoy.
Nicolae Ceausescu, 1918-89, (Roman.) Communist leader, head of state 1967-89; executed.
Austen Chamberlain, 1863-1937, (Br.) statesman; helped finalize Locarno Treaties, both 1925.
Neville Chamberlain, 1869-1940, (Br.) Conservative prime min. whose appeasement of Hitler led to Munich Pact.
Chiang Kai-shek, 1887-1975, (Chin.) Nationalist Chinese pres. whose government was driven from mainland to Taiwan.
Chiang Kai-shek, Madame, 1898-2003, (Chin.) highly influential wife of Nationalist Chinese leader Chiang Kai-shek.
Winston Churchill, 1874-1965, (Br.) prime min., soldier, author; guided Britain through WW2.

Galeazzo Ciano, 1903-44, (It.) fascist foreign minister; helped create Rome-Berlin Axis, executed by Mussolini.
Henry Clay, 1777-1852, (U.S.) "The Great Compromiser," one of the most influential pre-Civil War political leaders.
Georges Clemenceau, 1841-1929, (Fr.) twice prem., Wilson's antagonist at Paris Peace Conference after WW1.
DeWitt Clinton, 1769-1828, (U.S.) political leader; responsible for promoting the Erie Canal.
Robert Clive, 1725-74, (Br.) first administrator of Bengal; laid foundation for British Empire in India.
Jean Baptiste Colbert, 1619-83, (Fr.) statesman; influential under Louis XIV, created the French navy.
Bettino Craxi, 1934-2000, (It.) Italy's first post-WWII Socialist premier.
David Crockett, 1786-1836, (U.S.) frontiersman, congressman, died defending the Alamo.
Oliver Cromwell, 1599-1658, (Br.) Lord Protector of England, led parliamentary forces during Civil War.
Curzon of Kedleston, 1859-1925, (Br.) viceroy of India, foreign sec.; major force in post-WW1 world.
Édouard Daladier, 1884-1970, (Fr.) Radical Socialist politician, arrested by Vichy, interned by Germans until 1945.
Richard J. Daley, 1902-1976, (U.S.) Chicago mayor.
Georges Danton, 1759-94, (Fr.) leading French Rev. figure.
Jefferson Davis, 1808-89, (U.S.) pres. of the Confederacy.
Charles G. Dawes, 1865-1951, (U.S.) statesman, banker; advanced plan to stabilize post-WW1 German finances.
Alcide De Gasperi, 1881-1954, (It.) prime min.; founder of Christian Democratic party.
Charles De Gaulle, 1890-1970, (Fr.) general, statesman; first pres. of the Fifth Republic.
Deng Xiaoping, 1904-97, (Chin.) "paramount leader" of China; backed economic modernization.
Eamon De Valera, 1882-1975, (Ir.-U.S.) statesman; led fight for Irish independence.
Thomas E. Dewey, 1902-71, (U.S.) NY governor; twice loser in try for presidency.
Ngo Dinh Diem, 1901-63, (Viet.) South Vietnamese pres.; assassinated in government takeover.
Everett M. Dirksen, 1896-1969, (U.S.) Senate Republican minority leader, orator.
Benjamin Disraeli, 1804-81, (Br.) prime min.; considered founder of modern Conservative party.
Engelbert Dollfuss, 1892-1934, (Austrian) chancellor; assassinated by Austrian Nazis.
Andrea Doria, 1466-1560, (It.) Genoese admiral, statesman; called "Father of Peace" and "Liberator of Genoa."
Stephen A. Douglas, 1813-61, (U.S.) Democratic leader, orator; opposed Lincoln for the presidency.
Alexander Dubcek, 1921-92, (Czech.) statesman whose attempted liberalization was crushed, 1968.
John Foster Dulles, 1888-1959, (U.S.) sec. of state under Eisenhower, cold war policy-maker.
Abba Eban, 1915-2002, (Isr.) diplomat, foreign min. 1966-74.
Friedrich Ebert, 1871-1925, (Ger.) Social Democratic movement leader; 1st pres., Weimar Republic, 1919-25.
Sir Anthony Eden, 1897-1977, (Br.) foreign sec., prime min. during Suez invasion of 1956.
Ludwig Erhard, 1897-1977, (Ger.) economist, West German chancellor; led nation's economic rise after WW2.
King Fahid, 1921-2005, (Saudi Arab.) monarch since 1982, but inactive since 1995 stroke; encouraged U.S. relations.
Joao Baptista de Figueiredo, 1918-99, (Braz.) president of Brazil, restored the nation's democracy.
Hamilton Fish, 1808-93, (U.S.) sec. of state, successfully mediated disputes with Great Britain, Latin America.
James V. Forrestal, 1892-1949, (U.S.) sec. of navy, first sec. of defense.
Francisco Franco, 1892-1975, (Sp.) leader of rebel forces during Spanish Civil War and longtime ruler of Spain.
Benjamin Franklin, 1706-90, (U.S.) printer, publisher, author, inventor, scientist, diplomat.
Louis de Frontenac, 1620-98, (Fr.) governor of New France (Canada); encouraged explorations, fought Iroquois.
J. William Fulbright, 1905-95, (U.S.) U.S. senator; leading figure in U.S. foreign policy during cold war years.
Hugh Gaitskell, 1906-63, (Br.) Labour party leader; major force in reversing its stand for unilateral disarmament.
Albert Gallatin, 1761-1849, (U.S.) sec. of treasury; instrumental in negotiating end of War of 1812.
Léon Gambetta, 1838-82, (Fr.) statesman, politician; one of the founders of the Third Republic.
Indira Gandhi, 1917-84, (In.) daughter of Jawaharlal Nehru, prime min. of India, 1966-77, 1980-84; assassinated.
Mohandas K. Gandhi, 1869-1948, (In.) political leader, ascetic; led movement against British rule; assassinated.
Giuseppe Garibaldi, 1807-82, (It.) patriot, soldier; a leader in the Risorgimento, Italian unification movement.
William E. Gladstone, 1809-98, (Br.) prime min. 4 times; dominant force of Liberal party from 1868 to 1894.
Paul Joseph Goebbels, 1897-1945, (Ger.) Nazi propagandist, master of mass psychology.
Barry Goldwater, 1909-98 (U.S.) conservative U.S. senator and 1964 Republican presid. nominee.
Klement Gottwald, 1896-1953, (Czech.) Communist leader; ushered Communism into his country.
Alexander Hamilton, 1755-1804, (U.S.) first treasury sec.; champion of strong central government.
Dag Hammarskjold, 1905-61, (Swed.) statesman; UN sec.-general.
Hassan II, King, 1929-99, (Moroc.), ruler of Morocco,1962-99.
John Hay, 1838-1905, (U.S.) sec. of state; primarily associated with Open Door Policy toward China.
Sir Edward Heath, 1916-205, (Br.) Conserative prime min., 1970-74; promoted European unity.
Patrick Henry, 1736-99, (U.S.) major Revolutionary War figure, remarkable orator.
Édouard Herriot, 1872-1957, (Fr.) Radical Socialist leader; twice prem., pres. of National Assembly.
Theodor Herzl, 1860-1904, (Hung.) founded modern Zionism.
Heinrich Himmler, 1900-45, (Ger.) head of Nazi SS and Gestapo.
Paul von Hindenburg, 1847-1934, (Ger.) field marshal, WW1; 2nd pres. of Weimar Republic, 1925-34.
Adolf Hitler, 1889-1945, (Ger.) dictator; built Nazism, launched WW2, presided over the Holocaust.
Ho Chi Minh, 1890-1969, (Viet.) N Vietnamese pres., Vietnamese Communist leader.
Harry L. Hopkins, 1890-1946, (U.S.) New Deal administrator; closest adviser to FDR during WW2.
Edward M. House, 1858-1938, (U.S.) diplomat; confidential adviser to Woodrow Wilson.
Samuel Houston, 1793-1863, (U.S.) leader of struggle for Texas independence.
Cordell Hull, 1871-1955, (U.S.) sec. of state, 1933-44; initiated reciprocal trade to lower tariffs, helped organize UN.
Hubert H. Humphrey, 1911-78, (U.S.) MN Democrat; senator; vice pres., pres. candidate.
Hussein, King, 1935-99 (Jordan), peacemaker; ruler of Jordan, 1952-99.
Jinnah, Muhammad Ali, 1876-1948, (Pak.) founder, first governor-general of Pakistan.
Benito Juarez, 1806-72, (Mex.) rallied his country against foreign threats, sought to create democratic, federal republic.
Constantine Karamanlis, 1907-98, (Gr.) Greek prime min., restored democracy; later president.
Frank B. Kellogg, 1856-1937, (U.S.) sec. of state; negotiated Kellogg-Briand Pact to outlaw war.
Robert F. Kennedy, 1925-68, (U.S.) attorney general, senator; assassinated while seeking presidency.
Aleksandr Kerensky, 1881-1970, (Russ.) headed provisional government after Feb. 1917 revolution.
Ayatollah Ruhollah Khomeini, 1900-89, (Iranian), religious-political leader, spearheaded overthrow of shah, 1979.
Nikita Khrushchev, 1894-1971, (USSR) prem., first sec. of Communist party; initiated de-Stalinization.
Kim Il Sung, 1912-94, (Korean) N Korean dictator, 1948-94.
Lajos Kossuth, 1802-94, (Hung.) principal figure in 1848 Hungarian revolution.
Pyotr Kropotkin, 1842-1921, (Russ.) anarchist; championed the peasants but opposed Bolshevism.
Kublai Khan, c1215-94, (Mongol) emperor; founder of Yüan dynasty in China.
Béla Kun, 1886-c1939, (Hung.) member of 3rd Communist Internat.; tried to foment worldwide revolution.
Robert M. LaFollette, 1855-1925, (U.S.) Wisconsin public official; leader of progressive movement.
Fiorello La Guardia, 1882-1947, (U.S.) colorful NYC reform mayor.
Pierre Laval, 1883-1945, (Fr.) politician, Vichy foreign min.; executed for treason.
Andrew Bonar Law, 1858-1923, (Br.) Conservative party politician; led opposition to Irish home rule.
Vladimir Ilyich Lenin (Ulyanov), 1870-1924, (Russ.) revolutionary; founded Bolshevism; Soviet leader 1917-24.
Ferdinand de Lesseps, 1805-94, (Fr.) diplomat, engineer; conceived idea of Suez Canal.
Rene Levesque, 1922-87, (Can.) prem. of Quebec, 1976-85; led unsuccessful separartist campaign.
Maxim Litvinov, 1876-1951, (Pol.-Russ.) revolutionary, commissar of foreign affairs; favored cooperation with West.
Liu Shaoqi, c1898-1974, (Chin.) Communist leader; fell from grace during Cultural Revolution.
David Lloyd George, 1863-1945, (Br.) Liberal party prime min.; laid foundations for modern welfare state.
Henry Cabot Lodge, 1850-1924, (U.S.) Republican senator; led opposition to participation in League of Nations.
Huey P. Long, 1893-1935, (U.S.) Louisiana political demagogue, governor, U.S. senator; assassinated.

Rosa Luxemburg, 1871-1919, (Ger.) revolutionary; leader of the German Social Democratic party and Spartacus party.
J. Ramsay MacDonald, 1866-1937, (Br.) first Labour party prime min. of Great Britain.
Harold Macmillan, 1895-1986, (Br.) prime min. of Great Britain, 1957-63.
Joseph R. McCarthy, 1908-57, (U.S.) senator, extremist in searching out alleged Communists and pro-Communists.
Makarios III, 1913-77, (Cypriot) Greek Orthodox archbishop; first pres. of Cyprus.
Mao Zedong, 1893-1976, (Chin.) chief Chinese Marxist theorist, revolutionary, political leader; led Chinese revolution establishing his nation as Communist state.
Jean Paul Marat, 1743-93, (Fr.) revolutionary, politician; identified with radical Jacobins; assassinated.
José Martí, 1853-95, (Cub.) patriot, poet; leader of Cuban struggle for independence.
Jan Masaryk, 1886-1948, (Czech.) foreign min.; died by mysterious alleged suicide following Communist coup.
Thomas G. Masaryk, 1850-1937, (Czech.) statesman, philosopher; first pres. of Czechoslovak Republic.
Jules Mazarin, 1602-61, (Fr.) cardinal, statesman; prime min. under Louis XIII and queen regent Anne of Austria.
Giusseppe Mazzini, 1805-72, (It.), reformer dedicated to Risorgimento movement for renewal of Italy.
Tom Mboya, 1930-69, (Kenyan) political leader; instrumental in securing independence for Kenya.
Cosimo I de' Medici, 1519-74, (It.) Duke of Florence, grand duke of Tuscany.
Lorenzo de' Medici, the Magnificent, 1449-92, (It.) merchant prince; a towering figure in Italian Renaissance.
Catherine de Médicis, 1519-89, (Fr.) queen consort of Henry II, regent of France; influential in Catholic-Huguenot wars.
Golda Meir, 1898-1978, (Isr.) a founder of the state of Israel and prime min., 1969-74.
Klemens W. N. L. Metternich, 1773-1859, (Austrian) statesman; arbiter of post-Napoleonic Europe.
François Mitterrand, 1916-96, (Fr.) pres. of France, 1981-95.
Mobutu Sese Seko, 1930-97, (Zaire) longtime ruler of Zaire (now Congo) (1965-97); exiled after rebellion.
Guy Mollet, 1905-75, (Fr.) socialist politician, resistance leader.
Henry Morgenthau Jr., 1891-1967, (U.S.) sec. of treasury; fund-raiser for New Deal and U.S. WW2 activities.
Gouverneur Morris, 1752-1816, (U.S.) statesman, diplomat. financial expert, helped plan decimal coinage.
Daniel Patrick Moynihan 1927-2003, (U.S.) senator, diplomat, social scientist and author.
Benito Mussolini, 1883-1945, (It.) leader of the Italian fascist state; assassinated.
Imre Nagy, c1896-1958, (Hung.) Communist prem.; assassinated after Soviets crushed 1956 uprising.
Gamal Abdel Nasser, 1918-70, (Egypt.) leader of Arab unification, 2nd Egyptian pres.
Jawaharlal Nehru, 1889-1964, (In.) prime min.; guided India through its early years of independence.
Kwame Nkrumah, 1909-72, (Ghan.) 1st prime min., 1957-60, and pres., 1960-66, of Ghana.
Frederick North, 1732-92, (Br.) prime min.; his inept policies led to loss of American colonies.
Julius K. Nyerere, 1923?-99, (Tanz.) founding father, 1st pres., 1962-85, of Tanzania.
Daniel O'Connell, 1775-1847, (Ir.) nationalist political leader; known as The Liberator.
Omar, c581-644, Muslim leader; 2nd caliph, led Islam to become an imperial power.
Thomas P. (Tip) O'Neill Jr., 1912-94, (U.S.) U.S. congressman, Speaker of the House, 1977-86.
Ignace Paderewski, 1860-1941, (Pol.) statesman, pianist; composer, briefly prime min., an ardent patriot.
Viscount Palmerston, 1784-1865, (Br.) Whig-Liberal prime min., foreign min.; embodied British nationalism.
Andreas George Papandreou, 1919-1996, (Gk.) leftist politician, served 2 times as prem. (1981-89, 1993-96).
Georgios Papandreou, 1888-1968, (Gk.) Republican politician; served 3 times as prime min.
Franz von Papen, 1879-1969, (Ger.) politician; major role in overthrow of Weimar Republic and rise of Hitler.
Charles Stewart Parnell, 1846-1891, (Ir.) nationalist leader; "uncrowned king of Ireland."
Lester Pearson, 1897-1972, (Can.) diplomat, Liberal party leader, prime min.
Robert Peel, 1788-1850, (Br.) reformist prime min., founder of Conservative party.
Eva (Evita) Perón, 1919-52 (Arg.) highly influential 2nd wife of Juan Perón.
Juan Perón, 1895-1974, (Arg.) dynamic pres. of Argentina (1946-55, 1973-74).
Joseph Pilsudski, 1867-1935, (Pol.) statesman; instrumental in reestablishing Polish state in the 20th cent.
Charles Pinckney, 1757-1824, (U.S.) founding father; his Pinckney plan largely incorporated into Constitution.
Christian Pineau, 1905-95, (Fr.) leader of French Resistance during WW2; French foreign min., 1956-58.
William Pitt, the Elder, 1708-78, (Br.) statesman; the "Great Commoner," transformed Britain into imperial power.
William Pitt, the Younger, 1759-1806, (Br.) prime min. during French Revolutionary wars.
Georgi Plekhanov, 1857-1918, (Russ.) revolutionary, social philosopher; called "father of Russian Marxism."
Raymond Poincaré, 1860-1934, (Fr.) 9th pres. of the Republic; advocated harsh punishment of Germany after WW1.
Pol Pot, 1925-98, (Camb.) leader of Khmer Rouge; ruled Cambodia, 1975-79; responsible for mass deaths.
Georges Pompidou, 1911-74, (Fr.) Gaullist political leader; pres. 1969-74.
Grigori Potemkin, 1739-91, (Russ.) field marshal; favorite of Catherine II.
Yitzhak Rabin, 1922-95, (Isr.) military, political leader; prime min. of Israel, 1974-77, 1992-95; assassinated.
Edmund Randolph, 1753-1813, (U.S.) attorney; prominent in drafting, ratification of constitution.
John Randolph, 1773-1833, (U.S.) Southern planter; strong advocate of states' rights.
Jeannette Rankin, 1880-1973, (U.S.) pacifist; first woman member of U.S. Congress.
Walter Rathenau, 1867-1922, (Ger.) industrialist, statesman.
Sam Rayburn, 1882-1961, (U.S.) Democratic leader; representative for 47 years, House Speaker for 17.
Paul Reynaud, 1878-1966, (Fr.) statesman; prem. in 1940 at the time of France's defeat by Germany.
Syngman Rhee, 1875-1965, (Korean) first pres. of S Korea.
Cecil Rhodes, 1853-1902, (Br.) imperialist, industrial magnate; established Rhodes scholarships in his will.
Cardinal de Richelieu, 1585-1642, (Fr.) statesman, known as "red eminence;" chief minister to Louis XIII.
Maximilien Robespierre, 1758-94, (Fr.) leading figure in French Revolution and Reign of Terror.
Nelson Rockefeller, 1908-79, (U.S.) Republican governor of NY, 1959-73; U.S. vice pres., 1974-77.
George W. Romney, 1907-95, (U.S.) auto exec.; 3-term Republican governor of Michigan.
Eleanor Roosevelt, 1884-1962, (U.S.) influential First Lady, humanitarian, UN diplomat.
Elihu Root, 1845-1937, (U.S.) lawyer, statesman, diplomat; leading Republican supporter of the League of Nations.
Dean Rusk, 1909-95, (U.S.) statesman; sec. of state, 1961-69.
John Russell, 1792-1878, (Br.) Liberal prime min. during the Irish potato famine.
Anwar al-Sadat, 1918-81, (Egypt.) pres., 1970-1981, promoted peace with Israel; Nobel laureate; assassinated.
António de Oliveira Salazar, 1889-1970, (Port.) longtime dictator.
José de San Martin, 1778-1850, S Amer. revolutionary; protector of Peru.
Eisaku Sato, 1901-75, (Jpn.) prime min.; presided over Japan's post-WW2 emergence as major world power.
Abdul Aziz Ibn Saud, c1880-1953, (Saudi Arabia) king of Saudi Arabia, 1932-53.
Robert Schuman, 1886-1963, (Fr.) statesman; founded European Coal and Steel Community.
Carl Schurz, 1829-1906, (U.S.) German-American political leader, journalist, orator, dedicated reformer.
Kurt Schuschnigg, 1897-1977, (Austrian) chancellor; unsuccessful in stopping Austria's annexation by Germany.
William H. Seward, 1801-72, (U.S.) anti-slavery activist; as U.S. sec. of state purchased Alaska.
Carlo Sforza, 1872-1952, (It.) foreign min., anti-fascist.
Sitting Bull, c1831-90, (Nat. Am.) Sioux leader in Battle of Little Bighorn over George A. Custer, 1876.
Alfred E. Smith, 1873-1944, (U.S.) NY Democratic governor; first Roman Catholic to run for presidency.
Margaret Chase Smith, 1897-1995, (U.S.) congresswoman, senator; 1st woman elected to both houses of Congress.
Jan C. Smuts, 1870-1950, (S. African) statesman, philosopher, soldier, prime min.
Paul Henri Spaak, 1899-1972, (Belg.) statesman, socialist leader.
Joseph Stalin, 1879-1953, (USSR) Soviet dictator, 1924-53; instituted forced collectivization, massive purges, and labor camps, causing millions of deaths.
Edwin M. Stanton, 1814-69, (U.S.) sec. of war, 1862-68.
Edward R. Stettinius Jr., 1900-49, (U.S.) industrialist, sec. of state who coordinated aid to WW2 allies.
Adlai E. Stevenson, 1900-65, (U.S.) Democratic leader, diplomat, Illinois governor, presidenial candidate.
Henry L. Stimson, 1867-1950, (U.S.) statesman; served in 5 administrations, foreign policy adviser in 30s and 40s.
Sukarno, 1901-70, (Indon.) dictatorial first pres. of the Indonesian republic.

Sun Yat-sen, 1866-1925, (Chin.) revolutionary; leader of Kuomintang, regarded as the father of modern China.
Robert A. Taft, 1889-1953, (U.S.) conservative Senate leader, called "Mr. Republican."
Charles de Talleyrand, 1754-1838, (Fr.) statesman, diplomat; the major force of the Congress of Vienna of 1814-15.
U Thant, 1909-74 (Bur.) statesman, UN sec.-general.
Norman M. Thomas, 1884-1968, (U.S.) social reformer; 6 times Socialist party presidential candidate.
Josip Broz Tito, 1892-1980, (Yug.) pres. of Yugoslavia from 1953, WW2 guerrilla chief, postwar rival of Stalin.
Palmiro Togliatti, 1893-1964, (It.) major Italian Communist leader.
Hideki Tojo, 1885-1948, (Jpn.) statesman, soldier; prime min. during most of WW2.
François Toussaint L'Ouverture, c1744-1803, (Haitian) patriot, martyr; thwarted French colonial aims.
Leon Trotsky, 1879-1940, (Russ.) revolutionary, founded Red Army, expelled from party in conflict with Stalin; assassinated.
Pierre Elliott Trudeau, 1919-2000, (Can.) longtime liberal prime minister of Canada, 1968-79, 1980-84; achieved native Canadian constitution.
Rafael L. Trujillo Molina, 1891-1961, (Dom.) dictator of Dominican Republic, 1930-61; assassinated.
Moise K. Tshombe, 1919-69, (Cong.) pres. of secessionist Katanga, prem. of Congo.
William M. Tweed, 1823-78, (U.S.) politicial boss of Tammany Hall, NYC's Democratic political machine.
Walter Ulbricht, 1893-1973, (Ger.) Communist leader of German Democratic Republic.
Arthur H. Vandenberg, 1884-1951, (U.S.) senator; proponent of bipartisan anti-Communist foreign policy.
Eleutherios Venizelos, 1864-1936, (Gk.) most prominent Greek statesman of early 20th cent.
Hendrik F. Verwoerd, 1901-66, (S. African) prime min.; rigorously applied apartheid policy despite protest.
George Wallace, 1919-98, (U.S.) former segregationist governor of Alabama and presid. candidate.
Robert Walpole, 1676-1745, (Br.) statesman; generally considered Britain's first prime min.
Daniel Webster, 1782-1852, (U.S.) orator, politician; advocate of business interests during Jacksonian agrarianism.
Chaim Weizmann, 1874-1952, (Russ.-Isr.) Zionist leader, scientist; first Israeli pres.
Wendell L. Willkie, 1892-1944, (U.S.) Republican who tried to unseat FDR when he ran for his 3d term.
Harold Wilson, 1916-95, (Br.) Labour party leader; prime min., 1964-70, 1974-76.
Emiliano Zapata, c1879-1919, (Mex.) revolutionary; major influence on modern Mexico.
Todor Zhivkov, 1911-98, (Bulg.) Communist ruler of Bulgaria from 1954 until ousted in a 1989 coup.
Zhou Enlai, 1898-1976, (Chin.) diplomat, prime min.; a leading figure of the Chinese Communist party.

Scientists of the Past

Revised by Peter Barker, Prof. & Chair, Dept. of the Hist. of Science, Univ. of Oklahoma

For pre-modern scientists see also Philosophers and Religious Figures of the Past and Historical Figures chapter.

Albertus Magnus, c1200-1280, (Ger.) theologian, philosopher; helped found medieval study of natural science.
Alhazen (Ibn al-Haytham), c965-ca.1040, mathematician, astronomer; optical theorist.
Andre-Marie Ampère, 1775-1836, (Fr.) mathematician, chemist; founder of electrodynamics.
John V. Atanasoff, 1903-95, (U.S.) physicist; co-invented Atanasoff-Berry Computer (1939-41).
Amedeo Avogadro, 1776-1856, (It.) chemist, physicist; proposed that equal volumes of gas contain equal numbers of molecules, permitting determination of molecular weights.
John Bardeen, 1908-91, (U.S.) double Nobel laureate in physics (transistor, 1956; superconductivity, 1972).
A. H. Becquerel, 1852-1908, (Fr.) physicist; discovered radioactivity in uranium (1896).
Alexander Graham Bell, 1847-1922, (U.S.) inventor; first to patent and commercially exploit the telephone (1876).
Daniel Bernoulli, 1700-82, (Swiss) mathematician; developed fluid dynamics and kinetic theory of gases.
Clifford Berry, 1918-1963, (U.S.) collaborated with Atanasoff on the ABC computer (1939-41).
Jöns Jakob Berzelius, 1779-1848, (Swed.) chemist; developed modern chemical symbols and formulas, discovered selenium and thorium.
Henry Bessemer, 1813-98, (Br.) engineer; invented Bessemer steel-making process.
Hans Bethe, 1906-2005, (Ger.-U.S.) physicist; won Nobel Prize in 1967 for describing how stars generate energy.
Bruno Bettelheim, 1903-90, (Austrian-U.S.) psychoanalyst; studied disturbed children; *Uses of Enchantment* (1976).
Louis Blériot, 1872-1936, (Fr.) engineer; monoplane pioneer, first Channel flight (1909).
Franz Boas, 1858-1942, (Ger.-U.S.) founded modern anthropology; studied Pacific Coast tribes.
Niels Bohr, 1885-1962, (Dan.) atomic and nuclear physicist; founded quantum mechanics.
Max Born, 1882-1970, (Ger.) atomic and nuclear physicist; helped develop quantum mechanics.
Satyendranath Bose, 1894-1974, (Indian) physicist; forerunner of modern quantum theory for integral-spin particles.
Louis de Broglie, 1892-1987, (Fr.) physicist; proposed quantum wave-particle duality.
Robert Bunsen, 1811-99, (Ger.) chemist; pioneered spectroscopic analysis; discovered rubidium, caesium.
Luther Burbank, 1849-1926, (U.S.) naturalist; developed plant breeding into a modern science.
Vannevar Bush, 1890-1974, (U.S.) electrical engineer; developed differential analyzer, an early analogue computer; headed WWII Office of Scientific Res. and Dev.
Marvin Camras, 1916-95, (U.S.) inventor, electrical engineer; invented magnetic tape recording.
Alexis Carrel, 1873-1944, (Fr.) surgeon, biologist; developed methods of suturing blood vessels and transplanting organs.
Rachel Carson, 1907-64, (U.S.) marine biologist, environmentalist; *Silent Spring* (1962).
James Chadwick, 1891-1974, (Br.) physicist; discovered the neutron (1932); led Brit. Manhattan Project group in U.S..
Albert Claude, 1898-1983, (Belg.-U.S.) a founder of modern cell biology; determined role of mitochondria.
Nicolaus Copernicus, 1473-1543, (Pol.) first modern astronomer to propose sun as center of the planets' motions.
Jacques Yves Cousteau, 1910-1997, (Fr.) oceanographer; co-inventor, with E. Gagnan, of the Aqualung (1943).
Seymour Cray, 1925-96, (U.S.) computer industry pioneer; developed supercomputers.
Francis Crick, (1916-2004), (Br.) biophysicist; co-discoverer of genetic code; shared 1962 Nobel Prize.
Marie, 1867-1934 (Pol.-Fr.) and **Pierre Curie**, 1859-1906, (Fr.) physical chemists; pioneer investigators of radioactivity, discovered radium and polonium (1898).
Gottlieb Daimler, 1834-1900, (Ger.) engineer, inventor; pioneer automobile manufacturer.
John Dalton, 1766-1844, (Br.) chemist, physicist; formulated atomic theory, made first table of atomic weights.
Charles Darwin, 1809-82, (Br.) naturalist; established theory of organic evolution; *Origin of Species* (1859).
Lee De Forest, 1873-1961, (U.S.) inventor of triode, pioneer in wireless telegraphy, sound pictures, television.
Max Delbruck, 1906-81, (Ger.-U.S.) founded molecular biology.
Rudolf Diesel, 1858-1913, (Ger.) mechanical engineer; patented Diesel engine (1892).
Theodosius Dobzhansky, 1900-75, (Russ.-U.S.) biologist; reconciled genetics and natural selection.
Christian Doppler, 1803-53, (Austrian) physicist; showed change in wave frequency caused by motion of source, now known as Doppler effect.
J. Presper Eckert Jr., 1919-95, (U.S.) co-inventor, with Mauchly, of the ENIAC computer (1943-45).
Thomas A. Edison, 1847-1931, (U.S.) inventor; held more than 1,000 patents, including incandescent electric lamp.
Paul Ehrlich, 1854-1915, (Ger.) medical researcher in immunology and bacteriology; pioneered antitoxin production.
Albert Einstein, 1879-1955, (Ger.-U.S.) theoretical physicist; founded relativity theory, replacing Newton's theories of space, time, and gravity. Proved $E=mc^2$ (1905).
John F. Enders, 1897-1985, (U.S.) virologist, helped discover vaccines against polio, measles, mumps and chicken pox.
Erik Erikson, 1902-94, (U.S.) psychoanalyst, author; theory of developmental stages of life, *Childhood and Society* (1950).
Leonhard Euler, 1707-83, (Swiss) mathematician, physicist; pioneer of calculus, revived ideas of Fermat.
Gabriel Fahrenheit, 1686-1736, (Ger.) physicist; improved thermometers and introduced Fahrenheit temperature scale.
Michael Faraday, 1791-1867, (Br.) chemist, physicist; discovered electrical induction and invented dynamo (1831).
Philo T. Farnsworth, 1906-71, (U.S.) inventor; built first television system (San Francisco, 1928).
Pierre de Fermat, 1601-65, (Fr.) mathematician; founded modern theory of numbers.
Enrico Fermi, 1901-54, (It.-U.S.) nuclear physicist; demonstrated first controlled chain reaction (Chicago, 1942).

Richard Feynman, 1918-88, (U.S.) theoretical physicist, author; founder of Quantum Electrodynamics (QED).

Alexander Fleming, 1881-1955, (Br.) bacteriologist; discovered penicillin (1928).

Jean B. J. Fourier, 1768-1830, (fr.) introduced method of analysis in math and physics known as Fourier Series.

Sigmund Freud, 1856-1939, (Austrian) psychiatrist; founder of psychoanalysis. *Interpretation of Dreams* (1901).

Erich Fromm, 1900-1980, (U.S.) psychoanalyst. *Man for Himself* (1947).

Galileo Galilei, 1564-1642, (It.) physicist; used telescope to vindicate Copernicus, founded modern science of motion.

Luigi Galvani, 1737-98, (It.) physiologist; studied electricity in living organisms.

Carl Friedrich Gauss, 1777-1855, (Ger.) math. physicist; completed work of Fermat and Euler in number theory.

Joseph Gay-Lussac, 1778-1850, (Fr.) chemist, physicist; investigated behavior of gases, discovered boron.

Josiah W. Gibbs, 1839-1903, (U.S.) theoretical physicist, chemist; founded chemical thermodynamics.

Robert H. Goddard, 1882-1945, (U.S.) physicist; invented liquid fuel rocket (1926).

George W. Goethals, 1858-1928, (U.S.) chief engineer who completed Panama Canal (1907-14).

William C. Gorgas, 1854-1920, (U.S.) physician; pioneer in prevention of yellow fever and malaria.

Stephen Jay Gould, 1941-2002, (U.S.) paleontologist, evolutionary biologist, writer.

Ernest Haeckel, 1834-1919, (Ger.) zoologist, evolutionist; early Darwinist, introduced concept of "ecology."

Otto Hahn, 1879-1968, (Ger.) chemist; with Meitner discovered nuclear fission (1938).

Edmund Halley, 1656-1742, (Br.) astronomer; predicted return of 1682 comet ("Halley's Comet") in 1759.

William Harvey, 1578-1657, (Br.) physician, anatomist; discovered circulation of the blood (1628).

Werner Heisenberg, 1901-76, (Ger.) physicist; developed matrix mechanics and uncertainty principle (1927).

Hermann von Helmholtz, 1821-94, (Ger.) physicist, physiologist; formulated principle of conservation of energy.

William Herschel, 1738-1822, (Ger.-Br.) astronomer; discovered Uranus (1781).

Heinrich Hertz, 1857-94, (Ger.) physicist; discovered radio waves and photo-electric effect (1886-7).

David Hilbert, 1862-1943, (Ger.) mathematician; contributed to algebra, calculus and foundational studies (formalism).

Edwin P. Hubble, 1889-1953, (U.S.) astronomer; discovered observational evidence of expanding universe.

Alexander von Humboldt, 1769-1859, (Ger.) naturalist, author; explored S America, created ecology.

Edward Jenner, 1749-1823, (Br.) physician; pioneered vaccination, introduced term "virus."

James Joule, 1818-89, (Br.) physicist; found relation between heat and mechanical energy (conservation of energy).

Carl Jung, 1875-1961, (Swiss) psychiatrist; founder of analytical psychology.

Sister Elizabeth Kenny, 1886-1952, (Austral.) nurse; developed treatment for polio.

Johannes Kepler, 1571-1630, (Ger.) astronomer; discovered laws of planetary motion.

Al-Khawarizmi, early 9th cent., (Arab.), mathematician; regarded as founder of algebra.

Robert Koch, 1843-1910 (Ger.) bacteriologist; isolated bacterial causes of tuberculosis and other diseases.

Georges Köhler, 1946-95, (Ger.) immunologist; with Cesar Milstein he developed monoclonal antibody technique.

Jacques Lacan, 1901-81, (Fr.) influential psychoanalyst.

Joseph Lagrange, 1736-1813, (Fr.) geometer, astronomer; showed that gravity of earth and moon cancels creating stable points in space around them.

Jean B. Lamarck, 1744-1829, (Fr.) naturalist; forerunner of Darwin in evolutionary theory.

Pierre Simon de Laplace, 1749-1827, (Fr.) astronomer, physicist; proposed nebular origin for solar system.

Antoine Lavoisier, 1743-94, (Fr.) a founder of mod. chemistry.

Ernest O. Lawrence, 1901-58, (U.S.) physicist; invented the cyclotron.

Jerome Lejeune, 1927-94, (Fr.) geneticist; discovered chromosomal cause of Down syndrome (1959).

Louis 1903-72, and **Mary Leakey**, 1913-96, (Br.) early hominid paleoanthropologists; discovered remains in Africa.

Anton van Leeuwenhoek, 1632-1723, (Dutch) founder of microscopy.

Kurt Lewin, 1890-1947, (Ger.-U.S.) social psychologist; studied human motivation and group dynamics.

Justus von Liebig, 1803-73, (Ger.) founded quantitative organic chemistry.

Joseph Lister, 1827-1912, (Br.) physician; pioneered antiseptic surgery.

Hendrik Lorentz, 1853-1928 (Neth.), physicist, developed electron theory of matter, contrib. to relativity theory.

Konrad Lorenz, 1903-89, (Austrian) ethologist; pioneer in study of animal behavior.

Percival Lowell, 1855-1916, (U.S.) astronomer; predicted the existence of Pluto.

Louis, 1864-1948, and **Auguste Lumière**, 1862-1954, (Fr.) invented cinematograph and made first motion picture (1895).

Guglielmo Marconi, 1874-1937, (It.) physicist; developed wireless telegraphy.

John W. Mauchly, 1907-80, (U.S.) co-inventor, with Eckert, of computer ENIAC (1943-45).

James Clerk Maxwell, 1831-79, (Br.) physicist; unified electricity and magnetism; electromagnetic theory of light.

Maria Goeppert Mayer, 1906-72, (Ger.-U.S.) physicist; developed shell model of atomic nuclei.

Barbara McClintock, 1902-92, (U.S.) geneticist; showed that some genetic elements are mobile.

Lise Meitner, 1878-1968, (Austrian) co-discoverer, with Hahn, of nuclear fission (1938).

Gregor J. Mendel, 1822-84, (Austrian) botanist, monk; his experiments became the foundation of modern genetics.

Dmitri Mendeleyev, 1834-1907, (Russ.) chemist; established Periodic Table of the Elements.

Franz Mesmer, 1734-1815, (Ger.) physician; introduced hypnotherapy.

Albert A. Michelson, 1852-1931, (U.S.) physicist; invented interferometer.

Robert A. Millikan, 1868-1953, (U.S.) physicist; measured electronic charge.

Thomas Hunt Morgan, 1866-1945, (U.S.) geneticist, embryologist; established role of chromosomes in heredity.

Isaac Newton, 1642-1727, (Br.) natural philosopher; discovered laws of gravitation, motion; with Leibniz, founded calculus.

Robert N. Noyce, 1927-90, (U.S.) invented microchip.

J. Robert Oppenheimer, 1904-67, (U.S.) physicist; scientific director of Manhattan project.

Wilhelm Ostwald, 1853-1932, (Ger.) chemist, philosopher; main founder of modern physical chemistry.

Louis Pasteur, 1822-95, (Fr.) chemist; showed that germs cause disease and fermentation, originated pasteurization.

Linus C. Pauling, 1901-94, (U.S.) chemist; studied chemical bonds; campaigned for nuclear disarmament.

Jean Piaget, 1896-1980, (Swiss) psychologist; four-stage theory of intellectual development in children.

Max Planck, 1858-1947, (Ger.) physicist; introduced quantum hypothesis (1900).

Jules Henri Poincaré, 1854-1912 (Fr.), mathematician, founded algebraic topology, many other discoveries.

Walter S. Reed, 1851-1902, (U.S.) army physician; proved mosquitoes transmit yellow fever.

Theodor Reik, 1888-1969, (Austrian-U.S.) psychoanalyst, major Freudian disciple.

Bernhard Riemann, 1826-66, (Ger.) mathematician; developed non-Euclidean geometry used by Einstein.

Wilhelm Roentgen, 1845-1923, (Ger.) physicist; discovered X-rays (1895).

Carl Rogers, 1902-87, (U.S.) psychotherapist, author; originated nondirective therapy.

Ernest Rutherford, 1871-1937, (Br.) physicist; pioneer investigator of radioactivity, identified the atomic nucleus.

Albert B. Sabin, 1906-93, (Russ.-U.S.), developed oral polio live-virus vaccine.

Carl Sagan, 1934-96, (U.S.) astronomer, author.

Jonas Salk, 1914-95, (U.S.) developed first successful polio vaccine, widely used in U.S. after 1955.

Giovanni Schiaparelli, 1835-1910, (It.) astronomer; reported canals on Mars.

Erwin Schrödinger, 1887-1961, (Austrian) physicist; developed wave equation for quantum systems.

Glenn T. Seaborg, 1912-99, (U.S.) chemist, Nobel Prize winner (1951); codiscoverer of plutonium.

Harlow Shapley, 1885-1972, (U.S.) astronomer; mapped galactic clusters and position of Sun in our own galaxy.

B(urrhus) F(rederick) Skinner, 1904-89, (U.S.) psychologist; leading advocate of behaviorism.

Roger W. Sperry, 1913-94, (U.S.) neuorobiologist; established different functions of right and left sides of brain.

Benjamin Spock, 1903-98, (U.S.) pediatrician, child care expert; *Common Sense Book of Baby and Child Care.*

Charles P. Steinmetz, 1865-1923, (Ger.-U.S.) electrical engineer; developed basic ideas on alternating current.

Leo Szilard, 1898-1964, (Hung.-U.S.) physicist; helped on Manhattan project, later opposed nuclear weapons.

Edward Teller, 1908-2003, (Hung.-U.S.) physicist, aided on Manhattan project, had key role in development of H-bomb.

Nikola Tesla, 1856-1943, (Serb.-U.S.) invented electrical devices including a.c. dynamos, transformers and motors.

William Thomson (Lord Kelvin), 1824-1907, (Br.) physicist; aided in success of transatlantic telegraph cable (1865); proposed Kelvin absolute temperature scale.

Alan Turing, 1912-54, (Br.) mathematician; helped develop basis for computers.

Rudolf Virchow, 1821-1902, (Ger.) pathologist; pioneered the modern theory that diseases affect the body through cells.

Alessandro Volta, 1745-1827, (It.) physicist; electricity pioneer.

Werner von Braun, 1912-77, (Ger.-U.S.) developed rockets for warfare and space exploration.

John Von Neumann, 1903-57, (Hung.-U.S.) mathematician; originated game theory; basic design for modern computers.

Alfred Russell Wallace, 1823-1913, (Br.) naturalist; proposed concept of evolution independently of Darwin.

John B. Watson, 1878-1958, (U.S.) psychologist; a founder of behaviorism.

James E. Watt, 1736-1819, (Br.) mechanical engineer, inventor; invented modern steam engine (1765).

Alfred L. Wegener, 1880-1930, (Ger.) meteorologist, geophysicist; postulated continental drift.

Norbert Wiener, 1894-1964, (U.S.) mathematician; founder of cybernetics.

Sewall Wright, 1889-1988, (U.S.) evolutionary theorist; helped found population genetics.

Wilhelm Wundt, 1832-1920, (Ger.) founder of experimental psychology.

Ferdinand von Zeppelin, 1838-1917, (Ger.) soldier, aeronaut, airship designer.

Social Reformers, Activists, and Humanitarians of the Past

Jane Addams, 1860-1935, (U.S.) cofounder of Hull House; won Nobel Peace Prize, 1931.

Susan B. Anthony, 1820-1906, (U.S.) a leader in temperance, anti-slavery, and woman suffrage movements.

Thomas Barnardo, 1845-1905, (Br.) social reformer; pioneered in care of destitute children.

Clara Barton, 1821-1912, (U.S.) organized American Red Cross.

Henry Ward Beecher, 1813-87, (U.S.) clergyman, abolitionist.

Peter Benenson, 1921-2005, (Br.) activist, founded Amnesty International in 1961.

Amelia Bloomer, 1818-94, (U.S.) suffragette, social reformer.

William Booth, 1829-1912, (Br.) founded Salvation Army.

John Brown, 1800-59, (U.S.) abolitionist who led murder of 5 pro-slavery men, was hanged.

Frances Xavier (Mother) Cabrini, 1850-1917, (It.-U.S.) Italian-born nun; founded charitable institutions; first American canonized as a saint, 1946.

Carrie Chapman Catt, 1859-1947, (U.S.) suffragette.

Cesar Chavez, 1927-93, (U.S.) labor leader; helped establish United Farm Workers of America.

Clarence Darrow, 1857-1938, (U.S.) lawyer; defender of "underdog," opponent of capital punishment.

Dorothy Day, 1897-1980, (U.S.) founder of Catholic Worker movement.

Eugene V. Debs, 1855-1926, (U.S.) labor leader; led Pullman strike, 1894; 4-time Socialist presidential candidate.

Dorothea Dix, 1802-87, (U.S.) crusader for mentally ill.

Thomas Dooley, 1927-61, (U.S.) "jungle doctor," noted for efforts to supply medical aid to developing countries.

Marjory Stoneman Douglas, 1890-1998, (U.S.) writer and environmentalist; campaigned to save Florida Everglades.

William Lloyd Garrison, 1805-79, (U.S.) abolitionist.

Emma Goldman, 1869-1940, (Russ.-U.S.) published anarchist *Mother Earth,* birth-control advocate.

Samuel Gompers, 1850-1924, (U.S.) labor leader.

Michael Harrington, 1928-89, (U.S.) exposed poverty in affluent U.S. in *The Other America,* 1963.

Sidney Hillman, 1887-1946, (U.S.) labor leader; helped organize CIO.

Samuel G. Howe, 1801-76, (U.S.) social reformer; changed public attitudes toward the handicapped.

Helen Keller, 1880-1968, (U.S.) crusader for better treatment for the handicapped; deaf and blind herself.

Maggie Kuhn, 1905-95, (U.S.) founded Gray Panthers, 1970.

William Kunstler, 1919-95, (U.S.) civil liberties attorney.

John L. Lewis, 1880-1969, (U.S.) labor leader; headed United Mine Workers, 1920-60.

Karl Menninger, 1893-1990, (U.S.) with brother William founded Menninger Clinic and Menninger Foundation.

Lucretia Mott, 1793-1880, (U.S.) reformer, pioneer feminist.

Philip Murray, 1886-1952, (U.S.) Scottish-born labor leader.

Florence Nightingale, 1820-1910, (Br.) founder of modern nursing.

Emmeline Pankhurst, 1858-1928, (Br.) woman suffragist.

Walter Reuther, 1907-70, (U.S.) labor leader; headed UAW.

Jacob Riis, 1849-1914, (U.S.) crusader for urban reforms.

Margaret Sanger, 1883-1966, (U.S.) social reformer; pioneered the birth-control movement.

Earl of Shaftesbury (A. A. Cooper), 1801-85, (Br.) social reformer.

Elizabeth Cady Stanton, 1815-1902, (U.S.) woman suffrage pioneer.

Lucy Stone, 1818-93, (U.S.) feminist, abolitionist.

Mother Teresa of Calcutta, 1910-97, (Alban.) nun; founded order to care for sick, dying poor; 1979 Nobel Peace Prize.

Philip Vera Cruz, 1905-94, (Filipino-U.S.) helped to found the United Farm Workers Union.

William Wilberforce, 1759-1833, (Br.) social reformer; prominent in struggle to abolish the slave trade.

Frances E. Willard, 1839-98, (U.S.) temperance, women's rights leader.

Mary Wollstonecraft, 1759-97, (Br.) wrote *Vindication of the Rights of Women.*

Writers of the Present

Name (Birthplace)	Birthdate
Chinua Achebe (Ogidi, Nigeria)	11/16/30
Richard Adams (Newbury, Eng.)	5/9/20
Edward Albee (Wash., DC)	3/12/28
Isabel Allende (Lima, Peru)	8/2/42
Dorothy Allison (Greenville, SC)	4/11/49
Martin Amis (Oxford, Eng.)	8/25/49
Maya Angelou (St. Louis, MO)	4/4/28
Piers Anthony (Oxford, Eng.)	8/6/34
Jeffrey Archer (Somerset, Eng.)	4/15/40
Oscar Arias Sanchez (Heredia, Costa Rica)	9/13/41
John Ashbery (Rochester, NY)	7/28/27
Margaret Atwood (Ottawa, Ont.)	11/18/39
David Auburn (Chicago)	1969
Louis Auchincloss (Lawrence, NY)	9/27/17
Jean Auel (Chicago)	2/18/36
Paul Auster (Newark, NJ)	2/3/47
Alan Ayckbourn (Hampstead, Eng.)	4/12/39
Nicholson Baker (Rochester, NY)	1/7/57
Russell Banks (Newton, MA)	3/28/40
John Barth (Cambridge, MD)	5/27/30
Ann Beattie (Wash., DC)	9/8/47
Peter Benchley (NYC)	5/8/40
John Berendt (Syracuse, NY)	12/5/39
Thomas Berger (Cincinnati, OH)	7/20/24
Maeve Binchy (Dalkey, Ireland)	3/28/40
Judy Blume (Elizabeth, NJ)	2/12/38
T. Coraghessan Boyle (Peekskill, NY)	12/2/48

Name (Birthplace)	Birthdate
Ray Bradbury (Waukegan, IL)	8/22/20
Barbara Taylor Bradford (Leeds, Eng.)	5/10/33
Dan Brown (Exeter, NH),	6/22/64
Rita Mae Brown (Hanover, PA)	11/28/44
Christopher Buckley (NYC)	9/28/52
James Lee Burke (Houston, TX)	12/5/36
Augusten Burroughs (Pittsburgh, PA)	1965
Robert Olen Butler (Granite City, IL)	1/20/45
A. S. Byatt (Sheffield, England)	8/24/36
Hortense Calisher (NYC)	12/20/11
Ethan Canin (Ann Arbor, MI)	7/19/60
Peter Carey (Bacchus-Marsh, Victoria, Australia)	5/7/43
Caleb Carr (NYC)	5/19/63
Michael Chabon (Wash., DC)	5/19/63
Tracy Chevalier (Wash., DC)	10/62
Sandra Cisneros (Chicago)	12/20/54
Tom Clancy (Baltimore, MD)	4/12/47
Mary Higgins Clark (NYC)	12/24/29
Arthur C. Clarke (Minehead, Eng.)	12/16/29
Beverly Cleary (McMinnville, OR)	4/12/16
Paulo Coelho (Rio de Janeiro, Brazil)	8/24/47
J(ohn) M(axwell) Coetzee (Capetown, S. Africa)	2/9/40
Billy Collins (NYC)	3/22/41
Jackie Collins (London, Eng.)	10/4/41
Evan S. Connell (Kansas City, MO)	8/17/24

Name (Birthplace)	Birthdate
Pat Conroy (Atlanta, GA)	10/26/45
Robin Cook (NYC)	5/4/40
Patricia Cornwell (Miami, FL)	6/9/56
Harry Crews (Alma, GA)	6/6/35
Michael Crichton (Chicago)	10/23/42
Michael Cunningham (Cincinnati, Ohio)	11/6/52
Don DeLillo (NYC)	11/20/36
Nelson DeMille (NYC)	8/23/43
Joan Didion (Sacramento, CA)	12/5/34
E. L. Doctorow (NYC)	1/6/31
Takako Doi (Hyogo, Jap.)	11/30/28
Rita Dove (Akron, OH)	8/28/52
Roddy Doyle (Dublin, Ireland)	5/5/58
John Gregory Dunne (Hartford, CT)	5/25/32
Umberto Eco (Alessandria, Italy)	1/5/32
Bret Easton Ellis (Los Angeles, CA)	3/7/64
James Ellroy (Los Angeles)	3/4/48
Louise Erdrich (Little Falls, MN)	7/6/54
Laura Esquivel (Mexico City, Mexico)	9/30/51
Jeffrey Eugenides (Detroit, MI)	1960
Lawrence Ferlinghetti (Yonkers, NY)	3/24/19
Helen Fielding (Morley, Yorkshire, Eng.)	2/19/58
Ken Follet (Cardiff, Wales)	6/5/49
Dario Fo (San Giano, Italy)	3/26/26
Horton Foote (Wharton, TX)	3/14/16
Richard Ford (Jackson, MS)	2/16/44

Name (Birthplace)	Birthdate
Frederick Forsyth (Ashford, Eng.)	8/25/38
John Fowles (Leigh-on-Sea, Eng.)	3/31/26
Paula Fox (NYC)	4/22/23
Dick Francis (Tenby, Pembrokeshire, Wales)	10/31/20
Jonathan Franzen (Western Springs, IL)	8/17/59
Michael Frayn (London, Eng.)	9/8/33
Charles Frazier (Asheville, NC)	11/4/50
Marilyn French (NYC)	11/21/29
Brian Friel (Omagh, County Tyrone, N. Ireland)	1/9/29
Carlos Fuentes (Panama City, Panama)	11/11/28
Ernest J. Gaines (Oscar, LA)	1/15/33
Gabriel Garcia Marquez (Aracataca, Colombia)	3/6/28
Frank Gilroy (Bronx, NY)	10/13/25
Gail Godwin (Birmingham, AL)	6/18/37
William Goldman (Highland Park, IL)	8/12/31
Nadine Gordimer (Springs, S. Africa)	11/20/23
Mary Gordon (Far Rockaway, Long Island, NY)	12/8/49
Sue Grafton (Louisville, KY)	4/24/40
Günter Grass (Danzig, now Gdansk, Poland)	10/16/27
Shirley Ann Grau (New Orleans, LA)	7/8/29
John Grisham (Jonesboro, AR)	2/8/55
John Guare (NYC)	2/5/38
David Handler (Los Angeles)	9/14/52
David Hare (St. Leonards, Sussex, Eng.)	6/5/47
Jim Harrison (Grayling, MI)	12/11/37
Robert Hass (San Francisco, CA)	3/1/41
Vaclav Havel (Prague, Czech.)	10/5/36
Seamus Heaney (Mossbaum, Cty. Derry, N. Ire.)	4/13/39
Mark Helprin (NYC)	6/28/47
Carl Hiaasen (S. Florida)	3/12/53
Oscar Hijuelos (NYC)	8/24/51
Tony Hillerman (Sacred Heart, OK)	5/27/25
S. E. Hinton (Tulsa, OK)	7/22/50
Alice Hoffman (NYC)	3/16/52
John Irving (Exeter, NH)	3/2/42
Kazuo Ishiguro (Nagasaki, Japan)	11/8/54
John Jakes (Chicago)	3/31/32
P. D. James (Oxford, Eng.)	8/3/20
Ha Jih (Liaoning, China)	2/21/56
Erica Jong (NYC)	3/26/42
Garrison Keillor (Anoka, MN)	8/7/42
Thomas Keneally (Sydney, Austral.)	10/7/35
William Kennedy (Albany, NY)	1/16/28
Jamaica Kincaid (St. Johns, Antigua)	5/25/49
Stephen King (Portland, ME)	9/21/47
Barbara Kingsolver (Annapolis, MD)	4/8/55
Maxine Hong Kingston (Stockton, CA)	10/27/40
Galway Kinnell (Providence, RI)	2/1/27
Dean Koontz (Everett, PA)	7/9/45
Ted Kooser (Ames, IA)	4/25/39
Judith Krantz (NYC)	1/9/28
Maxine Kumin (Philadelphia, PA)	6/6/25
Milan Kundera (Brno, Czechoslovakia)	4/1/29
Stanley Kunitz (Worcester, MA)	7/29/05
Tony Kushner (NYC)	7/16/56
David Leavitt (Pittsburgh, PA)	6/23/61
John Le Carré (Poole, Eng.)	10/19/31
Harper Lee (Monroeville, AL)	4/28/26
Ursula K. Le Guin (Berkeley, CA)	10/21/29
Madeleine L'Engle (NYC)	11/29/18
Elmore Leonard (New Orleans, LA)	10/11/25
Doris Lessing (Kermanshah, Persia)	10/22/19
Jonathan Lethem (Bklyn, NY)	2/19/64
Ira Levin (NYC)	8/27/29
David Lodge (South London, Eng.)	1/28/35
Alison Lurie (Chicago)	9/3/26
Gregory Maguire (Albany, NY)	6/9/54
Naguib Mahfouz (Cairo, Egypt)	12/11/11
Norman Mailer (Long Branch, NJ)	1/31/23
David Mamet (Chicago)	11/30/47
Yann Martel (Salamanca, Spain)	6/25/63
Bobbie Ann Mason (nr. Mayfield, KY)	5/1/40
Peter Matthiessen (NYC)	5/22/27
Armistead Maupin (Wash., DC)	4/13/44
Cormac McCarthy (Providence, RI)	7/20/33
Frank McCourt (Bklyn, NY)	8/19/30
Colleen McCullough (Wellington, N.S.W., Austral.)	6/1/37
Alice McDermott (Bklyn, NY)	6/27/53
Ian McEwan (Aldershot, England)	6/21/48
Thomas McGuane (Wyandotte, MI)	12/11/39
Terry McMillan (Port Huron, MI)	10/18/51
Larry McMurtry (Wichita Falls, TX)	6/3/36
Terrence McNally (St. Petersburg, FL)	11/3/39
John McPhee (Princeton, NJ)	3/8/31
W(illiam) S(tanley) Merwin (NYC)	9/30/27
Toni Morrison (Lorain, OH)	2/18/31
Walter Mosley (Los Angeles, CA)	1/12/52
Andrew Motion (London)	10/26/52
Bharati Mukherjee (Calcutta, India)	7/27/40
Alice Munro (Wingham, Ont.)	7/10/31
Haruki Murakami (Kyoto, Japan)	1/12/49
V. S. Naipaul (Chaguanas, Trinidad)	8/17/32
Joyce Carol Oates (Lockport, NY)	6/16/38
Edna O'Brien (Tuamgraney, Ir.)	12/15/32
Tim O'Brien (Austin, MN)	10/1/46
Kenzaburo Oe (Uchiko, Japan)	1/31/35
Michael Ondaatje (Colombo, Sri Lanka)	9/12/43
Cynthia Ozick (NYC)	4/17/28
Grace Paley (NYC)	12/11/22
Robert B. Parker (Springfield, MA)	9/17/32
Suzan-Lori Parks (Fort Knox, KY)	5/10/63
Marge Piercy (Detroit, MI)	3/31/36
Robert Pinsky (Long Branch, NJ)	10/20/40
Harold Pinter (Hackney, East London, Eng.)	10/10/30
Reynolds Price (Macon, NC)	2/1/33
Richard Price (Bronx, NY)	10/12/49
E. Annie Proulx (Norwich, CT)	8/22/35
Philip Pullman (Norwich, Eng.)	10/19/46
Thomas Pynchon (Glen Cove, Long Island, NY)	5/8/37
David Rabe (Dubuque, IA)	3/10/40
Ishmael Reed (Chattanooga, TN)	2/22/38
Ruth Rendell (London, England)	2/17/30
Anne Rice (New Orleans, LA)	10/4/41
Adrienne Rich (Baltimore, MD)	5/16/29
Nora Roberts (Wash., DC)	10/10/50
Marilyn Robinson (Sandpoint, IL)	1944
Philip Roth (Newark, NJ)	3/19/33
J.K. Rowling (Chipping Sodbury, Eng.)	7/31/65
Norman Rush (Oakland, CA)	10/24/33
Salman Rushdie (Bombay, India)	6/19/47
Richard Russo (Johnstown, NY)	7/15/49
J. D. Salinger (NYC)	1/1/19
Jose Saramago (Azinhaga, Portugal)	11/16/22
Alice Sebold (Madison, WI)	1963
David Sedaris (Johnson City, NY)	12/26/56
Vikram Seth (Calcutta, India)	6/20/52
Sidney Sheldon (Chicago)	2/11/17
Sam Shepard (Ft. Sheridan, IL)	11/5/43
Neil Simon (Bronx, NY)	7/4/27
Jane Smiley (Los Angeles, CA)	9/26/49
Aleksandr Solzhenitsyn (Kislovodsk, Russia)	12/11/18
Wole Soyinka (Abeokuta, Nigeria)	7/13/34
Mickey Spillane (Bklyn, NY)	3/9/18
Danielle Steel (NYC)	8/14/47
Richard Stern (NYC)	2/25/28
Mary Stewart (Sunderland, Eng.)	9/17/16
R(obert) L(awrence) Stine (Columbus, OH)	10/8/43
Tom Stoppard (Zlin, Czech.)	7/3/37
Mark Strand (P.E.I., Can.)	4/11/34
William Styron (Newport News, VA)	6/11/25
Wislawa Szymborska (Kornik, Pol.)	7/2/23
Amy Tan (Oakland, CA)	2/19/52
Donna Tartt (Greenwood, MS)	12/23/63
Paul Theroux (Medford, MA)	4/10/41
Calvin Trillin (Kansas City, MO)	12/5/35
Scott F. Turow (Chicago)	4/12/49
Anne Tyler (Minneapolis, MN)	10/25/41
John Updike (Shillington, PA)	3/18/32
Mario Vargas Llosa (Arequipa, Peru)	3/28/36
Gore Vidal (West Point, NY)	10/3/25
Paula Vogel (Wash., DC)	11/16/51
Kurt Vonnegut Jr. (Indianapolis, IN)	11/11/22
Derek Walcott (Castries, Saint Lucia)	1/23/30
Alice Walker (Eatonton, GA)	2/9/44
Robert James Waller (Rockford, IA)	8/1/39
Joseph Wambaugh (East Pittsburgh, PA)	1/22/37
Wendy Wasserstein (Bklyn, NY)	10/18/50
Edmund White (Cincinnati, OH)	1/19/40
August Wilson (Pittsburgh, PA)	4/27/45
Lanford Wilson (Lebanon, MO)	4/13/37
Tom Wolfe (Richmond, VA)	3/2/31
Tobias Wolff (Birmingham, AL)	6/19/45
Herman Wouk (NYC)	5/27/15
Yevgeny Yevtushenko (Irkutsk, Russia)	7/18/33

Writers of the Past

See also Journalists of the Past, and Greeks and Romans in Historical Figures chapter.

Alice Adams, 1926-99, (U.S.) novelist, short-story writer. *Superior Woman.*

James Agee, 1909-55, (U.S.) novelist. *A Death in the Family.*

S(hmuel) Y(osef)Agnon, 1888-1970, (Is.) Hebrew novelist. *Only Yesterday.*

Conrad Aiken, 1889-1973, (U.S.) poet, critic. *Ushant.*

Anna Akhmatova, 1889-1966, (Russ.) poet. *Requiem.*

Louisa May Alcott, 1832-88, (U.S.) novelist. *Little Women.*

Sholom Aleichem, 1859-1916, (Russ.) Yiddish writer. *Tevye's Daughters, The Old Country.*

Vicente Aleixandre, 1898-1984, (Sp.) poet. *La destrucción o el amor, Dialogolos del conocimiento.*

Horatio Alger, 1832-1899, (U.S.) "rags-to-riches" books.

Jorge Amado, 1912-2001, (Brazil) novelist. *Dona Flor and Her Two Husbands, The Violent Land.*

Eric Ambler, 1909-98, (Br.) suspense novelist. *A Coffin for Dimitrios.*

Kingsley Amis, 1922-95, (Br.) novelist, critic. *Lucky Jim.*

Hans Christian Andersen, 1805-75, (Dan.) author of fairy tales. *The Ugly Duckling.*

Maxwell Anderson, 1888-1959, (U.S.) playwright. *What Price Glory?, High Tor, Winterset, Key Largo.*

Sherwood Anderson, 1876-1941, (U.S.) short-story writer. "Death in the Woods;" *Winesburg, Ohio.*

Reinaldo Arenas, 1943-1990, (Cuba) short-story writer, novelist. *Before Night Falls.*

Ludovico Ariosto, 1474-1533, (It.) poet. *Orlando Furioso.*

Matthew Arnold, 1822-88, (Br.) poet, critic. "Thrysis," "Dover Beach," "Culture and Anarchy."

Isaac Asimov, 1920-92, (U.S.) versatile writer, espec. of science-fiction. *I Robot.*

Miguel Angel Asturias, 1899-1974, (Guatemala) novelist. *El Señor Presidente.*

W(ystan) H(ugh) Auden, 1907-73, (Br.) poet, playwright, literary critic. "The Age of Anxiety."

Jane Austen, 1775-1817, (Br.) novelist. *Pride and Prejudice, Sense and Sensibility, Emma, Mansfield Park.*

Isaac Babel, 1894-1941, (Russ.) short-story writer, playwright. *Odessa Tales, Red Cavalry.*

James Baldwin, 1924-87, author, playwright. *The Fire Next Time, Blues for Mister Charlie.*

Honoré de Balzac, 1799-1850, (Fr.) novelist. *Le Père Goriot, Cousine Bette, Eugénie Grandet.*

James M. Barrie, 1860-1937, (Br.) playwright, novelist. *Peter Pan, Dear Brutus, What Every Woman Knows.*

Charles Baudelaire, 1821-67, (Fr.) poet. *Les Fleurs du Mal.*
L(yman) Frank Baum, 1856-1919, (U.S.) *Wizard of Oz* series.
Simone de Beauvoir, 1908-86, (Fr.) novelist, essayist. *The Second Sex, Memoirs of a Dutiful Daughter.*
Samuel Beckett, 1906-89, (Ir.) novelist, playwright. *Waiting for Godot, Endgame* (plays); *Murphy, Watt, Molloy* (novels).
Brendan Behan, 1923-64, (Ir.) playwright. *The Quare Fellow, The Hostage, Borstal Boy.*
Saul Bellow,1915-2005, (U.S.) novelist. *The Adventures of Augie March, Humboldt's Gift.*
Robert Benchley, 1889-1945, (U.S.) humorist.
Stephen Vincent Benét, 1898-1943, (U.S.) poet, novelist. *John Brown's Body.*
John Berryman, 1914-72, (U.S.) poet. *Homage to Mistress Bradstreet.*
Ambrose Bierce, 1842-1914, (U.S.) short-story writer, journalist. *In the Midst of Life, The Devil's Dictionary.*
Elizabeth Bishop, 1911-79, (U.S.) poet. *North and South—A Cold Spring.*
William Blake, 1757-1827, (Br.) poet, artist. *Songs of Innocence, Songs of Experience.*
Aleksandr Blok, 1880-1921, (Russ.) poet. "The Twelve", "The Scythians."
Giovanni Boccaccio, 1313-75, (It.) poet. *Decameron.*
Heinrich Böll, 1917-85, (Ger.) novelist, short-story writer. *Group Portrait With Lady.*
Jorge Luis Borges, 1900-86, (Arg.) short-story writer, poet, essayist. *Labyrinths.*
James Boswell, 1740-95, (Sc.) biographer. *The Life of Samuel Johnson.*
Pierre Boulle, 1913-94, (Fr.) novelist. *The Bridge Over the River Kwai, Planet of the Apes.*
Paul Bowles, 1910-99, (U.S.) novelist, short-story writer. *The Sheltering Sky*
Anne Bradstreet, c1612-72, (U.S.) poet. *The Tenth Muse Lately Sprung Up in America.*
Bertolt Brecht, 1898-1956, (Ger.) dramatist, poet. *The Threepenny Opera, Mother Courage and Her Children.*
Charlotte Brontë, 1816-55, (Br.) novelist. *Jane Eyre.*
Emily Brontë, 1818-48, (Br.) novelist. *Wuthering Heights.*
Elizabeth Barrett Browning, 1806-61, (Br.) poet. *Sonnets From the Portuguese, Aurora Leigh.*
Joseph Brodsky, 1940-96, (Russ.-U.S.) poet. *A Part of Speech, Less Than One, To Urania.*
Robert Browning, 1812-89, (Br.) poet. "My Last Duchess," "Fra Lippo Lippi," *The Ring and The Book.*
Pearl S. Buck, 1892-1973, (U.S.) novelist. *The Good Earth.*
Mikhail Bulgakov, 1891-1940, (Russ.) novelist, playwright. *The Heart of a Dog, The Master and Margarita.*
John Bunyan, 1628-88, (Br.) writer. *Pilgrim's Progress.*
Anthony Burgess, 1917-93, (Br.) author. *A Clockwork Orange.*
Frances Hodgson Burnett, 1849-1924, (Br.-U.S.) novelist. *The Secret Garden.*
Robert Burns, 1759-96, (Sc.) poet. "Flow Gently, Sweet Afton," "My Heart's in the Highlands," "Auld Lang Syne."
Edgar Rice Burroughs, 1875-1950, (U.S.) "Tarzan" books.
William S. Burroughs, 1914-97, (U.S.) novelist. *Naked Lunch.*
George Gordon, Lord Byron, 1788-1824, (Br.) poet. *Don Juan, Childe Harold, Manfred, Cain.*
Pedro Calderon de la Barca, 1600-81, (Sp.) playwright. *Life Is a Dream.*
Italo Calvino, 1923-85, (It.) novelist, short-story writer. *If on a Winter's Night a Traveler.*
Luis Vaz de Camoes, 1524?-80 (Port.) poet. *The Lusiads.*
Albert Camus, 1913-60, (Fr.) writer. *The Stranger, The Fall.*
Elias Canetti, 1905-94, (Bulg.) novelist, essayist. *Auto-Da-Fe.*
Karel Capek, 1890-1938, (Czech.) playwright, novelist, essayist. *R.U.R. (Rossum's Universal Robots).*
Truman Capote, 1924-84, (U.S.) author. *Other Voices, Other Rooms, Breakfast at Tiffany's, In Cold Blood.*
Lewis Carroll (Charles Dodgson), 1832-98, (Br.) writer, mathematician. *Alice's Adventures in Wonderland.*
Giacomo Casanova, 1725-98, (It.) adventurer, memoirist.
Willa Cather, 1873-1947, (U.S.) novelist. *O Pioneers!, My Ántonia, Death Comes for the Archbishop.*
Constantine Cavafy, 1863-1933, (Gr.) poet. "Ithaka", "Sensual Pleasures."
Camilo Jose Cela, 1916-2001, (Sp.) novelist. *The Family of Pascual Duarte, The Hive.*
Miguel de Cervantes Saavedra, 1547-1616, (Sp.) novelist, dramatist, poet. *Don Quixote.*
Raymond Chandler, 1888-1959, (U.S.) writer of detective fiction. Philip Marlowe series.
Geoffrey Chaucer, c1340-1400, (Br.) poet. *The Canterbury Tales, Troilus and Criseyde.*
John Cheever, 1912-82, (U.S.) novelist, short-story writer. *The Wapshot Scandal,* "The Country Husband."
Anton Chekhov, 1860-1904, (Russ.) short-story writer, dramatist. *Uncle Vanya, The Cherry Orchard, The Three Sisters.*
G(ilbert) K(eith) Chesterton, 1874-1936, (Br.) critic, novelist, relig. apologist. Father Brown series of mysteries.
Kate Chopin, 1851-1904, (U.S.) writer. *The Awakening.*
Agatha Christie, 1890-1976, (Br.) mystery writer; created Miss Marple, Hercule Poirot; *And Then There Were None, Murder on the Orient Express, Murder of Roger Ackroyd.*
James Clavell, 1924-94, (Br.-U.S.) novelist. *Shogun, King Rat.*
Jean Cocteau, 1889-1963, (Fr.) writer, visual artist, filmmaker. *The Beauty and the Beast, Les Enfants Terribles.*
Samuel Taylor Coleridge, 1772-1834, (Br.) poet, critic. "Kubla Khan," "The Rime of the Ancient Mariner."
(Sidonie) Colette, 1873-1954, (Fr.) novelist. *Claudine, Gigi.*
Wilkie Collins, 1824-89, (Br.) novelist. *The Moonstone.*
Joseph Conrad, 1857-1924, (Br.) novelist. *Lord Jim, Heart of Darkness, The Secret Agent.*
James Fenimore Cooper, 1789-1851, (U.S.) novelist. *Leatherstocking Tales, The Last of the Mohicans.*
Pierre Corneille, 1606-84, (Fr.) dramatist. *Medeé, Le Cid.*
Hart Crane, 1899-1932, (U.S.) poet. "The Bridge."
Stephen Crane, 1871-1900, (U.S.) novelist, short-story writer. *The Red Badge of Courage,* "The Open Boat."
E. E. Cummings, 1894-1962, (U.S.) poet. *Tulips and Chimneys.*
Roald Dahl, 1916-90, (Br.-U.S.) writer. *Charlie and the Chocolate Factory, James and the Giant Peach.*
Gabriele D'Annunzio, 1863-1938, (It.) poet, novelist, dramatist. *The Child of Pleasure, The Intruder, The Victim.*
Dante Alighieri, 1265-1321, (It.) poet. *The Divine Comedy.*
Robertson Davies, 1913-95, (Can.) novelist, playwright, essayist. Salterton, Deptford, and Cornish trilogies.
Daniel Defoe, 1660-1731, (Br.) writer. *Robinson Crusoe, Moll Flanders, Journal of the Plague Year.*
Charles Dickens, 1812-70, (Br.) novelist. *David Copperfield, Oliver Twist, Great Expectations, A Tale of Two Cities.*
Philip K. Dick, 1928-82, (U.S.) science fiction writer. *Do Androids Dream of Electric Sheep?*
James Dickey, 1923-1997, (U.S.) poet, novelist. *Deliverance.*
Emily Dickinson, 1830-86, (U.S.) lyric poet. "Because I could not stop for Death . . .," "Success is counted sweetest . . ."
Isak Dinesen (Karen Blixen), 1885-1962, (Dan.) author. *Out of Africa, Seven Gothic Tales, Winter's Tales.*
John Donne, 1573-1631, (Br.) poet. *Songs and Sonnets.*
José Donoso, 1924-96, (Chil.) surreal novelist and short-story writer. *The Obscene Bird of Night.*
John Dos Passos, 1896-1970, (U.S.) novelist. *U.S.A.*
Fyodor Dostoyevsky, 1821-81, (Russ.) novelist. *Crime and Punishment, The Brothers Karamazov, The Possessed.*
Arthur Conan Doyle, 1859-1930, (Br.) novelist. Sherlock Holmes mystery stories.
Theodore Dreiser, 1871-1945, (U.S.) novelist. *An American Tragedy, Sister Carrie.*
John Dryden, 1631-1700, (Br.) poet, dramatist, critic. *All for Love, Mac Flecknoe, Absalom and Achitophel.*
Alexandre Dumas, 1802-70, (Fr.) novelist, dramatist. *The Three Musketeers, The Count of Monte Cristo.*
Alexandre Dumas (fils), 1824-95, (Fr.) dramatist, novelist. *La Dame aux Camélias, Le Demi-Monde.*
Lawrence Durrell, 1912-90, (Br.) novelist, poet. *Alexandria Quartet.*
Ilya G. Ehrenburg, 1891-1967, (Russ.) writer. *The Thaw.*
George Eliot (Mary Ann Evans or Marian Evans), 1819-80, (Br.) novelist. *Silas Marner, Middlemarch.*
T(homas) S(tearns) Eliot, 1888-1965, (Br.) poet, critic. *The Waste Land,* "The Love Song of J. Alfred Prufrock."
Stanley Elkin, 1930-95, (U.S.) novelist, short story writer. *George Mills.*
Ralph Ellison, 1914-94, (U.S.), writer. *Invisible Man.*
Ralph Waldo Emerson, 1803-82, (U.S.) poet, essayist. "Brahma," "Nature," "The Over-Soul," "Self-Reliance."
James T. Farrell, 1904-79, (U.S.) novelist. *Studs Lonigan.*
William Faulkner, 1897-1962, (U.S.) novelist. *Sanctuary, Light in August, The Sound and the Fury, Absalom, Absalom!*
Edna Ferber, 1887-1968, (U.S.) novelist, short-story writer, playwright. *So Big, Cimarron, Show Boat.*
Henry Fielding, 1707-54, (Br.) novelist. *Tom Jones.*
F(rancis) Scott Fitzgerald, 1896-1940, (U.S.) short-story writer, novelist. *The Great Gatsby, Tender Is the Night.*
Gustave Flaubert, 1821-80, (Fr.) novelist. *Madame Bovary.*
Ian Fleming, 1908-64, (Br.) novelist; James Bond spy thrillers. *Dr. No, Goldfinger.*
Ford Madox Ford, 1873-1939, (Br.) novelist, critic, poet. *The Good Soldier.*
C(ecil) S(cott) Forester, 1899-1966, (Br.) writer. Horatio Hornblower books.
E(dward) M(organ) Forster, 1879-1970, (Br.) novelist. *A Passage to India, Howards End.*
Anatole France, 1844-1924, (Fr.) writer. *Penguin Island, My Friend's Book, The Crime of Sylvestre Bonnard.*
Robert Frost, 1874-1963, (U.S.) poet. "Birches," "Fire and Ice," "Stopping by Woods on a Snowy Evening."
William Gaddis, 1922-98, (U.S.) novelist. *The Recognitions.*

John Galsworthy, 1867-1933, (Br.) novelist, dramatist. *The Forsyte Saga.*
Federico Garcia Lorca, 1898-1936, (Sp.) poet, dramatist. *Blood Wedding.*
Erle Stanley Gardner, 1889-1970, (U.S.) mystery writer; created Perry Mason.
Jean Genet, 1911-86, (Fr.) playwright, novelist. *The Maids.*
Kahlil Gibran, 1883-1931, (Lebanese-U.S.) mystical novelist, essayist, poet. *The Prophet.*
André Gide, 1869-1951, (Fr.) writer. *The Immoralist, The Pastoral Symphony, Strait Is the Gate.*
Allen Ginsberg, 1926-1997, (U.S.) Beat poet. "Howl."
Jean Giraudoux, 1882-1944, (Fr.) novelist, dramatist. *Electra, The Madwoman of Chaillot, Ondine, Tiger at the Gate.*
Johann Wolfgang von Goethe, 1749-1832, (Ger.) poet, dramatist, novelist. *Faust, Sorrows of Young Werther.*
Nikolai Gogol, 1809-52, (Russ.) short-story writer, dramatist, novelist. *Dead Souls, The Inspector General.*
William Golding, 1911-93, (Br.) novelist. *Lord of the Flies.*
Oliver Goldsmith, 1728-74, (Br.-Ir.) dramatist, novelist. *The Vicar of Wakefield, She Stoops to Conquer.*
Maxim Gorky, 1868-1936, (Russ.) dramatist, novelist. *The Lower Depths.*
Robert Graves, 1895-1985, (Br.) poet, classical scholar, novelist. *I, Claudius; The White Goddess.*
Thomas Gray, 1716-71, (Br.) poet. "Elegy Written in a Country Churchyard," "The Progress of Poesy."
Julien Green, 1900-98, (U.S.-Fr.) expatriate American, French novelist. *Moira, Each Man in His Darkness.*
Graham Greene, 1904-91, (Br.) novelist. *The Power and the Glory, The Heart of the Matter, The Ministry of Fear.*
Zane Grey, 1872-1939, (U.S.) writer of Western stories.
Jakob Grimm, 1785-1863, (Ger.) philologist, folklorist; with brother **Wilhelm,** 1786-1859, collected *Grimm's Fairy Tales.*
Alex Haley, 1921-92, (U.S.) author. *Roots.*
Dashiell Hammett, 1894-1961, (U.S.) detective-story writer; created Sam Spade. *The Maltese Falcon, The Thin Man.*
Knut Hamsun, 1859-1952 (Nor.) novelist. *Hunger.*
Thomas Hardy, 1840-1928, (Br.) novelist, poet. *The Return of the Native, Tess of the D'Urbervilles, Jude the Obscure.*
Joel Chandler Harris, 1848-1908, (U.S.) Uncle Remus stories.
Moss Hart, 1904-61, (U.S.) playwright. *Once in a Lifetime, You Can't Take It With You, The Man Who Came to Dinner.*
Bret Harte, 1836-1902, (U.S.) short-story writer, poet. *The Luck of Roaring Camp.*
Jaroslav Hasek, 1883-1923, (Czech.) writer, playwright. *The Good Soldier Schweik.*
John Hawkes, 1925-98, (U.S.) experimental fiction writer. *The Goose on the Grave, Blood Oranges.*
Nathaniel Hawthorne, 1804-64, (U.S.) novelist, short-story writer. *The Scarlet Letter,* "Young Goodman Brown."
Heinrich Heine, 1797-1856, (Ger.) poet. *Book of Songs.*
Robert Heinlein, 1907-88, (U.S.) science fiction writer. *Stranger in a Strange Land.*
Joseph Heller, 1923-99, (U.S.) novelist. Catch-22.
Lillian Hellman, 1905-84, (U.S.) playwright, author of memoirs. *The Little Foxes, An Unfinished Woman, Pentimento.*
Ernest Hemingway, 1899-1961, (U.S.) novelist, short-story writer. *A Farewell to Arms, For Whom the Bell Tolls.*
O. Henry (W. S. Porter), 1862-1910, (U.S.) short-story writer. "The Gift of the Magi."
George Herbert, 1593-1633, (Br.) poet. "The Altar," "Easter Wings."
Zbigniew Herbert, 1924-98, (Pol.) poet. "Apollo and Marsyas."
Robert Herrick, 1591-1674, (Br.) poet. "To the Virgins to Make Much of Time."
John Hersey, 1914-93, (U.S.) novelist, journalist. *Hiroshima, A Bell for Adano.*
Hermann Hesse, 1877-1962, (Ger.) novelist, poet. *Death and the Lover, Steppenwolf, Siddhartha.*
James Hilton, 1900-54, (Br.) novelist. *Lost Horizon.*
Oliver Wendell Holmes, 1809-94, (U.S.) poet, novelist. *The Autocrat of the Breakfast-Table.*
Gerard Manley Hopkins, 1844-89, (Br.) poet. "Pied Beauty," "God's Grandeur."
A(lfred) E. Housman, 1859-1936, (Br.) poet. *A Shropshire Lad.*
William Dean Howells, 1837-1920, (U.S.) novelist, critic. *The Rise of Silas Lapham.*
Langston Hughes, 1902-67, (U.S.) poet, playwright. *The Weary Blues, One-Way Ticket, Shakespeare in Harlem.*
Ted Hughes, 1930-98, (Br.) British poet laureate, 1984-98. *Crow, The Hawk in the Rain.*
Victor Hugo, 1802-85, (Fr.) poet, dramatist, novelist. *Notre Dame de Paris, Les Misérables.*
Zora Neale Hurston, 1903-60, (U.S.) novelist, folklorist. *Their Eyes Were Watching God, Mules and Men.*
Aldous Huxley, 1894-1963, (Br.) writer. *Brave New World.*
Henrik Ibsen, 1828-1906, (Nor.) dramatist, poet. *A Doll's House, Ghosts, The Wild Duck, Hedda Gabler.*
William Inge, 1913-73, (U.S.) playwright. *Picnic; Come Back, Little Sheba; Bus Stop.*
Eugene Ionesco, 1910-94, (Fr.) surrealist dramatist. *The Bald Soprano, The Chairs.*
Washington Irving, 1783-1859, (U.S.) writer. "Rip Van Winkle," "The Legend of Sleepy Hollow."
Christopher Isherwood, 1904-1986, (Br.) novelist, playwright. *The Berlin Stories.*
Shirley Jackson, 1919-65, (U.S.) short-story writer. "The Lottery."
Henry James, 1843-1916, (U.S.) novelist, short-story writer, critic. *The Portrait of a Lady, The Ambassadors, Daisy Miller.*
Robinson Jeffers, 1887-1962, (U.S.) poet, dramatist. *Tamar and Other Poems, Medea.*
Samuel Johnson, 1709-84, (Br.) author, scholar, critic. *Dictionary of the English Language, Vanity of Human Wishes.*
Ben Jonson, 1572-1637, (Br.) dramatist, poet. *Volpone.*
James Joyce, 1882-1941, (Ir.) writer. *Ulysses, Dubliners, A Portrait of the Artist as a Young Man, Finnegans Wake.*
Ernst Junger, 1895-1998, (Ger.) novelist, essayist. *The Peace, On the Marble Cliff.*
Franz Kafka, 1883-1924, (Austro-Hung./Czech) novelist, short-story writer. *The Trial, The Castle,* "The Metamorphosis."
George S. Kaufman, 1889-1961, (U.S.) playwright. *The Man Who Came to Dinner, You Can't Take It With You.*
Yasunari Kawabata, 1899-1972, (Japan) novelist. *The Sound of the Mountains.*
Nikos Kazantzakis, 1883-1957, (Gk.) novelist. *Zorba the Greek, A Greek Passion.*
Alfred Kazin, 1915-98 (U.S.) author, critic, teacher. *On Native Grounds.*
John Keats, 1795-1821, (Br.) poet. "Ode on a Grecian Urn," "Ode to a Nightingale," "La Belle Dame Sans Merci."
Jack Kerouac, 1922-1969, (U.S.), author, Beat poet. *On the Road, The Dharma Bums,* "Mexico City Blues."
Joyce Kilmer, 1886-1918, (U.S.) poet. "Trees."
Rudyard Kipling, 1865-1936, (Br.) author, poet. "The White Man's Burden," "Gunga Din," *The Jungle Book.*
Jean de la Fontaine, 1621-95, (Fr.) poet. *Fables choisies.*
Pär Lagerkvist, 1891-1974, (Swed.) poet, dramatist, novelist. *Barabbas, The Sybil.*
Selma Lagerlöf, 1858-1940, (Swed.) novelist. *Jerusalem, The Ring of the Lowenskolds.*
Alphonse de Lamartine, 1790-1869, (Fr.) poet, novelist, statesman. *Méditations poétiques.*
Charles Lamb, 1775-1834, (Br.) essayist. *Specimens of English Dramatic Poets, Essays of Elia.*
Giuseppe di Lampedusa, 1896-1957, (It.) novelist. *The Leopard.*
William Langland, c1332-1400, (Eng.) poet. *Piers Plowman.*
Ring Lardner, 1885-1933, (U.S.) short-story writer, humorist.
Louis L'Amour, 1908-88, (U.S.) western author, screenwriter. *Hondo, The Cherokee Trail.*
D(avid) H(erbert) Lawrence, 1885-1930, (Br.) novelist. *Sons and Lovers, Women in Love, Lady Chatterley's Lover.*
Halldor Laxness, 1902-98, (Icelandic) novelist. *Iceland's Bell.*
Mikhail Lermontov, 1814-41, (Russ.) novelist, poet. "Demon," *Hero of Our Time.*
Alain-René Lesage, 1668-1747, (Fr.) novelist. *Gil Blas de Santillane.*
Gotthold Lessing, 1729-81, (Ger.) dramatist, philosopher, critic. *Miss Sara Sampson, Minna von Barnhelm.*
C(live) S(taples) Lewis, 1898-1963, (Br.) critic, novelist, religious writer. *Allegory of Love; The Lion, the Witch and the Wardrobe; Out of the Silent Planet.*
Sinclair Lewis, 1885-1951, (U.S.) novelist. *Babbitt, Main Street, Arrowsmith, Dodsworth.*
Li Po, 701-762 (China) poet. "Song Before Drinking," "She Spins Silk."
Vachel Lindsay, 1879-1931, (U.S.) poet. *General William Booth Enters Into Heaven, The Congo.*
Hugh Lofting, 1886-1947, (Br.) writer. Dr. Doolittle series.
Jack London, 1876-1916, (U.S.) novelist, journalist. *Call of the Wild, The Sea-Wolf, White Fang.*
Henry Wadsworth Longfellow, 1807-82, (U.S.) poet. *Evangeline, The Song of Hiawatha.*
Lope de Vega, 1562-1635, (Sp.) playwright. *Noche de San Juan, Maestro de Danzar.*
H(oward) P(hillips) Lovecraft, 1890-1937, (U.S.), novelist, short-story writer. "At the Mountains of Madness."
Amy Lowell, 1874-1925, (U.S.) poet, critic. "Lilacs."
James Russell Lowell, 1819-91, (U.S.) poet, editor. *Poems, The Biglow Papers.*
Robert Lowell, 1917-77, (U.S.) poet. "Lord Weary's Castle."
Joaquim Maria Machado de Assis, 1839-1908, (Brazil) novelist, poet. *The Posthumous Memoirs of Bras Cubas.*
Archibald MacLeish, 1892-1982, (U.S.) poet. *Conquistador.*
Bernard Malamud, 1914-86, (U.S.) short-story writer, novelist. "The Magic Barrel," *The Assistant, The Fixer.*
Stéphane Mallarmé, 1842-98, (Fr.) poet. *Poésies.*
Sir Thomas Malory, ?-1471, (Br.) writer. *Morte d'Arthur.*
Andre Malraux, 1901-76, (Fr.) novelist. *Man's Fate.*

Osip Mandelstam, 1891-1938, (Russ.) poet. *Stone, Tristia.*
Thomas Mann, 1875-1955, (Ger.) novelist, essayist. *Buddenbrooks, The Magic Mountain,* "Death in Venice."
Katherine Mansfield, 1888-1923, (Br.) short-story writer. "Bliss."
Christopher Marlowe, 1564-93, (Br.) dramatist, poet. *Tamburlaine the Great,* Dr. *Faustus, The Jew of Malta.*
Andrew Marvell, 1621-78, (Br.) poet. "To His Coy Mistress."
John Masefield, 1878-1967, (Br.) poet. "Sea Fever," "Cargoes," *Salt Water Ballads.*
Edgar Lee Masters, 1869-1950, (U.S.) poet, biographer. *Spoon River Anthology.*
W(illiam) Somerset Maugham, 1874-1965, (Br.) author. *Of Human* Bondage, *The Moon and Sixpence.*
Guy de Maupassant, 1850-93, (Fr.) novelist, short-story writer. "A Life," "Bel-Ami," "The Necklace."
François Mauriac, 1885-1970, (Fr.) novelist, dramatist. *Viper's Tangle, The Kiss to the Leper.*
Vladimir Mayakovsky, 1893-1930, (Russ.) poet, dramatist. *The Cloud in Trousers.*
Mary McCarthy, 1912-89, (U.S.) critic, novelist, memoirist. *Memories of a Catholic Girlhood.*
Carson McCullers, 1917-67, (U.S.) novelist. *The Heart Is a Lonely Hunter, Member of the Wedding.*
Herman Melville, 1819-91, (U.S.) novelist, poet. *Moby-Dick, Typee, Billy Budd, Omoo.*
George Meredith, 1828-1909, (Br.) novelist, poet. *The Ordeal of Richard Feverel, The Egoist.*
Prosper Mérimée, 1803-70, (Fr.) author. *Carmen.*
James Merrill, 1926-95, (U.S.) poet. *Divine Comedies.*
James Michener, 1907-97, (U.S.) novelist. *Tales of the South Pacific.*
Edna St. Vincent Millay, 1892-1950, (U.S.) poet. *The Harp Weaver and Other Poems.*
Arthur Miller,1915-2005, (U.S.) playwright. *The Crucible, After the Fall, Death of a Salesman.*
Henry Miller, 1891-1980, (U.S.) erotic novelist. *Tropic of Cancer.*
A(lan) A(lexander) Milne, 1882-1956, (Br.) author. *Winnie-the-Pooh.*
Czeslaw Milosz, 1911-2004, (Pol.) essayist, poet. "Esse," "Encounter."
John Milton, 1608-74, (Br.) poet, writer. *Paradise Lost, Comus, Lycidas, Areopagitica.*
Mishima Yukio (Hiraoka Kimitake), 1925-70, (Jpn.) writer. *Confessions of a Mask.*
Gabriela Mistral, 1889-1957, (Chil.) poet. *Sonnets of Death.*
Margaret Mitchell, 1900-49, (U.S.) novelist. *Gone With the Wind.*
Jean Baptiste Molière, 1622-73, (Fr.) dramatist. *Tartuffe, Le Misanthrope, Le Bourgeois Gentilhomme.*
Ferenc Molnár, 1878-1952, (Hung.) dramatist, novelist. *Liliom, The Guardsman, The Swan.*
Michel de Montaigne, 1533-92, (Fr.) essayist. *Essais.*
Eugenio Montale, 1896-1981, (It.) poet.
Brian Moore, 1921-99, (Ir.-U.S.) novelist. *The Lonely Passion of Judith Hearne.*
Clement C. Moore, 1779-1863, (U.S.) poet, educator. "A Visit From Saint Nicholas."
Marianne Moore, 1887-1972, (U.S.) poet.
Alberto Moravia, 1907-90, (It.) novelist, short-story writer. *The Time of Indifference.*
Sir Thomas More, 1478-1535, (Br.) writer, statesman, saint. *Utopia.*
Wright Morris, 1910-98 (U.S.) novelist. *My Uncle Dudley.*
Murasaki Shikibu, c978-1026, (Jpn.) novelist. *The Tale of Genji.*
Iris Murdoch, 1919-99 (Br.), novelist, philosopher. *The Sea, The Sea.*
Alfred de Musset, 1810-57, (Fr.) poet, dramatist. *La Confession d'un Enfant du Siècle.*
Vladimir Nabokov, 1899-1977, (Russ.-U.S.) novelist. *Lolita, Pale Fire.*
R.K. Narayan, 1906-2001, (India), novelist, *The Guide.*
Ogden Nash, 1902-71, (U.S.) poet of light verse.
Pablo Neruda, 1904-73, (Chil.) poet. *Twenty Love Poems and One Song of Despair, Toward the Splendid City.*
Patrick O'Brian, 1914-2000, (Br.) historical novelist. *Master and Commander, Blue at the Mizzen.*
Sean O'Casey, 1884-1964, (Ir.) dramatist. *Juno and the Paycock, The Plough and the Stars.*
Frank O'Connor (Michael Donovan), 1903-66, (Ir.) short-story writer. "Guests of a Nation."
Flannery O'Connor, 1925-64, (U.S.) novelist, short-story writer. *Wise Blood,* "A Good Man Is Hard to Find."
Clifford Odets, 1906-63, (U.S.) playwright. *Waiting for Lefty, Awake and Sing, Golden Boy, The Country Girl.*
John O'Hara, 1905-70, (U.S.) novelist, short-story writer. *From the Terrace, Appointment in Samarra, Pal Joey.*
Omar Khayyam, c1028-1122, (Per.) poet. *Rubaiyat.*
Eugene O'Neill, 1888-1953, (U.S.) playwright. *Emperor Jones, Anna Christie, Long Day's Journey Into Night.*
George Orwell (Eric Arthur Blair), 1903-50, (Br.) novelist, essayist. *Animal Farm, Nineteen Eighty-Four.*
John Osborne, 1929-95, (Br.) dramatist, novelist. *Look Back in Anger, The Entertainer.*
Wilfred Owen, 1893-1918 (Br.) poet. "Dulce et Decorum Est."
Dorothy Parker, 1893-1967, (U.S.) poet, short-story writer. *Enough Rope, Laments for the Living.*
Boris Pasternak, 1890-1960, (Russ.) poet, novelist. *Doctor Zhivago.*
Alan Paton, 1903-88, (S. Africa) novelist. *Cry, the Beloved Country.*
Octavio Paz, 1914-98, (Mex.) poet, essayist. *The Labyrinth of Solitude, They Shall Not Pass!, The Sun Stone.*
Samuel Pepys, 1633-1703, (Br.) public official, diarist.
S(idney) J(oseph) Perelman, 1904-79, (U.S.) humorist. *The Road to Miltown, Under the Spreading Atrophy.*
Charles Perrault, 1628-1703, (Fr.) writer. *Tales From Mother Goose* (*Sleeping Beauty, Cinderella*).
Petrarch (Francesco Petrarca), 1304-74, (It.) poet. *Africa, Trionfi, Canzoniere.*
Luigi Pirandello, 1867-1936, (It.) novelist, dramatist. *Six Characters in Search of an Author.*
Sylvia Plath, 1932-63, (U.S.) author, poet. *The Bell Jar.*
Edgar Allan Poe, 1809-49, (U.S.) poet, short-story writer, critic. "Annabel Lee," "The Raven," "The Purloined Letter."
Alexander Pope, 1688-1744, (Br.) poet. *The Rape of the Lock, The Dunciad, An Essay on Man.*
Katherine Anne Porter, 1890-1980, (U.S.) novelist, short-story writer. *Ship of Fools.*
Chaim Potok, 1929-2002, (U.S.) novelist. *The Chosen.*
Ezra Pound, 1885-1972, (U.S.) poet. *Cantos.*
Anthony Powell, 1905-2000, (Br.) novelist. *A Dance to the Music of Time* series.
J(ohn) B. Priestley, 1894-1984, (Br.) novelist, dramatist. *The Good Companions.*
Marcel Proust, 1871-1922, (Fr.) novelist. *Remembrance of Things Past.*
Aleksandr Pushkin, 1799-1837, (Russ.) poet, novelist. *Boris Godunov, Eugene Onegin.*
Mario Puzo, 1920-99, (U.S.) novelist. *The Godfather.*
François Rabelais, 1495-1553, (Fr.) writer. *Gargantua.*
Jean Racine, 1639-99, (Fr.) dramatist. *Andromaque, Phèdre, Bérénice, Britannicus.*
Ayn Rand, 1905-82, (Russ.-U.S.) novelist, moral theorist. *The Fountainhead, Atlas Shrugged.*
Terence Rattigan, 1911-77, (Br.) playwright. *Separate Tables, The Browning Version.*
Erich Maria Remarque, 1898-1970, (Ger.-U.S.) novelist. *All Quiet on the Western Front.*
Samuel Richardson, 1689-1761, (Br.) novelist. *Pamela; or Virtue Rewarded.*
Rainer Maria Rilke, 1875-1926, (Ger.) poet. *Life and Songs, Duino Elegies, Poems From the Book of Hours.*
Arthur Rimbaud, 1854-91, (Fr.) poet. *A Season in Hell.*
Edwin Arlington Robinson, 1869-1935, (U.S.) poet. "Richard Cory," "Miniver Cheevy," *Merlin.*
Theodore Roethke, 1908-63, (U.S.) poet. *Open House, The Waking, The Far Field.*
Romain Rolland, 1866-1944, (Fr.) novelist, biographer. *Jean-Christophe.*
Pierre de Ronsard, 1524-85, (Fr.) poet. *Sonnets pour Hélène, La Franciade.*
Christina Rossetti, 1830-94, (Br.) poet. "When I Am Dead, My Dearest."
Dante Gabriel Rossetti, 1828-82, (Br.) poet, painter. "The Blessed Damozel."
Edmond Rostand, 1868-1918, (Fr.) poet, dramatist. *Cyrano de Bergerac.*
Damon Runyon, 1880-1946, (U.S.) short-story writer, journalist. *Guys and Dolls, Blue Plate Special.*
John Ruskin, 1819-1900, (Br.) critic, social theorist. *Modern Painters, The Seven Lamps of Architecture.*
François Sagan, (Françoise quoirez) 1935-2004, (Fr.) novelist *Bonjour Tristesse.*
Antoine de Saint-Exupéry, 1900-44, (Fr.) writer. *Wind, Sand and Stars, The Little Prince.*
Saki, or H(ector) H(ugh) Munro, 1870-1916, (Br.) writer. *The Chronicles of Clovis.*
George Sand (Amandine Lucie Aurore Dupin), 1804-76, (Fr.) novelist. *Indiana, Consuelo.*
Carl Sandburg, 1878-1967, (U.S.) poet. *The People, Yes; Chicago Poems, Smoke and Steel, Harvest Poems.*
William Saroyan, 1908-81, (U.S.) playwright, novelist. *The Time of Your Life, The Human Comedy.*
Nathalie Sarraute, 1900-99, (Fr.) Nouveau Roman novelist. *Tropismes.*
May Sarton, 1914-95, (Belg.-U.S.) poet, novelist. *Encounter in April, Anger.*
Dorothy L. Sayers, 1893-1957, (Br.) mystery writer; created Lord Peter Wimsey.
Richard Scarry, 1920-94, (U.S.) author of children's books. *Richard Scarry's Best Story Book Ever.*

Friedrich von Schiller, 1759-1805, (Ger.) dramatist, poet, historian. *Don Carlos, Maria Stuart, Wilhelm Tell.*
Sir Walter Scott, 1771-1832, (Sc.) novelist, poet. *Ivanhoe.*
Jaroslav Seifert, 1902-86, (Czech.) poet.
Dr. Seuss (Theodor Seuss Geisel), 1904-91, (U.S.) children's book author and illustrator. *The Cat in the Hat.*
William Shakespeare, 1564-1616, (Br.) dramatist, poet. *Romeo and Juliet, Hamlet, King Lear, Julius Caesar,* sonnets.
Karl Shapiro, 1913-2000, (U.S.) poet. "Elegy for a Dead Soldier."
George Bernard Shaw, 1856-1950, (Ir.-Br.) playwright, critic. *St. Joan, Pygmalion, Major Barbara, Man and Superman.*
Mary Wollstonecraft Shelley, 1797-1851, (Br.) novelist, feminist. *Frankenstein. The Last Man.*
Percy Bysshe Shelley, 1792-1822, (Br.) poet. *Prometheus Unbound, Adonais,* "Ode to the West Wind," "To a Skylark."
Richard B. Sheridan, 1751-1816, (Br.) dramatist. *The Rivals, School for Scandal.*
Robert Sherwood, 1896-1955, (U.S.) playwright, biographer. *The Petrified Forest, Abe Lincoln in Illinois.*
Mikhail Sholokhov, 1906-84, (Russ.) writer. *The Silent Don.*
Georges Simenon (Georges Sims), 1903-89, (Belg.-Fr.) mystery writer; created Inspector Maigret.
Upton Sinclair, 1878-1968, (U.S.) novelist. *The Jungle.*
Isaac Bashevis Singer, 1904-91, (Pol.-U.S.) novelist, short-story writer, in Yiddish. *The Magician of Lublin.*
C(harles) P(ercy) Snow, 1905-80, (Br.) novelist, scientist. *Strangers and Brothers, Corridors of Power.*
Susan Sontag, 1933-2004, (U.S.) critic, essayist, novelist. *Notes on Camp, The Volcano Lover, In America.*
Stephen Spender, 1909-95, (Br.) poet, critic, novelist. *Twenty Poems,* "Elegy for Margaret."
Edmund Spenser, 1552-99, (Br.) poet. *The Faerie Queen.*
Johanna Spyri, 1827-1901, (Swiss) children's author. *Heidi.*
Christina Stead, 1903-83, (Austral.) novelist, short-story writer. *The Man Who Loved Children.*
Richard Steele, 1672-1729, (Br.) essayist, playwright, began the *Tatler* and *Spectator. The Conscious Lovers.*
Gertrude Stein, 1874-1946, (U.S.) writer. *Three Lives.*
John Steinbeck, 1902-68, (U.S.) novelist. *The Grapes of Wrath, Of Mice and Men, The Winter of Our Discontent.*
Stendhal (Marie Henri Beyle), 1783-1842, (Fr.) novelist. *The Red and the Black, The Charterhouse of Parma.*
Laurence Sterne, 1713-68, (Br.) novelist. *Tristram Shandy.*
Wallace Stevens, 1879-1955, (U.S.) poet. *Harmonium, The Man With the Blue Guitar, Notes Toward a Supreme Fiction.*
Robert Louis Stevenson, 1850-94, (Br.) novelist, poet, essayist. *Treasure Island, A Child's Garden of Verses.*
Bram Stoker, 1845-1910, (Br.) writer. *Dracula.*
Rex Stout, 1886-1975, (U.S.) mystery writer; created Nero Wolfe.
Harriet Beecher Stowe, 1811-96, (U.S.) novelist. *Uncle Tom's Cabin.*
Lytton Strachey, 1880-1932, (Br.) biographer, critic. *Eminent Victorians. Queen Victoria, Elizabeth and Essex.*
August Strindberg, 1849-1912, (Swed.) dramatist, novelist. *The Father, Miss Julie, The Creditors.*
Jonathan Swift, 1667-1745, (Br.) satirist, poet. *Gulliver's Travels,* "A Modest Proposal."
Algernon C. Swinburne, 1837-1909, (Br.) poet, dramatist. *Atalanta in Calydon.*
John M. Synge, 1871-1909, (Ir.) poet, dramatist. *Riders to the Sea, The Playboy of the Western World.*
Rabindranath Tagore, 1861-1941, (In.) author, poet. *Sadhana, The Realization of Life, Gitanjali.*
Booth Tarkington, 1869-1946, (U.S.) novelist. *Seventeen.*
Peter Taylor, 1917-94, (U.S.) novelist. A *Summons to Memphis.*
Sara Teasdale, 1884-1933, (U.S.) poet. *Helen of Troy and Other Poems, Rivers to the Sea.*
Alfred, Lord Tennyson, 1809-92, (Br.) poet. *Idylls of the King, In Memoriam,* "The Charge of the Light Brigade."
William Makepeace Thackeray, 1811-63, (Br.) novelist. *Vanity Fair, Henry Esmond, Pendennis.*
Dylan Thomas, 1914-53, (Welsh) poet. *Under Milk Wood, A Child's Christmas in Wales.*
Hunter S. Thompson, 1937-2005, (U.S.) author, journalist. *Hell's Angels, Fear and Loathing in Las Vegas.*
Henry David Thoreau, 1817-62, (U.S.) writer, philosopher, naturalist. *Walden,* "Civil Disobedience."
James Thurber, 1894-1961, (U.S.) humorist; "The Secret Life of Walter Mitty," *My Life and Hard Times.*
J(ohn) R(onald) R(euel) Tolkien, 1892-1973, (Br.) writer. *The Hobbit, Lord of the Rings* trilogy.
Leo Tolstoy, 1828-1910, (Russ.) novelist, short-story writer. *War and Peace, Anna Karenina,* "The Death of Ivan Ilyich."
Lionel Trilling, 1905-75 (U.S.) critic, author, teacher. *The Liberal Imagination.*
Anthony Trollope, 1815-82, (Br.) novelist. *The Warden, Barchester Towers,* the Palliser novels.
Ivan Turgenev, 1818-83, (Russ.) novelist, short-story writer. *Fathers and Sons, First Love, A Month in the Country.*
Amos Tutuola, 1920-97, (Nigerian) novelist. *The Palm-Wine Drunkard, My Life in the Bush of Ghosts.*
Mark Twain (Samuel Clemens), 1835-1910, (U.S.) novelist, humorist. *The Adventures of Huckleberry Finn.*
Sigrid Undset, 1881-1949, (Nor.) novelist, *Kristin Lavransdatter.*
Paul Valéry, 1871-1945, (Fr.) poet, critic. *La Jeune Parque, The Graveyard by the Sea.*
Paul Verlaine, 1844-96, (Fr.) Symbolist poet. *Songs Without Words.*
Jules Verne, 1828-1905, (Fr.) novelist. *Twenty Thousand Leagues Under the Sea.*
François Villon, 1431-63?, (Fr.) poet. *The Lays, The Grand Testament.*
Voltaire (F.M. Arouet), 1694-1778, (Fr.) writer of "philosophical romances"; philosopher, historian; *Candide.*
Robert Penn Warren, 1905-89, (U.S.) novelist, poet, critic. *All the King's Men.*
Evelyn Waugh, 1903-66, (Br.) novelist. *The Loved One, Brideshead Revisited, A Handful of Dust.*
H(erbert) G(eorge) Wells, 1866-1946, (Br.) novelist. *The Time Machine, The Invisible Man, The War of the Worlds.*
Eudora Welty, 1909-2001, (U.S.) Southern short story writer, novelist. "Why I Live at the P.O," "The Ponder Heart."
Rebecca West, 1893-1983, (Br.) novelist, critic, journalist. *Black Lamb and Grey Falcon.*
Edith Wharton, 1862-1937, (U.S.) novelist. *The Age of Innocence, The House of Mirth, Ethan Frome.*
E(lwyn) B(rooks) White, 1899-1985, (U.S.) essayist, novelist. *Charlotte's Web, Stuart Little.*
Patrick White, 1912-90, (Austral.) novelist. *The Tree of Man.*
T(erence) H(anbury) White, 1906-64, (Br.) author. *The Once and Future King, A Book of Beasts.*
Walt Whitman, 1819-92, (U.S.) poet. *Leaves of Grass.*
John Greenleaf Whittier, 1807-92, (U.S.) poet, journalist. *Snow-Bound.*
Oscar Wilde, 1854-1900, (Ir.) novelist, playwright. *The Picture of Dorian Gray, The Importance of Being Earnest.*
Laura Ingalls Wilder, 1867-1957, (U.S.) novelist. Little House on the Prairie series of children's books.
Thornton Wilder, 1897-1975, (U.S.) playwright. *Our Town, The Skin of Our Teeth, The Matchmaker.*
Tennessee Williams, 1911-83, (U.S.) playwright. *A Streetcar Named Desire, Cat on a Hot Tin Roof, The Glass Menagerie.*
William Carlos Williams, 1883-1963, (U.S.) poet, physician. *Tempers, Al Que Quiere! Paterson,* "This Is Just to Say."
Edmund Wilson, 1895-1972, (U.S.) critic, novelist. *Axel's Castle, To the Finland Station.*
P(elham) G(renville) Wodehouse, 1881-1975, (Br.-U.S.) humorist. The "Jeeves" novels, *Anything Goes.*
Thomas Wolfe, 1900-38, (U.S.) novelist. *Look Homeward, Angel; You Can't Go Home Again.*
Virginia Woolf, 1882-1941, (Br.) novelist, essayist. *Mrs. Dalloway, To the Lighthouse, A Room of One's Own.*
William Wordsworth, 1770-1850, (Br.) poet. "Tintern Abbey," "Ode: Intimations of Immortality," *The Prelude.*
Richard Wright, 1908-60, novelist, short-story writer. *Native Son, Black Boy, Uncle Tom's Children.*
Elinor Wylie, 1885-1928, (U.S.) poet. *Nets to Catch the Wind.*
William Butler Yeats, 1865-1939, (Ir.) poet, playwright. "The Second Coming," *The Wild Swans at Coole.*
Émile Zola, 1840-1902, (Fr.) novelist. *Nana, Thérese Raquin.*

Poets Laureate

There is no record of the origin of the office of Poet Laureate of England. Henry III (1216-72) reportedly had a Versificator Regis, or King's Poet, paid 100 shillings a year. Other poets said to have filled the role include Geoffrey Chaucer (d 1400), Edmund Spenser (d 1599), Ben Jonson (d 1637), and Sir William d'Avenant (d 1668). The first official English poet laureate was John Dryden, appointed 1668, for life (as was customary). Then came Thomas Shadwell, in 1689; Nahum Tate, 1692; Nicholas Rowe, 1715; Rev. Laurence Eusden, 1718; Colley Cibber, 1730; William Whitehead, 1757; Rev. Thomas Warton, 1785; Henry James Pye, 1790; Robert Southey, 1813; William Wordsworth, 1843; Alfred, Lord Tennyson, 1850; Alfred Austin, 1896; Robert Bridges, 1913; John Masefield, 1930; C. Day Lewis, 1968; Sir John Betjeman, 1972; Ted Hughes, 1984; Andrew Motion, 1999.

In U.S., appointment is by Librarian of Congress and is not for life: Robert Penn Warren, appointed 1986; Richard Wilbur, 1987; Howard Nemerov, 1988; Mark Strand, 1990; Joseph Brodsky, 1991; Mona Van Duyn, 1992; Rita Dove, 1993; Robert Hass, 1995; Robert Pinsky, 1997; Stanley Kunitz, 2000; Billy Collins, 2001; Louise Gluck, 2003; Ted Kooser, 2004.

Composers of Classical and Avant Garde Music

Carl Philipp Emanuel Bach, 1714-88, (Ger.) Cantatas, passions, numerous keyboard and instrumental works.
Johann Christian Bach, 1735-82, (Ger.) Concertos, operas, sonatas. Known as the "English" Bach.
Johann Sebastian Bach, 1685-1750, (Ger.) *St. Matthew Passion, The Well-Tempered Clavier.*
Samuel Barber, 1910-81, (U.S.) *Adagio for Strings, Vanessa.*
Béla Bartók, 1881-1945, (Hung.) *Concerto for Orchestra, The Miraculous Mandarin.*
Amy Beach (Mrs. H. H. A. Beach), 1867-1944, (U.S.) *The Year's at the Spring, Fireflies, The Chambered Nautilus.*
Ludwig van Beethoven, 1770-1827, (Ger.) Concertos (*Emperor*), sonatas (*Moonlight, Pathetique*), 9 symphonies.
Vincenzo Bellini, 1801-35, (It.) *I Puritani, La Sonnambula, Norma.*
Alban Berg, 1885-1935, (Austrian) *Wozzeck, Lulu.*
Hector Berlioz, 1803-69, (Fr.) *Damnation of Faust, Symphonie Fantastique, Requiem.*
Leonard Bernstein, 1918-90, (U.S.) *Chichester Psalms, Jeremiah Symphony, Mass.*
Georges Bizet, 1838-75, (Fr.) *Carmen, Pearl Fishers.*
Ernest Bloch, 1880-1959, (Swiss-U.S.) *Macbeth* (opera), *Schelomo, Voice in the Wilderness.*
Luigi Boccherini, 1743-1805, (It.) Chamber music and guitar pieces.
Alexander Borodin, 1833-87, (Russ.) *Prince Igor, In the Steppes of Central Asia, Polovtzian Dances.*
Pierre Boulez, b 1925, (Fr.) *LeVisage* nuptial, *Edats/Multiple, Domaines.*
Johannes Brahms, 1833-97, (Ger.) Liebeslieder Waltzes, *Acad. Festival Overture,* chamber music, 4 symphonies.
Benjamin Britten, 1913-76, (Br.) *Peter Grimes, Turn of the Screw, A Ceremony of Carols, War Requiem.*
Anton Bruckner, 1824-96, (Austrian) 9 symphonies.
Dietrich Buxtehude, 1637-1707, (Dan.) Organ works, vocal music.
William Byrd, 1543-1623, (Br.) Masses, motets.
John Cage, 1912-92, (U.S.) *Winter Music, Fontana Mix.*
Emmanuel Chabrier, 1841-94, (Fr.) *Le Roi Malgré Lui, España.*
Gustave Charpentier, 1860-1956, (Fr.) *Louise.*
Frédéric Chopin, 1810-49, (Pol.) Mazurkas, waltzes, etudes, nocturnes, polonaises, sonatas.
Aaron Copland, 1900-90, (U.S.) *Appalachian Spring, Fanfare for the Common Man, Lincoln Portrait.*
Claude Debussy, 1862-1918, (Fr.) *Pelleas et Melisande, La Mer, Prelude to the Afternoon of a Faun.*
Gaetano Donizetti, 1797-1848, (It.) Elixir of Love, Lucia di Lammermoor, Daughter of the Regiment.
Paul Dukas, 1865-1935, (Fr.) *Sorcerer's Apprentice.*
Antonin Dvorak, 1841-1904, (Czech.) *Songs My Mother Taught Me, Symphony in E Minor (From the New World).*
Edward Elgar, 1857-1934, (Br.) *Enigma Variations, Pomp and Circumstance.*
Manuel de Falla, 1876-1946, (Sp.) *El Amor Brujo, La Vida Breve, The Three-Cornered Hat.*
Gabriel Faurè, 1845-1924, (Fr.) *Requiem,* Elègie for Cello and Piano.
Cesar Franck, 1822-90, (Belg.) Symphony in D minor, Violin Sonata.
George Gershwin, 1898-1937, (U.S.) *Rhapsody in Blue, An American in Paris, Porgy and Bess.*
Philip Glass, b 1937, (U.S.) *Einstein on the Beach, The Voyage.*
Mikhail Glinka, 1804-57, (Russ.) *A Life for the Tsar, Ruslan and Ludmilla.*
Christoph W. Gluck, 1714-87, (Ger.) *Alceste, Iphigènie en Tauride.*
Charles Gounod, 1818-93, (Fr.) *Faust, Romeo and Juliet.*
Edvard Grieg, 1843-1907, (Nor.) *Peer Gynt Suite,* Concerto in A minor for piano.
George Frideric Handel, 1685-1759, (Ger.-Br.) *Messiah, Water Music.*
Howard Hanson, 1896-1981, (U.S.) Symphonies No. 1 (Nordic) and No. 2 (Romantic).
Roy Harris, 1898-1979, (U.S.) Symphonies.
(Franz) Joseph Haydn, 1732-1809, (Austrian) Symphonies (*Clock, London, Toy*), chamber music, oratorios.
Paul Hindemith, 1895-1963, (U.S.) *Mathis der Maler.*
Gustav Holst, 1874-1934, (Br.) *The Planets.*
Arthur Honegger, 1892-1955, (Fr.) *Judith, Le Roi David, Pacific 231.*
Alan Hovhaness, 1911-2000, (U.S.) Symphonies, *Magnificat.*
Engelbert Humperdinck, 1854-1921, (Ger.) *Hansel and Gretel.*
Charles Ives, 1874-1954, (U.S.) *Concord Sonata,* symphonies.
Aram Khachaturian, 1903-78, (Russ.) Ballets, piano pieces, *Sabre Dance.*
Zoltán Kodaly, 1882-1967, (Hung.) *Háry János, Psalmus Hungaricus.*
Fritz Kreisler, 1875-1962, (Austrian) *Caprice Viennois, Tambourin Chinois.*
Edouard Lalo, 1823-92, (Fr.) *Symphonie Espagnole.*
Ruggero Leoncavallo, 1857-1919, (It.) *Pagliacci.*
Franz Liszt, 1811-86, (Hung.) 20 Hungarian rhapsodies, symphonic poems.
Edward MacDowell, 1861-1908, (U.S.) *To a Wild Rose.*
Gustav Mahler, 1860-1911, (Austrian) *Das Lied von der Erde*; 9 complete symphonies.
Pietro Mascagni, 1863-1945, (It.) *Cavalleria Rusticana.*
Jules Massenet, 1842-1912, (Fr.) *Manon, Le Cid, Thaïs.*
Felix Mendelssohn, 1809-47, (Ger.) *A Midsummer Night's Dream, Songs Without Words,* violin concerto.
Gian-Carlo Menotti, b 1911, (It.-U.S.) *The Medium, The Consul, Amahl and the Night Visitors.*
Claudio Monteverdi, 1567-1643, (It.) Opera, masses, madrigals.
Modest Moussorgsky, 1839-81, (Russ.) *Boris Godunov, Pictures at an Exhibition.*
Wolfgang Amadeus Mozart, 1756-91, (Austrian) Chamber music, concertos, operas (*Magic Flute, Marriage of Figaro*), 41 symphonies.
Jacques Offenbach, 1819-80, (Fr.) *Tales of Hoffmann.*
Carl Orff, 1895-1982, (Ger.) *Carmina Burana.*
Johann Pachelbel, 1653-1706, (Ger.) Canon and Fugue in D major.
Ignacy Paderewski, 1860-1941, (Pol.) Minuet in G.
Niccolò Paganini, 1782-1840, (It.) Caprices for violin solo.
Giovanni Palestrina, c1525-94, (It.) Masses, madrigals.
Krzystof Penderecki, b 1933, (Pol.) *Psalmus, Polymorphia, De natura sonoris.*
Francis Poulenc, 1899-1963, (Fr.) *Dialogues des Carmèlites.*
Mel Powell, 1923-98, (U.S.) *Duplicates: A Concerto for Two Pianos and Orchestra, Cantilena Concertante.*
Sergei Prokofiev, 1891-1953, (Russ.) Classical Symphony, *Love for Three Oranges, Peter and the Wolf.*
Giacomo Puccini, 1858-1924, (It.) *La Boheme, Manon Lescaut, Tosca, Madama Butterfly.*
Henry Purcell, 1659-95, (Eng.) *Dido and Aeneas.*
Sergei Rachmaninoff, 1873-1943, (Russ.) Concertos, preludes (Prelude in C sharp minor), symphonies.
Maurice Ravel, 1875-1937, (Fr.) *Bolèro, Daphnis et Chloè,* Piano Concerto in D for Left Hand Alone.
Nikolai Rimsky-Korsakov, 1844-1908, (Russ.) *Golden Cockerel, Scheherazade, Flight of the Bumblebee.*
Gioacchino Rossini, 1792-1868, (It.) *Barber of Seville, Otello, William Tell.*
Camille Saint-Saëns, 1835-1921, (Fr.) *Carnival of Animals (The Swan), Samson and Delilah, Danse Macabre.*
Alessandro Scarlatti, 1660-1725, (It.) Cantatas, oratorios, operas.
Domenico Scarlatti, 1685-1757, (It.) Harpsichord works.
Alfred Schnittke, 1934-98 (Sov.-Ger.) *Life With an Idiot.*
Arnold Schoenberg, 1874-1951, (Austrian) *Pelleas and Melisande, Pierrot Lunaire, Verklärte Nacht.*
Franz Schubert, 1797-1828, (Austrian) Chamber music (*Trout Quintet*), lieder, symphonies (Unfinished).
Robert Schumann, 1810-56, (Ger.) *Die Frauenliebe und Leben, Träumerei.*
Dimitri Shostakovich, 1906-75, (Russ.) Symphonies, *Lady Macbeth of the District Mzensk.*
Jean Sibelius, 1865-1957, (Finn.) Finlandia.
Bedrich Smetana, 1824-84, (Czech.) *The Bartered Bride.*
Karlheinz Stockhausen, b 1928, (Ger.) *Kontra-Punkte, Kontakte for Electronic Instruments.*
Richard Strauss, 1864-1949, (Ger.) *Salome, Elektra, Der Rosenkavalier, Thus Spake Zarathustra.*
Igor Stravinsky, 1882-1971, (Russ.) *Noah and the Flood, The Rake's Progress, The Rite of Spring.*
Toru Takemitsu, 1930-96, (Jpn.) *Requiem for Strings, Dorian Horizon.*
Peter I. Tchaikovsky, 1840-93, (Russ.) *Nutcracker, Swan Lake, The Sleeping Beauty.*
Georg Philipp Telemann, 1681-1767, (Ger.) church music, orchestral suites, chamber music.
Virgil Thomson, 1896-1989, (U.S.) Opera, film music, *Four Saints in Three Acts.*
Dmitri Tiomkin, 1894-1979, (Russ.-U.S.) film scores, including *High Noon.*
Sir Michael Tippett, 1905-98, (Br.) *A Child of Our Time, The Midsummer Marriage, The Knot Garden.*
Ralph Vaughan Williams, 1872-1958, (Eng.) *Fantasiz on a Theme by Thomas Tallis,* symphonies, vocal music.
Giuseppe Verdi, 1813-1901, (It.) *Aida, Rigoletto, Don Carlo, Il Trovatore, La Traviata, Falstaff, Macbeth.*
Heitor Villa-Lobos, 1887-1959, (Brazil) *Bachianas Brasileiras.*
Antonio Vivaldi, 1678-1741, (It.) Concerto grossos (*The Four Seasons*).
Richard Wagner, 1813-83, (Ger.) *Rienzi, Tannhäuser, Lohengrin, Tristan und Isolde.*
Carl Maria von Weber, 1786-1826, (Ger.) *Der Freischutz.*

Composers of Operettas, Musicals, and Popular Music

Richard Adler, b 1921, (U.S.) *Pajama Game; Damn Yankees.*
Milton Ager, 1893-1979, (U.S.) I Wonder What's Become of Sally; Hard-Hearted Hannah; Ain't She Sweet?
Arthur Altman, 1910-94, (U.S.) *All or Nothing at All.*
Leroy Anderscn, 1908-75, (U.S.) Sleigh Ride, Blue Tango, Syncopated Clock.
Paul Anka, b 1941, (Can.) My Way; *Tonight Show* theme.
Harold Arlen, 1905-86, (U.S.) Stormy Weather; Over the Rainbow; Blues in the Night; That Old Black Magic.
Burt Bacharach, b 1928, (U.S.) Raindrops Keep Fallin' on My Head; Walk on By; What the World Needs Now Is Love.
Ernest Ball, 1878-1927, (U.S.) Mother Machree; When Irish Eyes Are Smiling.
Irving Berlin, 1888-1989, (U.S.) *Annie Get Your Gun; Call Me Madam;* God Bless America; White Christmas.
Leonard Bernstein, 1918-90, (U.S.) *On the Town; Wonderful Town; Candide; West Side Story.*
Eubie Blake, 1883-1983, (U.S.) *Shuffle Along;* I'm Just Wild About Harry.
Jerry Bock, b 1928, (U.S.) *Mr. Wonderful; Fiorello; Fiddler on the Roof; The Rothschilds.*
Carrie Jacobs Bond, 1862-1946, (U.S.) I Love You Truly.
Nacio Herb Brown, 1896-1964, (U.S.) Singing in the Rain; You Were Meant for Me; All I Do Is Dream of You.
Hoagy Carmichael, 1899-1981, (U.S.) Stardust; Georgia on My Mind; Old Buttermilk Sky.
George M. Cohan, 1878-1942, (U.S.) Give My Regards to Broadway; You're a Grand Old Flag; Over There.
Cy Coleman, b 1929, (U.S.) *Sweet Charity;* Witchcraft.
John Frederick Coots, 1895-1985, (U.S.) Santa Claus Is Coming to Town; You Go to My Head; For All We Know.
Noel Coward, 1899-1973, (Br.) *Bitter Sweet;* Mad Dogs and Englishmen; Mad About the Boy.
Neil Diamond, b 1941, (U.S.) I'm a Believer; Sweet Caroline.
Walter Donaldson, 1893-1947, (U.S.) My Buddy; Carolina in the Morning; Makin' Whoopee.
Vernon Duke, 1903-69, (U.S.) April in Paris.
Bob Dylan, b 1941, (U.S.) Blowin' in the Wind.
Gus Edwards, 1879-1945, (U.S.) School Days; By the Light of the Silvery Moon; In My Merry Oldsmobile.
Sherman Edwards, 1919-81, (U.S.) See You in September; Wonderful! Wonderful!
Duke Ellington, 1899-1974, (U.S.) Sophisticated Lady; Satin Doll; It Don't Mean a Thing; Solitude.
Sammy Fain, 1902-89, (U.S.) I'll Be Seeing You; Love Is a Many-Splendored Thing.
Fred Fisher, 1875-1942, (U.S.) Peg O' My Heart; Chicago.
Stephen Collins Foster, 1826-64, (U.S.) My Old Kentucky Home; Old Folks at Home, Beautiful Dreamer.
Rudolf Friml, 1879-1972, (Czech-U.S.) *The Firefly; Rose Marie; Vagabond King; Bird of Paradise.*
John Gay, 1685-1732, (Br.) *The Beggar's Opera.*
George Gershwin, 1898-1937, (U.S.) Someone to Watch Over Me; I've Got a Crush on You; Embraceable You.
Morton Gould, 1913-96, (U.S.) Fall River Suite, Holocaust Suite, Spirituals for Orchestra, Stringmusic.
Ferde Grofe, 1892-1972, (U.S.) Grand Canyon Suite.
Marvin Hamlisch, b 1944, (U.S.) The Way We Were; Nobody Does It Better; *A Chorus Line.*
Ray Henderson, 1896-1970, (U.S.) *George White's Scandals;* That Old Gang of Mine; Five Foot Two, Eyes of Blue.
Victor Herbert, 1859-1924, (Ir.-U.S.) *Mlle. Modiste; Babes in Toyland; The Red Mill; Naughty Marietta; Sweethearts.*
Jerry Herman, b 1933, (U.S.) *Hello Dolly; Mame.*
Brian Holland, b 1941, **Lamont Dozier,** b 1941, **Eddie Holland,** b 1939, (all U.S.) Heat Wave; Stop! In the Name of Love; Baby, I Need Your Loving.
Antonio Carlos Jobim, 1927-94, (Brazil) *The Girl From Ipanema; Desafinado; One Note Samba.*
Billy (William Martin) Joel, b 1949, (U.S.) *Just the Way You Are; Honesty;* Piano Man.
Scott Joplin, 1868-1917, (U.S.) Maple Leaf Rag; *Treemonisha.*
John Kander, b 1927, (U.S.) *Cabaret; Chicago; Funny Lady.*
Jerome Kern, 1885-1945, (U.S.) *Sally; Sunny; Show Boat.*
Carole King, b 1942, (U.S.) Will You Love Me Tomorrow?; Natural Woman; One Fine Day; Up on the Roof.
Burton Lane, 1912-1997, (U.S.) *Finian's Rainbow.*
Franz Lehar, 1870-1948, (Hung.) *Merry Widow.*
Jerry Leiber, & **Mike Stoller,** both b 1933, (both U.S.) Hound Dog; Searchin'; Yakety Yak; Love Me Tender.
Mitch Leigh, b 1928, (U.S.) *Man of La Mancha.*
John Lennon, 1940-80, & **Paul McCartney,** b 1942, (both Br.) I Want to Hold Your Hand; She Loves You.
Jay Livingston, 1915-2001 (U.S.) Mona Lisa; Que Sera, Sera.
Andrew Lloyd Webber, b 1948, (Br.) *Jesus Christ Superstar; Evita; Cats; The Phantom of the Opera.*
Frank Loesser, 1910-69, (U.S.) *Guys and Dolls; Where's Charley?; The Most Happy Fella; How to Succeed....*
Frederick Loewe, 1901-88, (Austrian-U.S.) *Brigadoon; Paint Your Wagon; My Fair Lady; Camelot.*
Henry Mancini, 1924-94, (U.S.) Moon River; Days of Wine and Roses; Pink Panther Theme.
Barry Mann, b 1939, & **Cynthia Weil,** b 1937, (both U.S.) You've Lost That Loving Feeling.
Jimmy McHugh, 1894-1969, (U.S.) Don't Blame Me; I'm in the Mood for Love; I Feel a Song Coming On.
Alan Menken, b 1949, (U.S.) *Little Shop of Horrors, Beauty and the Beast.*
Joseph Meyer, 1894-1987, (U.S.) If You Knew Susie; California, Here I Come; Crazy Rhythm.
Chauncey Olcott, 1858-1932, (U.S.) Mother Machree.
Jerome "Doc" Pomus, 1925-91, (U.S.) Save the Last Dance for Me; A Teenager in Love.
Cole Porter, 1893-1964, (U.S.) *Anything Goes; Kiss Me Kate; Can Can; Silk Stockings.*
Smokey Robinson, b 1940, (U.S.) Shop Around; My Guy; My Girl; Get Ready.
Richard Rodgers, 1902-79, (U.S.) *Oklahoma!; Carousel; South Pacific; The King and I; The Sound of Music.*
Sigmund Romberg, 1887-1951, (Hung.) *Maytime; The Student Prince; Desert Song; Blossom Time.*
Harold Rome, 1908-93, (U.S.) *Pins and Needles; Call Me Mister; Wish You Were Here; Fanny; Destry Rides Again.*
Vincent Rose, b 1880-1944, (U.S.) Avalon; Whispering; Blueberry Hill.
Harry Ruby, 1895-1974, (U.S.) Three Little Words; Who's Sorry Now?
Arthur Schwartz, 1900-84, (U.S.) *The Band Wagon;* Dancing in the Dark; By Myself; That's Entertainment.
Neil Sedaka, b 1939, (U.S.) Breaking Up Is Hard to Do.
Paul Simon, b 1942, (U.S.) Sounds of Silence; I Am a Rock; Mrs. Robinson; Bridge Over Troubled Waters.
Stephen Sondheim, b 1930, (U.S.) *A Little Night Music; Company; Sweeney Todd; Sunday in the Park With George.*
John Philip Sousa, 1854-1932, (U.S.) *El Capitan;* Stars and Stripes Forever.
Oskar Straus, 1870-1954, (Austrian) *Chocolate Soldier.*
Johann Strauss, 1825-99, (Austrian) *Gypsy Baron; Die Fledermaus;* waltzes: Blue Danube; Artist's Life.
Charles Strouse, b 1928, (U.S.) *Bye Bye, Birdie; Annie.*
Jule Styne, 1905-94, (Br.-U.S.) *Gentlemen Prefer Blondes; Bells Are Ringing; Gypsy; Funny Girl.*
Arthur S. Sullivan, 1842-1900, (Br.) *H.M.S. Pinafore; Pirates of Penzance; The Mikado.*
Deems Taylor, 1885-1966, (U.S.) *Peter Ibbetson.*
Harry Tobias, 1905-94, (U.S.) *I'll Keep the Lovelight Burning.*
Egbert van Alstyne, 1882-1951, (U.S.) In the Shade of the Old Apple Tree; Memories; Pretty Baby.
Jimmy Van Heusen, 1913-90, (U.S.) Moonlight Becomes You; Swinging on a Star; All the Way; Love and Marriage.
Albert von Tilzer, 1878-1956, (U.S.) I'll Be With You in Apple Blossom Time; Take Me Out to the Ball Game.
Harry von Tilzer, 1872-1946, (U.S.) Only a Bird in a Gilded Cage; On a Sunday Afternoon.
Fats Waller, 1904-43, (U.S.) Honeysuckle Rose; Ain't Misbehavin'.
Harry Warren, 1893-1981, (U.S.) You're My Everything; We're in the Money; I Only Have Eyes for You.
Jimmy Webb, b 1946, (U.S.) Up, Up and Away; By the Time I Get to Phoenix; Didn't We?; Wichita Lineman.
Kurt Weill, 1900-50, (Ger.-U.S.) *Threepenny Opera; Lady in the Dark; Knickerbocker Holiday; One Touch of Venus.*
Percy Wenrich, 1887-1952, (U.S.) When You Wore a Tulip; Moonlight Bay; Put On Your Old Gray Bonnet.
Richard A. Whiting, 1891-1938, (U.S.) Till We Meet Again; Sleepytime Gal; Beyond the Blue Horizon; My Ideal.
John Williams, b 1932, (U.S.) *Jaws; E.T.; Star Wars* series; *Raiders of the Lost Ark* series.
Meredith Willson, 1902-84, (U.S.) *The Music Man.*
Stevie Wonder, b 1950, (U.S.) You Are the Sunshine of My Life; Signed, Sealed, Delivered, I'm Yours.
Vincent Youmans, 1898-1946, (U.S.) *Two Little Girls in Blue; Wildflower; No, No, Nanette; Hit the Deck; Rainbow; Smiles.*

Lyricists

Howard Ashman, 1950-91, (U.S.) Little Shop of Horrors; The Little Mermaid.
Johnny Burke, 1908-84, (U.S.) Misty; Imagination.
Irving Caesar, 1895-1996, (U.S.) Swanee; Tea for Two; Just a Gigolo.
Sammy Cahn, 1913-93, (U.S.) High Hopes; Love and Marriage; The Second Time Around; It's Magic.
Leonard Cohen, b 1934, (Can.) Suzanne; Stranger Song.
Betty Comden, b 1919, (U.S.) and **Adolph Green,** 1915-2002, (U.S.) The Party's Over; Just in Time; New York, New York.
Hal David, b 1921, (U.S.) *What the World Needs Now Is Love.*
Buddy De Sylva, 1895-1950, (U.S.) When Day Is Done; Look for the Silver Lining; April Showers.
Howard Dietz, 1896-1983, (U.S.) Dancing in the Dark; You and the Night and the Music; That's Entertainment.
Al Dubin, 1891-1945, (U.S.) Tiptoe Through the Tulips; Anniversary Waltz; Lullaby of Broadway.
Fred Ebb, b 1936-2004, (U.S.) Cabaret; Zorba; Woman of the Year, Chicago.
Ray Evans, b 1915 (U.S.) Mona Lisa; Que Sera, Sera.
Dorothy Fields, 1905-74, (U.S.) On the Sunny Side of the Street; Don't Blame Me; The Way You Look Tonight.
Ira Gershwin, 1896-1983, (U.S.) The Man I Love; Fascinating Rhythm; S'Wonderful; Embraceable You.
William S. Gilbert, 1836-1911, (Br.) The Mikado; H.M.S. Pinafore; Pirates of Penzance.
Gerry Goffin, b 1939, (U.S.) Will You Love Me Tomorrow; Take Good Care of My Baby; Up on the Roof.
Mack Gordon, 1905-59, (Pol.-U.S.) You'll Never Know; The More I See You; Chattanooga Choo-Choo.
Oscar Hammerstein II, 1895-1960, (U.S.) Ol' Man River; Oklahoma!; Carousel.
E. Y. (Yip) Harburg, 1898-1981, (U.S.) Brother, Can You Spare a Dime; April in Paris; Over the Rainbow.
Sheldon Harnick, b 1924, (U.S.) Fiddler on the Roof, She Loves Me.
Lorenz Hart, 1895-1943, (U.S.) .) Isn't It Romantic; Blue Moon; Lover; Manhattan; My Funny Valentine.
DuBose Heyward, 1885-1940, (U.S.) Summertime.
Gus Kahn, 1886-1941, (U.S.) Memories; Ain't We Got Fun.
Alan J. Lerner, 1918-86, (U.S.) Brigadoon; My Fair Lady; Camelot; Gigi; On a Clear Day You Can See Forever.
Johnny Mercer, 1909-76, (U.S.) Blues in the Night; Come Rain or Come Shine; Laura; That Old Black Magic.
Bob Merrill, 1921-98, (U.S.) People; (How Much Is That) Doggie in the Window.
Jack Norworth, 1879-1959, (U.S.) Take Me Out to the Ball Game; Shine On Harvest Moon.
Mitchell Parish, 1901-93, (U.S.) Stardust; Stairway to the Stars.
Andy Razaf, 1895-1973, (U.S.) Honeysuckle Rose; Ain't Misbehavin'; S'posin'.
Leo Robin, 1900-84, (U.S.) Thanks for the Memory; Hooray for Love; Diamonds Are a Girl's Best Friend.
Paul Francis Webster, 1907-84, (U.S.) Secret Love; The Shadow of Your Smile; Love Is a Many-Splendored Thing.
Jack Yellen, 1892-1991, (U.S.) Down by the O-Hi-O; Ain't She Sweet; Happy Days Are Here Again.

Blues and Jazz Artists of the Past

Julian "Cannonball" Adderley, 1928-75, alto sax
Nat Adderley, 1931-2000, cornet
Henry "Red" Allen, 1908-67, trumpet
Louis "Satchmo" Armstrong, 1901-71, trumpet, singer, bandleader
Albert Ayler, 1936-70, tenor sax, alto sax
Mildred Bailey, 1907-51, singer
Chet Baker, 1929-88, trumpet, singer
Count Basie, 1904-84, bandleader, piano, composer
Sidney Bechet, 1897-1959, soprano sax, clarinet
Bix Beiderbecke, 1903-31, cornet, composer, piano
Bunny Berigan, 1908-42, trumpet
Barney Bigard, 1906-80, clarinet
Eubie Blake, 1883-1983, composer, piano
Art Blakey, 1919-90, drums, bandleader
Jimmy Blanton, 1921-42, bass
Charles "Buddy" Bolden, 1877-1931, cornet, pioneer bandleader
Lester Bowie, 1941-99, trumpet, composer, bandleader
Big Bill Broonzy, 1893-1958, blues singer, guitar
Clifford Brown, 1930-56, trumpet
Ray Brown, 1926-2002, bass
Don Byas, 1912-72, tenor sax
Charlie Byrd, 1925-99, guitarist; popularized bossa nova
Cab Calloway, 1907-94, bandleader, singer
Harry Carney, 1910-74, baritone sax, clarinet
Betty Carter, 1930-98, jazz singer
Sidney "Big Sid" Catlett, 1910-51, drums
Doc Cheatham, 1905-97, trumpet
Don Cherry, 1936-95, trumpet
Charlie Christian, 1916-42, guitar
Kenny "Klook" Clarke, 1914-85, drums
Buck Clayton, 1911-91, trumpet
Al Cohn, 1925-88, tenor sax
Cozy Cole, 1909-81, drums
John Coltrane, 1926-67, tenor sax, soprano sax, composer
Eddie Condon, 1905-73, guitar, bandleader
Tadd Dameron, 1917-65, piano, composer
Eddie "Lockjaw" Davis, 1921-86, tenor sax
Miles Davis, 1926-91, trumpet, composer
Wild Bill Davison, 1906-89, cornet
Paul Desmond, 1924-77, alto sax
Vic Dickenson, 1906-84, trombone
Willie Dixon, 1915-92, blues composer, bass
Johnny Dodds, 1892-1940, clarinet
Warren "Baby" Dodds, 1898-1959, drums
Eric Dolphy, 1928-64, alto sax, bass clarinet, flute
Jimmy Dorsey, 1904-57, alto sax, bandleader
Tommy Dorsey, 1905-56, trombone, bandleader
Billy Eckstine, 1914-93, singer, bandleader
Harry "Sweets" Edison, 1915-99, trumpet
Roy Eldridge, 1911-89, trumpet, singer
Duke Ellington, 1899-1974, piano, bandleader, composer
Bill Evans, 1929-80, piano
Gil Evans, 1912-88, composer, arranger, piano
Art Farmer, 1928-99, trumpet, flugelhorn
Ella Fitzgerald, 1917-96, singer
Tommy Flanagan, 1930-2001, piano
Erroll Garner, 1921-77, piano, composer
Stan Getz, 1927-91, tenor sax
Dizzy Gillespie, 1917-93, trumpet, composer, singer
Benny Goodman, 1909-86, clarinet, bandleader
Dexter Gordon, 1923-90, tenor sax
Stéphane Grappelli, 1908-97, violin
Bobby Hackett, 1915-76, trumpet, cornet
Lionel Hampton, 1908-2002, vibraphone, bandleader
W. C. Handy, 1873-1958, composer
Jimmy Harrison, 1900-31, trombone
Coleman Hawkins, 1904-69, tenor sax
Percy Heath, 1923-2005, bass
Fletcher Henderson, 1898-1952, bandleader, arranger
Woody Herman, 1913-87, clarinet, alto sax, bandleader
Jay C. Higginbotham, 1906-73, trombone
Earl "Fatha" Hines, 1903-83, piano
Milt Hinton, 1910-2000, bass
Al Hirt, 1922-99, trumpet
Johnny Hodges, 1906-70, alto sax
Billie Holiday, 1915-59, singer
John Lee Hooker, 1917-2001, blues guitar, singer
Sam "Lightnin" Hopkins, 1912-82, blues singer, guitar
Howlin' Wolf, 1910-1976, blues singer, harmonica, guitar
Alberta Hunter, 1895-1984, singer
Mahalia Jackson, 1911-72, gospel singer
Milt Jackson, 1923-99, vibraphone
Elmore James, 1918-63, blues singer, guitar
Blind Lemon Jefferson, 1897-1930, blues singer, guitar
Bunk Johnson, 1879-1949, trumpet
J.J. Johnson, 1924-2001, trombone
James P. Johnson, 1891-1955, piano, composer
Robert Johnson, 1912-38, blues singer, guitar
Elvin Jones, 1927-2004, drums
Jo Jones, 1911-85, drums
Philly Joe Jones, 1923-85, drums
Thad Jones, 1923-86, cornet, bandleader, composer
Scott Joplin, 1868-1917, ragtime composer
Louis Jordan, 1908-75, singer, alto sax
Stan Kenton, 1911-79, bandleader, composer, piano
Barney Kessel, 1923-2004, guitar
Albert King, 1923-92, blues guitar
John Kirby, 1908-52, bandleader, bass
Rahsaan Roland Kirk, 1936-77, saxophones, composer
Gene Krupa, 1909-73, drums, bandleader
Scott LaFaro, 1936-61, bass
Huddie Ledbetter (Lead Belly), 1888-1949, folk and blues singer, guitar
John Lewis, 1920-2001, piano, Modern Jazz Quartet founder
Mel Lewis, 1929-90, drums, bandleader
Jimmie Lunceford, 1902-47, bandleader

Machito (Frank Grillo), 1912-84, Latin percussion, singer, bandleader
Shelly Manne, 1920-84, drums, bandleader
Jimmy McPartland, 1907-91, trumpet
Carmen McRae, 1920-94, singer
Glenn Miller, 1904-44, trombone, bandleader
Charles Mingus, 1922-79, bass, composer, bandleader
Thelonious Monk, 1917-82, piano, composer
Wes Montgomery, 1925-68, guitar
"Jelly Roll" Morton, 1885-1941, composer, piano
Bennie Moten, 1894-1935, piano, bandleader
Gerry Mulligan, 1927-96, baritone sax, composer
"Fats" Navarro, 1923-50, trumpet
Red Nichols, 1905-65, cornet, bandleader
Red Norvo, 1908-99, vibraphone, xylophone, bandleader
Arturo "Chico" O'Farrill, 1921-2001, Latin composer, arranger
King Oliver, 1885-1938, cornet, band leader
Sy Oliver, 1910-88, arranger, composer
Kid Ory, 1886-1973, trombone, bandleader
Oran "Hot Lips" Page, 1908-54, trumpet, singer
Charlie "Bird" Parker, 1920-55, alto sax, composer
Joe Pass, 1929-94, guitar
Art Pepper, 1925-82, alto sax
Oscar Pettiford, 1922-60, bass
Bud Powell, 1924-66, piano
Chano Pozo, 1915-48, Cuban percussion, singer
Louis Prima, 1911-78, singer, bandleader
Tito Puente, 1923-2000, Latin percussion, bandleader
Gertrude "Ma" Rainey, 1886-1939, blues singer
Don Redman, 1900-64, composer, arranger
Django Reinhardt, 1910-53, guitar
Buddy Rich, 1917-87, drums
Red Rodney, 1928-94, trumpet
Jimmy Rowles, 1918-96, piano
Jimmy Rushing, 1903-72, blues and jazz singer
Pee Wee Russell, 1906-69, clarinet
Artie Shaw, 1910-2004, swing-era bandleader, clarinet
Zoot Sims, 1925-85, tenor sax
Zutty Singleton, 1898-1975, drums
Bessie Smith, 1894-1937, blues singer
Clarence "Pinetop" Smith, 1904-29, piano, singer; boogie woogie pioneer
Willie "The Lion" Smith, 1897-1973, piano, composer
Muggsy Spanier, 1906-67, cornet
Sonny Stitt, 1924-82, tenor sax, alto sax
Billy Strayhorn, 1915-67, composer, piano; Duke Ellington collaborator
Sun Ra, 1915?-93, bandleader, piano, composer
Art Tatum, 1910-56, piano
Art Taylor, 1929-95, drums
Jack Teagarden, 1905-64, trombone, singer
Mel Torme, 1925-99, singer ("the Velvet Fog")
Dave Tough, 1908-48, drums
Lennie Tristano, 1919-78, piano, composer
Joe Turner, 1911-85, blues singer
Sarah Vaughan, 1924-90, singer
Joe Venuti, 1904-78, violin
T-Bone Walker, 1910-75, blues guitar
Thomas "Fats" Waller, 1904-43, piano, singer, composer
Dinah Washington, 1924-63, singer
Grover Washington Jr., 1943-99, pop-jazz sax, composer
Ethel Waters, 1896-1977, jazz and blues singer
Muddy Waters, 1915-83, blues singer, songwriter
Julius Watkins, 1921-77, French horn
Chick Webb, 1902-39, bandleader, drums
Ben Webster, 1909-73, tenor sax
Junior Wells, 1934-98, blues singer, harmonica
Paul Whiteman, 1890-1967, bandleader
Charles "Cootie" Williams, 1910-85, trumpet, bandleader
Joe Williams, 1918-99, singer
Mary Lou Williams, 1910-81, piano, composer
Tony Williams, 1945-97, drums
John Lee "Sonny Boy" Williamson, 1914-48, blues singer, harmonica
Sonny Boy Williamson ("Rice" Miller), 1900?-65, blues singer, harmonica
Teddy Wilson, 1912-86, piano
Kai Winding, 1922-83, trombone
Jimmy Yancey, 1894-1951, piano
Lester "Pres" Young, 1909-59, tenor sax

Noted Country Music Artists of the Past and Present

Roy Acuff, 1903-92, fiddler, singer, songwriter; "Wabash Cannon Ball"
Alabama (Randy Owen, b 1949 ; Jeff Cook, b 1949 ; Teddy Gentry, b 1952 ; Mark Herndon, b 1955) "Feels So Right"
Eddy Arnold, b 1918 , singer, guitarist, the "Tennessee Plowboy"
Chet Atkins, 1924-2001, guitarist, composer, producer, helped create the "Nashville sound"
Gene Autry, 1907-98, first great singing movie cowboy; "Back in the Saddle Again"
Garth Brooks, b 1962, singer, songwriter; "Friends in Low Places"
Brooks & Dunn (Kix Brooks, b 1955 ; Ronnie Dunn, b 1953) "Hard Workin' Man"
Boudleaux and Felice Bryant (Boudleau, 1920-87; Felice, 1925-2003), songwriting team; "Hey Joe"
Glen Campbell, b 1936 , singer, instrumentalist, TV host; "Gentle on My Mind," "Rhinestone Cowboy"
Mary Chapin Carpenter, b 1958 , singer, songwriter; "I Feel Lucky"
Carter Family (original members,**"Mother" Maybelle** 1909-78; **A.P.,** 1891-1960, **Sara**, 1898-1979) "Wildwood Flower"
Johnny Cash, 1932-2003 , singer, songwriter; "I Walk the Line," "Ring of Fire," "Folsom Prison Blues"
Patsy Cline, 1932-63, singer; "Walkin' After Midnight," "Crazy," "Sweet Dreams"
John Denver, 1943-97, singer, songwriter; "Rocky Mountain High"
Dixie Chicks (Natalie Maines, b 1974 ; Martie Seidel, b 1969 ; Emily Erwin Robison, b 1972) "Wide Open Spaces," "Fly"
Dale Evans (Lucille Wood Smith), 1912-2001, singer, actress, married Roy Rogers
Flatt & Scruggs (Lester Flatt, 1914-79; Earl Scruggs, b 1924), guitar-banjo duo and soloists; "Foggy Mountain Breakdown"
Red Foley, 1910-68, singer; "Chattanoogie Shoe Shine Boy"
Tennessee Ernie Ford, 1919-91, singer, TV host; "Sixteen Tons"
Lefty Frizzell, 1928-75, singer, guitarist; "Long Black Veil"
Vince Gill, b 1957, singer, songwriter; "When I Call Your Name"
Merle Haggard, b 1937, singer, songwriter; "Okie from Muskogee"
Emmylou Harris, b 1947, singer, songwriter, folk-country crossover artist; "If I Could Only Win Your Love"
Faith Hill, b 1967, singer, songwriter, married Tim McGraw; "Wild One," "This Kiss," "Breathe"
Alan Jackson, b 1958, singer, songwriter, "Where Were You (When the World Stopped Turning)"
Waylon Jennings, 1937–2002, singer, songwriter, "outlaw country" pioneer; "Luckenbach, Texas"
George Jones, b 1931, singer, "He Stopped Loving Her Today"
The Judds (Naomi, 1946- ; Wynonna, 1964-), mother-daughter duo; Wynonna also a solo act
Alison Krauss, b 1971, bluegrass fiddler, singer, bandleader; "When You Say Nothing at All"
Kris Kristofferson, b 1936, singer, songwriter, actor; "Me and Bobby McGee"
Brenda Lee, b 1944, singer; "I'm Sorry"
Patty Loveless, b 1957, singer, songwriter; "How Can I Help You Say Goodbye"
Lyle Lovett, b 1957, singer, songwriter, bandleader, actor; "Cowboy Man"
Loretta Lynn, b 1935, singer, songwriter; "Coal Miner's Daughter"
Kathy Mattea, b 1959, singer, songwriter; "Eighteen Wheels and a Dozen Roses"
Reba McEntire, b 1955, singer, songwriter, actress; "Whoever's in New England"
Tim McGraw, b 1967, singer; "It's Your Love," with wife, Faith Hill
Roger Miller, 1936-92, singer, songwriter; "King of the Road"
Ronnie Milsap, b 1944, singer, songwriter; "There's No Gettin' Over Me"
Bill Monroe, 1911-96, singer, songwriter, mandolin player, "father of bluegrass music"; "Mule Skinner Blues"
Patsy Montana, 1908-96, yodeling/singing cowgirl; "I Want to Be a Cowboy's Sweetheart"
Willie Nelson, b 1933, singer, songwriter, actor; "On the Road Again"
Mark O'Connor, b 1961, fiddler, country-classical crossover composer
Dolly Parton, b 1946, singer, songwriter, actress; "Dollywood" theme park; "Here You Come Again," "9 to 5"
Minnie Pearl, 1912-96, comedienne, Grand Ole Opry star
Charley Pride, b 1938, singer, 1st African-American country star; "Kiss an Angel Good Mornin'"
Jim Reeves, 1923-64, singer, songwriter; "Four Walls"
Charlie Rich, 1932-95, singer, songwriter called the "Silver Fox"; "The Most Beautiful Girl"
LeAnn Rimes, b 1982, singer; "Blue"
Tex Ritter, 1905-74, singer, songwriter; "Jingle, Jangle, Jingle"

Marty Robbins, 1925-82, singer, songwriter; "A White Sport Coat and a Pink Carnation"
Jimmie Rodgers, 1897-1933, singer, songwriter; "T for Texas"
Kenny Rogers, b 1938, singer, songwriter; "The Gambler"
Roy Rogers (Leonard Slye), 1911-98, singer, actor, "King of the Cowboys," sang with Sons of the Pioneers.
Fred Rose, 1898-1954, songwriter, singer, producer; "Blue Eyes Cryin' in the Rain"
Ricky Skaggs, b 1954, singer, songwriter, bandleader; "Don't Cheat in Our Hometown"
Ralph Stanley, b 1927, singer, banjo player, "Man of Constant Sorrow"
George Strait, b 1952, singer, bandleader; "Ace in the Hole"
Merle Travis, 1917-83, singer, guitarist, songwriter; "Divorce Me C.O.D."
Randy Travis, b 1959, singer, songwriter; "Forever and Ever, Amen"
Ernest Tubb, 1914-84, singer, songwriter, guitarist; "Walking the Floor Over You"
Shania Twain, b 1965, singer, songwriter; "You're Still the One"
Conway Twitty, 1933-93, singer, songwriter; "Hello Darlin' "
Dottie West, 1932-91, singer, songwriter; "Here Comes My Baby"
Hank Williams Jr., b 1949, singer, songwriter; "Bocephus"; "All My Rowdy Friends (Have Settled Down)"
Hank Williams Sr., 1923-53, singer, songwriter; "Your Cheatin' Heart"
Bob Wills, 1905-75, Western Swing fiddler, singer, bandleader, songwriter; "New San Antonio Rose"
Tammy Wynette, 1942-98, singer; "Stand By Your Man"
Trisha Yearwood, b 1964, singer, songwriter; "How Do I Live"
Dwight Yoakam, b 1957, singer, songwriter, actor; "Ain't That Lonely Yet"

Dance Figures of the Past

Source: Reviewed by Gary Parks, Reviews editor, *Dance* magazine

Alvin Ailey, 1931-89, (U.S.) modern dancer, choreographer; melded modern dance and Afro-Caribbean techniques.
Frederick Ashton, 1904-88, (Br.) ballet choreographer; director of Great Britain's Royal Ballet, 1963-70.
Fred Astaire, 1899-1987, (U.S.) dancer, actor; teamed with dancer/actress
Ginger Rogers (1911-95) in movie musicals.
George Balanchine, 1904-83, (Russ.-U.S.) ballet choreographer, teacher; most influential exponent of the neoclassical style; founded, with Lincoln Kirstein, School of American Ballet and New York City Ballet.
Carlo Blasis, 1803-78, (It.) ballet dancer, choreographer, writer; his teaching methods are standards of classical dance.
August Bournonville, 1805-79, (Dan.) ballet dancer, choreographer, teacher; exuberant, light style.
Gisella Caccialanza, 1914-97, (U.S.) ballerina, charter member of Balanchine's American Ballet.
Enrico Cecchetti, 1850-1928, (It.) ballet dancer, leading dancer of Russia's Imperial Ballet; his technique was basis for Britain's Imperial Soc. of Teachers of Dancing.
Gower Champion, 1921-80, (U.S.) dancer, choreographer, director; with his wife **Marge,** b 1923, (U.S.) choreographed, danced in Broadway musicals and films.
John Cranko, 1927-73, (S. African) choreographer; created narrative ballets based on literary works.
Agnes de Mille, 1909-93, (U.S.) ballerina, choreographer; known for using American themes, she choreographed the ballet *Rodeo* and the musical *Oklahoma!*
Dame Ninette DeValois, 1898-2001, (Br.) choreographer, founding director London's Royal Ballet; *The Rake's Progress.*
Sergei Diaghilev, 1872-1929, (Russ.) impresario; founded Les Ballet Russes; saw ballet as an art unifying dance, drama, music, and decor.
Alexandra Danilova, 1903-97, (Russ.) ballerina; noted teacher at the School of American Ballet.
Isadora Duncan, 1877-1927, (U.S.) expressive dancer who united free movement with serious music; one of the founders of modern dance.
Fanny Elssler, 1810-84, (Austrian) ballerina of the Romantic era; known for dramatic skill, sensual style.
Michel Fokine, 1880-1942, (Russ.) ballet dancer, choreographer, teacher; rejected strict classicism in favor of dramatically expressive style.
Margot Fonteyn, 1919-91, (Br.) prima ballerina, Royal Ballet of Great Britain; famed performance partner of Rudolf Nureyev.
Bob Fosse, 1927-87, (U.S.) jazz dancer, choreographer, director; Broadway musicals and film.
Serge Golovine, 1924-98, (Fr.) ballet dancer with Grand Ballet du Marquis de Cuevas; choreographer.
Martha Graham, 1893-1991, (U.S.) modern dancer, choreographer; created and codified her own dramatic technique.
Martha Hill, 1901-95, (U.S.) educator; leading figure in modern dance; founded American Dance Festival.
Gregory Hines, 1946-2003, (U.S.) tap-dance innovator and master of improvisation.
Doris Humphrey, 1895-1958, (U.S.) modern dancer, choreographer, writer, teacher.
Robert Joffrey, 1930-88, (U.S.) ballet dancer, choreographer; cofounded with **Gerald Arpino,** b 1928, (U.S.), the Joffrey Ballet.
Kurt Jooss, 1901-79, (Ger.) choreographer, teacher; created expressionist works using modern and classical techniques.
Tamara Karsavina, 1885-1978, (Russ.) prima ballerina of Russia's Imperial Ballet and Diaghilev's Ballets Russes; partner of Nijinsky.
Nora Kaye, 1920-87, (U.S.) ballerina with Metropolitan Opera Ballet and Ballet Theater (now American Ballet Theatre).
Lincoln Kirstein, 1907-96 (U.S.) brought ballet as an art form to U.S.; founded, with George Balanchine, School of American Ballet and New York City Ballet.
Serge Lifar, 1905-86, (Russ.-Fr.) prem. danseur, choreographer; director of dance at Paris Opera, 1930-45, 1947-58.
José Limón, 1908-72, (Mex.-U.S.) modern dancer, choreographer, teacher; developed technique based on Humphrey.
Catherine Littlefield, 1908-51, (U.S.) ballerina, choreographer, teacher; pioneer of American ballet.
Léonide Massine, 1896-1979, (Russ.-U.S.) ballet dancer, choreographer; known for his "symphonic ballet."
Kenneth MacMillan, 1929-92, (Br.) dancer, choreographer; directed Royal Ballet of Great Britain 1970-77.
Dame Alicia Markova, 1910-2004, (Br.) ballerina; helped popularize ballet in U.S. and Britain; known for title role in *Giselle.*
Vaslav Nijinsky, 1890-50, (Russ.) prem. danseur, choreographer; leading member of Diaghilev's Ballets Russes; his ballets were revolutionary for their time.
Alwin Nikolais, 1910-93, (U.S.) modern choreographer; created dance theater utilizing mixed media effects.
Jean-George Noverre, 1727-1810, (Fr.) ballet choreographer, teacher, writer; "Shakespeare of the Dance."
Rudolf Nureyev, 1938-93, (Russ.) prem. danseur, choreographer; leading male dancer of his generation; director of dance at Paris Opera, 1983-89.
Ruth Page, 1903-91, (U.S.) ballerina, choreographer; danced and directed ballet at Chicago Lyric Opera.
Anna Pavlova, 1881-1931, (Russ.) prima ballerina; toured with her own company to world acclaim.
Marius Petipa, 1818-1910, (Fr.) ballet dancer, choreographer; ballet master of the Imperial Ballet; established Russian classicism as leading style of late 19th cent.
Pearl Primus, 1919-95, (Trinidad-U.S.) modern dancer, choreographer, scholar; combined African, Caribbean, and African-American styles.
Jerome Robbins, 1918-98, (U.S.) choreographer, director, dancer; *The King and I, West Side Story, Fiddler on the Roof*
Bill (Bojangles) Robinson, 1878-1949, (U.S.) famed tap dancer; called King of Tapology on stage and screen.
Ruth St. Denis, 1877-1968, (U.S.) influential interpretive dancer, choreographer, teacher.
Ted Shawn, 1891-1972, (U.S.) modern dancer, choreographer; formed dance company and school with Ruth St. Denis; established Jacob's Pillow Dance Festival.
Marie Taglioni, 1804-84, (It.) ballerina, teacher; in title role of *La Sylphide* established image of the ethereal ballerina.
Antony Tudor, 1908-87, (Br.) choreographer, teacher; exponent of the "psychological ballet."
Galina Ulanova, 1910-98, (Russ.) revered ballerina with Bolshoi Ballet.
Agrippina Vaganova, 1879-1951, (Russ.) ballet teacher, director; codified Soviet ballet technique that developed virtuosity; called "queen of variations."
Mary Wigman, 1886-1973, (Ger.) modern dancer, choreographer, teacher; influenced European expressionist dance.

Opera Singers of the Past

Frances Alda, 1883-1952, (N.Z.) soprano
Pasquale Amato, 1878-1942, (It.) baritone
Marian Anderson, 1897-1993, (U.S.) contralto
Jussi Björling, 1911-60, (Swed.) tenor
Lucrezia Bori, 1887-1960, (It.) soprano
Maria Callas, 1923-77, (U.S.) soprano
Emma Calvé, 1858-1942, (Fr.) soprano
Enrico Caruso, 1873-1921, (It.) tenor
Feodor Chaliapin, 1873-1938, (Russ.) bass
Boris Christoff, 1914-93, (Bulg.) bass
Franco Corelli, 1921-2003, (It.) tenor
Victoria De Los Angeles, 1923-2005, (Sp.) soprano
Giuseppe De Luca, 1876-1950, (It.) baritone
Fernando De Lucia, 1860-1925, (It.) tenor
Edouard De Reszke, 1853-1917, (Pol.) bass
Jean De Reszke, 1850-1925, (Pol.) tenor
Emmy Destinn, 1878-1930, (Czech.) soprano
Emma Eames, 1865-1952, (U.S.) soprano
(Carlo Broschi) Farinelli, 1705-82, (It.) castrato
Geraldine Farrar, 1882-1967, (U.S.) soprano
Eileen Farrell, 1920-2002, (U.S.) soprano
Kathleen Ferrier, 1912-53, (Eng.) contralto
Kirsten Flagstad, 1895-1962, (Nor.) soprano
Olive Fremstad, 1871-1951, (Swed.-U.S.) soprano
Amelita Galli-Curci, 1882-1963, (It.) soprano
Mary Garden, 1874-1967, (Br.) soprano
Nicolai Ghiaurov, 1929-2004, (Bulg.) bass
Beniamino Gigli, 1890-1957, (It.) tenor
Tito Gobbi, 1913-84, (It.) baritone
Giulia Grisi, 1811-69, (It.) soprano
Frieda Hempel, 1885-1955, (Ger.) soprano
Jerome Hines, 1921-2003, (U.S.) bass
Hans Hotter, 1909-2003, (Ger.) bass-baritone
Maria Jeritza, 1887-1982, (Czech.) soprano
Alexander Kipnis, 1891-1978, (Russ.-U.S.) bass
Dorothy Kirsten, 1910-1992, (U.S.) soprano
Alfredo Kraus, 1927-99, (Sp.) tenor
Luigi Lablache, 1794-1858, (It.) bass
Lilli Lehmann, 1848-1929, (Ger.) soprano
Lotte Lehmann, 1888-1976, (Ger.-U.S.) soprano
Jenny Lind, 1820-87, (Swed.) soprano
Maria Malibran, 1808-36, (Sp.) mezzo-soprano
Giovanni Martinelli, 1885-1969, (It.) tenor
John McCormack, 1884-1945, (Ir.) tenor
Nellie Melba, 1861-1931, (Austral.) soprano.
Lauritz Melchior, 1890-1973, (Dan.) tenor
Robert Merrill, 1919-2004, (U.S.) baritone
Zinka Milanov, 1906-89, (Yugo.) soprano
Lillian Nordica, 1857-1914, (U.S.) soprano
Giuditta Pasta, 1797-1865, (It.) soprano
Adelina Patti, 1843-1919, (It.) soprano
Peter Pears, 1910-86, (Eng.) tenor
Jan Peerce, 1904-84, (U.S.) tenor
Ezio Pinza, 1892-1957, (It.) bass
Lily Pons, 1898-1976, (Fr.) soprano
Rosa Ponselle, 1897-1981, (U.S.) soprano
Hermann Prey, 1929-98, (Ger.) baritone.
Elisabeth Rethberg, 1894-1976, (Ger.) soprano
Giovanni Battista Rubini, 1794-1854, (It.) tenor
Leonie Rysanek, 1926-1998, (Austrian) soprano
Bidú Sayão, 1902-99, (Braz.) soprano
Friedrich Schorr, 1888-1953, (Hung.) bass-baritone
Marcella Sembrich, 1858-1935, (Pol.) soprano
Eleanor Steber, 1916-90, (U.S.) soprano
Ferrucio Tagliavini, 1913-95, (It.) tenor
Renata Tebaldi, 1922-2004 (It.) soprano
Luisa Tetrazzini, 1871-1940, (It.) soprano
Lawrence Tibbett, 1896-1960, (U.S.) baritone
Tatiana Troyanos, 1938-93, (U.S.) mezzo-soprano
Richard Tucker, 1913-75, (U.S.) tenor
Pauline Viardot, 1821-1910, (Fr.) mezzo-soprano
William Warfield, 1920-2002, (U.S.) bass-baritone
Leonard Warren, 1911-60, (U.S.) baritone
Ljuba Welitsch, 1913-96, (Bulg.) soprano
Wolfgang Windgassen, 1914-74, (Ger.) tenor

Selected Rock and Roll, Rhythm and Blues, Rap Artists

Titles in quotation marks are singles; others are albums.

Aaliyah: "More than a Woman"
Paula Abdul: "Straight Up"
***AC/DC (2003):** "Back in Black"
Bryan Adams: "Cuts Like a Knife"
***Aerosmith (2001):** "Sweet Emotion"
Christina Aguilera: "What a Girl Wants"
Alice In Chains: "Heaven Beside You"
***The Allman Brothers Band (1995):** "Ramblin' Man"
***The Animals (1994):** "House of the Rising Sun"
Paul Anka: "Lonely Boy"
Fiona Apple: "Criminal"
Ashanti: "Foolish"
The Association: "Cherish"
Frankie Avalon: "Venus"
The B-52s: "Love Shack"
Bachman Turner Overdrive: "Takin' Care of Business"
Backstreet Boys: "I Want it That Way"
Bad Company: "Can't Get Enough"
Erykah Badu: "On and On"
***La Vern Baker (1991):** "I Cried a Tear"
***Hank Ballard and the Midnighters (1990):** "Work With Me, Annie"
***The Band (1994):** "The Weight"
Barenaked Ladies: "One Week"
***The Beach Boys (1988):** "Good Vibrations"
Beastie Boys: "(You Gotta) Fight for Your Right (to Party)"
***The Beatles (1988):** *Sgt. Pepper's Lonely Hearts Club Band*
Beck: "Loser"
***The Bee Gees (1997):** "Stayin' Alive"
Pat Benatar: "Hit Me With Your Best Shot"
Ben Folds Five: "Brick"
***Chuck Berry (1986):** "Johnny B. Goode"
The Big Bopper: "Chantilly Lace"
Björk: "Human Behavior"
The Black Crowes: "Hard to Handle"
Black Eyed Peas: *Elephunk*
Black Sabbath: "Paranoid"
***Bobby "Blue" Bland (1992):** "Turn On Your Love Light"
Mary J. Blige: *My Life*
Blind Faith: "Can't Find My Way Home"
Blink-182: "All the Small Things"
Blondie: "Heart of Glass"
Blood, Sweat, and Tears: "Spinning Wheel"
Blues Traveler: "Run-Around"
Gary "U.S." Bonds: "Quarter to Three"
Bon Jovi: "Livin' on a Prayer"
***Booker T. and the M.G.'s (1992):** "Green Onions"
Earl Bostic: "Flamingo"
Boston: "More Than A Feeling"
***David Bowie (1996):** "Space Oddity"
Boyz II Men: "I'll Make Love to You"
Toni Braxton: "Un-Break My Heart"
***James Brown (1986):** "Papa's Got a Brand New Bag"
***Ruth Brown (1993):** "Lucky Lips"
***Jackson Browne (2004):** "Doctor My Eyes"
***Buffalo Springfield (1997):** "For What It's Worth"
***Jimmy Buffett:** "Margaritaville"
***Solomon Burke (2001):** "Over and Over (Huggin' and Lovin')"
Bush: "Glycerine"
***The Byrds (1991):** "Turn! Turn! Turn!"
Mariah Carey: "Vision of Love"
The Carpenters: "(They Long to Be) Close to You"
The Cars: "Shake It Up"
***Johnny Cash (1992):** "I Walk the Line"
***Ray Charles (1986):** "Georgia on My Mind"
Cheap Trick: "Surrender"
Chicago: "Saturday in the Park"
Chubby Checker: "The Twist"
***Eric Clapton (2000):** "Layla"
***The Clash (2003):** "Rock the Casbah"
***The Coasters (1987):** "Yakety Yak"
***Eddie Cochran (1987):** "Summertime Blues"
Joe Cocker: "With a Little Help From My Friends"
Coldplay: "Politik"
Collective Soul: "The World I Know"
Phil Collins: "Against All Odds"
***Sam Cooke (1986):** "You Send Me"
Coolio: "Gangsta's Paradise"
Alice Cooper: "School's Out"
***Elvis Costello and the Attractions (2003):** "Alison"
Counting Crows: "Mr. Jones"
***Cream (1993):** "Sunshine of Your Love"
Creed: "Arms Wide Open"
***Creedence Clearwater Revival (1993):** "Proud Mary"
***Crosby, Stills, and Nash (1997):** "Suite: Judy Blue Eyes"
Sheryl Crow: "All I Want to Do"
The Cure: "Boys Don't Cry"
The Crystals: "Da Doo Ron Ron"
Cypress Hill: "Insane in the Brain"
Danny and the Juniors: "At the Hop"

***Bobby Darin (1990):** "Splish Splash"
Spencer Davis Group: "Gimme Some Lovin' "
Deep Purple: "Smoke on the Water"
Def Leppard: "Photograph"
***The Dells (2004):** "Oh, What a Night"
Depeche Mode: "Strange Love"
Destiny's Child: "Survivor"
***Bo Diddley (1987):** "Who Do You Love?"
***Dion and the Belmonts (1989):** "A Teenager in Love"
Celine Dion: "Because You Loved Me"
Dire Straits: "Money for Nothing"
DMX: "What's My Name"
***Fats Domino (1986):** "Blueberry Hill"
Donovan: "Mellow Yellow"
The Doobie Brothers: "What a Fool Believes"
***The Doors (1993):** "Light My Fire"
Dr. Dre: "Nothin' But a 'G' Thang"
***The Drifters (1988):** "Save the Last Dance for Me"
Duran Duran: "Hungry Like the Wolf"
***Bob Dylan (1988):** "Like a Rolling Stone"
***The Eagles (1998):** "Hotel California"
***Earth, Wind, and Fire (2000):** "Shining Star"
***Duane Eddy (1994):** "Rebel-Rouser"
Missy Elliott: "Sock It 2 Me"
Emerson, Lake, and Palmer: "Lucky Man"
Eminem: "The Real Slim Shady"
En Vogue: "Hold On"
Enya: *Shepherd Moons*
The Eurythmics: "Sweet Dreams (Are Made of This)"
Everclear: "Father Of Mine"
***The Everly Brothers (1986):** "Wake Up, Little Susie"
50 Cent (Curtis Jackson): *Get Rich Or Die Tryin'*
The Five Satins: "In the Still of the Night"
***The Flamingos (2001):** "I Only Have Eyes for You"
***Fleetwood Mac (1998):** *Rumours*
The Foo Fighters: "I'll Stick Around"
Foreigner: "Double Vision"
***The Four Seasons (1990):** "Sherry"
***The Four Tops (1990):** "I Can't Help Myself (Sugar Pie, Honey Bunch)"
***Aretha Franklin (1987):** "Respect"
Nelly Furtado: "I'm Like a Bird"
Peter Gabriel: "Shock the Monkey"
Marvin Gaye (1987): "I Heard It Through the Grapevine"
Genesis: "No Reply at All"
Goo Goo Dolls: "Iris"
Grand Funk Railroad: "We're an American Band"
Grand Master Flash and the Furious Five: "The Message"
***The Grateful Dead (1994):** "Uncle John's Band"
Macy Gray: "I Try"
***Al Green (1995):** "Let's Stay Together"
Green Day: "Time of Your Life"
The Guess Who: "American Woman"
Guns N' Roses: "Sweet Child o' Mine"
***Buddy Guy (2005):** *A Man and His Blues*
***Bill Haley and His Comets (1987):** "Rock Around the Clock"
Hall and Oates: "Kiss on My List"
Hanson: "MMMBop"
Juliana Hatfield: "Spin the Bottle"
***Isaac Hayes (2002):** "Theme from 'Shaft'"
Heart: "Barracuda"
***Jimi Hendrix (1992):** "Purple Haze"
Lauryn Hill: "Doo-Wop (That Thing)"
Hole: "Doll Parts"
The Hollies: "Long Cool Woman (In a Black Dress)"
***Buddy Holly (1986):** "Peggy Sue"
***John Lee Hooker (1991):** "Boogie Chillen"
Hootie and the Blowfish: *Cracked Rear View*
Whitney Houston: "I Will Always Love You"
***The Impressions (1991):** "For Your Precious Love"
Indigo Girls: "Closer to Fine"
INXS: "Need You Tonight"
***The Isley Brothers (1992):** "It's Your Thing"
***The Jackson Five (1997):** "ABC"
Janet Jackson: *Rhythm Nation*
***Michael Jackson (2001):** *Thriller*
***Etta James (1993):** "At Last"
Tommy James & The Shondells: "Crimson and Clover"
Jane's Addiction: "Jane Says"
Ja Rule: *Venni, Vetti, Vecci*
Jay and the Americans: "This Magic Moment"
Jay-Z: "Can I Live"
***Jefferson Airplane (1996):** "White Rabbit"
Jethro Tull: *Aqualung*
Joan Jett: "I Love Rock 'n' Roll"
Jewel: "You Were Meant for Me"
***Billy Joel (1999):** "Piano Man"
***Elton John (1994):** "Candle in the Wind"
***Little Willie John (1996):** "Sleep"
***Janis Joplin (1995):** "Me and Bobby McGee"
Journey: "Don't Stop Believin'"
K.C. and the Sunshine Band: "Get Down Tonight"
R. Kelly: "I Can't Sleep Baby (If I)"
Alicia Keys: "Fallin'"
Kid Rock: "Cowboy"
***B.B. King (1987):** "The Thrill Is Gone"
Carole King: *Tapestry*
***The Kinks (1990):** "You Really Got Me"
Kiss: "Rock 'n' Roll All Night"
***Gladys Knight and the Pips (1996):** "Midnight Train to Georgia"
Korn: "Blind"
Lenny Kravitz: "Are You Gonna Go My Way?"
***Led Zeppelin (1995):** "Stairway to Heaven"
***Brenda Lee (2002):** "I'm Sorry"
***John Lennon (1994):** "Imagine"
***Jerry Lee Lewis (1986):** "Whole Lotta Shakin' Going On"
Lil' Kim: "No Matter What They Say"
Limp Bizkit: "Break Stuff"
Linkin Park: "One Step Closer"
Little Anthony and the Imperials: "Tears on My Pillow"
***Little Richard (1986):** "Tutti Frutti"
Live: "Lightning Crashes"
L. L. Cool J: "Mama Said Knock You Out"
Jennifer Lopez: "Love Don't Cost a Thing"
***The Lovin' Spoonful (2000):** "Summer in the City"
***Frankie Lymon and the Teenagers (1993):** "Why Do Fools Fall in Love?"
Lynyrd Skynyrd: "Free Bird"
Madonna: "Material Girl"
Taj Mahal: "Going up to the Country, Paint My Mailbox Blue"
***The Mamas and the Papas (1998):** "Monday, Monday"
Aimee Mann: "Save Me"
Marilyn Manson: "Beautiful People"
***Bob Marley (1994):** *Exodus*
Maroon 5: *Songs About Jane*
***Martha and the Vandellas (1995):** "Dancin' in the Streets"
The Marvelettes: "Please, Mr. Postman"
Matchbox 20: "Push"
Dave Matthews Band: "Don't Drink the Water"
***Curtis Mayfield (1999):** "Superfly"
***Paul McCartney (1999):** "Band on the Run"
Don McLean: "American Pie"
***Clyde McPhatter (1987):** "A Lover's Question"
Meat Loaf: "Paradise by the Dashboard Light"
John (Cougar) Mellencamp: "Jack and Diane"
Men at Work: "Who Can It Be Now?"
Metallica: "Enter Sandman"
George Michael: "Faith"
***Joni Mitchell (1997):** "Both Sides Now"
Moby: "Bodyrock"
The Monkees: "I'm a Believer"
Moody Blues: "Nights in White Satin"
***The Moonglows (2000):** "Blue Velvet"
Alanis Morissette: "Ironic"
***Van Morrison (1993):** "Brown-Eyed Girl"
Nelly: *Country Grammar*
***Ricky Nelson (1987):** "Hello, Mary Lou"
Nine Inch Nails: "Closer"
Nirvana: *Nevermind*
No Doubt: *Rock Steady*
The Notorious B.I.G.: "Mo Money Mo Problems"
'N Sync: "Bye, Bye, Bye"
Oasis: "Wonderwall"
The Offspring: "Pretty Fly (for a White Guy)"
The O'Jays (2005): "Back Stabbers"
***Roy Orbison (1987):** "Oh, Pretty Woman"
Outkast: *Speakerboxxx*
Ozzy Osbourne: "Crazy Train"
***Parliament/Funkadelic (1997):** "One Nation Under a Groove"
Pearl Jam: "Jeremy"
***Carl Perkins (1987):** "Blue Suede Shoes"
Peter, Paul, and Mary: "Leaving on a Jet Plane"
***Tom Petty and the Heartbreakers (2002):** "Refugee"
Liz Phair: *Exile in Guyville*
Phish: "Sample in a Jar"
***Wilson Pickett (1991):** "Land of 1,000 Dances"
Pink: *Missundazstood!*
***Pink Floyd (1996):** *The Wall*
***Gene Pitney (2002):** "Only Love Can Break a Heart"
***The Platters (1990):** "The Great Pretender"
Poco: "Crazy Love"
***The Police (2003):** "Every Breath You Take"
Iggy Pop: "Lust for Life"
***Elvis Presley (1986):** "Love Me Tender"
***The Pretenders (2005):** "Back on the Chain Gang"
***Lloyd Price (1998):** "Stagger Lee"
***Prince (The Artist) (2004):** "Purple Rain"
Procol Harum: "A Whiter Shade of Pale"
Public Enemy: "Fight the Power"
Puff Daddy and the Family: *No Way Out*

***Queen (2001):** "Bohemian Rhapsody"
Radiohead: "Creep"
Rage Against the Machine: "Bulls on Parade"
***Bonnie Raitt (2000):** "Something to Talk About"
***The Ramones (2002):** "I Wanna Be Sedated"
***Otis Redding (1989):** "(Sittin' on) the Dock of the Bay"
Red Hot Chili Peppers: "Under the Bridge"
***Jimmy Reed (1991):** "Ain't That Loving You, Baby?"
Lou Reed: "Walk on the Wild Side"
R.E.M.: "Losing My Religion"
REO Speedwagon: "Can't Fight This Feeling"
Busta Rhymes: "What's It Gonna Be?"
***The Righteous Brothers (2003):** "You've Lost That Lovin' Feelin'"
Johnny Rivers: "Poor Side of Town"
***Smokey Robinson and the Miracles (1987):** "Shop Around"
***The Rolling Stones (1989):** "Satisfaction"
The Ronettes: "Be My Baby"
Linda Ronstadt: "You're No Good"
Run-D.M.C.: "Raisin' Hell"
Rush: "Tom Sawyer"
Sade: "Smooth Operator"
Salt-N-Pepa: "Shoop"
***Sam and Dave (1992):** "Soul Man"
***Santana (1998):** "Black Magic Woman"
Seal: "Kiss From a Rose"
Neil Sedaka: "Breaking Up Is Hard to Do"
***Bob Seger (2004):** "Old Time Rock & Roll"
The Sex Pistols: "Anarchy in the U.K."
Shaggy: "It Wasn't Me"
Shakira: "Whenever, Wherever"
Tupac Shakur: "How Do U Want It"
***Del Shannon (1999):** "Runaway"
***The Shirelles (1996):** "Soldier Boy"
Carly Simon: "You're So Vain"
***Paul Simon (2001):** "50 Ways to Leave Your Lover"
***Simon and Garfunkel (1990):** "Bridge Over Troubled Water"
Sisqo: "Thong Song"
***Percy Sledge (2005):** "When a Man Loves a Woman"
***Sly and the Family Stone (1993):** "Everyday People"
Smashing Pumpkins: "Today"
Patti Smith: "Because the Night"
Will Smith: "Gettin' Jiggy With It"
The Smiths: "This Charming Man"
Snoop Dogg: "Gin and Juice"
Sonic Youth: "Bull in the Heather"
Soundgarden: "Black Hole Sun"
Britney Spears: "Hit Me Baby One More Time"
Spice Girls: "Wannabe"
***Dusty Springfield (1999):** "I Only Want to Be With You"
***Bruce Springsteen (1999):** "Born to Run"
Squeeze (2001): "Tempted"
***Staple Singers (1999):** "I'll Take You There"
***Steely Dan (2001):** "Rikki Don't Lose That Number"
Steppenwolf: "Born to Be Wild"
***Rod Stewart (1994):** "Maggie Mae"
Sting: "If You Love Somebody, Set Them Free"
Stone Temple Pilots: "Plush"
Styx: "Come Sail Away"
Sublime: "What I Got"
The Sugar Hill Gang: "Rapper's Delight"
Donna Summer: "Bad Girls"
***The Supremes (1988):** "Stop! In the Name of Love"
***Talking Heads (2002):** "Once in a Lifetime"
***James Taylor (2001):** "You've Got a Friend"
***The Temptations (1989):** "My Girl"
Three Dog Night: "Joy to the World"
TLC: "Waterfalls"
T. Rex: "Bang a Gong (Get It On)"
***Traffic (2004):** Traffic
***Big Joe Turner (1987):** "Shake, Rattle & Roll"
***Ike and Tina Turner (1991):** "Proud Mary"
***Tina Turner:** "What's Love Got to Do With It?"
The Turtles: "Happy Together"
***U2 (2005):** "With or Without You"
Usher: "You Make Me Wanna"
***Ritchie Valens (2001):** "La Bamba"
Van Halen: "Running With the Devil"
Stevie Ray Vaughan: "Crossfire"
***The Velvet Underground (1996):** "Sweet Jane"
***Gene Vincent[1] (1998):** "Be-Bop-A-Lula"
Tom Waits: "Downtown Train"
The Wallflowers: "One Headlight"
Dionne Warwick: "I Say a Little Prayer"
***Muddy Waters (1987):** "I Can't Be Satisfied"
Mary Wells: "My Guy"
The White Stripes: "Seven Nation Army"
***The Who (1990):** *Tommy*
Lucinda Williams: *Car Wheels on a Gravel Road*
***Jackie Wilson (1987):** "That's Why"
***Stevie Wonder (1989):** "You Are the Sunshine of My Life"
Wu-Tang Clan: "Protect Ya Neck"
Weird Al Yankovic: Dare to Be Stupid
***The Yardbirds (1992):** "For Your Love"
Yes: "Roundabout"
***Neil Young (1995):** "Down by the River"
***The Young Rascals/The Rascals (1997):** "Good Lovin' "
***Frank Zappa[1]/Mothers of Invention (1995):** *Hot Rats*
John Zorn: *News for Lulu*
***ZZ Top (2004):** "Legs"

*Inducted into Rock and Roll Hall of Fame as performer between 1986 and 2005; year is in parentheses. (1) Only individual performer is in Rock and Roll Hall of Fame.

Entertainment Personalities of the Present

Living actors, musicians, dancers, singers, producers, directors, radio-TV performers.

Name	Birthplace	Birthdate
Abbado, Claudio	Milan, Italy	6/26/33
Abdul, Paula	San Fernando, CA	6/19/62
Abraham, F. Murray	Pittsburgh, PA	10/24/39
Adams, Bryan	Kingston, Ontario	11/5/59
Adams, Edie	Kingston, PA	4/16/29
Adjani, Isabelle	Paris, France	6/27/55
Ad-rock	South Orange, NJ	10/31/66
Affleck, Ben	Berkeley, CA	8/15/72
Aghdashloo, Shohreh	Tehran, Iran	1952
Aguilera, Christina	Staten Is., New York, NY	12/18/80
Agutter, Jenny	Taunton, Somerset, Eng.	12/20/52
Aiello, Danny	New York, NY	6/20/33
Aiken, Clay	Raleigh, NC	11/30/78
Aimee, Anouk	Paris, France	4/27/32
Albanese, Licia	Bari, Italy	7/22/13
Alberghetti, Anna Maria	Pesaro, Italy	5/15/36
Albert, Marv	Brooklyn, New York, NY	6/12/41
Alda, Alan	New York, NY	1/28/36
Alexander, Jane	Boston, MA	10/28/39
Alexander, Jason	Newark, NJ	9/23/59
Allen, Debbie	Houston, TX	1/16/50
Allen, Joan	Rochelle, IL	8/20/56
Allen, Karen	Carrollton, IL	10/5/51
Allen, Ted	Carmel, IN	5/20/65
Allen, Tim	Denver, CO	6/13/53
Allen, Woody	Brooklyn, NY	12/1/35
Alley, Kirstie	Wichita, KS	1/12/51
Allman, Gregg	Nashville, TN	12/8/47
Allyson, June	Bronx, New York, NY	10/7/17
Alonso, Maria Conchita	Cienfuegos, Cuba	6/29/57
Alpert, Herb	Los Angeles, CA	3/31/35
Altman, Robert	Kansas City, MO	2/20/25
Almodóvar, Pedro	Calzada de Calatrava, Spain	9/25/51
Ambrose, Lauren	New Haven, CT	2/20/78
Ames, Ed	Malden, Boston, MA	7/9/27
Amos, John	Newark, NJ	12/27/41
Amos, Tori	Newton, NC	8/22/63
Andre 3000	Atlanta, GA	5/27/75
Anderson, Gillian	Chicago, IL	8/9/68
Anderson, Harry	Newport, RI	10/14/52
Anderson, Ian	Dunfermline, Scotland	8/10/47
Anderson, Kevin	Gurnee, IL	1/13/60
Anderson, Loni	St. Paul, MN	8/5/46
Anderson, Lynn	Grand Forks, ND	9/26/47
Anderson, Melissa Sue	Berkeley, CA	9/26/62
Anderson, Pamela	Comox, Vancouver Isl., BC	7/1/67
Anderson, Richard	Long Branch, NJ	8/8/26
Anderson, Richard Dean	Minneapolis, MN	1/23/50
Anderson, Wes	Houston, TX	5/1/69
Andersson, Bibi	Stockholm, Sweden	11/11/35
Andress, Ursula	Bern, Switzerland	3/19/36
Andrews, Anthony	London, England	1/12/48
Andrews, Julie	Walton-on-Thames, Surrey, England	10/1/35
Andrews, Patty	Minneapolis, MN	2/16/20
Aniston, Jennifer	Sherman Oaks, CA	2/11/69
Anka, Paul	Ottawa, Ontario	7/30/41
Ann-Margret	Stockholm, Sweden	4/28/41
Anthony, Marc	New York, NY	9/16/68

Name	Birthplace	Birthdate
Antonioni, Michelangelo	Ferrara, Italy	9/29/12
Apple, Fiona	New York, NY	9/13/77
Applegate, Christina	Los Angeles, CA	11/25/71
Archer, Anne	Los Angeles, CA	8/25/47
Arkin, Adam	Brooklyn, NY	8/19/56
Arkin, Alan	New York, NY	3/26/34
Arnaz, Desi, Jr.	Hollywood, CA	1/19/53
Arnaz, Lucie	Hollywood, CA	7/17/51
Arness, James	Minneapolis, MN	5/26/23
Arnold, Eddy	Henderson, TN	5/15/18
Arnold, Tom	Ottumwa, IA	3/6/59
Arquette, David	Winchester, VA	9/8/71
Arquette, Patricia	Chicago, IL	4/8/68
Arquette, Rosanna	New York, NY	8/10/59
Arroyo, Martina	Harlem, New York, NY	2/2/37
Arthur, Beatrice	New York, NY	5/13/23
Ashanti (Douglas)	Glen Cove, NY	10/13/80
Ashley, Elizabeth	Ocala, FL	8/30/39
Asner, Ed	Kansas City, KS	11/15/29
Assante, Armand	New York, NY	10/4/49
Astin, John	Baltimore, MD	3/30/30
Atkins, Eileen	London, England	6/16/34
Atkins, Sharif	Pittsburgh, PA	1/29/75
Atkinson, Rowan	Newcastle-Upon-Tyne, Eng.	1/6/55
Attenborough, Richard	Cambridge, England	8/29/23
Auberjonois, Rene	New York, NY	6/1/40
Austin, Patti	New York, NY	8/10/48
Autry, Alan	Shreveport, LA	7/31/52
Avalon, Frankie	Philadelphia, PA	9/18/39
Aykroyd, Dan	Ottawa, Ontario	7/1/52
Azaria, Hank	Forest Hills, Queens, NY	4/25/64
Aznavour, Charles	Paris, France	5/22/24
Babyface (Kenneth Edmonds)	Indianapolis, IN	4/10/59
Bacall, Lauren	Bronx, New York, NY	9/16/24
Bacon, Kevin	Philadelphia, PA	7/8/58
Badalucco, Michael	Brooklyn, NY	12/20/54
Bader, Diedrich	Alexandria, VA	12/24/66
Badu, Erykah	Dallas, TX	2/26/71
Baez, Joan	Staten Island, NY	1/9/41
Bain, Conrad	Lethbridge, Alberta	2/4/23
Baio, Scott	Brooklyn, NY	9/22/61
Baker, Anita	Toledo, OH	1/26/58
Baker, Carroll	Johnstown, PA	5/28/31
Baker, Diane	Hollywood, CA	2/25/38
Baker, Joe Don	Groesbeck, TX	2/12/36
Baker, Kathy	Midland, TX	6/8/50
Baker, Kenny	Birmingham, England	8/24/34
Bakula, Scott	St. Louis, MO	10/9/54
Baldwin, Alec	Massapequa, NY	4/3/58
Baldwin, Daniel	Massapequa, NY	10/5/60
Baldwin, Stephen	Massapequa, NY	5/12/66
Baldwin, William	Massapequa, NY	2/21/63
Bale, Christian	Pembrokeshire, Wales	1/30/74
Ballard, Kaye	Cleveland, OH	11/20/26
Bana, Eric	Melbourne, Australia	8/9/68
Banderas, Antonio	Málaga, Spain	8/10/60
Banks, Elizabeth	Pittsfield, MA	2/10/75
Banks, Tyra	Los Angeles, CA	12/4/73
Bannon, Jack	Los Angeles, CA	6/14/40
Baranski, Christine	Buffalo, NY	5/2/52
Barbeau, Adrienne	Sacramento, CA	6/11/45
Bardem, Javier	Las Palmas, Canary Isl.	3/1/69
Bardot, Brigitte	Paris, France	9/28/34
Barker, Bob	Darrington, WA	12/12/23
Barkin, Ellen	Bronx, New York, NY	4/16/55
Barrie, Barbara	Chicago, IL	5/23/31
Barrino, Fantasia	High Point, NC	6/30/84
Barry, Gene	New York, NY	6/14/19
Barrymore, Drew	Los Angeles, CA	2/22/75
Bartoli, Cecilia	Rome, Italy	6/4/66
Barton, Misha	London, Eng.	1/24/86
Baryshnikov, Mikhail	Riga, Latvia	1/28/48
Basinger, Kim	Athens, GA	12/8/53
Bass, Lance	Laurel, MS	5/4/79
Bassett, Angela	Harlem, New York, NY	8/16/58
Bassey, Shirley	Cardiff, Wales	1/8/37
Bateman, Jason	Rye, NY	1/14/69
Bateman, Justine	Rye, NY	2/19/66
Bates, Kathy	Memphis, TN	6/28/48
Battle, Kathleen	Portsmouth, OH	8/13/48
Baxter, Meredith	Los Angeles, CA	6/21/47
Bean, Orson	Burlington, VT	7/22/28
Bean, Sean	Sheffield, England	4/17/59
Beatty, Ned	Louisville, KY	7/6/37
Beatty, Warren	Richmond, VA	3/30/37
Beauvais, Garcelle	St. Marc, Haiti	11/26/66
Beck (Hansen)	Los Angeles, CA	7/8/70
Beck, Jeff	Wallington, Surrey, Eng.	6/24/44
Beck, John	Chicago, IL	1/28/43
Beckinsale, Kate	London, England	7/26/73
Bedelia, Bonnie	New York, NY	3/25/48
Begley, Ed, Jr.	Los Angeles, CA	9/16/49
Behar, Joy	Brooklyn, NY	10/7/43
Belafonte, Harry	Harlem, New York, NY	3/1/27
Bell, Art	Camp Lejeune, NC	6/17/45
Bell, Catherine	London, England	8/14/68
Bello, Maria	Norristown, PA	4/18/67
Belmondo, Jean-Paul	Neuilly-sur-Seine, France	4/9/33
Belushi, Jim	Chicago, IL	6/15/54
Belzer, Richard	Bridgeport, CT	8/4/44
Benatar, Pat	Brooklyn, NY	1/10/53
Benedict, Dirk	Helena, MT	3/1/45
Benigni, Roberto	Misericordia, Italy	10/27/52
Bening, Annette	Topeka, KS	5/29/58
Benjamin, Richard	New York, NY	5/22/38
Bennett, Tony	Astoria, Queens, NY	8/3/26
Benson, George	Pittsburgh, PA	3/22/43
Benson, Robby	Dallas, TX	1/21/56
Berenger, Tom	Chicago, IL	5/31/50
Berfield, Justin	Ventura County, CA	2/25/86
Bergen, Candice	Beverly Hills, CA	5/9/46
Bergen, Polly	Knoxville, TN	7/14/30
Bergeron, Tom	Haverhill, MA	5/6/55
Bergman, Ingmar	Uppsala, Sweden	7/14/18
Berlinger, Warren	Brooklyn, NY	8/31/37
Berman, Shelley	Chicago, IL	2/3/26
Bernard, Crystal	Dallas, TX	9/30/64
Bernhard, Sandra	Flint, MI	6/6/55
Bernsen, Corbin	N. Hollywood, CA	9/7/54
Berry, Chuck	St. Louis, MO	10/18/26
Berry, Halle	Cleveland, OH	8/14/66
Berry, Ken	Moline, IL	11/3/33
Bertinelli, Valerie	Wilmington, DE	4/23/60
Bertolucci, Bernardo	Parma, Italy	3/16/40
Biafra, Jello	Boulder, CO	6/17/58
Bialik, Mayim	San Diego, CA	12/12/75
Big Boi	Savanah, GA	2/1/75
Biggs, Jason	Pompton Plains, NJ	5/12/78
Bikel, Theodore	Vienna, Austria	5/2/24
Billingsley, Barbara	Los Angeles, CA	12/22/22
Bilson, Rachel	Los Angeles, CA	8/25/81
Binoche, Juliette	Paris, France	3/9/64
Birch, Thora	Beverly Hills, CA	3/11/82
Birney, David	Washington, DC	4/23/39
Bishop, Joey	Bronx, NY	2/3/18
Bisset, Jacqueline	Weybridge, England	9/13/44
Bissett, Josie	Seattle, WA	10/5/70
Björk (Gudmundsdottir)	Reykjavik, Iceland	11/21/65
Black, Clint	Long Branch, NJ	2/4/62
Black, Jack	Los Angeles, CA	4/7/69
Black, Karen	Park Ridge, IL	7/1/42
Blades, Ruben	Panama City, Panama	7/16/48
Blair, Janet	Altoona, PA	4/23/21
Blair, Linda	St. Louis, MO	1/22/59
Blair, Selma	Southfield, MI	6/23/72
Blake, Robert	Nutley, NJ	9/18/33
Blanchett, Cate	Melbourne, Australia	5/14/69
Bledsoe, Tempestt	Chicago, IL	8/1/73
Bleeth, Yasmine	New York, NY	6/14/68
Blethyn, Brenda	Ramsgate, Kent, England	2/20/46
Blige, Mary J.	Bronx, NY	1/11/71
Bloom, Claire	London, England	2/15/31
Bloom, Orlando	Canterbury, England	1/13/77
Blyth, Ann	Mt. Kisco, NY	8/16/28
Bochco, Steven	New York, NY	12/16/43
Bocelli, Andrea	Lajatico, Italy	9/22/58
Bogdanovich, Peter	Kingston, NY	7/30/39
Bogosian, Eric	Woburn, MA	4/24/53
Bologna, Joseph	Brooklyn, NY	12/30/38
Bolton, Michael	New Haven, CT	2/26/53
Bonet, Lisa	San Francisco, CA	11/16/67
Bonham Carter, Helena	London, England	5/26/66
Bon Jovi, Jon	Sayreville, NJ	3/2/62
Bono (Vox)	Dublin, Ireland	5/10/60
Boone, Debby	Hackensack, NJ	9/22/56
Boone, Pat	Jacksonville, FL	6/1/34
Boreanaz, David	Buffalo, NY	5/16/71
Borgnine, Ernest	Hamden, CT	1/24/17
Bosco, Philip	Jersey City, NJ	9/26/30
Bosley, Tom	Chicago, IL	10/1/27
Bosson, Barbara	Charleroi, PA	11/1/39
Bostwick, Barry	San Mateo, CA	2/24/45
Bottoms, Timothy	Santa Barbara, CA	8/30/51
Bowen, Julie	Baltimore, MD	3/3/70
Bowie, David	London, England	1/8/47
Bowles, Peter	London, England	10/16/36

Name	Birthplace	Birthdate
Boxleitner, Bruce	Elgin, IL	5/12/50
Boy George	Bexleyheath, England	6/14/61
Boyle, Lara Flynn	Davenport, IA	3/24/70
Boyle, Peter	Philadelphia, PA	10/18/33
Bracco, Lorraine	Brooklyn, NY	10/2/55
Brady, Wayne	Orlando, FL	6/2/72
Braff, Zach	S. Orange, NJ	4/6/75
Branagh, Kenneth	Belfast, N. Ireland	12/10/60
Brandauer, Klaus Maria	Steiermark, Austria	6/22/44
Brandy (Norwood)	McComb, MS	2/11/79
Braschi, Nicoletta	Cesena, Italy	8/10/60
Bratt, Benjamin	San Francisco, CA	12/16/63
Braugher, Andre	Chicago, Il	7/1/62
Braxton, Toni	Severn, MD	10/7/66
Bremner, Ewen	Edinburgh, Scotland	1971
Brendon, Nicholas	Los Angeles, CA	4/12/71
Brennan, Eileen	Los Angeles, CA	9/3/35
Brenneman, Amy	Glastonbury, CT	6/22/64
Brenner, David	Philadelphia, PA	2/4/45
Brewer, Teresa	Toledo, OH	5/7/31
Bridges, Beau	Hollywood, CA	12/9/41
Bridges, Jeff	Los Angeles, CA	12/4/49
Brightman, Sarah	Berkhamstead, England	8/14/60
Brimley, Wilford	Salt Lake City, UT	9/27/34
Brinkley, Christie	Malibu, CA	2/2/54
Broadbent, Jim	Lincolnshire, England	5/24/49
Brochtrup, Bill	Inglewood, CA	3/7/63
Broderick, Matthew	New York, NY	3/21/62
Brody, Adam	San Diego, CA	12/15/79
Brody, Adrien	New York, NY	4/14/73
Brolin, James	Los Angeles, CA	7/18/40
Brooks, Albert	Beverly Hills, CA	7/22/47
Brooks, Garth	Tulsa, OK	2/7/62
Brooks, James L	North Bergen, NJ	5/9/40
Brooks, Mel	Brooklyn, NY	6/28/26
Brosnan, Pierce	Navan, Co. Meath, Ireland	5/16/53
Brown, Blair	Washington, DC	4/23/46
Brown, Bobby	Roxbury, Boston, MA	2/5/69
Brown, Bryan	Panania, Australia	6/23/47
Brown, James	Barnwell, SC	5/3/33
Browne, Jackson	Heidelberg, Germany	10/9/48
Browne, Roscoe Lee	Woodbury, NJ	5/2/25
Brubeck, Dave	Concord, CA	12/6/20
Bryson, Peabo	Greenville, SC	4/13/51
Buckley, Betty	Ft. Worth, TX	7/3/47
Buffett, Jimmy	Pascagoula, MS	12/25/46
Bujold, Genevieve	Montreal, Quebec	7/1/42
Bullock, Sandra	Arlington, VA	7/26/64
Bumbry, Grace	St. Louis, MO	1/4/37
Bundchen, Gisele	Horizontina, Brazil	7/20/80
Burghoff, Gary	Bristol, CT	5/24/43
Burke, Delta	Orlando, FL	7/30/56
Burnett, Carol	San Antonio, TX	4/26/33
Burns, Edward	Woodside, Queens, NY	1/29/68
Burrows, Darren E.	Winfield, KS	9/12/66
Burstyn, Ellen	Detroit, MI	12/7/32
Burton, LeVar	Landstuhl, W Germany	2/16/57
Burton, Tim	Burbank, CA	8/25/58
Buscemi, Steve	Brooklyn, NY	12/13/57
Busey, Gary	Goose Creek, TX	6/29/44
Busfield, Timothy	Lansing, MI	6/12/57
Butler, Brett	Montgomery, AL	1/30/58
Buttons, Red	Bronx, NY	2/5/19
Buzzi, Ruth	Westerly, RI	7/24/36
Bynes, Amanda	Thousand Oaks, CA	4/3/86
Byrne, David	Dumbarton, Scotland	5/14/52
Byrne, Gabriel	Dublin, Ireland	5/12/50
Caan, James	Bronx, NY	3/26/40
Caballe, Montserrat	Barcelona, Spain	4/12/33
Caesar, Sid	Yonkers, NY	9/8/22
Cage, Nicolas	Long Beach, CA	1/7/64
Cain, Dean	Mt. Clemens, MI	7/31/66
Caine, Michael	London, England	3/14/33
Caldwell, Sarah	Maryville, MO	3/6/24
Caldwell, Zoe	Hawthorne, Australia	9/14/33
Cameron, James	Kapuskasing, Ontario	8/16/54
Cameron, Kirk	Panorama City, CA	10/12/70
Camp, Hamilton	London, England	10/30/34
Campanella, Joseph	New York, NY	11/21/27
Campbell, Bruce	Royal Oak, MI	6/22/58
Campbell, Glen	Delight, AR	4/22/36
Campbell, Naomi	South London, England	5/22/70
Campbell, Neve	Guelph, Ontario	10/3/73
Campion, Jane	Waikanae, New Zealand	4/30/54
Cannell, Stephen J.	Pasadena, CA	5/2/41
Cannon, Dyan	Tacoma, WA	1/4/37
Capshaw, Kate	Ft. Worth, TX	11/3/53
Cara, Irene	New York, NY	3/18/64
Cardellini, Linda	Redwood City, CA	6/25/75
Cardinale, Claudia	Tunis, Tunisia	4/15/39
Carey, Drew	Cleveland, OH	5/23/58
Carey Jr., Harry	Saugus, CA	5/16/21
Carey, Mariah	Huntington, NY	3/27/70
Cariou, Len	Winnipeg, Canada	9/30/39
Carlin, George	Bronx, New York, NY	5/12/37
Carlisle Hart, Kitty	New Orleans, LA	9/3/10
Carlton, Vanessa	Milford, PA	8/16/80
Carlyle, Robert	Glasgow, Scotland	4/14/61
Carmen, Eric	Cleveland, OH	8/11/49
Caron, Leslie	Boulogne, France	7/1/31
Carpenter, John	Carthage, NY	1/16/48
Carpenter, Mary Chapin	Princeton, NJ	2/21/58
Carr, Vikki	El Paso, TX	7/19/41
Carradine, David	Hollywood, CA	12/8/36
Carradine, Keith	San Mateo, CA	8/8/49
Carreras, Jose	Barcelona, Spain	12/5/46
Carrere, Tia	Honolulu, HI	1/2/67
Carrey, Jim	Newmarket, Ontario	1/17/62
Carroll, Diahann	Bronx, NY	7/17/35
Carroll, Pat	Shreveport, LA	5/5/27
Carson, Lisa Nicole	Brooklyn, NY	7/12/69
Carter, Dixie	McLemoresville, TN	5/25/39
Carter, Jack	Brooklyn, New York, NY	6/24/23
Carter, Lynda	Phoenix, AZ	7/24/51
Carter, Nick	Jamestown, NY	1/28/80
Carter, Ron	Ferndale, MI	5/4/37
Cartwright, Nancy	Kettering, OH	10/25/59
Caruso, David	Forest Hills, Queens, NY	1/17/56
Carvey, Dana	Missoula, MT	6/2/55
Case, Sharon	Detroit, MI	2/9/71
Cash, Rosanne	Memphis, TN	5/24/55
Cassidy, David	New York, NY	4/12/50
Castellaneta, Dan	Chicago, IL	9/10/58
Castle-Hughes, Keisha	Donnybrook, W. Australia, Australia	3/24/90
Cates, Phoebe	New York, NY	7/16/63
Cattrall, Kim	Liverpool, England	8/21/56
Cavanagh, Tom	Ottawa, Canada	10/26/68
Cavett, Dick	Gibbon, NE	11/19/36
Cedric the Entertainer	Jefferson City, MO	4/24/64
Chabert, Lacey	Purvis, MS	9/30/82
Chalke, Sarah	Ottawa, Ontario	8/27/76
Chamberlain, Richard	Beverly Hills, CA	3/31/34
Chan, Jackie	Hong Kong	4/7/54
Channing, Carol	Seattle, WA	1/31/21
Channing, Stockard	New York, NY	2/13/44
Chaplin, Geraldine	Santa Monica, CA	7/31/44
Chapman, Tracy	Cleveland, OH	3/30/64
Chappelle, Dave	Washington, DC	8/24/73
Charisse, Cyd	Amarillo, TX	3/8/21
Charo	Murcia, Spain	1/15/41
Chase, Chevy	New York, NY	10/8/43
Chasez, Joshua (J.C.)	Washington, DC	8/8/76
Cheadle, Don	Kansas City, MO	11/29/64
Checker, Chubby	Spring Gulley, SC	10/3/41
Cher	El Centro, CA	5/20/46
Chianese, Dominic	Bronx, NY	2/24/31
Chiba, Sonny	Fukuoka, Kyushu, Japan	1/23/39
Chiklis, Michael	Lowell, MA	8/30/63
Cho, Margaret	San Francisco	12/5/68
Chong, Rae Dawn	Vancouver, B. C, Can.	2/28/61
Chong, Thomas	Edmonton, Alberta, Can.	5/24/38
Chow Yun-Fat	Hong Kong	5/18/55
Christensen, Hayden	Vancouver, B. C. Can.	4/19/81
Christensen, Helena	Copenhagen, Denmark	12/25/68
Christie, Julie	Chukua, Assam, India	4/14/40
Christopher, William	Evanston, IL	10/20/32
Chuck D.	New York, NY	8/1/60
Church, Charlotte	Llandaff, Cardiff, Wales	2/21/86
Church, Thomas Haden	El Paso, TX	6/17/61
Clapp, Gordon	North Conway, NH	9/24/48
Clapton, Eric	Surrey, England	3/30/45
Clark, Anthony	Lynchburg, VA	4/4/64
Clark, Dick	Mt. Vernon, NY	11/30/29
Clark, Petula	Ewell, Surrey, England	11/15/32
Clark, Roy	Meherrin, VA	4/15/33
Clarkson, Kelly	Burleson, TX	4/24/82
Clarkson, Patricia	New Orleans, LA	12/29/59
Clay, Andrew Dice	Brooklyn, NY	9/29/58
Clayburgh, Jill	New York, NY	4/30/44
Cleese, John	Weston-super-Mare, Eng.	10/27/39
Cliburn, Van	Shreveport, LA	7/12/34
Clooney, George	Lexington, KY	5/6/61
Close, Glenn	Greenwich, CT	3/19/47
Coen, Ethan	St. Louis Park, MN	9/21/57
Coen, Joel	St. Louis Park, MN	11/29/54
Cohen, Leonard	Montreal, Canada	9/21/34
Cohen, Sacha Baron	London, England	10/13/71

Name	Birthplace	Birthdate
Cole, Gary	Park Ridge, IL	9/20/57
Cole, Natalie	Los Angeles, CA	2/6/50
Cole, Olivia	Memphis, TN	11/26/42
Cole, Paula	Manchester, CT	4/5/68
Coleman, Dabney	Austin, TX	1/3/32
Coleman, Gary	Zion, IL	2/8/68
Coleman, Ornette	Fort Worth, TX	3/19/30
Collette, Toni	Blacktown, Australia	11/1/72
Collins, Joan	London, England	5/23/33
Collins, Judy	Seattle, WA	5/1/39
Collins, Pauline	Exmouth, England	9/3/40
Collins, Phil	London, England	1/30/51
Collins, Stephen	Des Moines, IA	10/1/47
Colvin, Shawn	Vermillion, SD	1/10/56
Combs, Sean "Diddy"	Harlem, NY	11/4/69
Comden, Betty	Brooklyn, NY	5/3/19
Connelly, Jennifer	Catskill Mountains, NY	12/12/70
Connery, Sean	Edinburgh, Scotland	8/25/30
Connick, Harry, Jr.	New Orleans, LA	9/11/67
Connolly, Kevin	New York, NY	3/5/74
Connors, Mike	Fresno, CA	8/15/25
Conrad, Robert	Chicago, IL	3/1/35
Conroy, Frances	Monroe, GA	11/13/53
Constantine, Michael	Reading, PA	5/22/27
Conti, Tom	Paisley, Scotland	11/22/41
Conway, Tim	Willoughby, OH	12/15/33
Cook, Barbara	Atlanta, GA	10/25/27
Coolidge, Rita	Nashville, TN	5/1/45
Coolio	Los Angeles, CA	8/1/63
Cooper, Alice	Detroit, MI	2/4/48
Cooper, Jackie	Los Angeles, CA	9/15/21
Copperfield, David	Metuchen, NJ	9/16/56
Coppola, Francis Ford	Detroit, MI	4/7/39
Coppola, Sofia	New York, NY	5/12/71
Corbett, John	Wheeling, WV	5/9/61
Corbin, Barry	Lamesa, TX	10/16/40
Cord, Alex	Floral Park, NY	5/3/33
Corea, Chick	Chelsea, MA	6/12/41
Corgan, Billy	Elk Grove, IL	3/17/67
Corley, Pat	Dallas, TX	6/1/30
Cornell, Chris	Seattle, WA	7/20/64
Corwin, Jeff	Halifax, Nova Scotia	7/11/67
Cosby, Bill	Philadelphia, PA	7/12/37
Costas, Bob	Queens, New York, NY	3/22/52
Costello, Elvis	London, England	8/25/54
Costner, Kevin	Compton, CA	1/18/55
Courtenay, Tom	Hull, England	2/25/37
Cowell, Simon	London, England	10/7/59
Cox, Brian	Dundee, Scotland	6/1/46
Cox, Nikki	Los Angeles, CA	6/2/78
Cox, Ronny	Cloudcroft, NM	7/23/38
Cox Arquette, Courteney	Birmingham, AL	6/15/64
Coyote, Peter	New York, NY	10/10/42
Cranston, Bryan	San Fernando Valley, CA	3/7/56
Crawford, Cindy	DeKalb, IL	2/20/66
Crawford, Michael	Salisbury, England	1/19/42
Crespin, Regine	Marseilles, France	2/23/26
Crosby, David	Los Angeles, CA	8/14/41
Cross, Ben	London, England	12/16/47
Cross, Marcia	Marlborough, MA	3/25/62
Crouse, Lindsay	New York, NY	5/12/48
Crow, Sheryl	Kennett, MO	2/11/62
Crowe, Cameron	Palm Springs, CA	7/13/57
Crowe, Russell	Wellington, New Zealand	4/7/64
Crowell, Rodney	Houston, TX	8/17/50
Crudup, Billy	Manhasset, NY	7/8/68
Cruise, Tom	Syracuse, NY	7/3/62
Cruz, Penelope	Madrid, Spain	4/28/74
Crystal, Billy	Long Beach, NY	3/14/47
Culkin, Kieran	New York, NY	9/30/82
Culkin, Macaulay	New York, NY	8/26/80
Culkin, Rory	New York, NY	7/21/89
Cullum, John	Knoxville, TN	3/2/30
Culp, Robert	Oakland, CA	8/16/30
Cummings, Constance	Seattle, WA	5/15/10
Curry, Tim	Cheshire, England	4/19/46
Curtin, Jane	Cambridge, MA	9/6/47
Curtis, Jamie Lee	Los Angeles, CA	11/22/58
Curtis, Tony	New York, NY	6/3/25
Cusack, Joan	New York, NY	10/11/62
Cusack, John	Evanston, IL	6/28/66
Cyrus, Billy Ray	Flatwoods, KY	8/25/61
Dafoe, Willem	Appleton, WI	7/22/55
Dahl, Arlene	Minneapolis, MN	8/11/28
Dale, Jim	Rothwell, England	8/15/35
Dalton, Abby	Las Vegas, NV	8/15/32
Dalton, Timothy	Colwyn Bay, Wales	3/21/46
Daltrey, Roger	London, England	3/1/44
Daly, Carson	Santa Monica, CA	6/22/73

Name	Birthplace	Birthdate
Daly, Timothy	New York, NY	3/1/56
Daly, Tyne	Madison, WI	2/21/46
Damon, Matt	Cambridge, MA	10/8/70
Damone, Vic	Brooklyn, NY	6/12/28
Danes, Claire	New York, NY	4/12/79
D'Angelo	Richmond, VA	2/11/74
D'Angelo, Beverly	Columbus, OH	11/15/54
Daniels, Anthony	Salisbury, England	2/21/46
Daniels, Charlie	Wilmington, NC	10/28/36
Daniels, Jeff	Athens, GA	2/19/55
Daniels, William	Brooklyn, NY	3/31/27
Danner, Blythe	Rosemont, PA	2/3/43
Danson, Ted	San Diego, CA	12/29/47
Danza, Tony	Brooklyn, New York, NY	4/21/51
Darby, Kim	Hollywood, CA	7/8/48
David, Larry	Brooklyn, NY	7/2/47
Davidson, John	Pittsburgh, PA	12/13/41
Davis, Ann B.	Schenectady, NY	5/5/26
Davis, Clifton	Chicago, IL	10/4/45
Davis, Geena	Wareham, MA	1/21/56
Davis, Hope	Englewood, NJ	3/23/64
Davis, Judy	Perth, Australia	4/23/55
Davis, Kristin	Boulder, CO	2/24/65
Davis, Mac	Lubbock, TX	1/21/42
Dawber, Pam	Farmington Hills, MI	10/18/51
Dawson, Richard	Gosport, Hampshire, Eng.	11/20/32
Dawson, Rosario	Bronx, New York, NY	5/9/79
Day, Doris	Cincinnati, OH	4/3/24
Day, Laraine	Roosevelt, UT	10/13/17
Day-Lewis, Daniel	London, England	4/29/57
Dean, Jimmy	Plainview, TX	8/10/28
Dearie, Blossom	E. Durham, NY	4/28/26
DeCarlo, Yvonne	Vancouver, BC	9/1/22
Dee, Ruby	Cleveland, OH	10/27/24
DeFranco, Buddy	Camden, NJ	2/17/23
DeGeneres, Ellen	Metairie, LA	1/26/58
DeHaven, Gloria	Los Angeles, CA	7/23/25
De Havilland, Olivia	Tokyo, Japan	7/1/16
Delaney, Kim	Philadelphia, PA	11/29/61
Delany, Dana	New York, NY	3/13/56
De la Rocha, Zack	Long Beach, CA	1/12/70
DeLaurentiis, Dino	Torre Annunziata, Italy	8/8/19
Delon, Alain	Sceaux, France	11/8/35
Del Toro, Benicio	Santurce, Puerto Rico	2/19/67
DeLuise, Dom	Brooklyn, NY	8/1/33
Demme, Jonathan	Baldwin, NY	2/22/44
De Mornay, Rebecca	Santa Rosa, CA	8/29/62
Dench, Judi	York, England	12/9/34
Deneuve, Catherine	Paris, France	10/22/43
De Niro, Robert	New York, NY	8/17/43
Dennehy, Brian	Bridgeport, CT	7/9/38
Denver, Bob	New Rochelle, NY	1/9/35
DePalma, Brian	Newark, NJ	9/11/40
Depardieu, Gerard	Chateauroux, France	12/27/48
Depp, Johnny	Owensboro, KY	6/9/63
Derek, Bo	Long Beach, CA	11/20/56
De Rossi, Portia	Melbourne, Victoria, Aust.	1/31/73
Dern, Bruce	Winnetka, IL	6/4/36
Dern, Laura	Santa Monica, CA	2/10/67
Devane, William	Albany, NY	9/5/39
DeVito, Danny	Neptune, NJ	11/17/44
DeWitt, Joyce	Wheeling, WV	4/23/49
Dey, Susan	Pekin, IL	12/10/52
Diamond, Neil	Brooklyn, NY	1/24/41
Diaz, Cameron	San Diego, CA	8/30/72
DiCaprio, Leonardo	Hollywood, CA	11/11/74
Dick, Andy	Charleston, SC	12/21/65
Dickinson, Angie	Kulm, ND	9/30/31
Diddley, Bo	McComb, MS	12/30/28
Diesel, Vin	New York, NY	7/18/67
Diggs, Taye	Essex Co., NJ	1/2/72
Diller, Phyllis	Lima, OH	7/17/17
Dillman, Bradford	San Francisco, CA	4/14/30
Dillon, Kevin	Mamaroneck, NY	8/16/65
Dillon, Matt	New Rochelle, NY	2/18/64
Dinklage, Peter	Mendham, NJ	6/11/69
Dion, Celine	Charlemagne, Quebec	3/30/68
Djalili, Omad	London, England	1965
Dobson, Kevin	Queens, New York, NY	3/18/43
Dogg, Snoop	Long Beach, CA	10/20/71
Doherty, Shannen	Memphis, TN	4/12/71
Dolenz, Mickey	Los Angeles, CA	3/8/45
Domingo, Placido	Madrid, Spain	1/21/41
Domino, Fats	New Orleans, LA	2/26/28
Donahue, Phil	Cleveland, OH	12/21/35
D'Onofrio, Vincent	Brooklyn, NY	6/30/59
Donovan (Leitch)	Glasgow, Scotland	5/10/46
Donovan, Tate	Tenafly, NJ	9/25/63
Dorn, Michael	Luling, TX	12/9/52

Name	Birthplace	Birthdate
Dorough, Howie	Orlando, FL	8/22/73
Dotrice, Roy	Guernsey, England	5/26/23
Douglas, Kirk	Amsterdam, NY	12/9/16
Douglas, Michael	New Brunswick, NJ	9/25/44
Dourdan, Gary	Philadelphia, PA	12/11/66
Dow, Tony	Hollywood, CA	4/13/45
Down, Lesley-Ann	London, England	3/17/54
Downey, Robert, Jr.	New York, NY	4/4/65
Downey, Roma	Derry, Northern Ireland	5/6/60
Downs, Hugh	Akron, OH	2/14/21
Drescher, Fran	Flushing, Queens, NY	9/30/57
Dreyfuss, Richard	Brooklyn, NY	10/29/47
Driver, Minnie	London, England	1/31/70
Dryer, Fred	Hawthorne, CA	7/6/46
Duchovny, David	New York, NY	8/7/60
Duff, Haylie	Houston, TX	2/19/85
Duff, Hilary	Houston, TX	9/28/87
Duffy, Julia	Minneapolis, MN	6/27/51
Duffy, Patrick	Townsend, MT	3/17/49
Duhamel, Josh	Minot, ND	11/14/72
Dukakis, Olympia	Lowell, MA	6/20/31
Duke, Patty	Elmhurst, NY	12/14/46
Dullea, Keir	Cleveland, OH	5/30/36
Dunaway, Faye	Bascom, FL	1/14/41
Duncan, Lindsay	Edinburgh, Scotland	11/7/50
Duncan, Sandy	Henderson, TX	2/20/46
Dunham, Katherine	Glen Ellyn, IL	6/22/10
Dunne, Griffin	New York, NY	6/8/55
Dunst, Kirsten	Point Pleasant, NJ	4/30/82
Durbin, Deanna	Winnipeg, Manitoba	12/4/21
Durning, Charles	Highland Falls, NY	2/28/23
Dussault, Nancy	Pensacola, FL	6/30/36
Dutton, Charles S.	Baltimore, MD	1/30/51
Duvall, Robert	San Diego, CA	1/5/31
Duvall, Shelley	Houston, TX	7/7/49
Dylan, Bob	Duluth, MN	5/24/41
Dylan, Jakob	New York, NY	12/9/69
Dysart, Richard	Brighton, MA	3/30/29
Dzundza, George	Rosenheim, Germany	7/19/45
Eads, George	Fort Worth, TX	3/1/67
Easton, Sheena	Bellshill, Scotland	4/27/59
Eastwood, Clint	San Francisco, CA	5/31/30
Ebert, Roger	Urbana, IL	6/18/42
Eden, Barbara	Tucson, AZ	8/23/34
Edwards, Anthony	Santa Barbara, CA	7/19/62
Edwards, Blake	Tulsa, OK	7/26/22
Edwards, Ralph	Merino, CO	6/13/13
Ehle, Jennifer	Winston-Salem, NC	12/29/69
Eichhorn, Lisa	Reading, PA	2/4/52
Eikenberry, Jill	New Haven, CT	1/21/47
Ekberg, Anita	Malmo, Sweden	9/29/31
Ekland, Britt	Stockholm, Sweden	10/6/42
Electra, Carmen	Cincinnati, OH	4/20/72
Elfman, Jenna	Los Angeles, CA	9/30/71
Elizabeth, Shannon	Houston, TX	9/7/73
Elizondo, Hector	New York, NY	12/22/36
Elliott, Bob	Boston, MA	3/26/23
Elliott, Chris	New York, NY	5/31/60
Elliott, Sam	Sacramento, CA	8/9/44
Elvira	Manhattan, KS	9/17/51
Eminem	St. Joseph, MO	10/17/72
Enberg, Dick	Mt. Clemens, MI	1/9/35
Englund, Robert	Glendale, CA	6/6/49
Enya	Gweedore, Ireland	5/17/61
Ephron, Nora	New York, NY	5/19/41
Ermey, R. Lee	Emporia, KS	3/24/44
Estefan, Gloria	Havana, Cuba	9/1/57
Estevez, Emilio	New York, NY	5/12/62
Estrada, Erik	New York, NY	3/16/49
Etheridge, Melissa	Leavenworth, KS	5/29/61
Evans, Linda	Hartford, CT	11/18/42
Evans, Robert	New York, NY	6/29/30
Everett, Chad	South Bend, IN	6/11/36
Everett, Rupert	Norfolk, England	5/29/59
Everly, Don	Brownie, KY	2/1/37
Everly, Phil	Chicago, IL	1/19/39
Evigan, Greg	South Amboy, NJ	10/14/53
Fabares, Shelley	Santa Monica, CA	1/19/44
Fabian (Forte)	Philadelphia, PA	2/6/43
Fabio	Milan, Italy	3/15/61
Fabray, Nanette	San Diego, CA	10/27/20
Fairchild, Morgan	Dallas, TX	2/3/50
Faison, Donald	New York, NY	6/22/74
Falana, Lola	Philadelphia, PA	9/11/43
Falco, Edie	Brooklyn, NY	7/5/63
Falk, Peter	New York, NY	9/16/27
Fallon, Jimmy	Brooklyn, NY	9/19/74
Farentino, James	Brooklyn, NY	2/24/38
Fargo, Donna	Mt. Airy, NC	11/10/49
Farina, Dennis	Chicago, IL	2/29/44
Farr, Jamie	Toledo, OH	7/1/34
Farrell, Colin	Dublin, Ireland	5/31/76
Farrell, Mike	St. Paul, MN	2/6/39
Farrell, Perry	Queens, NY	3/29/59
Farrelly, Bob	Cumberland, RI	6/17/58
Farrelly, Peter	Phoenixville, PA	12/17/56
Farrow, Mia	Los Angeles, CA	2/9/45
Fatone, Joey	Brooklyn, New York, NY	1/28/77
Faustino, David	Los Angeles, CA	3/3/74
Fawcett, Farrah	Corpus Christi, TX	2/2/47
Feinstein, Michael	Columbus, OH	9/7/56
Feldon, Barbara	Pittsburgh, PA	3/12/41
Feldshuh, Tovah	New York, NY	12/27/52
Feliciano, Jose	Lares, Puerto Rico	9/10/45
Fenn, Sherilyn	Detroit, MI	2/1/65
Ferrara, Jerry	Brooklyn, NY	11/29/79
Ferrell, Conchata	Charleston, WV	3/28/43
Ferrell, Will	Irvine, CA	7/16/67
Ferrer, Mel	Elberon, NJ	8/25/17
Feuerstein, Mark	New York, NY	6/8/71
Fey, Tina	Upper Darby, PA	5/18/70
Field, Sally	Pasadena, CA	11/6/46
Fiennes, Joseph	Salisbury, England	5/27/70
Fiennes, Ralph	Suffolk, England	12/22/62
Fierstein, Harvey	Brooklyn, NY	6/6/54
50 Cent	Queens, NY	7/6/76
Filicia, Thom	Syracuse, NY	5/17/69
Fincher, David	Denver, CO	5/10/62
Finney, Albert	Salford, England	5/9/36
Fiorentino, Linda	Philadelphia, PA	3/9/60
Firth, Colin	Grayshott, England	9/10/60
Firth, Peter	Bradford, Yorkshire, Eng.	10/27/53
Fischer-Dieskau, Dietrich	Berlin, Germany	5/28/25
Fishburne, Laurence	Augusta, GA	7/30/61
Fisher, Carrie	Beverly Hills, CA	10/21/56
Fisher, Eddie	Philadelphia, PA	8/10/28
Flack, Roberta	Black Mountain, NC	2/10/39
Flanagan, Fionnula	Dublin, Ireland	12/10/41
Flavor Flav	New York, NY	3/16/59
Fleetwood, Mick	Redruth, Cornwall, Eng.	6/24/42
Fleming, Rhonda	Hollywood, CA	8/10/23
Fletcher, Louise	Birmingham, AL	7/22/34
Flockhart, Calista	Freeport, IL	11/11/64
Florek, Dann	Flat Rock, MI	5/1/50
Foch, Nina	Leyden, Netherlands	4/20/24
Fogelberg, Dan	Peoria, IL	8/13/51
Fogerty, John	Berkeley, CA	5/28/45
Foley, Dave	Etobicoke, Ontario	1/4/63
Fonda, Bridget	Los Angeles, CA	1/27/64
Fonda, Jane	New York, NY	12/21/37
Fonda, Peter	New York, NY	2/23/40
Fontaine, Joan	Tokyo, Japan	10/22/17
Ford, Faith	Alexandria, LA	9/14/64
Ford, Glenn	Sainte-Christine, Quebec	5/1/16
Ford, Harrison	Des Plaines, IL	7/13/42
Forman, Milos	Caslav, Czechoslovakia	2/18/32
Forsythe, John	Penns Grove, NJ	1/29/18
Foster, Jodie	Los Angeles, CA	11/19/62
Fox, James	London, England	5/19/39
Fox, Jorja	New York, NY	7/7/68
Fox, Matthew	Crowheart, WY	7/14/66
Fox, Michael J.	Edmonton, Alberta	6/9/61
Fox, Vivica A.	Indianapolis, IN	7/30/64
Foxworth, Robert	Houston, TX	11/1/41
Foxworthy, Jeff	Atlanta, GA	9/6/58
Foxx, Jamie	Terrell, TX	12/13/67
Frampton, Peter	Kent, England	4/22/50
Franciosa, Anthony	East Harlem, NY, NY	10/25/28
Francis, Anne	Ossining, NY	9/16/30
Francis, Connie	Newark, NJ	12/12/38
Franco, James	Palo Alto, CA	4/19/78
Franken, Al	New York, NY	5/21/51
Franklin, Aretha	Memphis, TN	3/25/42
Franklin, Bonnie	Santa Monica, CA	1/6/44
Franz, Dennis	Maywood, IL	10/28/44
Fraser, Brendan	Indianapolis, IN	12/3/68
Freeman, Al, Jr.	San Antonio, TX	3/21/34
Freeman, Mona	Baltimore, MD	6/9/26
Freeman, Morgan	Memphis, TN	6/1/37
French, Dawn	Holyhead, Wales	10/11/57
Fricker, Brenda	Dublin, Ireland	2/17/45
Friedkin, William	Chicago, IL	8/29/39
Frost, David	Tenterden, England	4/7/39
Fry, Stephen	London, England	8/24/57
Fuentes, Daisy	Havana, Cuba	11/17/66
Fuller, Robert	Troy, NY	7/29/34
Funicello, Annette	Utica, NY	10/22/42
Furlong, Edward	Pasadena, CA	8/2/77

Name	Birthplace	Birthdate
Furtado, Nelly	Victoria, British Columbia	12/2/78
Gabor, Zsa Zsa	Budapest, Hungary	2/6/17
Gabriel, John	Niagara Falls, NY	5/25/31
Gabriel, Peter	Surrey, England	2/13/50
Gallagher, Peter	Armonk, NY	8/19/55
Gallo, Vincent	Buffalo, NY	4/11/62
Galway, James	Belfast, N. Ireland	12/8/39
Gandolfini, James	Westwood, NJ	9/18/61
Garagiola, Joe	St. Louis, MO	2/12/26
Garber, Victor	London, Ont.	3/16/49
Garcia, Andy	Havana, Cuba	4/12/56
Garfunkel, Art	Queens, New York, NY	11/5/41
Garland, Beverly	Santa Cruz, CA	10/17/26
Garner, James	Norman, OK	4/7/28
Garner, Jennifer	Houston, TX	4/17/72
Garofalo, Janeane	Newton, NJ	9/28/64
Garr, Teri	Lakewood, OH	12/11/49
Garrett, Betty	St. Joseph, MO	5/23/19
Garrett, Brad	Woodland Hills, CA	4/14/60
Garth, Jennie	Urbana, IL	4/3/72
Gatlin, Larry	Seminole, TX	5/2/48
Gavin, John	Los Angeles, CA	4/8/31
Gayle, Crystal	Paintsville, KY	1/9/51
Gaynor, Mitzi	Chicago, IL	9/4/31
Gazzara, Ben	New York, NY	8/28/30
Geary, Anthony	Coalville, UT	5/29/47
Geary, Cynthia	Jackson, MS	3/21/65
Gedda, Nicolai	Stockholm, Sweden	7/11/25
Gellar, Sarah Michelle	New York, NY	4/14/77
Gere, Richard	Philadelphia, PA	8/31/49
Gervais, Ricky	Reading, England	6/25/61
Getty, Estelle	New York, NY	7/25/23
Ghostley, Alice	Eve, MO	8/14/26
Giannini, Giancarlo	La Spezia, Italy	8/1/42
Gibb, Barry	Isle of Man, England	9/1/46
Gibb, Robin	Isle of Man, England	12/22/49
Gibbons, Leeza	Irmo, SC	3/26/57
Gibbs, Marla	Chicago, IL	6/14/31
Gibson, Deborah	Brooklyn, New York, NY	8/31/70
Gibson, Henry	Germantown, PA	9/21/35
Gibson, Mel	Peekskill, NY	1/3/56
Gibson, Thomas	Charleston, SC	7/3/62
Gifford, Frank	Santa Monica, CA	8/16/30
Gifford, Kathie Lee	Neuilly-sur-Seine, France	8/16/53
Gilbert, Sara	Santa Monica, CA	1/29/75
Gilbert, Melissa	Los Angeles, CA	5/8/64
Gilberto, Astrud	Salvador, Brazil	3/30/40
Gill, Vince	Norman, OK	4/12/57
Gillette, Anita	Baltimore, MD	8/16/36
Gilley, Mickey	Natchez, MS	3/9/36
Gilliam, Terry	Minneapolis, MN	11/22/40
Gilmour, David	Cambridge, England	3/6/44
Gilpin, Peri	Waco, TX	5/27/61
Ginty, Robert	New York, NY	11/14/48
Givens, Robin	New York, NY	11/27/64
Glaser, Paul Michael	Cambridge, MA	3/25/43
Gleeson, Brendan	Belfast, N. Ireland	11/9/55
Glenn, Scott	Pittsburgh, PA	1/26/42
Gless, Sharon	Los Angeles, CA	5/31/43
Glover, Crispin	New York, NY	9/20/64
Glover, Danny	San Francisco, CA	7/22/47
Glover, Julian	London, England	3/27/35
Glover, Savion	Newark, NJ	11/19/73
Godard, Jean Luc	Paris, France	12/3/30
Goldberg, Whoopi	New York, NY	11/13/55
Goldblum, Jeff	Pittsburgh, PA	10/22/52
Goldthwait, Bobcat	Syracuse, NY	5/26/62
Goldwyn, Tony	Los Angeles, CA	5/20/60
Gooding, Cuba, Jr.	Bronx, NY	1/2/68
Goodman, John	Affton, MO	6/20/52
Gordon-Levitt, Joseph	Los Angeles, CA	2/17/81
Gorme, Eydie	Bronx, NY	8/16/32
Gosselaar, Mark-Paul	Panorama City, CA	3/1/74
Gossett, Louis, Jr.	Brooklyn, NY	5/27/36
Gould, Elliott	Brooklyn, NY	8/29/38
Gould, Harold	Schenectady, NY	12/10/23
Goulet, Robert	Lawrence, MA	11/26/33
Gowdy, Curt	Green River, WY	7/31/19
Grace, Topher	New York, NY	7/19/78
Graham, Heather	Milwaukee, WI	1/29/70
Grammer, Kelsey	St. Thomas, Virgin Isl.	2/21/55
Granger, Farley	San Jose, CA	7/1/25
Grant, Amy	Augusta, GA	11/25/60
Grant, Hugh	London, England	9/9/60
Grant, Lee	New York, NY	10/31/27
Graves, Peter	Minneapolis, MN	3/18/26
Gray, Linda	Santa Monica, CA	9/12/40
Gray, Macy	Canton, OH	9/9/70
Grayson, Kathryn	Winston-Salem, NC	2/9/22

Name	Birthplace	Birthdate
Green, Al	Forrest City, AR	4/13/46
Green, Seth	Overbrook Park, PA	2/8/74
Green, Tom	Pembroke, Ontario	7/30/71
Greene, Shecky	Chicago, IL	4/8/26
Greenwood, Bruce	Noranda, Quebec	8/12/56
Gregory, Cynthia	Los Angeles, CA	7/8/46
Gregory, Dick	St. Louis, MO	10/12/32
Grenier, Adrian	Brooklyn, NY	7/10/76
Grey, Jennifer	New York, NY	3/26/60
Grey, Joel	Cleveland, OH	4/11/32
Grier, David Alan	Detroit, MI	6/30/55
Grier, Pam	Winston-Salem, NC	5/26/49
Gries, Jon	Glendale, CA	6/17/57
Griffin, Merv	San Mateo, CA	7/6/25
Griffith, Andy	Mount Airy, NC	6/1/26
Griffith, Melanie	New York, NY	8/9/57
Griffiths, Rachel	New Castle, Australia	2/20/68
Grimes, Tammy	Lynn, MA	1/30/34
Grint, Rupert	Hertfordshire, England	8/24/88
Grizzard, George	Roanoke Rapids, NC	4/1/28
Groban, Josh	Los Angeles, CA	2/27/81
Grodin, Charles	Pittsburgh, PA	4/21/35
Grohl, David	Warren, OH	1/14/69
Grosbard, Ulu	Antwerp, Belgium	1/9/29
Gross, Michael	Chicago, IL	6/21/47
Guest, Christopher	New York, NY	2/5/48
Guillaume, Robert	St. Louis, MO	11/30/37
Gumbel, Greg	New Orleans, LA	5/3/46
Guthrie, Arlo	Brooklyn, New York, NY	7/10/47
Guttenberg, Steve	Brooklyn, New York, NY	8/24/58
Guy, Buddy	Lettsworth, LA	7/30/36
Guy, Jasmine	Boston, MA	3/10/64
Gyllenhaal, Jake	Los Angeles, CA	12/19/80
Hackman, Gene	San Bernardino, CA	1/30/30
Hagerty, Julie	Cincinnati, OH	6/15/55
Haggard, Merle	Bakersfield, CA	4/6/37
Hagman, Larry	Fort Worth, TX	9/21/31
Haid, Charles	San Francisco, CA	6/2/43
Haines, Connie	Savannah, GA	1/20/22
Hale, Barbara	DeKalb, IL	4/18/22
Hall, Anthony Michael	West Roxbury, MA	4/14/68
Hall, Arsenio	Cleveland, OH	2/12/55
Hall, Daryl	Pottstown, PA	10/11/49
Hall, Deidre	Milwaukee, WI	10/31/47
Hall, Michael C.	Raleigh, NC	2/1/71
Hall, Monty	Winnipeg, Manitoba	8/25/21
Hall, Tom T.	Olive Hill, KY	5/25/36
Halliwell, Geri	Watford, England	8/6/72
Hamill, Mark	Oakland, CA	9/25/51
Hamilton, George	Memphis, TN	8/12/39
Hamilton, Linda	Salisbury, MD	9/26/56
Hamlin, Harry	Pasadena, CA	10/30/51
Hammer	Oakland, CA	3/29/63
Hammond, Darrell	Melbourne, FL	10/8/60
Hampshire, Susan	London, England	5/12/37
Hancock, Herbie	Chicago, IL	4/12/40
Hanks, Tom	Concord, CA	7/9/56
Hannah, Daryl	Chicago, IL	12/3/60
Hannigan, Alyson	Washington, DC	3/24/74
Hanson, Curtis	Reno, NV	3/24/45
Hanson, Isaac	Tulsa, OK	11/17/80
Hanson, Taylor	Tulsa, OK	3/14/83
Hanson, Zac	Tulsa, OK	10/22/85
Harden, Marcia Gay	La Jolla, CA	8/14/59
Hardison, Kadeem	New York, NY	7/24/66
Harewood, Dorian	Dayton, OH	8/6/50
Harmon, Angie	Highland Park, TX	8/10/72
Harmon, Mark	Burbank, CA	9/2/51
Harper, Ben	Claremont, CA	10/28/69
Harper, Jessica	Chicago, IL	10/10/49
Harper, Tess	Mammoth Springs, AR	8/15/50
Harper, Valerie	Suffern, NY	8/22/40
Harrelson, Woody	Midland, TX	7/23/61
Harrington, Pat	New York, NY	8/13/29
Harris, Barbara	Evanston, IL	7/25/35
Harris, Ed	Tenafly, NJ	11/28/50
Harris, Emmylou	Birmingham, AL	4/2/47
Harris, Julie	Grosse Pte. Park, MI	12/2/25
Harris, Neil Patrick	Albuquerque, NM	6/15/73
Harris, Rosemary	Ashby, England	9/19/30
Harris, Steve	Chicago, IL	12/3/65
Harrison, Gregory	Avalon, CA	5/31/50
Harry, Deborah	Miami, FL	7/1/45
Hart, Mary	Madison, SD	11/8/50
Hart, Melissa Joan	Sayville, NY	4/18/76
Hartley, Hal	Lindenhurst, NY	11/3/59
Hartley, Mariette	New York, NY	6/21/40
Hartman, David	Pawtucket, RI	5/19/35
Hartman Black, Lisa	Houston, TX	6/1/56

Name	Birthplace	Birthdate
Hartnett, Josh	San Francisco, CA	7/21/78
Harvey, P.J.	Yeovil, Somerset, England	10/9/69
Harvey, Steve	Welch, WV	11/23/56
Hasselhoff, David	Baltimore, MD	7/17/52
Hatcher, Teri	Sunnyvale, CA	12/8/64
Hatfield, Juliana	Wiscasset, ME	7/27/67
Hathaway, Anne	Brooklyn, NY	11/12/82
Hauer, Rutger	Breukelen, Netherlands	1/23/44
Havoc, June	Seattle, WA	11/8/16
Hawke, Ethan	Austin, TX	11/6/70
Hawn, Goldie	Washington, DC	11/21/45
Hayden, Melissa	Toronto, Ontario	4/25/23
Hayek, Salma	Coatzacoalcos, Mexico	9/2/66
Hayes, Isaac	Covington, TN	8/20/42
Hayes, Sean	Glen Ellyn, IL	6/26/70
Haynes, Roy	Roxbury, Boston, MA	3/13/26
Hays, Robert	Bethesda, MD	7/24/47
Head, Anthony Stewart	North London, England	2/20/54
Heard, John	Washington, DC	3/7/46
Hearn, George	St. Louis, MO	6/18/34
Heaton, Patricia	Bay Village, OH	3/4/58
Heche, Anne	Aurora, OH	5/25/69
Heder, Jon	Fort Collins, CO	10/26/77
Hedren, Tippi	Lafayette, MN	1/19/31
Helfgott, David	Melbourne, Australia	5/19/47
Helgenberger, Marg	Fremont, NE	11/16/58
Helmond, Katherine	Galveston, TX	7/5/34
Hemingway, Mariel	Mill Valley, CA	11/22/61
Hemsley, Sherman	Philadelphia, PA	2/1/38
Henderson, Florence	Dale, IN	2/14/34
Henderson, Skitch	Birmingham, England	1/27/18
Henley, Don	Gilmer, TX	7/22/47
Henner, Marilu	Chicago, IL	4/6/52
Hennessy, Jill	Edmonton, Alberta	11/25/68
Henry, Buck	New York, NY	12/9/30
Herman, Pee-Wee	Peekskill, NY	8/27/52
Herrmann, Edward	Washington, DC	7/21/43
Hershey, Barbara	Hollywood, CA	2/5/48
Hesseman, Howard	Lebanon, OR	2/27/40
Heston, Charlton	Evanston, IL	10/4/24
Hetfield, James	Downey, CA	8/3/63
Hewitt, Jennifer Love	Waco, TX	2/21/79
Hicks, Catherine	Scottsdale, AZ	8/6/51
Hill, Arthur	Melfort, Sask	8/1/22
Hill, Dulé	Orange, NJ	5/3/74
Hill, Faith	Jackson, MS	9/21/67
Hill, Lauryn	South Orange, NJ	5/25/75
Hill, Steven	Seattle, WA	2/24/22
Hillerman, John	Denison, TX	12/20/32
Hilton, Paris	New York, NY	2/17/81
Hines, Cheryl	Miami Beach, FL	9/21/65
Hingle, Pat	Denver, CO	7/19/24
Hirsch, Judd	New York, NY	3/15/35
Ho, Don	Kakaako, HI.	8/13/30
Hoffman, Dustin	Los Angeles, CA	8/8/37
Hoffman, Philip Seymour	Fairport, NY	7/23/67
Hogan, Paul	Lightning Ridge, New South Wales, Australia	10/8/39
Holbrook, Hal	Cleveland, OH	2/17/25
Holder, Geoffrey	Port of Spain, Trinidad	8/1/30
Holliday, Polly	Jasper, AL	7/2/37
Holliman, Earl	Delhi, LA	9/11/28
Holly, Lauren	Bristol, PA	10/28/63
Holm, Celeste	New York, NY	4/29/19
Holm, Ian	Ilford, England	9/12/31
Holmes, Katie	Toledo, OH	12/18/78
Hooks, Jan	Decatur, GA	4/23/57
Hopkins, Anthony	Port Talbot, South Wales	12/31/37
Hopkins, Bo	Greenville, SC	2/2/42
Hopkins, Telma	Louisville, KY	10/28/48
Hopper, Dennis	Dodge City, KS	5/17/36
Horne, Lena	Brooklyn, NY	6/30/17
Horne, Marilyn	Bradford, PA	1/16/34
Hornsby, Bruce	Williamsburg, VA	11/23/54
Horsley, Lee	Muleshoe, TX	5/15/55
Horton, Robert	Los Angeles, CA	7/29/24
Hoskins, Bob	Suffolk, England	10/26/42
Hounsou, Djimon	Benin	4/24/64
Houston, Whitney	Newark, NJ	8/9/63
Howard, Ken	El Centro, CA	3/28/44
Howard, Ron	Duncan, OK	3/1/54
Howell, C. Thomas	Van Nuys, CA	12/7/66
Howes, Sally Ann	London, England	7/20/30
Hudson, Kate	Los Angeles, CA	4/19/79
Huffman, Felicity	Bedford, NY	12/6/62
Hughes, Barnard	Bedford Hills, NY	7/16/15
Hulce, Tom	Whitewater, WI	12/6/53
Humperdinck, Engelbert	Madras, India	5/2/36
Humphries, Barry	Melbourne, Australia	2/17/34
Hunt, Bonnie	Chicago, IL	9/22/64
Hunt, Helen	Culver City, CA	6/15/63
Hunt, Linda	Morristown, NJ	4/2/45
Hunter, Holly	Conyers, GA	3/20/58
Hunter, Tab	New York, NY	7/11/31
Hurley, Elizabeth	Hampshire, England	6/10/65
Hurt, John	Chesterfield, England	1/22/40
Hurt, Mary Beth	Marshalltown, IA	9/26/48
Hurt, William	Washington, DC	3/20/50
Huston, Anjelica	Santa Monica, CA	7/8/51
Hutton, Betty	Battle Creek, MI	2/26/21
Hutton, Lauren	Charleston, SC	11/17/43
Hutton, Timothy	Malibu, CA	8/16/60
Hyman, Earle	Rocky Mount, NC	10/11/26
Ian, Janis	New York, NY	4/7/51
Ice Cube	Los Angeles, CA	6/15/69
Ice-T	Newark, NJ	2/16/58
Idle, Eric	S. Shields, England	3/29/43
Idol, Billy	Middlesex, England	11/30/55
Iglesias, Enrique	Madrid, Spain	5/8/75
Iglesias, Julio	Madrid, Spain	9/23/43
Iler, Robert	New York, NY	3/2/85
Iman	Mogadishu, Somalia	7/25/55
Imbruglia, Natalie	Sydney, Australia	2/4/75
Imperioli, Michael	Mount Vernon, NY	1/1/66
Imus, Don	Riverside, CA	7/23/40
Ingram, James	Akron, OH	2/16/56
Innes, Laura	Pontiac, MI	8/16/59
Ireland, Kathy	Glendale, CA	3/20/63
Irons, Jeremy	Isle of Wight, England	9/19/48
Irving, Amy	Palo Alto, CA	9/10/53
Irving, George S.	Springfield, MA	11/1/22
Irwin, Bill	Santa Monica, CA	4/11/50
Irwin, Steve	Beerwah, Queensl., Aust.	2/22/62
Ivey, Judith	El Paso, TX	9/4/51
Ivory, James	Berkeley, CA	6/7/28
Jackee (Harry)	Winston-Salem, NC	8/14/56
Jackman, Hugh	Sydney, Australia	10/12/68
Jackson, Anne	Allegheny, PA	9/3/26
Jackson, Glenda	Birkenhead, England	5/9/36
Jackson, Janet	Gary, IN	5/16/66
Jackson, Jermaine	Gary, IN	12/11/54
Jackson, Jonathan	Orlando, FL	5/11/82
Jackson, Joshua	Vancouver, Brit. Columbia	6/11/78
Jackson, Kate	Birmingham, AL	10/29/48
Jackson, La Toya	Gary, IN	5/29/56
Jackson, Michael	Gary, IN	8/29/58
Jackson, Peter	Wellington, New Zealand	10/31/61
Jackson, Samuel L.	Chattanooga, TN	12/21/48
Jacobi, Derek	London, England	10/22/38
Jagger, Mick	Dartford, England	7/26/43
James, Etta	Los Angeles, CA	1/25/38
James, Kevin	Mineola, NY	4/26/65
Janis, Conrad	New York, NY	2/11/28
Janney, Allison	Boston, MA	11/19/60
Janssen, Famke	Amsterdam, Netherlands	11/5/65
Jardine, Al	Lima, OH	9/3/42
Jarmusch, Jim	Akron, OH	1/22/53
Jarreau, Al	Milwaukee, WI	3/12/40
Jarrette, Keith	Allentown, PA	5/8/45
Jay Z	Brooklyn, NY	12/4/69
Jeffreys, Anne	Goldsboro, NC	1/26/23
Jett, Joan	Philadelphia, PA	9/22/60
Jewel (Kilcher)	Payson, UT	5/23/74
Jewison, Norman	Toronto, Ontario	7/21/26
Jillian, Ann	Cambridge, MA	1/29/50
Jillette, Penn	Greenfield, MA	3/5/55
Joel, Billy	Bronx, NY	5/9/49
Johansson, Scarlett	New York, NY	11/22/84
John, Elton	Pinner, Middlesex, Eng.	3/25/47
Johns, Glynis	Durban, S Africa	10/5/23
Johnson, Arte	Benton Harbor, MI	1/20/34
Johnson, Beverly	Buffalo, NY	10/13/52
Johnson, Don	Flatt Creek, MO	12/15/49
Johnson, Van	Newport, RI	8/25/16
Johnston, Bruce	Chicago, IL	6/24/44
Johnston, Kristen	Washington, DC	9/20/67
Jolie, Angelina	Los Angeles, CA	6/4/75
Jones, Charlie	Ft. Smith, AR	11/9/30
Jones, Cherry	Paris, TN	11/21/56
Jones, Davy	Manchester, England	12/30/45
Jones, Dean	Morgan City, AL	1/25/31
Jones, Elvin	Pontiac, MI	9/9/27
Jones, Gemma	London, England	12/4/42
Jones, George	Saratoga, TX	9/12/31
Jones, Grace	Spanishtown, Jamaica	5/19/52
Jones, Jack	Hollywood, CA	1/14/38
Jones, James Earl	Arkabutla, MS	1/17/31
Jones, Jennifer	Tulsa, OK	3/2/19

Name	Birthplace	Birthdate
Jones, Mick	London, England	6/26/55
Jones, Norah	New York, NY	3/30/79
Jones, Quincy	Chicago, IL	3/14/33
Jones, Shirley	Smithton, PA	3/31/34
Jones, Star	Badin, NC	3/24/62
Jones, Tom	Pontypridd, Wales	6/7/40
Jones, Tommy Lee	San Saba, TX	9/15/46
Jonze, Spike	Rockville, MD	10/22/69
Jourdan, Louis	Marseilles, France	6/19/19
Jovovich, Milla	Kiev, Ukraine	12/17/75
Judd, Ashley	Granada Hills, CA	4/19/68
Judd, Naomi	Ashland, KY	1/11/46
Judd, Wynonna	Ashland, KY	5/30/64
Kaczmarek, Jane	Milwaukee, WI	12/21/55
Kanaly, Steve	Burbank, CA	3/14/46
Kane, Carol	Cleveland, OH	6/18/52
Kaplan, Gabe	Brooklyn, NY	3/31/45
Karlen, John	Brooklyn, NY	5/28/33
Karn, Richard	Seattle, WA	2/17/56
Karras, Alex	Gary, IN	7/15/35
Kasem, Casey	Detroit, MI	4/27/32
Kattan, Chris	Sherman Oaks, CA	10/19/70
Kavner, Julie	Burbank, CA	9/7/51
Kazan, Lainie	New York, NY	5/15/42
Keach, Stacy	Savannah, GA	6/2/41
Keaton, Diane	Santa Ana, CA	1/5/46
Keaton, Michael	Pittsburgh, PA	9/9/51
Keener, Catherine	Miami FL	3/23/59
Keitel, Harvey	Brooklyn, NY	5/13/39
Keith, David	Knoxville, TN	5/8/54
Keith, Penelope	Sutton, Surrey, England	4/2/40
Kellerman, Sally	Long Beach, CA	6/2/37
Kelly, Jean Louisa	Worcester, MA	3/9/72
Kelly, R(obert)	Chicago, IL	1/8/67
Kennedy, George	New York, NY	2/18/25
Kennedy, Jamie	Upper Darby, PA	5/25/70
Kennedy, Jayne	Washington, DC	10/27/51
Kenny G	Seattle, WA	6/5/56
Kent, Allegra	Santa Monica, CA	8/11/37
Kercheval, Ken	Wolcottville, IN	7/15/35
Kerns, Joanna	San Francisco, CA	2/12/53
Kerr, Deborah	Helensburgh, Scotland	9/30/21
Keys, Alicia	New York, NY	1/25/81
Khan, Chaka	Great Lakes, IL	3/23/53
Kidder, Margot	Yellowknife, N.W.T.	10/17/48
Kidman, Nicole	Honolulu, HI	6/20/67
Kiel, Richard	Detroit, MI	9/13/39
Kilborn, Craig	Kansas City, KS	8/24/62
Kilmer, Val	Los Angeles, CA	12/31/59
Kimbrough, Charles	St. Paul, MN	5/23/36
Kimmel, Jimmy	Brooklyn, NY	11/13/67
King, B. B.	Itta Bena, MS	9/16/25
King, Carole	Brooklyn, NY	2/9/42
King, Larry	Brooklyn, NY	11/19/33
King, Perry	Alliance, OH	4/30/48
Kingsley, Ben	Scarborough, England	12/31/43
Kingston, Alex	London, England	3/11/63
Kinnear, Greg	Logansport, IN	6/17/63
Kinney, Kathy	Stevens Point, WI	11/3/53
Kinski, Nastassja	Berlin, W. Germany	1/24/60
Kirby, Bruno	New York, NY	4/28/49
Kirkland, Gelsey	Bethlehem, PA	12/29/52
Kirkpatrick, Chris	Clarion, PA	10/17/71
Kitt, Eartha	North, SC	1/17/27
Klein, Robert	Bronx, New York, NY	2/8/42
Kline, Kevin	St. Louis, MO	10/24/47
Klugman, Jack	Philadelphia, PA	4/27/22
Knight, Gladys	Atlanta, GA	5/28/44
Knight, Shirley	Goessel, KS	7/5/36
Knight, Wayne	New York, NY	8/7/55
Knightley, Keira	Teddington, England	3/26/85
Knopfler, Mark	Glasgow, Scotland	8/12/49
Knotts, Don	Morgantown, WV	7/21/24
Knowles, Beyoncé	Houston, TX	9/4/81
Knoxville, Johnny	Knoxville, TN	3/11/71
Konitz, Lee	Chicago, IL	10/13/27
Kopell, Bernie	New York, NY	6/21/33
Korman, Harvey	Chicago, IL	2/15/27
Kotto, Yaphet	New York, NY	11/15/37
Krakowski, Jane	Parsippany, NJ	10/11/68
Krause, Peter	Alexandria, MN	8/12/65
Kressley, Carson	Allentown, PA	11/11/69
Kretschmann, Thomas	Dessau, E. Germany	9/8/62
Kristofferson, Kris	Brownsville, TX	6/22/36
Kudrow, Lisa	Encino, CA	7/30/63
Kunis, Mila	Kiev, Ukraine, Soviet Union	8/14/83
Kuriyama, Chiaki	Tsuchiura, Ibaraki, Japan	10/10/84
Kurtz, Swoosie	Omaha, NE	9/6/44
Kutcher, Ashton	Cedar Rapids, IA	2/7/78

Name	Birthplace	Birthdate
Kwan, Nancy	Hong Kong	5/19/39
LaBelle, Patti	Philadelphia, PA	5/24/44
LaBeouf, Shia	Los Angeles, CA	6/11/86
Ladd, Cheryl	Huron, SD	7/12/51
Ladd, Diane	Meridian, MS	11/29/32
Lagasse, Emeril	Fall River, MA	10/15/59
Lahti, Christine	Royal Oak, MI	4/4/50
Laine, Cleo	Southall, England	10/28/27
Laine, Frankie	Chicago, IL	3/30/13
Lake, Ricki	Hastings-on-Hudson, NY	9/21/68
Lamas, Lorenzo	Santa Monica, CA	1/20/58
Lambert, Christopher	Great Neck, NY	3/29/57
Landau, Martin	Brooklyn, NY	6/20/28
Landis, John	Chicago, IL	8/3/50
Lane, Diane	New York, NY	1/22/65
Lane, Nathan	Jersey City, NJ	2/3/56
lang, k.d.	Consort, Alberta	11/2/61
Lang, Stephen	Queens, New York, NY	7/11/52
Lange, Jessica	Cloquet, MN	4/20/49
Langella, Frank	Bayonne, NJ	1/1/40
Lansbury, Angela	London, England	10/16/25
LaPaglia, Anthony	Adelaide, Australia	1/31/59
Laredo, Ruth	Detroit, MI	11/20/37
Larroquette, John	New Orleans, LA	11/25/47
LaSalle, Eriq	Hartford, CT	6/23/62
Lauper, Cyndi	Brooklyn, NY	6/20/53
Laurie, Piper	Detroit, MI	1/22/32
Lavigne, Avril	Napanee, Ontario	9/27/84
Lavin, Linda	Portland, ME	10/15/37
Law, Jude	London, England	12/29/72
Lawless, Lucy	Mount Albert, New Zealand	3/29/68
Lawrence, Carol	Melrose Park, IL	9/5/34
Lawrence, Joey	Montgomery, PA	4/20/76
Lawrence, Martin	Frankfurt, Germany	4/16/65
Lawrence, Steve	Brooklyn, NY	7/8/35
Lawrence, Vicki	Inglewood, CA	3/26/49
Leach, Robin	London, England	8/29/41
Leachman, Cloris	Des Moines, IA	4/30/26
Lear, Norman	New Haven, CT	7/27/22
Learned, Michael	Washington, DC	4/9/39
Leary, Denis	Worcester, MA	8/18/57
LeBlanc, Matt	Newton, MA	7/25/67
LeBon, Simon	Bushey, England	10/27/58
Ledger, Heath	Perth, Australia	4/4/79
Lee, Ang	Pingtung, Taiwan	10/23/54
Lee, Brenda	Lithonia, GA	12/11/44
Lee, Christopher	London, England	5/27/22
Lee, Jason	Huntington Beach, CA	4/25/70
Lee, Michele	Los Angeles, CA	6/24/42
Lee, Spike	Atlanta, GA	3/20/57
Leeves, Jane	London, England	4/18/61
Legrand, Michel	Paris, France	2/24/32
Leguizamo, John	Bogotá, Colombia	7/22/64
Leibman, Ron	New York, NY	10/11/37
Leigh, Janet	Merced, CA	7/6/27
Leigh, Jennifer Jason	Hollywood, CA	2/5/62
Leighton, Laura	Iowa City, IA	7/24/68
Lennox, Annie	Aberdeen, Scotland	12/25/54
Leno, Jay	New Rochelle, NY	4/28/50
Leonard, Robert Sean	Westwood, NJ	2/28/69
Leoni, Tea	New York, NY	2/25/66
Leslie, Joan	Detroit, MI	1/26/25
Leto, Jared	Bossier City, LA	12/26/71
Letterman, David	Indianapolis, IN	4/12/47
Levine, James	Cincinnati, OH	6/23/43
Levine, Ted	Parma, OH	5/29/58
Levinson, Barry	Baltimore, MD	4/6/42
Levy, Eugene	Hamilton, Ontario	12/17/46
Lewis, Al	New York, NY	4/30/10
Lewis, Huey	New York, NY	7/5/50
Lewis, Jason	Newport Beach, CA	6/25/71
Lewis, Jerry	Newark, NJ	3/16/26
Lewis, Jerry Lee	Ferriday, LA	9/29/35
Lewis, Juliette	San Fernando Valley, CA	6/21/73
Lewis, Richard	Brooklyn, NY	6/29/47
Li, Jet	Beijing, China	4/26/63
Light, Judith	Trenton, NJ	2/9/49
Lightfoot, Gordon	Orillia, Ontario	11/17/38
Lil' Kim	Brooklyn, NY	7/11/75
Linden, Hal	Bronx, New York, NY	3/20/31
Ling, Lisa	Sacramento, CA	8/30/73
Linkletter, Art	Moose Jaw, Sask., Can	7/17/12
Linn-Baker, Mark	St. Louis, MO	6/17/54
Linney, Laura	New York, NY	2/5/64
Liotta, Ray	Newark, NJ	12/18/55
Lithgow, John	Rochester, NY	10/19/45
Little, Rich	Ottawa, Ontario	11/26/38
Little Richard	Macon, GA	12/5/32
Littrell, Brian	Lexington, KY	2/20/75

Name	Birthplace	Birthdate
Liu, Lucy	Queens, NY	12/2/68
L. L. Cool J	St. Albans, Queens, NY	1/14/68
Lloyd, Christopher	Stamford, CT	10/22/38
Lloyd, Emily	North London, England	9/29/70
Lloyd Webber, Andrew	London, England	3/22/48
Locke, Sondra	Shelbyville, TN	5/28/47
Lockhart, June	New York, NY	6/25/25
Locklear, Heather	Westwood, CA	9/25/61
Loggia, Robert	Staten Island, NY	1/3/30
Loggins, Kenny	Everett, WA	1/7/48
Logue, Donal	Ottawa, Canada	2/27/66
Lohan, Lindsay	New York, NY	7/2/86
Lollobrigida, Gina	Subiaco, Italy	7/4/27
Lom, Herbert	Prague, Czechoslovakia	1/9/17
Lonergan, Kenneth	New York, NY	10/16/62
Long, Nia	Brooklyn, NY	10/30/70
Long, Shelley	Ft. Wayne, IN	8/23/49
Longoria, Eva	Corpus Christi, TX	3/15/75
Lopez, George	Mission Hills, CA	4/23/61
Lopez, Jennifer	Bronx, NY	7/24/70
Loren, Sophia	Rome, Italy	9/20/34
Loring, Gloria	New York, NY	12/10/46
Louis-Dreyfus, Julia	New York, NY	1/13/61
Love, Courtney	San Francisco, CA	7/9/64
Love, Mike	Baldwin Hills, CA	3/15/41
Lovett, Lyle	Klein, TX	11/1/57
Lovitz, Jon	Tarzana, CA	7/21/57
Loveless, Patty	Pikeville, KY	1/4/57
Lowe, Rob	Charlottesville, VA	3/17/64
Lowell, Carey	Huntington, NY	2/11/61
Lucas, George	Modesto, CA	5/14/44
Lucci, Susan	Scarsdale, NY	12/23/46
Luckinbill, Laurence	Ft. Smith, AR	11/21/34
Ludwig, Christa	Berlin, Germany	3/16/24
Luhrmann, Baz	Sydney, Australia	9/17/62
Lumet, Sidney	Philadelphia, PA	6/25/24
LuPone, Patti	Northport, NY	4/21/49
Lynch, David	Missoula, MT	1/20/46
Lynch, Susan	Corrinshego, N. Ireland,UK	6/5/71
Lynley, Carol	New York, NY	2/13/42
Lynn, Loretta	Butcher Hollow, KY	4/14/35
Lynn, Vera	London, England	3/20/17
Lynne, Shelby	Quantico, VA	10/22/68
Lyonne, Natasha	Great Neck, NY	4/4/79
Ma, Yo-Yo	Paris, France	10/7/55
Maazel, Lorin	Neuilly-sur-Seine, France	3/6/30
Mac, Bernie	Chicago, IL	10/5/58
MacArthur, James	Los Angeles, CA	12/8/37
Macchio, Ralph	Huntington, NY	11/4/62
MacCorkindale, Simon	Ely, England	2/12/52
MacDonald, Kelly	Glasgow, Scotland	2/23/76
MacDowell, Andie	Gaffney, SC	4/21/58
MacFarlane, Seth	Kent, CT	11/26/73
MacGraw, Ali	Pound Ridge, NY	4/1/38
MacGowan, Shane	Tunbridge, Kent, England	12/25/57
MacLachlan, Kyle	Yakima, WA	2/22/59
MacLaine, Shirley	Richmond, VA	4/24/34
MacLeod, Gavin	Mt. Kisco, NY	2/28/31
MacNee, Patrick	London, England	2/6/22
MacNeil, Cornell	Minneapolis, MN	9/24/22
MacNicol, Peter	Dallas, TX	4/10/54
MacPherson, Elle	Sydney, Australia	3/29/64
Macy, Bill	Revere, MA	5/18/22
Macy, William H.	Miami, FL	3/13/50
Madden, John	Austin, MN	4/10/36
Madigan, Amy	Chicago, IL	9/11/50
Madonna (Ciccone)	Bay City, MI	8/16/58
Madsen, Michael	Chicago, IL	9/25/58
Maguire, Tobey	Santa Monica, CA	6/27/75
Maher, Bill	New York, NY	1/20/56
Mahoney, John	Manchester, England	6/20/40
Majors, Lee	Wyandotte, MI	4/23/39
Malden, Karl	Gary, IN	3/22/12
Malick, Terrence	Ottawa, IL	11/30/43
Malick, Wendie	Buffalo, NY	12/13/50
Malina, Joshua	New York, NY	1/17/66
Malkovich, John	Christopher, IL	12/9/53
Malone, Dorothy	Chicago, IL	1/30/25
Mamet, David	Chicago, IL	11/30/47
Manchester, Melissa	Bronx, NY	2/15/51
Mandel, Howie	Toronto, Ontario	11/29/55
Mandrell, Barbara	Houston, TX	12/25/48
Mangione, Chuck	Rochester, NY	11/29/40
Manheim, Camryn	Caldwell, NJ	3/8/61
Manilow, Barry	Brooklyn, NY	6/17/46
Mann, Aimee	Richmond, VA	8/9/60
Manoff, Dinah	New York, NY	1/25/58
Manson, Marilyn	Canton, OH	1/5/69
Mantegna, Joe	Chicago, IL	11/13/47
Marceau, Marcel	Strasbourg, France	3/22/23
Marcil, Vanessa	Indio, CA	10/15/69
Margulies, Julianna	Spring Valley, NY	6/8/66
Marie, Constance	Hollywood, CA	9/9/69
Marin, Cheech	Los Angeles, CA	7/13/46
Marinaro, Ed	New York, NY	3/31/50
Markova, Alicia	London, England	12/1/10
Marriner, Neville	Lincoln, England	4/15/24
Marsalis, Branford	New Orleans, LA	8/26/60
Marsalis, Wynton	New Orleans, LA	10/18/61
Marsh, Jean	London, England	7/1/34
Marshall, Garry	Bronx, New York, NY	11/13/34
Marshall, Penny	Bronx, New York, NY	10/15/42
Marshall, Peter	Huntington, WV	3/30/27
Martin, Chris	Devon, England	3/22/77
Martin, Dick	Detroit, MI	1/30/22
Martin, Jesse L.	Rocky Mount, VA	1/18/69
Martin, Kellie	Riverside, CA	10/16/75
Martin, Ricky	San Juan, Puerto Rico	12/24/71
Martin, Steve	Waco, TX	8/14/45
Martin, Tony	Oakland, CA	12/25/13
Martins, Peter	Copenhagen, Denmark	10/27/46
Mason, Jackie	Sheboygan, WI	6/9/34
Mason, Marsha	St. Louis, MO	4/3/42
Masterson, Christopher	Long Island, NY	1/22/80
Masterson, Mary Stuart	New York, NY	6/28/66
Mastrantonio, Mary Elizabeth	Lombard, IL	11/17/58
Masur, Kurt	Brieg, Germany	7/18/27
Masur, Richard	New York, NY	11/20/48
Mathers, Jerry	Sioux City, IA	6/2/48
Matheson, Tim	Glendale, CA	12/31/47
Mathis, Johnny	Gilmer, TX	9/30/35
Matlin, Marlee	Morton Grove, IL	8/24/65
Matthews, Dave	Johannesburg, S. Africa	1/9/67
May, Elaine	Philadelphia, PA	4/21/32
Mayer, John	Bridgeport, CT	10/16/77
Mazar, Debi	Queens, NY	8/15/64
Mazursky, Paul	Brooklyn, NY	4/25/30
MCA	Brooklyn, NY	11/20/65
McAdams, Rachel	London, Ontario, Canada	10/7/86
McArdle, Andrea	Abington, PA	11/5/63
McBride, Patricia	Teaneck, NJ	8/23/42
McCallum, David	Glasgow, Scotland	9/19/33
McCarthy, Andrew	Westfield, NJ	11/29/62
McCarthy, Jenny	Chicago, IL	11/1/72
McCarthy, Kevin	Seattle, WA	2/15/14
McCartney, Paul	Liverpool, England	6/18/42
McCarver, Tim	Memphis, TN	10/16/41
McClanahan, Rue	Healdton, OK	2/21/34
McConaughey, Matthew	Uvalde, Texas	11/4/69
McCoo, Marilyn	Jersey City, NJ	9/30/43
McCormack, Eric	Toronto, Canada	4/18/63
McCormack, Mary	Plainsfield, NJ	2/8/69
McCrane, Paul	Philadelphia, PA	1/19/61
McDaniel, James	Washington, DC	3/25/58
McDermott, Dylan	Waterbury, CT	10/26/61
McDiarmid, Ian	Carnoustie, Tayside, Scotland	4/17/47
McDonald, Audra	Berlin, Germany	7/3/70
McDonnell, Mary	Wilkes-Barre, PA	4/28/52
McDormand, Frances	Illinois	6/23/57
McDowell, Malcolm	Leeds, England	6/13/43
McEntire, Reba	McAlester, OK	3/28/55
McFerrin, Bobby	New York, NY	3/11/50
McGavin, Darren	Spokane, WA	5/7/22
McGillis, Kelly	Newport Beach, CA	7/9/57
McGoohan, Patrick	Astoria, Queens, NY	3/19/28
McGovern, Elizabeth	Evanston, IL	7/18/61
McGovern, Maureen	Youngstown, OH	7/27/49
McGraw, Tim	Delhi, LA	5/1/67
McGregor, Ewan	Crieff, Scotland	3/31/71
McGuire, Al	New York, NY	9/7/31
McKean, Michael	New York, NY	10/17/47
McKechnie, Donna	Pontiac, MI	11/16/42
McKellen, Ian	Burnley, England	5/25/39
McKenzie, Benjamin	Austin, TX	9/12/78
McLachlan, Sarah	Halifax, Nova Scotia	1/28/68
McLean, A.J.	West Palm Beach, FL	1/9/78
McMahon, Ed	Detroit, MI	3/6/23
McNichol, Kristy	Los Angeles, CA	9/11/62
McPartland, Marian	Stough, England	3/20/20
McRaney, Gerald	Collins, MS	8/19/47
McShane, Ian	Blackburn, England	9/29/42
Meadows, Jayne	Wu Chang, China	9/27/20
Meara, Anne	Brooklyn, NY	9/20/29
Meat Loaf	Dallas, TX	9/27/51
Mehta, Zubin	Bombay, India	4/29/36
Mellencamp, John	Seymour, IN	10/7/51

Name	Birthplace	Birthdate
Meloni, Christopher	Washington, DC	4/2/61
Mendes, Sam	Redding, England	8/1/65
Mendes, Sergio	Niteroi, Brazil	2/11/41
Mercer, Marian	Akron, OH	11/26/35
Merchant, Natalie	Jamestown, NY	10/26/63
Merkerson, S. Epatha	Saginaw, MI	11/28/52
Merrill, Dina	New York, NY	12/9/25
Messing, Debra	Brooklyn, NY	8/15/68
Metcalf, Laurie	Carbondale, IL	6/16/55
Michael, George	London, England	6/25/63
Michaels, Al	Brooklyn, NY	11/12/44
Michaels, Lorne	Toronto, Canada	11/17/44
Midler, Bette	Honolulu, HI	12/1/45
Midori	Osaka, Japan	10/25/71
Mike D	Brooklyn, NY	11/20/65
Milano, Alyssa	Brooklyn, NY	12/19/72
Miles, Sarah	Ingatestone, England	12/31/41
Miles, Vera	near Boise City, OK	8/23/29
Miller, Dennis	Pittsburgh, PA	11/3/53
Miller, Mitch	Rochester, NY	7/4/11
Miller, Penelope Ann	Santa Monica, CA	1/13/64
Mills, Donna	Chicago, IL	12/11/43
Mills, Hayley	London, England	4/18/46
Milner, Martin	Detroit, MI	12/28/27
Milnes, Sherrill	Downers Grove, IL	1/10/35
Milsap, Ronnie	Robinsville, NC	1/16/44
Mimieux, Yvette	Hollywood, CA	1/8/42
Minghella, Anthony	Isle of Wight, England	1/6/54
Ming-Na	Macao	11/20/63
Minnelli, Liza	Los Angeles, CA	3/12/46
Minogue, Kylie	Melbourne, Australia	5/28/68
Mirren, Helen	London, England	7/26/45
Mitchell, Brian	Seattle, WA	10/31/58
Mitchell, Elizabeth	Los Angeles, CA	3/27/70
Mitchell, Joni	Fort McLeod, Alberta	11/7/43
Moby	Harlem, New York, NY	9/11/65
Modine, Matthew	Loma Linda, CA	3/22/59
Moffat, Donald	Plymouth, England	12/26/30
Moffo, Anna	Wayne, PA	6/27/34
Molina, Alfred	London, England	5/24/53
Molinaro, Al	Kenosha, WI	6/24/19
Moll, Richard	Pasadena, CA	1/13/43
Moloney, Janel	Woodland Hills, CA	10/3/69
Monica (Arnold)	College Park, GA	10/24/80
Mo'Nique	Woodlawn, MD	12/11/67
Montalban, Ricardo	Mexico City, Mexico	11/25/20
Moody, Ron	London, England	1/8/24
Moore, Demi	Roswell, NM	11/11/62
Moore, Julianne	Fort Bragg, NC	12/3/60
Moore, Mandy	Nashua, NH	4/10/84
Moore, Mary Tyler	Brooklyn, NY	12/29/36
Moore, Melba	New York, NY	10/29/45
Moore, Michael	Flint, MI	4/23/54
Moore, Roger	London, England	10/14/27
Moore, Terry	Los Angeles, CA	1/7/29
Morales, Esai	Brooklyn, NY	10/1/62
Moranis, Rick	Toronto, Ontario	4/18/54
Moreau, Jeanne	Paris, France	1/23/28
Moreno, Rita	Humacao, PR	12/11/31
Morgan, Harry	Detroit, MI	4/10/15
Moriarty, Michael	Detroit, MI	4/5/41
Morissette, Alanis	Ottawa, Ontario	6/1/74
Morita, Pat	Isleton, CA	6/28/32
Morris, Garrett	New Orleans, LA	2/1/37
Morrison, Van	Belfast, N. Ireland	8/31/45
Morrissey	Manchester, England	5/22/59
Morrow, Rob	New Rochelle, NY	9/21/62
Morse, David	Beverly, MA	10/11/53
Morse, Robert	Newton, MA	5/18/31
Mortensen, Viggo	New York, NY	10/20/58
Mortimer, Emily	London, England	12/1/71
Morton, Joe	Brooklyn, NY	10/18/47
Morton, Samantha	Nottingham, Enlgand	5/13/77
Moses, William	Los Angeles, CA	11/17/59
Moss, Carrie-Anne	Vancouver, B.C., Can.	8/21/67
Moss, Kate	Croydon, Surrey, England	1/16/74
Mueller-Stahl, Armin	Tilsit, E. Prussia	12/17/30
Muldaur, Diana	Brooklyn, NY	8/19/38
Mulgrew, Kate	Dubuque, IA	4/29/55
Mull, Martin	Chicago, IL	8/18/43
Mullally, Megan	Los Angeles, CA	11/12/58
Mullan, Peter	Peterhead, Scotland	1960
Mulroney, Dermot	Alexandria, VA	10/31/63
Muniz, Frankie	Ridgewood, NJ	12/5/85
Munsel, Patrice	Spokane, WA	5/14/25
Murphy, Ben	Jonesboro, AR	3/6/42
Murphy, Brittany	Atlanta, GA	11/10/77
Murphy, Donna	Queens, NY	3/7/58
Murphy, Eddie	Brooklyn, NY	4/3/61

Name	Birthplace	Birthdate
Murphy, Michael	Los Angeles, CA	5/5/38
Murray, Anne	Springhill, Nova Scotia	6/20/45
Murray, Bill	Wilmette, IL	9/21/50
Murray, Don	Hollywood, CA	7/31/29
Musburger, Brent	Portland, OR	5/26/39
Muti, Riccardo	Naples, Italy	7/28/41
Myers, Mike	Scarborough, Ontario	5/25/63
Nabors, Jim	Sylacauga, AL	6/12/30
Nagra, Parminder	Leicester, England	10/5/75
Nash, Graham	Blackpool, England	2/2/42
Naughton, James	Middletown, CT	12/6/45
Navarro, Dave	Santa Monica, CA	6/7/67
Neal, Patricia	Packard, KY	1/20/26
Nealon, Kevin	Bridgeport, CT	11/18/53
Neeson, Liam	Ballymena, N. Ireland	6/7/52
Neill, Sam	Ulster, N. Ireland	9/14/47
Nelligan, Kate	London, Ontario	3/16/51
Nelly	Austin, TX	11/2/74
Nelson, Craig T.	Spokane, WA	4/4/46
Nelson, Ed	New Orleans, LA	12/21/28
Nelson, Judd	Portland, ME	11/28/59
Nelson, Tracy	Santa Monica, CA	10/25/63
Nelson, Willie	Abbott, TX	4/30/33
Nero, Peter	Brooklyn, NY	5/22/34
Nesmith, Mike	Houston, TX	12/30/42
Nettleton, Lois	Oak Park, IL	8/16/29
Neuwirth, Bebe	Newark, NJ	12/31/58
Neville, Aaron	New Orleans, LA	1/24/41
Newhart, Bob	Oak Park, IL	9/5/29
Newman, Paul	Cleveland, OH	1/26/25
Newman, Randy	New Orleans, LA	11/28/43
Newton, Wayne	Norfolk, VA	4/3/42
Newton-John, Olivia	Cambridge, England	9/26/48
Nicholas, Denise	Detroit, MI	7/12/44
Nicholas, Fayard	Philadelphia, PA	10/20/14
Nichols, Mike	Berlin, Germany	11/6/31
Nicholson, Jack	Neptune, NJ	4/22/37
Nicks, Stevie	Phoenix, AZ	5/26/48
Nielsen, Connie	Copenhagen, Denmark	7/3/65
Nielsen, Leslie	Regina, Sask.	2/11/26
Nighy, Bill	Caterham, Surrey, Eng.	12/12/49
Nilsson, Birgit	Vastra Karup, Sweden	5/17/18
Nimoy, Leonard	Boston, MA	3/26/31
Nixon, Cynthia	New York, NY	4/9/66
Nolte, Nick	Omaha, NE	2/8/41
Noone, Peter	Manchester, England	11/5/47
Norman, Jessye	Augusta, GA	9/15/45
Norris, Chuck	Ryan, OK	3/10/40
North, Sheree	Hollywood, CA	1/17/33
Northam, Jeremy	Cambridge, Enlgand	12/1/61
Norton, Edward	Columbia, MD	8/18/69
Noth, Christopher	Madison, WI	11/13/54
Novak, Kim	Chicago, IL	2/13/33
Nuyen, France	Marseilles, France	7/31/39
Oates, John	New York, NY	4/7/49
Obradors, Jacqueline	San Fernando Valley, CA	10/6/66
O'Brian, Hugh	Rochester, NY	4/19/25
O'Brien, Conan	Brookline, MA	4/18/63
O'Brien, Margaret	Los Angeles, CA	1/15/37
Ocean, Billy	Fyzabad, Trinidad	1/21/50
O'Connor, Frances	Oxford, England	6/12/69
O'Connor, Sinead	Glenageary, Ireland	12/8/66
Odetta	Birmingham, AL	12/31/30
O'Donnell, Chris	Winnetka, IL	6/26/70
O'Donnell, Rosie	Commack, NY	3/21/62
O'Grady, Gail	Detroit, MI	1/23/63
O'Hara, Catherine	Toronto, Canada	3/4/54
O'Hara, Maureen	Dublin, Ireland	8/17/20
Oldman, Gary	South London, England	3/21/58
Olin, Ken	Chicago, IL	7/30/54
Olin, Lena	Stockholm, Sweden	3/22/55
Olmos, Edward James	E. Los Angeles, CA	2/24/47
Olsen, Ashley	Sherman Oaks, CA	6/13/86
Olsen, Mary-Kate	Sherman Oaks, CA	6/13/86
Olsen, Merlin	Logan, UT	9/15/40
Olson, Nancy	Milwaukee, WI	7/14/28
O'Malley, Mike	Boston, MA	10/31/69
O'Neal, Ryan	Los Angeles, CA	4/20/41
O'Neal, Tatum	Los Angeles, CA	11/5/63
O'Neill, Ed	Youngstown, OH	4/12/46
Ontkean, Michael	Vancouver, B.C.	1/24/46
Orlando, Tony	New York, NY	4/3/44
Ormond, Julia	Epsom, England	1/4/65
Osbourne, Jack	London, England	11/8/85
Osbourne, Kelly	London, England	10/27/84
Osbourne, Ozzy	Birmingham, England	12/3/48
Osbourne, Sharon	London, England	10/10/52
O'Shea, Milo	Dublin, Ireland	6/2/26
Oslin, K.T.	Crossett, AR	5/15/42

Name	Birthplace	Birthdate
Osment, Haley Joel	Los Angeles, CA	4/10/88
Osmond, Donny	Ogden, UT	12/9/57
Osmond, Marie	Ogden, UT	10/13/59
O'Toole, Annette	Houston, TX	4/1/53
O'Toole, Peter	Connemara, Ireland	8/2/32
Otto, Miranda	Brisbane, Australia	12/16/67
Owens, Buck	Sherman, TX	8/12/29
Oz, Frank	Herford, England	5/25/44
Ozawa, Seiji	Shenyang, China	9/1/35
Pacino, Al	East Harlem, NY	4/25/40
Packer, Billy	Wellsville, NY	2/25/40
Page, Bettie	Nashville, TN	4/22/23
Page, Jimmy	Heston, England	1/9/44
Page, Patti	Claremore, OK	11/8/27
Paget, Debra	Denver, CO	8/19/33
Paige, Janis	Tacoma, WA	9/16/22
Palance, Jack	Lattimer, PA	2/18/20
Palin, Michael	Sheffield, England	5/5/43
Palmer, Betsy	East Chicago, IN	11/1/29
Palmer, Geoffrey	London, England	6/4/27
Palminteri, Chazz	Bronx, NY	5/15/51
Paltrow, Gwyneth	Los Angeles, CA	9/28/72
Pantoliano, Joe	Hoboken, NJ	9/12/51
Papas, Irene	Chiliomodion, Greece	9/3/26
Paquin, Anna	Wellington, New Zealand	7/24/82
Parker, Alan	London, England	2/14/44
Parker, Eleanor	Cedarville, OH	6/26/22
Parker, Fess	Ft. Worth, TX	8/16/25
Parker, Jameson	Baltimore, MD	11/18/47
Parker, Jean	Dear Lodge, MT	8/11/15
Parker, Mary-Louise	Fort Jackson, SC	8/2/64
Parker, Sarah Jessica	Nelsonville, OH	3/25/65
Parsons, Estelle	Marblehead, MA	11/20/27
Parton, Dolly	Sevierville, TN	1/19/46
Patinkin, Mandy	Chicago, IL	11/30/52
Patric, Jason	Queens, NY	6/17/66
Patton, Will	Charleston, SC	6/14/54
Paul, Adrian	London, England	5/29/59
Paul, Les	Waukesha, WI	1/9/15
Paulson, Sarah	Tampa, FL	12/17/75
Pavarotti, Luciano	Modena, Italy	10/12/35
Paxton, Bill	Fort Worth, TX	5/17/55
Pearce, Guy	Ely, England	10/5/67
Peet, Amanda	New York, NY	1/11/72
Pendergrass, Teddy	Philadelphia, PA	3/26/50
Penn, Arthur	Philadelphia, PA	9/27/22
Penn, Sean	Burbank, CA	8/17/60
Penny, Joe	London, England	9/14/56
Perez, Rosie	Brooklyn, NY	9/6/64
Perkins, Elizabeth	Queens, NY	11/18/60
Perlman, Itzhak	Tel Aviv, Israel	8/31/45
Perlman, Rhea	Brooklyn, NY	3/31/48
Perlman, Ron	New York, NY	4/13/50
Perrine, Valerie	Galveston, TX	9/3/43
Perry, Luke	Fredericktown, OH	10/11/66
Perry, Mathew	Williamstown, MA	8/19/69
Persoff, Nehemiah	Jerusalem, Israel	8/2/20
Pesci, Joe	Newark, NJ	2/9/43
Peters, Bernadette	Queens, NY	2/28/48
Peters, Roberta	Bronx, NY	5/4/30
Petersen, Wolfgang	Emden, Germany	3/14/41
Peterson, Oscar	Montreal, Quebec	8/15/25
Petty, Lori	Chattanooga, TN	3/23/63
Petty, Tom	Gainesville, FL	10/20/50
Pfeiffer, Michelle	Santa Ana, CA	4/29/58
Philbin, Regis	New York, NY	8/25/31
Phair, Liz	New Haven, CT	4/17/67
Phillippe, Ryan	New Castle, DE	9/10/74
Phillips, Lou Diamond	Subic Bay, Philippines	2/17/62
Phillips, Mackenzie	Alexandria, VA	11/10/59
Phillips, Michelle	Long Beach, CA	6/4/44
Phillips, Sian	Bettws, Wales, UK	5/14/34
Phoenix, Joaquin	San Juan, Puerto Rico	10/28/74
Pickett, Wilson	Prattville, AL	3/18/41
Pierce, David Hyde	Albany, NY	4/3/59
Pinchot, Bronson	New York, NY	5/20/59
Pink (Alecia Moore)	Doylestown, PA	9/8/79
Pinkett Smith, Jada	Baltimore, MD	9/18/71
Pirner, David	Green Bay, WI	4/16/64
Piscopo, Joe	Passaic, NJ	6/17/51
Pitt, Brad	Shawnee, OK	12/18/63
Piven, Jeremy	New York, NY	7/26/65
Plant, Robert	W. Bromwich, England	8/20/48
Pleshette, Suzanne	New York, NY	1/31/37
Plowright, Joan	Brigg, England	10/28/29
Plummer, Amanda	New York, NY	3/23/57
Plummer, Christopher	Toronto, Ontario	12/13/27
Poitier, Sidney	Miami, FL	2/20/27
Polanski, Roman	Paris, France	8/18/33
Pollack, Sydney	Lafayette, IN	7/1/34
Ponti, Carlo	Milan, Italy	12/11/12
Pop, Iggy	Muskegon, MI	4/21/47
Portman, Natalie	Jerusalem, Israel	6/9/81
Posey, Parker	Baltimore, MD	11/8/68
Post, Markie	Palo Alto, CA	11/4/50
Poston, Tom	Columbus, OH	10/17/21
Potente, Franka	Dulmen, Germany	7/22/74
Potts, Annie	Nashville, TN	10/28/52
Povich, Maury	Bethesda, MD	1/17/39
Powell, Jane	Portland, OR	4/1/28
Powers, Stefanie	Hollywood, CA	11/2/42
Prentiss, Paula	San Antonio, TX	3/4/39
Prepon, Laura	Watchung, NJ	3/7/80
Presley, Priscilla	Brooklyn, NY	5/24/45
Preston, Billy	Houston, TX	9/9/46
Previn, Andre	Berlin, Germany	4/6/29
Price, Leontyne	Laurel, MS	2/10/27
Price, Molly	North Plainfield, NJ	12/15/66
Price, Ray	Perryville, TX	1/12/26
Pride, Charley	Sledge, MS	3/18/38
Priestley, Jason	Vancouver, Brit. Columbia	8/28/69
Prince (The Artist)	Minneapolis, MN	6/7/58
Prince, Faith	Augusta, GA	8/5/57
Principal, Victoria	Fukuoka, Japan	1/3/50
Prinze, Freddie, Jr.	Albuquerque, NM	3/8/76
Probst, Jeff	Wichita, KS	11/1/61
Proctor, Emily	Raleigh, NC	10/18/68
Prosky, Robert	Philadelphia, PA	12/13/30
Provine, Dorothy	Deadwood, SD	1/20/37
Pryce, Jonathan	Holywell, N. Wales	6/1/47
Pryor, Richard	Peoria, IL	12/1/40
Puck, Wolfgang	St. Veit, Austria	1/8/49
Pulliam, Keshia Knight	Newark, NJ	4/9/79
Pullman, Bill	Hornell, NY	12/17/53
Purcell, Sarah	Richmond, IN	10/8/48
Quaid, Dennis	Houston, TX	4/9/54
Quaid, Randy	Houston, TX	10/1/50
Queen Latifah	Newark, NJ	3/18/70
Quinn, Aidan	Chicago, IL	3/8/59
Quinn, Colin	Brooklyn, NY	8/15/59
Quinn, Martha	Albany, NY	5/11/59
Rachins, Alan	Cambridge, MA	10/3/42
Radcliffe, Daniel	London, England	7/23/89
Rae, Charlotte	Milwaukee, WI	4/22/26
Raffi	Cairo, Egypt	7/8/48
Rainer, Luise	Vienna, Austria	1/12/10
Raitt, Bonnie	Burbank, CA	11/8/49
Ramey, Samuel	Colby, KS	3/28/42
Ramirez, Efren	Los Angeles, CA	10/2/83
Ramone, Tommy	Budapest, Hungary	1/29/52
Randolph, Joyce	Detroit, MI	10/21/25
Raphael, Sally Jessy	Easton, PA	2/25/35
Rashad, Phylicia	Houston, TX	6/19/48
Ratzenberger, John	Bridgeport, CT	4/6/47
Raver, Kim	New York, NY	3/15/69
Rawls, Lou	Chicago, IL	12/1/35
Reddy, Helen	Melbourne, Australia	10/25/41
Redford, Robert	Santa Monica, CA	8/18/37
Redgrave, Lynn	London, England	3/8/43
Redgrave, Vanessa	London, England	1/30/37
Reed, Jerry	Atlanta, GA	3/20/37
Reed, Lou	Brooklyn, NY	3/2/42
Reed, Rex	Ft. Worth, TX	10/2/38
Reese, Della	Detroit, MI	7/6/31
Reeves, Keanu	Beirut, Lebanon	9/2/64
Reeves, Martha	Eufaula, AL	7/18/41
Regalbuto, Joe	Brooklyn, NY	8/24/49
Reid, Tara	Wyckoff, NJ	11/8/75
Reid, Tim	Norfolk, VA	12/19/44
Reid, Vernon	London, England	8/22/58
Reilly, Charles Nelson	New York, NY	1/13/31
Reilly, John C.	Chicago, IL	5/24/65
Reiner, Carl	Bronx, NY	3/20/22
Reiner, Rob	Bronx, NY	3/6/47
Reinhold, Judge	Wilmington, DE	5/21/57
Reinking, Ann	Seattle, WA	11/10/49
Reiser, Paul	New York, NY	3/30/57
Reitman, Ivan	Komarno, Czechoslovakia	10/26/46
Remini, Leah	Brooklyn, NY	6/15/70
Resnik, Regina	New York, NY	8/30/22
Reynolds, Burt	Waycross, GA	2/11/36
Reynolds, Debbie	El Paso, TX	4/1/32
Reznor, Trent	Mercer, PA	5/17/65
Rhames, Ving	Harlem, New York, NY	5/12/59
Rhymes, Busta	Brooklyn, NY	5/20/72
Ribisi, Giovanni	Los Angeles, CA	12/17/74
Ricci, Christina	Santa Monica, CA	2/12/80
Richards, Denise	Downers Grove, IL	2/17/71

Name	Birthplace	Birthdate
Richards, Keith	Dartford, Kent, England	12/18/43
Richards, Michael	Culver City, CA	7/24/49
Richardson, Ian	Edinburgh, Scotland	4/7/34
Richardson, Kevin	Lexington, KY	10/3/71
Richardson, Miranda	Lancashire, England	3/3/58
Richardson, Natasha	London, England	5/11/63
Richardson, Patricia	Bethesda, MD	2/23/51
Richie, Lionel	Tuskegee, AL	6/20/49
Richter, Andy	Grand Rapids, MI	8/28/66
Rickles, Don	Queens, NY	5/8/26
Rickman, Alan	Hammersmith, England	2/21/46
Riegert, Peter	New York, NY	4/11/47
Rigg, Diana	Doncaster, England	7/20/38
Rimes, LeAnn	Flowood, MS	8/28/82
Ringwald, Molly	Roseville, CA	2/18/68
Ripa, Kelly	Stratford, NJ	10/2/70
Rivera, Chita	Washington, DC	1/23/33
Rivera, Geraldo	New York, NY	7/4/43
Rivers, Joan	Brooklyn, NY	6/8/33
Roach, Max	New Land, NC	1/10/25
Robbins, Tim	W. Covina, CA	10/16/58
Roberts, Doris	St. Louis, MO	11/4/29
Roberts, Eric	Biloxi, MS	4/18/56
Roberts, Julia	Smyrna, GA	10/28/67
Roberts, Pernell	Waycross, GA	5/18/28
Roberts, Tony	New York, NY	10/22/39
Robertson, Cliff	La Jolla, CA	9/9/25
Robertson, Dale	Harrah, OK	7/14/23
Robinson, Smokey	Detroit, MI	2/19/40
Rochon, Lela	Torrance, CA	4/17/64
Rock, Chris	South Carolina	2/7/66
Rock, The	Hayward, CA	5/2/72
Rodgers, Jimmy	Camas, WA	9/18/33
Rodriguez, Jai	Brentwood, NY	6/22/77
Rodriguez, Johnny	Sabinal, TX	12/10/51
Rogan, Joe	Newark, NJ	8/11/67
Rogers, Kenny	Houston, TX	8/21/38
Rogers, Mimi	Coral Gables, FL	1/27/56
Rogers, Wayne	Birmingham, AL	4/7/33
Rohm, Elisabeth	Dusseldorf, Germany	4/28/73
Rollins, Henry	Washington, DC	2/13/61
Rollins, Sonny	Harlem, NY	9/7/30
Romano, Ray	Queens, NY	12/21/57
Romijn-Stamos, Rebecca	Berkeley, CA	11/6/72
Ronstadt, Linda	Tucson, AZ	7/15/46
Rooney, Mickey	Brooklyn, NY	9/23/20
Root, Stephen	Sarasota, FL	11/17/51
Rose, Axl	Lafayette, IN	2/6/62
Rose Marie	New York, NY	8/15/23
Roseanne	Salt Lake City, UT	11/3/52
Ross, Charlotte	Winnetka, IL	1/21/68
Ross, Diana	Detroit, MI	3/26/44
Ross, Katharine	Hollywood, CA	1/29/40
Rossdale, Gavin	London, England	10/30/67
Ross, Marion	Albert Lea, MN	10/25/28
Rossellini, Isabella	Rome, Italy	6/18/52
Rossum, Emmy	New York, NY	9/12/86
Rostropovich, Mstislav	Baku, Azerbaijan	3/27/27
Roth, David Lee	Bloomington, IN	10/10/55
Roth, Tim	London, England	5/14/61
Rotten, Johnny	London, England	1/31/56
Rourke, Mickey	Schenectady, NY	9/16/56
Routledge, Patricia	Birkenhead, England	2/17/29
Rowan, Kelly	Ottawa, Canada	1967
Rowlands, Gena	Cambria, WI	6/19/36
Rubinstein, John	Beverly Hills, CA	12/8/46
Rudner, Rita	Miami, FL	9/17/56
Ruehl, Mercedes	Queens, NY	2/28/48
Ruffalo, Mark	Kenosha, WI	11/22/67
Rupp, Debra Jo	Glendale, CA	2/24/51
Rush, Barbara	Denver, CO	1/4/27
Rush, Geoffrey	Toowoomba, Australia	7/6/51
Russell, Jane	Bemidji, MN	6/21/21
Russell, Ken	Southampton, England	7/3/27
Russell, Keri	Fountain Valley, CA	3/23/76
Russell, Kurt	Springfield, MA	3/17/51
Russel, Leon	Lawton, OK	4/2/41
Russell, Mark	Buffalo, NY	8/23/32
Russell, Nipsey	Atlanta, GA	10/13/24
Russell, Theresa	San Diego, CA	3/20/57
Russo, Rene	Burbank, CA	2/17/54
Rutherford, Ann	Toronto, Ontario	11/2/20
Ruttan, Susan	Oregon City, OR	9/16/50
Ryan, Meg	Fairfield, CT	11/19/61
Ryan, Roz	Detroit, MI	7/7/51
Rydell, Bobby	Philadelphia, PA	4/26/42
Ryder, Winona	Winona, MN	10/29/71
Sabato, Antonio, Jr.	Rome, Italy	2/29/72
Sade	Ibadan, Nigeria	1/16/59

Name	Birthplace	Birthdate
Sagal, Katey	Hollywood, CA	1/19/53
Saget, Bob	Philadelphia, PA	5/17/56
Sagnier, Ludivine	La Celle-St.-Cloud, France	7/3/79
Sahl, Mort	Montreal, Quebec	5/11/27
Saint, Eva Marie	Newark, NJ	7/4/24
St. James, Susan	Hollywood, CA	8/14/46
St. John, Jill	Los Angeles, CA	8/19/40
St. Patrick, Mathew	Philadelphia, PA	3/17/69
Sajak, Pat	Chicago, IL	10/26/46
Saks, Gene	New York, NY	11/8/21
Sales, Soupy	Franklinton, NC	1/8/26
Salonga, Lea	Manila, Philippines	2/22/71
Samms, Emma	London, England	8/28/60
Sandler, Adam	Brooklyn, NY	9/9/66
Sands, Julian	West Yorkshire, England	1/15/58
San Giacomo, Laura	West Orange, NJ	11/14/61
Santana, Carlos	Autlan, Mexico	7/20/47
Sara, Mia	Brooklyn, NY	6/19/67
Sarandon, Susan	New York, NY	10/4/46
Sarnoff, Dorothy	New York, NY	5/25/17
Sartain, Gailard	Tulsa, OK	9/18/46
Savage, Ben	Highland Park, IL	9/13/80
Savage, Fred	Highland Park, IL	7/9/76
Sawa, Devon	Vancouver, B.C., Can.	9/7/78
Saxon, John	Brooklyn, NY	8/5/35
Sayles, John	Schenectady, NY	9/28/50
Scacchi, Greta	Milan, Italy	2/18/60
Scaggs, Boz	Canton, OH	6/8/44
Scales, Prunella	Sutton Abinger, England	6/22/32
Scalia, Jack	Brooklyn, NY	11/10/51
Schallert, William	Los Angeles, CA	7/6/22
Scheider, Roy	Orange, NJ	11/10/35
Schell, Maximilian	Vienna, Austria	12/8/30
Schenkel, Chris	Bippus, IN	8/21/23
Schiff, Richard	Bethesda, MD	5/27/55
Schiffer, Claudia	Rheinbach, Germany	8/25/70
Schneider, John	Mt. Kisco, NY	4/8/54
Schneider, Rob	San Francisco, CA	10/31/63
Schram, Bitty	New York, NY	7/17/68
Schreiber, Liev	San Francisco, CA	10/4/67
Schroder, Rick	Staten Island, NY	4/13/70
Schwarzenegger, Arnold	Thal, Austria	7/30/47
Schwarzkopf, Elisabeth	Jarotschin, Poland	12/9/15
Schwimmer, David	Astoria, Queens, NY	11/2/66
Sciorra, Annabella	New York, NY	3/24/64
Scofield, Paul	Hurstpierpoint, England	1/21/22
Scolari, Peter	New Rochelle, NY	9/12/54
Scorsese, Martin	Flushing, Queens, NY	11/17/42
Scott, Lizabeth	Scranton, PA	9/29/22
Scott, Ridley	South Shields, England	11/30/37
Scott, Seann William	Cottage Grove, MN	10/3/76
Scott-Heron, Gil	Chicago, IL	4/1/49
Scott Thomas, Kristin	Redruth, England	5/24/60
Scotto, Renata	Savona, Italy	2/24/35
Scram, Bitty	New York, NY	7/17/68
Scully, Vin	Bronx, NY	11/29/27
Seacrest, Ryan	Atlanta, GA	12/24/74
Seagal, Steven	Lansing, MI	4/10/51
Secor, Kyle	Tacoma, WA	5/31/58
Sedaka, Neil	Brooklyn, NY	3/13/39
Seeger, Pete	New York, NY	5/3/19
Segal, George	Great Neck, NY	2/13/34
Seidelman, Susan	Abington, PA	12/11/52
Seinfeld, Jerry	Brooklyn, NY	4/29/54
Sellecca, Connie	Bronx, NY	5/25/55
Selleck, Tom	Detroit, MI	1/29/45
Severinsen, Doc	Arlington, OR	7/7/27
Sevigny, Chloë	Springfield, MA	11/18/74
Sewell, Rufus	London, England	10/29/67
Seymour, Jane	Hillingdon, England	2/15/51
Shackelford, Ted	Oklahoma City, OK	6/23/46
Shaffer, Paul	Thunder Bay, Ontario	11/28/49
Shakira	Barranquilla, Colombia	2/2/77
Shalhoub, Tony	Green Bay, WI	10/9/53
Shandling, Garry	Chicago, IL	11/29/49
Shankar, Ravi	Benares, India	4/7/20
Shannon, Molly	Shaker Heights, OH	9/16/64
Sharif, Omar	Alexandria, Egypt	4/10/32
Shatner, William	Montreal, Quebec	3/22/31
Shaughnessy, Charles	London, England	2/9/55
Shaver, Helen	St. Thomas, Ontario	2/24/51
Shea, John	N. Conway, NH	4/14/49
Shearer, Harry	Los Angeles, CA	12/23/43
Shearer, Moira	Dumfermline, Scotland	1/17/26
Shearing, George	London, England	8/13/19
Sheedy, Ally	New York, NY	6/13/62
Sheen, Charlie	Los Angeles, CA	9/3/65
Sheen, Martin	Dayton, OH	8/3/40
Sheindlin, Judge Judy	Brooklyn, NY	10/21/42

Name	Birthplace	Birthdate
Shelley, Carole	London, England	8/16/39
Shepard, Sam	Ft. Sheridan, IL	11/5/43
Shepherd, Cybill	Memphis, TN	2/18/50
Sheridan, Nicollette	Worthing, England	11/21/63
Shields, Brooke	New York, NY	5/31/65
Shire, Talia	Lake Success, NY	4/25/46
Short, Martin	Hamilton, Ontario	3/26/50
Show, Grant	Detroit, MI	2/27/62
Shue, Andrew	Washington, DE	2/20/67
Shue, Elisabeth	Wilmington, DE	10/6/63
Shyamalan, M. Night	Pondicherry, India	8/6/70
Siepi, Cesare	Milan, Italy	2/14/23
Sigler, Jamie-Lynn	Jericho, NY	5/15/81
Sikking, James B.	Los Angeles, CA	3/5/34
Sills, Beverly	Brooklyn, NY	5/25/29
Silver, Ron	New York, NY	7/2/46
Silverman, Jonathan	Beverly Hills, CA	8/5/66
Silverman, Sarah	Bedford, NH	12/70
Silverstone, Alicia	Hillsborough, CA	10/4/76
Simmons, Gene	Haifa, Israel	8/25/49
Simmons, Henry	Stamford, CT	7/1/70
Simmons, Jean	London, England	1/31/29
Simmons, Richard	New Orleans, LA	7/12/48
Simon, Carly	Riverdale, NY	6/25/45
Simon, Paul	Newark, NJ	10/13/41
Sinatra, Nancy	Jersey City, NJ	6/8/40
Sinbad	Benton Harbor, MI	11/10/56
Singleton, John	Los Angeles, CA	1/6/68
Sinise, Gary	Blue Island, IL	3/17/55
Sirico, Tony	Brooklyn, NY	7/29/42
Sisto, Jeremy	Grass Valley, CA	10/6/74
Sizemore, Tom	Detroit, MI	9/29/64
Skerritt, Tom	Detroit, MI	8/25/33
Skye, Ione	Hertfordshire, England	9/4/70
Slater, Christian	New York, NY	8/18/69
Slater, Helen	Massapequa, NY	12/15/63
Slezak, Erika	Hollywood, CA	8/5/46
Slick, Grace	Evanston, IL	10/30/39
Smirnoff, Yakov	Odessa, Ukraine	1/24/51
Smith, Allison	Bronx, NY	12/9/69
Smith, Jaclyn	Houston, TX	10/26/47
Smith, Keely	Norfolk, VA	3/9/32
Smith, Kevin	Red Bank, NJ	8/2/70
Smith, Maggie	Ilford, England	12/28/34
Smith, Patti	Chicago, IL	12/30/46
Smith, Robert	Blackpool, England	4/21/59
Smith, Will	West Philadelphia, PA	9/25/68
Smits, Jimmy	New York, NY	7/9/55
Smothers, Dick	Governor's Island, NY	11/20/38
Smothers, Tom	Governor's Island, NY	2/2/37
Snipes, Wesley	Orlando, FL	7/31/62
Snyder, Tom	Milwaukee, WI	5/12/36
Soderbergh, Steven	Atlanta, GA	1/14/63
Somers, Suzanne	San Bruno, CA	10/16/46
Sommer, Elke	Berlin, Germany	11/5/40
Sorbo, Kevin	Mound, MN	9/24/58
Sorvino, Mira	Tenafly, NJ	9/28/67
Sorvino, Paul	Brooklyn, NY	4/13/39
Soul, David	Chicago, IL	8/28/43
Spacek, Sissy	Quitman, TX	12/25/49
Spacey, Kevin	S. Orange, NJ	7/26/59
Spade, David	Birmingham, MI	7/22/64
Spader, James	Boston, MA	2/7/60
Spano, Joe	San Francisco, CA	7/7/46
Spears, Britney	Kentwood, LA	12/2/81
Spector, Phil	Bronx, NY	12/26/40
Spelling, Aaron	Dallas, TX	4/22/28
Spelling, Tori	Los Angeles, CA	5/16/73
Spencer, John	New York, NY	12/20/46
Spielberg, Steven	Cincinnati, OH	12/18/46
Spiner, Brent	Houston, TX	2/2/49
Springer, Jerry	London, England	2/13/44
Springfield, Rick	Sydney, Australia	8/23/49
Springsteen, Bruce	Freehold, NJ	9/23/49
Spurlock, Morgan	Parksburg, WV	11/7/70
Stafford, Jo	Coalinga, CA	11/12/17
Stahl, Nick	Harlingen, TX	12/5/79
Stahl, Richard	Detroit, MI	1/4/32
Stallone, Sylvester	New York, NY	7/6/46
Stamos, John	Cypress, CA	8/19/63
Stamp, Terence	Stepney, England	7/22/39
Stang, Arnold	Chelsea, MA	9/28/25
Stanton, Harry Dean	West Irvine, KY	7/14/26
Stapleton, Jean	New York, NY	1/19/23
Stapleton, Maureen	Troy, NY	6/21/25
Starr, Ringo	Liverpool, England	7/7/40
Steenburgen, Mary	Newport, AR	2/8/53
Stefani, Gwen	Anaheim, CA	10/3/69
Stein, Ben	Washington, DC	11/25/44
Stephens, James	Mt. Kisco, NY	5/18/51
Stern, Daniel	Bethesda, MD	8/28/57
Stern, Howard	Roosevelt, NY	1/12/54
Sternhagen, Frances	Washington, DC	1/13/30
Stevens, Andrew	Memphis, TN	6/10/55
Stevens, Cat	London, England	7/21/48
Stevens, Connie	Brooklyn, NY	8/8/38
Stevens, Rise	Bronx, NY	6/11/13
Stevens, Stella	Hot Coffee, MS	10/1/36
Stevenson, Parker	Philadelphia, PA	6/4/52
Stewart, French	Albuquerque, NM	2/20/64
Stewart, Jon	Trenton, NY	11/28/62
Stewart, Patrick	Mirfield, England	7/13/40
Stewart, Rod	London, England	1/10/45
Stiers, David Ogden	Peoria, IL	10/31/42
Stiles, Julia	New York, NY	3/28/81
Stiller, Ben	New York, NY	11/30/65
Stiller, Jerry	Brooklyn, NY	6/8/27
Stills, Stephen	Dallas, TX	1/3/45
Sting	Newcastle, England	10/2/51
Stipe, Michael	Decatur, GA	1/4/60
Stockwell, Dean	North Hollywood, CA	3/5/36
Stoltz, Eric	Whittier, CA	9/30/61
Stone, Dee Wallace	Kansas City, KS	12/14/48
Stone, Oliver	New York, NY	9/15/46
Stone, Sharon	Meadville, PA	3/10/58
Stookey, Paul	Baltimore, MD	12/30/37
Storch, Larry	New York, NY	1/8/23
Storm, Gale	Bloomington, TX	4/5/22
Stowe, Madeleine	Eagle Rock, CA	8/18/58
Strait, George	Pearsall, TX	5/18/52
Strasser, Robin	New York, NY	5/7/45
Stratas, Teresa	Toronto, Ontario	5/26/38
Strathairn, David	San Francisco, CA	1/26/49
Strauss, Peter	Croton-on-Hudson, NY	2/20/47
Streep, Meryl	Summit, NJ	6/22/49
Streisand, Barbra	Brooklyn, NY	4/24/42
Stringfield, Sherry	Colorado Springs, CO	6/24/67
Stritch, Elaine	Detroit, MI	2/2/26
Stroman, Susan	Wilmington, DE	10/17/54
Struthers, Sally	Portland, OR	7/28/48
Stuart, Gloria	Santa Monica, CA	7/4/10
Stuarti, Enzo	Rome, Italy	3/3/25
Studdard, Ruben	Birmingham, AL	9/12/78
Suchet, David	London, England	5/2/46
Sullivan, Erik Per	Worcester, MA	7/12/91
Sullivan, Susan	New York, NY	11/18/42
Sumac, Yma	Ichocan, Peru	9/10/27
Summer, Donna	Dorchester, MA	12/31/48
Sutherland, Donald	St. John, New Brunswick	7/17/34
Sutherland, Joan	Sydney, Australia	11/7/26
Sutherland, Kiefer	London, England	12/21/66
Suvari, Mena	Newport, RI	2/9/79
Swank, Hilary	Bellingham, WA	7/30/74
Swayze, Patrick	Houston, TX	8/18/52
Swinton, Tilda	London, England	11/5/60
Swit, Loretta	Passaic, NJ	11/4/37
Sykes, Wanda	Portsmouth, VA	3/7/64
Szmanda, Eric	Milwaukee, WI	7/24/75
T, Mr.	Chicago, IL	5/21/52
Takei, George	Los Angeles, CA	4/20/37
Tallchief, Maria	Fairfax, OK	1/24/25
Tamblyn, Amber	Santa Monica, CA	5/14/83
Tamblyn, Russ	Los Angeles, CA	12/30/34
Tarantino, Quentin	Knoxville, TN	3/27/63
Tautou, Audrey	Beaumont, France	8/9/78
Taylor, Billy	Greenville, NC	7/21/21
Taylor, Buck	Hollywood, CA	5/13/38
Taylor, Elizabeth	London, England	2/27/32
Taylor, James	Boston, MA	3/12/48
Taylor, Rip	Washington, DC	1/13/34
Taylor, Rod	Sydney, Australia	1/11/30
Taymor, Julie	Newton, MA	12/15/52
Te Kanawa, Kiri	Gisborne, New Zealand	3/6/44
Teller	Philadelphia, PA	2/14/48
Temple Black, Shirley	Santa Monica, CA	4/23/28
Tennant, Victoria	London, England	9/30/50
Tennille, Toni	Montgomery, AL	5/8/43
Tesh, John	Garden City, NY	7/9/52
Tharp, Twyla	Portland, IN	7/1/41
Thaxter, Phyllis	Portland, ME	11/20/21
Theron, Charlize	South Africa	8/7/75
Thicke, Alan	Kirkland Lake, Ontario	3/1/47
Thiessen, Tiffani	Long Beach, CA	1/23/74
Thomas, Jay	Kermit, TX	7/12/48

Name	Birthplace	Birthdate
Thomas, Jonathan Taylor	Bethlehem, PA	9/8/81
Thomas, Marlo	Deerfield, MI	11/21/38
Thomas, Michael Tilson	Hollywood, CA	12/21/44
Thomas, Philip Michael	Columbus, OH	5/26/49
Thomas, Richard	New York, NY	6/13/51
Thomas, Sean Patrick	Wilmington, DE	12/17/70
Thompson, Emma	London, England	4/15/59
Thompson, Jack	Sydney, Australia	8/31/40
Thompson, Lea	Rochester, MN	5/31/61
Thompson, Sada	Des Moines, IA	9/27/29
Thorne-Smith, Courtney	San Francisco, CA	11/8/67
Thornton, Billy Bob	Hot Springs, AR	8/4/55
Thurman, Uma	Boston, MA	4/29/70
Tiegs, Cheryl	Breckenridge, MN	9/25/47
Tierney, Maura	Boston, MA	2/3/65
Tillis, Mel	Tampa, FL	8/8/32
Tilly, Jennifer	Harbor City, CA	9/16/58
Tilly, Meg	Long Beach, CA	2/14/60
Timberlake, Justin	Memphis, TN	1/31/81
Todd, Richard	Dublin, Ireland	6/11/19
Tomei, Marisa	Brooklyn, NY	12/4/64
Tomlin, Lily	Detroit, MI	9/1/39
Tork, Peter	Washington, DC	2/13/42
Torn, Rip	Temple, TX	2/6/31
Townsend, Robert	Chicago, IL	2/6/57
Townshend, Peter	Chiswick, England	5/19/45
Travanti, Daniel J.	Kenosha, WI	3/7/40
Travers, Mary	Louisville, KY	11/7/37
Travis, Nancy	Astoria, Queens, NY	9/21/61
Travis, Randy	Marshville, NC	5/4/59
Travolta, John	Englewood, NJ	2/18/54
Trebek, Alex	Sudbury, Ontario	7/22/40
Tritt, Travis	Marietta, GA	2/9/63
Tucci, Stanley	Katonah, NY	1/11/60
Tucker, Chris	Decatur, GA	8/31/72
Tucker, Michael	Baltimore, MD	2/6/44
Tucker, Tanya	Seminole, TX	10/10/58
Tune, Tommy	Wichita Falls, TX	2/28/39
Turlington, Christy	Walnut Creek, CA	1/2/69
Turner, Ike	Clarksdale, MS	11/5/31
Turner, Janine	Lincoln, NE	12/6/62
Turner, Kathleen	Springfield, MO	6/19/54
Turner, Tina	Brownsville, TN	11/26/39
Turturro, John	Brooklyn, NY	2/28/57
Twain, Shania	Windsor, Ontario	8/28/65
Twiggy (Lawson)	London, England	9/19/49
Tyler, Liv	New York, NY	7/1/77
Tyler, Steven	Yonkers, NY	3/26/48
Tyson, Cicely	Harlem, NY	12/19/33
Uecker, Bob	Milwaukee, WI	1/26/35
Uggams, Leslie	New York, NY	5/25/43
Ullman, Tracey	Slough, England	12/30/59
Ullmann, Liv	Tokyo, Japan	12/16/39
Ulrich, Skeet	New York, NY	1/20/69
Underwood, Carrie	Checotah, OK	3/10/83
Underwood, Blair	Tacoma, WA	8/25/64
Usher (Raymond IV)	Chattanooga,TN	10/14/78
Vaccaro, Brenda	Brooklyn, NY	11/18/39
Vale, Jerry	Bronx, NY	7/8/32
Valente, Caterina	Paris, France	1/14/31
Valley, Mark	Ogdensburg, NY	12/24/64
Valli, Frankie	Newark, NJ	5/3/37
Van Ark, Joan	New York, NY	6/16/43
Vance, Courtney B.	Birmingham, MI	3/12/60
Van Damme, Jean-Claude	Brussels, Belgium	10/18/60
Van Der Beek, James	Chesire, CT	3/8/77
Van Doren, Mamie	Rowena, SD	2/6/31
Van Dyke, Dick	West Plains, MO	12/13/25
Van Dyke, Jerry	Danville, IL	7/27/31
Van Halen, Eddie	Nijmegen, Netherlands	1/26/55
Van Patten, Dick	Queens, NY	12/9/28
Van Peebles, Mario	Mexico City, Mexico	1/15/57
Van Sant, Gus	Louisville, KY	7/24/52
Van Zandt, Steven	Boston, MA	11/22/50
Vardalos, Nia	Winnipeg, Manit, Can.	9/24/62
Vaughn, Robert	New York, NY	11/22/32
Vaughn, Vince	Minneapolis, MN	3/28/70
Vedder, Eddie	Evanston, IL	12/23/64
Vega, Alexa	Miami, FL	8/27/88
Vereen, Ben	Miami, FL	10/10/46
Verrett, Shirley	New Orleans, LA	5/31/31
Vickers, Jon	Prince Albert, Sask.	10/29/26
Vieira, Meredith	Providence, RI	12/30/53
Vigoda, Abe	New York, NY	2/24/21
Vincent, Jan-Michael	Denver, CO	7/15/44
Vinton, Bobby	Canonsburg, PA	4/16/35
Visnjic, Goran	Sibenik, Yugo. (Croatia)	9/9/72
Vitale, Dick	East Rutherford, NJ	6/9/39
Voight, Jon	Yonkers, NY	12/29/38
Von Stade, Frederica	Somerville, NJ	6/1/45
Von Sydow, Max	Lund, Sweden	4/10/29
Von Trier, Lars	Copenhagen, Denmark	4/30/56
Wagner, Jack	Washington, MO	10/3/59
Wagner, Lindsay	Los Angeles, CA	6/22/49
Wagner, Robert	Detroit, MI	2/10/30
Wahl, Ken	Chicago, IL	2/14/56
Wahlberg, Mark	Dorchester, MA	6/5/71
Wain, Bea	Bronx, NY	4/30/17
Waite, Ralph	White Plains, NY	6/22/28
Waits, Tom	Pomona, CA	12/7/49
Walden, Robert	New York, NY	9/25/43
Walken, Christopher	Astoria, Queens, NY	3/31/43
Wallace, Marcia	Creston, IA	11/1/42
Wallach, Eli	Brooklyn, NY	12/7/15
Walter, Jessica	Brooklyn, NY	1/31/40
Ward, Fred	San Diego, CA	12/30/42
Ward, Sela	Meridian, MS	7/11/56
Ward, Simon	Kent, London, England	10/19/41
Warden, Jack	Newark, NJ	9/18/20
Warfield, Marsha	Chicago, IL	3/5/54
Warner, Malcolm-Jamal	Jersey City, NJ	8/18/70
Warren, Lesley Ann	New York, NY	8/16/46
Warwick, Dionne	East Orange, NJ	12/12/40
Washington, Denzel	Mt. Vernon, NY	12/28/54
Watanabe, Ken	Koide, Niigata, Japan	10/21/59
Waters, John	Baltimore, MD	4/22/46
Waters, Roger	Great Bookham, England	9/6/44
Waterston, Sam	Cambridge, MA	11/15/40
Watson, Emily	London, England	1/14/67
Watson, Emma	Oxford, England	4/15/90
Watts, Andre	Nuremberg, Germany	6/20/46
Watts, Naomi	Shoreham, England	9/28/68
Wayans, Damon	New York, NY	9/4/60
Wayans, Keenen Ivory	Brooklyn, NY	6/8/58
Wayans, Marlon	New York, NY	723/72
Wayans, Shawn	New York, NY	1/19/71
Weathers, Carl	New Orleans, LA	1/14/48
Weaver, Dennis	Joplin, MO	6/4/24
Weaver, Fritz	Pittsburgh, PA	1/19/26
Weaver, Sigourney	New York, NY	10/8/49
Weiland, Scott	Santa Cruz, CA	10/27/67
Weir, Peter	Sydney, Australia	8/8/44
Weisz, Rachel	London, England	3/7/71
Weitz, Bruce	Norwalk, CT	5/27/43
Welch, Raquel	Chicago, IL	9/5/40
Weld, Tuesday	New York, NY	8/27/43
Weller, Peter	Stevens Point, WI	6/24/47
Wells, Kitty	Nashville, TN	8/30/19
Wendt, George	Chicago, IL	10/17/48
West, Adam	Walla Walla, WA	9/19/28
West, Kayne	Atlanta, GA	6/8/77
West, Shane	Baton Rouge, LA	6/10/78
Wettig, Patricia	Cincinnati, OH	12/4/51
Whalley, Joanne	Manchester, England	8/25/64
Wheaton, Wil	Burbank, CA	7/29/72
Whitaker, Forest	Longview, TX	7/15/61
White, Betty	Oak Park, IL	1/17/22
White, Jack	Detroit, MI	7/9/75
White, Jaleel	Pasadena, CA	11/27/76
White, Vanna	N. Myrtle Beach, SC	2/18/57
Whitford, Bradley	Madison, WI	10/10/59
Whiting, Margaret	Detroit, MI	7/22/24
Whitman, Stuart	San Francisco, CA	2/1/26
Whitmore, James	White Plains, NY	10/1/21
Widmark, Richard	Sunrise, MN	12/26/14
Wiest, Dianne	Kansas City, MO	3/28/48
Wilder, Gene	Milwaukee, WI	6/11/33
Wilkinson, Tom	Leeds, England	12/12/48
Williams, Andy	Wall Lake, IA	12/3/27
Williams, Armstong	Marion, SC	2/5/59
Williams, Barry	Santa Monica, CA	9/30/54
Williams, Billy Dee	Harlem, NY	4/6/37
Williams, Cindy	Van Nuys, CA	8/22/47
Williams, Esther	Los Angeles, CA	8/8/23
Williams, Hal	Columbus, OH	12/14/38
Williams, Hank, Jr.	Shreveport, LA	5/26/49
Williams, JoBeth	Houston, TX	12/6/48
Williams, Kimberly	Rye, NY	9/14/71
Williams, Lucinda	Lake Charles, LA	1/26/53
Williams, Michelle	Kalispell, MT	9/9/80
Williams, Montel	Baltimore, MD	7/3/56
Williams, Paul	Omaha, NE	9/19/40
Williams, Robin	Chicago, IL	7/21/51
Williams, Treat	Rowayton, CT	12/1/51

Name	Birthplace	Birthdate
Williams, Vanessa	Tarrytown, NY	3/18/63
Williamson, Kevin	New Bern, NC	3/14/65
Williamson, Nicol	Hamilton, Scotland	9/14/38
Willis, Bruce	Idar-Oberstein, W. Germ.	3/19/55
Wilson, Brian	Hawthorne, CA	6/20/42
Wilson, Cassandra	Jackson, MS	12/4/55
Wilson, Demond	Valdosta, GA	10/13/46
Wilson, Elizabeth	Grand Rapids, MI	4/4/21
Wilson, Luke	Dallas, TX	9/21/71
Wilson, Nancy	Chillicothe, OH	2/20/37
Wilson, Owen	Dallas, TX	11/18/68
Windom, William	New York, NY	9/28/23
Winfrey, Oprah	Kosciusko, MS	1/29/54
Winger, Debra	Cleveland, OH	5/16/55
Winkler, Henry	New York, NY	10/30/45
Winningham, Mare	Phoenix, AZ	5/16/59
Winokur, Marissa Jaret	New York, NY	2/2/73
Winslet, Kate	Reading, England	10/5/75
Winter, Johnny	Beaumont,TX	2/23/44
Winters, Jonathan	Dayton, OH	11/11/25
Winters, Shelley	East St. Louis, IL	8/18/22
Winwood, Steve	Birmingham, England	5/12/48
Wiseman, Joseph	Montreal, Quebec	5/15/18
Withers, Jane	Atlanta, GA	4/12/26
Witherspoon, Reese	Nashville, TN	3/22/76
Witt, Alicia	Worcester, MA	8/21/75
Wolf, Scott	Boston, MA	6/4/68
Wonder, Stevie	Saginaw, MI	5/13/50
Wong, Faye	Beijing, China	8/8/69
Woo, John	Guangzhou, China	5/1/46
Wood, Elijah	Cedar Rapids, IA	1/28/81
Woodard, Alfre	Tulsa, OK	11/8/53
Woods, James	Vernal, UT	4/18/47
Woodward, Edward	Croyden, England	6/1/30
Woodward, Joanne	Thomasville, GA	2/27/30
Wopat, Tom	Lodi, WI	9/9/51
Wright, Martha	Seattle, WA	3/23/26
Wright, Max	Detroit, MI	8/2/43
Wright, Steven	New York, NY	12/6/55
Wright Penn, Robin	Dallas, TX	4/8/66
Wyatt, Jane	Campgaw, NJ	8/12/11
Wyle, Noah	Hollywood, CA	6/4/71
Wyman, Bill	London, England	10/24/36
Wyman, Jane	St. Joseph, MO	1/4/14
Yankovic, Weird Al	Lynwood, CA	10/23/59
Yanni	Kalamata, Greece	11/14/54
Yarbrough, Glenn	Milwaukee, WI	1/12/30
Yarrow, Peter	New York, NY	5/31/38
Yearwood, Trisha	Monticello, GA	9/19/64
Yoakam, Dwight	Pikesville, KY	10/23/56
York, Michael	Fulmer, England	3/27/42
York, Susannah	London, England	1/9/41
Young, Alan	North Shields, England	11/19/19
Young, Burt	New York, NY	4/30/40
Young, Neil	Toronto, Ontario	11/12/45
Young, Sean	Louisville, KY	11/20/59
Zane, Billy	Chicago, IL	2/24/66
Zeffirelli, Franco	Florence, Italy	2/12/23
Zellweger, Renee	Katy, TX	4/25/69
Zemeckis, Robert	Chicago, IL	5/14/52
Zerbe, Anthony	Long Beach, CA	5/20/36
Zeta-Jones, Catherine	Swansea, Wales	9/25/69
Zimbalist, Efrem, Jr.	New York, NY	11/30/18
Zimbalist, Stephanie	New York, NY	10/8/56
Zimmer, Kim	Grand Rapids, MI	2/2/55
Zukerman, Pinchas	Tel Aviv, Israel	7/16/48
Zuniga, Daphne	San Francisco, CA	10/28/62

Entertainment Personalities of the Past

See also other lists for some deceased entertainers not included here.

Name	Born	Died
Aaliyah	**1979**	**2001**
Abbott, Bud	**1895**	**1974**
Abbott, George	**1887**	**1995**
Acuff, Roy	**1903**	**1992**
Adams, Don	**1923**	**2005**
Adams, Joey	**1911**	**1999**
Adams, Maude	**1872**	**1953**
Adams, Mason	**1919**	**2005**
Adler, Jacob P	**1855**	**1926**
Adler, Luther	**1903**	**1984**
Adoree, Renee	**1898**	**1933**
Agar, John	**1921**	**2002**
Aherne, Brian	**1902**	**1986**
Ailey, Alvin	**1931**	**1989**
Akins, Claude	**1918**	**1994**
Albert, Eddie	**1908**	**2005**
Albertson, Frank	**1909**	**1964**
Albertson, Jack	**1907**	**1981**
Alda, Robert	**1914**	**1986**
Alexander, Ben	**1911**	**1969**
Allen, Fred	**1894**	**1956**
Allen, Gracie	**1906**	**1964**
Allen, Mel	**1913**	**1996**
Allen, Peter	**1944**	**1992**
Allen, Steve	**1921**	**2000**
Allgood, Sara	**1883**	**1950**
Ameche, Don	**1908**	**1993**
Ames, Leon	**1903**	**1993**
Amsterdam, Morey	**1908**	**1996**
Anderson, Judith	**1897**	**1992**
Anderson, Marian	**1902**	**1993**
Andre the Giant	**1946**	**1993**
Andrews, Dana	**1909**	**1992**
Andrews, Laverne	**1913**	**1967**
Andrews, Maxine	**1918**	**1995**
Angeli, Pier	**1933**	**1971**
Anita Louise	**1915**	**1970**
Arbuckle, Fatty (Roscoe)	**1887**	**1933**
Arden, Eve	**1908**	**1990**
Arlen, Richard	**1900**	**1976**
Arliss, George	**1868**	**1946**
Armetta, Henry	**1888**	**1945**
Armstrong, Louis	**1901**	**1971**
Arnaz, Desi	**1917**	**1986**
Arnold, Edward	**1890**	**1956**
Arquette, Cliff	**1905**	**1974**
Arthur, Jean	**1900**	**1991**
Ashcroft, Peggy	**1907**	**1991**
Astaire, Fred	**1899**	**1987**
Astor, Mary	**1906**	**1987**
Atkins, Chet	**1924**	**2001**
Atwill, Lionel	**1885**	**1946**
Auer, Mischa	**1905**	**1967**
Aumont, Jean-Pierre	**1911**	**2001**
Austin, Gene	**1900**	**1972**
Autry, Gene	**1907**	**1998**
Axton, Hoyt	**1938**	**1999**
Ayres, Lew	**1908**	**1996**
Backus, Jim	**1913**	**1989**
Bailey, Pearl	**1918**	**1990**
Bainter, Fay	**1892**	**1968**
Baker, Josephine	**1906**	**1975**
Baker, Stanley	**1927**	**1976**
Balanchine, George	**1904**	**1983**
Ball, Lucille	**1911**	**1989**
Balsam, Martin	**1919**	**1996**
Bancroft, Anne	**1931**	**2005**
Bancroft, George	**1882**	**1956**
Bankhead, Tallulah	**1903**	**1968**
Banks, Leslie	**1890**	**1952**
Bara, Theda	**1890**	**1955**
Barnes, Binnie	**1903**	**1998**
Barnett, Etta Moten	**1902**	**2004**
Barnum, Phineas T.	**1810**	**1891**
Barrymore, Ethel	**1879**	**1959**
Barrymore, John	**1882**	**1942**
Barrymore, Lionel	**1878**	**1954**
Barrymore, Maurice	**1848**	**1905**
Bartel, Paul	**1938**	**2000**
Barthelmess, Richard	**1897**	**1963**
Bartholomew, Freddie	**1924**	**1992**
Bartok, Eva	**1926**	**1998**
Barty, Billy	**1924**	**2000**
Basehart, Richard	**1914**	**1984**
Basie, Count	**1904**	**1984**
Bates, Alan	**1934**	**2003**
Bates, Clayton (Peg Leg)	**1907**	**1998**
Bates, Florence	**1888**	**1954**
Bavier, Francis	**1902**	**1989**
Baxter, Anne	**1923**	**1985**
Baxter, Warner	**1889**	**1951**
Beatty, Clyde	**1904**	**1965**
Beaumont, Hugh	**1909**	**1982**
Beavers, Louise	**1902**	**1962**
Beery, Noah, Sr.	**1884**	**1946**
Beery, Noah, Jr.	**1913**	**1994**
Beery, Wallace	**1889**	**1949**
Begley, Ed	**1901**	**1970**
Bel Geddes, Barbara	**1922**	**2005**
Bellamy, Ralph	**1904**	**1991**
Belushi, John	**1949**	**1982**
Benaderet, Bea	**1906**	**1968**
Bendix, William	**1906**	**1964**
Bennett, Constance	**1904**	**1965**
Bennett, Joan	**1910**	**1990**
Bennett, Michael	**1943**	**1987**
Benny, Jack	**1894**	**1974**
Benzell, Mimi	**1924**	**1970**
Berg, Gertrude	**1899**	**1966**
Bergen, Edgar	**1903**	**1978**
Bergman, Ingrid	**1915**	**1982**
Berkeley, Busby	**1895**	**1976**
Berle, Milton	**1908**	**2002**
Bernardi, Herschel	**1923**	**1986**
Berman, Lazar	**1930**	**2005**
Bernhardt, Sarah	**1844**	**1923**
Bernie, Ben	**1893**	**1943**
Berry, Jan	**1941**	**2004**
Bessell, Ted	**1939**	**1996**
Bickford, Charles	**1889**	**1967**
Big Bopper, The	**1930**	**1959**
Bing, Rudolf	**1902**	**1997**
Bissell, Whit	**1909**	**1996**
Bixby, Bill	**1934**	**1993**
Bjoerling, Jussi	**1911**	**1960**
Blackmer, Sidney	**1895**	**1973**
Blackstone, Harry	**1885**	**1965**
Blake, Amanda	**1931**	**1989**
Blaine, Vivian	**1921**	**1995**
Blanc, Mel	**1908**	**1989**
Blocker, Dan	**1928**	**1972**
Blondell, Joan	**1909**	**1979**
Blore, Eric	**1888**	**1959**
Blue, Ben	**1901**	**1975**
Blyden, Larry	**1925**	**1975**
Bogarde, Dirk	**1920**	**1999**
Bogart, Humphrey	**1899**	**1957**
Boland, Mary	**1880**	**1965**
Boles, John	**1895**	**1969**
Bolger, Ray	**1904**	**1987**
Bond, Ward	**1903**	**1960**
Bondi, Beulah	**1892**	**1981**
Bono, Sonny	**1935**	**1998**
Boone, Richard	**1917**	**1981**
Booth, Edwin	**1833**	**1893**
Booth, Junius Brutus	**1796**	**1852**
Booth, Shirley	**1898**	**1992**

Name	Born	Died
Borge, Victor	1909	2000
Bow, Clara	1905	1965
Bowes, Maj. Edward	1874	1946
Bowman, Lee	1914	1979
Brown, Les	1912	2001
Boxcar Willie	1931	1999
Boyd, Stephen	1928	1977
Boyd, William	1898	1972
Boyer, Charles	1899	1978
Bracken, Eddie	1915	2002
Brady, Alice	1893	1939
Brand, Neville	1921	1992
Brando, Marlon	1924	2004
Branigan, Laura	1957	2004
Brazzi, Rossano	1916	1994
Brennan, Walter	1894	1974
Brent, George	1904	1979
Brett, Jeremy	1935	1995
Brice, Fanny	1891	1951
Bridges, Lloyd	1913	1998
Broderick, Helen	1891	1959
Bronson, Charles	1921	2003
Brooks, Foster	1912	2001
Brown, Joe E.	1892	1973
Brown, Les	1912	2001
Bruce, Lenny	1925	1966
Bruce, Nigel	1895	1953
Bruce, Virginia	1910	1982
Brynner, Yul	1915	1985
Buchanan, Edgar	1903	1979
Buchholz, Horst	1933	2003
Buñuel, Luis	1900	1983
Buono, Victor	1938	1982
Burke, Billie	1885	1970
Burnette, Smiley	1911	1967
Burns, George	1896	1996
Burr, Raymond	1917	1993
Burton, Richard	1925	1984
Busch, Mae	1897	1946
Bushman, Francis X.	1883	1966
Butterworth, Charles	1896	1946
Byington, Spring	1893	1971
Cabot, Bruce	1904	1972
Cabot, Sebastian	1918	1977
Cagney, James	1899	1986
Calhern, Louis	1895	1956
Calhoun, Rory	1923	1999
Callas, Maria	1923	1977
Calloway, Cab	1907	1994
Cambridge, Godfrey	1933	1976
Campbell, Mrs. Patrick	1865	1940
Candy, John	1950	1994
Cantinflas	1911	1993
Cantor, Eddie	1892	1964
Capra, Frank	1897	1991
Carey, Harry	1878	1947
Carey, Macdonald	1913	1994
Carle, Frankie	1903	2001
Carney, Art	1918	2003
Carpenter, Karen	1950	1983
Carradine, John	1906	1988
Carrillo, Leo	1880	1961
Carroll, Leo G.	1892	1972
Carroll, Madeleine	1906	1987
Carroll, Nancy	1905	1965
Carson, Jack	1910	1963
Carson, Johnny	1925	2005
Carter, Benny	1907	2003
Carter, Nell	1948	2003
Caruso, Enrico	1873	1921
Casadesus, Gaby	1901	1999
Casals, Pablo	1876	1973
Cash, Johnny	1932	2003
Cash, June Carter	1929	2003
Cass, Peggy	1924	1999
Cassidy, Jack	1927	1976
Cassavetes, John	1929	1989
Castle, Irene	1893	1969
Castle, Vernon	1887	1918
Caulfield, Joan	1922	1991
Chaliapin, Feodor	1873	1938
Champion, Gower	1919	1980
Chandler, Jeff	1918	1961
Chaney, Lon	1883	1930
Chaney, Lon, Jr.	1905	1973
Chapin, Harry	1942	1981
Chaplin, Charles	1889	1977
Chapman, Graham	1941	1989
Charles, Ray	1930	2004

Name	Born	Died
Chase, Ilka	1905	1978
Chatterton, Ruth	1893	1961
Cherrill, Virginia	1908	1996
Chevalier, Maurice	1888	1972
Child, Julia	1912	2004
Clair, René	1898	1981
Clark, Bobby	1888	1960
Clark, Dane	1913	1998
Clark, Fred	1914	1968
Clayton, Jan	1917	1983
Clift, Montgomery	1920	1966
Cline, Patsy	1932	1963
Clooney, Rosemary	1928	2002
Clyde, Andy	1892	1967
Cobain, Kurt	1967	1994
Cobb, Lee J.	1911	1976
Coburn, Charles	1877	1961
Coburn, James	1928	2002
Coca, Imogene	1908	2001
Cochran, Steve	1917?	1965
Coco, James	1930	1987
Cody, Buffalo Bill	1846	1917
Cody, Iron Eyes	1907	1999
Cohan, George M.	1878	1942
Cohen, Myron	1902	1986
Colbert, Claudette	1903	1996
Cole, Nat "King"	1919	1965
Collins, Ray	1890	1965
Colman, Ronald	1891	1958
Columbo, Russ	1908	1934
Como, Perry	1912	2001
Conniff, Ray	1916	2002
Connors, Chuck	1921	1992
Conrad, William	1920	1994
Conried, Hans	1917	1982
Conte, Richard	1911	1975
Convy, Bert	1933	1991
Conway, Tom	1904	1967
Coogan, Jackie	1914	1984
Cook, Elisha, Jr.	1904	1995
Cooke, Alistair	1908	2004
Cooke, Sam	1935	1964
Cooper, Gary	1901	1961
Cooper, Gladys	1888	1971
Cooper, Melville	1896	1973
Corby, Ellen	1913	1999
Corelli, Franco	1923	2003
Corey, Jeff	1914	2002
Corio, Ann	1914	1999
Cornell, Katharine	1893	1974
Correll, Charles ("Andy")	1890	1972
Costello, Dolores	1905	1979
Costello, Lou	1906	1959
Cotten, Joseph	1905	1994
Coward, Noel	1899	1973
Cox, Wally	1924	1973
Crabbe, Buster	1908	1983
Crain, Jeanne	1925	2003
Crane, Bob	1928	1978
Crawford, Broderick	1911	1986
Crawford, Joan	1904	1977
Cregar, Laird	1914	1944
Crenna, Richard	1926	2003
Crews, Laura Hope	1880	1942
Crisp, Donald	1880	1974
Croce, Jim	1942	1973
Cronyn, Hume	1911	2003
Crosby, Bing	1903	1977
Crothers, Scatman	1910	1986
Cruz, Celia	1925	2003
Cugat, Xavier	1900	1990
Cukor, George	1899	1983
Cullen, Bill	1920	1990
Cummings, Robert	1908	1990
Currie, Finlay	1878	1968
Curtis, Keene	1923	2002
Curtis, Ken	1916	1991
Cushing, Peter	1913	1994
Dailey, Dan	1914	1978
Dandridge, Dorothy	1923	1965
Dangerfield, Rodney	1921	2004
Daniell, Henry	1894	1963
Daniels, Bebe	1901	1971
Darin, Bobby	1936	1973
Darnell, Linda	1921	1965
Darwell, Jane	1879	1967
Da Silva, Howard	1909	1986
Davenport, Harry	1866	1949
Davies, Marion	1897	1961

Name	Born	Died
Davis, Bette	1908	1989
Davis, Joan	1907	1961
Davis, Sammy Jr.	1925	1990
Davis, Ossie	1917	2005
Day, Dennis	1917	1988
Dean, James	1931	1955
Dee, Frances	1907	2004
Dee, Sandra	1942	2005
Defore, Don	1917	1993
Dekker, Albert	1905	1968
Del Rio, Dolores	1908	1983
Demarest, William	1892	1983
DeMille, Agnes	1905	1993
DeMille, Cecil B.	1881	1959
Denison, Michael	1915	1998
Denning, Richard	1914	1998
Dennis, Sandy	1937	1992
Denny, Reginald	1891	1967
Denver, Bob	1935	2005
Denver, John	1943	1997
Derek, John	1926	1998
DeSica, Vittorio	1901	1974
Devine, Andy	1905	1977
Dewhurst, Colleen	1924	1991
De Wilde, Brandon	1942	1972
De Wolfe, Billy	1907	1974
Diamond, Selma	1920	1985
Dietrich, Marlene	1901	1992
Digges, Dudley	1879	1947
Disney, Walt	1901	1966
Dix, Richard	1894	1949
Dmytryk, Edward	1908	1999
Donahue, Troy	1936	2001
Donat, Robert	1905	1958
Donlevy, Brian	1901?	1972
Dors, Diana	1931	1984
Dorsey, Tommy	1905	1956
Douglas, Melvyn	1901	1981
Douglas, Paul	1907	1959
Dove, Billie	1900	1998
Downey, Morton, Jr.	1933	2001
Doyle, David	1929	1997
Drake, Alfred	1914	1992
Draper, Ruth	1889	1956
Dresser, Louise	1881	1965
Dressler, Marie	1869	1934
Drew, Ellen	1915	2003
Drew, Mrs. John	1820	1897
Dru, Joanne	1923	1996
Duchin, Eddy	1909	1951
Duff, Howard	1917	1990
Duggan, Andrew	1923	1988
Dumbrille, Douglass	1890	1974
Dumont, Margaret	1889	1965
Duncan, Isadora	1878	1927
Dunn, James	1905	1967
Dunne, Irene	1898	1990
Dunnock, Mildred	1904	1991
Durante, Jimmy	1893	1980
Duryea, Dan	1907	1968
Duse, Eleanora	1858	1924
Dvorak, Ann	1912	1979
Eagels, Jeanne	1894	1929
Ebsen, Buddy	1908	2003
Eckstine, Billy	1914	1993
Eddington, Paul	1927	1995
Eddy, Nelson	1901	1967
Edelman, Herb	1933	1996
Edwards, Cliff	1897	1971
Edwards, Gus	1879	1945
Edwards, Vince	1928	1996
Egan, Richard	1923	1987
Eisenstein, Sergei	1898	1948
Elam, Jack	1916	2003
Ellington, Duke	1899	1974
Elliot, Cass	1941	1974
Elliott, Denholm	1922	1992
Ellis, Mary	1897	2003
Elman, Mischa	1891	1967
Errol, Leon	1881	1951
Evans, Dale	1912	2001
Evans, Edith	1888	1976
Evans, Maurice	1901	1989
Ewell, Tom	1909	1994
Fadiman, Clifton	1904	1999
Fairbanks, Douglas	1883	1939
Fairbanks, Douglas, Jr.	1909	2000
Falkenburg, Jinx	1919	2003
Farley, Chris	1964	1997

Name	Born	Died
Farmer, Frances	1914	1970
Farnsworth, Richard	1920	2000
Farnum, Dustin	1870	1929
Farnum, William	1876	1953
Farrar, Geraldine	1882	1967
Farrell, Charles	1901	1990
Farrell, Eileen	1920	2002
Farrell, Glenda	1904	1971
Fassbinder, Rainer Werner	1946	1982
Fay, Frank	1897	1961
Faye, Alice	1912	1998
Fazenda, Louise	1895	1962
Feld, Fritz	1900	1993
Feldman, Marty	1933	1982
Fell, Norman	1924	1998
Fellini, Federico	1920	1993
Fenneman, George	1919	1997
Ferrer, Jose	1912	1992
Fetchit, Stepin	1898	1985
Fiedler, Arthur	1894	1979
Fiedler, John	1925	2005
Field, Betty	1918	1973
Fields, Gracie	1898	1979
Fields, W.C.	1879	1946
Fields, Totie	1931	1978
Finch, Peter	1916	1977
Fine, Larry	1902	1975
Firkusny, Rudolf	1912	1994
Fiske, Minnie Maddern	1865	1932
Fitzgerald, Barry	1888	1961
Fitzgerald, Geraldine	1913	2005
Flagstad, Kirsten	1895	1962
Fleming, Art	1924	1995
Fleming, Eric	1925	1966
Flippen, Jay C.	1900	1971
Flynn, Errol	1909	1959
Flynn, Joe	1925	1974
Foley, Red	1910	1968
Fonda, Henry	1905	1982
Fontaine, Frank	1920	1978
Fontanne, Lynn	1887	1983
Fonteyn, Margot	1919	1991
Ford, John	1895	1973
Ford, Paul	1901	1976
Ford, Tennessee Ernie	1919	1991
Ford, Wallace	1899	1966
Forrest, Helen	1918	1999
Fosse, Bob	1927	1987
Foster, Phil	1914	1985
Foster, Preston	1901	1970
Foxx, Redd	1922	1991
Foy, Eddie	1857	1928
Franchi, Sergio	1933?	1990
Francis, Arlene	1908	2001
Francis, Kay	1903	1968
Franciscus, James	1934	1991
Frankenheimer, John	1930	2002
Frann, Mary	1943	1998
Frawley, William	1887	1966
Frederick, Pauline	1885	1938
French, Victor	1934	1989
Friganza, Trixie	1870	1955
Frisco, Joe	1890	1958
Froman, Jane	1907	1980
Fuller, Samuel	1912	1997
Funt, Allen	1914	1999
Furness, Betty	1916	1994
Gabin, Jean	1904	1976
Gable, Clark	1901	1960
Gabor, Eva	1920	1995
Garbo, Greta	1905	1990
Garcia, Jerry	1942	1995
Gardenia, Vincent	1922	1992
Gardner, Ava	1922	1990
Garfield, John	1913	1952
Garland, Judy	1922	1969
Garson, Greer	1904	1996
Gassman, Vittorio	1922	2000
Gaye, Marvin	1939	1984
Gaynor, Janet	1906	1984
Gebel-Williams, Gunther	1934	2001
Geer, Will	1902	1978
George, Gladys	1900	1954
Gibb, Andy	1958	1988
Gibb, Maurice	1949	2003
Gibson, Hoot	1892	1962
Gielgud, John	1904	2000
Gilbert, Billy	1894	1971
Gilbert, John	1895	1936
Gilford, Jack	1907	1990
Gillette, William	1855	1937
Gingold, Hermione	1897	1987
Gish, Dorothy	1898	1968
Gish, Lillian	1893	1993
Giulini, Carlos Maria	1914	2005
Gleason, Jackie	1916	1987
Gleason, James	1886	1959
Gluck, Alma	1884	1938
Gobel, George	1919	1991
Goddard, Paulette	1905	1990
Godfrey, Arthur	1903	1983
Godunov, Alexander	1949	1995
Goldwyn, Samuel	1882	1974
Gomez, Thomas	1905	1971
Goodman, Benny	1909	1986
Gorcey, Leo	1915	1969
Gordon, Gale	1906	1995
Gordon, Ruth	1896	1985
Gorshin, Frank	1934	2005
Gosden, Freeman ("Amos")	1899	1982
Gottschalk, Ferdinand	1869	1944
Gottschalk, Louis	1829	1869
Gould, Glenn	1932	1982
Gould, Morton	1913	1996
Grable, Betty	1916	1973
Graham, Martha	1894	1991
Graham, Virginia	1912	1998
Grahame, Gloria	1925	1981
Granger, Stewart	1913	1993
Grant, Cary	1904	1986
Granville, Bonita	1923	1988
Gray, Dolores	1924	2002
Gray, Spalding	1941	2004
Greco, Jose	1918	2001
Green, Adolph	1915	2002
Greene, Lorne	1915	1987
Greenstreet, Sydney	1879	1954
Greenwood, Charlotte	1890	1978
Greer, Jane	1924	2001
Gregory, James	1911	2002
Griffith, David Wark	1874	1948
Griffith, Hugh	1912	1980
Guardino, Harry	1925	1995
Guinness, Sir Alec	1914	2000
Guthrie, Woody	1912	1967
Gwenn, Edmund	1875	1959
Gwynne, Fred	1926	1993
Hackett, Buddy	1924	2003
Hackett, Joan	1934	1983
Hagen, Uta	1919	2004
Hale, Alan	1892	1950
Hale, Alan, Jr.	1918	1990
Haley, Bill	1925	1981
Haley, Jack	1899	1979
Hall, Huntz	1919	1999
Hall, Jon	1915	1979
Hamilton, Margaret	1902	1985
Hammerstein, Oscar	1847	1919
Hammerstein II, Oscar	1895	1960
Hampton, Lionel	1908	2002
Hardwicke, Cedric	1893	1964
Hardy, Oliver	1892	1957
Harlow, Jean	1911	1937
Harris, Phil	1904	1995
Harris, Richard	1930	2002
Harrison, George	1943	2001
Harrison, Rex	1908	1990
Hart, William S.	1870	1946
Hartman, Phil	1948	1998
Harvey, Laurence	1928	1973
Hatfield, Bobby	1940	2003
Haver, June	1926	2005
Hawkins, Jack	1910	1973
Hawkins, Screamin' Jay	1929	2000
Hawthorne, Nigel	1929	2001
Hayakawa, Sessue	1890	1973
Hayden, Sterling	1916	1986
Hayes, Gabby	1885	1969
Hayes, Helen	1900	1993
Hayes, Peter Lind	1915	1998
Hayward, Leland	1902	1971
Hayward, Louis	1909	1985
Hayward, Susan	1917	1975
Hayworth, Rita	1918	1987
Head, Edith	1907	1981
Healy, Ted	1896	1937
Heckart, Eileen	1919	2001
Heflin, Van	1910	1971
Heifetz, Jascha	1901	1987
Held, Anna	1873	1918
Hemingway, Margaux	1955	1996
Hemmings, David	1941	2003
Hendrix, Jimi	1942	1970
Henie, Sonja	1912	1969
Henreid, Paul	1908	1992
Henson, Jim	1936	1990
Hepburn, Audrey	1929	1993
Hepburn, Katharine	1907	2003
Hersholt, Jean	1886	1956
Hewett, Christopher	1922	2001
Hickey, William	1928	1997
Hickson, Joan	1906	1998
Hildegarde	1906	2005
Hill, Benny	1925	1992
Hill, George Roy	1921	2002
Hiller, Wendy	1912	2003
Hines, Gregory	1946	2003
Hines, Jerome	1921	2003
Hirt, Al	1922	1999
Hitchcock, Alfred	1899	1980
Hobson, Valerie	1917	1998
Hodiak, John	1914	1955
Holden, Fay	1894	1973
Holden, William	1918	1981
Holiday, Billie	1915	1959
Holliday, Judy	1922	1965
Holloway, Sterling	1905	1992
Holly, Buddy	1936	1959
Holt, Jack	1888	1951
Holt, Tim	1918	1973
Homolka, Oscar	1898	1978
Hooker, John Lee	1917	2001
Hoon, Shannon	1967	1995
Hope, Bob	1903	2003
Hopkins, Miriam	1902	1972
Hopper, DeWolf	1858	1935
Hopper, Hedda	1885	1966
Hopper, William	1915	1970
Horowitz, Vladimir	1904	1989
Horton, Edward Everett	1886	1970
Houdini, Harry	1874	1926
Houseman, John	1902	1988
Hovis, Larry	1936	2003
Howard (Horwitz), Curly	1903	1952
Howard, Eugene	1881	1965
Howard, Joe	1867	1961
Howard, Leslie	1890	1943
Howard (Horwitz), Moe	1897	1975
Howard (Horwitz), Shemp	1895	1955
Howard, Tom	1885	1955
Howard, Trevor	1916	1988
Howard, Willie	1885	1949
Hudson, Rock	1925	1985
Hull, Henry	1890	1977
Hull, Josephine	1886	1957
Humphrey, Doris	1895	1958
Hunter, Jeffrey	1925	1969
Hunter, Kim	1922	2002
Hunter, Ross	1921	1996
Husing, Ted	1901	1962
Hussey, Ruth	1911	2005
Huston, John	1906	1987
Huston, Walter	1884	1950
Hutchence, Michael	1960	1997
Hutton, Jim	1934	1979
Hutton, Robert	1920	1994
Hyde-White, Wilfrid	1903	1991
Ingram, Rex	1895	1969
Iturbi, Jose	1895	1980
Ireland, Jill	1936	1990
Ireland, John	1915	1992
Irving, Henry	1838	1905
Ives, Burl	1909	1995
Jack, Wolfman	1938	1995
Jackson, Joe	1875	1942
Jackson, Mahalia	1911	1972
Jackson, Milt	1922	1999
Jaeckel, Richard	1926	1997
Jaffe, Sam	1891	1984
Jagger, Dean	1903	1991
Jam Master Jay	1965	2003
James, Dennis	1917	1997
James, Harry	1916	1983
James, Rick	1948	2004
Janis, Elsie	1889	1956
Jannings, Emil	1886	1950
Janssen, David	1930	1980

Name	Born	Died
Jenkins, Allen	1900	1974
Jennings, Waylon	1937	2002
Jessel, George	1898	1981
Jeter, Michael	1952	2003
Johnson, Ben	1918	1996
Johnson, Celia	1908	1982
Johnson, Chic	1892	1962
Johnson, J.J.	1924	2001
Jolson, Al	1886	1950
Jones, Brian	1942	1969
Jones, Buck	1889	1942
Jones, Carolyn	1933	1983
Jones, Elvin	1927	2004
Jones, Henry	1912	1999
Jones, Spike	1911	1965
Joplin, Janis	1943	1970
Jordan, Richard	1938	1993
Jory, Victor	1902	1982
Joslyn, Allyn	1905	1981
Julia, Raul	1940	1994
Jump, Gordon	1932	2003
Jurado, Katy	1924	2002
Jurgens, Curt	1915	1982
Kahn, Madeline	1942	1999
Kane, Helen	1910	1966
Kanin, Garson	1912	1999
Karloff, Boris	1887	1969
Karns, Roscoe	1893	1970
Kaufman, Andy	1949	1984
Kaye, Danny	1913	1987
Kaye, Stubby	1918	1997
Kazan, Elia	1909	2003
Kean, Charles	1811	1868
Kean, Mrs. Charles	1806	1880
Kean, Edmund	1787	1833
Keaton, Buster	1895	1966
Keeler, Ruby	1910	1993
Keeshan, Bob (Captain Kangaroo)	1927	2004
Keel, Howard	1919	2005
Keith, Brian	1921	1997
Kellaway, Cecil	1894	1973
Kelley, DeForest	1920	1999
Kelly, Emmett	1898	1979
Kelly, Gene	1912	1996
Kelly, Grace	1929	1982
Kelly, Jack	1927	1992
Kelly, Nancy	1921	1985
Kelly, Patsy	1910	1981
Kelton, Pert	1907	1968
Kendall, Kay	1926	1959
Kennedy, Arthur	1914	1990
Kennedy, Edgar	1890	1948
Kibbee, Guy	1886	1956
Kilbride, Percy	1888	1964
Kiley, Richard	1922	1999
King, Alan	1927	2004
Kinski, Klaus	1926	1991
Kirby, George	1923	1995
Kirby, Durward	1912	2000
Kirsten, Dorothy	1910	1992
Klemperer, Werner	1919	2000
Knight, Ted	1923	1986
Kostelanetz, Andre	1901	1980
Kovacs, Ernie	1919	1962
Kramer, Stanley	1913	2001
Kruger, Otto	1885	1974
Kubrick, Stanley	1928	1999
Kulp, Nancy	1921	1991
Kurosawa, Akira	1910	1998
Kyser, Kay	1906	1985
Ladd, Alan	1913	1964
Lahr, Bert	1895	1967
Lake, Arthur	1905	1987
Lake, Veronica	1919	1973
Lamarr, Hedy	1913	2000
Lamas, Fernando	1915	1982
Lamour, Dorothy	1914	1996
Lancaster, Burt	1913	1994
Lanchester, Elsa	1902	1986
Lane, Pricilla	1917	1995
Landis, Carole	1919	1948
Landis, Jessie Royce	1904	1972
Landon, Michael	1936	1991
Lang, Fritz	1890	1976
Langdon, Harry	1884	1944
Lange, Hope	1931	2003
Langford, Frances	1914	2005
Langtry, Lillie	1853	1929
Lanza, Mario	1921	1959
LaRue, Lash (Alfred)	1917	1996
Lauder, Harry	1870	1950
Laughton, Charles	1899	1962
Laurel, Stan	1890	1965
Lawford, Peter	1923	1984
Lawrence, Gertrude	1898	1952
Lean, David	1908	1991
Lee, Bernard	1908	1981
Lee, Bruce	1940	1973
Lee, Canada	1907	1952
Lee, Gypsy Rose	1914	1970
Lee, Anna	1913	2004
Lee, Peggy	1920	2002
LeGallienne, Eva	1899	1991
Lehmann, Lotte	1888	1976
Leigh, Vivien	1913	1967
Leighton, Margaret	1922	1976
Lemmon, Jack	1925	2001
Lennon, John	1940	1980
Lenya, Lotte	1898	1981
Leonard, Eddie	1870	1941
Leonard, Sheldon	1907	1997
LeRoy, Mervyn	1900	1987
Levant, Oscar	1906	1972
Levene, Sam	1905	1980
Levenson, Sam	1911	1980
Lewis, Joe E.	1902	1971
Lewis, Shari	1934	1998
Lewis, Ted	1892	1971
Liberace	1919	1987
Lillie, Beatrice	1894	1989
Lind, Jenny	1820	1887
Lindfors, Viveca	1920	1995
Lindley, Audra	1918	1997
Linville, Larry	1939	2000
Little, Cleavon	1939	1992
Llewelyn, Desmond	1914	1999
Lloyd, Harold	1893	1971
Lloyd, Marie	1870	1922
Lockhart, Gene	1891	1957
Logan, Ella	1913	1969
Lombard, Carole	1909	1942
Lombardo, Guy	1902	1977
Long, Richard	1927	1974
Lopes, Lisa	1971	2002
Lopez, Vincent	1895	1975
Lord, Jack	1920?	1998
Lorne, Marion	1888	1968
Lorre, Peter	1904	1964
Loudon, Dorothy	1933	2003
Lovejoy, Frank	1912	1962
Lowe, Edmund	1890	1971
Loy, Myrna	1905	1993
Lubitsch, Ernst	1892	1947
Ludden, Allen	1918	1981
Lugosi, Bela	1882	1956
Lukas, Paul	1894	1971
Lundigan, William	1914	1975
Lunt, Alfred	1892	1977
Lupino, Ida	1918	1995
Lymon, Frankie	1942	1968
Lynde, Paul	1926	1982
Lynn, Diana	1926	1971
MacDonald, Jeanette	1903	1965
Mack, Ted	1904	1976
MacKenzie, Gisele	1927	2003
MacLane, Barton	1902	1969
MacMurray, Fred	1908	1991
MacRae, Gordon	1921	1986
Macready, George	1909	1973
Madison, Guy	1922	1996
Magnani, Anna	1908	1973
Mancini, Henry	1924	1994
Main, Marjorie	1890	1975
Malle, Louis	1932	1995
Mann, Herbie	1930	2003
Mansfield, Jayne	1932	1967
Mantovani, Annunzio	1905	1980
Marais, Jean	1913	1998
March, Fredric	1897	1975
March, Hal	1920	1970
Marchand, Nancy	1928	2000
Marley, Bob	1945	1981
Marshall, Brenda	1915	1992
Marshall, E.G.	1910	1998
Marshall, Herbert	1890	1966
Martin, Barney	1923	2005
Martin, Dean	1917	1995
Martin, Mary	1913	1990
Martin, Ross	1920	1981
Marvin, Lee	1924	1987
Marx, Arthur (Harpo)	1888	1964
Marx, Herbert (Zeppo)	1901	1979
Marx, Julius (Groucho)	1890	1977
Marx, Leonard (Chico)	1886	1961
Marx, Milton (Gummo)	1893	1977
Mason, James	1909	1984
Massey, Daniel	1933	1998
Massey, Raymond	1896	1983
Mastroianni, Marcello	1924	1996
Matthau, Walter	1920	2000
Mature, Victor	1916	1999
Maxwell, Marilyn	1921	1972
Mayer, Louis B.	1885	1957
Mayfield, Curtis	1942	1999
Maynard, Ken	1895	1973
Mayo, Virginia	1920	2005
Mazurki, Mike	1909	1990
McCambridge, Mercedes	1916	2004
McCartney, Linda	1941	1998
McClure, Doug	1935	1995
McCormack, John	1884	1945
McCrary, Tex	1910	2003
McCrea, Joel	1905	1990
McDaniel, Hattie	1895	1952
McDowall, Roddy	1928	1998
McFarland, George "Spanky"	1928	1993
McGuire, Dorothy	1916	2001
McHugh, Frank	1899	1981
McIntire, John	1907	1991
McKay, Gardner	1932	2001
McKern, Leo	1920	2002
McLaglen, Victor	1883	1959
McMahon, Horace	1907	1971
McNally, Stephen	1913	1994
McNeill, Don	1907	1996
McQueen, Butterfly	1911	1995
McQueen, Steve	1930	1980
Meader, Vaughn	1936	2004
Meadows, Audrey	1924	1996
Medford, Kay	1920	1980
Meek, Donald	1880	1946
Meeker, Ralph	1920	1988
Melba, Nellie	1861	1931
Melchior, Lauritz	1890	1973
Menjou, Adolphe	1890	1963
Menken, Helen	1902	1966
Menuhin, Yehudi	1916	1999
Mercouri, Melina	1925	1994
Mercury, Freddie	1946	1991
Meredith, Burgess	1909	1997
Merman, Ethel	1908	1984
Merrick, David	1911	2000
Merrill, Gary	1915	1990
Mifune, Toshiro	1920	1997
Milland, Ray	1905	1986
Miller, Ann	1923	2004
Miller, Glenn	1904	1944
Miller, Marilyn	1898	1936
Miller, Roger	1936	1992
Mills, Harry	1913	1982
Mills, Sir John	1908	2005
Minnevitch, Borrah	1903	1955
Mineo, Sal	1939	1976
Miner, Jan	1917	2004
Mingus, Charles	1922	1979
Miranda, Carmen	1913	1955
Mitchell, Cameron	1918	1994
Mitchell, Thomas	1892	1962
Mitchum, Robert	1917	1997
Mix, Tom	1880	1940
Monica, Corbett	1930	1998
Monroe, Marilyn	1926	1962
Monroe, Vaughn	1911	1973
Montand, Yves	1921	1991
Montez, Maria	1917	1951
Montgomery, Elizabeth	1933	1995
Montgomery, George	1916	2000
Montgomery, Robert	1904	1981
Moore, Clayton	1914	1999
Moore, Colleen	1900	1988
Moore, Dudley	1935	2002
Moore, Grace	1901	1947
Moore, Garry	1914	1993
Moore, Victor	1876	1962
Moorehead, Agnes	1906	1974

Name	Born	Died
Moreland, Mantan	1902	1973
Morgan, Dennis	1910	1994
Morgan, Frank	1890	1949
Morgan, Helen	1900	1941
Morgan, Henry	1915	1994
Morley, Robert	1908	1992
Morris, Chester	1901	1970
Morris, Greg	1934	1996
Morris, Howard	1919	2005
Morris, Wayne	1914	1959
Morrison, Jim	1943	1971
Morrow, Vic	1932	1982
Mostel, Zero	1915	1977
Mowbray, Alan	1897	1969
Mulhare, Edward	1923	1997
Mulligan, Gerry	1927	1996
Mulligan, Richard	1932	2000
Muni, Paul	1895	1967
Munshin, Jules	1915	1970
Murphy, Audie	1924	1971
Murphy, George	1902	1992
Murray, Arthur	1895	1991
Murray, Kathryn	1906	1999
Murray, Mae	1885	1965
Nagel, Conrad	1896	1970
Naish, J. Carroll	1900	1973
Naldi, Nita	1898	1961
Nance, Jack	1943	1997
Natwick, Mildred	1908	1994
Negri, Pola	1897	1987
Nelson, Harriet (Hilliard)	1909	1994
Nelson, Ozzie	1906	1975
Nelson, Rick	1940	1985
Nesbit, Evelyn	1885	1967
Newley, Anthony	1931	1999
Newton, Robert	1905	1956
Nicholas, Harold	1924	2000
Nijinsky, Vaslav	1890	1950
Nilsson, Anna Q.	1893	1974
Niven, David	1910	1983
Nolan, Lloyd	1902	1985
Normand, Mabel	1894	1930
Notorious B.I.G.	1972	1997
Novarro, Ramon	1899	1968
Nureyev, Rudolf	1938	1993
Oakie, Jack	1903	1978
Oakley, Annie	1860	1926
Oates, Warren	1928	1982
Oberon, Merle	1911	1979
O'Brien, Edmond	1915	1985
O'Brien, Pat	1899	1983
O'Connell, Arthur	1908	1981
O'Connell, Helen	1921	1993
O'Connor, Carroll	1924	2001
O'Connor, Donald	1925	2003
O'Connor, Una	1880	1959
O'Keefe, Dennis	1908	1968
O'Herlihy, Daniel	1919	2005
Oland, Warner	1880	1938
Olcott, Chauncey	1860	1932
Oliver, Edna May	1883	1942
Olivier, Laurence	1907	1989
Olsen, Ole	1892	1963
O'Neill, James	1849	1920
O'Neal, Ron	1937	2004
Orbach, Jerry	1935	2004
Orbison, Roy	1936	1988
Ormandy, Eugene	1899	1985
O'Sullivan, Maureen	1911	1998
Ouspenskaya, Maria	1876	1949
Owen, Reginald	1887	1972
Paar, Jack	1918	2004
Paderewski, Ignace	1860	1941
Page, Geraldine	1924	1987
Pakula, Alan	1928	1998
Pallette, Eugene	1889	1954
Palmer, Lilli	1914	1986
Palmer, Robert	1949	2003
Pangborn, Franklin	1894	1958
Parks, Bert	1914	1992
Parks, Larry	1914	1975
Pasternack, Josef A.	1881	1940
Pastor, Tony (vaudevillian)	1837	1908
Pastor, Tony (bandleader)	1907	1969
Patti, Adelina	1843	1919
Patti, Carlotta	1840	1889
Patrick, Gail	1911	1980
Pavlova, Anna	1885	1931
Paycheck, Johnny	1938	2003
Payne, John	1912	1989
Pearl, Minnie	1912	1996
Peck, Gregory	1916	2003
Peerce, Jan	1904	1984
Pendleton, Nat	1899	1967
Penner, Joe	1905	1941
Peppard, George	1928	1994
Perkins, Anthony	1932	1992
Perkins, Carl	1932	1998
Perkins, Marlin	1905	1986
Peters, Brock	1927	2005
Peters, Jean	1926	2000
Peters, Susan	1921	1952
Phillips, John	1935	2001
Phoenix, River	1970	1993
Piaf, Edith	1915	1963
Pickens, Slim	1919	1983
Pickford, Mary	1893	1979
Picon, Molly	1898	1992
Pidgeon, Walter	1897	1984
Pinza, Ezio	1892	1957
Pitts, Zasu	1898	1963
Plato, Dana	1964	1999
Pleasence, Donald	1919	1995
Pons, Lily	1904	1976
Ponselle, Rosa	1897	1981
Porter, Eric	1928	1995
Porter, Nyree Dawn	1940	2001
Powell, Dick	1904	1963
Powell, Eleanor	1912	1982
Powell, William	1892	1984
Power, Tyrone	1913	1958
Preminger, Otto	1905	1986
Presley, Elvis	1935	1977
Preston, Robert	1918	1987
Price, Vincent	1911	1993
Prima, Louis	1911	1978
Prinze, Freddie	1954	1977
Prowse, Juliet	1936	1996
Puente, Tito	1923	2000
Pyle, Denver	1920	1997
Quayle, Anthony	1913	1989
Questel, Mae	1908	1998
Quinn, Anthony	1915	2001
Quintero, José	1924	1999
Rabb, Ellis	1930	1998
Rabbit, Eddie	1941	1998
Radner, Gilda	1946	1989
Raft, George	1895	1980
Rains, Claude	1890	1967
Ralston, Esther	1902	1994
Raitt, John	1917	2005
Ramone, Dee Dee	1952	2002
Ramone, Joey	1951	2001
Ramone, Johnny	1951	2004
Rampal, Jean-Pierre	1922	2000
Randall, Tony	1920	2004
Randolph, John	1915	2004
Rathbone, Basil	1892	1967
Ratoff, Gregory	1897	1960
Ray, Aldo	1926	1991
Ray, Johnnie	1927	1990
Rayburn, Gene	1917	1999
Raye, Martha	1916	1994
Raymond, Gene	1908	1998
Reagan, Ronald	1911	2004
Redding, Otis	1941	1967
Redgrave, Michael	1908	1985
Reed, Donna	1921	1986
Reed, Oliver	1938	1999
Reed, Robert	1932	1992
Reeve, Christopher	1959	2004
Reeves, George	1914	1959
Reeves, Steve	1926	2000
Reinhardt, Max	1873	1943
Remick, Lee	1935	1991
Renaldo, Duncan	1904	1980
Rennie, Michael	1909	1971
Renoir, Jean	1894	1979
Rettig, Tommy	1941	1996
Reynolds, Marjorie	1923	1997
Rich, Charlie	1932	1995
Richardson, Ralph	1902	1983
Riddle, Nelson	1921	1985
Riefenstahl, Leni	1902	2003
Ripperton, Minnie	1947	1979
Ritchard, Cyril	1898	1977
Ritter, John	1948	2003
Ritter, Tex	1907	1974
Ritter, Thelma	1905	1969
Ritz, Al	1901	1965
Ritz, Harry	1906	1986
Ritz, Jimmy	1903	1985
Robards, Jason	1922	2000
Robbins, Jerome	1918	1998
Robbins, Marty	1925	1982
Robeson, Paul	1898	1976
Robinson, Bill	1878	1949
Robinson, Edward G.	1893	1973
Roche, Eugene	1928	2004
Rochester (E. Anderson)	1905	1977
Roddenberry, Gene	1921	1991
Rodgers, Jimmie	1897	1933
Rogers, Buddy	1904	1999
Rogers, Fred	1928	2003
Rogers, Ginger	1911	1995
Rogers, Roy	1911	1998
Rogers, Will	1879	1935
Roland, Gilbert	1905	1994
Rolle, Esther	1920?	1998
Rollins, Howard	1950	1996
Roman, Ruth	1924	1999
Romero, Cesar	1907	1994
Rooney, Pat	1880	1962
Rose, Billy	1899	1966
Rossellini, Roberto	1906	1977
Rowan, Dan	1922	1987
Rubinstein, Artur	1887	1982
Ruggles, Charles	1886	1970
Russell, Gail	1924	1961
Russell, Harold	1914	2002
Russell, Lillian	1861	1922
Russell, Rosalind	1911	1976
Rutherford, Margaret	1892	1972
Ryan, Irene	1903	1973
Ryan, Robert	1909	1973
Sabu	1924	1963
Sanford, Isabel	1917	2004
Sargent, Dick	1933	1994
St. Cyr, Lili	1917	1999
St. Denis, Ruth	1877	1968
Sakall, S.Z.	1884	1955
Sale (Chic), Charles	1885	1936
Sanders, George	1906	1972
Savalas, Telly	1924	1994
Schell, Maria	1926	2005
Schildkraut, Joseph	1895	1964
Schipa, Tito	1889	1965
Schlesinger, John	1926	2003
Schnabel, Artur	1882	1951
Schneider, Romy	1938	1982
Scott, George C.	1927	1999
Scott, Hazel	1920	1981
Scott, Martha	1914	2003
Scott, Randolph	1898	1987
Scott, Zachary	1914	1965
Scott-Siddons, Mrs.	1843	1896
Seberg, Jean	1938	1979
Seeley, Blossom	1892	1974
Segovia, Andres	1893	1987
Selena	1971	1995
Sellers, Peter	1925	1980
Selznick, David O.	1902	1965
Sennett, Mack	1884	1960
Senor Wences	1896	1999
Serling, Rod	1924	1975
Shakur, Tupac	1971	1996
Shaw, Robert (actor)	1927	1978
Shaw, Robert (conductor)	1916	1999
Shawn, Ted	1891	1972
Shean, Al	1868	1949
Shearer, Norma	1902	1983
Sheridan, Ann	1915	1967
Shore, Dinah	1917	1994
Short, Bobby	1924	2005
Shubert, Lee	1875	1953
Shull, Richard B.	1929	1999
Siddons, Mrs. Sarah	1755	1831
Sidney, Sylvia	1910	1999
Signoret, Simone	1921	1985
Silverheels, Jay	1912	1980
Silvers, Phil	1912	1985
Sim, Alastair	1900	1976
Simmons, Richard	1913	2003
Simone, Nina	1933	2003
Sims, Irene	1930	2001
Sinatra, Frank	1915	1998
Sinclair, Madge	1938	1995

Name	Born	Died
Singleton, Penny	1908	2003
Siskel, Gene	1946	1999
Sitka, Emil	1914	1998
Sjostrom, Victor	1879	1960
Skelton, Red	1913	1997
Skinner, Otis	1858	1942
Smith, Alexis	1921	1993
Smith, Buffalo Bob	1917	1998
Smith, C. Aubrey	1863	1948
Smith, Elliott	1969	2003
Smith, Jeff	1939	2004
Smith, Kate	1907	1986
Smith, Kent	1907	1985
Snodgress, Carrie	1946	2004
Snow, Hank	1914	1999
Solti, George	1912	1997
Sondergaard, Gale	1899	1985
Sothern, Ann	1909	2001
Sousa, John Philip	1854	1932
Sparks, Ned	1884	1957
Springfield, Dusty	1939	1999
Stack, Robert	1919	2003
Stander, Lionel	1908	1994
Stanley, Kim	1925	2001
Stanwyck, Barbara	1907	1990
Steiger, Rod	1925	2002
Sterling, Jan	1921	2004
Stern, Isaac	1920	2001
Stevens, Craig	1918	2000
Stevens, Inger	1934	1970
Stevens, Mark	1916	1994
Stevenson, McLean	1929	1996
Stewart, James	1908	1997
Stickney, Dorothy	1896	1998
Stokowski, Leopold	1882	1977
Stone, Lewis	1879	1953
Stone, Milburn	1904	1980
Straight, Beatrice	1918	2001
Strasberg, Lee	1901	1982
Strasberg, Susan	1938	1999
Strode, Woody	1914	1994
Strummer, Joe	1952	2002
Sturges, Preston	1898	1959
Sullavan, Margaret	1911	1960
Sullivan, Barry	1912	1994
Sullivan, Ed	1902	1974
Sullivan, Francis L.	1903	1956
Summerville, Slim	1892	1946
Swanson, Gloria	1899	1983
Swarthout, Gladys	1904	1969
Switzer, Carl "Alfalfa"	1926	1959
Talbot, Lyle	1904	1996
Talmadge, Norma	1893	1957
Tamiroff, Akim	1899	1972
Tandy, Jessica	1909	1994
Tanguay, Eva	1878	1947
Tati, Jacques	1908	1982
Taylor, Deems	1885	1966
Taylor, Dub	1907	1994
Taylor, Estelle	1899	1958
Taylor, Laurette	1887	1946
Taylor, Robert	1911	1969
Tebaldi, Renata	1922	2004
Terry, Ellen	1847	1928
Thalberg, Irving	1899	1936
Thaw, John	1942	2002
Thigpen, Lynne	1948	2003
Thomas, Danny	1912	1991
Thomas, John Charles	1892	1960
Thorndike, Sybil	1882	1976
Thulin, Ingrid	1926	2004
Tibbett, Lawrence	1896	1960
Tierney, Gene	1920	1991
Tiny Tim	1923	1996
Tippett, Sir Michael	1905	1998
Todd, Michael	1909	1958
Tomlinson, David	1917	2000
Tone, Franchot	1903	1968
Torme, Mel	1925	1999
Toscanini, Arturo	1867	1957
Tracy, Lee	1898	1968
Tracy, Spencer	1900	1967
Traubel, Helen	1903	1972
Travers, Henry	1874	1965
Treacher, Arthur	1894	1975
Tree, Herbert Beerbohm	1853	1917
Trevor, Claire	1909	2000
Truex, Ernest	1890	1973
Truffaut, Francois	1932	1984
Tucker, Forrest	1919	1986
Tucker, Richard	1913	1975
Tucker, Sophie	1884	1966
Turner, Lana	1920	1995
Turpin, Ben	1874	1940
Twelvetrees, Helen	1908	1958
Twitty, Conway	1933	1993
Urich, Robert	1947	2002
Ustinov, Peter	1921	2004
Valens, Ritchie	1941	1959
Valentino, Rudolph	1895	1926
Vallee, Rudy	1901	1986
Van, Bobby	1928	1980
Vance, Vivian	1912	1979
Van Cleef, Lee	1925	1989
Vandross, Luther	1951	2005
Van Fleet, Jo	1922	1996
Varney, Jim	1949	2000
Vaughan, Sarah	1924	1990
Veidt, Conrad	1893	1943
Velez, Lupe	1908	1944
Vera-Ellen	1926	1981
Verdon, Gwen	1925	2000
Vernon, Jackie	1925	1987
Vernon, John	1932	2005
Villechaize, Herve	1943	1993
Vincent, Gene	1935	1971
Vicious, Sid	1958	1979
Vinson, Helen	1907	1999
Von Stroheim, Erich	1885	1957
Von Zell, Harry	1906	1981
Walker, Junior	1942	1995
Walker, Nancy	1922	1992
Walker, Robert	1918	1951
Wallenda, Karl	1905	1978
Walsh, J. T.	1943	1998
Walsh, Raoul	1887	1980
Walston, Ray	1914	2001
Walter, Bruno	1876	1962
Ward, Helen	1916	1998
Waring, Fred	1900	1984
Warner, H. B.	1876	1958
Warrick, Ruth	1915	2005
Washington, Dinah	1924	1963
Waters, Ethel	1896	1977
Waxman, Al	1935	2001
Wayne, David	1914	1995
Wayne, John	1907	1979
Webb, Clifton	1891	1966
Webb, Jack	1920	1982
Weems, Ted	1901	1963
Weissmuller, Johnny	1904	1984
Welk, Lawrence	1903	1992
Welles, Orson	1915	1985
Wellman, William	1896	1975
Werner, Oskar	1922	1984
West, Mae	1893	1980
Weston, Jack	1924	1996
Whale, James	1889	1957
Wheeler, Bert	1895	1968
White, Barry	1944	2003
White, Jesse	1919	1997
White, Pearl	1889	1938
Whiteman, Paul	1891	1967
Whitty, May	1865	1948
Wickes, Mary	1910	1995
Wilde, Cornel	1918	1989
Wilder, Billy	1906	2002
Wilding, Michael	1912	1979
Williams, Bert	1877	1922
Williams, Guy	1924	1989
Williams, Hank Sr.	1923	1953
Wills, Bob	1905	1975
Wills, Chill	1903	1978
Wilson, Carl	1946	1998
Wilson, Dennis	1944	1983
Wilson, Dooley	1894	1953
Wilson, Flip	1933	1998
Wilson, Jackie	1934	1984
Wilson, Marie	1917	1972
Windsor, Marie	1919	2000
Winfield, Paul	1941	2004
Winninger, Charles	1884	1969
Wise, Robert	1914	2005
Withers, Grant	1904	1959
Wong, Anna May	1907	1961
Wood, Natalie	1938	1981
Wood, Peggy	1892	1978
Wooley, Sheb	1921	2003
Woolley, Monty	1888	1963
Worth, Irene	1916	2002
Wray, Fay	1907	2004
Wright, Teresa	1918	2005
Wyler, William	1902	1981
Wynette, Tammy	1942	1998
Wynn, Ed	1886	1966
Wynn, Keenan	1916	1986
Yankovic, Frank	1915	1998
York, Dick	1929	1992
Young, Clara Kimball	1890	1960
Young, Gig	1913	1978
Young, Loretta	1913	2000
Young, Robert	1907	1998
Young, Roland	1887	1953
Youngman, Henny	1906	1998
Zanuck, Darryl F.	1902	1979
Zapa, Frank	1940	1993
Zevon, Warren	1947	2003
Zinneman, Fred	1907	1997
Ziegfeld, Florenz	1869	1932
Zukor, Adolph	1873	1976

Original Names of Selected Entertainers

ALI G: Sacha Baron Cohen
EDIE ADAMS: Elizabeth Edith Enke
EDDIE ALBERT: Edward Albert Heimberger
ALAN ALDA: Alphonso D'Abruzzo
JASON ALEXANDER: Jay Greenspan
FRED ALLEN: John Sullivan
WOODY ALLEN: Allen Konigsberg
JUNE ALLYSON: Ella Geisman
ANDRE 3000: Andre Benjamin
JULIE ANDREWS: Julia Wells
EVE ARDEN: Eunice Quedens
BEATRICE ARTHUR: Bernice Frankel
JEAN ARTHUR: Gladys Greene
FRED ASTAIRE: Frederick Austerlitz
BABYFACE: Kenneth Edmonds
LAUREN BACALL: Betty Joan Perske
ERYKAH BADU: Erica Wright
ANNE BANCROFT: Anna Maria Italiano
GENE BARRY: Eugene Klass
PAT BENATAR: Patricia Andrejewski
TONY BENNETT: Anthony Benedetto
IRVING BERLIN: Israel Baline
JACK BENNY: Benjamin Kubelsky
BIG BOI: Antwan Patton
JOEY BISHOP: Joseph Gottlieb
THE BIG BOPPER: Jiles Perry "J.P." Richardson
BONO (VOX): Paul Hewson
VICTOR BORGE: Borge Rosenbaum
DAVID BOWIE: David Robert Jones
BOY GEORGE: George Alan O'Dowd
FANNY BRICE: Fanny Borach
CHARLES BRONSON: Charles Buchinski
ALBERT BROOKS: Albert Einstein
MEL BROOKS: Melvin Kaminsky
GEORGE BURNS: Nathan Birnbaum
ELLEN BURSTYN: Edna Gilhooley
RICHARD BURTON: Richard Jenkins
RED BUTTONS: Aaron Chwatt
NICOLAS CAGE: Nicholas Coppola
MICHAEL CAINE: Maurice Micklewhite
MARIA CALLAS: Maria Kalogeropoulos
CEDRIC THE ENTERTAINER: Cedric Kyles
JACKIE CHAN: Chan Kwong-Sung
CYD CHARISSE: Tula Finklea
RAY CHARLES: Ray Charles Robinson
CHUBBY CHECKER: Ernest Evans
CHUCK D: Carlton Ridenhour
CHER: Cherilyn Sarkisian
PATSY CLINE: Virginia Patterson Hensley
LEE J. COBB: Leo Jacoby

CLAUDETTE COLBERT: Lily Chauchoin
ALICE COOPER: Vincent Furnier
DAVID COPPERFIELD: David Kotkin
HOWARD COSELL: Howard Cohen
ELVIS COSTELLO: Declan McManus
LOU COSTELLO: Louis Cristillo
PETER COYOTE: Peter Cohon
MICHAEL CRAWFORD: Michael Dumble-Smith
TOM CRUISE: Thomas Mapother IV
TONY CURTIS: Bernard Schwartz
VIC DAMONE: Vito Farinola
RODNEY DANGERFIELD: Jacob Cohen
BOBBY DARIN: Walden Robert Cassotto
DORIS DAY: Doris von Kappelhoff
YVONNE DE CARLO: Peggy Middleton
SANDRA DEE: Alexandra Zuck
JOHN DENVER: Henry John Deutschendorf Jr.
BO DEREK: Mary Cathleen Collins
DANNY DEVITO: Daniel Michaeli
ANGIE DICKINSON: Angeline Brown
BO DIDDLEY: Elias Bates
PHYLLIS DILLER: Phyllis Driver
DMX: Earl Simmons
EARL TROY DONAHUE: Merle Johnson Jr.
KIRK DOUGLAS: Issur Danielovitch
MELVYN DOUGLAS: Melvyn Hesselberg
BOB DYLAN: Robert Zimmerman
BARBARA EDEN: Barbara Huffman
ELVIRA: Cassandra Peterson
EMINEM: Marshall Mathers
ENYA: Eithne Ni Bhraonian
DALE EVANS: Frances Smith
CHAD EVERETT: Raymond Cramton
DOUGLAS FAIRBANKS: Douglas Ullman
MORGAN FAIRCHILD: Patsy McClenny
JAMIE FARR: Jameel Farah
ALICE FAYE: Alice Jeanne Leppert
STEPIN FETCHIT: Lincoln Perry
W.C. FIELDS: William Claude Dukenfield
50 CENT: Curtis Jackson
BARRY FITZGERALD: William Shields
FLAVOR FLAV: William Drayton
JOAN FONTAINE: Joan de Havilland
JODIE FOSTER: Alicia Christian Foster
REDD FOXX: John Sanford
ANTHONY FRANCIOSA: Anthony Papaleo
ARLENE FRANCIS: Arlene Kazanjian
CONNIE FRANCIS: Concetta Franconero
GRETA GARBO: Greta Gustafsson
VINCENT GARDENIA: Vincent Scognamiglio
JOHN GARFIELD: Julius Garfinkle
JUDY GARLAND: Frances Gumm
JAMES GARNER: James Bumgarner
CRYSTAL GAYLE: Brenda Gayle Webb
KATHIE LEE GIFFORD: Kathie Epstein
WHOOPI GOLDBERG: Caryn Johnson
EYDIE GORME: Edith Gormezano
STEWART GRANGER: James Stewart
CARY GRANT: Archibald Leach
LEE GRANT: Lyova Rosenthal
ROBERT GUILLAUME: Robert Williams
BUDDY HACKETT: Leonard Hacker
HAMMER: Stanley Kirk Burrell
JEAN HARLOW: Harlean Carpentier
REX HARRISON: Reginald Carey
LAURENCE HARVEY: Larushka Skikne
HELEN HAYES: Helen Brown
SUSAN HAYWARD: Edythe Marriner
RITA HAYWORTH: Margarita Cansino
PEE-WEE HERMAN: Paul Reubenfeld
CHARLTON HESTON: John Charlton Carter
WILLIAM HOLDEN: William Beedle
BILLIE HOLIDAY: Eleanora Fagan
JUDY HOLLIDAY: Judith Tuvim
BOB HOPE: Leslie Townes Hope
HARRY HOUDINI: Ehrich Weiss
LESLIE HOWARD: Leslie Stainer
HOWLIN' WOLF: Chester Burnett
ROCK HUDSON: Roy Scherer Jr. (later Fitzgerald)
ENGELBERT HUMPERDINCK: Arnold Dorsey
KIM HUNTER: Janet Cole
BETTY HUTTON: Betty Thornberg
ICE CUBE: O'Shea Jackson
ICE-T: Tracy Morrow
BILLY IDOL: William Broad
JAY-Z: Shawn Carter
ANN JILLIAN: Anne Nauseda
ELTON JOHN: Reginald Dwight
DON JOHNSON: Donald Wayne
AL JOLSON: Asa Yoelson
JENNIFER JONES: Phylis Isley
TOM JONES: Thomas Woodward
SPIKE JONZE: Adam Spiegel
LOUIS JOURDAN: Louis Gendre
WYNONNA JUDD: Christina Ciminella
BORIS KARLOFF: William Henry Pratt
DANNY KAYE: David Kaminsky
DIANE KEATON: Diane Hall
MICHAEL KEATON: Michael Douglas
CHAKA KHAN: Yvette Stevens
CAROLE KING: Carole Klein
LARRY KING: Larry Zeiger
BEN KINGSLEY: Krishna Banji
TED KNIGHT: Tadeus Wladyslaw Konopka
CHERYL LADD: Cheryl Stoppelmoor
VERONICA LAKE: Constance Ockleman
HEDY LAMARR: Hedwig Kiesler
DOROTHY LAMOUR: Mary Leta Dorothy Slaton
MICHAEL LANDON: Eugene Orowitz
MARIO LANZA: Alfredo Cocozza
QUEEN LATIFAH: Dana Owens
STAN LAUREL: Arthur Jefferson
STEVE LAWRENCE: Sidney Leibowitz
BRENDA LEE: Brenda Mae Tarpley
GYPSY ROSE LEE: Rose Louise Hovick
MICHELLE LEE: Michelle Dusiak
PEGGY LEE: Norma Egstrom
JANET LEIGH: Jeanette Morrison
VIVIEN LEIGH: Vivian Hartley
HUEY LEWIS: Hugh Cregg
JERRY LEWIS: Joseph Levitch
LIL' KIM: Kimberly Denise Jones
CAROLE LOMBARD: Jane Peters
SOPHIA LOREN: Sophia Scicolone
PETER LORRE: Laszio Lowenstein
MYRNA LOY: Myrna Williams
BELA LUGOSI: Bela Ferenc Blasko
MOMS MABLEY: Loretta Mary Aitken
SHIRLEY MACLAINE: Shirley Beaty
ELLE MACPHERSON: Eleanor Gow
MADONNA: Madonna Louise Veronica Ciccone
LEE MAJORS: Harvey Lee Yeary
KARL MALDEN: Mladen Sekulovich
BARRY MANILOW: Barry Alan Pincus
JAYNE MANSFIELD: Vera Jane Palmer
MARILYN MANSON: Brian Warner
FREDRIC MARCH: Frederick Bickel
PETER MARSHALL: Pierre LaCock
WALTER MATTHAU: Walter Matuschanskayasky
DEAN MARTIN: Dino Crocetti
MEAT LOAF: Marvin Lee Aday
FREDDIE MERCURY: Frederick Bulsara
ETHEL MERMAN: Ethel Zimmerman
GEORGE MICHAEL: Georgios Panayiotou
RAY MILLAND: Reginald Truscott-Jones
ANN MILLER: Lucille Collier
HELEN MIRREN: Ilynea Lydia Mironoff
JONI MITCHELL: Roberta Joan Anderson
MOBY: Richard Melville Hall
MARILYN MONROE: Norma Jean Mortenson (later Baker)
YVES MONTAND: Ivo Livi
RON MOODY: Ronald Moodnick
DEMI MOORE: Demetria Guynes
GARRY MOORE: Thomas Garrison Morfit
RITA MORENO: Rosita Alverio
HARRY MORGAN: Harry Bratsburg
MR. T: Lawrence Tero
PAUL MUNI: Muni Weisenfreund
MIKE NICHOLS: Michael Igor Peschowsky
CHUCK NORRIS: Carlos Ray
NOTORIOUS B.I.G.: Christopher Wallace
HUGH O'BRIAN: Hugh Krampke
MAUREEN O'HARA: Maureen Fitzsimons
OZZY OSBOURNE: John Michael Osbourne
PATTI PAGE: Clara Ann Fowler
JACK PALANCE: Walter Palanuik
BERT PARKS: Bert Jacobson
MINNIE PEARL: Sarah Ophelia Cannon
BERNADETTE PETERS: Bernadette Lazzaro
EDITH PIAF: Edith Gassion
SLIM PICKENS: Louis Lindley
MARY PICKFORD: Gladys Smith
PAULA PRENTISS: Paula Ragusa
ROBERT PRESTON: Robert Preston Meservey
PRINCE: Prince Rogers Nelson
DEE DEE RAMONE: Douglas Colvin
JOEY RAMONE: Jeffrey Hyman
JOHNNY RAMONE: John Cummings
TOMMY RAMONE: Tom Erdelyi
TONY RANDALL: Leonard Rosenberg
MARTHA RAYE: Margaret O'Reed
DONNA REED: Donna Belle Mullenger
DELLA REESE: Delloreese Patricia Early
BUSTA RHYMES: Trevor Smith Jr.
JOAN RIVERS: Joan Sandra Molinsky
EDWARD G. ROBINSON: Emmanuel Goldenberg
THE ROCK: Dwayne Johnson
GINGER ROGERS: Virginia McMath
ROY ROGERS: Leonard Franklin Slye
MICKEY ROONEY: Joe Yule Jr.
JOHNNY ROTTEN: John Lydon
LILLIAN RUSSELL: Helen Leonard
MEG RYAN: Margaret Hyra
WINONA RYDER: Winona Horowitz
SADE: Helen Folsad Abu
SOUPY SALES: Milton Hines
SUSAN SARANDON: Susan Tomaling
SEAL: Samuel Sealhenry
RANDOLPH SCOTT: George Randolph Crane
JANE SEYMOUR: Joyce Frankenberg
OMAR SHARIF: Michael Shalhoub
CHARLIE SHEEN: Carlos Irwin Estevez
MARTIN SHEEN: Ramon Estevez
BEVERLY SILLS: Belle Silverman
TALIA SHIRE: Talia Coppola
PHIL SILVERS: Philip Silversmith
SINBAD: David Atkins
SNOOP DOGGY DOG: Calvin Broadus
ANN SOTHERN: Harriette Lake
ROBERT STACK: Robert Modini
BARBARA STANWYCK: Ruby Stevens
JEAN STAPLETON: Jeanne Murray
RINGO STARR: Richard Starkey
CONNIE STEVENS: Concetta Ingolia
STING: Gordon Sumner
JOE STRUMMER: John Graham Mellor
DONNA SUMMER: La Donna Gaines
RIP TAYLOR: Charles Elmer Jr.
ROBERT TAYLOR: Spangler Brugh
DANNY THOMAS: Muzyad Yakhoob, later Amos Jacobs
TINY TIM: Herbert Khaury
RIP TORN: Elmore Rual Torn Jr.
RANDY TRAVIS: Randy Traywick
SOPHIE TUCKER: Sophia Kalish
TINA TURNER: Annie Mae Bullock
TWIGGY: Leslie Hornby
CONWAY TWITTY: Harold Lloyd Jenkins
RUDOLPH VALENTINO: Rudolpho D'Antonguolla
FRANKIE VALLI: Frank Castelluccio
SID VICIOUS: John Simon Ritchie
JOHN WAYNE: Marion Morrison
CLIFTON WEBB: Webb Hollenbeck
RAQUEL WELCH: Raquel Tejada
GENE WILDER: Jerome Silberman
SHELLEY WINTERS: Shirley Schrift
STEVIE WONDER: Stevland Morris
JANE WYMAN: Sarah Jane Fulks
GIG YOUNG: Byron Barr
LORETTA YOUNG: Gretchen Michaels

ARTS AND MEDIA

Some Notable Movies, Sept. 2004 – Aug. 2005

Film	Stars	Director
Alexander	Colin Farrell, Anthony Hopkins, Angelina Jolie	Oliver Stone
Are We There Yet?	Ice Cube, Nia Long	Brian Levant
The Aviator	Cate Blanchett, Leonardo DiCaprio	Martin Scorsese
Batman Begins	Christian Bale, Michael Caine, Katie Holmes, Liam Neeson	Christopher Nolan
Bewitched	Will Farrell, Nicole Kidman, Shirley MacLaine	Nora Ephron
Blade Trinity	Jessica Biel, Kris Kristofferson, Ryan Reynolds, Wesley Snipes	David S. Goyer
Bridget Jones: The Edge of Reason	Colin Firth, Hugh Grant, Renée Zellweger	Beeban Kidron
Broken Flowers	Julie Delpy, Bill Murray, Sharon Stone, Jeffrey Wright	Jim Jarmusch
Charlie and the Chocolate Factory	Johnny Depp, Freddie Highmore	Tim Burton
Cinderella Man	Russell Crowe, Paul Giamatti, Renée Zellweger	Ron Howard
Closer	Jude Law, Clive Owen, Natalie Portman, Julia Roberts	Mike Nichols
Coach Carter	Samuel L. Jackson	Thomas Carter
Crash	Sandra Bullock, Don Cheadle, Matt Dillon, Jennifer Esposito	Paul Haggis
Diary of a Mad Black Woman	Kimberly Elise, Steve Harris, Tyler Perry	Darren Grant
The Dukes of Hazzard	Johnny Knoxville, Willie Nelson, Burt Reynolds, Seann William Scott, Jessica Simpson	Jay Chandrasekhar
Fantastic Four	Jessica Alba, Michael Chiklis, Chris Evans, Ioan Gruffudd, Julian McMahon	Tim Story
Fever Pitch	Drew Barrymore, Jimmy Fallon	Bobby & Peter Farrelly
Finding Neverland	Johnny Depp, Dustin Hoffman, Kate Winslet	Marc Forster
The 40-Year-Old Virgin	Steve Carell, Catherine Keener, Paul Rudd	Judd Apatow
Four Brothers	Andre Benjamin, Tyrese Gibson, Mark Wahlberg	John Singleton
The Grudge	Jason Behr, Sarah Michelle Gellar, Bill Pullman	Takashi Shimizu
Herbie: Fully Loaded	Michael Keaton, Lindsay Lohan	Angela Robinson
Hitch	Kevin James, Eva Mendes, Will Smith	Andy Tennant
The Hitchhiker's Guide to the Galaxy	Martin Freeman, Sam Rockwell	Garth Jennings
Hotel Rwanda	Don Cheadle, Nick Nolte, Sophie Okonedo	Terry George
House of Flying Daggers	Takeshi Kaneshiro, Andy Lau, Ziyi Zhang	Zhang Yimou
Hustle & Flow	Terrence DaShon Howard, Ludacris	Craig Brewer
I Heart Huckabees	Dustin Hoffman, Jason Schwartzman, Lily Tomlin	David O. Russell
In Good Company	Topher Grace, Scarlett Johansson, Dennis Quaid	Paul Weitz
The Incredibles	Holly Hunter, Samuel L. Jackson, Craig T. Nelson, Elizabeth Peña	Brad Bird
The Interpreter	Nicole Kidman, Sean Penn	Sidney Pollack
Kinsey	Laura Linney, Liam Neeson, Chris O'Donnell, Peter Sarsgaard	Bill Condon
Kung Fu Hustle	Stephen Chow, Qiu Yuen, Wah Yuen	Stephen Chow
Lemony Snicket's A Series of Unfortunate Events	Jim Carrey, Meryl Streep	Brad Silberling
The Life Aquatic with Steve Zissou	Cate Blanchett, Willem Dafoe, Anjelica Huston, Bill Murray, Owen Wilson	Wes Anderson
The Longest Yard	Burt Reynolds, Chris Rock, Adam Sandler	Peter Segal
Madagascar	Sacha Baron Cohen, Chris Rock, David Schwimmer, Jada Pinkett Smith, Ben Stiller	Eric Darnell, Tom McGrath
March of the Penguins	Morgan Freeman (narrator)	Luc Jacquet
Meet the Fockers	Blythe Danner, Robert De Niro, Dustin Hoffman, Ben Stiller, Barbra Streisand	Jay Roach
Million Dollar Baby	Clint Eastwood, Morgan Freeman, Hilary Swank	Clint Eastwood
Monster-in-Law	Jane Fonda, Jennifer Lopez, Wanda Sykes, Michael Vartan	Robert Luketic
The Motorcycle Diaries	Gael García Bernal, Rodrigo de la Serna	Walter Salles
Mr. and Mrs. Smith	Angelina Jolie, Brad Pitt, Vince Vaughn	Doug Liman
Murderball		Henry Alex Rubin, Dana Adam Shapiro
National Treasure	Justin Bartha, Sean Bean, Nicolas Cage, Harvey Keitel, Jon Voight	John Turteltaub
Ocean's Twelve	Don Cheadle, George Clooney, Matt Damon, Bernie Mac, Brad Pitt, Julia Roberts, Catherine Zeta-Jones	Steven Soderbergh
The Pacifier	Vin Diesel, Faith Ford, Lauren Graham, Carol Kane	Adam Shankman
The Phantom of the Opera	Gerard Butler, Minnie Driver, Miranda Richardson, Emmy Rossum	Joel Schumacher
Polar Express	Tom Hanks	Robert Zemeckis
Ray	Jamie Foxx, Regina King, Kerry Washington	Taylor Hackford
Red Eye	Rachel McAdams, Cillian Murphy	Wes Craven
Robots	Halle Berry, Jim Broadbent, Mel Brooks, Drew Carey, Greg Kinnear, Ewan McGregor, Robin Williams	Chris Wedge, Carlos Saldanha
Shall We Dance?	Richard Gere, Jennifer Lopez, Susan Sarandon, Stanley Tucci	Peter Chelsom
Shark Tale	Jack Black, Robert De Niro, Angelina Jolie, Martin Scorsese, Will Smith, Renée Zellweger	Bibo Bergeron, Vicky Jenson, Rob Letterman
Sideways	Thomas Hayden Church, Paul Giamatti, Virginia Madsen, Sandra Oh	Alexander Payne
Sin City	Jessica Alba, Rosario Dawson, Benicio Del Toro, Clive Owen, Mickey Rourke, Bruce Willis, Elijah Wood	Robert Rodriguez, Frank Miller, Quentin Tarantino
Spanglish	Cloris Leachman, Téa Leoni, Adam Sandler, Paz Vega	James L. Brooks
The SpongeBob SquarePants Movie	Alec Baldwin, David Hasselhoff, Scarlett Johansson, Tom Kenny, Jeffrey Tambor	Stephen Hillenburg
Star Wars: Episode 3– Revenge of the Sith	Hayden Christensen, Samuel L. Jackson, Christopher Lee, Ewan McGregor, Frank Oz, Natalie Portman	George Lucas
Team America: World Police	Trey Parker, Matt Stone	Trey Parker
War of the Worlds	Tom Cruise, Dakota Fanning, Tim Robbins	Steven Spielberg
Wedding Crashers	Rachel McAdams, Vince Vaughn, Christopher Walken, Owen Wilson	David Dobkin

IT'S A FACT: *March of the Penguins*, a nature documentary about the mating habits of Antarctica's emperor penguins, scored a surprising box office success in the summer of 2005. The English version was altered from the original French release, which had featured actors' voices speaking for the penguins in sometimes comical ways (replaced with traditional narration by Morgan Freeman). By Sept. 2005, the film had grossed $63.6 mil in the U.S. alone, making it the 2nd-highest-grossing documentary ever released in the U.S. (after *Fahrenheit 9/11*).

50 Top-Grossing Movies, 2004

Source: *Variety*, box-office grosses in the U.S. and Canada during calendar year 2004

Rank	Title	Gross (millions)
1.	Shrek 2	$436.7
2.	Spiderman 2	373.4
3.	The Passion of the Christ	370.3
4.	The Incredibles	251.7
5.	Harry Potter and the Prisoner of Azkaban	249.4
6.	The Day After Tomorrow	186.7
7.	The Bourne Supremacy	176.1
8.	Meet the Fockers	162.5
9.	Shark Tale	160.8
10.	The Polar Express	155.1
11.	National Treasure	154.5
12.	I, Robot	144.8
13.	Troy	133.3
14.	50 First Dates	120.8
15.	Van Helsing	120.1
16.	Fahrenheit 9/11	119.1
17.	DodgeBall: A True Underdog Story	114.3
18.	The Village	114.2
19.	The Grudge	110.2
20.	Ocean's Twelve	107.0
21.	Collateral	100.2
22.	Princess Diaries 2: Royal Engagement	95.2
23.	Lemony Snicket's A Series of Unfortunate Events	94.6
24.	Starsky & Hutch	88.2
25.	Along Came Polly	87.9
26.	Lord of the Rings: Return of the King	$86.6
27.	Mean Girls	86.1
28.	Anchorman	84.3
29.	Scooby Doo 2: Monsters Unleashed	84.2
30.	SpongeBob SquarePants	81.9
31.	The Notebook	81.0
32.	Alien vs. Predator	80.3
33.	Man on Fire	77.9
34.	The Terminal	77.1
35.	Garfield	75.4
36.	Ladder 49	73.9
37.	Christmas With the Kranks	73.1
38.	Ray	71.6
39.	White Chicks	69.1
40.	Hidalgo	67.3
41.	The Forgotten	66.6
42.	Kill Bill Vol. 2	66.2
43.	The Manchurian Candidate	66.0
44.	Barbershop 2	65.1
45.	Miracle	64.4
46.	Friday Night Lights	61.2
47.	The Stepford Wives	59.5
48.	Hellboy	59.0
49.	Dawn of the Dead	58.9
50.	Without a Paddle	58.1

National Film Registry, 1989-2004

Source: National Film Registry, Library of Congress

"Culturally, historically, or esthetically significant" American films placed on the registry. * = selected in 2004.

Abbott and Costello Meet Frankenstein (1948)
Adam's Rib (1949)
The Adventures of Robin Hood (1938)
The African Queen (1951)
Alien (1979)
All About Eve (1950)
All My Babies (1953)
All That Heaven Allows (1955)
All That Jazz (1979)
All Quiet on the Western Front (1930)
All the King's Men (1949)
An American in Paris (1951)
America, America (1963)
American Graffiti (1973)
A Movie (1958)
Annie Hall (1977)
Antonia: A Portrait of the Woman (1974)
The Apartment (1960)
Apocalypse Now (1979)
Atlantic City (1980)
The Awful Truth (1937)
The Bad and the Beautiful (1952)
Badlands (1973)
The Band Wagon (1953)
The Bank Dick (1940)
The Battle of San Pietro (1945)
Beauty and the Beast (1991)
Ben-Hur (1926)
Ben-Hur (1959)*
The Best Years of Our Lives (1946)
Big Business (1929)
The Big Parade (1925)
The Big Sleep (1946)
The Birth of a Nation (1915)
The Black Pirate (1926)
Blacksmith Scene (1893)
The Black Stallion (1979)
Blade Runner (1982)
The Blood of Jesus (1941)
The Blue Bird (1918)*
Bonnie and Clyde (1967)
Boyz N the Hood (1991)
Bride of Frankenstein (1935)
The Bridge on the River Kwai (1957)
Bringing Up Baby (1938)
Broken Blossoms (1919)
A Bronx Morning (1931)*
Butch Cassidy and the Sundance Kid (1969)
Cabaret (1972)
Carmen Jones (1954)
Casablanca (1942)
Castro Street (1966)
Cat People (1942)
Chan Is Missing (1982)
The Cheat (1915)
The Chechahcos (1924)
Chinatown (1974)
Chulas Fronteras (1976)
Citizen Kane (1941)
The City (1939)
City Lights (1931)
Civilization (1916)
Clash of the Wolves (1925)*
Cologne: From the Diary of Ray and Esther (1939)
The Conversation (1974)
The Cool World (1963)
Cops (1922)
A Corner in Wheat (1909)
The Court Jester (1956)*
The Crowd (1928)
Czechoslovakia 1968 (1968)
Daughters of the Dust (1991)*
David Holzman's Diary (1968)
The Day the Earth Stood Still (1951)
Dead Birds (1964)
The Deer Hunter (1978)
Destry Rides Again (1939)
Detour (1946)
Dickson Experimental Sound Film (1894-95)
D.O.A. (1950)*
Dodsworth (1936)
The Docks of New York (1928)
Dog Star Man (1964)
Don't Look Back (1967)
Do the Right Thing (1989)
Double Indemnity (1944)
Dracula (1931)
Dr. Strangelove (or, How I Learned to Stop Worrying and Love the Bomb)(1964)
Duck Amuck (1953)
Duck and Cover (1951)*
Duck Soup (1933)
Easy Rider (1969)
Eaux D'Artifice (1953)
El Norte (1983)
The Emperor Jones (1933)
Empire (1964)*
The Endless Summer (1966)
Enter the Dragon (1973)*
Eraserhead (1978)*
E.T.: The Extra-Terrestrial (1982)
Evidence of the Film (1913)
The Exploits of Elaine (1914)
The Fall of the House of Usher (1928)
Fantasia (1940)
Fatty's Tintype Tangle (1915)
Film Portrait (1970)
Five Easy Pieces (1970)
Flash Gordon serial (1936)
Footlight Parade (1933)
Force of Evil (1948)
The Forgotten Frontier (1931)
42nd Street (1933)
The Four Horsemen of the Apocalypse (1921)
Fox Movietone News: Jenkins Orphanage Band (1928)
Frankenstein (1931)
Frank Film (1973)
Freaks (1932)
The Freshman (1925)
From Here to Eternity (1953)
From the Manger to the Cross (1912)
From Stump to Ship (1930)
Fuji (1974)
Fury (1936)
Garlic is as Good as Ten Mothers (1980)*
The General (1927)
Gerald McBoing Boing (1951)
Gertie the Dinosaur (1914)
Gigi (1958)
The Godfather (1972)
The Godfather, Part II (1974)
Going My Way (1944)*
Gold Diggers of 1933 (1933)
The Gold Rush (1925)
Gone With the Wind (1939)
GoodFellas (1990)
The Graduate (1967)
The Grapes of Wrath (1940)
Grass (1925)
The Great Dictator (1940)
The Great Train Robbery (1903)
Greed (1924)
Gun Crazy (1949)
Gunga Din (1939)
Harlan County, U.S.A. (1976)
Harold and Maude (1972)

The Heiress (1949)
Hell's Hinges (1916)
High Noon (1952)
High School (1968)
Hindenburg Disaster Newsreel Footage (1937)
His Girl Friday (1940)
The Hitch-Hiker (1953)
Hoosiers (1986)
Hospital (1970)
The Hospital (1971)
The House in the Middle (1954)
How Green Was My Valley (1941)
How the West Was Won (1962)
The Hunters (1957)
The Hustler (1961)
I Am a Fugitive from a Chain Gang (1932)
The Immigrant (1917)
In the Heat of the Night (1967)
In the Land of the Head-Hunters aka In the Land of the War Canoes (1914)
Intolerance (1916)
Invasion of the Body Snatchers (1956)
It (1927)
It Happened One Night (1934)
It's a Wonderful Life (1946)
The Italian (1915)
Jailhouse Rock (1957)*
Jammin' the Blues (1944)
Jam Session (1942)
Jaws (1975)
Jazz on a Summer's Day (1959)
The Jazz Singer (1927)
Kannapolis, NC (1941)*
Killer of Sheep (1977)
King: A Filmed Record . . .Montgomery to Memphis (1970)
King Kong (1933)
The Kiss (1896)
Kiss Me Deadly (1955)
Knute Rockne, All American (1940)
Koyaanisqatsi (1983)
The Lady Eve (1941)
Lady Helen's Escapade (1909)*
Lady Windermere's Fan (1925)
Lambchops (1929)
The Land Beyond the Sunset (1912)
Lassie Come Home (1943)
The Last of the Mohicans (1920)
The Last Picture Show (1972)
Laura (1944)
Lawrence of Arabia (1962)
The Learning Tree (1969)
Let's All Go to the Lobby (1957)
Letter From an Unknown Woman (1948)
The Life and Death of 9413—A Hollywood Extra (1928)
Life and Times of Rosie the Riveter (1980)
The Life of Emile Zola (1937)
Little Caesar (1930)
The Little Fugitive (1953)
Little Miss Marker (1934)
The Living Desert (1953)
The Lost World (1925)
Louisiana Story (1948)
Love Finds Andy Hardy (1938)
Love Me Tonight (1932)
Magical Maestro (1952)
The Magnificent Ambersons (1942)
The Maltese Falcon (1941)
The Manchurian Candidate (1962)
Manhattan (1921)
Manhattan (1979)
March of Time: Inside Nazi Germany—1938 (1938)
Marian Anderson: The Lincoln Memorial Concert (1939)
Marty (1955)
M*A*S*H (1970)
Master Hands (1936)
Matrimony's Speed Limit (1913)
Mean Streets (1973)
Medium Cool (1969)
Meet Me in St. Louis (1944)
Melody Ranch (1940)
Memphis Belle (1944)
Meshes of the Afternoon (1943)
Midnight Cowboy (1969)
Mildred Pierce (1945)
The Miracle of Morgan's Creek (1944)
Miss Lulu Bett (1921)
Modern Times (1936)
Modesta (1956)
Morocco (1930)
Motion Painting No. 1 (1947)
Mr. Smith Goes to Washington (1939)
Multiple Sidosis (1970)
The Music Box (1932)
My Darling Clementine (1946)
My Man Godfrey (1936)
The Naked Spur (1953)
Nanook of the North (1922)
Nashville (1975)
National Lampoon's Animal House (1978)
National Velvet (1944)
Naughty Marietta (1935)
Network (1976)
A Night at the Opera (1935)
The Night of the Hunter (1955)
Night of the Living Dead (1968)
Ninotchka (1939)
North by Northwest (1959)
Nostalgia (1971)
Nothing but a Man (1964)
The Nutty Professor (1963)*
OffOn (1968)*
One Flew Over the Cuckoo's Nest (1975)
One Froggy Evening (1956)
On the Waterfront (1954)
The Outlaw Josey Wales (1976)
Out of the Past (1947)
The Ox-Bow Incident (1943)
Pass the Gravy (1928)
Paths of Glory (1957)
Patton (1970)
The Pearl (1948)
Peter Pan (1924)
Phantom of the Opera (1925)
The Philadelphia Story (1940)
Pinocchio (1940)
A Place in the Sun (1951)
Planet of the Apes (1968)
The Plow That Broke the Plains (1936)
Point of Order (1964)
The Poor Little Rich Girl (1917)
Popeye the Sailor Meets Sindbad the Sailor (1936)*
Porky in Wackyland (1938)
Powers of Ten (1978)
President McKinley Inauguration Footage (1901)
Primary (1960)
Princess Nicotine; or The Smoke Fairy (1909)
The Prisoner of Zenda (1937)
The Producers (1968)
Psycho (1960)
The Public Enemy (1931)
Pull My Daisy (1959)
Punch Drunks (1934)
Pups is Pups (Our Gang) (1930)*
Raging Bull (1980)
Raiders of the Lost Ark (1981)
Rear Window (1954)
Rebel Without a Cause (1955)
Red River (1948)
Regeneration (1915)
Republic Steel Strike Riots Newsreel Footage (1937)
Return of the Secaucus 7 (1980)
Ride the High Country (1962)
Rip Van Winkle (1896)
The River (1937)
Road to Morocco (1942)
Roman Holiday (1953)
Rose Hobart (1936)
Sabrina (1954)
Safety Last (1923)
Salesman (1969)
Salomé (1922)
Salt of the Earth (1954)
Scarface (1932)
Schindler's List (1993)*
The Searchers (1956)
Serene Velocity (1970)
Seven Brides for Seven Brothers (1954)*
Seventh Heaven (1927)
Shadow of a Doubt (1943)
Shadows (1959)
Shaft (1971)
Shane (1953)
She Done Him Wrong (1933)
Sherlock, Jr. (1924)
Sherman's March (1986)
Shock Corridor (1963)
The Shop Around the Corner (1940)
Show Boat (1936)
Show People (1928)
Singin' in the Rain (1952)
Sky High (1922)
Snow White (1933)
Snow White and the Seven Dwarfs (1937)
Some Like It Hot (1959)
The Son of the Sheik (1926)
The Sound of Music (1965)
Stagecoach (1939)
A Star Is Born (1954)
Star Theatre (1901)
Star Wars (1977)
Steamboat Willie (1928)
Stranger Than Paradise (1984)
A Streetcar Named Desire (1951)
Stormy Weather (1943)
Sullivan's Travels (1941)
Sunrise (1927)
Sunset Boulevard (1950)
Sweet Smell of Success (1957)
Swing Time (1936)*
Tabu (1931)
Tacoma Narrows Bridge Collapse (1940)
The Tall T (1957)
Tarzan and His Mate (1934)
Taxi Driver (1976)
The Ten Commandments (1956)
The Tell-Tale Heart (1953)
Tevye (1939)
Theodore Case Sound Tests: Gus Visser and His Singing Duck (1925)
There It Is (1928)*
The Thief of Bagdad (1924)
The Thin Blue Line (1988)
The Thing From Another World (1951)
The Thin Man (1934)
This Is Cinerama (1952)
This Is Spinal Tap (1984)
Through Navajo Eyes (series) (1966)
Tin Toy (1988)
To Be or Not To Be (1942)
To Fly (1976)
To Kill a Mockingbird (1962)
Tootsie (1982)
Topaz (1943-45)
Top Hat (1935)
Touch of Evil (1958)
Trance and Dance in Bali (1936-39)
The Treasure of the Sierra Madre (1948)
Trouble in Paradise (1932)
Tulips Shall Grow (1942)
Twelve O'Clock High (1949)
2001: A Space Odyssey (1968)
Unforgiven (1992)*
Verbena Tragica (1939)
Vertigo (1958)
The Wedding March (1928)
Westinghouse Works 1904 (1904)
West Side Story (1961)
What's Opera, Doc? (1957)
Where Are My Children? (1916)
White Heat (1949)
Why Man Creates (1968)
Why We Fight (Series/1943-45)
Wild and Wooly (1917)
The Wild Bunch (1969)
Wild River (1960)
Will Success Spoil Rock Hunter? (1957)
The Wind (1928)
Wings (1927)
Within Our Gates (1920)
The Wizard of Oz (1939)
Woman of the Year (1942)
A Woman Under the Influence (1974)
Woodstock (1970)
Yankee Doodle Dandy (1942)
Young Frankenstein (1974)
Young Mr. Lincoln (1939)
Zapruder Film (1963)

Top Movie Songs of All Time

In 2004, the American Film Institute published its list of top (American) movie songs of all time, based on a poll of jurors mostly from the film world. The top 10 are listed here.

Song	Movie	Year
1. "Over the Rainbow"	The Wizard of Oz	1939
2. "As Time Goes By"	Casablanca	1942
3. "Singin' in the Rain"	Singin' in the Rain	1952
4. "Moon River"	Breakfast at Tiffany's	1961
5. "White Christmas"	Holiday Inn	1942
6. "Mrs. Robinson"	The Graduate	1967
7. "When You Wish Upon a Star"	Pinocchio	1940
8. "The Way We Were"	The Way We Were	1973
9. "Stayin' Alive"	Saturday Night Fever	1977
10. "The Sound of Music"	The Sound of Music	1965

100 Best American Movies of All Time

Source: American Film Institute

Compiled in 1998 based on ballots sent to 1,500 figures, mostly from the film world. Criteria for judging included historical significance, critical recognition and awards, and popularity. The year each film was first released is in parentheses.

1. Citizen Kane (1941)
2. Casablanca (1942)
3. The Godfather (1972)
4. Gone With the Wind (1939)
5. Lawrence of Arabia (1962)
6. The Wizard of Oz (1939)
7. The Graduate (1967)
8. On the Waterfront (1954)
9. Schindler's List (1993)
10. Singin' in the Rain (1952)
11. It's a Wonderful Life (1946)
12. Sunset Boulevard (1950)
13. The Bridge on the River Kwai (1957)
14. Some Like It Hot (1959)
15. Star Wars (1977)
16. All About Eve (1950)
17. The African Queen (1951)
18. Psycho (1960)
19. Chinatown (1974)
20. One Flew Over the Cuckoo's Nest (1975)
21. The Grapes of Wrath (1940)
22. 2001: A Space Odyssey (1968)
23. The Maltese Falcon (1941)
24. Raging Bull (1980)
25. E.T.: The Extra-Terrestrial (1982)
26. Dr. Strangelove (1964)
27. Bonnie and Clyde (1967)
28. Apocalypse Now (1979)
29. Mr. Smith Goes to Washington (1939)
30. Treasure of the Sierra Madre (1948)
31. Annie Hall (1977)
32. The Godfather, Part II (1974)
33. High Noon (1952)
34. To Kill a Mockingbird (1962)
35. It Happened One Night (1934)
36. Midnight Cowboy (1969)
37. The Best Years of Our Lives (1946)
38. Double Indemnity (1944)
39. Doctor Zhivago (1965)
40. North by Northwest (1959)
41. West Side Story (1961)
42. Rear Window (1954)
43. King Kong (1933)
44. The Birth of a Nation (1915)
45. A Streetcar Named Desire (1951)
46. A Clockwork Orange (1971)
47. Taxi Driver (1976)
48. Jaws (1975)
49. Snow White and the Seven Dwarfs (1937)
50. Butch Cassidy and the Sundance Kid (1969)
51. The Philadelphia Story (1940)
52. From Here to Eternity (1953)
53. Amadeus (1984)
54. All Quiet on the Western Front (1930)
55. The Sound of Music (1965)
56. M*A*S*H (1970)
57. The Third Man (1949)
58. Fantasia (1940)
59. Rebel Without a Cause (1955)
60. Raiders of the Lost Ark (1981)
61. Vertigo (1958)
62. Tootsie (1982)
63. Stagecoach (1939)
64. Close Encounters of the Third Kind (1977)
65. The Silence of the Lambs (1991)
66. Network (1976)
67. The Manchurian Candidate (1962)
68. An American in Paris (1951)
69. Shane (1953)
70. The French Connection (1971)
71. Forrest Gump (1994)
72. Ben-Hur (1959)
73. Wuthering Heights (1939)
74. The Gold Rush (1925)
75. Dances With Wolves (1990)
76. City Lights (1931)
77. American Graffiti (1973)
78. Rocky (1976)
79. The Deer Hunter (1978)
80. The Wild Bunch (1969)
81. Modern Times (1936)
82. Giant (1956)
83. Platoon (1986)
84. Fargo (1996)
85. Duck Soup (1933)
86. Mutiny on the Bounty (1935)
87. Frankenstein (1931)
88. Easy Rider (1969)
89. Patton (1970)
90. The Jazz Singer (1927)
91. My Fair Lady (1964)
92. A Place in the Sun (1951)
93. The Apartment (1960)
94. Goodfellas (1990)
95. Pulp Fiction (1994)
96. The Searchers (1956)
97. Bringing Up Baby (1938)
98. Unforgiven (1992)
99. Guess Who's Coming to Dinner (1967)
100. Yankee Doodle Dandy (1942)

All-Time Top-Grossing American Movies[1]

Source: *Variety* magazine

Rank	Title (original release)	Gross[2]
1.	Titanic (1997)	$600.8
2.	Star Wars: Episode IV–A New Hope (1977)	461.0
3.	Shrek 2 (2004)	436.7
4.	E.T.: The Extra-Terrestrial (1982)	435.0
5.	Star Wars: Episode I–The Phantom Menace (1999)	431.1
6.	Spider-Man (2002)	403.7
7.	Star Wars: Episode III–Revenge of the Sith (2005)	379.4
8.	The Lord of the Rings: The Return of the King (2003)	377.0
9.	Spider-Man 2 (2004)	373.4
10.	The Passion of the Christ (2004)	370.3
11.	Jurassic Park (1993)	357.1
12.	The Lord of the Rings: The Two Towers (2002)	341.7
13.	Finding Nemo (2003)	339.7
14.	Forrest Gump (1994)	329.7
15.	The Lion King (1994)	328.5
16.	Harry Potter and the Sorcerer's Stone (2001)	317.6
17.	The Lord of the Rings: The Fellowship of the Ring (2001)	314.8
18.	Star Wars: Episode II–Attack of the Clones (2002)	310.7
19.	Star Wars: Episode VI–Return of the Jedi (1983)	309.2
20.	Independence Day (1996)	306.2
21.	Pirates of the Caribbean: The Curse of the Black Pearl (2003)	305.4
22.	The Sixth Sense (1999)	293.5
23.	Star Wars: Episode V–The Empire Strikes Back (1980)	290.3
24.	Home Alone (1990)	285.8
25.	The Matrix: Reloaded (2003)	$281.5
26.	Meet the Fockers (2004)	279.2
27.	Shrek (2001)	267.7
28.	Harry Potter and the Chamber of Secrets (2002)	262.0
29.	The Incredibles (2004)	261.4
30.	Dr. Seuss' How the Grinch Stole Christmas (2000)	260.0
31.	Jaws (1975)	260.0
32.	Monsters, Inc. (2001)	255.9
33.	Batman (1989)	251.2
34.	Men in Black (1997)	250.7
35.	Harry Potter and the Prisoner of Azkaban (2004)	249.4
36.	Toy Story 2 (1999)	245.9
37.	Bruce Almighty (2003)	242.7
38.	Raiders of the Lost Ark (1981)	242.4
39.	Twister (1996)	241.7
40.	My Big Fat Greek Wedding (2002)	241.4
41.	Ghostbusters (1984)	238.6
42.	Beverly Hills Cop (1984)	234.8
43.	Cast Away (2000)	233.6
44.	The Exorcist (1973)	232.7
45.	War of the Worlds (2005)	231.8
46.	The Lost World: Jurassic Park (1997)	229.1
47.	Signs (2002)	228.0
48.	Rush Hour 2 (2001)	226.2
49.	Mrs. Doubtfire (1993)	219.2
50.	Ghost (1990)	217.6

(1) Through Sept. 1, 2005. (2) Gross is in millions of absolute dollars based on box office sales in the U.S. and Canada. Rising ticket prices favor newer films. Revenues from re-releases are included.

WORLD ALMANAC EDITORS' PICKS
Most Terrifying Movie Villains of All Time

The editors of *The World Almanac* have ranked the following as the most terrifying movie villains in film history.

1. Darth Vader, *Star Wars* trilogy, 1977-1983
2. Dr. Hannibal Lecter, *The Silence of the Lambs*, 1991
3. The Wicked Witch of the West, *The Wizard of Oz*, 1939
4. Norman Bates, *Psycho*, 1960
5. HAL 9000, *2001: A Space Odyssey*, 1968
6. Jack Torrance, *The Shining*, 1980
7. Nurse Ratched, *One Flew Over the Cuckoo's Nest*, 1975
8. Count Dracula, *Dracula*, 1931
9. Mr. Potter, *It's a Wonderful Life*, 1946
10. The Shark, *Jaws*, 1975

Most Popular Movie Videos/DVDs

Source: Alexander & Associates/Video Flash, New York, NY

Note: Year given to distinguish from other films with the same title.

ALL TIME

Top Ten Rentals

VHS[1]

1. Top Gun
2. Pretty Woman
3. The Little Mermaid
4. Cinderella
5. Home Alone
6. Ghost
7. The Lion King
8. Forrest Gump
9. Terminator II: Judgment Day
10. Dances With Wolves

DVD[3]

1. The Fast and the Furious
2. The Matrix
3. Gladiator (2000)
4. The Lord of the Rings: The Fellowship of the Ring
5. Shrek
6. Training Day
7. Pearl Harbor (2001)
8. Black Hawk Down
9. Spider-Man (2002)
10. My Big Fat Greek Wedding

Top Ten Purchase Titles

VHS[2]

1. The Lion King
2. Cinderella
3. Snow White and the Seven Dwarfs
4. Forrest Gump
5. Aladdin
6. Toy Story
7. Jurassic Park
8. Pocahontas
9. Beauty and the Beast
10. The Little Mermaid

DVD[3]

1. The Lord of the Rings: The Fellowship of the Ring
2. Shrek
3. Harry Potter and the Sorcerer's Stone
4. Spider-Man (2002)
5. Gladiator (2000)
6. Monsters Inc.
7. The Fast and the Furious
8. The Matrix
9. Finding Nemo
10. A Knight's Tale

2004

Top Ten Purchase Titles

VHS

1. Pirates of the Caribbean: The Curse of the Black Pearl
2. Bruce Almighty
3. Brother Bear
4. Finding Nemo
5. Bad Boys 2
6. The Lord of the Rings: The Return of the King
7. Seabiscuit
8. The Lion King 1 1/2
9. Cheaper by the Dozen
10. The Passion of the Christ

DVD

1. Shrek 2
2. The Passion of the Christ
3. Finding Nemo
4. Pirates of the Caribbean: The Curse of the Black Pearl
5. The Day After Tomorrow
6. The Lord of the Rings: The Return of the King
7. Bad Boys 2
8. Seabiscuit
9. Spider-Man 2
10. Cheaper by the Dozen (2003)

Top Ten Rental Titles

VHS

1. Bruce Almighty
2. Cheaper by the Dozen (2003)
3. Pirates of the Caribbean: The Curse of the Black Pearl
4. Finding Nemo
5. School of Rock
6. Bad Boys 2
7. S.W.A.T
8. Gothika
9. Radio
10. Seabiscuit

DVD

1. The Day After Tomorrow
2. Man on Fire (2004)
3. Kill Bill Vol. 1
4. The Passion of the Christ
5. Shrek 2
6. 13 Going on 30
7. Pirates of the Caribbean: The Curse of the Black Pearl
8. Cheaper by the Dozen (2003)
9. Big Fish
10. Mean Girls

(1) March 1, 1987, to Dec. 31, 2004. (2) Feb. 16, 1988, to Dec. 31, 2004. (3) Jan. 1, 2000, to Dec. 31, 2004.

Top-Selling Video Games, 2004

Source: The NPD Group / NPD Funworld / Point-of-Sale; ranked by units sold.

Title, Platform

1. Grand Theft Auto: San Andreas, Sony PlayStation 2
2. Halo 2, Microsoft Xbox
3. Madden NFL 2005, Sony PlayStation 2
4. ESPN NFL 2K5, Sony PlayStation 2
5. Need For Speed: Underground 2, Sony PlayStation 2
6. Pokemon Fire Red, Nintendo Game Boy Advance
7. NBA Live 2005, Sony PlayStation 2
8. Spider-Man, The Movie 2, Sony PlayStation 2
9. Halo, Microsoft Xbox
10. ESPN NFL 2K5, Microsoft Xbox

Top 50 Record Long-Run Broadway Plays[1]

Source: The League of American Theatres and Producers, Inc., New York, NY; www.IBDB.com

	Title (Run)	Performances[2]
1.	Cats (1982-2000)	7,485
2.	*The Phantom of the Opera (1988-)	7,337
3.	Les Misérables (1987-2003)	6,680
4.	A Chorus Line (1975-90)	6,137
5.	Oh! Calcutta! (revival, 1976-89)	5,959
6.	*Beauty and the Beast (1994-)	4,662
7.	Miss Saigon (1991-2001)	4,092
8.	*Rent (1996-)	3,890
9.	*Chicago (revival, 1996-)	3,661
10.	42nd Street (1980-89)	3,486
11.	Grease (1972-80)	3,388
12.	*The Lion King (1997-)	3,253
13.	Fiddler on the Roof (1964-72)	3,242
14.	Life With Father (1939-47)	3,224
15.	Tobacco Road (1933-41)	3,182
16.	Hello, Dolly! (1964-70)	2,844
17.	My Fair Lady (1956-62)	2,717
18.	Annie (1977-83)	2,377
	Cabaret (revival, 1998-2004)	2,377
20.	Man of La Mancha (1965-71)	2,328
21.	Abie's Irish Rose (1922-27)	2,327
22.	Oklahoma! (1943-48)	2,212
23.	Smokey Joe's Cafe (1995-2000)	2,036
24.	Pippin (1972-77)	1,944
25.	South Pacific (1949-54)	1,925
26.	The Magic Show (1974-78)	1,920
27.	Aida (2000-04)	1,852
28.	Gemini (1977-81)	1,819
29.	*The Producers (2001-)	1,817
30.	Deathtrap (1978-82)	1,793
31.	Harvey (1944-49)	1,775
32.	Dancin' (1978-82)	1,774
33.	La Cage aux Folles (1983-87)	1,761
34.	Hair (1968-72)	1,750
35.	The Wiz (1975-79)	1,672
36.	Born Yesterday (1946-49)	1,642
37.	Crazy For You (1992-96)	1,622
38	*Mamma Mia! (2001-)	1,608
39.	Ain't Misbehavin' (1978-82)	1,604
40.	The Best Little Whorehouse in Texas (1978-82)	1,584
41.	Mary, Mary (1961-64)	1,572
42.	Evita (1979-83)	1,567
43.	The Voice of the Turtle (1943-48)	1,557
44.	Jekyll & Hyde (1997-2001)	1,543
45.	Barefoot in the Park (1963-67)	1,530
46.	42nd Street (revival, 2001-05)	1,524
47.	Dreamgirls (1981-85)	1,521
48.	Mame (1966-70)	1,508
49.	Grease (revival, 1994-98)	1,505
50.	Same Time, Next Year (1975-78)	1,453

*Still running Sept. 1, 2005. (1) Unless noted, listings reflect a play's first run on Broadway. (2) Number of performances through Sept. 1, 2005.

Broadway Season Statistics, 1959-2005

Source: The League of American Theatres and Producers, Inc., New York, NY

Season	Gross (mil $)	Attendance (mil)	Playing Weeks	New Productions
1959-1960	46	7.9	1,156	58
1960-1961	44	7.7	1,210	48
1961-1962	44	6.8	1,166	53
1962-1963	44	7.4	1,134	54
1963-1964	40	6.8	1,107	63
1964-1965	50	8.2	1,250	67
1965-1966	54	9.6	1,295	68
1966-1967	55	9.3	1,269	69
1967-1968	59	9.5	1,259	74
1968-1969	58	8.6	1,209	67
1969-1970	53	7.1	1,047	62
1970-1971	55	7.4	1,107	49
1971-1972	52	6.5	1,157	55
1972-1973	45	5.4	889	55
1973-1974	46	5.7	907	43
1974-1975	57	6.6	1,101	54
1975-1976	71	7.3	1,136	55
1976-1977	93	8.8	1,349	54
1977-1978	114	9.6	1,433	42
1978-1979	134	9.6	1,542	50
1979-1980	146	9.6	1,540	61
1980-1981	197	11.0	1,544	60
1981-1982	223	10.1	1,455	48
1982-1983	209	8.4	1,258	50
1983-1984	227	7.9	1,097	36
1984-1985	209	7.3	1,078	33
1985-1986	190	6.5	1,041	34
1986-1987	208	7.1	1,039	41
1987-1988	253	8.1	1,113	30
1988-1989	262	8.1	1,108	33
1989-1990	282	8.0	1,070	40
1990-1991	267	7.3	971	28
1991-1992	293	7.4	905	37
1992-1993	328	7.9	1,019	34
1993-1994	356	8.1	1,066	39
1994-1995	406	9.0	1,120	33
1995-1996	436	9.5	1,146	38
1996-1997	499	10.6	1,349	37
1997-1998	558	11.5	1,442	33
1998-1999	588	11.7	1,441	39
1999-2000	603	11.4	1,464	37
2000-2001	666	11.9	1,484	28
2001-2002	643	11.0	1,434	28
2002-2003	721	11.4	1,544	36
2003-2004	771	11.6	1,451	39
2004-2005	769	11.5	1,494	39

U.S. Symphony Orchestras[1]

Source: *Symphony* magazine, American Symphony Orchestra League

Symphony Orchestra[2]	Music Director[3]
Akron (OH)	Ya-Hui Wang
Alabama (Birmingham)	Christopher Confessore
American (New York, NY)	Leon Botstein
Arkansas (Little Rock)	David Itkin
Atlanta (GA)	Robert Spano
Austin (TX)	Peter Bay
Baltimore (MD)	Yuri Temirkanov
Baton Rouge Symphony (LA)	Timothy Muffitt
Boston (MA)	James Levine
Brooklyn Philharmonic Orch. (NY)	Michael Christie
Buffalo Philharmonic Orch. (NY)	JoAnn Falletta
Cedar Rapids (IA)	Christian Tiemeyer
Chamber Orch. of Philadelphia (PA)	Ignat Solzhenitsyn
Charlotte Symphony (NC)	Christof Perick
Chattanooga Symphony and Opera Assn. (TN)	Robert E. Bernhardt
Chicago (IL)	Daniel Barenboim
Chicago Sinfonietta (IL)	Paul Freeman
Cincinnati (OH)	Paavo Järvi
Cleveland Orch. (OH)	Franz Welser-Möst
Colorado (Denver)	Marin Alsop
Columbus (OH)	Gunther Herbig
Dallas (TX)	Andrew Litton
Dayton Philharmonic Orch. (OH)	Neal Gittleman
Delaware (Wilmington)	David Amato
Des Moines Symphony (IA)	Joseph S. Giunta
Detroit (MI)	Neeme Järvi
Elgin (IL)	Robert Hanson
Eos Orch. (NYC)	Jonathan Sheffer
Evansville Philharmonic Orch. (IN)	Alfred Savia
Florida Orchestra (Tampa)	Stefan Sanderling
Florida West Coast (Sarasota)	Leif Bjaland
Fort Wayne Philharmonic Orch. (IN)	Edvard Tchivzhel
Fort Worth (TX)	Miguel Harth-Bedoya
Grand Rapids Symphony (MI)	David Lockington
Grant Park Orchestra and Chorus (Chicago)	Carlos Kalmar
Greenville (SC)	Edvard Tchivzhel
Handel & Haydn Society (Boston)	Christopher Hogwood
Harrisburg Symphony Assn. (PA)	Stuart Malina
Hartford (CT)	Edward Cumming
Honolulu (HI)	Samuel Wong
Houston Symphony (TX)	Hans Graf
Indianapolis (IN)	Mario Venzago
Jacksonville (FL)	Fabio Mechetti
Kalamazoo (MI)	Raymond C. Harvey
Kansas City Symphony (MO)	Timothy Hankervich
Knoxville (TN)	Lucas Richman
Long Beach (CA)	Enrique Arturo Diemecke
Long Island Philharmonic	David S. Wiley
Los Angeles Chamber Orch. (CA)	Jeffrey Kahane
Los Angeles Philharmonic (CA)	Esa-Pekka Salonen
Louisiana Philharmonic Orch.	Carlos Miguel Prieto
Louisville Orchestra (KY)	Manning G. Warren III
Madison (WI)	John DeMain
Memphis (TN)	David Loebel
Milwaukee (WI)	Andreas Delfs
Minnesota Orch. (Minneapolis)	Osmo Vänskä
Mississippi (Jackson)	Crafton Beck
Music of the Baroque (Chicago)	Jane Glover
Monterey Symphony (Carmel, CA)	Max Bragado-Darman
Naples Philharmonic (FL)	Jorge Mester
NashvilleSymphony (TN)	Kenneth D. Schermerhorn
National (Washington, DC)	Leonard Slatkin
New Haven (CT)	Jung-Ho Pak
New Jersey (Newark)	Neeme Järvi
New Mexico (Albuquerque)	Guillermo Figueroa
New West (Thousand Oaks, CA)	Boris Brott
New York Philharmonic (NYC)	Lorin Maazel
New York Pops (NYC)	Skitch Henderson
North Carolina Symphony (Raleigh)	Grant Llewellyn
Northeastern Pennsylvania Philharmonic (Avoca)	Lawrence Loh
Oklahoma City Philharmonic (OK)	Joel A. Levine
Omaha Symphony (NE)	Victor Yampolsky
Oregon Symphony (Portland)	Carlos Kalmar
Orlando Philharmonic Orch. (FL)	Hal France
Orpheus Chamber Orch. (NYC)	Committee
Pasadena Symphony (CA)	Jorge Mester
Pacific Symphony (Santa Ana, CA)	Carl St. Clair
Peter Nero and The Philly Pops (PA)	Peter Nero
Philadelphia Orchestra (PA)	Christoph Eschenbach
Phoenix Symphony (AZ)	Michael Christie
Pittsburgh (PA)	Daniel Meyer
Portland (ME)	Toshiyuki Shimada
Puerto Rico (PR)	Guillermo Figueroa
Rhode Island Philharmonic (RI)	Larry Rachleff
Richmond Symphony (VA)	Mark Russell Smith
Rochester Philharmonic Orch. (NY)	Christopher Seaman
St. Louis (MO)	David Robertson
St. Paul Chamber Orchestra (MN)	Committee
San Antonio Symphony (TX)	Larry Rachleff
San Diego Symphony (CA)	Jahja Ling
San Francisco Symphony (CA)	Michael Tilson Thomas
Santa Rosa Symphony (CA)	Jeffrey Kahane
Seattle Symphony (WA)	Gerard Schwarz
Shreveport (LA)	Kermit Poling
Springfield (MA)	Kevin Rhodes
Spokane (WA)	Eckart Preu
Syracuse (NY)	Daniel Hege
Toledo (OH)	Stefan Sanderling
Tucson (AZ)	George Hanson
Utah Symphony and Opera (Salt Lake City)	Keith Lockhart
Virginia Symphony (VA)	JoAnn Falletta
Wichita (KS)	Andrew Sewell
West Virginia (Charleston)	Grant Cooper
Youngstown (OH)	Isaiah Jackson

(1) Includes only orchestras with annual expenses $1.65 mil or greater. (2) If only place name is given, add Symphony Orchestra. (3) General title; listed is highest-ranking member of conducting personnel.

U.S. Opera Companies[1]

Source: OPERA America, 1156 15th Street NW, Suite 810, Washington, DC 20005; as of Sept. 2005.

Anchorage Opera (AK); Ed Bourgeois
Arizona Opera (Tucson/Phoenix); Joel Revzen, gen./art. dir.
Atlanta Opera (GA); Dennis Hanthorn, gen. dir.
Austin Lyric Opera (TX); Richard Buckley, art. dir.
Baltimore Opera Company (MD); Michael Harrison, gen. dir.
Boston Lyric Opera (MA); Janice Mancini Del Sesto, gen. dir.
Central City Opera (CO); Pelham Pearce, gen. dir.
Chautauqua Opera (NY); Jay Lesenger, gen./art. dir.
Chicago Opera Theater (IL); Brian Dickie, gen. dir.
Cincinnati Opera (OH); Evans Mirageas, art. dir.
Cleveland Opera (OH); Robert Chumbley, gen. dir.
Connecticut Opera (Hartford); Willie Anthony Waters, gen./art. dir.
Dallas Opera (TX); Karen Stone, gen. dir.
Dayton Opera Association (OH); Thomas Bankston, art. dir.
Des Moines Metro Opera, Inc. (IA); Robert L. Larsen, art. dir.
Florentine Opera Company, Inc. (Milwaukee, WI); William Florescu, gen. dir.
Florida Grand Opera (Miami, FL); Robert M. Heuer, gen. dir.
Fort Worth Opera Association (TX); Darren Woods, gen. dir.
Glimmerglass Opera (Cooperstown, NY); Michael McLeod, gen. dir.
Hawaii Opera Theatre (Honolulu); Henry G. Akina, gen./art. dir.
Houston Grand Opera (TX); Anthony Freud, gen. dir.
Indianapolis Opera (IN); James Caraher, art. dir.
Kentucky Opera (Louisville); Deborah Sandler, gen. dir.
Knoxville Opera Company (TN); Brian Salesky, gen. dir.
Los Angeles Opera (CA); Plácido Domingo, art. dir.
Lyric Opera of Chicago (IL); William Mason, gen. dir.
Lyric Opera of Kansas City (MO); Evan R. Luskin, gen. dir.
Madison Opera (WI); John DeMain, art. dir.
Metropolitan Opera (New York, NY); James Levine, art. dir.
Michigan Opera Theatre (Detroit); David DiChiera, gen. dir.
Minnesota Opera Company (Minneapolis); Dale Johnson, art. dir.
Nashville Opera Association (TN); John Hoomes, gen./art. dir.
New Orleans Opera Association (LA); Robert Lyall, art. dir.
New York City Opera (NY); Paul Kellogg, gen./art. dir.
Opera Boston (MA); Carole Charnow, gen. dir.
Opera Carolina (Charlotte, NC); James Meena, gen. dir.
Opera Colorado (Denver); James Robinson, art. dir.
Opera Columbus (OH); William Boggs, art. dir.
Opera Company of Philadelphia (PA); Robert B. Driver, gen./art. dir.
OperaDelaware (Wilmington); Julie Van Blarcom, exec. dir.
Opera Memphis (TN); Michael Ching, art. dir.
Opera Omaha, Inc. (NE); Stewart Robertson, art. dir.
Opera Pacific (Irvine, CA); John DeMain, art. dir.
Opera Theatre of Saint Louis (MO); Charles MacKay, gen. dir.
Orlando Opera (FL); Robert Swedberg, gen. dir.
Palm Beach Opera, Inc. (FL); Maria Nagid, gen. dir.
Pittsburgh Opera (PA); Mark Weinstein, gen. dir.
Portland Opera (OR); Christopher Mattaliano, gen. dir.
Sacramento Opera (CA); Tim Rolek, art. dir.
San Diego Opera Association (CA); Ian D. Campbell, gen. dir.
San Francisco Opera (CA); David Gockley, gen. dir.
Santa Fe Opera (NM); Richard Gaddes, gen. dir.
Sarasota Opera (FL); Victor DeRenzi, art. dir.
Seattle Opera (WA); Speight Jenkins, gen. dir.
Skylight Opera Theatre (Milwaukee, WI); Bill Theisen, art. dir.
Syracuse Opera (NY); Richard McKee, art. dir.
Toledo Opera (OH); Renay Conlin, gen. dir.
Tulsa Opera (OK); Carol I. Crawford, gen. dir.
Utah Festival Opera (Logan); Michael Ballam, gen. dir.
Utah Symphony & Opera (Salt Lake City); Christopher McBeth, art. dir.
Virginia Opera; Peter Mark, art. dir.
Washington National Opera (DC); Plácido Domingo, gen. dir.

(1) Includes only opera companies with budgets of $1 million or more.

Some Notable U.S. Museums

This unofficial list of some of the largest (by budget) museums in the U.S. was compiled with the assistance of the American Association of Museums, a national association representing the concerns of the museum community. Association members also include zoos, aquariums, arboretums, botanical gardens, and planetariums, but these are not included in *The World Almanac* listing.

Museum	City	State
American Museum of Natural History	New York	NY
Amon Carter Museum of Western Art	Ft. Worth	TX
The Art Institute of Chicago	Chicago	IL
Brooklyn Museum of Art	Brooklyn	NY
Busch-Reisinger Museum	Cambridge	MA
California Academy of Sciences	San Francisco	CA
California Science Center	Los Angeles	CA
Carnegie Museums of Pittsburgh	Pittsburgh	PA
Chicago Historical Society	Chicago	IL
Children's Museum of Indianapolis	Indianapolis	IN
Cincinnati Art Museum	Cincinnati	OH
Cincinnati Museum Center	Cincinnati	OH
Cleveland Museum of Art	Cleveland	OH
Colonial Williamsburg	Williamsburg	VA
Corning Museum of Glass	Corning	NY
Dallas Museum of Art	Dallas	TX
Denver Art Museum	Denver	CO
Denver Museum of Nature and Science	Denver	CO
Detroit Institute of Arts	Detroit	MI
Exploratorium	San Francisco	CA
The Field Museum	Chicago	IL
Fine Arts Museums of San Francisco	San Francisco	CA
Franklin Institute	Philadelphia	PA
The Frick Collection	New York	NY
Harvard University Art Museums	Cambridge	MA
Henry F. Dupont Winterthur Museum	Winterthur	DE
Henry Ford Museum/Greenfield Village	Dearborn	MI
High Museum of Art	Atlanta	GA
Houston Museum of Natural Science	Houston	TX
Jamestown-Yorktown Foundation	Williamsburg	VA
Jewish Museum	New York	NY
L.A. County Museum of Art	Los Angeles	CA
Liberty Science Center, Liberty State Pk.	Jersey City	NJ
Maryland Science Center	Baltimore	MD
Mashantucket Pequot Museum and Research Center	Mashantucket	CT
Metropolitan Museum of Art	New York	NY
Milwaukee Public Museum	Milwaukee	WI
Minneapolis Institute of Art	Minneapolis	MN
Museum of African American History	Detroit	MI
Museum of the American West	Los Angeles	CA
Museum of Contemporary Art	Los Angeles	CA
Museum of Fine Arts	Boston	MA
Museum of Fine Arts	Houston	TX
Museum of Modern Art	New York	NY
Museum of New Mexico	Santa Fe	NM
Museum of Science	Boston	MA
Mystic Seaport Museum	Mystic	CT
National Air & Space Museum	Washington	DC
National Baseball Hall of Fame and Museum, Inc.	Cooperstown	NY
National Gallery of Art	Washington	DC
National Museum of American History	Washington	DC
National Museum of the American Indian	Washington	DC
National Museum of Natural History	Washington	DC
Nelson-Atkins Museum of Art	Kansas City	MO
New York Historical Society	New York	NY
New York State Museum	Albany	NY
Peabody Essex Museum	Salem	MA
Pennsylvania Historical & Museum Commission	Harrisburg	PA
Philadelphia Museum of Art	Philadelphia	PA
Public Museum of Grand Rapids	Grand Rapids	MI
Rock & Roll Hall of Fame and Museum Inc.	Cleveland	OH
San Diego Museum of Art	San Diego	CA
San Francisco Museum of Modern Art	San Francisco	CA
Science Museum of Minnesota	Saint Paul	MN
Scottsdale Museum of Contemp. Art	Scottsdale	AZ
St. Louis Science Center	St. Louis	MO
Toledo Museum of Art	Toledo	OH
U.S. Holocaust Memorial Museum	Washington	DC
Univ. of Pennsylvania Museum of Archaeology and Anthropology	Philadelphia	PA
Virginia Museum of Fine Arts	Richmond	VA
Wadsworth Atheneum	Hartford	CT
Walker Art Center	Minneapolis	MN
Whitney Museum of American Art	New York	NY

Best-Selling U.S. Magazines, 2004

Source: Audit Bureau of Circulations, Schaumburg, IL

General magazines, exclusive of comics; also excluding magazines that failed to file reports to ABC by press time. Based on total average paid circulation during the 6 months ending Dec. 31, 2004.

	Publication	Paid circ.
1.	AARP The Magazine	22,617,093
2.	AARP Bulletin	22,181,859
3.	Reader's Digest	10,081,577
4.	TV Guide	9,015,544
5.	Better Homes and Gardens	7,626,088
6.	National Geographic	5,475,135
7.	Good Housekeeping	4,639,941
8.	Woman's Day	4,209,130
9.	Family Circle	4,147,657
10.	Ladies' Home Journal	4,120,087
11.	Time	4,034,061
12.	People	3,652,022
13.	Sports Illustrated	3,324,631
14.	Home & Away	3,317,597
15.	Prevention	3,309,110
16.	Newsweek	3,125,971
17.	Playboy	3,051,344
18.	Cosmopolitan	2,982,508
19.	Southern Living	2,730,437
20.	Guideposts	2,659,733
21.	O, The Oprah Magazine	2,650,464
22.	Maxim	2,517,126
23.	Redbook	2,407,985
24.	Glamour	2,397,508
25.	Seventeen	2,108,292
26.	Game Informer	2,045,912
27.	Smithsonian	2,044,856
28.	Parenting	2,028,950
29.	U.S. News & World Report	2,014,422
30.	Parents	1,989,512
31.	Money	1,924,414
32.	Martha Stewart Living	1,894,134
33.	Real Simple	1,809,792
34.	ESPN The Magazine	1,792,359
35.	Entertainment Weekly	1,791,163
36.	Familyfun	1,739,121
37.	Country Living	1,728,962
38.	In Style	1,728,522
39.	Endless Vacation	1,695,852
40.	Cooking Light	1,680,573
41.	Men's Health	1,666,245
42.	Ebony	1,630,248
43.	YM	1,627,764
44.	Woman's World	1,622,084
45.	Shape	1,618,516
46.	Golf Digest	1,577,757
47.	Teen People	1,560,480
48.	Field & Stream	1,524,897
49.	First For Women	1,513,414
50.	Fitness	1,488,849
51.	US Weekly	1,475,010
52.	National Enquirer	1,473,815
53.	Popular Science	1,469,181
54.	Sunset	1,457,429
55.	Health	1,421,855
56.	Golf Magazine	1,417,683
57.	Cosmo Girl!	1,380,320
58.	Car and Driver	1,363,311
59.	Self	1,359,811
60.	Bon Appétit	1,344,109
61.	Stuff	1,312,588
62.	American Rifleman	1,306,704
63.	Star	1,300,076
64.	Country Home	1,270,819
65.	Rolling Stone	1,268,999
66.	Vogue	1,261,886
67.	FHM (For Him Magazine)	1,235,894
68.	Popular Mechanics	1,232,224
69.	Scholastic Parent & Child	1,220,312
70.	Family Handyman	1,146,459
71.	Weight Watchers	1,136,423
72.	Boys' Life	1,130,493
73.	Motor Trend	1,122,931
74.	Vanity Fair	1,118,847
75.	Elle	1,078,520
76.	Essence	1,063,645
77.	Scouting	1,039,345
78.	Lucky	1,036,495
79.	National Geographic International	1,032,278
80.	More	1,024,166
81.	In Touch Weekly	1,019,887
82.	New Yorker	1,018,962
83.	Allure	1,016,324
84.	PC World	1,006,480
85.	Home	1,002,402
86.	Traditional Home	993,001
87.	Businessweek	985,515
88.	Kiplinger's Personal Finance	972,270
89.	Gourmet	968,135
90.	Travel + Leisure	968,115
91.	American Hunter	967,678
92.	This Old House	963,101
93.	Jet	954,259
94.	Marie Claire	941,148
95.	Outdoor Life	937,895
96.	Food & Wine	927,118
97.	PC Magazine	926,275
98.	Forbes	924,518
99.	House & Garden	918,570
100.	Midwest Living	913,827

Some Notable New Books, 2004

Source: Reference and User Services Assn. and Young Adult Library Services Assn., divisions of the American Library Association, for books published in 2004

Fiction

The Lemon Table: Stories, Julian Barnes
The Half Brother, Lars Saabye Christensen
Birds Without Wings, Louis de Bernieres
I Sailed with Magellan, Stuart Dybek
The Swallows of Kabul, Yasmina Khadra
The Madonna of Excelsior, Zakes Mda
Cloud Atlas, David Mitchell
Runaway: Stories, Alice Munro
Popular Music from Vittula, Mikael Niemi
The Plot Against America, Philip Roth
Old School, Tobias Wolff

Nonfiction

Alexander Hamilton, Ron Chernow
One With Nineveh: Politics, Consumption, and the Human Future, Paul R. and Anne H. Ehrlich
Washington's Crossing (Pivotal Moments in American History), David Hackett Fischer
Pandora's Baby: How the First Test Tube Babies Sparked the Reproductive Revolution, Robin Marantz Henig
Chain of Command: The Road from 9/11 to Abu Ghraib, Seymour M. Hersh
Goya, Robert Hughes
The Year That Rocked the World, Mark Kurlansky
Outwitting History: The Amazing Adventures of a Man Who Rescued a Million Yiddish Books, Aaron Lansky
Civil Wars: A Battle for Gay Marriage, David Moats
The 9/11 Commission Report, National Commission on Terrorist Attacks
Sea of Glory: America's Voyage of Discovery, the U.S. Exploring Expedition, 1838-1842, Nathaniel Philbrick
The Ticket Out: Darryl Strawberry and the Boys of Crenshaw, Michael Sokolove
One Man's Castle: Clarence Darrow in Defense of the American Dream, Phyllis Vine

Poetry

The Collected Poetry of Nikki Giovanni: 1968-1998, Nikki Giovanni
Delights & Shadows, Ted Kooser

Young Adults

The Garden, Elsie V. Aidinoff
George Washington, Spymaster, Thomas B. Allen
Fire-Eaters, David Almond
Sign of the Qin: Outlaws of Moonshadow Marsh, No. 1, L.G. Bass.
With Courage and Cloth: Winning the Fight for a Woman's Right to Vote, Ann Bausum
Wake Up Our Souls: A Celebration of Black American Artists, Tonya Bolden
The Unthinkable Thoughts of Jacob Green, Joshua Braff
Doing It, Melvin Burgess
Al Capone Does My Shirts, Gennifer Choldenko
Daniel Half Human and the Good Nazi, David Chotjewitz
Splintering, Eireann Corrigan
Bucking the Sarge, Christopher Paul Curtis
The Blue Girl, Charles de Lint
Dr. Ernest Drake's Dragonology, ed. Dugald Steer
The Hollow Kingdom, Clare B. Dunkle
The Sea of Trolls, Nancy Farmer
The Oracle Betrayed, Catherine Fisher
Who Am I Without Him?: Stories About Girls and the Boys in Their Lives, Sharon Flake
Nothing to Lose, Alex Flinn
The Voice That Challenged a Nation: Marian Anderson and the Struggle for Equal Rights, Russell Freedman
Tending to Grace, Kimberly Newton Fusco
Gothic: Ten Dark Original Tales, Deborah Noyes
Andy Warhol: Prince of Pop, Jan Greenberg and Sandra Jordan
Donorboy, Brendan Halpin
Godless, Pete Hautman
The Race to Save the Lord God Bird, Phillip M. Hoose
Eagle Strike: An Alex Rider Adventure, Anthony Horowitz
Worlds Afire: The Hartford Circus Fire of 1944, Paul B. Janeczko
Mable Riley: A Reliable Record of Humdrum, Peril, and Romance, Marthe Jocelyn
Bird, Angela Johnson
A Fast and Brutal Wing, Kathleen Jeffrie Johnson
The Key to the Golden Firebird, Maureen Johnson
Margaux With an X, Ron Koertge
The Blue Mirror, Kathe Koja
The Outcasts of 19 Schuyler Place, E.L. Konigsburg

Yossel, April 19, 1943: A Story of the Warsaw Ghetto Uprising, Joe Kubert
A Crack in the Line, Michael Lawrence
B for Buster, Iain Lawrence
Heck, Superhero, Martine Leavitt
The Realm of Possibility, David Levithan
Saving Francesca, Melina Marchetta
Sunshine, Robin McKinley
An Earthly Knight, Janet McNaughton
A Dream of Freedom: The Civil Rights Movement from 1954 to 1968, Diane McWhorter
Curse of the Blue Tattoo: Being an Account of the Misadventures of Jacky Faber, Midshipman and Fine Lady, L.A. Meyer
Fleshmarket, Nicola Morgan
The Year of Secret Assignments, Jaclyn Moriarty
Private Peaceful, Michael Morpurgo
Here in Harlem: Poems in Many Voices, Walter Dean Myers
Bound, Donna Jo Napoli
Rock Star, Superstar, Blake Nelson
Airborn, Kenneth Oppel
The Teacher's Funeral: A Comedy in Three Parts, Richard Peck
Luna: A Novel, Julie Anne Peters
A Hat Full of Sky, Terry Pratchett
Under the Wolf, Under the Dog, Adam Rapp
Predator's Gold, Philip Reeve
Promises to Keep: How Jackie Robinson Changed America, Sharon Robinson
how i live now, Meg Rosoff
Sammy and Juliana in Hollywood, Benjamin Alire Saenz
Persepolis 2: The Story of a Return, Marjane Satrapi
Lizzie Bright and the Buckminster Boy, Gary D. Schmidt
It's a Bird, Steven T. Seagle
The Safe-Keeper's Secret, Sharon Shinn
The Schwa Was Here, Neal Shusterman
The Radioactive Boy Scout: The True Story of a Boy and His Backyard Nuclear Reactor, Ken Silverstein
One of Those Hideous Books Where the Mother Dies, Sonya Sones
Can't Get There from Here, Todd Strasser
Chanda's Secrets, Allan Stratton
The Golem's Eye: The Bartimaeus Trilogy, Book Two, Jonathan Stroud
Chief Sunrise, John McGraw, and Me, Timothy Tocher
Sky: A Novel in 3 Sets and an Encore, Roderick Townley
No Shame, No Fear, Ann Turnbull
Working Fire: The Making of an Accidental Fireman, Zac Unger
Montmorency: Thief, Liar, Gentleman?, Eleanor Updale
D-Day: The Greatest Invasion, Dan van der Vat
So B. It: A Novel, Sarah Weeks
Double Helix, Nancy Werlin
So Yesterday, Scott Westerfield
Fray, Joss Whedon
See You Down the Road, Kim Ablon Whitney
No Laughter Here, Rita Williams-Garcia
New Found Land: Lewis and Clark's Voyage of Discovery, Allan Wolf
The Haunting of Alaizabel Cray, Chris Wooding
Behind You, Jacqueline Woodson
Prince Across the Water, Jane Yolen and Robert J. Harris

Some Notable New Books for Children, 2004

Source: Association for Library Service to Children, a division of the American Library Association, for books published in 2004.

Younger Readers

Home, Jeannie Baker
Baby Danced the Polka, Karen Beaumont
Odd Boy Out: Young Albert Einstein, Don Brown
Guji Guji, Chih-Yuan Chen
The Neighborhood Mother Goose, Nina Crews
Hot Day on Abbott Avenue, Karen English
The Turn-Around, Upside-Down Alphabet Book, Lisa Campbell Ernst
Sidewalk Circus, Paul Fleischman
Where Is the Green Sheep?, Mem Fox
Kitten's First Full Moon, Kevin Henkes
Apples to Oregon, Deborah Hopkinson
Love and Roast Chicken, Barbara Knutson
The Red Book, Barbara Lehman
Ruby Lu, Brave and True, Lenore Look
Wow! City!, Robert Neubecker
If Not for the Cat, Jack Prelutsky
Tiger on a Tree, Anushka Ravishankar
Lemons Are Not Red, Laura Vaccaro Seeger
Wild About Books, Judy Sierra
Polar Bear Night, Lauren Thompson
Knuffle Bunny: A Cautionary Tale, Mo Willems
Teeth, Tails, & Tentacles, Christopher Wormell

Middle Readers

My Light, Molly Bang
César: ¡Sí, Se Puede! = Yes, We Can!, Carmen T. Bernier-Grand
The Crow-Girl, Bodil Bredsdorff
The Big House, Carolyn Coman
Millions, Frank Cottrell Boyce
Doodler Doodling, Rita Golden Gelman
Technically, It's Not My Fault: Concrete Poems, John Grandits
What Is Goodbye?, Nikki Grimes
The People Could Fly, Virginia Hamilton
The Cats in Krasinski Square, Karen Hesse
Merlin and the Making of the King, Margaret Hodges
The Star of Kazan, Eva Ibbotson
Mable Riley: A Reliable Record of Humdrum, Peril, and Romance, Marthe Jocelyn
Walt Whitman: Words for America, Barbara Kerley
Sélavi, That Is Life: A Haitian Story of Hope, Youme Landowne
Fish, L.S. Matthews
The Tarantula Scientist, Sy Montgomery
Remember: The Journey to School Integration, Toni Morrison
Mighty Jackie: The Strike-Out Queen, Marissa Moss
The Little Gentleman, Philippa Pearce
The Boy, the Bear, the Baron, the Bard, Gregory Rogers
Sequoyah: The Cherokee Man Who Gave His People Writing, James Rumford
George vs. George: The American Revolution as Seen from Both Sides, Rosalyn Schanzer
Science Verse, Jon Scieszka
Ellington Was Not a Street, Ntozake Shange
The Train of States, Peter Sís
Coming on Home Soon, Jacqueline Woodson

Older Readers

The Fire-Eaters, David Almond
With Courage and Cloth: Winning the Fight for a Woman's Right to Vote, Ann Bausum
Al Capone Does My Shirts, Gennifer Choldenko
Daniel Half Human and the Good Nazi, David Chotjewitz
Bucking the Sarge, Christopher Paul Curtis
Boy O'Boy, Brian Doyle
Remember D-Day: The Plan, the Invasion, Survivor Stories, Ronald J. Drez
The Sea of Trolls, Nancy Farmer
The Oracle Betrayed, Catherine Fisher
The Voice That Challenged a Nation: Marian Anderson and the Struggle for Equal Rights, Russell Freedman
The Race to Save the Lord God Bird, Phillip M. Hoose
Is This Forever, or What? Poems & Paintings from Texas, ed. Naomi Shihab Nye
Bird, Angela Johnson
Kira-Kira, Cynthia Kadohata
The Outcasts of 19 Schuyler Place, E.L. Konigsburg
Heck Superhero, Martine Leavitt
Indigo's Star, Hilary McKay
A Dream of Freedom: The Civil Rights Movement from 1954 to 1968, Diane McWhorter
Here in Harlem: Poems in Many Voices, Walter Dean Myers
Fortune's Bones: The Manumission Requiem, Marilyn Nelson
Airborn, Kenneth Oppel
The Teacher's Funeral: A Comedy in Three Parts, Richard Peck
A Hat Full of Sky, Terry Pratchett
Becoming Naomi León, Pam Muñoz Ryan
Lizzie Bright and the Buckminster Boy, Gary D. Schmidt
The Schwa Was Here, Neal Shusterman
The Shadows of Ghadames, Joëlle Stolz
So B. It, Sarah Weeks

All Ages

A Child's Christmas in Wales, Dylan Thomas
Under the Spell of the Moon: Art for Children from the World's Great Illustrators, ed. Patricia Aldana

WORLD ALMANAC QUICK QUIZ

According to Nielson Media Research, which group of people spend the least amount of time watching TV in an average week?

(a) Children, age 2-11 (b) Men, age 25-54 (c) Teens, age 12-17 (d) Women, age 55+

For the answer look in this chapter, or see page 1008.

Best-Selling Books, 2004

Source: Nielsen BookScan

Hardcover Fiction

1. *The Da Vinci Code*, Dan Brown
2. *The Five People You Meet in Heaven*, Mitch Albom
3. *Angels & Demons*, Dan Brown
4. *The Last Juror*, John Grisham
5. *The Rule of Four*, Ian Caldwell
6. *State of Fear*, Michael Crichton
7. *London Bridges*, James Patterson
8. *Trace*, Patricia Cornwell
9. *Song of Susannah*, Stephen King
10. *Glorious Appearing*, Tim LaHaye, Jerry B. Jenkins

Hardcover Nonfiction

1. *The South Beach Diet*, Arthur Agatston
2. *The Purpose-Driven® Life*, Rick Warren
3. *My Life*, Bill Clinton
4. *America (The Book)*, John Stewart & writers of "The Daily Show"
5. *He's Just Not That Into You*, Greg Behrendt, Liz Tuccillo
6. *Eats, Shoots & Leaves*, Lynne Truss
7. *The South Beach Diet Cookbook*, Arthur Agatston
8. *The Proper Care & Feeding of Husbands*, Laura C. Schlessinger
9. *The Ultimate Weight Solution*, Phil McGraw
10. *Plan of Attack*, Bob Woodward

Trade Paperback Fiction

1. *The Secret Life of Bees*, Sue Monk Kidd
2. *The Curious Incident of the Dog in the Night-Time*, Mark Haddon
3. *The Wedding*, Nicholas Sparks
4. *The Lovely Bones*, Alice Sebold
5. *Life of Pi*, Yann Martel
6. *One Hundred Years of Solitude*, Gabriel García Márquez
7. *The Kite Runner*, Khaled Hosseini
8. *Middlesex*, Jeffrey Eugenides
9. *The Time Traveler's Wife*, Audrey Niffenegger
10. *The Devil Wears Prada*, Lauren Weisberger

Trade Paperback Nonfiction

1. *The South Beach Diet Good Fats/Good Carbs Guide*, Arthur Agatston
2. *The 9/11 Commission Report*, National Commission on Terrorist Attacks
3. *Reading Lolita in Tehran*, Azar Nafisi
4. *1,000 Places to See Before You Die*, Patricia Schultz
5. *Rich Dad, Poor Dad*, Robert T. Kiyosaki
6. *What to Expect When You're Expecting*, Heidi Murkoff
7. *The Devil in the White City*, Erik Larson
8. *Tuesdays With Morrie*, Mitch Albom
9. *30-Minute Meals 2*, Rachael Ray
10. *A Child Called "It"*, Dave Pelzer

Mass Market

1. *Angels & Demons*, Dan Brown
2. *Deception Point*, Dan Brown
3. *Digital Fortress*, Dan Brown
4. *The Notebook*, Nicholas Sparks
5. *The King of Torts*, John Grisham
6. *Bleachers*, John Grisham
7. *Key of Valor*, Nora Roberts
8. *The Guardian*, Nicholas Sparks
9. *Blue Dahlia*, Nora Roberts
10. *The Last Juror*, John Grisham

Mass Market Nonfiction

1. *The Ultimate Weight Solution Food Guide*, Phil McGraw
2. *The Official Scrabble Players Dictionary*, Merriam-Webster
3. *Dr. Atkins' New Diet Revolution*, Robert C. Atkins
4. *Night*, Elie Wiesel
5. *The Atkins Essentials*, Atkins Health
6. *The New Comprehensive A-Z Crossword Dictionary*, Edy Garcia Schaffer
7. *How to Win Friends & Influence People*, Dale Carnegie
8. *Holy Blood, Holy Grail*, Michael Baigent
9. *The Merriam-Webster Dictionary*, Merriam-Webster
10. *Trump: The Art of the Deal*, Donald J. Trump

Almanacs, Atlases, & Annuals

1. *The World Almanac and Book of Facts 2005*, ed. Ken Park
2. *Old Farmer's Almanac 2005*, Old Farmer's Almanac
3. *The World Almanac and Book of Facts 2004*, ed. Ken Park
4. *Old Farmer's Almanac 2004*, Old Farmer's Almanac
5. *Encyclopaedia Britannica Almanac 2004*, Encyclopaedia Britannica
6. *Michelin North America Road Atlas 2004*, Michelin
7. *American Map Road Atlas 2004*, American Map Company
8. *Sports Illustrated 2005 Sports Almanac*, Eds. of Sports Illustrated
9. *The World Almanac 2004 Road Atlas*, Hammond World Atlas Corp.
10. *The Road Atlas 2004*, Rand McNally

Note: Ranks are based on point-of-sale totals from stores nationwide representing about 70% of the marketplace.

Leading U.S. Daily Newspapers, 2004

Source: 2005 *Editor & Publisher International Yearbook*

(Circulation as of Sept. 30, 2004; m = morning, e = evening, d=all day)

As of Feb. 1, 2005, the number of U.S. daily newspapers had risen to 1,457, for a net gain of 1 since Feb. 1, 2004. Average daily circulation fell by 559,213, from 55,185,351 in 2004 to 54,626,138. The overall number of Sunday papers dipped by 2, to 915. Average Sunday circulation as of Feb. 1, 2005, fell 741,682, or about 1.3%, from 58.5 million to 57.8 million.

	Newspaper		Circulation
1.	Arlington (VA) *USA Today*	(m)	2,220,863
2.	New York (NY) *Wall Street Journal*	(m)	2,106,774
3.	New York (NY) *Times*	(m)	1,121,057
4.	Los Angeles (CA) *Times*	(m)	902,164
5.	New York (NY) *Daily News*	(m)	715,052
6.	Washington (DC) *Post*	(m)	707,690
7.	New York (NY) *Post*	(m)	686,207
8.	Chicago (IL) *Tribune*	(m)	600,988
9.	Houston (TX) *Chronicle*	(m)	554,783
10.	Dallas (TX) *Morning News*	(m)	519,014
11.	San Francisco (CA) *Chronicle*	(d)	505,022
12.	Chicago (IL) *Sun-Times*	(m)	481,980
13.	Long Island (NY) *Newsday*	(m)	481,816
14.	Boston (MA) *Globe*	(m)	451,471
15.	Phoenix *Arizona Republic*	(m)	413,268
16.	Newark (NJ) *Star-Ledger*	(m)	400,042
17.	Atlanta (GA) *Journal-Constitution*	(m)	386,015
18.	Minneapolis (MN) *Star Tribune*	(m)	381,094
19.	Philadelphia (PA) *Inquirer*	(m)	368,883
20.	Cleveland (OH) *Plain Dealer*	(m)	354,309
21.	Detroit (MI) *Free Press*	(m)	348,838
22.	Portland (OR) *Oregonian*	(d)	337,707
23.	St. Petersburg (FL) *Times*	(m)	330,091
24.	Miami (FL) *Herald*	(m)	315,988
25.	San Diego (CA) *Union-Tribune*	(m)	311,324
26.	Orange County (CA) *Register*	(m)	303,418
27.	Sacramento (CA) *Bee*	(m)	293,705
28.	St. Louis (MO) *Post-Dispatch*	(m)	286,310
29.	Kansas City (MO) *Star*	(m)	275,747
30.	Denver (CO) *Post*	(m)	275,292
31.	Denver (CO) *Rocky Mountain News*	(m)	275,136
32.	Baltimore (MD) *Sun*	(m)	267,993
33.	San Jose (CA) *Mercury News*	(m)	263,067
34.	Orlando (FL) *Sentinel*	(d)	258,881
35.	New Orleans (LA) *Times-Picayune*	(m)	252,799
36.	Indianapolis (IN) *Star*	(m)	252,021
37.	Columbus (OH) *Dispatch*	(m)	251,045
38.	Boston (MA) *Herald*	(m)	240,759
39.	Milwaukee (WI) *Journal Sentinel*	(m)	240,581
40.	Pittsburgh (PA) *Post-Gazette*	(m)	238,860
41.	Fort Lauderdale *South Florida Sun-Sentinel*	(m)	236,190
42.	Seattle (WA) *Times*	(m)	231,051
43.	Tampa (FL) *Tribune*	(m)	226,573
44.	San Antonio (TX) *Express-News*	(m)	226,109
45.	Charlotte (NC) *Observer*	(m)	226,082
46.	Detroit (MI) *News*	(e)	224,215
47.	Fort Worth (TX) *Star-Telegram*	(m)	223,098
48.	Louisville (KY) *Courier-Journal*	(m)	207,665
49.	Norfolk (VA) *Virginian-Pilot*	(m)	200,055
50.	Oklahoma City (OK) *Daily Oklahoman*	(m)	197,507
51.	Buffalo (NY) *News*	(d)	196,429
52.	Omaha (NE) *World-Herald*	(d)	192,607
53.	Los Angeles (CA) *Investors Business Daily*	(m)	191,846
54.	Hartford (CT) *Courant*	(m)	191,500
55.	St. Paul (MN) *Pioneer Press*	(m)	191,264
56.	Richmond (VA) *Times-Dispatch*	(m)	184,950
57.	Cincinnati (OH) *Enquirer*	(m)	183,051
58.	Riverside (CA) *Press-Enterprise*	(m)	182,682
59.	Walnut Creek (CA) *Contra Costa Times*	(m)	182,647
60.	Little Rock (AR) *Democrat-Gazette*	(m)	182,391
61.	Los Angeles (CA) *Daily News*	(m)	178,404
62.	Austin (TX) *American-Statesman*	(m)	177,926
63.	Bergen County (NJ) *Record*	(m)	176,177

Newspaper		Circulation
64. Nashville (TN) *Tennessean*	(m)	170,361
65. West Palm Beach (FL) *Post*	(m)	168,257
66. Providence (RI) *Journal*	(m)	168,021
67. Rochester (NY) *Democrat and Chronicle*	(m)	166,727
68. Jacksonville *Florida Times-Union*	(m)	165,425
69. Raleigh (NC) *News & Observer*	(m)	164,294
70. Memphis (TN) *Commercial Appeal*	(m)	163,731
71. Neptune (NJ) *Asbury Park Press*	(m)	160,339
72. Fresno (CA) *Bee*	(m)	160,143
73. Las Vegas (NV) *Review-Journal*	(m)	159,507
74. Des Moines (IA) *Register*	(m)	152,800
75. Chicago (IL) *Daily Herald*	(m)	149,446
76. Seattle (WA) *Post-Intelligencer*	(m)	145,964
77. Birmingham (AL) *News*	(m)	145,506
78. Honolulu (HI) *Advertiser*	(d)	141,341
79. Westchester Co. (NY) *Journal News*	(m)	141,031
80. Toledo (OH) *Blade*	(m)	139,398
81. Grand Rapids (MI) *Press*	(e)	138,126
82. Tulsa (OK) *World*	(m)	137,231
83. Philadelphia (PA) *Daily News*	(m)	135,956
84. Akron (OH) *Beacon Journal*	(m)	135,002
85. Salt Lake City (UT) *Tribune*	(m)	133,025
86. Tacoma (WA) *News Tribune*	(m)	127,928
87. Los Angeles (CA) *La Opinion*	(m)	124,990
88. Dayton (OH) *Daily News*	(m)	122,639
89. Syracuse (NY) *Post-Standard*	(m)	118,962
90. Wilmington (DE) *News Journal*	(d)	115,641
91. Columbia (SC) *State*	(m)	115,464
92. Lexington (KY) *Herald-Leader*	(m)	114,234
93. Knoxville (TN) *News-Sentinel*	(m)	113,994
94. Allentown (PA) *Morning Call*	(m)	111,956
95. Sarasota (FL) *Herald-Tribune*	(m)	110,783
96. Greensburg (PA) *Tribune-Review*	(m)	108,109
97. Albuquerque (NM) *Journal*	(m)	107,306
98. Daytona Beach (FL) *News-Journal*	(m)	107,086
99. Worcester (MA) *Telegram & Gazette*	(m)	103,113
100. Stuart (FL) *Treasure Coast News/Press Tribune*	(m)	101,705

Leading Canadian Daily Newspapers, 2004

Source: 2004 *Editor & Publisher International Yearbook*

(Circulation as of Sept. 30, 2004; all morning papers)

Rank	Circulation
1. Toronto (ON) *Star*	464,838
2. Toronto (ON) *Globe and Mail*	317,954
3. Montreal (QC) *Le Journal*	265,168
4. Toronto (ON) *National Post*	243,966
5. Toronto (ON) *Sun*	194,011
6. Montreal (QC) *La Presse*	188,216
7. Vancouver (BC) *Sun*	172,486
8. Vancouver (BC) *Province*	154,590
9. Montreal (QC) *Gazette*	135,471
10. Ottawa (ON) *Citizen*	129,175

Top 25 News/Information Websites, July 2005

Source: comScore Media Metrix, Inc.

Rank	Visitors[1]
1. The Weather Channel	30,135,000
2. New York Times Digital	29,316,000
3. MSNBC	27,380,000
4. Yahoo! News	27,377,000
5. CNN	22,751,000
6. AOL News	20,031,000
7. Weatherbug Property	19,019,000
8. IBS Network	10,893,000
9. Knight Ridder Digital	8,667,000
10. Tribune Newspapers	7,883,000
11. USA Today Sites	7,762,000
12. WorldNow Sites	6,896,000
13. MSN Slate	5,846,000
14. Google News	5,839,000
15. Discovery.com	5,719,000
16. ABCNews Digital	5,607,000
17. FoxNews.com	5,529,000
18. CBS News	5,415,000
19. Military.com	4,883,000
20. Advance Publications, Inc	4,837,000
21. Accuweather.com	4,629,000
22. WashingtonPost.com	4,583,000
23. Legacy.com	4,070,000
24. Wunderground.com	3,622,000
25. BBC UKFS News (excl. home page)	3,361,000

(1) Number of unique visitors who visited Website at least once in July 2005.

U.S. Commercial Radio Stations, by Format, 1997-2005[1]

Source: The M Street Radio Directory, M Street Corporation, Littleton, NH © 2005; counts are for June of each year

Primary format	2005	2004	2003	2002	2001	1999	1998	1997
1. Country	2,019	2,047	2,088	2,131	2,190	2,306	2,368	2,491
2. News/Talk	1,324	1,282	1,224	1,179	1,139	1,159	1,131	1,111
3. Oldies	773	816	807	813	786	766	799	755
4. Spanish	703	665	628	603	574	536	493	474
5. Adult Contemporary (AC)	684	703	692	713	709	775	844	902
6. Top 40	502	497	491	474	468	401	379	358
7. Sports	497	469	429	388	338	256	251	220
8. Classic Rock	461	450	425	384	338	314	282	240
9. Adult Standards	405	460	497	547	569	595	561	551
10. Hot AC	380	416	399	395	369	325	281	260
11. Soft AC	324	322	336	340	375	382	368	346
12. Religion (Teaching, Variety)	318	336	347	332	356	363	356	404
13. Black Gospel	286	273	253	254	264	257	238	208
14. Rock	270	280	273	278	282	280	266	262
15. Classic Hits	262	229	237	258	265	222	192	172
16. Southern Gospel	207	208	207	240	255	269	273	255
17. Contemporary Christian	174	159	167	164	164	167	164	159
18. Urban AC	153	136	128	121	118	112	127	134
19. Modern Rock	152	165	169	147	140	136	145	137
20. R&B	150	159	189	193	183	166	171	169
Off Air	70	79	123	110	113	96	102	143
TOTAL OPERATING STATIONS[2]	**10,661**	**10,648**	**10,605**	**10,569**	**10,516**	**10,444**	**10,292**	**10,207**

(1) Data for 2000 unavailable. (2)Totals include stations that are changing or did not report format.

Top-Grossing North American Concert Tours, 1985-2004

Source: Pollstar, Fresno, CA

Rank	Artist (Year)	Total gross[1]	Cities/ Shows
1.	The Rolling Stones (1994)	$121.2	43/60
2.	Bruce Springsteen & The E. Street Band (2003)	115.9	30/47
3.	U2 (2001)	109.7	56/80
4.	Pink Floyd (1994)	103.5	39/59
5.	Paul McCartney (2002)	103.3	43/53
6.	The Rolling Stones (1989)	98.0	33/60
7.	The Rolling Stones (1997)	89.3	26/33
8.	The Rolling Stones (2002)	87.9	33/34
9.	Prince (2004)	87.4	69/96
10.	'N Sync (2001)	86.8	36/43
11.	Backstreet Boys (2001)	$82.1	73/98
12.	Celine Dion (2003)	80.5	1/145
13.	Celine Dion (2004)	80.4	1/154
14.	Tina Turner (2000)	80.2	88/95
15.	U2 (1997)	79.9	37/46
16.	Madonna (2004)	79.5	14/39
17.	The Eagles (1994)	79.4	32/54
18.	'N Sync (2000)	76.4	64/86
19.	The New Kids on the Block (1990)	74.1	122/152
20.	Cher (2002)	73.6	84/93

(1) In millions. Not adjusted for inflation.

Top-Selling Albums of All-Time[1]

Source: Recording Industry Assn. of America, Washington, DC

Rank	Title, Artist	Sales (in millions)
1.	*Eagles/Their Greatest Hits 1971-1975,* Eagles	28.0
2.	*Thriller,* Michael Jackson	27.0
3.	*The Wall,* Pink Floyd	23.0
4.	*Led Zeppelin IV,* Led Zeppelin	22.0
5.	*Back in Black,* AC/DC	21.0
	Greatest Hits Volume I & Volume II, Billy Joel	21.0
7.	*Come on Over,* Shania Twain	20.0
8.	*The Beatles,* The Beatles	19.0
	Rumours, Fleetwood Mac	19.0
10.	*Boston,* Boston	17.0
	The Bodyguard (soundtrack), Whitney Houston	17.0
12.	*The Beatles 1967-1970,* The Beatles	16.0
	No Fences, Garth Brooks	16.0
	Hotel California, Eagles	16.0
	Cracked Rear View, Hootie & the Blowfish	16.0
	Greatest Hits, Elton John	16.0
	Jagged Little Pill, Alanis Morissette	16.0
18.	*The Beatles 1962-1966,* The Beatles	15.0
	Saturday Night Fever (soundtrack), Bee Gees	15.0
	Double Live, Garth Brooks	15.0
	Appetite For Destruction, Guns 'N Roses	15.0
	Physical Graffiti, Led Zeppelin	15.0
	Dark Side of the Moon, Pink Floyd	15.0
	Supernatural, Santana	15.0
	Born in the U.S.A., Bruce Springsteen	15.0
26.	*Backstreet Boys,* Backstreet Boys	14.0
	Ropin' The Wind, Garth Brooks	14.0
	Bat Out of Hell, Meat Loaf	14.0
	Metallica, Metallica	14.0
	Simon & Garfunkel's Greatest Hits, Simon & Garfunkel	14.0
	...Baby One More Time, Britney Spears	14.0

(1) As of Aug. 2004; sales figures represent RIAA multi-platinum certifications, albums ranked by latest sales certification.

Sales of Recorded Music and Music Videos, by Units Shipped and Value, 1994-2004

Source: Recording Industry Assn. of America, Washington, DC
(in millions, net after returns)

FORMAT	1994	1995	1998	1999	2000	2001	2002	2003	2004	CHANGE 2003-04
Compact disc (CD)										
Units shipped	662.1	722.9	847.0	938.9	942.5	881.9	803.3	745.9	766.9	2.8%
Dollar value	8,464.5	9,377.4	11,416.0	12,816.3	13,214.5	12,909.4	12,044.1	11,232.9	11,446.5	1.9%
CD single										
Units shipped	9.3	21.5	56.0	55.9	34.2	17.3	4.5	8.3	3.1	–62.2%
Dollar value	56.1	110.9	213.2	222.4	142.7	79.4	19.6	35.9	14.9	–58.4%
Cassette										
Units shipped	345.4	272.6	158.5	123.6	76.0	45.0	31.1	17.2	5.2	–69.6%
Dollar value	2,976.4	2,303.6	1,419.9	1,061.6	626.0	363.4	209.8	108.1	23.6	–78.2%
Cassette single										
Units shipped	81.1	70.7	26.4	14.2	1.3	–1.5	–0.5	NA	NA	NA
Dollar value	274.9	236.3	94.4	48.0	4.6	–5.3	–1.6	NA	NA	NA
LP/EP										
Units shipped	1.9	2.2	3.4	2.9	2.2	2.3	1.7	1.5	1.3	–11.9%
Dollar value	17.8	25.1	34.0	31.8	27.7	27.4	20.5	21.7	19.2	–11.3%
Vinyl single										
Units shipped	11.7	10.2	5.4	5.3	4.8	5.5	4.4	3.8	3.5	–7.3%
Dollar value	47.2	46.7	25.7	27.9	26.3	31.4	24.9	21.5	19.8	–7.3%
Music video										
Units shipped	11.2	12.6	27.2	19.8	18.2	17.7	14.7	19.9	32.7	65.0%
Dollar value	231.1	220.3	508.0	376.7	281.9	329.2	288.4	399.9	607.2	51.8%
DVD audio										
Units shipped	—	—	—	—	—	0.3	0.4	0.4	0.35	–20.6%
Dollar value	—	—	—	—	—	6.0	8.5	8.0	64	–19.2%
SACD										
Units shipped	—	—	—	—	—	—	—	1.3	0.79	–39.6%
Dollar value	—	—	—	—	—	—	—	26.3	16.6	–36.9%
DVD video*										
Units shipped	—	—	0.5	2.5	3.3	7.9	10.7	17.5	29.01	66.0%
Dollar value	—	—	12.2	66.3	80.3	190.7	236.3	369.6	561.1	51.8%
TOTAL UNITS	**1,122.7**	**1,112.7**	**1,123.9**	**1,160.6**	**1,079.2**	**968.5**	**859.7**	**798.4**	**814.1**	**2.0%**
TOTAL VALUE	**12,068.0**	**12,320.3**	**13,711.2**	**14,584.7**	**14,323.7**	**13,740.9**	**12,614.2**	**11,854.4**	**12,154.7**	**2.5%**

* While broken out for this chart, DVD Video Product is included in the Music Video totals. Note: Exact figures for digital sales became available for the first time in 2004; 139.4 mil. singles and 4.5 mil. albums shipped that year; not included in totals shown.

Sales of Recorded Music and Music Videos, by Genre and Format, 1999-2004

Source: Recording Industry Assn. of America, Washington, DC
Breakdown is by percentage of sales revenue for all recorded music sold, ranked for 2004.

GENRE	2004	2003	2002	2001	2000	1999
Rock	23.9%	25.2%	24.7%	24.4%	24.8%	25.2%
Country	13.0	10.4	10.7	10.5	10.7	10.8
Rap/Hip-Hop	12.1	13.3	13.8	11.4	12.9	10.8
R&B/Urban[1]	11.3	10.6	11.2	10.6	9.7	10.5
Pop	10.0	8.9	9.0	12.1	11.0	10.3
Religious[2]	6.0	5.8	6.7	6.7	4.8	5.1
Children's	2.8	0.6	0.4	0.5	0.6	0.4
Jazz	2.7	.9	3.2	3.4	2.9	3.0
Classical	2.0	3.0	3.1	3.2	2.7	3.5
Oldies	1.4	1.3	0.9	0.8	0.9	0.7
Soundtracks	1.1	1.4	1.1	1.4	0.7	0.8
New Age	1.0	0.5	0.5	1.0	0.5	0.5
Other[3]	8.9	7.6	8.1	7.9	8.3	9.1
FORMAT						
Compact disc (CD)	90.3	87.8	90.5	89.2	89.3	83.2
Singles (all types)	2.4	2.4	1.9	2.4	2.5	5.4
Cassette	1.7	2.2	2.4	3.4	4.9	8.0
Digital download[4]	0.9	1.3	0.5	0.2	NA	NA
DVD audio	1.7	2.7	1.3	1.1	NA	NA
Music Videos/ DVDs[4]	1.0	0.6	0.7	1.1	0.8	0.9
LPs	0.9	0.5	0.7	0.6	0.5	0.5

(1) Includes R&B, blues, dance, disco, funk, fusion, Motown, reggae, soul. (2) Includes Christian, Gospel, Inspirational, Religious, and Spiritual. (3) "Other" includes big band, Broadway, comedy, contemporary, electronic, emo, ethnic, exercise, folk, gothic, grunge, holiday music, house music, humor, instrumental, language, latin, love songs, mix, mellow, modern, ska, spoken-word, standards, swing, Top-40, trip-hop. (4) 2001 is the first year that data were collected on digital download purchases, and that music video/DVD was recorded separately from audio DVD.

IT'S A FACT: The Recording Industry Association of America began certifying paid music downloads as gold, platinum, and multi-platinum for the first time in Oct. 2004. The hip-hop duo OutKast received the first multi-platinum honor, for 400,000 downloads of the song "Hey Ya!" The multi-platinum mark is set lower for downloads, which make up a small fraction of total music sales, though they are growing rapidly. In July 2005, Apple announced that its iTunes digital music site alone had surpassed 500 million song downloads since its launch in Apr. 2003.

Multi-Platinum and Platinum Awards for Recorded Music and Music Videos, 2004

Source: Recording Industry Assn. of America, Washington, DC

To achieve platinum status, an **album** must reach a minimum sale of 1 mil units in LPs, tapes, and CDs, with a manufacturer's dollar volume of at least $2 mil based on one-third of the suggested retail list price for each record, tape, or CD sold. To achieve multi-platinum status, an album must reach a minimum sale of at least 2 mil units in LPs, tapes, and CDs, with a manufacturer's dollar volume of at least $4 mil based on one-third of the list price.

Singles must sell 1 mil units to achieve a platinum award (created in 1976) and 2 mil to achieve a multi-platinum award (created in 1984). In 1999, the Diamond Award, honoring sales of 10 million or more copes of an album or single, was introduced. EP singles count as 2 units. Double-CD sets count as 2 units. **Music videos** (long form) must sell 100,000 units to qualify for a platinum award, more than 200,000 units for a multi-platinum award, and are recertified with each additional 100,000 sold. **Video singles**, which must have a maximum running time of 15 minutes and no more than 2 songs per title, must sell 50,000 units to qualify for a platinum award, at least 100,000 units to qualify for a multi-platinum award, and are recertified with each additional 50,000 sold. In Oct. 2004, digital gold (100,000 sold), platinum (200,000 sold), and multi-platinum (400,000 sold) awards were introduced.

Awards listed were for albums (released in 2004) and for music videos (released at any time) that were certified during the 2004 calendar year. Numbers in parentheses = millions sold. Alphabetized by artist's name.

Albums, Multi-Platinum

Elephunk, The Black Eyed Peas (2)
Genius Loves Company, Ray Charles (2)
When the Sun Goes Down, Kenny Chesney (3)
D12 World, D12 (2)
Destiny Fulfilled, Destiny's Child (2)
Encore, Eminem (4)
Feels Like Home, Norah Jones (4)
Greatest Hits 2, Toby Keith (2)
Happy People/U Saved Me, R. Kelly (3)
Under My Skin, Avril Lavigne (2)
Live Like You Were Dying, Tim McGraw (3)
Suit, Nelly (2)
Autobiography, Ashlee Simpson (3)
50 #1s, George Strait (5)
Greatest Hits, Shania Twain (2)
How to Dismantle an Atomic Bomb, U2 (3)
Confessions, Usher (8)
Now That's What I Call Music! Vol. 15, Various Artists (2)
Now That's What I Call Music! Vol. 16, Various Artists (3)
Now That's What I Call Music! Vol. 17, Various Artists (3)
The College Dropout, Kanye West (2)
Here for the Party, Gretchen Wilson (3)

Albums, Platinum

The Hunger for More, Lloyd Banks
To the 5 Boroughs, Beastie Boys
The Capitol Albums, Vol. 1, The Beatles
Horse of a Different Color, Big & Rich
License to Chill, Jimmy Buffett
Ray (Original Motion Picture Soundtrack), Ray Charles
Only You, Harry Connick Jr.
Hilary Duff, Hilary Duff
Chronicles of Life and Death, Good Charlotte
American Idiot, Green Day
Greatest Hits, Guns 'N Roses
A Crow Left of the Murder, Incubus
What I Do, Alan Jackson
Damita Jo, Janet Jackson
Unfinished Business, Jay-Z and R. Kelly
Jojo, Jojo
U Gotta Feel Me, Lil' Flip
Los Lonely Boys, Los Lonely Boys
La Trayectoria, Luny Tunes
Words & Music, John Mellencamp
Good News for People Who Love Bad News, Modest Mouse
Sweat, Nelly
With the Lights Out, Nirvana
Musicology, Prince
Feels Like Today, Rascal Flatts
R&G (Rhythm and Gangsta), Snoop Dogg
Greatest Hits: My Prerogative, Britney Spears
Love, Angel, Music, Baby, Gwen Stefani
Stardust...the Great American Songbook, Vol. 3, Rod Stewart
Kamikaze, Twista
Be Here, Keith Urban
The Best of Both Worlds, Van Halen
Contraband, Velvet Revolver

Music Videos, Multi-Platinum

Here Without You, 3 Doors Down (6)
Live at Donington, AC/DC (3)
The First U.S. Visit, The Beatles (2)
Live at Wembley, Beyoncé (2)
Hurt, Johnny Cash (2)
When the Sun Goes Down, Kenny Chesney (2)
Coldplay Live 2003, Coldplay (6)
Disclaimer II, Seether (5)
All Access Pass, Hilary Duff (2)
Anywhere But Home, Evanescence (5)
Live in New Orleans, Norah Jones (2)
The Reel Me, Jennifer Lopez (3)
Cunning Stunts, Metallica (3)
Everything, Alanis Morissette (4)
Live at the Garden, Pearl Jam (2)
Live at Pompeii, Pink Floyd (2)
'68 Comeback Special, Elvis Presley (2)
Live, Rascal Flatts (2)
Rush in Rio, Rush (4)
Live in Barcelona, Bruce Springsteen (4)
The Complete Masterworks, Tenacious D (5)
Concert for George, Various Artists (7)
Live on Broadway, Robin Williams (9)

Music Videos, Platinum

311 Day: Live in New Orleans, 311
Stripped: Live in the UK, Christina Aguilera
Not Today, Mary J. Blige
Live at Great Woods, Allman Brothers
The Complex Rock Tour Live, Blue Man Group
Red Dirt Road and Other Video Hits, Brooks & Dunn
Come Fly With Me, Michael Buble
Live From Atlanta, Casting Crowns
Road Case, Kenny Chesney
Greatest: The DVD, Duran Duran
The Best Present of All, Rob Evans
Live in Boston, Fleetwood Mac
Video Collection, Good Charlotte
Blue Wild Angel: Live at the Isle of Wight, Jimi Hendrix
Experience, Jimi Hendrix
Jimi Plays Berkeley, Jimi Hendrix
Number Ones, Michael Jackson
Greatest Hits DVD 1978-1997, Journey
5 Great Big Videos, Toby Keith
The R. in R&B: The Video Collection, R. Kelly
Show: A Night in the Life of Matchbox 20, Matchbox 20
Martina, Martina Mc Bride
The Videos, OutKast
The Way You Move/Hey Ya!, OutKast
aMotion, A Perfect Circle
Aloha From Hawaii, Elvis Presley
Britney Spears: In the Zone, Britney Spears
Greatest Hits: My Prerogative, Britney Spears
The Concert: Live at the MGM Grand, Barbra Streisand
Live Wire, Third Day
The Ghosts of Christmas Eve, Trans-Siberian Orchestra
Come on Over Video, Shania Twain
Platinum Collection, Shania Twain
Up Close and Personal, Shania Twain
Up! Live in Chicago, Shania Twain
Live at the Astoria, Steve Vai
Christmas in the Country, Various Artists
Harmony in the Heartland, Various Artists
Heaven, Various Artists
Now That's What I Call Music!, Various Artists
Now That's What I Call Music! Vol. 2, Various Artists
Oh My Glory, Various Artists
This is My Story, Various Artists
God Bless America, Various Artists
Beyond Ocean Avenue: Live at the Electric Factory, Yellowcard

U.S. Households With Cable Television, 1977-2004

Source: Nielsen Media Research

Year	Subscribers[1] (mil)	As % of households with TVs	Year	Subscribers[1] (mil)	As % of households with TVs	Year	Subscribers[1] (mil)	As % of households with TVs	Year	Subscribers[1] (mil)	As % of households with TVs
1977	12.2	16.6	1984	37.3	43.7	1991	55.8	60.6	1998	67.0	67.4
1978	13.4	17.9	1985	39.6	46.2	1992	57.3	61.5	1999	68.5	68.0
1979	14.9	19.4	1986	42.2	48.1	1993	58.8	62.5	2000	69.3	67.8
1980	17.7	22.6	1987	45.0	50.5	1994	60.5	63.4	2001	73.0	69.2
1981	23.2	28.3	1988	48.6	53.8	1995	63.0	65.7	2002	73.5	68.9
1982	29.2	35.0	1989	52.6	57.1	1996	64.6	66.7	2003	73.4	68.0
1983	34.1	40.5	1990	54.9	59.0	1997	65.9	67.3	2004	73.9	68.1

(1) Subscribers to basic cable service.

Number of Cable TV Systems,[1] 1975-2005

Source: *2005 Television and Cable Factbook*, Warren Communications News, Inc., Washington, DC; estimates as of Jan. 1

Year	Systems	Year	Systems	Year	Systems	Year	Systems	Year	Systems	Year	Systems	Year	Systems
1975	3,506	1980	4,225	1985	6,600	1990	9,575	1994	11,214	1998	10,845	2002	9,947
1976	3,681	1981	4,375	1986	7,500	1991	10,704	1995	11,218	1999	10,700	2003	9,339*
1977	3,832	1982	4,825	1987	7,900	1992	11,035	1996	11,119	2000	10,400	2004	8,869*
1978	3,875	1983	5,600	1988	8,500	1993	11,108	1997	10,950	2001	9,924	2005	8,409*
1979	4,150	1984	6,200	1989	9,050								

(1) The satellite-signal-receiving hardware, cable lines, and cable boxes that provide cable programming to homes within a geographic area. *Figures as of March of the year noted.

Top 20 Cable TV Networks, 2005

Source: *Cable Television Developments,* Natl. Cable Television Assn., April 2004; ranked by number of subscribers

Rank	Network[1]	Subscribers (mil)
1.	Discovery Channel (1985)	89.9
	ESPN (1979)	89.9
3.	CNN (Cable News Network) (1980)	89.4
	TNT (Turner Network Television) (1988)	89.4
5.	USA Network (1980)	89.2
6.	Nickelodeon (1979)	89.1
	TBS (Superstation) (1976)	89.1
	Spike TV[2] (2003)	89.1
9.	A&E Network (1984)	89.0
10.	LIFE (Lifetime Television) (1984)	88.9
11.	ESPN2 (1993)	88.8
	The Weather Channel (1982)	88.8
13.	TLC (The Learning Channel) (1980)	88.7
14.	MTV (Music Television) (1981)	88.5
15.	C-SPAN (Cable Satellite Public Affairs Network) (1979)	88.4
16.	Headline News (1982)	88.3
	Home & Garden Television (HGTV)	88.3
18.	ABC Family Channel[3] (2001)	88.3
19.	The History Channel (1995)	88.2
20.	QVC	88.1

Note: Data include noncable affiliates. (1) Date in parentheses is year service began. (2) Formerly The Nashville Network (1983-2000); The National Network (2000-2003); The New TNN (2003). (3) Began 1977 as the Family Channel; FOX Family Channel (1998-2000).

U.S. Television Set Owners, 2005

Source: Nielsen Media Research; Jan. 2005

Of the 106.9 million U.S. households that owned at least one TV set in 2005:

33% had 2 TV sets
46% had 3 or more TV sets
90% had a VCR
76% had a DVD player
68% received basic cable
42% received premium cable

Average U.S. Television Viewing Time, October 2004

Source: Nielsen Media Research (hours: minutes per week)

Group	Age	Total per week	M-F 7-10 AM	M-F 10 AM-4:00 PM	M-Sun. 8-11 PM	Sat. 7 AM-1 PM	M-F 11:30 PM-1 AM	Sunday 1-7:00 PM
Men	18+	31:45	1:43	3:52	9:02	0:52	1:37	1:53
	18-24	21:10	0:56	2:58	5:04	0:32	1:21	1:11
	25-54	30:55	1:37	3:21	8:53	0:53	1:40	1:53
	55+	38:28	2:20	5:20	11:19	0:57	1:35	2:13
Women	18+	36:29	2:26	5:51	9:50	0:57	1:43	1:38
	18-24	23:41	1:17	4:06	5:51	0:37	1:22	1:02
	25-54	34:56	2:22	5:12	9:26	0:58	1:46	1:35
	55+	44:01	3:03	7:42	12:05	1:04	1:47	1:56
Children	2-11	21:30	1:42	3:19	5:01	1:10	0:37	1:08
Teens	12-17	20:40	0:43	1:51	5:59	0:42	0:59	1:11
ALL VIEWERS		31:05	1:55	4:25	8:31	0:55	1:28	1:37

TV Viewing Shares, Broadcast Years 1990-2004[1]

Source: *Cable TV Facts,* Cable Advertising Bureau, New York, NY

	All Television Households[2]							All Cable Households[2]							Pay Cable Households[2]						
	'90	'95	'00	'01	'02	'03	'04	'90	'95	'00	'01	'02	'03	'04	'90	'95	'00	'01	'02	'03	'04
Network Affiliates[3]	55	48	44	42	39	31	37	46	41	40	37	35	28	33	43	38	37	35	33	25	30
Indep. TV Stations[4]	20	22	12	11	11	12	10	16	17	9	8	8	9	8	16	17	9	8	8	8	8
Public TV Stations	3	3	3	3	3	3	2	3	3	2	2	2	2	2	2	2	2	2	2	2	1
Basic Cable[5]	21	30	46	49	49	52	53	32	42	55	57	56	58	60	30	41	55	57	56	58	60
Pay Cable	6	6	6	6	6	6	6	10	8	7	7	7	7	7	18	15	11	11	12	12	13

Note: After 1998, Fox affiliates switched from Independent classification to Network Affiliates. (1) Broadcast years represent the 12-month period October-September. (2) Share figures refer to percentage of the viewing audience for all television viewing, 24 hours/day. As a result of multiset use and rounding of numbers, share figures add to more than 100. (3) Includes CBS, NBC, ABC, and FOX. (4) Includes WB, UPN, and PAX. (5) Includes ad-supported cable and all other cable (non-pay and non-ad-supported channels).

WORLD ALMANAC QUICK QUIZ

Of the 10 top-grossing North American concert tours, how many were headlined by the Rolling Stones?
(a) 8 (b) 4 (c) 2 (d) none

For the answer look in this chapter, or see page 1008.

Favorite Prime-Time Television Programs, 2004-05

Source: Nielsen Media Research

Data are for regularly scheduled network programs in 2004-05 season through May 25; ranked by average audience percentage. Average audience percentages, or ratings, are estimates of the percentage of all TV-owning households that are watching a particular program. Audience share percentages are estimates of the percentage of those watching TV that are tuned into a particular program. Tied programs are given the same rank.

Rank	Programs	Avg. Audience	Audience Share
1.	CSI	16.3%	25
2.	American Idol-Tuesday	15.8	24
3.	American Idol-Wednesday	15.3	23
4.	Desperate Housewives	14.3	21
5.	CSI: Miami	12.4	20
6.	Without a Trace	12.3	20
7.	Survivor: Palau	12.2	20
8.	Survivor: Vanuatu	11.7	18
9.	Grey's Anatomy	11.4	18
10.	Everybody Loves Raymond	10.9	16
11.	NFL Monday Night Football	10.8	18
12.	Two and a Half Men	10.5	15
13.	Apprentice 2	10.4	16
14.	E.R.	10.3	17
15.	Lost	9.8	15
	Cold Case	9.8	15
17.	60 Minutes	9.3	15
18.	Law & Order: SVU	9.2	15
19.	Apprentice 3	9.1	14
	Medium	9.1	14
21.	Extreme Makeover: Home Edition	9.0	14
	CSI: NY	9.0	15
23.	Law & Order	8.9	15
24.	NCIS	8.8	14
25.	NFL Monday Showcase	8.4	13
26.	House	8.2%	12
27.	Boston Legal	8.1	13
28.	Amazing Race 7	8.0	12
29.	Law & Order: Criminal Intent	7.9	12
	Fox NFL Sunday-Postgame	7.9	14
31.	Crossing Jordan	7.7	13
32.	CBS Sunday Movie	7.6	12
33.	Judging Amy	7.4	12
	Law & Order: Trial by Jury	7.4	13
	The West Wing	7.4	11
36.	Las Vegas	7.3	11
	Numb3rs	7.3	13
38.	Amazing Race: 6	7.2	11
	24	7.2	11
40.	Revelations	7.1	11
41.	Will & Grace	7.0	11
42.	The Biggest Loser	6.9	10
43.	Joey	6.8	11
44.	NYPD Blue	6.7	11
45.	Alias	6.6	10
	Still Standing	6.6	10
47.	Jag	6.5	11
	Wife Swap	6.5	11
	King of Queens	6.5	10
49.	According to Jim	6.5	10

Favorite Syndicated Programs, 2004-05

Source: Nielsen Media Research, Aug. 30, 2004-Aug. 14, 2005

Average audience percentages, or ratings, are estimates of the percentage of TV-owning households watching a program.

Rank	Program	Avg. audience (%)
1.	Wheel of Fortune	8.6
2.	Jeopardy	7.4
3.	Oprah Winfrey Show	7.1
4.	ESPN NFL Regular Season	6.6
5.	Everybody Loves Raymond	6.5
6.	Seinfeld (non-weekend)	5.8
7.	Seinfeld (weekend)	5.4
	ESPN NFL Regular Season 2	5.4
	Friends	5.4
10.	CSI	5.2
	Dr. Phil	5.2
12.	Warner Bros. Vol 32*	5.0
13.	Entertainment Tonight (non-weekend)	4.9
	Judge Judy	4.9
15.	Buena Vista III*	4.5
16.	Wheel of Fortune (weekend)	3.7
17.	Live With Regis and Kelly	3.5
18.	Everybody Loves Raymond (weekend)	3.4
	Warner Bros. Vol 34*	3.4
20.	Inside Edition	3.3
	Judge Joe Brown	3.3
	Who Wants to Be a Millionaire	3.3
	Warner Bros. Vol 35*	3.3
24.	Buena Vista VII*	3.1
	Malcolm in the Middle	3.1
	Warner Bros. Vol 33*	3.1
	Entertainment Tonight (weekend)	3.1
28.	That 70s Show	3.0
	King of the Hill	3.0
	Maury	3.0

* Represents a package of films sold for syndication.

Selected Reality TV Show Winners

Numbers in parenthesis represent the season/edition of the show.

The Amazing Race. Debuted Aug. 2001 on CBS. (1) Rob Frisbee & Brennan Swain; (2) Chris Luca & Alex Boylan; (3) Flo Pesenti & Zach Behr; (4) Reichen Lehmkuhl & Chip Arndt; (5) Chip & Kim McAllister; (6) Freddy Holliday & Kendra Bentley; (7) Uchenna & Joyce Agu.

American Idol. Debuted July 2002 on Fox. (1) Kelly Clarkson; (2) Ruben Studdard; (3) Fantasia Barrino; (4) Carrie Underwood.

America's Next Top Model. Debuted May 2003. (1) Adrianne Curry; (2) Yoanna House; (3) Eva Pigford; (4) Naima Mora.

The Apprentice. Debuted Jan. 2004 on NBC. (1) Bill Rancic; (2) Kelly Perdew; (3) Kendra Todd.

The Bachelor. Debuted Mar. 2002 on ABC. (1) Alex Michel chose Amanda Marsh; (2) Aaron Buerge chose Helene Eksterowicz; (3) Andrew Firestone chose Jen Schefft; (4) Bob Guiney chose Estella Gardinier; (5) Jesse Palmer chose Jessica Bowlin; (6) Byron Velvick chose Mary Delgado; (7) Charlie O'Connell chose Sarah Brice.

The Bachelorette. Debuted Jan. 2003 on ABC. (1) Trista Rehn chose Ryan Sutter; (2) Meredith Phillips chose Ian McKee; (3) Jen Schefft chose Jerry Ferris.

Big Brother. Debuted July 2000 on CBS. (1) Eddie McGee; (2) Will Kirby; (3) Lisa Donahue; (4) Jun Song; (5) Drew Daniel. (6) Maggie Ausburn.

Last Comic Standing. Debuted June 2003 on NBC. (1) Dat Phan; (2) John Heffron; (3) Alonzo Bodden.

Nashville Star. Debuted Mar. 2003 on USA Network.(1) Buddy Jewell; (2) Brad Cotter; (3) Erika Jo Heriges.

Project Runway. Debuted Dec. 2004 on Bravo. (1) Jay McCarroll.

Survivor. Debuted May 2000 on CBS. Borneo (1), Richard Hatch; Outback (2), Tina Wesson; Africa (3), Ethan Zohn; Marquesas (4), Vecepia Towery; Thailand (5), Brian Heidik; The Amazon (6), Jenna Morasca; Pearl Islands (7), Sandra Diaz-Twine; All-Stars (Panama) (8), Amber Brkich; Vanuatu (9), Chris Daugherty; Palau (10), Tom Westman.

Highest-Rated TV Shows of Each Season, 1950-51 to 2004-05

Source: Nielsen Media Research; regular series programs, Sept.-May season

Season	Program	Rating[1]	TV-owning households (in thousands)
1950-51	Texaco Star Theatre	61.6	10,320
1951-52	Godfrey's Talent Scouts	53.8	15,300
1952-53	I Love Lucy	67.3	20,400
1953-54	I Love Lucy	58.8	26,000
1954-55	I Love Lucy	49.3	30,700
1955-56	$64,000 Question	47.5	34,900
1956-57	I Love Lucy	43.7	38,900
1957-58	Gunsmoke	43.1	41,920
1958-59	Gunsmoke	39.6	43,950
1959-60	Gunsmoke	40.3	45,750
1960-61	Gunsmoke	37.3	47,200
1961-62	Wagon Train	32.1	48,555
1962-63	Beverly Hillbillies	36.0	50,300
1963-64	Beverly Hillbillies	39.1	51,600
1964-65	Bonanza	36.3	52,700
1965-66	Bonanza	31.8	53,850
1966-67	Bonanza	29.1	55,130
1967-68	Andy Griffith	27.6	56,670
1968-69	Rowan & Martin's Laugh-In	31.8	58,250
1969-70	Rowan & Martin's Laugh-In	26.3	58,500
1970-71	Marcus Welby, MD	29.6	60,100
1971-72	All in the Family	34.0	62,100
1972-73	All in the Family	33.3	64,800
1973-74	All in the Family	31.2	66,200
1974-75	All in the Family	30.2	68,500
1975-76	All in the Family	30.1	69,600
1976-77	Happy Days	31.5	71,200
1977-78	Laverne & Shirley	31.6	72,900
1978-79	Laverne & Shirley	30.5	74,500
1979-80	60 Minutes	28.2	76,300
1980-81	Dallas	31.2	79,900
1981-82	Dallas	28.4	81,500
1982-83	60 Minutes	25.5	83,300
1983-84	Dallas	25.7	83,800
1984-85	Dynasty	25.0	84,900
1985-86	Cosby Show	33.8	85,900
1986-87	Cosby Show	34.9	87,400
1987-88	Cosby Show	27.8	88,600
1988-89	Roseanne	25.5	90,400
1989-90	Roseanne	23.4	92,100
1990-91	Cheers	21.6	93,100
1991-92	60 Minutes	21.7	92,100
1992-93	60 Minutes	21.6	93,100
1993-94	Home Improvement	21.9	94,200
1994-95	Seinfeld	20.5	95,400
1995-96	E.R.	22.0	95,900
1996-97	E.R.	21.2	97,000
1997-98	Seinfeld	22.0	98,000
1998-99	E.R.	17.8	99,400
1999-2000	Who Wants to Be a Millionaire	18.6	100,800
2000-01	Survivor II	17.4	102,200
2001-02	Friends	15.3	105,500
2002-03	CSI	16.1	106,700
2003-04	CSI	15.9	108,400
2004-05	CSI	16.3	106,900

(1) Rating is percent of TV-owning households tuned in to the program. Data prior to 1988-89 exclude Alaska and Hawaii.

All-Time Highest-Rated Television Programs

Source: Nielsen Media Research, Jan. 1961-May 2005

Estimates exclude unsponsored or joint network telecasts (e.g., presidential addresses) or programs under 30 minutes long. Ranked by rating (percentage of TV-owning households tuned in to the program).

Rank	Program	Telecast date	Network	Rating (%)	Avg. households (in thousands)
1.	M*A*S*H (last episode)	2/28/83	CBS	60.2	50,150
2.	Dallas (Who Shot J.R.?)	11/21/80	CBS	53.3	41,470
3.	Roots-Pt. 8	1/30/77	ABC	51.1	36,380
4.	Super Bowl XVI	1/24/82	CBS	49.1	40,020
5.	Super Bowl XVII	1/30/83	NBC	48.6	40,480
6.	XVII Winter Olympics - 2nd Wed.	2/23/94	CBS	48.5	45,690
7.	Super Bowl XX	1/26/86	NBC	48.3	41,490
8.	Gone With the Wind-Pt. 1	11/7/76	NBC	47.7	33,960
9.	Gone With the Wind-Pt. 2	11/8/76	NBC	47.4	33,750
10.	Super Bowl XII	1/15/78	CBS	47.2	34,410
11.	Super Bowl XIII	1/21/79	NBC	47.1	35,090
12.	Bob Hope Christmas Show	1/15/70	NBC	46.6	27,260
13.	Super Bowl XIX	1/20/85	ABC	46.4	39,390
	Super Bowl XVIII	1/22/84	CBS	46.4	38,800
15.	Super Bowl XIV	1/20/80	CBS	46.3	35,330
16.	Super Bowl XXX	1/28/96	NBC	46.0	44,150
	ABC Theater (The Day After)	11/20/83	ABC	46.0	38,550
18.	Roots-Pt. 6	1/28/77	ABC	45.9	32,680
	The Fugitive	8/29/67	ABC	45.9	25,700
20.	Super Bowl XXI	1/25/87	CBS	45.8	40,030
21.	Roots-Pt. 5	1/27/77	ABC	45.7	32,540
22.	Super Bowl XXVIII	1/30/94	NBC	45.5	42,860
	Cheers (last episode)	5/20/93	NBC	45.5	42,360
24.	Ed Sullivan	2/9/64	CBS	45.3	23,240
25.	Super Bowl XXVII	1/31/93	NBC	45.1	41,990
26.	Bob Hope Christmas Show	1/14/71	NBC	45.0	27,050
27.	Roots-Pt. 3	1/25/77	ABC	44.8	31,900
28.	Super Bowl XXXII	1/25/98	NBC	44.5	43,630
29.	Super Bowl XV	1/25/81	NBC	44.4	34,540
	Super Bowl XI	1/9/77	NBC	44.4	31,610
31.	Super Bowl VI	1/16/72	CBS	44.2	27,450
32.	XVII Winter Olympics - 2nd Fri.	2/25/94	CBS	44.1	41,540
	Roots-Pt. 2	1/24/77	ABC	44.1	31,400
34.	Beverly Hillbillies	1/8/64	CBS	44.0	22,570
35.	Roots-Pt. 4	1/26/77	ABC	43.8	31,190
	Ed Sullivan	2/16/64	CBS	43.8	22,445
37.	Super Bowl XXIII	1/22/89	NBC	43.5	39,320
38.	Academy Awards	4/7/70	ABC	43.4	25,390
39.	Super Bowl XXXI	1/26/97	FOX	43.3	42,000
	Super Bowl XXXIV	1/30/00	ABC	43.3	43,620
41.	Thorn Birds-Pt. 3	3/29/83	ABC	43.2	35,990
42.	Thorn Birds-Pt. 4	3/30/83	ABC	43.1	35,900
43.	CBS NFC Championship	1/10/82	CBS	42.9	34,960
44.	Beverly Hillbillies	1/15/64	CBS	42.8	21,960
45.	Super Bowl VII	1/14/73	NBC	42.7	27,670

100 Leading U.S. Advertisers, 2004

Source: Reprinted with permission from Ad Age (http://www.adage.com). © 2005, Crain Communications Inc.
(in millions of dollars)

Rank	Advertiser	Ad spending
1.	General Motors Corp.	$3,997
2.	Procter & Gamble Co.	3,920
3.	Time Warner	3,283
4.	Pfizer	2,957
5.	SBC Communications	2,687
6.	DaimlerChrysler	2,462
7.	Ford Motor Co.	2,458
8.	Walt Disney Co.	2,242
9.	Verizon Communications	2,197
10.	Johnson & Johnson	2,176
11.	GlaxoSmithKline	1,828
12.	Sears Holdings Corp.	1,823
13.	Toyota Motor Corp.	1,821
14.	General Electric Co.	1,819
15.	Sony Corp.	1,665
16.	Nissan Motor Co	1,540
17.	Altria Group	1,399
18.	McDonald's Corp.	1,389
19.	L'Oreal	1,341
20.	Unilever	1,319
21.	Novartis	1,285
22.	PepsiCo	1,262
23.	Home Depot	1,256
24.	Merck & Co.	1,250
25.	U.S. Government	1,229
26.	Viacom	1,207
27.	Honda Motor Co.	1,205
28.	Sprint Corp.	1,114
29.	J.C. Penney Co.	1,095
30.	Estee Lauder Cos.	1,057
31.	Nestle	1,028
32.	Citigroup	1,001
33.	Microsoft Corp.	987
34.	Best Buy Co.	951
35.	General Mills	$913
36.	Target Corp.	904
37.	Hewlett-Packard Co.	899
38.	News Corp.	891
39.	Schering-Plough Corp	853
40.	Wal-Mart Stores	841
41.	Gillette Co.	837
42.	Wyeth	829
43.	Anheuser-Busch Cos.	817
44.	Cendant Corp.	803
45.	May Department Stores Co.	793
46.	Yum Brands	779
47.	Bristol-Myers Squibb Co.	773
48.	Dell	756
49.	Federated Department Stores	744
50.	Mars Inc.	740
51.	AstraZeneca	723
52.	American Express Co.	718
53.	Kroger Co.	686
54.	Sanofi-Aventis	674
55.	IAC/InterActiveCorp	648
56.	Kellogg Co.	647
57.	IBM Corp.	632
58.	Berkshire Hathaway	617
59.	Safeway	606
60.	Deutsche Telekom	604
61.	Diageo	594
62.	Eli Lilly & Co.	587
63.	Volkswagen	580
64.	Nextel Communications	576
65.	Nike	574
66.	Lowe's Cos.	542
67.	Burger King Corp.	542
68.	Coca-Cola Co.	541
69.	Hyundai Motor Co.	$534
70.	Kohl's Corp.	533
71.	Sara Lee Corp.	529
72.	Gap Inc.	526
73.	Clorox Co.	522
74.	Albertson's	512
75.	SC Johnson	511
76.	Visa International	505
77.	Capital One Financial Corp.	488
78.	Mattel	482
79.	SABMiller	471
80.	Doctor's Associates	463
81.	Bayer	459
82.	MasterCard International	445
83.	Wendy's International	436
84.	Campbell Soup Co.	425
85.	Mazda Motor Corp.	413
86.	BellSouth Corp.	405
87.	Limited Brands	399
88.	Bank of America Corp.	399
89.	AT&T Corp.	397
90.	DreamWorks SKG	380
91.	Cadbury Schweppes	375
92.	Mitsubishi Motors Corp.	374
93.	Allstate Corp.	374
94.	United Parcel Service	366
95.	ConAgra Foods	364
96.	Reckitt Benckiser	364
97.	Kia Motors Corp.	356
98.	Circuit City Stores	350
99.	Kimberly-Clark Corp.	342
100.	Molson Coors Brewing Co.	331

U.S. Ad SpendingCategories, 2004

Source: Reprinted with permission from Ad Age (http://www.adage.com). © 2005, Crain Communications Inc.
(in millions of dollars)

Category	Total	Mag.	Bus. Pub.	News-paper	Out-door	Televison Net-work	Spot	Syndi-cated	Spanish Lang.	Cable	Radio	Inter-net
Automotive	20,518	2,446	83	6,670	362	3,105	5,337	248	1,312	164	416	375
Retail	17,285	1,522	132	7,166	318	2,018	2,822	277	965	258	699	1,108
Telecom, Internet services, ISPs	9,059	551	216	2,209	168	1,542	1,241	180	880	290	420	1,362
Medicine & remedies	8,168	1,953	67	213	18	2,779	424	137	1,307	682	200	388
Financial services	7,344	906	235	1,642	220	1,418	610	70	922	185	221	915
Food, beverages & candy	6,840	1,631	112	51	78	2,127	657	205	1,331	430	140	79
General services	6,270	533	368	1,995	449	166	1,727	27	303	56	127	520
Personal care	5,528	1,977	46	25	16	1,657	184	144	823	562	42	53
Movies, recorded video & music	5,338	326	111	1,230	106	1,667	463	223	800	201	97	116
Direct response advertising	5,246	1,936	159	411	6	165	186	396	1,638	170	51	128
Airlines, hotels, car rental, travel	5,141	1,035	296	1,685	296	317	449	29	466	47	106	416
Government, politics, religion	4,767	308	39	432	128	1,206	1,474	448	358	45	185	145
Restaurants	4,418	177	2	176	204	1,429	1,371	126	567	197	147	22
Media	3,928	1,351	249	1,101	224	21	199	6	69	24	269	415
Apparel	2,589	1,848	94	39	24	248	26	7	186	31	18	69
Computers, software	2,467	518	806	225	23	299	26	0	127	4	34	406
Insurance	2,332	235	62	250	85	424	477	44	347	75	151	182
Home furnishings, appliances	2,051	861	259	72	6	330	93	4	319	51	21	37
Real estate	2,023	158	13	1,368	163	72	87	5	48	18	21	71
Beer, wine & liquor	1,976	528	15	73	169	588	116	45	317	38	45	44
Home supplies & cleaners	1,974	333	12	9	5	658	126	102	463	227	34	6
Education	1,500	136	251	268	56	3	433	0	95	10	18	230
Toys & games	1,132	114	91	5	2	269	18	6	481	56	6	86
Hardware & home building supplies	992	368	196	56	7	87	63	9	162	10	23	11
Sporting goods	492	350	2	19	4	63	7	0	38	1	1	8
Pet food & pet care	452	119	1	2	1	152	27	0	75	48	9	18
Shipping & freight	357	49	36	10	6	174	1	0	29	0	27	24
Gas & oil	353	66	10	17	34	65	33	3	71	7	43	5
Office equipment	334	83	74	23	1	82	2	0	31	21	10	7
Cigarettes & tobacco	319	250	5	10	0	5	1	3	1	1	3	40
Miscellaneous	3,948	760	1,186	1,001	36	341	110	3	291	23	61	137
Total	**135,141**	**23,426**	**5,228**	**28,451**	**3,213**	**23,473**	**18,789**	**2,745**	**14,818**	**3,931**	**3,644**	**7,421**

IT'S A FACT: *Everybody Loves Raymond* wrapped up its 9th and final season in 2005; about 32.9 mil viewers tuned in to bid farewell to the Barones when the finale aired on CBS May 16. The Emmy-winning series (2003-2005) was the only sitcom in the top 10-rated shows in 2005; a 30-second commercial spot on its finale sold for an average of $314,700.

AWARDS — MEDALS — PRIZES

The Alfred B. Nobel Prize Winners, 1901-2004

Alfred B. Nobel (1833-96) bequeathed $9 mil, the interest on which was to be distributed yearly to those judged to have most benefited humankind in physics, chemistry, medicine-physiology, literature, and promotion of peace. Prizes were first awarded in 1901. The 1st prize in economics was awarded in 1969, funded by Sweden's central bank. Each prize is now worth about 10 mil Swedish kroner (about $1.3 mil). If year is omitted, no award was given. For 2005 winners, see Table of Contents.

Physics

2004 David J. Gross, H. David Politzer, Frank Wilczek, U.S.
2003 Vitaly L. Ginzburg, Alexei A. Abrikosov, Russ., Anthony J. Leggett, UK
2002 Raymond Davis Jr., Riccardo Giacconi, U.S.; Masatoshi Koshiba, Jpn.
2001 Eric A. Cornell, Carl E. Wieman, U.S.; Wolfgang Ketterle, Ger.
2000 Jack S. Kilby, U.S.; Herbert Kroemer, Ger.-U.S.; Zhores I. Alferov, Russ.
1999 Gerardus 't Hooft and Martinus J. G. Veltman, Netherlands
1998 Robert B. Laughlin, U.S.; Horst L. Störmer, Ger.-U.S; Daniel C. Tsui, China-U.S.
1997 Steven Chu, William D. Phillips, U.S.; Claude Cohen-Tannoudji, Fr.
1996 David M. Lee, Douglas D. Osheroff, Robert C. Richardson, U.S.
1995 Martin Perl, Frederick Reines, U.S.
1994 Bertram N. Brockhouse, Can.; Clifford G. Shull, U.S.
1993 Joseph H. Taylor, Russell A. Hulse, U.S.
1992 Georges Charpak, Pol.-Fr.
1991 Pierre-Gilles de Gennes, Fr.
1990 Richard E. Taylor, Can.; Jerome I. Friedman, Henry W. Kendall, U.S.
1989 Norman F. Ramsey, U.S.; Hans G. Dehmelt, Ger.-U.S.; Wolfgang Paul, Ger.
1988 Leon M. Lederman, Melvin Schwartz, Jack Steinberger, U.S.
1987 K. Alex Müller, Switz.; J. Georg Bednorz, Ger.
1986 Ernest Ruska, Ger.; Gerd Binnig, Ger.; Heinrich Rohrer, Switz.
1985 Klaus von Klitzing, Ger.
1984 Carlo Rubbia, It.; Simon van der Meer, Neth.
1983 Subramanyan Chandrasekhar, William A. Fowler, U.S.
1982 Kenneth G. Wilson, U.S.
1981 Nicolaas Bloembergen, Arthur Schawlow, U.S.; Kai M. Siegbahn, Swed.
1980 James W. Cronin, Val L. Fitch, U.S.
1979 Steven Weinberg, Sheldon L. Glashow, U.S.; Abdus Salam, Pakistan
1978 Pyotr Kapitsa, USSR; Arno Penzias, Robert Wilson, U.S.
1977 John H. van Vleck, Philip W. Anderson, U.S.; Sir Nevill F. Mott, UK
1976 Burton Richter, Samuel C.C. Ting, U.S.
1975 Leo James Rainwater, U.S.; Ben Mottelson, U.S.-Den.; Aage Bohr, Den.
1974 Sir Martin Ryle, Antony Hewish, UK
1973 Ivar Giaever, U.S.; Leo Esaki, Jpn.; Brian D. Josephson, UK
1972 John Bardeen, Leon N. Cooper, John R. Schrieffer, U.S.
1971 Dennis Gabor, UK
1970 Louis Néel, Fr.; Hannes Alfvén, Swed.
1969 Murray Gell-Mann, U.S.
1968 Luis W. Alvarez, U.S.
1967 Hans A. Bethe, U.S.
1966 Alfred Kastler, Fr.
1965 Richard P. Feynman, Julian S. Schwinger, U.S.; Sin-Itiro Tomonaga, Jpn.
1964 Nicolay G. Basov, Aleksandr M. Prokhorov, USSR; Charles H. Townes, U.S.
1963 Maria Goeppert-Mayer, Eugene P. Wigner, U.S.; J. Hans D. Jensen, Ger.
1962 Lev D. Landau, USSR
1961 Robert Hofstadter, U.S.; Rudolf L. Mossbauer, Ger.
1960 Donald A. Glaser, U.S.
1959 Owen Chamberlain, Emilio G. Segre, U.S.
1958 Pavel Cherenkov, Il'ja Frank, Igor Y. Tamm, USSR
1957 Tsung-dao Lee, Chen Ning Yang, U.S.-China
1956 John Bardeen, Walter H. Brattain, William Shockley, U.S.
1955 Polykarp Kusch, Willis E. Lamb, U.S.
1954 Max Born, UK; Walter Bothe, Ger.
1953 Frits Zernike, Neth.
1952 Felix Bloch, Edward M. Purcell, U.S.
1951 Sir John D. Cockcroft, UK; Ernest T. S. Walton, Ire.
1950 Cecil F. Powell, UK
1949 Hideki Yukawa, Jpn.
1948 Patrick M. S. Blackett, UK
1947 Sir Edward V. Appleton, UK
1946 Percy W. Bridgman, U.S.
1945 Wolfgang Pauli, U.S.-Austria
1944 Isidor Isaac Rabi, U.S.
1943 Otto Stern, U.S.
1939 Ernest O. Lawrence, U.S.
1938 Enrico Fermi, It.-U.S.
1937 Clinton J. Davisson, U.S.; Sir George P. Thomson, UK
1936 Carl D. Anderson, U.S.; Victor F. Hess, Austria
1935 Sir James Chadwick, UK
1933 Paul A. M. Dirac, UK; Erwin Schrödinger, Austria
1932 Werner Heisenberg, Ger.
1930 Sir Chandrasekhara V. Raman, India
1929 Prince Louis-Victor de Broglie, Fr.
1928 Owen W. Richardson, UK
1927 Arthur H. Compton, U.S.; Charles T. R. Wilson, UK
1926 Jean B. Perrin, Fr.
1925 James Franck, Gustav Hertz, Ger.
1924 Karl M. G. Siegbahn, Swed.
1923 Robert A. Millikan, U.S.
1922 Niels Bohr, Den.
1921 Albert Einstein, Ger.-U.S.
1920 Charles E. Guillaume, Fr.-Switz.
1919 Johannes Stark, Ger.
1918 Max K. E. L. Planck, Ger.
1917 Charles G. Barkla, UK
1915 Sir William H. Bragg, Sir William L. Bragg, UK
1914 Max von Laue, Ger.
1913 Heike Kamerlingh Onnes, Neth.
1912 Nils G. Dalén, Swed.
1911 Wilhelm Wien, Ger.
1910 Johannes D. van der Waals, Neth.
1909 Carl F. Braun, Ger.; Guglielmo Marconi, It.
1908 Gabriel Lippmann, Fr.
1907 Albert A. Michelson, U.S.
1906 Sir Joseph J. Thomson, UK
1905 Philipp E. A. von Lenard, Ger.
1904 Lord Rayleigh (John W. Strutt), UK
1903 Antoine Henri Becquerel, Pierre Curie, Fr.; Marie Curie, Pol.-Fr.
1902 Hendrik A. Lorentz, Pieter Zeeman, Neth.
1901 Wilhelm C. Röntgen, Ger.

Chemistry

2004 Aaron Ciechanover, Avram Hershko, Isr.; Irwin Rose, U.S.
2003 Peter Agre, Roderick MacKinnon, U.S.
2002 John B. Fenn, U.S.; Koichi Tanaka, Jpn.; Kurt Wüthrich, Switz.
2001 K. Barry Sharpless, U.S.; William S. Knowles, U.S., Ryoji Noyori, Jpn.
2000 Alan J. Heeger, U.S.; Alan G. MacDiarmid, N. Zea.-U.S.; Hideki Shirakawa, Jpn.
1999 Ahmed H. Zewail, U.S.
1998 Walter Kohn, U.S.; John A. Pople, UK
1997 Paul D. Boyer, U.S., & John E. Walker, UK; Jens C. Skou, Den.
1996 Sir Harold W. Kroto, UK; Robert F. Curl Jr., Richard E. Smalley, U.S.
1995 Paul Crutzen, Neth.; Mario Molina, Mex.-U.S.; Sherwood Rowland, U.S.
1994 George A. Olah, U.S.
1993 Kary B. Mullis, U.S.; Michael Smith, UK-Can.
1992 Rudolph A. Marcus, Can.-U.S.
1991 Richard R. Ernst, Switz.
1990 Elias James Corey, U.S.
1989 Thomas R. Cech, Sidney Altman, U.S.
1988 Johann Deisenhofer, Robert Huber, Hartmut Michel, Ger.
1987 Donald J. Cram, Charles J. Pedersen, U.S.; Jean-Marie Lehn, Fr.
1986 Dudley Herschbach, Yuan T. Lee, U.S.; John C. Polanyi, Can.
1985 Herbert A. Hauptman, Jerome Karle, U.S.
1984 Robert Bruce Merrifield, U.S.
1983 Henry Taube, Can.
1982 Aaron Klug, UK-Lith.
1981 Kenichi Fukui, Jpn.; Roald Hoffmann, U.S.
1980 Paul Berg, Walter Gilbert, U.S.; Frederick Sanger, UK
1979 Herbert C. Brown, U.S.; Georg Wittig, Ger.
1978 Peter Mitchell, UK
1977 Ilya Prigogine, Belg.
1976 William N. Lipscomb, U.S.
1975 John Cornforth, Austral.-UK; Vladimir Prelog, Bosnia-Switz.
1974 Paul J. Flory, U.S.
1973 Ernst Otto Fischer, Ger.; Geoffrey Wilkinson, UK
1972 Christian B. Anfinsen, Stanford Moore, William H. Stein, U.S.
1971 Gerhard Herzberg, Can.
1970 Luis F. Leloir, Arg.
1969 Derek H. R. Barton, UK; Odd Hassel, Nor.
1968 Lars Onsager, U.S.
1967 Manfred Eigen, Ger.; Ronald G. W. Norrish, George Porter, UK
1966 Robert S. Mulliken, U.S.
1965 Robert B. Woodward, U.S.
1964 Dorothy C. Hodgkin, UK
1963 Giulio Natta, It.; Karl Ziegler, Ger.
1962 John C. Kendrew, Max F. Perutz, UK
1961 Melvin Calvin, U.S.
1960 Willard F. Libby, U.S.
1959 Jaroslav Heyrovsky, Czech.
1958 Frederick Sanger, UK
1957 Lord (Alexander R.) Todd, UK
1956 Sir Cyril N. Hinshelwood, UK; Nikolay N. Semenov, USSR
1955 Vincent du Vigneaud, U.S.
1954 Linus C. Pauling, U.S.
1953 Hermann Staudinger, Ger.
1952 Archer J. P. Martin, Richard L. M. Synge, UK
1951 Edwin M. McMillan, Glenn T. Seaborg, U.S.
1950 Kurt Alder, Otto P. H. Diels, Ger.
1949 William F. Giauque, U.S.
1948 Arne W. K. Tiselius, Swed.
1947 Sir Robert Robinson, UK
1946 James B. Sumner, John H. Northrop, Wendell M. Stanley, U.S.
1945 Artturi I. Virtanen, Fin.
1944 Otto Hahn, Ger.
1943 George de Hevesy, Hung.
1939 Adolf F. J. Butenandt, Ger.; Leopold Ruzicka, Switz.
1938 Richard Kuhn, Ger.
1937 Walter N. Haworth, UK; Paul Karrer, Switz.
1936 Peter J. W. Debye, Neth.
1935 Frédéric & Irene Joliot-Curie, Fr.

1934 Harold C. Urey, U.S.
1932 Irving Langmuir, U.S.
1931 Friedrich Bergius, Carl Bosch, Ger.
1930 Hans Fischer, Ger.
1929 Sir Arthur Harden, UK; Hans von Euler-Chelpin, Swed.
1928 Adolf O. R. Windaus, Ger.
1927 Heinrich O. Wieland, Ger.
1926 Theodor Svedberg, Swed.
1925 Richard A. Zsigmondy, Ger.
1923 Fritz Pregl, Austria
1922 Francis W. Aston, UK
1921 Frederick Soddy, UK
1920 Walther H. Nernst, Ger.
1918 Fritz Haber, Ger.
1915 Richard M. Willstätter, Ger.
1914 Theodore W. Richards, U.S.
1913 Alfred Werner, Switz.
1912 Victor Grignard, Paul Sabatier, Fr.
1911 Marie Curie, Pol.-Fr.
1910 Otto Wallach, Ger.
1909 Wilhelm Ostwald, Ger.
1908 Ernest Rutherford, UK
1907 Eduard Buchner, Ger.
1906 Henri Moissan, Fr.
1905 Adolf von Baeyer, Ger.
1904 Sir William Ramsay, UK
1903 Svante A. Arrhenius, Swed.
1902 Emil Fischer, Ger.
1901 Jacobus H. van't Hoff, Neth.

Physiology or Medicine

2004 Richard Axel, Linda B. Buck, U.S.
2003 Paul C. Lauterbur, U.S.; Sir Peter Mansfield, UK
2002 Sydney Brenner, John E. Sulston, UK; H. Robert Horvitz, U.S.
2001 Leland H. Hartwell, U.S.; R. Timothy (Tim) Hunt, Sir Paul M. Nurse, UK
2000 Arvid Carlsson, Swed.; Paul Greengard, U.S.; Eric R. Kandel, Austria-U.S.
1999 Günter Blobel, U.S.
1998 Robert F. Furchgott, Louis J. Ignarro, Ferid Murad, U.S.
1997 Stanley B. Prusiner, U.S.
1996 Peter C. Doherty, Austral.; Rolf M. Zinkernagel, Switz.
1995 Edward B. Lewis, Eric F. Wieschaus, U.S.; Christiane Nüsslein-Volhard, Ger.
1994 Alfred G. Gilman, Martin Rodbell, U.S.
1993 Phillip A. Sharp, U.S.; Richard J. Roberts, UK
1992 Edmond H. Fisher, Edwin G. Krebs, U.S.
1991 Edwin Neher, Bert Sakmann, Ger.
1990 Joseph E. Murray, E. Donnall Thomas, U.S.
1989 J. Michael Bishop, Harold E. Varmus, U.S.
1988 Gertrude B. Elion, George H. Hitchings, U.S; Sir James Black, UK
1987 Susumu Tonegawa, Jpn.
1986 Rita Levi-Montalcini, It.-U.S., Stanley Cohen, U.S.
1985 Michael S. Brown, Joseph L. Goldstein, U.S.
1984 César Milstein, UK-Arg.; Georges J. F. Köhler, Ger.; Niels K. Jerne, UK-Den.
1983 Barbara McClintock, U.S.
1982 Sune Bergström, Bengt Samuelsson, Swed.; John R. Vane, UK
1981 Roger W. Sperry, David H. Hubel, Torsten N. Wiesel, U.S.
1980 Baruj Benacerraf, George Snell, U.S.; Jean Dausset, Fr.
1979 Allan M. Cormack, U.S.; Godfrey N. Hounsfield, UK
1978 Daniel Nathans, Hamilton O. Smith, U.S.; Werner Arber, Switz.
1977 Rosalyn S. Yalow, Roger C.L. Guillemin, Andrew V. Schally, U.S.
1976 Baruch S. Blumberg, Daniel Carleton Gajdusek, U.S.
1975 David Baltimore, Howard Temin, U.S.; Renato Dulbecco, It.-U.S.
1974 Albert Claude, Lux.-U.S.; George Emil Palade, Rom.-U.S.; Christian de Duve, Belg.
1973 Karl von Frisch, Ger.; Konrad Lorenz, Austria; Nikolaas Tinbergen, UK
1972 Gerald M. Edelman, U.S.; Rodney R. Porter, UK
1971 Earl W. Sutherland Jr., U.S.
1970 Julius Axelrod, U.S.; Sir Bernard Katz, UK; Ulf von Euler, Swed.
1969 Max Delbrück, Alfred D. Hershey, Salvador Luria, U.S.
1968 Robert W. Holley, H. Gobind Khorana, Marshall W. Nirenberg, U.S.
1967 Ragnar Granit, Swed.; Haldan Keffer Hartline, George Wald, U.S.
1966 Charles B. Huggins, Peyton Rous, U.S.
1965 François Jacob, André Lwoff, Jacques Monod, Fr.
1964 Konrad E. Bloch, U.S.; Feodor Lynen, Ger.
1963 Sir John C. Eccles, Austral.; Alan L. Hodgkin, Andrew F. Huxley, UK
1962 Francis H. C. Crick, Maurice H. F. Wilkins, UK; James D. Watson, U.S.
1961 Georg von Békésy, U.S.
1960 Sir F. MacFarlane Burnet, Austral.; Peter B. Medawar, UK
1959 Arthur Kornberg, Severo Ochoa, U.S.
1958 George W. Beadle, Edward L. Tatum, Joshua Lederberg, U.S.
1957 Daniel Bovet, It.
1956 André F. Cournand, Dickinson W. Richards, U.S.; Werner Forssmann, Ger.
1955 Alex H. T. Theorell, Swed.
1954 John F. Enders, Frederick C. Robbins, Thomas H. Weller, U.S.
1953 Hans A. Krebs, UK; Fritz A. Lipmann, U.S.
1952 Selman A. Waksman, U.S.
1951 Max Theiler, U.S.
1950 Philip S. Hench, Edward C. Kendall, U.S.; Tadeus Reichstein, Switz.
1949 Walter R. Hess, Switz.; Antonio Moniz, Port.
1948 Paul H. Müller, Switz.
1947 Carl F. Cori, Gerty T. Cori, U.S.; Bernardo A. Houssay, Arg.
1946 Hermann J. Muller, U.S.
1945 Ernst B. Chain, Sir Alexander Fleming, Sir Howard W. Florey, UK
1944 Joseph Erlanger, Herbert S. Gasser, U.S.
1943 Henrik C. P. Dam, Den.; Edward A. Doisy, U.S.
1939 Gerhard Domagk, Ger.
1938 Corneille J. F. Heymans, Belg.
1937 Albert Szent-Gyorgyi, Hung.-U.S.
1936 Sir Henry H. Dale, UK; Otto Loewi, U.S.
1935 Hans Spemann, Ger.
1934 George R. Minot, William P. Murphy, G. H. Whipple, U.S.
1933 Thomas H. Morgan, U.S.
1932 Edgar D. Adrian, Sir Charles S. Sherrington, UK
1931 Otto H. Warburg, Ger.
1930 Karl Landsteiner, U.S.
1929 Christiaan Eijkman, Neth.; Sir Frederick G. Hopkins, UK
1928 Charles J. H. Nicolle, Fr.
1927 Julius Wagner-Jauregg, Austrian
1926 Johannes A. G. Fibiger, Den.
1924 Willem Einthoven, Neth.
1923 Frederick G. Banting, Can.; John J. R. Macleod, Scot.
1922 Archibald V. Hill, UK; Otto F. Meyerhof, Ger.
1920 Schack A. S. Krogh, Den.
1919 Jules Bordet, Belg.
1914 Robert Bárány, Austria
1913 Charles R. Richet, Fr.
1912 Alexis Carrel, Fr.
1911 Allvar Gullstrand, Swed.
1910 Albrecht Kossel, Ger.
1909 Emil T. Kocher, Switz.
1908 Paul Ehrlich, Ger.; Ilya Mechnikov, Fr.
1907 Charles L. A. Laveran, Fr.
1906 Camillo Golgi, It.; Santiago Ramon y Cajal, Spain
1905 Robert Koch, Ger.
1904 Ivan P. Pavlov, Russ.
1903 Niels R. Finsen, Den.
1902 Sir Ronald Ross, UK
1901 Emil A. von Behring, Ger.

Literature

2004 Elfriede Jelinek, Austria
2003 J.M. Coetzee, S. Afr.
2002 Imre Kertész, Hung.
2001 Sir V.S. Naipaul, UK
2000 Gao Xingjian, China-Fr.
1999 Günter Grass, Ger.
1998 Jose Saramago, Por.
1997 Dario Fo, It.
1996 Wislawa Szymborska, Pol.
1995 Seamus Heaney, Ire.
1994 Kenzaburo Oe, Jpn.
1993 Toni Morrison, U.S.
1992 Derek Walcott, W. Ind.
1991 Nadine Gordimer, S. Afr.
1990 Octavio Paz, Mex.
1989 Camilo José Cela, Spain
1988 Naguib Mahfouz, Egypt
1987 Joseph Brodsky, USSR-U.S.
1986 Wole Soyinka, Nigeria
1985 Claude Simon, Fr.
1984 Jaroslav Siefert, Czech.
1983 William Golding, UK
1982 Gabriel García Márquez, Colombia-Mex.
1981 Elias Canetti, Bulg.-UK
1980 Czeslaw Milosz, Pol.-U.S.
1979 Odysseus Elytis, Greece
1978 Isaac Bashevis Singer, U.S.
1977 Vicente Aleixandre, Spain
1976 Saul Bellow, U.S.
1975 Eugenio Montale, It.
1974 Eyvind Johnson, Harry Edmund Martinson, Swed.
1973 Patrick White, Austral.
1972 Heinrich Böll, Ger.
1971 Pablo Neruda, Chile
1970 Aleksandr I. Solzhenitsyn, USSR
1969 Samuel Beckett, Ire.
1968 Yasunari Kawabata, Jpn.
1967 Miguel Angel Asturias, Guat.
1966 Shmuel Yosef Agnon, Isr.; Nelly Sachs, Swed.
1965 Mikhail Sholokhov, USSR
1964 Jean-Paul Sartre, Fr. (declined)
1963 Giorgos Seferis, Greece
1962 John Steinbeck, U.S.
1961 Ivo Andric, Yugo.
1960 Saint-John Perse, Fr.
1959 Salvatore Quasimodo, It.
1958 Boris L. Pasternak, USSR (declined)
1957 Albert Camus, Fr.
1956 Juan Ramón Jiménez, Spain
1955 Halldór K. Laxness, Ice.
1954 Ernest Hemingway, U.S.
1953 Sir Winston Churchill, UK
1952 François Mauriac, Fr.
1951 Pär F. Lagerkvist, Swed.
1950 Bertrand Russell, UK
1949 William Faulkner, U.S.
1948 T.S. Eliot, UK
1947 André Gide, Fr.
1946 Hermann Hesse, Ger.-Switz.
1945 Gabriela Mistral, Chile
1944 Johannes V. Jensen, Den.
1939 Frans E. Sillanpää, Fin.
1938 Pearl S. Buck, U.S.
1937 Roger Martin du Gard, Fr.
1936 Eugene O'Neill, U.S.
1934 Luigi Pirandello, It.
1933 Ivan A. Bunin, USSR
1932 John Galsworthy, UK
1931 Erik A. Karlfeldt, Swed.
1930 Sinclair Lewis, U.S.
1929 Thomas Mann, Ger.
1928 Sigrid Undset, Nor.
1927 Henri Bergson, Fr.
1926 Grazia Deledda, It.
1925 George Bernard Shaw, Ire.-UK
1924 Wladyslaw S. Reymont, Pol.
1923 William Butler Yeats, Ire.
1922 Jacinto Benavente, Spain
1921 Anatole France, Fr.

1920 Knut Hamsun, Nor.
1919 Carl F. G. Spitteler, Switz.
1917 Karl A. Gjellerup, Henrik Pontoppidan, Den.
1916 Verner von Heidenstam, Swed.
1915 Romain Rolland, Fr.
1913 Rabindranath Tagore, India
1912 Gerhart Hauptmann, Ger.
1911 Maurice Maeterlinck, Belg.
1910 Paul J. L. Heyse, Ger.
1909 Selma Lagerlöf, Swed.
1908 Rudolf C. Eucken, Ger.
1907 Rudyard Kipling, UK
1906 Giosuè Carducci, It.
1905 Henryk Sienkiewicz, Pol.
1904 Fréderic Mistral, Fr.; José Echegaray y Eizaguirre, Spain
1903 Bjørnstjerne Bjørnson, Nor.
1902 Theodor Mommsen, Ger.
1901 Rene F. A. Sully Prudhomme, Fr.

Peace

2004 Wangari Maathai, Kenya
2003 Shirin Ebadi, Iran
2002 Jimmy Carter, U.S.
2001 UN; Kofi Annan, Ghana
2000 Kim Dae-Jung, S. Kor.
1999 Doctors Without Borders (Médecins Sans Frontières), Fr.
1998 John Hume, David Trimble, N. Ire.
1997 Jody Williams, U.S.; International Campaign to Ban Landmines
1996 Bishop Carlos Ximenes Belo, José Ramos-Horta, Timor-Leste
1995 Joseph Rotblat, Pol.-UK; Pugwash Conference
1994 Yasser Arafat, Pal.; Shimon Peres, Yitzhak Rabin, Isr.
1993 Frederik W. de Klerk, Nelson Mandela, S. Afr.
1992 Rigoberta Menchú Tum, Guat.
1991 Aung San Suu Kyi, Burm.
1990 Mikhail S. Gorbachev, USSR
1989 Dalai Lama, Tibet
1988 UN Peacekeeping Forces
1987 Oscar Arias Sánchez, Costa Rica
1986 Elie Wiesel, Rom.-U.S.
1985 Intl. Physicians for the Prevention of Nuclear War, U.S.
1984 Bishop Desmond Tutu, S. Afr.
1983 Lech Walesa, Pol.
1982 Alva Myrdal, Swed.; Alfonso García Robles, Mex.
1981 Office of UN High Com. for Refugees
1980 Adolfo Pérez Esquivel, Arg.
1979 Mother Teresa of Calcutta, Alb.-Ind.
1978 Anwar al-Sadat, Egypt; Menachem Begin, Isr.
1977 Amnesty International
1976 Mairead Corrigan, Betty Williams, N. Ire.
1975 Andrei Sakharov, USSR
1974 Eisaku Sato, Jpn.; Seán MacBride, Ire.
1973 Henry Kissinger, U.S.; Le Duc Tho, N. Viet. (Tho declined)
1971 Willy Brandt, Ger.
1970 Norman E. Borlaug, U.S.
1969 Intl. Labor Organization
1968 René Cassin, Fr.
1965 UN Children's Fund (UNICEF)
1964 Martin Luther King Jr., U.S.
1963 International Red Cross, League of Red Cross Societies
1962 Linus C. Pauling, U.S.
1961 Dag Hammarskjöld, Swed.
1960 Albert J. Lutuli, S. Afr.
1959 Philip J. Noel-Baker, UK
1958 Georges Pire, Belg.
1957 Lester B. Pearson, Can.
1954 Office of UN High Com. for Refugees
1953 George C. Marshall, U.S.
1952 Albert Schweitzer, Fr.
1951 Léon Jouhaux, Fr.
1950 Ralph J. Bunche, U.S.
1949 Lord John Boyd Orr of Brechin, UK
1947 Friends Service Council, UK; Amer. Friends Service Committee, U.S.
1946 Emily G. Balch, John R. Mott, U.S.
1945 Cordell Hull, U.S.
1944 International Red Cross
1938 Nansen International Office for Refugees
1937 Viscount Cecil of Chelwood, UK
1936 Carlos Saavedra Lamas, Arg.
1935 Carl von Ossietzky, Ger.
1934 Arthur Henderson, UK
1933 Sir Norman Angell, UK
1931 Jane Addams, Nicholas Murray Butler, U.S.
1930 Nathan Söderblom, Swed.
1929 Frank B. Kellogg, U.S.
1927 Ferdinand E. Buisson, Fr.; Ludwig Quidde, Ger.
1926 Aristide Briand, Fr.; Gustav Stresemann, Ger.
1925 Sir J. Austen Chamberlain, UK; Charles G. Dawes, U.S.
1922 Fridtjof Nansen, Nor.
1921 Karl H. Branting, Swed.; Christian L. Lange, Nor.
1920 Léon V.A. Bourgeois, Fr.
1919 Woodrow Wilson, U.S.
1917 International Red Cross
1913 Henri La Fontaine, Belg.
1912 Elihu Root, U.S.
1911 Tobias M.C. Asser, Neth.; Alfred H. Fried, Austria
1910 Permanent Intl. Peace Bureau
1909 Auguste M. F. Beernaert, Belg.; Paul H. B. B. d'Estournelles de Constant, Fr.
1908 Klas P. Arnoldson, Swed.; Fredrik Bajer, Den.
1907 Ernesto T. Moneta, It.; Louis Renault, Fr.
1906 Theodore Roosevelt, U.S.
1905 Baroness Bertha von Suttner, Austria
1904 Institute of International Law
1903 Sir William R. Cremer, UK
1902 Élie Ducommun, Charles A. Gobat, Switz.
1901 Jean H. Dunant, Switz.; Frédéric Passy, Fr.

Nobel Memorial Prize in Economic Science

2004 Finn E. Kydland, Nor.; Edward C. Prescott, U.S.
2003 Robert F. Engle, U.S.; Clive W.J. Granger, UK
2002 Daniel Kahneman, U.S.–Isr.; Vernon L. Smith, U.S.
2001 George A. Akerlof, A. Michael Spence, Joseph E. Stiglitz, U.S.
2000 James J. Heckman, Daniel L. McFadden, U.S.
1999 Robert A. Mundell, Can.
1998 Amartya Sen, India
1997 Robert C. Merton, U.S.; Myron S. Scholes, Can.-U.S.
1996 James A. Mirrlees, UK; William Vickrey, Can.-U.S.
1995 Robert E. Lucas Jr., U.S.
1994 John C. Harsanyi, John F. Nash, U.S.; Reinhard Selten, Ger.
1993 Robert W. Fogel, Douglass C. North, U.S.
1992 Gary S. Becker, U.S.
1991 Ronald H. Coase, UK-U.S.
1990 Harry M. Markowitz, William F. Sharpe, Merton H. Miller, U.S.
1989 Trygve Haavelmo, Nor.
1988 Maurice Allais, Fr.
1987 Robert M. Solow, U.S.
1986 James M. Buchanan, U.S.
1985 Franco Modigliani, It.-U.S.
1984 Richard Stone, UK
1983 Gerard Debreu, Fr.-U.S.
1982 George J. Stigler, U.S.
1981 James Tobin, U.S.
1980 Lawrence R. Klein, U.S.
1979 Theodore W. Schultz, U.S.; Sir Arthur Lewis, UK
1978 Herbert A. Simon, U.S.
1977 Bertil Ohlin, Swed.; James E. Meade, UK
1976 Milton Friedman, U.S.
1975 Tjalling Koopmans, Neth.-U.S.; Leonid Kantorovich, USSR
1974 Gunnar Myrdal, Swed.; Friedrich A. von Hayek, Austria
1973 Wassily Leontief, U.S.
1972 Kenneth J. Arrow, U.S.; John R. Hicks, UK
1971 Simon Kuznets, U.S.
1970 Paul A. Samuelson, U.S.
1969 Ragnar Frisch, Nor.; Jan Tinbergen, Neth.

Pulitzer Prizes in Journalism, Letters, and Music

Endowed by Joseph Pulitzer (1847-1911), publisher of the *New York World*, in a bequest to Columbia Univ. and awarded annually, in years shown, for work the previous year. Prizes are now $7,500 in each category, except Public Service (in Journalism), for which a medal is given. For letters and music, prizes in past years are listed; if a year is omitted, no award was given that year.

Journalism, 2005

Public Service: *LA Times*, for its series exposing medical problems and racial injustice at a major public hospital.

Breaking News Reporting: *The Star Ledger* (Newark, NJ) staff for coverage of the 2004 resignation of a NJ governor following revelations of his homosexual adultery.

Investigative Reporting: Nigel Jaquiss of *Willamette Week*, Portland, OR, for uncovering a former governor's long-concealed sexual misconduct.

Explanatory Reporting: Gareth Cook of *The Boston Globe*, for explaining the complex scientific and ethical dimensions of stem cell research.

Beat Reporting: Amy Dockser Marcus, *The Wall Street Journal*, for stories examining the world of cancer survivors.

National Reporting: Walt Bogdanich, *NY Times*, for stories about corporate cover-up of fatal accidents at railway crossings.

International Reporting: Kim Murphy, *LA Times*, for coverage of Russia's struggles with terrorism, the economy, and democracy. Dele Olojede of *Newsday*, Long Island, NY, for examining the Rwandan genocide's still-palpable effects.

Feature Writing: Julia Keller, *Chicago Tribune*, for reconstructing an account of a deadly tornado in Utica, IL.

Commentary: Connie Schultz, *The Plain Dealer*, Cleveland, OH, for columns voicing the concerns of the underprivileged.

Criticism: Joe Morgenstern, *The Wall Street Journal*, for film reviews.

Editorial Writing: Tom Philp, *The Sacramento Bee*, for editorials on reclaiming California's flooded Hetch Hetchy Valley.

Editorial Cartooning: Nick Anderson, *The Courier-Journal*, Louisville, KY.

Breaking News Photog.: Associated Press staff, for photographs of combat inside Iraqi cities.

Feature Photog.: Deanne Fitzmaurice, *San Francisco Chronicle*, for photo essay on an Oakland hospital's efforts to heal an injured Iraqi boy.

Letters

Fiction

1918—Ernest Poole, *His Family*
1919—Booth Tarkington, *The Magnificent Ambersons*
1921—Edith Wharton, *The Age of Innocence*
1922—Booth Tarkington, *Alice Adams*
1923—Willa Cather, *One of Ours*
1924—Margaret Wilson, *The Able McLaughlins*
1925—Edna Ferber, *So Big*
1926—Sinclair Lewis, *Arrowsmith* (refused prize)
1927—Louis Bromfield, *Early Autumn*
1928—Thornton Wilder, *Bridge of San Luis Rey*
1929—Julia M. Peterkin, *Scarlet Sister Mary*
1930—Oliver LaFarge, *Laughing Boy*
1931—Margaret Ayer Barnes, *Years of Grace*
1932—Pearl S. Buck, *The Good Earth*
1933—T. S. Stribling, *The Store*
1934—Caroline Miller, *Lamb in His Bosom*
1935—Josephine W. Johnson, *Now in November*
1936—Harold L. Davis, *Honey in the Horn*
1937—Margaret Mitchell, *Gone With the Wind*
1938—John P. Marquand, *The Late George Apley*
1939—Marjorie Kinnan Rawlings, *The Yearling*
1940—John Steinbeck, *The Grapes of Wrath*
1942—Ellen Glasgow, *In This Our Life*
1943—Upton Sinclair, *Dragon's Teeth*
1944—Martin Flavin, *Journey in the Dark*
1945—John Hersey, *A Bell for Adano*
1947—Robert Penn Warren, *All the King's Men*
1948—James A. Michener, *Tales of the South Pacific*
1949—James Gould Cozzens, *Guard of Honor*
1950—A. B. Guthrie Jr., *The Way West*
1951—Conrad Richter, *The Town*
1952—Herman Wouk, *The Caine Mutiny*
1953—Ernest Hemingway, *The Old Man and the* Sea
1955—William Faulkner, *A Fable*
1956—MacKinlay Kantor, *Andersonville*
1958—James Agee, *A Death in the Family*
1959—Robert Lewis Taylor, *The Travels of Jaimie McPheeters*
1960—Allen Drury, *Advise and Consent*
1961—Harper Lee, *To Kill a Mockingbird*
1962—Edwin O'Connor, *The Edge of Sadness*
1963—William Faulkner, *The Reivers*
1965—Shirley Ann Grau, *The Keepers of the House*
1966—Katherine Anne Porter, *Collected Stories*
1967—Bernard Malamud, *The Fixer*
1968—William Styron, *The Confessions of Nat Turner*
1969—N. Scott Momaday, *House Made of Dawn*
1970—Jean Stafford, *Collected Stories*
1972—Wallace Stegner, *Angle of Repose*
1973—Eudora Welty, *The Optimist's Daughter*
1975—Michael Shaara, *The Killer Angels*
1976—Saul Bellow, *Humboldt's Gift*
1978—James Alan McPherson, *Elbow Room*
1979—John Cheever, *The Stories of John Cheever*
1980—Norman Mailer, *The Executioner's Song*
1981—John Kennedy Toole, *A Confederacy of Dunces*
1982—John Updike, *Rabbit Is Rich*
1983—Alice Walker, *The Color Purple*
1984—William Kennedy, *Ironweed*
1985—Alison Lurie, *Foreign Affairs*
1986—Larry McMurtry, *Lonesome Dove*
1987—Peter Taylor, *A Summons to Memphis*
1988—Toni Morrison, *Beloved*
1989—Anne Tyler, *Breathing Lessons*
1990—Oscar Hijuelos, *The Mambo Kings Play Songs of Love*
1991—John Updike, *Rabbit at Rest*
1992—Jane Smiley, *A Thousand Acres*
1993—Robert Olen Butler, *A Good Scent From a Strange Mountain*
1994—E. Annie Proulx, *The Shipping News*
1995—Carol Shields, *The Stone Diaries*
1996—Richard Ford, *Independence Day*
1997—Steven Millhauser, *Martin Dressler: The Tale of an American Dreamer*
1998—Philip Roth, *American Pastoral*
1999—Michael Cunningham, *The Hours*
2000—Jhumpa Lahiri, *Interpreter of Maladies*
2001—Michael Chabon, *The Amazing Adventures of Kavalier & Clay*
2002—Richard Russo, *Empire Falls*
2003—Jeffrey Eugenides, *Middlesex*
2004—Edward P. Jones, *The Known World*
2005—Marilynne Robinson, *Gilead*

Drama

1918—Jesse Lynch Williams, *Why Marry?*
1920—Eugene O'Neill, *Beyond the Horizon*
1921—Zona Gale, *Miss Lulu Bett*
1922—Eugene O'Neill, *Anna Christie*
1923—Owen Davis, *Icebound*
1924—Hatcher Hughes, *Hell-Bent for Heaven*
1925—Sidney Howard, *They Knew What They Wanted*
1926—George Kelly, *Craig's Wife*
1927—Paul Green, *In Abraham's Bosom*
1928—Eugene O'Neill, *Strange Interlude*
1929—Elmer Rice, *Street Scene*
1930—Marc Connelly, *The Green Pastures*
1931—Susan Glaspell, *Alison's House*
1932—George S. Kaufman, Morrie Ryskind, and Ira Gershwin, *Of Thee I Sing*
1933—Maxwell Anderson, *Both Your Houses*
1934—Sidney Kingsley, *Men in White*
1935—Zoe Akins, *The Old Maid*
1936—Robert E. Sherwood, *Idiot's Delight*
1937—George S. Kaufman and Moss Hart, *You Can't Take It With You*
1938—Thornton Wilder, *Our Town*
1939—Robert E. Sherwood, *Abe Lincoln in Illinois*
1940—William Saroyan, *The Time of Your Life*
1941—Robert E. Sherwood, *There Shall Be No Night*
1943—Thornton Wilder, *The Skin of Our Teeth*
1945—Mary Chase, *Harvey*
1946—Russel Crouse and Howard Lindsay, *State of the Union*
1948—Tennessee Williams, *A Streetcar Named Desire*
1949—Arthur Miller, *Death of a Salesman*
1950—Richard Rodgers, Oscar Hammerstein 2nd and Joshua Logan, *South Pacific*
1952—Joseph Kramm, *The Shrike*
1953—William Inge, *Picnic*
1954—John Patrick, *Teahouse of the August Moon*
1955—Tennessee Williams, *Cat on a Hot Tin Roof*
1956—Frances Goodrich and Albert Hackett, *The Diary of Anne Frank*
1957—Eugene O'Neill, *Long Day's Journey Into Night*
1958—Ketti Frings, *Look Homeward, Angel*
1959—Archibald MacLeish, *J. B.*
1960—George Abbott, Jerome Weidman, Sheldon Harnick, and Jerry Bock, *Fiorello!*
1961—Tad Mosel, *All the Way Home*
1962—Frank Loesser and Abe Burrows, *How to Succeed in Business Without Really Trying*
1965—Frank D. Gilroy, *The Subject Was Roses*
1967—Edward Albee, *A Delicate Balance*
1969—Howard Sackler, *The Great White Hope*
1970—Charles Gordone, *No Place to Be Somebody*
1971—Paul Zindel, *The Effect of Gamma Rays on Man-in-the-Moon Marigolds*
1973—Jason Miller, *That Championship Season*
1975—Edward Albee, *Seascape*
1976—Michael Bennett, James Kirkwood, Nicholas Dante, Marvin Hamlisch, and Edward Kleban, *A Chorus Line*
1977—Michael Cristofer, *The Shadow Box*
1978—Donald L. Coburn, *The Gin Game*
1979—Sam Shepard, *Buried Child*
1980—Lanford Wilson, *Talley's Folly*
1981—Beth Henley, *Crimes of the Heart*
1982—Charles Fuller, *A Soldier's Play*
1983—Marsha Norman, *'night, Mother*
1984—David Mamet, *Glengarry Glen Ross*
1985—Stephen Sondheim and James Lapine, *Sunday in the Park With George*
1987—August Wilson, *Fences*
1988—Alfred Uhry, *Driving Miss Daisy*
1989—Wendy Wasserstein, *The Heidi Chronicles*
1990—August Wilson, *The Piano Lesson*
1991—Neil Simon, *Lost in Yonkers*
1992—Robert Schenkkan, *The Kentucky Cycle*
1993—Tony Kushner, *Angels in America: Millennium Approaches*
1994—Edward Albee, *Three Tall Women*
1995—Horton Foote, *The Young Man From Atlanta*
1996—Jonathan Larson, *Rent*
1998—Paula Vogel, *How I Learned to Drive*
1999—Margaret Edson, *Wit*
2000—Donald Margulies, *Dinner With Friends*
2001—David Auburn, *Proof*
2002—Suzan-Lori Parks, *Topdog/Underdog*
2003—Nilo Cruz, *Anna in the Tropics*
2004—Doug Wright, *I Am My Own Wife*
2005—John Patrick Shanley, *Doubt, a parable*

History (U.S.)

1917—J. J. Jusserand, *With Americans of Past and Present Days*
1918—James Ford Rhodes, *History of the Civil War*
1920—Justin H. Smith, *The War With Mexico*
1921—William Sowden Sims, *The Victory at Sea*
1922—James Truslow Adams, *The Founding of New England*

1923—Charles Warren, *The Supreme Court in United States History*
1924—Charles Howard McIlwain, *The American Revolution: A Constitutional Interpretation*
1925—Frederick L. Paxton, *A History of the American Frontier*
1926—Edward Channing, *A History of the U.S.*
1927—Samuel Flagg Bemis, *Pinckney's Treaty*
1928—V. L Parrington, *Main Currents in American Thought*
1929—Fred A. Shannon, *The Organization and Administration of the Union Army, 1861-65*
1930—Claude H. Van Tyne, *The War of Independence*
1931—Bernadotte E. Schmitt, *The Coming of the War, 1914*
1932—Gen. John J. Pershing, *My Experiences in the World War*
1933—Frederick J. Turner, *The Significance of Sections in American History*
1934—Herbert Agar, *The People's Choice*
1935—Charles McLean Andrews, *The Colonial Period of American History*
1936—Andrew C. McLaughlin, *The Constitutional History of the United States*
1937—Van Wyck Brooks, *The Flowering of New England*
1938—Paul Herman Buck, *The Road to Reunion, 1865-1900*
1939—Frank Luther Mott, *A History of American Magazines*
1940—Carl Sandburg, *Abraham Lincoln: The War Years*
1941—Marcus Lee Hansen, *The Atlantic Migration, 1607-1860*
1942—Margaret Leech, *Reveille in Washington*
1943—Esther Forbes, *Paul Revere and the World He Lived In*
1944—Merle Curti, *The Growth of American Thought*
1945—Stephen Bonsal, *Unfinished Business*
1946—Arthur M. Schlesinger Jr., *The Age of Jackson*
1947—James Phinney Baxter III, *Scientists Against Time*
1948—Bernard De Voto, *Across the Wide Missouri*
1949—Roy F. Nichols, *The Disruption of American Democracy*
1950—O. W. Larkin, *Art and Life in America*
1951—R. Carlyle Buley, *The Old Northwest: Pioneer Period 1815-1840*
1952—Oscar Handlin, *The Uprooted*
1953—George Dangerfield, *The Era of Good Feelings*
1954—Bruce Catton, *A Stillness at Appomattox*
1955—Paul Horgan, *Great River: The Rio Grande in North American History*
1956—Richard Hofstadter, *The Age of Reform*
1957—George F. Kennan, *Russia Leaves the War*
1958—Bray Hammond, *Banks and Politics in America—From the Revolution to the Civil War*
1959—Leonard D. White and Jean Schneider, *The Republican Era; 1869-1901*
1960—Margaret Leech, *In the Days of McKinley*
1961—Herbert Feis, *Between War and Peace: The Potsdam Conference*
1962—Lawrence H. Gibson, *The Triumphant Empire: Thunderclouds Gather in the West*
1963—Constance McLaughlin Green, *Washington: Village and Capital, 1800-1878*
1964—Sumner Chilton Powell, *Puritan Village: The Formation of a New England Town*
1965—Irwin Unger, *The Greenback Era*
1966—Perry Miller, *Life of the Mind in America*
1967—William H. Goetzmann, *Exploration and Empire: The Explorer and Scientist in the Winning of the American West*
1968—Bernard Bailyn, *The Ideological Origins of the American Revolution*
1969—Leonard W. Levy, *Origin of the Fifth Amendment*
1970—Dean Acheson, *Present at the Creation: My Years in the State Department*
1971—James McGregor Burns, *Roosevelt: The Soldier of Freedom*
1972—Carl N. Degler, *Neither Black nor White*
1973—Michael Kammen, *People of Paradox: An Inquiry Concerning the Origins of American Civilization*
1974—Daniel J. Boorstin, *The Americans: The Democratic Experience*
1975—Dumas Malone, *Jefferson and His Time*
1976—Paul Horgan, *Lamy of Santa Fe*
1977—David M. Potter, *The Impending Crisis*
1978—Alfred D. Chandler Jr., *The Visible Hand: The Managerial Revolution in American Business*
1979—Don E. Fehrenbacher, *The Dred Scott Case: Its Significance in American Law and Politics*
1980—Leon F. Litwack, *Been in the Storm So Long*
1981—Lawrence A. Cremin, *American Education: The National Experience, 1783-1876*
1982—C. Vann Woodward, ed., *Mary Chesnut's Civil War*
1983—Rhys L. Issac, *The Transformation of Virginia, 1740-1790*
1985—Thomas K. McCraw, *Prophets of Regulation*
1986—Walter A. McDougall, *The Heavens and the Earth*
1987—Bernard Bailyn, *Voyagers to the West*
1988—Robert V. Bruce, *The Launching of Modern American Science, 1846-1876*
1989—Taylor Branch, *Parting the Waters: America in the King Years, 1954-63*; and James M. McPherson, *Battle Cry of Freedom: The Civil War Era*
1990—Stanley Karnow, *In Our Image: America's Empire in the Philippines*
1991—Laurel Thatcher Ulrich, *A Midwife's Tale: The Life of Martha Ballard,* based on her diary, 1785-1812
1992—Mark E. Neely Jr., *The Fate of Liberty: Abraham Lincoln and Civil Liberties*
1993—Gordon S. Wood, *The Radicalism of the American Revolution*
1995—Doris Kearns Goodwin, *No Ordinary Time: Franklin and Eleanor Roosevelt: The Home Front in World War II*
1996—Alan Taylor, *William Cooper's Town: Power and Persuasion on the Frontier of the Early American Republic*
1997—Jack N. Rakove, *Original Meanings: Politics and Ideas in the Making of the Constitution*
1998—Edward J. Larson, *Summer for the Gods: The Scopes Trial and America's Continuing Debate Over Science and Religion*
1999—Edwin G. Burrows and Mike Wallace, *Gotham: A History of New York City to 1898*
2000—David M. Kennedy, *Freedom From Fear: The American People in Depression and War, 1929-1945*
2001—Joseph J. Ellis, *Founding Brothers: The Revolutionary Generation*
2002—Louis Menand, *The Metaphysical Club: A Story of Ideas in America*
2003—Rick Atkinson, *An Army at Dawn: The War in North Africa, 1942-1943*
2004—Steven Hahn, *A Nation Under Our Feet: Black Political Struggles in the Rural South from Slavery to the Great Migration*
2005—David Hackett Fischer, *Washington's Crossing*

Biography or Autobiography

1917—Laura E. Richards and Maude Howe Elliott, assisted by Florence Howe Hall, *Julia Ward Howe*
1918—William Cabell Bruce, *Benjamin Franklin, Self-Revealed*
1919—Henry Adams, *The Education of Henry Adams*
1920—Albert J. Beveridge, *The Life of John Marshall*
1921—Edward Bok, *The Americanization of Edward Bok*
1922—Hamlin Garland, *A Daughter of the Middle Border*
1923—Burton J. Hendrick, *The Life and Letters of Walter H. Page*
1924—Michael Pupin, *From Immigrant to Inventor*
1925—M. A. DeWolfe Howe, *Barrett Wendell and His Letters*
1926—Harvey Cushing, *Life of Sir William Osler*
1927—Emory Holloway, *Whitman: An Interpretation in Narrative*
1928—Charles Edward Russell, *The American Orchestra and Theodore Thomas*
1929—Burton J. Hendrick, *The Training of an American: The Earlier Life and Letters of Walter H. Page*
1930—Marquis James, *The Raven* (Sam Houston)
1931—Henry James, *Charles W. Eliot*
1932—Henry F. Pringle, *Theodore Roosevelt*
1933—Allan Nevins, *Grover Cleveland*
1934—Tyler Dennett, *John Hay*
1935—Douglas Southall Freeman, *R. E. Lee*
1936—Ralph Barton Perry, *The Thought and Character of William James*
1937—Allan Nevins, *Hamilton Fish: The Inner History of the Grant Administration*
1938—Divided between Odell Shepard, *Pedlar's Progress* (Bronson Alcott) and Marquis James, *Andrew Jackson*
1939—Carl Van Doren, *Benjamin Franklin*
1940—Ray Stannard Baker, *Woodrow Wilson, Life and Letters*
1941—Ola Elizabeth Winslow, *Jonathan Edwards*
1942—Forrest Wilson, *Crusader in Crinoline* (Harriet Beecher Stowe)
1943—Samuel Eliot Morison, *Admiral of the Ocean Sea* (Christopher Columbus)
1944—Carleton Mabee, *The American Leonardo: The Life of Samuel F. B. Morse*
1945—Russell Blaine Nye, *George Bancroft: Brahmin Rebel.*
1946—Linny Marsh Wolfe, *Son of the Wilderness* (John Muir)
1947—William Allen White, *Autobiography of William Allen White*
1948—Margaret Clapp, *Forgotten First Citizen: John Bigelow*
1949—Robert E. Sherwood, *Roosevelt and Hopkins*
1950—Samuel Flagg Bemis, *John Quincy Adams and the Foundations of American Foreign Policy*
1951—Margaret Louise Coit, *John C. Calhoun: American Portrait*
1952—Merlo J. Pusey, *Charles Evans Hughes*
1953—David J. Mays, *Edmund Pendleton, 1721-1803*
1954—Charles A. Lindbergh, *The Spirit of St. Louis*
1955—William S. White, *The Taft Story*
1956—Talbot F. Hamlin, *Benjamin Henry Latrobe*
1957—John F. Kennedy, *Profiles in Courage*
1958—Douglas Southall Freeman (I-VI), John Alexander Carroll and Mary Wells Ashworth (VII), *George Washington*
1959—Arthur Walworth, *Woodrow Wilson: American Prophet*
1960—Samuel Eliot Morison, *John Paul Jones*

1961—David Donald, *Charles Sumner and the Coming of the Civil War*
1963—Leon Edel, *Henry James: Vols. 2-3*
1964—Walter Jackson Bate, *John Keats*
1965—Ernest Samuels, *Henry Adams*
1966—Arthur M. Schlesinger Jr., *A Thousand Days*
1967—Justin Kaplan, *Mr. Clemens and Mark Twain*
1968—George F. Kennan, *Memoirs (1925-1950)*
1969—B. L. Reid, *The Man From New York: John Quinn and His Friends*
1970—T. Harry Williams, *Huey Long*
1971—Lawrence Thompson, *Robert Frost: The Years of Triumph, 1915-1938*
1972—Joseph P. Lash, *Eleanor and Franklin*
1973—W. A. Swanberg, *Luce and His Empire*
1974—Louis Sheaffer, *O'Neill, Son and Artist*
1975—Robert A. Caro, *The Power Broker: Robert Moses and the Fall of New York*
1976—R.W.B. Lewis, *Edith Wharton: A Biography*
1977—John E. Mack, *A Prince of Our Disorder: The Life of T. E. Lawrence*
1978—Walter Jackson Bate, *Samuel Johnson*
1979—Leonard Baker, *Days of Sorrow and Pain: Leo Baeck and the Berlin Jews*
1980—Edmund Morris, *The Rise of Theodore Roosevelt*
1981—Robert K. Massie, *Peter the Great: His Life and World*
1982—William S. McFeely, *Grant: A Biography*
1983—Russell Baker, *Growing Up*
1984—Louis R. Harlan, *Booker T. Washington*
1985—Kenneth Silverman, *The Life and Times of Cotton Mather*
1986—Elizabeth Frank, *Louise Bogan: A Portrait*
1987—David J. Garrow, *Bearing the Cross: Martin Luther King Jr. and the Southern Christian Leadership Conference*
1988—David Herbert Donald, *Look Homeward: A Life of Thomas Wolfe*
1989—Richard Ellmann, *Oscar Wilde*
1990—Sebastian de Grazia, *Machiavelli in Hell*
1991—Steven Naifeh and Gregory White Smith, *Jackson Pollock: An American Saga*
1992—Lewis B. Puller Jr., *Fortunate Son: The Healing of a Vietnam Vet*
1993—David McCullough, *Truman*
1994—David Levering Lewis, *W.E.B. DuBois: Biography of a Race, 1868-1919*
1995—Joan D. Hedrick, *Harriet Beecher Stowe: A Life*
1996—Jack Miles, *God: A Biography*
1997—Frank McCourt, *Angela's Ashes: A Memoir*
1998—Katharine Graham, *Personal History*
1999—A. Scott Berg, *Lindbergh*
2000—Stacy Schiff, *Véra (Mrs. Vladimir Nabokov)*
2001—David Levering Lewis, *W.E.B. Du Bois: The Fight for Equality and the American Century, 1919-1963*
2002—David McCullough, *John Adams*
2003—Robert Caro, *The Years of Lyndon Johnson: Master of the Senate*
2004—William Taubman, *Khrushchev: The Man and His Era*
2005—Mark Stevens and Annalyn Swan, *de Kooning: An American Master*

American Poetry

Before 1922, awards were funded by the Poetry Society.
1918—*Love Songs*, by Sara Teasdale;
1919—*Old Road to Paradise*, by Margaret Widdemer; *Corn Huskers*, by Carl Sandburg.
1922—Edwin Arlington Robinson, *Collected Poems*
1923—Edna St. Vincent Millay, *The Ballad of the Harp-Weaver; A Few Figs From Thistles; other works*
1924—Robert Frost, *New Hampshire: A Poem With Notes and Grace Notes*
1925—Edwin Arlington Robinson, *The Man Who Died Twice*
1926—Amy Lowell, *What's O'Clock*
1927—Leonora Speyer, *Fiddler's Farewell*
1928—Edwin Arlington Robinson, *Tristram*
1929—Stephen Vincent Benet, *John Brown's Body*
1930—Conrad Aiken, *Selected Poems*
1931—Robert Frost, *Collected Poems*
1932—George Dillon, *The Flowering Stone*
1933—Archibald MacLeish, *Conquistador*
1934—Robert Hillyer, *Collected Verse*
1935—Audrey Wurdemann, *Bright Ambush*
1936—Robert P. Tristram Coffin, *Strange Holiness*
1937—Robert Frost, *A Further Range*
1938—Marya Zaturenska, *Cold Morning Sky*
1939—John Gould Fletcher, *Selected Poems*
1940—Mark Van Doren, *Collected Poems*
1941—Leonard Bacon, *Sunderland Capture*
1942—William Rose Benet, *The Dust Which Is God*
1943—Robert Frost, *A Witness Tree*
1944—Stephen Vincent Benet, *Western Star*
1945—Karl Shapiro, *V-Letter and Other Poems*
1947—Robert Lowell, *Lord Weary's Castle*
1948—W. H. Auden, *The Age of Anxiety*
1949—Peter Viereck, *Terror and Decorum*
1950—Gwendolyn Brooks, *Annie Allen*
1951—Carl Sandburg, *Complete Poems*
1952—Marianne Moore, *Collected Poems*
1953—Archibald MacLeish, *Collected Poems*
1954—Theodore Roethke, *The Waking*
1955—Wallace Stevens, *Collected Poems*
1956—Elizabeth Bishop, *Poems, North and South*
1957—Richard Wilbur, *Things of This World*
1958—Robert Penn Warren, *Promises: Poems 1954-1956*
1959—Stanley Kunitz, *Selected Poems 1928-1958*
1960—W. D. Snodgrass, *Heart's Needle*
1961—Phyllis McGinley, *Times Three: Selected Verse From Three Decades*
1962—Alan Dugan, *Poems*
1963—William Carlos Williams, *Pictures From Breughel*
1964—Louis Simpson, *At the End of the Open Road*
1965—John Berryman, *77 Dream Songs*
1966—Richard Eberhart, *Selected Poems*
1967—Anne Sexton, *Live or Die*
1968—Anthony Hecht, *The Hard Hours*
1969—George Oppen, *Of Being Numerous*
1970—Richard Howard, *Untitled Subjects*
1971—William S. Merwin, *The Carrier of Ladders*
1972—James Wright, *Collected Poems*
1973—Maxine Winokur Kumin, *Up Country*
1974—Robert Lowell, *The Dolphin*
1975—Gary Snyder, *Turtle Island*
1976—John Ashbery, *Self-Portrait in a Convex Mirror*
1977—James Merrill, *Divine Comedies*
1978—Howard Nemerov, *Collected Poems*
1979—Robert Penn Warren, *Now and Then: Poems 1976-1978*
1980—Donald Justice, *Selected Poems*
1981—James Schuyler, *The Morning of the Poem*
1982—Sylvia Plath, *The Collected Poems*
1983—Galway Kinnell, *Selected Poems*
1984—Mary Oliver, *American Primitive*
1985—Carolyn Kizer, *Yin*
1986—Henry Taylor, *The Flying Change*
1987—Rita Dove, *Thomas and Beulah*
1988—William Meredith, *Partial Accounts*
1989—Richard Wilbur, *New and Collected Poems*
1990—Charles Simic, *The World Doesn't End*
1991—Mona Van Duyn, *Near Changes*
1992—James Tate, *Selected Poems*
1993—Louise Glück, *The Wild Iris*
1994—Yusef Komunyakaa, *Neon Vernacular*
1995—Philip Levine, *The Simple Truth*
1996—Jorie Graham, *The Dream of the Unified Field*
1997—Lisel Mueller, *Alive Together: New and Selected Poems*
1998—Charles Wright, *Black Zodiac*
1999—Mark Strand, *Blizzard of One*
2000—C. K. Williams, *Repair*
2001—Stephen Dunn, *Different Hours*
2002—Carl Dennis, *Practical Gods*
2003—Paul Muldoon, *Moy Sand and Gravel*
2004—Franz Wright, *Walking to Martha's Vineyard*
2005—Ted Kooser, *Delights & Shadows*

General Nonfiction

1962—Theodore H. White, *The Making of the President 1960*
1963—Barbara W. Tuchman, *The Guns of August*
1964—Richard Hofstadter, *Anti-Intellectualism in American Life*
1965—Howard Mumford Jones, *O Strange New World*
1966—Edwin Way Teale, *Wandering Through Winter*
1967—David Brion Davis, *The Problem of Slavery in Western Culture*
1968—Will and Ariel Durant, *Rousseau and Revolution*
1969—Norman Mailer, *The Armies of the Night;* Rene Jules Dubos, *So Human an Animal: How We Are Shaped by Surroundings and Events*
1970—Eric H. Erikson, *Gandhi's Truth*
1971—John Toland, *The Rising Sun*
1972—Barbara W. Tuchman, *Stilwell and the American Experience in China, 1911-1945*
1973—Frances FitzGerald, *Fire in the Lake: The Vietnamese and the Americans in Vietnam*; Robert Coles, *Children of Crisis,* Volumes II & III
1974—Ernest Becker, *The Denial of Death*
1975—Annie Dillard, *Pilgrim at Tinker Creek*
1976—Robert N. Butler, *Why Survive? Being Old in America*
1977—William W. Warner, *Beautiful Swimmers*
1978—Carl Sagan, *The Dragons of Eden*
1979—Edward O. Wilson, *On Human Nature*
1980—Douglas R. Hofstadter, *Gödel, Escher, Bach: An Eternal Golden Braid*
1981—Carl E. Schorske, *Fin-de-Siecle Vienna: Politics and Culture*
1982—Tracy Kidder, *The Soul of a New Machine*

1983—Susan Sheehan, *Is There No Place on Earth for Me?*
1984—Paul Starr, *Social Transformation of American Medicine*
1985—Studs Terkel, *The Good War*
1986—Joseph Lelyveld, *Move Your Shadow;* J. Anthony Lukas, *Common Ground*
1987—David K. Shipler, *Arab and Jew*
1988—Richard Rhodes, *The Making of the Atomic Bomb*
1989—Neil Sheehan, *A Bright Shining Lie: John Paul Vann and America in Vietnam*
1990—Dale Maharidge and Michael Williamson, *And Their Children After Them*
1991—Bert Holldobler and Edward O. Wilson, *The Ants*
1992—Daniel Yergin, *The Prize: The Epic Quest for Oil*
1993—Garry Wills, *Lincoln at Gettysburg*
1994—David Remnick, *Lenin's Tomb: The Last Days of the Soviet Empire*
1995—Jonathan Weiner, *The Beak of the Finch: A Story of Evolution in Our Time*
1996—Tina Rosenberg, *The Haunted Land: Facing Europe's Ghosts After Communism*
1997—Richard Kluger, *Ashes to Ashes: America's Hundred-Year Cigarette War, the Public Health, and the Unabashed Triumph of Philip Morris*
1998—Jared Diamond, *Guns, Germs, and Steel: The Fates of Human Societies*
1999—John McPhee, *Annals of the Former World*
2000—John W. Dower, *Embracing Defeat: Japan in the Wake of World War II*
2001—Herbert P. Bix, *Hirohito and the Making of Modern Japan*
2002—Diane McWhorter, *Carry Me Home: Birmingham, Alabama, the Climactic Battle of the Civil Rights Revolution*
2003—Samantha Power, *A Problem From Hell: America and the Age of Genocide*
2004—Anne Applebaum, *Gulag: A History*
2005—Steve Coll, *Ghost Wars*

Special Citation in Letters

1944—Richard Rodgers and Oscar Hammerstein II, for *Oklahoma!*
1957—Kenneth Roberts, for his historical novels
1960—*The Armada,* by Garrett Mattingly
1961—*American Heritage Picture History of the Civil War*
1973—*George Washington, Vols. I-IV*, by James Thomas Flexner
1977—Alex Haley, for *Roots*
1978—E.B. White
1984—Theodore Seuss Geisel (Dr. Seuss)
1992—Art Spiegleman, for *Maus*

Music

1943—William Schuman, *Secular Cantata No. 2, A Free Song*
1944—Howard Hanson, *Symphony No. 4, Op. 34*
1945—Aaron Copland, *Appalachian Spring*
1946—Leo Sowerby, *The Canticle of the Sun*
1947—Charles E. Ives, *Symphony No. 3*
1948—Walter Piston, *Symphony No. 3*
1949—Virgil Thomson, *Louisiana Story*
1950—Gian-Carlo Menotti, *The Consul*
1951—Douglas Moore, *Giants in the Earth*
1952—Gail Kubik, *Symphony Concertante*
1954—Quincy Porter, *Concerto for Two Pianos and Orchestra*
1955—Gian-Carlo Menotti, *The Saint of Bleecker Street*
1956—Ernest Toch, *Symphony No. 3*
1957—Norman Dello Joio, *Meditations on Ecclesiastes*
1958—Samuel Barber, *Vanessa*
1959—John La Montaine, *Concerto for Piano and Orchestra*
1960—Elliott Carter, *Second String Quartet*
1961—Walter Piston, *Symphony No. 7*
1962—Robert Ward, *The Crucible*
1963—Samuel Barber, *Piano Concerto No. 1*
1966—Leslie Bassett, *Variations for Orchestra*
1967—Leon Kirchner, *Quartet No. 3*
1968—George Crumb, *Echoes of Time and The River*
1969—Karel Husa, *String Quartet No. 3*
1970—Charles W. Wuorinen, *Time's Encomium*
1971—Mario Davidovsky, *Synchronisms No. 6*
1972—Jacob Druckman, *Windows*
1973—Elliott Carter, *String Quartet No. 3*
1974—Donald Martino, *Notturno*
1975—Dominick Argento, *From the Diary of Virginia Woolf*
1976—Ned Rorem, *Air Music*
1977—Richard Wernick, *Visions of Terror and Wonder*
1978—Michael Colgrass, *Deja Vu for Percussion and Orchestra*
1979—Joseph Schwantner, *Aftertones of Infinity*
1980—David Del Tredici, *In Memory of a Summer Day*
1982—Roger Sessions, *Concerto for Orchestra*
1983—Ellen T. Zwilich, *Three Movements for Orchestra*
1984—Bernard Rands, *Canti del Sole*
1985—Stephen Albert, *Symphony, RiverRun*
1986—George Perle, *Wind Quintet IV*
1987—John Harbison, *The Flight Into Egypt*
1988—William Bolcom, *12 New Etudes for Piano*
1989—Roger Reynolds, *Whispers Out of Time*
1990—Mel Powell, *Duplicates: A Concerto for Two Pianos and Orchestra*
1991—Shulamit Ran, *Symphony*
1992—Wayne Peterson, *The Face of the Night, The Heart of the Dark*
1993—Christopher Rouse, *Trombone Concerto*
1994—Gunther Schuller, *Of Reminiscences and Reflections*
1995—Morton Gould, *Stringmusic*
1996—George Walker, *Lilacs*
1997—Wynton Marsalis, *Blood on the Fields*
1998—Aaron Jay Kernis, *String Quartet No. 2*
1999—Melinda Wagner, *Concerto for Flute, Strings and Percussion*
2000—Lewis Spratlan, *Life is a Dream, Opera in Three Acts: Act II, Concert Version*
2001—John Corigliano, *Symphony No. 2 for String Orchestra*
2002—Henry Brant, *Ice Field*
2003—John Adams, *On the Transmigration of Souls*
2004—Paul Moravec, *Tempest Fantasy*
2005—Steven Stucky, *Second Concerto for Orchestra*

Special Citation in Music

1974—Roger Sessions
1976—Scott Joplin
1982—Milton Babbitt
1985—William Schuman
1998—George Gershwin
1999—Edward Kennedy "Duke" Ellington

National Book Awards, 1950-2004

The National Book Awards (known as American Book Awards 1980–86) are administered by the National Book Foundation and have been given annually in the years shown, since 1950. The prizes, each valued at $10,000, are awarded to U.S. citizens for works published in the U.S. In some years, multiple awards were given for nonfiction in various categories; in such cases, the history and biography (if any) or biography winner is listed. Selected additional awards in nonfiction and other 2004 awards are listed in footnotes.

Fiction

Year	Author, Title
1950	Nelson Algren, *The Man With the Golden Arm*
1951	William Faulkner, *The Collected Stories*
1952	James Jones, *From Here to Eternity*
1953	Ralph Ellison, *Invisible Man*
1954	Saul Bellow, *The Adventures of Augie March*
1955	William Faulkner, *A Fable*
1956	John O'Hara, *Ten North Frederick*
1957	Wright Morris, *The Field of Vision*
1958	John Cheever, *The Wapshot Chronicle*
1959	Bernard Malamud, *The Magic Barrel*
1960	Philip Roth, *Goodbye, Columbus*
1961	Conrad Richter, *The Waters of Kronos*
1962	Walker Percy, *The Moviegoer*
1963	J.F. Powers, *Morte d'Urban*
1964	John Updike, *The Centaur*
1965	Saul Bellow, *Herzog*
1966	Katherine Anne Porter, *The Collected Stories*
1967	Bernard Malamud, *The Fixer*
1968	Thornton Wilder, *The Eighth Day*
1969	Jerzy Kosinski, *Steps*
1970	Joyce Carol Oates, *Them*
1971	Saul Bellow, *Mr. Sammler's Planet*
1972	Flannery O'Connor, *The Complete Stories*
1973	John Barth, *Chimera*
1974	Thomas Pynchon, *Gravity's Rainbow*
1974	Isaac Bashevis Singer, *A Crown of Feathers*
1975	Robert Stone, *Dog Soldiers*
1976	William Gaddis, *JR*
1977	Wallace Stegner, *The Spectator Bird*
1978	Mary Lee Settle, *Blood Ties*
1979	Tim O'Brien, *Going After Cacciato*
1980	William Styron, *Sophie's Choice*
1981	Wright Morris, *Plains Song*
1982	John Updike, *Rabbit Is Rich*
1983	Alice Walker, *The Color Purple*
1984	Ellen Gilchrist, *Victory Over Japan*

Year	Author, Title
1985	Don DeLillo, *White Noise*
1986	E.L. Doctorow, *World's Fair*
1987	Larry Heinemann, *Paco's Story*
1988	Pete Dexter, *Paris Trout*
1989	John Casey, *Spartina*
1990	Charles Johnson, *Middle Passage*
1991	Norman Rush, *Mating*
1992	Cormac McCarthy, *All the Pretty Horses*
1993	E. Annie Proulx, *The Shipping News*
1994	William Gaddis, *A Frolic of His Own*
1995	Philip Roth, *Sabbath's Theater*
1996	Andrea Barrett, *Ship Fever and Other Stories*
1997	Charles Frazier, *Cold Mounatin*
1998	Alice McDermott, *Charming Billy*
1999	Ha Jin, *Waiting*
2000	Susan Sontag, *In America*
2001	Jonathan Franzen, *The Corrections*
2002	Julia Glass, *Three Junes*
2003	Shirley Hazzard, *The Great Fire*
2004	Lily Tuck, *The News from Paraguay*

Nonfiction

Year	Author, Title
1950	Ralph L. Rusk, *Ralph Waldo Emerson*
1951	Newton Arvin, *Herman Melville*
1952	Rachel Carson, *The Sea Around Us*
1953	Bernard A. De Voto, *The Course of an Empire*
1954	Bruce Catton, *A Stillness at Appomattox*
1955	Joseph Wood Krutch, *The Measure of Man*
1956	Herbert Kubly, *An American in Italy*
1957	George F. Kennan, *Russia Leaves the War*
1958	Catherine Drinker Bowen, *The Lion and the Throne*
1959	J. Christopher Herold, *Mistress to an Age: A Life of Madame De Stael*
1960	Richard Ellman, *James Joyce*
1961	William L. Shirer, *The Rise and Fall of the Third Reich*
1962	Lewis Mumford, *The City in History: Its Origins, Its Transformations, and Its Prospects*
1963	Leon Edel, *Henry James: Vol. II: The Conquest of London; Vol. III: The Middle Years*
1964	WIlliam H. McNeill, *The Rise of the West: A History of the Human Community*
1965	Louis Fisher, *The Life of Lenin*
1966	Arthur M. Schlesinger, Jr., *A Thousand Days: John F. Kennedy in the White House*
1967	Peter Gay, *The Enlightenment, An Interpretation Vol I: The Rise of Modern Paganism*
1968	George F. Kennan, *Memoirs: 1925–1950*[1]
1969	Winthrop D. Jordan, *White Over Black: American Attitudes Toward the Negro, 1550-1812*[2]
1970	T. Harry Williams, *Huey Long*[3]
1971	James MacGregor Burns, *Roosevelt: The Soldier of Freedom*
1972	Joseph P. Lash, *Eleanor and Franklin: The Story of Their Relationship, Based on Eleanor Roosevelt's Private Papers*
1973	James Thomas Flexner, *George Washington, Vol. IV: Anguish and Farewell, 1793-1799*[4]
1974	John Clive, *Macaulay, The Shaping of the Historian*; Douglas Day, *Malcolm Lowry: A Biography*[5]
1975	Richard B. Sewall, *The Life of Emily Dickinson*[6]
1976	David Brion Davis, *The Problem of Slavery in the Age of Revolution, 1770-1823*
1977	W.A. Swanberg, *Norman Thomas: The Last Idealist*[7]
1978	W. Jackson Bate, *Samuel Johnson*
1979	Arthur M. Schlesinger, Jr., *Robert Kennedy and His Times*
1980	Tom Wolfe, *The Right Stuff*
1981	Maxine Hong Kingston, *China Men*
1982	Tracy Kidder, *The Soul of a New Machine*
1983	Fox Butterfield, *China: Alive in the Bitter Sea*
1984	Robert V. Remini, *Andrew Jackson and the Course of American Democracy, 1833-1845*
1985	J. Anthony Lukas, *Common Ground: A Turbulent Decade in the Lives of Three American Families*
1986	Barry Lopez, *Arctic Dreams*
1987	Richard Rhodes, *The Making of the Atom Bomb*
1988	Neil Sheehan, *A Bright Shining Lie: John Paul Vann and America in Vietnam*
1989	Thomas L. Friedman, *From Beirut to Jerusalem*
1990	Ron Chernow, *The House of Morgan: An American Banking Dynasty and the Rise of Modern Finance*
1991	Orlando Patterson, *Freedom*
1992	Paul Monette, *Becoming a Man: Half a Life Story*
1993	Gore Vidal, *United States: Essays 1952-1992*
1994	Sherwin B. Nuland, *How We Die: Reflections on Life's Final Chapter*
1995	Tina Rosenberg, *The Haunted Land: Facing Europe's Ghosts After Communism*
1996	James Carroll, *An American Requiem: God, My Father, and the War That Came Between Us*
1997	Joseph J. Ellis, *American Sphinx: The Character of Thomas Jefferson*
1998	Edward Ball, *Slaves in the Family*
1999	John W. Dower, *Embracing Defeat: Japan in the Wake of World War II*
2000	Nathaniel Philbrick, *In the Heart of the Sea: The Tragedy of the Whaleship Essex*
2001	Andrew Solomon, *The Noonday Demon: An Atlas of Depression*
2002	Robert A. Caro, *Master of the Senate: The Years of Lyndon Johnson*
2003	Carlos Eire, *Waiting for Snow in Havana: Confessions of a Cuban Boy*
2004	Kevin Boyle, *Arc of Justice: A Saga of Race, Civil Rights, and Murder in the Jazz Age*[8]

(1) Science, Philosophy, and Religion: Jonathan Kozol, *Death at an Early Age.* (2) Arts & Letters: Norman Mailer, *The Armies of the Night: History as a Novel, The Novel as History.* (3) Arts & Letters: Lillian Hellman, *An Unfinished Woman: A Memoir.* (4) Contemp. Affairs: Frances FitzGerald, *Fire in the Lake: The Vietnamese and the Americans in Vietnam.* (5) Arts & Letters: Pauline Kael, *Deeper Into the Movies.* (6) Arts & Letters: Roger Shattuck, *Marcel Proust;* Lewis Thomas, *The Lives of a Cell: Notes of a Biology Watcher.* (7) Contemp. Thought: Bruno Bettelheim, *The Uses of Enchantment: The Meaning and Importance of Fairy Tales.* (8) **Other National Book Awards, 2004**: Poetry: Jean Valentine, *Door in the Mountain: New and Collected Poems.* Young People's Literature: Pete Hautman, *Godless.* Medal for Distinguished Contribution to American Letters: Judy Blume.

The Man Booker Prize for Fiction, 1969-2004

The Booker Prize for fiction, established in 1968, is awarded annually in October for what is judged the best full-length novel written in English by a citizen of the UK, the Commonwealth, or the Irish Republic. In 2002 sponsorship of the award was taken over by Man Group PLC, the name was changed to the Man Booker Prize, and the amount was increased from £20,000 to £50,000.

1969—P. H. Newby, *Something to Answer For*
1970—Bernice Rubens, *The Elected Member*
1971—V. S. Naipaul, *In a Free State*
1972—John Berger, *G*
1973—J. G. Farrell, *The Siege of Krishnapur*
1974—Nadine Gordimer, *The Conservationist;* Stanley Middleton, *Holiday*
1975—Ruth Prawer Jhabvala, *Heat & Dust*
1976—David Storey, *Saville*
1977—Paul Scott, *Staying On*
1978—Iris Murdoch, *The Sea*, The Sea
1979—Penelope Fitzgerald, *Offshore*
1980—William Golding, *Rites of Passage*
1981—Salman Rushdie, *Midnight's Children*
1982—Thomas Keneally, *Schindler's Ark*
1983—J. M. Coetzee, *Life and Times of Michael K*
1984—Anita Brookner, *Hotel du Lac*
1985—Keri Hulme, *The Bone People*
1986—Kingsley Amis, *The Old Devils*
1987—Penelope Lively, *Moon Tiger*
1988—Peter Carey, *Oscar and Lucinda*
1989—Kazuo Ishiguro, *The Remains of the Day*
1990—A. S. Byatt, *Possession*
1991—Ben Okri, *The Famished Road*
1992—Michael Ondaatje, *The English Patient;* Barry Unsworth, *Sacred Hunger*
1993—Roddy Doyle, *Paddy Clarke Ha Ha Ha*
1994—James Kelman, *How Late It Was, How Late*
1995—Pat Barker, *The Ghost Road*
1996—Graham Swift, *Last Orders*
1997—Arundhati Roy, *The God of Small Things*
1998—Ian McEwan, *Amsterdam*
1999—J. M. Coetzee, *Disgrace*
2000—Margaret Atwood, *The Blind Assassin*
2001—Peter Carey, *True History of the Kelly Gang*
2002—Yann Martel, *Life of Pi*
2003—DBC Pierre, *Vernon God Little*
2004—Alan Hollinghurst, *The Line of Beauty*

Newbery Medal Books, 1922-2005

The Newbery Medal was awarded annually in the years shown, by the Association for Library Service to Children, a division of the American Library Association, to the author of the most distinguished contribution to American literature for children.

Year	Book, Author
1922	*The Story of Mankind,* Hendrik Willem van Loon
1923	*The Voyages of Dr. Dolittle,* Hugh Lofting
1924	*The Dark Frigate,* Charles Boardman Hawes
1925	*Tales From Silver Lands,* Charles Joseph Finger
1926	*Shen of the Sea,* Arthur Bowie Chrisman
1927	*Smoky, the Cowhorse,* Will James
1928	*Gay-Neck,* Dhan Gopal Mukerji
1929	*The Trumpeter of Krakow,* Eric P. Kelly
1930	*Hitty, Her First Hundred Years,* Rachel Field
1931	*The Cat Who Went to Heaven,* Elizabeth Coatsworth
1932	*Waterless Mountain,* Laura Adams Armer
1933	*Young Fu of the Upper Yangtze,* Elizabeth Foreman Lewis
1934	*Invincible Louisa,* Cornelia Lynde Meigs
1935	*Dobry,* Monica Shannon
1936	*Caddie Woodlawn,* Carol Ryrie Brink
1937	*Roller Skates,* Ruth Sawyer
1938	*The White Stag,* Kate Seredy
1939	*Thimble Summer,* Elizabeth Enright
1940	*Daniel Boone,* James Daugherty
1941	*Call It Courage,* Armstrong Sperry
1942	*The Matchlock Gun,* Walter D. Edmonds
1943	*Adam of the Road,* Elizabeth Janet Gray
1944	*Johnny Tremain,* Esther Forbes
1945	*Rabbit Hill,* Robert Lawson
1946	*Strawberry Girl,* Lois Lenski
1947	*Miss Hickory,* Carolyn S. Bailey
1948	*Twenty-One Balloons,* William Pène Du Bois
1949	*King of the Wind,* Marguerite Henry
1950	*The Door in the Wall,* Marguerite de Angeli
1951	*Amos Fortune, Free Man,* Elizabeth Yates
1952	*Ginger Pye,* Eleanor Estes
1953	*Secret of the Andes,* Ann Nolan Clark
1954	*. . . And Now Miguel,* Joseph Krumgold
1955	*The Wheel on the School,* Meindert DeJong
1956	*Carry On, Mr. Bowditch,* Jean Lee Latham
1957	*Miracles on Maple Hill,* Virginia Sorensen
1958	*Rifles for Watie,* Harold Keith
1959	*The Witch of Blackbird Pond,* Elizabeth George Speare
1960	*Onion John,* Joseph Krumgold
1961	*Island of the Blue Dolphins,* Scott O'Dell
1962	*The Bronze Bow,* Elizabeth George Speare
1963	*A Wrinkle in Time,* Madeleine L'Engle
1964	*It's Like This, Cat,* Emily Cheney Neville
1965	*Shadow of a Bull,* Maja Wojciechowska
1966	*I, Juan de Pareja,* Elizabeth Borton de Trevino
1967	*Up a Road Slowly,* Irene Hunt
1968	*From the Mixed-Up Files of Mrs. Basil E. Frankweiler,* E. L. Konigsburg
1969	*The High King,* Lloyd Alexander
1970	*Sounder,* William H. Armstrong
1971	*The Summer of the Swans,* Betsy Byars
1972	*Mrs. Frisby and the Rats of NIMH,* Robert C. O'Brien
1973	*Julie of the Wolves,* Jean George
1974	*The Slave Dancer,* Paula Fox
1975	*M. C. Higgins the Great,* Virginia Hamilton
1976	*Grey King,* Susan Cooper
1977	*Roll of Thunder, Hear My Cry,* Mildred D. Taylor
1978	*Bridge to Terabithia,* Katherine Paterson
1979	*The Westing Game,* Ellen Raskin
1980	*A Gathering of Days,* Joan Blos
1981	*Jacob Have I Loved,* Katherine Paterson
1982	*A Visit to William Blake's Inn: Poems for Innocent and Experienced Travelers,* Nancy Willard
1983	*Dicey's Song,* Cynthia Voigt
1984	*Dear Mr. Henshaw,* Beverly Cleary
1985	*The Hero and the Crown,* Robin McKinley
1986	*Sarah, Plain and Tall,* Patricia MacLachlan
1987	*The Whipping Boy,* Sid Fleischman
1988	*Lincoln: A Photobiography,* Russell Freedman
1989	*Joyful Noise: Poems for Two Voices,* Paul Fleischman
1990	*Number the Stars,* Lois Lowry
1991	*Maniac Magee,* Jerry Spinelli
1992	*Shiloh,* Phyllis Reynolds Naylor
1993	*Missing May,* Cynthia Rylant
1994	*The Giver,* Lois Lowry
1995	*Walk Two Moons,* Sharon Creech
1996	*The Midwife's Apprentice,* Karen Cushman
1997	*The View From Saturday,* E. L. Konigsburg
1998	*Out of the Dust,* Karen Hesse
1999	*Holes,* Louis Sachar
2000	*Bud, Not Buddy,* Christopher Paul Curtis
2001	*A Year Down Yonder,* Richard Peck
2002	*A Single Shard,* Linda Sue Park
2003	*Crispin: The Cross of Lead,* Avi
2004	*The Tale of Despereaux: Being the Story of a Mouse, a Princess, Some Soup, and a Spool of Thread,* by Kate DiCamillo, illustrated by Timothy Basil Ering
2005	*Kira-Kira,* Cynthia Kadohata

Caldecott Medal Books, 1938-2005

The Caldecott Medal was awarded annually in the years shown, by the Association for Library Service to Children, a division of the American Library Association, to the illustrator of the most distinguished American picture book for children.

Year	Book, Illustrator
1938	*Animals of the Bible*, Dorothy P. Lathrop
1939	*Mei Li*, Thomas Handforth
1940	*Abraham Lincoln*, Ingri & Edgar Parin d'Aulaire
1941	*They Were Strong and Good*, Robert Lawson
1942	*Make Way for Ducklings*, Robert McCloskey
1943	*The Little House*, Virginia Lee Burton
1944	*Many Moons*, Louis Slobodkin
1945	*Prayer for a Child*, Elizabeth Orton Jones
1946	*The Rooster Crows*, Maude & Miska Petersham
1947	*The Little Island*, Leonard Weisgard
1948	*White Snow, Bright Snow*, Roger Duvoisin
1949	*The Big Snow*, Berta & Elmer Hader
1950	*Song of the Swallows*, Leo Politi
1951	*The Egg Tree*, Karherine Milhous
1952	*Finders Keepers*, Nicolas, pseud. (Nicholas Mordvinoff)
1953	*The Biggest Bear*, Lynd Ward
1954	*Madeline's Rescue*, Ludwig Bemelmans
1955	*Cinderella, or the Little Glass Slipper*, Marcia Brown
1956	*Frog Went A-Courtin'*, Feodor Rojankovsky
1957	*A Tree Is Nice*, Marc Simont
1958	*Time of Wonder*, Robert McCloskey
1959	*Chanticleer and the Fox,* Barbara Cooney
1960	*Nine Days to Christmas*, Marie Hall Ets
1961	*Baboushka and the Three Kings*, Nicolas Sidjakov
1962	*Once a Mouse*, Marcia Brown
1963	*The Snowy Day*, Ezra Jack Keats
1964	*Where the Wild Things Are*, Maurice Sendak
1965	*May I Bring a Friend?*, Beni Montressor
1966	*Always Room for One More*, Nonny Hogrogian
1967	*Sam, Bang, and Moonshine*, Evaline Ness
1968	*Drummer Hoff*, Ed Emberley
1969	*The Fool of the World and the Flying Ship*, Uri Shulevitz
1970	*Sylvester and the Magic Pebble*, William Steig
1971	*A Story A Story*, Gail E. Haley
1972	*One Fine Day*, Nonny Hogrogian
1973	*The Funny Little Woman*, Blair Lent
1974	*Duffy and the Devil*, Margot Zemach
1975	*Arrow to the Sun*, Gerald McDermott
1976	*Why Mosquitoes Buzz in People's Ears*, Leo & Diane Dillon
1977	*Ashanti to Zulu: African Traditions*, Leo & Diane Dillon
1978	*Noah's Ark*, Peter Spier
1979	*The Girl Who Loved Wild Horses*, Paul Goble
1980	*Ox-Cart Man*, Barbara Cooney
1981	*Fables*, Arnold Lobel
1982	*Jumanji*, Chris Van Allsburg
1983	*Shadow*, Marcia Brown
1984	*The Glorious Flight: Across the Channel with Louis Bleriot*, Alice and Martin Provensen
1985	*Saint George and the Dragon*, Trina Schart Hyman
1986	*The Polar Express*, Chris Van Allsburg
1987	*Hey, Al*, Richard Egielski
1988	*Owl Moon*, John Schoenherr
1989	*Song and Dance Man*, Stephen Grammell
1990	*Lon Po Po: A Red-Riding Hood Story From China*, Ed Young
1991	*Black and White*, David Macaulay
1992	*Tuesday*, David Wiesner

Year	Book, Illustrator
1993	*Mirette on the High Wire,* Emily Arnold McCully
1994	*Grandfather's Journey,* Allen Say
1995	*Smoky Night,* David Diaz
1996	*Officer Buckle and Gloria,* Peggy Rathmann
1997	*Golem,* David Wisniewski
1998	*Rapunzel,* Paul O. Zelinsky
1999	*Snowflake Bentley,* Mary Azarian
2000	*Joseph Had a Little Overcoat,* Simms Taback
2001	*So You Want to be President?,* David Small
2002	*The Three Pigs,* David Wiesner
2003	*My Friend Rabbit,* Eric Rohmann
2004	*The Man Who Walked Between the Towers,* Mordicai Gerstein
2005	*Kitten's First Full Moon,* Kevin Henkes

Miscellaneous Book Awards

(Awarded in 2005, unless otherwise noted)

Academy of American Poets Awards. Academy Fellowship, $25,000 stipend (2004): Jane Hirshfield. James Laughlin Award, $5,000: Jeff Clark, *Music and Suicide.* Walt Whitman Award, $5,000: Geri Doran, *Resin.* Harold Morton Landon Trans. Award, $1,000: Daryl Hine, *Works of Hesiod and the Homeric Hymns.* Lenore Marshall Poetry Prize, $25,000 (2004): Donald Revell, *My Mojave.* Raiziss/de Palchi Trans. Award (fellowship), $20,000 (2004): Ann Snodgrass, *Selected Poems of Vittorio Sereni.* Wallace Stevens Award, for poetry, $100,000 (2004): Mark Strand.

American Academy of Arts and Letters. Academy Awards in Literature ($7,500 each): Jim Grimsley, Joseph Harrison, Edward P. Jones, Donald Margulies, Charles Martin, Jeffrey Meyers, Stephen Orgel, Burton Watson. Benjamin H. Danks Award, $20,000: Edwidge Danticat. E. M. Forster Award, $15,000: Dennis O'Driscoll. Sue Kaufman Prize for First Fiction, $2,500: John Dalton, *Heaven Lake.* Gold Medal for Belles Lettres and Criticism: Joan Didion. William Dean Howells Medal: Shirley Hazzard, *The Great Fire.* Richard and Hinda Rosenthal Foundation Awards, $5,000: Jeff Talarigo, *The Pearl Diver.* Harold D. Vursell Memorial Award, $10,000: Ann Patchett. Rome Fellowships in Literature: Aaron Hamburger (writer), Craig Arnold (poet).

Bollingen Prize in Poetry, $75,000, by the Yale Univ. Library: Jay Wright.

Edgar Awards, by the Mystery Writers of America: Grand Master award: Marcia Muller. Best novel: *California Girl,* T. Jefferson Parker. First novel by an American author: *Country of Origin,* Don Lee. Best paperback original: *The Confession,* Domenic Stansberry. Best Critical/Biographical: *The New Annotated Sherlock Holmes: The Complete Short Stories,* ed. Leslie S. Klinger.

Golden Kite Awards, by Society of Children's Book Writers and Illustrators. Fiction: Christopher Paul Curtis, *Bucking the Sarge.* Nonfiction: Michael L. Cooper, *Dust to Eat: Drought and Depression in the 1930s.* Picture-illustration: Jean Cassels, *The Mysterious Collection of Dr. David Harleyson.* Picture book text: Deborah Hopkinson, *Apples to Oregon* (Nancy Carpenter, illus.).

Le Prix Goncourt, by Académie Goncourt (2004): Laurent Gaude, *Le Soleil des Scorta* (The Sun of the Scortas).

Hugo Awards, by the World Science Fiction Convention. Novel: *Jonathan Strange & Mr. Norrell,* Susanna Clarke. Novella: *The Concrete Jungle,* Charles Stross. Novelette: *The Faery Handbag,* Kelly Link. Short story: "Travels with My Cats," Mike Resnick. John W. Campbell Award for Best New Writer (not a Hugo): Elizabeth Bear.

Coretta Scott King Award, by American Library Assn., for African American authors and illustrators of outstanding books for children and young adults. Author: Toni Morrison, *Remember: The Journey to School Integration.* Illustrator: Kadir Nelson, *Ellington Was Not a Street.*

Lincoln Prize, by Lincoln and Soldiers Institute at Gettysburg College, for contribution to Civil War studies, $35,000 and bust of Lincoln (2005): Allen C. Guelzo, *Lincoln's Emancipation Proclamation: The End of Slavery in America.* 2nd place, $15,000: Harold Holzer, *Lincoln at Cooper Union.*

National Book Critics Circle Awards. Fiction: Marilynne Robinson, *Gilead.* Nonfiction: Diarmaid MacCulloch, *The Reformation: A History.* Criticism: Patricia Neate, *Where You're At: Notes From the Frontline of a Hip-Hop Planet.* Biography/Autobiography: Mark Stevens and Annalyn Swan, *De Kooning: An American Master.* Poetry: Adrienne Rich, *The School Among the Ruins.* Nona Balakian Citation for Excellence in Reviewing: David Orr. Ivan Sandrof Lifetime Achievement Award: Louis D. Rubin Jr.

Nebula Awards, by the Science Fiction Writers of America. Novel: *Paladin of Souls,* Lois McMaster Bujold. Novella: *The Green Leopard Plague,* Walter Jon Williams. Novelette: *Basement Magic,* Ellen Klages. Short story: "Coming to Terms," Eileen Gunn.

PEN/Faulkner Award, for fiction, $15,000: Ha Jin, *War Trash.*

Whitbread Book of the Year Award, by Whitbread PLC: £25,000: Andrea Levy, *Small Island.*

Journalism Awards, 2005

National Journalism Awards, by Scripps Howard Foundation, $10,000 each unless noted. Investigative Reporting ($25,000): *Los Angeles Times.* Public Service Reporting: *The Hartford Courant* (CT). Editorial Writing: Randy Bergmann, *Asbury Park Press* (Neptune, NJ). Commentary: Connie Schultz, *The Plain Dealer* (Cleveland). Human Interest Writing: Davan Maharaj, *Los Angeles Times.* Environmental Reporting: *The Sun* (San Bernardino, CA). Washington Reporting: Greg Jaffe, *The Wall Street Journal.* Business/Economics Reporting: *The Wall Street Journal.* Editorial Cartooning: Steve Sack, *Star Tribune* (Minneapolis). College Cartooning: Nathaniel R. Creekmore, *The Babbler,* Lipscomb Univ. (Nashville). Distinguished Service to the 1st Amendment: *The Dallas Morning News.* Photojournalism: Jim Gehrz, *Star Tribune* (Minneapolis). Web Reporting: DallasNews.com. Excellence in Electronic Media: (Radio) "This American Life," Chicago Public Radio/WBEZ; (TV/Cable) *The Age of Wal-Mart: Inside America's Most Powerful Company,* CNBC. Journalism Teacher of the Year: Sandra F. Chance, Univ. of Florida. Journalism Administrator of the Year: Will Norton Jr., Univ. of Nebraska-Lincoln.

National Magazine Awards, by American Society of Magazine Editors and Columbia Univ. Graduate School of Journalism. Gen. excel., circ. over 2 mil: *Glamour*; 1 mil-2 mil: *The New Yorker*; 500,000 to 1 mil: *Wired*; 250,000-500,000: *Martha Stewart Weddings*; 100,000-250,000: *Dwell*; under 100,000: *Print.* Personal service: *BabyTalk*; leisure interests: *Sports Illustrated*; reporting: *The New Yorker*; public interest: *The New Yorker*; feature writing: *Esquire*; profiles: *The New Yorker*; essays: *National Geographic*; columns/commentary: *National Journal*; criticism/reviews: *The New Yorker*; section: *Popular Science*; single-topic issue: *Newsweek*; design: *Kids: Fun Stuff to Do Together*; photography: *Gourmet*; photo essay: *Time*; fiction: *The Atlantic Monthly*; gen. excellence online: Style.com (www.style.com).

George Foster Peabody Awards, by Univ. of Georgia. *The Age of Wal-Mart: Inside America's Most Powerful Company,* CNBC. *The N-Word,* TRIO. *MOSAIC: World News from the Middle East,* Link TV. *Saluid es Vida...Enterate! (Lead a Healthy Life...Get the Facts!),* Univision. *Human Cargo,* Canadian Broadcasting Corp. *The War in Iraq,* NPR. *Takalani Sesame Presents talk to me,* Sesame Workshop and Kwasukasukela, SABC2, South Africa. *State of Play,* BBC America. *The Kumars at No. 4,* BBC America. *The Darfur Crisis,* BBC News. *Rwanda—Do the Scars Ever Fade?* Bill Brummel Productions, History Channel. *The Suffering of Sudan,* Channel One News. *60 Minutes II,* "Abuse at Abu Ghraib," CBS News. *On the Media,* WNYC Radio, New York. *Studio 360 American Icons,* "Herman Melville's Moby Dick," WNYC Radio and PRI, New York. *Leonard Bernstein: An American Life,* CultureWorks. *Let the Good Times Roll,* PRI. *To the Best of Our Knowledge,* Wisc. Public Radio and PRI. *Friends in High Places,* WTVF-TV, Nashville. *State of Denial,* WFAA-TV, Dallas. *Chesapeake Bay Pollution Investigation,* WBAL-TV, Baltimore. "The Bully Project," WITI-TV, Milwaukee. *American Experience: Tupperware!,* WGBH, Boston. "Indecision 2004," *The Daily Show with John Stewart,* Comedy Central. *Bus 174,* Cinemax. *Balseros,* Cinemax. *Beah: A Black Woman Speaks,* HBO. *Something the Lord Made,* HBO. *Deadwood,* HBO. *Black Sky: The Race for Space,* Discovery Channel. *Nursery Tap, Hip to Toe.* Individual Peabody Award: Grant Tinker.

Reuben Award, by National Cartoonists Society. For best cartoonist of 2004: Pat Brady.

WORLD ALMANAC QUICK QUIZ

Which of the following classic American movies did not win an Academy Award for Best Picture?

(a) *The Silence of the Lambs* (1991)
(b) *The French Connection* (1971)
(c) *Casablanca* (1943)
(d) *The Graduate* (1967)

For the answer look in this chapter, or see page 1008.

The Spingarn Medal, 1915-2005

The Spingarn Medal has been awarded annually since 1915 (except in 1938) by the National Assoc. for the Advancement of Colored People for outstanding achievement by an African American.

1915 Ernest E. Just
1916 Charles Young
1917 Harry T. Burleigh
1918 William S. Braithwaite
1919 Archibald H. Grimké
1920 W. E. B. Du Bois
1921 Charles S. Gilpin
1922 Mary B. Talbert
1923 George W.Carver
1924 Roland Hayes
1925 James W. Johnson
1926 Carter G. Woodson
1927 Anthony Overton
1928 Charles W. Chesnutt
1929 Mordecai W. Johnson
1930 Henry A. Hunt
1931 Richard B. Harrison
1932 Robert R. Moton
1933 Max Yergan
1934 William T. B. Williams
1935 Mary McLeod Bethune
1936 John Hope
1937 Walter White
1939 Marian Anderson
1940 Louis T. Wright
1941 Richard Wright
1942 A. Philip Randolph
1943 William H. Hastie
1944 Charles Drew
1945 Paul Robeson
1946 Thurgood Marshall
1947 Dr. Percy L. Julian
1948 Channing H. Tobias
1949 Ralph J. Bunche
1950 Charles H. Houston
1951 Mabel K. Staupers
1952 Harry T. Moore
1953 Paul R. Williams
1954 Theodore K. Lawless
1955 Carl Murphy
1956 Jack R. Robinson
1957 Martin Luther King Jr.
1958 Daisy Bates and the Little Rock Nine
1959 Duke Ellington
1960 Langston Hughes
1961 Kenneth B. Clark
1962 Robert C. Weaver
1963 Medgar W. Evers
1964 Roy Wilkins
1965 Leontyne Price
1966 John H. Johnson
1967 Edward W. Brooke
1968 Sammy Davis Jr.
1969 Clarence M. Mitchell Jr.
1970 Jacob Lawrence
1971 Leon H. Sullivan
1972 Gordon Parks
1973 Wilson C. Riles
1974 Damon Keith
1975 Henry (Hank) Aaron
1976 Alvin Ailey
1977 Alex Haley
1978 Andrew Young
1979 Rosa L. Parks
1980 Dr. Rayford W. Logan
1981 Coleman Young
1982 Dr. Benjamin E. Mays
1983 Lena Horne
1984 Thomas Bradley
1985 Bill Cosby
1986 Dr. Benjamin L. Hooks
1987 Percy E. Sutton
1988 Frederick D. Patterson
1989 Jesse Jackson
1990 L. Douglas Wilder
1991 Gen. Colin L. Powell
1992 Barbara Jordan
1993 Dorothy I. Height
1994 Maya Angelou
1995 John Hope Franklin
1996 A. Leon Higginbotham
1997 Carl T. Rowan
1998 Myrlie Evers-Williams
1999 Earl G. Graves Sr.
2000 Oprah Winfrey
2001 Vernon E. Jordan Jr.
2002 John Lewis
2003 Constance Baker Motley
2004 Robert L. Carter
2005 Oliver W. Hill

Miscellaneous Awards, 2005

(unless otherwise noted)

American Academy of Arts and Letters: Gold Medal for Painting: Jane Freilicher. Award for Distinguished Service to the Arts: James Levine. Arnold W. Brunner Memorial Prize in Architecture, $5,000: Shigeru Ban. Academy Awards, $7,500 each, in Architecture: Gisue Hariri & Mojgan Hariri, Toshiko Mori, Massimo & Lella Vignelli; in Art: Phong Bui, Kendall Buster, Lynn Davis, Judith Murray, Phoebe Washburn; in Music: Ross Bauer, Richard Festinger, David Glaser, Matthew Greenbaum. Jimmy Ernst Award in Art, $5,000: Richard Haas. Walter Hinrichsen Award (Music): Paul Yeon Lee. Charles Ives Fellowships in Music, $15,000: Edward Jacobs, Kurt Rohde. Goddard Lieberson Fellowships in Music, $15,000 each: Allen Anderson, Roger Briggs. Richard Rodgers Awards for the Musical Theater, $100,000 (staged readings): *Bringers*, Paul Libman and David Hudson; *Broadcast*, Scott Murphy and Nathan Christensen; *Red*, Brian Lowdermilk and Marcus Stevens. Richard and Hinda Rosenthal Foundation Award in Art, $5,000: Alessandra Esposito.

Congressional Gold Medal, by Congress: Jackie Robinson, March 2, 2005.

Intel Science Talent Search (formerly given by Westinghouse): First ($100,000 schol.): David Vigliarolo Bauer, Bronx, NY; second ($75,000 schol.): Timothy Frank Credo, Highland Park, IL; third ($50,000 schol.): Kelley Harris, Sacramento, CA.

John F. Kennedy Center for the Performing Arts Awards (Dec. 2004): Warren Beatty, Sir Elton John, Ossie Davis & Ruby Dee, Dame Joan Sutherland, John Williams.

Library of the Year Award, by Thomson Gale and *Library Journal.* Fayetteville Public Library, $10,000.

National Humanities Medal (formerly Charles Frankel Prize), by National Endowment for the Humanities. $5,000 each (2004): Marva Collins, Gertrude Himmelfarb, Hilton Kramer, Madeleine L'Engle, Harvey C. Mansfield, John Searle, Shelby Steele, U.S. Capitol Historical Society.

National Inventor of the Year Awards, by Intellectual Property Owners Education Foundation. Drs. Duane Burnett, John Clader, Sundeep Dugar, Brian McKittrick, & Stuart Rosenblum of Schering-Plough.

National Medal of the Arts, by the National Endowment for the Arts and the White House. Andrew W. Mellon Foundation, Ray Bradbury, Carlisle Floyd, Frederick Hart, Anthony Hecht, John Ruthven, Vincent Scully, Twyla Tharp.

Presidential Medal of Freedom, by the White House (Dec. 2004): L. Paul Bremer III, Tommy R. Franks, George J. Tenet.

Pritzker Architecture Prize, by the Hyatt Foundation, $100,000: Thom Mayne, U.S.

Teacher of the Year, by Council of Chief State School Officers and Scholastic, Inc.: Jason Kamras, John Philip Sousa Middle School, Washington, DC.

Templeton Prize for Progress Toward Research or Discoveries about Spiritual Realities, by Templeton Foundation, £795,000 (about $1.4 million): Charles Townes.

Miss America Winners, for 1921-2005

The Sept. 2005 Miss America pageant and award were postponed, with future pageants to be held in Jan. (starting in 2006) and broadcast by Country Music Television (CMT) rather than ABC, from a location to be determined, no longer Atlantic City.

1921	Margaret Gorman, Washington, DC
1922-23	Mary Campbell, Columbus, Ohio
1924	Ruth Malcolmson, Philadelphia, Pennsylvania
1925	Fay Lamphier, Oakland, California
1926	Norma Smallwood, Tulsa, Oklahoma
1927	Lois Delander, Joliet, Illinois
1933	Marion Bergeron, West Haven, Connecticut
1935	Henrietta Leaver, Pittsburgh, Pennsylvania
1936	Rose Coyle, Philadelphia, Pennsylvania
1937	Bette Cooper, Bertrand Island, New Jersey
1938	Marilyn Meseke, Marion, Ohio
1939	Patricia Donnelly, Detroit, Michigan
1940	Frances Marie Burke, Philadelphia, Pennsylvania
1941	Rosemary LaPlanche, Los Angeles, California
1942	Jo-Caroll Dennison, Tyler, Texas
1943	Jean Bartel, Los Angeles, California
1944	Venus Ramey, Washington, D.C.
1945	Bess Myerson, New York City, New York
1946	Marilyn Buferd, Los Angeles, California
1947	Barbara Walker, Memphis, Tennessee
1948	BeBe Shopp, Hopkins, Minnesota
1949	Jacque Mercer, Litchfield, Arizona
1951	Yolande Betbeze, Mobile, Alabama
1952	Coleen Kay Hutchins, Salt Lake City, Utah
1953	Neva Jane Langley, Macon, Georgia
1954	Evelyn Margaret Ay, Ephrata, Pennsylvania
1955	Lee Meriwether, San Francisco, California
1956	Sharon Ritchie, Denver, Colorado
1957	Marian McKnight, Manning, South Carolina
1958	Marilyn Van Derbur, Denver, Colorado
1959	Mary Ann Mobley, Brandon, Mississippi
1960	Lynda Lee Mead, Natchez, Mississippi
1961	Nancy Fleming, Montague, Michigan
1962	Maria Fletcher, Asheville, North Carolina
1963	Jacquelyn Mayer, Sandusky, Ohio
1964	Donna Axum, El Dorado, Arkansas
1965	Vonda Kay Van Dyke, Phoenix, Arizona
1966	Deborah Irene Bryant, Overland Park, Kansas
1967	Jane Anne Jayroe, Laverne, Oklahoma
1968	Debra Dene Barnes, Moran, Kansas
1969	Judith Anne Ford, Belvidere, Illinois
1970	Pamela Anne Eldred, Birmingham, Michigan
1971	Phyllis Ann George, Denton, Texas
1972	Laurie Lea Schaefer, Columbus, Ohio
1973	Terry Anne Meeuwsen, DePere, Wisconsin
1974	Rebecca Ann King, Denver, Colorado
1975	Shirley Cothran, Fort Worth, Texas
1976	Tawney Elaine Godin, Yonkers, New York
1977	Dorothy Kathleen Benham, Edina, Minnesota
1978	Susan Perkins, Columbus, Ohio
1979	Kylene Barker, Galax, Virginia
1980	Cheryl Prewitt, Ackerman, Mississippi
1981	Susan Powell, Elk City, Oklahoma
1982	Elizabeth Ward, Russellville, Arkansas
1983	Debra Maffett, Anaheim, California
1984	Vanessa Williams*, Milwood, New York
	Suzette Charles, Mays Landing, New Jersey
1985	Sharlene Wells, Salt Lake City, Utah

1986	Susan Akin, Meridian, Mississippi
1987	Kellye Cash, Memphis, Tennessee
1988	Kaye Lani Rae Rafko, Monroe, Michigan
1989	Gretchen Carlson, Anoka, Minnesota
1990	Debbye Turner, Columbia, Missouri
1991	Marjorie Vincent, Oak Park, Illinois
1992	Carolyn Suzanne Sapp, Honolulu, Hawaii
1993	Leanza Cornett, Jacksonville, Florida
1994	Kimberly Aiken, Columbia, South Carolina
1995	Heather Whitestone, Birmingham, Alabama
1996	Shawntel Smith, Muldrow, Oklahoma
1997	Tara Dawn Holland, Overland Park, Kansas
1998	Kate Shindle, Evanston, Illinois
1999	Nicole Johnson, Roanoke, Virginia
2000	Heather Renee French, Maysville, Kentucky
2001	Angela Perez Baraquio, Honolulu, Hawaii
2002	Katie Harman, Gresham, Oregon
2003	Erika Harold, Urbana, Illinois
2004	Ericka Dunlap, Orlando, Florida
2005	Deidre Downs, Birmingham, Alabama

* Resigned July 23, 1984.

Entertainment Awards

Tony (Antoinette Perry) Awards, 2005

Play: *Doubt*, by John Patrick Shanley
Musical: *Monty Python's Spamalot*
Book of a musical: Rachel Sheinkin, *The 25th Annual Putnam County Spelling Bee*
Actor, play: Bill Irwin, *Who's Afraid of Virginia Woolf?*
Actress, play: Cherry Jones, *Doubt*
Actor, musical: Norbert Leo Butz, *Dirty Rotten Scoundrels*
Actress, musical: Victoria Clark, *The Light in the Piazza*
Musical score: Adam Guettel, *The Light in the Piazza*
Director, play: Doug Hughes, *Doubt*
Director, musical: Mike Nichols, *Monty Python's Spamalot*
Play revival: *Glengarry Glen Ross*
Musical revival: *La Cage aux Folles*
Featured actor, play: Liev Schreiber, *Glengarry Glen Ross*
Featured actress, play: Adriane Lenox, *Doubt*
Featured actor, musical: Dan Fogler, *The 25th Annual Putnam County Spelling Bee*
Featured actress, musical: Sara Ramirez, *Monty Python's Spamalot*
Choreography: Jerry Mitchell, *La Cage aux Folles*
Costume design, play: Jess Goldstein, *The Rivals*
Costume design, musical: Catherine Zuber, *The Light in the Piazza*
Scenic design, play: Scott Pask, *The Pillowman*
Scenic design, musical: Michael Yeargan, *The Light in the Piazza*
Lighting design, play: Brian MacDeavitt, *The Pillowman*
Lighting design, musical: Christopher Akerlind, *The Light in the Piazza*
Orchestrations: Ted Sperling, Adam Guettel, & Bruce Couglin, *The Light in the Piazza*
Lifetime achievement: Edward Albee
Regional Theater: Theatre de la Jeune Lune, Minneapolis

Tony Awards, 1948-2005

Year	Play	Musical
1948	*Mister Roberts*	No Award
1949	*Death of a Salesman*	*Kiss Me Kate*
1950	*The Cocktail Party*	*South Pacific*
1951	*The Rose Tattoo*	*Guys and Dolls*
1952	*The Fourposter*	*The King and I*
1953	*The Crucible*	*Wonderful Town*
1954	*The Teahouse of the August Moon*	*Kismet*
1955	*The Desperate Hours*	*The Pajama Game*
1956	*The Diary of Anne Frank*	*Damn Yankees*
1957	*Long Day's Journey Into Night*	*My Fair Lady*
1958	*Sunrise at Campobello*	*The Music Man*
1959	*J.B.*	*Redhead*
1960	*The Miracle Worker*	(tie) *Fiorello!*, *The Sound of Music*
1961	*Becket*	*Bye, Bye Birdie*
1962	*A Man for All Seasons*	*How to Succeed in Business Without Really Trying*
1963	*Who's Afraid of Virginia Woolf?*	*A Funny Thing Happened on the Way to the Forum*
1964	*Luther*	*Hello, Dolly!*
1965	*The Subject Was Roses*	*Fiddler on the Roof*
1966	*Marat/Sade*	*Man of La Mancha*
1967	*The Homecoming*	*Cabaret*
1968	*Rosencrantz and Guildenstern Are Dead*	*Hallelujah, Baby!*
1969	*The Great White Hope*	*1776*
1970	*Borstal Boy*	*Applause*
1971	*Sleuth*	*Company*
1972	*Sticks and Bones*	*Two Gentleman of Verona*
1973	*That Championship Season*	*A Little Night Music*
1974	*The River Niger*	*Raisin*
1975	*Equus*	*The Wiz*
1976	*Travesties*	*A Chorus Line*
1977	*The Shadow Box*	*Annie*
1978	*Da*	*Ain't Misbehavin'*
1979	*The Elephant Man*	Sweeney Todd
1980	*Children of a Lesser God*	*Evita*
1981	*Amadeus*	*42nd Street*
1982	*The Life and Adventures of Nicholas Nickelby*	*Nine*
1983	*Torch Song Trilogy*	*Cats*
1984	*The Real Thing*	*La Cage aux Folles*
1985	*Biloxi Blues*	*Big River*
1986	*I'm Not Rappaport*	*The Mystery of Edwin Drood*
1987	*Fences*	*Les Miserables*
1988	*M. Butterfly*	*Phantom of the Opera*
1989	*The Heidi Chronicles*	*Jerome Robbins' Broadway*
1990	*The Grapes of Wrath*	*City of Angels*
1991	*Lost in Yonkers*	*The Will Rogers Follies*
1992	*Dancing at Lughnasa*	*Crazy for You*
1993	*Angels in America: Millennium Approaches*	*Kiss of the Spider Woman*
1994	*Angels in America: Perestroika*	*Passion*
1995	*Love! Valour! Compassion!*	*Sunset Boulevard*
1996	*Master Class*	*Rent*
1997	*The Last Night of Ballyhoo*	*Titanic*
1998	*Art*	*The Lion King*
1999	*Side Man*	*Fosse*
2000	*Copenhagen*	*Contact*
2001	*Proof*	*The Producers*
2002	*Edward Albee's The Goat or Who Is Sylvia?*	*Thoroughly Modern Millie*
2003	*Take Me Out*	*Hairspray*
2004	*I Am My Own Wife*	*Avenue Q*
2005	*Doubt*	*Monty Python's Spamalot*

2005 Selected Daytime Emmy Awards (for 2004-05 season)

Drama series: *General Hospital*, ABC
Actress: Erika Slezak, *One Life to Live*, ABC
Actor: Christian LeBlanc, *The Young and the Restless*, CBS
Sup. actress: Natalia Livingston, *General Hospital*, ABC
Sup. actor: Greg Rikaart, *The Young and the Restless*, CBS
Younger actress: Eden Riegel, *All My Children*, ABC
Younger actor: David Lago, *The Young and the Restless*, CBS
Drama series directing team: *General Hospital*, ABC
Drama series writing team: *As the World Turns*, CBS
Performer in children's series: Kevin Clash, *Sesame Street*, PBS
Performer in children's special: Stockard Channing, *Jack*, Showtime
Performer in an animated program: Henry Winkler, *Clifford's Puppy Days*, PBS
Game/audience participation show: *Jeopardy!*, syndicated
Game show host: Meredith Vieira, *Who Wants to Be a Millionaire*, synd.
Talk show: *The Ellen DeGeneres Show*, synd.
Talk show host: Ellen DeGeneres, *The Ellen DeGeneres Show.*
Outstanding service show host: (tie) Bobby Flay, *Boy Meets Grill*, and Michael Chiarello, *Easy Entertaining with Michael Chiarello*, Food Network
Lifetime Achievement Award: Merv Griffin

Selected 2005 Prime-Time Emmy Awards (for 2004-2005 TV season)

Drama series: *Lost*, ABC
Comedy series: *Everybody Loves Raymond*, CBS
Miniseries: *The Lost Prince (Masterpiece Theatre)*, PBS
Variety, music, or comedy series: *The Daily Show With Jon Stewart*, Comedy Central
Made-for-television movie: *Warm Springs*, HBO
Lead actor, drama: James Spader, *Boston Legal*, ABC
Lead actress, drama: Patricia Arquette, *Medium*, NBC
Lead actor, comedy: Tony Shalhoub, *Monk*, USA
Lead actress, comedy: Felicity Huffman, *Desperate Housewives*, ABC
Lead actor, miniseries/movie: Geoffrey Rush, *The Life and Death of Peter Sellers*, HBO
Lead actress, miniseries/movie: S. Epatha Merkerson, *Lackawanna Blues*, HBO
Sup. actor, drama: William Shatner, *Boston Legal*, ABC
Sup. actress, drama: Blythe Danner, *Huff*, HBO
Sup. actor, comedy: Brad Garrett, *Everybody Loves Raymond*,CBS
Sup. actress, comedy: Doris Roberts, *Everybody Loves Raymond*, CBS
Sup. actor, miniseries/movie: Paul Newman, *Empire Falls*, HBO
Sup. actress, miniseries/movie: Jane Alexander, *Warm Springs*, HBO
Individual performance, variety series/music program: Hugh Jackman, *The 58th Annual Tony Awards (2004)*, CBS
Reality/competition program: *The Amazing Race*, CBS

Prime-Time Emmy Awards, 1952-2005

The National Academy of Television Arts and Science presented the first Emmy Awards in 1949. Through the years, award categories have changed, but since 1952, the Academy has given out an outstanding comedy and drama award each year.

Year	Comedy	Drama
1952	*Red Skelton Show*, NBC	*Studio One*, CBS
1953	*I Love Lucy*, CBS	*Robert Montgomery Presents*, NBC
1954	*I Love Lucy*, CBS	*The U.S. Steel Hour*, ABC
1955	*Make Room for Daddy*, ABC	*The U.S. Steel Hour*, ABC
1956	*Phil Silvers Show*, CBS	*Producer's Showcase*, NBC
1957[1]	*Phil Silvers Show*, CBS	*Requiem for a Heavyweight*, CBS
1958	*Phil Silvers Show*, CBS	*Gunsmoke*, CBS
1959[2]	*Jack Benny Show*, CBS	*
1960	*Art Carney Special*, NBC	*Playhouse 90*, CBS
1961	*Jack Benny Show*, CBS	*Hallmark Hall of Fame: Macbeth*, NBC
1962	*Bob Newhart Show*, CBS	*The Defenders*, CBS
1963	*Dick Van Dyke Show*, CBS	*The Defenders*, CBS
1964	*Dick Van Dyke Show*, CBS	*The Defenders*, CBS
1965	*Dick Van Dyke Show*, CBS	*Hallmark Hall of Fame: The Magnificent Yankee*, NBC
1966	*Dick Van Dyke Show*, CBS	*The Fugitive*, ABC
1967	*The Monkees*, NBC	*Mission: Impossible*, CBS
1968	*Get Smart*, NBC	*Mission: Impossible*, CBS
1969	*Get Smart*, NBC	*NET Playhouse*, NET
1970	*My World and Welcome to It*, NBC	*Marcus Welby, M.D.*, ABC
1971	*All in the Family*, CBS	*The Bold Ones: "The Senator,"* NBC
1972	*All in the Family*, CBS	*Masterpiece Theatre: Elizabeth R*, PBS
1973	*All in the Family*, CBS	*The Waltons*, CBS
1974	*M*A*S*H*, CBS	*Masterpiece Theatre: Upstairs, Downstairs;* PBS
1975	*Mary Tyler Moore Show*, CBS	*Masterpiece Theatre: Upstairs, Downstairs;* PBS
1976	*Mary Tyler Moore Show*, CBS	*Police Story*, NBC
1977	*Mary Tyler Moore Show*, CBS	*Masterpiece Theatre: Upstairs, Downstairs;* PBS
1978	*All in the Family*, CBS	*The Rockford Files*, NBC
1979	*Taxi*, ABC	*Lou Grant*, CBS
1980	*Taxi*, ABC	*Lou Grant*, CBS
1981	*Taxi*, ABC	*Hill Street Blues*, NBC
1982	*Barney Miller*, ABC	*Hill Street Blues*, NBC
1983	*Cheers*, NBC	*Hill Street Blues*, NBC
1984	*Cheers*, NBC	*Hill Street Blues*, NBC
1985	*The Cosby Show*, NBC	*Cagney & Lacey*, CBS
1986	*Golden Girls*, NBC	*Cagney & Lacey*, CBS
1987	*Golden Girls*, NBC	*L.A. Law*, NBC
1988	*The Wonder Years*, ABC	*thirtysomething*, ABC
1989	*Cheers*, NBC	*L.A. Law*, NBC
1990	*Murphy Brown*, CBS	*L.A. Law*, NBC
1991	*Cheers*, NBC	*L.A. Law*, NBC
1992	*Murphy Brown*, CBS	*Northern Exposure*, CBS
1993	*Seinfeld*, NBC	*Picket Fences*, CBS
1994	*Frasier*, NBC	*Picket Fences*, CBS
1995	*Frasier*, NBC	*NYPD Blue*, ABC
1996	*Frasier*, NBC	*ER*, NBC
1997	*Frasier*, NBC	*Law & Order*, NBC
1998	*Frasier*, NBC	*The Practice*, ABC
1999	*Ally McBeal*, Fox	*The Practice*, ABC
2000	*Will & Grace*, NBC	*The West Wing*, NBC
2001	*Sex and the City*, HBO	*The West Wing*, NBC
2002	*Friends*, NBC	*The West Wing*, NBC
2003	*Everybody Loves Raymond*, CBS	*The West Wing*, NBC
2004	*Arrested Development*, Fox	*The Sopranos*, HBO
2005	*Everybody Loves Raymond*, CBS	*Lost*, ABC

(1) "Best Single Program of the Year," shown on *Playhouse 90*, which was named "Best New Series." (2) Beginning in 1959, Emmys awarded for work in the season encompassing the previous and current year. (*) *Playhouse 90* (CBS) was best drama of 1 hour or longer; *Alcoa-Goodyear Theatre* (NBC) was best drama of less than 1 hour.

2005 Golden Globe Awards

Film

Drama: *The Aviator*
Musical/comedy: *Sideways*
Actress, drama: Hilary Swank, *Million Dollar Baby*
Actor, drama: Leonardo DiCaprio, *The Aviator*
Actress, musical/comedy: Annette Bening, *Being Julia*
Actor, musical/comedy: Jamie Foxx, *Ray*
Sup. actress: Natalie Portman, *Closer*
Sup. actor: Clive Owen, *Closer*
Director: Clint Eastwood, *Million Dollar Baby*
Screenplay: Alexander Payne, Jim Taylor, *Sideways*
Foreign-language film: *The Sea Inside* (Spain)
Original score: Howard Shore, *The Aviator*
Original song: "Old Habits Die Hard," from *Alfie*, Mick Jagger, David A. Stewart
Cecil B. DeMille award for lifetime achievement: Robin Williams

Television

Series, drama: *Nip/Tuck*, FX
Actress, drama: Mariska Hargitay, *Law and Order: Special Victims Unit*, NBC
Actor, drama: Ian McShane, *Deadwood*, HBO
Series, musical/comedy: *Desperate Housewives*, ABC
Actress, musical/comedy: Teri Hatcher, *Desperate Housewives*, ABC
Actor, musical/comedy: Jason Bateman, *Arrested Development*, FOX
Miniseries, movie made for TV: *The Life and Death of Peter Sellers*, HBO
Actress, miniseries/movie: Glenn Close, *The Lion in Winter*, Showtime
Actor, miniseries/movie: Geoffrey Rush, *The Life and Death of Peter Sellers*, HBO
Sup. actress, series/miniseries/movie: Anjelica Huston, *Iron Jawed Angels*, HBO
Sup. actor, series/miniseries/movie: William Shatner, *Boston Legal*, ABC

2005 People's Choice Awards

Film

Picture: *Fahrenheit 9/11*
Drama: *The Passion of the Christ*
Comedy: *Shrek 2*
Movie stars: Johnny Depp, Julia Roberts
Action movie stars: Will Smith, Angelina Jolie

Music

Male performer: Usher
Female performer: Alicia Keys
Group or band: U2

Television

Drama: *CSI: Crime Scene Investigation*
Comedy: *Will & Grace*
Male performer: Matt LeBlanc, *Joey*
Female performer: Marg Helgenberger, *CSI*
New comedy: *Joey*
New drama: *Desperate Housewives*
Talk show host, daytime: Ellen DeGeneres
Talk show host, late-night: David Letterman
Reality program (competition): *American Idol*
Reality program (makeover): *Extreme Makeover: Home Edition*

Academy Awards (Oscars) for 1927-2004

Year	Picture	Actor	Actress	Sup. Actor[1]	Sup. Actress[1]	Director
1927-28	*Wings*	Emil Jannings, *The Way of All Flesh*	Janet Gaynor, *Seventh Heaven*			Frank Borzage, *Seventh Heaven*; Lewis Milestone, *Two Arabian Knights*
1928-29	*Broadway Melody*	Warner Baxter, *In Old Arizona*	Mary Pickford, *Coquette*			Frank Lloyd, *The Divine Lady*
1929-30	*All Quiet on the Western Front*	George Arliss *Disraeli*	Norma Shearer *The Divorcee*			Lewis Milestone *All Quiet on the Western Front*
1930-31	*Cimarron*	Lionel Barrymore *Free Soul*	Marie Dressler *Min and Bill*			Norman Taurog *Skippy*
1931-32	*Grand Hotel*	Fredric March *Dr. Jekyll and Mr. Hyde;* Wallace Beery *The Champ* (tie)	Helen Hayes *The Sin of Madelon Claudet*			Frank Borzage *Bad Girl*
1932-33	*Cavalcade*	Charles Laughton *The Private Life of Henry VIII*	Katharine Hepburn *Morning Glory*			Frank Lloyd *Cavalcade*
1934	*It Happened One Night*	Clark Gable *It Happened One Night*	Claudette Colbert *It Happened One Night*			Frank Capra *It Happened One Night*
1935	*Mutiny on the Bounty*	Victor McLaglen *The Informer*	Bette Davis *Dangerous*			John Ford *The Informer*
1936	*The Great Ziegfeld*	Paul Muni *Story of Louis Pasteur*	Luise Rainer *The Great Ziegfeld*	Walter Brennan *Come and Get It*	Gale Sondergaard *Anthony Adverse*	Frank Capra *Mr. Deeds Goes to Town*
1937	*Life of Emile Zola*	Spencer Tracy *Captains Courageous*	Luise Rainer *The Good Earth*	Joseph Schildkraut *Life of Emile Zola*	Alice Brady *In Old Chicago*	Leo McCarey *The Awful Truth*
1938	*You Can't Take It With You*	Spencer Tracy *Boys Town*	Bette Davis *Jezebel*	Walter Brennan *Kentucky*	Fay Bainter *Jezebel*	Frank Capra *You Can't Take It With You*
1939	*Gone With the Wind*	Robert Donat *Goodbye Mr. Chips*	Vivien Leigh *Gone With the Wind*	Thomas Mitchell *Stage Coach*	Hattie McDaniel *Gone With the Wind*	Victor Fleming *Gone With the Wind*
1940	*Rebecca*	James Stewart *The Philadelphia Story*	Ginger Rogers *Kitty Foyle*	Walter Brennan *The Westerner*	Jane Darwell *The Grapes of Wrath*	John Ford *The Grapes of Wrath*
1941	*How Green Was My Valley*	Gary Cooper *Sergeant York*	Joan Fontaine *Suspicion*	Donald Crisp *How Green Was My Valley*	Mary Astor *The Great Lie*	John Ford *How Green Was My Valley*
1942	*Mrs. Miniver*	James Cagney *Yankee Doodle Dandy*	Greer Garson *Mrs. Miniver*	Van Heflin *Johnny Eager*	Teresa Wright *Mrs. Miniver*	William Wyler *Mrs. Miniver*
1943	*Casablanca*	Paul Lukas *Watch on the Rhine*	Jennifer Jones *The Song of Bernadette*	Charles Coburn *The More the Merrier*	Katina Paxinou *For Whom the Bell Tolls*	Michael Curtiz *Casablanca*
1944	*Going My Way*	Bing Crosby *Going My Way*	Ingrid Bergman *Gaslight*	Barry Fitzgerald *Going My Way*	Ethel Barrymore *None But the Lonely Heart*	Leo McCarey *Going My Way*
1945	*The Lost Weekend*	Ray Milland *The Lost Weekend*	Joan Crawford *Mildred Pierce*	James Dunn *A Tree Grows in Brooklyn*	Anne Revere *National Velvet*	Billy Wilder *The Lost Weekend*
1946	*The Best Years of Our Lives*	Fredric March *The Best Years of Our Lives*	Olivia de Havilland *To Each His Own*	Harold Russell *The Best Years of Our Lives*	Anne Baxter *The Razor's Edge*	William Wyler *The Best Years of Our Lives*
1947	*Gentleman's Agreement*	Ronald Colman *A Double Life*	Loretta Young *The Farmer's Daughter*	Edmund Gwenn *Miracle on 34th Street*	Celeste Holm *Gentleman's Agreement*	Elia Kazan *Gentleman's Agreement*
1948	*Hamlet*	Laurence Olivier *Hamlet*	Jane Wyman *Johnny Belinda*	Walter Huston *Treasure of Sierra Madre*	Claire Trevor *Key Largo*	John Huston *Treasure of Sierra Madre*
1949	*All the King's Men*	Broderick Crawford *All the King's Men*	Olivia de Havilland *The Heiress*	Dean Jagger *Twelve O'Clock High*	Mercedes McCambridge *All the King's Men*	Joseph L. Mankiewicz *Letter to Three Wives*
1950	*All About Eve*	Jose Ferrer *Cyrano de Bergerac*	Judy Holliday *Born Yesterday*	George Sanders *All About Eve*	Josephine Hull *Harvey*	Joseph L. Mankiewicz *All About Eve*
1951	*An American in Paris*	Humphrey Bogart *The African Queen*	Vivien Leigh *A Streetcar Named Desire*	Karl Malden *A Streetcar Named Desire*	Kim Hunter *A Streetcar Named Desire*	George Stevens *A Place in the Sun*
1952	*The Greatest Show on Earth*	Gary Cooper *High Noon*	Shirley Booth *Come Back Little Sheba*	Anthony Quinn *Viva Zapata!*	Gloria Grahame *The Bad and the Beautiful*	John Ford *The Quiet Man*
1953	*From Here to Eternity*	William Holden *Stalag 17*	Audrey Hepburn *Roman Holiday*	Frank Sinatra *From Here to Eternity*	Donna Reed *From Here to Eternity*	Fred Zinnemann *From Here to Eternity*
1954	*On the Waterfront*	Marlon Brando *On the Waterfront*	Grace Kelly *The Country Girl*	Edmond O'Brien *The Barefoot Contessa*	Eva Marie Saint *On the Waterfront*	Elia Kazan *On the Waterfront*
1955	*Marty*	Ernest Borgnine *Marty*	Anna Magnani *The Rose Tattoo*	Jack Lemmon *Mister Roberts*	Jo Van Fleet *East of Eden*	Delbert Mann *Marty*
1956	*Around the World in 80 Days*	Yul Brynner *The King and I*	Ingrid Bergman *Anastasia*	Anthony Quinn *Lust for Life*	Dorothy Malone *Written on the Wind*	George Stevens *Giant*
1957	*The Bridge on the River Kwai*	Alec Guinness *The Bridge on the River Kwai*	Joanne Woodward *The Three Faces of Eve*	Red Buttons *Sayonara*	Miyoshi Umeki *Sayonara*	David Lean *The Bridge on the River Kwai*

Year	Picture	Actor	Actress	Sup. Actor[1]	Sup. Actress[1]	Director
1958	*Gigi*	David Niven *Separate Tables*	Susan Hayward *I Want to Live*	Burl Ives *The Big Country*	Wendy Hiller *Separate Tables*	Vincente Minnelli *Gigi*
1959	*Ben-Hur*	Charlton Heston *Ben-Hur*	Simone Signoret *Room at the Top*	Hugh Griffith *Ben-Hur*	Shelley Winters *Diary of Anne Frank*	William Wyler *Ben-Hur*
1960	*The Apartment*	Burt Lancaster *Elmer Gantry*	Elizabeth Taylor *Butterfield 8*	Peter Ustinov *Spartacus*	Shirley Jones *Elmer Gantry*	Billy Wilder *The Apartment*
1961	*West Side Story*	Maximilian Schell *Judgment at Nuremberg*	Sophia Loren *Two Women*	George Chakiris *West Side Story*	Rita Moreno *West Side Story*	Jerome Robbins, Robert Wise *West Side Story*
1962	*Lawrence of Arabia*	Gregory Peck *To Kill a Mockingbird*	Anne Bancroft *The Miracle Worker*	Ed Begley *Sweet Bird of Youth*	Patty Duke *The Miracle Worker*	David Lean *Lawrence of Arabia*
1963	*Tom Jones*	Sidney Poitier *Lilies of the Field*	Patricia Neal *Hud*	Melvyn Douglas *Hud*	Margaret Rutherford *The V.I.P.s*	Tony Richardson *Tom Jones*
1964	*My Fair Lady*	Rex Harrison *My Fair Lady*	Julie Andrews *Mary Poppins*	Peter Ustinov *Topkapi*	Lila Kedrova *Zorba the Greek*	George Cukor *My Fair Lady*
1965	*The Sound of Music*	Lee Marvin *Cat Ballou*	Julie Christie *Darling*	Martin Balsam *A Thousand Clowns*	Shelley Winters *A Patch of Blue*	Robert Wise *The Sound of Music*
1966	*A Man for All Seasons*	Paul Scofield *A Man for All Seasons*	Elizabeth Taylor *Who's Afraid of Virginia Woolf?*	Walter Matthau *The Fortune Cookie*	Sandy Dennis *Who's Afraid of Virginia Woolf?*	Fred Zinnemann *A Man for All Seasons*
1967	*In the Heat of the Night*	Rod Steiger *In the Heat of the Night*	Katharine Hepburn *Guess Who's Coming to Dinner*	George Kennedy *Cool Hand Luke*	Estelle Parsons *Bonnie and Clyde*	Mike Nichols *The Graduate*
1968	*Oliver!*	Cliff Robertson *Charly*	Katharine Hepburn *The Lion in Winter;* Barbra Streisand *Funny Girl* (tie)	Jack Albertson *The Subject Was Roses*	Ruth Gordon *Rosemary's Baby*	Sir Carol Reed *Oliver!*
1969	*Midnight Cowboy*	John Wayne *True Grit*	Maggie Smith *The Prime of Miss Jean Brodie*	Gig Young *They Shoot Horses, Don't They?*	Goldie Hawn *Cactus Flower*	John Schlesinger *Midnight Cowboy*
1970	*Patton*	George C. Scott *Patton* (refused)	Glenda Jackson *Women in Love*	John Mills *Ryan's Daughter*	Helen Hayes *Airport*	Franklin Schaffner *Patton*
1971	*The French Connection*	Gene Hackman *The French Connection*	Jane Fonda *Klute*	Ben Johnson *The Last Picture Show*	Cloris Leachman *The Last Picture Show*	William Friedkin *The French Connection*
1972	*The Godfather*	Marlon Brando *The Godfather* (refused)	Liza Minnelli *Cabaret*	Joel Grey *Cabaret*	Eileen Heckart *Butterflies Are Free*	Bob Fosse *Cabaret*
1973	*The Sting*	Jack Lemmon *Save the Tiger*	Glenda Jackson *A Touch of Class*	John Houseman *The Paper Chase*	Tatum O'Neal *Paper Moon*	George Roy Hill *The Sting*
1974	*The Godfather Part II*	Art Carney *Harry and Tonto*	Ellen Burstyn *Alice Doesn't Live Here Anymore*	Robert DeNiro *The Godfather Part II*	Ingrid Bergman *Murder on the Orient Express*	Francis Ford Coppola *The Godfather Part II*
1975	*One Flew Over the Cuckoo's Nest*	Jack Nicholson *One Flew Over the Cuckoo's Nest*	Louise Fletcher *One Flew Over the Cuckoo's Nest*	George Burns *The Sunshine Boys*	Lee Grant *Shampoo*	Milos Forman *One Flew Over the Cuckoo's Nest*
1976	*Rocky*	Peter Finch *Network*	Faye Dunaway *Network*	Jason Robards *All the President's Men*	Beatrice Straight *Network*	John G. Avildsen *Rocky*
1977	*Annie Hall*	Richard Dreyfuss *The Goodbye Girl*	Diane Keaton *Annie Hall*	Jason Robards *Julia*	Vanessa Redgrave *Julia*	Woody Allen *Annie Hall*
1978	*The Deer Hunter*	Jon Voight *Coming Home*	Jane Fonda *Coming Home*	Christopher Walken *The Deer Hunter*	Maggie Smith *California Suite*	Michael Cimino *The Deer Hunter*
1979	*Kramer vs. Kramer*	Dustin Hoffman *Kramer vs. Kramer*	Sally Field *Norma Rae*	Melvyn Douglas *Being There*	Meryl Streep *Kramer vs. Kramer*	Robert Benton *Kramer vs. Kramer*
1980	*Ordinary People*	Robert DeNiro *Raging Bull*	Sissy Spacek *Coal Miner's Daughter*	Timothy Hutton *Ordinary People*	Mary Steenburgen *Melvin & Howard*	Robert Redford *Ordinary People*
1981	*Chariots of Fire*	Henry Fonda *On Golden Pond*	Katharine Hepburn *On Golden Pond*	John Gielgud *Arthur*	Maureen Stapleton *Reds*	Warren Beatty *Reds*
1982	*Gandhi*	Ben Kingsley *Gandhi*	Meryl Streep *Sophie's Choice*	Louis Gossett Jr. *An Officer and a Gentleman*	Jessica Lange *Tootsie*	Richard Attenborough *Gandhi*
1983	*Terms of Endearment*	Robert Duvall *Tender Mercies*	Shirley MacLaine *Terms of Endearment*	Jack Nicholson *Terms of Endearment*	Linda Hunt *The Year of Living Dangerously*	James L. Brooks *Terms of Endearment*
1984	*Amadeus*	F. Murray Abraham *Amadeus*	Sally Field *Places in the Heart*	Haing S. Ngor *The Killing Fields*	Peggy Ashcroft *A Passage to India*	Milos Forman *Amadeus*
1985	*Out of Africa*	William Hurt *Kiss of the Spider Woman*	Geraldine Page *The Trip to Bountiful*	Don Ameche *Cocoon*	Anjelica Huston *Prizzi's Honor*	Sydney Pollack *Out of Africa*
1986	*Platoon*	Paul Newman *The Color of Money*	Marlee Matlin *Children of a Lesser God*	Michael Caine *Hannah and Her Sisters*	Dianne Wiest *Hannah and Her Sisters*	Oliver Stone *Platoon*
1987	*The Last Emperor*	Michael Douglas *Wall Street*	Cher *Moonstruck*	Sean Connery *The Untouchables*	Olympia Dukakis *Moonstruck*	Bernardo Bertolucci *The Last Emperor*
1988	*Rain Man*	Dustin Hoffman *Rain Man*	Jodie Foster *The Accused*	Kevin Kline *A Fish Called Wanda*	Geena Davis *The Accidental Tourist*	Barry Levinson *Rain Man*
1989	*Driving Miss Daisy*	Daniel Day-Lewis *My Left Foot*	Jessica Tandy *Driving Miss Daisy*	Denzel Washington *Glory*	Brenda Fricker *My Left Foot*	Oliver Stone *Born on the Fourth of July*
1990	*Dances With Wolves*	Jeremy Irons *Reversal of Fortune*	Kathy Bates *Misery*	Joe Pesci *Goodfellas*	Whoopi Goldberg *Ghost*	Kevin Costner *Dances With Wolves*
1991	*The Silence of the Lambs*	Anthony Hopkins *The Silence of the Lambs*	Jodie Foster *The Silence of the Lambs*	Jack Palance *City Slickers*	Mercedes Ruehl *The Fisher King*	Jonathan Demme *The Silence of the Lambs*
1992	*Unforgiven*	Al Pacino *Scent of a Woman*	Emma Thompson *Howards End*	Gene Hackman *Unforgiven*	Marisa Tomei *My Cousin Vinny*	Clint Eastwood *Unforgiven*

Year	Picture	Actor	Actress	Sup. Actor[1]	Sup. Actress[1]	Director
1993	*Schindler's List*	Tom Hanks *Philadelphia*	Holly Hunter *The Piano*	Tommy Lee Jones *The Fugitive*	Anna Paquin *The Piano*	Steven Spielberg *Schindler's List*
1994	*Forrest Gump*	Tom Hanks *Forrest Gump*	Jessica Lange *Blue Sky*	Martin Landau *Ed Wood*	Dianne Wiest *Bullets Over Broadway*	Robert Zemeckis *Forrest Gump*
1995	*Braveheart*	Nicolas Cage *Leaving Las Vegas*	Susan Sarandon *Dead Man Walking*	Kevin Spacey *The Usual Suspects*	Mira Sorvino *Mighty Aphrodite*	Mel Gibson *Braveheart*
1996	*The English Patient*	Geoffrey Rush *Shine*	Frances McDormand *Fargo*	Cuba Gooding Jr. *Jerry Maguire*	Juliette Binoche *The English Patient*	Anthony Minghella *The English Patient*
1997	*Titanic*	Jack Nicholson *As Good As It Gets*	Helen Hunt *As Good As It Gets*	Robin Williams *Good Will Hunting*	Kim Basinger *L.A. Confidential*	James Cameron *Titanic*
1998	*Shakespeare in Love*	Roberto Benigni *Life Is Beautiful*	Gwyneth Paltrow *Shakespeare in Love*	James Coburn *Affliction*	Judi Dench *Shakespeare in Love*	Steven Spielberg *Saving Private Ryan*
1999	*American Beauty*	Kevin Spacey *American Beauty*	Hilary Swank *Boys Don't Cry*	Michael Caine *The Cider House Rules*	Angelina Jolie *Girl, Interrupted*	Sam Mendes *American Beauty*
2000	*Gladiator*	Russell Crowe *Gladiator*	Julia Roberts *Erin Brockovich*	Benicio Del Toro *Traffic*	Marcia Gay Harden *Pollock*	Steven Soderbergh *Traffic*
2001	*A Beautiful Mind*	Denzel Washington *Training Day*	Halle Berry *Monster's Ball*	Jim Broadbent *Iris*	Jennifer Connelly *A Beautiful Mind*	Ron Howard *A Beautiful Mind*
2002	*Chicago*	Adrien Brody *The Pianist*	Nicole Kidman *The Hours*	Chris Cooper *Adaptation*	Catherine Zeta-Jones *Chicago*	Roman Polanski *The Pianist*
2003	*The Lord of the Rings: The Return of the King*	Sean Penn, *Mystic River*	Charlize Theron, *Monster*	Tim Robbins, *Mystic River*	Renée Zellweger, *Cold Mountain*	Peter Jackson, *The Lord of the Rings: The Return of the King*
2004	*Million Dollar Baby*	Jamie Foxx, *Ray*	Hilary Swank, *Million Dollar Baby*	Morgan Freeman, *Million Dollar Baby*	Cate Blanchett, *The Aviator*	Clint Eastwood, *Million Dollar Baby*

(1) These awards not given until 1936.

OTHER 2004 OSCAR WINNERS: Animated film: *The Incredibles.* Foreign film: *The Sea Inside*, Spain. Original screenplay: Charlie Kaufman, *Eternal Sunshine of the Spotless Mind.* Adapted screenplay: Alexander Payne & Jim Taylor, *Sideways.* Cinematography: Robert Richardson, *The Aviator.* Art direction: Dante Ferretti (art direction); Francesca Lo Schiavo (set decoration), *The Aviator.* Film editing: Thelma Schoonmaker, *The Aviator.* Original song: "Al Otro Lado del Rio," *The Motorcycle Diaries*, music and lyrics by Jorge Drexler. Original score: Jan A.P. Kaczmarek, *Finding Neverland.* Costume design: Sandy Powell, *The Aviator.* Makeup: Valli O'Reilly & Bill Corso, *Lemony Snicket's A Series of Unfortunate Events.* Sound mixing: Scott Millan, Greg Orloff, Bob Beemer, Steve Cantamessa, *Ray.* Documentary feature: Ross Kauffman & Zana Briski, *Born Into Brothels.* Documentary short subject: Robert Hudson & Bobby Houston, *Mighty Times: The Children's March.* Short film, live: Andrea Arnold, *Wasp.* Short film, animated: Chris Landreth, *Ryan.* Visual effects: John Dykstra, Scott Stokdyk, Anthony LaMolinara, John Frazier, *Spiderman 2.* Sound editing: Michael Silvers & Randy Thom, *The Incredibles.* Honorary Oscars: Sidney Lumet, Roger Mayer.

Other Film Awards Awarded in 2005

Cannes Film Festival Awards: Feature Films—Palme d'Or (Golden Palm): *L'Enfant (The Child)*, Jean-Pierre & Luc Dardenne, Belgium; Grand Prix: *Broken Flowers*, Jim Jarmusch, U.S.; Best Actress: Hanna Laslo, *Free Zone*, Israel; Best Actor: Tommy Lee Jones, *The Three Burials of Melquiades Estrada*, U.S.; Best Director: Michael Haneke, *Caché (Hidden)*, Austria; Best Screenplay: Guillermo Arriaga, *The Three Burials of Melquiades Estrada*; Jury Prize: *Shanghai Dreams*, Wang Xiaoshuai, China. Caméra d'Or (Golden Camera; first-time director's prize): (tie) *Sulanga Enu Pinisa (The Forsaken Land)*, Vimukthi Jayasundara, Sri Lanka; *Me and You and Everyone We Know*, Miranda July, U.S.

Short Films—Palme d'Or: *Podorozhni (Wayfarers)*, Igor Strembitskyy, Ukraine; Mention Spéciale: *Clara*, Van Sowerwine, Australia.

Director's Guild of America Awards: Feature film: Clint Eastwood, *Million Dollar Baby*; Documentary, Byambasuren Davaa & Luigi Falorni, *The Story of the Weeping Camel.*

Sundance Film Festival Awards: Grand Jury Prize: (drama) *Forty Shades of Blue,* Ira Sachs; (documentary) *Why We Fight*, Eugene Jarecki. Directing Award: (drama) Noah Baumbach, *The Squid and the Whale*; (doc.) Jeff Feuerzeig, *The Devil and Daniel Johnson.* Waldo Salt Screenwriting Award: Noah Baumbach, *The Squid and the Whale.* Audience Award: (drama): *Hustle & Flow*, Craig Brewer; (doc.) *Murderball*, Henry-Alex Rubin & Dana Adam Shapiro. Cinematography Award: (drama) Amelia Vincent, *Hustle & Flow*; (doc.) Gary Griffin, *The Education of Shelby Knox.* World Cinema Grand Jury Prize: (doc.) *Shape of the Moon*, Leonard Retel Helmrich (Neth.); (drama) *The Hero*, Zézé Gamboa (Ang./Port./Fr.). Special Jury Prize for Acting: Amy Adams, *Junebug*; Lou Pucci, *Thumbsucker.* Alfred P. Sloan Prize: *Grizzly Man*, Werner Herzog. Internat. Filmmakers Awards: Catalin Mitulescu, *How I Spent the End of the World* (Europe); Rodrigo Moreno, *The Minder* (Lat. Amer.); Richard Press, *Virtual Love* (U.S.); Mipo Oh, *Yomoyama Blues* (Japan). Short Filmmaking Jury Prize: *Family Portrait*, Patricia Riggen; *Wasp*, Andrea Arnold.

2005 MTV Video Music Awards

Video of the Year: Green Day, "Boulevard of Broken Dreams"
Best Male Video: Kanye West, "Jesus Walks"
Best Female Video: Kelly Clarkson, "Since U Been Gone"
Best Group Video: Green Day, "Boulevard of Broken Dreams"
Best Dance Video: Missy Elliott featuring Ciara & Fat Man Scoop, "Lose Control"
Best Pop Video: Kelly Clarkson, "Since U Been Gone"
Best R&B Video: Alicia Keys, "Karma"
Best Rap Video: Ludacris, "Number One Spot"
Best Rock Video: Green Day, "Boulevard of Broken Dreams"
Best Hip-Hop Video: Missy Elliott featuring Ciara & Fat Man Scoop, "Lose Control"
Best New Artist: The Killers, "Mr. Brightside"
Breakthrough Video: Gorillaz, "Feel Good INC."
Best Direction: Samuel Bayer for Green Day, "Boulevard of Broken Dreams"
Best Choreography: Gwen Stefani, "Hollaback Girl"
Best Special Effects: Gorillaz, "Feel Good INC."
Best Art Direction: Gwen Stefani, "What You Waiting For?"
Best Editing: Tim Royes for Green Day, "Boulevard of Broken Dreams"
Best Cinematography: Samuel Bayer for Green Day, "Boulevard of Broken Dreams"
Best Soundtrack From a Video Game: "Dance Dance Revolution Extreme"
Best MTV2 Video: Fall Out Boy, "Sugar, We're Goin' Down"
Viewers' Choice: Green Day, "American Idiot"

2005 Academy of Country Music Awards

Entertainer of the Year: Kenny Chesney
Album of the Year: *Be Here,* Keith Urban; Dann Huff and Keith Urban, producers
Single of the Year: "Live Like You Were Dying," Tim McGraw; Tim McGraw, Byron Gallimore, Darran Smith, producers
Top Female Vocalist: Gretchen Wilson
Top Male Vocalist: Keith Urban
Top Vocal Duo: Brooks & Dunn
Top Vocal Group: Rascal Flatts
Top New Artist: Gretchen Wilson
Video of the Year: "Whiskey Lullaby," Brad Paisley (featuring Alison Krauss); Don Lepore, producer; Rick Schroder, dir.
Song of the Year: "Live Like You Were Dying," Tim McGraw; written by Craig Wiseman and Tim Nichols
Vocal Event of the Year: "Whiskey Lullaby," Brad Paisley (featuring Alison Krauss); Frank Rogers, producer
Pioneer Award: Chris LeDoux
Humanitarian Award: Neal McCoy

Grammy Awards

Source: National Academy of Recording Arts & Sciences

Selected Grammy Awards for 2004

Record of the Year (single): "Here We Go Again," Ray Charles & Norah Jones
Album of the Year: *Genius Loves Company,* Ray Charles & various artists
Song of the Year: "Daughters," John Mayer
New artist: Maroon 5
Pop vocal perf., female: "Sunrise," Norah Jones
Pop vocal perf., male: "Daughters," John Mayer
Pop vocal perf., duo/group: "Heaven," Los Lonely Boys
Pop vocal album, traditional: *Stardust...The Great American Songbook Vol. III,* Rod Stewart
Pop instrumental album: *Henry Mancini: Pink Guitar*, various artists
Pop vocal album: *Genius Loves Company*, Ray Charles and various artists
Dance recording: "Toxic," Britney Spears
Rock vocal perf., solo: "Code of Silence," Bruce Springsteen
Rock vocal perf., duo/group: "Vertigo," U2
Rock instrumental perf.: "Mrs. O'Leary's Cow," Brian Wilson
Hard rock perf.: "Slither," Velvet Revolver
Metal perf.: "Whiplash," Motörhead
Rock song: "Vertigo," Bono, Adam Clayton, The Edge, and Larry Mullen (U2)
Rock album: *American Idiot,* Green Day
R&B vocal perf., female: "If I Ain't Got You," Alicia Keys
R&B vocal perf., male: "Call My Name," Prince
R&B vocal perf., duo/group: "My Boo," Usher & Alicia Keys
R&B song: "You Don't Know My Name," Alicia Keys, Harold Lilly, & Kanye West (Alicia Keys)
R&B album: *The Diary of Alicia Keys,* Alicia Keys
R&B album, contemporary: *Confessions,* Usher
Rap solo perf: "99 Problems," Jay-Z
Rap perf., duo/group: "Let's Get It Started," The Black Eyed Peas
Rap album: *The College Dropout*, Kanye West
Country vocal perf., female: "Redneck Woman," Gretchen Wilson
Country vocal perf., male: "Live Like You Were Dying," Tim McGraw
Country perf. with vocal, duo/group: "Top of the World," Dixie Chicks
Country song: "Live Like You Were Dying," Tim Nichols & Craig Wiseman (Tim McGraw)
Country album: *Van Lear Rose,* Loretta Lynn
Bluegrass album: *Brand New Strings,* Ricky Skaggs & Kentucky Thunder
Jazz album, vocal: *R.S.V.P. (Rare Songs, Very Personal),* Nancy Wilson
Jazz album, instr.: *Illuminations*, McCoy Tyner with Gary Bartz, Terence Blanchard, Christian McBride, & Lewis Nash
Jazz album, contemporary: *Unspeakable,* Bill Frisell
Blues album, contemporary: *Keep It Simple,* Keb' Mo'
Blues album, traditional: *Blues to the Bone,* Etta James
Folk album, contemporary: *The Revolution Starts...Now,* Steve Earle
Folk album, traditional: *Beautiful Dreamer: The Songs of Stephen Foster,* various artists
Reggae album: *True Love,* Toots & The Maytals
Latin pop album: *Amar Sin Mentiras,* Marc Anthony
Producer, non-classical: John Shanks
Classical album: *On the Transmigration of Souls*; Lorin Maazel, conductor; John Adams & Lawrence Rock, producers (Brooklyn Youth Chorus & New York Choral Artists; New York Philharmonic)
Classical vocal perf.: *Ives: Songs,* Susan Graham, mezzo soprano (Pierre-Laurent Aimard, Susan Graham)
Opera album: *Mozart: Le Nozze Di Figaro,* René Jacobs, conductor; Patrizia Ciofi, Véronique Gens, Simon Keenlyside, Angelika Kirchschlager, & Lorenzo Regazzo, singers; Martin Sauer, producer (Concerto Köln, various artists)

Grammy Awards for 1958-2004

Record of the Year (single)	Year	Album of the Year
Domenico Modugno, "Nel Blu Dipinto Di Blu (Volare)"	1958	Henry Mancini, *The Music From Peter Gunn*
Bobby Darin, "Mack the Knife"	1959	Frank Sinatra, *Come Dance With Me*
Percy Faith, "Theme From a Summer Place"	1960	Bob Newhart, *Button Down Mind*
Henry Mancini, "Moon River"	1961	Judy Garland, *Judy at Carnegie Hall*
Tony Bennett, "I Left My Heart in San Francisco"	1962	Vaughn Meader, *The First Family*
Henry Mancini, "The Days of Wine and Roses"	1963	Barbra Streisand, *The Barbra Streisand Album*
Stan Getz, Astrud Gilberto, "The Girl From Ipanema"	1964	Stan Getz, Astrud Gilberto, *Getz/Gilberto*
Herb Alpert, "A Taste of Honey"	1965	Frank Sinatra, *September of My Years*
Frank Sinatra, "Strangers in the Night"	1966	Frank Sinatra, *A Man and His Music*
5th Dimension, "Up, Up and Away"	1967	The Beatles, *Sgt. Pepper's Lonely Hearts Club Band*
Simon & Garfunkel, "Mrs. Robinson"	1968	Glen Campbell, *By the Time I Get to Phoenix*
5th Dimension, "Aquarius/Let the Sunshine In"	1969	Blood Sweat and Tears, *Blood, Sweat and Tears*
Simon & Garfunkel, "Bridge Over Troubled Water"	1970	Simon & Garfunkel, *Bridge Over Troubled Water*
Carole King, "It's Too Late"	1971	Carole King, *Tapestry*
Roberta Flack, "The First Time Ever I Saw Your Face"	1972	George Harrison and friends, *The Concert for Bangla Desh*
Roberta Flack, "Killing Me Softly With His Song"	1973	Stevie Wonder, *Innervisions*
Olivia Newton-John, "I Honestly Love You"	1974	Stevie Wonder, *Fulfillingness' First Finale*
Captain & Tennille, "Love Will Keep Us Together"	1975	Paul Simon, *Still Crazy After All These Years*
George Benson, "This Masquerade"	1976	Stevie Wonder, *Songs in the Key of Life*
Eagles, "Hotel California"	1977	Fleetwood Mac, *Rumours*
Billy Joel, "Just the Way You Are"	1978	Bee Gees, *Saturday Night Fever*
The Doobie Brothers, "What a Fool Believes"	1979	Billy Joel, *52nd Street*
Christopher Cross, "Sailing"	1980	Christopher Cross, *Christopher Cross*
Kim Carnes, "Bette Davis Eyes"	1981	John Lennon, Yoko Ono, *Double Fantasy*
Toto, "Rosanna"	1982	Toto, *Toto IV*
Michael Jackson, "Beat It"	1983	Michael Jackson, *Thriller*
Tina Turner, "What's Love Got to Do With It"	1984	Lionel Richie, *Can't Slow Down*
USA for Africa, "We Are the World"	1985	Phil Collins, *No Jacket Required*
Steve Winwood, "Higher Love"	1986	Paul Simon, *Graceland*
Paul Simon, "Graceland"	1987	U2, *The Joshua Tree*
Bobby McFerrin, "Don't Worry, Be Happy"	1988	George Michael, *Faith*
Bette Midler, "Wind Beneath My Wings"	1989	Bonnie Raitt, *Nick of Time*
Phil Collins, "Another Day in Paradise"	1990	Quincy Jones, *Back on the Block*
Natalie Cole, with Nat "King" Cole, "Unforgettable"	1991	Natalie Cole, with Nat "King" Cole, *Unforgettable*
Eric Clapton, "Tears in Heaven"	1992	Eric Clapton, *Unplugged*
Whitney Houston, "I Will Always Love You"	1993	Whitney Houston, *The Bodyguard*
Sheryl Crow, "All I Wanna Do"	1994	Tony Bennett, *MTV Unplugged*
Seal, "Kiss From a Rose"	1995	Alanis Morissette, *Jagged Little Pill*
Eric Clapton, "Change the World"	1996	Celine Dion, *Falling Into You*
Shawn Colvin, "Sunny Came Home"	1997	Bob Dylan, *Time Out of Mind*
Celine Dion, "My Heart Will Go On"	1998	Lauryn Hill, *The Miseducation of Lauryn Hill*
Santana featuring Rob Thomas, "Smooth"	1999	*Santana, Supernatural*
U2, "Beautiful Day"	2000	Steely Dan, *Two Against Nature*
U2, "Walk On"	2001	Various Artists, *O Brother, Where Art Thou?*
Norah Jones, "Don't Know Why"	2002	Norah Jones, *Come Away With Me*
Coldplay, "Clocks"	2003	OutKast, *Speakerboxxx/The Love Below*
Ray Charles & Norah Jones, "Here We Go Again"	2004	Ray Charles & Various Artists, *Genius Loves Company*

ENVIRONMENT AND NATURE

Greenhouse Effect and Global Warming

Source: U.S. Environmental Protection Agency

The Earth absorbs incoming solar radiation and emits thermal radiation back into space, but some of this thermal radiation is trapped by atmospheric "greenhouse gases" that warm Earth's surface and atmosphere (**"greenhouse effect"**). Naturally occurring greenhouse gases include carbon dioxide (CO_2), water vapor, methane (CH_4), nitrous oxide (N_2O), and ozone (O_3). Mostly artificial greenhouse gases include chlorofluorocarbons (CFCs), hydrochlorofluorocarbons (HCFCs), hydrofluorocarbons (HFCs), perfluorocarbons (PFCs), and sulfur hexafluoride (SF_6). (Several non-greenhouse gases—carbon monoxide [CO], oxides of nitrogen [NOX], and nonmethane volatile organic compounds [NMVOCs]—contribute indirectly to the greenhouse effect by producing greenhouse gases during chemical transformations and by influencing their atmospheric lifetimes.)

Levels of CO_2 are higher now than at any time in the past 400,000 years. They began rising over the past 2 centuries as a result of human activities such as the burning of fossil fuels (coal, oil, natural gas) and deforestation. During this time, atmospheric concentrations of CO_2, CH_4, and N_2O have risen sharply. Many scientists believe this buildup is a major cause of higher-than-normal average global temperatures since the 1990s. Over the 20th century **Earth's average temperature** rose about 1°F, and since the 1970s it has been rising at a faster rate. Some scientists believe the global temperature could rise by 2°F to 6°F over the 21st century. This could speed the melting of polar ice caps, inundate coastal lowlands, lead to stronger hurricanes, and cause major changes in crop production and natural habitats.

Delegates from over 150 nations adopted a proposal to limit emissions of CO_2, CH_4, N_2O, HFCs, PFCs, and SF_6 at a UN summit in Kyoto, Japan (Dec. 1997). Under the so-called **Kyoto Protocol**, the 38 participating industrial nations agreed to cut emissions by a collective 5.2% from 1990 levels by 2012. High-emissions nations could meet their targets by purchasing pollution credits from nations that exceed targeted cuts, and gain credits for "sinks," such as forests and croplands, that absorb CO_2 from the atmosphere. Cuts by developing nations were voluntary.

By 1999, 84 nations had signed the protocol, but the agreement could not be implemented until it was ratified by at least 55 countries responsible for at least 55% of developed nations' greenhouse emissions. This threshold was reached with Russia's Nov. 2004 ratification, and the protocol took effect on Feb. 16, 2005. As of Aug. 23, 2005, 154 nations responsible for 62% of developed nations' major greenhouse emissions had ratified the treaty. Among countries absent from the Kyoto Protocol were U.S. and Australia and developing nations such as China and India. Pres. Bill Clinton signed the agreement in 1998; however, it was not sent to the Senate for ratification because of dim prospects for approval.

Pres. George W. Bush opposed the agreement on the grounds that it did not bind developing nations and would hurt the U.S. economy. The Bush administration viewed global warming only as one among a set of concerns also including economic development, energy, security, and pollution, and has advocated urging technological innovations and providing tax incentives for companies, rather than mandatory limits. The U.S. accounts for 36% of developed nations' emissions.

U.S. Greenhouse Gas Emissions from Human Activities, 1990-2003

Source: U.S. Environmental Protection Agency

GAS AND MAJOR SOURCE(S)	1990	1998	1999	2000	2001	2002	2003	Percent Change
Carbon dioxide (CO_2)	**5,009.6**	**5,607.2**	**5,678.0**	**5,858.2**	**5,744.8**	**5,796.8**	**5,841.5**	**17**
Fossil fuel combustion	4,711.7	5,278.7	5,345.9	5,545.1	5,448.0	5,501.4	5,551.6	18
Methane (CH_4)	**605.3**	**569.1**	**557.3**	**554.2**	**546.8**	**542.5**	**545.0**	**–10**
Landfills	172.2	138.5	134.0	130.7	126.2	126.8	131.2	–23
Natural gas systems	128.3	131.8	127.4	132.1	131.8	130.6	125.9	–2
Enteric fermentation[1]	117.9	116.7	116.8	115.6	114.5	114.6	115.0	–2
Coal mining	81.9	62.8	58.9	56.2	55.6	52.4	53.8	34
Nitrous oxide (N_2O)	**382.0**	**407.8**	**382.1**	**401.9**	**385.8**	**380.5**	**376.7**	**1**
Agricultural soil management	253.0	267.7	243.4	263.9	257.1	252.6	253.5	0
Hydrofluorocarbons (HFCs), perfluorocarbons (PFCs), and sulfur hexafluoride (SF_6)[2]	**91.2**	**135.7**	**134.8**	**138.9**	**129.5**	**138.3**	**137.0**	**50**
TOTAL U.S. EMISSIONS	**6,088.1**	**6,719.7**	**6,752.2**	**6,953.2**	**6,806.9**	**6,858.1**	**6,900.2**	**13**
NET U.S. EMISSIONS[3]	**5,046.1**	**5,838.8**	**5,926.1**	**6,130.8**	**5,980.1**	**6,031.6**	**6,072.2**	**20**

Note: Emissions given in terms of equivalent emissions of carbon dioxide (CO_2), using units of teragrams of carbon dioxide equivalents (Tg CO_2 Eq.). (1) Digestive process of ruminent animals, such as cattle and sheep, producing methane as a by-product. (2) These gases have extremely high global warming potential, and PFCs and SF_6 have long atmospheric lifetimes. (3) Total emissions minus carbon dioxide absorbed by forests or other means.

Top 15 Nations Producing Carbon Dioxide Emissions, Ranked by 2003 Totals, 1980-2003

Source: U.S. Department of Energy

(million metric tons of carbon dioxide emitted from fossil fuel consumption)

Region/Country	1980	1985	1990	1995	2000	2002	2003	Percent change 1980-2003
United States	4,754.52	4,585.20	5,001.50	5,287.69	5,814.63	5,771.93	5,802.08	22
China	1,434.52	1,855.95	2,241.17	2,865.35	3,032.79	3,273.00	3,540.97	147
Russia[1]	3,027.53	3,496.77	3,792.16	1,590.82	1,555.11	1,546.04	1,606.42	–47
Japan	937.50	892.96	1,010.97	1,091.30	1,167.11	1,191.44	1,205.54	29
India	299.76	439.34	588.24	867.08	997.67	1,012.73	1,024.83	241
Germany	751.02	689.20	692.32	875.85	845.26	854.29	842.03	12
Canada	452.51	434.73	478.57	500.52	566.09	574.04	600.18	33
United Kingdom	608.30	588.25	598.58	555.00	550.85	558.17	564.56	–7
Korea, South	126.48	165.05	234.31	393.35	437.80	461.71	469.53	271
Italy	366.75	374.00	413.38	427.52	443.95	446.62	465.48	27
South Africa	234.19	298.81	295.48	344.10	383.89	380.43	411.25	76
France	487.89	394.61	370.37	372.65	399.79	403.37	409.18	–16
Mexico	231.43	270.46	300.09	318.70	380.03	368.72	404.72	75
Australia	198.31	224.59	262.77	287.70	355.75	371.39	376.83	90
Iran	119.52	164.72	201.79	260.13	317.89	362.48	372.00	211
World Total	**18,313.13**	**19,430.24**	**21,402.22**	**22,034.54**	**23,849.00**	**24,464.92**	**25,162.07**	**37**

(1) Numbers for 1980-90 are for the former Soviet Union. (2) Numbers for 1980-90 are for the former West Germany.

U.S. Greenhouse Gas Emissions, 2003

Source: U.S. Environmental Protection Agency

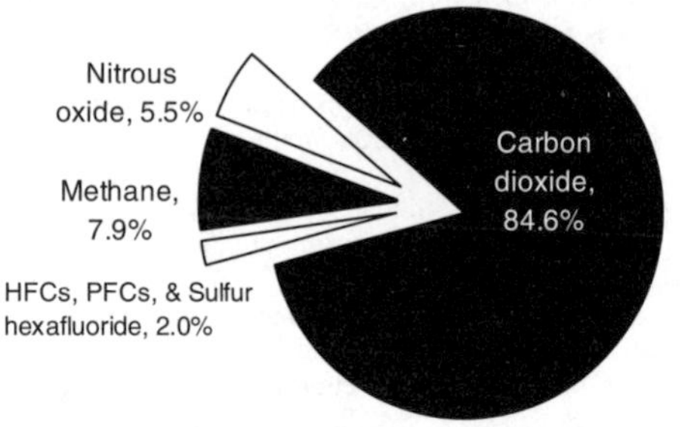

World Carbon Dioxide Emissions from the Use of Fossil Fuels, 2003

Source: U.S. Energy Information Administration

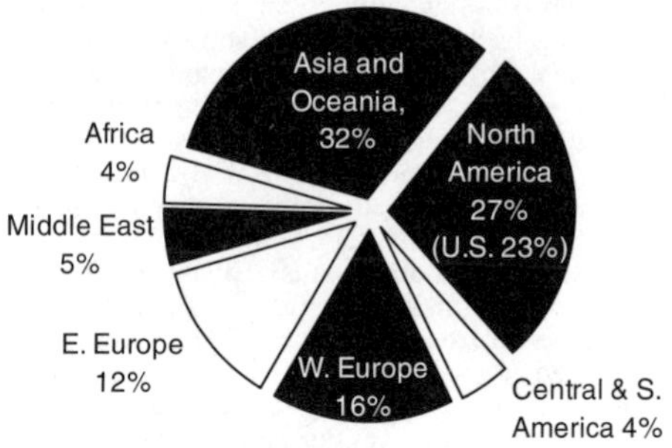

Atmospheric Concentration of CO_2, 1744-2004

Sources: Carbon Dioxide Information Analysis Center, Dept. of Energy

Year[1]	Concentration in ppm[2]	Year[1]	Concentration in ppm[2]	Year[1]	Concentration in ppm[2]	Year[1]	Concentration in ppm[2]	Year[1]	Concentration in ppm[2]
1744	277	1869	289	1915	301	1960	317	1990	354
1791	280	1878	290	1927	306	1970	326	2000	369
1816	284	1903	295	1943	308	1980	339	2004	377
1843	287								

(1) Measurements for the years 1744-1943 were derived from a 200m ice core sample drilled near Siple Station in Antarctica between 1983-84. Measurements from 1960-200 were taken directly from the atmosphere at Mauna Loa Observatory in Hawaii. (2) parts per million.

Average Global Temperatures, 1900-2004

Source: National Oceanic and Atmospheric Administration; in degrees Fahrenheit

1900-09	56.5	1930-39	57.0	1960-69	57.1	1990-99	57.6	2002	57.9
1910-19	56.6	1940-49	57.1	1970-79	57.0	2000	57.6	2003	57.9
1920-29	56.7	1950-59	57.1	1980-89	57.4	2001	57.8	2004	57.9

Note: The warmest year on record was 1998, when the average global temperature reached 58.0°F. The next-warmest years on record were 2002 through 2004.

Toxics Release Inventory, U.S., 2002-2003

Source: U.S. Environmental Protection Agency

Releases of toxic chemicals into the environment, by manner of release and industry sector; pollutant transfers by destination of transfer. Totals below may not add because of rounding.

	2002 mil lb	2003 mil lb
Pollutant releases		
Air releases	1,631	1,583
Surface water discharges	231	222
Underground injection	215	214
On-site land releases	1,735	1,420
Off-site releases	467	482
TOTAL on- and off-site releases	**4,280**	**3,920**
Pollutant transfers		
To recycling	1,986	1,870
To energy recovery	804	715
To treatment	276	288
To publicly owned treatment works	347	271
Other transfers	1	1
Off-site to disposal	596	599
TOTAL	**4,010**	**3,744**

Top industries, total releases	2002 %	2003 %
Metal mining	26	28
Electric utilities	23	24
Primary metals	16	11
Chemicals	12	12
Hazardous waste/solvent recovery	4	5
Paper	4	5
All others	15	15
Top carcinogens, air/water/land releases	**mil lb**	**mil lb**
Styrene	50	51
Formaldehyde	19	21
Acetaldehyde	14	14
Dichloromethane	12	9
Trichloroethylene	8	7
Ethylbenzene	7	7

Note: This information does not indicate whether (or to what degree) the public has been exposed to toxic chemicals.

Top 10 States, Total Toxics Releases, 2003

Source: U.S. Environmental Protection Agency

State	2003 mil lb	State	2003 mil lb	State	2003 mil lb	State	2003 mil lb
Alaska	540	Ohio	252	Pennsylvania	167	North Carolina	129
Nevada	409	Utah	242	Tennessee	143	**U.S. Total***	**4,439**
Texas	262	Indiana	235	Illinois	132		

*Total includes District of Columbia, Puerto Rico, American Samoa, Guam, Northern Marianas, and the Virgin Islands.

Air Pollution

Source: World Bank, *World Development Indicators 2005*

Air pollution is a major threat to health and the environment. **Winter smog**—made up of soot, dust, and sulfur dioxide—is associated with increases in deaths. Prolonged exposure to **particulate pollution** can lead to chronic respiratory illnesses and exacerbate heart disease. It causes an estimated 500,000 premature deaths in the world each year.

Emissions of sulfur dioxide and nitrogen oxides lead to **acid rain,** which spreads over long distances, upsetting the chemical balance of soils, trees, and plants. Direct exposure to high levels of sulfur dioxide or acid deposition causes **defoliation**.

Where **coal** is a primary fuel, high levels of urban air pollution may result. If the coal has a high sulfur content, widespread acid deposition may result. Combustion of **petroleum** products is another important cause of air pollution.

Air Pollution in Selected World Cities[1]

Particulate matter in the following table refers to smoke, soot, dust, and liquid droplets from combustion that are in the air—specifically, to particulates less than 10 microns in diameter capable of reaching deep into the respiratory tract. The level of particulates, an important indicator of air quality, is significantly affected by the state of technology and pollution controls. **Sulfur dioxide** is a pollutant formed when fossil fuels containing sulfur are burned. **Nitrogen dioxide** is a poisonous, pungent gas formed when nitric oxide combines with hydrocarbons and sunlight, producing a photochemical reaction. Nitrogen oxides are emitted by bacteria, nitrogenous fertilizers, aerobic decomposition of organic matter, biomass combustion, and, especially, burning fuel for vehicles and industrial activities.

Data in the following table are average concentrations based on reports from urban monitoring sites, measured in micrograms per cubic meter, mpcm; the figures give a general indication of air quality, but results should be interpreted with caution. World Health Organization standards for acceptable air quality are 50 mpcm for sulfur dioxide and 40 mpcm for nitrogen dioxide; the WHO has set no guidelines for acceptable levels of suspended particulate matter.

City and Country	Particulate matter	Sulfur dioxide	Nitrogen dioxide
Accra, Ghana	31	NA	NA
Amsterdam, Netherlands	37	10	58
Athens, Greece	50	34	64
Bangkok, Thailand	82	11	23
Barcelona, Spain	43	11	43
Beijing, China	106	90	122
Berlin, Germany	25	18	26
Cairo, Egypt	178	69	NA
Cape Town, South Africa	15	21	72
Caracas, Venezuela	18	33	57
Chicago, IL	27	14	57
Cordoba, Argentina	52	NA	97
Delhi, India	187	24	41
Kolkata (Calcutta), India	153	49	34
London, UK	23	25	77
Los Angeles, CA	38	9	74
Manila, Philippines	60	33	NA
Mexico City, Mexico	69	74	130
Milan, Italy	36	31	248
Montreal, Canada	22	10	42
Moscow, Russia	27	109	NA
Mumbai (Bombay), India	79	33	39
Nairobi, Kenya	49	NA	NA
New York, NY	23	26	79
Oslo, Norway	23	8	43
Paris, France	15	14	57
Prague, Czech Republic	27	14	33
Quito, Ecuador	34	22	NA
Rio de Janeiro, Brazil	40	129	NA
Rome, Italy	35	NA	NA
Seoul, South Korea	45	44	60
Sofia, Bulgaria	83	39	122
Sydney, Australia	22	28	81
Tokyo, Japan	43	18	68
Toronto, Canada	26	17	43
Warsaw, Poland	49	16	32

NA = Not available. (1) Data for particulates are for 1999 and come from the World Bank study, "The Human Cost of Air Pollution: New Estimates for Developing Countries;" data for sulfur dioxide and nitrogen dioxide are derived from WHO's Healthy Cities Air Management Information System and the World Resources Institute and were collected in 1998 or, if earlier, are the latest available.

Emissions of Principal Air Pollutants in the U.S., 1970-2003

Source: U.S. Environmental Protection Agency, Office of Air Quality Planning and Standards; in thousand tons; estimated

Polluant Emitted	1970	1975	1980	1985	1990	1995	2000	2001	2002	2003
Carbon monoxide	204,043	188,398	185,407	176,844	154,186	126,777	114,467	106,262	112,054	106,886
Nitrogen oxides[1]	26,883	26,377	27,079	25,757	25,529	24,956	22,598	21,549	21,102	20,728
Volatile org. compounds[1]	34,659	30,765	31,106	27,404	24,108	22,041	17,512	17,111	16,544	16,056
Particulate matter[2]	13,023	7,556	7,013	41,324	27,752	25,819	23,747	23,708	22,154	22,940
Sulfur dioxide	31,218	28,043	25,925	23,307	23,076	18,619	16,347	15,932	15,353	15,943
TOTAL[3]	**309,826**	**281,139**	**276,530**	**294,636**	**254,651**	**218,212**	**194,671**	**184,562**	**187,207**	**182,553**

(1) Ozone, a major air pollutant and the primary constituent of smog, is not emitted directly to the air but is formed by sunlight acting on emissions of nitrogen oxides and volatile organic compounds. (2) PM-10, particulates 10 microns or smaller in diameter. (3) Totals are rounded, as are components of totals.

Carbon Monoxide Emission Estimates, 1970-2003

Source: U.S. Environmental Protection Agency, Office of Air Quality Planning and Standards; in thousand tons

Source	1970	1975	1980	1985	1990	1995	2000	2001	2002	2003
Fuel combustion, elec. util.	237	276	322	291	363	372	484	485	499	530
Industrial processes[1]	10,610	8,304	7,700	5,894	5,572	5,631	3,628	3,782	3,830	3,900
Transportation	174,602	167,884	160,512	153,216	131,702	107,755	92,239	88,153	86,611	83,252
Fires	6,766	4,433	7,622	7,289	10,583	6,705	12,049	7,744	15,654	13,180
TOTAL[2]	**204,043**	**188,398**	**185,407**	**176,844**	**154,186**	**126,777**	**114,467**	**106,262**	**112,054**	**106,886**

(1) Includes industrial fuel combustion, chemical and allied manufacturing, metals processing, and petroleum and other industrial sectors. (2) Totals may not add because of rounding or because all categories are not listed.

Nitrogen Oxides Emission Estimates, 1970-2003

Source: U.S. Environmental Protection Agency, Office of Air Quality Planning and Standards; in thousand tons

Source	1970	1975	1980	1985	1990	1995	2000	2001	2002	2003
Fuel combustion, elec. util.	4,900	5,694	7,024	6,127	6,663	6,384	5,330	4,917	4,699	4,458
Industrial processes[1]	5,100	4,546	4,110	4,009	3,831	3,909	3,518	3,587	3,695	3,609
Transportation	15,276	15,029	14,846	14,508	13,373	12,989	12,560	11,930	11,452	11,484
TOTAL[2]	**26,883**	**26,377**	**27,079**	**25,757**	**25,529**	**24,956**	**22,598**	**21,549**	**21,102**	**20,728**

(1) Includes industrial fuel combustion, chemical and allied manufacturing, metals processing, and petroleum and other industrial sectors. (2) Totals may not add because of rounding or because all categories are not listed.

Sulfur Dioxide Emissions, 1970-2003

Source: U.S. Environmental Protection Agency, Office of Air Quality Planning and Standards; in thousand tons

Source	1970	1975	1980	1985	1990	1995	2000	2001	2002	2003
Fuel combustion, elec. util.	21,966	21,578	20,420	19,441	19,459	15,437	13,535	13,093	12,593,	13,157
Industrial processes[1]	7,093	4,683	3,774	2,428	1,852	1,588	1,376	1,422	1,363	1,363
Transportation	551	635	717	809	874	741	697	688	696	698
TOTAL[2]	**31,218**	**28,043**	**25,925**	**23,307**	**23,076**	**18,619**	**16,347**	**15,932**	**15,353**	**15,943**

(1) Includes industrial fuel combustion, chemical and allied manufacturing, metals processing, and petroleum and other industrial sectors. (2) Totals include miscellaneous sources not determined.

Air Quality of Selected U.S. Metropolitan Areas, 1990-2003

Source: U.S. Environmental Protection Agency, Office of Air Quality Planning and Standards

Data indicate the number of days metropolitan statistical areas failed to meet acceptable air-quality standards.

Metropolitan Statistical Area	1990	1995	1996	1997	1998	1999	2000	2001	2002	2003
Atlanta, GA	42	33	21	26	43	61	35	24	15	11
Bakersfield, CA	98	105	109	55	76	139	132	124	149	141
Baltimore, MD	28	36	28	30	51	41	23	33	42	20
Baton Rouge, LA	28	15	7	8	14	17	29	5	5	15
Boston, MA-NH	0	0	0	0	0	3	0	3	7	6
Chicago, IL	4	23	6	9	10	19	13	33	23	10
Cleveland-Lorain-Elyria, OH	10	24	16	10	20	36	21	29	30	17
Dallas, TX	0	0	0	0	0	0	0	0	3	0
Denver, CO	9	2	0	0	5	2	2	7	4	5
Detroit, MI	11	14	13	11	17	23	16	31	28	19
Fresno, CA	62	61	70	75	67	133	131	139	152	127
Greensboro-Winston Salem-High Point, NC	12	6	6	13	25	22	14	11	24	4
Houston, TX	51	65	26	47	38	51	42	27	21	31
Las Vegas, NV-AZ	4	0	2	0	0	0	1	4	2	5
Los Angeles-Long Beach, CA	171	113	94	60	56	60	87	89	81	88
Miami, FL	1	2	1	3	8	7	2	1	1	1
Minneapolis-St. Paul, MN-WI	3	4	0	0	0	0	5	5	1	1
New Haven-Meriden, CT	15	14	8	19	9	19	9	15	25	16
New York, NY	17	17	11	22	14	22	19	21	26	14
Orange County, CA	44	8	6	3	5	15	31	31	20	19
Philadelphia, PA-NJ	39	30	22	32	37	32	21	35	35	20
Phoenix-Mesa, AZ	12	22	15	12	14	10	11	7	9	9
Riverside-San Bernardino, CA	158	124	118	104	95	121	144	156	146	138
Sacramento, CA	56	32	27	2	20	47	34	39	46	22
St. Louis, MO-IL	22	34	20	15	23	31	20	20	34	13
Salt Lake City-Ogden, UT	5	4	8	1	12	13	20	27	33	10
San Diego, CA	96	48	31	14	33	33	31	31	19	20
San Francisco, CA	0	2	0	0	0	2	2	5	1	0
Seattle-Bellevue-Everett, WA	2	0	0	0	3	6	8	6	7	2
Washington, DC-MD-VA-WV	25	27	18	28	45	42	22	27	31	12

Hazardous Waste Sites in the U.S., 2005

Source: U.S. Environmental Protection Agency, *National Priorities List,* Sept. 2005

State/Territory	Proposed		Final		Total
	Gen	Fed	Gen	Fed	Number
Alabama	2	0	10	3	15
Alaska	0	0	1	5	6
Arizona	0	0	7	2	9
Arkansas	0	0	10	0	10
California	3	0	69	24	96
Colorado	2	0	14	3	19
Connecticut	1	0	14	1	16
Delaware	0	0	13	1	14
District of Columbia	0	0	0	1	1
Florida	1	0	44	6	51
Georgia	2	0	13	2	17
Hawaii	0	0	1	2	3
Idaho	3	0	4	2	9
Illinois	5	1	37	4	47
Indiana	1	0	29	0	30
Iowa	1	0	11	1	13
Kansas	1	1	9	1	12
Kentucky	0	0	13	1	14
Louisiana	3	0	11	1	15
Maine	0	0	9	3	12
Maryland	1	0	8	9	18
Massachusetts	2	0	24	7	33
Michigan	1	1	66	0	68
Minnesota	0	0	22	2	24
Mississippi	2	0	3	0	5
Missouri	0	0	23	3	26
Montana	1	0	14	0	15
Nebraska	2	0	11	1	14
Nevada	0	0	1	0	1
New Hampshire	1	0	19	1	21
New Jersey	2	0	105	8	115
New Mexico	1	0	11	1	13
New York	1	0	85	4	90
North Carolina	0	0	29	2	31
North Dakota	0	0	0	0	0
Ohio	5	2	27	3	37
Oklahoma	1	0	9	1	11
Oregon	0	0	9	2	11
Pennsylvania	2	0	88	6	96
Rhode Island	0	0	10	2	12
South Carolina	0	0	24	2	26
South Dakota	0	0	1	1	2
Tennessee	0	1	10	3	14
Texas	2	0	39	4	45
Utah	4	0	10	4	18
Vermont	0	0	11	0	11
Virginia	0	0	19	11	30
Washington	1	0	33	13	47
West Virginia	0	0	7	2	9
Wisconsin	1	0	37	0	38
Wyoming	0	0	1	1	2
Guam	0	0	1	1	2
Puerto Rico	1	0	9	1	11
Virgin Islands	0	0	2	0	2
Total	**56**	**6**	**1,087**	**158**	**1,307**

Note: Fed. = for hazardous waste produced by federal agency; Gen. = non-Fed. sites. Proposed = proposed for federal Superfund financing; Final = qualified for Superfund financing.

Renewable Energy Sources

Source: U.S. Department of Energy

Concern over the environmental impact of burning fossil fuels has helped spur interest in alternative fuels that are less polluting. And since the supply of fossil fuels is finite and diminishing, there is interest in "renewable" sources that do not deplete existing supplies. However, renewable energy sources still make up only a small share of U.S. domestic energy production (about 9%, or excluding hydropower about 5%). The major reason for this is their relatively higher cost (in some cases 2 to 4 times that of power obtained from traditional fuels). The following are the major renewable energy sources available.

Biomass is plant-derived material usable as a renewable energy source, including wood energy crops such as hybrid poplars and willow trees, agricultural crops including soybeans and corn, and animal and other wastes. Biomass is one of the two most common energy sources in the U.S. today. Forms of biomass such as wood can be burned to produce heat and generate electricity. Agricultural crops can be chemically converted into fuels such as ethanol and biodiesel; these are the only known renewable liquid energy sources, and may one day replace petroleum and fossil-fuel produced diesel. But bringing ethanol and biodiesel into wide use would require more energy-efficient methods of production and transportation. Overall, biomass fuels are much cleaner-burning than fossil fuels, though biomass fuels do produce carbon dioxide and other pollutants.

Geothermal energy is generated from heat from inside Earth. This form of energy is both clean and renewable. The technology has caught on in countries with substantial geothermal activity such as Iceland, where it accounts for 16% of electricity output and 86% of all energy used for home heating. In the U.S. the best sources for geothermal power are in the west, where there are many underground lakes of heated water; however, large-scale access would require drilling. A major goal in this field is to find a way to harness energy directly from magma (molten rock material), which has great potential because of its high temperature.

Hydrogen is the 3rd most abundant element on Earth. It does not naturally occur on Earth as a pure gas or liquid, but is always combined with other elements (such as with oxygen to form water or carbon to form methane). For energy use it is produced from hydrocarbons using heat, bacteria or algae through photosynthesis, or by using sunlight or electricity to split water into hydrogen and oxygen. Hydrogen batteries or "fuel cells" are already used by NASA on the space shuttle. In a fuel cell, electrons are released from the hydrogen atoms in a chemical reaction and flow through an external circuit as electricity. The protons then combine with oxygen (and some of the electrons in the electric current) to make heat and water suitable for drinking. Fuel cells do not run down, but work as long as hydrogen is supplied. Some experts think hydrogen will be the power source of the future. However, an infrastructure would need to be created for safe and cost-effective transportation and storage of hydrogen.

Hydropower, or hydroelectric power is generated by water flowing through turbines. It is one of the two most common renewable energy sources in the U.S. today. A dam on a river is a common hydropower producer. No harmful greenhouse gases are produced, but the dams needed to generate the power can harm river ecosystems. Researchers are working on turbine technologies that may maximize use of hydropower and reduce adverse environmental effects.

Ocean energy is generated in two ways. Thermal ocean energy uses the heat that the ocean absorbs from the sun to power generators, and sometimes drinkable desalinated water is a by-product. Mechanical ocean energy is generated by the movement of tides and waves through a turbine. In both cases, power generation is not very efficient with current technology. Much more research is needed to make thermal ocean energy generation a reality. Mechanical ocean energy requires large dams or breakwater-type structures called "tidal barrages" to be built, which could cause harm to coastal ecosystems.

Solar energy is generated using heat and light from the sun. Solar energy is an increasingly common source of electricity. Photovoltaic (PV) solar cells are made of semi-conducting materials that can directly convert sunlight to electricity without any harmful waste product. Solar collectors are made more efficient by using arrays of mirrors to concentrate the sun's rays onto PV panels. Another way of using sunlight is to heat water directly. According to the DOE, homes incorporating solar heating designs can save as much as 50% on heating bills. The downside to solar energy is that it depends heavily on a range of factors including location, time of year, and weather.

Wind energy uses wind turbines to produce energy. They are perched on high towers, usually 100 feet or higher, and often placed in large groups ("farms") to generate electricity for towns and cities. On a much smaller scale, stand-alone turbines are sometimes used by farmers and homeowners to generate supplemental electricity. In the past 20 years, government incentives in the form of tax credits to producers and incentives for homeowners have helped lower the price of wind power by 85%, making it a more feasible option. Some people object to wind farms because of their appearance or the noise the turbines make. Wind power raises few other environmental problems; but the turbines can pose a danger to birds. In addition, because weather is involved, consistent generation is a challenge.

Hurricane Katrina

Hurricane Katrina, which, in late Aug. 2005, devastated the Gulf Coast, and precipitated breaks in levees that flooded the city of New Orleans, created a number of environmental hazards, some of which posed risks to rescue workers, evacuees and returning residents. The storm also focused attention on the flooding threat associated with human development in coastal areas.

Tests of New Orleans floodwaters in September found dangerous levels of **E. coli bacteria and heavy metals** like lead, chromium and arsenic. E. coli, which was linked to the presence of fecal material, was one of several germs and viruses that caused gastrointestinal illnesses and infected wounds among flood victims. Heavy metals could lead to developmental defects and an increased cancer risk if enough were to be ingested. The floodwaters were also an ideal breeding ground for **mosquitoes**, which carried diseases like West Nile virus. Health officials planned to spray New Orleans with pesticide to curb that problem.

Oil spills were a major hazard in southern Louisiana, which was a hub for the petroleum industry. An early estimate put the amount of crude oil spilled because of Katrina at 6.5 million gallons. Oil-based fuels also leaked from flooded vehicles and gas stations, and household chemicals entered the water from containers floating amid the storm debris. Other possible sources of pollution included **flooded toxic waste sites and landfills**. All of these contaminants could cause skin and eye irritation, or nausea and light-headedness if fumes are inhaled. Long-term exposure could cause kidney damage, a raised cancer risk, and other problems.

Bodies of water like New Orleans's Lake Pontchartrain were expected to recover slowly from any damage caused by an influx of contaminated water from the land, however. Heavy metals would be trapped in sediment, and other substances would be flushed out by river water or tidal action. Similarly, **plant and animal habitats** disrupted by the storm, including freshwater marshes that were protected from the sea by levees, were expected to rebound eventually.

As the land dried, there was a danger that material left behind in mud deposits, as well as new growths of mold and fungi, could become **airborne irritants**. Recovery workers faced the daunting task of clearing away hundreds of thousands of rotting buildings and many acres of **contaminated silt**. Fortunately, the fecal bacteria was expected to die off after a short period.

A side-effect of the storm damage was an increase in **fuel prices**. In an effort to reduce pressure on the market, federal regulators temporarily relaxed pollution standards for fuels in many areas, making it easier for refiners to increase output.

The **flooding** raised questions about the **effectiveness of dikes and levees**. For decades, engineers had used such mechanisms to contain the Mississippi River, directing it along a fixed, easily navigable route to the sea. However, that meant the river's silt was flushed into the sea rather than spread across the natural floodplain. Robbed of replenishment, the land gradually subsided, leaving artificially protected areas like New Orleans in danger of catastrophic flooding. Outside the levees, Louisiana had lost about 1,900 square miles of **coastal wetlands** to the advancing sea since 1930, or about 25 square miles per year. Such marshes were a key defense against hurricanes, absorbing storm surges before they could reach developed areas. Another important barrier, the Chandeleur island chain, located 70 miles east of New Orleans in the Gulf of Mexico, was seriously eroded by Hurricane Katrina. Some people urged that more resources be devoted to restoration of the coastal marshes. The decades-long trend of increased building in vulnerable coastal communities also compounded weather-and flood-related problems.

Some scientists had been warning that **global warming** could be increasing the *intensity* of **hurricanes** worldwide by raising sea surface temperatures. The storms gather much of their energy from warm water. However, there was little evidence that warmer world oceans were increasing the overall *number* of hurricanes. A more established effect of global warming, melting polar ice caps and rising sea levels, added yet another threat to coastal cities like New Orleans.

Renewable Water Resources

Source: Food and Agriculture Organization, United Nations, 2005

Globally, water supplies are abundant, but they are unevenly distributed among and within countries. In some areas, water withdrawals are so high, relative to supply, that surface water supplies are shrinking and groundwater reserves are being depleted faster than they can be replenished by precipitation. The U.S. has a total of 2,818 cubic kilometers of internal renewable water resources, an actual total (which takes into account incoming water flow from outside the country) of 3,069 cubic kilometers, and 10,333 cubic meters per capita. Totals for all countries are 43,219 cubic kilometers of internal resources, 55,273 cubic kilometers of actual resources, and 8,549 cubic meters per capita.

These numbers, and those in the tables below, were published by the Food and Agriculture Organization in 2005; the tables draw upon studies done over a number of years and use 2000 population data.

Countries With Most Resources Per Capita

(ranked by per capita resources)

Country	Cubic meters per capita	Total cubic km
Iceland	582,191.8	170.0
Guyana	314,211.2	241.0
Suriname	277,904.3	122.0
Congo, Republic of	217,915.1	832.0
Papua New Guinea	137,251.5	801.0
Gabon	121,391.6	164.0
Canada	91,418.9	2902.0
Solomon Islands	91,038.7	44.7
Norway	83,919.2	382.0
New Zealand	83,760.2	327.0

Countries With Least Resources Per Capita*

(ranked by per capita resources, starting with the lowest)

Country/Territory	Cubic meters per capita	Total cubic km
Kuwait	7.7	(1)
United Arab Emirates	49.2	0.2
Bahamas	63.1	(1)
Qatar	85.6	0.1
Maldives	91.5	(1)
Saudi Arabia	96.3	2.4
Libya	106.0	0.6
Malta	127.5	0.1
Singapore	139.0	0.6
Jordan	156.8	0.9

* Data not available from all nations. (1) Less than 0.1 cubic km.

Some Endangered Animal Species

Source: Fish and Wildlife Service, U.S. Dept. of the Interior

Common name	Scientific name	Range
Albatross, Amsterdam	Diomedia amsterdamensis	Amsterdam Island, Indian Ocean
Antelope, giant sable	Hippotragus niger variani	Angola
Armadillo, giant	Pridontes maximus	Venezuela, Guyana to Argentina
Babirusa	Babyrousa babyrussa	Indonesia
Bandicoot, desert	Perameles eremiana	Australia
Bat, gray	Myotis grisescens	Central, southeastern U.S.
Bear, brown (grizzly)	Ursus arctos horribilis	Palearctic
Bison, wood	Bison bison athabascae	Canada, northwestern U.S.
Bobcat, Mexican	Felis rufus escuinapae	Central Mexico
Caiman, black	Melanosuchus niger	Amazon basin
Camel, Bactrian	Camelus bactrianus	Mongolia, China
Caribou, woodland	Rangifer tarandus caribou	Canada, Northwestern U.S.
Cheetah	Acinonyx jubatus	Africa to India
Chimpanzee, pygmy	Pan paniscus	Congo (formerly Zaire)
Condor, California	Gymnogyps californianus	U.S. (AZ, CA, OR), Mexico (Baja California)
Crane, whooping	Grus americana	Canada, Mexico, U.S. (Rocky Mts. to Carolinas)
Crocodile, American	Crocodylus acutus	U.S. (FL), Mexico, Caribbean Sea, Central and S America
Deer, Columbian white-tailed	Odocoileus virginianus leucurus	U.S. (OR, WA)
Dolphin, Chinese river	Lipotes vexillifer	China
Dugong	Dugong dugon	East Africa to southern Japan
Elephant, Asian	Elephas maximus	S central and southeastern Asia
Fox, northern swift	Vulpes velox hebes	Canada
Frog, Goliath	Conraua goliath	Cameroon, Equatorial Guinea, Gabon
Gorilla	Gorilla gorilla	Central and W Africa
Hartebeest, Tora	Alcelaphus buselaphus tora	Egypt, Ethiopia, Sudan
Hawk, Hawaiian	Buteo solitarius	U.S. (HI)
Hyena, brown	Hyaena brunnea	Southern Africa
Impala, black-faced	Aepyceros melampus petersi	Angola, Namibia
Kangaroo, Tasmanian forester	Macropus giganteus tasmaniensis	Australia (Tasmania)
Leopard	Panthera pardus	Africa and Asia
Lion, Asiatic	Panthera leo persica	Turkey to India
Manatee, West Indian	Trichechus manatus	Southeastern U.S., Caribbean Sea, Mexico
Monkey, spider	Ateles geoffroyi frontatus	Costa Rica, Nicaragua
Ocelot	Felis pardalis	U.S. (AZ, TX) to Central and S America
Orangutan	Pongo pygmaeus	Borneo, Sumatra
Ostrich, West African	Struthio camelus spatzi	W Sahara
Otter, marine	Lutra felina	Peru south to Straits of Magellan
Panda, giant	Ailuropoda melanoleuca	China
Panther, Florida	Felis concolor coryi	U.S. (FL)
Parakeet, golden	Aratinga guarouba	Brazil
Parrot, imperial	Amazona imperialis	West Indies (Dominica)
Penguin, Galapagos	Spheniscus mendiculus	Ecuador (Galapagos Islands)
Puma, eastern	Felis concolor couguar	Eastern N America (presumed extinct in wild)
Python, Indian	Python molurus molurus	Sri Lanka, India
Rat-kangaroo, brush-tailed	Bettongia penicillata	Australia
Rhinoceros, black	Diceros bicornis	Sub-Saharan Africa
Rhinoceros, northern white	Ceratotherium simum cottoni	Congo, Sudan, Uganda, Central African Rep.
Salamander, Chinese giant	Andrias davidianus	Western China
Sea-lion, Steller	Eumetopias jubatus	Alaska, Russia
Sheep, bighorn	Ovis canadensis	California
Squirrel, Carolina northern flying	Glaucomys sabrinus coloratus	U.S. (NC, TN)
Tiger	Panthera tigris	Asia
Tortoise, Galapagos	Geochelone elephantopus	Ecuador (Galapagos Islands)
Turtle, Plymouth red-bellied	Pseudemys rubriventris bangsi	U.S. (MA)
Whale, gray	Eschrichtius robustus	N Pacific Ocean
Whale, humpback	Megaptera novaeangliae	Oceania
Wolf, red	Canis rufus	U.S. (FL, NC, SC)

Common name	Scientific name	Range
Woodpecker, ivory-billed	Campephilus principalis	Cuba
Yak, wild	Bos grunniens mutus	China (Tibet), India
Zebra, mountain	Equus zebra zebra	South Africa

U.S. List of Endangered and Threatened Species, 2005

Source: Fish and Wildlife Service, U.S. Dept. of Interior; as of Sept. 2005

Group	Endangered U.S.	Endangered Foreign	Threatened U.S.	Threatened Foreign	Total species[1]	Species with recovery plans
Mammals	68	251	11	20	350	55
Birds	77	175	13	6	271	78
Reptiles	14	64	22	16	116	33
Amphibians	12	8	9	1	30	15
Fishes	71	11	43	1	126	95
Clams	62	2	8	0	72	69
Snails	24	1	11	0	36	23
Insects	35	4	9	0	48	31
Arachnids	12	0	0	0	12	5
Crustaceans	19	0	3	0	22	13
Animal subtotal	**394**	**516**	**129**	**44**	**1,083**	**417**
Flowering plants	571	1	143	0	715	583
Conifers & cycads	2	0	1	2	5	3
Ferns and allies	24	0	2	0	26	26
Lichens	2	0	0	0	2	2
Plant subtotal	**599**	**1**	**146**	**2**	**748**	**614**
GRAND TOTAL	**993**	**517**	**275**	**46**	**1,831**	**1,031**

(1) Some species are classified as both endangered and threatened. The table tallies these "dual status" species only once, as endangered, except for the olive ridley sea turtle, which is dual status but tallied as a U.S. threatened species. The other dual status species, all tallied as endangered, are: (U.S.) California tiger salamander, chinook salmon, gray wolf, green sea turtle, piping plover, roseate tern, sockeye salmon, steelhead, Steller sea lion; (non-U.S.) argali, chimpanzee, leopard, saltwater crocodile.

Classification

Source: *Funk & Wagnalls New Encyclopedia*

In biology, classification is the identification, naming, and grouping of organisms into a formal system. The 2 fields that are most directly concerned with classification are taxonomy and systematics. Although the 2 disciplines overlap considerably, taxonomy is more concerned with nomenclature (naming) and with constructing hierarchical systems, and systematics with uncovering evolutionary relationships. Two kingdoms of living forms, Plantae and Animalia, have been recognized since Aristotle established the first taxonomy in the 4th century BC. In addition, there are the following 3 kingdoms: Protista (one-celled organisms), Monera (bacteria and blue-green algae; also known as the kingdom Procaryotae), and Fungi. The 7 basic categories of classification (from most general to most specific) are: kingdom, phylum (or division), class, order, family, genus, and species. Below are 2 examples:

ZOOLOGICAL HIERARCHY

Kingdom	Phylum	Class	Order	Family	Genus	Species name	Common name
Animalia	Chordata	Mammalia	Primates	Hominidae	Homo	Homo sapiens	Human

BOTANICAL HIERARCHY

Kingdom	Division*	Class	Order	Family	Genus	Species name	Common name
Plantae	Magnoliophyta	Magnoliopsida	Magnoliales	Magnoliaceae	Magnolia	M. virginiana	Sweet Bay

* In botany, the division is generally used in place of the phylum.

Gestation, Longevity, and Incubation of Animals

Information reviewed by Ronald M. Nowak, author *Walker's Mammals of the World* (6th ed., Johns Hopkins University Press, 1999). Average longevity figures supplied by Ronald T. Reuther. These apply to animals in captivity; the potential life span of animals is rarely attained in nature. Figures on gestation and incubation are averages based on estimates.

ANIMAL	Gestation (days)	Average longevity (years)	Maximum longevity (yr-mo)
Ass	365	12	47
Baboon	187	20	45
Bear: Black	219	18	36-10
Grizzly	225	25	50
Polar	240	20	45
Beaver	105	5	50
Bison	285	15	40
Camel	406	12	50
Cat (domestic)	63	12	28
Chimpanzee	230	20	60
Chipmunk	31	6	10
Cow	284	15	30
Deer (white-tailed)	201	8	20
Dog (domestic)	61	12	20
Elephant (African)	660	35	70
Elephant (Asian)	645	40	77
Elk	250	15	26-8
Fox (red)	52	7	14
Giraffe	457	10	36-2
Goat (domestic)	151	8	18
Gorilla	258	20	54
Guinea pig	68	4	8
Hippopotamus	238	41	61
Horse	330	20	50
Kangaroo (gray)	36	7	24
Leopard	98	12	23
Lion	100	15	30
Monkey (rhesus)	166	15	37
Moose	240	12	27
Mouse (meadow)	21	3	4
Mouse (dom. white)	19	3	6
Opossum (American)	13	1	5
Pig (domestic)	112	10	27
Puma	90	12	20
Rabbit (domestic)	31	5	13
Rhinoceros (black)	450	15	45-10
Rhinoceros (white)	480	20	50
Sea lion (California)	350	12	34
Sheep (domestic)	154	12	20
Squirrel (gray)	44	10	23-6
Tiger	105	16	26-3
Wolf (maned)	63	5	15-8
Zebra (Grant's)	365	15	50

Incubation time (days)

Chicken	21
Duck	30
Goose	30
Pigeon	18
Turkey	26

Major Venomous Animals

Snakes

Asian pit viper — from 2 ft to 5 ft long; throughout Asia; reactions and mortality vary, but most bites cause tissue damage, and mortality is generally low.

Australian brown snake — 4 ft to 7 ft long; very slow onset of cardiac or respiratory distress; moderate mortality, but because death can be sudden and unexpected, it is the most dangerous of the Australian snakes; antivenom.

Barba Amarilla or fer-de-lance — up to 7 ft long; from tropical Mexico to Brazil; severe tissue damage common; moderate mortality; antivenom.

Black mamba — up to 14 ft long, fast-moving; S and C Africa; rapid onset of dizziness, difficulty breathing, erratic heartbeat; mortality high, nears 100% without antivenom.

Boomslang — less than 6 ft long; in African savannahs; rapid onset of nausea and dizziness, often followed by slight recovery and then sudden death from internal hemorrhaging; bites rare, mortality high; antivenom.

Bushmaster — up to 12 ft long; wet tropical forests of C and S America; few bites occur, but mortality rate is high.

Common or Asian cobra — 4 ft to 8 ft long; throughout southern Asia; considerable tissue damage, sometimes paralysis; mortality probably not more than 10%; antivenom.

Copperhead — less than 4 ft long; from New England to Texas; pain and swelling; very seldom fatal; antivenom seldom needed.

Coral snake — 2 ft to 5 ft long; in Americas south of Canada; bite may be painless; slow onset of paralysis, impaired breathing; mortalities rare, but high without antivenom and mechanical respiration.

Cottonmouth water moccasin — up to 5 ft long; wetlands of southern U.S. from Virginia to Texas. Rapid onset of severe pain, swelling; mortality low, but tissue destruction can be extensive; antivenom.

Death adder — less than 3 ft long; Australia; rapid onset of faintness, cardiac and respiratory distress; at least 50% mortality without antivenom.

Desert horned viper — in dry areas of Africa and western Asia; swelling and tissue damage; low mortality; antivenom.

European viper — 1 ft to 3 ft long; bleeding and tissue damage; mortality low; antivenom.

Gaboon viper — more than 6 ft long; fat; 2-in. fangs; south of the Sahara; massive tissue damage, internal bleeding; few recorded bites.

King cobra — up to 16 ft long; throughout southern Asia; rapid swelling, dizziness, loss of consciousness, difficulty breathing, erratic heartbeat; mortality varies sharply with amount of venom involved, but most bites involve nonfatal amounts; antivenom.

Krait — up to 5 ft long; in SE Asia; rapid onset of sleepiness; numbness; up to 50% mortality even with use of antivenom.

Puff adder — up to 5 ft long; fat; south of the Sahara and throughout the Middle East; rapid large swelling, great pain, dizziness; moderate mortality, often from internal bleeding; antivenom.

Rattlesnake — 2 ft to 6 ft long; throughout W Hemisphere; rapid onset of severe pain, swelling; mortality low, but amputation of affected digits is sometimes necessary; antivenom. Mojave rattler may produce temporary paralysis.

Ringhals, or spitting, cobra — 5 ft to 7 ft long; southern Africa; squirts venom through holes in front of fangs as a defense; venom is severely irritating, can cause blindness.

Russell's viper or tic-polonga — more than 5 ft long; throughout Asia; internal bleeding; bite reports common; moderate mortality rate; antivenom.

Saw-scaled or carpet viper — as much as 2 ft long; in dry areas from India to Africa; severe bleeding, fever; high mortality, causes more human fatalities than any other snake; antivenom.

Sea snakes — throughout Pacific, Indian oceans except NE Pacific; almost painless bite, variety of muscle pain, paralysis; mortality rate low, many bites not envenomed; some antivenoms.

Sharp-nosed pit viper or one hundred pace snake — up to 5 ft long; in S Vietnam, Taiwan, and China; the most toxic of Asian pit vipers; very rapid onset of swelling and tissue damage, internal bleeding; moderate mortality; antivenom.

Taipan — up to 11 ft long; in Australia and New Guinea; rapid paralysis with severe breathing difficulty; mortality nears 100% without antivenom.

Tiger snake — 2 ft to 6 ft long; S Australia; pain, numbness, mental disturbances with rapid paralysis; may be deadliest of all land snakes, but antivenom is quite effective.

Yellow or Cape cobra — 7 ft long; in S Africa; most toxic venom of any cobra; rapid onset of swelling, breathing and cardiac difficulties; mortality is high without treatment; antivenom.

Note: Not all bites by venomous snakes are actually envenomed. Any animal bite, however, carries the danger of tetanus, and anyone suffering a venomous snake bite should seek medical attention. Antivenoms do not cure; they are only an aid in the treatment of bites. Mortality rates above are for envenomed bites; low mortality, c. 2% or less; moderate, 2%-5%; high, 5%-15%.

Lizards

Gila monster — as much as 24 in. long, with heavy body and tail; in high desert in SW U.S. and N Mexico; immediate severe pain and transient low blood pressure; no recent mortality.

Mexican beaded lizard — similar to Gila monster, Mexican west coast; reaction and mortality rate similar to Gila monster.

Insects

Ants, bees, wasps, hornets, etc. Global distribution. Usual reaction is piercing pain in area of sting. Not directly fatal, except in cases of massive multiple stings. However, many people suffer allergic reactions — swelling and rashes — and a few may die within minutes from severe sensitivity to the venom (anaphylactic shock).

Spiders, Scorpions

Atrax spider — also known as funnel web spider; several varieties, often large; in Australia; slow onset of breathing, circulation difficulties; low mortality; antivenom.

Black widow — small, round-bodied with red hourglass marking; the widow and its relatives are found in tropical and temperate zones; severe musculoskeletal pain, weakness, breathing difficulty, convulsions; may be more serious in small children; low mortality; antivenom. The **redback** spider of Australia has the hourglass marking on its back, rather than on its front, but is otherwise identical to the black widow.

Brown recluse, or fiddleback, spider — small, oblong body; throughout U.S.; pain with later ulceration at place of bite; in severe cases fever, nausea, and stomach cramps; ulceration may last months; very low mortality.

Scorpion — crablike body with stinger in tail, various sizes, many varieties throughout tropical and subtropical areas; various symptoms may include severe pain spreading from the wound, numbness, severe agitation, cramps; severe reaction may include respiratory failure; low mortality, usually in children; antivenoms.

Tarantula — large, hairy spider found around the world; the American tarantula, and probably all other tarantulas, are harmless to humans, though their bite may cause some pain and swelling.

Sea Life

Cone-shell — mollusk in small, beautiful shell; in the S Pacific and Indian oceans; shoots barbs into victims; paralysis; low mortality.

Octopus — global distribution, usually in warm waters; all varieties produce venom, but only a few can cause death; rapid onset of paralysis with breathing difficulty.

Portuguese man-of-war — jellyfishlike, with tentacles up to 100 ft long; in most warm water areas; immediate severe pain; not directly fatal, though shock may cause death in rare cases.

Sea wasp — jellyfish, with tentacles up to 30 ft long, in the S Pacific; very rapid onset of circulatory problems; high mortality because of speed of toxic reaction; antivenom.

Stingray — several varieties of differing sizes; found in tropical and temperate seas and some fresh water; severe pain, rapid onset of nausea, vomiting, breathing difficulties; wound area may ulcerate, gangrene may appear; seldom fatal.

Stonefish — brownish fish that lies motionless as a rock on bottom in shallow water; throughout S Pacific and Indian oceans; extraordinary pain, rapid paralysis; low mortality; antivenom available, amount determined by number of puncture wounds; warm water relieves pain.

Speeds of Animals

Source: Natural History magazine. © American Museum of Natural History

ANIMAL	mph	ANIMAL	mph	ANIMAL	mph	ANIMAL	mph
Cheetah	70	Hyena	40	White-tailed deer	30	Wild turkey	15
Pronghorn antelope	61	Zebra	40	Wart hog	30	Squirrel	12
Wildebeest	50	Mongolian wild ass	40	Grizzly bear	30	Pig (domestic)	11
Lion	50	Greyhound	39.35	Cat (domestic)	30	Chicken	9
Thomson's gazelle	50	Whippet	35.50	Human	27.89	Spider (Tegenaria atrica)	1.17
Quarterhorse	47.5	Rabbit (domestic)	35	Elephant	25	Giant tortoise	0.17
Elk	45	Mule deer	35	Black mamba snake	20	Three-toed sloth	0.15
Cape hunting dog	45	Jackal	35	Six-lined race runner (lizard)	18	Garden snail	0.03
Coyote	43	Reindeer	32				
Gray fox	42	Giraffe	32				

Note: Most of these measurements are for maximum speeds over approximate quarter-mile distances. Exceptions are the lion and elephant, whose speeds were clocked in the act of charging; the whippet, which was timed over a 200-yd course; the cheetah, timed over a 100-yd distance; humans timed over a 15-yard segment of a 100-yard run; and the black mamba, six-lined race runner, spider, giant tortoise, three-toed sloth, and garden snail, which were measured over various small distances.

Top 50 American Kennel Club Registrations

Source: American Kennel Club, New York, NY; covers (new) dogs registered during calendar year shown

Breed	2004 Rank	2004 Number registered	2003 Rank	2003 Number registered
Labrador Retrievers	1	146,692	1	144,896
Golden Retrievers	2	52,550	2	52,520
German Shepherds	3	46,046	4	43,938
Beagles	4	44,555	3	45,021
Yorkshire Terriers	5	43,522	6	38,246
Dachshunds	6	40,770	5	39,468
Boxers	7	37,741	7	34,130
Poodles	8	32,671	8	32,162
Shih Tzu	9	28,958	9	26,926
Chihuahuas	10	24,850	10	24,923
Miniature Schnauzers	11	24,080	11	22,282
Pugs	12	23,152	12	21,337
Pomeranians	13	21,269	13	20,802
Bulldogs	14	19,396	16	16,732
Spaniels (Cocker)	15	18,553	14	19,020
Rottweilers	16	17,498	15	18,214
Boston Terriers	17	16,464	18	14,727
Shetland Sheepdogs	18	15,605	17	15,686
Maltese	19	13,683	20	12,645
Pointers (German Shorthaired)	20	12,799	21	12,266
Miniature Pinschers	21	12,697	19	13,155
Doberman Pinschers	22	11,724	22	11,549
Welsh Corgis (Pembroke)	23	11,230	24	10,333
Siberian Huskies	24	10,566	23	10,660
Basset Hounds	25	9,814	25	9,480
Bichons Frises	26	9,796	26	9,409
Great Danes	27	9,507	27	8,946
English Springer Spaniels	28	9,376	28	8,859
Weimaraners	29	9,010	29	8,763
Brittanys	30	8,151	30	7,751
West Highland White Terriers	31	7,744	31	7,407
Cavalier King Charles Spaniels	32	7,097	35	5,306
Mastiffs	33	6,439	33	5,654
Australian Shepherds	34	6,116	34	5,625
Papillons	35	6,019	36	5,143
Collies	36	5,485	32	5,679
St. Bernards	37	4,490	39	4,297
Pekingese	38	4,335	37	4,768
Lhasa Apsos	39	4,316	38	4,407
Neapolitan Mastiffs	40	4,164	154	0
Chinese Shar-Pei	41	3,924	40	4,100
Scottish Terriers	42	3,853	43	3,559
Cairn Terriers	43	3,750	42	3,706
Vizslas	44	3,616	45	3,178
Newfoundlands	45	3,505	46	3,134
Chesapeake Bay Retrievers	46	3,454	41	3,713
Bullmastiffs	47	3,433	48	2,943
Bernese Mountain Dogs	48	3,430	47	3,130
French Bulldogs	49	3,377	54	2,202
Bloodhounds	50	3,113	49	2,849

Breed Registration for Top 10 Pedigreed Cats, 1979-2004

Source: The Cat Fanciers' Association, Manasquan, NJ; ranked by new registrations, 2004.

Breed	2004	2003	2000	1995	1990	1979
Persian	18,176	20,431	25,524	44,735	60,661	25,819
Maine Coon	4,162	4,385	4,539	4,332	2,727	401
Exotic	2,838	2,720	2,094	1,610	1,311	289
Siamese	1,621	1,921	2,131	3,025	3,860	3,607
Abyssinian	1,462	1,417	1,683	2,469	2,702	1,524
Ragdoll	981	765	—	—	—	—
Birman	945	1,057	998	990	969	258
Oriental	854	952	1,085	1,237	1,288	260
American Shorthair	846	874	885	1,050	1,176	738
Tonkinese	717	864	803	780	618	—
TOTAL	**41,606**	**44,774**	**49,551**	**70,288**	**84,729**	**37,630**

Trees of the U.S.

Source: American Forests, Washington, DC

Approximately 826 native and naturalized species of trees are grown in the U.S. The oldest living tree is believed to be a bristlecone pine tree in California named Methuselah, estimated to be 4,700 years old. The world's largest known living tree, the General Sherman giant sequoia in California, weighs more than 6,167 tons—as much as 41 blue whales or 740 elephants.

Listed here are 10 largest National Champion trees as listed by American Forests.

10 Largest National Champion Trees

Tree Type	Girth at 4.5 ft. (in.)	Height (ft.)	Crown Spread (ft.)	Total Points*	Location
Giant sequoia (Gen. Sherman tree)	1,020	274	107	1,321	Sequoia National Park, CA
Coast redwood	950	321	75	1,290	Jedidiah Smith State Park, CA
Coast redwood	895	307	83	1,223	Jedidiah Smith State Park, CA
Coast redwood	867	311	101	1,203	Prairie Creek St. Pk., CA
Western red cedar	761	159	45	931	Olympic National Park, WA
Sitka spruce	668	191	96	833	Olympic National Park, WA
Sitka spruce	629	204	93	856	Kloochy Creek Park, OR
Douglas fir	600	200	71	809	Olympic National Park, WA
Douglas fir	512	301	65	829	Jedidiah Smith State Park, CA
Bluegum eucalyptus	586	141	126	759	Petrolia, CA

* American Forests uses a point system to determine the largest trees. The following calculation to determine a tree's total points: Trunk Circumference (in inches) + Height (in feet) + ¼ Average Crown Spread (in feet) = Total Points

SCIENCE AND TECHNOLOGY

Science News

Life Sciences news and glossary entries reviewed by Prof. Maura C. Flannery, St. John's Univ., NYC.
Physical Sciences news reviewed by Assoc. Prof. Matthew Strassler, Univ. of Washington, Seattle.

The following were some of the more newsworthy developments in Science in the past year. (See also the chapters on Astronomy, Computers and Telecommunications and Health.)

Life Science Developments

• Scientists found **soft tissue** in the thighbone of a 68-million-year old ***Tyrannosaurus rex*** from Montana's Hell Creek Formation. The groundbreaking discovery was reported in *Science* Mar. 25, 2005. Mary Schweitzer and colleagues at North Carolina State Univ. discovered blood vessels and other soft tissue fragments in the bone's cavity. The tissue's extraordinary state of preservation allowed researchers to find similarities between *T. rex* blood vessels and those of the modern-day ostrich. Further examination of the bone cavity revealed a structure that appears to be medullary bone. During ovulation, modern female birds develop medullary bone, which provides **calcium for the formation of eggshells**. Since only females produce this bone structure, the scientists concluded that the *T. rex* must have been a female that died near the end of her egg-laying cycle. This discovery, published in June 3 *Science*, establishes another **link between dinosaurs and living birds**.

• Paleontologist Yaoming Hu and associates found fossil remains of two mammals that lived about 130 million years ago in Liaoning, China, and that were **bigger than the largest known mammals** of that era. Their findings, reported in the Jan. 13 issue of *Nature,* challenge the traditional view that early mammals were rat-sized prey for dinosaurs and other animals. Remains of one of the mammals, called *Repenomamus giganticus*, was 50% bigger than the largest known mammals of the time. The young adult had a body over 3 feet long and weighed about 30 pounds. The other fossil, *R. robustus*, contained the remains of a small dinosaur in its belly, the first **evidence that mammals preyed on dinosaurs**.

• A report in *Nature* Feb. 24 announced the discovery of a new 6-foot-tall species of **raptor dinosaur** belonging to the group most closely related to birds. The fossils, found in the southern tip of South America, provide the first indication that this dinosaur group roamed the Southern Hemisphere.

• In the Feb. 17 issue of *Nature*, the Univ. of Utah's Frank Brown and colleagues reported that *Homo sapiens* appeared in Africa 65,000 years earlier than was previously believed. In 1967, Richard Leakey's group of paleontologists found bones of early humans buried in Ethiopia's Kibish rock formation. Based on technology available at that time, scientists dated the fossils as being 130,000 years old. Two modern techniques used by Brown's team pushed the date back to 195,000 years ago, making these the **oldest dated fossils of *Homo sapiens***.

• **The human family tree has a new branch.** Michael Morwood, Peter Brown, and their colleagues at the Univ. of New England (Armidale, Australia) described a startling newly discovered species in the Oct. 28, 2004, issue of *Nature*. Formally named *Homo floresiensis*, after the Indonesian island of Flores where their remains were discovered, these cousins to modern humans (*Homo sapiens*) stood just over 3 feet tall and exhibited significant intelligence by creating sophisticated tools and using fire. Scientists have assumed that the disappearance of Neanderthals about 25,000 to 30,000 years ago left *H. sapiens* as the lone intelligent humanoid species. It is now known that individuals of the *H. floresiensis* species, informally known as "**hobbits**," lived as recently as 18,000 years ago and, according to local folklore, might have persisted until the last century.

• The existence of the **ivory-billed woodpecker** (*Campephilus principalis*), previously believed to be extinct, in an eastern Arkansas swamp forest was confirmed by Cornell Univ.'s John Fitzpatrick and his team, according to the June 3 issue of *Science*. Once numbering in the tens of thousands, the woodpeckers stand about 20 inches tall and have wingspans of about 30 inches. During the obliteration of forests across the southeastern U.S., the birds began to disappear. The bird's reappearance suggests that other forest species thought to be extinct may reappear as well. See illustration, page 197.

• In another story of an animal comeback, for the first time in over 40 years, researchers caught a glimpse of endangered **snow leopards** on the southern slopes of Mt. Everest. Univ. of Illinois doctoral candidate Som Ale photographed the leopards in Oct. 2004 after tracking their prey, wild goats. Scientists hope that the sighting signals a growth in the snow leopard population.

• The discovery of a new species of rat-like animal that looks like a cross between a large dark rat and a squirrel led to the designation of a **whole new family, genus, and species**. As reported in the Dec. 2004 issue of *Systematics and Biodiversity*, conservation biologist Robert Timmins found the animal, the likes of which he had never seen, for sale at a central Laos food market. Scientists discover new rodent species at the rate of about one per year, but the discovery of a new family is rare. The new family is called *Laonastidae*; the genus is *Laonastes*; and the new species is called the Laotian rock rat (*Laonastes aenigmamus*).

• For the first time in 20 years, a **new species of African monkey** was discovered. As reported in *Science* May 20, Trevor Jones and Tim Davenport independently discovered the highland mangabey (*Lophocebus kipunji*) in Tanzania, while investigating sites hundreds of miles apart. They estimate that fewer than 1,000 of the animals live in highland forests.

• During the past decade, scientists discovered 35 new frog species in **Sri Lanka's rain forest**. In the June 30 issue of *The Raffles Bulletin of Zoology*, Sri Lanka's Wildlife Heritage Trust researcher Rohan Pethiyagoda and his group revealed that they have also found 17 new species of freshwater crabs. Other researchers have identified 50 new species of snails and 7 new lizards there.

• While investigating genetic mutations that enabled dogs to rapidly develop into over 100 breeds, the Univ. of Texas Southwestern Medical Center's John Fondon III discovered **an important mechanism of mammalian evolution**. His research, published in the Dec. 28, 2004, issue of the *Proceedings of the National Academy of Sciences USA*, shows a correlation between slight differences in the lengths of certain developmental genes and characteristics associated with dog breeds, such as muzzle shape. The differences in gene lengths are due to the occurrence of variable numbers of repeating segments of nucleotides. Changes in the number of repeating segments within a gene can alter the protein encoded by the gene such that the protein functions more or less efficiently. Humans, like dogs and other mammals, also carry these DNA "stutters" in developmental genes.

• Experts from 46 countries plan to create **databases that store species-specific DNA sequences** of animals and plants. Reporting in the Feb. 18 issue of *Science*, proponents of this effort envision a time when scientists can identify species by scanning biological samples, as if they were bar codes, with a portable device linked to DNA databases. This would reduce the need to classify an organism's species by examining morphology, a traditional method limited to certain life stages. Applications of this technology range from monitoring biodiversity to examining museum specimens to analyzing pollen grains left at a crime scene. By 2010, researchers hope to have identified species-specific DNA sequences for 15,000 marine and 8,000 freshwater fish, as well as 10,000 birds.

• Robert Pruitt and colleagues at Purdue Univ. announced in the Mar. 24 issue of *Nature* that plants seemingly **do not always obey the long-accepted laws of genetic inheritance** originally laid down 150 years ago by Austrian monk Gregor Mendel. It was previously believed that genes stably transmit traits from one generation to the next. The researchers examined *Arabidopsis* plants that carried a mutated gene, which prevented flowers from opening. Surprisingly, they found that some of the plants' offspring—produced by self-pollination—had open flowers and a restored, normal copy of the gene found not in the parental but in the grandparental generation. Further research could lead to the development of new methods to fight inherited diseases in humans.

• Scientists announced the **first successful cloning of a dog** in the Aug. 4 issue of *Nature*. Led by Woo Suk Hwang of Seoul National Univ., the team of scientists created two clones of an Afghan hound by taking DNA from the ear of an adult male and adding it to a harvested egg. One of the pups died soon after birth, but the other which appeared healthy, was hidden from the world for about 9 weeks until the cloning could be deemed successful. They named the clone "Snuppy," which stands for Seoul National University Puppy. Cloning dogs is difficult because canine eggs are very underdeveloped and almost unusable when they leave the ovaries. As they travel to the uterus they mature. The South Korean scientists were able to devise a way to harvest the mature eggs from the oviduct, before replacing their DNA with donor DNA to create the clone. A Labrador retriever served as the surrogate mother.

• A team headed by the Univ. of Michigan's Yehoash Raphael partially reversed deafness in experimental animals with **gene therapy,** marking the first time that anyone has biologically repaired hearing. As reported in the Mar. issue of *Nature Medicine*, the researchers injected a recombinant virus into the inner ears of guinea pigs that lacked cochlear sensory (hair) cells. The virus carried a gene that stimulated the non-sensory cells to develop into sensory hair cells which play a critical role in translating sound waves into electrical signals for the brain. The success in partially restoring hearing suggests that gene therapy may some day help people who have degenerated hair cells, the most common cause of sensorineural hearing loss.

• Two research teams reported comprehensive analyses of the **human X chromosome**. One team, headed by Mark Ross of England's Wellcome Trust Sanger Institute, sequenced 99.3% of the genetically active portions of the human X chromosome. The results, published in *Nature* Mar. 17, will enable scientists to examine over 1,000 protein-coding genes on the X chromosome. As reported in the Apr. issue of *Nature Genetics,* Johns Hopkins Univ.'s Akhilesh Pandey and colleagues explored the human X chromosome by searching for similarities between human protein-encoding genetic sequences and corresponding regions in chromosomes from chimpanzees, rats, mice, and pufferfish. The group found 43 potential new genes that encode proteins, including genes in chromosomal regions associated with mental retardation syndromes. Genetic analyses may accelerate research into diseases mapped to the X chromosome.

• A Seoul National Univ. research team, led by Woo Suk Hwang, created the first **human embryonic stem cells** that carry **DNA of specific individuals**. As reported in the June 17 issue of *Science*, the researchers replaced nuclei of donated eggs with nuclei taken from patients' cells. The transplanted nuclei contained the patients' genetic material, and in some cases, included genes responsible for genetic diseases. After switching nuclei, the researchers allowed embryos to develop for six days before harvesting stem cells. Scientists can use cells derived from donors with a genetic disorder to study the disease and investigate potential drugs for treatment. This may one day enable physicians to treat diseases by transplanting cells that genetically match the patient and thus prevent the patient's immune system from rejecting the cells.

• In the Apr. 22 issue of *Science*, Mark Roth and colleagues at Seattle's Fred Hutchinson Cancer Research Center reported a method for **inducing a mouse to enter a suspended animation-like state** by exposing the animal to hydrogen sulfide gas. Scientists have tried for years to put a mammal into a state of extreme metabolic slowdown or torpor, which is characterized by decreased heart rate, slowed breathing, and drop in body temperature. The Seattle researchers found that low concentrations of hydrogen sulfide gas induced torpor in mice, and that exposure to normal air revived the animals. Lowering the metabolic rate in humans could reduce damage from trauma—such as the consequences of a heart attack—and might improve **outcomes after surgery**.

• Artificial wetlands cleanse water at least as effectively as a natural marsh, according to a report published in the Dec. 30, 2004 issue of *Ecological Engineering*. Scientists have been developing **artificial replacements for disappearing natural wetlands**. These natural resources perform many vital functions, such as filtering phosphorous and nitrates from agricultural fertilizer before the chemicals pollute waterways. Over a 2-year period, William Mitsch and Daniel Fink of Ohio State Univ. examined a 3-acre wetland constructed as a series of basins that slope downward toward Ohio's Great Miami River. They found that the artificial wetland reduced levels of phosphorus and nitrates in runoff from nearby farm fields.

• Ecologists from The Woods Hole Research Center in Massachusetts led by Daniel Nepstad produced drought conditions in 2.2 acres of Amazonian rainforest using 6,000 plastic panels to divert rainwater from the ground over a 5-year period to study the **forest's response to drought**, according to a report in *Science* Apr. 15. The most detailed investigation of its kind, the research indicates that after 4 years of artificial drought, trees began to die. As more light reached the forest floor, leaf litter dried, and increased the risk of fire. The drought also reduced plant growth which decreased the forest's ability to store carbon. The Amazon rainforest removes and stores atmospheric carbon dioxide—a greenhouse gas. Several climate models predict that the Amazon will in the future experience increased droughts.—*Phill Jones*

Physical Sciences Developments

• New discoveries in the field of **nuclear fusion** made headlines in 2005. A team of UCLA physicists led by Seth Putterman reported evidence of **controlled nuclear fusion on a tabletop device**, in the April 28 issue of *Nature*. Their experiment produced free neutrons, which are often considered the ultimate sign of fusion. However, the fusion was not self-sustaining and therefore could not be used as a renewable power source. Fusion, which is the merger of light elements to form heavy ones, powers the Sun; producing a similar reaction on Earth could lead to an endless, cheap power supply. Any claims of "tabletop" fusion are hotly contested.

A Univ. of Illinois Urbana-Champlain team of chemists found that temperatures **inside collapsing bubbles** can be four times **as hot as the surface of the Sun**, according to research presented in the March 3 issue of *Nature*. The team, led by Ken Suslick, measured the temperature of collapsing xenon bubbles produced by ultra-high frequency sound waves in a flask of sulfuric acid. Bubbles formed this way give off intense flashes of heat and light as they collapse. As the gasses inside become compressed, plasma is formed. The light created is known as sonoluminescence. The team found the temperature on the surface of the plasma in the bubbles to be about 36,000°F (20,000°K), but they believe the temperature at the center of the reaction may be many times higher, possibly high enough create **nuclear fusion**. The researchers did not go so far as to say that their observations were direct signs of fusion, but some scientists have made controversial claims that such bubbles can start fusion.

• The **early universe** may have behaved **like a perfect liquid**, according to the research of several teams of particle physicists experimenting with hot, dense matter. Using the Relativistic Heavy Ion Collider at Brookhaven National Laboratory (a large particle accelerator) in Upton, NY, researchers smashed together gold atoms traveling near the speed of light. The collisions created an unexpected form of matter that is believed to have been present in the universe in its first few milliseconds of existence, called a quark-gluon plasma or perfect liquid. The plasma only existed for about 10-20 seconds before disintegrating into thousands of other particles. The scientists say it gives all the signs of being a perfectly-flowing liquid, not a loose gas, as most had expected. A perfect liquid is a liquid that has a very low viscosity. In the case of the quark-gluon plasma, its particles move uniformly (unlike conventional liquids whose particles move in different directions) so that it would look the same when viewed it from different directions. The loose-flowing liquid may explain why our universe appears to be so smooth and uniform in any direction we look. The finding may help scientists get an idea of the tremendously hot and dense conditions in the earliest microseconds, right after the Big Bang. The research was reported at an April conference of the American Physical Society in Tampa, FL.

• Roboticists have taken great steps recently toward creating **robots that can replicate themselves and interact better with their environment**. Cornell Univ. scientists created self-replicating robots using modular cubes they call "molecubes." As reported in the May 12 issue of *Nature*, the identical cubes, each 1,000 cubic cm, each contain the complete program for assembly and replication, and when mixed together, they form larger robots that can move, bend, and manipulate other robots.

French roboticists working with scientists at the Univ. of Michigan and Ohio State Univ. developed RABBIT, **a two-legged robot that can walk and balance** much like a human. As reported in the June *International Journal of Robotics Research*, the robot did not have human-shaped feet but had rounded bottoms on its legs that allowed the "feet" to rock as it took steps. The rounded-foot design makes it easier for the robot's computer-control program to keep the robot in balance, and allows the robot to move around easily. Aside from walking, RABBIT can recover from stumbles when tripped or shoved. The team says their work could lead to better human prosthetic feet and legs.

• Cockroaches are always sweeping the ground and walls with their antennae to figure out terrain contours and barriers. Engineers at Johns Hopkins Univ. **developed an artificial antenna** that let robots do the same thing. An onboard computer measured the tension of the antenna as it bent, which allowed the robot to discover the location and "feel" of obstacles, and adjust its own movements accordingly. Video cameras serve as "eyes" for most robots, but they generally do not work in the dark or when confronted with shiny surfaces. Navigation based on a sense of touch bypasses these problems. The findings were presented in April at the International Conference on Robotics and Automation, in Barcelona, Spain.

• The **chemistry of burning flames** has been studied for 150 years, but there is still much to learn about it. Researchers at Sandia National Laboratories in Livermore, CA, and colleagues from other institutions found an unsuspected but simple class of molecules called **enols** within flames according to a May report on the *Science Express* Web site. Enols are carbon compounds related to alcohols. The team of chemists who discovered them said they seem to be present in nearly all flames, and eluded discovery for so long because they have masses similar to other molecules present during combustion. The researchers used a new technique that allowed them to learn the structure and mass of the molecules. The enols and other intermediate compounds disappear quickly as the flame burns, but they play an important role in the burning process.

• Physicists have discovered a physical process that **could lead to new kinds of refrigeration.** Tammy Humphrey of U.C. Santa Cruz and Heiner Linke of the Univ. of Oregon showed in the April online version of *Nature Materials* how an electrochemical imbalance can be used to prevent heated regions from flowing into cold regions. Humphrey and Linke proposed a thermoelectric circuit that is good at conducting electrons, but poor at moving heat. The two physicists said quantum dots or tiny nanowires, which only let electrons have certain energy levels, could be designed to stop high-energy, heat-carrying electrons from passing. The dots and wires could absorb or redirect waste heat to a different location, where it can be converted again to electricity. Potential practical uses include converting the heat cast off by car engines, computer chips, and geothermal sources into electricity. Reversing the process could lead to quieter, smaller refrigerators, with no moving parts.

• A rare form of nickel had its lifetime measured, and the results will help astrophysicists understand how many of the **heaviest elements, like gold and lead**, are made in stars according to scientists in the U.S. and Germany as reported in the March 25 issue of *Physical Review Letters*. Using a high-energy particle accelerator, physicists produced **nickel-78**, a form of nickel whose atomic nucleus is perfectly packed with protons and neutrons, making it "noble" in a nuclear sense. Its lifetime, a mere 110 milliseconds, was four times shorter than predicted, meaning that making the heavier elements by nuclear fusion in explosions of stars called supernova is easier than thought. With the lifetime known, cosmologists will have to readjust their theories to explain the observed amounts of precious metals in the universe.

• When water is trapped in narrow pores called carbon nanotubes it **never freezes**, even when it's just a few degrees above absolute zero, according to physicists at the Argonne National Laboratory in Illinois. The findings, first published in the July 6 issue of *Physical Review Letters*, gave scientists an insight into **water's behavior at the molecular level** in a variety of physical and biological settings. **Carbon nanotubes** are hollow tubes of pure carbon with a diameter of only 1-2 nanometers. Inside such a narrow pore the water molecules must line up single file. In this arrangement the water molecules form fewer bonds with each other and continue to flow freely, despite the frigid temperature of -455° F, only 15° F (8° K) above absolute zero. The discovery shed light on how water flows in narrow plant roots and through aquaporin proteins, which control water's entry into cells.

• If people had the ability to see high-energy gamma rays with their own eyes on Dec. 27, 2004, they would have seen **an explosion brighter than the full Moon**. Astronomers from around the world detected a gamma-ray blast that came from a magnetar, a rare type of neutron star (a neutron star is made from the super-dense remains of a massive star that had collapsed, and has incredibly strong gravity), located 50,000 light years from Earth. Only 12 magnetars are known to exist in the Milky Way among the many neutron stars. The explosion, called a "star-quake," happened in our own galaxy, and gave astronomers, in astronomical terms, an up-close view.

The discovery provided scientists with a known source for mysterious short gamma-ray bursts, which come mostly from distant galaxies and have been very difficult to explain. Astrophysicists think that most short bursts come from mergers of two neutron stars, but the new observation reveals another source. Magnetars have **the strongest magnetic fields in the universe**—a thousand trillion times Earth's—which theoretically disrupt the star's surface and cause the bursts. The blast disrupted the Earth's ionosphere, but had it been as close as 10 light-years away, instead of 50,000, it would have destroyed the Earth's ozone layer and led to mass extinctions.

• A new metallic laminate may be a good replacement for the toxic metal beryllium and may serve as a **strong, lightweight metal for armor and aircraft**, according to an article in the March *Journal of Minerals, Metals and Materials Society*. Engineer Kenneth Vecchio, of the Univ. of California San Diego, has developed a strong metal made of titanium and aluminum. After heating and melting thin, stacked layers of titanium and aluminum together, Vecchio ended up with a laminate consisting of hard, almost ceramic layers of titanium aluminide and pliable layers of titanium alloy. He found the lightweight laminate was extremely tough—a tungsten bolt fired at 900 mph could not penetrate a ¾-inch sample.

• Light in the universe may arise from **tiny violations of Einstein's theory of relativity,** according to research published online in the March 22 issue of *Physical Review D*. Kostelecky, a physicist at the Univ. of Indiana, outlined a theory that says light is actually ripples in a field that permeates the empty space of the universe and violates Lorentz invariance. If that is true, there should be small detectable differences in light traveling in different directions as it goes with or against the field. This goes right back to the Michelson-Morley experiment of the 19th century, which attempted to detect the ether which was believed to permeate all space. These differences could be detected as Earth orbits the Sun or in particle accelerators. Kostelecky's theory goes against Einstein's well-tested theory of relativity, which says that light should travel at the same speed and have the same properties in any direction.—*Philip Downey*

WORLD ALMANAC QUICK QUIZ

Which of the following is not a real element?

(a) Adamantium	(b) Einsteinium
(c) Krypton	(d) Tin

For the answer look in this chapter, or see page 1008.

Some Laws of Physics

Isaac Newton's Laws of Motion

1. An object in motion moves at a constant velocity in a straight line unless acted upon by a force. Likewise, an object at rest will stay at rest. This is known as **inertia**.
2. The **acceleration** of an object is proportional to the force acting on it and inversely proportional to the mass of an object. This is best illustrated in the following equation:

   F=ma   Force equals mass times acceleration

3. For every **action**, there is an equal and opposite **reaction**.

Laws of Thermodynamics

1. Heat is a form of **energy**. Within a closed system energy must be conserved except in nuclear reactions or other extreme conditions. It is **neither created nor destroyed**.
2. Within a self-sustaining system, heat can never go from an area of low temperature to an area of high temperature. Disorder, or **entropy,** can only increase in closed system.
3. **Absolute zero** cannot be attained by any procedure in a finite number of steps. Absolute zero can be approached arbitrarily closely, but it can never be reached.

Two Basic Laws of Quantum Physics

1. Heisenberg's **uncertainty principle**: Certain pairs of observable quantities like energy and time, or position and momentum cannot be measured with complete accuracy simultaneously. Also known as indeterminacy principle.
2. Pauli's **exclusion principle**: Two electrons in an atom cannot simultaneously occupy the same quantum or energy state. This has since been shown to be true for many subatomic particles.

Science Glossary

This glossary covers some concepts that come up frequently in the news, in biology, chemistry, geology, and physics. See also Astronomy, Computers and Telecommunications, Environment, Health, Meteorology, Weights and Measures.

Biology

NOTE: For classification terms such as *kingdom, phylum,* etc., see Environment chapter.

Amino acid: one of about 20 similar small molecules that are the building blocks of proteins.

Antibiotic: a drug made from a substance produced by a bacterium, fungus, or other organism that battles bacterial infections and diseases, killing the bacteria or halting their growth.

Autoimmunity: a condition in which an individual's immune system reacts against his or her own tissues; leads to diseases such as lupus, diabetes, inflammatory bowel disease, rheumatoid arthritis.

Bacterium (plural, bacteria): one of a large, varied class of microscopic and simple, single-celled organisms; bacteria live almost everywhere—some forms cause disease, while others are useful in digestion and other natural processes.

Biodiversity: richness of variety of life forms—both plant and animal—in a given environment.

Cell: the smallest unit of life capable of living independently, or with other cells; usually bounded by a membrane; may include a nucleus and other specialized parts.

Cholesterol: a fatty substance in animal tissues; it is produced by the liver in humans, and is found in foods such as butter, eggs, and meat, and is an essential body constituent.

Chromosome: one of the rod-like structures in the nuclei of cells that carry genetic material (DNA).

Cloning: the process of copying a particular piece of DNA to allow it to be sequenced, studied, or used in some other way; can also refer to producing a genetic copy of an organism.

DNA (deoxyribonucleic acid): the chemical substance that carries genetic information, which determines the form and functioning of all living things.

Ecosystem: an interdependent community of living organisms and their climatic and geographical habitat.

Enzyme: a protein that promotes a particular chemical reaction in the body.

Estrogen: one of a group of hormones that promote development of female secondary sex characteristics and the growth and health of the female reproductive system; males also produce small amounts of estrogen.

Evolution: the process of gradual change that may occur as a species adapts to its environment; natural selection is the process by which evolution occurs.

Fight-or-flight response: the physical response that occurs in all animals when they encounter a threat; bodies release hormones, such as cortisol and epinephrine, that speed up the heart rate and increase blood flow to the muscles, allowing animals to fight enemies or run away.

Gene: a portion of a DNA molecule that provides the blueprint for the assembly of a protein.

Gene pool: the collection and total diversity of genes in an interbreeding population.

Gene therapy: a treatment in which scientists try to implant functioning genes into a person's cells so the genes can produce proteins that the person lacks or that help the person fight disease.

Genetic sequencing: the process of determining the order of subunits within a gene or even the order of all genes for an organism.

Genome: the complete set of an organism's genetic material.

Hormone: a substance secreted in one part of an organism that regulates the functioning of other tissues or organs.

Meiosis: the process of cell division that results in gametes (sperm or egg cells), all of which contain half the number of chromosomes as their precursor.

Metabolism: the sum total of the body's chemical processes providing energy for vital functions, and enabling new material to be synthesized.

Mitosis: the process by which a cell divides its nucleus and other cell materials into two duplicate daughter cells with the same DNA.

Neuron: a nerve cell, of the type found in the brain or spinal cord, that sends electrical and chemical messages to other cells.

Nucleus (plural: nuclei): the center of an atom; or the portion of a cell containing the chemical directions for functioning.

Organism: a living being.

Phenotype: the observable properties and characteristics of an organism arising at least in part from its genetic makeup.

Pheromone: a chemical secreted by an animal to influence the behavior of other members of its own species.

Placebo effect: a phenomenon in which patients show improvements even though they have taken a medically inactive substance, called a placebo.

Protein: a complex molecule made up of one or more chains of amino acids; essential to the structure and function of all cells.

RNA (ribonucleic acid): a complex molecule similar to the genetic material DNA, but usually single-stranded; several forms of RNA translate the genetic code of DNA and use that code to assemble proteins for structural and biological functions in the body.

Species: a population of organisms that breed with each other in nature and produce fertile offspring; other definitions of species exist to accommodate the diversity of life on Earth.

Stem cell: a cell that can give rise to other types of cells; for instance, bone marrow stem cells divide and produce different types of blood cells.

Steroid: type of hormone that freely enters cells (other hormones bind to cell surfaces); different varieties can suppress immune response or influence stress reaction, blood pressure, or sexual development; includes testosterone- and estrogen-related compounds.

Testosterone: a hormone that stimulates the development and maintenance of male sexual characteristics and the production of sperm; women also produce small amounts of testosterone.

Virus: a microscopic, often disease-causing, organism made of genetic material surrounded by a protein shell; can only reproduce inside a living cell.

WORLD ALMANAC QUICK QUIZ

Put these inventions in order from earliest to latest:
(a) pendulum clock (b) flush toilet
(c) electric battery (d) bubble gum
For the answer look in this chapter, or see page 1008.

Chemistry

Acid: a class of compound that contrasts with bases. Acids taste sour, turn litmus red/pink, and often produce hydrogen gas in contact with some metals. Acids donate protons (hydrogen atoms minus the electron) in chemical reactions.

Base: a substance that yields hydroxyl ions (OH-) when dissolved in water; any of a class of compounds whose aqueous solutions taste bitter, feel slippery, turn litmus blue, and react with acids to form salts; also known as **alkaline**.

Carbon fiber: an extremely strong, thin fiber made by pyrolyzing (decomposing by heat) synthetic fibers, such as rayon, until charred; used to make high-strength composites

Chlorofluorocarbon (CFC): one of a group of industrial chemicals that contain chlorine, fluorine, and carbon and have been found to damage Earth's ozone layer.

Element: a substance that cannot be chemically decomposed into simpler substances; the atoms of an element all have the same number of protons and electrons.

Isotope: an atom of a chemical element with the same number of protons in its nucleus as other atoms of that element, but with a different number of neutrons.

Molecule: the basic unit of a chemical compound, composed of two or more atoms bound together.

Osmosis: the transfer of a fluid from an area of higher concentration to an area of lower concentration, usually through a membrane.

Phase: any of the possible states of matter—solid, liquid, gas, or plasma—that change according to temperature and pressure.

Polymer: a huge molecule containing hundreds or thousands of smaller molecules arranged in repeating units.

Salt: a neutral compound produced by the reaction of an acid and a base.

Geology

Fault, tectonic: a crack or break in Earth's crust, often due to the slippage of tectonic plates past or over one another; usually geologically unstable.

Igneous: a type of rock formed by solidification from a molten state, especially from molten magma.

Magma: hot liquid rock material under Earth's crust, from which igneous rock is formed by cooling.

Metamorphic: in geology, the name given to sedimentary rocks or minerals that have recrystallized under the influence of heat and pressure since their original deposition.

Pangaea: a single super-continent that scientists believe broke apart about 170 million years ago to form the current continents.

Plate tectonics: theory that Earth's crust is made up of many separate rigid plates of rock that float on top of hot semi-liquid rock.

Sedimentary rock: rock formed by the buildup of material at the bottoms of bodies of water.

Physics

Absolute zero: the theoretical temperature at which all motion within a molecule stops, corresponding to –273.15° C (–459.67° F).

Antimatter: matter that consists of antiparticles, such as antiprotons, that have an opposite charge from normal particles; when matter meets antimatter, both are destroyed and their combined mass is converted to energy. Antimatter is created in certain radioactive decay processes, but appears to be present in only small amounts in the universe.

Atom: the basic unit of a chemical element.

Atomic mass: the total mass of an atom of a given element; atoms of the same element with different atomic masses (different numbers of neutrons, not protons) are called isotopes.

Atomic number: the number of protons in an atom of a given element of the periodic table; the characteristic that sets atoms of different elements apart.

Bose-Einstein condensate: a "super-atom" comprised of thousands of atoms super-cooled to within a few billionths of a degree of absolute zero and thus condensed into the lowest energy state; atoms bound in the BEC behave synchronously, giving the BEC wavelike properties.

Boson: force-carrying particles including photons, gluons, and the W and Z particles; one of the two primary categories of particles in the Standard Model, the other being fermions.

Dark energy: a mysterious, undefined energy leading to a repulsive force pervading all of space-time; proposed by cosmologists as counteracting gravity and accelerating the expansion of the universe; predicted to make up 65% of the universe's composition.

Dark matter: hypothetical, invisible matter that some scientists believe makes up 90% of the matter in the universe; its existence was proposed to account for otherwise inexplicable gravitational forces observed in space.

Doppler effect: a change in the frequency of sound, light, or radio waves caused by the motion of the source emitting the waves or the motion of the person or instrument perceiving the waves.

Electron: negatively charged particle that is the least massive electrically charged fundamental particle; the most common charged lepton in the Standard Model.

Energy: capacity to perform work. Energy can take various forms, such as potential energy, kinetic energy, chemical energy, etc.

Entropy: A measure of disorder in a system. According to the Second Law of Thermodynamics, disorder or entropy can only increase in a closed system.

Fermion: any one of a number of matter particles including electrons, protons, neutrons, and quarks; one of the two primary categories of particles in the Standard Model, the other being bosons.

Field: the effects of forces (gravitational, electric, etc.) are visualized and described mathematically by physicists in terms of fields, which show the strength and direction of a force at a given position.

Fission: a nuclear reaction that occurs when the nuclei of large, unstable atoms break apart, releasing large amounts of energy.

Force: In classical physics, a force is something that causes acceleration in a body, and can be thought of as a push or pull.

Fusion: a nuclear reaction occurring when atomic nuclei collide at high temperatures and combine to form one heavier atomic nucleus, releasing enormous energy in the process.

Gravity: an attractive force between any 2 objects or particles, proportional to the mass (or energy) of the objects; strength of the force decreases with greater distance; the only fundamental force still unaccounted for by the Standard Model.

Half-life: the time it takes for half of a given amount of a radioactive element to decay.

Hertz: a measure of frequency, or how many times a given event occurs per second; applied to sound waves, electrical current, microchip clock speeds; abbreviated as Hz.

Inertia: the tendency of an object to resist a change in its state of motion (i.e., to stay at rest if it is at rest, or to continue moving at a constant speed if it is moving at a constant speed). Inertia is proportional to mass, so a heavier object has more inertia.

Laser: light consisting of a cascade of photons all having the same wavelength; *laser* stands for Light Amplification by Stimulated Emission of Radiation.

Neutrino: a tiny fundamental particle with no electrical charge and very small mass that moves very quickly through the universe; comes in three varieties, or flavors, called electron, muon, and tau.

Neutron: a neutral particle found in the nuclei of atoms.

Particle accelerator: a large machine with a long tunnel in which atoms smash into each other at high speeds; physicists use these machines to study subatomic particles.

Photon: the elementary unit, or quantum, of light or electromagnetic radiation, having no mass or electrical charge; one of the fundamental force-carrying particles, or bosons, described by the Standard Model.

Plasma: a high-energy state of matter different from solid, liquid or gas in which atomic nuclei and the electrons orbiting them separate from each other.

Proton: a positively charged subatomic particle found in the nuclei of atoms.

Quantum: a natural unit of some physically measurable property, such as energy or electrical charge.

Quark: a fermion and a fundamental matter particle that makes up neutrons and protons, forming atomic nuclei; there are 6 different "flavors" of quarks grouped in pairs; up and down, charm and strange, top and bottom.

Radiation: energy emitted as rays or particles; radiation includes heat, light, ultraviolet rays, gamma rays, X rays, cosmic rays, alpha particles, beta particles, and the protons, neutrons, and electrons of radioactive atoms.

Relativity, general theory of: a theory of space-time proposed by Albert Einstein in 1915; gravitational and other forces are transmitted through the effects of the curvature of space-time.

Relativity, special theory of: Einstein's theory of space and time: all laws of physics are valid in all uniformly moving frames of reference and the speed of light in a vacuum is always the same, so long as the source and the observer are moving uniformly (not accelerating).

Standard Model: prevailing theory of fundamental particles and forces of matter; matter particles are fermions: either leptons or quarks; force-carrying particles are bosons: either gluons, W or Z bosons or photons; gravity has not yet been worked into the model.

String theory: a theory that seeks to unify quantum mechanics and general relativity, positing that the basic constituents of matter can best be understood not as point objects but as tiny closed loops ("strings").

Subatomic particle: one of the small particles, such as electrons, neutrons, and protons, which make up an atom.

Superconductivity: the property of certain materials, usually metals and chemically complex ceramics, to conduct electricity without resistance, generally at very cold temperatures.

Thermodynamics: the branch of physics that describes how energy, heat, and temperature flow in physical systems.

Ultraviolet radiation: a form of light, invisible to the human eye, that has a shorter wavelength and greater energy than visible light but a longer wavelength and less energy than X rays.

Virtual particle: subatomic particles that rapidly pop into and out of existence and can exert real forces; usually occur in particle-antiparticle pairs and are rapidly annihilated.

Chemical Elements, Atomic Numbers, Year Discovered

Reviewed by Darleane C. Hoffman, Ph.D., Lawrence Berkeley National Laboratory and Department of Chemistry, Univ. of California, Berkeley.

See Periodic Table of the Elements on page 314 for atomic weights.

Element	Symbol	Atomic number	Year discov.
Actinium	Ac	89	1899
Aluminum	Al	13	1825
Americium	Am	95	1944
Antimony	Sb	51	1450
Argon	Ar	18	1894
Arsenic	As	33	13th c.
Astatine	At	85	1940
Barium	Ba	56	1808
Berkelium	Bk	97	1949
Beryllium	Be	4	1798
Bismuth	Bi	83	15th c.
Bohrium	Bh	107	1981
Boron	B	5	1808
Bromine	Br	35	1826
Cadmium	Cd	48	1817
Calcium	Ca	20	1808
Californium	Cf	98	1950
Carbon	C	6	BC
Cerium	Ce	58	1803
Cesium	Cs	55	1860
Chlorine	Cl	17	1774
Chromium	Cr	24	1797
Cobalt	Co	27	1735
Copper	Cu	29	BC
Curium	Cm	96	1944
Darmstadtium	Ds	110	1995
Dubnium (Hahnium)[1]	Db (Ha)	105	1970
Dysprosium	Dy	66	1886
Einsteinium	Es	99	1952
Erbium	Er	68	1843
Europium	Eu	63	1901
Fermium	Fm	100	1953
Fluorine	F	9	1771
Francium	Fr	87	1939
Gadolinium	Gd	64	1886
Gallium	Ga	31	1875
Germanium	Ge	32	1886
Gold	Au	79	BC
Hafnium	Hf	72	1923
Hassium	Hs	108	1984
Helium	He	2	1868
Holmium	Ho	67	1878
Hydrogen	H	1	1766
Indium	In	49	1863
Iodine	I	53	1811
Iridium	Ir	77	1804
Iron	Fe	26	BC
Krypton	Kr	36	1898
Lanthanum	La	57	1839
Lawrencium	Lr	103	1961
Lead	Pb	82	BC
Lithium	Li	3	1817
Lutetium	Lu	71	1907
Magnesium	Mg	12	1829
Manganese	Mn	25	1774
Meitnerium	Mt	109	1982
Mendelevium	Md	101	1955
Mercury	Hg	80	BC
Molybdenum	Mo	42	1782
Neodymium	Nd	60	1885
Neon	Ne	10	1898
Neptunium	Np	93	1940
Nickel	Ni	28	1751
Niobium[2]	Nb	41	1801
Nitrogen	N	7	1772
Nobelium	No	102	1958
Osmium	Os	76	1804
Oxygen	O	8	1774
Palladium	Pd	46	1803
Phosphorus	P	15	1669
Platinum	Pt	78	1735
Plutonium	Pu	94	1941
Polonium	Po	84	1898
Potassium	K	19	1807
Praseodymium	Pr	59	1885
Promethium	Pm	61	1945
Protactinium	Pa	91	1917
Radium	Ra	88	1898
Radon	Rn	86	1900
Rhenium	Re	75	1925
Rhodium	Rh	45	1803
Roentgenium	Rg	111	1995
Rubidium	Rb	37	1861
Ruthenium	Ru	44	1845
Rutherfordium	Rf	104	1969
Samarium	Sm	62	1879
Scandium	Sc	21	1879
Seaborgium	Sg	106	1974
Selenium	Se	34	1817
Silicon	Si	14	1823
Silver	Ag	47	BC
Sodium	Na	11	1807
Strontium	Sr	38	1790
Sulfur	S	16	BC
Tantalum	Ta	73	1802
Technetium	Tc	43	1937
Tellurium	Te	52	1782
Terbium	Tb	65	1843
Thallium	Tl	81	1861
Thorium	Th	90	1828
Thulium	Tm	69	1879
Tin	Sn	50	BC
Titanium	Ti	22	1791
Tungsten (Wolfram)	W	74	1783
Uranium	U	92	1789
Vanadium	V	23	1830
Xenon	Xe	54	1898
Ytterbium	Yb	70	1878
Yttrium	Y	39	1794
Zinc	Zn	30	BC
Zirconium	Zr	40	1789

Note: 111 elements are listed here. The discovery of element 111 with a mass number of 272 was reported by S. Hofman *et al.* in 1995 and was approved by a Joint Working Party of the International Unions of Pure & Applied Chemistry (IUPAC) and Pure and Applied Physics (IUPAP) in 2003. The discoverers proposed the name Roentgenium with symbol Rg in early 2004 and it was confirmed by IUPAC in Nov. 2004. The discovery of element 112 by S. Hofman *et al.* in 1996 still awaits confirmation. Between 1999 and 2004, a multinational group and a Dubna/Lawrence Livermore National Laboratory group working in Dubna, Russia, have published evidence in refereed journals for observation of many isotopes of elements 112 through 116 and 118 has been reported. These reports all await confirmation and are shown in Italics in the periodic table. Evidence for Element 117 has not been published in refereed journals and is shown in parentheses. (1) The name Dubnium (Db) has been approved by IUPAC for element 105, but the name Hahnium (Ha) is used in most of the scientific literature before 1998 and is still sometimes used in the U.S. (2) Formerly Columbium.

WORLD ALMANAC QUICK QUIZ

Hans Geiger invented the Geiger counter, and Rudolph Diesel invented the diesel engine. Who invented the Polaroid Land Camera?

(a) Evan Polaroid (b) Edwin Land
(c) Antonio Camera (d) Walker Eastman

For the answer look in this chapter, or see page 1008.

Periodic Table of the Elements

Source: © 1996 Lawrence Berkeley National Laboratory

Parentheses indicate undiscovered elements.

Key: atomic number (14), atomic weight (28.09), symbol (Si), name (Silicon)

alkali metals	alkaline earth metals	transitional metals										other metals / nonmetals					noble gases
1 **H** Hydrogen 1.01																	2 **He** Helium 4.003
3 **Li** Lithium 6.94	4 **Be** Beryllium 9.01											5 **B** Boron 10.81	6 **C** Carbon 12.01	7 **N** Nitrogen 14.01	8 **O** Oxygen 15.999	9 **F** Fluorine 18.998	10 **Ne** Neon 20.18
11 **Na** Sodium 22.99	12 **Mg** Magnesium 24.31											13 **Al** Aluminum 26.98	14 **Si** Silicon 28.09	15 **P** Phosphorus 30.97	16 **S** Sulfur 32.06	17 **Cl** Chlorine 35.45	18 **Ar** Argon 39.95
19 **K** Potassium 39.10	20 **Ca** Calcium 40.08	21 **Sc** Scandium 44.96	22 **Ti** Titanium 47.90	23 **V** Vanadium 50.94	24 **Cr** Chromium 51.996	25 **Mn** Manganese 54.94	26 **Fe** Iron 55.85	27 **Co** Cobalt 58.93	28 **Ni** Nickel 58.70	29 **Cu** Copper 63.55	30 **Zn** Zinc 65.37	31 **Ga** Gallium 69.72	32 **Ge** Germanium 72.59	33 **As** Arsenic 74.92	34 **Se** Selenium 78.96	35 **Br** Bromine 79.90	36 **Kr** Krypton 83.80
37 **Rb** Rubidium 85.47	38 **Sr** Strontium 87.62	39 **Y** Yttrium 88.91	40 **Zr** Zirconium 91.22	41 **Nb** Niobium 92.91	42 **Mo** Molybdenum 95.94	43 **Tc** Technetium 98	44 **Ru** Ruthenium 101.07	45 **Rh** Rhodium 102.91	46 **Pd** Palladium 106.40	47 **Ag** Silver 107.87	48 **Cd** Cadmium 112.41	49 **In** Indium 114.82	50 **Sn** Tin 118.69	51 **Sb** Antimony 121.75	52 **Te** Tellurium 127.60	53 **I** Iodine 126.90	54 **Xe** Xenon 131.30
55 **Cs** Cesium 132.91	56 **Ba** Barium 137.33	57 **La** Lanthanum 138.91	72 **Hf** Hafnium 178.49	73 **Ta** Tantalum 180.95	74 **W** Tungsten 183.85	75 **Re** Rhenium 186.21	76 **Os** Osmium 190.20	77 **Ir** Iridium 192.22	78 **Pt** Platinum 195.09	79 **Au** Gold 196.97	80 **Hg** Mercury 200.59	81 **Tl** Thallium 204.37	82 **Pb** Lead 207.19	83 **Bi** Bismuth 208.98	84 **Po** Polonium 209	85 **At** Astatine 210	86 **Rn** Radon 222
87 **Fr** Francium 223	88 **Ra** Radium 226.03	89 **Ac** Actinium 227.03	104 **Rf** Rutherfordium 261	105 **Db (Ha)** Dubnium (Hahnium) 262	106 **Sg** Seaborgium 266	107 **Bh** Bohrium 267	108 **Hs** Hassium 269	109 **Mt** Meitnerium 268	110 **Ds** Darmstadtium 271	111 **Rg** Roentgenium 272	***112***	***113***	***114***	***115***	***116***	**(117)**	**118**

Lanthanide series	58 **Ce** Cerium 140.12	59 **Pr** Praseodymium 140.91	60 **Nd** Neodymium 144.24	61 **Pm** Promethium 145	62 **Sm** Samarium 150.35	63 **Eu** Europium 151.96	64 **Gd** Gadolinium 157.25	65 **Tb** Terbium 158.93	66 **Dy** Dysprosium 162.50	67 **Ho** Holmium 164.93	68 **Er** Erbium 167.26	69 **Tm** Thulium 168.93	70 **Yb** Ytterbium 173.04	71 **Lu** Lutetium 174.97
Actinide series	90 **Th** Thorium 232.04	91 **Pa** Protactinium 231.04	92 **U** Uranium 238.03	93 **Np** Neptunium 237.05	94 **Pu** Plutonium 244	95 **Am** Americium 243	96 **Cm** Curium 247	97 **Bk** Berkelium 247	98 **Cf** Californium 251	99 **Es** Einsteinium 252	100 **Fm** Fermium 257	101 **Md** Mendelevium 258	102 **No** Nobelium 259	103 **Lr** Lawrencium 262

Discoveries and Innovations: Chemistry, Physics, Biology, Medicine

	Date	Discoverer	Nationality
Acetylene gas	**1862**	Berthelot	French
ACTH	**1927**	Evans, Long	U.S.
Adrenalin	**1901**	Takamine	Japan
Aluminum, electrolytic process	**1886**	Hall	U.S.
Aluminum, isolated	**1825**	Oersted	Danish
Anesthesia, ether	**1842**	Long	U.S.
Anesthesia, local	**1885**	Koller	Austrian
Anesthesia, spinal	**1898**	Bier	German
Aniline dye	**1856**	Perkin	English
Anti-rabies	**1885**	Pasteur	French
Antiseptic surgery	**1867**	Lister	English
Antitoxin, diphtheria	**1891**	Von Behring	German
Argyrol	**1897**	Bayer	German
Arsphenamine	**1910**	Ehrlich	German
Aspirin	**1853**	Gerhardt	French
Atabrine	**1932**	Mietzsch, et al.	German
Atomic numbers	**1913**	Moseley	English
Atomic theory	**1803**	Dalton	English
Atomic time clock	**1948**	Lyons	U.S.
Atomic time clock, cesium beam	**1948**	Essen	English
Atom-smashing theory	**1919**	Rutherford	English
Bacitracin	**1943**	Johnson, Meleneyl	U.S.
Bacteria, description	**1676**	Leeuwenhoek	Dutch
Bleaching powder	**1798**	Tennant	English
Blood, circulation	**1628**	Harvey	English
Blood plasma storage (blood banks)	**1940**	Drew	U.S.
Bordeaux mixture	**1885**	Millardet	French
Bromine from the sea	**1826**	Balard	French
Calcium carbide	**1888**	Wilson	U.S.
Calculus	**1670**	Newton	English
Camphor synthetic	**1896**	Haller	French
Canning (food)	**1804**	Appert	French
Carbon oxides	**1925**	Fisher	German
Chemotherapy	**1909**	Ehrlich	German
Chloamphenicol	**1947**	Burkholder	U.S.
Chlorine	**1774**	Scheele	Swedish
Chloroform	**1831**	Guthrie, S.	U.S.
Chlortetracycline	**1948**	Duggen	U.S.
Classification of plants and animals	**1735**	Linnaeus	Swedish
Cloning, DNA	**1973**	Boyer, Cohen	U.S.
Cloning, mammal	**1996**	Wilmut, et al.	Scottish
Cocaine	**1860**	Niermann	German
Combustion explained	**1777**	Lavoisier	French
Conditioned reflex	**1914**	Pavlov	Russian
Cortisone	**1936**	Kendall	U.S.
Cortisone, synthesis	**1946**	Sarett	U.S.
Cosmic rays	**1910**	Gockel	Swiss
Cyanamide	**1905**	Frank, Caro	German
Cyclotron	**1930**	Lawrence	U.S.
DDT (not applied as insecticide until 1939)	**1874**	Zeidler	German
Deuterium	**1932**	Urey, Brickwedde, Murphy	U.S.
DNA (structure)	**1953**	Crick	English
		Watson	U.S.
		Wilkins	English
Electric resistance, law of	**1827**	Ohm	German
Electric waves	**1888**	Hertz	German
Electrolysis	**1852**	Faraday	English
Electromagnetism	**1819**	Oersted	Danish
Electron	**1897**	Thomson, J.	English
Electron diffraction	**1936**	Thomson	English
		G.Davisson	U.S.
Electroshock treatment	**1938**	Cerletti, Bini	Italian
Erythromycin	**1952**	McGuire	U.S.
Evolution, natural selection	**1858**	Darwin	English
Falling bodies, law of	**1590**	Galileo	Italian
Gases, law of combining volumes	**1808**	Gay-Lussac	French
Geometry, analytic	**1619**	Descartes	French
Gold, cyanide process for extraction	**1887**	MacArthur, Forest	British
Gravitation, law	**1687**	Newton	English
HIV (human immuno-deficiency virus)	**1984**	Montagnier	French
		Gallo	U.S.
Holograph	**1948**	Gabor	British
Human heart transplant	**1967**	Barnard	S. African
Indigo, synthesis of	**1880**	Baeyer	German
Induction, electric	**1830**	Henry	U.S.
Insulin	**1922**	Banting, Best, Macleod	Canadian, Scottish
Intelligence testing	**1905**	Binet, Simon	French
In vitro fertilization	**1978**	Steptoe, Edwards	English
Isoniazid	**1952**	Hoffmann-LaRoche	U.S.
		Domagk	German
Isotopes, theory	**1912**	Soddy	English
Laser	**1957**	Gould	U.S.
Light, velocity	**1675**	Roemer	Danish
Light, wave theory	**1690**	Huygens	Dutch
Lithography	**1796**	Senefelder	Bohemian
Logarithms	**1614**	Napier	Scottish
LSD-25	**1943**	Hoffman	Swiss
Mendelian laws	**1866**	Mendel	Austrian
Mercator projection (map)	**1568**	Mercator (Kremer)	Flemish
Methanol	**1661**	Boyle	Irish
Milk condensation	**1853**	Borden	U.S.
Molecular hypothesis	**1811**	Avogadro	Italian
Motion, laws of	**1687**	Newton	English
Neomycin	**1949**	Waksman, Lechevalier	U.S.
Neutron	**1932**	Chadwick	English
Nitric acid	**1648**	Glauber	German
Nitric oxide	**1772**	Priestley	English
Nitroglycerin	**1846**	Sobrero	Italian
Oil cracking process	**1891**	Dewar	U.S.
Oxygen	**1774**	Priestley	English
Oxytetracycline	**1950**	Finlay, et al.	U.S.
Ozone	**1840**	Schonbein	German
Paper, sulfite process	**1867**	Tilghman	U.S.
Paper, wood pulp, sulfate process	**1884**	Dahl	German
Penicillin	**1928**	Fleming	Scottish
practical use	**1941**	Florey, Chain	English
Periodic law and table of elements	**1869**	Mendeleyev	Russian
Physostigmine synthesis	**1935**	Julian	U.S.
Pill, birth-control	**1954**	Pincus, Rock	U.S.
Planetary motion, laws	**1609**	Kepler	German
Plutonium fission	**1940**	Kennedy, Wahl, Seaborg, Segre	U.S.
Polymyxin	**1947**	Ainsworth	English
Positron	**1932**	Anderson	U.S.
Proton	**1919**	Rutherford	N. Zealand
Psychoanalysis	**1900**	Freud	Austrian
Quantum theory	**1900**	Planck	German
Quasars	**1963**	Matthews, Sandage	U.S.
Quinine synthetic	**1946**	Woodward, Doering	U.S.
Radioactivity	**1896**	Becquerel	French
Radiocarbon dating	**1947**	Libby	U.S.
Radium	**1898**	Curie, Pierre	French
		Curie, Marie	Pol.-Fr.
Relativity theory	**1905**	Einstein	German
Reserpine	**1949**	Jal Vaikl	Indian
Schick test	**1913**	Schick	U.S.
Silicon	**1823**	Berzelius	Swedish
Smallpox eradication	**1979**	World Health Org.	UN
Streptomycin	**1944**	Waksman, et al	U.S.
Sulfanilamide	**1935**	Bovet, Trefouel	French
Sulfanilamide theory	**1908**	Gelmo	German
Sulfapyridine	**1938**	Ewins, Phelps	English
Sulfathiazole	**1939**	Fosbinder, Walter	U.S.
Sulfuric acid	**1831**	Phillips	English
Sulfuric acid, lead	**1746**	Roebuck	English
Syphilis test	**1906**	Wassermann	German
Thiacetazone	**1950**	Belmisch, Mietzsch, Domagk	German
Tuberculin	**1890**	Koch	German
Uranium fission theory	**1939**	Hahn, Meitner, Strassmann	German
		Bohr	Danish
		Fermi	Italian
		Einstein, Pegram, Wheeler	U.S.
Uranium fission, atomic reactor	**1942**	Fermi, Szilard	U.S.
Vaccine, measles	**1963**	Enders	U.S.
Vaccine, meningitis (first conjugate)	**1987**	Gordon, et al., Connaught Lab.	U.S.
Vaccine, polio	**1954**	Salk	U.S.
Vaccine, polio, oral	**1960**	Sabin	U.S.
Vaccine, rabies	**1885**	Pasteur	French
Vaccine, smallpox	**1796**	Jenner	English
Vaccine, typhus	**1909**	Nicolle	French
Vaccine, varicella	**1974**	Takahashi	Japan
Van Allen belts, radiation	**1958**	Van Allen	U.S.
Vitamin A	**1913**	McCollum, Davis	U.S.
Vitamin B	**1916**	McCollum	U.S.
Vitamin C	**1928**	Szent-Gyorgyi	Hungarian
		King	U.S.
Vitamin D	**1922**	McCollum	U.S.
Vitamin K	**1935**	Dam, Doisy	U.S.
Xerography	**1938**	Carlson	U.S.
X ray	**1895**	Roentgen	German

Inventions

Invention	Date	Inventor	Nationality
Adding machine	**1642**	Pascal	French
Adding machine	**1885**	Burroughs	U.S.
Aerosol spray	**1926**	Rotheim	Norwegian
Airbag	**1952**	Hetrick	U.S.
Air brake	**1868**	Westinghouse	U.S.
Air conditioning	**1902**	Carrier	U.S.
Air pump	**1654**	Guericke	German
Airplane, automatic pilot	**1912**	Sperry	U.S.
Airplane, experimental	**1896**	Langley	U.S.
Airplane, hydro	**1911**	Curtiss	U.S.
Airplane jet engine	**1939**	Ohain	German
Airplane with motor	**1903**	Wright Bros.	U.S.
Airship	**1852**	Giffard	French
Arc welder	**1919**	Thomson	U.S.
Aspartame	**1965**	Schlatter	U.S.
Autogyro	**1920**	de la Cierva	Spanish
Automobile, differential gear	**1885**	Benz	German
Automobile, electric	**1892**	Morrison	U.S.
Automobile, exp'mtl	**1864**	Marcus	Austrian
Automobile, gasoline	**1889**	Daimler	German
Automobile, gasoline	**1892**	Duryea	U.S.
Automobile magneto	**1897**	Bosch	German
Automobile muffler	**1904**	Pope	U.S.
Automobile self-starter	**1911**	Kettering	U.S.
Bakelite	**1907**	Baekeland	Belgian, U.S.
Balloon	**1783**	Montgolfier	French
Barometer	**1643**	Torricelli	Italian
Bicycle, modern	**1885**	Starley	English
Bifocal lens	**1780**	Franklin	U.S.
Bottle machine	**1895**	Owens	U.S.
Braille printing	**1829**	Braille	French
Bubble gum	**1928**	Diemer	U.S.
Burner, gas	**1855**	Bunsen	German
Calculating machine	**1833**	Babbage	English
Calculator, electronic pocket	**1972**	Merryman, Van Tassel	U.S.
Camera, Kodak	**1888**	Eastman, Walker	U.S
Camera, Polaroid Land	**1948**	Land	U.S.
Car coupler	**1873**	Janney	U.S.
Carburetor, gasoline	**1893**	Maybach	German
Carding machine	**1797**	Whittemore	U.S.
Carpet sweeper	**1876**	Bissell	U.S.
Cash register	**1879**	Ritty	U.S.
Cassette, audio	**1963**	Philips Co.	Dutch
Cassette, videotape	**1969**	Sony	Japanese
Cathode-ray tube	**1897**	Braun	German
CAT, or CT, scan	**1973**	Hounsfield	English
Cellophane	**1908**	Brandenberger	Swiss
Celluloid	**1870**	Hyatt	U.S.
Cement, Portland	**1824**	Aspdin	English
Chronometer	**1735**	Harrison	English
Circuit breaker	**1925**	Hilliard	U.S.
Circuit, integrated	**1959**	Kilby, Noyce, Texas Instr.	U.S.
Clock, pendulum	**1657**	Huygens	Dutch
Coaxial cable system	**1929**	Affel, Espensched	U.S.
Coffeemaker, automatic drip	**1963**	Bunn Corp.	U.S.
Compressed air rock drill	**1871**	Ingersoll	U.S.
Comptometer	**1887**	Felt	U.S.
Computer, automatic sequence	**1944**	Aiken, et al.	U.S.
Computer, electronic	**1942**	Atanasoff, Berry	U.S.
Computer, laptop	**1987**	Sinclair	English
Computer, mini	**1960**	Digital Corp	U.S.
Condenser microphone (telephone)	**1916**	Wente	U.S.
Contact lens, corneal	**1948**	Tuohy	U.S.
Contraceptive, oral	**1954**	Pincus, Rock	U.S.
Corn, hybrid	**1917**	Jones	U.S.
Cotton gin	**1793**	Whitney	U.S.
Cream separator	**1878**	DeLaval	Swedish
Cultivator, disc	**1878**	Mallon	U.S.
Cystoscope	**1878**	Nitze	German
Diapers, disposable	**1950**	Donovan	U.S.
Diesel engine	**1895**	Diesel	German
Disc, compact	**1972**	RCA	U.S.
Disc player, compact	**1979**	Sony, Philips Co.	Japan, Dutch
Dishwasher	**1893**	Cochrane	U.S.
Disk, floppy	**1970**	IBM	U.S.
Disk, video	**1972**	Philips Co.	Dutch
Dynamite	**1866**	Nobel	Swedish
Dynamo, contin. current	**1871**	Gramme	Belgian
Electric battery	**1800**	Volta	Italian
Electric fan	**1882**	Wheeler	U.S.
Electrocardiograph	**1903**	Einthoven	Dutch
Electroencephalograph	**1929**	Berger	German
Electromagnet	**1824**	Sturgeon	English
Electron spectrometer	**1944**	Deutsch, Elliott, Evans	U.S.
Electron tube multigrid	**1913**	Langmuir	U.S.
Electroplating	**1805**	Brugnatelli	Italian
Electrostatic generator	**1929**	Van de Graaff	U.S.
Elevator brake	**1852**	Otis	U.S.
Elevator, push button	**1922**	Larson	U.S.
Engine, automatic transmission	**1910**	Fottinger	German
Engine, coal-gas 4-cycle	**1876**	Otto	German
Engine, compression ignition	**1883**	Daimler	German
Engine, electric ignition	**1883**	Benz	German
Engine, gas, compound	**1926**	Eickemeyer	U.S.
Engine, gasoline	**1872**	Brayton, Geo.	U.S.
Engine, gasoline	**1889**	Daimler	German
Engine, jet	**1930**	Whittle	English
Engine, steam, piston	**1705**	Newcomen	English
Engine, steam, piston	**1769**	Watt	Scottish
Engraving, half-tone	**1852**	Talbot	U.S.
Fiberglass	**1938**	Owens-Corning	U.S.
Fiber optics	**1955**	Kapany	English
Fiber optic wire	**1970**	Keck, Maurer Schulz	U.S.
Filament, tungsten	**1913**	Coolidge	U.S.
Flanged rail	**1831**	Stevens	U.S.
Flatiron, electric	**1882**	Seely	U.S.
Food, frozen	**1923**	Birdseye	U.S.
Freon	**1930**	Midgley, et al.	U.S.
Furnace (for steel)	**1858**	Siemens	German
Galvanometer	**1820**	Sweigger	German
Garbage bag, polyethylene	**1950**	Wasylyk	Canadian
Gas discharge tube	**1922**	Hull	U.S.
Gas lighting	**1792**	Murdoch	Scottish
Gas mantle	**1885**	Welsbach	Austrian
Gasoline (lead ethyl)	**1922**	Midgley	U.S.
Gasoline, cracked	**1913**	Burton	U.S.
Gasoline, high octane	**1930**	Ipatieff	Russian
Geiger counter	**1913**	Geiger	German
Glass, laminated safety	**1909**	Benedictus	French
Glider	**1853**	Cayley	English
Gun, breechloader	**1811**	Thornton	U.S.
Gun, Browning	**1897**	Browning	U.S.
Gun, magazine	**1875**	Hotchkiss	U.S.
Gun, silencer	**1908**	Maxim, H.P.	U.S.
Guncotton	**1847**	Schoenbein	German
Gyrocompass	**1911**	Sperry	U.S.
Gyroscope	**1852**	Foucault	French
Harvester-thresher	**1818**	Lane	U.S.
Heart, artificial	**1982**	Jarvik	U.S.
Helicopter	**1939**	Sikorsky	U.S.
Hydrometer	**1768**	Baume	French
Iron lung	**1928**	Drinker, Slaw	U.S.
Kaleidoscope	**1817**	Brewster	Scottish
Kevlar	**1965**	Kwolek, Blades	U.S.
Kinetoscope	**1889**	Edison	U.S.
Lamp, arc	**1847**	Staite	English
Lamp, fluorescent	**1938**	General Electric, Westinghouse	U.S.
Lamp, incandescent	**1879**	Edison	U.S.
Lamp, incand., gas	**1913**	Langmuir	U.S.
Lamp, klieg	**1911**	Kliegl, A. & J.	U.S.
Lamp, mercury vapor	**1912**	Hewitt	U.S.
Lamp, miner's safety	**1816**	Davy	English
Lamp, neon	**1909**	Claude	French
Lathe, turret	**1845**	Fitch	U.S.
Launderette	**1934**	Cantrell	U.S.
Lens, achromatic	**1758**	Dollond	English
Lens, fused bifocal	**1908**	Borsch	U.S.
Leyden jar (condenser)	**1745**	von Kleist	German
Lightning rod	**1752**	Franklin	U.S.
Linoleum	**1860**	Walton	English
Linotype	**1884**	Mergenthaler	U.S.
Liquid Paper	**c.1951**	Graham	U.S.
Lock, cylinder	**1851**	Yale	U.S.
Locomotive, electric	**1851**	Vail	U.S.
Locomotive, exp'mtl	**1802**	Trevithick	English
Locomotive, exp'mtl	**1812**	Fenton, et al.	English
Locomotive, exp'mtl	**1814**	Stephenson	English
Locomotive, practical	**1829**	Stephenson	English
Locomotive, 1st U.S.	**1830**	Cooper, P.	U.S.
Loom, power	**1785**	Cartwright	English
Loudspeaker, dynamic	**1924**	Rice, Kellogg	U.S.
Machine gun	**1862**	Gatling	U.S.
Machine gun, improved	**1872**	Hotchkiss	U.S.
Machine gun (Maxim)	**1883**	Maxim, H.S.	U.S., Eng.
Magnet, electro	**1828**	Henry	U.S.

Invention	Date	Inventor	Nationality
Magnetic Resonance Imaging (MRI)	1971	Damadian	U.S.
Mantle, gas	1885	Welsbach	Austrian
Mason jar	1858	Mason, J.	U.S.
Match, friction	1827	Walker, J.	English
Mercerized textiles	1843	Mercer, J.	English
Meter, induction	1888	Shallenberger	U.S.
Metronome	1816	Malezel	German
Microcomputer	1973	Truong, et al.	French
Micrometer	1636	Gascoigne	English
Microphone	1877	Berliner	U.S.
Microprocessor	1971	Intel Corp.	U.S.
Microscope, compound	1590	Janssen	Dutch
Microscope, electronic	1931	Knoll, Ruska	German
Microscope, field ion	1951	Mueller	German
Microwave oven	1947	Spencer	U.S.
Minivan	1983	Chrysler	U.S.
Monitor, warship	1861	Ericsson	U.S.
Monotype	1887	Lanston	U.S.
Motor, AC	1892	Tesla	U.S.
Motor, DC.	1837	Davenport	U.S.
Motor, induction	1887	Tesla	U.S.
Motorcycle	1885	Daimler	German
Movie machine	1894	Jenkins	U.S.
Movie, panoramic	1952	Waller	U.S.
Movie, talking	1927	Warner Bros.	U.S.
Mower, lawn	1831	Budding, Ferrabee	English
Mowing machine	1822	Bailey	U.S.
Neoprene	1930	Carothers	U.S.
Nylon	1937	Du Pont lab	U.S.
Nylon synthetic	1930	Carothers	U.S.
Oil cracking furnace	1891	Gavrilov	Russian
Oil filled power cable	1921	Emanueli	Italian
Oleomargarine	1869	Mege-Mouries	French
Ophthalmoscope	1851	Helmholtz	German
Pacemaker	1952	Zoll	U.S.
Paper	105	Ts'ai	Chinese
Paper clip	1900	Waaler	Norwegian
Paper machine	1809	Dickinson	U.S.
Parachute	1785	Blanchard	French
Pen, ballpoint	1888	Loud	U.S.
Pen, fountain	1884	Waterman	U.S.
Pen, steel	1780	Harrison	English
Pendulum	1583	Galileo	Italian
Percussion cap	1807	Forsythe	Scottish
Phonograph	1877	Edison	U.S.
Photo, color	1892	Ives	U.S.
Photo film, celluloid	1893	Reichenbach	U.S.
Photo film, transparent	1884	Eastman, Goodwin	U.S.
Photoelectric cell	1895	Elster	German
Photocopier	1938	Carlson	U.S.
Photographic paper	1835	Talbot	English
Photography	1816	Niepce	French
Photography	1835	Talbot	English
Photography	1835	Daguerre	French
Photophone	1880	Bell	U.S.-Scot.
Phototelegraphy	1925	Bell Labs	U.S.
Piano	1709	Cristofori	Italian
Piano, player	1863	Fourneaux	French
Pin, safety	1849	Hunt	U.S.
Pistol (revolver)	1836	Colt	U.S.
Plow, cast iron	1785	Ransome	English
Plow, disc	1896	Hardy	U.S.
Pneumatic hammer	1890	King	U.S.
Post-it note	1980	3M	U.S.
Powder, smokeless	1884	Vieille	French
Printing press, rotary	1845	Hoe	U.S.
Printing press, web	1865	Bullock	U.S.
Propeller, screw	1804	Stevens	U.S.
Propeller, screw	1837	Ericsson	Swedish
Pulsars	1967	Bell	English
Punch card accounting	1889	Hollerith	U.S.
Radar	1940	Watson-Watt	Scottish
Radio, magnetic detector	1902	Marconi	Italian
Radio, signals	1895	Marconi	Italian
Radio amplifier	1906	De Forest	U.S.
Radio beacon	1928	Donovan	U.S.
Radio crystal oscillator	1918	Nicolson	U.S.
Radio receiver, cascade tuning	1913	Alexanderson	U.S.
Radio receiver, heterodyne	1913	Fessenden	U.S.
Radio transmitter triode modulation	1914	Alexanderson	U.S.
Radio tube diode	1904	Fleming	English
Radio tube oscillator	1915	De Forest	U.S.
Radio tube triode	1906	De Forest	U.S.
Radio FM, 2-path	1933	Armstrong	U.S.
Rayon (acetate)	1895	Cross	English
Rayon (cuprammonium)	1890	Despeissis	French
Rayon (nitrocellulose)	1884	Chardonnet	French

Invention	Date	Inventor	Nationality
Razor, electric	1917	Schick	U.S.
Razor, safety	1895	Gillette	U.S.
Reaper	1834	McCormick	U.S.
Record, cylinder	1887	Bell, Tainter	U.S.
Record, disc	1887	Berliner	U.S.
Record, long playing	1947	Goldmark	U.S.
Record, wax cylinder	1888	Edison	U.S.
Refrigerator car	1868	David	U.S.
Resin, synthetic	1931	Hill	English
Richter scale	1935	Richter	U.S.
Rifle, repeating	1860	Henry	U.S.
Rocket, liquid fuel	1926	Goddard	U.S.
Rollerblades	1980	Olson	U.S.
Rubber, vulcanized	1839	Goodyear	U.S.
Saccharin	1879	Remsen, Fahlberg	U.S.
Saw, circular	1777	Miller	English
Scotch tape	1930	Drew	U.S.
Seat belt	1959	Volvo	Swedish
Sewing machine	1846	Howe	U.S.
Shoe-lasting machine	1883	Matzeliger	U.S.
Shoe-sewing machine	1860	McKay	U.S.
Shrapnel shell	1784	Shrapnel	English
Shuttle, flying	1733	Kay	English
Sleeping-car	1865	Pullman	U.S.
Slide rule	1620	Oughtred	English
Smoke detector	1969	Smith, House	U.S.
Soap, hardwater	1928	Bertsch	German
Spectroscope	1859	Kirchoff, Bunsen	German
Spectroscope (mass)	1918	Dempster	U.S.
Spinning jenny	c.1764	Hargreaves	English
Spinning mule	1779	Crompton	English
Steamboat, exp'mtl	1778	Jouffroy	French
Steamboat, exp'mtl	1785	Fitch	U.S.
Steamboat, exp'mtl	1787	Rumsey	U.S.
Steamboat, exp'mtl	1803	Fulton	U.S.
Steamboat, exp'mtl	1804	Stevens	U.S.
Steamboat, practical	1802	Symington	Scottish
Steamboat, practical	1807	Fulton	U.S.
Steam car	1770	Cugnot	French
Steam turbine	1884	Parsons	English
Steel (converter)	1856	Bessemer	English
Steel alloy	1891	Harvey	U.S.
Steel alloy, high-speed	1901	Taylor, White	U.S.
Steel, manganese	1884	Hadfield	English
Steel, stainless	1916	Brearley	English
Stereoscope	1838	Wheatstone	English
Stethoscope	1819	Laennec	French
Stethoscope, binaural	1840	Cammann	U.S.
Stock ticker	1870	Edison	U.S.
Storage battery, rechargeable	1859	Plante	French
Stove, electric	1896	Hadaway	U.S.
Submarine	1891	Holland	U.S.
Submarine, even keel	1894	Lake	U.S.
Submarine, torpedo	1776	Bushnell	U.S.
Superconductivity	1957	Bardeen, Cooper, Schreiffer	U.S.
Superconductivity in ceramics at high temp	1986	Bednorz Muller	German Swiss
Synthesizer	1964	Moog	U.S.
Tank, military	1914	Swinton	English
Tape recorder, magnetic	1899	Poulsen	Danish
Teflon	1938	Du Pont	U.S.
Telegraph, magnetic	1837	Morse	U.S.
Telegraph, quadruplex	1864	Edison	U.S.
Telegraph, railroad	1887	Woods	U.S.
Telegraph, wireless high frequency	1895	Marconi	Italian
Telephone[1]	1871	Meucci	U.S.-Italian
Telephone[1]	1876	Bell	U.S.-Scot.
Telephone answering machine (1st practical)	1954	Hashimoto	Japanese
Telephone, automatic	1891	Strowger	U.S.
Telephone, cellular	1947	Bell Labs	U.S.
Telephone, cordless[2]	1950	Gross	U.S.
Telephone, radio	1900	Poulsen, Fessenden	Danish
Telephone, radio	1906	De Forest	U.S.
Telephone, radio, long dist.	1915	AT&T	U.S.
Telephone, recording	1898	Poulsen	Danish
Telephone amplifier	1912	De Forest	U.S.
Telescope	1608	Lippershey	Neth.
Telescope	1609	Galileo	Italian
Telescope, astronomical	1611	Kepler	German
Teletype	1928	Morkrum, Kleinschmidt	U.S.
Television, color	1928	Baird	Scottish
Television, electronic	1927	Farnsworth	U.S.
Television, iconoscope	1923	Zworykin	U.S.
Television, mech. scanner	1923	Baird	Scottish
Tesla Coil	1891	Tesla	U.S.

Invention	Date	Inventor	Nationality
Thermometer	1593	Galileo	Italian
Thermometer	1730	Reaumur	French
Thermometer, mercury	1714	Fahrenheit	German
Time recorder	1890	Bundy	U.S.
Tire, double-tube	1845	Thomson	Scottish
Tire, pneumatic	1888	Dunlop	Scottish
Toaster, automatic	1918	Strite	U.S.
Toilet, flush	1589	Harington	English
Tool, pneumatic	1865	Law	English
Torpedo, marine	1804	Fulton	U.S.
Tractor, crawler	1904	Holt	U.S.
Transformer, AC.	1885	Stanley	U.S.
Transistor	1947	Shockley, Brattain, Bardeen	U.S.
Trolley car, electric	1884-87	Van DePoele, Sprague	U.S.
Tungsten, ductile	1912	Coolidge	U.S.
Tupperware®	1945	Tupper	U.S.
Turbine, gas	1849	Bourdin	French
Turbine, hydraulic	1849	Francis	U.S.
Turbine, steam	1884	Parsons	English
Type, movable	1447	Gutenberg	German
Typewriter	1867	Sholes, Soule, Glidden	U.S.
Vacuum cleaner, electric	1907	Spangler	U.S.
Vacuum evaporating pan	1846	Rillieux	U.S.
Velcro	1948	de Mestral	Swiss
Video game ("Pong")	1972	Bushnell	U.S.
Video home system (VHS)	1975	Matsushita, JVC	Japanese
Washer, electric	1901	Fisher	U.S.
Welding, atomic hydrogen	1924	Langmuir, Palmer	U.S.
Welding, electric	1877	Thomson	U.S.
Windshield wiper	1903	Anderson	U.S.
Wind tunnel	1912	Eiffel	French
Wire, barbed	1874	Glidden	U.S.
Wrench, double-acting	1913	Owen	U.S.
X-ray tube	1913	Coolidge	U.S.
Zeppelin	1900	Zeppelin	German
Zipper, early model	1893	Judson	U.S.
Zipper, improved	1913	Sundback	Canadian

(1) While Alexander Graham Bell has traditionally been credited with invention of the telephone, which he patented, Antonio Meucci developed a working model before Bell. (2) Al Gross held a number of important early patents in the field of wireless communication; other people were also involved in the development of practical cordless telephones.

Top 30 Corporations Receiving U.S. Patents in 2004

Source: U.S. Patent and Trademark Office, U.S. Department of Commerce

Rank	Company	Number of patents
1.	International Business Machines Corporation	3,248
2.	Matsushita Electric Industrial Co., Ltd.	1,934
3.	Canon Kabushiki Kaisha	1,805
4.	Hewlett-Packard Development Company, L.P.	1,775
5.	Micron Technology, Inc.	1,760
6.	Samsung Electronics Co., Ltd.	1,604
7.	Intel Corporation	1,601
8.	Hitachi, Ltd.	1,514
9.	Toshiba Corporation	1,311
10.	Sony Corporation	1,305
11.	Fujitsu Limited	1,296
12.	Koninklijke Philips Electronics N.V.	1,217
13.	Fuji Photo Film Co., Ltd.	1,025
14.	General Electric Company	976
15.	Renesas Technology Corporation	913
16.	Robert Bosch GMBH	903
17.	Texas Instruments, Incorporated	898
18.	Seiko Epson Corporation	839
	Nec Corporation	813
20.	Advanced Micro Devices, Inc.	802
21.	Infineon Technologies Ag	785
22.	Mitsubishi Denki Kabushiki Kaisha	781
23.	Honda Giken Kogyo Kabushiki Kaisha (Honda Motor Co., Ltd.)	736
24.	Siemens Aktiengesellschaft	732
25.	Eastman Kodak Company	712
26.	Sun Microsystems, Inc.	678
27.	Denso Corporation	647
28.	Agilent Technologies, Inc.	645
29.	Microsoft Corporation	629
30.	Motorola, Inc.	563

Breaking the Sound Barrier; Speed of Sound

The prefix **Mach** is used to describe supersonic speed. It was named for Ernst Mach (1838-1916), a Czech-born Austrian physicist. When a plane moves at the speed of sound, it is Mach 1. When the plane is moving at twice the speed of sound, it is Mach 2. Mach may be defined as the ratio of the velocity of a rocket or a jet to the velocity of sound in the medium being considered.

When a plane passes the sound barrier—flying faster than sound travels—listeners in the area hear thunderclaps, but the pilot of the plane does not hear them.

Sound is produced by vibrations of an object and is transmitted by alternate increase and decrease in pressures that radiate outward through a material media of molecules—somewhat like waves spreading out on a pond after a rock has been tossed into it.

The **frequency of sound** is determined by the number of times the vibrating waves undulate per second and is measured in cycles per second. The slower the cycle of waves, the lower the frequency. As frequencies increase, the sound is higher in pitch. The human ear is usually not sensitive to frequencies of fewer than 20 vibrations per second or greater than about 20,000 vibrations per second—although this range varies among individuals.

Intensity, or loudness, is the strength of the pressure of these radiating waves and is measured in decibels. (See Weights and Measures.)

The **speed of sound** is generally defined as 1,088 feet per second at sea level at 32° F. It varies in other temperatures and in different media. Sound travels faster in water than in air, and even faster in iron and steel.

Light; Colors of the Spectrum

Light, a form of electromagnetic radiation similar to radiant heat, radio waves, and X rays, is emitted from a source in straight lines and spreads out over larger areas as it travels; light per unit area diminishes as the square of the distance.

The English mathematician and physicist Sir Isaac Newton (1642-1727) described light as an **emission of particles**; the Dutch astronomer, mathematician, and physicist Christiaan Huygens (1629-95) developed the theory that light travels by a **wave motion**. It is now believed that these 2 theories are essentially complementary, and the development of quantum theory has led to results where light acts like a series of particles in some experiments and like a wave in others.

The **speed of light** was first measured in a laboratory experiment by the French physicist Armand Hippolyte Louis Fizeau (1819-96). Today the speed of light is known very precisely as 299,792.458 km per sec (or 186,282.396 mi per sec) in a vacuum; in water the speed of light is about 25% less, and in glass, 33% less.

Color sensations are produced through the excitation of the retina of the eye by light vibrating at different frequencies. The different colors of the spectrum may be produced by viewing a light beam that is refracted by passage through a prism, which breaks the light into its wavelengths.

Customarily, the **primary colors** are taken to be the 6 monochromatic colors that occupy relatively large areas of the spectrum: red, orange, yellow, green, blue, and violet. Scientists have differed, however, in how many and which primary colors they recognized. The color sensation of **black** is due to complete lack of stimulation of the retina, that of **white** to complete stimulation.

The **infrared and ultraviolet rays**, below the red (long) end of the spectrum and above the violet (short) end of the spectrum, respectively, are invisible to the naked eye. Heat is the principal effect of the infrared rays, and chemical action that of the ultraviolet rays.

AEROSPACE

Memorable Moments in Human Spaceflight

Sources: National Aeronautics and Space Administration; Congressional Research Service; World Almanac research

The spaceflights listed are a selection of notable U.S. missions, by the National Aeronautics and Space Administration (NASA), unless otherwise noted, plus non-U.S. missions (shown with an asterisk). The non-U.S missions were sponsored by the USSR (later, the Commonwealth of Independent States and, from 1997, Russia) or by China. Dates are Eastern standard time. EVA = extravehicular activity. ASTP = Apollo-Soyuz Test Project. STS = Space Transportation System, NASA's name for the overall Shuttle program. Number of total flights by each crew member is given in parentheses when flight listed is not the first.

Launch Date	Mission[1]	Crew (no. of flights)	Duration (hr:min)	Remarks
4/12/61	*Vostok 1	Yuri A. Gagarin	1:48	**1st human orbital flight**
5/5/61	Mercury-Redstone 3	Alan B. Shepard Jr.	0:15	**1st American in space**
7/21/61	Mercury-Redstone 4	Virgil I. Grissom	0:15	Spacecraft sank, Grissom rescued
8/6/61	*Vostok 2	Gherman S. Titov	25:18	1st spaceflight of more than 24 hrs
2/20/62	Mercury-Atlas 6	John H. Glenn Jr.	4:55	**1st American in orbit;** 3 orbits
5/24/62	Mercury-Atlas 7	M. Scott Carpenter	4:56	Manual retrofire error caused 250-mi landing overshoot
8/11/62	*Vostok 3	Andrian G. Nikolayev	94:22	Vostok 3 and 4 made 1st group flight
8/12/62	*Vostok 4	Pavel R. Popovich	70:57	On 1st orbit, it came within 3 mi of Vostok 3
10/3/62	Mercury-Atlas 8	Walter M. Schirra Jr.	9:13	Landed 5 mi from target
5/15/63	Mercury-Atlas 9	L. Gordon Cooper	34:19	1st U.S. evaluation of effects of one day in space on a person; 22 orbits
6/14/63	*Vostok 5	Valery F. Bykovsky	119:06	Vostok 5 and 6 made 2nd group flight
6/16/63	*Vostok 6	Valentina V. Tereshkova	70:50	**1st woman in space**; passed within 3 mi of Vostok 5
10/12/64	*Voskhod 1	Vladimir M. Komarov, Konstantin P. Feoktistov, Boris B. Yegorov	24:17	1st 3-person orbital flight; 1st without space suits
3/18/65	*Voskhod 2	Pavel I. Belyayev, Aleksei A. Leonov	26:02	Leonov made **1st "space walk"** (10 min)
3/23/65	Gemini-Titan 3	Grissom (2), John W. Young	4:53	1st piloted spacecraft to change its orbital path
6/3/65	Gemini-Titan 4	James A. McDivitt, Edward H. White 2nd	97:56	White was 1st American to "walk in space" (36 min)
8/21/65	Gemini-Titan 5	Cooper (2), Charles Conrad Jr.	190:55	Longest-duration human flight to date
12/15/65	Gemini-Titan 6A	Schirra (2), Thomas P. Stafford	25:51	Completed 1st U.S. space rendezvous, with Gemini 7
12/4/65	Gemini-Titan 7	Frank Borman, James A. Lovell	330:35	Longest-duration Gemini flight
3/16/66	Gemini-Titan 8	Neil A. Armstrong, David R. Scott	10:41	**1st docking of one space vehicle with another;** mission aborted, control malfunction; 1st Pacific landing
6/3/66	Gemini-Titan 9A	Stafford (2), Eugene A. Cernan	72:21	Performed simulation of lunar module rendezvous
7/18/66	Gemini-Titan 10	Young (2), Michael Collins	70:47	1st use of Agena target vehicle's propulsion systems; 1st orbital docking
9/12/66	Gemini-Titan 11	Conrad (2), Richard F. Gordon Jr.	71:17	1st tethered flight; highest Earth-orbit altitude (850 mi)
11/11/66	Gemini-Titan 12	Lovell (2), Edwin E. "Buzz" Aldrin Jr.	94:34	Final Gemini mission; 5-hr EVA
4/23/67	*Soyuz 1	Komarov (2)	26:40	Crashed on reentry, killing Komarov
10/11/68	Apollo-Saturn 7	Schirra (3), Donn F. Eisele, R. Walter Cunningham	260:09	1st piloted flight of Apollo spacecraft command-service module only; live TV footage of crew
12/21/68	Apollo-Saturn 8	Borman (2), Lovell (3), William A. Anders	147:00	**1st lunar orbit** and piloted lunar return reentry (command-service module only); views of lunar surface televised to Earth
1/14/69	*Soyuz 4	Vladimir A. Shatalov	71:21	Docked with Soyuz 5
1/15/69	*Soyuz 5	Boris V. Volyanov, Aleksei S. Yeliseyev, Yevgeny V. Khrunov	72:54	Docked with 4; Yeliseyev and Khrunov transferred to Soyuz 4 via a spacewalk
3/3/69	Apollo-Saturn 9	McDivitt (2), D. Scott (2), Russell L. Schweickart	241:00	1st piloted flight of lunar module
5/18/69	Apollo-Saturn 10	Stafford (3), Young (3), Cernan (2)	192:03	1st lunar module orbit of Moon, 50,000 ft from Moon surface
7/16/69	Apollo-Saturn 11	Armstrong (2), Collins (2), Aldrin (2)	195:18	**1st lunar landing** made by Armstrong and Aldrin (7/20); collected 48.5 lb of soil, rock samples; lunar stay time 21:36:21
10/11/69	*Soyuz 6	Georgi S. Shonin, Valery N. Kubasov	118:43	1st welding of metals in space
10/12/69	*Soyuz 7	Anatoly V. Flipchenko, Vladislav N. Volkov, Viktor V. Gorbatko	118:40	Space lab construction test made; Soyuz 6, 7, and 8: 1st time 3 spacecraft, 7 crew members orbited the Earth at once
10/13/69	*Soyuz 8	Shatalov (2), Yeliseyev (2)	118:51	Part of space lab construction team
11/14/69	Apollo-Saturn 12	Conrad (3), Richard F. Gordon Jr. (2), Alan L. Bean	244:36	Conrad and Bean made **2nd Moon landing** (11/18); collected 74.7 lb of samples, lunar stay time 31:31
4/11/70	Apollo-Saturn 13	Lovell (4), Fred W. Haise Jr., John L. Swigert Jr.	142:54	Aborted after service module oxygen tank ruptured; crew returned in lunar module
6/1/70	*Soyuz 9	Nikolayev (2), Vitaliy I. Sevastyanov	424:59	Longest human spaceflight to date
1/31/71	Apollo-Saturn 14	A. Shepard (2), Stuart A. Roosa, Edgar D. Mitchell	216:01	Shepard and Mitchell made **3rd Moon landing** (2/3); collected 96 lb of lunar samples; lunar stay 33:31
4/19/71	*Salyut 12	(Occupied by Soyuz 11 crew)		**1st space station**
4/22/71	*Soyuz 10	Shatalov (3), Yeliseyev (3), Nikolay N. Rukavishnikov	47:46	**1st successful docking with a space station;** failed to enter space station
6/6/71	*Soyuz 11	Georgi T. Dobrovolskiy, V. Volkov (2), Viktor I. Patsayev	570:22	Docked and entered Salyut 1 space station; **crew died** during reentry from loss of pressurization
7/26/71	Apollo-Saturn 15	D. Scott (3), James B. Irwin, Alfred M. Worden	295:12	Scott and Irwin made **4th Moon landing** (7/30); 1st lunar rover use; 1st deep space walk; 170 lb of samples; 66:55 stay
4/16/72	Apollo-Saturn 16	Young (4), Charles M. Duke Jr., Thomas K. Mattingly 2nd	265:51	Young and Duke made **5th Moon landing** (4/20); collected 213 lb of lunar samples; lunar stay 71:2

Launch Date	Mission[1]	Crew (no. of flights)	Duration (hr:min)	Remarks
12/7/72	Apollo-Saturn 17	Cernan (3), Ronald E. Evans, Harrison H. Schmitt	301:51	Cernan and Schmitt made 6th and **last lunar landing** (12/11); collected 243 lb of samples; record lunar stay over 75 hrs
5/14/73[2]	Skylab 1	(Occupied by Skylab 2, 3, and 4 crews)		**1st U.S. space station**; fell out of orbit 7/11/79
5/25/73	Skylab 2	Conrad (4), Joseph P. Kerwin, Paul J. Weitz	672:49	1st Amer. piloted orbiting space station; crew repaired damage caused in boost
7/28/73	Skylab 3	Bean (2), Owen K. Garriott, Jack R. Lousma	1,427:09	Crew systems and operational tests; scientific activities; 3 EVAs, 13:44
11/16/73	Skylab 4	Gerald P. Carr, Edward G. Gibson, William Pogue	2,017:15	Final Skylab mission
7/15/75	*Soyuz 19 (ASTP)	Leonov (2), Kubasov (2)	143:31	U.S.-USSR joint flight; crews linked up in space (7/17), conducted experiments, shared meals, held a joint news conf.
7/15/75	Apollo (ASTP)	Vance Brand, Stafford (4), Donald K. Slayton	217:28	Joint flight with Soyuz 19
12/10/77	*Soyuz 26	Yuri V. Romanenko, Georgiy M. Grechko (2)	2,314:00	1st multiple docking to a space station (Soyuz 26 and 27 docked at Salyut 6)
1/10/78	*Soyuz 27	Vladimir A. Dzhanibekov	142:59	*See Soyuz 26*
3/2/78	*Soyuz 28	Aleksei A. Gubarev (2), Vladimir Remek	190:16	1st international crew launch; Remek was 1st Czech in space
4/12/81	Columbia (STS-1)	Young (5), Robert L. Crippen	54:21	**1st space shuttle** to fly into Earth's orbit
11/12/81	Columbia (STS-2)	Joe H. Engle, Richard H. Truly	54:13	1st scientific payload; 1st reuse of space shuttle
11/11/82	Columbia (STS-5)	Brand (2), Robert Overmyer, William Lenoir, Joseph Allen	122:14	1st 4-person crew
6/18/83	Challenger (STS-7)	Crippen (2), Frederick Hauck, Sally K. Ride, John M. Fabian, Norman Thagard	146:24	Ride was **1st U.S. woman in space**; 1st 5-person crew
6/27/83	*Soyuz T-9	Vladimir A. Lyakhov (2), Aleksandr Pavlovich	3,585:46	Docked at Salyut 7; 1st construction in space
8/30/83	Challenger (STS-8)	Truly (2), Daniel Brandenstein, William Thornton, Guion Bluford, Dale Gardner	145:09	Bluford was **1st African-American in space**
11/28/83	Columbia (STS-9)	Young (6), Brewster Shaw Jr., Robert Parker, Garriott (2), Byron Lichtenberg, Ulf Merbold	247:47	1st 6-person crew; 1st Spacelab mission
2/3/84	Challenger (41-B)	Brand (3), Robert Gibson, Ronald McNair, Bruce McCandless, Robert Stewart	191:16	1st untethered EVA
2/8/84	*Soyuz T-10B	Leonid Kizim, Vladimir Solovyov, Oleg Atkov	1,510:43	Docked with Salyut 7; crew set space duration record of 237 days
4/3/84	*Soyuz T-11	Yury Malyshev (2), Gennady Strekalov (3), Rakesh Sharma	4,365:48	Docked with Salyut 7; Sharma 1st Indian in space
4/6/84	Challenger (41-C)	Crippen (3), Francis R. Scobee, George D. Nelson, Terry J. Hart, James D. van Hoften	167:40	1st in-orbit satellite repair
7/17/84	*Soyuz T-12	Dzhanibekov (4), Svetlana Y. Savitskaya (2), Igor P. Volk	283:14	Docked at Salyut 7; Savitskaya was 1st woman to perform EVA
8/30/84	Discovery (41-D)	Henry W. Hartsfield (2), Michael L. Coats, Richard M. Mullane, Steven A. Hawley, Judith A. Resnik, Charles D. Walker	144:56	1st flight of U.S. nonastronaut (Walker)
10/5/84	Challenger (41-G)	Crippen (4), Jon A. McBride, Kathryn D. Sullivan, Ride (2), Marc Garneau, David C. Leestma, Paul D. Scully-Power	197:24	1st 7-person crew
11/8/84	Discovery (51-A)	Hauck (2); David M. Walker, Dr. Anna L. Fisher, J. Allen (2), D. Gardner (2)	191:45	1st satellite retrieval/repair
4/12/85	Discovery (51-D)	Karol J. Bobko, Donald E. Williams, Jake Garn, C. Walker (2), Jeffrey A. Hoffman, S. David Griggs, M. Rhea Seddon	167:55	Garn (R, UT) was **1st U.S. senator in space**
6/17/85	Discovery (51-G)	Brandenstein (2), John O. Creighton, Shannon W. Lucid, Steven R. Nagel, Fabian (2), Prince Sultan Salman al-Saud, Patrick Baudry	169:39	Launched 3 satellites; Salman al-Saud was 1st Arab in space; Baudry was 1st French person on U.S. mission
10/3/85	Atlantis (51-J)	Bobko (3), Ronald J. Grabe, David C. Hilmers, Stewart (2), William A. Pailes	97:47	1st Atlantis flight
10/30/85	Challenger (61-A)	Hartsfield (3), Nagel (2), Buchli (2), Bluford (2), Bonnie J. Dunbar, Wubbo J. Ockels, Richard Furrer, Ernst Messerschmid	168:45	1st 8-person crew; 1st German Spacelab mission
1/12/86	Columbia (61-C)	R. Gibson (2), Charles F. Bolden Jr., Hawley (2), G. Nelson (2), Franklin R. Chang-Diaz, Robert J. Cenker, Bill Nelson	146:04	B. Nelson was 1st U.S. representative in space; material and astronomy experiments conducted
1/28/86	Challenger (51-L)	Scobee (2), Michael J. Smith, Resnik (2), Ellison S. Onizuka (2), Ronald E. McNair, Gregory B. Jarvis, Christa McAuliffe	—	**Exploded 73 sec after liftoff**; all aboard were killed
2/20/86	*Mir[2]	—	—	***Mir* space station** with 6 docking ports **launched**
3/13/86	*Soyuz T-15	Kizim (3), Solovyov (2)	3,000:01	Ferry between stations; docked at *Mir*
2/5/87	*Soyuz TM-2	Romanenko (3), Aleksandr I. Laveikin	7,835:38	Romanenko set endurance record, since broken
7/22/87	*Soyuz TM-3	Aleksandr Viktorenko, Aleksandr Pavlovich Aleksandrov (2), Mohammed Faris	3,847:16	Docked with *Mir*; Faris 1st Syrian in space
9/29/88	Discovery (STS-26)	Hauck (3), Richard O. Covey (2), Hilmers (2), G. Nelson (2), John M. Lounge (2)	97:00	**1st shuttle flight since *Challenger* explosion** 1/28/86
5/4/89	Atlantis (STS-30)	D. Walker (2), Grabe (2), Thagard (2), Mary L. Cleave (2), Mark C. Lee	96:56	Launched Venus orbiter *Magellan*
10/18/89	Atlantis (STS-34)	Donald E. Williams (2), Michael J. McCulley, Lucid (2), Chang-Diaz (2), Ellen S. Baker	119:39	Launched Jupiter probe and orbiter *Galileo*
4/24/90	Discovery (STS-31)	McCandless (2), Sullivan (2), Loren J. Shriver (2), Bolden (2), Hawley (3)	121:16	**Launched Hubble Space Telescope**
10/6/90	Discovery (STS-41)	Richard N. Richards (2), Robert D. Cabana, Bruce E. Melnick, William M. Shepherd (2), Thomas D. Akers	98:10	Launched *Ulysses* spacecraft to investigate interstellar space and the Sun

Launch Date	Mission[1]	Crew (no. of flights)	Duration (hr:min)	Remarks
5/18/91	*Soyuz TM-12	Anatoly Artsebarskiy, Sergei Krikalev (2) (to *Mir*), Helen Sharman	3,471:22	Docked with *Mir;* Sharman 1st from United Kingdom in space
3/17/92	*Soyuz TM-14	Viktorenko (3) (to *Mir*), Alexandr Kaleri (to *Mir*), Klaus-Dietrich Flade, Aleksandr Volkov (3) (from *Mir*), Krikalev (2) (from *Mir*)	3,495:11	First human CIS space mission; docked with *Mir* 3/19; Viktorenko and Kaleri to *Mir,* Volkov and Krikalev from *Mir;* Krikalev was in space 313 days
5/7/92	Endeavour (STS-49)	Brandenstein (4), Kevin C. Chilton, Melnick (2), Pierre J. Thuot (2), Richard J. Hieb (2), Kathryn Thornton (2), Akers (2)	213:30	1st 3-person EVA; satellite recovery and redeployment
9/12/92	Endeavour (STS-47)	R. Gibson (4), Curtis L. Brown Jr., Lee (2), Jay Apt (2), N. Jan Davis, Mae Carol Jemison, Mamoru Mohri	190:30	Jemison was 1st black woman in space; Lee and Davis 1st married couple to travel together in space; 1st Japanese Spacelab
6/21/93	Endeavour (STS-57)	Grabe (4), Brian J. Duffy (2), G. David Low (3), Nancy J. Sherlock, Peter J. K. Wisoff, Janice E. Voss	239:46	Carried Spacelab commercial payload module
12/2/93	Endeavour (STS-61)	Covey (3), Kenneth D. Bowersox (2), Claude Nicollier (2), Story Musgrave (5), Akers (3), K. Thornton (3), Hoffman (4)	259:58	Hubble Space Telescope repaired; Akers set new U.S. EVA duration record (29 hr, 40 min)
2/3/94	Discovery (STS-60)	Bolden (3), Kenneth S. Reightier Jr. (2), Davis (2), Chang-Diaz (3), Ronald M. Sega, Krikalev (3)	199:10	Krikalev was 1st Russian on U.S. shuttle
7/1/94	*Soyuz TM-19	Yuri I. Malenchenko, Talgat A. Musabayev, Merbold (2) (from *Mir*)	3,022:53	Docked with *Mir;* Merbold from *Mir*
9/9/94	Discovery (STS-64)	Richards (4), L. Blaine Hammond Jr. (2), Jerry M. Linenger, Susan J. Helms (2), Carl J. Meade (3), Lee (3)	262:50	Performed atmospheric research; 1st untethered EVA in over 10 years
2/3/95	Discovery (STS-63)	James D. Wetherbee (3), Eileen M. Collins, Bernard A. Harris (2), C. Michael Foale (3), Janice E. Voss (2), V. Titov (4)	198:29	*Discovery* and Russian space station rendezvous
3/2/95	Endeavour (STS-67)	Stephen S. Oswald (3), William G. Gregory, Samuel T. Durrance (2), Ronald Parise (2), Wendy B. Lawrence, Tamara E. Jernigan (3), John M. Grunsfeld	399:09	Shuttle data made available on the Internet; astronomy research conducted
3/14/95	*Soyuz TM-21	Thagard (2), Vladimir Dezhurov, Strekalov (5)	2,688[3]	Docked with *Mir* 3/16/95; Thagard was 1st Amer. on the Russ. spacecraft; Valery Polyakov returned to Earth, 3/22/95, after record stay in space (439 days)
6/27/95	Atlantis (STS-71)	R. Gibson (5), Charles J. Precourt (2), E. Baker (3), Gregory J. Harbaugh (3), Dunbar (4), Anatoly Solovyev (4) (to *Mir*), Nikolai M. Budarin (to *Mir*), Thagard (5) (from *Mir*), Strekalov (from *Mir*), Dezhurov (from *Mir*)	269:47	**1st shuttle-*Mir* docking**; exchanged crew members with *Mir;* Thagard, with his stay on *Mir,* had spent 115 days in space
11/12/95	Atlantis (STS-74)	Kenneth D. Cameron (3), James D. Halsell Jr. (2), Chris Hadfield, Jerry L. Ross (5), William S. McArthur (2)	196:30	2nd shuttle-*Mir* docking (11/15-11/18); erected a 15-ft permanent docking tunnel to *Mir* for future use by U.S. orbiters
2/22/96	Columbia (STS-75)	Andrew M. Allen (3), Scott J. Horowitz, Chang-Diaz (5), Umberto Guidoni, Hoffman (5), Maurizio Cheli, Nicollier (3)	377:40	Lost an Italian satellite when its tether was severed; microgravity experiments performed; singe marks found on 2 O-rings
3/22/96	Atlantis (STS-76)	Chilton (3), Richard A. Searfoss (2), Sega (2), Michael R. Clifford (3), Linda Godwin (3), Lucid (5) (to *Mir*)	221:15	3rd shuttle-*Mir* docking (5 days); Lucid to *Mir,* 2-person EVA
9/16/96	Atlantis (STS-79)	Apt (4), Terry Wilcutt (2), WilliamReaddy (3), Akers (4), Carl E. Walz (3), Lucid (5) (from *Mir*), John E. Blaha (5) (to *Mir*)	243:19	Docked with *Mir* 9/18/96; exchanged crew members; **Lucid set U.S. and women's duration in space record (188 days)**
11/19/96	Columbia (STS-80)	Kenneth D. Cockrell (3), Kent V. Rominger (2), Jernigan (4), Thomas D. Jones (3), Musgrave (6)	423:53	Longest-duration shuttle flight; Musgrave 61, oldest thus far to fly in space; 2 science satellites deployed, retrieved
1/12/97	Atlantis (STS-81)	Michael A. Baker (4), Brent W. Jett (2), Wisoff (3), Grunsfeld (2), Marsha Ivins (4), Linenger (2) (to *Mir*), Blaha (5) (from *Mir*)	243:30	Docked with *Mir* 1/14-1/19/97; Linenger to *Mir;* Blaha from *Mir,* spent 128 days in space
2/11/97	Discovery (STS-82)	Bowersox (4), Horowitz (2), Joe Tanner (2), Hawley (4), Harbaugh (4), Lee (4), Steve Smith (2)	238:47	Increased capabilities of Hubble Space Telescope; 5 EVAs used to service it
5/15/97	Atlantis (STS-84)	Precourt (3), E. Collins (2), Jean-François Clervoy (2), Carlos Noriega, Ed Lu, Elena Kondakova, Foale (4) (to *Mir*), Linenger (2) (from *Mir*)	221:20	Docked with *Mir* 5/16-5/21; Foale to *Mir;* Linenger from *Mir,* 132 days in space, 2nd-longest time for an American; stay on *Mir* marked by troubles incl. fire 2/23
8/5/97	*Soyuz TM-26	Solovyev (5), Pavel Vinogradov	4,743:35	Docked with *Mir* 8/7/97; repaired damaged space station
8/7/97	Discovery (STS-85)	Brown (4), Rominger (3), Davis (3), Robert L. Curbeam Jr., Stephen K. Robinson, Bjarni V. Tryggvason	284:27	Deployed and retrieved satellite designed to study Earth's middle atmosphere; demonstrated robotic arm
9/25/97	Atlantis (STS-86)	Wetherbee (4), Michael J. Bloomfield, V. Titov (4), Scott Parazynski (2), Jean-Loup Chrétien (3), Lawrence (2), David A. Wolf (2) (to *Mir*), Foale (4) (from *Mir*)	236:24	Docked with *Mir* 9/27-10/3/97; delivered new computer to *Mir;* Wolf to *Mir;* Foale from *Mir;* stay on *Mir* marked by major collision with cargo ship 6/25
4/17/98	Columbia (STS-90)	Searfoss (3), Scott D. Altman, Richard M. Linnehan (2), Dafydd Rhys Williams, Kathryn P. Hire, Jay C. Buckey, James A. Pawelczyk	381:50	Studied effects of microgravity on the nervous systems of the crew and over 2,000 live animals; 1st surgery in space on animals meant to survive
6/2/98	Discovery (STS-91)	Precourt (4), Dominic L. Gorie, Lawrence (3), Chang-Diaz (6), Janet L. Kavandi, Valery Ryumin (4), A. Thomas (2) (from *Mir*)	235:53	Final docking mission with *Mir;* Thomas from *Mir,* 141 days in space
10/29/98	Discovery (STS-95)	Brown (5), Steven W. Lindsey (2), Parazynski (3), Robinson (2), Pedro Duque, Chiaki Mukai (2), Glenn (2)	213:44	Sen. John Glenn (D, OH), 77, was **oldest person to fly in space**; Duque was 1st Spaniard in space; experiments to study aging performed on Glenn

IT'S A FACT: Objects in low-Earth orbit, such as the space shuttle, must maintain a speed of about 17,000 mph to remain in orbit. The exact speed depends on altitude. A typical shuttle orbits at 115 to 400 miles above the Earth.

Launch Date	Mission[1]	Crew (no. of flights)	Duration (hr:min)	Remarks
12/4/98	Endeavour (STS-88)	Cabana (4), Frederick W. Sturckow, Nancy J. Currie (3), Ross (6), James H. Newman (3), Krivalev (4)	283:18	**1st assembly of International Space Station (ISS)**; attached U.S.-built *Unity* connecting module to Russian-built *Zarya* control module; 1st crew to enter ISS
7/23/99	Columbia (STS-93)	E. Collins (3), Jeffrey S. Ashby, Hawley (5), Catherine G. Coleman (2), Michel Tognini (2)	118:50	Collins was **1st woman to command a space shuttle**; deployed Chandra X-ray Observatory telescope
12/19/99	Discovery (STS-103)	Brown (6), Scott Kelly, S. Smith (3), Foale (5), Grunsfeld (3), Nicollier (4), Clervoy (3)	191:10	Replaced equipment on and upgraded Hubble Space Telescope; 3 EVAs
2/11/00	Endeavour (STS-99)	Kevin Kregel (4), Gorie (2), Kavandi (2), Janice E. Voss (5), Mohri (2), Gerhard P.J. Thiele	269:38	Used radar to make most complete topographic map of Earth's surface ever produced
5/19/00	Atlantis (STS-101)	Halsell (5), Horowitz (3), Helms (4), Yury Usachev (3), James S. Voss (4), Mary Ellen Weber (2), Jeffrey N. Williams	236:09	Serviced and resupplied ISS; boosted orbit of ISS to an altitude of about 238 mi; 1 EVA
9/8/00	Atlantis (STS-106)	Wilcutt (4), Altman (2), Lu (2), Richard A. Mastracchio, Daniel C. Burbank, Malenchenko (2), Boris V. Morukov	283:10	Prepared ISS for 1st permanent crew; 1 EVA by all 7 crew members
10/11/00	Discovery (STS-92)	Duffy (4), Pamela A. Melroy, Koichi Wakata (2), Leroy Chiao (3), Wisoff (4), Michael Lopez-Alegria (2), McArthur (3)	309:43	Installed framework structure on ISS, setting the stage for future additions; 4 EVAs
10/31/00	*Soyuz TM-204	Shepherd (4), Yuri Gidzenko (2), Krikalev (5)	—	Established **1st permanent manning of ISS** with 3-person crew for a 4-month stay
11/30/00	Endeavour (STS-97)	Jett (3), Bloomfield (2), Tanner (3), Marc Garneau (3), Noriega (2)	259:57	Delivered 17-ton solar arrays, batteries, and radiators to ISS; 3 EVAs
2/7/01	Atlantis (STS-98)	Cockrell (4), Ivins (5), Jones (4), Curbeam (2), Mark L. Polansky	309:20	Installed U.S. Destiny Laboratory Module on the ISS; 3 EVAs
3/8/01	Discovery (STS-102)	Wetherbee (5), James M. Kelly, Helms (4) (to ISS), James S. Voss (5) (to ISS), Paul Richards, Andrew S.W. Thomas (2), Usachev (4) (to ISS), Shepherd (4) (from ISS), Gidzenko (2) (from ISS), Krikalev (5) (from ISS)	307:49	Transported 2nd permanent crew (Voss, Helms, Usachev) to ISS and returned 1st crew to Earth; 2 EVAs
4/19/01	Endeavour (STS-100)	Rominger (5), John L. Phillips, Hadfield (2), Ashby (2), Parazynski (4), Guidoni (2), Yuri V. Lonchakov	285:30	Installed the Canadarm2, a robotic arm, and delivered supplies to ISS; 2 EVAs
7/12/01	Atlantis (STS-104)	Lindsey (3), Charles O. Hobaugh, Michael L. Gernhardt (4), Kavandi (3), James F. Reilly II(2)	259:58	Installed a Joint Airlock, with nitrogen and oxygen tanks to permit future spacewalks from the ISS; 3 EVAs
8/10/01	Discovery (STS-105)	Horowitz (4), Sturckow (2), Daniel Barry (3), Patrick G. Forrester, Culbertson (3) (to ISS), Dezhurov (2) (to ISS), Mikhail Tyurin (to ISS), Usachev, (4), Voss (5) (from ISS), Helms (5) (from ISS)	285:13	Transported Expedition 3 crew to ISS (Culbertson, Tyurin, Dezhurov) and returned Expedition 2 crew to Earth; 2 EVAs
12/5/01	Endeavour (STS-108)	Gorie (3), Mark Kelly, Godwin (4), Daniel Tani, Yury Onufrienko (2) (to ISS), Daniel Bursch (4) (to ISS), Walz (4) (to ISS), Culbertson (3) (from ISS), Dezhurov (2) (from ISS), Tyurin (from ISS)	283:36	Transported Expedition 4 crew to ISS (Onufrienko, Bursch, Walz) and returned Expedition 3 crew to Earth; deployed STARSHINE 2 satellite; 1 EVA
3/1/02	Columbia (STS-109)	Altman (3), Duane G. Carey, Grunsfeld (4), Currie (4), Linnehan (3), Newman (4), Michael J. Massimino	262:10	Installed powerful new camera and upgraded other equipment on Hubble Space Telescope; 5 EVAs
4/8/02	Atlantis (STS-110)	Bloomfield (3), Stephen N. Frick, Rex J. Walheim, Ellen Ochoa (4), Lee M.E. Morin, Ross (7), S. Smith (4)	259:42	Installed S0 Truss, backbone for expansion of ISS; Ross set records with 7th spaceflight, 9th spacewalk; 4 EVAs
6/5/02	Endeavour (STS-111)	Cockrell (5), Paul Lockhart, Chang-Diaz (7), Philippe Perrin, Valery Korzun (2) (to ISS), Peggy Whitson (to ISS), Sergei Treschev (to ISS), Onufrienko (2) (from ISS), Bursch (4) (from ISS), Walz (4) (from ISS)	332:35	Transported Expedition 5 crew to ISS (Korzun, Whitson, Treschev) and returned Expedition 4 crew to Earth; brought platform for ISS robot arm; 3 EVAs
10/7/02	Atlantis (STS 112)	Ashby (3), Melroy (2), Wolf (3), Sandy Magnus, Piers Sellers, Fyodor Yurchikhin	259:58	Installed S1 Truss to ISS; 3 EVAs
10/30/02	*Soyuz TMA-1	Sergei Zalyotin (2), Frank De Winne, Yuri Lonchakov (2)	—	1st launch of Soyuz TMA (Crew returned 11/10/02 on Soyuz TM-34 already docked at ISS)
11/23/02	Endeavour (STS 113)	Wetherbee (6), Lockhart (2), Lopez-Alegria (3), John Herrington, Bowersox (5) (to ISS), Budarin (3) (to ISS), Don Pettit (to ISS), Korzun (2) (from ISS), Whitson (from ISS), Treschev (from ISS)	330:47	Delivered Expedition 6 crew to ISS (Bowersox, Budarin, Pettit) and returned Expedition 5 crew to Earth; installed P1 Truss to ISS; 3 EVAs
1/16/03	Columbia (STS 107)	Rick Husband (2), William McCool, Michael Anderson (2), David Brown, Kalbana Chawla (2), Laurel Clark, Ilan Ramon	382:20	**Entire crew lost when *Columbia* burned up** during reentry, 2/1/03
10/15/03	*Shenzhou 5	Yang Liwei	21:00	**1st Chinese manned spacecraft**
6/21/04	SpaceShipOne	Mike Melvill	0:90	**1st privately funded manned spaceflight**[4]
7/26/05	Discovery (STS-121)	Lindsey (4), Kelly (2), Michael E. Fossum, Sellers (2), Lisa M. Nowak, Stephanie D. Wilson	333:32	**1st space shuttle flight since *Columbia* disaster**; tested new safety modifications to craft; delivered supplies to ISS

Note: As of Sept. 2005, there have been 114 space shuttle flights, 88 since the 1986 *Challenger* explosion, 1 since the 2003 loss of *Columbia*. Totals include the final (28th) *Columbia* flight. There are 3 remaining shuttles: *Discovery* (31 flights), *Atlantis* (26), and *Endeavour* (19); the *Challenger* completed 9 missions in all. Four Soviets have died during spaceflight: Vladimir Komarov was killed on *Soyuz 1* (1967) when parachute lines tangled during descent; the 3-person *Soyuz 11* crew (1971) was asphyxiated. Six Americans and an Israeli astronaut died aboard the *Columbia*; 7 Americans died in the *Challenger* explosion, and 3 astronauts—Virgil I. Grissom, Edward H. White, and Roger B. Chaffee—died in the Jan. 27, 1967, *Apollo 1* fire on the ground at Cape Canaveral, FL. (1) For shuttle flights, mission name is in parentheses following name of orbiter. (2) Space stations, such as the *Salyut*s and *Mir*, were used to house crews starting in 1971. (3) Approx. crew duration for Thagard's stay. Crew did not return together. (4) SpaceShipOne flew at least 100 km (62 mi) into space, 9/29/04, piloted by Mike Melvill, and 10/4/04, piloted by Brian Binnie, winning the $10 mil Ansari Prize for 1st private venture to accomplish this feat twice within 2 weeks.

U.S. Manned Space Program After *Columbia*

Following the Feb. 1, 2003, *Columbia* disaster, when the craft broke up on re-entry, all space shuttle flights were grounded. NASA formed a panel, the Columbia Accident Investigation Board (CAIB), to pinpoint the cause of the explosion and recommend future changes. In an Aug. 2003 report the CAIB said the accident was caused by a hole knocked in the heat shield on *Columbia*'s left wing by a chunk of foam insulation that had broken off from the external fuel tank during liftoff. During re-entry, hot gases entered the hole and melted *Columbia*'s fuselage causing its breakup. After analyzing the CAIB's recommendations, NASA began modifying the remaining shuttles, starting with *Discovery*. Safety improvements included a redesigned external tank, new sensors to register impact, and a boom with a camera to allow astronauts to inspect the shuttle in flight for any potential damage.

The modified *Discovery* was launched July 26, 2005, on a mission aimed mainly at testing the new safety modifications. Although the launch was successful in putting the shuttle into orbit, onboard cameras showed that foam insulation broke off from *Discovery*'s external fuel tank during launch. Luckily it did not strike the craft, as had the piece that broke off during the *Columbia* flight. But the problem that led to the Columbia disaster had apparently not been solved. NASA again suspended future shuttle missions until the fuel tank problem could be resolved.

During the *Discovery* flight, the crew visited the International Space Station and conducted 3 spacewalks, including an unprecedented excursion to the shuttle's underbelly to remove gap fillers from between the orbiter's heat-shielding tiles that had come loose, possibly during launch. The fear was that they could possibly cause overheating during re-entry. However, on Aug. 9, *Discovery* landed safely at Edwards Air Force Base, CA.

At the earliest, the next shuttle launch will not take place until Mar. 2006. Meanwhile, Pres. George W. Bush outlined his vision for space exploration after the shuttle, in a Jan. 2004 speech. Under the president's plan, the space shuttle would be retired in 2010 and replaced with a Crew Exploration Vehicle (CEV), able to carry up to 6 astronauts beyond low-Earth orbit (the space shuttle was designed to function only in a low-Earth orbit) to the Moon. The CEV would facilitate the building of lunar bases and future spacecraft that would ultimately bring humans to Mars. In Sept. 2005 NASA unveiled a $104 bil plan that would aim to get 4 people to the Moon, probably in 2018.

International Space Station

The International Space Station (ISS) is considered the largest cooperative scientific project in history.

16 cooperating nations: U.S., Russia, Canada, Belgium, Denmark, France, Germany, Italy, Netherlands, Norway, Spain, Sweden, Switzerland, United Kingdom, Japan, and Brazil.

Impact of *Columbia* disaster: The grounding of U.S. space shuttles after the *Columbia* disaster and then after *Discovery* in 2005 interrupted further assembly of the station. Since lower-capacity Russian *Soyuz* and *Progress* craft were the usual means of ferrying provisions and crew to and from Earth, the size of the crew aboard the ISS was reduced to 2. In 2005 the crew conducted repair and maintenance operations, with supplies delivered by Russian vehicles and the *Discovery* shuttle.

The station when completed:
- mass of 1,040,000 lb
- 356' x 290', with almost an acre of solar panels
- internal volume roughly equivalent to passenger cabin of a 747 jumbo jet
- 6 laboratories; living space for up to 7 people

Examples of research conducted or planned:
- growing living cells in a gravity-free environment
- studying the effects on humans of long-term exposure to reduced gravity
- studying large-scale long-term changes in Earth's environment by observing Earth from orbit

Summary of Worldwide Successful Launches, 1957-2004

Source: National Aeronautics and Space Administration

Year	Total[1]	Russia[2]	U.S.	ESA[3]	China	Japan	France	India	U.K.	Germany	Canada	Israel
1957-59	24	6	18	—	—	—	—	—	—	—	—	—
1960-69	1,035	399	614	2	—	—	4	—	1	—	—	—
1970-79	1,366	1,028	247	5	8	18	14	1	6	3	4	—
1980-89	1,431	1,132	191	14	16	26	5	9	4	7	5	—
1990-99	1,045	542	300	55	33	23	16	11	7	6	4	—
2000-04	317	126	114	37	25	7	0	5	0	0	0	2
TOTAL	**5,218**	**3,233**	**1,484**	**113**	**82**	**74**	**39**	**26**	**18**	**16**	**13**	**2**

(1) Includes launches sponsored by countries not shown. (2) Data for 1957-91 apply to the Soviet Union, for 1992-96 to the Commonwealth of Independent States, after 1996 to Russia. (3) European Space Agency.

Notable Proposed Space Missions

Source: National Aeronautics and Space Administration

Planned Launch	Mission	Purpose
Jan. 11, 2006	New Horizons (Pluto)	After a gravity boost from Jupiter in 2007, fly by Pluto in 2015, then go on to explore one or more Kuiper Belt objects.
June 17, 2006	Dawn	Orbit and study Vesta and Ceres, 2 of the biggest asteroids in the solar system.
July 2007	Planck-Herschel Satellite	Study the origins of the universe and "dark matter"; collect data to study whether the universe is finite or infinite.
Aug. 2007	Gamma-ray Large Area Space Telescope (GLAST)	High-energy gamma-ray observatory designed to study celestial gamma-ray sources such as black holes.
Aug. 2007	Phoenix Mars Lander	Land on or near Martian polar ice cap; study soil composition for chemical make-up and signs of life; monitor climate.
Oct. 2008	Lunar Reconnaissance Orbiter	Accurately map the surface of the moon; surface temperature mapping; assess lunar surface features for future landing sites.
2009	Mars Science Laboratory	Roving, long-range, long-duration science lab to study the Martian surface.

Notable U.S. Lunar and Planetary Science Missions

Source: National Aeronautics and Space Administration

Spacecraft	Launch date[1]	Mission	Remarks
Mariner 2	Aug. 27, 1962	Venus	Passed within 22,000 mi of Venus 12/14/62; contact lost 1/3/63 at 54 million mi
Ranger 7	July 28, 1964	Moon	Yielded over 4,000 photos of lunar surface
Mariner 4	Nov. 28, 1964	Mars	Passed behind Mars 7/14/65; took 22 photos from 6,000 mi
Ranger 8	Feb. 17, 1965	Moon	Yielded over 7,000 photos of lunar surface
Surveyor 3	Apr. 17, 1967	Moon	Scooped and tested lunar soil
Mariner 5	June 14, 1967	Venus	In solar orbit; closest Venus flyby 10/19/67
Mariner 6	Feb. 24, 1969	Mars	Came within 2,000 mi of Mars 7/31/69; collected data, photos
Mariner 7	Mar. 27, 1969	Mars	Came within 2,000 mi of Mars 8/5/69

Spacecraft	Launch date[1]	Mission	Remarks
Mariner 9	May 30, 1971	Mars	First craft to orbit Mars 11/13/71; sent back over 7,000 photos
Pioneer 10	Mar. 2, 1972	Jupiter	Passed Jupiter 12/4/73; exited the planetary system 6/13/83; transmission ended 3/31/97 at 6.39 billion mi
Pioneer 11	Apr. 5, 1973	Jupiter, Saturn	Passed Jupiter 12/3/74; Saturn 9/1/79; discovered an additional ring and 2 moons around Saturn; operating in outer solar system; transmission ended 9/95
Mariner 10	Nov. 3, 1973	Venus, Mercury	Passed Venus 2/5/74; arrived Mercury 3/29/74. 1st time gravity of 1 planet (Venus) used to whip spacecraft toward another (Mercury)
Viking 1	Aug. 20, 1975	Mars	Landed on Mars 7/20/76; did scientific research, sent photos; functioned 6 years
Viking 2	Sept. 9, 1975	Mars	Landed on Mars 9/3/76; functioned 3 years
Voyager 1	Sept. 5, 1977	Jupiter, Saturn	Encountered Jupiter 3/5/79, provided evidence of Jupiter ring; passed near Saturn 11/12/80; passed Pioneer 10 to become most distant human-made object 2/17/98
Voyager 2	Aug. 20, 1977	Jupiter, Saturn, Uranus, Neptune	Encountered Jupiter 7/9/79; Saturn 8/25/81; Uranus 1/24/86; Neptune 8/25/89
Pioneer Venus 1	May 20, 1978	Venus	Entered Venus orbit 12/4/78; spent 14 years studying planet; ceased operating 10/19/92
Pioneer Venus 2	Aug. 8, 1978	Venus	Encountered Venus 12/9/78; probes impacted on surface
Magellan	May 4, 1989	Venus	Landed on Venus 8/10/90; orbited and mapped Venus; monitored geological activity on surface; ceased operating 10/11/94
Galileo	Oct. 18, 1989	Jupiter	Used Earth's gravity to propel it toward Jupiter; encountered Venus Feb. 1990; encountered Jupiter 12/7/95; released probe to Jovian surface; encountered moons; disintegrated 9/21/03
Mars Global Surveyor	Nov. 7, 1996	Mars	Began orbiting Mars 9/11/97; began mapping survey of entire surface 3/9/99; discovered magnetism on planet; observed Martian moon Phobos; found evidence of liquid water in past 6/22/00
Mars Pathfinder	Dec. 4, 1996	Mars	Landed on Mars 7/4/97; rover *Sojourner* made measurements of the Martian climate and soil composition, sending thousands of surface images; ceased operating 9/27/97
Cassini-Huygens	Oct. 15, 1997	Saturn	Began orbiting Saturn 6/30/04; 4-year mission to study planet's atmosphere, rings, and moons; *Huygens* probe sched. to land on moon Titan 1/14/05.
Lunar Prospector	Jan. 6, 1998	Moon	Began orbiting Moon 1/11/98; mapped abundance of 11 elements on Moon's surface; discovered evidence of water-ice at both lunar poles; made 1st precise gravity map of entire lunar surface; crashed into crater near Moon's south pole 7/31/99 to end mission
Stardust	Feb. 7, 1999	Comet Wild-2	Reached comet 1/2/04; gathered dust samples; sched. to return them to Earth in 2006.
2001 Mars Odyssey	Apr. 7, 2001	Mars	Reached Mars 10/24/01; primary mission to study climate and geologic history completed 8/04; began extended mission.
Genesis	Aug. 8, 2001	Sun	Orbited Sun, collected particles from solar wind. Capsule containing specimens crashed to Earth 9/8/04 after a failure to deploy its drag chute; some samples survived.
Mars Exploration Rovers	June 7 & July 10, 2003	Mars	Rovers *Spirit* and *Opportunity* landed on Mars Jan. 2004, began studying the geology of the planet, focusing on history of water
MESSENGER	Mar. 2, 2004	Mercury	Due to reach Mercury in 2011 to map and study its surface.
Deep Impact	Jan. 12, 2005	Comet Tempel 1	Reached Tempel 1; deployed an impact probe which slammed into the comet on July 5; probe sent back pictures and analysis.
Mars Reconnaissance Orbiter	Aug. 12, 2005	Mars	Due to reach Mars in 2006, craft will take detailed images and look for topographical evidence that surface water once existed there.

(1) Coordinated Universal Time

Aircraft Operating Statistics

Source: Courtesy of Air Transport Association of America, Inc. Reprinted with permission. Copyright © 2003 by Air Transport Association of America, Inc. All rights reserved. Figures are averages for most commonly used models.

	No. of seats	Speed airborne (mph)	Flight length (mi)	Fuel (gal per hr)	Operating cost per hr
B747-200/300*	370	520	3,148	3,625	$9,153
B747-400	367	534	3,960	3,411	8,443
B747-100*	—	503	2,022	1,762	3,852
B747-F*	—	506	2,512	3,593	7,138
L-1011	325	494	2,023	1,981	8,042
DC-10*	286	497	1,637	2,405	7,374
B767-400	265	495	1,682	1,711	3,124
B-777	263	525	3,515	2,165	5,105
A330	261	509	3,559	1,407	3,076
MD-11*	261	515	2,485	2,473	7,695
A300-600*	235	460	947	1,638	6,518
B757-300	235	472	1,309	985	2,345
B767-300ER*	207	497	2,122	1,579	4,217
DC-8*	—	437	686	1,712	8,065
B757-200*	181	464	1,175	1,045	3,312
B767-200ER	175	487	1,987	1,404	3,873
A321	169	454	1,094	673	1,347
B737-800/900	151	454	1,035	770	2,248
MD-90	150	446	886	825	2,716
B727-200*	148	430	644	1,289	$4,075
B727-100*	—	417	468	989	13,667
A320	146	454	1,065	767	2,359
B737-400	141	409	646	703	2,595
MD-80	134	432	791	953	2,718
B737-700LR	132	441	879	740	1,692
B737-300/700	132	403	542	723	2,388
A319	122	442	904	666	1,913
A310-200*	—	455	847	1,561	8,066
B737-100/200	119	396	465	824	2,377
B717-200	112	339	175	573	3,355
B737-500	110	407	576	756	2,347
DC-9	101	387	496	826	2,071
F-100	87	398	587	662	2,303
B737-200C	55	387	313	924	3,421
ERJ-145	50	360	343	280	1,142
CRJ-145	49	397	486	369	1,433
ERJ-135	37	357	382	267	969
SD 340B	33	230	202	84	644

* Data include cargo operations.

IT'S A FACT: The gigantic Vehicle Assembly Building (VAB) at Cape Canaveral was built in 1966 for the purpose of vertically assembling the 365-foot Saturn V rockets—the biggest ever built—used during the Apollo missions. The VAB is 525 feet tall, 518 feet wide, and encloses a volume of 129,428,000 cubic feet. Spacecraft ready for launch exit the building through the VAB's huge 456-foot-high doors, which take 45 minutes to open. The building is now used to ready space shuttles for launch.

Some Notable Aviation Firsts[1]

1903 — On Dec. 17, near Kitty Hawk, NC, brothers Wilbur and Orville Wright made the 1st human-carrying, powered flight. Each made 2 flights; the longest, about 852 ft, lasted 59 sec.

1907 — U.S. airplane manufacturing company formed by Glenn H. Curtiss.

1908 — 1st airplane passenger, Lt. Frank P. Lahm, rode with Wilbur Wright in a brief (6 min, 24 sec) flight.

1911 — 1st transportation of mail by airplane officially approved by the U.S. Postal Service began on Sept. 23. It lasted one week. In 1918, limited scheduled airmail service began. By 1921, scheduled transcontinental airmail service began between New York City and San Francisco.

1914 — 1st scheduled passenger airline service began. It operated between St. Petersburg and Tampa, FL.

1919 — 1st airline food, a basket lunch, was served as part of a commercial airline service.

1930 — Ellen Church became 1st flight attendant.

1939 — On Aug. 27, the German Heinkel He 178 made the 1st successful flight powered by a jet engine.

1947 — Mach 1, the sound barrier was broken by Amer. Chuck Yeager in a Bell X-1 rocket-powered aircraft.

(1) Excludes notable around-the-world and international trips.

1947 — Largest airplane ever flown, Howard Hughes's "Spruce Goose," flew 1 mi at an altitude of 80 ft.

1953 — Jacqueline Cochran became 1st woman to fly faster than sound.

1960 — Convair B-58, 1st supersonic bomber, was introduced.

1968 — The supersonic speed of Mach 2 was accomplished for 1st time, in a Tupolev Tu-144. The plane had an approximate maximum speed of 1,200 mph.

1970 — The Tupolev Tu-144, during commercial transport, exceeded Mach 2. It reached about 1,335 mph at 53,475 ft.

1976 — The Concorde began 1st scheduled supersonic commercial service.

1977 — The Gossamer Condor successfully demonstrated human-powered flight, completing figure-8 course of 1.15 miles.

1979 — The human-powered Gossamer Albatross crossed the English Channel in 2 hr, 49 min.

1981 — Solar Challenger became the 1st solar-powered airplane to cross the English Channel.

2005 — The Airbus 380, the biggest-ever commercial jet, was unveiled. It was 240 ft. long, had a wingspan of 262 ft., and could seat a maximum of 840 passengers.

Some Notable Around-the-World and Intercontinental Trips

Aviator or Craft	From/To	Miles	Time	Date
J. Alcock-A.W. Brown [1]	Newfoundland/Ireland	1,960	16h 12m	June 14-15, 1919
2 U.S. Army airplanes	Seattle/Seattle	26,103	35d 01h 11m	1924
Richard E. Byrd, Floyd Bennett [2]	Spitsbergen (Nor.)/N. Pole	1,545	15h 30m	May 9, 1926
Amundsen-Ellsworth-Nobile Polar Expedition (in a dirigible)	Spitsbergen (Nor.)/over N. Pole to Teller, Alaska		80h	May 11-14,1926
E.S. Evans and L. Wells (*New York World*)	New York/NewYork	18,410[3]	28d 14h 36m 05s	June 16-July 14, 1926
Charles Lindbergh[4]	New York/Paris	3,610	33h 29m 30s	May 20-21, 1927
Amelia Earhart, W. Stultz, L. Gordon	Newfoundland/Wales		20h 40m	June 17-18, 1928
Graf Zeppelin	Friedrichshafen, Ger./Lakehurst, NJ	6,630	4d 15h 46m	Oct. 11-15, 1928
Graf Zeppelin	Friedrichshafen, Ger./Lakehurst, NJ	21,700	20d 04h	Aug. 14-Sept. 4, 1929
Wiley Post and Harold Gatty (Monoplane Winnie Mae)	New York/New York	15,474	8d 15h 51m	July 1, 1931
C. Pangborn-H. Herndon Jr.[5]	Misawa, Japan/Wenatchee, WA	4,458	41h 34m	Oct. 3-5, 1931
Amelia Earhart [6]	Newfoundland/Ireland	2,026	14h 56m	May 20-21, 1932
Wiley Post (Monoplane Winnie Mae)[7]	New York/New York	15,596	115h 36m 30s	July 15-22, 1933
Hindenburg Zeppelin	Lakehurst, NJ/Frankfort, Ger.		42h 53m	Aug. 9-11, 1936
Howard Hughes and 4 assistants	New York/New York	14,824	3d 19h 08m 10s	July 10-13, 1938
America, Pan American 4-engine Lockheed Constellation[8]	New York/New York	22,219	101h 32m	June 17-30, 1947
Col. Edward Eagan	New York/New York	20,559	147h 15m	Dec. 13, 1948
USAF B-50 Lucky Lady II (Capt. James Gallagher) [9]	Ft. Worth, TX/Ft. Worth, TX	23,452	94h 01m	Mar. 2, 1949
Col. D. Schilling, USAF [10]	England/Limestone, ME	3,300	10h 01m	Sept. 22, 1950
C.F. Blair Jr.	Norway/Alaska	3,300	10h 29m	May 29, 1951
Canberra Bomber [11]	N. Ireland/Newfoundland	2073	04h 34m	Aug. 26, 1952
	Newfoundland/N. Ireland	2073	03h 25m	Aug. 26, 1952
3 USAF B-52 Strato-fortresses [12]	Merced, CA/CA	24,325	45h 19m	Jan. 15-18, 1957
USSR TU-114 [13]	Moscow/New York	5,092	11h 06m	June 28, 1959
Peter Gluckmann (solo)	San Francisco/San Francisco	22,800	29d	Aug. 22-Sept. 20, 1959
Robert & Joan Wallick	Manila/Manila	23,129	5d 06h 17m 10s	June 2-7, 1966
Trevor K. Brougham	Darwin, Australia/Darwin	24,800	5d 05h 57m	Aug. 5-10, 1972
Arnold Palmer	Denver/Denver	22,985	57h 7m 12s	May 17-19, 1976
Boeing 747[14]	San Francisco/San Francisco	26,382	57h 25m 42s	Oct. 28-31, 1977
Richard Rutan & Jeana Yeager[15]	Edwards AFB, CA	24,986	09d 03m 44s	Dec. 14-23, 1986
Concorde	New York/New York	1,114 mph	31h 27m 49s	Aug. 15-16, 1995
Col. Douglas L. Raaberg and crew, B1 bomber[16]	Dyess AFB, Abilene, TX/ Dyess AFB	6,250	36h 13m 36s	June 3, 1995
Linda Finch[17]	Oakland, CA/Oakland, CA	26,000	73d	Mar. 17-May 28, 1997
Bertrand Piccard, Brian Jones[18]	Switzerland/Egypt	29,054.6	19d 21h 55m	Mar. 1-21, 1999
Steve Fossett[19]	Australia/Australia	21,109.6	14d 20h 01m	June 19-July 4, 2002
Steve Fossett[20]	Salina, KS/Salina, KS	26,366	67h 2m 38s	Mar. 1-Mar. 3, 2005

(1) Nonstop transatlantic flight. (2) Claim of reaching N. Pole in dispute; if claim is untrue, then Amundsen-Ellsworth-Nobile were the first to fly over N. Pole. (3) Includes mileage by train and auto, 4,110; by plane, 6,300; by steamship, 8,000. (4) Solo transatlantic flight in the Ryan monoplane "Spirit of St. Louis." (5) Nonstop transpacific flight. (6) First woman to complete a transoceanic solo flight. Earhart disappeared in the Pacific in 1937 while attempting an around-the-world flight. (7) First to fly solo around N circumference of the world and first to fly twice around the world. (8) Inception of regular commercial global air service. (9) First nonstop round-the-world flight, refueled 4 times in flight. (10) Nonstop jet transatlantic flight. (11) Transatlantic round trip on same day. (12) First nonstop global flight by jet planes; refueled in flight by KC-97 aerial tankers; average speed approx. 525 mph. (13) Nonstop between Moscow and New York. (14) Speed record around the world over both Earth's poles. (15) Circled Earth nonstop without refueling. (16) Refueled in flight 6 times. Tested B-1B bomber by bombing 3 pre-arranged target sites on 3 continents. (17) Followed the intended around-the-world flight route (1937) of Amelia Earhart. (18) First to circumnavigate the globe nonstop in a balloon. (19) First solo circumnavigation of globe nonstop in a balloon; time, dates, and distance are for complete flight, which exceeded circumnavigation because winds prevented landing. (20) First non-stop solo circumnavigation in an airplane without refueling.

ASTRONOMY

Edited by Lee T. Shapiro, Ph.D., Fellow of the Royal Astronomical Society

Celestial Events Summary, 2006

There are 4 **eclipses** in 2006: a total solar eclipse in March, an annular solar eclipse, and a partial lunar eclipse in September, and a penumbral lunar eclipse in March (which will pass mostly unnoticed). The path of the March total eclipse starts in the South Atlantic Ocean, crosses northern Africa, the Mediterranean Sea and central Asia, and ends in Mongolia. The September annular eclipse starts at the eastern coast of northern South America, crosses down the South Atlantic Ocean, and ends in the Indian Ocean. The shallow partial lunar eclipse of Sept. 7 will be best seen in Asia, Australia, much of Africa, and much of Europe.

The most likely viewing successes for **meteor showers** will be the Eta Aquarids in early May, the Orionids in October, and the Geminids in December. For the **planets**, at the start of the year Saturn is up most of the night, Jupiter rises after midnight, Mars is up at the start of the night setting after midnight, while Venus is low in the southwest. Venus is soon lost in the glare of the Sun and moves to the morning sky by the end of February. Jupiter gradually moves from the morning sky to also appearing in the evening sky. By June, Saturn and Mars are getting low in the west in the early evening while Jupiter is high prominent. In July Saturn disappears into sunset, and it appears in the morning sky in late August. By September Mars leaves the evening sky, and in October Venus leaves the morning sky. Jupiter leaves the evening sky in early November, and both Jupiter and Mars appear in the morning sky in December, where one can already see Saturn. Watch the close planet morning groupings of Mercury, Venus, and Saturn in August and Mercury, Mars, and Jupiter in December. The best opportunities for seeing Mercury occur in the 2nd half of February in the evening sky and in early December in the morning sky with the other bright planets except Venus.

The crescent **Moon,** with its light not overpowering, makes pretty pairings with the 2 brightest planets, Venus and Jupiter. Waxing crescent **pairings** are visible in the early evening soon after sunset, while waning crescent pairings are visible in the early morning rising shortly before sunrise. The waxing crescent Moon pairs with Venus in the early evening on the first of the year, then pairs with Jupiter in August, September, and October. The waning crescent Moon pairs with Venus in the morning in each of the months from late January through August. It also pairs with Jupiter in mid-December. Of special note is the pairing of the Moon with Venus nearby in late March, the triple grouping of the waxing crescent Moon, Mars, and Saturn at the beginning and end of May, and the very close pairing of Venus and Saturn in August; then in December Mars passes its "rival" the star Antares as the two of them are passed by the nearly quarter Moon.

Astronomical Positions and Constants

Two celestial bodies are in **conjunction** when they are due N and S of each other, either in **right ascension** (with respect to the N celestial pole) or in **celestial longitude** (with respect to the N ecliptic pole). Celestial bodies in conjunction will rise and set at nearly the same time. For the inner planets—Mercury and Venus—**inferior conjunction** occurs when either planet passes between Earth and the Sun, while **superior conjunction** occurs when either Mercury or Venus is on the far side of the Sun. Celestial bodies are in **opposition** when their Right Ascensions differ by exactly 12 hours, or when their Celestial Longitudes differ by 180°. In this case one of the 2 objects in opposition will rise while the other is setting. **Quadrature** refers to the arrangement where the coordinates of 2 bodies differ by exactly 90°. These terms may refer to the relative positions of any 2 bodies as seen from Earth, but one of the bodies is so frequently the Sun that mention of the Sun is omitted in that case.

When objects are in conjunction, the alignment is not perfect, and one is usually passing above or below the other. The geocentric angular separation between the Sun and an object is termed **elongation**. Elongation is limited only for Mercury and Venus; the greatest elongation for each of these bodies is approximately the time for longest observation. **Perihelion** is the point in an orbit that is nearest to the Sun, and **aphelion,** the point farthest from the Sun. **Perigee** is the point in an orbit that is nearest Earth, **apogee** the point that is farthest from Earth. An **occultation** of a planet or a star is an eclipse of it by some other body, usually the Moon. A **transit** of the Sun occurs when Mercury or Venus passes directly between Earth and the Sun, appearing to cross the disk of the Sun.

The following were adopted as part of the International Astronomical Union System of Astronomical Constants (1976): **Speed of light,** 299,792.458 km per sec., or about 186,282 statute mi per sec.; **solar parallax,** 8".794148; astronomical Unit (the mean distance between the Earth and the Sun), 149,597,870 km, or 92,955,807 mi; **constant of nutation,** 9".2025; and **constant of aberration,** 20".49552.

Celestial Events Highlights, 2006

(Coordinated Universal Time, or UTC—the standard time of the prime meridian)

January

Mercury visible low in the SE before sunrise, disappears from view by mid-month.

Venus is very low in the SW after sunset, disappears into the sunset before mid-month and reappears in the morning sky at the end of the month.

Mars is high in the E at sunset, setting after midnight.

Jupiter, rising after midnight, is in the S-SE before sunrise.

Saturn, rising shortly after sunset, is up most of the night.

Moon passes Venus on 1st and the 28th, Neptune on the 2nd and the 31st, Uranus on the 4th, Mars on the 8th, Saturn on the 15th, and Jupiter on the 23rd. **Watch for the thin waxing crescent Moon near Venus on the 1st and the thin waning crescent Moon near Venus on the 28th**.

Jan. 1—Pluto in Serpens Cauda the only divided constellation. Neptune in Capricornus and Uranus in Aquarius (all year). Saturn in Cancer. Jupiter in Libra. Mars in Aries. Venus in Capricornus. Sun in Sagittarius. Venus enters Sagittarius. Moon passes 7° S of Venus. **Mars at closest approach to the Earth this year.**

Jan. 2—Moon passes 4° S of Neptune.

Jan. 3—Quadrantid meteor shower from midnight until dawn.

Jan. 4—Moon passes 2° S of Uranus. Earth at perihelion, closest approach to the Sun.

Jan. 8—Moon passes 1.3° N of Mars.

Jan. 10—Mercury at aphelion.

Jan. 13—Venus at closest approach to the Earth this year.

Jan. 14—Venus at inferior conjunction, passes between the Earth and the Sun.

Jan. 15—Moon passes 4° N of Saturn.

Jan. 20—Sun enters Capricornus.

Jan. 21—Moon passes 0.6° N of the star Spica in the constellation Virgo, occults Spica like all occultations, visible only from some parts of Earth.

Jan. 23—Moon passes 5° S of Jupiter.

Jan. 24—Venus at perihelion.

Jan. 25—Moon passes 0.02° N of the star Antares in the constellation Scorpius, occults Antares.

Jan. 26—Mercury at superior conjunction, passes behind the Sun.

Jan. 27—Saturn at opposition. **Saturn at closest approach to the Earth this year.**

Jan. 28—Moon passes 12° S of Venus.

Jan. 31—Moon passes 1.7° S of Uranus.

February

Mercury reappears early in the month in the W-SW in the early evening, passes very close to Uranus on the 14th, and remains visible the rest of the month.

Venus is very low in the SW at the beginning of the month, slowly getting higher before sunrise.

Mars remains high in the S at sunset.

Jupiter, rising about midnight, is in the S before sunrise.

Saturn, low in the E-NE at sunset, is up most of the night.

Moon passes Mars on the 5th, Saturn on the 11th, Jupiter on the 20th and Neptune on the 26th. In the morning watch for the waning quarter Moon below Jupiter on the 20th.

Feb. 3—Venus stationary, resumes direct motion.

Feb. 5—Moon passes 2° N of Mars.

Feb. 6—Neptune at conjunction.

Feb. 7—Mars enters Taurus.

Feb. 11—Moon passes 4° N of Saturn.

Feb. 14—Mercury passes 0.03° N of Uranus.

Feb. 16—Sun enters Aquarius.

Feb. 18—Moon passes 0.4° N of Spica, occults Spica.

Feb. 20—Moon passes 5° S of Jupiter.

Feb. 21—Moon passes 0.2° S of Antares, occults Antares.

Feb. 22—Mercury at perihelion, closest to the Sun.

Feb. 24—Mercury at greatest eastern elongation of 18° (E of the Sun and sets after the Sun). Moon passes 10° S of Venus.

Feb. 26—Moon passes 4° S of Neptune.

March

Mercury disappears from the early evening sky early in the month to reappear in the early morning sky late in the month.

Venus, bright and low in the SE before sunrise, passes Neptune on the 26th.

Mars is high in the S after sunset.

Jupiter, rising a couple of hours after sunset, is prominent much of the night in the SW at sunrise.

Saturn is high in the E at sunset.

Moon passes Mercury on the 1st and 27th, Mars on the 6th, Saturn on the 10th, Jupiter on the 19th, Venus on the 25th, Neptune on the 26th, and Uranus on the 27th. Lunar occultation of the asteroid Ceres on the 25th should be visible from eastern N America. Look for waning crescent Moon near Mercury on the 27th with Venus nearby.

Mar. 1—Moon passes 4° S of Mercury. Uranus at conjunction.

Mar. 2—Mercury stationary, begins retrograde motion.

Mar. 5—Jupiter stationary, begins retrograde motion.

Mar. 6—Venus enters Capricornus. Moon passes 3° N of Mars.

Mar. 10—Moon passes 4° N of Saturn.

Mar. 11—Sun enters Pisces. Mars passes 7° N of the star Aldebaran in the constellation Taurus.

Mar. 12—Mercury at inferior conjunction, passes between the Earth and the Sun.

Mar. 14—Penumbral eclipse of the Moon, see details under Eclipses.

Mar. 17—Moon passes 0.3° N of Spica, occults Spica.

Mar. 19—Moon passes 5° S of Jupiter.

Mar. 20—Vernal equinox at 1:26 PM EST (18:26 UTC); **spring begins in the northern hemisphere, autumn in the southern hemisphere.** Venus enters Aquarius.

Mar. 21—Moon passes 0.3° S of Antares, occults Antares.

Mar. 24—Mercury stationary, resumes direct motion.

Mar. 25—Venus at greatest western elongation of 47° (W of the Sun, rises before the Sun). Moon passes 6° S of Venus.

Mar. 26—Moon passes 4° S of Neptune. Venus passes 1.9° N of Neptune.

Mar. 27—Venus enters Capricornus. Sun barely touches constellation of Cetus. Moon passes 1.4° S of Uranus and 2° S of Mercury, occults Uranus.

Mar. 29—Total eclipse of the Sun; see details under Eclipses. Pluto stationary, begins retrograde motion.

April

Mercury is in the morning sky very low in the E before sunrise all month.

Venus is prominent in the E-SE before sunrise, passing close to Uranus on the 18th.

Mars is high in the W after sunset.

Jupiter, rising about sunset, is prominent all night.

Saturn, high in the S at sunset, sets after midnight.

Moon passes Mars on the 3rd, Saturn on the 6th, Jupiter on the 15th, Neptune on the 22nd, Uranus and Venus on the 24th, and Mercury on the 26th. Look for the waxing crescent Moon near Mars on the 3rd and the waning crescent Moon near Venus on the 24th and two days later near Mercury on the 26th.

Apr. 3—Moon passes 4° N of Mars.

Apr. 4—Venus enters Aquarius.

Apr. 5—Saturn stationary, resumes direct motion.

Apr. 6—Moon passes 4° N of Saturn.

Apr. 7—Mercury at aphelion.

Apr. 8—Mercury at greatest western elongation of 28° (W of the Sun, rises before the Sun).

Apr. 13—Moon passes 0.3° N of Spica, occults Spica.

Apr. 14—Mars enters Gemini.

Apr. 15—Moon passes 5° S of Jupiter.

Apr. 17—Moon passes 0.2° S of Antares, occults Antares.

Apr. 18—Sun enters Aries. Venus passes 0.3° N of Uranus.

Apr. 22—Moon passes 4° S of Neptune. **Waning quarter moon interferes with observing the Lyrid meteor shower this morning.**

Apr. 24—Moon passes 1.2° S of Uranus and 0.5° S of Venus, occults Uranus and Venus.

Apr. 26—Moon passes 4° N of Mercury.

Apr. 28—Venus enters Pisces.

May

Mercury, very low in E-NE in the early morning, disappears into the glare of the Sun to emerge into the early evening sky at the end of the month.

Venus, still in the morning sky, moves from E-SE to E as the month progresses.

Mars, high in the W at sunset, sets before midnight.

Jupiter, rising about sunset, is prominent all night.

Saturn, high in the W-SW at sunset, sets before midnight.

Moon passes Mars on the 2nd, Saturn on the 4th, Neptune on the 19th, Uranus on the 21st, Venus on the 24th, and on the 31st passes Mars and Saturn for the second time this month. **Watch for the triple groupings of the crescent Moon, Mars, and Saturn on the 3rd and 31st.**

May 2—Moon passes 4° N of Mars.

May 4—Moon passes 4° N of Saturn. Jupiter at opposition.

May 5—Jupiter at closest approach to the Earth this year.

May 6—Eta Aquarid meteor shower from midnight until dawn.

May 9—Venus enters Cetus.

May 11—Moon passes 0.3° N of Spica, occults Spica.

May 12—Venus enters Pisces. Moon passes 5° S of Jupiter.

May 14—Sun enters Taurus. Moon passes 0.1° S of Antares, occults Antares.

May 17—Venus at aphelion.

May 18—Mercury at superior conjunction.

May 19—Moon passes 4° S of Neptune.

May 21—Mercury at perihelion. Moon passes 1° S of Uranus.

May 22—Neptune stationary, begins retrograde motion.

May 24—Moon passes 4° N of Venus.

May 25—Mars passes 5° S of the star Pollux in the constellation Gemini.

May 30—Mars enters Cancer.

May 31—Venus enters Aries. Moon passes 3° N of Mars and 4° N of Saturn.

June

Mercury, low in the W-NW, is in the evening sky all month, passes Pollux on the 20th.

Venus, still prominent in the morning sky, is now found in the W-NW.

Mars is getting low in the W after sunset and passes close to Saturn on the 17th.

Jupiter is in the SE at sunset, setting after midnight.

Saturn is getting low in the W-NW at sunset.

Moon passes Jupiter on the 8th, Neptune on the 15th, Uranus on the 17th, Venus on the 23rd, Mercury on the 27th, and Saturn and Mars on the 28th. Watch for the thin waxing crescent Moon grouped with Mercury, Saturn on Mars on the 27th and 28th.

June 7—Moon passes 0.1° N of Spica, occults Spica.

June 8—Moon passes 5° S of Jupiter.

June 10—Moon passes 0.1° S of Antares, occults Antares.

June 15—Moon passes 3° S of Neptune. Pluto at closest approach to the Earth this year.

June 16—Pluto at opposition.

June 17—Moon passes 0.6° S of Uranus, occults Uranus. Mars passes 0.6° N of Saturn.

June 18—Venus enters Taurus.

June 19—Uranus stationary, begins retrograde motion.

June 20—Mercury at greatest eastern elongation of 25°. Mercury passes 6° S of Pollux.

June 21—Northern solstice at 8:26 AM EDT (12:26 UTC); **summer begins in the northern hemisphere, winter in the southern hemisphere.** Sun enters Gemini.

June 23—Moon passes 6° N of Venus.

June 26—Mars at aphelion.

June 27—Moon passes 5° N of Mercury.

June 28—Moon passes 3° N of Saturn and 2° N of Mars.

July

Mercury is visible in the early evening sky early in the month and then disappears into the glow of the Sun.

Venus remains bright and low in the W-NW before sunrise, passing Aldebaran on the 2nd.

Mars is getting very low in the W after sunset, passing close to Regulus on the 22nd.

Jupiter, in the S at sunset, sets before midnight.

Saturn, very low in the W-NW at sunset, is disappearing into the glow of the Sun by the end of the month.

Moon passes Jupiter on the 6th, Neptune on the 13th, Uranus on the 14th, Venus on the 23rd, and Mars on the 27th. Watch for the thin waning crescent Moon above Venus on the 22nd and alongside Venus on the 23rd.

July 2—Mars enters Leo. Venus passes 4° N of Aldebaran.

July 3—Earth at aphelion.

July 4—Mercury stationary, begins retrograde motion. Mercury at aphelion. Moon passes 0.1° S of Spica, occults Spica.

July 6—Moon passes 5° S of Jupiter. Jupiter stationary, resumes direct motion.

July 8—Moon passes 0.2° S of Antares, occults Antares.

July 13—Moon passes 3° S of Neptune.

July 14—Moon passes 0.4° S of Uranus.

July 15—Mercury at closest approach to the Earth this year.

July 17—Venus enters Orion.

July 18—Mercury at inferior conjunction.

July 19—Venus enters Gemini.

July 20—Sun enters Cancer.

July 22—Mars passes 0.7° N of the star Regulus in the constellation of Leo.

July 23—Moon passes 6° N of Venus.

July 27—Moon passes 1.1° N of Mars, occults Mars.

July 28—Mercury stationary, resumes direct motion.

August

Mercury, in the morning sky for most of the month, passes Pollux on the 6th, makes a pretty pair with Venus for several days around the 10th, and passes close to Saturn on the 20th.

Venus, still prominent but lower in the W-NW, passes Pollux on the 8th. Watch planets live up to their name (wanderers) as first Mercury passes close to Saturn on the 20th and then Venus passes very close to Saturn on the 26th.

Mars, very low in the W at sunset, moving towards the glow of the Sun.

Jupiter is low in the SW at sunset.

Saturn re-emerges from the glow of the Sun, in the E–NE before sunrise.

Moon passes Jupiter on the 2nd and the 30th, Neptune on the 9th, Uranus on the 11th, Venus on the 22nd, and Mars on the 25th. Watch the thin waning crescent Moon paired with Venus the morning of the 22nd and the thin waxing crescent Moon paired very close to Mars on the 25th.

Aug. 1—Moon passes 0.4° S of Spica, occults Spica.

Aug. 2—Moon passes 5° S of Jupiter.

Aug. 4—Moon passes 0.4° S of Antares, occults Antares.

Aug. 6—Mercury passes 9° S of Pollux.

Aug. 7—Mercury at greatest western elongation of 19°. Saturn at conjunction.

Aug. 8—Venus passes 7° S of Pollux.

Aug. 9—Moon passes 3° S of Neptune.

Aug. 10—Neptune at closest approach to the Earth this year.

Aug. 11—Neptune at opposition. Venus enters Cancer. Sun enters Leo. Moon passes 0.3° S of Uranus, occults Uranus.

Aug. 13—Waning gibbous moon interferes with observing the Perseid meteor shower this morning.

Aug. 17—Mercury at perihelion.

Aug. 20—Mercury passes 0.5° N of Saturn.

Aug. 22—Moon passes 3° N of Venus.

Aug. 25—Moon passes 0.6° S of Mars, occults Mars.

Aug. 26—Venus passes 0.07° N of Saturn.

Aug. 27—Venus enters Leo.

Aug. 28—Moon passes 0.5° S of Spica.

Aug. 29—Mars enters Virgo.

Aug. 30—Saturn enters Leo. Moon passes 5° S of Jupiter.

September

Mercury returns to the evening sky during the 2nd half of the month, passing close to Mars on the 15th and Spica on the 27th.

Venus, getting lower in the E before sunrise, passes close to Regulus on the 5th.

Mars is lost in the glare of sunset early in the month.

Jupiter is low in the SW at sunset.

Saturn is gradually getting higher in the morning sky before sunrise.

Moon passes Neptune on the 5th, Uranus on the 7th, Saturn on the 19th, Mercury on the 24th, and Jupiter on the 26th. Watch the thin waxing crescent Moon pair with Mercury on the 24th and Jupiter on the 26th. Two eclipses this month with a partial lunar eclipse on the 7th and an annular solar eclipse on the 22nd.

Sept. 1—Moon passes 0.5° S of Antares, occults Antares. Mercury at superior conjunction.

Sept. 4—Uranus at closest approach to the Earth this year.

Sept. 5—Uranus at opposition. Pluto stationary, resumes direct motion. Moon passes 3° S of Neptune. Venus passes 0.8° N of Regulus.

Sept. 6—Venus at perihelion.

Sept. 7—Moon passes 0.4° S of Uranus, occults Uranus. **Partial eclipse of the Moon,** see details under Eclipses.

Sept. 15—Mercury passes 0.2° S of Mars.

Sept. 16—Sun enters Virgo.

Sept. 19—Moon passes 2° N of Saturn.

Sept. 22—Annular eclipse of the Sun; see details under Eclipses.

Sept. 23—Autumnal equinox at 12:03 AM EDT (4:03 UTC); **autumn begins in the northern hemisphere, spring in the southern hemisphere.**

Sept. 24—Moon passes 1.8° S of Mercury and 0.5° S of Spica, occults Spica.

Sept. 25—Venus enters Virgo.

Sept. 26—Moon passes 5° S of Jupiter.

Sept. 27—Mercury passes 1.3° N of Spica.

Sept. 28—Moon passes 0.5° S of Antares, occults Antares.

Sept. 30—Mercury at aphelion.

October

Mercury is low in the SW during the month passing Jupiter on the 25th and the 28th.

Venus, very low in the E, disappears into the glow of the Sun at mid-month.

Mars is hidden in the glare of the Sun this month.

Jupiter is getting even lower in the W-SW, becoming barely visible by the end of the month.

Saturn is high in the E before sunrise.

Moon passes Neptune on the 3rd and the 30th, Uranus on the 5th, Saturn on the 16th, and Jupiter and Mercury on the 24th. Watch the thin waxing crescent Moon tripled with Jupiter and Mercury on the 24th.

Oct. 1—Pluto enters Ophiuchus.

Oct. 3—Moon passes 3° S of Neptune.

Oct. 5—Moon passes 0.5° S of Uranus, occults Uranus.

Oct. 16—Moon passes 2° N of Saturn.

Oct. 17—Mercury at greatest eastern elongation of 25°.

Oct. 23—Mars at conjunction.

Oct. 24—Moon passes 5° S of Jupiter and 1.4° S of Mercury.

Oct. 25—Moon passes 0.4° S of Antares, occults Antares. Mercury passes 4° S of Jupiter.

Oct. 27—Venus at superior conjunction.

Oct. 28—Mercury passes 4° S of Jupiter.

Oct. 29—Mercury stationary, begins retrograde motion. Neptune stationary, resumes direct motion.

Oct. 30—Venus enters Libra. Moon passes 3° S of Neptune.

Oct. 31—Sun enters Libra.

November

Mercury, mainly visible in the 2nd half of the month in the morning low in the SW, transits the Sun on the 8th-9th. See precautions about observing this event under Eclipses.

Venus remains hidden in the glare of the Sun for this month.

Mars remains hidden in the glare of the Sun for this month.

Jupiter disappears in the glare of sunset at the start of the month.

Saturn, rising about midnight, is high in the S before sunrise.

Moon passes Uranus on the 1st and the 28th, Saturn on the 13th, Mercury on the 19th, and Neptune on the 26th. Watch the thin waning crescent Moon paired with Mercury on the morning of the 19th.

Nov. 1—Moon passes 0.5° S of Uranus, occults Uranus.

Nov. 4—Mars enters Libra.

Nov. 8—Mercury at inferior conjunction.

Nov. 8-9—Mercury transits the Sun; see details under Eclipses.

Nov. 13—Mercury at perihelion. Moon passes 1.6° N of Saturn.

Nov. 17—Mercury stationary, resumes direct motion.

Nov. 18—Venus enters Scorpius. Moon passes 0.6° S of Spica, occults Spica.

Nov. 19—Moon passes 6° S of Mercury.

Nov. 20—Uranus stationary, resumes direct motion.

Nov. 21—Jupiter at conjunction.

Nov. 23—Venus enters Ophiuchus. Sun enters Scorpius.

Nov. 25—Mercury at greatest western elongation of 20°.

Nov. 26—Moon passes 3° S of Neptune.

Nov. 28—Moon passes 0.3° S of Uranus, occults Uranus.

Nov. 29—Sun enters Ophiuchus.

December

Mercury appears in the morning sky, disappearing into the glare of sunrise after about 3 weeks, passing Mars on the 9th, close to Jupiter on the 10th, and Antares on the 14th.

Venus returns to the early evening sky very low in the SW just after sunset.

Mars appears in the early morning sky in the SE before sunrise, passing close to Jupiter on the 12th and its "rival" Antares on the 19th. Watch for a planet "dance" as Mercury, Mars, and Jupiter group together and take turns passing during the 10th to the 12th.

Jupiter appears in the early morning sky in the SE before sunrise.

Saturn, rising before midnight, is up for the rest of the night.

Moon passes Saturn the 10th, Jupiter on the 18th, Mars on the 19th, Neptune on the 24th, and Uranus on the 25th. Watch the thin waning crescent Moon paired with Jupiter on the 18th and then tripled with Mars and Antares on the 19th.

Dec. 4—Pluto enters Sagittarius.

Dec. 5—Jupiter enters Scorpius.

Dec. 6—Saturn stationary, begins retrograde motion.

Dec. 7—Mars enters Scorpius.

Dec. 8—Venus enters Sagittarius.

Dec. 9—Mercury passes 1° N of Mars.

Dec. 10—Moon passes 1.2° N of Saturn, occults Saturn. Mercury passes 0.1° N of Jupiter.

Dec. 12—Mars passes 0.8° S of Jupiter.

Dec. 14—Mercury passes 5° N of Antares. Geminid meteor shower from an hour after sunset until the moon rises.

Dec. 15—Moon passes 0.8° S of Spica, occults Spica.

Dec. 17—Mars enters Ophiuchus.

Dec. 18—Pluto at conjunction. Sun enters Sagittarius. Moon passes 6° S of Jupiter.

Dec. 19—Mars passes 4° N of Antares. Moon passes 0.4° S of Antares and 5° S of Mars, occults Antares.

Dec. 21—Southern Solstice at 7:22 PM EST (00:22 UTC, Dec. 22); **winter begins in the northern hemisphere, summer in the southern hemisphere.**

Dec. 24—Moon passes 3° S of Neptune.

Dec. 25—Moon passes 0.08° N of Uranus, occults Uranus.

Dec. 27—Mercury at aphelion.

Dec. 28—Jupiter enters Ophiuchus.

Meteorites and Meteor Showers

When a chunk of material, ice or rock, plunges into Earth's atmosphere and burns up in a fiery display, the event is a **meteor**. While the chunk of material is still in space, it is a **meteoroid**. If a portion of the material survives passage through the atmosphere and reaches the ground, the remnant on the ground is a **meteorite**.

Meteorites found on Earth are classified into types, depending on their composition: **irons**, those composed chiefly of iron, a small percentage of nickel, and traces of other metals such as cobalt; **stones**, stony meteors consisting of silicates; and **stony irons**, containing varying proportions of both iron and stone.

Serious study of meteorites as non-earth objects began in the 20th century. Scientists use sophisticated chemical analysis, X rays, and mass spectrography in determining their origin and composition. Although most meteorites are now believed to be fragments of asteroids or comets, geochemical studies have shown that a few Antarctic stones came from the Moon or from Mars, presumably ejected by the explosive impact of asteroids.

The **largest known meteorite**, estimated to weigh about 55 metric tons, is situated at Hoba West near Grootfontein, Namibia. The Manicouagan impact crater in Quebec, Canada, with an estimated diameter of 60 mi, is one of the largest crater structures still visible on the surface of the Earth. Although not visible to the eye, other still larger impact craters identified include the Vredefort crater in South Africa at 185 mi across and the Sudbury crater in Ontario, Canada, estimated at 125 mi across. The Bedout impact site off the NW coast of Australia gained attention in 2004, when scientists identified further evidence in support of the idea that it may be linked to the Permian extinction event 250 million years ago.

Meteor showers vary in strength, but usually the 3 best meteor showers of the year are the **Perseids**, around Aug. 13, the **Orionids**, around Oct. 21, and the **Geminids**, around Dec. 14. These showers feature meteors at the rate of about 60 per hour. Best observing conditions occur with the absence of moonlight, usually when the Moon's phase is between waning crescent Moon and waxing quarter Moon.

For most meteor showers the cometary debris is relatively uniformly scattered along the comet's orbit. However, in the case of the **Leonid** meteor shower, which occurs every year around Nov. 17-18, the cometary debris, from Comet Temple-Tuttle, seems to be bunched up in one stretch. Hence, most years when Earth crosses the orbit of this comet, the meteor shower produced is relatively weak. However, about every 33 years, Earth encounters the bunched-up debris. Sometimes the storm is a disappointment, as it was in 1899 and 1933; at other times it is a roaring success, as in 1833 and 1866. The Leonids stormed again more recently, producing rates of 1,000-3,000 meteors per hour in 2001. Best showers in 2006 are with the Eta Aquarids in early May after the waxing quarter Moon sets, and with the Orionids early morning in October near the time of new moon, and with the Geminids in December before the waning crescent moon rises. Typically, meteor showers are best observed after midnight, but the Geminids can be seen well before and after midnight.

Rising and Setting of Planets, 2006

In Coordinated Universal Time (0 in the *h* col. designates midnight)

Venus, 2006

	20° N Latitude		30° N Latitude		40° N Latitude		50° N Latitude		60° N Latitude	
	Rise	Set	Rise	Set	Rise	Set	Rise	Set	Rise	Set
Date	h m	h m	h m	h m	h m	h m	h m	h m	h m	h m
Jan. 1	7 48	18 57	8 04	18 42	8 23	18 23	8 49	17 56	9 33	17 13
11	6 45	17 58	6 59	17 44	7 16	17 27	7 40	17 03	8 18	16 25
21	5 39	16 55	5 52	16 42	6 09	16 26	6 31	16 03	7 07	15 27
31	4 46	16 03	5 00	15 50	5 16	15 34	5 38	15 11	6 14	14 35
Feb. 10	4 11	15 27	4 24	15 13	4 41	14 56	5 04	14 33	5 41	13 56
20	3 49	15 05	4 03	14 51	4 21	14 33	4 45	14 09	5 23	13 31
Mar. 2	3 37	14 53	3 52	14 39	4 09	14 22	4 33	13 58	5 11	13 19
12	3 31	14 49	3 45	14 36	4 02	14 19	4 24	13 56	5 01	13 19
22	3 28	14 50	3 40	14 38	3 55	14 23	4 16	14 02	4 49	13 30
Apr. 1	3 25	14 54	3 36	14 44	3 49	14 32	4 06	14 14	4 33	13 48
11	3 23	15 01	3 31	14 53	3 41	14 43	3 54	14 31	4 14	14 11
21	3 21	15 08	3 25	15 03	3 31	14 58	3 39	14 50	3 52	14 38
May 1	3 18	15 16	3 19	15 15	3 21	15 13	3 24	15 11	3 27	15 08
11	3 14	15 25	3 13	15 27	3 10	15 30	3 07	15 34	3 02	15 39
21	3 12	15 35	3 06	15 41	3 00	15 48	2 50	15 57	2 36	16 12
31	3 10	15 46	3 01	15 55	2 50	16 07	2 34	16 22	2 10	16 47
June 10	3 10	15 58	2 58	16 10	2 42	16 26	2 20	16 48	1 46	17 24
20	3 12	16 11	2 57	16 27	2 37	16 46	2 10	17 14	1 24	18 00
30	3 17	16 25	2 59	16 43	2 36	17 06	2 03	17 40	1 07	18 36
July 10	3 26	16 39	3 05	16 59	2 40	17 25	2 03	18 02	0 58	19 07
20	3 36	16 53	3 15	17 14	2 48	17 41	2 10	18 20	1 00	19 29
30	3 50	17 05	3 29	17 26	3 02	17 53	2 24	18 31	1 16	19 39
Aug. 9	4 05	17 16	3 45	17 35	3 20	18 00	2 45	18 35	1 43	19 36
19	4 20	17 23	4 03	17 41	3 41	18 02	3 11	18 32	2 19	19 23
29	4 36	17 28	4 22	17 42	4 04	18 00	3 40	18 24	3 00	19 03
Sept. 8	4 51	17 31	4 40	17 41	4 27	17 54	4 10	18 11	3 41	18 39
18	5 05	17 31	4 59	17 38	4 51	17 45	4 40	17 56	4 22	18 12
28	5 19	17 31	5 17	17 33	5 14	17 35	5 10	17 39	5 04	17 45
Oct. 8	5 33	17 30	5 35	17 27	5 37	17 25	5 40	17 21	5 45	17 16
18	5 46	17 29	5 53	17 23	6 00	17 15	6 11	17 04	6 26	16 48
28	6 01	17 30	6 12	17 19	6 25	17 06	6 42	16 49	7 09	16 21
Nov. 7	6 17	17 33	6 31	17 19	6 49	17 01	7 13	16 36	7 53	15 57
17	6 34	17 39	6 52	17 21	7 14	16 59	7 45	16 28	8 36	15 37
27	6 52	17 48	7 12	17 28	7 38	17 02	8 14	16 26	9 16	15 24
Dec. 7	7 09	18 01	7 31	17 39	7 59	17 11	8 38	16 32	9 48	15 22
17	7 25	18 16	7 47	17 54	8 15	17 26	8 55	16 46	10 06	15 35
27	7 39	18 33	8 00	18 12	8 26	17 46	9 04	17 09	10 09	16 03

Mars, 2006

	20° N Latitude		30° N Latitude		40° N Latitude		50° N Latitude		60° N Latitude	
	Rise	Set	Rise	Set	Rise	Set	Rise	Set	Rise	Set
Date	h m	h m	h m	h m	h m	h m	h m	h m	h m	h m
Jan. 1	13 21	2 18	13 06	2 33	12 48	2 51	12 21	3 18	11 39	4 00
11	12 52	1 51	12 36	2 07	12 16	2 27	11 48	2 55	11 02	3 41
21	12 25	1 28	12 08	1 45	11 46	2 06	11 16	2 36	10 26	3 27
31	12 00	1 07	11 42	1 25	11 19	1 48	10 47	2 21	9 52	3 16
Feb. 10	11 38	0 49	11 19	1 08	10 54	1 32	10 19	2 07	9 19	3 07
20	11 17	0 31	10 57	0 52	10 31	1 18	9 53	1 55	8 48	3 01
Mar. 2	10 58	0 15	10 36	0 37	10 09	1 04	9 30	1 44	8 18	2 55
12	10 40	23 59	10 18	0 23	9 49	0 51	9 08	1 33	7 51	2 49
22	10 23	23 45	10 00	0 09	9 31	0 39	8 48	1 21	7 27	2 42
Apr. 1	10 08	23 31	9 44	23 54	9 14	0 26	8 30	1 09	7 07	2 33
11	9 53	23 17	9 30	23 40	8 59	0 12	8 15	0 56	6 50	2 21
21	9 40	23 02	9 16	23 26	8 46	23 56	8 02	0 42	6 38	2 06
May 1	9 27	22 48	9 03	23 11	8 34	23 41	7 51	0 26	6 29	1 47
11	9 14	22 33	8 52	22 56	8 23	23 24	7 41	0 08	6 24	1 25
21	9 02	22 18	8 40	22 39	8 13	23 07	7 34	23 46	6 22	0 59
31	8 50	22 02	8 30	22 22	8 04	22 48	7 27	23 24	6 22	0 32
June 10	8 38	21 45	8 19	22 04	7 55	22 28	7 22	23 01	6 23	0 02
20	8 26	21 28	8 09	21 45	7 47	22 07	7 17	22 37	6 25	23 28
30	8 15	21 10	7 59	21 26	7 40	21 45	7 12	22 12	6 28	22 56
July 10	8 03	20 52	7 49	21 05	7 32	21 22	7 08	21 46	6 30	22 23
20	7 50	20 33	7 39	20 45	7 24	20 59	7 04	21 19	6 32	21 50
30	7 38	20 14	7 29	20 23	7 17	20 35	7 00	20 51	6 35	21 16
Aug. 9	7 26	19 54	7 19	20 02	7 09	20 11	6 57	20 23	6 37	20 42
19	7 14	19 35	7 08	19 40	7 02	19 46	6 53	19 55	6 39	20 08
29	7 01	19 15	6 58	19 18	6 55	19 21	6 49	19 26	6 41	19 34
Sept. 8	6 49	18 55	6 48	18 56	6 47	18 57	6 46	18 58	6 43	19 00
18	6 37	18 35	6 39	18 34	6 41	18 32	6 43	18 30	6 46	18 26
28	6 26	18 16	6 30	18 12	6 34	18 08	6 40	18 02	6 49	17 52
Oct. 8	6 15	17 57	6 21	17 51	6 28	17 44	6 38	17 34	6 52	17 19
18	6 04	17 39	6 12	17 31	6 22	17 21	6 36	17 07	6 57	16 46
28	5 54	17 22	6 04	17 11	6 17	16 58	6 34	16 41	7 01	16 14
Nov. 7	5 44	17 05	5 57	16 52	6 12	16 37	6 33	16 16	7 07	15 42
17	5 35	16 50	5 50	16 35	6 08	16 17	6 33	15 52	7 12	15 12
27	5 27	16 35	5 43	16 19	6 04	15 58	6 32	15 30	7 19	14 43
Dec. 7	5 19	16 22	5 37	16 04	6 00	15 41	6 32	15 09	7 24	14 16
17	5 12	16 10	5 32	15 50	5 56	15 26	6 31	14 51	7 30	13 52
27	5 05	15 59	5 26	15 39	5 52	15 13	6 29	14 36	7 33	13 31

Jupiter, 2006

	20° N Latitude		30° N Latitude		40° N Latitude		50° N Latitude		60° N Latitude	
	Rise	Set	Rise	Set	Rise	Set	Rise	Set	Rise	Set
Date	h m	h m	h m	h m	h m	h m	h m	h m	h m	h m
Jan. 1	2 22	13 41	2 35	13 28	2 50	13 13	3 12	12 51	3 46	12 17
11	1 49	13 07	2 02	12 54	2 19	12 38	2 41	12 16	3 16	11 40
21	1 16	12 33	1 29	12 19	1 46	12 02	2 09	11 40	2 45	11 03
31	0 41	11 57	0 55	11 43	1 12	11 26	1 35	11 03	2 12	10 26
Feb. 10	0 06	11 21	0 20	11 07	0 37	10 50	1 00	10 26	1 38	9 48
20	23 25	10 43	23 39	10 29	23 56	10 12	0 24	9 48	1 02	9 10
Mar. 2	22 46	10 05	23 01	9 51	23 18	9 34	23 42	9 10	0 24	8 31
12	22 07	9 25	22 21	9 11	22 38	8 54	23 02	8 30	23 40	7 52
22	21 26	8 45	21 40	8 31	21 57	8 14	22 20	7 50	22 58	7 12
Apr. 1	20 43	8 03	20 57	7 49	21 14	7 32	21 37	7 09	22 14	6 32
11	20 00	7 21	20 13	7 07	20 30	6 51	20 52	6 28	21 29	5 52
21	19 15	6 37	19 29	6 24	19 45	6 08	20 07	5 46	20 42	5 11
May 1	18 31	5 54	18 44	5 41	18 59	5 25	19 21	5 04	19 55	4 29
11	17 46	5 10	17 58	4 57	18 14	4 42	18 35	4 21	19 08	3 48
21	17 01	4 26	17 13	4 14	17 28	3 59	17 49	3 39	18 21	3 07
31	16 17	3 43	16 29	3 31	16 44	3 17	17 04	2 57	17 35	2 25
June 10	15 34	3 01	15 46	2 49	16 00	2 35	16 20	2 15	16 50	1 45
20	14 52	2 19	15 04	2 08	15 18	1 54	15 37	1 34	16 07	1 04
30	14 11	1 39	14 23	1 27	14 37	1 13	14 56	0 54	15 26	0 24
July 10	13 32	0 59	13 44	0 48	13 58	0 34	14 17	0 14	14 47	23 40
20	12 54	0 21	13 06	0 09	13 20	23 51	13 39	23 31	14 10	23 01
30	12 17	23 39	12 29	23 27	12 43	23 13	13 03	22 53	13 34	22 22
Aug. 9	11 41	23 03	11 53	22 51	12 08	22 36	12 29	22 15	13 01	21 43
19	11 07	22 27	11 19	22 15	11 35	21 59	11 55	21 38	12 28	21 05
29	10 33	21 52	10 46	21 39	11 02	21 23	11 23	21 02	11 58	20 28
Sept. 8	10 00	21 18	10 14	21 05	10 30	20 48	10 52	20 26	11 28	19 50
18	9 28	20 44	9 42	20 31	9 59	20 14	10 22	19 50	11 00	19 13
28	8 57	20 12	9 11	19 57	9 29	19 40	9 53	19 15	10 32	18 36
Oct. 8	8 26	19 39	8 41	19 24	9 00	19 06	9 25	18 41	10 05	18 00
18	7 56	19 07	8 12	18 52	8 30	18 33	8 57	18 07	9 39	17 24
28	7 26	18 35	7 42	18 20	8 02	18 00	8 29	17 33	9 13	16 48
Nov. 7	6 57	18 04	7 13	17 48	7 33	17 27	8 01	16 59	8 48	16 13
17	6 27	17 33	6 44	17 16	7 05	16 55	7 34	16 26	8 22	15 38
27	5 58	17 02	6 15	16 45	6 37	16 23	7 07	15 53	7 57	15 03
Dec. 7	5 28	16 31	5 46	16 13	6 08	15 51	6 39	15 20	7 31	14 29
17	4 59	16 00	5 17	15 42	5 40	15 19	6 12	14 48	7 05	13 54
27	4 29	15 29	4 48	15 11	5 11	14 47	5 43	14 15	6 38	13 20

Saturn, 2006

	20° N Latitude		30° N Latitude		40° N Latitude		50° N Latitude		60° N Latitude	
	Rise	Set	Rise	Set	Rise	Set	Rise	Set	Rise	Set
Date	h m	h m	h m	h m	h m	h m	h m	h m	h m	h m
Jan. 1	19 34	8 37	19 18	8 54	18 57	9 15	18 28	9 44	17 39	10 33
11	18 52	7 55	18 35	8 12	18 14	8 33	17 44	9 03	16 54	9 53
21	18 09	7 13	17 52	7 30	17 30	7 52	17 00	8 22	16 10	9 12
31	17 26	6 31	17 09	6 48	16 47	7 10	16 16	7 40	15 25	8 32
Feb. 10	16 43	5 49	16 26	6 06	16 03	6 28	15 32	6 59	14 40	7 52
20	16 00	5 07	15 43	5 24	15 20	5 47	14 49	6 18	13 56	7 11
Mar. 2	15 18	4 25	15 00	4 43	14 38	5 05	14 06	5 37	13 12	6 31
12	14 37	3 44	14 19	4 02	13 56	4 25	13 24	4 56	12 30	5 51
22	13 56	3 03	13 38	3 21	13 15	3 44	12 43	4 16	11 48	5 11
Apr. 1	13 16	2 23	12 58	2 41	12 35	3 04	12 02	3 37	11 08	4 31
11	12 37	1 44	12 18	2 02	11 55	2 25	11 23	2 57	10 28	3 52
21	11 58	1 05	11 40	1 24	11 17	1 46	10 45	2 18	9 50	3 13
May 1	11 20	0 27	11 02	0 45	10 40	1 08	10 08	1 40	9 13	2 35
11	10 44	23 46	10 26	0 08	10 03	0 30	9 31	1 02	8 38	1 56
21	10 07	23 10	9 50	23 27	9 27	23 50	8 56	0 25	8 03	1 18
31	9 32	22 33	9 14	22 51	8 52	23 13	8 21	23 44	7 29	0 40
June 10	8 57	21 57	8 39	22 15	8 18	22 36	7 47	23 07	6 56	0 02
20	8 22	21 22	8 05	21 39	7 44	22 00	7 14	22 30	6 23	23 21
30	7 48	20 47	7 31	21 03	7 10	21 24	6 40	21 54	5 51	22 43
July 10	7 14	20 12	6 57	20 28	6 37	20 49	6 08	21 17	5 20	22 05
20	6 40	19 37	6 24	19 53	6 04	20 13	5 35	20 41	4 49	21 28
30	6 06	19 02	5 50	19 18	5 31	19 37	5 03	20 05	4 18	20 50
Aug. 9	5 33	18 27	5 17	18 43	4 58	19 02	4 31	19 29	3 47	20 13
19	4 59	17 52	4 44	18 07	4 25	18 26	3 59	18 52	3 16	19 35
29	4 25	17 17	4 11	17 32	3 52	17 51	3 27	18 16	2 45	18 58
Sept. 8	3 51	16 42	3 37	16 57	3 19	17 15	2 54	17 40	2 13	18 20
18	3 17	16 07	3 03	16 21	2 46	16 39	2 21	17 03	1 42	17 42
28	2 43	15 32	2 29	15 45	2 12	16 02	1 48	16 26	1 09	17 05
Oct. 8	2 08	14 56	1 54	15 09	1 37	15 26	1 14	15 49	0 37	16 27
18	1 32	14 19	1 19	14 33	1 03	14 49	0 40	15 12	0 03	15 49
28	0 56	13 43	0 43	13 56	0 27	14 12	0 05	14 34	23 25	15 10
Nov. 7	0 20	13 05	0 07	13 18	23 47	13 34	23 25	13 56	22 49	14 32
17	23 38	12 28	23 26	12 40	23 10	12 56	22 48	13 18	22 13	13 53
27	23 00	11 49	22 47	12 02	22 32	12 18	22 10	12 40	21 35	13 15
Dec. 7	22 21	11 10	22 08	11 23	21 53	11 39	21 31	12 01	20 56	12 36
17	21 41	10 31	21 28	10 43	21 13	10 59	20 51	11 21	20 15	11 57
27	21 01	9 50	20 48	10 03	20 32	10 19	20 09	10 42	19 34	11 17

Brightest Stars

This table lists **stars of greatest visual magnitude** as seen in the night sky (the lower the number, the brighter the star). The common name of the star is in parentheses. Stars of variable magnitude are designated by v. Coordinates are for mid-2006. Greek letters in the star names indicate perceived degree of brightness within the constellation, alpha generally being the brightest, though there are some exceptions.

To find when the star is on the meridian, subtract Right Ascension of Mean Sun (see the table Greenwich Sidereal Time for 0h UTC) from the star's Right Ascension, first adding 24h to the latter if necessary. Mark this result PM if less than 12h; if greater than 12, subtract 12h and mark the remainder AM.

Star	Magnitude	Parallax "	Light-yrs	Right ascen. h	Right ascen. m	Declination ° '
α Canis Majoris (Sirius)	–1.44v	0.379	8.6	6	45.4	–16 43
α Carinae (Canopus)	–0.62v	0.010	313	6	24.1	–52 42
α Bootis (Arcturus)	–0.05v	0.089	37	14	16.0	+19 09
α Centauri (Rigel Kentaurus)	–0.01	0.742	4.4	14	40.1	–60 52
α Lyrae (Vega)	0.03v	0.129	25.3	18	37.2	+38 47
α Aurigae (Capella)	0.08v	0.077	42	5	17.1	+46 00
β Orionis (Rigel)	0.18v	0.004	773	5	14.8	– 8 11
α Canis Minoris (Procyon)	0.40	0.286	11.4	7	39.6	+ 5 13
α Eridani (Achernar)	0.45v	0.023	144	1	38.0	–57 12
α Orionis (Betelgeuse)	0.45v	0.008	427	5	55.5	+ 7 25
β Centauri (Hadar)	0.61v	0.006	525	14	4.3	–60 25
α Aquilae (Altair)	0.76v	0.194	16.8	19	51.1	+ 8 53
α Crucis (Acrux)	0.77	0.010	321	12	26.9	–63 08
α Tauri (Aldebaran)	0.87v	0.050	65	4	36.3	+16 31
α Virginis (Spica)	0.98v	0.012	262	13	25.5	–11 12
α Scorpii (Antares)	1.06v	0.005	604	16	29.8	–26 27
β Geminorum (Pollux)	1.16v	0.097	33.7	7	45.7	+28 01
α Piscis Austrinis (Fomalhaut)	1.17	0.130	25.1	22	58.0	–29 35
β Crucis (Becrux)	1.25v	0.009	352	12	48.1	–59 44
α Cygni (Deneb)	1.25v	0.001	3230	20	41.7	+45 18
α Leonis (Regulus)	1.36	0.042	77	10	08.7	+11 56
ε Canis Majoris (Adhara)	1.50v	0.008	431	6	58.9	–28 59
α Geminorum (Castor)	1.58	0.063	52	7	35.0	+31 53
γ Crucis (Gacrux)	1.59v	0.037	88	12	31.5	–57 09
λ Scorpii (Shaula)	1.62v	0.005	703	17	34.1	–37 07
γ Orionis (Bellatrix)	1.64v	0.013	243	5	25.5	+ 6 21
β Tauri (Elnath)	1.65	0.025	131	5	26.7	+28 37
β Carinae (Miaplacidus)	1.67v	0.029	111	9	13.2	–69 45
ε Orionis (Alnilam)	1.69v	0.002	1340	5	36.5	– 1 12
α Gruis (Al Nair)	1.73v	0.032	101	22	08.7	–46 56
ζ Orionis (Alnitak)	1.74	0.004	817	5	40.8	– 1 57
γ Velorum (Al Suhail)	1.75v	0.004	840	8	09.7	–47 21
ε Ursae Majoris (Alioth)	1.76v	0.040	81	12	54.3	+55 56
ε Sagittarii (Kaus Australis)	1.79	0.023	145	18	24.6	–34 23
α Persei (Mirfak)	1.79v	0.006	592	3	24.8	+49 53
α Ursae Majoris (Dubhe)	1.81	0.026	124	11	04.1	+61 43
δ Canis Majoris (Wezen)	1.83v	0.002	1790	7	08.6	–26 24
η Ursae Majoris (Alkaid)	1.85v	0.032	101	13	47.8	+49 17
ε Carinae (Avior)	1.86v	0.005	632	8	22.6	–59 32
θ Scorpii	1.86	0.012	272	17	37.8	–43 00
β Aurigae (Menkalinan)	1.90v	0.040	82	6	00.0	+44 57
α Trianguli Australis (Atria)	1.91v	0.008	415	16	49.4	–69 03
γ Geminorum (Alhena)	1.93	0.031	105	6	38.1	+16 24
δ Velorum	1.93	0.041	80	8	44.7	–54 42
α Pavonis (Peacock)	1.94v	0.018	183	20	26.2	–56 43
α Ursae Minoris (Polaris)	1.97v	0.008	431	2	37.9	+89 17
β Canis Majoris (Mirzam)	1.98v	0.007	499	6	23.0	–17 57
α Hydrae (Alphard)	1.99v	0.018	177	9	27.9	– 8 41
α Arietis (Hamal)	2.01	0.049	66	2	07.5	+23 30
γ Leonis (Algieba)	2.01v	0.026	126	10	20.0	+19 50
β Ceti (Deneb Kaitos)	2.04v	0.034	96	0	43.9	–17 57
σ Sagittarii (Nunki)	2.05v	0.015	224	18	55.7	–26 17
θ Centauri (Menkent)	2.06	0.054	61	14	07.1	–36 24
α Andromedae (Alpheratz)	2.07v	0.034	97	0	08.7	+29 07
β Andromedae (Mirach)	2.07v	0.016	199	1	10.1	+35 39
κ Orionis (Saiph)	2.07v	0.005	721	5	48.0	– 9 40
β Ursae Minoris (Kochab)	2.07v	0.026	126	14	50.8	+74 08
β Gruis	2.07v	0.019	170	22	43.1	–46 51
α Ophiuchi (Rasalhague)	2.08	0.070	47	17	35.3	+12 33
β Persei (Algol)	2.09v	0.035	93	3	08.6	+40 59
γ Andromedae (Almaak)	2.10	0.009	355	2	04.3	+42 22
β Leonis (Denebola)	2.14	0.090	36.2	11	49.4	+14 32
γ Cassiopeiae	2.15v	0.005	613	0	57.1	+60 45
γ Centauri	2.20	0.025	130	12	41.5	–48 58
ζ Puppis (Naos)	2.21v	0.002	1400	8	03.8	–40 01
ι Carinae (Tureis)	2.21	0.005	692	9	17.2	–59 18
α Coronae Borealis (Alphecca)	2.22v	0.044	75	15	35.0	+26 42
λ Velorum (Suhail)	2.23v	0.006	573	9	08.2	–43 28
ζ Ursae Majoris (Mizar)	2.23	0.042	78	13	24.2	+54 54
γ Cygni (Sadr)	2.23v	0.002	1520	20	22.5	+40 16
γ Draconis (Eltanin)	2.24v	0.022	148	17	56.8	+51 29
δ Orionis (Mintaka)	2.25v	0.004	916	5	32.3	– 0 18
β Cassiopeiae (Caph)	2.28v	0.060	54	0	09.5	+59 11
ε Scorpii	2.29	0.050	65	16	50.6	–34 18
ε Centauri	2.29v	0.009	376	13	40.3	–53 30
δ Scorpii (Dschubba)	2.29v	0.008	401	16	00.7	–22 39
α Lupi	2.30v	0.006	548	14	42.4	–47 25
η Centauri	2.33v	0.011	308	14	35.9	–42 11
β Ursae Majoris (Merak)	2.34	0.041	79	11	02.2	+56 21
ε Bootis (Izar)	2.35	0.016	210	14	45.0	+27 05
κ Scorpii	2.39v	0.007	464	17	43.0	–39 02

Morning and Evening Stars, 2006

(Coordinated Universal Time)

	Morning	Evening
Jan.	Mercury to Jan. 26 Venus from Jan. 14 Jupiter Saturn to Jan. 27 Pluto	Mercury from Jan. 26 Venus to Jan. 13 Mars Saturn from Jan. 27 Uranus Neptune
Feb.	Venus Jupiter Neptune from Feb. 6 Pluto	Mercury Mars Saturn Uranus Neptune to Feb. 6
Mar.	Mercury from Mar. 12 Venus Jupiter Uranus from Mar. 1 Neptune Pluto	Mercury to Mar. 12 Mars Saturn Uranus to Mar. 1
Apr.	Mercury Venus Jupiter Uranus Neptune Pluto	Mars Saturn
May	Mercury to May 18 Venus Jupiter to May 4 Uranus Neptune Pluto	Mercury from May 18 Mars Jupiter from May 4 Saturn
June	Venus Uranus Neptune Pluto to June 16	Mercury Mars Jupiter Saturn Pluto from June 16

	Morning	Evening
July	Mercury from July 18 Venus Uranus Neptune	Mercury to July 18 Mars Jupiter Saturn Pluto
Aug.	Mercury Venus Saturn from Aug. 7 Uranus Neptune to Aug. 11	Mars Jupiter Saturn to Aug. 7 Neptune from Aug. 11 Pluto
Sept.	Mercury to Sep. 1 Venus Saturn Uranus to Sep. 5	Mercury from Sep. 1 Mars Jupiter Uranus from Sep. 5 Neptune, Pluto
Oct.	Venus to Oct. 27 Mars from Oct. 23 Saturn	Mercury Venus from Oct. 27 Mars to Oct. 23 Jupiter Uranus Neptune Pluto
Nov.	Mercury from Nov. 8 Mars Jupiter from Nov. 21 Saturn	Mercury to Nov. 8 Venus Jupiter to Nov. 21 Uranus Neptune Pluto
Dec.	Mercury Mars Jupiter Saturn Pluto from Dec. 18	Venus Uranus Neptune Pluto to Dec. 18

Greenwich Sidereal Time for 0^h UTC, 2006

(Add 12 hours to obtain Right Ascension of Mean Sun)

Date	d	h	m
Jan.	1	6	42.0
	11	7	21.5
	21	8	00.9
	31	8	40.3
Feb.	10	9	19.7
	20	9	59.2
Mar.	2	10	38.6
	12	11	18.0
	22	11	57.4
Apr.	1	12	36.9
	11	13	16.3
	21	13	55.7
May	1	14	35.1
	11	15	14.6
	21	15	54.0
	31	16	33.6
June	10	17	12.8
	20	17	52.3
	30	18	31.7
July	10	19	11.1
	20	19	50.5
	30	20	30.0
Aug.	9	21	09.4
	19	21	48.8
	29	22	28.2
Sept.	8	23	07.7
	18	23	47.1
	28	0	26.5
Oct.	8	1	06.0
	18	1	45.4
	28	2	24.8
Nov.	7	3	04.2
	17	3	43.7
	27	4	23.1
Dec.	7	5	02.5
	17	5	41.9
	27	6	21.4

Aurora Borealis and Aurora Australis

The **Aurora Borealis,** also called the **Northern Lights**, is a broad display of rather faint light in the northern skies at night. The **Aurora Australis**, a similar phenomenon, appears at night in southern skies. The auroras are the result of particles from the Sun reacting with those in the Earth's atmosphere. The Sun produces a stream of charged particles, called the **solar wind**. These particles, mainly electrons and protons, approach Earth at speeds of up to 300 mi per second. In addition, there are interplanetary coronal mass ejections—large-scale, high-speed releases of as much as 10 bil tons of coronal material. Some of these particles are trapped by Earth's magnetic field, forming the **Van Allen belts**—2 donut-shaped radiation bands around Earth. Excess amounts of these charged particles, often produced by solar flares, follow Earth's magnetic lines of force toward Earth's magnetic poles. High in the atmosphere, collisions between these solar particles and terrestrial particles result in the glow in the upper atmosphere called the **aurora**. The glow may be vivid where the lines of magnetic force converge near the magnetic poles.

The aurora appears in a wide variety of forms. Sometimes it is seen as a quiet glow, almost foglike in character; sometimes as vertical streamers in which there may be considerable motion; sometimes as a series of luminous expanding arcs. There are many colors, with white, yellow, and red predominating. The auroras are most vivid and most frequently seen at about 20° from the magnetic poles. The Aurora Borealis is commonly seen along the northern coast of North America and eastern Europe. It has occasionally been seen as far south as Key West, FL, while the Aurora Australis has occasionally been seen as far north as Australia and New Zealand.

The auroral displays appear at heights ranging from 50 mi to about 600 mi and have given us a means of estimating the extent of Earth's atmosphere. The auroras are often accompanied by **magnetic storms** whose forces, also guided by the lines of force of Earth's magnetic field, disrupt electrical communication.

Largest Telescopes

Astronomers indicate the size of telescopes not by length or magnification, but by the diameter of the primary light-gathering component of the system—such as the lens or mirror. This measurement is a direct indication of the telescope's light-gathering power. The bigger the diameter, the fainter the objects you are able to detect. The Earth's atmosphere limits the resolution of what you see. That is why the Hubble Space Telescope, which is outside the atmosphere, can have better resolution than larger telescopes on the Earth.

Refracting (lens) telescopes are currently not made with lens diameters of more than 40 in. Mirror telescopes can be made less expensively than lens telescopes, so all modern large optical telescopes are made with mirrors. **Radio telescopes**, also reflecting telescopes, view at wavelengths not visible to optical telescopes or to the human eye. Radio telescopes are made larger than optical telescopes because larger diameters are required at longer wavelengths to obtain equivalent resolution. Arrays of telescopes are used to achieve even better resolution through a technique called interferometry. Originally developed for radio telescopes, the technique is now also used with optical and infrared telescopes.

Largest Refracting (lens) Optical Telescope: Yerkes Observatory—1 m (40 in), at Williams Bay, WI

Largest Reflecting (mirror) Optical/Infrared Telescope: Keck—9.8 m (32 ft), on Mauna Kea in Hawaii (segmented mirror; 2 equal-size telescopes)

Largest Infrared Interferometer: Four 8.2-m (27-ft) telescopes of the Very Large Telescope Interferometer (VLTI) with a 200-m (656-ft) baseline on Cerro Paranal in Chile

Largest Fully Steerable Radio Dish: Robert C. Byrd Green Bank Telescope—100 m x 110 m (328 ft x 361 ft), in West Virginia

Largest Single Radio Dish: Arecibo Observatory—305 m (1,000 ft), in Puerto Rico

Largest Radio Interferometer: Ten 25-m (82-ft) diameter telescopes of the Very Long Baseline Array (VLBA), dispersed from Hawaii to the Virgin Islands with a resolution equal to a radio dish of 8,600 km (5,000 mi), making it the highest resolution telescope in the solar system

Constellations

Culturally, constellations are imagined patterns among the stars that, in some cases, have been recognized through millennia. Knowledge of constellations was once necessary in order to function as an astronomer. For today's astronomers, constellations are simply areas on the entire sky in which interesting objects await observation and interpretation.

Because Western culture has prevailed in establishing modern science, equally viable and interesting constellations and celestial traditions of other cultures are not well known outside their regions of origin. Even the patterns with which we are most familiar today have undergone considerable change over the centuries.

Today, **88 constellations** are officially recognized. Although many have ancient origins, some are "modern," devised out of unclaimed stars by astronomers a few centuries ago. Unclaimed stars were those too faint or inconveniently placed to be included in the more prominent constellations. Stars in a constellation are not necessarily near each other; they are just located in the same direction on the celestial sphere.

When astronomers began to travel to South Africa in the 16th and 17th centuries, they found an unfamiliar sky that showed numerous brilliant stars. Thus, we find constellations in the southern hemisphere that depict technological marvels of the time, as well as some arguably traditional forms, such as the "fly."

Many of the commonly recognized constellations had their **origins** in ancient Asia Minor. These were adopted by the Greeks and Romans, who translated their names and stories into their own languages, modifying some details in the process. After the declines of these cultures, most such knowledge entered oral tradition or remained hidden in monastic libraries. From the 8th century, the Muslim explosion spread through the Mediterranean world. Wherever possible, everything was translated into Arabic to be taught in the universities the Muslims established all over their new-found world.

In the 13th century, Alfonso X of Castile, an avid student of astronomy, had Ptolemy's *Almagest* translated into Latin. It thus became widely available to European scholars. In the process, the constellation names were translated, but the star names were retained in their Arabic forms. Thus the names of many stars—e.g., Altair, Alnitak, Mirfak—have Arabic roots, although linguistic adaptation and the inaccuracies of transliteration have wrought changes.

Until the 1920s, astronomers used curved boundaries for the constellation areas. As these were rather arbitrary at best, the International Astronomical Union adopted new constellation boundaries that ran due north-south and east-west, filling the sky much as the contiguous states fill up the area of the "lower 48" United States.

Common names of stars often referred to parts of the traditional figures they represented: Deneb, the tail of the swan; Betelgeuse, the armpit of the giant. Avoiding traditional names, astronomers may label stars by using Greek letters, generally to denote order of brightness. Thus, the "alpha star" would generally be the brightest star of that constellation. The "of" implies possession, so the genitive (possessive) form of the constellation name is used, as in Alpha Orionis, the first star of Orion (Betelgeuse). Astronomers usually use a 3-letter abbreviation for the constellation name, as indicated here.

Within these boundaries, and occasionally crossing them, popular "asterisms" are recognized: the so-called Big Dipper is a small part of the constellation Ursa Major, the big bear; the Sickle is the traditional head and mane of Leo, the lion; the three stars of the Summer Triangle are each in a different constellation, with Vega in Lyra the lyre, Deneb in Cynus the swan, and Altair in Aquila the eagle; the northeast star of the Great Square of Pegasus is Alpha Andromedae.

Name	Genitive Case	Abbr.	Meaning
Andromeda	Andromedae	And	Chained Maiden
Antlia	Antliae	Ant	Air Pump
Apus	Apodis	Aps	Bird of Paradise
Aquarius	Aquarii	Aqr	Water Bearer
Aquila	Aquilae	Aql	Eagle
Ara	Arae	Ara	Altar
Aries	Arietis	Ari	Ram
Auriga	Aurigae	Aur	Charioteer
Boötes	Boötis	Boo	Herdsmen
Caelum	Caeli	Cae	Chisel
Camelopardalis	Camelopardalis	Cam	Giraffe
Cancer	Cancri	Cnc	Crab
Canes Venatici	Canum Venaticorum	CVn	Hunting Dogs
Canis Major	Canis Majoris	CMa	Greater Dog
Canis Minor	Canis Minoris	CMi	Littler Dog
Capricornus	Capricorni	Cap	Sea-goat
Carina	Carinae	Car	Keel
Cassiopeia	Cassiopeiae	Cas	Queen
Centaurus	Centauri	Cen	Centaur
Cepheus	Cephei	Cep	King
Cetus	Ceti	Cet	Whale
Chamaeleon	Chamaeleontis	Cha	Chameleon
Circinus	Circini	Cir	Compasses (art)
Columba	Columbae	Col	Dove
Coma Berenices	Comae Berenices	Com	Berenice's Hair
Corona Australis	Coronae Australis	CrA	Southern Crown
Corona Borealis	Coronae Borealis	CrB	Northern Crown
Corvus	Corvi	Crv	Crow
Crater	Crateris	Crt	Cup
Crux	Crucis	Cru	Cross (southern)
Cygnus	Cygni	Cyg	Swan
Delphinus	Delphini	Del	Dolphin
Dorado	Doradus	Dor	Goldfish
Draco	Draconis	Dra	Dragon
Equuleus	Equulei	Equ	Little Horse
Eridanus	Eridani	Eri	River
Fornax	Fornacis	For	Furnace
Gemini	Geminorum	Gem	Twins
Grus	Gruis	Gru	Crane (bird)
Hercules	Herculis	Her	Hercules
Horologium	Horologii	Hor	Clock
Hydra	Hydrae	Hya	Water Snake (female)
Hydrus	Hydri	Hyi	Water Snake (male)
Indus	Indi	Ind	Indian
Lacerta	Lacertae	Lac	Lizard
Leo	Leonis	Leo	Lion
Leo Minor	Leonis Minoris	LMi	Littler Lion
Lepus	Leporis	Lep	Hare
Libra	Librae	Lib	Balance
Lupus	Lupi	Lup	Wolf
Lynx	Lyncis	Lyn	Lynx
Lyra	Lyrae	Lyr	Lyre
Mensa	Mensae	Men	Table Mountain
Microscopium	Microscopii	Mic	Microscope
Monoceros	Monocerotis	Mon	Unicorn
Musca	Muscae	Mus	Fly
Norma	Normae	Nor	Square (rule)
Octans	Octantis	Oct	Octant
Ophiuchus	Ophiuchi	Oph	Serpent Bearer
Orion	Orionis	Ori	Hunter
Pavo	Pavonis	Pav	Peacock
Pegasus	Pegasi	Peg	Flying Horse
Perseus	Persei	Per	Hero
Phoenix	Phoenicis	Phe	Phoenix
Pictor	Pictoris	Pic	Painter
Pisces	Piscium	Psc	Fishes
Piscis Austrinus	Piscis Austrini	PsA	Southern Fish
Puppis	Puppis	Pup	Stern (deck)
Pyxis	Pyxidis	Pyx	Compass (sea)
Reticulum	Reticuli	Ret	Reticle
Sagitta	Sagittae	Sge	Arrow
Sagittarius	Sagittarii	Sgr	Archer
Scorpius	Scorpii	Sco	Scorpion
Sculptor	Sculptoris	Scl	Sculptor
Scutum	Scuti	Sct	Shield
Serpens	Serpentis	Ser	Serpent
Sextans	Sextantis	Sex	Sextant
Taurus	Tauri	Tau	Bull
Telescopium	Telescopii	Tel	Telescope
Triangulum	Trianguli	Tri	Triangle
Triangulum Australe	Trianguli Australis	TrA	Southern Triangle
Tucana	Tucanae	Tuc	Toucan
Ursa Major	Ursae Majoris	UMa	Greater Bear
Ursa Minor	Ursae Minoris	UMi	Littler Bear
Vela	Velorum	Vel	Sail
Virgo	Virginis	Vir	Maiden
Volans	Volantis	Vol	Flying Fish
Vulpecula	Vulpeculae	Vul	Fox

Eclipses, 2006

(in Coordinated Universal Time, standard time of the prime meridian)

There are 4 eclipses in 2006: a total eclipse of the Sun, an annular eclipse of the Sun, a partial eclipse of the Moon, and a penumbral eclipse of the Moon. There is also a rare transit of the Sun by Mercury this year.

Penumbral eclipses of the Moon have such a little effect on the appearance of the Moon that most people are unaware of them even when looking at the Moon. Unlike total or partial eclipses of the Moon, during a penumbral eclipse there is no distinct shadow (the umbra) observable on the Moon. An **annular eclipse of the Sun** occurs, because of the elipticity of the orbits of the Moon and the Earth, the Moon is far enough away from the Earth and the Earth close enough to the Sun, that the Moon's angular size is not quite large enough to block the Sun, and a ring of the central disk of the Sun, or annulus, can still be seen around the Moon even when the Moon is between the Earth and the Sun.

Occasionally the Moon is very close to the point where an annular eclipse rather than a total eclipse may occur. In such cases, the central phase of the eclipse may start as annular, then become solar, and near the end of the central phase again become total. Of course, all solar eclipses have partial phases, but a solar eclipse is called a partial solar eclipse only when it has no annular or total phase at all.

I. Penumbral eclipse of the Moon, March 14-15

Penumbral eclipses of the Moon are not very noticeable (see above). The beginning of this eclipse takes place over Asia, the full eclipse takes place over Africa and Europe, and the end of the eclipse takes place over N and S America.

Circumstances of the Eclipse

Event	Date	h	m
Penumbral eclipse begins	Mar. 14	21	21.5
Middle of eclipse	14	23	47.4
Penumbral eclipse ends	15	2	13.4

II. Total eclipse of the Sun, March 29

This path of totality begins off the eastern tip of S America, crosses the S Atlantic Ocean, crosses northern Africa, central Asia and ends in Mongolia. Partial phases will be visible in large portions of the Atlantic Ocean, Africa, Europe and western Asia.

Circumstances of the Eclipse

Event	Date	h	m
Eclipse begins	Mar. 29	7	36.8
Total eclipse begins	29	8	35.0
Middle of eclipse	29	10	11.2
Total eclipse ends	29	11	47.3
Eclipse ends	29	12	45.6

III. Partial eclipse of the Moon, Sept. 7

This will be a very shallow partial eclipse. Asia, Australia, most of Africa, and much of Europe will see all of the partial phases of the eclipse, while western Africa and parts of western Europe will miss some of the partial phase.

Circumstances of the Eclipse

Event	Date	h	m
Partial eclipse begins	Sept. 7	18	05.0
Middle of eclipse	7	18	51.3
Partial eclipse ends	7	19	37.6

IV. Annular eclipse of the Sun, Sept. 22

This annular solar eclipse is visible from S America, all but the northern Atlantic Ocean, eastern portions of Africa, about half of Antarctica, and a small part of the Indian Ocean.

Circumstances of the Eclipse

Event	Date	h	m
Eclipse begins	Sept 22	8	39.9
Annular eclipse begins	22	9	50.3
Middle of eclipse	22	11	40.0
Annular eclipse ends	22	13	29.7
Eclipse ends	22	14	40.2

V. Transit of the Sun by Mercury, Nov. 8-9

Since Mercury does not block the Sun, it is dangerous to observe this event directly or with optical aids. All of the transit is visible over much of the Pacific Ocean, far western N America, Hawaii, New Zealand, and the eastern edge of Australia. Most of N and S America see the beginning of the transit, while eastern Asia and the rest of Australia and Indonesia see the end of the transit.

Circumstances of the Transit

Event	Date	h	m
Ingress begins	Nov. 8	19	12.0
Least angular distance	8	21	41.0
Egress ends	9	0	10.1

Total Solar Eclipses, 2000-2030

Total solar eclipses actually take place nearly as often as total lunar eclipses; they occur at a rate of about 3 every 4 years, while total lunar eclipses come at a rate of about 5 every 6 years. But, total lunar eclipses are visible over at least half of the Earth, while total solar eclipses can be seen only along a very narrow path up to a few hundred miles wide and a few thousand miles long. Observing a total solar eclipse is thus a rarity for most people.

Solar eclipses can be dangerous to observe. This is not because the Sun emits more potent rays, but because the Sun is always dangerous to observe directly and people are particularly likely to stare at it during a solar eclipse.

	Duration[1]		Width	
Date	m	s	(mi)	Path of Totality
2001, June 21	4	56	125	Atlantic Ocean, Africa, Madagascar
2002, Dec. 4	2	4	54	S Africa, Indian Ocean, Australia
2003, Nov. 23	1	57	338	Antarctica
2005, Apr. 8h	0	42	17	Pacific Ocean, northwestern S America
2006, Mar. 29	4	7	118	Atlantic Ocean, Africa, Asia
2008, Aug. 1	2	27	157	Arctic Ocean, Asia
2009, July 22	6	39	160	Asia, Pacific Ocean
2010, July 11	5	20	164	Pacific Ocean, southern S America
2012, Nov. 13	4	2	112	N Australia, Pacific Ocean
2013, Nov. 3h	1	40	36	Atlantic Ocean, Africa
2015, Mar. 20	2	47	304	N Atlantic Ocean, Arctic Ocean
2016, Mar. 9	4	10	96	Indonesia, Pacific Ocean
2017, Aug. 21	2	40	71	Pacific Ocean, U.S., Atlantic Ocean
2019, July 2	4	33	125	S Pacific Ocean, S America
2020, Dec. 14	2	10	56	S Pacific Ocean, S America, S Atlantic Ocean
2021, Dec. 4	1	55	282	Antarctica, S Atlantic Ocean
2023, Apr. 20h	1	16	31	Indian Ocean, New Guinea, Pacific Ocean
2024, Apr. 8	4	28	127	Pacific Ocean, Mexico, N America, Atlantic Ocean
2026, Aug. 12	2	18	198	Arctic Ocean, Greenland, N Atlantic Ocean, Indian Ocean, Australia, New Zealand
2027, Aug. 2	6	23	161	N Atlantic Ocean, N Africa, Middle East, Indian Ocean
2028, July 22	5	9	145	Indian Ocean, Australia, New Zealand
2030, Nov. 25	3	44	105	S Pacific Ocean, S Africa, Indian Ocean, Australia

h = indicates annular-total hybrid eclipse. (1) Duration refers to length of time at optimal viewing area.

Total Solar Eclipses in the U.S. in the 21st Century

During the 21st century there will be 8 total solar eclipses visible somewhere in the continental U.S. The first comes after a long gap; the last total solar eclipse was on Feb. 26, 1979, in the northwestern U.S.

Date	Path of Totality	Date	Path of Totality
Aug. 21, 2017	Oregon to South Carolina	Mar. 30, 2052	Florida to Georgia
Apr. 8, 2024	Mexico to Texas and up through Maine	May 11, 2078	Louisiana to North Carolina
Aug. 23, 2044	Montana to North Dakota	May 1, 2079	New Jersey to the lower edge of New England
Aug. 12, 2045	N California to Florida	Sept. 14, 2099	North Dakota to Virginia

Beginnings of the Universe

One of the dominating astronomical discoveries of the 20th century was the realization that the galaxies of the universe all seem to be moving away from us. Doppler redshifts were observed for the spiral nebulae around 1920, even though they were not yet known to be galaxies. By the early 1930s, Edwin Hubble and M.L. Humason had established that the more distant a galaxy, the faster it was receding. It turned out that they are moving away not just from us but from one another—that is, **the universe is expanding**. Scientists conclude that the universe must once, very long ago, have been extremely compact and dense. The explosion of matter that gave birth to the universe is called the **Big Bang**.

On the subatomic level, according to this theory, there were vast changes of energy and matter and the way physical laws operated during the first 5 minutes. After those early minutes the percentages of the basic matter of the universe—hydrogen, helium, and lithium—were set. Everything was so compact and so hot that **radiation dominated the early universe** and there were no stable, un-ionized atoms. At first, the universe was opaque, in the sense that any energy emitted was quickly absorbed and then re-emitted by free electrons. **As the universe expanded, density and temperature continued to drop.** A few hundred thousand years after the Big Bang, the temperature dropped far enough that electrons and nuclei could combine to form stable atoms as the universe became transparent. Once that occurred, the radiation that had been trapped was free to escape.

In the 1940s, George Gamov and others predicted that astronomers should be able to see remnants of this escaped radiation. Astronomers were starting to search for this background radiation when physicists Arno Penzias and Robert Wilson, using a radio telescope, inadvertently beat them to the punch (the 2 were later awarded a Nobel Prize).

In 2003, NASA's Wilkinson Microwave Anisotropy Probe made measurements of the temperature of this **cosmic microwave background** radiation to within millionths of a degree. From these measurements, scientists were able to deduce that our universe is **13.7 bil years old** and that first-generation stars began to form a mere 200 mil years after the Big Bang.

A related mystery is that evidence suggests there is hidden matter and hidden energy that cannot be directly observed. This **dark matter** may be composed of gas, large numbers of cool, small objects, or even sub-atomic particles. The presence of dark matter is indicated by the rotation curves of galaxies and the dynamics of clusters of galaxies. Evidence for **dark energy** is derived from studies of distant Type Ia supernovae in far galaxies indicating that the expansion of the universe is accelerating, rather than slowing. The visible matter we see seems to constitute only about 4% of the total mass of the universe, while the rest of the mass of the universe is in the form of dark matter (23%) and dark energy (73%). Dark energy is a mysterious force that seems to work on the very fabric of the universe, spreading it apart.

Galaxies

The 20th century might be called the century of the galaxy. By the start of the century, more than 10,000 **nebulae**—cloud-like luminous objects in the sky—had been discovered. Some were correctly identified as star clusters and others as clouds of gas and dust. Those nebulae which were spiral or elliptical in shape were found in regions of the sky far from the glowing band that is our own Milky Way Galaxy. Immanuel Kant had written in 1775 that some of these fuzzy objects might be **"island universes"** apart from our own. But the idea remained speculative until 1923-24, when Edwin Hubble discovered the existence of variable stars in some of these nebulae. This provided conclusive evidence that these systems were outside our own "island universe," the Milky Way Galaxy.

Galaxies range in **size** from small dwarf elliptical ones, with perhaps 1 mil stars, to spiral galaxies containing 300 billion stars, to giant elliptical galaxies that may be home to more than 10 tril stars. The diameters of galaxies range from 3,000 light-years in dwarf elliptical galaxies to over 500,000 light-years in giant elliptical galaxies. It is estimated that the Milky Way galaxy is about 100,000 light-years in diameter with about 400 bil stars.

Galaxies also congregate into **clusters**. The smallest are poor clusters of only a few dozen galaxies, while the largest rich clusters may contain thousands of galaxies. The Milky Way is part of a poor cluster of about 3 dozen galaxies called the **Local Group**. The largest member of the Local Group is the Andromeda Galaxy, a spiral galaxy visible to the unaided eye in the constellation of Andromeda on a very dark night away from lights. The Milky Way is the second largest galaxy in this group; most other galaxies in our Local Group are small.

The Solar System

The planets of the solar system, in order of mean distance from the Sun, are **Mercury, Venus, Earth, Mars, Jupiter, Saturn, Uranus, Neptune,** and **Pluto** (Pluto sometimes nearer than Neptune). Both Uranus and Neptune are visible through good binoculars, but Pluto is so distant and small that only large telescopes or long-exposure photographs can make it visible. All the planets orbit or revolve counterclockwise around the Sun.

Because **Mercury and Venus** are nearer to the Sun than is Earth, their motions about the Sun appear from Earth as wide swings first to one side of the Sun then to the other, though both planets move continuously around the Sun in almost circular orbits. When their passage takes them either between Earth and the Sun or beyond the Sun as seen from Earth, they are invisible to us. Because of the geometry of the planetary orbits, Mercury and Venus require much less time to pass between Earth and the Sun than around the far side of the Sun; so their periods of visibility and invisibility are unequal.

The **planets that lie farther from the Sun** than does Earth may be seen for longer periods and are invisible only when so located in our sky so that they rise and set at about the same time as the Sun—and thus become overwhelmed by the Sun's brilliance. Though the giant planets emit their own energy, they are observed from Earth as a result of sunlight reflecting from their surfaces or cloud layers. On occasion, radio emissions from Jupiter exceed even those emitted by the Sun in intensity. Mercury and Venus, because they are between Earth and the Sun, show phases much as the Moon does. The planets farther from the Sun are always seen as full, although Mars does occasionally present a slightly gibbous phase—like the Moon when not quite full.

The **planets appear to move rapidly among the stars** because of being closer. The stars are also in motion, some at tremendous speeds, but they are so far away that their motion does not change their apparent positions in the heavens sufficiently to be perceived. The nearest star is about 9,000 times farther away than Neptune, the most distant giant planet in our solar system. The count for identified **moons** in the solar system stood at 154 in mid-2005, but the search for more moons continued.

Planets and the Sun, by Selected Characteristics

Sun and Planets	Radius: at unit distance[1] "	Radius: at mean least distance[2] "	Radius: in mi mean radius	Volume[3]	Mass[3]	Density[3]	Sidereal period d	h	m	s	Gravity at surface[3]	Reflecting power Pct°	Daytime surface temp. °F
Sun	959.5	976	432,500	1,304,000	333,000	0.26	25	9	7		28.0		+9,941
Mercury	3.36	6.5	1,516	0.0562	0.0553	0.98	58	15	36		0.38	0.11	845
Venus	8.34	33.0	3,760	0.857	0.815	0.95	243		30^R		0.91	0.65	867
Earth	8.78		3,959	1.000	1.000	1.00		23	56	4.2	1.00	0.37	59
Moon	2.40	986.2	1,079	0.0203	0.0123	0.61	27	7	43	40	0.16	0.12	260
Mars	4.67	12.8	2,106	0.151	0.107	0.71		24	37	22	0.38	0.15	–24
Jupiter	96.40	24.5	43,441	1,321	317.8	0.24		9	55	30	2.53	0.52	–162
Saturn	80.29	10.05	36,184	764	95.16	0.12		10	39	20	1.06	0.47	–218
Uranus	34.97	2.05	15,759	63.1	14.54	0.23		17	14	20^R	0.90	0.51	–323
Neptune	33.95	1.2	15,301	57.7	17.15	0.30		16	6	40	1.14	0.41	–330
Pluto	1.65	0.08	742	0.007	0.002	0.32	6	9	17	30^R	0.06	0.6	–369

(1) Angular radius, in seconds of arc, if object were seen at a distance of 1 astronomical unit. (2) Angular radius, in seconds of arc, when object is closest to Earth. (3) Earth = 1. R = Retrograde rotation.

Planet Superlatives

Largest, most massive planet	Jupiter	Most circular orbit	Venus
Fastest orbiting planet	Mercury	Slowest orbiting planet	Pluto
Fastest sidereal rotation	Jupiter	Slowest sidereal rotation	Venus
Longest (synodic) day	Mercury	Shortest (synodic) day	Jupiter
Rotational pole closest to ecliptic	Uranus	Hottest planet	Venus
Most moons	Jupiter	No moons	Mercury, Venus
Planet with largest moon	Jupiter	Planet with moon with most eccentric orbit	Neptune
Greatest average density	Earth	Lowest average density	Saturn
Tallest mountain	Mars	Deepest oceans	Jupiter
Strongest magnetic fields	Jupiter	Greatest amount of liquid, surface water	Earth

The Planets: Motion, Distance, and Brightness

Planet	Mean daily motion[1]	Orbital velocity mi per sec.[2]	Sidereal revolution days[3]	Synodic revolution days[4]	Distance from Sun in millions of mi Max.	Distance from Sun Min.	Distance from Earth in millions of mi Max.	Distance from Earth Min.	Light at[5] perihelion	Light at aphelion
Mercury	14,732	29.75	87.97	115.9	43.4	28.6	137.9	48.0	10.56	4.59
Venus	5,768	21.76	224.7	583.9	67.7	66.8	162.2	23.7	1.94	1.89
Earth	3,548	18.50	365.256	—	94.5	91.4	—	—	1.03	0.97
Mars	1,887	15.00	686.98	779.9	154.9	128.4	249.4	33.9	0.52	0.36
Jupiter	299	8.12	4,332.6	398.9	507.4	460.1	602	366	0.041	0.034
Saturn	120	6.02	10,759.2	378.1	941.1	840.4	1,031	743	0.012	0.0098
Uranus	42	4.23	30,685.4	369.7	1,866	1,703	1,962	1,605	0.0030	0.0025
Neptune	22	3.37	60,189.0	367.5	2,824	2,762	2,913	2,676	0.0011	0.0011
Pluto	14	2.93	90,465.0	366.7	4,583	2,757	4,682	2,669	0.0011	0.00041

(1) Average angular motion measured in seconds of arc per day. (2) Speed of revolution around Sun. (3) Number of Earth days to orbit Sun with respect to background stars. (4) Number of Earth days to get back to the same position in its orbit around Sun, relative to Earth. (5) Light at perihelion and aphelion is solar illumination measured in units of mean illumination at Earth.

Planets of the Solar System

Note: AU = astronomical unit (92.96 mil mi, mean distance of Earth from the Sun); **d** = 1 Earth synodic (solar) day (24 hrs); **synodic day** = rotation period of a planet measured with respect to the Sun (the "true" day, i.e. the time from midday to midday, or from sunrise to sunrise); **sidereal day** = the rotation period of a planet with respect to the stars

Mercury

Distance from Sun	
Perihelion	28.6 mil mi
Semi-major axis	0.387 AU
Aphelion	43.4 mil mi
Period of revolution around Sun	87.97 d
Orbital eccentricity	0.2056
Orbital inclination	7.00°
Synodic day (midday to midday)	175.94 d
Sidereal day	58.65 d
Rotational inclination	0.01°
Mass (Earth = 1)	0.0553
Mean radius	1,516 mi
Mean density (Earth = 1)	0.984
Natural satellites	0
Average surface temperature	333°F

Mercury, the nearest planet to the Sun, is the 2nd-smallest of the 9 known planets. Its diameter is 3,032 mi; its mean distance from the Sun is 35,980,000 mi.

Mercury moves with great speed around the Sun, averaging about 30 mi per second to complete its circuit in about 88 Earth days. Mercury takes nearly 59 days to rotate on its axis, thus exposing all its surface periodically to the Sun. Because its orbital period is only about 50% longer than its sidereal rotation, the solar (synodic) day on Mercury, or the time from one sunrise to the next, is about 176 days, twice as long as a Mercurian year. It is believed that the surface passing before the Sun may reach a temperature of about 845° F, while the temperature on the nighttime side may fall as low as –300° F.

Uncertainty about conditions on Mercury and its motion arises from its short angular distance from the Sun as seen from Earth. Mercury is too much in line with the Sun to be observed against a dark sky; it is always seen during either morning or evening twilight.

Mariner 10 passed Mercury 3 times in 1974 and 1975. Less than half of the surface was photographed, revealing cratering similar to that of the Moon. The most imposing feature on Mercury, the Caloris Basin, is a huge impact crater more than 800 mi in diameter. Mercury has a higher percentage of iron than any other planet. A very thin atmosphere of hydrogen and helium may be made up of gases of the solar wind temporarily concentrated by the presence of Mercury. The discovery of a weak but permanent magnetic field was a surprise to scientists. It has been held that both a fluid core and rapid rotation are necessary for the generation of a planetary magnetic field. Mercury may demonstrate the contrary; the field may reveal something about the history of Mercury. Radar mapping of Mercury with the Arecibo, NASA's Goldstone, and the NRAO's VLA have provided evidence of possible water ice near its poles.

In Aug. 2004, NASA launched its MESSENGER spacecraft, which will eventually fly by Mercury in 2008. In 2011, MESSENGER will orbit Mercury.

Venus

Distance from Sun	
Perihelion	66.8 mil mi
Semi-major axis	0.723 AU
Aphelion	67.7 mil mi
Period of revolution around Sun	224.70 d
Orbital eccentricity	0.0067
Orbital inclination	3.39°
Synodic day (midday to midday)	116.75 d (retrograde)
Sidereal day	243.02 d (retrograde)
Rotational inclination	177.4°
Mass (Earth = 1)	0.815
Mean radius	3,760 mi
Mean density (Earth = 1)	0.951
Natural satellites	0
Average surface temperature	867°F

Venus, slightly smaller than Earth, moves about the Sun at a mean distance of 67,240,000 mi in 225 Earth days. Its synodical revolution—its return to the same relationship with Earth and the Sun, which is a result of the combination of its own motion with that of Earth—is 584 days. As a result, every 19 months Venus is nearer to Earth than any other planet. Venus is covered with a dense, white, cloudy atmosphere that conceals whatever is below it. This same cloud reflects sunlight efficiently so that Venus is the 3rd-brightest object in the sky, exceeded only by the Sun and the Moon. Spectral analysis of sunlight reflected from Venus's cloud tops has shown features that can best be explained by identifying material of the clouds as sulfuric acid. The *Mariner 2* space probe in 1962 confirmed a high surface temperature. *Mariner 2* was unable to detect the existence of a magnetic field even as weak as 1/100,000 of Earth's.

Earth and Venus are about the same size and were presumably formed at the same time by the same general process and from the same mixture of chemical elements. However, measurements indicate that Venus has a surface temperature of about 867° F as a result of an extreme greenhouse effect. Due to the thick atmosphere, the temperature is essentially the same day and night.

In 1967, the Soviet *Venera 4* and the American *Mariner 5* space probes arrived at Venus within a few hours of each other. *Venera 4* dropped an instrument package into the Venusian atmosphere that was designed to land gently on the surface, but it ceased to transmit information when its temperature reading went above 500° F, about 20 mi above the surface. *Mariner 5*'s radio signals passed to Earth through Venus's atmosphere. The results showed that Venus's atmosphere is nearly all carbon dioxide (96.5%), with 3.5% nitrogen and trace amounts of sulfur dioxide, carbon monoxide, argon, water, helium, and neon. It exerts a pressure at the surface more than 90 times Earth's normal sea-level pressure.

Radio astronomers determined the rotation period of Venus to be 243 days clockwise—in other words, contrary to the spin of the other planets and contrary to its own motion around the Sun. This rate and sense of rotation makes for a solar day (sunrise to sunrise) on Venus of 116.8 Earth days. Any part of Venus will receive sunlight on its clouds for more than 58 days and then return to darkness for 58 days.

Carbon dioxide found in abundance in the atmosphere is rather opaque to certain ultraviolet wavelengths, enabling sensitive cameras to photograph the cloud cover. Soviet spacecraft discovered that the clouds are confined in a 12-mi layer 30 to 42 mi above the surface.

In 1978, two U.S. *Pioneer* probes confirmed expected high surface temperatures and high winds aloft. Winds of about 200 mph there may account for the transfer of heat into the night side despite the low rotation speed of the planet. However, at the surface, the winds are very slow. Soviet scientists in 1975 and later in 1982, obtained 4 photos of surface rocks. The *Pioneer* orbiter confirmed the cloud pattern and circulation shown by *Mariner 10*. Radar produced maps of the entire planet showing large craters, continent-size highlands, and extensive dry lowlands.

The Venus orbiter *Magellan* launched in 1989 used sophisticated radar techniques to observe Venus and map more than 99% of the surface. The spacecraft observed over 1,600 volcanoes and volcanic features, enabling creation of a 3-dimensional map. *Magellan* showed that more than 85% of the surface is covered by volcanic flows. Additionally, there are highly deformed mountain belts. Craters more than 20 mi wide are believed to have been caused by impacting bodies. Theia Mons, a huge shield volcano, has a diameter of over 600 mi and a height of over 3.5 mi. (The largest Hawaiian volcano is only about 125 mi in diameter, but rises nearly 5.5 mi from the ocean floor.

Erosion is a very slow process on Venus due to the extreme lack of water and features persist for long periods of time. There are indications of only restricted wind movement of dust and sand. No tectonic activity has been found similar to Earth's moving tectonic plates, but a system of global rift zones and numerous broad, low dome-like structures, called coronae, may be produced by the upwelling and subsidence of magma from the mantle. Volcanic surface features, such as vast lava plains, fields of small lava domes, and large shield volcanoes, are common. The few impact craters on Venus suggest that the surface is generally geologically young—less than 800 million years old.

A number of spacecraft missions have flown or will fly by Venus en route to their final destinations, including *Cassini* to Saturn in 1997 and MESSENGER to Mercury in 2006 and 2007. Approximately every 105-120 years, Venus and the Earth are in the proper positions so that Venus passes between the Earth and the Sun in a pair of transits 8 years apart. The second of the current pair of transits occurs in 2012.

Mars

Distance from Sun	
Perihelion	128.4 mil mi
Semi-major axis	1.524 AU
Aphelion	154.9 mil mi
Period of revolution around Sun	686.98 d (1.88 y)
Orbital eccentricity	0.0935
Orbital inclination	1.85°
Synodic day (midday to midday)	24h 39m 35s
Sidereal day	24h 37m 22s
Rotational inclination	25.19°
Mass (Earth = 1)	0.107
Mean radius	2,106 mi
Mean density (Earth = 1)	0.713
Natural satellites	2
Average surface temperature	–81° F

Mars's diameter is about 4,213 mi. Although its orbit is nearly circular, it is somewhat more eccentric than the orbits of most of the other planets, and Mars is more than 26 mil mi farther from the Sun at its most distant point compared to its closest approach. Mars takes 687 Earth days to make one circuit of the Sun, traveling at about 15 mi. per second. The planet rotates in almost the same period of time as Earth—24 hours and 37 minutes. Mars's mean distance from the Sun is 142 mil mi, so its temperature is lower than that on Earth. In 1965, *Mariner 4* became the first spacecraft to fly by Mars, reporting that atmospheric pressure on Mars is between 1% and 2% of Earth's atmospheric pressure. As with Venus, the atmosphere is composed largely of carbon dioxide. Mars is exposed to an influx of cosmic radiation about 100 times as intense as that on Earth. Mars's orbit and its speed in relation to Earth's position and speed bring it fairly close to Earth about every 2 years. Every 15-17 years the close approaches are especially favorable for observation. In 2003, Mars came within 34,646,418 mi, its closest approach to Earth in nearly 60,000 years.

Mars's axis of rotation is inclined from a vertical to the plane of its orbit about the Sun by about 25°, so Mars has seasons as does Earth. White caps form about the poles, growing in winter and shrinking in summer. These poles are believed to be both water ice and carbon dioxide ice. It is the carbon dioxide that comes and goes with the seasons. The water ice is apparently in many layers with dust between them, indicating climatic cycles.

The first space probes, to reach Mars in 1969-71, sent back photos of an alien world with valleys and nountains and other features clearly of volcanic origin. One of these is Olympus Mons, a shield volcano whose caldera is more than 40 mi wide and whose outer slopes are 300 mi in diameter; it stands 15 mi above the surrounding plain—the tallest known mountain in the solar system. Some features may have been produced by faulting and stretching of the surface. Valles Marineris, extending nearly 2,500 mi, is an example on a colossal scale. Many craters seem to have been produced by impacting bodies that may have come from the nearby asteroid belt. Features near the S pole may have been produced by glaciers no longer present.

In 1976, the U.S. landed 2 *Viking* spacecraft on Mars. Though the landers had devices to perform chemical analyses of the soil in search of evidence of life, results were inconclusive. The orbiters returned pictures of topographic features that scientists believe can be explained only if Mars once had large quantities of flowing water.

Two U.S. spacecraft—*Mars Pathfinder* and *Mars Global Surveyor*—reached Mars in 1997. *Pathfinder's* small movable robot, Sojourner, spent 3 months examining rocks. Geological results from *Pathfinder* indicate that in its beginning stages Mars melted to a sufficient extent to separate into dense and lighter layers. It also appears that the planet once had large amounts of flooding waters on its surface. *Surveyor* did extensive planet mapping and reported a very weak magnetic field. Its results support a view of the southern hemisphere of Mars covered with ancient craters like Earth's Moon. The northern hemisphere consists mainly of plains that are much younger and lower in elevation. Pictures from the *Surveyor* showed evidence of liquid water on Mars in recent times. The *Mars Odyssey* spacecraft, launched in 2001, detected evidence of the presence of water ice in the upper 3 feet of soil in a large area around the south pole.

In June 2003, the European Space Agency (ESA) launched the *Mars Express* spacecraft, its first probe to another planet. It reached Mars in Dec. 2003 and is performing remote sensing of Mars, including high-resolution photography in a search for subsurface water. The 3 orbiter spacecraft currently in orbit around Mars (*Mars Global Surveyor*, *Mars Odyssey*, and *Mars Express*) were joined by the *Mars Reconnaissance Orbiter*. Launched by NASA on Aug. 12, 2005, it will study the Martian climate and do high-resolution imagery.

Twin NASA spacecraft—*Spirit* and *Opportunity*—launched in mid-2003 made successful bouncing, airbag-wrapped landings on Mars in Jan. 2004. Spirit landed about 15° South of the Martian equator at Gusev Crater, a bowl-shaped feature larger than Connecticut, which may have held a lake far in the past. *Opportunity* landed 3 weeks later, about halfway around Mars at Meridiani Planum, a smooth plain. Both rovers have found evidence that liquid water once existed on Mars. As of mid-2005, they were still laboriously exploring the Martian surface, more than one year past their primary mission. In June 2005, *Spirit* took the first photo of a Martian meteor.

Mars has 2 satellites, discovered in 1877 by Asaph Hall. The outer satellite, Deimos, revolves around the planet in about 31 hours. The inner satellite, Phobos, whips around Mars in a little more than 7 hours, making 3 trips each Martian day. Since it orbits Mars faster than the planet rotates, Phobos rises in the W and sets in the E, opposite to what other bodies appear to do in the Martian sky. They are irregularly shaped and pitted with numerous craters. Phobos measures about 11 by 17 mi and Deimos about 7 by 9 mi.

Of the tens of thousands of meteorites found on Earth, about a dozen may have originated on Mars. In 1996, a NASA research team concluded that a meteorite found in 1984 on an Antarctic ice field might be a rock blasted from the surface of Mars containing microscopic structures that could form the building blocks of life. The meteorite has been age-dated to about 4.5 bil years. The scientists theorize that 3.5 bil years ago, Mars may have been warmer and wetter, and microscopic life may have formed and left evidence in the rock, including possible fossilized microscopic organisms. It is thought that 16 mil years ago a huge asteroid or comet struck Mars, blasting material, including this rock, into space. The rock may have entered Earth's atmosphere about 13,000 years ago, landing in Antarctica. The evidence is intriguing, but not conclusive, in suggesting that Mars once had microscopic life.

Jupiter

Distance from Sun	
Perihelion	460.1 mil mi
Semi-major axis	5.204 AU
Aphelion	507.4 mil mi
Period of revolution around Sun	11.862 y
Orbital eccentricity	0.0489
Orbital inclination	1.304°
Synodic day (midday to midday)	9h 55m 33s
Sidereal day	9h 55m 30s
Rotational inclination	3.13°
Mass (Earth = 1)	317.8
Mean radius	43,441 mi
Mean density (Earth = 1)	0.24
Natural satellites	63
Average temperature*	–162°F

*i.e., temperature where atmosphere pressure equals 1 Earth atmosphere.

Jupiter, largest of the planets, has an equatorial diameter of 88,846 mi, 11 times the diameter of Earth. Its polar diameter is more than 5,700 mi shorter. This noticeable oblateness is a result of the liquidity of the planet and its extremely rapid rotation rate—a Jupiter day is less than 10 Earth hours long. For a planet this size, this rotational speed is amazing. A point on Jupiter's equator moves at a speed of 22,000 mph, as compared with 1,000 mph for a point on Earth's equator. Jupiter is at an average distance of 484 mil mi from the Sun and takes almost 12 Earth years to make one complete circuit of the Sun.

The major chemical constituents of Jupiter's atmosphere are molecular hydrogen (H_2—90%) and helium (He—10%). Minor constituents include methane (CH_4), ammonia (NH_3), hydrogen deuteride (HD), ethane (C_2H_6), and water (H_2O).

The temperature at the tops of clouds may be about –280° F. The gases become denser with depth, until they may turn into a slush or slurry. There is no sharp interface between the gaseous atmosphere and the hydrogen ocean that accounts for most of Jupiter's volume. *Pioneer 10* and *11*, passing Jupiter in 1973 and 1974, provided evidence for considering Jupiter almost entirely liquid hydrogen. Jupiter apparently has a liquid hydrogen ocean more than 35,000 mi deep. It likely has a rocky core about the size of Earth, but 13 times more massive.

Jupiter's magnetic field is by far the strongest of any planet. Electrical activity caused by this field is so strong that it discharges billions of watts into Earth's magnetic field daily. At lower layers, under enormous pressure, the liquid hydrogen takes on the properties of a metal. It is likely that this liquid metallic hydrogen is the source for both Jupiter's persistent radio noise and for its improbably strong magnetic field.

Of Jupiter's 63 known satellites, 23 were found in 2003 through Earth-based observations. Four of the moons (in order from Jupiter), Io, Europa, Ganymede, and Callisto—all discovered by Galileo in 1610—are large and bright, rivaling Earth's Moon and Mercury in diameter. They move rapidly around Jupiter, and it is easy to observe their change of position from night to night using binoculars. The other satellites are much smaller, with 4 closer to Jupiter than Io, 5 between Ganymede and Callisto, and the rest farther out. Most of Jupiter's moons revolve around Jupiter clockwise as seen from the north, contrary to the motions of most satellites in the solar system and to the direction of revolution of planets around the Sun. These moons may be captured asteroids. Jupiter's mass is more than twice the mass of all the other planets, moons, and asteroids put together.

Photographs from *Pioneer 10* and *11* were far surpassed by those of *Voyager 1* and *2*, which arrived at Jupiter in 1979. The Great Red Spot exhibited internal counterclockwise rotation, and much turbulence was seen in adjacent material passing N or S of it. The satellites Amalthea, Io, Europa, Ganymede, and Callisto were photographed, some in great detail. Io has active volcanoes that probably have ejected material into a doughnut-shaped ring, or torus, enveloping its orbit about Jupiter. This is not to be confused with Jupiter's rings, the surprise of the *Voyager 1* mission. Since then, ground-based telescopes have imaged Jupiter's rings in the infrared.

In 1994, 21 large fragments of Comet Shoemaker-Levy 9 collided with Jupiter. Moving at 134,000 mph, stretched out like a 21-car freight train, the fragments impacted one after another. Massive plumes of gas erupted, and formed brilliant fire-balls. One of the largest chunks impacted with a force 100,000 times the power of the largest nuclear bomb ever detonated. It produced a plume 1,400 mi high and 5,000 mi wide and left a temporary dark discoloration larger than Earth.

The *Galileo* spacecraft went into orbit around Jupiter and released a probe over the Jovian atmosphere in Dec. 1995. The probe, traveling over 100,000 mph, plunged into Jupiter's atmosphere relaying information for 57.6 minutes. It revealed that Jupiter has thunderstorms many times larger than those on Earth, and provided evidence that Jupiter's rings are composed of small dust grains blasted off the 4 innermost moons by meteoroid impacts.

Galileo continued an extended mission to study the 4 large moons. Its observations show extensive ongoing volcanic eruptions on Io, with the volcanoes hotter than Earth's volcanoes. Europa may have a 30-mi-deep salty, liquid ocean beneath its icy crust, perhaps a small metallic core, and a very tenuous atmosphere. Ganymede has it own magnetic field produced by a molten core perhaps of iron sulfide. Callisto has the oldest, most heavily cratered surface in the solar system, a very thin atmosphere of carbon dioxide, and possibly a subsurface liquid ocean. In 2003, *Galileo* was intentionally plunged into Jupiter's atmosphere, destroying the spacecraft to prevent any accidental contamination of Europa's possible subsurface ocean.

Saturn

Distance from Sun	
Perihelion	840.44 mil mi
Semi-major axis	9.582 AU
Aphelion	941.07 mil mi
Period of revolution around Sun	29.458 y
Orbital eccentricity	0.0565
Orbital inclination	2.485°
Synodic day (midday to midday)	10h 39m 23s
Sidereal day	10h 39m 22s
Rotational Inclination	26.73°
Mass (Earth = 1)	95.159
Mean radius	36,184 mi
Mean density (Earth = 1)	0.125
Natural satellites	47
Average temperature*	–218° F

*i.e., temperature where atmosphere pressure equals 1 Earth atmosphere.

Saturn, last of the planets visible to the unaided eye, is almost twice as far from the Sun as Jupiter. It is 2nd in size to Jupiter, but its mass is much smaller. Saturn's specific gravity is less than that of water. Its diameter is almost 74,900 mi at the equator, while its polar diameter is more than 7,300 mi shorter. This noticeable oblateness is a result of the liquidity of the planet and its extremely rapid rate of rotation; a day is little more than 10 Earth hours long. Saturn's atmosphere is much like that of Jupiter, except that the temperature at the top of its cloud layer is at least 50° F colder. At about 300° F below zero, the ammonia would be frozen out of Saturn's clouds. The theoretical structure of Saturn resembles that of Jupiter; it likely has a small dense center surrounded by a layer of liquid and a deep atmosphere composed mostly of hydrogen (about 75%) and helium (about 25%), with traces of water, ammonia, methane, and rock.

Saturn's ring system begins about 4,000 mi above the visible disk of Saturn, lying above its equator and extending about 260,000 mi into space. The diameter of the ring system visible from Earth is about 170,000 mi; the rings are estimated to be about 700 feet thick. In 1973, radar observation showed the ring particles to be large chunks of material averaging a meter on a side. Later, *Voyager 1* and *2* observations showed the rings to be considerably more complex than had been believed.

Until *Pioneer 11* passed Saturn in 1979, only 10 satellites of the planet were known. *Pioneer 11* discovered 2 more, and 6 others were found in the *Voyager 1* and *2* flybys, which also yielded more information about Saturn's icy satellites. Twelve more moons were discovered in 2000, another one in 2003, and an astounding 15 in 2004. The *Cassini* spacecraft, in May 2005, discovered 2 moons, including a tiny moon in the Keeler Gap of Saturn's rings.

Launched in Oct. 1997, *Cassini*, with its tag-along companion *Huygens*, reached Saturn on July 1, 2004. The first spacecraft to orbit Saturn, *Cassini* was intended to remain for many years. On Jan. 14, 2005, the *Huygens* probe detached from *Cassini* and landed on Titan, Saturn's largest moon. Titan is the only moon in the solar system with a significant atmosphere. The photographs and data from *Huygens* showed a muddy surface, with possible deposits of water ice, channels carved by liquid methane springs, and an interesting boundary between light and dark material on the surface. Meanwhile, *Cassini* spotted a 270-mi-wide crater and observed a puzzling 300-mi-wide hot spot region on Titan. *Cassini* has also taken detailed looks at Saturn's rings, studied Saturn's auroras, and detected an atmosphere on Saturn's moon Enceladus.

Uranus

Distance from Sun	
Perihelion	1,703.4 mil mi
Semi-major axis	19.201 AU
Aphelion	1,866.4 mil mi
Period of revolution around Sun	84.01 y
Orbital eccentricity	0.0457
Orbital inclination	0.772°
Synodic day (midday to midday)	17h 14m 23s (retrograde)
Sidereal day	17h 14m 24s (retrograde)
Rotational inclination	97.77°
Mass (Earth = 1)	14.536
Mean radius	15,759mi
Mean density (Earth = 1)	0.230
Natural satellites	27
Average temperature*	–323° F

*i.e., temperature where atmosphere pressure equals 1 Earth atmosphere.

Uranus, discovered by Sir William Herschel on Mar. 13, 1781, lies 1.8 bil mi from the Sun, taking 84 years to make its circuit around our star. Uranus has a diameter of over 31,000 mi and spins once in some 17.4 hours, according to flyby magnetic data. One of the most fascinating features of Uranus is how far over it is tipped. Its N pole lies 98° from being directly up and down to its orbit plane. Thus, its seasons are extreme. When the Sun rises at the N pole, it stays up for 42 Earth years; then it sets, and the N pole is in darkness for 42 Earth years.

Uranus has 27 known moons, which have orbits lying in the plane of the planet's equator. Five moons are relatively large, while 22 are very small and were only discovered with the *Voyager 2* mission or in later observations. In the equatorial plane there is also a complex of 11 rings, 9 of which were discovered in 1978 by observers watching Uranus pass before a star.

In addition to photos of 10 very small satellites, *Voyager 2* returned detailed photos of the 5 large satellites. As in the case of other satellites newly observed in the *Voyager* program, these bodies proved to be quite different from one another and from any others. Miranda has grooved markings, reminiscent of Jupiter's Ganymede, but often arranged in a chevron pattern. Ariel shows rifts and channels. Umbriel is extremely dark, prompting some observers to regard its surface as among the oldest in the system. Titania has rifts and fractures, but not the evidence of flow found on Ariel. Oberon's main feature is its surface saturated with craters, unrelieved by other formations.

Uranus likely does not have a rocky core, but rather a mixture of rocks and assorted ices with about 15% hydrogen and a little helium. The atmosphere is about 83% hydrogen, 15% helium, and 2% methane. In addition to its rotational tilt, Uranus's magnetic field axis is tipped an incredible 58.6° from its rotational axis and is displaced about 30% of its radius away from the planet's center.

Neptune

Distance from the Sun	
Perihelion	2,761.7 mil mi
Semi-major axis	30.047 AU
Aphelion	2,824.5 mil mi
Period of revolution around Sun	164.79 y
Orbital eccentricity	0.0113
Orbital inclination	1.769°
Synodic day (midday to midday)	16h 6m 37s
Sidereal day	16h 6m 36s
Rotational inclination	28.32°
Mass (Earth = 1)	17.147
Mean radius	15,301 mi
Mean density (Earth = 1)	0.297
Natural satellites	13
Average temperature*	–330° F

*i.e., temperature where atmosphere pressure equals 1 Earth atmosphere.

Neptune lies at an average distance of 2.8 bil mi from the Sun. It was the last planet visited in *Voyager 2*'s epic 12-year trek (1977-89) from Earth.

As with other giant planets, Neptune may have no solid surface, or exact diameter. However, a mean value of 30,600 mi may be assigned to a diameter between atmosphere levels where the pressure is about the same as sea level on Earth. Astronomers use a determination of the rotation rate of the planet's magnetic field to indicate the internal rotation rate, which in the case of Neptune is 16.1 hours. Neptune orbits the Sun in 164.8 years in a nearly circular orbit. Discovered in 1846, Neptune will not have completed one full trip around the Sun since its discovery until 2010.

Voyager 2, which passed 3,000 mi from Neptune's N pole, found a magnetic field that is considerably asymmetric to the planet's structure, similar to, but not so extreme as, that found at Uranus. Neptune's magnetic field axis is tipped 46.9° from its rotational axis and is displaced more than 55% of its radius away from the planet's center. Neptune's atmosphere was seen to be quite blue, with quickly changing white clouds often suspended high above an apparent surface. There is a Great Dark Spot, reminiscent of the Great Red Spot of Jupiter. Observations with the Hubble Space Telescope have shown that the Great Dark Spot originally seen by *Voyager* has apparently dissipated, but a new dark spot has since appeared. Neptune's atmosphere is about 80% hydrogen, 19% helium, and 1% methane. Lightning and auroras have been found on other giant planets, but only the aurora phenomenon has been seen on Neptune. Some astronomers are actively seeking lightning on Neptune.

Six new satellites were discerned around Neptune by *Voyager 2*; 5 of them orbit Neptune in a half day or less. In 2002 astronomers who had used large telescopes in Chile and Hawaii announced the discovery of 3 more satellites. In 2003, 2 more moons, which orbit farther from their parent planet than any other moons, were discovered.

Nereid, found in 1949, has the highest orbital eccentricity (0.75) of any moon. Its long looping orbit suggests that it was captured rather than having been there from the beginning. Largest of Neptune's 13 satellites is Triton, the only large moon in a retrograde orbit, suggesting that it, too, was captured. Triton's large size, sufficient to raise significant tides on the planet, may one day, billions of years from now, cause Triton to come close enough to Neptune for it to be torn apart. Only about half of Triton has been observed, but its terrain shows cratering and a strange regional feature described as resembling the skin of a cantaloupe. Triton has a tenuous atmosphere of nitrogen with a trace of hydrocarbons and evidence of active geysers injecting material into it. At –390° F, the wintertime parts of Triton are the coldest regions yet found in the solar system.

Voyager 2 also confirmed the existence of 6 rings composed of very fine particles. There may be some clumpiness in the rings' structure. It is not known whether Neptune's satellites influence the formation or maintenance of the rings.

As with the other giant planets, Neptune is emitting more energy than it receives from the Sun. *Voyager* found the excess to be 2.7 times the solar contribution. Cooling from internal heat sources and from the heat of formation of the planets is thought to be responsible.

Pluto

Distance from Sun	
Perihelion	2,756.9 mil mi
Semi-major axis	39.482 AU
Aphelion	4,583.2 mil mi
Period of revolution around Sun	247.68 y
Orbital eccentricity	0.2488
Orbital inclination	17.16°
Synodic day (midday to midday)	6d 9h 17m (retrograde)
Sidereal day	6d 9h 18m (retrograde)
Rotational inclination	122.53°
Mass (Earth = 1)	0.0021
Mean radius	742.5 mi
Mean density (Earth = 1)	0.317
Natural satellites	1
Average surface temperature	–369°

Although Pluto on the average stays about 3.6 bil mi from the Sun and is currently the most distant planet, its orbit is very eccentric; it may get as close as 2.76 bil mi, and for about 20 years of its orbit, it is closer to the Sun than Neptune. Pluto takes 247.7 years to circumnavigate the Sun, a 3/2 resonance with Neptune.

About a century ago, a hypothetical planet was believed to lie beyond Neptune and Uranus because neither planet followed paths predicted by astronomers when all known gravitational influences were considered. In little more than a guess, a mass equal to Earth was assigned to the mysterious body, and mathematical searches were begun. Amid some controversy about the validity of the predictive process, Pluto was discovered nearly where it had been predicted to lie, by Clyde Tombaugh at the Lowell Observatory in Flagstaff, AZ, in 1930.

At the U.S. Naval Observatory in Flagstaff, in 1978, James Christy obtained a photograph of Pluto that was distinctly elongated. Repeated observations of this shape and its variation were convincing evidence of the discovery of a satellite of Pluto, now named Charon. Later observations showed its diameter to be 737 mi, just about half of Pluto's diameter of 1,485 mi. It orbits Pluto at a distance of 12,200 mi and takes 6.39 days to move around the planet. In this same length of time, Pluto and Charon both rotate once around their axes. The Pluto-Charon system thus appears to rotate as virtually a rigid body. This information allows the mass of Pluto to be calculated as 0.0021 of Earth. This mass makes its density about twice that of water. Theorists predict that Pluto has a rocky core, surrounded by a thick mantle of ice.

It is now clear that Pluto could not have influenced Neptune and Uranus to go astray. Besides being the smallest planet, Pluto is actually smaller than at least 7 of the solar system's moons, including Earth's moon. Although there may be additional solar system planets to be discovered and confirmed, astonomers no longer believe there are unexplained perturbations in the orbit of Uranus or Neptune that might be caused by another planet. Astronomers have found over 800 asteroid-size objects, somewhat beyond Pluto, in a region called the Kuiper Belt, where some comets are believed to originate.

Because the rotational axis of the system is tipped more than 120°, there is only an interval of a few years every 125 years when Pluto and Charon alternately eclipse each other. Both worlds are roughly spherical and have comparable densities. Large regions on Pluto are dark, others light; Pluto has spots and perhaps polar caps. Although extremely cold, Pluto appears to have a thin nitrogen–carbon dioxide–methane atmosphere, at least while it is closer to the Sun. When Pluto occulted a star, the star's light faded in such a way as to suggest it had passed through a haze layer lying above the planet's surface, indicating an inversion of temperatures and the possibility that Pluto has primitive weather.

A current controversy is the issue of Pluto's planet status. Pluto is clearly different from both the rocky terrestrial planets and the giant gaseous planets. Although many astronomers think it most closely resembles Kuiper Belt Objects (see Solar System Debris, page 343), and should be grouped with them, Pluto is still officially labeled a planet.

The Sun

The Sun has a mass and luminosity greater than that of 90% of the stars in our Milky Way galaxy. However, most of the stars that can be easily seen on a clear night are bigger and brighter than the Sun. It is the Sun's proximity to Earth that makes it appear tremendously large and bright. It is 400,000 times as bright as the full moon and gives Earth 6 mil times as much light as do all other stars put together. A series of nuclear fusion reactions, where hydrogen nuclei are converted to helium nuclei, powers the Sun and produces the heat and light that make life possible on Earth.

The Sun has a diameter of 865,000 mi and, on average, is 92,976,000 mi from Earth. It is 1.408 times as dense as water. The light of the Sun reaches Earth in 499 seconds, or in slightly more than 8 minutes. The average solar surface temperature has been measured at a value of 5,778 K, or about 9,941° F. The interior temperature of the Sun is theorized to be about 28,000,000° F.

When sunlight is analyzed with a spectroscope, it is found to consist of a continuous spectrum composed of all the colors of the rainbow in order, crossed by many dark lines. The dark "absorption lines" are produced by gaseous materials in the outer layers of the Sun. More than 60 of the natural terrestrial elements have been identified in the Sun, all in gaseous form because of the Sun's intense heat.

Spheres and Corona

The radiating surface of the Sun is called the **photosphere**; just above it is the **chromosphere**. The chromosphere is visible to the naked eye only at total solar eclipses, appearing then to be a pinkish-violet layer with occasional great prominences projecting above its general level. With proper instruments, the chromosphere can be seen or photographed whenever the Sun is visible without waiting for a total eclipse. Above the chromosphere is the **corona**, also visible to the naked eye only at times of total eclipse. Instruments also permit the brighter portions of the corona to be studied whenever conditions are favorable. The pearly light of the corona surges millions of miles from the Sun, where atoms of which it is composed are all in a state of extreme attenuation and high ionization that indicates temperatures nearly 2 mil° F.

Sunspots

Sunspots are dark, irregularly shaped regions whose diameters may reach tens of thousands of miles. There is an intimate connection between sunspots and the corona. At times of low sunspot activity, the fine streamers of the corona are longer above the Sun's equator than over the polar regions of the Sun; during periods of high sunspot activity, the corona extends fairly evenly outward from all regions of the Sun, but to a much greater distance in space. The average life of a sunspot group is 2 months, but some have lasted for more than a year.

Sunspots reach a low point, on average, every 11.3 years, with a peak of activity occurring irregularly between 2 successive minima. Launched in Dec. 1995, the SOHO spacecraft was designed to provide several years of study of the Sun from an orbit around it. The most recent solar maximum occurred in 2001; SOHO provided extraordinary views of the Sun's activity. The number of sunspots is now declining, heading towards solar minimum which should occur about 2006/2007.

Observations from SOHO show that magnetic arches, called **prominences**, extending tens of thousands of miles into the corona, may release enormous amounts of energy heating the corona. SOHO has also highlighted enormous releases of solar energy called **coronal mass ejections. Coronal holes** are regions where the corona appears dark in X rays. These are regions associated with open magnetic field lines, where the magnetic field lines project out into space instead of back towards the Sun, and it is in these regions where the high-speed solar wind originates. The solar wind carries the Sun's magnetic field, which is huge. In fact it is so large that it extends beyond the planets. This is called the **Interplanetary Magnetic Field** (IMF). Far past Pluto and the Kuiper Belt, the solar wind and the IMF lose their influence, and the boundary between them and interstellar space is called the **heliopause**.

The Moon

Distance from Earth	
Perigee	225,744 mi
Semi-major axis	238,855 mi
Apogee	251,966 mi
Period of revolution	27.322 d
Synodic orbital period (period of phases)	29.53 d
Orbital eccentricity	0.0549
Orbital inclination	5.145°
Sidereal day (rotation period	27.322 d
Rotational inclination	6.68°
Mass (Earth = 1)	0.0123
Mean radius	1,079 mi
Mean density (Earth = 1)	0.607
Average surface temperature	–100° F

The Moon completes a circuit around Earth in a period that averages 27 days, 7 hours, 43.2 minutes. This is the Moon's sidereal period. Because of the motion of the Moon in common with Earth around the Sun, the mean duration of the lunar month—the period from one New Moon to the next New Moon—is 29 days, 12 hours, 44.05 minutes. This is the Moon's synodic period.

The mean distance of the Moon from Earth is 238,855 mi. The orbit of the Moon about Earth is not circular but elliptical, and thus the actual distance varies considerably. The maximum distance from Earth that the Moon may reach is 251,966 mi and the least distance is 225,744 mi.

The Moon rotates on its axis in a period of time that is exactly equal to its sidereal revolution about Earth: 27.322 days. Thus the backside or farside of the Moon always faces away from Earth. But this does not mean that the backside is always dark. The farside of the Moon gets just as much direct sunlight as the nearside. At New Moon phase, the farside of the Moon is fully lit. With its long day and night, the daytime temperature can reach 260° F, while the coldest nighttime temperature may reach –280° F. This day-to-night contrast is exceeded only by that on Mercury.

The Moon's revolution about Earth is irregular because of its elliptical orbit. The Moon's rotation, however, is regular, and this, together with the irregular revolution, produces what is called "libration in longitude," which permits an observer on Earth to see first farther around the E side and then farther around the W side of the Moon. The Moon's variation N or S of the ecliptic permits one to see farther over first one pole and then the other of the Moon; this is called "libration in latitude." These two libration effects permit observers on Earth to see a total of about 60% of the Moon's surface over a period of time. The hidden side of the Moon was first photographed in 1959 by the Soviet space vehicle *Lunik III*. It has practically none of the large lava plains, called maria, so prominent on the nearside.

From 1969 through 1972, 6 American spacecraft brought 12 astronauts to walk on the surface of the Moon, and 3 additional missions either orbited or flew by the Moon. In 1998 NASA's *Lunar Prospector* spacecraft provided evidence for the presence of 300 mil metric tons of water ice at the lunar poles. *Lunar Prospector* results also indicate that the Moon has a small core, supporting the idea that most of the mass of the Moon was ripped away from the early Earth when a Mars-size object collided with Earth. *Smart-1*, which was launched in 2003 and entered lunar orbit late 2004, is the first spacecraft the European Space Agency (ESA) has sent to the Moon. The probe used solar electric primary propulsion, known also as ion engines, to reach the Moon and will carry out a complete program of scientific observations while in lunar orbit.

Tides on Earth are caused mainly by the Moon, because of its proximity to Earth. The ratio of the tide-raising power of the Moon to that of the Sun is 11 to 5.

Harvest Moon and Hunter's Moon

The Harvest Moon, the full Moon nearest the autumnal equinox, ushers in a period of several successive days when the Moon rises soon after sunset. This phenomenon gives farmers in temperate latitudes extra hours of light in which to harvest their crops before frost and winter. The 2006 Harvest Moon falls on Oct. 7 UTC. Harvest Moon in the southern hemisphere temperate latitudes falls on Mar. 14.

The next full Moon after Harvest Moon is called the Hunter's Moon; it is accompanied by a similar but less marked phenomenon. In 2006, the Hunter's Moon occurs on Nov. 5 in the northern hemisphere and on Apr. 13 in the southern hemisphere.

Moon's Perigee and Apogee, 2006

(Coordinated Universal Time, standard time of the prime meridian)

Perigee

Date	Hour	Date	Hour
Jan. 1	23	July 13	18
Jan. 30	8	Aug. 10	18
Feb. 27	20	Sept. 8	3
Mar. 28	7	Oct. 6	14
Apr. 25	11	Nov. 4	00
May 22	15	Dec. 2	00
June 16	17	Dec. 28	2

Apogee

Date	Hour	Date	Hour
Jan. 17	19	July 29	13
Feb. 14	1	Aug. 26	1
Mar. 13	2	Sept. 22	5
Apr. 9	13	Oct. 19	10
May 7	7	Nov. 15	23
June 4	2	Dec. 13	19
July 1	20		

Moon Phases, 2006

(Coordinated Universal Time, standard time of the prime meridian)

New Moon

Month	d	h	m
Jan.	29	14	15
Feb.	28	0	31
Mar.	29	10	15
Apr.	27	19	44
May	27	5	26
June	25	16	05
July	25	4	31
Aug.	23	19	10
Sept.	22	11	45
Oct.	22	5	14
Nov.	20	22	18
Dec.	20	14	01

Waxing Quarter

Month	d	h	m
Jan.	6	18	56
Feb.	5	6	29
Mar.	6	20	16
Apr.	5	12	01
May	5	5	13
June	3	23	06
July	3	16	37
Aug.	2	8	46
Aug.	31	22	56
Sept.	30	11	04
Oct.	29	21	25
Nov.	28	6	29
Dec.	27	14	48

Full Moon

Month	d	h	m
Jan.	14	9	48
Feb.	13	4	44
Mar.	14	23	35
Apr.	13	16	40
May	13	6	51
June	11	18	03
July	11	3	02
Aug.	9	10	54
Sept.	7	18	42
Oct.	7	3	13
Nov.	5	12	58
Dec.	5	0	25

Waning Quarter

Month	d	h	m
Jan.	22	15	14
Feb.	21	7	17
Mar.	22	19	10
Apr.	21	3	28
May	20	9	20
June	18	14	08
July	17	19	12
Aug.	16	1	51
Sept.	14	11	15
Oct.	14	0	26
Nov.	12	17	45
Dec.	12	14	32

Solar System Debris: Asteroids, Comets, Kuiper Belt, and the Oort Cloud

Asteroids

Besides planets, many smaller objects orbit the sun. **Asteroids** or minor planets are found mainly between the orbits of Mars and Jupiter, but some may be found outside this region. Though most are very small, the largest asteroid, Ceres, discovered in 1801, is 588 mi in diameter making it larger than 138 of the solar system's 154 known moons. It is smaller than any of the planets, but was initially assumed to be one. However, the next year Pallas was discovered, which led to a search for other such objects.

Some of these objects, or asteroids, are gravitationally locked with Jupiter and the Sun so that they have roughly the same orbit as Jupiter but either 60° ahead or behind the planet. These are the **Trojan asteroids.** Many of the smaller moons of the solar system, especially those in retrograde orbits, may be captured asteroids. Asteroids whose orbits either cross or come close to the Earth's orbit are labeled **Near Earth Asteroids** or NEAs. A handful of asteroids have actually been imaged by the Arecibo and Goldstone radio telescopes, and by the NEAR Shoemaker space probe, while the *Galileo* spacecraft imaged the asteroids Gaspra and Ida (including its moon Dactyl) on its way to Jupiter.

Comets

Comets are small icy bodies that orbit the Sun. When they approach the Sun, the energy from the Sun boils off material from the comet's icy nucleus, producing an enlarged head (or **coma**), and in many cases an extended tail. Because of the proximity to the Sun and the expanded head and tail, comets are brighter when near the Sun. For large comets, the head may be a 100,000 mi across and the tail more than a million mi long, though both are mainly empty space.

Comets have been known since ancient times; ultimately, British astronomer Edmund Halley (1656-1742) realized that a group of historical reports were just repeated visits of the same object. Comets are the only astronomical objects named after their discoverers. In 1986, the European spacecraft *Giotto* took the first close-up images of a comet's nucleus, specifically of Comet Halley, showing it had a peanut-shaped nucleus whose longest dimension was about 10 mi.

In 1995, Alan Hale and Thomas Bopp independently discovered a comet that was then beyond the orbit of Jupiter. It was the farthest comet ever discovered by amateurs and one of the brightest of all time. It also holds the record for length of naked-eye visibility—19 months—and is the most photographed comet in history.

In Sept. 2001, NASA's *Deep Space 1* flew within 1,500 mi of the Comet Borrelly and took pictures of the 6-mi-long nucleus of the comet. On Jan. 2, 2004, NASA's *Stardust* spacecraft flew within 150 mi of Comet Wild 2 taking pictures and capturing thousands of tiny cometary particles, which are scheduled to be returned to Earth in early 2006. NASA's *Deep Impact 2*, launched in Jan. 2005, was designed to observe and photograph Comet Tempel 1, and to release a probe intended to impact on the comet's surface. On July 3, 2005, *Deep Impact 2* released its camera-equipped, 816-pound, impact probe into the path of the comet, which 22 hours later slammed into the probe at a speed of nearly 23,000 mph on July 4 with a force roughly equal to 5 tons of TNT. The impact produced a huge flare that was observed by the *Deep Impact* flyby module, and by Earth-based and space-based observatories. Data was sent back by the probe for analysis. Based on the amount of material ejected into space during the impact, it was immediately evident that the comet surface was not as hard as had been thought. The Flyby part of the *Deep Impact 2* spacecraft remains intact and is scheduled to flyby Earth at the end of 2007 enroute to a possible future mission with another comet.

Kuiper Belt; Sedna; 2003 UB313

The **Kuiper Belt** is a donut-shaped region that extends from 30 to 100 AU from the Sun and is thought to be the source for short-period comets such as Comet Halley or Comet Swift-Tuttle. The more than 800 objects found in this region in recent years are called Kuiper Belt Objects (KBOs). It is estimated that there are more than 70,000 objects 60 mi in diameter or larger within the Kuiper Belt. A sub-group called Plutinos have physical and orbital characteristics similar to Pluto, except that they are smaller. Not including Pluto, which has a mean diameter of 1,491 mi, there are at least 7 KBOs larger than 500 mi in diameter.

In 2003 astronomers detected KBO 90 AU away at the time, possibly about 1,000 mi in diameter, with a highly elliptical orbit that can take it far beyond the Kuiper Belt, to about 880 AU from the Sun. It was named Sedna.

In 2005, astronomers announced the discovery of a Pluto-like KBO currently more than twice as far away from the Sun as Pluto and likely to be as large as or larger than Pluto. First photographed in 2003 and temporarily named 2003 UB313, it was discovered at its greatest distance from the Sun, 97 AU. In a mere 280 years (it takes 560 years to orbit) it will be at its closest, actually coming inside part of Pluto's orbit. There is a resemblance between Pluto, Neptune's large moon Triton, and this new object. Although its size is not well established, it may approach Triton's diameter of 1,690 mi. If Pluto continues to be labeled a planet, this object may deserve the same status.

Oort Cloud

The Oort Cloud is a vast spherical shell hypothesized to exist around the Sun. Astronomer Jan Oort proposed its existence as the origin for long-period comets that enter the inner part of the solar system where the planets orbit. As of yet, our technology is not sufficient to detect any members of the Oort Cloud, other than those comets that have been observed that indicate the most distant parts of their orbits may reach out to 50,000 AU. Recent examples of such long-period comets are Comet Hale-Bopp and Comet Hyakutake.

Searching for Planets

People have known of the existence of the 5 planets closest to the Sun since ancient times because they can be seen with the naked eye. However, the 3 farthest were discovered only since the invention of the telescope. The first, Uranus, was discovered in 1781 by the English astronomer William Herschel. Next, Neptune's existence and location were predicted through its action upon Uranus, by both John Couch Adams of England and Urbain Jean Joseph Le Verrier of France in 1845, leading to its discovery the following year. Finally, Pluto was discovered in 1930 by the American astronomer Clyde Tombaugh. Since then, many smaller objects have been found in the solar system, but none that are commonly classified as true planets.

During the last 10 years of the 20th century, astronomers began to detect the presence of planets orbiting stars other than the Sun. As of yet, They have not seen those objects, but merely inferred their existence by their effect on their parent star. The Sun is a typical star in many respects. With over 200 billion stars in the Milky Way, it seems plausible that many other stars might have planets.

Using the Doppler Effect to detect radial velocity changes in the motions of individual stars, astronomers are more likely to find high-mass planets in close and eccentric orbits around stars, because that situation produces larger and more noticeable changeseffects. As of mid-2005, astronomers had found 155 planets in 136 star systems where the planets are less than 13 times the mass of Jupiter (which is 318 times the mass of Earth). About 30 star systems may have planets less massive than Jupiter. In June 2005, astronomers reported detecting a planet that is only about 6 times the mass of the Earth, except t the planet orbits much closer to its parent star; Gliese 876 takes less than 2 days to complete one orbit.

In addition to the radial velocity method, astronomers are now using an optical gravitational lensing means of detecting extrasolar planets. Using this technique, Southern hemisphere astronomers found the most distant planet yet detected, about halfway to the center of our own Milky Way galaxy.

In 2005, astronomers obtained the first direct photograph of an extra-solar planet. The unnamed planet orbits a star called GQ Lupi, which is a star like our Sun but younger. The planet is about 100 AUs away from its star, and it is estimated to be about twice as massive as Jupiter.

Earth: Size, Computation of Time, Seasons

Distance from the Sun	
Perihelion	91.4 mil mi
Semi-major axis	1.0000 AU
Aphelion	94.5 mil mi
Period of revolution	365.256 d
Orbital eccentricity	0.0167
Orbital inclination	0.0°
Sidereal day (rotation period)	23h 56m 4.2s
Synodic day (midday to midday)	24h 0m 0s
Rotational inclination	23.45°
Mass (Earth = 1)	1.00
Mean radius	3,958.8 mi
Mean density (Earth = 1)	1.00
Natural satellites	1
Average surface temperature	59° F

Earth is the 5th-largest planet and the 3rd from the Sun. Its mass is 5.9736×10^{24} kg. Earth's equatorial diameter is 7,926 miles while its polar diameter is only 7,900 mi.

Size and Dimensions

Earth is considered a solid mass, yet it has a large, liquid iron, **magnetic core** with a radius of about 2,160 mi. Surprisingly, it has a solid **inner core** that may be a large iron crystal, with a radius of 760 mi. Around the core is a thick shell, or **mantle**, of dense rock. This mantle is composed of materials rich in iron and magnesium. It is somewhat plastic-like, and under slow steady pressure, it can flow like a liquid. The mantle, in turn, is covered by a thin **crust** forming the solid granite and basalt base of the continents and ocean basins. Over broad areas of Earth's surface, the crust has a thin cover of sedimentary rock such as sandstone, shale, and limestone formed by weathering and by deposits of sands, clays, and plant and animal remains.

The **temperature** inside the Earth increases about 1° F with every 100 to 200 feet in depth, in the upper 100 km of Earth, and reaches nearly 8,000-9,000° F at the center. The heat is believed to come from radioactivity in rocks, pressures within Earth, and the original heat of formation.

Atmosphere of Earth

Earth's atmosphere is a blanket composed of nitrogen, oxygen, and argon, in amounts of about 78%, 21%, and 1% by volume. Present in minute quantities are carbon dioxide, hydrogen, neon, helium, krypton, and xenon. Water vapor displaces other gases and varies from nearly zero to about 4% by volume. The atmosphere rests on Earth's surface with a weight equivalent to a layer of water 34 ft deep. For about 300,000 ft upward, the gases remain in the proportions stated. Gravity holds the gases to Earth. The weight of the air compresses it at the bottom so that the greatest density is at Earth's surface. Pressure and density decrease as height increases.

The lowest layer of the atmosphere extending up about 7.5 mi is the **troposphere**, which contains 90% of the air and the tallest mountains. This is also where most weather phenomena occur. The temperature drops with increasing height throughout this layer. The atmosphere for about 23 mi above the troposphere is the **stratosphere**, where the temperature generally increases with height. The stratosphere contains **ozone**, which prevents ultraviolet rays from reaching Earth's surface. Since there is very little convection in the stratosphere, jets regularly cruise in the lower parts to provide a smoother ride for passengers.

Above the stratosphere is the **mesosphere**, where the temperature again decreases with height for another 19 mi. Extending above the mesosphere to the outer fringes of the atmosphere is the **thermosphere**, a region where temperature once more increases with height to a value measured in thousands of degrees Fahrenheit. The lower portion of this region, extending from 50 to about 400 mi in altitude, is characterized by a high ion density and is thus called the **ionosphere**. Most meteors are in the lower thermosphere or the mesosphere at the time they are observed.

Longitude, Latitude

Position on the globe is measured by meridians and parallels. Meridians, which are imaginary lines drawn around Earth through the poles, determine **longitude**. The meridian running through Greenwich, England, is the **prime meridian** of longitude, and all others are either E or W. Parallels, which are imaginary circles parallel with the equator, determine **latitude**. The length of a degree of longitude varies as the cosine of the latitude. At the equator a degree of longitude is 69.171 statute mi; this is gradually reduced toward the poles. Value of a longitude degree at the poles is zero.

Latitude is reckoned by the number of degrees N or S of the **equator**, an imaginary circle on Earth's surface everywhere equidistant between the two poles. According to the International Astronomical Union, the length of a degree of latitude is 68.708 statute mi at the equator and varies slightly N and S because of the oblate form of the globe; at the poles it is 69.403 statute mi.

Definitions of Time

Earth rotates on its axis and follows an elliptical orbit around the Sun. The rotation makes the Sun appear to move across the sky from E to W. This rotation determines day and night, and the complete rotation, in relation to the Sun, is called the **apparent** or **true solar day**. A sundial thus measures **apparent solar time**. This length of time varies, but an average determines the mean solar day of 24 hours.

The mean solar day and **mean solar time** are in universal use for civil purposes. Mean solar time may be obtained from apparent solar time by correcting observations of the Sun for the **equation of time**. Mean solar time may be up to 16 minutes different from apparent solar time.

Sidereal time is the measure of time defined by the diurnal motion of the vernal equinox and is determined from observation of the meridian transits of stars. One complete rotation of Earth relative to the equinox is called the **sidereal day**. The **mean sidereal day** is 23 hours, 56 minutes, 4.091 seconds of mean solar time.

The interval required for Earth to make one absolute revolution around the Sun is a **sidereal** year; it consisted of 365 days, 6 hours, 9 minutes, and 9.5 seconds of mean solar time (approximately 24 hours per day) in 1900 and has been increasing at the rate of 0.0001 second annually.

The **tropical year**, upon which our calendar is based, is the interval between 2 consecutive returns of the Sun to the vernal equinox. The tropical year consisted of 365 days, 5 hours, 48 minutes, and 46 seconds in 1900. It has been decreasing at the rate of 0.530 second per century. The **calendar year** begins at 12 o'clock midnight precisely, local clock time, on the night of Dec. 31-Jan. 1. The day and the calendar month also begin at midnight by the clock.

On Jan. 1, 1972, the Bureau International des Poids et Mesures in Paris introduced **International Atomic Time** (TAI) as the most precisely determined time scale for astronomical usage. The fundamental unit of TAI in the international system of units is the second, defined as the duration of 9,192,631,770 periods of the radiation corresponding to the transition between 2 hyperfine levels of the ground state of the cesium 133 atom. **Coordinated Universal Time** (UTC), which serves as the basis for civil timekeeping and is the standard time of the prime meridian, is officially defined by a formula which relates UTC to mean sidereal time in Greenwich, England. (UTC has replaced GMT as the basis for standard time for the world.)

The Zones and Seasons

The 5 zones of Earth's surface are the Torrid, lying between the Tropics of Cancer and Capricorn; the N Temperate, between Cancer and the Arctic Circle; the S Temperate, between Capricorn and the Antarctic Circle; and the 2 Frigid Zones, between the Polar Circles and the Poles.

The inclination, or **tilt**, of Earth's axis, 23° 27′ away from a perpendicular to Earth's orbit of the Sun, determines the seasons. These are commonly marked in the N Temperate Zone, where spring begins at the vernal equinox, summer at the summer solstice, autumn at the autumnal equinox, and winter at the winter solstice. In the S Temperate Zone, the seasons are reversed. Spring begins at the autumnal equinox, summer at the winter solstice, etc.

The points at which the Sun crosses the equator are the **equinoxes**, when day and night are most nearly equal. The points at which the Sun is at a maximum distance from the equator are the **solstices**. Days and nights are then most unequal. However, at the equator, day and night are equal throughout the year.

In June, the North Pole is tilted 23° 27′ toward the Sun, and the days in the northern hemisphere are longer than the nights, while the days in the southern hemisphere are shorter than the nights. In Dec., the North Pole is tilted 23°27′ away from the Sun, and the situation is reversed.

The Seasons in 2006

In 2006 the 4 seasons begin in the northern hemisphere as shown. (Add 1 hour to Eastern Standard Time for Atlantic Time; subtract 1 hour for Central, 2 for Mountain, 3 for Pacific, 4 for Alaska, 5 for Hawaii-Aleutian. Also shown is Coordinated Universal Time.)

Seasons	Date	EST/EDT*	UTC
Vernal Equinox (spring)	Mar. 20	13:26	18:26
Northern Solstice (summer)	June 21	8:26	12:26
Autumnal Equinox (autumn)	Sept. 23	00:03*	4:03
Southern Solstice (winter)	Dec. 22	19:22	00:22

* Previous Day

Poles of Earth

The geographic (rotation) poles, or points where Earth's axis of rotation cuts the surface, are not absolutely fixed in the body of Earth. The pole of rotation describes an irregular curve about its mean position.

Two periods have been detected in this motion: (1) an annual period due to seasonal changes in barometric pressure, to load of ice and snow on the surface, and to other seasonal phenomena; (2) a period of about 14 months due to the shape and constitution of Earth. In addition, there are small but as yet unpredictable irregularities. The whole motion is so small that the actual pole at any time remains within a circle of 30 or 40 feet in radius centered at the mean position of the pole.

The pole of rotation for the time being is of course the pole having a latitude of 90° and an indeterminate longitude.

Magnetic Poles

Although Earth's magnetic field resembles that of an ordinary bar magnet, this magnetic field is probably produced by electric currents in the liquid currents of the Earth's outer core. The **north magnetic pole** of Earth is that region where the magnetic force is vertically downward, and the **south magnetic pole** is that region where the magnetic force is vertically upward. A compass placed at the magnetic poles experiences no directive force in azimuth (i.e., direction).

There are slow changes in the distribution of Earth's magnetic field. This slow temporal change is referred to as the secular change of the main magnetic field, and the magnetic poles shift due to this. The location of the N magnetic pole was first measured in 1831 at Cape Adelaide on the west coast of Boothia Peninsula in Canada's Northwest Territories (about latitude 70° N and longitude 96° W). Since then it has moved over 500 mi. It is now estimated to be at 82.7° N and 114.4°W, northwest of Ellef Ringnes Island in N Canada. Measurement for several decades by Canadian scientists indicates the motion of the pole has accelerated, now averaging about 25 mi per year.

The direction of the horizontal components of the magnetic field at any point is known as magnetic N at that point, and the angle by which it deviates E or W of true N is known as the magnetic declination.

A compass without error points in the direction of magnetic north. (In general, this is not the direction of the true rotational north pole.) If you follow the direction indicated by the N end of the compass, you will go along an irregular curve that eventually reaches the north magnetic pole (though not usually by a great-circle route). However, the action of the compass should not be thought of as due to any influence of the distant pole, but simply as an indication of the distribution of Earth's magnetism at the place of observation.

Rotation of Earth

The speed of rotation of Earth about its axis is slightly variable. The variations may be classified as:

(A) **Secular**. Tidal friction acts as a brake on the rotation and causes a slow secular increase in the length of the day, about 1 millisecond per century.

(B) **Irregular**. The speed of rotation may increase for a number of years, about 5 to 10, and then start decreasing. The maximum difference from the mean in the length of the day during a century is about 5 milliseconds. The accumulated difference in time has amounted to approximately 44 seconds since 1900. The cause is probably motion in the interior of Earth.

(C) **Periodic**. Seasonal variations exist with periods of 1 year and 6 months. The cumulative effect is such that each year, Earth is late about 30 milliseconds near June 1 and is ahead about 30 milliseconds near Oct. 1. The maximum seasonal variation in the length of the day is about 0.5 millisecond. It is believed that the principal cause of the annual variation is the seasonal change in the wind patterns of the northern and southern hemispheres. The semiannual variation is due chiefly to tidal action of the Sun, which distorts the shape of Earth slightly.

Calculation of Rise Times

The Daily Calendar on pages 347-58 contains rise and set times for the Sun and Moon for the Greenwich Meridian at N latitudes 20°, 30°, 40°, 50°, and 60°. From day to day, the values for the Sun at any particular latitude do not change very much. This means that whatever time the Sun rises or sets at the 0° meridian, it will rise or set at the same time at the Standard Time meridian of your time zone. Standard Time meridians occur every 15° of longitude (15° E and W, 30° E and W, etc.). The corrections necessary to observe that event from your location will be to account for your distance from the Standard Time meridian and for your latitude. Thus, if your latitude is about 45°, sunrise on Jan. 1, 2006, is roughly halfway between 7:22 and 7:59 A.M. on the Standard Time meridian for your time zone. If you are 7.5° west of your Standard Time meridian, sunrise will be about ½ hour later than this; if 7.5° east, about ½ hour earlier.

The Moon, however, moves its own diameter, about one-half degree, in an hour, or about 13.2° in one complete turn of Earth—one day. Most of this is eastward against the background stars of the sky, but some is also N or S movement. All this motion considerably affects the times of rise or set, as you can see from the adjacent entries in the table. Thus, it is necessary to take your longitude into account in addition to your latitude. If you have no need for total accuracy, simply note that the time will be between the 4 values (see example below) you find surrounding your location and the dates of interest.

The process of finding more accurate corrections is called interpolation. In the example, linear interpolation involving simple differences is used. In extreme cases, higher order interpolation should be used. If such cases are important to you, it is suggested that you plot the times, draw smooth curves through the plots, and interpolate by eye between the relevant curves. Some people find this exercise fun.

Let's find the times of the moonrise for the August Waxing Quarter Moon and sunset the same day at New Britain, CT.

First, where is New Britain, CT? Find New Britain's latitude and longitude in the the "Latitude, Longitude, and Altitude of U.S. and Canadian Cities" table on page 709. You must also know the time zone in which the city is located, which you can estimate from the "International Time Zones" map on page 480.

I. New Britain, CT: 41° 39′ 40″ N, 72° 46′ 48″ W

IA. Convert these values to decimals:
40/60 = 0.67
39 + 0.67 = 39.67
39.67/60 = 0.66
41 + 0.66 = 41.66 N
48/60 = 0.8
46 + 0.8 = 46.8
46.80/60 = 0.78
72 + 0.78 = 72.78 W

IB. Fraction New Britain lies between 40° and 50°:
41.66 - 40 = 1.66; 1.66/10 = 0.166

IC. Fraction world must turn between Greenwich and New Britain:
72.78/360 = 0.202

ID. New Britain is in the Eastern Standard Time zone and the EST meridian is 75°; thus 72.78 is 75 - 72.78 = 2.22° E of the Eastern Standard Meridian. In 24 hours, there are 24 x 60 = 1,440 minutes; 1,440/360 = 4 minutes for every degree around Earth. So events happen 4 x 2.22 = 8.9 minutes earlier in New Britain than at the 75° meridian. (If the location is W of the Standard Meridian, events happen later.)

IE. The values IB and IC are interpolates for New Britain; ID is the time correction from local to Standard time for New Britain. These values need never be calculated again for New Britain.

IIA. To find the time of moonrise we start from the table of Moon Phases, 2006 (p. 343). We see that August's first Waxing Quarter Moon occurs on August 2. We need the Greenwich times for moonset at latitudes 40° and 50°, and for August 2 and 3, the day of the Waxing Quarter Moon and the next day. These values are found in the Astronomy Daily Calendar 2006 (pp. 347-48); we then compute the difference between the two latitudes.

	20°	Diff.	30°
Aug. 2	12:58	0:31	13:29
Aug. 3	14:04	0:41	14:45

IIB. We want IB and the August 2 time difference:
0.166 x 31 = 5.1
Add this to the August 2, 40° rise time:
12:58 + 5.1 = 13:03.1
And for August 3:
0.166 x 41 = 6.8
Add this to the August 3, 40° rise time:
14:04 + 6.8 = 14:10.8
These 2 times are for the latitude of New Britain, but for the Greenwich meridian.

IIC. To get the time for New Britain meridian, take the difference between these 2 times just determined,
14:10.8 - 13:03.1 = 67.7 minutes,
and calculate what fraction of this 24-hour change took place while Earth turned between Greenwich and New Britain (See IC).
67.7 x 0.202 = 13.7 minutes after 13:03.1
Thus 13:03.1 + 13.7 = 13:16.8 is the time the Waxing Quarter Moon will rise in the local time of New Britain.

IID. But this happens 8.9 minutes (See ID) earlier by EST clock time at New Britain, thus
13:16.8 - 8.9 = 13:07.9 EST
But this is summer, and daylight time is in effect;
13:07.9 + 1:00 = 14:08 EDT is the rise time for the Waxing Quarter Moon at New Britain the afternoon of August 2, 2006.

IIIA. To find the time of sunset we need the Greenwich times for sunset at latitudes 40° and 50°. These values are found in the Astronomy Daily Calendar 2006; we then compute the difference between the two latitudes.

	20°	Diff.	30°
Aug. 2	19:13	0:28	19:41

IIIB. We want IB and the August 2 time difference:
0.166 x 28 = 4.6
Add this to the August 2, 40° set time:
19:13 + 4.6 = 19:17.6
This is the local time for the latitude of New Britain.

IIIC. But this happens 8.9 minutes (See ID) earlier by EST clock time at New Britain, thus
19:17.6 - 8.9 = 19:08.7
But daylight time is in effect;
19:09 + 1:00 = 20:09 is sunset at New Britain on August 2, 2006.

JANUARY 2006

1st Month **31 days**

Coordinated Universal Time (Greenwich Mean Time)

NOTE: For each day, numbers on first line indicate Sun; numbers on second line (except for Sun's distance) indicate Moon. Degrees are North Latitude.

Moon Phases: FM = Full Moon; LQ = Last (Waning) Quarter; NM = New Moon; FQ = First (Waxing) Quarter;
Sun's distance is in Astronomical Units

CAUTION: Must be converted to local time. For instructions see "Calculation of Rise Times," page 346.

Day of month, of week, of year	Sun on Meridian, Moon Phase h m s	Sun's Declination ° ′ Distance	20° Rise Sun Moon h m	20° Set Sun Moon h m	30° Rise Sun Moon h m	30° Set Sun Moon h m	40° Rise Sun Moon h m	40° Set Sun Moon h m	50° Rise Sun Moon h m	50° Set Sun Moon h m	60° Rise Sun Moon h m	60° Set Sun Moon h m
1 SU	12 03 33	– 23 02	6 35	17 32	6 56	17 11	7 22	16 45	7 59	16 09	9 02	15 05
1		.9834	7 59	19 09	8 24	18 46	8 55	18 16	9 40	17 34	10 48	14 15
2 MO	12 04 01	– 22 57	6 35	17 33	6 56	17 12	7 22	16 46	7 58	16 10	9 02	15 06
2		.9833	8 51	20 16	9 11	19 59	9 36	19 37	10 10	19 06	11 03	16 14
3 TU	12 04 29	– 22 51	6 36	17 33	6 56	17 13	7 22	16 47	7 58	16 11	9 01	15 08
3		.9833	9 38	21 20	9 51	21 09	10 08	20 55	10 32	20 36	11 07	18 13
4 WE	12 04 57	– 22 46	6 36	17 34	6 57	17 13	7 22	16 48	7 58	16 12	9 01	15 10
4		.9833	10 19	22 21	10 27	22 16	10 36	22 10	10 49	22 02	11 08	20 04
5 TH	12 05 24	– 22 39	6 36	17 35	6 57	17 14	7 22	16 49	7 58	16 13	9 00	15 11
5		.9833	10 57	23 19	10 58	23 20	11 00	23 22	11 03	23 25	11 08	21 49
6 FR	12 05 50	– 22 32	6 37	17 35	6 57	17 15	7 22	16 50	7 58	16 14	8 59	15 13
6	18 56 FQ	.9833	11 33	none	11 29	none	11 24	none	11 17	none	11 07	23 28
7 SA	12 06 16	– 22 25	6 37	17 36	6 57	17 16	7 22	16 51	7 57	16 16	8 58	15 15
7		.9833	12 10	0 16	12 00	0 24	11 48	0 33	11 31	0 46	11 06	none
8 SU	12 06 42	– 22 17	6 37	17 37	6 57	17 17	7 22	16 52	7 57	16 17	8 57	15 17
8		.9834	12 49	1 13	12 33	1 26	12 14	1 43	11 48	2 06	11 06	1 05
9 MO	12 07 07	– 22 09	6 37	17 37	6 57	17 17	7 22	16 53	7 56	16 18	8 56	15 19
9		.9834	13 31	2 11	13 10	2 29	12 44	2 53	12 08	3 26	11 06	2 44
10 TU	12 07 31	– 22 01	6 37	17 38	6 57	17 18	7 22	16 54	7 56	16 19	8 55	15 21
10		.9834	14 16	3 09	13 51	3 33	13 20	4 02	12 35	4 45	11 08	4 24
11 WE	12 07 55	– 21 52	6 37	17 38	6 57	17 19	7 21	16 55	7 55	16 21	8 54	15 23
11		.9834	15 06	4 08	14 38	4 35	14 03	5 09	13 12	5 59	11 12	6 06
12 TH	12 08 18	– 21 42	6 38	17 39	6 57	17 20	7 21	16 56	7 55	16 22	8 52	15 25
12		.9835	15 59	5 05	15 31	5 33	14 54	6 10	14 00	7 04	11 25	7 44
13 FR	12 08 41	– 21 32	6 38	17 40	6 57	17 21	7 21	16 57	7 54	16 24	8 51	15 27
13		.9835	16 54	5 59	16 27	6 26	15 52	7 02	15 00	7 55	12 00	9 04
14 SA	12 09 03	– 21 22	6 38	17 40	6 57	17 21	7 20	16 58	7 54	16 25	8 49	15 29
14	09 48 FM	.9836	17 50	6 48	17 26	7 13	16 54	7 46	16 09	8 32	13 10	9 46
15 SU	12 09 24	– 21 11	6 38	17 41	6 57	17 22	7 20	16 59	7 53	16 26	8 48	15 31
15		.9836	18 44	7 31	18 24	7 53	17 58	8 21	17 21	9 00	14 42	10 02
16 MO	12 09 45	– 21 00	6 38	17 42	6 57	17 23	7 20	17 00	7 52	16 28	8 46	15 34
16		.9837	19 36	8 10	19 20	8 28	19 01	8 50	18 33	9 20	16 16	10 07
17 TU	12 10 05	– 20 49	6 38	17 42	6 56	17 24	7 19	17 01	7 51	16 29	8 45	15 36
17		.9837	20 26	8 45	20 15	8 58	20 02	9 14	19 43	9 36	17 47	10 09
18 WE	12 10 24	– 20 37	6 38	17 43	6 56	17 25	7 19	17 02	7 50	16 31	8 43	15 38
18		.9838	21 15	9 18	21 09	9 26	21 02	9 36	20 52	9 49	19 14	10 10
19 TH	12 10 43	– 20 25	6 38	17 44	6 56	17 26	7 18	17 03	7 49	16 32	8 41	15 41
19		.9839	22 02	9 48	22 02	9 52	22 01	9 55	22 00	10 00	20 37	10 09
20 FR	12 11 01	– 20 12	6 38	17 44	6 56	17 27	7 18	17 05	7 48	16 34	8 39	15 43
20		.9840	22 50	10 19	22 55	10 17	23 01	10 14	23 09	10 11	21 59	10 08
21 SA	12 11 18	– 19 59	6 38	17 45	6 55	17 27	7 17	17 06	7 47	16 36	8 38	15 46
21		.9841	23 40	10 50	23 50	10 43	none	10 34	none	10 23	23 21	10 06
22 SU	12 11 34	– 19 45	6 38	17 46	6 55	17 28	7 17	17 07	7 46	16 37	8 36	15 48
22	15 14 LQ	.9842	none	11 23	none	11 11	0 02	10 56	0 19	10 36	none	10 05
23 MO	12 11 50	– 19 32	6 38	17 46	6 55	17 29	7 16	17 08	7 45	16 39	8 34	15 51
23		.9843	0 33	12 00	0 48	11 43	1 07	11 21	1 34	10 52	0 47	10 04
24 TU	12 12 04	– 19 18	6 37	17 47	6 54	17 30	7 15	17 09	7 44	16 40	8 32	15 53
24		.9844	1 29	12 42	1 49	12 20	2 15	11 53	2 52	11 13	2 18	10 03
25 WE	12 12 19	– 19 03	6 37	17 48	6 54	17 31	7 15	17 10	7 43	16 42	8 30	15 56
25		.9845	2 29	13 32	2 54	13 06	3 26	12 32	4 13	11 44	3 57	10 05
26 TH	12 12 32	– 18 48	6 37	17 48	6 54	17 32	7 14	17 12	7 42	16 44	8 28	15 58
26		.9846	3 33	14 29	4 01	14 01	4 37	13 24	5 31	12 29	5 44	10 10
27 FR	12 12 44	– 18 33	6 37	17 49	6 53	17 33	7 13	17 13	7 41	16 45	8 25	16 01
27		.9847	4 38	15 34	5 06	15 06	5 43	14 29	6 39	13 34	7 30	10 29
28 SA	12 12 56	– 18 17	6 37	17 49	6 53	17 34	7 12	17 14	7 39	16 47	8 23	16 03
28		.9848	5 40	16 43	6 06	16 18	6 41	15 45	7 30	14 57	8 43	11 30
29 SU	12 13 07	– 18 02	6 36	17 50	6 52	17 34	7 11	17 15	7 38	16 49	8 21	16 06
29	14 15 NM	.9850	6 36	17 53	6 59	17 33	7 27	17 07	8 07	16 30	9 09	13 21
30 MO	12 13 17	– 17 45	6 36	17 51	6 52	17 35	7 11	17 16	7 37	16 51	8 19	16 09
30		.9851	7 27	19 01	7 44	18 47	8 04	18 29	8 33	18 04	9 17	15 24
31 TU	12 13 26	– 17 29	6 36	17 51	6 51	17 36	7 10	17 18	7 35	16 52	8 17	16 11
31		.9852	8 12	20 06	8 22	19 58	8 35	19 49	8 52	19 36	9 19	17 23

FEBRUARY 2006

2nd Month **28 days**

Coordinated Universal Time (Greenwich Mean Time)

NOTE: For each day, numbers on first line indicate Sun; numbers on second line (except for Sun's distance) indicate Moon. Degrees are North Latitude.

Moon Phases: FM = Full Moon; LQ = Last (Waning) Quarter; NM = New Moon; FQ = First (Waxing) Quarter; Sun's distance is in Astronomical Units

CAUTION: Must be converted to local time. For instructions see "Calculation of Rise Times," page 346.

			20°		30°		40°		50°		60°	
Day of month, of week, of year	Sun on Meridian, Moon Phase h m s	Sun's Declination ° ′ Distance	Rise Sun Moon h m	Set Sun Moon h m	Rise Sun Moon h m	Set Sun Moon h m	Rise Sun Moon h m	Set Sun Moon h m	Rise Sun Moon h m	Set Sun Moon h m	Rise Sun Moon h m	Set Sun Moon h m
1 WE	12 13 35	– 17 12	6 36	17 52	6 50	17 37	7 09	17 19	7 34	16 54	8 14	16 14
32		.9854	8 52	21 07	8 56	21 06	9 01	21 05	9 08	21 04	9 19	19 15
2 TH	12 13 42	– 16 55	6 35	17 52	6 50	17 38	7 08	17 20	7 32	16 56	8 12	16 16
33		.9855	9 31	22 07	9 29	22 13	9 26	22 19	9 22	22 28	9 18	21 01
3 FR	12 13 49	– 16 38	6 35	17 53	6 49	17 39	7 07	17 21	7 31	16 57	8 09	16 19
34		.9856	10 09	23 06	10 00	23 17	9 50	23 32	9 37	23 52	9 17	22 43
4 SA	12 13 55	– 16 20	6 35	17 54	6 49	17 40	7 06	17 22	7 29	16 59	8 07	16 22
35		.9858	10 48	none	10 34	none	10 16	none	9 53	none	9 16	none
5 SU	12 14 00	– 16 02	6 34	17 54	6 48	17 40	7 05	17 24	7 28	17 01	8 05	16 24
36	06 29 FQ	.9859	11 29	0 05	11 10	0 22	10 46	0 44	10 12	1 14	9 16	0 24
6 MO	12 14 05	– 15 44	6 34	17 55	6 47	17 41	7 04	17 25	7 26	17 03	8 02	16 27
37		.9861	12 14	1 04	11 50	1 26	11 20	1 55	10 37	2 35	9 17	2 06
7 TU	12 14 08	– 15 25	6 33	17 55	6 47	17 42	7 03	17 26	7 25	17 04	8 00	16 30
38		.9862	13 02	2 03	12 35	2 29	12 01	3 02	11 10	3 52	9 20	3 50
8 WE	12 14 11	– 15 06	6 33	17 56	6 46	17 43	7 02	17 27	7 23	17 06	7 57	16 32
39		.9864	13 54	3 00	13 26	3 29	12 49	4 05	11 55	4 59	9 29	5 32
9 TH	12 14 13	– 14 47	6 32	17 56	6 45	17 44	7 00	17 28	7 21	17 08	7 54	16 35
40		.9866	14 49	3 55	14 21	4 23	13 45	5 00	12 52	5 54	9 54	6 59
10 FR	12 14 14	– 14 28	6 32	17 57	6 44	17 45	6 59	17 30	7 20	17 09	7 52	16 38
41		.9867	15 44	4 45	15 19	5 12	14 46	5 45	13 58	6 35	10 54	7 52
11 SA	12 14 14	– 14 08	6 31	17 57	6 43	17 45	6 58	17 31	7 18	17 11	7 49	16 40
42		.9869	16 39	5 30	16 17	5 53	15 49	6 23	15 09	7 04	12 22	8 12
12 SU	12 14 14	– 13 49	6 31	17 58	6 43	17 46	6 57	17 32	7 16	17 13	7 47	16 43
43		.9871	17 31	6 10	17 14	6 29	16 52	6 53	16 21	7 26	13 57	8 19
13 MO	12 14 12	– 13 29	6 30	17 58	6 42	17 47	6 56	17 33	7 15	17 15	7 44	16 45
44	04 44 FM	.9873	18 22	6 46	18 09	7 01	17 54	7 19	17 32	7 43	15 30	8 21
14 TU	12 14 10	– 13 08	6 30	17 59	6 41	17 48	6 54	17 34	7 13	17 16	7 41	16 48
45		.9875	19 11	7 19	19 03	7 29	18 54	7 41	18 42	7 57	16 58	8 22
15 WE	12 14 08	– 12 48	6 29	17 59	6 40	17 49	6 53	17 36	7 11	17 18	7 39	16 51
46		.9877	19 59	7 50	19 56	7 55	19 54	8 01	19 50	8 08	18 22	8 21
16 TH	12 14 04	– 12 27	6 29	18 00	6 39	17 49	6 52	17 37	7 09	17 20	7 36	16 53
47		.9879	20 46	8 21	20 49	8 20	20 53	8 20	20 58	8 19	19 44	8 20
17 FR	12 14 00	– 12 07	6 28	18 00	6 38	17 50	6 51	17 38	7 07	17 21	7 33	16 56
48		.9881	21 35	8 51	21 43	8 46	21 54	8 39	22 08	8 30	21 06	8 18
18 SA	12 13 55	– 11 46	6 28	18 01	6 37	17 51	6 49	17 39	7 05	17 23	7 30	16 59
49		.9883	22 26	9 23	22 39	9 12	22 56	9 00	23 20	8 42	22 30	8 16
19 SU	12 13 50	– 11 24	6 27	18 01	6 36	17 52	6 48	17 40	7 04	17 25	7 28	17 01
50		.9885	23 19	9 58	23 38	9 42	none	9 23	none	8 56	23 58	8 15
20 MO	12 13 44	– 11 03	6 26	18 01	6 35	17 52	6 47	17 41	7 02	17 27	7 25	17 04
51		.9887	none	10 37	none	10 16	0 02	9 51	0 35	9 15	none	8 14
21 TU	12 13 37	– 10 41	6 26	18 02	6 34	17 53	6 45	17 43	7 00	17 28	7 22	17 06
52	07 17 LQ	.9889	0 17	11 22	0 40	10 57	1 10	10 26	1 53	9 40	1 33	8 14
22 WE	12 13 30	– 10 20	6 25	18 02	6 34	17 54	6 44	17 44	6 58	17 30	7 19	17 09
53		.9892	1 17	12 14	1 44	11 46	2 19	11 10	3 11	10 17	3 14	8 16
23 TH	12 13 22	– 9 58	6 24	18 03	6 33	17 55	6 42	17 45	6 56	17 32	7 16	17 11
54		.9894	2 19	13 13	2 48	12 44	3 25	12 07	4 21	11 11	5 01	8 26
24 FR	12 13 13	– 9 36	6 24	18 03	6 31	17 55	6 41	17 46	6 54	17 33	7 13	17 14
55		.9896	3 21	14 19	3 49	13 51	4 25	13 16	5 19	12 23	6 32	9 01
25 SA	12 13 04	– 9 13	6 23	18 03	6 30	17 56	6 40	17 47	6 52	17 35	7 11	17 17
56		.9899	4 19	15 27	4 44	15 04	5 16	14 34	6 01	13 51	7 14	10 29
26 SU	12 12 54	– 8 51	6 22	18 04	6 29	17 57	6 38	17 48	6 50	17 37	7 08	17 19
57		.9901	5 12	16 36	5 32	16 18	5 57	15 56	6 32	15 24	7 27	12 28
27 MO	12 12 44	– 8 29	6 21	18 04	6 28	17 58	6 37	17 49	6 48	17 38	7 05	17 22
58		.9903	5 59	17 43	6 13	17 31	6 30	17 17	6 54	16 58	7 30	14 30
28 TU	12 12 33	– 8 06	6 21	18 05	6 27	17 58	6 35	17 50	6 46	17 40	7 02	17 24
59	00 31 NM	.9906	6 42	18 47	6 50	18 42	6 59	18 37	7 11	18 29	7 31	16 27

MARCH 2006

3rd Month **31 days**

Coordinated Universal Time (Greenwich Mean Time)

NOTE: For each day, numbers on first line indicate Sun; numbers on second line (except for Sun's distance) indicate Moon. Degrees are North Latitude.

Moon Phases: FM = Full Moon; LQ = Last (Waning) Quarter; NM = New Moon; FQ = First (Waxing) Quarter

Sun's distance is in Astronomical Units

CAUTION: Must be converted to local time. For instructions see "Calculation of Rise Times," page 346.

			20°		30°		40°		50°		60°	
Day of month, of week, of year	Sun on Meridian, Moon Phase h m s	Sun's Declination ° ′ Distance	Rise Sun Moon h m	Set Sun Moon h m	Rise Sun Moon h m	Set Sun Moon h m	Rise Sun Moon h m	Set Sun Moon h m	Rise Sun Moon h m	Set Sun Moon h m	Rise Sun Moon h m	Set Sun Moon h m
1 WE	12 12 22	− 7 43	6 20	18 05	6 26	17 59	6 34	17 52	6 44	17 42	6 59	17 27
60		.9908	7 23	19 49	7 24	19 51	7 25	19 54	7 26	19 58	7 30	18 17
2 TH	12 12 10	− 7 21	6 19	18 05	6 25	18 00	6 32	17 53	6 42	17 43	6 56	17 29
61		.9910	8 02	20 50	7 56	20 59	7 50	21 11	7 41	21 26	7 29	20 04
3 FR	12 11 57	− 6 58	6 18	18 06	6 24	18 00	6 31	17 54	6 40	17 45	6 53	17 32
62		.9913	8 42	21 52	8 30	22 07	8 16	22 26	7 57	22 52	7 28	21 50
4 SA	12 11 44	− 6 35	6 18	18 06	6 23	18 01	6 29	17 55	6 38	17 47	6 50	17 34
63		.9915	9 24	22 53	9 06	23 14	8 45	23 40	8 15	none	7 27	23 36
5 SU	12 11 31	− 6 11	6 17	18 06	6 22	18 02	6 28	17 56	6 36	17 48	6 47	17 37
64		.9918	10 08	23 54	9 46	none	9 18	none	8 38	0 17	7 27	none
6 MO	12 11 18	− 5 48	6 16	18 07	6 21	18 02	6 26	17 57	6 33	17 50	6 44	17 39
65	20 16 FQ	.9920	10 57	none	10 31	0 19	9 57	0 52	9 09	1 39	7 29	1 23
7 TU	12 11 03	− 5 25	6 15	18 07	6 20	18 03	6 25	17 58	6 31	17 52	6 41	17 42
66		.9923	11 49	0 54	11 21	1 22	10 44	1 58	9 50	2 51	7 34	3 11
8 WE	12 10 49	− 5 02	6 15	18 07	6 18	18 04	6 23	17 59	6 29	17 53	6 38	17 44
67		.9925	12 44	1 50	12 15	2 19	11 38	2 56	10 44	3 51	7 52	4 49
9 TH	12 10 34	− 4 38	6 14	18 08	6 17	18 04	6 22	18 00	6 27	17 55	6 35	17 47
68		.9928	13 39	2 42	13 12	3 10	12 38	3 45	11 48	4 36	8 39	5 55
10 FR	12 10 18	− 4 15	6 13	18 08	6 16	18 05	6 20	18 01	6 25	17 57	6 32	17 49
69		.9930	14 34	3 29	14 10	3 53	13 41	4 24	12 58	5 09	10 03	6 23
11 SA	12 10 03	− 3 51	6 12	18 08	6 15	18 06	6 18	18 02	6 23	17 58	6 29	17 52
70		.9933	15 27	4 10	15 08	4 31	14 44	4 57	14 10	5 33	11 38	6 31
12 SU	12 09 47	− 3 28	6 11	18 09	6 14	18 06	6 17	18 03	6 21	18 00	6 26	17 54
71		.9935	16 18	4 47	16 04	5 03	15 46	5 23	15 21	5 51	13 12	6 34
13 MO	12 09 30	− 3 04	6 10	18 09	6 13	18 07	6 15	18 04	6 19	18 01	6 23	17 57
72		.9938	17 07	5 21	16 58	5 32	16 47	5 46	16 31	6 05	14 41	6 35
14 TU	12 09 14	− 2 40	6 10	18 09	6 11	18 08	6 14	18 06	6 16	18 03	6 20	17 59
73	23 35 FM	.9941	17 55	5 53	17 51	5 59	17 47	6 07	17 40	6 17	16 07	6 34
15 WE	12 08 57	− 2 17	6 09	18 10	6 10	18 08	6 12	18 07	6 14	18 05	6 17	18 02
74		.9943	18 43	6 23	18 45	6 24	18 46	6 26	18 49	6 28	17 30	6 33
16 TH	12 08 40	− 1 53	6 08	18 10	6 09	18 09	6 10	18 08	6 12	18 06	6 14	18 04
75		.9946	19 32	6 54	19 38	6 50	19 47	6 45	19 58	6 39	18 52	6 31
17 FR	12 08 23	− 1 29	6 07	18 10	6 08	18 09	6 09	18 09	6 10	18 08	6 11	18 07
76		.9949	20 22	7 25	20 34	7 16	20 49	7 05	21 09	6 50	20 16	6 29
18 SA	12 08 05	− 1 06	6 06	18 10	6 07	18 10	6 07	18 10	6 08	18 09	6 08	18 09
77		.9952	21 15	7 59	21 32	7 45	21 53	7 27	22 24	7 04	21 43	6 27
19 SU	12 07 48	− 0 42	6 05	18 11	6 05	18 11	6 06	18 11	6 06	18 11	6 05	18 12
78		.9955	22 10	8 36	22 32	8 17	23 00	7 53	23 40	7 20	23 15	6 26
20 MO	12 07 30	− 0 18	6 04	18 11	6 04	18 11	6 04	18 12	6 03	18 13	6 02	18 14
79		.9957	23 09	9 19	23 35	8 55	none	8 25	none	7 43	none	6 25
21 TU	12 07 12	+ 0 05	6 03	18 11	6 03	18 12	6 02	18 13	6 01	18 14	5 59	18 16
80		.9960	none	10 07	none	9 40	0 08	9 06	0 58	8 15	0 54	6 27
22 WE	12 06 54	+ 0 29	6 03	18 12	6 02	18 12	6 01	18 14	5 59	18 16	5 56	18 19
81	19 10 LQ	.9963	0 09	11 03	0 38	10 34	1 15	9 56	2 10	9 01	2 38	6 32
23 TH	12 06 36	+ 0 53	6 02	18 12	6 01	18 13	5 59	18 15	5 57	18 17	5 53	18 21
82		.9966	1 09	12 04	1 38	11 35	2 15	10 59	3 11	10 04	4 17	6 53
24 FR	12 06 18	+ 1 17	6 01	18 12	5 59	18 14	5 57	18 16	5 55	18 19	5 50	18 24
83		.9969	2 07	13 09	2 34	12 43	3 08	12 11	3 57	11 23	5 17	7 58
25 SA	12 06 00	+ 1 40	6 00	18 12	5 58	18 14	5 56	18 17	5 52	18 21	5 47	18 26
84		.9972	3 00	14 15	3 23	13 54	3 51	13 28	4 31	12 51	5 36	9 46
26 SU	12 05 42	+ 2 04	5 59	18 13	5 57	18 15	5 54	18 18	5 50	18 22	5 44	18 29
85		.9975	3 48	15 21	4 05	15 06	4 26	14 48	4 55	14 22	5 42	11 44
27 MO	12 05 24	+ 2 27	5 58	18 13	5 56	18 16	5 53	18 19	5 48	18 24	5 41	18 31
86		.9978	4 32	16 25	4 43	16 17	4 56	16 07	5 14	15 53	5 43	13 40
28 TU	12 05 06	+ 2 51	5 57	18 13	5 55	18 16	5 51	18 20	5 46	18 25	5 38	18 34
87		.9980	5 13	17 27	5 17	17 26	5 23	17 24	5 30	17 22	5 42	15 31
29 WE	12 04 48	+ 3 14	5 56	18 13	5 53	18 17	5 49	18 21	5 44	18 27	5 35	18 36
88	10 15 NM	.9983	5 52	18 29	5 50	18 35	5 48	18 42	5 45	18 51	5 41	17 18
30 TH	12 04 30	+ 3 38	5 56	18 14	5 52	18 17	5 48	18 22	5 42	18 28	5 32	18 38
89		.9986	6 32	19 32	6 24	19 44	6 14	19 59	6 00	20 19	5 40	19 05
31 FR	12 04 12	+ 4 01	5 55	18 14	5 51	18 18	5 46	18 23	5 39	18 30	5 29	18 41
90		.9989	7 14	20 35	6 59	20 53	6 41	21 16	6 17	21 48	5 39	20 52

APRIL 2006

4th Month **30 days**

Coordinated Universal Time (Greenwich Mean Time)

NOTE: For each day, numbers on first line indicate Sun; numbers on second line (except for Sun's distance) indicate Moon. Degrees are North Latitude.

Moon Phases: FM = Full Moon; LQ = Last (Waning) Quarter; NM = New Moon; FQ = First (Waxing) Quarter

Sun's distance is in Astronomical Units

CAUTION: Must be converted to local time. For instructions see "Calculation of Rise Times," page 346.

Day of month, of week, of year	Sun on Meridian, Moon Phase h m s	Sun's Declination ° ′ Distance	20° Rise Sun Moon h m	20° Set Sun Moon h m	30° Rise Sun Moon h m	30° Set Sun Moon h m	40° Rise Sun Moon h m	40° Set Sun Moon h m	50° Rise Sun Moon h m	50° Set Sun Moon h m	60° Rise Sun Moon h m	60° Set Sun Moon h m
1 SA	12 03 54	+ 4 24	5 54	18 14	5 50	18 19	5 44	18 24	5 37	18 32	5 26	18 43
91		.9992	7 58	21 38	7 38	22 02	7 13	22 31	6 38	23 14	5 39	22 42
2 SU	12 03 36	+ 4 47	5 53	18 15	5 49	18 19	5 43	18 25	5 35	18 33	5 23	18 46
92		.9995	8 47	22 41	8 22	23 08	7 51	23 43	7 06	none	5 39	none
3 MO	12 03 19	+ 5 10	5 52	18 15	5 47	18 20	5 41	18 26	5 33	18 35	5 20	18 48
93		.9997	9 39	23 41	9 11	none	8 36	none	7 43	0 34	5 43	0 34
4 TU	12 03 01	+ 5 33	5 51	18 15	5 46	18 20	5 40	18 27	5 31	18 36	5 17	18 51
94		1.0000	10 35	none	10 06	0 09	9 29	0 46	8 33	1 41	5 54	2 22
5 WE	12 02 44	+ 5 56	5 50	18 15	5 45	18 21	5 38	18 28	5 29	18 38	5 14	18 53
95	12 01 FQ	1.0003	11 31	0 36	11 03	1 04	10 28	1 40	9 35	2 33	6 28	3 47
6 TH	12 02 27	+ 6 19	5 50	18 16	5 44	18 22	5 37	18 29	5 27	18 39	5 11	18 56
96		1.0006	12 27	1 25	12 02	1 51	11 31	2 24	10 45	3 11	7 42	4 28
7 FR	12 02 10	+ 6 42	5 49	18 16	5 43	18 22	5 35	18 30	5 24	18 41	5 08	18 58
97		1.0009	13 21	2 09	13 00	2 31	12 34	2 59	11 57	3 38	9 16	4 42
8 SA	12 01 53	+ 7 04	5 48	18 16	5 41	18 23	5 33	18 31	5 22	18 43	5 05	19 00
98		1.0012	14 13	2 47	13 57	3 05	13 37	3 27	13 09	3 58	10 52	4 46
9 SU	12 01 37	+ 7 27	5 47	18 16	5 40	18 23	5 32	18 32	5 20	18 44	5 02	19 03
99		1.0014	15 03	3 22	14 52	3 35	14 38	3 51	14 20	4 13	12 23	4 47
10 MO	12 01 20	+ 7 49	5 46	18 17	5 39	18 24	5 30	18 33	5 18	18 46	4 59	19 05
100		1.0017	15 51	3 54	15 45	4 02	15 38	4 12	15 29	4 25	13 50	4 47
11 TU	12 01 04	+ 8 11	5 45	18 17	5 38	18 25	5 29	18 34	5 16	18 47	4 56	19 08
101		1.0020	16 39	4 25	16 39	4 28	16 38	4 32	16 37	4 37	15 14	4 46
12 WE	12 00 49	+ 8 33	5 45	18 17	5 37	18 25	5 27	18 35	5 14	18 49	4 53	19 10
102		1.0023	17 28	4 55	17 32	4 53	17 38	4 51	17 46	4 47	16 36	4 44
13 TH	12 00 33	+ 8 55	5 44	18 18	5 36	18 26	5 26	18 36	5 12	18 50	4 50	19 13
103	16 40 FM	1.0026	18 18	5 27	18 28	5 19	18 40	5 11	18 58	4 59	17 59	4 42
14 FR	12 00 18	+ 9 17	5 43	18 18	5 35	18 26	5 24	18 37	5 10	18 52	4 47	19 15
104		1.0028	19 10	6 00	19 25	5 48	19 45	5 32	20 12	5 12	19 26	4 40
15 SA	12 00 03	+ 9 38	5 42	18 18	5 34	18 27	5 23	18 38	5 08	18 53	4 44	19 18
105		1.0031	20 05	6 36	20 26	6 19	20 52	5 57	21 29	5 27	20 57	4 39
16 SU	11 59 49	+ 10 00	5 41	18 18	5 32	18 28	5 21	18 39	5 06	18 55	4 41	19 20
106		1.0034	21 03	7 18	21 28	6 55	22 00	6 28	22 47	5 48	22 35	4 38
17 MO	11 59 35	+ 10 21	5 41	18 19	5 31	18 28	5 20	18 40	5 04	18 57	4 38	19 23
107		1.0037	22 03	8 05	22 31	7 38	23 07	7 05	none	6 17	none	4 39
18 TU	11 59 21	+ 10 42	5 40	18 19	5 30	18 29	5 18	18 41	5 02	18 58	4 35	19 25
108		1.0040	23 04	8 58	23 32	8 29	none	7 53	0 01	6 58	0 18	4 43
19 WE	11 59 08	+ 11 03	5 39	18 19	5 29	18 30	5 17	18 42	5 00	19 00	4 32	19 28
109		1.0043	none	9 57	none	9 28	0 10	8 51	1 06	7 55	2 00	4 58
20 TH	11 58 55	+ 11 24	5 38	18 20	5 28	18 30	5 15	18 43	4 58	19 01	4 29	19 30
110		1.0045	0 01	10 59	0 29	10 33	1 04	9 59	1 56	9 08	3 15	5 46
21 FR	11 58 43	+ 11 44	5 38	18 20	5 27	18 31	5 14	18 44	4 56	19 03	4 27	19 33
111	03 28 LQ	1.0048	0 54	12 04	1 18	11 41	1 49	11 13	2 32	10 31	3 43	7 22
22 SA	11 58 31	+ 12 05	5 37	18 20	5 26	18 31	5 12	18 45	4 54	19 04	4 24	19 35
112		1.0051	1 43	13 07	2 02	12 50	2 26	12 29	2 59	11 59	3 52	9 15
23 SU	11 58 20	+ 12 25	5 36	18 21	5 25	18 32	5 11	18 46	4 52	19 06	4 21	19 37
113		1.0054	2 26	14 10	2 40	13 59	2 56	13 45	3 19	13 27	3 54	11 08
24 MO	11 58 09	+ 12 45	5 36	18 21	5 24	18 33	5 10	18 47	4 50	19 08	4 18	19 40
114		1.0056	3 07	15 11	3 14	15 06	3 23	15 01	3 35	14 53	3 54	12 56
25 TU	11 57 58	+ 13 04	5 35	18 21	5 23	18 33	5 08	18 48	4 48	19 09	4 15	19 42
115		1.0059	3 45	16 11	3 47	16 13	3 48	16 16	3 50	16 19	3 53	14 41
26 WE	11 57 48	+ 13 24	5 34	18 22	5 22	18 34	5 07	18 49	4 46	19 11	4 12	19 45
116		1.0062	4 24	17 12	4 19	17 21	4 12	17 32	4 04	17 46	3 52	16 25
27 TH	11 57 39	+ 13 43	5 34	18 22	5 21	18 35	5 06	18 50	4 44	19 12	4 10	19 47
117	19 44 NM	1.0065	5 04	18 14	4 53	18 29	4 39	18 48	4 20	19 14	3 51	18 10
28 FR	11 57 30	+ 14 02	5 33	18 22	5 20	18 35	5 04	18 51	4 42	19 14	4 07	19 50
118		1.0067	5 47	19 18	5 30	19 39	5 08	20 05	4 39	20 43	3 51	19 58
29 SA	11 57 21	+ 14 21	5 32	18 23	5 19	18 36	5 03	18 52	4 40	19 15	4 04	19 52
119		1.0070	6 34	20 22	6 12	20 48	5 43	21 20	5 03	22 08	3 51	21 49
30 SU	11 57 14	+ 14 40	5 32	18 23	5 18	18 37	5 02	18 53	4 39	19 17	4 01	19 55
120		1.0072	7 26	21 25	6 59	21 53	6 26	22 29	5 36	23 23	3 53	23 41

MAY 2006

5th Month **31 days**

Coordinated Universal Time (Greenwich Mean Time)

NOTE: For each day, numbers on first line indicate Sun; numbers on second line (except for Sun's distance) indicate Moon. Degrees are North Latitude.

Moon Phases: FM = Full Moon; LQ = Last (Waning) Quarter; NM = New Moon; FQ = First (Waxing) Quarter

Sun's distance is in Astronomical Units

CAUTION: Must be converted to local time. For instructions see "Calculation of Rise Times," page 346.

Day of month, of week, of year	Sun on Meridian, Moon Phase h m s	Sun's Declination ° ′ Distance	20° Rise Sun Moon h m	20° Set Sun Moon h m	30° Rise Sun Moon h m	30° Set Sun Moon h m	40° Rise Sun Moon h m	40° Set Sun Moon h m	50° Rise Sun Moon h m	50° Set Sun Moon h m	60° Rise Sun Moon h m	60° Set Sun Moon h m
1 MO	11 57 06	+ 14 58	5 31	18 23	5 17	18 37	5 00	18 54	4 37	19 18	3 59	19 57
121		1.0075	8 21	22 24	7 53	22 52	7 16	23 29	6 22	none	4 00	none
2 TU	11 56 59	+ 15 16	5 30	18 24	5 17	18 38	4 59	18 55	4 35	19 20	3 56	20 00
122		1.0077	9 19	23 17	8 51	23 44	8 14	none	7 20	0 24	4 22	1 22
3 WE	11 56 53	+ 15 34	5 30	18 24	5 16	18 38	4 58	18 56	4 33	19 21	3 53	20 02
123		1.0080	10 16	none	9 50	none	9 17	0 18	8 29	1 08	5 20	2 24
4 TH	11 56 47	+ 15 52	5 29	18 25	5 15	18 39	4 57	18 57	4 32	19 23	3 50	20 05
124		1.0082	11 12	0 04	10 50	0 27	10 22	0 57	9 41	1 39	6 50	2 48
5 FR	11 56 42	+ 16 09	5 29	18 25	5 14	18 40	4 56	18 58	4 30	19 24	3 48	20 07
125	05 13 FQ	1.0085	12 05	0 45	11 48	1 04	11 26	1 28	10 54	2 02	8 28	2 56
6 SA	11 56 37	+ 16 26	5 28	18 25	5 13	18 40	4 54	18 59	4 28	19 26	3 45	20 10
126		1.0087	12 56	1 21	12 43	1 36	12 28	1 54	12 06	2 19	10 02	2 58
7 SU	11 56 33	+ 16 43	5 28	18 26	5 12	18 41	4 53	19 00	4 27	19 27	3 43	20 12
127		1.0089	13 45	1 54	13 37	2 04	13 28	2 16	13 15	2 33	11 30	2 58
8 MO	11 56 29	+ 17 00	5 27	18 26	5 12	18 42	4 52	19 01	4 25	19 29	3 40	20 15
128		1.0092	14 33	2 25	14 31	2 30	14 28	2 36	14 24	2 44	12 55	2 57
9 TU	11 56 26	+ 17 16	5 27	18 26	5 11	18 42	4 51	19 02	4 23	19 30	3 37	20 17
129		1.0094	15 21	2 56	15 24	2 56	15 27	2 55	15 32	2 55	14 17	2 56
10 WE	11 56 24	+ 17 32	5 26	18 27	5 10	18 43	4 50	19 03	4 22	19 32	3 35	20 20
130		1.0096	16 11	3 27	16 19	3 21	16 29	3 15	16 43	3 06	15 40	2 55
11 TH	11 56 22	+ 17 47	5 26	18 27	5 09	18 44	4 49	19 04	4 20	19 33	3 32	20 22
131		1.0099	17 02	3 59	17 16	3 49	17 32	3 36	17 56	3 19	17 05	2 53
12 FR	11 56 20	+ 18 03	5 25	18 28	5 09	18 44	4 48	19 05	4 19	19 35	3 30	20 24
132		1.0101	17 57	4 35	18 16	4 19	18 39	4 00	19 13	3 33	18 34	2 52
13 SA	11 56 20	+ 18 18	5 25	18 28	5 08	18 45	4 47	19 06	4 17	19 36	3 28	20 27
133	06 51 FM	1.0103	18 55	5 15	19 18	4 54	19 48	4 28	20 32	3 53	20 10	2 51
14 SU	11 56 19	+ 18 33	5 24	18 28	5 07	18 46	4 46	19 07	4 16	19 38	3 25	20 29
134		1.0105	19 56	6 00	20 23	5 36	20 57	5 04	21 49	4 19	21 53	2 51
15 MO	11 56 20	+ 18 47	5 24	18 29	5 07	18 46	4 45	19 08	4 14	19 39	3 23	20 31
135		1.0108	20 57	6 52	21 26	6 25	22 03	5 49	22 58	4 56	23 38	2 55
16 TU	11 56 20	+ 19 01	5 24	18 29	5 06	18 47	4 44	19 09	4 13	19 41	3 21	20 34
136		1.0110	21 56	7 51	22 24	7 22	23 00	6 45	23 54	5 49	none	3 06
17 WE	11 56 22	+ 19 15	5 23	18 30	5 06	18 48	4 43	19 10	4 12	19 42	3 18	20 36
137		1.0112	22 51	8 53	23 16	8 26	23 48	7 51	none	6 58	1 06	3 42
18 TH	11 56 24	+ 19 28	5 23	18 30	5 05	18 48	4 42	19 11	4 10	19 43	3 16	20 38
138		1.0114	23 41	9 57	none	9 34	none	9 03	0 34	8 19	1 47	5 06
19 FR	11 56 27	+ 19 41	5 23	18 30	5 04	18 49	4 42	19 12	4 09	19 45	3 14	20 41
139		1.0116	none	11 01	0 01	10 42	0 27	10 19	1 03	9 45	2 00	6 56
20 SA	11 56 30	+ 19 54	5 22	18 31	5 04	18 49	4 41	19 13	4 08	19 46	3 12	20 43
140	09 20 LQ	1.0118	0 25	12 02	0 40	11 50	0 59	11 34	1 24	11 12	2 04	8 48
21 SU	11 56 34	+ 20 07	5 22	18 31	5 03	18 50	4 40	19 14	4 07	19 47	3 10	20 45
141		1.0120	1 05	13 02	1 15	12 56	1 26	12 47	1 41	12 36	2 05	10 36
22 MO	11 56 38	+ 20 19	5 22	18 32	5 03	18 51	4 39	19 15	4 06	19 49	3 07	20 47
142		1.0122	1 44	14 01	1 47	14 01	1 51	14 00	1 56	14 00	2 05	12 19
23 TU	11 56 43	+ 20 31	5 22	18 32	5 02	18 51	4 38	19 15	4 04	19 50	3 05	20 50
143		1.0124	2 21	14 59	2 18	15 06	2 14	15 13	2 10	15 24	2 04	13 59
24 WE	11 56 48	+ 20 42	5 21	18 33	5 02	18 52	4 38	19 16	4 03	19 51	3 03	20 52
144		1.0126	2 59	15 59	2 50	16 12	2 39	16 27	2 25	16 49	2 03	15 40
25 TH	11 56 54	+ 20 53	5 21	18 33	5 02	18 52	4 37	19 17	4 02	19 52	3 02	20 54
145		1.0128	3 40	17 01	3 25	17 19	3 07	17 42	2 42	18 15	2 02	17 23
26 FR	11 57 00	+ 21 04	5 21	18 33	5 01	18 53	4 36	19 18	4 01	19 53	3 00	20 56
146		1.0130	4 24	18 04	4 04	18 28	3 38	18 58	3 03	19 41	2 02	19 10
27 SA	11 57 07	+ 21 14	5 21	18 34	5 01	18 54	4 36	19 19	4 00	19 55	2 58	20 58
147	05 26 NM	1.0132	5 13	19 08	4 48	19 35	4 17	20 09	3 32	21 01	2 04	21 01
28 SU	11 57 15	+ 21 24	5 21	18 34	5 01	18 54	4 35	19 20	3 59	19 56	2 56	21 00
148		1.0133	6 07	20 09	5 39	20 37	5 04	21 14	4 12	22 09	2 09	22 48
29 MO	11 57 22	+ 21 34	5 20	18 35	5 00	18 55	4 35	19 20	3 58	19 57	2 54	21 02
149		1.0135	7 05	21 05	6 36	21 33	6 00	22 08	5 05	23 01	2 23	none
30 TU	11 57 31	+ 21 43	5 20	18 35	5 00	18 55	4 34	19 21	3 58	19 58	2 53	21 04
150		1.0137	8 03	21 55	7 36	22 21	7 02	22 52	6 10	23 38	3 03	0 10
31 WE	11 57 39	+ 21 52	5 20	18 35	5 00	18 56	4 34	19 22	3 57	19 59	2 51	21 05
151		1.0138	9 01	22 39	8 37	23 01	8 07	23 27	7 23	none	4 23	0 49

JUNE 2006

6th Month **30 days**

Coordinated Universal Time (Greenwich Mean Time)

NOTE: For each day, numbers on first line indicate Sun; numbers on second line (except for Sun's distance) indicate Moon. Degrees are North Latitude.

Moon Phases: FM = Full Moon; LQ = Last (Waning) Quarter; NM = New Moon; FQ = First (Waxing) Quarter

Sun's distance is in Astronomical Units

CAUTION: Must be converted to local time. For instructions see "Calculation of Rise Times," page 346.

Day of month, of week, of year	Sun on Meridian, Moon Phase h m s	Sun's Declination ° ′ Distance	20° Rise Sun Moon h m	20° Set Sun Moon h m	30° Rise Sun Moon h m	30° Set Sun Moon h m	40° Rise Sun Moon h m	40° Set Sun Moon h m	50° Rise Sun Moon h m	50° Set Sun Moon h m	60° Rise Sun Moon h m	60° Set Sun Moon h m
1 TH	11 57 48	+ 22 00	5 20	18 36	4 59	18 56	4 33	19 23	3 56	20 00	2 50	21 07
152		1.0140	9 56	23 18	9 36	23 35	9 12	23 55	8 37	0 04	6 00	1 02
2 FR	11 57 58	+ 22 09	5 20	18 36	4 59	18 57	4 33	19 23	3 55	20 01	2 48	21 09
153		1.0141	10 48	23 53	10 33	none	10 15	none	9 50	0 23	7 37	1 07
3 SA	11 58 08	+ 22 16	5 20	18 36	4 59	18 57	4 33	19 24	3 55	20 02	2 47	21 11
154	23 06 FQ	1.0143	11 38	none	11 28	0 04	11 16	0 19	11 00	0 38	9 08	1 08
4 SU	11 58 18	+ 22 24	5 20	18 37	4 59	18 58	4 32	19 25	3 54	20 03	2 45	21 12
155		1.0144	12 26	0 25	12 22	0 31	12 16	0 40	12 09	0 51	10 35	1 08
5 MO	11 58 28	+ 22 30	5 20	18 37	4 59	18 58	4 32	19 25	3 53	20 04	2 44	21 14
156		1.0146	13 14	0 55	13 14	0 57	13 15	0 59	13 17	1 02	11 57	1 07
6 TU	11 58 39	+ 22 37	5 20	18 38	4 59	18 59	4 32	19 26	3 53	20 05	2 43	21 15
157		1.0147	14 02	1 26	14 08	1 22	14 16	1 18	14 26	1 13	13 19	1 06
7 WE	11 58 50	+ 22 43	5 20	18 38	4 58	18 59	4 31	19 27	3 52	20 06	2 42	21 17
158		1.0148	14 52	1 57	15 04	1 49	15 18	1 38	15 37	1 25	14 42	1 04
8 TH	11 59 01	+ 22 49	5 20	18 38	4 58	19 00	4 31	19 27	3 52	20 06	2 41	21 18
159		1.0149	15 46	2 31	16 02	2 18	16 23	2 01	16 53	1 38	16 09	1 03
9 FR	11 59 13	+ 22 54	5 20	18 39	4 58	19 00	4 31	19 28	3 52	20 07	2 40	21 19
160		1.0151	16 43	3 09	17 04	2 51	17 32	2 28	18 11	1 55	17 42	1 02
10 SA	11 59 24	+ 22 59	5 20	18 39	4 58	19 01	4 31	19 28	3 51	20 08	2 39	21 20
161		1.0152	17 43	3 53	18 09	3 30	18 42	3 00	19 30	2 19	19 22	1 02
11 SU	11 59 36	+ 23 04	5 20	18 39	4 58	19 01	4 31	19 29	3 51	20 09	2 38	21 21
162	18 03 FM	1.0153	18 45	4 43	19 13	4 16	19 50	3 42	20 44	2 52	21 08	1 04
12 MO	11 59 49	+ 23 08	5 20	18 40	4 58	19 01	4 31	19 29	3 51	20 09	2 38	21 22
163		1.0154	19 47	5 40	20 15	5 11	20 52	4 35	21 46	3 40	22 47	1 12
13 TU	12 00 01	+ 23 11	5 20	18 40	4 58	19 02	4 31	19 30	3 51	20 10	2 37	21 23
164		1.0155	20 45	6 43	21 11	6 15	21 44	5 39	22 33	4 45	23 47	1 37
14 WE	12 00 14	+ 23 15	5 20	18 40	4 58	19 02	4 31	19 30	3 50	20 10	2 37	21 24
165		1.0156	21 37	7 48	21 59	7 23	22 27	6 51	23 06	6 04	none	2 45
15 TH	12 00 26	+ 23 18	5 20	18 41	4 58	19 02	4 31	19 30	3 50	20 11	2 36	21 25
166		1.0157	22 24	8 53	22 40	8 33	23 01	8 08	23 30	7 31	0 07	4 32
16 FR	12 00 39	+ 23 20	5 21	18 41	4 59	19 03	4 31	19 31	3 50	20 11	2 36	21 26
167		1.0158	23 06	9 56	23 16	9 42	23 30	9 24	23 48	8 59	0 14	6 27
17 SA	12 00 52	+ 23 22	5 21	18 41	4 59	19 03	4 31	19 31	3 50	20 12	2 36	21 26
168		1.0159	23 44	10 57	23 49	10 49	23 55	10 39	none	10 25	0 16	8 18
18 SU	12 01 05	+ 23 24	5 21	18 41	4 59	19 03	4 31	19 31	3 50	20 12	2 36	21 27
169	14 08 LQ	1.0160	none	11 56	none	11 54	none	11 51	0 03	11 48	0 16	10 03
19 MO	12 01 18	+ 23 25	5 21	18 42	4 59	19 04	4 31	19 32	3 50	20 12	2 36	21 27
170		1.0161	0 21	12 53	0 20	12 58	0 19	13 03	0 17	13 11	0 15	11 43
20 TU	12 01 31	+ 23 26	5 21	18 42	4 59	19 04	4 31	19 32	3 50	20 13	2 36	21 28
171		1.0162	0 59	13 52	0 51	14 02	0 43	14 15	0 31	14 33	0 14	13 22
21 WE	12 01 44	+ 23 26	5 21	18 42	4 59	19 04	4 31	19 32	3 51	20 13	2 36	21 28
172		1.0162	1 37	14 51	1 24	15 08	1 08	15 28	0 47	15 57	0 13	15 02
22 TH	12 01 58	+ 23 26	5 22	18 42	5 00	19 04	4 31	19 32	3 51	20 13	2 36	21 28
173		1.0163	2 19	15 53	2 01	16 14	1 38	16 42	1 06	17 21	0 13	16 45
23 FR	12 02 11	+ 23 26	5 22	18 42	5 00	19 04	4 32	19 33	3 51	20 13	2 36	21 28
174		1.0164	3 06	16 55	2 42	17 21	2 13	17 54	1 31	18 42	0 14	18 32
24 SA	12 02 24	+ 23 25	5 22	18 43	5 00	19 05	4 32	19 33	3 51	20 13	2 37	21 28
175		1.0164	3 57	17 56	3 30	18 25	2 56	19 01	2 06	19 55	0 17	20 20
25 SU	12 02 37	+ 23 24	5 22	18 43	5 00	19 05	4 32	19 33	3 52	20 13	2 37	21 28
176	16 05 NM	1.0165	4 53	18 54	4 24	19 23	3 48	19 59	2 54	20 52	0 27	21 53
26 MO	12 02 49	+ 23 22	5 23	18 43	5 01	19 05	4 33	19 33	3 52	20 13	2 38	21 28
177		1.0165	5 51	19 47	5 23	20 13	4 47	20 46	3 54	21 35	0 54	22 48
27 TU	12 03 02	+ 23 20	5 23	18 43	5 01	19 05	4 33	19 33	3 53	20 13	2 38	21 27
178		1.0166	6 49	20 33	6 24	20 56	5 52	21 25	5 05	22 05	2 00	23 08
28 WE	12 03 14	+ 23 18	5 23	18 43	5 01	19 05	4 33	19 33	3 53	20 13	2 39	21 27
179		1.0166	7 45	21 14	7 24	21 33	6 58	21 55	6 19	22 27	3 33	23 16
29 TH	12 03 27	+ 23 15	5 24	18 43	5 02	19 05	4 34	19 33	3 54	20 13	2 40	21 26
180		1.0166	8 39	21 51	8 23	22 04	8 02	22 21	7 33	22 43	5 11	23 18
30 FR	12 03 39	+ 23 12	5 24	18 43	5 02	19 05	4 34	19 33	3 54	20 13	2 41	21 26
181		1.0167	9 30	22 24	9 19	22 32	9 05	22 43	8 45	22 57	6 45	23 19

JULY 2006

7th Month **31 days**

Coordinated Universal Time (Greenwich Mean Time)

NOTE: For each day, numbers on first line indicate Sun; numbers on second line (except for Sun's distance) indicate Moon. Degrees are North Latitude.

Moon Phases: FM = Full Moon; LQ = Last (Waning) Quarter; NM = New Moon; FQ = First (Waxing) Quarter

Sun's distance is in Astronomical Units

CAUTION: Must be converted to local time. For instructions see "Calculation of Rise Times," page 346.

Day of month, of week, of year	Sun on Meridian, Moon Phase h m s	Sun's Decli-nation ° ′ Distance	20° Rise Sun Moon h m	20° Set Sun Moon h m	30° Rise Sun Moon h m	30° Set Sun Moon h m	40° Rise Sun Moon h m	40° Set Sun Moon h m	50° Rise Sun Moon h m	50° Set Sun Moon h m	60° Rise Sun Moon h m	60° Set Sun Moon h m
1 SA	12 03 50	+ 23 08	5 24	18 43	5 02	19 05	4 35	19 33	3 55	20 12	2 42	21 25
182		1.0167	10 19	22 54	10 13	22 58	10 05	23 02	9 54	23 08	8 14	23 18
2 SU	12 04 02	+ 23 04	5 24	18 44	5 03	19 05	4 35	19 33	3 56	20 12	2 43	21 24
183		1.0167	11 06	23 25	11 05	23 23	11 04	23 21	11 02	23 19	9 38	23 17
3 MO	12 04 13	+ 22 59	5 25	18 44	5 03	19 05	4 36	19 32	3 56	20 12	2 44	21 23
184	16 37 FQ	1.0167	11 54	23 55	11 58	23 49	12 03	23 41	12 10	23 30	11 00	23 15
4 TU	12 04 24	+ 22 54	5 25	18 44	5 04	19 05	4 36	19 32	3 57	20 11	2 45	21 22
185		1.0167	12 43	none	12 52	none	13 04	none	13 20	23 43	12 21	23 14
5 WE	12 04 34	+ 22 49	5 25	18 44	5 04	19 05	4 37	19 32	3 58	20 11	2 47	21 21
186		1.0167	13 34	0 28	13 49	0 16	14 07	0 02	14 32	23 58	13 45	23 13
6 TH	12 04 45	+ 22 43	5 26	18 44	5 05	19 05	4 37	19 32	3 59	20 10	2 48	21 20
187		1.0167	14 29	1 03	14 48	0 47	15 13	0 26	15 48	none	15 14	23 12
7 FR	12 04 54	+ 22 37	5 26	18 44	5 05	19 05	4 38	19 31	3 59	20 10	2 50	21 19
188		1.0167	15 27	1 44	15 51	1 23	16 22	0 56	17 07	0 18	16 50	23 13
8 SA	12 05 04	+ 22 31	5 26	18 44	5 05	19 04	4 39	19 31	4 00	20 09	2 51	21 18
189		1.0167	16 29	2 31	16 56	2 05	17 31	1 33	18 24	0 46	18 33	23 18
9 SU	12 05 13	+ 22 24	5 27	18 43	5 06	19 04	4 39	19 31	4 01	20 09	2 53	21 17
190		1.0166	17 31	3 25	18 00	2 57	18 37	2 21	19 32	1 27	20 18	23 32
10 MO	12 05 21	+ 22 17	5 27	18 43	5 06	19 04	4 40	19 30	4 02	20 08	2 54	21 15
191		1.0166	18 32	4 26	18 59	3 57	19 34	3 21	20 26	2 25	21 39	none
11 TU	12 05 29	+ 22 09	5 28	18 43	5 07	19 04	4 41	19 30	4 03	20 07	2 56	21 14
192	03 02 FM	1.0166	19 28	5 32	19 52	5 05	20 22	4 31	21 05	3 41	22 12	0 19
12 WE	12 05 37	+ 22 01	5 28	18 43	5 07	19 04	4 41	19 29	4 04	20 07	2 58	21 12
193		1.0166	20 18	6 39	20 37	6 17	21 00	5 49	21 32	5 08	22 23	1 56
13 TH	12 05 44	+ 21 53	5 28	18 43	5 08	19 03	4 42	19 29	4 05	20 06	2 59	21 11
194		1.0165	21 03	7 45	21 16	7 29	21 31	7 08	21 53	6 39	22 26	3 53
14 FR	12 05 51	+ 21 44	5 29	18 43	5 08	19 03	4 43	19 28	4 06	20 05	3 01	21 09
195		1.0165	21 43	8 48	21 50	8 38	21 58	8 26	22 09	8 08	22 26	5 50
15 SA	12 05 57	+ 21 35	5 29	18 43	5 09	19 03	4 44	19 28	4 07	20 04	3 03	21 07
196		1.0165	22 22	9 49	22 22	9 45	22 23	9 41	22 24	9 34	22 26	7 40
16 SU	12 06 03	+ 21 25	5 29	18 43	5 10	19 02	4 44	19 27	4 08	20 03	3 05	21 06
197		1.0164	22 59	10 48	22 54	10 51	22 47	10 54	22 38	10 59	22 25	9 24
17 MO	12 06 08	+ 21 15	5 30	18 42	5 10	19 02	4 45	19 27	4 10	20 02	3 07	21 04
198	19 12 LQ	1.0164	23 38	11 47	23 26	11 56	23 12	12 07	22 53	12 22	22 24	11 05
18 TU	12 06 13	+ 21 05	5 30	18 42	5 11	19 02	4 46	19 26	4 11	20 01	3 09	21 02
199		1.0163	none	12 46	none	13 01	23 40	13 20	23 11	13 46	22 24	12 46
19 WE	12 06 17	+ 20 55	5 31	18 42	5 11	19 01	4 47	19 25	4 12	20 00	3 11	21 00
200		1.0163	0 18	13 47	0 01	14 07	none	14 33	23 34	15 09	22 24	14 28
20 TH	12 06 21	+ 20 44	5 31	18 42	5 12	19 01	4 48	19 25	4 13	19 59	3 13	20 58
201		1.0162	1 03	14 48	0 41	15 13	0 13	15 44	none	16 31	22 26	16 14
21 FR	12 06 24	+ 20 32	5 31	18 41	5 12	19 00	4 48	19 24	4 14	19 58	3 15	20 56
202		1.0161	1 52	15 49	1 26	16 16	0 53	16 52	0 05	17 45	22 33	18 01
22 SA	12 06 27	+ 20 21	5 32	18 41	5 13	19 00	4 49	19 23	4 16	19 57	3 18	20 54
203		1.0161	2 45	16 47	2 17	17 16	1 41	17 52	0 47	18 47	22 52	19 39
23 SU	12 06 29	+ 20 09	5 32	18 41	5 14	18 59	4 50	19 22	4 17	19 55	3 20	20 52
204		1.0160	3 42	17 41	3 14	18 08	2 37	18 43	1 43	19 33	23 43	20 48
24 MO	12 06 30	+ 19 56	5 32	18 40	5 14	18 59	4 51	19 22	4 18	19 54	3 22	20 50
205		1.0159	4 40	18 29	4 14	18 53	3 40	19 23	2 50	20 07	none	21 16
25 TU	12 06 31	+ 19 44	5 33	18 40	5 15	18 58	4 52	19 21	4 19	19 53	3 24	20 47
206	04 31 NM	1.0158	5 37	19 12	5 14	19 31	4 45	19 56	4 04	20 31	1 09	21 26
26 WE	12 06 32	+ 19 31	5 33	18 40	5 15	18 57	4 53	19 20	4 21	19 51	3 26	20 45
207		1.0157	6 31	19 49	6 13	20 04	5 50	20 23	5 18	20 49	2 47	21 29
27 TH	12 06 31	+ 19 18	5 34	18 39	5 16	18 57	4 54	19 19	4 22	19 50	3 29	20 43
208		1.0156	7 23	20 23	7 10	20 34	6 54	20 46	6 31	21 03	4 23	21 30
28 FR	12 06 30	+ 19 04	5 34	18 39	5 16	18 56	4 54	19 18	4 23	19 49	3 31	20 40
209		1.0155	8 13	20 55	8 05	21 00	7 55	21 06	7 41	21 15	5 54	21 29
29 SA	12 06 29	+ 18 50	5 34	18 38	5 17	18 56	4 55	19 17	4 25	19 47	3 33	20 38
210		1.0154	9 01	21 25	8 58	21 25	8 54	21 26	8 49	21 26	7 20	21 28
30 SU	12 06 27	+ 18 36	5 35	18 38	5 18	18 55	4 56	19 16	4 26	19 46	3 36	20 36
211		1.0153	9 48	21 55	9 50	21 50	9 53	21 44	9 57	21 37	8 42	21 27
31 MO	12 06 24	+ 18 21	5 35	18 38	5 18	18 54	4 57	19 15	4 28	19 44	3 38	20 33
212		1.0152	10 36	22 26	10 43	22 16	10 53	22 05	11 05	21 48	10 03	21 25

AUGUST 2006

8th Month **31 days**

Coordinated Universal Time (Greenwich Mean Time)

NOTE: For each day, numbers on first line indicate Sun; numbers on second line (except for Sun's distance) indicate Moon. Degrees are North Latitude.

Moon Phases: FM = Full Moon; LQ = Last (Waning) Quarter; NM = New Moon; FQ = First (Waxing) Quarter

Sun's distance is in Astronomical Units

CAUTION: Must be converted to local time. For instructions see "Calculation of Rise Times," page 346.

Day of month, of week, of year	Sun on Meridian, Moon Phase h m s	Sun's Declination ° ′ Distance	20° Rise Sun Moon h m	20° Set Sun Moon h m	30° Rise Sun Moon h m	30° Set Sun Moon h m	40° Rise Sun Moon h m	40° Set Sun Moon h m	50° Rise Sun Moon h m	50° Set Sun Moon h m	60° Rise Sun Moon h m	60° Set Sun Moon h m
1 TU	12 06 20	+ 18 06	5 35	18 37	5 19	18 53	4 58	19 14	4 29	19 43	3 40	20 31
213		1.0150	11 25	23 00	11 38	22 45	11 54	22 27	12 16	22 02	11 25	21 23
2 WE	12 06 16	+ 17 51	5 36	18 37	5 19	18 53	4 59	19 13	4 30	19 41	3 43	20 28
214	08 46 FQ	1.0149	12 18	23 37	12 35	23 18	12 58	22 53	13 29	22 19	12 51	21 22
3 TH	12 06 12	+ 17 36	5 36	18 36	5 20	18 52	5 00	19 12	4 32	19 40	3 45	20 26
215		1.0148	13 13	none	13 36	23 56	14 04	23 26	14 45	22 43	14 23	21 22
4 FR	12 06 06	+ 17 20	5 36	18 36	5 21	18 51	5 01	19 11	4 33	19 38	3 47	20 23
216		1.0146	14 12	0 20	14 38	none	15 12	none	16 02	23 17	16 01	21 24
5 SA	12 06 01	+ 17 04	5 37	18 35	5 21	18 50	5 02	19 10	4 35	19 36	3 50	20 21
217		1.0145	15 13	1 10	15 42	0 43	16 19	0 08	17 14	none	17 45	21 32
6 SU	12 05 54	+ 16 48	5 37	18 34	5 22	18 50	5 03	19 08	4 36	19 35	3 52	20 18
218		1.0143	16 14	2 07	16 43	1 38	17 20	1 01	18 14	0 06	19 21	21 58
7 MO	12 05 47	+ 16 31	5 37	18 34	5 22	18 49	5 04	19 07	4 38	19 33	3 54	20 15
219		1.0142	17 13	3 11	17 39	2 43	18 12	2 07	19 00	1 13	20 15	23 13
8 TU	12 05 39	+ 16 14	5 38	18 33	5 23	18 48	5 05	19 06	4 39	19 31	3 57	20 13
220		1.0140	18 06	4 18	18 28	3 53	18 54	3 22	19 32	2 36	20 32	none
9 WE	12 05 31	+ 15 57	5 38	18 33	5 24	18 47	5 06	19 05	4 40	19 30	3 59	20 10
221	10 54 FM	1.0139	18 54	5 26	19 10	5 06	19 29	4 42	19 56	4 07	20 37	1 06
10 TH	12 05 22	+ 15 40	5 38	18 32	5 24	18 46	5 07	19 04	4 42	19 28	4 02	20 07
222		1.0137	19 38	6 32	19 47	6 19	19 58	6 02	20 14	5 40	20 38	3 06
11 FR	12 05 13	+ 15 22	5 39	18 31	5 25	18 45	5 08	19 02	4 43	19 26	4 04	20 05
223		1.0135	20 18	7 35	20 21	7 29	20 24	7 21	20 29	7 10	20 38	5 02
12 SA	12 05 03	+ 15 05	5 39	18 31	5 25	18 44	5 08	19 01	4 45	19 24	4 06	20 02
224		1.0134	20 57	8 37	20 53	8 37	20 49	8 38	20 44	8 38	20 37	6 53
13 SU	12 04 52	+ 14 47	5 39	18 30	5 26	18 43	5 09	19 00	4 46	19 22	4 09	19 59
225		1.0132	21 36	9 38	21 26	9 45	21 14	9 53	20 59	10 05	20 36	8 39
14 MO	12 04 41	+ 14 28	5 40	18 29	5 27	18 42	5 10	18 58	4 48	19 21	4 11	19 56
226		1.0130	22 17	10 39	22 01	10 52	21 42	11 08	21 16	11 31	20 35	10 23
15 TU	12 04 30	+ 14 10	5 40	18 29	5 27	18 41	5 11	18 57	4 49	19 19	4 14	19 54
227		1.0129	23 01	11 40	22 40	11 59	22 14	12 23	21 37	12 57	20 35	12 07
16 WE	12 04 17	+ 13 51	5 40	18 28	5 28	18 40	5 12	18 56	4 51	19 17	4 16	19 51
228	01 51 LQ	1.0127	23 49	12 42	23 24	13 06	22 52	13 36	22 06	14 20	20 36	13 55
17 TH	12 04 05	+ 13 32	5 41	18 27	5 28	18 39	5 13	18 54	4 52	19 15	4 19	19 48
229		1.0125	none	13 43	none	14 11	23 37	14 46	22 44	15 38	20 40	15 43
18 FR	12 03 52	+ 13 13	5 41	18 27	5 29	18 38	5 14	18 53	4 54	19 13	4 21	19 45
230		1.0123	0 41	14 42	0 13	15 11	none	15 48	23 36	16 43	20 53	17 28
19 SA	12 03 38	+ 12 53	5 41	18 26	5 30	18 37	5 15	18 51	4 55	19 11	4 23	19 42
231		1.0121	1 37	15 37	1 08	16 05	0 31	16 41	none	17 34	21 31	18 48
20 SU	12 03 24	+ 12 34	5 41	18 25	5 30	18 36	5 16	18 50	4 57	19 09	4 26	19 39
232		1.0120	2 34	16 27	2 07	16 52	1 32	17 24	0 40	18 10	22 50	19 25
21 MO	12 03 10	+ 12 14	5 42	18 24	5 31	18 35	5 17	18 49	4 58	19 07	4 28	19 37
233		1.0118	3 31	17 11	3 07	17 32	2 36	17 59	1 51	18 36	none	19 37
22 TU	12 02 54	+ 11 54	5 42	18 24	5 31	18 34	5 18	18 47	5 00	19 05	4 31	19 34
234		1.0116	4 26	17 49	4 06	18 06	3 41	18 27	3 06	18 56	0 27	19 41
23 WE	12 02 39	+ 11 34	5 42	18 23	5 32	18 33	5 19	18 46	5 01	19 03	4 33	19 31
235	19 10 NM	1.0113	5 18	18 24	5 03	18 36	4 45	18 51	4 19	19 11	2 04	19 42
24 TH	12 02 23	+ 11 13	5 42	18 22	5 32	18 32	5 20	18 44	5 03	19 01	4 35	19 28
236		1.0111	6 08	18 56	5 58	19 03	5 46	19 12	5 30	19 23	3 36	19 42
25 FR	12 02 07	+ 10 53	5 43	18 21	5 33	18 31	5 21	18 43	5 04	18 59	4 38	19 25
237		1.0109	6 57	19 27	6 52	19 29	6 46	19 31	6 38	19 34	5 03	19 40
26 SA	12 01 50	+ 10 32	5 43	18 20	5 34	18 30	5 22	18 41	5 06	18 57	4 40	19 22
238		1.0107	7 44	19 57	7 45	19 54	7 45	19 50	7 46	19 45	6 26	19 39
27 SU	12 01 33	+ 10 11	5 43	18 20	5 34	18 29	5 23	18 40	5 07	18 55	4 43	19 19
239		1.0105	8 32	20 27	8 37	20 19	8 44	20 09	8 54	19 56	7 48	19 37
28 MO	12 01 16	+ 9 50	5 43	18 19	5 35	18 27	5 24	18 38	5 09	18 53	4 45	19 16
240		1.0103	9 20	20 59	9 31	20 46	9 45	20 30	10 03	20 08	9 09	19 35
29 TU	12 00 58	+ 9 29	5 44	18 18	5 35	18 26	5 25	18 37	5 10	18 51	4 47	19 13
241		1.0100	10 11	21 35	10 27	21 17	10 47	20 55	11 15	20 24	10 33	19 34
30 WE	12 00 40	+ 9 08	5 44	18 17	5 36	18 25	5 26	18 35	5 12	18 49	4 50	19 10
242		1.0098	11 04	22 15	11 25	21 52	11 51	21 24	12 29	20 44	12 02	19 33
31 TH	12 00 21	+ 8 46	5 44	18 16	5 36	18 24	5 27	18 33	5 13	18 47	4 52	19 07
243	22 56 FQ	1.0095	12 00	23 01	12 25	22 34	12 57	22 01	13 44	21 12	13 36	19 34

SEPTEMBER 2006

9th Month **30 days**

Coordinated Universal Time (Greenwich Mean Time)

NOTE: For each day, numbers on first line indicate Sun; numbers on second line (except for Sun's distance) indicate Moon. Degrees are North Latitude.

Moon Phases: FM = Full Moon; LQ = Last (Waning) Quarter; NM = New Moon; FQ = First (Waxing) Quarter

Sun's distance is in Astronomical Units

CAUTION: Must be converted to local time. For instructions see "Calculation of Rise Times," page 346.

Day of month, of week, of year	Sun on Meridian, Moon Phase h m s	Sun's Declination ° ′ Distance	20° Rise Sun Moon h m	20° Set Sun Moon h m	30° Rise Sun Moon h m	30° Set Sun Moon h m	40° Rise Sun Moon h m	40° Set Sun Moon h m	50° Rise Sun Moon h m	50° Set Sun Moon h m	60° Rise Sun Moon h m	60° Set Sun Moon h m
1 FR	12 00 02	+ 8 24	5 44	18 15	5 37	18 23	5 27	18 32	5 15	18 44	4 54	19 04
244		1.0093	12 59	23 53	13 27	23 24	14 03	22 48	14 57	21 53	15 17	19 38
2 SA	11 59 43	+ 8 03	5 45	18 15	5 37	18 22	5 28	18 30	5 16	18 42	4 57	19 01
245		1.0091	13 59	none	14 28	none	15 05	23 46	16 01	22 50	16 57	19 52
3 SU	11 59 24	+ 7 41	5 45	18 14	5 38	18 20	5 29	18 29	5 18	18 40	4 59	18 58
246		1.0088	14 57	0 52	15 25	0 23	16 00	none	16 52	none	18 11	20 40
4 MO	11 59 04	+ 7 19	5 45	18 13	5 38	18 19	5 30	18 27	5 19	18 38	5 01	18 55
247		1.0086	15 52	1 56	16 16	1 29	16 46	0 55	17 29	0 05	18 39	22 19
5 TU	11 58 44	+ 6 57	5 45	18 12	5 39	18 18	5 31	18 26	5 21	18 36	5 04	18 52
248		1.0083	16 42	3 02	17 00	2 40	17 24	2 12	17 56	1 31	18 48	none
6 WE	11 58 23	+ 6 34	5 45	18 11	5 40	18 17	5 32	18 24	5 22	18 34	5 06	18 49
249		1.0081	17 27	4 09	17 40	3 53	17 55	3 32	18 17	3 03	18 50	0 16
7 TH	11 58 03	+ 6 12	5 46	18 10	5 40	18 16	5 33	18 22	5 24	18 32	5 09	18 46
250	18 42 FM	1.0078	18 09	5 14	18 15	5 04	18 23	4 52	18 33	4 35	18 50	2 14
8 FR	11 57 42	+ 5 50	5 46	18 09	5 41	18 14	5 34	18 21	5 25	18 29	5 11	18 43
251		1.0076	18 49	6 18	18 49	6 15	18 49	6 11	18 48	6 06	18 49	4 08
9 SA	11 57 22	+ 5 27	5 46	18 08	5 41	18 13	5 35	18 19	5 27	18 27	5 13	18 40
252		1.0073	19 30	7 21	19 23	7 25	19 14	7 29	19 03	7 35	18 48	5 57
10 SU	11 57 00	+ 5 04	5 46	18 07	5 42	18 12	5 36	18 17	5 28	18 25	5 16	18 37
253		1.0071	20 11	8 24	19 58	8 34	19 42	8 47	19 20	9 05	18 47	7 45
11 MO	11 56 39	+ 4 42	5 46	18 07	5 42	18 11	5 37	18 16	5 30	18 23	5 18	18 34
254		1.0068	20 55	9 27	20 36	9 44	20 13	10 05	19 40	10 34	18 46	9 33
12 TU	11 56 18	+ 4 19	5 47	18 06	5 43	18 09	5 38	18 14	5 31	18 21	5 20	18 31
255		1.0065	21 43	10 31	21 19	10 53	20 49	11 22	20 06	12 02	18 46	11 24
13 WE	11 55 57	+ 3 56	5 47	18 05	5 43	18 08	5 39	18 12	5 32	18 18	5 23	18 28
256		1.0063	22 35	11 35	22 08	12 01	21 33	12 35	20 42	13 25	18 49	13 16
14 TH	11 55 36	+ 3 33	5 47	18 04	5 44	18 07	5 40	18 11	5 34	18 16	5 25	18 25
257	11 15 LQ	1.0060	23 31	12 36	23 02	13 05	22 25	13 42	21 30	14 37	18 58	15 07
15 FR	11 55 14	+ 3 10	5 47	18 03	5 44	18 06	5 41	18 09	5 35	18 14	5 27	18 22
258		1.0058	none	13 33	none	14 02	23 25	14 38	22 31	15 33	19 25	16 41
16 SA	11 54 53	+ 2 47	5 48	18 02	5 45	18 04	5 42	18 07	5 37	18 12	5 30	18 19
259		1.0055	0 28	14 25	0 01	14 51	none	15 25	23 41	16 13	20 33	17 31
17 SU	11 54 32	+ 2 24	5 48	18 01	5 45	18 03	5 43	18 06	5 38	18 10	5 32	18 16
260		1.0052	1 26	15 10	1 00	15 33	0 28	16 02	none	16 42	22 08	17 48
18 MO	11 54 10	+ 2 00	5 48	18 00	5 46	18 02	5 43	18 04	5 40	18 07	5 34	18 13
261		1.0050	2 21	15 50	2 00	16 09	1 33	16 31	0 55	17 03	23 46	17 54
19 TU	11 53 49	+ 1 37	5 48	17 59	5 47	18 01	5 44	18 03	5 41	18 05	5 37	18 10
262		1.0047	3 14	16 26	2 58	16 40	2 37	16 56	2 08	17 19	none	17 55
20 WE	11 53 28	+ 1 14	5 48	17 58	5 47	17 59	5 45	18 01	5 43	18 03	5 39	18 07
263		1.0044	4 05	16 59	3 53	17 07	3 39	17 18	3 19	17 32	1 19	17 55
21 TH	11 53 06	+ 0 51	5 49	17 57	5 48	17 58	5 46	17 59	5 44	18 01	5 41	18 03
264		1.0042	4 53	17 29	4 47	17 33	4 39	17 37	4 29	17 43	2 48	17 54
22 FR	11 52 45	+ 0 27	5 49	17 56	5 48	17 57	5 47	17 58	5 46	17 59	5 44	18 00
265	11 45 NM	1.0039	5 41	17 59	5 40	17 58	5 38	17 56	5 37	17 54	4 12	17 52
23 SA	11 52 24	+ 0 04	5 49	17 56	5 49	17 56	5 48	17 56	5 47	17 56	5 46	17 57
266		1.0036	6 28	18 30	6 33	18 23	6 38	18 15	6 44	18 05	5 34	17 50
24 SU	11 52 03	− 0 19	5 49	17 55	5 49	17 54	5 49	17 54	5 49	17 54	5 48	17 54
267		1.0033	7 17	19 01	7 26	18 50	7 37	18 36	7 53	18 17	6 55	17 48
25 MO	11 51 42	− 0 43	5 49	17 54	5 50	17 53	5 50	17 53	5 50	17 52	5 51	17 51
268		1.0030	8 07	19 36	8 21	19 19	8 39	18 59	9 04	18 31	8 18	17 47
26 TU	11 51 22	− 1 06	5 50	17 53	5 50	17 52	5 51	17 51	5 52	17 50	5 53	17 48
269		1.0027	8 59	20 14	9 18	19 53	9 42	19 26	10 17	18 49	9 45	17 46
27 WE	11 51 02	− 1 30	5 50	17 52	5 51	17 51	5 52	17 49	5 54	17 48	5 55	17 45
270		1.0025	9 54	20 57	10 17	20 32	10 48	20 00	11 32	19 14	11 17	17 46
28 TH	11 50 41	− 1 53	5 50	17 51	5 52	17 49	5 53	17 48	5 55	17 45	5 58	17 42
271		1.0022	10 51	21 46	11 18	21 18	11 53	20 42	12 44	19 49	12 55	17 48
29 FR	11 50 21	− 2 16	5 50	17 50	5 52	17 48	5 54	17 46	5 57	17 43	6 00	17 39
272		1.0019	11 49	22 41	12 18	22 12	12 55	21 35	13 51	20 39	14 35	17 57
30 SA	11 50 02	− 2 34	5 51	17 49	5 53	17 47	5 55	17 44	5 58	17 41	6 03	17 36
273	11 04 FQ	1.0016	12 46	23 41	13 14	23 13	13 51	22 38	14 45	21 44	16 01	18 28

OCTOBER 2006

10th Month **31 days**

Coordinated Universal Time (Greenwich Mean Time)

NOTE: For each day, numbers on first line indicate Sun; numbers on second line (except for Sun's distance) indicate Moon. Degrees are North Latitude.

Moon Phases: FM = Full Moon; LQ = Last (Waning) Quarter; NM = New Moon; FQ = First (Waxing) Quarter

Sun's distance is in Astronomical Units

CAUTION: Must be converted to local time. For instructions see "Calculation of Rise Times," page 346.

			20°		30°		40°		50°		60°	
Day of month, of week, of year	**Sun on Meridian, Moon Phase h m s**	**Sun's Declination ° ′ Distance**	**Rise Sun Moon h m**	**Set Sun Moon h m**	**Rise Sun Moon h m**	**Set Sun Moon h m**	**Rise Sun Moon h m**	**Set Sun Moon h m**	**Rise Sun Moon h m**	**Set Sun Moon h m**	**Rise Sun Moon h m**	**Set Sun Moon h m**
1 SU	11 49 42	– 3 03	5 51	17 48	5 53	17 46	5 56	17 43	6 00	17 39	6 05	17 33
274		1.0013	13 40	none	14 06	none	14 39	23 49	15 26	23 03	16 44	19 46
2 MO	11 49 23	– 3 26	5 51	17 47	5 54	17 45	5 57	17 41	6 01	17 37	6 07	17 30
275		1.0010	14 31	0 44	14 52	0 20	15 19	none	15 56	none	16 57	21 35
3 TU	11 49 04	– 3 49	5 51	17 47	5 54	17 43	5 58	17 40	6 03	17 35	6 10	17 27
276		1.0007	15 17	1 49	15 32	1 29	15 52	1 05	16 19	0 30	17 01	23 29
4 WE	11 48 45	– 4 13	5 52	17 46	5 55	17 42	5 59	17 38	6 04	17 32	6 12	17 24
277		1.0004	15 59	2 53	16 09	2 40	16 21	2 23	16 37	2 00	17 02	none
5 TH	11 48 27	– 4 36	5 52	17 45	5 56	17 41	6 00	17 36	6 06	17 30	6 15	17 21
278		1.0001	16 40	3 56	16 43	3 49	16 47	3 41	16 52	3 29	17 01	1 22
6 FR	11 48 09	– 4 59	5 52	17 44	5 56	17 40	6 01	17 35	6 07	17 28	6 17	17 18
279		.9998	17 20	4 59	17 16	4 59	17 12	4 59	17 07	4 59	17 00	3 11
7 SA	11 47 51	– 5 22	5 52	17 43	5 57	17 39	6 02	17 33	6 09	17 26	6 19	17 15
280	03 13 FM	.9995	18 01	6 02	17 51	6 09	17 39	6 17	17 23	6 29	16 59	4 59
8 SU	11 47 34	– 5 45	5 53	17 42	5 57	17 37	6 03	17 32	6 10	17 24	6 22	17 12
281		.9993	18 45	7 06	18 28	7 20	18 09	7 37	17 41	8 00	16 58	6 47
9 MO	11 47 18	– 6 08	5 53	17 41	5 58	17 36	6 04	17 30	6 12	17 22	6 24	17 09
282		.9990	19 32	8 12	19 11	8 32	18 43	8 57	18 05	9 32	16 58	8 38
10 TU	11 47 01	– 6 30	5 53	17 41	5 59	17 35	6 05	17 28	6 14	17 20	6 27	17 06
283		.9987	20 25	9 18	19 58	9 43	19 25	10 15	18 37	11 01	17 00	10 33
11 WE	11 46 46	– 6 53	5 53	17 40	5 59	17 34	6 06	17 27	6 15	17 18	6 29	17 03
284		.9984	21 21	10 23	20 52	10 51	20 16	11 27	19 22	12 21	17 06	12 30
12 TH	11 46 30	– 7 16	5 54	17 39	6 00	17 33	6 07	17 25	6 17	17 15	6 31	17 00
285		.9981	22 19	11 24	21 51	11 53	21 14	12 30	20 20	13 25	17 24	14 17
13 FR	11 46 16	– 7 38	5 54	17 38	6 00	17 32	6 08	17 24	6 18	17 13	6 34	16 57
286		.9978	23 18	12 19	22 52	12 47	22 18	13 21	21 28	14 12	18 16	15 29
14 SA	11 46 02	– 8 01	5 54	17 37	6 01	17 31	6 09	17 22	6 20	17 11	6 36	16 55
287	00 26 LQ	.9976	none	13 08	23 53	13 32	23 24	14 02	22 42	14 45	19 47	15 56
15 SU	11 45 48	– 8 23	5 55	17 37	6 02	17 29	6 10	17 21	6 21	17 09	6 39	16 52
288		.9973	0 15	13 50	none	14 10	none	14 34	23 57	15 09	21 26	16 04
16 MO	11 45 35	– 8 45	5 55	17 36	6 02	17 28	6 11	17 19	6 23	17 07	6 41	16 49
289		.9970	1 09	14 27	0 51	14 42	0 29	15 01	none	15 26	23 02	16 07
17 TU	11 45 22	– 9 07	5 55	17 35	6 03	17 27	6 12	17 18	6 25	17 05	6 44	16 46
290		.9967	2 01	15 00	1 48	15 11	1 31	15 23	1 09	15 40	none	16 07
18 WE	11 45 10	– 9 29	5 56	17 34	6 04	17 26	6 13	17 16	6 26	17 03	6 46	16 43
291		.9965	2 50	15 32	2 42	15 37	2 32	15 43	2 18	15 52	0 32	16 06
19 TH	11 44 59	– 9 51	5 56	17 34	6 04	17 25	6 14	17 15	6 28	17 01	6 49	16 40
292		.9962	3 38	16 02	3 35	16 02	3 31	16 02	3 27	16 03	1 57	16 05
20 FR	11 44 49	– 10 13	5 56	17 33	6 05	17 24	6 15	17 14	6 30	16 59	6 51	16 37
293		.9959	4 25	16 32	4 27	16 27	4 30	16 21	4 34	16 14	3 19	16 03
21 SA	11 44 39	– 10 34	5 57	17 32	6 06	17 23	6 17	17 12	6 31	16 57	6 54	16 34
294		.9956	5 13	17 03	5 21	16 53	5 30	16 41	5 43	16 25	4 41	16 02
22 SU	11 44 30	– 10 55	5 57	17 32	6 06	17 22	6 18	17 11	6 33	16 55	6 56	16 32
295	05 14 NM	.9953	6 03	17 37	6 15	17 22	6 31	17 04	6 53	16 39	6 03	16 00
23 MO	11 44 21	– 11 17	5 58	17 31	6 07	17 21	6 19	17 09	6 34	16 54	6 59	16 29
296		.9951	6 54	18 14	7 12	17 54	7 34	17 30	8 06	16 56	7 29	15 59
24 TU	11 44 13	– 11 38	5 58	17 30	6 08	17 20	6 20	17 08	6 36	16 52	7 01	16 26
297		.9948	7 49	18 56	8 11	18 32	8 40	18 02	9 21	17 19	9 00	15 59
25 WE	11 44 06	– 11 58	5 58	17 30	6 09	17 19	6 21	17 07	6 38	16 50	7 04	16 23
298		.9945	8 46	19 43	9 12	19 16	9 45	18 41	10 35	17 51	10 36	16 01
26 TH	11 43 59	– 12 19	5 59	17 29	6 09	17 18	6 22	17 05	6 39	16 48	7 06	16 21
299		.9942	9 43	20 36	10 12	20 07	10 48	19 30	11 43	18 35	12 16	16 08
27 FR	11 43 54	– 12 40	5 59	17 28	6 10	17 17	6 23	17 04	6 41	16 46	7 09	16 18
300		.9940	10 40	21 34	11 09	21 06	11 46	20 29	12 41	19 35	13 47	16 30
28 SA	11 43 48	– 13 00	6 00	17 28	6 11	17 17	6 24	17 03	6 43	16 44	7 11	16 15
301		.9937	11 35	22 35	12 01	22 09	12 35	21 36	13 25	20 48	14 44	17 32
29 SU	11 43 44	– 13 20	6 00	17 27	6 11	17 16	6 25	17 02	6 44	16 42	7 14	16 12
302	21 25 FQ	.9934	12 25	23 37	12 48	23 16	13 17	22 49	13 58	22 10	15 04	19 11
30 MO	11 43 41	– 13 40	6 00	17 27	6 12	17 15	6 27	17 00	6 46	16 41	7 17	16 10
303		.9931	13 11	none	13 29	none	13 51	none	14 22	23 35	15 11	21 00
31 TU	11 43 38	– 13 59	6 01	17 26	6 13	17 14	6 28	16 59	6 48	16 39	7 19	16 07
304		.9929	13 53	0 39	14 05	0 23	14 20	0 03	14 40	none	15 12	22 49

NOVEMBER 2006

11th Month **30 days**

Coordinated Universal Time (Greenwich Mean Time)

NOTE: For each day, numbers on first line indicate Sun; numbers on second line (except for Sun's distance) indicate Moon. Degrees are North Latitude.

Moon Phases: FM = Full Moon; LQ = Last (Waning) Quarter; NM = New Moon; FQ = First (Waxing) Quarter

Sun's distance is in Astronomical Units

CAUTION: Must be converted to local time. For instructions see "Calculation of Rise Times," page 346.

Day of month, of week, of year	Sun on Meridian, Moon Phase h m s	Sun's Declination ° ′ Distance	20° Rise Sun Moon h m	20° Set Sun Moon h m	30° Rise Sun Moon h m	30° Set Sun Moon h m	40° Rise Sun Moon h m	40° Set Sun Moon h m	50° Rise Sun Moon h m	50° Set Sun Moon h m	60° Rise Sun Moon h m	60° Set Sun Moon h m
1 WE	11 43 36	– 14 19	6 01	17 26	6 14	17 13	6 29	16 58	6 49	16 37	7 22	16 05
305		.9926	14 32	1 40	14 39	1 30	14 46	1 18	14 56	1 02	15 12	none
2 TH	11 43 34	– 14 38	6 02	17 25	6 14	17 12	6 30	16 57	6 51	16 36	7 24	16 02
306		.9923	15 11	2 40	15 11	2 37	15 11	2 33	15 11	2 28	15 12	0 35
3 FR	11 43 34	– 14 57	6 02	17 25	6 15	17 12	6 31	16 56	6 53	16 34	7 27	15 59
307		.9921	15 51	3 41	15 44	3 45	15 36	3 49	15 26	3 55	15 11	2 19
4 SA	11 43 34	– 15 16	6 03	17 24	6 16	17 11	6 32	16 54	6 54	16 32	7 29	15 57
308		.9918	16 33	4 44	16 20	4 54	16 04	5 06	15 43	5 23	15 10	4 03
5 SU	11 43 36	– 15 34	6 03	17 24	6 17	17 10	6 33	16 53	6 56	16 31	7 32	15 54
309	12 58 FM	.9916	17 18	5 48	16 59	6 05	16 36	6 26	16 04	6 55	15 10	5 51
6 MO	11 43 38	– 15 52	6 04	17 23	6 18	17 09	6 34	16 52	6 58	16 29	7 35	15 52
310		.9913	18 09	6 55	17 45	7 17	17 15	7 46	16 32	8 26	15 11	7 43
7 TU	11 43 40	– 16 10	6 04	17 23	6 18	17 09	6 36	16 51	6 59	16 27	7 37	15 49
311		.9911	19 05	8 02	18 37	8 29	18 02	9 03	17 11	9 53	15 15	9 40
8 WE	11 43 44	– 16 28	6 05	17 22	6 19	17 08	6 37	16 50	7 01	16 26	7 40	15 47
312		.9908	20 04	9 07	19 36	9 36	18 59	10 12	18 04	11 07	15 27	11 35
9 TH	11 43 49	– 16 45	6 05	17 22	6 20	17 07	6 38	16 49	7 03	16 24	7 42	15 45
313		.9906	21 05	10 07	20 38	10 35	20 03	11 11	19 11	12 04	16 02	13 09
10 FR	11 43 54	– 17 02	6 06	17 22	6 21	17 07	6 39	16 48	7 04	16 23	7 45	15 42
314		.9904	22 05	11 00	21 40	11 25	21 10	11 57	20 25	12 44	17 20	13 55
11 SA	11 44 00	– 17 19	6 06	17 21	6 22	17 06	6 40	16 47	7 06	16 22	7 47	15 40
315		.9901	23 01	11 45	22 41	12 07	22 16	12 34	21 41	13 11	19 00	14 11
12 SU	11 44 07	– 17 36	6 07	17 21	6 22	17 06	6 41	16 46	7 08	16 20	7 50	15 38
316	17 45 LQ	.9899	23 54	12 25	23 39	12 42	23 21	13 03	22 55	13 31	20 39	14 16
13 MO	11 44 15	– 17 52	6 08	17 21	6 23	17 05	6 43	16 46	7 09	16 19	7 52	15 35
317		.9897	none	13 00	none	13 12	none	13 27	none	13 47	22 13	14 18
14 TU	11 44 24	– 18 08	6 08	17 21	6 24	17 04	6 44	16 45	7 11	16 17	7 55	15 33
318		.9895	0 45	13 32	0 35	13 39	0 23	13 48	0 06	13 59	23 40	14 17
15 WE	11 44 34	– 18 23	6 09	17 20	6 25	17 04	6 45	16 44	7 12	16 16	7 57	15 31
319		.9892	1 33	14 03	1 28	14 05	1 23	14 07	1 15	14 10	none	14 17
16 TH	11 44 45	– 18 39	6 09	17 20	6 26	17 04	6 46	16 43	7 14	16 15	8 00	15 29
320		.9890	2 20	14 33	2 21	14 30	2 22	14 26	2 22	14 21	1 03	14 15
17 FR	11 44 56	– 18 54	6 10	17 20	6 27	17 03	6 47	16 42	7 16	16 14	8 02	15 27
321		.9888	3 08	15 04	3 14	14 56	3 21	14 46	3 30	14 33	2 24	14 14
18 SA	11 45 08	– 19 08	6 10	17 20	6 27	17 03	6 48	16 42	7 17	16 13	8 05	15 25
322		.9886	3 57	15 37	4 08	15 24	4 21	15 08	4 40	14 46	3 46	14 12
19 SU	11 45 22	– 19 22	6 11	17 20	6 28	17 02	6 49	16 41	7 19	16 11	8 07	15 23
323		.9884	4 48	16 13	5 04	15 55	5 24	15 33	5 52	15 02	5 10	14 11
20 MO	11 45 36	– 19 36	6 12	17 19	6 29	17 02	6 51	16 40	7 20	16 10	8 10	15 21
324	22 18 NM	.9882	5 42	16 53	6 03	16 31	6 29	16 03	7 07	15 23	6 39	14 11
21 TU	11 45 50	– 19 50	6 12	17 19	6 30	17 02	6 52	16 40	7 22	16 09	8 12	15 19
325		.9880	6 39	17 39	7 04	17 13	7 35	16 40	8 22	15 52	8 14	14 13
22 WE	11 46 06	– 20 03	6 13	17 19	6 31	17 01	6 53	16 39	7 23	16 08	8 15	15 17
326		.9878	7 37	18 31	8 05	18 03	8 40	17 27	9 34	16 33	9 54	14 18
23 TH	11 46 22	– 20 16	6 13	17 19	6 32	17 01	6 54	16 39	7 25	16 07	8 17	15 15
327		.9876	8 35	19 29	9 04	19 00	9 41	18 24	10 36	17 29	11 30	14 36
24 FR	11 46 39	– 20 28	6 14	17 19	6 32	17 01	6 55	16 38	7 27	16 06	8 19	15 13
328		.9874	9 31	20 29	9 58	20 03	10 33	19 29	11 24	18 39	12 40	15 25
25 SA	11 46 57	– 20 41	6 15	17 19	6 33	17 01	6 56	16 38	7 28	16 05	8 22	15 12
329		.9872	10 22	21 31	10 46	21 09	11 17	20 40	12 00	19 59	13 09	16 56
26 SU	11 47 16	– 20 52	6 15	17 19	6 34	17 00	6 57	16 37	7 29	16 05	8 24	15 10
330		.9870	11 09	22 32	11 28	22 15	11 52	21 53	12 26	21 22	13 19	18 43
27 MO	11 47 35	– 21 04	6 16	17 19	6 35	17 00	6 58	16 37	7 31	16 04	8 26	15 09
331		.9868	11 51	23 32	12 05	23 20	12 22	23 06	12 46	22 46	13 22	20 30
28 TU	11 47 55	– 21 14	6 17	17 19	6 36	17 00	6 59	16 36	7 32	16 03	8 28	15 07
332	06 29 FQ	.9866	12 30	none	12 39	none	12 49	none	13 02	none	13 23	22 14
29 WE	11 48 16	– 21 25	6 17	17 19	6 36	17 00	7 00	16 36	7 34	16 02	8 30	15 06
333		.9865	13 08	0 31	13 10	0 25	13 13	0 19	13 16	0 09	13 22	23 55
30 TH	11 48 37	– 21 35	6 18	17 19	6 37	17 00	7 01	16 36	7 35	16 02	8 33	15 04
334		.9863	13 46	1 29	13 42	1 30	13 37	1 31	13 31	1 33	13 22	none

DECEMBER 2006

12th Month **31 days**

Coordinated Universal Time (Greenwich Mean Time)

NOTE: For each day, numbers on first line indicate Sun; numbers on second line (except for Sun's distance) indicate Moon. Degrees are North Latitude.

Moon Phases: FM = Full Moon; LQ = Last (Waning) Quarter; NM = New Moon; FQ = First (Waxing) Quarter

Sun's distance is in Astronomical Units

CAUTION: Must be converted to local time. For instructions see "Calculation of Rise Times," page 346.

Day of month, of week, of year	Sun on Meridian, Moon Phase h m s	Sun's Declination ° ′ Distance	20° Rise Sun Moon h m	20° Set Sun Moon h m	30° Rise Sun Moon h m	30° Set Sun Moon h m	40° Rise Sun Moon h m	40° Set Sun Moon h m	50° Rise Sun Moon h m	50° Set Sun Moon h m	60° Rise Sun Moon h m	60° Set Sun Moon h m
1 FR	11 48 59	– 21 45	6 19	17 19	6 38	17 00	7 02	16 35	7 36	16 01	8 35	15 03
335		.9861	14 25	2 28	14 15	2 36	14 02	2 45	13 46	2 57	13 21	1 35
2 SA	11 49 22	– 21 54	6 19	17 19	6 39	17 00	7 03	16 35	7 38	16 01	8 37	15 02
336		.9859	15 07	3 30	14 51	3 44	14 32	4 01	14 04	4 24	13 21	3 16
3 SU	11 49 45	– 22 03	6 20	17 20	6 40	17 00	7 04	16 35	7 39	16 00	8 39	15 01
337		.9858	15 55	4 34	15 33	4 54	15 06	5 18	14 29	5 53	13 21	5 02
4 MO	11 50 09	– 22 11	6 20	17 20	6 40	17 00	7 05	16 35	7 40	16 00	8 40	14 59
338		.9856	16 48	5 40	16 22	6 05	15 49	6 36	15 02	7 22	13 24	6 54
5 TU	11 50 34	– 22 19	6 21	17 20	6 41	17 00	7 06	16 35	7 42	15 59	8 42	14 58
339	00 25 FM	.9855	17 46	6 47	17 18	7 14	16 42	7 50	15 48	8 43	13 32	8 49
6 WE	11 50 59	– 22 27	6 22	17 20	6 42	17 00	7 07	16 35	7 43	15 59	8 44	14 58
340		.9853	18 47	7 49	18 19	8 18	17 43	8 54	16 49	9 48	13 54	10 36
7 TH	11 51 24	– 22 34	6 22	17 20	6 43	17 00	7 08	16 35	7 44	15 59	8 46	14 57
341		.9852	19 49	8 47	19 23	9 13	18 50	9 47	18 02	10 37	14 52	11 46
8 FR	11 51 50	– 22 41	6 23	17 21	6 43	17 00	7 09	16 35	7 45	15 58	8 47	14 56
342		.9851	20 48	9 36	20 26	10 00	19 59	10 29	19 20	11 10	16 27	12 14
9 SA	11 52 17	– 22 47	6 23	17 21	6 44	17 00	7 10	16 35	7 46	15 58	8 49	14 55
343		.9849	21 44	10 20	21 27	10 38	21 06	11 01	20 37	11 34	18 10	12 23
10 SU	11 52 44	– 22 53	6 24	17 21	6 45	17 01	7 11	16 35	7 47	15 58	8 51	14 55
344		.9848	22 36	10 57	22 25	11 11	22 10	11 28	21 50	11 51	19 47	12 27
11 MO	11 53 11	– 22 58	6 25	17 22	6 45	17 01	7 11	16 35	7 48	15 58	8 52	14 54
345		.9847	23 26	11 31	23 19	11 40	23 11	11 51	23 00	12 05	21 18	12 27
12 TU	11 53 39	– 23 03	6 25	17 22	6 46	17 01	7 12	16 35	7 49	15 58	8 53	14 54
346	14 32 LQ	.9846	none	12 02	none	12 06	none	12 11	none	12 17	22 43	12 27
13 WE	11 54 07	– 23 07	6 26	17 22	6 47	17 01	7 13	16 35	7 50	15 58	8 55	14 53
347		.9845	0 14	12 33	0 12	12 31	0 11	12 30	0 09	12 28	none	12 26
14 TH	11 54 36	– 23 11	6 26	17 23	6 47	17 02	7 14	16 35	7 51	15 58	8 56	14 53
348		.9844	1 01	13 03	1 05	12 57	1 10	12 49	1 16	12 39	0 05	12 25
15 FR	11 55 04	– 23 15	6 27	17 23	6 48	17 02	7 15	16 36	7 52	15 58	8 57	14 53
349		.9843	1 49	13 35	1 58	13 24	2 09	13 10	2 25	12 51	1 26	12 23
16 SA	11 55 33	– 23 18	6 28	17 23	6 49	17 02	7 15	16 36	7 53	15 58	8 58	14 53
350		.9842	2 39	14 09	2 53	13 53	3 11	13 33	3 35	13 06	2 49	12 22
17 SU	11 56 03	– 23 21	6 28	17 24	6 49	17 03	7 16	16 36	7 53	15 59	8 59	14 53
351		.9841	3 32	14 48	3 51	14 27	4 15	14 01	4 49	13 25	4 16	12 22
18 MO	11 56 32	– 23 23	6 29	17 24	6 50	17 03	7 16	16 37	7 54	15 59	9 00	14 53
352		.9840	4 28	15 32	4 51	15 07	5 21	14 36	6 04	13 51	5 48	12 23
19 TU	11 57 02	– 23 24	6 29	17 25	6 51	17 04	7 17	16 37	7 55	15 59	9 01	14 53
353		.9840	5 26	16 23	5 53	15 55	6 27	15 20	7 18	14 28	7 26	12 27
20 WE	11 57 32	– 23 25	6 30	17 25	6 51	17 04	7 18	16 37	7 55	16 00	9 01	14 54
354	14 01 NM	.9839	6 25	17 19	6 54	16 51	7 30	16 14	8 25	15 19	9 06	12 39
21 TH	11 58 02	– 23 26	6 30	17 26	6 52	17 04	7 18	16 38	7 56	16 00	9 02	14 54
355		.9838	7 23	18 20	7 51	17 53	8 27	17 18	9 20	16 26	10 29	13 15
22 FR	11 58 32	– 23 26	6 31	17 26	6 52	17 05	7 19	16 38	7 56	16 01	9 02	14 55
356		.9837	8 17	19 23	8 42	18 59	9 14	18 29	10 00	17 45	11 12	14 35
23 SA	11 59 02	– 23 26	6 31	17 27	6 53	17 06	7 19	16 39	7 57	16 01	9 03	14 55
357		.9837	9 06	20 26	9 27	20 07	9 53	19 43	10 30	19 10	11 27	16 21
24 SU	11 59 32	– 23 26	6 32	17 27	6 53	17 06	7 20	16 39	7 57	16 02	9 03	14 56
358		.9836	9 51	21 27	10 06	21 14	10 25	20 57	10 51	20 35	11 32	18 11
25 MO	12 00 02	– 23 24	6 32	17 28	6 53	17 07	7 20	16 40	7 58	16 03	9 03	14 57
359		.9836	10 31	22 26	10 41	22 19	10 52	22 10	11 08	21 58	11 33	19 58
26 TU	12 00 31	– 23 23	6 33	17 28	6 54	17 07	7 20	16 41	7 58	16 03	9 04	14 58
360		.9835	11 09	23 24	11 12	23 23	11 17	23 22	11 23	23 21	11 33	21 39
27 WE	12 01 01	– 23 21	6 33	17 29	6 54	17 08	7 21	16 41	7 58	16 04	9 04	14 59
361	14 48 FQ	.9835	11 46	none	11 43	none	11 41	none	11 37	none	11 32	23 19
28 TH	12 01 30	– 23 18	6 34	17 30	6 55	17 08	7 21	16 42	7 58	16 05	9 04	15 00
362		.9834	12 23	0 22	12 15	0 27	12 05	0 34	11 52	0 43	11 32	none
29 FR	12 02 00	– 23 15	6 34	17 30	6 55	17 09	7 21	16 43	7 58	16 06	9 03	15 01
363		.9834	13 03	1 21	12 49	1 32	12 32	1 47	12 08	2 07	11 31	0 57
30 SA	12 02 28	– 23 11	6 34	17 31	6 55	17 10	7 22	16 44	7 59	16 07	9 03	15 02
364		.9833	13 47	2 22	13 28	2 40	13 03	3 02	12 29	3 33	11 31	2 39
31 SU	12 02 57	– 23 07	6 35	17 31	6 56	17 10	7 22	16 44	7 59	16 07	9 03	15 03
365		.9833	14 37	3 26	14 12	3 48	13 42	4 17	12 58	4 59	11 33	4 25

CALENDAR

Julian and Gregorian Calendars; Leap Year; Century

The **Julian calendar**, under which all Western nations measured time until AD 1582, was authorized by Julius Caesar in 46 BC. It called for a year of 365¼ days, starting in January, with every 4th year being a **leap year** of 366 days. St. Bede, an Anglo-Saxon monk also known as the Venerable Bede, announced in AD 730 that the Julian year was 11 min, 14 sec too long, a cumulative error of about a day every 128 years, but nothing was done about this for centuries.

By 1582 the accumulated error was estimated at 10 days. In that year Pope Gregory XIII decreed that the day following Oct. 4, 1582, should be called Oct. 15, thus dropping 10 days and initiating the **Gregorian calendar**.

The Gregorian calendar continued a system devised by the monk Dionysius Exiguus (6th century), starting from the first year following the birth of Jesus Christ, which was inaccurately taken to be year 753 in the Roman calendar. Leap years were continued but, to prevent further displacements, centesimal years (years ending in 00) were made common years, not leap years, unless divisible by 400. Under this plan, **1600** and **2000** were leap years (as was **2004**); 1700, 1800, and 1900 were not.

The Gregorian calendar was adopted at once by France, Italy, Spain, Portugal, and Luxembourg. Within 2 years most German Catholic states, Belgium, and parts of Switzerland and the Netherlands were brought under the new calendar, and Hungary followed in 1587. The rest of the Netherlands, along with Denmark and the German Protestant states, made the change in 1699-1700.

The British government adopted the Gregorian calendar and imposed it on all its possessions, including the American colonies, in 1752, decreeing that the day following Sept. 2, 1752, should be called Sept. 14, a loss of 11 days. All dates preceding were marked OS, for Old Style. In addition, New Year's Day was moved to Jan. 1 from Mar. 25 (under the old reckoning, for example, Mar. 24, 1700, had been followed by Mar. 25, 1701). Thus George Washington's birthdate, which was Feb. 11, 1731, OS, became Feb. 22, 1732, NS (New Style). In 1753 Sweden also went Gregorian.

In 1793 the French revolutionary government adopted a calendar of 12 months of 30 days with 5 extra days in September of each common year and a 6th every 4th year. Napoleon reinstated the Gregorian calendar in 1806.

The Gregorian system later spread to non-European regions, replacing traditional calendars at least for official purposes. Japan in 1873, Egypt in 1875, China in 1912, and Turkey in 1925 made the change, usually in conjunction with political upheaval. In China, the republican government began reckoning years from its 1911 founding. After 1949, the People's Republic adopted the Common, or Christian Era, year count, even for the traditional lunar calendar, which is also retained. In 1918 the Soviet Union decreed that the day after Jan. 31, 1918, OS, would be Feb. 14, 1918, NS. Greece changed over in 1923. For the first time in history, all major nations had one calendar. The Russian Orthodox church and some other Christian sects retained the Julian calendar.

To convert from the Julian to the Gregorian calendar, add 10 days to dates Oct. 5, 1582, through Feb. 28, 1700; after that date add 11 days through Feb. 28, 1800; 12 days through Feb. 28, 1900; and 13 days through Feb. 28, 2100.

A **century** consists of 100 consecutive years. The 1st century AD may be said to have run from the years 1 through 100. The 20th century by this reckoning consisted of the years 1901 through 2000 and technically ended Dec. 31, 2000, as did the 2nd millennium AD. The 21st century thus technically began Jan. 1, 2001.

For a **Perpetual Calendar,** see pages 362-63.

Gregorian Calendar

Choose the desired year from the table below or from the Perpetual Calendar (for years 1803 to 2080). The number after each year designates which calendar to use for that year, as shown in the Perpetual Calendar—see pages 362-63. (The Gregorian calendar was inaugurated Oct. 15, 1582. From that date to Dec. 31, 1582, use calendar 6.)

1583-1802

1583	7	1603	4	1623	1	1643	5	1663	2	1683	6	1703	2	1723	6	1743	3	1763	7	1783	4
1584	8	1604	12	1624	9	1644	13	1664	10	1684	14	1704	10	1724	14	1744	11	1764	8	1784	12
1585	3	1605	7	1625	4	1645	1	1665	5	1685	2	1705	5	1725	2	1745	6	1765	3	1785	7
1586	4	1606	1	1626	5	1646	2	1666	6	1686	3	1706	6	1726	3	1746	7	1766	4	1786	1
1587	5	1607	2	1627	6	1647	3	1667	7	1687	4	1707	7	1727	4	1747	1	1767	5	1787	2
1588	13	1608	10	1628	14	1648	11	1668	8	1688	12	1708	8	1728	12	1748	9	1768	13	1788	10
1589	1	1609	5	1629	2	1649	6	1669	3	1689	7	1709	3	1729	7	1749	4	1769	1	1789	5
1590	2	1610	6	1630	3	1650	7	1670	4	1690	1	1710	4	1730	1	1750	5	1770	2	1790	6
1591	3	1611	7	1631	4	1651	1	1671	5	1691	2	1711	5	1731	2	1751	6	1771	3	1791	7
1592	11	1612	8	1632	12	1652	9	1672	13	1692	10	1712	13	1732	10	1752	14	1772	11	1792	8
1593	6	1613	3	1633	7	1653	4	1673	1	1693	5	1713	1	1733	5	1753	2	1773	6	1793	3
1594	7	1614	4	1634	1	1654	5	1674	2	1694	6	1714	2	1734	6	1754	3	1774	7	1794	4
1595	1	1615	5	1635	2	1655	6	1675	3	1695	7	1715	3	1735	7	1755	4	1775	1	1795	5
1596	9	1616	13	1636	10	1656	14	1676	11	1696	8	1716	11	1736	8	1756	12	1776	9	1796	13
1597	4	1617	1	1637	5	1657	2	1677	6	1697	3	1717	6	1737	3	1757	7	1777	4	1797	1
1598	5	1618	2	1638	6	1658	3	1678	7	1698	4	1718	7	1738	4	1758	1	1778	5	1798	2
1599	6	1619	3	1639	7	1659	4	1679	1	1699	5	1719	1	1739	5	1759	2	1779	6	1799	3
1600	14	1620	11	1640	8	1660	12	1680	9	1700	6	1720	9	1740	13	1760	10	1780	14	1800	4
1601	2	1621	6	1641	3	1661	7	1681	4	1701	7	1721	4	1741	1	1761	5	1781	2	1801	5
1602	3	1622	7	1642	4	1662	1	1682	5	1702	1	1722	5	1742	2	1762	6	1782	3	1802	6

The Julian Period

How many days have you lived? To determine this, multiply your age by 365, add the number of days since your last birthday, and account for all leap years. Chances are your calculations will go wrong somewhere. Astronomers, however, find it convenient to express dates and time intervals in days rather than in years, months, and days. This is done by placing events within the Julian period.

The Julian period was devised in 1582 by the French classical scholar Joseph Scaliger (1540-1609), and it was named after his father, Julius Caesar Scaliger, not after the Julian calendar as might be supposed.

Scaliger began with a zero hour, or starting time, of noon on Jan. 1, 4713 BC (on the Julian calendar). This was the most recent time that 3 major chronological cycles began on the same day: (1) the 28-year solar cycle, after which dates in the Julian calendar (e.g., Feb. 11) return to the same days of the week (e.g., Monday); (2) the 19-year lunar cycle, after which the phases of the moon return to the same dates of the year; and (3) the 15-year indiction cycle, used in ancient Rome to regulate taxes.

It will take 7,980 years to complete the period, the product of 28, 19, and 15.

Noon of Dec. 31, 2005, will be Julian Date (JD) 2,453,736; that many days will have passed since the start of the Julian period. The JD at noon of any date in 2006 may be found by adding to this figure the day of the year for that date, which can be obtained from the left half of the "How Far Apart Are Two Dates?" chart on the next page.

Julian Calendar

To find which of the 14 calendars of the Perpetual Calendar (pages 362-63) applies to any year under the Julian system, find the century for the desired year in the 3 leftmost columns below. Read across and find the year in the 4 top rows. Then read down. The number in the intersection is the calendar designation for that year. For some years and countries the Julian new year did not start Jan. 1; to find the correct Perpetual Calendar for Britain and its possessions, you can generally add one year for dates from Jan. 1-Mar. 24. For example, to look up Feb. 2, 1705, Old Style, use the year 1706.

Year (last 2 figures of desired year)

				01	02	03	04	05	06	07	08	09	10	11	12	13	14	15	16	17	18	19	20	21	22	23	24	25	26	27	28
				29	30	31	32	33	34	35	36	37	38	39	40	41	42	43	44	45	46	47	48	49	50	51	52	53	54	55	56
				57	58	59	60	61	62	63	64	65	66	67	68	69	70	71	72	73	74	75	76	77	78	79	80	81	82	83	84
Century			**00**	85	86	87	88	89	90	91	92	93	94	95	96	97	98	99													
0	**700**	**1400**	12	7	1	2	10	5	6	7	8	3	4	5	13	1	2	3	11	6	7	1	9	4	5	6	14	2	3	4	12
100	**800**	**1500**	11	6	7	1	9	4	5	6	14	2	3	4	12	7	1	2	10	5	6	7	8	3	4	5	13	1	2	3	11
200	**900**	**1600**	10	5	6	7	8	3	4	5	13	1	2	3	11	6	7	1	9	4	5	6	14	2	3	4	12	7	1	2	10
300	**1000**	**1700**	9	4	5	6	14	2	3	4	12	7	1	2	10	5	6	7	8	3	4	5	13	1	2	3	11	6	7	1	9
400	**1100**	**1800**	8	3	4	5	13	1	2	3	11	6	7	1	9	4	5	6	14	2	3	4	12	7	1	2	10	5	6	7	8
500	**1200**	**1900**	14	2	3	4	12	7	1	2	10	5	6	7	8	3	4	5	13	1	2	3	11	6	7	1	9	4	5	6	14
600	**1300**	**2000**	13	1	2	3	11	6	7	1	9	4	5	6	14	2	3	4	12	7	1	2	10	5	6	7	8	3	4	5	13

How Far Apart Are Two Dates?

This table covers a range of 2 years. To use, **find the numbers in the tables for each date and subtract** the smaller from the larger. Example—to find the number of days from Mar. 15, 2006, to Sept. 22, 2007, subtract 74 from 630; the result is 556. For leap years, such as 2004, where Feb. 29 intervenes, one day must be then added; thus Feb. 4, 2003, and Mar. 13, 2004, were 403 days apart.

First Year

Date	Jan.	Feb.	Mar.	April	May	June	July	Aug.	Sept.	Oct.	Nov.	Dec.
1	1	32	60	91	121	152	182	213	244	274	305	335
2	2	33	61	92	122	153	183	214	245	275	306	336
3	3	34	62	93	123	154	184	215	246	276	307	337
4	4	35	63	94	124	155	185	216	247	277	308	338
5	5	36	64	95	125	156	186	217	248	278	309	339
6	6	37	65	96	126	157	187	218	249	279	310	340
7	7	38	66	97	127	158	188	219	250	280	311	341
8	8	39	67	98	128	159	189	220	251	281	312	342
9	9	40	68	99	129	160	190	221	252	282	313	343
10	10	41	69	100	130	161	191	222	253	283	314	344
11	11	42	70	101	131	162	192	223	254	284	315	345
12	12	43	71	102	132	163	193	224	255	285	316	346
13	13	44	72	103	133	164	194	225	256	286	317	347
14	14	45	73	104	134	165	195	226	257	287	318	348
15	15	46	74	105	135	166	196	227	258	288	319	349
16	16	47	75	106	136	167	197	228	259	289	320	350
17	17	48	76	107	137	168	198	229	260	290	321	351
18	18	49	77	108	138	169	199	230	261	291	322	352
19	19	50	78	109	139	170	200	231	262	292	323	353
20	20	51	79	110	140	171	201	232	263	293	324	354
21	21	52	80	111	141	172	202	233	264	294	325	355
22	22	53	81	112	142	173	203	234	265	295	326	356
23	23	54	82	113	143	174	204	235	266	296	327	357
24	24	55	83	114	144	175	205	236	267	297	328	358
25	25	56	84	115	145	176	206	237	268	298	329	359
26	26	57	85	116	146	177	207	238	269	299	330	360
27	27	58	86	117	147	178	208	239	270	300	331	361
28	28	59	87	118	148	179	209	240	271	301	332	362
29	29	—	88	119	149	180	210	241	272	302	333	363
30	30	—	89	120	150	181	211	242	273	303	334	364
31	31	—	90	—	151	—	212	243	—	304	—	365

Second Year

Date	Jan.	Feb.	Mar.	April	May	June	July	Aug.	Sept.	Oct.	Nov.	Dec.
1	366	397	425	456	486	517	547	578	609	639	670	700
2	367	398	426	457	487	518	548	579	610	640	671	701
3	368	399	427	458	488	519	549	580	611	641	672	702
4	369	400	428	459	489	520	550	581	612	642	673	703
5	370	401	429	460	490	521	551	582	613	643	674	704
6	371	402	430	461	491	522	552	583	614	644	675	705
7	372	403	431	462	492	523	553	584	615	645	676	706
8	373	404	432	463	493	524	554	585	616	646	677	707
9	374	405	433	464	494	525	555	586	617	647	678	708
10	375	406	434	465	495	526	556	587	618	648	679	709
11	376	407	435	466	496	527	557	588	619	649	680	710
12	377	408	436	467	497	528	558	589	620	650	681	711
13	378	409	437	468	498	529	559	590	621	651	682	712
14	379	410	438	469	499	530	560	591	622	652	683	713
15	380	411	439	470	500	531	561	592	623	653	684	714
16	381	412	440	471	501	532	562	593	624	654	685	715
17	382	413	441	472	502	533	563	594	625	655	686	716
18	383	414	442	473	503	534	564	595	626	656	687	717
19	384	415	443	474	504	535	565	596	627	657	688	718
20	385	416	444	475	505	536	566	597	628	658	689	719
21	386	417	445	476	506	537	567	598	629	659	690	720
22	387	418	446	477	507	538	568	599	630	660	691	721
23	388	419	447	478	508	539	569	600	631	661	692	722
24	389	420	448	479	509	540	570	601	632	662	693	723
25	390	421	449	480	510	541	571	602	633	663	694	724
26	391	422	450	481	511	542	572	603	634	664	695	725
27	392	423	451	482	512	543	573	604	635	665	696	726
28	393	424	452	483	513	544	574	605	636	666	697	727
29	394	—	453	484	514	545	575	606	637	667	698	728
30	395	—	454	485	515	546	576	607	638	668	699	729
31	396	—	455	—	516	—	577	608	—	669	—	730

Signs of the Zodiac

The **zodiac** is the apparent yearly path of the sun among the stars as viewed from earth, and was divided by the ancients into 12 equal sections or signs, each named for the constellation situated within its limits in ancient times. Astrologers claim that the temperament and destiny of each individual depend on the zodiac sign under which the person was born and the relationships between the planets at that time and throughout life.

Below are the 12 traditional signs and the traditional range of dates pertaining to each:

♈ **Aries** (Ram), March 21– April 19

♉ **Taurus** (Bull), April 20– May 20

♊ **Gemini** (Twins), May 21– June 21

♋ **Cancer** (Crab), June 22– July 22

♌ **Leo** (Lion), July 23– August 22

♍ **Virgo** (Maiden), August 23– September 22

♎ **Libra** (Balance), September 23– October 23

♏ **Scorpio** (Scorpion), October 24– November 21

♐ **Sagittarius** (Archer), November 22– December 21

♑ **Capricorn** (Goat), December 22– January 19

♒ **Aquarius** (Water Bearer), January 20 – February 18

♓ **Pisces** (Fishes), February 19 – March 20

WORLD ALMANAC QUICK QUIZ

Which of these traditional anniversary gifts is for the couple longest married?

(a) pearl (b) emerald (c) silver (d) fur

For the answer look in this chapter, or see page 1008.

Calendar for the Year 2006

JANUARY

S	M	T	W	T	F	S
1	2	3	4	5	6	7
8	9	10	11	12	13	14
15	16	17	18	19	20	21
22	23	24	25	26	27	28
29	30	31				

FEBRUARY

S	M	T	W	T	F	S
			1	2	3	4
5	6	7	8	9	10	11
12	13	14	15	16	17	18
19	20	21	22	23	24	25
26	27	28				

MARCH

S	M	T	W	T	F	S
			1	2	3	4
5	6	7	8	9	10	11
12	13	14	15	16	17	18
19	20	21	22	23	24	25
26	27	28	29	30	31	

APRIL

S	M	T	W	T	F	S
						1
2	3	4	5	6	7	8
9	10	11	12	13	14	15
16	17	18	19	20	21	22
23	24	25	26	27	28	29
30						

MAY

S	M	T	W	T	F	S
	1	2	3	4	5	6
7	8	9	10	11	12	13
14	15	16	17	18	19	20
21	22	23	24	25	26	27
28	29	30	31			

JUNE

S	M	T	W	T	F	S
				1	2	3
4	5	6	7	8	9	10
11	12	13	14	15	16	17
18	19	20	21	22	23	24
25	26	27	28	29	30	

JULY

S	M	T	W	T	F	S
						1
2	3	4	5	6	7	8
9	10	11	12	13	14	15
16	17	18	19	20	21	22
23	24	25	26	27	28	29
30	31					

AUGUST

S	M	T	W	T	F	S
		1	2	3	4	5
6	7	8	9	10	11	12
13	14	15	16	17	18	19
20	21	22	23	24	25	26
27	28	29	30	31		

SEPTEMBER

S	M	T	W	T	F	S
					1	2
3	4	5	6	7	8	9
10	11	12	13	14	15	16
17	18	19	20	21	22	23
24	25	26	27	28	29	30

OCTOBER

S	M	T	W	T	F	S
1	2	3	4	5	6	7
8	9	10	11	12	13	14
15	16	17	18	19	20	21
22	23	24	25	26	27	28
29	30	31				

NOVEMBER

S	M	T	W	T	F	S
			1	2	3	4
5	6	7	8	9	10	11
12	13	14	15	16	17	18
19	20	21	22	23	24	25
26	27	28	29	30		

DECEMBER

S	M	T	W	T	F	S
					1	2
3	4	5	6	7	8	9
10	11	12	13	14	15	16
17	18	19	20	21	22	23
24	25	26	27	28	29	30
31						

Federal Holidays and Other Notable Dates, 2006

Some dates may be subject to change.

The days marked on the calendar above and shown below *in italics* are U.S. federal holidays, designated by the president or Congress and applicable to federal employees and the District of Columbia. Most U.S. states also observe these holidays, and many states observe others; practices vary from state to state. In most states the secretary of state's office can provide details.

January

1 *New Year's Day*
2 Sugar Bowl; Fiesta Bowl; Cotton Bowl
3 Orange Bowl
10 Eid al-Adha (Festival of Sacrifice)
16 *Martin Luther King Jr. Day* (3rd Mon. in Jan.)
16-29 Australian Open tennis tournament
26 Australia Day, Australia
29 Chinese New Year
30 Muharram 1 (Islamic New Year), 1st full day

February

2 Groundhog Day
5 Super Bowl XL (Detroit, MI); Constitution Day, Mexico
10-26 2006 Winter Olympics (Turin, Italy)
12 Lincoln's Birthday; NFL Pro Bowl
13-14 Westminster Dog Show
14 Valentine's Day
19 Daytona 500; NBA All-Star Game
20 *Washington's Birthday* (observed), *Presidents' Day*, or *Washington-Lincoln Day* (3rd Mon. in Feb.)
25-28 Carnival, Brazil
28 Mardi Gras

March

1 Ash Wednesday
4 Iditarod Trail Sled Dog Race begins
5 Academy Awards
13 Commonwealth Day, Canada
14 Purim (Feast of Lots), 1st full day
17 St. Patrick's Day
20 First day of spring (Northern Hemisphere)
21 Benito Juárez's Birthday, Mexico

April

1 April Fool's Day
2 Daylight Saving Time begins in U.S.
3 NCAA men's basketball championship
4 NCAA women's basketball championship
6-9 Masters golf tournament
13 Passover (commemorates exodus of Israelites from Egypt)
14 Good Friday
16 Easter
17 Patriots' Day; Boston Marathon
22 Earth Day
23 Orthodox Easter
26 Administrative Professionals Day
27 Take Our Daughters and Sons to Work Day
28 Arbor Day, U.S.

May

1 May Day
2 National Teacher Day, U.S.
5 Cinco de Mayo (Battle of Puebla Day), Mexico; Buddha's Birthday, Korea, Hong Kong
6 Kentucky Derby
14 Mother's Day
20 Armed Forces Day; Preakness Stakes
22 Victoria Day, Canada
29-June 11 French Open tennis tournament
29 *Memorial Day*, or *Decoration Day* (last Mon. in May)
31 Dragon Boat Festival, China

June

10 Belmont Stakes
14 Flag Day, U.S.
15-18 U.S. Open golf tournament
18 Father's Day
21 First day of summer (Northern Hemisphere)
26-July 9 Wimbledon tennis tournament

July

1 Canada Day
4 *Independence Day*
7–14 Running of the Bulls (Pamplona, Spain)
14 Bastille Day, France
20-23 British Open golf tournament

August

17-20 PGA Championship
30 St. Rose of Lima, Peru

September

4 *Labor Day,* U.S. (1st Monday in Sept.); Labor Day, Canada
10 Grandparents' Day, U.S.
16 Independence Day, Mexico
17 Citizenship Day, U.S.
19 San Gennaro, Italy
23 First day of autumn (Northern Hemisphere); Rosh Hashanah (New Year), 1st full day; Ramadan (month of fasting), 1st full day

October

2 U.S. Supreme Court session begins; Yom Kippur (Day of Atonement)
3 German Unification Day, Germany
9 *Columbus Day* (2nd Mon. in Oct.); Thanksgiving Day, Canada
12 Día de la Raza, Spain, Mexico
24 United Nations Day
29 Daylight Saving Time ends in U.S.
31 Halloween

November

1 All Saints' Day
2 Día de los Muertos, Mexico
5 Guy Fawkes Day, UK; New York City Marathon
7 Election Day (1st Tues. after 1st Mon. in Nov.; observed in some states)
11 *Veterans Day*; Remembrance Day, Canada, UK
15 Shichi-Go-San (Seven-Five-Three), Japan
23 *Thanksgiving Day, U.S.* (4th Thurs. in Nov.)

December

10 Nobel Prizes awarded (winners announced in Oct.)
12 Día de la Virgen de Guadalupe, Mexico
16-23 Hanukkah (Festival of Lights)
21 First day of winter (Northern Hemisphere)
25 *Christmas Day*
26 Boxing Day, Australia, Canada, New Zealand, UK
26-Jan. 1 Kwanzaa

Perpetual Calendar

The number shown for each year indicates which Gregorian calendar to use. For 1583-1802, see "Gregorian Calendar" on page 359. For 1803-20, use numbers for 1983-2000, respectively. For Julian Calendar, see "Julian Calendar" on page 360.

1821....2	1847....6	1873....4	1899....1	1925....5	1951....2	1977....7	2003....4	2029....2	2055....6
1822....3	1848...14	1874....5	1900....2	1926....6	1952...10	1978....1	2004...12	2030....3	2056...14
1823....4	1849....2	1875....6	1901....3	1927....7	1953....5	1979....2	2005....7	2031....4	2057....2
1824...12	1850....3	1876...14	1902....4	1928....8	1954....6	1980...10	2006....1	2032...12	2058....3
1825....7	1851....4	1877....2	1903....5	1929....3	1955....7	1981....5	2007....2	2033....7	2059....4
1826....1	1852...12	1878....3	1904...13	1930....4	1956....8	1982....6	2008...10	2034....1	2060...12
1827....2	1853....7	1879....4	1905....1	1931....5	1957....3	1983....7	2009....5	2035....2	2061....7
1828...10	1854....1	1880...12	1906....2	1932...13	1958....4	1984....8	2010....6	2036...10	2062....1
1829....5	1855....2	1881....7	1907....3	1933....1	1959....5	1985....3	2011....7	2037....5	2063....2
1830....6	1856...10	1882....1	1908...11	1934....2	1960...13	1986....4	2012....8	2038....6	2064...10
1831....7	1857....5	1883....2	1909....6	1935....3	1961....1	1987....5	2013....3	2039....7	2065....5
1832....8	1858....6	1884...10	1910....7	1936...11	1962....2	1988...13	2014....4	2040....8	2066....6
1833....3	1859....7	1885....5	1911....1	1937....6	1963....3	1989....1	2015....5	2041....3	2067....7
1834....4	1860....8	1886....6	1912....9	1938....7	1964...11	1990....2	2016...13	2042....4	2068....8
1835....5	1861....3	1887....7	1913....4	1939....1	1965....6	1991....3	2017....1	2043....5	2069....3
1836...13	1862....4	1888....8	1914....5	1940....9	1966....7	1992...11	2018....2	2044...13	2070....4
1837....1	1863....5	1889....3	1915....6	1941....4	1967....1	1993....6	2019....3	2045....1	2071....5
1838....2	1864...13	1890....4	1916...14	1942....5	1968....9	1994....7	2020...11	2046....2	2072...13
1839....3	1865....1	1891....5	1917....2	1943....6	1969....4	1995....1	2021....6	2047....3	2073....1
1840...11	1866....2	1892...13	1918....3	1944...14	1970....5	1996....9	2022....7	2048...11	2074....2
1841....6	1867....3	1893....1	1919....4	1945....2	1971....6	1997....4	2023....1	2049....6	2075....3
1842....7	1868...11	1894....2	1920...12	1946....3	1972...14	1998....5	2024....9	2050....7	2076...11
1843....1	1869....6	1895....3	1921....7	1947....4	1973....2	1999....6	2025....4	2051....1	2077....6
1844....9	1870....7	1896...11	1922....1	1948...12	1974....3	2000...14	2026....5	2052....9	2078....7
1845....4	1871....1	1897....6	1923....2	1949....7	1975....4	2001....2	2027....6	2053....4	2079....1
1846....5	1872....9	1898....7	1924...10	1950....1	1976...12	2002....3	2028...14	2054....5	2080....9

1 2006

JANUARY

S	M	T	W	T	F	S
1	2	3	4	5	6	7
8	9	10	11	12	13	14
15	16	17	18	19	20	21
22	23	24	25	26	27	28
29	30	31				

FEBRUARY

S	M	T	W	T	F	S
			1	2	3	4
5	6	7	8	9	10	11
12	13	14	15	16	17	18
19	20	21	22	23	24	25
26	27	28				

MARCH

S	M	T	W	T	F	S
			1	2	3	4
5	6	7	8	9	10	11
12	13	14	15	16	17	18
19	20	21	22	23	24	25
26	27	28	29	30	31	

APRIL

S	M	T	W	T	F	S
						1
2	3	4	5	6	7	8
9	10	11	12	13	14	15
16	17	18	19	20	21	22
23	24	25	26	27	28	29
30						

MAY

S	M	T	W	T	F	S
	1	2	3	4	5	6
7	8	9	10	11	12	13
14	15	16	17	18	19	20
21	22	23	24	25	26	27
28	29	30	31			

JUNE

S	M	T	W	T	F	S
				1	2	3
4	5	6	7	8	9	10
11	12	13	14	15	16	17
18	19	20	21	22	23	24
25	26	27	28	29	30	

JULY

S	M	T	W	T	F	S
						1
2	3	4	5	6	7	8
9	10	11	12	13	14	15
16	17	18	19	20	21	22
23	24	25	26	27	28	29
30	31					

AUGUST

S	M	T	W	T	F	S
		1	2	3	4	5
6	7	8	9	10	11	12
13	14	15	16	17	18	19
20	21	22	23	24	25	26
27	28	29	30	31		

SEPTEMBER

S	M	T	W	T	F	S
					1	2
3	4	5	6	7	8	9
10	11	12	13	14	15	16
17	18	19	20	21	22	23
24	25	26	27	28	29	30

OCTOBER

S	M	T	W	T	F	S
1	2	3	4	5	6	7
8	9	10	11	12	13	14
15	16	17	18	19	20	21
22	23	24	25	26	27	28
29	30	31				

NOVEMBER

S	M	T	W	T	F	S
			1	2	3	4
5	6	7	8	9	10	11
12	13	14	15	16	17	18
19	20	21	22	23	24	25
26	27	28	29	30		

DECEMBER

S	M	T	W	T	F	S
					1	2
3	4	5	6	7	8	9
10	11	12	13	14	15	16
17	18	19	20	21	22	23
24	25	26	27	28	29	30
31						

2 2001/2007

JANUARY

S	M	T	W	T	F	S
	1	2	3	4	5	6
7	8	9	10	11	12	13
14	15	16	17	18	19	20
21	22	23	24	25	26	27
28	29	30	31			

FEBRUARY

S	M	T	W	T	F	S
				1	2	3
4	5	6	7	8	9	10
11	12	13	14	15	16	17
18	19	20	21	22	23	24
25	26	27	28			

MARCH

S	M	T	W	T	F	S
				1	2	3
4	5	6	7	8	9	10
11	12	13	14	15	16	17
18	19	20	21	22	23	24
25	26	27	28	29	30	31

APRIL

S	M	T	W	T	F	S
1	2	3	4	5	6	7
8	9	10	11	12	13	14
15	16	17	18	19	20	21
22	23	24	25	26	27	28
29	30					

MAY

S	M	T	W	T	F	S
		1	2	3	4	5
6	7	8	9	10	11	12
13	14	15	16	17	18	19
20	21	22	23	24	25	26
27	28	29	30	31		

JUNE

S	M	T	W	T	F	S
					1	2
3	4	5	6	7	8	9
10	11	12	13	14	15	16
17	18	19	20	21	22	23
24	25	26	27	28	29	30

JULY

S	M	T	W	T	F	S
1	2	3	4	5	6	7
8	9	10	11	12	13	14
15	16	17	18	19	20	21
22	23	24	25	26	27	28
29	30	31				

AUGUST

S	M	T	W	T	F	S
			1	2	3	4
5	6	7	8	9	10	11
12	13	14	15	16	17	18
19	20	21	22	23	24	25
26	27	28	29	30	31	

SEPTEMBER

S	M	T	W	T	F	S
						1
2	3	4	5	6	7	8
9	10	11	12	13	14	15
16	17	18	19	20	21	22
23	24	25	26	27	28	29
30						

OCTOBER

S	M	T	W	T	F	S
	1	2	3	4	5	6
7	8	9	10	11	12	13
14	15	16	17	18	19	20
21	22	23	24	25	26	27
28	29	30	31			

NOVEMBER

S	M	T	W	T	F	S
				1	2	3
4	5	6	7	8	9	10
11	12	13	14	15	16	17
18	19	20	21	22	23	24
25	26	27	28	29	30	

DECEMBER

S	M	T	W	T	F	S
						1
2	3	4	5	6	7	8
9	10	11	12	13	14	15
16	17	18	19	20	21	22
23	24	25	26	27	28	29
30	31					

3 2002

JANUARY

S	M	T	W	T	F	S
		1	2	3	4	5
6	7	8	9	10	11	12
13	14	15	16	17	18	19
20	21	22	23	24	25	26
27	28	29	30	31		

FEBRUARY

S	M	T	W	T	F	S
					1	2
3	4	5	6	7	8	9
10	11	12	13	14	15	16
17	18	19	20	21	22	23
24	25	26	27	28		

MARCH

S	M	T	W	T	F	S
					1	2
3	4	5	6	7	8	9
10	11	12	13	14	15	16
17	18	19	20	21	22	23
24	25	26	27	28	29	30
31						

APRIL

S	M	T	W	T	F	S
	1	2	3	4	5	6
7	8	9	10	11	12	13
14	15	16	17	18	19	20
21	22	23	24	25	26	27
28	29	30				

MAY

S	M	T	W	T	F	S
			1	2	3	4
5	6	7	8	9	10	11
12	13	14	15	16	17	18
19	20	21	22	23	24	25
26	27	28	29	30	31	

JUNE

S	M	T	W	T	F	S
						1
2	3	4	5	6	7	8
9	10	11	12	13	14	15
16	17	18	19	20	21	22
23	24	25	26	27	28	29
30						

JULY

S	M	T	W	T	F	S
	1	2	3	4	5	6
7	8	9	10	11	12	13
14	15	16	17	18	19	20
21	22	23	24	25	26	27
28	29	30	31			

AUGUST

S	M	T	W	T	F	S
				1	2	3
4	5	6	7	8	9	10
11	12	13	14	15	16	17
18	19	20	21	22	23	24
25	26	27	28	29	30	31

SEPTEMBER

S	M	T	W	T	F	S
1	2	3	4	5	6	7
8	9	10	11	12	13	14
15	16	17	18	19	20	21
22	23	24	25	26	27	28
29	30					

OCTOBER

S	M	T	W	T	F	S
		1	2	3	4	5
6	7	8	9	10	11	12
13	14	15	16	17	18	19
20	21	22	23	24	25	26
27	28	29	30	31		

NOVEMBER

S	M	T	W	T	F	S
					1	2
3	4	5	6	7	8	9
10	11	12	13	14	15	16
17	18	19	20	21	22	23
24	25	26	27	28	29	30

DECEMBER

S	M	T	W	T	F	S
1	2	3	4	5	6	7
8	9	10	11	12	13	14
15	16	17	18	19	20	21
22	23	24	25	26	27	28
29	30	31				

4 2003

JANUARY

S	M	T	W	T	F	S
			1	2	3	4
5	6	7	8	9	10	11
12	13	14	15	16	17	18
19	20	21	22	23	24	25
26	27	28	29	30	31	

FEBRUARY

S	M	T	W	T	F	S
						1
2	3	4	5	6	7	8
9	10	11	12	13	14	15
16	17	18	19	20	21	22
23	24	25	26	27	28	

MARCH

S	M	T	W	T	F	S
						1
2	3	4	5	6	7	8
9	10	11	12	13	14	15
16	17	18	19	20	21	22
23	24	25	26	27	28	29
30	31					

APRIL

S	M	T	W	T	F	S
		1	2	3	4	5
6	7	8	9	10	11	12
13	14	15	16	17	18	19
20	21	22	23	24	25	26
27	28	29	30			

MAY

S	M	T	W	T	F	S
				1	2	3
4	5	6	7	8	9	10
11	12	13	14	15	16	17
18	19	20	21	22	23	24
25	26	27	28	29	30	31

JUNE

S	M	T	W	T	F	S
1	2	3	4	5	6	7
8	9	10	11	12	13	14
15	16	17	18	19	20	21
22	23	24	25	26	27	28
29	30					

JULY

S	M	T	W	T	F	S
		1	2	3	4	5
6	7	8	9	10	11	12
13	14	15	16	17	18	19
20	21	22	23	24	25	26
27	28	29	30	31		

AUGUST

S	M	T	W	T	F	S
					1	2
3	4	5	6	7	8	9
10	11	12	13	14	15	16
17	18	19	20	21	22	23
24	25	26	27	28	29	30
31						

SEPTEMBER

S	M	T	W	T	F	S
	1	2	3	4	5	6
7	8	9	10	11	12	13
14	15	16	17	18	19	20
21	22	23	24	25	26	27
28	29	30				

OCTOBER

S	M	T	W	T	F	S
			1	2	3	4
5	6	7	8	9	10	11
12	13	14	15	16	17	18
19	20	21	22	23	24	25
26	27	28	29	30	31	

NOVEMBER

S	M	T	W	T	F	S
						1
2	3	4	5	6	7	8
9	10	11	12	13	14	15
16	17	18	19	20	21	22
23	24	25	26	27	28	29
30						

DECEMBER

S	M	T	W	T	F	S
	1	2	3	4	5	6
7	8	9	10	11	12	13
14	15	16	17	18	19	20
21	22	23	24	25	26	27
28	29	30	31			

5 2009

JANUARY

S	M	T	W	T	F	S
				1	2	3
4	5	6	7	8	9	10
11	12	13	14	15	16	17
18	19	20	21	22	23	24
25	26	27	28	29	30	31

FEBRUARY

S	M	T	W	T	F	S
1	2	3	4	5	6	7
8	9	10	11	12	13	14
15	16	17	18	19	20	21
22	23	24	25	26	27	28

MARCH

S	M	T	W	T	F	S
1	2	3	4	5	6	7
8	9	10	11	12	13	14
15	16	17	18	19	20	21
22	23	24	25	26	27	28
29	30	31				

APRIL

S	M	T	W	T	F	S
			1	2	3	4
5	6	7	8	9	10	11
12	13	14	15	16	17	18
19	20	21	22	23	24	25
26	27	28	29	30		

MAY

S	M	T	W	T	F	S
					1	2
3	4	5	6	7	8	9
10	11	12	13	14	15	16
17	18	19	20	21	22	23
24	25	26	27	28	29	30
31						

JUNE

S	M	T	W	T	F	S
	1	2	3	4	5	6
7	8	9	10	11	12	13
14	15	16	17	18	19	20
21	22	23	24	25	26	27
28	29	30				

JULY

S	M	T	W	T	F	S
			1	2	3	4
5	6	7	8	9	10	11
12	13	14	15	16	17	18
19	20	21	22	23	24	25
26	27	28	29	30	31	

AUGUST

S	M	T	W	T	F	S
						1
2	3	4	5	6	7	8
9	10	11	12	13	14	15
16	17	18	19	20	21	22
23	24	25	26	27	28	29
30	31					

SEPTEMBER

S	M	T	W	T	F	S
		1	2	3	4	5
6	7	8	9	10	11	12
13	14	15	16	17	18	19
20	21	22	23	24	25	26
27	28	29	30			

OCTOBER

S	M	T	W	T	F	S
				1	2	3
4	5	6	7	8	9	10
11	12	13	14	15	16	17
18	19	20	21	22	23	24
25	26	27	28	29	30	31

NOVEMBER

S	M	T	W	T	F	S
1	2	3	4	5	6	7
8	9	10	11	12	13	14
15	16	17	18	19	20	21
22	23	24	25	26	27	28
29	30					

DECEMBER

S	M	T	W	T	F	S
		1	2	3	4	5
6	7	8	9	10	11	12
13	14	15	16	17	18	19
20	21	22	23	24	25	26
27	28	29	30	31		

6 2010

JANUARY

S	M	T	W	T	F	S
					1	2
3	4	5	6	7	8	9
10	11	12	13	14	15	16
17	18	19	20	21	22	23
24	25	26	27	28	29	30
31						

FEBRUARY

S	M	T	W	T	F	S
	1	2	3	4	5	6
7	8	9	10	11	12	13
14	15	16	17	18	19	20
21	22	23	24	25	26	27
28						

MARCH

S	M	T	W	T	F	S
	1	2	3	4	5	6
7	8	9	10	11	12	13
14	15	16	17	18	19	20
21	22	23	24	25	26	27
28	29	30	31			

APRIL

S	M	T	W	T	F	S
				1	2	3
4	5	6	7	8	9	10
11	12	13	14	15	16	17
18	19	20	21	22	23	24
25	26	27	28	29	30	

MAY

S	M	T	W	T	F	S
						1
2	3	4	5	6	7	8
9	10	11	12	13	14	15
16	17	18	19	20	21	22
23	24	25	26	27	28	29
30	31					

JUNE

S	M	T	W	T	F	S
		1	2	3	4	5
6	7	8	9	10	11	12
13	14	15	16	17	18	19
20	21	22	23	24	25	26
27	28	29	30			

JULY

S	M	T	W	T	F	S
				1	2	3
4	5	6	7	8	9	10
11	12	13	14	15	16	17
18	19	20	21	22	23	24
25	26	27	28	29	30	31

AUGUST

S	M	T	W	T	F	S
1	2	3	4	5	6	7
8	9	10	11	12	13	14
15	16	17	18	19	20	21
22	23	24	25	26	27	28
29	30	31				

SEPTEMBER

S	M	T	W	T	F	S
			1	2	3	4
5	6	7	8	9	10	11
12	13	14	15	16	17	18
19	20	21	22	23	24	25
26	27	28	29	30		

OCTOBER

S	M	T	W	T	F	S
					1	2
3	4	5	6	7	8	9
10	11	12	13	14	15	16
17	18	19	20	21	22	23
24	25	26	27	28	29	30
31						

NOVEMBER

S	M	T	W	T	F	S
	1	2	3	4	5	6
7	8	9	10	11	12	13
14	15	16	17	18	19	20
21	22	23	24	25	26	27
28	29	30				

DECEMBER

S	M	T	W	T	F	S
			1	2	3	4
5	6	7	8	9	10	11
12	13	14	15	16	17	18
19	20	21	22	23	24	25
26	27	28	29	30	31	

7 2005

JANUARY
S	M	T	W	T	F	S
						1
2	3	4	5	6	7	8
9	10	11	12	13	14	15
16	17	18	19	20	21	22
23	24	25	26	27	28	29
30	31					

FEBRUARY
S	M	T	W	T	F	S
		1	2	3	4	5
6	7	8	9	10	11	12
13	14	15	16	17	18	19
20	21	22	23	24	25	26
27	28					

MARCH
S	M	T	W	T	F	S
		1	2	3	4	5
6	7	8	9	10	11	12
13	14	15	16	17	18	19
20	21	22	23	24	25	26
27	28	29	30	31		

APRIL
S	M	T	W	T	F	S
					1	2
3	4	5	6	7	8	9
10	11	12	13	14	15	16
17	18	19	20	21	22	23
24	25	26	27	28	29	30

MAY
S	M	T	W	T	F	S
1	2	3	4	5	6	7
8	9	10	11	12	13	14
15	16	17	18	19	20	21
22	23	24	25	26	27	28
29	30	31				

JUNE
S	M	T	W	T	F	S
			1	2	3	4
5	6	7	8	9	10	11
12	13	14	15	16	17	18
19	20	21	22	23	24	25
26	27	28	29	30		

JULY
S	M	T	W	T	F	S
					1	2
3	4	5	6	7	8	9
10	11	12	13	14	15	16
17	18	19	20	21	22	23
24	25	26	27	28	29	30
31						

AUGUST
S	M	T	W	T	F	S
	1	2	3	4	5	6
7	8	9	10	11	12	13
14	15	16	17	18	19	20
21	22	23	24	25	26	27
28	29	30	31			

SEPTEMBER
S	M	T	W	T	F	S
				1	2	3
4	5	6	7	8	9	10
11	12	13	14	15	16	17
18	19	20	21	22	23	24
25	26	27	28	29	30	

OCTOBER
S	M	T	W	T	F	S
						1
2	3	4	5	6	7	8
9	10	11	12	13	14	15
16	17	18	19	20	21	22
23	24	25	26	27	28	29
30	31					

NOVEMBER
S	M	T	W	T	F	S
		1	2	3	4	5
6	7	8	9	10	11	12
13	14	15	16	17	18	19
20	21	22	23	24	25	26
27	28	29	30			

DECEMBER
S	M	T	W	T	F	S
				1	2	3
4	5	6	7	8	9	10
11	12	13	14	15	16	17
18	19	20	21	22	23	24
25	26	27	28	29	30	31

8

JANUARY
S	M	T	W	T	F	S
1	2	3	4	5	6	7
8	9	10	11	12	13	14
15	16	17	18	19	20	21
22	23	24	25	26	27	28
29	30	31				

FEBRUARY
S	M	T	W	T	F	S
			1	2	3	4
5	6	7	8	9	10	11
12	13	14	15	16	17	18
19	20	21	22	23	24	25
26	27	28	29			

MARCH
S	M	T	W	T	F	S
				1	2	3
4	5	6	7	8	9	10
11	12	13	14	15	16	17
18	19	20	21	22	23	24
25	26	27	28	29	30	31

APRIL
S	M	T	W	T	F	S
1	2	3	4	5	6	7
8	9	10	11	12	13	14
15	16	17	18	19	20	21
22	23	24	25	26	27	28
29	30					

MAY
S	M	T	W	T	F	S
		1	2	3	4	5
6	7	8	9	10	11	12
13	14	15	16	17	18	19
20	21	22	23	24	25	26
27	28	29	30	31		

JUNE
S	M	T	W	T	F	S
					1	2
3	4	5	6	7	8	9
10	11	12	13	14	15	16
17	18	19	20	21	22	23
24	25	26	27	28	29	30

JULY
S	M	T	W	T	F	S
1	2	3	4	5	6	7
8	9	10	11	12	13	14
15	16	17	18	19	20	21
22	23	24	25	26	27	28
29	30	31				

AUGUST
S	M	T	W	T	F	S
			1	2	3	4
5	6	7	8	9	10	11
12	13	14	15	16	17	18
19	20	21	22	23	24	25
26	27	28	29	30	31	

SEPTEMBER
S	M	T	W	T	F	S
						1
2	3	4	5	6	7	8
9	10	11	12	13	14	15
16	17	18	19	20	21	22
23	24	25	26	27	28	29
30						

OCTOBER
S	M	T	W	T	F	S
	1	2	3	4	5	6
7	8	9	10	11	12	13
14	15	16	17	18	19	20
21	22	23	24	25	26	27
28	29	30	31			

NOVEMBER
S	M	T	W	T	F	S
				1	2	3
4	5	6	7	8	9	10
11	12	13	14	15	16	17
18	19	20	21	22	23	24
25	26	27	28	29	30	

DECEMBER
S	M	T	W	T	F	S
						1
2	3	4	5	6	7	8
9	10	11	12	13	14	15
16	17	18	19	20	21	22
23	24	25	26	27	28	29
30	31					

9

JANUARY
S	M	T	W	T	F	S
	1	2	3	4	5	6
7	8	9	10	11	12	13
14	15	16	17	18	19	20
21	22	23	24	25	26	27
28	29	30	31			

FEBRUARY
S	M	T	W	T	F	S
				1	2	3
4	5	6	7	8	9	10
11	12	13	14	15	16	17
18	19	20	21	22	23	24
25	26	27	28	29		

MARCH
S	M	T	W	T	F	S
					1	2
3	4	5	6	7	8	9
10	11	12	13	14	15	16
17	18	19	20	21	22	23
24	25	26	27	28	29	30
31						

APRIL
S	M	T	W	T	F	S
	1	2	3	4	5	6
7	8	9	10	11	12	13
14	15	16	17	18	19	20
21	22	23	24	25	26	27
28	29	30				

MAY
S	M	T	W	T	F	S
			1	2	3	4
5	6	7	8	9	10	11
12	13	14	15	16	17	18
19	20	21	22	23	24	25
26	27	28	29	30	31	

JUNE
S	M	T	W	T	F	S
						1
2	3	4	5	6	7	8
9	10	11	12	13	14	15
16	17	18	19	20	21	22
23	24	25	26	27	28	29
30						

JULY
S	M	T	W	T	F	S
	1	2	3	4	5	6
7	8	9	10	11	12	13
14	15	16	17	18	19	20
21	22	23	24	25	26	27
28	29	30	31			

AUGUST
S	M	T	W	T	F	S
				1	2	3
4	5	6	7	8	9	10
11	12	13	14	15	16	17
18	19	20	21	22	23	24
25	26	27	28	29	30	31

SEPTEMBER
S	M	T	W	T	F	S
1	2	3	4	5	6	7
8	9	10	11	12	13	14
15	16	17	18	19	20	21
22	23	24	25	26	27	28
29	30					

OCTOBER
S	M	T	W	T	F	S
		1	2	3	4	5
6	7	8	9	10	11	12
13	14	15	16	17	18	19
20	21	22	23	24	25	26
27	28	29	30	31		

NOVEMBER
S	M	T	W	T	F	S
					1	2
3	4	5	6	7	8	9
10	11	12	13	14	15	16
17	18	19	20	21	22	23
24	25	26	27	28	29	30

DECEMBER
S	M	T	W	T	F	S
1	2	3	4	5	6	7
8	9	10	11	12	13	14
15	16	17	18	19	20	21
22	23	24	25	26	27	28
29	30	31				

10 2008

JANUARY
S	M	T	W	T	F	S
		1	2	3	4	5
6	7	8	9	10	11	12
13	14	15	16	17	18	19
20	21	22	23	24	25	26
27	28	29	30	31		

FEBRUARY
S	M	T	W	T	F	S
					1	2
3	4	5	6	7	8	9
10	11	12	13	14	15	16
17	18	19	20	21	22	23
24	25	26	27	28	29	

MARCH
S	M	T	W	T	F	S
						1
2	3	4	5	6	7	8
9	10	11	12	13	14	15
16	17	18	19	20	21	22
23	24	25	26	27	28	29
30	31					

APRIL
S	M	T	W	T	F	S
		1	2	3	4	5
6	7	8	9	10	11	12
13	14	15	16	17	18	19
20	21	22	23	24	25	26
27	28	29	30			

MAY
S	M	T	W	T	F	S
				1	2	3
4	5	6	7	8	9	10
11	12	13	14	15	16	17
18	19	20	21	22	23	24
25	26	27	28	29	30	31

JUNE
S	M	T	W	T	F	S
1	2	3	4	5	6	7
8	9	10	11	12	13	14
15	16	17	18	19	20	21
22	23	24	25	26	27	28
29	30					

JULY
S	M	T	W	T	F	S
		1	2	3	4	5
6	7	8	9	10	11	12
13	14	15	16	17	18	19
20	21	22	23	24	25	26
27	28	29	30	31		

AUGUST
S	M	T	W	T	F	S
					1	2
3	4	5	6	7	8	9
10	11	12	13	14	15	16
17	18	19	20	21	22	23
24	25	26	27	28	29	30
31						

SEPTEMBER
S	M	T	W	T	F	S
	1	2	3	4	5	6
7	8	9	10	11	12	13
14	15	16	17	18	19	20
21	22	23	24	25	26	27
28	29	30				

OCTOBER
S	M	T	W	T	F	S
			1	2	3	4
5	6	7	8	9	10	11
12	13	14	15	16	17	18
19	20	21	22	23	24	25
26	27	28	29	30	31	

NOVEMBER
S	M	T	W	T	F	S
						1
2	3	4	5	6	7	8
9	10	11	12	13	14	15
16	17	18	19	20	21	22
23	24	25	26	27	28	29
30						

DECEMBER
S	M	T	W	T	F	S
	1	2	3	4	5	6
7	8	9	10	11	12	13
14	15	16	17	18	19	20
21	22	23	24	25	26	27
28	29	30	31			

11

JANUARY
S	M	T	W	T	F	S
			1	2	3	4
5	6	7	8	9	10	11
12	13	14	15	16	17	18
19	20	21	22	23	24	25
26	27	28	29	30	31	

FEBRUARY
S	M	T	W	T	F	S
						1
2	3	4	5	6	7	8
9	10	11	12	13	14	15
16	17	18	19	20	21	22
23	24	25	26	27	28	29

MARCH
S	M	T	W	T	F	S
1	2	3	4	5	6	7
8	9	10	11	12	13	14
15	16	17	18	19	20	21
22	23	24	25	26	27	28
29	30	31				

APRIL
S	M	T	W	T	F	S
			1	2	3	4
5	6	7	8	9	10	11
12	13	14	15	16	17	18
19	20	21	22	23	24	25
26	27	28	29	30		

MAY
S	M	T	W	T	F	S
					1	2
3	4	5	6	7	8	9
10	11	12	13	14	15	16
17	18	19	20	21	22	23
24	25	26	27	28	29	30
31						

JUNE
S	M	T	W	T	F	S
	1	2	3	4	5	6
7	8	9	10	11	12	13
14	15	16	17	18	19	20
21	22	23	24	25	26	27
28	29	30				

JULY
S	M	T	W	T	F	S
			1	2	3	4
5	6	7	8	9	10	11
12	13	14	15	16	17	18
19	20	21	22	23	24	25
26	27	28	29	30	31	

AUGUST
S	M	T	W	T	F	S
						1
2	3	4	5	6	7	8
9	10	11	12	13	14	15
16	17	18	19	20	21	22
23	24	25	26	27	28	29
30	31					

SEPTEMBER
S	M	T	W	T	F	S
		1	2	3	4	5
6	7	8	9	10	11	12
13	14	15	16	17	18	19
20	21	22	23	24	25	26
27	28	29	30			

OCTOBER
S	M	T	W	T	F	S
				1	2	3
4	5	6	7	8	9	10
11	12	13	14	15	16	17
18	19	20	21	22	23	24
25	26	27	28	29	30	31

NOVEMBER
S	M	T	W	T	F	S
1	2	3	4	5	6	7
8	9	10	11	12	13	14
15	16	17	18	19	20	21
22	23	24	25	26	27	28
29	30					

DECEMBER
S	M	T	W	T	F	S
		1	2	3	4	5
6	7	8	9	10	11	12
13	14	15	16	17	18	19
20	21	22	23	24	25	26
27	28	29	30	31		

12 2004

JANUARY
S	M	T	W	T	F	S
				1	2	3
4	5	6	7	8	9	10
11	12	13	14	15	16	17
18	19	20	21	22	23	24
25	26	27	28	29	30	31

FEBRUARY
S	M	T	W	T	F	S
1	2	3	4	5	6	7
8	9	10	11	12	13	14
15	16	17	18	19	20	21
22	23	24	25	26	27	28
29						

MARCH
S	M	T	W	T	F	S
	1	2	3	4	5	6
7	8	9	10	11	12	13
14	15	16	17	18	19	20
21	22	23	24	25	26	27
28	29	30	31			

APRIL
S	M	T	W	T	F	S
				1	2	3
4	5	6	7	8	9	10
11	12	13	14	15	16	17
18	19	20	21	22	23	24
25	26	27	28	29	30	

MAY
S	M	T	W	T	F	S
						1
2	3	4	5	6	7	8
9	10	11	12	13	14	15
16	17	18	19	20	21	22
23	24	25	26	27	28	29
30	31					

JUNE
S	M	T	W	T	F	S
		1	2	3	4	5
6	7	8	9	10	11	12
13	14	15	16	17	18	19
20	21	22	23	24	25	26
27	28	29	30			

JULY
S	M	T	W	T	F	S
				1	2	3
4	5	6	7	8	9	10
11	12	13	14	15	16	17
18	19	20	21	22	23	24
25	26	27	28	29	30	31

AUGUST
S	M	T	W	T	F	S
1	2	3	4	5	6	7
8	9	10	11	12	13	14
15	16	17	18	19	20	21
22	23	24	25	26	27	28
29	30	31				

SEPTEMBER
S	M	T	W	T	F	S
			1	2	3	4
5	6	7	8	9	10	11
12	13	14	15	16	17	18
19	20	21	22	23	24	25
26	27	28	29	30		

OCTOBER
S	M	T	W	T	F	S
					1	2
3	4	5	6	7	8	9
10	11	12	13	14	15	16
17	18	19	20	21	22	23
24	25	26	27	28	29	30
31						

NOVEMBER
S	M	T	W	T	F	S
	1	2	3	4	5	6
7	8	9	10	11	12	13
14	15	16	17	18	19	20
21	22	23	24	25	26	27
28	29	30				

DECEMBER
S	M	T	W	T	F	S
			1	2	3	4
5	6	7	8	9	10	11
12	13	14	15	16	17	18
19	20	21	22	23	24	25
26	27	28	29	30	31	

13

JANUARY
S	M	T	W	T	F	S
					1	2
3	4	5	6	7	8	9
10	11	12	13	14	15	16
17	18	19	20	21	22	23
24	25	26	27	28	29	30
31						

FEBRUARY
S	M	T	W	T	F	S
	1	2	3	4	5	6
7	8	9	10	11	12	13
14	15	16	17	18	19	20
21	22	23	24	25	26	27
28	29					

MARCH
S	M	T	W	T	F	S
		1	2	3	4	5
6	7	8	9	10	11	12
13	14	15	16	17	18	19
20	21	22	23	24	25	26
27	28	29	30	31		

APRIL
S	M	T	W	T	F	S
					1	2
3	4	5	6	7	8	9
10	11	12	13	14	15	16
17	18	19	20	21	22	23
24	25	26	27	28	29	30

MAY
S	M	T	W	T	F	S
1	2	3	4	5	6	7
8	9	10	11	12	13	14
15	16	17	18	19	20	21
22	23	24	25	26	27	28
29	30	31				

JUNE
S	M	T	W	T	F	S
			1	2	3	4
5	6	7	8	9	10	11
12	13	14	15	16	17	18
19	20	21	22	23	24	25
26	27	28	29	30		

JULY
S	M	T	W	T	F	S
					1	2
3	4	5	6	7	8	9
10	11	12	13	14	15	16
17	18	19	20	21	22	23
24	25	26	27	28	29	30
31						

AUGUST
S	M	T	W	T	F	S
	1	2	3	4	5	6
7	8	9	10	11	12	13
14	15	16	17	18	19	20
21	22	23	24	25	26	27
28	29	30	31			

SEPTEMBER
S	M	T	W	T	F	S
				1	2	3
4	5	6	7	8	9	10
11	12	13	14	15	16	17
18	19	20	21	22	23	24
25	26	27	28	29	30	

OCTOBER
S	M	T	W	T	F	S
						1
2	3	4	5	6	7	8
9	10	11	12	13	14	15
16	17	18	19	20	21	22
23	24	25	26	27	28	29
30	31					

NOVEMBER
S	M	T	W	T	F	S
		1	2	3	4	5
6	7	8	9	10	11	12
13	14	15	16	17	18	19
20	21	22	23	24	25	26
27	28	29	30			

DECEMBER
S	M	T	W	T	F	S
				1	2	3
4	5	6	7	8	9	10
11	12	13	14	15	16	17
18	19	20	21	22	23	24
25	26	27	28	29	30	31

14 2000

JANUARY
S	M	T	W	T	F	S
						1
2	3	4	5	6	7	8
9	10	11	12	13	14	15
16	17	18	19	20	21	22
23	24	25	26	27	28	29
30	31					

FEBRUARY
S	M	T	W	T	F	S
		1	2	3	4	5
6	7	8	9	10	11	12
13	14	15	16	17	18	19
20	21	22	23	24	25	26
27	28	29				

MARCH
S	M	T	W	T	F	S
			1	2	3	4
5	6	7	8	9	10	11
12	13	14	15	16	17	18
19	20	21	22	23	24	25
26	27	28	29	30	31	

APRIL
S	M	T	W	T	F	S
						1
2	3	4	5	6	7	8
9	10	11	12	13	14	15
16	17	18	19	20	21	22
23	24	25	26	27	28	29
30						

MAY
S	M	T	W	T	F	S
	1	2	3	4	5	6
7	8	9	10	11	12	13
14	15	16	17	18	19	20
21	22	23	24	25	26	27
28	29	30	31			

JUNE
S	M	T	W	T	F	S
				1	2	3
4	5	6	7	8	9	10
11	12	13	14	15	16	17
18	19	20	21	22	23	24
25	26	27	28	29	30	

JULY
S	M	T	W	T	F	S
						1
2	3	4	5	6	7	8
9	10	11	12	13	14	15
16	17	18	19	20	21	22
23	24	25	26	27	28	29
30	31					

AUGUST
S	M	T	W	T	F	S
		1	2	3	4	5
6	7	8	9	10	11	12
13	14	15	16	17	18	19
20	21	22	23	24	25	26
27	28	29	30	31		

SEPTEMBER
S	M	T	W	T	F	S
					1	2
3	4	5	6	7	8	9
10	11	12	13	14	15	16
17	18	19	20	21	22	23
24	25	26	27	28	29	30

OCTOBER
S	M	T	W	T	F	S
1	2	3	4	5	6	7
8	9	10	11	12	13	14
15	16	17	18	19	20	21
22	23	24	25	26	27	28
29	30	31				

NOVEMBER
S	M	T	W	T	F	S
			1	2	3	4
5	6	7	8	9	10	11
12	13	14	15	16	17	18
19	20	21	22	23	24	25
26	27	28	29	30		

DECEMBER
S	M	T	W	T	F	S
					1	2
3	4	5	6	7	8	9
10	11	12	13	14	15	16
17	18	19	20	21	22	23
24	25	26	27	28	29	30
31						

IT'S A FACT: Guy Fawkes Day, which celebrates the foiling of a plot by Catholics to blow up the British parliament in 1605, in protest against anti-Catholic laws, is observed on Nov. 5 in Britain. The name comes from that of the chief conspirator; traditional holiday celebrations include fireworks, bonfires, and effigy-burning.

Chinese Calendar, Asian Festivals

Source: Chinese Information and Culture Center, New York, NY

The Chinese calendar (like the Jewish and Islamic calendars (see the Religion chapter) is a lunar calendar. It is divided into 12 months of 29 or 30 days (compensating for the lunar month's mean duration of 29 days, 12 hr, 44.05 min). This calendar is synchronized with the solar year by the addition of extra months at fixed intervals.

The Chinese calendar runs on a 60-year cycle. The cycles 1876-1935 and 1936-95, with the years grouped under their 12 animal designations, are printed below, along with the first 24 years of the current cycle. This cycle began in 1996 and will last until 2055. Feb. 9, 2005, marks the beginning of the year 4703 in the Chinese calendar, and is designated the Year of the Rooster. Readers can find the animal name for the year of their birth in the chart below. (Note: The first 3-7 weeks of each Western year belong to the previous Chinese year and animal designation.)

Both the Western (Gregorian) and traditional lunar calendars are used publicly in China and in North and South Korea, and 2 New Year's celebrations are held. In Taiwan, in overseas Chinese communities, and in Vietnam, the lunar calendar is used only to set the dates for traditional festivals, with the Gregorian system in general use.

The 4-day Chinese New Year, Hsin Nien, the 3-day Vietnamese New Year festival, Tet, and the 3-to-4-day Korean festival, Suhl, begin at the 2nd new moon after the winter solstice. The new moon in the Far East, which is west of the International Date Line, may be a day later than the new moon in the U.S. The festivals may start, therefore, anywhere between Jan. 21 and Feb. 19 of the Gregorian calendar.

Rat	Ox	Tiger	Hare (Rabbit)	Dragon	Snake	Horse	Sheep (Goat)	Monkey	Rooster	Dog	Pig
1876	1877	1878	1879	1880	1881	1882	1883	1884	1885	1886	1887
1888	1889	1890	1891	1892	1893	1894	1895	1896	1897	1898	1899
1900	1901	1902	1903	1904	1905	1906	1907	1908	1909	1910	1911
1912	1913	1914	1915	1916	1917	1918	1919	1920	1921	1922	1923
1924	1925	1926	1927	1928	1929	1930	1931	1932	1933	1934	1935
1936	1937	1938	1939	1940	1941	1942	1943	1944	1945	1946	1947
1948	1949	1950	1951	1952	1953	1954	1955	1956	1957	1958	1959
1960	1961	1962	1963	1964	1965	1966	1967	1968	1969	1970	1971
1972	1973	1974	1975	1976	1977	1978	1979	1980	1981	1982	1983
1984	1985	1986	1987	1988	1989	1990	1991	1992	1993	1994	1995
1996	1997	1998	1999	2000	2001	2002	2003	2004	2005	2006	2007
2008	2009	2010	2011	2012	2013	2014	2015	2016	2017	2018	2019

Other Calendars, Year and New Year's

Era	Year	Begins in 2006
Byzantine	7515	Sept. 14
Jewish	5767	Sept. 22[1]
Roman (Ab Urbe Condita)	2759	Jan. 14
Nabonassar (Babylonian)	2755	Apr. 23
Japanese (starts at 0 with new emperor)	18	Jan. 1
Grecian (Seleucidae)	2318	Sept. 14 or Oct. 14
Diocletian	1723	Sept. 11
Indian (Saka)	1928	Mar. 22
Islamic/Muslim (Hijra)	1427	Jan. 29/30[2]
Chinese (Year of the Dog)	4704	Jan. 29

(1) Year begins at sunset. (2) Year begins at moon crescent.

Chronological Cycles, 2006

Dominical Letter	A	Roman Indiction	14	Solar Cycle	27
Golden Number (Lunar Cycle)	12	Epact	0	Julian Period (year of)	6719

Special Months

Every year there are many thousands of special months, days, and weeks as a result of anniversaries, official proclamations, and promotional events, both trivial and serious. Here are a few of the special months:

January: Jump Out of Bed Month, National Mentoring Month, National Poverty in America Awareness Month

February: Black History Month, American Heart Month, Library Lovers Month, Youth Leadership Month, Return Shopping Carts to the Supermarket Month

March: Irish-American Heritage Month, Women's History Month, American Red Cross Month, National Frozen Foods Month, National Talk With Your Teen About Sex Month

April: National Child Abuse Prevention Month, National Humor Month, Stress Awareness Month, Grange Month

May: Clean Air Month, Get Caught Reading Month, National Barbecue Month, Asian Pacific American Heritage Month, National Mental Health Month

June: National Candy Month, Gay and Lesbian Pride Month, Potty Training Awareness Month, National Safety Month

July: Cell Phone Courtesy Month, National Hot Dog Month, Women's Motorcycle Month

August: Black Business Month, National Inventors' Month, Happiness Happens Month, National Toddler Month

September: Library Card Sign-Up Month, National Hispanic Heritage Month (Sept. 15-Oct. 15), National Biscuit Month

October: National Domestic Violence Awareness Month, National Breast Cancer Awareness Month, Diversity Awareness Month, National Popcorn Poppin' Month

November: National AIDS Awareness Month, National American Indian Heritage Month, National Adoption Month, American Diabetes Month, Peanut Butter Lovers' Month

December: Universal Human Rights Month, National Drunk and Drugged Driving Prevention Month, National Tie Month, Colorectal Cancer Education and Awareness Month

Wedding Anniversaries

The traditional names for wedding anniversaries go back many years in social usage and have been used to suggest types of appropriate anniversary gifts. Traditional products for gifts are listed here in capital letters, with a few allowable revisions in parentheses, followed by common modern gifts in each category.

1st	PAPER, clocks	**9th**	POTTERY (CHINA), leather goods	**25th**	SILVER, sterling silver
2nd	COTTON, china	**10th**	TIN, ALUMINUM, diamond	**30th**	PEARL, diamond
3rd	LEATHER, crystal, glass	**11th**	STEEL, fashion jewelry	**35th**	CORAL (JADE), jade
4th	LINEN (SILK), appliances	**12th**	SILK, pearls, colored gems	**40th**	RUBY, ruby
5th	WOOD, silverware	**13th**	LACE, textiles, furs	**45th**	SAPPHIRE, sapphire
6th	IRON, wood objects	**14th**	IVORY, gold jewelry	**50th**	GOLD, gold
7th	WOOL (COPPER), desk sets	**15th**	CRYSTAL, watches	**55th**	EMERALD, emerald
8th	BRONZE, linens, lace	**20th**	CHINA, platinum	**60th**	DIAMOND, diamond

Birthstones

Source: Jewelry Industry Council

MONTH	Ancient	Modern
January	Garnet	Garnet
February	Amethyst	Amethyst
March	Jasper	Bloodstone or Aquamarine
April	Sapphire	Diamond
May	Agate	Emerald
June	Emerald	Pearl, Moonstone, or Alexandrite
July	Onyx	Ruby
August	Carnelian	Sardonyx or Peridot
September	Chrysolite	Sapphire
October	Aquamarine	Opal or Tourmaline
November	Topaz	Topaz
December	Ruby	Turquoise or Zircon

Standard Time, Daylight Saving Time, and Others

Source: National Imagery and Mapping Agency; U.S. Dept. of Transportation
See also Time Zone map, page 460.

Standard Time

Standard Time is reckoned from the Prime Meridian of Longitude in Greenwich, England. The world is divided into 24 zones, each 15 deg of arc, or one hour in time apart. The Greenwich meridian (0 deg) extends through the center of the initial zone, and the zones to the east are numbered from 1 to 12, with the prefix "minus" indicating the number of hours to be subtracted to obtain Greenwich Time. Each zone extends 7.5 deg on either side of its central meridian.

Westward zones are similarly numbered, but prefixed "plus," showing the number of hours that must be added to get Greenwich Time. Although these zones apply generally to sea areas, the Standard Time maintained in many countries does not coincide with zone time. A graphical representation of the zones is shown on the Standard Time Zone Chart of the World (WOBZC76) published by the National Imagery and Mapping Agency. This chart is available from the Federal Aviation Administration (FAA), 6501 Lafayette Avenue, Riverdale, MD 20737-1199; telephone: (800) 638-8972.

The U.S. and possessions are divided into 10 Standard Time zones. Each zone is approximately 15 deg of longitude in width. All places in each zone use, instead of their own local time, the time counted from the transit of the "mean sun" across the Standard Time meridian that passes near the middle of that zone. These time zones are designated as Atlantic, Eastern, Central, Mountain, Pacific, Alaska, Hawaii-Aleutian, Samoa, Wake Island, and Guam; the time in these zones is reckoned from the 60th, 75th, 90th, 105th, 120th, 135th, 150th, and 165th meridians west of Greenwich and the 165th and 150th meridians east of Greenwich. The time zone line wanders to conform to local geographical regions. The time in the various zones in the U.S. and U.S. territories west of Greenwich is earlier than Greenwich Time by 4, 5, 6, 7, 8, 9, 10, and 11 hours, respectively. However, Wake Island and Guam cross the International Date Line and are 12 and 10 hours later than Greenwich Time, respectively.

24-Hour Time

Twenty-four-hour time is widely used in scientific work throughout the world. In the U.S. it is also used in operations of the armed forces. In Europe it is frequently used by the transportation networks in preference to the 12-hour AM and PM system. With the 24-hour system the day begins at midnight, and times are designated 00:00 through 23:59.

International Date Line

The Date Line, approximately coinciding with the 180th meridian, separates the calendar dates. The date must be advanced one day when crossing in a westerly direction and set back one day when crossing in an easterly direction. The Date Line frequently deviates from the 180th meridian because of decisions made by individual nations affected. The line is deflected eastward through the Bering Strait and westward of the Aleutians to prevent separating these areas by date. The line is deflected eastward of the Tonga and New Zealand Islands in the South Pacific for the same reason. More recently it was deflected much farther eastward to include all of Kiribati. The line is established by international custom; there is no international authority prescribing its exact course.

Daylight Saving Time

Daylight Saving Time is achieved by advancing the clock one hour. Daylight Saving Time in the U.S. begins each year at 2 AM on the first Sunday in Apr. and ends at 2 AM on the last Sunday in Oct. In accordance with a 2005 energy bill passed by Congress, which will take effect in 2007, daylight saving time will be extended by 4 weeks, and will be observed from the 2nd Sunday in Mar. to the first Sunday in Nov.

Daylight Saving Time was first observed in the U.S. during World War I, and then again during World War II. In the intervening years, some states and communities observed Daylight Saving Time, using whatever beginning and ending dates they chose. In 1966, Congress passed the Uniform Time Act, which provided that any state or territory that chooses to observe Daylight Saving Time must begin and end on the federal dates. Any state could, by law, exempt itself; a 1972 amendment to the act authorized states split by time zones to observe Daylight Saving Time in one time zone and standard time in the other time zone. Currently, Arizona, Hawaii, Puerto Rico, the U.S. Virgin Islands, and American Samoa do not observe Daylight Saving Time. On Apr. 2, 2006, all of Indiana will observe Daylight Saving Time for the first time.

Congress and the secretary of transportation both have authority to change time zone boundaries. Since 1966 there have been a number of changes to U.S. time zone boundaries. In addition, efforts to conserve energy have prompted various changes in the times that Daylight Saving Time is observed.

Daylight Saving Time: International Usage

Adjusting clock time so as to gain the added daylight on summer evenings is common throughout the world.

Canada, which extends over 6 time zones, generally observes Daylight Saving Time from the first Sunday of Apr. until the last Sunday of Oct. Saskatchewan remains on standard time all year. Communities elsewhere in Canada also may exempt themselves from Daylight Saving Time. Mexico, which occupies 3 time zones, observes Daylight Saving Time during the same period as most of Canada.

Member nations of the European Union (EU) observe a "summer-time period," the EU's version of Daylight Saving Time, from the last Sunday of Mar. until the last Sunday in Oct.

Russia, which extends over 11 time zones, maintains its Standard Time 1 hour fast for its zone designation. Additionally, it proclaims Daylight Saving Time from the last Sunday in Mar. until the 4th Sunday in Oct.

China, which extends across 5 time zones, has decreed that the entire country be placed on Greenwich Time plus 8 hours. Daylight Saving Time is not observed. Japan, which lies within one time zone, also does not modify its legal time during the summer months.

Many countries in the Southern Hemisphere maintain Daylight Saving Time, generally from Oct. to Mar.; however, most countries near the equator do not deviate from Standard Time.

IT'S A FACT: In 1863, Pres. Abraham Lincoln proclaimed the last Thursday in November a national day of Thanksgiving. Pres. Franklin D. Roosevelt changed it to the fourth Thursday, in order to allow for a longer holiday shopping season when there are five Thursdays in the month.

WORLD ALMANAC QUICK QUIZ

Bill Clinton, George W. Bush, Donald Trump, and Steven Spielberg were all born in 1946, which is what year according to the Chinese calendar?

(a) Year of the Lotus (b) Year of the Snake (c) Year of the Dog (d) Year of the Panda

For the answer look in this chapter, or see page 1008.

Standard Time Differences—World Cities

The time indicated in the table is fixed by law and is called the legal time or, more generally, Standard Time. Use of Daylight Saving Time varies widely. *Indicates morning of the following day. At 12:00 noon, Eastern Standard Time, the Standard Time (in 24-hour time) in selected cities is as follows:

Addis Ababa	20 00
Amsterdam	18 00
Ankara	19 00
Athens	19 00
Auckland	5 00*
Baghdad	20 00
Bangkok	0 00*
Beijing	1 00*
Belfast	17 00
Belgrade	18 00
Berlin	18 00
Bogotá	12 00
Bombay (Mumbai)	22 30
Brussels	18 00
Bucharest	19 00
Budapest	18 00
Buenos Aires	14 00
Cairo	19 00
Calcutta (Kolkata)	22 30
Cape Town	19 00
Caracas	13 00
Casablanca	17 00
Copenhagen	18 00
Dhaka	23 00
Dublin	17 00
Edinburgh	17 00
Geneva	18 00
Helsinki	19 00
Ho Chi Minh City	0 00*
Hong Kong	1 00*
Islamabad	22 00
Istanbul	19 00
Jakarta	0 00*
Jerusalem	19 00
Johannesburg	19 00
Kabul	21 50
Karachi	22 00
Kathmandu	22 45
Kiev	19 00
Lagos	18 00
Lima	12 00
Lisbon	17 00
London	17 00
Madrid	18 00
Manila	1 00*
Mecca	20 00
Melbourne	3 00*
Montevideo	14 00
Moscow	20 00
Munich	18 00
Nagasaki	2 00*
Nairobi	20 00
New Delhi	22 30
Oslo	18 00
Paris	18 00
Prague	18 00
Quito	12 00
Rio de Janeiro	14 00
Riyadh	20 00
Rome	18 00
St. Petersburg	20 00
Santiago	13 00
Sarajevo	18 00
Seoul	2 00*
Shanghai	1 00*
Singapore	1 00*
Stockholm	18 00
Sydney	3 00*
Taipei	1 00*
Tashkent	22 00
Tehran	20 30
Tel Aviv	19 00
Tokyo	2 00*
Vladivostok	3 00*
Vienna	18 00
Warsaw	18 00
Wellington	5 00*
Yangon (Rangoon)	23 30
Yokohama	2 00*
Zurich	18 00

Standard Time Differences—North American Cities

At 12:00 noon, Eastern Standard Time, the Standard Time in selected North American cities is as follows:

Akron, OH	12 00 Noon
Albuquerque, NM	10 00 AM
Anchorage, AK	8 00 AM
Atlanta, GA	12 00 Noon
Austin, TX	11 00 AM
Baltimore, MD	12 00 Noon
Birmingham, AL	11 00 AM
Bismarck, ND	11 00 AM
Boise, ID	10 00 AM
Boston, MA	12 00 Noon
Buffalo, NY	12 00 Noon
Butte, MT	10 00 AM
Calgary, Alta.	10 00 AM
Charleston, SC	12 00 Noon
Charleston, WV	12 00 Noon
Charlotte, NC	12 00 Noon
Charlottetown, PEI.	1 00 PM
Chattanooga, TN	12 00 Noon
Cheyenne, WY	10 00 AM
Chicago, IL	11 00 AM
Cleveland, OH	12 00 Noon
Colorado Spr., CO	10 00 AM
Columbus, OH	12 00 Noon
Dallas, TX	11 00 AM
*Dawson, Yuk.	9 00 AM
Dayton, OH	12 00 Noon
Denver, CO	10 00 AM
Des Moines, IA	11 00 AM
Detroit, MI	12 00 Noon
Duluth, MN	11 00 AM
Edmonton, Alta.	10 00 AM
El Paso, TX	10 00 AM
Erie, PA	12 00 Noon
Evansville, IN	11 00 AM
Fairbanks, AK	8 00 AM
Flint, MI	12 00 Noon
*Fort Wayne, IN	12 00 Noon
Frankfort, KY	12 00 Noon
Havana, Cuba	12 00 Noon
Helena, MT	10 00 AM
*Honolulu, HI	7 00 AM
Houston, TX	11 00 AM
Indianapolis, IN	12 00 Noon
Jacksonville, FL	12 00 Noon
Juneau, AK	8 00 AM
Kansas City, MO	11 00 AM
*Kingston, Jamaica	12 00 Noon
Knoxville, TN	12 00 Noon
Las Vegas, NV	9 00 AM
Lexington, KY	12 00 Noon
Lincoln, NE	11 00 AM
Little Rock, AR	11 00 AM
Los Angeles, CA	9 00 AM
Louisville, KY	12 00 Noon
Mexico City, Mexico	11 00 AM
Memphis, TN	11 00 AM
Miami, FL	12 00 Noon
Milwaukee, WI	11 00 AM
Minneapolis, MN	11 00 AM
Mobile, AL	11 00 AM
Montreal, Que	12 00 Noon
Nashville, TN	11 00 AM
Nassau, Bahamas	12 00 Noon
New Haven, CT	12 00 Noon
New Orleans, LA	11 00 AM
New York, NY	12 00 Noon
Nome, AK	8 00 AM
Norfolk, VA	12 00 Noon
Oklahoma City, OK	11 00 AM
Omaha, NE	11 00 AM
Ottawa, Ont.	12 00 Noon
*Panama City, Panama	12 00 Noon
Peoria, IL	11 00 AM
*Phoenix, AZ	10 00 AM
Pierre, SD	11 00 AM
Pittsburgh, PA	12 00 Noon
*Regina, Sask.	11 00 AM
Reno, NV	9 00 AM
Richmond, VA	12 00 Noon
Rochester, NY	12 00 Noon
Sacramento, CA	9 00 AM
St. John's, Nfld.	1 30 PM
St. Louis, MO	11 00 AM
St. Paul, MN	11 00 AM
Salt Lake City, UT	10 00 AM
San Antonio, TX	11 00 AM
San Diego, CA	9 00 AM
San Francisco, CA	9 00 AM
San Jose, CA	9 00 AM
*San Juan, PR	1 00 PM
Santa Fe, NM	10 00 AM
Savannah, GA	12 00 Noon
Seattle, WA	9 00 AM
Shreveport, LA	11 00 AM
Sioux Falls, SD	11 00 AM
Spokane, WA	9 00 AM
Tampa, FL	12 00 Noon
Toledo, OH	12 00 Noon
Topeka, KS	11 00 AM
Toronto, Ont.	12 00 Noon
*Tucson, AZ	10 00 AM
Tulsa, OK	11 00 AM
Vancouver, BC	9 00 AM
Washington, DC	12 00 Noon
Wichita, KS	11 00 AM
Wilmington, DE	12 00 Noon
Winnipeg, Man.	11 00 AM

Note: This same table can be used for Daylight Saving Time when it is in effect, but allowance must be made for cities that do not observe it; they are marked with an asterisk (*). Daylight Saving Time is one hour later than Standard Time. As of Aug. 2005, Indiana was split between the Central and Eastern Time Zones. Following the decision to impose Daylight Saving Time statewide as of Apr. 2006, Indiana was petitioning the Department of Transportation to determine any changes to the time zone boundaries in the state.

WEIGHTS AND MEASURES

Source: National Institute of Standards and Technology, U.S. Dept. of Commerce

The International System of Units (SI)

Two systems of weights and measures coexist in the U.S. today: the **U.S. Customary System** and the **International System of Units** (SI, after the initials of Systême International). SI, **commonly identified with the metric system,** is actually a more complete, coherent version of it. Throughout U.S. history, the Customary System (inherited from, but now different from, the British Imperial System) has been generally used; federal and state legislation has given it, through implication, standing as the primary weights and measures system. The metric system, however, is the only system that Congress has ever specifically sanctioned. An 1866 law reads:

"It shall be lawful throughout the United States of America to employ the weights and measures of the metric system; and no contract or dealing, or pleading in any court, shall be deemed invalid or liable to objection because the weights or measures expressed or referred to therein are weights or measures of the metric system."

Since that time, use of the metric system in the U.S. has slowly and steadily increased, particularly in the scientific community, the pharmaceutical industry, and the manufacturing sector—the last motivated by the practice in international commerce, in which the metric system is now predominantly used.

On Feb. 10, 1964, the National Bureau of Standards (now known as the National Institute of Standards and Technology) issued the following statement:

"Henceforth it shall be the policy of the National Bureau of Standards to use the units of the International System (SI), as adopted by the 11th General Conference on Weights and Measures (October 1960), except when the use of these units would obviously impair communication or reduce the usefulness of a report."

On Dec. 23, 1975, Pres. Gerald R. Ford signed the Metric Conversion Act of 1975. It defines the metric system as being the International System of Units as interpreted in the U.S. by the secretary of commerce. The Trade Act of 1988 and other legislation declare the metric system the preferred system of weights and measures for U.S. trade and commerce, call for the federal government to adopt metric specifications, and mandate the Commerce Dept. to oversee the program. However, the metric system has still not become the system of choice for most Americans' daily use.

The following 7 units serve as the base units for the system: **length**—meter; **mass**—kilogram; **time**—second; **electric current**—ampere; **thermodynamic temperature**—kelvin; **amount of substance**—mole; and **luminous intensity**—candela.

Frequently Used Conversions

Boldface indicates exact values. For greater accuracy, use the "multiply by" number in parentheses. For weights, *avdp* is an abbreviation for avoirdupois weight, the system of weights applied to all goods except medicines, precious metals, and precious stones (see p.370). For more detailed tables, see pp.369-372.

U.S. Customary to Metric

	If you have:	Multiply by:		To get:
Length	inches	**25.4**		millimeters
	inches	**2.54**		centimeters
	inches	**0.0254**		meters
	feet	0.3	(**0.3048**)	meters
	yards	0.9	(**0.9144**)	meters
	miles[1]	1.6	(**1.609344**)	kilometers
Area	sq. inches	6.5	(**6.4516**)	sq. cm.
	sq. feet	0.09	(0.09290341)	sq. meters
	sq. yards	0.84	(0.83612736)	sq. meters
	acres	0.4	(0.4046873)	hectares
	sq. miles	2.6	(2.58998811)	sq. kilometers
Weight	ounces (avdp)	28	(**28.349523125**)	grams
	pounds (avdp)	454	(**453.59237**)	grams
	pounds (avdp)	0.45	(**0.45359237**)	kilograms
	short tons[2]	0.91	(**0.90718474**)	metric tons
	long tons[3]	1	(**1.0160469088**)	metric tons
Liquid meas.	ounces	0.03	(0.02957353)	liters
	cups	0.24	(0.23658824)	liters
	pints	0.47	(0.473176473)	liters
	quarts	0.95	(0.946352946)	liters
	gallons	3.79	(3.785411784)	liters

Metric to U.S. Customary

	If you have:	Multiply by:		To get:
Length	millimeters	0.04	(0.03937)	inches
	centimeters	0.4	(0.3937)	inches
	meters	39	(39.37)	inches
	meters	3.3	(3.280840)	feet
	meters	1.1	(1.093613)	yards
	kilometers	0.6	(0.621371)	miles
Area	sq. cm.	0.16	(0.15500)	sq. inches
	sq. meters	10.8	(10.76391)	sq. feet
	sq. meters	1.2	(1.195990)	sq. yards
	hectares	2.5	(2.471044)	acres
	sq. kilometers	0.39	(0.386102)	sq. miles
Weight	grams	0.035	(0.03527396)	ounces (avdp)
	grams	0.002	(0.00220462)	pounds (avdp)
	kilograms	2.2	(2.204623)	pounds (avdp)
	metric tons	1.1	(1.102311)	short tons[2]
	metric tons	0.98	(0.9842065)	long tons[3]
Liquid meas.	liters	33.8	(33.81402)	ounces
	liters	4.2	(4.226752)	cups
	liters	2.1	(2.113376)	pints
	liters	1.1	(1.056688)	quarts
	liters	0.26	(0.264172)	gallons

(1) Statute mile. (2) A short ton is 2,000 pounds. (3) A long ton is 2,240 pounds.

Temperature Conversions

The left-hand column below gives a temperature according to the **Celsius** scale, and the right-hand gives the same temperature according to the **Fahrenheit** scale. The lowest number on each scale is equivalent to absolute zero, the temperature at which all motion within a molecule would stop.

For temperatures not shown: To convert Fahrenheit to Celsius by formula, subtract 32 degrees and divide by 1.8; to convert Celsius to Fahrenheit, multiply by 1.8 and add 32 degrees.

Note: Although the term *centigrade* is still frequently used, the International Committee on Weights and Measures and the National Institute of Standards and Technology have recommended since 1948 that this scale be called *Celsius*.

Celsius	Fahrenheit	Celsius	Fahrenheit	Celsius	Fahrenheit	Celsius	Fahrenheit	Celsius	Fahrenheit
–273.15	–459.67	–45.6	–50	–1.1	30	30	86	66	150
–250	–418	–40	–40	0	32	32.2	90	70	158
–200	–328	–34.4	–30	4.4	40	35	95	80	176
–184	–300	–30	–22	10	50	37	98.6	90	194
–157	–250	–28.9	–20	15.6	60	37.8	100	93	200
–150	–238	–23.3	–10	20	68	40	104	100	212
–129	–200	–20	–4	21.1	70	43	110	121	250
–101	–150	–17.8	0	23.9	75	49	120	149	300
–100	–148	–12.2	10	25	77	50	122	150	302
–73.3	–100	–10	14	26.7	80	54	130	200	392
–50	–58	–6.7	20	29.4	85	60	140	300	572

IT'S A FACT: Despite his reputation as "vertically-challenged," the French emperor Napoleon Bonaparte I (1769-1821) was actually of average height. Autopsy examinations put his height at 5'2" in the French unit of measure *(pieds de roi)*, and when autopsy details were made public, the units were not converted to the English standard. Dubbed *le petit caporal* by the French—an endearing term, rather than a physical description—Napoleon actually stood about 5'6½", or slightly above average height for a Frenchman at the time.

Boiling and Freezing Points

Water boils at 212° F (100° C) at sea level. For every 550 feet above sea level, boiling point of water is lower by about 1° F. Methyl alcohol boils at 148° F. Average human oral temperature, 98.6° F. **Water freezes** at 32° F (0° C).

Mathematical Formulas

Note: The value of π (the Greek letter pi) is approximately 3.14159265 (equal to the ratio of the circumference of a circle to the diameter). The equivalence is typically rounded further to 3.1416 or 3.14.

To find the CIRCUMFERENCE of a:

Circle — Multiply the diameter by π.

To find the AREA of a:

Circle — Multiply the square of the radius (equal to ½ the diameter) by π.
Rectangle — Multiply the length of the base by the height.
Sphere (surface) — Multiply the square of the radius by π and multiply by 4.
Square — Square the length of one side.
Trapezoid — Add the 2 parallel sides, multiply by the height, and divide by 2.
Triangle — Multiply the base by the height, divide by 2.

To find the VOLUME of a:

Cone — Multiply the square of the radius of the base by π, multiply by the height, and divide by 3.
Cube — Cube the length of one edge.
Cylinder — Multiply the square of the radius of the base by π and multiply by the height.
Pyramid — Multiply the area of the base by the height and divide by 3.
Rectangular Prism — Multiply the length by the width by the height.
Sphere — Multiply the cube of the radius by π, multiply by 4, and divide by 3.

Playing Cards and Dice Chances

5-Card Poker Hands

Hand	Number possible	Odds against
Royal flush	4	649,739 to 1
Other straight flush	36	72,192 to 1
Four of a kind	624	4,164 to 1
Full house	3,744	693 to 1
Flush	5,108	508 to 1
Straight	10,200	254 to 1
Three of a kind	54,912	46 to 1
Two pairs	123,552	20 to 1
One pair	1,098,240	4 to 3 (1.37 to 1)
Nothing	1,302,540	1 to 1
TOTAL	**2,598,960**	

Bridge

The odds—against suit distribution in a hand of 4-4-3-2 are about 4 to 1, against 5-4-2-2 about 8 to 1, against 6-4-2-1 about 20 to 1, against 7-4-1-1 about 254 to 1, against 8-4-1-0 about 2,211 to 1, and against 13-0-0-0 about 158,753,389,899 to 1.

Dice

(probabilities on 2 dice)

Total	Odds against (single toss)	Total	Odds against (single toss)
2	35 to 1	8	31 to 5
3	17 to 1	9	8 to 1
4	11 to 1	10	11 to 1
5	8 to 1	11	17 to 1
6	31 to 5	12	35 to 1
7	5 to 1		

Large Numbers

No. of zeros	U.S.	British[1], French, German
6	million	million
9	billion	milliard
12	trillion	billion
15	quadrillion	1,000 billion
18	quintillion	trillion
21	sextillion	1,000 trillion
24	septillion	quadrillion
27	octillion	1,000 quadrillion
30	nonillion	quintillion
33	decillion	1,000 quintillion
36	undecillion	sextillion
39	duodecillion	1,000 sextillion
42	tredecillion	septillion
45	quattuordecillion	1,000 septillion
48	quindecillion	octillion
51	sexdecillion	1,000 octillion
54	septendecillion	nonillion
57	octodecillion	1,000 nonillion
60	novemdecillion	decillion
63	vigintillion	1,000 decillion
100	googol	googol
303	centillion	—
600	—	centillion
googol	googolplex	googolplex

(1) In recent years, it has become more common in Britain to use U.S. terminology for large numbers.

Prime Numbers

A prime number is a positive integer that is divisible only by two positive integers, 1 and itself.

Prime Numbers to 1,009

	2	3	5	7	11	13	17	19	23
29	31	37	41	43	47	53	59	61	67
71	73	79	83	89	97	101	103	107	109
113	127	131	137	139	149	151	157	163	167
173	179	181	191	193	197	199	211	223	227
229	233	239	241	251	257	263	269	271	277
281	283	293	307	311	313	317	331	337	347
349	353	359	367	373	379	383	389	397	401
409	419	421	431	433	439	443	449	457	461
463	467	479	487	491	499	503	509	521	523
541	547	557	563	569	571	577	587	593	599
601	607	613	617	619	631	641	643	647	653
659	661	673	677	683	691	701	709	719	727
733	739	743	751	757	761	769	773	787	797
809	811	821	823	827	829	839	853	857	859
863	877	881	883	887	907	911	919	929	937
941	947	953	967	971	977	983	991	997	1,009

Common Fractions Reduced to Decimals

8ths	16ths	32nds	64ths	8ths	16ths	32nds	64ths	8ths	16ths	32nds	64ths	8ths	16ths	32nds	64ths
			1 = 0.015625				17 = 0.265625				33 = 0.515625				49 = 0.765625
		1	2 = 0.03125			9	18 = 0.28125			17	34 = 0.53125			25	50 = 0.78125
			3 = 0.046875				19 = 0.296875				35 = 0.546875				51 = 0.796875
	1	2	4 = 0.0625		5	10	20 = 0.3125			18	36 = 0.5625		13	26	52 = 0.8125
			5 = 0.078125				21 = 0.328125				37 = 0.578125				53 = 0.828125
		3	6 = 0.09375			11	22 = 0.34375			19	38 = 0.59375			27	54 = 0.84375
			7 = 0.109375				23 = 0.359375				39 = 0.609375				55 = 0.859375
1	2	4	8 = 0.125	3	6	12	24 = 0.375	5	10	20	40 = 0.625	7	14	28	56 = 0.875
			9 = 0.140625				25 = 0.390625				41 = 0.640625				57 = 0.890625
		5	10 = 0.15625			13	26 = 0.40625			21	42 = 0.65625			29	58 = 0.90625
			11 = 0.171875				27 = 0.421875				43 = 0.671875,				59 = 0.921875
	3	6	12 = 0.1875		7	14	28 = 0.4375		11	22	44 = 0.6875		15	30	60 = 0.9375
			13 = 0.203125				29 = 0.453125				45 = 0.703125				61 = 0.953125
		7	14 = 0.21875			15	30 = 0.46875			23	46 = 0.71875			31	62 = 0.96875
			15 = 0.234375				31 = 0.484375				47 = 0.734375				63 = 0.984375
2	4	8	16 = 0.25	4	8	16	32 = 0.5	6	12	24	48 = 0.75	8	16	32	64 = 1.0

Roman Numerals

I — 1	IV — 4	VII — 7	X — 10	XX — 20	L — 50	C — 100	D — 500
II — 2	V — 5	VIII — 8	XI — 11	XXX — 30	LX — 60	CC — 200	CM — 900
III — 3	VI — 6	IX — 9	XIX — 19	XL — 40	XC — 90	CD — 400	M — 1,000

Note: The numerals V, X, L, C, D, or M shown with a horizontal line on top denote 1,000 times the original value.

Ancient Measures

Biblical

Cubit............ = 21.8 inches
Omer .... = 0.45 peck
= 3.964 liters
Ephah........... = 10 omers
Shekel .... = 0.497 ounce
= 14.1 grams

Greek

Cubit .... = 18.3 inches
Stadion .... = 607.2 or 622 feet
Obolos.......... = 715.38 milligrams
Drachma .... = 4.2923 grams
Mina .... = 0.9463 pound
Talent .... = 60 mina

Roman

Cubit............ = 17.5 inches
Stadium .... = 202 yards
As, libra, pondus........ = 325.971 grams
= 0.71864 pound

Metric System Prefixes

The following prefixes, in combination with the basic unit names, provide the multiples and submultiples in the metric system. For example, the unit name *meter*, with the prefix *kilo* added, produces *kilometer*, meaning "1,000 meters."

Prefix	Symbol	Multiples	Equivalent
yotta	Y	10^{24}	septillionfold
zetta	Z	10^{21}	sextillionfold
exa	E	10^{18}	quintillionfold
peta	P	10^{15}	quadrillionfold
tera	T	10^{12}	trillionfold
giga	G	10^{9}	billionfold
mega	M	10^{6}	millionfold
kilo	k	10^{3}	thousandfold
hecto	h	10^{2}	hundredfold
deka	da	10	tenfold

Prefix	Symbol	Multiples	Equivalent
deci	d	10^{-1}	tenth part
centi	c	10^{-2}	hundredth part
milli	m	10^{-3}	thousandth part
micro	µ	10^{-6}	millionth part
nano	n	10^{-9}	billionth part
pico	p	10^{-12}	trillionth part
femto	f	10^{-15}	quadrillionth part
atto	a	10^{-18}	quintillionth part
zepto	z	10^{-21}	sextillionth part
yocto	y	10^{-24}	septillionth part

Tables of Metric Weights and Measures

(**Note:** The metric system generally uses the term *mass* instead of *weight*. Mass is a measure of an object's inertial property, or the amount of matter it contains. Weight is a measure of the force exerted on an object by gravity or the force needed to support it. Also, the metric system does not make a distinction between "dry volume" and "liquid volume.")

Length

10 millimeters (mm) .... = 1 centimeter (cm)
10 centimeters .... = 1 decimeter (dm)
= 100 millimeters
10 decimeters.............. = 1 meter (m)
= 1,000 millimeters
10 meters.................. = 1 dekameter (dam)
10 dekameters .... = 1 hectometer (hm)
= 100 meters
10 hectometers .... = 1 kilometer (km)
= 1,000 meters

Area

100 square millimeters (mm^2) = 1 square centimeter (cm^2)
10,000 square centimeters.... = 1 square meter (m^2)
= 1,000,000 square millimeters
100 square meters .... = 1 are (a)
100 ares................... = 1 hectare (ha)
= 10,000 square meters
100 hectares .... = 1 square kilometer (km^2)
= 1,000,000 square meters

Volume

10 milliliters (mL) .... = 1 centiliter (cL)
10 centiliters............... = 1 deciliter (dL)
= 100 milliliters
10 deciliters .... = 1 liter (L)
= 1,000 milliliters
10 liters .... = 1 dekaliter (daL)
10 dekaliters .... = 1 hectoliter (hL)
= 100 liters
10 hectoliters.............. = 1 kiloliter (kL)
= 1,000 liters

Volume (Cubic Measure)

1,000 cubic millimeters (mm^3) = 1 cubic centimeter (cm^3)
1,000 cubic centimeters ..... = 1 cubic decimeter (dm^3)
= 1,000,000 cubic millimeters
1,000 cubic decimeters ...... = 1 cubic meter (m^3)
= 1 stere
= 1,000,000 cubic centimeters
= 1,000,000,000 cubic millimeters

Weight (Mass)

10 milligrams (mg).......... = 1 centigram (cg)
10 centigrams .... = 1 decigram (dg)
= 100 milligrams
10 decigrams............... = 1 gram (g)
= 1,000 milligrams
10 grams .... = 1 dekagram (dag)
10 dekagrams .... = 1 hectogram (hg)
= 100 grams
10 hectograms.............. = 1 kilogram (kg)
= 1,000 grams
1,000 kilograms............ = 1 metric ton (t)

Table of U.S. Customary Weights and Measures

Length

12 inches (in)	= 1 foot (ft)
3 feet	= 1 yard (yd)
5½ yards	= 1 rod (rd), pole, or perch (16½ feet)
40 rods	= 1 furlong (fur)
	= 220 yards
	= 660 feet
8 furlongs	= 1 statute mile (mi)
	= 1,760 yards
	= 5,280 feet
3 miles	= 1 league (land)
	= 5,280 yards
	= 15,840 feet
6076.11549 feet	= 1 international nautical mile

Volume (Liquid Measure)

When necessary to distinguish the liquid pint or quart from the dry pint or quart, the word *liquid* or the abbreviation *liq* is used in combination with the name or abbreviation of the liquid unit.

4 gills (gi)	= 1 pint (pt)
	= 28.875 cubic inches
2 pints	= 1 quart (qt)
	= 57.75 cubic inches
4 quarts	= 1 gallon (gal)
	= 231 cubic inches
	= 8 pints
	= 32 gills

Volume (Dry Measure)

When necessary to distinguish the dry pint or quart from the liquid pint or quart, the word *dry* is used in combination with the name or abbreviation of the dry unit.

2 pints (pt)	= 1 quart (qt)
	= 67.2006 cubic inches
8 quarts	= 1 peck (pk)
	= 537.605 cubic inches
	= 16 pints
4 pecks	= 1 bushel (bu)
	= 2,150.42 cubic inches
	= 32 quarts

Area

Squares and cubes of units are sometimes abbreviated by using superscripts. For example, ft^2 means square foot, and ft^3 means cubic foot.

144 square inches	= 1 square foot (ft^2)
9 square feet	= 1 square yard (yd^2)
	= 1,296 square inches
30 ¼ square yards	= 1 square rod (rd^2)
	= 272¼ square feet
160 square rods	= 1 acre
	= 4,840 square yards
	= 43,560 square feet
640 acres	= 1 square mile (mi^2)
1 mile square	= 1 section (of land)
6 miles square	= 1 township
	= 36 sections
	= 36 square miles

Cubic Measure

1 cubic foot (ft^3)	= 1,728 cubic inches (in^3)
27 cubic feet	= 1 cubic yard (yd^3)

Gunter's, or Surveyor's, Chain Measure

7.92 inches (in)	= 1 link
100 links	= 1 chain (ch)
	= 4 rods
	= 66 feet
80 chains	= 1 statute mile (mi)
	= 320 rods
	= 5,280 feet

Avoirdupois Weight

When necessary to distinguish the avoirdupois ounce or pound from the troy ounce or pound, the word *avoirdupois* or the abbreviation *avdp* is used in combination with the name or abbreviation of the avoirdupois unit. The *grain* is the same in avoirdupois and troy weight.

27 $^{11}/_{32}$ grains	= 1 dram (dr)
16 drams	= 1 ounce (oz)
	= 437 ½ grains
16 ounces	= 1 pound (lb)
	= 256 drams
	= 7,000 grains
100 pounds	= 1 hundredweight (cwt)*
20 hundredweights	= 1 ton
	= 2,000 pounds*

In *gross* or *long* measure, the following values are recognized.

112 pounds	= 1 gross or long hundredweight*
20 gross or long hundredweights	= 1 gross or long ton
	= 2,240 pounds*

*When the terms *hundredweight* and *ton* are used unmodified, they are commonly understood to mean the 100-pound hundredweight and the 2,000-pound ton, respectively; these units may be designated *net* or *short* when necessary to distinguish them from the corresponding units in gross or long measure.

Troy Weight

24 grains	= 1 pennyweight (dwt)
20 pennyweights	= 1 ounce troy (oz t)
	= 480 grains
12 ounces troy	= 1 pound troy (lb t)
	= 240 pennyweights
	= 5,760 grains

Tables of Equivalents

In this table it is necessary to distinguish between the *international* and the *survey* foot. The international foot, defined in 1959 as exactly equal to 0.3048 meter, is shorter than the old survey foot by exactly 2 parts in 1 million. The survey foot is still used in data expressed in feet in geodetic surveys within the U.S. In this table the survey foot is indicated with capital letters.

When the name of a unit is enclosed in brackets, e.g., [1 hand], either (1) the unit is not in general current use in the U.S. or (2) the unit is believed to be based on custom and usage rather than on formal definition.

Equivalents involving decimals are, in most instances, rounded to the 3rd decimal place; exact equivalents are so designated.

Lengths

1 angstrom (Å)	= 0.1 nanometer (exactly)
	= 0.000 1 micrometer (exactly)
	= 0.000 000 1 millimeter (exactly)
	= 0.000 000 004 inch
1 cable's length	= 120 fathoms (exactly)
	= 720 FEET (exactly)
	= 219 meters
1 centimeter (cm)	= 0.3937 inch
1 chain (ch) (Gunter's or surveyor's)	= 66 FEET (exactly)
	= 20.1168 meters
1 chain (engineer's)	= 30.48 meters (exactly)
	= 100 feet
1 decimeter (dm)	= 3.937 inches
1 degree (geographical)	= 364,566.929 feet
	= 69.047 miles (avg.)
	= 111.123 kilometers (avg.)
of latitude	= 68.708 miles at equator
	= 69.403 miles at poles
of longitude	= 69.171 miles at equator
1 dekameter (dam)	= 32.808 feet
1 fathom	= 6 FEET (exactly)
	= 1.8288 meters
1 foot (ft)	= 0.3048 meters (exactly)
	= 0.015 chains (surveyors)
1 furlong (fur)	= 660 FEET (exactly)
	= $^1/_8$ statute mile (exactly)
	= 201.168 meters
[1 hand] (height measure for horses from ground to top of shoulders)	= 4 inches
1 inch (in)	= 2.54 centimeters (exactly)
1 kilometer (km)	= 0.621371 mile
	= 3,280.8 feet
1 league (land)	= 3 statute miles (exactly)
	= 4.828 kilometers
1 link (Gunter's or surveyor's)	= 7.92 inches (exactly)
	= 0.201 meter
1 link (engineer's)	= 1 foot
	= 0.305 meter
1 meter (m)	= 39.37 inches
	= 1.09361 yards

1 micrometer (μm) = 0.001 millimeter (exactly)
= 0.00003937 inch

1 mil = 0.001 inch (exactly)
= 0.0254 millimeter (exactly)

1 mile (mi) (statute or land) = 5,280 FEET (exactly)
= 1.609344 kilometers (exactly)

1 international nautical mile (nmi) = 1.852 kilometers (exactly)
= 1.150779 statute miles
= 6,076.11549 feet

1 millimeter (mm) = 0.03937 inch

1 nanometer (nm) = 0.001 micrometer (exactly)
= 0.00000003937 inch

1 pica (typography) = 12 points

1 point (typography) = 0.013 837 inch (exactly)
= 0.351 millimeter

1 rod (rd), pole, or perch = 16½ FEET (exactly)
= 5.029 meters

1 yard (yd) = 0.9144 meter (exactly)

Areas or Surfaces

1 acre = 43,560 square FEET (exactly)
= 4,840 square yards
= 0.405 hectare

1 are (a) = 119.599 square yards
= 0.025 acre

1 bolt (cloth measure):
length = 100 yards (on modern looms)
width = 45 or 60 inches

1 hectare (ha) = 2.471 acres

[1 square (building)] = 100 square feet

1 square centimeter (cm^2) = 0.155 square inch

1 square decimeter (dm^2) = 15.500 square inches

1 square foot (ft^2) = 929.030 square centimeters

1 square inch (in^2) = 6.4516 square centimeters (exactly)

1 square kilometer (km^2) = 247.104 acres
= 0.386102 square mile

1 square meter (m^2) = 1.196 square yards
= 10.764 square feet

1 square mile (mi^2) = 258.999 hectares

1 square millimeter (mm^2) = 0.002 square inch

1 square rod (rd^2), sq. pole, or sq. perch = 25.293 square meters

1 square yard (yd^2) = 0.836127 square meter

Capacities or Volumes

1 barrel (bbl), liquid = 31 to 42 gallons*

*There are a variety of "barrels" established by law or usage. For example: federal taxes on fermented liquors are based on a barrel of 31 gallons; many state laws fix the "barrel for liquids" as 31½ gallons; one state fixes a 36-gallon barrel for cistern measurement; federal law recognizes a 40-gallon barrel for "proof spirits"; by custom, 42 gallons constitute a barrel of crude oil or petroleum products for statistical purposes, and this equivalent is recognized "for liquids" by 4 states.

1 barrel (bbl), standard for fruits, vegetables, and other dry commodities except dry cranberries = 7,056 cubic inches
= 1 barrel (bbl), standard for fruits

1 barrel (bbl), standard, cranberry = 86 $^{45}/_{64}$ dry quarts
= 2.709 bushels, struck measure = 5,826 cubic inches

1 board foot (lumber measure) = a foot-square board 1 inch thick

1 bushel (bu) (U.S.) (struck measure) = 2,150.42 cubic inches (exactly)
= 35.239 liters

[1 bushel, heaped (U.S.)] = 2,747.715 cubic inches
= 1.278 bushels, struck measure*

*Frequently recognized as 1¼ bushels, struck measure.

[1 bushel (bu) (British Imperial) (struck measure)] = 1.032 U.S. bushels, struck measure
= 2,219.36 cubic inches

1 cord (cd) firewood = 128 cubic feet (exactly)

1 cubic centimeter (cm^3) = 0.061 cubic inch

1 cubic decimeter (dm^3) = 61.024 cubic inches

1 cubic inch (in^3) = 0.554 fluid ounce
= 4.433 fluid drams
= 16.387 cubic centimeters

1 cubic foot (ft^3) = 7.481 gallons
= 28.317 cubic decimeters

1 cubic meter (m^3) = 1.308 cubic yards

1 cubic yard (yd^3) = 0.765 cubic meter

1 cup, measuring = 8 fluid ounces (exactly)
= ½ liquid pint (exactly)

[1 dram, fluid (fl dr) (British)] = 0.961 U.S. fluid dram
= 0.217 cubic inch
= 3.552 milliliters

1 dekaliter (daL) = 2.642 gallons
= 1.135 pecks

1 gallon (gal) (U.S.) = 231 cubic inches (exactly)
= 3.785 liters
= 0.833 British gallon
= 128 U.S. fluid ounces (exactly)

[1 gallon (gal) British Imperial] = 277.42 cubic inches
= 1.201 U.S. gallons
= 4.546 liters
= 160 British fluid ounces (exactly)

1 gill (gi) = 7.219 cubic inches
= 4 fluid ounces (exactly)
= 0.118 liter

1 hectoliter (hL) = 26.418 gallons
= 2.838 bushels

1 liter (L) (1 cubic decimeter exactly) = 1.057 liquid quarts
= 0.908 dry quart
= 61.024 cubic inches

1 milliliter (mL) (1 cu cm exactly) = 0.271 fluid dram
= 16.231 minims
= 0.061 cubic inch

1 ounce, liquid (U.S.) = 1.805 cubic inches
= 29.574 milliliters
= 1.041 British fluid ounces

[1 ounce, fluid (fl oz) (British)] = 0.961 U.S. fluid ounce
= 1.734 cubic inches
= 28.412 milliliters

1 peck (pk) = 8.810 liters

1 pint (pt), dry = 33.600 cubic inches
= 0.551 liter

1 pint (pt), liquid = 28.875 cubic inches (exactly)
= 0.473 liter

1 quart (qt), dry (U.S.) = 67.201 cubic inches
= 1.101 liters
= 0.969 British quart

1 quart (qt), liquid (U.S.) = 57.75 cubic in (exactly)
= 0.946 liter
= 0.833 British quart

[1 quart (qt) (British)] = 69.354 cubic inches
= 1.032 U.S. dry quarts
= 1.201 U.S. liquid quarts

1 tablespoon = 3 teaspoons*(exactly)
= 4 fluid drams
= ½ fluid ounce (exactly)

1 teaspoon = $^1/_3$ tablespoon*(exactly)
= 1 $^1/_3$ fluid drams*

*The equivalent "1 teaspoon = 1 $^1/_3$ fluid drams" has been found to correspond more closely with the actual capacities of teaspoons in use than the equivalent "1 teaspoon = 1 fluid dram" which is given by many dictionaries.

Weights or Masses

1 assay ton** (AT) = 29.167 grams

**Used in assaying. The assay ton bears the same relation to the milligram that a ton of 2,000 pounds avoirdupois bears to the ounce troy; hence, the weight in milligrams of precious metal obtained from one assay ton of ore gives directly the number of troy ounces to the net ton.

1 bale (cotton measure) = 500 pounds in U.S.
= 750 pounds in Egypt

1 carat (c) = 200 milligrams (exactly)
= 3.086 grains

1 dram avoirdupois (dr avdp) = 27 $^{11}/_{32}$ (= 27.344) grains
= 1.772 grams

1 gamma (g) = 1 microgram (exactly), see below

1 grain = 64.7989 milligrams

1 gram = 15.432 grains
= 0.035 ounce, avoirdupois

1 hundredweight, gross or long*** (gross cwt) = 112 pounds (exactly)
= 50.802 kilograms

1 hundredweight, net or short (cwt or net cwt) = 100 pounds (exactly)
= 45.359 kilograms

1 kilogram (kg) = 2.20462 pounds

1 microgram (μg) = 0.000001 gram (exactly)

1 milligram (mg) .... = 0.015 grain
1 ounce, avoirdupois (oz avdp) = 437.5 grains (exactly)
= 0.911 troy ounce
= 28.3495 grams
1 ounce, troy (oz t).......... = 480 grains (exactly)
= 1.097 avoirdupois ounces
= 31.103 grams
1 pennyweight (dwt) .... = 1.555 grams
1 pound, avoirdupois (lb avdp) = 7,000 grains (exactly)
= 1.215 troy pounds
= 453.59237 grams (exactly)
1 pound, troy (lb t) .... = 5,760 grains (exactly)
= 0.823 pound, avoirdupois
= 373.242 grams

1 stone, (avdp) .... = 14 pounds avdp (exactly)
= 6.350 kilograms
1 ton, gross or long***(gross ton) = 2,240 pounds (exactly)
= 1.12 net tons (exactly)
= 1.016 metric tons

***The gross or long ton and hundredweight are used commercially in the U.S. to only a limited extent, usually in restricted industrial fields. These units are the same as the British ton and hundredweight.

1 ton, metric (t) .... = 2,204.623 pounds
= 0.984 gross ton
= 1.102 net tons
1 ton, net or short (sh ton).... = 2,000 pounds (exactly)
= 0.893 gross ton
= 0.907 metric ton

Electrical Units

The **watt** is the unit of power (electrical, mechanical, thermal, etc.). Electrical power is given by the product of the voltage and the current.

Energy is sold by the **joule,** but in common practice the billing of electrical energy is expressed in terms of the **kilowatt-hour,** which is 3,600,000 joules or 3.6 megajoules.

The **horsepower** is a nonmetric unit sometimes used in mechanics. It is equal to 746 watts.

The **ohm** is the unit of electrical resistance and represents the physical property of a conductor that offers a resistance to the flow of electricity, permitting just 1 ampere to flow at 1 volt of pressure.

Measures of Force and Pressure

Dyne = force necessary to accelerate a 1-gram mass 1 centimeter per second squared = 0.000072 poundal

Poundal = force necessary to accelerate a 1-pound mass 1 foot per second squared = 13,825.5 dynes = 0.138255 newtons

Newton = force needed to accelerate a 1-kilogram mass 1 meter per second squared

Pascal (pressure) = 1 newton per square meter = 0.020885 pound per square foot

Atmosphere (air pressure at sea level) = 2,116.102 pounds per square foot = 14.6952 pounds per square inch = 1.0332 kilograms per square centimeter = 101,323 newtons per square meter

Spirits Measures

Pony............. = 0.5 jigger
Shot .... = 0.667 jigger
= 1.0 ounce
Jigger .... = 1.5 shots
Pint .... = 16 shots
= 0.625 fifth
Fifth .... = 25.6 shots
= 1.6 pints
= 0.8 quart
= 0.75706 liter

Quart .... = 32 shots
= 1.25 fifths
Magnum.......... = 2 quarts
= 2.49797 bottles (wine)

For champagne and brandy only:
Jeroboam .... = 6.4 pints
= 1.6 magnum
= 0.8 gallon

For champagne only:
Rehoboam ....= 3 magnums
Methuselah.........= 4 magnums
Salmanazar ....= 6 magnums
Balthazar ....= 8 magnums
Nebuchadnezzar ....= 10 magnums
Wine bottle (standard)........= 0.800633 quart
= 0.7576778 liter

Miscellaneous Modern Measures

Caliber—the diameter of a gun bore. In the U.S., caliber is traditionally expressed in hundredths of inches, e.g., .22. In Britain, caliber is often expressed in thousandths of inches, e.g., .270. Now it is commonly expressed in millimeters, e.g., the 5.56 mm M16 rifle. Heavier weapons' caliber has long been expressed in millimeters, e.g., the 155 mm howitzer. Naval guns' caliber refers to the barrel length as a multiple of the bore diameter. A 5-inch, 50-caliber naval gun has a 5-inch bore and a barrel length of 250 inches.

Decibel (dB)—a measure of the relative loudness or intensity of sound. A 20-decibel sound is 10 times louder than a 10-decibel sound; 30 decibels is 100 times louder; 40 decibels is 1,000 times louder, etc.

One decibel is the smallest difference between sounds detectable by the human ear. A 120-decibel sound is painful.

10 decibels	– a light whisper
20	– quiet conversation
30	– normal conversation
40	– light traffic
50	– typewriter, loud conversation
60	– noisy office
70	– normal traffic, quiet train
80	– rock music, subway
90	– heavy traffic, thunder
100	– jet plane at takeoff

Em—a printer's measure designating the square width of any given type size. Thus, an em of 10-point type is 10 points. An en is half an em.

Gauge—a measure of shotgun bore diameter. Gauge numbers originally referred to the number of lead balls just fitting the gun barrel diameter required to make a pound. Thus, a 16-gauge shotgun's bore was smaller than a 12-gauge shotgun's. Today, an international agreement assigns millimeter measures to each gauge, e.g.:

Gauge	Bore diameter (in mm)	Gauge	Bore diameter (in mm)
6.....	23.34	14	17.60
10.....	19.67	16	16.81
12.....	18.52	20	15.90

Horsepower—the power needed to lift 550 pounds 1 foot in 1 second or to lift 33,000 pounds 1 foot in 1 minute. Equivalent to 746 watts or 2,546.0756 Btu/h.

Karat or carat—a measure of fineness for gold equal to $^1/_{24}$ part of pure gold in an alloy. Thus 24-karat gold is pure; 18-karat gold is ¼ alloy. The *carat* is also used as a unit of weight for precious stones; it is equal to 200 milligrams or 3.086 grains.

Knot—a measure of the speed of ships. A knot equals 1 nautical mile per hour.

Quire—25 sheets of paper

Ream—500 sheets of paper

WORLD ALMANAC QUICK QUIZ

Which of these is not a metric system unit of length?

(a) zettameter (b) yoctometer (c) petameter (d) blottometer

For the answer look in this chapter, or see page 1008.

COMPUTERS AND TELECOMMUNICATIONS

Computer Milestones

Devices for performing calculations are nothing new—the abacus, a frame with wires on which beads are moved back and forth (still used today in some parts of the world), traces its origins back to ancient times. But the marvels of electronic miniaturization that are modern PCs are a relatively recent development. They are the descendants of vacuum-tube devices introduced in the early 20th century. Here are some early **landmark events in computer history**:

• 1623: German mathematician Wilhelm Schickard developed the **1st mechanical calculator**, capable of adding, subtracting, multiplying, and dividing.

• 1642: French mathematician Blaise Pascal built the 1st of more than 4 dozen copies of an **adding and subtracting machine** that he invented.

• 1801: French inventor Joseph Marie Jacquard demonstrated a new control system for looms. He **"programmed"** the loom, communicating desired weaving operations to the machine via patterns of holes in paper cards.

• 1833-71: British mathematician and scientist Charles Babbage used the Jacquard punch-card system in his design for a sophisticated, programmable **"Analytical Engine"** that foreshadowed basic features of today's computers. Babbage's conception was beyond the capabilities of the technology of his time, and the machine remained unfinished at his death in 1871.

• 1889: American engineer Herman Hollerith patented an electromechanical **punch-card tabulating system** that facilitated the handling of large amounts of statistical data and quickly found use in censuses in the U.S. and other countries.

• 1911: Hollerith's Tabulating Machine Company merged with 2 other enterprises to form the Computing-Tabulating-Recording Company, renamed in 1924 the International Business Machines (**IBM**).

• 1941: German engineer Konrad Züse completed the Z3, the **1st fully functional digital computer** to be **controlled by a program;** the Z3 was not electronic—it was based on electrical switches called relays.

• 1942: Iowa State College physicist John Vincent Atanasoff and his assistant Clifford Berry completed a working model of the **1st fully electronic computer,** using vacuum tubes, which could operate much more quickly than relays; the rudimentary machine was not programmable.

• 1944: IBM and Harvard Professor Howard Aiken completed the **1st large-scale automatic digital computer**, the Mark I, a relay-based machine 55 feet long and 8 feet high.

• 1943: British scientists built the **Colossus,** an electronic computer designed specifically for breaking German codes.

• 1946: **Eniac** (for Electronic Numerical Integrator and Computer), a 30-ton room-sized electronic computer with over 18,000 vacuum tubes, was completed by physicist John Mauchly and engineer J. Presper Eckert at the University of Pennsylvania for the U.S. Army. Eniac could be programmed to do different tasks, although programming could take a couple of days, since cables had to be plugged in and switches set by hand.

• 1951: Eckert and Mauchly's **Univac** ("Universal Automatic Computer") became the 1st computer commercially available in the U.S.; the 1st customer: the Census Bureau. CBS-TV used a Univac in 1952 to predict election results.

• 1969-71: The powerful **Unix operating system**, was developed at Bell Laboratories; later versions became widely used on large computers and formed the basis for the popular Linux and Macintosh OS X operating systems for personal computers.

• 1971: Intel released the 4004, the 1st commerical **microprocessor** (an entire computer processing unit on a chip).

• 1973: The Alto computer, developed at Xerox's Palo Alto Research Center, became operational, implementing many features used years later in commerical personal computers, including a **graphical user interface** (GUI) featuring windows, icons, a mouse, and pointers.

• 1975: The **1st widely marketed personal computer**, the MITS Altair 8800, was introduced in kit form, with no keyboard and no video display, for under $400.

• 1975: **Microsoft** was founded by college dropouts Bill Gates and Paul Allen.

• 1976: The **1st word-processing program** for personal computers, the Electric Pencil, was written.

• 1976: **Apple** Computer Company was founded by Steven Jobs and Stephen Wozniak.

• 1977: Apple introduced the **Apple II;** capable of displaying text and graphics in color, the machine enjoyed phenomenal success.

• 1981: **IBM** unveiled its **"Personal Computer,"** which used Microsoft's DOS (disk operating system).

• 1984: Apple introduced the 1st **Macintosh**. The easy-to-use Macintosh came with a proprietary operating system and was the 1st popular computer to have a GUI (graphical user interface) and a mouse.

• 1990: Microsoft released **Windows** 3.0, the 1st workable version of its own GUI.

• 1991: **Linux** was invented for the personal computer by Helsinki Univ. student Linus Torvalds and made available for free.

• 1996: The **Palm Pilot**, the 1st widely successful handheld computer and personal information manager, arrived.

• 1997: The IBM computer **Deep Blue** beat world chess champion Garry Kasparov in a 6-game match, 3.5-2.5.

• 2000: **Microsoft** was found guilty of **antitrust violations** by a a federal district judge, who ordered the company split into 2 parts, an outcome later avoided through a settlement in which Microsoft accepted certain restrictions on its competitive practices.

• 2001: Apple introduced the **Unix-based operating system** OS X for the **Macintosh**.

• 2002: The total number of **personal computers** (PCs), including desktop and laptop machines of all types, shipped by manufacturers since 1975 reached 1 bil, according to computer industry research firm Gartner Dataquest.

• 2004: The European Union found **Microsoft** guilty of **anticompetitive practices** and fined the company 497 mil euros (over $600 mil); Microsoft was also ordered to share certain details of its Windows operating system with other software producers and to introduce a stripped-down version of Windows.

• 2005: **Apple** announced it would start using **Intel microprocessors** in its Macintosh computers beginning in 2006. The Macintosh traditionally used microprocessors of a different design than the chips made by Intel and other companies that were found in the more than 90% of PCs running Microsoft Windows.

About the Internet

Internet Milestones

The **Internet** is a vast and rapidly growing computer network of computer networks. In 1994, a total of 3 mil people (most of them in the U.S.) made use of it; by early 2004, estimates of the number of users worldwide ranged as high as 934 mil (Computer Industry Almanac, Inc.).

The Internet is not owned or funded by any one institution, organization, or government. It has no CEO and is not a commercial service. Its development is guided by the Internet Society (ISOC), composed of volunteers. The ISOC appoints the Internet Architecture Board (IAB), which oversees issues of standards, network resources, etc.

IT'S A FACT: According to a 2005 survey of 10,000 workers conducted by America Online and Salary.com, the average worker wastes just over 2 hours a day at work, which in salary terms, adds up to about $759 bil in lost productivity. What was their main time-wasting activity? According to 44.7% of respondents, it was surfing the Internet.

Major historical highlights:

• 1969: **ARPANET**, an experimental 4-computer network, was established by the Advanced Research Projects Agency (ARPA) of the U.S. Defense Dept. 2 years later, ARPANET linked about 2 dozen computers ("hosts") at 15 sites, including MIT and Harvard.

• 1978: The 1st **spam**, or junk e-mail, message was sent over ARPANET.

• 1983: The protocol, or set of communications rules, known as **TCP/IP**, became the main networking protocol of ARPANET. TCP/IP facilitates connection between networks, and its adoption was tantamount to the birth of the Internet.

• 1983: The military portion of ARPANET was moved onto the MILNET.

• 1986: The U.S. National Science Foundation (NSF) launched **NSFNET**, the 1st large-scale network using Internet techonology.

• 1988: **Internet Relay Chat** (IRC) was developed by Finnish student Jarkko Oikarinen, enabling people to communicate via the Internet in "real time."

• 1988: A **"worm"** crafted by Cornell Univ graduate student Robert Morris, Jr., infected thousands of computers, shutting many down and causing millions of dollars of damage—the 1st known case of large-scale damage caused by a computer virus spread via the Internet.

• 1989: The World—the **1st commercial Internet service** provider supplying dial-up access—appeared.

• 1989-90: Tim Berners-Lee invented the **World Wide Web.** Begun as an environment in which scientists at the European Center for Nuclear Research in Switzerland could share information, it gradually evolved into a medium with text, graphics, audio, animation, and video.

• 1990: ARPANET was disbanded.

• 1991: The NSFNET was opened to commercial traffic.

• 1991: Berners-Lee introduced the **1st browser**, or software for accessing the Web.

• 1993: The U.S. National Center for Supercomputing Applications released versions of **Mosaic**, the 1st Web browser able to present both text and images in a single page, for Microsoft Windows, Unix systems running the X Window GUI, and the Apple Macintosh.

• 1994: Netscape Communications released the **Netscape Navigator** browser.

• 1995: Microsoft released its **Internet Explorer** browser but initially failed to make a dent in Netscape's dominance of the browser market. By 1998, Netscape's market share had fallen below 50%, while Internet Explorer's exceeded 25% and was growing rapidly.

• 1996: A group of universities launched **Internet2**, an advanced, high-performance network for the research community and a test bed for development of new capabilities that might find use in the commercial Internet.

• 1998: Under a contract with the U.S. Dept. of Commerce, the nonprofit Internet Corporation for Assigned Numbers and Names (ICANN) took over the management of such basic Internet functions as assignment of **domain names** and Internet (IP) addresses.

• 1999: Release of the free **Napster** file-sharing service enabled users to easily exchange files containing music or other content without regard to copyright restrictions. In 2001 a court ordered Napster to suspend operations; Napster users, however, switched to other file-sharing services, such as Morpheus and KaZaA. (Napster was later reconstituted as a for-pay music download service.)

• 2003: Niue, a self-governing Pacific island associated with New Zealand, became the 1st "country" to offer free **nationwide wireless access** to the Internet (using Wi-Fi technology).

• 2005: U.S. federal agents shut down the Elite Torrents network, part of the BitTorrent system for distributing files via peer-to-peer Internet connections, after it made available copies of the Star Wars film *Revenge of the Sith* even before the movie officially opened in theaters.

Internet Addresses

The fundamental part of an address on the Internet is called the domain. The final part of a domain name, known as the **top-level domain**, is its most basic part. For example, in *The World Almanac*'s e-mail address—Walmanac@waegroup.com—com is the top-level domain. ("Walmanac" is *The World Almanac*'s "username.") So-called generic top-level domains, consisting of 3 or more letters, include:

Domain	What It Is
.aero	an organization in the air-transport industry
.biz	a business
.com	generally a commercial organization, business, or company
.coop	a nonprofit business cooperative, such as a rural electric coop
.edu	a 4-year higher-educational institution
.gov	a nonmilitary U.S. governmental entity, usually federal
.info	an informational site for an individual or organization, without restriction
.int	an international organization
.jobs	information about employment, such as job openings
.mil	a U.S. military organization
.museum	a museum
.name	an individual
.net	suggested for a network administration, but actually used by a wide variety of sites
.org	suggested for a nonprofit organization, but actually used by a wide variety of sites
.pro	a professional, such as an accountant, lawyer or physician
.travel	information about travel
.xxx	a sexually explicit site

Domain names with 2 letters are generally for countries or regions. The **top-level domain** .us, for instance, is available to persons, organizations, and entities in the U.S. More examples: .eu (European Union), .jp (Japan), .ru (Russia), .uk (United Kingdom).

As of mid-2005, negotiations were under way to establish additional generic top-level domains, among them .cat (for Catalan language and culture), .post (postal services), and .mobi (content for mobile devices).

Safety and Security on the Internet

Common sense dictates some basic security rules:

• Pick passwords that are difficult to guess, preferably consisting of both letters and numbers, and perhaps also other symbols (if permitted). It's a bad idea to use the same password at multiple Websites.

• Do not give out your phone number, address, credit card number, or other personal information, unless needed for a transaction at a site you trust.

• If you feel someone is being threatening or dangerous, inform your Internet service provider.

• Use protective "firewall," antivirus, and antispyware software to guard your system against attacks by hackers. Be sure to keep the software up to date.

• Be careful about opening e-mail from unknown correspondents.

• If you have programs that can make use of macros—bits of auxiliary coding that are meant to play a helpful role but can be taken advantage of by some viruses—make sure the programs' macro virus protection (if any) is turned on. Keep macros disabled if you do not know what you might want to use them for.

• Users of so-called **peer-to-peer** (P2P) file-sharing networks, such as KaZaA, should open up only part of their computer system to sharing—not the entire hard drive.

• Security flaws turn up from time to time in operating systems, Web browsers, and other software, and when the manufacturers provide **patches** to solve the problem, it is usually advisable to install these fixes. If a fix is not available for a serious security problem, you may want to consider switching to an alternative program.

Malware. Software designed to harm a computer system—such as a virus (malicious code carried within a program) or a worm (a self-contained malicious program)—may be picked up from the Internet or elsewhere, received on a disk, or communicated via e-mail.

IT'S A FACT: About 88% of U.S. Internet users 15 years old and older use it for e-mail, 77% to search for product and service information, 67% for news, weather, or sports information, 52% for shopping, 38% for playing games, and 28% for banking, according to a survey taken in 2003 by the National Telecommunications and Information Administration.

Some malicious software may install a "back door" on an infected system, giving access to a hacker; may attempt to turn off any antivirus program on the system; or may try to log the user's keystrokes.

A **Trojan horse** is computer code concealed within harmless code or data that is capable of taking control and causing damage. It can be used to mount a massive **"denial-of-service"** attack, which overwhelms targeted computers by inundating them with messages. The infected computers, acting under hacker control without their owners' knowledge, are called **zombies**, and the network of zombie computers that carry out the attack is called a **botnet**.

Spyware—software that observes your computer activity without your knowledge—is often regarded as a type of malware. Spyware programs may gain entry to your machine via a Trojan horse. They may record your keystrokes and report passwords or other personal information to a hacker. Some may flood your screen with ads.

Phishing. A popular scam is **phishing**—the use of a forged e-mail message purportedly from a respectable organization, such as a bank, to elicit such personal data. The e-mail typically contains a hyperlink that leads to a fabricated Website resembling the site of the ostensible sender. A simple way to avoid falling victim to a phishing scam is to refuse to click on links in e-mails from companies where you have an account. If you want to visit such a company's website, open your browser and manually enter the site's normal address.

Spam. Junk e-mail, or **spam**, can be a time-wasting annoyance or worse—spam may hawk pornography or products dangerous to health, seek to defraud the recipient, may carry a destructive virus, or turn the recipient's machine into a zombie that stores illicit material, takes part in a denial-of-service attack, or distributes spam. Net administrators worry that the flood of spam may cause delays or even a breakdown in the flow of Internet traffic.

In 2003 Congress enacted a law that attempted to restrict spam, but it had little effect on the ever-increasing volume of spam received on e-mail accounts.

While filtering software can help reduce the deluge of spam—some e-mail programs include filters—it is not completely accurate. Experts recommend that you be wary of revealing your e-mail address as you surf the Web.

New Tools Enhance Searching

Billions of Web pages are indexed by powerful search engines, often giving you what you want in seconds. But sometimes a search yields too many hits to digest or fails to come up with anything useful. Below are some of the **recent improvements made by prominent search engines**, notably the 3 most commonly used—Google, Yahoo!, and Microsoft's MSN Search.

• Microsoft launched a **revamped MSN Search** in early 2005. It draws on such resources as Microsoft's *Encarta Encyclopedia* and MSN Music, and may precede the usual list of Web links with a "direct answer" to the search question. Depending on what is asked, the answer might be a single word, a definition, a capsule biography, or a calculation result.

Aerial or satellite photographs of the earth's surface have been offered before, but 2005 saw major new initiatives in this area that supplemented search-engine mapping features. Google came out with **Google Maps**, based largely on the imaging/mapping offerings of Keyhole, a company it acquired in 2004. This product presents satellite views of streets with local data overlays. Google also released a downloadable program called **Google Earth** that works with Google Maps and allows for angled views of streets and relief maps (a free version can be downloaded from earth.google.com). Microsoft developed its own **"Virtual Earth"** service, which works much like Google Maps. Meanwhile, in early 2005, Amazon's A9 began supplementing its "yellow page" local search results for certain major cities with street-front photos of the businesses searched. The feature is called **Block View** because it permits the user to scroll along a block.

• In 2005 both Google and Yahoo! introduced the capability to store search histories and results online for later reference. Google dubbed its program **"My Search History."** Yahoo!'s, called **"My Web,"** includes the capability to annotate saved search pages and to share pages with others. Other recent experiments by Yahoo! include new services for refining the search process. Yahoo!'s **Mindset** search allows the user to specify whether the search results should be more commercial in character or more informational.

• Some other new features were a little farther in the future. **Google Print**, which will take years to implement, searches not websites but the contents of printed works, and the results include information on where copies of the works may be obtained. In addition to publishers, several major libraries have agreed to let Google scan books for this program. Limited access to the content of printed books is also available through the **A9** search engine introduced by Amazon.com in 2004; A9 permits users to make notes in a "search diary."

• Many software developers and hobbyists co-opt the output of a search engine like Google or Yahoo! for their own purposes or improve on it in some way. **Housingmaps.com** uses Google maps to show locations of sale and rental offerings posted in the popular Craigslist (www.craigslist.org) for more than two dozen U.S. and Canadian metropolitan areas. Scroogle removes ads from the search results on Google (www.scroogle.org/cgi-bin/scraper.htm) or Yahoo! (www.scroogle.org/scraper7.html).

For more information about new search features based on Yahoo!, visit next.yahoo.com and research.yahoo.com. For a rundown on Google's beta projects, go to labs.google.com. MSN Search's home page is at search. msn.com.

Emerging Computer Technologies

Progress in miniaturization and computing power in recent decades has been impressive. But there are physical limits to the ways electrons can be shunted around tiny circuits in a wafer of silicon. For this reason, researchers have been looking into alternative technologies that might someday deliver performance unthinkable with traditional semiconductors. Some of the most interesting approaches deal with the very small—the **world of molecules** and the even more minuscule **subatomic realm** where the strange laws of quantum mechanics come into play.

Molecules

Among molecules with a high profile in computer-technology research, the two most intriguing are the **carbon nanotube** and **DNA** (deoxyribonucleic acid), the basic vehicle of heredity in the biological world.

Nanotube Devices: Carbon nanotubes have a simple structure and astounding physical characteristics. They consist of carbon atoms, which may be arranged in a hexagonal pattern—like chicken wire. This chicken wire structure is rolled up to form a tube that may be as narrow as 1 nanometer. (A nanometer is one-billionth of a meter, or 0.0000000000254 inch, that is, about 50,000 times thinner than a human hair.) Carbon nanotubes are extraordinarily strong and hard. They are resistant to heat, cold, magnetism, and radiation. Depending on how their atoms are arranged, they can be fine conductors of electricity or, conversely, they may resist its flow. The tiny tubes potentially offer a way to **overcome the limitations of** the **silicon chips and copper wires** used in today's computers.

Engineers have already developed carbon nanotube transistors that can carry as much as 1,000 times the current accommodated by the copper wires used in silicon chips. Today's computer processors, however, may have a billion transistors or more. Still to be solved are the problems of how to make similarly enormous numbers of high-quality nanotubes and how to arrange them in circuits—while keeping costs down.

Nanotubes' potential is enormous. Their use in computer storage and memory devices raises the prospect of ultra-high capacity hard drives as well as fast random-access memory (RAM) that, unlike today's RAM chips, would not lose its contents when the power is turned off. Such storage devices could make possible instant-booting computers, handheld computers with upwards of 10 gigabytes of memory, and MP3 players that hold exponentially more songs than today's devices.

DNA Computing: DNA carries a living organism's genetic code. Instead of the 0 and 1 used in computers' binary code, the genetic code uses four basic units called bases, which pack a lot of information into a single strand of DNA. They are usually symbolized A, C, G, and T. In an organism, this information is used, with the help of RNA (ribonucleic acid, a molecule related to DNA) and enzymes, to make proteins as well as replicate DNA molecules. Researchers who would like to employ DNA in computing see particularly great potential in using multiple DNA molecules "in parallel," thereby generating enormous computing power, since a trillion or more strands of DNA could be contained in a space as small as a drop of water.

The **first demonstration of the manipulation of DNA** to solve a simple mathematical problem was made in 1994 by Univ. of Southern California computer scientist Leonard M. Adleman. In 2001, researchers at the Weizmann Institute of Science in Israel created a test-tube computer able to do elementary computations; DNA played the role of software governing the action of enzymes (the "hardware").

Aside from its rudimentary capabilities, this test-tube computer was rather impractical because accessing the results required substantial equipment. To get around this limitation, the Israeli scientists developed a computer that would not only compute but would act on the results. In 2004, they reported the creation of a DNA test-tube computer that could detect the presence of cancer genes and thereupon release a drug. Meanwhile, in 2003 a pair of U.S. scientists developed the first interactive DNA computing system, an enzyme-driven device called MAYA that played unbeatable tic-tac-toe. Its human opponent made moves by putting DNA into little wells making up the game board; each well contained enzymes that acted as "logic gates" controlling the device's response to the input data.

Quantum Effects

Much of the buzz associated with quantum computing in recent years has been about computing systems that take advantage of the peculiarities of quantum mechanics to implement parallel processing on an extravagantly huge scale. Conventional computers operate in a binary universe where statements are either true or false, switches are either on or off. In this universe, the bit, the basic unit of information, has a value of either 1 or 0. In the quantum world, a quantum bit, or qubit, can be both on and off at the same time. The two states are said to be "superposed." Because of this simultaneity of values, a quantum computer using 300 qubits could, in theory, speedily carry out more calculations than the number of atoms in the known universe.

Scientists **working to build a practical quantum computer** have to confront a number of difficulties. For example, there is the question of how to physically implement qubits. Another big issue is how to extract the results; in the quantum world, the mere act of observing or measuring can cause superposed states to collapse into one state.

The first demonstration of a working quantum computer was carried out by California researchers in 1998. The experimental device had just two qubits: the carbon and hydrogen atoms in a molecule of chloroform, which were manipulated with a variation on the magnetic resonance imaging used in medicine. Subsequent quantum computing experiments have been done with slightly more qubits, but the problems solved by the devices have been only rudimentary. A variety of methods have been proposed for constructing quantum computers, including, recently, the use of carbon nanotubes as mechanical cubits.

Cryptography of the Future

Today's encryption systems for protecting information transmitted via such channels as the Internet tend to rely on mathematical problems that would take an enormous—hopefully unfeasible—amount of time and effort to solve. For example, one of the most popular encryption methods, called **RSA** (from the initials of its inventors), depends on the fact that it is very hard to find the prime factors of a very large number—that is, the prime numbers that produce the number when multiplied by each other.

This approach works for now, but **what if mathematicians make a breakthrough?** As it happens, one of the most celebrated unsolved problems in mathematics, the so-called Riemann hypothesis, deals with the pattern that might lurk behind the seeming randomness of prime numbers. The Clay Mathematics Institute of Cambridge, MA, has promised $1 mil to anyone who can prove the hypothesis. A successful proof could lead to development of an easy way to find the factors of large primes, thereby bringing, notes British mathematician Marcus du Sautoy, "the whole of e-commerce to its knees overnight." A proof was proposed by U.S. mathematician Louis de Branges in 2004, but it is exceedingly abstruse and has yet to be verified.

Another potential threat to secure encryption comes from **quantum computing**. In 1994, Bell Laboratories computer scientist Peter Shor demonstrated that a sizable quantum computer, because of its unconventional properties, could find the factors of a large number reasonably quickly.

Paradoxically, quantum physics could also become the savior of secure encryption. So-called quantum cryptography, whose origins date back to the late 1980s, utilizes such fundamental quantum concepts as the **Heisenberg uncertainty principle** (it is impossible to measure one property of a quantum system without perturbing a second one) and the principle of entanglement (two separate quantum systems that interacted at one time may still share some information). The keys required for encrypting and decrypting messages are represented in this instance by a pattern of particles of light, or photons, with certain characteristics. Interception by an eavesdropper will leave obvious traces, revealing that the key has been detected. In theory, surreptitious eavesdropping would be impossible.

The **first commercial quantum-cryptographic systems** came on the market in 2003, for communication between two points. Transmission over large distances remained a major hurdle—as of early 2005, 90 mi or so was the farthest achieved. The first network to use quantum cryptography went into operation in 2004, connecting several sites in the Boston area by underground optical fiber links, over which encryption keys are sent. A wireless link was added in 2005.

Called the DARPA Quantum Network, the project was funded by the Pentagon's Defense Advanced Research Projects Agency (DARPA) and built by BBN Technologies, the company that played the lead role in the creation of ARPANET, the forerunner of the Internet. The purpose of the project was to foster the development of hardware and software facilitating quantum cryptography over a network and to demonstrate its practicality.

Internet Lingo

The following abbreviations are sometimes used on the Internet documents and in e-mail.

BTW	By the way	**GOK**	God only knows	**LOL**	Laughing out loud
CBLO	See below	**GTG**	Got to go	**PLS**	Please
F2F	Face to face; a personal meeting	**HHOK**	Ha, ha—only kidding	**ROTFL**	Rolling on the floor laughing
FCOL	For crying out loud	**IMHO**	In my humble opinion	**TAFN**	That's all for now
FWIW	For what it's worth	**IMO**	In my opinion	**TTFN**	Ta-ta for now

Emoticons, or **smileys**, are a series of typed characters that, when turned sideways, resemble a face and express an emotion. Here are some smileys often encountered on the Internet.

:-)	Smile	:-D	Laugh	:-(	Unhappy	:-b..	Drooling		
;-)	Wink	:-*	Kiss	:-o	Surprised	{*}	A hug and a kiss		

Nations With the Most Personal Computers in Use

Source: Computer Industry Almanac, Inc., for year end 2004

Rank	Country	PCs In Use[1]	% of Worldwide Total
1.	United States	223.8	27.2
2.	Japan	69.2	8.4
3.	China	53.0	6.5
4.	Germany	46.3	5.6
5.	United Kingdom	35.9	4.4
6.	France	29.4	3.6
7.	South Korea	26.2	3.2
8.	Italy	22.7	2.8
9.	Canada	22.4	2.7
10.	Brazil	19.4	2.4
11.	Russia	19.0	2.3
12.	Australia	13.7	1.7
13.	India	13.0	1.6
14.	Mexico	11.2	1.4
15.	Netherlands	11.1	1.4
	Worldwide Total	**822.2**	**100**

(1) In millions.

Nations With the Most Internet Users

Source: Computer Industry Almanac, Inc., for year end 2004

Rank	Country	Internet Users[1]	% of Worldwide Users
1.	United States	185,550	19.9
2.	China	99,800	10.7
3.	Japan	78,050	8.4
4.	Germany	41,880	4.5
5.	India	36,970	4.0
6.	United Kingdom	33,110	3.5
7.	South Korea	31,670	3.4
8.	Italy	25,530	2.7
9.	France	25,470	2.7
10.	Brazil	22,320	2.4
11.	Russia	21,230	2.3
12.	Canada	20,450	2.2
13.	Mexico	13,880	1.5
14.	Spain	13,440	1.4
15.	Australia	13,010	1.4
	Worldwide Total	**934,480**	**100**

(1) In thousands.

U.S. Internet and Broadband Users, by Selected Characteristics[1]

Source: National Telecommunications and Information Administration, U.S. Dept. of Commerce; data as of Oct. 2003.

	Internet Users	Living in Broadband Households[2]
OF TOTAL POPULATION	**58.7%**	**22.8%**
By Race/Ethnicity		
White	65.1	25.7
Black	45.6	14.2
Asian Amer. & Pac. Isl.	63.1	34.2
Hispanic (of any race)	37.2	12.6
By Employment Status		
Employed	70.7	26.0
Not Employed	42.8	16.1
By Family Income		
Less than $15,000	31.2	7.5
$15,000 - $24,999	38.0	9.3
$25,000 - $34,999	48.9	13.4
$35,000 - $49,999	62.1	19.0
$50,000 - $74,999	71.8	27.9
$75,000 & above	82.9	45.4
By Education		
Less than High School	15.5%	5.9%
High School Diploma/GED	44.5	14.5
Some College	68.6	23.7
Bachelor's Degree	84.9	34.9
Beyond Bachelor's Degree	88.0	38.0
By Age Group		
3-4	19.9	22.0
5-9	42.0	24.1
10-13	67.3	25.8
14-17	78.8	28.3
18-24	70.6	25.5
In School	86.7	33.8
Not in School	58.2	19.0
25-49	68.0	25.9
50+	44.8	15.9

(1) All data are for persons 3 yrs. old or older. (2) Percent of persons in stated population living in a house with broadband, i.e. high-speed internet connections that allow 1 or more users to be online simultaneously. — = not available or not applicable.

Most-Visited Websites, June 2005

Source: comScore Media Metrix, Inc.

Rank	Website*	Visitors[1]
1.	Time Warner Network	118,516
2.	Yahoo! Sites	118,248
3.	MSN-Microsoft Sites	112,235
4.	Google Sites	79,960
5.	eBay	64,065
6.	Amazon Sites	40,092
7.	Ask Jeeves	39,821
8.	Viacom Online	32,258
9.	Vendare Media	31,290
10.	Verizon Communications Corp.	31,213
11.	CNET Networks	31,128
12.	Walt Disney Internet Group (WDIG)	29,853
13.	New York Times Digital	29,057
14.	Monster Worldwide	28,319
15.	The Weather Channel	28,023
16.	Expedia Travel	26,049
17.	Lycos, Inc.	25,463
18.	Wal-Mart	22,650
19.	Real.com Network	22,392
20.	Trip Network Inc.	20,917

*In some cases, represents an aggregation of commonly owned domain names. (1) Number of visitors, in thousands, who visited Website at least once in June 2005.

IT'S A FACT: Notebook personal computers accounted for 24% of all personal computers used in the world, and nearly 27% of those used in the U.S. as of 2003, according to the *Computer Industry Almanac.*

Internet Directory to Selected Sites

The Websites listed are but a sampling of what is available. For some others, see; the Where to Get Help directory (Health), Business Directory (Consumer Information), Sports Directory, Travel and Tourism, Associations and Societies, 100 Most Populous U.S. Cities, States of the U.S., U.S. Government, and Nations of the World.

Online Service Providers

America Online
www.aol.com
CompuServe
www.compuserve.com
EarthLink
www.earthlink.net
Microsoft Network
www.msn.com
Juno
www.juno.com
SBC Yahoo!
sbc.yahoo.com

Directories

Addresses.com
www.addresses.com
Bigfoot (e-mail addresses and white page listings)
www.bigfoot.com
InfoSpace, the Ultimate Directory
www.infospace.com
People Search
people.yahoo.com
Switchboard, the People and Business Directory
www.switchboard.com

Security and Screening

Anti-Phishing Working Group
www.antiphishing.org
The National Fraud Information Center
www.fraud.org
National Cyber Security Alliance
www.staysafeonline.info
U.S. Computer Emergency Readiness Team (CERT)
www.us-cert.gov

Auctions

eBay
www.ebay.com
uBid Online Auction
www.ubid.com
Yahoo! Auctions
auctions.shopping.yahoo.com

Audio/Video

MP3.com
www.mp3.com
Real Networks
www.real.com

Bookstores

Amazon.com Inc.
www.amazon.com
AddAll Book Search
www.addall.com
Barnes and Noble
www.barnesandnoble.com
Powell's City of Books
www.powells.com

Chat Sites

America Online
www.aim.com
Excite
communicate.excite.com
IVILLAGE: The Women's Network
www.ivillage.com
Yahoo
chat.yahoo.com

Children's Sites

(*See also Family Resources*)

American Library Association-Great Web Sites for Kids
www.ala.org/parentspage/greatsites/amazing.htm
FirstGov for Kids
www.kids.gov
Nick.com (Nickelodeon)
www.nick.com
Scholastic
www.scholastic.com/kids
Sports Illustrated for Kids
www.siforkids.com
Time for Kids
www.timeforkids.com
Weekly Reader
www.weeklyreader.com
World Almanac for Kids
www.worldalmanacforkids.com
Yahooligans (for homework help sites)
www.yahooligans.com

Economic Data

Bureau of Economic Analysis
www.bea.doc.gov
Bureau of Labor Statistics
www.bls.gov
Economics Statistics Briefing Room
www.whitehouse.gov/fsbr/esbr.html
Economy at a Glance
stats.bls.gov/eag/
Office of Management and Budget
www.gpoaccess.gov/usbudget
Statistical Abstract of the United States (a sampling)
www.census.gov/statab/www
STAT-USA/Internet (a subscription-based government service)
www.stat-usa.gov/stat-usa.html

Entertainment

Eonline
www.eonline.com
The Internet Movie Database
www.imdb.com
Movies.com
www.movies.go.com
The Movie Times
www.the-movie-times.com
Variety
www.variety.com

Family Resources

(*See also Children's Sites*)

Babies Online
www.babiesonline.com
BabyCenter
www.babycenter.com
FamilyFun.Com
familyfun.go.com
KidsHealth.org
www.kidshealth.org
KidSource Online
www.kidsource.com
Parenthood.com
www.parenthood.com
Parenting on iVillage
www.parenting.ivillage.com
Screen It! Entertainment Reviews for Parents
www.screenit.com
Zero to Three
www.zerotothree.org

Greeting Cards, Electronic

Blue Mountain Arts
www.bluemountain.com
Egreetings Network
www.egreetings.com
E-CARDS
www.ecards.com
1001 Postcards
www.postcards.org
123 Greetings
www.123greetings.com

Health

CenterWatch Clinical Trials Listing Service
www.centerwatch.com
Drugstore.com
www.drugstore.com
Healthfinder
www.healthfinder.gov
MayoClinic.com
www.mayoclinic.com
The Merck Manual
www.merck.com
National Institutes of Health
health.nih.gov
WebMD
www.webmd.com

Job Search Sites

CareerBuilder.com
www.careerbuilder.com
Hotjobs
hotjobs.yahoo.com
Monster
www.monster.com

Money Management

Internal Revenue Service
www.irs.gov
American Stock Exchange
www.amex.com
E*TRADE
www.etrade.com
MarketWatch
www.marketwatch.com
NASDAQ
www.nasdaq.com
New York Stock Exchange
www.nyse.com

Music

All Music Guide
www.allmusic.com
MusicMoz (the open music project)
www.musicmoz.org
BBC Music
www.bbc.co.uk/music
Classical Net
www.classical.net

Online Maps/Directions

MapQuest
www.mapquest.com
Google Maps
maps.google.com
Multimap.com
www.multimap.com

News

The Associated Press
www.ap.org
BBC Online
news.bbc.co.uk
Cable News Network
www.cnn.com
Fox News
www.foxnews.com
Los Angeles Times
www.latimes.com
MSNBC
www.msnbc.com
The New York Times on the Web
www.nytimes.com
NPR
www.npr.org
Reuters
www.reuters.com
USA Today
www.usatoday.com
Wall Street Journal
www.wsj.com
Washington Post
www.washingtonpost.com
World Press Review Online
www.worldpress.org

Reference

CIA Publications and Reports
www.odci.gov/cia/publications
Explore the Internet; The Library of Congress
www.loc.gov
Great Books Online
www.bartleby.com
Libweb: Library Servers via WWW
sunsite.berkeley.edu/Libweb
Merriam-Webster Online
www.m-w.com
yourDictionary.com
www.yourdictionary.com
Refdesk
www.refdesk.com
Roget's Thesaurus
www.thesaurus.com
Snopes.com (evaluates rumors, urban legends)
www.snopes.com

Shopping Sites

Overstock.com
www.overstock.com
Buy.com
www.buy.com

Sports

ESPN
www.espn.go.com
Sporting News
www.sportingnews.com
Sports Illustrated
www.sportsillustrated.cnn.com
Sports Network
www.sportsnetwork.com

Weather

National Weather Service
www.nws.noaa.gov
NationalCenter for Environmental Prediction (includes links to Storm Prediction Center sites)
www.ncep.noaa.gov
Weather Channel
www.weather.com

Weddings/Registries

Weddings/Registries
www.theknot.com

Selected Fun and Odd Websites[1]

The following is a sampling of odd or humorous Websites selected by the editors of *The World Almanac.*

Name	URL	Description
Baby Name Wizard	babynamewizard.com/namevoyager	See which names were popular and when.
Condiment Museum	www.clearfour.com/condiment	Online museum exhibiting condiment packets from around the world.
Cursor Thief	gprime.net/flash.php/cursorthieflive	He takes your cursor and throws it into a pile.
Four Word Film Reviews	www.fwfr.com	Movie reviews in 4 words or less.
Fred Society	www.fredsociety.com	Dedicated to preserving the name "Fred".
Hold the Button	www.holdthebutton.com	See how long you can hold down your mouse button.
Insect Recipes	www.ent.iastate.edu/misc/insectsasfood.html	Real food recipes with insects for ingredients.
Men Who Look Like Kenny Rogers	menwholooklikekennyrogers.com	Their photos, plus "Kenny spotting tips," etc.
Museum of Hoaxes	www.museumofhoaxes.com/top100.html	The truth behind the lies.
Music Plasma	www.musicplasma.com	See a map of musicians' influences.
Oracle of Bacon	oracleofbeacon.org	The popular Kevin Bacon movie game made easy.
Salary Compensation	swz.salary.com/salarytimer/layoutscripts/stml_start.asp	Compare yours to earnings of rich celebrities.
Stare Sally Down	www.stairwell.com/stare	A staring contest against a website.
Street Mattress	www.streetmattress.com	Photos of mattresses in the streets.
Traveling Pee Wee	www.travelingpeewee.com	Pee Wee Herman dolls photographed in various locations.
Twinkies Project	www.twinkiesproject.com	Testing the limits of twinkies.

(1) These sites were viewed by the editors, but content is subject to change and *The World Almanac* cannot take responsibility for contents.

The monthly World Almanac e-newsletter provides updates on interesting Websites, as well as on current events, offbeat news, celebrity birthdays, and obituaries, among other features. To subscribe, visit www.worldalmanac.com or e-mail newsletter@waegroup.com.

Top-Selling Software, 2004-2005

Source: The NPD Group/NPD Techworld
(based on unit U.S. sales, June 2004-June 2005[1])

All Software

1. TurboTax 2004 Deluxe, Intuit
2. Norton Antivirus 2005, Symantec
3. TurboTax 2004 Multi State 45, Intuit
4. Norton Internet Security 2005, Symantec
5. MS Office 2003 Student/Teacher Ed, Microsoft
6. Norton Internet Security 2005/Password Manager 2004 Bundle, Symantec
7. Norton Antivirus 2004, Symantec
8. Norton Antivirus 2005 Upgr, Symantec
9. Acrobat 6.0 Acad, Adobe
10. Spy Sweeper, Webroot

Business

1. MS Office 2003 Student/Teacher Ed, Microsoft
2. MS Office 2003 Pro SELECT Lic Acad, Microsoft
3. Clnt Management Suite Flex Lic, Altiris
4. MS Campus Agreement 3.1 Lic, Microsoft
5. MS Exchange Svr 2003 Clnt Acc OPEN Lic, Microsoft
6. MS Exchange Svr 2003 Clnt Acc SELECT Lic Govt, Microsoft
7. Clnt Management Suite 5.5 Mnt Lic, Altiris
8. M7 Exchange Svr 2003 Clnt Acc SELECT Lic Acad, Microsoft
9. MS Exchange Svr 2003 Clnt Acc SELECT Lic, Microsoft
10. MS Office 2003 Pro SELECT Lic, Microsoft

Home Education

1. Dora The Explorer Animal Adventures, Atari
2. Mavis Beacon Teaches Typing 16.0, Riverdeep Interactive
3. Instant Immersion Spanish JC, Topics Entertainment
4. Sponge Bob Square Pants: Typing, Riverdeep Interactive
5. I Spy Spooky Mansion Deluxe, Scholastic
6. Strawberry Shortcake: Amazing Cookie Party, Riverdeep Interactive
7. Adventure Workshop 1st-3rd Grade 5.0, Riverdeep Interactive
8. Adventure Workshop 4th-6th Grade 5.0, Riverdeep Interactive
9. Instant Immersion Spanish, Topics Entertainment
10. Jumpstart Advanced Third Grade 2003, Knowledge Adventure

Finance

1. TurboTax 2004 Deluxe, Intuit
2. TurboTax 2004 Multi State 45, Intuit
3. Taxcut 2004 Deluxe, Block Financial
4. TurboTax 2004, Intuit
5. TurboTax 2004 Premier, Intuit
6. Taxcut 2004 State, Block Financial
7. Quicken 2005, Intuit
8. Quicken 2005 Deluxe, Intuit
9. Taxcut 2004, Block Financial
10. QuickBooks 2005 Pro, Intuit

Imaging/Graphics

1. Acrobat 6.0 Acad, Adobe
2. Print Shop 20.0 Deluxe, Riverdeep Interactive
3. Adobe Photoshop Elements 3.0, Adobe
4. Print Perfect DVD JC, Cosmi
5. MS Digital Image 10.0 Suite, Microsoft
6. Print Shop 20.0 Essentials, Riverdeep Interactive
7. Printmaster 16.0 Platinum, Riverdeep Interactive
8. Hallmark Card Studio 2005 Deluxe, Nova Development
9. Printmaster 16.0 Gold, Riverdeep Interactive
10. Art Explosion Scrapbook Factory 2.0 Deluxe, Nova Development

Operating System

1. MS Windows XP Home Ed Upgr, Microsoft
2. MS Windows Svr 2003 Clnt Acc SELECT Lic, Microsoft
3. MS Windows Svr 2003 Clnt Acc OPEN Lic, Microsoft
4. MS Windows XP Pro Upgr, Microsoft
5. MS Windows Svr 2003 Clnt Acc SELECT Lic Acad, Microsoft
6. MS Windows XP Home Ed, Microsoft
7. MS Windows Svr 2003 Clnt Acc OPEN Lic Acad, Microsoft
8. MS Windows Svr 2003 TS Clnt Acc OPEN Lic, Microsoft
9. Mac OS X 10.4 Tiger, Apple
10. MS Windows XP Pro, Microsoft

PC Games

1. The Sims 2, Electronic Arts
2. World Of Warcraft, Vivendi Universal
3. Half-Life 2, Vivendi Universal
4. Doom 3, Activision
5. The Sims 2 Special Edition, Electronic Arts
6. The Sims Deluxe, Electronic Arts
7. Roller Coaster Tycoon 3, Atari
8. The Sims 2 University Expansion Pack, Electronic Arts
9. MS Zoo Tycoon 2, Microsoft
10. Rome: Total War, Activision

Personal Productivity

1. MS Streets & Trips 2005, Microsoft
2. Easy Media Creator 7.0, Roxio
3. DVD Ripper JC, Cosmi
4. Nero 6 Ultra Edition, Ahead Software
5. Marine Aquarium 2.0, Encore
6. MS Streets & Trips 2005 w/GPS Locator, Microsoft
7. MS Works 8.0, Microsoft
8. MS Works Suite 2005, Microsoft
9. MS Streets & Trips 2004, Microsoft
10. Bible Library Deluxe JC, Valusoft (THQ)

System Utilities

1. Norton Antivirus 2005, Symantec
2. Norton Internet Security 2005, Symantec
3. Norton Internet Security 2005/Password Manager 2004 Bundle, Symantec
4. Norton Antivirus 2004, Symantec
5. Norton Antivirus 2005 Upgr, Symantec
6. Spy Sweeper, Webroot
7. Spy Sweeper Tech Bench, Webroot
8. Norton Internet Security 2004, Symantec
9. Norton System Works 2005, Symantec
10. VirusScan 9.0, McAfee Inc.

(1) Some widely used software is often bundled with computers when sold; these are not included in sales figures above.

TELECOMMUNICATIONS

Worldwide Telecommunications: Market Data (1990-2003)

Source: © International Telecommunication Union

	1990	1998	1999	2000	2001	2002[3]	2003[4]
Total market revenue (billions of U.S. $)[1]	$508	$1,015	$1,123	$1,210	$1,232	$1,295	$1,370
Intl. phone traffic (billions of minutes)[2]	33	89	100	118	127	135	140
Main telephone lines (millions)	520	846	905	983	1,053	1,129	1,210
Mobile cellular subscriptions (millions)	11	318	490	740	955	1,155	1,341

(1) Revenue from installation, subscription, and local, trunk, and international call charges. (2) From 1994 including traffic between countries of the former Soviet Union. (3) Estimate. (4) Preliminary.

Worldwide Use of Cellular Telephones, Year-End 2004

Source: © International Telecommunication Union, estimated; top countries or regions ranked by subscriptions per 100 pop.

Country/Region	Subscriptions (thousands)	per 100 pop.
Taiwan	25,089.6	110.8
Luxembourg	473.0	106.1
Hong Kong	7,241.4	105.8
Italy	55,918.0	101.8
Iceland	279.1	96.6
Czech Republic	9,708.7	96.5
Israel	6,334.0	95.5
Spain	37,506.7	91.6
Norway	4,163.4	90.9
Portugal	9,341.4	90.4
Finland	4,700.0	90.1
Sweden	7,949.0	88.9
Denmark	4,785.3	88.7
Austria	7,094.5	87.9
Slovenia	1,739.1	87.1
Ireland	3,400.0	84.5
Switzerland	6,172.0	84.3
United Kingdom	49,677.0	84.1
Macao	364.0	81.5
Singapore	3,312.6	79.6
Belgium	8,135.5	78.6

Country/Region	Subscriptions (thousands)	per 100 pop.
Germany	64,800.0	78.5
Greece	8,936.2	78.0
Netherlands	12,500.0	76.8
United Arab Emirates	2,972.3	73.6
Malta	290.0	72.5
Australia	14,347.0	72.0
France	41,683.1	69.6
South Korea	33,591.8	69.4
Slovak Republic	3,678.8	68.4
Seychelles	54.5	68.2
Japan	86,658.6	68.0
Hungary	6,862.8	67.6
Lithuania	2,169.9	66.6
Estonia	881.0	65.0
New Zealand	2,599.0	64.8
Bahrain	443.1	63.8
Qatar	376.5	59.0
Cyprus	417.9	58.4
Croatia	2,553.0	58.4
Kuwait	1,420.0	57.8

Country/Region	Subscriptions (thousands)	per 100 pop.
United States	**158,722.0**	**54.3**
Jamaica	1,400.0	53.3
Latvia	1,219.6	52.9
Barbados	140.0	51.9
Antigua & Barbuda	38.2	49.0
Poland	17,400.0	45.1
Malaysia	11,124.1	44.2
Chile	6,445.7	42.8
Canada	13,221.8	41.7
Turkey	27,887.5	40.8
Brunei	137.0	40.1
Bahamas	121.8	39.0
Mauritius	462.4	37.9
French Polynesia	90.0	37.5
South Africa	16,860.0	36.4
Albania	1,100.0	35.8
New Caledonia	80.0	35.7
Serbia and Montenegro	3,634.6	33.8
WORLD	**1,340,667.7**	**21.9**

U.S. Cellular Telephone Subscribership, 1985–2004[1]

Source: The CTIA Semi-Annual Wireless Industry Survey. Used with permission of CTIA; in thousands of subscriptions[2]

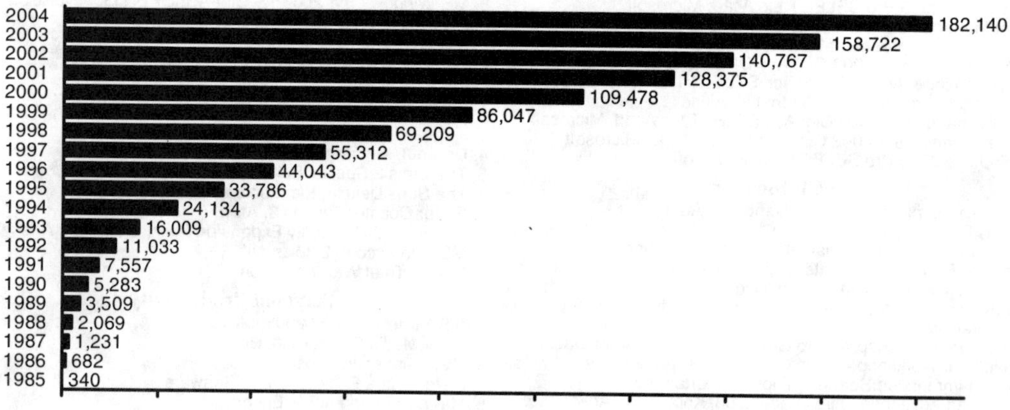

(1) In December. (2) Data may differ slightly from other sources.

U.S. Sales and Household Penetration, Selected Products[1], 1985-2004

Source: Consumer Electronics Association

	1985		1990		1995		2000		2003		2004	
	Sales[2]	% of all households	Sales[2]	% of all households	Sales[2]	% of all households	Sales[2]	% of all households	Sales[2]	% of all households	Sales[2]	% of all households
Cordless telephones	$280	11	$842	28	$1,141	55	$1,307	80	$1,268	82	$1,134	83
Pagers	—	—	118	1	300	11	750	23	729	17	675	13
Modems/Fax modems	10	0	191	2.7	770	16	1,564	55	1,419	64	1,386	64
Telephone answering devices	325	7	827	35	1,077	57	984	75	1,210	78	1,274	78
Cellular phones	116	0.10	1,098	5	2,574	29	8,995	60	9,163	70	10,538	70

(1) Data may differ slightly from other sources. (2) In millions of dollars.

Telephone Area Codes, by Number

As of Aug. 2005. For area codes listed by place, see pages 491-524.

Area Code	Location or Service
201	New Jersey
202	District of Columbia
203	Connecticut
204	Manitoba
205	Alabama
206	Washington
207	Maine
208	Idaho
209	California
210	Texas
211	Community Info.
212	New York
213	California
214	Texas
215	Pennsylvania
216	Ohio
217	Illinois
218	Minnesota
219	Indiana
224	Illinois
225	Louisiana
226	Ontario
228	Mississippi
229	Georgia
231	Michigan
234	Ohio
239	Florida
240	Maryland
242	Bahamas
246	Barbados
248	Michigan
250	British Columbia
251	Alabama
252	North Carolina
253	Washington
254	Texas
256	Alabama
260	Indiana
262	Wisconsin
264	Anguilla
267	Pennsylvania
268	Antigua/Barbuda
269	Michigan
270	Kentucky
276	Virginia
281	Texas
284	British Virgin Islands
289	Ontario
301	Maryland
302	Delaware
303	Colorado
304	West Virginia
305	Florida
306	Saskatchewan
307	Wyoming
308	Nebraska
309	Illinois
310	California
311	Non-Emergency Access
312	Illinois
313	Michigan
314	Missouri
315	New York
316	Kansas
317	Indiana
318	Louisiana
319	Iowa
320	Minnesota
321	Florida
323	California
325	Texas
330	Ohio
334	Alabama
336	North Carolina
337	Louisiana
339	Massachusetts
340	U.S. Virgin Islands
345	Cayman Islands
347	New York
351	Massachusetts
352	Florida
360	Washington
361	Texas
386	Florida
401	Rhode Island
402	Nebraska
403	Alberta
404	Georgia
405	Oklahoma
406	Montana
407	Florida
408	California
409	Texas
410	Maryland
411	Directory Assistance
412	Pennsylvania
413	Massachusetts
414	Wisconsin
415	California
416	Ontario
417	Missouri
418	Quebec
419	Ohio
423	Tennessee
425	Washington
430	Texas
432	Texas
434	Virginia
435	Utah
438	Quebec
440	Ohio
441	Bermuda
443	Maryland
450	Quebec
456	Inbound International
469	Texas
473	Grenada
478	Georgia
479	Arkansas
480	Arizona
484	Pennsylvania
500	Personal Comm. Serv.
501	Arkansas
502	Kentucky
503	Oregon
504	Louisiana
505	New Mexico
506	New Brunswick
507	Minnesota
508	Massachusetts
509	Washington
510	California
511	Traffic Info.
512	Texas
513	Ohio
514	Quebec
515	Iowa
516	New York
517	Michigan
518	New York
519	Ontario
520	Arizona
530	California
540	Virginia
541	Oregon
551	New Jersey
559	California
561	Florida
562	California
563	Iowa
567	Ohio
570	Pennsylvania
571	Virginia
573	Missouri
574	Indiana
580	Oklahoma
585	New York
586	Michigan
600	(Canadian Services)
601	Mississippi
602	Arizona
603	New Hampshire
604	British Columbia
605	South Dakota
606	Kentucky
607	New York
608	Wisconsin
609	New Jersey
610	Pennsylvania
611	Repair Service
612	Minnesota
613	Ontario
614	Ohio
615	Tennessee
616	Michigan
617	Massachusetts
618	Illinois
619	California
620	Kansas
623	Arizona
626	California
630	Illinois
631	New York
636	Missouri
641	Iowa
646	New York
647	Ontario
649	Turks & Caicos Islands
650	California
651	Minnesota
660	Missouri
661	California
662	Mississippi
664	Montserrat
670	N. Mariana Islands
671	Guam
678	Georgia
682	Texas
684	American Samoa
700	IC Services
701	North Dakota
702	Nevada
703	Virginia
704	North Carolina
705	Ontario
706	Georgia
707	California
708	Illinois
709	Newfoundland
710	U.S. Government
711	TRS Access
712	Iowa
713	Texas
714	California
715	Wisconsin
716	New York
717	Pennsylvania
718	New York
719	Colorado
720	Colorado
724	Pennsylvania
727	Florida
731	Tennessee
732	New Jersey
734	Michigan
740	Ohio
754	Florida
757	Virginia
758	St. Lucia
760	California
763	Minnesota
765	Indiana
767	Dominica
769	Mississippi
770	Georgia
772	Florida
773	Illinois
774	Massachusetts
775	Nevada
778	British Columbia
780	Alberta
781	Massachusetts
784	St. Vincent & Gren.
785	Kansas
786	Florida
787	Puerto Rico
800	Toll-Free Service
801	Utah
802	Vermont
803	South Carolina
804	Virginia
805	California
806	Texas
807	Ontario
808	Hawaii
809	Dominican Republic
810	Michigan
811	Business Office
812	Indiana
813	Florida
814	Pennsylvania
815	Illinois
816	Missouri
817	Texas
818	California
819	Quebec
828	North Carolina
829	Dominican Republic
830	Texas
831	California
832	Texas
843	South Carolina
845	New York
847	Illinois
848	New Jersey
850	Florida
856	New Jersey
857	Massachusetts
858	California
859	Kentucky
860	Connecticut
862	New Jersey
863	Florida
864	South Carolina
865	Tennessee
866	Toll-Free Service
867	Yukon, NW Terr., Nunavut
868	Trinidad & Tobago
869	St. Kitts & Nevis
870	Arkansas
876	Jamaica
877	Toll-Free Service
878	Pennsylvania
881	Toll-Free Service
882	Toll-Free Service
888	Toll-Free Service
900	Premium Service
901	Tennessee
902	Nova Scotia
903	Texas
904	Florida
905	Ontario
906	Michigan
907	Alaska
908	New Jersey
909	California
910	North Carolina
911	Emergency
912	Georgia
913	Kansas
914	New York
915	Texas
916	California
917	New York
918	Oklahoma
919	North Carolina
920	Wisconsin
925	California
928	Arizona
931	Tennessee
936	Texas
937	Ohio
939	Puerto Rico
940	Texas
941	Florida
947	Michigan
949	California
951	California
952	Minnesota
954	Florida
956	Texas
970	Colorado
971	Oregon
972	Texas
973	New Jersey
978	Massachusetts
979	Texas
980	North Carolina
985	Louisiana
989	Michigan

CONSUMER INFORMATION

Business Directory

Listed below are major U.S. corporations offering products and services to consumers. Information as of Sept. 2005. Alphabetization is by first key word. Listings generally include examples of products offered.

Company Name; Address; Telephone Number; Website; Top Executive; Business, Products, or Services.

A&P: *see* Great Atlantic & Pacific Tea Co.

Abbott Laboratories; 100 Abbott Park Rd., Abbott Park, IL 60064; (847) 937-6100; www.abbott.com; Miles D. White; develops and manuf. pharmaceutical, nutritional, and hospital prods.

Aetna, Inc.; 151 Farmington Ave., Hartford, CT 06156; (860) 273-0123; www.aetna.com; John W. Rowe; health insurance, financial services.

AFLAC; 1932 Wynnton Rd., Columbus, GA 31999; (706) 323-3431; www.aflac.com; Daniel Amos; health and life insurance.

Alaska Air Group; 19300 International Blvd., Seattle, WA 98188; (206) 392-5040; www.alaskaair.com; William Ayer; air travel (Alaska Air, Horizon Air).

Alberto-Culver; 2525 Armitage Ave., Melrose Park, IL 60160; (708) 450-3000; www.alberto.com; Carol Lavin Bernick; hair care (VO5), consumer prods. (Mrs. Dash, Sugar Twin), personal care prods. (St. Ives), Sally Beauty Supply stores.

Albertson's, Inc.; 250 Parkcenter Blvd., Boise, ID 83706; (208) 395-6200; www.albertsons.com; Lawrence R. Johnston; supermarkets.

Alcoa Inc.; 201 Isabella St., Pittsburgh, PA 15212; (412) 553-4545; www.alcoa.com; Alain J.P. Belda; aluminum products; aerospace & automotive components; industrial materials/tools.

Allegheny Technologies, Inc.; 1000 Six PPG Place, Pittsburgh, PA 15222-5479; (412) 394-2800; www.allegheny techologies.com; L. Patrick Hassey; electronics, aerospace, industrial; specialty metals.

Allied Waste Industries; 15880 N. Greenway-Hayden Loop, Suite 100, Scottsdale, AZ 85260; (480) 627-2700; www.allied waste.com; John Jay Zillmer; solid waste management.

Allstate Corp.; 2775 Sanders Rd., Northbrook, IL 60062; (847) 402-5000; www.allstate.com; Edward Liddy; property/casualty, life insurance.

Altria Group, Inc.; 120 Park Ave., NY, NY 10017; (917) 663-4000; www.altria.com; www.kraft.com. Louis C. Camilleri; cigarettes (largest U.S. tobacco company; Marlboro, Merit, Virginia Slims); Kraft Foods products (Jell-O, Maxwell House, Kool-Aid, Oscar Mayer, Tang, Cheez Whiz and Velveeta, Post cereals, Tombstone Pizza, and Toblerone chocolate); Nabisco products (Oreo, Chips Ahoy! cookies, Ritz, Triscuit crackers, Mallomars). (Philip Morris Companies, Inc., changed its name to Altria, 1/27/03).

Amazon.com Inc.; 1200 12th Ave. S., Suite 1200 Seattle, WA 98144; (206) 266-1000; www.amazon.com; Jeff Bezos; online books, electronics, photo, and home and garden products.

Amerada Hess Corp.; 1185 Ave. of the Americas, NY, NY 10036; (212) 997-8500; www.hess.com; John B. Hess; integrated international oil co.

American Electric Power; 1 Riverside Plaza, Columbus, OH 43215; (614) 716-1000; www.aep.com; Michael G. Morris; utilities.

American Express Co.; 200 Vesey St., NY, NY 10285; (212) 640-2000; www.americanexpress.com; Kenneth Chenault; travel, financial, and information services.

American Greetings Corp.; 1 American Rd., Cleveland, OH 44144; (216) 252-7300; www.americangreetings.com; Zev Weiss; greeting cards, stationery, party goods, gift items.

American Home Products: *see* Wyeth.

American Intl. Group; 70 Pine St., NY, NY 10270; (212) 770-7000; www.aig.com; Martin J. Sullivan; insurance, financial services.

American Standard; One Centennial Ave., P.O. Box 6820, Piscataway, NJ 08855; (732) 980-6000; www.americanstandard.com; Frederic M. Poses; bathroom and kitchen fixtures and fittings, air conditioning systems, vehicle control systems.

AMR Corp.; 4333 Amon Carter Blvd., Ft. Worth, TX 76155; (817) 963-1234; www.aa.com; Gerard J. Arpey; air transportation (American Airlines, American Eagle); acquired assets of Trans World Air Lines Inc. in 2001.

Anheuser-Busch Cos., Inc.; 1 Busch Pl., St. Louis, MO 63118; (314) 577-2000; www.anheuser-busch.com; August A. Busch 3rd; world's largest brewer (Budweiser, Michelob, Busch, O'Doul's), aluminum can manuf. and recycling, theme parks.

AOL Time Warner Inc.: *see* Time Warner, Inc.

Apple Computer, Inc.; 1 Infinite Loop, Cupertino, CA 95014-2084; (408) 996-1010; www.apple.com; Steve Jobs; manuf. of personal computers, software, peripherals.

Aramark Corp.; Aramark Tower, 1101 Market St., Philadelphia, PA 19107; (215) 238-3000; www.aramark.com; Joseph Neubauer; food and support services, uniforms and career apparel, child care and early education.

Archer Daniels Midland Co.; 4666 Faries Pkwy., Decatur, IL 62525; (217) 424-5200; www.admworld.com; G. Allen Andreas; agricultural commodities and prods.

Armstrong World Industries, Inc.; 2500 Columbia Ave., Lancaster, PA 17604; (717) 397-0611; www.armstrong.com; Michael D. Lockhart; interior furnishings, specialty prods.

Arvinmeritor Industries, Inc.; 2135 West Maple Road, Troy, MI 48084; (248) 435-1000; www.arvinmeritor.com; Charles G. McClure; auto emission and ride control systems.

Ashland Inc.; 50 E. RiverCenter, P.O. Box 391, Covington, KY 41011; (859) 815-3333; www.ashland.com; James J. O' Brien Jr.; petroleum producer and refiner (Valvoline), chemicals, road construction.

AT&T Corp.; One AT&T Way, Bedminster, NJ 07921; (908) 221-2000; www.att.com; David W. Dorman; communications, global information management.

AutoNation; 110 S.E. 6th St., Ft. Lauderdale, FL 33301; (954) 769- 6000; www.autonation.com; Michael Jackson; new and used auto vehicles; auto parts, maintenance, and repair; auto protection products.

Avon Prods., Inc.; 1345 Ave. of Americas, NY, NY 10105; (212) 282-5000; www.avon.com; Andrea Jung; cosmetics, fragrances, toiletries, fashion jewelry, gift items, casual apparel, lingerie.

Bank of America Corp.; Bank of America Corporate Center, 100 N. Tryon St., Charlotte, NC 28255; (704) 386-5000; www.bankofamerica.com; Kenneth D. Lewis; major U.S. bank; acquired FleetBoston, 4/1/2004; agreed to acquire MBNA, June 2005.

Bank One Corp.; 1 Bank One Plaza, Chicago, IL 60670; (302) 732-4000; www.bankone.com; James Dimon; banking and financial services, credit card services, investment management. Merged with JP Morgan Chase on 7/1/04.

Barnes & Noble, Inc.; 122 Fifth Ave., New York, NY 10011; (212) 633-3300; www.bn.com; Steve Riggio; leading U.S. bookstore chain (Barnes & Noble, B. Dalton stores), publishing (Sterling Pub. Co.).

Bausch & Lomb Inc.; One Bausch & Lomb Place, Rochester, NY 14604; (585) 338-6000; www.bausch.com; Ronald L. Zarrella; vision and health-care prods., accessories.

Baxter International Inc.; 1 Baxter Pkwy., Deerfield, IL 60015; (847) 948-2000; www.baxter.com; Robert Parkinson Jr.; health care prods. & services.

Bear Stearns Cos. Inc.; 383 Madison Ave., NY, NY 10179; (212) 272-2000; www.bearstearns.com; James E. Cayne; investment banking, securities trading, brokerage.

Becton, Dickinson & Co.; 1 Becton Dr., Franklin Lakes, NJ 07417; (201) 847-6800; www.bd.com; E.J. Ludwig; medical, laboratory, diagnostic prods.

BellSouth Corp.; 1155 Peachtree St. NE, Atlanta, GA 30309; (404) 249-2000; www.bellsouth.com; F. Duane Ackerman; telephone service in southern U.S.

Berkshire Hathaway Inc.; 1440 Kiewit Plaza, Omaha, NE 68131; (402) 346-1400; www.berkshirehathaway.com; Warren E. Buffett; subsidiaries include GEICO Direct insurance, Johns Manville building materials, Fruit of the Loom underwear, Dairy Queen restaurants/desserts, Benjamin Moore paints.

Bertelsmann AG; Carl-Bertelsmann-Strasse 270, D-33311 Gütersloh, Germany; +49-5241-80-0; www.bertelsmann.de; Gunter Thielen; largest trade book publisher (Random House: Knopf, Ballantine, Bantam, Crown, Doubleday), largest music company.

Best Buy Co., Inc.; 7601 Penn Ave. S., Richfield, MN 55423; (612) 291-1000; www.bestbuy.com; Richard Schulze; retailer of software, appliances, electronics, cameras, home office equipment.

Black & Decker Corp.; 701 E. Joppa Rd., Towson, MD 21286; (410) 716-3900; www.bdk.com; Nolan D. Archibald; manuf. power tools (DeWalt, Black & Decker), household prods. (Kwikset locks, Price Pfister faucets, Black & Decker small appliances).

H & R Block, Inc.; 4400 Main St., Kansas City, MO 64111; (816) 753-6900; www.hrblock.com; Mark A. Ernst; tax return preparation.

Blockbuster Inc.; 1201 Elm St., Dallas, TX 75270; (214) 854-3000; www.blockbuster.com; John F. Antioco; DVD rentals.

Boeing Co.; 100 N. Riverside Plaza, Chicago, IL 60606; (312) 544-2000; www.boeing.com; W. James McNerney Jr.; leading manufacturer of commercial, jet aircraft.

Boise Cascade; 1111 W. Jefferson St., Boise, ID 83702; (208) 384-6161; www.bc.com; William Thomas Stevens; distributor of office products & building materials; paper, wood prods.

The Brink's Co.; 1801 Bayberry Ct., Richmond, VA 23226; (804) 289-9600; www.brinkscompany.com; Michael T. Dan; security (alarm systems, armored cars).

Bristol-Myers Squibb Co.; 345 Park Ave., NY, NY 10154; (212) 546-4000; www.bms.com; Peter R. Dolan; drugs (Bufferin, Comtrex, Pravachol, TAXOL), nutritionals (Enfamil infant formula, Boost energy drink).

Brown-Forman Corp.; 850 Dixie Hwy,, Louisville, KY 40210; (502) 585-1100; www.brown-forman.com; Owsley Brown 2nd; distilled spirits (Jack Daniel's, Southern Comfort), wines (Bolla, Fetzer, Korbel), china and crystal (Dansk, Lenox), Gorham, Kirk Steiff silver prods., Hartmann luggage.

Brown Shoe Co., Inc.; 8300 Maryland Ave., P.O. Box 29, St. Louis, MO 63105; (314) 854-4000; www.brownshoe.com; Ronald A. Fromm; manuf. and retailer (Famous Footwear) of women's, men's, and children's shoes (Buster Brown, Naturalizer, Dr. Scholl's).

Brunswick Corp.; 1 N. Field Ct., Lake Forest, IL 60045; (847) 735-4700; www.brunswick.com; George Buckley; largest U.S. maker of leisure and recreation prods., incl. marine, camping, fitness, and fishing equip.; bowling centers and equip.

Burger King Corp.; 5505 Blue Lagoon Dr., Miami, FL 33126; (305) 378-3000; www.burgerking.com; Greg Brenneman; fast-food restaurants.

Burlington Industries; 804 Green Valley Rd., Greensboro, NC 27408; (336) 379-2000; www.burlington.com; Joseph L. Gorga; fabrics and textile products.

Burlington Northern Santa Fe Inc.; 2650 Lou Menk Dr., Ft. Worth, TX 76131; (817) 352-1000; www.bnsf.com; Matthew Rose; one of the largest U.S. rail transportation cos.

Cablevision Systems Corp.; 1111 Stewart Ave., Bethpage, NY 11714; (516) 803-2300; www.cablevision.com; James L. Dolan; cable & VoIP provider. CATV (AMC, Fuse, IFC, WE); sports teams (NY Knicks, NY Rangers)

Cadbury Schweppes; 25 Berkeley Sq., London, W1J 6HB, UK; +44 20 7409 1313; www.cadburyschweppes.com; John M. Sunderland; 3rd-largest beverage producer; candies, gum.

Campbell Soup Co.; One Campbell Pl., Camden, NJ 08103; (856) 342-4800; www.campbellsoup.com; Douglas R. Conant; soups, Franco-American spaghetti, V8 vegetable juice, Prego spaghetti sauce, Pepperidge Farm, Pace sauces.

Caterpillar Inc.; 100 N.E. Adams St., Peoria, IL 61629; (309) 675-1000; www.cat.com; James W. Owens; world's largest producer of earth moving equip.

Chase Manhattan Corp.: *see* JPMorgan Chase & Co. Inc.

Chevron Corp.; 6001 Bollinger Canyon Rd., San Ramon, CA 94583; (925) 842-1000; www.chevron. com; David J. O'Reilly; 2nd-largest U.S.-based oil co; acquired Unocal, 8/10/05.

Chiquita Brands International, Inc.; 250 E. 5th St., Cincinnati, OH 45202; (513) 784-8000; www.chiquita.com; Fernando Aguirre; bananas, fruits, vegetables.

Church & Dwight Co., Inc.; 469 N. Harrison St., Princeton, NJ 08543; (609) 683-5900; www.churchdwight.com; R.A. Davies 3rd; world's largest producer of sodium bicarbonate (Arm & Hammer); household products (Brillo, Fresh'n Soft, other Arm & Hammer products); personal care products (Arrid antiperspirant, Pearl Drops, Nair, Trojan condoms, First Response pregnancy test).

CIGNA Corp.; 1 Liberty Pl., Philadelphia, PA 19192; (215) 761-1000; www.cigna.com; H. Edward Hanway; insurance holding co.

Circuit City Stores, Inc.; 9950 Mayland Dr., Richmond, VA 23233; (804) 527-4000; www.circuitcity.com; W. Alan McCollough; retailer of electronic, audio/video equip., consumer appliances.

Cisco Systems; 170 West Tasman Dr., San Jose, CA 95134; (408) 526-4000; www.cisco.com; John Chambers; networking and communication products.

Citigroup; 399 Park Ave., NY, NY 10043; (212) 559-1000; www.citigroup.com; Sanford I. Weill; diversified financial services.

Clear Channel Communications, Inc.; 200 E. Basse Rd., San Antonio, TX 78209; (210) 822-2828; www.clearchannel.com; Mark P. Mays; largest radio station owner in U.S. (1,200 stations); outdoor advertising (billboards, mass transit ads).

Clorox Co.; 1221 Broadway, Oakland, CA 94612; (510) 271-7000; www.clorox.com; Gerald E. Johnston; retail consumer prods. (Clorox, Formula 409, Pine-Sol, S.O.S., Soft Scrub cleansers; Armor All, STP, Rain Dance automotive prods.; Scoop Away, Fresh Step cat litters; Kingsford charcoal briquets; Hidden Valley dressing; K.C. Masterpiece barbecue sauce; Brita water systems)

Coca-Cola Co.; 1 Coca-Cola Plaza, Atlanta, GA 30313; (404) 676-2121; www.cocacola.com; E. Neville Isdell; world's largest soft drink co. (Coca-Cola, Sprite, Nestea), world's largest dist. of juice prods. (Minute Maid, Hi-C, Fruitopia).

Colgate-Palmolive Co.; 300 Park Ave., NY, NY 10022; (212) 310-2000; www.colgate.com; Reuben Mark; soap (Palmolive, Irish Spring), detergent (Fab, Ajax), toothpaste (Colgate), Hill's pet food.

Comcast Corp.; 1500 Market St., Philadelphia, PA 19102; 215-665-1700; www.comcast.com; Brian L. Roberts; largest U.S. cable company; broadband cable, internet, and voice services. Some programming, incl. E!, Golf Channel, et al.

Compaq Computer Corp.: *see* Hewlett-Packard Co.

CompUSA Inc.; 14951 N. Dallas Pkwy., Dallas, TX 75254; (972) 982-4000; www.compusa.com; Larry Mondry; largest U.S. superstore retailer of microcomputers and peripherals.

Computer Sciences Corp.; 2100 E. Grand Ave., El Segundo, CA 90245; (310) 615-0311; www.csc.com; Van B. Honeycutt; technology services.

ConAgra Foods, Inc.; 1 ConAgra Dr., Omaha, NE 68102; (402) 595-4000; www.conagra.com; Bruce Rohde; 2nd-largest U.S. food processor (Armour, Bumble Bee, Butterball, Chef Boyardee, Healthy Choice frozen dinners, Egg Beaters, Reddi-Wip).

ConocoPhillips Co.; 600 North Dairy Ashford, P.O. Box 2197, Houston, TX 77079; (281) 293-1000; www.conocophillips.com; James J. Mulva; oil and petrochemical co. Formed by merger of Conoco and Phillips Petroleum, 8/30/02. Third-largest U.S. integrated energy company.

Continental Airlines, Inc.; 1600 Smith St. HQS11, Houston, TX 77002; (713) 324-5242; www.continental.com; Larry Kellner; air transportation.

Corning Inc.; 1 Riverfront Plaza, Corning, NY 14831; (607) 974-9000; www.corning.com; James R. Houghton; telecommunications, specialty materials, optical fiber and cable.

Costco Wholesale Corp.; 999 Lake Dr., Issaquah, WA 98027; (425) 313-8100; www.costco.com; James D. Sinegal; wholesale-membership warehouses.

Crane Co.; 100 First Stamford Place, Stamford, CT 06902; (203) 363-7300; www.craneco.com; Eric C. Fast; manuf. fluid control devices, vending machines, fiberglass panels, aircraft brakes.

A. T. Cross Co.; 1 Albion Rd., Lincoln, RI 02865; (401) 333-1200; www.cross.com; David Whalen; writing instruments.

Crown Holdings; 1 Crown Way, Philadelphia, PA 19154-4599; (215) 698-5100; www.crowncork.com; John W. Conway; leading supplier of packaging prods.

CSX Corp.; 500 Water St., 15th Fl., Jacksonville, FL 32202; (904) 359-3200; www.csx.com; Michael J. Ward; rail, ocean, barge freight transport.

CVS Corp.; 1 CVS Dr., Woonsocket, RI 02895; (401) 765-1500; www.CVS.com; Thomas M. Ryan; acquired Eckerd Corp. in August 2004, to become nation's largest drugstore chain.

Dana Corp.; 4500 Dorr St., Toledo, OH 43615; (419) 535-4500; www.dana.com; Michael Burns; truck and auto parts, supplies.

Darden Restaurants; 5900 Lake Ellenor Dr., Orlando, FL 32809; (407) 245-4000; www.darden.com; Joe Lee; chain restaurants (Red Lobster, Olive Garden, Bahama Breeze, Smokey Bones BBQ Sports Bar).

Dean Foods Co.; 2515 McKinney Ave., Ste. 1200, Dallas, TX 75201; 214-303-3400; www.deanfoods.com; Gregg L. Engles; milk and specialty dairy products (Land O'Lakes, Horizon Organic, Silk soymilk), salad dressings (Marie's), pickles.

Deere & Co.; One John Deere Pl., Moline, IL 61265; (309) 765-8000; www.deere.com; Robert W. Lane; world's largest manuf. of farm equip.; also makes industrial equip., and lawn and garden tractors.

Dell Inc.; 1 Dell Way, Round Rock, TX 78682; (512) 338-4400; www.dell.com; Michael S. Dell; laptop and desktop computers.

Delphi Corp.; 5725 Delphi Dr., Troy, MI 48098; (248) 813-2000; www.delphi.com; Robert S. Miller Jr.; automotive systems, audio systems, mobile electronics.

Delta Air Lines, Inc.; P.O. Box 20706, Atlanta, GA 30320; (404) 715-2600; www.delta.com; Gerald Grinstein; air transportation.

Dial Corp.; 15501 N. Dial Blvd., Scottsdale, AZ 85260-1619; (480) 754-3425; www.dialcorp.com; Bradley A. Casper; consumer prods. (Dial soap, Purex detergent, Armour Star meats, Renuzit air fresheners).

Diebold, Inc; 5995 Mayfair Rd., P.O. Box 3077, North Canton, OH 44720; (330) 490-4000; www.diebold.com; Walden W. O'Dell; manuf. ATMs, security systems and prods.

Dillard's; 1600 Cantrell Rd., Little Rock, AR 72201; (501) 376-5200; www.dillards.com; William Dillard 2nd; 2nd-largest dept. store chain in U.S.

Walt Disney Co.; 500 S. Buena Vista St., Burbank, CA 91521-7320; (818) 560-1000; www.disney.com; Michael D. Eisner; motion pictures, television (ESPN, ABC, SoapNet, Disney Channel, Lifetime), radio stations, theme parks (Walt Disney World, Disneyland) and resorts, publishing, recordings, retailing (Disney Stores).

Dole Food Co., Inc.; One Dole Drive, Westlake Village, CA 91362; (818) 879-6600; www.dole.com; David H. Murdock; food prods., fresh fruits and vegetables.

R. R. Donnelley & Sons Co.; 111 S. Wacker Dr., Chicago, IL 60606; (312) 326-8000; www.rrdonnelley.com; Mark A. Angelson; largest commercial printer in N. America; photo/graphics, translation; printer of *The World Almanac.*

Dow Chemical Co.; 2030 Dow Center, Midland, MI 48674; (989) 636-1000; www.dow.com; Andrew M. Liveris; chemicals, plastics (world's 2nd-largest chemical co. after merger, 2/7/01, with Union Carbide).

Dow Jones & Co., Inc.; 200 Liberty St., NY, NY 10281; (212) 416-2000; www.dowjones.com; Peter R. Kann; financial news service, publishing (*Wall Street Journal, Barron's*, Ottaway Newspapers).

Duke Energy Corp.; 526 S. Church St., Charlotte, NC 28202; 704-594-6200; www.duke-energy.com; Paul M. Anderson; natural gas, uilities, pipelines, fiber optics.

Dun & Bradstreet Corp.; 103 JFK Parkway, Short Hills, NJ 07078; (973) 921-5500; www.dnb.com; Steven Alesio; business information, publishing ("Yellow Pages" phone books).

Duracell: *see* Gillette.

E. I. du Pont de Nemours & Co. (Dupont); 1007 Market St., Wilmington, DE 19898; (302) 774-1000; www.dupont.com; Charles Holliday; largest U.S. chemical co.; petroleum, consumer prods.

Eastman Kodak Co.; 343 State St., Rochester, NY 14650-0205; (585) 724-4000; www.kodak.com; D. Carp; world's largest producer of photographic prods.

Eaton Corp.; 1111 Superior Ave., Cleveland, OH 44114; (216) 523-5000; www.eaton.com; Alexander Cutler; manuf. of vehicle powertrain components, controls.

eBay Inc.; 2145 Hamilton Ave., San Jose, CA 95125; (408) 376-7400; www.ebay.com; Meg C. Whitman; online auctions.

Eckerd Corp.: *see* CVS Corp.

Edison Intl.; 2244 Walnut Grove Ave., P.O. Box 800, Rosemead, CA 91770; (626) 302-2222; www.edisonx.com; John Bryson; electric utilities.

Electronic Arts Inc.; 209 Redwood Shores Pkwy, Redwood City, CA 94065; (650) 628-1500; www.ea.com; Larry Probst III; leading U.S. video game publisher.

Electronic Data Systems; 5400 Legacy Dr., Plano, TX 75024; (972) 604-6000; www.eds.com; Michael Jordan; management consulting, e-solutions, software.

Eli Lilly and Co.; Lilly Corporate Center, Indianapolis, IN 46285; 317-276-2000; www.lilly.com; Sidney Taurel; pharmaceutical research, development, and manufacturing (Prozac, Stratera, Evista, Cialis).

El Paso Corp.; 1001 Louisiana Street, Houston, TX 77002; (713) 420-2600; www.elpaso.com; Ronald L. Kuehn Jr.; diversified energy company primarily engaged in interstate transmission of natural gas.

EMC Corp.; 176 South St., Hopkinton, MA 01748; (877) 362-6973; www.emc.com; Mike Ruettgers; data storage and protection.

Emerson Electric Co.; 8000 West Florissant Avenue, St. Louis, MO 63136; (314) 553-2000; www.gotoemerson.com; David Farr; electrical, electronics prods. & systems.

Energizer Holdings Inc.; 533 Maryville Univ. Dr., St. Louis, MO 63141; (314) 985-2000; www.energizer.com; Ward M. Klein; batteries, flashlights, lanterns.

Exelon Corp.; 10 S. Dearborn St., 37th Fl., Chicago, IL 60680; www.exeloncorp.com; 312-394-7398; John W. Rowe; electricity generation and distribution; nat. gas.

Exxon Mobil Corp.; 5959 Las Colinas Blvd., Irving, TX 75039-2298; (972) 444-1000; www.exxonmobil.com; Lee Raymond; world's 2nd-largest publicly owned integrated oil co.

Fannie Mae; 3900 Wisconsin Ave. NW, Washington, DC 20016; (202) 752-7000; www.fanniemae.com; Daniel H. Mudd; largest U.S. provider of residential mortgage funds.

Fedders Corp.; 505 Martinsville Road, P.O. Box 813, Liberty Corner, NJ 07938; (908) 604-8686; www.fedders.com; Salvatore Giordano Jr; manuf. of room air conditioners (Fedders, Airtemp), dehumidifiers.

Federated Dept. Stores; 7 W. 7th St., Cincinnati, OH 45202; (513) 579-7000; www.Federated-fds.com; Terry J. Lundgren; dept. stores (Macy's, Bloomingdale's); merged with May Dept. Stores (Lord & Taylor, Marshall Field's), 2/28/05.

FedEx Corp.; 942 S. Shady Grove Rd., Memphis, TN 38120; (901) 818-7500; www.fedex.com; F. W. Smith; express delivery service.

First Data Corp.; 6200 S. Quebec St., Greenwood Village, CO, 80111; (303) 967-8000; www.firstdatacorp.com; Charles Fote; info. retrieval, data processing.

FirstEnergy Corp.; 76 S. Main St., Akron, OH 44308; 800-633-4766; www.firstenergycorp.com; Anthony J. Alexander; public utility company; provides electricity and natural gas.

FleetBoston Financial Corp.: *see* Bank of America.

Fleetwood Enterprises, Inc.; 3125 Myers St., Riverside, CA 92503; (951) 351-3500; www.fleetwood.com; Elden L. Smith; manufactured homes, recreational vehicles.

Fluor Corp.; One Enterprise Dr., Aliso Viejo, CA 92656; (949) 349-2000; www.fluor.com; Alan L. Boeckmann; largest international engineering and construction co. in U.S.

Foot Locker, Inc.; formerly Venator Group, 112 West 34th St., NY, NY 10120; (212) 720-3700; www.footlocker-inc.com; Matthew D. Serra; operates retail stores: shoes (Kinney), apparel (Eastbay), athletic footwear (Foot Locker), athletic merchandise (Champs).

Ford Motor Co.; 1 American Rd., Dearborn, MI 48126; (313) 322-3000; www.ford.com; William Clay Ford Jr.; 2nd-largest auto manufacturer, motor vehicle sales (Ford, Lincoln-Mercury, Volvo), rentals (Hertz).

Fortune Brands, Inc.; 300 Tower Parkway, Lincolnshire, IL 60069; (847) 484-4400; www.fortunebrands.com; Norman H. Wesley; spirits and wine (Jim Beam), hardware, office prods., golf and leisure prods. (Titleist, Cobra, FootJoy).

Freddie Mac; 8200 Jones Branch Dr., McLean, VA 22102; (703) 903-2000; www.freddiemac.com; Dick Syron; residential mortgage provider.

Fruit of the Loom, Inc.; 1 Fruit of the Loom Dr., Bowling Green, KY 42103; (270) 781-6400; www.fruit.com; John B. Holland; manuf. of underwear, activewear. A subsidiary of Berkshire Hathaway, acquired 4/30/02.

Gannett Co., Inc.; 7950 Jones Branch Dr., McLean, VA 22107; (703) 854-6000; www.gannett.com; D.H. McCorkindale; newspaper publishing (*USA Today*), network and cable TV.

Gap Inc.; Two Folsom St., San Francisco, CA 94105; (415) 952-4400; www.gap.com; Robert Fisher; casual apparel retailer (Gap, Banana Republic, Old Navy).

Gateway Inc.; 7565 Irvine Ctr. Dr., Irvine, CA 92618; (949) 471-7000; www.gateway.com; Wayne Inouye; personal computers.

General Dynamics; 2941 Fairview Park Drive, Ste. 100, Falls Church, VA 22042; (703) 876-3000; www.generaldyn.com; Nicholas D. Chabraja; nuclear submarines (Trident, Seawolf), armored vehicles, combat systems, computing devices, defense systems.

General Electric Co.; 3135 Easton Tpke., Fairfield, CT 06828; (203) 373-2211; www.ge.com; Jeffrey Immelt; electrical, electronic equip., radio and TV broadcasting (NBC, Bravo, USA, Telemundo), aircraft engines, power generation, appliances.

General Mills, Inc.; One General Mills Blvd., Minneapolis, MN 55426; (763) 764-7600; www.generalmills.com; S. W. Sanger; foods (Total, Wheaties, Cheerios, Chex, Hamburger Helper, Betty Crocker, Bisquick).

General Motors; 300 Renaissance Center, Detroit, MI 48265; (313) 556-5000; www.gm.com; G. Richard Wagoner Jr.; world's largest auto manuf. (Chevrolet, Pontiac, Cadillac, Buick).

Genuine Parts Co.; 2999 Circle 75 Pkwy., Atlanta, GA 30339; (770) 953-1700; www.genpt.com; Thomas C. Gallagher; distributes auto replacement parts (NAPA).

Georgia-Pacific Corp.; 133 Peachtree St. NE, Atlanta, GA 30303; (404) 652-4000; www.gp.com; A. D. Correll; manuf. of paper and wood prods.

Gillette; Prudential Tower Bldg., Boston, MA 02199; (617) 421-7000; www.gillette.com; James M. Kilts; personal care prods. (Sensor, Atra razors, Oral-B toothbrushes, Right Guard, Soft & Dri), appliances (Braun), batteries (Duracell); proposed merger with Procter & Gamble approved by shareholders, 7/12/05.

Goldman Sachs Group; 85 Broad Street, NY, NY 10004; (212) 902-1000; www.goldmansachs.com; Henry M. Paulson Jr.; investment banking, asset management, securities services.

The Goodyear Tire & Rubber Co.; 1144 E. Market St., Akron, OH 44316; (330) 796-2121; www.goodyear.com; Robert Keegan; world's largest rubber manuf.; tires and other auto prods.

Google, Inc.; 1600 Amphitheatre Pkwy., Mountain View, CA 94043; (650) 623-4000; www.google.com; Eric E. Schmidt; internet search engine/media company.

W. R. Grace & Co.; 7500 Grace Dr., Columbia, MD 21044; (410) 531-4000; www.grace.com; Paul J. Norris; chemicals, construction prods.

Great Atlantic & Pacific Tea Co. (A&P); 2 Paragon Dr., Montvale, NJ 07645; (201) 573-9700; www.aptea.com; Christian Haub; supermarkets (A&P, Waldbaum's, Kohl's, Dominion).

Halliburton Co.; 5 Houston Center, 1401 McKinney, Houston, TX 77010; (713) 759-2600; www.halliburton.com; Dave Lesar; energy, engineering, and construction services.

Harley-Davidson, Inc.; 3700 W. Juneau Avenue, Milwaukee, WI 53208; (414) 342-4680; www.harley-davidson.com; Jeffrey Bleustein; manuf. of motorcycles, parts, and accessories.

Harrah's Entertainment, Inc.; One Harrah's Court, Las Vegas, NV 89119; (702) 407-6000; www.harrahs.com; Gary W. Loveman; casino-hotels and riverboats; merged with Park Place Entertainment, Jan. 2005.

Hartford Financial Services Group, Inc.; Hartford Plaza, 690 Asylum Ave., Hartford, CT 06115; (860) 547-5000; www.thehartford.com; Ramani Ayer; insurance, financial services.

Hartmarx; 101 N. Wacker Dr., Chicago, IL 60606; (312) 372-6300; www.hartmarx.com; Homi Patel; apparel manuf. (Hart Schaffner & Marx, Hickey Freeman, Claiborne, Tommy Hilfiger, Pierre Cardin, Perry Ellis).

Hasbro, Inc.; 1027 Newport Ave., Pawtucket, RI 02862; (401) 431-8697; www.hasbro.com; Alan G. Hassenfeld; toy and game manuf. (Milton Bradley, Playskool, G. I. Joe, Parker Bros., Tiger Electronics, Play-Doh).

HCA Inc.; 1 Park Plaza, Nashville, TN 37203; (615) 344-9551; www.hcahealthcare.com; Jack O. Bovender Jr.; largest hospital mgmt. co. in the U.S.

H. J. Heinz Co.; 600 Grant St., Pittsburgh, PA 15219; (412) 456-5700; www.heinz.com; William R. Johnson; foods (StarKist, Ore-Ida, 57 Varieties), pet food (Kibbles 'n Bits, 9 Lives), Weight Watchers.

Hershey Co.; 100 Crystal A Dr., Hershey, PA 17033; (717) 534-6799; www.hersheys.com; Richard H. Lenny; largest U.S. producer of chocolate and confectionery prods. (Reese's, Kit Kat, Mounds, Almond Joy, Cadbury, Jolly Rancher, Twizzlers, Milk Duds, Good & Plenty).

Hewlett-Packard Co.; 3000 Hanover St., Palo Alto, CA 94304; (650) 857-1501; www.hp.com; Mark V. Hurd; manuf. computers, electronic prods. and systems. (On 5/3/02 Hewlett-Packard acquired Compaq Computer Co.)

Hillenbrand Industries, Inc.; 700 State Rte. 46 E, Batesville, IN 47006; (812) 934-7000; www.hillenbrand.com; Rolf A. Classon; manuf. caskets, adjustable hospital beds.

Hilton Hotels Corp.; 9336 Civic Center Dr., Beverly Hills, CA 90210; (310) 278-4321; www.hiltonworldwide.com; Stephen F. Bollenbach; hotels, casinos.

Home Depot, Inc.; 2455 Paces Ferry Rd. NW, Atlanta, GA 30339; (770) 433-8211; www.homedepot.com; Robert L. Nardelli; retail building supply, home improvement warehouse stores.

Honeywell Inc.; 101 Columbia Road, Morristown, NJ 07962; (973) 455-2000; www.honeywell.com; David Cote; industrial and home control systems, aerospace guidance systems.

Hormel Foods Corp.; 1 Hormel Pl., Austin, MN 55912-3680; (507) 437-5611; www.hormel.com; Joel W. Johnson; meat processor, pork and beef prods. (SPAM, Dinty Moore, Little Sizzlers).

Houghton Mifflin Co.; 222 Berkeley St., Boston, MA 02116; (617) 351-5000; www.hmco.com; Anthony Lucki; publisher of textbooks, reference, general interest books.

Huffy Corp.; 225 Byers Rd., Miamisburg, OH 45342; (937) 866-6251; www.huffy.com; Jay Muskovich; largest U.S. bicycle manuf.; sports and hardware equip.

Humana, Inc.; 500 W. Main Street, P.O. Box 1438, Louisville, KY 40202; (502) 580-1000; www.humana.com; David A. Jones; managed healthcare service provider, related specialty products.

Illinois Toolworks; 3600 West Lake Ave., Glenview, IL 60026; (847) 724-7500; www.itwinc.com; W. James Farrell; food equip. (Hobart), home appliances and cookware (West Bend).

Ingersoll-Rand; 155 Chestnut Ridge Road, Montvale, NJ 07645; (201) 573-0123; www.irco.com; Herbert L. Henkel; industrial machinery.

Intel Corp.; 2200 Mission College Blvd., Santa Clara, CA 95052-8119; (408) 765-8080; www.intel.com; Paul S. Otellini; manuf. integrated circuits (Pentium).

International Business Machines Corp. (IBM); One New Orchard Rd., Armonk, NY 10504; (914) 499-1900; www.ibm.com; Samuel Palmisano; world's largest supplier of advanced information processing technology equip., services.

International Paper Co.; 400 Atlantic St., Stamford, CT 06921; (203) 541-8000; www.paper.com; John Faraci; world's largest paper/forest prods. co.; chemicals, packaging.

Interstate Bakeries Corp.; 12 E. Armour Blvd., Kansas City, MO 64111; (816) 502-4000; www.interstatebakeriescorp.com; Antonio C. Alvarez II; baked goods wholesaler, distributor (Wonder, Hostess, Dolly Madison, Beefsteak, Home Pride).

J. Crew Group, Inc.; 770 Broadway, NY, NY 10003; (212) 209-2500; www.jcrew.com; Millard S. Drexler; apparel and accessories, retail and mail order.

Jet Blue Airways; 118-29 Queens Blvd., Forest Hills, NY 11375; (800) JETBLUE; www.jetblue.com; David Neeleman; air travel.

Jo-Ann Stores, Inc.; 5555 Darrow Rd., Hudson, OH 44236; (330) 656-2600; www.joann.com; Alan Rosskamm; nation's largest specialty fabric and craft stores (Jo-Ann Fabric and Crafts, Jo-Ann etc.).

Johnson & Johnson; 1 Johnson & Johnson Plaza, New Brunswick, NJ 08933; (732) 524-0400; www.jnj.com; William Weldon; surgical dressings (Band-Aid), pharmaceuticals (Tylenol), toiletries (Neutrogena).

S.C. Johnson & Son, Inc.; 1525 Howe St., Racine, WI 53403; (262) 260-2000; www.scjohnson.com; H. Fisk Johnson; cleaning and other household prods. (Johnson's Wax, Windex, Pledge, Fantastik, Raid, Off!, Shout, Glade, Scrubbing Bubbles, Ziploc bags).

Johnson Controls, Inc.; 5757 N. Green Bay Avenue, Milwaukee, WI 53201; (414) 524-1200; www. johnsoncontrols.com; John Barth; fire protection services, auto seats and batteries.

Jones Apparel Group, Inc.; 250 Rittenhouse Circle, Bristol, PA 19007; 215-785-4000; www.jny.com; Peter Boneparth; apparel (Jones New York, Gloria Vanderbilt), shoes (Nine West, Anne Klein), retail and outlet stores.

Jostens Inc.; 5501 American Blvd. W., Minneapolis, MN 55437; (952) 830-3300; www.jostens.com; Michael L. Bailey; school rings, yearbooks, plaques.

JPMorgan Chase & Co. Inc; 270 Park Ave., NY, NY 10017; (212) 270-6000; www.jpmorganchase.com; William Harrison Jr.; global financial firm. (Merged with Bank One Corp., 7/1/04.)

Kellogg Co.; One Kellogg Sq., Battle Creek, MI 49016; (269) 961-2000; www.kelloggcompany.com; James M. Jennes; world's largest mfgr. of ready-to-eat cereals, other food prods. (Frosted Flakes, Rice Krispies, Froot Loops, Pop-Tarts, Nutri-Grain, Eggo).

Kelly Services, Inc.; 999 West Big Beaver Rd., Troy, MI 48084; (248) 362-4444; www.kellyservices.com; Terence Adderley; temporary staffing services.

Kimberly-Clark Corp.; 351 Phelps Dr. , Dallas, TX 75038; (972) 281-1200; www.kimberly-clark.com; Thomas Falk; personal care prods. (Kleenex, Scott, Cottonelle, Huggies, Viva, Kotex).

Kmart Corp.: *see* Sears Holdings.

Knight Ridder, Inc.; 50 W. San Fernando Street, San Jose, CA 95113-2413; (408) 938-7700; www.kri.com; P.A. Ridder; newspaper publishing.

Kraft Foods, Inc.: *see* Altria Group, Inc.

Kroger Co.; 1014 Vine St., Cincinnati, OH 45202; (513) 762-4000; www.kroger.com; David Dillon; largest U.S. retail grocery chain, convenience stores, mall jewelry stores.

(Estee) Lauder Cos.; 767 5th Ave., NY, NY 10153; (212) 572-4200; www.esteelauder.com; William P. Lauder; cosmetics (Clinique), fragrance prods. (Aramis, Aveda, Tommy Hilfiger).

La-Z-Boy Inc.; 1284 N. Telegraph Rd., Monroe, MI 48162; (734) 242-1444; www.lazboy.com; Kurt L. Darrow; reclining chairs, other furniture.

Leggett & Platt, Inc.; No. 1 Leggett Rd., Carthage, MO 64836; (417) 358-8131; www.leggett.com; Felix E. Wright; furniture and furniture components, industrial materials, automotive seating suspension, train and cable control systems.

Lehman Bros. Holdings, Inc.; 745 7th Ave., NY, NY 10019; (212) 526-7000; www.lehman.com; Richard S. Fuld Jr.; investment bank.

Levi Strauss & Co; 1155 Battery St., San Francisco, CA 94111; (415) 501-6000; www.levistrauss.com; Robert D. Haas; blue jeans, casual sportswear.

Lexmark Intl., Inc.; 740 W. New Circle Rd., Lexington, KY 40550; (800) 539-6275; www.lexmark.com; Paul J. Curlander; computer printers and peripherals.

Liberty Mutual Group; 175 Berkeley St., Boston, MA 02116; (617) 357-9500; www.libertymutual.com; Edmund F. Kelly; auto, home, and life insurance.

Limited Brands; 3 Limited Pkwy., P.O. Box 16000, Columbus, OH 43216; (614) 415-7000; www.limitedbrands.com; Leslie H. Wexner; apparel stores (Lane Bryant, Lerner, Limited, Express, Victoria's Secret, Henri Bendel), home decor (White Barn Candle Co., Bath & Body Works).

Liz Claiborne, Inc.; 1441 Bway., New York, NY 10018; (212) 354-4900; Paul R. Charron; women's apparel (Ellen Tracy, Laundry, Crazy Horse, Dana Buchman).

L.L.Bean, Inc.; 15 Casco St., Freeport, ME 04033-0001; (207) 865-4761; www.llbean.com; Chris McCormick; outdoor apparel and footwear.

Lockheed Martin Corp.; 6801 Rockledge Dr., Bethesda, MD 20817; (301) 897-6000; www.lockheedmartin.com; Robert J. Stevens; commercial and military aircraft, electronics, missiles.

Loews Corp.; 667 Madison Ave., NY, NY 10021; (212) 521-2000; www.loews.com; James S. Tisch; tobacco prods. (Kent, True, Newport), watches (Bulova), hotels, insurance (CNA Financial), offshore drilling (Diamond).

Longs Drug Stores, Inc.; 141 N. Civic Dr., P.O. Box 5222, Walnut Creek, CA 94596; (925) 937-1170; www.longs.com; Warren Bryant; drug store chain.

Lowe's Cos., Inc; 1605 Curtis Bridge Rd., N. Wilkesboro, NC 28656; (336) 658-4000; www.lowes.com; Robert A. Niblock; building materials and home improvement superstores.

Luby's, Inc.; 13111 Northwest Fwy., Ste. 600, Houston, TX 77040; (713) 329-6800; www.lubys.com; Christopher Pappas; operates cafeterias in S and SW.

Lucent Technologies, Inc.; 600 Mountain Ave., Murray Hill, NJ 07974; (908) 582-8500; www.lucent.com; Patricia Russo; leading developer, designer, and manuf. of telecommunications systems, software, and prods.

Mandalay Resort Group: *see* MGM MIRAGE.

Manpower Inc.; 5301 N. Ironwood Rd., Milwaukee, WI 53217; (414) 961-1000; www.manpower.com; Jeffrey A. Joerres; 2nd-largest non-gov't. employment services co. in the world.

Marathon Oil Corp.; 5555 San Felipe Rd., Houston, TX 77056; (713) 629-6600; www.marathon.com; Thomas J. Usher; integrated oil co. (Became independent co. 1/1/02 after being separated from USX-Marathon Group; United States Steel Corp. created as a result of a spin-off from USX.)

Marriott International, Inc.; One Marriott Drive, Washington, DC 20058; (301) 380-3000; www.marriott.com; John Willard Marriott Jr; hotels, retirement communities, food service dist.

Masco Corp.; 21001 Van Born Rd., Taylor, MI 48180; (313) 274-7400; www.masco.com; Richard A. Manoogian; manuf. kitchen, bathroom prods. (Delta, Peerless faucets; Fieldstone, Merillat cabinets).

MassMutual Financial Group; 1295 State St., Springfield, MA 01111; (800) 767-1000; www.massmutual.com; James R. Birle; financial planning and investment, life insurance.

Mattel, Inc.; 333 Continental Blvd., El Segundo, CA 90245; (310) 252-2000; www.mattel.com; Robert A. Eckert; largest U.S. toymaker (Barbie, Fisher-Price, Hot Wheels, Matchbox, American Girls).

May Department Stores Co.: *see* Federated Dept. Stores.

Maytag Corp.; 403 W. Fourth St. N., Newton, IA 50208; (641) 792-7000; www.maytag.com; Ralph F. Hake; major appliance mfgr. (Magic Chef, Admiral, Jenn-Air), Hoover vacuum cleaners, floor care systems; agreed to be acquired by Whirlpool, 8/22/05.

MBNA Corp.; 1100 N. King St., Wilmington, DE 19884; (302) 453-9930; www.mbna.com; Randy Lerner; financial services; *see* Bank of America.

McDonald's Corp.; McDonald's Plaza, Oak Brook, IL 60523; (630) 623-3000; www.mcdonalds.com; James A. Skinner; fast-food restaurants.

McGraw-Hill Cos.; 1221 Ave. of the Americas, NY, NY 10020; (212) 512-2000; www.mcgraw-hill.com; Harold (Terry) McGraw 3rd; book, textbooks, magazine publishing (*Business Week*), information and financial services (Standard & Poor's), TV stations.

MCI, Inc.; 22001 Loudoun County Pkwy., Ashburn, VA 20147; (703) 886-5600; www.mci.com; Michael D. Capellas; long-distance telephone service.

McKesson Corp.; 1 Post St., San Francisco, CA 94104; (415) 983-8300; www.mckesson.com; John Hammergren; distributor of drugs and toiletries; provides software and services in U.S.; bottled water.

MeadWestvaco Corp.; One High Ridge Park, Stamford, CT 06905; (203) 461-7400; www.meadwestvaco.com; John A. Luke Jr.; printing and writing paper, paperboard, packaging, shipping containers.

Medco Health Solutions, Inc.; 100 Parsons Pond Dr., Franklin Lakes, NJ 07417; (201) 269-3400; www.medco.com; David B. Snow Jr.; pharmacy benefits management.

Medtronic, Inc.; 710 Medtronic Pkwy. NE, Minneapolis, MN 55432; (763) 514-4000; www.medtronic.com; Art Collins Jr.; world's largest manuf. of implantable biomedical devices.

Merck & Co., Inc.; P.O. Box 100, Whitehouse Station, NJ 08889-0100; (908) 423-1000; www.merck.com; Dick Clark; pharmaceuticals (Pepcid, Zocor), animal health care prods.

Meredith Corp.; 1716 Locust St., Des Moines, IA 50309; (515) 284-3000; www.meredith.com; William T. Kerr; magazine publishing (*Better Homes and Gardens*, *Ladies' Home Journal*), book publishing, broadcasting.

Merrill Lynch & Co., Inc.; 4 World Financial Ctr., NY, NY 10080; (212) 449-1000; www.ml.com; Stan O' Neal; securities broker, financial services.

Metropolitan Life Ins. Co.; 200 Park Ave., NY, NY 10166; (212) 578-2211; www.metlife.com; Bob H. Benmosche; insurance, financial services.

MGM MIRAGE; 3600 S. Las Vegas Blvd., Las Vegas, NV 89109; (702) 791-7111; www.mirage.com; J. Terrence Lanni; hotel-casino operator (Mirage, Treasure Island, Golden Nugget); acquired Mandalay Resort Group, 4/25/05.)

Microsoft Corp.; One Microsoft Way, Redmond, WA 98052-6399; (425) 882-8080; www.microsoft.com; William H. Gates; largest independent software maker (Windows, Word, Excel).

Mobil Corp.: *see* Exxon Mobil Corp.

Miller Brewing Co.: W. Highland Blvd. Milwaukee, WI 53208; (414) 931-2000; Norman J. Adami; brewer (Miller, sharps); subsidiary of SABMiller plc.

Mittal Steel USA; 3210 Watling St., East Chicago, IN; (219) 399-1200; www.mittalsteel.com; Lakshmi N. Mittal; subsidiary of Mittal Steel Co., N.V., World's largest steel co.

Molson Coors Brewing Co.; 311 Tenth St., Golden, CO 80401; (303) 279-6565; www.molsoncoors.com; W. Leo Kiely III; brewer (Coors, Killian's, Molson, Zima). Formed by merger of Adolph Coors and Molson, 2/9/05.

Morgan Stanley; 1585 Broadway, NY, NY 10036; (212) 761-4000; www.msdw.com; John J. Mack; diversified financial services, major U.S. credit-card issuer.

Motorola, Inc.; 1303 E. Algonquin Rd., Schaumburg, IL 60196; (847) 576-5000; www.motorola.com; Edward Zander; electronic equipment and components; integrated communication devices.

Nabisco: *see* Altria Group., Inc.

National Semiconductor Corp.; 2900 Semiconductor Dr., P.O. Box 58090; Santa Clara, CA 95052-8090; (408) 721-5000; www.national.com; Brian L. Halla; manuf. of semiconductors, integrated circuits.

Nationwide Mutual Insurance Co.; One Nationwide Plaza, Columbus, OH 43215; (800) 882-2822; www.nation wide.com; W.G. Jurgensen; life insurance and financial services.

Navistar Intl. Corp.; 4201 Winfield Rd., P.O. Box 1488, Warrenville, IL 60555; (630) 735-2143; www.navistar.com; Daniel Ustian; manuf. heavy-duty trucks, parts, school buses.

NCR Corp.; 1700 S. Patterson Blvd., Dayton, OH 45479; (937) 445-5000; www.ncr.com; James M. Ringler; computer hardware and software, computer services and supplies.

Nestlé USA, Inc.; 800 North Brand Blvd., Glendale, CA 91203; (818) 549-6000; www.nestleusa.com; Joe Weller; candy (Baby Ruth, Raisinets), beverages (Nestea, Juicy Juice, Perrier), frozen foods (Stouffer's). Owned by Nestlé SA in Switzerland; world's largest producer of pet foods (Purina, Alpo, Friskies).

Netflix, Inc.; 970 University Ave., Los Gatos, CA 95032; (408) 317-3700; www.netflix.com; Reed Hastings; online DVD rentals.

New York Life Insurance Co.; 51 Madison Ave., New York, NY 10010; 212-576-7000; www.newyorklife.com; Seymour (Sy) Sternberg; life insurance, annuities, mutual funds.

New York Times Co.; 229 W. 43rd St., NY, NY 10036; (212) 556-1234; www.nytco.com; A. O. Sulzberger Jr.; newspapers (*New York Times, Boston Globe*), radio and TV stations, magazines (*Golf Digest*).

Newell Rubbermaid Inc.; 10 B Glenlake Pkwy, Ste. 600, Atlanta, GA 30328; (770) 407-3800; www.newellco.com; William D. Marohn; housewares (Anchor Hocking, Rubbermaid); hair accessories (Goody); writing utensils (Eberhard Faber, Sharpie); childrens' prods. (Little Tikes, Graco).

News Corp.; 1211 Ave. of the Americas, 8th fl., New York, NY 10036; (212) 852-7017; www.newscorp.com; K. Rupert Murdoch; newspapers, magazines, book publishing (Harper Collins), TV and CATV stations (FOX, Fox News Channel, FX), film (20th Century Fox, Fox Searchlight).

Nextel Communications, Inc.: *see* Sprint Nextel Corp.

NIKE, Inc.; 1 Bowerman Dr., Beaverton, OR 97005; (503) 671-6453; www.Nike.com; Philip H. Knight; #1 in world athletic footware market.

Nordstrom, Inc.; 1617 6th Ave., Seattle, WA 98101; (206) 628-2111; www.nordstrom.com; Bruce A. Nordstrom; upscale dept. store chain.

Norfolk Southern Corp.; Three Commercial Pl., Norfolk, VA 23510; (757) 629-2600; www.nscorp.com; David R. Goode; operates railway, freight carrier.

Northrop Grumman Corp; 1840 Century Park East, Los Angeles, CA 90067; (310) 553-6262; www.northgrum.com; Ronald D. Sugar; aircraft, electronics, data systems, information systems, missiles. (Northrop Grumman acquired TRW, 12/12/02.)

Northwest Airlines Corp.; 2700 Lone Oak Pkwy., Eagan, MN 55121; (612) 726-2111; www.nwa.com; Gary L. Wilson; air transportation.

Northwestern Mutual Life Insurance Co.; 720 E. Wisconsin Ave., Milwaukee, WI 53202; (414) 271-1444; www.north westernmutual.com; Edward J. Zore; life insurance, investment products and services, annuities.

Occidental Petroleum Corp.; 10889 Wilshire Blvd., Los Angeles, CA 90024; (310) 208-8800; www.oxy.com; Ray R. Irani; oil, natural gas, chemicals, plastics, fertilizers.

Office Depot, Inc.; 2200 Old Germantown Rd., Delray Beach, FL 33445; (561) 438-4800; www.officedepot.com; Steve Odland; retail office supply stores.

Omnicom Group Inc.; 437 Madison Ave., NY, NY 10022; (212) 415-3600; www.omnicomgroup.com; Bruce Crawford; advertising, market services, interactive/digital media.

Oracle Corp.; 500 Oracle Pkwy., Redwood Shores, CA 94065; (650) 506-7000; www.oracle.com; Jeffrey O. Henley; database and file management software.

Owens Corning; 1 Owens Corning Parkway, Toledo, OH 43659; (419) 248-8000; www.owenscorning.com; Michael H. Thaman; world leader in advanced glass, composite materials.

Owens-Illinois; 1 SeaGate, Toledo, OH 43666; (419) 247-5000; Steven McCracken; www.o-i.com; one of the world's largest producers of glass and plastic packaging.

Oxford Health Plans: *see* UnitedHealth Group.

Pacific Gas & Electric Corp. (PG&E); One Market, Spear Tower, Ste. 2400, San Francisco, CA 94105; (415) 267-7000; www.pgecorp.com; Robert D. Glynn Jr.; energy supplier.

PaineWebber Group, Inc.: *see* UBS.

Park Place Entertainment: *see* Harrah's Entertainment.

J.C. Penney Co.; 6501 Legacy Dr., Plano, TX 75024; (972) 431-1000; www.jcpenney.com; Myron E. Ulman III; dept. stores, catalog sales, drug stores (Eckerd, Fay's), insurance.

Pennzoil-Quaker State Co. (SOPUS Products); Pennzoil Pl., P.O. Box 2967, Houston, TX 77252-2967; (800) 990-9811; www.pennzoil.com; motor, gear, and transmission oils; grease; air and oil filters; cleaning and hydraulic fluids. Acquired by Royal Dutch/Shell Group (based in Neth.) 10/1/2002; U.S. affiliate is Shell Oil Co.

Pepsi Americas, Inc.; 4000 Dain Rauscher Plaza, 60 S. Sixth St., Minneapolis, MN 55402; (612) 661-4000; americas.com; Robert C. Pohlad; intl. beverage distributor, esp. Pepsi products.

PepsiCo, Inc.; 700 Anderson Hill Rd., Purchase, NY 10577; (914) 253-2000; www.pepsico.com; Steven S. Reinemund; soft drinks (Pepsi-Cola, Mountain Dew), fruit juice (Tropicana), FritoLay snacks (Ruffles, Lay's, Fritos, Doritos, Rold Gold), Quaker Oats.

Pfizer, Inc.; 235 E. 42nd St., NY, NY 10017; (212) 573-2323; www.pfizer.com; Henry McKinnell Jr.; pharmaceuticals (Diflucan, Viagra, Zithromax), hospital, agricultural, chemical prods., consumer prods. (Visine, Desitin, Benadryl, Listerine, Lubriderm, Schick, Sudafed, Zantac 75, BenGay). (Co. merged with Warner-Lambert 6/19/01; acquired Pharmacia Corp. 4/16/03.)

Pharmacia Corp.: *see* Pfizer, Inc.

Philip Morris Cos. Inc.: see Altria Group, Inc.

Phillips-Van Heusen Corp.; 200 Madison Ave., NY, NY 10016; (212) 381-3500; www.pvh.com; Bruce J. Klatsky; designer of apparel (IZOD, Geoffrey Beene, DKNY, Kenneth Cole). (Acquired Calvin Klein 2/12/03.)

Pitney Bowes, Inc.; 1 Elmcroft Rd., Stamford, CT 06926; (203) 356-5000; www.pb.com; Michael J. Critelli; world's largest mfgr. of postage meters and mailing equip.

Plains All American Pipeline, L.P.; 333 Clay St., Ste. 1600, Houston, TX 77002; (800) 564-3036; www.plainsallamerican.com; Greg L. Armstrong; oil transportation, storage.

Polaroid Corp.; 1265 Main St., Bldg. W3, Waltham, MA 02451; (781) 386-2000; www.polaroid.com; Jacques A. Nasser; photographic equip. and supplies, optical goods.

Polo Ralph Lauren Corp.; 650 Madison Ave., NY, NY 10022; (212) 318-7000; www.polo.com; Ralph Lauren; men's and women's apparel.

PPG Industries, Inc.; 1 PPG Place, Pittsburgh, PA 15272; (412) 434-3131; www.ppg.com; Charles E. Bunch; glass prods., silicas, fiberglass, chemicals; world's leading supplier of automobile/industrial coatings.

Procter & Gamble Co.; 1 Procter & Gamble Plaza, Cincinnati, OH 45202; (513) 983-1100; www.pg.com; Alan Lafley; soaps and detergents (Ivory, Cheer, Tide, Mr. Clean, Comet, Zest); toiletries (Crest, Scope, Head & Shoulders, Noxzema, Oil of Olay, Old Spice); pharmaceuticals (NyQuil, Pepto-Bismol, Vicks cough medicines); foods (Folgers coffee, Pringles); paper prods. (Charmin toilet tissues, Bounty towels, Tampax tampons, Pampers & Luvs disposable diapers); Cover Girl and Max Factor cosmetics, Clairol haircare; proposed merger with Gillette approved by shareholders, 7/12/05.

Prudential Financial, Inc.; 751 Broad St., Newark, NJ 07102; (973) 802-6000; www.prudential.com; Arthur F. Ryan; insurance, financial services.

Publix Super Markets Inc.; 3300 Publix Corporate Pkwy., Lakeland, FL 33811; (863) 688-1188; www.publix.com; Howard M. Jenkins; chain of supermarkets.

Quaker Oats Co.: *see* PepsiCo, Inc.

Qwest Communications, Inc.; 1801 California St., Denver, CO 80202; (303) 992-1400; www.qwest.com; Richard Notebaert; telecommunications, wireless, and directory services for most of western and southwestern U.S.

Radio Shack; 300 Radio Shack Circle, Fort Worth, TX 76102; (817) 415-3011; www.radioshack.com; Leonard H. Roberts; consumer electronics retailer (Computer City, Radio Shack).

Ralcorp Holdings, Inc.; 800 Market St., St. Louis, MO 63101; (314) 877-7000; www.ralcorp.com; William Stiritz; private-label breakfast cereals, snack foods, baby food (Beech-Nut).

Ralston Purina: *see* Nestlé Purina PetCare.

Raytheon Co.; 870 Winter St., Waltham, MA 02451; (781) 522-3000; www.raytheon.com; William Swanson; defense systems, electronics.

Reader's Digest Assn., Inc.; Reader's Digest Road, Pleasantville, NY 10570; (914) 238-1000; www.rd.com; Thomas Ryder; direct-mail marketer of magazines, books, other media.

Reebok Intl., Ltd.; 1895 J.W. Foster Blvd., Canton, MA 02021; (781) 401-5000; www.reebok.com; Paul Fireman; athletic and leisure footwear, appare; agreement pending for Germany's Adidas-Saloman AG to acquire Reebok.

Revlon, Inc.; 237 Park Ave., NY, NY 10017; (212) 527-4000; www.revlon.com; Ronald O. Perelman; cosmetics, skin care.

Reynolds American Inc.; 401 N. Main St., Winston-Salem, NC 27102; (336) 741-2000; www.reynoldsamerican.com; Andrew J. Schindler; 2nd-largest U.S. producer of cigarettes (Winston, Salem, Camel). On 7/30/04, RJ Reynolds merged with Brown & Williamson Tobacco Corp. to form co.

Rite Aid Corp.; 30 Hunter Lane, Camp Hill, PA 17011-2404; (717) 761-2633; www.riteaid.com; Robert G. Miller; discount drug stores.

Rockwell Auto; 777 E. Wisconsin Ave., Suite 1400, Milwaukee, WI 53202; (414) 212-5200; www.rockwell.com; Keith D. Nosbusch; diversified high-tech. co. (world leader in electronic controls).

Rohm & Haas Co.; 100 Independence Mall West, Philadelphia, PA 19106; (215) 592-3000; www.rohmhaas.com; Raj Gupta; adhesives and sealants, process chemicals, automotive coatings; salt (Morton, Windsor).

Ryder System, Inc.; 3600 NW 82nd Ave., Miami, FL 33166; (305) 500-3726; www.ryder.com; Gregory T. Swienton; truck-leasing service.

Safeway Inc.; 5918 Stoneridge Mall Rd., Pleasanton, CA 94588-3229; (925) 467-3000; www.safeway.com; Steven A. Burd; supermarkets.

Sara Lee Corp.; Three First National Plaza, Chicago, IL 60602; (312) 726-2600; www.saralee.com; C. Steven McMillan; baked goods, fresh and processed meats (Ball Park, Jimmy Dean, Hillshire Farms, Kahn's), hosiery, intimate apparel, and knitwear (Hanes, L'eggs, Playtex, Champion).

SBC Communications, Inc.; 175 E. Houston, San Antonio, TX 78205; (210) 821-4105; www.sbc.com; Edward Whitacre Jr.; telephone services (Ameritech, Southwestern Bell, Pacific Bell).

Schering-Plough Corp.; 2000 Galloping Hill Rd., Kenilworth, NJ 07033; (908) 298-4000; www.sch-plough.com; Fred Hassan; pharmaceuticals (Claritin, Proventil), consumer prods. (Afrin, Coppertone), animal health prods.

Sears Holdings Co.; 3333 Beverly Rd., Hoffman Estates, IL 60179; (847) 286-2500; www.searshc.com; Eddie Lampert; 3rd largest U.S. retailer; formed by merger of Kmart and Sears, Mar. 2005.

Sears, Roebuck and Co.: *see* Sears Holdings.

Shaw Industries, Inc.: *see* Berkshire Hathaway Inc.

Shell Oil Co.: *see* Pennzoil-Quaker State Co.

Sherwin-Williams Co.; 101 Prospect Ave. NW, Cleveland, OH 44115-1075; (216) 566-2000; www.sherwin.com; Christopher Connor; largest North American paint and varnish producer (Dutch Boy, Pratt & Lambert, Martha Stewart, Minwax).

Smithfield Foods, Inc.; 200 Commerce St., Smithfield, VA 23430; (757) 365-3000; www.smithfieldfoods.com; Joseph Luter III; pork and processed meat products.

J. M. Smucker Co.; One Strawberry Lane, Orrville, OH 44667; (330) 682-3000; www.smuckers.com; Timothy P. Smucker; preserves, jams, jellies (Dickinson's), toppings (Magic Shell), syrups, juices, Jif peanut butter, Crisco oil

Smurfit-Stone Container Corp.; 150 N. Michigan Ave., Chicago, IL 60601; (312) 346-6600; www.smurfit-stone.net; Patrick J. Moore; industry leader for corrugated containers, paper bags and sacks.

Southwest Airlines Co.; 2702 Love Field Dr., Dallas, TX 75235; (214) 792-4000; www.southwest.com; Herb Kelleher; air transportation.

Sprint Nextel Corp.; 6200 Sprint Pkwy., Overland Park, KS 66251; (800) 829-0965; www.sprint.com; Tim Donahue; wireless, long-distance, and local telecommunications; merged with Nextel, 8/12/05.

Staples, Inc; 500 Staples Dr., Framingham, MA 01702; (508) 253-5000; www.staples.com; Ron Sargent; office-supply superstores.

Starbucks Corp.; 2401 Utah Ave. S., Seattle, WA 98134; (206) 447-1575; www.starbucks.com; Howard Schultz; coffee and tea producers, retail coffee and tea stores.

Starwood Hotels and Resorts Worldwide; 1111 Westchester Ave., White Plains, NY 10604; (914) 640-8100; www.starwood.com; Bruce Duncan; hotels and leisure company (Westin, Sheraton, W Hotels).

State Farm Mutual Automobile Ins. Co.; 1 State Farm Plaza, Bloomington, IL 61710; (309) 766-2311; www.statefarm.com; Edward B. Rust Jr.; major insurance co.

Stride Rite Corp.; 191 Spring St., Lexington, MA 02420; (617) 824-6000; www.striderite.com; David Chamberlain; high-quality children's footwear (Keds, Sperry Top-Sider) and eyewear.

Sun Microsystems, Inc.; 4150 Network Circle, Santa Clara, CA 95054; (800) 555-9SUN; www.sun.com; Scott G. McNealy; supplier of network-based distributed computer systems.

Sunoco, Inc.; Ten Penn Ctr., 1801 Market St., Philadelphia, PA 19103-1699; (215) 977-3000; www.sunocoinc.com; John G. Drosdick; energy resources co., markets Sunoco gasoline.

SUPERVALU Inc.; 11840 Valley View Rd., Eden Prairie, MN 55344; (952) 828-4000; www.supervalu.com; Jeffrey Noddle; food wholesaler, retailer.

Sysco Corp.; 1390 Enclave Pkwy, Houston, TX 77077-2099; (281) 584-1390; www.sysco.com; Richard J. Schnieders; leading U.S. food distributor.

Target Corp.; 1000 Nicollet Mall, Minneapolis, MN 55403; (612) 304-6073; www.targetcorp.com; Robert J. Ulrich; department, specialty stores (Target, Marshall Field's, Mervyn's California).

Tenneco Automotive, Inc.; 500 N. Field Drive, Lake Forest, IL 60045; (847) 482-5000; www.tenneco-automotive.com; Mark P. Frissora; automotive parts (Monroe, Walker).

Texas Instruments Inc.; 12500 TI Blvd., Dallas, TX 75243; (800) 336-5236; www.ti.com; T. J. Engibous; electronics, semiconductors, software.

Textron, Inc.; 40 Westminster St., Providence, RI 02903; (401) 421-2800; www.textron.com; Lewis B. Campbell; aerospace, industrial, automotive prods., financial services.

3M Company; 3M Center, St. Paul, MN 55144-1000; (612) 733-1110; www.3m.com; Robert S. Morrison; abrasives, adhesives, electrical, health care, cleaning (Scotch-Brite, O-Cel-O sponges), printing, consumer prods. (Scotch Tape, Post-it).

TIAA-CREF; 730 Third Ave., NY, NY 10017; (212) 490-9000; www.tiaa-cref.com; Herb Allison; financial services provider.

Timberland Company; 200 Domain Dr., Stratham, NH 03885; (603) 772-9500; www.timberland.com; Sidney Swartz; footwear, apparel, accessories.

Time Warner Inc.; One Time Warner Ctr., New York, NY 10019; (212) 484-8000; www.timewarner.com; Richard D. Parsons; world's largest Internet online service; magazine publishing (*Time, Sports Illustrated, Fortune, Money, People,* DC Comics), TV and CATV (WB Network, HBO, Cinemax, CNN, TBS, TNT), book publishing (Little, Brown; Warner Books), motion pictures (Warner Bros., New Line Cinema), recordings, sports teams (Atlanta Braves, Atlanta Hawks), (America Online and Time Warner completed the largest corporate merger in history in 2001, becoming the largest media company in the U.S. Dropped "AOL" from name, 9/18/03.)

The TJX Cos., Inc.; 770 Cochituate Rd., Framingham, MA 01701; (508) 390-1000; www.tjx.com; Edmond English; world's largest off-price apparel retailer (T.J. Maxx, Marshalls).

Tootsie Roll Industries, Inc.; 7401 S. Cicero Ave., Chicago, IL 60629; (773) 838-3400; www.tootsie.com; Melvin Gordon; candy (Tootsie Roll, Mason Dots, Charms, Sugar Daddy, Charleston Chew, Junior Mints).

Toro Co.; 8111 Lyndale Ave. S, Bloomington, MN 55420; (952) 888-8801; www.toro.com; Kendrick B. Melrose; lawn and turf maintenance (Lawn-Boy), snow removal equipment, lighting and irrigation systems.

Toys "R" Us; 1 Geoffrey Way, Wayne, NJ 07470; (973) 617-3500; www.toysrus.com; Rick Markee; children's specialty retailer (Toys "R" Us, Kids "R" Us, Babies "R" Us, Imaginarium).

Trans World Airlines, Inc.: *see* AMR Corp.

Triarc Cos., Inc.; 280 Park Ave., NY, NY 10017; (212) 451-3000; www.triarc.com; Nelson Peltz; fast-food restaurants (Arby's).

Tribune Co.; 435 N. Michigan Ave., Chicago, IL 60611; (312) 222-9100; www.tribune.com; Dennis J. FitzSimons; newspapers (*Los Angeles Times, Chicago Tribune, Newsday, Hoy*), magazines (*Field & Stream, Popular Science*), broadcasting (incl. WGN-TV and 23 other stations), Chicago Cubs baseball team.

Trinity Industries, Inc.; 2525 Stemmons Fwy., Dallas, TX 75207; (214) 631-4420; www.trin.net; Timothy R. Wallace; manufactures metal prods., rail and freight prods.

TRW Inc.: *see* Northrop Grumman.

TWA: *see* AMR Corp.

Tyco Intl., Ltd.; 9 Roszel Rd., Princeton, NJ 08540; (609) 720-4200; www.tyco.com; Edward Breen; fire protection systems, pipes, power cables, medical supplies, packaging.

Tyson Foods, Inc.; 2210 West Oaklawn Dr., Springdale, AR 72762; (479) 290-4000 www.tysonfoodsinc.com; John Tyson; fresh and processed poultry and beef, pork, and seafood prods. (Holly Farms, Weaver, Louis Kemp, IBP).

UAL Corp.; 1200 E. Algonquin Rd., Elk Grove Twp., IL 60007; (847) 700-4000; www.ual.com; Glenn Tilton; air transportation (United Airlines).

UBS AG; Bahnhofstrasse 45, CH-8098 Zurich, Switzerland; +41-44-234-4111; www.ubs.com; Marcel Ospel; financial services.

Unilever US; 800 Sylvan Ave., Englewood Cliffs, NJ 07632; (877) 995-4483; www.unilever.com; Niall Fitzgerald and Anthony Burgmans; food (Hellmann's mayonnaise, Knorr soups, Ragu pasta sauce, Wish-Bone salad dressing, Lipton Tea, Skippy Peanut Butter, Slim-Fast), hygiene prods. (Dove, Q-Tips, Vaseline). Owned by Unilever NV (Neth.) and Unilever PLC (UK).

Union Carbide Corp.: *see* Dow Chemical Co.

Union Pacific Corp.; 1400 Dodge St., Omaha, NE, 68179; (402) 544-5000; www.up.com; Richard Davidson; largest railroad, trucking co. in U.S.

Unisys Corp.; Unisys Way, Blue Bell, PA 19424-0001; (215) 986-4011; www.unisys.com; Lawrence A. Weinbach; designs, manuf. computer information systems and related prods..

UnitedHealth Group Corp.; P.O. Box 1459, Minneapolis, MN 55440; (800) 328-5979; www.unitedhealthgroup.com; William W. McGuire; owns, manages health maintenance organizations; acquired Oxford Health Plans, July 2004; agreed to acquire PacifiCare, July 2005.

United Parcel Service Inc.; 55 Glenlake Pkwy. NE, Atlanta, GA 30328; (404) 828-6000; www.ups.com; Michael L. Eskew; courier services.

United States Steel Corp.; 600 Grant St., Pittsburgh, PA 15219-2800; (412) 433-1121; www.ussteel.com; Thomas J. Usher; steel, tin prods. (Became separate co. 1/1/02 as a result of a spin-off from USX-Marathon Group; rest of corp. became Marathon Oil Corp.)

United Technologies Corp.; One Financial Plaza, Hartford, CT 06101; (860) 728-7000; www.utc.com; George David; aerospace, industrial prods. and services (Carrier, Otis Elevator, Pratt & Whitney, Sikorsky Aircraft).

Unocal Corp.; 2141 Rosecrans Ave., Ste. 4000, El Segundo, CA 90245; (310) 726-7600; www.unocal.com; Charles R. Williamson; integrated oil co.; announced plans to merge with Chevron, 4/4/05.

US Airways Group, Inc.; 2345 Crystal Dr., Arlington, VA 22227; (703) 872-7000; www.usairways.com; David G. Bronner; air transportation.

UST Inc.; 100 W. Putnam Ave., Greenwich, CT 06830; (203) 661-1100; www.ustinc.com; Vincent A. Gierer Jr.; smokeless tobacco (Copenhagen, Skoal), pipe tobacco, wine (Chateau St. Michelle, Conn Creek, Columbia Crest).

Verizon Communications; 1095 Avenue of the Americas, New York, NY 10036; (212) 395-2121; www.verizon.com; Ivan Seidenberg; largest U.S. wireline and wireless provider; world's lgst. provider of print and on-line directory info. (co. formed from merger of Bell Atlantic and GTE, 6/30/00.)

V.F. Corp.; 105 Corporate Center Blvd., Greensboro, NC 27408; (336) 424-6000; www.vfc.com; Mackey J. McDonald; apparel (Lee, Wrangler, Vanity Fair, Jantzen).

Viacom, Inc.; 1515 Broadway, NY, NY 10036; (212) 258-6000; www.viacom.com; Sumner Redstone; TV and CATV (CBS, UPN, TNN, BET, Comedy Central, Showtime, MTV, VH1, Nickelodeon); book publishing (Simon & Schuster); produces, distributes movies, TV shows (Paramount); radio stations (Infinity), theme parks. (Announced plans to become two separate cos.—Viacom and CBS Corp.—6/14/05.)

Visteon Corp.; One Village Ctr. Dr., Van Buren Twp., MI 48111; (313) 755-2800; www.visteon.com; Mike Johnston; automotive parts manufacturing, architectural glass.

Wachovia Corp.; One Wachovia Center, Charlotte, NC 28288; (704) 374-6565; www.wachovia.com; G. Kennedy Thompson; financial services provider.

Walgreen Co.; 200 Wilmot Rd., Deerfield, IL 60015; (847) 914-2500; www.walgreens.com; David W. Bernauer; drugstore chain.

Wal-Mart Stores, Inc.; 702 SW 8th St., Bentonville, AR 72716; (479) 273-4000; www.walmart.com; S. Robson Walton; world's largest retailer; discount stores, wholesale clubs.

Washington Post Co.; 1150 15th St. NW, Washington, DC 20071; (202) 334-6000; www.washpostco.com; Donald E. Graham; newspapers, *Newsweek* magazine, Salon.com, TV and CATV stations, Kaplan Educational Centers.

Waste Management; 1001 Fannin St., Suite 4000, Houston, TX 77002; (713) 512-6200; www.wm.com; David P. Steiner; N. America's largest solid waste collection and disposal co.

WellPoint Inc.; ;120 Monument Circle, Indianapolis, IN 46204; (317) 488-6000; www.wellpoint.com; Leonard D. Schaeffer; HMOs and PPOs, incl. Blue Cross Blue Shield (in CA, GA, MI, WI), HealthLink, and UNICARE. (Merged with Anthem, Inc. Nov. 30, 2004).

Wells Fargo & Co.; 420 Montgomery St., San Francisco, CA 94163; (800) 869-3557; www.wellsfargo.com; Dick Kovacevich; banking, financial services.

Wendy's Intl., Inc; One Dave Thomas Blvd., Dublin, OH 43017; (614) 764-3100; www.wendys.com; John T. Schuessler; quick-serve restaurants.

Weyerhaeuser Co.; P.O. Box 9777, Federal Way, WA 98063; (253) 924-2345; www.weyerhaeuser.com; Steven R. Rogel; world's largest private owner of softwood timber, distrib. paper and wood prods.

Whirlpool Corp.; 2000 N. M-63, Benton Harbor, MI 49022; (269) 923-5000; www.whirlpoolcorp.com; Jeff M. Fettig; world's largest manuf. of major home appliances (KitchenAid, Kenmore, Roper). Signed an agreement ot acquire Maytag, 8/22/05.

Winn-Dixie Stores, Inc.; 5050 Edgewood Ct., Jacksonville, FL 32254; (904) 783-5000; www.winn-dixie.com; H. Jay Skelton; supermarkets (Winn Dixie, Save RIte, ThriftWay).

Winnebago Industries, Inc.; P.O. Box 152, Forest City, IA 50436; (641) 585-3535; www.winnebagoind.com; Bruce D. Hertzke; manuf. of motor homes, recreational vehicles.

WRC Media Inc.; 512 Seventh Ave., New York, NY 10018; (212) 768-1150; www.wrcmedia.com; Martin E. Kenney Jr.; publisher of educational and reference media; World Almanac, Facts On File News Services, Funk & Wagnalls, Gareth Stevens Publishing, CompassLearning, Weekly Reader.

Wm. Wrigley Jr. Co.; 410 N. Michigan Ave., Chicago, IL 60611; (312) 644-2121; www.wrigley.com; William Wrigley Jr.; world's largest mfgr. of chewing gum.

Wyeth; 5 Giralda Farms, Madison, NJ 07940; (973) 660-5000; www.wyeth.com; Robert Essner; prescription and over-the-counter drugs (Advil, Chap Stick, Robitussin).

Xerox Corp.; 800 Long Ridge Road, Stamford, CT 06904; (203) 968-3000; www.xerox.com; Anne Mulcahy; copiers, printers, document publishing equip.

Yahoo! Inc.; 701 First Ave. Sunnyvale, CA 94089; (408) 349-3300; www.yahoo.com; Terry Semel; internet media company.

Yum! Brands, Inc.; 1441 Gardiner Lane, Louisville, KY 40213; (502) 874-8300; www.yum.com; David C. Novak; quick-serve restaurants (Pizza Hut, KFC, Taco Bell).

Who Owns What: Familiar Consumer Products and Services

The following is a partial list of well-known consumer brands with their (U.S.) parent companies. Among brands not listed are many brands whose parent companies have the same or a similar name (e.g., Colgate is product of Colgate-Palmolive Co.). For company contact information, see Business Directory on previous pages.

A&W Rootbeer: Cadbury Schweppes
ABC broadcasting: Walt Disney
Admiral appliances: Maytag
Advil: Wyeth
Ajax cleanser: Colgate-Palmolive
Almond Joy candy bar: Hershey
American Girl: Mattel
Arm & Hammer: Church & Dwight
Arrid antiperspirant: Church & Dwight
Aunt Jemima Pancake mix: PepsiCo (Quaker Oats)
Aunt Millie's pasta sauce: H.J. Heinz
Banana Republic stores: Gap Inc.
Band-Aids: Johnson & Johnson
Barbie dolls: Mattel
BENGAY: Pfizer
Betty Crocker prods.: General Mills
Boston Market: McDonald's
Bounty paper towels: Procter & Gamble
Brillo soap pads: Church & Dwight
Brita water systems: Clorox
Budweiser beer: Anheuser-Busch
Bulova watches: Loews
Business Week magazine: McGraw-Hill
Butterball: ConAgra
Cap'n Crunch cereal: PepsiCo (Quaker Oats)
Calphalon cookware: Newell Rubbermaid
Camel cigarettes: Reynolds American
CBS Broadcasting: Viacom
Charmin toilet tissue: Procter & Gamble
Cheer detergent: Procter & Gamble
Cheerios cereal: General Mills
Cheez Whiz: Altria (Kraft)
Chef Boyardee: ConAgra
Chipotle Mexican Grill restaurants: McDonald's
Chips Ahoy!: Altria (Nabisco)
Cinemax: Time Warner
Clairol hair prods.: Procter & Gamble
Clinique: Estee Lauder
CNN: Time Warner
Combat insecticides: Henkel
Coppertone sun care prods.: Schering-Plough
Crest toothpaste: Procter & Gamble
Crisco shortening: J.M. Smucker
DC Comics: Time Warner
Dr. Pepper: Cadbury Schweppes
Doritos chips: PepsiCo
Dove soaps: Unilever
Duracell batteries: Gillette
Dutch Boy paints: Sherwin-Williams
Efferdent dental cleanser: Pfizer
ESPN: Walt Disney
Fab detergent: Colgate-Palmolive
Fantastik: S.C. Johnson
Febreeze: Proctor & Gamble
Fisher Price Toys: Mattel
Folger's coffee: Procter & Gamble
Formula 409 spray cleaner: Clorox
Fox News Channel: NewsCorp.
Fortune magazine: Time Warner
Friskies Cat Food: Nestlé
Frito-Lays snacks: PepsiCo
Fruitopia drinks: Coca-Cola
Gatorade: PepsiCo
Glad Prods.: Clorox
Godiva chocolate: Campbell Soup
Haagen-Dazs: General Mills
Halcion: Pfizer
Halls coughdrops: Cadbury–Schweppes
Hamburger Helper: General Mills
Hanes hosiery: Sara Lee
HBO: Time Warner
Head and Shoulders shampoo: Procter & Gamble
Healthtex: Lollytogs
Hellmann's mayonnaise: Unilever Bestfoods
Hertz car rental: Ford
Hi-C fruit drinks: Coca-Cola
Hidden Valley prods.: Clorox
Hillshire Farm meats: Sara Lee
Holly Farms: Tyson Foods
Hot Wheels/Matchbox cars: Mattel
Hostess cupcakes: Interstate Bakeries
Huggies diapers: Kimberly-Clark
Irish Spring: Colgate-Palmolive
Ivory soap: Procter & Gamble
Jack Daniel's Whiskey: Brown-Forman
Jell-O: Altria (Kraft)
Jenn-Air stoves: Maytag
Jif peanut butter: J.M. Smucker
Jim Beam bourbon: Fortune Brands
Keds footwear: Stride Rite
Kent cigarettes: Loews
KFC restaurants: Yum! Brands
Kibbles 'n Bits pet foods: Del Monte
KitchenAid appliances: Whirlpool
Kit Kat candy: Hershey
Kleenex: Kimberly-Clark
Knorr soups: Unilever
Kool-Aid: Altria (Kraft)
Ladies Home Journal magazine: Meredith
Lee jeans: V.F. Corp.
L'eggs hosiery: Sara Lee
Lenox china: Brown-Forman
LifeSavers candy: Altria (Kraft)
Lipton tea: Unilever
Listerine mouthwash: Pfizer
Lord & Taylor: Federated Dept. Stores
Marlboro cigarettes: Altria (Philip Morris)
Max Factor beauty products: Procter & Gamble
Maxwell House coffee: Altria (Kraft)
Metamucil: Procter & Gamble
Michelob beer: Anheuser-Busch
Miller beer: Miiller Brewing (SABMiller)
Milton Bradley games: Hasbro
Minute Maid juices: Coca-Cola
Mr. Clean: Procter & Gamble
Monroe automotive parts: Tenneco Automotive
MTV: Viacom
Nature Valley granola bars: General Mills
NBC broadcasting: General Electric
Neutrogena soap: Johnson & Johnson
Newport cigarettes: Loews
Newsweek magazine: Washington Post
Nickelodeon TV: Viacom
9 Lives cat food: Del Monte
Olay: Procter & Gamble
Old Navy Clothing: Gap Inc.
Oreo cookies: Altria (Nabisco)
Oscar Mayer meats: Altria (Kraft)
Pampers: Procter & Gamble
Pantene Shampoos: Procter & Gamble
Parker Bros. games: Hasbro
People magazine: Time Warner
Pepperidge Farm prods.: Campbell Soup
Pepto-Bismol: Procter & Gamble
Philadelphia Cream Cheese: Altria (Kraft)
Pillsbury: General Mills
Pine-Sol cleaner: Clorox
Pizza Hut restaurants: Yum! Brands
Planters nuts: Altria (Kraft)
Playskool toys: Hasbro
Playtex apparel: Sara Lee
Post cereals: Altria (Kraft)
Post-it notes: 3M
Prego pasta sauce: Campbell Soup
Prozac: Eli Lilly
Purina pet foods: Nestlé
Q-Tips: Unilever
Ragu sauce: Unilever
Reese's candy: Hershey
Rice-A-Roni: PepsiCo (Quaker Oats)
Rice Krispies: Kellogg Co.
Right Guard deodorant: Gillette
Ritz crackers: Altria (Nabisco)
Robitussin: Wyeth
Rogaine hair growth aide: Pfizer
Ruffles chips: PepsiCo
Schick razors: Energizer
Scope mouthwash: Procter & Gamble
Scotch tape: 3M
Scott tissue: Kimberly-Clark
Simon & Schuster publishing: Viacom
Skippy peanut butter: Unilever
Slimfast: Unilever
SnackWell's cookies: Altria (Nabisco)
S.O.S. cleanser: Clorox
Southern Comfort liquor: Brown-Forman
SPAM meat: Hormel Foods
Sports Illustrated magazine: Time Warner
Sprite soda: Coca-Cola
StarKist tuna: Del Monte
Swanson broth: Campbell Soup
Swiffer: Procter & Gamble
Taco Bell restaurants: Yum! Brands
Tampax tampons: Procter & Gamble
Thomas' English muffins: Unilever
Tide detergent: Procter & Gamble
Time magazine: Time Warner
Titleist: Fortune Brands
Tombstone pizza: Altria (Kraft)
Triscuits: Altria (Nabisco)
Trojan condoms: Church & Dwight
Tropicana juice: PepsiCo
Tylenol: Johnson & Johnson
USA Today newspaper: Gannett
V8 vegetable juice: Campbell Soup
Vanity Fair apparel: V.F. Corp.
Vaseline: Unilever
Velveeta cheese prods.: Altria (Kraft)
VH-1: Viacom
Viagra: Pfizer
Vicks cold medicines: Procter & Gamble
Victoria's Secret stores: Limited Brands
Visine eye drops: Pfizer
Wall Street Journal: Dow Jones
Weekly Reader: WRC Media
Weight Watchers: H.J. Heinz
Wheaties cereal: General Mills
Windex: S.C. Johnson
Windows software applications: Microsoft
Wise snacks: Palladium Equity
Wonderbra: Sara Lee
Wonder bread: Interstate Bakeries
The World Almanac: WRC Media
Zest soap: Procter & Gamble
Ziploc storage bags: S.C. Johnson

WORLD ALMANAC QUICK QUIZ

Which of the following restaurant chains is not owned by Yum! Brands?

(a) Pizza Hut (b) KFC (c) Boston Market (d) Taco Bell

For the answer look in this chapter, or see page 1008.

Top Brands in Selected Categories, 2004-2005[1]

Source: Information Resources, Inc., a Chicago-based marketing research company; figures for 12-month period ending 7/10/05.

Beer

	Sales	Market Share (%)
Bud Light	$1,341,192,448	15.6
Budweiser	842,264,256	9.8
Miller Lite	705,604,608	8.2
Coors Light	587,700,096	6.8
Corona Extra	428,456,544	5.0

Chocolate Candies

	Sales	Market Share (%)
Hersheys	$82,520,500	10.1
M & Ms	80,408,780	9.9
Reeses	79,572,650	9.8
Snickers	71,265,600	8.7
Kit Kat	39,873,000	4.9

Ready-to-Eat Cold Cereals

	Sales	Market Share (%)
Private Label	$543,791,104	8.9
General Mills Cheerios	290,276,256	4.8
General Mills Honey Nut Cheerios	247,846,192	4.1
Kelloggs Frosted Flakes	247,822,032	4.1
Post Honey Bunches of Oats	238,938,960	3.9

Ground Coffee (excluding Decaf)

	Sales	Market Share (%)
Folgers	$390,322,240	23.2
Maxwell House	249,905,040	14.8
Starbucks	162,782,000	9.7
Private Label	124,868,520	7.4
Folgers Coffee House	96,879,560	5.8

Cookies

	Sales	Market Share (%)
Nabisco Oreo	$197,957,900	5.4
Nabisco Chips Ahoy	116,844,700	3.2
Nabisco Double Stuf Oreo	115,742,800	3.2
Pepperidge Farm Distinctive Milano	79,525,900	2.2
Nabisco Chewy Chips Ahoy	74,308,190	2.0

Ice Cream

	Sales	Market Share (%)
Private Label	$836,673,600	20.8
Breyers	546,809,984	13.6
Dreyers Edy's Grand	436,553,984	10.9
Blue Bell	246,846,800	6.1
Haagen Dazs	230,708,912	5.7

Paper Towels

	Sales	Market Share (%)
Bounty	$878,719,232	40.3
Private Label	391,788,800	18.0
Brawny	252,610,576	11.6
Scott	224,814,400	10.3
Kleenex Viva	170,498,112	7.8

Frozen Pizza

	Sales	Market Share (%)
Di Giorno	$521,529,056	19.8
Tombstone	274,237,795	10.4
Red Baron	254,580,960	9.7
Private Label	184,509,312	7.0
Freschetta	177,193,520	6.7

Salad Dressing

	Sales	Market Share (%)
Kraft	$251,519,808	18.4
Wishbone	164,900,080	12.1
Ken's Steakhouse	128,101,768	9.4
Private Label	124,076,824	9.1
Hidden Valley Ranch	109,796,384	8.0

Toothpaste

	Sales	Market Share (%)
Crest	$159,536,100	13.5
Colgate Total	101,523,100	8.6
Colgate	99,235,460	8.4
Crest Whitening Expressions	69,262,700	5.8
Sensodyne	57,436,920	4.8

(1) For all categories brands are ranked by dollar sales at supermarkets, drugstores, and mass merchandisers, excluding Wal-Mart.

Most Visited Shopping Websites, July 2005

Source: comScore Media Metrix, Inc.

Rank	Website[1]	Visitors[2]
1.	eBay	61,715,000
2.	Amazon Sites	41,982,000
3.	Wal-Mart	22,641,000
4.	Shopping.com Sites	22,391,000
5.	Target	20,537,000
6.	Apple Computer, Inc.	17,438,000
7.	Overstock.com	17,177,000
8.	Yahoo! Stores	16,674,000
9.	Shopzilla.com Sites	16,386,000
10.	Dell	14,239,000
11.	Ticketmaster	14,050,000
12.	Moviefone	12,653,000
13.	Cingular.com	12,473,000
14.	AmericanGreetings Property	12,418,000
15.	Best Buy Sites	11,815,000
16.	Yahoo! Shopping	11,510,000
17.	Nextag.com Sites	11,272,000
18.	The Home Depot, Inc.	10,326,000
19.	JCPenney Sites	9,678,000
20.	Netflix.com	9,959,000

(1) May include affiliated Websites not shown. (2) Unique visitors (visited Website at least once in July 2005).

The Annual Cost of Raising a Child Born in 2004

Source: Center for Nutrition Policy and Promotion, U.S. Dept. of Agriculture

Estimated annual expenditures in 2004 dollars for a child born in 2004, by income group, for each year to age 17, assuming an average inflation rate of 3.1%. Estimates are for the younger child in a 2-parent family with 2 children, for the overall U.S.

	Income group[1]		
Year (Age)	Lowest	Middle	Highest
2004 (<1)	$7,040	$9,840	$14,620
2005 (1)	7,250	10,140	15,070
2006 (2)	7,480	10,450	15,530
2007 (3)	7,890	11,070	16,370
2008 (4)	8,130	11,410	16,870
2009 (5)	8,380	11,760	17,380
2010 (6)	8,680	12,010	17,620
2011 (7)	8,950	12,380	18,150
2012 (8)	9,220	12,760	18,710
2013 (9)	9,460	12,990	18,960
2014 (10)	$9,750	$13,380	$19,540
2015 (11)	10,050	13,790	20,140
2016 (12)	11,570	15,260	21,900
2017 (13)	11,930	15,720	22,570
2018 (14)	12,290	16,200	23,250
2019 (15)	12,550	17,110	24,810
2020 (16)	12,940	17,630	25,570
2021 (17)	13,330	18,170	26,350
TOTAL	**$176,890**	**$242,070**	**$353,410**

(1) In 2004, lowest annual income group included those households earning less than $41,700 (average in this range = $26,100); middle income covered those earning $41,700-$70,199 (average = $55,500); highest income group had earnings of $70,200 or more (average = $105,100).

How to Obtain Birth, Death, Marriage, Divorce Records

The pamphlet "Where to Write for Vital Records: Births, Deaths, Marriages, and Divorces" (Stock # 017-022-01539-1) is available from the U.S. Government Printing Office (GPO) at a cost of $4.25. Orders can also be placed by calling (202) 512-1800, by mail at Superintendent of Documents, P.O. Box 371954, Pittsburgh, PA 15250, or on the Website bookstore.gpo.gov.

The complete pamphlet and other vital records information can also be accessed online at www.cdc.gov/nchs/howto/w2w/w2welcom.htm

Median Price of Existing Single-Family Homes, by Metropolitan Area, 2003-2005

Source: National Association of REALTORS®

Median prices are based on all transactions within the time period shown.

Metropolitan Area	2003	2004	2nd Qtr. 2005
Akron, OH	$116,700	$116,900	$119,800
Albany/Schenectady/Troy, NY	141,600	161,300	176,100
Albuquerque, NM	138,400	145,400	171,700
Allentown/Bethlehem/ Easton, PA	184,700	207,300	249,100
Amarillo, TX	95,700	97,100	107,400
Anaheim/Santa Ana (Orange Cnty.), CA	487,000	627,300	696,100
Appleton/Oshkosh/Neenah, WI	118,600	122,900	129,600
Atlanta/Sandy Springs/ Marietta, GA	152,400	156,900	166,500
Atlantic City, NJ	166,500	197,900	244,900
Austin/Round Rock, TX	156,700	154,700	166,800
Baltimore/Towson, MD	180,000	217,000	264,700
Baton Rouge, LA	121,200	127,700	135,400
Beaumont/Port Arthur, TX	88,400	93,500	96,500
Birmingham, AL	137,500	146,600	156,100
Boise City/Nampa, ID	130,600	135,900	161,800
Boston/Cambridge/Quincy, MA	358,500	389,700	418,500
Boulder, CO	313,000	325,300	346,200
Buffalo/Niagara Falls, NY	90,500	95,000	97,500
Canton/Massillon, OH	114,400	115,200	NA
Cedar Rapids, IA	122,800	129,500	131,600
Champaign/Urbana, IL	122,600	127,200	137,600
Charleston, SC	168,900	183,500	193,600
Charleston, WV	110,900	111,300	121,700
Charlotte/Gastonia/ Concord, NC/SC	151,500	168,000	NA
Chattanooga, TN/GA	116,700	125,400	130,500
Chicago/Naperville/Joliet, IL	220,300	240,100	263,600
Cincinnati/Middletown, OH/KY/IN	138,900	142,500	148,500
Cleveland/Elyria/Mentor, OH	NA	136,400	144,700
Colorado Springs, CO	184,500	187,600	214,200
Columbia, SC	123,600	123,400	133,700
Columbus, OH	146,300	146,700	155,900
Corpus Christi, TX	102,100	112,700	123,000
Cumberland, MD/WV	69,500	72,700	88,600
Dallas/Ft. Worth/Arlington, TX	138,400	138,200	149,100
Davenport/Moline/ Rock Island, IA/IL	100,600	107,800	133,900
Dayton, OH	114,600	115,800	119,400
Daytona Beach/Deltona/ Ormond Beach, FL	124,900	148,600	194,000
Denver/Aurora, CO	238,200	239,100	248,400
Des Moines, IA	133,900	140,800	145,100
Detroit/Warren/Livonia, MI	NA	161,000	169,200
Dover, DE	128,300	150,100	176,300
Durham, NC	NA	149,000	198,500
Elmira, NY	77,900	78,800	NA
El Paso, TX	92,900	94,700	108,900
Erie, PA	89,900	98,600	98,500
Eugene/Springfield, OR	151,700	164,900	192,400
Fargo/Moorhead, ND/MN	115,100	124,200	132,600
Farmington, NM	127,200	134,600	151,800
Ft. Wayne, IN	93,200	96,600	102,800
Gainesville, FL	145,000	159,000	178,800
Gary/Hammond, IN	119,200	122,600	129,600
Grand Rapids, MI	129,900	132,900	139,000
Green Bay, WI	137,300	143,300	159,200
Greensboro/Winston-Salem/ High Point, NC	137,300	139,800	148,000
Greenville, SC	136,900	135,800	143,200
Hartford, CT	207,900	231,600	257,700
Honolulu, HI	380,000	460,000	577,800
Houston/Baytown/ Sugar Land, TX	136,400	136,000	142,500
Indianapolis, IN	121,100	121,700	124,600
Jackson, MS	110,700	118,100	131,700
Jacksonville, FL	131,600	150,700	166,600
Kalamazoo/Portage, MI	123,400	123,100	122,600
Kansas City, MO/KS	144,200	150,000	157,100
Knoxville, TN	130,500	132,200	143,400
Lansing/East Lansing, MI	133,600	137,900	143,600
Las Vegas/Paradise, NV	179,200	266,400	300,100
Lexington/Fayette, KY	133,400	138,700	144,800
Lincoln, NE	131,500	134,400	138,300
Little Rock-N. Little Rock, AR	104,800	108,400	118,900
Los Angeles Area, CA	354,700	446,400	474,800
Louisville, KY/IN	$131,700	$131,500	$136,800
Madison, WI	183,800	200,800	220,100
Memphis, TNAR/MS	133,800	136,200	150,100
Miami/Ft. Lauderdale/ Miami Beach, FL	231,600	286,400	371,600
Milwaukee/Waukesha/ W. Allis, WI	182,100	197,100	216,800
Minneapolis/St. Paul, MN/WI	199,600	217,400	237,700
Mobile, AL	109,100	115,200	129,100
Montgomery, AL	115,700	116,600	133,300
Nashville/Davidson, TN	NA	145,400	159,700
New Haven/Milford, CT	223,900	249,200	283,800
New Orleans/Metairie/Kenner, LA	130,800	137,400	152,600
New York/N. New Jersey/ Long Island, NY/NJ	343,500	385,900	452,700
New York: Nassau/Suffolk, NY	364,500	413,500	467,700
New York: Newark/Union, NJ/PA	336,300	375,800	414,400
Ocala, FL	NA	110,100	135,300
Oklahoma City, OK	103,000	131,300	115,700
Omaha, NE/IA	128,100	131,300	137,300
Orlando, FL	145,100	169,600	232,200
Pensacola/Ferry Pass/ Brent, FL	116,400	131,100	163,600
Peoria, IL	93,100	96,300	110,500
Philadelphia/Camden/ Wilmington, PA/NJ/DE/MD	168,800	185,100	211,000
Phoenix/Mesa/Scottsdale, AZ	152,500	169,400	243,400
Pittsburgh, PA	108,200	113,400	118,500
Portland/S. Portland/ Biddeford, ME	193,100	224,800	247,200
Portland/Vancouver/Beaverton, OR/WA	188,900	206,500	238,000
Providence/New Bedford/ Fall River, RI	242,900	276,900	291,600
Raleigh/Cary, NC	162,000	169,900	185,200
Reno/Sparks, NV	204,900	284,300	357,400
Richmond, VA	155,100	170,700	198,400
Riverside/San Bernardino/ Ontario, CA	221,000	296,400	367,600
Rochester, NY	99,400	103,600	122,700
Rockford, IL	99,400	103,600	122,700
Sacramento/Arden-Arcade/ Roseville, CA	247,600	317,600	377,400
Saint Louis, MO/IL	123,000	128,700	141,900
Salem, OR	150,600	154,600	172,000
Salt Lake City, UT	148,000	158,000	169,900
San Antonio, TX	118,100	122,700	134,000
San Diego/Carlsbad/ San Marcos, CA	424,900	551,600	605,600
San Francisco Bay Area, CA	558,100	641,700	726,900
Sarasota/Bradenton/Venice, FL	193,300	255,700	367,800
Seattle/Tacoma/Bellevue, WA	239,100	284,600	310,300
Shreveport/Bossier City, LA	100,700	110,600	125,100
Sioux Falls, SD	123,200	129,200	137,700
South Bend/Mishawaka, IN	91,100	93,600	102,100
Spartanburg, SC	109,200	110,800	118,700
Spokane, WA	120,300	128,500	158,600
Springfield, IL	101,000	103,300	109,000
Springfield, MA	162,300	180,300	197,900
Springfield, MO	NA	114,100	NA
Syracuse, NY	95,000	98,400	108,700
Tallahassee, FL	137,100	152,500	163,300
Tampa/St. Petersburg/ Clearwater, FL	138,100	159,700	195,000
Toledo, OH	111,400	113,500	118,600
Topeka, KS	97,300	102,100	103,100
Trenton/Ewing, NJ	212,400	234,200	267,700
Tucson, AZ	156,300	177,300	228,500
Tulsa, OK	110,400	113,100	117,400
Washington/Arlington/ Alexandria, DC/MD/VA	277,900	339,800	429,200
Waterloo/Cedar Falls, IA	91,300	95,200	100,700
Wichita, KS	100,500	103,900	106,300
Worcester, MA	252,600	275,900	292,300
Yakima, WA	123,400	129,900	134,800
Youngstown/Warren/ Boardman, OH/PA	NA	86,000	82,900
United States	**$170,000**	**$184,100**	**$208,500**

NA = Not available.

U.S. Home Ownership Rates, by Selected Characteristics, 1997, 2005[1]

Source: Bureau of the Census, U.S. Dept. of Commerce

Region	1997	2005	Age	1997	2005	Race/Ethnicity[2]	1997	2005	Income	1997	2005
Northeast	62.4%	64.7%	Under 35	38.6%	42.8%	White, non-Hispanic	72.1%	75.6%	Median family income or more	80.8%	84.4%
Midwest	70.3	73.4	35-44	66.3	68.7	Black	44.4	48.0	Below median family income	50.0	52.7
South	68.1	70.4	45-54	75.6	76.3	Hispanic	43.3	49.2	**TOTAL U.S.**	**65.7%**	**68.6%**
West	59.9	63.8	55-64	80.3	81.3	Other	52.7	58.0			
			65+	79.1	80.3						

(1) In 2005, figures are for 2nd quarter of the year. Not seasonally-adjusted. (2) Hispanic householders may be of any race. "Other" includes householders reporting Asian, Native Hawaiian/Pacific Islander, and Native American/AK Native, as well as combinations of two or more races/ethnicities.

Housing Affordability, U.S., 1990-2005

Source: National Association of REALTORS®

Year	Median priced existing home	Average mortgage rate[1]	Monthly principal & interest payment	Payment as percentage of median monthly income
1990	$92,000	10.04%	$648	22.0%
1991	97,100	9.30	642	21.4
1992	99,700	8.11	591	19.3
1993	103,100	7.16	558	18.1
1994	107,200	7.47	598	18.5
1995	110,500	7.85	639	18.9
1996	115,800	7.71	661	18.8
1997	121,800	7.68	693	18.7
1998	$128,400	7.10%	$690	17.4%
1999	133,300	7.33	733	18.0
2000	139,000	8.03	818	19.3
2001	147,800	7.03	789	18.4
2002	158,100	6.55	804	18.3
2003	170,000	5.74	793	17.8
2004	184,100	5.72	857	18.9
2005[2]	208,500	5.83	982	20.7

(1) All figures assume a down payment of 20% of the home price. Based on effective rate on loans closed on existing homes for the period shown. (2) Preliminary, as of the 2nd quarter of fiscal year 2005.

Identity Theft

Source: Federal Trade Commission; Dept. of Justice

Identity theft and fraud are crimes in which a person wrongfully obtains and uses deception or fraud to take advantage of another person's personal data, usually for financial gain. Identifying information—such as Social Security, bank account, and credit card numbers—can be used without permission to remove funds from bank and other financial accounts. In the worst-case scenario, an identity thief could mirror a person's identity altogether, creating new accounts and vast debts, and even committing other crimes in the victim's name.

In 2004, the Federal Trade Commission (FTC) received 246,570 identity theft complaints from U.S. law enforcement and consumers, up 15% from 2003. The U.S. Dept. of Justice made identity theft and identity fraud federal offenses in 1998.

Identity Theft Prevention

You can take these simple steps (acronym, **SCAM**) to reduce your vulnerability to identity theft.

• **Be stingy** about revealing personal information to others unless you have a reason to trust them. Adopt a "need to know" basis for revealing personal data. Keep information printed on personal bank checks to a minimum. If someone contacts you via telephone or the Internet and offers a prize but asks for personal data, ask them to mail you a form, and check the company with the Better Business Bureau (www.bbb.org). When traveling, have mail held at the local post office or have a trusted person collect your mail. Be careful when throwing out documents that contain personal information.

• **Check** financial information often for irregular activity, and review statements for any charges or transactions that should not be there. Statements for your bank and credit card accounts should arrive monthly; if not, contact the company or financial institution.

• **Ask** for a copy of your credit report periodically, and review it to confirm that no unknown accounts have been opened in your name. Free annual credit reports are now available by visiting www.annualcreditreport.com, or calling 877-322-8228. Note: Do not contact the credit bureaus directly for this.

• **Maintain** careful records. Keep monthly statements and cancelled checks or their copies for at least a year. These can be useful if you need to dispute a transaction.

Identity Theft Recovery

If you think you have become a victim of identity theft or fraud, take action immediately.

• Contact one of the three major credit bureaus to have them place a fraud alert in your file. This will require that creditors contact you before opening new accounts in your name or changing information on existing accounts. Once the alert is activated, the other two credit bureaus will be notified.

• Get a copy of your credit report and review it closely. Close any accounts that have been tampered with or opened fraudulently. Speak with someone in the fraud/security department of each creditor, and follow up in writing, with copies of supporting documents. Victims of identity theft have the right to request that those debts incurred through fraud are blocked from future credit reports. An ID Theft affidavit, accepted by most credit companies, is available online at www.ftc. gov/bcp/conline/pubs/credit/affidavit.pdf

• Report the crime to local police or police in the community where the theft took place. Report the theft to the FTC at www.consumer.gov/idtheft or 877-IDTHEFT. You can also report to the FTC in writing at the Identity Theft Clearinghouse, Federal Trade Commission, 600 Pennsylvania Ave. NW, Washington, DC 20580.

• Obtain copies of fraudulent credit and account applications from the three major credit bureaus and give copies to the police.

• Contact the Social Security Administration (www.ssa.gov) if you suspect your social security number is being used.

Credit Bureau Contacts

Equifax. Reports: 800-685-1111; fraud alerts: 800-525-6285. P.O. Box 740241, Atlanta, GA 30374-0241. www.equifax.com

Experian (formerly TRW). Reports and fraud alerts: 888-EXPERIAN. Reports: P.O. Box 2002, Allen, TX 75013; fraud alerts: P.O. Box 9530, Allen, TX 75013. www.experian.com

Trans Union. Reports: 800-888-4213; P.O. Box 1000, Chester, PA 19022. Fraud alerts: 800-680-7289; P.O. Box 6790, Fullerton, CA 92634. www.transunion.com

IT'S A FACT: According to a Federal Trade Commission survey published in Sept. 2003, the average victim of identity theft was taken for around $500, and spent about 30 hours resolving problems that the theft had caused. If the thief had opened new accounts in the person's name (as opposed to illegally using existing accounts), the average cost to the victim jumped to $1,180 and the amount of time spent resolving problems doubled.

POSTAL INFORMATION

Note: As of Sept. 2005, a 5.4% increase of all domestic rates was pending with the Postal Rate Commission. If the new rates are approved, the price of a standard First-Class Mail stamp would increase from 37¢ to 39¢. The proposed rates were to be implemented no sooner than Jan. 2006.

Basic U.S. Postal Service

The Postal Reorganization Act, creating a government-owned postal service under the executive branch and replacing the old Post Office Department, was signed into law by Pres. Richard Nixon, Aug. 12, 1970. The service officially came into being on July 1, 1971. The U.S. Postal Service is governed by an 11-person Board of Governors. Nine of the members are appointed by the president, with Senate approval. These 9 choose a postmaster general. The board and the postmaster general choose the 11th member, who serves as deputy postmaster general. An independent Postal Rate Commission of 5 members, appointed by the president, reviews and rules on proposed postal rate increases submitted by the Board of Governors.

U.S. Domestic Rates

(Domestic rates apply to the U.S., to its territories and possessions, and to APOs and FPOs.)

First-Class Mail

First-Class Mail includes written matter such as letters, postal cards, and postcards (private mailing cards), plus all other matter wholly or partly in writing, whether sealed or unsealed, except book manuscripts, periodical articles and music, manuscript copy accompanying proofsheets or corrected proofsheets of the same, and the writing authorized by law on matter of other classes. Also included: matter sealed or closed against inspection, bills, and statements of accounts.

Written letters and matter sealed against inspection cost **37¢** for first ounce or fraction, 23¢ for each additional ounce or fraction up to and including 13 ounces. U.S. Postal Service cards cost 23¢ for postage, with a 2¢ fee for the card. Private postcards postage is **23¢**. Presort and automation-compatible mail can qualify for lower rates if certain piece minimums, mailing permits, and other requirements are met.

Express Mail

Express Mail provides guaranteed expedited service for any mailable article (up to 70 lbs and not over 108 in. in combined length and girth). Offers next day delivery by noon to most destinations; no extra charge for Saturday, Sunday, or holiday delivery. Second-day service is available to locations not on the Next Day Delivery Network. The basic rate for Express Mail weighing up to 8 oz is **$13.65**. All rates include insurance up to $100, shipment receipt, and record of delivery at the destination post office. Express Mail tracking is available on the USPS Web site (www.usps.com).

Express Mail Flat Rate: $13.65, regardless of weight, if matter fits into a special Postal Service flat-rate envelope.

Scheduled pickup service is available for **$12.50** per stop, regardless of the number of pieces or service used (e.g., Express Mail, Priority Mail, or Parcel Post can be picked up together).

Contact your local post office for further information.

Standard Mail

Standard Mail is limited to items less than 16 ounces such as solicitations, newsletters, advertising materials, books, cassettes, and other merchandise. A minimum volume of 200 pieces or 50 lbs of such items is necessary, and specific bulk mail preparation and sortation requirements apply.

The minimum rate per piece for pieces 3.3 ounces or less is $0.268 for basic letters and $0.344 for basic nonletters. Contact your post office for the discounts offered for automation, presorted, carrier route, destination entry, and other discounts. Separate rates are available for some nonprofit organizations.

Any mailer who uses a permit imprint is required to pay a one-time $150 fee plus an annual (calendar year) fee of $150. Additional standards apply to mailings of nonidentical-weight pieces.

Priority Mail

Due to expeditious handling and transportation, Priority Mail is delivered in 1-3 days, on average. Priority Mail may include any mailable article up to 70 lbs and not over 108 in. in length and girth combined, whether sealed or unsealed, including written and other First Class material.

Packages weighing less than 15 lbs and measuring over 84 in., but less than 108 in., in length and girth combined cost the same as a 15-lb parcel mailed to the same zone. Scheduled pickup service costs an additional $12.50 per stop, regardless of the number of pieces or service used (e.g. Express Mail, Priority Mail, or Parcel Post can be picked up together).

Priority Mail Flat Rate: $3.85, regardless of weight, if matter fits into a special Postal Service flat-rate envelope. **$7.75**, regardless of weight (under 70 lbs), if matter fits into a special Postal Service flat-rate box.

Priority Mail Rates

Weight not over (lbs)	ZONES 1-3	4	5	6	7	8
1	$3.85	$3.85	$3.85	$3.85	$3.85	$3.85
2	3.95	4.55	4.90	5.05	5.40	5.75
3	4.75	6.05	6.85	7.15	7.85	8.55
4	5.30	7.05	8.05	8.50	9.45	10.35
5	5.85	8.00	9.30	9.85	11.00	12.15
6	6.30	8.85	9.90	10.05	11.30	12.30
7	6.80	9.80	10.65	11.00	12.55	14.05
8	7.35	10.75	11.45	11.95	13.80	15.75
9	7.90	11.70	12.20	12.90	15.05	17.50
10	8.40	12.60	13.00	14.00	16.30	19.20
11	8.95	13.35	13.75	15.15	17.55	20.90
12	9.50	14.05	14.50	16.30	18.80	22.65
13	10.00	14.75	15.30	17.50	20.05	24.35
14	10.55	15.45	16.05	18.60	21.25	26.05
15(1)	11.05	16.20	16.85	19.75	22.50	27.80

(1) See postmaster for pieces over 15 lbs.

Periodicals

Periodicals include newspapers and magazines.

For the general public, the applicable Package Services or First-Class postage is paid for periodicals.

For publishers, rates vary according to (1) whether item is sent to same county, (2) percentage of editorial and advertising matter, (3) whether the publishing org. is nonprofit or produces educational material for use in classrooms, (4) weight, (5) distance, (6) level of presort, (7) automation compatibility.

Package Services

Package Services, formerly "Standard Mail (B)," is any mailable matter that is not included in First-Class or Periodicals (unless permitted or required by regulations). There are currently four subclasses of Package Services: Parcel Post, Bound Printed Matter, Media Mail (formerly "Special Standard Mail"), and Library Mail.

The post office determines charges for Package Services according to the weight of the package in pounds and the zone distance shipped (Media Mail and Library Mail rates are determined by weight alone). There is no minimum weight; see separate headings for maximum weight. Presort and automation-compatible mail for all Package Services can qualify for lower rates if certain piece minimums, mailing permits, and other requirements are met. Contact your local post office for further information. Package Services is not sealed against postal inspection.

Parcel Post

Parcel Post is any Package Services not mailed as Bound Print Matter, Media Mail, or Library Mail. Any Package Services matter may be mailed at the Parcel Post rates, subject to these basic standards: not to exceed 70 lbs or 130 in. in combined length and girth (packages over 84 in., but not more than 130 in. in combined length and girth and under 15 lbs are subject to the 15 lb "balloon rate"). All fractions of a pound are counted as a full pound. Parcel Post subclass consists of two basic retail rate categories and three drop-shipped categories, the latter collectively known as Parcel Select.

Parcel Post Basic Rate Schedule

(Inter BMC/ASF ZIP codes only, machinable[1] parcels, no discount, no surcharge)

Weight not over	ZONES 1 & 2	3	4	5	6	7	8
1 lb.	$3.69	$3.75	$3.75	$3.75	$3.75	$3.75	$3.75
2	3.85	3.85	4.14	4.14	4.49	4.49	4.49
3	4.65	4.65	5.55	5.65	5.71	5.77	6.32
4	4.86	5.20	6.29	6.93	7.14	7.20	7.87
5	5.03	5.71	6.94	7.75	8.58	8.64	9.43
6	5.63	6.01	7.44	8.50	9.52	9.90	11.49
7	5.80	6.28	7.91	9.20	10.35	11.39	12.83
8	5.98	6.53	8.30	9.84	11.11	12.54	15.04
9	6.11	6.76	8.74	10.45	11.83	13.38	17.04
10	6.28	7.57	9.10	11.01	12.50	14.17	18.14
11	6.41	7.80	9.47	11.54	13.13	14.92	19.15
12	6.54	8.01	9.80	12.04	13.72	15.62	20.10
13	6.67	8.19	10.12	12.51	14.28	16.27	20.99
14	6.80	8.42	10.43	12.95	14.81	16.90	21.84
15	6.92	8.61	10.73	13.38	15.31	17.49	22.64
16	7.02	8.79	11.00	13.78	15.79	18.05	23.41
17	7.15	8.94	11.28	14.16	16.24	18.59	24.13
18	7.25	9.11	11.52	14.52	16.68	19.09	24.82
19	7.37	9.28	11.77	14.87	17.09	19.58	25.48
20[2]	7.46	9.43	11.98	15.20	17.48	20.05	26.12

(1) Machinable parcels must be: not less than 6 in. long, 3 in. high, and .25 in. thick or more than 34 in. long, 17 in. high, and 17 in. thick; at least 6 oz. but not more than 35 lbs. (2) Consult postmaster for pieces greater than 20 lbs.

Library Mail

(minimum weight: none; maximum weight: 70 lbs)

Applies to books, printed music, bound academic theses, periodicals, sound recordings, museum materials, and other library materials mailed between schools, colleges, universities, public libraries, museums, veteran and fraternal organizations, and nonprofit religious, educational, scientific, and labor organizations or associations (or to or from these organizations). Advertising restrictions apply. All packages must be marked "Library Mail," and may not exceed 108 in. in combined length and girth. Contact your local post office for further information.

Rates are calculated by weight only. Single-piece rates are: $1.35, up to 1 lb; 40¢ for each additional pound or fraction, to 7 lbs; additional pounds thereafter, 29¢ each.

Media Mail

(minimum weight: none; maximum weight: 70 lbs)

Formerly "Special Standard Mail." Applies to books of at least 8 printed pages; 16-mm or narrower-width films; printed music; printed test materials; sound recordings, playscripts, and manuscripts for books; printed educational charts; loose-leaf pages and binders consisting of medical information; computer-readable media. Advertising restrictions apply. Packages must be marked "Media Mail" and may not exceed 108 in. in combined length and girth. Contact your local post office for further information.

Rates are calculated by weight only. Single-piece rates are: $1.42, up to 1 lb; 42¢ for each additional pound or fraction, to 7 lbs; additional pounds thereafter, 30¢ each.

Bound Printed Matter

(minimum weight: none; maximum weight: 15 lbs)

Applies to advertising, promotional, directory, or editorial material that is bound by permanent fastening and consists of sheets of which at least 90% are imprinted by any process other than handwriting or typewriting. Does not include stationery (or pads of blank forms) or personal correspondence. Packages may not exceed 108 in. in combined length and girth, marked "Bound Printed Matter" or "BPM."

Bound Printed Matter Rates

(zone rate for flat single pieces; parcels pay 8¢ more)

Weight not over	ZONES 1 & 2	3	4	5	6	7	8
1.0 lb.	$1.79	$1.84	$1.88	$1.96	$2.03	$2.12	$2.29
1.5	1.79	1.84	1.88	1.96	2.03	2.12	2.29
2.0	1.86	1.92	1.98	2.08	2.18	2.30	2.52
2.5	1.93	2.01	2.08	2.21	2.33	2.48	2.76
3.0	2.00	2.09	2.18	2.33	2.48	2.66	2.99
3.5	2.07	2.18	2.28	2.46	2.63	2.84	3.23
4.0	2.14	2.26	2.38	2.58	2.78	3.02	3.46
4.5	2.21	2.35	2.48	2.71	2.93	3.20	3.70
5.0	2.28	2.43	2.58	2.83	3.08	3.38	3.93
6.0	2.42	2.60	2.78	3.08	3.38	3.74	4.40
7.0	2.56	2.77	2.98	3.33	3.68	4.10	4.87
8.0	2.70	2.94	3.18	3.58	3.98	4.46	5.34
9.0	2.84	3.11	3.38	3.83	4.28	4.82	5.81
10.0	2.98	3.28	3.58	4.08	4.58	5.18	6.28
11.0	3.12	3.45	3.78	4.33	4.88	5.54	6.75
12.0	3.26	3.62	3.98	4.58	5.18	5.90	7.22
13.0	3.40	3.79	4.18	4.83	5.48	6.26	7.69
14.0	3.54	3.96	4.38	5.08	5.78	6.62	8.16
15.0	3.68	4.13	4.58	5.33	6.08	6.98	8.63

Domestic Mail Special Services

Insured Mail

Applicable to Standard Mail, Package Services, and First-Class or Priority Mail items eligible to be mailed as Package Services. Matter for sale addressed to prospective purchasers who have not ordered it or authorized its sending cannot be insured. **Note:** for Express Mail, insurance is included up to $100. Add $1.00 per $100 or fraction thereof over $100 up to $5,000.

Declared Value	Insured Mail Fee[1]
$0.01 to $50.00	$1.30
$50.01 to $100.00	2.20
$100.01 to $200.00	3.20
$200.01 to $300.00	4.20
$300.01 to $400.00	5.20
$400.01 to $500.00	6.20
$500.01 to $600.00	7.20
$600.01 to $700.00	8.20
$700.01 to $800.00	9.20
$800.01 to $900.00	10.20
$900.01 to $1,000.00	11.20
$1,000.01 to $5,000.00	11.20 plus $1.00 per each $100 or fraction thereof over $1,000 in desired coverage

(1) In addition to postage. (Maximum liability is $5,000.) See postmaster for details on bulk discounts.

Special Handling

Provides preferential handling, but not preferential delivery, to the extent practicable in dispatch and transportation. Available for First-Class Mail, Priority Mail, and Package Services for the following surcharge: up to 10 lb, $5.95; over 10 lb, $8.25 Pieces must be marked "Special Handling."

Delivery Confirmation

Applies to First-Class Mail parcels, Priority Mail, and Package services. Available for purchase at the time of mailing only. Provides mailer with the date and time an article was delivered and, if delivery was attempted but not successful, the date and time of the attempt. Electronic confirmation is available for barcoded matter.

Manual confirmation is available for retail purchasers on the Internet (www.usps.com) or toll-free by phone (800-222-1811).

Priority Mail fees: manual, 45¢; electronic, free. First-Class Mail parcels and Package Services fees: manual, 55¢; electronic, 13¢. Standard Mail fee: electronic, 13¢.

IT'S A FACT: "Franked" mail is mail that bears the signature (or a facsimile) of an authorized person and can therefore be sent without postage. The vice president and members of Congress, among others, have the privilege of franking while in office, though scores of conditions are attached. Former presidents and their spouses enjoy lifetime franking privileges; the only restriction is that the franked mail must be nonpolitical in nature.

Registered Mail

Provides sender with mailing receipt, and a delivery record is maintained. Only matter prepaid with postage at First Class or priority mail rates may be registered. Stamps or meter stamps must be attached. The face of the article must be at least 5" long, 3½" high.

Declared Value	Fee
$0.00	$7.50
$0.01 to $100.00	8.00
$100.01 to $500.00	8.85
$500.01 to $1,000.00	9.70
$1,000.01 to $2,000.00	10.55
$2,000.01 to $3,000.00	11.40
$3,000.01 to $4,000.00	12.25
$4,000.01 to $5,000.00	13.10
$5,000.01 to $6,000.00	13.95
$6,000.01 to $7,000.00	14.80
$7,000.01 to $8,000.00	15.65
$8,000.01 to $9,000.00	16.50
$9,000.01 to $10,000.00	17.35
$10,000.01 to $25,000.00	17.35 plus $0.85 for each $1,000 or fraction thereof over $10,000
$25,000.01 to $1 million	30.10 plus $0.85 for each $1,000 or fraction thereof over $25,000
$1 million to $5 million	858.85 plus $0.85 for each $1,000 or fraction thereof over $1 million
Over $15 million	12,758.85 plus any additional amount determined by the Postal Service

Note: The mailer is required to declare the value of mail presented for registration. Fee for articles with declared value over $0.00 up to $25,000 includes insurance; fee is in addition to postage.

C.O.D. Unregistered: Applicable to First Class, Priority Mail, Express Mail, and Package Services. Items must be sent as bona fide orders or be in conformity with agreements between senders and addressees. Maximum amount collectible is $1,000.

C.O.D. Registered: For details, consult postmaster.

Certified mail: Available for any matter having no intrinsic value on which First Class or Priority Mail postage is paid. A receipt is furnished at the time of mailing, and evidence of delivery is obtained. Basic fee is $2.30 in addition to regular postage. Return receipt and restricted delivery available upon payment of additional fees. No indemnity.

Forwarding Addresses

To obtain a forwarding address, the mailer must write on the envelope or the cover "Address Correction Requested." The destination post office then will check for a forwarding address on file and, if available, provide it for 70¢ per manual correction, 20¢ per automated correction.

International Mail Special Services

Registration: Available to practically all countries for letter-post items only. Fee $7.50. The maximum indemnity payable is $43.93. To Canada only, the fee is $8.00, providing indemnity for loss up to $100, $8.85 for loss up to $500, and $9.70 for loss up to $1,000. Contact your post office for more details.

Return Receipt: Shows to whom and when delivered; Fee: $1.75 (must be purchased at time of mailing).

Air Mail: Available daily to practically all countries.

Aerogrammes — Aerogrammes are letter sheets that can be folded into the form of an envelope and sealed. Intended for personal communication only and may not include enclosures. Fee: 70¢ from U.S. to all countries.

Air mail postcards (single) — 50¢ to Canada and Mexico; 70¢ to all other countries.

International Reply Coupons (IRC): Provide foreign addressees with a prepaid means of responding to communications initiated by a U.S. sender. Each IRC is equivalent to the destination country's minimum postage rate for an unregistered airmail letter. Fee: $1.75 per coupon.

Restricted Delivery: Available to many countries for registered mail; some limitations. Fee: $3.50.

Insurance: Available to many countries for loss of or damage to items paid at parcel post rate. Consult postmaster for indemnity limits for individual countries.

Limit of indemnity Not over	Fees Canada[1]	All other countries[1]
$50	$1.30	$1.85
100	2.20	2.60
200	3.20	3.60
300	4.20	4.60
400	5.20	5.60
500	6.20	6.60
600	7.20	7.60
700	8.20	8.60
800		9.60
900		10.60
1,000[2]		11.60

(1) Not all countries insure items up to the amounts listed in the table. Canada does not insure items for more than $675. (2) For amounts more than $1,000, add $1.00 for each $100 or fraction.

Post Office-Authorized 2-Letter State Abbreviations

The abbreviations below are approved by the U.S. Postal Service for use in addresses.

Alabama	AL	Hawaii	HI	Missouri	MO	Pennsylvania	PA
Alaska	AK	Idaho	ID	Montana	MT	Puerto Rico	PR
American Samoa	AS	Illinois	IL	Nebraska	NE	Rhode Island	RI
Arizona	AZ	Indiana	IN	Nevada	NV	South Carolina	SC
Arkansas	AR	Iowa	IA	New Hampshire	NH	South Dakota	SD
California	CA	Kansas	KS	New Jersey	NJ	Tennessee	TN
Colorado	CO	Kentucky	KY	New Mexico	NM	Texas	TX
Connecticut	CT	Louisiana	LA	New York	NY	Utah	UT
Delaware	DE	Maine	ME	North Carolina	NC	Vermont	VT
District of Columbia	DC	Marshall Islands[1]	MH	North Dakota	ND	Virgin Islands	VI
Federated States of Micronesia[1]	FM	Maryland	MD	Northern Mariana Is.	MP	Virginia	VA
		Massachusetts	MA	Ohio	OH	Washington	WA
Florida	FL	Michigan	MI	Oklahoma	OK	West Virginia	WV
Georgia	GA	Minnesota	MN	Oregon	OR	Wisconsin	WI
Guam	GU	Mississippi	MS	Palau[1]	PW	Wyoming	WY

(1) Although an independent nation, this country is currently subject to domestic rates and fees.

Canadian Province and Territory Postal Abbreviations

Source: Canada Post

Alberta	AB	Newfoundland and Labrador	NF	Nunavut	NU	Quebec	QC[1]
British Columbia	BC	Northwest Territories	NT	Ontario	ON	Saskatchewan	SK
Manitoba	MB	Nova Scotia	NS	Prince Edward Island	PE	Yukon Territory	YT
New Brunswick	NB						

(1) PQ is also acceptable.

SOCIAL SECURITY

Old-Age, Survivors, and Disability Insurance; Medicare; Supplemental Security Income

Source: Social Security Administration; World Almanac research; provisions shown are as under current law, Sept. 2005

Social Security Benefits

Social Security benefits are based on a worker's **primary insurance amount (PIA)**, which is related by law to the average indexed monthly earnings (AIME) on which Social Security contributions have been paid. The full PIA is payable to a retired worker at age 65 (or a certain number of months after the 65th birthday, depending on year of birth) and to an entitled disabled worker at any age. Spouses and children of retired or disabled workers and survivors of deceased workers receive set proportions of the PIA subject to a family maximum amount.

The PIA is calculated by applying varying percentages to succeeding parts of the AIME. The formula is adjusted annually to reflect changes in average annual wages.

Automatic increases in Social Security benefits are initiated for December of each year, assuming the Consumer Price Index (CPI) for the 3rd calendar quarter of the year increased relative to the base quarter, which is either the 3rd calendar quarter of the preceding year or the quarter in which an increase legislated by Congress became effective. The size of the benefit increase is determined by the percentage rise of the CPI between the quarters measured.

The **average monthly benefit** payable to all retired workers amounted to $955 in Dec. 2004. The average benefit for disabled workers in that month amounted to $894.

Minimum and maximum monthly retired-worker benefits payable to individuals who retired at age 65[1]

	Minimum benefit[2]		Maximum benefit[2]	
Year attaining age 65	Paid at retirement	Payable as of Dec. 2004	Payable at retirement	Payable effective Dec. 2004
1970	$64.00	$333.30	(3)	(4)
1980	133.90	333.30	$572.00	$1,397.80
1990	(5)	(5)	975.00	1,395.30
1995	(5)	(5)	1,199.10	1,424.70
1996	(5)	(5)	1,248.90	1,493.30
1997	(5)	(5)	1,326.60	1,422.20
1998	(5)	(5)	1,342.80	1,480.40
1999	(5)	(5)	1,373.10	1,494.40
2000	(5)	(5)	1,434.80	1,526.30
2001	(5)	(5)	1,536.70	1,576.60
2002	(5)	(5)	1,660.50	1,683.70
2003	(5)	(5)	1,741.10	1,777.60
2004	(5)	(5)	1,784.80	1,832.90

(1) Assumes retirement at beginning of year. (2) The final benefit amount payable is rounded to next lower $1 (if not already a multiple of $1). (3) Benefits $196.40 for women and $189.80 for men. (4) Benefits $1,003.40 for women and $968.90 for men. (5) Minimum eliminated for workers who reached age 62 after 1981.

Amount of Work Required

To qualify for benefits, the worker generally must have worked a certain length of time in covered employment. Just how long depends on when the worker reaches age 62 or, if earlier, when he or she dies or becomes disabled. A person born after 1929 who dies, becomes disabled, or reaches age 62 after 1991 must have had at least 10 years work credit to qualify for full benefits.

A person is **fully insured** who has 1 quarter of coverage for every year after 1950 (or year age 21 is reached, if later) up to but not including the year the worker reaches 62, dies, or becomes disabled. In 2005, a person earns 1 quarter of coverage for each $920 of annual earnings in covered employment, up to 4 quarters per year.

To receive **disability benefits**, the worker, in addition to being fully insured, must generally have credit for 20 quarters of coverage out of the 40 calendar quarters before he or she became disabled. A disabled blind worker need meet only the fully insured requirement. Persons disabled before age 31 can qualify with a briefer period of coverage. Certain survivor benefits are payable if the deceased worker had 6 quarters of coverage in the 13 quarters preceding death.

Contribution and benefit base

Calendar year	OASDI[1]	HI[2]	Calendar year	OASDI[1]	HI[2]
1990	$51,300	$51,300	1999	$72,600	no limit
1992	55,500	130,200	2000	76,200	no limit
1993	57,600	135,000	2001	80,400	no limit
1994	60,600	no limit	2002	84,900	no limit
1995	61,200	no limit	2003	87,000	no limit
1996	62,700	no limit	2004	87,900	no limit
1997	65,400	no limit	2005	90,000	no limit
1998	68,400	no limit	2006	93,000 (est.)	no limit

(1) Old-Age, Survivors, and Disability Ins. (2) Hospital Ins.

Tax-rate schedule

(percentage of covered earnings)

Year	Total	OASDI	HI
	(for employees and employers, each)		
1979-80	6.13	5.08	1.05
1981	6.65	5.35	1.30
1982-83	6.70	5.40	1.30
1984	7.00	5.70	1.30
1985	7.05	5.70	1.35
1986-87	7.15	5.70	1.45
1988-89	7.51	6.06	1.45
1990 and after	7.65	6.20	1.45
	For self-employed		
1979-80	8.10	7.05	1.05
1981	9.30	8.00	1.30
1982-83	9.35	8.05	1.30
1984	14.00	11.40	2.60
1985	14.10	11.40	2.70
1986-87	14.30	11.40	2.90
1988-89	15.02	12.12	2.90
1990 and after	15.30	12.40	2.90

What Aged Workers Receive

A person may receive monthly old-age benefits when he or she has enough work in covered employment and has reached retirement age—age 62 for reduced benefit, the age below for full benefits.

Full-Benefit Retirement Age (FRA) by Birth Year

Year of Birth	FRA	Year of Birth	FRA
1937 or earlier	65	1943-1954	66
1938	65 and 2 months	1955	66 and 2 months
1939	65 and 4 months	1956	66 and 4 months
1940	65 and 6 months	1957	66 and 6 months
1941	65 and 8 months	1958	66 and 8 months
1942	65 and 10 months	1959	66 and 10 months
		1960	67

Note: If born on Jan. 1, refer to the previous birth year.

In 2000, the retirement **earnings test** was eliminated beginning with the month when the beneficiary reaches **full-benefit retirement age (FRA)**. A person at and above FRA no longer has benefits reduced because of earnings. However, in the calendar year a beneficiary reaches FRA, benefits are reduced $1 for every $3 of earnings above the limit allowed by law ($31,800 in 2005) for the months prior to FRA. For years before the beneficiary attains FRA, the reduction is $1 for every $2 of earnings over the exempt amount ($12,000 for year 2005).

For workers who reached age 65 between 1982 and 1989, Social Security benefits are raised by 3% for each year for which the worker between ages 65 and 70 (72 before 1984) failed to receive benefits, whether because of earnings from work or because the worker had not applied for benefits. The **delayed retirement credit** is 1% per year for workers who reached age 65 before 1982. The delayed retirement credit is scheduled to rise to 8% per year by 2008. The rate for workers who reached age 65 in 1998-99 is 5.5%; 2000-01, 6.0%; 2002-03, 6.5%; 2004-05, 7.0%. For 2006-07 it is 7.5%.

For workers retiring early, before full retirement age, benefits are **permanently reduced** 5/9 of 1% for each month before FRA, up to 36 months. If the number of months exceeds 36, then the benefit is further reduced 5/12 of 1% per month.

For example, when FRA reaches 67, for workers who retire at exactly age 62, there are a total of 60 months of reduction.

The reduction for the first 36 months is 5/9 of 36%, or 20%. The reduction for the remaining 24 months is 5/12 of 24%, or 10%. Thus, when the FRA reaches 67, the amount of reduction at age 62 will be 30%. The nearer to FRA the worker is when he or she begins collecting a benefit, the larger the benefit will be.

Benefits for Worker's Spouse

A person not receiving his or her own benefits may receive benefits as a spouse. The spouse of a worker who is getting Social Security retirement or disability payments may become entitled to an insurance benefit of **one-half of the worker's PIA** when he or she reaches full retirement age. Reduced spouse's benefits are available at age 62 and are permanently reduced 25/36 of 1% for each month before FRA, up to 36 months. If the number of months exceeds 36, then the benefit is further reduced 5/12 of 1% per month. Benefits are also payable to the aged divorced spouse of an insured worker if he or she was married to the worker for at least 10 years.

Benefits for Children of Workers

If a retired or disabled worker has a child under age 18, the **child** will normally get a benefit equal to half of the worker's unreduced benefit. So will the worker's spouse, even if under age 62, if he or she is **caring for an entitled child** of the worker who is under 16 or became disabled before age 22. However, total benefits paid on a worker's earnings record are subject to a maximum. (Total monthly benefits paid to the family of a worker who retired in 2005 at FRA and always had the maximum earnings creditable under Social Security cannot exceed $3,394.10.)

When entitled children reach age 18, their benefits generally stop, but a child disabled before age 22 may get a benefit as long as the disability meets the definition in the law. Benefits will be paid until age 19 to a child attending elementary or secondary school full-time.

Benefits may also be paid to a grandchild or step-grandchild of a worker or of his or her spouse, in special circumstances.

OASDI Beneficiaries

Beneficiaries	May 2005	May 2004	May 2003	May 2002
total (in thousands)[1]	**48,068**	**47,378**	**46,771**	**46,190**
Aged 65 and over, total	33,811	33,400	33,179	32,953
Retired workers	27,413	27,014	26,680	26,352
Survivors and dependents	6,286	6,386	6,498	6,601
Under age 65, total	14,257	13,978	13,592	13,236
Retired workers	2,809	2,668	2,645	2,660
Disabled workers	6,239	6,035	5,702	5,337
Survivors and dependents	5,209	5,275	8,579	5,198
Total monthly benefits (in millions)	**$42,074**	**$39,960**	**$38,244**	**$36,885**

(1) Totals may not add because of rounding or incomplete enumeration.

What Disabled Workers Receive

A worker who becomes unable to work may be eligible for a monthly **disability benefit**. Benefits continue until it is determined that the individual is no longer disabled. When a disabled-worker beneficiary reaches FRA (65 years, 6 months in 2005), the disability benefit becomes a retired-worker benefit. In 2005, there were 112,000 disabled worker beneficiaries aged 65 and older who had not reached FRA.

Benefits generally like those for dependents of retired-worker beneficiaries may be paid to dependents of disabled beneficiaries. However, the maximum family benefit in disability cases is generally lower than in retirement cases.

Survivor Benefits

If an insured worker should die, one or more types of benefits may be payable to survivors, again subject to a maximum family benefit as described above.

1. If claiming benefits at age 65, the **surviving spouse** will receive a benefit equal to 100% of the deceased worker's PIA. Benefits claimed before FRA are reduced for age with a maximum reduction of 28.5 percent at age 60. However, for those whose spouses claimed their benefits before age 65, these are limited to the reduced amount the worker would be getting if alive, but not less than 82.5% of the worker's PIA. Remarriage after the worker's death ends the surviving spouse's benefit rights. However, if the widow(er) marries and the marriage is ended, he or she regains benefit rights. (A marriage after age 60, age 50 if disabled, is deemed not to have occurred for benefit purposes.) Survivor benefits may also be paid to a divorced spouse if the marriage lasted for at least 10 years.

Disabled widows and widowers may under certain circumstances qualify for benefits after attaining age 50 at the rate of 71.5% of the deceased worker's PIA. The widow or widower must have become totally disabled before or within 7 years after the spouse's death or the last month in which he or she received mother's or father's insurance benefits.

2. There is a benefit for each **child under age 18**. The monthly benefit for each child of a deceased worker is ¾ of the amount the worker would have received if he or she had lived and drawn full retirement benefits. A child with a disability that began before age 22 may also receive benefits. Also, a child may receive benefits until reaching age 19 if he or she is in full-time attendance at an elementary or secondary school.

3. There is a **mother's or father's benefit** for the widow(er) if children of the worker under age 16 are in his or her care. The benefit is 75% of the PIA, and it continues until the youngest child reaches age 16, at which time payments stop even if the child's benefit continues. However, if the widow(er) has a disabled child beneficiary age 16 or over in care, benefits may continue.

4. **Dependent parents** may be eligible for benefits if they have been receiving at least half their support from the worker before his or her death, have reached age 62, and (except in certain circumstances) have not remarried since the worker's death. Each parent gets 75% of the worker's PIA; if only one parent survives, the benefit is 82%.

5. A **lump sum** cash payment of **$255** is made when there is a spouse who was living with the worker or a spouse or child eligible for immediate monthly survivor benefits.

Self-Employed Workers

A self-employed person who has **net earnings of $400** or more in a year must report such earnings for Social Security tax and credit purposes. The person reports net returns from the business. Income from real estate, savings, dividends, loans, pensions, or insurance policies are not included unless it is part of the business.

A self-employed person receives 1 quarter of coverage for each $920 (for 2005), up to a maximum of 4 quarters.

The nonfarm self-employed have the option of reporting their earnings as $^2/_3$ of their gross income from self-employment, but not more than $1,600 a year and not less than their actual net earnings. This option can be used only if actual net earnings from self-employment income are less than $1,600, and may be used only 5 times. Also, the self-employed person must have actual net earnings of $400 or more in 2 of the 3 taxable years immediately preceding the year in which he or she uses the option.

When a person has both taxable wages and earnings from self-employment, wages are credited for Social Security purposes first; only as much self-employment income as brings total earnings up to the current taxable maximum becomes subject to the self-employment tax.

Farm Owners and Workers

Self-employed farmers whose gross annual earnings from farming are **$2,400** or less may report 2/3 of their gross earnings instead of net earnings for Social Security purposes. Farmers whose gross income is over $2,400 and whose net earnings are less than $1,600 can report $1,600. Cash or crop shares received from a tenant or share farmer count if the owner participated materially in production or management. The self-employed farmer pays contributions at the same rate as other self-employed persons.

Agricultural employees. A worker's earnings from farm work count toward benefits (1) if the employer pays the worker $150 or more in cash during the year; or (2) if the employer spends $2,500 or more in the year for agricultural labor. Under these rules a person gets credit for 1 calendar quarter for each $920 in cash pay in 2005.

Foreign farm workers admitted to the U.S. on a temporary basis are not covered.

Household Workers

Anyone 18 or older employed as maid, cook, laundry worker, nurse, babysitter, chauffeur, gardener, or other worker in the house of another is covered by Social Security if paid **$1,400** or more in cash in calendar year 2005 by any one employer. Room and board do not count, but transportation costs count if paid in cash. The job need not be regular or full-time. The employee should get a Social Security card at the Social Security office and show it to the employer.

The employer deducts the amount of the employee's Social Security tax from the worker's pay, adds an identical amount as the employer's Social Security tax, and sends the total amount to the federal government.

Medicare Coverage

The Medicare health insurance program provides acute-care coverage for Social Security and Railroad Retirement beneficiaries age 65 and over, for persons entitled for 24 months to receive Social Security or Railroad Retirement disability benefits, and for certain persons with end-stage kidney disease. What follows is a basic description and may not cover all circumstances.

The **basic Medicare plan**, available nationwide, is a fee-for-service arrangement, where the beneficiary may use any provider accepting Medicare; some services are not covered and there are some out-of-pocket costs.

Under **Medicare Advantage** (formerly Medicare + Choice), persons eligible for Medicare may have the option of getting services through a health maintenance organization (HMO) or other **managed care** plan. Any such plan must provide at least the same benefits, except for hospice services, and may provide added benefits—such as lower or no deductibles and coverage for some prescription drugs—but is usually subject to restrictions in choice of health care providers. In some plans services by outside providers are still covered for an extra out-of-pocket cost. Also available as options in some areas are Medicare-approved private fee-for-service plans and Medicare medical savings accounts.

Hospital insurance (Part A). The basic hospital insurance program pays covered services for hospital and posthospital care including the following:

- All necessary inpatient hospital care for the first 60 days of each benefit period, except for a deductible ($912 in 2005). For days 61-90, Medicare pays for services over and above a coinsurance amount ($228 per day in 2005). After 90 days, the beneficiary has 60 lifetime reserve days for which Medicare helps pay. The coinsurance amount for reserve days was $456 in 2005.
- Up to 100 days of care in a skilled-nursing facility in each benefit period. Hospital insurance pays for all covered services for the first 20 days; for the 21-100th day, the beneficiary pays coinsurance ($114 per day in 2005).
- Part-time home health care provided by nurses or other health workers.
- Limited coverage of hospice care for individuals certified to be terminally ill.

There is a premium for this insurance in certain cases.

Medical insurance (Part B). Elderly persons can receive benefits under this supplementary program only if they sign up for them and agree to a monthly premium ($78.20 if you sign up upon being eligible in 2005). The federal government pays the rest of the cost. The Part B deductible was $110 in 2005; beginning in 2006, the deductible will rise in proportion to the increase in average cost of Part B services to beneficiaries. After the deductible, the medical insurance program usually pays 80% of the approved amount for the following services:

- Covered services received from a doctor in his or her office, in a hospital, in a skilled-nursing facility, at home, or in other locations.
- Medical and surgical services, including anesthesia.
- Diagnostic tests and procedures that are part of the patient's treatment.
- Radiology and pathology services by doctors while the individual is a hospital inpatient or outpatient.
- Other services such as X rays, services of a doctor's office nurse, drugs and biologicals that cannot be self-administered, transfusions of blood and blood components, medical supplies, physical/occupational therapy and speech pathology services.

In addition to the above, certain other tests or preventive measures are now covered without an additional premium. These include a "Welcome to Medicare" physical exam and related services, mammograms, bone mass measurement, colo-rectal cancer screening, and flu shots. Routine physical exams, dental care, hearing aids, and routine eye care are generally not covered under the basic plan. There is limited coverage for nonhospital treatment of mental illness.

To get medical insurance (Part B), persons approaching age 65 may enroll in the **7-month period** that includes 3 months before the 65th birthday, the month of the birthday, and 3 months after the birthday, but if they want coverage to begin in the month they reach age 65, they must enroll in the 3 months before their birthday. Persons not enrolling within their first enrollment period may enroll later, but only during the first 3 months of each year (coverage begins July 1). Their premium may be 10% higher for each 12-month period elapsed since they first could have enrolled.

The monthly premium is deducted from the cash benefit for persons receiving Social Security, Railroad Retirement, or Civil Service retirement benefits. Income from the medical premiums and the federal matching payments are put in a Supplementary Medical Insurance Trust Fund, from which benefits and administrative expenses are paid.

Prescription Drug Coverage (Part D). Starting Jan. 1, 2006, a Medicare prescription drug plan will provide insurance coverage for prescription drugs. Medicare recipients pay a monthly premium (around $32.20 in 2006, depending on the provider) and a portion of drug costs. **Enrollment is scheduled to take place Nov. 15, 2005-May 15, 2005**, and is optional. Coverage varies depending on the drug plan selected.

Further details are available on the Internet at www.medicare.gov or by calling 1-800-MEDICARE (1-800-633-4227).

Medicare card. Persons qualifying for hospital insurance under Social Security receive a health insurance card similar to cards now used by Blue Cross and other health insurers. The card indicates whether the individual has taken out medical insurance protection. It is to be shown to the hospital, skilled-nursing facility, home health agency, doctor, or whoever provides the covered services.

Payments are generally made only in the 50 states, Puerto Rico, Virgin Islands, Guam, and American Samoa.

Social Security Financing

Social Security is paid for by a tax on certain earnings (for 2005, on earnings up to $90,000) for **Old Age, Survivors, and Disability Insurance** and on all earnings (no upper limit) for Hospital Insurance with the **Medicare** Program; the taxable earnings base for OASDI has been adjusted annually to reflect increases in average wages. The employed worker and his or her employer share Social Security taxes equally.

Employers remit amounts withheld from employee wages for Social Security and income taxes to the Internal Revenue Service; employer Social Security taxes are also payable at the same time. (Self-employed workers pay Social Security taxes when filing their regular income tax forms.) The Social Security taxes (along with revenues arising from partial taxation of the Social Security benefits of certain high-income people) are transferred to the Social Security Trust Funds—the Federal Old-Age and Survivors Insurance (OASI) Trust Fund, the Federal Disability Insurance (DI) Trust Fund, and the Federal Hospital Insurance (HI) Trust Fund; they can be used only to pay benefits, the cost of rehabilitation services, and administrative expenses. Money not immediately needed for these purposes is by law invested in obligations of the federal government, which must pay interest on the money borrowed and must repay the principal when the obligations are redeemed or mature.

Supplemental Security Income

On Jan. 1, 1974, the **Supplemental Security Income (SSI)** program established by the 1972 Social Security Act amendments replaced the former federal grants to states for aid to the needy aged, blind, and disabled in the 50 states and the District of Columbia. The program provides both for federal payments, based on uniform national standards and eligibility requirements, and for state supplementary payments varying from state to state. The Social Security Administration administers the federal payments financed from general funds of the Treasury—and the state supplements as well, if the state elects to have its supplementary program federally administered. States may supplement the federal payment for all recipients and must supplement it for persons otherwise adversely affected by the transition from the former public assistance programs. In May 2005, the number of persons receiving federally administered payments was 7,092,426 and the payments totaled $3.3 billion.

The **maximum** monthly federal SSI payment for individuals with no other countable income, living in their own household, was $579 in 2005. For couples the maximum payment was $869.

Social Security Statement

On Oct. 1, 1999, the Social Security Administration initiated the mailing of an annual *Social Security Statement* to all workers age 25 and older not already receiving benefits. Workers will automatically receive statements about 3 months before their birth month. The statement provides estimates of potential monthly Social Security retirement, disability, and survivor benefits as well as a record of lifetime earnings. The statement also gives workers an easy way to determine whether their earnings are accurately posted in Social Security records.

For further information contact the Social Security Administration toll-free at 1-800-772-1213 or visit its website at www.socialsecurity.gov

Examples of Monthly Benefits Available

Description of benefit or beneficiary	For low earnings ($16,470 in 2005)[1, 2]	For avg. earnings ($36,600 in 2005)[2]	For max. earnings ($90,000 in 2005)
Primary insurance amount (worker retiring at 65.5)	$776.90	$1,281.10	$1,939.00
Maximum family benefit (worker retiring at 65.5)	1,165.40	2,338.30	3,394.10
Maximum family disability benefit (worker disabled at 55; in 2004)*	1,085.40	1,907.70	2,997.40
Disabled worker (worker disabled at 55)			
Worker alone	772.30	1,271.80	1,998.30
Worker, spouse, and 1 child	1,084.00	1,905.00	2,996.00
Retired worker claiming benefits at age 62:			
Worker alone[3]	598.00	986.00	1,493.00
Worker with spouse claiming benefits at—			
Age 65 or over	984.00	1,622.00	2,456.00
Age 62[3]	878.00	1,447.00	2,191.00
Widow or widower claiming benefits at—			
Age 65 and 2 months or over[4]	776.00	1,281.00	1,939.00
Age 60 (spouse died at 65 without receiving reduced benefits)	555.00	915.00	1,386.00
Disabled widow or widower claiming benefits at age 50-59[5]	555.00	915.00	1,386.00
1 surviving child	582.00	960.00	1,454.00
Widow or widower age 65 or over and 1 child[6]	1,164.00	2,241.00	3,325.00
Widowed mother or father and 1 child[6]	1,164.00	1,920.00	2,908.00
Widowed mother or father and 2 children[6]	1,164.00	2,337.00	3,393.00

Effective Jan. 2005. *Assumes work beginning at age 22. (1) 45% of average. (2) Estimate. (3) Assumes maximum reduction. (4) A widow(er)'s benefit amount is limited to the amount the spouse would have been receiving if still living, but not less than 82.5% of the Primary Insurance Amount (PIA). (5) Effective Jan. 1984, disabled widow(er)s claiming a benefit at ages 50-59 receive a benefit equal to 71.5% of the PIA. (6) Based on worker dying at age 65.

Social Security Trust Funds

Old-Age and Survivors Insurance Trust Fund, 1940-2004

(in millions)

	INCOME					DISBURSEMENTS					
Fiscal year[1]	Total	Net contributions[2]	Income from taxing benefits	Payments from the Treasury fund[3]	Net interest[4]	Total	Benefit payments[5]	Administrative expenses	Transfers to Railroad Retirement program	Net increase in fund[6]	Fund at end of period
1940	$592	$550	—	—	$42	$28	$16	$12	—	$564	$1,745
1950	2,367	2,106	—	$4	257	784	727	57	—	1,583	12,893
1960	10,360	9,843	—	—	517	11,073	10,270	202	$600	−713	20,829
1970	31,746	29,955	—	442	1,350	27,321	26,268	474	579	4,425	32,616
1980	100,051	97,608	—	557	1,886	103,228	100,626	1,160	1,442	−3,177	24,566
1990	278,607	261,506	2,924	34	14,143	223,481	218,948	1,564	2,969	55,126	203,445
1995	326,067	289,529	5,114	7	31,417	294,456	288,607	1,797	4,052	31,611	447,946
1997	386,465	342,312	6,462	3	37,689	318,548	312,862	1,998	3,688	67,916	567,395
1998	415,666	364,871	8,595	2	42,198	329,953	324,256	2,034	3,662	85,713	653,108
1999	446,956	389,933	10,172	1	46,849	337,894	332,369	1,843	3,681	109,062	762,170
2000	484,228	418,219	12,476	—	53,532	353,396	347,868	1,990	3,538	130,832	893,003
2001	513,834	440,819	11,771	—	61,243	372,996	367,654	2,069	3,273	140,837	1,033,840
2002	529,257	448,133	12,597	414	68,113	389,546	383,942	2,111	3,493	139,711	1,173,551
2003	542,343	456,014	12,340	—	73,990	402,814	396,710	2,522	3,580	139,530	1,313,080
2004	556,523	466,807	13,269	1	76,446	417,053	411,148	2,274	3,628	139,470	1,452,550

(1) Fiscal years 1980 and later consist of the 12 months ending on Sept. 30 of each year. Fiscal years prior to 1977 consisted of the 12 months ending on June 30 of each year. (2) Beginning in 1983, includes transfers from general fund of Treasury representing contributions that would have been paid on deemed wage credits for military service in 1957 and later, if such credits were considered covered wages. (3) Includes payments (a) in 1947-52 and in 1967 and later, for costs of noncontributory wage credits for military service performed before 1957; (b) in 1972-83, for costs of deemed wage credits for military service performed after 1956; and (c) in 1969 and later, for costs of benefits to certain uninsured persons who attained age 72 before 1968. (4) Net interest includes net profits or losses on marketable investments. Beginning in 1967, administrative expenses were charged currently to the trust fund on an estimated basis, with a final adjustment, including interest, made in the next fiscal year. The amounts of these interest adjustments are included in net interest. For years prior to 1967, the method of accounting for administrative expenses is described in the 1970 Annual Report. Beginning in Oct. 1973, the figures shown include relatively small amounts of gifts to the fund. During 1983-91, interest paid from the trust fund to the general fund on advance tax transfers is reflected. (5) Beginning in 1967, includes payments for vocational rehabilitation services furnished to disabled persons receiving benefits because of their disabilities. Beginning in 1983, amounts are reduced by amount of reimbursement for unnegotiated benefit checks. (6) Net change in assets during fiscal year, including amounts borrowed or repaid by other funds.

Disability Insurance Trust Fund, 1960-2004

(in millions)

	INCOME					DISBURSEMENTS					
Fiscal year[1]	Total	Net contri-butions[2]	Income from taxing benefits	Payments from the Treasury fund[3]	Net interest[4]	Total	Benefit pay-ments[5]	Admini-strative expenses	Transfers to Railroad Retirement program	Net increase in fund[6]	Fund at end of period
1960...	$1,034	$987	—	—	$47	$533	$528	$32	$–27	$501	$2,167
1970...	4,380	4,141	—	$16	223	2,954	2,795	149	10	1,426	5,104
1980...	17,376	16,805	—	118	453	15,320	14,998	334	–12	2,056	7,680
1990...	28,215	27,291	$158	—	766	25,124	24,327	717	80	3,091	11,455
1995	70,209	67,987	335	—	1,888	41,374	40,234	1,072	68	28,835	35,206
2000...	77,023	70,001	756	—	6,266	56,008	54,244	1,608	159	21,014	113,752
2001...	82,079	74,611	732	–836	7,573	59,930	58,098	1,762	10	22,149	135,901
2002...	85,720	76,067	936	—	8,717	66,364	64,138	2,005	154	19,356	155,258
2003...	87,909	77,431	919	—	9,559	71,907	69,716	1,968	167	16,002	171,260
2004...	90,105	79,269	1,047	—	9,789	78,471	76,139	2,070	215	11,634	182,893

* Less than $50 million. (1) Fiscal years 1977 and later consist of the 12 months ending Sept. 30 of each year. Fiscal years prior to 1977 consisted of the 12 months ending June 30 of each year. (2) Beginning in 1983, includes transfers from general fund of Treasury representing contributions that would have been paid on deemed wage credits for military service in 1957 and later, if such credits were considered to be covered wages. (3) Includes payments (a) for costs of noncontributory wage credits for military service performed before 1957; and (b) in 1972-83, for costs of deemed wage credits for military service performed after 1956. (4) Net interest includes net profits or losses on marketable investments. Administrative expenses are charged currently to the trust fund on an estimated basis, with a final adjustment, including interest, made in the following fiscal year. Figures shown include relatively small amounts of gifts to the fund. During the years 1983-91, interest paid from the trust fund to the general fund on advance tax transfers is reflected. (5) Includes payments for vocational rehabilitation services. Beginning in 1983, amounts are reduced by amount of reimbursement for unnegotiated benefit checks. (6) Net change in assets during fiscal year, including amounts borrowed or repaid by other funds. **NOTE:** Totals may not add because of rounding.

Supplementary Medical Insurance Trust Fund (Medicare SMI), 1975-2004

(in millions)

	INCOME				DISBURSEMENTS				
Fiscal year[1]	Premium from participants	Government contri-butions[2]	Interest and other income[3]	Total Income	Benefit payments[4]	Admini-strative expenses	Total disburse-ments	Net increase in fund	Balance in fund at end of year[5]
1975..	$1,887	$2,330	$106	$4,322	$3,765	$404	$4,170	$152	$1,424
1980..	2,928	6,932	416	10,275	10,144	593	10,737	–462	4,532
1990..	11,494[6]	33,210	1,434[6]	46,138[6]	41,498	1,524[6]	43,022[6]	3,115	14,527[6]
1995..	19,244	36,988	1,937	58,169	63,491	1,722	65,213	–7,045	13,874
2000..	20,515	65,561	3,164	89,239	87,212[7]	1,780	88,992	247	45,896
2001..	22,307	69,838	3,191	95,336	97,466[7]	1,986	99,452	–4,116	41,780
2002..	24,427	78,318	2,960	105,705	106,995[7]	1,830	108,825	–3,121	38,659
2003..	26,834	80,905	2,455	110,194	121,699[7]	2,356	124,055	–13,861	24,799
2004..	30,341	94,734	1,730	126,805	131,673	2,817	134,490	–7,684	17,114

(1) Fiscal year 1975 consists of the 12 months ending on June 30, 1975; fiscal years 1980 and later consist of the 12 months ending on Sept. 30 of each year. (2) Includes Part B general fund matching payments, Part D subsidiary costs (for the transitional assistance provision in 2004), and certain interest-adjustment items. (3) Other income includes recoveries of amounts reimbursed from the trust fund that are not obligations of the trust fund and other miscellaneous income. (4) Includes costs of Peer Review Organizations from 1983 to 2001, and costs of Quality Improvement Organizations beginning in 2002. (5) The financial status of SMI depends on both the assets and the liabilities of the trust fund. (6) Includes the impact of the Medicare Catastrophic Coverage Act of 1988. (7) Benefit payments less monies transferred from the HI trust fund for home health agency costs, as provided for by PL 105-33. **NOTE:** Totals do not necessarily equal sums of rounded components.

Hospital Insurance Trust Fund (Medicare HI), 1975-2004

(in millions)

	INCOME								DISBURSEMENTS				
Fisc. year[1]	Payroll taxes	Income from taxation of benefits	Transfers from railroad retire-ment acct.	Reim-bursement for uninsured persons	Premiums from voluntary enrollees	Pymts. for military wage credits	Interest on invest-ments and other income[2]	Total income	Benefit pymts.[3]	Admini-strative expenses[4]	Total disburse-ments	Net increase in fund	Fund at end of year
1975	$11,291	—	$132	$481	$6	$48	$609	$12,568	$10,353	$259	$10,612	$1,956	$9,870
1980	23,244	—	244	697	17	141	1,072	25,415	23,790	497	24,288	1,127	14,490
1990	70,655	—	367	413	113	107	7,908	79,563	65,912	774	66,687	12,876	95,631
1995	98,053	$3,913	396	462	998	61	10,963	114,847	113,583	1,300	114,883	–36	129,520
2000	137,738	8,787	465	470	1,392	2	10,827	159,681	127,934[6]	2,350	130,284	29,397	168,084
2001	151,931	4,903	470	453	1,440	–1,175[7]	12,993	171,014	139,356[6]	2,368	141,723	29,290	197,374
2002	151,575	10,946	425	442	1,525	0	14,850	179,762	145,566[6]	2,464	148,031	31,731	229,105
2003	149,839	8,318	396	393	1,598	0	14,758	175,813	151,250[6]	2,541	153,792	22,021	251,127
2004	153,448	8,577	419	365	1,799	173	16,034	180,815	164,079	2,920	166,998	13,816	264,943

(1) Fiscal year 1975 consists of the 12 months ending on June 30, 1975; fiscal years 1980 and later consist of the 12 months ending Sept. 30 of each year. (2) Other income includes recoveries of amounts reimbursed from the trust fund that are not obligations of the trust fund, receipts from the fraud and abuse control program, and a small amount of miscellaneous income. (3) Includes costs of Peer Review Organizations from 1983 through 2001 (beginning with the implementation of the Prospective Payment System on Oct. 1, 1983), and costs of Quality Improvement Organizations beginning in 2002. (4) Includes costs of experiments and demonstration projects. Beginning in 1997, includes fraud and abuse control expenses, as provided for by PL 104-191. (5) Includes the lump-sum general revenue adjustment of $–2,366 mil, as provided for by PL 98-21. (6) Includes monies transferred to the SMI trust fund for home health agency costs, as provided for by PL 105-33. (7) Includes the lump-sum general review adjustment of –$1,117 million, as provided for by sec. 151 of PL 98-21. **NOTE:** Totals do not necessarily equal sums of rounded components.

TAXES

Federal Income Tax

Source: George W. Smith III, CPA, Managing Partner, George W. Smith & Company, P.C.

New 2004 Legislation

On Oct. 4, 2004, Pres. George W. Bush signed the Working Families Tax Relief Act. This law is estimated to provide $146 bil in tax cuts for individuals and businesses. Several weeks later he signed the American Jobs Creation Act into law; the 650-page act added 34 new Internal Revenue Code sections and amended more than 270 sections of the code.

Highlights of the 2004 Law

Tax Deductions. Individual taxpayers who elect to itemize can deduct the greater of their state and local income taxes or their state and local sales taxes on Schedule A.

Child Tax Credit. Congress kept the child tax credit at $1,000 in 2004. It will remain through 2010, canceling a provision that would have cut it to $700.

Filing Jointly. The standard deduction for married taxpayers filing jointly will remain double the standard deduction for single taxpayers through 2010. The 15% tax bracket amount that applies to married taxpayers will be double the 15% tax bracket amount for single taxpayers through 2010.

Vehicle Credits. Taxpayers who buy an electric vehicle may qualify for a tax credit up to a maximum of $4,000. Qualifying clean-fuel automobiles were allowed a maximum deduction of $2,000. The IRS certified the 2006 Lexus RX 400h gasoline-electric sport utility vehicle and Toyota Highlander as eligible for the clean-burning fuel $2,000 special deduction. Cars that qualify in 2005 also include the Toyota Prius, Honda Insight, Honda Civic Hybrid, Honda Accord Hybrid, and Ford Escape Hybrid.

Donated Vehicles. Starting in 2005 taxpayers can deduct only the amount of gross proceeds received by the charity from the sale of the donor's vehicle. For tax deduction purposes, individuals who donate their vehicles to charity no longer can use the "blue book" value.

Military. For tax years ending after Oct. 4, 2004, Congress treats excludable combat pay as earned income for purposes of the refundable earned income credit.

Collections. Congress also authorized the IRS to hire private contractors to collect unpaid taxes. The IRS anticipates that private collection agencies could recover up to $1.4 bil in unpaid taxes.

Citizenship. Congress closed a tax loophole that allowed wealthy individuals to relinquish their American citizenship and claim they were moving to a foreign tax haven. The law in effect states that if the individual is not really going to leave the country, the U.S. is going to tax the person.

Jobs and Growth Tax Relief Reconciliation Act of 2003

The 10-year, $350 bil package was the 3rd-largest tax cut in U.S. history.

Rate Reductions. The 2003 Act reduced individual tax rates to 25%, 28%, 33%, and a maximum rate of 35%. Unless Congress decides otherwise, the rates will revert to pre-2001 levels after 2010.

Dividend Income. Congress reduced the maximum tax rate from 38.6% to 15% for qualifying dividends paid after 2002. For taxpayers in the 10% and 15% tax brackets the rates were reduced to 5%. After 2008 dividends will be taxed at the rates they were prior to 2003.

Capital Gains. The maximum long-term (held more than one year) capital gains tax rate was reduced from 20% to 15% starting May 6, 2003. The lower 10% income tax rate dropped further to 5%. This provision expires at the end of 2008. Depending on the taxpayer's income there are higher capital gain rates on collectibles such as works of art, antiques, gold and silver, gems, stamps, and coins. For 2006 these capital gain rates are 5%, 15%, 25%, and 28%.

Other Recent Tax Laws

The Economic Growth and Tax Relief Reconciliation Act of 2001 added 440 changes to the Internal Revenue Tax Code over a 10-year period. The Job Creation and Worker Assistance Act of 2002 contained over $120 bil in tax cuts and incentives.

Classroom Materials. Elementary and secondary school teachers, principals, and counselors who buy school books or other teaching materials and supplies with their own money are allowed to deduct up to $250 of these expenses as a page-one adjustment to gross income. This deduction was extended through 2005.

Dependent Care. The maximum expense eligible for the dependent care tax credit was increased from $2,400 to $3,000 for one qualifying child or other dependent incapable of self-care, and from $4,800 to $6,000 for 2 or more dependents. The phase-out limitations for higher income also increased.

Adoption. The maximum adoption credit was increased, adjusted annually for inflation. For 2005 the credit is $10,630 per child. The exclusion from income of employer-provided adoption assistance starts to phase out at $159,450 of adjusted gross income. The credit can also be claimed for a special needs adoption whether or not the taxpayer has qualified adoption expenses.

Exemptions. The phasing out of the personal exemption and Schedule A itemized deductions for higher income taxpayers will be reduced by 1/3 in 2006 and 2007, 2/3 for 2008 and 2009, and totally eliminated in 2010.

Student Loans. The income phase-out range for the interest deduction up to $2,500 on student loans was increased to $50,000-$65,000 for single taxpayers and $100,000-$130,000 for married taxpayers filing jointly.

College. This educational deduction increased to $4,000 for qualified college tuition and related expenses. The expenses are deductible even if the taxpayer does not itemize. This deduction is repealed after 2005.

Visiting Your Tax Preparer

In 2006 the IRS predicts that over 65% of all individual income tax returns will be prepared by paid tax professionals. Here are some things to keep in mind when visiting your tax preparer.

- Time spent with your preparer may affect your bill. If you bring in the proverbial shoebox full of jumbled records and deductions, it may cost you extra to have professionals organize your records.
- Review last year's tax return. Make notes of any changes since then such as marriage, divorce, number of dependents, retirement, job changes, additional income, new deductions, etc.
- Prepare a list of questions in advance.
- Organize your records with income items first. Next, have your itemized deductions ready and in sequence (medical, taxes, interest, charitable, and other miscellaneous deductions). Save questionable items for last.
- Don't be afraid to discuss your tax situation with the preparer, especially any unusual circumstances.
- Advise your preparer if you're waiting to recieve additional records. He or she can start preparation of your tax return and include the missing data later.
- Don't hesitate to call the preparer if you receive additional information at a later time. However, if you call after the return is completed, changes may cost you additional fees.
- Review your tax return before signing it. Ask questions about any item you don't understand. Remember, must sign the return will be responsible for what it contains.
- Make sure your preparer signs the return.

IT'S A FACT: The average federal income tax refund given out by the IRS on 2004 returns received through June 17, 2005, was $2,110, up 2.4% from 2004. 95.4 mil taxpayers received refunds, down 1.5% from the previous year. The total dollar amount received by taxpayers was $201.4 bil, a 1% increase.

Recent IRS Rulings and Other Tax Matters

Combat. Military personnel serving in combat zones, deployed in "contingency operations," or hospitalized outside the United States as a result of injuries sustained while deployed, do not have to file tax returns until 180 days after they return home.

Same Sex Marriage. The IRS ruled that it is unlawful for same-sex couples to file their federal taxes under any married status, even if the jurisdiction in which the couple lives recognizes such marriages.

Weight Loss. The IRS allows a medical deduction for costs of certain weight-loss programs. Participation must be for treatment of a physician-diagnosed disease, including obesity. No deduction is allowed for purely cosmetic reasons or special diet foods.

Tax Tip. According to the IRS, the cost of home exercise equipment qualifies as a tax-deductible medical expense if prescribed by a doctor to treat obesity or illness.

Eye Surgery. The cost of certain kinds of eye surgery (radial keratomy, LASIK, etc.) to improve vision is allowed as a medical deduction.

Smoking. Taxpayers can deduct two types of aids for quitting cigarette smoking as a medical expense: (1) participation in a smoking-cessation program, and (2) prescription drugs to alleviate the effects of nicotine withdrawal. Over-the-counter products such as nicotine patches and chewing gum remain nondeductible.

Cell Phones. Cell phone expenses can be deducted as an employee business expense if the phone is used for the convenience of the employer and the use is a condition of employment.

Tax Tip. Revenues received from a garage sale usually do not result in taxable income. In most cases, the item that was sold cost more than the revenue received. Also, losses are considered personal and therefore not deductible.

Day Camp. If both spouses work, the cost of summer day camp may qualify for the child care credit.

Alimony. Payments to an individual under a written separation agreement constitute alimony for federal tax purposes even if the separation agreement is not enforceable under state law.

Whoops! Penalties and fines paid to a governmental agency or department are not deductible. This includes parking and speeding tickets as well as penalties for a late filing of a tax return.

Death Benefits. Qualified accelerated death benefits paid under a life insurance contract to terminally ill persons (certified as expected to die within 24 months) are excludable from gross income. A similar exclusion applies to the sale or assignment of insurance death benefits to another person.

Sale of Residence. Married couples filing jointly who have lived in their principal residence for at least 2 years out of the last 5-year period can exclude up to $500,000 in gain from the sale of their residence. Single taxpayers can exclude a gain up to $250,000.

Tax Tip. Rental income (for instance, a summer cottage or personal residence rented to players in a major golf tournament) is *not* taxable if it is rented for fewer than 15 days during the year.

Domestic Workers. The annual threshold dollar amount for reporting and paying Social Security and federal unemployment taxes on domestic employees, including nannies and housekeepers, remains at $1,400 in 2005. Household workers under 18 are exempt unless household work is their principal occupation.

Mileage. The mileage allowance deduction for driving to obtain medical treatment or for automobile costs incurred in a job-related move increased from 14 cents to 15 cents per mile in 2005, while cars used for volunteer work in charities remain at 14 cents per mile. The standard mileage rate for business use of autos, including leased cars, increased to 40.5 cents from 37.5 cents.

Investment Expenses. Investors can take a miscellaneous deduction on Schedule A for investment and custodial fees, trust administration fees, cost of investment advice, financial newspapers and reports, and other expenses incurred in managing their investment portfolio. However, they cannot deduct expenses for attending a convention, seminar, or similar meeting.

"Hands Off". In a unanimous 2005 decision, the U.S. Supreme Court held that individual retirement accounts (IRAs) are beyond the reach of creditors. This includes IRA assets of taxpayers who have filed for bankruptcy. Their retirement savings are also protected.

Innocent Spouse. The IRS Reform Act provides a separate liability section for spouses who are divorced, legally separated, or living apart for at least 12 months. In effect, this legislation prevents a former spouse from being held liable for the other spouse's tax liability and misdeeds.

Children. If a dependent child with taxable income cannot file an income tax return, the parent, guardian, or other legally responsible person must file a return for the child. Parents may elect to include on their income tax return the dividend and interest income of a dependent child under age 14 whose unearned income is more than $800 and gross income is less than $8,000. Form 8814, Parent's Election to Report Child's Interest and Dividends, must be attached to the parents' tax return.

Full-Time Student. A taxpayer may not claim a dependency exemption in 2005 for an individual who qualifies as a full-time student and is over age 23 at the end of the year, unless the student's gross income is less than $3,200.

Hobbies. Qualifying long-term gains for collectibles such as art, antiques, jewelry, stamps, and coins are taxed at a maximum 28%.

Frivolous Returns. Taxpayers who file frivolous income tax returns face a $500 penalty and may be subject to civil penalties of 20-75% of the underpaid tax. Those who pursue frivolous tax cases in the courts may face a penalty of up to $25,000, in addition to the taxes, interest, and civil penalties they may owe.

Tax Tip. The income ceiling for using the short and simple Form 1040EZ and the somewhat longer Form 1040A has been increased from less than $50,000 to $100,000. This change means about 1.6 mil more taxpayers may be eligible to file these user-friendly forms.

Income Tax Filing and Payment Dates

Filing Dates. The due date for filing a 2005 Form 1040, 1040A, or 1040EZ U.S. Individual Income Tax Return is Mon., Apr. 17, 2006. (The 15th falls on a Saturday.)

Estimated Taxes. Due dates for filing individual quarterly federal estimated tax payments for 2005, Form 1040-ES, are: 1st quarter, Mon, Apr. 17, 2006; 2nd quarter, Thurs., June 15; 3rd quarter, Fri., Sept. 15; and 4th quarter, Mon., Jan. 15, 2007. Different filing dates may apply for state and local tax payments.

Refunds. Individuals can call the IRS's toll-free number at 1-800-829-4477 for a recorded message or visit the IRS Web site at www.irs.gov to check on the status of their expected refund. Taxpayers may have refunds deposited directly into their bank accounts.

Need More Time? Individuals who cannot file their 2005 tax return by the due date may apply for an automatic 4-month extension to Aug. 15, 2006. Although the extension is automatic, Form 4868 must be filed no later than Apr. 17, 2006 to qualify. Extensions may also be obtained using the IRS's e-file or calling 1-888-796-1074. Approximately nine million extensions were filed by April 15, 2005, for 2004 tax returns.

Filing Penalties. The IRS can levy 2 potential penalties when a return is filed after the due date with a balance owing: one penalty is for failing to file a timely tax return, the other is for failure to pay the tax when due. In addition, interest will be charged on any unpaid tax balance.

Installment Payments. Depending on the amount of tax owed, taxpayers may apply for monthly installment payments by attaching Form 9465 to their tax return. There is a filing fee if the request is approved.

Statute of Limitations. Taxpayers have until Apr. 15, 2006 (not April 17), to file their 2002 federal tax return to claim a refund. After that date any tax or withholding refund for the year 2002, including the refundable earned income tax credit they may have coming, will be lost.

IT'S A FACT: Pres. George W. Bush and First Lady Laura Bush reported an adjusted gross income of $784,219 for 2004. Their taxable income, after deductions, was $672,788, with a tax liability of $207,307.

IRS Services and Information

Tax Questions: 1-800-829-1040

Website: www.irs.gov

Fax: 1-703-368-9694

Forms/Publications: 1-800-829-3676

English/Spanish. The IRS provides videotaped instructions both in English and in Spanish at participating libraries. Many IRS publications and tax forms, including instructions, are also printed in Spanish. For more information, call 1-800-TAX-FORM and ask for the free IRS Publication *1SP, Derechos del Contribuyente*.

Hearing Impaired. The IRS telephone service for hearing impaired persons is available for taxpayers with access to TDD equipment. The toll-free number is 1-800-829-4059.

Electronic Filing. The IRS reported that through June 17, 2005, 66.9 mil income tax returns were filed using e-file, the IRS's computerized submission system. This represented almost an 11% increase over 2004.

Individual Income Tax Rates and Tax Brackets

Taxable Income And Rates For 2005

Tax Rate	Single	Married Filing Separately	Married Filing Jointly or Qualifying Widow(er)	Head of Household	Estates and Trusts
10%	$1 to $7,300	$1 to $7,300	$1 to $14,600	$1 to $10,450	$0 to $2,000
15%	$7,301 to $29,700	$7,301 to $29,700	$14,601 to $59,400	$10,451 to $39,800	$2,001 to $4,700
25%	$29,701 to $71,950	$29,701 to $59,975	$59,401 to $119,950	$39,801 to $102,800	$4,701 to $7,150
28%	$71,951 to $150,150	$59,976 to $91,400	$119,951 to $182,800	$102,801 to $166,450	$7,151 to $9,750
33%	$150,151 to $326,450	$91,401 to $163,225	$182,801 to $326,450	$166,451 to $326,450	More than $9,750
35%	More than $326,450	More than $163,225	More than $326,450	More than $326,450	

"Kiddie Tax." If a child under age 14 has net investment income exceeding $1,600 for 2005, the excess is taxed at the parents' top marginal tax rate.

Exemptions

Dollar Amounts. The personal exemption amount for each taxpayer, spouse, and dependent for 2005 is $3,200, a $100 increase from 2004. These exemption amounts are adjusted each year for cost of living.

Phase-out. The exemption deduction for higher-income taxpayers begins to be phased out when their income exceeds certain threshold dollar amounts, adjusted annually for cost of living. Each exemption is reduced by 2% for each $2,500 ($1,250 for married persons filing separately) or fraction thereof by which adjusted gross income for year 2005 exceeds the following:

Married filing jointly	$218,950
Qualifying widow(er)	$218,950
Head of household	$182,450
Single	$145,950
Married filing separately	$109,475

These phase-out regulations will be repealed in 2010.

Standard Deductions

The standard deduction is a flat dollar amount that is subtracted from the adjusted gross income of taxpayers who do not itemize deductions.

2005 Standard Deduction Amount

Single	$5,000
Married filing jointly or qualifying widow(er)	$10,000
Married filing separately	$5,000
Head of household	$7,300

These figures are not applicable if an individual can be claimed as a dependent on another person's tax return.

Standard Deduction for Dependents. An individual reported as a dependent on another person's 2005 income tax return generally may claim on his or her own tax return only the greater of $800 or the sum of $250 plus earned income not to exceed the regular standard deduction.

Taxpayers in 2005 who are 65 or older and/or blind may claim an additional standard deduction:

Single or head of household, 65 or older OR blind	$1,250
Single or head of household, 65 or older AND blind	$2,500
Married filing jointly or qualifying widow(er), 65 or older OR blind (per person)	$1,000
Married filing jointly or qualifying widow(er), 65 or older AND blind (per person)	$2,000
Married filing separately, 65 or older OR blind	$1,000
Married filing separately, 65 or older AND blind	$2,000

Adjustments to Income

Traditional IRA. The maximum tax-deferred Individual Retirement Arrangement (IRA) deduction for a married couple filing jointly is $8,000 for 2005. Each spouse can contribute up to $4,000 annually even if one spouse has little or no income. Individuals age 50 or older can fund an additional "catch-up" amount of $500 through 2005. However, there are income limitations and phase-outs.

Withdrawals. There is a 10% penalty for IRA distributions before age 59½. Distributions paid to the beneficiary due to a disability or death of the owner are not to be subject to this penalty, nor are payments for certain unreimbursed medical expenses, higher-education expenses, or first-time home buyer acquisition costs (up to $10,000).

Tax Tip. The early IRA distribution penalty is waived if the owner takes a series of substantially equal payments for the longer of 5 years or until the owner reaches 59½ years old.

Roth IRA. Although contributions paid into a Roth IRA are not deductible, distributions of funds including investment earnings held in the account for 5 years or longer and distributed after age 59½ are free both of income tax and the 10% early withdrawal penalty at the time of distribution.

Withdrawals in less than 5 years can be subject both to income tax and the 10% withdrawal penalty regardless of age. However, earnings withdrawn for "qualified higher education expenses" of the taxpayer, spouse, or any child or grandchild of the taxpayer or spouse are taxable but not subject to the early withdrawal penalty.

Age 70½ Plus. The owner of a traditional IRA (or a SIMPLE plan, pension or profit sharing plan account) must begin receiving distributions by Apr. 1 of the calendar year following the year in which he or she reaches age 70½, even if the individual is not retired. However, any employee who works beyond age 70½ and is not a 5% or more owner of the business can continue to defer profit sharing and pension plan distributions.

IRA Publication. For more information on IRAs call the IRS at 1-800-829-3676 for a free copy of Publication 590, Individual Retirement Arrangements (IRA).

Reminder. States may not impose an income tax on retirement income if the person is no longer a resident of the state where the taxpayer earned these benefits.

Itemized Deductions

If the total amount of itemized deductions is more than the standard deduction, taxpayers generally should itemize their deductions on Schedule A, Form 1040. The following examples are just a few of the deductions that may be itemized; some are subject to income limitations.

Medical expenses that exceed 7.5% of the taxpayer's adjusted gross income are deductible. Medicines, birth control pills, and insulin qualify if prescribed by a doctor. Cosmetic surgery for congenital abnormality, for personal injury from an accident or trauma, or for a disfiguring disease also are allowed as a medical deduction. Also, long-term care insurance premiums, up to certain annual limits based on age, are deductible.

Mortgage interest paid on a primary residence or a second home are deductible. However, there are limitations on mortgages in excess of $1 mil. Interest on home equity loans also is deductible, but only covering the first $1 mil of equity debt. Credit card interest is not deductible.

Tax Tip. "Points" (up-front fees paid to obtain a lower interest rate) must usually be spread over the life of the loan. But points on initial mortgages may be fully deductible in the year they're paid.

Taxes. State and local income taxes or, if higher, sales taxes. Don't overlook real estate and personal property taxes.

Personal losses. Casualty and theft losses are deductible, but subject to the $100 and 10% limitation rule for each occurrence.

Charitable contributions. Taxpayers deducting individual contributions of $250 or more must obtain written substantiation from the charity.

Certain miscellaneous expenses are deductible, but only the amount that exceeds 2% of adjusted gross income. These include investment expenses, union and professional dues, cost of tax preparation, safe-deposit box rental fees, and certain expenses for a job search.

Miscellaneous expenses also include unreimbursed employee business expenses such as travel, automobile, telephone, and gifts. However, only 50% of the cost of customer meals and entertainment is deductible.

Moving Expenses. Taxpayers who change jobs or are transferred, usually can deduct part of their moving expenses, including travel and the cost of the moving of household goods, but not meals. The mileage rate for automobiles used in the move increased to 15 cents per mile in 2005.

Tax Credits

A tax *deduction* reduces a taxpayer's taxable income, whereas tax *credits* reduce dollar-for-dollar the amount of tax owed.

Earned Income Credit. Lower-income workers who maintain a household may be eligible for an earned income credit. It is based on total earned income such as wages, commissions, and tips. The Tax Relief Act extended the definition of qualifying children to include descendants of stepchildren and eliminated the one-year residency requirement for foster children.

The phase-out range of the earned income credit increased for joint filers by an additional $1,000 starting in 2002, up to a maximum increase of $3,000 in 2008. Starting in 2009 the credit will be adjusted annually for the cost of living. After 2010 all these changes will expire.

The Hope Scholarship Credit applies to qualified tuition and expenses for the first 2 years of postsecondary education in a degree or certificate program at an eligible institution. However, it does not apply to room and board or cost of books. The credit can be as high as $1,500.

The Lifetime Learning Credit is available for taxpayers whose postsecondary education expenses are not eligible for the Hope credit. The credit is 20% of tuition and other qualifying expenses paid for by the taxpayer, spouse, or dependents up to a total credit of $2,000 (20% of $10,000 in expenses) for all entitled students who are enrolled in an eligible educational institution. The credit begins to phase out for higher income levels.

Adoption Credit. The adoption credit for qualified expenses increased in 2005. The credit limit is per person, not per year, and is adjusted annually for inflation.

Taxable Social Security Benefits

Earnings Limitations. Social Security recipients who have not reached full retirement age lose $1 of their benefits for every $2 of earned income over $12,000.

Taxable Benefits. Up to 50% of Social Security benefits may be taxable if the person's total income is: over $25,000 but less than $34,000 for a single individual, head of household, qualifying widow(er), or a married person who is filing separately if spouses lived apart all year; or over $32,000 but less than $44,000 for married individuals filing jointly. For higher incomes, 85% of Social Security benefits may become taxable.

Good News. *Social Security benefits are not taxable if they are the only income received during the year.*

Alternative Minimum Tax

Ticking Time Bomb. The Alternative Minimum Tax (AMT) was established in 1969 to prevent people with very high incomes from using special tax breaks to pay little or no tax. It was never indexed for inflation. Because of changes in the tax law, it affects more and more middle-income taxpayers every year. The IRS projects that 20 mil taxpayers by 2006, and 30 mil by 2010, could be liable for the AMT.

The instructions included with tax forms 1040 and 1040A provide help for individuals to determine whether they are subject to the AMT. Form 6251, Alternative Minimum Tax, is used to figure out how much tax is owed.

Estate and Gift Taxes

Exclusion. The Tax Relief Reconciliation Act of 2001 increased the estate tax exclusion from $675,000 to $1 mil in 2002 and 2003, $1.5 mil in 2004 and 2005, $2 mil in 2006 through 2008, and $3.5 mil in 2009.

Estate Tax Rates. For 2001 the maximum tax rate on the value of an estate was 55%, reduced to 50% in 2002. Starting in 2005, the tax rate was further reduced to 47% and will continue to decrease until 2007 when the maximum will be 45%, and will remain at 45% until 2009. All estate taxes are repealed for the year 2010. Unless new legislation is passed prior to 2011, the estate laws revert to 2001 provisions.

Resident Alien. The estate of a resident alien is subject to the same rules as that of an American citizen. All property owned worldwide is subject to the U.S. estate tax rules and regulations.

Gifting. Citizens, resident and non-resident aliens can make tax-free gifts of up to $11,000 each year to as many individuals as he or she chooses; twice that amount with consent of the spouse even if only one spouse does the gifting.

Lifetime Gifting. A $1 mil gift tax exclusion is the limit an individual is allowed to give to other individuals (not charities) during his or her lifetime before having to pay gift taxes. The annual $11,000 gifts are not included in the gift tax exclusion.

IRS Tax Audits

The IRS projects that over 130 mil individual income tax returns will be filed for 2005. For 2004 the IRS said it audited 1,008,000 individual tax returns, less than 1% of the returns filed.

Needless to say, the agency is very good at selecting returns that will yield additional taxes. If the IRS concludes that you owe more and you disagree with the findings, you can meet with a supervisor. If you still do not agree, you can appeal to a separate Appeals Office or to the U.S. Tax Court.

For more information about audits, call the IRS at 1-800-829-3676 for its free Publication 556, Examination of Returns, Appeal Rights, and Claims for Refund. Or visit www.irs.gov

Enforcement. Out of the $10.5 bil from the current budget reserved for the IRS, approximately $4.4 bil has been set aside for enforcement and collection.

Your Rights as a Taxpayer

Congress has enacted "taxpayer bill of rights" legislation and created an Office of the Taxpayer Advocate within the IRS, with authority to order IRS personnel to issue refund checks and meet deadlines for resolving disputes. Taxpayer advocates can be contacted at 1-877-777-4778 (1-800-829-4059 for TTY/TDD). The IRS must pay legal fees if the taxpayer wins the case and the IRS cannot show it was "substantially justified" in pursuing it.

To confidentially report misconduct, waste, fraud, or abuse by an IRS employee, you can call 1-800-366-4484.

For more information ask for IRS Publication 1, Your Rights as a Taxpayer, by calling 1-800-TAX-FORM for a free copy.

Federal Outlays to States Per Dollar of Tax Revenue Received

Source: The Tax Foundation

(figures for fiscal year 2003; revised; ranked highest to lowest)

State	Outlay	State	Outlay	State	Outlay	State	Outlay	State	Outlay
District of Columbia	$6.59	Kentucky	$1.52	Arizona	$1.23	Ohio	$1.02	Colorado	$0.80
New Mexico	1.99	South Dakota	1.49	Utah	1.19	Florida	1.00	New York	0.80
Alaska	1.89	Oklahoma	1.48	Vermont	1.14	Oregon	1.00	California	0.78
Mississippi	1.83	Arkansas	1.47	Wyoming	1.13	Texas	0.98	Massachusetts	0.78
West Virginia	1.82	Louisiana	1.47	Kansas	1.13	Indiana	0.96	Illinois	0.73
North Dakota	1.75	South Carolina	1.36	North Carolina	1.09	Georgia	0.95	Nevada	0.70
Alabama	1.69	Maine	1.36	Pennsylvania	1.08	Washington	0.90	Minnesota	0.70
Montana	1.60	Maryland	1.34	Rhode Island	1.06	Michigan	0.86	Connecticut	0.65
Virginia	1.58	Idaho	1.32	Iowa	1.06	Wisconsin	0.84	New Hampshire	0.64
Hawaii	1.58	Missouri	1.31	Nebraska	1.06	Delaware	0.82	New Jersey	0.57
		Tennessee	1.29						

State Government Personal Income Tax Rates, 2005

Source: Reproduced with permission from *CCH State Tax Guide*, published and copyrighted by CCH Inc., 2700 Lake Cook Road, Riverwoods, IL 60015

Alaska, Florida, Nevada, South Dakota, Texas, Washington, and Wyoming did not have state income taxes and are thus not listed. Tax rates apply in stages—for example, a single person in Arizona making \$60,000 in taxable income would pay 2.87% on the first \$10,000 of income, 3.2% on the next \$15,000, etc. For further details, see notes at end of table.

Alabama
Single, Head of household, & Married filing separately
- \$0 to \$500 ... 2%
- \$501 to \$3,000 ... 4%
- \$3,001 and over ... 5%

Married filing jointly
- \$0 to \$1,000 ... 2%
- \$1,001 to \$6,000 ... 4%
- \$6,001 and over ... 5%

Arizona[1]
Single & Married filing separately
- \$0 to \$10,000 ... 2.87%
- \$10,001 to \$25,000 ... 3.2%
- \$25,001 to \$50,000 ... 3.74%
- \$50,001 to \$150,000 ... 4.72%
- \$150,001 and over ... 5.04%

Married filing jointly and Head of household
- \$0 to \$20,000 ... 2.87%
- \$20,001 to \$50,000 ... 3.2%
- \$50,001 to \$100,000 ... 3.74%
- \$100,001 to \$300,000 ... 4.72%
- \$300,001 and over ... 5.04%

Arkansas[2,3]
Single, Head of household, Married filing jointly, & Married filing separately
- \$0 to \$3,399 ... 1%
- \$3,400 to \$6,799 ... 2.5%
- \$6,800 to \$10,299 ... 3.5%
- \$10,300 to \$17,099 ... 4.5%
- \$17,100 to \$28,499 ... 6%
- \$28,500 and over ... 7%

California[1, 2]
Single & Married filing separately
- \$0 to \$6,319 ... 1%
- \$6,320 to \$14,979 ... 2%
- \$14,980 to \$23,641 ... 4%
- \$23,642 to \$32,819 ... 6%
- \$32,820 to \$41,476 ... 8%
- \$41,477and over ... 9.3%

Head of household
- \$0 to \$12,644 ... 1%
- \$12,645 to \$29,959 ... 2%
- \$29,960 to \$38,619 ... 4%
- \$38,620 to \$47,796 ... 6%
- \$47,797 to \$56,456 ... 8%
- \$56,457 and over ... 9.3%

Married filing jointly and surviving spouse
- \$0 to \$12,638 ... 1%
- \$12,639 to \$29,958 ... 2%
- \$29,959 to \$47,282 ... 4%
- \$47,282 to \$65,638 ... 6%
- \$65,639 to \$82,952 ... 8%
- \$82,953 and over ... 9.3%

Colorado
4.63% of federal taxable income.

Connecticut
Single & Married filing separately
- \$0 to \$10,000 ... 3%
- \$10,001 and over ... 5%

Head of household
- \$0 to \$16,000 ... 3%
- \$16,001 and over ... 5%

Married filing jointly and surviving spouse
- \$0 to \$20,000 ... 3%
- \$20,001 and over ... 5%

Delaware
Single, Head of household, Married filing jointly, & Married filing separately
- \$2,000 to \$5,000 ... 2.2%
- \$5,001 to \$10,000 ... 3.9%
- \$10,001 to \$20,000 ... 4.8%
- \$20,001 to \$25,000 ... 5.2%
- \$25,001 to \$60,000 ... 5.55%
- \$60,001 and over ... 5.95%

District of Columbia
Single, Head of household, Married filing jointly, & Married filing separately
- \$0 to \$10,000 ... 5%
- \$10,001 to \$30,000 ... 7.5%
- \$30,001 and over ... 9.3%

Georgia
Single
- \$0 to \$750 ... 1%
- \$751 to \$2,250 ... 2%
- \$2,251 to \$3,750 ... 3%
- \$3,751 to \$5,250 ... 4%
- \$5,251 to \$7,000 ... 5%
- \$7,001 and over ... 6%

Head of household, Married filing jointly, or surviving spouse
- \$0 to \$1,000 ... 1%
- \$1,001 to \$3,000 ... 2%
- \$3,001 to \$5,000 ... 3%
- \$5,001 to \$7,000 ... 4%
- \$7,001 to \$10,000 ... 5%
- \$10,001 and over ... 6%

Married filing separately
- \$0 to \$500 ... 1%
- \$501 to \$1,500 ... 2%
- \$1,501 to \$2,500 ... 3%
- \$2,501 to \$3,500 ... 4%
- \$3,501 to \$5,000 ... 5%
- \$5,001 and over ... 6%

Hawaii
Single & Married filing separately
- \$0 to \$2,000 ... 1.4%
- \$2,001 to \$4,000 ... 3.2%
- \$4,001 to \$8,000 ... 5.5%
- \$8,001 to \$12,000 ... 6.4%
- \$12,001 to \$16,000 ... 6.8%
- \$16,001 to \$20,000 ... 7.2%
- \$20,001 to \$30,000 ... 7.6%
- \$30,001 to \$40,000 ... 7.9%
- \$40,001 and over ... 8.25%

Head of household
- \$0 to \$3,000 ... 1.4%
- \$3,001 to \$6,000 ... 3.2%
- \$6,001 to \$12,000 ... 5.5%
- \$12,001 to \$18,000 ... 6.4%
- \$18,001 to \$24,000 ... 6.8%
- \$24,001 to \$30,000 ... 7.2%
- \$30,001 to \$45,000 ... 7.6%
- \$45,001 to \$60,000 ... 7.9%
- \$60,001 and over ... 8.25%

Married filing jointly and surviving spouse
- \$0 to \$4,000 ... 1.4%
- \$4,001 to \$8,000 ... 3.2%
- \$8,001 to \$16,000 ... 5.5%
- \$16,001 to \$24,000 ... 6.4%
- \$24,001 to \$32,000 ... 6.8%
- \$32,001 to \$40,000 ... 7.2%
- \$40,001 to \$60,000 ... 7.6%
- \$60,001 to \$80,000 ... 7.9%
- \$80,001 and over ... 8.25%

Idaho[1, 2, 3]
Single & Married filing separately
- \$0 to \$1,128 ... 1.6%
- \$1,129 to \$2,257 ... 3.6%
- \$2,258 to \$3,386 ... 4.1%
- \$3,387 to \$4,514 ... 5.1%
- \$4,515 to \$5,643 ... 6.1%
- \$5,644 to \$8,465 ... 7.1%
- \$8,279 to \$22,074 ... 7.4%
- \$22,577 and over ... 7.8%

Head of household, Married filing jointly, or surviving spouse
- \$0 to \$2,257 ... 1.6%
- \$2,258 to \$4,514 ... 3.6%
- \$4,515 to \$6,772 ... 4.1%
- \$6,773 to \$9,030 ... 5.1%
- \$9,031 to \$11,287 ... 6.1%
- \$11,288 to \$16,932 ... 7.1%
- \$16,933 to \$45,152 ... 7.4%
- \$45,153 and over ... 7.8%

Illinois
3% of taxable net income

Indiana
3.4% of adjusted gross income

Iowa[2]
Single, Head of household, Married filing jointly, & Married filing separately
- \$0 to \$1,269 ... 0.36%
- \$1,270 to \$2,538 ... 0.72%
- \$2,539 to \$5,076 ... 2.43%
- \$5,077 to \$11,421 ... 4.5%
- \$11,422 to \$19,035 ... 6.12%
- \$19,036 to \$25,380 ... 6.48%
- \$25,381 to \$38,070 ... 6.8%
- \$38,071 to \$57,105 ... 7.92%
- \$57,106 and over ... 8.98%

Kansas
Single, Head of household, & Married filing separately
- \$0 to \$15,000 ... 3.5%
- \$15,001 to \$30,000 ... 6.25%
- \$30,001 and over ... 6.45%

Married filing jointly
- \$0 to \$30,000 ... 3.5%
- \$30,001 to \$60,000 ... 6.25%
- \$60,001 and over ... 6.45%

Kentucky
Single, Head of household, Married filing jointly, & Married filing separately
- \$0 to \$3,000 ... 2%
- \$3,001 to \$4,000 ... 3%
- \$4,001 to \$5,000 ... 4%
- \$5,001 to \$8,000 ... 5%
- \$8,001 and over ... 6%

Louisiana[1]
Single, Head of household, & Married filing separately
- \$0 to \$12,500 ... 2%
- \$12,501 to \$25,000 ... 4%
- \$25,001 and over ... 6%

Married filing jointly
- \$0 to \$25,000 ... 2%
- \$25,001 to \$50,000 ... 4%
- \$50,001 and over ... 6%

Maine[2]
Single & Married filing separately
- \$0 to \$4,449 ... 2%
- \$4,450 to \$8,849 ... 4.5%
- \$8,850 to \$17,699 ... 7%
- \$17,770 and over ... 8.5%

Head of household
- \$0 to \$6,649 ... 2%
- \$6,650 to \$13,249 ... 4.5%
- \$13,250 to \$26,599 ... 7%
- \$26,600 and over ... 8.5%

Married filing jointly
- \$0 to \$8,899 ... 2%
- \$8,900 to \$17,699 ... 4.5%
- \$17,700 to \$35,449 ... 7%
- \$35,450 and over ... 8.5%

Maryland
Single, Head of household, Married filing jointly, & Married filing separately
- \$0 to \$1,000 ... 2%
- \$1,001 to \$2,000 ... 3%
- \$2,001 to \$3,000 ... 4%
- \$3,001 and over ... 4.75%

Massachusetts
- Short-term capital gains ... 12%
- All other income ... 5.3%

Michigan
3.9% of taxable income

Minnesota[2]
Single
- \$0 to \$19,890 ... 5.35%
- \$19,891 to \$65,330 ... 7.05%
- \$65,331 and over ... 7.85%

Head of household
- \$0 to \$24,490 ... 5.35%
- \$24,491 to \$98,390 ... 7.05%
- \$98,391 and over ... 7.85%

Married filing jointly
- \$0 to \$29,070 ... 5.35%
- \$29,071 to \$115,510 ... 7.05%
- \$115,511 and over ... 7.85%

Married filing separately
- \$0 to \$14,540 ... 5.35%
- \$14,541 to \$57,760 ... 7.05%
- \$57,761 and over ... 7.85%

Mississippi
Single, Head of household, Married filing jointly, & Married filing separately
- \$0 to \$5,000 ... 3%
- \$5,001 to \$10,000 ... 4%
- \$10,001 and over ... 5%

Missouri
Single, Head of household, Married filing jointly, & Married filing separately
- \$0 to \$1,000 ... 1.5%
- \$1,001 to \$2,000 ... 2%
- \$2,001 to \$3,000 ... 2.5%
- \$3,001 to \$4,000 ... 3%
- \$4,001 to \$5,000 ... 3.5%
- \$5,001 to \$6,000 ... 4%
- \$6,001 to \$7,000 ... 4.5%
- \$7,001 to \$8,000 ... 5%
- \$8,001 to \$9,000 ... 5.5%
- \$9,001 and over ... 6%

Montana[2,3]
Single, Head of household, Married filing jointly, & Married filing separately
- \$0 to \$2,299 ... 1%
- \$2,300 to \$4,099 ... 2%
- \$4,100 to \$6,199 ... 3%
- \$6,200to \$8,399 ... 4%
- \$8,400 to \$10,799 ... 5%
- \$10,800 to \$13,899 ... 6%
- \$3,900 and over ... 6.9%

Nebraska
Single
- \$0 to \$2,400 ... 2.56%
- \$2,401 to \$17,000 ... 3.57%
- \$17,001 to \$26,500 ... 5.12%
- \$26,501 and over ... 6.84%

Head of household
- \$0 to \$3,800 ... 2.56%
- \$3,801 to \$24,000 ... 3.57%
- \$24,001 to \$35,000 ... 5.12%
- \$35,001 and over ... 6.84%

Married filing jointly
- \$0 to \$4,000 ... 2.56%
- \$4,001 to \$30,000 ... 3.57%
- \$30,001 to \$46,750 ... 5.12%
- \$46,751 and over ... 6.84%

Married filing separately
- \$0 to \$2,000 ... 2.56%
- \$2,001 to \$15,000 ... 3.57%
- \$15,001 to \$23,375 ... 5.12%
- \$23,376 and over ... 6.84%

New Hampshire
5% on interest and dividends only

New Jersey
Single & Married filing separately
- \$0 to \$20,000 ... 1.4%
- \$20,001 to \$35,000 ... 1.75%
- \$35,001 to \$40,000 ... 3.5%
- \$40,001 to \$75,000 ... 5.525%
- \$75,001 to \$500,000 ... 6.37%
- \$500,001 and over ... 8.97%

Head of household & Married filing jointly
- \$0 to \$20,000 ... 1.4%
- \$20,001 to \$50,000 ... 1.75%
- \$50,001 to \$70,000 ... 2.45%
- \$70,001 to \$80,000 ... 3.5%
- \$80,001 to \$150,000 ... 5.525%
- \$150,001 to \$500,000 ... 6.37%
- \$500,001 and over ... 8.97%

New Mexico[1]
Single
- \$0 to \$5,500 ... 1.7%
- \$5,501 to \$11,000 ... 3.2%
- \$11,001 to \$16,000 ... 4.7%
- \$16,001 and over ... 6%

Head of household
- \$0 to \$7,000 ... 1.7%
- \$7,001 to \$14,000 ... 3.2%
- \$14,001 to \$20,000 ... 4.7%
- \$20,001 and over ... 6%

Married filing jointly
- \$0 to \$8,000 ... 1.7%
- \$8,001 to \$16,000 ... 3.2%
- \$16,001 to \$24,000 ... 4.7%
- \$24,001 and over ... 6%

Married filing separately
- \$0 to \$4,000 ... 1.7%
- \$4,001 to \$8,000 ... 3.2%
- \$8,001 to \$12,000 ... 4.7%
- \$12,001 and over ... 6%

New York

Single & Married filing separately
$0 to $8,000 . . . . 4%
$8,001 to $11,000 . . . . . 4.5%
$11,001 to $13,000 . . . 5.25%
$13,001 to $20,000 . . . . 5.9%
$20,001 to $100,000 . . 6.85%
$100,001 to $500,000 . 7.25%
$500,001 and over 7.7%

Head of Household
$0 to $11,000 . . . . 4%
$11,001 to $15,000 . . . . 4.5%
$15,001 to $17,000 . . . 5.25%
$17,001 to $30,000 . . . . 5.9%
$30,001 to $125,000 . . 6.85%
$125,001 to $500,000 . 7.25%
$500,001 and over 7.7%

Married filing jointly
$0 to $16,000 . . . . 4%
$16,001 to $22,000 . . . . 4.5%
$22,001 to $26,000 . . . 5.25%
$26,001 to $40,000 . . . . 5.9%
$40,001 to $150,000 . . 6.85%
$150,001 to $500,000 . 7.25%
$500,001 and over 7.7%

North Carolina

Single
$0 to $12,750 . . . . 6%
$12,751 to $60,000 . . . . . 7%
$60,001 to $120,000 . . 7.75%
$120,001 and over 8.25%

Head of household
$0 to $17,000 . . . . 6%
$17,001 to $80,000 . . . . . 7%
$80,001 to $160,000 . . 7.75%
$160,001 and over 8.25%

Married filing jointly
$0 to $21,250 . . . . 6%
$21,251 to $100,000 . . . . 7%
$100,001 to $200,000 . 7.75%
$200,001 and over 8.25%

Married filing separately
$0 to $10,625 . . . . 6%
$10,626 to $50,000 . . . . . 7%
$50,001 to $100,000 . . 7.75%
$100,001 and over 8.25%

North Dakota[2]

Single
$0 to $29,700 . . . . 2.1%
$29,701 to $71,950 . . . 3.92%
$71,951 to $150,150 . . 4.34%
$150,151 to $326,450 . 5.04%
$326,451 and over 5.54%

Head of Household
$0 to $39,800 . . . . 2.1%
$39,801 to $102,800 . . 3.92%
$102,801 to $166,450 . 4.34%
$166,451 to $326,450 . 5.04%
$326,451 and over . . . 5.54%

Married filing jointly
$0 to $49,600 . . . . 2.1%
$49,601 to $119,950 . . 3.92%
$119,951 to $182,800 . 4.34%
$182,801 to $326,450 . 5.04%
$326,451 and over . . . 5.54%

Married filing separately
$0 to $24,800 . . . . 2.1%
$24,801 to $59,975 . . . 3.92%
$59,976 to $91,400 . . . 4.34%
$91,401 to $163,225 . . 5.04%
$163,226 and over . . . 5.54%

Ohio

Single, Head of household, Married filing jointly, & Married filing separately
$0 to $5,000 . . . . 0.712%
$5,001 to $10,000 . . . 1.424%
$10,001 to $15,000 . . 2.847%
$15,001 to $20,000 . . 3.559%
$20,001 to $40,000 . . . 4.27%
$40,001 to $80,000 . . 4.983%
$80,001 to $100,000 . 5.693%
$100,001 to $200,000 . 6.61%
$200,001 and over . . 7.185%

Oklahoma

Single & Married filing separately
$0 to $1,000 . . . . 0.5%
$1,001 to $2,500 . . . . 1%
$2,501 to $3,750 . . . . 2%
$3,751 to $4,900 . . . . 3%
$4,901 to $6,200 . . . . 4%
$6,201 to $7,700 . . . . 5%
$7,701 to $10,000 . . . . 6%
$10,001 and over 6.65%

Head of household & Married filing jointly
$0 to $2,000 . . . . 0.5%
$2,001 to $5,000 . . . . 1%
$5,001 to $7,500 . . . . 2%
$7,501 to $9,800 . . . . 3%
$9,801 to $12,200 . . . . 4%
$12,201 to $15,000 . . . . . . 5%
$15,001 to $21,000 . . . . . . 6%
$21,001 and over 6.65%

Oregon[2]

Single & Married filing separately
$0 to $2,650 . . . . 5%
$2,651 to $6,650 . . . . 7%
$6,651 and over 9%

Married filing jointly and Head of household
$0 to $5,200 . . . . 5%
$5,201 to $13,000 . . . . . . 7%
$13,001 and over 9%

Pennsylvania

3.07% of taxable compensation, net profits, net gains from the sale of property, rent, royalties, dividends, interest, etc.

Rhode Island

Generally, 25% of the federal income tax rates, including capital gains and other special rates for types of income in effect before enactment of the 2001 Economic Growth and Tax Relief Reconciliation Act

South Carolina[2,3]

Single, Head of household, Married filing jointly, & Married filing separately
$0 to $2,530 . . . . 2.5%
$2,531 to $5,060 . . . . 3%
$5,061 to $7,590 . . . . 4%
$7,591 to $10,120 . . . . . . 5%
$10,121 to $12,650 . . . . . 6%
$12,651 and over 7%

Tennessee

6% of interest and dividends

Utah

Single & Married filing separately
$0 to $863 . . . . 2.3%
$864 to $1,726 . . . . 3.3%
$1,727 to $2,588 . . . . . . 4.2%
$2,589 to $3,450 . . . . . . 5.2%
$3,451 to $4,313 . . . . 6%
$4,314 and over 7%

Head of household & Married filing jointly
$0 to $1,726 . . . . 2.3%
$1,727 to $3,450 . . . . . . 3.3%
$3,451 to $5,176 . . . . . . 4.2%
$5,177 to $6,900 . . . . . . 5.2%
$6,901 to $8,626 . . . . 6%
$8,627 and over 7%

Vermont[2,3]

Single
$0 to $29,050 . . . . 3.6%
$29,051 to $70,350 . . . . 7.2%
$70,351 to $146,750 . . . 8.5%
$146,751 to $319,100 . . 9.0%
$319,101 and over 9.5%

Head of Household
$0 to $38,900 . . . . 3.6%
$38,901 to $100,500 . . . 7.2%
$100,501 to $162,700 . . 8.5%
$162,701 to $319,100 . . 9.0%
$319,101 and over 9.5%

Married filing jointly
$0 to $48,500 . . . . 3.6%
$48,501 to $117,250 . . . 7.2%
$117,251 to $178,650 . . 8.5%
$178,651 to $819,100 . . 9.0%
$319,101 and over 9.5%

Married filing separately
$0 to $24,250 . . . . 3.6%
$24,231 to $58,625 . . . . 7.2%
$58,626 to $89,325 . . . . 8.5%
$89,326 to $159,550 . . . 9.0%
$159,551 and over 9.5%

Virginia

Single, Head of household, Married filing jointly, & Married filing separately
$0 to $3,000 . . . . 2%
$3,001 to $5,000 . . . . 3%
$5,001 to $17,000 . . . . 5%
$17,001 and over 5.75%

West Virginia

Single, Head of household, & Married filing jointly
$0 to $10,000 . . . . 3%
$10,001 to $25,000 . . . . . . 4%
$25,001 to $40,000 . . . . 4.5%
$40,001 to $60,000 . . . . . . 6%
$60,001 and over 6.5%

Married filing separately
$0 to $5,000 . . . . 3%
$5,001 to $12,500 . . . . 4%
$12,501 to $20,000 . . . . 4.5%
$20,001 to $30,000 . . . . . . 6%
$30,001 and over 6.5%

Wisconsin[1, 2]

Single and Head of household
$0 to $8,840 . . . . 4.6%
$8,841 to $17,680 . . . . 6.15%
$17,631 to $132,580 . . . 6.5%
$132,581 and over . . . 6.75%

Married filing jointly
$0 to $11,780 . . . . 4.6%
$11,781 to $23,570 . . . 6.15%
$23,571 to $176,770 . . . 6.5%
$176,771 and over . . . 6.75%

Married filing separately
$0 to $5,890 . . . . 4.6%
$5,891 to $11,780 . . . . 6.15%
$11,781 to $88,390 . . . . 6.5%
$88,91 and over 6.75%

(1) Community property state in which one-half of the community income is usually taxable to each spouse. (2) Brackets indexed for inflation annually. (3) 2005 adjusted brackets not currently available. Bracketed rates listed are for 2004. **Colorado:** Alternative minimum tax imposed. Qualified taxpayers may pay alternative tax of 0.5% of gross receipts from sales. **Connecticut:** Resident estates and trusts are subject to the 5% income tax rate. Additional state minimum tax imposed on resident individuals, trusts, and estates is equal to the amount by which the minimum tax exceeds the basic income tax (the lesser of (a) 19% of adjusted federal tentative minimum tax, or (b) 5.5% of adjusted federal alternative minimum taxable income). Separate provisions apply for non- and part-year resident individuals, trusts, and estates. **Idaho:** Each person (joint returns deemed one person) filing a return pays additional $10. **Illinois:** Additional personal property replacement tax of 1.5% of net income is imposed on partnerships, trusts, and S corporations. **Indiana:** Counties may impose an adjusted gross income tax on residents at .5%, .75%, or 1%, and at .25% on nonresidents or a county option income tax at rates ranging between .2% and 1%, with the rate on nonresidents equal to one-fourth of the rate on residents. **Iowa:** An alternative minimum tax of 6.7% of alternative minimum income if the minimum tax exceeds the taxpayer's regular income tax liability. The minimum tax is 75% of the maximum regular tax rate. **Maine:** Additional state minimum tax is imposed equal to the amount by which the state minimum tax (27% of adjusted federal tentative minimum tax) exceeds Maine income tax liability, other than withholding tax liability. **Michigan:** Persons with business activity allocated or apportioned to Michigan are also subject to a single business tax on an adjusted tax base. **Minnesota:** A 6.4% alternative minimum tax is imposed. **Montana:** Minimum tax, $1. **Nebraska:** The tax rates in the schedules are determined by multiplying the primary rate set by the legislature by the following factors for the brackets, from lowest to highest bracket. For tax years beginning on or after Jan. 1, 2003, the respective factors are: 0.6932, 0.9646, 1.3846, and 1.848. For tax years beginning before Jan. 1, 2003, the respective factors are: 0.6784, 0.9432, 1.3541, and 1.8054. The figure obtained for each bracket is rounded to the nearest hundredth of 1%. One rate schedule is to be established for each federal filing status (Sec. 77-2715.02). **New Mexico:** Qualified taxpayers may pay alternative tax of 0.75% of gross receipts from New Mexico sales. **New York:** A supplemental tax is imposed to recapture the tax table benefit. The supplemental tax is calculated in accordance with NY Tax Law Sec. 601(d). Special provisions apply for tax years beginning in 2003, 2004, 2005 because of the temporary increase in the state personal income tax rates for taxpayers at higher income levels. **Oklahoma:** Rates given are for taxpayers not deducting federal income tax. Rates for married individuals filing jointly, surviving spouses, and heads of households deducting federal income tax range from .50% of the first $2,000 to 10% of income over $24,000. For single individuals and married individuals filing separately deducting federal income tax, rates range from .50% of the first $1,000 to 10% of income over $16,000. **Vermont:** The tax amount in the schedules is increased by 24% of a taxpayer's federal tax liability for: additional taxes assessed due to early withdrawals from qualified retirement plans, individual retirement accounts, and medical savings accounts; recapture of the federal investment tax credit; or tax on qualified lump-sum distributions of pension income not included in federal taxable income. The amount of tax is decreased by 24% of the reduction in the taxpayer's federal liability due to farm income averaging. **West Virginia:** Minimum tax equal to the excess by which 25% of any federal minimum tax or alternative minimum tax for the taxable year exceeds the sum of the primary tax for West Virginia personal income tax purposes for the taxable year. **Wisconsin:** A permanant recycling surcharge is imposed on individuals, estates, partnerships, and trusts with at least $4 million in gross receipts, except those entities engaged only in farming, at the rate of the greater of $25 or .2% of net business income as allocated or apportioned to Wisconsin. The maximum surcharge is $9,800. An individual, estate, trust, or partnership engaged in farming with more than $1 million in gross receipts is subject to a surcharge of $25.

ASSOCIATIONS AND SOCIETIES

Source: World Almanac questionnaire; World Almanac research

Selected list, generally by first distinctive **key word** in each title; e.g., Retired Persons, American Association of. Listed by acronym when that is the official name. Founding year in parentheses; figure after ZIP code = membership as reported. Information, especially website addresses, subject to change. For other organizations, see Directory of Sports Organizations; Where to Get Help in Health chapter; Membership of Religious Groups in Religion chapter; Major International Organizations in Nations chapter.

AAA (American Automobile Assn.) (1902), 1000 AAA Dr., Box 28, Heathrow, FL 32746; www.aaa.com
AARP. See Retired Persons, American Assn. of
Abortion Federation, National (1977), 1755 Massachusetts Ave. NW, Ste. 600, Washington, DC 20036; 400 institutions; www.prochoice.org
Academies, Natl. (1863), 500 Fifth St. NW, Washington, DC 20001; approx. 6,000; www.nationalacademies.org
Accountants, American Institute of Certified Public (1887), 1211 Ave. of the Americas, New York, NY 10036; 336,000+; www.aicpa.org
Actuaries, Society of (1949), 475 N. Martingale Rd., Ste. 600, Schaumburg, IL 60173; 17,000; www.soa.org
Administrative Professionals, Intl. Assn. of (1942), 10502 NW Ambassador Dr., Kansas City, MO 64195-0404; 40,000; www.iaap-hq.org
Collegiate Schools of Business, Assn. to Advance (AACSB) (1916), 777 S. Harbour Island Blvd., Ste. 750, Tampa, FL 33602; 950+ institutions; www.aacsb.edu
Advancement and Support of Education, Council for (1974); 1307 New York Ave. NW, Ste. 1000, Washington, DC 20005; 3,000 schools; www.case.org
Aeronautic Assn., Natl. (1922), 1737 King St., Ste. 220, Alexandria, VA 22314; 3,000; www.naa-usa.org
Aerospace Industries Assn. of America Inc. (1919), 1000 Wilson Blvd., Ste. 1700, Arlington, VA 22209; 104 cos.; www.aia-aerospace.org
Aerospace Medical Assn. (1929), 320 S. Henry St., Alexandria, VA 22314; 3,100; www.asma.org
AFCEA (Armed Forces Communications and Electronics Assn.) (1946), 4400 Fair Lakes Ct., Fairfax, VA 22033; 20,000 indiv., 11,000 corp.; www.afcea.org
African-American Life and History, Assn. for the Study of (1915), CB Powell Building, 525 Bryant St., Ste. C142, Washington, DC 20059; 3,500; www.asalh.org
AFS Intercultural Programs USA (1947), 198 Madison Ave., 8th Fl., New York, NY 10016; www.afs.org/usa
Agricultural Engineers, American Soc. of (ASAE) (1907), 2950 Niles Road, St. Joseph, MI 49085; 9,000; www.asae.org
Air & Waste Management Assn. (1907), One Gateway Center, 3rd Fl., 420 Fort Duquesne Blvd., Pittsburgh, PA 15222; 9,000+; www.awma.org
Aircraft Owners and Pilots Assn. (1939), 421 Aviation Way, Frederick, MD 21701; 400,000+; www.aopa.org
Air Force Assn. (1946), 1501 Lee Hwy., Arlington, VA 22209; 230+ chapt.; www.afa.org
Al-Anon/Alateen (1951), 1600 Corporate Landing Pkwy., Virginia Beach, VA 23454; www.al-anon.alateen.org
Alcoholics Anonymous (AA) (1935), Box 459, Grand Central Station, New York, NY 10163; 2,000,000+; www.aa.org
Alcoholism and Drug Dependence, Inc., Natl. Council on (1944), 22 Cortlandt St., Ste. 801, New York, NY 10007; 100 affil.; www.ncadd.org
Alexander Graham Bell Assn. for the Deaf & Hard of Hearing (1890), 3417 Volta Pl. NW, Washington, DC 20007; 5,000; www.agbell.org
Allergy, Asthma, and Immunology, American Academy of (1943), 555 E. Wells St., Ste. 2100, Milwaukee, WI 53202; 6,000; www.aaaai.org
Alpha Delta Kappa (1947), 1615 W. 92nd St., Kansas City, MO 64114; 46,563; www.alphadeltakappa.org
Alpha Lambda Delta, Natl. (1924), P.O. Box 4403, Macon, GA 31208-4403; 650,000; www.nationalald.org
Alzheimer's Assn. (1980), 225 N. Michigan Ave., 17th Fl., Chicago, IL 60611; 81 chapt.; www.alz.org
AMBUCS, Inc., Natl. (1922), 4285 Regency Court, High Point, NC 27265; 6,000; www.ambucs.com
American. See also other entries under next major word in title.
American Federation of Labor & Congress of Industrial Oranizations (AFL-CIO) (1955), 815 16th St. NW, Washington, DC 20006; 9 mil+; www.aflcio.org
American Indians, Natl. Congress of (1944), 1301 Connecticut Ave. NW, Ste. 200, Washington, DC 20036; 262 member tribes; www.ncai.org
American-Islamic Relations, Council on (1994), 453 New Jersey Ave. SE, Washington, DC 20003; www.cair-net.org
American Legion (1919), P.O. Box 1055, 700 N. Pennsylvania St., Indianapolis, IN 46206; 3 mil.; www.legion.org
American Legion Auxiliary (1919), 777 N. Meridian St., 3rd Floor, Indianapolis, IN 46204; 1 mil; www.legion-aux.org
AmeriCares Foundation (1982), 88 Hamilton Ave., Stamford, CT 06902; www.americares.org
AMIDEAST (formerly American Mideast Educational & Training Services) (1951), 1730 M St. NW, Ste. 1100, Washington, DC 20036; www.amideast.org
Amnesty Intl. USA (1961), 5 Penn Plaza, 14th Fl., New York, NY 10001; 320,000+; www.amnestyusa.org
AMVETS (American Veterans) (1943); **AMVETS Natl. Auxiliary** (1946), 4647 Forbes Blvd., Lanham, MD 20706; 250,000; www.amvets.org
Amusement Parks and Attractions, Intl. Assn. of (IAAPA) (1918), 1448 Duke St., Alexandria, VA 22316; 4,000+; www.iaapa.org
Animals, American Society for Prevention of Cruelty to (ASPCA) (1866), 424 E. 92nd St., New York, NY 10128; 750,000; www.aspca.org
Animals, People for the Ethical Treatment of (PETA) (1980), 501 Front St., Norfolk, VA 23510; 850,000; www.peta.org
Animal Welfare Institute (1951), P.O. Box 3650, Washington, DC 20027; 22,000; www.awionline.org
Anthropological Assn., American (1902), 2200 Wilson Blvd., Ste. 600, Arlington, VA 22201; 11,500; www.aaanet.org
Antiquarian Society, American (1812), 185 Salisbury St., Worcester, MA 01609; 800; www.americanantiquarian.org
APICS (Assn. for Operations Mgmt.) (1957), 5301 Shawnee Rd., Alexandria, VA 22312- 2317; 60,000; www.apics.org
Appalachian Mountain Club (1876), 5 Joy St., Boston, MA 02108; 90,000+; www.outdoors.org
Appalachian Trail Conference (1925), 799 Washington St., P.O. Box 807, Harpers Ferry, WV 25425; 125,000; www.appalachiantrail.org
Arbitration Assn., American (1926), 335 Madison Ave., 10th Fl., New York, NY 10017; 8,000; www.adr.org
Arc of the United States, The (1950), 1010 Wayne Avenue, Ste. 650, Silver Spring, MD 20910; 140,000; www.thearc.org
Archaeological Institute of America (1879), 656 Beacon St., 4th Fl., Boston, MA 02215; 9,000; www.archaeological.org
Architects, American Institute of (1857), 1735 New York Ave. NW, Washington, DC 20006; 74,000; www.aia.org
Army, Assn. of the United States (1950), 2425 Wilson Blvd., Arlington, VA 22201; 130 chapt.; www.ausa.org
Arthritis Foundation (1948), 1330 W. Peachtree St., Ste. 100, Atlanta, GA 30309; www.arthritis.org
Arts, Americans for the (1996), 1000 Vermont Ave. NW, 6th Fl., Washington, DC 20005; 1,500; www.artsusa.org
Arts and Sciences, American Academy of (1780), 136 Irving St., Cambridge, MA 02138; 4,600 fellows; www.amacad.org
ASPCA. See Animals, Amer. Soc. for Prev. of Cruelty to.
Associated Press (1848), 450 W. 33rd St., New York, NY 10001; 3,700 staff, 1,500+ newspapers, 5,000+ U.S. broadcast stations; www.ap.org
Astrologers, Inc., American Federation of (AFA, Inc.) (1938), 6535 South Rural Road, Tempe, AZ 85283; 4,000; www.astrologers.com
Astronautical Society, American (1954), 6352 Rolling Mill Pl., #102, Springfield, VA 22152; 1,500; www.astronautical.org
Astronomical Society, American (1899), 2000 Florida Ave. NW, Ste. 400, Washington, DC 20009; 6,400+; www.aas.org
Atheists, American (1963), P.O. Box 5733, Parsippany, NJ 07054; 2,300; www.atheists.org
Audubon Soc., Natl. (1905), 700 Broadway, New York, NY 10003; 600,000; www.audubon.org
Authors Guild, The (1912), 31 E. 28th St., New York, NY 10016; 8,200; www.authorsguild.org
Authors Registry, The (1995), 31 E. 28th St., New York, NY 10016; 30,000; www.authorsregistry.org
Autism Soc. of America (1965), 7910 Woodmont Ave., Ste. 300, Bethesda, MD 20814; 24,000; www.autism-society.org
Autograph Collectors Club, Universal (1965), P.O. Box 6181, Washington, DC 20044-6181; 1,300; www.uacc.org
Automobile, Aerospace, and Agricultural Implement Workers of America, United, The Intl. Union (UAW) (1935), 8000 E. Jefferson Ave., Detroit, MI 48214; 710,000; www.uaw.org
Automobile Club of America, Antique (1935), 501 W. Governor Road, P.O. Box 417, Hershey, PA 17033; 60,000; www.aaca.org
Automobile License Plate Collectors Assn. (1954), 118 Quaker Rd. Hampton, VA 23669; ; 3,000; www.alpca.org
Badminton Assn., USA (1938), One Olympic Plaza, Colorado Springs, CO 80909; 3,000; www.usabadminton.org
Bald-Headed Men of America (1973), 102 Bald Dr., Morehead City, NC 28557; approx. 22,000; baldusa.org

IT'S A FACT: The American Coaster Enthusiasts, a group dedicated to roller coaster "conservation, appreciation, knowledge, and enjoyment," was founded in 1978 by 3 reuniting roller coaster marathoners. The year before, in a publicity stunt for the 1977 movie *Roller Coaster*, the founders and other coaster lovers had met at King's Dominion amusement park in Doswell, VA. Several of the marathoners lasted nearly a week riding and sleeping on the Rebel Yell roller coaster, shattering the previous world record.

Bankers of America, Independent Community (1930), One Thomas Circle NW, Ste. 400, Washington, DC 20005; 5,000; www.icba.org

Bar Assn., American (1878), 321 N. Clark St., Chicago, IL 60610; 400,000+; www.abanet.org

Bar Assn., Federal (1920), 2215 M Street NW, Washington, DC 20037; 16,000; www.fedbar.org

Barbershop Harmony Society (1938), 7930 Sheridan Rd., Kenosha, WI 53143; 30,000; www.spebsqsa.org

Baseball Congress, American Amateur (1935), 100 W. Broadway, Farmington, NM 87401; 14,500 teams; www.aabc.us

Baseball Congress, Natl. (1934), 300 S. Sycamore, Wichita, KS 67213; www.nbcbaseball.com

Baseball Research, Inc., Society for American (1971), 812 Huron Road E #719, Cleveland, OH 44115; 6,800; www.sabr.org

Battleship Assn., American (1964), P.O. Box 711247, San Diego, CA 92171; 1,025

Beer Can Collectors of America (1970), 747 Merus Ct., Fenton, MO 63026; 4,000; www.bcca.com

Beta Gamma Sigma Honor Society (1913), 125 Weldon Pkwy., Maryland Heights, MO 63043; 360,000; www.betagammasigma.org

Beta Sigma Phi (1931), 1800 W. 91st Pl., Kansas City, MO 64114; 200,000; www.betasigmaphi.org

Better Business Bureaus, Council of (1970), 4200 Wilson Blvd., Suite 800, Arlington, VA 22203; 120 bureaus; www.bbb.org

Bible Society, American (1816), 1865 Broadway, New York, NY 10023; 136 societies; www.americanbible.org

Biblical Literature, Society of (1880), 825 Houston Mill Rd., Ste. 350, Atlanta, GA 30329; 6,000; www.sbl-site.org

Big Brothers/Big Sisters of America (1904), 230 N. 13th St., Philadelphia, PA 19107; 470 agencies; bbbsa.org

Biochemistry and Molecular Biology, American Society for (1906), 9650 Rockville Pike, Bethesda, MD 20814; 11,900; www.asbmb.org

Biological Sciences, American Institute of (1947), 1444 I St. NW, Ste. 200, Washington, DC 20005; 240,000; www.aibs.org

Blind, American Council of the (1961), 1155 15th St. NW, Ste. 1004, Washington, DC 20005; 71 orgs.; www.acb.org

Blind, Natl. Federation of the (1940), 1800 Johnson St., Baltimore, MD 21230; 50,000+; www.nfb.org

Blinded Veterans Assn. (1958), 477 H St. NW, Washington, DC 20001; 10,035; www.bva.org

Blindness America, Prevent (1908), 211 W. Wacker Dr., Ste. 1700, Chicago, IL 60606; 50,000; www.preventblindness.org

B'nai B'rith Intl. (1843), 2020 K St. NW, 7th Fl., Washington, DC 20006; 180,000; www.bnaibrith.org

Boat Owners Assn. of the U.S. (1966), 880 S. Pickett St., Alexandria, VA 22304; 575,000; www.boatUS.com

Bookplate Collectors & Designers, Amer. Soc. of (1922), P.O. Box 14964, Tucson, AZ 85732; 250; www.bookplate.org

Boy Scouts of America (1910), P.O. Box 152079, Irving, TX 75015; 4 mil+; www.scouting.org

Boys & Girls Clubs of America (1906), 1230 W. Peachtree St. NW, Atlanta, GA 30309; 4.4 mil; www.bgca.org

Bread for the World (1974), 50 F St. NW, Ste. 500, Washington, DC 20001; 54,000; www.bread.org

Brewing Chemists, American Society of (1934), 3340 Pilot Knob Road, St. Paul, MN 55121; 800+; www.asbcnet.org

Broadcasters, Natl. Assn. of (1923), 1771 N St. NW, Washington, DC 20036; www.nab.org

Business Women's Assn., American (1949), 9100 Ward Pkwy., P.O. Box 8728, Kansas City, MO 64114; 55,000; www.abwa.org

Button Society, Natl. (1938), 2733 Juno Pl., Akron, OH 44333-4137; 3,500+

Camp Fire USA (formerly Camp Fire Boys & Girls) (1910), 4601 Madison Ave., Kansas City, MO 64112; 750,000; www.campfireusa.org

Camping Assn., American (1910), 5000 State Rd. 67 N., Martinsville, IN 46151; 7,000+; www.acacamps.org

Cancer Society, American (1913), 1599 Clifton Rd. NE, Atlanta, GA 30329; 3,400 local offices; www.cancer.org

Cartoonists Society, Natl. (1948), 1133 West Morse Blvd., Ste. 201, Winter Park, FL 32789; 600; www.reuben.org

Cat Fanciers' Assn., The (1906), P.O. Box 1005, Manasquan, NJ 08736; 657 clubs; www.cfainc.org

Catholic Bishops, United States Conference of (1966), 3211 4th St. NE, Washington, DC 20017; 402 members, 350 staff; www.nccbuscc.org

Catholic Church Extension Society of the USA (1905), 150 S. Wacker Dr., 20th Fl., Chicago, IL 60606; www.catholic-extension.org

Catholic Daughters of the Americas (1903), 10 West 71st St., New York, NY 10023; 95,000; www.catholicdaughters.org

Catholic Educational Assn., Natl. (1904), 1077 30th St. NW, Ste. 100, Washington, DC 20007; 200,000; www.ncea.org

Catholic Historical Soc., American (1884), 263 S. Fourth St., Philadelphia, PA 19106-3819; 450; www.amchs.org

Catholic Library Association (1921), 100 North St., Ste. 224, Pittsfield, MA 01201-5109; 1,000; www.cathla.org

Catholic War Veterans, USA Inc. (1935), 441 N. Lee St., Alexandria, VA 22314-2301; 20,000; cwv.org

Ceramic Society, The American (1899), 735 Ceramic Pl., Westerville, OH 43081; 7,500; www.ceramics.org

Cerebral Palsy, Inc., United (1949), 1660 L St. NW, Ste. 700, Washington, DC 20036; 100 affiliates; www.ucp.org

Computing Professionals, Institute for Certification of (1973), 2350 E. Devon Ave., Ste. 115, Des Plaines, IL 60018-4610; 50,000; www.iccp.org

Chamber of Commerce of the U.S.A. (1912), 1615 H St. NW, Washington, DC 20062; 215,000; www.uschamber.com

Chamber Music Players, Inc., Amateur (1969), 1123 Broadway, Rm. 304, New York, NY 10010; 5,200; www.acmp.net

Chemical Society, American (1876), 1155 16th St. NW, Washington, DC 20036; 158,000; www.chemistry.org

Chemistry Council, American (1872), 1300 Wilson Blvd., Arlington, VA 22209; 170 cos.; www.americanchemistry.com

Chess Federation, U.S. (1939), P.O. Box 3967, Crossville, TN 38557; 90,000+; www.uschess.org

Chiefs of Police, Intl. Assn. of (1893), 515 N. Washington St., Alexandria, VA 22314; 20,000+; www.theiacp.org

Childhood Education Intl., Assn. for (1892), 17904 Georgia Ave., Ste. 215, Olney, MD 20832; 12,000; www.acei.org

Children's Aid Society (1912), 105 E. 22nd St., New York, NY 10010; www.childrensaid.org

Children's Book Council, The (1945), 12 W. 37th St., 2nd Fl., New York, NY 10018; 75 publishers; www.cbcbooks.org

Child Welfare League of America (1920), 440 First St. NW, 3rd Fl., Washington, DC 20001; 900 agencies; www.cwla.org

Chiropractic Assn., American (1963), 1701 Clarendon Blvd., Arlington, VA 22209; 18,000; www.amerchiro.org

Chris-Craft Antique Boat Club (1973), 217 S. Adams St., Tallahassee, FL 32301-1734; 3,000; www.chris-craft.org

Christian Children's Fund (1938), 2821 Emerywood Pkwy., Richmond, VA 23294; 159 staff; www.christianchildrensfund.org

Cities, Natl. League of (1924), 1301 Pennsylvania Ave. NW, Ste. 550, Washington, DC 20004; 1,600+; www.nlc.org

Civil Air Patrol (1941), 105 S. Hansell St., Bldg. 714, Maxwell AFB, AL 36112; 58,000; www.cap.gov

Civil Engineers, American Society of (1852), 1801 Alexander Bell Dr., Reston, VA 20191; 123,000+; www.asce.org

Civil Liberties Union, American (ACLU) (1920), 125 Broad St., 18th Fl., New York, NY 10004; 400,000; www.aclu.org

Coaster Enthusiasts, American (1978), 13355 10th Ave. N, Ste. 108, Minneapolis, MN 55441; 8,000; www.aceonline.org

Coast Guard Combat Veterans Assn. (1985), P.O. Box 544, Westfield Center, OH 44251; 1,800; www.aug.edu/~libwrw/cgcva/cgcva.htm

Collectors, Natl. Assn. of (1996), 18222 Flower Hill Way, #299, Gaithersburg, MD 20879; 30,000; collectors.org

Co-dependents Anonymous (1986), P.O. Box 33577; Phoenix, AZ 85067; www.codependents.org

College Admission Counseling, Natl. Assn. for (1937), 1631 Prince Street, Alexandria, VA 22314; 8,000; www.nacac.com

College Board, The (1900), 45 Columbus Ave., New York, NY 10023; 4,700 inst.; www.collegeboard.org

College Music Society, The (1958), 312 East Pine St., Missoula, MT 59802; 8,800; www.music.org

Colleges and Universities, Assn. of American (1915), 1818 R St. NW, Washington, DC 20009; 1,000+ institutions; www.aacu.org

Collegiate Schools of Business, Assn. to Advance (AACSB) (1916), 777 S. Harbour Island Blvd., Ste. 750, Tampa, FL

Colonial Dames XVII Century, Natl. Soc. (1915), 1300 New Hampshire Ave. NW, Washington, DC 20036; 13,000+; www.colonialdames17c.net

Commercial Law League of America (1895), 70 E. Lake St., Ste. 630, Chicago, IL 60601; 4,000; www.clla.org
Common Cause (1970), 1250 Connecticut Ave. NW, Ste. 600, Washington, DC 20036; 300,000+; www.commoncause.org
Communication Assn., Natl. (1914), 1765 N St. NW, Washington, DC, 20036; 7,700; www.natcom.org
Community & Justice, National Conference for (1927), 475 Park Ave. S.; New York, NY 10016; 55 offices; www.nccj.org
Community Colleges, American Assn. of (1920), One Dupont Circle NW, Ste. 410, Washington, DC 20036; 1,100 inst; www.aacc.nche.edu
Composers, Authors & Publishers, American Soc. of (ASCAP) (1914), One Lincoln Plaza, New York, NY 11217; 200,000; www.ascap.com
Composers/USA, Natl. Assn. of (1933), P.O. Box 49256, Barrington Station, Los Angeles, CA 90049; 400+; www.musicusa.org/nacusa
Computing Machinery, Assn. for (1947), 1515 Broadway, 17th Fl., New York, NY 10036; 78,000+; www.acm.org
Computing Professionals, Institute for Certification of (1973), 2350 E. Devon Ave., Ste. 115, Des Plaines, IL 60018-4610; 50,000; www.iccp.org
Concerned Women for America (1979), 1015 Fifteenth St. NW, Ste. 1100, Washington, DC 20005; 500,000; www.cwfa.org
Congress of Racial Equality (CORE) (1942), 817 Broadway, 3rd Floor, New York, NY 10003; 82,000; www.core-online.org
Conscientious Objectors, Central Committee for (1948), 405 14th St., #205, Oakland, CA 94612; www.objector.org
Construction Inspectors, Assn. of (1974), 1224 N. Nokomis NE, Alexandria, MN 56308; 1,000; www.iami.org/aci
Construction Specifications Institute (1948); 99 Canal Center Plaza, Ste. 300, Alexandria, VA 22301; 17,000; www.csi net.org
Consumer Federation of America (1968), 1424 16th St. NW, Ste. 604, Washington, DC 20036; 300 member organizations; www.consumerfed.org
Consumer Interests, American Council on (ACCI) (1953), 415 S. Duff Ave. Ste. C, Ames, IA 50010-6600; 750; www.consumerinterests.org
Consumers Union of the U.S. (1936), 101 Truman Ave., Yonkers, NY 10703; 405,990; www.consumersunion.org
Contract Bridge League, American (1937), 2990 Airways Blvd., Memphis, TN 38116; 160,000; www.acbl.org
Co-op America (1982), 1612 K St. NW, Ste. 600, Washington, DC 20006; 50,000 indiv., 2,500 cos.; www.coopamerica.org
Correctional Assn., American (1870), 4380 Forbes Blvd., Lanham, MD 20706; 20,000; www.aca.org
Cosmetology Assn., Natl. (1921); 401 N. Michigan Ave., Chicago, IL 60611; 25,000; www.ncacares.org
Counseling Assn., American (1952), 5999 Stevenson Ave., Alexandria, VA 22304; 52,000; www.counseling.org
Country Music Assn. (1958), One Music Circle S., Nashville, TN 37203; 5,500; www.CMAworld.com
Craft & Hobby Assn.(2004), 319 E. 54th St., Elmwood Park, NJ 07407; 4,900; www.hobby.org
Crime and Delinquency, Natl. Council on (1907), 1970 Broadway, Ste. 500, Oakland, CA 94612; 300+; www.nccdcrc.org
Croplife America (1933), 1156 15th St. NW, Ste. 400, Washington, DC 20005; 80 cos.; www.croplifeamerica.org
Cryogenic Soc. of America, Inc. (1964), 1033 South Blvd., Ste. 13, Oak Park, IL 60302; 500; www.cryogenicsociety.org
Customs Brokers and Forwarders Assn. of America, Inc., Natl. (1897), 1200 18th St. NW, Ste. 901, Washington, DC 20036; 700; www.ncbfaa.org
Cystic Fibrosis Foundation (1955), 6931 Arlington Rd., Bethesda, MD 20814; 30,000; www.cff.org
Dark-Sky Association, Intl. (1988), 3225 N. First Ave., Tucson, AZ 85719-2103; 10,629; www.darksky.org
Daughters of the American Revolution Natl. Society (1890), 1776 D Street NW, Washington, DC 20006; 168,000; www.dar.org
Daughters of the Confederacy, United (1894), 328 North Blvd., Richmond, VA 23220; 25,000; www.hqudc.org
Deaf, Natl. Assn. of the (1880), 814 Thayer Ave., Ste. 250, Silver Spring, MD 20910; 16,500; www.nad.org
Defenders of Wildlife (1947), 1130 17th St. NW, Washington, DC 20030; 480,000; www.defenders.org
Delta Kappa Gamma Society Intl. (1929), 416 W. 12th St., Austin, TX 78767; 136,000; www.deltakappagamma.org
Democratic Natl. Committee (1848), 430 S. Capitol St. SE, Wash., DC 20003; 447 elected mem.; www.democrats.org
Dental Assn., American (1859), 211 E. Chicago Ave., Chicago, IL 60611; 152,000; www.ada.org
Diabetes Assn., American (1940), 1701 North Beauregard St., Alexandria, VA 22311; 416,967; www.diabetes.org
Dialect Society, American (1889), c/o Allan Metcalf, English Dept., MacMurray College, 447 E. College Ave., Jacksonville, IL 62650; 500; www.americandialect.org
Directors Guild of America (1936), 7920 Sunset Blvd., Los Angeles, CA 90046; 12,700+; www.dga.org
Disabled American Veterans (1932), 3725 Alexandria Pike, Cold Spring, KY 41076; 1,000,000; www.dav.org
Disabled Sports USA (1967), 451 Hungerford Dr., Ste. 100, Rockville, MD 20850; 60,000+; www.dsusa.org
Doctors Without Borders/Médecins Sans Frontières (1971), 333 Seventh Ave., 2nd Fl., New York, NY 10001; 3,400+ missions; www.doctorswithoutborders.org
Down Syndrome Society, Natl. (1979), 666 Broadway, 8th Fl., New York, NY 10012; 30,000; www.ndss.org
Ducks Unlimited (1937), One Waterfowl Way, Memphis, TN 38120; 620,000; www.ducks.org
Eagles, Fraternal Order of (1898), 1623 Gateway Circle South, Grove City, OH 43123; 700 chapt.; www.foe.com
Easter Seals (1919), 230 W. Monroe St., Ste. 1800, Chicago, IL 60606; www.easterseals.org
Eastern Star, General Grand Chapter, Order of the (1876), 1618 New Hampshire Ave. NW, Washington, DC 20009; 1 mil.; www.easternstar.org
Edsel Club (1967), 19296 Tuckaway Ct., N. Fort Myers, FL 33903; 300; www.edselworld.com
Education, American Council on (1918), One Dupont Circle NW, Ste. 800, Washington, DC 20036; 1,800 org.; www.acenet.edu
Education, Council for Advancement & Support of (1974), 1307 New York Ave. NW, Ste 1000, Washington, DC 20005; 3,000+ schools; www.case.org
Education of Young Children, Natl. Assn. for the (1926), 1509 16th St. NW, Washington, DC 20036; 100,000; www.naeyc.org
Educators for World Peace, Intl. Assn. of (1973), P.O. Box 3282, Mastin Lake Station, Huntsville, AL 35810; 35,000; www.iaewp.org
Egalitarian Communities, Federation of (1978), 1309 13th Ave. S., Seattle, WA 98144; 14 comm.; www.thefec.org
88th Infantry Division Assn. (1946), 11 Lovett Ave., Brockton, MA 02301-1750; 4,200; www.88infdiv.org
84th Infantry Div. Railsplitter Soc., (1945), P.O. Box 827, Sioux Falls, SD 57101-0827; 2,115
82nd Airborne Division Assn., Inc. (1946), P.O. Box 9308, Fayetteville, NC 28311; 27,000+; www.82ndassociation.org
Electrical and Electronics Engineers, Institute of (1963), 445 Hoes Lane, Piscataway, NJ 08854; 365,000; www.ieee.org
Electrical Manufacturers Assn., Natl. (1926), 1300 N. 17th St., Ste. 1847, Rosslyn, VA 22209; 400 cos.; www.nema.org
Electrochemical Society, Inc., The (ECS, Inc.) (1902), 65 South Main St., Bldg. D, Pennington, NJ 08534-2839; 8,000+; www.electrochem.org
Electronics Technicians, Intl. Soc. of Certified (1980), 3608 Pershing Ave., Ft. Worth, TX 76107; 46,000; www.iscet.org
Elks of the U.S.A., Benevolent and Protective Order of (1868), 2750 N. Lakeview Ave., Chicago, IL 60614; 2,100 chapt.; www.elks.org
Energy Engineers, Assn. of (1977), 4025 Pleasantdale Rd., Ste. 420, Atlanta, GA 30340; 9,000; www.aeecenter.org
Engineers, Natl. Society of Professional (1934), 1420 King St., Alexandria, VA 22314; 60,000; www.nspe.org
English Inc., U.S. (1983), 1747 Pennsylvania Ave. NW, Washington, DC 20006; 1.7 mil; www.usenglish.org
English-Speaking Union of the U.S. (1920), 144 E. 39th St., New York, NY 10036; 10,000; www.englishspeakingunion.org
Entomological Society of America (1953), 10001 Derekwood Ln., Ste 100, Lanham, MD 20706-4876; 5,700; www.entsoc.org
Environmental Assessment Association (1972), 1224 North Nokomis NE, Alexandria, MN 56308; 5,000; www.iami.org/eaa
Environmental Health Assn., Natl. (1937), 720 S. Colorado Blvd., Ste. 970-S, Denver, CO 80246; approx. 5,000; www.neha.org
Esperanto League for North America Inc. (1953), P.O. Box 1129, El Cerrito, CA 94530; 700; www.esperanto-usa.org
Experimental Aircraft Assn. (1953), P.O. Box 3086, Oshkosh, WI 54903; 170,000+; www.eaa.org
Ex-Prisoners of War, American (1942), 3201 E. Pioneer Pkwy., #40, Arlington, TX 76010; 27,000; www.axpow.org
Fairs & Expositions, Intl. Assn. of (1885), P.O. Box 985, Springfield, MO 65809; 2,900; www.fairsandexpos.com
Family, Career and Com. Leaders of Am. (1945), 1910 Association Dr., Reston, VA 20791; 220,000; www. fcclainc.org
Family Physicians, American Academy of (1947), P.O. Box 11210, Shawnee Mission, KS 66207; 94,000; www.aafp.org
Family Relations, Natl. Council on (1938), 3989 Central Avenue NE, Suite 550, Minneapolis, MN 55421; 4,000; www.ncfr.org
Farm Bureau, American (1919), 600 Maryland Ave. SW, Ste. 800, Washington, DC 20024; 5 mil+ families; www.fb.org
Farmers of America Org., Natl. Future (1929), P.O. Box 68960, Indianapolis, IN 46268; 476,000+; www.ffa.org
Farmers Union, Natl. (1902), 11900 E. Cornell Ave., Aurora, CO 80014; 250,000; www.nfu.org

WORLD ALMANAC QUICK QUIZ

Which of these associations can boast the highest membership?
(a) International Wizard of Oz Club (b) North American Ventriloquists Association
(c) International Brotherhood of Magicians (d) American Guild of Organists
For the answer look in this chapter, or see page 1008.

Fat Acceptance, Inc., Natl. Assn. to Advance (NAAFA) (1969), P.O. Box 22510, Oakland, CA 94609; 50 chapt.; www.naafa.org

Feminists for Life of America (1972), 733 15th St. NW, Ste. 1100, Wash., DC 20005; c. 5,000; www.feministsforlife.org

Financial Professionals, Assn. for (formerly Treasury Management Assn.) (1979), 7315 Wisconsin Ave., Ste. 600W, Bethesda, MD 20814; 14,000; www.AFPonline.org

Financial Service Professionals, Soc. of (1928), 17 Campus Blvd, Newtown Square, PA 19073; 22,000; www.financialpro.org

Financial Women Intl. (1921 as Natl. Assoc. of Bank Women), 1027 W. Roselawn Ave., Roseville, MN 55113; 2,000+; www.fwi.org

Fire Chiefs, Intl. Assn. of (1873), 4025 Fair Ridge Dr., Ste. 300, Fairfax, VA 22033; 12,000; www.iafc.org

Fire Protection Assn., Natl. (NFPA) (1896), 1 Batterymarch Park, Quincy, MA 02169; 75,000; www.nfpa.org

Fire Protection Engineers, Soc. of (1950), 7315 Wisconsin Avenue, Ste. 1225W, Bethesda, MD 20814; 3,500; www.sfpe.org

First Candle/SIDSAlliance (1987), 1314 Bedford Ave., Ste. 210, Baltimore, MD 21208; www. sidsalliance.org

Fisheries Soc., American (1870), 5410 Grosvenor Ln., Ste. 110, Bethesda, MD 20814; 100 chapt.; www.fisheries.org

Fleet Reserve Association (1924), 125 N. West St., Alexandria, VA 22314-2754; 122,000; www.fra.org

Food and Commercial Workers Intl. Union, United (UFCW) (1979), 1775 K St. NW, Washington, DC 2006; 1.4 mil; www.ufcw.org

Food Technologists, Institute of (1939), 525 W. Van Buren, Ste. 1000, Chicago, IL 60607; 27,000; www.ift.org

Foreign Study, The American Institute for (1964), River Plaza, 9 W. Broad St., Stamford, CT 06902; 1 mil+; www.aifs.com

Foreign Trade Council, Inc., Natl. (1914), 1625 K St. NW, Washington, DC 20006; 300 companies.; www.nftc.org

Forensic Sciences, American Academy of (1948), P.O. Box 669, Colorado Springs, CO 80901; 5,600; www.aafs.org

Foresters, Society of American (1900), 5400 Grosvenor La., Bethesda, MD 20814; 17,500; www.safnet.org

Forest History Society (1946), 701 Wm. Vickers Ave., Durham, NC 27701-3162; 1,500; www.foresthistory.org

4-H Clubs (1914), CSREES/USDA, 1400 Independence Ave. SW, Washington, DC 20250; 7 mil; www.4h-usa.org

Freedom From Religion Foundation (1978), P.O. Box 750, Madison, WI 53701; 6,000; www.ffrf.org

Freedom of Information Center (1958), Missouri School of Journalism, 133 Neff Annex, Columbia, MO 65211-0012; foi.missouri.edu

Freemasonry, Scottish Rite of, Supreme Council Ancient and Accepted Scottish Rite of, Northern Masonic Jurisdiction (1872), P.O. Box 519, Lexington, MA 02420; 270,000; www.supremecouncil.org

Freemasonry, Scottish Rite of, Supreme Council Ancient and Accepted Scottish Rite of, Southern Jurisdiction (1802), 1733 16th St. NW, Washington, DC 20009-3103; 350,000; www.srmason-sj.org

Free Men, Natl. Coalition of (1977), P.O. Box 582023, Minneapollis, MN 55458; 2,000; www.ncfm.org

Free Press Readership Council, American (2001), 1433 Pennsylvania Ave., S.E., Washington, DC 20003; 4,500; www.americanfreepress.net

French Institute/Alliance Française (1971), 22 E. 60th St., New York, NY 10022; 7,000; www.fiaf.org

Frozen Food Institute, American (1942), 2000 Corporate Ridge, Suite 1000, McLean, VA 22102; 505; www.affi.com

Funeral Consumers Alliance (FAMSA) (1963), P.O. Box 10, Hinesburg, VT 05461; 120 soc.; www.funerals.org/famsa

Future Business Leaders of America/Phi Beta Lambda, Inc. (1942), 1912 Association Dr., Reston, VA 20191; 233,000; www.fbla-pbl.org

Gamblers Anonymous (1957), P.O. Box 17173, Los Angeles, CA 90017; approx. 30,000; www.gamblersanonymous.org

Garden Club of America (1913), 14 E. 60th St., New York, NY 10022; 18,000; www.gcamerica.org

Garden Clubs, Inc., National Council of State (1929), 4401 Magnolia Ave., St. Louis, MO 63110; 217,233; www.gardenclub.org

Gay and Lesbian Task Force, Natl. (1973), 1325 Massachusetts Ave. NW, Ste. 600, Washington, DC 20005; 20,000; www.thetaskforce.org

Genealogical Society, Natl. (1903), 3108 Columbia Pike, Ste. 300, Arlington, VA 22204; 11,000; www.ngsgenealogy.org

General Contractors of America, The Associated (1918), 333 John Carlyle St., Ste. 200, Alexandria, VA 22314; 33,000+ cos.; www.agc.org

Genetic Association, American (1903), P.O. Box 257, Buckeystown, MD 21717; www.theaga.org

Geographers, Assn. of American (1904), 1710 16th St. NW, Washington, DC 20009; 7,500+; www.aag.org

Geographic Education, Natl. Council for (1915), 206-A Martin Hall, Jacksonville State Univ., Jacksonville, AL 36265; 2,500; www.ncge.org

Geographic Society, Natl. (1888), 1145 17th St. NW, Washington, DC 20036; 9.2 mil.; www.nationalgeographic.com

Geographical Society, The American (1851), 120 Wall St., Ste. 100, New York, NY 10005; 1,000; www.amergeog.org

Geological Society of America (1888), P.O. Box 9140, Boulder, CO 80301; 18,500; www.geosociety.org

Geriatrics Society, American (1942), 350 5th Ave., Ste. 801, New York, NY 10118; 6,800+; www.americangeriatrics.org

Gideons Intl. (1899), P.O. Box 140800, Nashville, TN 37214; 236,000+; www.gideons.org

Gifted Children, Natl. Assn. for (1954), 1707 L Street NW, Suite 550, Washington, DC 20036; 8,000; www.nagc.org

Girl Scouts of the U.S.A. (1912), 420 5th Ave., New York, NY 10018; 3.7 mil; www.girlscouts.org

Golf Assn., U.S. (1894), P.O. Box 708, Far Hills, NJ 07931; 750,000; www.usga.org

Gospel Music Assn. (1964), 1205 Division St., Nashville, TN 37203; 4,200; www.gospelmusic.org

Governors' Assn., Natl. (1908), Hall of the States, 444 N. Capitol, Ste. 267, Washington, DC 20001; 55 govs.; www.nga.org

Grange Patrons of Husbandry, Natl. (1867), 1616 H Street NW, Washington, DC 20006; 300,000; www.nationalgrange.org

Graphic Arts, American Institute of (1914), 164 5th Ave., New York, NY 10010; 16,000; www.aiga.org

Gray Panthers (1970), 733 15th St. NW, Ste 437, Washington, DC 20005; approx. 20,000; www.graypanthers.org

Green Mountain Club, The (1910), 4711 Waterbury-Stowe Rd., Waterbury Center, VT 05677; 9,000+; www.greenmountainclub.org

Green Party (1984), P.O. Box 3568, Eureka, CA 95502; www.greenparty.org

Greenpeace, Inc. (1971), 702 H St. NW, Suite 300, Washington, DC 20001; 2.8 mil; www.greenpeaceusa.org.

Ground Water Assn., Natl. (1948), 601 Dempsey Rd., Westerville, OH 43081; 15,000; www.ngwa.org

Guide Dog Foundation for the Blind, Inc. (1946), 371 E. Jericho Turnpike, Smithtown, NY 11787; www.guidedog.org

Hadassah, the Women's Zionist Organization of America (1912), 50 W. 58th St., New York, NY 10019; 300,000+; www.hadassah.org

Handball Assn., U.S. (1951), 2333 N. Tucson Blvd., Tucson, AZ 85716; 8,500; www.ushandball.org

Health Council, Natl. (1920), 1730 M St. NW, Ste. 500, Washington, DC 20036; 115 org.; www.nationalhealthcouncil.org

Hearing Society, Intl. (1951), 16880 Middlebelt Rd., Ste. 4, Livonia, MI 48154; 54 chapt.; www.ihsinfo.org

Heart Assn., American (1924), 7272 Greenville Ave., Dallas, TX 75231; 22.5 mil.; www.americanheart.org

Heating, Refrigerating & Air-Conditioning Engineers, Inc., American Soc. of (1894), 1791 Tullie Cir. NE, Atlanta, GA 30329; 55,000; www.ashrae.org

Helicopter Society, American (1944), 271 N. Washington St., Alexandria, VA 22314, 6,000; www.vtol.org

Hemispheric Affairs, Council on (1975), 1250 Connecticut Ave. NW, Ste. 1C, Washington, DC 20036; 4,000; www.coha.org

Highpointers Club (1986), P.O. Box 1496, Golden, CO 80402; 2,600; www.highpointers.org

High School Band Directors Hall of Fame, Natl. (1985), 400 E. Agency St., Roberta, GA 31078; 27; www.hsbanddirectorhallof fame.com

Hiking Society, American (1976), 1422 Fenwick Lane, Silver Spring, MD 20910; 170 clubs; www.americanhiking.org

Historic Preservation, Natl. Trust for (1949), 1785 Massachusetts Avenue NW, Washington, DC 20036; 270,000; www.nationaltrust.org

Historical Assn., American (1884), 400 A St. SE, Washington, DC 20003; 14,000; www.historians.org

Historical Society, United States (1971), 7433 Whitepine Rd., Richmond, VA 23237; 250,000; www.ushsdolls.com

Hockey, U.S.A. (1936), 1775 Bob Johnson Dr., Colorado Springs, CO 80906; 592,000; www.usahockey.com.

Home Builders, Natl. Assn. of (1942), 1201 15th St. NW, Washington, DC 20005; 220,000; www.nahb.org

Homeless, Natl. Coalition for the (1984), 2201 P St. NW, Ste. 600, Washington, DC 20037; 2,500; www.nationalhomeless.org

Honor Society, Natl. (1921), 1904 Association Dr., Reston, VA 20191; 1 mil+; www.nhs.us

Horse Council, American (1969), 1616 H St. NW, 7th Fl., Washington, DC 20006; 195 org., 1,800 ind.; www.horsecouncil.org

Hospital Assn., American (1898), 1 N. Franklin, Chicago, IL 60606; 5,000 hosp., 37,000 indiv. members; www.aha.org

Hostelling Intl. USA (1934), 8401 Colesville Rd, Ste. 600, Silver Spring, MD 20910; 100 affil.; www.hiayh.org

Hotel & Motel Assn., American (1910), 1201 New York Ave. NW, #600, Washington, DC 20005; 10,000+; www.ahma.com

Hot Rod Assn., Natl. (1951), 2035 Financial Way, Glendora, CA 91741; 80,000; www.nhra.com

Housing Inspection Foundation (1979), 1224 N. Nokomis NE, Alexandria, MN 56308; 1,800; www.iami.org/hif

Huguenot Society, Natl. (1951), 9033 Lyndale Ave. S, #108, Bloomington, MN 55420; 3,800; www.huguenot.netnation.com

Humane Society of the U.S. (1954), 2100 L St. NW, Washington, DC 20037; 650,000; www.hsus.org

Human Resource Management, Society for (SHRM) (1948), 1800 Duke St., Alexandria, VA 22314; 190,000; www.shrm.org

Illustrators, Inc., Society of (1901), 128 E. 63rd St., New York, NY 10021-7303; 900; www.societyillustrators.org

Industrial and Applied Mathematics, Society for (1952), 3600 Univ. City Science Center, Philadelphia, PA 19104; 10,000; www.siam.org

Industrial Designers Society of America (1965), 45195 Business Ct., Ste. 250, Dulles, VA 20166; 3,300; www.idsa.org

Industrial Security, American Soc. for (1955), 1625 Prince St., Alexandria, VA 22314; 33,000; www.asisonline.org

Insurance Assn., American (1866), 1130 Connecticut Avenue NW, Suite 1000, Washington, DC 20036; 450 companies; www.aiadc.org

Intellectual Property Owners Assn. (1972), 1255 23rd St. NW, Ste. 200, Washington, DC 20037; 350; www.ipo.org

Intelligence Officers, Assn. of Former (1975), 6723 Whittier Ave., Ste. 303A, McLean, VA 22101; 22 chapt.; www. afio.com

Intercollegiate Athletics, Natl. Assn. of (1937), 23500 W. 105th St., P.O. Box 1325, Olathe, KS 66051; 300 member coll./univ.; www.naia.org

Interfaith Alliance, The (1994), 1331 H St., 11th Floor, Washington, DC 20005-4706; 150,000; www.interfaithalliance.org

Interior Designers, American Society of (1975), 608 Massachusetts Avenue NE, Washington, DC 20002; 38,000; www.asid.org

International. See also other organizations under next major word in title.

Intl. Education, Institute of (1919), 809 United Nations Plaza, 7th Fl., New York, NY 10017; 800 coll./univ.; www.iie.org

Intl. Educational Exchange, Council on (1947), 7 Custom House St., 3rd Fl., Portland, ME 04101; 240 member groups; www.ciee.org

Intl. Educators, Assn. of (NAFSA) (1948), 1307 New York Ave. NW, 8th Fl., Washington, DC 20005; 9,000; www.nafsa.org

Intl. Law, American Society of (1906), 2223 Massachusetts Ave. NW, Washington, DC 20008; 4,000; www.asil.org

Inventors, American Soc. of (1953), P.O. Box 58426, Philadelphia, PA 19102; 150; www.asoi.org

Investigative Pathology, American Soc. for (1900), 9650 Rockville Pike, Bethesda, MD 20814; 1,718; www.asip.org

Investors Corp., Natl. Assn. of (1951), P.O. Box 220, Royal Oak, MI 48068; 220,000; www.better-investing.org

Irish American Cultural Inst. (1962), 1 Lackawanna Pl., Morristown, NJ 07960; 20 chapt.; www.irishaci.org

Jail Assn., American (1981), 1135 Professional Ct., Hagerstown, MD 21740; 4,500; www.corrections.com/aja

Japanese-American Citizens League (1929), 1765 Sutter St., San Francisco, CA 94115; 21,000; www.jacl.org

Jewish Committee, American (1906), 165 E. 65th St., New York, NY 10022; 125,000; www.ajc.org

Jewish Community Centers Assn. of North America (1917), 15 E. 26th St., New York, NY 10010; 1,000,000+; www.jcca.org

Jewish Congress, American (1918), 15 E. 84th St., New York, NY 10028; 50,000; www.ajcongress.org

Jewish War Veterans of the U.S.A. (1896), 1811 R St. NW, Washington, DC 20009; 37,000; jwv.org

Jewish Women, Natl. Council of (1893), 53 W. 23rd St., 6th Fl., New York, NY 10010; 90,000; www.ncjw.org

John Birch Society (1958), P.O. Box 8040, Appleton, WI 54912; www.jbs.org

Joint Action in Community Service (JACS) (1967), 5225 Wisconsin Ave. NW, Ste. 404, Washington, DC 20015; www.jacsinc.org

Journalists, Society of Professional (1909), 3909 N. Meridian St., Indianapolis, IN 46208; 9,000; spj.org

Journalists and Authors, American Society of (1948), 1501 Broadway, Ste. 302, New York, NY 10036; 1,000+; www.asja.org

Judicature Society, American (1913), Opperman Ctr., 2700 University Ave., Des Moines, IA 50311; 5,500; www.ajs.org

Jugglers Assn., Intl. (1947), P.O. Box 112550, Carrollton, TX, 75011; 2,500; www.juggle.org

Junior Achievement, Inc. (1919), One Education Way, Colorado Springs, CO 80906; www.ja.org

Junior Auxiliaries, Natl. Assn. of (1941), 845 South Main St., Greenville, MS 38701; 12,876; www.najanet.org

Junior Chamber of Commerce, U.S. (1920), P.O. Box 7, Tulsa, OK 74102; 200,000; www.usjaycees.org

Junior College Athletic Assn., Natl. (1937), P.O. Box 7305, Colorado Springs, CO 80933; 520; www.njcaa.org

Junior Honor Society, Natl. (1929), 1904 Association Dr., Reston, VA 20191; 1 mil+; www.njhs.us

Junior Leagues, Assn. of (1921), 90 Williams St., Ste. 200, New York, NY 10038; 294 leagues; www.ajli.org

Kidney Fund, The American (1971), 6110 Executive Blvd., Ste. 1010, Rockville, MD 20852; www.akfinc.org

Kiwanis International (1915), 3636 Woodview Trace, Indianapolis, IN 46268; 500,000+; www.kiwanis.org

Knights of Columbus (1882), One Columbus Plaza, New Haven, CT 06510-4000; 1.6 mil; www.kofc.org

Knights of Pythias, (1864), 59 Coddington Street, #202, Quincy, MA 02169; www.pythias.org

La Leche League Intl. (1957), P.O. Box 4079, Schaumburg, IL 60168; 26,000; www.lalecheleague.org

Lady Bird Johnson Wildflower Center (1982), 4801 La Crosse Avenue, Austin, TX 78739; 22,000; www.wildflower.org

Landscape Architects, American Society of (1899), 636 Eye St. NW, Washington, DC 20001; 15,200; www.asla.org

Law Libraries, American Assn. of (1906), 53 W. Jackson Blvd., #940, Chicago, IL 60604; 5,000; www.aallnet.org

Learned Societies, American Council of (1919), 633 Third Ave., New York, NY 10017; 64 societies; www.acls.org

Legal Administrators, Assn. of (1971), 75 Tri-State Intl., Ste. 222, Lincolnshire, IL 60069-4435; 9,900; www.alanet.org

Legal Secretaries, Natl. Assn. of (NALS) (1929), 314 E 3rd St., Ste. 210, Tulsa, OK 74120; 8,500; www.nals.org

Legion of Valor Museum (1991), 2425 Fresno St., Fresno, CA 93721; 700+; www.legionofvalormuseum.org

Leprosy Missions, Inc., American (1906), One Alm Way, Greenville, SC 29601; www.leprosy.org

Leukemia and Lymphoma Society (1949), 1311 Mamaroneck Ave., White Plains, NY 10605; www.lls.org

Lewis and Clark Trail Heritage Foundation. (1969), P.O. Box 3434, Great Falls, MT 59403; 3,600; www.lewisandclark.org

Libertarian Party (1971), 2600 Virginia Ave. NW, Ste. 100, Washington, DC 20037; 224,000; www.lp.org

Libraries Assn., Special (1909), 331 S. Patrick St., Alexandria, VA 22314; 12,000+; www.sla.org

Library Assn., American (1876), 50 E. Huron St., Chicago, IL 60611; 66,700+; www.ala.org

Lifesaving Assn., U.S. (1964), PO Box 366, Huntington Beach, CA 92648; 11,000; www.usla.org

Lighter-Than-Air Society (1952), 526 S. Main St., Akron, OH 44306; 1,000; www.blimpinfo.com

Linguistic Society of America (1924), 1325 18th St. NW, Ste. 211, Washington, DC 20036; 5,000 indiv.; www.lsadc.org

Lions Clubs, Intl., Assn. of (1917), 300 W. 22nd St., Oak Brook, IL 60523; 1,400,000; www.lionsclubs.org

Little League Baseball, Inc. (1939), P.O. Box 3489, S. Williamsport, PA 17701; 4 mil, www.littleleague.org

Little People of America, Inc. (1961), 5289 NE Elam Young Pkwy, Ste. F100, Hillsboro, OR 97124; 8,000+; www.lpaonline.org

Logistics, Intl. Society of (SOLE) (1966), 8100 Professional Pl., Ste. 111, Hyattsville, MD 20785; 3,500; www.sole.org

London Club (1975), Route One, Lecompton, KS 66050; 100+

Lung Assn., American (1904), 61 Broadway, 6th Fl., New York, NY 10006; www.lungusa.org
Magazine Publishers of America (1919), 810 Seventh Ave., 24th Fl., New York, NY 10019; 1,200 titles; www.magazine.org
Magicians, Intl. Brotherhood of (1922), 11155 S. Towne Sq., Ste. B, St. Louis, MO 63123; 15,000; www.magician.org
Management Accountants, Institute of (1919), 10 Paragon Dr., Montvale, NJ 07645; 75,000; www.imanet.org
Management Assn., American (1923), 1601 Broadway, New York, NY 10019; 700,000; www.amanet.org
Manufacturers, Natl. Assn. of (1895), 1331 Pennsylvania Ave. NW, Washington, DC 20004; 14,000 cos.; www.nam.org
March of Dimes Birth Defects Foundation (1938), 1275 Mamaroneck Avenue, White Plains, NY 10605; 3 mil; www.marchofdimes.com
Marine Corps League (1937), P.O. Box 3070, Merrifield, VA 22116-3070; 60,000+; www.mcleague.org
Marketing Assn., Am. (1915), 311 S. Wacker Dr., Ste. 5800, Chicago, IL 60606; 38,000; www.marketingpower.com
Master Brewers Association of the Americas (1887), 3340 Pilot Knob Rd., St. Paul, MN 55121; 3,500; www.mbaa.com
Materials and Process Engineering, Soc. for the Advancement of (1944), 1161 Park View Dr., Covina, CA 91724; 5,000; www.sampe.org
Mathematical Society, American (1888), P.O. Box 3297, Plymouth, MA 02361; 30,000; www.ams.org
Mayflower Descendants, General Society of (1897), P.O. Box 3297, Plymouth, MA 02361; 26,000; www.mayflower.org
Mayors, U.S. Conference of (1932), 1620 Eye St. NW, Washington, DC 20006; 1,183; www.usmayors.org
Mechanical Engineers, American Soc. of (1880), 3 Park Ave., New York, NY 10016; 120,000; www.asme.org
Medical Assn., American (1847), 515 N. State St., Chicago, IL 60610; 300,000; www.ama-assn.org
Medical Library Assn. (1898), 65 E. Wacker Pl., Ste. 1900, Chicago, IL 60602; 3,600; www.mlanet.org
MENC: The Natl. Assn. for Music Education (formerly Music Educators Natl. Conference) (1907), 1806 Robert Fulton Dr., Reston, VA 20191; 120,000; www.menc.org
Mended Hearts, Inc. (1950), 7272 Greenville Ave., Dallas, TX 75231; 460 hospitals; www.mendedhearts.org
Mensa, Ltd., American (1960), 1229 Corporate Dr. W, Arlington, TX 76006; 50,000; www.us.mensa.org
Mental Health Assn., Natl. (1909), 2001 N. Beauregard St., 12th Fl., Alexandria, VA 22311; 340 affiliates; www.nmha.org
Mentally Ill, Natl. Alliance for the (1979), Colonial Place Three, 2107 Wilson Blvd. Ste. 300, Arlington, VA 22201; 220,000; www.nami.org
Merrill's Marauders Assn. (1947), 11244 N. 33rd St., Phoenix, AZ 85028-2723; 1,698; www.marauder.org
Meteorological Society, American (1919), 45 Beacon St., Boston, MA 02108; 11,000+; www.ametsoc.org
Metric Assn., Inc., U.S. (1916), 10245 Andasol Ave., Northridge, CA 91325-1504; 1,200; www.metric.org
Microbiology, American Society for (1899), 1752 N. St. NW, Washington, DC 20036; 40,000; www.asm.org
Military Officers Assn. (1940), 201 N. Washington St., Alexandria, VA 22314; 370,000; www.moaa.org
Military Order of the Purple Heart of the USA (1958), 5413-B Backlick Road, Springfield, VA 22151; 36,765; www.purpleheart.org
Military Order of the World Wars (1919), 435 N. Lee St., Alexandria, VA 22314; 155 chapt.; www.militaryorder.net
Military Surgeons of the U.S., Assn. of (1898), 9320 Old Georgetown Road, Bethesda, MD 20814; 10,000+; www.amsus.org
Missing and Exploited Children, Natl. Center for (1984), The Charles B. Wang International Children's Building, 699 Prince St., Alexandria, VA 22314; www.missingkids.com
Model Railroad Assn., Natl. (1935), 4121 Cromwell Rd., Chattanooga, TN 37421-2119; 20,500; www.nmra.org
Modern Language Assn. of America (1883), 26 Broadway, 3rd Fl., New York, NY 10004; 30,000+; www.mla.org
Molecular Plant-Microbe Interactions, Intl. Soc. for (1990), 3340 Pilot Knob Rd., St. Paul, MN 55121; 450; www.ismpminet.org
Moose Intl., Inc. (1888), 155 S. International Dr., Mooseheart, IL 60539; 1.5 mil; www.mooseintl.org
Mothers of Twins Clubs, Natl. Organization of (1963), P.O. Box 700860, Plymouth, MI 48170; 23,000; www.nomotc.org
Motion Picture Arts & Sciences, Academy of (1927), 8949 Wilshire Blvd., Beverly Hills, CA 90211; 6,000; www.oscars.org
Motion Picture & Television Engineers, Soc. of (1916), 595 W. Hartsdale Ave., White Plains, NY 10607; 10,000; www.smpte.org
Motorcyclist Assn., American (1924), 13515 Yarmouth Dr., Pickerington, OH 43147; 260,000+; www.amadirectlink.com
Motorists Association, Natl. (1982), 402 W. 2nd St., Waunakee, WI 53597; 6,000; www.motorists.org
Multiple Sclerosis Society, Natl. (1946), 733 3rd Ave,. 6th Fl., New York, NY 10017; 497,000; www.nationalmssociety.org
Muscular Dystrophy Assn., Inc. (1950), 3300 E. Sunrise Dr., Tucson, AZ 85718; 2 mil. volunteers; www.mdausa.org
Museums, American Assn. of (1906), 1575 Eye St. NW, Ste. 400, Washington, DC 20005; 16,000 indiv., 3,100 institutions; www.aam-us.org
Music Teachers Natl. Assn. (1876), 441 Vine St., Ste. 505, Cincinnati, OH 45202; 24,000; www.mtna.org
Musicological Society, American (1934), 201 S. 34th St., Philadelphia, PA 19104-6313; 3,300; www.ams-net.org
Muzzle Loading Rifle Assn., Natl. (1933), P.O. Box 67, Friendship, IN 47021; 18,000; www.nmlra.org
Myasthenia Gravis Foundation of America (1952), 1821 University Ave. W., Ste S256, St. Paul, MN 55104; www.myasthenia.org
Mystery Writers of America, Inc. (1945), 17 E. 47th St., 6th Fl., New York, NY 10017; 2,235; www.mysterywriters.org
NA'AMAT USA (1921), 350 Fifth Ave., Ste. 4700, New York, NY 10118; 25,000; www.naamat.org
Name Society, American (1951), c/o Michael McGoff, Vice Provost, Provost's Office, SUNY Binghamton, Binghamton, NY 13902; 700; www.wtsn.binghamton.edu/ANS
Narcotics Anonymous World Services (1953), P.O Box 9999, Van Nuys, CA 94109; 20,000 groups; www.na.org
National. See other organizations under next major word in title.
Natl. Assn. for the Advancement of Colored People (NAACP) (1909), 4805 Mt. Hope Dr., Baltimore, MD 21215; www.naacp.org
National Guard Assn. of the U.S. (1878), One Massachusetts Ave. NW, Washington, DC 20001; 45,000; www.ngaus.org
Nature Conservancy, The (1951), 4245 N. Fairfax Drive, Ste. 100, Arlington, VA 22203; 1 mil; nature.org
Naval Institute, U.S. (1873), 291 Wood Rd., Annapolis, MD 21402; 70,000; www.usni.org
Naval Reserve Assn. (1954), 1619 King St., Alexandria, VA 22314; 23,000; www.navy-reserve.org
Navy League of the United States (1902), 2300 Wilson Blvd., Arlington,VA 22201-3308; 75,000; www.navyleague.org
Negro College Fund, United (1944), 8260 Willow Oaks Corporate Dr., Fairfax, VA 22031; 39 institutions; www.uncf.org
Neurofibromatosis Foundation, Natl. (1978), 95 Pine St., 16th Fl., New York, NY 10005; 24,000; www.nf.org
Newspaper Assn. of America (NAA) (1992), 1921 Gallows Rd., Ste. 600, Vienna, VA 22182-3900; 2,000+; www.naa.org
Ninety-Nines (Intl. Organization of Women Pilots) (1929), 4300 Amelia Earhart Rd., Oklahoma City, OK 73159; 6,000; www.ninety-nines.org
Non-Commissioned Officers Assn. (1960), 610 Madison St., Alexandria, VA 22314; 160,000; www.ncoausa.org
NOT-SAFE: Nat'l Organization Taunting Safety and Fairness Everywhere (1984), P.O. Box 5743-WS, Santa Barbara, CA 93150; 9,110; www.notsafe.org
Notaries, American Society of (1965), P.O. Box 5707, Tallahassee, FL 32314; approx. 20,000; www.notaries.org
Nuclear Society, American (1954), 555 N. Kensington Ave., La Grange Park, IL 60526; 10,500; www.ans.org
Nude Recreation, American Assn. for (1931), 1703 N. Main St., Kissimmee, FL 34744; almost 50,000; www.aanr.com
Numismatic Assn., American (1891), 818 N. Cascade Ave., Colorado Springs, CO 80903; 30,000; www.money.org
Numismatic Society, American (1858), 96 Fulton St., New York, NY 10038; 2,127; www.amnumsoc.org
Nurses Assn., American (ANA) (1897), 8515 Georgia Ave., Ste. 400, Silver Spring, MD 20910; 2.7 mil; www.nursingworld.org
Nursing, Natl. League for (1952), 61 Broadway, New York, NY 10006; 5,000; www.nln.org
Ocean Conservancy (1972), 2029 K St., Wash.,DC 20006; 500,000; www.oceanconservancy.org
Odd Fellows, Independent Order of (1819), 422 Trade St., Winston-Salem, NC 27101; 250,000; www.ioof.org
Optimist Intl. (1919), 4494 Lindell Blvd., St. Louis, MO 63108; 105,000; www.optimist.org
Optometric Assn., American (1918), 243 N. Lindbergh Blvd., St. Louis, MO 63141; 32,904; www.aoa.org
Organ Sharing, United Network for (1984), P.O. Box 2484, Richmond, VA 23218; 408; www.unos.org
Organists, American Guild of (1896), 475 Riverside Dr., Ste. 1260, New York, NY 10115; 20,000; www.agohq.org
Oriental Society, American (1842), Univ. of Michigan, Hatcher Graduate Library, 110D, Ann Arbor, MI 48109; 1,350; www.umich.edu/~aos
ORT Inc., American (Org. for Rehabilitation Through Training) (1922), 817 Broadway, 10th Fl., New York, NY 10003; 10,000; www.aort.org

IT'S A FACT: The American Political Items Collectors (APIC) were influential in passing the Hobby Protection Act (1973), which requires that imitations of buttons and other collectible Americana be clearly marked as reproductions.

Ornithologists' Union, American (1883), 1313 Dolley Madison Blvd., Ste. 402, McLean, VA 22101; 4,000; www.aou.org
Overeaters Anonymous (1960) P.O. Box 44020, Rio Rancho, NM 87124-4020; www.oa.org
Oxfam America (1970) 26 West St., Boston, MA 02111; 150,000; www.oxfamamerica.org
Paralyzed Veterans of America (1946), 801 18th St. NW, Washington, DC 20006; 18,000; www.pva.org
Parapsychology Institute of America (1971), P.O. Box 5442, Babylon, NY, 11707; 400
Parents Without Partners, Inc. (1957), 1650 South Dixie Hwy, Ste. 510, Boca Raton, FL 33432; 200 chapt.; www.parentswithoutpartners.org
Parkinson's Disease Foundation, Inc. (1957), 710 W. 168th St., New York, NY 10032; 100,000; www.pdf.org
Parliamentarians, Natl. Assn. of (1930), 213 S. Main St., Independence, MO 64050; 4,000; www.parliamentarians.org
Peace Corps (1961), 1111 20th St., NW, Washington, DC 20526; 178,000; www.peacecorps.gov
Pearl Harbor History Associates, Inc. (1986), P.O. Box 1007, Stratford, CT 06615; 275; www.pearlharbor-history.org
PEN American Center, Inc. (1921), 588 Broadway, Ste. 303, New York, NY 10012; 2,900; www.pen.org
Pen Friends, Intl. (1967), 500 University Ave., #2415, Honolulu, HI 96826; 300,000; www.pen-pals.net
Pen Women, Natl. League of American (1897), 1300 17th St. NW, Washington, DC 20036; 3,569: www.americanpenwomen.org
People for the Ethical Treatment of Animals. See Animals.
Performance Improvement, Intl. Society for (1962), 1400 Spring St., Ste. 260, Silver Spring, MD 20910; 6,000; www. ispi.org
Petroleum Institute, American (1919), 1220 L St. NW, Washington, DC 20005; 400 companies; www.api.org
Pharmacists Assn., American (1852), 2215 Constitution Ave. NW, Washington, DC 20037; 50,000; www.aphanet.org, www.pharmacist.com
Phi Beta Kappa Society (1776), 1606 New Hampshire Ave. NW, Washington, DC 20009; 270 inst.; www.pbk.org
Phi Kappa Phi, Honor Society of (1897), P.O. Box 16000, LSU Baton Rouge, Baton Rouge, LA 70893; 120,000+; www.phikappaphi.org
Phi Theta Kappa Int'l. Honor Society (1918), 1625 Eastover Drive, Jackson, MS 39211; 800,000; www.ptk.org
Philatelic Society, American (1886), 100 Match Factory Place, Bellefonte, PA 16823; 44,000+; www.stamps.org
Philological Association, American (1869), Univ. of Penn., 292 Logan Hall, 249 S. 36th St., Philadelphia, PA, 19104-6304; 3,100; www.apaclassics.org
Philosophical Assn., American (1900), 31 Amstel Ave., Univ. of Delaware, Newark, DE 19716; 11,097; www.apa.udel.edu/apa
Physical Therapy Assn., American (1921), 1111 N. Fairfax St., Alexandria, VA 22314; 66,000; www.apta.org
Physically Handicapped, Inc., Natl. Assn. of the (1958), Scarlet Oaks, 440 Lafayette Ave., #GA4, Cincinnati, OH 45220-1022; approx. 400; www.naph.net
Physics, American Inst. of (1931), One Physics Ellipse, College Park, MD 20740; 13 soc. and org.; www.aip.org
Physiological Society, American (1887), 9650 Rockville Pike, Bethesda, MD 20814-3991; 10,500; www.the-aps.org
Phytopathological Society, American (1908), 3340 Pilot Knob Rd., St. Paul, MN 55121; 5,000; www.apsnet.org
Pilgrims Natl. Soc., Sons and Daughters of (1909), 3917 Heritage Dr., #104, Bloomington, MN 55437-2633; 2,000; www.nssdp.org
Pilot Intl. & Pilot Intl. Foundation (1921), P.O. Box 4844, Macon, GA 31208; 25,000; www.pilotinternational.org
Planetary Society (1979), 65 N. Catalina Ave., Pasadena, CA 91106; approx. 70,000; www.planetary.org
Planned Parenthood Federation of America, Inc. (1916), 434 West 33rd Street, New York, NY 10001; www.plannedparenthood.org
Plastics Engineers, Society of (1942), 14 Fairfield Dr., P.O. Box 403, Brookfield, CT 06804; 25,000+; www.4spe.org
Poetry Society of America (1910), 15 Gramercy Park, New York, NY 10003; approx. 3,000; www.poetrysociety.org
Poets, The Academy of American (1934), 588 Broadway, Ste. 604, New York, NY 10012; 8,000; www.poets.org
Police Assn., Intl. (1950 in UK, 1962 in U.S.), 100 Chase Ave., Yonkers, NY 10703; 291,000+; www.ipa-usa.org
Political Items Collectors, American (1945), P.O. Box 5632, Derwood, MD 20855; 3,000; apic.us
Political Science, Academy of (1886), 475 Riverside Drive, Ste. 1274, New York, NY 10115; 5,825; www.psqonline.org
Political & Social Science, American Academy of (1889), 3814 Walnut St., Univ. of Penn., Philadelphia, PA 19104; 400; www.aapss.org
Polo Assn., U.S. (1890), 771 Corporate Dr., Ste. 505, Lexington, KY 40503; 3,737; www.uspolo.org
Population Assn. of America (1931), 8630 Fenton St., Ste. 722, Silver Spring, MD 20910; 3,000; www.popassoc.org
Population Connection (formerly Zero Population Growth) (1968), 1400 16th St. NW, Ste 320, Washington, DC 20036; www.populationconnection.org
Postal Stationery Society, United (1945) P.O. Box 3982, Chester, VA 23831; 1,100; www.upss.org
Postcard Dealers, Inc., International Federation of (1979), P.O. Box 1765, Manassas, VA 20109; 202
Postmasters of the U.S., Natl. League of (1887), 1023 N. Royal St., Alexandria, VA 22314; 95 clubs; www.postmasters.org
Postmasters of the U.S., Natl. Assn. of (1898), 8 Herbert St., Arlington, VA 22305; 95 clubs, www.napus.org
Power Boat Assn., American (1903), 17640 Nine Mile Rd., Eastpointe, MI 48021; 6,000; www.apba-racing.com
Press Club, National (1908), 529 14th St., 13th Fl., NW, Washington, DC 20045; 4,000; www.press.org
Printing Industries of America, Inc. (1887), 200 Deer Run Rd., Sewickley, PA 15143; 12,000; www.gain.net
Procrastinators Club of America (1956), P.O. Box 712, Bryn Athyn, PA 19009; 14,500; www.geocities.com/procrastinators_club_of_america
Professional Ball Players of America, Assn. of (1924), 1820 W. Orangewood Ave., Ste. 206, Orange, CA 92868; 11,000; www.apbpa.org
ProLiteracy Worldwide (2002), 1320 Jamesville Ave., Syracuse, NY 13210; 1,200 affiliates; www.proliteracy.org
Psoriasis Foundation, Natl. (1968), 6600 SW 92nd Ave., Ste. 300, Portland, OR 97223; 33,000; www.psoriasis.org
Psychiatric Assn., American (1844), 1000 Wilson Blvd., Suite 1825, Arlington, VA 22209-3901; 37,000; www.psych.org
Psychical Research, American Society for (1885), 5 W. 73rd St., New York, NY 10023; www.aspr.com
Psychological Assn., American (1892), 750 1st St. NE, Washington, DC 20002; 150,000; www.apa.org
PTA, Natl. (1897), 541 N. Fairbanks Ct., Ste. 1300, Chicago, IL 60611; 5,896,672; www.pta.org
Public Administration, American Soc. for (1939), 1120 G St. NW, Washington, DC 20005; 9,000+; www.aspanet.org
Public Health Assn., American (1872), 800 I St. NW, Washington, DC 20001; 50,000+; www.apha.org
Publishers, Assn. of American (1970), 71 5th Ave., New York, NY 10003; 300+; www.publishers.org
Quill and Scroll Society (1926), School of Journalism, The University of Iowa, Iowa City, IA 52242; www.uiowa.edu/~quill-sc
Quota International, Inc. (1919), 1420 21st St. NW, Washington, DC 20036; 7,000+; www.quota.org
Rabbis, Central Conference of American (1889), 355 Lexington Ave., New York, NY 10017; 1,800; ccarnet.org
Radio and Television Society Foundation, Intl. (1939), 420 Lexington Ave., Ste. 1601, New York, NY 10170; 1,787; www.irts.org
Radio Relay League, American (1914), 225 Main St., Newington, CT 06111; 152,000; www.arrl.org
Railway Historical Society, Natl. (1935), 100 N. 17th St., Ste. 1203, Philadelphia, PA 19103; app. 17,000+; www.nrhs.com
Range Management, Society for (1948), 445 Union Blvd., Ste. 230, Lakewood, CO 80228; 3,700; www.rangelands.org/srm.shtml
Reading Assn., Intl. (1956), 800 Barksdale Rd., P.O. Box 8139, Newark, DE 19714; 350,000; www.reading.org
Real Estate Appraisers, Natl. Assn. of (1966) 1224 N. Nokomis NE, Alexandria, MN 56308; 3,000; www.iami.org/narea
Real Estate Institute, Intl. (1975), 1224 N. Nokomis, Alexandria, MN 56308; 700; www.iami.org/irei
Recreation and Park Assn., Natl. (1965), 22377 Belmont Ridge Rd., Ashburn, VA 20148; 21,000; www.nrpa.org
Recycling Coalition, Natl. (1978), 1325 G St., NW, Washington, DC, 20005; 4,000; www.nrc-recycle.org
Red Cross, American Natl. (1881), 2025 E St. NW, Washington, DC 20006; 1.3 mil volunteers; www.redcross.org
Reform Party of the U.S.A. (1996), P.O. Box 126437, Ft. Worth, TX 76126; 500,000; www.reformparty.org
Refugee Committee, American (1978), 430 Oak Grove St., Ste. 204, Minneapolis, MN 55403; www.archq.org
Rehabilitation Assn., Natl. (1925), 633 S. Washington St., Alexandria, VA 22310-4109; approx. 11,000; www.nationalrehab.org

Religion, American Academy of (1909), 825 Houston Mill Rd., Suite 300, Atlanta, GA 30329; 9,000; www.aarweb.org
Renaissance Society of America (1954), (CUNY) 365 5th. Ave., Rm. 5400, New York, NY 10016; 3,000; www.rsa.org
Republican National Committee (1856), 310 1st St. SE, Washington, DC 20003; www.rnc.org
Reserve Officers Assn. of the U.S. (1922), One Constitution Ave. NE, Washington, DC 20002; 75,000; www.roa.org
Retail Federation, Natl. (1908), 325 7th St. NW, Ste. 1100, Washington, DC 20004; 50,000; www.nrf.com
Retired Persons, American Assn. of (1958), 601 E St. NW, Washington, DC 20049; 35 mil+; www.aarp.org
Reye's Syndrome Foundation, Natl. (1974), 426 N. Lewis St., Bryan, OH 43506-0829; 5,000+; www.reyessyndrome.org
Richard III Society, Inc. (1961), 11000 Anaheim Ave., Albuquerque, NM 87122; 4,000; www.r3.org
Rifle Assn., Natl. (1871), 11250 Waples Mill Rd., Fairfax, VA 22030; approx 3 mil; www.nra.org
Road & Transportation Builders Assn., American (1902), The ARTBA Building, 1010 Massachusetts Ave. NW, Washington, DC 20001; 5,000+; www.artba.org
Roller Sports, U.S.A. (1937), 4730 South St., Lincoln, NE 68506; 30,000; www.usarollersports.org
Rose Society, American (1892), P.O. Box 30000, Shreveport, LA 71130; 20,000; www.ars.org
Rotary Intl. (1905), One Rotary Center, 1560 Sherman Ave., Evanston, IL 60201; 1,220,543; www.rotary.org
Running Assn., American (1968), 4405 East West Hwy, Ste. 405, Bethesda, MD 20814; 15,000; www.americanrunning.org
Safety Council, Natl. (1913), 1121 Spring Lake Dr., Itasca, IL 60143; 46,000 member facilities; www.nsc.org
Safety Engineers, American Soc. of (1911), 1800 E. Oakton St., Des Plaines, IL 60018; 32,000; www.asse.org
Save-the-Redwoods League (1918), 114 Sansome St., Ste. 1200, San Francisco, CA 94104; 40,000; www.savetheredwoods.org
School Administrators, American Assn. of (1865), 801 N. Quincy St., Ste 700, Arlington, VA 22203; 13,000+; www.aasa.org
Science, American Assn. for the Advancement of (1848), 1200 New York Ave. NW, Washington, DC 20005; approx. 10 mil.; www.aaas.org
Science Fiction Society, World (1939), P.O. Box 426159, Kendall Square Station, Cambridge, MA 02142; 10,000; www.wsfs.org
Sciences, Natl. Academy of (1863), 500 5th St. NW, Washington, DC 20001; 2,000+; www.nas.edu
Science Teachers Assn., Natl. (1944), 1840 Wilson Blvd., Arlington, VA 22201; 55,000; www.nsta.org
Science Writers, Natl. Assn. of (1955), P.O. Box 890, Hedgesville, WV 25427; 2,400; www.nasw.org
Scrabble® Assn., Natl. (1978), P.O. Box 700, 403 Front St., Greenport, NY 11944; 10,000+; www.scrabble-assoc.com
Screen Actors Guild (1933), 5757 Wilshire Blvd., Los Angeles, CA 90036; 120,000; www.sag.com
2nd Air Division Assn. of the 8th Air Force (1950), P.O. Box 484, Elkhorn, WI 53121-0484; 4,000
Secular Humanism, Council for (1980), P.O. Box 664, Amherst, NY 14226; 24,000; www.secularhumanism.org
Separation of Church & State, Americans United for (1947), 518 C St. NE, Washington, DC 20002; 75,000+; www.au.org
Sharkhunters Intl. (1983), P.O. Box 1539-WS, Hernando, FL 34442; 6,900; www.sharkhunters.com
Shipbuilders Council of America (1920), 1455 F St., NW, Ste. 225, Washington, DC 20005; 43 member cos; www.shipbuilders.org
Ships in Bottles Assn. of America (1982), P.O. Box 180550, Coronado, CA 92178; 250; www.shipsinbottles.org
Shriners of North America, The (1872), 2900 Rocky Point Dr., Tampa, FL 33607; approx 500,000+; www.shrinershq.org
Sierra Club (1892), 85 2nd St., 2nd Fl., San Francisco, CA 94105; 750,000+; www.sierraclub.org
Sigma Beta Delta (1994) P.O. Box 210570, St. Louis, MO 63121-0570; 20,000; www.sigmabetadelta.org
Skeet Shooting Assn., Natl. (1934), 5931 Roft Rd., San Antonio, TX 78253; 20,000; www.mynssa.com
Small Business United, Natl. (1937), 1156 15th St. NW, Ste. 1100, Washington, DC 20005; 150,000+; www.nsba.biz
Sociological Assn., American (1905), 1307 New York Avenue NW, Suite 700, Washington, DC 20005; 14,000; www.asanet.org
Softball Assn., Amateur (1933), 2801 NE 50th St., Oklahoma City, OK 73111; 245,000+ teams; www.softball.org
Software and Information Industry Assn. (1999), 1090 Vermont Ave. NW, 6th Fl., Wash. DC 20005; 750 cos.; www.siia.net
Soldiers', Sailors', Marines' and Airmen's Club (1919), 283 Lexington Ave., New York, NY 10016; www.ssmaclub.org
Songwriters Guild of America (1931), 209 10th Ave. S., Ste. 534, Nashville, TN 37203; 5,000+; www.songwritersguild.com
Sons of the American Colonists, Natl. Society of (1970) 5611 N. 15th St., Arlington, VA 22205-0482; 250
Sons of the American Legion (1932), P.O. Box 1055, Indianapolis, IN 46206; 287,000; www.sal.legion.org
Sons of the American Revolution, Natl. Society of (1889), 1000 S. 4th St., Louisville, KY 40203; 26,000; www.sar.org
Sons of Confederate Veterans (1896), P.O. Box 59, Columbia, TN 38402; 35,000; www.scv.org
Sons of Italy in America, Order (1905), 219 E St. NE, Washington, DC 20002; 600,000; www.osia.org
Sons of Norway (1895), 1455 W. Lake St., Minneapolis, MN 55408; 61,600; www.sofn.com
Southern Christian Leadership Conference (1957), P.O. Box 89128, Atlanta, GA 30312; 1 mil.; sclcnational.org
Space Society, Natl. (1974), 1620 Eye St. NW, Ste. 615, Washington, DC 20006; 22,000+; www.nss.org
Speech-Language-Hearing Assn., American (1925), 10801 Rockville Pike, Rockville, MD 20852; 118,000; www.asha.org
Speedskating, U.S. (1966), P.O. Box 450639, Westlake, OH 44145; 1,800; www.usspeedskating.org
Speleological Society, Natl. (1941), 2813 Cave Ave., Huntsville, AL 35810; 12,000; www.caves.org
Sports Car Club of America (1944), P.O. Box 19400, Topeka, KS 66619; 60,000; www.scca.org
Sportscasters Assn., The American (1980), 225 Broadway, Ste. 2030, New York, NY 10007; 500+; americansportscastersonline.com
State, County, and Municipal Employees, American Federation of (AFSCME) (1936), 1625 L St. NW, Washington, DC 20036; 1.4 mil; www.afscme.org
State & Local History, American Assn. for (1940), 1717 Church St., Nashville, TN 37203; 6,100; www.aaslh.org
State Governments, Council of (1933), 2760 Research Park Drive, P.O. Box 11910, Lexington, KY 40578; 50 states, 4 territories; www.csg.org
Steamship Historical Society of America, Inc. (1935), 300 Ray Dr., Ste. 4, Providence, RI 02906; 3,400; www.sshsa.org
Steelworkers of America, United (USWA) (1942), 5 Gateway Center, Pittsburgh, PA 15222; 1.2 mil; www.uswa.org
Stock Exchange, American (1911), 86 Trinity Pl., New York, NY 10006; www.amex.com
Stock Exchange, New York (1792), 11 Wall St., New York, NY 10005; www.nyse.com
Stock Exchange, Philadelphia (1790), 1900 Market St., Philadelphia, PA 19103; www.phlx.com
Student Councils, Natl. Assn. of (1931) 1904 Association Dr., Reston, VA 20191; 17,000 councils; www.nasc.us
Stuttering Assn., Natl. (1977), 119 W. 40th St., 14th Fl, New York, NY 10018; 2,800; www.nsastutter.org
Supreme Court Historical Society (1974), Opperman House, 224 East Capitol St. NE, Washington, DC 20003; 5,700; www.supremecourthistory.org
Surgeons, American College of (1913), 633 N. Saint Clair St., Chicago, IL 60611; 64,000; www.facs.org
Symphony Orchestra League, American (1942), 33 W. 60th St., 5th Fl., New York, NY 10023; 900; www.symphony.org
Table Tennis Assn., U.S. (1933), One Olympic Plaza, Colorado Springs, CO 80909; 8,000+; www.usatt.org
Tall Buildings and Urban Habitat, Council on (1969), Illinois Inst. of Tech., S.R. Crown Hall, 3360 S. State St., Chicago, IL 60616; 1,400; www.ctbuh.org
Tau Beta Pi Association (1885), P.O. Box 2697, Knoxville, TN 37901; 477,318; www.tbp.org
Tax Administrators, Federation of (1937), 444 N. Capitol St. NW, Ste. 348, Washington, DC 20001; www.taxadmin.org
Tax Foundation (1937), 2001 L. St. NW, Ste. 1050, Washington, DC 20036; 50 U.S. states; www.taxfoundation.org
Taxpayers Union, Natl. (1969), 108 N. Alfred St., Alexandria, VA 22314; 335,000; www.ntu.org
Teachers, American Federation of (AFT) (1916), 555 New Jersey Ave. NW, Wash., DC 20001; 1.3 mil; www.aft.org
Teachers of English, Natl. Council of (1911), 1111 W. Kenyon Rd., Urbana, IL 61801; 60,000; www.ncte.org
Teachers of English to Speakers of Other Languages (1966), 700 S. Washington St., Ste. 200, Alexandria, VA 22314; 13,441; www.tesol.org
Teachers of French, American Assn. of (1927), Southern Illinois University, Mailcode 4510, Carbondale, IL 62901; 9,500; www.frenchteachers.org
Teachers of German, American Assn. of (1926), 112 Haddontowne Ct. #104, Cherry Hill, NJ 08034; 6,000; www.aatg.org
Teachers of Mathematics, Natl. Council of (1920), 1906 Association Dr., Reston, VA 20191; 100,000; www.nctm.org
Teachers of Singing, Natl. Assn. of (1944), 4745 Sutton Park Ct., Ste. 201, Jacksonville, FL 32224; 6,000; www.nats.org
Teachers of Spanish & Portuguese, American Assn. of (1917), 423 Exton Commons, Exton, PA, 19341; 11,522; www.aatsp.org

Teamsters, Intl. Brotherhood of (IBT) (1903), 25 Louisiana Ave. NW, Washington, DC 20001; 1.4 mil; www.teamster.org
TelecomPioneers (1911), P.O. Box 13888, Denver, CO 80201; 625,000; www.telecom-pioneers.com
Television Academy, Natl. (1957), 111 W. 57th St., Ste. 600, New York, NY 10019; www.emmyonline.org
Term Limits, U.S. (1992), 240 Waukegan Rd., Ste. 200, Glenview, IL 60025; www.termlimits.org
Theodore Roosevelt Assn. (1920), P.O. Box 719, Oyster Bay, NY 11771; 2,500; www.theodoreroosevelt.org
Theological Library Assn., American (1946), 250 S. Wacker Dr., Ste. 1600, Chicago, IL 60606; 1,000+; www.atla.com
Theological Schools in the U.S. and Canada, Assn. of (1918), 10 Summit Park Dr., Pittsburgh, PA 15275; 251; www.ats.edu
Theosophical Society in America (1875), P.O. Box 270, Wheaton, IL 60189; 5,000; www.theosophical.org
Therapy Dogs Intl., Inc (1976), 88 Bartley Rd., Flanders, NJ 07836; 12,200; www.tdi-dog.org
Thoreau Society (1941), 55 Old Bedford Rd., Concord, MA 01742; 1,700+; www.thoreausociety.org
Thoroughbred Racing Assns. (1942), 420 Fair Hill Dr., Ste. 1, Elkton, MD 21921; 49 racing assoc.; www.tra-online.com
Tin Can Sailors (1976), P.O. Box 100, Somerset, MA 02726; 24,000; www.destroyers.org
Titanic Historical Society & Museum (1963), 208 Main St., Indian Orchard, MA 01151-0053; 4,328; www.titanichistoricalsociety.org
Toastmasters Intl. (1924), P.O. Box 9052, Mission Viejo, CA 92690; 200,000+; www.toastmasters.org
Topical Assn., American (1949), P.O. Box 57, Arlington, TX, 76004-0057; 3,300; americantopicalassn.org
Toy Industry Assn., Inc. (1916), 1115 Broadway, Suite 400, New York, NY 10010; 400+ cos.; www.toy-tma.org
Transportation Alternatives (1973), 127 W. 26th St., Ste. 1002, New York, NY 10001; 5,000; www.transalt.org
Transportation Engineers, Inst. of (1930), 1099 14th St. NW, Suite 300-W, Washington, DC 20005; 16,000; www.ite.org
Trapshooting Assn. of America, Amateur (1900), 601 W. National Road, Vandalia, OH 45377; 54,208; www.shootata.com
Travel Agents, American Soc. of (1931), 1101 King St., Ste. 200, Alexandria, VA 22314; 20,000+; www.astanet.com
Travelers Protective Assn. of America (1890), 3755 Lindell Blvd., St. Louis, MO 63108; 91,008; www.tpahq.org
Truck Historical Soc., American (1971), P.O. Box 901611, Kansas City, MO 64190; 22,000+; www.aths.org
Tuberous Sclerosis Alliance (1974), 801 Roeder Rd., Ste. 750, Silver Spring, MD 20910; approx. 2,000; www.tsalliance.org
UFOs, Natl. Investigations Committee on (1967) 21601 Devonshire St., #217, Chatsworth, CA 91311; 250; www.nicufo.org
Underwriters (CPCU), Soc. of Chartered Property and Casualty (1944), 720 Providence Rd., Malvern, PA 19355; 24,800; www.cpcusociety.org
UNICEF, U.S. Fund for (1947), 333 E. 38th St., New York, NY 10016; www.unicefusa.org
United. See also other entries under next major word in title.
Uniformed Services, Natl. Assn. for (1968), 5535 Hempstead Way, Springfield, VA 22151; 202,780; www.naus.org
United Nations Assn. of the U.S.A. (1943), 801 2nd Ave., 2nd Fl., New York, NY 10017; 20,000; www.unausa.org
United Order True Sisters, Inc. (1846), Linton Intl. Plaza, 600 Linton Blvd, Ste. 6, Delray Beach, FL 33444; approx. 2,000; uots.org
United Press Intl. (1907), 1510 H St. NW, Washington, DC 20005; www.upi.com
United Way of America (1918), 701 N. Fairfax St., Alexandria, VA 22314; approx. 1,400 org.; national.unitedway.org
Universities, Assn. of American (1900), 1200 New York Ave., NW, Ste. 550, Washington, DC 20005; 62 coll/univ.; www.aau.edu
University Women, American Assn. of (1881), 1111 16th St. NW, Washington, DC 20036; 100,000+; www.aauw.org
Urban League, Natl. (1910), 120 Wall St., New York, NY 10005; 100 local affiliates; www.nul.org
USO World Headquarters (1941), 2111 Wilson Blvd., Ste. 1200, Arlington, VA 22201; www.uso.org
USS *Forrestal* CVA/CV/AVT-59 Assn., Inc. (1990), 300 Cassady Avenue, Virginia Beach, VA 23452; 2,600; www.ussforrestal.org
USS *Idaho* Assn. (1957), P.O. Box 711247, San Diego, CA 92171; 231
USS *Los Angeles CA-135* Assn. (1977), c/o Myron Shoemaker, 1240 Hendrick Dr. #K4, Carbondale, CO 81623; 365; www.uss-la-ca135.org
USS *Missouri* Memorial Assn., Inc. (1994), P.O. Box 879, Aiea, HI 96701; 1,500; www.ussmissouri.org
Ventriloquists, North American Assn. of (1944), P.O. Box 420, Littleton, CO 80160; 1,450; www.maherstudios.com/naav.htm
Veterans of Foreign Wars of the U.S. (1899), 406 W. 34th St., Kansas City, MO 64111; 1.8 mil+.; www.vfw.org
Veterans of Foreign Wars of the U.S., Ladies Auxiliary to the (1914), 406 W. 34th St., Kansas City, MO 64111; 616,439; www.ladiesauxvfw.org
Veterans of the Vietnam War, Inc. (1978), 805 S. Township Blvd., Pittston, PA 18640-3327; 15,000; www.vvnw.org
Veterinary Medical Assn., American (1863), 1931 N. Meacham Rd., Schaumburg, IL 60173; 72,000; www.avma.org
Victorian Society in America (1966), 205 S Camac St., Philadelphia, PA 19107; 3,000; www.victoriansociety.org
Volleyball, USA (1928), 715 S. Circle Dr., Colorado Springs, CO 80910; 191,000; www.usavolleyball.org
Volunteers of America (1896), 1660 Duke St., Alexandria, VA 22314; 14,000 staff, 70,000 volunteers; www.voa.org
War Mothers, American (1917), 5415 Connecticut Ave., NW, Ste. L-30, Washington, DC 20015; 500
Watch & Clock Collectors, Inc., Natl. Assn. of (NAWCC) (1943), 514 Poplar St., Columbia, PA 17512; 27,000; www.nawcc.org
Watercolor Society, American (1866), 47 5th Ave., New York, NY 10003; 480; www.americanwatercolorsociety.com
Water Environment Federation (1928), 601 Wythe St., Alexandria, VA 22314; 76 assns.; www.wef.org
Water Works Assn., American (1881), 6666 W. Quincy Ave., Denver, CO 80235; 57,000; www.awwa.org
Wheelchair Sports, USA (1956), 1668 320th Way, Earlham, IA 50072; 4,000; www.wsusa.org
Wildlife Federation, Natl. (1936),11100 Wildlife Center Dr., Reston, VA, 20190; 4 mil.; www.nwf.org
Wildlife Management Institute (1911), 1146 19th St. NW, Ste. 700, Washington, DC 20036; 300; www.wildlifemanagementinstitute.org
Wizard of Oz Club, Intl. (1957), P.O. Box 26249, San Francisco, CA 94126; 1,300+; www.ozclub.org
Women, Natl. Organization for (NOW) (1966), 1100 H St. NW, 3rd Fl., Washington, DC 20005; 500,000; www.now.org
Women and Families, Natl. Partnership for (1971), 1875 Connecticut Ave. NW, Ste. 650, Washington, DC 20009; 2,000; www.nationalpartnership.org
Women Artists, Inc., Natl. Assn. of (1889), 80 5th Ave., Ste. 1405, New York, NY 10011; 800+; www.nawanet.org
Women in Communications, The Association for (1909 as Theta Sigma Phi), 780 Ritchie Hwy., Ste. 28-S, Severna Park, MD 21146; 4,000+; www.womcom.org
Women Engineers, Society of (1950), 230 E. Ohio St., Ste. 400, Chicago, IL 60611; 17,000; www.swe.org
Women in Radio and Television Inc., Amer. (1951), 8405 Greensboro Dr., Ste. 800, McLean, VA 22102; www.awrt.org
Women's Army Corps Veterans Assn. (1946), P.O. Box 5577, Ft. McClellan, AL 36205; 4,500; www.armywomen.org
Women's Christian Temperance Union, Natl. (1874), 1730 Chicago Ave., Evanston, IL 60201; www.wctu.org
Women's Clubs, General Federation of (1890), 1734 N St. NW, Washington, DC, 20036; 180,000 U.S.; www.gfwc.org
Women Voters of the U.S., League of (1920), 1730 M St. NW, Ste. 1000, Washington, DC 20036; 130,000; www.lwv.org
Woodmen of America, Modern (1883), 1701 1st Ave., Rock Island, IL 61201; 750,000; www.modern-woodmen.org
Workmen's Circle (1900), 45 E. 33rd St., New York, NY 10016; 35,000; www.circle.org
World Council of Churches, U.S. Office (1948), 475 Riverside Drive, Rm. 1371, New York, NY 10115; 330+ denominations, www.wcc-usa.org.
World Federalist Assn. (1947), 418 7th St. SE, Washington, DC 20003; 11,000
World Future Society (1966), 7910 Woodmont Ave., Ste. 450, Bethesda, MD 20814; 25,000; www.wfs.org
World Learning (1954), Kipling Rd., P.O. Box 676, Brattleboro, VT 05302-0676; 100,000; www.worldlearning.org
World Wildlife Fund (1961), 1250 24th St. NW, Washington, DC 20037; 1.2 mil+; www.worldwildlife.org
Writers Guild of America, West (1933), 7000 W. Third St., Los Angeles, CA 90048; 10,500; www.wga.org
YMCA (Young Men's Christian Assn.) of the U.S.A. (1851) 101 N. Wacker Dr., Chicago, IL 60606; 18.9 mil.; www.ymca.net
YWCA (Young Women's Christian Assn.) of the U.S.A. (1858), 1015 18th St. NW, Ste. 1100, Washington, DC 20036; approx. 2 mil; www.ywca.org
Zionist Organization of America (1897), 4 E. 34th St., New York, NY 10016; 50,000; www.zoa.org
Zoo and Aquarium Assn., American (1924), 8403 Colesville Road, Suite 710, Silver Spring, MD 20910; 212 institutions, 5,500 individuals; www.aza.org

100 MOST POPULOUS U.S. CITIES

Source: Bureau of Labor Statistics: employment; Bureau of Econ. Analysis: per cap. income; other data U.S. Census Bureau.

Included here are the 100 most populous U.S. cities, using 2004 Census Bureau estimates. Population rank indicated by figure in parentheses. (Two cities joined the list in 2004—Reno, NV and San Bernadino, CA; dropping off were Yonkers, NY, and Tacoma, WA). Most data are for the city proper. Some statistics, where noted, apply to the whole Metropolitan Statistical Area (MSA). Employment figures are for 2004; per capita income figures for 2003. Mayors are as of Sept. 2005. Inc.=incorporated; est.=established. **Note:** Websites are as of Sept. 2005 and subject to change. For a listing of the 100 largest U.S. cities, ranked by population, see p. 479.

Akron, Ohio

Population (2004): 212,179 (88); **Pop. density**: 3,417 per. sq. mi.; **Pop. change (2000-2004)**: -2.3%. **Area:** 62.1 sq. mi. **Employment (2004):** 98,282 employed; 6.9% unemployed. **Per capita income (MSA):** $30,878; increase (2002-2003): +3.1%.

Mayor: Donald L. Plusquellic, Democrat

History: settled 1825; inc. as city 1865; located on Ohio-Erie Canal and is a port of entry; polymer center of the Americas.

Transportation: 1 airport; major trucking industry; Conrail, Amtrak; metro transit system. **Communications:** 1 TV, 8 radio stations; 1 daily newspaper. **Medical facilities:** 4 hosp.; specialized children's treatment center. **Educational facilities:** 4 univ. and colleges; 68 pub. schools. **Further information:** Greater Akron Chamber, One Cascade Plaza, 17th Floor, Akron, OH 44308; www.ci.akron.oh.us; www.greaterakronchamber.org

Albuquerque, New Mexico

Population (2004): 484,246 (33); **Pop. density**: 2,681 per. sq. mi.; **Pop. change (2000-2004)**: +7.9%. **Area:** 180.6 sq. mi. **Employment (2004):** 239,182 employed; 5.1% unemployed. **Per capita income (MSA):** $28,519; increase (2002-2003): +2.3%.

Mayor: Martin Chavez, Democrat

History: founded 1706 by the Spanish; inc. 1890.

Transportation: 1 intl. airport; 1 railroad; 11 bus service/charters. **Communications:** 13 TV, 32 radio stations. **Medical facilities:** 6 major hosp. **Educational facilities:** 1 univ., 25 colleges. **Further information:** Albuquerque Convention & Visitors Bureau, PO Box 26866, Albuquerque, NM 87125-6866; www.itsatrip.org; www.cabq.gov/a-z.org

Anaheim, California

Population (2004): 333,776 (54); **Pop. density**: 6,826 per. sq. mi.; **Pop. change (2000-2004)**: +1.8%. **Area:** 48.9. **Employment (2004):** 162,379 employed; 5.5% unemployed. **Per capita income (MSA):** $33,347; increase (2002-2003): +2.4%.

Mayor: Curt Pringle, Republican

History: founded 1857; inc. 1870; home of Disneyland Resort, Mighty Ducks of Anaheim, and the Anaheim Angels.

Transportation: Amtrak, Metrolink (2 sta.), OCTA bus service, Greyhound. **Communications:** 2 TV, 2 radio stations (MSA). **Medical facilities:** 4 hosp.; 5 medical centers. **Educational facilities:** 13 univ. and colleges; 39 elem., 11 junior high, 10 high schools (MSA). **Further information:** City Hall, 200 South Anaheim Blvd., Ste. 733, Anaheim, CA 92805; www.anaheim.net

Anchorage, Alaska

Population (2004): 272,687 (68); **Pop. density:** 161 per sq. mi; **Pop. change (2000-2004)**: +4.8%. **Area:** 1697.2 sq. mi. **Employment (2004):** 137,114 employed; 5.9% unemployed. **Per capita income (MSA):** $36,083; increase (2002-2003): +1.5%.

Mayor: Mark Begich, Democrat

History: founded 1914 as a construction camp for railroad; HQ of Alaska Defense Command, WWII; severely damaged in earthquake 1964, now rebuilt; current population center of Alaska.

Transportation: 1 intl. airport; 1 railroad; transit system, 1 port. **Communications:** 9 TV, 28 radio stations. **Medical facilities:** 4 hosp. **Educational facilities:** 3 univ., 1 college, 91 pub. schools. **Further information:** Anchorage Chamber of Commerce, 441 W. 5th Ave., Ste. 300, Anchorage, AK 99501-2309; www.ci.anchorage.ak.us; www.anchoragechamber.org

Arlington, Texas

Population (2004): 359,467 (50); **Pop. density**: 3,752 per sq. mi; **Pop. change (2000–2004):** +8.0%. **Area:** 95.8 sq. mi. **Employment (2004):** 192,358 employed; 5.3% unemployed. **Per capita income (MSA):** $33,790; increase (2002-2003): +0.1%.

Mayor: Robert Cluck, Non-Partisan

History: settled in 1840s; inc. 1884.

Transportation: 1 intl. airport; 1 rail line, Union Pacific. **Communications:** 11 TV, 44 radio stations. **Medical facilities:** 2 hosp. **Educational facilities:** 1 univ., 1 junior college; 60 pub. schools. **Further information:** Arlington Chamber of Commerce, 505 East Border, Arlington, TX 76010; City of Arlington, 101 W. Abram, Arlington, TX 76010; www.ci.arlington.tx.us; www.arling ontx.com

Atlanta, Georgia

Population (2004): 419,122 (42); **Pop. density**: 3,182 per sq. mi; **Pop. change (2000-2004)**: +0.6%. **Area:** 131.7 sq. mi. **Employment (2004):** 182,532 employed; 7.7% unemployed. **Per capita income (MSA):** $33,308; increase (2002-2003): +0.1%.

Mayor: Shirley Franklin, Democrat

History: founded as "Terminus" 1837; renamed Atlanta 1845; inc. 1847; played major role in Civil War; became permanent state capital 1877; birthplace of civil rights movement; host to 1996 Centennial Olympic Games.

Transportation: 1 intl. airport; 3 railroad lines; MARTA bus and rapid rail service. **Communications:** 14 TV, 56 radio stations; 29 cable TV cos. **Medical facilities:** 61 hosp.; VA hosp.; U.S. Centers for Disease Control and Prevention; American Cancer Society. **Educational facilities:** 43 colleges, univ., seminaries, junior colleges; 85 pub. schools. **Further information:** Metro Atlanta Chamber of Commerce, 235 Andrew Young Intl. Blvd. NW, Atlanta, GA 30303; www.metroatlantachamber.com; www.atlantaga.gov

Aurora, Colorado

Population (2004): 291,843 (60); **Pop. density**: 2,048 per sq. mi; **Pop. change (2000-2004)**: +5.6%. **Area:** 142.5 sq. mi. **Employment (2004):** 151,620 employed; 6.8% unemployed. **Per capita income (MSA):** $39,203; increase (2002-2003): +0.7%.

Mayor: Ed Tauer, Non-Partisan

History: early growth stimulated by presence of military bases; fast-growing trade, technology, and medical science center.

Transportation: adjacent to Denver Intl. Airport; bus system. **Communications:** 1 TV station. **Medical facilities:** Major pub. univ. medical center; 2 pub. hosp. **Educational facilities:** 1 univ., 4 community and junior colleges, 2 technical colleges; 68 pub. schools, 4 private schools. **Further information:** Aurora Planning Dept., 15151 E. Alameda Pkwy., Aurora, CO 80012; www.auroragov.org; www.aurorachamber.org

Austin, Texas

Population (2004): 681,804 (16); **Pop. density**: 2,711 per sq. mi; **Pop. change (2000-2004)**: +3.8%. **Area:** 251.5 sq. mi. **Employment (2004):** 386,141 employed; 5.5% unemployed. **Per capita income (MSA):** $31,135; increase (2002-2003): +0.7%.

Mayor: Will Wynn, Non-Partisan

History: first permanent settlement 1835; capital of Rep. of Texas 1839; named after Stephen Austin; inc. 1840.

Transportation: 1 intl. airport; 2 railroads. **Communications:** 8 TV, 29 radio stations. **Medical facilities:** 15 hosp. **Educational facilities:** 5 univ. and colleges. **Further information:** Greater Austin Chamber, 210 Barton Springs Rd., Ste. 400, Austin, TX 78704; www.ci.austin.tx.us; www.austinchamber.com

Bakersfield, California

Population (2004): 283,936 (62); **Pop. density:** 2,511 per sq. mi; **Pop. change (2000-2004)**: +14.9%. **Area:** 113.1 sq. mi. **Employment (2004):** 126,063 employed; 6.8% unemployed. **Per capita income (MSA):** $22,947; increase (2002-2003): +1.4%.

Mayor: Harvey Hall, Non-Partisan

History: named after Col. Thomas Baker, an early settler; inc. 1898.

Transportation: 2 airports; 3 railroads; Amtrak; Greyhound buses; local bus system. **Communications:** 8 TV, 29 radio stations. **Medical facilities:** 9 major hosp.; 9 convalescent, 1 psychiatric, 3 physical rehab., 5 urgent care facilities; 3 clinics. **Educational facilities:** 9 univ., 1 community college, 14 vocational schools, 1 adult school, 15 elem. school districts, 14 high schools (Kern County). **Further information:** Greater Bakersfield Chamber of Commerce, 1725 Eye St., PO Box 1947, Bakersfield, CA 93303; www.bakersfieldchamber.org

Baltimore, Maryland

Population (2004): 636,251 (18); **Pop. density:** 7,874 per sq. mi; **Pop. change (2000-2004):** –2.3%. **Area:** 80.8 sq. mi. **Employment (2004):** 250,382 employed; 7.4% unemployed. **Per capita income (MSA):** $36,733; increase (2002-2003): +2.2%.

Mayor: Martin O'Malley, Democrat

History: founded by Maryland legislature 1729; inc. 1797; War of 1812 British bombing of Ft. McHenry (1814) inspired Francis Scott Key to write "Star-Spangled Banner"; birthplace of America's railroads 1828; rebuilt after fire 1904; site of National Aquarium 1981.

Transportation: 1 major airport; 3 railroads; bus system; subway system; light rail system; Inner Harbor water taxi system; 2 underwater tunnels. **Communications:** 6 TV, 25 radio stations. **Medical facilities:** 31 hosp.; 2 major medical centers. **Educational facilities:** over 30 univ. and colleges; 186 pub. schools. **Further information:** Greater Baltimore Committee, 111 S. Calvert St., Ste. 1700, Baltimore, MD 21202-6180; www.ci.baltimore.md.us; www.baltimore.org

IT'S A FACT: One might think that the city of Buffalo was named after the animal, but historians think otherwise. In 1780, Seneca Indians established a village on the site of the future city in an area long visited by French explorers, and named it for a nearby stream known as Buffalo Creek. But the likely origin of the stream's name was not the animal, but a corruption of the French term *beau fleuve*, which means "beautiful river."

Baton Rouge, Louisiana

Population (2004): 224,097 (80); **Pop. density:** 2,918 per sq. mi; **Pop. change (2000-2004)**: –1.6%. **Area:** 76.8 sq. mi. **Employment (2004):** 102,165 employed; 7.1% unemployed. **Per capita income (MSA):** $26,921; increase (2002-2003): +2.3%.

Mayor: Melvin "Kip" Holden, Democrat

History: claimed by Spain at time of Louisiana Purchase 1803; est. independence by rebellion 1810; inc. as town 1817; became state capital 1849; Union-held most of Civil War.

Transportation: 1 airport, 5 airlines; 1 bus line; 3 railroad trunk lines. **Communications:** 5 TV, 19 radio stations. **Medical facilities:** 5 hosp. **Educational facilities:** 107 pub., 52 nonpublic schools; 2 univ., 1 Community College, 1 Technical College. **Further information:** The Chamber of Greater Baton Rouge, PO Box 3217, Baton Rouge, LA 70821; www.brgov.com; www.brchamber.org

Birmingham, Alabama

Population (2004): 233,149 (76); **Pop. density:** 1,555 per sq. mi; **Pop. change (2000-2004)**: –4.0%. **Area:** 149.9 sq. mi. **Employment (2004):** 102,198 employed; 8.2% unemployed. **Per capita income (MSA):** $31,540; increase (2002-2003): +2.7%.

Mayor: Bernard Kincaid, Democrat

History: settled 1871 at the intersection of 2 major railroads, within proximity of elements needed for iron and steel production.

Transportation: 1 intl. airport; 4 major rail freight lines, Amtrak; 1 bus line; 75 truck line terminals; 5 air cargo cos.; 7 barge lines; 5 interstate highways. **Communications:** 7 TV, 32 radio stations; 1 educational TV, 1 educational radio station. **Medical facilities:** 16, including the Univ. of Alabama at Birmingham Medical Center; VA hosp. **Educational facilities:** 1 pub., 2 private univ.; 4 private colleges, 3 private law schools. **Further information:** Birmingham Area Chamber of Commerce, 2027 First Ave. N, Birmingham, AL 35203; www.birminghamchamber.com; www.informationbirmingham.com

Boston, Massachusetts

Population (2004): 569,165 (24); **Pop. density:** 11,760 per sq. mi; **Pop. change (2000-2004)**: –3.4%. **Area:** 48.4 sq. mi. **Employment (2004):** 279,883 employed; 5.5% unemployed. **Per capita income (MSA):** $43,135; increase (2002-2003): +1.4%.

Mayor: Thomas M. Menino, Democrat

History: settled 1630 by John Winthrop; capital of Mass. Bay Colony; figured strongly in Am. Revolution, earning distinction as the "Cradle of Liberty"; inc. 1822.

Transportation: 1 major airport; 2 railroads; city rail and subway system; 3 underwater tunnels; port. **Communications:** 12 TV, 21 radio stations. **Medical facilities:** 31 hosp.; 8 major medical research centers. **Educational facilities:** 30 univ. and colleges. **Further information:** Greater Boston Convention and Visitors Bureau, 2 Copley Pl., Suite 105, Boston, MA 02116; www.bostonusa.com

Buffalo, New York

Population (2004): 282,864 (63); **Pop. density:** 6,967 per sq. mi; **Pop. change (2000-2004)**: –3.3%. **Area:** 40.6 sq. mi. **Employment (2004):** 116,290 employed; 7.3% unemployed. **Per capita income (MSA):** $29,145; increase (2002-2003): +3.3%.

Mayor: Anthony M. Masiello, Democrat

History: settled 1780 by Seneca Indians; raided twice by British, War of 1812; served as western terminus for Erie Canal, became a center for trade and manufacturing; inc. 1832; last stop on the Underground Railroad; key point for Canada-U.S. political, trade, and social relations.

Transportation: 1 intl. airport; 4 Class I railroads; Amtrak metro rail system; water service to Great Lakes-St. Lawrence Seaway system and Atlantic seaboard. **Communications:** 11 TV, 27 radio stations. **Medical facilities:** 16 hosp., 40 research centers. **Educational facilities:** 15 colleges and univ.; 400 pub. and private schools. **Further information:** Buffalo Niagara Visitor Center, Market Arcade/Walden Galleria, 617 Main Street, Buffalo, NY 14203; www.ci.buffalo.ny.us; buffaloniagara.org

Chandler, Arizona

Population (2004): 223,991 (81); **Pop. density:** 3,869 per sq. mi; **Pop. change (2000-2004)**: +26.8%. **Area:** 57.9 sq. mi. **Employment (2004):** 110,262 employed; 3.4% unemployed. **Per capita income (MSA):** $29,590; increase (2002-2003): +1.7%.

Mayor: Boyd W. Dunn, Non-Partisan

History: town formed 1912; population doubled in 1990s as "the high-tech oasis of the Silicon Desert."

Transportation: 1 municipal airport; mass transit system. **Communications:** 2 TV, 3 newspapers. **Medical facilities:** 1 medical center. **Educational facilities:** 2 univ., 2 community coll.; 26 elem., 7 junior high, 4 high schools; 13 charter schools **Further information:** Chandler Chamber, 25 South Arizona Pl., Suite 201, Chandler, AZ 85225; www.chandlerchamber.com; chandleraz.gov

Charlotte, North Carolina

Population (2004): 594,359 (20); **Pop. density:** 2,453 per sq. mi; **Pop. change (2000-2004)**: +9.9%. **Area:** 242.3 sq. mi. **Employment (2004):** 307,936 employed; 5.5% unemployed. **Per capita income (MSA):** $33,251; increase (2002-2003): +0.6%.

Mayor: Patrick McCrory, Republican

History: settled by Scotch-Irish immigrants 1740s; inc. 1768 and named after Queen Charlotte, George III's wife; scene of first major U.S. gold discovery 1799.

Transportation: 1 airport; 2 major railway lines; 1 bus line; 605 trucking firms. **Communications:** 12 TV, 28 radio stations. **Medical facilities:** 10 hosp., 2 medical centers. **Educational facilities:** 9 univ., 9 colleges, 89 elem. schools, 31 middle schools, 17 high schools. **Further information:** Chamber of Commerce, PO Box 32785, Charlotte, NC 28232; www.charlottechamber.com

Chesapeake, Virginia

Population (2004): 214,725 (86); **Pop. density:** 630.2 per sq. mi; **Pop. change (2000-2004)**: +7.8%. **Area:** 340.7 sq. mi. **Employment (2004):** 102,281 employed; 3.7% unemployed. **Per capita income (MSA):** $29,337; increase (2002-2003): +2.4%.

Mayor: Dalton S. Edge, Non-Partisan

History: region settled in 1620s with first English colonies on banks of Elizabeth River; home to Great Dismal Swamp Canal, first envisioned by George Washington in 1763; Battle of Great Bridge fought here Dec. 1775; inc. as a city 1963.

Transportation: Freight rail service; bus service; 2 regional airports. **Communications:** 9 TV, 48 radio stations (serving Hampton Roads community). **Medical facilities:** 1 hosp. **Educational facilities:** 9 colleges and univ.; 49 pub. schools and educational centers. **Further information:** City of Chesapeake, Public Communications Dept., 306 Cedar Rd., Chesapeake, VA 23322; www.cityofchesapeake.net

Chicago, Illinois

Population (2004): 2,862,244 (3); **Pop. density:** 12,604 per sq. mi; **Pop. change (2000-2004)**: –1.2%. **Area:** 227.1 sq. mi. **Employment (2004):** 1,233,434 employed; 7.2% unemployed. **Per capita inc. (MSA):** $35,464; increase (2002-2003): +1.1%

Mayor: Richard M. Daley, Democrat

History: site acquired from Indians 1795; significant white settlement began with Erie Canal 1825; chartered as city 1837; boomed with arrival of railroads and canal to Mississippi R.; one-third of city destroyed by fire 1871; major grain and livestock market.

Transportation: 2 airports; major railroad system, trucking industry. **Communications:** 15 TV, 35 radio stations. **Medical facilities:** over 41 hosp. **Educational facilities:** 63 insts. of higher learning. **Further information:** Chicagoland Chamber of Commerce, 1 IBM Plaza, Ste. 2800, Chicago, IL 60611; www.cityofchicago.org; www.chicagolandchamber.org

Chula Vista, California

Population (2004): 204,879 (92); **Pop. density:** 4,190 per sq. mi; **Pop. change (2000-2004)**: +18%. **Area:** 48.9 sq. mi. **Employment (2004):** 82,023 employed; 5.5% unemployed. **Per capita income (MSA):** $35,841; increase (2002-2003): +2.7%.

Mayor: Stephen C. Padilla, Non-Partisan

History: visited by Spanish in 1542; became part of Spanish land grant in 1795; came into the U.S. during the Mexican War in 1847; inc. 1911. WWII brought aircraft industry and growth.

Transportation: bus system; DART. **Communications**: See San Diego, CA. **Medical facilities:** 2 hosp. **Educational facilities:** 39 elementary, 7 middle, 3 junior high, 10 senior high, 5 colleges and univ. **Further Information:** Chula Vista Chamber of Commerce, 233 Fourth Ave., Chula Vista, CA 91910. www.chulavistachamber.org

Cincinnati, Ohio

Population (2004): 314,154 (58); **Pop. density:** 4,028 per sq. mi; **Pop. change (2000-2004)**: –5.2%. **Area:** 78.0 sq. mi. **Employment (2004):** 147,874 employed; 6.4% unemployed. **Per capita income (MSA):** $32,979; increase (2002-2003): +2.5%.

Mayor: Charlie Luken, Democrat

History: founded 1788 and named after the Society of Cincinnati, an organization of Revolutionary War officers; chartered as village 1802; inc. as city 1819.

Transportation: 1 intl. airport; 3 railroads; 2 bus systems. **Communications:** 7 TV, 25 radio stations. **Medical facilities:** 28 hosp.; Cincinnati Children's Hosp. Medical Center; VA hosp.

Educational facilities: 4 univ., 12 colleges, 8 technical & 2-year colleges. **Further information:** Chamber of Commerce, 300 Carew Tower, 441 Vine St., Cincinnati, OH 45202; www.cincinnatichamber.com; www.cincinnatiusa.org

Cleveland, Ohio

Population (2004): 458,684 (36); **Pop. density:** 5,911 per sq. mi; **Pop. change (2000-2004)**: –4.1%. **Area:** 77.6 sq. mi. **Employment (2004):** 178,437 employed; 8.2% unemployed. **Per capita income (MSA):** $33,196; increase (2002-2003): +3.0%.

Mayor: Jane Campbell, Democrat

History: surveyed in 1796; given recognition as village 1815, inc. as city 1836; annexed Ohio City 1854.

Transportation: 1 intl. airport; rail service; major port; rapid transit system. **Communications:** 9 TV, 21 radio stations. **Medical facilities:** 14 hosp. **Educational facilities:** 8 univ. and colleges; 127 pub. schools. **Further information:** Greater Cleveland Growth Assn., Tower City Center, 50 Pub. Square, Suite 200, Cleveland, OH 44113-2291; www.clevelandgrowth.com; www.city.cleveland.oh.us

Colorado Springs, Colorado

Population (2004): 369,363 (49); **Pop. density:** 1,989 per sq. mi; **Pop. change (2000-2004)**: +2.3%. **Area:** 185.7 sq. mi. **Employment (2004):** 192,844 employed; 5.5% unemployed. **Per capita income (MSA):** $30,736; increase (2002-2003): +1.3%.

Mayor: Lionel Rivera, Non-Partisan

History: city founded in 1871 at the foot of Pike's Peak; inc. 1872.

Transportation: 1 municipal airport; 1 bus line. **Communications:** 9 TV, 28 radio stations. **Medical facilities:** 5 hosp. **Educational facilities:** 11 univ., 5 colleges. **Further information:** Chamber of Commerce, 2 N. Cascade, Ste. 110, Colorado Springs, CO 80901; www.springsgov.com; www.coloradospringschamber.org

Columbus, Ohio

Population (2004): 730,008 (15); **Pop. density:** 3,471 per sq. mi; **Pop. change (2000-2004)**: +2.6%. **Area:** 210.3 sq. mi. **Employment (2004):** 386,756 employed; 5.4% unemployed. **Per capita income (MSA):** $32,930; increase (2002-2003): +1.9%.

Mayor: Michael B. Coleman, Democrat

History: first settlement 1797; laid out as new capital 1812 with current name; became city 1834.

Transportation: 6 airports; 2 railroads; 2 intercity bus lines. **Communications:** 8 TV, 32 radio stations. **Medical facilities:** 17 hosp. **Educational facilities:** 11 univ. and colleges; 8 technical/2-year schools; 150 pub. schools (95 elem., 26 middle, 19 high, 10 special-purpose). **Further information:** Greater Columbus Chamber of Commerce, 37 N. High St., Columbus, OH 43215. Experience Columbus, 90 N. High St., Columbus, OH 43215; www.columbus-chamber.org; www.experiencecolumbus.org

Corpus Christi, Texas

Population (2004): 281,196 (64); **Pop. density:** 1,819 per sq. mi; **Pop. change (2000-2004)**: +1.3%. **Area:** 154.6 sq. mi. **Employment (2004):** 132,194 employed; 6.1% unemployed. **Per capita income (MSA):** $25,696; increase (2002-2003): +3.6%.

Mayor: Henry Garrett, Non-Partisan

History: settled 1839 and inc. 1852.

Transportation: 1 intl. airport; 2 bus lines, metro bus system; 3 freight railroads. **Communications:** 6 TV, 17 radio stations. **Medical facilities:** 14 hosp. including a children's center. **Educational facilities:** 1 univ., 1 college. **Further information:** Corpus Christi Regional Economic Development Corp., PO Box 2724, Corpus Christi, TX 78403; www.ccredc.com; www.ci.corpuschristi.tx.us

Dallas, Texas

Population (2004): 1,210,393 (9); **Pop. density:** 3,534 per sq. mi; **Pop. change (2000–2004):** +1.8%. **Area:** 342.5 sq. mi. **Employment (2004):** 574,888 employed; 8.1% unemployed. **Per capita income (MSA):** $33,790; increase (2002-2003): +0.1%.

Mayor: Laura Miller, Non-Partisan

History: first settled 1841; platted 1846; inc. 1871; developed as the financial and commercial center of Southwest; headquarters of regional Federal Reserve Bank; major center for distribution and high-tech manufacturing.

Transportation: 1 intl. airport, 1 regional airport; Amtrak; transit system. **Communications:** 17 TV, 52 radio stations. **Medical facilities:** 19 general hosp.; major medical center. **Educational facilities:** 218 pub. schools, 12 univ. and colleges, 3 community college campuses. **Further information:** Greater Dallas Chamber, Resource Center, 700 N. Pearl St., Ste. 1200, Dallas, TX 75201; www.dallaschamber.org; www.dallascityhall.com

Denver, Colorado

Population (2004): 556,835 (25); **Pop. density:** 3,630 per sq. mi; **Pop. change (2000-2004)**: +0.4%. **Area:** 153.4 sq. mi. **Employment (2004):** 286,112 employed; 6.7% unemployed. **Per capita income (MSA):** $39,203; increase (2002-2003): +0.7%.

Mayor: John W. Hickenlooper, Democrat

History: settled 1858 by gold prospectors and miners; inc. 1861; became territorial capital 1867; growth spurred by gold and silver boom; became financial, industrial, cultural center of Rocky Mt. region.

Transportation: 1 intl. airport, 3 corporate reliever airports; 5 rail freight lines, Amtrak; 1 bus line. **Communications:** 14 TV, 29 radio stations. **Medical facilities:** 20 hosp. **Educational facilities:** 15 four-yr. colleges and univ.; 8 two-yr. and community colleges. **Further information:** Denver Metro Chamber of Commerce, 1445 Market St., Denver, CO 80202-1729; www. denverchamber.org

Detroit, Michigan

Population (2004) 900,198 (11); **Pop. density:** 6,486 per sq. mi; **Pop. change (2000-2004)**: –5.4%. **Area:** 138.8 sq. mi. **Employment (2004):** 326,153 employed; 14% unemployed. **Per capita income (MSA):** $35,972; increase (2002-2003): +4.2%.

Mayor: Kwame M. Kilpatrick, Democrat

History: founded by French 1701; controlled by British 1760; acquired by U.S. 1796; destroyed by fire 1805; inc. as city 1815; capital of state 1837-47; auto manufacturing began 1890.

Transportation: 1 intl. airport, 1 general aviation airport; 10 railroads (4 Class I); major intl. port; pub. transit system. **Communications:** 4 TV, 6 radio stations. **Medical facilities:** 13 hosp.; 3 major medical centers. **Educational facilities:** 2 univ., 3 colleges, 1 community college. **Further information:** Detroit Regional Chamber, One Woodward Ave., PO Box 33840, Detroit, MI 48232-0840; www.detroitchamber.com

Durham, North Carolina

Population (2004): 201,726 (95); **Pop. density:** 2,132 per sq. mi; **Pop. change (2000–2004)**: +7.9%. **Area:** 94.6 sq. mi. **Employment (2004)**: 100,959 employed; 4.8% unemployed. **Per capita income (MSA):** $31,466; increase (2002-2003): +1.0%

Mayor: William V. Bell, Non-Partisan

History: Inc. 1869; Trinity College moved to Durham in 1892, renamed Duke Univ. in 1924.

Transportation: 2 area bus systems; 1 airport; 1 train station. **Communications:** 34 radio stations; 6 TV stations. **Medical facilities:** 8 hosp. **Educational facilities:** 45 pub. schools, plus private and charter schools; 1 comm. col.; school of nursing; 2 univ. **Further information:** Durham Convention and Visitors Bureau, 101 E. Morgan St., Durham, NC 2770-3333; www.durham-nc.com

El Paso, Texas

Population (2004): 592,099 (21); **Pop. density:** 2,377 per sq. mi; **Pop. change (2000-2004)**: +5.0%. **Area:** 249.1 sq. mi. **Employment (2004):** 230,441 employed; 7.5% unemployed. **Per capita income (MSA):** $20,875; increase (2002-2003): +3.0%.

Mayor: John Cook, Non-Partisan

History: first settled 1598; inc. 1873; arrival of railroad 1881 boosted city's population and industries.

Transportation: 1 intl. airport; 2 rail providers; 2 interstate highways; 4 intl. ports of entry. **Communications:** 12 TV, 21 radio stations. **Medical facilities:** 8 hosp.; 8 rehabilitation; 11 specialty centers. **Educational facilities:** 5 univ., 2 colleges; 2 grad. and doctoral programs. **Further information:** Greater El Paso Chamber of Commerce, 10 Civic Center Plaza, El Paso, TX 79901; www.elpaso.org

Fort Wayne, Indiana

Population (2004): 219,351 (84); **Pop. density:** 2,777 per sq. mi; **Pop. change (2000–2004)**: +6.6%. **Area:** 79.0 sq. mi. **Employment (2004):** 100,976 employed; 6.7% unemployed. **Per capita income (MSA):** $29,943; increase (2002-2003): +1.9%.

Mayor: Graham A. Richard, Democrat

History: French fort 1680; U.S. fort 1794; settled by 1832; inc. 1840 prior to Wabash-Erie canal completion 1843.

Transportation: 2 airports; 3 railroads; 6 bus lines. **Communications:** 6 TV, 25 radio stations, 11 newspapers. **Medical facilities:** 8 regional hosp.; VA hosp. **Educational facilities:** 5 univ., 4 colleges, 3 bus. schools; 92 pub. schools. **Further information:** Chamber of Commerce, 826 Ewing Street, Fort Wayne, IN 46802-2182; www.fwchamber.org

IT'S A FACT: During its early history, Cleveland was actually "Cleaveland." The city was named for General Moses Cleaveland, who founded the city in 1796, and was known as Cleaveland until 1832, when the local newspaper, the *Cleveland Advertiser*, dropped the "a" so that the paper's name would fit onto the masthead. The new spelling stuck.

Fort Worth, Texas

Population (2004): 603,337 (19); **Pop. density:** 2,063 per sq. mi; **Pop. change (2000-2004)**: +12.8%. **Area:** 292.5 sq. mi. **Employment (2004):** 262,205 employed; 7.3% unemployed. **Per capita income (MSA):** $33,790; increase (2002-2003): +0.1%.

Mayor: Mike Moncrief, Non-Partisan

History: established as military post 1849; inc. 1873; oil discovered 1917.

Transportation: 2 intl. airport, 1 industrial airport; 4 major railroads, Amtrak; local bus service; 1 transcontinental, 1 intrastate bus lines. **Communications:** 15 TV, 95 local radio stations. **Medical facilities:** 10 hosp.; 1 children's hosp.; 4 government hosp. **Educational facilities:** 5 univ. and colleges. **Further information:** Chamber of Commerce, 777 Taylor St. #900, Fort Worth, TX 76102; www.fortworthgov.org; www.fortworthchamber.com

Fremont, California

Population (2004): 202,373 (94); **Pop. density:** 2,63p per sq. mi; **Pop. change (2000-2004)**: –0.5%. **Area:** 76.7 sq. mi. **Employment (2004):** 104,741 employed; 4.3% unemployed. **Per capita income (MSA):** $46,958; increase (2002-2003): +1.3%.

Mayor: Bob Wasserman, Non-Partisan

History: area first settled by Spanish 1769; inc. 1956 with consolidation of 5 communities.

Transportation: intracity bus line; Bay Area Rapid Transit System (southern terminal). **Communications:** 1 radio station. **Medical facilities:** 2 hosp.; 2 major medical facilities; 18 clinics. **Educational facilities:** 1 community college; 42 pub. schools. **Further information:** Chamber of Commerce, 39488 Stevenson Place, Suite 100, Fremont, CA 94539; www.fremontbusiness.com

Fresno, California

Population (2004): 457,719 (37); **Pop. density:** 4,384 per sq. mi; **Pop. change (2000-2004)**: +7.0%. **Area:** 104.4 sq. mi. **Employment (2004):** 194,758 employed; 9.7% unemployed. **Per capita income (MSA):** $24,277; increase (2002-2003): +1.9%.

Mayor: Alan Autry, Non-Partisan

History: founded 1872; inc. as city 1885.

Transportation: 1 municipal airport; Amtrak; 1 bus line; intracity bus system. **Communications:** 15 TV, 23 radio stations. **Medical facilities:** 17 general hosp. **Educational facilities:** 9 colleges; 102 pub. schools. **Further information:** Greater Fresno Area Chamber of Commerce, PO Box 1469, Fresno, CA 93716-1469; www.fresnochamber.com; fresno-online.com

Garland, Texas

Population (2004): 217,176 (85); **Pop. density:** 3,803 per sq. mi; **Pop. change (2000-2004)**: +0.7%. **Area:** 57.1 sq. mi. **Employment (2004):** 110,179 employed; 5.7% unemployed. **Per capita income (MSA):** $33,790; increase (2002-2003): +0.1%.

Mayor: Bob Day, Democrat

History: settled 1850s; inc. 1891.

Transportation: 30 min. from Dallas/Ft. Worth Intl. Airport; 2 railroads. **Communications:** 14 local TV (Dallas/Ft. Worth), 25+ radio stations. **Medical facilities:** 2 hosp.; 348 beds. **Educational facilities:** 3 univ., 2 community colleges; 64 pub. schools. **Further information:** Chamber of Commerce, 914 S. Garland Ave., Garland, TX 75040; www.garlandchamber.com

Glendale, Arizona

Population (2004): 235,591 (75); **Pop. density:** 4,230 per sq. mi; **Pop. change (2000-2004)**: +7.7%. **Area:** 55.7 sq. mi. **Employment (2004):** 123,080 employed; 4.5% unemployed. **Per capita income (MSA):** $29,590; increase (2002-2003): +1.8%.

Mayor: Elaine M. Scruggs, Non-Partisan

History: est. 1892; inc. 1910.

Transportation: 1 local airport. **Communications:** 12 TV stations, 40 radio stations. **Medical facilities:** 3 hosp. **Educational facilities:** 12 institutes of higher education, 9 pub. school districts. **Further information:** City of Glendale Marketing/Communications Department, 5850 W. Glendale Ave, Glendale, AZ 85301; www.glendaleaz.com

Glendale, California

Population (2004): 201,326 (96); **Pop. density:** 6,579 per sq. mi; **Pop. change (2000–2004)**: +3.3%. **Area:** 30.6 sq. mi. **Employment (2004):** 97,231 employed, 5.7% unemployed. **Per capita income (MSA):** $33,347; increase (2002-2003): +2.4%.

Mayor: Rafi Manoukian, Non-Partisan

History: became a town in 1887; inc. 1906.

Transportation: near Los Angeles Intl. airport; 1 local airport; commuter trains, Amtrak; bus system. **Communications:** 21 TV, 70 radio stations. **Medical facilities:** 3 hosp; other facilities. **Educational facilities:** 1 community college; 29 pub. schools. **Further information:** City of Glendale Public Information Officer, 613 E. Broadway, Glendale, CA 91206; www.ci.glendale.ca.us

WORLD ALMANAC QUIZ

Which California city is among the top 10 fastest-shrinking big cities (population over 200,000)?

(a) Los Angeles (b) Fresno
(c) San Francisco (d) San Bernardino

For the answer look in this chapter, or see page 1008.

Greensboro, North Carolina

Population (2004): 231,543 (77); **Pop. density:** 2,212 per sq. mi; **Pop. change (2000-2004)**: +3.4%. **Area:** 104.7 sq. mi. **Employment (2004):** 117,607 employed; 5.7% unemployed. **Per capita income (MSA):** $28,940; increase (2002-2003): +1.4%.

Mayor: Keith Holliday, Non-Partisan

History: settled 1749; site of Revolutionary War conflict 1781 between Generals Nathanael Greene and Cornwallis; inc. 1807, origin of civil rights sit-in movement.

Transportation: 1 intl. airport; 2 railroads; Trailways/Greyhound bus service. **Communications:** all cable TV stations; 11 radio stations. **Medical facilities:** 4 hosp. **Educational facilities:** 2 univ., 4 colleges; 94 pub. schools. **Further information:** Chamber of Commerce, PO Box 3246, Greensboro, NC 27402; www.greensboro-nc.gov; www.greensboro.com

Henderson, Nevada

Population (2004): 224,829 (78); **Pop. density:** 2,821 per sq. mi; **Pop. change (2000-2004)**: 28.2%. **Area:** 79.7 sq. mi. **Employment (2004):** 110,972 employed; 3.2% unemployed. **Per capita income (MSA):** $30,961; increase (2002-2003): +3.5%.

Mayor: James B. Gibson, Non-Partisan.

History: early growth spurred by World War II magnesium mining; inc. 1953.

Transportation: Henderson Executive Airport; Citizens Area Transit (CAT) public transportation. **Communications:** 9 TV stations; 38 radio stations. **Medical facilities:** 3 hosp.; medical center facilities. **Educational facilities:** 5 coll.; 2 vocational schools; 23 elem., 5 middle, 6 high schools. **Further information:** City of Henderson Public Information Office, 240 Water St., Henderson, NV 89015; www.cityofhenderson.gov; www.hendersonchamber.com

Hialeah, Florida

Population (2004): 224,522 (79); **Pop. density:** 11,694 per sq. mi; **Pop. change (2000-2004)**: –0.8%. **Area:** 19.2 sq. mi. **Employment (2004):** 93,515 employed; 6.8% unemployed. **Per capita income (MSA):** $33,094; increase (2002-2003): +1.8%.

Mayor: Raul L. Martinez, Democrat

History: founded 1917, inc. 1925; industrial and residential city NW of Miami; Hialeah Park Horse Racing Track.

Transportation: 5 mi from Miami Intl. Airport; access to Port of Miami; Amtrak; 2 rail freight lines; Metrorail, Metrobus systems. **Communications:** 5 TV, 7 radio stations. **Medical facilities:** 4 hosp. (30 more in the area). **Educational facilities:** 8 univ. and colleges, 25 pub., 39 private schools. **Further information:** Hialeah-Dade Development, Inc., 501 Palm Ave., Hialeah, FL 33010; www.ci.hialeah.fl.us; www.hddi.org

Honolulu, Hawaii

Population (2004): 377,260 (47); **Pop. density:** 4,402 per sq. mi; **Pop. change (2000-2004)**: +1.5%. **Area:** 85.7 sq. mi. **Employment (2004):** 417,985; employed, 3.2% unemployed. **Per capita income (2004):** $32,463; increase (2002-2003): +3.0%.

Mayor: Mufi Hannemann, Non-Partisan

History: harbor entered by Europeans 1778; declared capital of kingdom by King Kamehameha III 1850; Pearl Harbor naval base attacked by Japanese Dec. 7, 1941.

Transportation: 1 major airport; 3 commercial harbors. **Communications:** 16 TV, 38 radio stations. **Medical facilities:** 10 acute, 26 long-term care facilities. **Educational facilities:** 7 univ., 7 community colleges; 169 pub. schools, 88 private schools, 9 charter schools. **Further information:** Hawaii Visitors and Convention Bureau, 2270 Kalakaua Ave., 8th Fl., Honolulu, HI 96815; www.co.honolulu.hi.us; www.gohawaii.com

Houston, Texas

Population (2004): 2,012,626 (4); **Pop. density:** 3,474 per sq. mi; **Pop. change (2000-2004)**: +3.0%. **Area:** 579.4 sq. mi. **Employment (2004):** 951,782; employed; 7.4% unemployed. **Per capita income (MSA):** $34,578; increase (2002-2003): +0.5%.

Mayor: Bill White, Non-Partisan

History: founded 1836; inc. 1837; capital of Repub. of Texas 1837-39; developed rapidly after construction of channel to Gulf of Mexico 1914; world center of oil and natural gas technology.

Transportation: 3 commercial airports; 2 mainline railroads; major bus and rail transit system; major intl. port. **Communications:** 18 TV, 67 radio stations. **Medical facilities:** 75 hosp. (Harris Co.); major medical center. **Educational facilities:** 35 univ. and colleges (Harris Co.) **Further information:** Greater Houston Partnership, 1200 Smith St., Houston, TX 77002-4400; www.houston.org; www.cityofhouston.gov

Indianapolis, Indiana

Population (2004): 784,242 (12); **Pop. density:** 2,169 per sq. mi; **Pop. change (2000-2004)**: +0.3%. **Area:** 361.5 sq. mi. **Employment (2004):** 406,055 employed; 5.5% unemployed. **Per capita income (MSA):** $33,618; increase (2002-2003): +1.9%.

Mayor: Bart Peterson, Democrat

History: settled 1820; became capital 1825.

Transportation: 1 intl. airport; 5 railroads; 3 interstate bus lines. **Communications:** 11 TV, 16 radio stations. **Medical facilities:** 21 hosp.; 1 major medical and research center. **Educational facilities:** 8 univ. and colleges; major pub. library system. **Further information:** Greater Indianapolis Chamber of Commerce, 111 Monument Circle, Ste. 1950, Indianapolis, IN 46204; www.ci.indianapolis.in.us; www.indychamber.com

Jacksonville, Florida

Population (2004): 777,704 (13); **Pop. density:** 1,026 per sq. mi; **Pop. change (2000-2004)**: +5.7%. **Area:** 757.7 sq. mi. **Employment (2004):** 367,821 employed; 5.3% unemployed. **Per capita income (MSA):** $30,525; increase (2002-2003): +2.5%.

Mayor: John Peyton, Republican

History: settled 1816 as Cowford; renamed after Andrew Jackson 1822; inc. 1832; rechartered 1851; scene of conflicts in Seminole and Civil wars.

Transportation: 1 intl. airport; 3 railroads; 2 interstate bus lines; 2 seaports. **Communications:** 7 TV, 34 radio stations. **Medical facilities:** 11 hosp. **Educational facilities:** 7 univ., 5 colleges, 1 community college; 278 pub. schools, 114 private schools. **Further information:** Chamber of Commerce, 3 Independent Drive, Jacksonville, FL 32202; www.expandinjax.com; www.myjaxchamber.com; www.coj.net

Jersey City, New Jersey

Population (2004): 239,079 (72); **Pop. density:** 16,046 per sq. mi; **Pop. change (2000-2004)**: –0.4 %. **Area:** 14.9 sq. mi. **Employment (2004):** 103,979 employed; 7% unemployed. **Per capita income (MSA):** $40,899; increase (2002-2003): +1.8%.

Mayor: Jerramiah Healy, Democrat

History: site bought from Indians 1630; chartered as town by British 1668; scene of Revolutionary War conflict 1779; chartered under present name 1838; important station on Underground Railroad.

Transportation: Intercity bus and subway system; ferry service to Manhattan. **Communications:** see New York, NY. **Medical facilities:** 4 hosp. **Educational facilities:** 3 colleges. **Further information:** Hudson County Chamber of Commerce, 660 Newark Ave., Ste. 220, Jersey City, NJ 07306; www.jerseycityonline.com

Kansas City, Missouri

Population (2004): 444,387 (39); **Pop. density:** 1,418 per sq. mi; **Pop. change (2000-2004)**: +0.6%. **Area:** 313.5 sq. mi. **Employment (2004):** 221,794 employed; 7.5% unemployed. **Per capita income (MSA):** $33,335; increase (2002-2003): +1.4%.

Mayor: Kay Barnes, Non-Partisan

History: settled by 1838 at confluence of the Missouri and Kansas rivers; inc. 1850.

Transportation: 1 intl. airport; a major rail center; more than 300 motor freight carriers; 7 barge lines. **Communications:** 9 TV, 43 radio stations. **Medical facilities:** 50 hosp.; 2 VA hosp. **Educational facilities:** 22 univ. and colleges. **Further information:** Greater Kansas City Chamber of Commerce, 911 Main St., Ste. 2600, Kansas City, MO 64105; www.kcchamber.com

Laredo, Texas

Population (2004): 203,212 (93); **Pop. density:** 2,589 per sq. mi; **Pop. change (2000–2004):** +15.1 %. **Area:** 78.5 sq. mi. **Employment (2004)**: 72,990 employed; 6.5% unemployed. **Per capita income (MSA):** $17,060; increase (2002-2003): +2.5%

Mayor: Elizabeth G. Flores, Democrat

History: founded by Spanish colonists in 1755; part of U.S. from 1848; fast growth fueled by immigration; became principal port of entry into Mexico.

Transportation: 1 intl. airport; 2 railroads; 3 interstate bus lines, 2 local bus lines. **Communications:** 3 TV, 10 radio stations; 2 newspapers. **Medical facilities:** 3 hosp. **Educational facilities:** 1 univ., 1 community college; 62 public schools, 29 private schools; 7 vocational training centers. **Further information:** Laredo Chamber of Commerce, P.O. Box 790, Laredo, TX 78042; www.laredochamber.com

Las Vegas, Nevada

Population (2004): 534,847 (29); **Pop. density:** 4,721 per sq. mi; **Pop. change (2000-2004)**: +11.8%. **Area:** 113.3 sq. mi. **Employment (2004):** 266,075 employed; 4.6% unemployed. **Per capita income (MSA):** $30,961; increase (2002-2003): +3.5%.

Mayor: Oscar B. Goodman, Democrat

History: occupied by Mormons 1855-57; bought by railroad 1903; city of Las Vegas inc. 1911; gambling legalized 1931.

Transportation: 1 intl. airport; 1 railroad; monorail; bus system. **Communications:** 21 TV, 44 radio stations. **Medical facilities:** 11 hosp. **Educational facilities:** 1 univ., 2 state colleges; 277 pub. schools in area. **Further information:** Las Vegas Chamber of Commerce, 3720 Howard Hughes Parkway, Las Vegas, NV 89109-0937; www.lvchamber.com; www.lasvegasnevada.gov

Lexington, Kentucky

Population (2004): 266,358 (69); **Pop. density:** 936 per sq. mi; **Pop. change (2000-2004)**: +2.2%. **Area:** 284.5 sq. mi. **Employment (2004):** 140,688 employed; 3.9% unemployed. **Per capita income (MSA):** $32,118; increase (2002-2003): +3.0%.

Mayor: Teresa Ann Isaac, Non-Partisan

History: site was founded and named in 1775 by hunters after the site of the opening battle of the Revolutionary War at Lexington, Mass.; settled 1779; chartered 1782; inc. as a city 1832.

Transportation: 6 comm. airlines; 2 railroads; city buses. **Communications:** 5 TV, 20 radio stations. **Medical facilities:** 5 general, 5 specialized hosp. **Educational facilities:** 2 univ., 4 colleges, 53 public schools: 6 high schools, 10 middle schools, 35 elementary schools, 2 technology schools. **Further information:** Commerce Lexington, 330 E. Main St., Lexington, KY 40507; www.commercelexington.com

Lincoln, Nebraska

Population (2004): 236,146 (74); **Pop. density:** 3,166 per sq. mi; **Pop. change (2000-2004)**: +4.7%. **Area:** 74.6 sq. mi. **Employment (2004):** 137,355 employed; 3.6% unemployed. **Per capita income (MSA):** $30,855; increase (2002-2003): +2.5%.

Mayor: Coleen J. Seng, Non-Partisan

History: originally called Lancaster; chosen state capital 1867, renamed after Abraham Lincoln; inc. 1869.

Transportation: 1 airport; Greyhound; Amtrak, 2 railroads. **Communications:** 3 TV, 15 radio stations. **Medical facilities:** 6 hosp. including VA, rehabilitation facilities. **Educational facilities:** 3 univ., 3 voc.-tech./business colleges; 55 pub., 30 private schools, 3 focus programs. **Further information:** Chamber of Commerce, PO Box 83006, Lincoln, NE 68501-3006; www.lincoln.org; www.lcoc.com

Long Beach, California

Population (2004): 476,564 (34); **Pop. density:** 9,456 per sq. mi; **Pop. change (2000-2004)**: +3.3%. **Area:** 50.4 sq. mi. **Employment (2004):** 215,264; employed; 7.3% unemployed. **Per capita income (MSA):** $33,347; increase (2002-2003): +2.4%.

Mayor: Beverly O'Neill, Non-Partisan

History: settled as early as 1784 by Spanish; by 1884 present site developed on harbor; inc. 1888; oil discovered 1921.

Transportation: 1 airport; 3 railroads; major intl. port; 4 bus co. with 40 bus lines, light rail service. **Communications:** 1 radio station, 1 CATV franchise. **Medical facilities:** 5 hosp. **Educational facilities:** 1 univ., 1 community college (2 campuses); 87 pub. schools in district. **Further information:** Long Beach City Hall, 333 W. Ocean Blvd., Long Beach, CA 90802; www.ci.long-beach.ca.us; www.lbchamber.com

Los Angeles, California

Population (2004): 3,845,541 (2); **Pop. density:** 8,198 per sq. mi; **Pop. change (2000–2004)**: +4.1%. **Area:** 469.1 sq. mi. **Employment (2004):** 1,737,476 employed; 7.3% unemployed. **Per capita income (MSA):** $33,347; increase (2002-2003): +2.4%.

Mayor: Antonio Villaraigosa, Democrat

History: founded by Spanish 1781; captured by U.S. 1846; inc. 1850; grew rapidly after coming of railroads, 1876 & 1885; Hollywood a district of L.A.

Transportation: 1 intl. airport; 3 railroads; major freeway system; intracity bus and rail system. **Communications:** 21 TV, 83 radio stations. **Medical facilities:** 822 hosp. and clinics in metro. area. **Educational facilities:** 158 univ. and colleges (incl. junior, community, and other); 1,858 pub. schools; 1,120 private schools. **Further information:** Los Angeles Area Chamber of Commerce, 350 S. Bixel St., PO Box 513696, Los Angeles, CA 90051-1696; www.ci.la.ca.us; www.lachamber.org

Louisville, Kentucky

Population (2004): 556,332 (26); **Pop. density:** 1,141 per sq. mi; **Pop. change (2000-2004):** 0.9%. **Area:** 386 sq. mi. **Employment (2004):** 332,773 employed; 5.2% unemployed. **Per capita income (MSA):** $32,485; increase (2002-2003): +2.9%.

Mayor: Jerry Abramson, Democrat

History: settled 1778; named for Louis XVI of France; inc. 1828; base for Union forces in Civil War.

Transportation: 1 municipal airport, 2 private-craft airport; 1 terminal, 4 trunk-line railroads; metro bus line, Greyhound station; 5 barge lines. **Communications:** 6 TV, 21 radio stations, 2 educational. **Medical facilities:** 23 hosp. **Educational facilities:** 10 univ. and colleges, 32 business and vocational schools. **Further information:** Greater Louisville, Inc. Metro Chamber of Commerce, 614 W. Main St., Louisville, KY 40202; www.greaterlouisville.com

Lubbock, Texas

Population (2004): 207,852 (89); **Pop. density:** 1,811 per sq. mi; **Pop. change (2000-2004)**: 4.2%. **Area:** 114.8 sq. mi. **Employment (2004):** 108,497 employed; 4.7% unemployed. **Per capita income (MSA):** $25,085; increase (2002-2003): +1.8%.

Mayor: Mark McDougal, Non-Partisan

History: settled 1879; laid out 1891; inc. 1909 through merger of two towns.

Transportation: 1 intl. airport; 2 railroads, bus line. **Communications:** 9 TV, 25 radio stations. **Medical facilities:** 7 hosp. **Educational facilities:** 3 univ., 1 junior college; 51 pub. schools. **Further information:** Chamber of Commerce, 1301 Broadway, Lubbock, TX 79401; www.ci.lubbock.tx.us; www.lubbockchamber.com

Madison, Wisconsin

Population (2004): 220,332 (83); **Pop. density:** 3,207 per sq. mi; **Pop. change (2000-2004)**: +5.9%. **Area:** 68.7 sq. mi. **Employment (2004):** 136,982 employed; 3.2% unemployed. **Per capita income (MSA):** $35,471; increase (2002-2003): +2.5%.

Mayor: Dave Cieslewicz, Non-Partisan

History: first white settlement 1832; selected as site for state capital, named after James Madison, 1836; chartered 1856.

Transportation: 1 airport, 11 airlines; 1 intracity, 3 intercity bus systems; 3 freight rail lines. **Communications:** 10 TV, 26 radio stations, 3 cable providers. **Medical facilities:** 6 hosp., 92 clinics. **Educational facilities:** 7 colleges and univ., including main branch of Univ. of Wisconsin; 30 elem. schools, 11 middle schools, 5 high schools. **Further information:** Greater Madison Chamber of Commerce, PO Box 71, Madison, WI 53701-0071; www.cityofmadison.com; www.madisonchamber.com

Memphis, Tennessee

Population (2004): 671,929 (17); **Pop. density:** 2,406 per sq. mi; **Pop. change (2000-2004)**: +3.4%. **Area:** 279.3 sq. mi. **Employment (2004):** 279,595 employed; 7.7% unemployed. **Per capita income (MSA):** $31,677; increase (2002-2003): +2.9%.

Mayor: Willie W. Herenton, Democrat

History: French, Spanish, and U.S. forts by 1797; settled by 1819; inc. as town 1826, as city 1840; surrendered charter to state 1879 after yellow fever epidemics; rechartered as city 1893.

Transportation: 1 intl. airport; 5 railroads; 1 bus system. **Communications:** 7 TV, 32 radio stations. **Medical facilities:** 20 hosp. **Educational facilities:** 17 univ. and colleges; 191public schools. **Further information:** Memphis Regional Chamber, 22 N. Front St., 2nd Floor, Memphis, TN 38101; www.ci.memphis.tn.us; www.memphischamber.com

Mesa, Arizona

Population (2004): 437,454 (41); **Pop. density:** 3,500 per sq. mi; **Pop. change (2000-2004)**: +10.4%. **Area:** 125.0 sq. mi. **Employment (2004):** 220,501 employed; 5.8% unemployed. **Per capita income (MSA):** $29,590; increase (2002-2003): +1.8%.

Mayor: Keno Hawker, Non-Partisan

History: founded by Mormons 1878; inc. 1883; population boomed fivefold 1960-80.

Transportation: 2 local airports; metro bus service. **Medical facilities:** 6 major hosp. **Educational facilities:** 5 univ., 7 colleges; 82 pub. schools. **Further information:** Convention and Visitor's Bureau and Mesa Chamber of Commerce, 120 N. Center, Mesa, AZ 85201; www.mesacvb.com; www.mesachamber.org; www.cityofmesa.org

Miami, Florida

Population (2004): 379,724 (46); **Pop. density:** 10,637 per sq. mi; **Pop. change (2000-2004)**: +4.8%. **Area:** 35.7 sq. mi. **Employment (2004):** 147,766 employed; 7.5% unemployed. **Per capita income (MSA):** $33,094; increase (2002-2003): +1.8%.

Mayor: Manuel A. Diaz, Independent

History: site of fort 1836; settlement began 1870; inc. 1896, modern city developed into financial and recreation center; land speculation in 1920s added to city's growth, as did Cuban, Central and South American, and Haitian immigration since 1960.

Transportation: 1 intl. airport; seaport; Amtrak, transit rail system; 2 bus lines; 65 truck lines. **Communications:** 9 commercial, 2 educational TV stations; 48 radio stations. **Medical facilities:** 8 hosp.; VA hosp. **Educational facilities:** 6 univ. and colleges. **Further information:** Greater Miami Chamber of Commerce, Omni Intl. Complex, 1601 Biscayne Blvd., Miami, FL 33132; www.greatermiami.com; www.ci.miami.fl.us

Milwaukee, Wisconsin

Population (2004): 583,624 (22); **Pop. density:** 6,073 per sq. mi; **Pop. change (2000-2004)**: –2.2%. **Area:** 96.1 sq. mi. **Employment (2004):** 254,607 employed; 7.7% unemployed. **Per capita income (MSA):** $35,133; increase (2002-2003): +2.2%.

Mayor: Tom Barrett, Democrat

History: Indian trading post by 1674; settlement began 1835; inc. as city 1848; famous beer industry.

Transportation: 1 intl. airport; 3 railroads; major port; 4 bus lines. **Communications:** 12 TV, 37 radio stations. **Medical facilities:** 7 hosp.; major medical center. **Educational facilities:** 7 univ. and colleges, 182 pub. schools. **Further information:** Visit Milwaukee, 648 N. Plankinton Ave, Milwaukee, WI 53703; www.visitmilwaukee.org

Minneapolis, Minnesota

Population (2004): 373,943 (48); **Pop. density:** 6,811 per sq. mi; **Pop. change (2000-2004)**: –2.3%. **Area:** 54.9 sq. mi. **Employment (2004):** 212,894 employed; 5.1% unemployed. **Per capita income (MSA):** $38,601; increase (2002-2003): 2.2%.

Mayor: R.T. Rybak, Democrat

History: site visited by Hennepin 1680; included in area of military reservations 1819; inc. 1867.

Transportation: 1 intl. airport; 5 railroads. **Communications:** 7 TV, 30 radio stations. **Medical facilities:** 7 hosp., incl. leading heart hosp. at Univ. of Minnesota. **Educational facilities:** 10 univ. and colleges; 121 pub., 28 private schools. **Further information:** City of Minneapolis Office of Pub. Affairs, 323M City Hall, 350 S. 5th Street, Minneapolis, MN 55415; www.ci.minneapolis.mn.us

Modesto, California

Population (2004): 206,769 (90); **Pop. density:** 5,776 per sq. mi; **Pop. change (2000-2004)**: 9.5%. **Area:** 35.8 sq. mi. **Employment (2004):** 90,438 employed; 7.8% unemployed. **Per capita income (MSA):** $24,276; increase (2002-2003): +2.1%.

Mayor: Jim Ridenour, Republican

History: founded 1870 after the Gold Rush of 1849 brought an influx of settlers to the region; recent growth boosted by agriculture and immigration.

Transportation: 1 airport. **Communications:** 8 TV, 15 radio stations. **Medical facilities:** 2 hospitals. **Educational facilities:** 1 junior college, 5 public high schools. **Further information:** Modesto Convention & Visitor Bureau, 1150 Ninth St., Ste. C, Modesto, CA 95354; www.visitmodesto.com

Montgomery, Alabama

Population (2004): 200,983 (97); **Pop. density:** 1,293 per sq. mi; **Pop. change (2000-2004)**: –0.3%. **Area:** 155.4 sq. mi. **Employment (2004):** 90,383 employed; 5.8% unemployed. **Per capita income (MSA):** $28,881; increase (2002-2003): +3.9%.

Mayor: Bobby N. Bright, Democrat

History: inc. as town 1819, as city 1837; became state capital 1846; first capital of Confederacy 1861.

Transportation: 3 airlines; 2 railroads; 2 bus lines; Alabama R. navigable to Gulf of Mexico. **Communications:** 4 TV, 2 CATV, 1 public TV, 16 radio stations. **Medical facilities:** 3 major hosp.; VA and 32 clinics. **Educational facilities:** 8 colleges and univ.; 35 pub., 35 private schools. **Further information:** Montgomery Area Chamber of Commerce, PO Box 79, Montgomery, AL 36101; www.montgomerychamber.com

Nashville, Tennessee

Population (2004): 546,719 (28); **Pop. density:** 1,151 per sq. mi; **Pop. change (2000–2004):** +0.2%. **Area:** 473.3 sq. mi. **Employment (2004):** 292,276 employed; 4.4% unemployed. **Per capita income (MSA):** $33,368; increase (2002-2003): +3.2%.

Mayor: Bill Purcell, Non-Partisan

History: settled 1779; first chartered 1806; became permanent state capital 1843; home of Grand Ole Opry.

Transportation: 1 airport; 1 railroad; bus line; transit system of buses and trolleys. **Communications:** 11 TV, 34 radio stations. **Medical facilities:** 14 hosp.; VA and speech-hearing center. **Educational facilities:** 17 universities and colleges, 129 pub. schools. **Further information:** Chamber of Commerce, 211 Commerce St., Ste 100, Nashville, TN 37201; www.nashvillechamber.com

Newark, New Jersey

Population (2004): 280,451 (65); **Pop. density:** 11,784 per sq. mi; **Pop. change (2000–2004):** 2.5%. **Area:** 23.8 sq. mi. **Employment (2004):** 92,467employed; 10.4% unemployed. **Per capita income (MSA):** $40,899; increase (2002-2003): +1.8%.

Mayor: Sharpe James, Democrat

History: settled by Puritans 1666; used as supply base by Washington 1776; inc. as town 1833, as city 1836.

Transportation: 1 intl. airport; 1 intl. seaport, 4 railroads; bus system; subways. **Communications:** 5 TV, 6 radio stations within city limits, 1 daily newspaper, 8 weekly newspapers. **Medical facilities:** 5 hosp. **Educational facilities:** 5 univ. and colleges; 58 pub. elementary schools, 13 junior and senior high schools, 10 special schools, 2 vocational schools, and 40 private schools. **Further information:** Newark Public Information Office, City of Newark, 920 Broad St., Newark, NJ 07102; www.ci.newark.nj.us; www.rbp.org

New Orleans, Louisiana

New Orleans was devastated by flooding Aug. 30 in the wake of Hurricane Katrina. Almost the entire population was eventually evacuated, with thousands relocated in nearby cities, including Baton Rouge, LA; Houston, TX; and San Antonio, TX. See Table of Contents and Index for further coverage.

Population (2004): 462,269 (35); **Pop. density:** 2,560 per sq. mi; **Pop. change (2000–2004):** –4.6%. **Area:** 180.6 sq. mi. **Employment (2004):** 189,726 employed; 5.2% unemployed. **Per capita income (MSA):** $30,092; increase (2002-2003): +3.4%.

Mayor: C. Ray Nagin, Democrat

History: founded by French 1718; became major seaport on Mississippi R.; acquired by U.S. as part of Louisiana Purchase 1803; inc. as city 1805; Americans defeated British forces at the Battle of New Orleans in 1815.

Transportation: 2 airports; major railroad center; street car and bus lines. **Communications:** 8 TV, 26 radio stations. **Medical facilities:** 22 hosp.; 2 major research centers. **Educational facilities:** 10 univ. and 9 colleges. **Further information:** New Orleans Metropolitan Convention & Visitors Bureau, Inc., 1520 Sugar Bowl Dr., New Orleans, LA 70112; www.neworleanscvb.com; www.cityofno.com

New York, New York

Population (2004): 8,104,079 (1); **Pop. density:** 26,720 per sq. mi; **Pop. change (2000–2004):** +1.2%. **Area:** 303.3 sq. mi. **Employment (2004):** 3,457,022 employed; 7.1% unemployed. **Per capita income (MSA):** $40,899; increase (2002-2003): +1.8%.

Mayor: Michael Bloomberg, Republican

History: trading post established 1624; British took control from Dutch 1664 and named city New York; briefly U.S. capital; Washington inaugurated as president 1789; under new charter, 1898, city expanded to include 5 boroughs: The Bronx, Brooklyn, Queens, and Staten Island, as well as Manhattan; Sept. 11, 2001, terrorist attack destroyed World Trade Center, killed about 2,800.

Transportation: 3 intl. airports serve area; 2 rail terminals; major subway network that includes 28 routes; 244 bus routes; ferry system; 4 underwater tunnels. **Communications:** 17 TV, 67 radio stations. **Medical facilities:** 79 hosp.; 6 academic medical centers. **Educational facilities:** 54 univ. and colleges; 1,198 pub. schools. **Further information:** Convention and Visitors Bureau, 810 Seventh Ave., New York, NY 10019; www.nyc.gov; www.nycvisit.com

Norfolk, Virginia

Population (2004): 237,835 (73); **Pop. density:** 4,429 per sq. mi; **Pop. change (2000–2004):** +1.5%. **Area:** 53.7 sq. mi. **Employment (2004):** 94,543 employed, 5.4% unemployed. **Per capita income (MSA):** $29,337; increase (2002-2003): +2.4%.

Mayor: Paul D. Fraim, Non-Partisan.

History: founded 1682; burned by patriots to prevent capture by British during Revolutionary War; rebuilt and inc. as town 1805, as city 1845; site of world's largest naval base; major east coast commercial port and cruise terminal.

Transportation: 1 intl. airport; 2 railroads; Amtrak; bus system; free downtown shuttle. **Communications:** 13 TV, 6 city-access TV, 27 radio stations. **Medical facilities:** 6 hosp. **Educational facilities:** 2 univ., 2 colleges, 1 medical school; 59 pub. schools. **Further information:** Norfolk Convention and Visitors Bureau, 232 E. Main St., Norfolk, VA 23510; www.norfolk.va.us; www.norfolkcvb.com

Oakland, California

Population (2004): 397,976 (44); **Pop. density:** 7,094 per sq. mi; **Pop. change (2000–2004):** –0.4%. **Area:** 56.1 sq. mi. **Employment (2004):** 178,066 employed; 9.2% unemployed. **Per capita income (MSA):** $46,958; increase (2002-2003): +1.3%.

Mayor: Jerry Brown, Non-Partisan

History: area settled by Spanish 1820; inc. as city under present name 1854.

Transportation: 1 intl. airport; western terminus for 2 railroads; underground, 75-mi underwater subway. **Communications:** 1 TV, 3 radio stations in city. **Medical facilities:** 10 hosp. in MSA. **Educational facilities:** 12 East Bay colleges and univ.; 81 pub. schools. **Further information:** Oakland Metropolitan Chamber of Commerce, 475 14th St., Oakland, CA 94612-1903; www.oaklandchamber.com; www.oaklandnet.com

Oklahoma City, Oklahoma

Population (2004): 528,042 (31); **Pop. density:** 870 per sq. mi; **Pop. change (2000–2004):** +4.3%. **Area.** 607.0 sq. mi. **Employment (2004):** 249,852 employed; 5.0% unemployed. **Per capita income (MSA):** $28,958; increase (2002-2003): +2.7%.

Mayor: Mick Cornett, Non-Partisan

History: settled during land rush in Midwest 1889; inc. 1890; became capital 1910; oil discovered 1928. Bomb in 1995 destroyed federal office bldg., killed 168 people.

Transportation: 1 intl. airport; 2 railroad; pub. transit system; 1 major bus line. **Communications:** 6 TV, 23 radio stations. **Medical facilities:** 26 hosp. **Educational facilities:** 20 univ. and colleges; 83 pub., 37 private schools. **Further information:** Chamber of Commerce, Economic Development Division, 123 Park Ave., Oklahoma City, OK 73102; www.okcchamber.com; www.okccvb.org; www.greateroklahomacity.com.

Omaha, Nebraska

Population (2004): 409,416 (43); **Pop. density:** 3,539 per sq. mi; **Pop. change (2000–2004):** +5.0%. **Area:** 115.7 sq. mi. **Employment (2004):** 213,586 employed; 4.8% unemployed. **Per capita income (MSA):** $33,537; increase (2002-2003): +2.3%.

Mayor: Mike Fahey, Democrat

History: founded 1854; inc. 1857; large food-processing, telecommunications, information-processing center.

Transportation: 10 major airlines; 3 major railroads; intercity bus line. **Communications:** 7 TV, 18 radio stations. **Medical facilities:** 11 hosp.; institute for cancer research. **Educational facilities:** 5 univ., 6 colleges; 243 pub., 78 private schools. **Further information:** Greater Omaha Chamber of Commerce, 1301 Harney St., Omaha, NE 68102; www.ci.omaha.ne.us; www.accessomaha.com

Orlando, Florida

Population (2004): 205,648 (91); **Pop. density:** 2,199 per sq. mi; **Pop. change (2000–2004):** +10.6%. **Area:** 93.5 sq. mi. **Employment (2004):** 108,875 employed; 4.6% unemployed. **Per capita income (MSA):** $28,114; increase (2002-2003): +2.6%.

Mayor: Buddy Dyer, Democrat.

History: Fort Gatlin built just south of present-day Orlando in 1838; name changed from Jernigan to Orlando, 1856; inc. 1875; Walt Disney World opened in 1971.

Transportation: 1 intl. airport; 2 bus lines. **Medical facilities:** 6 hosp. **Communications**: 7 TV, 20 radio stations. **Educational facilities:** 153 public schools; 4 tech schools; 5 colleges and univ.**Further Information:** Orlando/Orange County Convention and Visitors Bureau, 8723 International Dr., Suite 101, Orlando, FL 32819. www.orlandoinfo.com

Philadelphia, Pennsylvania

Population (2004): 1,470,151 (5); **Pop. density:** 10,882 per sq. mi; **Pop. change (2000–2004):** –3.1%. **Area:** 135.1 sq. mi. **Employment (2004):** 584,547 employed; 7.5% unemployed. **Per capita income (MSA):** $37,059; increase (2002-2003): +3.2%.

Mayor: John F. Street, Democrat

History: first settled by Swedes 1638; Swedes surrendered to Dutch 1654; settled by English and Scottish Quakers 1678; named Philadelphia 1682; chartered 1701; Continental Congresses convened 1774, 1775; Declaration of Independence signed here 1776; national capital 1790-1800; state capital 1683-1799.

Transportation: 1 major airport; 3 railroads; major freshwater port; subway, el, rail commuter, bus, and streetcar system. **Communications:** 2 major daily newspapers, 14 TV, 102 radio stations. **Medical facilities:** 41 hosp. **Educational facilities:** 27 univ. and colleges. **Further information:** Greater Philadelphia Chamber of Commerce, Business Information Center, 200 South Broad St., Suite 700, Philadelphia PA 19102; www.phila.gov; www.philachamber.com

Phoenix, Arizona

Population (2004): 1,418,041 (6); **Pop. density:** 2,986 per sq. mi; **Pop. change (2000–2004):** +7.3%. **Area:** 474.9 sq. mi. **Employment (2004):** 725,688 employed; 5.2% unemployed. **Per capita income (MSA):** $29,590; increase (2002-2003): +1.8%.

Mayor: Phil Gordon, Democrat

History: founded 1867; inc. as city 1881; became territorial capital 1889.

Transportation: 1 intl. airport; 2 transcontinental and 10 intrastate railroads; transcontinental bus line; pub. transit system. **Communications:** 12 TV, 17 radio stations. **Medical facilities:** 8 hosp., 1 medical research center. **Educational facilities:** 36 institutions of higher learning; 380 pub. schools (247 elem. and junior high schools, 35 senior high schools, 98 charter schools). **Further information:** Greater Phoenix Chamber of Commerce, 201 N. Central Ave., 27th fl., Phoenix, AZ 85073; www.phoenix.gov; www.phoenix chamber.com

WORLD ALMANAC QUICK QUIZ

Of the top 10 fastest-growing cities with a population of over 200,000, how many are located east of the Mississippi River?

(a) 1 (b) 2 (c) 5 (d) 10

For the answer look in this chapter, or see page 1008.

Pittsburgh, Pennsylvania

Population (2004): 322,450 (56); **Pop. density:** 5,800 per sq. mi; **Pop. change (2000–2004):** –3.6%. **Area:** 55.6 sq. mi. **Employment (2004):** 147,394 employed; 5.9% unemployed. **Per capita income (MSA):** $33,015; increase (2002-2003): +2.6%.

Mayor: Tom J. Murphy, Democrat

History: settled around Ft. Pitt 1758; inc. as city 1816; has one of the largest inland ports; by Civil War, already a center for iron production.

Transportation: 1 intl. airport; 20 railroads; 2 bus lines; trolley/subway system. **Communications:** 6 TV, 26 radio stations. **Medical facilities:** 35 hosp.; VA installation. **Educational facilities:** 3 univ., 6 colleges; 93 pub. schools. **Further information:** Greater Pittsburgh Convention & Visitors Bureau, Regional Enterprise Tower, 30th Floor, 425 Sixth Ave., Pittsburgh, PA 15219; Pittsburgh Regional Alliance, Regional Enterprise Tower, 36th Floor, 425 Sixth Ave., Pittsburgh, PA 15219; www.visitpittsburgh.com; www.pittsburghregion.org

Plano, Texas

Population (2004): 245,411 (71); **Pop. density:** 3,428 per sq. mi; **Pop. change (2000–2004):** +10.5%. **Area:** 71.6 sq. mi. **Employment (2004):** 146,346 employed; 4.8% unemployed. **Per capita income (MSA):** $33,790; increase (2002-2003): +0.1%.

Mayor: Pat Evans, Non-Partisan

History: settled 1846; inc. as city 1873.

Transportation: DART bus line; 2 DART (Dallas Area Rapid Transit) stations. **Communications:** 2 TV,1 radio station. **Medical facilities:** 2 full service hosp., 4 medical treatment centers. **Educational facilities:** 5 institutions of higher learning, 64 pub. schools. **Further information:** City of Plano Public Information Dept. 1520 K Ave., Suite 320, Plano, TX 75074; Plano Chamber of Commerce, PO Drawer 940287, Plano, TX 75094-0287; www.plano.gov; www.planochamber.org

Portland, Oregon

Population (2004): 533,492 (30); **Pop. density:** 3,972 per sq. mi; **Pop. change (2000–2004):** +0.8%. **Area:** 134.3 sq. mi. **Employment (2004):** 278,864 employed; 7.7% unemployed. **Per capita income (MSA):** $32,152; increase (2002-2003): +0.5%.

Mayor: Tom Potter, Non-Partisan

History: settled by pioneers 1845; developed as trading center, aided by California Gold Rush 1849; city chartered 1851.

Transportation: 1 intl. airport; 2 major rail freight lines, Amtrak; mass transit bus, light rail, and street car system; marine port. **Com-munications:** 9 TV, 27 radio stations. **Medical facilities:** 12 hosp.; VA hosp. **Educational facilities:** 25 univ. and colleges, 1 community college. **Further information:** Portland Business Alliance, 520 SW Yamhill St., Ste. 100, Portland, OR 97204; www.portlandalliance.com

Raleigh, North Carolina

Population (2004): 326,653 (55); **Pop. density:** 2,850 per sq. mi; **Pop. change (2000–2004):** +18.3%. **Area:** 114.6 sq. mi. **Employment (2004):** 164,647 employed; 4.9% unemployed. **Per capita income (MSA):** $33,627; increase (2002-2003): +0.2%.

Mayor: Charles Meeker, Democrat

History: named after Sir Walter Raleigh; site chosen for capital 1788; laid out 1792; inc. 1795; occupied by Gen. Sherman 1865.

Transportation: 1 intl. airport, 10 airlines, 6 commuter airlines; 3 railroads; 2 bus lines. **Communications:** 8 TV, 31 radio stations. **Medical facilities:** 3 hosp. **Educational facilities:** 6 univ. and colleges; 1 community college; 140 pub. schools (county). **Further information:** Chamber of Commerce, 800 S. Salisbury St., PO Box 2978, Raleigh, NC 27602; www.raleigh-wake.org; www.raleighchamber.org

Reno, Nevada

Population (2004): 197,963 (100); **Pop. density:** 2,865 per sq. mi; **Pop. change (2000–2004):** +9.7%. **Area:** 69.1 sq. mi. **Employment (2004):** 103,878 employed; 4.5% unemployed. **Per capita income (MSA):** $38,155; increase (2002-2003): +3.1%.

Mayor: Robert Cashell, Republican

History: Founded in 1857. Originally named Lakes Crossing. Name changed to Reno, after a Union Civil War general, in 1868 with the arrival of the transcontinental railroad.

Transportation: 2 airports; local and national bus lines; Amtrak, Union Pacific Railroad. **Communications:** 4 TV, 7 radio stations. **Medical Facilities:** 3 hosp. **Educational Facilities:** 58 public schools; 1 univ. **Further information:** City of Reno, NV PO Box 1900, Reno, NV 89505; www.cityofreno.com

Riverside, California

Population (2004): 288,384 (61); **Pop. density:** 3,693 per sq. mi; **Pop. change (2000–2004):** +13.0%. **Area:** 78.1 sq. mi. **Employment (2004):** 134,176 employed; 5.8% unemployed. **Per capita income (MSA):** $24,526; increase (2002-2003): +1.7%.

Mayor: Ronald O. Loveridge, Non-Partisan

History: founded 1870; inc. 1886; known for its citrus industry; home of the parent navel orange tree and the historic Mission Inn.

Transportation: municipal airport, intl. airport nearby; rail freight lines, commuter line; trolley/bus system; interstate freeways. **Communications:** 15 TV, 47 radio stations. **Medical facilities:** 3 hosp.; many clinics. **Educational facilities:** 3 univ., 1 community college. **Further information:** Chamber of Commerce, 3985 University Avenue, Riverside, CA 92501; www.ci.riverside.ca.us; www.riverside-chamber.com

Rochester, New York

Population (2004): 212,481 (87); **Pop. density:** 5,935 per sq. mi; **Pop. change (2000–2004):** –3.3%. **Area:** 35.8 sq. mi. **Employment (2004):** 90,389 employed; 6.9% unemployed. **Per capita income (MSA):** $31,057; increase (2002-2003): +2.9%.

Mayor: William A. Johnson Jr., Democrat

History: first permanent settlement 1812; inc. as village 1817, as city 1834; developed as Erie Canal town.

Transportation: 1 intl. airport; Amtrak; 2 bus lines; intracity transit service; Port of Rochester. **Communications:** 6 TV, 19 radio stations. **Medical facilities:** 8 general hosp. **Educational facilities:** 11 colleges, 3 community colleges. **Further information:** Rochester Business Alliance, 150 State St., Rochester, NY 14614; www.rochesterbusinessalliance.com; www.ci.rochester.ny.us

Sacramento, California

Population (2004): 454,330 (38); **Pop. density:** 4,675 per sq. mi; **Pop. change (2000–2004):** +11.6%. **Area:** 97.2 sq. mi. **Employment (2004):** 195,409 employed; 6.5% unemployed. **Per capita income (MSA):** $31,425; increase (2002-2003): +1.8%.

Mayor: Heather Fargo, Non-Partisan

History: settled 1839; important trading center during California Gold Rush 1840s; became state capital 1854.

Transportation: international, executive, and cargo airports; 2 mainline transcontinental rail carriers; bus and light rail system; Port of Sacramento. **Communications:** 8 TV, 34 radio stations; 3 cable TV cos. **Medical facilities:** 15 major hosp. **Educational facilities:** 7 colleges and univ., 5 community colleges, 81 pub. schools. **Further information:** Sacramento Metropolitan Chamber of Commerce, 917 Seventh St., Sacramento, CA 95814; www.metrochamber.org; www.cityofsacramento.org

St. Louis, Missouri

Population (2004): 343,279 (52); **Pop. density:** 5,546 per sq. mi; **Pop. change (2000–2004):** –1.4%. **Area:** 61.9 sq. mi. **Employment (2004):** 144,526 employed; 9.1% unemployed. **Per capita income (MSA):** $33,535; increase (2002-2003): +2.2%.

Mayor: Francis Slay, Democrat

History: founded 1764 as a fur trading post by French; acquired by U.S. 1803; chartered as city 1822; became independent city 1876; lies on Mississippi R., near confluence with Missouri R.

Transportation: 2 intl. airports; 2d largest rail center, 7 trunk-line railroads; 3d largest inland port; Amtrak; Greyhound; bus & light rail; 32 barge lines, 550 motor freight carriers. **Communications:** 8 TV, 19 radio stations. **Medical facilities:** 8 hosp., incl. 2 teaching hosp.; VA hosp., 2 pediatric hosp. **Educational facilities:** 8 univ., 13 colleges and seminaries; 63 public schools; 29 parochial schools; 5 magnet/charter high schools. **Further information:** St. Louis Planning & Urban Design Agency, 1015 Locust St., Ste. 1200, St. Louis, MO 63101; stlouis.missouri.org

St. Paul, Minnesota

Population (2004): 276,963 (67); **Pop. density:** 5,246 per sq. mi; **Pop. change (2000–2004):** –3.5%. **Area:** 52.8 sq. mi. **Employment (2004):** 145,224 employed; 5.4% unemployed. **Per capita income (MSA):** $38,601; increase (2002-2003): +2.2%.

Mayor: Randy C. Kelly, Democrat

History: founded in early 1840s as "Pig's Eye Landing"; became capital of the Minnesota territory 1849 and chartered as St. Paul 1854.

Transportation: 1 intl., 1 business airport; 6 major rail lines; 2 interstate bus lines; pub. transit system. **Communications:** 9 TV, 47 radio stations. **Medical facilities:** 6 hosp. **Educational facilities:** 5 univ., 5 colleges; 1 technical, 3 law schools, 1 art and design college; 65 public, 39 private schools. **Further information:** St. Paul Area Chamber of Commerce, 401 N. Robert St., Ste. 150, St. Paul, MN 55101; www.visitsaintpaul.com; www.stpaulcvb.org

St. Petersburg, Florida

Population (2004): 249,090 (70); **Pop. density:** 4,179 per sq. mi; **Pop. change (2000–2004):** +0.3%. **Area:** 59.6 sq. mi. **Employment (2004):** 125,869 employed; 5.2% unemployed. **Per capita income (MSA):** $29,881; increase (2002-2003): +1.0%.

Mayor: Rick Baker, Non-Partisan

History: founded 1888; inc. 1903.

Transportation: 1 municipal, 2 intl. airports; Amtrak bus connection; county-wide public bus system; downtown 'Looper' bus service; has largest municipal marina in Florida; 1 cruise port. **Communications:** 17 TV, 41 radio stations in area, 2 daily newspapers. **Medical facilities:** 4 major hosp.; VA hosp. **Educational facilities:** 1 univ., 1 college, 1 law school; 27 elem., 9 middle, 5 high schools; 3 alternative/vocational schools; 100 private schools. **Further information:** City of St. Petersburg , PO Box 2842, St. Petersburg, FL 33731; www.stpete.org

San Antonio, Texas

Population (2004): 1,236,249 (8); **Pop. density:** 3,033 per sq. mi; **Pop. change (2000–2004):** +8.0%. **Area:** 407.6 sq. mi. **Employment (2004):** 548,054 employed; 6.1% unemployed. **Per capita income (MSA):** $27,381; increase (2002-2003): +2.0%.

Mayor: Phil Hardberger, Democrat

History: first Spanish garrison 1718; Battle at the Alamo in 1836; city subsequently captured by Texans; inc. 1837; 1st town meeting in Texas took place here in 1845.

Transportation: 1 intl. airport; 2 railroads; 3 bus lines; pub. transit system. **Communications:** 14 TV, 49 radio stations. **Medical facilities:** 22 hosp.; major medical center. **Educational facilities:** 18 univ. and colleges; 16 pub. school districts. **Further information:** Chamber of Commerce, PO Box 1628, San Antonio, TX 78296; www.sachamber.org; www.sanantonio.gov

San Bernadino, California

Population (2004): 198,406 (99); **Pop. density:** 3,374 per sq. mi; **Pop. change (2000–2004):** +7.0%. **Area:** 58.8 sq. mi. **Employment (2004):** 74,171 employed; 7.7% unemployed. **Per capita income (MSA):** $24,526; increase (2002-2003): +1.7%.

Mayor: Judith Valles, Democrat

History: Named by Spanish Franciscan missionaries in 1810. Major Mormon settlement in the 1850s, later recalled to Utah. Population grew in 1860s when gold was discovered nearby. Later became a transportation hub. Inc. 1854.

Transportation: 2 intl. airports; commuter rail; local bus lines.**Communications:** 1 TV, 21 radio stations. **Medical facilities:** 10 hosp. **Educational facilities:** 3 univ.; 66 public schools. **Further information:** San Bernardino Convention & Visitors Bureau 201 North "E" Street, Suite 103, San Bernardino, CA 92401; www.san-bernardino.com

San Diego, California

Population (2004): 1,263,756 (7); **Pop. density:** 3,897 per sq. mi; **Pop. change (2000–2004):** +3.3%. **Area:** 324.3 sq. mi. **Employment (2004):** 633,932 employed; 4.7% unemployed. **Per capita income (MSA):** $35,841; increase (2002-2003): +2.7%.

Mayor: Toni Atkins, Democrat

History: claimed by the Spanish 1542; first mission est. 1769; scene of conflict during Mexican-American War 1846; inc. 1850.

Transportation: 1 major airport; 1 railroad; major freeway system; bus system; trolley system. **Communications:** 9 TV, 25 radio stations, 2 cable providers. **Medical facilities:** 17 hosp. **Educational facilities:** 25 colleges and univ.; 177 pub. schools. **Further information:** San Diego Regional Chamber of Commerce, 402 W. Broadway, Ste. 1000, San Diego, CA 92101; www.sannet.gov; www.sdchamber.org

San Francisco, California

Population (2004): 744,230 (14); **Pop. density:** 15,936 per sq. mi; **Pop. change (2000–2004):** -4.2%. **Area:** 46.7 sq. mi. **Employment (2004):** 400,897; employed; 5.9% unemployed. **Per capita income (MSA):** $46,958; decrease (2002-2003): –1.3%.

Mayor: Gavin Newsom, Non-Partisan

History: nearby Farallon Islands sighted by Spanish 1542; city settled by 1776; claimed by U.S. 1846; became a major city during California Gold Rush 1849; inc. as city 1850; earthquake devastated city 1906.

Transportation: 1 major airport; intracity railway system; 2 railway transit systems; bus and railroad service; ferry system; 1 underwater tunnel. **Communications:** 8 TV; 8 radio stations. **Medical facilities:** 16 hosp. **Educational facilities:** 18 univ. and colleges, 113 pub. schools, 5 charter schools. **Further information:** San Francisco Convention & Visitors Bureau, 201 3rd St., Ste. 900, San Francisco, CA 94103; www.ci.sf.ca.us; www.sfchamber.com; www.sfvisitor.org

San Jose, California

Population (2004): 904,522 (10); **Pop. density:** 5,172 per sq. mi; **Pop. change (2000–2004):** +1.1%. **Area:** 174.9 sq. mi. **Employment (2004):** 401,861 employed; 7.4% unemployed. **Per capita income (MSA):** $46,072; increase (2002-2003): +0.1%.

Mayor: Ron Gonzales, Democrat

History: founded by the Spanish 1777 between San Francisco and Monterey; state cap. 1849-51; inc. 1850.

Transportation: 1 intl. airport; 2 railroads; light rail system; bus system. **Communications:** 9 TV, 15 radio stations. **Medical facilities:** 6 hosp. **Educational facilities:** 6 univ. and colleges. **Further information:** San Jose Convention and Visitors Bureau, 408 Almaden Blvd., San Jose, CA 95110; www.sanjoseca.gov; www.sanjose.org

WORLD ALMANAC QUICK QUIZ

What is the biggest city in terms of area in the top 100 most populous U.S. cities?

(a) Los Angeles (b) Anchorage
(c) Houston (d) New York City

For the answer look in this chapter, or see page 1008.

Santa Ana, California

Population (2004): 342,715 (53); **Pop. density:** 12,646 per sq. mi; **Pop. change (2000–2004):** +1.4%. **Area:** 27.1 sq. mi. **Employment (2004):** 145,044 employed; 6.9% unemployed. **Per capita income (MSA):** $33,347; increase (2002-2003): +2.3%.

Mayor: Miguel Pulido, Non-Partisan

History: founded 1769; inc. as city 1869.

Transportation: 1 airport; 5 major freeways including main Los Angeles-San Diego artery; Amtrak. **Communications:** 14 TV, 28 radio stations. **Medical facilities:** 4 hosp. **Educational facilities:** 1 community college. **Further information:** Santa Ana Chamber of Commerce, 2020 N. Broadway, 2nd floor, Santa Ana, CA 92706; www.santaanachamber.com

Scottsdale, Arizona

Population (2004): 221,792 (82); **Pop. density:** 1,204 per sq. mi; **Pop. change (2000–2004):** +9.4%. **Area:** 184.2 sq. mi. **Employment (2004):** 124,367 employed; 3.2% unemployed. **Per capita income (MSA):** $29,590; increase (2002-2003): +1.7%.

Mayor: Mary Manross, Democrat

History: founded 1888 by Army Chaplain Winfield Scott; inc. June 25, 1951; Frank Lloyd Wright built winter home here (Taliesin West); slogan "West's Most Western Town," by Mayor Malcolm White, adopted 1951.

Transportation: 1 intl. airport in area, 1 local airport; regional bus system; local bus system; taxi system. **Communications:** 12 TV, 45 radio stations. **Medical facilities:** 2 general hospitals; Mayo Clinic. **Educational facilities:** 1 univ. nearby, 1 community college; 3 unified school districts. **Further information:** Scottsdale Convention and Visitors Bureau, 4343 N. Scottsdale Rd., Ste. 170, Scottsdale, AZ 85251; www.scottsdaleaz.gov; www.scottsdalecvb.com

Seattle, Washington

Population (2004): 571,480 (23); **Pop. density:** 6,811 per sq. mi; **Pop. change (2000–2004):** +1.4%. **Area:** 83.9 sq. mi. **Employment (2004):** 321,598 employed; 5.5% unemployed. **Per capita income (MSA):** $39,008; increase (2002-2003): +1.7%.

Mayor: Greg Nickels, Democrat

History: settled 1851; inc. 1869; suffered severe fire 1889; played prominent role during Alaska Gold Rush 1897; growth followed opening of Panama Canal 1914; center of aircraft industry WWII.

Transportation: 2 intl. airport; 2 railroads; ferries serve Puget Sound, Alaska, Canada. **Communications:** 7 TV, 29 radio stations. **Medical facilities:** 40 hosp. **Educational facilities:** 7 univ., 6 colleges, 11 community colleges. **Further information:** Greater Seattle Chamber of Commerce, 1301 5th Ave., Ste. 2500, Seattle, WA 98101-2611; www.ci.seattle.wa.us; www.seattlechamber.com

Shreveport, Louisiana

Population (2004): 198,675 (98); **Pop. density:** 1,927 per sq. mi; **Pop. change (2000–2004):** –0.7%. **Area:** 103.1 sq. mi. **Employment (2004):** 85,281 employed; 6.7% unemployed. **Per capita income (MSA):** $27,507; increase (2002-2003): +4.1%.

Mayor: Keith Hightower, Democrat

History: founded 1836 near site of a 180-mi logjam cleared by Capt. Henry Shreve; inc. 1839; oil discovered 1905.

Transportation: 2 airports, over 40 flights daily; 3 bus lines. **Communications:** 6 TV, 20 radio stations. **Medical facilities:** 16 hosp. **Educational facilities:** 2 univ., 4 colleges; approx. 100 pub. schools. **Further information:** Chamber of Commerce, PO Box 20074, 400 Edwards St., Shreveport, LA 71120; www.shreveportchamber.org

Stockton, California

Population (2004): 279,888 (66); **Pop. density:** 5,117 per sq. mi; **Pop. change (2000–2004):** + 14.8%. **Area:** 54.7 sq. mi. **Employment (2004):** 106,066; employed; 10.4% unemployed. **Per capita income (MSA):** $24,397; increase (2002-2003): +1.3%.

Mayor: Ed Chavez, Non-Partisan

History: site purchased 1842; settled 1849; inc. 1850; chief distributing point for agric. products of San Joaquin Valley.

Transportation: 1 airport; deepwater inland seaport; 4 railroads; 2 bus lines, county bus system. **Communications:** 5 TV stations. **Medical facilities:** 4 hosp.; regional burn, cancer, heart centers. **Educational facilities:** 9 univ. and colleges; 58 pub. schools. **Further information:** Chamber of Commerce, 445 W. Weber Ave., Ste. 220, Stockton, CA 95203; www.stocktongov.com; www.stocktonchamber.org

Tampa, Florida

Population (2004): 321,772 (57); **Pop. density:** 2,870 per sq. mi; **Pop. change (2000–2004):** +6.0%. **Area:** 112.1 sq. mi. **Employment (2004):** 155,770 employed; 5.4% unemployed. **Per capita income (MSA):** $29,881; increase (2002-2003): +1.0%.

Mayor: Pam Iorio, Non-Partisan

History: U.S. army fort on site 1824; inc. 1851; Ybor City National Historical Landmark district.

Transportation: 1 intl. airport; Port of Tampa; CSX rail, Amtrak Rail; bus system; downtown streetcar. **Communications:** 17 TV, 57 radio stations. **Medical facilities:** 21 hosp. **Educational facilities:** 5 univ. and colleges; 193 pub. schools. **Further information:** Greater Tampa Chamber of Commerce, 615 Channelside Drive, Ste. 108, P.O. Box 420, Tampa, FL 33602; www.tampachamber.com

Toledo, Ohio

Population (2004): 304,973 (59); **Pop. density:** 3,784 per sq. mi; **Pop. change (2000–2004):** –2.8%. **Area:** 80.6 sq. mi. **Employment (2004):** 136,468 employed; 7.9% unemployed. **Per capita income (MSA):** $29,963; increase (2002-2003): +4.5%.

Mayor: Jack Ford, Democrat

History: site of Ft. Industry 1794; Battles of Ft. Meigs and Ft. Timbers 1812; figured in "Toledo War" 1835-36 between Ohio and Michigan over borders; inc. 1837.

Transportation: 7 major airlines; 4 railroads; 53 motor freight lines; 16 interstate bus lines. **Communications:** 6 TV, 22 radio stations. **Medical facilities:** 5 major hosp. complexes. **Educational facilities:** 6 univ. and colleges. **Further information:** Toledo Area Chamber of Commerce, 300 Madison Ave., Ste. 200, Toledo, OH 43604; www.toledochamber.com

Tucson, Arizona

Population (2004): 512,023 (32); **Pop. density:** 2,630 per sq. mi; **Pop. change (2000–2004):** +5.2%. **Area:** 194.7 sq. mi. **Employment (2004):** 242,666 employed; 5.1% unemployed. **Per capita income (MSA):** $25,906; increase (2002-2003): +3.0%.

Mayor: Robert E. Walkup, Republican

History: settled 1775 by Spanish as a presidio; acquired by U.S. in Gadsden Purchase 1853; inc. 1877.

Transportation: 1 intl. airport; 2 railroads; 1 bus system, 1 trolley. **Communications:** 10 TV, 34 radio stations. **Medical facilities:** 12 hosp. **Educational facilities:** 1 univ., 1 community college; 216 pub. schools. **Further information:** Tucson Metropolitan Chamber of Commerce, PO Box 991, Tucson, AZ 85702; www.ci.tucson.az.us; www.tucsonchamber.org

Tulsa, Oklahoma

Population (2004): 383,764 (45); **Pop. density:** 2,107 per sq. mi; **Pop. change (2000–2004):** –2.4%. **Area:** 182.6 sq. mi. **Employment (2004):** 194,171 employed; 5.4% unemployed. **Per capita income (MSA):** $30,908; increase (2002-2003): +1.0%.

Mayor: Bill LaFortune, Republican

History: settled in 1836 by Creek Indians; modern town founded 1882 and inc. 1898; oil discovered early 20th century; emerging as telecommunications hub.

Transportation: 1 intl. airport; 5 rail lines; 5 bus lines; transit bus system. **Communications:** 7 TV, 31 radio stations. **Medical facilities:** 10 hosp. **Educational facilities:** 8 univ. and colleges; 85 pub., 39 private schools. **Further information:** Tulsa Metro Chamber, 2 West 2nd Tower II, Ste. 150, Tulsa, OK 74103; www.tulsachamber.com; www.cityoftulsa.org

Virginia Beach, Virginia

Population (2004): 440,098 (40); **Pop. density:** 1,772 per sq. mi; **Pop. change (2000–2004):** +3.5%. **Area:** 248.3 sq. mi. **Employment (2004):** 210,724 employed; 3.6% unemployed. **Per capita income (MSA):** $29,337; increase (2002-2003): +2.4%.

Mayor: Meyera E. Oberndorf, Independent

History: area founded by Capt. John Smith 1607; formed by merger with Princess Anne Co. 1963.

Transportation: 1 airport; 2 railroads; 1 bus line; pub. transit system. **Communications:** 8 TV, 44 radio stations. **Medical facilities:** 2 hosp. **Educational facilities:** 1 univ., 2 colleges; 87 pub. schools. **Further information:** Virginia Beach Dept. of Economic Development, 222 Central Park Ave., Suite 1000, Virginia Beach, VA 23462; Virginia Beach Convention and Visitors Bureau, 2100 Parks Ave., Virginia Beach, VA 23451; www.yesvirginiabeach.com; www.vbfun.com

Washington, District of Columbia

Population (2004): 553,523 (27); **Pop. density:** 9,015 per sq. mi; **Pop. change (2000–2004):** –3.2%. **Area:** 61.4 sq. mi. **Employment (2004):** 274,465 employed, 8.2% unemployed. **Per capita income (MSA):** $44,056; increase (2002-2003): +2.5%.

Mayor: Anthony A. Williams, Democrat

History: U.S. capital; site at Potomac R. chosen by George Washington 1790 on land ceded from VA and MD (portion S of Potomac returned to VA 1846); Congress first met 1800; inc. 1802; sacked by British, War of 1812; 125 killed during Sept. 11, 2001 terrorist attack on the Pentagon.

Transportation: 3 intl. airports in area; Amtrak, 6 other passenger & cargo rail lines; Metrobus/Metrorail transit system; bus line. **Communications:** 5 TV, 61 radio stations. **Medical facilities:** 16 hosp. **Educational facilities:** 10 univ. and colleges. **Further information:** DC Chamber of Commerce, 1213 K Street NW, Washington, DC 20005; www.dc.gov; www.dcchamber.org

Wichita, Kansas

Population (2004): 353,823 (51); **Pop. density:** 2,606 per sq. mi; **Pop. change (2000–2004):** +2.8%. **Area:** 135.8 sq. mi. **Employment (2004):** 172,604 employed; 6.8% unemployed. **Per capita income (MSA):** $30,060; increase (2002-2003): +0.6%.

Mayor: Carlos Mayans, Non-Partisan

History: founded 1864; inc. 1871.

Transportation: 2 airports; 3 major rail freight lines; 2 bus lines. **Communications:** 80 TV, 34 radio stations. **Medical facilities:** 7 hosp., 2 psychiatric rehab. centers. **Educational facilities:** 3 univ., 1 medical school; 96 pub. schools. **Further information:** Chamber of Commerce, 350 W. Douglas Ave., Wichita, KS 67202; www.wichitakansas.org; www.wichita.gov; www.gwedc.org

Fastest-Growing Big Cities*

City	2004 population	2000 population	% change
1. Henderson, NV	224,829	175,381	28.2
2. Chandler, AZ	223,991	176,581	26.8
3. Raleigh, NC	326,653	276,093	18.3
4. Chula Vista, CA	204,879	173,556	18.0
5. Laredo, TX	203,212	176,576	15.1
6. Bakersfield, CA	283,936	247,057	14.9
7. Stockton, CA	279,888	243,771	14.8
8. Riverside, CA	288,384	255,166	13.0
9. Fort Worth, TX	603,337	534,694	12.8
10. Las Vegas, NV	534,847	478,434	11.8

Fastest-Shrinking Big Cities*

City	2004 population	2000 population	% change
1. Detroit, MI	900,198	951,270	–5.4
2. CIncinnati, OH	314,154	331,285	–5.2
3. New Orleans, LA	462,269	484,674	–4.6
4. San Francisco, CA	744,230	776,733	–4.2
5. Cleveland, OH	458,684	478,403	–4.1
6. Birmingham, AL	233,149	242,820	–4.0
8. Pittsburgh, PA	322,450	334,563	–3.6
8. St. Paul , MN	276,963	287,151	–3.5
9. Boston , MA	569,165	589,141	–3.4
10. Buffalo, NY	282,864	292,648	–3.3

*Among those with populations of 200,000 or more, based on 2004 U.S. Census Bureau estimates.

Percent of Population by Race and Hispanic Origin, 10 Largest Cities,[1] 2000

City	White	Black or African-Amer.	Amer. Indian, Alaska Native	Asian	Hawaiian & Other Pacific Isl.	Some other race[2]	Two or more races	Hispanic or Latino (of any race)
1. New York, NY	44.7	26.6	0.5	9.8	0.1	13.4	4.9	27.0
2. Los Angeles, CA	46.9	11.2	0.8	10.0	0.2	25.7	5.2	46.5
3. Chicago, IL	42.0	36.8	0.4	4.3	0.1	13.6	2.9	26.0
4. Houston, TX	49.3	25.3	0.4	5.3	0.1	16.5	3.1	37.4
5. Philadelphia, PA	45.0	43.2	0.3	4.5	0.0	4.8	2.2	8.5
6. Phoenix, AZ	71.1	5.1	2.0	2.0	0.1	16.4	3.3	34.1
7. San Diego, CA	60.2	7.9	0.6	13.6	0.5	12.4	4.8	25.4
8. Dallas, TX	50.8	25.9	0.5	2.7	0.0	17.2	2.7	35.6
9. San Antonio, TX	67.7	6.8	0.8	1.6	0.1	19.3	3.7	58.7
10. San Jose, CA	47.5	3.5	0.8	26.9	0.4	15.9	5.0	30.2

(1) Top 10 cities as determined by 2004 Census Bureau estimates. (2) Persons who, instead of checking off a race shown, filled in a designation under "some other race."

STATES AND OTHER AREAS OF THE U.S.

Sources: Population: U.S. Commerce Dept., Bureau of the Census—Census 2000: April 1, 2000, and July 2004 est. (including armed forces stationed in the state). Area: Bureau of the Census, Geography Division; forested land: Agriculture Dept., Forest Service. Lumber production: Bureau of the Census, Industry Division; mineral production: Dept. of Interior, Office of Mineral Information; commercial fishing: Commerce Dept., Natl. Marine Fisheries Service; new private housing: Bureau of the Census, Residential Construction Branch. Personal per capita income: Commerce Dept., Bureau of Economic Analysis; sales tax: CCH Inc.; unemployment: Labor Dept., Bureau of Labor Statistics. Tourism: Travel Association of America. Lottery figures (not all states have a lottery): North American Assn. of State and Provincial Lotteries, for local fiscal year. Finance: Federal Deposit Insurance Corp. Federal employees: Labor Dept., Office of Personnel Management. Energy: Energy Dept., Energy Information Administration. Other information from sources in individual states. Some data on Outlying U.S. Areas & Other Islands provided by the CIA World Factbook.

NOTE: Population density is for land area only. Categories under racial distribution may not add to 100% due to rounding. "Nat. AK" (Native Alaskans) includes Eskimos and Aleuts. **Hispanic population may be any race** and is dispersed among racial categories, besides being listed separately. Nonfuel mineral values for some states exclude small amounts to avoid disclosing proprietary data. Categories under employment distribution are not all-inclusive. Commercial bank and savings institution figures are for FDIC-insured institutions only. Notable federal facilities marked with an asterisk (*) have been recommended for realignment or closure by the U.S. Dept. of Defense. **Famous Persons lists may include nonnatives** associated with the state as well as persons born there. Website addresses listed may not be official state sites and are not endorsed by *The World Almanac;* all website addresses are subject to change.

Alabama (AL)

Heart of Dixie, Camellia State

People. Population (2004 est.): 4,530,182; rank: 23; **net change** (2003-2004): 0.6%. **Pop. density:** 89.3 per sq mi. **Racial distribution** (2003): 71.3% white; 26.4% black; 0.8% Asian; 0.5% Native American/Nat. AK; 0.04% Hawaiian/Pacific Islander; 2 or more races, 0.9%. **Hispanic pop.** (any race): 2.0%.

Geography. Total area: 52,419 sq mi; rank: 30. **Land area:** 50,744 sq mi; rank: 28. **Acres forested:** 23.0 mil. **Location:** East South Central state extending N-S from Tenn. to the Gulf of Mexico; E of the Mississippi River. **Climate:** long, hot summers; mild winters; generally abundant rainfall. **Topography:** coastal plains, including Prairie Black Belt, give way to hills, broken terrain; highest elevation, 2,407 ft. **Capital:** Montgomery.

Economy. Chief industries: pulp & paper, chemicals, electronics, apparel, textiles, primary metals, lumber and wood products, food processing, fabricated metals, automotive tires, oil and gas exploration. **Chief manuf. goods:** electronics, cast iron & plastic pipe, fabricated steel products, ships, paper products, chemicals, steel, mobile homes, fabrics, poultry processing, soft drinks, furniture, tires. **Chief crops**: cotton, greenhouse & nursery, peanuts, sweet potatoes, potatoes and other vegetables. **Livestock:** (Jan. 2005) 1.32 mil. cattle/calves; (Dec. 2004) 180,000 hogs/pigs, 14.3 mil. chickens (excl. broilers), 1.1 bil. broilers. **Timber/lumber** (est. 2003): 2.4 bil bd. ft.; pine, hardwoods. **Nonfuel minerals** (est. 2004): $982 mil.; cement (portland), stone (crushed), lime, sand and gravel (construction), cement (masonry). **Commercial fishing** (2003): $39.5 mil. **Chief port:** Mobile. **Gross state product** (2004): $138.5 bil. **Sales tax** (2005): 4.0%. **Employment distrib**. (May 2005): 18.8% govt.; 19.7% trade/trans./util.; 15.4% mfg.; 10.2% ed./health serv.; 10.6% prof./bus. serv. 8.5% leisure/hosp. 5.0% finance; 5.4% constr.; 4.2% other serv.; 1.6% info. **Unemployment** (2004): 5.6%. **Per cap. pers. income** (2004): $27,795. **New private housing** (2004): 26,896 units/$3.4 bil. **Commercial banks** (2004): 165; **deposits**: $60.9 bil. **Savings institutions** (2004): 13; **deposits**: $1.7 bil. **Principal internat. airports at:** Birmingham, Huntsville. **Tourism expends.** (2003): $5.5 bil.

Federal govt. Fed. civ. employees (Mar. 2004): 35,695; **avg. salary:** $60,364. **Notable fed. facilities:** Marshall Space Flight Ctr.; *Maxwell/Gunter AFB; Ft. Rucker; Intern'l. Fertilizer Development Ctr.; Navy Station & U.S. Corps of Engineers; Redstone Arsenal.

Energy. Electricity production (est. 2004, kWh by source): Coal: 73.9 bil; Petroleum: 106 mil; Gas: 8.1 bil; Hydroelectric: 10.5 bil; Nuclear: 31.6 bil.

State data. Motto: We dare defend our rights. **Flower:** Camellia. **Bird:** Yellowhammer. **Tree:** Southern Longleaf pine. **Song:** Alabama. **Entered union** Dec. 14, 1819; rank, 22nd. **State fair:** Regional and county fairs held in Sept. and Oct.; no state fair.

History. Alabama was inhabited by the Creek, Cherokee, Chickasaw, Alabama, and Choctaw peoples when the Europeans arrived. The first Europeans were Spanish explorers in the early 1500s. The French made the first permanent settlement on Mobile Bay, 1702. France later gave up the entire region to England under the Treaty of Paris, 1763. Spanish forces took control of the Mobile Bay area, 1780, and it remained Spanish until U.S. troops seized the area, 1813. Most of present-day Alabama was held by the Creeks until Gen. Andrew Jackson broke their power, 1814, and they were removed to Oklahoma Territory. The state seceded, 1861, and the Confederate states were organized Feb. 4, at Montgomery, the first capital; it was readmitted, 1868.

Tourist attractions. First White House of the Confederacy, Civil Rights Memorial, Alabama Shakespeare Festival, all Montgomery; Ivy Green, Helen Keller's birthplace, Tuscumbia; Civil Rights Museum, statue of Vulcan, Birmingham; Carver Museum, Tuskegee; W. C. Handy Home, Museum, & Library, Florence; Alabama Space and Rocket Center, Huntsville; Moundville State Monument, Moundville; Pike Pioneer Museum, Troy; USS *Alabama* Memorial Park, Mobile; Russell Cave Natl. Monument, near Bridgeport: a detailed record of occupancy by humans from about 10,000 BC to AD 1650.

Famous Alabamians. Hank Aaron, Tallulah Bankhead, Hugo L. Black, Paul "Bear" Bryant, George Washington Carver, Nat King Cole, William C. Handy, Bo Jackson, Helen Keller, Coretta Scott King, Harper Lee, Joe Louis, Willie Mays, John Hunt Morgan, Jim Nabors, Jesse Owens, Condoleezza Rice, George Wallace, Booker T. Washington, Hank Williams.

Tourist information. Bureau of Tourism and Travel, 401 Adams Avenue, Suite 126, Montgomery, AL 36103; 1-800-ALABAMA out of state. **Website:** www.tourism.state.al.us

Website. www.alabama.gov

Alaska (AK)

The Last Frontier (unofficial)

People. Population (2004 est.): 655,435; rank: 47; **net change** (2003-2004): 1.1%. **Pop. density:** 1.2 per sq mi. **Racial distribution** (2003): 70.8% white; 3.9% black; 4.2% Asian; 15.8% Native American/Nat. AK; 0.6% Hawaiian/Pacific Islander; 2 or more races, 4.7%. **Hispanic pop.** (any race): 4.6%.

Geography. Total area: 663,267 sq mi; rank: 1. **Land area:** 571,951 sq mi; rank: 1. **Acres forested:** 126.9 mil. **Location:** NW corner of North America, bordered on E by Canada. **Climate:** SE, SW, and central regions, moist and mild; far north extremely dry. Extended summer days, winter nights, throughout. **Topography:** includes Pacific and Arctic mountain systems, central plateau, and Arctic slope. Mt. McKinley, 20,320 ft, is the highest point in North America. **Capital:** Juneau.

Economy. Chief industries: petroleum, tourism, fishing, mining, forestry, transportation, aerospace. **Chief manuf. goods:** fish products, lumber & pulp, furs. **Chief crops:** greenhouse products, barley, oats, hay, potatoes, lettuce, aquaculture. **Livestock:** (Jan. 2005) 14,500 cattle/calves; (Dec. 2004) 1,700 hogs/pigs. **Timber/lumber:** figs. undisclosed; spruce, yellow cedar, hemlock. **Nonfuel minerals** (est. 2004): $1.3 bil.; zinc, gold, lead, sand and gravel (construction), silver. **Commercial fishing** (2003): $989.8 mil. **Chief ports:** Anchorage, Dutch Harbor, Kodiak, Seward, Skagway, Juneau, Sitka, Valdez, Wrangell. **Gross state product** (2004): $33.9 bil. **Sales tax** (2005): none. **Employment distrib.** (May 2005): 26.7% govt.; 20.6% trade/trans./util.; 3.3% mfg.; 11.7% ed./health serv.; 7.6% prof./bus. serv. 10.2% leisure/hosp. 4.8% finance; 5.9% constr.; 3.6% other serv.; 2.2% info. **Unemployment** (2004): 7.5%. **Per cap. pers. income** (2004): $34,454. **New private housing** (2004): 3,264 units/$535 mil. **Commercial banks** (2004): 7; **deposits**: $5.6 bil. **Savings institutions** (2004): 2; **deposits**: $308 mil. **Principal internat. airports at:** Anchorage, Fairbanks, Juneau. **Tourism expends.** (2003): $1.4 bil.

Federal govt. Fed. civ. employees (Mar. 2004): 12,053; **avg. salary:** $53,499. **Notable fed. facilities:** *Ft. Richardson; Ft. Wainwright; *Elmendorf AFB; *Eilson AFB.

IT'S A FACT: Alaska's population has a higher proportion of males to females than any other U.S. state (103.2 males for every 100 females). Only five U.S. states have populations that are more male than female (the others are Nevada, Colorado, Wyoming, and Utah). In the U.S. population as a whole, males are outnumbered by a ratio of 100 to 95.8.

Energy. Electricity production (est. 2004, kWh by source): Coal: 211 mil; Petroleum: 565 mil; Gas: 3.2 bil; Hydroelectric: 1.6 bil; Other: 1 mil.

State data. Motto: North to the future. **Flower:** Forget-Me-Not. **Bird:** Willow ptarmigan. **Tree:** Sitka spruce. **Song:** Alaska's Flag. **Entered union** Jan. 3, 1959; rank, 49th. **State fair** at Palmer; late Aug.-early Sept.

History. Early inhabitants were the Tlingit-Haida people and tribes of the Athabascan family. The Aleut and Inuit (Eskimo), who probably arrived about 12,000 years ago from Siberia, lived in the coastal areas. Vitus Bering, a Danish explorer working for Russia, was the first European to land in Alaska, 1741. The first permanent Russian settlement was established on Kodiak Island, 1784. In 1799, the Russian-American Co. controlled the region, and the first chief manager, Aleksandr Baranov, set up headquarters at Archangel, near present-day Sitka. Sec. of State William H. Seward bought Alaska from Russia for $7.2 mil in 1867, a bargain some called "Seward's Folly." In 1896, gold was discovered in the Klondike region, and the famed gold rush began. Alaska became a territory in 1912.

Tourist attractions. Inside Passage; Portage Glacier; Mendenhall Glacier; Ketchikan Totems; Glacier Bay Natl. Park and Preserve; Denali Natl. Park, one of N. America's great wildlife sanctuaries, surrounding Mt. McKinley, N. America's highest peak; Mt. Roberts Tramway, Juneau; Pribilof Islands fur seal rookeries; restored St. Michael's Russian Orthodox Cathedral, Sitka; White Pass & Yukon Route railroad; Skagway; Katmai Natl. Park & Preserve.

Famous Alaskans. Tom Bodett, Susan Butcher, Ernest Gruening, Jewel (Kilcher), Gov. Tony Knowles, Sydney Laurence, Libby Riddles, Jefferson "Soapy" Smith.

Tourist information. Alaska Travel Industry Association, 2600 Cordova St., Ste. 201, Anchorage, AK 99503; 1-800-862-5275. **Website:** www.travelalaska.com

Website. www.state.ak.us

Arizona (AZ)

Grand Canyon State

People. Population (2004 est.): 5,743,834; rank: 18; **net change** (2003-2004): 3.0%. **Pop. density:** 50.6 per sq mi. **Racial distribution** (2003): 87.7% white; 3.3% black; 2.0% Asian; 5.3% Native American/Nat. AK; 0.2% Hawaiian/Pacific Islander; 2 or more races, 1.5%. **Hispanic pop.** (any race): 27.8%.

Geography. Total area: 113,998 sq mi; rank: 6. **Land area:** 113,635 sq mi; rank: 6. **Acres forested:** 19.4 mil. **Location:** in the southwestern U.S. **Climate:** clear and dry in the southern regions and northern plateau; high central areas have heavy winter snows. **Topography:** Colorado plateau in the N, containing the Grand Canyon; Mexican Highlands running diagonally NW to SE; Sonoran Desert in the SW. **Capital:** Phoenix.

Economy. Chief industries: manufacturing, construction, tourism, mining, agriculture. **Chief manuf. goods:** electronics, printing & publishing, foods, prim. & fabric. metals, aircraft and missiles, apparel. **Chief crops:** cotton, lettuce, cauliflower, broccoli, sorghum, barley, corn, wheat, citrus fruits. **Livestock:** (Jan. 2005) 910,000 cattle/calves, 100,000 sheep/lambs; (Dec. 2004) 136,000 hogs/pigs. **Timber/lumber** (est. 2003): 60 mil bd. ft.; pine, fir, spruce. **Nonfuel minerals** (est. 2004): $3.0 bil.; copper, sand and gravel (construction), cement (portland), molybdenum concentrates, stone (crushed). **Gross state product** (2004): $199.7 bil. **Sales tax** (2005): 5.6%. **Employment distrib.** (May 2005): 16.9% govt.; 19.3% trade/trans./util.; 7.1% mfg.; 11.1% ed./health serv.; 14.0% prof./bus. serv. 10.4% leisure/hosp. 6.8% finance; 8.5% constr.; 3.6% other serv.; 1.9% info. **Unemployment** (2004): 5.0%. **Per cap. pers. income** (2004): $28,442. **New private housing** (2004): 89,323 units/$13.1 bil. **Commercial banks** (2004): 61; **deposits**: $56.3 bil. **Savings institutions** (2004): 17; **deposits**: $5.5 bil. **Lottery** (2004): total sales: $366.6 mil; net income: $107.8 mil. **Principal internat. airports at:** Phoenix, Tucson. **Tourism expends.** (2003): $9.2 bil.

Federal govt. Fed. civ. employees (Mar. 2004): 32,822; **avg. salary:** $51,372. **Notable fed. facilities:** *Luke, Davis-Monthan AF bases; *Ft. Huachuca Army Base; Yuma Proving Grounds.

Energy. Electricity production (est. 2004, kWh by source): Coal: 39.4 bil; Petroleum: 39 mil; Gas: 6.0 bil; Hydroelectric: 6.8 bil; Nuclear: 28.1 bil; Other: 46 mil.

State data. Motto: Ditat Deus (God enriches). **Flower:** Blossom of the Saguaro cactus. **Bird:** Cactus wren. **Tree:** Paloverde. **Song:** Arizona. **Entered union** Feb. 14, 1912; rank, 48th. **State fair** at Phoenix; Oct.-early Nov.

History. Anasazi, Mogollon, and Hohokam civilizations inhabited the area c 300 BC-AD 1300, later Pueblo peoples; Navajo and Apache came c 15th cent. Marcos de Niza, a Franciscan, and Estevanico, a former black slave, explored, 1539; Spanish explorer Francisco Vásquez de Coronado visited, 1540. Eusebio Francisco Kino, a Jesuit missionary, taught Indians 1692-1711, and left missions. Tubac, a Spanish fort, became the first European settlement, 1752. Spain ceded Arizona to Mexico, 1821. The U.S. took over, 1848, after the Mexican War. The area below the Gila River was obtained from Mexico in the Gadsden Purchase, 1853. Arizona became a territory, 1863. Apache wars ended with Geronimo's surrender, 1886.

Tourist attractions. The Grand Canyon; Painted Desert; Petrified Forest Natl. Park; Canyon de Chelly; Meteor Crater; London Bridge, Lake Havasu City; Biosphere 2, Oracle; Navajo Natl. Monument; Sedona.

Famous Arizonans. Bruce Babbitt, Cochise, Alice Cooper, Geronimo, Barry Goldwater, Zane Grey, Carl Hayden, George W. P. Hunt, Helen Jacobs, Bil Keane, Percival Lowell, John McCain, William H. Pickering, John J. Rhodes, Morris Udall, Stewart Udall, Frank Lloyd Wright.

Tourist information. Arizona Office of Tourism, 1110 W. Washington St., Ste. 155, Phoenix, AZ 85007; 1-866-275-5816. **Website:** www.arizonaguide.com

Website. www.az.gov

Arkansas (AR)

The Natural State, The Razorback State

People. Population (2004 est.): 2,752,629; rank: 32; **net change** (2003-2004): 0.9%. **Pop. density:** 52.9 per sq mi. **Racial distribution** (2003): 81.0% white; 16.2% black; 0.9% Asian; 0.7% Native American/Nat. AK; 0.1% Hawaiian/Pacific Islander; 2 or more races, 1.1%. **Hispanic pop.** (any race): 3.7%.

Geography. Total area: 53,179 sq mi; rank: 29. **Land area:** 52,068 sq mi; rank: 27. **Acres forested:** 18.8 mil. **Location:** in the west south-central U.S. **Climate:** long, hot summers, mild winters; generally abundant rainfall. **Topography:** eastern delta and prairie, southern lowland forests, and the northwestern highlands, which include the Ozark Plateaus. **Capital:** Little Rock.

Economy. Chief industries: manufacturing, agriculture, tourism, forestry. **Chief manuf. goods:** food products, chemicals, lumber, paper, plastics, electric motors, furniture, auto components, airplane parts, apparel, machinery, steel. **Chief crops:** rice, soybeans, cotton, tomatoes, grapes, apples, commercial vegetables, peaches, wheat. **Livestock:** (Jan. 2005) 1.9 mil. cattle/calves; (Dec. 2004) 330,000 hogs/pigs, 24.0 mil. chickens (excl. broilers), 1.2 bil. broilers. **Timber/lumber** (est. 2003): 2.8 bil bd. ft.; oak, hickory, gum, cypress, pine. **Nonfuel minerals** (est. 2004): $514 mil.; bromine, stone (crushed), cement (portland), sand and gravel (construction), lime. **Chief ports:** Little Rock, Pine Bluff, Osceola, Helena, Fort Smith, Van Buren, Camden, Dardanelle, North Little Rock, West Memphis, Crossett, McGehee, Morrilton. **Gross state product** (2004): $80.1 bil. **Sales tax** (2005): 6%. **Employment distrib.** (May 2005): 17.5% govt.; 20.7% trade/trans./util.; 17.2% mfg.; 12.4% ed./health serv.; 9.3% prof./bus. serv. 8.1% leisure/hosp. 4.4% finance; 4.5% constr.; 3.5% other serv.; 1.7% info. **Unemployment** (2004): 5.7%. **Per cap. pers. income** (2004): $25,725. **New private housing** (2004): 15,486 units/$1.7 bil. **Commercial banks** (2004): 171; **deposits**: $37.2 bil. **Savings institutions** (2004): 8; **deposits**: $1.5 bil. **Principal internat. airport at:** Blytheville. **Tourism expends.** (2003): $ 4.0 bil.

Federal govt. Fed. civ. employees (Mar. 2004): 11,791; **avg. salary:** $50,972. **Notable fed. facilities:** Nat'l. Ctr. for Toxicological Research, Jefferson; Pine Bluff Arsenal, Little Rock AFB.

Energy. Electricity production (est. 2004, kWh by source): Coal: 25.2 bil; Gas: 339 mil; Hydroelectric: 3.6 bil; Nuclear: 15.5 bil.

IT'S A FACT: The median value of an owner-occupied home in California as of 2004 was $391,102–the highest in the nation, and nearly 5 times that of a home in Arkansas, which had the lowest median home value ($79,006).

State data. Motto: Regnat Populus (The people rule). **Flower:** Apple blossom. **Bird:** Mockingbird. **Tree:** Pine. **Song:** Arkansas. **Entered union** June 15, 1836; rank, 25th. **State fair** at Little Rock; late Sept.-early Oct.

History. Quapaw, Caddo, Osage, Cherokee, and Choctaw peoples lived in the area at the time of European contact. The first European explorers were de Soto, 1541; Marquette and Jolliet, 1673; and La Salle, 1682. The first settlement was by the French under Henri de Tonty, 1686, at Arkansas Post. In 1762, the area was ceded by France to Spain, then given back again, 1800, and was part of the Louisiana Purchase, 1803. It was made a territory, 1819. Arkansas seceded in 1861, only after the Civil War began; more than 10,000 Arkansans fought on the Union side.

Tourist attractions. Hot Springs Natl. Park (water ranging from 95°F-147°F); Eureka Springs; Ozark Folk Center, Blanchard Caverns, both near Mountain View; Crater of Diamonds (only U.S. diamond mine) near Murfreesboro; Toltec Mounds Archeological State Park, Little Rock; Buffalo Natl. River; Mid-America Museum, Hot Springs; Pea Ridge National Military Park, Pead Ridge; Tanyard Springs, Morrilton; Wiederkehr Wine Village, Wiederkehr Village.

Famous Arkansans. Daisy Bates, Dee Brown, Paul "Bear" Bryant, Glen Campbell, Johnny Cash, Hattie Caraway, Wesley Clark, Bill Clinton, "Dizzy" Dean, Orval Faubus, James W. Fulbright, John Grisham, John H. Johnson, Douglas MacArthur, John L. McClellan, James S. McDonnell, Scottie Pippen, Dick Powell, Brooks Robinson, Billy Bob Thornton, Winthrop Rockefeller, Mary Steenburgen, Edward Durell Stone, Sam Walton, Archibald Yell.

Tourist Information. Arkansas Dept. of Parks & Tourism, 1 Capitol Mall, Little Rock, AR 72201; 1-800-NATURAL. **Website:** www.arkansas.com

Website. www.state.ar.us

California (CA)

Golden State

People. Population (2004 est.): 35,893,799; rank: 1; **net change** (2003-2004): 1.2%. **Pop. density:** 230.2 per sq mi. **Racial distribution** (2003): 77.5%; white; 6.9% black; 11.7% Asian; 1.2% Native American/Nat. AK; 0.4% Hawaiian/Pacific Islander; 2 or more races, 2.3% **Hispanic pop.** (any race): 34.3%.

Geography. Total area: 163,696 sq mi; rank: 3. **Land area:** 155,959 sq mi; rank: 3. **Acres forested:** 40.2 mil. **Location:** on western coast of the U.S. **Climate:** moderate temperatures and rainfall along the coast; extremes in the interior. **Topography:** long mountainous coastline; central valley; Sierra Nevada on the east; desert basins of the southern interior; rugged mountains of the north. **Capital:** Sacramento.

Economy. Chief industries: agriculture, tourism, apparel, electronics, telecommunications, entertainment. **Chief manuf. goods:** electronic and electrical equip., computers, industrial machinery, transportation equip. and instruments, food. **Chief crops**: milk and cream, grapes, cotton, flowers, oranges, rice, nursery products, hay, tomatoes, lettuce, strawberries, almonds, asparagus. **Livestock:** (Jan. 2005) 5.4 mil. cattle/calves, 670,000 sheep/lambs; (Dec. 2004) 140,000 hogs/pigs, 24.6 mil. chickens (excl. broilers). **Timber/lumber** (est. 2003): 2.6 bil bd. ft.; fir, pine, redwood, oak. **Nonfuel minerals** (est. 2004): $3.6 bil.; sand and gravel (construction), cement (portland), stone (crushed), boron minerals, soda ash. **Commercial fishing** (2003): $130.3 mil. **Chief ports:** Long Beach, Los Angeles, San Diego, Oakland, San Francisco, Sacramento, Stockton. **Gross state product** (2004): $1,543.8 bil. **Sales tax** (2005): 7.25%. **Employment distrib.** (May 2005): 16.5% govt.; 18.6% trade/trans./util.; 10.4% mfg.; 10.8% ed./health serv.; 14.5% prof./bus. serv. 10.1% leisure/hosp. 6.2% finance; 6.0% constr.; 3.5% other serv.; 3.3% info. **Unemployment** (2004): 6.2%. **Per cap. pers. income** (2004): $35,019. **New private housing** (2004): 203,724 units/$36.6 bil. **Commercial banks** (2004): 288; **deposits**: $465.3 bil. **Savings institutions** (2004): 40; **deposits**: $205.7 bil. **Lottery** (2004): total sales: $2.9 bil; net income: $1.0 bil. **Principal internat. airports at:** Fresno, Los Angeles, Oakland, Ontario, Sacramento, San Diego, San Francisco, San Jose. **Tourism expends.** (2003): $61.1 bil.

Federal govt. Fed. civ. employees (Mar. 2004): 143,772; **avg. salary:** $60,904. **Notable fed. facilities:** Vandenberg, *Beale, Travis AF bases; San Diego Naval Sta.; Pt. Loma Naval Sub Base; *USMC Camp Pendleton; Lawrence Livermore Natl. Lab; Berkeley Natl. Lab; NASA Jet Propulsion Lab; Edwards AFB (NASA Dryden Flight Research Ctr., AF Flight Test Ctr.); San Francisco Mint.

Energy. Electricity production (est. 2004, kWh by source): Coal: 55 mil; Gas: 10.1 bil; Hydroelectric: 33.3 bil; Nuclear: 30.3 bil; Other: 1.3 bil.

State data. Motto: Eureka (I have found it). **Flower:** Golden poppy. **Bird:** California valley quail. **Tree:** California redwood. **Song:** I Love You, California. **Entered union** Sept. 9, 1850; rank, 31st. **State fair** at Sacramento; late Aug.-early Sept.

History. Early inhabitants included more than 100 different Native American tribes with multiple dialects. The first European explorers were Cabrillo, 1542, and Drake, 1579. The first settlement was the Spanish Alta California mission at San Diego, 1769, first in a string founded by Franciscan Father Junípero Serra. U.S. traders and settlers arrived in the 19th cent. and staged the Bear Flag revolt, 1846, in protest against Mexican rule; later that year U.S. forces occupied California. At the end of the Mexican War, Mexico ceded the territory to the U.S., 1848; that same year gold was discovered, and the famed gold rush began.

Tourist attractions. The *Queen Mary*, Long Beach; Palomar Mountain; Disneyland, Anaheim; Getty Center, Los Angeles; Tournament of Roses and Rose Bowl, Pasadena; Universal Studios, Hollywood; Long Beach Aquarium of the Pacific; Golden State Museum, Sacramento; San Diego Zoo; Yosemite Valley; Lassen and Sequoia-Kings Canyon natl. parks; Lake Tahoe; Mojave and Colorado deserts; San Francisco Bay; Napa Valley; Monterey Peninsula; oldest living things on earth believed to be a stand of Bristlecone pines in the Inyo National Forest, est. 4,700 years old; world's tallest tree, 365-ft "National Geographic Society" coast redwood, in Humboldt Redwoods State Park.

Famous Californians. Edmund G. (Pat) Brown, Jerry Brown, Luther Burbank, Julia Child, Ted Danson, Cameron Diaz, Leonardo DiCaprio, Joe DiMaggio, Dianne Feinstein, John C. Fremont, Robert Frost, Tom Hanks, Bret Harte, William Randolph Hearst, Helen Hunt, Jack Kemp, Monica Lewinsky, Jack London, George Lucas, Mark McGwire, Marilyn Monroe, John Muir, Richard M. Nixon, George S. Patton Jr., Gregory Peck, Nancy Pelosi, Ronald Reagan, Sally K. Ride, William Saroyan, Father Junípero Serra, O.J. Simpson, Kevin Spacey, Leland Stanford, John Steinbeck, Arnold Schwarzenegger, Shirley Temple, Earl Warren, Ted Williams, Serena Williams, Venus Williams, Tiger Woods.

California Division of Tourism. P.O. Box 1499, Sacramento, CA 95812-1499;1-800-862-2543. **Website:** www.gocalif.ca.gov

Website. www.state.ca.us

Colorado (CO)

Centennial State

People. Population (2004 est.): 4,601,403; rank: 22; **net change** (2003-2004): 1.2%. **Pop. density:** 44.4 per sq mi. **Racial distribution** (2003): 90.2% white; 4.2% black; 2.6% Asian; 1.1% Native American/Nat. AK; 0.1% Hawaiian/Pacific Islander; 2 or more races, 1.8% **Hispanic pop.** (any race): 18.6%.

Geography. Total area: 104,094 sq mi; rank: 8. **Land area:** 103,718 sq mi; rank: 8. **Acres forested:** 21.6 mil. **Location:** in W central U.S. **Climate:** low relative humidity, abundant sunshine, wide daily, seasonal temp. ranges; alpine conditions in the high mountains. **Topography:** eastern dry high plains; hilly to mountainous central plateau; western Rocky Mountains of high ranges, with broad valleys, deep, narrow canyons. **Capital:** Denver.

Economy. Chief industries: manufacturing, construction, government, tourism, agriculture, aerospace, electronics equipment. **Chief manuf. goods:** computer equip. & instruments, foods, machinery, aerospace products. **Chief crops:** corn, wheat, hay, sugar beets, barley, potatoes, apples, peaches, pears, dry edible beans, sorghum, onions, oats, sunflowers, vegetables. **Livestock:** (Jan. 2005) 2.5 mil. cattle/calves, 365,000 sheep/lambs; (Dec. 2004) 800,000 hogs/pigs, 5.0 mil. chickens (excl. broilers). **Timber/lumber** (est. 2003): 139 mil bd. ft.; oak, ponderosa pine, Douglas fir. **Nonfuel minerals** (est. 2004): $762 mil.; sand and gravel (construction), cement (portland), molybdenum concentrates, gold, stone (crushed). **Gross state product** (2004): $200.0 bil. **Sales tax** (2005): 2.9%. **Employment distrib.** (May 2005): 16.9% govt.; 18.5% trade/trans./util.; 6.9% mfg.; 10.1% ed./health serv.; 14.0% prof./bus. serv. 11.2% leisure/hosp. 7.1% finance; 7.2% constr.; 4.0% other serv.; 3.5% info. **Unemployment** (2004): 5.5%.

Per cap. pers. income (2004): $36,063. **New private housing** (2004): 46,360 units/$8.0 bil. **Commercial banks** (2004): 190; **deposits**: $55.3 bil. **Savings institutions** (2004): 16; **deposits**: $9.2 bil. **Lottery** (2004): total sales: $401.3 mil; net income: $104.1 mil. **Principal internat. airport at:** Denver. **Tourism expends.** (2003): $9.2 bil.

Federal govt. Fed. civ. employees (Mar. 2004): 33,627; **avg. salary:** $62,289. **Notable fed. facilities:** *U.S. Air Force Academy; U.S. Mint; Ft. Carson; Natl. Renewable Energy Labs; U.S. Rail Transportation Test Ctr.; Cheyenne Mtn. Operations Ctr. (NORAD, U.S. Space Comm.); Denver Federal Ctr.; Natl. Ctr. for Atmospheric Research; Natl. Instit. for Standards in Technology; Natl. Wildlife Res. Ctr.; NOAA Env. Technology Lab.

Energy. Electricity production (est. 2004, kWh by source): Coal: 35.4 bil; Petroleum: 15 mil; Gas: 4.2 bil; Hydroelectric: 1.2 bil; Other: 54 mil.

State data. Motto: Nil Sine Numine (Nothing Without Providence). **Flower:** Rocky Mountain columbine. **Bird:** Lark bunting. **Tree:** Colorado blue spruce. **Song:** Where the Columbines Grow. **Entered union:** Aug. 1, 1876; rank 38th. **State fair** at Pueblo; mid-Aug.—early Sept.

History. Early civilization centered around the Mesa Verde c 2,000 years ago; later, Ute, Pueblo, Cheyenne, and Arapaho peoples lived in the area. The region was claimed by Spain, but passed to France. The U.S. acquired eastern Colorado in the Louisiana Purchase, 1803. Lt. Zebulon M. Pike explored the area, 1806, discovering the peak that bears his name. After the Mexican War, 1846-48, U.S. immigrants settled in the east, former Mexicans in the south. Gold was discovered in 1858, causing a population boom. Displaced Native Americans protested, resulting in the so-called Sand Creek Massacre, 1864, where more than 200 Cheyenne and Arapaho were killed. All Native Americans were later removed to Oklahoma Territory.

Tourist attractions. Rocky Mountain and Black Canyon of the Gunnison natl. parks; Aspen Ski Resort; Garden of the Gods, Colorado Springs; Great Sand Dunes, Dinosaur, and Colorado natl. monuments; Pikes Peak and Mt. Evans highways; Mesa Verde Natl. Park (ancient Anasazi Indian cliff dwellings); Grand Mesa Natl. Forest; mining towns of Central City, Silverton, Cripple Creek; Burlington's Old Town; Bent's Fort, outside La Junta; Georgetown Loop Historic Mining Railroad Park, Cumbres & Toltec Scenic Railroad; limited stakes gaming in Central City, Blackhawk, Cripple Creek, Ignacio, and Towaoe.

Famous Coloradans. Tim Allen, Frederick Bonfils, Henry Brown, Molly Brown, William N. Byers, M. Scott Carpenter, Lon Chaney, Jack Dempsey, Mamie Eisenhower, Douglas Fairbanks, Barney Ford, Scott Hamilton, John Kerry, Chief Ourey, "Baby Doe" Tabor, Lowell Thomas, Byron R. White, Paul Whiteman.

State Chamber of Commerce. 1776 Lincoln, Ste. 1200, Denver, CO 80203. Phone: 303-831-7411

Tourist information. Colorado Tourism Office, 1625 Broadway, Ste. 1700, Denver, CO 80202; 1-800-COLORADO. **Website:** www.colorado.com

Website. www.colorado.gov

Connecticut (CT)

Constitution State, Nutmeg State

People. Population (2004 est.): 3,503,604; rank: 29; **net change** (2003-2004): 0.5%. **Pop. density:** 722.9 per sq mi. **Racial distribution** (2003): 85.4% white; 10.0% black; 2.9% Asian; 0.3% Native American/Nat. AK; 0.1% Hawaiian/Pacific Islander; 2 or more races, 1.3%. **Hispanic pop.** (any race): 10.1%.

Geography. Total area: 5,543 sq mi; rank: 48. **Land area:** 4,845 sq mi; rank: 48. **Acres forested:** 1.9 mil. **Location:** New England state in NE corner of the U.S. **Climate:** moderate; winters avg. slightly below freezing; warm, humid summers. **Topography:** western upland, the Berkshires, in the NW, highest elevations; narrow central lowland N-S; hilly eastern upland drained by rivers. **Capital:** Hartford.

Economy. Chief industries: manufacturing, retail trade, government, services, finances, insurance, real estate. **Chief manuf. goods:** aircraft engines and parts, submarines, helicopters, machinery and computer equipment, electronics and electrical equipment, medical instruments, pharmaceuticals. **Chief crops:** nursery stock, Christmas trees, mushrooms, vegetables, sweet corn, tobacco, apples. **Livestock:** (Jan. 2005) 56,000 cattle/calves; (Dec. 2004) 4,200 hogs/pigs, 3.6 mil. chickens (excl. broilers). **Timber/lumber** (est. 2003): 44 mil bd. ft.; oak, birch, beech, maple. **Nonfuel minerals** (est. 2004): $132 mil.; stone (crushed), sand and gravel (construction), stone (dimension), clays (common), gemstones. **Commercial fishing** (2003): $29.8 mil. Chief ports: New Haven, Bridgeport, New London. **Gross state product** (2004): $187.1 bil. **Sales tax** (2005): 6.0%. **Employment distrib.** (May 2005): 14.7% govt.; 18.6% trade/trans./util.; 11.8% mfg.; 16.2% ed./health serv.; 11.8% prof./bus. serv. 8.0% leisure/hosp. 8.4% finance; 4.3% constr.; 3.8% other serv.; 2.3% info. **Unemployment** (2004): 4.9%. **Per cap. pers. income** (2004): $45,398. **New private housing** (2004): 11,939 units/$2.1 bil. **Commercial banks** (2004): 35; **deposits**: $42.7 bil. **Savings institutions** (2004): 37; **deposits**: $31.1 bil. **Lottery** (2004): total sales: $907.7 mil; net income: $280.8 mil. **Principal internat. airport at:** Windsor Locks. **Tourism expends.** (2003): $6.7 bil.

Federal govt. Fed. civ. employees (Mar. 2004): 6,970; **avg. salary:** $61,242. **Notable fed. facilities:** U.S. Coast Guard Academy; *Navy Sub Base New London.

Energy. Electricity production (est. 2002, kWh, by source): Petroleum: 8 mil; Hydroelectric: 32 mil; Other: 143 mil.

State data. Motto: Qui Transtulit Sustinet (He who transplanted still sustains). **Flower:** Mountain laurel. **Bird:** American robin. **Tree:** White oak. **Song:** Yankee Doodle. **Fifth** of the 13 original states to ratify the Constitution, Jan. 9, 1788. **State Fair:** largest fair at Durham, late Sept.; no state fair.

History. At the time of European contact, inhabitants of the area were Algonquian peoples, including the Mohegan and Pequot. Dutch explorer Adriaen Block was the first European visitor, 1614. By 1634, settlers from Plymouth Bay had started colonies along the Connecticut River; in 1637 they defeated the Pequots. The Colony of Connecticut was chartered by England, 1662, adding New Haven, 1665. In the American Revolution, Connecticut Patriots fought in most major campaigns, while Connecticut privateers captured British merchant ships.

Tourist attractions. Mark Twain House, Hartford; Yale University's Art Gallery, Peabody Museum, both in New Haven; Mystic Seaport; Mystic Marine Life Aquarium; P. T. Barnum Museum, Bridgeport; Gillette Castle, Hadlyme; U.S.S. *Nautilus* Memorial, Groton (1st nuclear-powered submarine); Mashantucket Pequot Museum & Research Center, Foxwoods Resort & Casino, both in Ledyard; Mohegan Sun, Uncasville; Lake Compounce, Bristol.

Famous "Nutmeggers." Ethan Allen, Phineas T. Barnum, Samuel Colt, Jonathan Edwards, Nathan Hale, Katharine Hepburn, Isaac Hull, Robert Mitchum, J. Pierpont Morgan, Ralph Nader, Israel Putnam, Wallace Stevens, Harriet Beecher Stowe, Mark Twain, Noah Webster, Eli Whitney.

Tourist information. Connecticut Commission on Culture and Tourism, One Financial Plaza, 755 Main St., Hartford, CT 06103; 1-800-CTBOUND. **Website:** www.ctbound.org

Website. www.ct.gov

Delaware (DE)

First State, Diamond State

People. Population (2004 est.): 830,364; rank: 45; **net change** (2003-2004): 1.5%. **Pop. density:** 425.4 per sq mi. **Racial distribution** (2003): 76.3% white; 19.5% black; 2.5% Asian; 0.4% Native American/Nat. AK; 0.1% Hawaiian/Pacific Islander; 2 or more races, 1.3%. **Hispanic pop.** (any race): 5.3%.

Geography. Total area: 2,489 sq mi; rank: 49. **Land area:** 1,954 sq mi; rank: 49. **Acres forested:** 0.4 mil. **Location:** occupies the Delmarva Peninsula on the Atlantic coastal plain. **Climate:** moderate. **Topography:** Piedmont plateau to the N, sloping to a near sea-level plain. **Capital:** Dover.

Economy. Chief industries: chemicals, agriculture, finance, poultry, shellfish, tourism, auto assembly, food processing, transportation equipment. **Chief manuf. goods:** nylon, apparel, luggage, foods, autos, processed meats and vegetables, railroad & aircraft equipment. **Chief crops:** soybeans, potatoes, corn, mushrooms, lima beans, green peas, barley, cucumbers, wheat, corn, grain sorghum, greenhouse & nursery. **Livestock:** (Jan. 2005) 23,000 cattle/calves; (Dec. 2004) 15,000 hogs/pigs, 240.7 mil. broilers. **Timber/lumber:** figs. undisclosed; hardwoods and softwoods. **Nonfuel minerals** (est. 2004): $20.8 mil.; sand and gravel (construction), magnesium compounds, gemstones. **Commercial fishing** (2003): $5.2 mil. **Chief ports:** Wilmington. **Gross state product** (2004): $54.5 bil. **Sales tax** (2005): none. **Employment distrib.** (May 2005): 14.2% govt.; 18.8% trade/trans./util.; 8.0% mfg.; 12.3% ed./health serv.; 14.5% prof./bus. serv. 9.7% leisure/hosp. 10.2% finance; 6.4% constr.; 4.3% other serv.; 1.5% info. **Unemployment** (2004): 4.1%. **Per cap.**

pers. income (2004): $35,861. **New private housing** (2004): 7,940 units/$897 mil. **Commercial banks** (2004): 34; **deposits**: $68.8 bil. **Savings institutions** (2004): 9; **deposits**: $37.0 bil. **Lottery** (2004): total sales: $640.9 mil; net income: $222.0 mil. **Principal internat. airport at:** Philadelphia/Wilmington. **Tourism expends.** (2003): $1.1 bil.

Federal govt. Fed. civ. employees (Mar. 2004): 2,583; **avg. salary:** $53,017. **Notable fed. facilities:** Dover AFB, Federal Wildlife Refuge, Bombay Hook.

Energy. Electricity production (est. 2004, kWh by source): Petroleum: 162 mil; Gas: 9 mil.

State data. Motto: Liberty and independence. **Flower:** Peach blossom. **Bird:** Blue hen chicken. **Tree:** American holly. **Song:** Our Delaware. **First** of original 13 states to ratify the Constitution, Dec. 7, 1787. **State fair** at Harrington; end of July.

History. The Lenni Lenape (Delaware) people lived in the region at the time of European contact. Henry Hudson located the Delaware R., 1609, and in 1610, English explorer Samuel Argall entered Delaware Bay, naming the area after Virginia's governor, Lord De La Warr. The Dutch first settled near present Lewes, 1631, but the colony was destroyed by Indians. Swedes settled at Fort Christina (now Wilmington), 1638. Dutch settled anew, 1651, near New Castle and seized the Swedish settlement, 1655, only to lose all Delaware and New Netherland to the British, 1664. After 1682, Delaware became part of Pennsylvania, and in 1704 it was granted its own assembly. In 1776, it adopted a constitution as the state of Delaware. Although it remained in the Union during the Civil War, Delaware retained slavery until abolished by the 13th Amendment in 1865.

Tourist attractions. Ft. Christina Monument, site of founding of New Sweden, Holy Trinity (Old Swedes) Church, erected 1698, the oldest Protestant church in the U.S. still in use, Wilmington; Hagley Museum, Winterthur Museum and Gardens, both near Wilmington; historic district, New Castle; John Dickinson "Penman of the Revolution" home, Dover; Rehoboth Beach, "nation's summer capital," Rehoboth; Dover Downs Intl. Speedway.

Famous Delawareans. Thomas F. Bayard, Joseph Biden, Henry Seidel Canby, E. I. du Pont, John P. Marquand, Howard Pyle, Caesar Rodney.

Tourist Information. Delaware Tourism Office, 99 Kings Highway, Dover, DE 19901. 1-866-2VISITDE. **Website:** www.visitdelaware.net

Website. www.delaware.gov

Florida (FL)

Sunshine State

People. Population (2004 est.): 17,397,161; rank: 4; **net change** (2003-2004): 2.3%. **Pop. density:** 322.7 per sq mi. **Racial distribution** (2003): 80.6% white; 15.9% black; 1.9% Asian; 0.4% Native American/Nat. AK; 0.1% Hawaiian/Pacific Islander; 2 or more races, 1.2%. **Hispanic pop.** (any race): 18.6%.

Geography. Total area: 65,755 sq mi; rank: 22. **Land area:** 53,927 sq mi; rank: 26. **Acres forested:** 16.3 mil. **Location:** peninsula jutting southward 500 mi between the Atlantic and the Gulf of Mexico. **Climate:** subtropical N of Bradenton-Lake Okeechobee-Vero Beach line; tropical S of line. **Topography:** land is flat or rolling; highest point is 345 ft in the NW. **Capital:** Tallahassee.

Economy. Chief industries: tourism, agriculture, manufacturing, construction, services, international trade. **Chief manuf. goods:** electric & electronic equipment, transportation equipment, food, printing & publishing, chemicals, instruments, industrial machinery. **Chief crops:** citrus fruits, vegetables, melons, greenhouse and nursery products, potatoes, sugarcane, strawberries. **Livestock:** (Jan. 2005) 1.74 mil. cattle/calves; (Dec. 2004) 20,000 hogs/pigs, 13.1 mil. chickens (excl. broilers), 78.5 mil. broilers. **Timber/lumber** (est. 2003): 860 mil bd. ft.; pine, cypress, cedar **Nonfuel minerals** (est. 2004): $2.2 bil.; phosphate rock, stone (crushed), cement (portland), sand and gravel (construction), cement (masonry). **Commercial fishing** (2003): $171.8 mil. **Chief ports:** Pensacola, Tampa, Manatee, Miami, Port Everglades, Jacksonville, St. Petersburg, Canaveral. **Gross state product** (2004): $594.5 bil. **Sales tax** (2005): 6.0%. **Employment distrib.** (May 2005): 14.2% govt.; 19.7% trade/trans./util.; 5.1% mfg.; 12.2% ed./health serv.; 17.5% prof./bus. serv. 11.5% leisure/hosp. 6.6% finance; 6.7% constr.; 4.2% other serv.; 2.2% info. **Unemployment** (2004): 4.8%. **Per cap. pers. income** (2004): $31,455. **New private housing** (2004): 251,613 units/$35.9 bil. **Commercial banks** (2004): 300; **deposits**: $248.6 bil. **Savings institutions** (2004): 53; **deposits**: $58.3 bil. **Lottery** (2004): total sales: $3.1 bil; net income: $1.1 bil. **Principal internat. airports at:** Daytona Beach, Ft. Lauderdale/Hollywood, Ft. Myers, Jacksonville, Key West, Miami, Orlando, St. Petersburg/Clearwater, Sarasota/Bradenton, Tampa, West Palm Beach. **Tourism expends.** (2003): $42.9 bil.

Federal govt. Fed. civ. employees (Mar. 2004): 70,684; **avg. salary:** $56,151. **Notable fed. facilities:** John F. Kennedy Space Ctr., NASA-Kennedy Space Ctr.'s Spaceport USA; Eglin AFB; MacDill AFB; *Pensacola NAS; Jacksonville NAS; Mayport Naval Sta.

Energy. Electricity production (est. 2004, kWh by source): Coal: 57.5 bil; Petroleum: 29.3 bil; Gas: 66.0 bil; Hydroelectric: 200 mil; Nuclear: 31.2 bil; Other: 122 mil.

State data. Motto: In God we trust. **Flower:** Orange blossom. **Bird:** Mockingbird. **Tree:** Sabal palmetto palm. **Song:** Old Folks at Home. **Entered union** Mar. 3, 1845; rank, 27th. **State fair** at Tampa; early Feb.

History. The original inhabitants of Florida included the Timucua, Apalachee, and Calusa peoples. Later the Seminole migrated from Georgia to Florida, becoming dominant there in the early 18th cent. The first European to see Florida was Ponce de León, 1513. France established a colony, Fort Caroline, on the St. John River, 1564. Spain settled St. Augustine, 1565, and Spanish troops massacred most of the French. Britain's Sir Francis Drake burned St. Augustine, 1586. In 1763, Spain ceded Florida to Great Britain, which held the area briefly, 1763-83, before returning it to Spain. After Andrew Jackson led a U.S. invasion, 1818, Spain ceded Florida to the U.S., 1819. The Seminole War, 1835-42, resulted in removal of most Native Americans to Oklahoma Territory. Florida seceded from the Union, 1861, and was readmitted in 1868.

Tourist attractions. Miami Beach; St. Augustine, oldest permanent European settlement in U.S.; Castillo de San Marcos, St. Augustine; Walt Disney World's Magic Kingdom, EPCOT Center, Disney-MGM Studios, and Animal Kingdom, all near Orlando; Sea World, Universal Studios, near Orlando; Spaceport USA, Kennedy Space Center; Everglades Natl. Park; Ringling Museum of Art, Ringling Museum of the Circus, both in Sarasota; Cypress Gardens, Winter Haven; Busch Gardens, Tampa; U.S. Astronaut Hall of Fame, Mariana Caverns; Church St. Station, Orlando; Silver Springs, Ocala.

Famous Floridians. Edna Buchanan, Jeb Bush, Marjory Stoneman Douglas, Henry M. Flagler, Carl Hiaasen, Zora Neale Hurston, James Weldon Johnson, MacKinlay Kantor, John D. MacDonald, Chief Osceola, Claude Pepper, Henry B. Plant, A. Philip Randolph, Marjorie Kinnan Rawlings, Janet Reno, Joseph W. Stilwell, Charles P. Summerall, Ben Vereen.

Tourist information. Visit Florida, 661 E. Jefferson St., Tallahassee, FL 32301; (1-888-7FLA-USA). **Website:** www.visitflorida.com

Website. www.myflorida.com

Georgia (GA)

Empire State of the South, Peach State

People. Population (2004 est.): 8,829,383; rank: 9; **net change** (2003-2004): 1.8%. **Pop. density:** 153.4 per sq mi. **Racial distribution** (2003): 67.5% white; 28.7% black; 2.4% Asian; 0.3% Native American/Nat. AK; 0.1% Hawaiian/Pacific Islander; 2 or more races, 1.0%. **Hispanic pop.** (any race): 6.2%.

Geography. Total area: 59,425 sq mi; rank: 24. **Land area:** 57,906 sq mi; rank: 21. **Acres forested:** 24.4 mil. **Location:** South Atlantic state. **Climate:** maritime tropical air masses dominate in summer; polar air masses in winter; E central area drier. **Topography:** most southerly of the Blue Ridge Mts. cover NE and N central; central Piedmont extends to the fall line of rivers; coastal plain levels to the coast flatlands. **Capital:** Atlanta.

Economy. Chief industries: services, manufacturing, retail trade. **Chief manuf. goods:** textiles, apparel, food, and kindred products, pulp & paper products. **Chief crops:** peanuts, cotton, corn, tobacco, hay, soybeans. **Livestock:** (Jan. 2005) 1.21 mil. cattle/calves; (Dec. 2004) 275,000 hogs/pigs, 29.4 mil. chickens (excl. broilers), 1.3 bil. broilers. **Timber/lumber** (est. 2003): 2.8 bil bd. ft.; pine, hardwood. **Nonfuel minerals** (est. 2004): $1.8 bil.; clays (kaolin), stone (crushed), clays (fuller's earth), cement (portland), sand and gravel (construction). **Commercial fishing** (2003): $13.5 mil. **Chief ports:** Savannah, Brunswick. **Gross state product** (2004): $340.7 bil. **Sales tax** (2005): 4.0%. **Employment distrib.** (May 2005): 16.6% govt.; 20.9% trade/trans./util.; 11.2% mfg.; 10.6% ed./health serv.; 13.2% prof./bus. serv. 9.4% leisure/hosp. 5.6% finance; 5.1% constr.; 4.0% other serv.; 3.0% info.

Unemployment (2004): 4.6%. **Per cap. pers. income** (2004): $30,051. **New private housing** (2004): 105,554 units/ $12.6 bil. **Commercial banks** (2004): 344; **deposits**: $126.4 bil. **Savings institutions** (2004): 24; **deposits**: $5.7 bil. **Lottery** (2004): total sales: $2.7 bil; net income: $782.7 mil. **Principal internat. airports at:** Atlanta, Savannah. **Tourism expends.** (2003): $14.5 bil.

Federal govt. Fed. civ. employees (Mar. 2004): 64,282. **avg. salary:** $57,216. **Notable fed. facilities:** Dobbins AFB; Ft. Benning; Ft. Gordon; *Ft. Gillem; Ft. Stewart; King's Bay Naval Base; Moody AFB; *Navy Supply Corps School; *Ft. McPherson; Fed. Law Enforcement Training Ctr., Glynco, Robins AFB; Centers for Disease Control.

Energy. Electricity production (est. 2004, kWh by source): Coal: 79.3 bil; Petroleum: 157 mil; Gas: 2.1 bil; Hydroelectric: 3.4 bil; Nuclear: 33.7 bil..

State data. Motto: Wisdom, justice and moderation. **Flower:** Cherokee rose. **Bird:** Brown thrasher. **Tree:** Live oak. **Song:** Georgia On My Mind. **Fourth** of the 13 original states to ratify the Constitution, Jan. 2, 1788. **State fair** at Macon, late Sept.-Oct.

History. Creek and Cherokee peoples were early inhabitants of the region. The earliest known European settlement was the Spanish mission of Santa Catalina, 1566, on Saint Catherines Island. Gen. James Oglethorpe established a colony at Savannah, 1733, for the poor and religiously persecuted. Oglethorpe defeated a Spanish army from Florida at Bloody Marsh, 1742. In the American Revolution, Georgians seized the Savannah armory, 1775, and sent the munitions to the Continental Army. They fought seesaw campaigns with Cornwallis's British troops, twice liberating Augusta and forcing final evacuation by the British from Savannah, 1782. The Cherokee were removed to Oklahoma Territory, 1832-38, and thousands died on the long march, known as the Trail of Tears. Georgia seceded from the Union, 1861, and was invaded by Union forces, 1864, under Gen. William T. Sherman, who took Atlanta, Sept. 2, and proceeded on his famous "march to the sea," ending in Dec., in Savannah. Georgia was readmitted, 1870.

Tourist attractions. State Capitol, Stone Mt. Park, Six Flags Over Georgia, Kennesaw Mt. Natl. Battlefield Park, Martin Luther King Jr. Natl. Historic Site, Underground Atlanta, Jimmy Carter Library & Museum, all Atlanta; Chickamauga and Chattanooga Natl. Military Park, near Dalton; Chattahoochee Natl. Forest; alpine village of Helen; Dahlonega, site of America's first gold rush; Brasstown Bald Mt.; Lake Lanier; Franklin D. Roosevelt's Little White House, Warm Springs; Callaway Gardens, Pine Mt.; Andersonville Natl. Historic Site; Okefenokee Swamp, near Waycross; Jekyll Island; St. Simons Island; Cumberland Island Natl. Seashore; historic riverfront district, Savannah.

Famous Georgians. Kim Basinger, Griffin Bell, James Bowie, James Brown, Erskine Caldwell, Jimmy Carter, Ray Charles, Lucius D. Clay, Ty Cobb, James Dickey, John C. Fremont, Newt Gingrich, Joel Chandler Harris, "Doc" Holliday, Holly Hunter, Alan Jackson, Jasper Johns, Martin Luther King Jr., Gladys Knight, Sidney Lanier, Little Richard, Juliette Gordon Low, Margaret Mitchell, Sam Nunn, Flannery O'Connor, Otis Redding, Burt Reynolds, Julia Roberts, Jackie Robinson, Clarence Thomas, Travis Tritt, Ted Turner, Carl Vinson, Alice Walker, Herschel Walker, Joseph Wheeler, Joanne Woodward, Trisha Yearwood, Andrew Young.

Tourist Information. Dept. of Economic Development, 75 Fifth St., NW, Ste. 1200, Atlanta, GA 30308; 1-800-VISITGA. **Website:** www.georgia.org/tourism

Website. www.georgia.gov

Hawai'i (HI)

Aloha State

People. Population (2004 est.): 1,262,840; rank: 42; **net change** (2003-2004): 1.1%. **Pop. density:** 196.6 per sq mi. **Racial distribution** (2003): 25.9% white; 2.4% black; 42.1% Asian; 0.3% Native American/Nat. AK; 9.2% Hawaiian/Pacific Islander; 2 or more races, 20.1%. **Hispanic pop.** (any race): 7.6%.

Geography. Total area: 10,931 sq mi; rank: 43. **Land area:** 6,423 sq mi; rank: 47. **Acres forested:** 1.7 mil. **Location:** Hawaiian Islands lie in the North Pacific, 2,397 mi SW from San Francisco. **Climate:** subtropical, with wide variations in rainfall; Waialeale, on Kaua'i, wettest spot in U.S. (annual rainfall 460 in.) **Topography:** islands are tops of a chain of submerged volcanic mountains; active volcanoes: Mauna Loa, Kilauea. **Capital:** Honolulu.

Economy. Chief industries: tourism, defense, sugar, pineapples. **Chief manuf. goods:** processed sugar, canned pineapple, clothing, foods, printing & publishing. **Chief crops:** sugar, pineapples, macadamia nuts, fruits, coffee, vegetables, floriculture. **Livestock:** (Jan. 2005) 155,000 cattle/ calves; (Dec. 2004) 22,000 hogs/pigs, 598,000 chickens (excl. broilers). **Timber/lumber:** figs. undisclosed. **Nonfuel minerals** (est. 2004): $74.8 mil.; stone (crushed), sand and gravel (construction), gemstones. **Commercial fishing** (2003): $52.4 mil. **Chief ports:** Honolulu, Hilo, Kailua. **Gross state product** (2004): $50.1 bil. **Sales tax** (2005): 4.0%. **Employment distrib.** (May 2005): 20.5% govt.; 19.4% trade/ trans./util.; 2.6% mfg.; 11.6% ed./health serv.; 12.1% prof./ bus. serv. 17.7% leisure/hosp. 4.9% finance; 5.4% constr.; 4.1% other serv.; 1.8% info. **Unemployment** (2004): 3.3%. **Per cap. pers. income** (2004): $32,160. **New private housing** (2004): 8,785 units/$1.7 bil. **Commercial banks** (2004): 7; **deposits**: $17.8 bil. **Savings institutions** (2004): 3; **deposits**: $5.2 bil. **Principal internat. airports at:** Hilo, Honolulu, Kailua, Kahului. **Tourism expends.** (2003): $7.5 bil.

Federal govt. Fed. civ. employees (Mar. 2004): 20,758; **avg. salary:** $52,057. **Notable fed. facilities:** Pearl Harbor Naval Shipyard; *Hickam AFB; Schofield Barracks; Ft. Shafter; Marine Corps Base-Kaneohe Bay; Barbers Point NAS; Wheeler AFB; Prince Kuhio Federal Bldg.

Energy. Electricity production (est. 2004, kWh by source): Petroleum: 6.8 bil; Other: 1 mil.

State data. Motto: The life of the land is perpetuated in righteousness. **Flower:** Yellow hibiscus. **Bird:** Hawaiian goose. **Tree:** Kukui (Candlenut). **Song:** Hawai'i Pono'i. **Entered union** Aug. 21, 1959; rank, 50th. **State fair:** at O'ahu, late July–early Aug.

History. Polynesians from islands 2,000 mi to the south settled the Hawaiian Islands, probably between AD 300 and AD 600. The first European visitor was British captain James Cook, 1778. Between 1790 and 1810, the islands were united politically under the leadership of a native king, Kamehameha I, whose four successors—all bearing the name Kamehameha—ruled the kingdom from his death, 1819, until the end of the dynasty, 1872. Missionaries arrived, 1820, bringing Western culture. King Kamehameha III and his chiefs created the first constitution and a legislature that set up a public school system. Sugar production began, 1835, and it became the dominant industry. In 1893, Queen Liliuokalani was deposed, and a republic was instituted, 1894, headed by Sanford B. Dole. Annexation by the U.S. came in 1898. The Japanese attack on Pearl Harbor, Dec. 7, 1941, brought the U.S. into World War II.

Tourist attractions. Hawaii Volcanoes, Haleakala natl. parks; Natl. Memorial Cemetery of the Pacific, Waikiki Beach, Diamond Head, Honolulu; U.S.S. *Arizona* Memorial, Pearl Harbor; Hanauma Bay; Polynesian Cultural Center, Laie; Nu'uanu Pali; Waimea Canyon; Wailoa and Wailuku River state parks.

Famous Islanders. Bernice Pauahi Bishop, Tia Carrere, Father Damien de Veuster, Don Ho, Duke Kahanamoku, King Kamehameha, Brook Mahealani Lee, Daniel K. Inouye, Jason Scott Lee, Queen Liliuokalani, Bette Midler, Ellison Onizuka.

Tourist Information. Hawaii Visitors and Conventions Bureau, 2270 Kalakaua Ave., Ste. 801, Honolulu, HI 96815; 1-800-GOHAWAII. **Website:** www.gohawaii.com

Website. www.hawaii.gov

Idaho (ID)

Gem State

People. Population (2004 est.): 1,393,262; rank: 39; **net change** (2003-2004): 1.9%. **Pop. density:** 16.8 per sq mi. **Racial distribution** (2003): 95.5% white; 0.6% black; 1.1% Asian; 1.4% Native American/Nat. AK; 0.1% Hawaiian/Pacific Islander; 2 or more races, 1.4%. **Hispanic pop.** (any race): 8.7%.

Geography. Total area: 83,570 sq mi; rank: 14. **Land area:** 82,747 sq mi; rank: 11. **Acres forested:** 21.6 mil. **Location:** northwestern Mountain state bordering on British Columbia. **Climate:** tempered by Pacific westerly winds; drier, colder, continental climate in SE; altitude an important factor. **Topography:** Snake R. plains in the S; central region of mountains, canyons, gorges (Hells Canyon, 7,900 ft, deepest in N. America); subalpine northern region. **Capital:** Boise.

Economy. Chief industries: manufacturing, agriculture, tourism, lumber, mining, electronics. **Chief manuf. goods:** electronic components, computer equipment, processed foods, lumber and wood products, chemical products, primary metals, fabricated metal products, machinery. **Chief**

crops: potatoes, peas, dry beans, sugar beets, alfalfa seed, lentils, wheat, hops, barley, plums and prunes, mint, onions, corn, cherries, apples, hay. **Livestock:** (Jan. 2005) 2.07 mil. cattle/calves, 270,000 sheep/lambs; (Dec. 2004) 21,000 hogs/pigs, 1.2 chickens (excl. broilers). **Timber/lumber:** 1.8 bil. bd. ft; pine, fir, spruce. **Nonfuel minerals** (est. 2004): $322 mil.; phosphate rock, sand and gravel (construction), molybdenum concentrates, silver, cement (portland). **Chief port:** Lewiston. **Gross state product** (2004): $43.4 bil. **Sales tax** (2005): 6.0%. **Employment distrib.** (May 2005): 19.5% govt.; 19.7% trade/trans./util.; 10.2% mfg.; 11.1% ed./health serv.; 12.7% prof./bus. serv. 9.3% leisure/hosp. 4.7% finance; 7.3% constr.; 3.1% other serv.; 1.8% info. **Unemployment** (2004): 4.7%. **Per cap. pers. income** (2004): $27,098. **New private housing** (2004): 17,606 units/$2.5 bil. **Commercial banks** (2004): 26; **deposits**: $11.5 bil. **Savings institutions** (2004): 8; **deposits**: $2.3 bil. **Lottery** (2004): total sales: $109.3 mil; net income: $23.0 mil. **Tourism expends.** (2003): $2.2 bil.

Federal govt. Fed. civ. employees (Mar. 2004): 8,056; **avg. salary:** $54,292. **Notable fed. facilities:** Idaho Natl. Engineering Lab; *Mountain Home AFB.

Energy. Electricity production (est. 2004, kWh by source): Gas: 49 mil; Hydroelectric: 7.7 bil.

State data. Motto: Esto Perpetua (It is perpetual). **Flower:** Syringa. **Bird:** Mountain bluebird. **Tree:** White pine. **Song:** Here We Have Idaho. **Entered union** July 3, 1890; rank, 43rd. **State fair** at Boise, late Aug.; at Blackfoot, early Sept.

History. Early inhabitants were Shoshone, Northern Paiute, Bannock, and Nez Percé peoples. White exploration of the region began with Lewis and Clark, 1805-6. Next came fur traders, setting up posts, 1809-34, and missionaries, 1830s-50s. Mormons made their first permanent settlement at Franklin, 1860. Idaho's gold rush began the same year and brought thousands of permanent settlers. Most remarkable of the Indian wars was the 1,700-mi trek, 1877, of Chief Joseph and the Nez Percé, pursued by U.S. troops through 3 states and caught just short of the Canadian border. The Idaho territory was organized, 1863. Idaho adopted a progressive constitution and became a state, 1890.

Tourist attractions. Hells Canyon, deepest gorge in N. America; World Center for Birds of Prey; Craters of the Moon; Sun Valley, in Sawtooth Mts.; Crystal Falls Cave; Shoshone Falls; Lava Hot Springs; Lake Pend Oreille; Lake Coeur d'Alene; Sawtooth Natl. Recreation Area; River of No Return Wilderness Area; Redfish Lake.

Famous Idahoans. William E. Borah, Frank Church, Lou Dobbs, Fred T. Dubois, Chief Joseph, Harmon Killebrew, Ezra Pound, Sacagawea, Picabo Street, Lana Turner.

Tourist information. Division of Tourism Development, 700 W. State St., Boise, ID 83720; 1-800-842-5858. **Website:** www. visitid.org

Website. www.state.id.us

Illinois (IL)

Prairie State

People. Population (2004 est.): 12,713,634; rank: 5; **net change** (2003-2004): 0.5%. **Pop. density:** 228.8 per sq mi. **Racial distribution** (2003): 79.5% white; 15.2% black; 4.0% Asian; 0.3% Native American/Nat. AK; 0.1% Hawaiian/Pacific Islander; 2 or more races, 1.0%. **Hispanic pop.** (any race): 13.6%.

Geography. Total area: 57,914 sq mi; rank: 25. **Land area:** 55,584 sq mi; rank: 24. **Acres forested:** 4.3 mil. **Location:** East North Central state; western, southern, and eastern boundaries formed by Mississippi, Ohio, and Wabash rivers, respectively. **Climate:** temperate; typically cold, snowy winters, hot summers. **Topography:** prairie and fertile plains throughout; open hills in the southern region. **Capital:** Springfield.

Economy. Chief industries: services, manufacturing, travel, wholesale and retail trade, finance, insurance, real estate, construction, health care, agriculture. **Chief manuf. goods:** machinery, electric and electronic equipment, prim. & fabric. metals, chemical products, printing & publishing, food and kindred products. **Chief crops:** corn, soybeans, wheat, sorghum, hay. **Livestock:** (Jan. 2005) 1.38 mil. cattle/calves, 69,000 sheep/lambs; (Dec. 2004) 4.0 mil. hogs/pigs, 4.9 mil. chickens (excl. broilers). **Timber/lumber** (est. 2003): 131 mil bd. ft.; oak, hickory, maple, cottonwood. **Nonfuel minerals** (est. 2004): $1.0 bil.; stone (crushed), cement (portland), sand and gravel (construction), sand and gravel (industrial), lime. **Chief ports:** Chicago. **Gross state product** (2004): $528.9 bil. **Sales tax** (2005): 6.25%. **Employment distrib.** (May 2005): 14.5% govt.; 20.1% trade/trans./util.; 11.8% mfg.; 12.5% ed./health serv.; 14.0% prof./bus. serv. 9.1% leisure/hosp. 6.8% finance; 4.6% constr.; 4.4% other serv.; 2.0% info. **Unemployment** (2004): 6.2%. **Per cap. pers. income** (2004): $34,351. **New private housing** (2004): 62,576 units/$9.6 bil. **Commercial banks** (2004): 689; **deposits:** $248.9 bil. **Savings institutions** (2004): 111; **deposits**: $32.9 bil. **Lottery** (2004): total sales: $1.7 bil; net income: $570.1 mil. **Principal internat. airports at:** Chicago. **Tourism expends.** (2003): $21.6 bil.

Federal govt. Fed. civ. employees (Mar. 2004): 42,809; **avg. salary:** $62,388. **Notable fed. facilities:** Fermi Natl. Accelerator Lab; Argonne Natl. Lab; *Rock Island Arsenal; *Great Lakes Naval Station, Scott AFB.

Energy. Electricity production (est. 2004, kWh by source): Coal: 19.1 bil; Petroleum: 23 mil; Gas: 130 mil; Hydroelectric: 51 mil; Other: 6 mil.

State data. Motto: State sovereignty—national union. **Flower:** Native violet. **Bird:** Cardinal. **Tree:** White oak. **Song:** Illinois. **Entered union** Dec. 3, 1818; rank, 21st. **State fair** at Springfield, mid-Aug.; DuQuoin, late Aug.

History. Seminomadic Algonquian peoples, including the Peoria, Illinois, Kaskaskia, and Tamaroa, lived in the region at the time of European contact. Fur traders were the first Europeans in Illinois, followed shortly by Jolliet and Marquette, 1673, and La Salle, 1680, who built a fort near present-day Peoria. The first settlements were French, at Cahokia, near present-day St. Louis, 1699, and Kaskaskia, 1703. France ceded the area to Britain, 1763, and in 1778, American Gen. George Rogers Clark took Kaskaskia from the British without a shot. Defeat of Native American tribes in the Black Hawk War, 1832, and growth of railroads brought change to the area. In 1787, it became part of the Northwest Territory. Post-Civil War Illinois became a center for the labor movement as bitter strikes, such as the Haymarket Square riot, occurred in 1885-86.

Tourist attractions. Chicago museums and parks; Lincoln shrines at Springfield, New Salem, Sangamon County; Cahokia Mounds, Collinsville; Starved Rock State Park; Crab Orchard Wildlife Refuge; Mormon settlement at Nauvoo; Fts. Kaskaskia, Chartres, Massac (parks); Shawnee Natl. Forest, Southern Illinois; Illinois State Museum, Springfield; Dickson Mounds Museum, between Havana and Lewistown.

Famous Illinoisans. Jane Addams, John Ashcroft, Saul Bellow, Jack Benny, Ray Bradbury, Gwendolyn Brooks, William Jennings Bryan, St. Frances Xavier Cabrini, Hillary Rodham Clinton, Clarence Darrow, John Deere, Stephen A. Douglas, James T. Farrell, George W. Ferris, Marshall Field, Betty Friedan, Benny Goodman, Ulysses S. Grant, Dennis Hastert, Ernest Hemingway, Charlton Heston, Wild Bill Hickok, Henry J. Hyde, Abraham Lincoln, Vachel Lindsay, Edgar Lee Masters, Oscar Mayer, Cyrus McCormick, Ronald Reagan, Donald Rumsfeld, Carl Sandburg, Adlai Stevenson, James Watson, Frank Lloyd Wright, Philip Wrigley.

Tourist information. Illinois Dept. of Commerce and Economic Opportunity, 620 E. Adams St., 4th fl., Springfield, IL 62701; 1-800-2-CONNECT. **Website:** www.enjoyillinois.com

Website. www.illinois.gov

Indiana (IN)

Hoosier State

People. Population (2004 est.): 6,237,569; rank: 14; **net change** (2003-2004): 0.6%. **Pop. density:** 173.9 per sq mi. **Racial distribution** (2003): 88.9% white; 8.6% black; 1.2% Asian; 0.3% Native American/Nat. AK; 0.04% Hawaiian/Pacific Islander; 2 or more races, 1.0%. **Hispanic pop.** (any race): 3.9%.

Geography. Total area: 36,418 sq mi; rank: 38. **Land area:** 35,867 sq mi; rank: 38. **Acres forested:** 4.5 mil. **Location:** East North Central state; Lake Michigan on N border. **Climate:** 4 distinct seasons with a temperate climate. **Topography:** hilly southern region; fertile rolling plains of central region; flat, heavily glaciated north; dunes along Lake Michigan shore. **Capital:** Indianapolis.

Economy: Chief industries: manufacturing, services, agriculture, government, wholesale and retail trade, transportation and public utilities. **Chief manuf. goods:** primary metals, transportation equipment, motor vehicles & equip., industrial machinery & equipment, electronic & electric equipment. **Chief crops:** corn, soybeans, wheat, nursery and greenhouse products, vegetables, popcorn, fruit, hay, tobacco, mint. **Livestock:** (Jan. 2005) 850,000 cattle/calves, 50,000 sheep/lambs; (Dec. 2004) 3.15 mil. hogs/pigs, 30.7 mil. chickens (excl. broilers). **Timber/lumber** (est. 2003): 321 mil bd. ft.; oak, tulip, beech, sycamore. **Nonfuel minerals** (est. 2004):

$774 mil.; stone (crushed), cement (portland), sand and gravel (construction), lime, cement (masonry). **Chief ports:** Burns Harbor, Portage; Southwind Maritime, Mt. Vernon; Clark Maritime, Jeffersonville. **Gross state product** (2004): $227.3 bil. **Sales tax** (2005): 6.0%. **Employment distrib.** (May 2005): 14.6% govt.; 19.4% trade/trans./util.; 19.2% mfg.; 12.6% ed./health serv.; 9.1% prof./bus. serv. 9.7% leisure/hosp. 4.8% finance; 5.2% constr.; 3.8% other serv.; 1.4% info. **Unemployment** (2004): 5.2%. **Per cap. pers. income** (2004): $30,094. **New private housing** (2004): 38,825 units/$5.6 bil. **Commercial banks** (2004): 167; **deposits**: $70.1 bil. **Savings institutions** (2004): 59; **deposits**: $11.0 bil. **Lottery** (2004): total sales: $734.9 mil; net income: $199.4 mil. **Principal internat. airports at:** Indianapolis, Ft. Wayne. **Tourism expends.** (2003): $6.7 bil.

Federal govt. Fed. civ. employees (Mar. 2004): 18,595; **avg. salary:** $56,381. **Notable fed. facilities:** Nav. Surface Warfare Ctr., Crane Div.

Energy. Electricity production (est. 2004, kWh by source): Coal: 112.8 bil; Petroleum: 137 mil; Gas: 975 mil; Hydroelectric: 434 mil.

State data. Motto: Crossroads of America. **Flower:** Peony. **Bird:** Cardinal. **Tree:** Tulip poplar. **Song:** On the Banks of the Wabash, Far Away. **Entered union** Dec. 11, 1816; rank, 19th. **State fair** at Indianapolis; mid-Aug.

History. When the Europeans arrived, Miami, Potawatomi, Kickapoo, Piankashaw, Wea, and Shawnee peoples inhabited the area. A French trading post was built, 1731-32, at Vincennes. La Salle visited the present South Bend area, 1679 and 1681. The first French fort was built near present-day Lafayette, 1717. France ceded the area to Britain, 1763. During the American Revolution, American Gen. George Rogers Clark captured Vincennes, 1778, and defeated British forces, 1779. At war's end, Britain ceded the area to the U.S. Miami Indians defeated U.S. troops twice, 1790, but were beaten, 1794, at Fallen Timbers by Gen. Anthony Wayne. At Tippecanoe, 1811, Gen. William H. Harrison defeated Tecumseh's Indian confederation. The Delaware, Potawatomi, and Miami were moved farther west, 1820-1850.

Tourist attractions. Lincoln Log Cabin Historic Site, near Charleston; George Rogers Clark Park, Vincennes; Wyandotte Cave; Tippecanoe Battlefield Memorial Park; Benjamin Harrison home; Indianapolis 500 raceway and museum, all Indianapolis; Indiana Dunes, near Chesterton; National College Football Hall of Fame, South Bend; Hoosier Nat'l. Forest, south-central Indiana.

Famous "Hoosiers." Larry Bird, Ambrose Burnside, Hoagy Carmichael, Jim Davis, James Dean, Eugene V. Debs, Theodore Dreiser, Paul Dresser, Jeff Gordon, Benjamin Harrison, Gil Hodges, Michael Jackson, David Letterman, Carole Lombard, John Mellencamp, Jane Pauley, Cole Porter, Gene Stratton Porter, Ernie Pyle, Dan Quayle, James Whitcomb Riley, Oscar Robertson, Red Skelton, Booth Tarkington, Kurt Vonnegut, Lew Wallace, Wendell L. Willkie, Wilbur Wright.

Tourist Information. Indiana Office of Tourism Development, 1 North Capital, Suite 100, Indianapolis, IN 46204; 1-888-ENJOYIN. **Website:** www.in.gov/enjoyindiana

Website. www.in.gov

Iowa (IA)

Hawkeye State

People. Population (2004 est.): 2,954,451; rank: 30; **net change** (2003-2004): 0.4%. **Pop. density:** 52.9 per sq mi. **Racial distribution** (2003): 94.9% white; 2.3% black; 1.6% Asian; 0.4% Native American/Nat. AK; 0.1% Hawaiian/Pacific Islander; 2 or more races, 0.9%. **Hispanic pop.** (any race): 3.1%.

Geography. Total area: 56,272 sq mi; rank: 26. **Land area:** 55,869 sq mi; rank: 23. **Acres forested:** 2.1 mil. **Location:** West North Central state bordered by Mississippi R. on the E and Missouri R. on the W. **Climate:** humid, continental. **Topography:** Watershed from NW to SE; soil especially rich and land level in the N central counties. **Capital:** Des Moines.

Economy. Chief industries: agriculture, communications, construction, finance, insurance, trade, services, manufacturing. **Chief manuf. goods:** processed food products, tires, farm machinery, electronic products, appliances, household furniture, chemicals, fertilizers, auto accessories. **Chief crops:** silage and grain corn, soybeans, oats, hay. **Livestock:** (Jan. 2005) 3.6 mil. cattle/calves, 245,000 sheep/lambs; (Dec. 2004) 16.1 mil. hogs/pigs, 57.5 mil. chickens (excl. broilers). **Timber/lumber** (est. 2003): 77 mil bd. ft.; red cedar. **Nonfuel minerals** (est. 2004): $533 mil.; cement (portland), stone (crushed), sand and gravel (construction), gypsum (crude), lime. **Gross state product** (2004): $114.3 bil. **Sales tax** (2005): 5.0%. **Employment distrib.** (May 2005): 16.9% govt.; 20.7% trade/trans./util.; 15.2% mfg.; 13.1% ed./health serv.; 7.2% prof./bus. serv. 9.2% leisure/hosp. 6.7% finance; 4.7% constr.; 3.8% other serv.; 2.3% info. **Unemployment** (2004): 4.8%. **Per cap. pers. income** (2004): $30,560. **New private housing** (2004): 16,192 units/$2.2 bil. **Commercial banks** (2004): 408; **deposits**: $44.9 bil. **Savings institutions** (2004): 26; **deposits**: $6.4 bil. **Lottery** (2004): total sales: $209.9 mil; net income: $55.1 mil. **Principal internat. airport at:** Des Moines. **Tourism expends.** (2003): $4.6 bil.

Federal govt. Fed. civ. employees (Mar. 2004): 7,268; **avg. salary:** $52,354. **Notable fed. facilities:** Ames Lab; Natl. Animal Disease Ctr.

Energy. Electricity production (est. 2004, kWh by source): Coal: 33.7 bil; Petroleum: 61 mil; Gas: 422 mil; Hydroelectric: 931 mil; Nuclear: 4.9 bil; Other: 46 mil.

State data. Motto: Our liberties we prize, and our rights we will maintain. **Flower:** Wild rose. **Bird:** Eastern goldfinch. **Tree:** Oak. **Rock:** Geode. **Entered union** Dec. 28, 1846; rank, 29th. **State fair** at Des Moines; mid-Aug.

History. Early inhabitants were Mound Builders who dwelt on Iowa's fertile plains. Later, Woodland tribes including the Iowa and Yankton Sioux lived in the area. The first Europeans, Marquette and Jolliet, gave France its claim to the area, 1673. In 1762, France ceded the region to Spain, but Napoleon took it back, 1800. It became part of the U.S. through the Louisiana Purchase, 1803. Native American Sauk and Fox tribes moved into the area from states farther east but relinquished their land in defeat, after the 1832 uprising led by the Sauk chieftain Black Hawk. By mid-19th cent. they were forced to move on to Kansas. Iowa became a territory in 1838, and entered as a free state, 1846, strongly supporting the Union.

Tourist attractions. Herbert Hoover birthplace and library, West Branch; Effigy Mounds Natl. Monument, prehistoric Indian burial site, Marquette; Amana Colonies; Grant Wood's paintings and memorabilia, Davenport Municipal Art Gallery; Living History Farms, Des Moines; Adventureland, Altoona; Boone & Scenic Valley Railroad, Boone; Greyhound Parks, in Dubuque and Council Bluffs; Prairie Meadows horse racing, Altoona; riverboat cruises and casino gambling, Mississippi and Missouri Rivers; Iowa Great Lakes, Okoboji.

Famous Iowans. Tom Arnold, Johnny Carson, Marquis Childs, Buffalo Bill Cody, Mamie Dowd Eisenhower, Bob Feller, George Gallup, Susan Glaspell, James Norman Hall, Harry Hansen, Herbert Hoover, Ann Landers, Glenn Miller, Lillian Russell, Billy Sunday, James A. Van Allen, Abigail Van Buren, Carl Van Vechten, Henry Wallace, John Wayne, Meredith Willson, Grant Wood.

Tourist information. Iowa Tourism Office, Iowa Dept. of Economic Development, 200 E. Grand Ave., Des Moines, IA 50309; 1-888-472-6035. **Website:** www.traveliowa.com

Website. www.iowa.gov

Kansas (KS)

Sunflower State

People. Population (2004 est.): 2,735,502; rank: 33; **net change** (2003-2004): 0.4%. **Pop. density:** 33.4 per sq mi. **Racial distribution** (2003): 89.3% white; 6.0% black; 2.1% Asian; 1.0% Native American/Nat. AK; 0.1% Hawaiian/Pacific Islander; 2 or more races, 1.6%. **Hispanic pop.** (any race): 7.8%.

Geography. Total area: 82,277 sq mi; rank: 15. **Land area:** 81,815 sq mi; rank: 13. **Acres forested:** 1.5 mil. **Location:** West North Central state, with Missouri R. on E. **Climate:** temperate but continental, with great extremes between summer and winter. **Topography:** hilly Osage Plains in the E; central region level prairie and hills; high plains in the W. **Capital:** Topeka.

Economy. Chief industries: manufacturing, finance, insurance, real estate, services. **Chief manuf. goods:** transportation equipment, machinery & computer equipment, food and kindred products, printing & publishing. **Chief crops:** wheat, sorghum, corn, hay, soybeans, sunflowers. **Livestock:** (Jan. 2005) 6.65 mil. cattle/calves, 106,000 sheep/lambs; (Dec. 2004) 1.72 mil. hogs/pigs. **Timber/lumber**: figs. undisclosed; oak, walnut. **Nonfuel minerals** (est. 2004): $741 mil.; cement (portland), helium (Grade-A), salt, stone (crushed), helium (crude). **Chief ports:** Kansas City. **Gross state product** (2004): $99.1 bil. **Sales tax** (2005): 5.3%. **Employment distrib.** (May 2005): 19.5% govt.; 19.2% trade/trans./util.; 13.2% mfg.; 12.0% ed./health serv.; 9.8% prof./bus. serv. 8.5% leisure/hosp. 5.2% finance; 5.0% constr.; 4.0% other serv.; 3.0% info. **Unemployment** (2004): 5.5%.

Per cap. pers. income (2004): $30,811. **New private housing** (2004): 13,651 units/$1.8 bil. **Commercial banks** (2004): 373; **deposits**: $38.2 bil. **Lottery** (2004): total sales: $224.2 mil; net income: $73.0 mil. **Savings institutions** (2004): 21; **deposits**: $8.4 bil. **Principal internat. airport at:** Kansas City. **Tourism expends.** (2003): $3.8 bil.

Federal govt. Fed. civ. employees (Mar. 2004): 15,410; **avg. salary:** $54,104. **Notable fed. facilities:** Fts. Riley, Leavenworth; Leavenworth Fed. Pen.; McConnell AFB; Colmery-O'Neal Veterans Hospital.

Energy. Electricity production (est. 2004, kWh by source): Coal: 34.6 bil; Petroleum: 856 mil; Gas: 942 mil; Nuclear: 10.1 bil; Other: 1 mil.

State data. Motto: Ad Astra per Aspera (To the stars through difficulties). **Flower:** Native sunflower. **Bird:** Western meadowlark. **Tree:** Cottonwood. **Song:** Home on the Range. **Entered union** Jan. 29, 1861; rank, 34th. **State fair** at Hutchinson; begins Friday after Labor Day.

History. When Coronado first explored the area, Wichita, Pawnee, Kansa, and Osage peoples lived there. These Native Americans—hunters who also farmed—were joined on the Plains by the nomadic Cheyenne, Arapaho, Comanche, and Kiowa about 1800. French explorers established trading between 1682 and 1739, and the U.S. took over most of the area in the Louisiana Purchase, 1803. After 1830, thousands of eastern Native Americans were removed to Kansas. Kansas became a territory, 1854. Violent incidents between pro- and antislavery settlers caused the territory to be known as "Bleeding Kansas." It eventually entered the Union as a free state, 1861. Railroad construction after the war made Abilene and Dodge City terminals of large cattle drives from Texas.

Tourist attractions. Eisenhower Center, Abilene; Agricultural Hall of Fame and Natl. Center, Bonner Springs; Dodge City-Boot Hill & Frontier Town; Old Cowtown Museum, Wichita; Ft. Scott and Ft. Larned, restored 1800s cavalry forts; Kansas Cosmosphere and Space Center, Hutchinson; Woodlands Racetrack, Kansas City; U.S. Cavalry Museum, Ft. Riley; NCAA Visitors Center, Shawnee; Heartland Park Raceway, Topeka.

Famous Kansans. Kirstie Alley, Roscoe "Fatty" Arbuckle, Ed Asner, Gwendolyn Brooks, John Brown, George Washington Carver, Wilt Chamberlain, Walter P. Chrysler, Glenn Cunningham, John Stuart Curry, Robert Dole, Amelia Earhart, Wyatt Earp, Dwight D. Eisenhower, Ron Evans, Maurice Greene, Wild Bill Hickok, Cyrus Holliday, Dennis Hopper, William Inge, Don Johnson, Walter Johnson, Nancy Landon Kassebaum, Buster Keaton, Emmett Kelly, Alf Landon, Edgar Lee Masters, Hattie McDaniel, Oscar Micheaux, Carry Nation, Georgia Neese-Gray, Charlie Parker, Gordon Parks, Jim Ryun, Barry Sanders, Vivian Vance, William Allen White, Jess Willard.

Tourist information. Kansas Dept. of Commerce, Travel and Tourism Div., 1000 SW Jackson St., Ste. 100, Topeka, KS 66612; 1-800-2KANSAS. **Website:** www.travelks.com

Website. www.accesskansas.org

Kentucky (KY)

Bluegrass State

People. Population (2004 est.): 4,145,922; rank: 26; **net change** (2003-2004): 0.7%. **Pop. density:** 104.7 per sq mi. **Racial distribution** (2003): 90.3% white; 7.6% black; 0.9% Asian; 0.2% Native American/Nat. AK; 0.1% Hawaiian/Pacific Islander; 2 or more races, 1.0%. **Hispanic pop.** (any race): 1.7%.

Geography. Total area: 40,409 sq mi; rank: 37. **Land area:** 39,728 sq mi; rank: 36. **Acres forested:** 12.7 mil. **Location:** East South Central state, bordered on N by Illinois, Indiana, Ohio; on E by West Virginia and Virginia; on S by Tennessee; on W by Missouri. **Climate:** moderate, with plentiful rainfall. **Topography:** mountainous in E; rounded hills of the Knobs in the N; Bluegrass, heart of state; wooded rocky hillsides of the Pennyroyal; Western Coal Field; the fertile Purchase in the SW. **Capital:** Frankfort.

Economy. Chief industries: manufacturing, services, finance, insurance and real estate, retail trade, public utilities. **Chief manuf. goods:** transportation & industrial machinery, apparel, printing & publishing, food products, electric & electronic equipment. **Chief crops:** tobacco, corn, soybeans. **Livestock:** (Jan. 2005) 2.25 mil. cattle/calves, 32,000 sheep/lambs; (Dec. 2004) 350,000 hogs/pigs, 7.0 mil. chickens (excl. broilers), 290.8 mil. broilers. **Timber/lumber** (est. 2002): 659 mil bd. ft.; hardwoods, pines. **Nonfuel minerals** (est. 2004): $674 mil.; stone (crushed), lime, cement (portland), sand and gravel (construction), clays (ball). **Chief ports:** Paducah, Louisville, Covington, Owensboro, Ashland, Henderson County, Lyon County, Hickman-Fulton County. **Gross state product** (2004): $135.4 bil. **Sales tax** (2005): 6.0%. **Employment distrib.** (May 2005): 17.2% govt.; 20.5% trade/trans./util.; 14.6% mfg.; 12.8% ed./health serv.; 9.1% prof./bus. serv. 9.3% leisure/hosp. 4.7% finance; 4.8% constr.; 4.4% other serv.; 1.5% info. **Unemployment** (2004): 5.3%. **Per cap. pers. income** (2004): $27,709. **New private housing** (2004): 22,384 units/$2.6 bil. **Commercial banks** (2004): 236; **deposits**: $54.5 bil. **Savings institutions** (2004): 29; **deposits**: $2.4 bil. **Lottery** (2004): total sales: $725.3 mil; net income: $193.5 mil. **Principal internat. airports at:** Covington/Cincinnati, Louisville. **Tourism expends.** (2003): $5.4 bil.

Federal govt. Fed. civ. employees (Mar. 2004): 20,783; **avg. salary:** $49,526. **Notable fed. facilities:** U.S. Gold Bullion Depository, Ft. Knox; Ft. Campbell; Fed. Correctional Institution, Lexington.

Energy. Electricity production (est. 2004, kWh by source): Coal: 78.7 bil; Petroleum: 90 mil; Gas: 399 mil; Hydroelectric: 3.8 bil; Other: 16 mil.

State data. Motto: United we stand, divided we fall. **Flower:** Goldenrod. **Bird:** Cardinal. **Tree:** Tulip Poplar. **Song:** My Old Kentucky Home. **Entered union** June 1, 1792; rank, 15th. **State fair** at Louisville, late Aug.

History. The area was predominantly hunting grounds for Shawnee, Wyandot, Delaware, and Cherokee peoples. Explored by Americans Thomas Walker and Christopher Gist, 1750-51, Kentucky was the first area west of the Alleghenies settled by American pioneers. The first permanent settlement was Harrodsburg, 1774. Daniel Boone blazed the Wilderness Trail through the Cumberland Gap and founded Ft. Boonesborough, 1775. Conflicts with Native Americans, spurred by the British, were unceasing until, during the American Revolution, Gen. George Rogers Clark captured British forts in Indiana and Illinois, 1778. In 1792, Virginia dropped its claims to the region, and it became the 15th state. Although officially a Union state, Kentuckians had divided loyalties during the Civil War and were forced to choose sides; its slaves were freed only after the adoption of the 13th Amendment to the U.S. Constitution, 1865.

Tourist attractions. Kentucky Derby; Louisville; Land Between the Lakes Natl. Recreation Area, Kentucky Lake and Lake Barkley; Mammoth Cave Natl. Park; Echo River, 360 ft below ground; Lake Cumberland; Lincoln's birthplace, Hodgenville; My Old Kentucky Home State Park, Bardstown; Cumberland Gap Natl. Historical Park, Middlesboro; Kentucky Horse Park, Lexington; Shaker Village, Pleasant Hill.

Famous Kentuckians. Muhammad Ali, John James Audubon, Alben W. Barkley, Daniel Boone, Louis D. Brandeis, John C. Breckinridge, Kit Carson, Albert B. "Happy" Chandler, Henry Clay, Jefferson Davis, D. W. Griffith, "Casey" Jones, Abraham Lincoln, Mary Todd Lincoln, Thomas Hunt Morgan, Carry Nation, Col. Harland Sanders, Diane Sawyer, Adlai Stevenson, Jesse Stuart, Zachary Taylor, Hunter S. Thompson, Robert Penn Warren, Whitney Young Jr.

Tourist Information. Kentucky Dept. of Tourism, Capital Plaza Tower, 22nd fl., 500 Mero St., Frankfort, KY 40601; 1-800-225-TRIP. **Website:** www.kentuckytourism.com

Website. www.kentucky.gov

Louisiana (LA)

Pelican State

See Index and Table of Contents for coverage of Hurricane Katrina.

People. Population (2004 est.): 4,515,770; rank: 24; **net change** (2003-2004): 0.5%. **Pop. density:** 104.2 per sq mi. **Racial distribution** (2003): 64.2% white; 32.9% black; 1.4% Asian; 0.6% Native American/Nat. AK; 0.04% Hawaiian/Pacific Islander; 2 or more races, 0.8%. **Hispanic pop.** (any race): 2.6%.

Geography. Total area: 51,840 sq mi; rank: 31. **Land area:** 43,562 sq mi; rank: 33. **Acres forested:** 13.8 mil. **Location:** West South Central state on the Gulf Coast. **Climate:** subtropical, affected by continental weather patterns. **Topography:** lowlands of marshes and Mississippi R. flood plain; Red R. Valley lowlands; upland hills in the Florida Parishes; average elevation, 100 ft. **Capital:** Baton Rouge.

Economy. Chief industries: wholesale and retail trade, tourism, manufacturing, construction, transportation, communication, public utilities, finance, insurance, real estate, mining. **Chief manuf. goods:** chemical products, foods, transportation equipment, electronic equipment, petroleum products, lumber, wood, and paper. **Chief crops:** soybeans, sugarcane, rice, corn, cotton, sweet potatoes, pecans, sorghum, aquaculture. **Livestock:** (Jan. 2005) 860,000 cattle/calves; (Dec. 2004) 16,000 hogs/pigs, 2.6 mil. chickens (excl.

broilers). **Timber/lumber** (est. 2003): 1.4 bil bd. ft.; pines, hardwoods, oak. **Nonfuel minerals** (est. 2004): $364 mil.; salt, sand and gravel (construction), stone (crushed), sand and gravel (industrial), lime. **Commercial fishing** (2003): $294.0. **Chief ports:** New Orleans, Baton Rouge, Lake Charles, Port of S. Louisiana (La Place), Shreveport, Plaquemine, St. Bernard, Alexandria. **Gross state product** (2004): $152.0 bil. **Sales tax** (2005): 4.0%. **Employment distrib.** (May 2005): 19.9% govt.; 19.7% trade/trans./util.; 7.8% mfg.; 13.1% ed./health serv.; 9.6% prof./bus. serv. 10.8% leisure/hosp. 5.4% finance; 6.1% constr.; 3.8% other serv.; 1.5% info. **Unemployment** (2004): 5.7%. **Per cap. pers. income** (2004): $27,581. **New private housing** (2004): 23,510 units/$2.4 bil. **Commercial banks** (2004): 146; **deposits**: $51.6 bil. **Savings institutions** (2004): 31; **deposits**: $3.6 bil. **Lottery** (2004): total sales: $340.1 mil; net income: $121.2 mil. **Principal internat. airport at:** New Orleans. **Tourism expends.** (2003): $9.1 bil.

Federal govt. Fed. civ. employees (Mar. 2004): 19,931; **avg. salary:** $53,285. **Notable federal facilities:** Strategic Petroleum Reserve, Michoud Assembly Plant, Southern Regional Research Ctr., U.S. Army Corps of Engineers, all New Orleans; Ft. Polk (Joint Readiness Training Ctr.); Barksdale AFB; New Orleans NAS.

Energy. Electricity production (est. 2004, kWh by source): Coal: 11.3 bil; Petroleum: 1.9 bil; Gas: 12.9 bil; Nuclear: 17.1 bil.

State data. Motto: Union, justice, and confidence. **Flower:** Magnolia. **Bird:** Eastern brown pelican. **Tree:** Cypress. **Song:** Give Me Louisiana. **Entered union** Apr. 30, 1812; rank, 18th. **State fair** at Shreveport; Oct.

History. Caddo, Tunica, Choctaw, Chitimacha, and Chawash peoples lived in the region at the time of European contact. Europeans Cabeza de Vaca and Panfilo de Narvaez first visited, 1530. The region was claimed for France by La Salle, 1682. The first permanent settlement was by the French at Biloxi, now in Mississippi, 1699. France ceded the region to Spain, 1762, took it back, 1800, and sold it to the U.S., 1803, in the Louisiana Purchase. During the American Revolution, Spanish Louisiana aided the Americans. Admitted as a state in 1812, Louisiana was the scene of the Battle of New Orleans, 1815.

Louisiana Creoles are descendants of early French and/or Spanish settlers. About 4,000 Acadians, French settlers in Nova Scotia, Canada, were forcibly transported by the British to Louisiana in 1755 (an event commemorated in Longfellow's "Evangeline") and settled near Bayou Teche; their descendants became known as Cajuns. Another group, the Islenos, were descendants of Canary Islanders brought to Louisiana by a Spanish governor in 1770. Traces of Spanish and French survive in local dialects.

Tourist attractions. French Quarter and other New Orleans attractions *(many attractions did not suffer major damage from Hurricane Katrina and, as of late Sept., were making plans to reopen).* Battle of New Orleans site; Longfellow-Evangeline Memorial Park, St. Martinville; Kent House Museum, Alexandria; Hodges Gardens, Natchitoches, USS *Kidd* Memorial, Baton Rouge.

Famous Louisianans. Louis Armstrong, Pierre Beauregard, Judah P. Benjamin, Braxton Bragg, Kate Chopin, Johnnie Cochraw, Harry Connick Jr., Ellen DeGeneres, Fats Domino, Lillian Hellman, Grace King, Elmore Leonard, Bob Livingston, Huey Long, Eli & Peyton Manning, Wynton Marsalis, Leonidas K. Polk, Anne Rice, Henry Miller Shreve, Britney Spears, Edward D. White Jr.

Tourist information. Louisiana Office of Tourism, 1051 N. 3rd St., Baton Rouge, LA 70804-9291; 1-800-677-4082. **Website:** www.louisianatravel.com

Website. www.louisiana.gov

Maine (ME)

Pine Tree State

People. Population (2004 est.): 1,317,253; rank: 40; **net change** (2003-2004): 0.6%. **Pop. density:** 42.7 per sq mi. **Racial distribution** (2003): 97.1% white; 0.6% black; 0.8% Asian; 0.6% Native American/Nat. AK; 0.04% Hawaiian/Pacific Islander; 2 or more races, 0.9%. **Hispanic pop.** (any race): 0.8%.

Geography. Total area: 35,385 sq mi; rank: 39. **Land area:** 30,862 sq mi; rank: 39. **Acres forested:** 17.7 mil. **Location:** New England state at northeastern tip of U.S. **Climate:** Southern interior and coastal, influenced by air masses from the S and W; northern clime harsher, avg. over 100 in. snow in winter. **Topography:** Appalachian Mts. extend through state; western borders have rugged terrain; long sand beaches on southern coast; northern coast mainly rocky promontories, peninsulas, fjords. **Capital:** Augusta.

Economy. Chief industries: manufacturing, agriculture, fishing, services, trade, government, finance, insurance, real estate, construction. **Chief manuf. goods:** paper & wood products, transportation equipment. **Chief crops:** potatoes, aquaculture products. **Livestock:** (Jan. 2005) 92,000 cattle/calves; (Dec. 2004) 5,000 hogs/pigs, 4.3 mil. chickens (excl. broilers). **Timber/lumber** (est. 2003): 947 mil bd. ft.; pine, spruce, fir. **Nonfuel minerals** (est. 2004): $122 mil.; sand and gravel (construction), cement (portland), stone (crushed), stone (dimension), peat. **Commercial fishing** (2003): $283.8 mil. **Chief ports:** Searsport, Portland, Eastport. **Gross state product** (2004): $43.3 bil. **Sales tax** (2005): 5.0%. **Employment distrib.** (May 2005): 17.5% govt.; 20.1% trade/trans./util.; 9.9% mfg.; 18.3% ed./health serv.; 8.1% prof./bus. serv. 9.8% leisure/hosp. 5.5% finance; 5.2% constr.; 3.3% other serv.; 1.9% info. **Unemployment** (2004): 4.6%. **Per cap. pers. income** (2004): $30,566. **New private housing** (2004): 9,267 units/$1.2 bil. **Commercial banks** (2004): 19; **deposits**: $10.1 bil. **Savings institutions** (2004): 23; **deposits**: $6.6 bil. **Lottery** (2004): total sales: $185.9 mil; net income: $42.5 mil. **Principal internat. airports at:** Bangor, Portland. **Tourism expends.** (2003): $2.0 bil.

Federal govt. Fed. civ. employees (Mar. 2004): 9,083; **avg. salary:** $53,208. **Notable fed. facilities:** Kittery Naval Shipyard; *Brunswick NAS.

Energy. Electricity production (est. 2002, kWh, by source): Hydroelectric: 6 mil.

State data. Motto: Dirigo (I direct). **Flower:** White pine cone and tassel. **Bird:** Chickadee. **Tree:** Eastern white pine. **Song:** State of Maine Song. **Entered union** Mar. 15, 1820; rank, 23rd. **State fair:** at Bangor, late July; at Skowhegan, mid-Aug.

History. When the Europeans arrived, Maine was inhabited by Algonquian peoples including the Abnaki, Penobscot, and Passamaquoddy. Maine's rocky coast was believed to have been explored by the Cabots, 1498-99. French settlers arrived, 1604, at the St. Croix River, English, c 1607, on the Kennebec; both settlements failed. Maine was made part of Massachusetts, 1691. In the American Revolution, a Maine regiment fought at Bunker Hill. A British fleet destroyed Falmouth (now Portland), 1775, but the British ship *Margaretta* was captured near Machiasport. In 1820, Maine broke off and became a separate state.

Tourist attractions. Acadia Natl. Park, Bar Harbor, on Mt. Desert Island; Old Orchard Beach; Portland's Old Port; Kennebunkport; Common Ground Country Fair; Portland Headlight; Baxter State Pk.; Freeport/L. L. Bean.

Famous "Down Easters." Leon Leonwood (L.L.) Bean, James G. Blaine, Cyrus H. K. Curtis, Hannibal Hamlin, Sarah Jewett, Stephen King, Henry Wadsworth Longfellow, Sir Hiram and Hudson Maxim, Edna St. Vincent Millay, George Mitchell, Edmund Muskie, Judd Nelson, Edwin Arlington Robinson, Joan Benoit Samuelson, Liv Tyler, Kate Douglas Wiggin, Ben Ames Williams.

Tourist Information. Maine Office of Tourism, 59 State House Station, Augusta, ME 04333; 1-888-MAINE45 (from within the United States and Canada). **Website:** www.visitmaine.com

Website. www.state.me.us

Maryland (MD)

Old Line State, Free State

People. Population (2004 est.): 5,558,058; rank: 19; **net change** (2003-2004): 0.8%. **Pop. density:** 572.3 per sq mi. **Racial distribution** (2003): 65.6% white; 28.1% black; 4.5% Asian; 0.3% Native American/Nat. AK; 0.1% Hawaiian/Pacific Islander; 2 or more races, 1.4%. **Hispanic pop.** (any race): 4.8%.

Geography. Total area: 12,407 sq mi; rank: 42. **Land area:** 9,774 sq mi; rank: 42. **Acres forested:** 2.6 mil. **Location:** South Atlantic state stretching from the Ocean to the Allegheny Mts. **Climate:** continental in the west; humid subtropical in the east. **Topography:** Eastern Shore of coastal plain and Maryland Main of coastal plain, piedmont plateau, and the Blue Ridge, separated by the Chesapeake Bay. **Capital:** Annapolis.

Economy. Chief industries: manufacturing, biotechnology and information technology, services, tourism. **Chief manuf. goods:** electric and electronic equipment; food and kindred products, chemicals and allied products, printed materials. **Chief crops:** greenhouse and nursery products, soybeans, corn. **Livestock:** (Jan. 2005) 235,000 cattle/calves,

23,000 sheep/lambs; (Dec. 2004) 26,000 hogs/pigs, 4.6 mil. chickens (excl. broilers), 284.6 mil. broilers. **Timber/lumber** (est. 2003): 275 mil bd. ft.; hardwoods. **Nonfuel minerals** (est. 2004): $478 mil.; cement (portland), stone (crushed), sand and gravel (construction), cement (masonry), stone (dimension). **Commercial fishing** (2003): $49.0 mil. **Chief port:** Baltimore. **Gross state product** (2004): $226.5 bil. **Sales tax** (2005): 5.0%. **Employment distrib.** (May 2005): 18.4% govt.; 18.2% trade/trans./util.; 5.4% mfg.; 13.8% ed./health serv.; 15.1% prof./bus. serv. 9.4% leisure/hosp. 6.1% finance; 7.0% constr.; 4.6% other serv.; 2.0% info. **Unemployment** (2004): 4.2%. **Per cap. pers. income** (2004): $39,247. **New private housing** (2004): 29,225 units/$3.9 bil. **Commercial banks** (2004): 92; **deposits**: $66.8 bil. **Savings institutions** (2004): 55; **deposits**: $15.3 bil. **Lottery** (2004): total sales: $1.4 bil; net income: $458.4 mil. **Principal internat. airport at:** Baltimore. **Tourism expends.** (2003): $9.0 bil.

Federal govt. Fed. civ. employees (Mar. 2004): 104,087; **avg. salary:** $72,636. **Notable fed. facilities:** U.S. Naval Academy; Natl. Agriculture Res. Ctr.; Ft. Meade, Aberdeen Proving Ground; Goddard Space Flight Ctr.; Natl. Institutes of Health; Natl. Inst. of Standards & Technology; Food & Drug Administration; Bureau of the Census; Natl. Naval Med. Ctr., Bethesda; Natl. Marine Fisheries Serv.; Natl. Oceanic and Atmospheric Admin.

Energy. Electricity production (est. 2002, kWh, by source): Petroleum: 28 mil; Gas: 3 mil.

State data. Motto: Fatti Maschii, Parole Femine (Manly deeds, womanly words). **Flower:** Black-eyed Susan. **Bird:** Baltimore oriole. **Tree:** White oak. **Song:** Maryland, My Maryland. **Seventh** of the original 13 states to ratify the U.S. Constitution, Apr. 28, 1788. **State fair** held at Timonium; late Aug.-early Sept.

History. Europeans encountered Algonquian-speaking Nanticoke and Piscataway and Iroquois-speaking Susquehannock when they first visited the area. Italian explorer Verrazano visited the Chesapeake region in the early 16th cent. English Capt. John Smith explored and mapped the area, 1608. William Claiborne set up a trading post on Kent Island in Chesapeake Bay, 1631. King Charles I granted land to Cecilius Calvert, Lord Baltimore, 1632; Calvert's brother Leonard, with about 200 settlers, founded St. Marys, 1634. The bravery of Maryland troops in the American Revolution, as at the Battle of Long Island, won the state its nickname "The Old Line State." In the War of 1812, when a British fleet tried to take Ft. McHenry, Marylander Francis Scott Key wrote "The Star-Spangled Banner," 1814. Although a slave-holding state, Maryland remained with the Union during the Civil War and was the site of the battle of Antietam, 1862, which halted Gen. Robert E. Lee's march north.

Tourist attractions. The Preakness at Pimlico track, Baltimore; The Maryland Million at Laurel Race Course; Ocean City; restored Ft. McHenry, near which Francis Scott Key wrote "The Star-Spangled Banner"; Edgar Allan Poe house, Ravens Football at Memorial Stadium, Camden Yards, Natl. Aquarium, Harborplace, all Baltimore; Antietam Battlefield, near Hagerstown; South Mountain Battlefield; U.S. Naval Academy, Annapolis; Maryland State House, Annapolis, 1772, the oldest still in legislative use in the U.S.

Famous Marylanders. John Astin, Benjamin Banneker, Tom Clancy, Jonathan Demme, Francis Scott Key, H. L. Mencken, Kweisi Mfume, Ogden Nash, Charles Willson Peale, William Pinkney, Edgar Allan Poe, Cal Ripken Jr., Babe Ruth, Upton Sinclair, Roger B. Taney, John Waters, Montel Williams.

Tourist Information. Maryland Office of Tourism Development, 217 E. Redwood St., 9th Fl., Baltimore, MD 21202; 1-800-MDISFUN. **Website:** www.mdisfun.org

Website. www.maryland.gov

Massachusetts (MA)

Bay State, Old Colony

People. Population (2004 est.): 6,416,505; rank: 13; **net change** (2003-2004): -0.1%. **Pop. density:** 818.2 per sq mi. **Racial distribution** (2003): 87.2% white; 6.7% black; 4.4% Asian; 0.3% Native American/Nat. AK; 0.1% Hawaiian/Pacific Islander; 2 or more races, 1.2%. **Hispanic pop.** (any race): 7.4%.

Geography. Total area: 10,555 sq mi; rank: 44. **Land area:** 7,840 sq mi; rank: 45. **Acres forested:** 3.1 mil. **Location:** New England state along Atlantic seaboard. **Climate:** temperate, with colder and drier clime in western region. **Topography:** jagged indented coast from Rhode Island around Cape Cod; flat land yields to stony upland pastures near central region and gentle hilly country in west; except in west, land is rocky, sandy, and not fertile. **Capital:** Boston.

Economy. Chief industries: services, trade, manufacturing. **Chief manuf. goods:** electric and electronic equipment, instruments, industrial machinery and equipment, printing and publishing, fabricated metal products. **Chief crops:** cranberries, greenhouse, nursery, vegetables. **Livestock:** (Jan. 2005) 48,000 cattle/calves; (Dec. 2004) 12,000 hogs/pigs, 307,000 chickens (excl. broilers). **Timber/lumber:** (2003 est.) 60 mil bd. ft.; white pine, oak, other hard woods. **Nonfuel minerals** (est. 2004): $221 mil.; stone (crushed), sand and gravel (construction), lime, stone (dimension), clays (common). **Commercial fishing** (2003): $291.6 mil. **Chief ports:** Boston, Fall River, New Bedford, Salem, Gloucester, Plymouth. **Gross state product** (2004): $317.7 bil. **Sales tax** (2005): 5.0%. **Employment distrib.** (May 2005): 12.9% govt.; 17.8% trade/trans./util.; 9.7% mfg.; 18.2% ed./health serv.; 14.3% prof./bus. serv. 9.4% leisure/hosp. 6.8% finance; 4.5% constr.; 3.6% other serv.; 2.6% info. **Unemployment** (2004): 5.1%. **Per cap. pers. income** (2004): $41,801. **New private housing** (2004): 21,044 units/$3.5 bil. **Commercial banks** (2004): 47; **deposits**: $108.2 bil. **Savings institutions** (2004): 169; **deposits**: $64.5 bil. **Lottery** (2004): total sales: $4.4 bil. **Principal internat. airport at:** Boston. **Tourism expends.** (2003): $10.0 bil.

Federal govt. Fed. civ. employees (Mar. 2004): 25,118; **avg. salary:** $61,351. **Notable fed. facilities:** Thomas P. O'Neill Jr. Fed. Bldg., J.W. McCormack Bldg., JFK Fed. Bldg., *Natick Army Soldier Systems Ctr.

Energy. Electricity production (est. 2004, kWh by source): Coal: 938 mil; Petroleum: 259 mil; Gas: 136 mil.

State data. Motto: Ense Petit Placidam Sub Libertate Quietem (By the sword we seek peace, but peace only under liberty). **Flower:** Mayflower. **Bird:** Chickadee. **Tree:** American elm. **Song:** All Hail to Massachusetts. **Sixth** of the original 13 states to ratify Constitution, Feb. 6, 1788. **State Fair** at Springfield, mid-Sept.–early Oct.

History. Early inhabitants were the Algonquian, Nauset, Wampanoag, Massachuset, Pennacook, Nipmuc, and Pocumtuc peoples. Pilgrims settled in Plymouth, 1620, giving thanks for their survival with the first Thanksgiving Day, 1621. About 20,000 new settlers arrived, 1630-40. Native American relations with the colonists deteriorated leading to King Philip's War, 1675-76, which the colonists won, ending Native American resistance. Demonstrations against British restrictions set off the Boston Massacre, 1770, and the Boston Tea Party, 1773. The first bloodshed of American Revolution was at Lexington, 1775.

Tourist attractions. Provincetown artists' colony; Cape Cod; Plymouth Rock, Plimouth Plantation, *Mayflower II*, all Plymouth; Freedom Trail, Isabella Stewart Gardner Museum, Museum of Fine Arts, Children's Museum, Museum of Science, New England Aquarium, JFK Library, Boston Ballet, Boston Pops, Boston Symphony Orchestra, all Boston; Tanglewood, Jacob's Pillow Dance Festival, Hancock Shaker Village, Berkshire Scenic Railway Museum, Norman Rockwell Museum, Edith Wharton and Herman Melville homes, all in the Berkshires; Salem; Old Sturbridge Village; Deerfield Historic District; Walden Pond; Naismith Memorial Basketball Hall of Fame, Springfield.

Famous "Bay Staters." John Adams, John Quincy Adams, Samuel Adams, Louisa May Alcott, Horatio Alger, Susan B. Anthony, Crispus Attucks, Clara Barton, Alexander Graham Bell, Stephen Breyer, George H. W. Bush, John Cheever, E. E. Cummings, Emily Dickinson, Charles Eliot, Ralph Waldo Emerson, William Lloyd Garrison, Edward Everett Hale, John Hancock, Nathaniel Hawthorne, Oliver Wendell Holmes, Winslow Homer, Elias Howe, John F. Kennedy, John Kerry, Jack Lemmon, James Russell Lowell, Cotton Mather, Samuel F. B. Morse, Edgar Allan Poe, Paul Revere, Norman Rockwell, Dr. Seuss (Theodore Seuss Geisel), Henry David Thoreau, Barbara Walters, James McNeil Whistler, John Greenleaf Whittier.

Tourist information. Massachusetts Office of Travel & Tourism, 10 Park Plaza, Ste. 4510, Boston, MA 02116; 1-800-227-MASS. **Website:** www.massvacation.com

Website. www.mass.gov

Michigan (MI)

Great Lakes State, Wolverine State

People. Population (2004 est.): 10,112,620; rank: 8; **net change** (2003-2004): 0.3%. **Pop. density:** 178.5 per sq mi. **Racial distribution** (2003): 81.5% white; 14.4% black; 2.2% Asian; 0.6% Native American/Nat. AK; 0.04% Hawaiian/Pacific Islander; 2 or more races, 1.4%. **Hispanic pop.** (any race): 3.5%.

Geography. Total area: 96,716 sq mi; rank: 11. **Land area:** 56,804 sq mi; rank: 22. **Acres forested:** 19.3 mil. **Location:** East North Central state bordering on 4 of the 5 Great Lakes, divided into an Upper and Lower Peninsula by the Straits of Mackinac, which link lakes Michigan and Huron. **Climate:** well-defined seasons tempered by the Great Lakes. **Topography:** low rolling hills give way to northern tableland of hilly belts in Lower Peninsula; Upper Peninsula is level in the east, with swampy areas; western region is higher and more rugged. **Capital:** Lansing.

Economy. Chief industries: manufacturing, services, tourism, agriculture, forestry/lumber. **Chief manuf. goods:** automobiles, transportation equipment, machinery, fabricated metals, food products, plastics, office furniture. **Chief crops:** corn, wheat, soybeans, dry beans, hay, potatoes, sweet corn, apples, cherries, sugar beets, blueberries, cucumbers, Niagra grapes. **Livestock:** (Jan. 2005) 1.01 mil. cattle/calves, 83,000 sheep/lambs; (Dec. 2004) 940,000 hogs/pigs, 9.3 chickens (excl. broilers). **Timber/lumber** (est. 2003): 759 mil bd. ft.; maple, oak, aspen. **Nonfuel minerals** (est. 2004): $1.5 bil.; cement (portland), sand and gravel (construction), iron ore (usable), stone (crushed), salt. **Commercial fishing** (2003): $5.7 mil. **Chief ports:** Detroit, Saginaw River, Escanaba, Muskegon, Sault Ste. Marie, Port Huron, Marine City. **Gross state product** (2004): $372.8 bil. **Sales tax** (2005): 6.0%. **Employment distrib.** (May 2005): 16.0% govt.; 18.3% trade/trans./util.; 15.4% mfg.; 12.6% ed./health serv.; 13.0% prof./bus. serv. 9.5% leisure/hosp. 5.0% finance; 4.4% constr.; 4.1% other serv.; 1.5% info. **Unemployment** (2004): 7.1%. **Per cap. pers. income** (2004): $31,954. **New private housing** (2004): 53,933 units/$7.5 bil. **Commercial banks** (2004): 173; **deposits**: $124.8 bil. **Savings institutions** (2004): 22; **deposits**: $11.3 bil. **Lottery** (2004): total sales: $2.0 bil; net income: $645.0 mil. **Principal internat. airports at:** Detroit, Flint, Grand Rapids, Kalamazoo, Lansing, Saginaw. **Tourism expends.** (2003): $12.0 bil.

Federal govt. Fed. civ. employees (Mar. 2004): 23,582; **avg. salary:** $60,536. **Notable fed. facilities:** Isle Royal, Sleeping Bear Dunes national parks.

Energy. Electricity production (est. 2004, kWh by source): Coal: 67.4 bil; Petroleum: 707 mil; Gas: 666 mil; Hydroelectric: 1.5 bil; Nuclear: 30.6 bil; Other: 35 mil.

State data. Motto: Si Quaeris Peninsulam Amoenam, Circumspice (If you seek a pleasant peninsula, look about you). **Flower:** Apple blossom. **Bird:** Robin. **Tree:** White pine. **Song:** Michigan, My Michigan. **Entered union** Jan. 26, 1837; rank, 26th. **State fair** at Detroit, late Aug.–early Sept.; Upper Peninsula (Escanaba), mid-Aug.

History. Early inhabitants were the Ojibwa, Ottawa, Miami, Potawatomi, and Huron. French fur traders and missionaries visited the region, 1616, set up a mission at Sault Ste. Marie, 1641, and a settlement there, 1668. French settlements were taken over, 1763, by the British, who crushed a Native American uprising led by Ottawa chieftain Pontiac that same year. Treaty of Paris ceded territory to U.S., 1783, but British remained until 1796. The British seized Ft. Mackinac and Detroit, 1812. After Oliver H. Perry's Lake Erie victory and William H. Harrison's victory near the Thames River, 1813, the British retreated to Canada. The opening of the Erie Canal, 1825, and new land laws and Native American cessions led the way for a flood of settlers.

Tourist attractions. Henry Ford Museum, Greenfield Village, both in Dearborn; Frederick Meijer Gardens and Sculpture Park, Grand Rapids; Michigan Space Center, Jackson; Tahquamenon *(Hiawatha)* Falls; DeZwaan windmill and Tulip Festival, Holland; "Soo Locks," St. Mary's Falls Ship Canal, Sault Ste. Marie, Kalamazoo Aviation History Museum; Mackinac Island; Kellogg's Cereal City USA, Battle Creek; Museum of African-American History, Motown Historical Museum, both Detroit.

Famous Michiganders. Ralph Bunche, Francis Ford Coppola, Paul de Kruif, Thomas Edison, Edna Ferber, Gerald R. Ford, Henry Ford, Aretha Franklin, Edgar Guest, Lee Iacocca, Robert Ingersoll, Magic Johnson, Casey Kasem, Will Kellogg, Ring Lardner, Elmore Leonard, Charles Lindbergh, Joe Louis, Madonna, Malcolm X, Terry McMillan, Michael Moore, Pontiac, Gilda Radner, Diana Ross, Glenn Seaborg, Tom Selleck, Sinbad (David Adkins), John Smoltz, Lily Tomlin, Stewart Edward White, Serena Williams.

Tourist Information. Michigan Economic Development Corp., 300 N. Washington Square, Lansing, MI 48913. Phone: 1-888-78GREAT. **Website:** travel.michigan.org

Website. www.michigan.gov

Minnesota (MN)

North Star State, Gopher State

People. Population (2004 est.): 5,100,958; rank: 21; **net change** (2003-2004): 0.7%. **Pop. density:** 64.1 per sq mi. **Racial distribution** (2003): 90.2% white; 3.9% black; 3.3% Asian; 1.2% Native American/Nat. AK; 0.1% Hawaiian/Pacific Islander; 2 or more races, 1.4%. **Hispanic pop.** (any race): 3.3%.

Geography. Total area: 86,939 sq mi; rank: 12. **Land area:** 79,610 sq mi; rank: 14. **Acres forested:** 16.7 mil. **Location:** West North Central state bounded on the E by Wisconsin and Lake Superior, on the N by Canada, on the W by the Dakotas, and on the S by Iowa. **Climate:** northern part of state lies in the moist Great Lakes storm belt; the western border lies at the edge of the semi-arid Great Plains. **Topography:** central hill and lake region covering approx. half the state; to the NE, rocky ridges and deep lakes; to the NW, flat plain; to the S, rolling plains and deep river valleys. **Capital:** St. Paul.

Economy. Chief industries: agribusiness, forest products, mining, manufacturing, tourism. **Chief manuf. goods:** food, chemical and paper products, industrial machinery, electric and electronic equipment, computers, printing & publishing, scientific and medical instruments, fabricated metal products, forest products. **Chief crops:** corn, soybeans, wheat, sugar beets, hay, barley, potatoes, sunflowers. **Livestock:** (Jan. 2005) 2.4 mil. cattle/calves, 145,000 sheep/lambs; (Dec. 2004) 6.5 mil. hogs/pigs, 14.5 mil. chickens (excl. broilers), 46.3 mil. broilers. **Timber/lumber** (est. 2003): 257 mil bd. ft.; needle-leaves and hardwoods. **Nonfuel minerals** (est. 2004): $1.6 bil.; iron ore (usable), sand and gravel (construction), stone (crushed), sand and gravel (industrial), stone (dimension). **Commercial fishing** (2003): $228,000. **Chief ports:** Duluth, St. Paul, Minneapolis. **Gross state product** (2004): $225.6 bil. **Sales tax** (2005): 6.5%. **Employment distrib.** (May 2005): 15.5% govt.; 19.3% trade/trans./util.; 12.7% mfg.; 14.3% ed./health serv.; 11.2% prof./bus. serv. 8.9% leisure/hosp. 6.6% finance; 4.8% constr.; 4.3% other serv.; 2.2% info. **Unemployment** (2004): 4.7%. **Per cap. pers. income** (2004): $35,861. **New private housing** (2004): 40,832 units/$6.3 bil. **Commercial banks** (2004): 480; **deposits**: $91.1 bil. **Savings institutions** (2004): 30; **deposits**: $3.3 bil. **Lottery** (2004): total sales: $386.9 mil; net income: $100.0 mil. **Principal internat. airport at:** Minneapolis-St. Paul. **Tourism expends.** (2003): $8.0 bil.

Federal govt. Fed. civ. employees (Mar. 2004): 14,313; **avg. salary:** $58,304.

Energy. Electricity production (est. 2004, kWh by source): Coal: 31.3 bil; Petroleum: 50 mil; Gas: 970 mil; Hydroelectric: 793 mil; Nuclear: 13.3 bil; Other: 387 mil.

State data. Motto: L'Etoile du Nord (The star of the north). **Flower:** Pink and white lady's-slipper. **Bird:** Common loon. **Tree:** Red pine. **Song:** Hail! Minnesota. **Entered union** May 11, 1858; rank, 32nd. **State fair** at St. Paul/Minneapolis; late Aug.-early Sept.

History. Dakota Sioux were early inhabitants of the area, and in the 16th cent., the Ojibwa began moving in from the east. French fur traders Médard Chouart and Pierre Esprit Radisson entered the region in the mid-17th cent. In 1679, French explorer Daniel Greysolon, sieur Duluth, claimed the entire region in the name of France. Britain took the area east of the Mississippi, 1763. The U.S. took over that portion after the American Revolution and in 1803, gained the western area in the Louisiana Purchase. The U.S. built Ft. St. Anthony (now Ft. Snelling), 1819, and in 1837, bought Native American lands, spurring an influx of settlers from the east. In 1849, the Territory of Minnesota was created. Sioux Indians staged a bloody uprising, the Battle of Woods Lake, 1862, and were driven from the state.

Tourist attractions. Minneapolis Institute of Arts, Walker Art Center, Minneapolis Sculpture Garden, Minnehaha Falls (inspiration for Longfellow's *Hiawatha),* Guthrie Theater, Minneapolis; Ordway Theater, St. Paul; Voyageurs Natl. Park; Mayo Clinic, Rochester; St. Paul Winter Carnival; North Shore (of Lake Superior).

Famous Minnesotans. Warren Burger, Ethan and Joel Coen, William O. Douglas, Bob Dylan, F. Scott Fitzgerald, Al Franken, Judy Garland, Cass Gilbert, Hubert Humphrey, Garrison Keillor, Sister Elizabeth Kenny, Jessica Lange, Sinclair Lewis, Paul Manship, Roger Maris, E. G. Marshall, William and Charles Mayo, Eugene McCarthy, Walter F. Mondale, Prince (Rodgers Nelson), Charles Schulz, Harold Stassen, Thorstein Veblen, Jesse Ventura, Paul Wellstone.

Tourist Information. Explore Minnesota Tourism, Metro Square, 121 7th Pl. E., Ste. 100, St. Paul, MN 55101. Phone: 1-888-TOURISM. **Website:** www.exploreminnesota.com

Website. www.state.mn.us

Mississippi (MS)

Magnolia State

See Index and Table of Contents for coverage of Hurricane Katrina.

People. Population (2004 est.): 2,902,966; rank: 31; **net change** (2003-2004): 0.7%. **Pop. density:** 61.9 per sq mi. **Racial distribution** (2003): 61.2% white; 36.9% black; 0.8% Asian; 0.4% Native American/Nat. AK; 0.03% Hawaiian/Pacific Islander; 2 or more races, 0.6%. **Hispanic pop.** (any race): 1.5%.

Geography. Total area: 48,430 sq mi; rank: 32. **Land area:** 46,907 sq mi; rank: 31. **Acres forested:** 18.6 mil. **Location:** East South Central state bordered on the W by the Mississippi R. and on the S by the Gulf of Mexico. **Climate:** semi-tropical, with abundant rainfall, long growing season, and extreme temperatures unusual. **Topography:** low, fertile delta between the Yazoo and Mississippi rivers; loess bluffs stretching around delta border; sandy gulf coastal terraces followed by piney woods and prairie; rugged, high sandy hills in extreme NE followed by Black Prairie Belt, Pontotoc Ridge, and flatwoods into the north central highlands. **Capital:** Jackson.

Economy. Chief industries: warehousing & distribution, services, manufacturing, government, wholesale and retail trade. **Chief manuf. goods:** chemicals & plastics, food & kindred products, furniture, lumber & wood products, electrical machinery, transportation equipment. **Chief crops:** cotton, rice, soybeans. **Livestock:** (Jan. 2005) 1.07 mil. cattle/calves; (Dec. 2004) 315,000 hogs/pigs, 11.1 mil. chickens (excl. broilers), 827.8 mil. broilers. **Timber/lumber** (est. 2003): 2.6 bil bd. ft.; pine, oak, hardwoods. **Nonfuel minerals** (est. 2004): $189 mil.; sand and gravel (construction), clays (fuller's earth), stone (crushed), cement (portland), sand and gravel (industrial). **Commercial fishing** (2003): $45.5 mil. **Chief ports:** Pascagoula, Vicksburg, Gulfport, Natchez, Greenville. **Gross state product** (2004): $76.2 bil. **Sales tax** (2005): 7.0%. **Employment distrib.** (May 2005): 21.5% govt.; 19.5% trade/trans./util.; 15.8% mfg.; 10.8% ed./health serv.; 7.4% prof./bus. serv. 11.2% leisure/hosp. 4.1% finance; 4.4% constr.; 3.3% other serv.; 1.3% info. **Unemployment** (2004): 6.2%. **Per cap. pers. income** (2004): $24,650. **Commercial banks** (2004): 102; **deposits**: $32.9 bil. **Savings institutions** (2004): 9; **deposits**: $566 mil. **New private housing** (2004): 13,903 units/$1.4 bil. **Principal internat. airport at:** Jackson. **Tourism expends.** (2003): $5.4 bil.

Federal govt. Fed. civ. employees (Mar. 2004): 16,734; **avg. salary:** $53,242. **Notable fed. facilities:** Columbus AFB; *Keesler AFB; Meridian NAS; NASA Stennis Space Ctr.; Army Corps of Engineers Waterways Experiment Sta.; Naval Constr. Battalion Ctr., Gulfport.

Energy. Electricity production (est. 2004, kWh by source): Coal: 14.3 bil; Petroleum: 2.8 bil; Gas: 5.4 bil; Nuclear: 10.2 bil.

State data. Motto: Virtute et Armis (By valor and arms). **Flower:** Magnolia. **Bird:** Mockingbird. **Tree:** Magnolia. **Song:** Go, Mississippi! **Entered union** Dec. 10, 1817; rank, 20th. **State fair** at Jackson; early Oct.

History. Early inhabitants of the region were Choctaw, Chickasaw, and Natchez peoples. Hernando de Soto explored the area, 1540, and sighted the Mississippi River, 1541. Robert La Salle traced the river from Illinois to its mouth and claimed the entire valley for France, 1682. The first settlement was the French Ft. Maurepas, near Ocean Springs, 1699. The area was ceded to Britain, 1763; American settlers followed. During the American Revolution, Spain seized part of the area, remaining even after the U.S. acquired title at the end of the conflict; Spain finally moved out, 1798. The Territory of Mississippi was formed, 1798. Mississippi seceded, 1861. Union forces captured Corinth and Vicksburg and destroyed Jackson and much of Meridian. Mississippi was readmitted to the Union in 1870.

Tourist attractions. Vicksburg Natl. Military Park and Cemetery, other Civil War sites; Hattiesburg; Natchez Trace; Indian mounds; Antebellum homes; pilgrimages in Natchez and some 25 other cities; The Elvis Presley Birthplace & Museum, Tupelo; Smith Robertson Museum, Mynelle Gardens, both Jackson; Mardi Gras and Shrimp Festival, both in Biloxi; Gulf Islands Natl. Seashore.

Famous Mississippians. Margaret Walker Alexander, Dana Andrews, Jimmy Buffett, Hodding Carter III, Bo Diddley, William Faulkner, Brett Favre, Shelby Foote, Morgan Freeman, John Grisham, Fannie Lou Hamer, Jim Henson, Faith Hill, John Lee Hooker, Robert Johnson, James Earl Jones, B. B. King, L. Q. C. Lamar, Trent Lott, Gerald McRaney, Willie Morris, Walter Payton, Elvis Presley, Leontyne Price, Charley Pride, LeAnn Rimes, Muddy Waters, Eudora Welty, Tennessee Williams, Oprah Winfrey, Johnny Winter, Richard Wright, Tammy Wynette.

Tourist Information. Mississippi Division of Tourism. PO Box 849, Jackson, MS 39205-0849; 1-888-SEE-MISS. **Website:** www.visitmississippi.org

Website. www.ms.gov

Missouri (MO)

Show Me State

People. Population (2004 est.): 5,754,618; rank: 17; **net change** (2003-2004): 0.6%. **Pop. density:** 83.5 per sq mi. **Racial distribution** (2003): 85.3% white; 11.6% black; 1.3% Asian; 0.5% Native American/Nat. AK; 0.1% Hawaiian/Pacific Islander; 2 or more races, 1.3%. **Hispanic pop.** (any race): 2.3%.

Geography. Total area: 69,704 sq mi; rank: 21. **Land area:** 68,886 sq mi; rank: 18. **Acres forested:** 14.0 mil. **Location:** West North Central state near the geographic center of the conterminous U.S.; bordered on the E by the Mississippi R., on the NW by the Missouri R. **Climate:** continental, susceptible to cold Canadian air, moist, warm gulf air, and drier SW air. **Topography:** rolling hills, open, fertile plains, and well-watered prairie N of the Missouri R.; south of the river land is rough and hilly with deep, narrow valleys; alluvial plain in the SE; low elevation in the west. **Capital:** Jefferson City.

Economy. Chief industries: agriculture, manufacturing, aerospace, tourism. **Chief manuf. goods:** transportation equipment, food and related products, electrical and electronic equipment, chemicals. **Chief crops:** soybeans, corn, wheat, hay. **Livestock:** (Jan. 2005) 4.45 mil. cattle/calves, 65,000 sheep/lambs; (Dec. 2004) 2.9 mil. hogs/pigs, 9.4 mil. chickens (excl. broilers). **Timber/lumber** (est. 2003): 530 mil bd. ft.; oak, hickory. **Nonfuel minerals** (est. 2004): $1.5 bil.; stone (crushed), cement (portland), lead, lime, sand and gravel (construction). **Gross state product** (2004): $203.2 bil. **Sales tax** (2005): 4.225%. **Employment distrib.** (May 2005): 16.1% govt.; 19.6% trade/trans./util.; 11.5% mfg.; 13.3% ed./health serv.; 11.1% prof./bus. serv. 10.1% leisure/hosp. 6.1% finance; 5.1% constr.; 4.4% other serv.; 2.3% info. **Unemployment** (2004): 5.7%. **Per cap. pers. income** (2004): $30,608. **New private housing** (2004): 31,036 units/$3.9 bil. **Commercial banks** (2004): 362; **deposits**: $82.8 bil. **Savings institutions** (2004): 35; **deposits**: $4.3 bil. **Lottery** (2004): total sales: $791.5 mil; net income: $230.3 mil. **Principal internat. airports at:** Kansas City, St. Louis. **Tourism expends.** (2003): $9.2 bil.

Federal govt. Fed. civ. employees (Mar. 2004): 32,792; **avg. salary:** $53,083. **Notable fed. facilities:** Federal Reserve banks; *Ft. Leonard Wood; Jefferson Barracks Natl. Cem.; Whiteman AFB.

Energy. Electricity production (est. 2004, kWh by source): Coal: 74.5 bil; Petroleum: 68 mil; Gas: 1.9 bil; Hydroelectric: 1.4 bil; Nuclear: 7.8 bil; Other: 107 mil.

State data. Motto: Salus Populi Suprema Lex Esto (The welfare of the people shall be the supreme law). **Flower:** Hawthorn. **Bird:** Bluebird. **Tree:** Dogwood. **Song:** Missouri Waltz. **Entered union** Aug. 10, 1821; rank, 24th. **State fair** at Sedalia; 3rd week in Aug.

History. Early inhabitants of the region were Algonquian Sauk, Fox, and Illinois and Siouan Osage, Missouri, Iowa, and Kansa peoples. Hernando de Soto visited 1541. French hunters and lead miners made the first settlement c 1735, at Ste. Genevieve. The territory was ceded to Spain by the French, 1763, then returned to France, 1800. The U.S. acquired Missouri as part of the Louisiana Purchase, 1803. The influx of white settlers drove Native American tribes to the Kansas and Oklahoma territories; most were gone by 1836. The fur trade and the Santa Fe Trail provided prosperity; St. Louis became the gateway for pioneers heading West. Missouri entered the Union as a slave state, 1821. Though it remained with the Union, pro- and anti-slavery forces battled there during the Civil War.

Tourist attractions. Silver Dollar City, Branson; Mark Twain Area, Hannibal; Pony Express Museum, St. Joseph; Harry S. Truman Library, Independence; Gateway Arch, St. Louis; Worlds of Fun, Kansas City; Lake of the Ozarks; Churchill Mem., Fulton; State Capitol, Jefferson City.

WORLD ALMANAC QUICK QUIZ

After Rhode Island, which is the next smallest state in the Union by area?

(a) Connecticut (b) Hawaii (c) New Hampshire (d) Delaware

For the answer look in this chapter, or see page 1008.

Famous Missourians. Maya Angelou, Robert Altman, Burt Bacharach, Josephine Baker, Scott Bakula, Thomas Hart Benton, Tom Berenger, Yogi Berra, Chuck Berry, George Caleb Bingham, Daniel Boone, Omar Bradley, William Burroughs, Kate Capshaw, Dale Carnegie, George Washington Carver, Bob Costas, Walter Cronkite, Walt Disney, T. S. Eliot, Richard Gephardt, John Goodman, Betty Grable, Edwin Hubble, Jesse James, Rush Limbaugh, Marianne Moore, Reinhold Niebuhr, J. C. Penney, John J. Pershing, Brad Pitt, Joseph Pulitzer, Ginger Rogers, Bess Truman, Harry S. Truman, Kathleen Turner, Tina Turner, Mark Twain, Dick Van Dyke, Tennessee Williams, Lanford Wilson, Shelley Winters, Jane Wyman.

Tourist Information. Missouri Division of Tourism. P.O. Box 1055, Jefferson City, MO 65102; 1-800-519-2100. **Website:** www.missouritourism.org

Website. www.state.mo.us

Montana (MT)

Treasure State

People. Population (2004 est.): 926,865; rank: 44; **net change** (2003-2004): 0.9%. **Pop. density:** 6.4 per sq mi. **Racial distribution** (2003): 90.9% white; 0.4% black; 0.6% Asian; 6.5% Native American/Nat. AK; 0.1% Hawaiian/Pacific Islander; 2 or more races, 1.5%. **Hispanic pop.** (any race): 2.1%.

Geography. Total area: 147,042 sq mi; rank: 4. **Land area:** 145,552 sq mi; rank: 4. **Acres forested:** 23.3 mil. **Location:** Mountain state bounded on the E by the Dakotas, on the S by Wyoming, on the SSW by Idaho, and on the N by Canada. **Climate:** colder, continental climate with low humidity. **Topography:** Rocky Mts. in western third of the state; eastern two-thirds gently rolling northern Great Plains. **Capital:** Helena.

Economy. Chief industries: agriculture, timber, mining, tourism, oil and gas. **Chief manuf. goods:** food products, wood & paper products, primary metals, printing & publishing, petroleum and coal products. **Chief crops:** wheat, barley, sugar beets, hay, oats. **Livestock:** (Jan. 2005) 2.35 mil. cattle/calves, 305,000 sheep/lambs; (Dec. 2004) 165,000 hogs/pigs, 480,000 chickens (excl. broilers). **Timber/lumber** (est. 2003): 1.2 bil bd. ft.; Douglas fir, pines, larch. **Nonfuel minerals** (est. 2004): $582 mil.; gold, palladium, platinum, sand and gravel (construction), cement (portland). **Gross state product** (2004): $27.7 bil. **Sales tax** (2005): none. **Employment distrib.** (May 2005): 21.3% govt.; 20.7% trade/trans./util.; 4.6% mfg.; 13.1% ed./health serv.; 8.1% prof./bus. serv. 13.1% leisure/hosp. 5.1% finance; 6.1% constr.; 4.1% other serv.; 1.9% info. **Unemployment** (2004): 4.4%. **Per cap. pers. income** (2004): $26,857. **New private housing** (2004): 5,475 units/$452 mil. **Commercial banks** (2004): 80; **deposits**: $11.5 bil. **Savings institutions** (2004): 3; **deposits**: $426 mil. **Lottery** (2004): total sales: $36.7 mil; net income: $8.1 mil. **Principal internat. airports at:** Billings, Missoula. **Tourism expends.** (2003): $2.1 bil.

Federal govt. Fed. civ. employees (Mar. 2004): 8,971; **avg. salary:** $52,261. **Notable fed. facilities:** Malmstrom AFB; Ft. Peck, Hungry Horse, Libby, Yellowtail dams; numerous missile silos.

Energy. Electricity production (est. 2004, kWh by source): Coal: 293 mil; Gas: 4 mil; Hydroelectric: 5.7 bil.

State data. Motto: Oro y Plata (Gold and silver). **Flower:** Bitterroot. **Bird:** Western meadowlark. **Tree:** Ponderosa pine. **Song:** Montana. **Entered union** Nov. 8, 1889; rank, 41st. **State fair** at Great Falls; late July-early Aug.

History. Cheyenne, Blackfoot, Crow, Assiniboin, Salish (Flatheads), Kootenai, and Kalispel peoples were early inhabitants of the area. French explorers visited the region, 1742. The U.S. acquired the area partly through the Louisiana Purchase, 1803, partly through explorations of Lewis and Clark, 1805-6. Fur traders and missionaries established posts early 19th cent. Gold was discovered, 1863, and the Montana territory was established, 1864. Indian uprisings reached their peak with the Battle of Little Bighorn, 1876. Chief Joseph and the Nez Percé tribe surrendered here, 1877, after long trek across the state. Mining activity and the coming of the Northern Pacific Railway, 1883, brought population growth. Copper wealth from the Butte pits resulted in the turn of the century "War of Copper Kings" as factions fought for control of "the richest hill on earth."

Tourist attractions. Glacier Natl. Park; Yellowstone Natl. Park; Museum of the Rockies, Bozeman; Museum of the Plains Indian, Blackfeet Reservation, near Browning; Little Bighorn Battlefield Natl. Monument and Custer Natl. Cemetery; Flathead Lake; Helena; Lewis and Clark Caverns State Park, near Whitehall; Lewis and Clark Interpretive Center, Great Falls.

Famous Montanans. Dana Carvey, Gary Cooper, Marcus Daly, Chet Huntley, Will James, Myrna Loy, David Lynch, Mike Mansfield, Brent Musburger, Jeannette Rankin, Charles M. Russell, Lester Thurow.

Tourist Information. Travel Montana, Dept. of Commerce, PO Box 200533, 301 S. Park, Helena, MT 59601; 1-800-VISITMT. **Website:** www.visitmt.org

Website. www.state.mt.us

Nebraska (NE)

Cornhusker State

People. Population (2004 est.): 1,747,214; rank: 38; **net change** (2003-2004): 0.6%. **Pop. density:** 22.7 per sq mi. **Racial distribution** (2003): 92.1% white; 4.2% black; 1.6% Asian; 0.9% Native American/Nat. AK; 0.1% Hawaiian/Pacific Islander; 2 or more races, 1.1%. **Hispanic pop.** (any race): 6.1%.

Geography. Total area: 77,354 sq mi; rank: 16. **Land area:** 76,872 sq mi; rank: 15. **Acres forested:** 0.9 mil. **Location:** West North Central state with the Missouri R. for a NE and E border. **Climate:** continental semi-arid. **Topography:** till plains of the central lowland in the eastern third rising to the Great Plains and hill country of the north central and NW. **Capital:** Lincoln.

Economy. Chief industries: agriculture, manufacturing. **Chief manuf. goods:** processed foods, industrial machinery, printed materials, electric and electronic equipment, primary and fabricated metal products, transportation equipment. **Chief crops:** corn, sorghum, soybeans, hay, wheat, dry beans, oats, potatoes, sugar beets. **Livestock:** (Jan. 2005) 6.35 mil. cattle/calves, 97,000 sheep/lambs; (Dec. 2004) 2.85 mil. hogs/pigs, 14.0 mil. chickens (excl. broilers), 4.3 mil. broilers. **Timber/lumber** (est. 2003): 17 mil bd. ft.; oak, hickory, and elm. **Nonfuel minerals** (est. 2004): $94.8 mil.; cement (portland), stone (crushed), sand and gravel (construction), cement (masonry), lime. **Chief ports:** Omaha, Sioux City, Brownville, Blair, Plattsmouth, Nebraska City. **Gross state product** (2004): $67.9 bil. **Sales tax** (2005): 5.5%. **Employment distrib.** (May 2005): 17.4% govt.; 21.4% trade/trans./util.; 10.5% mfg.; 13.6% ed./health serv.; 10.2% prof./bus. serv. 8.8% leisure/hosp. 6.8% finance; 5.3% constr.; 3.7% other serv.; 2.3% info. **Unemployment** (2004): 3.8%. **Per cap. pers. income** (2004): $31,339. **New private housing** (2004): 11,597 units/$1.3 bil. **Commercial banks** (2004): 265; **deposits**: $29.4 bil. **Savings institutions** (2004): 16; **deposits**: $3.5 bil. **Lottery** (2004): total sales: $92.6 mil; net income: $19.7 mil. **Tourism expends.** (2003): $2.8 bil.

Federal govt. Fed. civ. employees (Mar. 2004): 8,624; **avg. salary:** $53,537. **Notable fed. facilities:** *Offutt AFB.

Energy. Electricity production (est. 2004, kWh by source): Coal: 20.3 bil; Petroleum: 18 mil; Gas: 297 mil; Hydroelectric: 1.0 bil; Nuclear: 10.2 bil; Other: 3 mil.

State data. Motto: Equality before the law. **Flower:** Goldenrod. **Bird:** Western meadowlark. **Tree:** Cottonwood. **Song:** Beautiful Nebraska. **Entered union** Mar. 1, 1867; rank, 37th. **State fair** at Lincoln; Aug.-Sept.

History. When the Europeans first arrived, Pawnee, Ponca, Omaha, and Oto peoples lived in the region. Spanish and French explorers and fur traders visited the area prior to its acquisition in the Louisiana Purchase, 1803. Lewis and Clark passed through, 1804-6. The first permanent settlement was Bellevue, near Omaha, 1823. The region was gradually settled, despite the 1834 Indian Intercourse Act, which declared Nebraska Indian country and excluded white settlement. Conflicts with settlers eventually forced Native Americans to move to reservations. Many Civil War veterans settled under free land terms of the 1862 Homestead Act; as agriculture grew, struggles followed between homesteaders and ranchers.

Tourist attractions. State Museum (Elephant Hall), State Capitol, both Lincoln; Stuhr Museum of the Prairie Pioneer, Grand Island; Museum of the Fur Trade, Chadron; Henry Doorly Zoo, Joslyn Art Museum, both Omaha; Ashfall Fossil Beds, Strategic Air Command Museum, Ashland; Boys Town, west of Omaha; Arbor Lodge State Park, Nebraska City; Buffalo Bill Ranch State Hist. Park, North Platte; Pioneer Village, Minden; Oregon Trail landmarks; Scotts Bluff Natl. Monument; Chimney Rock Natl. Historic Site; Ft. Robinson; Hastings Museum, Hastings.

Famous Nebraskans. Grover Cleveland Alexander, Fred Astaire, Marlon Brando, Charles W. Bryan, William Jennings Bryan, Warren Buffett, Johnny Carson, Willa Cather, Dick Cavett, Dick Cheney, William F. "Buffalo Bill" Cody, Loren Eiseley, Rev. Edward J. Flanagan, Henry Fonda, Gerald R. Ford, Bob Gibson, Rollin Kirby, Harold Lloyd, Malcolm X, J. Sterling Morton, John Neihardt, Nick Nolte, George Norris, Tom Osborne, John J. Pershing, Roscoe Pound, Chief Red Cloud, Mari Sandoz, Robert Taylor, Darryl F. Zanuck.

Tourist Infomation. Nebraska Division of Travel and Tourism, PO Box 98907, Lincoln, NE 68509-8907; 1-877-NEBRASKA. **Website:** www.visitnebraska.org

Website. www.state.ne.us

Nevada (NV)

Sagebrush State, Battle Born State, Silver State

People. Population (2004 est.): 2,334,771; rank: 35; **net change** (2003-2004): 4.1%. **Pop. density:** 21.3 per sq mi. **Racial distribution** (2003): 84.1% white; 6.9% black; 4.7% Asian; 1.5% Native American/Nat. AK; 0.04% Hawaiian/Pacific Islander; 2 or more races, 2.4%. **Hispanic pop.** (any race): 21.9%.

Geography. Total area: 110,561 sq mi; rank: 7. **Land area:** 109,826 sq mi; rank: 7. **Acres forested:** 10.2 mil. **Location:** Mountain state bordered on N by Oregon and Idaho, on E by Utah and Arizona, on SE by Arizona, and on SW and W by California. **Climate:** semi-arid and arid. **Topography:** rugged N-S mountain ranges; highest elevation, Boundary Peak, 13,140 ft; southern area is within the Mojave Desert; lowest elevation, Colorado River at southern tip of state, 479 ft. **Capital:** Carson City.

Economy. Chief industries: gaming, tourism, mining, manufacturing, government, retailing, warehousing, trucking. **Chief manuf. goods:** food products, plastics, chemicals, aerospace products, lawn and garden irrigation equipment, seismic and machinery-monitoring devices. **Chief crops:** hay, alfalfa seed, potatoes, onions, garlic, barley, wheat. **Livestock:** (Jan. 2005) 500,000 cattle/calves, 70,000 sheep/lambs; (Dec. 2004) 5,500 hogs/pigs. **Timber/lumber** (est. 2003): <0.5 mil bd. ft.; piñon, juniper, other pines. **Nonfuel minerals** (est. 2004): $3.3 bil.; gold, sand and gravel (construction), lime, stone (crushed), diatomite. **Gross state product** (2004): $99.4 bil. **Sales tax** (2005): 6.5%. **Employment distrib.** (May 2005): 12.0% govt.; 17.1% trade/trans./util.; 3.8% mfg.; 6.9% ed./health serv.; 11.7% prof./bus. serv. 27.0% leisure/hosp. 5.3% finance; 10.9% constr.; 3.2% other serv.; 1.2% info. **Unemployment** (2004): 4.3%. **Per cap. pers. income** (2004): $33,405. **New private housing** (2004): 44,663 units/$5.4 bil. **Commercial banks** (2004): 42; **deposits**: $36.8 bil. **Savings institutions** (2004): 10; **deposits**: $3.7 bil. **Principal internat. airports at:** Las Vegas, Reno. **Tourism expends.** (2003): $19.3 bil.

Federal govt. Fed. civ. employees (Mar. 2004): 9,048; **avg. salary:** $55,901. **Notable fed. facilities:** Nevada Test Site; *Hawthorne Army Depot; Nellis AFB and Range Complex; Fallon NAS; Natl. Wild Horse and Burro Ctr. at Palomino Valley.

Energy. Electricity production (est. 2004, kWh by source): Coal: 18.3 bil; Petroleum: 96 mil; Gas: 4.5 bil; Hydroelectric: 1.6 bil.

State data. Motto: All for our country. **Flower:** Sagebrush. **Bird:** Mountain bluebird. **Trees:** Single-leaf piñon and bristlecone pine. **Song:** Home Means Nevada. **Entered union** Oct. 31, 1864; rank, 36th. **State fair** at Reno; late Aug.

History. Shoshone, Paiute, Bannock, and Washoe peoples lived in the area at the time of European contact. Nevada was first explored by Spaniards, 1776. Hudson's Bay Co. trappers explored the north and central region, 1825; trader Jedediah Smith crossed the state, 1826-27. The area was acquired by the U.S., 1848, at the end of the Mexican War. The first settlement, Mormon Station, now Genoa, was established, 1849. Discovery of the Comstock Lode, rich in gold and silver, 1859, spurred a population boom. In the early 20th cent., Nevada adopted progressive measures such as the initiative, referendum, recall, and woman suffrage.

Tourist attractions. Legalized gambling at: Lake Tahoe, Reno, Las Vegas, Laughlin, Elko County, and elsewhere. Hoover Dam; Lake Mead; Great Basin Natl. Park; Valley of Fire State Park; Virginia City; Red Rock Canyon Natl. Conservation Area; Liberace Museum, the Las Vegas Strip, Guinness World of Records Museum, Lost City Museum, Overton, Lamoille Canyon, Pyramid Lake, all Las Vegas. Skiing near Lake Tahoe.

Famous Nevadans. Andre Agassi, Walter Van Tilburg Clark, George Ferris, Sarah Winnemucca Hopkins, Paul Laxalt, Dat So La Lee, John William Mackay, Anne Martin, Pat McCarran, Key Pittman, William Morris Stewart.

Tourist information. Commission on Tourism, 401 N. Carson St., Carson City, NV 89701; 1-800-NEVADA8. **Website:** www.travelnevada.com

Website. www.nv.gov

New Hampshire (NH)

Granite State

People. Population (2004 est.): 1,299,500; rank: 41; **net change** (2003-2004): 0.8%. **Pop. density:** 144.9 per sq mi. **Racial distribution** (2003): 96.3% white; 0.9% black; 1.6% Asian; 0.3% Native American/Nat. AK; 0.04% Hawaiian/Pacific Islander; 2 or more races, 0.9%. **Hispanic pop.** (any race): 1.8%.

Geography. Total area: 9,350 sq mi; rank: 46. **Land area:** 8,968 sq mi; rank: 44. **Acres forested:** 4.8 mil. **Location:** New England state bounded on S by Massachusetts, on W by Vermont, on N and NW by Canada, on E by Maine and the Atlantic Ocean. **Climate:** highly varied, due to its nearness to high mountains and ocean. **Topography:** low, rolling coast followed by countless hills and mountains rising out of a central plateau. **Capital:** Concord.

Economy. Chief industries: tourism, manufacturing, agriculture, trade, mining. **Chief manuf. goods:** machinery, electrical and electronic products, plastics, fabricated metal products. **Chief crops:** dairy products, nursery & greenhouse products, hay, vegetables, fruit, maple syrup & sugar products. **Livestock:** (Jan. 2005) 40,000 cattle/calves; (Dec. 2004) 3,600 hogs/pigs, 251,000 chickens (excl. broilers). **Timber/lumber** (est. 2003): 240 mil bd. ft.; white pine, hemlock, oak, birch. **Nonfuel minerals** (est. 2004): $64.6 mil.; sand and gravel (construction), stone (crushed), stone (dimension), gemstones. **Commercial fishing** (2003): $15.1 mil. **Chief ports:** Portsmouth, Hampton, Rye. **Gross state product** (2004): $52.1 bil. **Sales tax** (2005): none. **Employment distrib.** (May 2005): 14.7% govt.; 22.1% trade/trans./util.; 12.6% mfg.; 15.2% ed./health serv.; 8.8% prof./bus. serv. 10.5% leisure/hosp. 6.0% finance; 4.9% constr.; 3.1% other serv.; 2.0% info. **Unemployment** (2004): 3.8%. **Per cap. pers. income** (2004): $37,040. **New private housing** (2004): 8,952 units/$1.3 bil. **Commercial banks** (2004): 20; **deposits**: $18.8 bil. **Savings institutions** (2004): 20; **deposits**: $10.6 bil. **Lottery** (2004): total sales: $237.1 mil; net income: $71.5 mil. **Tourism expends.** (2003): $2.7 bil.

Federal govt. Fed. civ. employees (Mar. 2004): 3,224; **avg. salary:** $70,174. **Notable fed. facilities:** U.S. Army Cold Regions Res. & Engineering Lab.

Energy. Electricity production (est. 2004, kWh by source): Coal: 4.0 bil; Petroleum: 1.8 bil; Hydroelectric: 314 mil.

State data. Motto: Live free or die. **Flower:** Purple lilac. **Bird:** Purple finch. **Tree:** White birch. **Song:** Old New Hampshire. **Ninth** of the original 13 states to ratify the Constitution, June 21, 1788. **State Fair:** Many agricultural fairs statewide, July through Sept.; no State fair.

History. Algonquian-speaking peoples, including the Pennacook, lived in the region when the Europeans arrived. The first explorers to visit the area were England's Martin Pring, 1603, and France's Champlain, 1605. The first settlement was Odiorne's Point (now port of Rye), 1623. Native American conflicts were ended, 1759, by Robert Rogers' Rangers. Before the American Revolution, New Hampshire residents seized a British fort at Portsmouth, 1774, and drove the royal governor out, 1775. New Hampshire became the first colony to adopt its own constitution, 1776. Three regiments served in the Continental Army, and scores of privateers raided British shipping.

Tourist attractions. Mt. Washington, highest peak in Northeast; Lake Winnipesaukee; White Mt. National Forest; Crawford, Franconia—famous for the Old Man of the Mountain, described by Hawthorne as the Great Stone Face, Pinkham notches, all White Mt. region; the Flume, a spectacular gorge; the aerial tramway, Cannon Mt.; Strawbery Banke, Portsmouth; Shaker Village, Canterbury; Saint-Gaudens, Natl. Historic Site, Cornish; Mt. Monadnock.

Famous New Hampshirites. Salmon P. Chase, Ralph Adams Cram, Mary Baker Eddy, Daniel Chester French, Robert Frost, Horace Greeley, Sarah Buell Hale, Franklin Pierce, Augustus Saint-Gaudens, Adam Sandler, Alan Shepard, David H. Souter, Daniel Webster.

Tourist information. Division of Travel & Tourism Development, 172 Pembroke Rd., Concord, NH 03302-1856; 1-800-FUNINNH, ext. 169. **Website:** www.visitnh.gov

Website. www.state.nh.us

New Jersey (NJ)

Garden State

People. Population (2004 est.): 8,698,879; rank: 10; **net change** (2003-2004): 0.7%. **Pop. density:** 1,175.6 per sq mi. **Racial distribution** (2003): 77.3% white; 14.5% black; 6.5% Asian; 0.3% Native American/Nat. AK; 0.1% Hawaiian/Pacific Islander; 2 or more races, 1.2%. **Hispanic pop.** (any race):14.5%.

Geography. Total area: 8,721 sq mi; rank: 47. **Land area:** 7,417 sq mi; rank: 46. **Acres forested:** 2.1 mil. **Location:** Middle Atlantic state bounded on N and E by New York and Atlantic Ocean, on S and W by Delaware and Pennsylvania. **Climate:** moderate, with marked difference bet. NW and SE extremities. **Topography:** Appalachian Valley in the NW also has highest elevation, High Pt., 1,801 ft; Appalachian Highlands, flat-topped NE-SW mountain ranges; Piedmont Plateau, low plains broken by high ridges (Palisades) rising 400-500 ft; Coastal Plain, covering three-fifths of state in SE, rises from sea level to gentle slopes. **Capital:** Trenton.

Economy. Chief industries: pharmaceuticals/drugs, telecommunications, biotechnology, printing & publishing. **Chief manuf. goods:** chemicals, electronic equipment, food. **Chief crops:** nursery/greenhouse, tomatoes, blueberries, peaches, peppers, cranberries, soybeans. **Livestock:** (Jan. 2005) 44,000 cattle/calves; (Dec. 2004) 11,000 hogs/pigs, 2.1 mil. chickens (excl. broilers). **Timber/lumber:** figs. undisclosed; pine, cedar, mixed hardwoods. **Nonfuel minerals** (est. 2004): $330 mil.; stone (crushed), sand and gravel (construction), sand and gravel (industrial), greensand marl, peat. **Commercial fishing** (2003): $120.6 mil. **Chief ports:** Newark, Elizabeth, Hoboken, Camden. **Gross state product** (2004): $415.9 bil. **Sales tax** (2005): 6.0%. **Employment distrib.** (May 2005): 16.0% govt.; 21.8% trade/trans./util.; 8.1% mfg.; 13.8% ed./health serv.; 14.5% prof./bus. serv. 8.4% leisure/hosp. 6.9% finance; 4.1% constr.; 3.9% other serv.; 2.4% info. **Unemployment** (2004): 4.8%. **Per cap. pers. income** (2004): $41,332. **New private housing** (2004): 35,638 units/$4.3 bil. **Commercial banks** (2004): 94; **deposits**: $154.0 bil. **Savings institutions** (2004): 79; **deposits**: $57.3 bil. **Lottery** (2004): total sales: $2.2 bil; net income: $793.0 mil. **Principal internat. airports at:** Atlantic City, Newark. **Tourism expends.** (2003): $14.7 bil.

Federal govt. Fed. civ. employees (Mar. 2004): 27,223; **avg. salary:** $66,118. **Notable fed. facilities:** McGuire AFB; Ft. Dix; *Ft. Monmouth; Picatinny Arsenal; *Lakehurst Naval Air Engineering Ctr.; FAA William J.Hughes Technical Ctr.

Energy. Electricity production (est. 2004, kWh by source): Coal: 1.7 bil; Petroleum: 111 mil; Gas: 36 mil.

State data. Motto: Liberty and prosperity. **Flower:** Purple violet. **Bird:** Eastern goldfinch. **Tree:** Red oak. **Third** of the original 13 states to ratify the Constitution, Dec. 18, 1787. **State fair** at Augusta; late July-early Aug.

History. The Lenni Lenape (Delaware) peoples lived in the region and had mostly peaceful relations with European colonists, who arrived after the explorers Verrazano, 1524, and Hudson, 1609. The first permanent European settlement was Dutch, at Bergen (now Jersey City), 1660. When the British took New Netherland, 1664, the area between the Delaware and Hudson Rivers was given to Lord John Berkeley and Sir George Carteret. During the American Revolution, New Jersey was the scene of nearly 100 battles, large and small, including Trenton, 1776; Princeton, 1777; Monmouth, 1778.

Tourist attractions. 127 mi of beaches; Miss America Pageant, Atlantic City; Grover Cleveland birthplace, Caldwell; Cape May Historic District; Edison Natl. Historic Site, W. Orange; Six Flags Great Adventure, Jackson; Liberty State Park, Jersey City; Meadowlands Sports Complex, E. Rutherford; Pine Barrens wilderness area; Princeton University; numerous Revolutionary War historical sites; State Aquarium, Camden.

Famous New Jerseyans. Jason Alexander, Count Basie, Judy Blume, Jon Bon Jovi, Bill Bradley, Aaron Burr, Grover Cleveland, James Fenimore Cooper, Stephen Crane, Danny DeVito, Thomas Edison, Albert Einstein, James Gandolfini, Allen Ginsberg, Alexander Hamilton, Ed Harris, Whitney Houston, Buster Keaton, Joyce Kilmer, Norman Mailer, Jack Nicholson, Thomas Paine, Dorothy Parker, Joe Pesci, Molly Pitcher, Paul Robeson, Philip Roth, Antonin Scalia, Wally Schirra, H. Norman Schwarzkopf, Frank Sinatra, Bruce Springsteen, Martha Stewart, Meryl Streep, Dave Thomas, John Travolta, Walt Whitman, William Carlos Williams, Woodrow Wilson.

Tourist Information. New Jersey Commerce and Economic Growth Commission, PO Box 820, Trenton, NJ 08625-0820; 1-800-VISITNJ. **Website:** www.visitnj.org

Website. www.state.nj.us

New Mexico (NM)

Land of Enchantment

People. Population (2004 est.): 1,903,289; rank: 36; **net change** (2003-2004): 1.3%. **Pop. density:** 15.7 per sq mi. **Racial distribution** (2003): 84.9% white; 2.3% black; 1.3% Asian; 10.0% Native American/Nat. AK; 0.1% Hawaiian/Pacific Islander; 2 or more races, 1.5%. **Hispanic pop.** (any race): 43.2%.

Geography. Total area: 121,589 sq mi; rank: 5. **Land area:** 121,356 sq mi; rank: 5. **Acres forested:** 16.7 mil. **Location:** southwestern state bounded by Colorado on the N, Oklahoma, Texas, and Mexico on the E and S, and Arizona on the W. **Climate:** dry, with temperatures rising or falling 5× F with every 1,000 ft elevation. **Topography:** eastern third, Great Plains; central third, Rocky Mts. (85% of the state is over 4,000-ft elevation); western third, high plateau. **Capital:** Santa Fe.

Economy. Chief industries: government, services, trade. **Chief manuf. goods:** foods, machinery, apparel, lumber, printing, transportation equipment, electronics, semiconductors. **Chief crops:** hay, onions, chiles, greenhouse nursery, pecans, cotton. **Livestock:** (Jan. 2005) 1.5 mil. cattle/calves, 145,000 sheep/lambs; (Dec. 2004) 2,500 hogs/pigs. **Timber/lumber** (est. 2003): 76 mil bd. ft.; ponderosa pine, Douglas fir. **Nonfuel minerals** (est. 2004): $811 mil.; potash, copper, sand and gravel (construction), cement (portland), stone (crushed). **Gross state product** (2004): $60.9 bil. **Sales tax** (2005): 5.0%. **Employment distrib.** (May 2005): 25.3% govt.; 17.1% trade/trans./util.; 4.4% mfg.; 13.1% ed./health serv.; 11.4% prof./bus. serv. 10.5% leisure/hosp. 4.4% finance; 6.6% constr.; 3.6% other serv.; 1.8% info. **Unemployment** (2004): 5.7%. **Per cap. pers. income** (2004): $26,191. **New private housing** (2004): 12,793 units/$1.8 bil. **Commercial banks** (2004): 57; **deposits**: $16.2 bil. **Savings institutions** (2004): 10; **deposits**: $2.0 bil. **Lottery** (2004): total sales: $148.7 mil; net income: $35.9 mil. **Principal internat. airport at:** Albuquerque. **Tourism expends.** (2003): $4.1 bil.

Federal govt. Fed. civ. employees (Mar. 2004): 21,700; **avg. salary:** $54,650. **Notable fed. facilities:** Kirtland, *Cannon, *Holloman AF bases; Los Alamos Natl. Lab; *White Sands Missile Range; Natl. Solar Observatory; Natl. Radio Astronomy Observatory, Sandia Natl. Labs.

Energy. Electricity production (est. 2004, kWh by source): Coal: 29.3 bil; Petroleum: 29 mil; Gas: 2.9 bil; Hydroelectric: 263 mil.

State data. Motto: Crescit Eundo (It grows as it goes). **Flower:** Yucca. **Bird:** Roadrunner. **Tree:** Piñon. **Song:** O, Fair New Mexico; Asi Es Nuevo Mexico. **Entered union** Jan. 6, 1912; rank, 47th. **State fair** at Albuquerque; mid-Sept.

History. Early inhabitants were peoples of the Mogollon and Anasazi civilizations, followed by the Pueblo peoples, Anasazi descendants. The nomadic Navajo and Apache tribes arrived c 15th cent. Franciscan Marcos de Niza and a former black slave, Estevanico, explored the area, 1539, seeking gold. First settlements were at San Juan Pueblo, 1598, and Santa Fe, 1610. Settlers alternately traded and fought with the Apache, Comanche, and Navajo. Trade on the Santa Fe Trail to Missouri started, 1821. The Mexican War was declared in May 1846; Gen. Stephen Kearny took Santa Fe without firing a shot, Aug. 18, 1846, declaring New Mexico part of the U.S. All Hispanic New Mexicans and Pueblo became U.S. citizens by terms of the 1848 treaty ending the war, but Congress denied the area statehood and created the territory of New Mexico, 1850. Pancho Villa raided Columbus, 1916, and U.S. troops were sent to the area. The world's first atomic bomb was exploded near Alamogordo, south of Santa Fe, 1945.

Tourist attractions. Carlsbad Caverns Natl. Park, with the largest natural underground chamber in the world; Santa Fe, oldest capital in U.S.; White Sands Natl. Monument, the largest gypsum deposit in the world; Chaco Culture National Historical Park; Acoma Pueblo, the "sky city," built atop a 357-ft mesa; Taos; Taos Art Colony; Taos Ski Valley; Ute Lake State Park; Shiprock.

Famous New Mexicans. Ben Abruzzo, Maxie Anderson, Jeff Bezos, Billy (the Kid) Bonney, Kit Carson, Bob Foster, Peter Hurd, Tony Hillerman, Archbishop Jean Baptiste Lamy, Nancy Lopez, Bill Mauldin, Georgia O'Keeffe, Bill Richardson, Kim Stanley, Al Unser, Bobby Unser, Lew Wallace.

Tourist information. New Mexico Dept. of Tourism, 491 Old Santa Fe Tr., Santa Fe, NM 87501; 1-800-733-6396, ext. 0643. **Website:** www.newmexico.org

Website. www.state.nm.us

New York (NY)

Empire State

People. Population (2004 est.): 19,227,088; rank: 3; **net change** (2003-2004): 0.1%. **Pop. density:** 407.2 per sq mi. **Racial distribution** (2003): 73.6% white; 17.8% black; 6.5% Asian; 0.6% Native American/Nat. AK; 0.1% Hawaiian/Pacific Islander; 2 or more races, 1.4%. **Hispanic pop.** (any race): 16.3%.

Geography. Total area: 54,556 sq mi; rank: 27. **Land area:** 47,214 sq mi; rank: 30. **Acres forested:** 18.4 mil. **Location:** Middle Atlantic state, bordered by the New England states, Atlantic Ocean, New Jersey and Pennsylvania, Lakes Ontario and Erie, and Canada. **Climate:** variable; the SE region moderated by the ocean. **Topography:** highest and most rugged mountains in the NE Adirondack upland; St. Lawrence-Champlain lowlands extend from Lake Ontario NE along the Canadian border; Hudson-Mohawk lowland follows the flows of the rivers N and W, 10-30 mi wide; Atlantic coastal plain in the SE; Appalachian Highlands, covering half the state westward from the Hudson Valley, include the Catskill Mts., Finger Lakes; plateau of Erie-Ontario lowlands. **Capital:** Albany.

Economy. Chief industries: manufacturing, finance, communications, tourism, transportation, services. **Principal manuf. goods:** books & periodicals, clothing & apparel, pharmaceuticals, machinery, instruments, toys & sporting goods, electronic equipment, automotive & aircraft components. **Chief crops:** apples, grapes, strawberries, cherries, pears, onions, potatoes, cabbage, sweet corn, green beans, cauliflower, field corn, hay, wheat, oats, dry beans. **Chief farm prods.:** milk, cheese, maple syrup, wine. **Livestock:** (Jan. 2005) 1.41 mil. cattle/calves, 75,000 sheep/lambs; (Dec. 2004) 84,000 hogs/pigs, 5.5 mil. chickens (excl. broilers), 2.6 mil. broilers. **Timber/lumber** (est. 2003): 460 mil bd. ft.; birch, sugar and red maple, basswood, hemlock, pine, oak, ash. **Nonfuel minerals** (est. 2004): $1.1 bil.; stone (crushed), cement (portland), salt, sand and gravel (construction), wollastonite. **Commercial fishing** (2003): $51.7 mil. **Chief ports:** New York, Buffalo, Albany. **Gross state product** (2004): $899.7 bil. **Sales tax** (2005): 4.0%. **Employment distrib.** (May 2005): 17.6% govt.; 17.4% trade/trans./util.; 6.8% mfg.; 18.2% ed./health serv.; 12.5% prof./bus. serv. 8.0% leisure/hosp. 8.2% finance; 3.8% constr.; 4.2% other serv.; 3.2% info. **Unemployment** (2004): 5.8%. **Per cap. pers. income** (2004): $38,228. **New private housing** (2004): 55,093 units/ $7.1 bil. **Commercial banks** (2004): 158; **deposits**: $537.1 bil. **Savings institutions** (2004): 70; **deposits**: $95.7 bil. **Lottery** (2004): total sales: $5.8 bil; net income: $1.9 bil. **Principal internat. airports at:** Albany, Buffalo, New York, Newburgh, Rochester, Syracuse. **Tourism expends.** (2003): $27.7 bil.

Federal govt. Fed. civ. employees (Mar. 2004): 58,958; **avg. salary:** $59,700. **Notable fed. facilities:** West Point Military Academy; Merchant Marine Academy; Ft. Drum; *Rome Labs.; Watervliet Arsenal; Brookhaven Natl. Lab.

Energy. Electricity production (est. 2004, kWh by source): Coal: 1.7 bil; Petroleum: 9.2 bil; Gas: 6.4 bil; Hydroelectric: 21.4 bil; Nuclear: 1.9 bil.

State data. Motto: Excelsior (Ever upward). **Flower:** Rose. **Bird:** Bluebird. **Tree:** Sugar maple. **Song:** I Love New York. **Eleventh** of the original 13 states to ratify the Constitution, July 26, 1788. **State fair** at Syracuse; late Aug.-early Sept.

History. Algonquians including the Mahican, Wappinger, and Lenni Lenape inhabited the region, as did the Iroquoian Mohawk, Oneida, Onondaga, Cayuga, and Seneca tribes, who established the League of the Five Nations. In 1609, Henry Hudson visited the river named for him, and Champlain explored the lake named for him. The first permanent settlement was Dutch, near present-day Albany, 1624. New Amsterdam was settled, 1626, at the S tip of Manhattan Island. A British fleet seized New Netherland, 1664. Ninety-two of the 300 or more engagements of the American Revolution were fought in New York, including the Battle of Bemis Heights-Saratoga, 1777, a turning point of the war. Completion of Erie Canal, 1825, established the state as a gateway to the West. The first women's rights convention was held in Seneca Falls, 1848.

Tourist attractions. New York City; Adirondack and Catskill Mts.; Finger Lakes; Great Lakes; Thousand Islands; Niagara Falls; Saratoga Springs; Philipsburg Manor, Sunnyside (Washington Irving's home), the Dutch Church of Sleepy Hollow, all in Tarrytown area; Corning Glass Center and Steuben factory, Corning; Fenimore House, Natl. Baseball Hall of Fame and Museum, both in Cooperstown; Ft. Ticonderoga overlooking Lakes George and Champlain; Empire State Plaza, Albany; Lake Placid; Franklin D. Roosevelt Natl. Historic Site, including the Roosevelt Library, Hyde Park; Long Island beaches; Theodore Roosevelt estate, Sagamore Hill, Oyster Bay; Turning Stone Casino.

Famous New Yorkers. Woody Allen, Susan B. Anthony, James Baldwin, Lucille Ball, Ann Bancroft, L. Frank Baum, Milton Berle, Humphrey Bogart, Barbara Boxer, Mel Brooks, Benjamin Cardozo, De Witt Clinton, Peter Cooper, Aaron Copland, Tom Cruise, Robert De Niro, George Eastman, Millard Fillmore, Lou Gehrig, George and Ira Gershwin, Ruth Bader Ginsburg, Rudolph Giuliani, Jackie Gleason, Stephen Jay Gould, Julia Ward Howe, Charles Evans Hughes, Washington Irving, Henry and William James, John Jay, Michael Jordan, Edward Koch, Fiorello LaGuardia, Herman Melville, Arthur Miller, J. Pierpont Morgan Jr., Eddie Murphy, Joyce Carol Oates, Carroll O'Connor, Rosie O'Donnell, Eugene O'Neill, Jerry Orbach, George Pataki, Colin Powell, Nancy Reagan, John D. Rockefeller, Nelson Rockefeller, John Roberts, Richard Rodgers, Ray Romano, Eleanor Roosevelt, Franklin D. Roosevelt, Theodore Roosevelt, Tim Russert, J. D. Salinger, Caroline Kennedy Schlossberg, Jerry Seinfeld, Al Sharpton, Paul Simon, Alfred E. Smith, Elizabeth Cady Stanton, Barbra Streisand, Donald Trump, William (Boss) Tweed, Martin Van Buren, Luther Vandross, Gore Vidal, Denzel Washington, Edith Wharton, Walt Whitman.

Tourist information. Empire State Development, Travel Information Center, 1 Commerce Plaza, Albany, NY 12245; 1-800-CALLNYS from U.S. states and territories and Canada; 1-518-474-4116 from other areas. **Website:** www.iloveny.com

Website. www.state.ny.us

North Carolina (NC)

Tar Heel State, Old North State

People. Population (2004 est.): 8,541,221; rank: 11; **net change** (2003-2004): 1.4%. **Pop. density:** 175.4 per sq mi. **Racial distribution** (2003): 74.1% white; 21.9% black; 1.7% Asian; 1.3% Native American/Nat. AK; 0.1% Hawaiian/Pacific Islander; 2 or more races, 1.0%. **Hispanic pop.** (any race): 5.6%.

Geography. Total area: 53,819 sq mi; rank: 28. **Land area:** 48,711 sq mi; rank: 29. **Acres forested:** 19.3 mil. **Location:** South Atlantic state bounded by Virginia, South Carolina, Georgia, Tennessee, and the Atlantic Ocean. **Climate:** subtropical in SE, medium-continental in mountain region; tempered by the Gulf Stream and the mountains in W. **Topography:** coastal plain and tidewater, two-fifths of state, extending to the fall line of the rivers; piedmont plateau, another two-fifths, of gentle to rugged hills; southern Appalachian Mts. contains the Blue Ridge and Great Smoky Mts. **Capital:** Raleigh.

Economy. Chief industries: manufacturing, agriculture, tourism. **Chief manuf. goods:** food products, textiles, industrial machinery and equipment, electrical and electronic equipment, furniture, tobacco products, apparel. **Chief crops:** tobacco, cotton, soybeans, corn, food grains, wheat, peanuts, sweet potatoes. **Livestock:** (Jan. 2005) 870,000 cattle/ calves, 20,000 sheep/lambs; (Dec. 2004) 9.8 mil. hogs/pigs, 17.7 mil. chickens (excl. broilers), 720.2 mil. broilers. **Timber/ lumber** (est. 2003): 2.5 bil bd. ft.; yellow pine, oak, hickory, poplar, maple. **Nonfuel minerals** (est. 2004): $822 mil.; stone (crushed), phosphate rock, sand and gravel (construction), sand and gravel (industrial), feldspar. **Commercial fishing** (2003): $83.0 mil. **Chief ports:** Morehead City, Wilmington. **Gross state product** (2004): $335.4 bil. **Sales tax** (2005): 4.5%. **Employment distrib.** (May 2005): 17.1% govt.; 18.6% trade/trans./util.; 14.8% mfg.; 11.8% ed./health serv.; 11.3% prof./bus. serv. 9.2% leisure/hosp. 5.0% finance; 5.8% constr.; 4.4% other serv.; 1.8% info. **Unemployment** (2004): 5.5%. **Per cap. pers. income** (2004): $29,246. **New private**

housing (2004): 92,411 units/$12.5 bil. **Commercial banks** (2004): 89; **deposits**: $158.6 bil. **Savings institutions** (2004): 41; **deposits**: $5.3 bil. **Principal internat. airports at:** Charlotte, Greensboro, Raleigh/Durham, Wilmington. **Tourism expends.** (2003): $12.6 bil.

Federal govt. Fed. civ. employees (Mar. 2004): 32,406; **avg. salary:** $52,523. **Notable fed. facilities:** Ft. Bragg; *Camp LeJeune Marine Base; U.S. EPA R&D Labs, *Cherry Point Marine Corps Air Station; Natl. Humanities Ctr.; Natl. Inst. of Environmental Health Science; Natl. Ctr. for Health Statistics Lab, Research Triangle Park.

Energy. Electricity production (est. 2004, kWh by source): Coal: 72.0 bil; Petroleum: 248 mil; Gas: 2.0 bil; Hydroelectric: 3.6 bil; Nuclear: 40.1 bil.

State data. Motto: Esse Quam Videri (To be rather than to seem). **Flower:** Dogwood. **Bird:** Cardinal. **Tree:** Pine. **Song:** The Old North State. **Twelfth** of the original 13 states to ratify the Constitution, Nov. 21, 1789. **State fair** at Raleigh; mid-Oct.

History. Algonquian, Siouan, and Iroquoian peoples lived in the region at the time of European contact. The first English colony in America was the first of 2 established by Sir Walter Raleigh on Roanoke Island, 1585 and 1587. The first group returned to England; the second, the "Lost Colony," disappeared without a trace. Permanent settlers came from Virginia, c 1660. Roused by British repression, the colonists drove out the royal governor, 1775. The province's congress was the first to vote for independence; ten regiments were furnished to the Continental Army. Cornwallis's forces were defeated at Kings Mountain, 1780, and forced out after Guilford Courthouse, 1781. The state seceded in 1861, and provided more troops to the Confederacy than any other state; readmitted in 1868.

Tourist attractions. Cape Hatteras and Cape Lookout natl. seashores; Great Smoky Mts.; Guilford Courthouse and Moore's Creek parks; 66 American Revolution battle sites; Bennett Place, near Durham, where Gen. Joseph Johnston surrendered the last Confederate army to Gen. William Sherman; Ft. Raleigh, Roanoke Island, where Virginia Dare, first child of English parents in the New World, was born Aug. 18, 1587; Wright Brothers Natl. Memorial, Kitty Hawk; Battleship *North Carolina*, Wilmington; NC Zoo, Asheboro; NC Symphony, NC Museum, Raleigh; Carl Sandburg Home, Hendersonville, Biltmore House & Gardens, Asheville.

Famous North Carolinians. David Brinkley, Robert Byrd, Shirley Caesar, John Coltrane, Rick Dees, Elizabeth Hanford Dole, John Edwards, Ava Gardner, Richard J. Gatling, Billy Graham, Andy Griffith, O. Henry, Andrew Jackson, Andrew Johnson, Michael Jordan, Wm. Rufus King, Charles Kuralt, Meadowlark Lemon, Dolley Madison, Thelonious Monk, Edward R. Murrow, Arnold Palmer, Richard Petty, James K. Polk, Charlie Rose, Carl Sandburg, Enos Slaughter, Dean Smith, James Taylor, Thomas Wolfe.

Tourist information. North Carolina Division of Tourism, Film & Sports Development, 301 N. Wilmington St., Raleigh, NC 27601; 1-800-VISITNC. **Website:** www.visitnc.com

Website. www.nc.gov

North Dakota (ND)

Peace Garden State

People. Population (2004 est.): 634,366; rank: 48; **net change** (2003-2004): 0.2%. **Pop. density:** 9.2 per sq mi. **Racial distribution** (2003): 92.5% white; 0.8% black; 0.7% Asian; 4.9% Native American/Nat. AK; 0.04% Hawaiian/Pacific Islander; 2 or more races, 1.0%. **Hispanic pop.** (any race): 1.3%.

Geography. Total area: 70,700 sq mi; rank: 19. **Land area:** 68,976 sq mi; rank: 17. **Acres forested:** 0.7 mil. **Location:** West North Central state, situated exactly in the middle of North America, bounded on the N by Canada, on the E by Minnesota, on the S by South Dakota, on the W by Montana. **Climate:** continental, with a wide range of temperature and moderate rainfall. **Topography:** Central Lowland in the E comprises the flat Red River Valley and the Rolling Drift Prairie; Missouri Plateau of the Great Plains on the W. **Capital:** Bismarck.

Economy. Chief industries: agriculture, mining, tourism, manufacturing, telecommunications, energy, food processing. **Chief manuf. goods:** farm equipment, processed foods, fabricated metal, high-tech. electronics. **Chief crops:** spring wheat, durum, barley, flaxseed, oats, potatoes, dry edible beans, honey, soybeans, sugar beets, sunflowers, hay. **Livestock:** (Jan. 2005) 1.71 mil. cattle/calves, 105,000 sheep/lambs; (Dec. 2004) 169,000 hogs/pigs. **Timber/lumber** (est. 2003): 1 mil bd. ft.; oak, ash, cottonwood, aspen. **Nonfuel minerals** (est. 2004): $52.3 mil.; sand and gravel (construction), lime, stone (crushed), clays (common), sand and gravel (industrial). **Gross state product** (2004): $23.6 bil. **Sales tax** (2005): 5.0%. **Employment distrib.** (May 2005): 22.3% govt.; 21.5% trade/trans./util.; 7.3% mfg.; 14.2% ed./health serv.; 7.1% prof./bus. serv. 9.3% leisure/hosp. 5.4% finance; 5.4% constr.; 4.3% other serv.; 2.2% info. **Unemployment** (2004): 3.4%. **Per cap. pers. income** (2004): $31,398. **New private housing** (2004): 4,128 units/$423 mil. **Commercial banks** (2004): 108; **deposits**: $10.7 bil. **Savings institutions** (2004): 2; **deposits**: $671 mil. **Lottery** (2004): total sales: $5.8 mil. **Principal internat. airport at:** Fargo. **Tourism expends.** (2003): $1.2 bil.

Federal govt. Fed. civ. employees (Mar. 2004): 5,517; **avg. salary:** $50,482. **Notable fed. facilities:** Strategic Air Command Base; Northern Prairie Wildlife Res. Ctr.; Garrison Dam; Theodore Roosevelt Natl. Park; Grand Forks Energy Res. Ctr.; Ft. Union Natl. Historic Site.

Energy. Electricity production (est. 2004, kWh by source): Coal: 29.3 bil; Petroleum: 31 mil; Hydroelectric: 1.5 bil; Other: 6 mil.

State data. Motto: Liberty and union, now and forever, one and inseparable. **Flower:** Wild prairie rose. **Bird:** Western meadowlark. **Tree:** American elm. **Song:** North Dakota Hymn. **Entered union** Nov. 2, 1889; rank, 39th. **State fair** at Minot; July.

History. At the time of European contact, the Ojibwa, Yanktonai and Teton Sioux, Mandan, Arikara, and Hidatsa peoples lived in the region. Pierre de Varennes was the first French fur trader in the area, 1738, followed later by the English. The U.S. acquired half the territory in the Louisiana Purchase, 1803. Lewis and Clark built Ft. Mandan, near present-day Stanton, 1804-5, and wintered there. In 1818, American ownership of the other half was confirmed by agreement with Britain. The first permanent settlement was at Pembina, 1812. Missouri River steamboats reached the area, 1832, the first railroad, 1873, bringing many homesteaders. The "bonanza farm" craze of the 1870s-80s attracted many settlers. The state was first to hold a national Presidential primary, 1912.

Tourist attractions. North Dakota Heritage Center, Bismarck; Bonanzaville, Fargo; Ft. Union Trading Post Natl. Historic Site; Lake Sakakawea; Intl. Peace Garden; Theodore Roosevelt Natl. Park, including Elkhorn Ranch, Badlands; Ft. Abraham Lincoln State Park and Museum, near Mandan; Dakota Dinosaur Museum, Dickinson; Knife River Indian Villages-National Historic Site.

Famous North Dakotans. Maxwell Anderson, Angie Dickinson, John Bernard Flannagan, Phil Jackson, Louis L'Amour, Peggy Lee, Eric Sevareid, Ann Sothern, Vilhjalmur Stefansson, Lawrence Welk.

Tourist Information. North Dakota Tourism Division, Century Center, 1600 E. Century Ave., Ste 2, Bismarck, ND 58503; 1-800-HELLO-ND. **Website:** www.ndtourism.com

Website. www.discovernd.com

Ohio (OH)

Buckeye State

People. Population (2004 est.): 11,459,011; rank: 7; **net change** (2003-2004): 0.2%. **Pop. density:** 280.1 per sq mi. **Racial distribution** (2003): 85.4% white; 11.7% black; 1.4% Asian; 0.2% Native American/Nat. AK; 0.03% Hawaiian/Pacific Islander; 2 or more races, 1.2%. **Hispanic pop.** (any race): 2.0%.

Geography. Total area: 44,825 sq mi; rank: 34. **Land area:** 40,948 sq mi; rank: 35. **Acres forested:** 7.9 mil. **Location:** East North Central state bounded on the N by Michigan and Lake Erie; on the E and S by Pennsylvania, West Virginia, and Kentucky; on the W by Indiana. **Climate:** temperate but variable; weather subject to much precipitation. **Topography:** generally rolling plain; Allegheny plateau in E; Lake Erie plains extend southward; central plains in the W. **Capital:** Columbus.

Economy. Chief industries: manufacturing, trade, services. **Chief manuf. goods:** transportation equipment, machinery, primary and fabricated metal products. **Chief crops:** corn, hay, winter wheat, oats, soybeans. **Livestock:** (Jan. 2005) 1.3 mil. cattle/calves, 142,000 sheep/lambs; (Dec. 2004) 1.45 mil. hogs/pigs, 36.0 mil. chickens (excl. broilers), 41.6 mil. broilers. **Timber/lumber** (est. 2003): 386 mil bd. ft.; oak, ash, maple, walnut, beech. **Nonfuel minerals** (est. 2004): $1.1 bil.; stone (crushed), sand and gravel (construction), salt, lime, cement (portland). **Commercial fishing** (2003): $3.0 mil. **Chief ports:** Toledo, Conneaut, Cleveland,

Ashtabula. **Gross state product** (2004): $418.3 bil. **Sales tax** (2005): 5.5%. **Employment distrib.** (May 2005): 15.0% govt.; 18.8% trade/trans./util.; 15.1% mfg.; 13.8% ed./health serv.; 11.8% prof./bus. serv. 9.4% leisure/hosp. 5.7% finance; 4.4% constr.; 4.2% other serv.; 1.7% info. **Unemployment** (2004): 6.1%. **Per cap. pers. income** (2004): $31,322. **New private housing** (2004): 58,568 units/$7.7 bil. **Commercial banks** (2004): 203; **deposits**: $171.4 bil. **Savings institutions** (2004): 115; **deposits**: $28.8 bil. **Lottery** (2004): total sales: $2.2 bil; net income: $648.1 mil. **Principal internat. airports at:** Akron, Cincinnati, Cleveland, Columbus, Dayton. **Tourism expends.** (2003): $12.4 bil.

Federal govt. Fed. civ. employees (Mar. 2004): 41,791; **avg. salary:** $62,683. **Notable fed. facilities:** Wright Patterson AFB; Defense Supply Ctr., Columbus; *NASA John H. Glenn Res. Ctr.; Portsmouth Gaseous Diffusion Plant; Lima Army Tank Plant.

Energy. Electricity production (est. 2004, kWh by source): Coal: 124.8 bil; Petroleum: 311 mil; Gas: 343 mil; Hydroelectric: 419 mil; Nuclear: 15.9 bil.

State data. Motto: With God, all things are possible. **Flower:** Scarlet carnation. **Bird:** Cardinal. **Tree:** Buckeye. **Song:** Beautiful Ohio. **Entered union** Mar. 1, 1803; rank, 17th. **State fair** at Columbus; Aug.

History. Wyandot, Delaware, Miami, and Shawnee peoples sparsely occupied the area when the first Europeans arrived. La Salle visited the region, 1669, and France claimed the area, 1682. Around 1730, traders from Pennsylvania and Virginia entered the area; the French and their Native American allies sought to drive them out. France ceded its claim, 1763, to Britain. During the American Revolution, George Rogers Clark seized British posts and held the region, until Britain gave up its claim, 1783, in the Treaty of Paris. The region became U.S. territory after the American Revolution. First organized settlement was at Marietta, 1788. Indian warfare ended with Anthony Wayne's victory at Fallen Timbers, 1794. In the War of 1812, Oliver Hazard Perry's victory on Lake Erie and William Henry Harrison's invasion of Canada, 1813, ended British incursions.

Tourist attractions. Mound City Group, a group of 24 prehistoric Indian burial mounds in Hopewell Culture Natl. Historical Park; Neil Armstrong Air and Space Museum, Wapakoneta; Air Force Museum, Dayton; Pro Football Hall of Fame, Canton; King's Island amusement park, Mason; Lake Erie Islands, Cedar Point amusement park, both Sandusky; birthplaces, homes of, and memorials to U.S. Pres. W. H. Harrison, Grant, Garfield, Hayes, McKinley, Harding, Taft, B. Harrison; Amish Region, Tuscarawas/Holmes counties; German Village, Columbus; Sea World, Aurora; Jack Nicklaus Sports Center, Mason; Bob Evans Farm, Rio Grande; Rock and Roll Hall of Fame and Museum, Cleveland.

Famous Ohioans. Sherwood Anderson, Neil Armstrong, George Bellows, Halle Berry, Ambrose Bierce, Erma Bombeck, Drew Carey, Hart Crane, George Custer, Clarence Darrow, Paul Laurence Dunbar, Thomas Edison, Clark Gable, John Glenn, Zane Grey, Bob Hope, William Dean Howells, Toni Morrison, Jack Nicklaus, Jesse Owens, Jack Paar, Pontiac, Eddie Rickenbacker, John D. Rockefeller Sr. and Jr., Roy Rogers, Pete Rose, Arthur Schlesinger Jr., Gen. William Sherman, Steven Spielberg, Gloria Steinem, Harriet Beecher Stowe, Charles Taft, Robert A. Taft, William H. Taft, Tecumseh, James Thurber, Ted Turner, Orville and Wilbur Wright.

Tourist Information. Division of Travel and Tourism, 77 S. High St., PO Box 1001, Columbus, OH 43216; 1-800-BUCKEYE. **Website:** www.discoverohio.com

Website. www.ohio.gov

Oklahoma (OK)

Sooner State

People. Population (2004 est.): 3,523,553; rank: 28; **net change** (2003-2004): 0.5%. **Pop. density:** 51.3 per sq mi. **Racial distribution** (2003): 78.4% white; 7.9% black; 1.6% Asian; 8.0% Native American/Nat. AK; 0.1% Hawaiian/Pacific Islander; 2 or more races, 4.0%. **Hispanic pop.** (any race): 5.7%.

Geography. Total area: 69,898 sq mi; rank: 20. **Land area:** 68,667 sq mi; rank: 19. **Acres forested:** 7.7 mil. **Location:** West South Central state bounded on the N by Colorado and Kansas; on the E by Missouri and Arkansas; on the S and W by Texas and New Mexico. **Climate:** temperate; southern humid belt merging with colder northern continental; humid eastern and dry western zones. **Topography:** high plains predominate in the W, hills and small mountains in the E; the east central region is dominated by the Arkansas R. Basin, and the Red R. Plains, in the S. **Capital:** Oklahoma City.

Economy. Chief industries: manufacturing, mineral and energy exploration and production, agriculture, services. **Chief manuf. goods:** nonelectrical machinery, transportation equipment, food products, fabricated metal products. **Chief crops:** wheat, cotton, hay, peanuts, grain sorghum, soybeans, corn, pecans. **Livestock:** (Jan. 2005) 5.4 mil. cattle/calves, 70,000 sheep/lambs; (Dec. 2004) 2.4 mil. hogs/pigs, 5.4 mil. chickens (excl. broilers), 243.8 mil. broilers. **Timber/lumber:** figs. undisclosed; pine, oak, hickory. **Nonfuel minerals** (est. 2004): $498 mil.; stone (crushed), cement (portland), sand and gravel (construction), sand and gravel (industrial), iodine (crude). **Chief ports:** Catoosa, Muskogee. **Gross state product** (2004): $107.2 bil. **Sales tax** (2005): 4.5%. **Employment distrib.** (May 2005): 21.0% govt.; 18.4% trade/trans./util.; 9.4% mfg.; 12.1% ed./health serv.; 11.2% prof./bus. serv. 8.8% leisure/hosp. 5.7% finance; 4.2% constr.; 4.9% other serv.; 2.1% info. **Unemployment** (2004): 4.8%. **Per cap. pers. income** (2004): $28,089. **New private housing** (2004): 17,169 units/$2.1 bil. **Commercial banks** (2004): 278; **deposits**: $42.6 bil. **Savings institutions** (2004): 7; **deposits**: $3.7 bil. **Principal internat. airports at:** Oklahoma City, Tulsa. **Tourism expends.** (2003): $4.2 bil.

Federal govt. Fed. civ. employees (Mar. 2004): 33,421; **avg. salary:** $52,855. **Notable fed. facilities:** FAA Mike Monroney Aeronautical Ctr.; *Altus AFB; Tinker AFB; Vance AFB; Ft. Sill; Natl. Inst. for Petroleum & Energy Res.; Natl. Severe Storms Lab.

Energy. Electricity production (est. 2004, kWh by source): Coal: 31.2 bil; Petroleum: 15 mil; Gas: 14.1 bil; Hydroelectric: 2.6 bil.

State data. Motto: Labor Omnia Vincit (Labor conquers all things). **Flower:** Mistletoe. **Bird:** Scissor-tailed flycatcher. **Tree:** Redbud. **Song:** Oklahoma! **Entered union** Nov. 16, 1907; rank, 46th. **State fair** at Oklahoma City; last 2 full weeks of Sept.

History. The region was sparsely inhabited by Native American tribes when Coronado, the first European, arrived in 1541; in the 16th and 17th cent., French traders visited. Part of the Louisiana Purchase, 1803, Oklahoma was established as Indian Territory (but not given territorial government). It became home to the "Five Civilized Tribes"—Cherokee, Choctaw, Chickasaw, Creek, and Seminole—after the forced removal of Indians from the eastern U.S., 1828-46. The land was also used by Comanche, Osage, and other Plains Indians. As white settlers pressed west, land was opened for homesteading by runs and lottery, the first run on Apr. 22, 1889. The most famous run was to the Cherokee Outlet, 1893.

Tourist attractions. Cherokee Heritage Center, Tahlequah; Oklahoma City Natl. Memorial; White Water Bay and Frontier City theme pks., both Oklahoma City; Will Rogers Memorial, Claremore; Natl. Cowboy Hall of Fame and Remington Park Race Track, both Oklahoma City; Ft. Gibson Stockade, near Muskogee; Ouachita Natl. Forest; Tulsa's art deco district; Wichita Mts. Wildlife Refuge, Lawton; Woolaroc Museum & Wildlife Preserve, Bartlesville; Sequoyah's Home Site, near Sallisaw; Philbrook Museum of Art and Gilcrease Museum, both Tulsa.

Famous Oklahomans. Troy Aikman, Carl Albert, Gene Autry, Johnny Bench, William "Hopalong Cassidy" Boyd, Garth Brooks, Lon Chaney, L. Gordon Cooper, Walter Cronkite, Jerome "Dizzy" Dean, Ralph Ellison, John Hope Franklin, James Garner, Geronimo, Woody Guthrie, Paul Harvey, Ron Howard, Gen. Patrick J. Hurley, Ben Johnson, Jeane Kirkpatrick, Louis L'Amour, Shannon Lucid, Mickey Mantle, Reba McEntire, Wiley Post, Tony Randall, Oral Roberts, Will Rogers, Sam Snead, Barry Switzer, Maria Tallchief, Jim Thorpe, J.C. Watts Jr.

Tourist Information. Travel and Tourism Division, 120 N. Robinson, 6th fl., Oklahoma City, OK 73152-2002; 1-800-652-6552. **Website:** www.travelok.com

Website. www.ok.gov

Oregon (OR)

Beaver State

People. Population (2004 est.): 3,594,586; rank: 27; **net change** (2003-2004): 0.8%. **Pop. density:** 37.5 per sq mi. **Racial distribution** (2003): 90.8% white; 1.8% black; 3.4% Asian; 1.4% Native American/Nat. AK; 0.3% Hawaiian/Pacific Islander; 2 or more races, 2.3%. **Hispanic pop.** (any race): 9.2%.

Geography. Total area: 98,381 sq mi; rank: 9. **Land area:** 95,997 sq mi; rank: 10. **Acres forested:** 29.7 mil. **Location:** Pacific state, bounded on N by Washington; on E by Idaho; on S by Nevada and California; on W by the Pacific. **Climate:** coastal mild and humid climate; continental dryness and extreme temperatures in the interior. **Topography:** Coast Range of rugged mountains; fertile Willamette R. Valley to E and S; Cascade Mt. Range of volcanic peaks E of the valley; plateau E of Cascades, remaining two-thirds of state. **Capital:** Salem.

Economy. Chief industries: manufacturing, services, trade, finance, insurance, real estate, government, construction. **Chief manuf. goods:** electronics & semiconductors, lumber & wood products, metals, transportation equipment, processed food, paper. **Chief crops:** greenhouse, hay, wheat, grass seed, potatoes, onions, Christmas trees, pears, mint. **Livestock:** (Jan. 2005) 1.43 mil. cattle/calves, 225,000 sheep/lambs; (Dec. 2004) 27,000 hogs/pigs, 3.7 mil. chickens (excl. broilers). **Timber/lumber** (est. 2003): 6.1 bil bd. ft.; Douglas fir, hemlock, ponderosa pine. **Nonfuel minerals** (est. 2004): $356 mil.; sand and gravel (construction), stone (crushed), cement (portland), diatomite, lime. **Commercial fishing** (2003): $85.5 mil. **Chief ports:** Portland, Astoria, Coos Bay. **Gross state product** (2004): $128.1 bil. **Sales tax** (2005): none. **Employment distrib.** (May 2005): 17.2% govt.; 19.9% trade/trans./util.; 12.3% mfg.; 12.2% ed./health serv.; 11.0% prof./bus. serv. 9.9% leisure/hosp. 6.0% finance; 5.3% constr.; 3.6% other serv.; 2.1% info. **Unemployment** (2004): 7.4%. **Per cap. pers. income** (2004): $29,971. **New private housing** (2004): 28,396 units/$4.5 bil. **Commercial banks** (2004): 48; **deposits**: $31.0 bil. **Savings institutions** (2004): 7; **deposits**: $8.1 bil. **Lottery** (2004): total sales: $893.3 mil; net income: $387.1 mil. **Principal internat. airports at:** Portland, Medford. **Tourism expends.** (2003): $5.6 bil.

Federal govt. Fed. civ. employees (Mar. 2004): 18,440; **avg. salary:** $56,305. **Notable fed. facilities:** Bonneville Power Administration.

Energy. Electricity production (est. 2004, kWh by source): Coal: 3.5 bil; Petroleum: 20 mil; Gas: 2.6 bil; Hydroelectric: 32.7 bil.

State data. Motto: She flies with her own wings. **Flower:** Oregon grape. **Bird:** Western meadowlark. **Tree:** Douglas fir. **Song:** Oregon, My Oregon. **Entered union** Feb. 14, 1859; rank, 33rd. **State fair** at Salem; 12 days ending with Labor Day.

History. More than 100 Native American tribes inhabited the area at the time of European contact, including the Chinook, Yakima, Cayuse, Modoc, and Nez Percé. Capt. Robert Gray sighted and sailed into the Columbia River, 1792; Lewis and Clark, traveling overland, wintered at its mouth, 1805-6; John Jacob Astor established a trading post in the Columbia River region, 1811. Settlers arrived in the Williamette Valley, 1834. In 1843, the first large wave of settlers arrived via the Oregon Trail. Early in the 20th cent., the "Oregon System"—political reforms that included the initiative, referendum, recall, direct primary, and woman suffrage—was adopted.

Tourist attractions. John Day Fossil Beds Natl. Monument; Columbia River Gorge; Timberline Lodge, Mt. Hood Natl. Forest; Crater Lake Natl. Park; Oregon Dunes Natl. Recreation Area; Ft. Clatsop Natl. Memorial; Oregon Caves Natl. Monument; Oregon Museum of Science and Industry, Portland; Shakespearean Festival, Ashland; High Desert Museum, Bend; Multnomah Falls; Diamond Lake; "Spruce Goose," Evergreen Aviation Museum, McMinnville.

Famous Oregonians. Ernest Bloch, Bill Bowerman, Ernest Haycox, Chief Joseph, Ken Kesey, Phil Knight, Ursula K. Le Guin, Edwin Markham, Tom McCall, Dr. John McLoughlin, Joaquin Miller, Bob Packwood, Linus Pauling, Steve Prefontaine, John Reed, Alberto Salazar, Mary Decker Slaney, William Simon U'Ren.

Tourist information. Oregon Tourism Commission, 670 Hawthorne SE, Ste. 240, Salem, OR 97301; 1-800-547-7842. **Website:** www.traveloregon.com

Website. www.oregon.gov

Pennsylvania (PA)

Keystone State

People. Population (2004 est.): 12,406,292; rank: 6; **net change** (2003-2004): 0.3%. **Pop. density:** 276.9 per sq mi. **Racial distribution** (2003): 86.4% white; 10.3% black; 2.1% Asian; 0.2% Native American/Nat. AK; 0.04% Hawaiian/Pacific Islander; 2 or more races, 0.9%. **Hispanic pop.** (any race): 3.4%.

Geography. Total area: 46,055 sq mi; rank: 33. **Land area:** 44,817 sq mi; rank: 32. **Acres forested:** 16.9 mil. **Location:** Middle Atlantic state, bordered on the E by the Delaware R.; on the S by the Mason-Dixon Line; on the W by West Virginia and Ohio; on the N/NE by Lake Erie and New York. **Climate:** continental with wide fluctuations in seasonal temperatures. **Topography:** Allegheny Mts. run SW to NE, with Piedmont and Coast Plain in the SE triangle; Allegheny Front a diagonal spine across the state's center; N and W rugged plateau falls to Lake Erie Lowland. **Capital:** Harrisburg.

Economy. Chief industries: agribusiness, advanced manufacturing, health care, travel & tourism, depository institutions, biotechnology, printing & publishing, research & consulting, trucking & warehousing, transportation by air, engineering & management, legal services. **Chief manuf. goods:** fabricated metal products; industrial machinery & equipment, transportation equipment, rubber & plastics, electronic equipment, chemicals & pharmaceuticals, lumber & wood products, stone, clay, & glass products. **Chief crops:** corn, hay, mushrooms, apples, potatoes, winter wheat, oats, vegetables, tobacco, grapes, peaches. **Livestock:** (Jan. 2005) 1.63 mil. cattle/calves, 100,000 sheep/lambs; (Dec. 2004) 1.08 mil. hogs/pigs, 27.9 mil. chickens (excl. broilers), 133.5 mil. broilers. **Timber/lumber** (est. 2003): 1.1 bil bd. ft.; pine, oak, maple. **Nonfuel minerals** (est. 2004): $1.4 bil.; stone (crushed), cement (portland), sand and gravel (construction), lime, cement (masonry). **Commercial fishing** (2003): $39,000. **Chief ports:** Philadelphia, Pittsburgh, Erie. **Gross state product** (2004): $468.8 bil. **Sales tax** (2005): 6.0%. **Employment distrib.** (May 2005): 13.4% govt.; 19.6% trade/trans./util.; 11.9% mfg.; 17.7% ed./health serv.; 11.3% prof./bus. serv. 8.7% leisure/hosp. 5.9% finance; 4.5% constr.; 4.7% other serv.; 1.9% info. **Unemployment** (2004): 5.5%. **Per cap. pers. income** (2004): $33,348. **New private housing** (2004): 48,214 units/$6.3 bil. **Commercial banks** (2004): 186; **deposits**: $151.1 bil. **Savings institutions** (2004): 102; **deposits**: $59.6 bil. **Lottery** (2004): total sales: $2.4 bil; net income: $818.7 mil. **Principal internat. airports at:** Allentown, Harrisburg, Philadelphia, Pittsburgh, Wilkes-Barre/Scranton. **Tourism expends.** (2003): $15.2 bil.

Federal govt. Fed. civ. employees (Mar. 2004): 62,821; **avg. salary:** $54,754. **Notable fed. facilities:** Carlisle Barracks; Army War College; Naval Inventory Control Point, Phila. and Mechanicsbrg; Defense Personnel Supply Ctr., Phila.; Defense Distribution Ctr., New Cumberland; Tobyhanna Army Depot; Letterkenny Army Depot; *NAS Willow Grove; 911th Air Wing, Pittsburgh; Naval Surface Warfare Ctr., Phila.; *Charles E. Kelly Support Facility.

Energy. Electricity production (est. 2004, kWh by source): Coal: 18.4 bil; Petroleum: 28 mil; Hydroelectric: 1.5 bil; Nuclear: 14.0 bil.

State data. Motto: Virtue, liberty and independence. **Flower:** Mountain laurel. **Bird:** Ruffed grouse. **Tree:** Hemlock. **Song:** Pennsylvania. **Second** of the original 13 states to ratify the Constitution, Dec. 12, 1787. **State fair** at Harrisburg; 2nd week in Jan. at State Farm Show Complex.

History. At the time of European contact, Lenni Lenape (Delaware), Shawnee and Iroquoian Susquehannocks, Erie, and Seneca occupied the region. Swedish explorers established the first permanent settlement, 1643, on Tinicum Island. In 1655, the Dutch seized the settlement but lost it to the British, 1664. The region was given by Charles II to William Penn, 1681. Philadelphia ("brotherly love") was the capital of the colonies during most of the American Revolution, and of the U.S., 1790-1800. Philadelphia was taken by the British, 1777; Washington's troops encamped at Valley Forge in the bitter winter of 1777-78. The Declaration of Independence, 1776, and the Constitution, 1787, were signed in Philadelphia. The Civil War battle of Gettysburg, July 1-3, 1863, marked a turning point, favoring Union forces.

Tourist attractions. Independence Natl. Historic Park, Franklin Institute Science Museum, Philadelphia Museum of Art, all in Philadelphia; Valley Forge Natl. Historic Park; Gettysburg Natl. Military Park; Pennsylvania Dutch Country; Hershey; Duquesne Incline, Carnegie Institute, Heinz Hall, all in Pittsburgh; Pocono Mts.; Pennsylvania's Grand Canyon, Tioga County; Allegheny Natl. Forest; Laurel Highlands; Presque Isle State Park; Fallingwater, Mill Run; Johnstown; SteamTown U.S.A., Scranton; State Flagship Niagara, Erie; Oil Heritage Region, Northwest PA.

Famous Pennsylvanians. Marian Anderson, Maxwell Anderson, George Blanda, James Buchanan, Andrew Carnegie, Rachel Carson, Perry Como, Bill Cosby, Thomas Eakins, Stephen Foster, Benjamin Franklin, Robert Fulton, Martha Graham, Milton Hershey, Gene Kelly, Grace Kelly (Princess Grace of Monaco), Dan Marino, George C. Marshall, Chris Matthews, John J. McCloy, Margaret Mead, Andrew W. Mellon, Joe Montana, Stan Musial, Joe Namath, John O'Hara, Arnold Palmer, Robert E. Peary, Mike Piazza, Tom Ridge, Mary Roberts Rinehart, Fred Rogers, Betsy Ross, Will Smith, Jimmy Stewart, Jim Thorpe, Johnny Unitas, John Updike, Honus Wagner, Andy Warhol, Benjamin West.

Tourist Information. Department of Community and Economic Development, Office of Tourism, 400 North St.,4th Fl., Harrisburg, PA 17120-0225; 1-800-VISITPA. **Website:** www.experiencepa.co

Website. www.state.pa.us

Rhode Island (RI)

Little Rhody, Ocean State

People. Population (2004 est.): 1,080,632; rank: 43; **net change** (2003-2004): 0.4%. **Pop. density:** 1,041.3 per sq mi. **Racial distribution** (2003): 89.2% white; 5.9% black; 2.7% Asian; 0.6% Native American/Nat. AK; 0.1% Hawaiian/Pacific Islander; 2 or more races, 1.4%. **Hispanic pop.** (any race): 9.5%.

Geography. Total area: 1,545 sq mi; rank: 50. **Land area:** 1,045 sq mi; rank: 50. **Acres forested:** 0.4 mil. **Location:** New England state. **Climate:** invigorating and changeable. **Topography:** eastern lowlands of Narragansett Basin; western uplands of flat and rolling hills. **Capital:** Providence.

Economy. Chief industries: services, manufacturing. **Chief manuf. goods:** costume jewelry, toys, machinery, textiles, electronics. **Chief crops:** nursery products, turf & vegetable production. **Livestock:** (Jan. 2005) 5,500 cattle/calves; (Dec. 2004) 2,000 hogs/pigs. **Timber/lumber:** figs. undisclosed. **Nonfuel minerals** (est. 2004): $37.2 mil.; sand and gravel (construction), stone (crushed), sand and gravel (industrial), gemstones. **Commercial fishing** (2003): $63.1 mil. **Chief ports:** Providence, Quonset Point, Newport. **Gross state product** (2004): $41.9 bil. **Sales tax** (2005): 7.0%. **Employment distrib.** (May 2005): 13.5% govt.; 15.8% trade/trans./util.; 11.1% mfg.; 19.5% ed./health serv.; 11.2% prof./bus. serv. 10.6% leisure/hosp. 7.1% finance; 4.3% constr.; 4.7% other serv.; 2.2% info. **Unemployment** (2004): 5.2%. **Per cap. pers. income** (2004): $33,733. **New private housing** (2004): 2,457 units/$363 mil. **Commercial banks** (2004): 11; **deposits**: $16.2 bil. **Savings institutions** (2004): 12; **deposits**: $3.7 bil. **Lottery** (2004): total sales: $1.5 bil; net income: $281.0 mil. **Tourism expends.** (2003): $1.4 bil.

Federal govt. Fed. civ. employees (Mar. 2004): 6,120; **avg. salary:** $66,594. **Notable fed. facilities:** Naval War College; Naval Underwater Warfare Ctr.; Natl. Marine Fisheries Lab; EPA Environmental Res. Lab.

Energy. Electricity production (est. 2002, kWh, by source): Petroleum: 8 mil.

State data. Motto: Hope. **Flower:** Violet. **Bird:** Rhode Island red. **Tree:** Red maple. **Song:** Rhode Island. **Thirteenth** of original 13 states to ratify the Constitution, May 29, 1790. **State fair** at Richmond; mid-Aug.

History. When the Europeans arrived Narragansett, Niantic, Nipmuc, and Wampanoag peoples lived in the region. Verrazano visited the area, 1524. The first permanent settlement was founded at Providence, 1636, by Roger Williams, who was exiled from the Massachusetts Bay Colony; Anne Hutchinson, also exiled, settled Portsmouth, 1638. Quaker and Jewish immigrants seeking freedom of worship began arriving, 1650s-60s. The colonists broke the power of the Narragansett in the Great Swamp Fight, 1675, the decisive battle in King Philip's War. British trade restrictions angered colonists, and they burned the British customs vessel *Gaspee*, 1772. The colony became the first to formally renounce all allegiance to King George III, May 4, 1776. Initially opposed to joining the Union, Rhode Island was the last of the 13 colonies to ratify the Constitution, 1790.

Tourist attractions. Newport mansions; yachting races including Newport to Bermuda; Block Island; Touro Synagogue, oldest in U.S., Newport; first Baptist Church in America, Providence; Slater Mill Historic Site, Pawtucket; Gilbert Stuart birthplace, Saunderstown.

Famous Rhode Islanders. Ambrose Burnside, George M. Cohan, Nelson Eddy, Jabez Gorham, Nathanael Greene, Christopher and Oliver La Farge, John McLaughlin, Matthew C. and Oliver Hazard Perry, Gilbert Stuart.

Tourist Information. Rhode Island Tourism Division, 1 W. Exchange St., Providence, RI 02903; 1-800-556-2484. **Website:** www.visitrhodeisland.com

Website. www.state.ri.us

South Carolina (SC)

Palmetto State

People. Population (2004 est.): 4,198,068; rank: 25; **net change** (2003-2004): 1.2%. **Pop. density:** 139.4 per sq mi. **Racial distribution** (2003): 67.7% white; 30.0% black; 1.1% Asian; 0.4% Native American/Nat. AK; 0.1% Hawaiian/Pacific Islander; 2 or more races, 0.8%. **Hispanic pop.** (any race): 2.8%.

Geography. Total area: 32,020 sq mi; rank: 40. **Land area:** 30,109 sq mi; rank: 40. **Acres forested:** 12.5 mil. **Location:** South Atlantic state, bordered by North Carolina on the N; Georgia on the SW and W; the Atlantic Ocean on the E, SE, and S. **Climate:** humid subtropical. **Topography:** Blue Ridge province in NW has highest peaks; piedmont lies between the mountains and the fall line; coastal plain covers two-thirds of the state. **Capital:** Columbia.

Economy. Chief industries: tourism, agriculture, manufacturing. **Chief manuf. goods:** textiles, chemicals and allied products, machinery and fabricated metal products, apparel and related products. **Chief crops:** tobacco, cotton, soybeans, corn, wheat, peaches, tomatoes. **Livestock:** (Jan. 2005) 435,000 cattle/calves; (Dec. 2004) 300,000 hogs/pigs, 7.0 mil. chickens (excl. broilers), 204.5 mil. broilers. **Timber/lumber** (est. 2003): 1.4 bil bd. ft.; pine, oak. **Nonfuel minerals** (est. 2004): $586 mil.; cement (portland), stone (crushed), cement (masonry), sand and gravel (construction), clays (kaolin). **Commercial fishing** (2003): $29.1 mil. **Chief ports:** Charleston, Georgetown, Royal. **Gross state product** (2004): $135.3 bil. **Sales tax** (2005): 5.0%. **Employment distrib.** (May 2005): 18.5% govt.; 19.5% trade/trans./util.; 14.4% mfg.; 9.3% ed./health serv.; 10.2% prof./bus. serv. 11.6% leisure/hosp. 5.1% finance; 6.1% constr.; 3.6% other serv.; 1.5% info. **Unemployment** (2004): 6.8%. **Per cap. pers. income** (2004): $27,172. **New private housing** (2004): 43,059 units/ $5.5 bil. **Commercial banks** (2004): 83; **deposits**: $43.2 bil. **Savings institutions** (2004): 24; **deposits**: $4.9 bil. **Lottery** (2004): total sales: $950.0 mil; net income: $290.1 mil. **Principal internat. airports at:** Charleston, Greenville/Spartanburg, Myrtle Beach. **Tourism expends.** (2003): $7.2 bil.

Federal govt. Fed. civ. employees (Mar. 2004): 16,249; **avg. salary:** $53,680. **Notable fed. facilities:** Polaris Submarine Base; Barnwell Nuclear Power Plant; Ft. Jackson; Parris Island; Savannah River Plant.

Energy. Electricity production (est. 2004, kWh by source): Coal: 38.5 bil; Petroleum: 199 mil; Gas: 2.5 bil; Hydroelectric: 1.9 bil; Nuclear: 51.2 bil; Other: 14 mil.

State data. Motto: Dum Spiro Spero (While I breathe, I hope). **Flower:** Yellow jessamine. **Bird:** Carolina wren. **Tree:** Palmetto. **Song:** Carolina. **Eighth** of the original 13 states to ratify the Constitution, May 23, 1788. **State fair** at Columbia; mid-Oct.

History. At the time of European settlement, Cherokee, Catawba, and Muskogean peoples lived in the area. The first English colonists settled near the Ashley River, 1670, and moved to the site of Charleston, 1680. The colonists seized the government, 1775, and the royal governor fled. The British took Charleston, 1780, but were defeated at Kings Mountain that same year, and at Cowpens and Eutaw Springs, 1781. In the 1830s, South Carolinians, angered by federal protective tariffs, adopted the Nullification Doctrine, holding that a state can void an act of Congress. The state was the first to secede from the Union, 1860, and Confederate troops fired on and forced the surrender of U.S. troops at Ft. Sumter, in Charleston Harbor, launching the Civil War. South Carolina was readmitted,1868.

Tourist attractions. Historic Charleston; Ft. Sumter Natl. Monument, in Charleston Harbor; Charleston Museum, est. 1773, oldest museum in U.S.; Middleton Place, Magnolia Plantation, Cypress Gardens, Drayton Hall, all near Charleston; other gardens at Brookgreen, Edisto, Glencairn; Myrtle Beach; Hilton Head Island; Revolutionary War battle sites; Andrew Jackson State Park & Museum; South Carolina State Museum, Columbia; Riverbanks Zoo, Columbia.

Famous South Carolinians. Charles Bolden, James F. Byrnes, John C. Calhoun, Joe Fraizer, DuBose Heyward, Ernest F. Hollings, Andrew Jackson, Jesse Jackson, "Shoeless" Joe Jackson, James Longstreet, Francis Marion, Andie McDowell, Ronald McNair, Charles Pinckney, John Rutledge, Thomas Sumter, Strom Thurmond, John B. Watson.

Tourist information. SC Dept. of Parks, Recreation, & Tourism, 1205 Pendleton St., Rm. 505, Columbia, SC 29201; 803-734-0122; 1-800-346-3634. **Website:** www.discoversouthcarolina.com

Website. www.myscgov.com

South Dakota (SD)

Coyote State, Mount Rushmore State

People. Population (2004 est.): 770,883; rank: 46; **net change** (2003-2004): 0.8%. **Pop. density:** 10.2 per sq mi. **Racial distribution** (2003): 88.8% white; 0.8% black; 0.7% Asian; 8.4% Native American/Nat. AK; 0.04% Hawaiian/Pacific Islander; 2 or more races, 1.2%. **Hispanic pop.** (any race): 1.5%.

Geography. Total area: 77,116 sq mi; rank: 17. **Land area:** 75,885 sq mi; rank: 16. **Acres forested:** 1.6 mil. **Location:** West North Central state bounded on the N by North Dakota; on the E by Minnesota and Iowa; on the S by Nebraska; on the W by Wyoming and Montana. **Climate:** characterized by extremes of temperature, persistent winds, low precipitation and humidity. **Topography:** Prairie Plains in the E; rolling hills of the Great Plains in the W; the Black Hills, rising 3,500 ft, in the SW corner. **Capital:** Pierre.

Economy. Chief industries: agriculture, services, manufacturing. **Chief manuf. goods:** food and kindred products, machinery, electric and electronic equipment. **Chief crops:** corn, soybeans, oats, wheat, sunflowers, sorghum. **Livestock:** (Jan. 2005) 3.75 mil. cattle/calves, 375,000 sheep/lambs; (Dec. 2004) 1.33 mil. hogs/pigs, 3.7 mil. chickens (excl. broilers). **Timber/lumber:** figs. undisclosed; ponderosa pine. **Nonfuel minerals** (est. 2004): $210 mil.; cement (portland), sand and gravel (construction), stone (crushed), gold, stone (dimension). **Gross state product** (2004): $29.4 bil. **Sales tax** (2005): 4.0%. **Employment distrib.** (May 2005): 19.7% govt.; 20.2% trade/trans./util.; 10.1% mfg.; 14.5% ed./health serv.; 6.0% prof./bus. serv. 10.8% leisure/hosp. 7.1% finance; 5.6% constr.; 4.1% other serv.; 1.7% info. **Unemployment** (2004): 3.5%. **Per cap. pers. income** (2004): $30,856. **New private housing** (2004): 5,800 units/$686 mil. **Commercial banks** (2004): 92; **deposits**: $52.3 bil. **Savings institutions** (2004): 6; **deposits**: $965 mil. **Lottery** (2004): total sales: $664.4 mil; net income: $114.8 mil. **Tourism expends.** (2003): $1.5 bil.

Federal govt. Fed. civ. employees (Mar. 2004): 7,059; **avg. salary:** $49,605. **Notable fed. facilities:** *Ellsworth AFB, Corp of Engineers, Nat'l Park Service.

Energy. Electricity production (est. 2004, kWh by source): Coal: 3.6 bil; Petroleum: 17 mil; Gas: 104 mil; Hydroelectric: 3.6 bil; Other: 5 mil.

State data. Motto: Under God, the people rule. **Flower:** Pasqueflower. **Bird:** Chinese ring-necked pheasant. **Tree:** Black Hills spruce. **Song:** Hail, South Dakota. **Entered union** Nov. 2, 1889; rank, 40th. **State fair** at Huron; early Sept.

History. At the time of first European contact, Mandan, Hidatsa, Arikara, and Sioux lived in the area. The French Verendrye brothers explored the region, 1742-43. The U.S. acquired the area, 1803, in the Louisiana Purchase. Lewis and Clark passed through the area, 1804-6. In 1817 a trading post was opened at Fort Pierre, which later became the site of the first European settlement in South Dakota. Gold was discovered, 1874, in the Black Hills on the great Sioux reservation; the "Great Dakota Boom" began in 1879. Conflicts with Native Americans led to the Great Sioux Agreement, 1889, which established reservations and opened up more land for white settlement. The massacre of Native American families at Wounded Knee, 1890, ended Sioux resistance.

Tourist attractions. Black Hills; Mt. Rushmore; Needles Highway; Harney Peak, tallest E. of Rockies; Deadwood, 1876 Gold Rush town; Custer State Park; Jewel Cave Natl. Monument; Badlands Natl. Park "moonscape"; "Great Lakes of S. Dakota"; Ft. Sisseton; Great Plains Zoo & Museum, Sioux Falls; Corn Palace, Mitchell; Wind Cave Natl. Park; Crazy Horse Memorial, mountain carving in progress.

Famous South Dakotans. Sparky Anderson, Black Elk, Bob Barker, Tom Brokaw, Crazy Horse, Thomas Daschle, Myron Floren, Mary Hart, Cheryl Ladd, Dr. Ernest O. Lawrence, George McGovern, Billy Mills, Allen Neuharth, Pat O'Brien, Sitting Bull.

Tourist information. Department of Tourism and State Development, Capitol Lake Plaza, 711 E. Wells Ave., c/o 500 E. Capitol Ave., Pierre, SD 57501-5070; 1-800-SDAKOTA. **Website:** www.travelsd.com

Website. www.state.sd.us

Tennessee (TN)

Volunteer State

People. Population (2004 est.): 5,900,962; rank: 16; **net change** (2003-2004): 1.0%. **Pop. density:** 143.2 per sq mi. **Racial distribution** (2003): 80.8% white; 16.7% black; 1.2% Asian; 0.3% Native American/Nat. AK; 0.1% Hawaiian/Pacific Islander; 2 or more races, 0.9%. **Hispanic pop.** (any race): 2.5%.

Geography. Total area: 42,143 sq mi; rank: 36. **Land area:** 41,217 sq mi; rank: 34. **Acres forested:** 14.4 mil. **Location:** East South Central state bounded on the N by Kentucky and Virginia; on the E by North Carolina; on the S by Georgia, Alabama, and Mississippi; on the W by Arkansas and Missouri. **Climate:** humid continental to the N; humid subtropical to the S. **Topography:** rugged country in the E; the Great Smoky Mts. of the Unakas; low ridges of the Appalachian Valley; the flat Cumberland Plateau; slightly rolling terrain and knobs of the Interior Low Plateau, the largest region; Eastern Gulf Coastal Plain to the W, laced with streams; Mississippi Alluvial Plain, a narrow strip of swamp and flood plain in the extreme W. **Capital:** Nashville.

Economy. Chief industries: manufacturing, trade, services, tourism, finance, insurance, real estate. **Chief manuf. goods:** chemicals, food, transportation equipment, industrial machinery & equipment, fabricated metal products, rubber/plastic products, paper & allied products, printing & publishing. **Chief crops:** tobacco, cotton, lint, soybeans, grain, corn. **Livestock:** (Jan. 2005) 2.17 mil. cattle/calves, 23,000 sheep/lambs; (Dec. 2004) 215,000 hogs/pigs, 2.4 mil. chickens (excl. broilers), 195.9 mil. broilers. **Timber/lumber:** (est. 2003): 925 mil bd. ft.; red oak, white oak, yellow poplar, hickory. **Nonfuel minerals** (est. 2004): $660 mil.; stone (crushed), cement (portland), sand and gravel (construction), zinc, clays (ball). **Chief ports:** Memphis, Nashville, Chattanooga, Knoxville. **Gross state product** (2004): $216.9 bil. **Sales tax** (2005): 7.0%. **Employment distrib.** (May 2005): 15.3% govt.; 21.6% trade/trans./util.; 15.1% mfg.; 11.9% ed./health serv.; 11.1% prof./bus. serv. 9.6% leisure/hosp. 5.3% finance; 4.4% constr.; 3.8% other serv.; 1.8% info. **Unemployment** (2004): 5.4%. **Per cap. pers. income** (2004): $30,005. **New private housing** (2004): 44,652 units/$5.8 bil. **Commercial banks** (2004): 210; **deposits**: $86.5 bil. **Savings institutions** (2004): 23; **deposits**: $3.7 bil. **Lottery** (2004): total sales: $427.7 mil; net income: $123.7 mil. **Principal internat. airports at:** Memphis, Nashville. **Tourism expends.** (2003): $10.6 bil.

Federal govt. Fed. civ. employees (Mar. 2004): 33,143; **avg. salary:** $55,661. **Notable fed. facilities:** Tennessee Valley Authority; Oak Ridge Nat'l. Lab; Arnold Engineering Development Ctr.; Ft. Campbell; Naval Support Activity, Mid-South.

Energy. Electricity production (est. 2004, kWh by source): Coal: 56.6 bil; Petroleum: 165 mil; Gas: 174 mil; Hydroelectric: 9.6 bil; Nuclear: 28.6 bil; Other: 4 mil.

State data. Motto: Agriculture and commerce. **Flower:** Iris. **Bird:** Mockingbird. **Tree:** Tulip poplar. **Songs:** My Homeland, Tennessee; When It's Iris Time in Tennessee; My Tennessee; Tennessee Waltz; Rocky Top. **Entered union** June 1, 1796; rank, 16th. **State fair** at Nashville; mid-Sept.

History. When the first European explorers arrived, Creek and Yuchi peoples lived in the area; the Cherokee moved into the region in the early 18th cent. Spanish explorers first visited the area, 1541. English traders crossed the Great Smokies from the east while France's Marquette and Jolliet sailed down the Mississippi on the west, 1673. The first permanent settlement was by Virginians on the Watauga River, 1769. During the American Revolution, the colonists helped win the Battle of Kings Mountain (NC), 1780, and joined other eastern campaigns. The state seceded from the Union, 1861, and saw many Civil War engagements, but 30,000 soldiers fought for the Union. Tennessee was readmitted in 1866, the only former Confederate state not to have a postwar military government.

Tourist attractions. Reelfoot Lake; Lookout Mountain, Chattanooga; Fall Creek Falls; Great Smoky Mountains Natl. Park; Lost Sea, Sweetwater; Cherokee Natl. Forest; Cumberland Gap Natl. Park; Andrew Jackson's home, the Hermitage, near Nashville; homes of Pres. Polk and Andrew Johnson; American Museum of Science and Energy, Oak Ridge; Parthenon, Grand Old Opry, Opryland USA, all Nashville; Dollywood theme park, Pigeon Forge; Tennessee Aquarium, Chattanooga; Graceland, home of Elvis Presley, Memphis; Alex Haley Home and Museum, Henning; Casey Jones Home and Museum, Jackson.

Famous Tennesseans. Roy Acuff, Davy Crockett, David Farragut, Ernie Ford, Aretha Franklin, Morgan Freeman, Bill Frist, Al Gore Jr., Alex Haley, William C. Handy, Sam Houston, Cordell Hull, Andrew Jackson, Andrew Johnson, Casey Jones, Estes Kefauver, Grace Moore, Dolly Parton, Minnie Pearl, James Polk, Elvis Presley, Dinah Shore, Bessie Smith, Fred Thompson, Hank Williams Jr., Alvin York.

Tourist information. Dept. of Tourist Development, Wm. Snodgrass/Tennessee Tower, 312 8th Ave., 25th Fl., Nashville, TN 37243; 1-615-741-2159. **Website:** www.tnvacation.com

Website. www.tn.gov

IT'S A FACT: Texas, already a land of superlatives, was granted one more in 2005—containing (surprisingly) the most lakes of any of the lower 48 states—at least by one scientific count. Bill Renwick, chair of the geography department at Miami Univ. in Ohio, conducted a count that considered a lake as any body of water (natural or artificial) big enough (roughly 100 feet in diameter) to be seen by a satellite. Some of Renwick's lakes may be mere ponds to his critics, but they all have ecological significance according to him. Texas tops the list, with 296,976 lakes, followed by Florida, Oklahoma, Kansas, and Missouri. Minnesota, the "Land of 10,000 Lakes," only ranks 7th on Renwick's list, with about ten times the number of lakes it traditionally claims.

Texas (TX)

Lone Star State

People. Population (2004 est.): 22,490,022; rank: 2; **net change** (2003-2004): 1.7%. **Pop. density:** 86.0 per sq mi. **Racial distribution** (2003): 83.6% white; 11.6% black; 3.1% Asian; 0.7% Native American/Nat. AK; 0.1% Hawaiian/Pacific Islander; 2 or more races, 1.0%. **Hispanic pop.** (any race): 34.2%.

Geography. Total area: 268,581 sq mi; rank: 2. **Land area:** 261,797 sq mi; rank: 2. **Acres forested:** 17.1 mil. **Location:** Southwestern state, bounded on the SE by the Gulf of Mexico; on the SW by Mexico, separated by the Rio Grande; surrounding states are Louisiana, Arkansas, Oklahoma, New Mexico. **Climate:** extremely varied; driest region is the Trans-Pecos; wettest is the NE. **Topography:** Gulf Coast Plain in the S and SE; North Central Plains slope upward with some hills; the Great Plains extend over the Panhandle, are broken by low mountains; the Trans-Pecos is the southern extension of the Rockies. **Capital:** Austin.

Economy. Chief industries: manufacturing, trade, oil and gas extraction, services. **Chief manuf. goods:** industrial machinery and equipment, foods, electrical and electronic products, chemicals and allied products, apparel. **Chief crops:** cotton, grains (wheat), sorghum grain, vegetables, citrus and other fruits, greenhouse/nursery, pecans, peanuts. **Chief farm products:** milk, eggs. **Livestock:** (Jan. 2005) 13.8 mil. cattle/calves, 1.07 mil. sheep/lambs; (Dec. 2004) 980,000 hogs/pigs, 24.6 mil. chickens (excl. broilers), 620.7 mil. broilers. **Timber/lumber** (est. 2003): 1.7 bil bd. ft.; pine, cypress. **Nonfuel minerals** (est. 2004): $2.4 bil.; cement (portland), stone (crushed), sand and gravel (construction), lime, salt. **Commercial fishing** (2003): $168.3 mil. **Chief ports:** Houston, Galveston, Brownsville, Beaumont, Port Arthur, Corpus Christi. **Gross state product** (2004): $880.9 bil. **Sales tax** (2005): 6.25%. **Employment distrib.** (May 2005): 17.6% govt.; 20.3% trade/trans./util.; 9.2% mfg.; 12.2% ed./health serv.; 11.5% prof./bus. serv. 9.5% leisure/hosp. 6.2% finance; 5.7% constr.; 3.8% other serv.; 2.4% info. **Unemployment** (2004): 6.1%. **Per cap. pers. income** (2004): $30,222. **New private housing** (2004): 186,664 units/$21.4 bil. **Commercial banks** (2004): 679; **deposits**: $267.0 bil. **Savings institutions** (2004): 49; **deposits**: $43.4 bil. **Lottery** (2004): total sales: $2.9 bil; net income: $839.3 mil. **Principal internat. airports at:** Amarillo, Austin, Corpus Christi, Dallas/Ft. Worth, El Paso, Houston, San Antonio. **Tourism expends.** (2003): $31.5 bil.

Federal govt. Fed. civ. employees (Mar. 2004): 108,071; **avg. salary:** $55,726. **Notable fed. facilities:** *Ft. Hood, Kelly AFB; Ft. Sam Houston; NASA Johnson Space Ctr.; Naval Air Training School; Corpus Christi NAS; Kingsville NAS; Ft. Worth Western Currency Facility.

Energy. Electricity production (est. 2004, kWh by source): Coal: 63.9 bil; Petroleum: 71 mil; Gas: 26.4 bil; Hydroelectric: 1.0 bil; Other: 2 mil.

State data. Motto: Friendship. **Flower:** Bluebonnet. **Bird:** Mockingbird. **Tree:** Pecan. **Song:** Texas, Our Texas. **Entered union** Dec. 29, 1845; rank, 28th. **State fair** at Dallas; late Sept.-mid-Oct.

History. At the time of European contact, Native American tribes in the region were numerous and diverse in culture. Coahuiltecan, Karankawa, Caddo, Jumano, and Tonkawa peoples lived in the area, and during the 19th cent., the Apache, Comanche, Cherokee, and Wichita arrived. Spanish explorer Pineda sailed along the Texas coast, 1519; Cabeza de Vaca and Coronado visited the interior, 1541. Spaniards made the first settlement at Ysleta, near El Paso, 1682. Americans moved into the land early in the 19th cent. Mexico, of which Texas was a part, won independence from Spain, 1821; Santa Anna became dictator in 1835; Texans rebelled. Santa Anna wiped out defenders of the Alamo, 1836; Sam Houston's Texans defeated Santa Anna at San Jacinto, and independence was proclaimed that same year. The Republic of Texas, with Sam Houston as its first president, functioned as a nation until 1845, when it was admitted to the Union.

Tourist attractions. Padre Island Natl. Seashore; Big Bend, Guadalupe Mts. natl. parks; The Alamo; Ft. Davis; Six Flags Amusement Park; Sea World and Fiesta Texas, both in San Antonio; San Antonio Missions Natl. Historical Park; Cowgirl Hall of Fame, Fort Worth; Lyndon B. Johnson Natl. Historical Park, marking his birthplace, boyhood home, and ranch, near Johnson City; Lyndon B. Johnson Library and Museum, Austin; Texas State Aquarium, Corpus Christi; Kimball Art Museum, Fort Worth; George Bush Library, College Station.

Famous Texans. Lance Armstrong, Stephen F. Austin, Lloyd Bentsen, James Bowie, Carol Burnett, George H. W. Bush, George W. Bush, Joan Crawford, J. Frank Dobie, Dwight D. Eisenhower, Morgan Fairchild, Farrah Fawcett, Sam Houston, Howard Hughes, Kay Bailey Hutchison, Molly Ivins, Lyndon B. Johnson, Tommy Lee Jones, Janis Joplin, Barbara Jordan, Mary Martin, Chester Nimitz, Sandra Day O'Connor, H. Ross Perot, Katherine Ann Porter, Dan Rather, Sam Rayburn, Ann Richards, Sissy Spacek, Kenneth Starr, George Strait.

Tourist Information. Texas Tourism, P.O. Box 12428, Austin, TX 78711; 1-800-8888TEX. **Website:** www.traveltex.com

Website. www.state.tx.us

Utah (UT)

Beehive State

People. Population (2004 est.): 2,389,039; rank: 34; **net change** (2003-2004): 1.6%. **Pop. density:** 29.1 per sq mi. **Racial distribution** (2003): 93.6% white; 1.0% black; 1.9% Asian; 1.4% Native American/Nat. AK; 0.8% Hawaiian/Pacific Islander; 2 or more races, 1.3%. **Hispanic pop.** (any race): 9.9%.

Geography. Total area: 84,899 sq mi; rank: 13. **Land area:** 82,144 sq mi; rank: 12. **Acres forested:** 15.7 mil. **Location:** Middle Rocky Mountain state; its southeastern corner touches Colorado, New Mexico, and Arizona, and is the only spot in the U.S. where 4 states join. **Climate:** arid; ranging from warm desert in SW to alpine in NE. **Topography:** high Colorado plateau is cut by brilliantly colored canyons of the SE; broad, flat, desert-like Great Basin of the W; the Great Salt Lake and Bonneville Salt Flats to the NW; Middle Rockies in the NE run E-W; valleys and plateaus of the Wasatch Front. **Capital:** Salt Lake City.

Economy. Chief industries: services, trade, manufacturing, government, transportation, utilities. **Chief manuf. goods:** medical instruments, electronic components, food products, fabricated metals, transportation equipment, steel and copper. **Chief crops:** hay, corn, wheat, barley, apples, potatoes, cherries, onions, peaches, pears. **Livestock:** (Jan. 2005) 860,000 cattle/calves, 270,000 sheep/lambs; (Dec. 2004) 690,000 hogs/pigs, 3.9 mil. chickens (excl. broilers). **Timber/lumber** (est. 2003): 51 mil bd. ft.; aspen, spruce, pine. **Nonfuel minerals** (est. 2004): $1.7 bil.; copper, cement (portland), salt, gold, sand and gravel (construction). **Commercial fishing** (2003): $15.6 mil. **Gross state product** (2004): $82.4 bil. **Sales tax** (2005): 4.75%. **Employment distrib.** (May 2005): 18.0% govt.; 19.7% trade/trans./util.; 10.3% mfg.; 11.0% ed./health serv.; 12.8% prof./bus. serv. 9.1% leisure/hosp. 5.8% finance; 7.0% constr.; 3.0% other serv.; 2.7% info. **Unemployment** (2004): 5.2%. **Per cap. pers. income** (2004): $26,606. **New private housing** (2004): 24,891 units/$3.4 bil. **Commercial banks** (2004): 66; **deposits**: $95.8 bil. **Savings institutions** (2004): 7; **deposits**: $6.2 bil.**Principal internat. airport at:** Salt Lake City. **Tourism expends.** (2003): $3.7 bil.

Federal govt. Fed. civ. employees (Mar. 2004): 27,018; **avg. salary:** $50,538. **Notable fed. facilities:** *Hill AFB; Tooele Army Depot; Army Dugway Proving Ground.

Energy. Electricity production (est. 2004, kWh by source): Coal: 35.9 bil; Petroleum: 44 mil; Gas: 1.0 bil; Hydroelectric: 494 mil; Other: 195 mil.

State data. Motto: Industry. **Flower:** Sego lily. **Bird:** Seagull. **Tree:** Blue spruce. **Song:** Utah, This is the Place. **Entered union** Jan. 4, 1896; rank, 45th. **State fair** at Salt Lake City; Sept.

History. Ute, Gosiute, Southern Paiute, and Navajo peoples lived in the region at the time of European contact. Spanish Franciscans visited the area, 1776; American fur traders followed. Permanent settlement began with the arrival of the Mormons, 1847; they made the arid land bloom and created a prosperous economy. The State of Deseret was organized in 1849, and asked admission to the Union. In 1850, Congress established the region as the territory of Utah, and Brigham Young was appointed governor. The Union Pacific and Central Pacific

railroads met near Promontory Point, May 10, 1869, creating the first transcontinental railroad. Statehood was not achieved until 1896, after a long period of controversy over the Mormon Church's doctrine of polygamy, which it discontinued in 1890.

Tourist attractions. Temple Square, Mormon Church headquarters, Salt Lake City; Great Salt Lake; Zion, Canyonlands, Bryce Canyon, Arches, and Capitol Reef natl. parks; Dinosaur, Rainbow Bridge, Timpanogos Cave, and Natural Bridges natl. monuments; Lake Powell; Flaming Gorge Natl. Recreation Area.

Famous Utahans. Maude Adams, Ezra Taft Benson, John Moses Browning, Mariner Eccles, Philo Farnsworth, James Fletcher, David M. Kennedy, J. Willard Marriott, Merlin Olsen, Osmond family, Ivy Baker Priest, George Romney, Roseanne, Wallace Stegner, Brigham Young, Loretta Young.

Tourist information. Utah Travel Council, Council Hall, Salt Lake City, UT 84114; 1-800-200-1160 or 1-800-UTAH-FUN. **Website:** www.utah.com

Website. www.utah.gov

Vermont (VT)

Green Mountain State

People. Population (2004 est.): 621,394; rank: 49; **net change** (2003-2004): 0.3%. **Pop. density:** 67.2 per sq mi. **Racial distribution** (2003): 96.9% white; 0.6% black; 1.0% Asian; 0.4% Native American/Nat. AK; 0.07% Hawaiian/Pacific Islander; 2 or more races, 1.1%. **Hispanic pop.** (any race): 0.9%.

Geography. Total area: 9,614 sq mi; rank: 45. **Land area:** 9,250 sq mi; rank: 43. **Acres forested:** 4.6 mil. **Location:** northern New England state. **Climate:** temperate, with considerable temperature extremes; heavy snowfall in mountains. **Topography:** Green Mts. N-S backbone 20-36 mi wide; avg. altitude 1,000 ft. **Capital:** Montpelier.

Economy. Chief industries: manufacturing, tourism, agriculture, trade, finance, insurance, real estate, government. **Chief manuf. goods:** machine tools, furniture, scales, books, computer components, speciality foods. **Chief crops:** dairy products, apples, maple syrup, greenhouse/nursery, vegetables and small fruits. **Livestock:** (Jan. 2005) 275,000 cattle/calves; (Dec. 2004) 2,000 hogs/pigs, 225,000 chickens (excl. broilers). **Timber/lumber** (est. 2003): 182 mil bd. ft.; pine, spruce, fir, hemlock. **Nonfuel minerals** (est. 2004): $69.1 mil.; stone (dimension), stone (crushed), sand and gravel (construction), talc (crude), gemstones. **Gross state product** (2004): $22.1 bil. **Sales tax** (2005): 6.0%. **Employment distrib.** (May 2005): 18.0% govt.; 19.1% trade/trans./util.; 12.1% mfg.; 17.7% ed./health serv.; 7.1% prof./bus. serv. 9.9% leisure/hosp. 4.4% finance; 5.9% constr.; 3.4% other serv.; 2.1% info. **Unemployment** (2004): 3.7%. **Per cap. pers. income** (2004): $32,770. **New private housing** (2004): 3,906 units/$452 mil. **Commercial banks** (2004): 17; **deposits**: $7.9 bil. **Savings institutions** (2004): 7; **deposits**: $1.2 bil. **Lottery** (2004): total sales: $92.3 mil; net income: $19.5 mil. **Principal internat. airport at:** Burlington. **Tourism expends.** (2003): $1.4 bil.

Federal govt. Fed. civ. employees (Mar. 2004): 3,696; **avg. salary:** $51,723.

Energy. Electricity production (est. 2004, kWh by source): Petroleum: 9 mil; Gas: 3 mil; Hydroelectric: 345 mil; Other: 227 mil.

State data. Motto: Freedom and unity. **Flower:** Red clover. **Bird:** Hermit thrush. **Tree:** Sugar maple. **Song:** These Green Mountains. **Entered union** Mar. 4, 1791; rank, 14th. **State fair** at Rutland; early Sept.

History. Before the arrival of the Europeans, Abnaki and Mahican peoples lived in the region. Champlain explored the lake that bears his name, 1609. The first American settlement was Ft. Dummer, 1724, near Brattleboro. During the American Revolution, Ethan Allen and the Green Mountain Boys captured Ft. Ticonderoga (NY), 1775; John Stark defeated part of Burgoyne's forces near Bennington, 1777. In the War of 1812, Thomas MacDonough defeated a British fleet on Lake Champlain off Plattsburgh (NY), 1814.

Tourist attractions. Shelburne Museum; Rock of Ages Quarry, Graniteville; Vermont Marble Exhibit, Proctor; Bennington Battle Monument; Pres. Calvin Coolidge homestead, Plymouth; Maple Grove Maple Museum, St. Johnsbury; Ben & Jerry's Factory, Waterbury.

Famous Vermonters. Ethan Allen, Chester A. Arthur, Calvin Coolidge, Howard Dean, John Deere, George Dewey, John Dewey, Stephen A. Douglas, Dorothy Canfield Fisher, James Fisk, James Jeffords, Rudy Vallee.

Chamber of Commerce. PO Box 37, Montpelier, VT 05601.

Tourist information. Vermont Dept. of Tourism and Marketing, 6 Baldwin St., Drawer 33, Montpelier, VT 05633-1301; 1-800-VERMONT. **Website:** www.vermontvacation.com

Website. www.vermont.gov

Virginia (VA)

Old Dominion

People. Population (2004 est.): 7,459,827; rank: 12; **net change** (2003-2004): 1.3%. **Pop. density:** 188.5 per sq mi. **Racial distribution** (2003): 73.9% white; 20.0% black; 4.2% Asian; 0.3% Native American/Nat. AK; 0.1% Hawaiian/Pacific Islander; 2 or more races, 1.5%. **Hispanic pop.** (any race): 5.3%.

Geography. Total area: 42,774 sq mi; rank: 35. **Land area:** 39,594 sq mi; rank: 37. **Acres forested:** 16.1 mil. **Location:** South Atlantic state bounded by the Atlantic Ocean on the E and surrounded by North Carolina, Tennessee, Kentucky, West Virginia, and Maryland. **Climate:** mild and equable. **Topography:** mountain and valley region in the W, including the Blue Ridge Mts.; rolling piedmont plateau; tidewater, or coastal plain, including the eastern shore. **Capital:** Richmond.

Economy. Chief industries: services, trade, government, manufacturing, tourism, agriculture. **Chief manuf. goods:** food processing, transportation equipment, printing, textiles, electronic & electrical equipment, industrial machinery & equipment, lumber & wood products, chemicals, rubber & plastics, furniture. **Chief crops:** tobacco, grain corn, soybeans, winter wheat, peanuts, lint & seed cotton. **Livestock:** (Jan. 2005) 1.64 mil. cattle/calves, 61,000 sheep/lambs; (Dec. 2004) 375,000 hogs/pigs, 4.9 mil. chickens (excl. broilers), 263.0 mil. broilers. **Timber/lumber** (est. 2003): 1.4 bil bd. ft.; pine and hardwoods. **Nonfuel minerals** (est. 2004): $868 mil.; stone (crushed), cement (portland), sand and gravel (construction), lime, clays (fuller's earth). **Commercial fishing** (2003): $130.7 mil. **Chief ports:** Hampton Roads, Richmond, Alexandria. **Gross state product** (2004): $326.6 bil. **Sales tax** (2005): 5.0%. **Employment distrib.** (May 2005): 18.1% govt.; 18.0% trade/trans./util.; 8.2% mfg.; 10.7% ed./health serv.; 16.1% prof./bus. serv. 9.0% leisure/hosp. 5.3% finance; 6.6% constr.; 5.0% other serv.; 2.7% info. **Unemployment** (2004): 3.7%. **Per cap. pers. income** (2004): $35,477. **New private housing** (2004): 61,238 units/$7.9 bil. **Commercial banks** (2004): 150; **deposits**: $113.0 bil. **Savings institutions** (2004): 18; **deposits**: $34.8 bil. **Lottery** (2004): total sales: $1.3 bil; net income: $408.1 mil. **Principal internat. airports at:** Arlington, Norfolk, Loudon, Richmond, Newport News. **Tourism expends.** (2003): $13.9 bil.

Federal govt. Fed. civ. employees (Mar. 2004): 119,184; **avg. salary:** $67,482. **Notable fed. facilities:** Pentagon; Norfolk Naval Sta., Shipyard; Marine Corps Base; Langley AFB; NASA Langley Res. Ctr.; CIA George Bush Ctr. for Intelligence, Langley; Quantico USMC Base; FBI Academy (Quantico); Dahlgren Nav. Surface Warfare Ctr. & Lab; USDA Food and Nutrition Serv.; U.S. Geological Survey Natl. Ctr.

Energy. Electricity production (est. 2004, kWh by source): Coal: 28.0 bil; Petroleum: 4.7 bil; Gas: 4.2 bil; Hydroelectric: 1.3 bil; Nuclear: 28.3 bil.

State data. Motto: Sic Semper Tyrannis (Thus always to tyrants). **Flower:** Dogwood. **Bird:** Cardinal. **Tree:** Dogwood. **Song Emeritus:** Carry Me Back to Old Virginia. **Tenth** of the original 13 states to ratify the Constitution, June 25, 1788. **State fair** at Richmond; late Sept.-early Oct.

History. Living in the area at the time of European contact were the Cherokee and Susquehanna and the Algonquians of the Powhatan Confederacy. English settlers founded Jamestown, 1607. Virginians took over much of the government from royal governor Dunmore, 1775, forcing him to flee. Virginians under George Rogers Clark freed the Ohio-Indiana-Illinois area of British forces. Benedict Arnold burned Richmond and Petersburg for the British, 1781. That same year, Britain's Cornwallis was trapped at Yorktown and surrendered, ending the American Revolution. Virginia seceded from the Union, 1861, and Richmond became the capital of the Confederacy. Hampton Roads, off the Virginia coast, was the site of the famous naval battle of the USS *Monitor* and CSS *Virginia* (Merrimac), 1862. Virginia was readmitted, 1870.

Tourist attractions. Colonial Williamsburg; Busch Gardens, Williamsburg; Wolf Trap Farm, near Falls Church; Arlington Natl. Cemetery; Mt. Vernon, home of George Washington; Jamestown Festival Park; Yorktown; Jefferson's Monticello, Charlottesville; Robert E. Lee's birthplace, Stratford Hall, and grave, Lexington; Appomattox; Shenandoah Natl. Park; Blue Ridge Parkway; Virginia Beach; Paramount's King's Dominion, near Richmond.

Famous Virginians. Richard E. Byrd, James B. Cabell, Henry Clay, Jubal Early, Jerry Falwell, William Henry Harrison, Patrick Henry, A.P. Hill, Thomas Jefferson, Joseph E. Johnston, Robert E. Lee, Meriwether Lewis and William Clark, James Madison, John Marshall, George Mason, James Monroe, George Pickett, Pocahontas, Edgar Allan Poe, John Randolph, Walter Reed, Rev. Pat Robertson, John Smith, J.E.B. Stuart, William Styron, Zachary Taylor, John Tyler, Maggie Walker, Booker T. Washington, George Washington, L. Douglas Wilder, Woodrow Wilson.

Tourist Information. Virginia Tourism Corp., 901 E. Byrd St., Richmond, VA 23219; 1-800-VISITVA. **Website:** www.virginia.org

Website. www.virginia.gov

Washington (WA)

Evergreen State

People. Population (2004 est.): 6,203,788; rank: 15; **net change** (2003-2004): 1.2%. **Pop. density:** 93.2 per sq mi. **Racial distribution** (2003): 85.5% white; 3.5% black; 6.0% Asian; 1.6% Native American/Nat. AK; 0.4% Hawaiian/Pacific Islander; 2 or more races, 2.9%. **Hispanic pop.** (any race): 8.3%.

Geography. Total area: 71,300 sq mi; rank: 18. **Land area:** 66,544 sq mi; rank: 20. **Acres forested:** 21.8 mil. **Location:** Pacific state bordered by Canada on the N; Idaho on the E; Oregon on the S; and the Pacific Ocean on the W. **Climate:** mild, dominated by the Pacific Ocean and protected by the Cascades. **Topography:** Olympic Mts. on NW peninsula; open land along coast to Columbia R.; flat terrain of Puget Sound Lowland; Cascade Mts. region's high peaks to the E; Columbia Basin in central portion; highlands to the NE; mountains to the SE. **Capital:** Olympia.

Economy. Chief industries: advanced technology, aerospace, biotechnology, intl. trade, forestry, tourism, recycling, agriculture & food processing. **Chief manuf. goods:** computer software, aircraft, pulp & paper, lumber and plywood, aluminum, processed fruits and vegetables, machinery, electronics. **Chief crops:** apples, potatoes, hay, farm forest products. **Livestock:** (Jan. 2005) 1.08 mil. cattle/calves, 46,000 sheep/lambs; (Dec. 2004) 26,000 hogs/pigs, 5.9 mil. chickens (excl. broilers). **Timber/lumber** (est. 2003): 5.1 mil bd. ft.; Douglas fir, hemlock, cedar, pine. **Nonfuel minerals** (est. 2004): $447 mil.; sand and gravel (construction), cement (portland), stone (crushed), diatomite, lime. **Commercial fishing** (2003): $170.2 mil. **Chief ports:** Seattle, Tacoma, Vancouver, Kelso-Longview. **Gross state product** (2004): $259.8 bil. **Sales tax** (2005): 6.5%. **Employment distrib.** (May 2005): 19.4% govt.; 19.1% trade/trans./util.; 9.7% mfg.; 12.0% ed./health serv.; 11.3% prof./bus. serv. 9.5% leisure/hosp. 5.5% finance; 6.2% constr.; 3.7% other serv.; 3.3% info. **Unemployment** (2004): 6.2%. **Per cap. pers. income** (2004): $35,299. **New private housing** (2004): 48,595 units/ $7.4 bil. **Commercial banks** (2004): 93; **deposits**: $58.6 bil. **Savings institutions** (2004): 24; **deposits**: $28.9 bil. **Lottery** (2004): total sales: $481.4 mil; net income: $117.3 mil. **Principal internat. airports at:** Seattle/Tacoma, Spokane, Boeing Field. **Tourism expends**. (2003): $8.0 bil.

Federal govt. Fed. civ. employees (Mar. 2004): 45,538; **avg. salary:** $58,124. **Notable fed. facilities:** Bonneville Power Admin.; Ft. Lewis; *McChord AFB; Hanford Nuclear Reservation; Bremerton Naval Shipyards; *Naval Sub Base, Bangor; Naval Sta., Everett; Pacific Northwest Natl. Lab.

Energy. Electricity production (est. 2004, kWh by source): Petroleum: 8 mil; Gas: 2.4 bil; Hydroelectric: 70.8 bil; Nuclear: 9.0 bil; Other: 518 mil.

State data. Motto: Alki (By and by). **Flower:** Western rhododendron. **Bird:** Willow goldfinch. **Tree:** Western hemlock. **Song:** Washington, My Home. **Entered union** Nov. 11, 1889; rank, 42nd. **State fairs:** 5 area fairs, in Aug. and Sept.; no state fair.

History. At the time of European contact, many Native American tribes lived in the area, including the Nez Percé, Spokan, Yakima, Cayuse, Okanogan, Walla Walla, and Colville peoples, who lived in the interior region, and the Nooksak, Chinook, Nisqually, Clallam, Makah, Quinault, and Puyallup peoples, who inhabited the coastal area. Spain's Bruno Hezeta sailed the coast, 1775. In 1792, British naval officer George Vancouver mapped Puget Sound area, and that same year, American Capt. Robert Gray sailed up the Columbia River. Canadian fur traders set up Spokane House, 1810. Americans under John Jacob Astor established a post at Ft. Okanogan, 1811, and missionary Marcus Whitman settled near Walla Walla, 1836. Final agreement on the border of Washington and Canada was made with Britain, 1846, and Washington became part of the Oregon Territory, 1848. Gold was discovered, 1855.

Tourist attractions. Seattle Waterfront, Seattle Center and Space Needle, Museum of Flight, Underground Tour, all Seattle; Mt. Rainier, Olympic, and North Cascades natl. parks; Mt. St. Helens; Puget Sound; San Juan Islands; Grand Coulee Dam; Columbia R. Gorge Natl. Scenic Area; Spokane's Riverfront Park.

Famous Washingtonians. Raymond Carver, Kurt Cobain, Bing Crosby, William O. Douglas, Bill Gates, Jimi Hendrix, Henry M. Jackson, Gary Larson, Mary McCarthy, Robert Motherwell, Edward R. Murrow, Theodore Roethke, Ann Rule, Hilary Swank, Julia Sweeney, Adam West, Marcus Whitman, Minoru Yamasaki.

Tourist information. WA State Tourism, 128 10th Ave. SW, Olympia, WA 98504; 1-800-544-1800. **Website:** www.experiencewashington.com

Website. www.access.wa.gov

West Virginia (WV)

Mountain State

People. Population (2004 est.): 1,815,354; rank: 37; **net change** (2003-2004): 0.2%. **Pop. density:** 75.4 per sq mi. **Racial distribution** (2003): 95.0% white; 3.3% black; 0.6% Asian; 0.2% Native American/Nat. AK; 0.03% Hawaiian/Pacific Islander; 2 or more races, 0.8%. **Hispanic pop.** (any race): 0.7%.

Geography. Total area: 24,230 sq mi; rank: 41. **Land area:** 24,078 sq mi; rank: 41. **Acres forested:** 12.1 mil. **Location:** South Atlantic state bounded on the N by Ohio, Pennsylvania, Maryland; on the S and W by Virginia, Kentucky, Ohio; on the E by Maryland and Virginia. **Climate:** humid continental climate except for marine modification in the lower panhandle. **Topography:** ranging from hilly to mountainous; Allegheny Plateau in the W, covers two-thirds of the state; mountains here are the highest in the state, over 4,000 ft. **Capital:** Charleston.

Economy. Chief industries: manufacturing, services, mining, tourism. **Chief manuf. goods:** machinery, plastic & hardwood prods., fabricated metals, chemicals, aluminum, automotive parts, steel. **Chief crops:** apples, peaches, hay, tobacco, corn, wheat, oats. **Chief farm products:** dairy products, eggs. **Livestock:** (Jan. 2005) 405,000 cattle/calves, 31,000 sheep/lambs; (Dec. 2004) 10,000 hogs/pigs, 2.3 mil. chickens (excl. broilers), 86.4 mil. broilers. **Timber/lumber** (est. 2003): 655 mil bd. ft.; oak, yellow poplar, hickory, walnut, cherry. **Nonfuel minerals** (est. 2004): $179 mil.; stone (crushed), cement (portland), sand and gravel (industrial), lime, salt. **Chief port:** Huntington. **Gross state product** (2004): $49.8 bil. **Sales tax** (2005): 6.0%. **Employment distrib.** (May 2005): 19.5% govt.; 18.4% trade/trans./util.; 8.4% mfg.; 14.9% ed./health serv.; 7.8% prof./bus. serv. 9.4% leisure/hosp. 4.0% finance; 5.2% constr.; 7.5% other serv.; 1.6% info. **Unemployment** (2004): 5.3%. **Per cap. pers. income** (2004): $25,872. **New private housing** (2004): 5,317 units/ $660 mil. **Commercial banks** (2004): 84; **deposits**: $21.8 bil. **Savings institutions** (2004): 7; **deposits**: $840 mil. **Lottery** (2004): total sales: $1.3 bil.; net income: $512.1 mil. **Tourism expends.** (2003): $1.8 bil.

Federal govt. Fed. civ. employees (Mar. 2004): 12,605; **avg. salary:** $55,544. **Notable fed. facilities:** Natl. Radio Astronomy Observatory; Bureau of Public Debt Bldg.; Harpers Ferry Natl. Park; Correctional Institution for Women; FBI Identification Ctr.

Energy. Electricity production (est. 2004, kWh by source): Coal: 58.7 bil; Petroleum: 233 mil; Gas: 3 mil; Hydroelectric: 256 mil; Other: 15 mil.

> ***IT'S A FACT:*** All U.S. states impose a tax on gasoline. As of July 2005, Wisconsin had the highest per-gallon tax on gasoline, taking 32.9 cents for every gallon pumped. The Badger State was followed closely by Washington (31 cents per gallon), Rhode Island (30 cents per gallon), and Ohio (28 cents per gallon). Georgia had the lowest gasoline tax rate in mid-2005, charging only 7.5 cents tax per gallon.

State data. Motto: Montani Semper Liberi (Mountaineers are always free). **Flower:** Big rhododendron. **Bird:** Cardinal. **Tree:** Sugar maple. **Songs:** The West Virginia Hills; This Is My West Virginia; West Virginia, My Home, Sweet Home. **Entered union** June 20, 1863; rank, 35th. **State fair** at Lewisburg (Fairlea); late Aug.

History. Sparsely inhabited at the time of European contact, the area was primarily Native American hunting grounds. British explorers Thomas Batts and Robert Fallam reached the New River, 1671. Early American explorers included George Washington, 1753, and Daniel Boone. In the fall of 1774, frontiersmen defeated an allied Indian uprising at Point Pleasant. The area was part of Virginia and often objected to rule by the eastern part of the state. When Virginia seceded in 1861, the Wheeling Convention repudiated the act and created a new state, Kanawha, later renamed West Virginia. It was admitted to the Union 1863.

Tourist attractions. Harpers Ferry Natl. Historic Park; Science and Cultural Center, Charleston; White Sulphur (in Greenbrier) and Berkeley Springs mineral water spas; New River Gorge, Fayetteville; Winter Place, Exhibition Coal Mine, both Beckley; Monongahela Natl. Forest; Fenton Glass, Williamstown; Viking Glass, New Martinsville; Blenko Glass, Milton; Sternwheel Regatta, Charleston; Mountain State Forest Festival; Snowshoe Ski Resort, Slaty Fork; Canaan State Park, Davis; Mountain State Arts & Crafts Fair, Ripley; Ogle Bay, Wheeling; White water rafting, several locations.

Famous West Virginians. Newton D. Baker, Pearl Buck, John W. Davis, Thomas "Stonewall" Jackson, Don Knotts, Dwight Whitney Morrow, Michael Owens, Mary Lou Retton, Walter Reuther, Cyrus Vance, Jerry West, Charles "Chuck" Yeager.

Tourist information. West Virginia Division of Tourism, 90 MacCorkle Ave., SW, South Charleston, WV 25303; 1-800-CALLWVA. **Website:** www.wvtourism.com

Website. www.wv.gov

Wisconsin (WI)

Badger State

People. Population (2004 est.): 5,509,026; rank: 20; **net change** (2003-2004): 0.6%. **Pop. density:** 101.5 per sq mi. **Racial distribution** (2003): 90.1% white; 5.9% black; 2.0% Asian; 0.9% Native American/Nat. AK; 0.04% Hawaiian/Pacific Islander; 2 or more races, 1.0%. **Hispanic pop.** (any race): 3.9%.

Geography. Total area: 65,498 sq mi; rank: 23. **Land area:** 54,310 sq mi; rank: 25. **Acres forested:** 16.0 mil. **Location:** East North Central state, bounded on the N by Lake Superior and Upper Michigan; on the E by Lake Michigan; on the S by Illinois; on the W by the St. Croix and Mississippi rivers. **Climate:** long, cold winters and short, warm summers tempered by the Great Lakes. **Topography:** narrow Lake Superior Lowland plain met by Northern Highland, which slopes gently to the sandy crescent Central Plain; Western Upland in the SW; 3 broad parallel limestone ridges running N-S are separated by wide and shallow lowlands in the SE. **Capital:** Madison.

Economy. Chief industries: services, manufacturing, trade, government, agriculture, tourism. **Chief manuf. goods:** food products, motor vehicles & equip., paper products, medical instruments and supplies, printing, plastics. **Chief crops:** corn, hay, soybeans, potatoes, cranberries, sweet corn, peas, oats, snap beans. **Chief farm products:** milk, butter, cheese, canned and frozen vegetables. **Livestock:** (Jan. 2005) 3.35 mil. cattle/calves, 85,000 sheep/lambs; (Dec. 2004) 430,000 hogs/pigs, 6.5 mil. chickens (excl. broilers), 33.8 mil. broilers. **Timber/lumber** (est. 2003): 535 mil bd. ft.; maple, birch, oak, evergreens. ft. **Nonfuel minerals** (est. 2004): $487 mil.; stone (crushed), sand and gravel (construction), lime, sand and gravel (industrial), stone (dimension). **Commercial fishing** (2003): $4.1 mil. **Chief ports:** Superior, Ashland, Milwaukee, Green Bay, Kewaunee, Pt. Washington, Manitowoc, Sheboygan, Marinette, Kenosha. **Gross state product** (2004): $211.7 bil. **Sales tax** (2005): 5.0%. **Employment distrib.** (May 2005): 14.9% govt.; 19.0% trade/trans./util.; 17.6% mfg.; 13.5% ed./health serv.; 8.8% prof./bus. serv. 9.2% leisure/hosp. 5.6% finance; 4.7% constr.; 4.8% other serv.; 1.8% info. **Unemployment** (2004): 4.9%. **Per cap. pers. income** (2004): $32,157. **New private housing** (2004): 41,112 units/$5.5 bil. **Commercial banks** (2004): 280; **deposits**: $79.4 bil. **Savings institutions** (2004): 42; **deposits**: $16.7 bil. **Lottery** (2004): total sales: $482.9 mil. **Principal internat. airports at:** Green Bay, Milwaukee. **Tourism expends.** (2003): $7.2 bil.

Federal govt. Fed. civ. employees (Mar. 2004): 11,637. **avg. salary:** $53,348. **Notable fed. facilities:** *Ft. McCoy.

Energy. Electricity production (est. 2004, kWh by source): Coal: 41.1 bil; Petroleum: 66 mil; Gas: 636 mil; Hydroelectric: 2.3 bil; Nuclear: 11.9 bil; Other: 308 mil.

State data. Motto: Forward. **Flower:** Wood violet. **Bird:** Robin. **Tree:** Sugar maple. **Song:** On, Wisconsin! **Entered union** May 29, 1848; rank, 30th. **State fair** at State Fair Park, West Allis; early Aug.

History. At the time of European contact, Ojibwa, Menominee, Winnebago, Kickapoo, Sauk, Fox, and Potawatomi peoples inhabited the region. Jean Nicolet was the first European to see the Wisconsin area, arriving in Green Bay, 1634; French missionaries and fur traders followed. The British took over, 1763. The U.S. won the land after the American Revolution, but the British were not ousted until after the War of 1812. Lead miners came next, then farmers. In 1816, the U.S. government built a fort at Prairie du Chien on Wisconsin's border with Iowa. Native Americans in the area rebelled against the seizure of their tribal lands in the Black Hawk War of 1832, but treaties from 1829 to 1848, transferred all land titles in Wisconsin to the U.S. government. Railroads were started in 1851, serving growing wheat harvests and iron mines. Some 96,000 soldiers served the Union cause during the Civil War.

Tourist attractions. Old Wade House and Carriage Museum, Greenbush; Villa Louis, Prairie du Chien; Circus World Museum, Baraboo; Wisconsin Dells; Old World Wisconsin, Eagle; Door County peninsula; Chequamegon and Nicolet national forests; Lake Winnebago; House on the Rock, Dodgeville; Monona Terrace, Madison.

Famous Wisconsinites. Don Ameche, Carrie Chapman Catt, Willem Dafoe, Edna Ferber, Hamlin Garland, King Camp Gillette, Harry Houdini, Robert La Follette, Alfred Lunt, Pat O'Brien, Georgia O'Keeffe, William H. Rehnquist, John Ringling, Donald K. "Deke" Slayton, Spencer Tracy, Thorstein Veblen, Orson Welles, Laura Ingalls Wilder, Thornton Wilder, Frank Lloyd Wright.

Tourist information. Wisconsin Dept. of Tourism, 201 W. Washington Ave., Madison, WI 53708-8690; 1-800-432-TRIP. **Website:** www.travelwisconsin.com

Website. www.wisconsin.gov

Wyoming (WY)

Equality State, Cowboy State

People. Population (2004 est.): 506,529; rank: 51; **net change** (2003-2004): 0.9%. **Pop. density:** 5.2 per sq mi. **Racial distribution** (2003): 94.7% white; 0.9% black; 0.7% Asian; 2.4% Native American/Nat. AK; 0.07% Hawaiian/Pacific Islander; 2 or more races, 1.2%. **Hispanic pop.** (any race): 6.8%.

Geography. Total area: 97,814 sq mi; rank: 10. **Land area:** 97,100 sq mi; rank: 9. **Acres forested:** 11.0 mil. **Location:** Mountain state lying in the high western plateaus of the Great Plains. **Climate:** semi-desert conditions throughout; true desert in the Big Horn and Great Divide basins. **Topography:** the eastern Great Plains rise to the foothills of the Rocky Mts.; the Continental Divide crosses the state from the NW to the SE. **Capital:** Cheyenne.

Economy. Chief industries: mineral extraction, oil, natural gas, tourism and recreation, agriculture. **Chief manuf. goods:** refined petroleum, wood, stone, clay products, foods, electronic devices, sporting apparel, and aircraft. **Chief crops:** wheat, beans, barley, oats, sugar beets, hay. **Livestock:** (Jan. 2005) 1.35 mil. cattle/calves, 450,000 sheep/lambs; (Dec. 2004) 114,000 hogs/pigs, 17,000 chickens (excl. broilers). **Timber/lumber** (est. 2003): 160 mil bd. ft.; ponderosa & lodgepole pine, Douglas fir, Engelmann spruce. **Nonfuel minerals** (est. 2004): $1.1 bil.; soda ash, clays (bentonite), helium (Grade-A), cement (portland), sand and gravel (construction). **Gross state product** (2004):

$24.3 bil. **Sales tax** (2005): 4.0%. **Employment distrib.** (May 2005): 25.4% govt.; 19.0% trade/trans./util.; 3.5% mfg.; 8.4% ed./health serv.; 6.0% prof./bus. serv. 12.0% leisure/hosp. 4.1% finance; 7.9% constr.; 3.8% other serv.; 1.6% info. **Unemployment** (2004): 3.9%. **Per cap. pers. income** (2004): $34,306. **New private housing** (2004): 2,990 units/$529 mil. **Commercial banks** (2004): 47; **deposits**: $7.6 bil. **Savings institutions** (2004): 4; **deposits**: $314 mil. **Principal internat. airport at:** Casper. **Tourism expends.** (2003): $1.7 bil.

Federal govt. Fed. civ. employees (Mar. 2004): 4,870; **avg. salary:** $51,079. **Notable fed. facilities:** Warren AFB.

Energy. Electricity production (est. 2004, kWh by source): Coal: 42.5 bil; Petroleum: 42 mil; Gas: 127 mil; Hydroelectric: 631 mil; Other: 15 mil.

State data. Motto: Equal Rights. **Flower:** Indian Paintbrush. **Bird:** Western Meadowlark. **Tree:** Plains Cottonwood. **Song:** Wyoming. **Entered union** July 10, 1890; rank, 44th. **State fair** at Douglas; late Aug.

History. Shoshone, Crow, Cheyenne, Oglala Sioux, and Arapaho peoples lived in the area at the time of European contact. France's François and Louis La Verendrye were the first Europeans to see the region, 1743. John Colter, an American, was first to traverse Yellowstone area, 1807-8. Trappers and fur traders followed in the 1820s. Forts Laramie and Bridger became important stops on the pioneer trails to the West Coast. Population grew after the Union Pacific crossed the state, 1868. Women won the vote, for the first time in the U.S., from the Territorial Legislature, 1869. Disputes between large land owners and small ranchers culminated in the Johnson County Cattle War, 1892; federal troops were called in to restore order.

Tourist attractions. Yellowstone Natl. Park, the first U.S. national park, est. 1872; Grand Teton Natl. Park; Natl. Elk Refuge; Devils Tower Natl. Monument; Fort Laramie Natl. Historic Site and nearby pioneer trail ruts; Buffalo Bill Historical Center, Cody; Cheyenne Frontier Days, Cheyenne.

Famous Wyomingites. James Bridger, William F. "Buffalo Bill" Cody, Curt Gowdy, Esther Hobart Morris, Jackson Pollock, Nellie Tayloe Ross.

Tourist information. Wyoming Travel and Tourism, I-25 at College Dr., Cheyenne, WY 82002; 1-800-CALLWYO. **Website:** www.wyomingtourism.org

Website. www.state.wy.us

District of Columbia (DC)

People. Population (2004 est.): 553,523; rank: 50; **net change** (2003-2004): -0.7%. **Pop. density:** 9,057.0 per sq mi. **Racial distribution** (2003): 36.2% white; 58.8% black; 3.1% Asian; 0.4% Native American/Nat. AK; 0.07% Hawaiian/Pacific Islander; 2 or more races, 1.4%. **Hispanic pop.** (any race): 9.4%.

Geography. Total area: 68 sq mi; rank: 50. **Land area:** 61 sq mi; rank: 51. **Location:** at the confluence of the Potomac and Anacostia rivers, flanked by Maryland on the N, E, and SE and by Virginia on the SW. **Climate:** hot humid summers, mild winters. **Topography:** low hills rise toward the N away from the Potomac R. and slope to the S; highest elevation, 410 ft, lowest Potomac R., 1 ft.

Economy. Chief industries: government, service, tourism. **Gross product** (2004): $75.3 bil. **Sales tax** (2005): 5.75%. **Employment distrib.** (May 2005): 33.6% govt.; 4.1% trade/trans./util.; 0.4% mfg.; 13.6% ed./health serv.; 21.5% prof./bus. serv. 8.1% leisure/hosp. 4.6% finance; 1.8% constr.; 8.9% other serv.; 3.4% info. **Unemployment** (2004): 8.2%. **Per cap. pers. income** (2004): $51,803. **New private housing** (2004): 1,936 units/$225 mil. **Commercial banks** (2004): 19; **deposits**: $16.0 bil. **Savings institutions** (2004): 8; **deposits**: $2.6 bil. **Lottery** (2004): total sales: $245.0 mil; net income: $75.8 mil. **Principal internat. airports at:** Arlington (VA), Dulles (VA). **Tourism expends.** (2003): $4.3 bil.

Federal govt. Fed. civ. employees (Mar. 2004): 150,631; **avg. salary:** $79,680.

Energy. Electricity production (2000, kWh, by source): Petroleum: 95 mil; Other: 28 mil.

District data. Motto: Justitia omnibus (Justice for all). **Flower:** American beauty rose. **Tree:** Scarlet oak. **Bird:** Wood thrush.

History. The District of Columbia, coextensive with the city of Washington, is the seat of the U.S. federal government. It lies on the west central edge of Maryland on the Potomac River, opposite Virginia. Its area was originally 100 sq mi taken from the sovereignty of Maryland and Virginia. Virginia's portion south of the Potomac was given back to that state in 1846.

The 23rd Amendment (1961) granted residents the right to vote for president and vice president for the first time since 1800 and gave them 3 members in the Electoral College. The first such votes were cast in Nov. 1964.

Congress, which has legislative authority over the District under the Constitution, established in 1874 a government of 3 commissioners appointed by the president. The Reorganization Plan of 1967 substituted a single appointive commissioner (also called mayor), assistant, and 9-member City Council. Funds were still appropriated by Congress; residents had no vote in local government, except to elect school board members. In Sept. 1970, Congress approved legislation giving the District one delegate to the House of Representatives, who can vote in committee but not on the floor. The first delegate was elected 1971.

In May 1974, voters approved a congressionally drafted charter giving them the right to elect their own mayor and a 13-member city council; the first took office Jan. 2, 1975. The district won the right to levy taxes; Congress retained power to veto council actions and approve the city budget.

Proposals for a "federal town" for the deliberations of the Continental Congress were made in 1783, 4 years before the adoption of the Constitution. Rivalry between Northern and Southern delegates over the site appeared in the First Congress, 1789. John Adams, presiding officer of the Senate, cast the deciding vote of that body for Germantown, PA. In 1790 Congress compromised by making Philadelphia the temporary capital for 10 years. The Virginia members of the House wanted a permanent capital on the eastern bank of the Potomac, while the Southerners opposed having the nation assume the war debts of the 13 original states as provided under the Assumption Bill, fathered by Alexander Hamilton. Hamilton and Jefferson arranged a compromise: the Virginia men voted for the Assumption Bill, and the Northerners conceded the capital to the Potomac. Pres. Washington chose the site in Oct. 1790 and persuaded landowners to sell their holdings to the government. The capital was named Washington.

Washington appointed Pierre Charles L'Enfant, a Frenchman, to plan the capital on an area not more than 10 mi square. The L'Enfant plan, for streets 100 to 110 ft. wide and one avenue 400 ft. wide and a mile long, seemed grandiose and foolhardy, but Washington endorsed it. When L'Enfant ordered a wealthy landowner to remove his new manor house because it obstructed a vista, and demolished it when the owner refused, Washington stepped in and dismissed the architect. Andrew Ellicott, who was working on surveying the area, finished the official map and design of the city. Ellicott was assisted by Benjamin Banneker, a distinguished black architect and astronomer.

On Sept. 18, 1793, Pres. Washington laid the cornerstone of the north wing of the Capitol. On June 3, 1800, Pres. John Adams moved to Washington, and on June 10, Philadelphia ceased to be the temporary capital. The City of Washington was incorporated in 1802; the District of Columbia was created as a municipal corporation in 1874, embracing Washington, Georgetown, and Washington County.

Tourist attractions: *See* Washington, DC, Capital of the U.S., page 455.

Famous Washingtonians: Edward Albee, Frederick Douglass, John Foster Dulles, Duke Ellington, Al Gore, Katherine Grahm, Goldie Hawn, J. Edgar Hoover, Pete Sampras, John Philip Sousa.

Tourist information. Washington, DC Convention and Tourism Corp., 901 7th St NW, 4th Fl., Washington, D.C., 20001-3719; 202-789-7000. **Website:** www.washington.org

Website. www.dc.gov

WORLD ALMANAC QUICK QUIZ

Of the following former slaveholding border states, which is the only one to have seceded from the Union during the Civil War?

(a) Delaware (b) Tennessee (c) Maryland (d) Missouri

For the answer look in this chapter, or see page 1008.

OUTLYING U.S. AREAS

American Samoa (AS)

People. Population (July 2005 est.): 57,881. **Population growth rate** (2004-2005 est.): -0.11%. **Pop. density** (2005): 752 per sq mi. **Major ethnic groups:** Samoan 89%, Caucasian 2%, Tongan 4%, other 5%. **Languages:** Samoan, English.

Total area: 77 sq mi. **Land area:** 77 sq. mi. **Capital:** Pago Pago, Island of Tutuila. **Motto:** Samoa Muamua le Atua (In Samoa, God Is First). **Song:** Amerika Samoa. **Flower:** Paogo (Ula-fala). **Plant:** Ava. Boasting spectacular scenery and delightful South Seas climate, American Samoa is the most southerly of all lands under U.S. sovereignty. It is an unincorporated territory consisting of 7 small islands of the Samoan group: **Tutuila, Aunu'u, Manu'a Group (Ta'u, Olosega, Ofu), and Rose** and **Swains Island.** The islands are 2,300 mi SW of Honolulu.

Economy. Chief industries: tuna fishing and processing, trade, services, tourism. **Chief crops:** giant taro, taro, yams, copra, coconuts, breadfruits, bananas. **Livestock** (2004): 103 cattle; 10,500 hogs/pigs, 38,000 chickens. **Commercial fishing** (2000): $2 mil. **Gross domestic product** (2000 est.): $500 mil. **Commercial banks** (2004): 2; **deposits**: $142 mil. **Principal airport at:** Pago Pago.

Energy. Electricity production (2001): 130 mil. kWh

A tripartite agreement between Great Britain, Germany, and the U.S. in 1899 gave the U.S. sovereignty over the eastern islands of the Samoan group; these islands became American Samoa. Local chiefs ceded Tutuila and Aunu'u to the U.S. in 1900, and the Manu'a group and Rose Island in 1904; Swains Island was annexed in 1925. Samoa (Western), comprising the larger islands of the Samoan group, was a New Zealand mandate and UN Trusteeship until it became independent Jan. 1, 1962 (now called Samoa).

Tutuila and Aunu'u have an area of 53 sq mi. Ta'u has an area of 17 sq mi, and the islets of Ofu and Olosega, 5 sq mi with a population of a few thousand. Swains Island has nearly 2 sq mi and a population of about 100.

About 70% of the land is bush and mountains. Chief exports are fish products, especially tuna. Taro, breadfruit, yams, coconuts, pineapples, oranges, and bananas are also produced.

From 1900 to 1951, American Samoa was under the jurisdiction of the U.S. Navy. Since 1951, it has been under the Interior Dept. On Jan. 3, 1978, the first popularly elected Samoan governor and lieutenant governor were inaugurated. Previously, the governor was appointed by the Secretary of the Interior. American Samoa has a bicameral legislature and elects a delegate to the House of Representatives, with no vote except in committees.

The American Samoans are of Polynesian origin. They are nationals of the U.S.; approximately 20,000 live in Hawaii, 65,000 in California and Washington.

Tourist information. Office of Tourism, Dept. of Commerce, American Samoa Govt., P.O. Box 1147, Pago Pago, AS 96799; 684-699-9411. **Website:** www.washington.org

Website. www.amsamoa.com

Guam (GU)

Where America's Day Begins

People. Population (July 2005 est.): 168,564. **Population growth rate** (2004-2005 est.): 1.5%. **Pop. density** (2005): 795 per sq mi. **Ethnic distrib.** (2000): 37.1% Chamorro, 26.3% Filipino, 11.3% other Pacific Islander, 6.9% white, 6.3% Asian, 2.3% other, 9.8% two or more race/ethnicities. **Languages:** English, Chamorro, Philippine/other Pacific Island languages.

Geography. Total area: 212 sq mi. **Land area:** 212 sq. mi. **Location:** largest and southernmost of the Mariana Islands in the West Pacific, 3,700 mi W of Hawaii. **Climate:** tropical, with temperatures from 70° to 90° F; avg. annual rainfall, about 70 in. **Topography:** coralline limestone plateau in the N; southern chain of low volcanic mountains sloping gently to the W, more steeply to coastal cliffs on the E; general elevation, 500 ft; highest point, Mt. Lamlam, 1,334 ft. **Capital:** Hagatna.

Economy. Chief industries: U.S. military, tourism, construction, shipping, concrete products, printing & publishing. **Chief manuf. goods:** textiles, foods. **Chief crops:** cabbages, eggplants, cucumber, long beans, tomatoes, bananas, coconuts, watermelon, yams, cantaloupe, papayas, maize, sweet potatoes. **Livestock** (2001): 130 cattle; 5,100 hogs/pigs, 200,000 chickens. **Commercial fishing** (2000): $1.3 mil. **Chief port:** Apra Harbor. **Gross domestic product** (2000 est.): $3.2 bil. **Employment distrib.** (2000 est.): 26% govt.; 24% trade; 40% serv.; 10% indust. **Unemployment** (2000 est.): 15%. **Per capita income** (2000 est.): $21,000. **Commercial banks** (2004): 6; **deposits**: $1.5 bil. **Savings institutions** (2004): 1; **deposits**: $55 mil. **Principal internat. airport at:** Hagatna. **Tourism expends.** (1995): $4.9 bil.

Energy. Electricity production (2002): 835 mil. kWh

Federal govt. Federal employees (1990): 7,200. **Notable fed. facilities:** Anderson AFB; naval, air, and port bases.

Misc. data. Flower: Puti Tai Nobio (Bougainvillea). **Bird:** Toto (Fruit dove). **Tree:** Ifit (Intsiabijuga). **Song:** Stand Ye Guamanians.

History. Guam was probably settled by voyagers from the Indonesian-Philippine archipelago by 3rd cent. BC. Pottery, rice cultivation, and megalithic technology show strong East Asian cultural influence. Centralized, village clan-based communities engaged in agriculture and offshore fishing. The estimated population by the early 16th cent. was 50,000-75,000. Magellan arrived in the Marianas Mar. 6, 1521. They were colonized in 1668 by Spanish missionaries, who named them the Mariana Islands in honor of Maria Anna, queen of Spain. When Spain ceded Guam to the U.S., it sold the other Marianas to Germany. Japan obtained a League of Nations mandate over the German islands in 1919; in Dec. 1941 it seized Guam, which was retaken by the U.S. in July-August 1944.

Guam is a self-governing organized unincorporated U.S. territory. The Organic Act of 1950 provided for a governor, elected to a 4-year term, and a 21-member unicameral legislature, elected biennially by the residents, who are American citizens. In 1970, the first governor was elected. In 1972, a U.S. law gave Guam one delegate to the U.S. House of Representatives who has a voice but no vote, except in committees.

Guam's quest to change its status to a U.S. Commonwealth began in the late 1970s. The Guam Commission on Self-Determination, created in 1984, developed a draft Commonwealth Act. In 1993, legislation proposing a change of status was submitted to the U.S. Congress. In 1994, the U.S. Congress passed legislation transferring 3,200 acres of land on Guam from federal to local control.

Tourist attractions. Tropical climate, oceanic marine environment; annual mid-Aug. Merizo Water Festival; Tarzan Falls; beaches; water sports; duty-free port shopping.

Website: ns.gov.gu

Tourism website. ns.gov.gu/visiting.html

Commonwealth of the Northern Mariana Islands (MP)

People. Population (July 2005 est.): 80,362. **Population growth rate** (2004-2005 est.): 2.61%. **Pop. density** (2004): 424.8 per sq mi. **Ethnic distrib.** (2000): 56.3% Asian, 36.3% Pacific Islander, 1.8% white, 0.8% other, 4.8% two or more races/ethnicities. **Languages:** Philippine languages, Chinese, English, Chamorro.

Total area: 184.2 sq mi. **Land area:** 184.2 sq mi. Located in the perpetually warm climes between Guam and the Tropic of Cancer, the 14 islands of the Northern Marianas form a 300-mi. long archipelago. The indigenous population is concentrated on the 3 largest of the 6 inhabited islands: **Saipan,** the seat of government and commerce, **Rota,** and **Tinian. Capital:** Saipan.

Economy. Chief industries: tourism, manufacturing, construction, apparel, handicrafts. **Chief manuf. goods:** apparel, stone, clay and glass products. **Chief crops:** coconuts, fruits, and vegetables. **Livestock**: (1998): 1,789 cattle; 831 hogs/pigs, 29,409 chickens. **Commercial fishing** (2000): $938,365. **Chief ports:** Saipan, Tinian. **Gross domestic product** (2000 est., incl. U.S. subsidy): $900 mil. **Employment distrib.** (1999 est.): 35% manuf.; 18% managerial; 16% serv. **Unemployment** (1999): 4.3%. **Commercial banks** (2004): 3; **deposits**: $513 mil. **Savings institutions** (2004): 1; **deposits**: $9 mil. **Tourism expends.** (1997): $585 mil.

The people of the Northern Marianas are predominantly of Chamorro cultural extraction, although Carolinians and immigrants from other areas of E. Asia and Micronesia have also settled in the islands. English is among the several languages commonly spoken. Pursuant to the Covenant of 1976, which established the Northern Marianas as a commonwealth in political union with the U.S., most of the indigenous population and many domiciliaries of these islands achieved U.S. citizenship on Nov. 3, 1986, when the U.S. terminated its administration of the UN trusteeship as it affected the Northern Marianas. From July 18, 1947, the U.S. had administered the

Northern Marianas under a trusteeship agreement with the UN Security Council.

The Northern Mariana Islands has been self-governing since 1978, when a constitution drafted and adopted by the people became effective and a popularly elected bicameral legislature (2-year term), with offices of governor (4-year term) and lieut. governor, was inaugurated.

Website: www.gov.mp

Tourism website. www.mymarianas.com

Commonwealth of Puerto Rico (PR)

(Estado Libre Asociado de Puerto Rico)

People. Population (2004 est.): 3,894,855 (about 3.4 mil. more Puerto Ricans reside in the mainland U.S.). **Population growth rate:** (2003-2004): 0.4%. **Pop. density:** 1,137.4 per sq mi. . **Racial distribution** (2000): 80.5% white; 8.0% black; 0.2% Asian; 0.4% Native American/Nat. AK; 6.8% other; 2 or more races, 4.2%. **Hispanic pop.** (any race): 98.8%. **Languages:** Spanish and English are joint official languages.

Geography. Total area: 3,515 sq mi. **Land area:** 3,459 sq mi. **Location:** island lying between the Atlantic to the N and the Caribbean to the S; it is easternmost of the West Indies group called the Greater Antilles, of which Cuba, Hispaniola, and Jamaica are the larger islands. **Climate:** mild, with a mean temperature of 77°F. **Topography:** mountainous throughout three-fourths of its rectangular area, surrounded by a broken coastal plain; highest peak, Cerro de Punto, 4,390 ft. **Capital:** San Juan.

Economy. Chief industries: manufacturing, service, tourism. **Chief manuf. goods:** pharmaceuticals, apparel, electronics, food products. **Chief crops:** coffee, plantains, pineapples, sugarcane, bananas. **Livestock** (2004): 420,000 cattle; 100,000 hogs/pigs, (Dec. 2004) 1.7 mil. chickens (excl. broilers). **Nonfuel minerals** (est. 2000): $159 mil.; mostly portland cement, crushed stone. **Commercial fishing** (2000): $6.4 mil. **Chief ports:** San Juan, Ponce, Mayagüez. **Gross domestic product:** (2004 est.) $69.0 bil. **Employment distrib.** (May 2005): 29.5% govt.; 17.6% trade/trans./util.; 11.3% mfg.; 9.9% ed./health serv.; 9.8% prof./bus. serv. 6.7% leisure/hosp. 4.5% finance; 6.4% constr.; 2.2% other serv.; 2.2% info. **Unemployment** (mid-2005): 10.9%. **Per capita pers. income** (2004): $12,031. **Commercial banks** (2004): 12; **deposits**: $44.4 bil. **Lottery** (2004): total sales: $344.0 mil; net income: 128.8. **Principal airports at:** San Juan, Ponce, Mayagüez, Aguadilla. **Tourism expends.** (2002): $2.5 bil.

Federal govt. Fed. civ. employees (1997): 13,874. **Notable fed. facilities:** U.S. Naval Station at Roosevelt Roads; P.R. Natl. Guard Training Area at Camp Santiago, and at Ft. Allen, Juana Diaz; Sabana SECA Communications Ctr. (U.S. Navy); *U.S. Army Station at Ft. Buchanan.

Energy. Electricity production (2002): 22.1 bil kWh

Misc. data. Motto: Joannes Est Nomen Eius (John is his name). **Flower:** Maga. **Bird:** Reinita. **Tree:** Ceiba. **National anthem:** La Borinqueña.

History. Puerto Rico (or Borinquen, after the original Arawak Indian name, Boriquen) was visited by Columbus on his second voyage, Nov. 19, 1493. In 1508, the Spanish arrived.

Sugarcane was introduced, 1515, and slaves were imported 3 years later. Gold mining petered out, 1570. Spaniards fought off a series of British and Dutch attacks; slavery was abolished, 1873. Under the treaty of Paris, Puerto Rico was ceded to the U.S. after the Spanish-American War, 1898. In 1952 the people voted in favor of Commonwealth status.

The Commonwealth of Puerto Rico is a self-governing part of the U.S. with a primarily Hispanic culture. The island's citizens have virtually the same control over their internal affairs as do the 50 states of the U.S. However, they do not vote in national general elections, only in national primaries.

Puerto Rico is represented in the U.S. House of Representatives by a Resident Commissioner who has a voice but no vote, except in committees.

No federal income tax is collected from residents on income earned from local sources in Puerto Rico. Nevertheless, as part of the U.S. legal system, Puerto Rico is subject to the provisions of the U.S. Constitution; most federal laws apply as they do in the 50 states.

Puerto Rico's famous "Operation Bootstrap," begun in the late 1940s, succeeded in changing the island from "The Poorhouse of the Caribbean" to an area with the highest per capita income in Latin America. This program encouraged manufacturing and development of the tourist trade by selective tax exemption, low-interest loans, and other incentives. Despite the marked success of Puerto Rico's development efforts over an extended period of time, per capita income in Puerto Rico is low in comparison to that of the 50 states.

Tourist attractions. Ponce Museum of Art; Forts El Morro and San Cristobal; Old Walled City of San Juan; Arecibo Observatory; Cordillera Central and state parks; El Yunque Rain Forest; San Juan Cathedral; Porta Coeli Chapel and Museum of Religious Art, Interamerican Univ., San Germán; Condado Convention Center; Casa Blanca, Ponce de León family home, Puerto Rican Family Museum of 16th and 17th centuries, and Fine Arts Center all in San Juan.

Cultural facilities and events. Festival Casals classical music concerts, mid-June; Puerto Rico Symphony Orchestra at Music Conservatory; Botanical Garden and Museum of Anthropology, Art, and History at the University of Puerto Rico; Institute of Puerto Rican Culture, at the Dominican Convent; and many popular festivals.

Famous Puerto Ricans. Julia de Burgos, Marta Casals Istomin, Pablo Casals, José Celso Barbosa, Orlando Cepeda, Roberto Clemente, José de Diego, José Feliciano, Doña Felisa Rincón de Gautier, Luis A. Ferré, José Ferrer, Commodore Diégo E. Hernández, Miguel Hernández Agosto, Rafael Hernández (El Jibarito), Rafael Hernández Colón, Raúl Julía, René Marqués, Ricky Martin, Concha Meléndez, Rita Moreno, Luis Muñoz Marín, Luis Palés Matos, Adm. Horacio Rivero.

Chamber of Commerce. La Princesa Bldg., #2 Paseo la Princesa, Old San Juan, PR 00902; 800-866-7827. **Website:** www.gobierno.pr (site is in Spanish).

Tourism Website. www.gotopuertorico.com

Virgin Islands (VI)

St. John, St. Croix, St. Thomas

People. Population (July 2005 est.): 108,708. **Population growth rate** (2004-2005 est.): –0.07%. **Pop. density** (2005): 805.2 per sq mi. **Ethnic distrib.** (2000): 76.2% black, 13.1% white, 1.1% Asian, 6.1% other races, 3.5% two or more races. **Languages:** English (official), Spanish, Creole.

Geography. Total area: 136 sq mi. **Land area:** 135 sq mi. **Location:** 3 larger and 50 smaller islands and cays in the S and W of the V.I. group (British V.I. colony to the N and E), which is situated 70 mi E of Puerto Rico, located W of the Anegada Passage, a major channel connecting the Atlantic Ocean and the Caribbean Sea. **Climate:** subtropical; the sun tempered by gentle trade winds; humidity is low; average temperature, 78° F. **Topography:** St. Thomas is mainly a ridge of hills running E and W, and has little tillable land; St. Croix rises abruptly in the N but slopes to the S to flatlands and lagoons; St. John has steep, lofty hills and valleys with little level tillable land. **Capital:** Charlotte Amalie, St.Thomas.

Economy. Chief industries: tourism, rum distilling, alumina, petroleum refining, watch assembly, textiles, electronics, printing & publishing. **Chief manuf. goods:** rum, textiles, pharmaceuticals, perfumes, stone, glass & clay products. **Chief crops:** vegetables, horticulture, fruits and nuts. **Livestock** (2004): 8,000 cattle; 2,600 hogs/pigs, 35,000 chickens. **Minerals:** sand, gravel. **Chief ports:** Cruz Bay, St. John; Frederiksted and Christiansted, St. Croix; Charlotte Amalie, St. Thomas. **Principal internat. airports on:** St. Thomas, St. Croix. **Gross domestic product** (2002 est.): $2.5 bil. **Unemployment** (2003 est.): 9.3%. **Per capita income** (2001 est.): $19,000. **Commercial banks** (2004): 4; **deposits**: $1.7 bil.

Energy. Electricity production (2002): 1.0 bil. kWh

Misc. data. Flower: Yellow elder or yellow trumpet, local designation Ginger Thomas. **Bird:** Yellow breast. **Song:** Virgin Islands March.

History. The islands were visited by Columbus in 1493. Spanish forces, 1555, defeated the Caribes and claimed the territory; by 1596 the native population was annihilated. First permanent settlement in the U.S. territory, 1672, by the Danes; U.S. purchased the islands, 1917, for defense purposes.

The Virgin Islands has a republican form of government, headed by a governor and lieut. governor elected, since 1970, by popular vote for 4-year terms. There is a 15-member unicameral legislature, elected by popular vote for a 2-year term. Residents of the V.I. have been U.S. citizens since 1927. Since 1973 they have elected a delegate to the U.S. House of Representatives, who has a voice but no vote, except in committees.

Tourist attractions. Magens Bay, St. Thomas; duty-free shopping; Virgin Islands Natl. Park, beaches, Indian relics, and evidence of colonial Danes.

Tourist information. Dept. of Economic Development & Agriculture: St. Thomas, P.O. Box 6400, St. Thomas, VI 00804; St. Croix, P.O. Box 4535, Christiansted, St. Croix 00820. **Website:** www.usvitourism.vi

Website. www.usvi.net

Other Islands

Navassa lies between Jamaica and Haiti, 100 mi south of Guantanamo Bay, Cuba, in the Caribbean; it covers about 2 sq mi, is reserved by the U.S. for a lighthouse, and is uninhabited. It is administered by the U.S. Coast Guard.

Wake Atoll, and its neighboring atolls, **Wilkes** and **Peale,** lie in the Pacific Ocean on the direct route from Hawaii to Hong Kong, about 2,300 mi W of Honolulu and 1,290 mi E of Guam. The group is 4.5 mi long, 1.5 mi wide, and totals less than 3 sq mi in land area. The U.S. flag was hoisted over Wake Atoll, July 4, 1898; formal possession taken Jan. 17, 1899. Wake was administered by the U.S. Air Force, 1972-94. The population consists of about 200 persons.

Midway Atoll, acquired in 1867, consists of 2 atolls, **Sand** and **Eastern,** in N Pacific 1,150 mi. NW of Honolulu, with an area of about 2 sq mi, administered by the U.S. Navy. There is no indigenous population; total pop. is about 450. **Johnston Atoll,** 717 mi WSW of Honolulu, area 1 sq mi, is operated by the Defense Nuclear Agency, and the Fish and Wildlife Service, U.S. Dept. of the Interior; its population is about 396. **Kingman Reef,** 920 mi S of Hawaii, is under Navy control. **Howland, Jarvis,** and **Baker Islands,** 1,400-1,650 mi SW of Honolulu, uninhabited since World War II, are under the Interior Dept. **Palmyra** is an atoll about 1,000 mi S of Hawaii, area, 5 sq mi. Privately owned, it is under the Interior Dept.

WASHINGTON, DC, CAPITAL OF THE U.S.

Most attractions are free. All times are subject to change. For more details call the Washington, DC, Convention and Visitors Association at 1-800-422-8644, or check out the website at: www.washington.org

Bureau of Engraving and Printing

The **Bureau of Engraving and Printing** of the U.S. Treasury Dept. is the headquarters for the making of U.S. paper money. Public tours are offered Mon.-Fri., 9-10:45 AM, 12:30-2 PM, except on federal holidays. 14th and C Sts. SW. Phone: 866-874-2330.

Website. www.moneyfactory.com

Capitol

The **United States Capitol** was originally designed by Dr. William Thornton, an amateur architect, who submitted a plan in 1793 that won him $500 and a city lot. Three other architects designed or supervised the construction of the Capitol before its completion.

The present cast iron dome at its greatest exterior height measures 135 ft 5 in. and is topped by the bronze Statue of Freedom, which stands 19½ ft and weighs 14,985 lb. On its base are the words *E Pluribus Unum* ("Out of Many, One").

The Capitol is open to the public, for guided tours only, from 9 AM to 4:30 PM. It is closed Jan. 1, Thanksgiving Day, and Dec. 25.

To observe debate while Congress is in session, those living in the U.S. may obtain tickets from their U.S. representative or senator. Visitors from other countries may obtain passes at the Capitol. Between Constitution & Independence Aves., at Pennsylvania Ave. Phone: 202-225-6827.

Website. www.aoc.gov

Federal Bureau of Investigation

The **Federal Bureau of Investigation** offers guided one-hour tours of its headquarters. Visitors learn about the history of the FBI and see weapons confiscated from famous gangsters, photos of most-wanted fugitives, the DNA laboratory, goods forfeited/seized in narcotics operations, and a sharpshooting demonstration.

Tours have been suspended for building renovation. J. Edgar Hoover Bldg., Pennsylvania Ave., between 9th and 10th Sts. NW. Phone: 202-324-3447.

Website. www.fbi.gov

Folger Shakespeare Library

The **Folger Shakespeare Library,** on Capitol Hill, is a research institution holding rare books and manuscripts of the Renaissance period and the largest collection of Shakespearean materials in the world. Exhibit may be visited Mon.-Sat., 10 AM-4 PM, 201 E. Capitol St., SE , Phone: 202-544-4600.

Website. www.folger.edu

Holocaust Memorial Museum

The **U.S. Holocaust Memorial Museum** opened on Apr. 21, 1993. The museum documents the events of the Holocaust through permanent and temporary displays, interactive videos, and special lectures. The permanent exhibition is not recommended for children under age 11.

The museum is open daily, 10 AM-5:30 PM, except Yom Kippur and Dec. 25, and extended hours Tues. and Thurs. (10 AM-7:50 PM) from Apr.-June. A limited number of free tickets are available at the door; advance tickets may be ordered for a small fee at 800-400-9373. 100 Raoul Wallenberg Pl. SW. Phone: 202-488-0400.

Website. www.ushmm.org

Jefferson Memorial

Dedicated in 1943, the **Thomas Jefferson Memorial** stands on the south shore of the Tidal Basin in West Potomac Park. It is a circular stone structure that combines architectural elements of the dome of the Pantheon in Rome and the rotunda designed by Jefferson for the Univ. of Virginia.

The memorial is open daily, 8 AM-midnight; closed Dec. 25. Has elevator and curb ramps for handicapped. Phone: 202-426-6841.

Website. www.nps.gov/thje

John F. Kennedy Center

The **John F. Kennedy Center for the Performing Arts** opened Sept. 8, 1971. Designed by Edward Durell Stone, it includes an opera house, a concert hall, several theaters, 2 restaurants, and a library. Free tours are available Mon.-Fri., 10 AM-5 PM and Sat. & Sun., 10 AM-1 PM. 2700 F St. NW. Phone: 202-467-4600, or 1-800-444-1324.

Website. www.kennedy-center.org

Korean War Veterans Memorial

Dedicated on July 27, 1995, the **Korean War Veterans Memorial** honors Americans who served in the Korean War. Situated at the west end of the Mall, the triangular-shaped stone and steel memorial features a multiservice formation of 19 combat-ready troops clad in ponchos with the wind at their back. A granite wall, with images of men and women who served, juts into a pool of water, the Pool of Remembrance.

The memorial is open 8 AM-11:45 pm; closed Dec. 25. French Dr., SW across from Lincoln Memorial. Phone: 202-426-6841.

Website. www.nps.gov/kwvm

Library of Congress

Established by and for Congress in 1800, the **Library of Congress** extends its services to other government agencies and libraries, scholars, and the general public, and now serves as the national library. It contains over 80 mil. items in 470 languages.

Exhibit halls are open to the public Mon.-Fri., 8:30 AM-9:30 PM; Sat., 8:30 AM-6:30 PM. The Library is closed all federal holidays. 101 Independence Ave., SE. Phone: 202-707-8000.

Website. www.loc.gov

Lincoln Memorial

Designed by Henry Bacon, the **Lincoln Memorial** in West Potomac Park is a large marble hall enclosing a statue of Abraham Lincoln seated on an armchair. The memorial was dedicated May 30, 1922. The statue was designed by Daniel Chester French and sculpted by French and the Piccirilli brothers. The text of the Gettysburg Address is in the south chamber; that of Lincoln's Second Inaugural speech is in the north chamber. Each is engraved on a stone tablet.

The memorial is open daily 8 AM-midnight, and is wheelchair-accessible. W. Potomac Park at 23rd St. NW. Phone: 202-426-6841.

Website. www.nps.gov/linc

National Archives and Records

Original copies of the Declaration of Independence, the Constitution, and the Bill of Rights are on display in the **National Archives** Exhibition Hall. The National Archives also holds other valuable U.S. government records and historic maps, photographs, and manuscripts. Central Research and Microfilm Research Rooms are also available to the public for genealogical research.

Exhibition Hall open daily 10 AM-5:30PM (later in spring and summer). 7th & Pennsylvania Ave. NW. Phone: 866-325-7208.

Website. www.archives.gov

National Gallery of Art

The **National Gallery of Art** was established by Congress, Mar. 24, 1937, and opened Mar. 17, 1941. The original West building was designed by John Russell Pope. The East building, opened in 1978, was designed by I. M. Pei. Open daily, Mon.-Sat. 10 AM-5 PM, Sunday 11 AM-6 PM. Closed Jan. 1 and Dec. 25. 4th & Constitution Ave NW. Phone: 202-737-4215.

Website. www.nga.gov

Franklin Delano Roosevelt Memorial

Opened May 2, 1997, the **FDR Memorial** features 9 bronze sculptural ensembles depicting FDR, Eleanor Roosevelt, and events from the Great Depression and World War II. This 7.5-acre memorial is located near the Tidal Basin in a park-like setting and is wheelchair accessible.

Grounds, staffed daily, 8 AM-midnight, except Dec. 25. 1850 W. Basin Dr. SW. Phone: 202-426-6841.

Website. www.nps.gov/fdrm

Smithsonian Institution

The **Smithsonian Institution,** established in 1846, is the world's largest museum complex and consists of 14 museums and the National Zoo. It holds some 100 mil artifacts and specimens in its trust. The **Smithsonian Information Center** is located in "the Castle" on the Mall. Also on the Mall are the **National Museum of American History,** the **National Museum of Natural History,** the **National Air and Space Museum,** the **Hirshhorn Museum and Sculpture Garden,** the **Arthur M. Sackler Gallery,** the **National Museum of African Art,** the **Freer Gallery of Art,** and the **Arts and Industries Building.** Near the Sackler Gallery is the **Enid A. Haupt Garden.** Located nearby are the **National Postal Museum,** the **National Museum of American Art,** the **National Portrait Gallery,** and the **Renwick Gallery.** Farther away, at 1901 Fort Place SE, is the **Anacostia Museum.**

Most museums are open daily, except Dec. 25, 10 AM-5:30 PM. Phone: 202-357-2020.

Website. www.si.edu

Vietnam Veterans Memorial

Originally dedicated on Nov. 13, 1982, the **Vietnam Veterans Memorial** recognizes the men and women who served in the armed forces in the Vietnam War. The names of more than 58,000 Americans who lost their lives or remain missing are inscribed on a V-shaped black-granite wall, designed by Maya Ying Lin.

Since 1982, 2 additions have been made to the Memorial. The 1st, dedicated on Nov. 11, 1984, is the Frederick Hart sculpture *Three Servicemen*. On Nov. 11, 1993, the Vietnam Women's Memorial, designed by Glenna Goodacre, was dedicated, honoring the more than 11,500 women who served in Vietnam.

The memorial is open 8 AM-midnight daily. Constitution Ave. & Bacon Dr. NW. Phone: 202-426-6841.

Website. www.nps.gov/vive

Washington Monument

The **Washington Monument,** dedicated in 1885, is a tapering shaft, or obelisk, of white marble, 555 ft, 5 $^1/_8$ inches in height and 55 ft, 1½ in. square at base. Eight small windows, 2 on each side, are located at the 500-ft level.

Open daily (except Dec. 25), 9 AM-4:45 PM. Free timed passes are available; passes are available in advance for a small fee. 15th & Constitution Ave. NW. Phone: 202-426-6841.

Website. www.nps.gov/wash

White House

The **White House,** the President's residence, stands on 18 acres on the south side of Pennsylvania Ave., between the Treasury and the old Executive Office Building. The walls are of sandstone, quarried at Aquia Creek, VA. On Aug. 24, 1814, during Madison's administration, the house was burned by the British, but it was rebuilt by Oct. 1817 and painted white, giving rise to the name "White House."

The White House is normally open for free self-guided tours Tues.-Sat., 7:30 AM-12:30 pm. (Tour requests must be made at least one month in advance through your member of Congress.) Only the public rooms on the ground floor and state floor may be visited. 1600 Pennsylvania Ave. The White House Visitor Center at 1450 Pennsylvania Ave. is open daily 7:30 AM - 4 PM. Phone: 202-456-7041.

Website. www.whitehouse.gov

National World War II Memorial

The **National WWII Memorial** is dedicated to the approx. 16 mil. veterans who served and the more than 400,000 who died in the war. It rests on 7.4 acres of land at the east end of the reflecting pool on the Mall. The memorial opened on April 29, 2004, and was dedicated on May 29.

At the north and south entrances are 43-ft. archways, representing the Atlantic and Pacific theaters. Inside the grounds is a large, oval plaza with a wall of 4,000 gold stars; each represents 100 American deaths. Fifty-six pillars ringing the center represent the states, territories, and District of Columbia. There is also a garden enclosed by a stone wall (called the "Circle of Remembrance").

The memorial is wheelchair-accessible and open daily, 24 hours a day, except Dec. 25. Located on 17th St. between Constitution and Independence Aves. Phone: 202-619-7222.

Website. www.nps.gov/nwwm

Attractions Near Washington, DC

Arlington National Cemetery

Arlington National Cemetery, on the former Custis-Lee estate in Arlington, VA, is the site of the **Tomb of the Unknowns** and is the final resting place of Pres. John F. Kennedy and his wife, Jacqueline Bouvier Kennedy Onassis. An eternal flame burns over the grave site. Many other famous Americans are buried at Arlington, as well as more than 200,000 U.S. military personnel, from every major war.

North of the National Cemetery stands the **U.S. Marine Corps War Memorial**, also known as Iwo Jima. The memorial is a bronze statue of the raising of the U.S. flag on Mt. Suribachi, Feb. 23, 1945, during World War II, executed by Felix de Weldon from the photograph by Joe Rosenthal.

On the southern side of the Memorial Bridge, near the cemetery entrance, a memorial honoring the women in the military was dedicated, Oct. 18, 1997. The **Women in Military Service for America Memorial** is a granite monument, 30 ft. high and 226 ft. in diameter, with the Great Seal of the U.S. in the center.

Open daily, 8 AM-5 PM (8 AM-7 PM., Apr.-Sept.), Arlington, VA. Phone: 703-607-8000.

Website. www.arlingtoncemetery.org

Mount Vernon

Mount Vernon, George Washington's estate, is on the south bank of the Potomac R., 16 mi from Washington, DC, in northern Virginia. The present house is an enlargement of one apparently built on the site by Augustine Washington, who lived there 1735-38. His son Lawrence came there in 1743; he died in 1752 and was succeeded as proprietor by his half-brother, George Washington. The estate has been restored to its 18th-century appearance and includes many original furnishings. Washington and his wife, Martha, are buried on the grounds.

Open 365 days, 8 AM-5 PM, Apr.-Aug., 9 AM-5 PM, Sept., Oct., Mar.; 9 AM-4 PM, Nov.-Feb. Phone: 703-780-2000, or 1-800-429-1520. Admission: adults $11, seniors (62+) $10.50, children (6-11) $5, age 5 and under free.

Website. www.mountvernon.org

The Pentagon

The **Pentagon,** headquarters of the Dept. of Defense, is the largest office building in the U.S. Situated in Arlington, VA, it houses more than 23,000 employees in offices occupying 3,705,793 sq ft. The building was severely damaged when struck by a plane Sept. 11, 2001.

Tours available to schools, educational organizations, and other select groups by reservation only. Arlington, VA (I-395 South to Boundary Channel Drive exit). Pentagon tour office: 703-697-1776.

Website. www.defenselink.mil/pubs/pentagon

AFGHANISTAN
ALBANIA
ALGERIA
ANDORRA
ANGOLA
ANTIGUA AND BARBUDA
ARGENTINA
ARMENIA
AUSTRALIA
AUSTRIA
AZERBAIJAN
THE BAHAMAS
BAHRAIN
BANGLADESH
BARBADOS
BELARUS
BELGIUM
BELIZE
BENIN
BHUTAN
BOLIVIA
BOSNIA AND HERZEGOVINA
BOTSWANA
BRAZIL
BRUNEI
BULGARIA
BURKINA FASO
BURUNDI
CAMBODIA
CAMEROON
CANADA
CAPE VERDE
CENTRAL AFRICAN REPUBLIC
CHAD
CHILE
CHINA
COLOMBIA
COMOROS
CONGO, DEM. REP. OF THE
CONGO REPUBLIC
COSTA RICA
CÔTE D'IVOIRE
CROATIA
CUBA
CYPRUS
CZECH REPUBLIC
DENMARK
DJIBOUTI
DOMINICA
DOMINICAN REPUBLIC
ECUADOR
EGYPT
EL SALVADOR
EQUATORIAL GUINEA
ERITREA

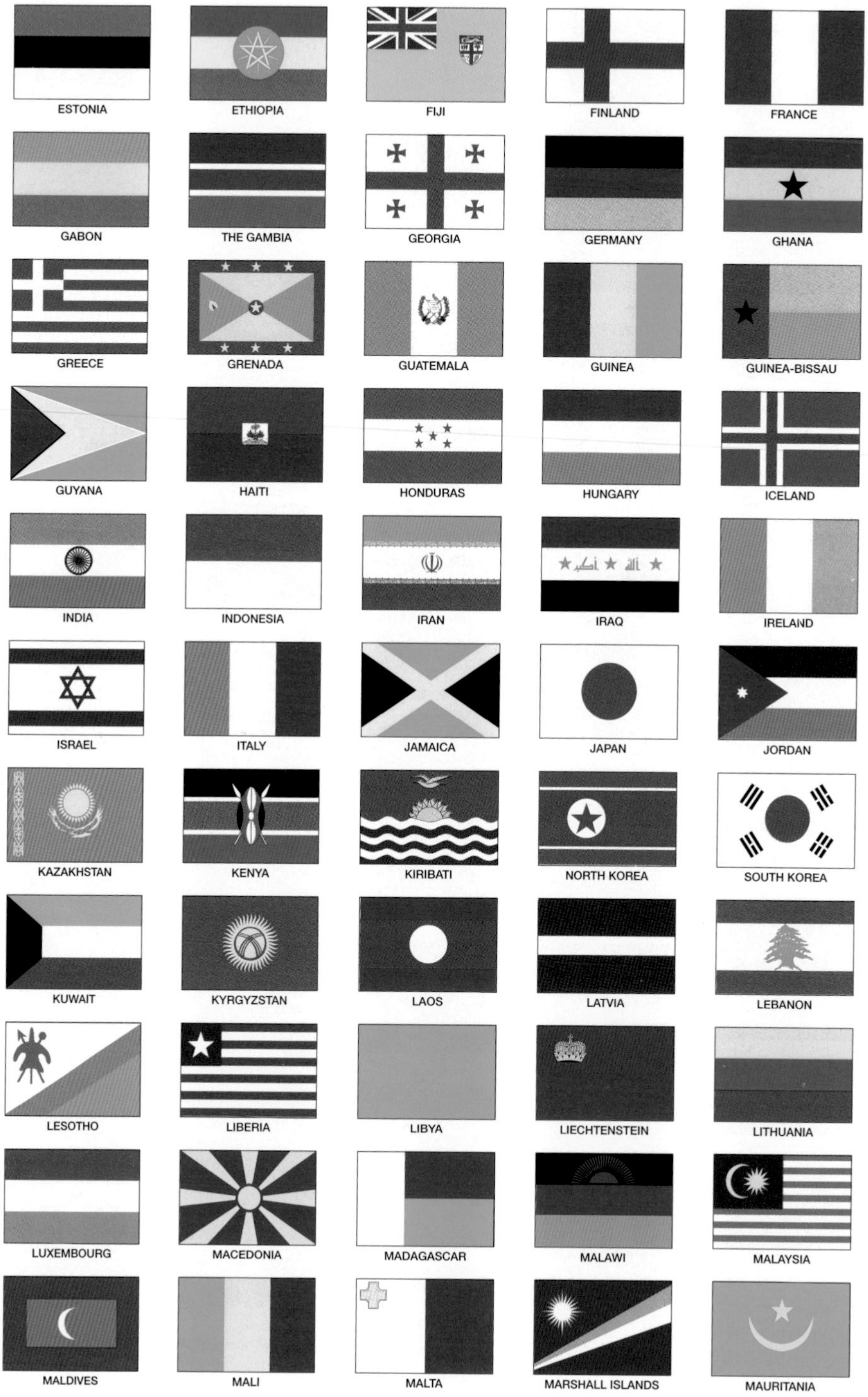
ESTONIA
ETHIOPIA
FIJI
FINLAND
FRANCE
GABON
THE GAMBIA
GEORGIA
GERMANY
GHANA
GREECE
GRENADA
GUATEMALA
GUINEA
GUINEA-BISSAU
GUYANA
HAITI
HONDURAS
HUNGARY
ICELAND
INDIA
INDONESIA
IRAN
IRAQ
IRELAND
ISRAEL
ITALY
JAMAICA
JAPAN
JORDAN
KAZAKHSTAN
KENYA
KIRIBATI
NORTH KOREA
SOUTH KOREA
KUWAIT
KYRGYZSTAN
LAOS
LATVIA
LEBANON
LESOTHO
LIBERIA
LIBYA
LIECHTENSTEIN
LITHUANIA
LUXEMBOURG
MACEDONIA
MADAGASCAR
MALAWI
MALAYSIA
MALDIVES
MALI
MALTA
MARSHALL ISLANDS
MAURITANIA

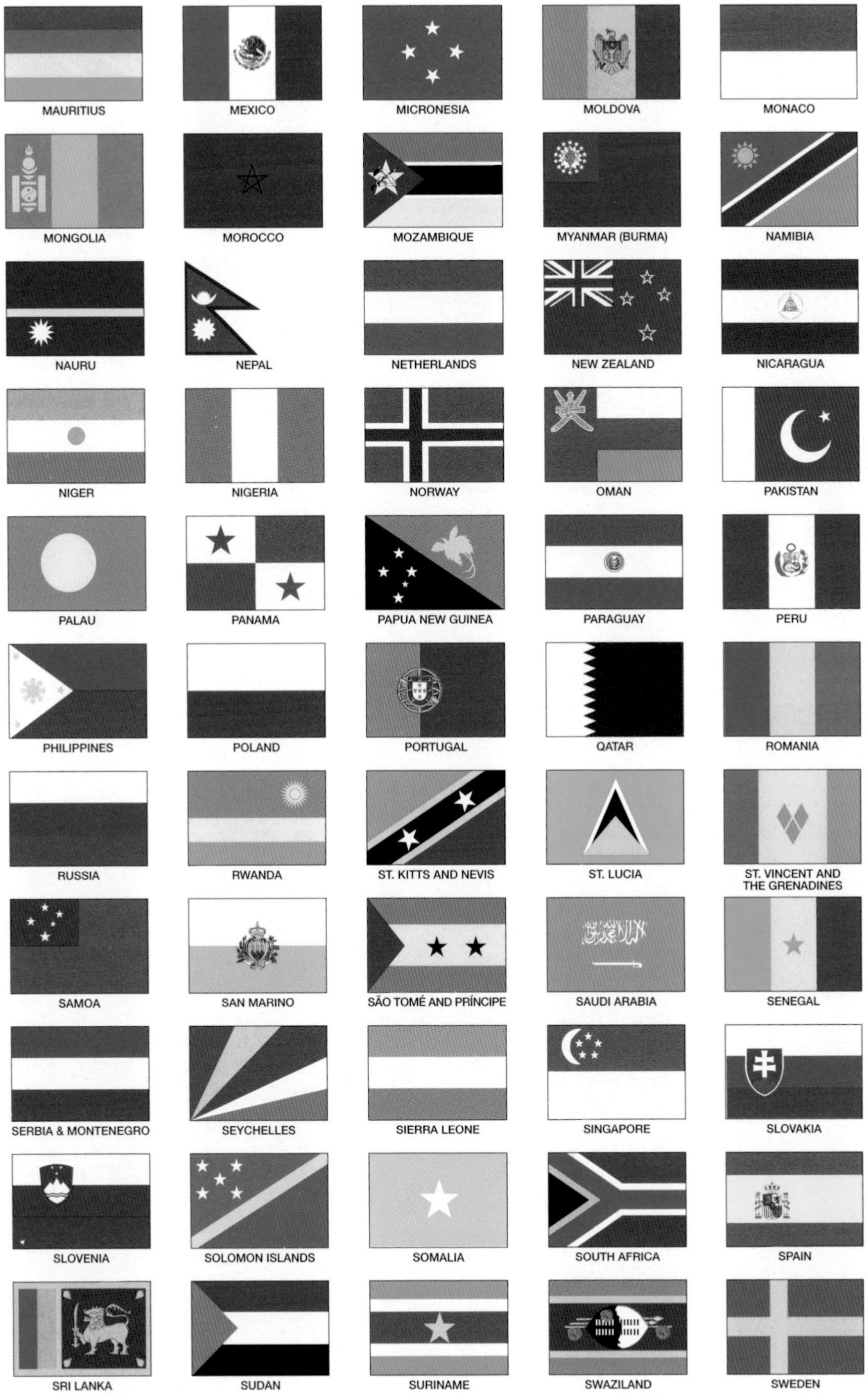
MAURITIUS
MEXICO
MICRONESIA
MOLDOVA
MONACO
MONGOLIA
MOROCCO
MOZAMBIQUE
MYANMAR (BURMA)
NAMIBIA
NAURU
NEPAL
NETHERLANDS
NEW ZEALAND
NICARAGUA
NIGER
NIGERIA
NORWAY
OMAN
PAKISTAN
PALAU
PANAMA
PAPUA NEW GUINEA
PARAGUAY
PERU
PHILIPPINES
POLAND
PORTUGAL
QATAR
ROMANIA
RUSSIA
RWANDA
ST. KITTS AND NEVIS
ST. LUCIA
ST. VINCENT AND THE GRENADINES
SAMOA
SAN MARINO
SÃO TOMÉ AND PRÍNCIPE
SAUDI ARABIA
SENEGAL
SERBIA & MONTENEGRO
SEYCHELLES
SIERRA LEONE
SINGAPORE
SLOVAKIA
SLOVENIA
SOLOMON ISLANDS
SOMALIA
SOUTH AFRICA
SPAIN
SRI LANKA
SUDAN
SURINAME
SWAZILAND
SWEDEN

SWITZERLAND

SYRIA

TAIWAN

TAJIKISTAN

TANZANIA

THAILAND

TIMOR-LESTE
EAST TIMOR

TOGO

TONGA

TRINIDAD AND TOBAGO

TUNISIA

TURKEY

TURKMENISTAN

TUVALU

UGANDA

UKRAINE

UNITED ARAB EMIRATES

UNITED KINGDOM

UNITED STATES

URUGUAY

UZBEKISTAN

VANUATU

VATICAN CITY

VENEZUELA

VIETNAM

YEMEN

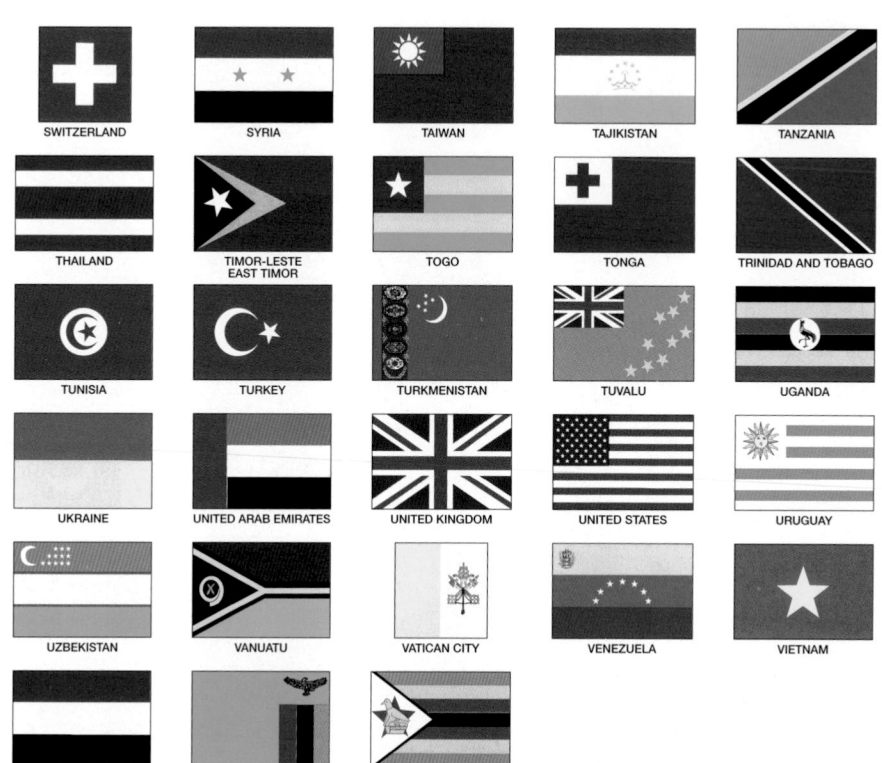

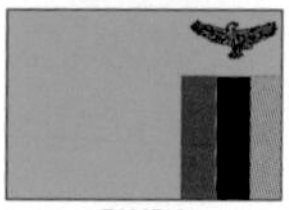
ZAMBIA

ZIMBABWE

INTERNATIONAL TIME ZONES

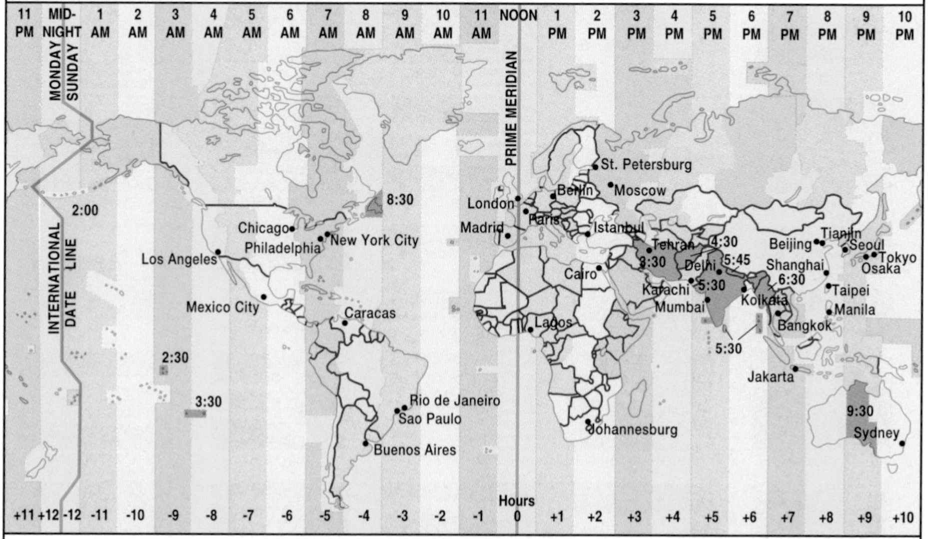

The world is divided into 24 time zones, each 15° longitude wide. The longitudinal meridian passing through Greenwich, England, is the starting point, and is called the *prime meridian.* The 12th zone is divided by the 180th meridian (International Date Line). When the line is crossed going west, the date is advanced one day; when crossed going east, the date becomes a day earlier.

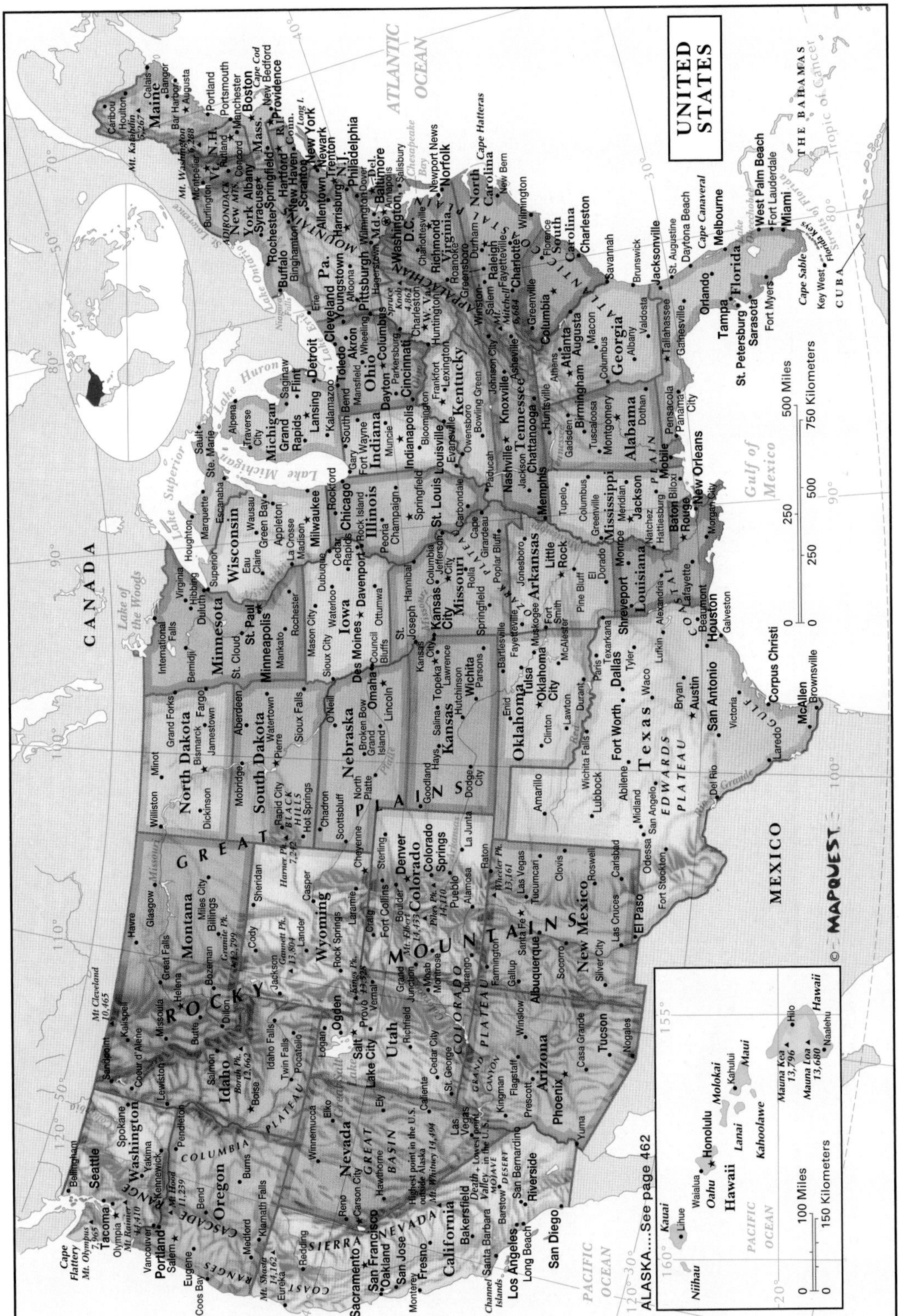
UNITED STATES
CANADA
MEXICO
ATLANTIC OCEAN
PACIFIC OCEAN
Gulf of Mexico
THE BAHAMAS
CUBA
Tropic of Cancer
Lake Superior
Lake Michigan
Lake Huron
Lake Erie
Lake Ontario
Lake of the Woods
Washington
Oregon
California
Nevada
Idaho
Montana
Wyoming
Utah
Arizona
Colorado
New Mexico
North Dakota
South Dakota
Nebraska
Kansas
Oklahoma
Texas
Minnesota
Iowa
Missouri
Arkansas
Louisiana
Wisconsin
Illinois
Michigan
Indiana
Ohio
Kentucky
Tennessee
Mississippi
Alabama
Georgia
Florida
South Carolina
North Carolina
Virginia
W. Va.
Pa.
New York
Vt.
N.H.
Maine
Mass.
R.I.
Conn.
N.J.
Del.
Md.
D.C.
ROCKY MOUNTAINS
GREAT PLAINS
CASCADE RANGE
COAST RANGES
SIERRA NEVADA
COLUMBIA PLATEAU
GREAT BASIN
COLORADO PLATEAU
EDWARDS PLATEAU
OZARK PLATEAU
APPALACHIAN MOUNTAINS
ATLANTIC COASTAL PLAIN
GULF COASTAL PLAIN
ALASKA....See page 462
Hawaii
PACIFIC OCEAN
Niihau
Kauai
Oahu
Honolulu
Molokai
Lanai
Maui
Kahoolawe
Mauna Kea 13,796
Mauna Loa 13,680
0 100 Miles
0 150 Kilometers
0 250 500 Miles
0 250 500 750 Kilometers
© MAPQUEST

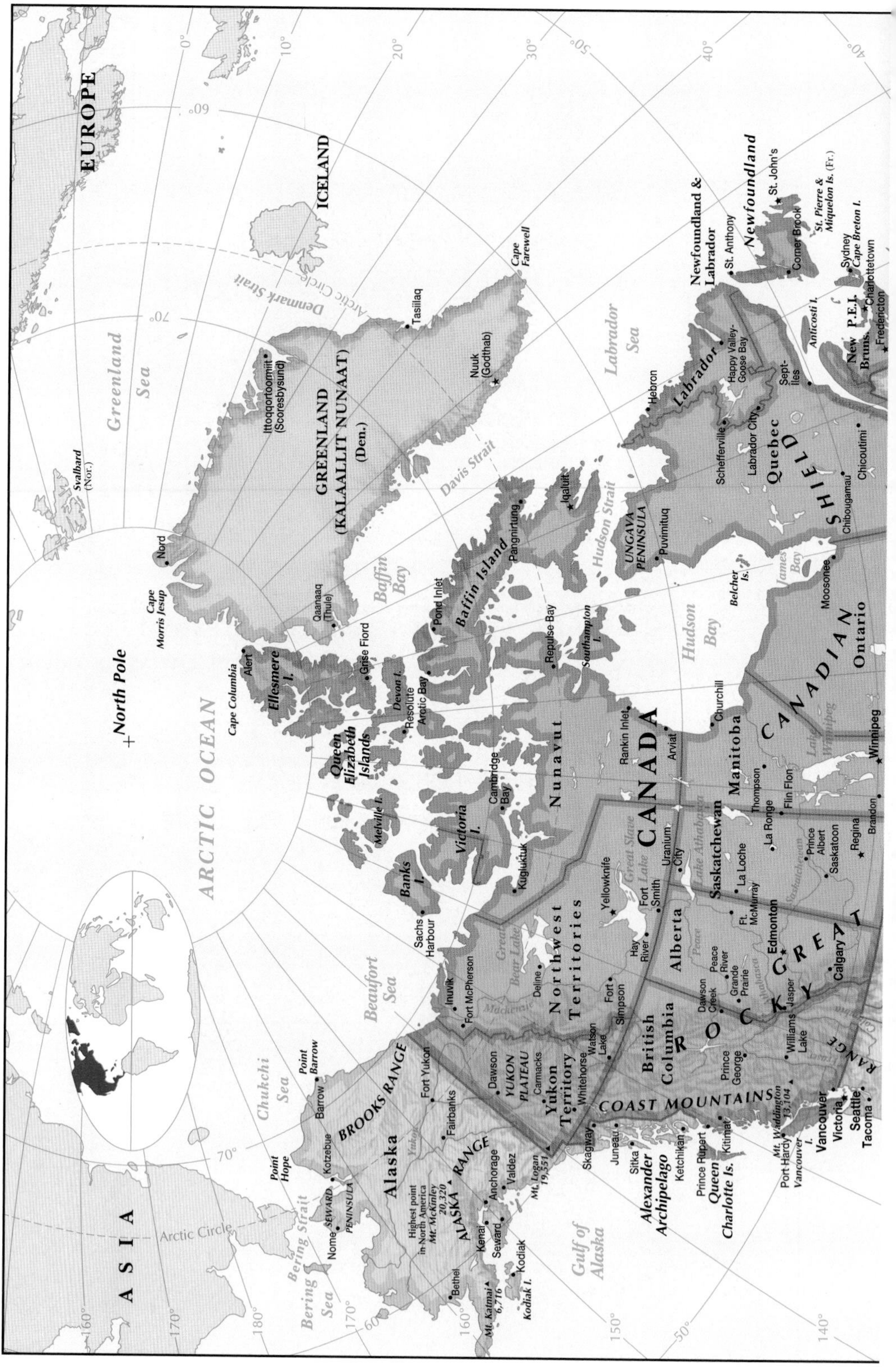
EUROPE
ICELAND
Greenland Sea
Svalbard (Nor.)
GREENLAND (KALAALLIT NUNAAT) (Den.)
Ittoqqortoormiit (Scoresbysund)
Tasiilaq
Cape Farewell
Denmark Strait
Arctic Circle
Nuuk (Godthab)
Davis Strait
Labrador Sea
Nord
Cape Morris Jesup
North Pole
ARCTIC OCEAN
Cape Columbia
Alert
Ellesmere I.
Qaanaaq (Thule)
Baffin Bay
Grise Fiord
Devon I.
Resolute
Arctic Bay
Pond Inlet
Baffin Island
Pangnirtung
Iqaluit
Hudson Strait
UNGAVA PENINSULA
Puvirnituq
Hebron
Labrador
Newfoundland & Labrador
St. Anthony
Newfoundland
St. John's
Corner Brook
St. Pierre & Miquelon Is. (Fr.)
Sydney
Cape Breton I.
Charlottetown
Fredericton
New Bruns.
P.E.I.
Anticosti I.
Sept-Iles
Happy Valley-Goose Bay
Schefferville
Labrador City
Quebec
SHIELD
Chibougamau
Chicoutimi
James Bay
Belcher Is.
Moosonee
Hudson Bay
Southampton I.
Repulse Bay
Queen Elizabeth Islands
Melville I.
Banks I.
Victoria I.
Cambridge Bay
Nunavut
Rankin Inlet
CANADA
Arviat
Churchill
Manitoba
CANADIAN
Ontario
Lake Winnipeg
Winnipeg
Thompson
Flin Flon
Brandon
Regina
Saskatoon
Prince Albert
La Ronge
La Loche
Saskatchewan
Lake Athabasca
Uranium City
Fort Smith
Great Slave Lake
Yellowknife
Kugluktuk
Sachs Harbour
Beaufort Sea
Inuvik
Fort McPherson
Great Bear Lake
Deline
Northwest Territories
Hay River
Fort Simpson
Alberta
Ft. McMurray
Edmonton
Calgary
Peace River
Grande Prairie
Dawson Creek
Jasper
ROCKY
GREAT
British Columbia
Prince George
Williams Lake
Watson Lake
Whitehorse
Yukon Territory
Carmacks
Dawson
YUKON PLATEAU
Fort Yukon
Fairbanks
Alaska
BROOKS RANGE
Point Barrow
Barrow
Chukchi Sea
Point Hope
Kotzebue
SEWARD PENINSULA
Nome
Bering Strait
Bering Sea
ASIA
Bethel
Mt. Katmai 6,716
Kodiak I.
Kodiak
Kenai
Seward
Anchorage
Valdez
Highest point in North America Mt. McKinley 20,320
ALASKA RANGE
Mt. Logan 19,551
Gulf of Alaska
Skagway
Juneau
Sitka
Alexander Archipelago
Ketchikan
Prince Rupert
Queen Charlotte Is.
Kitimat
Mt. Waddington 13,104
Port Hardy
Vancouver I.
Vancouver
Victoria
Seattle
Tacoma
COAST MOUNTAINS
RANGE

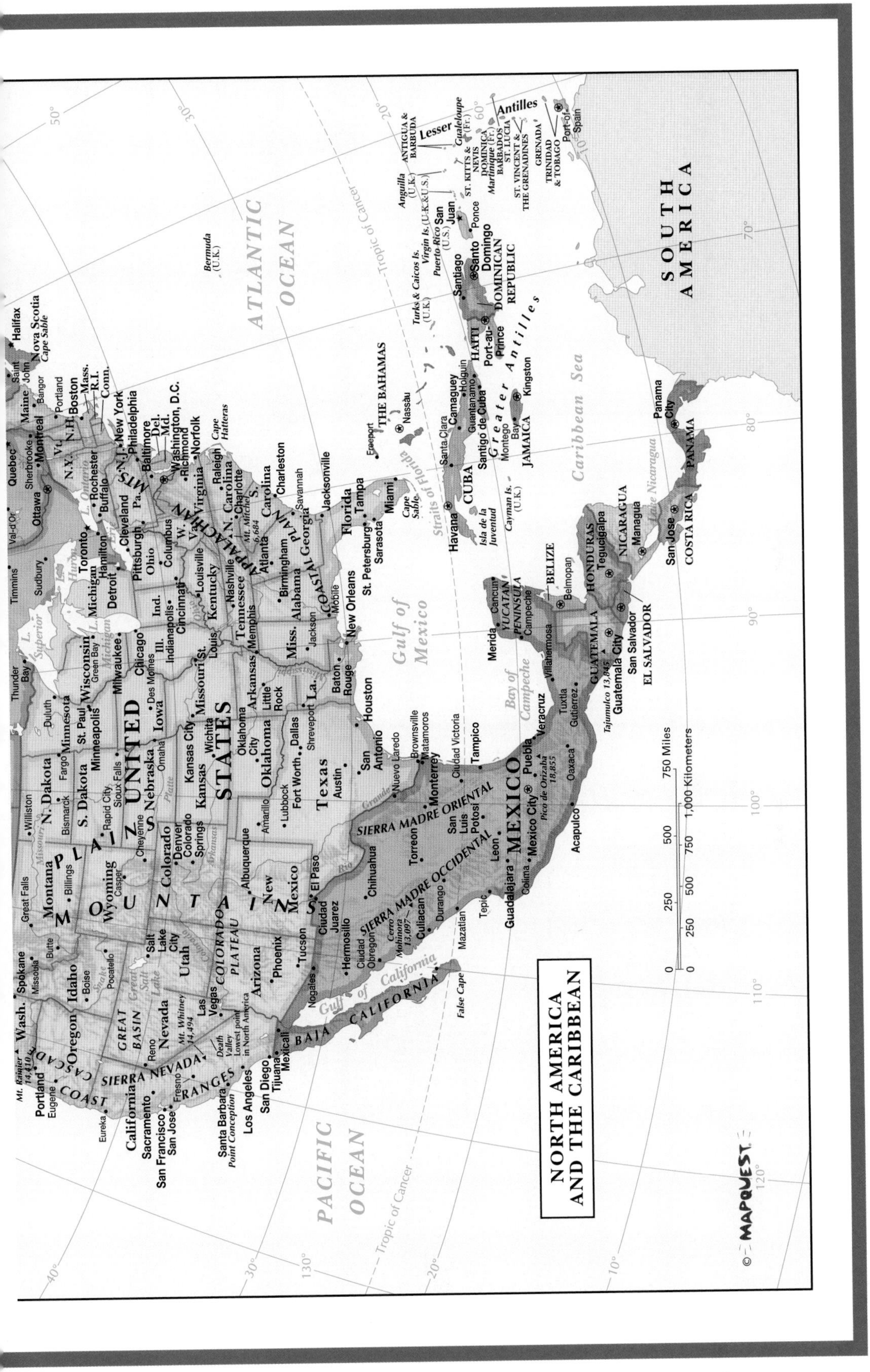

NORTH AMERICA AND THE CARIBBEAN
ATLANTIC OCEAN
PACIFIC OCEAN
Gulf of Mexico
Caribbean Sea
Bay of Campeche
Gulf of California
Tropic of Cancer
UNITED STATES
MEXICO
SOUTH AMERICA
CUBA
THE BAHAMAS
HAITI
DOMINICAN REPUBLIC
JAMAICA
BELIZE
GUATEMALA
HONDURAS
EL SALVADOR
NICARAGUA
COSTA RICA
PANAMA
Greater Antilles
Lesser Antilles
ROCKY MOUNTAINS
GREAT PLAINS
COASTAL PLAIN
APPALACHIAN MTS.
SIERRA NEVADA
COAST RANGES
CASCADE
GREAT BASIN
COLORADO PLATEAU
SIERRA MADRE ORIENTAL
SIERRA MADRE OCCIDENTAL
BAJA CALIFORNIA
YUCATAN PENINSULA
Bermuda (U.K.)
Turks & Caicos Is. (U.K.)
Puerto Rico
Virgin Is. (U.K.&U.S.)
Anguilla (U.K.)
ANTIGUA & BARBUDA
Guadeloupe (Fr.)
ST. KITTS & NEVIS
DOMINICA
Martinique (Fr.)
ST. LUCIA
BARBADOS
ST. VINCENT & THE GRENADINES
GRENADA
TRINIDAD & TOBAGO
Cayman Is. (U.K.)
Isla de la Juventud
Straits of Florida
Mt. Rainier 14,410
Mt. Whitney 14,494
Death Valley Lowest point in North America
Mt. Mitchell 6,684
Pico de Orizaba 18,855
Cerro Mohinora 13,097
Tajumulco 13,845
Cape Hatteras
Cape Sable
Point Conception
False Cape
0 250 500 750 Miles
0 250 500 750 1,000 Kilometers
© MAPQUEST

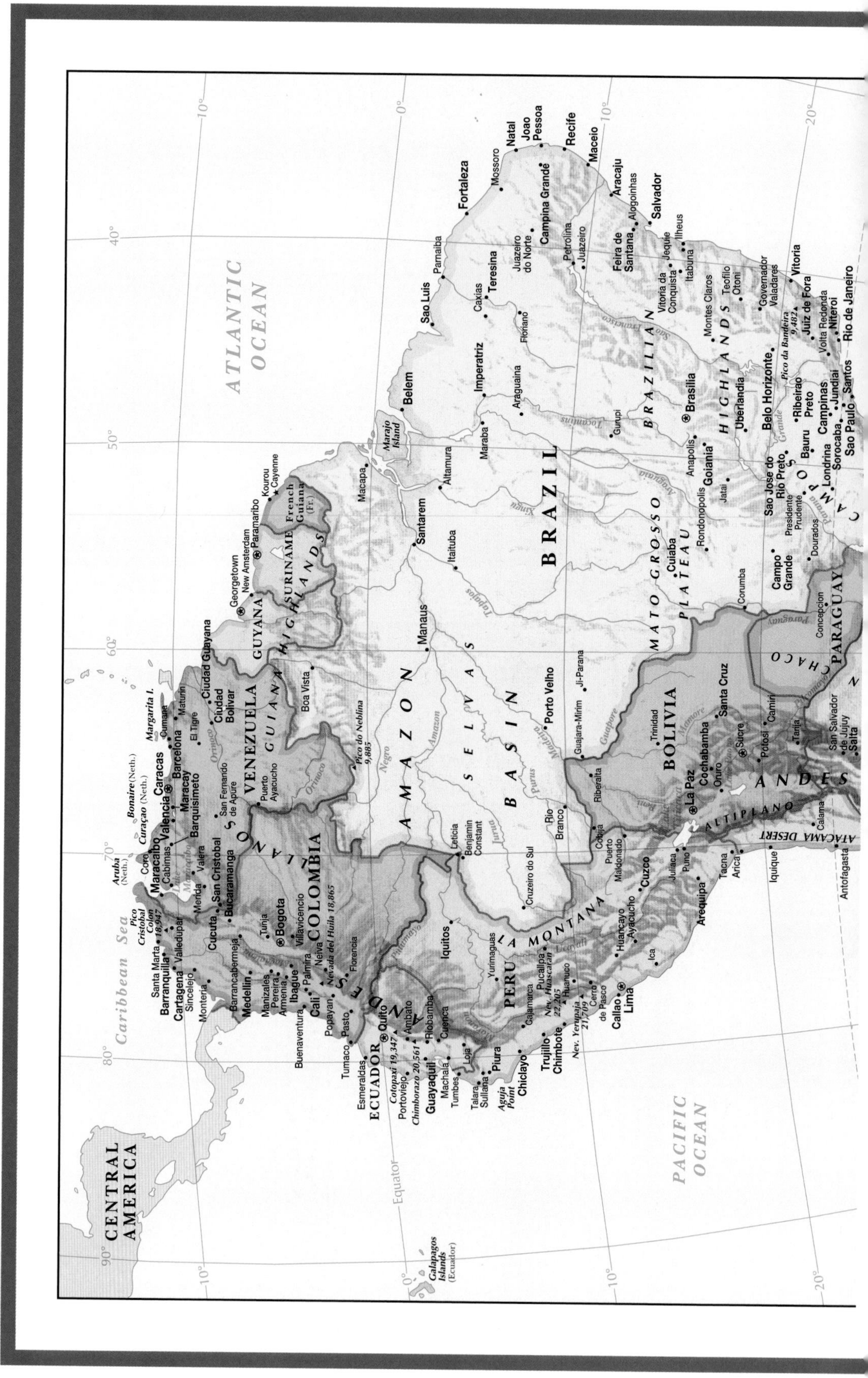
CENTRAL AMERICA
Caribbean Sea
ATLANTIC OCEAN
PACIFIC OCEAN
Equator
Galapagos Islands (Ecuador)
Aruba (Neth.)
Bonaire (Neth.)
Curaçao (Neth.)
Margarita I.
Pico Cristobal Colon 18,947
Santa Marta
Barranquilla
Cartagena
Sincelejo
Monteria
Valledupar
Maracaibo
Coro
Cabimas
Caracas
Valencia
Maracay
Barquisimeto
Barcelona
Cumana
Maturin
El Tigre
Ciudad Guayana
Ciudad Bolivar
San Fernando de Apure
Puerto Ayacucho
VENEZUELA
LLANOS
GUIANA HIGHLANDS
Merida
Valera
San Cristobal
Cucuta
Bucaramanga
Barrancabermeja
Medellin
Manizales
Pereira
Armenia
Ibague
Tunja
Bogota
Villavicencio
COLOMBIA
Nevada del Huila 18,865
Neiva
Palmira
Cali
Buenaventura
Popayan
Pasto
Florencia
Tumaco
Esmeraldas
ECUADOR
Quito
Cotopaxi 19,347
Chimborazo 20,561
Portoviejo
Ambato
Riobamba
Guayaquil
Cuenca
Machala
Tumbes
Loja
Talara
Sullana
Piura
Aguja Point
Chiclayo
Trujillo
Chimbote
Cajamarca
Nev. Huascaran 22,205
Nev. Yerupaja 21,709
Huanuco
Cerro de Pasco
Callao
Lima
Ica
Huancayo
Ayacucho
Cuzco
Pucallpa
Yurimaguas
Iquitos
PERU
LA MONTANA
ANDES
Arequipa
Juliaca
Puno
Tacna
Arica
Iquique
Antofagasta
Calama
ATACAMA DESERT
ALTIPLANO
La Paz
Oruro
Cochabamba
Sucre
Potosi
Tarija
Camiri
Santa Cruz
Trinidad
Riberalta
Cobija
Puerto Maldonado
BOLIVIA
San Salvador de Jujuy
Salta
Guajara-Mirim
Porto Velho
Ji-Parana
Rio Branco
Cruzeiro do Sul
Leticia
Benjamin Constant
Pico do Neblina 9,885
AMAZON BASIN
SELVAS
Manaus
Boa Vista
GUYANA
Georgetown
New Amsterdam
SURINAME
Paramaribo
French Guiana (Fr.)
Kourou
Cayenne
Macapa
Marajo Island
Belem
Santarem
Itaituba
Altamura
Maraba
Imperatriz
Araguaina
Sao Luis
Parnaiba
Teresina
Caxias
Floriano
Fortaleza
Mossoro
Natal
Joao Pessoa
Campina Grande
Recife
Maceio
Juazeiro do Norte
Petrolina
Juazeiro
Aracaju
Alagoinhas
Salvador
Feira de Santana
Jequie
Ilheus
Itabuna
Vitoria da Conquista
BRAZIL
BRAZILIAN HIGHLANDS
MATO GROSSO PLATEAU
Gurupi
Brasilia
Anapolis
Goiania
Cuiaba
Rondonopolis
Jatai
Corumba
Campo Grande
Dourados
Presidente Prudente
Sao Jose do Rio Preto
Bauru
Londrina
Uberlandia
Montes Claros
Teofilo Otoni
Governador Valadares
Vitoria
Belo Horizonte
Pico da Bandeira 9,482
Juiz de Fora
Volta Redonda
Niteroi
Rio de Janeiro
Ribeirao Preto
Campinas
Jundiai
Sorocaba
Sao Paulo
Santos
PARAGUAY
Concepcion
CHACO
CAMPOS

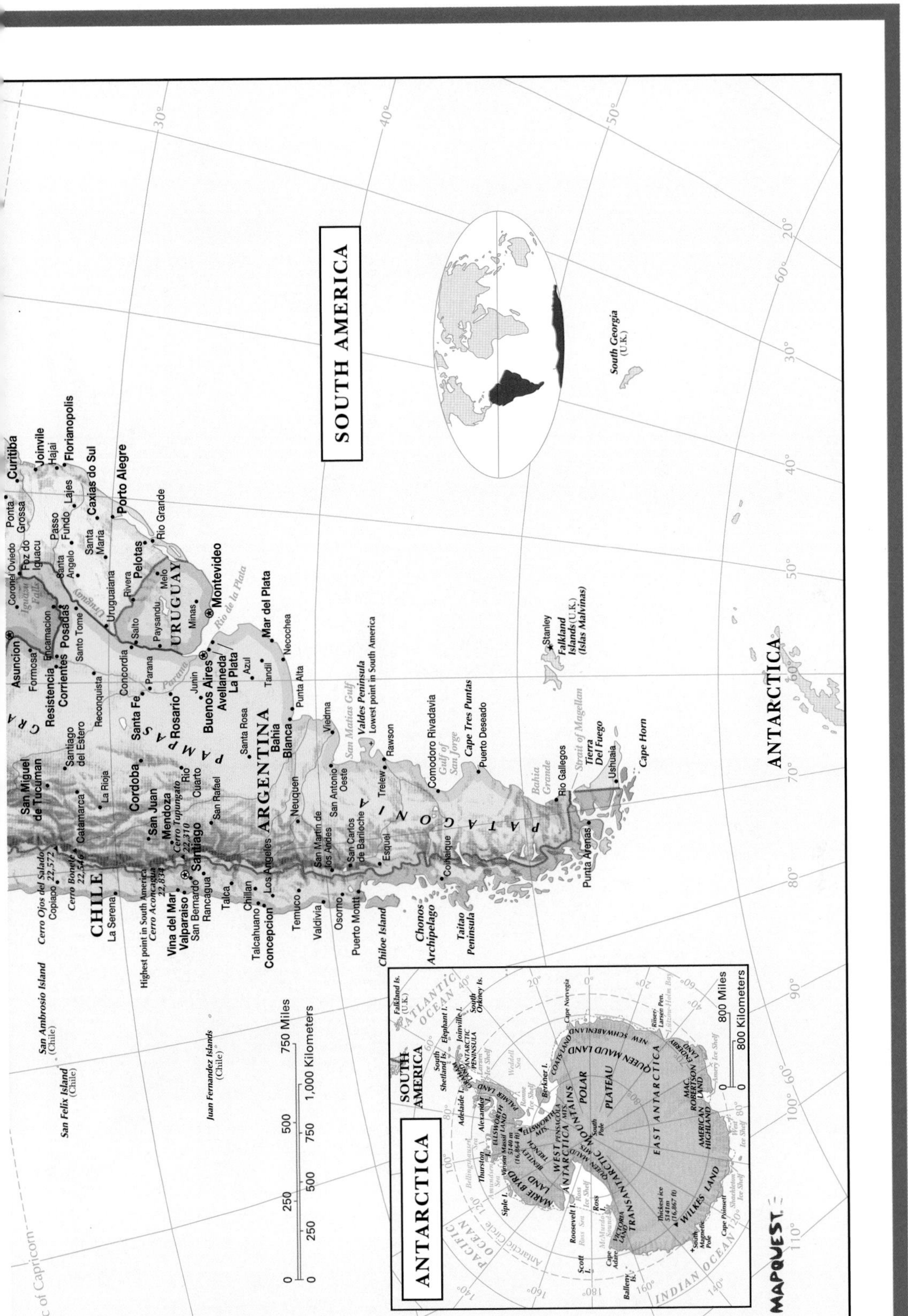
SOUTH AMERICA
ANTARCTICA
CHILE
ARGENTINA
URUGUAY
PATAGONIA
PAMPAS
Tropic of Capricorn
San Ambrosio Island (Chile)
San Felix Island (Chile)
Juan Fernandez Islands (Chile)
Cerro Ojos del Salado 22,572
Cerro Bonete 22,546
Highest point in South America Cerro Aconcagua 22,834
Cerro Tupungato 22,310
Copiapo
La Serena
Vina del Mar
Valparaiso
San Bernardo
Santiago
Rancagua
Talca
Chillan
Talcahuano
Concepcion
Los Angeles
Temuco
Valdivia
Osorno
Puerto Montt
Chiloe Island
Chonos Archipelago
Taitao Peninsula
Coihaique
Esquel
San Carlos de Bariloche
San Martin de los Andes
Neuquen
San Antonio Oeste
Trelew
Rawson
Viedma
San Matias Gulf
Valdes Peninsula
Lowest point in South America
Comodoro Rivadavia
Gulf of San Jorge
Cape Tres Puntas
Puerto Deseado
Bahia Grande
Rio Gallegos
Strait of Magellan
Punta Arenas
Tierra Del Fuego
Ushuaia
Cape Horn
Falkland Islands (U.K.) (Islas Malvinas)
Stanley
South Georgia (U.K.)
San Miguel de Tucuman
Catamarca
La Rioja
Santiago del Estero
Cordoba
San Juan
Mendoza
San Rafael
Rio Cuarto
Santa Rosa
Bahia Blanca
Punta Alta
Santa Fe
Rosario
Parana
Reconquista
Concordia
Junin
Buenos Aires
Avellaneda
La Plata
Azul
Tandil
Mar del Plata
Necochea
Rio de la Plata
Montevideo
Minas
Paysandu
Salto
Rivera
Melo
Asuncion
Formosa
Resistencia
Corrientes
Encarnacion
Posadas
Santo Tome
Uruguaiana
Santa Maria
Santa Angelo
Passo Fundo
Lajes
Caxias do Sul
Porto Alegre
Pelotas
Rio Grande
Coronel Oviedo
Foz do Iguacu
Iguazu Falls
Ponta Grossa
Curitiba
Joinvile
Hajai
Florianopolis
Uruguay
Parana
0 250 500 750 Miles
0 250 500 750 1,000 Kilometers
SOUTH AMERICA
Falkland Is. (U.K.)
ATLANTIC OCEAN
South Shetland Is.
Elephant I.
Joinville I.
South Orkney Is.
ANTARCTIC PENINSULA
GRAHAM LAND
PALMER LAND
Adelaide I.
Alexander I.
ELLSWORTH LAND
Vinson Massif 5140 m (16,864 ft)
Thurston I.
Bellingshausen Sea
Amundsen Sea
Ronne Ice Shelf
Weddell Sea
Berkner I.
COATS LAND
Cape Norvegia
QUEEN MAUD LAND
NEW SCHWABENLAND
ELLSWORTH MTS.
PENSACOLA MTS.
WEST ANTARCTICA
POLAR PLATEAU
South Pole
QUEEN MAUD MTS.
TRANSANTARCTIC MOUNTAINS
EAST ANTARCTICA
ENDERBY LAND
MAC. ROBERTSON LAND
AMERICAN HIGHLAND
Amery Ice Shelf
West Ice Shelf
Riiser-Larsen Pen.
MARIE BYRD LAND
Siple I.
Roosevelt I.
Ross Sea
Ross Ice Shelf
Ross I.
McMurdo Sound
VICTORIA LAND
Thickest ice 5141 m (16,867 ft)
WILKES LAND
Shackleton Ice Shelf
Cape Poinsett
South Magnetic Pole
Cape Adare
Scott I.
Balleny Is.
PACIFIC OCEAN
INDIAN OCEAN
Antarctic Circle
0 800 Miles
0 800 Kilometers
© MAPQUEST

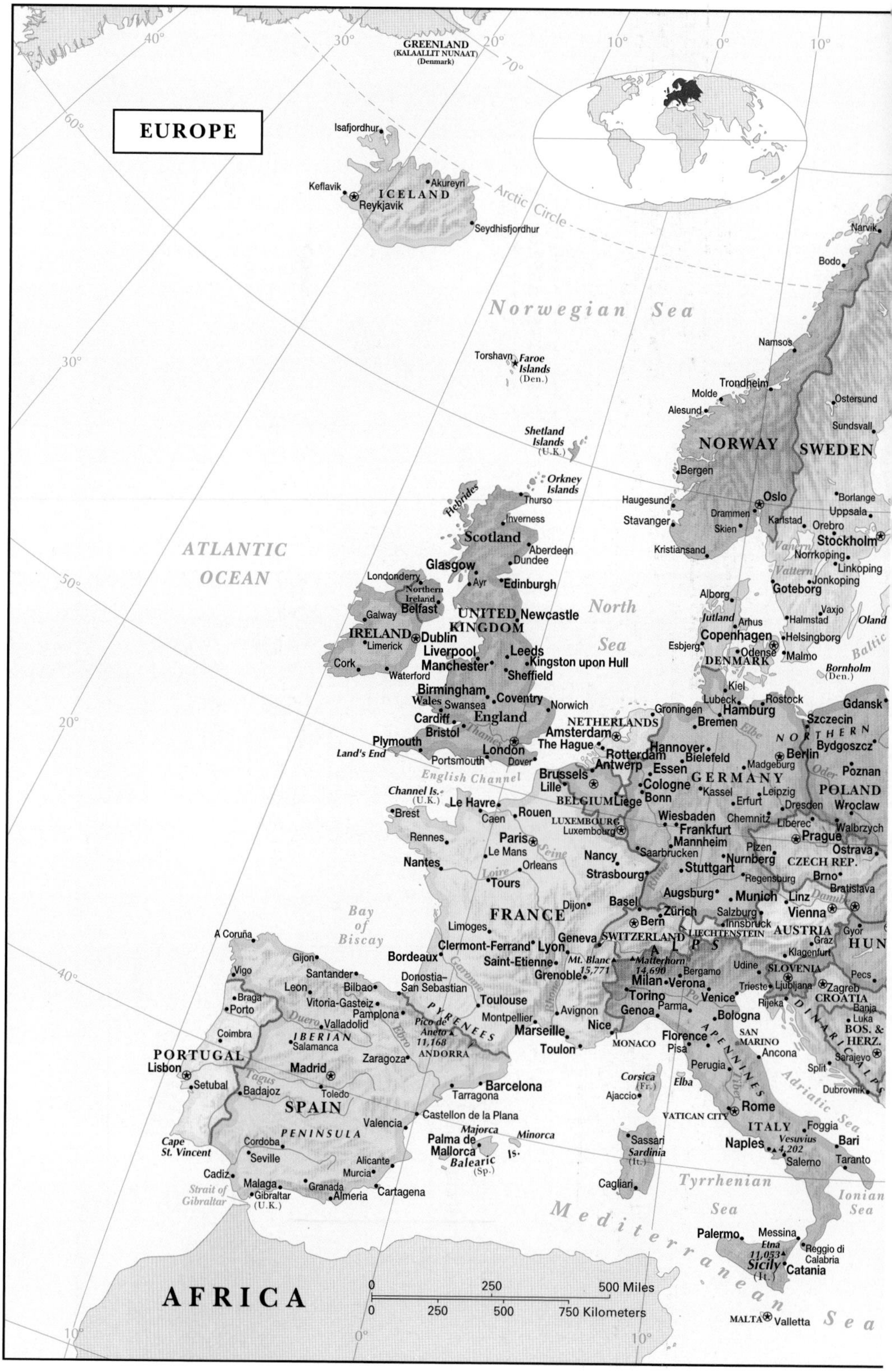
EUROPE
GREENLAND
(KALAALLIT NUNAAT)
(Denmark)
Arctic Circle
Isafjordhur
Keflavik
ICELAND
Akureyri
Reykjavik
Seydhisfjordhur
Norwegian Sea
Torshavn
Faroe Islands
(Den.)
Shetland Islands
(U.K.)
Orkney Islands
Thurso
Hebrides
Inverness
Scotland
Aberdeen
Dundee
Glasgow
Ayr
Edinburgh
ATLANTIC OCEAN
Londonderry
Northern Ireland
Belfast
Galway
IRELAND
Dublin
Limerick
Cork
Waterford
UNITED KINGDOM
Newcastle
Liverpool
Manchester
Leeds
Kingston upon Hull
Sheffield
Birmingham
Coventry
Wales
Swansea
Cardiff
Bristol
England
Norwich
Plymouth
Land's End
London
Portsmouth
Dover
Thames
North Sea
English Channel
Channel Is.
(U.K.)
Narvik
Bodo
Namsos
Trondheim
Molde
Alesund
Ostersund
Sundsvall
NORWAY
SWEDEN
Bergen
Haugesund
Stavanger
Oslo
Drammen
Skien
Kristiansand
Karlstad
Borlange
Uppsala
Orebro
Stockholm
Vanern
Norrkoping
Vattern
Linkoping
Jonkoping
Goteborg
Alborg
Jutland
Arhus
Halmstad
Vaxjo
Oland
Copenhagen
Helsingborg
Esbjerg
Odense
Malmo
DENMARK
Baltic
Bornholm
(Den.)
Kiel
Lubeck
Rostock
Hamburg
Gdansk
Groningen
Bremen
NETHERLANDS
Amsterdam
The Hague
Rotterdam
Hannover
Bielefeld
Berlin
Szczecin
NORTHERN
Bydgoszcz
Elbe
Antwerp
Essen
Madgeburg
Oder
Poznan
Brussels
Lille
GERMANY
Cologne
Kassel
Leipzig
POLAND
BELGIUM
Liege
Bonn
Erfurt
Dresden
Wroclaw
LUXEMBOURG
Luxembourg
Wiesbaden
Chemnitz
Liberec
Walbrzych
Frankfurt
Prague
Mannheim
Plzen
Ostrava
Saarbrucken
Nurnberg
CZECH REP.
Stuttgart
Regensburg
Brno
Bratislava
Augsburg
Munich
Linz
Danube
Vienna
Salzburg
Innsbruck
AUSTRIA
Graz
Gyor
HUN
LIECHTENSTEIN
Klagenfurt
Le Havre
Brest
Caen
Rouen
Rennes
Paris
Seine
Le Mans
Nantes
Loire
Orleans
Tours
Nancy
Strasbourg
Rhine
Dijon
Basel
Zurich
Bern
SWITZERLAND
FRANCE
Bay of Biscay
Limoges
Clermont-Ferrand
Lyon
Geneva
Bordeaux
Saint-Etienne
Mt. Blanc
15,771
Matterhorn
14,690
ALPS
Bergamo
Udine
SLOVENIA
Pecs
Grenoble
Milan
Verona
Trieste
Ljubljana
Zagreb
CROATIA
Donostia-San Sebastian
Garonne
Rhone
Torino
Po
Venice
Rijeka
DINARIC ALPS
Banja Luka
Toulouse
Avignon
Genoa
Parma
Bologna
BOS. & HERZ.
Montpellier
Nice
SAN MARINO
Sarajevo
Pico de Aneto
11,168
PYRENEES
Marseille
MONACO
Florence
Ancona
Split
ANDORRA
Toulon
Pisa
APENNINES
Perugia
Dubrovnik
Corsica
(Fr.)
Elba
Ajaccio
Tiber
Adriatic Sea
VATICAN CITY
Rome
ITALY
Foggia
Sassari
Sardinia
(It.)
Naples
Vesuvius
4,202
Bari
Salerno
Taranto
Cagliari
Tyrrhenian Sea
Ionian Sea
Palermo
Messina
Etna
11,053
Reggio di Calabria
Sicily
(It.)
Catania
MALTA
Valletta
Mediterranean Sea
A Coruña
Gijon
Santander
Vigo
Leon
Bilbao
Braga
Porto
Vitoria-Gasteiz
Pamplona
Duero
Valladolid
Ebro
Coimbra
IBERIAN
Salamanca
PORTUGAL
Lisbon
Madrid
Zaragoza
Setubal
Tagus
Toledo
Barcelona
Badajoz
Tarragona
SPAIN
Castellon de la Plana
Valencia
PENINSULA
Majorca
Minorca
Palma de Mallorca
Balearic Is.
(Sp.)
Cape St. Vincent
Cordoba
Seville
Alicante
Murcia
Cadiz
Malaga
Granada
Almeria
Cartagena
Gibraltar
(U.K.)
Strait of Gibraltar
AFRICA
0
250
500 Miles
0
250
500
750 Kilometers
40°
30°
20°
10°
0°
10°
70°
60°
30°
50°
20°
40°
10°
0°
10°

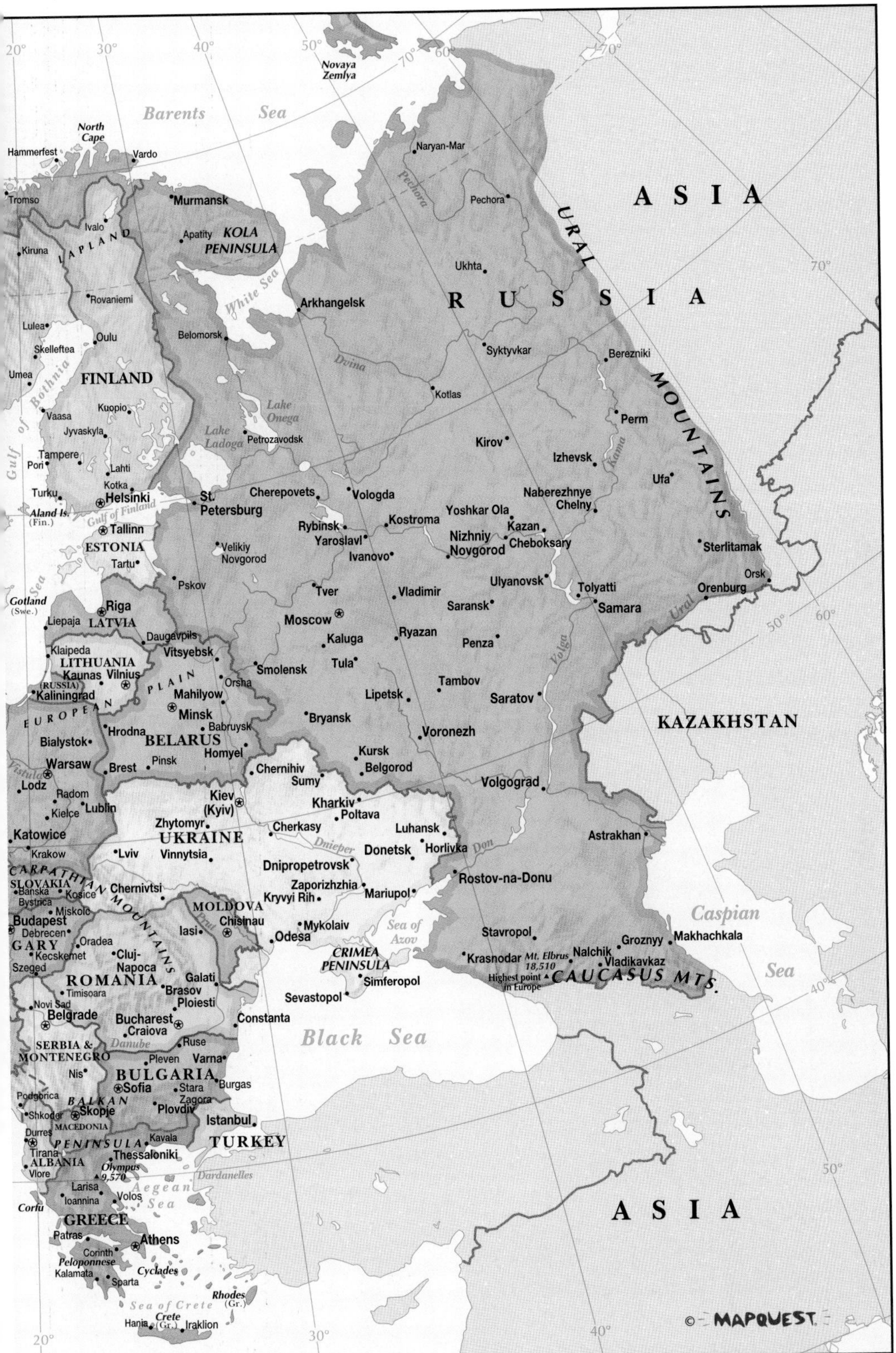
20°
30°
40°
50°
60°
70°
Novaya Zemlya
Barents Sea
North Cape
Hammerfest
Vardo
Tromso
Murmansk
Naryan-Mar
Pechora
Pechora
ASIA
URAL MOUNTAINS
Ivalo
Apatity
KOLA PENINSULA
Kiruna
LAPLAND
White Sea
Ukhta
Rovaniemi
Arkhangelsk
RUSSIA
Lulea
Oulu
Belomorsk
Skelleftea
Dvina
Syktyvkar
Bereznik
Umea
FINLAND
Gulf of Bothnia
Lake Onega
Kotlas
Kuopio
Vaasa
Jyvaskyla
Lake Ladoga
Petrozavodsk
Perm
Kirov
Izhevsk
Kama
Tampere
Pori
Lahti
Ufa
Kotka
Turku
Helsinki
Cherepovets
Vologda
Naberezhnye Chelny
Aland Is. (Fin.)
Gulf of Finland
St. Petersburg
Yoshkar Ola
Tallinn
Rybinsk
Kostroma
Kazan
Nizhniy Novgorod
Cheboksary
ESTONIA
Yaroslavl
Sterlitamak
Velikiy Novgorod
Ivanovo
Tartu
Orsk
Pskov
Tver
Ulyanovsk
Tolyatti
Orenburg
Gotland (Swe.)
Vladimir
Riga
Samara
Saransk
Ural
LATVIA
Moscow
Liepaja
Daugavpils
Ryazan
Kaluga
Penza
Klaipeda
Vitsyebsk
LITHUANIA
Smolensk
Tula
Volga
(RUSSIA)
Kaunas
Vilnius
Orsha
Tambov
Kaliningrad
PLAIN
Mahilyow
Lipetsk
Saratov
EUROPEAN
Minsk
Bryansk
KAZAKHSTAN
Babruysk
Hrodna
BELARUS
Voronezh
Bialystok
Kursk
Homyel
Vistula
Warsaw
Brest
Pinsk
Chernihiv
Belgorod
Sumy
Volgograd
Lodz
Radom
Kiev (Kyiv)
Kharkiv
Kielce
Lublin
Poltava
Zhytomyr
Cherkasy
Luhansk
Astrakhan
Katowice
UKRAINE
Dnieper
Horlivka
Donetsk
Don
Lviv
Vinnytsia
Krakow
Dnipropetrovsk
Rostov-na-Donu
CARPATHIAN MOUNTAINS
SLOVAKIA
Chernivtsi
Zaporizhzhia
Banska Bystrica
Kosice
Kryvyi Rih
Mariupol
MOLDOVA
Miskolc
Caspian Sea
Budapest
Prut
Chisinau
Mykolaiv
Sea of Azov
Iasi
Stavropol
Groznyy
Makhachkala
Debrecen
Odesa
HUNGARY
Oradea
Cluj-Napoca
CRIMEA PENINSULA
Krasnodar
Mt. Elbrus 18,510 Highest point in Europe
Nalchik
Vladikavkaz
Kecskemet
Szeged
ROMANIA
Galati
Simferopol
CAUCASUS MTS.
Timisoara
Brasov
Sevastopol
Novi Sad
Ploiesti
Belgrade
Bucharest
Constanta
Craiova
Black Sea
SERBIA & MONTENEGRO
Danube
Ruse
Pleven
Varna
BULGARIA
Nis
Sofia
Burgas
Podgorica
BALKAN
Stara Zagora
Skopje
Shkoder
Plovdiv
Istanbul
MACEDONIA
Durres
PENINSULA
Kavala
TURKEY
Tirana
Thessaloniki
ALBANIA
Olympus 9,570
Vlore
Dardanelles
Larisa
Ioannina
Volos
Aegean Sea
Corfu
GREECE
ASIA
Patras
Athens
Corinth
Peloponnese
Kalamata
Sparta
Cyclades
Rhodes (Gr.)
Sea of Crete
Crete (Gr.)
Hania
Iraklion
© MAPQUEST

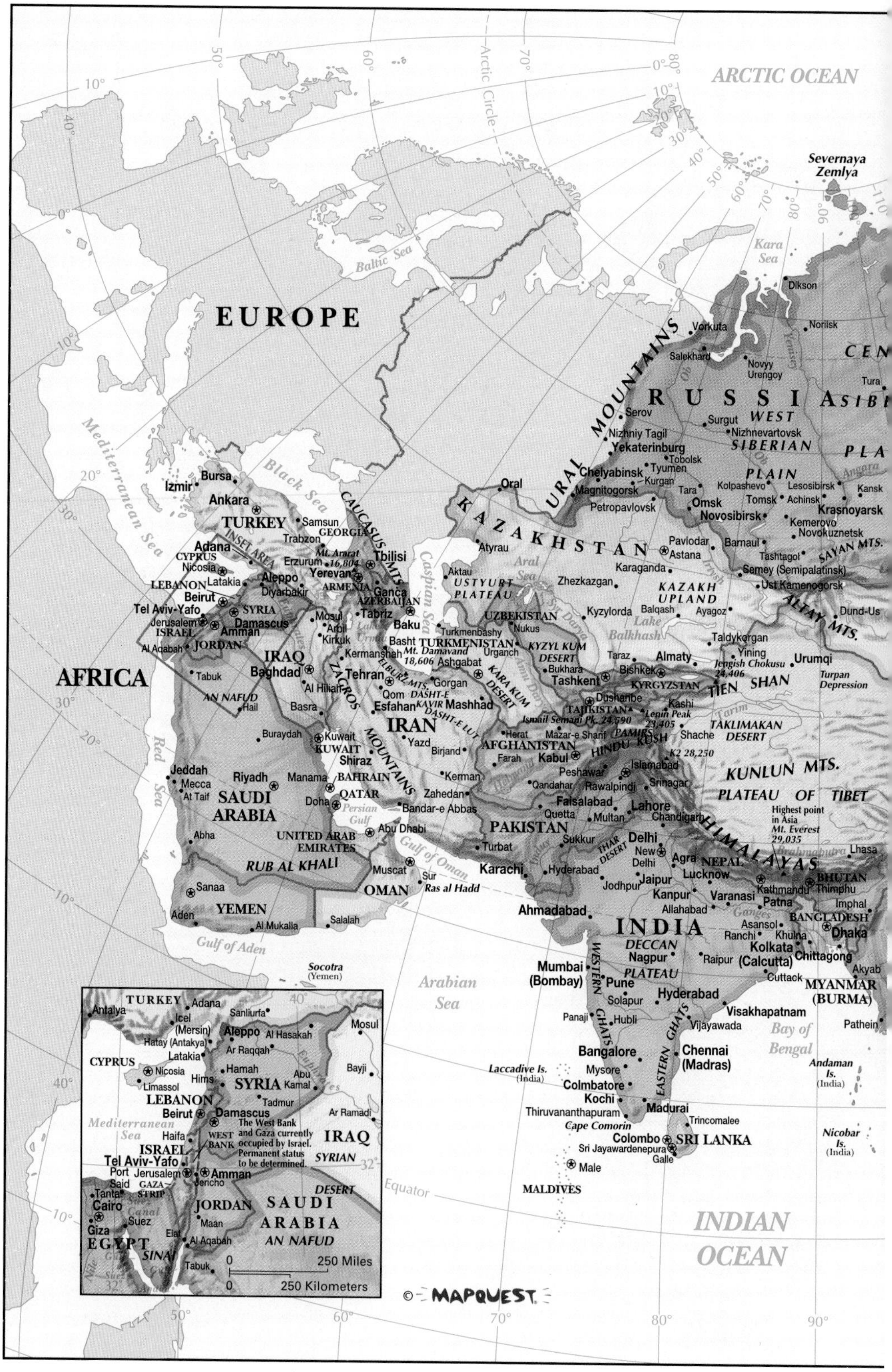
ARCTIC OCEAN
Severnaya Zemlya
Kara Sea
Dikson
Norilsk
Baltic Sea
EUROPE
Arctic Circle
Vorkuta
Salekhard
Novyy Urengoy
Tura
URAL MOUNTAINS
RUSSIA
Serov
Surgut
WEST SIBERIAN PLAIN
Nizhnevartovsk
Nizhniy Tagil
Yekaterinburg
Tobolsk
Tyumen
Chelyabinsk
Kurgan
Magnitogorsk
Tara
Kolpashevo
Lesosibirsk
Kansk
Achinsk
Krasnoyarsk
Tomsk
Omsk
Novosibirsk
Kemerovo
Novokuznetsk
Petropavlovsk
Oral
KAZAKHSTAN
Pavlodar
Astana
Barnaul
Tashtagol
SAYAN MTS.
Semey (Semipalatinsk)
Ust Kamenogorsk
Karaganda
Zhezkazgan
KAZAKH UPLAND
ALTAY MTS.
Dund-Us
Atyrau
Aktau
USTYURT PLATEAU
Aral Sea
Kyzylorda
Balqash
Ayagoz
Lake Balkhash
Taldykorgan
Mediterranean Sea
Black Sea
Bursa
Izmir
Ankara
TURKEY
Samsun
Trabzon
GEORGIA
CAUCASUS MTS.
INSET AREA
Adana
CYPRUS
Nicosia
Mt. Ararat 16,804
Erzurum
Tbilisi
Yerevan
ARMENIA
Ganca
AZERBAIJAN
Caspian Sea
LEBANON
Latakia
Aleppo
Diyarbakir
Beirut
Tel Aviv-Yafo
SYRIA
Jerusalem
Damascus
ISRAEL
Amman
JORDAN
Al Aqabah
Mosul
Arbil
Kirkuk
Tabriz
Baku
Turkmenbashy
UZBEKISTAN
Nukus
KYZYL KUM DESERT
Bukhara
Tashkent
Taraz
Almaty
Bishkek
KYRGYZSTAN
Yining
Jengish Chokusu 24,406
Urumqi
Turpan Depression
TIEN SHAN
Basht
TURKMENISTAN
Mt. Damavand 18,606
Urganch
Ashgabat
KARA KUM DESERT
Dushanbe
TAJIKISTAN
Kashi
Lenin Peak 23,405
Ismail Semani Pk. 24,590
PAMIRS
Tarim
TAKLIMAKAN DESERT
AFRICA
IRAQ
Baghdad
Kermanshah
Tehran
ELBURZ MTS.
Gorgan
Qom
DASHT-E KAVIR
Mashhad
DASHT-E LUT
ZAGROS MOUNTAINS
Esfahan
IRAN
Yazd
Birjand
Herat
Mazar-e Sharif
AFGHANISTAN
HINDU KUSH
Shache
Farah
Kabul
K2 28,250
Tabuk
AN NAFUD
Hail
Al Hillah
Basra
Buraydah
Kuwait
KUWAIT
Shiraz
Islamabad
Peshawar
Srinagar
KUNLUN MTS.
Jeddah
Mecca
At Taif
Red Sea
Riyadh
SAUDI ARABIA
Manama
BAHRAIN
Doha
QATAR
Persian Gulf
Kerman
Zahedan
Qandahar
Rawalpindi
PLATEAU OF TIBET
Faisalabad
Lahore
Quetta
Multan
Chandigarh
Highest point in Asia Mt. Everest 29,035
Bandar-e Abbas
Abu Dhabi
UNITED ARAB EMIRATES
PAKISTAN
Sukkur
THAR DESERT
Delhi
New Delhi
Brahmaputra
Lhasa
HIMALAYAS
Abha
RUB AL KHALI
Gulf of Oman
Turbat
Karachi
Hyderabad
Agra
NEPAL
Lucknow
Kathmandu
BHUTAN
Thimphu
Muscat
Sur
Ras al Hadd
Jaipur
Jodhpur
Kanpur
Varanasi
Patna
Imphal
Sanaa
OMAN
Ahmadabad
Allahabad
Ganges
BANGLADESH
YEMEN
Asansol
Dhaka
Aden
Al Mukalla
Salalah
INDIA
Ranchi
Khulna
Gulf of Aden
DECCAN PLATEAU
Kolkata (Calcutta)
Chittagong
Nagpur
Raipur
Akyab
Socotra (Yemen)
Mumbai (Bombay)
WESTERN GHATS
Pune
Cuttack
MYANMAR (BURMA)
Arabian Sea
Solapur
Hyderabad
Visakhapatnam
Panaji
Hubli
Vijayawada
Pathein
Bay of Bengal
Bangalore
EASTERN GHATS
Chennai (Madras)
Mysore
Andaman Is. (India)
Laccadive Is. (India)
Coimbatore
Kochi
Madurai
Thiruvananthapuram
Cape Comorin
Trincomalee
Nicobar Is. (India)
Colombo
SRI LANKA
Sri Jayawardenepura
Galle
Male
MALDIVES
Equator
INDIAN OCEAN
TURKEY
Adana
Antalya
Icel (Mersin)
Sanliurfa
Mosul
Hatay (Antakya)
Aleppo
Al Hasakah
Ar Raqqah
Latakia
Euphrates
CYPRUS
Nicosia
Hamah
Abu Kamal
Bayji
Limassol
Hims
SYRIA
Tadmur
LEBANON
Beirut
Damascus
Ar Ramadi
Mediterranean Sea
The West Bank and Gaza currently occupied by Israel. Permanent status to be determined.
Haifa
WEST BANK
IRAQ
ISRAEL
SYRIAN DESERT
Tel Aviv-Yafo
Port Said
Jerusalem
Amman
Jericho
Tanta
GAZA STRIP
Cairo
Suez Canal
JORDAN
SAUDI ARABIA
Suez
Maan
Giza
Elat
Al Aqabah
AN NAFUD
EGYPT
SINAI
Nile
Tabuk
0 250 Miles
0 250 Kilometers
© MAPQUEST

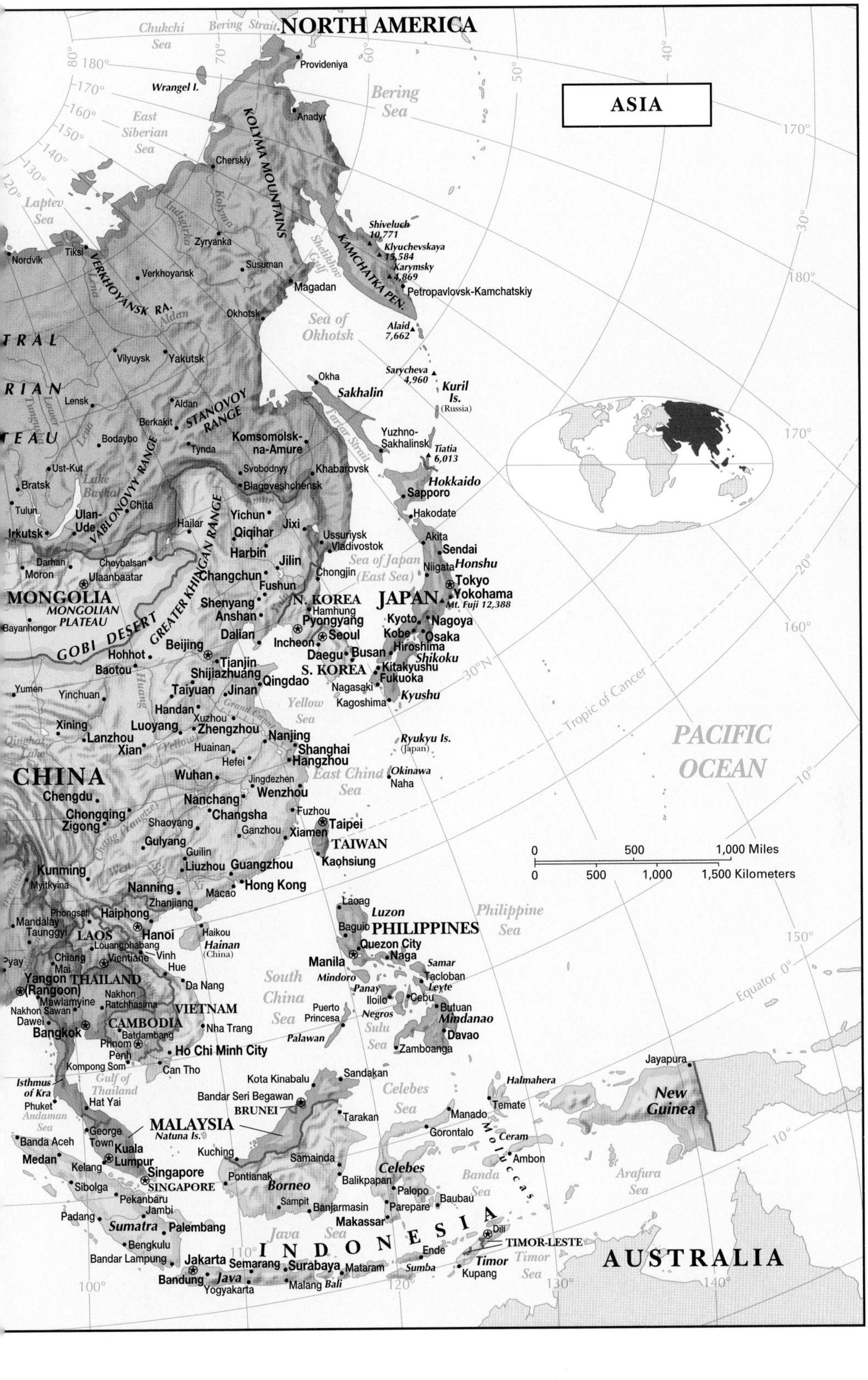

ASIA
NORTH AMERICA
Chukchi Sea
Bering Strait
Provideniya
Wrangel I.
Bering Sea
East Siberian Sea
Anadyr
KOLYMA MOUNTAINS
Cherskiy
Laptev Sea
Indigirka
Kolyma
Zyryanka
Shelikhov Gulf
KAMCHATKA PEN.
Shiveluch 10,771
Klyuchevskaya 15,584
Karymsky 4,869
Petropavlovsk-Kamchatskiy
Nordvik
Tiksi
VERKHOYANSK RA.
Verkhoyansk
Lena
Susuman
Magadan
Aldan
Okhotsk
Sea of Okhotsk
Alaid 7,662
TRAL
Vilyuysk
Yakutsk
RIAN
Sarycheva 4,960
Kuril Is. (Russia)
Okha
Sakhalin
Lensk
Aldan
STANOVOY RANGE
Berkakit
Tatar Strait
EAU
Bodaybo
Tynda
Komsomolsk-na-Amure
Yuzhno-Sakhalinsk
Tiatia 6,013
Ust-Kut
Svobodnyy
Khabarovsk
Bratsk
Lake Baykal
YABLONOVYY RANGE
Blagoveshchensk
Hokkaido
Sapporo
Tulun
Chita
Ulan-Ude
Yichun
Hakodate
Irkutsk
Hailar
Qiqihar
Jixi
Ussuriysk
Vladivostok
Akita
Sendai
Harbin
Darhan
Moron
Choybalsan
Ulaanbaatar
Jilin
Chongjin
Sea of Japan (East Sea)
Niigata
Honshu
Changchun
Fushun
Tokyo
Yokohama
Mt. Fuji 12,388
MONGOLIA
MONGOLIAN PLATEAU
GREATER KHINGAN RANGE
Shenyang
Anshan
N. KOREA
Hamhung
Pyongyang
JAPAN
Bayanhongor
Kyoto
Kobe
Nagoya
Osaka
GOBI DESERT
Dalian
Incheon
Seoul
Hiroshima
Beijing
Hohhot
Daegu
Busan
Shikoku
Baotou
Tianjin
S. KOREA
Kitakyushu
Fukuoka
30°N
Yumen
Shijiazhuang
Qingdao
Nagasaki
Yinchuan
Taiyuan
Jinan
Kagoshima
Kyushu
Tropic of Cancer
Handan
Yellow Sea
Xuzhou
Grand Canal
Xining
Luoyang
Zhengzhou
Nanjing
Ryukyu Is. (Japan)
PACIFIC OCEAN
Lanzhou
Xian
Huainan
Shanghai
Hefei
Hangzhou
CHINA
Wuhan
Jingdezhen
East China Sea
Okinawa
Naha
Chengdu
Nanchang
Wenzhou
Chongqing
Zigong
Shaoyang
Changsha
Fuzhou
Taipei
Ganzhou
Xiamen
TAIWAN
Gulyang
Guilin
Kaohsiung
0 500 1,000 Miles
0 500 1,000 1,500 Kilometers
Kunming
Liuzhou
Guangzhou
Myitkyina
Nanning
Hong Kong
Macao
Zhanjiang
Laoag
Luzon
Philippine Sea
Phongsali
Haiphong
Mandalay
Taunggyi
LAOS
Hanoi
Haikou
Baguio
PHILIPPINES
Louangphabang
Hainan (China)
Quezon City
Chiang Mai
Vientiane
Vinh
Manila
Naga
Hue
Samar
Yangon (Rangoon)
THAILAND
South China Sea
Mindoro
Tacloban
Da Nang
Leyte
Nakhon Ratchasima
Panay
Mawlamyine
Iloilo
Cebu
Nakhon Sawan
VIETNAM
Puerto Princesa
Negros
Butuan
Dawei
CAMBODIA
Nha Trang
Mindanao
Bangkok
Batdambang
Sulu Sea
Davao
Phnom Penh
Palawan
Zamboanga
Equator 0°
Ho Chi Minh City
Jayapura
Kompong Som
Can Tho
Kota Kinabalu
Sandakan
Isthmus of Kra
Gulf of Thailand
Halmahera
Bandar Seri Begawan
New Guinea
Celebes Sea
Phuket
Hat Yai
BRUNEI
Ternate
Andaman Sea
Tarakan
Manado
MALAYSIA
George Town
Natuna Is.
Gorontalo
Moluccas
Ceram
Banda Aceh
Kuala Lumpur
Kuching
Ambon
Medan
Kelang
Samainda
Celebes
Singapore
Pontianak
Sibolga
SINGAPORE
Borneo
Balikpapan
Banda Sea
Arafura Sea
Pekanbaru
Palopo
Baubau
Jambi
Sampit
Banjarmasin
Parepare
Padang
Sumatra
Palembang
Java Sea
Makassar
Dili
INDONESIA
Bengkulu
Ende
TIMOR-LESTE
Bandar Lampung
Jakarta
Semarang
Surabaya
Mataram
Sumba
Timor
Timor Sea
AUSTRALIA
Bandung
Java
Malang
Bali
Kupang
Yogyakarta

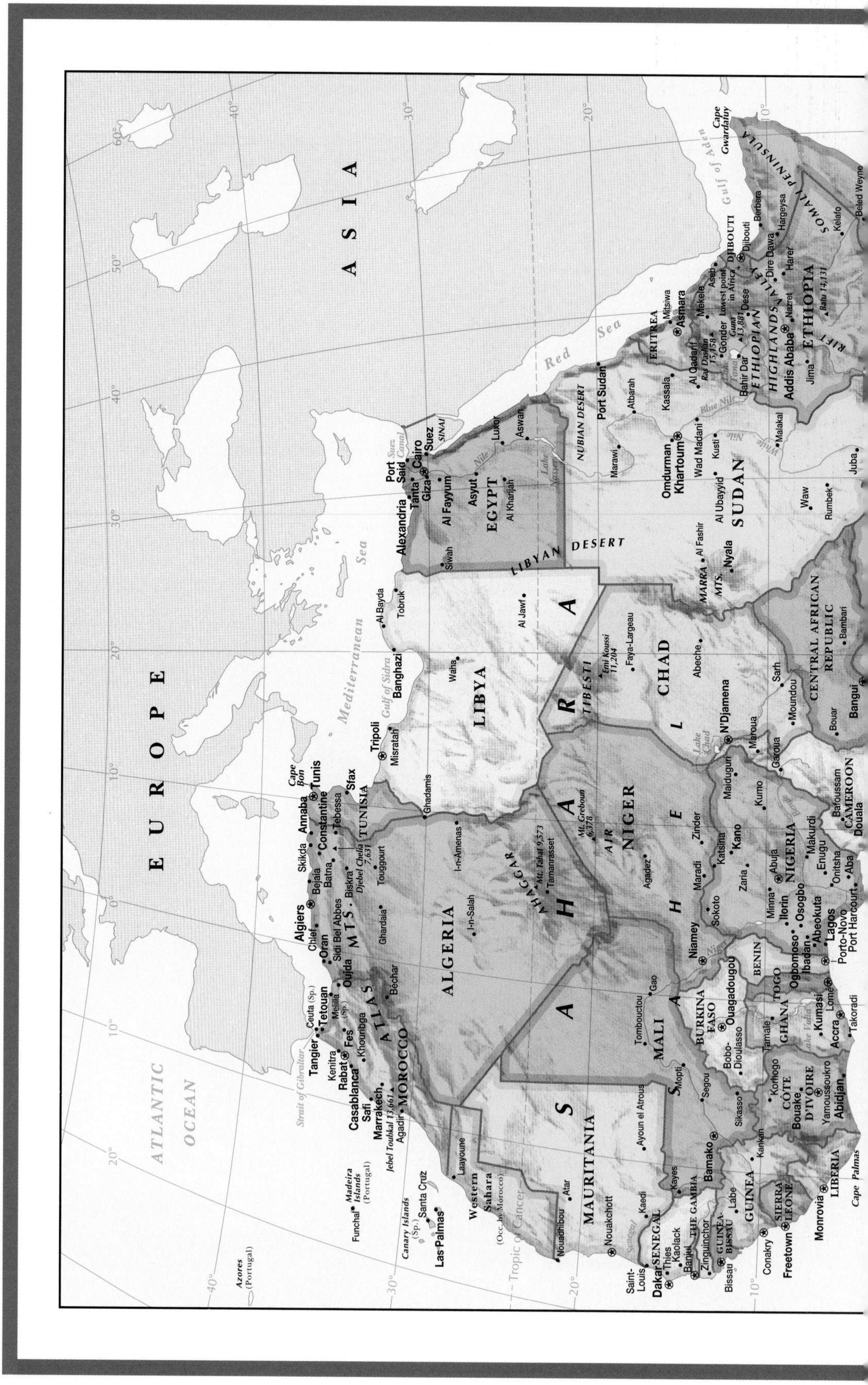
EUROPE
ASIA
ATLANTIC OCEAN
Mediterranean Sea
Red Sea
Gulf of Aden
Gulf of Sidra
Strait of Gibraltar
Tropic of Cancer
Azores (Portugal)
Madeira Islands (Portugal)
Funchal
Canary Islands (Sp.)
Santa Cruz
Las Palmas
SAHARA
LIBYAN DESERT
NUBIAN DESERT
ATLAS MTS.
AHAGGAR
TIBESTI
AIR
MARRA MTS.
SINAI
ETHIOPIAN HIGHLANDS
RIFT VALLEY
SOMALI PENINSULA
Cape Bon
Cape Gwardafuy
Cape Palmas
Jebel Toubkal 13,661
Djebel Chelia 7,631
Mt. Tahat 9,573
Mt. Greboun 6,378
Emi Koussi 11,204
Ras Dashan 15,158
Lake Nasser
Lake Chad
Lake Volta
Lake Tana
Suez Canal
Nile
Blue Nile
White Nile
Niger
Senegal
MOROCCO
Tangier
Ceuta (Sp.)
Tetouan
Melilla (Sp.)
Kenitra
Rabat
Fes
Casablanca
Khouribga
Safi
Marrakech
Agadir
Western Sahara (Occ. by Morocco)
Layoune
ALGERIA
Algiers
Oran
Chlef
Sidi Bel Abbes
Oujda
Bechar
Bejaia
Batna
Skikda
Annaba
Constantine
Tebessa
Biskra
Touggourt
Ghardaia
In-Salah
In-Amenas
Tamanrasset
TUNISIA
Tunis
Sfax
LIBYA
Tripoli
Misratah
Ghadamis
Banghazi
Al Bayda
Tobruk
Waha
Al Jawf
EGYPT
Alexandria
Port Said
Cairo
Giza
Suez
Tanta
Al Fayyum
Asyut
Al Kharijah
Luxor
Aswan
Siwah
SUDAN
Port Sudan
Atbarah
Marawi
Kassala
Omdurman
Khartoum
Wad Madani
Kusti
Al Ubayyid
Al Fashir
Nyala
Al Qadarif
Malakal
Waw
Rumbek
Juba
ERITREA
Asmara
Mitsiwa
Aseb
DJIBOUTI
Djibouti
ETHIOPIA
Mekele
Gonder
Bahir Dar
Dese
Dire Dawa
Harer
Nazret
Addis Ababa
Jima
Batu 14,131
Lowest point in Africa
Gaua -3,881
SOMALIA
Berbera
Hargeysa
Kelafo
Beled Weyne
CHAD
Faya-Largeau
Abeche
N'Djamena
Sarh
Moundou
CENTRAL AFRICAN REPUBLIC
Bambari
Bangui
Bouar
NIGER
Agadez
Zinder
Maradi
Niamey
MALI
Tombouctou
Gao
Mopti
Segou
Bamako
Sikasso
Kayes
MAURITANIA
Nouakchott
Nouadhibou
Atar
Ayoun el Atrous
Kaedi
SENEGAL
Saint-Louis
Dakar
Thies
Kaolack
THE GAMBIA
Banjul
Ziguinchor
GUINEA-BISSAU
Bissau
GUINEA
Conakry
Labe
Kankan
SIERRA LEONE
Freetown
LIBERIA
Monrovia
CÔTE D'IVOIRE
Korhogo
Bouake
Yamoussoukro
Abidjan
BURKINA FASO
Ouagadougou
Bobo-Dioulasso
GHANA
Tamale
Kumasi
Accra
Takoradi
TOGO
Lome
BENIN
Porto-Novo
NIGERIA
Sokoto
Katsina
Kano
Zaria
Maiduguri
Minna
Abuja
Ilorin
Ogbomoso
Osogbo
Ibadan
Abeokuta
Lagos
Makurdi
Enugu
Onitsha
Aba
Port Harcourt
CAMEROON
Garoua
Maroua
Kumo
Bafoussam
Douala
10°
20°
30°
40°
50°
60°
0°

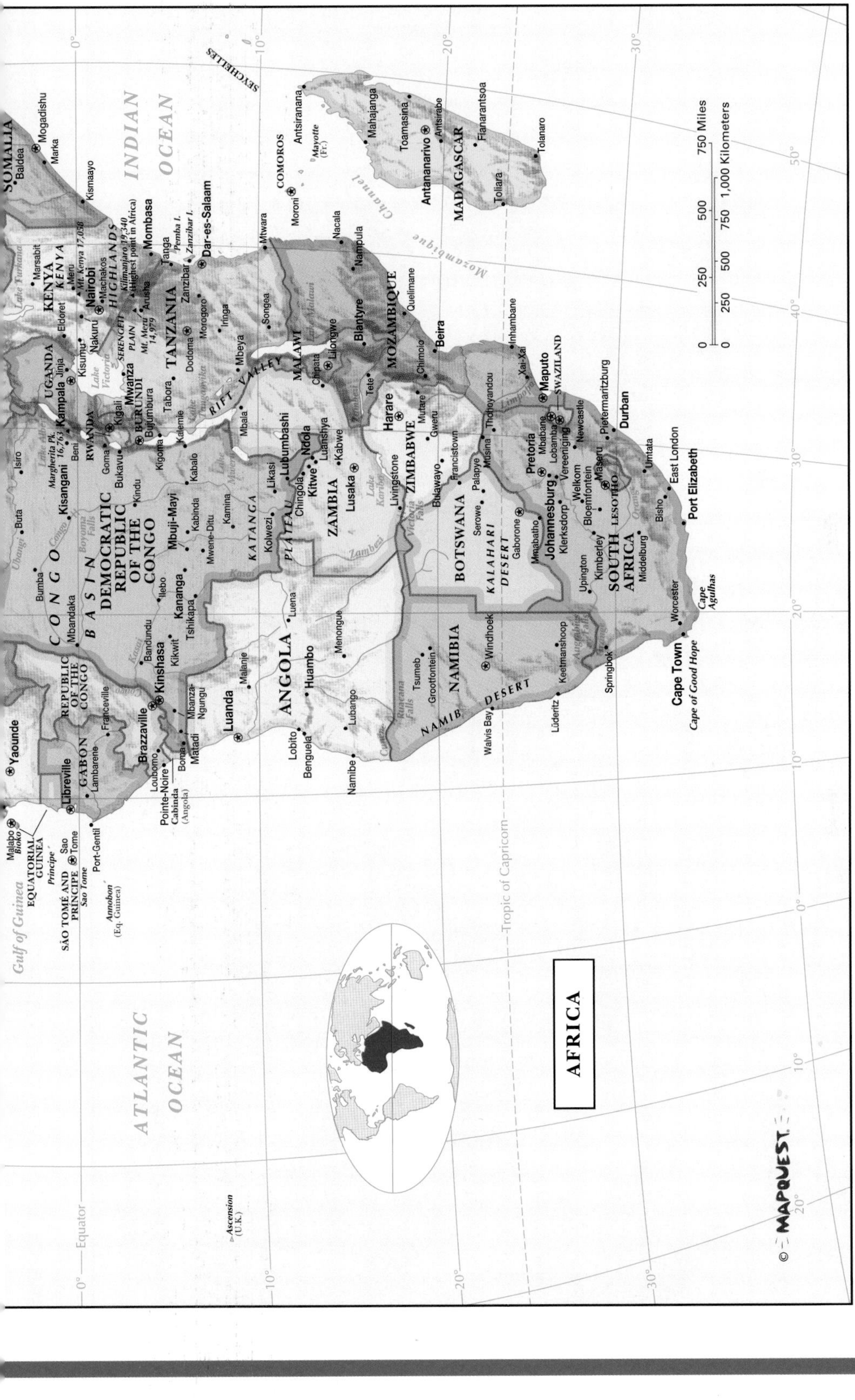
AFRICA
ATLANTIC OCEAN
INDIAN OCEAN
Gulf of Guinea
Equator
Tropic of Capricorn
SOMALIA
Mogadishu
Marka
Baldea
Kismaayo
KENYA
Marsabit
Nairobi
Mombasa
Eldoret
Nakuru
Kisumu
Machakos
Meru
Mt. Kenya 17,058
KENYA HIGHLANDS
Kilimanjaro 19,340 (highest point in Africa)
UGANDA
Kampala
Jinja
Lake Victoria
RWANDA
Kigali
BURUNDI
Bujumbura
TANZANIA
Dar-es-Salaam
Dodoma
Tanga
Zanzibar
Zanzibar I.
Pemba I.
Arusha
Mt. Meru 14,979
Mwanza
SERENGETI PLAIN
Tabora
Kigoma
Morogoro
Iringa
Mbeya
Songea
Mtwara
RIFT VALLEY
MALAWI
Lilongwe
Blantyre
Chipata
Lake Malawi
MOZAMBIQUE
Maputo
Beira
Nampula
Nacala
Quelimane
Chimoio
Tete
Inhambane
Xai-Xai
Mozambique Channel
COMOROS
Moroni
Mayotte (Fr.)
SEYCHELLES
MADAGASCAR
Antananarivo
Antsiranana
Mahajanga
Toamasina
Antsirabe
Fianarantsoa
Toliara
Tolanaro
DEMOCRATIC REPUBLIC OF THE CONGO
CONGO BASIN
Kinshasa
Kisangani
Mbandaka
Bumba
Buta
Isiro
Goma
Bukavu
Kindu
Kalemie
Kabalo
Kabinda
Mbuji-Mayi
Kananga
Tshikapa
Ilebo
Bandundu
Kikwit
Matadi
Boma
Mbanza-Ngungu
Lubumbashi
Likasi
Kolwezi
Kamina
KATANGA PLATEAU
Mwene-Ditu
Beni
Margherita Pk. 16,763
REPUBLIC OF THE CONGO
Brazzaville
Pointe-Noire
Loubomo
Franceville
GABON
Libreville
Lambarene
Port-Gentil
Yaounde
EQUATORIAL GUINEA
Malabo
Bioko
SÃO TOMÉ AND PRINCIPE
Sao Tome
Principe
Annobon (Eq. Guinea)
Cabinda (Angola)
ANGOLA
Luanda
Huambo
Lobito
Benguela
Lubango
Namibe
Malanje
Luena
Menongue
ZAMBIA
Lusaka
Ndola
Kitwe
Chingola
Luanshya
Kabwe
Livingstone
Victoria Falls
Lake Kariba
Zambezi
ZIMBABWE
Harare
Bulawayo
Mutare
Gweru
BOTSWANA
Gaborone
Francistown
Serowe
Palapye
KALAHARI DESERT
NAMIBIA
Windhoek
Walvis Bay
Lüderitz
Keetmanshoop
Tsumeb
Grootfontein
NAMIB DESERT
SOUTH AFRICA
Pretoria
Johannesburg
Cape Town
Durban
Port Elizabeth
East London
Bloemfontein
Kimberley
Upington
Springbok
Worcester
Middelburg
Welkom
Klerksdorp
Vereeniging
Newcastle
Pietermaritzburg
Umtata
Bisho
Mmabatho
Thohoyandou
Musina
LESOTHO
Maseru
SWAZILAND
Mbabane
Lobamba
Cape of Good Hope
Cape Agulhas
Ascension (U.K.)
0 250 500 750 Miles
0 250 500 750 1,000 Kilometers
© MAPQUEST

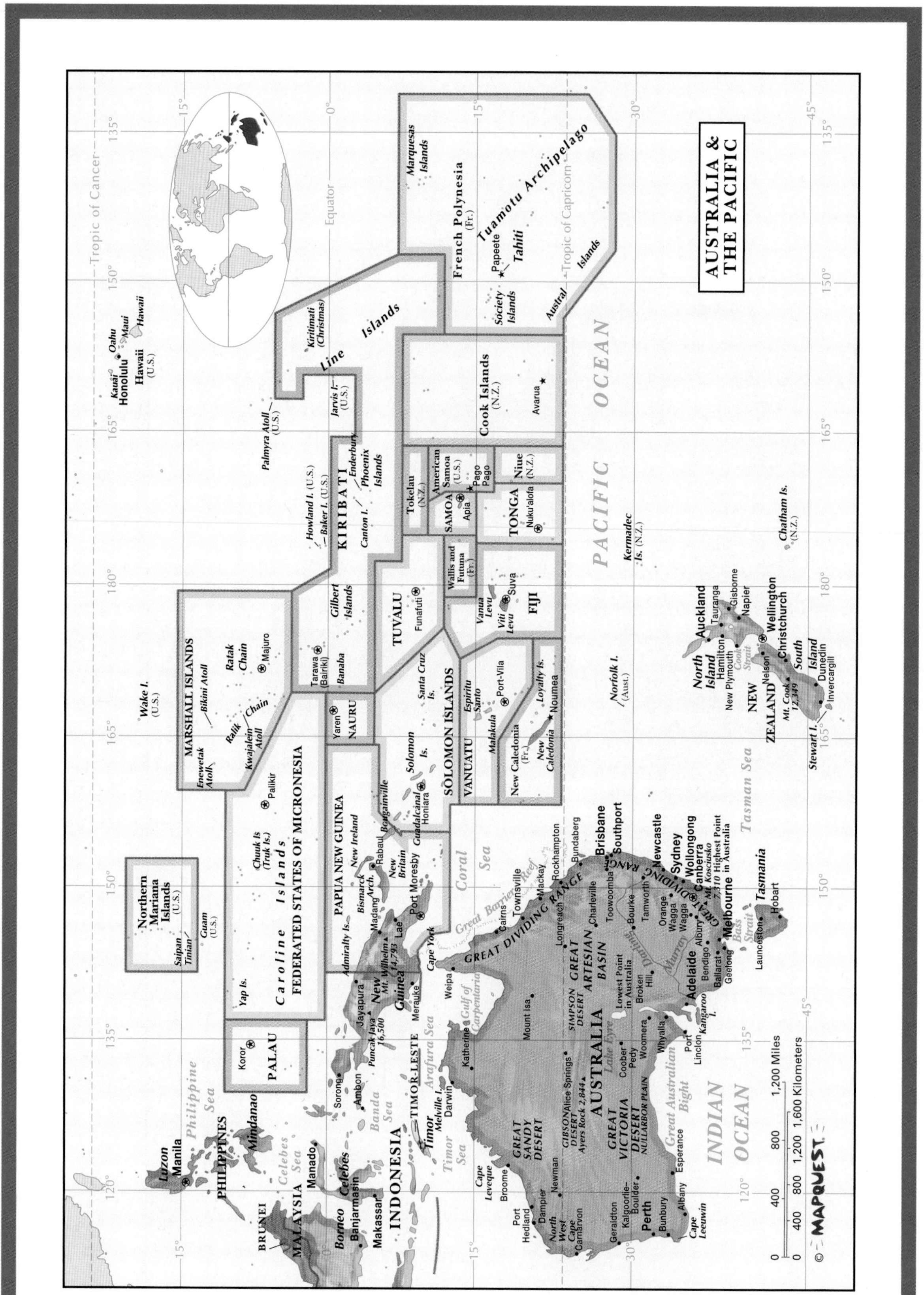
AUSTRALIA & THE PACIFIC
PACIFIC OCEAN
INDIAN OCEAN
AUSTRALIA
NEW ZEALAND
PAPUA NEW GUINEA
INDONESIA
PHILIPPINES
MALAYSIA
BRUNEI
TIMOR-LESTE
PALAU
FEDERATED STATES OF MICRONESIA
MARSHALL ISLANDS
NAURU
KIRIBATI
TUVALU
SOLOMON ISLANDS
VANUATU
FIJI
SAMOA
TONGA
French Polynesia (Fr.)
Cook Islands (N.Z.)
Northern Mariana Islands (U.S.)
Hawaii (U.S.)
Tropic of Cancer
Equator
Tropic of Capricorn
Coral Sea
Tasman Sea
Arafura Sea
Timor Sea
Banda Sea
Celebes Sea
Philippine Sea
Great Australian Bight
GREAT DIVIDING RANGE
GREAT SANDY DESERT
GREAT VICTORIA DESERT
GIBSON DESERT
SIMPSON DESERT
GREAT ARTESIAN BASIN
NULLARBOR PLAIN
Canberra
Sydney
Melbourne
Brisbane
Perth
Adelaide
Darwin
Hobart
Wellington
Auckland
Christchurch
Port Moresby
Honiara
Port-Vila
Suva
Apia
Nuku'alofa
Funafuti
Tarawa (Bairiki)
Majuro
Palikir
Koror
Yaren
Manila
Honolulu
Papeete
0 400 800 1,200 Miles
0 400 800 1,200 1,600 Kilometers
© MAPQUEST

UNITED STATES POPULATION

Census Bureau Numbers Provide a View of Life in America

by Charles Louis Kincannon, Director, U.S. Census Bureau

As the United States reaches the midpoint of the century's 1st decade, a number of trends have become increasingly prominent. For starters, the population continues to shift to the South and also to the West. The nation is also rapidly becoming more diverse, with steady increases in the number of people of Hispanic or Asian ancestry and numbers of immigrants. The population is more educated than ever before. And more and more money is being spent on housing. Here is a more detailed look at the key trends.

Hispanic Population Grows

Hispanics are the nation's largest and fastest-growing minority group. The Hispanic population reached 41.3 million as of July 1, 2004, becoming the first minority group to pass the 40-million population mark.

Hispanics, who may be of any race, accounted for about half the national population growth of 2.9 million between July 1, 2003, and July 1, 2004. The Hispanic growth rate, 3.6%, was more than three times that of the total population.

Moving South and West

The nation's total population is inching closer to the 300-million mark. It grew by 1% (2.9 million people) between July 1, 2003, and July 1, 2004, reaching 293.7 million. The population is projected to pass the 300-million mark by mid-2007.

With a growth rate of 4.1% between 2003 and 2004, Nevada was the fastest-growing state for the 18th consecutive year; four nearby states, all Western, joined Nevada in the top 10: Arizona (2nd), Idaho (4th), Utah (7th), and New Mexico (10th). The remaining top 10 fastest-growing states were all coastal: Florida (3rd), Georgia (5th), Texas (6th), Delaware (8th), and North Carolina (9th).

California remained the most populous state, with 35.9 million people in 2004. Next came Texas with 22.5 million; New York was 3rd with 19.2 million.

Flagler County, FL, on the Atlantic coast between Daytona Beach and Jacksonville, was the nation's fastest-growing county over the 2003-2004 period, experiencing a 10.1% population increase. In fact, Florida had 14 of the nation's 100 fastest-growing counties, including Flagler's neighbor, St. Johns, which ranked 9th. Half of the remaining top 10 fastest-growing counties were located in either the South or West: Loudoun, VA, near Washington, DC, ranked 3rd in growth; Lampasas, TX (north of Austin), 6th; Lyon, NV (near Carson City), 7th; and Camden, NC (south of Norfolk, VA), 8th.

Rounding out the top 10 fastest-growing counties were four in the Midwest: Kendall, IL (in the Chicago area), 2nd; Hanson, SD, and Lincoln, SD (both near Sioux Falls), 4th and 5th, respectively; and Dallas, IA (west of Des Moines), 10th.

Port St. Lucie, FL, had the fastest growth rate among large cities (population of 100,000 or more). Located on the Atlantic coast between Cape Canaveral and West Palm Beach, Port St. Lucie saw its population grow 12%, to 118,396. It was joined on the list of the 10 fastest-growing cities by two others in the Sunshine State: Cape Coral (ranking 5th) and Miramar (8th).

California had four cities in the top 10: Elk Grove (2nd), Moreno Valley (6th), Rancho Cucamonga (9th), and Roseville (10th). Two cities in Arizona were in the top 10—Gilbert (4th) and Chandler (7th)—and, relatively nearby, North Las Vegas, NV, was 3rd. Elk Grove, Miramar, and Roseville each became eligible for this list for the first time, as all three passed the 100,000-population threshold between 2003 and 2004.

Looking Ahead: More Migration South and West

If current trends continue, three states—Florida, California and Texas—will account for nearly half (46%) of total U.S. population growth between 2000 and 2030. Consequently, Florida, now the 4th most populous state, will edge past New York into 3rd place in total population by 2011, while California and Texas will continue to rank 1st and 2nd.

Florida, California, and Texas are each projected to gain more than 12 million people between 2000 and 2030. Arizona, projected to add 5.6 million people, and North Carolina, with 4.2 million, would round out the top five numerical gainers. As a result, Arizona and North Carolina would move into the top 10 by 2030—Arizona rising from 20th place in 2000 to 10th place in 2030, and North Carolina from 11th to 7th place. Michigan and New Jersey are projected to drop out of the top 10.

The projections indicate that the top five fastest-growing states between 2000 and 2030 by percent will be Nevada (114%), Arizona (109%), Florida (80%), Texas (60%), and Utah (56%). Based on these projections, 88% of the nation's population growth between 2000 and 2030 would occur in the South and West, which would be home to all of the 10 fastest-growing states. The share of the population living in the South and West would increase from 58% in 2000 to 65% in 2030, while the share in the Northeast and Midwest would decline from 42% to 35%.

Diversity Abounds

The nation's foreign-born population numbered 34.2 million in 2004, accounting for 11.7% of the total population. The total number of foreign-born is 2.3% higher than in 2003. In 1920, when Ellis Island was nearing the end of its peak years, there were only 13.9 million foreign-born. These made up 13.2% of the population—not much different from now—but the percentages dipped between then and now, to 6.9% in 1950 and 4.7% in 1970.

Of the 2004 foreign-born population, 52.4% were born in Latin America, 27.0% in Asia, 14.3% in Europe, and the remainder in other regions of the world, such as Africa and Oceania. In 1920, Europe was the starting point for a majority of the foreign-born population.

Second-generation Americans, natives with one or both parents born in a foreign country, numbered 30.4 million, or 11% of the total U.S. population.

A Better-Educated Populace

In 2004, 84% of those age 25 or older reported they had completed at least high school and 27% had attained at least a bachelor's degree—both record highs.

Educational attainment levels show a clear relation to earning potential: in 2004, workers 18 and over without a high school diploma earned $18,734 on average, those with only a high school diploma earned $27,915, bachelor's degree holders earned an average of $51,206 a year, while workers with advanced degrees made an average of $74,602.

The number of students enrolled in elementary and high school in 2003—49.5 million—surpassed the previous all-time high of 48.7 million set in 1970, when baby boomers still filled schools. After peaking in 1970, total elementary and high school enrollment fell during the 1970s and early 1980s. In addition to an increase in births during the late 1980s, immigration has also contributed to the growth of the student population. In 2003, more than 1 in 5 students had at least one foreign-born parent.

Income Stable, Poverty Up

Real median household income in 2004 was $44,389, unchanged in real terms since 2003. At the same time, the nation's official poverty rate rose from 12.7% in 2003 to 13.1% in the same period. The number of people with health insurance increased by 2.0 million to 245.3 million—84.3% of the U.S. population; 59.8% of the population is covered by employment-based insurance. The number without any insurance coverage rose by 0.8 million to 45.8 million.

Home Values Continue to Rise

According to the American Community Survey, the national median home value in 2004 was about $151,366, up nearly 5.5% from 2003, while the percentage of million-dollar homes increased from 1% to 1.4% since 2003. Despite this, home-ownership also increased 0.3%, with 67.1% of all housing units being owner-occupied. This number varies greatly by state. Minnesota (75.3%) and Michigan (74.7%) had the greatest percentage of homes that were owner-occupied. New York (55.6%) and the District of Columbia (43.6%) had the lowest percentage.

In 2004, California led the nation with the highest median home value ($391,102), followed by Hawaii ($364,840), the

District of Columbia ($334,702), and Massachusetts ($331,200). In contrast, states with the lowest median home values were Arkansas ($79,006), Mississippi ($79,023), West Virginia ($81,826), and North Dakota ($84,354). For percentage increase in value from 2003 to 2004, the District of Columbia topped the list (35%), followed by Nevada (19%), New Jersey (19%), Rhode Island (17%), and California (17%).

Of the 236 counties with populations of 250,000 or more, San Mateo ($678,433), San Francisco ($661,904), and Santa Clara ($602,727)—all in California—had some of the highest median home values in 2004. New York County closely followed ($600,250). Among counties with the least expensive homes were Hidalgo ($56,087), Cameron ($58,621), and El Paso ($73,647), Nueces ($78,018), and Bell ($83,778), all in Texas.

San Francisco ($661,904) also had the most expensive median home values among the 70 large cities with populations of 250,000 or more in 2004. Also among those with the highest median home values were three other California cities—San Jose ($554,244), San Diego ($481,829), and Oakland ($426,497).

Smaller Households, Later Marriages

The proportion of households that are family groups has remained stable; it was 67.2% in 2004.

Married-couple families comprise 50.2% of all households, and only 44% of these married-couple families have children under age 18 in their home. In families with children at home, there are many "stay-at-home" parents: about 5.7 million of them in 2004. There were a little under 5.6 million mothers and 147,000 stay-at-home fathers.

Since the mid-1990s, the percentages of single mothers and single fathers have also remained fairly constant. Female head-of-households with no husband present account for 23.8% of families with children under 18.

Of course, many households do not contain families—two or more people living together and related to one another. The proportion of households consisting of one person living alone increased from about 17% in 1970 to 26% in 2004. Unmarried-partner households accounted for 4.2% of all households, up from 2.9% in 1996.

Since the 1970s, people have been marrying later, a trend that has continued through 2004. In 2004, the median ages at first marriage were 25.8 years for women and 27.4 years for men, up from 20.8 years and 23.2 years, respectively, in 1970. As a result, the proportion of young, never-married adults has risen dramatically. For women ages 20 to 24, it more than doubled, from 36% to 75.4%; and for women ages 30 to 34, it quadrupled, from 6% to 23.7%.

As a result of these societal changes, the nation's households are smaller today. In 2004, only 10% of all households contained five or more people, a drop from 21% in 1970. In 2004, 60% of households had one or two people, compared to 46% in 1970.

Longer and More "Extreme Commutes"

According to the American Community Survey, Americans spend more than 100 hours commuting to work each year. This exceeds the two weeks of paid vacation time (80 hours) typically taken by workers over the course of a year.

For the nation as a whole, the average daily commute to work lasted about 24.7 minutes in 2004, up from 24.3 in 2003. Of the 236 counties with populations of 250,000 or more, Queens (41.2 minutes), Bronx (40.6 minutes), and Kings (40.3 minutes)—all in New York—experienced the longest average commute-to-work times. Additionally, workers living in Prince William County, VA (39.2 minutes) and Montgomery County, MD (33.3 minutes)—suburban counties located within the Washington, DC, metropolitan area—also faced some of the longest commutes.

In a ranking of large cities (with populations of 250,000 or more), New York (38.4 minutes), Chicago (35.0 minutes), Philadelphia (33.7 minutes), Newark (32.3 minutes), and Los Angeles (30 minutes) had among the nation's highest average commute times.

In 2003 (the last year for which data were available), cities with "extreme commutes" were highlighted. Among the 10 cities with the highest average commuting times, New York and Baltimore lay claim to having the highest percentage of people with "extreme" commutes; 5.6% of their commuters spent 90 or more minutes each day getting to work. Other cities with a large percentage of workers with extreme commutes include Newark, NJ (5.2%); Riverside, CA (5.0%); Los Angeles (3.0%), Philadelphia (2.9%); and Chicago (2.5%). Nationally, just 2.0% of workers faced extreme commutes to their jobs.

The Census: Looking Back

The U.S. census is conducted every 10 years as mandated by the Constitution, Article I, Section 2. The primary purpose is to apportion seats in the House of Representatives and determine state legislative district boundaries. The data are also critical for a vast array of government programs at every level, and for providing demographic information to individuals and businesses.

The first U.S. census, which counted 3.9 million people, was conducted in 1790, shortly after George Washington became president. It counted the number of free white males age 16 and over, the number under 16 (to measure how many men might be available for military service), the number of free white females, all other free persons (including any American Indians who paid taxes), and slaves. It took 18 months to collect the data, often on unofficial sheets of paper supplied by U.S. marshals. In contrast to today's pledge of confidentiality, the 1790 census results were publicly displayed. The 1790 census resulted in an increase of 41 seats (65 to 106) in the House of Representatives.

As the nation expanded, so did the scope of the census data. The first inquiry on manufactures was made in 1810. Questions on agriculture, mining, and fisheries were added in 1840. In 1850, the census included inquiries on social issues—taxation, churches, pauperism, and crime.

The 1880 census had so many questions that it took the full 10 years between censuses to publish all the results. Because of this delay, Congress limited the 1900 census to questions on population, manufactures, agriculture, and mortality. (Many of the dropped topics reappeared in later censuses.)

For many years, the undertaking of each census had to be authorized by a specific act of Congress. In 1954, Congress specified the laws under which the Census Bureau operates in Title 13 of the U.S. Code. This title delineates the basic scope of the census, the requirements for the public to provide information as well as for the Bureau to keep information confidential, and the penalties for violating any of these obligations.

Today, the secretary of commerce (and through that individual, the Census Bureau) is directed by law to take censuses of population, housing, agriculture, irrigation, manufactures, mineral industries, other businesses (wholesale trade, retail trade, services), construction, transportation, and governments at stated intervals, and may take surveys related to any of these subjects.

U.S. marshals supervised their assistants' enumeration of the first 9 censuses and reported to the president (1790), the secretary of state (1800-1840), or the secretary of the interior (1850-1870). There was no continuity of personnel from one census to the next. However, in 1902, Congress authorized the president to set up a permanent Census Office in the Interior Dept. In 1903, the agency was transferred to the new Dept. of Commerce and Labor, and when the department split in 1913, the Bureau of the Census was placed in the Commerce Dept.

The Census Bureau began using statistical sampling techniques in the 1940s, computers in the 1950s, and mail enumeration in the 1960s, all as part of an effort to publish more data sooner and at a lower cost, and with less burden on the public. For the 2010 Census, the Census Bureau planned to continue mailing questionnaires to most housing units in the country, but to use handheld computers, rather than paper and pencil, in doing follow-up interviews at nonresponding households.

U.S. Area and Population, 1790-2000

Source: Bureau of the Census, U.S. Dept. of Commerce

	AREA			POPULATION			
						Increase over preceding census	
Census date	**Gross Area**	**Land Area**	**Water Area**	**Number**	**Per sq mi of land**	**Number**	**%**
1790 (Aug. 2)	891,364	864,746	26,618	3,929,214	4.5	—	—
1800 (Aug. 4)	891,364	864,746	26,618	5,308,483	6.1	1,379,269	35.1
1810 (Aug. 6)	1,722,685	1,681,828	40,857	7,239,881	4.3	1,931,398	36.4
1820 (June 1)	1,792,552	1,749,462	43,090	9,638,453	5.5	2,398,572	33.1
1830 (June 1)	1,792,552	1,749,462	43,090	12,866,020[2]	7.4	3,227,567	33.5
1840 (June 1)	1,792,552	1,749,462	43,090	17,068,953[2]	9.8	4,203,433	32.7
1850 (June 1)	2,991,655	2,940,042	51,613	23,191,876	7.9	6,122,423	35.9
1860 (June 1)	3,021,295	2,969,640	51,655	31,443,321	10.6	8,251,445	35.6
1870 (June 1)	3,612,299	3,540,705	71,594	38,558,371	10.9	7,115,050	22.6
1880 (June 1)	3,612,299	3,540,705	71,594	50,189,209	14.2	11,630,838	30.2
1890 (June 1)	3,612,299	3,540,705	71,594	62,979,766	17.8	12,790,557	25.5
1900 (June 1)	3,618,770	3,547,314	71,456	76,212,168	21.5	13,232,402	21.0
1910 (Apr. 15)	3,618,770	3,547,045	71,725	92,228,496	26.0	16,016,328	21.0
1920 (Jan. 1)	3,618,770	3,546,931	71,839	106,021,537	29.9	13,793,041	15.0
1930 (Apr. 1)	3,618,770	3,551,608	67,162	123,202,624	34.7	17,181,087	16.2
1940 (Apr. 1)	3,618,770	3,554,608	64,162	132,164,569	37.2	8,961,945	7.3
1950 (Apr. 1)	3,618,770	3,552,206	66,564	151,325,798	42.6	19,161,229	14.5
1960 (Apr. 1)	3,618,770	3,540,911	77,859	179,323,175	50.6	27,997,377	18.5
1970 (Apr. 1)	3,618,770	3,536,855	81,915	203,302,031	57.5	23,978,856	13.4
1980 (Apr. 1)	3,618,770	3,539,289	79,481	226,542,203	64.0	23,240,172	11.4
1990 (Apr. 1)	3,717,796[1]	3,536,278	181,518[1]	248,709,873	70.3	22,167,670	9.8
2000 (Apr. 1)	3,794,085	3,537,440	256,648[1]	281,421,906	79.6	32,712,033	13.2

(1) 1990 figure includes inland, coastal, and Great Lakes water. 2000 figure includes additional territorial water as determined by presidential decree in Dec. 1998. Data before 1990 cover inland water only. (2) The U.S. total includes persons (5,318 in 1830 and 6,100 in 1840) on public ships in the service of the U.S. not credited to any region, division, or state. **NOTE:** Percent changes are computed on the basis of change in population since the preceding census date, so the period covered is not always exactly 10 years. Population density figures given for various years represent the area within the boundaries of the U.S. that was under the jurisdiction on the date in question—including, in some cases, considerable areas not organized or settled and not actually covered by the census. In 1870, for example, Alaska was not covered by the census, but its area is included in density calculations. Population figures shown here may reflect corrections made to the initial tabulated census counts.

Congressional Apportionment

Source: Bureau of the Census, U.S. Dept. of Commerce; by census year

	2000	**1990**	**1980**	**1970**	**1950**	**1900**	**1850**
AL.....	7	7	7	7	9	9	7
AK	1	1	1	1	NA	NA	NA
AZ.....	8	6	5	4	2	NA	NA
AR	4	4	4	4	6	7	2
CA	53	52	45	43	30	8	2
CO	7	6	6	5	4	3	NA
CT	5	6	6	6	6	5	4
DE	1	1	1	1	1	1	1
FL.....	25	23	19	15	8	3	1
GA	13	11	10	10	10	11	8
HI	2	2	2	2	1	NA	NA
ID	2	2	2	2	2	1	NA
IL	19	20	22	24	25	25	9
IN	9	10	10	11	11	13	11
IA	5	5	6	6	8	11	2
KS	4	4	5	5	6	8	NA
KY	6	6	7	7	8	11	10
LA.....	7	7	8	8	8	7	4
ME	2	2	2	2	3	4	6
MD	8	8	8	8	7	6	6
MA	10	10	11	12	14	14	11
MI.....	15	16	18	19	18	12	4
MN	8	8	8	8	9	9	2
MS	4	5	5	5	6	8	5
MO	9	9	9	10	11	16	7

	2000	**1990**	**1980**	**1970**	**1950**	**1900**	**1850**
MT.....	1	1	2	2	2	1	NA
NE.....	3	3	3	3	4	6	NA
NV.....	3	2	2	1	1	1	NA
NH.....	2	2	2	2	2	2	3
NJ	13	13	14	15	14	10	5
NM.....	3	3	3	2	2	NA	NA
NY.....	29	31	34	39	43	37	33
NC.....	13	12	11	11	12	10	8
ND.....	1	1	1	1	2	2	NA
OH.....	18	19	21	23	23	21	21
OK.....	5	6	6	6	6	5	NA
OR.....	5	5	5	4	4	2	1
PA	19	21	23	25	30	32	25
RI......	2	2	2	2	2	2	2
SC	6	6	6	6	6	7	6
SD	1	1	1	2	2	2	NA
TN	9	9	9	8	9	10	10
TX	32	30	27	24	22	16	2
UT	3	3	3	2	2	1	NA
VT	1	1	1	1	1	2	3
VA	11	11	10	10	10	10	13
WA.....	9	9	8	7	7	3	NA
WV.....	3	3	4	4	6	5	NA
WI	8	9	9	9	10	11	3
WY.....	1	1	1	1	1	1	NA
TOTAL	**435**	**435**	**435**	**435**	**435**	**391**	**237**

Note: NA = Not applicable.

The Constitution, in Article 1, Section 2, provided for a census of the population every 10 years to establish a basis for apportionment of representatives among the states. This apportionment largely determines the number of electoral votes allotted to each state.

The number of representatives of each state in Congress is determined by the state's population, but each state is entitled to one representative regardless of population. A congressional apportionment has been made after each decennial census except that of 1920. (The year given above is the year of the census on which apportionment for the next election year is based.) Prior to 1870, $^3/_5$ the number of slaves were added to the total free population. Indians "not taxed" were excluded until 1940.

Under provisions of a law that became effective Nov. 15, 1941, representatives are apportioned by the method of equal proportions. In the application of this method, the apportionment is made so that the average population per representative has the least possible variation between one state and any other.

The first House of Representatives, in 1789, had 65 members, as provided by the Constitution. Of these, the largest numbers were from Virginia (19), Massachusetts (14), and Pennsylvania (13).

As the nation's population grew, the number of representatives was increased, but the total membership of the House has been fixed at 435 since the apportionment based on the 1910 census.

U.S. Population by Official

STATE	1790[1]	1800[1]	1810[1]	1820[1]	1830[1]	1840	1850	1860	1870	1880	1890	1900
AL...	....	1	9	128	310	590,756	771,623	964,201	996,992	1,262,505	1,513,401	1,828,697
AK ..	....	....	....	....	....	....	....	....	....	33,426	32,052	63,592
AZ...	....	....	....	....	....	....	....	....	9,658	40,440	88,243	122,931
AR ..	....	....	1	14	30	97,574	209,897	435,450	484,471	802,525	1,128,211	1,311,564
CA ..	....	....	....	....	....	....	92,597	379,994	560,247	864,694	1,213,398	1,485,053
CO ..	....	....	....	....	....	....	....	34,277	39,864	194,327	413,249	539,700
CT ..	238	251	262	275	298	309,978	370,792	460,147	537,454	622,700	746,258	908,420
DE ..	59	64	73	73	77	78,085	91,532	112,216	125,015	146,608	168,493	184,735
DC ..	....	8	16	23	30	33,745	51,687	75,080	131,700	177,624	230,392	278,718
FL...	....	....	....	....	35	54,477	87,445	140,424	187,748	269,493	391,422	528,542
GA ..	83	163	252	341	517	691,392	906,185	1,057,286	1,184,109	1,542,180	1,837,353	2,216,331
HI...	....	....	....	....	....	....	....	....	....	....	....	154,001
ID...	....	....	....	....	....	....	....	....	14,999	32,610	88,548	161,772
IL ...	....	....	12	55	157	476,183	851,470	1,711,951	2,539,891	3,077,871	3,826,352	4,821,550
IN ...	....	6	25	147	343	685,866	988,416	1,350,428	1,680,637	1,978,301	2,192,404	2,516,462
IA ...	....	....	....	....	....	43,112	192,214	674,913	1,194,020	1,624,615	1,912,297	2,231,853
KS ..	....	....	....	....	....	....	....	107,206	364,399	996,096	1,428,108	1,470,495
KY ..	74	221	407	564	688	779,828	982,405	1,155,684	1,321,011	1,648,690	1,858,635	2,147,174
LA...	....	....	77	153	216	352,411	517,762	708,002	726,915	939,946	1,118,588	1,381,625
ME ..	97	152	229	298	399	501,793	583,169	628,279	626,915	648,936	661,086	694,466
MD ..	320	342	381	407	447	470,019	583,034	687,049	780,894	934,943	1,042,390	1,188,044
MA ..	379	423	472	523	610	737,699	994,514	1,231,066	1,457,351	1,783,085	2,238,947	2,805,346
MI...	....	....	5	9	32	212,267	397,654	749,113	1,184,059	1,636,937	2,093,890	2,420,982
MN ..	....	....	....	....	....	....	6,077	172,023	439,706	780,773	1,310,283	1,751,394
MS ..	....	8	31	75	137	375,651	606,526	791,305	827,922	1,131,597	1,289,600	1,551,270
MO ..	....	....	20	67	140	383,702	682,044	1,182,012	1,721,295	2,168,380	2,679,185	3,106,665
MT ..	....	....	....	....	....	....	....	....	20,595	39,159	142,924	243,329
NE ..	....	....	....	....	....	....	....	28,841	122,993	452,402	1,062,656	1,066,300
NV ..	....	....	....	....	....	....	....	6,857	42,491	62,266	47,355	42,335
NH ..	142	184	214	244	269	284,574	317,976	326,073	318,300	346,991	376,530	411,588
NJ...	184	211	246	278	321	373,306	489,555	672,035	906,096	1,131,116	1,444,933	1,883,669
NM ..	....	....	....	....	....	....	61,547	93,516	91,874	119,565	160,282	195,310
NY ..	340	589	959	1,373	1,919	2,428,921	3,097,394	3,880,735	4,382,759	5,082,871	6,003,174	7,268,894
NC ..	394	478	556	639	736	753,419	869,039	992,622	1,071,361	1,399,750	1,617,949	1,893,810
ND ..	....	....	....	....	....	....	....	....	2,405[2]	36,909	190,983	319,146
OH ..	....	45	231	581	938	1,519,467	1,980,329	2,339,511	2,665,260	3,198,062	3,672,329	4,157,545
OK ..	....	....	....	....	....	....	....	....	....	....	258,657	790,391
OR ..	....	....	....	....	....	....	12,093	52,465	90,923	174,768	317,704	413,536
PA ..	434	602	810	1,049	1,348	1,724,033	2,311,786	2,906,215	3,521,951	4,282,891	5,258,113	6,302,115
RI...	69	69	77	83	97	108,830	147,545	174,620	217,353	276,531	345,506	428,556
SC ..	249	346	415	503	581	594,398	668,507	703,708	705,606	995,577	1,151,149	1,340,316
SD ..	....	....	....	....	....	....	....	4,837[2]	11,776[2]	98,268	348,600	401,570
TN ..	36	106	262	423	682	829,210	1,002,717	1,109,801	1,258,520	1,542,359	1,767,518	2,020,616
TX...	....	....	....	....	....	....	212,592	604,215	818,579	1,591,749	2,235,527	3,048,710
UT ..	....	....	....	....	....	....	11,380	40,273	86,786	143,963	210,779	276,749
VT...	85	154	218	236	281	291,948	314,120	315,098	330,551	332,286	332,422	343,641
VA ..	692	808	878	938	1,044	1,025,227	1,119,348	1,219,630	1,225,163	1,512,565	1,655,980	1,854,184
WA ..	....	....	....	....	....	....	1,201	11,594	23,955	75,116	357,232	518,103
WV ..	56	79	105	137	177	224,537	302,313	376,688	442,014	618,457	762,794	958,800
WI...	....	....	....	....	....	30,945	305,391	775,881	1,054,670	1,315,497	1,693,330	2,069,042
WY ..	....	....	....	....	....	....	....	....	9,118	20,789	62,555	92,531
U.S. ..	**3,929**	**5,308**	**7,240**	**9,638**	**12,866[3]**	**17,068,953[3]**	**23,191,876**	**31,443,321**	**38,558,371**	**50,189,209**	**62,979,766**	**76,212,168**

Note: Where possible, population shown is that of the 2000 area of the state. Members of the Armed Forces overseas or other U.S. nationals abroad are not included. Totals revised to include corrections of initial tabulated counts. (1) Totals for 1790 through 1830 are in thousands. (2) 1860 figure is for Dakota Territory; 1870 figures are for parts of Dakota Territory. (3) Includes persons (5,318 in 1830 and 6,100 in 1840) on public ships in the service of the U.S. not credited to any region, division, or state.

Estimated Population of American Colonies, 1630–1780

Source: Bureau of the Census, U.S. Dept. of Commerce; in thousands

Colony	1630	1650	1670	1690	1700	1720	1740	1750	1770	1780
TOTAL	**4.6**	**50.4**	**111.9**	**210.4**	**250.9**	**466.2**	**905.6**	**1,170.8**	**2,148.1**	**2,780.4**
Maine (counties)[1]	0.4	1.0	...	...	...	...	...	...	31.3	49.1
New Hampshire[2]	0.5	1.3	1.8	4.2	5.0	9.4	23.3	27.5	62.4	87.8
Vermont[3]	...	...	...	...	...	...	...	...	10.0	47.6
Plymouth and Massachusetts[1,2,4]	0.9	15.6	35.3	56.9	55.9	91.0	151.6	188.0	235.3	268.6
Rhode Island[2]	...	0.8	2.2	4.2	5.9	11.7	25.3	33.2	58.2	52.9
Connecticut[2]	...	4.1	12.6	21.6	26.0	58.8	89.6	111.3	183.9	206.7
New York[2]	0.4	4.1	5.8	13.9	19.1	36.9	63.7	76.7	162.9	210.5
New Jersey[2]	...	...	1.0	8.0	14.0	29.8	51.4	71.4	117.4	139.6
Pennsylvania[2]	...	...	...	11.4	18.0	31.0	85.6	119.7	240.1	327.3
Delaware[2]	...	0.2	0.7	1.5	2.5	5.4	19.9	28.7	35.5	45.4
Maryland[2]	...	4.5	13.2	24.0	29.6	66.1	116.1	141.1	202.6	245.5
Virginia[2]	2.5	18.7	35.3	53.0	58.6	87.8	180.4	231.0	447.0	538.0
North Carolina[2]	...	...	3.8	7.6	10.7	21.3	51.8	73.0	197.2	270.1
South Carolina[2]	...	...	0.2	3.9	5.7	17.0	45.0	64.0	124.2	180.0
Georgia[2]	...	...	...	...	...	...	2.0	5.2	23.4	56.1
Kentucky[5]	...	...	...	...	...	...	...	...	15.7	45.0
Tennessee[6]	...	...	...	...	...	...	...	...	1.0	10.0

(1) For 1660–1750, Maine counties are included with Massachusetts. Maine was part of Massachusetts until it became a separate state in 1820. (2) One of the original 13 states. (3) Admitted to statehood in 1791. (4) Plymouth became a part of the Province of Massachusetts in 1691. (5) Admitted to statehood in 1792. (6) Admitted to statehood in 1796.

Census, 1790–2000

1910	1920	1930	1940	1950	1960	1970	1980	1990	2000
2,138,093	2,348,174	2,646,248	2,832,961	3,061,743	3,266,740	3,444,354	3,894,025	4,040,587	4,447,100
64,356	55,036	59,278	72,524	128,643	226,167	302,583	401,851	550,043	626,932
204,354	334,162	435,573	499,261	749,587	1,302,161	1,775,399	2,716,546	3,665,228	5,130,632
1,574,449	1,752,204	1,854,482	1,949,387	1,909,511	1,786,272	1,923,322	2,286,357	2,350,725	2,673,400
2,377,549	3,426,861	5,677,251	6,907,387	10,586,223	15,717,204	19,971,069	23,667,764	29,760,021	33,871,648
799,024	939,629	1,035,791	1,123,296	1,325,089	1,753,947	2,209,596	2,889,735	3,294,394	4,301,261
1,114,756	1,380,631	1,606,903	1,709,242	2,007,280	2,535,234	3,032,217	3,107,564	3,287,116	3,405,565
202,322	223,003	238,380	266,505	318,085	446,292	548,104	594,338	666,168	783,600
331,069	437,571	486,869	663,091	802,178	763,956	756,668	638,432	606,900	572,059
752,619	968,470	1,468,211	1,897,414	2,771,305	4,951,560	6,791,418	9,746,961	12,937,926	15,982,378
2,609,121	2,895,832	2,908,506	3,123,723	3,444,578	3,943,116	4,587,930	5,462,982	6,478,216	8,186,453
191,874	255,881	368,300	422,770	499,794	632,772	769,913	964,691	1,108,229	1,211,537
325,594	431,866	445,032	524,873	588,637	667,191	713,015	944,127	1,006,749	1,293,953
5,638,591	6,485,280	7,630,654	7,897,241	8,712,176	10,081,158	11,110,285	11,427,409	11,430,602	12,419,293
2,700,876	2,930,390	3,238,503	3,427,796	3,934,224	4,662,498	5,195,392	5,490,214	5,544,159	6,080,485
2,224,771	2,404,021	2,470,939	2,538,268	2,621,073	2,757,537	2,825,368	2,913,808	2,776,755	2,926,324
1,690,949	1,769,257	1,880,999	1,801,028	1,905,299	2,178,611	2,249,071	2,364,236	2,477,574	2,688,418
2,289,905	2,416,630	2,614,589	2,845,627	2,944,806	3,038,156	3,220,711	3,660,324	3,685,296	4,041,769
1,656,388	1,798,509	2,101,593	2,363,880	2,683,516	3,257,022	3,644,637	4,206,116	4,219,973	4,468,976
742,371	768,014	797,423	847,226	913,774	969,265	993,722	1,125,043	1,227,928	1,274,923
1,295,346	1,449,661	1,631,526	1,821,244	2,343,001	3,100,689	3,923,897	4,216,933	4,781,468	5,296,486
3,366,416	3,852,356	4,249,614	4,316,721	4,690,514	5,148,578	5,689,170	5,737,093	6,016,425	6,349,097
2,810,173	3,668,412	4,842,325	5,256,106	6,371,766	7,823,194	8,881,826	9,262,044	9,295,297	9,938,444
2,075,708	2,387,125	2,563,953	2,792,300	2,982,483	3,413,864	3,806,103	4,075,970	4,375,099	4,919,479
1,797,114	1,790,618	2,009,821	2,183,796	2,178,914	2,178,141	2,216,994	2,520,770	2,573,216	2,844,658
3,293,335	3,404,055	3,629,367	3,784,664	3,954,653	4,319,813	4,677,623	4,916,766	5,117,073	5,595,211
376,053	548,889	537,606	559,456	591,024	674,767	694,409	786,690	799,065	902,195
1,192,214	1,296,372	1,377,963	1,315,834	1,325,510	1,411,330	1,485,333	1,569,825	1,578,385	1,711,263
81,875	77,407	91,058	110,247	160,083	285,278	488,738	800,508	1,201,833	1,998,257
430,572	443,083	465,293	491,524	533,242	606,921	737,681	920,610	1,109,252	1,235,786
2,537,167	3,155,900	4,041,334	4,160,165	4,835,329	6,066,782	7,171,112	7,365,011	7,730,188	8,414,350
327,301	360,350	423,317	531,818	681,187	951,023	1,017,055	1,303,302	1,515,069	1,819,046
9,113,614	10,385,227	12,588,066	13,479,142	14,830,192	16,782,304	18,241,391	17,558,165	17,990,455	18,976,457
2,206,287	2,559,123	3,170,276	3,571,623	4,061,929	4,556,155	5,084,411	5,880,095	6,628,637	8,049,313
577,056	646,872	680,845	641,935	619,636	632,446	617,792	652,717	638,800	642,200
4,767,121	5,759,394	6,646,697	6,907,612	7,946,627	9,706,397	10,657,423	10,797,603	10,847,115	11,353,140
1,657,155	2,028,283	2,396,040	2,336,434	2,233,351	2,328,284	2,559,463	3,025,487	3,145,585	3,450,654
672,765	783,389	953,786	1,089,684	1,521,341	1,768,687	2,091,533	2,633,156	2,842,321	3,421,399
7,665,111	8,720,017	9,631,350	9,900,180	10,498,012	11,319,366	11,800,766	11,864,720	11,881,643	12,281,054
542,610	604,397	687,497	713,346	791,896	859,488	949,723	947,154	1,003,464	1,048,319
1,515,400	1,683,724	1,738,765	1,899,804	2,117,027	2,382,594	2,590,713	3,120,729	3,486,703	4,012,012
583,888	636,547	692,849	642,961	652,740	680,514	666,257	690,768	696,004	754,844
2,184,789	2,337,885	2,616,556	2,915,841	3,291,718	3,567,089	3,926,018	4,591,023	4,877,185	5,689,283
3,896,542	4,663,228	5,824,715	6,414,824	7,711,194	9,579,677	11,198,655	14,225,513	16,986,510	20,851,820
373,351	449,396	507,847	550,310	688,862	890,627	1,059,273	1,461,037	1,722,850	2,233,169
355,956	352,428	359,611	359,231	377,747	389,881	444,732	511,456	562,758	608,827
2,061,612	2,309,187	2,421,851	2,677,773	3,318,680	3,966,949	4,651,448	5,346,797	6,187,358	7,078,515
1,141,990	1,356,621	1,563,396	1,736,191	2,378,963	2,853,214	3,413,244	4,132,353	4,866,692	5,894,121
1,221,119	1,463,701	1,729,205	1,901,974	2,005,552	1,860,421	1,744,237	1,950,186	1,793,477	1,808,344
2,333,860	2,632,067	2,939,006	3,137,587	3,434,575	3,951,777	4,417,821	4,705,642	4,891,769	5,363,675
145,965	194,402	225,565	250,742	290,529	330,066	332,416	469,557	453,588	493,782
92,228,496	**106,021,537**	**123,202,624**	**132,164,569**	**151,325,798**	**179,323,175**	**203,302,031**	**226,542,203**	**248,709,873**	**281,421,906**

U.S. Center of Population, 1790–2000

Source: Bureau of the Census, U.S. Dept. of Commerce

The U.S. Center of Population is considered here as the center of population gravity, or that point upon which the U.S. would balance if it were a rigid plane without weight and the population distributed thereon, with each individual assumed to have equal weight and to exert an influence on a central point proportional to his or her distance from that point. The 2000 center is 12.1 miles south and 32.5 miles west of the 1990 center of population, and is more than 1,000 miles from the 1790 center.

	N Lat			W Long			
YEAR	°	′	″	°	′	″	APPROXIMATE LOCATION
1790	39	16	30	76	11	12	23 miles east of Baltimore, MD
1800	39	16	6	76	56	30	18 miles west of Baltimore, MD
1810	39	11	30	77	37	12	40 miles northwest by west of Washington, DC (in VA)
1820	39	5	42	78	33	0	16 miles east of Moorefield, WV[1]
1830	38	57	54	79	16	54	19 miles west–southwest of Moorefield, WV[1]
1840	39	2	0	80	18	0	16 miles south of Clarksburg, WV[1]
1850	38	59	0	81	19	0	23 miles southeast of Parkersburg, WV[1]
1860	39	0	24	82	48	48	20 miles south by east of Chillicothe, OH
1870	39	12	0	83	35	42	48 miles east by north of Cincinnati, OH
1880	39	4	8	84	39	40	8 miles west by south of Cincinnati, OH (in KY)
1890	39	11	56	85	32	53	20 miles east of Columbus, IN
1900	39	9	36	85	48	54	6 miles southeast of Columbus, IN
1910	39	10	12	86	32	20	In the city of Bloomington, IN
1920	39	10	21	86	43	15	8 miles south–southeast of Spencer, Owen Co., IN
1930	39	3	45	87	8	6	3 miles northeast of Linton, Greene Co., IN
1940	38	56	54	87	22	35	2 miles southeast by east of Carlisle, Haddon township, Sullivan Co., IN
1950 (incl. Alaska & Hawaii)	38	48	15	88	22	8	3 miles northeast of Louisville, Clay Co., IL
1960	38	35	58	89	12	35	6½ miles northwest of Centralia, Clinton Co., IL
1970	38	27	47	89	42	22	5 miles east southeast of Mascoutah, St. Clair Co., IL
1980	38	8	13	90	34	26	¼ mile west of De Soto, Jefferson Co., MO
1990	37	52	20	91	12	55	9.7 miles northwest of Steelville, MO
2000	37	41	49	91	48	34	2.8 miles east of Edgar Springs, MO

(1) West Virginia was set off from Virginia on Dec. 31, 1862, and was admitted as a state on June 20, 1863.

Population by State, 2000, 2004

Source: Bureau of the Census, U.S. Dept. of Commerce

Rank	State	2004 population	2000 population	Percent change 2000-2004	Rank	State	2004 population	2000 population	Percent change 2000-2004
1.	California	35,893,799	33,871,653	6.0	27.	Oregon	3,594,586	3,421,432	5.1
2.	Texas	22,490,022	20,851,790	7.9	28.	Oklahoma	3,523,553	3,450,654	2.1
3.	New York	19,227,088	18,976,821	1.3	29.	Connecticut	3,503,604	3,405,584	2.9
4.	Florida	17,397,161	15,982,820	8.8	30.	Iowa	2,954,451	2,926,382	1.0
5.	Illinois	12,713,634	12,419,570	2.4	31.	Mississippi	2,902,966	2,844,656	2.0
6.	Pennsylvania	12,406,292	12,281,054	1.0	32.	Arkansas	2,752,629	2,673,398	3.0
7.	Ohio	11,459,011	11,353,143	0.9	33.	Kansas	2,735,502	2,688,814	1.7
8.	Michigan	10,112,620	9,938,480	1.8	34.	Utah	2,389,039	2,233,198	7.0
9.	Georgia	8,829,383	8,186,517	7.8	35.	Nevada	2,334,771	1,998,257	16.8
10.	New Jersey	8,698,879	8,414,347	3.4	36.	New Mexico	1,903,289	1,819,046	4.6
11.	North Carolina	8,541,221	8,046,451	6.1	37.	West Virginia	1,815,354	1,808,350	0.4
12.	Virginia	7,459,827	7,078,483	5.4	38.	Nebraska	1,747,214	1,711,265	2.1
13.	Massachusetts	6,416,505	6,349,097	1.1	39.	Idaho	1,393,262	1,293,956	7.7
14.	Indiana	6,237,569	6,080,506	2.6	40.	Maine	1,317,253	1,274,923	3.3
15.	Washington	6,203,788	5,894,141	5.3	41.	New Hampshire	1,299,500	1,235,786	5.2
16.	Tennessee	5,900,962	5,689,262	3.7	42.	Hawaii	1,262,840	1,211,537	4.2
17.	Missouri	5,754,618	5,596,683	2.8	43.	Rhode Island	1,080,632	1,048,319	3.1
18.	Arizona	5,743,834	5,130,632	12.0	44.	Montana	926,865	902,195	2.7
19.	Maryland	5,558,058	5,296,485	4.9	45.	Delaware	830,364	783,600	6.0
20.	Wisconsin	5,509,026	5,363,704	2.7	46.	South Dakota	770,883	754,844	2.1
21.	Minnesota	5,100,958	4,919,485	3.7	47.	Alaska	655,435	626,931	4.5
22.	Colorado	4,601,403	4,301,997	7.0	48.	North Dakota	634,366	642,200	–1.2
23.	Alabama	4,530,182	4,447,100	1.9	49.	Vermont	621,394	608,827	2.1
24.	Louisiana	4,515,770	4,468,958	1.0	50.	District of Columbia	553,523	572,059	–3.2
25.	South Carolina	4,198,068	4,011,848	4.6	51.	Wyoming	506,529	493,782	2.6
26.	Kentucky	4,145,922	4,042,209	2.6		**Total Resident Pop[1]**	**293,655,404**	**281,423,231**	**4.3**

(1)Resident population excludes military personnel and others living abroad and allocated to the state in total population count.

Density of Population by State, 1930–2000

Source: Bureau of the Census, U.S. Dept. of Commerce
(per square mile, land area only)

STATE	1930	1960	1980	1990	2000	STATE	1930	1960	1980	1990	2000
AL	51.8	64.2	76.6	79.6	87.6	MT	3.7	4.6	5.4	5.5	6.2
AK*	.1	0.4	0.7	1.0	1.1	NE	18.0	18.4	20.5	20.5	22.3
AZ	3.8	11.5	23.9	32.3	45.2	NV	.8	2.6	7.3	10.9	18.2
AR	35.2	34.2	43.9	45.1	51.3	NH	51.6	67.2	102.4	123.7	137.8
CA	36.2	100.4	151.4	190.8	217.2	NJ	537.3	805.5	986.2	1,042.0	1,134.5
CO	10.0	16.9	27.9	31.8	41.5	NM	3.5	7.8	10.7	12.5	15.0
CT	328.0	520.6	637.8	678.4	702.9	NY	262.6	350.6	370.6	381.0	401.9
DE	120.5	225.2	307.6	340.8	401.0	NC	64.5	93.2	120.4	136.1	165.2
DC	7,981.5	12,523.9	10,132.3	9,882.8	9,378.0	ND	9.7	9.1	9.4	9.3	9.3
FL	27.1	91.5	180.0	239.6	296.4	OH	161.6	236.6	263.3	264.9	277.3
GA	49.7	67.8	94.1	111.9	141.4	OK	34.6	33.8	44.1	45.8	50.3
HI*	57.5	98.5	150.1	172.5	188.6	OR	9.9	18.4	27.4	29.6	35.6
ID	5.4	8.1	11.5	12.2	15.6	PA	213.8	251.4	264.3	265.1	274.0
IL	136.4	180.4	205.3	205.6	223.4	RI	649.8	819.3	897.8	960.3	1,003.2
IN	89.4	128.8	152.8	154.6	169.5	SC	56.8	78.7	103.4	115.8	133.2
IA	44.1	49.2	52.1	49.7	52.4	SD	9.1	9.0	9.1	9.2	9.9
KS	22.9	26.6	28.9	30.3	32.9	TN	62.4	86.2	111.6	118.3	138.0
KY	65.2	76.2	92.3	92.8	101.7	TX	22.1	36.4	54.3	64.9	79.6
LA	46.5	72.2	94.5	96.9	102.6	UT	6.2	10.8	17.8	21.0	27.2
ME	25.7	31.3	36.3	39.8	41.3	VT	38.8	42.0	55.2	60.8	65.8
MD	165.0	313.5	428.7	489.2	541.9	VA	60.7	99.6	134.7	156.3	178.8
MA	537.4	657.3	733.3	767.6	809.8	WA	23.3	42.8	62.1	73.1	88.6
MI	84.9	137.7	162.6	163.6	175.0	WV	71.8	77.2	80.8	74.5	75.1
MN	32.0	43.1	51.2	55.0	61.8	WI	53.7	72.6	86.5	90.1	98.8
MS	42.4	46.0	53.4	54.9	60.6	WY	2.3	3.4	4.9	4.7	5.1
MO	52.4	62.6	71.3	74.3	81.2	**U.S.**	**41.2**	**50.6**	**64.0**	**70.3**	**79.6**

* For purposes of comparison, Alaska and Hawaii are included in above tabulation for 1930, even though not states then.

25 Largest Counties, by Population, 2000, 2004

Source: Bureau of the Census, U.S. Dept of Commerce

County	2004 Population	2000 Population	Percent change	County	2004 Population	2000 Population	Percent change
Los Angeles County, CA	9,937,739	9,519,330	4.4	King County, WA	1,777,143	1,737,044	2.3
Cook County, IL	5,327,777	5,376,745	–0.9	Broward County, FL	1,754,893	1,623,018	8.1
Harris County, TX	3,644,285	3,400,578	7.2	Santa Clara County, CA	1,685,188	1,682,585	0.2
Maricopa County, AZ	3,501,001	3,072,149	14.0	Clark County, NV	1,650,671	1,375,738	20.0
Orange County, CA	2,987,591	2,846,289	5.0	Tarrant County, TX	1,588,088	1,537,372	9.8
San Diego County, CA	2,931,714	2,813,833	4.2	New York County, NY	1,562,723	1,446,219	1.6
Kings County, NY	2,475,290	2,465,525	0.4	Bexar County, TX	1,493,965	1,392,931	7.3
Miami–Dade County, FL	2,363,600	2,253,779	4.9	Suffolk County, NY	1,475,488	1,419,369	4.0
Dallas County, TX	2,294,706	2,218,774	3.4	Philadelphia County, PA	1,470,151	1,517,550	–3.1
Queens County, NY	2,237,216	2,229,379	0.4	Middlesex County, MA	1,464,628	1,466,394	–0.1
Wayne County, MI	2,016,202	2,061,162	–2.2	Alameda County, CA	1,455,235	1,443,741	0.8
San Bernardino County, CA	1,921,131	1,709,434	12.4	Bronx County, NY	1,365,536	1,334,749	2.5
Riverside County, CA	1,871,950	1,545,387	21.1				

Note on least populated counties: The following are the ten smallest counties by 2004 population: Loving County, TX (52); Kalawao County, HI (126); King County, TX (323); Arthur County, NE (402); Kenedy County, TX (407); Petroleum County, MT (492); Blaine County, NE (518); McPherson County, NE (524); San Juan County, CO (575); and Loup County, NE (712).

Metropolitan Area Populations, 1990–2000

Source: Bureau of the Census, U.S. Dept. of Commerce
(MSAs ranked by Census 2000 population counts)

Metropolitan Statistical Areas (MSAs) are defined for federal statistical use by the Office of Management and Budget (OMB), with technical assistance from the Bureau of the Census. These definitions have been revised periodically, and were last modified in 2000. The list below was released in Dec. 2003. MSAs must have at least one urbanized area of 50,000 inhabitants or more, plus an adjacent area closely integrated socially and economically with the core as measured by commuting ties. A new category, Micropolitan Statistical Areas (not listed here)—must in general have at least one urban cluster with a population of at least 10,000 but no more than 50,000. Some metropolitan areas with populations of 2.5 million or more may, under certain circumstances, be subdivided into smaller groupings of counties referred to as "metropolitan divisions."

The Office of Management and Budget has designated 361 MSAs in the U.S. and 8 MSAs in Puerto Rico.

Applying the 2003 OMB revisions to 2000 census figures showed that the nation in that year had 49 metropolitan areas of at least 1 mil people, including 6 that had reached that size since 1990. The 49 areas had 149.2 mil people, or 53% of the U.S. population, in 2000. In all, about 236.2 mil people resided in MSAs in 2000, 83.9% of the total U.S. population. This was an increase of 28.9 mil (13.9%) since 1990.

Rank	Metropolitan Statistical Area (MSA)	Population 2000	Population 1990	Percent Change 1990-2000
1	New York–Northern New Jersey–Long Island, NY–NJ–PA	18,323,002	16,846,046	8.8
2	Los Angeles–Long Beach–Santa Ana, CA	12,365,627	11,273,720	9.7
3	Chicago–Naperville–Joliet, IL–IN–WI	9,098,316	8,182,076	11.2
4	Philadelphia–Camden–Wilmington, PA–NJ–DE	5,687,147	5,435,468	4.6
5	Dallas–Fort Worth–Arlington, TX	5,161,544	3,989,294	29.4
6	Miami–Fort Lauderdale–Miami Beach, FL	5,007,564	4,056,100	23.5
7	Washington–Arlington–Alexandria, DC–VA–MD	4,796,183	4,122,914	16.3
8	Houston–Baytown–Sugar Land, TX	4,715,407	3,767,335	25.2
9	Detroit–Warren–Livonia, MI	4,452,557	4,248,699	4.8
10	Boston–Cambridge–Quincy, MA–NH	4,391,344	4,133,895	6.2
11	Atlanta–Sandy Springs–Marietta, GA	4,247,981	3,069,425	38.4
12	San Francisco–Oakland–Fremont, CA	4,123,740	3,686,592	11.9
13	Riverside–San Bernardino–Ontario, CA	3,254,821	2,588,793	25.7
14	Phoenix–Mesa–Scottsdale, AZ	3,251,876	2,238,480	45.3
15	Seattle–Tacoma–Bellevue, WA	3,043,878	2,559,164	18.9
16	Minneapolis–St. Paul–Bloomington, MN–WI	2,968,806	2,538,834	16.9
17	San Diego–Carlsbad–San Marcos, CA	2,813,833	2,498,016	12.6
18	St. Louis, MO–IL	2,698,687	2,580,897	4.6
19	Baltimore–Towson, MD	2,552,994	2,382,172	7.2
20	Pittsburgh, PA	2,431,087	2,468,289	–1.5
21	Tampa–St. Petersburg–Clearwater, FL	2,395,997	2,067,959	15.9
22	Denver–Aurora, CO	2,179,240	1,666,883	30.7
23	Cleveland–Elyria–Mentor, OH	2,148,143	2,102,248	2.2
24	Cincinnati–Middletown, OH–KY–IN	2,009,632	1,844,917	8.9
25	Portland–Vancouver–Beaverton, OR–WA	1,927,881	1,523,741	26.5
26	Kansas City, MO–KS	1,836,038	1,636,528	12.2
27	Sacramento–Arden–Arcade–Roseville, CA	1,796,857	1,481,102	21.3
28	San Jose–Sunnyvale–Santa Clara, CA	1,735,819	1,534,274	13.1
29	San Antonio, TX	1,711,703	1,407,745	21.6
30	Orlando, FL	1,644,561	1,224,852	34.3
31	Columbus, OH	1,612,694	1,405,168	14.8
32	Providence–New Bedford–Fall River, RI–MA	1,582,997	1,509,789	4.8
33	Virginia Beach–Norfolk–Newport News, VA–NC	1,576,370	1,449,389	8.8
34	Indianapolis, IN	1,525,104	1,294,217	17.8
35	Milwaukee–Waukesha–West Allis, WI	1,500,741	1,432,149	4.8
36	Las Vegas–Paradise, NV	1,375,765	741,459	85.5
37	Charlotte–Gastonia–Concord, NC–SC	1,330,448	1,024,643	29.8
38	New Orleans–Metairie–Kenner, LA	1,316,510	1,264,391	4.1
39	Nashville–Davidson–Murfreesboro, TN	1,311,789	1,048,216	25.1
40	Austin–Round Rock, TX	1,249,763	846,227	47.7
41	Memphis, TN–MS–AR	1,205,204	1,067,263	12.9
42	Buffalo–Niagara Falls, NY	1,170,111	1,189,288	–1.6
43	Louisville, KY–IN	1,161,975	1,055,973	10.0
44	Hartford–West Hartford–East Hartford, CT	1,148,618	1,123,678	2.2
45	Jacksonville, FL	1,122,750	925,213	21.4
46	Richmond, VA	1,096,957	949,244	15.6
47	Oklahoma City, OK	1,095,421	971,042	12.8
48	Birmingham–Hoover, AL	1,052,238	956,844	10.0
49	Rochester, NY	1,037,831	1,002,410	3.5
50	Salt Lake City, UT	968,858	768,075	26.1
51	Bridgeport–Stamford–Norwalk, CT	882,567	827,645	6.6
52	Honolulu, HI	876,156	836,231	4.8
53	Tulsa, OK	859,532	761,019	12.9
54	Dayton, OH	848,153	843,835	0.5
55	Tucson, AZ	843,746	666,880	26.5
56	Albany–Schenectady–Troy, NY	825,875	809,443	2.0
57	New Haven–Milford, CT	824,008	804,219	2.5
58	Fresno, CA	799,407	667,490	19.8
59	Raleigh–Cary, NC	797,071	541,100	47.3
60	Omaha–Council Bluffs, NE–IA	767,041	685,797	11.8
61	Oxnard–Thousand Oaks–Ventura, CA	753,197	669,016	12.6
62	Worcester, MA	750,963	709,705	5.8
63	Grand Rapids–Wyoming, MI	740,482	645,914	14.6
64	Allentown–Bethlehem–Easton, PA–NJ	740,395	686,688	7.8
65	Albuquerque, NM	729,649	599,416	21.7
66	Baton Rouge, LA	705,973	623,853	13.2
67	Akron, OH	694,960	657,575	5.7
68	Springfield, MA	680,014	672,970	1.0
69	El Paso, TX	679,622	591,610	14.9
70	Bakersfield, CA	661,645	543,477	21.7

Population of 100 Largest U.S. Cities, 1850–2004

Source: Bureau of the Census, U.S. Dept. of Commerce; ranked by estimated 2004 population

Rank	City	2004	2000	1990	1980	1970	1950	1900	1850
1.	New York, NY	8,104,079	8,008,654	7,322,564	7,071,639	7,895,563	7,891,957	3,437,202	696,115
2.	Los Angeles, CA	3,845,541	3,694,742	3,485,398	2,968,528	2,811,801	1,970,358	102,479	1,610
3.	Chicago, IL	2,862,244	2,896,047	2,783,726	3,005,072	3,369,357	3,620,962	1,698,575	29,963
4.	Houston, TX	2,012,626	1,953,633	1,630,553	1,595,138	1,233,535	596,163	44,633	2,396
5.	Philadelphia, PA	1,470,151	1,517,550	1,585,577	1,688,210	1,949,996	2,071,605	1,293,697	121,376
6.	Phoenix, AZ	1,418,041	1,321,190	983,403	789,704	584,303	106,818	5,544	...
7.	San Diego, CA	1,263,756	1,223,429	1,110,549	875,538	697,471	334,387	17,700	...
8.	San Antonio, TX	1,236,249	1,151,305	935,933	785,940	654,153	408,442	53,321	3,488
9.	Dallas, TX	1,210,393	1,188,589	1,006,877	904,599	844,401	434,462	42,638	...
10.	San Jose, CA	904,522	895,193	782,248	629,400	459,913	95,280	21,500	...
11.	Detroit, MI	900,198	951,270	1,027,974	1,203,368	1,514,063	1,849,568	285,704	21,019
12.	Indianapolis, IN[1]	784,242	781,864	741,952	700,807	736,856	427,173	169,164	8,091
13.	Jacksonville, FL[1]	777,704	735,617	635,230	540,920	504,265	204,517	28,429	1,045
14.	San Francisco, CA	744,230	776,733	723,959	678,974	715,674	775,357	342,782	34,776
15.	Columbus, OH	730,008	711,265	632,910	565,021	540,025	375,901	125,560	17,882
16.	Austin, TX	681,804	656,562	465,622	345,890	253,539	132,459	22,258	629
17.	Memphis, TN	671,929	650,100	610,337	646,174	623,988	396,000	102,320	8,841
18.	Baltimore, MD	636,251	651,154	736,014	786,741	905,787	949,708	508,957	169,054
19.	Fort Worth, TX	603,337	541,099	447,619	385,164	393,455	278,778	26,688	...
20.	Charlotte, NC	594,359	557,834	395,934	315,474	241,420	134,042	18,091	1,065
21.	El Paso, TX	592,099	563,657	515,342	425,259	322,261	130,485	15,906	...
22.	Milwaukee, WI	583,624	596,974	628,088	636,297	717,372	637,392	285,315	20,061
23.	Seattle, WA	571,480	563,376	516,259	493,846	530,831	467,591	80,671	...
24.	Boston, MA	569,165	589,141	574,283	562,994	641,071	801,444	560,892	136,881
25.	Denver, CO	556,835	553,693	467,610	492,686	514,678	415,786	133,859	...
26.	Louisville, KY[1]	556,332	256,207	269,063	298,694	361,706	369,129	204,731	43,194
27.	Washington, DC	553,523	572,059	606,900	638,432	756,668	802,178	278,718	40,001
28.	Nashville, TN[1]	546,719	545,535	510,784	455,651	426,029	174,307	80,865	10,165
29.	Las Vegas, NV	534,847	479,639	258,295	164,674	125,787	24,624	...	...
30.	Portland, OR	533,492	529,184	437,319	368,148	379,967	373,628	90,426	...
31.	Oklahoma City, OK	528,042	506,129	444,719	404,014	368,164	243,504	10,037	...
32.	Tucson, AZ	512,023	487,341	405,390	330,537	262,933	45,454	7,531	...
33.	Albuquerque, NM	484,246	448,948	384,736	332,920	244,501	96,815	6,238	...
34.	Long Beach, CA	476,564	461,522	429,433	361,498	358,879	250,767	2,252	...
35.	New Orleans, LA	462,269	484,674	496,938	557,927	593,471	570,445	287,104	116,375
36.	Cleveland, OH	458,684	477,472	505,616	573,822	750,879	914,808	381,768	17,034
37.	Fresno, CA	457,719	428,873	354,202	217,491	165,655	91,669	12,470	...
38.	Sacramento, CA	454,330	407,018	369,365	275,741	257,105	137,572	29,282	6,820
39.	Kansas City, MO	444,387	441,545	435,146	448,028	507,330	456,622	163,752	...
40.	Virginia Beach, VA	440,098	425,257	393,069	262,199	172,106	5,390	...	...
41.	Mesa, AZ	437,454	397,776	288,091	152,404	63,049	16,790	722	...
42.	Atlanta, GA	419,122	416,441	394,017	425,022	495,039	331,314	89,872	2,572
43.	Omaha, NE	409,416	391,019	335,795	313,939	346,929	251,117	102,555	...
44.	Oakland, CA	397,976	399,484	372,242	339,337	361,561	384,575	66,960	...
45.	Tulsa, OK	383,764	393,120	367,302	360,919	330,350	182,740	1,390	...
46.	Miami, FL	379,724	362,437	358,548	346,681	334,859	249,276	1,681	...
47.	Honolulu, HI[2]	377,260	371,657	365,272	365,048	324,871	248,034	39,306	...
48.	Minneapolis, MN	373,943	382,747	368,383	370,951	434,400	521,718	202,718	...
49.	Colorado Springs, CO	369,363	360,988	281,140	215,105	135,517	45,472	21,085	...
50.	Arlington, TX	359,467	332,969	261,721	160,113	90,229	7,692	1,079	...
51.	Wichita, KS	353,823	351,150	304,011	279,838	276,554	168,279	24,671	...
52.	St. Louis, MO	343,279	348,189	396,685	452,801	622,236	856,796	575,238	77,860
53.	Santa Ana, CA	342,715	337,977	293,742	204,023	155,710	45,533	4,933	...
54.	Anaheim, CA	333,776	328,071	266,406	219,494	166,408	14,556	1,456	...
55.	Raleigh, NC	326,653	282,956	207,951	150,255	122,830	65,679	13,643	4,518
56.	Pittsburgh, PA	322,450	334,563	369,879	423,959	520,089	676,806	321,616	46,601
57.	Tampa, FL	321,772	303,463	280,015	271,577	277,714	124,681	15,839	...
58.	Cincinnati, OH	314,154	331,285	364,040	385,409	453,514	503,998	325,902	115,435
59.	Toledo, OH	304,973	313,782	332,943	354,635	383,062	303,616	131,822	3,829
60.	Aurora, CO	291,843	275,923	222,103	158,588	74,974	11,421	202	...
61.	Riverside, CA	288,384	255,175	226,505	170,591	140,089	46,764	7,973	...
62.	Bakersfield, CA	283,936	243,082	174,820	105,611	69,515	34,784	4,836	...
63.	Buffalo, NY	282,864	292,648	328,123	357,870	462,768	580,132	352,387	42,261
64.	Corpus Christi, TX	281,196	277,496	257,453	232,134	204,525	108,287	4,703	...
65.	Newark, NJ	280,451	272,537	275,221	329,248	381,930	438,776	246,070	38,894
66.	Stockton, CA	279,888	243,771	210,943	148,283	109,963	70,853	17,506	...
67.	St. Paul, MN	276,963	286,840	272,235	270,230	309,866	311,349	163,065	1,112
68.	Anchorage, AK	272,687	260,283	226,338	174,431	48,081	11,254	...	...
69.	Lexington, KY	266,358	260,512	225,366	204,165	108,137	55,534	26,369	8,159
70.	St. Petersburg, FL	249,090	248,408	238,629	238,647	216,159	96,738	1,575	...
71.	Plano, TX	245,411	222,008	128,713	72,331	17,872	2,126	1,304	...
72.	Jersey City, NJ	239,079	240,055	228,537	223,532	260,350	299,017	206,433	6,856
73.	Norfolk, VA	237,835	234,403	261,229	266,979	307,951	213,513	46,624	14,326
74.	Lincoln, NE	236,146	225,638	191,972	171,932	149,518	98,884	40,169	...
75.	Glendale, AZ	235,591	218,831	148,134	96,988	36,228	8,179	...	...
76.	Birmingham, AL	233,149	242,790	265,968	284,413	300,910	326,037	38,415	...
77.	Greensboro, NC	231,543	224,047	183,521	155,642	144,076	74,389	10,035	...
78.	Henderson, NV	224,829	175,406	64,942	23,376	16,400	5,717	...	...
79.	Hialeah, FL	224,522	226,419	188,004	145,254	102,452	19,676	...	...
80.	Baton Rouge, LA	224,097	228,520	219,531	220,394	165,921	125,629	11,269	3,905
81.	Chandler, AZ	223,991	176,643	89,862	29,673	13,763	3,799	...	...
82.	Scottsdale, AZ	221,792	202,596	130,069	88,364	67,823	2,032	...	...
83.	Madison, WI	220,332	208,903	191,262	170,616	171,809	96,056	19,164	1,525
84.	Fort Wayne, IN	219,351	220,483	173,072	172,391	178,269	133,607	45,115	4,282
85.	Garland, TX	217,176	215,794	180,650	138,857	81,437	10,571	819	...

Rank	City	2004	2000	1990	1980	1970	1950	1900	1850
86.	Chesapeake, VA	214,725	199,184	151,976	114,486	89,580	...	...	...
87.	Rochester, NY	212,481	219,773	231,636	241,741	295,011	332,488	162,608	36,403
88.	Akron, OH	212,179	217,070	223,019	237,177	275,425	274,605	42,728	3,266
89.	Lubbock, TX	207,852	199,572	186,206	174,361	149,101	71,747	...	...
90.	Modesto, CA	206,769	188,864	164,730	106,963	61,712	17,389	2,024[3]	...
91.	Orlando, FL	205,648	190,914	164,693	128,394	99,006	52,367	2,481	...
92.	Chula Vista, CA	204,879	173,553	135,163	83,927	67,901	31,339	...	...
93.	Laredo, TX	203,212	177,322	122,899	91,449	69,024	51,910	13,429	...
94.	Fremont, CA	202,373	203,413	173,339	131,945	100,869	...	...	...
95.	Durham, NC	201,726	187,316	136,611	100,831	95,438	71,311	6,679	...
96.	Glendale, CA	201,326	194,973	180,038	139,060	133,000	96,000	...	...
97.	Montgomery, AL	200,983	201,607	187,106	177,857	133,386	106,525	30,346	8,728
98.	Shreveport, LA	198,675	200,172	198,525	206,989	182,064	127,206	16,013	1,728
99.	San Bernardino, CA	198,406	185,240	170,036	118,794	106,869	63,058	6,150	NA[4]
100.	Reno, NV	197,963	180,901	134,230	100,756	72,863	32,497	4,500	—

(1) Indianapolis, IN; Jacksonville, FL; Louisville, KY; and Nashville, TN, are parts of consolidated city–county governments. Populations of other incorporated places in the county have been excluded from the population totals shown here. For years that predate the establishment of a consolidated city–county government, city population is shown. (2) Locations in Hawaii are called "census designated places (CDPs)." Although these areas are not incorporated, they are recognized for census purposes as large urban places. Honolulu CDP is coextensive with Honolulu Judicial District within the city and county of Honolulu. (3) Estimated. (4) The earliest census figure for San Bernardino is 940, in 1860.

Mobility, by Selected Characteristics, 2003–04

Source: 2004 Annual Social and Economic Supplement to Current Population Survey, Bureau of the Census, U.S. Dept. of Commerce

(numbers in thousands)

	Total no. of movers[1]	MOVED TO: Same county	Diff. county, same state	Diff. state	Abroad
Marital status					
Married, spouse present	11,499	6,156	2,499	2,399	445
Married, spouse absent	721	372	119	128	102
Widowed	926	535	179	189	23
Divorced	3,303	2,001	658	610	34
Separated	1,089	733	190	143	23
Never married	12,364	7,118	2,463	2,347	436
Educational attainment[2]					
Less than 9th grade	1,214	732	188	159	135
Grades 9-12, no diploma	2,008	1,311	305	324	68
High school grad.	6,289	3,762	1,270	1,109	148
Some college or AA degree	5,610	3,147	1,209	1,163	91
Bachelor's degree	4,229	2,165	943	955	166
Prof. or graduate degree	2,035	943	367	576	149

	Total no. of movers[1]	MOVED TO: Same county	Diff. county, same state	Diff. state	Abroad
Income[3]					
Under $5,000	3,343	1,793	679	723	149
$5,000–$9,999	3,208	1,949	569	580	110
$10,000–$19,999	6,225	3,770	1,099	1,225	131
$20,000–$29,999	4,631	2,650	1,037	849	97
$30,000–$39,999	3,164	1,753	760	600	51
$40,000–$49,999	1,956	1,040	472	391	53
$50,000–$59,999	1,144	638	278	219	10
$60,000–$74,999	1,111	611	266	214	20
$75,000–$99,999	769	423	153	180	12
$100,000 and over	849	457	142	210	40
Ownership status					
Owner	14,841	8,303	3,398	2,824	316
Renter	24,154	14,248	4,443	4,505	957
ALL MOVERS[4]	**38,995**	**22,551**	**7,842**	**7,330**	**1,272**

(1) People who moved to a new residence in the 12 months preceding the survey, made in Feb.-Apr. 2004. (2) People 25 years and older. (3) People 15 years and older. (4) People 1 year and older.

U.S. Population, by Age, Sex, and Household, 2000

Source: Bureau of the Census, U.S. Dept. of Commerce; 2000 Census

	Number	%
Total population	**281,421,906**	**100**
AGE		
Under 5 years	19,175,798	6.8
5 to 9 years	20,549,505	7.3
10 to 14 years	20,528,072	7.3
15 to 19 years	20,219,890	7.2
20 to 24 years	18,964,001	6.7
25 to 34 years	39,891,724	14.2
35 to 44 years	45,148,527	16.0
45 to 54 years	37,677,952	13.4
55 to 59 years	13,469,237	4.8
60 to 64 years	10,805,447	3.8
65 to 74 years	18,390,986	6.5
75 to 84 years	12,361,180	4.4
85 years and over	4,239,587	1.5
18 years and over	209,128,094	74.3
Male	100,994,367	35.9
Female	108,133,727	38.4
21 years and over	196,899,193	70.0
62 years and over	41,256,029	14.7
65 years and over	34,991,753	12.4
SEX		
Male	138,053,563	49.1
Female	143,368,343	50.9
HOUSEHOLDS BY TYPES		
Total Households	105,480,101	100.0
Family households (families)	71,787,347	68.1
Married–couple families	54,493,232	51.7
Female householder, no husband present	12,900,103	12.2
Nonfamily households	33,692,754	31.9
Householder living alone	27,230,075	25.8
Householder 65 years and over	9,722,857	9.2
Persons living in households	273,643,273	97.2
Persons per household	2.59	NA
Persons living in group quarters	7,778,633	2.8
Institutionalized persons	4,059,039	1.4
Other persons in group quarters	3,719,594	1.3

NA = Not applicable.

IT'S A FACT: Of the 70 largest cities in 2004, New Orleans, LA, ranked as the place where U.S.-born residents were most likely to also be natives of their state—88% were. Of all states, Louisiana and New York had the highest percentage of U.S.-born residents still living in the state where they were born—82%. The states with the lowest percentage of U.S-born residents who were also state natives were Arizona and Nevada, each with only 28%.

U.S. Foreign-Born Population

Source: Bureau of the Census, U.S. Dept. of Commerce; total population based on Current Population Survey

Percentage of Population That Is Foreign-Born, 1900–2004

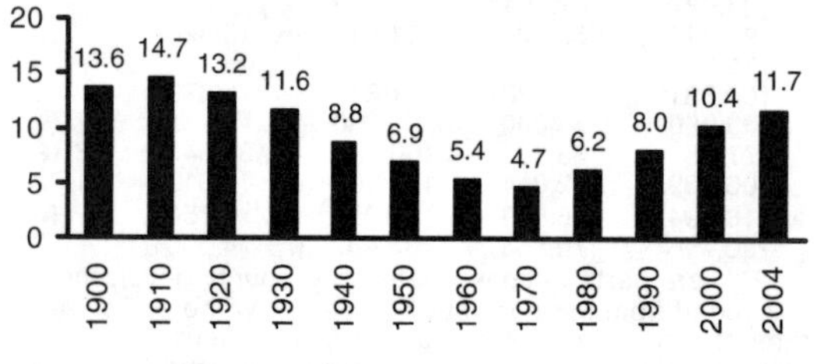

U.S. Foreign–Born Population by Regional Origin, 1995–2004

Region	2004 (thous.)	2004 % of totals	2000 (thous.)	1995 (thous.)
Europe	4,661	13.6	4,355	3,937
Under 18	327	10.6	250	232
Asia	8,685	25.4	7,246	6,121
Under 18	649	20.9	657	767
Latin America	18,314	53.5	14,477	11,777
Under 18	1,836	59.2	1,684	1,481
Other	2,584	7.5	2,301	2,658
Under 18	285	9.2	245	275
ALL REGIONS	**34,244**	**100.0**	**28,379**	**24,493**
Under 18	**3,098**	**100.0**	**2,837**	**2,726**

Foreign–Born Population: Top Countries of Origin, 1880, 1920, 1960, 1980, 2000

Source: Bureau of the Census, U.S. Dept. of Commerce
(totals in thousands; % is percent of all foreign-born)

1880			1920			1960			1980			2000		
Country	**No.**	**%**	**Country**	**No.**	**%**	**Country**	**No.**	**%**	**Country**	**No.**	**%**	**Country**	**No.**	**%**
Germany	1,967	29.4	Germany	1,686	12.1	Italy	1,257	12.9	Mexico	2,199	15.6	Mexico	9,177	29.5
Ireland	1,855	27.8	Italy	1,610	11.6	Germany	990	10.2	Germany	849	6.0	China[2]	1,519	4.9
Gr. Britain	918	13.7	U.S.S.R.	1,400	10.1	Canada	952	9.8	Canada	843	6.0	Philippines	1,369	4.4
Canada	717	10.7	Poland	1,140	8.2	Gr. Britain	765	7.9	Italy	832	5.9	India	1,023	3.3
Sweden	194	2.9	Canada	1,138	8.2	Poland	748	7.7	Gr. Britain	649	4.6	Vietnam	988	3.2
Norway	182	2.7	Gr. Britain	1,135	8.2	U.S.S.R.	691	7.1	Cuba	608	4.3	Cuba	873	2.8
France	107	1.6	Ireland	1,037	7.5	Mexico	576	5.9	Poland	418	3.0	Korea[3]	864	2.8
China[1]	104	1.6	Sweden	626	4.5	Ireland	339	3.5	U.S.S.R.	406	2.9	Canada	821	2.6
Switzerland	89	1.3	Austria	576	4.1	Austria	305	3.1	China[1]	286	2.0	El Salvador	817	2.6
Czech.	85	1.3	Mexico	486	3.5	Hungary	245	2.5	Japan	222	1.6	Germany	707	2.3
Total	**6,680**		Total	**13,921**		**Total**	**9,738**		**Total**	**14,080**		**Total**	**28,379**	

(1) Prior to 1980, includes Taiwan. (2) Includes Hong Kong, Taiwan, and Paracel Islands. (3) Includes N. and S. Korea.

Languages Spoken at Home by the U.S. Population[1], 2000

Source: Bureau of the Census, U.S. Dept. of Commerce
(as of Apr. 1, in thousands; based on 2000 Census of Population and Housing)

Language	Speakers (thousands)	Language	Speakers (thousands)	Language	Speakers (thousands)
Total U.S. pop. 5 years and older	**262,375**	Italian	1,008	Urdu	263
Speak only English	215,424	Korean	894	Gujarathi	236
Speak other language	**46,952**	Russian	706	Serbo-Croatian	234
Spanish or Spanish Creole	28,101	Polish	667	Armenian	203
Chinese	2,022	Arabic	615	Hebrew	195
French (inc. Patois, Cajun)	1,644	Portuguese or Portuguese Creole	565	Mon-Khmer, Cambodian	182
German	1,383	Japanese	478	Navajo	178
Tagalog	1,224	Greek	365	Miao, Hmong	168
Vietnamese	1,010	Hindi	317	Laotian	149
		Persian	312	Thai	120
				Hungarian	118

(1) 5 years and older

Immigrants Admitted, by State of Intended Residence, 2004

Source: Bureau of Citizenship and Immigration Services, U.S. Dept. of Homeland Security
(fiscal year 2004)

STATE	Immigrants	STATE	Immigrants	STATE	Immigrants	STATE	Immigrants
Alabama	2,139	Iowa	3,984	New Jersey	50,303	Vermont	790
Alaska	1,219	Kansas	4,041	New Mexico	3,024	Virginia	21,695
Arizona	19,297	Kentucky	3,624	New York	102,390	Washington	19,442
Arkansas	2,251	Louisiana	2,998	North Carolina	10,718	West Virginia	583
California	252,920	Maine	1,264	North Dakota	578	Wisconsin	5,257
Colorado	10,923	Maryland	20,253	Ohio	11,599	Wyoming	295
Connecticut	12,138	Massachusetts	27,676	Oklahoma	3,506	Guam	1,272
Delaware	1,671	Michigan	18,334	Oregon	8,389	Northern Mariana Islands	69
Dist. of Columbia	2,110	Minnesota	11,708	Pennsylvania	18,232	Puerto Rico	4,754
Florida	75,644	Mississippi	1,252	Rhode Island	3,689	U.S. Virgin Isls.	878
Georgia	16,286	Missouri	6,782	South Carolina	2,496	Armed Services Posts	114
Hawaii	6,347	Montana	419	South Dakota	727	Other or unknown	109
Idaho	2,229	Nebraska	2,954	Tennessee	5,620	**Total**	**946,142**
Illinois	46,314	Nevada	8,758	Texas	91,799		
Indiana	5,929	New Hampshire	2,198	Utah	4,255		

WORLD ALMANAC QUICK QUIZ

Three of these states each saw population increases of more than 5% from 2000 to 2004. One saw a decrease in population over that same period. Which one was it?

(a) North Dakota (b) Idaho (c) Virginia (d) Washington

For the answer look in this chapter, or see page 1008.

Immigrants Admitted, by Top 50 Metropolitan Areas of Intended Residence, 2003

Source: Bureau of Citizenship and Immigration Services, U.S. Dept. of Homeland Security

(fiscal year 2003)

Metropolitan Statistical Area (MSA)	Number	Percentage
TOTAL Immigrants admitted to U.S.	**703,542**	**100%**
New York, NY	71,536	10.2
Los Angeles-Long Beach, CA	64,422	9.2
Chicago, IL	29,815	4.2
Washington, DC-MD-VA-WV	29,768	4.2
Miami, FL	21,047	3.0
Houston, TX	15,357	2.2
Orange County, CA	15,167	2.2
Oakland, CA	13,704	1.9
Boston, MA-NH	13,526	1.9
San Jose, CA	12,992	1.8
San Francisco, CA	12,797	1.8
San Diego, CA	12,777	1.8
Dallas, TX	12,057	1.7
Seattle-Bellevue-Everett, WA	11,351	1.6
Fort Lauderdale, FL	10,738	1.5
Riverside-San Bernardino, CA	10,710	1.5
Nassau-Suffolk, NY	10,358	1.5
Philadelphia, PA-NJ	10,166	1.4
Newark, NJ	10,160	1.4
Detroit, MI	9,162	1.3
Bergen-Passaic, NJ	9,080	1.3
Middlesex-Somerset-Hunterdon, NJ	8,578	1.2
Atlanta, GA	8,481	1.2
Phoenix-Mesa, AZ	7,464	1.1
Minneapolis-St. Paul, MN-WI	7,110	1.0
Denver, CO	6,903	1.0
Portland-Vancouver, OR-WA	6,002	0.9
Sacramento, CA	5,909	0.8
Jersey City, NJ	5,908	0.8
Las Vegas, NV-AZ	5,135	0.7
Baltimore, MD	4,974	0.7
West Palm Beach-Boca Raton, FL	4,809	0.7
Orlando, FL	4,110	0.6
Tampa-St. Petersburg-Clearwater, FL	4,064	0.6
Fresno, CA	3,991	0.6
Honolulu, HI	3,733	0.5
St. Louis, MO-IL	3,596	0.5
Fort Worth-Arlington, TX	3,577	0.5
Austin-San Marcos, TX	3,425	0.5
San Antonio, TX	3,184	0.5
Columbus, OH	3,166	0.5
Kansas City, MO-KS	3,097	0.4
Ventura, CA	2,967	0.4
Hartford, CT	2,899	0.4
Raleigh-Durham-Chapel Hill, NC	2,740	0.4
San Juan-Bayamon, PR	2,692	0.4
Providence-Fall River-Warwick, RI-MA	2,679	0.4
Cleveland-Lorain-Elyria, OH	2,634	0.4
McAllen-Edinburg-Mission, TX	2,595	0.4
Bakersfield, CA	2,514	0.4
Non-MSA	36,853	5.2
Other & Unknown	131,063	18.6

Projections of Total U.S. Population, by Age, 2010–50

Source: Bureau of the Census, U.S. Dept. of Commerce

Age	2010 Pop.[1]	2010 % Distrib.	2020 Pop.[1]	2020 % Distrib.	2030 Pop.[1]	2030 % Distrib.	2040 Pop.[1]	2040 % Distrib.	2050 Pop.[1]	2050 % Distrib.
TOTAL	**308,936**	**100**	**335,805**	**100**	**363,584**	**100**	**391,946**	**100**	**419,854**	**100**
Under 5 years	21,426	6.9	22,932	6.8	24,272	6.7	26,299	6.7	28,080	6.7
5–14 years	40,473	13.1	44,478	13.2	47,329	13.0	50,503	12.9	54,495	13.0
15–24 years	43,012	13.9	42,229	12.6	46,639	12.8	49,721	12.7	52,869	12.6
25–34 years	41,646	13.5	45,065	13.4	44,935	12.4	49,755	12.7	52,804	12.6
35–44 years	41,121	13.3	42,816	12.8	46,676	12.8	47,008	12.0	51,796	12.3
45–54 years	44,827	14.5	40,921	12.2	42,902	11.8	46,981	12.0	47,383	11.3
55–64 years	36,186	11.7	42,732	12.7	39,378	10.8	41,629	10.6	45,721	10.9
65 years and over	40,244	13.0	54,632	16.3	71,453	19.7	80,050	20.4	86,706	20.7
85 years and over	6,123	2.0	7,269	2.2	9,603	2.6	15,409	3.9	20,861	5.0

NOTE: Estimates of U.S. population consistent with the 2000 decennial census, as enumerated. All figures shown are for July 1 of the given year, exclude Armed Forces and U.S. citizens residing overseas, and are based on middle series projections for births, deaths, and immigration. Percentage distribution may not equal 100, because of overlapping categories shown and rounding. (1) In thousands.

The Elderly U.S. Population, 1900–2030

Source: Bureau of the Census, U.S. Dept. of Commerce

Year[1]	65 AND OVER Number[2]	65 AND OVER Percent	85 AND OVER Number[2]	85 AND OVER Percent
1900	3,080	4.1	122	0.2
1910	3,949	4.3	167	0.2
1920	4,933	4.7	210	0.2
1930	6,634	5.4	272	0.2
1940	9,019	6.8	365	0.3
1950	12,269	8.1	577	0.4
1960	16,560	9.2	929	0.5
1970	19,980	9.8	1,409	0.7
1980	25,550	11.3	2,240	1.0
1990	31,079	12.5	3,021	1.2
1995[3]	33,619	12.8	3,685	1.4
2000	34,992	12.4	4,240	1.5
2001[3]	35,338	12.4	4,430	1.6
2002[3]	35,608	12.4	4,570	1.6
2003[3]	35,919	12.4	4,713	1.6
2004[3]	36,294	12.4	4,860	1.7
2010[4]	40,244	13.0	6,123	2.0
2020[4]	54,632	16.3	7,269	2.2
2030[4]	71,453	19.6	9,603	2.6

NOTE: Figures for 1900 to 1950 exclude Alaska and Hawaii. (1) Date of Census. (2) Resident population, in thousands. (3) Estimate for July 1 of year indicated. (4) Projected.

Disability Status of the Elderly (65 and Over)[1], 2000

Source: Bureau of the Census, U.S. Dept. of Commerce

(as of Apr. 1, in thousands; based on 2000 Census of Population and Housing)

	Number	%
Population 65 years and over	**33,347**	**100.0**
With a disability[2]	13,978	41.9
Sensory disability	4,738	14.2
Physical disability	9,546	28.6
Mental disability[3]	3,593	10.8
Self-care disability[4]	3,184	9.5
Go-outside-home disability[5]	6,796	20.4
With no disability	19,369	58.1

(1) Non-institutionalized. (2) Persons with 1 or more disabilities. (3) Learning, remembering, or concentrating. (4) Dressing, bathing, or getting around inside the home. (5) Going outside the home alone to shop or visit a doctor's office.

Young Adults Living at Home or Dormitory in the U.S., 1960–2004

Source: Bureau of the Census, U.S. Dept. of Commerce
(numbers in thousands)

	18–24 years old							25–34 years old					
		Male		Female					Male		Female		
YEAR	Total	At home[1]	%	Total	At home[1]	%	YEAR	Total	At home[1]	%	Total	At home[1]	%
1960	6,842	3,583	52	7,876	2,750	35	1960	10,896	1,185	11	11,587	853	7
1970	10,398	5,641	54	11,959	4,941	41	1970	11,929	1,129	9	12,637	829	7
1980	14,278	7,755	54	14,844	6,336	43	1980	18,107	1,894	10	18,689	1,300	7
1985	13,695	8,172	60	14,149	6,758	48	1985	20,184	2,685	13	20,673	1,661	8
1990	12,450	7,232	58	12,860	6,135	48	1990	21,462	3,213	15	21,779	1,774	8
1995	12,545	7,328	58	12,613	5,896	47	1995	20,589	3,166	15	20,800	1,759	8
1996	12,402	7,327	59	12,441	5,955	48	1996	20,390	3,213	16	20,528	1,810	9
1997	12,534	7,501	60	12,452	6,006	48	1997	20,039	2,909	15	20,217	1,745	9
1998	12,633	7,399	59	12,568	5,974	48	1998	19,526	2,845	15	19,828	1,680	8
1999	12,936	7,440	58	13,031	6,389	49	1999	18,924	2,636	14	19,551	1,690	9
2000	13,291	7,593	57	13,242	6,232	47	2000	18,563	2,387	13	19,222	1,602	8
2001[2]	13,412	7,385	55	13,361	6,068	45	2001[2]	19,308	2,520	13	19,527	1,583	8
2002[2]	13,696	7,575	55	13,602	6,252	46	2002[2]	19,220	2,610	14	19,428	1,618	8
2003[2]	13,811	7,537	55	13,592	5,753	42	2003[2]	19,543	2,554	13	19,659	968	5
2004[2]	14,165	7,922	56	13,611	5,779	42	2004[2]	19,553	2,543	13	19,587	995	5

(1) Includes young adults living in their parent(s)' home and unmarried college students living in a dormitory. (2) Data for 2001 and later use population controls based on Census 2000 and an expanded sample of households.

Grandchildren Living in the Home of Their Grandparents, 1970–2004

Source: Bureau of the Census, U.S. Dept. of Commerce (numbers in thousands)

		Grandchildren living with grandparents				
			WITH PARENT(S) PRESENT			
YEAR	Total children under 18	Total	Both parents present	Mother only present	Father only present	Without parent(s) present
1970	69,276	2,214	363	817	78	957
1980	63,369	2,306	310	922	86	988
1990	64,137	3,155	467	1,563	191	935
1995	70,254	3,965	427	1,876	195	1,466
1996	70,908	4,060	467	1,943	220	1,431
1997	70,983	3,894	554	1,785	247	1,309
1998	71,377	3,989	503	1,827	241	1,417
1999	71,703	3,919	535	1,803	250	1,331
2000	72,012	3,842	531	1,732	220	1,359
2001[1]	72,006	3,844	510	1,755	231	1,348
2002[1]	72,321	3,681	477	1,658	275	1,274
2003[1]	73,001	3,767	547	1,576	227	1,416
2004[1]	73,205	4,050	526	1,761	259	1,504

(1) Data for 2001-2004 are based on Census 2000 figures and an expanded sample of households.

Living Arrangements of Children, 1970–2004

Source: Bureau of the Census, U.S. Dept. of Commerce
(excludes persons under 18 years of age who maintained households or resided in group quarters)

		Percentage of children who live with—							
			MOTHER ONLY						
Race, Hispanic origin, and year	Number (1,000)	BOTH PARENTS	Total	Divorced	Married Spouse absent	Single[1]	Widowed	FATHER ONLY	NEITHER PARENT
White									
1970	58,790	90	8	3	3	Z	2	1	2
1980	52,242	83	14	7	4	1	2	2	2
1990	51,390	79	16	8	4	3	1	3	2
1998	56,118	74	18	8	4	5	1	5	3
1999	56,265	74	18	NA	NA	NA	NA	4	3
2000	56,455	75	17	NA	NA	NA	NA	4	3
2001	56,135	75	18	8	1	5	1	4	3
2002	58,276	75	18	8	1	5	1	5	3
2003	55,920	74	18	8	1	5	1	5	3
2004	55,902	74	18	8	1	6	1	4	3
Black									
1970	9,422	59	30	5	16	4	4	2	10
1980	9,375	42	44	11	16	13	4	2	12
1990	10,018	38	51	10	12	27	2	4	8
1998	11,407	36	51	9	9	32	1	4	9
1999	11,425	35	51	NA	NA	NA	NA	4	10
2000	11,412	38	49	NA	NA	NA	NA	4	9
2001	11,578	38	48	8	2	30	2	5	10
2002	11,646	39	48	9	2	31	1	5	8
2003	11,340	36	51	11	2	30	1	5	9
2004	11,424	35	50	9	2	31	2	6	9
Hispanic[2]									
1970	4,006[3]	78	NA	NA	NA	NA	NA	NA	NA
1980	5,459	75	20	6	8	4	2	2	4
1990	7,174	67	27	7	10	8	2	3	3
1998	10,857	64	27	6	8	12	1	4	5
1999	11,236	63	27	NA	NA	NA	NA	5	5
2000	11,613	65	25	NA	NA	NA	NA	4	5
2001	12,446	65	25	6	2	11	1	5	6
2002	12,817	65	25	6	2	11	1	5	5
2003	13,284	65	25	5	2	11	1	6	5
2004	13,752	65	25	6	1	11	1	5	5

NA = Not available. Z = Less than 0.5%. (1) Never married. (2) Hispanic persons may be of any race. (3) All persons under 18 years old.

Population, by Sex, Race, Residence, and Median Age, 1790–2004

Source: Bureau of the Census, U.S. Dept. of Commerce

(in thousands, except as indicated)

	SEX		RACE				RESIDENCE		MEDIAN AGE (years)		
				Black or Afr. Am.							
	Male	Female	White	Number	Percent	Other[5]	Urban	Rural	All races	White	Black
Conterminous U.S.[1]											
1790 (Aug. 2)	NA	NA	3,172	757	19.3	NA	202	3,728	NA	NA	NA
1810 (Aug. 6)	NA	NA	5,862	1,378	19.0	NA	525	6,714	NA	16.0	NA
1820 (Aug. 7)	4,897	4,742	7,867	1,772	18.4	NA	693	8,945	16.7	16.6	17.2
1840 (June 1)	8,689	8,381	14,196	2,874	16.8	NA	1,845	15,224	17.8	17.9	17.6
1860 (June 1)	16,085	15,358	26,923	4,442	14.1	79	6,217	25,227	19.4	19.7	17.5
1870 (June 1)	19,494	19,065	33,589	4,880	12.7	89	9,902	28,656	20.2	20.4	18.5
1880 (June 1)	25,519	24,637	43,403	6,581	13.1	172	14,130	36,026	20.9	21.4	18.0
1890 (June 1)	32,237	30,711	55,101	7,489	11.9	358	22,106	40,841	22.0	22.5	17.8
1900 (June 1)	38,816	37,178	66,809	8,834	11.6	351	30,160	45,835	22.9	23.4	19.4
1920 (Jan. 1)	53,900	51,810	94,821	10,463	9.9	427	54,158	51,553	25.3	25.5	22.3
1930 (Apr. 1)	62,137	60,638	110,287	11,891	9.7	597	68,955	53,820	26.5	26.9	23.5
1940 (Apr. 1)	66,062	65,608	118,215	12,866	9.8	589	74,424	57,246	29.0	29.5	25.3
United States											
1950 (Apr. 1)	74,833	75,864	135,150	15,045	9.9	1,131	96,467	54,230	30.2	30.7	26.2
1960 (Apr. 1)	88,331	90,992	158,832	18,872	10.5	1,620	125,269	54,054	29.5	30.3	23.5
1970 (Apr. 1)[2]	98,912	104,300	177,749	22,580	11.1	2,883	149,647	53,565	28.1	28.9	22.4
1980 (Apr. 1)[3]	110,053	116,493	194,713	26,683	11.8	5,150	167,051	59,495	30.0	30.9	24.9
1985 (July 1, est.)	115,730	122,194	202,031	28,569	12.0	7,324	NA	NA	31.4	32.3	26.6
1990 (Apr. 1)	121,239	127,470	199,686	29,986	12.1	9,233	187,053	61,656	32.9	34.4	28.1
1991 (July 1, est.)	122,984	129,122	210,979	31,107	12.3	10,020	NA	NA	33.1	34.1	28.1
1992 (July 1, est.)	124,506	130,496	212,885	31,670	12.4	10,446	NA	NA	33.4	34.4	28.5
1993 (July 1, est.)	125,938	131,858	214,760	32,168	12.5	10,867	NA	NA	33.7	34.7	28.7
1994 (July 1, est.)	127,216	133,076	216,413	32,653	12.5	11,227	NA	NA	34.0	35.0	29.0
1995 (July 1, est.)	128,569	134,321	218,149	33,095	12.6	11,646	NA	NA	34.3	35.3	29.2
1996 (July 1, est.)	129,746	135,434	219,686	33,514	12.6	11,979	NA	NA	34.6	35.7	29.5
1997 (July 1, est.)	131,018	136,618	221,334	33,947	12.7	12,355	NA	NA	34.9	36.0	29.7
1998 (July 1, est.)	132,263	137,766	222,932	34,370	12.7	12,727	NA	NA	35.3	36.3	29.9
1999 (July 1, est.)	133,352	139,526	224,692	34,903	12.8	13,283	NA	NA	35.5	36.6	30.1
2000 (Apr. 1)[4]	138,054	143,368	228,105	35,816	12.7	13,716	222,361	59,061	35.3	36.6	30.0
2001 (July 1, est.)[4]	140,009	145,085	230,502	36,247	12.7	14,291	NA	NA	35.6	36.9	30.3
2002 (July 1, est.)[4]	141,533	146,441	232,369	36,676	12.7	14,749	NA	NA	35.7	37.1	30.5
2003 (July 1, est.)[4]	143,037	147,773	234,196	37,099	12.8	15,207	NA	NA	35.9	37.3	30.6
2004 (June 1, est.)[4]	144,537	149,118	236,058	37,502	12.8	15,657	NA	NA	36.0	37.5	30.8

NA = Not available. **NOTE:** For 2000 "urban" includes residents of Urban Areas (densely settled areas with 50,000 or more inhabitants); or Urban Clusters (densely settled areas with at least 2,500 but fewer than 50,000). These definitions differ from previous Census years. (1) Excludes Alaska and Hawaii. (2) The revised 1970 resident population count is 203,302,031, which incorporates changes due to errors found after tabulations were completed. The race and sex data shown here reflect the official 1970 census count; the residence data come from the tabulated count. (3) The race data shown for Apr. 1, 1980, have been modified. (4) Race data for 2000–2004 are for one race alone. (5) "Other" consists of American Indians, Alaska Natives, Asians, and Pacific Islanders.

U.S. Population by Race and Latino or Hispanic Origin, 1990–2000

	2000 Census		1990 Census		% increase, 1990 – 2000	
	One race only	One race or more[3]	Number	% of total pop.	Using one race only for 2000[4]	Using one race only or in combination for 2000[4]
RACE[1]						
Total U.S. population[2]	281,421,906	281,421,906	248,709,873	100.0	13.2	13.2
White	211,460,626	216,930,975	199,686,070	80.3	5.9	8.6
Black or African American	34,658,190	36,419,434	29,986,060	12.1	15.6	21.5
American Indian and Alaska Native	2,475,956	4,119,301	1,959,234	0.8	26.4	110.3
Asian	10,242,998	11,898,828	6,908,638	2.8	48.3	72.2
Native Hawaiian and other Pac. Isl.	398,835	874,414	365,024	0.1	9.3	139.5
Some other race	15,359,073	18,521,486	9,804,847	3.9	56.6	88.9
HISPANIC OR LATINO AND RACE						
Total U.S. population[2]	281,421,906	281,421,906	248,709,873	100.0	13.2	13.2
Hispanic or Latino (of any race)[2]	35,305,818	35,305,818	22,354,059	9.0	57.9	57.9
Not Hispanic or Latino[2]	246,116,088	246,116,088	226,355,814	91.0	8.7	8.7
White	194,552,774	198,177,900	188,128,296	75.6	3.4	5.3
Black or African American	33,947,837	35,383,751	29,216,293	11.7	16.2	21.1
American Indian and Alaska Native	2,068,883	3,444,700	1,793,773	0.7	15.3	92.0
Asian	10,123,169	11,579,494	6,642,481	2.7	52.4	74.3
Native Hawaiian and other Pac. Isl.	353,509	748,149	325,878	0.1	8.5	129.6
Some other race	467,770	1,770,645	249,093	0.1	87.8	610.8

(1) Because individuals could report only one race in 1990 and could report more than one race in 2000, and because of other changes in the census questionnaire, the race data for 1990 and 2000 are not directly comparable. (2) The data for the total U.S. population, Hispanic or Latino population, and total Not Hispanic or Latino population are not affected by the changes cited in (1). Hispanic or Latino persons may be of any race. (3) Alone or in combination with one or more of the other five races listed. (4) Columns 5 and 6 provide, respectively, a "minimum–maximum" range for the percent increase in population for each race between 1990 and 2000.

WORLD ALMANAC QUICK QUIZ

Three of these states topped the 2004 list for percentage of total population that were of two or more races. Which state had the lowest percentage of people of two or more races?

(a) Alaska (b) Hawaii (c) Mississippi (d) Oklahoma

For the answer look in this chapter, or see page 1008.

IT'S A FACT: In four U.S. states the "minority" population (defined by the Census Bureau as all those except non-Hispanic whites) is now really the "majority." Population estimates for July 1, 2004, show that Texas had a minority population of 50.2%, joining three other "minority-majority" states. Hawaii's population was 77% minority, and New Mexico and California had minority populations of 57% and 56%, respectively. Five states had minority populations of around 40%: Arizona, Georgia, Maryland, Mississippi, and New York.

U.S. Population Growth by Race and Hispanic Origin, 1970-2020[1]

Source: U.S. Census Bureau; figures in millions

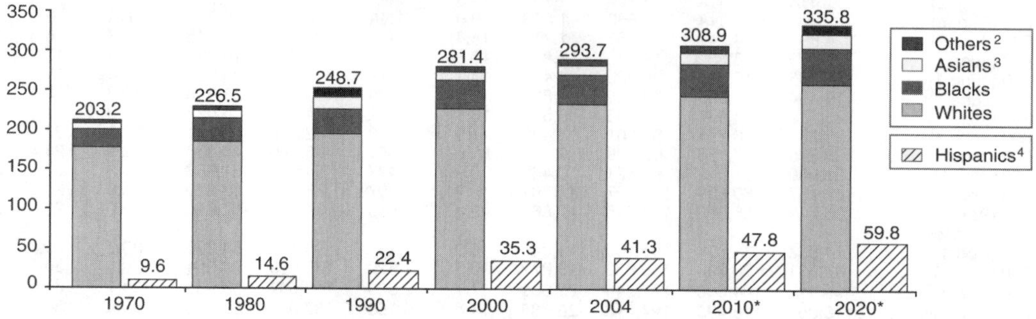

*Projected. (1) Totals may not add to 100% because of rounding. Because of changes in census questions and methods, data on race and Hispanic origin may not be wholly comparable over time. (2)Includes American Indians, Alaska Natives, and other races. From 2000 on, this category also includes Native Hawaiians, other Pacific Islanders, and persons reporting 2 or more races. (3) Figures for 1970-90 include Pacific Islanders. (4) May be of any race.

Race and Minority Group Populations by Age, 2004

Source: U.S. Census Bureau; resident population

Hispanic Americans were the youngest of the population groups below, with a median age of 26.9 in 2004. The median age for blacks was 30.8; for Asians, 34.1; and for whites, 37.5.

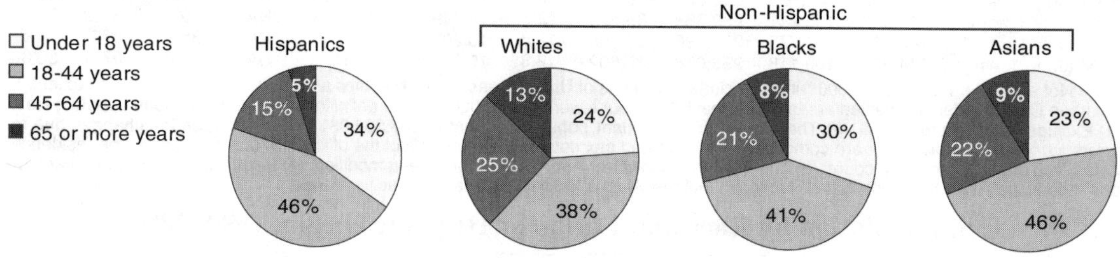

Educational Attainment of the U.S. Population 25 Years of Age and Over, 2004

Source: U.S. Census Bureau

Group	Pop. (in thousands)	High school grad. or more	Some college or more	Bachelor's degree or more
Hispanics (of any race)	21,596	58.4%	30.7%	12.1%
Non-Hispanic whites	154,150	85.8%	53.7%	28.2%
Blacks	20,812	80.6%	44.6%	17.6%
Asians	7,970	86.8%	67.0%	49.4%
U.S. Total	186,877	85.2%	53.1%	27.7%

Race and Minority Groups-Percentage by State

Source: U.S. Census Bureau, 2004 American Community Survey, except where noted

Non-Hispanic White Population Percentage by State, 2004

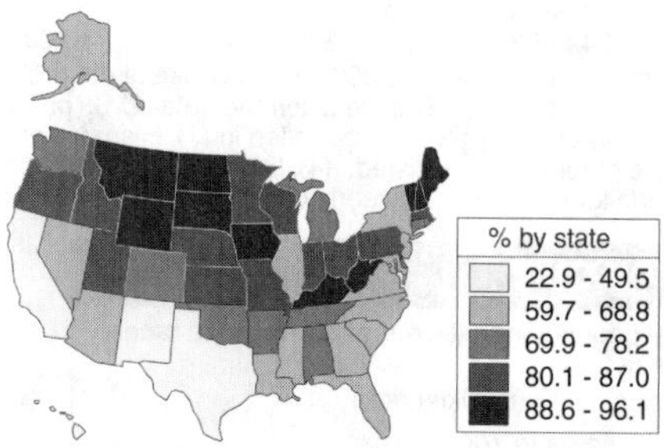

Latino Population Percentage by State, 2000

Source: Population Reference Bureau

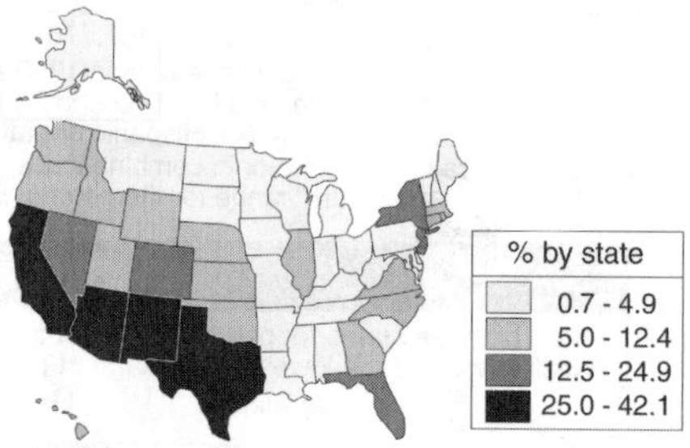

American Indian and Alaska Native Population Percentage by State, 2004

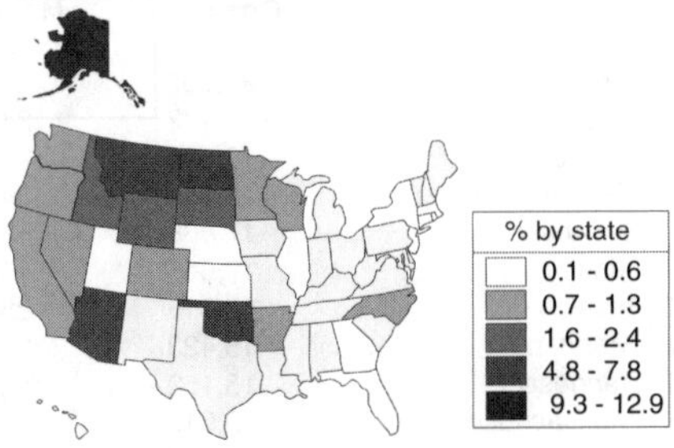

Asian Population Percentage by State, 2004

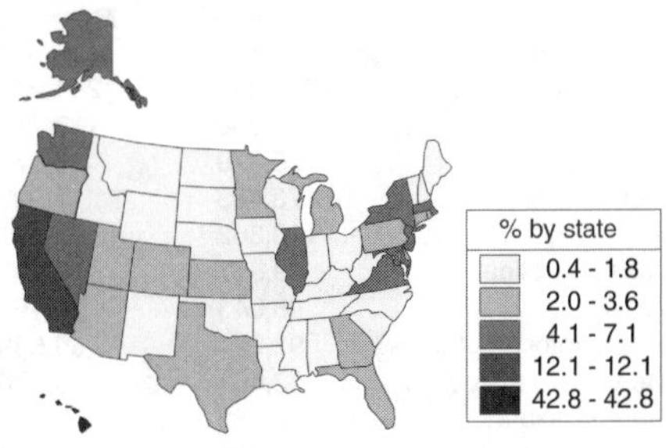

Black Population Percentage by State, 2004

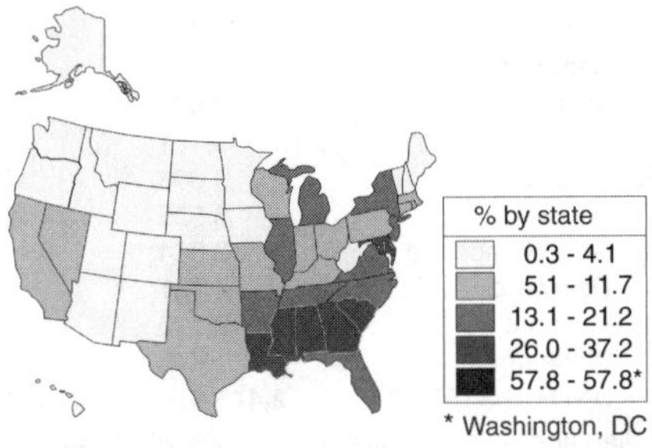

Two or More Races Population Percentage by State, 2004

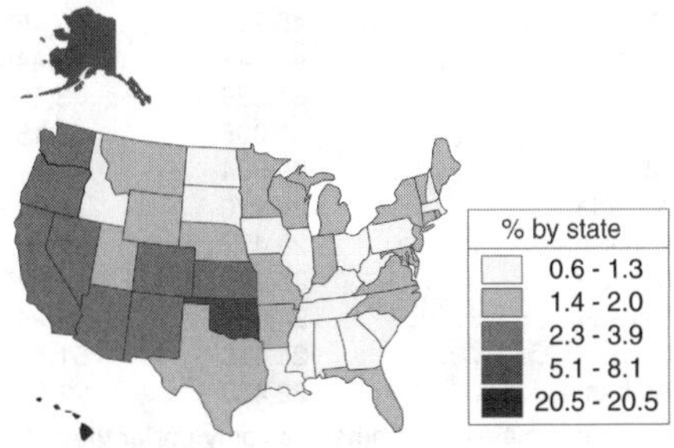

Hispanic Voting Power

Source: U.S. Census Bureau, 2004 American Community Survey. More information is available from the Census Bureau's Annual Population Estimates Program, at www.census.gov/popest/estimates.php

Data compiled by the Tomás Rivera Policy Institute at the Univ. of Southern California show that Latino voter turnout in presidential elections increased from 2,453,000 in 1980 to 5,934,000 by 2000. In the Nov. 2004 U.S. election, the Latino turnout rose to 7,587,000. Two candidates, Mel Martinez of Florida and Ken Salazar of Colorado, were elected as, respectively, the fourth and fifth Latino senators in U.S. history.

Two states—California and Texas—account for more than half of all Hispanic registered voters. In Florida, a hotly contested state in recent elections, the proportion of registered Hispanics to all registered voters is approaching 1 in 8. Except for Cubans, most Hispanic-Americans are Democrats or independents.

According to the National Association of Latino Elected and Appointed Officials (NALEO), the number of elected Hispanic officeholders at all levels of government rose from 3,128 in 1984 to 5,041 in 2005; during the same period, the number of Hispanics in Congress increased from 9 to 25, including 2 in the U.S. Senate.

Top 10 States in Hispanic Percent of All Registered Voters, 2004

Source: Univision

Rank	State (electoral votes)	Hispanics Registered	% of Elig. Hispanic Reg.	Hispanic % of All Reg. Voters
1.	New Mexico (5) . .	259,000	56.1	32.5
2.	Texas (34)	2,035,000	60.0	21.7
3.	Arizona (10)	331,000	49.3	16.4
4.	California (55) . . .	2,032,000	55.0	14.6
5.	Florida (27)	857,000	63.4	12.0
6.	Colorado (9).	213,000	57.0	10.7
7.	New York (31) . . .	606,000	56.0	7.3
8.	Nevada (5).	59,000	47.2	7.1
9.	New Jersey (15). .	218,000	61.4	5.4
10.	Illinois (21)	267,000	65.5	4.6

Party Affiliation of Latino Voters by Origin, 2004

Source: Pew Hispanic Center/Kaiser Family Foundation

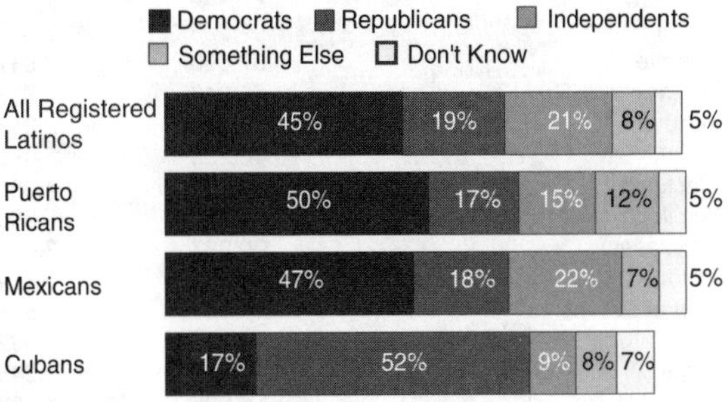

The Undocumented Population

Source: Pew Hispanic Center

The number of unauthorized migrants as of mid-2005 was approaching 11 million, according to the Pew Hispanic Center, with more unauthorized migrants than new legal immigrants arriving each year since the mid-1990s. Most of the unauthorized population lives in families, and a quarter had at least some college education. At least 6.3 million unauthorized workers were employed as of March 2004, making up 4.3% of the work force, though it has been illegal for employers to hire undocumented workers since 1986. Of unauthorized workers, the top occupations were service (33%), construction and extractive industries (17%), production, installation, and repair (16%), sales and administrative support (13%), management, business, and professional (10%), and transportation and material moving (8%). While 3% of the total work in agriculture, unauthorized workers account for 11% of all farm workers.

U.S. States Ranked by American Indian and Alaska Native Population, 2000

Source: Bureau of the Census, U.S. Dept. of Commerce

Rank	State	One race only[1]	More than one race[2]
1.	California	333,346	294,216
2.	Oklahoma	273,230	118,719
3.	Arizona	255,879	36,673
4.	New Mexico	173,483	17,992
5.	Texas	118,362	97,237
6.	North Carolina	99,551	32,185
7.	Alaska	98,043	21,198
8.	Washington	93,301	65,639
9.	New York	82,461	89,120
10.	South Dakota	62,283	5,998
11.	Michigan	58,479	65,933
12.	Montana	56,068	10,252
13.	Minnesota	54,967	26,107
14.	Florida	53,541	64,339
15.	Wisconsin	47,228	22,158
16.	Oregon	45,211	40,456
17.	Colorado	44,241	35,448
18.	North Dakota	31,329	3,899
19.	Illinois	31,006	42,155
20.	Utah	29,684	10,761
21.	Nevada	26,420	15,802
22.	Louisiana	25,477	17,401
23.	Missouri	25,076	35,023
24.	Kansas	24,936	22,247
25.	Ohio	24,486	51,589
26.	Alabama	22,430	22,019
27.	Georgia	21,737	31,460
28.	Virginia	21,172	31,692
29.	New Jersey	19,492	29,612
30.	Pennsylvania	18,348	34,302
31.	Arkansas	17,808	19,194
32.	Idaho	17,645	9,592
33.	Indiana	15,815	23,448
34.	Maryland	15,423	24,014
35.	Tennessee	15,152	24, 036
36.	Massachusetts	15,015	23,035
37.	Nebraska	14,896	7,308
38.	South Carolina	13,718	13,738
39.	Mississippi	11,652	7,903
40.	Wyoming	11,133	3,879
41.	Connecticut	9,639	14,849
42.	Iowa	8,989	9,257
43.	Kentucky	8,616	15,936
44.	Maine	7,098	6,058
45.	Rhode Island	5,121	5,604
46.	West Virginia	3,606	7,038
47.	Hawaii	3,535	21,347
48.	New Hampshire	2,964	4,921
49.	Delaware	2,731	3,338
50.	Vermont	2,420	3,976
51.	Washington, DC	1,713	3,062
	UNITED STATES	**2,475,956**	**1,643,345**

(1) Respondents classified themselves only under the category "American Indian and Alaska Native" on Census 2000. (2) Respondents classified themselves as "American Indian and Alaska Native" in combination with one or more other races.

Largest American Indian and Alaska Native Tribes in the U.S., 2000

Source: Bureau of the Census, U.S. Dept. of Commerce

Based on self-identification in Census 2000. Some respondents reported themselves as members of two or more tribes and/or as American Indian or Alaska Native in combination with one or more other races. The last column is the sum of preceding columns.

	American Indian and Alaska Native alone		American Indian and Alaska Native in combination with one or more races		American Indian and Alaska Native tribe alone or in any combination
Tribe[1]	One tribe reported	Two or more tribes reported	One tribe reported	Two or more tribes reported	
ALL AMERICAN INDIANS	**2,416,410**	**59,546**	**1,582,860**	**60,485**	**4,119,301**
Cherokee	281,069	18,793	390,902	38,769	729,533
Navajo	269,202	6,789	19,491	2,715	298,197
Canadian and Latin American	108,802	2,236	79,499	2,233	192,770
Sioux	108,272	4,794	35,179	5,115	153,360
Chippewa	105,907	2,730	38,635	2,397	149,669
Choctaw	87,349	9,552	50,123	11,750	158,774
Pueblo	59,533	3,527	9,943	1,082	74,085
Apache	57,060	7,917	24,947	6,909	96,833
Lumbee	51,913	642	4,934	379	57,868
Iroquois	45,212	2,318	29,763	3,529	80,822
Creek	40,223	5,495	21,652	3,940	71,310
Blackfeet	27,104	4,358	41,389	12,899	85,750
Yup'ik	21,212	895	1,996	134	24,237
Chickasaw	20,887	3,014	12,025	2,425	38,351
Tohono O'Odham	17,466	714	1,748	159	20,087
Inupiat Eskimo	16,047	845	2,282	191	19,365
Potawatomi	15,817	592	8,602	584	25,595
Yaqui	15,224	1,245	5,184	759	22,412
Tlingit-Haida	14,825	1,059	6,047	434	22,365
Alaskan Athabascan	14,520	815	3,218	285	18,838
Seminole	12,431	2,982	9,505	2,513	27,431
Cheyenne	11,191	1,365	4,655	993	18,204
Puget Sound Salish	11,034	226	3,212	159	14,631
Comanche	10,120	1,568	6,120	1,568	19,376
Paiute	9,705	1,163	2,315	349	13,532

(1) Ranked by totals shown in first column.

IT'S A FACT: Most Native Americans and Alaska Natives speak English at home. However, the 2000 Census counted 353,340 people (over age 5) who speak a Native American language at home. The most common Native American language spoken at home was Navajo, with 173,800 speakers. Among Cherokees, the most populous tribe, only 12,009 people (over age 5) reported that they spoke the Cherokee language at home.

Children by Relationship to Householder, 2000

Source: Bureau of the Census, U.S. Dept. of Commerce
(numbers in thousands; totals may not add due to rounding)

	All Ages		Under 6		6-17 yrs		18 yrs +	
	Total	%	Total	%	Total	%	Total	%
Children of householder	83,714	100	20,120	100	44,532	100	19,062	100
Adopted children	2,059	2.5	389	1.9	1,197	2.7	473	25
Stepchildren	4,385	5.2	328	1.6	2,964	6.7	1,092	5.7
Biological children	77,271	92.3	19,402	96.4	40,371	90.7	17,497	91.8

Block Grants for Welfare (Temporary Assistance for Needy Families), Fiscal Year 2004

Source: Office of Family Assistance, Admin. for Children and Families, U.S. Dept. of Health and Human Services

State	Total Federal and State TANF Expenditures, 2004[1]	2004 Average Monthly Expenditure per Family	Recipient	2004 Average Monthly Number of Families	Recipients	Children
Alabama	$114,195	$496.82	$209.72	19,154	45,377	35,526
Alaska	76,237	1,289.61	461.43	4,926	13,768	9,377
Arizona	305,055	512.94	221.11	49,559	114,970	84,342
Arkansas	41,521	345.23	154.75	10,023	22,360	16,756
California	6,177,941	1,127.36	466.69	456,666	1,103,152	899,753
Colorado	211,832	1,207.16	462.57	14,623	38,162	27,725
Connecticut	434,877	1,749.00	847.08	20,720	42,782	30,545
Delaware	53,521	790.37	350.54	5,643	12,723	9,669
Dist. of Columbia	168,634	818.11	322.24	17,177	43,610	32,605
Florida	877,066	1,272.06	628.95	57,457	116,208	94,661
Georgia	535,343	838.34	359.08	53,215	124,239	96,515
Hawaii	127,601	1,199.61	464.19	8,864	22,908	16,194
Idaho	41,470	1,869.60	1,014.92	1,848	3,405	2,714
Illinois	981,155	2,292.88	918.50	35,660	89,018	73,008
Indiana	313,987	517.22	199.55	50,589	131,125	100,649
Iowa	163,222	743.83	303.93	18,286	44,753	31,006
Kansas	156,063	776.57	298.01	16,747	43,640	29,954
Kentucky	196,430	459.43	209.39	35,629	78,174	57,932
Louisiana	252,078	1,118.72	461.62	18,777	45,506	37,274
Maine	102,409	878.67	320.22	9,713	26,651	18,191
Maryland	349,569	1,145.53	490.73	25,430	59,362	44,919
Massachusetts	681,214	1,141.00	527.44	49,753	107,630	75,134
Michigan	1,281,075	1,344.00	503.14	79,432	212,182	155,420
Minnesota	401,786	975.01	379.18	34,340	88,302	63,374
Mississippi	102,733	455.51	201.63	18,795	42,459	31,298
Missouri	300,308	610.69	251.23	40,979	99,613	70,646
Montana	44,888	711.65	261.88	5,256	14,284	9,578
Nebraska	88,945	679.97	277.10	10,901	26,749	19,255
Nevada	68,447	644.91	272.19	8,844	20,956	16,147
New Hampshire	60,054	827.40	356.66	6,049	14,032	9,673
New Jersey	888,893	1,655.70	687.77	44,739	107,703	80,282
New Mexico	132,567	628.03	240.54	17,590	45,926	32,479
New York	4,195,899	2,377.83	1,039.92	147,050	336,236	240,973
North Carolina	437,816	969.03	473.10	37,651	77,119	60,408
North Dakota	34,473	937.64	364.99	3,064	7,871	5,499
Ohio	833,955	821.72	373.09	84,574	186,272	139,988
Oklahoma	194,597	1,142.06	473.77	14,199	34,229	26,441
Oregon	242,993	1,093.12	478.01	18,525	42,362	31,476
Pennsylvania	1,191,955	1,127.11	429.52	88,128	231,260	165,972
Rhode Island	155,200	1,051.95	405.07	12,295	31,929	22,282
South Carolina	38,375	191.77	82.92	16,676	38,567	29,481
South Dakota	28,981	879.82	402.43	2,745	6,001	5,016
Tennessee	236,231	273.15	103.54	72,069	190,132	135,852
Texas	767,926	608.33	256.35	105,197	249,634	200,280
Utah	113,643	1,047.47	411.54	9,041	23,012	16,468
Vermont	68,524	1,182.12	465.89	4,831	12,257	7,850
Virginia	278,532	2,461.53	863.40	9,430	26,883	17,250
Washington	588,581	878.10	358.68	55,858	136,747	95,980
West Virginia	149,855	843.06	351.19	14,813	35,559	25,124
Wisconsin	492,734	1,825.50	756.00	22,493	54,314	42,676
Wyoming	39,845	9,439.68	5,249.66	352	633	555
2004 Totals	**25,821,230**	**1,082.66**	**449.78**	**1,987,476**	**4,784,042**	**3,617,569**
2003 Totals	**26,339,994**	**1,092.33**	**447.99**	**2,009,468**	**4,899,677**	**3,691,479**
2002 Totals	**25,414,383**	**1,039.38**	**418.01**	**2,037,618**	**5,066,574**	**3,790,207**
2001 Totals	**25,667,381**	**1,024.57**	**400.86**	**2,087,646**	**5,335,891**	**3,968,499**
2000 Totals	**24,780,711**	**926.32**	**353.72**	**2,229,315**	**5,838,043**	**4,303,943**
1999 Totals	**23,114,572**	**720.45**	**267.99**	**2,673,610**	**7,187,658**	**NA**
1998 Totals	**22,036,420**	**573.92**	**208.91**	**3,199,700**	**8,790,149**	**NA**
1997 Totals	**19,010,190**	**402.42**	**144.87**	**3,936,610**	**10,935,125**	**NA**

NOTE: Under 1996 legislation, the Aid to Families with Dependent Children (AFDC) program was converted to this state block-grant program. (1) In thousands. FY 2004 covers period from Oct. 2003 to Sept. 2004. NA = Not available.

Adults Receiving TANF[1] (Welfare) Funds, by Employment Status, Fiscal Year 2003

Source: Office of Family Assistance, Admin. for Children and Families, U.S. Dept. of Health and Human Services

STATE	Adults	Employed
AL	9,786	25.7%
AK	4,845	29.1
AZ	30,481	15.2
AR	6,829	13.1
CA	244,124	26.6
CO	9,593	17.8
CT	12,819	31.7
DE	3,042	23.2
DC	10,853	22.5
FL	24,140	17.1
GA	31,426	11.5
Guam	NA	NA
HI	7,825	34.1
ID	637	30.1
IL	17,846	27.4
IN	34,524	46.2
IA	17,138	40.6
KS	11,823	12.8
KY	21,210	18.6
LA	11,767	24.4%
ME	7,202	29.2
MD	16,037	8.3
MA	32,609	12.2
MI	52,143	25.5
MN	27,310	28.1
MS	11,832	13.7
MO	29,144	24.1
MT	5,982	28.0
NE	7,520	15.1
NV	6,002	4.8
NH	4,386	28.5
NJ	25,566	16.7
NM	13,168	27.4
NY	92,644	17.9
NC	19,535	18.1
ND	2,640	33.7
OH	48,446	23.8
OK	8,752	10.8
OR	10,965	11.8%
PA	56,643	17.1
Puerto Rico	16,575	3.3
RI	10,633	27.8
SC	13,629	22.0
SD	1,146	19.0
TN	51,86	18.0
TX	73,797	27.5
UT	6,217	23.5
VT	4,574	22.4
Virgin Islands	381	2.9
VA	5,884	33.0
WA	41,411	33.4
WV	13,087	17.5
WI	10,039	14.8
WY	103	11.2
U.S.	**1,248,570**	**22.9**

NA = Not available. (1) TANF = the state block grant program known as Temporary Assistance for Needy Families.

Marital Status of the U.S. Population, 1990-2004

Source: U.S. Bureau of the Census, Dept. of Commerce

Marital status	Total				Male				Female			
	1990	1995	2000	2004	1990	1995	2000	2004	1990	1995	2000	2004
Total pop.[1]	**181.8**	**191.6**	**201.8**	**227.3**	**86.9**	**92.0**	**96.9**	**110.0**	**95.0**	**99.6**	**104.9**	**117.3**
Never married	40.4	43.9	48.2	65.9	22.4	24.6	26.1	35.9	17.9	19.3	22.1	30.0
Married	112.6	116.7	120.1	126.0	55.8	57.7	59.6	63.5	56.7	58.9	60.4	63.3
Widowed	13.8	13.4	13.7	13.8	2.3	2.3	2.6	2.6	11.5	11.1	11.1	11.1
Divorced	15.1	17.6	19.8	21.8	6.3	7.4	8.5	9.0	8.8	10.3	11.3	12.8
Percent of total pop.[1]												
Never married	22.2	22.9	23.9	29.0	25.8	26.8	27.0	32.6	18.9	19.4	21.1	25.6
Married	61.9	60.9	59.5	55.4	64.3	62.7	61.5	56.8	59.7	59.2	57.6	54.0
Widowed	7.6	7.0	6.8	6.1	2.7	2.5	2.7	2.4	12.1	11.1	10.5	9.5
Divorced	8.3	9.2	9.8	9.6	7.2	8.0	8.8	8.2	9.3	10.3	10.8	10.9

(1) Aged 15 and older. Totals may not add because of rounding.

U.S. Households Headed by Couples, 1960-2004

Source: Bureau of the Census, U.S. Dept. of Commerce

(based on 2004 Current Population Survey and earlier reports; numbers in thousands[1])

YEAR	Total	Married-couple households	% of Total	Unmarried-couple households[2]	% of Total
1960	52,799	39,254	74	439	0.8
1970	63,401	44,728	71	523	0.8
1980	80,776	49,112	61	1,589	2.0
1981	82,368	49,294	60	1,808	2.2
1982	83,527	49,630	59	1,863	2.2
1983	83,918	49,908	59	1,891	2.3
1984	85,407	50,090	59	1,988	2.3
1985	86,789	50,350	58	1,983	2.3
1986	88,458	50,933	58	2,220	2.5
1987	89,479	51,537	58	2,334	2.6
1988	91,124	51,675	57	2,588	2.8
1989	92,830	52,100	56	2,764	3.0
1990	93,347	52,317	56	2,856	3.1
1991	94,312	52,147	55	3,039	3.2
1992	95,669	52,457	55	3,308	3.5
1993	96,426	53,090	55	3,510	3.6
1994	97,107	53,171	55	3,661	3.8
1995	98,990	53,858	54	3,668	3.7
1996	99,627	53,567	54	3,958	4.0
1997	101,018	53,604	53	4,130	4.1
1998	102,528	54,317	53	4,236	4.1
1999	103,874	54,770	53	4,486	4.3
2000	104,705	55,311	53	4,736	4.5
2001	108,209	56,592	52	4,893	4.5
2002	109,297	56,747	52	4,898	4.5
2003	111,278	57,320	52	5,054	4.5
2004	112,000	57,719	52	5,080	4.5

(1) Data may differ from Census figures. (2) Does not include same-sex couples or families living in U.S. military barracks or emergency/homeless shelters.

Unmarried-Partner Households by Sex of Partners, 2000

Source: Bureau of the Census, U.S. Dept. of Commerce

(as of Apr. 1; based on 2000 Census of Population and Housing)

Household	Number
Total U.S. households	**105,480,101**
Unmarried-partner households	5,475,768
Male householder and male partner	301,026
Male householder and female partner	2,615,119
Female householder and female partner	293,365
Female householder and male partner	2,266,258
All other households	100,004,333

Note: Does not include families living in U.S. military barracks or emergency/homeless shelters.

WORLD ALMANAC QUICK QUIZ

What were the percentages of the population over the age of 65 in 1900 and 2000, respectively?

(a) 4.1%, 12.4% (b) 8.1%, 10.2% (c) 10.2%, 8.1% (d) 12.4%, 4.1%

For the answer look in this chapter, or see page 1008.

U.S. Places of 5,000 or More Population–With ZIP and Area Codes

Source: U.S. Bureau of the Census, Dept. of Commerce; NeuStar Inc.

The following is a list of places of 5,000 or more inhabitants recognized by the Bureau of the Census, U.S. Dept. of Commerce, based on July 1, 2004 Census Bureau estimates. Also given are 1990 census populations. This list includes **places that are incorporated** under the laws of their respective states as cities, boroughs, towns, and villages, as well as boroughs in Alaska and towns in the 6 New England states, New York, and Wisconsin. Townships are not included.

Places that the Census Bureau designates as **"census designated places" (CDPs)** are also included; these are marked (c). The Census Bureau does not calculate estimates for CDPs; for these places, the 2000 Census figure is given, in *italics*, in place of the 2004 estimate. CDP boundaries can change from one census to another.

This list also includes, in *italics*, **minor civil divisions (MCDs)**, for Connecticut, Maine, Massachusetts, New Hampshire, Rhode Island, and Vermont. MCDs are not incorporated and not recognized as CDPs, but are often the primary political or administrative divisions of a county.

An **asterisk** (*) denotes that the ZIP code given is for general delivery; named streets and/or P.O. boxes within the community may differ; consult www.usps.com. Telephone **area codes** are given in parentheses. Some regions have 2 or more area codes intermixed (where new customers receive the newer area code); these are known as **overlays**. States where this occurs are noted. When 2 or more area codes are listed for one place, consult local operators for assistance. Area codes based on latest information as of Aug. 2005. For a listing in numerical order of specific area codes in the U.S., Canada, and the Caribbean, see Computers and Telecommunications chapter, page 382.

For some places listed, no area code and/or ZIP code is available. — = Not available.

Alabama

ZIP	Place	Area Code	2004	1990
*35007	Alabaster	(205)	26,830	14,619
*35950	Albertville	(256)	18,251	14,507
*35010	Alexander City	(256)	14,971	14,917
*36420	Andalusia	(334)	8,593	9,269
*36201	Anniston	(256)	23,822	26,638
35016	Arab	(256)	7,397	6,321
*35611	Athens	(256)	20,316	16,901
*36502	Atmore	(251)	7,572	8,046
35954	Attalla	(256)	6,395	6,859
*36830	Auburn	(334)	48,348	33,830
36507	Bay Minette	(251)	7,819	7,168
*35020	Bessemer	(205)	28,727	33,581
*35201	Birmingham	(205)	233,149	265,347
*35956	Boaz	(256)	7,739	6,928
*36426	Brewton	(251)	5,400	5,885
35040	Calera	(205)	5,920	2,136
35243	Cahaba Heights (c)	(205)	*5,203*	4,778
*35215	Center Point (c)	(205)	*15,130*	22,658
36611	Chickasaw	(251)	6,063	6,651
*35045	Clanton	(205)	8,217	7,669
*35055	Cullman	(256)	14,544	13,367
36526	Daphne	(251)	18,115	11,291
*35601	Decatur	(256)	54,528	49,917
36732	Demopolis	(334)	7,301	7,512
*36301	Dothan	(334)	61,287	54,131
*36330	Enterprise	(334)	22,231	20,119
*36027	Eufaula	(334)	13,521	13,220
35064	Fairfield	(205)	11,866	12,200
*36532	Fairhope	(251)	14,602	9,189
*35630	Florence	(256)	36,258	36,426
*36535	Foley	(251)	10,421	4,937
35214	Forestdale (c)	(205)	*10,509*	10,395
*35967	Fort Payne	(256)	13,435	11,838
36362	Fort Rucker (c)	(334)	*6,052*	7,593
35068	Fultondale	(205)	6,812	6,400
*35901	Gadsden	(256)	37,640	42,523
35071	Gardendale	(205)	12,532	9,251
35905	Glencoe	(256)	5,253	4,687
35235	Grayson Valley (c)	(205)	*5,447*	—
36037	Greenville	(334)	7,078	7,847
*36542	Gulf Shores	(251)	6,295	3,261
35976	Guntersville	(256)	7,641	7,038
35570	Hamilton	(205)	6,503	6,171
35640	Hartselle	(256)	12,866	11,114
35080	Helena	(205)	12,433	4,303
*35209	Homewood	(205)	24,259	23,644
*35244	Hoover	(205)	66,346	39,988
*35023	Hueytown	(205)	15,313	15,280
*35801	Huntsville	(256)	164,146	159,880
35210	Irondale	(205)	9,653	9,458
36545	Jackson	(251)	5,309	5,819
36265	Jacksonville	(256)	8,716	10,283
*35501	Jasper	(205)	13,907	13,553
35242	Lake Purdy (c)	(205)	*5,799*	1,840
36863	Lanett	(334)	7,598	8,985
35094	Leeds	(205)	11,020	10,009
*35758	Madison	(256)	35,012	14,792
35228	Midfield	(205)	5,402	5,559
36054	Millbrook	(334)	13,248	6,046
*36601	Mobile	(251)	192,759	199,973
*36460	Monroeville	(251)	6,686	6,993
35115	Montevallo	(205)	5,082	4,239
*36104	Montgomery	(334)	200,983	190,350
35004	Moody	(205)	9,817	4,921
35811	Moores Mill (c)	(256)	*5,178*	3,362
*35223	Mountain Brook	(205)	20,747	19,810
*35661	Muscle Shoals	(256)	12,395	9,611
*35476	Northport	(205)	20,451	17,297
35121	Oneonta	(205)	6,314	4,844
*36801	Opelika	(334)	23,483	22,122
36467	Opp	(334)	6,651	7,011
36203	Oxford	(256)	15,648	9,537
*36360	Ozark	(334)	14,953	13,030
35124	Pelham	(205)	18,113	9,356
*35125	Pell City	(205)	10,602	7,945
*36867	Phenix City	(334)	28,936	25,311
35126	Pinson (c)	(205)	*5,033*	10,987
35127	Pleasant Grove	(205)	10,377	8,458
*36067	Prattville	(334)	27,500	19,816
36610	Prichard	(251)	27,622	34,320
*35906	Rainbow City	(256)	8,807	7,667
36274	Roanoke	(334)	6,599	6,362
*35653	Russellville	(256)	8,797	7,812
36206	Saks (c)	(256)	*10,698*	11,138
36571	Saraland	(251)	12,603	11,784
36572	Satsuma	(251)	5,930	5,194
*35768	Scottsboro	(256)	14,806	13,786
*36701	Selma	(334)	19,618	23,755
35660	Sheffield	(256)	9,300	10,380
35907	Southside	(256)	7,633	5,580
*36527	Spanish Fort	(251)	5,611	3,732
*35150	Sylacauga	(256)	12,883	12,520
*35160	Talladega	(256)	17,090	18,175
35217	Tarrant	(205)	6,792	8,046
*36081	Troy	(334)	13,737	13,051
35173	Trussville	(205)	15,744	8,283
*35401	Tuscaloosa	(205)	80,181	77,866
35674	Tuscumbia	(256)	8,172	8,413
36083	Tuskegee	(334)	11,741	12,257
*36854	Valley	(334)	8,863	9,556
*35216	Vestavia Hills	(205)	31,012	19,550
*36092	Wetumpka	(334)	6,620	4,670

Alaska (907)

ZIP	Place	2004	1990
*99501	Anchorage	272,687	226,338
*99559	Bethel	6,106	4,674
*99708	College (c)	*11,402*	11,249
99702	Eielson AFB (c)	*5,400*	5,251
*99701	Fairbanks	30,435	30,843
99603	Homer	5,252	3,660
*99801	Juneau	31,118	26,751
*99611	Kenai	7,379	6,327
*99901	Ketchikan	7,423	8,263
99654	Knik-Fairview (c)	*7,049*	272
*99615	Kodiak	6,264	6,365
99654	Lakes (c)	*6,706*	—
99645	Palmer	6,163	2,901
*99835	Sitka	8,849	8,588
*99654	Wasilla	7,738	4,028

Arizona

ZIP	Place	Area Code	2004	1990
*85220	Apache Junction	(480)	33,457	18,092
85323	Avondale	(623)	59,180	17,595
85653	Avra Valley (c)	(520)	*5,038*	3,403
86351	Big Park (c)	(928)	*5,245*	3,024
85603	Bisbee	(520)	6,044	6,288
*85326	Buckeye	(623)	9,271	4,436
*86442	Bullhead City	(928)	37,568	21,951
86322	Camp Verde	(928)	10,033	6,243
85704	Casas Adobes (c)	(520)	*54,011*	—
*85738	Catalina (c)	(520)	*7,025*	4,864
85718	Catalina Foothills (c)	(520)	*53,794*	—
*85222	Casa Grande	(520)	31,192	19,076
*85225	Chandler	(480)	223,991	89,862
86323	Chino Valley	(928)	9,160	4,837
85228	Coolidge	(520)	8,238	6,934
86326	Cottonwood	(928)	10,424	5,918
86326	Cottonwood-Verde Village (c)	(928)	*10,610*	7,037
86327	Dewey-Humboldt (c)	(928)	*6,295*	3,640
*85607	Douglas	(520)	16,706	13,908
85746	Drexel Heights (c)	(520)	*23,849*	—
85335	El Mirage	(623)	20,914	5,001
85231	Eloy	(520)	10,695	7,211
*86004	Flagstaff	(928)	57,038	45,857
*85232	Florence	(520)	17,198	7,321
85705	Flowing Wells (c)	(520)	*15,050*	14,013
85367	Fortuna Foothills (c)	(928)	*20,478*	7,737

ZIP	Place	Area Code	2004	1990
*85268	Fountain Hills	(480)	22,557	10,030
*85234	Gilbert	(480)	156,917	29,149
*85301	Glendale	(623)	235,591	147,070
*85501	Globe	(928)	7,204	6,062
85219	Gold Camp (c)	(480)	*6,029*	—
85338	Goodyear	(623)	37,496	6,258
*85614	Green Valley (c)	(520)	*17,283*	13,231
85283	Guadalupe	(480)	5,254	5,458
86025	Holbrook	(928)	5,101	4,770
*86401	Kingman	(928)	24,174	13,208
*86403	Lake Havasu City	(928)	53,204	24,363
85653	Marana	(520)	23,099	2,565
*85201	Mesa	(480)	437,454	289,199
*86440	Mohave Valley (c)	(928)	*13,694*	6,962
86401	New Kingman-Butler (c)	(928)	*14,810*	11,627
*85087	New River (c)	(623)	*10,740*	—
*85621	Nogales	(520)	20,619	19,489
*85737	Oro Valley	(520)	37,653	9,024
*86040	Page	(928)	6,818	6,598
85253	Paradise Valley	(480)	14,330	11,903
*85541	Payson	(928)	14,473	8,377
*85345	Peoria	(623)	132,487	51,080
*85034	Phoenix	(602)	1,418,041	988,015
85743	Picture Rocks (c)	(520)	*8,139*	4,026
*86301	Prescott	(928)	38,930	26,592
*86314	Prescott Valley	(928)	30,231	8,904
85242	Queen Creek	(480)	13,866	2,639
*85546	Safford	(928)	8,945	7,359
85349	San Luis	(928)	20,539	4,212
*85251	Scottsdale	(480)	221,792	130,099
*86336	Sedona	(928)	11,067	7,720
*85901	Show Low	(928)	9,453	5,020
*85635	Sierra Vista	(520)	40,820	32,983
85650	Sierra Vista Southeast (c)	(520)	9,042	9,237
85350	Somerton	(928)	5,564	5,293
85713	South Tucson	(520)	38,930	5,171
*85351	Sun City (c)	(623)	*38,309*	38,126
*85375	Sun City West (c)	(623)	*26,344*	15,997
85248	Sun Lakes (c)	(480)	*11,936*	6,578
*85374	Surprise	(623)	60,686	7,122
85749	Tanque Verde (c)	(520)	*16,195*	—
*85282	Tempe	(480)	160,676	141,993
85736	Three Points (c)	(520)	*5,273*	2,175
85353	Tolleson	(623)	5,948	4,483
86045	Tuba City (c)	(928)	*8,225*	7,323
*85726	Tucson	(520)	512,023	415,444
85735	Tucson Estates (c)	(520)	*9,755*	2,662
85941	Whiteriver (c)	(928)	*5,220*	3,775
*85390	Wickenburg	(928)	5,550	4,515
86047	Winslow	(928)	9,901	9,279
*85364	Yuma	(928)	83,322	56,966

Arkansas

ZIP	Place	Area Code	2004	1990
*71923	Arkadelphia	(870)	10,665	10,014
*72501	Batesville	(870)	9,549	9,187
72012	Beebe	(501)	5,474	4,809
*72714	Bella Vista (c)	(479)	*16,582*	9,083
*72015	Benton	(501)	24,695	18,177
72712	Bentonville	(479)	27,765	11,257
*72315	Blytheville	(870)	16,868	22,523
*72022	Bryant	(501)	12,543	5,940
72023	Cabot	(501)	19,607	8,319
*71701	Camden	(870)	12,342	14,701
72830	Clarksville	(479)	8,156	5,833
*72032	Conway	(501)	50,358	26,481
71635	Crossett	(870)	5,935	6,282
71832	De Queen	(870)	5,836	4,633
72065	East End (c)	(501)	*5,623*	—
*71730	El Dorado	(870)	20,682	23,146
*72701	Fayetteville	(479)	64,190	42,247
*72335	Forrest City	(870)	14,242	13,364
*72901	Fort Smith	(479)	81,849	72,798
72936	Greenwood	(479)	7,657	3,984
*72601	Harrison	(870)	12,563	9,936
*72543	Heber Springs	(501)	6,862	5,628
72342	Helena	(870)	5,748	7,491
*71801	Hope	(870)	10,462	9,768
*71901	Hot Springs	(501)	37,245	33,095
*71909	Hot Springs Village (c)	(501)	*8,397*	6,361
*72076	Jacksonville	(501)	30,600	29,101
*72401	Jonesboro	(870)	58,799	46,535
*72201	Little Rock	(501)	184,081	175,727
72745	Lowell	(479)	6,674	1,224
*71753	Magnolia	(870)	10,458	11,151
*72104	Malvern	(501)	8,994	9,236
72364	Marion	(870)	9,409	4,405
*72113	Maumelle	(501)	13,273	6,714
71953	Mena	(479)	5,586	5,475
*71655	Monticello	(870)	9,188	8,119
72110	Morrilton	(501)	6,561	6,551
*72653	Mountain Home	(870)	11,709	9,027
72112	Newport	(870)	7,321	7,459
*72114	North Little Rock	(501)	59,474	61,829
72370	Osceola	(870)	8,226	9,165
*72450	Paragould	(870)	23,397	18,540
*71601	Pine Bluff	(870)	53,419	57,140
72455	Pocahontas	(870)	6,698	6,151
*72756	Rogers	(479)	44,885	24,692
*72801	Russellville	(479)	25,179	21,260
*72143	Searcy	(501)	20,429	15,180
*72120	Sherwood	(501)	22,564	18,890
72761	Siloam Springs	(479)	13,246	8,151
*72764	Springdale	(479)	55,971	29,945
72160	Stuttgart	(870)	9,377	10,420
71854	Texarkana	(870)	29,494	22,631
72472	Trumann	(870)	6,883	6,346
*72956	Van Buren	(479)	20,637	14,899
71671	Warren	(870)	6,342	6,455
72390	West Helena	(870)	7,932	10,137
*72301	West Memphis	(870)	28,117	28,259
*71602	White Hall	(870)	5,089	3,849
72396	Wynne	(870)	8,463	8,187

California

ZIP	Place	Area Code	2004	1990
92301	Adelanto	(760)	21,642	6,815
*91376	Agoura Hills	(818)	22,863	20,396
*94501	Alameda	(510)	71,136	73,979
94507	Alamo (c)	(925)	*15,626*	12,277
94706	Albany	(510)	16,216	16,327
*91802	Alhambra	(626)	87,995	82,087
92656	Aliso Viejo	(949)	41,468	7,612
90249	Alondra Park (c)	(310)	*8,622*	12,215
*91901	Alpine (San Diego Co.) (c)	(619)	*13,143*	9,695
*91003	Altadena (c)	(626)	*42,610*	42,658
95945	Alta Sierra (c)	(530)	*6,522*	5,709
95127	Alum Rock (c)	(408)	*13,479*	—
94589	American Canyon	(707)	13,887	7,734
*92803	Anaheim	(714)	333,776	266,406
96007	Anderson	(530)	10,375	8,299
*94509	Antioch	(925)	100,923	62,195
*92307	Apple Valley	(760)	62,639	46,079
*95003	Aptos (c)	(831)	*9,396*	9,061
*91006	Arcadia	(626)	55,992	48,284
*95521	Arcata	(707)	16,929	15,211
95825	Arden-Arcade (c)	(916)	*96,025*	92,040
*93420	Arroyo Grande	(805)	16,183	14,432
*90701	Artesia	(562)	16,782	15,464
93203	Arvin	(661)	14,404	9,286
94577	Ashland (c)	(510)	*20,793*	16,590
*93422	Atascadero	(805)	27,158	23,138
94027	Atherton	(650)	7,127	7,163
95301	Atwater	(209)	26,370	22,282
*95603	Auburn	(530)	12,775	10,653
95202	August (c)	(209)	*7,808*	6,376
93204	Avenal	(559)	16,681	9,770
91746	Avocado Heights (c)	(626)	*15,148*	14,232
91702	Azusa	(626)	283,936	41,203
*93302	Bakersfield	(661)	78,887	176,264
91706	Baldwin Park	(626)	28,686	69,330
92220	Banning	(951)	23,528	20,572
*92312	Barstow	(760)	16,681	21,472
94565	Bay Point (c)	(925)	*21,534*	17,453
—	Bayview-Montalvin (c)	(510)	*5,004*	3,988
93402	Baywood-Los Osos (c)	(805)	*14,351*	14,377
95903	Beale AFB (c)	(530)	*5,115*	6,912
92223	Beaumont	(951)	18,115	9,685
*90201	Bell	(323)	37,779	34,365
*90706	Bellflower	(562)	74,964	61,815
*90202	Bell Gardens	(213)/(323)/(562)	45,372	42,315
94002	Belmont	(650)	24,449	24,165
94510	Benicia	(707)	26,828	24,437
*94704	Berkeley	(510)	101,517	102,724
92203	Bermuda Dunes (c)	(760)	*6,229*	4,571
*90210	Beverly Hills	(213)/(310)/(323)	35,088	31,971
92314	Big Bear City (c)	(909)	*5,779*	4,920
92315	Big Bear Lake	(909)	6,127	5,351
94526	Blackhawk-Camino Tassajara (c)	(925)	*10,048*	6,199
92316	Bloomington (c)	(951)	*19,318*	15,116
*92225	Blythe	(760)	22,428	10,835
93637	Bonadelle Ranchos-Madera Ranchos (c)	(559)	*7,300*	5,705
*91902	Bonita (c)	(619)	*12,401*	12,542
92021	Bostonia (c)	(619)	*15,169*	13,670
95416	Boyes Hot Springs (c)	(707)	*6,665*	5,973
92227	Brawley	(760)	22,255	18,923
*92822	Brea	(562)/(714)	38,522	32,873
*94513	Brentwood	(925)	39,827	7,563
—	Bret Harte (c)	(209)	*5,161*	—
*90622	Buena Park	(714)	79,357	68,784
*91510	Burbank (Los Angeles Co.)	(818)	104,114	93,649
—	Burbank (Santa Clara Co.) (c)	(408)	*5,239*	4,902
*94010	Burlingame	(650)	27,420	26,666
*91372	Calabasas	(818)	21,629	16,577
*92231	Calexico	(760)	34,326	18,633
*93504	California City	(760)	11,422	5,955
92320	Calimesa	(909)	7,497	6,654
92233	Calipatria	(760)	7,678	2,701
94515	Calistoga	(707)	5,207	4,468
*93010	Camarillo	(805)	60,890	52,297
93428	Cambria (c)	(805)	*6,232*	5,382
95682	Cameron Park (c)	(530)	*14,549*	11,897
*95008	Campbell	(408)	37,013	36,088
92054	Camp Pendleton North (c)	(760)	*8,197*	10,373
92055	Camp Pendleton South (c)	(760)	*8,854*	11,299
92587	Canyon Lake	(951)	11,161	9,991

ZIP	Place	Area Code	2004	1990
95010	Capitola	(831)	9,640	10,171
*92008	Carlsbad	(760)	89,042	63,292
*95608	Carmichael (c)	(916)	*49,742*	48,702
*93013	Carpinteria	(805)	13,829	13,747
*90745	Carson	(310)	93,733	83,995
92077	Casa de Oro-Mt. Helix (c)	(619)	*18,874*	30,727
*94546	Castro Valley (c)	(510)	*57,292*	48,619
95012	Castroville (c)	(831)	*6,724*	95012
*92235	Cathedral City	(760)	50,756	30,085
95307	Ceres	(209)	38,546	26,413
90703	Cerritos	(562)	52,898	53,244
91724	Charter Oak (c)	(626)	*9,027*	8,858
94541	Cherryland (c)	(510)	*13,837*	11,088
*95926	Chico	(530)	70,204	39,970
*91708	Chino	(909)	76,042	59,682
91709	Chino Hills	(909)	75,622	37,868
93610	Chowchilla	(559)	15,693	5,930
*91910	Chula Vista	(619)	204,879	135,160
91702	Citrus (c)	(626)	*10,581*	9,481
*95621	Citrus Heights	(916)	87,383	107,439
91711	Claremont	(909)	35,097	32,610
94517	Clayton	(925)	11,126	7,317
95422	Clearlake	(707)	14,513	11,804
95425	Cloverdale	(707)	7,844	4,924
*93612	Clovis	(559)	82,374	50,323
92236	Coachella	(760)	30,194	16,896
93210	Coalinga	(559)	17,102	8,212
*92324	Colton	(909)	51,382	40,213
95932	Colusa	(530)	5,855	4,934
90040	Commerce	(323)	13,405	12,135
*90221	Compton	(310)	96,235	90,454
*94520	Concord	(925)	124,328	111,308
*93212	Corcoran	(559)	22,434	13,360
*96021	Corning	(530)	7,079	5,870
92877	Corona	(951)	145,398	75,943
*92118	Coronado	(619)	23,774	26,540
*94925	Corte Madera	(415)	9,177	8,272
*92628	Costa Mesa	(714)/(949)	110,411	96,357
94931	Cotati	(707)	7,089	5,714
92679	Coto de Caza (c)	(949)	*13,057*	2,853
94556	Country Club (c)	(209)	*9,462*	9,325
*91722	Covina	(626)	48,091	43,332
92325	Crestline (c)	(909)	25,191	8,594
90201	Cudahy	(323)	39,896	22,817
*90230	Culver City	(310)	51,405	38,793
*95014	Cupertino	(408)	47,614	39,967
90630	Cypress	(714)	48,091	42,655
*94015	Daly City	(415)/(650)	100,620	92,088
*92629	Dana Point	(949)	36,019	31,896
*94526	Danville	(925)	42,199	31,306
*95616	Davis	(530)	63,722	46,322
90250	Del Aire (c)	(310)	*9,012*	8,040
*93215	Delano	(661)	43,988	22,762
95315	Delhi (c)	(209)	*8,022*	3,280
*92240	Desert Hot Springs	(760)	58,326	11,668
91765	Diamond Bar	(909)	18,479	53,672
93618	Dinuba	(559)	43,988	12,743
95620	Dixon	(707)	16,710	10,417
90239	Downey	(562)	110,318	91,444
94514	Discovery Bay (c)	(925)	*8,981*	5,351
*91009	Duarte	(626)	22,273	20,716
94568	Dublin	(925)	36,995	23,229
*95938	Durham (c)	(530)	*5,220*	4,784
93219	Earlimart (c)	(661)	*6,583*	5,881
90220	East Compton (c)	(310)	*9,286*	7,967
—	East Foothills (c)	(408)	*8,133*	14,898
92343	East Hemet (c)	(951)	*14,823*	17,611
90638	East La Mirada (c)	(562)	*9,538*	9,367
90022	East Los Angeles (c)	(323)	*124,283*	126,379
94303	East Palo Alto	(650)	32,042	23,451
91107	East Pasadena (c)	(626)	*6,045*	5,910
93257	East Porterville (c)	(559)	*6,730*	5,790
91775	East San Gabriel (c)	(626)	*14,512*	12,736
*93524	Edwards AFB (c)	(661)	*5,909*	7,423
*92020	El Cajon	(619)	93,987	88,918
*92244	El Centro	(760)	38,350	31,405
94530	El Cerrito	(510)	23,138	22,869
95762	El Dorado Hills (c)	(916)	*18,016*	6,395
94018	El Granada (c)	(650)	*5,724*	4,426
*91734	El Monte	(626)	122,123	106,162
*93446	El Paso de Robles	(805)	26,887	18,583
93030	El Rio (c)	(805)	*6,193*	6,419
90245	El Segundo	(310)	16,492	15,223
*94803	El Sobrante (c)	(510)	*12,260*	9,852
*95624	Elk Grove	(916)	100,760	17,483
*94608	Emeryville	(510)	8,023	5,740
*92024	Encinitas	(760)	60,057	55,406
95320	Escalon	(209)	6,937	4,437
*92025	Escondido	(760)	135,462	108,648
*95501	Eureka	(707)	25,803	27,025
93221	Exeter	(559)	9,842	7,276
*94930	Fairfax	(415)	7,159	6,931
94533	Fairfield	(707)	103,949	78,650
95628	Fair Oaks (c)	(916)	*28,008*	26,867
94541	Fairview (c)	(510)	*9,470*	9,045
*92028	Fallbrook (c)	(760)	*29,100*	22,095
93223	Farmersville	(559)	9,583	6,235
*93015	Fillmore	(805)	14,967	11,992
93622	Firebaugh	(559)	6,937	4,429
90001	Florence-Graham (c)	(323)	*60,197*	57,147
95828	Florin (c)	(916)	*27,653*	24,330
*95630	Folsom	(916)	63,960	29,802
*92334	Fontana	(909)	158,715	87,535
95841	Foothill Farms (c)	(916)	*17,426*	17,135
92610	Foothill Ranch (c)	(949)	*10,899*	—
95437	Fort Bragg	(707)	6,878	6,078
95540	Fortuna	(707)	10,995	8,788
94404	Foster City	(650)	28,847	28,176
*92728	Fountain Valley	(714)	56,352	53,691
95019	Freedom (c)	(831)	*6,000*	8,361
*94537	Fremont	(510)	202,373	173,339
*93706	Fresno	(559)	457,719	354,091
*92834	Fullerton	(714)	133,439	114,144
95632	Galt	(209)	22,965	8,889
*90247	Gardena	(310)	59,727	51,481
95205	Garden Acres (c)	(209)	*9,747*	8,547
*92842	Garden Grove	(714)	167,347	142,965
*95020	Gilroy	(408)	44,356	31,487
92509	Glen Avon (c)	(951)	*14,853*	12,663
*91209	Glendale	(818)	201,326	180,038
*91741	Glendora	(626)	50,889	47,832
93561	Golden Hills (c)	(661)	*7,434*	5,423
95670	Gold River (c)	(916)	*8,023*	—
*93116	Goleta	(805)	28,181	—
93926	Gonzales	(831)	8,482	4,660
92324	Grand Terrace	(951)	12,349	10,946
95746	Granite Bay (c)	(916)	*19,388*	—
*95945	Grass Valley	(530)	11,986	9,048
93927	Greenfield	(831)	12,845	7,464
95948	Gridley	(530)	5,648	4,631
93433	Grover Beach	(805)	13,036	11,602
93434	Guadalupe	(805)	5,989	5,479
95322	Gustine	(209)	5,340	4,137
91745	Hacienda Heights (c)	(626)	*53,122*	52,354
94019	Half Moon Bay	(650)	12,208	8,886
*93230	Hanford	(559)	46,820	30,463
90716	Hawaiian Gardens	(562)	15,406	13,639
*90250	Hawthorne	(310)/(323)	86,279	71,349
*94544	Hayward	(510)	140,795	114,705
95448	Healdsburg	(707)	11,130	9,469
92546	Hemet	(951)	66,563	43,366
94547	Hercules	(510)	23,425	16,829
90254	Hermosa Beach	(310)	19,537	18,219
*92340	Hesperia	(760)	73,376	50,418
92346	Highland	(909)	50,236	34,439
94010	Hillsborough	(650)	10,600	10,667
*95023	Hollister	(831)	36,330	19,318
92250	Holtville	(760)	5,505	4,820
91720	Home Gardens (c)	(951)	*9,461*	7,780
95326	Hughson	(209)	5,907	2,918
*92647	Huntington Beach	(714)	195,305	181,519
90255	Huntington Park	(323)	62,979	56,129
93234	Huron	(559)	6,997	4,766
92251	Imperial	(760)	9,612	4,113
*91932	Imperial Beach	(619)	26,710	26,512
*92201	Indio	(760)	63,326	36,850
*90301	Inglewood	(310)/(323)	115,313	109,602
—	Interlaken (c)	(831)	*7,328*	6,404
95640	Ione	(209)	7,577	6,516
*92619	Irvine	(714)/(949)	178,317	110,330
93117	Isla Vista (c)	(805)	*18,344*	20,395
91935	Jamul (c)	(619)	*5,920*	2,258
94914	Kentfield (c)	(415)	*6,351*	6,030
93630	Kerman	(559)	10,238	5,448
93930	King City	(831)	11,162	7,634
93631	Kingsburg	(559)	11,049	7,245
*91011	La Canada Flintridge	(818)	21,063	19,378
90045	Ladera Heights (c)	(310)	*6,568*	6,316
94549	Lafayette	(925)	24,665	23,366
—	Laguna (c)	(916)	*34,309*	9,828
*92652	Laguna Beach	(949)	24,250	23,170
*92654	Laguna Hills	(949)	32,380	22,719
*92607	Laguna Niguel	(949)	64,946	44,723
—	Laguna West-Lakeside (c)	—	*8,414*	—
*92654	Laguna Woods	(949)	18,306	—
*90631	La Habra	(562)/(949)	59,803	51,263
90631	La Habra Heights	(562)	5,988	6,226
92352	Lake Arrowhead (c)	(909)	*8,934*	6,539
*92531	Lake Elsinore	(951)	37,009	19,733
92630	Lake Forest	(949)	77,012	56,036
92530	Lakeland Village (c)	(909)	*5,626*	5,159
*93535	Lake Los Angeles (c)	(661)	*11,523*	7,977
95453	Lakeport	(707)	5,230	4,567
92040	Lakeside(c)	(619)	*19,560*	39,412
*90714	Lakewood	(562)	81,088	73,553
*91941	La Mesa	(619)	53,855	52,911
*90638	La Mirada	(562)/(714)	49,636	40,452
93241	Lamont (c)	(661)	*13,296*	11,517
*93539	Lancaster	(661)	128,928	97,300
90623	La Palma	(562)/(714)	15,935	15,392
—	La Presa (c)	(619)	*32,721*	—
*91747	La Puente	(626)	42,058	36,955
*92253	La Quinta	(760)	35,363	11,215
95401	La Riviera (c)	(916)	*10,273*	10,986
95403	Larkfield-Wikiup (c)	(707)	*7,479*	6,779
*94939	Larkspur	(415)	11,797	11,068
92688	Las Flores (c)	(949)	*5,625*	—
95330	Lathrop	(209)	12,642	6,841
91750	La Verne	(909)	33,146	30,843
*90260	Lawndale	(310)	32,436	27,331

ZIP	Place	Area Code	2004	1990
*91945	Lemon Grove	(619)	24,537	23,984
93245	Lemoore	(559)	22,231	13,622
90304	Lennox (c)	(310)	*22,950*	22,757
95648	Lincoln	(916)	28,134	7,248
95901	Linda (c)	(530)	*13,474*	13,033
93247	Lindsay	(559)	10,734	8,338
95062	Live Oak (Santa Cruz Co.) (c)	(831)	*16,628*	15,212
95953	Live Oak (Sutter Co.)	(530)	6,552	4,320
*94550	Livermore	(925)	77,983	56,741
95334	Livingston	(209)	12,093	7,317
*95240	Lodi	(209)	61,961	51,874
92354	Loma Linda	(951)	20,332	18,470
90717	Lomita	(310)	20,549	19,442
*93436	Lompoc	(805)	40,908	37,649
*90801	Long Beach	(310)/(562)	476,564	429,321
95650	Loomis	(916)	6,375	5,705
*90720	Los Alamitos	(562)/(949)	11,780	11,788
*94022	Los Altos	(650)	26,992	26,599
94022	Los Altos Hills	(650)	8,122	7,514
*90086	Los Angeles	(213)/(310)/(323)/(818)	3,845,541	3,485,557
93635	Los Banos	(209)	31,830	14,519
*95030	Los Gatos	(408)	27,930	27,357
94903	Lucas Valley-Marinwood (c)	(415)	*6,357*	5,982
90262	Lynwood	(213)/(310)/(323)	27,930	61,945
93250	Mc Farland	(661)	10,074	7,005
95521	McKinleyville (c)	(707)	*13,599*	10,749
*93638	Madera	(559)	50,043	29,283
93637	Madera Acres (c)	(559)	*7,741*	5,245
95954	Magalia (c)	(530)	*10,569*	8,987
*90265	Malibu	(310)	13,305	11,730
93546	Mammoth Lakes	(760)	7,259	4,785
*90266	Manhattan Beach	(310)	36,321	32,063
*95336	Manteca	(209)	61,407	40,773
93933	Marina	(831)	19,324	26,512
*90291	Marina del Rey (c)	(310)	*8,176*	7,431
94553	Martinez	(925)	36,305	31,800
95901	Marysville	(530)	12,518	12,324
—	Mayflower Village (c)		*5,081*	4,978
90270	Maywood	(323)	28,816	27,893
93640	Mendota	(559)	8,858	6,821
*94025	Menlo Park	(650)	29,759	28,403
92359	Mentone (c)	(909)	*7,803*	5,675
*95340	Merced	(209)	72,487	56,155
94030	Millbrae	(650)	20,419	20,414
*94941	Mill Valley	(415)	13,359	13,029
*95035	Milpitas	(408)	62,698	50,690
91752	Mira Loma (c)	(951)	*17,617*	15,786
*93641	Miramonte (c)	(805)	*7,177*	7,744
*92690	Mission Viejo	(949)	96,253	79,464
*95350	Modesto	(209)	206,769	164,746
*91017	Monrovia	(626)	38,174	35,733
91763	Montclair	(909)	35,245	28,434
90640	Montebello	(323)	63,700	59,564
*93940	Monterey	(831)	29,669	31,954
*91754	Monterey Park	(323)/(626)/(818)	62,398	60,738
*93021	Moorpark	(805)	35,894	25,494
*94556	Moraga	(925)	16,797	15,987
*92552	Moreno Valley	(951)	166,290	118,779
*95037	Morgan Hill	(408)	34,885	23,928
*93442	Morro Bay	(805)	10,309	9,664
*94041	Mountain View	(650)	69,011	67,365
*92564	Murrieta	(951)	74,513	18,557
92407	Muscoy (c)	(714)	*8,919*	7,541
*94558	Napa	(707)	75,465	61,865
*91950	National City	(619)	54,572	54,249
92363	Needles	(760)	5,346	5,475
94560	Newark	(510)	42,511	37,861
95360	Newman	(209)	8,552	4,158
*92658	Newport Beach	(949)	79,957	66,643
93444	Nipomo (c)	(805)	*12,626*	7,109
91760	Norco	(951)	26,668	23,302
*90650	Norwalk	(562)	106,683	94,279
95603	North Auburn (c)	(530)	*11,847*	10,301
94025	North Fair Oaks (c)	(650)	*15,440*	13,912
95660	North Highlands (c)	(916)	*44,187*	42,105
*94947	Novato	(415)	49,238	47,585
95361	Oakdale	(209)	17,679	11,978
*94617	Oakland	(510)	397,976	372,242
94561	Oakley	(925)	26,818	18,374
93445	Oceano (c)	(805)	*7,260*	6,169
*92056	Oceanside	(760)	167,438	128,090
93308	Oildale (c)	(661)	*27,885*	26,553
*93023	Ojai	(805)	170,057	7,613
95961	Olivehurst (c)	(530)	*11,061*	9,738
*91761	Ontario	(909)	8,046	133,179
95060	Opal Cliffs (c)	(831)	*6,458*	5,940
*92863	Orange	(714)	133,819	110,658
93646	Orange Cove	(559)	9,325	5,604
95662	Orangevale (c)	(916)	*26,705*	26,266
*93457	Orcutt (c)	(805)	*28,830*	—
94563	Orinda	(925)	18,176	16,642
95963	Orland	(530)	6,601	5,052
93647	Orosi (c)	(559)	*7,318*	5,486
*95965	Oroville	(530)	13,209	11,885
*93030	Oxnard	(805)	183,587	142,560
94044	Pacifica	(650)	37,182	37,670
93950	Pacific Grove	(831)	15,280	16,117
95968	Palermo (c)	(530)	*5,720*	5,260
*93590	Palmdale	(661)	131,153	73,314
*92260	Palm Desert	(760)	46,615	23,252
*92262	Palm Springs	(760)	46,436	40,144
*94303	Palo Alto	(650)	56,862	55,900
*90274	Palos Verdes Estates	(310)	13,868	13,512
*95969	Paradise	(530)	26,671	25,401
90723	Paramount	(562)	56,899	47,669
95823	Parkway-So. Sacramento (c)	(916)	*36,468*	31,903
93648	Parlier	(559)	12,981	7,938
*91109	Pasadena	(323)/(626)/(818)	144,068	131,586
	Paso Robles. *See* El Paso de Robles			
95363	Patterson	(209)	14,793	8,626
92509	Pedley (c)	(951)	*11,207*	8,869
*92572	Perris	(951)	45,793	21,500
*94952	Petaluma	(707)	55,359	43,166
—	Phoenix Lake-Cedar Ridge (c)	—	*5,123*	3,569
*90660	Pico Rivera	(562)	65,198	59,177
*94611	Piedmont	(510)	10,713	10,602
94564	Pinole	(510)	19,272	17,460
*93449	Pismo Beach	(805)	8,473	7,669
94565	Pittsburg	(925)	62,600	47,607
*92871	Placentia	(714)	49,949	41,259
95667	Placerville	(530)	10,151	8,286
94523	Pleasant Hill	(925)	33,529	31,583
*94566	Pleasanton	(925)	65,951	50,570
*91769	Pomona	(909)	155,448	131,700
*93257	Porterville	(559)	44,011	29,521
*93041	Port Hueneme	(805)	22,041	20,322
92679	Portola Hills (c)	(949)	*6,391*	2,677
*92064	Poway	(858)	48,977	43,396
93907	Prunedale (c)	(831)	*16,432*	7,393
*93551	Quartz Hill (c)	(661)	*9,890*	9,626
92065	Ramona (c)	(760)	*15,691*	13,040
*95670	Rancho Cordova (c)	(916)	*56,508*	48,731
*91729	Rancho Cucamonga	(909)	159,346	101,409
92270	Rancho Mirage	(760)	16,230	9,778
90275	Rancho Palos Verdes	(310)	42,310	41,667
91941	Rancho San Diego (c)	(619)	*20,155*	6,977
92688	Rancho Santa Margarita	(949)	50,004	11,390
96080	Red Bluff	(530)	13,911	12,363
*96049	Redding	(530)	88,573	66,176
*92373	Redlands	(909)	69,682	62,667
*90277	Redondo Beach	(310)	66,683	60,167
*94063	Redwood City	(650)	73,346	66,072
93654	Reedley	(559)	22,264	15,791
*92377	Rialto	(909)	99,659	72,395
*94802	Richmond	(510)	102,318	86,019
*93556	Ridgecrest	(760)	25,854	28,295
95003	Rio del Mar (c)	(831)	*9,198*	8,919
95673	Rio Linda (c)	(916)	*10,466*	9,481
94571	Rio Vista	(707)	6,556	3,488
95366	Ripon	(209)	12,980	7,455
95367	Riverbank	(209)	20,207	8,591
*92502	Riverside	(951)	288,384	226,546
*95677	Rocklin	(916)	48,637	18,806
*94572	Rodeo (c)	(510)	*8,717*	7,589
*94928	Rohnert Park	(707)	41,966	36,326
*90274	Rolling Hills Estates	(310)	7,990	7,789
93560	Rosamond (c)	(661)	*14,349*	7,430
—	Rosedale (c)	(805)	*8,445*	4,673
95407	Roseland (c)	(707)	*6,369*	8,779
*91770	Rosemead	(626)	55,296	51,638
95826	Rosemont (c)	(916)	*22,904*	22,851
*95678	Roseville	(916)	103,609	44,685
90720	Rossmoor (c)	(714)	*10,298*	9,893
91748	Rowland Heights (c)	(626)	*48,553*	42,647
*92519	Rubidoux (c)	(951)	*29,180*	24,367
92382	Running Springs (c)	(909)	*5,125*	4,195
*95814	Sacramento	(916)	454,330	369,365
94574	Saint Helena	(707)	6,026	4,990
95368	Salida (c)	(209)	*12,560*	4,499
*93907	Salinas	(831)	148,183	108,777
*94960	San Anselmo	(415)	12,110	11,735
*92401	San Bernardino	(909)	198,406	170,036
*94066	San Bruno	(650)	39,661	38,961
*93001	San Buenaventura (Ventura)	(805)	104,068	92,557
*94070	San Carlos	(650)	26,915	26,382
*92674	San Clemente	(949)	59,550	41,100
*92138	San Diego	(619)/(858)	1,263,756	1,110,623
*92065	San Diego Country Estates (c)	(760)	*9,262*	6,874
91773	San Dimas	(909)	36,067	32,398
*91341	San Fernando	(818)	24,355	22,580
*94142	San Francisco	(415)	744,230	723,959
*91778	San Gabriel	(626)	41,260	37,120
93657	Sanger	(559)	21,040	16,839
*92581	San Jacinto	(951)	28,043	17,614
*95113	San Jose	(408)	904,522	782,224
*92690	San Juan Capistrano	(949)	34,882	26,183
*94577	San Leandro	(510)	79,183	68,223
*93401	San Luis Obispo	(805)	44,032	41,958
*92069	San Marcos	(760)	68,347	38,974
*91108	San Marino	(626)	13,272	12,959
*94402	San Mateo	(650)	91,275	85,619
94806	San Pablo	(510)	31,041	25,158
*94915	San Rafael	(415)	55,560	48,410
94583	San Ramon	(925)	45,616	35,303
*92711	Santa Ana	(714)/(949)	342,715	293,827
*93102	Santa Barbara	(805)	87,370	85,571
*95050	Santa Clara	(408)	104,001	93,613
*91380	Santa Clarita	(661)	164,800	120,050
*95060	Santa Cruz	(831)	54,213	49,711
90670	Santa Fe Springs	(562)	17,060	15,520

ZIP	Place	Area Code	2004	1990
*93454	Santa Maria	(805)	83,756	61,552
*90401	Santa Monica	(310)	87,823	86,905
*93060	Santa Paula	(805)	28,732	25,062
*95402	Santa Rosa	(707)	153,636	113,261
*92071	Santee	(619)	52,577	52,902
*95070	Saratoga	(408)	29,633	28,061
*94965	Sausalito	(415)	7,228	7,152
*95066	Scotts Valley	(831)	11,205	8,667
90740	Seal Beach	(562)	24,459	25,098
93955	Seaside	(831)	34,130	38,826
*95472	Sebastopol	(707)	7,685	7,008
93662	Selma	(559)	21,919	14,757
—	Shackelford (c)	—	*5,170*	—
*93263	Shafter	(661)	14,155	9,404
*96019	Shasta Lake	(916)	10,117	8,821
*91025	Sierra Madre	(626)	11,023	10,762
*90806	Signal Hill	(562)	10,698	8,371
*93065	Simi Valley	(805)	118,893	100,218
92075	Solana Beach	(858)	12,860	12,956
93960	Soledad	(831)	26,325	13,426
*93463	Solvang	(805)	5,225	4,741
95476	Sonoma	(707)	9,680	8,168
95073	Soquel (c)	(831)	*5,081*	9,188
91733	South El Monte	(626)	21,801	20,850
90280	South Gate	(323)/(562)	99,627	86,284
*96151	South Lake Tahoe	(530)	23,926	21,586
95965	South Oroville (c)	(530)	*7,695*	7,463
*91030	So. Pasadena	(213)/(323)/626)/(818)	25,048	23,936
*94080	South San Francisco	(650)	59,897	54,312
91770	South San Gabriel (c)	(626)	*7,595*	7,700
91744	South San Jose Hills (c)	(626)	*20,218*	17,814
90605	South Whittier (c)	(562)	*55,193*	49,514
95991	South Yuba City (c)	(530)	*12,651*	8,816
*91977	Spring Valley (c)	(619)	*26,663*	55,331
*94309	Stanford (c)	(650)	*13,315*	18,097
90680	Stanton	(714)	37,923	30,491
*95208	Stockton	(209)	279,888	210,943
95375	Strawberry (c)	(209)	*5,302*	4,377
*94585	Suisun City	(707)	26,945	22,704
*92586	Sun City (c)	(951)	*17,773*	14,930
*94086	Sunnyvale	(408)	128,012	117,324
*96130	Susanville	(530)	18,043	12,130
93268	Taft	(661)	9,076	5,902
94941	Tamalpais-Homestead Val. (c)	(415)	*10,691*	9,601
94806	Tara Hills (c)	(510)	*5,332*	4,998
*93581	Tehachapi	(661)	11,653	6,182
*92589	Temecula	(951)	82,083	27,177
91780	Temple City	(626)	36,911	31,153
95965	Thermalito (c)	(530)	*6,045*	5,646
*91359	Thousand Oaks	(805)	125,054	104,381
92276	Thousand Palms (c)	(760)	*5,120*	4,122
94920	Tiburon	(415)	8,691	7,554
*90503	Torrance	(310)	142,841	133,107
95376	Tracy	(209)	76,900	33,558
*96161	Truckee	(916)	15,451	8,848
*93274	Tulare	(559)	48,697	33,249
*95380	Turlock	(209)	65,484	42,224
*92781	Tustin	(714)/(949)	68,612	50,689
92705	Tustin Foothills (c)	(714)	*24,044*	24,358
*92277	Twentynine Palms	(760)	30,081	11,821
92278	Twentynine Palms Base (c)	(760)	*8,413*	10,606
95060	Twin Lakes (c)	(831)	*5,533*	5,379
*95482	Ukiah	(707)	15,580	14,632
94587	Union City	(510)	68,938	53,762
*91785	Upland	(909)	73,526	63,374
*95687	Vacaville	(707)	94,303	71,476
91744	Valinda (c)	(626)	*21,776*	18,735
*94590	Vallejo	(707)	118,349	109,199
92343	Valle Vista (c)	(951)	*10,488*	8,751
92082	Valley Center (c)	(760)	*7,323*	1,711
93437	Vandenberg AFB (c)	(805)	*6,151*	9,846
93436	Vandenberg Village (c)	(805)	*5,802*	5,971
*92393	Victorville	(760)	82,790	50,103
90043	View Park-Windsor Hills (c)	(310)	*10,958*	11,769
92861	Villa Park	(714)	6,069	6,299
—	Vincent (c)	—	*15,097*	13,713
—	Vineyard (c)	—	*10,109*	—
*93291	Visalia	(559)	104,655	75,659
*92083	Vista	(760)	91,585	71,861
—	Waldon (c)	—	*5,133*	—
*91788	Walnut	(626)	31,607	29,105
*94596	Walnut Creek	(925)	64,822	60,569
90255	Walnut Park (c)	(213)	*16,180*	14,722
93280	Wasco	(661)	23,240	12,412
95386	Waterford	(209)	8,119	4,771
*95076	Watsonville	(831)	47,152	31,099
90044	West Athens (c)	(310)	*9,101*	8,859
90502	West Carson (c)	(310)	*21,138*	20,143
90247	West Compton (c)	(310)	*5,435*	5,451
*91790	West Covina	(626)	108,668	96,226
90069	West Hollywood	(310)/(323)	36,933	36,118
*91359	Westlake Village	(805)	8,584	7,455
*92685	Westminster	(714)	89,855	78,293
—	West Modesto (c)	—	*6,096*	—
90047	Westmont (c)	(323)	*31,623*	31,044
91746	West Puente Valley (c)	(626)	*22,589*	20,254
*95691	West Sacramento	(916)	39,351	28,898
*90606	West Whittier-Los Nietos (c)	(562)	*25,129*	24,164
*90605	Whittier	(562)	85,509	77,671
92595	Wildomar (c)	(951)	*14,064*	10,411
*95490	Willits	(707)	5,098	5,027
90222	Willowbrook (c)	(323)	*34,138*	32,772
95988	Willows	(530)	6,299	5,988
95492	Windsor	(707)	24,751	12,002
—	Winter Gardens (c)	—	*19,771*	—
95694	Winters	(530)	6,838	4,639
95388	Winton (c)	(209)	*8,832*	7,559
92504	Woodcrest (c)	(951)	*8,342*	7,796
93286	Woodlake	(559)	7,082	5,678
*95695	Woodland	(530)	51,693	40,230
94061	Woodside	(650)	5,284	5,034
*92885	Yorba Linda	(714)	63,660	52,422
96097	Yreka	(530)	7,166	6,948
*95991	Yuba City	(530)	52,124	27,385
92399	Yucaipa	(909)	47,864	32,819
*92286	Yucca Valley	(760)	19,031	16,539

Colorado

Area code (720) overlays area code (303). See introductory note.

ZIP	Place	Area Code	2004	1990
*80840	Air Force Academy (c)	(719)	*7,526*	9,062
*81101	Alamosa	(719)	8,545	7,579
80401	Applewood (c)	(303)	*7,123*	11,069
*80004	Arvada	(303)	102,562	89,261
*81611	Aspen	(970)	5,717	5,049
*80017	Aurora	(303)	291,843	222,103
81620	Avon	(970)	6,363	1,798
—	Berkley (c)	—	*10,743*	—
80513	Berthoud	(970)	5,055	3,087
*80908	Black Forest (c)	(719)	*13,247*	8,143
*80302	Boulder	(303)	92,196	85,127
*80601	Brighton	(303)	26,927	14,203
*80020	Broomfield	(303)	42,901	24,638
80723	Brush	(970)	5,219	4,165
*81212	Canon City	(719)	15,813	12,687
81623	Carbondale	(970)	5,706	3,004
—	Castle Pines (c)	(303)	*5,958*	—
*80104	Castle Rock	(303)	32,709	8,710
80120	Castlewood (c)	(303)	*25,567*	24,392
*80015	Centennial	(303)	98,245	—
*80110	Cherry Hills Village	(303)	6,092	5,245
81222	Cimarron Hills (c)	(719)	369,363	11,160
81520	Clifton (c)	(970)	29,734	12,671
*80903	Colorado Springs	(719)	8,252	280,430
80120	Columbine (c)	(303)	9,220	23,969
*80022	Commerce City	(303)	8,064	16,466
81321	Cortez	(970)	556,835	7,284
*81625	Craig	(970)	15,020	8,091
81416	Delta	(970)	98,245	3,789
*80202	Denver	(303)	6,092	467,610
80022	Derby (c)	(303)	369,363	6,043
*81301	Durango	(970)	29,734	12,439
80214	Edgewater	(303)	5,273	4,613
81632	Edwards (c)	(970)	*8,257*	—
*80110	Englewood	(303)	32,432	29,396
80516	Erie	(303)	10,064	1,258
*80517	Estes Park	(970)	5,790	3,184
80620	Evans	(970)	16,314	5,876
*80439	Evergreen (c)	(303)	11,809	7,582
80221	Federal Heights	(303)	11,809	9,342
*80504	Firestone	(303)	5,756	1,358
80913	Fort Carson (c)	(719)	126,967	11,309
*80525	Fort Collins	(970)	126,967	87,491
80621	Fort Lupton	(970)	7,089	5,159
*80701	Fort Morgan	(970)	10,992	9,068
80817	Fountain	(719)	15,663	10,754
*80530	Frederick	(303)	6,034	988
81521	Fruita	(970)	6,816	4,045
81504	Fruitvale (c)	(303)	*6,936*	5,222
*81601	Glenwood Springs	(970)	8,475	6,561
*80401	Golden	(303)	17,436	13,127
*81501	Grand Junction	(970)	44,693	32,893
*80631	Greeley	(970)	84,815	60,454
*80111	Greenwood Village	(303)	12,678	7,589
80501	Gunbarrel (c)	(303)	5,319	9,388
*81230	Gunnison	(970)	5,319	4,636
80163	Highlands Ranch (c)	(303)	6,406	10,181
80534	Johnstown	(970)	7,307	1,579
80127	Ken Caryl (c)	(303)	5,319	24,391
80026	Lafayette	(303)	6,406	14,708
81050	La Junta	(719)	7,307	7,678
*80226	Lakewood	(303)	141,301	126,475
81052	Lamar	(719)	8,531	8,343
*80126	Littleton	(303)	40,456	33,711
*80124	Lone Tree	(303)	7,863	1,261
*80501	Longmont	(303)	80,627	51,976
80027	Louisville	(303)	18,493	12,363
*80538	Loveland	(970)	57,784	37,357
80829	Manitou Springs	(719)	5,038	4,540
80543	Milliken	(970)	5,202	1,605
*81401	Montrose	(970)	14,771	8,854
*80233	Northglenn	(303)	33,234	27,195
80649	Orchard Mesa (c)	(303)	*6,456*	5,977
*80134	Parker	(303)	36,962	5,450
*81003	Pueblo	(719)	103,621	98,640
81007	Pueblo West (c)	(719)	*16,899*	4,386
81503	Redlands (c)	(970)	*8,043*	9,355
81650	Rifle	(970)	7,683	4,858
*81201	Salida	(719)	5,491	4,737

ZIP	Place	Area Code	2004	1990
80911	Security-Widefield (c)	(719)	*29,845*	23,822
80110	Sheridan	(303)	5,491	4,976
80221	Sherrelwood (c)	(303)	*17,657*	16,636
80122	Southglenn (c)	(303)	*43,520*	43,087
*80477	Steamboat Springs	(970)	9,344	6,695
80751	Sterling	(970)	12,730	10,362
—	Stonegate (c)	—	*6,284*	—
80906	Stratmoor (c)	(719)	*6,650*	5,854
80027	Superior	(303)	10,404	255
—	The Pinery (c)	(303)	*7,253*	4,885
*80229	Thornton	(303)	102,072	55,031
81082	Trinidad	(719)	9,047	8,580
81251	Twin Lakes (c)	(719)	*6,301*	—
80229	Welby (c)	(303)	*12,973*	10,218
*80030	Westminster	(303)	104,759	74,619
*80033	Wheat Ridge	(303)	31,411	29,419
*80550	Windsor	(970)	13,832	5,062
*80863	Woodland Park	(719)	6,645	4,610
80132	Woodmoor (c)	(719)	*7,177*	3,858

Connecticut

See introductory note.

ZIP	Place	Area Code	2004	1990
06401	Ansonia	(203)	18,844	18,403
06001	*Avon*	(860)	16,709	13,937
06403	*Beacon Falls*	(203)	5,524	5,083
06037	*Berlin*	(860)	19,322	16,787
06524	*Bethany*	(203)	5,331	—
06801	*Bethel*	(203)	18,566	17,541
06002	*Bloomfield*	(860)	19,803	19,483
06043	*Bolton*	(860)	5,199	—
06405	*Branford*	(203)	29,136	27,603
06405	Branford Center (c)	(203)	*5,735*	5,688
*06602	Bridgeport	(203)	139,910	141,686
*06010	Bristol	(860)	61,005	60,640
06804	*Brookfield*	(203)	16,037	14,113
06234	*Brooklyn*	(860)	7,487	6,681
*06013	*Burlington*	(860)	8,808	7,026
06019	*Canton*	(860)	9,413	8,268
06331	*Canterbury*	(860)	5,020	
06040	Central Manchester (c)	(860)	*30,595*	30,934
*06410	*Cheshire*	(203)	29,187	25,684
06410	Cheshire Village (c)	(203)	*5,789*	5,759
06413	*Clinton*	(860)	13,645	12,767
*06415	*Colchester*	(860)	15,158	10,980
06237	*Columbia*	(860)	5,228	4,510
06340	Conning Towers-Nautilus Pk. (c)	(860)	*10,241*	10,013
06238	*Coventry*	(860)	12,108	10,063
06416	*Cromwell*	(860)	13,471	12,286
*06810	Danbury	(203)	78,263	65,585
06820	*Darien*	(203)	19,921	18,196
06418	Derby	(203)	12,608	12,199
06422	*Durham*	(860)	7,134	5,732
06423	*East Haddam*	(860)	8,711	6,676
*06424	*East Hampton*	(860)	11,660	10,428
*06108	*East Hartford*	(860)	49,596	50,452
*06512	*East Haven*	(203)	28,710	26,144
06026	*East Granby*	(860)	5,028	4,302
06333	*East Lyme*	(860)	18,537	15,340
06612	*Easton*	(203)	7,482	6,303
*06088	*East Windsor*	(860)	10,185	10,081
06029	*Ellington*	(860)	13,952	11,197
*06082	*Enfield*	(860)	45,539	45,532
06426	*Essex*	(860)	6,800	5,904
*06825	*Fairfield*	(203)	58,407	53,418
*06032	*Farmington*	(860)	24,507	20,608
06033	*Glastonbury*	(860)	32,789	27,901
06033	Glastonbury Center (c)	(860)	*7,157*	7,082
*06035	*Granby*	(860)	10,869	9,369
*06830	*Greenwich*	(203)	61,972	58,441
06351	*Griswold*	(860)	11,087	10,384
*06340	Groton Naval Base	(860)	9,715	9,837
06340	*Groton*	(860)	40,002	45,144
06437	*Guilford*	(203)	22,082	19,848
06438	*Haddam*	(860)	7,459	6,769
*06514	*Hamden*	(203)	58,626	52,434
*06101	Hartford	(860)	124,848	139,739
06791	*Harwinton*	(860)	5,495	5,228
06248	*Hebron*	(860)	9,047	7,079
06037	Kensington (c)	(860)	*8,541*	8,306
*06239	*Killingly*	(860)	16,940	15,889
06419	*Killingworth*	(860)	6,373	4,814
06249	*Lebanon*	(860)	7,145	6,041
06339	*Ledyard*	(860)	15,003	14,913
*06759	*Litchfield*	(860)	8,531	8,365
06443	*Madison*	(203)	18,698	15,485
*06040	*Manchester*	(860)	55,390	51,618
*06250	*Mansfield*	(860)	23,324	21,103
06447	*Marlborough*	(860)	6,094	5,535
*06450	Meriden	(203)	59,136	59,479
*06762	*Middlebury*	(203)	6,745	6,145
06457	Middletown	(860)	47,157	42,762
*06460	Milford	(203)	52,726	48,168
06468	*Monroe*	(203)	19,614	16,896
06353	*Montville*	(860)	19,718	16,673
06770	Naugatuck	(203)	31,805	30,625
*06050	New Britain	(860)	71,699	75,491
*06840	*New Canaan*	(203)	19,839	17,864
06812	*New Fairfield*	(203)	14,179	12,911
06057	*New Hartford*	(860)	6,548	5,769
*06511	New Haven	(203)	124,829	130,474
*06101	*Newington*	(860)	29,695	29,208
06320	New London	(860)	26,319	28,540
06776	*New Milford*	(860)	28,211	23,629
06470	*Newtown*	(203)	26,299	20,779
06471	*North Branford*	(203)	14,228	12,996
06473	*North Haven*	(203)	23,628	22,247
06359	*North Stonington*	(860)	5,165	4,907
*06856	Norwalk	(203)	84,401	78,331
06360	Norwich	(860)	36,645	37,391
06779	Oakville (c)	(860)	*8,618*	8,741
06371	*Old Lyme*	(860)	7,483	6,535
06475	*Old Saybrook*	(860)	10,535	9,552
06477	*Orange*	(203)	13,572	12,830
06478	*Oxford*	(203)	10,729	8,685
06379	Pawcatuck (c)	(860)	*5,474*	5,289
06374	*Plainfield*	(860)	15,174	14,363
06062	*Plainville*	(860)	17,461	17,392
06782	*Plymouth*	(860)	12,067	11,822
06480	*Portland*	(860)	9,264	8,418
06712	*Prospect*	(203)	9,161	7,775
*06260	*Putnam*	(860)	9,079	9,031
06260	Putnam District (c)	(860)	*6,746*	6,835
06896	*Redding*	(203)	8,572	7,927
*06877	Ridgefield (c)	(203)	*7,212*	6,363
06877	*Ridgefield*	(203)	24,131	20,919
06066	Rockville (c)	(860)	*7,708*	—
06067	*Rocky Hill*	(860)	18,528	16,554
*06483	*Seymour*	(203)	16,045	14,288
06484	Shelton	(203)	39,321	35,418
06082	Sherwood Manor (c)	(860)	*5,689*	6,357
*06070	*Simsbury*	(860)	23,496	22,023
06070	Simsbury Center (c)	(860)	*5,603*	5,577
06071	*Somers*	(860)	10,870	9,108
06488	*Southbury*	(203)	19,279	15,818
06489	*Southington*	(860)	41,397	38,518
*06074	*South Windsor*	(860)	25,270	22,090
06082	Southwood Acres (c)	(860)	*8,067*	8,963
*06075	*Stafford*	(860)	11,743	11,091
*06904	Stamford	(203)	120,226	108,056
06378	*Stonington*	(860)	18,206	16,919
*06268	Storrs (c)	(860)	*10,996*	12,198
*06602	*Stratford*	(203)	50,182	49,389
*06078	*Suffield*	(860)	14,217	11,427
*06786	Terryville (c)	(860)	*5,360*	5,426
*06787	*Thomaston*	(860)	7,857	6,947
06277	*Thompson*	(860)	9,157	8,668
06082	Thompsonville (c)	(860)	*8,125*	8,458
06084	*Tolland*	(860)	14,264	11,001
*06790	Torrington	(860)	35,930	33,687
06611	*Trumbull*	(203)	35,013	32,016
06066	*Vernon*	(860)	29,206	29,841
*06492	*Wallingford*	(203)	44,331	40,822
06492	Wallingford Center (c)	(203)	*17,509*	17,827
*06702	Waterbury	(203)	108,429	108,961
*06385	*Waterford*	(860)	19,034	17,930
06795	*Watertown*	(860)	22,178	20,456
06498	*Westbrook*	(860)	6,583	5,414
*06101	*West Hartford*	(860)	61,424	60,110
06516	West Haven	(203)	53,087	54,021
06883	*Weston*	(203)	10,239	8,648
*06880	*Westport*	(203)	26,320	24,410
*06101	*Wethersfield*	(860)	26,398	25,651
06226	Willimantic (c)	(860)	*15,823*	14,746
06279	*Willington*	(860)	6,198	5,979
06897	*Wilton*	(203)	17,909	15,989
*06094	*Winchester*	(860)	10,781	11,524
*06280	*Windham*	(860)	23,014	22,039
*06095	*Windsor*	(860)	28,565	27,817
06096	*Windsor Locks*	(860)	12,256	12,358
*06098	Winsted (c)	(860)	*7,321*	8,254
*06716	*Wolcott*	(203)	16,024	13,700
06525	*Woodbridge*	(203)	9,249	7,924
06798	*Woodbury*	(203)	9,557	8,131
06281	*Woodstock*	(860)	7,685	6,008

Delaware (302)

ZIP	Place	2004	1990
19701	Bear (c)	*17,593*	—
19713	Brookside (c)	*14,806*	15,307
19703	Claymont (c)	*9,220*	9,800
*19901	Dover	33,618	27,630
*19809	Edgemoor (c)	*5,992*	5,853
19805	Elsmere	5,722	5,935
19702	Glasgow (c)	*12,840*	—
19707	Hockessin (c)	*12,902*	—
19709	Middletown	7,619	3,834
19963	Milford	7,088	6,032
*19711	Newark	29,821	26,463
19800	Pike Creek (c)	*19,751*	10,163
19973	Seaford	6,939	5,689
19977	Smyrna	6,808	5,231
*19899	Wilmington	72,784	71,529
19720	Wilmington Manor (c)	*8,262*	8,568

District of Columbia (202)

ZIP	Place	2004	1990
*20090	Washington	553,523	606,900

Florida

Area code (321) overlays area code (407). Area code (754) overlays (954). Area code (786) overlays (305). See introductory note.

ZIP	Place	Area Code	2004	1990
*32615	Alachua	(386)	7,020	4,667
*32714	Altamonte Springs	(407)	40,786	35,167
—	Andover (c)	(305)	8,489	6,251
33572	Apollo Beach (c)	(813)	7,444	6,025
*32712	Apopka	(407)	32,062	13,611
*34266	Arcadia	(863)	7,114	6,488
*32233	Atlantic Beach	(904)	13,553	11,636
33823	Auburndale	(863)	12,154	8,846
*33160	Aventura	(305)	27,236	14,914
*33825	Avon Park	(863)	8,797	8,078
32807	Azalea Park (c)	(407)	11,073	8,926
*33830	Bartow	(863)	15,824	14,716
33154	Bay Harbor Islands	(305)	5,125	4,703
—	Bay Hill (c)	(407)	5,177	5,346
34667	Bayonet Point (c)	(727)	23,577	21,860
33507	Bayshore Gardens (c)	(941)	17,350	17,062
33589	Beacon Square (c)	(727)	7,263	6,265
34233	Bee Ridge (c)	(941)	8,744	6,406
*33756	Bellair-MeadowbrookTerrace (c)	(904)	16,539	15,606
33430	Belle Glade	(561)	15,318	16,177
*32802	Belle Isle	(407)	6,307	5,272
*34420	Belleview (c)	(352)	21,201	19,386
*34465	Beverly Hills (c)	(352)	8,317	6,163
33043	Big Pine Key (c)	(305)	5,032	4,206
*33509	Bloomingdale (c)	(813)	19,839	13,912
33433	Boca Del Mar (c)	(561)	21,832	17,754
*33431	Boca Raton	(561)	78,069	61,486
*34135	Bonita Springs	(239)	35,850	13,600
33547	Boyette (c)	(813)	64,775	—
*33436	Boynton Beach	(561)	64,775	46,284
*34206	Bradenton	(941)	53,136	43,769
*33509	Brandon (c)	(813)	77,895	57,985
32503	Brent (c)	(850)	22,257	21,624
33317	Broadview Park (c)	(954)	6,798	6,109
33313	Broadview-Pompano Park (c)	(954)	5,314	5,230
*34601	Brooksville	(352)	7,487	7,589
33142	Brownsville (c)	(305)	14,393	15,607
32404	Callaway	(850)	14,510	12,253
32920	Cape Canaveral	(321)	9,826	8,014
*33920	Cape Coral	(239)	127,985	74,991
*33055	Carol City (c)	(305)	59,443	53,331
*32707	Casselberry	(407)	24,142	20,736
—	Cedar Grove	(850)	5,351	1,479
33401	Century Village (c)	(305)	7,616	8,363
—	Cheval (c)	(813)	7,602	—
33624	Citrus Park (c)	(813)	20,226	—
*32966	Citrus Ridge (c)	(772)	12,015	—
*33758	Clearwater	(727)	108,606	98,669
*34711	Clermont	(352)	11,125	6,910
33440	Clewiston	(863)	6,972	6,085
*32922	Cocoa	(321)	16,693	17,710
*32931	Cocoa Beach	(321)	12,588	12,123
*32922	Cocoa West (c)	(321)	5,921	6,160
*33097	Coconut Creek	(954)	48,889	27,269
33064	Collier Manor-Cresthaven (c)	(954)	7,741	7,322
33801	Combee Settlement (c)	(863)	5,436	5,463
32809	Conway (c)	(407)	14,394	13,159
*33328	Cooper City	(954)	29,446	21,335
*33114	Coral Gables	(305)	42,459	40,091
*33075	Coral Springs	(954)	128,355	78,864
33157	Coral Terrace (c)	(305)	24,380	23,255
33015	Country Club (c)	(305)	36,310	3,408
—	Country Walk (c)	(305)	10,653	—
*32536	Crestview	(850)	16,826	9,886
33803	Crystal Lake (c)	(863)	5,341	5,300
*33157	Cutler (c)	(305)	17,390	16,201
*33157	Cutler Ridge (c)	(305)	24,781	21,268
33884	Cypress Gardens (c)	(863)	8,844	9,188
33919	Cypress Lake (c)	(239)	12,072	10,491
*33525	Dade City	(352)	6,615	5,633
*33004	Dania Beach	(954)	28,479	—
*33329	Davie	(954)	82,579	47,143
*32114	Daytona Beach	(386)	64,422	61,991
*32713	DeBary	(386)	16,211	9,327
*33441	Deerfield Beach	(954)	65,694	46,997
*32433	DeFuniak Springs	(850)	5,141	5,200
*32720	De Land	(386)	22,857	16,622
*33444	Delray Beach	(561)	64,150	47,184
*32783	Deltona	(407)	79,749	49,429
*32541	Destin	(850)	12,162	8,090
32819	Doctor Phillips (c)	(407)	9,548	7,963
*33178	Doral (c)	(305)	20,438	3,126
*34698	Dunedin	(727)	36,632	34,427
33610	East Lake (c)	(813)	29,394	—
33610	East Lake-Orient Park (c)	(813)	5,703	6,171
—	East Perrine (c)	(305)	7,079	—
*32132	Edgewater	(386)	20,721	15,351
32542	Eglin AFB (c)	(850)	8,082	8,347
—	Egypt Lake-Leto (c)	(813)	32,782	—
34680	Elfers (c)	(727)	13,161	12,356
*34295	Englewood (c)	(941)	16,196	15,025
32534	Ensley (c)	(850)	18,752	16,362
33928	Estero (c)	(239)	9,503	3,177
*32726	Eustis	(352)	17,235	12,856
32804	Fairview Shores (c)	(305)	13,898	13,192
*32034	Fernandina Beach	(904)	11,241	8,765
32730	Fern Park (c)	(407)	8,318	8,294
32514	Ferry Pass (c)	(850)	27,176	26,301
*32136	Flagler Beach	(386)	5,228	3,851
*33034	Florida City	(305)	8,363	5,978
32960	Florida Ridge (c)	(772)	15,217	12,218
32714	Forest City (c)	(407)	12,612	10,638
*33310	Fort Lauderdale	(954)	164,578	149,238
33841	Fort Meade	(863)	5,761	5,151
*33902	Fort Myers	(239)	52,901	44,947
*33931	Fort Myers Beach	(239)	6,780	9,284
*33922	Fort Myers Shores (c)	(239)	5,793	5,460
*34981	Fort Pierce	(772)	37,959	36,830
*33452	Fort Pierce North (c)	(772)	7,386	5,833
*34982	Fort Pierce South (c)	(772)	5,672	5,320
*32548	Fort Walton Beach	(850)	19,992	21,407
—	Fountainbleau (c)	(305)	59,549	—
*32259	Fruit Cove (c)	(904)	16,077	5,904
34232	Fruitville (c)	(941)	12,741	9,808
33823	Fussels Corner (c)	(863)	5,313	3,840
*32602	Gainesville	(352)	108,856	91,482
33534	Gibsonton (c)	(813)	8,752	7,706
32960	Gifford (c)	(772)	7,599	6,278
33138	Gladeview (c)	(954)	14,468	15,637
33143	Glenvar Heights (c)	(305)	16,243	14,823
34116	Golden Gate (c)	(239)	20,951	14,148
33055	Golden Glades (c)	(305)	32,623	25,474
33411	Golden Lakes (c)	(561)	6,694	3,867
32733	Goldenrod (c)	(407)	12,871	12,362
32560	Gonzalez (c)	(850)	11,365	7,669
33170	Goulds (c)	(305)	7,453	7,284
—	Greater Carrollwood (c)	(813)	33,519	—
33624	Greater Northdale (c)	(813)	20,461	16,318
—	Greater Sun Center (c)	(813)	16,321	—
*33454	Greenacres	(561)	32,019	18,683
32043	Green Cove Springs	(904)	5,990	4,497
*32561	Gulf Breeze	(850)	6,333	5,530
33581	Gulf Gate Estates (c)	(941)	11,647	11,622
*33737	Gulfport	(727)	12,740	11,709
*33844	Haines City	(863)	14,530	11,683
*33009	Hallandale Beach	(305)/(954)	36,349	30,997
33434	Hamptons at Boca Raton (c)	(561)	11,306	11,686
34442	Hernando (c)	(352)	8,253	2,103
*33010	Hialeah	(305)	224,522	188,008
*33016	Hialeah Gardens	(305)	19,969	7,727
*33455	Hobe Sound (c)	(772)	11,376	11,507
*34690	Holiday (c)	(727)	21,904	19,360
*32125	Holly Hill	(386)	12,586	11,141
*33022	Hollywood	(954)	144,535	121,720
*34218	Holmes Beach	(941)	5,100	4,826
*33030	Homestead	(305)	37,957	26,694
34447	Homosassa Springs (c)	(352)	12,458	6,271
*34667	Hudson (c)	(727)	12,765	7,344
—	Hunters Creek (c)	(407)	9,369	—
*34142	Immokalee (c)	(239)	19,763	14,120
32937	Indian Harbour Beach	(321)	8,503	6,933
32963	Indian River Estates (c)	(772)	5,793	4,858
33785	Indian Rocks Beach	(727)	5,255	3,963
34956	Indiantown (c)	(772)	5,588	4,794
*34450	Inverness	(352)	7,287	5,797
—	Inverness Highlands South (c)	(352)	5,781	—
33880	Inwood (c)	(863)	6,925	6,824
33908	Iona (c)	(239)	11,756	9,565
*33036	Islamorada, Village of Islands	(305)	6,772	1,220
33162	Ives Estates (c)	(305)	17,586	13,531
*32203	Jacksonville	(904)	777,704	635,230
*32250	Jacksonville Beach	(904)	21,353	17,839
33880	Jan Phyl Village (c)	(863)	5,633	5,308
33568	Jasmine Estates (c)	(727)	18,213	17,136
*34957	Jensen Beach (c)	(772)	11,100	9,884
*33458	Jupiter	(561)	46,752	26,753
33183	Kendale Lakes (c)	(305)	56,901	48,524
*33256	Kendall (c)	(305)	75,226	87,271
—	Kendall West (c)	(305)	38,034	—
33149	Key Biscayne	(305)	10,324	8,854
33037	Key Largo (c)	(305)	11,886	11,336
—	Keystone (c)	(813)	14,627	—
*33040	Key West	(305)	24,768	24,832
*33573	Kings Point (c)	(305)	12,207	12,422
*34744	Kissimmee	(407)	56,153	30,337
*32159	Lady Lake	(352)	13,042	8,071
—	Lake Butter (c)	—	7,062	—
*32055	Lake City	(386)	10,699	9,626
*33804	Lakeland	(863)	88,357	70,576
33801	Lakeland Highlands (c)	(863)	12,557	9,972
32569	Lake Lorraine (c)	(850)	7,106	6,779
33054	Lake Lucerne (c)	(305)	9,132	9,478
33612	Lake Magdalene (c)	(813)	28,755	15,973
*32746	Lake Mary	(407)	13,918	5,929
*33403	Lake Park	(561)	9,080	6,704
—	Lakes by the Bay (c)	(305)	9,055	5,615
32073	Lakeside (c)	(904)	30,927	29,137
*33853	Lake Wales	(863)	11,802	9,670
34951	Lakewood Park (c)	(772)	10,458	7,211
*33461	Lake Worth	(561)	35,485	28,564
—	Lake Worth Corridor (c)	—	18,663	—
*34639	Land O'Lakes (c)	(813)	20,971	7,892
*33465	Lantana	(561)	10,389	8,392
*33770	Largo	(727)	71,704	65,910
*33062	Lauderdale-by-the-Sea	(954)	5,968	4,014
*33313	Lauderdale Lakes	(954)	31,639	27,341

ZIP	Place	Area Code	2004	1990
*33313	Lauderhill	(954)	59,542	49,015
34272	Laurel (c)	(941)	*8,393*	8,245
*34461	Lecanto (c)	(352)	*5,161*	1,243
*34748	Leesburg	(352)	18,079	14,783
*33936	Lehigh Acres (c)	(239)	*33,430*	13,611
*33033	Leisure City (c)	(305)	*22,152*	19,379
*33074	Lighthouse Point	(954)	11,212	10,378
*32060	Live Oak	(386)	6,828	6,332
32810	Lockhart (c)	(407)	*12,944*	11,636
34228	Longboat Key	(941)	7,622	5,937
*32750	Longwood	(407)	13,571	13,316
*33549	Lutz (c)	(813)	*17,081*	10,552
32444	Lynn Haven	(850)	14,663	9,270
33919	McGregor (c)	(904)	*7,136*	*6,504*
32063	Macclenny	(904)	5,030	3,966
*32751	Maitland	(407)	14,099	8,932
33550	Mango (c)	(813)	*8,842*	8,700
33050	Marathon	(305)	10,002	8,857
*34145	Marco Island	(239)	15,828	—
*33093	Margate	(954)	55,152	42,985
*32446	Marianna	(850)	6,200	6,292
32824	Meadow Woods (c)	(407)	*11,286*	4,876
33811	Medulla (c)	(863)	*6,637*	3,977
*32901	Melbourne	(321)	75,366	60,034
32666	Melrose Park (c)	(954)	*7,114*	6,477
33561	Memphis (c)	(941)	*7,264*	6,760
*32953	Merritt Island (c)	(321)	*36,090*	32,886
*33101	Miami	(305)	379,724	358,648
*33152	Miami Beach	(305)	89,104	92,639
*33014	Miami Lakes	(305)	22,688	12,750
*33153	Miami Shores	(305)	10,195	10,084
*33266	Miami Springs	(305)	13,422	13,268
32976	Micco (c)	(772)	*9,498*	8,757
*32068	Middleburg (c)	(904)	*10,338*	6,223
*32570	Milton	(850)	8,044	7,216
32754	Mims (c)	(321)	*9,147*	9,412
*34755	Minneola	(352)	7,253	1,515
*33023	Miramar	(954)	101,486	40,663
*32757	Mount Dora	(352)	10,658	7,294
32526	Myrtle Grove (c)	(850)	*17,211*	17,402
*34102	Naples	(239)	21,480	19,505
34113	Naples Manor (c)	(239)	*5,186*	4,574
34102	Naples Park (c)	(239)	*6,741*	8,002
32266	Neptune Beach	(904)	7,120	6,816
*34653	New Port Richey	(727)	16,675	14,044
33552	New Port Richey East (c)	(727)	*9,916*	9,683
*32168	New Smyrna Beach	(386)	21,464	16,549
*32578	Niceville	(850)	12,515	10,509
33269	Norland (c)	(305)	*22,995*	22,109
33308	North Andrews Gardens (c)	(954)	*9,656*	9,002
33141	North Bay Village	(305)	6,819	5,383
*33918	North Fort Myers (c)	(239)	*40,214*	30,027
*33068	North Lauderdale	(954)	34,403	26,473
*33261	North Miami	(305)	58,750	50,001
*33160	North Miami Beach	(305)	39,921	35,361
*33408	North Palm Beach	(561)	12,645	11,538
*34287	North Port	(941)	35,272	11,973
34234	North Sarasota (c)	(941)	*6,738*	6,702
33307	Oakland Park	(305)	31,512	26,326
33860	Oak Ridge (c)	(407)	*22,349*	15,388
*34478	Ocala	(352)	48,901	42,045
32548	Ocean City (c)	(850)	*5,594*	5,422
34761	Ocoee	(407)	28,248	12,778
*33163	Ojus (c)	(305)	*16,642*	15,519
*34972	Okeechobee	(863)	5,784	4,943
34677	Oldsmar	(813)	13,706	8,361
*33265	Olympia Heights (c)	(305)	*13,452*	37,792
*33054	Opa-Locka	(305)	15,327	15,283
33054	Opa-Locka North (c)	(305)	*6,224*	6,568
*32763	Orange City	(386)	7,172	5,372
*32073	Orange Park	(904)	9,243	9,488
*32802	Orlando	(407)	205,648	164,674
32811	Orlo Vista (c)	(407)	*6,047*	5,990
*32174	Ormond Beach	(386)	37,929	29,721
32074	Ormond By-The-Sea (c)	(386)	*8,430*	8,157
*32765	Oviedo	(407)	28,802	11,114
32571	Pace (c)	(850)	*7,393*	6,277
33476	Pahokee	(561)	6,459	6,822
*32177	Palatka	(386)	10,796	10,447
*32905	Palm Bay	(321)	88,758	62,543
33480	Palm Beach	(561)	9,860	9,814
*33408	Palm Beach Gardens	(561)	44,315	24,139
*34990	Palm City (c)	(772)	*20,097*	3,925
*32135	Palm Coast	(386)	44,427	14,287
*34221	Palmetto	(941)	13,132	9,268
33157	Palmetto Estates (c)	(305)	*13,675*	12,293
*34683	Palm Harbor (c)	(727)	*59,248*	50,256
*33601	Palm River-Clair Mel (c)	(813)	*17,589*	13,691
*33406	Palm Springs	(561)	14,690	9,763
33012	Palm Springs North (c)	(305)	*5,460*	5,300
32082	Palm Valley (c)	(904)	*19,860*	9,960
*32401	Panama City	(850)	37,079	34,396
*32417	Panama City Beach	(850)	10,199	4,051
*33067	Parkland	(954)	20,556	3,773
34108	Pelican Bay (c)	—	*5,686*	—
*33021	Pembroke Park	(954)	5,415	4,933
*33029	Pembroke Pines	(954)	150,104	65,566
*32502	Pensacola	(850)	54,734	59,198
*32347	Perry	(850)	6,703	7,151
32839	Pine Castle (c)	(407)	*8,803*	8,276
33156	Pinecrest	(305)	19,432	—
32858	Pine Hills (c)	(407)	*41,764*	35,322
33324	Pine Island Ridge (c)	(954)	*5,199*	5,244
*33781	Pinellas Park	(727)	47,166	43,571
*34465	Pine Ridge (c)	(352)	*5,490*	—
33168	Pinewood (c)	(305)	*16,523*	15,518
*33318	Plantation	(954)	85,497	66,814
*33566	Plant City	(813)	30,906	22,754
*34758	Poinciana (c)	(407)	*13,647*	—
*33060	Pompano Beach	(954)	88,874	72,411
33064	Pompano Beach Highlands (c)	(954)	*6,505*	17,915
*33952	Port Charlotte (c)	(941)	*46,451*	41,535
*32129	Port Orange	(904)	52,793	35,399
32927	Port St. John (c)	(321)	*12,112*	8,933
*34981	Port St. Lucie	(772)	118,396	55,761
34983	Port St. Lucie-River Park (c)	(772)	*5,175*	4,874
34992	Port Salerno (c)	(772)	*10,141*	7,786
*33032	Princeton (c)	(305)	*10,090*	7,073
*33950	Punta Gorda	(941)	17,215	10,637
*32351	Quincy	(850)	6,975	7,452
*33156	Richmond Heights (c)	(305)	*8,479*	8,583
—	Richmond West (c)	(305)	*28,082*	—
34231	Ridge Wood Heights (c)	(941)	*5,028*	4,851
*33569	Riverview (c)	(813)	*12,035*	6,478
*33419	Riviera Beach	(561)	32,522	27,646
*32955	Rockledge	(321)	23,295	16,023
33947	Rotonda (c)	(941)	*6,574*	3,576
*33411	Royal Palm Beach	(561)	30,371	15,532
*33570	Ruskin (c)	(813)	*8,321*	6,046
*34695	Safety Harbor	(727)	17,550	15,120
*32084	Saint Augustine	(904)	12,157	11,695
32080	Saint Augustine Beach	(904)	5,650	3,830
32086	Saint Augustine South (c)	(904)	*5,035*	4,218
*34769	Saint Cloud	(407)	22,385	12,684
*33706	Saint Pete Beach	(727)	10,027	9,200
*33733	Saint Petersburg	(727)	249,090	240,318
33912	San Carlos Park (c)	(239)	*16,317*	11,785
33432	Sandalfoot Cove (c)	(305)	*16,582*	14,214
*32771	Sanford	(407)	45,460	32,387
33957	Sanibel	(239)	6,102	5,468
*34230	Sarasota	(941)	53,349	50,897
33577	Sarasota Springs (c)	(941)	*15,875*	16,088
32937	Satellite Beach	(321)	9,840	9,889
33055	Scott Lake (c)	(305)	*14,401*	14,588
*32958	Sebastian	(772)	18,671	10,248
*33870	Sebring	(863)	10,076	8,841
*33584	Seffner (c)	(813)	*5,467*	5,371
*33770	Seminole	(813)	18,226	9,251
34610	Shady Hills (c)	(727)	*7,798*	—
*34242	Siesta Key (c)	(941)	*7,150*	7,772
34472	Silver Springs Shores (c)	(352)	*6,690*	6,421
32809	Sky Lake (c)	(407)	*5,651*	6,202
32703	South Apopka (c)	(407)	*5,800*	6,360
33505	South Bradenton (c)	(941)	*21,587*	20,398
32121	South Daytona	(386)	13,758	12,488
34266	Southeast Arcadia (c)	(863)	*6,064*	4,145
34277	Southgate (c)	(941)	*7,455*	7,324
34233	South Gate Ridge (c)	(941)	*5,655*	5,924
—	South Highpoint (c)	(727)	*8,839*	—
*33243	South Miami	(305)	11,274	10,404
33157	South Miami Heights (c)	(305)	*33,522*	30,030
33707	South Pasadena	(727)	5,745	5,644
32937	South Patrick Shores (c)	(321)	*8,913*	10,249
34230	South Sarasota (c)	(941)	*5,314*	5,298
33595	South Venice (c)	(941)	*13,539*	11,951
*33331	Southwest Ranches	(954)	7,342	—
32206	Springfield	(850)	8,990	8,719
*34604	Spring Hill (c)	(352)	*69,078*	31,117
32091	Starke	(904)	5,769	5,226
*34994	Stuart	(772)	15,728	11,936
34446	Sugarmill Woods (c)	(352)	*6,409*	4,073
33160	Sunny Isles Beach	(305)	15,399	—
*33325	Sunrise	(954)	90,227	65,683
*33283	Sunset (c)	(305)	*17,150*	15,810
33144	Sweetwater	(305)	13,992	13,909
*32301	Tallahassee	(850)	156,612	124,773
*33320	Tamarac	(954)	59,278	44,822
33144	Tamiami (c)	(305)	*54,788*	33,845
*33601	Tampa	(813)	321,772	280,015
*34689	Tarpon Springs	(727)	22,554	17,874
32778	Tavares	(352)	11,368	7,488
*33687	Temple Terrace	(813)	21,694	16,444
33469	Tequesta	(561)	5,828	4,499
33186	The Crossings (c)	(305)	*23,557*	—
—	The Hammocks (c)	(305)	*47,379*	—
*32159	The Villages (c)	(352)	*8,333*	—
33592	Thonotosassa (c)	(813)	*6,091*	—
—	Three Lakes (c)	(305)	*6,955*	—
33025	Timber Pines (c)	(352)	*5,840*	3,182
*32780	Titusville	(321)	42,614	39,394
32615	Town 'n' Country (c)	(813)	*72,523*	60,946
*33706	Treasure Island	(727)	7,521	7,266
32817	Union Park (c)	(407)	*10,191*	6,890
33024	University (c)	(813)	*30,736*	—
—	University Park (c)	(305)	*26,538*	—
32401	Upper Grand Lagoon (c)	(850)	*10,889*	7,855
32580	Valparaiso	(850)	6,336	6,316
*33594	Valrico (c)	(813)	*6,582*	—
34231	Vamo (c)	(941)	*5,285*	3,325

ZIP	Place	Area Code	2004	1990
*34285	Venice	(941)	19,990	17,052
33595	Venice Gardens (c)	(941)	*7,466*	7,701
*32960	Vero Beach	(772)	17,209	17,350
32960	Vero Beach South (c)	(772)	*20,362*	16,973
33901	Villas (c)	(239)	*11,346*	9,898
32507	Warrington (c)	(850)	*15,207*	16,040
32791	Wekiva Springs (c)	(407)	*23,169*	23,026
*33414	Wellington	(561)	49,976	20,670
33543	Wesley Chapel (c)	(813)	*5,691*	—
—	West and East Lealman (c)	(727)	*21,753*	—
33626	Westchase (c)	(813)	*11,116*	—
33165	Westchester (c)	(305)	*30,271*	29,883
33409	Westgate-Belvedere Homes (c)	(561)	*8,134*	6,880
33138	West Little River (c)	(305)	*32,498*	33,575
*32912	West Melbourne	(321)	13,797	8,398
*33144	West Miami	(305)	5,925	5,727
*33326	Weston	(954)	63,534	—
*33416	West Palm Beach	(561)	95,344	67,764
32505	West Pensacola (c)	(850)	*21,939*	22,107
33157	West Perrine (c)	(305)	*8,600*	—
34208	West Samoset (c)	(941)	*5,507*	3,819
—	West Vero Corridor (c)	(772)	*7,695*	—
33168	Westview (c)	(305)	*9,692*	9,668
33165	Westwood Lakes (c)	(305)	*12,005*	11,522
33496	Whisper Walk (c)	(561)	*5,135*	3,037
32821	Williamsburg (c)	(407)	*6,736*	3,093
*33305	Wilton Manors	(954)	12,844	11,804
33803	Winston (c)	(813)	*9,024*	9,118
*34787	Winter Garden	(407)	22,070	9,863
*33880	Winter Haven	(863)	27,855	24,725
*32789	Winter Park	(407)	26,608	24,260
*32707	Winter Springs	(407)	31,972	22,151
32547	Wright (c)	(850)	*21,697*	18,945
34972	Yeehaw Junction (c)	(407)	*21,778*	—
*32097	Yulee (c)	(904)	*8,392*	6,915
*33540	Zephyrhills	(813)	11,854	8,220
33541	Zephyrhills West (c)	(813)	*5,242*	4,249

Georgia

Area code (678) overlays (770). Area code (762) overlays (706). See introductory note.

ZIP	Place	Area Code	2004	1990
*30101	Acworth	(770)	18,093	4,519
31620	Adel	(229)	5,454	5,093
*31706	Albany	(229)	76,253	78,804
*30004	Alpharetta	(770)	34,245	13,002
*31709	Americus	(229)	16,737	16,516
*30603	Athens-Clarke County[1]	(706)	102,744	86,522
*30301	Atlanta	(404)	419,122	393,929
30011	Auburn	(770)	6,937	3,139
*30903	Augusta-Richmond County[2]	(706)	191,326	186,616
*30168	Austell	(770)	6,517	4,173
*39818	Bainbridge	(229)	12,106	10,803
30204	Barnesville	(770)	5,905	4,747
30032	Belvedere Park (c)	(404)	*18,945*	18,089
31723	Blakely	(229)	5,485	5,595
30110	Bremen	(770)	5,272	4,353
*31520	Brunswick	(912)	15,978	16,433
*30518	Buford	(404)	10,966	8,771
*39827	Cairo	(229)	9,363	9,035
*30701	Calhoun	(706)	13,103	7,135
31730	Camilla	(229)	5,605	5,124
30032	Candler-McAfee (c)	(404)	*28,294*	29,491
*30114	Canton	(770)	15,094	4,817
*30117	Carrollton	(770)	21,010	16,029
*30120	Cartersville	(770)	17,403	12,037
30125	Cedartown	(770)	9,729	7,976
31028	Centerville	(770)	5,549	3,509
30366	Chamblee	(404)	9,112	7,668
30021	Clarkston	(404)	7,107	5,385
30337	College Park	(404)	18,353	20,645
*31908	Columbus	(706)	182,850	178,683
*30529	Commerce	(770)	5,636	4,108
30288	Conley (c)	(404)	*6,188*	5,528
*30013	Conyers	(404)	12,147	7,380
*31015	Cordele	(229)	11,557	10,833
—	Country Club Estates (c)	—	*7,594*	7,500
*30014	Covington	(770)	13,464	9,860
*30040	Cumming	(770)	5,443	2,798
*30132	Dallas	(770)	7,697	2,810
*30720	Dalton	(706)	31,478	22,218
*31742	Dawson	(229)	5,035	5,295
*30030	Decatur	(404)	18,251	17,304
31520	Dock Junction (c)	(912)	*6,951*	7,094
*30362	Doraville	(404)	10,032	7,626
*31533	Douglas	(912)	10,916	10,464
*30134	Douglasville	(404)	26,461	11,635
30333	Druid Hills (c)	(404)	*12,741*	12,174
*31021	Dublin	(478)	16,689	16,312
*30096	Duluth	(404)	24,255	9,821
*30356	Dunwoody (c)	(404)	*32,808*	26,302
31023	Eastman	(478)	5,393	5,153
30364	East Point	(404)	35,457	34,595
*31024	Eatonton	(706)	6,789	6,479
30809	Evans (c)	(706)	*17,727*	13,713
30213	Fairburn	(770)	7,005	4,013
30060	Fair Oaks (c)	(404)	*8,443*	6,996
30535	Fairview (c)	(706)	*6,601*	6,444
*30214	Fayetteville	(404)	13,858	5,827
31750	Fitzgerald	(229)	8,864	8,901
*30297	Forest Park	(404)	21,184	16,958
31905	Fort Benning South (c)	(706)	*11,737*	14,617
30742	Fort Oglethorpe	(706)	8,431	5,880
*31313	Fort Stewart (c)	(912)	*11,205*	13,774
31030	Fort Valley	(478)	8,234	8,198
*30501	Gainesville	(770)	31,107	17,885
*31418	Garden City	(912)	9,773	7,410
31754	Georgetown (c)	(912)	*10,599*	5,554
30316	Gresham Park (c)	(404)	*9,215*	9,000
*30223	Griffin	(770)	23,397	21,325
30813	Grovetown	(706)	6,919	3,596
30354	Hapeville	(404)	5,448	5,483
*31313	Hinesville	(912)	30,566	21,596
—	Irondale (c)	—	*7,727*	3,352
*31546	Jesup	(912)	9,743	8,958
*30144	Kennesaw	(404)	27,433	8,936
31548	Kingsland	(912)	11,588	6,089
30728	La Fayette	(706)	6,801	6,655
*30240	LaGrange	(706)	26,955	25,574
*30045	Lawrenceville	(404)	26,925	17,250
*30047	Lilburn	(404)	11,419	9,295
30052	Loganville	(770)	8,551	3,180
30126	Mableton (c)	(404)	*29,733*	25,725
30253	McDonough	(770)	13,622	2,929
*31201	Macon	(478)	94,990	107,365
*30060	Marietta	(404)	60,547	44,129
30907	Martinez (c)	(706)	*27,749*	33,731
—	Midway-Hardwick (c)	—	*5,135*	4,910
*31061	Milledgeville	(478)	19,268	17,727
*30655	Monroe	(770)	11,903	9,759
*30260	Morrow	(770)	5,100	5,074
*31768	Moultrie	(229)	14,792	14,865
30087	Mountain Park (c)	(404)	*11,753*	11,025
*30263	Newnan	(770)	22,520	12,497
*30071	Norcross	(404)	9,518	5,947
30319	North Atlanta (c)	(404)	*38,579*	27,812
30033	North Decatur (c)	(404)	*15,270*	13,936
30033	North Druid Hills (c)	(404)	*18,852*	14,170
30032	Panthersville (c)	(404)	*11,791*	9,874
*30269	Peachtree City	(404)	33,810	19,027
31069	Perry	(478)	10,660	9,452
31322	Pooler	(912)	9,223	4,649
30127	Powder Springs	(404)	14,300	6,862
30074	Redan (c)	(404)	*33,841*	24,376
31324	Richmond Hill	(912)	8,798	2,934
31326	Rincon	(912)	5,987	2,992
*30274	Riverdale	(404)	15,611	9,495
*30161	Rome	(706)	35,551	30,425
*30077	Roswell	(404)	85,044	47,986
31558	Saint Marys	(912)	16,187	8,204
31522	Saint Simons (c)	(912)	*13,381*	12,026
31082	Sandersville	(478)	6,048	6,290
30358	Sandy Springs (c)	(404)	*85,781*	67,842
*31402	Savannah	(912)	129,808	137,812
30079	Scottdale (c)	(404)	*9,803*	8,636
—	Skidaway Island (c)	(912)	*6,914*	4,495
*30080	Smyrna	(404)	45,755	32,453
*30078	Snellville	(404)	18,782	12,084
*30458	Statesboro	(912)	24,604	20,770
30281	Stockbridge	(404)	12,541	3,359
*30086	Stone Mountain	(404)	7,095	6,544
30518	Sugar Hill	(404)	14,982	4,519
30024	Suwanee	(770)	10,956	2,412
30401	Swainsboro	(478)	7,153	7,361
31791	Sylvester	(229)	5,936	6,023
30286	Thomaston	(706)	9,426	9,127
*31792	Thomasville	(229)	18,526	17,554
30824	Thomson	(706)	6,787	6,862
*31794	Tifton	(229)	16,197	14,215
*30577	Toccoa	(706)	9,225	8,720
*30084	Tucker (c)	(404)	*26,532*	25,781
30290	Tyrone	(770)	5,228	2,724
30291	Union City	(404)	13,355	9,347
*31603	Valdosta	(229)	45,373	40,038
*30474	Vidalia	(912)	10,868	11,118
30180	Villa Rica	(770)	8,930	3,916
30339	Vinings (c)	(404)	56,305	7,417
*31088	Warner Robins	(478)	15,187	43,861
*31501	Waycross	(912)	15,187	16,410
30830	Waynesboro	(706)	5,919	5,669
—	Whitemarsh Island (c)	(912)	*5,824*	2,824
31410	Wilmington Island (c)	(912)	*14,213*	11,230
30680	Winder	(770)	12,083	7,373
*30188	Woodstock	(770)	17,214	4,361

(1) Athens merged with Clarke County in 1991. The 2004 and 1990 populations are for all of Clarke County except Winterville and Bogart, which are part of the county but are also separate incorporated places.
(2) Augusta merged with Richmond County in 1996. The 2004 and 1990 populations are for all of Richmond County except Blythe and Hephzibah, which are part of the county but are also separate incorporated places.

Hawaii (808)

ZIP	Place	2004	1990
—	Ahuimanu (c)	*8,506*	8,387
96701	Aiea (c)	*9,019*	8,906
96706	Ewa Beach(c)	*14,650*	14,315
—	Haiku-Pauwela (c)	*6,578*	4,509
—	Halawa (c)	*13,891*	13,408
96778	Hawaiian Paradise Park (c)	*7,051*	3,389
96853	Hickam Housing (c)	*5,471*	6,553
*96720	Hilo (c)	*40,759*	37,808
96725	Holualoa (c)	*6,107*	3,834
*96820	Honolulu (c)	380,149	377,059
*96732	Kahului (c)	*20,146*	16,889
96734	Kailua (Hawaii Co.) (c)	*9,870*	9,126
96863	Kailua (Honolulu Co.) (c)	*36,513*	36,818
96740	Kalaoa (c)	*6,794*	4,490
96744	Kaneohe (c)	*34,970*	35,448
—	Kaneohe Station (c)	*11,827*	11,662
96746	Kapaa (c)	*9,472*	8,149
96753	Kihei (c)	*16,749*	11,107
*96761	Lahaina (c)	*9,118*	9,073
96766	Lihue (c)	*5,674*	5,536
96792	Maili (c)	*5,943*	6,059
96792	Makaha (c)	*7,753*	7,990
96706	Makakilo (c)	*13,156*	9,828
96768	Makawao (c)	*6,327*	5,405
96789	Mililani Town (c)	*28,608*	29,359
96792	Nanakuli (c)	*10,814*	9,575
96761	Napili-Honokowai (c)	*6,788*	4,332
96782	Pearl City (c)	*30,976*	30,993
96788	Pukalani (c)	*7,380*	5,879
96857	Schofield Barracks (c)	*14,428*	19,597
—	Village Park (c)	*9,625*	7,407
*96786	Wahiawa (c)	*16,151*	17,386
96792	Waianae (c)	*10,506*	8,758
—	Waihee-Waiehu (c)	*7,310*	4,004
96753	Wailea-Makena (c)	*5,671*	3,799
96793	Wailuku (c)	*12,296*	10,688
—	Waimalu (c)	*29,371*	29,967
96796	Waimea (c)	*7,028*	5,972
96797	Waipahu (c)	*33,108*	31,435
96797	Waipio (c)	*11,672*	11,812
96786	Waipio Acres (c)	*5,298*	5,304

Idaho (208)

ZIP	Place	2004	1990
*83401	Ammon	9,763	5,002
83221	Blackfoot	10,707	9,646
*83707	Boise	190,122	126,685
83318	Burley	9,180	8,702
*83605	Caldwell	32,718	18,586
83202	Chubbuck	10,492	7,794
*83814	Coeur d'Alene	38,388	24,561
83616	Eagle	16,176	3,327
83617	Emmett	5,981	4,601
*83714	Garden City	11,173	6,369
83333	Hailey	7,462	3,575
83835	Hayden	11,086	4,888
*83402	Idaho Falls	52,148	43,973
83338	Jerome	8,377	6,529
*83634	Kuna	9,460	1,955
83501	Lewiston	31,028	28,082
*83642	Meridian	44,962	9,596
*83843	Moscow	21,900	18,398
*83647	Mountain Home	11,427	7,913
83648	Mountain Home AFB (c)	*8,894*	5,936
*83653	Nampa	68,156	28,365
83661	Payette	7,418	5,672
*83201	Pocatello	50,723	46,117
*83854	Post Falls	21,351	7,349
83858	Rathdrum	5,605	2,014
*83440	Rexburg	24,733	14,298
*83350	Rupert	5,303	5,455
*83864	Sandpoint	7,647	5,561
*83301	Twin Falls	37,619	27,634
83672	Weiser	5,415	4,571

Illinois

Area code (224) overlays area code (847). See introductory note.

ZIP	Place	Area Code	2004	1990
60101	Addison	(630)	37,040	32,053
*60102	Algonquin	(847)	28,223	11,764
60803	Alsip	(708)	19,239	18,227
62002	Alton	(618)	29,774	33,060
62906	Anna	(618)	5,075	4,805
60002	Antioch	(847)	11,223	6,105
*60005	Arlington Heights	(847)	75,181	75,463
*60505	Aurora	(630)	166,614	99,672
*60010	Barrington	(847)	10,170	9,538
*60103	Bartlett	(630)	37,773	19,395
61607	Bartonville	(309)	6,164	6,555
*60510	Batavia	(630)	26,901	17,076
*60083	Beach Park	(847)	12,104	9,492
62618	Beardstown	(217)	5,749	5,270
*62220	Belleville	(618)	41,429	42,806
60104	Bellwood	(708)	19,754	20,241
61008	Belvidere	(815)	23,797	16,059
*60106	Bensenville	(630)	20,594	17,767
62812	Benton	(618)	6,904	7,216
60163	Berkeley	(708)	5,063	5,137
60402	Berwyn	(708)	52,000	45,426
62010	Bethalto	(618)	9,670	9,507
*60108	Bloomingdale	(630)	21,903	16,614
*61701	Bloomington	(309)	69,282	51,889
*60406	Blue Island	(708)	23,010	21,203
*60440	Bolingbrook	(630)	66,206	40,843
60538	Boulder Hill (c)	(630)	16,627	8,894
60914	Bourbonnais	(815)	13,608	13,929
60915	Bradley	(815)	37,040	10,954
60408	Braidwood	(815)	5,965	3,584
60455	Bridgeview	(708)	15,061	14,402
*60153	Broadview	(708)	7,951	8,538
60513	Brookfield	(708)	18,678	18,876
60089	Buffalo Grove	(847)	43,152	36,417
60459	Burbank	(708)	27,741	27,600
60527	Burr Ridge	(630)	10,822	8,247
62206	Cahokia	(618)	15,794	17,550
60409	Calumet City	(708)	38,172	37,840
*60643	Calumet Park	(708)	8,207	8,418
61520	Canton	(309)	14,933	13,959
*62901	Carbondale	(618)	24,790	27,033
62626	Carlinville	(217)	5,771	5,416
62821	Carmi	(618)	5,393	5,735
*60188	Carol Stream	(630)	40,267	31,759
60110	Carpentersville	(847)	35,980	23,049
62918	Carterville	(618)	5,016	3,630
60013	Cary	(847)	18,717	10,025
62801	Centralia	(618)	13,775	14,476
62207	Centreville	(618)	5,912	7,489
*61821	Champaign	(217)	70,306	63,502
60410	Channahon	(815)	11,038	4,266
61920	Charleston	(217)	20,204	20,398
62629	Chatham	(217)	9,514	6,074
62233	Chester	(618)	7,932	8,204
*60607	Chicago	(312)/(773)	2,862,244	2,783,726
*60411	Chicago Heights	(708)	31,688	32,966
60415	Chicago Ridge	(708)	13,728	13,643
61523	Chillicothe	(309)	5,814	5,959
60804	Cicero	(708)	83,102	67,436
60514	Clarendon Hills	(630)	8,257	6,994
61727	Clinton	(217)	7,288	7,437
62234	Collinsville	(618)	25,384	22,424
61241	Colona	(309)	5,202	2,237
62236	Columbia	(618)	8,689	5,524
60478	Country Club Hills	(708)	16,283	15,431
60525	Countryside	(708)	5,853	5,961
60435	Crest Hill	(815)	18,025	10,999
60445	Crestwood	(708)	11,255	10,823
60417	Crete	(708)	8,490	6,773
61610	Creve Coeur	(309)	5,277	5,938
*60014	Crystal Lake	(815)	40,496	24,692
*61832	Danville	(217)	33,069	33,828
60561	Darien	(630)	22,923	20,556
*62525	Decatur	(217)	78,751	83,900
60015	Deerfield	(847)	19,426	17,327
60115	DeKalb	(815)	41,532	35,076
*60018	Des Plaines	(847)	56,229	53,414
61021	Dixon	(815)	15,452	15,134
60419	Dolton	(708)	24,765	23,956
*60515	Downers Grove	(630)	49,302	47,464
62832	Du Quoin	(618)	6,389	6,697
62024	East Alton	(618)	6,680	7,063
61244	East Moline	(309)	21,114	20,147
*61611	East Peoria	(309)	22,502	21,378
*62201	East St. Louis	(618)	30,266	40,944
*62025	Edwardsville	(618)	23,953	14,582
62401	Effingham	(217)	12,413	11,927
*60120	Elgin	(847)	97,761	77,014
*60009	Elk Grove Village	(847)	34,136	33,429
60126	Elmhurst	(630)	44,352	42,029
60707	Elmwood Park	(708)	24,653	23,206
*60201	Evanston	(847)	74,811	73,233
60805	Evergreen Park	(708)	20,086	20,874
*62837	Fairfield	(618)	5,291	5,439
*62208	Fairview Heights	(618)	15,805	14,768
60422	Flossmoor	(708)	9,389	8,651
*60130	Forest Park	(708)	15,251	14,918
60020	Fox Lake	(847)	10,367	7,539
60021	Fox River Grove	(847)	5,085	3,629
60423	Frankfort	(815)	14,667	7,180
—	Frankfort Square (c)	(815)	*7,766*	6,227
*60131	Franklin Park	(847)	18,701	18,485
61032	Freeport	(815)	25,771	25,840
60030	Gages Lake (c)	(847)	*10,415*	8,349
*61401	Galesburg	(309)	32,408	33,530
61254	Geneseo	(309)	6,430	5,990
60134	Geneva	(630)	22,913	12,625
62034	Glen Carbon	(618)	11,714	7,774
60022	Glencoe	(847)	8,936	8,499
*60139	Glendale Heights	(630)	32,729	27,915
*60137	Glen Ellyn	(630)	27,214	24,919
*60025	Glenview	(847)	44,655	38,436
60425	Glenwood	(708)	8,693	9,289
62035	Godfrey	(618)	16,974	15,675
—	Goodings Grove (c)	(815)	*17,084*	14,054
62040	Granite City	(618)	31,223	32,766
60030	Grayslake	(847)	20,459	7,388
62246	Greenville	(618)	7,095	5,108
60031	Gurnee	(847)	30,709	13,715

ZIP	Place	Area Code	2004	1990
60133	Hanover Park	(630)	37,391	32,918
62946	Harrisburg	(618)	9,685	9,318
60033	Harvard	(815)	8,855	5,975
*60426	Harvey	(708)	29,030	29,771
*60656	Harwood Heights	(708)	8,259	7,680
60047	Hawthorn Woods	(847)	6,793	4,423
60429	Hazel Crest	(708)	14,555	13,334
62948	Herrin	(618)	11,503	10,857
*60457	Hickory Hills	(708)	13,652	13,021
62249	Highland	(618)	9,040	7,546
*60035	Highland Park	(847)	31,221	30,575
60040	Highwood	(847)	5,494	5,358
*60162	Hillside	(708)	7,858	7,672
*60521	Hinsdale	(630)	17,632	16,029
*60195	Hoffman Estates	(847)	49,823	46,363
*60491	Homer Glen	(708)	24,138	—
*60430	Homewood	(708)	19,112	19,278
60942	Hoopeston	(217)	5,812	5,871
60142	Huntley	(847)	15,065	2453
*60067	Inverness	(847)	7,009	6,516
60042	Island Lake	(847)	8,423	4,449
60143	Itasca	(630)	8,432	6,947
*62650	Jacksonville	(217)	19,674	19,327
62052	Jerseyville	(618)	8,068	7,382
*60050	Johnsburg	(815)	6,165	—
*60436	Joliet	(815)	129,519	77,217
60458	Justice	(708)	12,649	11,137
60901	Kankakee	(815)	26,996	27,541
61443	Kewanee	(309)	12,670	12,969
60525	La Grange	(708)	15,557	15,362
60526	La Grange Park	(708)	12,857	12,861
*60010	Lake Barrington	(847)	5,033	3,855
60044	Lake Bluff	(847)	6,234	5,486
60045	Lake Forest	(847)	20,922	17,836
*60102	Lake in the Hills	(847)	28,220	5,882
60046	Lake Villa	(847)	8,296	2,857
*60047	Lake Zurich	(847)	19,325	14,927
60438	Lansing	(708)	27,574	28,131
61301	La Salle	(815)	9,584	9,717
*60439	Lemont	(630)	14,643	7,359
*60048	Libertyville	(847)	21,665	19,174
62656	Lincoln	(217)	15,078	15,418
60069	Lincolnshire	(847)	6,553	4,928
*60645	Lincolnwood	(847)	12,101	11,365
60046	Lindenhurst	(847)	14,353	8,044
60532	Lisle	(630)	22,321	19,584
62056	Litchfield	(217)	6,759	6,883
*60441	Lockport	(815)	20,587	9,401
60148	Lombard	(630)	42,975	39,408
*60047	Long Grove	(847)	7,688	4,747
*61130	Loves Park	(815)	22,560	15,457
60411	Lynwood	(708)	7,622	6,535
60534	Lyons	(708)	10,480	9,828
*60050	McHenry	(815)	23,997	16,343
*61115	Machesney Park	(815)	21,415	19,042
61455	Macomb	(309)	18,782	19,952
61853	Mahomet	(217)	5,469	3,499
60950	Manteno	(815)	7,193	3,709
60152	Marengo	(815)	7,219	4,768
62959	Marion	(618)	16,853	14,597
*60426	Markham	(708)	12,348	13,136
62062	Maryville	(618)	6,246	2,576
*62258	Mascoutah	(618)	5,717	5,511
*60443	Matteson	(708)	14,668	11,378
61938	Mattoon	(217)	17,671	18,441
*60153	Maywood	(708)	26,081	27,139
*60160	Melrose Park	(708)	22,734	20,859
61342	Mendota	(815)	7,133	7,017
62960	Metropolis	(618)	6,422	6,734
60445	Midlothian	(708)	14,072	14,372
61264	Milan	(309)	5,257	5,753
60447	Minooka	(815)	6,365	2,561
60448	Mokena	(708)	16,529	6,128
*61265	Moline	(309)	42,927	43,080
61462	Monmouth	(309)	9,337	9,489
60538	Montgomery	(630)	10,459	4,487
61856	Monticello	(217)	5,197	4,775
60450	Morris	(815)	12,479	10,274
61550	Morton	(309)	15,599	13,799
60053	Morton Grove	(847)	22,383	22,373
62863	Mount Carmel	(618)	7,713	8,287
60056	Mount Prospect	(847)	55,028	53,168
62864	Mount Vernon	(618)	16,337	17,082
60060	Mundelein	(847)	32,651	21,224
62966	Murphysboro	(618)	8,380	9,176
*60540	Naperville	(630)	140,106	85,806
60451	New Lenox	(815)	22,528	9,698
60714	Niles	(847)	29,617	28,375
*61761	Normal	(309)	49,287	40,023
*60634	Norridge	(708)	14,159	14,459
60542	North Aurora	(630)	13,677	6,010
*60062	Northbrook	(708)	34,209	32,565
*60064	North Chicago	(847)	33,271	34,978
60093	Northfield	(847)	5,577	4,924
60164	Northlake	(708)	11,473	12,505
60546	North Riverside	(708)	6,455	6,180
*60521	Oak Brook	(630)	8,892	9,087
60452	Oak Forest	(708)	28,078	26,202
*60303	Oak Lawn	(708)	54,257	56,182
*60303	Oak Park	(708)	50,993	53,648
62269	O'Fallon	(618)	24,547	16,064
62450	Olney	(618)	8,494	8,873
60477	Orland Hills	(708)	7,345	5,510
*60462	Orland Park	(708)	54,781	35,720
60543	Oswego	(630)	20,946	3,949
61350	Ottawa	(815)	18,684	17,574
*60067	Palatine	(847)	66,401	41,554
60463	Palos Heights	(708)	12,440	11,478
60465	Palos Hills	(708)	17,399	17,803
62557	Pana	(217)	5,578	5,796
61944	Paris	(217)	8,907	9,105
60085	Park City	(847)	6,781	4,677
60466	Park Forest	(708)	23,189	24,656
60068	Park Ridge	(847)	37,185	37,075
*61554	Pekin	(309)	33,286	32,254
*61601	Peoria	(309)	112,720	113,508
61616	Peoria Heights	(309)	6,357	6,930
61354	Peru	(815)	9,834	9,302
62274	Pinckneyville	(618)	5,439	3,372
*60544	Plainfield	(815)	24,647	4,557
60545	Plano	(630)	5,855	5,104
61764	Pontiac	(815)	11,409	11,428
62040	Pontoon Beach	(618)	6,033	4,013
61356	Princeton	(815)	7,509	7,197
60070	Prospect Heights	(847)	16,544	15,236
*62301	Quincy	(217)	39,669	39,682
61866	Rantoul	(217)	12,604	17,212
60471	Richton Park	(708)	12,879	10,523
60827	Riverdale	(708)	14,759	13,671
60305	River Forest	(708)	11,371	11,669
60171	River Grove	(708)	10,293	9,961
60546	Riverside	(708)	8,578	8,774
60472	Robbins	(708)	6,435	7,498
62454	Robinson	(618)	6,547	6,740
61068	Rochelle	(815)	9,641	8,769
61071	Rock Falls	(815)	9,451	9,669
*61125	Rockford	(815)	38,807	142,815
*61201	Rock Island	(309)	8,578	40,630
61072	Rockton	(815)	5,381	2,928
60008	Rolling Meadows	(847)	23,990	22,598
*60446	Romeoville	(815)	35,020	14,101
61073	Roscoe	(815)	6,344	2,079
60172	Roselle	(630)	23,367	20,803
60073	Round Lake	(847)	12,166	3,550
60073	Round Lake Beach	(847)	28,208	16,406
60073	Round Lake Park	(847)	6,201	4,045
*60174	Saint Charles	(630)	32,134	22,636
62881	Salem	(618)	7,679	7,470
60548	Sandwich	(815)	6,850	5,607
60411	Sauk Village	(708)	10,490	10,734
*60194	Schaumburg	(847)	73,346	68,586
*60176	Schiller Park	(847)	11,726	11,189
*62269	Shiloh	(618)	9,909	2,655
*60436	Shorewood	(815)	10,987	6,264
61282	Silvis	(309)	7,423	6,926
*60077	Skokie	(847)	63,965	59,432
61080	South Beloit	(815)	5,437	4,072
60177	South Elgin	(847)	20,746	7,474
60473	South Holland	(708)	21,731	22,105
*62703	Springfield	(217)	114,738	105,412
60081	Spring Grove	(815)	5,085	1,066
61362	Spring Valley	(815)	5,342	5,246
62088	Staunton	(618)	5,060	4,806
60475	Steger	(708)	10,201	9,251
61081	Sterling	(815)	15,454	15,142
*60402	Stickney	(708)	5,955	5,678
60165	Stone Park	(708)	5,057	4,383
60107	Streamwood	(630)	37,125	31,197
61364	Streator	(815)	13,995	14,121
60554	Sugar Grove	(630)	7,541	2,123
60501	Summit	(708)	10,391	9,971
*62221	Swansea	(618)	11,842	8,201
60178	Sycamore	(815)	14,010	9,896
62568	Taylorville	(217)	11,318	11,133
60477	Tinley Park	(708)	56,274	37,115
62294	Troy	(618)	9,204	6,194
60466	University Park	(708)	7,897	6,204
*61801	Urbana	(217)	39,178	36,383
62471	Vandalia	(618)	6,817	6,114
60061	Vernon Hills	(847)	23,446	15,319
60181	Villa Park	(630)	22,795	22,279
60555	Warrenville	(630)	13,293	11,389
61571	Washington	(309)	12,394	10,136
*62204	Washington Park	(618)	5,785	7,431
62298	Waterloo	(618)	8,982	5,030
60970	Watseka	(815)	5,553	5,424
60084	Wauconda	(847)	10,104	6,294
*60085	Waukegan	(847)	91,602	69,481
60154	Westchester	(708)	16,367	17,301
*60185	West Chicago	(630)	26,063	14,808
60118	West Dundee	(847)	7,428	3,728
60558	Western Springs	(708)	12,562	11,956
62896	West Frankfort	(618)	8,259	8,526
60559	Westmont	(630)	24,820	21,402
*60187	Wheaton	(630)	54,979	51,441
60090	Wheeling	(847)	36,766	29,911
60527	Willowbrook	(630)	8,949	8,651
60480	Willow Springs	(708)	6,029	4,509
60091	Wilmette	(847)	27,104	26,694
60481	Wilmington	(815)	5,791	4,743

ZIP	Place	Area Code	2004	1990
60190	Winfield	(630)	9,655	7,096
60093	Winnetka	(847)	12,473	12,210
60096	Winthrop Harbor	(847)	6,966	6,240
60097	Wonder Lake (c)	(815)	*7,463*	6,664
*60191	Wood Dale	(630)	13,388	12,394
60517	Woodridge	(630)	33,943	26,359
62095	Wood River	(618)	11,085	11,490
60098	Woodstock	(815)	21,556	14,368
60482	Worth	(708)	10,718	11,208
60560	Yorkville	(630)	9,556	3,974
60099	Zion	(847)	24,086	19,783

Indiana

ZIP	Place	Area Code	2004	1990
46001	Alexandria	(765)	5,977	5,709
*46011	Anderson	(765)	57,942	59,518
46703	Angola	(260)	7,795	5,851
46706	Auburn	(260)	12,661	9,386
46123	Avon	(317)	8,220	—
47006	Batesville	(812)	6,365	4,720
47421	Bedford	(812)	13,570	13,817
46107	Beech Grove	(317)	14,236	13,383
*47408	Bloomington	(812)	68,779	62,735
46714	Bluffton	(260)	9,457	9,104
47601	Boonville	(812)	6,830	6,686
47834	Brazil	(812)	8,244	7,640
47025	Bright (c)	(812)	*5,405*	3,945
46112	Brownsburg	(317)	17,622	7,751
*46032	Carmel	(317)	58,198	25,380
46303	Cedar Lake	(219)	9,722	8,885
47111	Charlestown	(812)	7,971	5,889
46304	Chesterton	(219)	11,570	9,118
*47129	Clarksville	(812)	21,136	19,838
46725	Columbia City	(260)	7,764	5,883
*47201	Columbus	(812)	39,251	33,948
47331	Connersville	(765)	14,445	15,550
*47933	Crawfordsville	(765)	15,088	13,584
*46307	Crown Point	(219)	21,822	17,728
46229	Cumberland	(317)	5,343	4,557
46122	Danville	(317)	7,091	4,345
46733	Decatur	(260)	9,506	8,642
46517	Dunlap (c)	(574)	*5,887*	5,705
*46311	Dyer	(219)	14,793	10,923
46312	East Chicago	(219)	31,237	33,892
*46515	Elkhart	(574)	51,878	44,661
47429	Ellettsville	(812)	5,170	3,275
46036	Elwood	(765)	9,263	9,494
*47708	Evansville	(812)	117,156	126,272
*46038	Fishers	(317)	54,330	7,189
*46802	Fort Wayne	(260)	219,351	195,680
*46041	Frankfort	(765)	16,441	14,754
46131	Franklin	(317)	21,201	12,932
46738	Garrett	(260)	5,767	5,349
*46401	Gary	(219)	99,516	116,646
46933	Gas City	(765)	5,868	6,311
*46526	Goshen	(574)	30,555	23,794
46530	Granger (c)	(574)	*28,284*	20,241
46135	Greencastle	(765)	10,011	8,984
46140	Greenfield	(317)	16,048	11,657
47240	Greensburg	(812)	10,462	9,286
*46142	Greenwood	(317)	40,813	26,507
46319	Griffith	(219)	16,806	17,914
*46320	Hammond	(219)	79,985	84,236
47348	Hartford City	(765)	6,702	6,960
*46322	Highland	(219)	23,290	23,696
46342	Hobart	(219)	27,510	24,440
47542	Huntingburg	(812)	5,890	5,236
46750	Huntington	(260)	17,040	16,389
*46206	Indianapolis	(317)	784,242	731,278
*47546	Jasper	(812)	13,533	10,030
*47130	Jeffersonville	(812)	28,640	24,016
46755	Kendallville	(260)	9,995	7,984
*46902	Kokomo	(765)	46,070	44,996
*47901	Lafayette	(765)	59,753	45,933
—	Lakes of the Four Seasons (c)	(219)	*7,291*	6,556
46405	Lake Station	(219)	13,657	13,899
*46350	La Porte	(219)	20,982	21,507
46226	Lawrence	(317)	40,878	26,849
46052	Lebanon	(765)	14,560	12,059
47441	Linton	(812)	5,819	5,814
46947	Logansport	(574)	19,350	16,865
46356	Lowell	(219)	7,896	6,430
47250	Madison	(812)	12,335	12,006
*46952	Marion	(765)	30,830	32,607
46151	Martinsville	(765)	11,739	11,677
*46401	Merrillville	(219)	31,258	27,257
*46360	Michigan City	(219)	32,179	33,822
*46544	Mishawaka	(574)	48,385	42,635
47960	Monticello	(574)	5,549	5,237
46158	Mooresville	(317)	10,826	5,779
47620	Mount Vernon	(812)	7,320	7,217
*47302	Muncie	(765)	67,166	71,170
46321	Munster	(219)	22,240	19,949
46550	Nappanee	(574)	6,840	5,474
*47150	New Albany	(812)	36,877	36,322
47362	New Castle	(765)	18,944	17,753
46774	New Haven	(260)	13,638	11,234
*46060	Noblesville	(317)	35,438	17,655
46962	North Manchester	(260)	6,046	6,383

ZIP	Place	Area Code	2004	1990
47265	North Vernon	(812)	6,454	5,129
47130	Oak Park (c)	(812)	*5,379*	5,630
*46970	Peru	(765)	12,856	12,843
46168	Plainfield	(317)	22,564	14,953
46563	Plymouth	(574)	10,728	8,291
46368	Portage	(219)	35,269	29,062
46304	Porter	(219)	5,155	3,242
47371	Portland	(260)	6,249	6,483
47670	Princeton	(812)	8,659	8,127
47978	Rensselaer	(219)	6,209	5,045
*47374	Richmond	(765)	37,943	38,705
46975	Rochester	(574)	6,424	5,969
46173	Rushville	(765)	5,785	5,533
46373	Saint John	(219)	9,975	4,921
47167	Salem	(812)	6,417	5,619
46375	Schererville	(219)	27,451	20,155
47170	Scottsburg	(812)	6,034	5,334
47172	Sellersburg	(812)	6,078	5,936
47274	Seymour	(812)	18,704	15,605
46176	Shelbyville	(765)	17,848	15,347
*46624	South Bend	(574)	105,494	105,511
46383	South Haven (c)	(219)	*5,619*	6,112
46224	Speedway	(317)	12,570	13,092
47586	Tell City	(812)	7,698	8,088
*47808	Terre Haute	(812)	57,224	57,475
46072	Tipton	(765)	5,337	4,751
*46383	Valparaiso	(219)	28,750	24,414
47591	Vincennes	(812)	18,105	19,867
46992	Wabash	(260)	11,342	12,127
*46580	Warsaw	(574)	12,672	10,968
47501	Washington	(812)	11,304	10,864
46074	Westfield	(317)	11,911	3,304
*46580	West Lafayette	(765)	28,609	26,144
46391	Westville	(219)	5,062	5,234
46077	Zionsville	(317)	10,650	6,207

Iowa

ZIP	Place	Area Code	2004	1990
50511	Algona	(515)	5,562	6,015
50009	Altoona	(515)	12,107	7,242
*50010	Ames	(515)	52,319	47,198
52205	Anamosa	(319)	5,634	5,100
*50021	Ankeny	(515)	34,439	18,482
50022	Atlantic	(712)	6,987	7,432
52722	Bettendorf	(563)	31,615	28,139
*50036	Boone	(515)	12,856	12,392
52601	Burlington	(319)	25,579	27,208
51401	Carroll	(712)	9,949	9,579
*50613	Cedar Falls	(319)	36,343	34,298
*52401	Cedar Rapids	(319)	122,206	108,772
52544	Centerville	(641)	5,798	5,936
*50616	Charles City	(641)	7,641	7,878
51012	Cherokee	(712)	5,121	6,026
51632	Clarinda	(712)	5,493	5,104
50428	Clear Lake	(641)	7,962	8,183
*52732	Clinton	(563)	27,319	29,201
50325	Clive	(515)	13,598	7,446
52241	Coralville	(319)	17,528	10,347
*51501	Council Bluffs	(712)	59,347	54,315
50801	Creston	(641)	7,389	7,911
*52802	Davenport	(563)	98,355	95,333
52101	Decorah	(563)	8,070	8,063
51442	Denison	(712)	7,386	6,604
*50318	Des Moines	(515)	194,311	193,189
52742	De Witt	(563)	5,176	4,514
*52001	Dubuque	(563)	57,504	57,538
51334	Estherville	(712)	6,401	6,720
*52556	Fairfield	(641)	9,459	9,955
50501	Fort Dodge	(515)	25,723	26,057
52627	Fort Madison	(319)	10,944	11,614
51534	Glenwood	(712)	5,536	4,960
50111	Grimes	(515)	5,795	2,653
*50112	Grinnell	(641)	9,312	8,902
*51537	Harlan	(712)	5,195	5,148
52233	Hiawatha	(319)	6,565	5,354
50644	Independence	(319)	6,014	5,972
50125	Indianola	(515)	13,714	11,340
*52240	Iowa City	(319)	63,027	59,735
50126	Iowa Falls	(641)	5,091	5,435
50131	Johnston	(515)	11,770	4,702
52632	Keokuk	(319)	10,845	12,451
*50138	Knoxville	(641)	7,545	8,232
51031	Le Mars	(712)	9,318	8,454
52057	Manchester	(563)	5,085	5,137
52060	Maquoketa	(563)	6,048	6,130
52302	Marion	(319)	29,825	20,422
50158	Marshalltown	(641)	26,057	25,178
*50401	Mason City	(641)	28,177	29,040
52641	Mount Pleasant	(319)	8,770	7,959
52761	Muscatine	(563)	22,713	22,881
50201	Nevada	(515)	6,249	6,009
50208	Newton	(641)	15,696	14,799
52317	North Liberty	(319)	7,638	2,926
50211	Norwalk	(515)	7,723	5,726
50662	Oelwein	(319)	6,352	6,691
51041	Orange City	(712)	5,713	4,940
52577	Oskaloosa	(641)	10,945	10,600
52501	Ottumwa	(641)	24,680	24,488
50219	Pella	(641)	10,182	9,270

ZIP	Place	Area Code	2004	1990
50220	Perry	(515)	8,642	6,652
*50317	Pleasant Hill	(515)	5,991	3,671
*51566	Red Oak	(712)	5,976	6,264
*51601	Shenandoah	(712)	5,256	5,572
51250	Sioux Center	(712)	6,579	5,074
*51101	Sioux City	(712)	83,680	80,505
51301	Spencer	(712)	11,063	11,066
50588	Storm Lake	(712)	9,981	8,769
*50322	Urbandale	(515)	33,379	23,775
52349	Vinton	(319)	5,199	5,103
52353	Washington	(319)	7,174	7,074
*50701	Waterloo	(319)	66,767	66,467
50263	Waukee	(515)	8,467	2,512
50677	Waverly	(319)	9,092	8,539
50595	Webster City	(515)	8,105	7,894
*50265	West Des Moines	(515)	51,363	31,702

Kansas

ZIP	Place	Area Code	2004	1990
67410	Abilene	(785)	6,397	6,242
67002	Andover	(316)	8,617	4,204
67005	Arkansas City	(620)	11,753	12,762
66002	Atchison	(913)	10,185	10,656
67010	Augusta	(316)	8,560	7,848
*66952	Bel Aire	(316)	6,530	3,695
66012	Bonner Springs	(913)	6,892	6,413
66720	Chanute	(620)	9,043	9,488
67337	Coffeyville	(620)	10,504	12,917
67701	Colby	(785)	5,145	5,510
66901	Concordia	(785)	5,392	6,152
67037	Derby	(316)	20,326	14,691
*67801	Dodge City	(620)	25,762	21,129
67042	El Dorado	(316)	12,717	11,495
66801	Emporia	(620)	26,639	25,512
66442	Fort Riley North (c)	(785)	*8,114*	12,848
66701	Fort Scott	(620)	8,048	8,362
*67846	Garden City	(620)	27,312	24,097
*66030	Gardner	(913)	12,937	4,277
67530	Great Bend	(620)	14,851	15,427
*67601	Hays	(785)	19,841	18,632
67060	Haysville	(316)	9,627	8,364
*67501	Hutchinson	(620)	41,047	39,308
67301	Independence	(620)	9,407	10,030
66749	Iola	(620)	6,083	6,351
*66441	Junction City	(785)	16,806	20,642
*66102	Kansas City	(913)	145,004	151,521
66043	Lansing	(913)	10,117	7,120
*66044	Lawrence	(785)	81,873	65,608
*66048	Leavenworth	(913)	35,290	38,495
*66209	Leawood	(913)	29,504	19,693
*66214	Lenexa	(913)	42,615	34,110
*67901	Liberal	(620)	20,218	16,573
67460	McPherson	(620)	13,681	12,422
*66502	Manhattan	(785)	47,916	43,081
*66202	Merriam	(913)	10,774	11,819
*66201	Mission	(913)	9,772	9,504
67110	Mulvane	(316)	5,575	4,683
*67114	Newton	(316)	18,154	16,700
*66061	Olathe	(913)	108,390	63,402
66067	Ottawa	(785)	12,499	10,667
*66204	Overland Park	(913)	162,728	111,790
66071	Paola	(913)	5,161	4,698
*67219	Park City	(316)	7,000	5,081
67357	Parsons	(620)	11,291	11,919
*66762	Pittsburg	(620)	19,152	17,789
*66208	Prairie Village	(913)	21,511	23,186
67124	Pratt	(620)	6,397	6,687
66205	Roeland Park	(913)	6,997	7,706
*67401	Salina	(785)	45,988	42,299
*66203	Shawnee	(913)	56,178	37,962
*66601	Topeka	(785)	121,809	119,883
67880	Ulysses	(620)	5,769	5,474
67147	Valley Center	(316)	5,369	4,272
67152	Wellington	(620)	8,277	8,517
*67202	Wichita	(316)	353,823	304,017
67156	Winfield	(620)	12,005	11,931

Kentucky

ZIP	Place	Area Code	2004	1990
41001	Alexandria	(859)	8,016	5,592
*41101	Ashland	(606)	21,586	23,622
40004	Bardstown	(502)	10,897	6,712
*41073	Bellevue	(859)	6,091	6,997
*40403	Berea	(859)	12,738	9,129
42101	Bowling Green	(270)	51,294	41,688
40218	Buechel (c)	(502)	*7,272*	7,081
41005	Burlington (c)	(859)	*10,779*	6,070
42718	Campbellsville	(270)	10,752	9,592
*42330	Central City	(270)	5,823	4,979
40701	Corbin	(606)	8,111	7,644
41011	Covington	(859)	43,010	43,646
41031	Cynthiana	(859)	6,243	6,497
40422	Danville	(859)	15,428	14,454
*41074	Dayton	(859)	5,619	6,576
40243	Douglass Hills	(502)	5,624	5,431
*41017	Edgewood	(859)	9,012	8,143
*42701	Elizabethtown	(270)	23,190	18,167
41018	Elsmere	(859)	8,054	6,847
*41018	Erlanger	(859)	16,746	15,979
40118	Fairdale (c)	(502)	*7,658*	6,563
40291	Fern Creek (c)	(502)	*17,870*	16,406
41139	Flatwoods	(606)	7,659	7,799
*41042	Florence	(859)	25,449	18,586
42223	Fort Campbell North (c)	(270)	*14,338*	18,861
40121	Fort Knox (c)	(270)	*12,377*	21,495
41017	Fort Mitchell	(859)	7,693	7,438
41075	Fort Thomas	(859)	15,733	16,032
41011	Fort Wright	(859)	5,493	6,404
*40601	Frankfort	(502)	27,281	26,535
*42134	Franklin	(270)	8,071	7,607
40324	Georgetown	(502)	19,732	11,414
*42141	Glasgow	(270)	13,829	12,777
40330	Harrodsburg	(859)	8,041	7,335
*42420	Henderson	(270)	27,574	25,945
*41076	Highland Heights	(859)	6,326	4,223
40228	Highview (c)	(502)	*15,161*	14,814
40129	Hillview	(502)	7,253	6,119
*42240	Hopkinsville	(270)	28,953	29,809
41051	Independence	(859)	17,940	10,444
*40269	Jeffersontown	(502)	26,232	23,223
*40031	La Grange	(502)	5,966	3,901
40342	Lawrenceburg	(502)	9,396	5,911
40033	Lebanon	(270)	5,884	5,695
*42754	Leitchfield	(270)	6,419	4,965
*40507	Lexington	(859)	266,358	225,366
*40741	London	(606)	7,767	5,757
*40232	Louisville	(502)	556,332	269,555
*40252	Lyndon	(502)	10,270	8,037
42431	Madisonville	(270)	19,340	18,693
42066	Mayfield	(270)	10,252	9,935
41056	Maysville	(606)	9,011	8,113
40965	Middlesborough	(606)	10,192	11,328
*40253	Middletown	(502)	6,040	5,016
42633	Monticello	(606)	6,080	5,357
40351	Morehead	(606)	7,589	8,357
40353	Mount Sterling	(859)	6,122	5,362
40047	Mount Washington	(502)	8,718	5,256
42071	Murray	(270)	15,270	14,442
40219	Newburg (c)	(502)	*20,636*	21,647
*41071	Newport	(859)	16,086	18,871
*40356	Nicholasville	(859)	22,878	13,603
41042	Oakbrook (c)	(859)	*7,726*	4,113
42262	Oak Grove	(502)	7,601	2,863
*40259	Okolona (c)	(502)	*17,807*	18,902
*42301	Owensboro	(270)	54,900	53,577
*42003	Paducah	(270)	25,545	27,256
*40361	Paris	(859)	9,284	8,730
*41501	Pikeville	(606)	6,304	6,324
*40268	Pleasure Ridge Park (c)	(502)	*25,776*	25,131
42445	Princeton	(270)	6,412	6,940
*40160	Radcliff	(502)	21,617	19,778
*40475	Richmond	(859)	30,008	21,183
42276	Russellville	(270)	7,235	7,454
40216	Saint Dennis (c)	(502)	*9,177*	10,326
*40207	Saint Matthews	(502)	17,374	15,691
*40066	Shelbyville	(502)	10,622	6,155
40165	Shepherdsville	(502)	8,737	4,805
40256	Shively	(502)	15,258	15,535
*42501	Somerset	(606)	11,972	10,735
41015	Taylor Mill	(859)	6,786	5,530
*40272	Valley Station (c)	(502)	*22,946*	22,840
*40383	Versailles	(859)	7,498	7,269
41017	Villa Hills	(859)	7,809	7,370
40769	Williamsburg	(606)	5,107	5,493
40390	Wilmore	(859)	5,845	4,215
*40391	Winchester	(859)	16,412	15,799

Louisiana

ZIP	Place	Area Code	2004	1990
*70510	Abbeville	(337)	11,683	11,769
*71301	Alexandria	(318)	45,971	49,049
70032	Arabi (c)	(504)	*8,093*	8,787
70094	Avondale (c)	(504)	*5,441*	5,813
70714	Baker	(225)	13,386	13,087
71220	Bastrop	(318)	12,661	13,916
*70821	Baton Rouge	(225)	224,097	219,531
*70364	Bayou Cane (c)	(985)	*17,046*	15,876
*70037	Belle Chasse (c)	(504)	*9,848*	8,512
*70427	Bogalusa	(985)	12,908	14,280
*71111	Bossier City	(318)	59,611	52,721
70517	Breaux Bridge	(337)	7,556	6,694
70094	Bridge City (c)	(504)	*8,323*	8,327
70518	Broussard	(337)	6,538	3,213
70811	Brownfields (c)	(225)	*5,222*	5,229
71292	Brownsville-Bawcomville (c)	(318)	*7,616*	7,397
70520	Carencro	(337)	6,083	5,518
*70043	Chalmette (c)	(504)	*32,069*	31,860
70443	Claiborne (c)	(318)	*9,830*	8,300
*70433	Covington	(985)	8,882	7,691
*70526	Crowley	(337)	13,797	13,983
70345	Cut Off (c)	(985)	*5,635*	5,325
*70726	Denham Springs	(225)	10,106	8,381
70634	De Ridder	(337)	9,847	10,475
70047	Destrehan (c)	(985)	*11,260*	8,031
70346	Donaldsonville	(225)	7,565	7,949
70458	Eden Isle (c)	(985)	*6,261*	3,768

ZIP	Place	Area Code	2004	1990
70072	Estelle (c)	(504)	*15,880*	14,091
70535	Eunice	(337)	11,569	11,162
71459	Fort Polk South (c)	(337)	*11,000*	10,911
70538	Franklin	(337)	7,984	9,004
70354	Galliano (c)	(985)	*7,356*	4,294
70810	Gardere (c)	(225)	*8,992*	7,209
*70737	Gonzales	(225)	8,399	7,208
*70053	Gretna	(504)	17,178	17,208
*70401	Hammond	(985)	18,044	15,871
70123	Harahan	(504)	9,774	9,927
*70058	Harvey (c)	(504)	*22,226*	21,222
*70360	Houma	(985)	32,022	30,495
70544	Jeanerette	(337)	6,006	6,205
70121	Jefferson (c)	(504)	*11,843*	14,521
70546	Jennings	(337)	10,674	11,305
70548	Kaplan	(337)	5,132	4,535
*70062	Kenner	(504)	70,252	72,033
*70501	Lafayette	(337)	111,966	101,865
*70601	Lake Charles	(337)	70,819	70,580
71254	Lake Providence (c)	(318)	*5,104*	5,380
*70068	Laplace (c)	(985)	*27,684*	24,194
*70373	Larose (c)	(985)	*7,306*	5,772
*71446	Leesville	(337)	6,259	7,638
70070	Luling (c)	(985)	*11,512*	2,803
*70471	Mandeville	(985)	11,511	7,474
71052	Mansfield	(318)	5,496	5,389
71351	Marksville	(318)	5,696	5,526
*70072	Marrero (c)	(504)	*36,165*	36,671
70075	Meraux (c)	(504)	*10,192*	8,849
70812	Merrydale (c)	(225)	*10,427*	10,395
*70009	Metairie (c)	(504)	*146,136*	149,428
*71055	Minden	(318)	13,281	13,661
*71207	Monroe	(318)	52,141	54,909
*70380	Morgan City	(985)	12,153	14,531
70611	Moss Bluff (c)	(337)	*10,535*	8,039
*71457	Natchitoches	(318)	17,916	16,609
*70560	New Iberia	(337)	32,499	31,828
*70140	New Orleans	(504)	462,269	496,938
71463	Oakdale	(318)	7,984	6,837
70810	Oak Hills Place (c)	(225)	*7,996*	5,479
70817	Old Jefferson (c)	(225)	*5,631*	4,531
*70570	Opelousas	(337)	22,865	19,091
70392	Patterson	(985)	5,179	5,166
*71360	Pineville	(318)	13,784	15,308
*70764	Plaquemine	(225)	6,748	7,101
70454	Ponchatoula	(985)	5,591	5,499
70767	Port Allen	(225)	5,154	6,277
70605	Prien (c)	(337)	*7,215*	6,448
70394	Raceland (c)	(985)	*10,224*	5,564
70578	Rayne	(337)	8,472	8,502
71037	Red Chute (c)	(318)	*5,984*	5,431
70084	Reserve (c)	(985)	*9,111*	8,847
70123	River Ridge (c)	(504)	*14,588*	14,800
*71270	Ruston	(318)	20,665	20,071
70776	Saint Gabriel	(225)	5,476	3,854
70582	Saint Martinville	(337)	7,005	7,226
70087	Saint Rose (c)	(504)	*6,540*	6,259
70395	Schriever (c)	(985)	*5,880*	4,958
70583	Scott	(337)	8,058	4,912
70817	Shenandoah (c)	(318)	*17,070*	13,429
*71102	Shreveport	(318)	198,675	198,518
*70458	Slidell	(985)	26,845	24,124
71075	Springhill	(318)	5,209	5,668
*70663	Sulphur	(337)	19,747	20,125
*71282	Tallulah	(318)	8,597	8,526
70056	Terrytown (c)	(504)	*25,430*	23,787
*70301	Thibodaux	(985)	14,501	14,125
70056	Timberlane (c)	(504)	*11,405*	12,614
70810	Village Saint George (c)	(225)	*6,993*	6,242
70586	Ville Platte	(337)	8,287	9,037
70092	Violet (c)	(504)	*8,555*	8,574
70094	Waggaman (c)	(504)	*9,435*	9,405
70785	Walker	(225)	5,551	3,846
*71291	West Monroe	(318)	12,990	14,096
*70094	Westwego	(504)	10,537	11,218
71483	Winnfield	(318)	5,386	6,138
71295	Winnsboro	(318)	5,111	5,755
70592	Youngsville	(337)	5,016	
70791	Zachary	(225)	12,070	9,036

Maine (207)

See introductory note.

ZIP	Place	2004	1990
*04210	Auburn	23,551	24,309
*04330	Augusta	18,631	21,325
*04401	Bangor	31,595	33,181
04609	*Bar Harbor*	5,071	4,443
04530	Bath	9,394	9,799
04915	Belfast	6,840	6,355
03901	*Berwick*	7,011	5,995
*04005	Biddeford	21,842	20,710
04412	Brewer	9,110	9,021
04009	Bridgton (c)	5,023	1,995
04011	Brunswick (c)	*14,816*	14,683
04011	*Brunswick*	21,529	20,906
04093	*Buxton*	7,913	6,494
*04843	*Camden*	5,354	5,060
04107	*Cape Elizabeth*	9,013	8,854
04736	Caribou	8,279	9,415
04021	*Cumberland*	7,440	5,836
03903	*Eliot*	6,328	5,329
04605	Ellsworth	6,937	5,975
04937	*Fairfield*	6,600	6,718
04105	*Falmouth*	10,582	7,610
04938	*Farmington*	7,416	7,436
*04032	*Freeport*	7,966	6,905
04345	Gardiner	6,232	6,746
04038	*Gorham*	15,013	11,856
04039	*Gray*	7,178	5,904
04444	*Hampden*	6,609	5,974
04079	*Harpswell*	5,222	5,012
*04730	Houlton (c)	*5,270*	5,627
04730	*Houlton*	6,361	6,613
04043	*Kennebunk*	11,263	8,004
03904	*Kittery*	10,183	9,372
04027	*Lebanon*	5,334	—
*04240	Lewiston	35,776	39,757
04457	*Lincoln*	5,265	5,587
*04250	*Lisbon*	9,236	9,457
04462	*Millinocket*	5,145	6,956
04462	Millinocket (c)	*5,190*	6,922
04260	*New Gloucester*	5,145	3,878
04963	*Oakland*	6,096	5,595
04064	*Old Orchard Beach*	9,222	7,789
04064	Old Orchard Beach (c)	*8,856*	7,789
04468	Old Town	8,066	8,317
04473	*Orono*	9,142	10,573
04473	Orono (c)	*8,253*	9,789
04274	Poland	5,097	4,342
*04101	Portland	63,905	64,157
04769	Presque Isle	9,402	10,550
04841	Rockland	7,666	7,972
04276	*Rumford*	6,449	7,078
04072	Saco	18,090	15,181
04073	Sanford (c)	*10,133*	10,296
04073	*Sanford*	21,666	20,463
*04074	*Scarborough*	18,459	12,518
04976	Skowhegan (c)	*6,696*	6,990
04976	*Skowhegan*	8,798	8,725
03908	*South Berwick*	7,197	5,877
*04106	South Portland	23,513	23,163
04084	*Standish*	9,712	7,678
04086	Topsham (c)	*6,271*	6,147
04086	*Topsham*	9,623	8,746
04282	*Turner*	5,243	4,293
04572	*Waldoboro*	5,092	4,601
04087	*Waterboro*	7,015	4,510
*04901	Waterville	15,897	17,173
04090	*Wells*	9,906	7,778
*04092	Westbrook	16,004	16,121
*04062	*Windham*	15,448	13,020
04901	Winslow (c)	*7,743*	5,436
04901	*Winslow*	7,908	7,997
04364	*Winthrop*	6,394	5,968
04096	*Yarmouth*	8,290	7,862
03909	*York*	13,390	9,818

Maryland

Area code (240) overlays area code (301). Area code (443) overlays (410). See introductory note.

ZIP	Place	Area Code	2004	1990
21001	Aberdeen	(410)	14,204	13,087
20607	Accokeek (c)	(301)	*7,349*	4,477
*20783	Adelphi (c)	(301)	*14,998*	13,524
20762	Andrews AFB (c)	(410)	*7,925*	10,228
*21401	Annapolis	(410)	36,217	33,195
21227	Arbutus (c)	(410)	*20,116*	19,750
*21012	Arnold (c)	(410)	*23,422*	20,261
*20916	Aspen Hill (c)	(301)	*50,228*	45,494
21220	Ballenger Creek (c)	(410)	*13,518*	5,546
*21203	Baltimore	(410)	636,251	736,014
*21014	Bel Air	(410)	9,882	8,942
21050	Bel Air North (c)	(410)	*25,798*	14,880
21014	Bel Air South (c)	(410)	*39,711*	26,421
*20705	Beltsville (c)	(301)	*15,690*	14,476
—	Bennsville (c)	—	*7,325*	—
*20814	Bethesda (c)	(301)	*55,277*	62,936
20710	Bladensburg	(301)	7,920	8,064
*20715	Bowie	(301)	53,840	37,642
21220	Bowleys Quarters (c)	(410)	*6,314*	5,595
21225	Brooklyn Park (c)	(410)	*10,938*	10,987
*21716	Brunswick	(301)	5,225	5,091
*20866	Burtonsville (c)	(301)	*7,305*	5,853
20619	California (c)	(410)	*9,307*	7,626
20705	Calverton (c)	(301)	*12,610*	12,046
21613	Cambridge	(410)	10,826	11,514
*20748	Camp Springs (c)	(301)	*17,968*	16,392
21401	Cape St. Clair (c)	(410)	*8,022*	7,878
21234	Carney (c)	(410)	*28,264*	25,578
*21228	Catonsville (c)	(410)	*39,820*	35,233
20657	Chesapeake Ranch Estates-Drum Point (c)	(301)	*11,503*	5,423
*20784	Cheverly	(301)	6,661	6,023
*20815	Chevy Chase (c)	(301)	*9,381*	8,559
20782	Chillum (c)	(301)	*34,252*	31,309

ZIP	Place	Area Code	2004	1990
20735	Clinton (c)	(301)	26,064	19,987
20904	Cloverly (c)	(301)	7,835	7,904
21030	Cockeysville (c)	(410)	19,388	18,668
*20914	Colesville (c)	(301)	19,810	18,819
*20740	College Park	(301)	25,350	23,714
*21045	Columbia (c)	(410)/(301)	88,254	75,883
20743	Coral Hills (c)	(410)	10,720	11,032
—	Cresaptown-Bel Air (c)	—	5,884	4,586
21114	Crofton (c)	(410)	20,091	12,781
*21502	Cumberland	(301)	20,957	23,712
20872	Damascus (c)	(301)	11,430	9,817
*20874	Darnestown (c)	(301)	6,378	—
*20747	District Heights	(301)	6,296	6,711
21222	Dundalk (c)	(410)	62,306	65,800
*21601	Easton	(410)	12,845	9,372
20737	East Riverdale (c)	(301)	14,961	14,187
21219	Edgemere (c)	(410)	9,248	9,226
21040	Edgewood (c)	(410)	23,378	23,903
21784	Eldersburg (c)	(410)	27,741	9,720
21075	Elkridge (c)	(410)	22,042	12,953
*21921	Elkton	(410)	14,067	9,073
*21043	Ellicott City (c)	(410)	56,397	41,396
21221	Essex (c)	(410)	39,078	40,872
20904	Fairland (c)	(301)	21,738	19,828
21047	Fallston (c)	(410)	8,427	5,730
21061	Ferndale (c)	(410)	16,056	16,355
—	Forest Glen (c)	—	7,344	—
*20747	Forestville (c)	(301)	12,707	16,731
20755	Fort Meade (c)	(301)	9,882	12,509
*20744	Fort Washington (c)	(301)	23,845	24,032
*21701	Frederick	(301)	57,009	40,186
20744	Friendly (c)	(301)	10,938	9,028
21532	Frostburg	(301)	8,139	8,069
*20877	Gaithersburg	(301)	58,091	39,676
21117	Garrison (c)	(410)	7,969	5,045
*20874	Germantown (c)	(301)	55,419	41,145
*20706	Glenarden	(301)	6,568	5,025
*21061	Glen Burnie (c)	(410)	38,922	37,305
20769	Glenn Dale (c)	(301)	12,609	9,689
—	Goddard (c)	—	5,554	4,576
—	Greater Landover (c)	—	22,900	—
20772	Greater Upper Marlboro (c)	—	18,720	11,528
*20770	Greenbelt	(301)	22,176	20,561
21122	Green Haven (c)	(410)	17,415	14,416
21771	Green Valley (c)	(301)	12,262	9,424
*21740	Hagerstown	(301)	37,536	35,306
21740	Halfway (c)	(301)	10,065	8,873
21074	Hampstead	(410)	5,417	2,608
21211	Hampton (c)	—	5,004	4,926
21078	Havre de Grace	(410)	11,605	8,952
20748	Hillcrest Heights (c)	(301)	16,359	17,136
*20780	Hyattsville	(301)	15,186	13,864
20794	Jessup (c)	(410)	7,865	6,537
21085	Joppatowne (c)	(410)	11,391	11,084
—	Kemp Mill (c)	—	9,956	—
*20772	Kettering (c)	(301)	11,008	9,901
—	Lake Arbor (c)	—	8,533	—
*21122	Lake Shore (c)	(410)	13,065	13,269
*20787	Langley Park (c)	(301)	16,214	17,474
20706	Lanham-Seabrook (c)	(301)	18,190	16,792
21227	Lansdowne-Baltimore Highlands (c)	—	15,724	15,509
20646	La Plata	(301)	8,109	5,841
20772	Largo (c)	(301)	8,408	9,475
*20707	Laurel	(301)	21,048	19,086
20653	Lexington Park (c)	(410)	11,021	9,943
—	Linganore-Bartonsville (c)	—	12,529	4,079
21090	Linthicum (c)	(410)	7,539	7,547
21207	Lochearn (c)	(410)	25,269	25,240
21037	Londontowne (c)	(410)	7,595	6,992
*21093	Lutherville-Timonium (c)	(410)	15,814	16,442
*20748	Marlow Heights (c)	(301)	6,059	5,885
20772	Marlton (c)	(301)	7,798	5,523
20724	Maryland City (c)	(301)	6,814	6,813
21093	Mays Chapel (c)	(410)	11,427	10,132
21220	Middle River (c)	(410)	23,958	24,616
21207	Milford Mill (c)	(410)	26,527	22,547
*20717	Mitchellville (c)	(301)	9,611	12,593
*20886	Montgomery Village (c)	(301)	38,051	32,315
21771	Mount Airy	(301)/(410)	8,202	3,730
20712	Mount Rainier	(301)	8,739	7,954
20784	New Carrollton	(301)	13,029	12,002
*20815	North Bethesda (c)	(301)	38,610	29,656
20895	North Kensington (c)	(301)	8,940	8,607
20707	North Laurel (c)	(301)	20,468	15,008
20878	North Potomac (c)	(301)	23,044	18,456
*21842	Ocean City	(410)	7,137	5,146
21811	Ocean Pines (c)	(410)	10,496	4,251
21113	Odenton (c)	(410)	20,534	12,833
*20832	Olney (c)	(301)	31,438	23,019
21206	Overlea (c)	(410)	12,148	12,137
21117	Owings Mills (c)	(410)	20,193	9,474
*20750	Oxon Hill-Glassmanor (c)	(301)	35,355	35,794
21234	Parkville (c)	(410)	31,118	31,617
21401	Parole (c)	(410)	14,031	10,054
*21122	Pasadena (c)	(410)	12,093	10,012
21128	Perry Hall (c)	(410)	28,705	22,723
*21282	Pikesville (c)	(410)	29,123	24,815
20837	Poolesville	(301)	5,447	3,796
*20850	Potomac (c)	(301)	44,822	45,634
21227	Pumphrey (c)	(410)	5,317	5,483
21133	Randallstown (c)	(301)	30,870	26,277
—	Redland (c)	(301)	16,998	16,145
*21136	Reisterstown (c)	(410)	22,438	19,314
*20737	Riverdale Park	(301)	6,612	4,843
21017	Riverside (c)	—	6,128	—
*21122	Riviera Beach (c)	(410)	12,695	11,376
*20850	Rockville	(301)	57,100	44,830
20772	Rosaryville (c)	(301)	12,322	8,976
21237	Rosedale (c)	(410)	19,199	18,703
—	Rossmoor (c)	—	7,569	6,182
21221	Rossville (c)	(410)	11,515	9,492
*20602	Saint Charles (c)	(301)	33,379	28,717
*21801	Salisbury	(410)	26,148	20,592
*20763	Savage-Guilford (c)	(410)	12,918	9,669
20743	Seat Pleasant	(301)	5,052	5,354
21144	Severn (c)	(410)	35,076	24,499
21146	Severna Park (c)	(410)	28,507	25,879
20764	Shady Side (c)	(301)	5,559	4,107
*20907	Silver Spring (c)	(301)	76,540	76,046
21061	South Gate (c)	(410)	28,672	27,564
20895	South Kensington (c)	(301)	7,887	8,777
20707	South Laurel (c)	(301)	20,479	18,591
21666	Stevensville (c)	(410)	5,880	1,862
*20752	Suitland-Silver Hills (c)	(301)	33,515	35,111
*20913	Takoma Park	(301)	17,591	16,724
21787	Taneytown	(410)	5,421	3,695
*20748	Temple Hills (c)	(301)	7,792	6,865
21788	Thurmont	(301)	5,995	3,398
*21204	Towson (c)	(410)	51,793	49,445
—	Travilah (c)	(301)	7,442	—
*20602	Waldorf (c)	(301)	22,312	15,058
20743	Walker Mill (c)	(301)	11,104	10,920
21793	Walkersville	(301)	5,564	4,145
*21157	Westminster	(410)	17,562	13,060
*20902	Wheaton-Glenmont (c)	(301)	57,694	53,720
21162	White Marsh (c)	(410)	8,485	8,183
20903	White Oak (c)	(301)	20,973	18,671
21207	Woodlawn (c) (Baltimore Co.)	(410)	36,079	32,907
21284	Woodlawn (c) (Pr. George's Co.)	(410)	6,251	5,329
—	Woodmore (c)	(240)/(301)	6,077	2,874

Massachusetts

Area code (339) overlays area code (781). Area code (351) overlays (978). Area code (774) overlays (508). Area code (857) overlays (617). See introductory note.

ZIP	Place	Area Code	2004	1990
02351	*Abington*	(781)	16,264	13,817
*01720	*Acton*	(978)	20,660	17,872
*02743	*Acushnet*	(508)	10,582	9,554
01220	*Adams*	(413)	8,508	9,445
01220	Adams (c)	(413)	5,784	6,356
01001	Agawam	(413)	28,616	27,323
01913	*Amesbury*	(978)	16,737	14,997
01913	Amesbury (c)	(978)	12,327	12,109
*01002	*Amherst*	(413)	34,255	35,228
*01002	Amherst Center (c)	(413)	17,050	17,824
*01810	Andover (c)	(978)	7,900	8,242
*01810	*Andover*	(978)	32,141	29,151
*02205	*Arlington*	(781)	41,546	44,630
01430	*Ashburnham*	(978)	5,901	5,433
01721	*Ashland*	(508)	15,528	12,066
*01331	*Athol*	(978)	11,673	11,451
*01331	Athol (c)	(978)	8,370	8,732
02703	Attleboro	(508)	43,506	38,383
01501	*Auburn*	(508)	16,381	15,005
*01432	*Ayer*	(978)	7,212	6,871
*02630	Barnstable	(508)	48,535	40,949
01005	*Barre*	(978)	5,357	1,094
*01730	*Bedford*	(781)	12,519	12,996
01007	*Belchertown*	(413)	13,846	10,579
02019	*Bellingham*	(508)	15,762	14,877
*02478	*Belmont*	(781)	23,604	24,720
02779	*Berkley*	(508)	6,351	4,237
01915	Beverly	(978)	40,166	38,195
*01821	*Billerica*	(978)	39,951	37,609
01504	*Blackstone*	(508)	9,055	8,023
—	Bliss Corner (c)	(508)	5,466	4,908
*02205	Boston	(617)	569,165	574,283
*02532	*Bourne*	(508)	19,516	16,064
01719	Boxborough	(978)	5,044	3,343
01921	*Boxford*	(978)	8,221	6,266
*02185	*Braintree*	(781)	33,873	33,836
02631	*Brewster*	(508)	10,368	8,440
*02324	Bridgewater (c)	(508)	6,664	7,242
*02324	*Bridgewater*	(508)	25,723	21,249
*02303	Brockton	(508)	95,009	92,788
*02446	*Brookline*	(617)	56,188	54,718
*01803	*Burlington*	(781)	23,223	23,302
*02139	Cambridge	(617)	100,771	95,802
02021	*Canton*	(781)	21,505	18,530
*02330	*Carver*	(508)	11,492	10,590
01507	*Charlton*	(508)	12,295	9,576
02633	*Chatham*	(508)	6,860	6,579
01824	*Chelmsford*	(978)	33,769	32,383
02150	Chelsea	(617)	33,227	28,710
*01020	Chicopee	(413)	54,838	56,632
01510	*Clinton*	(978)	13,890	13,222
01510	Clinton (c)	(978)	7,884	7,943

ZIP	Place	Area Code	2004	1990
01778	Cochituate (c)	(508)	*6,768*	6,046
02025	*Cohasset*	(781)	7,274	7,075
01742	*Concord*	(978)	16,919	17,076
*01226	*Dalton*	(413)	6,736	7,155
01923	*Danvers*	(978)	25,659	24,174
*02714	*Dartmouth*	(508)	31,317	27,244
*02026	*Dedham*	(781)	23,225	23,782
02638	*Dennis*	(508)	16,123	13,864
02715	*Dighton*	(508)	6,628	5,631
01516	*Douglas*	(508)	7,762	5,438
02030	*Dover*	(508)	5,657	4,915
01826	*Dracut*	(978)	28,681	25,594
01571	*Dudley*	(508)	10,775	9,540
*02332	*Duxbury*	(781)	14,691	13,895
02333	*East Bridgewater*	(508)	13,692	11,104
02536	East Falmouth (c)	(508)	*6,615*	5,577
02642	*Eastham*	(508)	5,622	4,462
01027	Easthampton	(413)	16,089	15,537
*01028	*East Longmeadow*	(413)	14,811	13,367
*02334	*Easton*	(508)	23,061	19,807
02149	Everett	(617)	37,195	35,701
02719	*Fairhaven*	(508)	16,335	16,132
*02722	Fall River	(508)	92,526	92,703
*02540	*Falmouth*	(508)	33,806	27,960
01420	Fitchburg	(978)	39,910	41,194
02035	*Foxborough*	(508)	16,354	14,637
02035	Foxborough (c)	(508)	*5,509*	5,706
*01701	*Framingham*	(508)	65,598	64,989
02038	Franklin	(508)	30,192	22,095
02702	*Freetown*	(508)	8,971	8,522
*01440	Gardner	(978)	20,967	20,125
01833	*Georgetown*	(978)	7,961	6,384
*01930	Gloucester	(978)	30,817	28,716
01519	*Grafton*	(508)	16,297	13,035
01033	*Granby*	(413)	6,339	5,565
01230	*Great Barrington*	(413)	7,434	7,725
*01301	*Greenfield*	(413)	17,926	18,666
*01301	Greenfield (c)	(413)	*13,716*	14,016
*01450	*Groton*	(978)	10,369	7,511
01834	*Groveland*	(978)	6,472	5,214
02338	*Halifax*	(781)	7,781	6,526
*01936	*Hamilton*	(978)	8,426	7,280
01036	*Hampden*	(413)	5,316	—
*02339	*Hanover*	(781)	13,853	11,912
*02341	*Hanson*	(781)	9,898	9,028
01451	*Harvard*	(978)	6,083	12,329
02645	*Harwich*	(508)	12,809	10,275
*01830	Haverhill	(978)	60,482	51,418
*02018	Hingham (c)	(781)	*5,352*	5,454
*02043	*Hingham*	(781)	21,198	19,821
02343	*Holbrook*	(781)	10,832	11,041
01520	*Holden*	(508)	16,595	14,628
01746	*Holliston*	(508)	13,919	12,926
*01040	Holyoke	(413)	40,058	43,704
01747	*Hopedale*	(508)	6,222	5,666
01748	*Hopkinton*	(508)	14,031	9,191
01749	*Hudson*	(978)	18,726	17,233
01749	Hudson (c)	(978)	*14,388*	14,267
02045	*Hull*	(781)	11,320	10,466
02601	Hyannis (c)	(508)	*11,050*	14,120
01938	*Ipswich*	(978)	13,374	11,873
02364	Kingston (c)	(781)	*5,380*	4,774
02364	*Kingston*	(781)	12,345	9,045
02347	*Lakeville*	(508)	10,533	7,785
01523	*Lancaster*	(978)	6,719	6,661
*01842	Lawrence	(978)	71,858	70,207
*01238	*Lee*	(413)	5,888	5,849
01524	*Leicester*	(508)	10,904	10,191
01240	*Lenox*	(413)	5,162	5,069
01453	Leominster	(978)	41,911	38,145
*02420	*Lexington*	(781)	30,419	28,974
01773	*Lincoln*	(781)	8,000	7,666
01460	*Littleton*	(978)	8,578	7,051
*01028	*Longmeadow*	(413)	15,631	15,467
*01853	Lowell	(978)	103,655	103,439
01056	*Ludlow*	(413)	21,934	18,820
01462	*Lunenburg*	(978)	9,980	9,117
*01901	Lynn	(781)	89,485	81,245
01940	*Lynnfield*	(781)	11,640	11,049
02148	Malden	(781)	55,340	53,884
01944	*Manchester-by-the-Sea*	(978)	5,370	5,286
*02048	*Mansfield*	(508)	22,998	16,568
02048	Mansfield Center (c)	(508)	*7,320*	7,170
01945	*Marblehead*	(781)	24,817	19,971
02738	*Marion*	(508)	5,310	4,496
01752	Marlborough	(508)	37,699	31,813
*02050	*Marshfield*	(781)	24,775	21,531
02649	*Mashpee*	(508)	14,301	7,884
02739	*Mattapoisett*	(508)	6,467	5,850
01754	*Maynard*	(978)	10,322	10,325
02052	Medfield (c)	(508)	*6,670*	5,985
02052	*Medfield*	(508)	12,397	10,531
*02155	Medford	(781)	54,197	57,407
02053	*Medway*	(508)	12,886	9,931
02176	Melrose	(781)	26,533	28,150
01756	*Mendon*	(508)	5,761	—
01860	*Merrimac*	(978)	6,321	5,166
01844	Methuen	(978)	44,845	39,990
*02346	*Middleborough*	(508)	21,121	17,867
02346	Middleborough Center (c)	(508)	*6,913*	6,837
01949	*Middleton*	(978)	9,107	4,921
01757	*Milford*	(508)	27,410	25,355
01757	Milford (c)	(508)	*24,230*	23,339
*01527	*Millbury*	(508)	13,376	12,228
02054	*Millis*	(508)	7,997	7,613
02186	*Milton*	(617)	25,855	25,725
01057	*Monson*	(413)	8,684	7,776
01351	*Montague*	(413)	8,443	8,316
*02584	*Nantucket*	(508)	10,124	6,012
01760	*Natick*	(508)	32,113	30,510
*02494	*Needham*	(781)	29,022	27,557
*02740	New Bedford	(508)	93,979	99,922
01951	*Newbury*	(978)	6,886	5,623
01950	Newburyport	(978)	17,552	16,317
*02456	Newton	(617)	83,802	82,585
02056	*Norfolk*	(508)	10,492	9,259
01247	North Adams	(413)	14,167	16,797
01059	North Amherst (c)	(413)	*6,019*	6,239
*01060	Northampton	(413)	28,930	11,929
01845	*North Andover*	(978)	27,979	29,289
*02760	*North Attleborough*	(508)	28,176	22,792
02760	North Attleborough Center (c)	(508)	*16,796*	16,178
01532	Northborough (c)	(508)	*6,257*	5,761
01532	*Northborough*	(508)	14,320	13,371
01534	*Northbridge*	(508)	13,882	12,002
*01864	*North Reading*	(978)	13,980	25,038
02060	North Scituate (c)	(781)	*5,065*	4,891
*02766	*Norton*	(508)	19,157	14,265
02061	*Norwell*	(781)	10,390	9,279
02062	*Norwood*	(781)	28,548	28,700
02065	Ocean Bluff-Brant Rock (c)	(781)	*5,100*	4,541
*01364	*Orange*	(978)	7,563	7,312
02653	*Orleans*	(508)	6,474	5,838
01540	Oxford (c)	(508)	*5,899*	5,969
01540	*Oxford*	(508)	13,735	12,588
01069	*Palmer*	(413)	12,902	12,054
*01960	Peabody	(978)	50,370	47,264
*02359	*Pembroke*	(781)	17,715	14,544
01463	*Pepperell*	(978)	11,434	10,098
01866	Pinehurst (c)	(978)	*6,941*	6,614
*01201	Pittsfield	(413)	44,285	48,622
02762	*Plainville*	(508)	7,926	6,871
*02360	Plymouth (c)	(508)	*7,658*	7,258
*02360	*Plymouth*	(508)	54,604	45,608
*02169	Quincy	(617)	89,909	84,985
02368	*Randolph*	(781)	30,748	30,093
*02767	*Raynham*	(508)	13,324	9,867
01867	*Reading*	(781)	23,362	22,539
02769	*Rehoboth*	(508)	11,137	8,656
02151	Revere	(781)	46,169	42,786
02770	Rochester	(508)	5,202	3,921
02370	*Rockland*	(781)	17,861	16,123
01966	Rockport (c)	(978)	*5,606*	5,448
01966	*Rockport*	(978)	7,805	7,482
01969	*Rowley*	(978)	5,720	4,452
01543	*Rutland*	(508)	7,245	4,936
*01970	Salem	(978)	41,912	38,091
01952	*Salisbury*	(978)	8,159	6,882
*02563	*Sandwich*	(508)	20,826	15,489
01906	*Saugus*	(781)	26,762	25,549
02066	Scituate (c)	(781)	*5,069*	5,180
*02066	*Scituate*	(781)	18,195	16,786
02771	*Seekonk*	(508)	13,730	13,046
02067	*Sharon*	(781)	17,347	15,517
02067	Sharon (c)	(781)	*5,941*	5,893
01464	*Shirley*	(978)	7,601	6,118
*01545	*Shrewsbury*	(508)	33,161	24,146
*02725	*Somerset*	(508)	18,692	17,655
*02143	Somerville	(617)	75,621	76,210
01002	South Amherst (c)	(413)	*5,039*	5,053
01073	*Southampton*	(413)	5,772	4,478
*01772	*Southborough*	(508)	9,549	6,628
01550	*Southbridge*	(508)	17,314	17,816
01550	Southbridge (c)	(508)	*12,878*	13,631
01075	*South Hadley*	(413)	17,181	16,685
01077	*Southwick*	(413)	9,428	7,667
01562	Spencer (c)	(508)	*6,032*	6,306
01562	*Spencer*	(508)	12,014	11,645
*01101	Springfield	(413)	152,091	156,983
01564	*Sterling*	(978)	7,742	6,481
02180	*Stoneham*	(781)	21,781	22,203
02072	*Stoughton*	(781)	26,902	26,777
01775	*Stow*	(978)	6,119	5,328
*01566	*Sturbridge*	(508)	8,692	7,775
01776	*Sudbury*	(978)	17,164	14,358
01590	*Sutton*	(508)	8,878	6,824
01907	*Swampscott*	(781)	14,433	13,650
02777	*Swansea*	(508)	16,317	15,411
*02780	Taunton	(508)	56,648	49,832
01468	*Templeton*	(978)	7,322	6,438
01876	*Tewksbury*	(978)	29,130	27,266
01983	*Topsfield*	(978)	6,228	5,754
01469	*Townsend*	(978)	9,326	8,496
01879	*Tyngsborough*	(978)	11,387	8,642
01568	*Upton*	(508)	6,262	4,677
01569	*Uxbridge*	(508)	12,243	10,415
01880	*Wakefield*	(781)	24,562	24,825
*02081	Walpole (c)	(508)	*5,867*	5,495
02081	*Walpole*	(508)	22,518	20,223
*02451	Waltham	(781)	59,232	57,878

ZIP	Place	Area Code	2004	1990
01082	Ware (c)	(413)	*6,174*	6,533
01082	*Ware*	(413)	10,022	9,808
02571	*Wareham*	(508)	21,090	19,232
*02471	Watertown	(781)	32,603	33,284
01778	*Wayland*	(508)	13,063	11,874
01570	*Webster*	(508)	16,880	16,196
01570	Webster (c)	(508)	*11,600*	11,849
*02457	*Wellesley*	(781)	26,515	26,615
*01581	*Westborough*	(508)	18,737	14,133
01583	*West Boylston*	(508)	7,616	6,611
02379	*West Bridgewater*	(508)	6,844	6,389
01742	West Concord (c)	(978)	*5,632*	5,761
*01085	Westfield	(413)	40,559	38,372
01886	*Westford*	(978)	21,475	16,392
*01473	*Westminster*	(978)	7,302	6,191
02493	*Weston*	(781)	11,595	10,200
02790	*Westport*	(508)	14,741	13,852
*01089	*West Springfield*	(413)	28,048	27,537
02090	*Westwood*	(781)	14,020	12,557
02673	West Yarmouth (c)	(508)	*6,460*	5,409
*02188	*Weymouth*	(781)	54,202	54,063
01588	Whitinsville (c)	(508)	*6,340*	5,639
02382	*Whitman*	(781)	14,351	13,240
01095	*Wilbraham*	(413)	13,938	12,635
01267	*Williamstown*	(413)	8,272	8,220
01887	*Wilmington*	(978)	21,568	17,651
01475	*Winchendon*	(978)	10,037	8,805
01890	*Winchester*	(781)	21,167	20,267
02152	*Winthrop*	(617)	17,461	18,127
*01801	Woburn	(781)	37,448	35,943
*01613	Worcester	(508)	175,966	169,759
*02093	*Wrentham*	(508)	11,086	9,006
*02675	*Yarmouth*	(508)	24,972	21,174
02675	Yarmouth Port (c)	(508)	*5,395*	4,271

Michigan

Area code (947) overlays area code (248). See introductory note.

ZIP	Place	Area Code	2004	1990
49221	Adrian	(517)	21,977	22,097
49224	Albion	(517)	9,184	10,066
49401	Allendale (c)	(616)	*11,555*	6,950
*48101	Allen Park	(313)	28,481	31,092
*48801	Alma	(989)	9,308	9,034
49707	Alpena	(989)	10,939	11,354
*48106	Ann Arbor	(734)	113,567	109,608
*48321	Auburn Hills	(248)	20,737	17,076
*49016	Battle Creek	(269)	53,399	53,516
*48707	Bay City	(989)	35,317	38,936
48505	Beecher (c)	(810)	*12,793*	14,465
*48809	Belding	(616)	5,870	5,969
*49022	Benton Harbor	(269)	10,851	12,818
49022	Benton Heights (c)	(269)	*5,458*	5,465
48072	Berkley	(248)	15,236	16,960
48025	Beverly Hills	(248)	10,186	10,610
49307	Big Rapids	(231)	10,852	12,603
*48012	Birmingham	(248)	19,217	19,997
*48301	Bloomfield (c)	(248)	*43,021*	42,137
48722	Bridgeport (c)	(989)	*7,849*	8,569
*48116	Brighton	(810)	7,116	5,686
48601	Buena Vista (c)	(989)	*7,845*	8,196
*48509	Burton	(810)	30,926	27,437
49601	Cadillac	(231)	10,135	10,104
*48184	Canton (c)	(734)	*76,366*	57,047
48724	Carrollton (c)	(989)	*6,602*	6,521
48015	Center Line	(586)	8,362	9,026
48813	Charlotte	(517)	9,046	8,083
49721	Cheboygan	(231)	5,208	4,997
*48017	Clawson	(248)	12,443	13,874
*48046	Clinton (c)	(517)	*95,648*	85,866
49036	Coldwater	(517)	10,821	9,607
49321	Comstock Park (c)	(616)	*10,674*	6,530
49508	Cutlerville (c)	(616)	*15,114*	11,228
48423	Davison	(810)	5,410	5,693
*48120	Dearborn	(313)	95,470	89,286
*48127	Dearborn Heights	(313)	56,828	60,838
*48231	Detroit	(313)	900,198	1,027,974
49047	Dowagiac	(269)	5,968	6,418
*49506	East Grand Rapids	(616)	10,482	10,807
*48826	East Lansing	(517)	46,678	50,677
48021	Eastpointe	(586)	33,384	35,283
49001	Eastwood (c)	(269)	*6,265*	6,340
48827	Eaton Rapids	(517)	5,279	4,695
48229	Ecorse	(313)	10,896	12,180
49829	Escanaba	(906)	12,752	13,659
49022	Fair Plain (c)	(269)	*7,828*	8,051
*48333	Farmington	(248)	10,146	10,170
*48333	Farmington Hills	(248)	80,787	74,614
48430	Fenton	(810)	11,911	8,434
48220	Ferndale	(248)	21,666	25,084
48134	Flat Rock	(734)	9,501	7,290
*48501	Flint	(810)	119,716	140,925
48433	Flushing	(810)	8,197	8,542
49506	Forest Hills (c)	(616)	*20,942*	16,690
48026	Fraser	(586)	15,130	13,899
48623	Freeland (c)	(989)	*5,147*	1,421
*48135	Garden City	(734)	29,310	31,846
48173	Gibraltar	(734)	5,095	4,297
49837	Gladstone	(906)	5,266	4,565
48439	Grand Blanc	(810)	7,984	7,760
49417	Grand Haven	(616)	10,733	11,951
48837	Grand Ledge	(517)	7,808	7,562
*49501	Grand Rapids	(616)	195,115	189,126
*49418	Grandville	(616)	16,680	15,624
48838	Greenville	(616)	8,282	8,101
48138	Grosse Ile (c)	(734)	*10,894*	9,781
*48230	Grosse Pointe	(313)	5,504	5,681
48230	Grosse Pointe Farms	(313)	9,468	10,092
48230	Grosse Pointe Park	(313)	12,064	12,857
48230	Grosse Pointe Woods	(313)	16,546	17,715
*48212	Hamtramck	(313)	22,241	18,372
48225	Harper Woods	(313)	13,952	14,903
48625	Harrison (c)	(989)	*24,461*	24,685
48840	Haslett (c)	(517)	*11,283*	10,230
49058	Hastings	(269)	7,151	6,549
48030	Hazel Park	(248)	18,553	20,051
48203	Highland Park	(313)	15,675	20,121
49242	Hillsdale	(517)	8,026	8,175
*49423	Holland	(616)	34,606	30,745
48442	Holly	(248)	6,347	5,595
48842	Holt (c)	(517)	*11,315*	11,744
*49931	Houghton	(906)	7,010	7,498
*48844	Howell	(517)	9,734	8,147
49426	Hudsonville	(616)	7,091	6,170
48070	Huntington Woods	(248)	5,998	6,419
48141	Inkster	(313)/(734)	29,239	30,772
48846	Ionia	(616)	12,359	10,349
*49801	Iron Mountain	(906)	7,995	8,525
49938	Ironwood	(906)	5,808	6,849
*49849	Ishpeming	(906)	6,544	7,200
*49204	Jackson	(517)	35,133	37,425
*49428	Jenison (c)	(616)	*17,211*	17,882
*49001	Kalamazoo	(269)	73,960	80,277
*49518	Kentwood	(616)	46,538	37,826
49802	Kingsford	(906)	5,442	5,480
48144	Lambertville (c)	(734)	*9,299*	7,860
*48901	Lansing	(517)	116,941	127,321
48446	Lapeer	(810)	9,362	7,759
48146	Lincoln Park	(313)	38,744	41,832
*48150	Livonia	(734)	98,936	100,850
49431	Ludington	(231)	8,349	8,507
48071	Madison Heights	(248)	30,510	32,196
49660	Manistee	(231)	6,714	6,734
49855	Marquette	(906)	20,664	21,977
*49068	Marshall	(269)	7,359	6,941
48040	Marysville	(810)	9,982	8,515
48854	Mason	(517)	7,870	6,768
48122	Melvindale	(313)	10,719	11,216
49858	Menominee	(906)	8,866	9,398
*48640	Midland	(989)	42,145	38,053
48160	Milan	(734)	5,149	4,040
*48381	Milford	(248)	6,449	5,500
*48161	Monroe	(734)	21,690	22,902
*48046	Mount Clemens	(586)	17,108	18,405
*48804	Mount Pleasant	(989)	25,651	23,299
*49440	Muskegon	(231)	39,954	39,809
49444	Muskegon Heights	(231)	11,807	13,176
*48047	New Baltimore	(586)	10,857	5,798
*49120	Niles	(269)	11,876	12,458
49505	Northview (c)	(616)	*14,730*	13,712
*48167	Northville	(248)	6,384	6,226
*49441	Norton Shores	(231)	51,934	21,755
*48376	Novi	(248)	29,074	32,998
48237	Oak Park	(248)	29,074	30,468
*48805	Okemos (c)	(517)	*22,805*	20,216
*48867	Owosso	(989)	15,532	16,322
49770	Petoskey	(231)	6,227	6,056
48170	Plymouth	(734)	8,877	9,560
48170	Plymouth Township (c)	(734)	*27,798*	23,646
*48343	Pontiac	(248)	67,582	71,136
*49081	Portage	(269)	45,210	41,042
*48061	Port Huron	(810)	31,710	33,694
*48239	Redford (c)	(313)	*51,622*	54,387
48062	Richmond	(586)	5,538	4,028
48218	River Rouge	(313)	9,367	11,314
*48192	Riverview	(734)	12,909	13,894
*48308	Rochester	(248)	11,217	7,130
*48306	Rochester Hills	(248)	69,480	61,766
48174	Romulus	(313)/(734)	23,609	22,897
48066	Roseville	(586)	47,960	51,412
*48068	Royal Oak	(248)	58,573	65,410
*48605	Saginaw	(989)	59,045	69,512
48604	Saginaw Township North (c)	(989)	*24,994*	23,018
48603	Saginaw Township South (c)	(989)	*13,801*	13,987
48079	Saint Clair	(810)	5,945	5,116
*48080	Saint Clair Shores	(313)	5,945	68,107
48879	Saint Johns	(989)	61,864	7,392
49085	Saint Joseph	(269)	7,493	9,214
48880	Saint Louis	(989)	8,701	3,828
48176	Saline	(734)	8,859	6,663
*49783	Sault Sainte Marie	(906)	14,157	14,689
49455	Shelby (c)	(231)	*65,159*	48,655
48609	Shields (c)	(989)	6,590	6,634
*48037	Southfield	(248)	77,491	75,727
48195	Southgate	(734)	29,919	30,771
49090	South Haven	(269)	5,144	5,563

ZIP	Place	Area Code	2004	1990
48178	South Lyon	(248)	11,017	6,479
48161	South Monroe (c)	(734)	*6,370*	5,266
49015	Springfield	(269)	5,237	5,582
*48311	Sterling Heights	(586)	127,476	117,810
49091	Sturgis	(269)	11,120	10,130
48473	Swartz Creek	(810)	5,300	4,851
48180	Taylor	(313)/(734)	65,383	70,811
49286	Tecumseh	(517)	8,773	7,462
48182	Temperance (c)	(734)	*7,757*	6,542
49093	Three Rivers	(269)	7,126	7,464
*49684	Traverse City	(231)	14,508	15,155
48183	Trenton	(734)	19,468	20,586
*48099	Troy	(248)	81,432	72,884
49534	Walker	(616)	23,315	17,279
*48390	Walled Lake	(248)	6,877	6,278
*48090	Warren	(586)	136,118	144,864
*48329	Waterford (c)	(248)	*73,150*	66,692
48917	Waverly (c)	(517)	*16,194*	15,614
48184	Wayne	(734)	18,780	19,899
*48323	West Bloomfield Township (c)	(248)	*64,862*	54,843
*48185	Westland	(313)/(734)	86,316	84,724
49009	Westwood (c)	(269)	*9,122*	8,957
48189	Whitmore Lake (c)	(734)	*6,574*	3,251
48393	Wixom	(248)	13,514	8,550
48183	Woodhaven	(734)	12,853	11,631
*48192	Wyandotte	(734)	27,247	30,938
*49509	Wyoming	(616)	70,205	63,891
*48197	Ypsilanti	(734)	22,492	24,846
49464	Zeeland	(616)	5,645	5,417

Minnesota

ZIP	Place	Area Code	2004	1990
56007	Albert Lea	(507)	17,819	18,310
55301	Albertville	(763)	5,489	1,252
56308	Alexandria	(320)	10,231	8,029
*55304	Andover	(763)	29,450	15,216
*55303	Anoka	(612)/(763)	17,797	17,192
55124	Apple Valley	(952)	49,606	34,598
*55112	Arden Hills	(651)	9,567	9,199
55912	Austin	(507)	23,507	21,926
*56425	Baxter	(218)	7,067	3,695
*56601	Bemidji	(218)	13,016	11,165
55309	Big Lake	(763)	8,422	3,113
*55014	Blaine	(651)/(763)	52,137	38,975
*55420	Bloomington	(952)	81,875	86,335
*56401	Brainerd	(218)	13,746	12,353
*55429	Brooklyn Center	(763)	27,851	28,887
*55443	Brooklyn Park	(763)	67,927	56,381
55313	Buffalo	(763)	12,801	7,302
*55337	Burnsville	(651)/(952)	59,384	51,288
55008	Cambridge	(763)	6,762	5,094
55316	Champlin	(763)	23,293	16,849
55317	Chanhassen	(952)	22,977	11,736
55318	Chaska	(952)	21,694	11,339
55014	Circle Pines	(763)/(651)	5,065	4,704
55720	Cloquet	(218)	11,463	10,885
55421	Columbia Heights	(612)/(763)	18,258	18,910
*55433	Coon Rapids	(763)	62,721	52,978
*55340	Corcoran	(763)	5,700	5,199
55016	Cottage Grove	(651)	32,146	22,935
56716	Crookston	(218)	7,946	8,119
*55428	Crystal	(763)	21,883	23,788
*56501	Detroit Lakes	(218)	7,864	7,141
*55806	Duluth	(218)	85,556	85,493
*55121	Eagan	(651)/(952)	64,105	47,409
*55005	East Bethel	(763)	11,856	8,050
56721	East Grand Forks	(218)	7,676	8,658
*55344	Eden Prairie	(612)/(952)	60,430	39,311
*55424	Edina	(952)	46,081	46,075
55330	Elk River	(763)	20,224	11,143
*56031	Fairmont	(507)	10,548	11,265
*55113	Falcon Heights	(651)	5,432	5,380
55021	Faribault	(507)	21,924	17,085
55024	Farmington	(651)/(952)	17,344	5,940
*56537	Fergus Falls	(218)	13,715	12,362
55025	Forest Lake	(651)	16,948	5,833
*55432	Fridley	(763)	26,942	28,335
55336	Glencoe	(320)	5,534	4,648
*55427	Golden Valley	(763)	20,200	20,971
*55744	Grand Rapids	(218)	8,046	7,976
*55304	Ham Lake	(763)	14,559	8,924
55033	Hastings	(651)	20,353	15,478
*55810	Hermantown	(218)	8,376	6,761
*55746	Hibbing	(218)	16,706	18,046
*55343	Hopkins	(952)	16,957	16,529
55038	Hugo	(651)	9,258	4,417
55350	Hutchinson	(320)	13,521	11,459
56649	International Falls	(218)	6,338	8,325
*55076	Inver Grove Heights	(651)	32,338	22,477
55944	Kasson	(507)	5,210	3,514
55947	La Crescent	(507)	5,063	4,311
55041	Lake City	(651)	5,313	4,490
55042	Lake Elmo	(651)	7,692	5,900
*55044	Lakeville	(952)	49,440	24,854
*55014	Lino Lakes	(651)	19,123	8,807
55355	Litchfield	(320)	6,665	6,041
*55117	Little Canada	(651)	9,680	8,971
56345	Little Falls	(320)	8,191	7,371
55115	Mahtomedi	(651)	8,086	5,633
*56001	Mankato	(507)	34,463	31,459
*55311	Maple Grove	(763)	58,628	38,736
*55109	Maplewood	(651)	35,528	30,954
56258	Marshall	(507)	12,409	12,023
*55118	Mendota Heights	(651)	11,378	9,388
*55440	Minneapolis	(612)/(763)/(952)	373,943	368,383
*55345	Minnetonka	(952)	50,077	48,370
55359	Minnetrista	(952)	5,234	3,439
56265	Montevideo	(320)	5,300	5,499
*55362	Monticello	(763)	10,412	5,045
*56560	Moorhead	(218)	33,390	32,295
56267	Morris	(320)	5,195	5,613
55364	Mound	(952)	9,411	9,634
55112	Mounds View	(763)	12,360	12,541
55112	New Brighton	(651)	21,145	22,207
*54427	New Hope	(763)	19,983	21,853
56071	New Prague	(952)	6,115	3,575
56073	New Ulm	(507)	13,705	13,132
55056	North Branch	(651)/(763)	10,016	4,267
55057	Northfield	(507)	18,567	14,684
*56002	North Mankato	(507)	12,134	10,662
55109	North Saint Paul	(651)	11,600	12,376
*55128	Oakdale	(651)	27,571	18,377
*55011	Oak Grove	(763)	7,602	5,488
*55323	Orono	(952)	7,744	7,285
*55330	Otsego	(763)	10,057	5,219
55060	Owatonna	(507)	23,707	19,386
*55446	Plymouth	(763)	69,797	50,889
55372	Prior Lake	(952)	21,286	11,482
55303	Ramsey	(763)	20,735	12,408
55066	Red Wing	(651)	15,907	15,134
56283	Redwood Falls	(507)	5,332	4,859
55423	Richfield	(612)	33,911	35,710
55422	Robbinsdale	(763)	13,490	14,396
*55901	Rochester	(507)	93,284	70,729
55374	Rogers	(763)	5,938	722
55068	Rosemount	(651)/(952)	17,997	8,622
*55113	Roseville	(651)	32,695	33,485
*55418	Saint Anthony	(612)	7,670	7,727
*56301	Saint Cloud	(320)	64,337	48,812
55070	Saint Francis	(763)	6,929	2,479
*56374	Saint Joseph	(320)	5,386	3,294
*55426	Saint Louis Park	(952)	43,607	43,787
55376	Saint Michael	(763)	13,505	2,506
*55101	Saint Paul	(651)	276,963	272,235
55071	Saint Paul Park	(651)	5,021	4,965
56082	Saint Peter	(507)	10,358	9,481
56377	Sartell	(320)	12,303	5,409
56379	Sauk Rapids	(320)	11,381	7,823
55378	Savage	(952)	25,714	9,906
*55379	Shakopee	(612)	29,321	11,739
55126	Shoreview	(651)	26,991	24,587
*55331	Shorewood	(952)	7,476	5,913
*55075	South Saint Paul	(651)	19,478	20,197
55432	Spring Lake Park	(763)	6,809	6,532
55976	Stewartville	(507)	5,495	4,520
*55082	Stillwater	(651)	17,171	13,882
*56701	Thief River Falls	(218)	8,349	8,010
*55127	Vadnais Heights	(651)	12,869	11,041
55386	Victoria	(952)	5,393	2,354
*55792	Virginia	(218)	8,783	9,432
55387	Waconia	(952)	8,339	3,498
*56387	Waite Park	(320)	6,857	5,020
56093	Waseca	(507)	9,467	8,385
*55118	West Saint Paul	(651)	19,183	19,248
*55110	White Bear Lake	(651)	24,051	24,622
56201	Willmar	(320)	18,205	17,531
*55987	Winona	(507)	26,451	25,435
*55125	Woodbury	(651)	50,020	20,075
56187	Worthington	(507)	11,087	9,977

Mississippi

Area code (769) overlays area code (601). See introductory note.

ZIP	Place	Area Code	2004	1990
39730	Aberdeen	(662)	6,274	6,837
38821	Amory	(662)	6,829	7,093
38606	Batesville	(662)	7,674	6,403
*39520	Bay Saint Louis	(228)	8,293	8,063
*39530	Biloxi	(228)	50,115	46,319
38829	Booneville	(662)	8,705	7,955
*39042	Brandon	(601)	18,631	11,089
*39601	Brookhaven	(601)	9,854	10,243
39272	Byram (c)	(601)	*7,386*	—
39046	Canton	(601)	12,826	11,723
*38614	Clarksdale	(662)	19,467	21,180
*38732	Cleveland	(662)	12,897	15,384
*39056	Clinton	(601)	24,392	21,847
39429	Columbia	(601)	6,453	6,815
*39701	Columbus	(662)	24,791	23,799

ZIP	Place	Area Code	2004	1990
*38834	Corinth	(662)	14,222	11,820
39059	Crystal Springs	(601)	5,907	5,643
39525	Diamondhead (c)	(228)	*5,912*	2,661
39540	Diberville	(228)	7,757	6,566
39232	Flowood	(601)	6,448	2,770
39074	Forest	(601)	6,012	5,062
39553	Gautier	(228)	16,853	10,088
*38701	Greenville	(662)	38,979	45,226
*38930	Greenwood	(662)	17,439	18,906
*38901	Grenada	(662)	14,492	10,864
39564	Gulf Hills (c)	(228)	*5,900*	5,004
*39501	Gulfport	(228)	71,851	64,045
*39401	Hattiesburg	(601)	46,442	45,325
38632	Hernando	(662)	9,420	3,125
*38635	Holly Springs	(662)	8,009	7,261
38637	Horn Lake	(662)	21,764	9,069
*38751	Indianola	(662)	11,449	11,809
*39205	Jackson	(601)	179,298	202,062
39090	Kosciusko	(662)	7,359	6,986
*39440	Laurel	(601)	18,186	18,827
38756	Leland	(662)	5,184	6,366
39560	Long Beach	(228)	17,258	15,804
39339	Louisville	(662)	6,774	7,165
*39648	McComb	(601)	13,127	11,797
*39110	Madison	(601)	16,462	7,471
*39302	Meridian	(601)	38,833	41,036
*39563	Moss Point	(228)	15,318	17,837
*39120	Natchez	(601)	17,272	19,460
38652	New Albany	(662)	7,913	6,775
*39564	Ocean Springs	(228)	17,698	15,221
38654	Olive Branch	(662)	26,516	3,567
38655	Oxford	(662)	13,301	10,026
*39567	Pascagoula	(228)	25,873	25,899
39571	Pass Christian	(228)	6,758	5,557
*39288	Pearl	(601)	23,039	19,588
39465	Petal	(601)	7,761	7,883
39350	Philadelphia	(601)	7,361	6,758
39466	Picayune	(601)	10,750	10,633
38863	Pontotoc	(662)	5,758	4,570
39218	Richland	(601)	6,993	4,014
*39157	Ridgeland	(601)	21,577	11,714
38663	Ripley	(662)	5,536	5,371
—	Saint Martin (c)	(228)	*6,676*	6,349
38668	Senatobia	(601)	6,751	4,772
*38671	Southaven	(662)	36,244	18,705
*39759	Starkville	(662)	21,964	18,458
*38801	Tupelo	(662)	35,418	30,685
*39180	Vicksburg	(601)	25,776	26,886
39576	Waveland	(228)	7,120	5,369
39367	Waynesboro	(601)	5,144	5,143
—	West Hattiesburg (c)	(601)	*6,305*	5,450
39773	West Point	(662)	11,858	8,489
38967	Winona	(662)	5,086	5,965
39194	Yazoo City	(662)	11,936	12,427

Missouri

ZIP	Place	Area Code	2004	1990
63123	Affton (c)	(314)	*20,535*	21,106
63010	Arnold	(636)	20,146	18,828
65605	Aurora	(417)	7,145	6,459
*63011	Ballwin	(636)	30,778	27,054
63012	Barnhart (c)	(314)	*6,108*	4,911
63137	Bellefontaine Neighbors	(314)	10,732	10,918
64012	Belton	(816)	23,793	18,145
*63134	Berkeley	(314)	9,740	12,250
63033	Black Jack	(314)	6,942	6,131
*64015	Blue Springs	(816)	49,467	40,103
*65613	Bolivar	(417)	9,759	6,845
65233	Boonville	(660)	8,608	7,095
63334	Bowling Green	(573)	5,102	3,046
*65615	Branson	(417)	6,315	3,706
63144	Brentwood	(314)	7,443	8,150
*63044	Bridgeton	(314)	15,382	17,732
64429	Cameron	(816)	9,322	6,782
*63701	Cape Girardeau	(573)	35,993	34,475
64834	Carl Junction	(417)	6,139	4,123
64836	Carthage	(417)	13,003	10,747
*63830	Caruthersville	(573)	6,505	7,389
63834	Charleston	(573)	5,166	5,131
*63017	Chesterfield	(636)	47,110	42,325
64601	Chillicothe	(660)	8,697	8,799
*63105	Clayton	(314)	15,944	13,926
64735	Clinton	(660)	9,443	8,703
*65201	Columbia	(573)	89,593	69,133
*63128	Concord (c)	(314)	11,757	19,859
63126	Crestwood	(314)	16,642	11,229
63141	Creve Coeur	(314)	6,431	12,289
*63366	Dardenne Prairie	(636)	89,593	1,769
*63135	Dellwood	(314)	5,084	5,245
63020	De Soto	(636)	6,541	5,993
*63131	Des Peres	(636)	8,607	8,395
63841	Dexter	(573)	7,547	7,506
*63011	Ellisville	(636)	9,389	7,183
63025	Eureka	(636)	8,794	4,683
64024	Excelsior Springs	(816)	11,324	10,373
63640	Farmington	(573)	14,807	11,596
*63135	Ferguson	(314)	21,677	22,290
63028	Festus	(636)	10,438	8,105
*63033	Florissant	(314)	51,583	51,038
65473	Fort Leonard Wood (c)	(573)	*13,666*	15,863
65251	Fulton	(573)	11,879	10,033
*64118	Gladstone	(816)	27,182	26,243
63137	Glasgow Village (c)	(573)	*5,234*	5,199
63122	Glendale	(314)	5,643	5,945
64029	Grain Valley	(816)	7,986	1,898
64030	Grandview	(816)	24,848	24,973
63401	Hannibal	(573)	17,719	18,004
64701	Harrisonville	(816)	9,592	7,696
*63042	Hazelwood	(314)	25,651	15,512
*64050	Independence	(816)	111,023	112,301
63755	Jackson	(573)	12,751	9,256
*65101	Jefferson City	(573)	38,671	35,517
63136	Jennings	(314)	15,056	15,841
*64801	Joplin	(417)	46,830	41,175
*64108	Kansas City	(816)	444,387	434,829
64060	Kearney	(816)	6,937	1,790
63857	Kennett	(573)	11,005	10,941
63501	Kirksville	(660)	17,057	17,152
63122	Kirkwood	(314)	27,156	28,318
63124	Ladue (St. Louis Co.)	(314)	8,305	8,795
63367	Lake Saint Louis	(636)	12,893	7,536
65536	Lebanon	(417)	12,865	9,983
*64063	Lee's Summit	(816)	78,659	46,418
63125	Lemay (c)	(314)	*17,215*	18,005
*64068	Liberty	(816)	28,528	20,459
63552	Macon	(660)	5,399	5,571
*63011	Manchester	(636)	19,059	6,506
63143	Maplewood	(314)	8,911	9,962
65340	Marshall	(660)	12,103	12,711
65706	Marshfield	(417)	6,553	4,374
63043	Maryland Heights	(314)	25,407	25,440
64468	Maryville	(816)	10,511	10,663
63129	Mehlville (c)	(314)	*28,822*	27,557
65265	Mexico	(573)	10,965	11,290
65270	Moberly	(660)	13,745	12,839
65708	Monett	(417)	8,137	6,529
63026	Murphy (c)	(636)	*9,048*	9,342
*64850	Neosho	(417)	10,961	9,254
64772	Nevada	(417)	8,434	8,597
65714	Nixa	(417)	14,617	4,893
63121	Normandy	(314)	5,085	4,480
64075	Oak Grove	(816)	6,654	4,565
63129	Oakville (c)	(314)	*35,309*	31,750
63366	O'Fallon	(636)	67,009	17,427
63132	Olivette	(314)	7,458	7,573
63114	Overland	(314)	16,272	17,987
65721	Ozark	(417)	14,457	4,401
*63069	Pacific	(636)	5,805	4,350
*63601	Park Hills	(573)	8,419	7,866
*63775	Perryville	(573)	7,803	6,933
64080	Pleasant Hill	(816)	6,491	3,827
*63901	Poplar Bluff	(573)	16,678	16,841
64083	Raymore	(816)	14,414	5,592
*64133	Raytown	(816)	29,348	30,601
65738	Republic	(417)	9,936	6,290
64085	Richmond	(816)	6,043	5,738
63117	Richmond Heights	(314)	9,376	10,448
*65401	Rolla	(573)	17,411	14,090
63074	Saint Ann	(314)	13,235	14,449
*63301	Saint Charles	(636)	61,411	50,634
63114	Saint John	(314)	6,635	7,502
*64501	Saint Joseph	(816)	72,628	71,852
*63166	Saint Louis	(314)	343,279	396,685
*63376	Saint Peters	(636)	53,907	40,660
*63126	Sappington (c)	(314)	*7,287*	10,917
*65301	Sedalia	(660)	20,196	19,800
63119	Shrewsbury	(314)	6,459	6,416
63801	Sikeston	(573)	17,057	17,641
64089	Smithville	(816)	6,606	2,525
63138	Spanish Lake (c)	(314)	*21,337*	20,322
*65801	Springfield	(417)	150,704	140,494
63080	Sullivan	(573)	6,579	5,661
63127	Sunset Hills	(314)	8,377	4,915
63011	Town and Country	(314)	10,851	10,944
64683	Trenton	(660)	6,033	6,129
63379	Troy	(314)	8,951	3,811
63084	Union	(636)	8,626	6,196
63130	University City	(314)	37,493	40,087
63088	Valley Park	(636)	6,409	4,165
64093	Warrensburg	(660)	17,452	15,244
63383	Warrenton	(636)	6,281	3,564
63090	Washington	(636)	13,955	11,367
64870	Webb City	(417)	10,553	7,538
63119	Webster Groves	(314)	23,076	22,992
*63304	Weldon Spring	(636)	5,341	1,470
63385	Wentzville	(636)	14,601	4,640
*65775	West Plains	(417)	11,112	9,214
*63011	Wildwood	(314)	34,588	16,742

Montana (406)

ZIP	Place	2004	1990
59711	Anaconda-Deer Lodge County	9,088	10,356
59714	Belgrade	7,046	3,422
*59101	Billings	96,977	81,125
*59718	Bozeman	32,414	22,660
*59701	Butte	32,393	33,336
59901	Evergreen (c)	*6,215*	4,109
*59401	Great Falls	56,503	55,125
59501	Havre	9,460	10,201
*59601	Helena	27,196	24,609
—	Helena Valley Southeast (c)	*7,141*	4,601
—	Helena Valley West Central (c)	*6,983*	6,327
*59901	Kalispell	17,381	11,917
59044	Laurel	6,339	5,686
59457	Lewistown	6,116	6,097
59047	Livingston	7,062	6,701
59301	Miles City	8,315	8,461
*59801	Missoula	61,790	42,918
59801	Orchard Homes (c)	*5,199*	10,317
59937	Whitefish	6,151	4,368

Nebraska

ZIP	Place	Area Code	2004	1990
69301	Alliance	(308)	8,351	9,765
68310	Beatrice	(402)	12,963	12,352
*68108	Bellevue	(402)	47,347	39,240
*68008	Blair	(402)	7,706	6,860
69337	Chadron	(308)	5,402	5,588
68108	Chalco (c)	(402)	*10,736*	7,337
*68601	Columbus	(402)	20,881	19,480
68333	Crete	(402)	6,332	4,841
68022	Elkhorn	(402)	8,040	1,398
*68025	Fremont	(402)	25,272	23,680
69341	Gering	(308)	7,740	7,946
*68802	Grand Island	(308)	44,287	39,487
*68901	Hastings	(402)	23,404	22,837
*68949	Holdrege	(308)	5,481	5,671
*68847	Kearney	(308)	28,640	24,396
68128	La Vista	(402)	14,685	9,992
68850	Lexington	(308)	10,056	6,600
*68501	Lincoln	(402)	236,146	191,972
69001	McCook	(308)	7,742	8,112
68410	Nebraska City	(402)	7,067	6,547
*68701	Norfolk	(402)	24,072	21,476
*69101	North Platte	(308)	23,944	22,605
68113	Offutt AFB (c)	(402)	*8,901*	—
*68005	Omaha	(402)	409,416	344,463
*68046	Papillion	(402)	19,497	13,892
68048	Plattsmouth	(402)	7,075	6,415
68127	Ralston	(402)	6,220	6,236
68661	Schuyler	(402)	5,364	4,052
*69361	Scottsbluff	(308)	14,767	13,711
68434	Seward	(402)	6,664	5,641
*69162	Sidney	(308)	6,381	5,959
68776	South Sioux City	(402)	12,142	9,677
68787	Wayne	(402)	5,179	5,142
68467	York	(402)	7,796	7,940

Nevada

ZIP	Place	Area Code	2004	1990
*89005	Boulder City	(702)	15,246	12,567
*89701	Carson City	(775)	55,974	40,443
89403	Dayton (c)	(775)	*5,907*	2,217
*89801	Elko	(775)	16,230	14,836
—	Enterprise (c)		*14,676*	6,412
*89406	Fallon	(775)	7,959	6,430
89408	Fernley	(775)	10,505	5,164
89410	Gardnerville Ranchos (c)	(775)	*11,054*	7,455
*89015	Henderson	(702)	224,829	64,948
*89450	Incline Village-Crystal Bay c)	(775)	*9,952*	7,119
*89125	Las Vegas	(702)	534,847	258,877
*89028	Laughlin (c)	(702)	*7,076*	4,791
89506	Lemmon Valley-Golden Valley(c)	(702)	*6,855*	—
*89024	Mesquite	(702)	12,631	1,871
89040	Moapa Valley (c)	(702)	*5,784*	3,444
89191	Nellis AFB (c)	(702)	*8,896*	8,377
*89030	North Las Vegas	(702)	158,748	47,849
*89041	Pahrump (c)	(775)	*24,631*	7,424
89109	Paradise (c)	(775)	*186,070*	124,682
*89501	Reno	(775)	197,963	134,230
89436	Spanish Springs (c)	(775)	*9,018*	—
*89431	Sparks	(775)	81,014	53,367
89815	Spring Creek (c)	(702)	*10,548*	5,866
—	Spring Valley (c)	(702)	*117,390*	51,726
89110	Sunrise Manor (c)	(702)	*156,120*	95,362
89433	Sun Valley (c)	(775)	*19,461*	11,391
89101	Winchester (c)	(702)	*26,958*	23,365

New Hampshire (603)

See introductory note.

ZIP	Place	2004	1990
03275	Allenstown	5,022	4,649
03031	*Amherst*	11,566	9,068
03811	*Atkinson*	6,638	5,188
03032	Auburn	5,037	4,085
03825	*Barrington*	8,071	6,164
03110	*Bedford*	20,480	12,563
03220	*Belmont*	7,230	5,796
03570	Berlin	10,484	11,824
03304	*Bow*	7,961	5,500
03743	Claremont	13,344	13,902
*03301	Concord	42,345	36,006
03818	*Conway*	9,093	7,940
03038	Derry (c)	22,661	20,446
03038	*Derry*	34,371	29,603
*03820	Dover	28,495	25,042
03824	Durham (c)	12,904	9,236
03824	*Durham*	13,080	11,818
03042	*Epping*	6,023	5,162
03833	Exeter (c)	9,759	9,556
03833	*Exeter*	14,709	12,481
03835	*Farmington*	6,296	5,739
03235	Franklin	8,683	8,304
03246	*Gilford*	7,436	5,867
03045	*Goffstown*	17,536	14,621
03841	*Hampstead*	8,700	6,732
*03842	Hampton (c)	9,126	7,989
*03842	*Hampton*	15,363	12,278
03755	Hanover Compact (c)	8,162	6,538
03755	*Hanover*	11,124	9,212
03244	*Hillsborough*	5,274	4,698
03049	*Hollis*	7,603	5,705
03106	*Hooksett*	13,064	9,002
03229	*Hopkinton*	5,602	4,806
03051	Hudson (c)	7,814	7,626
03051	*Hudson*	24,310	19,530
03452	*Jaffrey*	5,647	5,361
*03431	Keene	22,955	22,430
03848	*Kingston*	6,216	5,591
*03246	Laconia	17,133	15,743
*03766	Lebanon	12,655	12,183
03052	*Litchfield*	8,130	5,516
03561	*Littleton*	6,116	5,827
03053	Londonderry (c)	11,417	10,114
03053	*Londonderry*	24,406	19,781
*03103	Manchester	109,310	99,332
03253	*Meredith*	6,493	4,837
03054	*Merrimack*	26,577	22,156
03055	Milford (c)	8,293	8,015
03055	*Milford*	14,558	11,795
*03060	Nashua	87,411	79,662
03857	Newmarket (c)	5,124	4,917
03857	*Newmarket*	8,880	7,157
03773	*Newport*	6,472	6,110
03076	*Pelham*	12,310	9,408
03275	*Pembroke*	7,260	6,561
03458	*Peterborough*	6,069	5,239
03102	Pinardville (c)	5,779	4,654
03865	*Plaistow*	7,809	7,316
03264	*Plymouth*	6,225	5,811
*03801	Portsmouth	20,786	25,925
03077	*Raymond*	10,027	8,713
03461	*Rindge*	6,137	4,941
*03867	Rochester	29,757	26,630
03870	*Rye*	5,248	—
03079	*Salem*	29,399	25,746
03873	*Sandown*	5,641	—
03874	*Seabrook*	8,376	6,503
03878	Somersworth	11,736	11,249
03106	South Hooksett (c)	5,282	3,638
03885	*Stratham*	6,892	4,955
03275	Suncook (c)	5,362	5,214
03446	*Swanzey*	7,086	6,236
03281	*Weare*	8,542	6,193
03087	*Windham*	12,452	9,000
03894	*Wolfeboro*	6,572	4,807

New Jersey

Area code (551) overlays area code (201). Area code (848) overlays (732). Area code (862) overlays (973). See introductory note.

ZIP	Place	Area Code	2004	1990
*08201	Absecon	(609)	7,905	7,298
07401	Allendale	(201)	6,799	5,900
07712	Asbury Park	(732)	16,819	16,799
08034	Ashland (c)		*8,375*	—
*08401	Atlantic City	(609)	40,580	37,986
08106	Audubon	(856)	9,070	9,205
07001	Avenel (c)	(732)	*17,552*	15,504
—	Barclay-Kingston (c)		*10,728*	—
08007	Barrington	(856)	7,036	6,792
07002	Bayonne	(201)	60,748	61,464
08722	Beachwood	(732)	10,740	9,324
07109	Belleville (c)	(973)	*35,928*	34,213
*08031	Bellmawr	(856)	11,184	12,603
*07719	Belmar	(732)	6,033	5,877
07621	Bergenfield	(201)	26,210	24,458
07922	Berkeley Heights (c)	(908)	*13,407*	11,980
08009	Berlin	(856)	7,595	5,672
07924	Bernardsville	(908)	7,597	6,597
07403	Bloomingdale	(973)	7,699	7,530
07603	Bogota	(201)	8,208	7,824
07005	Boonton	(973)	8,468	8,343
08805	Bound Brook	(732)	10,174	9,487
08302	Bridgeton	(856)	22,727	18,942
08203	Brigantine	(609)	12,769	11,354
08015	Browns Mills (c)	(609)	*11,257*	11,429

ZIP	Place	Area Code	2004	1990
07828	Budd Lake (c)	(973)	*8,100*	7,272
08016	Burlington	(609)	9,833	9,835
07405	Butler	(973)	8,118	7,392
*07006	Caldwell	(973)	7,594	7,542
*08101	Camden	(856)	79,948	87,492
07072	Carlstadt	(201)	6,019	5,510
08069	Carney's Point (c)	(856)	*6,914*	8,443
07008	Carteret	(732)	21,523	19,025
07009	Cedar Grove (c)	(973)	*12,300*	12,053
07928	Chatham	(973)	8,428	8,007
08002	Cherry Hill Mall (c)	(856)	*13,238*	—
07066	Clark (c)	(732)/(908)	*14,597*	14,629
08312	Clayton	(856)	7,424	6,155
07010	Cliffside Park	(201)	23,012	20,393
*07015	Clifton	(973)	79,944	71,984
07624	Closter	(201)	8,623	8,094
08108	Collingswood	(856)	14,138	15,289
07067	Colonia (c)	(732)	*17,811*	18,238
07016	Cranford (c)	(908)	*22,578*	22,633
07626	Cresskill	(201)	8,212	7,558
08759	Crestwood Village (c)	(732)	*8,392*	8,030
08810	Dayton (c)	(732)	*6,235*	4,321
*07801	Dover	(973)	18,463	15,115
07628	Dumont	(201)	17,571	17,187
08812	Dunellen	(732)	6,995	6,528
08816	East Brunswick (c)	(732)	*46,756*	43,548
*07019	East Orange	(973)	68,930	73,552
07073	East Rutherford	(201)/(973)	8,754	7,902
*07724	Eatontown	(732)	14,139	13,800
08043	Echelon (c)	(856)	*10,440*	—
07020	Edgewater	(201)	9,358	5,001
*08818	Edison (c)	(732)/(908)	*97,687*	88,680
*07207	Elizabeth	(908)	124,724	110,002
07630	Emerson	(201)	7,339	6,930
*07631	Englewood	(201)	26,353	24,850
07632	Englewood Cliffs	(201)	5,655	5,634
08002	Erlton-Ellisburg (c)		*8,168*	—
08618	Ewing (c)	(609)	*35,707*	34,185
07004	Fairfield (Essex Co.) (c)	(973)	*7,063*	7,615
07704	Fair Haven	(732)	5,961	5,270
07410	Fair Lawn	(201)/(973)	31,613	30,548
07022	Fairview (Bergen Co.)	(201)	13,561	10,733
07023	Fanwood	(908)	7,255	7,115
08518	Florence-Roebling (c)	(609)	*8,200*	8,564
07932	Florham Park	(973)	12,556	8,521
08863	Fords (c)	(732)	*15,032*	14,392
08640	Fort Dix (c)	(609)	*7,464*	10,205
07024	Fort Lee	(201)	37,310	31,997
07416	Franklin (Sussex Co.)	(973)	5,233	4,977
07417	Franklin Lakes	(201)	11,260	9,873
07728	Freehold	(732)	11,527	10,742
07026	Garfield	(862)/(973)	29,833	26,727
08028	Glassboro	(856)	19,177	15,614
07028	Glen Ridge	(973)	7,123	7,076
07452	Glen Rock	(201)	11,525	10,883
*08030	Gloucester City	(856)	11,608	12,649
—	Greentree (c)		*11,536*	—
07093	Guttenberg	(201)	11,011	8,268
*07602	Hackensack	(201)	43,681	37,049
07840	Hackettstown	(908)	9,339	8,120
08033	Haddonfield	(856)	11,596	11,633
08035	Haddon Heights	(856)	7,453	7,860
*07508	Haledon	(973)	8,440	6,951
08037	Hammonton	(609)	13,280	12,208
07029	Harrison	(973)	14,164	13,425
07604	Hasbrouck Heights	(201)	11,679	11,488
*07506	Hawthorne	(973)	18,378	17,084
07422	Highland Lake (c)	(973)	*5,051*	4,550
08904	Highland Park	(732)	14,172	13,279
07732	Highlands	(732)	5,072	4,849
08520	Hightstown	(609)	5,326	5,126
07642	Hillsdale	(201)	10,138	9,750
07205	Hillside (c)	(908)/(973)	*21,747*	21,044
07030	Hoboken	(201)	40,175	33,397
08753	Holiday City-Berkeley (c)	(732)	*13,884*	14,293
07843	Hopatcong	(973)	16,035	15,586
07111	Irvington (c)	(973)	*60,695*	59,774
08830	Iselin (c)	(732)	*16,698*	16,141
08831	Jamesburg	(732)	6,524	5,294
*07303	Jersey City	(201)	239,079	228,517
07734	Keansburg	(732)	10,739	11,069
*07032	Kearny	(201)/(973)	39,496	34,874
08824	Kendall Park (c)	(908)	*9,006*	7,127
07033	Kenilworth	(908)	7,764	7,574
07735	Keyport	(732)	7,570	7,586
07405	Kinnelon	(973)	9,542	8,470
07871	Lake Mohawk (c)	(973)	*9,755*	8,930
08701	Lakewood (c)	(732)	*36,065*	26,095
08879	Laurence Harbor (c)	(732)	*6,227*	6,361
*08733	Leisure Village West-Pine Lake Park (c)	(732)	*11,085*	10,139
07605	Leonia	(201)	8,911	8,365
07035	Lincoln Park	(973)	10,894	10,978
07738	Lincroft (c)	(732)	*6,255*	6,193
07036	Linden	(732)/(908)	40,004	36,701
08021	Lindenwold	(856)	17,297	18,734
08221	Linwood	(609)	7,415	6,866
07424	Little Falls (c)	(973)	*10,855*	11,294
07643	Little Ferry	(201)	10,840	9,989
07739	Little Silver	(732)	6,191	5,721
07039	Livingston (c)	(973)	*27,391*	26,609
07644	Lodi	(201)/(973)	24,336	22,355
07740	Long Branch	(732)	31,526	28,658
07071	Lyndhurst (c)	(201)	*19,383*	18,262
08641	McGuire AFB (c)	(609)	*6,478*	7,580
07940	Madison	(973)	16,005	15,850
08859	Madison Park (c)	(732)	*6,929*	7,490
08736	Manasquan	(732)	6,286	5,369
08835	Manville	(908)	10,416	10,567
07040	Maplewood (c)	(973)	*23,868*	21,756
08402	Margate City	(609)	8,627	8,431
08053	Marlton (c)	(856)	*10,260*	10,228
07747	Matawan	(732)	8,919	9,239
07607	Maywood	(201)	9,505	9,536
07945	Mendham	(973)	5,160	4,890
08619	Mercerville-Hamilton Sq. (c)	(609)	*26,419*	26,873
08840	Metuchen	(732)	13,335	12,804
08846	Middlesex	(732)	13,967	13,055
07432	Midland Park	(201)	6,953	7,047
07041	Millburn (c)	(973)	*19,765*	18,630
08850	Milltown	(732)	7,148	6,968
08332	Millville	(856)	27,611	25,992
*07042	Montclair (c)	(973)	*38,977*	37,729
07645	Montvale	(201)	7,321	6,946
08057	Moorestown-Lenola (c)	(856)	*13,860*	13,242
07751	Morganville (c)	(732)	*11,255*	—
07950	Morris Plains	(973)	5,563	5,219
*07960	Morristown	(973)	18,842	16,189
07092	Mountainside	(908)	6,660	6,657
07856	Mount Arlington	(973)	5,139	3,630
08087	Mystic Islands (c)	(609)	*8,694*	7,400
07753	Neptune City	(732)	5,373	4,997
*07102	Newark	(973)	280,451	275,221
*08901	New Brunswick	(732)	50,010	41,711
07646	New Milford	(201)	16,397	15,990
07974	New Providence	(908)	11,981	11,439
07860	Newton	(973)	8,382	7,521
07031	North Arlington	(201)	15,254	13,790
08902	North Brunswick Twp. (c)	(732)	*36,287*	31,287
07006	North Caldwell	(973)	7,354	6,706
08225	Northfield	(609)	8,054	7,305
*07508	North Haledon	(973)	8,812	7,987
*07060	North Plainfield	(908)	21,135	18,820
07648	Norwood	(201)	6,223	4,858
07110	Nutley (c)	(973)	*27,362*	27,099
07436	Oakland	(201)	13,707	11,997
*08050	Ocean Acres (c)	(609)	*13,155*	5,587
08226	Ocean City	(609)	15,506	15,512
07757	Oceanport	(732)	5,832	6,146
08857	Old Bridge (c)	(732)	*22,833*	22,151
07675	Old Tappan	(201)	5,869	4,254
07649	Oradell	(201)	8,041	8,024
*07051	Orange (c)	(973)	*32,868*	29,925
07650	Palisades Park	(201)	18,301	14,536
08065	Palmyra	(856)	7,672	7,056
*07652	Paramus	(201)	26,624	25,004
07656	Park Ridge	(201)	8,970	8,102
07055	Passaic	(973)	68,662	58,041
*07510	Paterson	(973)	150,869	140,891
08066	Paulsboro	(856)	6,110	6,577
*08110	Pennsauken (c)	(856)	*35,737*	34,738
08070	Pennsville (c)	(856)	*11,657*	12,218
*08861	Perth Amboy	(732)	48,823	41,967
08865	Phillipsburg	(908)	15,070	15,757
08021	Pine Hill	(856)	11,221	9,854
08071	Pitman	(856)	9,271	9,365
*07061	Plainfield	(908)	47,987	46,577
*08232	Pleasantville	(609)	19,113	16,027
08742	Point Pleasant	(732)	19,821	18,177
08742	Point Pleasant Beach	(732)	5,408	5,112
07442	Pompton Lakes	(973)	11,389	10,539
*08540	Princeton	(609)	13,590	12,016
—	Princeton Meadows (c)	(609)	*13,436*	—
*07508	Prospect Park	(973)	5,802	5,053
07065	Rahway	(732)	27,578	25,325
08057	Ramblewood (c)	(856)	*6,003*	6,181
07446	Ramsey	(201)	14,601	13,228
—	Ramtown (c)	(732)	*5,932*	—
*08869	Raritan	(908)	6,401	5,798
*07701	Red Bank	(732)	11,940	10,636
07657	Ridgefield	(201)	11,005	9,996
07660	Ridgefield Park	(201)	12,822	12,454
*07451	Ridgewood	(201)/(973)	24,916	24,152
07456	Ringwood	(973)	12,769	12,623
07661	River Edge	(201)	10,966	10,603
07866	Rockaway	(973)	6,437	6,243
07068	Roseland	(973)	5,341	4,847
07203	Roselle	(908)	21,415	20,314
07204	Roselle Park	(908)	13,296	12,805
07760	Rumson	(732)	7,271	6,701
08078	Runnemede	(856)	8,511	9,042
07070	Rutherford	(201)	18,084	17,790
08079	Salem	(856)	5,787	6,883
*08872	Sayreville	(732)	42,663	34,998
*07094	Secaucus	(201)	15,663	14,061
08083	Somerdale	(856)	5,162	5,440
08244	Somers Point	(609)	11,731	11,216
08876	Somerville	(908)	12,434	11,632

ZIP	Place	Area Code	2004	1990
08879	South Amboy	(732)	8,008	7,851
07080	South Plainfield	(732)/(908)	23,034	20,489
*08882	South River	(732)	16,025	13,692
08884	Spotswood	(732)	8,215	7,983
07762	Spring Lake Heights	(732)	5,190	5,341
08084	Stratford	(856)	7,201	7,614
*07901	Summit	(908)	21,267	19,757
07670	Tenafly	(201)	14,214	13,326
*07724	Tinton Falls	(732)	16,206	12,361
*07512	Totowa	(973)	10,360	10,177
*08650	Trenton	(609)	85,379	88,675
07083	Union (Union Co.) (c)	(908)	66,167	50,024
07735	Union Beach	(732)	6,750	6,156
*07087	Union City	(201)	66,167	58,012
07458	Upper Saddle River	(201)	8,362	7,198
08406	Ventnor City	(609)	12,831	11,005
*08360	Vineland	(856)	58,009	54,780
07463	Waldwick	(201)	9,664	9,757
07057	Wallington	(201)/(973)	11,558	10,828
07465	Wanaque	(201)/(973)	10,440	9,711
07882	Washington	(908)	6,885	6,474
07069	Watchung	(908)	5,789	5,110
*07091	Westfield	(732)/(908)	30,062	28,870
07764	West Long Branch	(732)	8,241	7,690
07093	West New York	(201)	46,231	38,125
*07675	Westwood	(201)	11,051	10,446
07885	Wharton	(973)	6,239	5,405
08260	Wildwood	(609)	5,211	4,484
*08096	Woodbury	(856)	10,437	10,904
07677	Woodcliff Lake	(201)	5,886	5,303
07075	Wood-Ridge	(201)/(973)	7,657	7,506

New Mexico (505)

ZIP	Place	2004	1990
*88310	Alamogordo	36,211	27,596
*87101	Albuquerque	484,246	384,915
88021	Anthony (c)	*7,904*	5,160
*88210	Artesia	10,553	10,610
87410	Aztec	6,906	5,480
87002	Belen	6,946	6,547
87004	Bernalillo	6,956	5,864
87413	Bloomfield	7,240	5,214
*88220	Carlsbad	25,417	24,952
88021	Chaparral (c)	*6,117*	2,962
*88101	Clovis	33,063	30,954
87048	Corrales	7,616	5,453
*88030	Deming	14,647	11,422
—	El Cerro-Monterey Park (c)	*5,483*	—
—	Eldorado at Santa Fe (c)	*5,799*	2,260
*87532	Espanola	9,709	8,389
*87401	Farmington	42,421	33,997
*87301	Gallup	19,715	19,157
87020	Grants	9,041	8,626
*88240	Hobbs	28,708	29,121
87417	Kirtland (c)	*6,190*	3,552
*88001	Las Cruces	79,524	62,360
*87701	Las Vegas	14,031	14,753
87544	Los Alamos (c)	*11,909*	11,455
87002	Los Chaves (c)	*5,033*	3,872
87031	Los Lunas	11,748	6,013
*87107	Los Ranchos de Albuquerque	5,495	5,075
88260	Lovington	9,553	9,322
87107	North Valley (c)	*11,923*	12,507
*88130	Portales	11,214	10,690
87740	Raton	7,036	7,372
*87124	Rio Rancho	61,953	32,512
*88201	Roswell	45,074	44,260
*88345	Ruidoso	8,691	4,600
*87501	Santa Fe	68,041	56,537
87420	Shiprock c)	*8,156*	7,687
*88061	Silver City	9,911	10,683
87801	Socorro	8,724	8,159
87105	South Valley (c)	*39,060*	35,701
*88063	Sunland Park	13,934	8,179
87571	Taos	5,062	4,065
87901	Truth or Consequences	7,163	6,221
*88401	Tucumcari	5,476	6,827
87544	White Rock (c)	*6,045*	6,192
87327	Zuni Pueblo (c)	*6,367*	5,857

New York

Area code (347) overlays area code (718). Area codes (646) and (917) overlay (212). See introductory note.

ZIP	Place	Area Code	2004	1990
*10901	Airmont	(845)	8,619	7,674
*12201	Albany	(518)	94,226	100,031
11507	Albertson (c)	(516)	*5,200*	5,166
14411	Albion	(585)	5,836	5,863
*11701	Amityville	(516)/(631)	9,557	9,286
12010	Amsterdam	(518)	17,928	20,714
12603	Arlington (c)	(845)	*12,481*	11,948
*13021	Auburn	(315)	28,080	31,258
11702	Babylon	(631)	12,736	12,249
11510	Baldwin (c)	(516)	*23,455*	22,719
11510	Baldwin Harbor (c)	(516)	*8,147*	7,899
13027	Baldwinsville	(315)	7,173	6,591
12020	Ballston Spa	(518)	5,587	5,194
*14020	Batavia	(585)	15,830	16,310
14810	Bath	(607)	5,622	5,801
11705	Bayport (c)	(631)	*8,662*	7,702
11706	Bay Shore (c)	(631)	*23,852*	21,279
11709	Bayville	(516)	7,154	7,193
12508	Beacon	(845)	14,762	13,243
11710	Bellmore (c)	(516)	*16,441*	16,438
11714	Bethpage (c)	(516)	*16,543*	15,761
*13902	Binghamton	(607)	45,864	53,008
10913	Blauvelt (c)	(845)	*5,207*	4,838
11716	Bohemia (c)	(631)	*9,871*	9,556
11717	Brentwood (c)	(631)	*53,917*	45,218
10510	Briarcliff Manor	(914)	7,900	7,070
14610	Brighton (c)	(585)	*35,584*	34,455
14420	Brockport	(585)	8,136	8,749
10708	Bronxville	(914)	6,503	6,028
*14240	Buffalo	(716)	282,864	328,175
11933	Calverton (c)	(631)	*5,704*	4,759
*14424	Canandaigua	(585)	11,363	10,725
13617	Canton	(315)	6,101	6,379
11514	Carle Place (c)	(516)	*5,247*	5,107
10512	Carmel Hamlet (c)	(845)	*5,650*	4,800
11516	Cedarhurst	(516)	6,113	5,716
11720	Centereach (c)	(631)	*27,285*	26,720
11934	Center Moriches (c)	(631)	*6,655*	5,987
11721	Centerport (c)	(631)	*5,446*	5,333
11722	Central Islip (c)	(516)	*31,950*	26,028
10514	Chappaqua (c)	(914)	*9,468*	—
14225	Cheektowaga (c)	(716)	*79,988*	84,387
*10977	Chestnut Ridge	(845)	7,891	7,517
12047	Cohoes	(518)	15,211	16,825
12205	Colonie	(518)	8,102	8,019
11725	Commack (c)	(631)	*36,367*	36,124
10920	Congers (c)	(845)	*8,303*	8,003
11726	Copiague (c)	(631)	*21,922*	20,769
11727	Coram (c)	(631)	*34,923*	30,111
*14830	Corning	(607)	10,608	11,938
13045	Cortland	(607)	18,713	19,801
*10520	Croton-on-Hudson	(914)	7,862	7,018
11729	Deer Park (c)	(631)	*28,316*	28,840
12054	Delmar (c)	(518)	*8,292*	8,360
14043	Depew	(716)	16,003	17,673
11746	Dix Hills (c)	(631)	*26,024*	25,849
10522	Dobbs Ferry	(914)	16,003	9,940
*14048	Dunkirk	(716)	12,627	13,989
14052	East Aurora	(585)/(716)	6,442	6,647
10709	Eastchester (c)	(914)	*18,564*	18,537
12302	East Glenville (c)	(518)	*6,064*	6,518
*11576	East Hills	(516)	6,797	6,746
11730	East Islip (c)	(631)	*14,078*	14,325
11758	East Massapequa (c)	(516)	*19,565*	19,550
11554	East Meadow (c)	(516)	*37,461*	36,909
11731	East Northport (c)	(631)	*20,845*	20,411
11772	East Patchogue (c)	(631)	*20,824*	20,195
14445	East Rochester	(585)	6,441	6,932
11518	East Rockaway	(516)	10,327	10,152
11786	East Shoreham (c)	(631)	*5,809*	5,461
*14901	Elmira	(607)	30,073	33,724
11003	Elmont (c)	(516)	*32,657*	28,612
11731	Elwood (c)	(631)	*10,916*	10,916
*13760	Endicott	(607)	12,749	13,531
13762	Endwell (c)	(607)	*11,706*	12,602
13219	Fairmount (c)	(315)	*10,795*	12,266
14450	Fairport	(585)	5,640	5,943
—	Fairview (c)	(845)	*5,421*	4,811
*11735	Farmingdale	(516)	8,692	8,022
*11001	Floral Park	(516)	15,850	15,947
13603	Fort Drum(c)	(315)	*12,123*	11,578
11768	Fort Salonga (c)	(631)	*9,634*	9,176
11010	Franklin Square (c)	(516)	*29,342*	28,205
14063	Fredonia	(716)	10,705	10,436
11520	Freeport	(516)	43,726	39,894
13069	Fulton	(315)	11,643	12,929
*11530	Garden City	(516)	21,848	21,675
11040	Garden City Park (c)	(516)	*7,554*	7,437
14624	Gates-North Gates (c)	(585)	*15,138*	14,995
14454	Geneseo	(585)	7,846	7,187
14456	Geneva	(315)	13,558	14,143
11542	Glen Cove	(516)	26,787	24,149
12801	Glens Falls	(518)	14,166	15,023
12801	Glens Falls North (c)	(518)	*8,061*	7,978
12078	Gloversville	(518)	15,277	16,656
10924	Goshen	(845)	5,436	5,255
*11021	Great Neck	(516)	9,615	8,745
11020	Great Neck Plaza	(516)	6,979	5,897
14616	Greece (c)	(585)	*14,614*	15,632
11740	Greenlawn (c)	(631)	*13,286*	13,208
*10583	Greenville (Westchester Co.) (c)	(914)	*8,648*	9,528
14075	Hamburg	(716)	9,741	10,442
11946	Hampton Bays (c)	(631)	*12,236*	7,893
10528	Harrison	(914)	25,553	23,308
10530	Hartsdale (c)	(914)	*9,830*	9,587
10706	Hastings-on-Hudson	(914)	7,757	8,000
*11788	Hauppauge (c)	(631)	*20,100*	19,750
10927	Haverstraw	(845)	10,136	9,438
10532	Hawthorne (c)	(845)	*5,083*	4,764
*11551	Hempstead	(516)	53,145	45,982
13350	Herkimer	(315)	7,295	7,945
11557	Hewlett (c)	(516)	*7,060*	6,620
*11802	Hicksville (c)	(516)	*41,260*	40,174
12528	Highland (c)	(845)	*5,060*	4,492
10977	Hillcrest (c)	(845)	*7,106*	6,447

ZIP	Place	Area Code	2004	1990
14468	Hilton	(585)	5,960	5,216
14843	Hornell	(607)	8,800	9,877
*14845	Horseheads	(607)	6,425	6,802
12534	Hudson	(518)	7,220	8,034
12839	Hudson Falls	(518)	6,909	7,651
11743	Huntington (c)	(631)	18,403	18,243
11746	Huntington Station (c)	(631)	29,910	28,247
13357	Ilion	(315)	8,374	8,888
11096	Inwood (c)	(516)	9,325	7,767
14617	Irondequoit (c)	(585)	52,354	52,322
10533	Irvington	(914)	6,655	6,348
11751	Islip (c)	(631)	20,575	18,924
11752	Islip Terrace (c)	(631)	5,641	5,530
*14850	Ithaca	(607)	29,952	29,541
*14702	Jamestown	(716)	30,695	34,681
10535	Jefferson Valley-Yorktown (c)	(914)	14,891	14,118
11753	Jericho (c)	(516)	13,045	13,141
13790	Johnson City	(607)	15,084	16,578
12095	Johnstown	(518)	8,557	9,058
*14217	Kenmore	(716)	15,749	17,180
11754	Kings Park (c)	(631)	16,146	17,773
11024	Kings Point	(516)	5,200	4,843
*12401	Kingston	(845)	23,219	23,095
10950	Kiryas Joel	(845)	17,651	7,437
14218	Lackawanna	(716)	18,394	20,585
10512	Lake Carmel (c)	(845)	8,663	8,489
11755	Lake Grove	(631)	10,646	9,612
10547	Lake Mohegan (c)	(914)	5,979	—
11779	Lake Ronkonkoma (c)	(631)	19,701	18,997
11552	Lakeview (c)	(516)	5,607	5,476
*14086	Lancaster	(716)	11,594	11,940
10538	Larchmont	(914)	6,527	6,181
11559	Lawrence	(516)	6,541	6,513
11756	Levittown (c)	(516)	53,067	53,286
11757	Lindenhurst	(631)	28,426	26,879
13365	Little Falls	(315)	5,062	5,829
*14094	Lockport	(716)	21,504	24,426
11561	Long Beach	(516)	35,553	33,510
11563	Lynbrook	(516)	19,795	19,208
12953	Malone	(518)	5,958	6,777
11565	Malverne	(516)	8,866	9,054
10543	Mamaroneck	(914)	18,463	17,325
11030	Manhasset (c)	(516)	8,362	7,718
11050	Manorhaven	(516)	6,329	5,672
11949	Manorville (c)	(631)	11,131	6,198
11758	Massapequa (c)	(516)	22,652	22,018
11762	Massapequa Park	(516)	17,400	18,044
13662	Massena	(315)	10,911	11,716
11950	Mastic (c)	(631)	15,436	13,778
11951	Mastic Beach (c)	(631)	11,543	10,293
13211	Mattydale (c)	(315)	6,367	6,418
—	Mechanicstown (c)	(845)	6,061	—
12118	Mechanicville	(518)	5,019	5,249
11763	Medford (c)	(631)	21,985	21,274
14103	Medina	(585)/(716)	6,312	6,686
11747	Melville (c)	(631)	14,533	12,586
11566	Merrick (c)	(516)	22,764	23,042
11953	Middle Island (c)	(631)	9,702	7,848
*10940	Middletown	(845)	26,117	24,160
11764	Miller Place (c)	(631)	10,580	9,315
11501	Mineola	(516)	19,129	19,005
*10950	Monroe	(845)	8,129	6,672
10952	Monsey (c)	(845)	14,504	13,986
*12701	Monticello	(845)	6,565	6,597
10970	Mount Ivy (c)	(845)	6,536	6,013
10549	Mount Kisco	(914)	10,057	9,108
11766	Mount Sinai (c)	(631)	8,734	8,023
*10551	Mount Vernon	(914)	68,321	67,153
12590	Myers Corner (c)	(845)	5,546	5,599
10954	Nanuet (c)	(845)	16,707	14,065
11767	Nesconset (c)	(631)	11,992	10,712
14513	Newark	(315)	9,481	9,849
*12550	Newburgh	(845)	28,551	26,454
11590	New Cassel (c)	(516)	13,298	10,257
10956	New City (c)	(845)	34,038	33,673
*11040	New Hyde Park	(516)	9,518	9,728
12561	New Paltz	(845)	6,285	5,470
*10802	New Rochelle	(914)	72,985	67,265
10977	New Square	(845)	5,920	2,623
*12550	New Windsor (c)	(845)	9,077	8,898
*10001	New York	(212)/(718)	8,104,079	7,322,564
*14302	Niagara Falls	(716)	53,708	61,840
11701	North Amityville (c)	(631)	16,572	13,849
11703	North Babylon (c)	(631)	17,877	18,081
11706	North Bay Shore (c)	(631)	14,992	12,799
11710	North Bellmore (c)	(516)	20,079	19,707
11713	North Bellport (c)	(631)	9,007	8,182
11757	North Lindenhurst (c)	(631)	11,767	10,563
11758	North Massapequa (c)	(516)	19,152	19,365
11566	North Merrick (c)	(516)	11,844	12,113
11040	North New Hyde Park (c)	(516)	14,542	14,359
11772	North Patchogue (c)	(631)	7,825	7,374
11768	Northport	(631)	7,664	7,572
13212	North Syracuse	(315)	6,793	7,363
14120	North Tonawanda	(716)	32,188	34,989
11580	North Valley Stream (c)	(516)	15,789	14,574
11793	North Wantagh (c)	(516)	12,156	12,276
13815	Norwich	(607)	7,296	7,613
10960	Nyack	(845)	6,734	6,558
11769	Oakdale (c)	(631)	8,075	7,875
11572	Oceanside (c)	(516)	32,733	32,423
13669	Ogdensburg	(315)	11,486	13,521
11804	Old Bethpage (c)	(516)	5,400	5,610
14760	Olean	(585)/(716)	14,972	16,946
13421	Oneida	(315)	10,977	10,850
13820	Oneonta	(607)	13,099	13,954
12550	Orange Lake (c)	(845)	6,085	5,196
10562	Ossining	(914)	23,656	22,582
13126	Oswego	(315)	18,407	19,195
11771	Oyster Bay (c)	(516)	6,826	6,687
11772	Patchogue	(631)	12,026	11,060
10965	Pearl River (c)	(845)	15,553	15,314
10566	Peekskill	(914)	23,782	19,536
10803	Pelham	(914)	6,403	5,443
10803	Pelham Manor	(914)	5,434	6,413
14527	Penn Yan	(315)	5,119	5,248
11714	Plainedge (c)	(516)	9,195	8,739
11803	Plainview (c)	(516)	25,637	26,207
*12901	Plattsburgh	(518)	19,218	21,255
*10570	Pleasantville	(914)	7,167	6,592
10573	Port Chester	(914)	27,902	24,728
11777	Port Jefferson	(631)	7,971	7,455
11776	Port Jefferson Station (c)	(631)	7,527	7,232
*12771	Port Jervis	(845)	9,161	9,060
11050	Port Washington (c)	(516)	15,215	15,387
*13676	Potsdam	(315)	9,697	10,251
*12601	Poughkeepsie	(845)	30,348	28,844
12144	Rensselaer	(518)	7,784	8,255
11961	Ridge (c)	(631)	13,380	11,734
11901	Riverhead (c)	(631)	10,513	8,814
*14692	Rochester	(585)	212,481	230,356
*11571	Rockville Centre	(516)	24,392	24,727
11778	Rocky Point (c)	(631)	10,185	8,596
*13440	Rome	(315)	34,551	44,350
11779	Ronkonkoma (c)	(631)	20,029	20,391
11575	Roosevelt (c)	(516)	15,854	15,030
11577	Roslyn Heights (c)	(516)	6,295	6,405
12303	Rotterdam (c)	(518)	20,536	21,228
10580	Rye	(914)	15,067	14,936
10573	Rye Brook	(914)	9,395	7,765
11780	Saint James (c)	(631)	13,268	12,703
14779	Salamanca	(716)	5,926	6,566
13454	Salisbury (c)	(315)	12,341	12,226
12866	Saratoga Springs	(518)	27,686	25,001
11782	Sayville (c)	(631)	16,735	16,550
10583	Scarsdale	(914)	17,888	16,987
*12301	Schenectady	(518)	61,125	65,566
10940	Scotchtown (c)	(845)	8,954	8,765
12302	Scotia	(518)	7,882	7,359
11579	Sea Cliff	(516)	5,032	5,054
11783	Seaford (c)	(516)	15,791	15,597
11507	Searingtown (c)	(516)	5,034	5,020
11784	Selden (c)	(631)	21,861	20,608
13148	Seneca Falls	(315)	6,897	7,370
10591	Sleepy Hollow[1]	(914)	9,903	8,152
11787	Smithtown (c)	(631)	26,901	25,638
13209	Solvay	(315)	6,676	6,717
11789	Sound Beach (c)	(631)	9,807	9,102
11735	South Farmingdale (c)	(516)	15,061	15,377
14850	South Hill (c)	(607)	6,003	5,423
11746	South Huntington (c)	(631)	9,465	9,624
14094	South Lockport (c)	(716)	8,552	7,112
11971	Southold (c)	(631)	5,465	5,192
14904	Southport (c)	(607)	7,396	7,753
11581	South Valley Stream (c)	(516)	5,638	5,328
10977	Spring Valley	(845)	25,542	21,802
*11790	Stony Brook (c)	(631)	13,727	13,726
10980	Stony Point (c)	(845)	11,744	10,587
*10901	Suffern	(845)	10,984	11,055
11791	Syosset (c)	(516)	18,544	18,967
*13220	Syracuse	(315)	143,101	163,860
10983	Tappan (c)	(845)	6,757	6,867
10591	Tarrytown	(914)	11,402	10,739
11776	Terryville (c)	(631)	10,589	10,275
10594	Thornwood (c)	(914)	5,980	7,025
*14150	Tonawanda	(716)	15,515	17,284
*12180	Troy	(518)	48,162	54,269
10707	Tuckahoe	(914)	6,257	6,302
11553	Uniondale (c)	(516)	23,011	20,328
*13504	Utica	(315)	59,684	68,637
10595	Valhalla (c)	(914)	5,379	—
10989	Valley Cottage (c)	(845)	9,269	9,007
*11582	Valley Stream	(516)	36,131	33,946
—	Viola (c)		5,931	4,504
11792	Wading River (c)	(631)	6,668	5,317
12586	Walden	(845)	6,762	5,836
12590	Wappingers Falls	(845)	5,032	4,605
11793	Wantagh (c)	(516)	18,971	18,567
10990	Warwick	(845)	6,590	5,984
10992	Washingtonville	(845)	6,271	4,906
13165	Waterloo	(315)	5,142	5,116
*13601	Watertown	(315)	26,240	29,429
12189	Watervliet	(518)	9,992	11,061
14580	Webster	(585)	5,149	5,464
10952	Wesley Hills	(845)	5,064	4,308
*11704	West Babylon (c)	(631)	43,452	42,410
*11590	Westbury	(516)	14,259	13,060
14905	West Elmira (c)	(607)	5,136	5,218
12801	West Glens Falls (c)	(518)	6,721	5,964
10993	West Haverstraw	(845)	10,314	9,183

ZIP	Place	Area Code	2004	1990
11743	West Hills (c)	(631)	*5,607*	5,849
11795	West Islip (c)	(631)	*28,907*	28,419
12203	Westmere (c)	(518)	*7,188*	6,750
*10996	West Point (c)	(845)	*7,138*	8,024
11796	West Sayville (c)	(631)	*5,003*	4,680
14224	West Seneca (c)	(716)	*45,943*	47,866
13219	Westvale (c)	(315)	*5,166*	5,952
11798	Wheatley Heights (c)	(631)	*5,013*	5,027
*10602	White Plains	(914)	56,509	48,718
*14231	Williamsville	(716)	5,377	5,583
11596	Williston Park	(516)	7,173	7,516
11797	Woodbury (c)	(516)	*9,010*	8,008
11598	Woodmere (c)	(516)	*16,447*	15,578
11798	Wyandach (c)	(631)	*10,546*	8,950
11980	Yaphank (c)	(631)	*5,025*	4,637
*10702	Yonkers	(914)	197,126	188,082
10598	Yorktown Heights (c)	(914)	*7,972*	7,690

(1) North Tarrytown changed its name to Sleepy Hollow on Dec. 12, 1996.

North Carolina

Area code (980) overlays area code (704). See introductory note.

ZIP	Place	Area Code	2004	1990
*28001	Albemarle	(704)	15,390	14,940
*27502	Apex	(919)	27,509	4,789
27263	Archdale	(336)	9,272	6,975
*27203	Asheboro	(336)	23,215	16,362
*28802	Asheville	(828)	70,400	63,379
28012	Belmont	(704)	8,786	8,434
28016	Bessemer City	(704)	5,120	4,698
28711	Black Mountain	(828)	7,598	7,156
*28607	Boone	(828)	13,286	12,949
28712	Brevard	(828)	6,650	5,452
*27215	Burlington	(336)	46,645	39,498
27509	Butner (c)	(919)	5,192	4,679
28428	Carolina Beach	(910)	16,429	4,002
27510	Carrboro	(919)	101,265	12,134
*27511	Cary	(919)	49,368	44,394
*27514	Chapel Hill	(919)	594,359	38,719
*28204	Charlotte	(704)	5,430	419,558
28021	Cherryville	(704)	12,173	4,756
*27520	Clayton	(919)	15,390	4,756
27012	Clemmons	(336)	16,276	5,982
*28328	Clinton	(910)	8,695	8,385
*28025	Concord	(704)	59,960	29,591
28613	Conover	(828)	6,982	5,311
28031	Cornelius	(704)	17,875	2,581
*28036	Davidson	(704)	8,343	4,046
*28334	Dunn	(910)	9,790	9,258
*27701	Durham	(919)	201,726	138,894
*27288	Eden	(336)	15,754	15,238
27932	Edenton	(252)	5,031	5,268
*27909	Elizabeth City	(252)	17,811	16,087
27244	Elon	(336)	7,077	4,394
*28302	Fayetteville	(910)	125,241	75,850
28043	Forest City	(828)	7,314	7,475
*28307	Fort Bragg (c)	(910)	*29,183*	34,744
27526	Fuquay-Varina	(919)	11,110	4,447
27529	Garner	(919)	21,772	14,716
*28052	Gastonia	(704)	68,292	54,725
*27530	Goldsboro	(919)	38,774	40,736
27253	Graham	(336)	13,494	10,368
*27420	Greensboro	(336)	231,543	185,125
*27834	Greenville	(252)	68,687	46,274
*28540	Half Moon (c)	(910)	*6,645*	6,306
28345	Hamlet	(910)	5,834	6,722
*28532	Havelock	(252)	22,369	20,300
*27536	Henderson	(252)	16,243	15,655
*28739	Hendersonville	(828)	11,232	7,284
*28603	Hickory	(828)	40,112	28,474
*27260	High Point	(336)	92,857	69,428
27278	Hillsborough	(919)	5,302	4,263
27540	Holly Springs	(919)	13,740	1,203
28348	Hope Mills	(910)	12,529	8,272
*28070	Huntersville	(704)	34,332	3,014
28079	Indian Trail	(704)	15,610	1,942
*28540	Jacksonville	(910)	72,335	78,031
—	James City (c)	(252)	*5,420*	4,279
*28081	Kannapolis	(704)	38,547	31,592
*27284	Kernersville	(336)	20,486	11,860
27948	Kill Devil Hills	(252)	6,425	4,238
27021	King	(336)	6,256	4,059
—	Kings Grant (c)	—	*7,738*	—
28086	Kings Mountain	(704)	10,634	8,768
*28502	Kinston	(252)	22,917	25,295
27545	Knightdale	(919)	6,137	1,884
*28352	Laurinburg	(910)	15,792	16,131
*28645	Lenoir	(828)	17,943	16,337
27023	Lewisville	(336)	9,379	6,433
*27292	Lexington	(336)	20,472	16,583
*28092	Lincolnton	(704)	10,194	6,955
*28358	Lumberton	(910)	21,314	18,656
28403	Masonboro (c)	(910)	*11,812*	7,010
*28105	Matthews	(704)	23,897	13,756
27302	Mebane	(919)	8,760	4,754
—	Mills River	(828)	5,871	—
28227	Mint Hill	(704)	17,480	13,637
*28110	Monroe	(704)	28,422	18,623
*28115	Mooresville	(704)	20,122	9,563
28557	Morehead City	(252)	8,485	6,473
*28655	Morganton	(828)	17,176	15,085
27560	Morrisville	(919)	11,595	1,022
*27030	Mount Airy	(336)	8,420	7,156
28120	Mount Holly	(704)	9,639	7,710
—	Murraysville (c)	—	*7,279*	—
—	Myrtle Grove (c)	—	*7,125*	4,275
*28562	New Bern	(252)	23,368	20,728
28658	Newton	(828)	12,881	11,134
*28465	Oak Island	(910)	7,281	—
—	Ogden (c)	—	*5,481*	3,228
27565	Oxford	(919)	8,506	7,965
*28374	Pinehurst	(910)	10,998	5,825
28399	Piney Green (c)	(910)	*11,658*	8,999
*27611	Raleigh	(919)	326,653	218,859
*27320	Reidsville	(336)	14,780	14,085
27870	Roanoke Rapids	(252)	16,397	15,722
*28379	Rockingham	(910)	9,323	9,399
*27801	Rocky Mount	(252)	56,351	53,078
*27573	Roxboro	(336)	8,760	7,332
28704	Royal Pines (c)	—	*5,334*	4,418
28601	Saint Stephens (c)	(828)	*9,439*	8,734
*28144	Salisbury	(704)	26,519	23,626
*27330	Sanford	(919)	23,469	18,881
27576	Selma	(919)	6,502	4,600
*28150	Shelby	(704)	21,275	15,460
27344	Siler City	(919)	8,078	4,808
—	Silver Lake (c)	—	*5,788*	4,071
27577	Smithfield	(919)	11,702	10,180
*28387	Southern Pines	(910)	11,556	9,213
28052	South Gastonia (c)	(704)	*5,433*	5,487
28390	Spring Lake	(910)	8,199	7,552
*28677	Statesville	(704)	24,489	20,647
27358	Summerfield	(336)	7,124	2,051
27886	Tarboro	(252)	10,583	11,037
*27360	Thomasville	(336)	25,752	15,915
27370	Trinity	(336)	6,831	5,469
28110	Unionville	(704)	6,053	—
*27587	Wake Forest	(919)	17,390	5,832
27889	Washington	(252)	9,764	9,160
*28786	Waynesville	(828)	9,415	7,282
28104	Weddington	(704)	7,982	3,803
28472	Whiteville	(910)	5,150	5,340
27892	Williamston	(252)	5,678	5,870
*28402	Wilmington	(910)	93,292	55,530
*27893	Wilson	(252)	46,507	38,400
*27102	Winston-Salem	(336)	191,523	162,292

North Dakota (701)

ZIP	Place	2004	1990
*58501	Bismarck	56,619	49,272
58301	Devils Lake	6,842	7,782
*58601	Dickinson	15,686	16,097
*58102	Fargo	91,048	74,084
*58201	Grand Forks	48,984	49,417
*58401	Jamestown	14,925	15,571
58554	Mandan	16,969	15,177
*58701	Minot	35,149	34,544
*58701	Minot AFB (c)	*7,599*	9,095
58072	Valley City	6,446	7,163
*58075	Wahpeton	8,411	8,751
58078	West Fargo	17,581	12,287
*58801	Williston	12,191	13,136

Ohio

Area code (234) overlays area code (330). Area code (567) overlays (419). See introductory note.

ZIP	Place	Area Code	2004	1990
45810	Ada	(419)	5,882	5,428
*44309	Akron	(330)	212,179	223,019
44601	Alliance	(330)	23,268	23,376
44001	Amherst	(440)	11,805	10,332
44805	Ashland	(419)	21,627	20,079
*44004	Ashtabula	(440)	20,353	21,633
45701	Athens	(740)	21,824	21,265
44202	Aurora	(330)	14,357	9,192
44515	Austintown (c)	(330)	*31,627*	32,371
44011	Avon	(440)	14,880	7,337
44012	Avon Lake	(440)	20,233	15,066
44203	Barberton	(330)	27,362	27,623
44140	Bay Village	(440)	15,439	17,000
44122	Beachwood	(216)	11,680	10,644
45434	Beavercreek	(937)	39,421	33,626
—	Beckett Ridge (c)	—	*8,663*	4,505
44146	Bedford	(216)/(440)	13,583	14,822
*44146	Bedford Heights	(216)/(440)	11,015	12,131
45305	Bellbrook	(937)	7,010	6,511
43311	Bellefontaine	(937)	13,034	12,126
44811	Bellevue	(419)	8,091	8,157
45714	Belpre	(740)	6,585	6,796
44017	Berea	(440)	18,276	19,051
43209	Bexley	(614)	12,411	13,088
43004	Blacklick Estates (c)	(614)	*9,518*	10,080
*45242	Blue Ash	(513)	11,917	11,923
*44513	Boardman (c)	(330)	29,454	38,596
44513	Boardman (c)	(330)	*37,215*	38,596
*43402	Bowling Green	(419)	29,454	28,303

ZIP	Place	Area Code	2004	1990
44141	Brecksville	(440)	13,377	11,818
45211	Bridgetown North (c)	(513)	20,296	11,748
45211	Bridgetown North (c)	(513)	*12,569*	11,748
44147	Broadview Heights	(440)	13,377	12,219
44144	Brooklyn	(216)	29,454	11,706
44142	Brook Park	(216)/(440)	20,296	22,865
45309	Brookville	(937)	5,305	4,621
44212	Brunswick	(330)	34,929	28,218
43506	Bryan	(419)	8,389	8,348
44820	Bucyrus	(419)	12,949	13,496
*43725	Cambridge	(740)	11,657	11,748
44405	Campbell	(330)	8,991	10,038
44614	Canal Fulton	(330)	5,069	4,157
43110	Canal Winchester	(614)	5,381	2,652
44406	Canfield	(330)	7,191	5,409
*44711	Canton	(330)	79,905	84,161
45005	Carlisle	(937)	5,621	4,872
*45822	Celina	(419)	10,268	9,945
*45458	Centerville (Montgomery Co.)	(937)	23,122	21,082
44024	Chardon	(440)	5,283	4,446
45211	Cheviot	(513)	8,399	9,616
45601	Chillicothe	(740)	22,039	21,923
*45202	Cincinnati	(513)	314,154	364,114
43113	Circleville	(740)	13,365	11,666
45315	Clayton	(937)	13,215	713
*44101	Cleveland	(216)	458,684	505,616
*44118	Cleveland Heights	(216)	48,643	54,052
43410	Clyde	(419)	6,101	6,087
44408	Columbiana	(330)	5,731	4,961
*43216	Columbus	(614)	730,008	632,945
44030	Conneaut	(440)	12,693	13,241
44410	Cortland	(330)	6,675	5,652
43812	Coshocton	(740)	11,650	12,193
45238	Covedale (c)	(513)	*6,360*	6,669
*44222	Cuyahoga Falls	(330)	50,515	48,950
*45401	Dayton	(937)	160,293	182,011
45236	Deer Park	(513)	5,681	6,181
43512	Defiance	(419)	16,076	16,787
43015	Delaware	(740)	30,012	19,966
45833	Delphos	(419)	6,860	7,093
*45247	Dent (c)	(513)	*7,612*	6,416
44622	Dover	(330)	512,498	11,329
45663	Dry Run (c)	(614)	*6,553*	5,389
*43016	Dublin	(614)/(740)	34,301	16,366
*44112	East Cleveland	(216)	25,924	33,096
*44095	Eastlake	(440)	19,901	21,161
43920	East Liverpool	(330)	12,539	13,654
45320	Eaton	(937)	8,215	7,396
*44035	Elyria	(440)	56,175	56,746
*45322	Englewood	(937)	12,598	11,402
*44117	Euclid	(216)	50,398	54,875
45324	Fairborn	(937)	32,411	31,300
*45011	Fairfield	(513)	42,379	39,709
*44334	Fairlawn	(330)	7,238	5,779
44126	Fairview Park	(440)	16,754	18,028
*45839	Findlay	(419)	40,175	35,703
45224	Finneytown (c)	(513)	*13,492*	13,096
45240	Forest Park	(513)	18,381	18,621
45230	Forestville (c)	(513)	*10,978*	9,185
44830	Fostoria	(419)	13,611	14,971
45005	Franklin	(513)	12,246	11,026
43420	Fremont	(419)	17,181	17,619
43230	Gahanna	(614)	32,791	23,898
44833	Galion	(419)	11,423	11,859
*44125	Garfield Heights	(216)	29,445	31,739
44041	Geneva	(440)	6,495	6,597
*45325	Germantown	(937)	5,170	4,916
44420	Girard	(330)	10,594	11,304
44044	Grafton	(440)	6,415	3,423
43212	Grandview Heights	(614)	6,331	7,010
43023	Granville	(740)	5,241	4,315
44232	Green	(330)	23,433	19,179
*45123	Greenfield	(937)	5,132	5,172
45331	Greenville	(937)	13,267	12,863
45253	Groesbeck (c)	(513)	*7,202*	6,684
43123	Grove City	(614)	30,502	19,661
*45011	Hamilton	(513)	60,996	61,438
45030	Harrison	(513)	7,584	7,520
43056	Heath	(740)	8,761	7,231
44134	Highland Heights	(440)	8,563	6,249
43026	Hilliard	(614)/(740)	26,449	11,794
45133	Hillsboro	(937)	6,684	6,235
44484	Howland Center (c)	(330)	*6,481*	6,732
44425	Hubbard	(330)	8,057	8,248
45424	Huber Heights	(937)	38,229	38,696
*44236	Hudson	(330)	23,054	5,159
44839	Huron	(419)	7,692	7,067
44131	Independence	(216)/(440)	7,038	6,500
45638	Ironton	(740)	11,337	12,751
45640	Jackson	(740)	6,251	6,167
*44240	Kent	(330)	27,601	28,835
43326	Kenton	(419)	8,255	8,356
43606	Kenwood (c)	(513)	*7,423*	7,469
*45429	Kettering	(937)	55,903	60,569
*44094	Kirtland	(440)	7,106	5,881
44107	Lakewood	(216)	53,971	59,718
43130	Lancaster	(740)	35,933	34,507
45039	Landen (c)	(513)	*12,766*	9,263
45036	Lebanon	(513)	19,370	10,461
*45802	Lima	(419)	39,333	45,553
43228	Lincoln Village (c)	(614)	*9,482*	9,958
43138	Logan	(740)	7,087	6,725
43140	London	(614)/(740)	9,328	7,807
*44052	Lorain	(440)	67,915	71,245
44641	Louisville	(330)	9,294	8,087
*45140	Loveland	(513)	11,285	10,122
44124	Lyndhurst	(216)/(440)	14,600	15,982
*44056	Macedonia	(330)	10,147	7,509
—	Mack South (c)		*5,837*	5,767
45243	Madeira	(513)	8,464	9,141
*44901	Mansfield	(419)	50,557	50,627
44137	Maple Heights	(216)	25,068	27,089
45750	Marietta	(740)	14,295	15,026
*43302	Marion	(740)	37,136	34,075
43935	Martins Ferry	(740)	7,027	8,003
*43040	Marysville	(937)	16,787	10,362
45040	Mason	(513)	27,958	11,450
*44646	Massillon	(330)	32,055	30,969
43537	Maumee	(419)	14,472	15,561
44124	Mayfield Heights	(440)	18,538	19,847
*44256	Medina	(330)	26,564	19,231
*44060	Mentor	(440)	51,332	47,491
44060	Mentor-on-the-Lake	(216)	8,293	8,271
*45343	Miamisburg	(937)	19,809	17,834
44130	Middleburg Heights	(216)/(440)	15,527	14,702
*45042	Middletown	(513)	51,804	46,758
45150	Milford	(513)	6,366	5,660
*45050	Monroe	(513)	9,362	5,380
45242	Montgomery	(513)	10,147	9,733
—	Montrose-Ghent (c)	—	*5,261*	4,906
45439	Moraine	(937)	6,741	5,989
45231	Mount Healthy	(513)	6,813	7,580
43050	Mount Vernon	(740)	16,019	14,550
44262	Munroe Falls	(330)	5,327	5,359
*43545	Napoleon	(419)	9,173	8,884
45764	Nelsonville	(740)	5,446	4,563
43054	New Albany	(614)	5,333	1,621
*43055	Newark	(740)	46,745	44,396
45344	New Carlisle	(937)	5,652	6,049
44663	New Philadelphia	(330)	17,470	15,698
44446	Niles	(330)	20,194	21,128
45239	Northbrook (c)	(513)	*11,076*	11,471
*44720	North Canton	(330)	16,796	14,904
45239	North College Hill	(513)	9,528	11,002
45251	Northgate (c)	(513)	*8,016*	7,864
44057	North Madison (c)	(440)	*8,451*	8,699
44070	North Olmsted	(440)	33,105	34,204
45502	Northridge (c) (Clark Co.)	(937)	*6,853*	5,939
45414	Northridge (c) (Montgomery Co.)	(937)	*8,487*	9,448
*44039	North Ridgeville	(440)	25,204	21,564
44133	North Royalton	(440)	29,497	23,197
*43619	Northwood	(419)	5,493	5,506
44203	Norton	(330)	11,596	11,477
44857	Norwalk	(419)	16,457	14,731
*45212	Norwood	(513)	20,405	23,674
*45873	Oakwood	(973)	8,817	8,957
44074	Oberlin	(440)	8,248	8,191
44138	Olmsted Falls	(440)	8,500	6,741
44862	Ontario	(419)	5,262	4,026
*43616	Oregon	(419)	19,269	18,334
44667	Orrville	(330)	8,502	7,955
45056	Oxford	(513)	22,317	19,013
44077	Painesville	(440)	17,599	15,769
*44129	Parma	(216)/(440)	82,672	87,876
44130	Parma Heights	(216)/(440)	20,954	21,448
43062	Pataskala	(740)	12,348	3,046
*44124	Pepper Pike	(216)/(440)	5,851	6,185
44646	Perry Heights (c)	(330)	*8,900*	9,055
*43551	Perrysburg	(419)	16,947	12,551
43147	Pickerington	(614)/(740)	14,968	5,668
45356	Piqua	(937)	20,774	20,612
—	Pleasant Run (c)	—	*5,267*	4,964
44319	Portage Lakes (c)	(330)	*9,870*	13,373
*43452	Port Clinton	(419)	6,329	7,106
*45662	Portsmouth	(740)	20,100	22,676
43065	Powell	(614)	9,716	2,154
44266	Ravenna	(330)	11,503	12,069
*45215	Reading	(513)	10,521	12,038
43068	Reynoldsburg	(614)/(740)	32,943	25,748
44143	Richmond Heights	(216)/(440)	10,623	9,611
44270	Rittman	(330)	6,312	6,147
45431	Riverside	(937)	22,869	1,471
44116	Rocky River	(440)	19,910	20,410
43460	Rossford	(419)	6,387	5,861
43950	Saint Clairsville	(740)	5,036	5,136
45885	Saint Marys	(419)	8,253	8,441
44460	Salem	(330)	12,063	12,233
*44870	Sandusky	(419)	26,977	29,764
44870	Sandusky South (c)	(419)	*6,599*	6,336
44131	Seven Hills	(216)/(440)	28,084	12,339
*44122	Shaker Heights	(216)	13,299	30,955

ZIP	Place	Area Code	2004	1990
*45241	Sharonville	(513)	9,171	13,121
44054	Sheffield Lake	(440)	9,480	9,825
44875	Shelby	(419)	12,063	9,610
44878	Shiloh (c)	(419)	*11,272*	11,607
*45365	Sidney	(937)	20,149	18,710
44139	Solon	(440)	22,309	18,548
*44121	South Euclid	(216)	22,504	23,866
45066	Springboro	(513)	15,780	6,574
45246	Springdale	(513)	9,950	10,621
*45501	Springfield	(937)	63,609	70,487
*43952	Steubenville	(740)	19,512	22,125
44224	Stow	(330)	34,394	27,998
44241	Streetsboro	(330)	13,900	9,932
*44136	Strongsville	(440)	44,315	35,308
44471	Struthers	(330)	11,321	12,284
—	Summerside (c)	—	*5,523*	4,573
43560	Sylvania	(419)	18,905	17,489
44278	Tallmadge	(330)	17,180	14,870
45243	The Village of Indian Hill	(513)	5,653	5,383
44883	Tiffin	(419)	17,509	18,604
45371	Tipp City	(937)	9,301	6,483
*43601	Toledo	(419)	304,973	332,943
43964	Toronto	(740)	5,487	6,127
45067	Trenton	(513)	10,294	6,189
*45426	Trotwood	(937)	26,800	29,358
*45373	Troy	(937)	22,183	19,478
44087	Twinsburg	(330)	17,286	9,606
44683	Uhrichsville	(740)	5,685	5,604
45322	Union	(937)	5,708	5,531
*44122	University Heights	(216)	13,553	14,787
*43221	Upper Arlington	(614)	31,860	34,128
43351	Upper Sandusky	(419)	6,459	5,906
43078	Urbana	(937)	11,615	11,353
45377	Vandalia	(937)	14,304	13,872
45891	Van Wert	(419)	10,533	10,922
*44089	Vermilion	(440)	10,971	11,127
*44281	Wadsworth	(330)	19,707	15,718
*45895	Wapakoneta	(419)	9,531	9,214
*44481	Warren	(330)	46,235	50,793
*44122	Warrensville Heights	(216)	14,444	15,884
*43160	Washington	(740)	13,302	13,080
43566	Waterville	(419)	5,146	4,594
43567	Wauseon	(419)	7,303	6,322
45692	Wellston	(740)	6,052	6,049
*45449	West Carrollton City	(937)	13,299	14,403
*43081	Westerville	(614)	34,846	30,269
44145	Westlake	(440)	31,535	27,018
45694	Wheelersburg (c)	(740)	*6,471*	5,113
43213	Whitehall	(614)	18,258	20,572
45239	White Oak (c)	(513)	*13,277*	12,430
44092	Wickliffe	(440)	13,355	14,558
*44890	Willard	(419)	6,851	6,210
*44094	Willoughby	(440)	22,493	20,510
*44094	Willoughby Hills	(440)	8,524	8,427
*44095	Willowick	(440)	14,175	15,269
45177	Wilmington	(937)	12,356	11,199
45459	Woodbourne-Hyde Park (c)	(937)	*7,910*	7,837
44691	Wooster	(330)	25,605	22,427
43085	Worthington	(614)	13,335	14,869
45433	Wright-Patterson AFB (c)	(937)	*6,656*	8,579
*45215	Wyoming	(513)	7,856	8,128
45385	Xenia	(937)	23,768	24,836
*44501	Youngstown	(330)	77,713	95,732
*43701	Zanesville	(740)	25,324	26,778

Oklahoma

ZIP	Place	Area Code	2004	1990
*74820	Ada	(580)	15,840	15,765
*73521	Altus	(580)	20,393	21,910
73717	Alva	(580)	5,034	5,495
73005	Anadarko	(405)	6,563	6,586
*73401	Ardmore	(580)	24,341	23,079
*74003	Bartlesville	(918)	34,638	34,256
73008	Bethany	(405)	19,871	20,075
74008	Bixby	(918)	17,729	9,502
74631	Blackwell	(580)	7,357	7,538
*74012	Broken Arrow	(918)	84,399	58,082
74015	Catoosa	(918)	6,020	2,954
*73018	Chickasha	(405)	16,463	14,988
73020	Choctaw	(405)	10,276	8,545
*74017	Claremore	(918)	16,994	13,280
73601	Clinton	(580)	8,368	9,298
74429	Coweta	(918)	8,135	6,159
74023	Cushing	(918)	8,325	7,218
*73115	Del City	(405)	22,029	23,928
*73533	Duncan	(580)	22,207	21,732
*74701	Durant	(580)	14,780	12,929
*73034	Edmond	(405)	73,080	52,310
*73644	Elk City	(580)	10,442	10,428
73036	El Reno	(405)	15,952	15,414
*73701	Enid	(580)	46,626	45,309
74033	Glenpool	(918)	8,542	6,688
*74344	Grove	(918)	5,668	4,020
73044	Guthrie	(405)	10,505	10,440
73942	Guymon	(580)	10,730	7,803
74437	Henryetta	(918)	6,076	5,872
74848	Holdenville	(405)	5,619	4,893
74743	Hugo	(580)	5,568	5,978
74745	Idabel	(580)	6,944	6,957
74037	Jenks	(918)	12,079	7,484
*73501	Lawton	(580)	88,214	80,561
*74501	McAlester	(918)	17,783	16,739
*74354	Miami	(918)	13,464	13,142
*73140	Midwest City	(405)	54,822	52,267
*73153	Moore	(405)	46,208	40,318
*74401	Muskogee	(918)	38,846	37,708
73064	Mustang	(405)	15,168	10,434
73065	Newcastle	(405)	5,957	4,214
73068	Noble	(405)	5,381	4,710
*73069	Norman	(405)	100,923	80,071
*73125	Oklahoma City	(405)	528,042	444,724
74447	Okmulgee	(918)	12,854	13,441
*74055	Owasso	(918)	22,582	11,151
73075	Pauls Valley	(405)	6,195	6,150
73077	Perry	(580)	5,125	4,978
*74601	Ponca City	(580)	25,224	26,359
74953	Poteau	(918)	8,024	7,210
*74361	Pryor Creek	(918)	9,173	8,327
73080	Purcell	(405)	5,713	4,784
74955	Sallisaw	(918)	8,536	7,122
74063	Sand Springs	(918)	17,642	15,339
*74066	Sapulpa	(918)	19,803	18,074
*74868	Seminole	(405)	6,895	7,071
*74801	Shawnee	(405)	29,746	26,017
74070	Skiatook	(918)	6,087	4,910
*74074	Stillwater	(405)	40,731	36,676
*74464	Tahlequah	(918)	15,710	10,586
74873	Tecumseh	(405)	6,488	5,750
73120	The Village	(405)	9,907	10,353
*74103	Tulsa	(918)	383,764	367,302
73089	Tuttle	(405)	5,070	2,807
74301	Vinita	(918)	5,949	5,804
*74467	Wagoner	(918)	7,866	6,894
*73123	Warr Acres	(405)	9,551	9,288
73096	Weatherford	(580)	9,736	10,124
*73801	Woodward	(580)	11,864	12,340
*73099	Yukon	(405)	21,596	20,935

Oregon

Area code (971) overlays area code (503). See introductory note.

ZIP	Place	Area Code	2004	1990
*97321	Albany	(541)	43,889	33,523
*97006	Aloha (c)	(503)	*41,741*	34,284
97601	Altamont (c)	(541)	*19,603*	18,591
97520	Ashland	(541)	20,755	16,252
97103	Astoria	(503)	9,758	10,069
97814	Baker City	(541)	9,746	9,140
*97005	Beaverton	(503)	82,907	53,307
*97701	Bend	(541)	62,937	23,740
97415	Brookings	(541)	6,121	4,400
97013	Canby	(503)	14,715	8,990
97225	Cedar Hills (c)	(503)	*8,949*	9,294
97291	Cedar Mill (c)	(503)	*12,597*	9,697
97502	Central Point	(541)	15,152	7,512
97058	City of the Dalles	(541)	11,948	11,021
97015	Clackamas (c)	(503)	*5,177*	2,578
97420	Coos Bay	(541)	15,565	15,076
97113	Cornelius	(503)	10,346	6,148
*97333	Corvallis	(541)	50,380	44,757
*97424	Cottage Grove	(541)	8,631	7,403
97338	Dallas	(503)	13,461	9,422
97524	Eagle Point	(541)	6,959	3,026
*97440	Eugene	(541)	142,681	112,733
97024	Fairview	(503)	9,255	2,588
97439	Florence	(541)	7,664	5,171
97116	Forest Grove	(503)	19,261	13,559
97301	Four Corners (c)	(503)	*13,922*	12,156
97223	Garden Home-Whitford (c)	(503)	*6,931*	6,652
97027	Gladstone	(503)	12,131	10,152
*97526	Grants Pass	(541)	27,195	17,503
97470	Green (c)	(541)	*6,174*	5,076
*97030	Gresham	(503)	95,376	68,285
*97015	Happy Valley	(503)	7,264	1,552
97303	Hayesville (c)	(503)	14,439	14,318
97303	Hayesville (c)	(503)	*18,222*	14,318
97838	Hermiston	(541)	81,854	10,047
*97123	Hillsboro	(503)	6,362	37,598
97031	Hood River	(541)	95,376	4,632
97351	Independence	(503)	7,552	4,425
97222	Jennings Lodge (c)	(503)	*7,036*	6,530
97448	Junction City	(541)	5,229	3,961
97307	Keizer	(503)	34,414	21,884
*97601	Klamath Falls	(541)	19,694	17,737
97850	La Grande	(541)	12,371	11,766
*97034	Lake Oswego	(503)	36,368	30,576
97739	La Pine (c)	(541)	*5,799*	—
97355	Lebanon	(541)	13,515	10,950
97367	Lincoln City	(541)	7,526	5,903
97128	McMinnville	(503)	28,973	17,894
97741	Madras	(541)	5,146	3,443
*97501	Medford	(541)	68,099	47,021
97862	Milton-Freewater	(541)	6,462	5,533
*97269	Milwaukie	(503)	20,755	18,670
97038	Molalla	(503)	6,315	3,651
97361	Monmouth	(503)	8,389	6,288
97132	Newberg	(503)	20,280	13,086

ZIP	Place	Area Code	2004	1990
*97365	Newport	(541)	9,627	8,437
97459	North Bend	(541)	9,658	9,614
97268	Oak Grove (c)	(503)	*12,808*	12,576
—	Oak Hills (c)	—	*9,050*	6,450
—	Oatfield (c)	—	*15,750*	15,348
97914	Ontario	(541)	11,152	9,394
97045	Oregon City	(503)	29,767	14,698
97801	Pendleton	(541)	16,605	15,142
*97208	Portland	(503)	533,492	485,975
97754	Prineville	(541)	8,575	5,355
97225	Raleigh Hills (c)	(503)	*5,865*	6,066
97756	Redmond	(541)	18,017	7,165
—	Redwood (c)	—	*5,844*	3,702
—	Rockcreek (c)	—	*9,404*	8,282
97470	Roseburg	(541)	20,447	18,389
97470	Roseburg North (c)	(541)	*5,473*	6,831
97051	Saint Helens	(503)	11,432	7,535
*97309	Salem	(503)	146,120	107,793
97055	Sandy	(503)	7,544	4,154
97056	Scappoose	(503)	5,706	3,550
97138	Seaside	(503)	6,023	5,359
97378	Sheridan	(503)	5,526	3,950
97140	Sherwood	(503)	14,540	3,093
97381	Silverton	(503)	8,116	5,635
*97477	Springfield	(541)	55,048	44,664
97383	Stayton	(503)	7,125	5,011
—	Sunnyside (c)	(503)	*6,791*	4,423
97479	Sutherlin	(541)	7,256	5,020
97386	Sweet Home	(541)	8,297	6,850
97540	Talent	(541)	5,813	3,274
*97281	Tigard	(503)	46,860	29,435
97060	Troutdale	(503)	14,711	7,852
97062	Tualatin	(503)	25,268	14,664
97882	Umatilla	(541)	6,054	3,058
97225	West Haven-Sylvan (c)	(503)	*7,147*	6,009
97068	West Linn	(503)	25,051	16,389
*97225	West Slope (c)	(503)	*6,442*	7,959
97503	White City (c)	(541)	*5,466*	5,891
97070	Wilsonville	(503)	15,514	7,510
97071	Woodburn	(503)	22,147	13,404

Pennsylvania

Area code (267) overlays area code (215). Area code (484) overlays (610). Area code (878) overlays (412). See introductory note.

ZIP	Place	Area Code	2004	1990
15001	Aliquippa	(724)	11,270	13,374
*18105	Allentown	(610)	106,732	105,301
*16603	Altoona	(814)	47,832	51,881
19002	Ambler	(215)	6,386	6,609
15003	Ambridge	(724)	7,439	8,133
18403	Archbald	(570)	6,267	6,291
19003	Ardmore (c)	(610)	*12,616*	12,646
15210	Arlington Heights (c)	(412)	*5,132*	4,768
15068	Arnold	(724)	5,463	6,113
19407	Audubon (c)	(610)	*6,549*	6,328
15202	Avalon	(412)	5,044	5,784
—	Back Mountain (c)	—	19,138	—
—	Back Mountain (c)	—	*26,690*	—
15234	Baldwin	(412)	5,282	21,923
*18013	Bangor	(610)	9,525	5,383
15010	Beaver Falls	(724)	6,199	10,687
16823	Bellefonte	(814)	8,367	6,358
15202	Bellevue	(412)	10,493	9,126
18603	Berwick	(570)	32,670	10,976
15102	Bethel Park	(412)	72,441	33,823
*18016	Bethlehem	(610)	5,184	71,427
19508	Birdsboro	(610)	6,841	4,222
18447	Blakely	(570)	12,805	7,222
*17815	Bloomsburg	(570)	19,138	12,439
19422	Blue Bell (c)	(215)/(610)	*6,395*	6,091
19061	Boothwyn (c)	(610)	*5,206*	5,069
16701	Bradford	(814)	8,752	9,625
15227	Brentwood	(412)	9,964	10,823
15017	Bridgeville	(412)	5,094	5,445
19007	Bristol	(215)	9,869	10,405
19015	Brookhaven	(610)	7,866	8,570
19008	Broomall (c)	(610)	*11,046*	10,930
*16001	Butler	(724)	14,626	15,714
15419	California	(724)	5,707	5,748
*17011	Camp Hill	(717)	7,465	7,831
15317	Canonsburg	(724)	8,825	9,200
18407	Carbondale	(570)	9,423	10,664
*17013	Carlisle	(717)	18,074	18,419
15106	Carnegie	(412)	8,220	9,278
15108	Carnot-Moon (c)	(412)	*10,637*	10,187
15234	Castle Shannon	(412)	8,395	9,135
18032	Catasauqua	(610)	6,548	6,662
17201	Chambersburg	(717)	18,026	16,647
*19013	Chester	(610)	36,922	41,856
15025	Clairton	(412)	8,174	9,656
16214	Clarion	(814)	6,084	6,457
18411	Clarks Summit	(570)	5,035	5,433
16830	Clearfield	(814)	6,387	6,633
19018	Clifton Heights	(610)	6,648	7,111
19320	Coatesville	(610)	11,386	11,038
19023	Collingdale	(610)	8,524	9,175
17109	Colonial Park (c)	(717)	*13,259*	13,777
17512	Columbia	(717)	10,159	10,701
15425	Connellsville	(724)	8,739	9,229
*19428	Conshohocken	(610)	7,745	8,064
15108	Coraopolis	(412)	5,848	6,747
16407	Corry	(814)	6,638	7,216
15205	Crafton	(412)	6,387	7,188
19021	Croydon (c)	(215)	*9,993*	9,967
19023	Darby	(610)	10,085	11,140
19036	Darby Twp. (c)	(610)	*9,622*	10,955
19333	Devon-Berwyn (c)	(610)	*5,067*	5,019
18519	Dickson City	(570)	6,007	6,276
15033	Donora	(724)	5,462	5,928
15216	Dormont	(412)	8,845	9,772
*19335	Downingtown	(610)	7,859	7,749
18901	Doylestown	(215)	8,222	8,575
19026	Drexel Hill (c)	(610)	*29,364*	29,744
15801	Du Bois	(814)	7,869	8,286
*18512	Dunmore	(570)	13,672	15,403
15110	Duquesne	(412)	6,988	8,525
19401	East Norriton (c)	(610)	*13,211*	13,324
*18042	Easton	(610)	26,267	26,276
18301	East Stroudsburg	(570)	10,404	8,781
17402	East York (c)	(717)	*8,782*	8,487
—	Economy	(724)	9,361	9,305
*16412	Edinboro	(814)	6,879	7,736
17022	Elizabethtown	(717)	11,920	9,952
16117	Ellwood City	(724)	8,366	8,894
*18049	Emmaus	(610)	11,325	11,157
17025	Enola (c)	(717)	*5,627*	5,961
17522	Ephrata	(717)	13,180	12,133
*16501	Erie	(814)	103,925	108,718
18643	Exeter	(570)	6,036	5,691
19030	Fairless Hills (c)	(215)	*8,365*	9,026
16121	Farrell	(724)	6,058	6,835
19053	Feasterville-Trevose (c)	(215)	*6,525*	6,696
16063	Fernway (c)	(724)	*12,188*	9,072
19032	Folcroft	(610)	6,910	7,506
19033	Folsom (c)	(610)	*8,072*	8,173
15221	Forest Hills	(412)	6,526	7,335
15238	Fox Chapel	(412)	5,307	5,319
16323	Franklin	(814)	6,947	7,329
—	Franklin Park	(412)	11,708	10,109
18052	Fullerton (c)	(610)	*14,268*	13,127
*17325	Gettysburg	(717)	7,891	7,025
19036	Glenolden	(610)	7,336	7,260
19038	Glenside (c)	(215)	*7,914*	8,704
*15601	Greensburg	(724)	15,579	16,318
16125	Greenville	(724)	6,346	6,734
16127	Grove City	(412)	7,800	8,240
15101	Hampton Twp. (c) (Allegheny Co.)	(412)	*17,526*	15,568
*17331	Hanover	(717)	14,916	14,399
19438	Harleysville (c)	(215)	*8,795*	7,405
*17105	Harrisburg	(717)	47,635	52,376
15065	Harrison Twp. (c) (Allegheny Co.)	(412)	*10,934*	11,763
19040	Hatboro	(215)	7,329	7,382
*18201	Hazleton	(570)	22,319	24,730
18055	Hellertown	(610)	5,587	5,662
16148	Hermitage	(724)	16,549	15,260
17033	Hershey (c)	(717)	*12,771*	11,860
16648	Hollidaysburg	(814)	5,376	5,624
16001	Homeacre-Lyndora (c)	(724)	*6,685*	7,511
19044	Horsham (c)	(215)	*14,779*	15,051
*16652	Huntingdon	(814)	6,879	6,843
*15701	Indiana	(724)	14,925	15,174
15644	Jeannette	(724)	10,309	11,221
15025	Jefferson Hills	(412)	9,679	—
*15907	Johnstown	(814)	22,772	28,124
15108	Kennedy Twp. (c)	(412)	*7,504*	7,152
19348	Kennett Square	(610)	5,300	5,218
19406	King of Prussia (c)	(610)	*18,511*	18,406
18704	Kingston	(570)	13,284	14,507
19443	Kulpsville (c)	(215)	*8,005*	5,183
19530	Kutztown	(610)	5,144	4,704
*17604	Lancaster	(717)	55,182	55,551
19446	Lansdale	(215)	16,014	16,362
19050	Lansdowne	(610)	10,827	11,712
15650	Latrobe	(724)	8,711	9,265
17540	Leacock-Leola-Bareville (c)	(717)	*6,625*	5,685
*17042	Lebanon	(717)	23,925	24,800
18235	Lehighton	(610)	5,536	5,914
*19055	Levittown (c)	(215)	*53,966*	55,362
*17837	Lewisburg	(570)	5,597	5,785
17044	Lewistown	(717)	8,692	9,341
17112	Linglestown (c)	(717)	*6,414*	5,862
19353	Lionville-Marchwood (c)	(610)	*6,298*	6,468
17543	Lititz	(717)	9,022	8,280
17745	Lock Haven	(570)	8,983	9,230
17011	Lower Allen (c)	(717)	*6,619*	6,329
15068	Lower Burrell	(724)	12,521	12,251
15237	McCandless Twp. (c)	(412)	*29,022*	28,781
*15134	McKeesport	(412)	23,053	26,016
15136	McKees Rocks	(412)	6,305	7,691
19002	Maple Glen (c)	(215)	*7,042*	5,881
*16335	Meadville	(814)	13,360	14,318
*17055	Mechanicsburg	(717)	8,843	9,452
*19063	Media	(610)	5,469	5,957
17057	Middletown (Dauphin Co.)	(717)	9,001	9,254
18017	Middletown (c) (Northampton Co.)	(610)	*7,378*	6,866
17551	Millersville	(717)	7,493	8,099
17847	Milton	(570)	6,507	6,746
15061	Monaca	(724)	6,059	6,739
15062	Monessen	(724)	8,397	9,901

ZIP	Place	Area Code	2004	1990
18936	Montgomeryville (c)	(215)	*12,031*	9,114
18507	Moosic	(570)	5,706	5,397
19067	Morrisville (Bucks Co.)	(215)	9,864	9,765
18707	Mountain Top (c)	(570)	*15,269*	—
17851	Mount Carmel	(570)	6,104	7,196
17552	Mount Joy	(717)	6,906	6,398
15228	Mount Lebanon (c)	(412)	*33,017*	34,414
15120	Munhall	(412)	11,697	13,158
*15146	Municipality of Monroeville	(412)	28,486	29,169
15668	Municipality of Murrysville	(724)	19,407	17,240
18634	Nanticoke	(570)	10,471	12,267
18064	Nazareth	(610)	6,017	5,713
19086	Nether Providence Twp. (c)	(610)	*13,456*	12,730
15066	New Brighton	(724)	6,367	6,854
*16108	New Castle	(724)	25,308	28,334
17070	New Cumberland	(717)	7,162	7,665
17557	New Holland	(717)	5,181	4,484
*15068	New Kensington	(724)	14,245	15,894
*19403	Norristown	(610)	30,873	30,754
18067	Northampton	(610)	9,647	8,717
15104	North Braddock	(412)	6,098	7,036
15137	North Versailles (c)	(412)	*11,125*	13,294
16421	Northwest Harborcreek (c)	(814)	*8,658*	7,485
19074	Norwood	(610)	5,873	6,162
15139	Oakmont	(412)	6,672	6,961
15238	O'Hara Twp. (c)	(412)	*8,856*	9,096
16301	Oil City	(814)	11,060	11,949
18518	Old Forge	(570)	8,578	8,834
19075	Oreland (c)	(215)	*5,509*	5,695
18071	Palmerton	(610)	5,289	5,394
17078	Palmyra	(717)	6,998	6,910
19301	Paoli (c)	(610)	*5,425*	5,277
16801	Park Forest Village (c)	(814)	*8,830*	6,703
17331	Parkville (c)	(717)	*6,593*	5,009
17112	Paxtonia (c)	(570)	*5,254*	4,862
15235	Penn Hills (c)	(412)	*46,809*	57,632
19096	Penn Wynne (c)	(610)	*5,382*	5,807
18944	Perkasie	(215)	8,771	7,878
*19104	Philadelphia	(215)	1,470,151	1,585,577
*19460	Phoenixville	(610)	14,976	15,066
*15233	Pittsburgh	(412)	322,450	369,879
*18640	Pittston	(570)	7,753	9,389
15236	Pleasant Hills	(412)	8,065	8,884
15239	Plum	(412)	26,684	25,609
18651	Plymouth	(570)	6,214	7,134
19462	Plymouth Meeting (c)	(610)	*5,593*	6,241
*19464	Pottstown	(610)	21,665	21,831
17901	Pottsville	(570)	14,881	16,603
17109	Progress (c)	(717)	*9,647*	9,654
19076	Prospect Park	(610)	6,466	6,764
15767	Punxsutawney	(814)	6,130	6,782
18951	Quakertown	(215)	8,864	8,982
19087	Radnor Twp. (c)	(610)	*30,878*	27,676
*19612	Reading	(610)	80,727	78,380
17356	Red Lion	(717)	6,087	6,130
18954	Richboro (c)	(215)	*6,678*	5,141
19078	Ridley Park	(610)	7,069	7,592
15237	Ross Twp. (c)	(412)	*32,551*	35,102
15857	Saint Marys	(814)	14,081	14,020
19464	Sanatoga (c)	(610)	*7,734*	3,723
18840	Sayre	(570)	5,642	5,791
17972	Schuylkill Haven	(570)	5,336	5,610
15106	Scott Twp. (c)	(412)	*17,288*	20,413
*18505	Scranton	(570)	73,928	81,805
17870	Selinsgrove	(570)	5,374	5,384
15116	Shaler Twp. (c)	(412)	*29,757*	33,694
17872	Shamokin	(570)	7,652	9,184
*16146	Sharon	(724)	15,652	17,533
19079	Sharon Hill	(610)	5,359	5,771
17976	Shenandoah	(570)	5,354	6,221
19607	Shillington	(610)	5,020	5,062
17404	Shiloh (c)	(717)	*10,192*	5,315
17257	Shippensburg	(717)	5,611	5,331
*15501	Somerset	(814)	6,573	6,454
18964	Souderton	(215)	6,735	5,957
15129	South Park Twp. (c)	(814)	*14,340*	14,292
17702	South Williamsport	(570)	6,228	6,496
19064	Springfield (c) (Delaware Co.)	(610)	*23,677*	25,326
*16804	State College	(814)	39,311	38,981
17113	Steelton	(717)	5,707	5,152
15136	Stowe Twp. (c)	(412)	*6,706*	9,202
18360	Stroudsburg	(570)	6,157	5,312
—	Sugarcreek	(814)	5,167	5,532
*17801	Sunbury	(570)	10,171	11,591
19081	Swarthmore	(610)	6,172	6,157
15218	Swissvale	(412)	9,192	10,637
18252	Tamaqua	(570)	6,827	7,943
18517	Taylor	(570)	6,262	6,941
16354	Titusville	(814)	5,895	6,434
19401	Trooper (c)	(610)	*6,061*	7,370
15145	Turtle Creek	(412)	5,791	6,556
16686	Tyrone	(814)	5,398	5,743
15401	Uniontown	(724)	12,065	12,034
19063	Upper Providence Twp. (c)	(610)	*10,509*	9,477
15241	Upper Saint Clair (c)	(412)	*20,053*	19,023
15690	Vandergrift	(724)	5,250	5,904
19013	Village Green-Green Ridge (c)	(610)	*8,279*	9,026
*16365	Warren	(814)	9,780	11,122
15301	Washington (Wash. Co.)	(724)	14,849	15,864
17268	Waynesboro	(717)	9,688	9,578
17315	Weigelstown (c)	(717)	*10,117*	8,665
*19380	West Chester	(610)	17,701	18,041
19380	West Goshen (c)	(610)	*8,472*	8,948
*15122	West Mifflin	(412)	21,563	23,644
—	Westmont	(814)	5,277	5,789
19401	West Norriton (c)	(610)	*14,901*	15,209
15229	West View	(412)	6,969	7,734
18052	Whitehall (Allegheny Co.)	(412)	13,923	14,451
15131	White Oak	(412)	8,288	8,761
*18703	Wilkes-Barre	(570)	41,559	47,523
15221	Wilkinsburg	(412)	18,302	21,080
15145	Wilkins Twp. (c)	(412)	*6,917*	7,487
*17701	Williamsport	(570)	30,175	31,933
19090	Willow Grove (c)	(215)	*16,234*	16,325
17584	Willow Street (c)	(717)	*7,258*	5,817
15025	Wilson	(412)	7,733	7,830
19094	Woodlyn (c)	(610)	*10,036*	10,151
19038	Wyndmoor (c)	(215)	*5,601*	5,682
19610	Wyomissing	(610)	11,142	7,332
19050	Yeadon	(610)	11,535	11,980
*17405	York	(717)	40,043	42,192

Rhode Island (401)

See introductory note.

ZIP	Place	2004	1990
02806	*Barrington*	*16,836*	15,849
02809	*Bristol*	24,741	21,625
02830	*Burrillville*	16,493	16,230
02863	Central Falls	19,292	17,637
02813	*Charlestown*	8,266	6,478
02816	*Coventry*	35,072	31,083
02864	*Cumberland*	33,794	29,038
02864	Cumberland Hill (c)	*7,738*	6,379
*02905	Cranston	81,986	76,060
02818	*East Greenwich*	13,594	11,865
02914	East Providence	49,765	50,380
02822	*Exeter*	6,289	5,461
02814	*Glocester*	10,551	9,227
02828	Greenville (c)	*8,626*	8,303
02833	*Hopkinton*	8,120	6,873
02835	*Jamestown*	5,697	4,999
02919	*Johnston*	29,299	26,542
02881	Kingston (c)	*5,446*	6,504
02865	*Lincoln*	22,188	18,045
02842	*Middletown*	17,032	19,460
02882	*Narragansett*	16,945	15,004
02840	Newport	26,136	28,227
02843	Newport East (c)	*11,463*	11,080
02852	*North Kingstown*	27,221	23,786
02908	*North Providence*	33,329	32,090
02896	*North Smithfield*	11,026	10,497
*02860	Pawtucket	74,330	72,644
02871	*Portsmouth*	17,309	16,857
*02904	Providence	176,365	160,728
02812	*Richmond*	7,728	5,351
02857	*Scituate*	10,941	9,796
02917	*Smithfield*	21,811	19,163
02879	*South Kingstown*	29,275	24,612
02878	Tiverton (c)	*7,282*	7,259
02878	*Tiverton*	15,464	14,312
02864	Valley Falls (c)	*11,599*	11,175
*02879	Wakefield-Peacedale (c)	*8,468*	7,134
02885	*Warren*	11,412	11,385
*02886	Warwick	87,365	85,427
02891	Westerly (c)	*17,682*	16,477
02891	*Westerly*	23,747	21,605
02817	*West Greenwich*	5,657	—
02893	*West Warwick*	30,114	29,268
02895	Woonsocket	44,654	43,877

South Carolina

ZIP	Place	Area Code	2004	1990
29620	Abbeville	(864)	5,777	5,778
*29801	Aiken	(803)	27,299	20,386
*29621	Anderson	(864)	25,715	26,385
*29070	Batesburg-Leesville	(803)	5,547	6,107
29841	Belvedere (c)	(803)	*5,631*	6,133
29512	Bennettsville	(843)	9,260	10,095
29611	Berea (c)	(864)	*14,158*	13,535
29902	Burton (c)	(843)	*7,180*	6,917
29020	Camden	(803)	6,975	6,696
29033	Cayce	(803)	12,418	10,824
—	Centerville (c)	(573)	*5,181*	4,866
*29402	Charleston	(843)	104,883	88,256
29520	Cheraw	(843)	5,428	5,553
29706	Chester	(803)	6,273	7,158
*29631	Clemson	(864)	12,074	11,145
29325	Clinton	(864)	8,985	9,603
*29201	Columbia	(803)	116,331	110,734
*29526	Conway	(843)	13,293	9,819
*29532	Darlington	(843)	6,575	7,310
29204	Dentsville (c)	(803)	*13,009*	11,839
29536	Dillon	(843)	6,437	6,829
*29640	Easley	(864)	18,643	15,179
—	Five Forks (c)	—	*8,064*	—
*29501	Florence	(843)	30,883	29,913
29206	Forest Acres	(803)	10,127	7,181
*29715	Fort Mill	(803)	8,041	4,930
29644	Fountain Inn	(864)	6,584	4,388

ZIP	Place	Area Code	2004	1990
*29341	Gaffney	(864)	12,969	13,149
29605	Gantt (c)	(864)	*13,962*	13,891
29576	Garden City (c)	(843)	*9,357*	6,305
*29442	Georgetown	(843)	8,926	9,517
29445	Goose Creek	(843)	32,250	24,692
*29602	Greenville	(864)	56,291	58,256
*29646	Greenwood	(864)	22,242	20,807
*29650	Greer	(864)	20,416	10,322
*29406	Hanahan	(843)	13,376	13,176
*29550	Hartsville	(843)	7,429	8,372
*29928	Hilton Head Island	(843)	34,371	23,694
29621	Homeland Park (c)	(864)	*6,337*	6,569
29063	Irmo	(803)	11,181	11,284
29456	Ladson (c)	(843)	*13,264*	13,540
29560	Lake City	(843)	6,618	7,153
*29720	Lancaster	(803)	8,472	8,914
29902	Laurel Bay (c)	(843)	*6,625*	4,972
29360	Laurens	(864)	9,834	9,694
*29072	Lexington	(803)	12,610	4,046
29566	Little River (c)	(843)	*7,027*	3,470
29078	Lugoff (c)	(803)	*6,278*	3,211
29571	Marion	(843)	7,029	7,658
29662	Mauldin	(864)	18,604	11,662
*29461	Moncks Corner	(843)	6,348	5,599
*29465	Mount Pleasant	(843)	56,350	30,108
29576	Murrells Inlet (c)	(843)	*5,519*	3,334
*29575	Myrtle Beach	(803)	25,410	24,848
29108	Newberry	(803)	10,700	10,543
*29841	North Augusta	(803)	19,095	15,684
*29410	North Charleston	(843)	84,271	70,304
*29582	North Myrtle Beach	(843)	13,160	8,731
29565	Oak Grove (c)	(803)	*8,183*	7,173
*29115	Orangeburg	(803)	12,895	13,772
29935	Port Royal	(843)	9,188	2,985
—	Parker (c)	—	*10,760*	11,072
—	Powderville (c)	—	*5,362*	—
29072	Red Bank (c)	(803)	*8,811*	5,950
29020	Red Hill (c)	(843)	*10,509*	6,112
*29730	Rock Hill	(803)	57,902	42,112
29417	Saint Andrews (c)	(843)	*21,814*	25,692
29609	Sans Souci (c)	(864)	*7,836*	7,612
*29678	Seneca	(864)	7,958	7,726
29210	Seven Oaks (c)	(803)	*15,755*	15,722
*29681	Simpsonville	(864)	14,924	11,744
29577	Socastee (c)	(843)	*14,295*	10,426
*29306	Spartanburg	(864)	38,599	43,479
*29483	Summerville	(843)	34,241	22,519
*29150	Sumter	(803)	39,671	40,977
29687	Taylors (c)	(864)	*20,125*	19,619
29379	Union	(864)	8,377	9,840
29607	Wade Hampton (c)	(864)	*20,458*	20,014
29488	Walterboro	(843)	5,516	5,595
29611	Welcome (c)	(864)	*6,390*	6,560
*29169	West Columbia	(803)	13,029	10,974
29206	Woodfield (c)	(803)	*9,238*	8,862
29745	York	(803)	7,028	6,709

South Dakota (605)

ZIP	Place	2004	1990
*57401	Aberdeen	24,196	24,995
57005	Brandon	6,813	3,545
*57006	Brookings	18,705	16,270
*57350	Huron	11,198	12,448
57042	Madison	6,163	6,257
57301	Mitchell	14,887	13,798
57501	Pierre	13,983	12,906
*57701	Rapid City	61,459	54,523
*57701	Rapid Valley (c)	61,459	5,968
*57101	Sioux Falls	136,695	100,836
*57783	Spearfish	9,205	6,966
57785	Sturgis	6,379	5,537
57069	Vermillion	9,975	10,034
57201	Watertown	20,207	17,623
*57078	Yankton	13,491	12,703

Tennessee

ZIP	Place	Area Code	2004	1990
37701	Alcoa	(865)	8,365	6,400
*37303	Athens	(423)	13,719	12,054
*38184	Bartlett	(901)	42,865	27,038
37660	Bloomingdale (c)	(423)	*10,350*	10,953
*37027	Brentwood	(615)	30,586	16,392
*37621	Bristol	(423)	24,933	23,421
38012	Brownsville	(731)	10,705	10,017
*37401	Chattanooga	(423)	154,853	152,393
*37642	Church Hill	(423)	6,222	5,208
*37040	Clarksville	(931)	108,972	75,542
*37311	Cleveland	(423)	37,746	32,236
*37716	Clinton	(865)	9,348	8,960
37315	Collegedale	(423)	7,166	5,048
*38017	Collierville	(901)	36,562	14,501
37663	Colonial Heights (c)	(423)	*7,067*	6,716
*38401	Columbia	(931)	33,599	28,583
*38501	Cookeville	(931)	27,648	21,744
38019	Covington	(901)	8,989	7,487
*38555	Crossville	(931)	9,955	6,930
37321	Dayton	(423)	6,439	5,671
*37055	Dickson	(615)	12,760	10,487
*38024	Dyersburg	(731)	17,406	16,321
37411	East Brainerd (c)	(423)	*14,132*	11,594
37412	East Ridge	(423)	20,010	21,101
*37643	Elizabethton	(423)	13,993	13,087
37650	Erwin	(423)	5,840	5,318
37062	Fairview	(615)	6,771	4,210
*37922	Farragut	(865)	18,985	12,802
37334	Fayetteville	(931)	6,996	7,158
—	Forest Hills	(615)	5,031	—
*37064	Franklin	(615)	48,191	20,098
37066	Gallatin	(615)	25,653	18,794
*38138	Germantown	(901)	37,555	33,159
*37072	Goodlettsville	(615)	15,111	11,219
37073	Greenbrier	(615)	5,928	3,062
*37743	Greeneville	(423)	15,302	13,532
37215	Green Hill (c)	(615)	*7,068*	6,763
37748	Harriman	(865)	6,757	7,119
37341	Harrison (c)	(423)	*7,630*	7,191
37074	Hartsville-Trousdale	(615)	7,484	2,222
38340	Henderson	(731)	5,964	4,760
*37075	Hendersonville	(615)	43,866	32,188
38343	Humboldt	(731)	9,332	9,651
*38301	Jackson	(731)	61,772	49,145
37760	Jefferson City	(865)	7,925	5,875
*37601	Johnson City	(423)	57,812	50,354
*37662	Kingsport	(423)	44,070	40,457
37763	Kingston	(423)	5,439	4,552
*37950	Knoxville	(865)	178,118	169,761
*37766	La Follette	(423)	8,155	7,201
*37086	La Vergne	(615)	24,811	7,496
38464	Lawrenceburg	(931)	10,865	10,397
*37087	Lebanon	(615)	22,452	15,208
*37771	Lenoir City	(865)	7,403	6,147
37091	Lewisburg	(931)	10,782	9,879
38351	Lexington	(731)	7,605	5,810
37352	Lynchburg	(931)	5,978	4,721
38201	McKenzie	(731)	5,475	5,168
*37110	McMinnville	(931)	13,108	11,194
*38101	Memphis	(901)	671,929	618,652
37343	Middle Valley (c)	(423)	*11,854*	12,255
38358	Milan	(731)	7,796	7,512
37072	Millersville	(615)	6,085	2,575
*38053	Millington	(901)	10,399	17,866
*37813	Morristown	(423)	25,462	22,513
37645	Mount Carmel	(423)	5,218	4,268
*37122	Mount Juliet	(615)	17,296	5,389
38058	Munford	(901)	5,418	2,944
*37130	Murfreesboro	(615)	81,511	44,922
*37202	Nashville	(615)	546,719	488,366
*37821	Newport	(423)	7,268	7,123
*37830	Oak Ridge	(865)	27,298	27,310
37363	Ooltewah (c)	(423)	*5,681*	4,903
38242	Paris	(731)	9,860	9,332
*37862	Pigeon Forge	(865)	5,561	3,027
37148	Portland	(615)	10,087	5,539
38478	Pulaski	(931)	7,845	7,916
37415	Red Bank	(423)	11,865	12,320
38063	Ripley	(731)	7,772	6,634
37854	Rockwood	(865)	5,440	5,348
38372	Savannah	(731)	7,131	6,547
*37862	Sevierville	(865)	14,101	7,178
37865	Seymour (c)	(865)	*8,850*	7,026
*37160	Shelbyville	(931)	17,981	14,042
37377	Signal Mountain	(423)	7,207	7,034
37167	Smyrna	(615)	31,925	14,720
*37379	Soddy-Daisy	(423)	11,970	8,240
37311	South Cleveland (c)	(423)	*6,216*	5,372
37172	Springfield	(615)	15,683	11,227
37174	Spring Hill	(931)	14,431	1,464
37874	Sweetwater	(423)	5,925	5,066
*37388	Tullahoma	(931)	18,677	16,761
*38261	Union City	(731)	10,824	10,513
37188	White House	(615)	8,428	2,987
37398	Winchester	(931)	7,668	6,305

Texas

Area codes (281) and (832) overlay area code (713). Area code (430) overlays (903). Area code (682) overlays (817). Area codes (972) and (469) overlay (214). See introductory note.

ZIP	Place	Area Code	2004	1990
*79604	Abilene	(325)	114,807	106,707
—	Abram-Perezville (c)	—	*5,444*	3,999
75001	Addison	(214)	13,778	8,783
78516	Alamo	(956)	15,928	8,352
78209	Alamo Heights	(210)	7,307	6,502
77039	Aldine (c)	(713)	*13,979*	11,133
*78332	Alice	(361)	19,445	19,788
*75002	Allen	(214)	66,341	19,315
*79830	Alpine	(432)	6,079	5,622
78574	Alton	(956)	6,786	3,048
—	Alton North (c)	—	*5,051*	—
*77511	Alvin	(713)	22,142	19,220
*79105	Amarillo	(806)	180,791	157,571
78750	Anderson Mill (c)	—	*8,953*	9,468
79714	Andrews	(432)	9,463	10,678
*77515	Angleton	(979)	18,704	17,140
*78336	Aransas Pass	(361)	8,817	7,180
*76004	Arlington	(817)	359,467	261,717
77346	Atascocita (c)	(281)	*35,757*	—

ZIP	Place	Area Code	2004	1990
*75751	Athens	(903)	12,364	10,982
75551	Atlanta	(214)	5,616	6,118
*78712	Austin	(512)	681,804	472,020
*76020	Azle	(817)	10,301	8,868
77518	Bacliff (c)	(409)	19,343	5,549
75180	Balch Springs	(214)	19,343	17,406
78602	Bastrop	(512)	7,006	4,044
*77414	Bay City	(979)	18,381	18,170
*77520	Baytown	(713)	67,321	63,843
*77707	Beaumont	(409)	112,294	114,323
*76021	Bedford	(817)	48,417	43,762
*78102	Beeville	(361)	13,586	13,547
*77401	Bellaire	(713)	16,948	13,844
*76715	Bellmead	(254)	9,636	8,336
76513	Belton	(254)	14,838	12,463
*76126	Benbrook	(817)	21,646	19,564
*79720	Big Spring	(432)	24,524	23,093
*78006	Boerne	(830)	7,395	4,361
75418	Bonham	(903)	10,439	6,688
*79007	Borger	(806)	13,400	15,675
76230	Bowie	(940)	5,470	4,990
76825	Brady	(325)	5,446	5,946
76424	Breckenridge	(254)	5,628	5,665
—	Briar (c)	—	*5,350*	3,899
*77833	Brenham	(979)	14,044	11,952
77611	Bridge City	(409)	8,729	8,010
76426	Bridgeport	(940)	5,404	3,581
79316	Brownfield	(806)	9,302	9,560
*78520	Brownsville	(956)	161,225	107,027
*76801	Brownwood	(325)	19,467	18,387
78717	Brushy Creek (c)	(903)	*15,371*	5,833
*77801	Bryan	(979)	66,316	55,002
76354	Burkburnett	(940)	10,513	10,145
*76028	Burleson	(817)	27,932	16,113
78611	Burnet	(512)	5,415	3,423
76520	Cameron	(254)	5,863	5,635
—	Cameron Park (c)	—	*5,961*	3,802
79835	Canutillo (c)	(915)	*5,129*	4,442
*79015	Canyon	(806)	13,060	11,365
78130	Canyon Lake (c)	(830)	*16,870*	9,975
78834	Carrizo Springs	(830)	5,576	5,745
*75006	Carrolton	(214)	117,823	82,169
75633	Carthage	(903)	6,713	6,496
*75104	Cedar Hill	(214)	40,219	19,988
*78613	Cedar Park	(512)	45,360	5,161
75935	Center	(936)	5,713	4,950
77530	Channelview (c)	(713)	*29,685*	25,564
79201	Childress	(940)	6,575	5,055
78108	Cibolo	(210)	5,847	1,757
—	Cinco Ranch (c)	(281)	*11,196*	—
*76031	Cleburne	(817)	28,803	22,205
*77327	Cleveland	(713)	8,053	7,124
77015	Cloverleaf (c)	(713)	*23,508*	18,230
77531	Clute	(979)	10,763	9,467
*77840	College Station	(979)	72,186	52,443
76034	Colleyville	(817)	21,720	12,724
*75428	Commerce	(903)	8,669	6,825
*77301	Conroe	(936)	43,402	27,675
78109	Converse	(210)	12,014	8,887
*75019	Coppell	(214)	38,939	16,881
76522	Copperas Cove	(254)	29,997	24,079
*76205	Corinth	(940)	17,212	3,944
*78469	Corpus Christi	(361)	281,196	257,428
*75110	Corsicana	(903)	25,858	22,911
75835	Crockett	(936)	7,054	7,024
76036	Crowley	(817)	9,337	6,974
78839	Crystal City	(830)	7,173	8,263
77954	Cuero	(361)	6,725	6,700
79022	Dalhart	(806)	7,127	6,246
*75221	Dallas	(214)	1,210,393	1,007,618
77535	Dayton	(936)	6,529	5,042
76234	Decatur	(214)	5,907	4,245
77536	Deer Park	(713)	28,647	27,424
*78840	Del Rio	(830)	35,816	30,705
*75020	Denison	(903)	23,379	21,505
*76201	Denton	(940)	98,288	66,270
*75115	De Soto	(214)	43,050	30,544
75941	Diboll	(936)	5,461	4,341
77539	Dickinson	(281)	17,749	11,692
78537	Donna	(956)	15,611	12,652
79029	Dumas	(806)	13,819	12,871
*75138	Duncanville	(214)	35,346	35,008
76135	Eagle Mountain (c)	(817)	*6,599*	5,847
*78852	Eagle Pass	(830)	24,847	20,651
*78539	Edinburg	(956)	58,448	31,091
77957	Edna	(361)	5,887	5,436
—	Eidson Road (c)	—	*9,348*	—
77437	El Campo	(979)	10,928	10,511
78621	Elgin	(512)	8,007	4,846
*79910	El Paso	(915)	592,099	515,342
78543	Elsa	(956)	6,369	5,242
*75119	Ennis	(214)	18,551	13,869
*76039	Euless	(817)	50,575	38,149
76140	Everman	(817)	5,794	5,672
79838	Fabens (c)	(915)	*8,043*	5,599
*78015	Fair Oaks Ranch	(210)	5,527	1,886
78355	Falfurrias	(361)	5,101	5,788
*75381	Farmers Branch	(214)	26,706	24,250
78114	Floresville	(830)	6,744	5,247
*75022	Flower Mound	(214)	62,209	15,527
76119	Forest Hill	(817)	13,275	11,482
75126	Forney	(214)	8,775	4,070
79906	Fort Bliss (c)	(915)	*8,264*	13,915
76544	Fort Hood (c)	(254)	*33,711*	35,580
79735	Fort Stockton	(432)	7,320	8,524
*76161	Fort Worth	(817)	603,337	447,619
78624	Fredericksburg	(830)	10,087	6,934
*77541	Freeport	(979)	12,759	11,389
*77546	Friendswood	(281)	32,717	22,814
*75034	Frisco	(214)	62,372	6,138
*76240	Gainesville	(940)	16,361	14,256
77547	Galena Park	(713)	10,341	10,033
*77550	Galveston	(409)	57,355	59,067
*75040	Garland	(214)	217,176	180,635
*76528	Gatesville	(254)	15,732	11,492
*78626	Georgetown	(512)	36,462	14,840
78942	Giddings	(979)	5,436	4,093
*75644	Gilmer	(903)	5,071	4,822
75647	Gladewater	(903)	6,261	6,027
75154	Glenn Heights	(214)	8,647	4,564
78629	Gonzales	(830)	7,400	6,527
—	Greatwood (c)	—	*6,640*	—
76450	Graham	(940)	8,680	8,986
*76048	Granbury	(817)	6,814	4,045
*75051	Grand Prairie	(214)	140,320	99,606
*76051	Grapevine	(817)	47,265	29,407
*75401	Greenville	(903)	25,149	23,071
77619	Groves	(409)	15,147	16,744
*75147	Gun Barrel City	(903)	5,901	3,526
*76117	Haltom City	(817)	40,132	32,856
*76548	Harker Heights	(254)	20,255	12,932
*78550	Harlingen	(956)	61,589	48,746
75032	Heath	(214)	6,115	2,128
78023	Helotes	(210)	5,852	1,556
77445	Hempstead	(979)	6,264	3,598
*75652	Henderson	(903)	11,417	11,139
79045	Hereford	(806)	14,458	14,745
76643	Hewitt	(254)	12,679	8,983
78557	Hidalgo	(956)	10,073	3,292
*75205	Highland Park	(214)	8,810	8,739
77562	Highlands (c)	(713)	*7,089*	6,632
75067	Highland Village	(214)	14,589	7,027
76645	Hillsboro	(254)	8,905	7,072
77563	Hitchcock	(409)	7,147	5,868
—	Homestead Meadows South (c)	—	*6,807*	—
78861	Hondo	(830)	8,481	6,018
*79927	Horizon City	(915)	7,797	2,308
*77052	Houston	(281)/(713)/(832)	2,012,626	1,654,348
*77338	Humble	(713)	14,757	12,060
*77340	Huntsville	(936)	35,840	30,628
*76053	Hurst	(817)	37,893	33,574
78634	Hutto	(512)	5,588	—
78362	Ingleside	(361)	9,156	5,696
76367	Iowa Park	(940)	6,222	6,072
*75015	Irving	(214)	194,547	155,037
77029	Jacinto City	(713)	10,048	9,343
75766	Jacksonville	(903)	14,138	12,765
75951	Jasper	(409)	7,540	7,160
*77040	Jersey Village	(713)	7,162	4,826
78729	Jollyville (c)	(512)	*15,813*	15,206
76058	Joshua	(817)	5,376	3,634
*77449	Katy	(713)	13,012	8,004
75142	Kaufman	(214)	7,769	5,251
76059	Keene	(817)	5,731	3,944
*76248	Keller	(817)	34,915	13,683
76060	Kennedale	(817)	6,495	4,096
79745	Kermit	(432)	5,308	6,875
*78028	Kerrville	(830)	21,477	17,384
*75662	Kilgore	(903)	11,619	11,066
*76540	Killeen	(254)	96,943	63,535
*78363	Kingsville	(361)	25,257	25,276
78219	Kirby	(210)	8,675	8,326
78640	Kyle	(512)	14,053	2,225
78236	Lackland AFB (c)	(210)	*7,123*	9,352
76705	Lacy-Lakeview	(254)	5,827	3,617
78559	La Feria	(956)	6,832	4,360
78645	Lago Vista	(512)	5,425	2,199
—	La Homa (c)	—	*10,433*	1,403
75065	Lake Dallas	(940)	6,894	3,656
77566	Lake Jackson	(979)	27,022	22,771
*78734	Lakeway	(512)	8,404	4,044
77568	La Marque	(409)	13,733	14,120
79331	Lamesa	(806)	9,383	10,809
76550	Lampasas	(512)	7,883	6,382
*75146	Lancaster	(214)	30,304	22,117
*77571	La Porte	(713)	33,265	27,923
*78041	Laredo	(956)	203,212	122,893
*77573	League City	(281)	57,981	30,159
*78641	Leander	(512)	15,874	3,354
*78268	Leon Valley	(210)	9,376	9,581
*79336	Levelland	(806)	12,771	13,986
*75067	Lewisville	(214)	89,142	46,521

ZIP	Place	Area Code	2004	1990
77575	Liberty	(936)	8,304	7,690
75068	Little Elm	(214)	14,884	1,242
79339	Littlefield	(806)	6,360	6,489
*78233	Live Oak	(210)	10,023	10,023
*77351	Livingston	(936)	6,381	5,019
78644	Lockhart	(512)	13,523	9,205
*75606	Longview	(903)	75,306	70,311
*79408	Lubbock	(806)	207,852	186,206
*75901	Lufkin	(936)	33,500	30,210
78648	Luling	(830)	5,418	4,661
77657	Lumberton	(409)	9,381	6,640
*78501	McAllen	(956)	120,743	84,021
*75070	McKinney	(214)	88,409	21,283
76063	Mansfield	(817)	34,735	15,615
*78654	Marble Falls	(830)	6,059	4,017
76661	Marlin	(254)	6,298	6,386
*75670	Marshall	(903)	23,671	23,682
78368	Mathis	(361)	5,346	5,423
77477	Meadows Place	(281)/(713)	5,770	4,663
78570	Mercedes	(956)	14,164	12,694
*75149	Mesquite	(214)	129,710	101,484
76667	Mexia	(254)	6,743	6,933
*79701	Midland	(432)	98,082	89,343
76065	Midlothian	(214)	11,599	5,040
*76067	Mineral Wells	(940)	16,854	14,935
*78572	Mission	(956)	57,812	28,653
—	Mission Bend (c)	—	*30,831*	24,945
*77489	Missouri City	(713)	66,587	36,143
79756	Monahans	(432)	6,403	8,101
*75455	Mount Pleasant	(903)	14,610	12,291
*75094	Murphy	(214)	9,596	1,603
*75961	Nacogdoches	(936)	30,647	30,872
*77868	Navasota	(936)	7,287	6,296
77627	Nederland	(409)	16,837	16,192
*78130	New Braunfels	(830)	44,931	27,334
—	New Territory (c)	(281)	*13,861*	—
*76161	North Richland Hills	(817)	60,483	45,895
—	Nurillo (c)	—	*5,056*	—
*79761	Odessa	(432)	92,844	89,699
*77630	Orange	(409)	18,140	19,370
77465	Palacios	(361)	5,234	4,418
*75801	Palestine	(903)	17,869	18,042
*18520	Palmhurst	(956)	5,027	—
—	Palmview South (c)	—	*6,219*	—
*79065	Pampa	(806)	16,702	19,959
*75460	Paris	(903)	26,578	24,799
*77501	Pasadena	(713)	144,174	119,604
*77581	Pearland	(713)	52,402	18,927
78061	Pearsall	(830)	7,685	6,924
78721	Pecan Grove (c)	—	*13,551*	9,502
79772	Pecos	(432)	8,419	12,069
79070	Perryton	(806)	7,884	7,619
*78660	Pflugerville	(512)	25,911	4,444
78577	Pharr	(956)	56,839	32,921
*79072	Plainview	(806)	21,995	21,698
*75074	Plano	(214)	245,411	127,885
78064	Pleasanton	(830)	9,220	7,678
*77640	Port Arthur	(409)	56,727	58,551
78578	Port Isabel	(956)	5,391	4,740
78374	Portland	(361)	15,584	12,224
77979	Port Lavaca	(361)	11,759	10,886
77651	Port Neches	(409)	13,224	12,908
78579	Progreso	(956)	5,049	2,808
*78580	Raymondville	(956)	9,456	8,880
75154	Red Oak	(214)	6,444	3,660
76028	Rendon (c)	(817)	*9,022*	7,658
*75080	Richardson	(214)	99,263	74,840
*76118	Richland Hills	(817)	8,101	7,978
*77469	Richmond	(713)	13,001	10,042
78043	Rio Bravo	(956)	5,755	—
78582	Rio Grande City	(956)	13,403	10,725
76114	River Oaks	(817)	6,944	6,580
76701	Robinson	(254)	8,711	7,111
78380	Robstown	(361)	12,614	12,849
76567	Rockdale	(512)	6,027	5,235
*78382	Rockport	(361)	8,694	5,619
*75087	Rockwall	(214)	26,696	10,486
78584	Roma	(956)	10,698	8,059
77471	Rosenberg	(713)	29,470	20,183
*78681	Round Rock	(512)	82,040	30,923
*75088	Rowlett	(214)	52,779	23,260
75785	Rusk	(903)	5,234	4,366
75048	Sachse	(214)	16,077	5,346
*76179	Saginaw	(817)	16,874	8,551
*76902	San Angelo	(325)	88,112	84,462
*78265	San Antonio	(210)	1,236,249	976,514
78586	San Benito	(956)	24,387	20,125
79849	San Elizario (c)	(915)	*11,046*	4,385
76266	Sanger	(940)	5,847	3,602
78589	San Juan	(956)	29,741	12,561
*78666	San Marcos	(512)	44,628	28,738
*77510	Santa Fe	(409)	10,371	8,429
*78154	Schertz	(210)	24,975	10,597
77586	Seabrook	(281)	10,856	6,685
75159	Seagoville	(214)	11,071	8,969
77474	Sealy	(979)	5,936	4,541
*78155	Seguin	(830)	24,212	18,692
79360	Seminole	(432)	5,881	6,342
—	Shady Hollow (c)	—	*5,140*	—
*75090	Sherman	(903)	36,578	31,584
77656	Silsbee	(409)	6,620	6,368
78387	Sinton	(361)	5,517	5,549
79364	Slaton	(806)	5,873	6,078
*79549	Snyder	(325)	10,542	12,195
79927	Socorro	(915)	28,029	22,995
77587	South Houston	(713)	16,350	14,207
76092	Southlake	(817)	24,490	7,082
*77373	Spring (c)	(713)	*36,385*	33,111
*77477	Stafford	(713)	18,794	8,395
*76401	Stephenville	(254)	15,416	13,502
*77478	Sugar Land	(713)	73,721	33,712
*75482	Sulphur Springs	(903)	15,081	14,062
79556	Sweetwater	(325)	10,882	11,967
76574	Taylor	(512)	14,636	11,472
*76501	Temple	(254)	54,505	46,150
*75160	Terrell	(214)	16,914	12,490
78209	Terrell Hills	(210)	5,088	4,592
*75501	Texarkana	(903)	35,492	32,294
*77590	Texas City	(409)	43,535	40,822
*75056	The Colony	(214)	36,316	22,113
77387	The Woodlands (c)	(713)	*55,649*	29,205
—	Timberwood Park (c)	(210)	*5,889*	2,578
*77375	Tomball	(713)	9,853	6,370
76262	Trophy Club	(817)	7,269	3,922
*75702	Tyler	(903)	89,552	75,450
*78148	Universal City	(830)	15,821	13,057
75205	University Park	(214)	23,686	22,259
*78801	Uvalde	(830)	16,233	14,729
*76384	Vernon	(940)	11,165	12,001
*77901	Victoria	(361)	61,677	55,076
*77662	Vidor	(409)	11,293	10,935
*76702	Waco	(254)	118,093	103,590
75501	Wake Village	(903)	5,178	4,761
76148	Watauga	(817)	23,649	20,009
*75165	Waxahachie	(214)	24,654	17,984
*76086	Weatherford	(817)	22,343	14,804
77598	Webster	(281)	8,905	4,678
78728	Wells Branch (c)	—	*11,271*	7,094
*78596	Weslaco	(956)	31,081	22,739
—	West Livingston (c)	—	*6,612*	—
79764	West Odessa (c)	(432)	*17,799*	16,568
77005	West University Place	(713)	14,820	12,920
77488	Wharton	(979)	9,412	9,011
75791	Whitehouse	(903)	6,820	4,018
75693	White Oak	(903)	6,023	5,136
76108	White Settlement	(817)	15,652	15,472
*76307	Wichita Falls	(940)	100,929	96,259
78239	Windcrest	(210)	5,100	5,331
—	Windemere (c)	—	*6,868*	3,207
76712	Woodway	(254)	8,750	8,695
75098	Wylie	(214)	25,743	8,716
77995	Yoakum	(361)	5,720	5,611

Utah

ZIP	Place	Area Code	2004	1990
84004	Alpine	(801)	7,896	3,492
84003	American Fork	(801)	22,387	15,722
84065	Bluffdale	(801)	6,087	2,142
*84010	Bountiful	(801)	41,173	37,544
84302	Brigham City	(435)	17,149	15,644
84109	Canyon Rim (c)	(801)	*10,428*	10,527
*84720	Cedar City	(435)	22,224	13,443
84062	Cedar Hills	(801)	5,813	708
84014	Centerville	(801)	14,670	11,500
*84015	Clearfield	(801)	27,227	21,435
84015	Clinton	(801)	16,447	7,945
84121	Cottonwood Heights (c)	(801)	*27,569*	28,766
84121	Cottonwood West (c)	(801)	*18,727*	17,476
84020	Draper	(801)	33,042	7,143
84043	Eagle Mountain	(801)	8,190	30
84109	East Millcreek (c)	(801)	*21,385*	21,184
84025	Farmington	(801)	13,882	9,049
84029	Grantsville	(435)	7,077	4,500
84032	Heber	(435)	8,800	4,782
84065	Herriman	(801)	7,826	—
84003	Highland	(801)	12,332	5,007
*84117	Holladay	(801)	19,311	14,095
84737	Hurricane	(435)	9,748	3,915
84319	Hyrum	(435)	6,463	4,829
84738	Ivins	(435)	6,404	1,639
84037	Kaysville	(801)	21,749	13,961
84118	Kearns (c)	(801)	*33,659*	28,374
*84041	Layton	(801)	61,205	41,784
84043	Lehi	(801)	25,665	8,475
84042	Lindon	(801)	8,489	3,818
—	Little Cottonwood Creek Valley (c)	(801)	*7,221*	5,042
*84321	Logan	(435)	45,517	32,771
84044	Magna (c)	(801)	*22,770*	17,829
84664	Mapleton	(801)	6,129	3,572
84047	Midvale	(801)	27,019	11,886
84109	Millcreek (c)	(801)	*30,377*	32,230
84117	Mount Olympus (c)	(801)	*7,103*	7,413

ZIP	Place	Area Code	2004	1990
*84157	Murray	(801)	43,328	31,274
84648	Nephi	(435)	5,034	3,515
84341	North Logan	(435)	6,692	3,775
*84404	North Ogden	(801)	16,328	11,593
84054	North Salt Lake	(801)	9,555	6,464
*84401	Ogden	(801)	78,519	63,943
—	Oquirrh (c)	(801)	*10,390*	7,593
*84057	Orem	(801)	88,619	67,561
*84060	Park City	(435)	7,882	4,468
*84651	Payson	(801)	14,542	9,510
84062	Pleasant Grove	(801)	27,116	13,476
*84404	Pleasant View	(801)	6,048	3,597
84501	Price	(435)	8,197	8,712
84332	Providence	(435)	5,351	3,344
*84601	Provo	(801)	99,624	86,835
84701	Richfield	(435)	7,048	5,593
84405	Riverdale	(801)	7,896	6,419
*84065	Riverton	(801)	30,119	11,261
*84067	Roy	(801)	35,308	24,560
*84770	Saint George	(435)	59,780	28,572
*84101	Salt Lake City	(801)	178,605	159,928
*84070	Sandy	(801)	89,979	75,240
84765	Santa Clara	(435)	5,661	2,323
84655	Santaquin	(801)	5,815	2,522
84043	Saratoga Springs	(801)	5,389	—
84335	Smithfield	(435)	7,801	5,566
84095	South Jordan	(801)	36,791	12,215
84403	South Ogden	(801)	15,130	12,105
84165	South Salt Lake	(801)	21,510	10,129
*84403	South Weber	(801)	5,486	2,853
84660	Spanish Fork	(801)	22,839	11,272
84663	Springville	(801)	21,507	13,950
84098	Summit Park (c)	—	*6,597*	—
84015	Sunset	(801)	5,000	5,128
84075	Syracuse	(801)	16,158	4,658
84118	Taylorsville	(801)	58,179	51,550
84074	Tooele	(435)	27,903	13,887
84337	Tremonton	(435)	6,205	4,262
*84078	Vernal	(435)	7,939	6,640
84780	Washington	(435)	11,521	4,198
84405	Washington Terrace	(801)	8,395	8,189
84401	West Haven	(801)	5,237	—
*84084	West Jordan	(801)	89,011	42,915
84015	West Point	(801)	7,046	4,258
*84170	West Valley City	(801)	112,678	86,969
84070	White City (c)	(801)	*5,988*	6,506
*84087	Woods Cross	(801)	7,859	5,384

Vermont (802)

See introductory note.

ZIP	Place	2004	1990
05641	Barre	9,141	9,482
05641	*Barre*	7,905	7,411
05201	Bennington (c)	*9,168*	9,532
05201	*Bennington*	15,473	16,451
*05301	*Brattleboro*	11,944	12,241
*05301	Brattleboro (c)	*8,289*	8,612
*05401	Burlington	38,934	39,127
*05446	*Colchester*	17,177	14,731
*05451	Essex Junction	19,065	16,498
05047	*Hartford*	10,698	9,404
05465	*Jericho*	5,067	1,405
05849	*Lyndon*	5,587	5,371
05753	Middlebury (c)	*6,252*	6,007
*05753	*Middlebury*	8,172	8,034
05468	*Milton*	10,065	8,404
*05602	Montpelier	8,013	8,247
05661	*Morristown*	5,502	4,733
05855	Newport	5,118	4,434
05663	*Northfield*	5,787	5,610
—	Randolph	5,031	—
—	Rockingham	5,175	—
*05701	Rutland	17,080	18,230
*05478	Saint Albans	5,812	7,339
05478	*Saint Albans City*	7,548	4,606
05819	Saint Johnsbury (c)	*6,319*	6,424
05819	*Saint Johnsbury*	7,560	7,608
05482	*Shelburne*	6,984	5,871
*05403	South Burlington	16,460	12,809
05156	*Springfield*	8,957	9,579
05488	*Swanton*	6,423	5,636
05676	*Waterbury*	5,164	4,614
05495	*Williston*	8,224	4,887
05404	Winooski	6,365	6,649

Virginia

Area code (571) overlays area code (703). See introductory note.

ZIP	Place	Area Code	2004	1990
*24210	Abingdon	(276)	7,938	7,003
*22313	Alexandria	(703)	128,206	111,182
22003	Ananndale (c)	(703)	*54,994*	50,975
22554	Aquia Harbour (c)	(703)	*7,856*	6,308
*22210	Arlington (c)	(703)	186,117	170,897
23005	Ashland	(804)	6,943	5,864
*22041	Bailey's Crossroads (c)	(703)	*23,166*	19,507
24523	Bedford	(540)	6,229	6,177
22306	Belle Haven (c)	(757)	*6,269*	6,427
24219	Big Stone Gap	(276)	5,833	4,847
*24060	Blacksburg	(540)	39,212	34,590
24605	Bluefield	(304)	5,030	5,363
23235	Bon Air (c)	(804)	*16,213*	16,413
22812	Bridgewater	(540)	5,301	3,918
*24203	Bristol	(276)	17,308	18,426
24416	Buena Vista	(540)	6,230	6,406
—	Bull Run (c)	(703)	*11,337*	5,525
*22150	Burke (c)	(703)	*57,737*	57,734
24018	Cave Spring (c)	(540)	*24,941*	24,053
*20120	Centreville (c)	(703)	*48,661*	26,585
*20151	Chantilly (c)	(703)	*41,041*	29,337
*22906	Charlottesville	(434)	36,605	40,475
*23320	Chesapeake	(757)	214,725	151,982
*23831	Chester (c)	(804)	*17,890*	14,986
*24073	Christiansburg	(540)	17,495	15,004
24078	Collinsville (c)	(276)	*7,777*	7,280
23834	Colonial Heights	(804)	17,511	16,064
24426	Covington	(540)	6,256	7,198
*22701	Culpeper	(540)	11,070	8,581
22193	Dale City (c)	(703)	*55,971*	47,170
*24541	Danville	(434)	46,371	53,056
23228	Dumbarton (c)	(804)	*6,674*	8,526
22027	Dunn Loring (c)	(703)	*7,861*	6,509
23222	East Highland Park (c)	(804)	*12,488*	11,850
23847	Emporia	(434)	5,674	5,479
23803	Ettrick (c)	(804)	*5,627*	5,290
*22030	Fairfax	(703)	22,062	19,894
*22046	Falls Church	(703)	10,781	9,522
*23901	Farmville	(434)	7,011	6,505
24551	Forest (c)	(434)	*8,006*	5,624
22060	Fort Belvoir (c)	(703)	*7,176*	8,590
22308	Fort Hunt (c)	(703)	*12,923*	12,989
23801	Fort Lee (c)	(804)	*7,269*	6,895
22310	Franconia (c)	(703)	*31,907*	19,882
23851	Franklin	(757)	8,471	7,864
*22404	Fredericksburg	(540)	20,458	19,027
22630	Front Royal	(540)	14,210	11,880
24333	Galax	(276)	6,657	6,699
*23060	Glen Allen (c)	(804)	*12,562*	9,010
23062	Gloucester Point (c)	(804)	*9,429*	8,509
22066	Great Falls (c)	(703)	*8,549*	6,945
22306	Groveton (c)	(703)	*21,296*	19,997
*23670	Hampton	(757)	145,951	133,811
*22801	Harrisonburg	(540)	41,066	30,707
*20170	Herndon	(703)	21,666	16,139
23075	Highland Springs (c)	(804)	*15,137*	13,823
24019	Hollins (c)	(540)	*14,309*	13,305
23860	Hopewell	(804)	22,369	23,101
22303	Huntington (c)	(703)	*8,325*	7,489
22306	Hybla Valley (c)	(703)	*16,721*	15,491
22043	Idylwood (c)	(703)	*16,005*	14,710
22042	Jefferson (c)	(703)	*27,422*	25,782
22041	Lake Barcroft (c)	(703)	*8,906*	8,686
22963	Lake Monticello (c)	(434)	*6,852*	2,331
22191	Lake Ridge (c)	(540)	*30,404*	23,862
23228	Lakeside (c)	(804)	*11,157*	12,081
23060	Laurel (c)	(804)	*14,875*	13,011
*20175	Leesburg	(703)	34,828	16,202
24450	Lexington	(540)	6,910	6,959
22312	Lincolnia (c)	(703)	*15,788*	13,041
—	Linton Hall (c)	—	*8,620*	—
*22079	Lorton (c)	(703)	*17,786*	15,385
*24506	Lynchburg	(434)	64,932	66,049
*22101	McLean (c)	(703)	*38,929*	38,168
24572	Madison Heights (c)	(434)	*11,584*	11,700
*20110	Manassas	(703)	37,615	27,957
20113	Manassas Park	(703)	11,519	6,734
22030	Mantua (c)	(703)	*7,485*	6,804
24354	Marion	(276)	6,168	6,630
*24112	Martinsville	(276)	15,039	16,162
*23111	Mechanicsville (c)	(804)	*30,464*	22,027
*22116	Merrifield (c)	(703)	*11,170*	8,399
—	Montclair (c)	—	*15,728*	11,399
23231	Montrose (c)	(804)	*7,018*	6,405
22121	Mount Vernon (c)	(703)	*28,582*	27,485
22122	Newington (c)	(703)	*19,784*	17,965
*23607	Newport News	(757)	181,913	171,439
*23501	Norfolk	(757)	237,835	261,250
22151	North Springfield (c)	(703)	*9,173*	8,996
22124	Oakton (c)	(703)	*29,348*	24,610
*23804	Petersburg	(804)	32,757	37,027
22043	Pimmit Hills (c)	(703)	*6,152*	6,019
23662	Poquoson	(757)	11,700	11,005
*23707	Portsmouth	(757)	99,291	103,910
24301	Pulaski	(540)	9,169	9,985
22134	Quantico Station (c)	(703)	*6,571*	7,425
*24141	Radford	(540)	14,770	15,940
*20190	Reston (c)	(703)	*56,407*	48,556
*23232	Richmond	(804)	192,494	202,798
*24022	Roanoke	(540)	92,352	96,509
24281	Rose Hill (c)	(276)	*15,058*	12,675
*24153	Salem	(540)	24,347	23,797
22044	Seven Corners (c)	(703)	*8,701*	7,280
*23430	Smithfield	(757)	6,784	4,686

ZIP	Place	Area Code	2004	1990
24592	South Boston	(434)	8,151	6,997
*22150	Springfield (c)	(703)	30,417	23,706
*24402	Staunton	(540)	23,840	24,461
24477	Stuarts Draft (c)	(540)	8,367	5,087
23162	Sudley (c)	(540)	7,719	7,321
*23434	Suffolk	(757)	76,586	52,143
24502	Timberlake (c)	(434)	10,683	10,314
22172	Triangle (c)	(703)	5,500	4,740
23229	Tuckahoe (c)	(804)	43,242	42,629
22101	Tysons Corner (c)	(703)	18,540	13,124
*22180	Vienna	(703)	14,850	14,852
24179	Vinton	(540)	7,742	7,643
*23450	Virginia Beach	(757)	440,098	393,089
*20186	Warrenton	(540)	8,295	4,882
22980	Waynesboro	(540)	20,755	18,549
22110	West Gate (c)	(703)	7,493	6,565
22152	West Springfield (c)	(703)	28,378	28,126
*23185	Williamsburg	(757)	11,465	11,409
*22601	Winchester	(540)	24,779	21,947
24592	Wolf Trap (c)	(703)	14,001	13,133
*22191	Woodbridge (c)	(703)	31,941	26,401
—	Wyndham (c)	—	6,176	—
24382	Wytheville	(276)	7,917	8,036
22110	Yorkshire (c)	(703)	6,732	5,699

Washington

ZIP	Place	Area Code	2004	1990
98520	Aberdeen	(360)	16,364	16,565
98036	Alderwood Manor (c)	(425)	15,329	22,945
*98221	Anacortes	(360)	15,764	11,451
98223	Arlington	(360)	14,491	4,037
98335	Artondale (c)	(253)	8,630	7,141
*98002	Auburn	(253)	44,980	33,650
98110	Bainbridge Island	(206)	21,910	—
98315	Bangor Trident Base (c)	(360)	7,253	3,702
98604	Battle Ground	(360)	13,001	3,758
*98009	Bellevue	(425)	116,914	95,213
*98225	Bellingham	(360)	72,992	52,179
*98390	Bonney Lake	(360)	14,142	7,494
*98011	Bothell	(425)	30,671	12,575
*98337	Bremerton	(360)	35,967	38,142
98036	Brier	(425)	6,319	5,633
98178	Bryn Mawr-Skyway (c)	(206)	13,977	12,514
*98166	Burien	(206)	30,887	27,507
98233	Burlington	(360)	7,837	4,349
—	Camano (c)	—	13,347	—
98607	Camas	(360)	16,089	6,762
98055	Cascade-Fairwood (c)	(425)	34,580	30,107
98531	Centralia	(360)	15,250	12,101
98532	Chehalis	(360)	7,181	6,527
99004	Cheney	(509)	10,076	7,723
99403	Clarkston	(509)	7,266	6,753
—	Clarkston Heights-Vineland (c)	—	6,117	2,832
99324	College Place	(509)	8,779	6,308
98072	Cottage Lake (c)	(206)	24,330	—
99218	Country Homes (c)	(509)	5,203	5,126
98042	Covington	(253)	16,205	—
*98198	Des Moines	(206)	28,847	20,830
99213	Dishman (c)	(509)	10,031	9,671
98019	Duvall	(425)	5,655	2,640
—	East Hill-Meridian (c)	—	29,308	42,696
98366	East Port Orchard (c)	(360)	5,116	5,409
98056	East Renton Highlands (c)	(425)	13,264	13,218
98802	East Wenatchee	(509)	8,721	3,886
98801	East Wenatchee Bench (c)	(509)	13,658	12,539
*98371	Edgewood	(253)	9,598	8,702
*98020	Edmonds	(425)	39,601	30,743
98387	Elk Plain (c)	—	15,697	12,197
*98926	Ellensburg	(509)	16,385	12,360
98022	Enumclaw	(360)	10,940	7,243
98823	Ephrata	(509)	7,096	5,349
*98201	Everett	(425)	96,101	70,937
99218	Fairwood (c)	(509)	6,764	5,807
*98002	Federal Way	(253)	81,356	67,535
98685	Felida (c)	(360)	5,683	3,109
98248	Ferndale	(360)	9,736	5,398
99336	Finley (c)	(509)	5,770	4,897
98466	Fircrest	(253)	6,016	5,270
98597	Five Corners (c)	—	12,207	6,776
98433	Fort Lewis (c)	(253)	19,089	22,224
98373	Frederickson (c)	(206)	5,758	3,502
*98329	Gig Harbor	(253)	6,597	3,236
98338	Graham (c)	(253)	8,739	—
98930	Grandview	(509)	8,619	7,169
99016	Green Acres (c)	(509)	5,158	4,626
98660	Hazel Dell North (c)	(360)	9,261	6,924
98665	Hazel Dell South (c)	(360)	6,605	5,796
98025	Hobart (c)	—	6,251	—
—	Hockinson (c)	(360)	5,136	—
98550	Hoquiam	(360)	9,036	8,972
98011	Inglewood-Finn Hill (c)	(425)	22,661	29,132
*98027	Issaquah	(425)	15,570	7,786
98626	Kelso	(360)	11,820	11,767
98028	Kenmore	(425)	19,353	8,917
*99336	Kennewick	(509)	60,118	42,148
*98031	Kent	(253)/(425)	81,631	37,960
98033	Kingsgate (c)	(425)	12,222	14,259
*98033	Kirkland	(425)	45,557	40,059
*98509	Lacey	(360)	32,981	19,279
98155	Lake Forest Park	(206)	12,474	4,031
98002	Lakeland North (c)	(253)	15,085	14,402
98002	Lakeland South (c)	(253)	11,436	9,027
—	Lake Morton-Berrydale (c)	—	9,659	—
98665	Lake Shore (c)	(360)	6,670	6,268
98258	Lake Stevens	(425)	7,238	3,435
*98498	Lakewood	(253)	58,070	55,937
—	Lea Hill (c)	—	10,871	6,876
98632	Longview	(360)	35,943	31,499
98264	Lynden	(360)	10,456	5,709
*98046	Lynnwood	(425)	33,418	28,637
98290	Maltby (c)	(360)	8,267	—
98038	Maple Valley	(425)	14,286	1,211
98012	Martha Lake (c)	(425)	12,633	10,155
*98270	Marysville	(360)	28,804	12,248
98040	Mercer Island	(206)	22,182	20,816
98444	Midland (c)	(253)	7,414	5,587
*98082	Mill Creek	(425)	13,506	7,180
—	Mill Plain (c)	(360)	7,400	—
98354	Milton	(253)	6,238	4,995
98661	Minnehaha (c)	(360)	7,689	9,661
98272	Monroe	(360)	15,178	4,275
98837	Moses Lake	(509)	16,453	11,235
98043	Mountlake Terrace	(425)	20,310	19,320
*98273	Mount Vernon	(360)	28,821	17,647
—	Mount Vista (c)	—	5,770	—
98275	Mukilteo	(425)	19,434	11,575
*98059	Newcastle	(425)	9,015	4,649
*98166	Normandy Park	(206)	6,200	6,794
—	North Creek (c)	—	25,742	23,236
98270	North Marysville (c)	(425)	21,161	18,711
*98277	Oak Harbor	(360)	21,660	17,176
*98501	Olympia	(360)	43,982	33,729
99214	Opportunity (c)	(509)	25,065	22,326
98662	Orchards (c)	(360)	17,852	—
*99327	Othello	(509)	6,106	4,638
99027	Otis Orchards-East Farms (c)	(360)	6,318	5,811
98047	Pacific	(253)	5,649	4,622
—	Paine Field-Lake Stickney (c)	—	24,383	18,670
98444	Parkland (c)	(253)	24,053	20,882
98366	Parkwood (c)	(360)	7,213	6,853
*99301	Pasco	(509)	42,290	20,337
—	Picnic Point-North Lynnwood (c)	—	22,953	—
*98362	Port Angeles	(360)	18,635	17,710
*98366	Port Orchard	(360)	7,983	4,984
98368	Port Townsend	(360)	8,810	7,001
98370	Poulsbo	(360)	7,435	4,848
98390	Prairie Ridge (c)	—	11,688	8,278
99350	Prosser	(509)	5,153	4,492
*99163	Pullman	(509)	25,022	23,478
*98371	Puyallup	(253)	35,496	23,878
98848	Quincy	(509)	5,345	3,738
*98052	Redmond	(425)	46,965	35,800
*98058	Renton	(425)	54,807	41,688
*99352	Richland	(509)	43,427	32,315
98188	Riverton-Boulevard Park (c)	(206)	11,188	15,337
98686	Salmon Creek (c)	(360)	16,767	11,989
*98074	Sammamish	(425)	34,269	—
*98148	SeaTac	(206)	25,155	22,760
*98101	Seattle	(206)/(425)	571,480	516,259
—	Seattle Hill-Silver Firs (c)	—	35,311	—
98284	Sedro-Woolley	(360)	9,857	6,333
98942	Selah	(509)	6,716	5,113
98584	Shelton	(360)	8,946	7,241
*98133	Shoreline	(206)	51,950	46,979
*98315	Silverdale (c)	(360)	15,816	7,660
*98290	Snohomish	(360)	8,596	6,499
*98065	Snoqualmie	(425)	5,257	1,546
98373	South Hill (c)	—	31,623	12,963
98387	Spanaway (c)	(253)	21,588	15,001
*99210	Spokane	(509)	196,721	177,165
*99211	Spokane Valley	(509)	81,189	—
98388	Steilacoom	(253)	6,144	5,728
*98371	Summit (c)	(253)	8,041	6,312
*98390	Sumner	(253)	9,121	7,535
98944	Sunnyside	(509)	14,216	11,238
*98402	Tacoma	(253)	196,094	176,664
98501	Tanglewilde-Thompson Place (c)	(360)	5,670	6,061
—	Terrace Heights (c)	—	6,447	4,223
98948	Toppenish	(509)	9,204	7,419
*98138	Tukwila	(206)	16,992	14,506
*98501	Tumwater	(360)	13,182	9,976
*98901	Union Gap	(509)	5,704	3,120
—	Union Hill-Novelty Hill (c)		11,265	—
98467	University Place	(253)	30,399	26,724
*98661	Vancouver	(360)	155,053	62,065
*98013	Vashon (c)	(206)	10,123	—
99037	Veradale (c)	(509)	9,387	7,836
99362	Walla Walla	(509)	30,272	26,482
—	Waller (c)	—	9,200	6,415
—	Walnut Grove (c)	—	7,164	3,906
98671	Washougal	(360)	10,134	4,764
*98801	Wenatchee	(509)	29,022	21,746
—	West Lake Sammamish (c)	—	5,937	6,087
98258	West Lake Stevens (c)	(425)	18,071	12,453
*99353	West Richland	(509)	9,510	3,962
99181	West Valley (c)	—	10,433	6,594
98166	White Center (c)	(206)	20,975	20,531
*98072	Woodinville	(425)	9,590	7,628
*98903	Yakima	(509)	80,891	58,427

West Virginia (304)

ZIP	Place	2004	1990
*25801	Beckley	16,994	18,274
24701	Bluefield	11,222	12,756
26330	Bridgeport	7,462	6,837
26201	Buckhannon	5,866	5,909
*25301	Charleston	51,685	57,287
*26507	Cheat Lake (c)	*6,396*	3,992
*26301	Clarksburg	16,522	17,970
25301	Cross Lanes (c)	*10,353*	10,878
25064	Dunbar	7,837	8,697
26241	Elkins	7,020	7,494
*26554	Fairmont	18,992	20,210
26354	Grafton	5,389	5,524
*25704	Huntington	49,891	54,844
25526	Hurricane	5,788	4,461
26726	Keyser	5,502	5,870
*25401	Martinsburg	15,635	14,073
*26505	Morgantown	28,160	25,879
26041	Moundsville	9,695	10,753
26155	New Martinsville	5,760	6,705
25143	Nitro	6,782	6,851
*25901	Oak Hill	7,372	6,812
*26101	Parkersburg	32,159	33,862
—	Pea Ridge (c)	*6,363*	6,535
24740	Princeton	6,243	7,043
25177	Saint Albans	11,173	12,241
*25303	South Charleston	12,869	13,645
25569	Teays Valley (c)	*12,704*	8,436
*26105	Vienna	10,767	10,862
26062	Weirton	19,691	22,124
26003	Wheeling	29,891	34,882

Wisconsin

ZIP	Place	Area Code	2004	1990
54301	Allouez	(920)	15,043	14,431
54720	Altoona	(715)	6,469	5,889
54409	Antigo	(715)	8,344	8,284
*54911	Appleton	(920)	70,293	65,695
54806	Ashland	(715)	8,382	8,695
*54304	Ashwaubenon	(920)	17,050	16,376
53913	Baraboo	(608)	10,771	9,203
53916	Beaver Dam	(920)	15,015	14,196
54311	Bellevue Town (c)	(920)	*14,386*	7,541
*53511	Beloit	(608)	35,803	35,571
54923	Berlin	(920)	5,265	5,371
*53045	Brookfield	(262)	39,890	35,184
*53209	Brown Deer	(414)	11,895	12,236
53105	Burlington	(262)	11,043	8,851
53012	Cedarburg	(262)	11,303	10,086
*54729	Chippewa Falls	(715)	12,721	12,749
53110	Cudahy	(414)	18,112	18,659
53532	De Forest	(608)	8,183	4,882
53018	Delafield	(262)	6,740	5,347
53115	Delavan	(262)	8,315	6,073
54115	De Pere	(920)	22,875	16,594
*54703	Eau Claire	(715)	62,576	56,806
53534	Edgerton	(608)	5,025	4,254
53121	Elkhorn	(262)	8,540	5,337
53122	Elm Grove	(262)	6,235	6,261
*53711	Fitchburg	(608)	21,821	15,648
*54935	Fond du Lac	(920)	42,408	37,755
53538	Fort Atkinson	(920)	11,870	10,213
53217	Fox Point	(414)	6,813	7,238
53132	Franklin	(414)	32,405	21,855
53022	Germantown	(262)	19,104	13,658
*53209	Glendale	(414)	13,008	14,088
53024	Grafton	(262)	11,588	9,340
*54303	Green Bay	(920)	101,100	96,466
53129	Greendale	(414)	13,995	15,128
*53220	Greenfield	(414)	35,865	33,403
*53130	Hales Corners	(414)	7,580	7,623
53027	Hartford	(262)	12,625	8,188
53029	Hartland	(262)	8,595	6,906
54313	Hobart	—	5,695	4,284
54636	Holmen	(608)	7,080	3,220
*54303	Howard	(920)	15,774	9,874
*54016	Hudson	(715)	10,754	6,378
53037	Jackson	(262)	5,884	2,603
*53545	Janesville	(608)	61,604	52,210
53549	Jefferson	(920)	7,509	6,078
54130	Kaukauna	(920)	14,463	11,982
*53140	Kenosha	(262)	93,798	80,426
54136	Kimberly	(920)	6,262	5,406
—	Kronenwetter	—	6,002	4,850
*54601	La Crosse	(608)	50,695	51,140
53147	Lake Geneva	(262)	7,445	5,979
54140	Little Chute	(920)	10,791	9,207
53558	McFarland	(608)	7,254	5,232
*53714	Madison	(608)	220,332	190,766
*54220	Manitowoc	(920)	33,906	32,521
54143	Marinette	(715)	11,374	11,843
*54449	Marshfield	(715)	18,644	19,293
54952	Menasha	(920)	16,363	14,711
*53051	Menomonee Falls	(262)	33,877	26,840
54751	Menomonie	(715)	15,195	13,547
*53097	Mequon	(262)	23,793	18,885
54452	Merrill	(715)	10,153	9,860
53562	Middleton	(608)	15,956	13,785
53563	Milton	(608)	5,429	4,574
*53201	Milwaukee	(414)	583,624	628,088
*53716	Monona	(608)	7,817	8,637
53566	Monroe	(608)	10,583	10,241
53572	Mount Horeb	(608)	6,111	4,182
53406	Mount Pleasant	(262)	25,389	20,884
53149	Mukwonago	(262)	6,700	4,495
53150	Muskego	(414)	22,600	16,813
*54956	Neenah	(920)	24,557	23,219
*53186	New Berlin	(262)	38,719	33,592
54961	New London	(920)	7,024	6,658
54017	New Richmond	(715)	7,493	5,106
53154	Oak Creek	(414)	32,155	19,513
53066	Oconomowoc	(262)	13,528	10,993
54650	Onalaska	(608)	15,622	12,201
53575	Oregon	(608)	8,237	4,519
*54901	Oshkosh	(920)	63,515	55,006
53072	Pewaukee (city)	(262)	12,709	—
53072	Pewaukee (village)	(262)	8,924	5,287
53818	Platteville	(608)	9,850	9,862
*53158	Pleasant Prairie	(262)	18,483	12,037
54467	Plover	(715)	11,155	8,176
53073	Plymouth	(920)	8,151	6,769
53901	Portage	(608)	10,010	8,640
53074	Port Washington	(262)	10,890	9,338
53821	Prairie du Chien	(608)	5,863	5,657
*53401	Racine	(262)	80,108	84,298
*53959	Reedsburg	(608)	8,368	5,834
54501	Rhinelander	(715)	7,753	7,382
54401	Rib Mountain (c)	(715)	*6,059*	4,634
54868	Rice Lake	(715)	8,354	7,998
53581	Richland Center	(608)	5,208	5,018
54971	Ripon	(920)	7,287	7,241
54022	River Falls	(715)	13,019	10,610
54474	Rothschild	(715)	5,034	3,310
*53235	Saint Francis	(414)	9,373	9,245
54166	Shawano	(715)	8,372	7,598
*53081	Sheboygan	(920)	49,020	49,587
53085	Sheboygan Falls	(920)	7,215	5,823
53211	Shorewood	(414)	13,351	14,116
53172	South Milwaukee	(414)	21,051	20,958
54656	Sparta	(608)	8,793	7,788
*54481	Stevens Point	(715)	24,283	23,002
53589	Stoughton	(608)	12,692	8,786
54235	Sturgeon Bay	(920)	9,290	9,176
53177	Sturtevant	(262)	5,706	3,803
*54173	Suamico	(920)	9,960	5,214
*53590	Sun Prairie	(608)	24,464	15,352
54880	Superior	(715)	26,947	27,134
53089	Sussex	(262)	9,687	5,039
54660	Tomah	(608)	8,614	7,572
53181	Twin Lakes	(262)	5,420	3,989
*54241	Two Rivers	(920)	12,163	13,030
53593	Verona	(608)	9,938	5,374
*53094	Watertown	(920)	22,824	19,142
*53186	Waukesha	(262)	67,258	56,894
53597	Waunakee	(608)	9,983	5,897
54981	Waupaca	(715)	5,837	4,946
53963	Waupun	(920)	10,552	8,844
*54403	Wausau	(715)	37,173	37,060
*53213	Wauwatosa	(414)	45,602	49,366
*53214	West Allis	(414)	59,508	63,221
*53095	West Bend	(262)	29,302	24,470
*54476	Weston	(715)	12,736	9,714
*53217	Whitefish Bay	(414)	13,672	14,272
53190	Whitewater	(262)	14,215	12,636
53185	Wind Lake (c)	(262)	*5,202*	3,748
*54494	Wisconsin Rapids	(715)	17,845	18,245

Wyoming (307)

ZIP	Place	2004	1990
*82609	Casper	51,240	46,765
*82009	Cheyenne	55,362	50,008
82414	Cody	9,050	7,897
82633	Douglas	5,489	5,076
*82930	Evanston	11,407	10,904
*82716	Gillette	22,260	17,545
*82935	Green River	11,807	12,711
*83002	Jackson	8,966	4,708
82520	Lander	6,888	7,023
*82072	Laramie	26,441	26,687
82435	Powell	5,250	5,292
*82301	Rawlins	8,633	9,380
82501	Riverton	9,389	9,202
*82901	Rock Springs	18,746	19,050
82801	Sheridan	16,118	13,904
82240	Torrington	5,560	5,651

Populations and Areas of Counties and States

Source: U.S. Bureau of the Census, Dept. of Commerce; World Almanac research

Counties are the primary legal divisions of most states and generally are functioning governmental units. In **Alaska**, however, the chief units of local government are boroughs; outside the boroughs there are "census areas," delineated for statistical purposes. In **Louisiana**, the primary legal divisions are known as parishes.

State population figures are estimates for July 1, 2004. **For counties**, July 1, 2004, population estimates and Apr. 1, 1990, decennial census figures are given. **Land areas** are from 2000 census. County areas may not add to state areas because of rounding.

Alabama

(67 counties, 50,744 sq. mi. land; pop. 4,530,182)

County	County seat or courthouse	2004 Pop.	1990 Pop.	Land area sq. mi.
Autauga	Prattville	47,468	34,222	596
Baldwin	Bay Minette	156,701	98,280	1,596
Barbour	Clayton	28,557	25,417	885
Bibb	Centreville	21,317	16,598	623
Blount	Oneonta	54,988	39,248	646
Bullock	Union Springs	11,229	11,042	625
Butler	Greenville	20,764	21,892	777
Calhoun	Anniston	112,425	116,032	608
Chambers	Lafayette	35,567	36,876	597
Cherokee	Centre	24,525	19,543	553
Chilton	Clanton	41,466	32,458	694
Choctaw	Butler	15,238	16,018	914
Clarke	Grove Hill	27,422	27,240	1,238
Clay	Ashland	14,092	13,252	605
Cleburne	Heflin	14,458	12,730	553
Coffee	Elba	45,041	40,240	679
Colbert	Tuscumbia	54,824	51,666	595
Conecuh	Evergreen	13,453	14,054	851
Coosa	Rockford	11,368	11,063	652
Covington	Andalusia	36,875	36,478	1,034
Crenshaw	Luverne	13,610	13,635	610
Cullman	Cullman	79,189	67,613	738
Dale	Ozark	49,122	49,633	561
Dallas	Selma	44,884	48,130	981
De Kalb	Fort Payne	66,935	54,651	778
Elmore	Wetumpka	71,944	49,210	621
Escambia	Brewton	38,336	35,518	947
Etowah	Gadsden	103,250	99,840	535
Fayette	Fayette	18,273	17,962	628
Franklin	Russellville	30,823	27,814	636
Geneva	Geneva	25,599	23,647	576
Greene	Eutaw	9,746	10,153	646
Hale	Greensboro	18,275	15,498	644
Henry	Abbeville	16,699	15,374	562
Houston	Dothan	92,947	81,331	580
Jackson	Scottsboro	53,821	47,796	1,079
Jefferson	Birmingham	658,495	651,520	1,113
Lamar	Vernon	14,975	15,715	605
Lauderdale	Florence	87,515	79,661	669
Lawrence	Moulton	34,418	31,513	693
Lee	Opelika	120,714	87,146	609
Limestone	Athens	69,387	54,135	568
Lowndes	Hayneville	13,210	12,658	718
Macon	Tuskegee	23,179	24,928	611
Madison	Huntsville	293,072	238,912	805
Marengo	Linden	22,084	23,084	977
Marion	Hamilton	30,267	29,830	741
Marshall	Guntersville	84,781	70,832	567
Mobile	Mobile	400,526	378,643	1,233
Monroe	Monroeville	23,725	23,968	1,026
Montgomery	Montgomery	222,559	209,085	790
Morgan	Decatur	113,211	100,043	582
Perry	Marion	11,522	12,759	719
Pickens	Carrollton	20,401	20,699	881
Pike	Troy	29,396	27,595	671
Randolph	Wedowee	22,603	19,881	581
Russell	Phenix City	49,262	46,860	641
Saint Clair	Ashville & Pell City	70,245	49,811	634
Shelby	Columbiana	165,677	99,363	795
Sumter	Livingston	14,141	16,174	905
Talladega	Talladega	80,277	74,109	740
Tallapoosa	Dadeville	40,861	38,826	718
Tuscaloosa	Tuscaloosa	167,104	150,500	1,324
Walker	Jasper	70,005	67,670	794
Washington	Chatom	17,906	16,694	1,081
Wilcox	Camden	12,958	13,568	889
Winston	Double Springs	24,475	22,053	614

Alaska

(27 divisions, 571,951 sq. mi. land; pop. 655,435)

Census Division	2004 Pop.	1990 Pop.	Land area sq. mi.
Aleutians East Borough	2,695	2,464	6,988
Aleutians West Census Area	5,407	9,478	4,397
Anchorage Municipality	272,687	226,338	1,697
Bethel Census Area	16,964	13,660	40,633
Bristol Bay Borough	1,103	1,410	505
Denali Borough	1,943	1,682	12,750
Dillingham Census Area	4,924	4,010	18,675
Fairbanks North Star Borough	85,930	77,720	7,366
Haines Borough	2,233	2,117	2,344
Juneau Borough	31,118	26,752	2,717
Kenai Peninsula Borough	51,563	40,802	16,013
Ketchikan Gateway Borough	13,248	13,828	1,233
Kodiak Island Borough	13,276	13,309	6,560
Lake and Peninsula Borough	1,584	1,666	23,782
Matanuska-Susitna Borough	72,278	39,683	24,682
Nome Census Area	9,363	8,288	23,001
North Slope Borough	7,002	5,986	88,817
Northwest Arctic Borough	7,545	6,106	35,898
Prince of Wales-Outer Ketchikan Census Area	5,779	6,278	7,411
Sitka Borough	8,849	8,588	2,874
Skagway-Hoonah-Angoon Census Area	3,136	3,679	7,896
Southeast Fairbanks Census Area	5,997	5,925	24,815
Valdez-Cordova Census Area	9,964	9,920	34,319
Wade Hampton Census Area	7,508	5,789	17,194
Wrangell-Petersburg Census Area	6,297	7,042	5,835
Yakutat Borough	708	725	7,650
Yukon-Koyukuk Census Area	6,334	6,798	145,900

Arizona

(15 counties, 113,635 sq. mi. land; pop. 5,743,834)

County	County seat or courthouse	2004 Pop.	1990 Pop.	Land area sq. mi.
Apache	Saint Johns	68,903	61,591	11,205
Cochise	Bisbee	124,013	97,624	6,169
Coconino	Flagstaff	122,754	96,591	18,617
Gila	Globe	51,422	40,216	4,768
Graham	Safford	32,993	26,554	4,629
Greenlee	Clifton	7,501	8,008	1,847
La Paz	Parker	19,898	13,844	4,500
Maricopa	Phoenix	3,501,001	2,122,101	9,203
Mohave	Kingman	179,981	93,497	13,312
Navajo	Holbrook	106,455	77,674	9,953
Pima	Tucson	907,059	666,957	9,186
Pinal	Florence	214,359	116,397	5,370
Santa Cruz	Nogales	40,784	29,676	1,238
Yavapai	Prescott	190,628	107,714	8,123
Yuma	Yuma	176,083	106,895	5,514

Arkansas

(75 counties, 52,068 sq. mi. land; pop. 2,752,629)

County	County seat or courthouse	2004 Pop.	1990 Pop.	Land area sq. mi.
Arkansas	DeWitt & Stuttgart	20,130	21,653	988
Ashley	Hamburg	23,687	24,319	921
Baxter	Mountain Home	39,827	31,186	554
Benton	Bentonville	179,756	97,530	846
Boone	Harrison	35,253	28,297	591
Bradley	Warren	12,348	11,793	651
Calhoun	Hampton	5,539	5,826	628
Carroll	Berryville & Eureka Springs	26,555	18,623	630
Chicot	Lake Village	13,287	15,713	644
Clark	Arkadelphia	23,105	21,437	865
Clay	Corning & Piggott	16,759	18,107	639
Cleburne	Heber Springs	25,045	19,411	553
Cleveland	Rison	8,842	7,781	595
Columbia	Magnolia	24,751	25,691	766
Conway	Morrilton	20,589	19,151	556
Craighead	Jonesboro & Lake City	86,191	68,956	711
Crawford	Van Buren	56,578	42,493	595
Crittenden	Marion	51,488	49,939	610
Cross	Wynne	19,079	19,225	616
Dallas	Fordyce	8,662	9,614	667
Desha	Arkansas City	14,665	16,798	765
Drew	Monticello	18,524	17,369	828
Faulkner	Conway	95,113	60,006	647
Franklin	Charleston & Ozark	18,064	14,897	610
Fulton	Salem	11,909	10,037	618
Garland	Hot Springs	92,141	73,397	677
Grant	Sheridan	17,242	13,948	632
Greene	Paragould	38,975	31,804	578
Hempstead	Hope	23,469	21,621	729
Hot Spring	Malvern	30,627	26,115	615
Howard	Nashville	14,478	13,569	587
Independence	Batesville	34,648	31,192	764
Izard	Melbourne	13,329	11,364	581
Jackson	Newport	17,285	18,944	634
Jefferson	Pine Bluff	82,656	85,487	885
Johnson	Clarksville	23,713	18,221	662
Lafayette	Lewisville	8,221	9,643	527
Lawrence	Walnut Ridge	17,410	17,455	587
Lee	Marianna	11,724	13,053	602
Lincoln	Star City	14,368	13,690	561
Little River	Ashdown	13,254	13,966	532
Logan	Booneville & Paris	22,899	20,557	710
Lonoke	Lonoke	58,678	39,268	766

County	County seat or courthouse	2004 Pop.	1990 Pop.	Land area sq. mi.
Madison	Huntsville	14,685	11,618	837
Marion	Yellville	16,383	12,001	598
Miller	Texarkana	42,468	38,467	624
Mississippi	Blytheville & Osceola	48,485	57,525	898
Monroe	Clarendon	9,415	11,333	607
Montgomery	Mount Ida	9,282	7,841	781
Nevada	Prescott	9,620	10,101	620
Newton	Jasper	8,484	7,666	823
Ouachita	Camden	27,361	30,574	732
Perry	Perryville	10,456	7,969	551
Phillips	Helena	24,309	28,830	693
Pike	Murfreesboro	10,973	10,086	603
Poinsett	Harrisburg	25,339	24,664	758
Polk	Mena	20,092	17,347	859
Pope	Russellville	55,933	45,883	812
Prairie	Des Arc & De Valls Bluff	9,186	9,518	646
Pulaski	Little Rock	365,913	349,773	771
Randolph	Pocahontas	18,411	16,558	652
Saint Francis	Forrest City	28,225	28,497	634
Saline	Benton	89,234	64,183	723
Scott	Waldron	11,003	10,205	894
Searcy	Marshall	8,050	7,841	667
Sebastian	Fort Smith & Greenwood	117,786	99,590	536
Sevier	De Queen	16,120	13,637	564
Sharp	Ash Flat	17,491	14,109	604
Stone	Mountain View	11,700	9,775	607
Union	El Dorado	44,595	46,719	1,039
Van Buren	Clinton	16,579	14,008	712
Washington	Fayetteville	174,077	113,409	950
White	Searcy	70,658	54,676	1,034
Woodruff	Augusta	8,135	9,520	587
Yell	Danville & Dardanelle	21,318	17,759	928

California

(58 counties, 155,959 sq. mi. land; pop. 35,893,79)

County	County seat or courthouse	2004 Pop.	1990 Pop.	Land area sq. mi.
Alameda	Oakland	1,455,235	1,304,347	738
Alpine	Markleeville	1,190	1,113	739
Amador	Jackson	37,837	30,039	593
Butte	Oroville	212,968	182,120	1,639
Calaveras	San Andreas	45,939	31,998	1,020
Colusa	Colusa	20,339	16,275	1,151
Contra Costa	Martinez	1,009,144	803,731	720
Del Norte	Crescent City	28,351	23,460	1,008
El Dorado	Placerville	172,889	125,995	1,711
Fresno	Fresno	866,772	667,479	5,963
Glenn	Willows	27,488	24,798	1,315
Humboldt	Eureka	128,529	119,118	3,572
Imperial	El Centro	152,448	109,303	4,175
Inyo	Independence	18,244	18,281	10,203
Kern	Bakersfield	734,846	544,981	8,141
Kings	Hanford	142,561	101,469	1,391
Lake	Lakeport	64,446	50,631	1,258
Lassen	Susanville	34,661	27,598	4,557
Los Angeles	Los Angeles	9,937,739	8,863,052	4,061
Madera	Madera	138,951	88,090	2,136
Marin	San Rafael	246,045	230,096	520
Mariposa	Mariposa	18,003	14,302	1,451
Mendocino	Ukiah	88,551	80,345	3,509
Merced	Merced	237,005	178,403	1,929
Modoc	Alturas	9,599	9,678	3,944
Mono	Bridgeport	12,766	9,956	3,044
Monterey	Salinas	414,629	355,660	3,322
Napa	Napa	132,339	110,765	754
Nevada	Nevada City	97,660	78,510	958
Orange	Santa Ana	2,987,591	2,410,668	789
Placer	Auburn	307,004	172,796	1,404
Plumas	Quincy	21,359	19,739	2,554
Riverside	Riverside	1,871,950	1,170,413	7,207
Sacramento	Sacramento	1,352,445	1,066,789	966
San Benito	Hollister	56,243	36,697	1,389
San Bernardino	San Bernardino	1,921,131	1,418,380	20,053
San Diego	San Diego	2,931,714	2,498,016	4,200
San Francisco	San Francisco	744,230	723,959	47
San Joaquin	Stockton	649,868	480,628	1,399
San Luis Obispo	San Luis Obispo	254,566	217,162	3,304
San Mateo	Redwood City	699,216	649,623	449
Santa Barbara	Santa Barbara	401,851	369,608	2,737
Santa Clara	San Jose	1,685,188	1,497,577	1,291
Santa Cruz	Santa Cruz	250,633	229,734	445
Shasta	Redding	177,816	147,036	3,785
Sierra	Downieville	3,490	3,318	953
Siskiyou	Yreka	44,891	43,531	6,287
Solano	Fairfield	412,970	339,469	829
Sonoma	Santa Rosa	468,450	388,222	1,576
Stanislaus	Modesto	498,355	370,522	1,494
Sutter	Yuba City	86,760	64,409	603
Tehama	Red Bluff	60,075	49,625	2,951
Trinity	Weaverville	13,671	13,063	3,179
Tulare	Visalia	401,502	311,932	4,824
Tuolumne	Sonora	56,962	48,456	2,235
Ventura	Ventura	797,699	669,016	1,845
Yolo	Woodland	184,364	141,212	1,013
Yuba	Marysville	64,631	58,234	631

Colorado

(64 counties, 103,718 sq. mi. land; pop. 4,601,403)

County	County seat or courthouse	2004 Pop.	1990 Pop.	Land area sq. mi.
Adams[1]	Brighton	389,857	265,038	1,192
Alamosa	Alamosa	15,088	13,617	723
Arapahoe	Littleton	522,812	391,572	803
Archuleta	Pagosa Springs	11,615	5,345	1,350
Baca	Springfield	4,121	4,556	2,556
Bent	Las Animas	5,610	5,048	1,514
Boulder[1]	Boulder	278,917	225,339	742
Broomfield[2]	Broomfield	42,901	NA	27
Chaffee	Salida	16,936	12,684	1,013
Cheyenne	Cheyenne Wells	2,030	2,397	1,781
Clear Creek	Georgetown	9,223	7,619	395
Conejos	Conejos	8,398	7,453	1,287
Costilla	San Luis	3,603	3,190	1,227
Crowley	Ordway	5,486	3,946	789
Custer	Westcliffe	3,841	1,926	739
Delta	Delta	29,774	20,980	1,142
Denver	Denver	556,835	467,549	153
Dolores	Dove Creek	1,788	1,504	1,067
Douglas	Castle Rock	237,963	60,391	840
Eagle	Eagle	46,299	21,928	1,688
Elbert	Kiowa	554,574	9,646	1,851
El Paso	Colorado Springs	22,488	397,014	2,126
Fremont	Canon City	47,425	32,273	1,533
Garfield	Glenwood Springs	48,503	29,974	2,947
Gilpin	Central City	4,883	3,070	150
Grand	Hot Sulphur Springs	13,253	7,966	1,847
Gunnison	Gunnison	14,166	10,273	3,239
Hinsdale	Lake City	810	467	1,118
Huerfano	Walsenburg	7,755	6,009	1,591
Jackson	Walden	1,454	1,605	1,613
Jefferson[1]	Golden	526,351	438,430	772
Kiowa	Eads	1,444	1,688	1,771
Kit Carson	Burlington	7,723	7,140	2,161
Lake	Leadville	7,717	6,007	377
La Plata	Durango	46,468	32,284	1,692
Larimer	Fort Collins	268,872	186,136	2,601
Las Animas	Trinidad	15,353	13,765	4,772
Lincoln	Hugo	5,746	4,529	2,586
Logan	Sterling	20,909	17,567	1,839
Mesa	Grand Junction	127,253	93,145	3,328
Mineral	Creede	932	558	876
Moffat	Craig	13,468	11,357	4,742
Montezuma	Cortez	24,795	18,672	2,037
Montrose	Montrose	36,674	24,423	2,241
Morgan	Fort Morgan	28,129	21,939	1,285
Otero	La Junta	19,605	20,185	1,263
Ouray	Ouray	4,139	2,295	540
Park	Fairplay	16,833	7,174	2,201
Phillips	Holyoke	4,576	4,189	688
Pitkin	Aspen	14,700	12,661	970
Prowers	Lamar	14,062	13,347	1,640
Pueblo	Pueblo	150,171	123,051	2,389
Rio Blanco	Meeker	6,071	6,051	3,221
Rio Grande	Del Norte	12,414	10,770	912
Routt	Steamboat Springs	21,012	14,088	2,362
Saguache	Saguache	7,029	4,619	3,168
San Juan	Silverton	575	745	387
San Miguel	Telluride	7,116	3,653	1,287
Sedgwick	Julesburg	2,539	2,690	548
Summit	Breckenridge	24,950	12,881	608
Teller	Cripple Creek	21,677	12,468	557
Washington	Akron	4,656	4,812	2,521
Weld[1]	Greeley	219,257	131,821	3,992
Yuma	Wray	9,779	8,954	2,366

NA = Not available. (1) Parts of these counties were taken to create Broomfield County in 2001. (2) Created in 2001.

Connecticut

(8 counties, 4,845 sq. mi. land; pop. 3,503,604)

County	County seat or courthouse	2004 Pop.	1990 Pop.	Land area sq. mi.
Fairfield	Bridgeport	903,291	827,645	626
Hartford	Hartford	875,602	851,783	735
Litchfield	Litchfield	189,246	174,092	920
Middlesex	Middletown	162,295	143,196	369
New Haven	New Haven	845,694	804,219	606
New London	New London	266,466	254,957	666
Tolland	Rockville	146,667	128,699	410
Windham	Putnam	114,343	102,525	513

Delaware

(3 counties, 1,954 sq. mi. land; pop. 830,364)

County	County seat or courthouse	2004 Pop.	1990 Pop.	Land area sq. mi.
Kent	Dover	138,752	110,993	590
New Castle	Wilmington	519,396	441,946	426
Sussex	Georgetown	172,216	113,229	938

District of Columbia

(61 sq. mi. land; pop. 553,523)

Has no counties; coextensive with city of Washington.

Florida

(67 counties, 53,927 sq. mi. land; pop. 17,397,161)

County	County seat or courthouse	2004 Pop.	1990 Pop.	Land area sq. mi.
Alachua	Gainesville	223,090	181,596	874
Baker	Macclenny	24,019	18,486	585
Bay	Panama City	157,949	126,994	764
Bradford	Starke	27,622	22,515	293
Brevard	Titusville	519,387	398,978	1,018
Broward	Fort Lauderdale	1,754,893	1,255,531	1,205
Calhoun	Blountstown	13,185	11,011	567
Charlotte	Punta Gorda	157,134	110,975	694
Citrus	Inverness	130,465	93,513	584
Clay	Green Cove Springs	164,394	105,986	601
Collier	Naples	296,678	152,099	2,025
Columbia	Lake City	61,889	42,613	797
De Soto	Arcadia	34,892	23,865	637
Dixie	Cross City	14,294	10,585	704
Duval	Jacksonville	821,338	672,971	774
Escambia	Pensacola	298,859	262,445	662
Flagler	Bunnell	69,005	28,701	485
Franklin	Apalachicola	10,123	8,967	544
Gadsden	Quincy	46,107	41,116	516
Gilchrist	Trenton	16,024	9,667	349
Glades	Moore Haven	11,131	7,591	774
Gulf	Port Saint Joe	13,816	11,504	555
Hamilton	Jasper	14,184	10,930	515
Hardee	Wauchula	27,987	19,499	637
Hendry	La Belle	38,163	25,773	1,153
Hernando	Brooksville	150,370	101,115	478
Highlands	Sebring	93,127	68,432	1,028
Hillsborough	Tampa	1,101,261	834,054	1,051
Holmes	Bonifay	19,011	15,778	482
Indian River	Vero Beach	124,114	90,208	503
Jackson	Marianna	47,692	41,375	916
Jefferson	Monticello	14,502	11,296	598
Lafayette	Mayo	7,482	5,578	543
Lake	Tavares	260,788	152,104	953
Lee	Fort Myers	514,295	335,113	804
Leon	Tallahassee	243,867	192,493	667
Levy	Bronson	37,330	25,912	1,118
Liberty	Bristol	7,406	5,569	836
Madison	Madison	19,093	16,569	692
Manatee	Bradenton	296,385	211,707	741
Marion	Ocala	291,322	194,835	1,579
Martin	Stuart	137,956	100,900	556
Miami-Dade	Miami	2,363,600	1,937,194	1,946
Monroe	Key West	78,284	78,024	997
Nassau	Fernandina Beach	63,157	43,941	652
Okaloosa	Crestview	181,460	143,777	936
Okeechobee	Okeechobee	38,988	29,627	774
Orange	Orlando	989,926	677,491	907
Osceola	Kissimmee	219,544	107,728	1,322
Palm Beach	West Palm Beach	1,243,230	863,503	1,974
Pasco	Dade City	407,799	281,131	745
Pinellas	Clearwater	928,537	851,659	280
Polk	Bartow	524,389	405,382	1,874
Putnam	Palatka	72,511	65,070	722
Saint Johns	Saint Augustine	152,473	83,829	609
Saint Lucie	Fort Pierce	226,816	150,171	572
Santa Rosa	Milton	138,276	81,961	1,017
Sarasota	Sarasota	355,477	277,776	572
Seminole	Sanford	391,449	287,521	308
Sumter	Bushnell	60,705	31,577	546
Suwannee	Live Oak	37,681	26,780	688
Taylor	Perry	19,291	17,111	1,042
Union	Lake Butler	14,673	10,252	240
Volusia	De Land	478,670	370,737	1,103
Wakulla	Crawfordville	27,179	14,202	607
Walton	De Funiak Springs	48,477	27,759	1,058
Washington	Chipley	21,940	16,919	580

Georgia

(159 counties, 57,906 sq. mi. land; pop. 8,829,383)

County	County seat or courthouse	2004 Pop.	1990 Pop.	Land area sq. mi.
Appling	Baxley	17,966	15,744	509
Atkinson	Pearson	8,011	6,213	338
Bacon	Alma	10,330	9,566	285
Baker	Newton	4,248	3,615	343
Baldwin	Milledgeville	45,207	39,530	258
Banks	Homer	15,685	10,308	234
Barrow	Winder	56,418	29,721	162
Bartow	Cartersville	86,972	55,915	459
Ben Hill	Fitzgerald	17,343	16,245	252
Berrien	Nashville	16,680	14,153	452
Bibb	Macon	155,170	150,137	250
Bleckley	Cochran	12,047	10,430	217
Brantley	Nahunta	15,542	11,077	444
Brooks	Quitman	16,367	15,398	494
Bryan	Pembroke	27,535	15,438	442
Bulloch	Statesboro	60,344	43,125	682
Burke	Waynesboro	23,189	20,579	830
Butts	Jackson	22,362	15,326	187
Calhoun	Morgan	6,102	5,013	280
Camden	Woodbine	45,108	30,167	630
Candler	Metter	10,193	7,744	247
Carroll	Carrollton	101,577	71,422	499
Catoosa	Ringgold	59,845	42,464	162
Charlton	Folkston	10,698	8,496	781
Chatham	Savannah	238,518	216,774	438
Chattahoochee	Cusseta	13,506	16,934	249
Chattooga	Summerville	26,554	22,236	313
Cherokee	Canton	174,680	90,204	424
Clarke	Athens	103,951	87,594	121
Clay	Fort Gaines	3,317	3,364	195
Clayton	Jonesboro	264,951	181,436	143
Clinch	Homerville	6,949	6,160	809
Cobb	Marietta	654,005	447,745	340
Coffee	Douglas	39,379	29,592	599
Colquitt	Moultrie	43,763	36,645	552
Columbia	Appling	100,589	66,031	290
Cook	Adel	16,255	13,456	229
Coweta	Newnan	105,376	53,853	443
Crawford	Knoxville	12,888	8,991	325
Crisp	Cordele	22,028	20,011	274
Dade	Trenton	15,992	13,183	174
Dawson	Dawsonville	19,064	9,429	211
Decatur	Bainbridge	28,615	25,517	597
DeKalb	Decatur	675,725	546,174	268
Dodge	Eastman	19,501	17,607	500
Dooly	Vienna	11,604	9,901	393
Dougherty	Albany	95,681	96,321	330
Douglas	Douglasville	107,217	71,120	199
Early	Blakely	12,091	11,854	511
Echols	Statenville	4,101	2,334	404
Effingham	Springfield	44,661	25,687	479
Elbert	Elberton	20,908	18,949	369
Emanuel	Swainsboro	22,093	20,546	686
Evans	Claxton	11,248	8,724	185
Fannin	Blue Ridge	21,613	15,992	386
Fayette	Fayetteville	101,333	62,415	197
Floyd	Rome	94,009	81,251	513
Forsyth	Cumming	131,865	44,083	226
Franklin	Carnesville	21,453	16,650	263
Fulton	Atlanta	814,438	648,776	529
Gilmer	Ellijay	26,755	13,368	427
Glascock	Gibson	2,631	2,357	144
Glynn	Brunswick	71,357	62,496	422
Gordon	Calhoun	49,077	35,067	356
Grady	Cairo	24,280	20,279	458
Greene	Greensboro	15,652	11,793	388
Gwinnett	Lawrenceville	700,794	352,910	433
Habersham	Clarkesville	38,978	27,622	278
Hall	Gainesville	160,925	95,434	394
Hancock	Sparta	9,811	8,908	473
Haralson	Buchanan	28,069	21,966	282
Harris	Hamilton	26,788	17,788	464
Hart	Hartwell	23,369	19,712	232
Heard	Franklin	11,290	8,628	296
Henry	McDonough	159,506	58,741	323
Houston	Perry	123,753	89,208	377
Irwin	Ocilla	9,936	8,649	357
Jackson	Jefferson	49,540	30,005	342
Jasper	Monticello	12,866	8,453	370
Jeff Davis	Hazlehurst	12,820	12,032	333
Jefferson	Louisville	16,883	17,408	528
Jenkins	Millen	8,680	8,247	350
Johnson	Wrightsville	9,586	8,329	304
Jones	Gray	26,235	20,739	394
Lamar	Barnesville	16,410	13,038	185
Lanier	Lakeland	7,463	5,531	187
Laurens	Dublin	46,708	39,988	812
Lee	Leesburg	29,913	16,250	356
Liberty	Hinesville	61,748	52,745	519
Lincoln	Lincolnton	8,398	7,442	211
Long	Ludowici	10,928	6,202	401
Lowndes	Valdosta	95,787	75,981	504
Lumpkin	Dahlonega	23,925	14,573	284
McDuffie	Thomson	21,517	20,119	260
McIntosh	Darien	11,138	8,634	433
Macon	Oglethorpe	13,935	13,114	403
Madison	Danielsville	27,312	21,050	284

County	County seat or courthouse	2004 Pop.	1990 Pop.	Land area sq. mi.
Marion	Buena Vista	7,112	5,590	367
Meriwether	Greenville	22,750	22,411	503
Miller	Colquitt	6,165	6,280	283
Mitchell	Camilla	23,838	20,275	512
Monroe	Forsyth	23,428	17,113	396
Montgomery	Mount Vernon	8,970	7,379	245
Morgan	Madison	17,012	12,883	350
Murray	Chatsworth	40,556	26,147	344
Muscogee	Columbus	182,850	179,280	216
Newton	Covington	81,524	41,808	276
Oconee	Watkinsville	28,940	17,618	186
Oglethorpe	Lexington	13,557	9,763	441
Paulding	Dallas	105,936	41,611	313
Peach	Fort Valley	24,665	21,189	151
Pickens	Jasper	27,771	14,432	232
Pierce	Blackshear	16,720	13,328	343
Pike	Zebulon	15,750	10,224	218
Polk	Cedartown	40,267	33,815	311
Pulaski	Hawkinsville	9,837	8,108	247
Putnam	Eatonton	19,746	14,137	345
Quitman	Georgetown	2,467	2,210	152
Rabun	Clayton	16,011	11,648	371
Randolph	Cuthbert	7,331	8,023	429
Richmond	Augusta	196,265	189,719	324
Rockdale	Conyers	76,821	54,091	131
Schley	Ellaville	4,041	3,590	168
Screven	Sylvania	15,336	13,842	648
Seminole	Donalsonville	9,268	9,010	238
Spalding	Griffin	60,886	54,457	198
Stephens	Toccoa	24,988	23,436	179
Stewart	Lumpkin	4,981	5,654	459
Sumter	Americus	32,873	30,232	485
Talbot	Talbotton	6,587	6,524	393
Taliaferro	Crawfordville	1,896	1,915	195
Tattnall	Reidsville	22,994	17,722	484
Taylor	Butler	8,985	7,642	377
Telfair	McRae	12,913	11,000	441
Terrell	Dawson	10,950	10,653	335
Thomas	Thomasville	43,989	38,943	548
Tift	Tifton	40,178	34,998	265
Toombs	Lyons	26,775	24,072	367
Towns	Hiawassee	10,133	6,754	167
Treutlen	Soperton	7,045	5,994	201
Troup	La Grange	61,201	55,532	414
Turner	Ashburn	9,400	8,703	286
Twiggs	Jeffersonville	10,449	9,806	360
Union	Blairsville	19,607	11,993	323
Upson	Thomaston	28,105	26,300	325
Walker	La Fayette	63,379	58,310	447
Walton	Monroe	71,941	38,586	329
Ware	Waycross	35,615	35,471	902
Warren	Warrenton	6,254	6,078	286
Washington	Sandersville	21,061	19,112	680
Wayne	Jesup	28,198	22,356	645
Webster	Preston	2,326	2,263	210
Wheeler	Alamo	6,588	4,903	298
White	Cleveland	23,595	13,006	242
Whitfield	Dalton	89,461	72,462	290
Wilcox	Abbeville	8,691	7,008	380
Wilkes	Washington	10,583	10,597	471
Wilkinson	Irwinton	10,191	10,228	447
Worth	Sylvester	22,008	19,744	570

Hawaii

(5 counties, 6,423 sq. mi. land; pop. 1,262,840)

County	County seat or courthouse	2004 Pop.	1990 Pop.	Land area sq. mi.
Hawaii	Hilo	162,971	120,317	4,028
Honolulu	Honolulu	899,593	836,231	600
Kalawao[1]		126	130	13
Kauai	Lihue	61,929	51,177	622
Maui	Wailuku	138,221	100,374	1,159

(1) Administered by state government.

Idaho

(44 counties, 82,747 sq. mi. land; pop. 1,393,262)

County	County seat or courthouse	2004 Pop.	1990 Pop.	Land area sq. mi.
Ada	Boise	332,523	205,775	1,055
Adams	Council	3,451	3,254	1,365
Bannock	Pocatello	75,672	66,026	1,113
Bear Lake	Paris	6,323	6,084	971
Benewah	Saint Maries	8,961	7,937	776
Bingham	Blackfoot	43,205	37,583	2,095
Blaine	Hailey	21,103	13,552	2,645
Boise	Idaho City	7,362	3,509	1,902
Bonner	Sandpoint	39,872	26,622	1,738
Bonneville	Idaho Falls	89,653	72,207	1,868
Boundary	Bonners Ferry	10,396	8,332	1,269
Butte	Arco	2,838	2,918	2,233
Camas	Fairfield	1,013	727	1,075
Canyon	Caldwell	158,038	90,076	590
Caribou	Soda Springs	7,213	6,963	1,766
Cassia	Burley	21,393	19,532	2,566
Clark	Dubois	906	762	1,765
Clearwater	Orofino	8,393	8,505	2,461
Custer	Challis	4,114	4,133	4,925
Elmore	Mountain Home	28,878	21,205	3,078
Franklin	Preston	12,199	9,232	665
Fremont	Saint Anthony	12,263	10,937	1,867
Gem	Emmett	15,963	11,844	563
Gooding	Gooding	14,346	11,633	731
Idaho	Grangeville	15,616	13,768	8,485
Jefferson	Rigby	20,782	16,543	1,095
Jerome	Jerome	19,279	15,138	600
Kootenai	Coeur d'Alene	122,350	69,795	1,245
Latah	Moscow	35,169	30,617	1,077
Lemhi	Salmon	7,820	6,899	4,564
Lewis	Nez Perce	3,753	3,516	479
Lincoln	Shoshone	4,326	3,308	1,206
Madison	Rexberg	30,782	23,674	472
Minidoka	Rupert	19,229	19,361	760
Nez Perce	Lewiston	37,823	33,754	849
Oneida	Malad City	4,143	3,492	1,200
Owyhee	Murphy	10,998	8,392	7,678
Payette	Payette	21,587	16,434	408
Power	American Falls	7,483	7,086	1,406
Shoshone	Wallace	12,827	13,931	2,634
Teton	Driggs	7,253	3,439	450
Twin Falls	Twin Falls	67,935	53,580	1,925
Valley	Cascade	7,970	6,109	3,678
Washington	Weiser	10,059	8,550	1,456

Illinois

(102 counties, 55,584 sq. mi. land; pop. 12,713,634)

County	County seat or courthouse	2004 Pop.	1990 Pop.	Land area sq. mi.
Adams	Quincy	66,916	66,090	857
Alexander	Cairo	9,191	10,626	236
Bond	Greenville	17,980	14,991	380
Boone	Belvidere	48,490	30,806	281
Brown	Mount Sterling	6,805	5,836	306
Bureau	Princeton	35,155	35,688	869
Calhoun	Hardin	5,190	5,322	254
Carroll	Mount Carroll	16,339	16,805	444
Cass	Virginia	13,816	13,437	376
Champaign	Urbana	184,369	173,025	997
Christian	Taylorville	35,322	34,418	709
Clark	Marshall	16,906	15,921	502
Clay	Louisville	14,186	14,460	469
Clinton	Carlyle	36,065	33,944	474
Coles	Charleston	51,528	51,644	508
Cook	Chicago	5,327,777	5,105,044	946
Crawford	Robinson	20,059	19,464	444
Cumberland	Toledo	11,066	10,670	346
DeKalb	Sycamore	16,597	77,932	634
De Witt	Clinton	95,503	16,516	398
Douglas	Tuscola	19,942	19,464	417
DuPage	Wheaton	928,718	781,689	334
Edgar	Paris	19,276	19,595	624
Edwards	Albion	6,758	7,440	222
Effingham	Effingham	34,575	31,704	479
Fayette	Vandalia	21,649	20,893	716
Ford	Paxton	14,270	14,275	486
Franklin	Benton	39,464	40,319	412
Fulton	Lewiston	37,633	38,080	866
Gallatin	Shawneetown	6,178	6,909	324
Greene	Carrollton	14,532	15,317	543
Grundy	Morris	41,069	32,337	420
Hamilton	McLeansboro	8,400	8,499	435
Hancock	Carthage	19,405	21,373	795
Hardin	Elizabethtown	4,725	5,189	178
Henderson	Oquawka	8,046	8,096	379
Henry	Cambridge	50,552	51,159	823
Iroquois	Watseka	30,666	30,787	1,116
Jackson	Murphysboro	58,271	61,067	588
Jasper	Newton	10,018	10,609	494
Jefferson	Mount Vernon	40,389	37,020	571
Jersey	Jerseyville	22,320	20,539	369
Jo Daviess	Galena	22,594	21,821	601
Johnson	Vienna	12,997	11,347	345
Kane	Geneva	472,482	317,471	520
Kankakee	Kankakee	107,188	96,255	677
Kendall	Yorkville	72,548	39,413	321
Knox	Galesburg	53,884	56,393	716
Lake	Waukegan	692,895	516,418	448
La Salle	Ottawa	112,335	106,913	1,135
Lawrence	Lawrenceville	15,994	15,972	372
Lee	Dixon	35,742	34,392	725
Livingston	Pontiac	39,041	39,301	1,044
Logan	Lincoln	30,738	30,798	618
McDonough	Macomb	32,393	35,244	589
McHenry	Woodstock	296,389	183,241	604
McLean	Bloomington	158,006	129,180	1,184
Macon	Decatur	110,980	117,206	581
Macoupin	Carlinville	49,067	47,679	864
Madison	Edwardsville	264,350	249,238	725
Marion	Salem	40,567	41,561	572
Marshall	Lacon	13,198	12,846	386
Mason	Havana	15,941	16,269	539

County	County seat or courthouse	2004 Pop.	1990 Pop.	Land area sq. mi.
Massac	Metropolis	15,283	14,752	239
Menard	Petersburg	12,703	11,164	314
Mercer	Aledo	16,973	17,290	561
Monroe	Waterloo	30,491	22,422	388
Montgomery	Hillsboro	30,392	30,728	704
Morgan	Jacksonville	36,053	36,397	569
Moultrie	Sullivan	14,403	13,930	336
Ogle	Oregon	53,686	45,957	759
Peoria	Peoria	182,418	182,827	620
Perry	Pinckneyville	22,733	21,412	441
Piatt	Monticello	16,483	15,548	440
Pike	Pittsfield	17,086	17,577	830
Pope	Golconda	4,311	4,373	371
Pulaski	Mound City	6,987	7,523	201
Putnam	Hennepin	6,111	5,730	160
Randolph	Chester	33,360	34,583	578
Richland	Olney	15,859	16,545	360
Rock Island	Rock Island	147,771	148,723	427
Saint Clair	Belleville	259,132	262,852	664
Saline	Harrisburg	26,245	26,551	383
Sangamon	Springfield	192,042	178,386	868
Schuyler	Rushville	7,002	7,498	437
Scott	Winchester	5,430	5,644	251
Shelby	Shelbyville	22,437	22,261	759
Stark	Toulon	6,145	6,534	288
Stephenson	Freeport	48,147	48,052	564
Tazewell	Pekin	129,132	123,692	649
Union	Jonesboro	18,191	17,619	416
Vermilion	Danville	82,786	88,257	899
Wabash	Mount Carmel	12,606	13,111	223
Warren	Monmouth	17,796	19,181	543
Washington	Nashville	15,124	14,965	563
Wayne	Fairfield	16,903	17,241	714
White	Carmi	15,239	16,522	495
Whiteside	Morrison	60,031	60,186	685
Will	Joliet	613,849	357,313	837
Williamson	Marion	63,094	57,733	423
Winnebago	Rockford	286,788	252,913	514
Woodford	Eureka	36,967	32,653	528

Indiana

(92 counties, 35,867 sq. mi. land; pop. 6,237,569)

County	County seat or courthouse	2004 Pop.	1990 Pop.	Land area sq. mi.
Adams	Decatur	33,815	31,095	339
Allen	Fort Wayne	342,168	300,836	657
Bartholomew	Columbus	72,987	63,657	407
Benton	Fowler	9,139	9,441	406
Blackford	Hartford City	13,841	14,067	165
Boone	Lebanon	50,847	38,147	423
Brown	Nashville	15,228	14,080	312
Carroll	Delphi	20,331	18,809	372
Cass	Logansport	40,417	38,413	413
Clark	Jeffersonville	100,706	87,774	375
Clay	Brazil	27,210	24,705	358
Clinton	Frankfort	34,148	30,974	405
Crawford	English	11,167	9,914	306
Daviess	Washington	30,245	27,533	431
Dearborn	Lawrenceburg	48,583	38,835	305
Decatur	Greensburg	24,970	23,645	373
De Kalb	Auburn	41,524	35,324	363
Delaware	Muncie	117,774	119,659	393
Dubois	Jasper	40,771	36,616	430
Elkhart	Goshen	191,768	156,198	464
Fayette	Connersville	24,934	26,015	215
Floyd	New Albany	71,543	64,404	148
Fountain	Covington	17,671	17,808	396
Franklin	Brookville	22,852	19,580	386
Fulton	Rochester	20,581	18,840	369
Gibson	Princeton	33,286	31,913	489
Grant	Marion	71,543	74,169	414
Greene	Bloomfield	33,500	30,410	542
Hamilton	Noblesville	231,760	108,936	398
Hancock	Greenfield	60,915	45,527	306
Harrison	Corydon	36,376	29,890	485
Hendricks	Danville	123,476	75,717	408
Henry	New Castle	47,809	48,139	393
Howard	Kokomo	84,615	80,827	293
Huntington	Huntington	38,124	35,427	383
Jackson	Brownstown	41,959	37,730	509
Jasper	Rensselaer	31,624	24,823	560
Jay	Portland	21,654	21,512	384
Jefferson	Madison	32,110	29,797	361
Jennings	Vernon	28,401	23,661	377
Johnson	Franklin	125,864	88,109	320
Knox	Vincennes	38,442	39,884	516
Kosciusko	Warsaw	75,667	65,294	538
Lagrange	Lagrange	36,515	29,477	380
Lake	Crown Point	490,844	475,594	497
La Porte	La Porte	109,755	107,066	598
Lawrence	Bedford	46,398	42,836	449
Madison	Anderson	130,602	130,669	452
Marion	Indianapolis	863,596	797,159	396
Marshall	Plymouth	46,732	42,182	444
Martin	Shoals	10,467	10,369	336
Miami	Peru	35,955	36,897	376
Monroe	Bloomington	121,013	108,978	394
Montgomery	Crawfordsville	37,937	34,436	505
Morgan	Martinsville	69,424	55,920	406
Newton	Kentland	14,421	13,551	402
Noble	Albion	47,297	37,877	411
Ohio	Rising Sun	5,849	5,315	87
Orange	Paoli	19,718	18,409	400
Owen	Spencer	23,074	17,281	385
Parke	Rockville	17,254	15,410	445
Perry	Tell City	18,999	19,107	381
Pike	Petersburg	12,938	12,509	336
Porter	Valparaiso	154,961	128,932	418
Posey	Mount Vernon	26,990	25,968	409
Pulaski	Winamac	13,825	12,780	434
Putnam	Greencastle	36,786	30,315	480
Randolph	Winchester	26,697	27,148	453
Ripley	Versailles	27,549	24,616	446
Rush	Rushville	18,028	18,129	408
Saint Joseph	South Bend	266,431	247,052	457
Scott	Scottsburg	23,604	20,991	190
Shelby	Shelbyville	43,717	40,307	413
Spencer	Rockport	20,310	19,490	399
Starke	Knox	22,903	22,747	309
Steuben	Angola	33,722	27,446	309
Sullivan	Sullivan	21,862	18,993	447
Switzerland	Vevay	9,508	7,738	221
Tippecanoe	Lafayette	152,042	130,598	500
Tipton	Tipton	16,605	16,119	260
Union	Liberty	7,226	6,976	162
Vanderburgh	Evansville	173,157	165,058	235
Vermillion	Newport	16,500	16,773	257
Vigo	Terre Haute	103,195	106,107	403
Wabash	Wabash	34,169	35,069	413
Warren	Williamsport	8,760	8,176	365
Warrick	Boonville	55,465	44,920	384
Washington	Salem	27,882	23,717	514
Wayne	Richmond	69,778	71,951	404
Wells	Bluffton	27,963	25,948	370
White	Monticello	24,846	23,265	505
Whitley	Columbia City	31,955	27,651	336

Iowa

(99 counties, 55,869 sq. mi. land; pop. 2,954,451)

County	County seat or courthouse	2004 Pop.	1990 Pop.	Land area sq. mi.
Adair	Greenfield	7,932	8,409	569
Adams	Corning	4,320	4,866	424
Allamakee	Waukon	14,759	13,855	640
Appanoose	Centerville	13,616	13,743	496
Audubon	Audubon	6,486	7,334	443
Benton	Vinton	26,638	22,429	716
Black Hawk	Waterloo	126,078	123,798	567
Boone	Boone	26,478	25,186	571
Bremer	Waverly	23,455	22,813	438
Buchanan	Independence	21,046	20,844	571
Buena Vista	Storm Lake	20,156	19,965	575
Butler	Allison	15,071	15,731	580
Calhoun	Rockwell City	10,571	11,508	570
Carroll	Carroll	20,898	21,423	569
Cass	Atlantic	14,266	15,128	564
Cedar	Tipton	18,255	17,444	580
Cerro Gordo	Mason City	45,029	46,733	568
Cherokee	Cherokee	12,470	14,098	577
Chickasaw	New Hampton	12,632	13,295	505
Clarke	Osceola	9,223	8,287	431
Clay	Spencer	16,869	17,585	569
Clayton	Elkader	18,291	19,054	779
Clinton	Clinton	49,872	51,040	695
Crawford	Denison	16,925	16,775	714
Dallas	Adel	49,591	29,755	586
Davis	Bloomfield	8,703	8,312	503
Decatur	Leon	8,538	8,338	532
Delaware	Manchester	18,067	18,035	578
Des Moines	Burlington	40,857	42,614	416
Dickinson	Spirit Lake	16,672	14,909	381
Dubuque	Dubuque	91,000	86,403	608
Emmet	Estherville	10,604	11,569	396
Fayette	West Union	21,170	21,843	731
Floyd	Charles City	16,535	17,058	501
Franklin	Hampton	10,731	11,364	582
Fremont	Sidney	7,734	8,226	511
Greene	Jefferson	10,049	10,045	568
Grundy	Grundy Center	12,380	12,029	503
Guthrie	Guthrie Center	11,586	10,935	591
Hamilton	Webster City	16,276	16,071	577
Hancock	Garner	11,801	12,638	571
Hardin	Eldora	18,150	19,094	569
Harrison	Logan	15,821	14,730	697
Henry	Mount Pleasant	20,258	19,226	434
Howard	Cresco	9,834	9,809	473
Humboldt	Dakota City	10,044	10,756	434
Ida	Ida Grove	7,437	8,365	432
Iowa	Marengo	16,030	14,630	586
Jackson	Maquoketa	20,264	19,950	636
Jasper	Newton	37,718	34,795	730
Jefferson	Fairfield	16,022	16,310	435
Johnson	Iowa City	116,097	96,119	614

County	County seat or courthouse	2004 Pop.	1990 Pop.	Land area sq. mi.
Jones	Anamosa	20,646	19,444	575
Keokuk	Sigourney	11,276	11,624	579
Kossuth	Algona	16,378	18,591	973
Lee	Fort Madison & Keokuk	36,726	38,687	517
Linn	Cedar Rapids	197,262	168,767	717
Louisa	Wapello	12,132	11,592	402
Lucas	Chariton	9,719	9,070	431
Lyon	Rock Rapids	11,752	11,952	588
Madison	Winterset	14,957	12,483	561
Mahaska	Oskaloosa	22,199	21,532	571
Marion	Knoxville	32,766	30,001	554
Marshall	Marshalltown	39,503	38,276	572
Mills	Glenwood	15,039	13,202	437
Mitchell	Osage	10,970	10,928	469
Monona	Onawa	9,730	10,034	693
Monroe	Albia	7,861	8,114	433
Montgomery	Red Oak	11,398	12,076	424
Muscatine	Muscatine	42,557	39,907	439
O'Brien	Primghar	14,428	15,444	573
Osceola	Sibley	6,791	7,267	399
Page	Clarinda	16,249	16,870	535
Palo Alto	Emmetsburg	9,778	10,669	564
Plymouth	Le Mars	24,925	23,388	864
Pocahontas	Pocahontas	8,112	9,525	578
Polk	Des Moines	393,184	327,140	569
Pottawattamie	Council Bluffs	89,236	82,628	954
Poweshiek	Montezuma	19,036	19,033	585
Ringgold	Mount Ayr	5,284	5,420	538
Sac	Sac City	10,828	12,324	576
Scott	Davenport	160,141	150,973	458
Shelby	Harlan	12,764	13,230	591
Sioux	Orange City	32,180	29,903	768
Story	Nevada	80,404	74,252	573
Tama	Toledo	17,948	17,419	721
Taylor	Bedford	6,689	7,114	534
Union	Creston	11,993	12,750	424
Van Buren	Keosauqua	7,710	7,676	485
Wapello	Ottumwa	35,798	35,696	432
Warren	Indianola	42,560	36,033	572
Washington	Washington	21,300	19,612	569
Wayne	Corydon	6,594	7,067	526
Webster	Fort Dodge	39,288	40,342	715
Winnebago	Forest City	11,391	12,122	400
Winneshiek	Decorah	21,188	20,847	690
Woodbury	Sioux City	103,113	98,276	873
Worth	Northwood	7,715	7,991	400
Wright	Clarion	13,648	14,269	581

Kansas

(105 counties, 81,815 sq. mi. land; pop. 2,735,502)

County	County seat or courthouse	2004 Pop.	1990 Pop.	Land area sq. mi.
Allen	Iola	13,949	14,638	503
Anderson	Garnett	8,191	7,803	583
Atchison	Atchison	16,848	16,932	432
Barber	Medicine Lodge	4,999	5,874	1,134
Barton	Great Bend	27,367	29,382	894
Bourbon	Fort Scott	15,066	14,966	637
Brown	Hiawatha	10,362	11,128	571
Butler	El Dorado	61,828	50,580	1,428
Chase	Cottonwood Falls	3,068	3,021	776
Chautauqua	Sedan	4,178	4,407	642
Cherokee	Columbus	21,950	21,374	587
Cheyenne	Saint Francis	2,979	3,243	1,020
Clark	Ashland	2,343	2,418	975
Clay	Clay Center	8,597	9,158	644
Cloud	Concordia	9,779	11,023	716
Coffey	Burlington	8,759	8,404	630
Comanche	Coldwater	1,903	2,313	788
Cowley	Winfield	35,772	36,915	1,126
Crawford	Girard	38,060	35,582	593
Decatur	Oberlin	3,274	4,021	894
Dickinson	Abilene	19,132	18,958	848
Doniphan	Troy	8,062	8,134	392
Douglas	Lawrence	102,786	81,798	457
Edwards	Kinsley	3,308	3,787	622
Elk	Howard	3,117	3,327	647
Ellis	Hays	27,060	26,004	900
Ellsworth	Ellsworth	6,350	6,586	716
Finney	Garden City	39,271	33,070	1,302
Ford	Dodge City	33,278	27,463	1,099
Franklin	Ottawa	26,049	21,994	574
Geary	Junction City	25,111	30,453	385
Gove	Gove	2,845	3,231	1,071
Graham	Hill City	2,745	3,543	898
Grant	Ulysses	7,685	7,159	575
Gray	Cimarron	5,980	5,396	869
Greeley	Tribune	1,415	1,774	778
Greenwood	Eureka	7,538	7,847	1,140
Hamilton	Syracuse	2,654	2,388	996
Harper	Anthony	6,238	7,124	801
Harvey	Newton	33,769	31,028	539
Haskell	Sublette	4,272	3,886	577
Hodgeman	Jetmore	2,089	2,177	860
Jackson	Holton	13,169	11,525	656
Jefferson	Oskaloosa	18,906	15,905	536
Jewell	Mankato	3,422	4,251	909
Johnson	Olathe	496,691	355,021	477
Kearny	Lakin	4,515	4,027	871
Kingman	Kingman	8,390	8,292	863
Kiowa	Greensburg	3,084	3,660	722
Labette	Oswego	22,269	23,693	649
Lane	Dighton	1,950	2,375	717
Leavenworth	Leavenworth	72,439	64,371	463
Lincoln	Lincoln	3,416	3,653	719
Linn	Mound City	9,775	8,254	599
Logan	Oakley	2,827	3,081	1,073
Lyon	Emporia	35,717	34,732	851
McPherson	McPherson	29,413	27,268	900
Marion	Marion	13,010	12,888	943
Marshall	Marysville	10,402	11,705	903
Meade	Meade	4,592	4,247	978
Miami	Paola	29,712	23,466	577
Mitchell	Beloit	6,564	7,203	700
Montgomery	Independence	34,975	38,816	645
Morris	Council Grove	5,977	6,198	697
Morton	Elkhart	3,269	3,480	730
Nemaha	Seneca	10,458	10,446	718
Neosho	Erie	16,555	17,035	572
Ness	Ness City	3,080	4,033	1,075
Norton	Norton	5,799	5,947	878
Osage	Lyndon	17,091	15,248	704
Osborne	Osborne	4,100	4,867	892
Ottawa	Minneapolis	6,175	5,634	721
Pawnee	Larned	6,795	7,555	754
Phillips	Phillipsburg	5,583	6,590	886
Pottawatomie	Westmoreland	18,871	16,128	844
Pratt	Pratt	9,417	9,702	735
Rawlins	Atwood	2,765	3,404	1,070
Reno	Hutchinson	63,676	62,389	1,254
Republic	Belleville	5,224	6,482	716
Rice	Lyons	10,497	10,610	727
Riley	Manhattan	63,069	67,139	610
Rooks	Stockton	5,386	6,039	888
Rush	LaCrosse	3,466	3,842	718
Russell	Russell	6,978	7,835	885
Saline	Salina	53,943	49,301	720
Scott	Scott City	4,691	5,289	718
Sedgwick	Wichita	463,802	403,662	999
Seward	Liberal	23,237	18,743	640
Shawnee	Topeka	171,716	160,976	550
Sheridan	Hoxie	2,614	3,043	895
Sherman	Goodland	6,218	6,926	1,056
Smith	Smith Center	4,179	5,078	895
Stafford	Saint John	4,512	5,365	792
Stanton	Johnson	2,374	2,333	680
Stevens	Hugoton	5,520	5,048	728
Sumner	Wellington	25,272	25,841	1,182
Thomas	Colby	7,801	8,258	1,075
Trego	WaKeeney	3,158	3,694	888
Wabaunsee	Alma	6,938	6,603	797
Wallace	Sharon Springs	1,579	1,821	914
Washington	Washington	6,107	7,073	898
Wichita	Leoti	2,360	2,758	719
Wilson	Fredonia	9,946	10,289	574
Woodson	Yates Center	3,553	4,116	501
Wyandotte	Kansas City	156,487	162,026	151

Kentucky

(120 counties, 39,728 sq. mi. land; pop. 4,145,922)

County	County seat or courthouse	2004 Pop.	1990 Pop.	Land area sq. mi.
Adair	Columbia	17,575	15,360	407
Allen	Scottsville	18,541	14,628	346
Anderson	Lawrenceburg	20,099	14,571	203
Ballard	Wickliffe	8,295	7,902	251
Barren	Glasgow	39,473	34,001	491
Bath	Owingsville	11,538	9,692	279
Bell	Pineville	29,672	31,506	361
Boone	Burlington	101,354	57,589	246
Bourbon	Paris	19,623	19,236	291
Boyd	Catlettsburg	49,743	51,096	160
Boyle	Danville	28,241	25,590	182
Bracken	Brooksville	8,707	7,766	203
Breathitt	Jackson	15,937	15,703	495
Breckinridge	Hardinsburg	19,168	16,312	572
Bullitt	Shepherdsville	66,645	47,567	299
Butler	Morgantown	13,364	11,245	428
Caldwell	Princeton	12,879	13,232	347
Calloway	Murray	34,789	30,735	386
Campbell	Newport	87,256	83,866	152
Carlisle	Bardwell	5,310	5,238	192
Carroll	Carrollton	10,344	9,292	130
Carter	Grayson	27,459	24,340	411
Casey	Liberty	16,059	14,211	446
Christian	Hopkinsville	70,649	68,941	721
Clark	Winchester	34,377	29,496	254
Clay	Manchester	24,254	21,746	471
Clinton	Albany	9,558	9,135	197
Crittenden	Marion	8,999	9,196	362
Cumberland	Burkesville	7,168	6,784	306
Daviess	Owensboro	92,587	87,189	462

County	County seat or courthouse	2004 Pop.	1990 Pop.	Land area sq. mi.
Edmonson	Brownsville	11,921	10,357	303
Elliott	Sandy Hook	6,835	6,455	234
Estill	Irvine	15,164	14,614	254
Fayette	Lexington	266,358	225,366	285
Fleming	Flemingsburg	14,480	12,292	351
Floyd	Prestonsburg	42,379	43,586	394
Franklin	Frankfort	48,142	44,143	210
Fulton	Hickman	7,357	8,271	209
Gallatin	Warsaw	7,979	5,393	99
Garrard	Lancaster	16,163	11,579	231
Grant	Williamstown	24,317	15,737	260
Graves	Mayfield	37,401	33,550	556
Grayson	Leitchfield	25,004	21,050	504
Green	Greensburg	11,667	10,371	289
Greenup	Greenup	37,274	36,796	346
Hancock	Hawesville	8,459	7,864	189
Hardin	Elizabethtown	96,066	89,240	628
Harlan	Harlan	31,927	36,574	467
Harrison	Cynthiana	18,256	16,248	310
Hart	Munfordville	18,237	14,890	416
Henderson	Henderson	45,426	43,044	440
Henry	New Castle	15,771	12,823	289
Hickman	Clinton	5,172	5,566	244
Hopkins	Madisonville	46,818	46,126	551
Jackson	McKee	13,622	11,955	346
Jefferson	Louisville	700,030	665,123	385
Jessamine	Nicholasville	42,313	30,508	173
Johnson	Paintsville	23,856	23,248	262
Kenton	Covington	152,890	142,005	162
Knott	Hindman	17,582	17,906	352
Knox	Barbourville	31,912	29,676	388
Larue	Hodgenville	13,485	11,679	263
Laurel	London	55,993	43,438	436
Lawrence	Louisa	16,048	13,998	419
Lee	Beattyville	7,786	7,422	210
Leslie	Hyden	12,043	13,642	404
Letcher	Whitesburg	24,677	27,000	339
Lewis	Vanceburg	13,820	13,029	484
Lincoln	Stanford	24,821	20,096	336
Livingston	Smithland	9,762	9,062	316
Logan	Russellville	27,048	24,416	556
Lyon	Eddyville	8,205	6,624	216
McCracken	Paducah	64,700	62,879	251
McCreary	Whitley City	17,055	15,603	428
McLean	Calhoun	9,982	9,628	254
Madison	Richmond	76,208	57,508	441
Magoffin	Salyersville	13,456	13,077	309
Marion	Lebanon	18,728	16,499	346
Marshall	Benton	30,813	27,205	305
Martin	Inez	12,328	12,526	231
Mason	Maysville	16,937	16,666	241
Meade	Brandenburg	28,300	24,170	309
Menifee	Frenchburg	6,766	5,092	204
Mercer	Harrodsburg	21,493	19,148	251
Metcalfe	Edmonton	10,165	8,963	291
Monroe	Tompkinsville	11,660	11,401	331
Montgomery	Mount Sterling	23,629	19,561	199
Morgan	West Liberty	14,360	11,648	381
Muhlenberg	Greenville	31,752	31,318	475
Nelson	Bardstown	40,406	29,710	423
Nicholas	Carlisle	7,076	6,725	197
Ohio	Hartford	23,565	21,105	594
Oldham	La Grange	52,100	33,263	189
Owen	Owenton	11,300	9,035	352
Owsley	Booneville	4,749	5,036	198
Pendleton	Falmouth	15,134	12,062	281
Perry	Hazard	29,762	30,283	342
Pike	Pikeville	67,080	72,584	788
Powell	Stanton	13,615	11,686	180
Pulaski	Somerset	58,727	49,489	662
Robertson	Mount Olivet	2,308	2,124	100
Rockcastle	Mount Vernon	16,782	14,803	318
Rowan	Morehead	22,176	20,353	281
Russell	Jamestown	16,838	14,716	254
Scott	Georgetown	38,029	23,867	285
Shelby	Shelbyville	37,219	24,824	384
Simpson	Franklin	16,891	15,145	236
Spencer	Taylorsville	14,822	6,801	186
Taylor	Campbellsville	23,479	21,146	270
Todd	Elkton	11,863	10,940	376
Trigg	Cadiz	13,249	10,361	443
Trimble	Bedford	9,047	6,090	149
Union	Morganfield	15,708	16,557	345
Warren	Bowling Green	97,168	77,720	545
Washington	Springfield	11,266	10,441	301
Wayne	Monticello	20,400	17,468	459
Webster	Dixon	14,130	13,955	335
Whitley	Williamsburg	37,566	33,326	440
Wolfe	Campton	7,045	6,503	223
Woodford	Versailles	23,961	19,955	191

Louisiana

(64 parishes, 43,562 sq. mi. land; pop. 4,515,770)

Parish	Parish seat or courthouse	2004 Pop.	1990 Pop.	Land area sq. mi.
Acadia	Crowley	59,168	55,882	655
Allen	Oberlin	25,407	21,226	765
Ascension	Donaldsonville	87,164	58,214	292
Assumption	Napoleonville	23,234	22,753	339
Avoyelles	Marksville	41,981	39,159	832
Beauregard	De Ridder	34,094	30,083	1,160
Bienville	Arcadia	15,361	16,232	811
Bossier	Benton	104,080	86,088	839
Caddo	Shreveport	251,506	248,253	882
Calcasieu	Lake Charles	184,961	168,134	1,071
Caldwell	Columbia	10,837	9,806	529
Cameron	Cameron	9,681	9,260	1,313
Catahoula	Harrisonburg	10,627	11,065	704
Claiborne	Homer	16,471	17,405	755
Concordia	Vidalia	19,724	20,828	696
De Soto	Mansfield	26,231	25,668	877
East Baton Rouge	Baton Rouge	412,633	380,105	455
East Carroll	Lake Providence	8,954	9,709	421
East Feliciana	Clinton	20,950	19,211	453
Evangeline	Ville Platte	35,451	33,274	664
Franklin	Winnsboro	20,812	22,387	624
Grant	Colfax	19,139	17,526	645
Iberia	New Iberia	74,449	68,297	575
Iberville	Plaquemine	32,497	31,049	619
Jackson	Jonesboro	15,278	15,859	570
Jefferson	Gretna	453,590	448,306	307
Jefferson Davis	Jennings	31,235	30,722	652
Lafayette	Lafayette	195,707	164,762	270
Lafourche	Thibodaux	92,157	85,860	1,085
La Salle	Jena	14,161	13,662	624
Lincoln	Ruston	42,382	41,745	471
Livingston	Livingston	105,653	70,523	648
Madison	Tallulah	12,996	12,463	624
Morehouse	Bastrop	30,551	31,938	794
Natchitoches	Natchitoches	38,741	37,254	1,255
Orleans	New Orleans	462,269	496,938	181
Ouachita	Monroe	148,355	142,191	611
Plaquemines	Pointe a la Hache	28,969	25,575	845
Pointe Coupee	New Roads	22,537	22,540	557
Rapides	Alexandria	128,013	131,556	1,323
Red River	Coushatta	9,606	9,526	389
Richland	Rayville	20,485	20,629	558
Sabine	Many	23,616	22,646	865
Saint Bernard	Chalmette	65,554	66,631	465
Saint Charles	Hahnville	50,073	42,437	284
Saint Helena	Greensburg	10,309	9,874	408
Saint James	Convent	21,146	20,879	246
Saint John the Baptist	Edgard	45,581	39,996	219
Saint Landry	Opelousas	89,635	80,312	929
Saint Martin	Saint Martinville	50,453	44,097	740
Saint Mary	Franklin	52,189	58,086	613
Saint Tammany	Covington	213,553	144,500	854
Tangipahoa	Amite	105,158	85,709	790
Tensas	Saint Joseph	6,176	7,103	602
Terrebonne	Houma	106,523	96,982	1,255
Union	Farmerville	22,894	20,796	878
Vermilion	Abbeville	54,751	50,055	1,174
Vernon	Leesville	49,545	61,961	1,328
Washington	Franklinton	44,161	43,185	670
Webster	Minden	41,254	41,989	595
West Baton Rouge	Port Allen	21,880	19,419	191
West Carroll	Oak Grove	11,963	12,093	359
West Feliciana	Saint Francisville	15,108	12,915	406
Winn	Winnfield	16,151	16,498	950

Maine

(16 counties, 30,862 sq. mi. land; pop. 1,317,253)

County	County seat or courthouse	2004 Pop.	1990 Pop.	Land area sq. mi.
Androscoggin	Auburn	107,022	105,259	470
Aroostook	Houlton	73,390	86,936	6,672
Cumberland	Portland	273,505	243,135	836
Franklin	Farmington	29,736	29,008	1,698
Hancock	Ellsworth	53,556	46,948	1,588
Kennebec	Augusta	120,645	115,904	868
Knox	Rockland	41,008	36,310	366
Lincoln	Wiscasset	35,236	30,357	456
Oxford	South Paris	56,614	52,602	2,078
Penobscot	Bangor	148,196	146,601	3,396
Piscataquis	Dover-Foxcroft	17,525	18,653	3,966
Sagadahoc	Bath	36,927	33,535	254
Somerset	Skowhegan	51,584	49,767	3,927
Waldo	Belfast	38,392	33,018	730
Washington	Machias	33,558	35,308	2,568
York	Alfred	200,359	164,587	991

Maryland

(23 counties, 1 ind. city, 9,774 sq. mi. land; pop. 5,558,058)

County	County seat or courthouse	2004 Pop.	1990 Pop.	Land area sq. mi.
Allegany	Cumberland	73,871	74,946	425
Anne Arundel	Annapolis	508,572	427,239	416
Baltimore	Towson	780,821	692,134	599
Calvert	Prince Frederick	86,474	51,372	215
Caroline	Denton	31,058	27,035	320
Carroll	Westminster	166,159	123,372	449
Cecil	Elkton	95,526	71,347	348

County	County seat or courthouse	2004 Pop.	1990 Pop.	Land area sq. mi.
Charles	La Plata	135,807	101,154	461
Dorchester	Cambridge	30,912	30,236	558
Frederick	Frederick	217,653	150,208	663
Garrett	Oakland	30,124	28,138	648
Harford	Bel Air	235,594	182,132	440
Howard	Ellicott City	266,738	187,328	252
Kent	Chestertown	19,582	17,842	279
Montgomery	Rockville	921,690	762,875	496
Prince George's	Upper Marlboro	842,967	722,705	485
Queen Anne's	Centreville	45,078	33,953	372
Saint Mary's	Leonardtown	94,921	75,974	361
Somerset	Princess Anne	25,863	23,440	327
Talbot	Easton	35,017	30,549	269
Washington	Hagerstown	139,624	121,393	458
Wicomico	Salisbury	88,782	74,339	377
Worcester	Snow Hill	48,974	35,028	473
Independent City				
Baltimore		636,251	736,014	81

Massachusetts

(14 counties, 7,840 sq. mi. land; pop. 6,416,505)

County	County seat or courthouse	2004 Pop.	1990 Pop.	Land area sq. mi.
Barnstable	Barnstable	228,683	186,605	396
Berkshire	Pittsfield	132,486	139,352	931
Bristol	Taunton	548,176	506,325	556
Dukes	Edgartown	15,669	11,639	104
Essex	Salem	738,984	670,080	501
Franklin	Greenfield	72,235	70,086	702
Hampden	Springfield	461,844	456,310	618
Hampshire	Northampton	153,894	146,568	529
Middlesex	East Cambridge	1,464,628	1,398,468	823
Nantucket	Nantucket	10,124	6,012	48
Norfolk	Dedham	653,617	616,087	400
Plymouth	Plymouth	490,655	435,276	661
Suffolk	Boston	666,022	663,906	59
Worcester	Worcester	779,488	709,711	1,513

Michigan

(83 counties, 56,804 sq. mi. land; pop. 10,112,620)

County	County seat or courthouse	2004 Pop.	1990 Pop.	Land area sq. mi.
Alcona	Harrisville	11,646	10,145	674
Alger	Munising	9,760	8,972	918
Allegan	Allegan	112,477	90,509	827
Alpena	Alpena	30,739	30,605	574
Antrim	Bellaire	24,500	18,185	477
Arenac	Standish	17,321	14,906	367
Baraga	L'Anse	8,728	7,954	904
Barry	Hastings	59,371	50,057	556
Bay	Bay City	109,480	111,723	444
Benzie	Beulah	17,466	12,200	321
Berrien	Saint Joseph	163,125	161,378	571
Branch	Coldwater	46,444	41,502	507
Calhoun	Marshall	139,067	135,982	709
Cass	Cassopolis	51,761	49,477	492
Charlevoix	Charlevoix	26,665	21,468	417
Cheboygan	Cheboygan	27,289	21,398	716
Chippewa	Sault Sainte Marie	38,791	34,604	1,561
Clare	Harrison	31,838	24,952	567
Clinton	Saint Johns	68,800	57,893	571
Crawford	Grayling	14,870	12,260	558
Delta	Escanaba	38,380	37,780	1,170
Dickinson	Iron Mountain	27,345	26,831	766
Eaton	Charlotte	107,056	92,879	576
Emmet	Petoskey	33,277	25,040	468
Genesee	Flint	443,947	430,459	640
Gladwin	Gladwin	27,172	21,896	507
Gogebic	Bessemer	17,029	18,052	1,102
Grand Traverse	Traverse City	82,752	64,273	465
Gratiot	Ithaca	42,396	38,982	570
Hillsdale	Hillsdale	47,470	43,431	599
Houghton	Houghton	35,568	35,446	1,012
Huron	Bad Axe	34,948	34,951	837
Ingham	Mason	280,073	281,912	559
Ionia	Ionia	64,378	57,024	573
Iosco	Tawas City	26,873	30,209	549
Iron	Crystal Falls	12,587	13,175	1,166
Isabella	Mount Pleasant	64,481	54,624	574
Jackson	Jackson	162,973	149,756	707
Kalamazoo	Kalamazoo	240,724	223,411	562
Kalkaska	Kalkaska	17,204	13,497	561
Kent	Grand Rapids	593,898	500,631	856
Keweenaw	Eagle River	2,204	1,701	541
Lake	Baldwin	11,881	8,583	567
Lapeer	Lapeer	92,510	74,768	654
Leelanau	Leland	22,163	16,527	348
Lenawee	Adrian	101,768	91,476	751
Livingston	Howell	177,538	115,645	568
Luce	Newberry	6,850	5,763	903
Mackinac	Saint Ignace	11,383	10,674	1,022
Macomb	Mount Clemens	822,660	717,400	480
Manistee	Manistee	25,090	21,265	544
Marquette	Marquette	64,874	70,887	1,821
Mason	Ludington	29,074	25,537	495
Mecosta	Big Rapids	42,394	37,308	556
Menominee	Menominee	25,174	24,920	1,044
Midland	Midland	84,615	75,651	521
Missaukee	Lake City	15,286	12,147	567
Monroe	Monroe	152,552	133,600	551
Montcalm	Stanton	63,627	53,059	708
Montmorency	Atlanta	10,498	8,936	548
Muskegon	Muskegon	174,401	158,983	509
Newaygo	White Cloud	49,892	38,206	842
Oakland	Pontiac	1,213,339	1,083,592	873
Oceana	Hart	28,415	22,455	540
Ogemaw	West Branch	21,919	18,681	564
Ontonagon	Ontonagon	7,538	8,854	1,312
Osceola	Reed City	23,842	20,146	566
Oscoda	Mio	9,348	7,842	565
Otsego	Gaylord	24,513	17,957	515
Ottawa	Grand Haven	252,351	187,768	566
Presque Isle	Rogers City	14,306	13,743	660
Roscommon	Roscommon	26,103	19,776	521
Saginaw	Saginaw	209,062	211,946	809
Saint Clair	Port Huron	170,916	145,607	724
Saint Joseph	Centreville	62,964	58,913	504
Sanilac	Sandusky	44,828	39,928	964
Schoolcraft	Manistique	8,874	8,302	1,178
Shiawassee	Corunna	73,125	69,770	539
Tuscola	Caro	58,646	55,498	812
Van Buren	Paw Paw	78,541	70,060	611
Washtenaw	Ann Arbor	339,191	282,937	710
Wayne	Detroit	2,016,202	2,111,687	614
Wexford	Cadillac	31,494	26,360	565

Minnesota

(87 counties, 79,610 sq. mi. land; pop. 5,100,958)

County	County seat or courthouse	2004 Pop.	1990 Pop.	Land area sq. mi.
Aitkin	Aitkin	16,031	12,425	1,819
Anoka	Anoka	319,950	243,641	424
Becker	Detroit Lakes	31,817	27,881	1,310
Beltrami	Bemidji	42,263	34,384	2,505
Benton	Foley	38,099	30,185	408
Big Stone	Ortonville	5,602	6,285	497
Blue Earth	Mankato	57,409	54,044	752
Brown	New Ulm	26,763	26,984	611
Carlton	Carlton	33,639	29,259	860
Carver	Chaska	82,122	47,915	357
Cass	Walker	28,460	21,791	2,018
Chippewa	Montevideo	12,659	13,228	583
Chisago	Center City	48,349	30,521	418
Clay	Moorhead	52,905	50,422	1,045
Clearwater	Bagley	8,437	8,309	995
Cook	Grand Marais	5,317	3,868	1,451
Cottonwood	Windom	11,961	12,694	640
Crow Wing	Brainerd	59,431	44,249	997
Dakota	Hastings	379,058	275,210	570
Dodge	Mantorville	19,355	15,731	440
Douglas	Alexandria	34,628	28,674	634
Faribault	Blue Earth	15,642	16,937	714
Fillmore	Preston	21,321	20,777	861
Freeborn	Albert Lea	31,971	33,060	708
Goodhue	Red Wing	45,496	40,690	758
Grant	Elbow Lake	6,118	6,246	546
Hennepin	Minneapolis	1,120,897	1,032,431	557
Houston	Caledonia	19,890	18,497	558
Hubbard	Park Rapids	18,849	14,939	922
Isanti	Cambridge	36,546	25,921	439
Itasca	Grand Rapids	44,316	40,863	2,665
Jackson	Jackson	11,234	11,677	702
Kanabec	Mora	16,056	12,802	525
Kandiyohi	Willmar	41,191	38,761	796
Kittson	Hallock	4,820	5,767	1,097
Koochiching	International Falls	13,863	16,299	3,102
Lac qui Parle	Madison	7,756	8,924	765
Lake	Two Harbors	11,218	10,415	2,099
Lake of the Woods	Baudette	4,404	4,076	1,297
Le Sueur	Le Center	27,166	23,239	449
Lincoln	Ivanhoe	6,178	6,890	537
Lyon	Marshall	24,703	24,789	714
McLeod	Glencoe	36,190	32,030	492
Mahnomen	Mahnomen	5,081	5,044	556
Marshall	Warren	10,015	10,993	1,772
Martin	Fairmont	21,044	22,914	709
Meeker	Litchfield	23,277	20,846	609
Mille Lacs	Milaca	25,079	18,670	574
Morrison	Little Falls	32,689	29,604	1,125
Mower	Austin	38,998	37,385	712
Murray	Slayton	8,995	9,660	704
Nicollet	Saint Peter	30,829	28,076	452
Nobles	Worthington	20,477	20,098	715
Norman	Ada	7,085	7,975	876
Olmsted	Rochester	133,283	106,470	653
Otter Tail	Fergus Falls	57,931	50,714	1,980
Pennington	Thief River Falls	13,545	13,306	617
Pine	Pine City	28,116	21,264	1,411
Pipestone	Pipestone	9,579	10,491	466
Polk	Crookston	31,123	32,589	1,970
Pope	Glenwood	11,227	10,745	670
Ramsey	Saint Paul	499,498	485,760	156

County	County seat or courthouse	2004 Pop.	1990 Pop.	Land area sq. mi.
Red Lake	Red Lake Falls	4,289	4,525	432
Redwood	Redwood Falls	16,201	17,254	880
Renville	Olivia	16,701	17,673	983
Rice	Faribault	60,418	49,183	498
Rock	Luverne	9,579	9,806	483
Roseau	Roseau	16,308	15,026	1,663
Saint Louis	Duluth	198,136	198,232	6,225
Scott	Shakopee	114,794	57,846	357
Sherburne	Elk River	78,762	41,945	436
Sibley	Gaylord	15,230	14,366	589
Stearns	Saint Cloud	141,055	119,324	1,345
Steele	Owatonna	35,166	30,729	430
Stevens	Morris	9,935	10,634	562
Swift	Benson	11,478	10,724	744
Todd	Long Prairie	24,647	23,363	942
Traverse	Wheaton	3,871	4,463	574
Wabasha	Wabasha	22,215	19,744	525
Wadena	Wadena	13,603	13,154	535
Waseca	Waseca	19,270	18,079	423
Washington	Stillwater	216,660	145,860	392
Watonwan	Saint James	11,390	11,682	435
Wilkin	Breckenridge	6,784	7,516	751
Winona	Winona	49,046	47,828	626
Wright	Buffalo	106,889	68,710	661
Yellow Medicine	Granite Falls	10,580	11,684	758

Mississippi

(82 counties, 46,907 sq. mi. land; pop. 2,902,966)

County	County seat or courthouse	2004 Pop.	1990 Pop.	Land area sq. mi.
Adams	Natchez	32,591	35,356	460
Alcorn	Corinth	35,230	31,722	400
Amite	Liberty	13,418	13,328	730
Attala	Kosciusko	19,653	18,481	735
Benton	Ashland	7,844	8,046	407
Bolivar	Cleveland & Rosedale	38,928	41,875	876
Calhoun	Pittsboro	14,864	14,908	587
Carroll	Carrollton & Vaiden	10,517	9,237	628
Chickasaw	Houston & Okolona	19,318	18,085	502
Choctaw	Ackerman	9,601	9,071	419
Claiborne	Port Gibson	11,546	11,370	487
Clarke	Quitman	17,634	17,313	691
Clay	West Point	21,650	21,120	409
Coahoma	Clarksdale	29,202	31,665	554
Copiah	Hazlehurst	29,151	27,592	777
Covington	Collins	20,225	16,527	414
De Soto	Hernando	130,587	67,910	478
Forrest	Hattiesburg	74,469	68,314	467
Franklin	Meadville	8,411	8,377	565
George	Lucedale	20,838	16,673	478
Greene	Leakesville	13,166	10,220	713
Grenada	Grenada	22,736	21,555	422
Hancock	Bay Saint Louis	45,933	31,760	477
Harrison	Gulfport	192,393	165,365	581
Hinds	Jackson & Raymond	249,987	254,441	869
Holmes	Lexington	21,148	21,604	756
Humphreys	Belzoni	10,628	12,134	418
Issaquena	Mayersville	1,978	1,909	413
Itawamba	Fulton	23,310	20,017	532
Jackson	Pascagoula	135,436	115,243	727
Jasper	Bay Springs & Paulding	18,005	17,114	676
Jefferson	Fayette	9,456	8,653	519
Jefferson Davis	Prentiss	13,087	14,051	408
Jones	Ellisville & Laurel	65,662	62,031	694
Kemper	De Kalb	10,338	10,356	766
Lafayette	Oxford	40,745	31,826	631
Lamar	Purvis	43,262	30,424	497
Lauderdale	Meridian	77,449	75,555	704
Lawrence	Monticello	13,445	12,458	431
Leake	Carthage	22,306	18,436	583
Lee	Tupelo	78,102	65,579	450
Leflore	Greenwood	36,146	37,341	592
Lincoln	Brookhaven	33,701	30,278	586
Lowndes	Columbus	60,487	59,308	502
Madison	Canton	81,973	53,794	717
Marion	Columbia	25,440	25,544	542
Marshall	Holly Springs	35,498	30,361	706
Monroe	Aberdeen	37,947	36,582	764
Montgomery	Winona	11,721	12,387	407
Neshoba	Philadelphia	29,511	24,800	570
Newton	Decatur	22,165	20,291	578
Noxubee	Macon	12,283	12,604	695
Oktibbeha	Starkville	41,309	38,375	458
Panola	Batesville & Sardis	35,373	29,996	684
Pearl River	Poplarville	51,835	38,714	811
Perry	New Augusta	12,236	10,865	647
Pike	Magnolia	39,260	36,882	409
Pontotoc	Pontotoc	28,099	22,237	497
Prentiss	Booneville	25,745	23,278	415
Quitman	Marks	9,715	10,490	405
Rankin	Brandon	128,380	87,161	775
Scott	Forest	28,656	24,137	609
Sharkey	Rolling Fork	6,083	7,066	428
Simpson	Mendenhall	27,784	23,953	589
Smith	Raleigh	15,857	14,798	636
Stone	Wiggins	14,445	10,750	445
Sunflower	Indianola	33,392	35,129	694
Tallahatchie	Charleston & Sumner	14,255	15,210	644
Tate	Senatobia	26,133	21,432	404
Tippah	Ripley	20,979	19,523	458
Tishomingo	Iuka	19,051	17,683	424
Tunica	Tunica	10,066	8,164	455
Union	New Albany	26,449	22,085	415
Walthall	Tylertown	15,193	14,352	404
Warren	Vicksburg	49,113	47,880	587
Washington	Greenville	59,567	67,935	724
Wayne	Waynesboro	21,227	19,517	810
Webster	Walthall	10,116	10,222	422
Wilkinson	Woodville	10,182	9,678	677
Winston	Louisville	19,797	19,433	607
Yalobusha	Coffeeville & Water Valley	13,337	12,033	467
Yazoo	Yazoo City	28,211	25,506	919

Missouri

(114 counties, 1 ind. city, 68,886 sq. mi. land; pop. 5,754,618)

County	County seat or courthouse	2004 Pop.	1990 Pop.	Land area sq. mi.
Adair	Kirksville	24,666	24,577	567
Andrew	Savannah	16,834	14,632	435
Atchison	Rockport	6,302	7,457	545
Audrain	Mexico	25,658	23,599	693
Barry	Cassville	35,314	27,547	779
Barton	Lamar	13,070	11,312	594
Bates	Butler	16,965	15,025	848
Benton	Warsaw	18,519	13,859	706
Bollinger	Marble Hill	12,341	10,619	621
Boone	Columbia	141,367	112,379	685
Buchanan	Saint Joseph	84,825	83,083	410
Butler	Poplar Buff	40,989	38,765	698
Caldwell	Kingston	9,204	8,380	429
Callaway	Fulton	42,086	32,809	839
Camden	Camdenton	38,702	27,495	655
Cape Girardeau	Jackson	70,730	61,633	579
Carroll	Carrollton	10,129	10,748	695
Carter	Van Buren	5,963	5,515	508
Cass	Harrisonville	91,593	63,808	699
Cedar	Stockton	13,894	12,093	476
Chariton	Keytesville	8,142	9,202	756
Christian	Ozark	64,273	32,644	563
Clark	Kahoka	7,356	7,547	507
Clay	Liberty	197,588	153,411	396
Clinton	Plattsburg	20,683	16,595	419
Cole	Jefferson City	71,996	63,579	391
Cooper	Boonville	17,259	14,835	565
Crawford	Steelville	23,647	19,173	743
Dade	Greenfield	7,829	7,449	490
Dallas	Buffalo	16,328	12,646	542
Daviess	Gallatin	8,166	7,865	567
De Kalb	Maysville	12,488	9,967	424
Dent	Salem	15,067	13,702	754
Douglas	Ava	13,546	11,876	815
Dunklin	Kennett	32,488	33,112	546
Franklin	Union	98,234	80,603	923
Gasconade	Hermann	15,612	14,006	521
Gentry	Albany	6,523	6,854	492
Greene	Springfield	247,932	207,949	675
Grundy	Trenton	10,183	10,536	436
Harrison	Bethany	8,816	8,469	725
Henry	Clinton	22,701	20,044	702
Hickory	Hermitage	9,167	7,335	399
Holt	Oregon	5,087	6,034	462
Howard	Fayette	9,940	9,631	466
Howell	West Plains	37,995	31,447	928
Iron	Ironton	10,329	10,726	551
Jackson	Independence	660,095	633,234	605
Jasper	Carthage	109,460	90,465	640
Jefferson	Hillsboro	210,397	171,380	657
Johnson	Warrensburg	50,669	42,514	830
Knox	Edina	4,199	4,482	506
Laclede	Lebanon	33,617	27,158	766
Lafayette	Lexington	33,134	31,107	629
Lawrence	Mount Vernon	36,710	30,236	613
Lewis	Monticello	10,261	10,233	505
Lincoln	Troy	45,816	28,892	630
Linn	Linneus	13,281	13,885	620
Livingston	Chillicothe	14,269	14,592	535
McDonald	Pineville	22,363	16,938	540
Macon	Macon	15,554	15,345	804
Madison	Fredericktown	11,948	11,127	497
Maries	Vienna	8,877	7,976	528
Marion	Palmyra	28,410	27,682	438
Mercer	Princeton	3,618	3,723	454
Miller	Tuscumbia	24,624	20,700	592
Mississippi	Charleston	13,697	14,442	413
Moniteau	California	15,042	12,298	417
Monroe	Paris	9,467	9,104	646
Montgomery	Montgomery City	12,085	11,355	537

County	County seat or courthouse	2004 Pop.	1990 Pop.	Land area sq. mi.
Morgan	Versailles	20,263	15,574	597
New Madrid	New Madrid	18,969	20,928	678
Newton	Neosho	54,775	44,445	626
Nodaway	Maryville	21,754	21,709	877
Oregon	Alton	10,441	9,470	791
Osage	Linn	13,324	12,018	606
Ozark	Gainesville	9,431	8,598	742
Pemiscot	Caruthersville	19,571	21,921	493
Perry	Perryville	18,289	16,648	475
Pettis	Sedalia	39,753	35,437	685
Phelps	Rolla	41,726	35,248	673
Pike	Bowling Green	18,403	15,969	673
Platte	Platte City	80,967	57,867	420
Polk	Bolivar	28,320	21,826	637
Pulaski	Waynesville	44,478	41,307	547
Putnam	Unionville	5,074	5,079	518
Ralls	New London	9,682	8,476	471
Randolph	Huntsville	25,120	24,370	482
Ray	Richmond	23,937	21,968	569
Reynolds	Centerville	6,603	6,661	811
Ripley	Doniphan	13,839	12,303	629
Saint Charles	Saint Charles	320,734	212,751	560
Saint Clair	Osceola	9,540	8,457	677
Sainte Genevieve	Sainte Genevieve	60,724	16,037	502
Saint Francois	Farmington	18,264	48,904	449
Saint Louis	Clayton	1,009,235	993,508	508
Saline	Marshall	23,059	23,523	756
Schuyler	Lancaster	4,348	4,236	308
Scotland	Memphis	4,907	4,822	438
Scott	Benton	40,891	39,376	421
Shannon	Eminence	8,381	7,613	1,004
Shelby	Shelbyville	6,709	6,942	501
Stoddard	Bloomfield	29,773	28,895	827
Stone	Galena	30,720	19,078	463
Sullivan	Milan	6,938	6,326	651
Taney	Forsyth	41,939	25,561	632
Texas	Houston	24,476	21,476	1,179
Vernon	Nevada	20,383	19,041	834
Warren	Warrenton	27,809	19,534	431
Washington	Potosi	23,955	20,380	760
Wayne	Greenville	13,112	11,543	761
Webster	Marshfield	34,133	23,753	593
Worth	Grant City	2,294	2,440	267
Wright	Hartville	18,177	16,758	682
Independent City				
Saint Louis		343,279	396,685	62

Montana

(56 counties, 145,552 sq. mi. land; pop. 926,865)

County	County seat or courthouse	2004 Pop.	1990 Pop.	Land area sq. mi.
Beaverhead	Dillon	8,845	8,424	5,542
Big Horn	Hardin	13,005	11,337	4,995
Blaine	Chinook	6,668	6,728	4,226
Broadwater	Townsend	4,530	3,318	1,191
Carbon	Red Lodge	9,755	8,080	2,048
Carter	Ekalaka	1,324	1,503	3,340
Cascade	Great Falls	79,849	77,691	2,698
Chouteau	Fort Benton	5,575	5,452	3,973
Custer	Miles City	11,454	11,697	3,783
Daniels	Scobey	1,844	2,266	1,426
Dawson	Glendive	8,635	9,505	2,373
Deer Lodge	Anaconda	9,088	10,356	737
Fallon	Baker	2,774	3,103	1,620
Fergus	Lewistown	11,539	12,083	4,339
Flathead	Kalispell	81,217	59,218	5,098
Gallatin	Bozeman	75,637	50,484	2,606
Garfield	Jordan	1,218	1,589	4,668
Glacier	Cut Bank	13,508	12,121	2,995
Golden Valley	Ryegate	1,117	912	1,175
Granite	Philipsburg	2,853	2,548	1,727
Hill	Havre	16,376	17,654	2,896
Jefferson	Boulder	10,857	7,939	1,657
Judith Basin	Stanford	2,191	2,282	1,870
Lake	Polson	27,919	21,041	1,494
Lewis & Clark	Helena	57,972	47,495	3,461
Liberty	Chester	2,020	2,295	1,430
Lincoln	Libby	19,101	17,481	3,613
McCone	Circle	1,775	2,276	2,643
Madison	Virginia City	7,079	5,989	3,587
Meagher	White Sulphur Springs	1,977	1,819	2,392
Mineral	Superior	3,879	3,315	1,220
Missoula	Missoula	99,018	78,687	2,598
Musselshell	Roundup	4,515	4,106	1,867
Park	Livingston	15,791	14,515	2,802
Petroleum	Winnett	492	519	1,654
Phillips	Malta	4,201	5,163	5,140
Pondera	Conrad	6,148	6,433	1,625
Powder River	Broadus	1,785	2,090	3,297
Powell	Deer Lodge	6,873	6,620	2,326
Prairie	Terry	1,147	1,383	1,737
Ravalli	Hamilton	39,376	25,010	2,394
Richland	Sidney	9,112	10,716	2,084
Roosevelt	Wolf Point	10,660	10,999	2,356
Rosebud	Forsyth	9,270	10,505	5,012
Sanders	Thompson Falls	10,945	8,669	2,762
Sheridan	Plentywood	3,620	4,732	1,677
Silver Bow	Butte	33,093	33,941	718
Stillwater	Columbus	8,391	6,536	1,795
Sweet Grass	Big Timber	3,699	3,154	1,855
Teton	Choteau	6,283	6,271	2,273
Toole	Shelby	5,094	5,046	1,911
Treasure	Hysham	745	874	979
Valley	Glasgow	7,270	8,239	4,921
Wheatland	Harlowton	2,068	2,246	1,423
Wibaux	Wibaux	971	1,191	889
Yellowstone	Billings	134,717	113,419	2,635

Nebraska

(93 counties, 76,872 sq. mi. land; pop. 1,747,214)

County	County seat or courthouse	2004 Pop.	1990 Pop.	Land area sq. mi.
Adams	Hastings	30,913	29,625	563
Antelope	Neligh	7,111	7,965	857
Arthur	Arthur	402	462	715
Banner	Harrisburg	762	852	746
Blaine	Brewster	518	675	711
Boone	Albion	5,831	6,667	687
Box Butte	Alliance	11,388	13,130	1,075
Boyd	Butte	2,267	2,835	540
Brown	Ainsworth	3,430	3,657	1,221
Buffalo	Kearney	43,406	37,447	968
Burt	Tekamah	7,490	7,868	493
Butler	David City	8,813	8,601	584
Cass	Plattsmouth	25,671	21,318	559
Cedar	Hartington	9,059	10,131	740
Chase	Imperial	3,961	4,381	895
Cherry	Valentine	6,071	6,307	5,961
Cheyenne	Sidney	9,902	9,494	1,196
Clay	Clay Center	6,778	7,123	573
Colfax	Schuyler	10,498	9,139	413
Cuming	West Point	9,786	10,117	572
Custer	Broken Bow	11,515	12,270	2,576
Dakota	Dakota City	20,612	16,742	264
Dawes	Chadron	8,746	9,021	1,396
Dawson	Lexington	24,532	19,940	1,013
Deuel	Chappell	2,019	2,237	440
Dixon	Ponca	6,110	6,143	476
Dodge	Fremont	36,066	34,500	534
Douglas	Omaha	482,112	416,444	331
Dundy	Benkelman	2,202	2,582	920
Fillmore	Geneva	6,462	7,103	576
Franklin	Franklin	3,425	3,938	575
Frontier	Stockville	2,875	3,101	975
Furnas	Beaver City	5,128	5,553	718
Gage	Beatrice	23,436	22,794	855
Garden	Oshkosh	2,170	2,460	1,704
Garfield	Burwell	1,838	2,141	570
Gosper	Elwood	2,034	1,928	458
Grant	Hyannis	670	769	776
Greeley	Greeley	2,537	3,006	569
Hall	Grand Island	54,862	48,925	546
Hamilton	Aurora	9,484	8,862	544
Harlan	Alma	3,641	3,810	553
Hayes	Hayes Center	1,115	1,222	713
Hitchcock	Trenton	3,021	3,750	710
Holt	O'Neill	10,858	12,599	2,413
Hooker	Mullen	749	793	721
Howard	Saint Paul	6,722	6,057	569
Jefferson	Fairbury	8,090	8,759	573
Johnson	Tecumseh	4,563	4,673	376
Kearney	Minden	6,880	6,629	516
Keith	Ogallala	8,401	8,584	1,061
Keya Paha	Springview	938	1,029	773
Kimball	Kimball	3,783	4,108	952
Knox	Center	8,995	9,564	1,108
Lancaster	Lincoln	261,545	213,641	839
Lincoln	North Platte	34,979	32,508	2,564
Logan	Stapleton	710	878	571
Loup	Taylor	703	683	570
McPherson	Tryon	504	546	859
Madison	Madison	35,752	32,655	573
Merrick	Central City	8,101	8,062	485
Morrill	Bridgeport	5,252	5,423	1,424
Nance	Fullerton	3,751	4,275	441
Nemaha	Auburn	7,067	7,980	409
Nuckolls	Nelson	4,833	5,786	575
Otoe	Nebraska City	15,488	14,252	616
Pawnee	Pawnee City	2,842	3,317	432
Perkins	Grant	3,081	3,367	883
Phelps	Holdrege	9,632	9,715	540
Pierce	Pierce	7,692	7,827	574
Platte	Columbus	31,245	29,820	678
Polk	Osceola	5,408	5,655	439
Red Willow	McCook	11,131	11,705	717
Richardson	Falls City	8,884	9,937	553
Rock	Bassett	1,579	2,019	1,008
Saline	Wilber	14,275	12,715	575
Sarpy	Papillion	135,973	102,583	241
Saunders	Wahoo	20,344	18,285	754
Scotts Bluff	Gering	36,631	36,025	739

County	County seat or courthouse	2004 Pop.	1990 Pop.	Land area sq. mi.
Seward	Seward	16,656	15,450	575
Sheridan	Rushville	5,817	6,750	2,441
Sherman	Loup City	3,175	3,718	566
Sioux	Harrison	1,447	1,549	2,067
Stanton	Stanton	6,520	6,244	430
Thayer	Hebron	5,498	6,635	575
Thomas	Thedford	642	851	713
Thurston	Pender	7,134	6,936	394
Valley	Ord	4,521	5,169	568
Washington	Blair	19,605	16,607	390
Wayne	Wayne	9,214	9,364	443
Webster	Red Cloud	3,876	4,279	575
Wheeler	Bartlett	811	948	575
York	York	14,228	14,428	576

Nevada

(16 counties, 1 ind. city, 109,826 sq. mi. land; pop. 2,334,771)

County	County seat or courthouse	2004 Pop.	1990 Pop.	Land area sq. mi.
Churchill	Fallon	24,355	17,938	4,929
Clark	Las Vegas	1,650,671	741,368	7,910
Douglas	Minden	45,394	27,637	710
Elko	Elko	44,551	33,463	17,179
Esmeralda	Goldfield	830	1,344	3,589
Eureka	Eureka	1,414	1,547	4,176
Humboldt	Winnemucca	16,893	12,844	9,648
Lander	Battle Mountain	5,112	6,266	5,494
Lincoln	Pioche	4,286	3,775	10,634
Lyon	Yerington	43,230	20,001	1,994
Mineral	Hawthorne	4,912	6,475	3,756
Nye	Tonopah	37,714	17,781	18,147
Pershing	Lovelock	6,405	4,336	6,037
Storey	Virginia City	3,737	2,526	263
Washoe	Reno	380,754	254,667	6,342
White Pine	Ely	8,539	9,264	8,876
Independent City				
Carson City		55,974	40,443	143

New Hampshire

(10 counties, 8,968 sq. mi. land; pop. 1,299,500)

County	County seat or courthouse	2004 Pop.	1990 Pop.	Land area sq. mi.
Belknap	Laconia	60,858	49,216	401
Carroll	Ossipee	46,762	35,410	934
Cheshire	Keene	76,872	70,121	707
Coos	Lancaster	33,511	34,828	1,800
Grafton	Woodsville	84,169	74,929	1,713
Hillsborough	Nashua	398,574	335,838	876
Merrimack	Concord	145,542	120,240	934
Rockingham	Brentwood	292,526	245,845	695
Strafford	Dover	118,217	104,233	369
Sullivan	Newport	42,469	38,592	537

New Jersey

(21 counties, 7,417 sq. mi. land; pop. 8,698,879)

County	County seat or courthouse	2004 Pop.	1990 Pop.	Land area sq. mi.
Atlantic	Mays Landing	268,693	224,327	561
Bergen	Hackensack	902,998	825,380	234
Burlington	Mount Holly	449,685	395,066	805
Camden	Camden	516,282	502,824	222
Cape May	Cape May Court House	100,758	95,089	255
Cumberland	Bridgeton	151,183	138,053	489
Essex	Newark	796,684	777,964	126
Gloucester	Woodbury	271,806	230,082	325
Hudson	Jersey City	606,240	553,099	47
Hunterdon	Flemington	129,746	107,852	430
Mercer	Trenton	365,271	325,759	226
Middlesex	New Brunswick	785,095	671,712	310
Monmouth	Freehold	636,298	553,192	472
Morris	Morristown	488,173	421,330	469
Ocean	Toms River	553,251	433,203	636
Passaic	Paterson	500,427	470,872	185
Salem	Salem	65,346	65,294	338
Somerset	Somerville	316,750	240,222	305
Sussex	Newton	152,218	130,936	521
Union	Elizabeth	531,957	493,819	103
Warren	Belvidere	110,018	91,675	358

New Mexico

(33 counties, 121,356 sq. mi. land; pop. 1,903,289)

County	County seat or courthouse	2004 Pop.	1990 Pop.	Land area sq. mi.
Bernalillo	Albuquerque	593,765	480,577	1,166
Catron	Reserve	3,440	2,563	6,928
Chaves	Roswell	61,635	57,849	6,071
Cibola	Grants	27,549	23,794	4,539
Colfax	Raton	13,831	12,925	3,757
Curry	Clovis	45,662	42,207	1,406
DeBaca	Fort Sumner	2,035	2,252	2,325
Dona Ana	Las Cruces	186,095	135,510	3,807
Eddy	Carlsbad	51,688	48,605	4,182
Grant	Silver City	29,443	27,676	3,966
Guadalupe	Santa Rosa	4,530	4,156	3,030
Harding	Mosquero	774	987	2,125
Hidalgo	Lordsburg	5,186	5,958	3,446
Lea	Lovington	56,231	55,765	4,393
Lincoln	Carrizozo	20,727	12,219	4,831
Los Alamos	Los Alamos	18,796	18,115	109
Luna	Deming	26,129	18,110	2,965
McKinley	Gallup	72,425	60,686	5,449
Mora	Mora	5,212	4,264	1,931
Otero	Alamogordo	63,282	51,928	6,627
Quay	Tucumcari	9,483	10,823	2,875
Rio Arriba	Tierra Amarilla	40,710	34,365	5,858
Roosevelt	Portales	18,165	16,702	2,449
Sandoval	Bernalillo	102,120	63,319	3,709
San Juan	Aztec	124,166	91,605	5,514
San Miguel	Las Vegas	29,514	25,743	4,717
Santa Fe	Santa Fe	138,705	98,928	1,909
Sierra	Truth or Consequences	12,961	9,912	4,180
Socorro	Socorro	18,177	14,764	6,646
Taos	Taos	31,464	23,118	2,203
Torrance	Estancia	16,864	10,285	3,345
Union	Clayton	3,827	4,124	3,830
Valencia	Los Lunas	68,698	45,235	1,068

New York

(62 counties, 47,214 sq. mi. land; pop. 19,227,088)

County	County seat or courthouse	2004 Pop.	1990 Pop.	Land area sq. mi.
Albany	Albany	298,432	292,812	523
Allegany	Belmont	50,575	50,470	1,030
Bronx[1]	Bronx	1,365,536	1,203,789	42
Broome	Binghamton	197,696	212,160	707
Cattaraugus	Little Valley	83,179	84,234	1,310
Cayuga	Auburn	81,916	82,313	693
Chautauqua	Mayville	137,267	141,895	1,062
Chemung	Elmira	89,984	95,195	408
Chenango	Norwich	51,861	51,768	894
Clinton	Plattsburgh	81,875	85,969	1,039
Columbia	Hudson	63,668	62,982	636
Cortland	Cortland	49,006	48,963	500
Delaware	Delhi	47,328	47,352	1,446
Dutchess	Poughkeepsie	293,395	259,462	802
Erie	Buffalo	936,318	968,584	1,044
Essex	Elizabethtown	38,901	37,152	1,797
Franklin	Malone	51,009	46,540	1,631
Fulton	Johnstown	55,463	54,191	496
Genesee	Batavia	59,689	60,060	494
Greene	Catskill	49,195	44,739	648
Hamilton	Lake Pleasant	5,227	5,279	1,720
Herkimer	Herkimer	63,858	65,809	1,411
Jefferson	Watertown	111,467	110,943	1,272
Kings[1]	Brooklyn	2,475,290	2,300,664	71
Lewis	Lowville	26,564	26,796	1,275
Livingston	Geneseo	64,819	62,372	632
Madison	Wampsville	70,407	69,166	656
Monroe	Rochester	735,177	713,968	659
Montgomery	Fonda	49,283	51,981	405
Nassau	Mineola	1,339,641	1,287,873	287
New York[1]	New York	1,562,723	1,487,536	23
Niagara	Lockport	218,060	220,756	523
Oneida	Utica	234,962	250,836	1,213
Onondaga	Syracuse	459,805	468,973	780
Ontario	Canandaigua	103,504	95,101	644
Orange	Goshen	370,352	307,571	816
Orleans	Albion	44,138	41,846	391
Oswego	Oswego	123,776	121,785	953
Otsego	Cooperstown	62,518	60,390	1,003
Putnam	Carmel	100,570	83,941	231
Queens[1]	Jamaica	2,237,216	1,951,598	109
Rensselaer	Troy	154,077	154,429	654
Richmond[1]	Saint George	463,314	378,977	58
Rockland	New City	293,626	265,475	174
Saint Lawrence	Canton	111,306	111,974	2,686
Saratoga	Ballston Spa	212,706	181,276	812
Schenectady	Schenectady	148,042	149,285	206
Schoharie	Schoharie	32,012	31,840	622
Schuyler	Watkins Glen	19,505	18,662	329
Seneca	Waterloo	35,075	33,683	325
Steuben	Bath	98,814	99,088	1,393
Suffolk	Riverhead	1,475,488	1,321,339	912
Sullivan	Monticello	76,110	69,277	970
Tioga	Owego	51,535	52,337	519
Tompkins	Ithaca	100,135	94,097	476
Ulster	Kingston	181,779	165,380	1,126
Warren	Lake George	65,147	59,209	869
Washington	Hudson Falls	62,807	59,330	835
Wayne	Lyons	93,861	89,123	604
Westchester	White Plains	942,444	874,866	433
Wyoming	Warsaw	42,986	42,507	593
Yates	Penn Yan	24,669	22,810	338

(1) New York City comprises 5 counties: Bronx, Kings (Brooklyn), New York (Manhattan), Queens, and Richmond (Staten Island).

IT'S A FACT: For the period 1990 to 2000, Burke County, ND, was the fastest-shrinking county in the U.S., losing 25.3% of its population. Subject to extremes of weather and the long-term economic stagnation that has produced population declines through much of the Northern Great Plains, the county, which shares a border with Saskatchewan, saw its population fall to 2,074 people in 2004. Population had peaked at 9,998 in 1930.

North Carolina

(100 counties, 48,711 sq. mi. land; pop. 8,541,221)

County	County seat or courthouse	2004 Pop.	1990 Pop.	Land area sq. mi.
Alamance	Graham	138,462	108,213	430
Alexander	Taylorsville	34,842	27,544	260
Alleghany	Sparta	10,835	9,590	235
Anson	Wadesboro	25,109	23,474	532
Ashe	Jefferson	25,224	22,209	426
Avery	Newland	17,786	14,867	247
Beaufort	Washington	45,794	42,283	828
Bertie	Windsor	19,539	20,388	699
Bladen	Elizabethtown	33,007	28,663	875
Brunswick	Bolivia	84,575	50,985	855
Buncombe	Asheville	215,680	174,357	656
Burke	Morganton	89,466	75,740	507
Cabarrus	Concord	146,135	98,935	364
Caldwell	Lenoir	78,960	70,709	472
Camden	Camden	8,437	5,904	241
Carteret	Beaufort	62,034	52,407	520
Caswell	Yanceyville	23,673	20,662	425
Catawba	Newton	149,466	118,412	400
Chatham	Pittsboro	57,023	38,979	683
Cherokee	Murphy	25,289	20,170	455
Chowan	Edenton	14,504	13,506	173
Clay	Hayesville	9,467	7,155	215
Cleveland	Shelby	98,258	84,958	465
Columbus	Whiteville	54,703	49,587	935
Craven	New Bern	91,599	81,812	708
Cumberland	Fayetteville	308,489	274,713	653
Currituck	Currituck	22,067	13,736	262
Dare	Manteo	33,518	22,746	384
Davidson	Lexington	153,775	126,688	552
Davie	Mocksville	38,006	27,859	265
Duplin	Kenansville	51,778	39,995	818
Durham	Durham	239,733	181,844	290
Edgecombe	Tarboro	54,713	56,692	505
Forsyth	Winston-Salem	320,919	265,855	410
Franklin	Louisburg	53,520	36,414	492
Gaston	Gastonia	194,459	174,769	356
Gates	Gatesville	10,936	9,305	341
Graham	Robbinsville	8,075	7,196	292
Granville	Oxford	52,878	38,341	531
Greene	Snow Hill	20,219	15,384	265
Guilford	Greensboro	438,795	347,431	649
Halifax	Halifax	56,034	55,516	725
Harnett	Lillington	101,542	67,833	595
Haywood	Waynesville	56,256	46,948	554
Henderson	Hendersonville	95,361	69,747	374
Hertford	Winton	23,551	22,317	353
Hoke	Raeford	39,262	22,856	391
Hyde	Swan Quarter	5,521	5,411	613
Iredell	Statesville	136,924	93,205	576
Jackson	Sylva	34,975	26,835	491
Johnston	Smithfield	141,640	81,306	792
Jones	Trenton	10,404	9,361	472
Lee	Sanford	49,162	41,370	257
Lenoir	Kinston	58,424	57,274	400
Lincoln	Lincolnton	67,952	50,319	299
McDowell	Marion	43,285	35,681	442
Macon	Franklin	31,412	23,504	516
Madison	Marshall	19,951	16,953	449
Martin	Williamston	24,796	25,078	461
Mecklenburg	Charlotte	771,617	511,211	526
Mitchell	Bakersville	15,850	14,433	221
Montgomery	Troy	27,501	23,359	492
Moore	Carthage	80,026	59,000	698
Nash	Nashville	90,710	76,677	540
New Hanover	Wilmington	173,554	120,284	199
Northampton	Jackson	21,624	21,004	536
Onslow	Jacksonville	154,297	149,838	767
Orange	Hillsborough	117,515	93,662	400
Pamlico	Bayboro	12,814	11,368	337
Pasquotank	Elizabeth City	36,806	31,298	227
Pender	Burgaw	45,117	28,855	871
Perquimans	Hertford	11,762	10,447	247
Person	Roxboro	36,941	30,180	392
Pitt	Greenville	140,587	108,480	652
Polk	Columbus	19,021	14,458	238
Randolph	Asheboro	136,230	106,546	787
Richmond	Rockingham	46,648	44,511	474
Robeson	Lumberton	126,469	105,170	949
Rockingham	Wentworth	92,517	86,064	566
Rowan	Salisbury	134,317	110,605	511
Rutherford	Rutherfordton	63,570	56,956	564
Sampson	Clinton	62,379	47,297	945
Scotland	Laurinburg	36,230	33,763	319
Stanly	Albemarle	58,927	51,765	395
Stokes	Danbury	45,390	37,224	452
Surry	Dobson	72,293	61,704	537
Swain	Bryson City	13,146	11,268	528
Transylvania	Brevard	29,525	25,520	378
Tyrrell	Columbia	4,130	3,856	390
Union	Monroe	153,652	84,210	637
Vance	Henderson	43,774	38,892	254
Wake	Raleigh	719,520	426,311	832
Warren	Warrenton	19,890	17,265	429
Washington	Plymouth	13,335	13,997	348
Watauga	Boone	42,457	36,952	313
Wayne	Goldsboro	114,245	104,666	553
Wilkes	Wilkesboro	67,095	59,393	757
Wilson	Wilson	76,091	66,061	371
Yadkin	Yadkinville	37,292	30,488	336
Yancey	Burnsville	18,158	15,419	312

North Dakota

(53 counties, 68,976 sq. mi. land; pop. 634,366)

County	County seat or courthouse	2004 Pop.	1990 Pop.	Land area sq. mi.
Adams	Hettinger	2,429	3,174	988
Barnes	Valley City	11,133	12,545	1,492
Benson	Minnewaukan	6,968	7,198	1,381
Billings	Medora	825	1,108	1,151
Bottineau	Bottineau	6,846	8,011	1,669
Bowman	Bowman	3,101	3,596	1,162
Burke	Bowbells	2,074	3,002	1,104
Burleigh	Bismarck	72,585	60,131	1,633
Cass	Fargo	128,615	102,874	1,765
Cavalier	Langdon	4,376	6,064	1,488
Dickey	Ellendale	5,456	6,107	1,131
Divide	Crosby	2,208	2,899	1,260
Dunn	Manning	3,437	4,005	2,010
Eddy	New Rockford	2,601	2,951	630
Emmons	Linton	3,913	4,830	1,510
Foster	Carrington	3,492	3,983	635
Golden Valley	Beach	1,770	2,108	1,002
Grand Forks	Grand Forks	64,923	70,683	1,438
Grant	Carson	2,623	3,549	1,659
Griggs	Cooperstown	2,515	3,303	709
Hettinger	Mott	2,541	3,445	1,132
Kidder	Steele	2,563	3,332	1,351
La Moure	La Moure	4,504	5,383	1,147
Logan	Napoleon	2,099	2,847	993
McHenry	Towner	5,630	6,528	1,874
McIntosh	Ashley	3,129	4,021	975
McKenzie	Watford City	5,499	6,383	2,742
McLean	Washburn	8,815	10,457	2,110
Mercer	Stanton	8,434	9,808	1,045
Morton	Mandan	25,339	23,700	1,926
Mountrail	Stanley	6,530	7,021	1,824
Nelson	Lakota	3,445	4,410	982
Oliver	Center	1,875	2,381	724
Pembina	Cavalier	8,190	9,238	1,119
Pierce	Rugby	4,357	5,052	1,018
Ramsey	Devils Lake	11,450	12,681	1,185
Ransom	Lisbon	5,828	5,921	863
Renville	Mohall	2,477	3,160	875
Richland	Wahpeton	17,626	18,148	1,437
Rolette	Rolla	13,823	12,772	902
Sargent	Forman	4,110	4,549	859
Sheridan	McClusky	1,476	2,148	972
Sioux	Fort Yates	4,141	3,761	1,094
Slope	Amidon	742	907	1,218
Stark	Dickinson	22,116	22,832	1,338
Steele	Finley	2,062	2,420	712
Stutsman	Jamestown	20,928	22,241	2,221
Towner	Cando	2,575	3,627	1,025
Traill	Hillsboro	8,366	8,752	862
Walsh	Grafton	11,646	13,840	1,282
Ward	Minot	56,224	57,921	2,013
Wells	Fessenden	4,658	5,864	1,271
Williams	Williston	19,278	21,129	2,070

Ohio

(88 counties, 40,048 sq. mi. land; pop. 11,459,011)

County	County seat or courthouse	2004 Pop.	1990 Pop.	Land area sq. mi.
Adams	West Union	28,398	25,371	584
Allen	Lima	106,873	109,755	404
Ashland	Ashland	54,058	47,507	424
Ashtabula	Jefferson	103,152	99,880	702
Athens	Athens	63,187	59,549	507
Auglaize	Wapakoneta	46,938	44,585	401
Belmont	Saint Clairsville	69,366	71,074	537
Brown	Georgetown	44,239	34,966	492

County	County seat or courthouse	2004 Pop.	1990 Pop.	Land area sq. mi.
Butler	Hamilton	346,560	291,479	467
Carroll	Carrollton	29,576	26,521	395
Champaign	Urbana	39,645	36,019	429
Clark	Springfield	142,613	147,538	400
Clermont	Batavia	188,614	150,094	452
Clinton	Wilmington	42,280	35,444	411
Columbiana	Lisbon	111,519	108,276	532
Coshocton	Coshocton	37,039	35,427	564
Crawford	Bucyrus	45,961	47,870	402
Cuyahoga	Cleveland	1,351,009	1,412,140	458
Darke	Greenville	53,260	53,617	600
Defiance	Defiance	39,038	39,350	411
Delaware	Delaware	142,503	66,929	442
Erie	Sandusky	78,992	76,781	255
Fairfield	Lancaster	136,063	103,468	505
Fayette	Washington Court House	28,134	27,466	407
Franklin	Columbus	1,088,971	961,437	540
Fulton	Wauseon	42,919	38,498	407
Gallia	Gallipolis	31,256	30,954	469
Geauga	Chardon	94,602	81,087	404
Greene	Xenia	152,233	136,731	415
Guernsey	Cambridge	41,304	39,024	522
Hamilton	Cincinnati	814,611	866,228	407
Hancock	Findlay	73,602	65,536	531
Hardin	Kenton	32,171	31,111	470
Harrison	Cadiz	15,938	16,085	404
Henry	Napoleon	29,382	29,108	417
Highland	Hillsboro	42,610	35,728	553
Hocking	Logan	28,838	25,533	423
Holmes	Millersburg	41,273	32,849	423
Huron	Norwalk	60,404	56,238	493
Jackson	Jackson	33,411	30,230	420
Jefferson	Steubenville	71,420	80,298	410
Knox	Mount Vernon	57,785	47,473	527
Lake	Painesville	232,061	215,500	228
Lawrence	Ironton	62,705	61,834	455
Licking	Newark	152,866	128,300	687
Logan	Bellefontaine	46,616	42,310	458
Lorain	Elyria	294,324	271,126	493
Lucas	Toledo	450,632	462,361	340
Madison	London	41,113	37,078	465
Mahoning	Youngstown	249,755	264,806	415
Marion	Marion	66,310	64,274	404
Medina	Medina	165,077	122,354	422
Meigs	Pomeroy	23,286	22,987	429
Mercer	Celina	41,075	39,443	463
Miami	Troy	100,797	93,184	407
Monroe	Woodsfield	15,063	15,497	456
Montgomery	Dayton	550,063	573,809	462
Morgan	McConnelsville	14,941	14,194	418
Morrow	Mount Gilead	34,247	27,749	406
Muskingum	Zanesville	85,669	82,068	665
Noble	Caldwell	14,021	11,336	399
Ottawa	Port Clinton	41,407	40,029	255
Paulding	Paulding	19,486	20,488	416
Perry	New Lexington	35,040	31,557	410
Pickaway	Circleville	53,656	48,248	502
Pike	Waverly	28,294	24,249	441
Portage	Ravenna	154,764	142,585	492
Preble	Eaton	42,553	40,113	425
Putnam	Ottawa	34,718	33,819	484
Richland	Mansfield	128,096	126,137	497
Ross	Chillicothe	74,466	69,330	688
Sandusky	Fremont	61,948	61,963	409
Scioto	Portsmouth	77,046	80,327	612
Seneca	Tiffin	57,789	59,733	551
Shelby	Sidney	48,517	44,915	409
Stark	Canton	381,229	367,585	576
Summit	Akron	547,314	514,990	413
Trumbull	Warren	220,486	227,795	616
Tuscarawas	New Philadelphia	92,221	84,090	568
Union	Marysville	44,487	31,969	437
Van Wert	Van Wert	29,276	30,464	410
Vinton	McArthur	13,352	11,098	414
Warren	Lebanon	189,276	113,973	400
Washington	Marietta	62,577	62,254	635
Wayne	Wooster	113,577	101,461	555
Williams	Bryan	38,912	36,956	422
Wood	Bowling Green	123,278	113,269	617
Wyandot	Upper Sandusky	22,878	22,254	406

Oklahoma

(77 counties, 68,667 sq. mi. land; pop. 3,523,553)

County	County seat or courthouse	2004 Pop.	1990 Pop.	Land area sq. mi.
Adair	Stilwell	21,657	18,421	576
Alfalfa	Cherokee	5,810	6,416	867
Atoka	Atoka	14,255	12,778	978
Beaver	Beaver	5,474	6,023	1,814
Beckham	Sayre	19,347	18,812	902
Blaine	Watonga	11,290	11,470	928
Bryan	Durant	37,758	32,089	909
Caddo	Anadarko	30,167	29,550	1,278
Canadian	El Reno	95,505	74,409	900
Carter	Ardmore	47,087	42,919	824
Cherokee	Tahlequah	44,106	34,049	751
Choctaw	Hugo	15,451	15,302	774
Cimarron	Boise City	2,897	3,301	1,835
Cleveland	Norman	222,074	174,253	536
Coal	Coalgate	5,928	5,780	518
Comanche	Lawton	110,514	111,486	1,069
Cotton	Walters	6,514	6,651	637
Craig	Vinita	14,873	14,104	761
Creek	Sapulpa	68,666	60,915	956
Custer	Arapaho	25,230	26,897	987
Delaware	Jay	39,088	28,070	741
Dewey	Taloga	4,667	5,551	1,000
Ellis	Arnett	3,932	4,497	1,229
Garfield	Enid	57,282	56,735	1,058
Garvin	Pauls Valley	27,229	26,605	807
Grady	Chickasha	48,176	41,747	1,101
Grant	Medford	4,824	5,689	1,001
Greer	Mangum	5,849	6,559	639
Harmon	Hollis	2,997	3,793	538
Harper	Buffalo	3,397	4,063	1,039
Haskell	Stigler	12,088	10,940	577
Hughes	Holdenville	14,016	13,014	807
Jackson	Altus	27,182	28,764	803
Jefferson	Waurika	6,460	7,010	759
Johnston	Tishomingo	10,440	10,032	645
Kay	Newkirk	46,761	48,056	919
Kingfisher	Kingfisher	14,176	13,212	903
Kiowa	Hobart	9,879	11,347	1,015
Latimer	Wilburton	10,647	10,333	722
Le Flore	Poteau	49,161	43,270	1,586
Lincoln	Chandler	32,386	29,216	958
Logan	Guthrie	36,301	29,011	744
Love	Marietta	9,133	7,788	515
McClain	Purcell	29,070	22,795	570
McCurtain	Idabel	34,046	33,433	1,852
McIntosh	Eufaula	19,939	16,779	620
Major	Fairview	7,363	8,055	957
Marshall	Madill	13,860	10,829	371
Mayes	Pryor	39,274	33,366	656
Murray	Sulphur	12,682	12,042	418
Muskogee	Muskogee	70,626	68,078	814
Noble	Perry	11,233	11,045	732
Nowata	Nowata	10,717	9,992	565
Okfuskee	Okemah	11,637	11,551	625
Oklahoma	Oklahoma City	680,815	599,611	709
Okmulgee	Okmulgee	39,890	36,490	697
Osage	Pawhuska	45,181	41,645	2,251
Ottawa	Miami	32,737	30,561	471
Pawnee	Pawnee	16,834	15,575	569
Payne	Stillwater	69,675	61,507	686
Pittsburg	McAlester	43,950	40,950	1,306
Pontotoc	Ada	35,007	34,119	720
Pottawatomie	Shawnee	67,111	58,760	788
Pushmataha	Antlers	11,715	10,997	1,397
Roger Mills	Cheyenne	3,259	4,147	1,142
Rogers	Claremore	79,042	55,170	675
Seminole	Wewoka	24,679	25,412	633
Sequoyah	Sallisaw	40,578	33,828	674
Stephens	Duncan	42,826	42,299	874
Texas	Guymon	20,296	16,419	2,037
Tillman	Frederick	8,785	10,384	872
Tulsa	Tulsa	569,148	503,341	570
Wagoner	Wagoner	63,054	47,883	563
Washington	Bartlesville	49,027	48,066	417
Washita	Cordell	11,512	11,441	1,003
Woods	Alva	8,570	9,103	1,287
Woodward	Woodward	18,741	18,976	1,242

Oregon

(36 counties, 95,997 sq. mi. land; pop. 3,594,586)

County	County seat or courthouse	2004 Pop.	1990 Pop.	Land area sq. mi.
Baker	Baker City	16,470	15,317	3,068
Benton	Corvallis	79,357	70,811	676
Clackamas	Oregon City	363,276	278,850	1,868
Clatsop	Astoria	36,340	33,301	827
Columbia	Saint Helens	46,971	37,557	657
Coos	Coquille	63,739	60,273	1,600
Crook	Prineville	21,424	14,111	2,979
Curry	Gold Beach	22,100	19,327	1,627
Deschutes	Bend	134,479	74,976	3,018
Douglas	Roseburg	103,152	94,649	5,037
Gilliam	Condon	1,817	1,717	1,204
Grant	Canyon City	7,380	7,853	4,529
Harney	Burns	7,132	7,060	10,134
Hood River	Hood River	21,155	16,903	522
Jackson	Medford	192,992	146,387	2,785
Jefferson	Madras	19,868	13,676	1,781
Josephine	Grants Pass	79,920	62,649	1,640

County	County seat or courthouse	2004 Pop.	1990 Pop.	Land area sq. mi.
Klamath	Klamath Falls	65,098	57,702	5,944
Lake	Lakeview	7,382	7,186	8,136
Lane	Eugene	331,594	282,912	4,554
Lincoln	Newport	45,277	38,889	980
Linn	Albany	107,410	91,227	2,292
Malheur	Vale	31,425	26,038	9,887
Marion	Salem	301,841	228,483	1,184
Morrow	Heppner	11,681	7,625	2,032
Multnomah	Portland	672,161	583,887	435
Polk	Dallas	67,565	49,541	741
Sherman	Moro	1,712	1,918	823
Tillamook	Tillamook	24,922	21,570	1,102
Umatilla	Pendleton	73,436	59,249	3,215
Union	La Grande	24,406	23,598	2,037
Wallowa	Enterprise	6,976	6,911	3,145
Wasco	The Dalles	23,669	21,683	2,381
Washington	Hillsboro	488,253	311,554	724
Wheeler	Fossil	1,483	1,396	1,715
Yamhill	McMinnville	90,723	65,551	716

Pennsylvania

(67 counties, 44,817 sq. mi. land; pop. 12,406,292)

County	County seat or courthouse	2004 Pop.	1990 Pop.	Land area sq. mi.
Adams	Gettysburg	98,322	78,274	520
Allegheny	Pittsburgh	1,250,867	1,336,449	730
Armstrong	Kittanning	71,395	73,478	654
Beaver	Beaver	178,601	186,093	434
Bedford	Bedford	50,230	47,919	1,015
Berks	Reading	391,640	336,523	859
Blair	Hollidaysburg	127,468	130,542	526
Bradford	Towanda	62,569	60,967	1,151
Bucks	Doylestown	617,558	541,174	607
Butler	Butler	180,663	152,013	789
Cambria	Ebensburg	148,496	163,062	688
Cameron	Emporium	5,652	5,913	397
Carbon	Jim Thorpe	61,194	56,803	381
Centre	Bellefonte	140,476	124,812	1,108
Chester	West Chester	465,795	376,389	756
Clarion	Clarion	41,123	41,699	602
Clearfield	Clearfield	82,913	78,097	1,147
Clinton	Lock Haven	37,486	37,182	891
Columbia	Bloomsburg	65,015	63,202	486
Crawford	Meadville	89,890	86,166	1,013
Cumberland	Carlisle	221,397	195,257	550
Dauphin	Harrisburg	253,282	237,813	525
Delaware	Media	555,040	547,658	184
Elk	Ridgway	34,064	34,878	829
Erie	Erie	282,355	275,575	802
Fayette	Uniontown	145,651	145,351	790
Forest	Tionesta	4,994	4,802	428
Franklin	Chambersburg	134,864	121,082	772
Fulton	McConnellsburg	14,641	13,837	438
Greene	Waynesburg	40,133	39,550	576
Huntingdon	Huntingdon	45,995	44,164	874
Indiana	Indiana	89,062	89,994	829
Jefferson	Brookville	45,952	46,083	655
Juniata	Mifflintown	23,391	20,625	392
Lackawanna	Scranton	209,932	219,097	459
Lancaster	Lancaster	487,332	422,822	949
Lawrence	New Castle	93,374	96,246	360
Lebanon	Lebanon	124,489	113,744	362
Lehigh	Allentown	326,050	291,130	347
Luzerne	Wilkes-Barre	313,431	328,149	891
Lycoming	Williamsport	118,542	118,710	1,235
McKean	Smethport	44,708	47,131	982
Mercer	Mercer	119,797	121,003	672
Mifflin	Lewistown	46,210	46,197	412
Monroe	Stroudsburg	158,925	95,681	609
Montgomery	Norristown	774,029	678,193	483
Montour	Danville	18,069	17,735	131
Northampton	Easton	282,554	247,110	374
Northumberland	Sunbury	92,879	96,771	460
Perry	New Bloomfield	44,652	41,172	554
Philadelphia	Philadelphia	1,470,151	1,585,577	135
Pike	Milford	54,117	28,032	547
Potter	Coudersport	17,950	16,717	1,081
Schuylkill	Pottsville	147,670	152,585	778
Snyder	Middleburg	38,112	36,680	331
Somerset	Somerset	79,515	78,218	1,075
Sullivan	Laporte	6,413	6,104	450
Susquehanna	Montrose	42,047	40,380	823
Tioga	Wellsboro	41,849	41,126	1,134
Union	Lewisburg	42,720	36,176	317
Venango	Franklin	56,285	59,381	675
Warren	Warren	42,576	45,050	883
Washington	Washington	205,738	204,584	857
Wayne	Honesdale	49,561	39,944	729
Westmoreland	Greensburg	368,660	370,321	1,025
Wyoming	Tunkhannock	28,168	28,076	397
York	York	401,613	339,574	904

Rhode Island

(5 counties, 1,045 sq. mi. land; pop. 1,080,632)

County	County seat or courthouse	2004 Pop.	1990 Pop.	Land area sq. mi.
Bristol	Bristol	52,989	48,859	25
Kent	East Greenwich	172,120	161,143	170
Newport	Newport	85,003	87,194	104
Providence	Providence	641,883	596,270	413
Washington	West Kingston	128,637	109,998	333

South Carolina

(46 counties, 30,110 sq. mi. land; pop. 4,198,068)

County	County seat or courthouse	2004 Pop.	1990 Pop.	Land area sq. mi.
Abbeville	Abbeville	26,308	23,862	508
Aiken	Aiken	148,960	120,991	1,073
Allendale	Allendale	11,061	11,727	408
Anderson	Anderson	173,550	145,177	718
Bamberg	Bamberg	15,952	16,902	393
Barnwell	Barnwell	23,404	20,293	548
Beaufort	Beaufort	135,725	86,425	587
Berkeley	Moncks Corner	149,668	128,658	1,098
Calhoun	Saint Matthews	15,287	12,753	380
Charleston	Charleston	326,762	295,159	919
Cherokee	Gaffney	53,782	44,506	393
Chester	Chester	33,563	32,170	581
Chesterfield	Chesterfield	43,289	38,575	799
Clarendon	Manning	33,157	28,450	607
Colleton	Walterboro	39,595	34,377	1,056
Darlington	Darlington	67,577	61,851	561
Dillon	Dillon	31,289	29,114	405
Dorchester	Saint George	107,004	83,060	575
Edgefield	Edgefield	24,794	18,360	502
Fairfield	Winnsboro	24,142	22,295	687
Florence	Florence	129,679	114,344	800
Georgetown	Georgetown	59,790	46,302	815
Greenville	Greenville	401,174	320,127	790
Greenwood	Greenwood	67,519	59,567	456
Hampton	Hampton	21,301	18,186	560
Horry	Conway	217,608	144,053	1,134
Jasper	Ridgeland	21,193	15,487	656
Kershaw	Camden	55,491	43,599	726
Lancaster	Lancaster	63,135	54,516	549
Laurens	Laurens	70,218	58,132	715
Lee	Bishopville	20,500	18,437	410
Lexington	Lexington	231,057	167,526	699
McCormick	McCormick	10,133	8,868	360
Marion	Marion	35,086	33,899	489
Marlboro	Bennettsville	28,147	29,716	480
Newberry	Newberry	37,209	33,172	631
Oconee	Walhalla	69,057	57,494	625
Orangeburg	Orangeburg	90,779	84,804	1,106
Pickens	Pickens	112,475	93,896	497
Richland	Columbia	334,609	286,321	756
Saluda	Saluda	18,870	16,441	452
Spartanburg	Spartanburg	264,230	226,793	811
Sumter	Sumter	105,943	101,276	665
Union	Union	28,862	30,337	514
Williamsburg	Kingstree	35,372	36,815	934
York	York	183,762	131,497	682

South Dakota

(66 counties, 75,885 sq. mi. land; pop. 770,883)

County	County seat or courthouse	2004 Pop.	1990 Pop.	Land area sq. mi.
Aurora	Plankinton	2,935	3,135	708
Beadle	Huron	16,051	18,253	1,259
Bennett	Martin	3,522	3,206	1,185
Bon Homme	Tyndall	7,071	7,089	563
Brookings	Brookings	28,159	25,207	794
Brown	Aberdeen	34,812	35,580	1,713
Brule	Chamberlain	5,185	5,485	819
Buffalo	Gannvalley	2,080	1,759	471
Butte	Belle Fourche	9,273	7,914	2,249
Campbell	Mound City	1,604	1,965	736
Charles Mix	Lake Andes	9,099	9,131	1,098
Clark	Clark	3,953	4,403	958
Clay	Vermillion	13,059	13,186	412
Codington	Watertown	25,914	22,698	688
Corson	McIntosh	4,372	4,195	2,473
Custer	Custer	7,665	6,179	1,558
Davison	Mitchell	19,009	17,503	435
Day	Webster	5,865	6,978	1,029
Deuel	Clear Lake	4,264	4,522	624
Dewey	Timber Lake	6,115	5,523	2,303
Douglas	Armour	3,301	3,746	434
Edmunds	Ipswich	4,097	4,356	1,146
Fall River	Hot Springs	7,352	7,353	1,740
Faulk	Faulkton	2,438	2,744	1,000
Grant	Milbank	7,598	8,372	683
Gregory	Burke	4,332	5,359	1,016

County	County seat or courthouse	2004 Pop.	1990 Pop.	Land area sq. mi.
Haakon	Philip	1,998	2,624	1,813
Hamlin	Hayti	5,575	4,974	507
Hand	Miller	3,405	4,272	1,437
Hanson	Alexandria	3,786	2,994	435
Harding	Buffalo	1,244	1,669	2,671
Hughes	Pierre	16,774	14,817	741
Hutchinson	Olivet	7,672	8,262	813
Hyde	Highmore	1,614	1,696	861
Jackson	Kadoka	2,900	2,811	1,869
Jerauld	Wessington Springs	2,096	2,425	530
Jones	Murdo	1,090	1,324	971
Kingsbury	De Smet	5,476	5,925	838
Lake	Madison	10,913	10,550	563
Lawrence	Deadwood	22,300	20,655	800
Lincoln	Canton	31,437	15,427	578
Lyman	Kennebec	3,977	3,638	1,640
McCook	Salem	5,886	5,688	575
McPherson	Leola	2,739	3,228	1,137
Marshall	Britton	4,354	4,844	838
Meade	Sturgis	24,856	21,878	3,471
Mellette	White River	2,089	2,137	1,306
Miner	Howard	2,623	3,272	570
Minnehaha	Sioux Falls	157,366	123,809	810
Moody	Flandreau	6,590	6,507	520
Pennington	Rapid City	92,631	81,343	2,776
Perkins	Bison	3,137	3,932	2,872
Potter	Gettysburg	2,487	3,190	866
Roberts	Sisseton	10,056	9,914	1,101
Sanborn	Woonsocket	2,626	2,833	569
Shannon	(Attached to Fall River)	13,346	9,902	2,094
Spink	Redfield	6,981	7,981	1,504
Stanley	Fort Pierre	2,802	2,453	1,443
Sully	Onida	1,434	1,589	1,007
Todd	(Attached to Tripp)	9,738	8,352	1,388
Tripp	Winner	6,075	6,924	1,614
Turner	Parker	8,635	8,576	617
Union	Elk Point	13,357	10,189	460
Walworth	Selby	5,514	6,087	708
Yankton	Yankton	21,521	19,252	522
Ziebach	Dupree	2,658	2,220	1,962

Tennessee

(95 counties, 41,217 sq. mi. land; pop. 5,900,962)

County	County seat or courthouse	2004 Pop.	1990 Pop.	Land area sq. mi.
Anderson	Clinton	72,244	68,250	338
Bedford	Shelbyville	41,233	30,411	474
Benton	Camden	16,517	14,524	395
Bledsoe	Pikeville	12,785	9,669	406
Blount	Maryville	113,744	85,962	559
Bradley	Cleveland	91,196	73,712	329
Campbell	Jacksboro	40,507	35,079	480
Cannon	Woodbury	13,339	10,467	266
Carroll	Huntingdon	29,364	27,514	599
Carter	Elizabethton	58,622	51,505	341
Cheatham	Ashland City	38,032	27,140	303
Chester	Henderson	15,773	12,819	289
Claiborne	Tazewell	30,726	26,137	434
Clay	Celina	8,006	7,238	236
Cocke	Newport	34,675	29,141	434
Coffee	Manchester	50,172	40,343	429
Crockett	Alamo	14,553	13,378	265
Cumberland	Crossville	50,084	34,736	682
Davidson	Nashville	572,475	510,786	502
Decatur	Decaturville	11,650	10,472	334
De Kalb	Smithville	18,213	14,360	305
Dickson	Charlotte	45,339	35,061	490
Dyer	Dyersburg	37,621	34,854	511
Fayette	Somerville	33,624	25,559	705
Fentress	Jamestown	17,023	14,669	499
Franklin	Winchester	40,702	34,923	555
Gibson	Trenton	48,124	46,315	603
Giles	Pulaski	29,255	25,741	611
Grainger	Rutledge	21,928	17,095	280
Greene	Greeneville	64,718	55,832	622
Grundy	Altamont	14,465	13,362	361
Hamblen	Morristown	59,489	50,480	161
Hamilton	Chattanooga	310,371	285,536	542
Hancock	Sneedville	6,643	6,739	222
Hardeman	Bolivar	28,164	23,377	668
Hardin	Savannah	25,931	22,633	578
Hawkins	Rogersville	55,851	44,565	487
Haywood	Brownsville	19,614	19,437	533
Henderson	Lexington	26,269	21,844	520
Henry	Paris	31,506	27,888	562
Hickman	Centerville	23,612	16,754	613
Houston	Erin	7,992	7,018	200
Humphreys	Waverly	18,141	15,813	532
Jackson	Gainesboro	11,146	9,297	309
Jefferson	Dandridge	47,593	33,016	274
Johnson	Mountain City	18,049	13,766	298
Knox	Knoxville	400,061	335,749	508
Lake	Tiptonville	7,656	7,129	163
Lauderdale	Ripley	26,828	23,491	470
Lawrence	Lawrenceburg	40,864	35,303	617
Lewis	Hohenwald	11,418	9,247	282
Lincoln	Fayetteville	32,141	28,157	570
Loudon	Loudon	42,237	31,255	229
McMinn	Athens	50,981	42,383	430
McNairy	Selmer	25,152	22,422	560
Macon	Lafayette	21,401	15,906	307
Madison	Jackson	94,397	77,982	557
Marion	Jasper	27,661	24,683	498
Marshall	Lewisburg	27,991	21,539	375
Maury	Columbia	74,692	54,812	613
Meigs	Decatur	11,524	8,033	195
Monroe	Madisonville	42,070	30,541	635
Montgomery	Clarksville	142,204	100,498	539
Moore	Lynchburg	5,978	4,696	129
Morgan	Wartburg	20,132	17,300	522
Obion	Union City	32,393	31,717	545
Overton	Livingston	20,419	17,636	433
Perry	Linden	7,673	6,612	415
Pickett	Byrdstown	4,881	4,548	163
Polk	Benton	16,041	13,643	435
Putnam	Cookeville	65,963	51,373	401
Rhea	Dayton	29,792	24,344	316
Roane	Kingston	52,920	47,227	361
Robertson	Springfield	59,322	41,492	476
Rutherford	Murfreesboro	210,025	118,570	619
Scott	Huntsville	21,838	18,358	532
Sequatchie	Dunlap	12,361	8,863	266
Sevier	Sevierville	77,270	51,050	592
Shelby	Memphis	908,175	826,330	755
Smith	Carthage	18,413	14,143	314
Stewart	Dover	12,795	9,479	458
Sullivan	Blountville	152,498	143,596	413
Sumner	Gallatin	141,611	103,281	529
Tipton	Covington	54,722	37,568	459
Trousdale	Hartsville	7,484	5,920	114
Unicoi	Erwin	17,703	16,549	186
Union	Maynardville	18,884	13,694	224
Van Buren	Spencer	5,471	4,846	273
Warren	McMinnville	39,559	32,992	433
Washington	Jonesborough	110,996	92,336	326
Wayne	Waynesboro	16,869	13,935	734
Weakley	Dresden	33,733	31,972	580
White	Sparta	23,857	20,090	377
Williamson	Franklin	146,935	81,021	583
Wilson	Lebanon	97,891	67,675	571

Texas

(254 counties, 261,797 sq. mi. land; pop. 22,490,022)

County	County seat or courthouse	2004 Pop.	1990 Pop.	Land area sq. mi.
Anderson	Palestine	56,117	48,024	1,071
Andrews	Andrews	12,840	14,338	1,501
Angelina	Lufkin	81,492	69,884	802
Aransas	Rockport	24,041	17,892	252
Archer	Archer City	9,274	7,973	910
Armstrong	Claude	2,163	2,021	914
Atascosa	Jourdanton	42,696	30,533	1,232
Austin	Bellville	25,800	19,832	653
Bailey	Muleshoe	6,662	7,064	827
Bandera	Bandera	19,754	10,562	792
Bastrop	Bastrop	68,608	38,263	888
Baylor	Seymour	3,933	4,385	871
Bee	Beeville	33,046	25,135	880
Bell	Belton	250,324	191,073	1,060
Bexar	San Antonio	1,493,965	1,185,394	1,247
Blanco	Johnson City	9,101	5,972	711
Borden	Gail	683	799	899
Bosque	Meridian	18,002	15,125	989
Bowie	Boston	90,248	81,665	888
Brazoria	Angleton	271,130	191,707	1,386
Brazos	Bryan	156,275	121,862	586
Brewster	Alpine	9,226	8,653	6,193
Briscoe	Silverton	1,716	1,971	900
Brooks	Falfurrias	7,753	8,204	943
Brown	Brownwood	38,183	34,371	944
Burleson	Caldwell	17,057	13,625	666
Burnet	Burnet	40,286	22,677	996
Caldwell	Lockhart	36,498	26,392	546
Calhoun	Port Lavaca	20,569	19,053	512
Callahan	Baird	13,314	11,859	899
Cameron	Brownsville	371,825	260,120	906
Camp	Pittsburg	12,011	9,904	198
Carson	Panhandle	6,478	6,576	923
Cass	Linden	30,012	29,982	937
Castro	Dimmitt	7,687	9,070	898
Chambers	Anahuac	28,227	20,088	599
Cherokee	Rusk	48,091	41,049	1,052
Childress	Childress	7,613	5,953	710

County	County seat or courthouse	2004 Pop.	1990 Pop.	Land area sq. mi.
Clay	Henrietta	11,231	10,024	1,098
Cochran	Morton	3,340	4,377	775
Coke	Robert Lee	3,715	3,424	899
Coleman	Coleman	8,738	9,710	1,260
Collin	McKinney	627,938	264,036	848
Collingsworth	Wellington	3,046	3,573	919
Colorado	Columbus	20,767	18,383	963
Comal	New Braunfels	91,806	51,832	561
Comanche	Comanche	13,616	13,381	938
Concho	Paint Rock	3,744	3,044	991
Cooke	Gainesville	38,626	30,777	874
Coryell	Gatesville	75,074	64,226	1,052
Cottle	Paducah	1,748	2,247	901
Crane	Crane	3,849	4,652	786
Crockett	Ozona	3,950	4,078	2,807
Crosby	Crosbyton	6,645	7,304	900
Culberson	Van Horn	2,727	3,407	3,812
Dallam	Dalhart	6,175	5,461	1,505
Dallas	Dallas	2,294,706	1,852,691	880
Dawson	Lamesa	14,383	14,349	902
Deaf Smith	Hereford	18,510	19,153	1,497
Delta	Cooper	5,506	4,857	277
Denton	Denton	530,597	273,644	889
DeWitt	Cuero	20,354	18,840	909
Dickens	Dickens	2,711	2,571	904
Dimmit	Carrizo Springs	10,221	10,433	1,331
Donley	Clarendon	3,939	3,696	930
Duval	San Diego	12,669	12,918	1,793
Eastland	Eastland	18,379	18,488	926
Ector	Odessa	124,488	118,934	901
Edwards	Rocksprings	2,013	2,266	2,120
Ellis	Waxahachie	713,126	85,167	940
El Paso	El Paso	128,710	591,610	1,013
Erath	Stephenville	33,704	27,991	1,086
Falls	Marlin	17,765	17,712	769
Fannin	Bonham	32,620	24,804	891
Fayette	La Grange	22,513	20,095	950
Fisher	Roby	4,096	4,842	901
Floyd	Floydada	7,330	8,497	992
Foard	Crowell	1,551	1,794	707
Fort Bend	Richmond	442,620	225,421	875
Franklin	Mount Vernon	10,066	7,802	286
Freestone	Fairfield	18,597	15,818	877
Frio	Pearsall	16,386	13,472	1,133
Gaines	Seminole	14,563	14,123	1,502
Galveston	Galveston	271,743	217,396	398
Garza	Post	5,094	5,143	896
Gillespie	Fredericksburg	22,502	17,204	1,061
Glasscock	Garden City	1,334	1,447	901
Goliad	Goliad	7,104	5,980	854
Gonzales	Gonzales	19,281	17,205	1,068
Gray	Pampa	21,409	23,967	928
Grayson	Sherman	115,933	95,019	934
Gregg	Longview	115,035	104,948	274
Grimes	Anderson	25,241	18,843	794
Guadalupe	Seguin	99,620	64,873	711
Hale	Plainview	36,029	34,671	1,005
Hall	Memphis	3,735	3,905	903
Hamilton	Hamilton	8,115	7,733	836
Hansford	Spearman	5,207	5,848	920
Hardeman	Quanah	4,374	5,283	695
Hardin	Kountze	50,347	41,320	894
Harris	Houston	3,644,285	2,818,101	1,729
Harrison	Marshall	62,727	57,483	899
Hartley	Channing	5,423	3,634	1,462
Haskell	Haskell	5,592	6,820	903
Hays	San Marcos	119,359	65,614	678
Hemphill	Canadian	3,336	3,720	910
Henderson	Athens	79,184	58,543	874
Hidalgo	Edinburg	658,248	383,545	1,570
Hill	Hillsboro	35,157	27,146	962
Hockley	Levelland	22,781	24,199	908
Hood	Granbury	46,492	28,981	422
Hopkins	Sulphur Springs	33,201	28,833	782
Houston	Crockett	23,303	21,375	1,231
Howard	Big Spring	32,879	32,343	903
Hudspeth	Sierra Blanca	3,300	2,915	4,571
Hunt	Greenville	81,781	64,343	841
Hutchinson	Stinnett	22,617	25,689	887
Irion	Mertzon	1,738	1,629	1,051
Jack	Jacksboro	8,981	6,981	917
Jackson	Edna	14,400	13,039	829
Jasper	Jasper	35,609	31,102	937
Jeff Davis	Fort Davis	2,253	1,946	2,264
Jefferson	Beaumont	248,223	239,389	904
Jim Hogg	Hebbronville	5,062	5,109	1,136
Jim Wells	Alice	40,807	37,679	865
Johnson	Cleburne	143,418	97,165	729
Jones	Anson	20,093	16,490	931
Karnes	Karnes City	15,458	12,455	750
Kaufman	Kaufman	85,377	52,220	786
Kendall	Boerne	27,214	14,589	662
Kenedy	Sarita	407	460	1,457
Kent	Jayton	744	1,010	902
Kerr	Kerrville	45,675	36,304	1,106
Kimble	Junction	4,563	4,122	1,251
King	Guthrie	323	354	912
Kinney	Brackettville	3,337	3,119	1,363
Kleberg	Kingsville	31,357	30,274	871
Knox	Benjamin	3,893	4,837	849
Lamar	Paris	49,710	43,949	917
Lamb	Littlefield	14,520	15,072	1,016
Lampasas	Lampasas	20,718	13,521	712
La Salle	Cotulla	5,945	5,254	1,489
Lavaca	Hallettsville	18,945	18,690	970
Lee	Giddings	16,536	12,854	629
Leon	Centerville	16,106	12,665	1,072
Liberty	Liberty	74,821	52,726	1,160
Limestone	Groesbeck	22,763	20,946	909
Lipscomb	Lipscomb	3,074	3,143	932
Live Oak	George West	11,694	9,556	1,036
Llano	Llano	18,143	11,631	935
Loving	Mentone	52	107	673
Lubbock	Lubbock	251,018	222,636	899
Lynn	Tahoka	6,156	6,758	892
McCulloch	Brady	8,108	8,778	1,069
McLennan	Waco	222,439	189,123	1,042
McMullen	Tilden	853	817	1,113
Madison	Madisonville	13,203	10,931	470
Marion	Jefferson	11,115	9,984	381
Martin	Stanton	4,448	4,956	915
Mason	Mason	3,844	3,423	932
Matagorda	Bay City	38,092	36,928	1,114
Maverick	Eagle Pass	50,436	36,378	1,280
Medina	Hondo	42,269	27,312	1,328
Menard	Menard	2,285	2,252	902
Midland	Midland	120,344	106,611	900
Milam	Cameron	25,204	22,946	1,017
Mills	Goldthwaite	5,130	4,531	748
Mitchell	Colorado City	9,402	8,016	910
Montague	Montague	19,503	17,274	931
Montgomery	Conroe	362,382	182,201	1,044
Moore	Dumas	20,333	17,865	900
Morris	Daingerfield	13,079	13,200	255
Motley	Matador	1,307	1,532	989
Nacogdoches	Nacogdoches	60,249	54,753	947
Navarro	Corsicana	48,243	39,926	1,008
Newton	Newton	14,345	13,569	933
Nolan	Sweetwater	15,129	16,594	912
Nueces	Corpus Christi	317,513	291,145	836
Ochiltree	Perryton	9,143	9,128	918
Oldham	Vega	2,140	2,278	1,501
Orange	Orange	84,873	80,509	356
Palo Pinto	Palo Pinto	27,325	25,055	953
Panola	Carthage	22,865	22,035	801
Parker	Weatherford	100,336	64,785	904
Parmer	Farwell	9,933	9,863	882
Pecos	Fort Stockton	15,949	14,675	4,764
Polk	Livingston	46,397	30,687	1,057
Potter	Amarillo	118,410	97,841	909
Presidio	Marfa	7,639	6,637	3,856
Rains	Emory	11,066	6,715	232
Randall	Canyon	109,062	89,673	914
Reagan	Big Lake	3,064	4,514	1,175
Real	Leakey	2,995	2,412	700
Red River	Clarksville	13,650	14,317	1,050
Reeves	Pecos	11,842	15,852	2,636
Refugio	Refugio	7,640	7,976	770
Roberts	Miami	863	1,025	924
Robertson	Franklin	16,136	15,511	855
Rockwall	Rockwall	58,260	25,604	129
Runnels	Ballinger	10,943	11,294	1,051
Rusk	Henderson	47,973	43,735	924
Sabine	Hemphill	10,407	9,586	490
San Augustine	San Augustine	8,923	7,999	528
San Jacinto	Coldspring	24,678	16,372	571
San Patricio	Sinton	68,187	58,749	692
San Saba	San Saba	6,086	5,401	1,134
Schleicher	Eldorado	2,779	2,990	1,311
Scurry	Snyder	16,084	18,634	903
Shackelford	Albany	3,232	3,316	914
Shelby	Center	26,156	22,034	794
Sherman	Stratford	3,095	2,858	923
Smith	Tyler	186,414	151,309	928
Somervell	Glen Rose	7,453	5,360	187
Starr	Rio Grande City	59,832	40,518	1,223
Stephens	Breckenridge	9,523	9,010	895
Sterling	Sterling City	1,305	1,438	923
Stonewall	Aspermont	1,405	2,013	919
Sutton	Sonora	4,097	4,135	1,454
Swisher	Tulia	7,854	8,133	900
Tarrant	Fort Worth	1,588,088	1,170,103	863
Taylor	Abilene	125,108	119,655	916
Terrell	Sanderson	957	1,410	2,358
Terry	Brownfield	12,576	13,218	890
Throckmorton	Throckmorton	1,632	1,880	912
Titus	Mount Pleasant	29,224	24,009	411
Tom Green	San Angelo	103,772	98,458	1,522
Travis	Austin	869,868	576,407	989
Trinity	Groveton	14,345	11,445	693
Tyler	Woodville	20,806	16,646	923
Upshur	Gilmer	37,397	31,370	588
Upton	Rankin	3,147	4,447	1,242
Uvalde	Uvalde	26,616	23,340	1,557
Val Verde	Del Rio	47,410	38,721	3,170
Van Zandt	Canton	51,996	37,944	849

County	County seat or courthouse	2004 Pop.	1990 Pop.	Land area sq. mi.
Victoria	Victoria	85,777	74,361	883
Walker	Huntsville	62,217	50,917	787
Waller	Hempstead	34,757	23,374	514
Ward	Monahans	10,358	13,115	835
Washington	Brenham	31,248	26,154	609
Webb	Laredo	219,464	133,239	3,357
Wharton	Wharton	41,594	39,955	1,090
Wheeler	Wheeler	4,787	5,879	914
Wichita	Wichita Falls	127,321	122,378	628
Wilbarger	Vernon	14,184	15,121	971
Willacy	Raymondville	20,231	17,705	597
Williamson	Georgetown	317,938	139,551	1,123
Wilson	Floresville	36,726	22,650	807
Winkler	Kermit	6,714	8,626	841
Wise	Decatur	55,539	34,679	905
Wood	Quitman	40,357	29,380	650
Yoakum	Plains	7,348	8,786	800
Young	Graham	17,938	18,126	922
Zapata	Zapata	13,154	9,279	997
Zavala	Crystal City	11,700	12,162	1,298

Utah

(29 counties, 82,144 sq. mi. land; pop. 2,389,039)

County	County seat or courthouse	2004 Pop.	1990 Pop.	Land area sq. mi.
Beaver	Beaver	6,077	4,765	2,590
Box Elder	Brigham City	44,810	36,485	5,723
Cache	Logan	97,467	70,183	1,165
Carbon	Price	19,689	20,228	1,478
Daggett	Manila	926	690	698
Davis	Farmington	261,208	187,941	304
Duchesne	Duchesne	15,004	12,645	3,238
Emery	Castle Dale	10,723	10,332	4,452
Garfield	Panguitch	4,427	3,980	5,174
Grand	Moab	8,712	6,620	3,682
Iron	Parowan	36,285	20,789	3,298
Juab	Nephi	9,009	5,817	3,392
Kane	Kanab	6,178	5,169	3,992
Millard	Fillmore	12,305	11,333	6,589
Morgan	Morgan	7,614	5,528	609
Piute	Junction	1,393	1,277	758
Rich	Randolph	2,054	1,725	1,029
Salt Lake	Salt Lake City	935,295	725,956	737
San Juan	Monticello	14,015	12,621	7,820
Sanpete	Manti	23,649	16,259	1,588
Sevier	Richfield	19,455	15,431	1,910
Summit	Coalville	33,843	15,518	1,871
Tooele	Tooele	49,688	26,601	6,930
Uintah	Vernal	26,671	22,211	4,477
Utah	Provo	403,352	263,590	1,998
Wasatch	Heber City	18,139	10,089	1,177
Washington	Saint George	109,924	48,560	2,427
Wayne	Loa	2,494	2,177	2,460
Weber	Ogden	208,633	158,330	576

Vermont

(14 counties, 9,250 sq. mi. land; pop. 621,394)

County	County seat or courthouse	2004 Pop.	1990 Pop.	Land area sq. mi.
Addison	Middlebury	36,865	32,953	770
Bennington	Bennington	36,956	35,845	676
Caledonia	Saint Johnsbury	30,464	27,846	651
Chittenden	Burlington	149,286	131,761	539
Essex	Guildhall	6,654	6,405	665
Franklin	Saint Albans	47,556	39,980	637
Grand Isle	North Hero	7,643	5,318	83
Lamoille	Hyde Park	24,418	19,735	461
Orange	Chelsea	29,189	26,149	689
Orleans	Newport	27,372	24,053	698
Rutland	Rutland	63,616	62,142	933
Washington	Montpelier	59,068	54,928	689
Windham	Newfane	44,284	41,588	789
Windsor	Woodstock	58,023	54,055	971

Virginia

(95 counties, 39 ind. cities, 39,594 sq. mi. land; pop. 7,459,827)

County	County seat or courthouse	2004 Pop.	1990 Pop.	Land area sq. mi.
Accomack	Accomac	39,358	31,703	455
Albemarle	Charlottesville	88,726	68,177	723
Alleghany[1]	Covington	16,737	12,815	445
Amelia	Amelia Court House	11,929	8,787	357
Amherst	Amherst	31,981	28,578	475
Appomattox	Appomattox	13,913	12,300	334
Arlington	Arlington	186,117	170,895	26
Augusta	Staunton	68,774	54,557	970
Bath	Warm Springs	4,984	4,799	532
Bedford	Bedford	63,788	45,553	755
Bland	Bland	7,034	6,514	359
Botetourt	Fincastle	31,777	24,992	543
Brunswick	Lawrenceville	18,194	15,987	566
Buchanan	Grundy	25,200	31,333	504
Buckingham	Buckingham	15,919	12,873	581
Campbell	Rustburg	51,695	47,499	504
Caroline	Bowling Green	24,019	19,217	533
Carroll	Hillsville	29,495	26,519	476
Charles City	Charles City	7,120	6,282	183
Charlotte	Charlotte Court House	12,412	11,688	475
Chesterfield	Chesterfield	282,925	209,599	426
Clarke	Berryville	13,852	12,101	177
Craig	New Castle	5,139	4,372	331
Culpeper	Culpeper	40,192	27,791	381
Cumberland	Cumberland	9,178	7,825	298
Dickenson	Clintwood	16,177	17,620	332
Dinwiddie	Dinwiddie	25,173	22,279	504
Essex	Tappahannock	10,339	8,689	258
Fairfax	Fairfax	1,003,157	818,310	395
Fauquier	Warrenton	63,255	48,700	650
Floyd	Floyd	14,464	11,965	381
Fluvanna	Palmyra	23,644	12,429	287
Franklin	Rocky Mount	49,841	39,549	692
Frederick	Winchester	66,611	45,723	415
Giles	Pearisburg	16,989	16,366	357
Gloucester	Gloucester	37,262	30,131	217
Goochland	Goochland	18,753	14,163	284
Grayson	Independence	16,490	16,278	443
Greene	Stanardsville	17,024	10,297	157
Greensville	Emporia	11,496	8,553	295
Halifax	Halifax	36,362	36,030	819
Hanover	Hanover	96,054	63,306	473
Henrico	Richmond	276,479	217,878	238
Henry	Collinsville	56,940	56,942	382
Highland	Monterey	2,482	2,635	416
Isle of Wight	Isle of Wight	32,774	25,053	316
James City	Williamsburg	55,502	34,779	143
King and Queen	King and Queen Court House	6,775	6,289	316
King George	King George	19,355	13,527	180
King William	King William	14,334	10,913	275
Lancaster	Lancaster	12,030	10,896	133
Lee	Jonesville	23,846	24,496	437
Loudoun	Leesburg	239,156	86,185	520
Louisa	Louisa	28,802	20,325	497
Lunenburg	Lunenburg	13,085	11,419	432
Madison	Madison	13,134	11,949	321
Mathews	Mathews	9,226	8,348	86
Mecklenburg	Boydton	32,493	29,241	624
Middlesex	Saluda	10,489	8,653	130
Montgomery	Christiansburg	83,959	73,913	388
Nelson	Lovingston	14,902	12,778	472
New Kent	New Kent	15,552	10,466	210
Northampton	Eastville	13,303	13,061	207
Northumberland	Heathsville	12,893	10,524	192
Nottoway	Nottoway	15,625	14,993	315
Orange	Orange	28,970	21,421	342
Page	Luray	23,730	21,690	311
Patrick	Stuart	19,239	17,473	483
Pittsylvania	Chatham	61,752	55,672	971
Powhatan	Powhatan	25,866	15,328	261
Prince Edward	Farmville	20,326	17,320	353
Prince George	Prince George	34,313	27,390	266
Prince William	Manassas	336,586	214,954	338
Pulaski	Pulaski	35,152	34,496	321
Rappahannock	Washington	7,171	6,622	267
Richmond	Warsaw	8,990	7,273	191
Roanoke	Salem	87,679	79,278	251
Rockbridge	Lexington	21,084	18,350	600
Rockingham	Harrisonburg	70,218	57,482	851
Russell	Lebanon	28,893	28,667	475
Scott	Gate City	22,982	23,204	537
Shenandoah	Woodstock	38,032	31,636	512
Smyth	Marion	32,538	32,370	452
Southampton	Courtland	17,585	17,022	600
Spotsylvania	Spotsylvania	111,850	57,397	401
Stafford	Stafford	111,021	62,255	270
Surry	Surry	6,970	6,145	279
Sussex	Sussex	11,914	10,248	491
Tazewell	Tazewell	44,753	45,960	520
Warren	Front Royal	34,377	26,142	214
Washington	Abingdon	52,030	45,887	563
Westmoreland	Montross	17,039	15,480	229
Wise	Wise	41,744	39,573	404
Wythe	Wytheville	28,013	25,471	463
York	Yorktown	60,885	42,434	106

Independent Cities

	2004 Pop.	1990 Pop.	Land area sq. mi.
Alexandria	128,206	111,183	15
Bedford	6,229	6,176	7
Bristol	17,308	18,426	13
Buena Vista	6,230	6,406	7
Charlottesville	36,605	40,470	10
Chesapeake	214,725	151,982	341
Colonial Heights	17,511	16,064	7
Covington	6,256	7,352	6
Danville	46,371	53,056	43
Emporia	5,674	5,556	7
Fairfax	22,062	19,945	6
Falls Church	10,781	9,464	2
Franklin	8,471	8,392	8

Independent Cities	2004 Pop.	1990 Pop.	Land area sq. mi.
Fredericksburg	20,458	19,033	11
Galax	6,657	6,745	8
Hampton	145,951	133,773	52
Harrisonburg	41,066	30,707	18
Hopewell	22,369	23,101	10
Lexington	6,910	6,959	2
Lynchburg	64,932	66,120	49
Manassas	37,615	27,757	10
Manassas Park	11,519	6,798	2
Martinsville	15,039	16,162	11
Newport News	181,913	171,477	68
Norfolk	237,835	261,250	54
Norton	3,753	4,247	8
Petersburg	32,757	37,071	23
Poquoson	11,700	11,005	16
Portsmouth	99,291	103,910	33
Radford	14,770	15,940	10
Richmond	192,494	202,713	60
Roanoke	92,352	96,487	43
Salem	24,347	23,835	15
Staunton	23,840	24,581	20
Suffolk	76,586	52,143	400
Virginia Beach	440,098	393,089	248
Waynesboro	20,755	18,549	15
Williamsburg	11,465	11,600	9
Winchester	24,779	21,947	9

(1) The independent city of Clifton Forge became part of Alleghany County in 2001.

Washington

(39 counties, 66,544 sq. mi. land; pop. 6,203,788)

County	County seat or courthouse	2004 Pop.	1990 Pop.	Land area sq. mi.
Adams	Ritzville	16,596	13,603	1,925
Asotin	Asotin	20,831	17,605	635
Benton	Prosser	155,991	112,560	1,703
Chelan	Wenatchee	68,987	52,250	2,921
Clallam	Port Angeles	67,867	56,210	1,739
Clark	Vancouver	392,403	238,053	628
Columbia	Dayton	4,187	4,024	869
Cowlitz	Kelso	96,189	82,119	1,139
Douglas	Waterville	34,427	26,205	1,821
Ferry	Republic	7,565	6,295	2,204
Franklin	Pasco	59,472	37,473	1,242
Garfield	Pomeroy	2,311	2,248	711
Grant	Ephrata	79,981	54,798	2,681
Grays Harbor	Montesano	70,338	64,175	1,917
Island	Coupeville	79,293	60,195	208
Jefferson	Port Townsend	28,110	20,406	1,814
King	Seattle	1,777,143	1,507,305	2,126
Kitsap	Port Orchard	239,138	189,731	396
Kittitas	Ellensburg	35,721	26,725	2,297
Klickitat	Goldendale	19,855	16,616	1,872
Lewis	Chehalis	71,539	59,358	2,408
Lincoln	Davenport	10,412	8,864	2,311
Mason	Shelton	53,637	38,341	961
Okanogan	Okanogan	39,444	33,350	5,268
Pacific	South Bend	21,246	18,882	933
Pend Oreille	Newport	12,474	8,915	1,400
Pierce	Tacoma	745,411	586,203	1,679
San Juan	Friday Harbor	15,190	10,035	175
Skagit	Mount Vernon	111,064	79,545	1,735
Skamania	Stevenson	10,549	8,289	1,656
Snohomish	Everett	644,274	465,628	2,089
Spokane	Spokane	435,644	361,333	1,764
Stevens	Colville	41,310	30,948	2,478
Thurston	Olympia	224,673	161,238	727
Wahkiakum	Cathlamet	3,755	3,327	264
Walla Walla	Walla Walla	57,354	48,439	1,271
Whatcom	Bellingham	180,167	127,780	2,120
Whitman	Colfax	40,146	38,775	2,159
Yakima	Yakima	229,094	188,823	4,296

West Virginia

(55 counties, 24,078 sq. mi. land; pop. 1,815,354)

County	County seat or courthouse	2004 Pop.	1990 Pop.	Land area sq. mi.
Barbour	Philippi	15,476	15,699	341
Berkeley	Martinsburg	89,362	59,253	321
Boone	Madison	25,721	25,870	503
Braxton	Sutton	14,950	12,998	513
Brooke	Wellsburg	24,785	26,992	89
Cabell	Huntington	94,801	96,827	282
Calhoun	Grantsville	7,415	7,885	281
Clay	Clay	10,424	9,983	342
Doddridge	West Union	7,418	6,994	320
Fayette	Fayetteville	47,049	47,952	664
Gilmer	Glenville	6,982	7,669	340
Grant	Petersburg	11,537	10,428	477
Greenbrier	Lewisburg	34,886	34,693	1,021
Hampshire	Romney	21,542	16,498	642
Hancock	New Cumberland	31,507	35,233	83
Hardy	Moorefield	13,209	10,977	583
Harrison	Clarksburg	68,303	69,371	416
Jackson	Ripley	28,477	25,938	466
Jefferson	Charles Town	47,663	35,926	210
Kanawha	Charleston	195,218	207,619	903
Lewis	Weston	17,132	17,223	382
Lincoln	Hamlin	22,564	21,382	437
Logan	Logan	36,502	43,032	454
McDowell	Welch	24,726	35,233	535
Marion	Fairmont	56,453	57,249	310
Marshall	Moundsville	34,722	37,356	307
Mason	Point Pleasant	25,941	25,178	432
Mercer	Princeton	62,070	64,980	420
Mineral	Keyser	27,145	26,697	328
Mingo	Williamson	27,389	33,739	423
Monongalia	Morgantown	83,918	75,509	361
Monroe	Union	13,568	12,406	473
Morgan	Berkeley Springs	15,810	12,128	229
Nicholas	Summersville	26,276	26,775	649
Ohio	Wheeling	45,410	50,871	106
Pendleton	Franklin	7,897	8,054	698
Pleasants	St. Marys	7,441	7,546	131
Pocahontas	Marlinton	8,995	9,008	940
Preston	Kingwood	29,856	29,037	648
Putnam	Winfield	53,836	42,835	346
Raleigh	Beckley	79,175	76,819	607
Randolph	Elkins	28,495	27,803	1,040
Ritchie	Harrisville	10,486	10,233	454
Roane	Spencer	15,359	15,120	484
Summers	Hinton	13,809	14,204	361
Taylor	Grafton	16,202	15,144	173
Tucker	Parsons	7,046	7,728	419
Tyler	Middlebourne	9,365	9,796	258
Upshur	Buckhannon	23,996	22,867	355
Wayne	Wayne	42,515	41,636	506
Webster	Webster Springs	9,849	10,729	556
Wetzel	New Martinsville	17,048	19,258	359
Wirt	Elizabeth	5,835	5,192	233
Wood	Parkersburg	87,100	86,915	367
Wyoming	Pineville	24,698	28,990	501

Wisconsin

(72 counties, 54,310 sq. mi. land; pop. 5,509,026)

County	County seat or courthouse	2004 Pop.	1990 Pop.	Land area sq. mi.
Adams	Friendship	20,444	15,682	648
Ashland	Ashland	16,719	16,307	1,044
Barron	Barron	45,595	40,750	863
Bayfield	Washburn	15,173	14,008	1,476
Brown	Green Bay	237,166	194,594	529
Buffalo	Alma	13,824	13,584	684
Burnett	Siren	16,565	13,084	822
Calumet	Chilton	43,765	34,291	320
Chippewa	Chippewa Falls	58,924	52,360	1,010
Clark	Neillsville	34,103	31,647	1,216
Columbia	Portage	54,800	45,088	774
Crawford	Prairie du Chien	16,998	15,940	573
Dane	Madison	453,582	367,085	1,202
Dodge	Juneau	88,057	76,559	882
Door	Sturgeon Bay	28,302	25,690	483
Douglas	Superior	44,045	41,758	1,309
Dunn	Menomonie	41,477	35,909	852
Eau Claire	Eau Claire	94,226	85,183	638
Florence	Florence	5,032	4,590	488
Fond du Lac	Fond du Lac	98,663	90,083	723
Forest	Crandon	9,950	8,776	1,014
Grant	Lancaster	49,647	49,266	1,148
Green	Monroe	34,650	30,339	584
Green Lake	Green Lake	19,210	18,651	354
Iowa	Dodgeville	23,384	20,150	763
Iron	Hurley	6,681	6,153	757
Jackson	Black River Falls	19,610	16,588	987
Jefferson	Jefferson	78,497	67,783	557
Juneau	Mauston	25,529	21,650	768
Kenosha	Kenosha	158,435	128,181	273
Kewaunee	Kewaunee	20,676	18,878	343
La Crosse	La Crosse	108,754	97,904	453
Lafayette	Darlington	16,293	16,074	634
Langlade	Antigo	20,957	19,505	873
Lincoln	Merrill	30,236	26,993	883
Manitowoc	Manitowoc	81,864	80,421	592
Marathon	Wausau	127,733	115,400	1,545
Marinette	Marinette	43,364	40,548	1,402
Marquette	Montello	14,973	12,321	455
Menominee	Keshena	4,559	4,075	358
Milwaukee	Milwaukee	928,018	959,212	242
Monroe	Sparta	42,376	36,633	901
Oconto	Oconto	37,631	30,226	998
Oneida	Rhinelander	37,189	31,679	1,125
Outagamie	Appleton	169,337	140,510	640
Ozaukee	Port Washington	86,025	72,894	232
Pepin	Durand	7,404	7,107	232

County	County seat or courthouse	2004 Pop.	1990 Pop.	Land area sq. mi.
Pierce	Ellsworth	38,342	32,765	576
Polk	Balsam Lake	43,886	34,773	917
Portage	Stevens Point	67,358	61,405	806
Price	Phillips	15,447	15,600	1,253
Racine	Racine	194,188	175,034	333
Richland	Richland Center	18,433	17,521	586
Rock	Janesville	156,512	139,510	720
Rusk	Ladysmith	15,274	15,079	913
Saint Croix	Hudson	74,339	50,251	722
Sauk	Baraboo	57,119	46,975	838
Sawyer	Hayward	16,911	14,181	1,256
Shawano	Shawano	41,209	37,157	893
Sheboygan	Sheboygan	113,958	103,877	514
Taylor	Medford	19,757	18,901	975
Trempealeau	Whitehall	27,492	25,263	734
Vernon	Viroqua	28,702	25,617	795
Vilas	Eagle River	22,230	17,707	874
Walworth	Elkhorn	98,334	75,000	555
Washburn	Shell Lake	16,631	13,772	810
Washington	West Bend	124,502	95,328	431
Waukesha	Waukesha	377,193	304,715	556
Waupaca	Waupaca	52,746	46,104	751
Waushara	Wautoma	23,818	19,385	626
Winnebago	Oshkosh	159,008	140,320	439
Wood	Wisconsin Rapids	75,195	73,605	793

Wyoming

(23 counties, 97,100 sq. mi. land; pop. 506,529)

County	County seat or courthouse	2004 Pop.	1990 Pop.	Land area sq. mi.
Albany	Laramie	31,473	30,797	4,273
Big Horn	Basin	11,416	10,525	3,137
Campbell	Gillette	36,721	29,370	4,797
Carbon	Rawlins	15,271	16,659	7,896
Converse	Douglas	12,515	11,128	4,255
Crook	Sundance	6,006	5,294	2,859
Fremont	Lander	36,310	33,662	9,182
Goshen	Torrington	12,286	12,373	2,225
Hot Springs	Thermopolis	4,598	4,809	2,004
Johnson	Buffalo	7,657	6,145	4,166
Laramie	Cheyenne	85,296	73,142	2,686
Lincoln	Kemmerer	15,626	12,625	4,069
Natrona	Casper	69,010	61,226	5,340
Niobrara	Lusk	2,272	2,499	2,626
Park	Cody	26,516	23,178	6,942
Platte	Wheatland	8,666	8,145	2,085
Sheridan	Sheridan	27,163	23,562	2,523
Sublette	Pinedale	6,654	4,843	4,883
Sweetwater	Green River	37,758	38,823	10,425
Teton	Jackson	18,964	11,173	4,008
Unita	Evanston	19,772	18,705	2,082
Washakie	Worland	7,939	8,388	2,240
Weston	Newcastle	6,640	6,518	2,398

Population of Outlying Areas

Source: Bureau of the Census, U.S. Dept. of Commerce; World Almanac research

Population estimates for July 1, 2004, are given for Puerto Rican municipios (a municipio is the governmental unit that is the primary legal subdivision of Puerto Rico; the Census Bureau treats the municipio as the statistical equivalent of a county). All other population counts and all land area figures are from the 2000 census. Because only selected areas are shown, the population and land area figures may not equal the total reported.

ZIP codes with an asterisk (*) are general delivery ZIP codes. Consult the local postmaster or www.usps.com for more specific delivery information. Wake Atoll, Johnston Atoll, and Midway Atoll receive mail through APO and FPO addresses.

Commonwealth of Puerto Rico

ZIP code	Municipio	2004 Pop.	Land area sq. mi.
*00601	Adjuntas	18,970	67
00602	Aguada	43,948	31
*00605	Aguadilla	66,277	37
00703	Aguas Buenas	30,137	31
00705	Aibonito	26,938	31
00610	Añasco	29,292	39
*00613	Arecibo	102,117	126
00714	Arroyo	19,176	15
00617	Barceloneta	22,725	19
00794	Barranquitas	29,914	34
*00958	Bayamón	225,121	44
00623	Cabo Rojo	49,584	70
*00726	Caguas	142,556	59
00627	Camuy	37,261	46
00729	Canóvanas	45,369	33
*00984	Carolina	187,767	45
*00963	Cataño	27,763	5
*00737	Cayey	47,563	52
00735	Ceiba	18,254	29
00638	Ciales	20,326	67
00739	Cidra	45,054	36
00769	Coamo	38,729	78
00782	Comerío	19,854	28
00783	Corozal	38,004	43
00775	Culebra	1,972	12
00646	Dorado	34,995	23
00738	Fajardo	41,860	30
00650	Florida	13,655	15
00653	Guánica	22,456	37
*00785	Guayama	45,097	65
00656	Guayanilla	23,510	42
*00970	Guaynabo	102,169	27
00778	Gurabo	39,371	28
00659	Hatillo	40,879	42
00660	Hormigüeros	17,032	11
*00791	Humacao	60,161	45
00662	Isabela	46,060	55
00664	Jayuya	17,858	45
00795	Juana Díaz	52,143	60
00777	Juncos	38,287	27
00667	Lajas	27,170	60
00669	Lares	36,108	61
00670	Las Marías	11,612	46
00771	Las Piedras	36,603	34
00772	Loíza	33,509	19
00773	Luquillo	20,329	26
00674	Manatí	47,501	45
00606	Maricao	6,519	37
00707	Maunabo	12,854	21
*00681	Mayagüez	97,350	78
00676	Moca	41,841	50
00687	Morovis	31,430	39
00718	Naguabo	24,082	52
00719	Naranjito	30,235	27
00720	Orocovis	24,660	63
00723	Patillas	20,301	47
00624	Peñuelas	28,037	44
*00732	Ponce	185,744	115
00678	Quebradillas	26,713	23
00677	Rincón	15,577	14
00745	Río Grande	54,423	61
00637	Sabana Grande	26,878	36
00751	Salinas	31,943	69
00683	San Germán	37,732	55
*00936	San Juan	433,319	48
00754	San Lorenzo	42,806	53
00685	San Sebastián	45,857	70
00757	Santa Isabel	22,376	34
*00954	Toa Alta	70,950	27
*00950	Toa Baja	95,432	23
*00976	Trujillo Alto	80,431	21
00641	Utuado	35,437	113
00692	Vega Alta	38,911	28
*00694	Vega Baja	63,710	46
00765	Vieques	9,253	51
00766	Villalba	29,277	35
00767	Yabucoa	40,061	55
00698	Yauco	47,680	68
TOTAL		**3,894,855**	**3,425**

Commonwealth of the Northern Mariana Islands

ZIP code	Municipality	2000 Pop.	Land area sq. mi.
96950	Northern Islands	6	60
96951	Rota	3,283	33
96950	Saipan	62,392	45
96952	Tinian	3,540	42
TOTAL		**69,221**	**179**

Other U.S. External Territories

ZIP code	Location	2000 Pop.	Land area sq. mi.
	American Samoa		
96799	American Samoa	57,291	77
	Guam		
*96910	Agaña Hts.	3,940	1
96928	Agat	5,656	10
*96910	Asan	2,090	6
*96913	Barrigada	8,652	8
96924	Chalan Pago-Ordot	5,923	6
96929	Dededo	42,980	31
*96910	Hagatña	1,100	1
96915	Inarajan	3,052	19
96913	Mangilao	13,313	10
96915	Merizo	2,163	6
*96910	Mongmong-Toto-Maite	5,845	2
96915	Piti	1,666	7
96915	Santa Rita	7,500	16
96910	Sinajana	2,853	1
96915	Talofofo	3,215	18
*96913	Tamuning	18,012	6
96915	Umatac	887	6
96929	Yigo	19,474	35
96915	Yona	6,484	20
TOTAL		**154,805**	**210**
	Virgin Islands		
00820	Saint Croix	53,234	83
*00820	Christiansted	2,637	
*00841	Frederiksted	732	
*00830	Saint John	4,197	20
*00804	Saint Thomas	51,181	31
*00802	Charlotte Amalie	11,004	
TOTAL		**108,612**	**134**

UNITED STATES FACTS

Superlative U.S. Statistics[1]

Source: U.S. Geological Survey, Dept. of the Interior; U.S. Bureau of the Census, Dept. of Commerce; World Almanac research

Total Area for 50 states and Washington, DC (Land, 3,537,440 sq mi; Water, 256,648 sq mi) . . . 3,794,085 sq mi[2]

Largest state	Alaska	663,267 sq mi
Smallest state	Rhode Island	1,545 sq mi
Largest county (excluding Alaska)	San Bernardino County, CA	20,105 sq mi
Smallest county	Arlington County, VA[3]	26 sq mi
Largest incorporated city	Sitka, AK	4,812 sq mi
Northernmost city	Barrow, AK	71° 17′ N
Northernmost point	Point Barrow, AK	71° 23′ N
Southernmost city	Hilo, HI	19° 44′ N
Southernmost settlement	Naalehu, HI	19° 03′ N
Southernmost point	Ka Lae (South Cape), Island of Hawaii	18° 55′ N (155°41′ W)
Easternmost city	Eastport, ME	66° 59′05″ W
Easternmost settlement[4]	Amchitka Isl., AK	179° 15′ E
Easternmost point[4]	Pochnoi Point, on Semisopochnoi Isl., AK	179° 46′ E
Westernmost city	Atka, AK	174° 12′ W
Westernmost settlement	Adak Station, AK	176° 39′ W
Westernmost point	Amatignak Isl., AK	179° 06′ W
Highest settlement	Climax, CO	11,360 ft
Lowest settlement	Calipatria, CA	–184 ft
Highest point on Atlantic coast	Cadillac Mountain, Mount Desert Isl., ME	1,530 ft
Oldest national park	Yellowstone National Park (1872), WY, MT, ID	2,219,791 acres
Largest national park	Wrangell-St. Elias, AK	8,323,148 acres
Highest waterfall	Yosemite Falls—Total in 3 sections. (Upper Yosemite Fall, 1,430 ft; Cascades, 675 ft; Lower Yosemite Fall, 320 ft)	2,425 ft
Longest river system	Mississippi-Missouri-Red Rock	3,710 mi
Highest mountain	Mount McKinley (Denali), AK	20,320 ft
Lowest point	Death Valley, CA	–282 ft
Deepest lake	Crater Lake, OR	1,932 ft
Rainiest spot	Mount Waialeale, HI	Annual avg rainfall 460 in
Largest gorge	Grand Canyon, Colorado River, AZ	277 mi long, 600 ft to 18 mi wide, 1 mi deep
Deepest gorge	Hells Canyon, Snake River, OR-ID	7,900 ft
Largest dam	New Cornelia Tailings, Ten Mile Wash, AZ[5]	274,026,000 cu yds material used
Tallest building	Sears Tower, Chicago, IL	1,450 ft
Largest building	Boeing Manufacturing Plant, Everett, WA	472,000,000 cu ft; covers 98 acres
Largest office building	Pentagon, Arlington, VA	77,025,000 cu ft; covers 29 acres
Tallest structure	TV tower, Blanchard, ND	2,063 ft
Longest bridge span	Verrazano-Narrows, NY	4,260 ft
Highest bridge	Royal Gorge, CO	1,053 ft above water
Deepest well	Gas well, Washita County, OK	31,441 ft

The 48 Contiguous States

Total Area for 48 states and Washington, DC (Land, 2,959,066 sq mi; Water, 160,824 sq mi) . . . 3,119,887 sq mi[2]

Largest state	Texas	268,581 sq mi
Northernmost city	Bellingham, WA	48°46′ N
Northernmost settlement	Angle Inlet, MN	49°21′ N
Northernmost point	Northwest Angle, MN	49°23′ N
Southernmost city	Key West, FL	24°33′ N
Southernmost mainland city	Florida City, FL	25°27′ N
Southernmost point	Key West, FL	24°33′ N
Easternmost settlement	Lubec, ME	66°58′49 W
Easternmost point	West Quoddy Head, ME	66°57′W
Westernmost town	La Push, WA	124°38′ W
Westernmost point	Cape Alava, WA	124°44′ W
Highest mountain	Mount Whitney, CA	14,494 ft

(1) All areas are total area, including water, unless otherwise noted. (2) Does not add, because of rounding. (3) Smallest county by land area is New York County (Manhattan) at 23 sq mi; its total area including water is 34 square miles. Superlative shown is for smallest total area. (4) Alaska's Aleutian Islands extend into the eastern hemisphere and thus technically contain the easternmost point and settlement in the U.S. (5) The New Cornelia Tailings Dam is a privately owned industrial dam composed of tailings, remnants of a mining process.

Geodetic Datum of North America

In July 1986, the National Oceanic and Atmospheric Administration's National Geodetic Survey (NGS), in cooperation with Canada and Mexico, completed readjustment and redefinition of the system of latitudes and longitudes. The resulting North American Datum of 1983 (NAD 83) replaces the North American Datum of 1927, as well as local reference systems for Hawaii and for Puerto Rico and the Virgin Islands. The change was prompted by Hawaii's increased need for accurate co-ordinate information. To facilitate use of satellite surveying and navigation systems, such as the Global Positioning System (GPS), the new datum was redefined using the Geodetic Reference System 1980 as the reference ellipsoid because this model more closely approximates the true size and shape of the earth. In addition, the origin of the coordinate system is referenced to the mass center of the earth to coincide with the orbital orientation of the GPS satellites. Positional changes resulting from the datum redefinition can reach 330 ft in the continental U.S., Canada, and Mexico. Changes that exceed 660 ft can be expected in Alaska, Puerto Rico, and the Virgin Islands. Hawaii's coordinates changed about 1,300 ft.

Additional Statistical Information About the U.S.

The annual *Statistical Abstract of the United States,* published by U.S. Dept. of Commerce, contains additional data. For information, write Supt. of Documents, Government Printing Office, PO Box 371954, Pittsburgh, PA 15250-7954, or call (202) 512-1800. For electronic products, write U.S. Dept. of Commerce, U.S. Census Bureau, PO Box 277943, Atlanta, GA 30384-7943, or call (301) 763-INFO (4636). Parts of *The Statistical Abstract* can be viewed on the Internet at www.census.gov/statab/www

IT'S A FACT: The Pentagon, the largest office building in the U.S. and the headquarters of the Dept. of Defense, contains 17.5 miles of hallways and three times the floor space of the Empire State Building. But because of the efficient layout, it only takes about 7 minutes to walk between any two points. Along the way, one might ride one of 19 elevators, climb one of 131 stairways, or drink from any of 691 water fountains.

Highest and Lowest Altitudes in U.S. States and Territories

Source: U.S. Geological Survey, Dept. of the Interior

(Minus sign means below sea level.)

State	HIGHEST POINT Name	County	Elev. (ft)	LOWEST POINT Name	County	Elev. (ft)
Alabama	Cheaha Mountain	Cleburne	2,407	Gulf of Mexico		Sea level
Alaska	Mount McKinley	Denali	20,320	Pacific Ocean		Sea level
Arizona	Humphreys Peak	Coconino	12,633	Colorado R	Yuma	70
Arkansas	Magazine Mountain	Logan	2,753	Ouachita R	Ashley-Union	55
California	Mount Whitney	Inyo-Tulare	14,494	Death Valley	Inyo	–282
Colorado	Mount Elbert	Lake	14,433	Arikaree R	Yuma	3,315
Connecticut	S. slope of Mt. Frissell	Litchfield	2,380	Long Island Sound		Sea level
Delaware	On Ebright Road	New Castle	448	Atlantic Ocean		Sea level
Dist. of Columbia	Tenleytown	N W part	410	Potomac R		1
Florida	Britton Hill	Walton	345	Atlantic Ocean		Sea level
Georgia	Brasstown Bald	Towns-Union	4,784	Atlantic Ocean		Sea level
Guam	Mount Lamlam	Agat District	1,332	Pacific Ocean		Sea level
Hawaii	Mauna Kea	Hawaii	13,796	Pacific Ocean		Sea level
Idaho	Borah Peak	Custer	12,662	Snake R	Nez Perce	710
Illinois	Charles Mound	Jo Daviess	1,235	Mississippi R	Alexander	279
Indiana	Hoosier Hill	Wayne	1,257	Ohio R	Posey	320
Iowa	Hawkeye Point	Osceola	1,670	Mississippi R	Lee	480
Kansas	Mount Sunflower	Wallace	4,039	Verdigris R	Montgomery	679
Kentucky	Black Mountain	Harlan	4,145	Mississippi R	Fulton	257
Louisiana	Driskill Mountain	Bienville	535	New Orleans	Orleans	–8
Maine	Mount Katahdin	Piscataquis	5,268	Atlantic Ocean		Sea level
Maryland	Hoye-Crest	Garrett	3,360	Atlantic Ocean		Sea level
Massachusetts	Mount Greylock	Berkshire	3,491	Atlantic Ocean		Sea level
Michigan	Mount Arvon	Baraga	1,979	Lake Erie	Monroe	571
Minnesota	Eagle Mountain	Cook	2,301	Lake Superior		602
Mississippi	Woodall Mountain	Tishomingo	806	Gulf of Mexico		Sea level
Missouri	Taum Sauk Mt.	Iron	1,772	St. Francis R	Dunklin	230
Montana	Granite Peak	Park	12,799	Kootenai R	Lincoln	1,800
Nebraska	Panorama Point	Kimball	5,424	Missouri R	Richardson	840
Nevada	Boundary Peak	Esmeralda	13,143	Colorado R	Clark	479
New Hampshire	Mt. Washington	Coos	6,288	Atlantic Ocean		Sea level
New Jersey	High Point	Sussex	1,803	Atlantic Ocean		Sea level
New Mexico	Wheeler Peak	Taos	13,161	Red Bluff Res.	Eddy	2,842
New York	Mount Marcy	Essex	5,344	Atlantic Ocean		Sea level
North Carolina	Mount Mitchell	Yancey	6,684	Atlantic Ocean		Sea level
North Dakota	White Butte	Slope	3,506	Red R of the North	Pembina	750
Ohio	Campbell Hill	Logan	1,550	Ohio R	Hamilton	455
Oklahoma	Black Mesa	Cimarron	4,973	Little R	McCurtain	289
Oregon	Mount Hood	Clackamas-Hood R.	11,239	Pacific Ocean		Sea level
Pennsylvania	Mt. Davis	Somerset	3,213	Delaware R	Delaware	Sea level
Puerto Rico	Cerro de Punta	Ponce District	4,390	Atlantic Ocean		Sea level
Rhode Island	Jerimoth Hill	Providence	812	Atlantic Ocean		Sea level
Samoa	Lata Mountain	Tau Island	3,160	Pacific Ocean		Sea level
South Carolina	Sassafras Mountain	Pickens	3,560	Atlantic Ocean		Sea level
South Dakota	Harney Peak	Pennington	7,242	Big Stone Lake	Roberts	966
Tennessee	Clingmans Dome	Sevier	6,643	Mississippi R	Shelby	178
Texas	Guadalupe Peak	Culberson	8,749	Gulf of Mexico		Sea level
Utah	Kings Peak	Duchesne	13,528	Beaver Dam Wash	Washington	2,000
Vermont	Mount Mansfield	Lamoille	4,393	Lake Champlain		95
Virginia	Mount Rogers	Grayson-Smyth	5,729	Atlantic Ocean		Sea level
Virgin Islands	Crown Mountain	St. Thomas Island	1,556	Atlantic Ocean		Sea level
Washington	Mount Rainier	Pierce	14,411	Pacific Ocean		Sea level
West Virginia	Spruce Knob	Pendleton	4,863	Potomac R	Jefferson	240
Wisconsin	Timms Hill	Price	1,951	Lake Michigan		579
Wyoming	Gannett Peak	Fremont	13,804	Belle Fourche R	Crook	3,099

U.S. Coastline by States

Source: National Oceanic and Atmospheric Administration, U.S. Dept. of Commerce

(in statute miles)

	Coastline[1]	Shoreline[2]
ATLANTIC COAST	**2,069**	**28,673**
Connecticut	0	618
Delaware	28	381
Florida	580	3,331
Georgia	100	2,344
Maine	228	3,478
Maryland	31	3,190
Massachusetts	192	1,519
New Hampshire	13	131
New Jersey	130	1,792
New York	127	1,850
North Carolina	301	3,375
Pennsylvania	0	89
Rhode Island	40	384
South Carolina	187	2,876
Virginia	112	3,315

	Coastline[1]	Shoreline[2]
GULF COAST	**1,631**	**17,141**
Alabama	53	607
Florida	770	5,095
Louisiana	397	7,721
Mississippi	44	359
Texas	367	3,359
PACIFIC COAST	**7,623**	**40,298**
Alaska	5,580	31,383
California	840	3,427
Hawaii	750	1,052
Oregon	296	1,410
Washington	157	3,026
ARCTIC COAST	**1,060**	**2,521**
UNITED STATES	**12,383**	**88,633**

(1) Figures are lengths of general outline of seacoast. Measurements were made with a unit measure of 30 minutes of latitude on charts as near the scale of 1:1,200,000 as possible. Coastline of sounds and bays is included to a point where they narrow to width of unit measure, and includes the distance across at such point. (2) Figures obtained in 1939-40 with a recording instrument on the largest-scale charts and maps then available. Shoreline of outer coast, offshore islands, sounds, bays, rivers, and creeks is included to the head of tidewater or to a point where tidal waters narrow to a width of 100 ft.

States: Capitals, Key Dates, Geographic Data

The 13 colonies that declared independence from Great Britain and fought the War of Independence (American Revolution) became the 13 original states. They were (in the order in which they ratified the Constitution): Delaware, Pennsylvania, New Jersey, Georgia, Connecticut, Massachusetts, Maryland, South Carolina, New Hampshire, Virginia, New York, North Carolina, and Rhode Island.

			Entered Union		Extent in miles		Area in sq mi			
State	Settled[1]	Capital	Date	Order	Long (approx. mean)	Wide (approx. mean)	Land	Water	Total	Rank in area[2]
AL	1702	Montgomery	Dec. 14, 1819	22	330	190	50,744	1,675	52,419	30
AK	1784	Juneau	Jan. 3, 1959	49	1,480[3]	810	571,951	91,316	663,267	1
AZ	1776	Phoenix	Feb. 14, 1912	48	400	310	113,635	364	113,998	6
AR	1686	Little Rock	June 15, 1836	25	260	240	52,068	1,110	53,179	29
CA	1769	Sacramento	Sept. 9, 1850	31	770	250	155,959	7,736	163,696	3
CO	1858	Denver	Aug. 1, 1876	38	380	280	103,718	376	104,094	8
CT	1634	Hartford	Jan. 9, 1788	5	110	70	4,845	699	5,543	48
DE	1638	Dover	Dec. 7, 1787	1	100	30	1,954	536	2,489	49
DC	NA	NA	NA	NA	. . .	. . .	61	7	68	51
FL	1565	Tallahassee	Mar. 3, 1845	27	500	160	53,927	11,828	65,755	22
GA	1733	Atlanta	Jan. 2, 1788	4	300	230	57,906	1,519	59,425	24
HI	1820	Honolulu	Aug. 21, 1959	50	. . .	. . .	6,423	4,508	10,931	43
ID	1842	Boise	July 3, 1890	43	570	300	82,747	823	83,570	14
IL	1720	Springfield	Dec. 3, 1818	21	390	210	55,584	2,331	57,914	25
IN	1733	Indianapolis	Dec. 11, 1816	19	270	140	35,867	551	36,418	38
IA	1788	Des Moines	Dec. 28, 1846	29	310	200	55,869	402	56,272	26
KS	1727	Topeka	Jan. 29, 1861	34	400	210	81,815	462	82,277	15
KY	1774	Frankfort	June 1, 1792	15	380	140	39,728	681	40,409	37
LA	1699	Baton Rouge	Apr. 30, 1812	18	380	130	43,562	8,278	51,840	31
ME	1624	Augusta	Mar. 15, 1820	23	320	190	30,862	4,523	35,385	39
MD	1634	Annapolis	Apr. 28, 1788	7	250	90	9,774	2,633	12,407	42
MA	1620	Boston	Feb. 6, 1788	6	190	50	7,840	2,715	10,555	44
MI	1668	Lansing	Jan. 26, 1837	26	490	240	56,804	39,912	96,716	11
MN	1805	St. Paul	May 11, 1858	32	400	250	79,610	7,329	86,939	12
MS	1699	Jackson	Dec. 10, 1817	20	340	170	46,907	1,523	48,430	32
MO	1735	Jefferson City	Aug. 10, 1821	24	300	240	68,886	818	69,704	21
MT	1809	Helena	Nov. 8, 1889	41	630	280	145,552	1,490	147,042	4
NE	1823	Lincoln	Mar. 1, 1867	37	430	210	76,872	481	77,354	16
NV	1849	Carson City	Oct. 31, 1864	36	490	320	109,826	735	110,561	7
NH	1623	Concord	June 21, 1788	9	190	70	8,968	382	9,350	46
NJ	1660	Trenton	Dec. 18, 1787	3	150	70	7,417	1,304	8,721	47
NM	1610	Santa Fe	Jan. 6, 1912	47	370	343	121,356	234	121,589	5
NY	1614	Albany	July 26, 1788	11	330	283	47,214	7,342	54,556	27
NC	1660	Raleigh	Nov. 21, 1789	12	500	150	48,711	5,108	53,819	28
ND	1812	Bismarck	Nov. 2, 1889	39	340	211	68,976	1,724	70,700	19
OH	1788	Columbus	Mar. 1, 1803	17	220	220	40,948	3,877	44,825	34
OK	1889	Oklahoma City	Nov. 16, 1907	46	400	220	68,667	1,231	69,898	20
OR	1811	Salem	Feb. 14, 1859	33	360	261	95,997	2,384	98,381	9
PA	1682	Harrisburg	Dec. 12, 1787	2	283	160	44,817	1,239	46,055	33
RI	1636	Providence	May 29, 1790	13	40	30	1,045	500	1,545	50
SC	1670	Columbia	May 23, 1788	8	260	200	30,109	911	32,020	40
SD	1859	Pierre	Nov. 2, 1889	40	380	210	75,885	1,232	77,116	17
TN	1769	Nashville	June 1, 1796	16	440	120	41,217	926	42,143	36
TX	1682	Austin	Dec. 29, 1845	28	790	660	261,797	6,784	268,581	2
UT	1847	Salt Lake City	Jan. 4, 1896	45	350	270	82,144	2,755	84,899	13
VT	1724	Montpelier	Mar. 4, 1791	14	160	80	9,250	365	9,614	45
VA	1607	Richmond	June 25, 1788	10	430	200	39,594	3,180	42,774	35
WA	1811	Olympia	Nov. 11, 1889	42	360	240	66,544	4,756	71,300	18
WV	1727	Charleston	June 20, 1863	35	240	130	24,078	152	24,230	41
WI	1766	Madison	May 29, 1848	30	310	260	54,310	11,188	65,498	23
WY	1834	Cheyenne	July 10, 1890	44	360	280	97,100	713	97,814	10

Note: Land and water areas may not add to totals because of rounding. NA = Not applicable. (1) First permanent settlement by Europeans. (2) Rank is based on total area as shown. (3) Aleutian Islands and Alexander Archipelago not included.

The Continental Divide of the U.S.

The Continental Divide of the U.S., also known as the Great Divide, is located at the watershed created by the mountain ranges, or tablelands, of the Rocky Mountains. This watershed separates the waters that drain easterly into the Atlantic Ocean and its marginal seas, such as the Gulf of Mexico, from those waters that drain westerly into the Pacific Ocean. The majority of easterly flowing water in the U.S. drains into the Gulf of Mexico before reaching the Atlantic Ocean. The majority of westerly flowing water, before reaching the Pacific Ocean, drains either through the Columbia River or through the Colorado River, which flows into the Gulf of California before reaching the Pacific Ocean.

The location and route of the Continental Divide across the U.S. can briefly be described as follows:

Beginning at the U.S.-Mexican boundary, near long. 108° 45′ W, the Divide, in a northerly direction, crosses New Mexico along the W edge of the Rio Grande drainage basin, entering Colorado near long. 106° 41′ W.

From there by a very irregular route north across Colorado along the W summits of the Rio Grande and of the Arkansas, the South Platte, and the North Platte river basins, and across Rocky Mountain National Park, entering Wyoming near long. 106° 52′ W.

From there in a northwesterly direction, forming the W rims of the North Platte, the Big Horn, and the Yellowstone river basins, crossing the SW portion of Yellowstone National Park.

From there in a westerly and then a northerly direction forming the common boundary of Idaho and Montana, to a point on said boundary near long. 114° 00′ W.

From there northeasterly and northwesterly through Montana and the Glacier National Park, entering Canada near long. 114° 04′ W.

WORLD ALMANAC QUICK QUIZ

Of the following recent U.S. presidents, who is the only one to have a National Historic Site named for him?
(a) Jimmy Carter (b) Ronald Reagan (c) George H.W. Bush (d) Bill Clinton

For the answer look in this chapter, or see page 1008.

Chronological List of Territories, With State Admissions to Union

Source: National Archives and Records Service

Name of territory	Date of act creating territory	When act took effect	Admission as state	Yrs. terr.
Northwest Territory[1]	July 13, 1787	No fixed date	Mar. 1, 1803[2]	16
Territory southwest of River Ohio	May 26, 1790	No fixed date	June 1, 1796[3]	6
Mississippi	Apr. 7, 1798	When president acted	Dec. 10, 1817	19
Indiana	May 7, 1800	July 4, 1800	Dec. 11, 1816	16
Orleans	Mar. 26, 1804	Oct. 1, 1804	Apr. 30, 1812[4]	7
Michigan	Jan. 11, 1805	June 30, 1805	Jan. 26, 1837	31
Louisiana-Missouri[5]	Mar. 3, 1805	July 4, 1805	Aug. 10, 1821	16
Illinois	Feb. 3, 1809	Mar. 1, 1809	Dec. 3, 1818	9
Alabama	Mar. 3, 1817	When MS became a state	Dec. 14, 1819	2
Arkansas	Mar. 2, 1819	July 4, 1819	June 15, 1836	17
Florida	Mar. 30, 1822	No fixed date	Mar. 3, 1845	23
Wisconsin	Apr. 20, 1836	July 3, 1836	May 29, 1848	12
Iowa	June 12, 1838	July 3, 1838	Dec. 28, 1846	8
Oregon	Aug. 14, 1848	Date of act	Feb. 14, 1859	10
Minnesota	Mar. 3, 1849	Date of act	May 11, 1858	9
New Mexico	Sept. 9, 1850	On president's proclamation	Jan. 6, 1912	61
Utah	Sept. 9, 1850	Date of act	Jan. 4, 1896	46
Washington	Mar. 2, 1853	Date of act	Nov. 11, 1889	36
Nebraska	May 30, 1854	Date of act	Mar. 1, 1867	12
Kansas	May 30, 1854	Date of act	Jan. 29, 1861	6
Colorado	Feb. 28, 1861	Date of act	Aug. 1, 1876	15
Nevada	Mar. 2, 1861	Date of act	Oct. 31, 1864	3
Dakota	Mar. 2, 1861	Date of act	Nov. 2, 1889	28
Arizona	Feb. 24, 1863	Date of act	Feb. 14, 1912	49
Idaho	Mar. 3, 1863	Date of act	July 3, 1890	27
Montana	May 26, 1864	Date of act	Nov. 8, 1889	25
Wyoming	July 25, 1868	When officers were qualified	July 10, 1890	22
Alaska[6]	May 17, 1884	No fixed date	Jan. 3, 1959	75
Oklahoma	May 2, 1890	Date of act	Nov. 16, 1907	17
Hawaii	Apr. 30, 1900	June 14, 1900	Aug. 21, 1959	59

(1) Included what is now Ohio, Indiana, Illinois, Michigan, Wisconsin, E Minnesota. (2) Ohio was the first state of NW territory admitted. (3) Admitted as the state of Tennessee. (4) Admitted as the state of Louisiana. (5) The act creating Missouri Territory (June 4, 1812) became effective Dec. 7, 1812. (6) Although the May 17, 1884, act actually constituted Alaska as a district, it was often referred to as a territory, and administered as such. The Territory of Alaska was formally organized by an act of Aug. 24, 1912.

Geographic Centers, U.S. and Each State

Source: U.S. Geological Survey, Dept. of the Interior

There is no generally accepted definition of geographic center and no uniform method for determining it. Following the U.S. Geological Survey, the geographic center of an area is defined here as the center of gravity of the surface, or that point on which the surface would balance if it were a plane of uniform thickness. All locations in the following list are approximate.

No marked or monumented point has been officially established by any government agency as the geographic center of the 50 states, the conterminous U.S. (48 states), or the North American continent. A group of private citizens erected a monument in Lebanon, KS, marking it as geographic center of the conterminous U.S., and a cairn erected in Rugby, ND, asserts that location as the center of the North American continent.

Geographic centers as reported by the U.S. Geological Survey are indicated below:

United States, including Alaska and Hawaii—W of Castle Rock, Butte County, SD; lat. 44° 58′ N, long. 103° 46′ W
Conterminous U.S. (48 states)—Near Lebanon, Smith Co., Kansas, lat. 39° 50′ N, long. 98° 35′ W
North American continent—6 mi W of Balta, Pierce County, North Dakota; lat. 48° 10′ N, long. 100° 10′ W
Alabama—Chilton, 12 mi SW of Clanton
Alaska—lat. 63° 50′ N, long. 152° W; approx. 60 mi NW of Mt. McKinley
Arizona—Yavapai, 55 mi E-SE of Prescott
Arkansas—Pulaski, 12 mi NW of Little Rock
California—Madera, 38 mi E of Madera
Colorado—Park, 30 mi NW of Pikes Peak
Connecticut—Hartford, at East Berlin
Delaware—Kent, 11 mi S of Dover
District of Columbia—Near 4th and L Sts. NW
Florida—Hernando, 12 mi N-NW of Brooksville
Georgia—Twiggs, 18 mi SE of Macon
Hawaii—lat. 20° 15′ N, long. 156° 20′ W, off Maui Is.
Idaho—Custer, SW of Challis
Illinois—Logan, 28 mi NE of Springfield
Indiana—Boone, 14 mi N-NW of Indianapolis
Iowa—Story, 5 mi NE of Ames
Kansas—Barton, 15 mi NE of Great Bend
Kentucky—Marion, 3 mi N-NW of Lebanon
Louisiana—Avoyelles, 3 mi SE of Marksville
Maine—Piscataquis, 18 mi N of Dover
Maryland—Prince George's, 4.5 mi NW of Davidsonville
Massachusetts—Worcester, N part of city
Michigan—Wexford, 5 mi N-NW of Cadillac
Minnesota—Crow Wing, 10 mi SW of Brainerd
Mississippi—Leake, 9 mi W-NW of Carthage
Missouri—Miller, 20 mi SW of Jefferson City
Montana—Fergus, 11 mi W of Lewistown
Nebraska—Custer, 10 mi NW of Broken Bow
Nevada—Lander, 26 mi SE of Austin
New Hampshire—Belknap, 3 mi E of Ashland
New Jersey—Mercer, 5 mi SE of Trenton
New Mexico—Torrance, 12 mi S-SW of Willard
New York—Madison, 12 mi S of Oneida and 26 mi SW of Utica
North Carolina—Chatham, 10 mi NW of Sanford
North Dakota—Sheridan, 5 mi SW of McClusky
Ohio—Delaware, 25 mi N-NE of Columbus
Oklahoma—Oklahoma, 8 mi N of Oklahoma City
Oregon—Crook, 25 mi S-SE of Prineville
Pennsylvania—Centre, 2.5 mi SW of Bellefonte
Rhode Island—Kent, 1 mi S-SW of Crompton
South Carolina—Richland, 13 mi SE of Columbia
South Dakota—Hughes, 8 mi NE of Pierre
Tennessee—Rutherford, 5 mi NE of Murfreesboro
Texas—McCulloch, 15 mi NE of Brady
Utah—Sanpete, 3 mi N of Manti
Vermont—Washington, 3 mi E of Roxbury
Virginia—Buckingham, 5 mi SW of Buckingham
Washington—Chelan, 10 mi W-SW of Wenatchee
West Virginia—Braxton, 4 mi E of Sutton
Wisconsin—Wood, 9 mi SE of Marshfield
Wyoming—Fremont, 58 mi E-NE of Lander

International Boundary Lines of the U.S.

The length of the N boundary of the conterminous U.S.—the U.S.-Canadian border, excluding Alaska—is 3,987 mi according to the U.S. Geological Survey, Dept. of the Interior. The length of the Alaskan-Canadian border is 1,538 mi. The U.S.-Mexican border, from the Gulf of Mexico to the Pacific Ocean, is about 1,933 mi (1963 boundary agreement).

Origins of the Names of U.S. States

Source: State officials, Smithsonian Institution, and Topographic Division, U.S. Geological Survey, Dept. of the Interior

Alabama—Indian for tribal town, later a tribe (Alabamas or Alibamons) of the Creek confederacy.

Alaska—Russian version of Aleutian (Eskimo) word, *alakshak*, for "peninsula," "great lands," or "land that is not an island."

Arizona—Spanish version of Pima Indian word for "little spring place," or Aztec *arizuma*, meaning "silver-bearing."

Arkansas—Algonquin name for the Quapaw Indians, meaning "south wind."

California—Bestowed by the Spanish conquistadors (possibly by Cortez). It was the name of an imaginary island, an earthly paradise, in *Las Serges de Esplandian*, a Spanish romance written by Montalvo in 1510. *Baja California* (Lower California, in Mexico) was first visited by Spanish in 1533. The present U.S. state was called *Alta* (Upper) *California*.

Colorado—From Spanish for "red," first applied to Colorado River.

Connecticut—From Mohican and other Algonquin words meaning "long river place."

Delaware—Named for Lord De La Warr, early governor of Virginia; first applied to river, then to Indian tribe (Lenni-Lenape), and the state.

District of Columbia—For Christopher Columbus, 1791.

Florida—Named by Ponce de Leon *Pascua Florida*, "Flowery Easter," on Easter Sunday, 1513.

Georgia—For King George II of England, by James Oglethorpe, colonial administrator, 1732.

Hawaii—Possibly derived from native word for homeland, *Hawaiki* or *Owhyhee*.

Idaho—Said to be a coined name with an invented meaning: "gem of the mountains"; originally suggested for the Pikes Peak mining territory (Colorado), then applied to the new mining territory of the Pacific Northwest. Another theory suggests *Idaho* may be a Kiowa Apache term for the Comanche.

Illinois—French for *Illini* or "land of *Illini*," Algonquin word meaning "men" or "warriors."

Indiana—Means "land of the Indians."

Iowa—Indian word variously translated as "here I rest" or "beautiful land." Named for the Iowa R., which was named for the Iowa Indians.

Kansas—Sioux word for "south wind people."

Kentucky—Indian word that is variously translated as "dark and bloody ground," "meadowland," and "land of tomorrow."

Louisiana—Part of territory called Louisiana by Sieur de La Salle for French King Louis XIV.

Maine—From Maine, ancient French province. Also: descriptive, referring to the mainland as distinct from the many coastal islands.

Maryland—For Queen Henrietta Maria, wife of Charles I of England.

Massachusetts—From Indian tribe named after "large hill place" identified by Capt. John Smith as being near Milton, MA.

Michigan—From Chippewa words, *mici gama*, meaning "great water," after the lake of the same name.

Minnesota—From Dakota Sioux word meaning "cloudy water" or "sky-tinted water" of the Minnesota River.

Mississippi—Probably Chippewa; *mici zibi*, "great river" or "gathering-in of all the waters." Also: Algonquin word, *messipi*.

Missouri—An Algonquin Indian term meaning "river of the big canoes."

Montana—Latin or Spanish for "mountainous."

Nebraska—From Omaha or Otos Indian word meaning "broad water" or "flat river," describing the Platte River.

Nevada—Spanish, meaning "snow-clad."

New Hampshire—Named, 1629, by Capt. John Mason of Plymouth Council for his home county in England.

New Jersey—The Duke of York, 1664, gave a patent to John Berkeley and Sir George Carteret to be called Nova Caesaria, or New Jersey, after England's Isle of Jersey.

New Mexico—Spaniards in Mexico applied term to land north and west of Rio Grande in the 16th century.

New York—For Duke of York and Albany, who received patent to New Netherland from his brother Charles II and sent an expedition to capture it, 1664.

North Carolina—In 1619 Charles I gave a large patent to Sir Robert Heath to be called Province of Carolana, from *Carolus*, Latin name for Charles. A new patent was granted by Charles II to Earl of Clarendon and others. Divided into North and South Carolina, 1710.

North Dakota—*Dakota* is Sioux for "friend" or "ally."

Ohio—Iroquois word for "fine or good river."

Oklahoma—Choctaw word meaning "red man," proposed by Rev. Allen Wright, Choctaw-speaking Indian.

Oregon—Origin unknown. One theory holds that the name may have been derived from that of the Wisconsin River, shown on a 1715 French map as "Ouaricon-sint."

Pennsylvania—William Penn, the Quaker who was made full proprietor of this area by King Charles II in 1681, suggested "Sylvania," or "woodland," for his tract. The king's government owed Penn's father, Admiral William Penn, 16,000 pounds, and the land was granted as partial settlement. Charles II added the "Penn" to Sylvania, against the desires of the modest proprietor, in honor of the admiral.

Puerto Rico—Spanish for "rich port."

Rhode Island—Exact origin is unknown. One theory notes that Giovanni de Verrazano recorded an island about the size of Rhodes in the Mediterranean in 1524, but others believe the state was named *Roode Eylandt* by Adriaen Block, Dutch explorer, because of its red clay.

South Carolina—See North Carolina.

South Dakota—See North Dakota.

Tennessee—*Tanasi* was the name of Cherokee villages on the Little Tennessee River. From 1784 to 1788 this was the State of Franklin, or Frankland.

Texas—Variant of word used by Caddo and other Indians meaning "friends" or "allies," and applied to them by the Spanish in eastern Texas. Also written *Texias*, *Tejas*, *Teysas*.

Utah—From a Navajo word meaning "upper," or "higher up," as applied to a Shoshone tribe called Ute. Spanish form is *Yutta*. The English is *Uta* or *Utah*. Proposed name *Deseret*, "land of honeybees," from Book of Mormon, was rejected by Congress.

Vermont—From French words *vert* (green) and *mont* (mountain). The Green Mountains were said to have been named by Samuel de Champlain. When the state was formed, 1777, Dr. Thomas Young suggested combining *vert* and *mont* into Vermont.

Virginia—Named by Sir Walter Raleigh, who fitted out the expedition of 1584, in honor of Queen Elizabeth, the Virgin Queen of England.

Washington—Named after George Washington. When the bill creating the Territory of Columbia was introduced in the 32nd Congress, the name was changed to Washington because of the existence of the District of Columbia.

West Virginia—So named when western counties of Virginia refused to secede from the U.S. in 1863.

Wisconsin—An Indian name, spelled *Ouisconsin* and *Mesconsing* by early chroniclers. Believed to mean "grassy place" in Chippewa. Congress made it *Wisconsin*.

Wyoming—From the Algonquin words for "large prairie place," "at the big plains," or "on the great plain."

Territorial Sea of the U.S.

According to a Dec. 27, 1988, proclamation by Pres. Ronald Reagan: "The territorial sea of the United States henceforth extends to 12 nautical miles from the baselines of the United States determined in accordance with international law. In accordance with international law, as reflected in the applicable provisions of the 1982 United Nations Convention on the Law of the Sea, within the territorial sea of the United States, the ships of all countries enjoy the right of innocent passage and the ships and aircraft of all countries enjoy the right of transit passage through international straits."

Major Accessions of Territory by the U.S.

Source: U.S. Dept. of the Interior; Bureau of the Census, U.S. Dept. of Commerce

Not including territories such as Panama Canal Zone and the Philippines which are no longer under U.S. jurisdiction; area figures are for total area and may differ from figure s for current areas given elsewhere.

	Acquisition date	Area (sq mi)
Territory in 1790[1]	NA	888,685
Louisiana Purchase	1803	827,192
Purchase of Florida	1819	58,560
Other areas from Spain	1819	13,443
Texas	1845	390,143
Oregon Territory	1846	285,580
Mexican Cession	1848	529,017
Gadsden Purchase	1853	29,640
Alaska	1867	586,412
Hawaii	1898	6,450
Puerto Rico[2]	1899	3,435
Guam[3]	1899	212
American Samoa[4]	1900	76
U.S. Virgin Islands	1917	133
Northern Marianas[5]	1986	179

NA = Not applicable. (1) Includes that part of a drainage basin of Red River of the North, S of 49th parallel, sometimes considered part of Louisiana Purchase. (2) Ceded by Spain in 1898, ratified in 1899, and became the Commonwealth of Puerto Rico by Act of Congress on July 25, 1952. (3) Acquired in 1898; ratified 1899. (4) Acquired in 1899; ratified 1900. (5) Formerly a part of the U.S. administered Trust Territory of the Pacific Islands; became a U.S. commonwealth, Nov. 3, 1986.

Federally Owned Land, by State

Source: Office of Governmentwide Policy, General Services Administration; as of Sept. 30, 2004

State	Total acreage[1]	Federal acreage[2]	% federal acreage[2]
Alabama	32,678,400	513,913.0	1.57
Alaska	365,481,600	252,495,811.3	69.09
Arizona	72,688,000	34,933,236.1	48.06
Arkansas	33,599,360	2,407,948.0	7.17
California	100,206,720	45,393,237.5	45.30
Colorado	66,485,760	24,354,712.8	36.63
Connecticut	3,135,360	13,937.7	0.44
Delaware	1,265,920	25,874.4	2.04
District of Columbia	39,040	9,630.6	24.67
Florida	34,721,280	2,858,781.8	8.23
Georgia	37,295,360	1,409,406.3	3.78
Hawaii	4,105,600	796,725.5	19.41
Idaho	52,933,120	26,565,411.8	50.19
Illinois	35,795,200	641,959.0	1.79
Indiana	23,158,400	463,244.6	2.00
Iowa	35,860,480	273,954.3	0.76
Kansas	52,510,720	631,351.2	1.20
Kentucky	25,512,320	1,378,677.1	5.40
Louisiana	28,867,840	1,474,788.4	5.11
Maine	19,847,680	208,421.8	1.05
Maryland	6,319,360	178,526.9	2.83
Massachusetts	5,034,880	93,950.1	1.87
Michigan	36,492,160	3,637,873.4	9.97
Minnesota	51,205,760	2,873,517.4	5.61
Mississippi	30,222,720	2,196,940.3	7.27
Missouri	44,248,320	2,224,787.8	5.03
Montana	93,271,040	27,910,151.8	29.92
Nebraska	49,031,680	665,481.4	1.36
Nevada	70,264,320	59,362,642.5	84.48
New Hampshire	5,768,960	775,665.1	13.45
New Jersey	4,813,440	148,440.8	3.08
New Mexico	77,766,400	32,483,876.5	41.77
New York	30,680,960	233,533.4	0.76
North Carolina	31,402,880	3,710,338.3	11.82
North Dakota	44,452,480	1,185,776.9	2.67
Ohio	26,222,080	448,381.4	1.71
Oklahoma	44,087,680	1,586,148.3	3.60
Oregon	61,598,720	32,715,514.1	53.11
Pennsylvania	28,804,480	719,863.6	2.50
Rhode Island	677,120	2,923.0	0.43
South Carolina	19,374,080	560,955.9	2.90
South Dakota	48,881,920	3,028,002.7	6.19
Tennessee	26,727,680	865,836.9	3.24
Texas	168,217,600	3,130,345.0	1.8
Utah	52,696,960	30,271,905.2	57.45
Vermont	5,936,640	443,249.2	7.4
Virginia	25,496,320	2,534,177.6	9.94
Washington	42,693,760	12,949,661.7	30.33
West Virginia	15,410,560	1,146,210.8	7.44
Wisconsin	35,011,200	1,971,901.8	5.63
Wyoming	62,343,040	26,391,487.2	42.33
Total	**2,271,343,360**	**653,299,090.2**	**28.76**

Note: Totals do not include inland water. (1) Bureau of the Census, U.S. Dept. of Commerce figures. (2) Excludes trust properties.

Special Recreation Areas Administered by the U.S. Forest Service, 2005

Source: U.S. Forest Service, Dept. of Agriculture

NHL=National Historic Landmark; NS(A)=Nat. Scenic (Area); NM=National Monument; NP=National Preserve; NRA=National Recreation Area; NVM=Nat. Volcanic Monument; SRA=Scenic Recreation Area

Area name	Location	Estab.	Acres
Admiralty Island NM	AK	1980	978,881
Allegheny NRA	PA	1984	23,063
Arapaho NRA	CO	1978	30,690
Beech Creek NS & Botanic Area	OK	1988	7,500
Cascade Head NS Research Area	OR	1974	6,630
Columbia River Gorge NSA	OR-WA	1986	63,150
Coosa Bald NSA	GA	1991	7,100
Ed Jenkins NRA	GA	1991	23,166
Flaming Gorge NRA	UT-WY	1968	189,825
Giant Sequoia NM	CA	2000	327,769
Grand Island NRA	MI	1990	12,961
Grey Towers NHL	PA	1963	102
Hells Canyon NRA	OR-ID	1975	536,648
Indian Nations NS & Wildlife Area	OK	1988	40,051
Jemez NRA	NM	1993	57,000
Land Between the Lakes NRA	KY-TN	1998	170,000
Misty Fiords NM	AK	1980	2,293,428
Mono Basin NSA	CA	1984	115,600
Mount Baker NRA	WA	1984	8,473
Mount Pleasant NSA	VA	1994	7,580
Mount Rogers NRA	VA	1966	114,520
Mount St. Helens NVM	WA	1989	112,593
Newberry NVM	OR	1990	54,822
North Cascades NSA	WA	1984	87,600
Opal Creek SRA	OR	1996	13,000
Oregon Dunes NRA	OR	1972	27,212
Pine Ridge NRA	NE	1986	6,600
Rattlesnake NRA	MT	1980	59,119
Santa Rosa and San Jacinto Mts. NM	CA	2000	272,000
Sawtooth NRA	ID	1972	729,322
Smith River NRA	CA	1990	305,169
Spring Mt. NRA	NV	1993	316,000
Spruce Knob-Seneca Rocks NRA	WV	1965	57,237
Valles Caldera NP	NM	2000	88,900
Whiskeytown-Shasta-Trinity NRA	CA	1965	176,367
White Rocks NRA	VT	1984	36,400
Winding Stair Mt. NRA	OK	1988	25,890

20 Most-Visited Sites in the National Park System, 2004

Source: National Park Service, Dept. of the Interior

Attendance at all areas administered by the National Park Service in 2004 totaled 276,908,337 recreation visits.

Site (location)	Recreation visits
Blue Ridge Parkway (NC-VA)	17,999,116
Golden Gate National Recreation Area (CA)	13,270,547
Great Smoky Mountains National Park (NC-TN)	9,167,046
Gateway National Recreation Area (NJ-NY)	8,228,573
Lake Mead National Recreation Area (AZ-NV)	7,819,984
George Washington Memorial Pkwy (VA-MD-DC)	7,227,909
Natchez Trace Parkway (MS-AL-TN)	5,389,227
National World War II Memorial	5,382,498
Delaware Water Gap Natl. Recreation Area (NJ-PA)	5,052,264
Grand Canyon National Park (AZ)	4,326,234
Gulf Islands National Seashore (FL-MS)	4,241,477
Cape Cod National Seashore (MA)	4,106,840
Independence National Historical Park (PA)	4,087,918
San Francisco Maritime Natl. Historical Park (CA)	4,055,479
Lincoln Memorial (DC)	3,988,650
Vietnam Veterans Memorial (DC)	3,789,889
Statue of Liberty National Monument (NJ-NY)	3,618,053
Korean War Memorial	3,610,796
Colonial National Historical Park (VA)	3,327,573
Cuyahoga Valley National Park (OH)	3,306,175

National Parks, Other Areas Administered by National Park Service

Dates when sites were authorized for initial protection by Congress or by presidential proclamation are given in parentheses. If different, the date the area got its current designation, or was transferred to the National Park Service, follows. Gross area in acres, as of Sept. 30, 2004, follows date(s). Over 84 mil acres of federal land are now administered by the National Park Service.

NATIONAL PARKS

Acadia, ME (1916/1929) 47,390. Includes Mount Desert Isl., half of Isle au Haut, Schoodic Peninsula on mainland. Highest elevation on Eastern seaboard.

American Samoa, AS (1988) 9,000. Features a paleotropical rain forest and a coral reef. No federal facilities.

Arches, UT (1929/1971) 76,519. Contains giant red sandstone arches and other products of erosion.

Badlands, SD (1929/1978) 242,756. Reformations and native prairie. Animal fossils 23-37 mil years old.

Big Bend, TX (1935) 801,163. Rio Grande, Chisos Mts.

Biscayne, FL (1968/1980) 172,924. Aquatic park encompassing chain of islands south of Miami.

Black Canyon of the Gunnison, CO (1933/1999) 32,950. Has a canyon 2,900 ft deep and 40 ft wide at its narrowest part.

Bryce Canyon, UT (1923/1928) 35,835. Spectacularly colorful and unusual display of erosion effects.

Canyonlands, UT (1964) 337,598. At junction of Colorado and Green rivers; extensive evidence of prehistoric Indians.

Capitol Reef, UT (1937/1971) 241,904. A 70-mi uplift of sandstone cliffs dissected by high-walled gorges.

Carlsbad Caverns, NM (1923/1930) 46,766. Largest known caverns; not yet fully explored.

Channel Islands, CA (1938/1980) 249,561. Sea lion breeding place, nesting sea birds, unique plants.

Crater Lake, OR (1902) 183,224. Extraordinary blue lake in the crater of Mt. Mazama, a volcano that erupted about 7,700 years ago; deepest U.S. lake.

Cuyahoga Valley, OH (1974/2000) 32,861. Rural landscape along Ohio and Erie Canal system between Akron and Cleveland.

Death Valley, CA-NV (1933/1994) 3,372,402. Large desert area. Includes the lowest point in the Western Hemisphere; also includes Scotty's Castle.

Denali, AK (1917/1980) 4,740,912. Name changed from Mt. McKinley National Park. Contains highest mountain in U.S.; wildlife.

Dry Tortugas, FL (1935/1992) 64,701. Formerly Ft. Jefferson National Monument.

Everglades, FL (1934) 1,508,538. Largest remaining subtropical wilderness in continental U.S.

Gates of the Arctic, AK (1978/1984) 7,523,898. Vast wilderness in north central region. Limited federal facilities.

Glacier, MT (1910) 1,013,572. Superb Rocky Mt. scenery, numerous glaciers and glacial lakes. Part of Waterton-Glacier Intl. Peace Park established by U.S. and Canada in 1932.

Glacier Bay, AK (1925/1986) 3,224,840. Great tidewater glaciers that move down mountainsides and break up into the sea; much wildlife.

Grand Canyon, AZ (1893/1919) 1,217,403. Most spectacular part of Colorado River's greatest canyon.

Grand Teton, WY (1929) 309,995. Most impressive part of the Teton Mts., winter feeding ground of largest American elk herd.

Great Basin, NV (1922/1986) 77,180. Includes Wheeler Pk., Lexington Arch, and Lehman Caves.

Great Smoky Mountains, NC-TN (1926/1934) 521,752. Largest Eastern mountain range, magnificent forests.

Guadalupe Mountains, TX (1966) 86,416. Extensive Permian limestone fossil reef; tremendous earth fault.

Haleakala, HI (1916/1960) 29,094. Dormant volcano on Maui with large colorful craters.

Hawaii Volcanoes, HI (1916/1961) 323,431. Contains Kilauea and Mauna Loa, active volcanoes.

Hot Springs, AR (1832/1921) 5,550. Bathhouses are furnished with thermal waters from the park's 47 hot springs; these waters are used for bathing and drinking.

Isle Royale, MI (1931) 571,790. Largest island in Lake Superior, noted for its wilderness area and wildlife.

Joshua Tree, CA (1936/1994) 789,745. Desert region includes Joshua trees, other plant and animal life.

Katmai, AK (1918/1980) 3,674,530. "Valley of Ten Thousand Smokes," scene of 1912 volcanic eruption.

Kenai Fjords, AK (1978/1980) 669,983. Abundant marine mammals, birdlife; the Harding Icefield, one of the 4 major icecaps in U.S.

Kings Canyon, CA (1890/1940) 461,901. Mountain wilderness, dominated by Kings River Canyons and High Sierra; contains giant sequoias.

Kobuk Valley, AK (1978/1980) 1,750,717. Contains geological and recreational sites. Limited federal facilities.

Lake Clark, AK (1978/1980) 2,619,733. Across Cook Inlet from Anchorage. A scenic wilderness rich in fish and wildlife. Limited federal facilities.

Lassen Volcanic, CA (1907/1916) 106,372. Contains Lassen Peak, recently active volcano, and other volcanic phenomena.

Mammoth Cave, KY (1926/1941) 52,830. 144 mi of surveyed underground passages, beautiful natural formations, river 300 ft below surface.

Mesa Verde, CO (1906) 52,122. Most notable and best preserved prehistoric cliff dwellings in the U.S.

Mount Rainier, WA (1899) 235,625. Greatest single-peak glacial system in the U.S.

North Cascades, WA (1968) 504,781. Spectacular mountainous region with many glaciers, lakes.

Olympic, WA (1909/1938) 922,651. Mountain wilderness containing finest remnant of Pacific Northwest rain forest, active glaciers, Pacific shoreline, rare elk.

Petrified Forest, AZ (1906/1962) 93,533. Extensive petrified wood and Indian artifacts. Contains part of Painted Desert.

Redwood, CA (1968) 112,512. 40 mi of Pacific coastline, groves of ancient redwoods and world's tallest trees.

Rocky Mountain, CO (1915) 265,828. On the Continental Divide; includes peaks over 14,000 ft.

Saguaro, AZ (1933/1994) 91,440. Part of the Sonoran Desert; includes the giant saguaro cacti, unique to the region.

Sequoia, CA (1890) 404,051. Groves of giant sequoias, highest mountain in conterminous U.S.—Mt. Whitney (14,494 ft). World's largest tree.

Shenandoah, VA (1926) 199,045. Portion of the Blue Ridge Mts.; overlooks Shenandoah Valley; Skyline Drive.

Theodore Roosevelt, ND (1947/1978) 70,447. Contains part of T.R.'s ranch and scenic badlands.

Virgin Islands, VI (1956) 14,689. Authorized to cover 75% of St. John Isl. and Hassel Isl.; lush growth, lovely beaches, Carib Indian petroglyphs, evidence of colonial Danes.

Voyageurs, MN (1971) 218,200. Abundant lakes, forests, wildlife, canoeing, boating.

Wind Cave, SD (1903) 28,295. Limestone caverns in Black Hills. Extensive wildlife includes a herd of bison.

Wrangell-St. Elias, AK (1978/1980) 8,323,148. Largest area in park system, most peaks over 16,000 ft, abundant wildlife; day's drive east of Anchorage. Limited federal facilities.

Yellowstone, ID-MT-WY (1872) 2,219,791. World's first national park. World's greatest geyser area has about 10,000 geysers and hot springs; spectacular falls and impressive canyons of the Yellowstone River; grizzly bear, moose, and bison.

Yosemite, CA (1890) 761,266. Yosemite Valley, the nation's highest waterfall, grove of sequoias, and mountains.

Zion, UT (1909/1919) 146,598. Unusual shapes and landscapes resulting from erosion and faulting; evidence of past volcanic activity; Zion Canyon has sheer walls ranging up to 2,640 ft.

NATIONAL HISTORICAL PARKS

Adams, MA (1946/1998) 24. Home of Pres. John Adams, John Quincy Adams, and celebrated descendants.

Appomattox Court House, VA (1930/1954) 1,774. Where Lee surrendered to Grant.

Boston, MA (1974) 43. Includes Faneuil Hall, Old North Church, Bunker Hill, Paul Revere House.

Cane River Creole (and heritage area), LA (1994) 207. Preserves the Creole culture as it developed along the Cane R.

Cedar Creek and Belle Grove, VA (2002) 3,593. Civil War battle site and an antebellum plantation in the Shenandoah Valley.

Chaco Culture, NM (1907/1980) 33,960. Ruins of pueblos built by prehistoric Indians.

Chesapeake and Ohio Canal, MD-DC-WV (1938/1971) 19,586. 184-mi historic canal; DC to Cumberland, MD.

Colonial, VA (1930/1936) 8,677. Includes most of Jamestown Isl., site of first successful English colony; Yorktown, site of Cornwallis's surrender to George Washington; and the Colonial Parkway.

Cumberland Gap, KY-TN-VA (1940) 20,508. Mountain pass of the Wilderness Road, which carried the first great migration of pioneers into America's interior.

Dayton Aviation Heritage, OH (1992) 86. Commemorates the area's aviation heritage.

George Rogers Clark, Vincennes, IN (1966) 26. Commemorates American defeat of British in West during Revolution.

Harpers Ferry, MD-VA-WV (1944/1963) 2,504. At the confluence of the Shenandoah and Potomac rivers, the site of John Brown's 1859 raid on the Army arsenal.

Hopewell Culture, OH (1923/1992) 1,170. Formerly Mound City Group National Monument.

Independence, PA (1948) 45. Contains several properties associated with the American Revolution and the founding of the U.S. Includes Independence Hall.

Jean Laffite (and preserve), LA (1907/1978) 20,005. Includes Chalmette, site of 1815 Battle of New Orleans; French Quarter.

Kalaupapa, HI (1980) 10,779. Molokai's former leper colony site and other historic areas.

IT'S A FACT: In July 2005, fears that lichen growing on the presidential faces might cause features to break or crumble off induced the park to give Mount Rushmore National Monument its first scouring since it was completed in 1940. Armed with hot water blasters and silicon sealant, park rangers dangled from rope harnesses—to avoid obscuring visitors' views—and scrubbed the 60-ft granite likeness of Presidents Washington, Jefferson, Lincoln, and Theodore Roosevelt.

Kaloko-Honokohau, HI (1978) 1,161. Preserves the native culture of Hawaii. No federal facilities.

Keweenaw, MI (1992) 1,869. Site of first significant copper mine in U.S. Federal facilities are under development.

Klondike Gold Rush, AK-WA (1976) 13,191. Alaskan Trails in 1898 Gold Rush. Museum in Seattle.

Lowell, MA (1978) 141. Textile mills, canal, 19th-cent. structures; park shows planned city of Industrial Revolution.

Lyndon B. Johnson, TX (1969/1980) 1,570. President's birthplace, boyhood home, ranch.

Marsh-Billings-Rockefeller, VT (1992) 643. Boyhood home of conservationist George Perkins Marsh. No federal facilities.

Minute Man, MA (1959) 971. Where the Minute Men battled the British, Apr. 19, 1775. Also contains Hawthorne's home.

Morristown, NJ (1933) 1,711. Sites of important military encampments during the American Revolution; Washington's headquarters, 1777, 1779-80.

Natchez, MS (1988) 105. Mansions, townhouses, and villas related to history of Natchez.

New Bedford Whaling, MA (1996) 34. Preserves structures and relics associated with the city's 19th-cent. whaling industry.

New Orleans Jazz, LA (1994) 5. Preserves, educates, and interprets jazz as it has evolved in New Orleans.

Nez Perce, ID (1965) 2,495. Illustrates the history and culture of the Nez Perce Indian country (38 separate sites).

Pecos, NM (1965/1990) 6,670. Ruins of ancient Pueblo of Pecos, archaeological sites, and 2 associated Spanish colonial missions from the 17th and 18th centuries.

Pu'uhonua o Honaunau, HI (1955/1978) 420. Until 1819, a sanctuary for Hawaiians vanquished in battle and for those guilty of crimes or breaking taboos.

Rosie the Riveter WWII Home Front, CA (2000) 145. Built on site that was a shipyard employing thousands of women in WWII; commemorates women who worked in war-time industries.

Salt River Bay (and ecological preserve), St. Croix, VI (1992) 978. The only site known where, 500 years ago, members of a Columbus party landed on what is now territory of the U.S.

San Antonio Missions, TX (1978) 826. Four of finest Spanish missions in U.S., 18th-cent. irrigation system.

San Francisco Maritime, CA (1988) 50. Artifacts, photographs, and historic vessels related to the development of the Pacific Coast.

San Juan Island, WA (1966) 1,752. Commemorates peaceful relations between the U.S., Canada, and Great Britain since the 1872 boundary disputes.

Saratoga, NY (1938) 3,392. Scene of a major 1777 battle that became a turning point in the American Revolution.

Sitka, AK (1910/1972) 112. Scene of last major resistance of the Tlingit Indians to the Russians, 1804.

Tumacacori, AZ (1908/1990) 360. Historic Spanish mission building stands near site first visited by Father Kino in 1691.

Valley Forge, PA (1976) 3,466. Continental Army campsite in 1777-78 winter.

War in the Pacific, GU (1978) 2,037. Seven distinct units illustrating the Pacific theater of WWII. Limited federal facilities.

Women's Rights, NY (1980) 7. Seneca Falls site where Lucretia Mott, Elizabeth Cady Stanton began rights movement in 1848.

NATIONAL BATTLEFIELDS

Antietam, MD (1890/1978) 3,252. Battle here ended first Confederate invasion of North, Sept. 17, 1862.

Big Hole, MT (1910/1963) 1,011. Site of major battle with Nez Perce Indians, Aug. 9-10, 1877.

Cowpens, SC (1929/1972) 842. American Revolution battlefield, Jan. 17, 1781.

Fort Donelson, TN-KY (1928/1985) 552. Site of first major Union victory, Feb. 14-16, 1862.

Fort Necessity, PA (1931/1961) 903. Site of first battle of French and Indian War, July 3, 1754.

Monocacy, MD (1934/1976) 1,647. Civil War battle in defense of Washington, DC, fought here, July 9, 1864.

Moores Creek, NC (1926/1980) 88. 1776 battle between Patriots and Loyalists commemorated here.

Petersburg, VA (1926/1962) 2,739. Scene of 10-month Union campaigns, 1864-65.

Stones River, TN (1927/1960) 709. Scene of battle that began federal offensive to trisect the Confederacy, Dec. 31, 1862-Jan. 2, 1863.

Tupelo, MS (1929/1961) 1. Site of crucial battle over Sherman's supply line, July 15-15, 1865.

Wilson's Creek, MO (1960/1970) 1,750. Scene of Civil War battle for control of Missouri, Aug. 10, 1861.

NATIONAL BATTLEFIELD PARKS

Kennesaw Mountain, GA (1917/1935) 2,884. Site of two major battles of Atlanta campaign in Civil War.

Manassas, VA (1940) 5,073. Scene of two battles in Civil War, 1861 and 1862.

Richmond, VA (1936) 2,517. Site of battles defending Confederate capital.

NATIONAL BATTLEFIELD SITE

Brices Cross Roads, MS (1929) 1. Civil War battlefield.

NATIONAL MILITARY PARKS

Chickamauga and Chattanooga, GA-TN (1890) 9,038. Site of major Confederate victory, 1863.

Fredericksburg and Spotsylvania County, VA (1927/1933) 8,374. Sites of several major Civil War battles and campaigns.

Gettysburg, PA (1895/1933) 5,990. Site of decisive Confederate defeat in North, July 1863, and of Gettysburg Address.

Guilford Courthouse, NC (1917/1933) 229. American Revolution battle site.

Horseshoe Bend, AL (1956) 2,040. On Tallapoosa River, where Gen. Andrew Jackson's forces broke the power of the Upper Creek Indian Confederacy on March 27, 1814.

Kings Mountain, SC (1931/1933) 3,945. Site of American Revolution battle, fought on Oct. 7, 1780.

Pea Ridge, AR (1956) 4,300. Scene of Civil War battle.

Shiloh, TN (1894/1933) 5,060. Major Civil War battlesite; includes some well-preserved Indian burial mounds.

Vicksburg, MS (1899/1933) 1,795. Union victory gave North control of the Mississippi and split the Confederate forces.

NATIONAL MEMORIALS

Arkansas Post, AR (1960) 758. First permanent French settlement in the lower Mississippi River valley.

Arlington House, the Robert E. Lee Memorial, VA (1925/1972) 28. Lee's home overlooking the Potomac.

Chamizal, El Paso, TX (1966/1974) 55. Commemorates 1963 settlement of 99-year border dispute with Mexico.

Coronado, AZ (1941/1952) 4,750. Commemorates first European exploration of the Southwest.

DeSoto, FL (1948) 27. Commemorates 16th-cent. Spanish explorations.

Federal Hall, NY (1939/1955) 0.45. First seat of U.S. government under the Constitution.

Fort Caroline, FL (1950) 138. On St. Johns River, overlooks site of a French Huguenot colony.

Fort Clatsop, OR (1958) 1,415. Lewis and Clark encampment, 1805-6.

Franklin Delano Roosevelt, DC (1982) 8. Statues of Pres. Roosevelt and Eleanor Roosevelt; waterfalls and gardens.

General Grant, NY (1958) 0.76. Tomb of Grant and wife.

Hamilton Grange, NY (1962) 1. Home of Alexander Hamilton.

Jefferson National Expansion Memorial, St. Louis, MO (1935) 91. Commemorates westward expansion.

Johnstown Flood, PA (1964) 164. Commemorates tragic flood of 1889.

Korean War Veterans, DC (1986) 2. Dedicated in 1995; honors those who served in the Korean War.

Lincoln Boyhood, IN (1962) 200. Lincoln grew up here.

Lincoln Memorial, DC (1911/1933) 107. Marble statue of the 16th U.S. president.

Lyndon B. Johnson Memorial Grove on the Potomac, DC (1973) 17. Overlooks the Potomac R.; vista of the Capitol.

Mount Rushmore, SD (1925) 1,278. World-famous sculpture of 4 presidents.

Oklahoma City, OK (1997) 3.3. Commemorates site of April 19, 1995, bombing which killed 168.

Perry's Victory and International Peace Memorial, Put-in-Bay, OH (1936/1972) 25. The world's most massive Doric column, constructed 1912-15, promotes pursuit of peace through arbitration and disarmament.

Roger Williams, Providence, RI (1965) 5. Memorial to founder of Rhode Island.

Thaddeus Kosciuszko, PA (1972) 0.02. Memorial to Polish hero of American Revolution.

Theodore Roosevelt Island, DC (1932/1933) 89. Statue of Roosevelt in wooded island sanctuary.

Thomas Jefferson Memorial, DC (1934) 18. Statue of Jefferson in an inscribed circular, colonnaded structure.

USS *Arizona*, HI (1980) 11. Memorializes American losses at Pearl Harbor.

Vietnam Veterans, DC (1980) 2. Black granite wall inscribed with names of those missing or killed in action in Vietnam War.

Washington Monument, DC (1848/1933) 106. Obelisk honoring the first U.S. president.

Wright Brothers, NC (1927/1953) 428. Site of first powered flight.

NATIONAL HISTORIC SITES

Abraham Lincoln Birthplace, Hodgenville, KY (1916/1959) 345. Memorial building, sinking spring.

Allegheny Portage Railroad, PA (1964) 1,296. Linked the Pennsylvania Canal system and the West.

Andersonville, Andersonville, GA (1970) 515. Noted Civil War prisoner-of-war camp.

Andrew Johnson, Greeneville, TN (1935/1963) 17. Two homes and the tailor shop of the 17th U.S. president.

Bent's Old Fort, CO (1960) 799. Reconstruction of S Plains outpost.

Boston African-American, MA (1980) 0.59. Pre-Civil War black history structures.

Brown v. Board of Education, KS (1992) 2. Commemorates the landmark 1954 U.S. Supreme Court decision.

Carl Sandburg Home, Flat Rock, NC (1968) 264. Poet's home.

Charles Pinckney, SC (1988) 28. Statesman's farm.

Christiansted, St. Croix, VI (1952/1961) 27. Commemorates Danish colony.

Clara Barton, MD (1974) 9. Home of founder of American Red Cross.

Edgar Allan Poe, PA (1978/1980) 0.52. Writer's home.

Edison, West Orange, NJ (1955/1962) 21. Inventor's home and laboratory.

Eisenhower, Gettysburg, PA (1967) 690. Home of 34th president.

Eleanor Roosevelt, Hyde Park, NY (1977) 181. The former first lady's personal retreat.

Eugene O'Neill, Danville, CA (1976) 13. Playwright's home.

First Ladies, Canton, OH (2000) 0.33. Library devoted to America's first ladies.

Ford's Theatre, DC (1866/1970) 0.29. Includes theater, now restored, where Lincoln was assassinated, house where he died, and Lincoln Museum.

Fort Bowie, AZ (1964) 999. Focal point of operations against Geronimo and the Apaches.

Fort Davis, TX (1961) 474. Frontier outpost in West Texas.

Fort Laramie, WY (1938/1960) 833. Military post on Oregon Trail.

Fort Larned, KS (1964/1966) 718. Military post on Santa Fe Trail.

Fort Point, San Francisco, CA (1970) 29. West Coast fortification.

Fort Raleigh, NC (1941) 513. First attempted English settlement in North America.

Fort Scott, KS (1965/1978) 17. Commemorates U.S. frontier of 1840s and '50s.

Fort Smith, AR-OK (1961) 75. Active post during 1817-90.

Fort Union Trading Post, MT-ND (1966) 444. Principal fur-trading post on upper Missouri, 1829-67.

Fort Vancouver, WA (1948/1961) 210. Headquarters for Hudson's Bay Company in 1825. Early political seat.

Frederick Douglass, DC (1962/1988) 9. Home of famous black abolitionist, writer, and orator.

Frederick Law Olmsted, MA (1979) 7. Home of famous city planner.

Friendship Hill, PA (1978) 675. Home of Albert Gallatin, Jefferson's and Madison's secretary of treasury.

Golden Spike, UT (1957) 2,735. Commemorates completion of first transcontinental railroad in 1869.

Grant-Kohrs Ranch, MT (1972) 1,618. Ranch house and part of 19th-cent. ranch.

Hampton, MD (1948) 62. 18th-cent. Georgian mansion.

Harry S. Truman, MO (1983) 7. Home of Pres. Truman after 1919.

Herbert Hoover, West Branch, IA (1965) 187. Birthplace and boyhood home of 31st president.

Home of Franklin D. Roosevelt, Hyde Park, NY (1944) 800. FDR's birthplace, home, and "summer White House."

Hopewell Furnace, PA (1938/1985) 848. 19th-cent. iron-making village.

Hubbell Trading Post, AZ (1965) 160. Still active today.

James A. Garfield, Mentor, OH (1980) 8. Home of 20th president.

Jimmy Carter, GA (1987) 71. Birthplace and home of 39th president.

John Fitzgerald Kennedy, Brookline, MA (1967) 0.09. Birthplace and childhood home of 35th president.

John Muir, Martinez, CA (1964) 345. Home of early conservationist and writer.

Knife River Indian Villages, ND (1974) 1,758. Remnants of villages last occupied by Hidatsa and Mandan Indians.

Lincoln Home, Springfield, IL (1971) 12. Lincoln's residence at the time he was elected 16th president, 1860.

Little Rock Central High School, AR (1998) 27. Commemorates 1957 desegregation during which federal troops had to be called in to protect 9 black students.

Longfellow, Cambridge, MA (1972) 2. Poet's home, 1837-82; Washington's headquarters during Boston siege, 1775-76.

Maggie L. Walker, VA (1978) 1. Richmond home of black leader and bank president, daughter of an ex-slave.

Manzanar, Lone Pine, CA (1992) 814. Commemorates Manzanar War Relocation Ctr., a Japanese-American internment camp during WWII. No federal facilities.

Martin Luther King Jr., Atlanta, GA (1980) 39. Birthplace, grave, church of the civil rights leader. Limited federal facilities.

Martin Van Buren, NY (1974) 40. Lindenwald, home of 8th president, near Kinderhook.

Mary McLeod Bethune Council House, DC (1982/1991). Commemorates Bethune's leadership in the black women's movement.

Minuteman Missile, SD (1999) 15. Missile launch facilities dating back to the Cold War era.

Nicodemus, KS (1996) 161. Only remaining western town established by African-Americans during Reconstruction.

Ninety Six, SC (1976) 1,022. Colonial trading village.

Palo Alto Battlefield, TX (1978) 3,407. Scene of first battle of the Mexican War.

Pennsylvania Avenue, DC (1965) Also includes area next to the road between Capitol and White House, encompassing Ford's Theatre and other structures.

Puukohola Heiau, HI (1972) 86. Ruins of temple built by King Kamehameha.

Sagamore Hill, Oyster Bay, NY (1962) 83. Home of Pres. Theodore Roosevelt from 1885 until his death in 1919.

Saint-Gaudens, Cornish, NH (1964) 148. Home, studio, and gardens of American sculptor Augustus Saint-Gaudens.

Saint Paul's Church, NY, NY (1943) 6. Site associated with John Peter Zenger's "freedom of press" trial.

Salem Maritime, MA (1938) 9. Only port never seized from the patriots by the British. Major fishing and whaling port.

Sand Creek Massacre, Sand Creek, CO (2000) 12,583. Site where over 100 Cheyenne and Arapaho Indians were killed by U.S. soldiers in 1864.

San Juan, PR (1949) 75. 16th-cent. Span. fortifications.

Saugus Iron Works, MA (1974) 9. Reconstructed 17th-cent. colonial ironworks.

Springfield Armory, MA (1974) 55. Small-arms manufacturing center for nearly 200 years.

Steamtown, PA (1986) 62. Railyard, roadhouse, repair shops of former Delaware, Lackawanna & Western Railroad.

Theodore Roosevelt Birthplace, New York, NY (1962) 0.11. Reconstructed brownstone.

Theodore Roosevelt Inaugural, Buffalo, NY (1966) 1. Wilcox House where he took oath of office, 1901.

Thomas Stone, MD (1978) 328. Home of signer of Declaration of Independence, built in 1771.

Tuskegee Airmen, AL (1998) 90. Airfield where pilots of all-black air corps unit of WWII received flight training.

Tuskegee Institute, AL (1974) 58. College founded by Booker T. Washington in 1881 for blacks.

Ulysses S. Grant, St. Louis Co., MO (1989) 10. Home of Grant during pre-Civil War years.

Vanderbilt Mansion, Hyde Park, NY (1940) 212. Mansion of 19th-cent. financier.

Washita Battlefield, OK (1996) 315. Scene of Nov. 27, 1868, battle between Plains tribes and the U.S. army.

Weir Farm, Wilton, CT (1990) 74. Home and studio of American impressionist painter J. Alden Weir.

Whitman Mission, WA (1936/1963) 139. Mission site of Marcus and Narcissa Whitman.

William Howard Taft, Cincinnati, OH (1969) 3. Birthplace and early home of the 27th president.

NATIONAL MONUMENTS

Name	State	Year[1]	Acreage
Agate Fossil Beds	NE	1965	3,055
Alibates Flint Quarries	TX	1965	1,371
Aniakchak[2]	AK	1978	137,176
Aztec Ruins	NM	1923	318
Bandelier	NM	1916	33,677
Booker T. Washington	VA	1956	239
Buck Island Reef	VI	1961	19,015
Cabrillo	CA	1913	160
Canyon de Chelly	AZ	1931	83,840
Cape Krusenstern[3]	AK	1978	649,085
Capulin Volcano	NM	1916	793
Casa Grande Ruins	AZ	1889	473
Castillo de San Marcos	FL	1924	20
Castle Clinton	NY	1946	1
Cedar Breaks	UT	1933	6,155
Chiricahua	AZ	1924	11,985
Colorado	CO	1911	20,534
Craters of the Moon National Monument and Preserve	ID	1924	714,727
Devils Postpile	CA	1911	798

Name	State	Year[1]	Acreage
Devils Tower	WY	1906	1,347
Dinosaur	CO-UT	1915	210,278
Effigy Mounds	IA	1949	2,526
El Malpais	NM	1987	114,277
El Morro	NM	1906	1,279
Florissant Fossil Beds	CO	1969	5,998
Fort Frederica	GA	1936	241
Fort Matanzas	FL	1924	300
Fort McHenry National Monument and Historic Shrine	MD	1925	43
Fort Pulaski	GA	1924	5,623
Fort Stanwix	NY	1935	16
Fort Sumter	SC	1948	200
Fort Union	NM	1954	721
Fossil Butte	WY	1972	8,198
George Washington Birthplace	VA	1930	662
George Washington Carver	MO	1943	210
Gila Cliff Dwellings	NM	1907	533
Governors Island	NY	2001	23
Grand Portage	MN	1951	710
Great Sand Dunes National Monument and Preserve	CO	2000	84,670
Hagerman Fossil Beds[3]	ID	1988	4,351
Hohokam Pima[4]	AZ	1972	1,690
Homestead National Monument of America	NE	1936	211
Hovenweep	CO-UT	1923	785
Jewel Cave	SD	1908	1,274
John Day Fossil Beds	OR	1974	13,944
Lava Beds	CA	1925	46,560
Little Big Horn Battlefield	MT	1879	765
Minidoka Internment [2]	ID	2001	73
Montezuma Castle	AZ	1906	858
Muir Woods	CA	1908	554
Natural Bridges	UT	1908	7,636
Navajo	AZ	1909	360
Ocmulgee	GA	1934	702
Oregon Caves	OR	1909	488
Organ Pipe Cactus	AZ	1937	330,689
Petroglyph	NM	1990	7,232
Pinnacles	CA	1908	24,514
Pipe Spring	AZ	1923	40
Pipestone	MN	1937	282
Poverty Point[2]	LA	1988	911
Rainbow Bridge[3]	UT	1910	160
Russell Cave	AL	1961	310
Salinas Pueblo Missions	NM	1909	1,071
Scotts Bluff	NE	1919	3,005
Statue of Liberty	NJ-NY	1924	58
Sunset Crater Volcano	AZ	1930	3,040
Timpanogos Cave	UT	1922	250
Tonto	AZ	1907	1,120
Tuzigoot	AZ	1939	812
Virgin Islands Coral Reef	VI	2001	13,893
Walnut Canyon	AZ	1915	3,579
White Sands	NM	1933	143,733
Wupatki	AZ	1924	35,422
Yucca House[4]	CO	1919	34

NATIONAL PRESERVES

Name	State	Year[1]	Acreage
Aniakchak	AK	1978	464,118
Bering Land Bridge	AK	1978	2,697,393
Big Cypress	FL	1974	720,567
Big Thicket	TX	1974	97,205
Denali	AK	1917	1,334,118
Gates of the Arctic	AK	1978	948,608
Glacier Bay	AK	1925	58,406
Katmai	AK	1918	418,699
Lake Clark	AK	1978	1,410,292
Little River Canyon[2]	AL	1992	13,633
Mojave	CA	1994	1,534,819
Noatak	AK	1978	6,569,904
Tallgrass Prairie	KS	1996	10,894
Timucuan Ecological & Historic Preserve[3]	FL	1988	46,287
Wrangell-St. Elias	AK	1978	4,852,753
Yukon-Charley Rivers[3]	AK	1978	2,526,512

NATIONAL SEASHORES

Name	State	Year[1]	Acreage
Assateague Island	MD-VA	1965	39,727
Canaveral	FL	1975	57,662
Cape Cod	MA	1961	43,608
Cape Hatteras	NC	1937	30,351
Cape Lookout	NC	1966	28,243
Cumberland Island	GA	1972	36,415
Fire Island	NY	1964	19,578
Gulf Islands	FL-MS	1971	137,991
Padre Island	TX	1962	130,434
Point Reyes	CA	1962	71,068

NATIONAL PARKWAYS

Name	State	Year[1]	Acreage
Blue Ridge	NC-VA	1933	93,390
George Washington Memorial	VA-MD-DC	1930	7,193
John D. Rockefeller Jr. Mem.	WY	1972	23,777
Natchez Trace	MS-AL-TN	1938	51,982

NATIONAL LAKESHORES

Name	State	Year[1]	Acreage
Apostle Islands	WI	1970	69,372
Indiana Dunes	IN	1966	15,067
Pictured Rocks	MI	1966	73,236
Sleeping Bear Dunes	MI	1970	71,198

NATIONAL RESERVES

Name	State	Year[1]	Acreage
City of Rocks[3]	ID	1988	14,107
Ebey's Landing[3]	WA	1978	19,324

NATIONAL RIVERS

Name	State	Year[1]	Acreage
Big South Fork Natl. R and Recreation Area	KY-TN	1976	125,310
Buffalo	AR	1972	94,293
Mississippi Natl. R and Recreation Area	MN	1988	53,775
New River Gorge	WV	1978	72,189
Niobrara	NE-SD	1991	23,074
Ozark	MO	1964	80,785

NATIONAL WILD AND SCENIC RIVERS

Name	State	Year[1]	Acreage
Alagnak	AK	1980	30,665
Bluestone[2]	WV	1978	4,310
Delaware	NY-NJ-PA	1978	1,973
Great Egg Harbor	NJ	1992	43,311
Missouri	NE-SD	1991	34,159
Obed	TN	1976	5,174
Rio Grande[2]	TX	1978	9,600
Saint Croix	MN-WI	1968	67,459
Upper Delaware	NY-PA	1978	75,000

NATIONAL RECREATION AREAS

Name	State	Year[1]	Acreage
Amistad	TX	1965	58,500
Bighorn Canyon	MT-WY	1966	120,296
Boston Harbor Islands	MA	1996	1,482
Chattahoochee R.	GA	1978	9,271
Chickasaw	OK	1902	9,889
Curecanti	CO	1965	41,972
Delaware Water Gap	NJ-PA	1965	66,740
Gateway	NJ-NY	1972	26,607
Gauley R.[3]	WV	1988	11,507
Glen Canyon	AZ-UT	1958	1,254,429
Golden Gate	CA	1972	74,820
Lake Chelan	WA	1968	61,947
Lake Mead	AZ-NV	1936	1,495,664
Lake Meredith	TX	1965	44,978
Lake Roosevelt[5]	WA	1946	100,390
Ross Lake	WA	1968	117,575
Santa Monica Mts.[3]	CA	1978	154,095
Whiskeytown-Shasta-Trinity	CA	1965	42,503

NATIONAL SCENIC TRAIL

Name	State	Year[1]	Acreage
Appalachian	ME to GA	1968	227,001
Natchez Trace	MS-TN	1983	10,995
Potomac Heritage	MD-DC-VA-PA	1983	NA

PARKS (no other classification)

Name	State	Year[1]	Acreage
Catoctin Mountain	MD	1954	5,810
Constitution Gardens	DC	1974	52
Fort Washington	MD	1930	341
Greenbelt	MD	1950	1,176
National Capital	DC	1933	6,631
National Mall	DC	1933	146
Piscataway	MD	1961	4,695
Prince William Forest	VA	1948	19,377
Rock Creek	DC	1890	1,755
White House	DC	1933	18
Wolf Trap Farm Park for the Performing Arts	VA	1966	130

INTERNATIONAL HISTORIC SITE

Name	State	Year[1]	Acreage
Saint Croix Island[3]	ME	1949	45

NA=Not available. (1) Year first designated. (2) No federal facilities. (3) Limited federal facilities. (4) Not open to the public. (5) Formerly Coulee Dam National Recreation Area.

UNITED STATES HISTORY

This chapter includes the following sections:

Chronology of Events

1492

Christopher Columbus and crew sighted land Oct. 12 in present-day Bahamas.

1497

John Cabot explored northeast coast to Delaware.

1513

Juan Ponce de León explored Florida coast.

1524

Giovanni da Verrazano led French expedition along coast from Carolina north to Nova Scotia; entered New York harbor.

1526

San Miguel de Guadalupe, **first European settlement** in what became U.S. territory, was established in the summer off S. Carolina coast; abandoned in Oct.

1539

Hernando de Soto landed in Florida May 28; crossed Mississippi River, **1541.**

1540

Francisco Vásquez de Coronado explored Southwest north of Rio Grande. Hernando de Alarcón reached Colorado River; Don Garcia Lopez de Cardenas reached Grand Canyon. Others explored California coast.

1562

First French colony in what became U.S. territory was founded on Parris Island off S. Carolina coast; abandoned, **1564.**

1565

St. Augustine, FL, founded Sept. 8 by Pedro Menéndez. Razed by Francis Drake, **1586.**

1579

Francis Drake entered San Francisco Bay and claimed region for Britain.

1585

"Lost colony" sponsored by **Sir Walter Raleigh** was founded on **Roanoke Island**, off N. Carolina coast; settlers found to have vanished, **1590.**

1587

Virginia Dare (on Roanoke Island) became first infant born in the Thirteen Colonies of English parents.

1607

Capt. John Smith and 105 cavaliers in 3 ships landed on Virginia coast, started first permanent English settlement in New World at **Jamestown.**

1609

Henry Hudson, English explorer of Northwest Passage, employed by Dutch, sailed into New York Harbor in Sept., and up Hudson to Albany. **Samuel de Champlain** explored Lake Champlain, to the north.

Spaniards settled **Santa Fe, NM.**

1619

House of Burgesses, first representative assembly in New World, elected July 30 at Jamestown, VA.

First black laborers—indentured servants—in English N. American colonies, landed by Dutch at Jamestown in Aug. Chattel slavery legally recognized, **1650.**

1620

Pilgrims, Puritan separatists, left Plymouth, England, Sept. 16 on *Mayflower;* reached Cape Cod Nov. 19; 103 passengers landed Dec. 26 at Plymouth. **Mayflower Compact**, signed Nov. 11, was agreement to form a self-government. Half of colony died during harsh winter.

1624

Dutch colonies started in Albany and in New York area, where **New Netherland** was established in May.

1626

Peter Minuit bought **Manhattan** for Dutch West India Co. from Man-a-hat-a Indians during summer for goods valued at $24; named island **New Amsterdam.**

1630

Settlement of **Boston** established by Massachusetts colonists led by **John Winthrop**.

William Bradford began his chronicle *History of the Plymouth Plantation*; in the Mass. Bay Colony **John Winthrop** began *The History of New England.*

1634

Maryland founded as Catholic colony under charter to Lord Baltimore. Religious toleration granted **1649.**

1635

Boston Latin School, oldest U.S. public school in continuous existence, founded Apr. 23.

1636

Roger Williams founded Providence, RI, in June, as a democratically ruled colony with separation of church and state. Charter granted, **1644.**

Harvard College founded; oldest institution of higher learning in U.S.

1640

First book was printed in America, the so-called Bay Psalm Book.

1647

Liberal constitution drafted in Rhode Island.

First law in America providing for **free compulsory basic education** enacted in Massachusetts.

1660

British Parliament passed First **Navigation Act** Dec. 1, regulating colonial commerce to suit English needs.

1661

A version of the New Testament translated into Algonquian became the **first Bible** printed in the colonies.

1664

British troops **Sept. 8 seized New Netherland** from Dutch. Charles II granted New Netherland and city of New Amsterdam to brother, Duke of York; both renamed **New York.** Dutch recaptured colony **1673,** but ceded it to Britain Nov. 10, **1674.**

1670

Charles Town, South Carolina, was founded by English colonists in Apr.

1673

Jacques **Marquette** and Louis **Jolliet** reached the upper **Mississippi** and traveled down it.

Regular **mail service** on horseback was instituted Jan. 1 between New York and Boston.

1674

Future **Salem witch trial** judge Samuel Sewall began a renowned diary covering events through 1729.

1676

Nathaniel Bacon led planters against autocratic British Gov. Sir William Berkeley, burned Jamestown, VA, Sept. 19. Rebellion collapsed when Bacon died; 23 followers executed.

Bloody **Indian war** in New England ended Aug. 12. **King Philip,** Wampanoag chief, and Narragansett Indians killed.

1678

A book of poetry by **Anne Bradstreet** was published posthumously in Massachusetts.

1679

A **fire** destroyed 150 houses in **Boston**.

1681

John Bunyan's *The Pilgrim's Progress* published in America; became a best-seller.

1682

Robert Cavelier, Sieur de La Salle, claimed lower Mississippi River country for France, called it Louisiana Apr. 9. Had French outposts built in Illinois and Texas, **1684.** Killed during mutiny, **1687.**

William Penn arrived in **Pennsylvania.**

Spanish colonists became the **first Europeans** to settle in **Texas**, at the site of present-day El Paso.

1683

William Penn signed treaty with Delaware Indians Apr. 23, and made payment for Pennsylvania lands. The **first German colonists** in America settled near Philadelphia.

1689

New York's English colonial governor, **Sir Edmund Andros**, resigned after an armed uprising in **Boston** on Apr. 18.

1690

The **New England Primer** came into use in elementary schools.

The **first colonial newspaper**, *Publick Occurrences*, was published by Benjamin Harris, but promptly shut down for lack of official permission.

Whaling began large-scale operations in Nantucket.

1692

Witchcraft delusion at Salem, MA; 20 alleged witches executed by special court.

1696

Capt. William Kidd arrested and sent to England; hanged for piracy, **1701.**

1697

The Essays of Sir Francis Bacon, published in England in 1597, was published in America; it became a best-seller.

1699

French settlements made in Mississippi, Louisiana.

1702

Legislation enacted making the Church of England the **established church** in Maryland.

1704

Indians attacked Deerfield, MA, Feb. 28-29; killed 40, carried off 100.

Boston News Letter, **first regular newspaper,** started by John Campbell, postmaster.

1709

British-colonial troops captured French fort, Port Royal, Nova Scotia, in **Queen Anne's War 1701-13.** France yielded Nova Scotia by treaty, **1713.**

1712

Slaves revolted in New York Apr. 6; 21 were executed. Second rising, **1741;** 13 slaves hanged, 13 burned, 71 deported.

1716

First theater in colonies opened in Williamsburg, VA.

1726

Poor people **rioted** in Philadelphia.

Great Awakening religious revival began.

1731

America's **first circulating library** founded in Philadelphia by Benjamin Franklin.

1732

Benjamin Franklin published the first ***Poor Richard's Almanack;*** published annually to **1757.**

Last of the 13 colonies, **Georgia,** chartered.

1733

Influenza epidemic swept through New York City and Philadelphia.

1735

Editor **John Peter Zenger acquitted** Aug. 5 in New York of libeling British governor by criticizing his conduct in office.

1739

A series of **slave uprisings** put down in South Carolina.

1741

Famous sermon "Sinners in the Hands of an Angry God," delivered at Enfield, MA, July 8, by **Jonathan Edwards**, a major figure in the revivalist **Great Awakening**.

Capt. Vitus Bering reached Alaska.

1744

King George's War pitted British and colonials vs. French. Colonials captured Louisburg, Cape Breton Is., June 17, **1745**. Returned to France **1748** by Treaty of Aix-la-Chapelle.

1752

Benjamin Franklin, flying kite in thunderstorm, proved lightning is electricity June 15; invented lightning rod.

Liberty Bell, cast in England, was delivered to Pennsylvania.

1754

Delegates from 7 colonies to **Albany**, NY, **Congress**, July 19, approved a "Plan of Union" by Benjamin Franklin; but plan was rejected by the colonies.

French and Indian War began when French occupied Ft. Duquesne (Pittsburgh). British moved Acadian French from Nova Scotia to Louisiana Oct. 8, **1755.** British captured Québec Sept. 18, **1759**, in battles in which French Gen. Joseph de Montcalm and British Gen. James Wolfe were killed. Peace pact signed Feb. 10, **1763.** French lost Canada and Midwest.

1757

The first **street lights** appeared in Philadelphia.

1764

Sugar Act, Apr. 5, placed duties on lumber, foodstuffs, molasses, and rum in colonies, to pay French and Indian War debts.

1765

Stamp Act, enacted by Parliament Mar. 22, required revenue stamps to help fund royal troops. Nine colonies, at **Stamp Act Congress** in New York Oct. 7-25, adopted Declaration of Rights. Stamp Act **repealed** Mar. 17, **1766.**

Quartering Act, requiring colonists to house British troops, went into effect Mar. 24.

1767

Townshend Acts levied taxes on glass, painter's lead, paper, and tea. In **1770** all duties except on tea were repealed.

1770

British troops fired Mar. 5 into Boston mob, killed 5 including **Crispus Attucks,** a black man, reportedly leader of group; later called **Boston Massacre.**

1773

East India Co. tea ships turned back at Boston, New York, and Philadelphia in May. Cargo ship burned at Annapolis Oct. 14; cargo thrown overboard at **Boston Tea Party** Dec. 16, to protest the tea tax.

First museum in the colonies was officially established in Charleston, SC; later named the **Charleston** Museum.

1774

"Intolerable Acts" of Parliament curtailed Massachusetts self-rule; barred use of Boston harbor till tea was paid for.

First Continental Congress held in Philadelphia Sept. 5-Oct. 26; called for civil disobedience against British.

Rhode Island abolished slavery.

1775

Patrick Henry addressed Virginia convention, Mar. 23, said, "Give me liberty or give me death."

Paul Revere and William Dawes Apr. 18 rode to alert Patriots that British were on their way to Concord to destroy arms. At **Lexington**, MA, Apr. 19, Minutemen lost 8. On return from **Concord**, British took 273 casualties.

Col. Ethan Allen (joined by Col. Benedict Arnold) captured **Ft. Ticonderoga, NY,** May 10; also Crown Point. Colonials headed for **Bunker Hill,** fortified Breed's Hill, Charlestown, MA. Repulsed British under Gen. William Howe twice before retreating June 17.

Continental Congress June 15 named **George Washington** commander in chief. Established a postal system, July 26; **Benjamin Franklin** became the first postmaster general.

1776

Common Sense, famous pro-independence pamphlet by Thomas Paine, was published Jan. 10; quickly sold some 100,000 copies.

France and Spain each agreed May 2 to provide arms.

In Continental Congress June 7, Richard Henry Lee (VA) moved "that these united colonies are and of right ought to be free and independent states." Resolution adopted July 2. **Declaration of Independence** approved July 4.

Col. William Moultrie's batteries at **Charleston, SC,** repulsed British sea attack June 28. Washington lost **Battle of Long Island** Aug. 27; evacuated New York.

Nathan Hale executed as spy by British Sept. 22.

Brig. Gen. Arnold's **Lake Champlain** fleet was defeated at Valcour Oct. 11, but British returned to Canada. Howe failed to destroy Washington's army at White Plains Oct. 28. Hessians captured Ft. Washington, Manhattan, and 3,000 men Nov. 16; captured Ft. Lee, NJ, Nov. 18.

Washington, in Pennsylvania, recrossed **Delaware River** Dec. 25-26, defeated Hessians at Trenton, NJ, Dec. 26.

1777

Washington defeated Lord Cornwallis at **Princeton** Jan. 3.

Continental Congress, June 14, authorized an **American flag**, the Stars and Stripes.

Maj. Gen. John Burgoyne's force of 8,000 from Canada, captured **Ft. Ticonderoga** July 6. Americans beat back Burgoyne at Bemis Heights Oct. 7, cut off British escape route. Burgoyne surrendered 5,000 men at **Saratoga,** NY, Oct. 17.

Articles of Confederation adopted by Continental Congress Nov. 15.

1778

France signed treaty of aid with U.S. Feb. 6. Sent fleet; British evacuated Philadelphia in consequence, June 18.

1779

George Rogers Clark took Vincennes in **Feb.**

John Paul Jones on the *Bonhomme Richard* defeated *Serapis* in British North Sea waters, Sept. 23.

1780

Charleston, SC, fell to the British May 12, but a British force was defeated near **Kings Mountain, NC,** Oct. 7 by militiamen.

Benedict Arnold found to be a traitor Sept. 23. Arnold escaped, made brigadier general in British army.

1781

Articles of Confederation took effect Mar. 1.

Bank of North America incorporated May 26.

Cornwallis retired to **Yorktown, VA.** Adm. Francois Joseph de Grasse landed 3,000 French and stopped British fleet in **Hampton Roads.** Washington and Jean Baptiste de Rochambeau joined forces, arrived near Williamsburg Sept. 26. Siege of Cornwallis began Oct. 6; **Cornwallis surrendered** Oct. 19.

1782

New **British** cabinet agreed in March to **recognize U.S.** independence. Preliminary agreement signed in Paris Nov. 30.

Use of the **scarlet letter A**, sewn on clothing or branded on skin of adulterers, was **discontinued** in New England.

1783

Massachusetts Supreme Court declared **slavery** illegal in that state.

Britain, U.S. signed **Paris peace treaty** Sept. 3 recognizing American independence (Congress ratified it Jan. 14, **1784**).

Washington ordered army disbanded Nov. 3, bade farewell to his officers at **Fraunces Tavern,** New York City, Dec. 4.

First regular daily newspaper, *Pennsylvania Evening Post,* went on sale in Philadelphia, May 30.

Noah Webster published *American Spelling Book.*

1784

Thomas Jefferson's proposal to **ban slavery** in new territory after 1802 was narrowly defeated Mar. 1.

First successful daily newspaper, ***Pennsylvania Packet & General Advertiser***, published Sept. 21.

1785

Regular **stagecoach routes** established between Albany, New York City, and Philadelphia.

1786

Delegates from 5 states at **Annapolis, MD,** Sept. 11-14 asked Congress to call a constitutional convention.

1787

Shays's Rebellion of debt-ridden farmers in Massachusetts failed Jan. 25.

Northwest Ordinance adopted July 13 by Continental Congress for Northwest Territory, N of Ohio River, W of New York; made rules for statehood. Guaranteed freedom of religion, support for schools, no slavery.

Constitutional convention opened at Philadelphia May 25, with Washington presiding. Constitution accepted by delegates Sept. 17; **Delaware** became 1st state to ratify it, Dec. 7; **Pennsylvania** and **New Jersey** followed. Ratification by 9th state, New Hampshire, June 21, **1788,** meant adoption; declared in effect Mar. 4, **1789.**

Federalist Papers first appeared in *NY Independent Journal.*

1788

A large fire in New Orleans, then a Spanish territory, destroyed much of the city Mar. 21.

The **Constitution was adopted** June 21 after being ratified by the requisite 9th state (New Hampshire); also ratified by **Georgia, Connecticut, Massachusetts, Maryland, S. Carolina, Virginia,** and **New York** throughout the year.

First U.S. senators elected Sept. 30, from Pennsylvania.

Settlers founded future cities Cincinnati, OH; Dubuque, IA; and Charleston, WV.

1789

George Washington chosen president by all electors voting (73 eligible, 69 voting, 4 absent); **John Adams, vice president**, got 34 votes. **First Congress** met at Federal Hall, New York City, and declared Constitution in effect, Mar. 4; Washington **inaugurated** there Apr. 30; first inaugural ball held May 7.

Tammany Hall founded as benevolent organization, May 12.

U.S. **State Dept**. established by Congress July 27. (Thomas **Jefferson** installed as first secretary of state Feb. **1790**.) **War Dept**. created, Aug. 7, with Henry **Knox** to be secretary; **Treasury Dept.** created Sept. 2, with Alexander **Hamilton** to be secretary.

Supreme Court created by Federal Judiciary Act, Sept. 24; **John Jay** confirmed by Congress as first Supreme Court **chief justice,** Sept. 26. Congress submitted **Bill of Rights** to states, Sept. 25.

1790

Congress, Mar. 1, authorized decennial **U.S. census; Naturalization Act** (2-year residency) passed Mar. 26.

John Carroll consecrated as **1st American Catholic bishop**, Aug. 15.

Congress met in **Philadelphia**, new temporary capital, Dec. 6.

1791

Bill of Rights went into effect Dec. 15.

1792

Coinage Act established **U.S. Mint** in Philadelphia Apr. 2.

Gen. **"Mad" Anthony Wayne** made commander in Ohio-Indiana area, trained "American Legion," established string of forts. Routed Indians at Fallen Timbers on Maumee River Aug. 20, **1794,** checked British at Fort Miami, OH.

White House cornerstone laid Oct. 13.

1793

Washington inaugurated for 2nd term, Mar. 4, having received 132 electoral votes; John **Adams** again became vice president, having received the 2nd highest total, 77.

Washington declared **U.S. neutrality**, Apr. 22, in war between Britain and France.

Eli Whitney invented **cotton gin,** reviving Southern slavery.

1794

Whiskey Rebellion, W Pennsylvania farmers protesting liquor tax of **1791,** suppressed by federal militia in Sept.

Jay's controversial **treaty** with Britain signed Nov. 19, ratified June 24, **1795.**

1795

U.S. bought peace from **Algerian pirates** by paying $1 mil ransom for 115 seamen Sept. 5, followed by annual tributes.

Gen. Wayne signed peace with Indians at Fort Greenville.

University of North Carolina became first operating state university.

1796

Washington's Farewell Address as president delivered Sept. 17. Warned against permanent alliances with foreign powers, big public debt, large military establishment, and devices of "small, artful, enterprising minority."

1797

U.S. **frigate *United States*** launched at Philadelphia July 10; ***Constellation*** at Baltimore Sept. 7; ***Constitution*** (Old Ironsides) at Boston Sept. 20.

John Adams inaugurated as 2nd president Mar. 4, after having received 71 electoral votes; **Thomas Jefferson** became vice president having received 68.

1798

Alien & Sedition Acts passed by Federalists June-July; intended to silence political opposition.

War with France threatened over French raids on U.S. shipping and rejection of U.S. diplomats. Navy (45 ships) and 365 privateers captured 84 French ships. USS *Constellation* took French warship *Insurgente,* **1799.** Napoleon stopped French raids after becoming First Consul.

1799

Washington died at Mount Vernon Dec. 14.

1800

Federal government moved to **Washington, DC.**

1801

John Marshall named Supreme Court chief justice, Jan. 20.

Thomas Jefferson, who had received same number of electoral votes as Aaron Burr in 1800 election, won out over Burr in **House** vote reached Feb. 17; Burr named vice president.

Tripoli declared war June 10 against U.S., which refused added tribute to commerce-raiding Arab corsairs. Land and naval campaigns forced Tripoli to negotiate **peace** June 4, **1805.**

Oldest U.S. art institution, Pennsylvania Academy of Fine Arts, founded.

1802

Congress established the U.S. Military Academy at **West Point**, N.Y.

1803

Supreme Court, in ***Marbury v Madison*** case, for the first time overturned a U.S. law Feb. 24.

Napoleon sold all of **Louisiana,** stretching to Canadian border, to U.S., for $11,250,000 in bonds, plus $3,750,000 indemnities to American citizens with claims against France. U.S. took title Dec. 20. Purchase doubled U.S. area.

1804

Lewis and Clark expedition ordered by Pres. Thomas Jefferson to explore what is now northwest U.S. Started from St. Louis May 14; ended Sept. 23, **1806.**

Vice Pres. **Aaron Burr shot Alexander Hamilton** in a duel July 11 in Weehawken, NJ; Hamilton died next day.

1805

U.S. Marines aided by Arab mercenaries, Apr. 27, captured Tripolitan port of Derna, major victory in war against **Barbary pirates;** inspiration for "to the shores of Tripoli" in Marines Corps song.

1807

Robert Fulton made first practical steamboat trip; left New York City Aug. 17, reached Albany, 150 mi, in 32 hr.

Embargo Act banned all trade with foreign countries, forbidding ships to set sail for foreign ports Dec. 22.

1808

Slave importation outlawed. Some 250,000 slaves were illegally imported **1808-60.**

1810

Third U.S. Census found a population of 7,239,881. The black population was put at 1,378,110, of whom 186,746 were free citizens.

1811

William Henry Harrison, governor of Indiana, defeated Indians under the Prophet, in battle of **Tippecanoe** Nov. 7.

Cumberland Road begun at Cumberland, MD; became important route to West.

About 400 **slaves revolted** in Louisiana, killing the son of a plantation owner and marching on **New Orleans.** The insurrection was suppressed; some 75 slaves killed.

1812

War of 1812 had 3 main causes: Britain seized U.S. ships trading with France; Britain seized 4,000 naturalized U.S. sailors by **1810;** Britain armed Indians who raided western border. U.S. stopped trade with Europe **1807** and **1809.** Trade with Britain only was stopped **1810.**

Unaware that Britain had raised the blockade against France 2 days before, **Congress declared war** June 18.

USS *Essex* captured *Alert* Aug. 13; USS *Constitution* destroyed *Guerriere* Aug. 19; USS *Wasp* took *Frolic* Oct. 18; USS *United States* defeated *Macedonian* off Azores Oct. 25; USS *Constitution* beat *Java* Dec. 29. British took Detroit Aug. 16.

1813

Oliver H. Perry defeated British fleet at **Battle of Lake Erie,** Sept. 10. U.S. won Battle of the Thames, Ontario, Oct. 5, but failed in Canadian invasion attempts. York (Toronto) and Buffalo were burned.

1814

British landed in Maryland in Aug., defeated U.S. force Aug. 24, **burned Capitol and White House.** Maryland militia stopped British advance Sept. 12. Bombardment of Ft. McHenry, Baltimore, for 25 hours, Sept. 13-14, by British fleet failed; Francis Scott Key wrote words to **"The Star-Spangled Banner."**

Troops under Andrew Jackson defeated Creek Indians led by Chief Weatherford at **Battle of Horshoe Bend in Alabama**, Mar. 29, ending Creek Indian War (1813-14).

U.S. won naval **Battle of Lake Champlain** Sept. 11. Peace treaty with Great Britain signed at Ghent Dec. 24.

1815

Some 5,300 British, unaware of peace treaty, attacked U.S. entrenchments near **New Orleans,** Jan. 8. British had more than 2,000 casualties; Americans lost 71.

U.S. flotilla finally ended piracy by **Algiers, Tunis, Tripoli** by Aug. 6.

1816

Second **Bank of the U.S.** chartered Apr. 10.

The **American Colonization Society**, which sought to address slavery issue by transporting freed blacks to Africa, formed in Washington, DC, Dec. **1816**-Jan. **1817**.

1817

William Cullen Bryant's poem **"Thanatopsis"** published.

Thomas Hopkins Gallaudet established the **first free public school for the deaf** in Hartford, CT.

1818

Connecticut **expanded suffrage among white male voters**. Massachusetts followed suit in 1820, and New York in 1821, reducing or eliminating property qualifications.

1819

Spain ceded **Florida** to U.S. Feb. 22.

American steamship ***Savannah*** made first part-steam-powered, part-sail-powered crossing of Atlantic: Savannah, GA, to Liverpool, England, 29 days.

Washington Irving's *Sketch Book* became a best-seller.

1820

First organized **immigration of blacks to Africa** from U.S. began with 86 free blacks sailing Feb. to Sierra Leone.

Henry Clay's **Missouri Compromise** bill passed by Congress Mar. 3. Slavery was allowed in Missouri, but not elsewhere west of the Mississippi River north of 36°30′ latitude (the southern line of Missouri). Repealed **1854.**

1821

Emma Willard founded Troy Female Seminary, first U.S. women's college.

Stephen Austin established the **first American community in Texas**, San Felipe de Austin.

The Spy, a novel by James Fenimore Cooper set during the American Revolution, was published and became a best-seller.

1822

Tension between sports and academics surfaced when Yale College Pres. Timothy Dwight **banned a primitive form of football,** setting fines for violators.

1823

Monroe Doctrine, opposing European intervention in the Americas, enunciated by Pres. James Monroe Dec. 2. The **Hudson River School**, painters who focused on the beauties of nature, began to come to public attention.

1824

Pawtucket, RI, **weavers strike,** first such action by women.

Slavery abolished in the state of Illinois Aug. 2.

1825

After a deadlocked election, **John Quincy Adams** was elected president by the U.S. House, Feb. 9.

Erie Canal opened; first boat left Buffalo Oct. 26, reached New York City Nov. 4.

John Stevens, of Hoboken, NJ, built and operated first experimental **steam locomotive** in U.S.

1826

Thomas **Jefferson** and John **Adams** both died July 4.

James Fenimore Cooper's *The Last of the Mohicans* published.

1827

Massachusetts passed a law providing for **tax-supported public high schools**, the first state to do so.

1828

South Carolina Dec. 19 declared the right of state **nullification of federal laws,** opposing the "Tariff of Abominations."

Noah Webster published his *American Dictionary of the English Language.*

Baltimore & Ohio, the first U.S. passenger railroad, begun July 4.

1829

Andrew Jackson inaugurated as president, Mar. 4.

1830

Famous **debate** Jan. 27 between Sen. **Daniel Webster** (MA) and Robert Hayne (SC), on state right to nullify federal law.

Mormon church organized by Joseph Smith in Fayette, NY, Apr. 6.

Pres. Jackson, May 28, signed **Indian Removal Act,** providing land and some pay to Indians agreeing to resettle in West.

1831

William Lloyd Garrison began **abolitionist newspaper** *The Liberator* Jan. 1.

Nat Turner, black slave in Virginia, led local **slave rebellion,** starting Aug. 21; 57 whites killed. Troops called in, 100 slaves killed, Turner captured, tried, hanged Nov. 11.

1832

Black Hawk War (IL-WI) Apr.-Sept. pushed Sauk and Fox Indians west across Mississippi.

1833

American Anti-Slavery Society founded in Philadelphia, Dec. 4.

Oberlin College became first in U.S. to adopt coeducation.

1835

Liberty Bell cracked July 8, tolling death of Chief Justice **John Marshall**.

Seminole Indians in Florida under Osceola began attacks Nov. 1, protesting forced removal. The unpopular war ended Aug. 14, **1842;** most of the Indians were sent to Oklahoma.

Texas proclaimed right to secede from Mexico; Sam Houston put in command of Texas army, Nov. 2-4.

Gold discovered on **Cherokee land** in Georgia. Indians forced to cede lands, Dec. 20, and to cross Mississippi.

1836

Texans besieged at Alamo in San Antonio by Mexicans under Santa Anna, Feb. 23-Mar. 6; entire garrison killed. Texas independence declared, Mar. 2. At San Jacinto Apr. 21, Sam Houston and Texans defeated Mexicans.

Ralph Waldo Emerson published his first work, *Nature,* espousing his philosophy of **transcendentalism**.

Marcus Whitman, H. H. Spaulding, and wives reached Fort Walla Walla on Columbia River, OR. **First white women to cross plains.**

1838

Cherokee Indians made **"Trail of Tears"** as they were removed from Georgia to Oklahoma starting Oct.

1841

First emigrant **wagon train for California,** 47 persons, left Independence, MO, May 1, reached California Nov. 4.

Edgar Allan Poe published one of the first American detective stories, *The Murders in the Rue Morgue.*

Brook Farm commune set up by New England Transcendentalist intellectuals. Lasted to **1846.**

1842

Webster-Ashburton Treaty signed Aug. 9, fixing the U.S.-Canada border in Maine and Minnesota.

First use of **anesthetic** (sulfuric ether gas).

Settlement of Oregon began via **Oregon Trail.**

1843

More than 1,000 settlers left Independence, MO, for **Oregon** May 22, arrived Oct.

1844

First message over first **telegraph line** sent May 24 by inventor Samuel F.B. Morse from Washington to Baltimore: "What hath God wrought!"

1845

Congress **overrode a presidential veto** for the first time, Mar. 3, after Pres. John Tyler vetoed a tariff bill.

Texas Congress **voted for annexation** by U.S., July 4. U.S. Congress admitted Texas to Union, Dec. 29.

Edgar Allan Poe's poem "The Raven" published.

1846

Mexican War began after Pres. James K. Polk ordered Gen. Zachary Taylor to seize disputed Texan land settled by Mexicans. After border clash, U.S. declared war May 13; Mexico May 23.

Bear flag of **Republic of California** raised by American settlers at Sonoma June 14.

About 12,000 U.S. troops took Vera Cruz Mar. 27, **1847,** and Mexico City Sept. 14, **1847.** By **treaty,** signed Feb. 2, **1848**, war was ended, and Mexico ceded claims to Texas, California, and other territory.

Treaty with Britain June 15 set **boundary in Oregon** territory at 49th parallel (extension of existing line). Expansionists had used slogan "54° 40′ or fight." The term **"manifest destiny,"** coined by a journalist in **1845**, also came into play.

Mormons, after violent clashes with settlers over polygamy, left Nauvoo, IL, for West under Brigham Young; settled July **1847** at **Salt Lake City, UT.**

Elias Howe invented **sewing machine.**

1847

First **adhesive U.S. postage stamps** on sale July 1; Benjamin Franklin 5¢, Washington 10¢.

Ralph Waldo Emerson published first book of poems; **Henry Wadsworth Longfellow** published *Evangeline.*

1848

Gold discovered Jan. 24 in California; 80,000 prospectors emigrated in **1849.**

Lucretia Mott and Elizabeth Cady Stanton led **Seneca Falls, NY, Women's Rights Convention** July 19-20.

1850

Sen. Henry Clay's **Compromise of 1850** admitted California as 31st state Sept. 9, with slavery forbidden; made Utah and New Mexico territories; made Fugitive Slave Law more harsh; ended District of Columbia slave trade.

Nathaniel Hawthorne's *The Scarlet Letter* published.

1851

Herman Melville's *Moby-Dick* published.

1852

Uncle Tom's Cabin, by Harriet Beecher Stowe, published as a book.

1853

Comm. Matthew C. Perry, U.S.N., received by Japan, July 14; negotiated **treaty to open Japan** to U.S. ships.

New York City hosted **first World's Fair** in the U.S., beginning July 14.

Stephen Foster published "My Old Kentucky Home."

1854

Republican Party formed at Ripon, WI, Feb. 28. Opposed Kansas-Nebraska Act (became law May 30), which left issue of slavery to vote of settlers.

Henry David Thoreau published *Walden.*

Treaty ratified with Mexico Apr. 25, providing for purchase of a strip of land **(Gadsden Purchase).**

1855

Walt Whitman published *Leaves of Grass.*

First railroad train crossed **Mississippi River** on the river's first bridge, Rock Island, IL-Davenport, IA, Apr. 21.

1856

Republican Party's first nominee for president, **John C. Fremont,** defeated. Abraham Lincoln made 50 speeches for him.

Lawrence, KS, sacked May 21 by proslavery group; abolitionist **John Brown** led antislavery men against Missourians at **Osawatomie, KS,** Aug. 30.

The **first** U.S. **kindergarten** was opened, in Watertown, WI.

1857

Dred Scott decision by Supreme Court Mar. 6 held that slaves did not become free in a free state, Congress could not bar slavery from a territory, and blacks could not be citizens.

Currier & Ives issued their first print.

1858

First **Atlantic cable** completed, by Cyrus W. Field Aug. 5.

Lincoln-Douglas debates in Illinois, Aug. 21-Oct. 15.

1859

First commercially productive **oil well,** drilled near Titusville, PA, by Edwin L. Drake Aug. 27.

Abolitionist **John Brown,** with 21 men, seized U.S. Armory at **Harpers Ferry** Oct. 16. U.S. Marines captured raiders, killing several. Brown hanged for treason Dec. 2.

1860

Approximately 20,000 **New England shoe workers** went on strike Feb. 22 and won higher wages.

Abraham Lincoln, Republican, elected president Nov. 6 in 4-way race.

First **Pony Express** between Sacramento, CA, and St. Joseph, MO, started Apr. 3.

1861

Seven southern states set up **Confederate States of America** Feb. 8, with Jefferson Davis as president, captured federal arsenals and forts. **Civil War** began as Confederates fired on **Ft. Sumter** in Charleston, SC, Apr. 12, capturing it Apr. 14.

Pres. **Lincoln** called for 75,000 volunteers Apr. 15. By May, 11 states had seceded. Lincoln blockaded Southern ports Apr. 19, cutting off vital exports, aid.

Confederates repelled Union forces at first **Battle of Bull Run,** July 21.

First **transcontinental telegraph line** was put in operation.

1862

Union forces were victorious in Western campaigns, took **New Orleans** May 1. Battles in East were largely inconclusive despite heavy casualties. The Battle of **Antietam,** in western Maryland Sept. 17, was the bloodiest one-day battle of the war; each side lost over 2,000 men.

Homestead Act approved May 20; it granted free farms to settlers.

Land Grant Act approved July 7, providing for public land sale to benefit agricultural education; eventually led to establishment of state university systems.

1863

Pres. Lincoln issued **Emancipation Proclamation** Jan. 1, freeing "all slaves in areas still in rebellion."

Entire **Mississippi River** was in Union hands by July 4. Union forces won a major victory at **Gettysburg, PA,** July 1-3. Lincoln gave his **Gettysburg Address** Nov. 19.

Confederate forces under siege surrendered **Vicksburg** to Union forces under Gen. Ulysses S. Grant, July 4.

In **draft riots** in New York City about 1,000 were killed or wounded; some blacks were hanged by mobs July 13-16.

Pres. Lincoln declared **Thanksgiving** to be a national holiday.

1864

Gen. William Tecumseh **Sherman marched through Georgia,** taking Atlanta Sept. 1, Savannah Dec. 22.

Sand Creek massacre of Cheyenne and Arapaho Indians Nov. 29. Soldiers drove Indians out of village; about 150 killed.

1865

Gen. Robert E. Lee surrendered 27,800 Confederate troops to Gen. Grant at **Appomattox** Court House, VA, Apr. 9. J. E. Johnston surrendered 31,200 to Sherman at Durham Station, NC, Apr. 18. Last rebel troops surrendered May 26.

Pres. Lincoln was shot Apr. 14 by John Wilkes Booth in Ford's Theater, Washington, DC; died the following morning. Vice Pres. **Andrew Johnson** was sworn in as president. Booth was hunted down; fatally wounded, perhaps by his own hand, Apr. 26. Four co-conspirators hanged July 7.

13th Amendment, abolishing slavery, ratified Dec. 6.

1866

Ku Klux Klan formed secretly in South to terrorize blacks who voted. Disbanded **1869-71.** A 2nd Klan organized **1915.**

Congress took control of Southern **Reconstruction,** backed freedmen's rights in legislation vetoed by Johnson; veto overridden by Congress, Apr. 9.

1867

Alaska sold to U.S. by Russia for $7.2 mil Mar. 30, through efforts of Sec. of State William H. Seward.

The **Grange** was organized Dec. 4, to protect farmer interests.

Horatio Alger published first book, *Ragged Dick.*

1868

Pres. **Johnson** tried to remove Edwin M. Stanton, secretary of war; was impeached by House Feb. 24 for violation of Tenure of Office Act; acquitted by Senate Mar.-May.

14th Amendment, providing for citizenship of all persons born or naturalized in U.S., ratified July 9.

Louisa May Alcott published *Little Women.*

The World Almanac, a publication of the *New York World,* appeared for the first time.

1869

Financial **"Black Friday"** in New York Sept. 24; caused by attempt to "corner" gold.

Transcontinental railroad completed; golden spike driven at Promontory, UT, May 10, marking the junction of Central Pacific and Union Pacific.

Knights of Labor formed in Philadelphia. By **1886,** this labor union had 700,000 members nationally.

Woman suffrage law passed in Wyoming Territory Dec. 10.

1870

15th Amendment, making race no bar to voting rights, ratified Feb. 8.

First U.S. boardwalk completed, in Atlantic City, NJ.

U.S. Weather Bureau founded.

1871

Great fire destroyed **Chicago** Oct. 8-11.

National Rifle Association founded.

1872

Amnesty Act restored civil rights to citizens of the South May 22, except for 500 Confederate leaders.

Congress established first national park—**Yellowstone.**

James McNeill Whistler painted famous portrait known informally as **"Whistler's Mother."**

1873

First U.S. **postal card** issued May 1.

Jesse James and his gang robbed their first passenger train July 21.

Banks failed, panic began in Sept. Depression lasted 5 years.

"Boss" William Tweed of New York City convicted Nov. 19 of stealing public funds. He died in jail in **1878.**

New York's Bellevue Hospital started **first nursing school.**

1874

Women's Christian Temperance Union established in Cleveland.

The **first** U.S. public **zoo** was established in Philadelphia.

1875

Congress passed **Civil Rights Act** Mar. 1, giving equal rights to blacks in public accommodations and jury duty. Act invalidated in **1883** by Supreme Court.

First **Jim Crow** segregation law enacted, in Tennessee.

First **Kentucky Derby** held May 17.

1876

Samuel J. Tilden, Democrat, received majority of popular votes for president over **Rutherford B. Hayes,** Republican, but 22 electoral votes were in dispute; issue left to Congress. Congress agreed to certify Hayes as winner in Feb. **1877** after Republicans agreed to end federal Reconstruction of South.

Alexander Graham Bell patented the telephone Mar. 7

Col. **George A. Custer** and 264 soldiers of the 7th Cavalry killed June 25 in "last stand," Battle of the **Little Big Horn,** MT, in Sioux Indian War.

1877

Molly Maguires, Irish terrorist society in Scranton, PA, mining areas, was broken up by the hanging, June 21, of 11 leaders for murders of mine officials and police.

Pres. Rutherford B. Hayes sent troops in violent national **railroad strike.**

1878

First commercial **telephone** exchange opened, New Haven, CT, Jan. 28.

Thomas A. Edison founded **Edison Electric Light Co.** on Oct. 15.

1879

F. W. Woolworth opened his first five-and-ten store, in Utica, NY, Feb. 22.

Henry George published *Progress & Poverty,* advocating single tax on land.

French actress **Sarah Bernhardt** made her U.S. debut Nov. 8 at New York City's Booth Theater.

1880

Chinese Exclusion Treaty signed with China, Nov. 17, providing for restitution of Chinese nationals entering U.S.

Lew Wallace's ***Ben Hur*** published.

1881

Clara Barton May 21 founded the **American Red Cross.**

Pres. **James A. Garfield shot** in Washington, DC, July 2; died Sept. 19.

Famous gun battle between the Earp brothers and outlaw rustlers, Oct. 26 near the **OK Corral**, Tombstone, AZ.

Booker T. Washington founded Tuskegee Institute for blacks.

Helen Hunt Jackson published *A Century of Dishonor*, about mistreatment of Indians.

1882

Chinese Exclusion Act, barring Chinese immigration, passed by Congress May 6.

1883

Pendleton Act passed Jan. 16, reformed civil service.

Northern Pacific Railroad completed, Sept. 8.

Brooklyn Bridge opened May 24.

Buffalo Bill Cody's Wild West Show began its 30-year touring run.

1884

First **long-distance** telephone call completed, Mar. 27, between Boston and New York.

First roller coaster in the U.S. opened at Coney Island in New York City.

Mark Twain's masterpiece, *The Adventures of Huckleberry Finn*, appeared.

1885

Washington Monument dedicated Feb. 21

Postal rates lowered to 2 cents an ounce.

1886

Haymarket riot and bombing, May 4, followed bitter labor battles for 8-hour day in Chicago; 7 police and 4 workers died. Eight anarchists found guilty Aug. 20; 4 hanged Nov. 11.

Coca-Cola first sold, May 8 at Jacob's Pharmacy in Atlanta.

Geronimo, Apache Indian, surrendered Sept. 4, ending last major Indian war.

Statue of Liberty dedicated Oct. 28.

American Federation of Labor (AFL) formed Dec. 8 by 25 craft unions.

1887

Interstate Commerce Act enacted Feb. 4.

Pres. Grover Cleveland signed the **Hatch Act**, Mar. 2, establishing agriculture experiment stations across the U.S.

Eugene Field published poem **"Little Boy Blue."**

1888

Great blizzard struck eastern U.S. Mar. 11-14, causing about 400 deaths.

Ernest Thayer's poem **"Casey at the Bat"** was recited for the first time in public, at a New York City theater in May.

1889

U.S. opened Oklahoma to white settlement Apr. 22; within 24 hours **claims for 2 mil acres** were staked by 50,000 "sooner" settlers.

Johnstown, PA, flood May 31; 2,200 lives lost.

Electric lights installed at the White House.

1890

Battle of **Wounded Knee,** SD, Dec. 29, the last major conflict between Indians and U.S. troops. About 200 Indian men, women, and children and 29 soldiers were killed.

Sherman Antitrust Act passed July 2, began federal effort to curb monopolies.

Jacob Riis published *How the Other Half Lives,* about city slums.

Poems of **Emily Dickinson** published, 4 years after her death.

1891

Forest Reserve Act, Mar. 3, let president close public forest land to settlement for establishment of national parks.

Carnegie Hall, in New York City, opened May 5.

1892

Ellis Island, in New York Bay, opened Jan. 1 to receive immigrants.

Homestead, PA, strike at Carnegie steel mills; 7 guards and 11 strikers and spectators shot to death July 6.

Heavyweight **James J. Corbett** KO'd John L. Sullivan Sept. 7, in first title bout to use padded gloves.

1893

Columbian Exposition, blockbuster world's fair, held May-Oct. in Chicago.

Financial panic began, led to 4-year depression.

Mormon Temple dedicated in Salt Lake City, UT.

1894

Thomas A. Edison's kinetoscope, for motion pictures (invented **1887**), given first public showing Apr. 14.

Jacob S. Coxey led army of unemployed from the Midwest, reaching Washington, DC, Apr. 30. Coxey arrested May 1 for trespassing on Capitol grounds; his army disbanded.

Pullman strike began May 11 at a railroad car plant in Chicago.

Milton Hershey started **Hershey Chocolate Company**.

1895

"America the Beautiful" appeared for 1st time, in church publication, July 4.

Stephen Crane's *The Red Badge of Courage* published.

1896

William Jennings Bryan delivered "Cross of Gold" speech July 8; won Democratic Party nomination.

Supreme Court, in ***Plessy v. Ferguson***, May 18, approved racial segregation under the "separate but equal" doctrine.

John Philip Sousa composed "Stars and Stripes Forever" on Dec. 25.

1897

Olney-Pauncefote Treaty signed with **Britain,** Jan. 11, giving wide scope to arbitration in settling disputes; never ratified by U.S.

John J. McDermott won **first Boston Marathon** Apr. 19.

First Klondike **gold** arrived in San Francisco July 14.

Coal miners' **strike** settled Sept. 11, after more than 20 miners fired on and killed by lawmen.

1898

U.S. **battleship *Maine*** blown up Feb. 15 at Havana; 260 killed.

U.S. blockaded Cuba Apr. 22 in aid of independence forces. U.S. declared **war on Spain** Apr. 24; destroyed Spanish fleet in **Philippines** May 1; took **Guam** June 20.

Puerto Rico taken by U.S. July 25-Aug. 12. Spain agreed Dec. 10 to cede Philippines, Puerto Rico, and Guam, and approved independence for Cuba.

Annexation of **Hawaii** signed by Pres. William McKinley, July 7.

1899

Filipino insurgents, unable to get recognition of independence from U.S., started guerrilla war Feb. 4. Their leader, Emilio Aguinaldo, captured May 23, **1901.** Philippine Insurrection ended **1902.** 20,000 Filipino troops killed, and some 200,000 civilian deaths, mostly from disease and starvation.

Pres. McKinley signed **treaty** officially ending Spanish-America War, Feb. 10.

U.S. declared **Open Door Policy** Sept. 6, to make China an open international market.

John Dewey published *The School and Society,* advocating "progressive education."

Pianist Scott Joplin's "Maple Leaf Rag" was published, popularizing **ragtime**.

1900

Carry Nation, Kansas antisaloon agitator, began raiding with hatchet.

U.S. helped suppress **"Boxer Rebellion"** in Beijing.

International Ladies' Garment Workers Union was founded in New York City June 3.

Eastman Kodak Co. introduced the **Brownie camera**, popularizing picture-taking.

1901

Texas had first significant **oil strike**, Jan. 10.

Pres. **McKinley was shot** Sept. 6 in Buffalo, NY, by an anarchist, Leon Czolgosz; died Sept. 14. Vice Pres. Theodore **Roosevelt** sworn in as youngest-ever president, age 42 years, 11 months.

Booker T. Washington published ***Up From Slavery.***

1902

Permanent Bureau of the **Census** established Mar. 6.

U.S. withdrew troops from **Cuba** May 20, and Cuba became independent.

Helen Keller autobiography appeared in serial form.

1903

Treaty between U.S. and Colombia to have U.S. dig **Panama Canal** signed Jan. 22, rejected by Colombia. Panama declared independence from Colombia with U.S. support Nov. 3; recognized by Pres. Theodore Roosevelt Nov. 6. U.S., Panama signed **canal treaty** Nov. 18.

Wisconsin set first **direct primary** voting system, May 23.

Henry Ford founded Ford Motor Co., June 16.

Boston defeated Pittsburgh, 5 games to 3, Oct. 13 in the **first modern World Series**.

First successful flight in heavier-than-air mechanically propelled airplane by **Orville Wright** Dec. 17 near Kitty Hawk, NC, 120 ft. in 12 secs. Later flight same day by **Wilbur Wright,** 852 ft. in 59 secs. Improved plane patented, **1906.**

Fire in Iroquois Theater, Chicago, killed about 600, Dec. 30

Great Train Robbery, pioneering film, produced.

1904

St. Louis hosted **first Olympics** in U.S., July 1-Nov. 23.

First section of New York **subway** system opened, Oct. 27.

Ida Tarbell published muckraking *The History of the Standard Oil Company.*

Henry James's last great novel, *The Golden Bowl,* appeared.

1905

Industrial Workers of the World (Wobblies) founded by radicals in Chicago, June 27.

First **Rotary Club** founded in Chicago.

1906

Upton Sinclair published ***The Jungle***.

San Francisco earthquake and fire, Apr. 18-19, left 503 dead, $350 mil damages.

Pure Food and Drug Act and Meat Inspection Act both passed June 30.

1907

Financial panic and depression started Mar. 13.

First round-world cruise of U.S. **"Great White Fleet":** 16 battleships, 12,000 men.

1908

Springfield, IL, torn by anti-black **rioting**, Aug. 14-15.

Henry Ford introduced **Model T** car, priced at $850, Oct. 1.

1909

Adm. Robert E. Peary claimed to have reached **North Pole** Apr. 6 on 6th attempt, accompanied by Matthew Henson, a black man, and 4 Eskimos; may have fallen short.

National Conference on the Negro convened May 30, leading to founding of National Association for the Advancement of Colored People.

1910

Boy Scouts of America founded Feb. 8.

In a famous speech in Kansas, Aug. 10, former Pres. Roosevelt called for a **"new nationalism."**

1911

Supreme Court dissolved **Standard Oil** Co. May 15.

Building holding New York City's **Triangle Shirtwaist** Co. factory caught fire Mar. 25; 146 died.

First **transcontinental airplane flight** (with numerous stops) by C. P. Rodgers, New York to Pasadena, CA, Sept. 17-Nov. 5; time in air 82 hr., 4 min.

1912

American Girl Guides founded Mar. 12; name changed in **1913** to **Girl Scouts.**

U.S. sent Marines Aug. 14 to **Nicaragua,** which was in default of loans to U.S. and Europe.

1913

16th Amendment, authorizing federal income tax, ratified Feb. 3.

NY Armory Show brought modern art to U.S. Feb. 17.

17th Amendment, providing for direct popular election of U.S. senators, ratified Apr. 8.

Federal Reserve System was authorized Dec. 23, in a major reform of U.S. banking and finance.

Charles Beard published his *Economic Interpretation of the Constitution.*

1914

Ford Motor Co. raised basic wage rates from $2.40 for 9-hr. day to $5 for 8-hr. day, Jan. 5.

When U.S. sailors were arrested at Tampico, Mexico, Apr. 9, Atlantic fleet was sent to **Veracruz,** occupied city.

Pres. Woodrow Wilson proclaimed **U.S. neutrality** in the European war, Aug. 4.

Panama Canal was officially opened Aug. 15.

The **Clayton Antitrust Act** was passed Oct. 15, strengthening federal antimonopoly powers.

1915

First transcontinental **telephone call,** New York to San Francisco, was completed Jan. 25, by Alexander Graham Bell and Thomas A. Watson.

British ship ***Lusitania*** sunk May 7 by German submarine; 128 American passengers lost (Germany had warned passengers in advance). As a result of U.S. campaign, Germany issued apology and promise of payments, Oct. 5. Pres. Wilson asked for a military fund increase, Dec. 7.

U.S. troops landed in **Haiti,** July 28. Haiti became a virtual U.S. protectorate under Sept. 16 treaty.

D.W. Griffith's film ***The Birth of a Nation*** released.

1916

Gen. John J. **Pershing entered Mexico** to pursue Francisco (Pancho) Villa, who had raided U.S. border areas. Forces withdrawn Feb. 5, **1917.**

Rural Credits Acts passed July 17, followed by Warehouse Act Aug. 11; both provided financial aid to farmers.

Bomb exploded during **San Francisco** Preparedness Day parade July 22, killed 10. Thomas J. Mooney, labor organizer, and Warren K. Billings, shoe worker, were convicted **1917;** both later pardoned.

U.S. bought **Virgin Islands** from Denmark Aug. 4.

Jeannette Rankin (R, MT) elected as **first-ever female** member of U.S. **House**.

U.S. established military government in the **Dominican Republic** Nov. 29.

Trade and loans to **European allies** soared during the year.

1917

Germany, suffering from British blockade, declared almost unrestricted **submarine warfare** Jan. 31. U.S. cut diplomatic ties with Germany Feb. 3, and formally **declared war** Apr. 6.

Jones Act, passed Mar. 2, made **Puerto Rico U.S. territory**, its inhabitants U.S. citizens.

Conscription law was passed May 18. First U.S. troops arrived in Europe June 26.

18th Amendment to the Constitution, providing for **prohibition** of manufacture, sale, or transportation of alcoholic beverages, was submitted to the states by Congress Dec. 18.

1918

Pres. Wilson set out his **14 Points** as basis for peace, Jan. 8.

More than 1 mil **American troops** were in Europe by July. Allied counteroffensive launched at Château-Thierry July 18. War ended with signing of **armistice** Nov. 11.

Influenza epidemic killed an estimated 20 mil worldwide, 548,000 in U.S.

1919

18th **(prohibition)** Amendment, ratified Jan. 16, to take effect in 1 year.

First **transatlantic flight,** by U.S. Navy seaplane, left Rockaway, NY, May 8, stopped at Newfoundland, Azores, Lisbon May 27.

Boston police strike Sept. 9; National Guard breaks strike.

About 250 **alien radicals** were deported Dec. 22.

Sherwood Anderson published *Winesburg, Ohio.*

1920

In national **Red Scare,** some 2,700 Communists, anarchists, and other radicals were arrested Jan.-May.

League of Women Voters founded Feb. 14.

Senate refused Mar. 19 to ratify the **League of Nations Covenant.**

Radicals Nicola **Sacco** and Bartolomeo **Vanzetti** accused of killing 2 men in Massachusetts payroll holdup Apr. 15. Found guilty **1921.** A 6-year campaign for their release failed; both were executed Aug. 23, **1927.** Verdict repudiated **1977,** by proclamation of Gov. Michael Dukakis.

19th Amendment ratified Aug. 18, giving women the vote.

First regular licensed **radio broadcasting** begun Aug. 20.

Wall St., New York City, **bomb** explosion killed 30, injured 100, did $2 mil damage, Sept. 16.

Sinclair Lewis's *Main Street,* **F. Scott Fitzgerald's** *This Side of Paradise,* **Edith Wharton's** *The Age of Innocence* published.

1921

Congress sharply **curbed immigration,** set national quota system May 19.

Joint congressional resolution declaring **peace with Germany, Austria,** and **Hungary** signed July 2 by Pres. Warren G. Harding; treaties were signed in Aug.

In so-called **Black Sox** scandal, 8 Chicago **White Sox players** were banned from baseball Aug. 4 for conspiring with gamblers to throw the **1919** World Series.

Limitation of Armaments Conference met in Washington, DC, Nov. 12-Feb. 6, **1922.** Major powers agreed to curtail naval construction, outlaw poison gas, restrict submarine attacks on merchant vessels, respect integrity of China.

Ku Klux Klan began revival with violence against Catholics in North, South, and Midwest.

1922

Violence during **coal-mine strike** at Herrin, IL, June 22-23 cost 36 lives, including those of 21 nonunion miners.

Reader's Digest founded.

T. S. Eliot's *The Waste Land* published in London.

1923

First **sound-on-film motion picture,** *Phonofilm*, shown at Rivoli Theater, New York City, beginning in April.

Pres. Calvin Coolidge addressed Congress, Dec. 6; **first** official **broadcast** of a presidential speech.

1924

Law approved by Congress June 15 making all **Native Americans U.S. citizens.**

Nellie Tayloe Ross elected governor of Wyoming Nov. 9; inaugurated as nation's first woman governor Jan. 5, **1925.** **Miriam (Ma) Ferguson** elected governor of Texas Nov. 9; installed Jan. 20, **1925.**

George Gershwin wrote *Rhapsody in Blue.*

1925

John T. Scopes found guilty of having taught **evolution** in Dayton, TN, high school, fined $100 and costs, July 24.

F. Scott Fitzgerald's *The Great Gatsby* appeared.

1926

Dr. Robert H. Goddard demonstrated practicality of rockets, Mar. 16 at Auburn, MA, with first **liquid-fuel rocket**; rocket traveled 184 ft. in 2.5 sec.

Congress established **Army Air Corps** July 2.

Air Commerce Act passed Nov. 2, providing federal aid for airlines and airports.

Ernest Hemingway's *The Sun Also Rises* published.

1927

About 1,000 **marines landed in China** Mar. 5 to protect property in civil war.

Capt. **Charles A. Lindbergh** left Roosevelt Field, NY, May 20 alone in plane ***Spirit of St. Louis*** on first New York-Paris nonstop flight. Reached Le Bourget airfield May 21, 3,610 mi in 33½ hours.

The Jazz Singer, with **Al Jolson,** demonstrated part-talking pictures in New York City Oct. 6.

Show Boat opened in New York Dec. 27.

1928

Amelia Earhart became first woman to fly across the Atlantic, June 17.

Herbert Hoover elected president Nov. 6, defeating New York Gov. **Alfred E. Smith,** a Catholic.

1929

"St. Valentine's Day massacre" in Chicago Feb. 14; gangsters killed 7 rivals.

Farm price stability aided by **Agricultural Marketing Act,** passed June 15.

Albert B. Fall, former secretary of the interior, was convicted of accepting bribe of $100,000 in the leasing of the **Elk Hills (Teapot Dome)** naval oil reserve; sentenced Nov. 1 to a year in prison and fined $100,000.

Stock market crash Oct. 29 marked end of past prosperity as stock prices plummeted. Stock losses for **1929-31** estimated at $50 bil; worst American depression began.

Thomas Wolfe published *Look Homeward, Angel.* **William Faulkner** published *The Sound and the Fury.*

1930

London **Naval Reduction Treaty** signed by U.S., Britain, Italy, France, and Japan Apr. 22; in effect Jan. 1, **1931;** expired Dec. 31, **1936.**

Hawley-Smoot Tariff signed; rate hikes slash world trade.

Sinclair Lewis became the first American to win a **Nobel Prize in literature**.

1931

Empire State Building opened in New York City May 1.

Al Capone was convicted of tax evasion Oct. 17.

Pearl Buck published *The Good Earth.*

1932

Reconstruction Finance Corp. established Jan. 22 to stimulate banking and business. Unemployment at 12 mil.

19-month-old **Charles Lindbergh Jr. was kidnapped** Mar. 1; found dead May 12. Bruno Hauptmann found guilty in trial Jan.-Feb. **1935;** executed Apr. 3, **1936.**

Bonus March on Washington, DC, launched May 29 by World War I veterans demanding Congress pay their bonus in full.

Franklin D. Roosevelt elected president for the first time in Democratic landslide, Nov. 8.

Chicago Bears won **first NFL title game** Dec. 18, defeating the Portsmouth (OH) Spartans, 9–0.

1933

Pres. Roosevelt named **Frances Perkins** U.S. secretary of labor; first woman in U.S. cabinet.

All **banks in the U.S. ordered closed** by Pres. Roosevelt Mar. 6.

In a "100 days" special session, Mar. 9-June 16, Congress passed **New Deal** social and economic measures, including measures to regulate banks, distribute funds to the jobless, create jobs, raise agricultural prices, and set wage and production standards for industry.

Tennessee Valley Authority created by act of Congress, May 18.

Gold standard dropped by U.S.; announced by Pres. Roosevelt Apr. 19, ratified by Congress June 5.

Prohibition ended in the U.S. as 36th state ratified 21st Amendment Dec. 5.

Pres. Roosevelt foreswore armed intervention in **western hemisphere** nations, Dec. 26.

1934

Pres. Roosevelt signed law creating the **Securities and Exchange Commission**, June 6.

U.S. troops pulled out of **Haiti,** Aug. 6.

1935

Boulder Dam (later renamed Hoover Dam) completed, May 29.

Works Progress Administration **(WPA)** instituted May 6. Rural Electrification Administration created May 11. National Industrial Recovery Act struck down by Supreme Court May 27.

Comedian **Will Rogers** and aviator Wiley Post killed Aug. 15 in Alaska plane crash.

Social Security Act passed by Congress Aug. 14.

Huey Long, senator from Louisiana and national political leader, **shot** Sept. 8; died Sept. 10.

George Gershwin's ***Porgy and Bess*** opened Oct. 10 in New York.

Committee for Industrial Organization (CIO; later Congress of Industrial Organizations) formed to expand industrial unionism Nov. 9.

1936

Jesse Owens won 4 gold medals at the Berlin **Olympics** in August.

Baseball Hall of Fame founded in Cooperstown, NY.

Margaret Mitchell published *Gone With the Wind.*

1937

Hindenburg exploded May 6 landing at Lakehurst, NJ.

Golden Gate Bridge opened, May 27.

Joe Louis knocked out James J. Braddock, became world heavyweight champ June 22.

Amelia Earhart, aviator, and copilot Fred Noonan lost July 2 near Howland Island, in the Pacific.

Pres. Roosevelt asked for 6 additional Supreme Court justices; **"packing" plan** defeated.

Auto, steel labor unions won first big contracts.

1938

Naval Expansion Act passed May 17.

National minimum wage enacted June 25.

Orson Welles radio dramatization of **Martian invasion,** *War of the Worlds,* Oct. 30, caused scare.

Seabiscuit beat *War Admiral* in match race of the century, at Pimlico track, MD, Nov. 1.

Artist **"Grandma Moses"** discovered.

Thornton Wilder's ***Our Town*** produced on Broadway.

1939

Pres. Roosevelt asked for **defense budget hike** in Jan.

New York World's Fair opened Apr. 30, closed Oct. 31; reopened May 11, **1940,** ended Oct. 21.

Lou Gehrig, seriously ill, said farewell to fans at Yankee Stadium, July 4.

Albert Einstein alerted Pres. Roosevelt to **A-bomb** possibilities in Aug. 2 letter.

U.S. declared its neutrality in European war Sept. 5.

Roosevelt proclaimed a limited **national emergency** Sept. 8, an unlimited emergency May 27, **1941.** Both ended by Pres. Harry Truman, Apr. 28, **1952.**

John Steinbeck published *The Grapes of Wrath.*

Pocket books appeared in U.S.

Gone With the Wind and ***The Wizard of Oz*** films released.

1940

U.S. okayed sale of **surplus war materiel** to Britain June 3; announced transfer of 50 overaged destroyers Sept. 3.

First **peacetime military draft** in U.S. history approved, Sept. 14.

40-hour work week went into effect, Oct. 24.

Roosevelt elected Nov. 5 to 3rd term as president.

Richard Wright published *Native Son.*

1941

Four Freedoms termed essential by Pres. Roosevelt in speech to Congress Jan. 6: freedom of speech and religion, freedom from want and fear.

Lend-Lease Act signed Mar. 11 provided $7 bil in military credits for Britain. Lend-Lease for USSR approved in Nov.

The **Atlantic Charter,** 8-point declaration of principles, issued by Roosevelt and British Prime Min. Winston Churchill, Aug. 14.

Japan attacked **Pearl Harbor,** Hawaii, 7:55 AM Hawaiian time, Dec. 7; called by Roosevelt "a date that will live in infamy"; 19 ships sunk or damaged, 2,300 dead. U.S. declared war on Japan Dec. 8, on Germany and Italy Dec. 11.

Japanese invaded Philippines, Dec. 22; Wake Island fell, Dec. 23.

1942

Japanese troops took **Bataan** peninsula Apr. 8, **Corregidor** May 6.

Federal government forcibly moved 110,000 **Japanese-Americans** from West Coast to detention camps. Exclusion lasted 3 years.

Battle of **Midway** June 4-7 was Japan's first major defeat.

Marines landed on **Guadalcanal** Aug. 7; last Japanese not expelled until Feb. 9, **1943.**

U.S., Britain invaded **North Africa** Nov. 8.

First **nuclear chain reaction** (fission of uranium isotope U-235) produced at Univ. of Chicago, under physicists Arthur Compton, Enrico Fermi, others, Dec. 2.

1943

Oklahoma! opened Mar. 31 on Broadway.

War contractors barred from **racial discrimination,** May 27.

Pres. Roosevelt signed June 10 pay-as-you-go income tax bill. Starting July 1, wage and salary earners were subject to a **paycheck withholding** tax.

Race riot in Detroit June 21; 34 dead, 700 injured. Riot in Harlem section of New York City Aug. 2; 6 killed.

U.S., Britain invaded **Sicily** July 9, Italian **mainland** Sept. 3.

Marines in Nov. recaptured the **Gilbert Islands,** captured by Japan in **1941** and **1942.**

1944

U.S., Allied forces invaded Europe at **Normandy** on "D Day," June 6, in greatest amphibious landing in history. **Battle of the Bulge**, failed Nazi counteroffensive, waged Dec. 16, 1944, to Jan. 28, 1945; 500,000 Americans fought.

GI Bill of Rights signed by Pres. Roosevelt June 22, providing benefits for veterans.

Representatives of the U.S. and other major powers met at **Dunbarton Oaks**, Washington, DC, Aug. 21-Oct. 7, to work out formation of postwar world organization that became the **United Nations.**

U.S. forces landed on **Leyte,** Philippines, Oct. 20.

Roosevelt elected to 4th term as president, Nov. 7.

Federal Highway Act passed by Congress, Nov. 29, creating national system of **interstate highways.**

1945

Yalta Conference met in the Crimea, USSR, Feb. 4-11. Roosevelt, Churchill, and Soviet leader Joseph Stalin agreed that their 3 countries, plus France, would occupy Germany and that the Soviet Union would enter war against Japan.

Marines landed on **Iwo Jima** Feb. 19, won control Mar. 16 after heavy casualties. U.S. forces invaded **Okinawa** Apr. 1, captured Okinawa June 21.

Pres. Roosevelt died in Warm Springs, GA, Apr. 12; Vice Pres. **Harry S. Truman** became president.

Germany surrendered May 7; May 8 proclaimed V-E Day.

First **atomic bomb,** produced at Los Alamos, NM, exploded at Alamogordo, NM, July 16. Bomb dropped on **Hiroshima** Aug. 6, with about 75,000 people killed; bomb dropped on **Nagasaki** Aug. 9, killing about 40,000. Japan agreed to surrender Aug. 14; formally surrendered Sept. 2.

Empire State Building struck accidentally by Army B-25 bomber, July 28, killing 13.

At **Potsdam Conference,** July 17-Aug. 2, leaders of U.S., USSR, and Britain agreed on disarmament of Germany, occupation zones, war crimes trials.

U.S. forces entered **Korea** south of 38th parallel to displace Japanese Sept. 8.

Gen. Douglas MacArthur took over supervision of Japan Sept. 9.

1946

Steel strike by 750,000 started Jan. 21, settled in 4 weeks. Strike by 400,000 **mine workers** began Apr. 1 (settled May 29); other industries followed.

At a speech at a Fulton, MO, college, Mar. 5, Winston Churchill employed the phrase **"iron curtain."**

Atomic bomb tested off Bikini Atoll in Pacific, July 1.

Philippines given independence by U.S. July 4.

Mother Frances Xavier Cabrini 1st American to be canonized, July 7.

Dr. Benjamin Spock's ***Baby and Child Care*** published as 1946-64 **baby boom** began.

1947

Pres. Truman asked Congress for financial and military aid for Greece and Turkey to help combat Communist subversion (**Truman Doctrine),** Mar. 12. Approved May 15.

UN Security Council voted Apr. 2 to place under **U.S. trusteeship** the Pacific islands formerly mandated to Japan.

Jackie Robinson joined the Brooklyn Dodgers Apr. 11, breaking the color barrier in major league baseball.

The **Marshall Plan,** for U.S. aid to European countries, was proposed by Sec. of State George C. Marshall June 5. Congress authorized some $12 bil in next 4 years.

Taft-Hartley Labor Act restricting labor union power was vetoed by Truman June 20; Congress overrode the veto.

Air Force Capt. **Chuck Yeager** broke the sound barrier, Oct. 14, in X-1 rocket plane.

1948

USSR halted all surface traffic into **W. Berlin,** June 23; in response, U.S. and British troops launched an **airlift.** Soviet blockade halted May 12, **1949;** airlift ended Sept. 30.

Organization of American States founded Apr. 30.

Alger Hiss indicted Dec. 15 for perjury, after denying he had passed secret documents to Whittaker Chambers to go to a **Communist spy ring.** Convicted Jan. 21, **1950.**

Pres. Truman, elected Nov. 2, defeating Gov. Thomas E. Dewey in a historic upset.

Kinsey Report on sexuality in the human male published.

1949

NATO established Aug. 24 by U.S., Canada, and 10 Western European nations, agreeing that an armed attack against one would be considered an attack against all.

Eleven leaders of **U.S. Communist Party** convicted Oct. 14 of advocating violent overthrow of U.S. government; sentenced to prison. Supreme Court upheld convictions **1951.**

Pres. Truman Oct. 26 signed legislation raising federal **minimum wage** from 40¢ an hour to 75¢.

Arthur Miller's *Death of a Salesman* opened on Broadway.

1950

Masked bandits robbed **Brink's, Inc.,** Boston express office, Jan. 17 of $2.8 mil. Case solved **1956;** 8 sentenced to life.

Pres. Truman authorized production of the **H-bomb** Jan. 31.

North Korean forces invaded **South Korea** June 25. UN asked for troops to restore peace.

Truman ordered Air Force and Navy to Korea June 27. Truman approved ground forces, air strikes against **North Korea** June 30.

U.S. sent 35 military advisers to **South Vietnam** June 27, and agreed to aid anti-Communist government.

Army seized all railroads Aug. 27 on Truman's order to prevent a general strike; returned to owners in **1952.**

U.S. forces landed at Inchon Sept. 15; UN force took Pyongyang Oct. 20, reached China border Nov. 20; China sent troops across border Nov. 26.

Two members of **Puerto Rican nationalist** movement tried to kill Pres. Truman Nov. 1.

U.S. banned shipments Dec. 8 to Communist **China** and to Asiatic ports trading with it.

Your Show of Shows debuted on TV.

Peanuts comic strip appeared.

David Riesman's ***The Lonely Crowd*** published.

1951

Sen. Estes Kefauver led Senate probe into organized crime.

22nd Amendment, limiting **presidential term of office,** ratified Feb. 27.

Julius Rosenberg, his wife, **Ethel**, and Morton Sobell found guilty Mar. 29 of conspiracy to commit wartime **espionage**. Rosenbergs received death penalty. Sobell sentenced to 30 years; released **1969.**

Gen. Douglas MacArthur removed from Korea command Apr. 11 by Pres. Truman, for unauthorized policy statements.

Korea cease-fire talks began in July; lasted 2 years. Fighting ended July 27, **1953.**

The U.S., Australia, and New Zealand signed **Anzus** mutual security pact Sept. 1.

Transcontinental TV began Sept. 4 with Pres. Truman's address at Japanese Peace Treaty Conference in San Francisco.

Japanese peace treaty signed in San Francisco Sept. 8 by U.S., Japan, and 47 other nations.

J. D. Salinger published *Catcher in the Rye.*

1952

Seizure of nation's steel mills was ordered by Pres. Truman Apr. 8 to avert a strike. Ruled illegal by Supreme Court June 2.

Peace contract between West Germany, U.S., Great Britain, and France was signed May 26.

The last racial and ethnic barriers to naturalization removed, June 26-27, with passage of **Immigration and Naturalization Act of 1952.**

Richard Nixon, as vice-pres. candidate, gave **"Checkers" speech,** Sept. 23.

Puerto Rico proclaimed commonwealth July 25, after referendum Mar. 3.

First **hydrogen device** explosion Nov. 1 in Pacific.

1953

Federal jury in New York convicted 13 **Communist** leaders on conspiracy charges, Jan. 20.

Julius and Ethel Rosenberg executed in the Sing Sing Prison electric chair, Ossining, NY, June 19, for betraying nuclear secrets to Soviet Union.

Korean War armistice signed July 27.

California Gov. **Earl Warren** was sworn in Oct. 5 as 14th **chief justice** of U.S. Supreme Court.

1954

Nautilus, first atomic-powered submarine, was launched at Groton, CT, Jan. 21.

Five members of Congress were **wounded** in the House Mar. 1 by 4 **Puerto Rican independence supporters** who fired at random from a spectators' gallery.

At televised **Army-McCarthy hearings,** Apr. 22-June 17, before a Senate subcommittee, Army officials accused Sen. Joseph McCarthy (R, WI) of seeking preferential treatment for a draftee, and McCarthy accused the Army of hindering probe of Communist infiltration into the Army.

Racial segregation in public schools unanimously ruled unconstitutional by Supreme Court May 17, in *Brown* v. *Board of Education of Topeka.*

Southeast Asia Treaty Organization **(SEATO)** formed by defense pact signed in Manila Sept. 8 by U.S., Britain, France, Australia, New Zealand, Philippines, Pakistan, and Thailand.

Condemnation of **Sen. McCarthy** voted by Senate, 67-22, Dec. 2, for abuse of the Senate during hearings and debates.

Ernest Hemingway won Nobel Prize.

1955

U.S. agreed Feb. 12 to help train **South Vietnamese** army.

Supreme Court ordered **"all deliberate speed"** in integration of public schools, May 31.

A **summit meeting** of leaders of U.S., Britain, France, and USSR took place July 18-23 in Geneva, Switzerland.

Rosa Parks refused Dec. 1 to give her seat to a white man on a **bus in Montgomery, AL**. Bus segregation ordinance declared unconstitutional by a federal court following **boycott** organized by **Rev. Martin Luther King Jr**.

America's 2 largest labor organizations merged Dec. 5, creating the **AFL-CIO**.

1956

Massive resistance to Supreme Court desegregation rulings was called for Mar. 12 by 101 Southern congressmen.

U.S. Supreme Court, Apr. 23, unanimously ruled against **racial segregation** on intrastate buses.

Federal-Aid **Highway Act** signed June 29, inaugurating interstate highway system.

First transatlantic **telephone cable** activated Sept. 25.

On Oct. 8, in Game 5, Yankee right-hander Don Larsen pitched the only **World Series perfect game.**

My Fair Lady opened on Broadway in Mar., Eugene O'Neill's ***Long Day's Journey Into Night*** opened in Nov.

1957

Congress approved first **civil rights bill** for blacks since Reconstruction, Apr. 29, to protect voting rights.

The U.S. surgeon general July 12 said studies showed a "direct link" between cigarette **smoking and lung cancer**.

National Guardsmen, called out by Arkansas Gov. Orval Faubus Sept. 4, barred 9 black students from entering all-white high school in **Little Rock.** Faubus complied Sept. 21 with federal court order to remove Guardsmen, but the blacks were ordered to withdraw by local authorities. Pres. Eisenhower sent troops Sept. 24 to enforce court order.

Jack Kerouac published *On the Road.*

1958

First U.S. **earth satellite** to go into orbit, ***Explorer I,*** launched by Army Jan. 31 at Cape Canaveral, FL; discovered Van Allen radiation belt.

U.S. Marines sent to **Lebanon** to protect elected government from threatened overthrow July-Oct.

Nuclear sub ***Nautilus*** made first undersea crossing of the **North Pole** Aug. 5.

Presidential aide **Sherman Adams resigned** Sept. 22 over a scandal involving alleged improper gifts.

First domestic **jet airline** passenger service in U.S. opened by National Airlines Dec. 10 between New York and Miami.

1959

Alaska admitted as 49th state, Jan. 3; **Hawaii** admitted as 50th Aug. 21.

St. Lawrence Seaway opened Apr. 25.

Vice Pres. **Richard Nixon**, on tour of USSR, held so-called kitchen debate, July 24, with Soviet Prem. **Nikita Khrushchev** at U.S. exhibit in Moscow.

Prem. **Khrushchev** paid unprecedented visit to U.S. Sept. 15-27; made transcontinental tour.

Pres. Eisenhower issued an injunction Oct. 12, upheld and made effective by the Supreme Court Nov. 7, ending a record 116-day **steel strike**.

In a **quiz show scandal**, Columbia Univ. Prof. Charles Van Doren admitted to a U.S. House subcommittee Nov. 2 that he had been coached before appearances on NBC-TV's *21* in 1956; he had won $129,000.

1960

Sit-ins began Feb. 1 when 4 black college students in Greensboro, NC, refused to move from a Woolworth lunch counter when denied service. By Sept. **1961** over 70,000 students, whites and blacks, had participated in sit-ins.

Congress approved a strong **voting rights act** Apr. 21.

A U.S. **U-2 reconnaissance plane** was shot down in the Soviet Union May 1; pilot Gary Powers captured. The incident led to cancellation of a Paris summit conference.

Vice Pres. Richard Nixon and Sen. John F. Kennedy faced each other Sept. 26 in the first in a series of televised **debates. Kennedy defeated Nixon** to win presidency, Nov. 8.

U.S. announced Dec. 15 it backed rightist group in **Laos,** which took power the next day.

1961

U.S. severed diplomatic and consular relations with **Cuba** Jan. 3, after disputes over nationalizations of U.S. firms, U.S. military presence at Guantanamo base. Invasion of Cuba's **Bay of Pigs** Apr. 17 by Cuban exiles directed by U.S. unsuccessfully attempted to overthrow the regime of Prem. Fidel Castro.

Peace Corps created by executive order, Mar. 1.

23rd Amendment, giving **District of Columbia** citizens the right to vote in presidential elections, ratified Mar. 29.

Commander Alan B. Shepard Jr. was rocketed from Cape Canaveral, FL, in a Mercury capsule May 5, in first U.S.-crewed suborbital space flight.

"Freedom Rides" from Washington, DC, across deep South were launched May 20 to **protest segregation** in interstate transportation.

Pres. Kennedy, May 27, signed bill creating **Alliance for Progress**, for Latin America.

John Updike's *Rabbit, Run* published.

1962

Lt. Col. John H. Glenn Jr. became first American in orbit Feb. 20 when he circled the earth 3 times in the Mercury capsule ***Friendship 7***.

Pres. John F. Kennedy said Feb. 14 that U.S. military advisers in **Vietnam** would fire if fired upon.

In *Baker v. Carr*, Mar. 26, Supreme Court backed **"one-man one-vote"** apportionment of seats in state legislatures.

James Meredith became first black student at University of Mississippi Oct. 1 after 3,000 troops put down riots.

A Soviet **offensive missile buildup in Cuba** was revealed Oct. 22 by Pres. Kennedy, who ordered a naval and air quarantine on shipment of offensive military equipment to the island. He and Soviet Prem. Khrushchev agreed Oct. 28 on formula to end crisis. Kennedy announced Nov. 2 that missile bases in Cuba were being dismantled.

Rachel Carson's *Silent Spring* launched environmentalist movement.

1963

In *Gideon v. Wainwright,* Mar. 18, Supreme Court ruled that all **criminal defendants** must have counsel.

University of Alabama **desegregated** after Gov. **George Wallace** stepped aside when confronted by federally deployed National Guard troops June 11.

Civil rights leader **Medgar Evers** assassinated June 12.

Supreme Court ruled, June 17 that laws requiring **recitation of the Lord's Prayer** or Bible verses in public schools were unconstitutional.

President **Kennedy**, on Europe trip, addressed huge crowd in **West Berlin**, June 23.

A limited **nuclear test-ban treaty** was agreed upon July 25 by the U.S., the Soviet Union, and Britain.

March for civil rights began May 2 in Birmingham, AL, led to desegegregation accord, which in turn sparked rioting and violence.

On Aug. 28, 200,000 joined in **March on Washington, DC,** in support of **black demands** for equal rights led by **Rev. Martin Luther King Jr.;** highlight was "I have a dream" speech by **King.**

16th St. Baptist Church in Birmingham, AL, bombed Sept. 15 in racial violence; 4 black girls killed.

South Vietnam Pres. **Ngo Dinh Diem assassinated** Nov. 2; U.S. had earlier withdrawn support.

Pres. Kennedy shot and fatally wounded Nov. 22 as he rode in a motorcade through downtown Dallas, TX. Vice Pres. **Lyndon B. Johnson sworn in** as president. **Lee Harvey Oswald arrested** and charged with the murder; he was shot and fatally wounded Nov. 24. **Jack Ruby,** a nightclub owner, was convicted of Oswald's murder; he died in **1967,** while awaiting retrial following reversal of his conviction.

Betty Friedan's *Feminine Mystique* was published.

1964

Panama suspended relations with U.S. Jan. 9 after riots. U.S. offered Dec. 18 to negotiate a new canal treaty.

The **Beatles** arrived in U.S. for first time, appeared Feb. 9 on CBS-TV's *Ed Sullivan Show*.

Supreme Court ordered Feb. 17 that **congressional districts** have equal populations.

U.S. reported May 27 it was sending military planes to **Laos.**

Omnibus **civil rights bill** signed by Pres. Johnson July 2, banning discrimination in voting, jobs, public accommodations.

Three **civil rights workers** were reported missing in Mississippi June 22; found buried Aug. 4. Twenty-one white men were arrested. On Oct. 20, **1967**, an all-white federal jury convicted 7 of conspiracy in the slayings.

Congress Aug. 7 passed the **Tonkin Gulf Resolution,** authorizing presidential action in Vietnam, after N Vietnamese boats reportedly attacked 2 U.S. destroyers Aug. 2.

Congress approved **War on Poverty** bill Aug. 11, providing for a domestic Peace Corps **(VISTA),** a **Job Corps,** and antipoverty funding.

The **Warren Commission** released Sept. 27 a report concluding that Lee Harvey Oswald was solely responsible for the Kennedy assassination.

Pres. Johnson was elected to a full term, Nov. 3, defeating Republican **Sen. Barry Goldwater** (AZ) in a landslide.

Verrazano-Narrows Bridge opened in New York City Nov. 21.

1965

In State of the Union address Jan. 4, Pres. Johnson outlined plans for his **"Great Society."**

Pres. Johnson in Feb. ordered continuous **bombing of North Vietnam** below 20th parallel.

Malcolm X assassinated Feb. 21 at New York City rally.

Some 14,000 U.S. troops sent to **Dominican Republic** during civil war Apr. 28. All troops withdrawn by next year.

March from Selma to Montgomery, AL, begun Mar. 21 by Rev. Martin Luther King Jr. to demand federal protection of **blacks' voting rights.** New **Voting Rights Act** signed Aug. 6.

Bill establishing **Medicare,** government health insurance program for elderly, signed by Pres. Johnson July 30.

Los Angeles riot by blacks living in **Watts** area resulted in 34 deaths and $200 mil in property damage Aug. 11-16.

National **immigration** quota system abolished Oct. 3.

Electric power failure blacked out most of northeastern U.S., parts of 2 Canadian provinces the night of Nov. 9-10.

1966

U.S. forces began firing into **Cambodia** May 1.

Bombing of Hanoi area of N Vietnam by U.S. planes began June 29. By Dec. 31, 385,300 U.S. troops were stationed in S Vietnam, plus 60,000 offshore and 33,000 in Thailand.

U.S. Supreme Court ruled June 13, in ***Miranda*** *v. Arizona,* that suspects must be read their rights before police questioning.

Medicare began July 1.

Charles Whitman, 25, **killed 13 students** from a tower at the **Univ. of Texas**, Austin, Aug. 1, before being shot dead by police.

U.S. **Dept. of Transportation** created, Oct. 15.

Edward Brooke (R, MA) elected Nov. 8 as first black U.S. senator in 85 years.

Robert C. Weaver named secretary of newly created Dept. of Housing and Urban Development **(HUD)**, becoming **1st black cabinet member**.

1967

Green Bay Packers beat Kansas City Chiefs, 35-10, in **first Super Bowl,** Jan. 15 in Los Angeles.

Black U.S. Rep. **Adam Clayton Powell** (D, NY) was denied his seat Mar. 1 because of charges he misused government funds. Reelected in **1968,** he was seated, but fined $25,000 and stripped of his seniority.

Pres. Johnson and Soviet Prem. Aleksei Kosygin met June 23 and 25 at **Glassboro State College** in NJ; agreed not to let any crisis push them into war.

25th Amendment, providing for **presidential succession,** was ratified Feb. 10.

Riots by blacks in **Newark, NJ,** July 12-17 killed 26, injured 1,500; more than 1,000 arrested. In **Detroit, MI,** July 23-30, 43 died; 2,000 injured, 5,000 left homeless by rioting, looting, burning in city's black neighborhoods.

An **antiwar march** on Washington, Oct. 21-22, drew 50,000 participants.

Thurgood Marshall was sworn in Oct. 2 as first black U.S. Supreme Court Justice. **Carl B. Stokes** (D, Cleveland) and **Richard G. Hatcher** (D, Gary, IN) were elected first black mayors of major U.S. cities Nov. 7.

1968

USS *Pueblo* and 83-man crew seized in Sea of Japan Jan. 23 by North Koreans; 82 men released Dec. 22.

"Tet offensive": Communist troops attacked Saigon, 30 province capitals Jan. 30, suffered heavy casualties.

Pres. Johnson **curbed bombing** of North Vietnam Mar. 31. Peace talks began in Paris May 10. All bombing of North halted Oct. 31.

Martin Luther King Jr., 39, assassinated Apr. 4 in Memphis, TN. **James Earl Ray,** an escaped convict, pleaded guilty to the slaying, was sentenced to 99 years.

Students at **Columbia** Univ., Apr. 23-24, seized school buildings in protest demonstrations.

Sen. Robert F. Kennedy (D, NY), 42, **shot** June 5 in Los Angeles, after celebrating presidential primary victories. Died June 6. Sirhan Bishara Sirhan convicted of murder, **1969;** death sentence commuted to life in prison, **1972.**

Vice Pres. **Hubert Humphrey nominated** for president by Democrats **at convention in Chicago,** marked by clash between police and **antiwar protesters**, Aug. 26-29. The Republican nominee, **Richard Nixon, won** the **presidency,** defeating Hubert Humphrey in a close race Nov. 5.

Apollo 8 **orbited moon** in 5-day mission, Dec. 21-27.

1969

Expanded 4-party **Vietnam peace talks** began Jan. 18. U.S. force peaked at 543,400 in April. Withdrawal started July 8. Pres. Nixon set Vietnamization policy Nov. 3.

Earl Warren retired upon swearing in **Warren Burger**, June 23, as Supreme Court chief justice.

U.S. astronaut **Neil Armstrong,** commander of the *Apollo 11* mission, became the first person to **set foot on the moon,** July 20; followed by astronaut **Edwin "Buzz" Aldrin;** astronaut **Michael Collins** remained aboard command module.

Woodstock music festival near Bethel, NY, drew 300,000-500,000 people, Aug. 15-18.

Anti-Vietnam-War **demonstrations** held in cities across the U.S. marking Vietnam Mortatorium day, Oct. 15; on Nov. 15, some 250,000 marched in Washington, DC.

Massacre of hundreds of civilians by U.S. troops at **My Lai, South Vietnam,** in **1968** incident reported Nov. 16.

Sesame Street launched on public TV.

1970

A federal jury Feb. 18 found the **"Chicago 7"** antiwar activists innocent of conspiring to incite riots during the 1968 **Democratic National Convention.** However, 5 were convicted of crossing state lines with intent to incite riots.

Millions of Americans participated in antipollution demonstrations Apr. 22 to mark the **first Earth Day.**

U.S. and South Vietnamese forces crossed **Cambodian** borders Apr. 30 to get at enemy bases.

Four students were killed May 4 at **Kent State** Univ. in Ohio by National Guardsmen during a protest against the war. In protest at **Jackson State** Univ. in Mississippi police fired on protesters; 2 killed.

Two **women generals,** the first in U.S. history, were named by Pres. Nixon May 15.

A **postal reform** measure was signed Aug. 12, creating an independent U.S. Postal Service.

Pres. Nixon, Dec. 31, signed **clean air bill** calling for development of a cleaner auto engine and national air quality standards for 10 major pollutants.

Doonesbury comic strip launched in 30 papers.

1971

Charles Manson and 3 of his cult followers were found guilty Jan. 25 of first-degree murder in **1969** slaying of actress Sharon Tate and 6 others.

Pres. Nixon, Apr. 14, relaxed 20-year trade embargo with **China**.

The 26th Amendment, lowering the **voting age to 18** in all elections, was ratified June 30.

A court-martial jury Mar. 29 convicted **Lt. William L. Calley Jr.** in murder of 22 South Vietnamese at **My Lai** on Mar. 16, **1968.** He was sentenced to life imprisonment Mar. 31 later reduced to 20 years.

Publication of classified **Pentagon papers** on U.S. involvement in Vietnam was begun June 13 by the *New York Times*. Supreme Court June 30 upheld, 6-3, the right of the *Times* and *Washington Post* to publish the documents.

Pres. Nixon, Aug. 15, instituted a 90-day **wage and price** freeze.

U.S. bombers struck massively in North Vietnam for 5 days starting Dec. 26 in retaliation for alleged violations of agreements reached prior to the 1968 bombing halt.

1972

Pres. Nixon arrived in **Beijing** Feb. 21 for an 8-day visit to China, in a "journey for peace;" a joint communiqué released Feb. 27 called for increased Sino-U.S. contracts.

By a vote of 84 to 8, the Senate, Mar. 22, approved **Equal Rights Amendment** banning **discrimination** on the basis of sex, and sent the measure to the states for ratification.

North Vietnamese forces launched the biggest attacks in 4 years across the demilitarized zone Mar. 30. The U.S. responded Apr. 15 by resumption of bombing of Hanoi and Haiphong after a 4-year lull.

Pres. Nixon announced May 8 the mining of **North Vietnam ports.** Last U.S. combat troops left Aug. 11.

Gov. **George C. Wallace** (AL), campaigning for president at a Laurel, MD, shopping center May 15, **was shot** and seriously wounded. Arthur Bremer **convicted** Aug. 4, sentenced to 63 years for shooting Wallace and 3 others.

In **first visit of a U.S. president to Moscow,** Pres. Nixon arrived May 22 for summit talks with Kremlin leaders that culminated in a landmark strategic arms pact **(SALT I)**.

Five men were arrested June 17 for breaking into the offices of the Democratic National Committee in the **Watergate** office complex in Washington, DC.

Supreme Court in *Furman* v. *Georgia* June 29 ruled capital punishment as currently practiced was unconstitutional.

Mark Spitz won 7 gold medals in world record times, at the Munich Olympics in Sept.

Pres. **Nixon** was **reelected** Nov. 7 in a landslide, carrying 49 states to defeat Democratic Sen. George McGovern (SD).

The **Dow Jones** Industrial Average closed above 1,000 for the first time, Nov. 14.

Full-scale **bombing of North Vietnam** resumed after Paris peace negotiations reached an impasse Dec. 18.

1973

Five of 7 defendants in **Watergate** break-in trial pleaded guilty Jan. 11 and 15; the other 2 were convicted Jan. 30.

In **Roe *v.* Wade,** Supreme Court ruled, 7-2, Jan. 22, that states may not ban **abortions** during **first 3 months of pregnancy** and may regulate, but may not ban, abortions during 2nd trimester.

Wounded Knee, SD, occupied in protest by activists in American Indian Movement, Feb. 27.

WORLD ALMANAC QUICK QUIZ

Can you match the event with the year?
a. 1848; b. 1868; c. 1888; d. 1908

(1) The World Almanac was published for the first time.
(2) Henry Ford introduced the Model T, at a price tag of $850.
(3) Gold was discovered in California.
(4) A Great Blizzard caused about 400 deaths in northeastern U.S.

For the answer look in this chapter, or see page 1008.

Four-party **Vietnam peace pacts** were signed in Paris Jan. 27, and North Vietnam released some 590 U.S. prisoners by Apr. 1. Last U.S. troops left Mar. 29.

End of the military **draft** announced Jan. 27.

Top **Nixon aides** H. R. Haldeman, John D. Ehrlichman, and John Dean and Attorney Gen. Richard Kleindienst **resigned** Apr. 30, amid charges of White House efforts to obstruct justice in the Watergate case.

Skylab, 1st U.S. space station, launched May 14.

Secretariat became first Triple Crown winner since Citation in 1948, after winning Belmont Stakes June 9 in record time.

John Dean, former Nixon counsel, told Senate hearings June 25 that Nixon, his staff and campaign aides, and the Justice Dept. had conspired to cover up **Watergate** facts.

The U.S. officially ceased bombing in **Cambodia** at midnight Aug. 14 in accord with a June congressional action.

Vice Pres. Spiro Agnew, Oct. 10, **resigned** and pleaded no contest to a charge of tax evasion on payments made to him by contractors when he was governor of Maryland. **Gerald R. Ford,** Oct. 12, became **first appointed vice president** under the 25th Amendment; sworn in Dec. 6.

A total ban on **oil exports** to the U.S. was imposed by Arab oil-producing nations Oct. 19-21 after the outbreak of an Arab-Israeli war. The ban was lifted Mar. 18, **1974.**

The **"Saturday Night Massacre"** occurred Oct. 20, when Pres. Nixon ordered **Attorney Gen. Elliot Richardson** to fire **Watergate special prosecutor Archibald Cox**, who had sought the handover of Nixon's subpoenaed White House tapes. Richardson refused to comply and resigned; **Dep. Attorney Gen. William Ruckelshaus** refused and was fired. **Solicitor Gen. Robert Bork, as acting attorney gen.,** then fired Cox. **Leon Jaworski** named Nov. 1 by the Nixon administration to succeed Cox.

Congress overrode Nov. 7 Pres. Nixon's veto of the **war powers** bill, which curbed president's power to commit forces to hostilities abroad without congressional approval.

1974

On Apr. 8, **Hank Aaron** of the Atlanta Braves hit his 715th career **home run** to break **Babe Ruth's** record.

Impeachment hearings opened May 9 against Pres. Nixon by the House Judiciary Committee.

John D. Ehrlichman and 3 **White House "plumbers"** found guilty July 12 of conspiring to violate the civil rights of Pentagon Papers leaker Daniel Ellsberg's psychiatrist by breaking into his office.

Supreme Court ruled, 8-0, July 24 that Nixon had to turn over **64 tapes** of White House conversations.

House Judiciary Committee, in televised hearings July 24-30, recommended 3 **articles of impeachment** against Pres. Nixon, involving conspiracy to obstruct justice in the Watergate cover-up, abuses of power and defiance of committee subpoenas. The House voted Aug. 20, 412-3, to accept the committee report, which included the impeachment articles.

Pres. Nixon announced his resignation, Aug. 8, and **resigned** Aug. 9; his support in Congress had begun to collapse Aug. 5, after release of tapes appearing to implicate him in Watergate cover-up. **Vice Pres. Ford** was **sworn in** Aug. 9 as 38th U.S. president.

Ford, Aug. 20, nominated Nelson **Rockefeller** to be **vice president**; he was sworn in Dec. 10.

A **pardon** to ex-Pres. Nixon for any federal crimes he committed while president issued by Pres. Ford Sept. 8.

1975

Found guilty of Watergate cover-up charges Jan. 1 were ex-Atty. Gen. John Mitchell and ex-presidential advisers H. R. Haldeman and John Ehrlichman.

U.S. launched **evacuation** of Americans and some South Vietnamese **from Saigon** Apr. 29 as Communist forces completed takeover of South Vietnam; **South Vietnamese** government officially **surrendered** Apr. 30.

U.S. merchant ship ***Mayaguez*** and its crew of 39 were seized by Cambodian forces in Gulf of Siam May 12. In rescue operation, U.S. Marines attacked Tang Island, planes bombed air base; Cambodia surrendered ship and crew.

Congress voted $405 mil for **South Vietnam refugees** May 16; 140,000 were flown to the U.S.

Illegal CIA operations described by panel headed by Vice Pres. **Rockefeller** June 10.

Publishing heiress **Patricia (Patty) Hearst,** kidnapped Feb. 5, **1974**, by "Symbionese Liberation Army" militants, captured in San Francisco Sept. 18 with others. She was convicted Mar. 20, **1976**, of bank robbery.

1976

In **"right to die"** case, NJ Supreme Court Mar. 31 allowed comatose **Karen Ann Quinlan** to be removed from respirator; she survived, dying in a nursing home in **1985.**

Supreme Court **reinstated death penalty,** July 2, subject to conditions.

U.S. celebrated **200th anniversary of independence** July 4, with festivals, parades, and New York City's Operation Sail, a gathering of tall ships from around the world.

"Legionnaire's disease" killed 29 persons who attended an American Legion convention July 21-24 in Philadelphia.

Viking II set down on **Mars'** Utopia Plains Sept. 3, following the successful landing by *Viking I* July 20.

Two U.S. officers on routine mission near DMZ slain by **North Korean soldiers,** Aug. 18; North Korea stated "regret," Aug. 21.

1977

Pres. Jimmy Carter Jan. 21 pardoned most Vietnam War **draft evaders.**

Convicted murderer **Gary Gilmore executed** by a Utah firing squad Jan. 17; first exercise of capital punishment in the U.S. since **1967.**

Natural gas shortage, caused by severe winter weather, led Congress Feb. 2 to approve emergency federal allocation program.

Pres. Carter signed an act Aug. 4 creating a new cabinet-level **Energy Department.**

Elvis Presley died Aug. 16.

FBI Dec. 7 released 40,000 pages of previously secret files relating to **Kennedy assassination**.

George Lucas's first ***Star Wars*** film produced.

1978

Crippling 110-day coal miners **strike** ended Mar. 25 with ratification of new contract.

Senate voted, 68-32, Apr. 18 to turn over **Panama Canal** to Panama on Dec. 31, **1999**; a Mar. 16 vote had given approval to a treaty guaranteeing the area's neutrality after the year 2000.

Californians, June 6, approved **Proposition 13,** a state constitutional amendment slashing property taxes.

Supreme Court, June 28, ruled against **racial quotas** in *Bakke* v. *University of California*.

Egyptian Pres. Anwar al-**Sadat** and Israeli Prem. Menachem **Begin** reached accord on "framework for peace," Sept. 17, after Carter-mediated talks at **Camp David**.

New York's Chemical Bank Dec. 20 led move to raise **prime interest rate** to near-record 11.75%.

1979

Former Atty. Gen. John Mitchell, last of 25 persons still jailed for crimes relating to **Watergate scandal**, released Jan. 19.

Partial meltdown released radioactive material Mar. 28, at nuclear reactor on **Three Mile Island** near Middletown, PA.

American Airlines DC-10 **jetliner crashed** May 25 after takeoff from Chicago, killing 275 persons.

In a speech July 15, Pres. Carter spoke of a national **"crisis of confidence"** and outlined a proposed 10-year $140 bil program to **reduce U.S. dependence on foreign oil.**

Federal government announced, Nov. 1, a $1.5 bil loan-guarantee plan to aid the ailing **Chrysler Corp.**

Some 90 people, including 63 Americans, **taken hostage,** Nov. 4, at **American embassy in Tehran,** Iran, by militant followers of **Ayatollah Khomeini.** He demanded return of former Shah Muhammad Reza Pahlavi, who was undergoing medical treatment in New York City.

1980

Pres. Carter announced, Jan. 4, economic sanctions against the USSR, in retaliation for Soviet invasion of Afghanistan. At Carter's request, **U.S. Olympic Committee** voted, Apr. 12, against U.S. participation in Moscow Summer Olympics.

Lake Placid, NY, hosted the **Winter Olympics** for the 2nd time. The U.S. hockey team defeated the heavily favored Russian team Feb. 22 en route to winning the gold medal.

Eight Americans killed and 5 wounded, Apr. 24, **in ill-fated** attempt to **rescue hostages** held by Iranian militants.

Mt. St. Helens, in Washington state, **erupted** May 18. The blast, with others May 25 and June 12, left 57 dead.

In a sweeping victory, Nov. 4, **Ronald Reagan** (R) was elected 40th president, defeating incumbent Pres. Carter. Republicans gained control of the Senate.

Former Beatle **John Lennon** was shot and **killed**, Dec. 8, in New York City.

1981

Minutes after Reagan's inauguration Jan. 20, the **52 Americans** held **hostage in Iran** for 444 days were **freed.**

Pres. Reagan was **shot and seriously wounded**, Mar. 30, in Washington, DC; also seriously wounded were a Secret Service agent, a policeman, and Press Sec. **James Brady. John W. Hinckley Jr.** arrested, found not guilty by reason of insanity in **1982,** committed to mental institution.

World's first reusable spacecraft, the **space shuttle *Columbia***, was sent into space, Apr. 12.

Congress, July 29, passed Pres. Reagan's **tax-cut legislation,** expected to save taxpayers $750 bil over 5 years.

Federal air traffic controllers, Aug. 3, began an illegal **nationwide strike.** Most defied a back-to-work order and were dismissed by Pres. Reagan Aug. 5.

In a 99-0 vote, the Senate confirmed, Sept. 21, appointment of **Sandra Day O'Connor** as **first woman justice** of U.S. Supreme Court.

1982

The 13-year-old lawsuit against **AT&T** by the **Justice Dept.** was settled Jan. 8. AT&T agreed to give up the 22 Bell System companies and was allowed to expand.

The Equal Rights Amendment was **defeated** after a 10-year struggle, when the deadline for ratification expired June 30.

Centers for Disease Control, July 16, reported evidence of growing **AIDS epidemic**, responsible for 184 U.S. deaths since 1st reported in U.S. in June **1981.**

The economy showed signs of recovery from the **recession** that began in mid-**1981,** as the **Dow Jones** Industrial Average Oct. 13 hit 1016.93, its highest level in 18 months.

The most expensive **strike** in sports history ended, Nov. 16, when **NFL** players and team owners settled.

Space shuttle ***Columbia*** completed its first operational flight, Nov. 16.

A retired dentist, **Dr. Barney B. Clark,** 61, became first recipient of a **permanent artificial heart,** Dec. 2; he died Mar. 23, **1983,** after 112 days.

EPA administrator Anne Gorsuch was **cited for contempt** by the House Dec. 16, after refusing to produce certain documents concerning the Superfund.

1983

Pres. Reagan, Jan. 3, declared Times Beach, MO, a federal disaster area because of toxic **dioxin** in the soil.

The Commerce Dept. Jan 19 reported that average real **GNP** in the recessionary year **1982** fell 1.8% from **1981** levels, the **worst decline** since 1946.

Harold Washington was elected Apr. 12 as the first African-American **mayor of Chicago**.

On Apr. 20, **Pres. Reagan** signed a compromise bipartisan bill designed to save **Social Security** from bankruptcy.

Sally Ride became the first American **woman** to travel in **space,** June 18, when the **space shuttle *Challenger*** was launched from Cape Canaveral, FL.

On Sept. 1, **a South Korean passenger jet** infringing on Soviet air space and apparently misidentified was **shot down;** 269 people, including 61 Americans, were killed.

On Oct. 23, 241 **U.S. Marines and sailors** were killed in Lebanon when a TNT-laden suicide bomb blew up Marine headquarters at **Beirut** International Airport.

U.S. troops, with a small force from 6 **Caribbean** nations, invaded **Grenada** Oct. 25. In a few days, Grenadian militia and Cuban "construction workers" were overcome, U.S. citizens evacuated, and the **Marxist regime deposed.**

1984

Seven **regional companies** took over **local telephone service** from AT&T, Jan. 1.

On the space shuttle *Challenger*, launched on its 4th trip Feb. 3, two austronauts became **first humans to fly free of a spacecraft.**

On May 7, American **Vietnam war** veterans reached an out-of-court **settlement with 7 chemical companies** in a class-action suit over the herbicide **Agent Orange.**

Former Vice Pres. **Walter Mondale** won the **Democratic presidential nomination,** June 6; he chose **Rep. Geraldine Ferraro** (D, NY) as candidate for **vice president.**

Pres. Reagan signed a bill July 17 cutting federal transportation aid to states that keep their **drinking age** under 21.

Pres. **Reagan** was **reelected** Nov. 6 in a Republican **landslide,** carrying 49 states for a record 525 electoral votes.

Bernhard Goetz shot and wounded 4 allegedly menacing teenage boys, on a NYC subway train, Dec. 22; later was acquitted of major charges but was successfully sued.

1985

Visiting Germany, Pres. Reagan, May 5, laid wreath at concentration camp site and also at a **Bitburg** cemetery, where some Nazis lay.

Philadelphia police bombed a rowhouse occupied by **MOVE anarchists**, May 13; 11 were killed, and fire damaged 2 blocks of houses.

On June 14 a **TWA jet was seized** by terrorists after takeoff from Athens; 153 passengers and crew held hostage for 17 days; 1 U.S. serviceman killed.

Reversing an earlier decision to market "new" coke, the **Coca-Cola Co.** said, July 10, it would resume marketing soda made under its original "Classic" formula.

"Live Aid," a rock concert broadcast around the world July 13, raised $70 mil for starving peoples of Africa.

On Oct. 7, **4 Palestinian hijackers seized** Italian cruise ship ***Achille Lauro*** in the Mediterranean and held it hostage for 2 days; one American, Leon Klinghoffer, was killed.

For first time in 6 years U.S. and Soviet leaders met at **summit in Geneva**, Nov. 19-20.

General Electric agreed Dec. 11 to buy RCA Corp. for $6.28 bil.

1986

On Jan. 20, for the first time, the U.S. officially observed **Martin Luther King Jr. Day.**

The space shuttle ***Challenger*** **exploded** 73 seconds after liftoff, Jan. 28, **killing 6 astronauts and Christa McAuliffe,** a New Hampshire teacher, on board.

In a 4-day extravaganza in July, the U.S. celebrated the 100th birthday of the **Statue of Liberty**.

Congress completed action Oct. 2 overriding a veto to place conomic **sanctions on South Africa**.

The Senate confirmed, Sept. 17, Reagan's nomination of **William Rehnquist** as chief justice and **Antonin Scalia** as associate justice of the Supreme Court.

Press reports in early Nov. broke first news of the **Iran-contra scandal,** involving secret U.S. sale of arms to Iran.

Ivan Boesky, accused of insider trading, agreed, Nov. 14, to plead guilty to an unspecified criminal count.

Robert Penn Warren was named by the Library of Congress as America's **first poet laureate**.

1987

Pres. Reagan produced the nation's first **trillion-dollar budget**, Jan. 5.

Dow Jones closed above 2,000 for first time, Jan. 8.

The U.S. government, Mar. 20, approved, for the first time, the use of a drug in the fight against AIDS (AZT).

Nearly **1.4 mil illegal aliens** met May 4 deadline for applying for **amnesty** under a new federal policy.

An **Iraqi missile killed 37 sailors** on the frigate USS *Stark* in the Persian Gulf, May 17. Iraq called it an accident.

Public hearings by Senate and House committees investigating the **Iran-contra affair** were held May-Aug. Lt. Col. **Oliver North** said he had believed all his activities were authorized by his superiors. Pres. Reagan, Aug. 12, denied knowing of a diversion of funds to the contras.

The 200th anniversary of the **U.S. Constitution** signing was observed, Sept. 17, in Philadelphia and around the U.S.

Wall Street crashed, Oct. 19, with the Dow Jones plummeting a record 508 points to 1738, ending a bull market that began in mid-**1982.**

Pres. Reagan and Soviet leader **Mikhail Gorbachev,** Dec. 8, signed a **pact to dismantle** all 1,752 U.S. and 859 Soviet **missiles** with a 300- to 3,400-mi. range.

1988

In a report issued May 16, Surgeon Gen. C. Everett Koop declared that **cigarettes** were addictive.

Congress approved, in June, the greatest expansion yet of **Medicare** benefits, to protect the **elderly and disabled** against "catastrophic" medical costs.

Much of the U.S. suffered worst **drought** in over 50 years; by late June half the nation's agricultural counties had been declared disaster areas.

A missile, fired from **U.S. Navy warship *Vincennes,*** in the Persian Gulf, mistakenly struck a commercial **Iranian airliner**, July 3, killing all 290.

George H. W. Bush was **elected** 41st U.S. **president**, Nov. 8, decisively defeating Gov. **Michael Dukakis** (MA).

Pan Am Flight 103 exploded and crashed, due to a terrorist bomb, into the town of **Lockerbie, Scotland,** Dec. 21, killing all 259 people aboard and 11 on the ground.

Drexel Burnham Lambert agreed, Dec. 21, **to plead guilty** to insider trading and other violations, and **pay penalties of $650 mil,** the largest such settlement ever.

1989

Major oil spill occurred when the ***Exxon Valdez*** struck Bligh Reef in Alaska's Prince William Sound, Mar. 24.

Former National Security Council staff member **Oliver North** was convicted, May 4, on charges related to **Iran-contra** scandal. Conviction thrown out on appeal in **1991** because of his immunized testimony.

A measure to **rescue the savings and loan industry** was signed into law, Aug. 9, by Pres. Bush.

Army Gen. Colin Powell was nominated Aug. 10 by Pres. Bush, as **chairman of the Joint Chiefs of Staff;** he became the first black to hold the post.

Pete Rose, a baseball legend, was **banned** from the game for life Aug. 24, for involvement with gamblers.

Hurricane Hugo swept through the Caribbean and the Carolinas Sept. 10-22, causing at least 40 deaths and $6 bil in damage in the Carolinas alone.

Just before a World Series game, Oct. 17, an **earthquake** struck the **San Francisco Bay area,** causing 62 deaths.

L. Douglas Wilder (D) elected governor of Virginia, the **first U.S. black governor** since Reconstruction.

U.S. troops invaded Panama, Dec. 20, overthrowing the government of **Manuel Noriega.** Noriega, wanted by U.S. authorities on drug charges, surrendered Jan. 3, **1990.**

1990

Junk bond financier Michael Milkin pleaded guilty to fraud related charges, Apr. 14; agreed to pay $500 mil in restitution; sentenced Nov. 21 to 10 years in prison.

Justice William Brennan announced, July 20, his resignation from the U.S. Supreme Court; his replacement, **Judge David Souter,** was confirmed Sept. 27.

Pres. Bush signed **Americans With Disabilities Act** on July 26, barring discrimination against the disabled.

Operation Desert Shield forces left for **Saudi Arabia,** Aug. 7, to defend that country following the **invasion** of its neighbor **Kuwait by Iraq,** Aug. 2.

Pres. Bush signed, Nov. 5, a bill to **reduce budget deficits** $500 bil over 5 years, by spending curbs and tax hikes.

Pres. Bush Nov. 15 signed into law a strengthened version of the 1970 **Clean Air Act.**

1991

The **U.S. and its allies defeated Iraq** in the **Persian Gulf War** and liberated Kuwait, which Iraq had overrun in Aug. **1990.** On Jan. 17, the allies launched a devastating **air attack.** In a **rapid ground war** starting Feb. 24, which lasted just 100 hours, the U.S.-led forces killed or captured thousands of Iraqi soldiers and sent the rest into retreat before Pres. Bush ordered a cease-fire Feb. 27.

An 8-month **recession** showed signs of having ended in Mar. **The Dow Jones** Industrial Average closed above **3000** for first time, Apr. 17

Justice **Thurgood Marshall**, first black to sit on U.S. Supreme Court, June 17, announced plans **to retire**.

U.S. **House bank** ordered closed Oct. 3 after revelations that House members had written 8,331 bad checks.

The **Senate approved,** Oct. 15, nomination of **Clarence Thomas** to the Supreme Court, despite allegations of sexual harassment against him by **Anita Hill,** a former aide. He became the 2nd African-American to serve on the Court, replacing retiring Justice **Thurgood Marshall,** the 1st black.

Charles Keating convicted of securities fraud Dec. 4. The prosecution asserted that as chairman of an S&L he had induced investors to buy $250 mil in uninsured bonds.

1992

Retail giant **R.H. Macy & Co.** filed for bankruptcy, Jan. 27. **Trans World Airlines,** Jan. 31, became the latest major U.S. carrier to file for bankruptcy.

Riots swept South-Central **Los Angeles** Apr. 29, after **jury acquitted 4 white policemen** on all but one count in videotaped 1991 beating of black motorist **Rodney King.** Death toll in the L.A. violence was put at 52.

The **27th Amendment**, regarding congressional pay raises, became part of the Constitution May 7 when it was ratified by the 38th state, Michigan.

Hurricane Andrew ravaged South Florida and Louisiana Aug. 24-26, killing 23 people.

White supremacist and fugitive Randall Weaver surrendered Aug. 31 after an 11-day FBI **siege** at his **Ruby Ridge,** ID, cabin, during which his wife and son and a deputy sheriff were killed in exchanges of gunfire.

Bill Clinton (D) was **elected** 42nd president, Nov. 3, defeating **Pres. Bush** (R) and independent **Ross Perot.**

A UN-sanctioned military force, led by U.S. troops, arrived in **Somalia** Dec. 9.

Presidents of U.S., Canada, and Mexico Dec. 17 signed North American Free Trade Agreement.

More than 1.1 million votes were cast in an election to choose a portrait of the late **Elvis Presley** (died 1977) for a **U.S. postage stamp**.

1993

A bomb exploded in a parking garage beneath the **World Trade Center** in New York City, Feb. 26, killing 6 people. Two Islamic militants were convicted in the bombing, Nov. 12, **1997**. Four men were found guilty, Mar. 4, **1994**.

Janet Reno became the first woman U.S. attorney general Mar. 12.

Four federal agents were killed, Feb. 28, during an unsuccessful raid on the **Branch Davidian compound near Waco, TX.** A 51-day siege by federal agents ended Apr. 19, when the compound **burned down,** leaving more than 70 cult members dead. 11 **cult** members were acquitted Feb. 26, **1994,** of charges in the deaths of the federal agents. U.S. agents were cleared of wrong doing in 2000.

A federal jury, Apr. 17, found **2 Los Angeles police officers guilty** and 2 not guilty of violating the civil rights of motorist **Rodney King** in **1991** beating incident.

Defense Sec. Les Aspin, Apr. 28, removed restrictions on aerial **combat roles by women** in the armed forces.

In a May 14 **plebiscite** voters in Puerto Rico supported continuing commonwealth status with U.S.

A **"motor-voter" bill** was signed by Pres. Clinton, May 20, allowing citizens to register to vote by mail when applying for a driver's license or certain benefits.

"The Great Flood of 1993" inundated 8 mil acres in 9 Midwestern states in summer, leaving 50 dead.

Pres. Clinton July 2 approved recommendations that 33 major U.S. **military bases** be **closed.** On July 19 he announced a **"don't ask, don't tell, don't pursue"** policy for homosexuals in the U.S. military.

Judge Ruth Bader Ginsburg was sworn in, Aug. 10, as 107th justice of the Supreme Court.

Pres. Clinton, Aug. 10, signed a measure designed to **cut federal budget deficits** $496 bil over 5 years, through spending cuts and new taxes.

The **"Brady Bill,"** a major gun-control measure, was signed into law by Pres. Clinton Nov. 30.

1994

North American Free Trade Agreement took effect Jan. 1.

A predawn **earthquake** struck the **Los Angeles** area, Jan. 17, claiming 61 lives and causing widespread devastation.

Pres. Clinton Feb. 3 lifted 19-year ban on U.S. **trade with Vietnam.**

Kenneth Starr named Aug. 5 as independent counsel to probe **Whitewater affair;** congressional committees, late July, began Whitewater hearings.

Byron De La Beckwith convicted Feb. 5 of the **1963** murder of civil rights leader **Medgar Evers.**

Longtime CIA officer **Aldrich Ames** and his wife were **charged** Feb. 21 **with spying**. Under a plea bargain, he received life in prison, while she drew 63 months.

U.S. troops, Mar. 25, officially ended peacekeeping and humanitarian aid mission in **Somalia** begun in **1992.**

Major league **baseball players went on strike,** following Aug. 11 games; World Series canceled; strike ended Apr. 25, **1995**.

Senate Majority Leader George Mitchell (D, ME), Sept. 26, dropped efforts to pass Pres. Clinton's **health-care reform** package.

1995

When the 104th Congress opened, Jan. 4, **Sen. Bob Dole** (R, KS) became **Senate majority leader** and **Rep. Newt Gingrich** (R, GA) was elected **House Speaker.** A bill to end Congress's exemption from federal labor laws, first in a series of measures in Republicans' **"Contract With America,"** cleared Congress Jan. 17; signed into law Jan. 23.

Clinton invoked emergency powers, Jan. 31, to extend a **$20 bil loan** to help **Mexico** avert financial collapse.

The last UN peacekeeping troops withdrew from **Somalia** Feb. 28-Mar. 3, with the aid of U.S. Marines. In **Haiti,** peacekeeping responsibilities were transferred from U.S. to UN forces Mar. 31, with the U.S. providing 2,400 soldiers.

A truck **bomb** exploded outside **a federal office building in Oklahoma City** Apr. 19, **killing 168** people in all, in deadliest terrorist attack yet on U.S. soil; **Timothy McVeigh** was 1st and key suspect arrested, Apr. 21.

The U.S. space shuttle *Atlantis* made the first in a series of **dockings with** Russian space station ***Mir,*** June 29-July 4.

A U.S. **F-16 fighter jet** piloted by Air Force Capt. **Scott O'Grady** was **shot down** over Bosnia and Herzegovina June 2; O'Grady was **rescued** by U.S. Marines 6 days later.

The U.S. announced on July 11 that it was reestablishing diplomatic **relations with Vietnam.**

Former football star **O. J. Simpson** found **not guilty** Oct. 3 of the **June 1994** murders of his former wife, Nicole Brown Simpson, and her friend Ron Goldman.

Ten Muslim militants convicted in New York, Oct. 1, in a failed plot to blow up **UN Headquarters** and other buildings and assassinate political leaders.

Shannon Faulkner won a legal fight to gain admission to the previously all-male cadet corps of **The Citadel,** Aug. 11, though she dropped out after a few days of training.

Hundreds of thousands of African-American men participated in **"Million Man March"** and rally in Washington, DC, Oct. 16, organized by Rev. Louis Farrakhan.

The federal **55-mile-per-hour speed limit** was **repealed** by a measure signed Nov. 28.

After talks outside Dayton, OH, **warring parties in Bosnia and Herzegovina reached agreement** Nov. 21 to end their conflict; treaty was signed Dec. 14, after which first of some 20,000 **U.S. peacekeeping troops** arrived in Bosnia.

Five Americans were among 7 **killed,** Nov. 13, in bombing of a U.S. military post in **Riyadh, Saudi Arabia.**

A budget impasse between Congress and Pres. Clinton led to a partial **government shutdown** beginning Nov. 14. Operations resumed Nov. 20 under continuing resolutions.

1996

Senate, Jan. 26, approved, 87-4, the Second Strategic Arms Reduction Treaty (**START II**).

On Feb. 24 **Cuban jets shot down** 2 civilian planes owned by a Cuban exile group; 4 killed. Cuba claimed its territory was violated; U.S., Feb. 26, tightened embargo.

John Salvi found guilty, Mar. 18, in the **1994 murder** of receptionists at 2 **abortion clinics** in Brookline, MA.

Congress, in Mar., approved a **"line item veto"** bill, but it was struck down by the Supreme Court, June 25, **1998**.

James and Susan McDougal were convicted May 28 of fraud and conspiracy in the Whitewater case. Arkansas Gov. **Jim Guy Tucker** was convicted of similar charges by the same jury.

The antitax **Freemen** surrendered to federal authorities June 13 after an 81-day standoff near Jordan, MT; 4 were convicted, July 8, **1998**, of conspiring to defraud banks.

Republicans June 12 chose Sen. **Trent Lott** (MS) as new majority leader to replace Sen. **Robert Dole,** who resigned, June 11, to focus on his presidential campaign.

A **bomb** exploded at a military complex near Dhahran, **Saudi Arabia,** June 25, killing 19 American servicemen.

On July 27 **a bomb exploded** in Atlanta, GA, near the **Olympics;** one person was directly killed.

Major **welfare reform bill** was signed into law Aug. 22.

Shannon Lucid, Sept. 26, completed a space voyage of 188 days, a record for women and for U.S. astronauts.

Pres. Clinton was reelected to 2nd term, Nov. 5.

1997

Bombs were detonated at **abortion clinics** in Tulsa, OK, Jan. 1, in Atlanta on Jan. 16, and again at the first site in Tulsa on Jan. 19; 6 people were injured.

Newt Gingrich (R, GA) was reelected Speaker of the U.S. House Jan. 7, but was fined and reprimanded by colleagues for alleged misuse of tax-exempt donations.

Madeleine Albright was sworn in as secretary of state Jan. 23, becoming the first woman to head State Dept.

Harold Nicholson, a former CIA official, pleaded guilty, Mar. 3, to spying for Russia.

39 members of the **Heaven's Gate religious cult** found dead in a house in Rancho Santa Fe, CA, Mar. 26, in an apparent mass suicide.

Timothy McVeigh convicted of conspiracy and murder, June 2, in **1995** Oklahoma City bombing.

On **Oct. 27,** the **Dow Jones** fell 554.26 points, largest 1-day point decline yet. On Oct. 28, the Dow rebounded, surging 337.17 points, largest-yet single-day point advance.

Islamic militants **Ramzi Ahmed Yousef** and **Eyad Ismoil Yousef** convicted, Nov. 12, in the **1993** bombing of the World Trade Center in New York City.

On Nov. 19, **Bobbi McCaughey**, 29, delivered the first set of live septuplets to survive more than a month.

Terry Nichols convicted Dec. 23 on charges related to the **1995 Oklahoma City bombing**.

1998

It was reported Jan. 21 that Whitewater independent counsel Kenneth Starr had evidence of a **sexual relationship** between **Pres. Clinton** and onetime White House intern Monica Lewinsky. Clinton denied it.

Theodore Kaczynski, the **"Unabomber,"** arrested in Montana in 1993, pleaded guilty Jan. 22 in California and New Jersey bombings that killed 3 people and injured 2.

The state of Texas, Feb. 3, executed its first female convict in 135 years—**Karla Faye Tucker**.

2 youths aged 11 and 13 were arrested, Mar. 24, in the killing of 4 schoolgirls and a teacher outside a **Jonesboro, AR,** school; later committed to a juvenile detention center.

On Apr. 25, First Lady **Hillary Rodham Clinton** provided videotaped testimony at the White House for the Little Rock, AR, grand jury in the **Whitewater** case.

Monica Lewinsky, Aug. 6, testified to having had a sexual relationship with **Pres. Clinton,** but said she was never asked to lie. In grand jury testimony and an address to the nation, Aug. 17, **Clinton** acknowledged an inappropriate relationship with Lewinsky. On Sept. 9, independent counsel **Kenneth Starr** sent the House what he called "credible information that may constitute grounds" for impeachment.

Mark McGwire, Sept. 8, hit his 62nd **home run** of the season, breaking **Roger Maris's** season record.

On Sept. 30, Pres. Clinton announced a **budget surplus** of $70 billion for fiscal year 1998, the first since 1969.

Terrorist **bombs** in **U.S. embassies** in Nairobi, Kenya, and Dar-es-Salaam, Tanzania, killed at least 257, Aug. 7. The U.S. launched **retaliatory strikes**, Aug. 20, against alleged terrorist-related targets in Afghanistan and Sudan.

The House Judiciary Committee, Oct. 5, voted 21-16 along party lines to recommend that the Clinton **impeachment** investigation proceed. The House concurred Oct. 8, voting 258-176; 31 Democrats voted yes.

John Glenn, 77, first U.S. astronaut to orbit Earth, returned to space Oct. 29-Nov. 7, aboard the shuttle *Discovery*.

Pres. Clinton, Nov. 13, settled a suit by agreeing to pay $850,000 to **Paula Corbin Jones.** She alleged that he had made an unwanted sexual advance to her in 1991.

The country's 4 largest **tobacco** companies, in a settlement, Nov. 23, with 46 states, the District of Columbia, and 4 territories, agreed to pay $206 bil over 25 years to cover public health costs related to smoking.

The U.S. House, Dec. 19, approved 2 articles of **impeachment** charging **Pres. Clinton** with grand jury perjury (228-206) and obstruction of justice (221-212) in a cover-up of his sexual relationship with **Monica Lewinsky;** 2 other impeachment articles failed.

1999

J. Dennis Hastert (IL) was elected Speaker of the House for the 106th Congress, Jan. 6.

Pres. Clinton's impeachment trial—the 2nd such trial in U.S. history—began in the GOP-controlled Senate Jan. 7. He was acquitted, Feb. 12. The perjury article failed, with 45 votes; the obstruction of justice article drew a 50-50 vote, with a two-thirds vote needed for conviction.

Dr. Jack Kevorkian, who claimed he had helped 130 people kill themselves, convicted of 2nd-degree murder Mar. 26 in one death; sentenced to 10-25 years in prison.

Two men were convicted in the **1998** beating death of **Matthew Shepard,** an openly homosexual student at the Univ. of Wyoming.

Eric Harris, 18, and Dylan Klebold, 17, killed 12 fellow students and a teacher Apr. 20 at **Columbine** High School in Littleton, CO, then shot themselves fatally.

One NYC police officer pleaded guilty to 6 charges, May 25, and another was convicted on an assault charge, June 8, in connection with the **1997** torture and sodomizing of Haitian immigrant **Abner Louima** in a police station.

John F. Kennedy Jr., son of the former president, died in a plane crash July 16, along with his wife and sister-in-law.

The **Dow Jones** closed the year at a **record** level of 11,497.12—25.2% above the **1998** close.

2000

Across the U.S., midnight **celebrations** marked the changeover to the **year 2000** on Jan. 1; the feared **Y2K** computer glitch caused only minor problems.

America Online Inc. announced Jan. 10 that it would buy **Time Warner Inc.**, in the largest merger to date. The FTC approved it Dec. 14.

Teams of scientists from the U.S. and Britain announced jointly, June 26, that they had determined the structure of the **human genome.**

Following a bitter legal controversy, 6-year-old Cuban **Elián González** was returned to Cuba June 28, 7 months after he was rescued from a boat wreck off the coast of Florida.

The Justice Dept., July 21, cleared U.S. agents of any wrongdoing in a **1993** assault on the compound of the Branch Davidian religious sect in **Waco,** TX.

Tiger Woods, 24, became the youngest to win all 4 of golf's majors, with record score in British Open July 23.

17 U.S. sailors were killed Oct. 12 in terrorist bombing of the **USS *Cole*,** refueling in Aden, Yemen.

The U.S. Food and Drug Administration announced, Sept. 28, approval of **RU-486,** a pill that induces abortions.

On **election night,** Nov. 7, the winner of Florida's 25 deciding electoral votes remained uncertain. The Florida Supreme Court, Dec. 8, ordered a manual recount of all ballots that did not have a vote for president recorded by machine. On Dec. 12, the U.S. Supreme Court reversed that decision. Vice Pres. Gore conceded the presidential election to Gov. **George W. Bush** (TX) in a televised address, Dec. 13.

2001

Congress, Jan. 6, certified **George W. Bush** as president by an electoral vote of 271- 266 (1 Gore elector abstained).

AOL-Time Warner merger completed, Jan. 11.

Outgoing Pres. Clinton issued 176 pardons and commutations, Jan. 20, including that of **Marc Rich**, a fugitive commodities trader whose ex-wife was a financial backer.

George W. Bush, was sworn in as 43rd president Jan. 20.

FBI agent **Robert Hanssen** arrested Feb. 20 and charged 2 days later with spying for the Soviet Union and Russia.

A **U.S. Navy spy plane** collided with a Chinese fighter plane over the South China Sea Apr. 1, killing the fighter pilot. The 24 U.S. crew members were detained in Hainan until U.S. officials expressed apology, Apr. 12.

Sen. James Jeffords (R, VT) announced May 24 he was leaving his party, giving Democrats control of the Senate.

Congress approved, May 26, a $1.35 trillion **tax cut** spread over 10 years.

Oklahoma City bomber **Timothy McVeigh** was executed June 11 by lethal injection in Terre Haute, IN.

Rep. **Gary Condit** (D, CA) in a TV interview Aug. 23 denied involvement in the Apr. 30 disappearance of intern **Chandra Levy,** with whom he had had an affair. Levy's remains were later found in a DC park.

Bush announced Aug. 9 he would allow federal funding of limited **stem-cell research** using human embryos.

On the morning of **Sept. 11,** 2 hijacked commercial airliners struck and destroyed the twin towers of the **World Trade Center** in New York City, in the worst-ever **terrorist attack** on American soil. A 3rd hijacked plane destroyed a portion of the **Pentagon** and a 4th crashed in **Pennsylvania.** Some 3,000 people were killed, including about 2,800 at the World Trade Center. U.S. observed a national day of mourning, Sept. 14.

Congress, Sept. 21, approved a $15 bil bailout package for the **airline industry.**

The **U.S.** and **Britain** Oct. 7 launched a sustained air strike campaign against Afghan-based terrorist organization **al-Qaeda** and the country's ruling Taliban militia.

On Oct. 7, San Francisco Giant outfielder **Barry Bonds** hit his **73rd** home run for a single season record.

Pres. Bush created a new **Office of Homeland Security,** Oct. 8, and signed a federal **antiterrorism bill** Oct. 26.

5 people died and 14 became ill from exposure to **anthrax** traveling through the U.S. mail, Oct. 5-Nov. 21.

The **Taliban** surrendered Kabul, the Afghan capital, Nov. 13, and fled from Kandahar, their stronghold, Dec. 7.

Leading energy-trading company **Enron** became the largest firm thus far to file for bankruptcy, Dec. 2.

The U.S. government, Dec. 11, indicted **Zacarias Moussaoui** as an alleged conspirator in the Sept. 11 attacks.

Pres. Bush announced Dec. 13 that the U.S. would withdraw from the 1972 **Antiballistic Missile Treaty**.

Pres. Bush, Dec. 28, formally granted permanent normal trade status to **China**, as of Jan. 1, 2002.

Taliban member **John Walker Lindh,** a U.S. citizen, was captured Dec. 2 by U.S. forces in Afghanistan.

2002

Taliban and al-Qaeda fighters captured in Afghanistan were flown to a U.S. **naval base at Guantanamo Bay** in Cuba, with the first 20 arriving Jan. 11.

A House committee Jan. 14 released parts of a letter from Sherron Watkins, an **Enron** employee, to CEO Kenneth Lay, warning him the company could "implode" in scandal. Lay resigned Jan. 23. Congress, Jan. 24, began public hearings into the **Enron** bankruptcy.

In his first State of the Union address, Jan. 29, Pres. Bush called Iran, Iraq, and North Korea part of an **"axis of evil."**

Eight U.S. troops were killed Mar. 2-4 in an assault against Taliban and al-Qaeda forces in eastern Afghanistan. By Mar. 6, 1,200 U.S. troops were involved in the mission, **Operation Anaconda,** which ended Mar. 12.

A final independent prosecutor's report Mar. 20 found **insufficient evidence** that Pres. Clinton or his wife had committed any crime in connection with **Whitewater.**

Pres. Bush Mar. 27 signed into law a major **campaign-finance** reform bill.

A ceremonial last girder was removed May 30 from the site of the **World Trade Center** towers in New York, signaling the end of a massive clean-up and recovery operation.

Coleen Rowley testified before a congressional committee June 6 that Washington FBI agents had stymied investigative efforts in Minneapolis.

U.S. **Roman Catholic bishops**, meeting in Dallas, TX, June 13-15, approved stringent policies dealing with priests who sexually abuse minors; revised rules formulated with Vatican approval were adopted by the bishops Nov. 13.

The **Arthur Andersen** accounting firm was convicted of obstruction of justice by a federal jury, June 15.

WorldCom announced June 25 that it had overstated its cash flow by billions; on July 21, it displaced Enron Corp. as the largest U.S. company to declare bankruptcy.

On July 4, an Egyptian-born gunman killed 2 people near an **El Al ticket counter** at the L.A. international airport; he was shot dead by an El Al guard.

A dramatic **rescue** operation July 28 saved the lives of 9 miners trapped in a Pennsylvania **coal mine**.

Pres. Bush told the **UN General Assembly** Sept. 12 that he would work with the Security Council to deal with the threat posed by **Iraqi weapons** of mass destruction.

Richard Reid pleaded guilty Oct. 4 to all charges stemming from an incident aboard a Paris-to-Miami flight in Dec. 2001, when he tried to ignite **explosives in his shoes.**

Four men were arrested in **Portland, OR**, Oct. 4, charged with plotting to join **al-Qaeda** and Taliban forces; a 5th suspect was later arrested in Malaysia. On Oct. 9, the head of an Islamic charity, the Benevolence International Foundation, was charged with funneling money to al-Qaeda.

Former Pres. **Jimmy Carter** was named Oct. 10 as winner of the 2002 **Nobel Peace Prize**

On Oct. 10-11 the House, 296-133, and Senate, 77-23, gave Bush **backing** for using **military force** against Iraq.

The Bush administration revealed Oct. 16 that **North Korea** had acknowledged it was developing nuclear arms.

Two men were arrested Oct. 24 in connection with a series of random **sniper shootings** in the Washington, DC, area that left 10 dead.

Sen. **Paul Wellstone** (D, MN) died in a plane crash near Eveleth, MN, Oct. 25, with his wife, daughter, and 5 others.

Pres Bush, Oct. 29, signed a measure providing $3.9 bil to the states to fix shortcomings in their **election process**.

An antitrust settlement between **Microsoft** Corp. and U.S. Justice Dept. was approved Nov. 1 by a federal judge.

Republicans emerged from elections, Nov. 5, with a majority in the Senate and an increased margin in the House.

Rep. **Nancy Pelosi** (CA) was elected by House Democrats Nov. 14 to head their caucus in the new Congress, the **first woman** to lead either party in the House.

Some 50 mil people in 8 states and the province of Ontario

Pres. **Bush** Nov. 25 signed legislation creating a cabinet-level Dept. of **Homeland Security**.

Cardinal Bernard Law, Dec. 13, resigned as archbishop of Boston after he had been blamed by many for allegedly covering up instances of a child sexual-abuse by Catholic priests.

On Dec. 16, Pres. Bush named former NJ Gov. Thomas Kean (R) to chair a national **commission** investigating the Sept. 11, 2001, **attacks**.

Bush, Dec. 17, ordered the Pentagon to proceed with construction of a limited **missile defense shield**.

Trent Lott (R, MS), just chosen as majority leader in the new Senate, **bowed out** Dec. 20, amid furor over a comment apparently supporting segregation; Sen. **Bill Frist** (R, TN) was elected as leader Dec. 23.

2003

On Jan. 10-11, shortly before leaving office, Gov. George Ryan (R, IL) pardoned or commuted death sentences of 171 **convicts on death row.**

The Senate, Jan. 22, approved, 94-0, Pres. Bush's nomination of Tom Ridge to be **secretary of homeland security.**

The **space shuttle *Columbia* broke apart in space** Feb. 1 over southwestern U.S. during its descent toward a planned landing; all 7 crew members were killed. An official report issued Aug. 26 found the immediate cause was foam breaking off after liftoff and damaging the left wing; it also cited a "broken safety culture" at NASA.

The Senate, Mar. 6, approved, 95-0, the **Strategic Offensive Reductions Treaty** signed in 2002 by leaders of the U.S. and Russia. It required the 2 countries to reduce their deployed nuclear warheads to 1,700-2,200 by 2012.

On Apr. 3, **U.S. Marines** crossed the Tigris River and moved close to Baghdad. By Apr. 8, major government buildings had been occupied and **organized resistance had dropped away**. With the collapse of the regime, services in major cities were disrupted, and **looting** became widespread. Pres. Bush, speaking from the aircraft carrier *Abraham Lincoln*, declared on May 1 that **major combat operations had ended**. However, insurgents continued to mount attacks against both military and civilan targets.

Nine Democrats seeking their party's nomination for president in 2004 **debated** in Columbia, SC, May 3.

The *New York Times*, May 11, published a long story documenting major deceptions and inaccuracies by reporter **Jayson Blair**.

Pres. Bush signed a measure May 28 providing **$318 bil in tax cuts** over 10 years.

Under a settlement in a private antitrust suit brought by Netscape (a unit of AOL), **Microsoft** agreed May 29 to pay **AOL Time Warner** $750 mil.

On June 23, the Supreme Court, voting 5-4, **upheld an affirmative action program** providing preference to minorities for admission to the Univ. of Michigan law school. But the Court, 6-3, rejected an undergraduate affirmative action program at the university that employed numerical formulas.

The Labor Dept. reported July 3 that June **unemployment** had climbed to a 9-year high of 6.4%. Since Feb. 2001, the economy had lost almost 2.6 mil jobs.

The Senate Nov. 3 approved by voice vote the **$87.5 bil** that Pres. Bush sought **for U.S. military forces** in Iraq and for helping to rebuild the country. The House had given its approval, 298-121, on Oct. 31.

A **U.S.-led military offensive aimed at ousting Saddam Hussein** in Iraq got underway Mar. 19, when 40 Tomahawk cruise missiles hit **targets in Baghdad**; strikes continued in succeeding nights. U.S. forces Mar. 21 seized major **oil fields near Basra**. On Apr. 1, U.S. forces announced the rescue from an Iraqi hospital of injured Army Pfc. **Jessica Lynch**, one of a group of soldiers ambushed near Nasiriyah.

Forest fires in southern California in late October laid waste to over 700,000 acres and destroyed 3,000 homes.

U.S. soldiers killed 2 once-powerful **sons of Saddam Hussein** in a gun battle in Mosul, N Iraq, July 22.

A **power failure** spread rapidly through Ohio, Michigan, and the Northeast, as well as eastern Canada, on Aug. 14. were left without electricity for as long as 2 days.

WORLD ALMANAC QUICK QUIZ

Can you match the event with the year?
a. 1966; b. 1976; c. 1986; d. 1996

(1) The U.S. celebrated the 200th anniversary of the Declaration of Independence.
(2) The U.S. celebrated the 100th birthday of the Statue of Liberty.
(3) Shannon Lucid completed a 188-day voyage in space, a record for a U.S. astronaut and for women.
(4) The Supreme Court ruled in Miranda v. Arizona that suspects arrested by police must be read their rights before being questioned.

For the answer look in this chapter, or see page 1008.

John Geoghan, a **former priest** incarcerated for child sex abuse, was **strangled at a state prison** in Shirley, MA, Aug. 23, apparently by another inmate.

On Sept. 9, the Roman Catholic archdiocese of Boston and lawyers representing about 550 victims of **sexual abuse** by priests announced a **settlement** worth up to $85 mil.

Richard Grasso, chairman and CEO of the New York Stock Exchange, resigned under fire, Sept. 17.

California voters Oct. 7 voted to recall Gov. Gray Davis (D) from office and replace him with actor-turned-politician **Arnold Schwarzenegger** (R).

The Rev. V. Gene Robinson was consecrated Nov. 2 as Episcopal bishop of New Hampshire, becoming the **first openly gay prelate** in the Episcopal Church U.S.A.

A Virginia jury Nov. 17 found **John Muhammad** guilty in the **sniper attacks** that plagued the Washington, DC, area in 2002; he was sentenced to death. Another VA jury found **Lee Malvo** guilty of 2 counts of murder in the attacks, Dec. 18; he was sentenced to life in prison without parole.

The Massachusetts Supreme Judicial Court, in a controversial 4-3 decision Nov. 18, held that **gay couples** had a **right to marry** under the state constitution.

Saddam Hussein was captured by U.S. military forces Dec. 13, in an underground hideout southeast of Tikrit.

The Bush administration announced Dec. 23 that a Holstein in Washington State had tested positive for **mad-cow disease**; the animal, the first in the U.S. to be so identified, had been slaughtered.

Major stock indexes showed big gains for 2003. The Dow Jones had risen 25%, the NASDAQ by 50%.

2004

Sen. John Kerry (MA) became the Democratic frontrunner in the candidacy for the presidency by winning the Jan. 19 Iowa caucus and the Jan. 27 New Hampshire primary.

On Feb. 1 the New England Patriots beat the Carolina Panthers 32-29 in Super Bowl XXXVIII. During the **halftime show**, Justin Timberlake tore Janet Jackson's top garment, exposing her breast in what was called a **"wardrobe malfunction."**

On Feb. 12, **San Francisco** began issuing **marriage licenses** to thousands of **same-sex couples**. On Mar. 11, the state supreme court issued a stay blocking the practice.

Media entrepreneur **Martha Stewart** was **convicted** Mar. 5 of conspiracy and obstruction of justice. She was sentenced July 16 to 5 months in prison.

The **National World War II Memorial**, located on the National Mall in Washington, DC, opened to the public April 29. It was dedicated May 29.

Photos showing humiliating **abuse by American soldiers of prisoners in Iraq** emerged Apr. 30, provoking outrage.

Pres. Bush announced June 3 that he had accepted the **resignation of CIA Director** George Tenet, effective July 11.

Ronald Reagan, 40th president of the U.S., died at his home in Los Angeles June 5. He had been diagnosed with Alzheimer's disease in 1994.

In one of the biggest upsets in NBA history, the **Detroit Pistons won the 2004 NBA championship**, June 15, after they defeated the Los Angeles Lakers, 4 games to 1.

Connecticut Gov. John Rowland (R), facing impeachment amid federal corruption charges, announceds his **resignation**, effective July 1. He pleaded guilty Dec. 23 to one charge of corruption.

The U.S.-led coalition formally **transferred power to an interim Iraqi government** on June 28.

The 9/11 Commission Report, released to the public July 22, summarized what was known about the events of that day and called for a **restructuring** of the U.S. **intelligence operations**.

In Boston, July 26-29, **Democrats nominated Sen. John Kerry** for president and Sen. John Edwards (NC) for vice president.

Lance Armstrong won the Tour de France for a record-setting **6th consecutive year** July 25.

The **Statue of Liberty reopened** Aug. 3 having been closed for nearly two years following the terrorist attacks on Sept. 11, 2001. Extensive security and safety upgrades were completed to accommodate visitors.

Four hurricanes—Charley, Frances, Ivan, and Jeanne-hit **Florida** and surrounding states in a 6-week period, Aug. 13-Sept. 25. The storms were blamed for over 50 deaths and more than $20 bil in damage in the U.S. Flooding was severe in neighboring states Alabama, Georgia, Louisiana, and S. Carolina.

New Jersey Gov. James McGreevey (D) Aug. 12 announced his **resignation**, effective Nov. 15, citing an extramarital affair with another man.

Pres. **Bush** and Vice Pres. **Cheney** were renominated Sept. 1 on the **Republican ticket** at the party convention in New York.

The number of U.S. soldiers killed in the Iraqi conflict **reached 1,000** on Sept. 7, including 755 in combat.

CBS, Sept. 8, aired a story on *60 Minutes* in which it claimed to have obtained documents showing that **Pres. Bush** had failed to meet his responsibilities while a member of the **National Guard** in the 1970s. However, **serious doubts** were cast on the validity of the documents, and on Sept. 20, veteran CBS Evening News managing editor and anchorman, **Dan Rather**, admitted on air they could not be authenticated.

The Senate, Sept. 22, confirmed Rep. **Porter Goss** (R, FL) as the new **CIA director**.

The **Supreme Court** announced Oct. 25 that **Chief Justice William H. Rehnquist** was being treated for thyroid cancer. He did not attend oral arguments at the Court for the remainder of the year.

Sweeping their last 8 games, the **Boston Red Sox** Oct. 27 **won the World Series** for the first time since 1918.

Pres. George W. Bush won reelection on Tuesday Nov. 2, capturing 31 states with 286 electoral votes, just 16 more than the 270 needed. In the **Senate, Republicans gained 4 seats** for a new 55-44 majority as a result of the election. **Republicans won a majority in the House** of Representatives for the 6th consecutive election. After two runoff races were held in Louisiana, the newly elected House had 232 Republicans, 202 Democrats, and 1 independent.

On Nov. 14, **U.S. forces took control** of the Iraqi city of **Fallujah**, after a week-long campaign against insurgents who had controlled the city.

In an episode broadcast Nov. 30, **Ken Jennings** ended his record-setting **75-game winning streak** on *Jeopardy!*, leaving the show with over $2.5 million in prize money.

Pres. Bush signed an **intelligence reform bill** Dec. 17, based on findings of the 9-11 Commission. The new law created a **director of national intelligence** to oversee the nation's intelligence agencies.

Patrick Henry's Speech to the Virginia Convention

The following is an excerpt from Patrick Henry's speech to the Virginia Convention, which met at St. John's Church in Richmond, on Mar. 23, 1775, to react to British oppression.

Gentlemen may cry, peace, peace—but there is no peace. The war is actually begun! The next gale that sweeps from the north will bring to our ears the clash of resounding arms! Our brethren are already in the field! Why stand we here idle? What is it that gentlemen wish? What would they have? Is life so dear, or peace so sweet, as to be purchased at the price of chains and slavery? Forbid it, Almighty God! I know not what course others may take; but as for me, give me liberty, or give me death!

How the Declaration of Independence Was Adopted

On June 7, 1776, Richard Henry Lee, who had issued the first call for a congress of the colonies, introduced in the Continental Congress at Philadelphia a resolution declaring "that these United Colonies are, and of right ought to be, free and independent states, that they are absolved from all allegiance to the British Crown, and that all political connection between them and the state of Great Britain is, and ought to be, totally dissolved."

The resolution, seconded by John Adams on behalf of the Massachusetts delegation, came up again on June 10 when a committee of 5, headed by Thomas Jefferson, was appointed to express the purpose of the resolution in a declaration of independence. The other 4 were John Adams, Benjamin Franklin, Robert R. Livingston, and Roger Sherman.

Drafting the Declaration was assigned to Jefferson, who worked on a portable desk of his own construction in a room at Market and 7th Sts. The committee reported the result on June 28, 1776. The members of the Congress suggested a number of changes, which Jefferson called "deplorable." They didn't approve Jefferson's arraignment of the British people and King George III for encouraging and fostering the slave trade, which Jefferson called "an execrable commerce." They made 86 changes, eliminating 480 words and leaving 1,337. In the final form, capitalization was erratic. Jefferson had written that men were endowed with "inalienable" rights; in the final copy it came out as "unalienable" and has been thus ever since.

The Lee-Adams resolution of independence was adopted by 12 "yeas" on July 2—the actual date of the act of independence. The Declaration, which explains the act, was adopted July 4.

After the Declaration was adopted, July 4, 1776, it was turned over to John Dunlap, printer, to be printed on broadsides. The original copy was lost and one of his broadsides was attached to a page in the journal of the Congress. It was read aloud July 8 in Philadelphia, PA, Easton, PA, and Trenton, NJ. On July 9 at 6 PM it was read by order of Gen. George Washington to the troops assembled on the Common in New York City (City Hall Park).

The Continental Congress of July 19, 1776, adopted the following resolution:

"Resolved, That the Declaration passed on the 4th, be fairly engrossed on parchment with the title and stile of 'The Unanimous Declaration of the thirteen United States of America' and that the same, when engrossed, be signed by every member of Congress."

Not all delegates who signed the engrossed Declaration were present on July 4. Robert Morris (PA), William Williams (CT), and Samuel Chase (MD) signed on Aug. 2; Oliver Wolcott (CT), George Wythe (VA), Richard Henry Lee (VA), and Elbridge Gerry (MA) signed in August and September; Matthew Thornton (NH) joined the Congress Nov. 4 and signed later. Thomas McKean (DE) rejoined Washington's army before signing and said later that he signed in 1781.

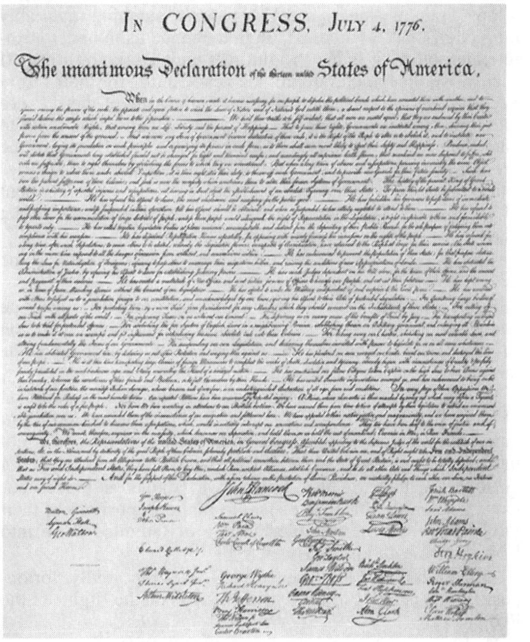
IN CONGRESS, JULY 4, 1776.

The unanimous Declaration of the ... States of America,

Charles Carroll of Carrollton was appointed a delegate by Maryland on July 4, 1776, presented his credentials July 18, and signed the engrossed Declaration on Aug. 2. Born Sept. 19, 1737, he was 95 years old and the last surviving signer when he died on Nov. 14, 1832.

Two Pennsylvania delegates who did not support the Declaration on July 4 were replaced. The 4 New York delegates did not have authority from their state to vote on July 4. On July 9, the New York state convention authorized its delegates to approve the Declaration, and the Congress was so notified on July 15, 1776. The 4 signed the Declaration on Aug. 2.

The original engrossed Declaration is preserved in the National Archives Building in Washington, DC.

Declaration of Independence

The Declaration of Independence was adopted by the Continental Congress in Philadelphia on July 4, 1776. John Hancock was president of the Congress, and Charles Thomson was secretary. A copy of the Declaration, engrossed on parchment, was signed by members of Congress on and after Aug. 2, 1776. On Jan. 18, 1777, Congress ordered that "an authenticated copy, with the names of the members of Congress subscribing the same, be sent to each of the United States, and that they be desired to have the same put upon record." Authenticated copies were printed in broadside form in Baltimore, where the Continental Congress was then in session. The following text is that of the original printed by John Dunlap at Philadelphia for the Continental Congress. The original is on display at the National Archives in Washington, DC.

IN CONGRESS, July 4, 1776.
A DECLARATION
By the REPRESENTATIVES of the
UNITED STATES OF AMERICA,
In GENERAL CONGRESS assembled

When in the Course of human Events, it becomes necessary for one People to dissolve the Political Bands which have connected them with another, and to assume among the Powers of the Earth, the separate and equal Station to which the Laws of Nature and of Nature's God entitle them, a decent Respect to the Opinions of Mankind requires that they should declare the causes which impel them to the Separation.

We hold these Truths to be self-evident, that all Men are created equal, that they are endowed by their Creator with certain unalienable Rights, that among these are Life, Liberty, and the Pursuit of Happiness—That to secure these Rights, Governments are instituted among Men, deriving their just Powers

WORLD ALMANAC QUICK QUIZ

U.S. senators were originally elected by state legislatures, not by the public. In what year was the method changed?

(a) 1795 (b) 1832
(c) 1868 (d) 1913

For the answer look in this chapter, or see page 1008.

from the Consent of the Governed, that whenever any Form of Government becomes destructive of these Ends, it is the Right of the People to alter or to abolish it, and to institute new Government, laying its Foundation on such Principles, and organizing its Powers in such Form, as to them shall seem most likely to effect their Safety and Happiness. Prudence, indeed, will dictate that Governments long established should not be changed for light and transient Causes; and accordingly all Experience hath shewn, that Mankind are more disposed to suffer, while Evils are sufferable, than to right themselves by abolishing the Forms to which they are accustomed. But when a long Train of Abuses and Usurpations, pursuing invariably the same Object, evinces a Design to reduce them under absolute Despotism, it is their Right, it is their Duty, to throw off such Government, and to provide new Guards for their future Security. Such has been the patient Sufferance of these Colonies; and such is now the Necessity which constrains them to alter their former Systems of Government. The History of the present King of Great-Britain is a History of repeated Injuries and Usurpations, all having in direct Object the Establishment of an absolute Tyranny over these States. To prove this, let Facts be submitted to a candid World.

He has refused his Assent to Laws, the most wholesome and necessary for the public Good.

He has forbidden his Governors to pass Laws of immediate and pressing Importance, unless suspended in their Operation till his Assent should be obtained; and when so suspended, he has utterly neglected to attend to them.

He has refused to pass other Laws for the Accommodation of large Districts of People, unless those People would relinquish the Right of Representation in the Legislature, a Right inestimable to them, and formidable to Tyrants only.

He has called together Legislative Bodies at Places unusual, uncomfortable, and distant from the Depository of their Public Records, for the sole Purpose of fatiguing them into Compliance with his Measures.

He has dissolved Representative Houses repeatedly, for opposing with manly Firmness his Invasions on the Rights of the People.

He has refused for a long Time, after such Dissolutions, to cause others to be elected; whereby the Legislative Powers, incapable of Annihilation, have returned to the People at large for their exercise; the State remaining in the mean time exposed to all the Dangers of Invasion from without, and Convulsions within.

He has endeavoured to prevent the Population of these States; for that Purpose obstructing the Laws for Naturalization of Foreigners; refusing to pass others to encourage their Migrations hither, and raising the Conditions of new Appropriations of Lands.

He has obstructed the Administration of Justice, by refusing his Assent to Laws for establishing Judiciary Powers.

He has made Judges dependent on his Will alone, for the Tenure of their Offices, and the Amount and payment of their Salaries.

He has erected a Multitude of new Offices, and sent hither Swarms of Officers to harrass our People, and eat out their Substance.

He has kept among us, in Times of Peace, Standing Armies, without the consent of our Legislatures.

He has affected to render the Military independent of, and superior to the Civil Power.

He has combined with others to subject us to a Jurisdiction foreign to our Constitution, and unacknowledged by our Laws; giving his Assent to their Acts of pretended Legislation:

For quartering large Bodies of Armed Troops among us:

For protecting them, by a mock Trial, from Punishment for any Murders which they should commit on the Inhabitants of these States:

For cutting off our Trade with all Parts of the World:

For imposing Taxes on us without our Consent:

For depriving us, in many Cases, of the Benefits of Trial by Jury:

For transporting us beyond Seas to be tried for pretended Offences:

For abolishing the free System of English Laws in a neighbouring Province, establishing therein an arbitrary Government, and enlarging its Boundaries, so as to render it at once an Example and fit Instrument for introducing the same absolute Rule into these Colonies:

For taking away our Charters, abolishing our most valuable Laws, and altering fundamentally the Forms of our Governments:

For suspending our own Legislatures, and declaring themselves invested with Power to legislate for us in all Cases whatsoever.

He has abdicated Government here, by declaring us out of his Protection and waging War against us.

He has plundered our Seas, ravaged our Coasts, burnt our towns, and destroyed the Lives of our People.

He is, at this Time, transporting large Armies of foreign Mercenaries to complete the works of Death, Desolation, and Tyranny, already begun with circumstances of Cruelty and Perfidy, scarcely paralleled in the most barbarous Ages, and totally unworthy the Head of a civilized Nation.

He has constrained our fellow Citizens taken Captive on the high Seas to bear Arms against their Country, to become the Executioners of their Friends and Brethren, or to fall themselves by their Hands.

He has excited domestic Insurrections amongst us, and has endeavoured to bring on the Inhabitants of our Frontiers, the merciless Indian Savages, whose known Rule of Warfare, is an undistinguished Destruction, of all Ages, Sexes and Conditions.

In every stage of these Oppressions we have Petitioned for Redress in the most humble Terms: Our repeated Petitions have been answered only by repeated Injury. A Prince, whose Character is thus marked by every act which may define a Tyrant, is unfit to be the Ruler of a free People.

Nor have we been wanting in Attentions to our British Brethren. We have warned them from Time to Time of Attempts by their Legislature to extend an unwarrantable Jurisdiction over us. We have reminded them of the Circumstances of our Emigration and Settlement here. We have appealed to their native Justice and Magnanimity, and we have conjured them by the Ties of our common Kindred to disavow these Usurpations, which, would inevitably interrupt our Connections and Correspondence. They too have been deaf to the Voice of Justice and of Consanguinity. We must, therefore, acquiesce in the Necessity, which denounces our Separation, and hold them, as we hold the rest of Mankind, Enemies in War, in Peace, Friends.

We, therefore, the Representatives of the UNITED STATES OF AMERICA, in General Congress, Assembled, appealing to the Supreme Judge of the World for the Rectitude of our Intentions, do, in the Name, and by Authority of the good People of these Colonies, solemnly Publish and Declare, That these United Colonies are, and of Right ought to be, Free and Independent States; that they are absolved from all Allegiance to the British Crown, and that all political Connection between them and the State of Great-Britain, is and ought to be totally dissolved; and that as Free and Independent States, they have full Power to levy War, conclude Peace, contract Alliances, establish Commerce, and to do all other Acts and Things which Independent States may of right do. And for the support of this declaration, with a firm Reliance on the Protection of Divine Providence, we mutually pledge to each other our lives, our Fortunes, and our sacred Honor.

JOHN HANCOCK, President

Attest.

CHARLES THOMSON, Secretary.

IT'S A FACT: Rhode Island, the last of the original 13 colonies to ratify the Constitution, was the only state that didn't send delegates to the Constitutional Convention in 1787. Rhode Island did not ratify the document until May 29, 1790, after Congress threatened to treat it as a foreign nation and impose duties on its exports to other states.

Signers of the Declaration of Independence

Delegate (state)	Occupation	Birthplace	Born	Died
Adams, John (MA)	Lawyer	Braintree (Quincy), MA	Oct. 30, 1735	July 4, 1826
Adams, Samuel (MA)	Political leader	Boston, MA	Sept. 27, 1722	Oct. 2, 1803
Bartlett, Josiah (NH)	Physician, judge	Amesbury, MA	Nov. 21, 1729	May 19, 1795
Braxton, Carter (VA)	Farmer	Newington Plantation, VA	Sept. 10, 1736	Oct. 10, 1797
Carroll, Chas. of Carrollton (MD)	Lawyer	Annapolis, MD	Sept. 19, 1737	Nov. 14, 1832
Chase, Samuel (MD)	Judge	Princess Anne, MD	Apr. 17, 1741	June 19, 1811
Clark, Abraham (NJ)	Surveyor	Roselle, NJ	Feb. 15, 1726	Sept. 15, 1794
Clymer, George (PA)	Merchant	Philadelphia, PA	Mar. 16, 1739	Jan. 23, 1813
Ellery, William (RI)	Lawyer	Newport, RI	Dec. 22, 1727	Feb. 15, 1820
Floyd, William (NY)	Soldier	Brookhaven, NY	Dec. 17, 1734	Aug. 4, 1821
Franklin, Benjamin (PA)	Printer, publisher	Boston, MA	Jan. 17, 1706	Apr. 17, 1790
Gerry, Elbridge (MA)	Merchant	Marblehead, MA	July 17, 1744	Nov. 23, 1814
Gwinnett, Button (GA)	Merchant	Down Hatherly, England	c. 1735	May 19, 1777
Hall, Lyman (GA)	Physician	Wallingford, CT	Apr. 12, 1724	Oct. 19, 1790
Hancock, John (MA)	Merchant	Braintree (Quincy), MA	Jan. 12, 1737	Oct. 8, 1793
Harrison, Benjamin (VA)	Farmer	Berkeley, VA	Apr. 5, 1726	Apr. 24, 1791
Hart, John (NJ)	Farmer	Stonington, CT	c. 1711	May 11, 1779
Hewes, Joseph (NC)	Merchant	Princeton, NJ	Jan. 23, 1730	Nov. 10, 1779
Heyward, Thos. Jr. (SC)	Lawyer, farmer	St. Luke's Parish, SC	July 28, 1746	Mar. 6, 1809
Hooper, William (NC)	Lawyer	Boston, MA	June 28, 1742	Oct. 14, 1790
Hopkins, Stephen (RI)	Judge, educator	Providence, RI	Mar. 7, 1707	July 13, 1785
Hopkinson, Francis (NJ)	Judge, author	Philadelphia, PA	Sept. 21, 1737	May 9, 1791
Huntington, Samuel (CT)	Judge	Windham County, CT	July 3, 1731	Jan. 5, 1796
Jefferson, Thomas (VA)	Lawyer	Shadwell, VA	Apr. 13, 1743	July 4, 1826
Lee, Francis Lightfoot (VA)	Farmer	Westmoreland County, VA	Oct. 14, 1734	Jan. 11, 1797
Lee, Richard Henry (VA)	Farmer	Westmoreland County, VA	Jan. 20, 1732	June 19, 1794
Lewis, Francis (NY)	Merchant	Llandaff, Wales	Mar., 1713	Dec. 31, 1802
Livingston, Philip (NY)	Merchant	Albany, NY	Jan. 15, 1716	June 12, 1778
Lynch, Thomas Jr. (SC)	Farmer	Winyah, SC	Aug. 5, 1749	(at sea) 1779
McKean, Thomas (DE)	Lawyer	New London, PA	Mar. 19, 1734	June 24, 1817
Middleton, Arthur (SC)	Farmer	Charleston, SC	June 26, 1742	Jan. 1, 1787
Morris, Lewis (NY)	Farmer	Morrisania (Bronx County), NY	Apr. 8, 1726	Jan. 22, 1798
Morris, Robert (PA)	Merchant	Liverpool, England	Jan. 20, 1734	May 9, 1806
Morton, John (PA)	Judge	Ridley, PA	1724	Apr., 1777
Nelson, Thos. Jr. (VA)	Farmer	Yorktown, VA	Dec. 26, 1738	Jan. 4, 1789
Paca, William (MD)	Judge	Abingdon, MD	Oct. 31, 1740	Oct. 23, 1799
Paine, Robert Treat (MA)	Judge	Boston, MA	Mar. 11, 1731	May 12, 1814
Penn, John (NC)	Lawyer	Near Port Royal, VA	May 17, 1741	Sept. 14, 1788
Read, George (DE)	Judge	Near North East, MD	Sept. 18, 1733	Sept. 21, 1798
Rodney, Caesar (DE)	Judge	Dover, DE	Oct. 7, 1728	June 29, 1784
Ross, George (PA)	Judge	New Castle, DE	May 10, 1730	July 14, 1779
Rush, Benjamin (PA)	Physician	Byberry, PA (Philadelphia)	Dec. 24, 1745	Apr. 19, 1813
Rutledge, Edward (SC)	Lawyer	Charleston, SC	Nov. 23, 1749	Jan. 23, 1800
Sherman, Roger (CT)	Lawyer	Newton, MA	Apr. 19, 1721	July 23, 1793
Smith, James (PA)	Lawyer	Dublin, Ireland	c. 1719	July 11, 1806
Stockton, Richard (NJ)	Lawyer	Near Princeton, NJ	Oct. 1, 1730	Feb. 28, 1781
Stone, Thomas (MD)	Lawyer	Charles County, MD	1743	Oct. 5, 1787
Taylor, George (PA)	Ironmaster	Ireland	1716	Feb. 23, 1781
Thornton, Matthew (NH)	Physician	Ireland	1714	June 24, 1803
Walton, George (GA)	Judge	Prince Edward County, VA	1741	Feb. 2, 1804
Whipple, William (NH)	Merchant, judge	Kittery, ME	Jan. 14, 1730	Nov. 28, 1785
Williams, William (CT)	Merchant	Lebanon, CT	Apr. 23, 1731	Aug. 2, 1811
Wilson, James (PA)	Judge	Carskerdo, Scotland	Sept. 14, 1742	Aug. 28, 1798
Witherspoon, John (NJ)	Clergyman, educator	Gifford, Scotland	Feb. 5, 1723	Nov. 15, 1794
Wolcott, Oliver (CT)	Judge	Windsor, CT	Dec. 1, 1726	Dec. 1, 1797
Wythe, George (VA)	Lawyer	Elizabeth City Co. (Hampton), VA	1726	June 8, 1806

Origin of the Constitution

The War of Independence was conducted by delegates from the original 13 states, called the Congress of the United States of America and known as the Continental Congress. In 1777 the Congress submitted to the legislatures of the states the Articles of Confederation and Perpetual Union, which were ratified by New Hampshire, Massachusetts, Rhode Island, Connecticut, New York, New Jersey, Pennsylvania, Delaware, Virginia, North Carolina, South Carolina, Georgia, and finally, in 1781, Maryland.

The first article read: "The stile of this confederacy shall be the United States of America." This did not signify a sovereign nation, because the states delegated only those powers they could not handle individually, such as to wage war, make treaties, and contract debts for general expenses (e.g. paying the army). Taxes for payment of such debts were levied by the individual states. The president signed himself "President of the United States in Congress assembled," but here the United States were considered in the plural, a cooperating group.

When the war was won, it became evident that a stronger federal union was needed. The Congress left the initiative to the legislatures. Virginia in Jan. 1786 appointed commissioners to meet with representatives of other states; delegates from Virginia, Delaware, New York, New Jersey, and Pennsylvania met at Annapolis. Alexander Hamilton prepared their call asking delegates from all states to meet in Philadelphia in May 1787 "to render the Constitution of the federal government adequate to the exigencies of the union." Congress endorsed the plan on Feb. 21, 1787. Delegates were appointed by all states except Rhode Island.

The convention met on May 14, 1787. George Washington was chosen president (presiding officer). The states certified 65 delegates, but 10 did not attend. The work was done by 55, not all of whom were present at all sessions. Of the 55 attending delegates, 16 failed to sign, and 39 actually signed Sept. 17, 1787, some with reservations. Some historians have said 74 delegates (9 more than the 65 actually certified) were named and 19 failed to attend. These 9 additional persons refused the appointment, were never delegates, and were never counted as absentees. Washington sent the Constitution to Congress, and that body, Sept. 28, 1787, ordered it sent to the legislatures, "in order to be submitted to a convention of delegates chosen in each state by the people thereof."

The Constitution was ratified by votes of state conventions as follows: Delaware, Dec. 7, 1787, unanimous; Pennsylvania, Dec. 12, 1787, 43 to 23; New Jersey, Dec. 18, 1787, unanimous; Georgia, Jan. 2, 1788, unanimous; Connecticut, Jan. 9, 1788, 128 to 40; Massachusetts, Feb. 6, 1788, 187 to 168; Maryland, Apr. 28, 1788, 63 to 11; South Carolina, May 23, 1788, 149 to 73; New Hampshire, June 21, 1788, 57 to 46; Virginia, June 25, 1788, 89 to 79; New York, July 26, 1788, 30 to 27. Nine states were needed to establish the operation of the Constitution "between the states so ratifying the same," and New Hampshire was the 9th state. The government did not declare the Constitution in effect until the first Wednesday in Mar. 1789, which was Mar. 4. After that, North Carolina ratified it on Nov. 21, 1789, 194 to 77; and Rhode Island, May 29, 1790, 34 to 32. Vermont in convention ratified it on Jan. 10, 1791, and by act of Congress approved on Feb. 18, 1791, was admitted into the Union as the 14th state, Mar. 4, 1791.

Constitution of the United States

The Original 7 Articles

The text of the Constitution given here (except for Amendment XXVII) is from the pocket-size edition of the Constitution published by the U.S. Government Printing Office as a result of a congressional resolution to print the Constitution in its original form as amended through July 5, 1971. *Text in brackets* indicates that an item has been superseded or amended, or provides background information. **Boldface text preceding** an article, section, or amendment is a brief summary, added by *The World Almanac*.

PREAMBLE

We, the People of the United States, in Order to form a more perfect Union, establish Justice, insure domestic Tranquility, provide for the common defence, promote the general Welfare, and secure the Blessings of Liberty to ourselves and our Posterity, do ordain and establish this Constitution for the United States of America.

ARTICLE I.

Section 1—Legislative powers; in whom vested:

All legislative Powers herein granted shall be vested in a Congress of the United States, which shall consist of a Senate and House of Representatives.

Section 2—House of Representatives, how and by whom chosen. Qualifications of a Representative. Representatives and direct taxes, how apportioned. Enumeration. Vacancies to be filled. Power of choosing officers, and of impeachment.

The House of Representatives shall be composed of Members chosen every second Year by the People of the several States, and the Electors in each State shall have the Qualifications requisite for Electors of the most numerous Branch of the State Legislature.

No person shall be a Representative who shall not have attained to the Age of twenty-five Years, and been seven Years a Citizen of the United States, and who shall not, when elected, be an Inhabitant of that State in which he shall be chosen.

[Representatives and direct taxes shall be apportioned among the several States which may be included within this Union, according to their respective Numbers, which shall be determined by adding to the whole Number of free Persons, including those bound to Service for a Term of Years, and excluding Indians not taxed, three-fifths of all other persons.] [The previous sentence was superseded by Amendment XIV, section 2.] The actual Enumeration shall be made within three Years after the first Meeting of the Congress of the United States, and within every subsequent Term of ten Years, in such Manner as they shall by Law direct. The Number of Representatives shall not exceed one for every thirty Thousand, but each State shall have at Least one Representative; and until such enumeration shall be made, the State of New Hampshire shall be entitled to chuse three, Massachusetts eight, Rhode-Island and Providence Plantations one, Connecticut five, New-York six, New Jersey four, Pennsylvania eight, Delaware one, Maryland six, Virginia ten, North Carolina five, South Carolina five, and Georgia three.

When vacancies happen in the Representation from any State, the Executive Authority thereof shall issue Writs of Election to fill such Vacancies.

The House of Representatives shall chuse their Speaker and other Officers; and shall have the sole Power of Impeachment.

Section 3—Senators, how and by whom chosen. How classified. Qualifications of a Senator. President of the Senate, his right to vote. President pro tem., and other officers of the Senate, how chosen. Power to try impeachments. When President is tried, Chief Justice to preside. Sentence.

The Senate of the United States shall be composed of two Senators from each State, *[chosen by the Legislature thereof] [the preceding five words were superseded by Amendment XVII, section 1]* for six Years; and each Senator shall have one Vote.

Immediately after they shall be assembled in Consequence of the first Election, they shall be divided as equally as may be into three Classes. The Seats of the Senators of the first Class shall be vacated at the Expiration of the second Year, of the second Class at the Expiration of the fourth Year, and of the third Class at the Expiration of the Sixth year, so that one-third may be chosen every second Year; *[and if Vacancies happen by Resignation, or otherwise, during the Recess of the Legislature of any State, the Executive thereof may make temporary Appointments until the next Meeting of the Legislature, which shall then fill such Vacancies.] [The words in parentheses were superseded by Amendment XVII, section 2.]*

No person shall be a Senator who shall not have attained to the Age of thirty Years, and been nine Years a Citizen of the United States, and who shall not, when elected, be an Inhabitant of that State for which he shall be chosen.

The Vice President of the United States shall be President of the Senate, but shall have no Vote, unless they be equally divided.

The Senate shall chuse their other Officers, and also a President pro tempore, in the absence of the Vice President, or when he shall exercise the Office of President of the United States.

The Senate shall have the sole Power to try all Impeachments. When sitting for that Purpose, they shall be on Oath or Affirmation. When the President of the United States is tried, the Chief Justice shall preside: And no Person shall be convicted without the Concurrence of two thirds of the Members present.

Judgment in Cases of Impeachment shall not extend further than to removal from Office, and disqualification to hold and enjoy any Office of honor, Trust or Profit under the United States: but the Party convicted shall nevertheless be liable and subject to Indictment, Trial, Judgment and Punishment, according to Law.

Section 4—Times, etc., of holding elections, how prescribed. One session each year.

The Times, Places and Manner of holding Elections for Senators and Representatives, shall be prescribed in each State by the Legislature thereof; but the Congress may at any time by Law make or alter such Regulations, except as to the Place of Chusing Senators.

The Congress shall assemble at least once in every Year, and such Meeting shall *[be on the first Monday in December,] [The words in parentheses were superseded by Amendment XX, section 2.]* unless they shall by Law appoint a different Day.

Section 5—Membership, quorum, adjournments, rules. Power to punish or expel. Journal. Time of adjournments, how limited, etc.

Each House shall be the Judge of the Elections, Returns and Qualifications of its own Members, and a Majority of each shall constitute a Quorum to do Business; but a smaller number may adjourn from day to day, and may be authorized to compel the Attendance of absent Members, in such manner, and under such Penalties as each House may provide.

Each House may determine the Rules of its Proceedings, punish its members for disorderly Behavior, and, with the Concurrence of two thirds, expel a Member.

Each House shall keep a Journal of its Proceedings, and from time to time publish the same, excepting such Parts as may in their Judgment require Secrecy; and the Yeas and

Nays of the Members of either House on any question shall, at the Desire of one fifth of those Present, be entered on the Journal.

Neither House, during the Session of Congress, shall, without the Consent of the other, adjourn for more than three days, nor to any other Place than that in which the two Houses shall be sitting.

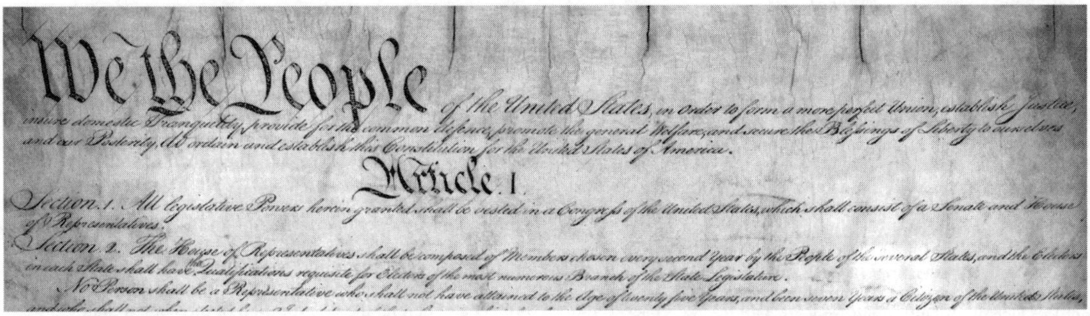

Section 6—Compensation, privileges, disqualifications in certain cases.

The Senators and Representatives shall receive a Compensation for their Services, to be ascertained by Law, and paid out of the Treasury of the United States. They shall in all Cases, except Treason, Felony and Breach of the Peace, be privileged from Arrest during their Attendance at the Session of their respective Houses, and in going to and returning from the same; and for any Speech or Debate in either House, they shall not be questioned in any other Place.

No Senator or Representative shall, during the Time for which he was elected, be appointed to any civil Office under the Authority of the United States, which shall have been created, or the Emoluments whereof shall have been encreased during such time; and no Person holding any Office under the United States, shall be a Member of either House during his Continuance in Office.

Section 7—House to originate all revenue bills. Veto. Bill may be passed by two-thirds of each House, notwithstanding, etc. Bill, not returned in ten days, to become a law. Provisions as to orders, concurrent resolutions, etc.

All bills for raising Revenue shall originate in the House of Representatives; but the Senate may propose or concur with Amendments as on other Bills.

Every Bill which shall have passed the House of Representatives and the Senate, shall, before it become a Law, be presented to the President of the United States; If he approve he shall sign it, but if not he shall return it, with his Objections to that House in which it shall have originated, who shall enter the Objections at large on their Journal, and proceed to reconsider it. If after such Reconsideration two thirds of that House shall agree to pass the Bill, it shall be sent, together with the Objections, to the other House, by which it shall likewise be reconsidered, and if approved by two thirds of that House, it shall become a Law. But in all such Cases the Votes of both Houses shall be determined by Yeas and Nays, and the Names of the Persons voting for and against the Bill shall be entered on the Journal of each House respectively. If any Bill shall not be returned by the President within ten Days (Sundays excepted) after it shall have been presented to him, the Same shall be a Law, in like Manner as if he had signed it, unless the Congress by their Adjournment prevent its Return, in which Case it shall not be a Law.

Every order, Resolution, or Vote to which the Concurrence of the Senate and House of Representatives may be necessary (except on a question of Adjournment) shall be presented to the President of the United States; and before the Same shall take Effect, shall be approved by him, or being disapproved by him, shall be repassed by two thirds of the Senate and House of Representatives, according to the Rules and Limitations prescribed in the Case of a Bill.

Section 8—Powers of Congress.

The Congress shall have Power To lay and collect Taxes, Duties, Imposts and Excises, to pay the Debts and provide for the common Defence and general Welfare of the United States; but all Duties, Imposts and Excises shall be uniform throughout the United States;

To borrow money on the credit of the United States;

To regulate Commerce with foreign Nations, and among the several States, and with the Indian Tribes;

To establish an uniform Rule of Naturalization, and uniform Laws on the subject of Bankruptcies throughout the United States;

To coin Money, regulate the Value thereof, and of foreign Coin, and fix the Standard of Weights and Measures;

To provide for the Punishment of counterfeiting the Securities and current Coin of the United States;

To establish Post Offices and post Roads;

To promote the Progress of Science and useful Arts, by securing for limited Times to Authors and Inventors the exclusive Right to their respective Writings and Discoveries;

To constitute Tribunals inferior to the supreme Court;

To define and punish Piracies and Felonies committed on the high Seas, and Offenses against the Law of Nations;

To declare War, grant Letters of Marque and Reprisal, and make Rules concerning Captures on Land and Water;

To raise and support Armies, but no Appropriation of Money to that Use shall be for a longer Term than two Years;

To provide and maintain a Navy;

To make Rules for the Government and Regulation of the land and naval Forces;

To provide for calling forth the Militia to execute the Laws of the Union, suppress Insurrections and repel Invasions;

To provide for organizing, arming, and disciplining the Militia, and for governing such Part of them as may be employed in the Service of the United States, reserving to the States respectively, the Appointment of the Officers, and the Authority of training the Militia according to the discipline prescribed by Congress;

To exercise exclusive Legislation in all Cases whatsoever, over such District (not exceeding ten Miles square) as may, by Cession of particular States, and the acceptance of Congress, become the Seat of the Government of the United States, and to exercise like Authority over all Places purchased by the Consent of the Legislature of the State in which the Same shall be, for the Erection of Forts, Magazines, Arsenals, dock-Yards, and other needful Buildings;—And

To make all Laws which shall be necessary and proper for carrying into Execution the foregoing Powers, and all other Powers vested by this Constitution in the Government of the United States, or in any Department or Officer thereof.

Section 9—Provision as to migration or importation of certain persons. Habeas corpus, bills of attainder, etc. Taxes, how apportioned. No export duty. No commercial preference. Money, how drawn from Treasury, etc. No titular nobility. Officers not to receive presents, etc.

The Migration or Importation of such Persons as any of the States now existing shall think proper to admit, shall not be prohibited by the Congress prior to the Year one thousand eight hundred and eight, but a tax or duty may be imposed on such Importation, not exceeding ten dollars for each Person.

The privilege of the Writ of Habeas Corpus shall not be suspended, unless when in Cases of Rebellion or Invasion the public Safety may require it.

No Bill of Attainder or ex post facto Law shall be passed.

No capitation, or other direct, Tax shall be laid, unless in Proportion to the Census or Enumeration herein before directed to be taken. *[Modified by Amendment XVI.]*

No Tax or Duty shall be laid on Articles exported from any State.

No Preference shall be given by any Regulation of Commerce or Revenue to the Ports of one State over those of another: nor shall Vessels bound to, or from, one State, be obliged to enter, clear, or pay Duties in another.

No Money shall be drawn from the Treasury, but in Consequence of Appropriations made by Law; and a regular Statement and Account of the Receipts and Expenditures of all public Money shall be published from time to time.

No Title of Nobility shall be granted by the United States: and no Person holding any Office of Profit or Trust under them, shall, without the Consent of the Congress, accept of any present, Emolument, Office, or Title, of any kind whatever, from any King, Prince, or foreign State.

Section 10—States prohibited from the exercise of certain powers.

No State shall enter into any Treaty, Alliance, or Confederation; grant Letters of Marque and Reprisal; coin Money; emit Bills of Credit; make any Thing but gold and silver Coin a Tender in Payment of Debts; pass any Bill of Attainder, ex post facto Law, or Law impairing the Obligation of Contracts, or grant any Title of Nobility.

No State shall, without the Consent of the Congress, lay any Imposts or Duties on Imports or Exports, except what may be absolutely necessary for executing its inspection Laws: and the net Produce of all Duties and Imposts, laid by any State on Imports or Exports, shall be for the Use of the Treasury of the United States; and all such Laws shall be subject to the Revision and Control of the Congress.

No State shall, without the Consent of Congress, lay any duty of Tonnage, keep Troops, or Ships of War in time of Peace, enter into any Agreement or Compact with another State, or with a foreign Power, or engage in War, unless actually invaded, or in such imminent Danger as will not admit of delay.

ARTICLE II.

Section 1—President: his term of office. Electors of President; number and how appointed. Electors to vote on same day. Qualification of President. On whom his duties devolve in case of his removal, death, etc. President's compensation. His oath of office.

The executive Power shall be vested in a President of the United States of America. He shall hold his Office during the Term of four Years, and, together with the Vice President, chosen for the same Term, be elected, as follows.

Each State shall appoint, in such Manner as the Legislature thereof may direct, a Number of Electors, equal to the whole Number of Senators and Representatives to which the State may be entitled in the Congress: but no Senator or Representative, or Person holding an Office of Trust or Profit under the United States, shall be appointed an Elector.

[The Electors shall meet in their respective States, and vote by Ballot for two persons, of whom one at least shall not be an Inhabitant of the same State with themselves. And they shall make a List of all the Persons voted for, and of the Number of Votes for each; which List they shall sign and certify, and transmit sealed to the Seat of the Government of the United States, directed to the President of the Senate. The President of the Senate shall, in the Presence of the Senate and House of Representatives, open all the Certificates, and the Votes shall then be counted. The Person having the greatest Number of Votes shall be the President, if such Number be a Majority of the whole Number of Electors appointed; and if there be more than one who have such Majority, and have an equal Number of Votes, then the House of Representatives shall immediately chuse by Ballot one of them for President; and if no Person have a Majority, then from the five highest on the List the said House shall in like Manner chuse the President. But in chusing the President, the Votes shall be taken by States, the Representation from each State having one Vote; a quorum for this Purpose shall consist of a Member or Members from two thirds of the States, and a Majority of all the States shall be necessary to a Choice. In every Case, after the Choice of the President, the Person having the greatest Number of Votes of the Electors shall be the Vice President. But if there should remain two or more who have equal Votes, the Senate shall chuse from them by Ballot the Vice-President.]

[This clause was superseded by Amendment XII.]

The Congress may detemine the Time of chusing the Electors, and the Day on which they shall give their Votes; which Day shall be the same throughout the United States.

No person except a natural born Citizen, or a Citizen of the United States, at the time of the Adoption of this Constitution, shall be eligible to the Office of President; neither shall any Person be eligible to that Office who shall not have attained to the Age of thirty-five Years, and been fourteen Years a Resident within the United States.

[For qualification of the Vice President, see Amendment XII.]

In Case of the Removal of the President from Office, or of his Death, Resignation, or Inability to discharge the Powers and Duties of the said Office, the same shall devolve on the Vice President, and the Congress may by Law, provide for the Case of Removal, Death, Resignation or Inability, both of the President and Vice President, declaring what Officer shall then act as President, and such Officer shall act accordingly, until the Disability be removed, or a President shall be elected.

[This clause has been modified by Amendments XX and XXV.]

The President shall, at stated Times, receive for his Services, a Compensation, which shall neither be encreased nor diminished during the Period for which he shall have been elected, and he shall not receive within that Period any other Emolument from the United States, or any of them.

Before he enter on the Execution of his Office, he shall take the following Oath or Affirmation:–"I do solemnly swear (or affirm) that I will faithfully execute the Office of President of the United States, and will to the best of my Ability, preserve, protect and defend the Constitution of the United States."

Section 2—President to be Commander-in-Chief. He may require opinions of cabinet officers, etc., may pardon. Treaty-making power. Nomination of certain officers. When President may fill vacancies.

The President shall be Commander in Chief of the Army and Navy of the United States, and of the Militia of the several States, when called into the actual Service of the United States; he may require the Opinion in writing, of the principal Officer in each of the executive Departments, upon any subject relating to the Duties of their respective Offices, and he shall have Power to Grant Reprieves and Pardons for Offenses against the United States, except in Cases of Impeachment.

He shall have Power, by and with the Advice and Consent of the Senate, to make Treaties, provided two-thirds of the Senators present concur; and he shall nominate, and by and with the Advice and Consent of the Senate, shall appoint Ambassadors, other public Ministers and Consuls, Judges of the supreme Court, and all other Officers of the United States, whose Appointments are not herein otherwise provided for, and which shall be established by Law: but the Congress may by Law vest the Appointment of such inferior Officers, as they think proper, in the President alone, in the Courts of Law, or in the Heads of Departments.

The President shall have Power to fill up all Vacancies that may happen during the Recess of the Senate, by granting Commissions which shall expire at the End of their next Session.

Section 3—President shall communicate to Congress. He may convene and adjourn Congress, in case of disagreement, etc. Shall receive ambassadors, execute laws, and commission officers.

He shall from time to time give to the Congress Information of the State of the Union, and recommend to their Consideration such Measures as he shall judge necessary and expedient; he may, on extraordinary Occasions, convene both Houses, or either of them, and in Case of Disagreement between them, with Respect to the Time of Adjournment, he may adjourn them to such Time as he shall think proper; he shall receive Ambassadors and other public Ministers; he shall take Care that the Laws be faithfully executed, and shall Commission all the Officers of the United States.

Section 4—All civil offices forfeited for certain crimes.

The President, Vice President and all civil Officers of the United States, shall be removed from Office on Impeachment for, and Conviction of, Treason, Bribery, or other high Crimes and Misdemeanors.

ARTICLE III.

Section 1—Judicial powers, tenure. compensation.

The judicial Power of the United States, shall be vested in one supreme Court, and in such inferior Courts as the Congress may from time to time ordain and establish. The Judges, both of the supreme and inferior Courts, shall hold their Offices during good Behaviour, and shall, at stated Times, receive for their Services, a Compensation, which shall not be diminished during their Continuance in Office.

Section 2—Judicial power; to what cases it extends. Original jurisdiction of Supreme Court; appellate jurisdiction. Trial by jury, etc. Trial, where.

The judicial Power shall extend to all Cases, in Law and Equity, arising under this Constitution, the Laws of the United States, and Treaties made, or which shall be made, under their Authority;–to all Cases affecting Ambassadors, other public Ministers and Consuls;–to all Cases of admiralty and maritime Jurisdiction;–to Controversies to which the United States shall be a Party;–to Controversies between two or more States;–between a State and Citizens of another State;–between Citizens of different States;–between Citizens of the same State claiming Lands under Grants of different States, and between a State, or the Citizens thereof, and foreign States, Citizens or Subjects.

[This section is modified by Amendment XI.]

In all Cases affecting Ambassadors, other public Ministers and Consuls, and those in which a State shall be Party, the supreme Court shall have original Jurisdiction. In all the other Cases before mentioned, the supreme Court shall have appellate Jurisdiction, both as to Law and Fact, with such Exceptions, and under such Regulations as the Congress shall make.

The trial of all Crimes, except in Cases of Impeachment, shall be by Jury; and such Trial shall be held in the State where the said Crimes shall have been committed; but when not committed within any State, the Trial shall be at such Place or Places as the Congress may by Law have directed.

Section 3—Treason Defined. Proof of, Punishment of.

Treason against the United States, shall consist only in levying War against them, or in adhering to their Enemies, giving them Aid and Comfort. No Person shall be convicted of Treason unless on the Testimony of two Witnesses to the same overt Act, or on Confession in open Court.

The Congress shall have Power to declare the Punishment of Treason, but no Attainder of Treason shall work Corruption of Blood, or Forfeiture except during the Life of the Person attainted.

ARTICLE IV.

Section 1—Each State to give credit to the public acts, etc., of every other State.

Full Faith and Credit shall be given in each State to the public Acts, Records, and judicial Proceedings of every other State. And the Congress may by general Laws prescribe the Manner in which such Acts, Records and Proceedings shall be proved, and the Effect thereof.

The judicial Power of the United States, shall be vested in one supreme Court, and in such inferior Courts as the Congress may from time to time ordain and establish. The Judges, both of the supreme and inferior Courts, shall hold their Offices during good Behaviour, and shall, at stated Times, receive for their Services, a Compensation, which shall not be diminished during their Continuance in Office.

Section 2—Privileges of citizens of each State. Fugitives from justice to be delivered up. Persons held to service having escaped, to be delivered up.

The Citizens of each State shall be entitled to all Privileges and Immunities of Citizens in the several States.

A Person charged in any State with Treason, Felony, or other Crime, who shall flee from Justice, and be found in another State, shall on demand of the executive Authority of the State from which he fled, be delivered up, to be removed to the State having Jurisdiction of the Crime.

[No Person held to Service or Labour in one State, under the Laws thereof, escaping into another, shall, in Consequence of any Law or Regulation therein, be discharged from such Service or Labour, but shall be delivered up on Claim of the Party to whom such Service or Labour may be due.] [This clause was superseded by Amendment XIII.]

Section 3—Admission of new States. Power of Congress over territory and other property.

New States may be admitted by the Congress into this Union; but no new State shall be formed or erected within the Jurisdiction of any other State; nor any State be formed by the Junction of two or more States, or parts of States, without the Consent of the Legislatures of the States concerned as well as of the Congress.

The Congress shall have Power to dispose of and make all needful Rules and Regulations respecting the Territory or other Property belonging to the United States; and nothing in this Constitution shall be so construed as to Prejudice any Claims of the United States, or of any particular State.

Section 4—Republican form of government guaranteed. Each State to be protected.

The United States shall guarantee to every State in this Union a Republican Form of Government, and shall protect each of them against Invasion; and on Application of the Legislature, or of the Executive (when the Legislature cannot be convened) against domestic Violence.

ARTICLE V.

Constitution: how amended; proviso.

The Congress, whenever two-thirds of both Houses shall deem it necessary, shall propose Amendments to this Constitution, or, on the Application of the Legislatures of two-thirds of the several States, shall call a Convention for proposing Amendments, which, in either Case, shall be valid to all Intents and Purposes, as part of this Constitution, when ratified by the Legislatures of three-fourths of the several States, or by Conventions in three-fourths thereof, as the one or the other Mode of Ratification may be proposed by the Congress: Provided that no Amendment which may be made prior to the Year One thousand eight hundred and eight shall in any Manner affect the first and fourth Clauses in the Ninth Section of the first Article; and that no State, without its Consent, shall be deprived of its equal Suffrage in the Senate.

ARTICLE VI.

Certain debts, etc., declared valid. Supremacy of Constitution, treaties, and laws of the United States. Oath to support Constitution, by whom taken. No religious test.

All Debts contracted and Engagements entered into, before the Adoption of this Constitution, shall be as valid against the United States under this Constitution, as under the Confederation.

This Constitution, and the Laws of the United States which shall be made in Pursuance thereof; and all Treaties made, or which shall be made, under the Authority of the United States, shall be the supreme Law of the Land; and the Judges in every State shall be bound thereby, any Thing in the Constitution or Laws of any State to the Contrary notwithstanding.

The Senators and Representatives before mentioned, and the Members of the several State Legislatures, and all executive and judicial Officers, both of the United States and of the several States, shall be bound by Oath or Affirmation, to support this Constitution; but no religious Test shall ever be required as a Qualification to any Office or public Trust under the United States.

ARTICLE VII.

What ratification shall establish Constitution.

The Ratification of the Conventions of nine States shall be sufficient for the Establishment of this Constitution between the States so ratifying the Same.

Done in Convention by the Unanimous Consent of the States present the Seventeenth Day of September in the Year of our Lord one thousand seven hundred and Eighty seven and of the Independence of the United States of America the Twelfth.

In Witness whereof We have hereunto subscribed our Names.

Go WASHINGTON, Presidt and deputy from Virginia

New Hampshire—John Langdon, Nicholas Gilman

Massachusetts—Nathaniel Gorham, Rufus King

Connecticut—Wm. Saml. Johnson, Roger Sherman

New York—Alexander Hamilton

New Jersey—Wil: Livingston, David Brearley, Wm. Paterson, Jona: Dayton

Pennsylvania—B Franklin, Thomas Mifflin, Robt Morris, Geo. Clymer, Thos. FitzSimons, Jared Ingersoll, James Wilson, Gouv Morris

Delaware—Geo: Read, Gunning Bedford jun, John Dickinson, Richard Bassett, Jaco: Broom

Maryland—James McHenry, Dan of St Thos. Jenifer, Danl Carroll

Virginia—John Blair, James Madison Jr.

North Carolina—Wm. Blount, Rich'd Dobbs Spaight, Hu Williamson

South Carolina—J. Rutledge, Charles Cotesworth Pinckney, Charles Pinckney, Pierce Butler

Georgia—William Few, Abr Baldwin

Attest: William Jackson, Secretary.

IT'S A FACT: Since 1952, the original pages of the Constitution have been on public display at the National Archives in Washington, DC. Each page is sealed in a special light-filtering glass case that contains a mixture of helium and water vapor to preserve the paper. Only pages one and four are displayed daily, and at night, they are lowered into a steel and concrete-reinforced vault. The entire Constitution is displayed only once a year, on Sept.17, the anniversary of its signing in 1787.

Ten Original Amendments: The Bill of Rights

In force Dec. 15, 1791

[The First Congress, at its first session in the City of New York, Sept. 25, 1789, submitted to the states 12 amendments to clarify certain individual and state rights not named in the Constitution. They are generally called the Bill of Rights.

Influential in framing these amendments was the Declaration of Rights of Virginia, written by George Mason (1725-1792) in 1776. Mason, a Virginia delegate to the Constitutional Convention, did not sign the Constitution and opposed its ratification on the ground that it did not sufficiently oppose slavery or safeguard individual rights.

In the preamble to the resolution offering the proposed amendments, Congress said: "The conventions of a number of the States having at the time of their adopting the Constitution, expressed a desire, in order to prevent misconstruction or abuse of its powers, that further declaratory and restrictive clauses should be added, and as extending the ground of public confidence in the government will best insure the beneficent ends of its institution, be it resolved," etc.

Ten of these amendments, now commonly known as one to 10 inclusive, but originally 3 to 12 inclusive, were ratified by the states as follows: New Jersey, Nov. 20, 1789; Maryland, Dec. 19, 1789; North Carolina, Dec. 22, 1789; South Carolina, Jan. 19, 1790; New Hampshire, Jan. 25, 1790; Delaware, Jan. 28, 1790; New York, Feb. 27, 1790; Pennsylvania, Mar. 10, 1790; Rhode Island, June 7, 1790; Vermont, Nov. 3, 1791; Virginia, Dec. 15, 1791; Massachusetts, Mar. 2, 1939; Georgia, Mar. 18, 1939; Connecticut, Apr. 19, 1939. These original 10 ratified amendments follow as Amendments I to X inclusive.

Of the two original proposed amendments that were not ratified promptly by the necessary number of states, the first related to apportionment of Representatives; the second, relating to compensation of members of Congress, was ratified in 1992 and became Amendment 27.]

AMENDMENT I.

Religious establishment prohibited. Freedom of speech, of press, right to assemble and to petition.

Congress shall make no law respecting an establishment of religion, or prohibiting the free exercise thereof; or abridging the freedom of speech, or of the press; or the right of the people peaceably to assemble, and to petition the Government for a redress of grievances.

AMENDMENT II.

Right to keep and bear arms.

A well regulated Militia, being necessary to the security of a free State, the right of the people to keep and bear Arms, shall not be infringed.

AMENDMENT III.

Conditions for quarters for soldiers.

No Soldier shall, in time of peace be quartered in any house, without the consent of the Owner, nor in time of war, but in a manner to be prescribed by law.

AMENDMENT IV.

Protection from unreasonable search and seizure.

The right of the people to be secure in their persons, houses, papers, and effects, against unreasonable searches and seizures, shall not be violated, and no Warrants shall issue, but upon probable cause, supported by Oath or affirmation, and particularly describing the place to be searched, and the persons or things to be seized.

AMENDMENT V.

Provisions concerning prosecution and due process of law. Double jeopardy restriction. Private property not to be taken without compensation.

No person shall be held to answer for a capital, or otherwise infamous crime, unless on a presentment or indictment of a Grand Jury, except in cases arising in the land or naval forces, or in the Militia, when in actual service in time of War or public danger; nor shall any person be subject for the same offence to be twice put in jeopardy of life or limb; nor shall be compelled in any criminal case to be a witness against himself, nor be deprived of life, liberty, or property, without due process of law; nor shall private property be taken for public use, without just compensation.

AMENDMENT VI.

Right to speedy trial, witnesses, etc.

In all criminal prosecutions, the accused shall enjoy the right to a speedy and public trial, by an impartial jury of the State and district wherein the crime shall have been committed, which district shall have been previously ascertained by law, and to be informed of the nature and cause of the accusation; to be confronted with the witnesses against him; to have compulsory process for obtaining witnesses in his favor, and to have the Assistance of Counsel for his defence.

AMENDMENT VII.

Right of trial by jury.

In suits at common law, where the value in controversy shall exceed twenty dollars, the right of trial by jury shall be preserved, and no fact tried by a jury, shall be otherwise reexamined in any Court of the United States, than according to the rules of the common law.

AMENDMENT VIII.

Excessive bail or fines; cruel and unusual punishment.

Excessive bail shall not be required, nor excessive fines imposed, nor cruel and unusual punishments inflicted.

AMENDMENT IX.

Rule of construction of Constitution.

The enumeration in the Constitution, of certain rights, shall not be construed to deny or disparage others retained by the people.

AMENDMENT X.

Rights of States under Constitution.

The powers not delegated to the United States by the Constitution, nor prohibited by it to the States, are reserved to the States respectively, or to the people.

Amendments Since the Bill of Rights

AMENDMENT XI.

Judicial powers construed.

The Judicial power of the United States shall not be construed to extend to any suit in law or equity, commenced or prosecuted against one of the United States by Citizens of another State, or by Citizens or Subjects of any Foreign State.

[This amendment was proposed to the Legislatures of the several States by the Third Congress on March. 4, 1794, and was declared to have been ratified in a message from the President to Congress, dated Jan. 8, 1798.

[It was on Jan. 5, 1798, that Secretary of State Pickering received from 12 of the States authenticated ratifications, and informed President John Adams of that fact.

[As a result of later research in the Department of State, it is now established that Amendment XI became part of the Constitution on Feb. 7, 1795, for on that date it had been ratified by 12 States as follows:

[1. New York, Mar. 27, 1794. 2. Rhode Island, Mar. 31, 1794. 3. Connecticut, May 8, 1794. 4. New Hampshire, June 16, 1794. 5. Massachusetts, June 26, 1794. 6. Vermont, between Oct. 9, 1794, and Nov. 9, 1794. 7. Virginia, Nov. 18, 1794. 8. Georgia, Nov. 29, 1794. 9. Kentucky, Dec. 7, 1794. 10. Maryland, Dec. 26, 1794. 11. Delaware, Jan. 23, 1795. 12. North Carolina, Feb. 7, 1795.

[On June 1, 1796, more than a year after Amendment XI had become a part of the Constitution—but before anyone was officially aware of this—Tennessee had been admitted as a State; but not until Oct. 16, 1797, was a certified copy of the resolution of Congress proposing the amendment sent to the Governor of Tennessee, John Sevier, by Secretary of State Pickering, whose office was then at Trenton, New Jersey, because of the epidemic of yellow fever at Philadelphia; it seems, however, that the Legislature of Tennessee took no action on Amendment XI, owing doubtless to the fact that public announcement of its adoption was made soon thereafter.

[Besides the necessary 12 States, one other, South Carolina, ratified Amendment XI, but this action was not taken until Dec. 4, 1797; the two remaining States, New Jersey and Pennsylvania, failed to ratify.]

AMENDMENT XII.

Manner of choosing President and Vice-President.

[Proposed by Congress Dec. 9, 1803; ratified June 15, 1804.]

The Electors shall meet in their respective states and vote by ballot for President and Vice-President, one of whom, at least, shall not be an inhabitant of the same state with themselves; they shall name in their ballots the person voted for as President, and in distinct ballots the person voted for as Vice-President, and they shall make distinct lists of all persons voted for as President, and of all persons voted for as Vice-President, and of the number of votes for each, which lists they shall sign and certify, and transmit sealed to the seat of the government of the United States, directed to the President of the Senate;–The President of the Senate shall, in presence of the Senate and House of Representatives, open all the certificates and the votes shall then be counted;—The person having the greatest number of votes for President, shall be the President, if such number be a majority of the whole number of Electors appointed; and if no person have such majority, then from the persons having the highest numbers not exceeding three on the list of those voted for as President, the House of Representatives shall choose immediately, by ballot, the President. But in choosing the President, the votes shall be taken by states, the representation from each state having one vote; a quorum for this purpose shall consist of a member or members from two-thirds of the states, and a majority of all the states shall be necessary to a choice. *[And if the House of Representatives shall not choose a President whenever the right of choice shall devolve upon them, before the fourth day of March next following, then the Vice-President shall act as President, as in the case of the death or other constitutional disability of the President.] [The words in parentheses were superseded by Amendment XX, section 3.]* The person having the greatest number of votes as Vice-President, shall be the Vice-President, if such number be a majority of the whole number of Electors appointed, and if no person have a majority, then from the two highest numbers on the list, the Senate shall choose the Vice-President; a quorum for the purpose shall consist of two-thirds of the whole number of Senators, and a majority of the whole number shall be necessary to a choice. But no person constitutionally ineligible to the office of President shall be eligible to that of Vice-President of the United States.

THE RECONSTRUCTION AMENDMENTS

[Amendments XIII, XIV, and XV are commonly known as the Reconstruction Amendments, inasmuch as they followed the Civil War, and were drafted by Republicans who were bent on imposing their own policy of reconstruction on the South. Post-bellum legislatures there—Mississippi, South Carolina, Georgia, for example—had set up laws which, it was charged, were contrived to perpetuate Negro slavery under other names.]

AMENDMENT XIII.

Slavery abolished.

[Proposed by Congress Jan. 31, 1865; ratified Dec. 6, 1865. The amendment, when first proposed by a resolution in Congress, was passed by the Senate, 38 to 6, on Apr. 8, 1864, but was defeated in the House, 95 to 66 on June 15, 1864. On reconsideration by the House, on Jan. 31, 1865, the resolution passed, 119 to 56. It was approved by President Lincoln on Feb. 1, 1865, although the Supreme Court had decided in 1798 that the President has nothing to do with the proposing of amendments to the Constitution, or their adoption.]

1. Neither slavery nor involuntary servitude, except as a punishment for crime whereof the party shall have been duly convicted, shall exist within the United States, or any place subject to their jurisdiction.

2. Congress shall have power to enforce this article by appropriate legislation.

AMENDMENT XIV.

Citizenship rights not to be abridged.

[The following amendment was proposed to the Legislatures of the several states by the 39th Congress, June 13, 1866, ratified July 9, 1868, and declared to have been ratified in a proclamation by the Secretary of State, July 28, 1868.]

[The 14th amendment was adopted only by virtue of ratification subsequent to earlier rejections. Newly constituted legislatures in both North Carolina and South Carolina (respectively July 4 and 9, 1868), ratified the proposed amendment, although earlier legislatures had rejected the proposal. The Secretary of State issued a proclamation, which, though doubtful as to the effect of attempted withdrawals by Ohio and New Jersey, entertained no doubt as to the validity of the ratification by North and South Carolina. The following day (July 21, 1868), Congress passed a resolution which declared the 14th Amendment to be a part of the Constitution and directed the Secretary of State so to promulgate it. The Secretary waited, however, until the newly constituted Legislature of Georgia had ratified the amendment, subsequent to an earlier rejection, before the promulgation of the ratification of the new amendment.]

1. All persons born or naturalized in the United States, and subject to the jurisdiction thereof, are citizens of the United States and of the State wherein they reside. No State shall make or enforce any law which shall abridge the privileges or immunities of citizens of the United States; nor shall any State deprive any person of life, liberty, or property, without due process of law; nor deny to any person within its jurisdiction the equal protection of the laws.

2. Representatives shall be apportioned among the several States according to their respective numbers, counting the whole number of persons in each State, excluding Indians not taxed. But when the right to vote at any election for the choice of electors for President and Vice-President of the United States, Representatives in Congress, the Executive and Judicial officers of a State, or the members of the Legislature thereof, is denied to any of the male inhabitants of such State, being twenty-one years of age, and citizens of the United States, or in any way abridged, except for participation in rebellion, or other crime, the basis of representation therein shall be reduced in the proportion which the number of such male citizens shall bear to the whole number of male citizens twenty-one years of age in such State.

3. No person shall be a Senator or Representative in Congress, or elector of President and Vice-President, or hold any office, civil or military, under the United States, or under any State, who, having previously taken an oath, as a member of Congress, or as an officer of the United States, or as a member of any State legislature, or as an executive or judicial officer of any State, to support the Constitution of the United States, shall have engaged in insurrection or rebellion against the same, or given aid or comfort to the enemies thereof. But Congress may by a vote of two-thirds of each House, remove such disability.

4. The validity of the public debt of the United States, authorized by law, including debts incurred for payment of pensions and bounties for services in suppressing insurrection or rebellion, shall not be questioned. But neither the United States nor any State shall assume or pay any debt or obligation incurred in aid of insurrection or rebellion against the United States, or any claim for the loss or emancipation of any slave; but all such debts, obligations and claims shall be held illegal and void.

The Congress shall have power to enforce, by appropriate legislation, the provisions of this article.

AMENDMENT XV.

Race no bar to voting rights.

[The following amendment was proposed to the legislatures of the several States by the 40th Congress, Feb. 26, 1869, and ratified Feb. 8, 1870.]

1. The right of citizens of the United States to vote shall not be denied or abridged by the United States or by any State on account of race, color, or previous condition of servitude–

2. The Congress shall have power to enforce this article by appropriate legislation.

AMENDMENT XVI.

Income taxes authorized.

[Proposed by Congress July 12, 1909; ratified Feb. 3, 1913.]

The Congress shall have power to lay and collect taxes on incomes, from whatever source derived, without apportionment among the several States, and without regard to any census or enumeration.

AMENDMENT XVII.

United States Senators to be elected by direct popular vote.

[Proposed by Congress May 13, 1912; ratified Apr. 8, 1913.]

The Senate of the United States shall be composed of two Senators from each State, elected by the people thereof, for six years; and each Senator shall have one vote. The electors in each State shall have the qualifications requisite for electors of the most numerous branch of the State legislatures.

When vacancies happen in the representation of any State in the Senate, the executive authority of such State shall issue writs of election to fill such vacancies: *Provided,* That the legislature of any State may empower the executive thereof to make temporary appointments until the people fill the vacancies by election as the legislature may direct.

This amendment shall not be so construed as to affect the election or term of any Senator chosen before it becomes valid as part of the Constitution.

AMENDMENT XVIII.

Liquor prohibition amendment.

[Proposed by Congress Dec. 18, 1917; ratified Jan. 16, 1919. Repealed by Amendment XXI, effective Dec. 5, 1933.]

1. After one year from the ratification of this article the manufacture, sale, or transportation of intoxicating liquors within, the importation thereof into, or the exportation thereof from the United States and all territory subject to the jurisdiction thereof for beverage purposes is hereby prohibited.

2. The Congress and the several States shall have concurrent power to enforce this article by appropriate legislation.

3. This article shall be inoperative unless it shall have been ratified as an amendment to the Constitution by the legislatures of the several States as provided in the Constitution, within seven years from the date of the submission hereof to the States by the Congress.

[The total vote in the Senates of the various States was 1,310 for, 237 against—84.6% dry. In the lower houses of the States the vote was 3,782 for, 1,035 against—78.5% dry.

[The amendment ultimately was adopted by all the States except Connecticut and Rhode Island.]

AMENDMENT XIX.

Giving nationwide suffrage to women.

[Proposed by Congress June 4, 1919; ratified Aug. 18, 1920.]

The right of citizens of the United States to vote shall not be denied or abridged by the United States or by any State on account of sex.

Congress shall have power to enforce this Article by appropriate legislation.

AMENDMENT XX.

Terms of President and Vice President to begin on Jan. 20; those of Senators, Representatives, Jan. 3.

[Proposed by Congress Mar. 2, 1932; ratified Jan. 23, 1933.]

1. The terms of the President and Vice President shall end at noon on the 20th day of January, and the terms of Senators and Representatives at noon on the 3d day of January, of the years in which such terms would have ended if this article had not been ratified; and the terms of their successors shall then begin.

2. The Congress shall assemble at least once in every year, and such meeting shall begin at noon on the 3d day of January, unless they shall by law appoint a different day.

3. If, at the time fixed for the beginning of the term of the President, the President elect shall have died, the Vice President elect shall become President. If a President shall not have been chosen before the time fixed for the beginning of his term, or if the President elect shall have failed to qualify, then the Vice President elect shall act as President until a President shall have qualified; and the Congress may by law provide for the case wherein neither a President elect nor a Vice President elect shall have qualified, declaring who shall then act as President, or the manner in which one who is to act shall be selected, and such person shall act accordingly until a President or Vice President shall have qualified.

4. The Congress may by law provide for the case of the death of any of the persons from whom the House of Representatives may choose a President whenever the right of choice shall have devolved upon them, and for the case of the death of any of the persons from whom the Senate may choose a Vice President whenever the right of choice shall have devolved upon them.

5. Sections 1 and 2 shall take effect on the 15th day of October following the ratification of this article (Oct. 1933).

6. This article shall be inoperative unless it shall have been ratified as an amendment to the Constitution by the legislatures of three-fourths of the several States within seven years from the date of its submission.

AMENDMENT XXI.

Repeal of Amendment XVIII.

[Proposed by Congress Feb. 20, 1933; ratified Dec. 5, 1933.]

1. The eighteenth article of amendment to the Constitution of the United States is hereby repealed.

2. The transportation or importation into any State, Territory, or possession of the United States for delivery or use therein of intoxicating liquors, in violation of the laws thereof, is hereby prohibited.

3. This article shall be inoperative unless it shall have been ratified as an amendment to the Constitution by conventions in the several States, as provided in the Constitution, within seven years from the date of the submission hereof to the States by the Congress.

AMENDMENT XXII.

Limiting Presidential terms of office.

[Proposed by Congress Mar. 24, 1947; ratified Feb. 27, 1951.]

1. No person shall be elected to the office of the President more than twice, and no person who has held the office of President, or acted as President, for more than two years of a term to which some other person was elected President shall be elected to the office of the President more than once. But this Article shall not apply to any person holding the office of President when this Article was proposed by the Congress, and shall not prevent any person who may be holding the office of President, or acting as President, during the term within which this Article becomes operative from holding the office of President or acting as President during the remainder of such term.

2. This article shall be inoperative unless it shall have been ratified as an amendment to the Constitution by the legislatures of three-fourths of the several States within seven years from the date of its submission to the States by the Congress.

AMENDMENT XXIII.

Presidential vote for District of Columbia.

[Proposed by Congress June 16, 1960; ratified Mar. 29, 1961.]

1. The District constituting the seat of Government of the United States shall appoint in such manner as the Congress may direct:

A number of electors of President and Vice President equal to the whole number of Senators and Representatives in Congress to which the District would be entitled if it were a State, but in no event more than the least populous State; they shall be in addition to those appointed by the States, but they shall be considered, for the purposes of the election of President and Vice President, to be electors appointed by a State; and they shall meet in the District and perform such duties as provided by the twelfth article of amendment.

2. The Congress shall have power to enforce this article by appropriate legislation.

AMENDMENT XXIV.

Barring poll tax in federal elections.

[Proposed by Congress Aug. 27, 1962; ratified Jan. 23, 1964.]

1. The right of citizens of the United States to vote in any primary or other election for President or Vice President, for electors for President or Vice President, or for Senator or Representative in Congress, shall not be denied or abridged by the United States or any State by reason of failure to pay any poll tax or other tax.

2. The Congress shall have power to enforce this article by appropriate legislation.

AMENDMENT XXV.

Presidential disability and succession.

[Proposed by Congress July 6, 1965; ratified Feb. 10, 1967.]

1. In case of the removal of the President from office or of his death or resignation, the Vice President shall become President.

2. Whenever there is a vacancy in the office of the Vice President, the President shall nominate a Vice President who shall take office upon confirmation by a majority vote of both houses of Congress.

3. Whenever the President transmits to the President pro tempore of the Senate and the Speaker of the House of Representatives his written declaration that he is unable to discharge the powers and duties of his office, and until he transmits to them a written declaration to the contrary, such powers and duties shall be discharged by the Vice President as Acting President.

4. Whenever the Vice President and a majority of either the principal officers of the executive departments or of such other

body as Congress may by law provide, transmit to the President pro tempore of the Senate and the Speaker of the House of Representatives their written declaration that the President is unable to discharge the powers and duties of his office, the Vice President shall immediately assume the powers and duties of the office as Acting President.

Thereafter, when the President transmits to the President pro tempore of the Senate and the Speaker of the House of Representatives his written declaration that no inability exists, he shall resume the powers and duties of his office unless the Vice President and a majority of either the principal officers of the executive department or of such other body as Congress may by law provide, transmit within four days to the President pro tempore of the Senate and the Speaker of the House of Representatives their written declaration that the President is unable to discharge the powers and duties of his office. Thereupon Congress shall decide the issue, assembling within forty-eight hours for that purpose if not in session. If the Congress, within twenty-one days after receipt of the latter written declaration, or, if Congress is not in session, within twenty-one days after Congress is required to assemble, determines by two-thirds vote of both Houses that the President is unable to discharge the powers and duties of his office, the Vice President shall continue to discharge the same as Acting President; otherwise, the President shall resume the powers and duties of his office.

AMENDMENT XXVI.

Lowering voting age to 18 years.

[Proposed by Congress Mar. 23, 1971; ratified June 30, 1971.]

1. The right of citizens of the United States, who are eighteen years of age or older, to vote shall not be denied or abridged by the United States or by any State on account of age.

2. The Congress shall have the power to enforce this article by appropriate legislation.

AMENDMENT XXVII.

Congressional pay.

[Proposed by Congress Sept. 25, 1789; ratified May 7, 1992.]

No law, varying the compensation for the services of the Senators and Representatives, shall take effect, until an election of Representatives shall have intervened.

How a Bill Becomes a Law

A senator or representative introduces a bill in Congress by sending it to the clerk of the House or the Senate, who assigns it a number and title. This procedure is termed the first reading. The clerk then refers the bill to the appropriate committee of the Senate or House.

If the committee opposes the bill, it will table, or kill, it. Otherwise, the committee holds hearings to listen to opinions and facts offered by members and other interested people. The committee then debates the bill and possibly offers amendments. A vote is taken, and if favorable, the bill is sent back to the clerk of the House or Senate.

The clerk reads the bill to the house—the second reading. Members may then debate the bill and suggest amendments.

After debate and possibly amendment, the bill is given a third reading, simply of the title, and put to a voice or roll-call vote.

If passed, the bill goes to the other house, where it may be defeated or passed, with or without amendments. If defeated, the bill dies. If passed with amendments, a conference committee made up of members of both houses works out the differences and arrives at a compromise.

After passage of the final version by both houses, the bill is sent to the president. If the president signs it, the bill becomes a law. The president may, however, veto the bill by refusing to sign it and sending it back to the house where it originated, with reasons for the veto.

The Capitol

The president's objections are then read and debated, and a roll-call vote is taken. If the bill receives less than a two-thirds majority, it is defeated. If it receives at least two-thirds, it is sent to the other house. If that house also passes it by at least a two-thirds majority, the 1 veto is overridden, and the bill becomes a law.

If the president neither signs nor vetoes the bill within 10 days—not including Sundays—it automatically becomes a law even without the president's signature. However, if Congress has adjourned within those 10 days, the bill is automatically killed; this indirect rejection is termed a pocket veto.

Note: Under "line-item veto" legislation effective Jan. 1, 1997, the president was authorized, under certain circumstances, to veto a bill in part, but the legislation was found unconstitutional by the Supreme Court, June 25, 1998.

Confederate States and Secession

The American Civil War (1861-65) grew out of sectional disputes over the continued existence of slavery in the South and the contention of Southern legislators that the states retained many rights, including the right to secede.

The war was not fought by state against state but by one federal regime against another, the Confederate government in Richmond assuming control over the economic, political, and military life of the South, under protest from Georgia and South Carolina.

South Carolina voted an ordinance of secession from the Union, repealing its 1788 ratification of the U.S. Constitution on Dec. 20, 1860, to take effect on Dec. 24. Other states seceded in 1861. Their votes in conventions were: Mississippi, Jan. 9, 84-15; Florida, Jan. 10, 62-7; Alabama, Jan. 11, 61-39; Georgia, Jan. 19, 208-89; Louisiana, Jan. 26, 113-17; Texas, Feb. 1, 166-7, ratified by popular vote on Feb. 23 (for 34,794, against 11,325); Virginia, Apr. 17, 88-55, ratified by popular vote on May 23 (for 128,884; against 32,134); Arkansas, May 6, 69-1; Tennessee, May 7, ratified by popular vote on June 8 (for 104,019, against 47,238); North Carolina, May 21.

Missouri Unionists stopped secession in conventions Feb. 28 and Mar. 9. The legislature condemned secession Mar. 7. Under the protection of Confederate troops, secessionist members of the legislature adopted a resolution of secession at Neosho, Oct. 31. The Confederate Congress seated the secessionists' representatives.

Kentucky did not secede, and its government remained Unionist. In a part of the state occupied by Confederate troops, Kentuckians approved secession, and the Confederate Congress admitted their representatives.

The Maryland legislature voted against secession Apr. 27, 53-13. Delaware did not secede. Western Virginia held conventions at Wheeling, named a pro-Union governor on June 11, 1861, and was admitted to the Union as West Virginia on June 20, 1863. Its constitution provided for gradual abolition of slavery.

Confederate Government

Forty-two delegates from South Carolina, Georgia, Alabama, Mississippi, Louisiana, and Florida met in convention at Montgomery, AL, on Feb. 4, 1861. They adopted a provisional constitution of the Confederate States of America and elected Jefferson Davis (MS) as provisional president and Alexander H. Stephens (GA) as provisional vice president.

A permanent constitution was adopted Mar. 11. It abolished the African slave trade, but it did not bar interstate commerce in slaves. On July 20 the Congress moved to Richmond, VA. Davis was elected president in October and was inaugurated on Feb. 22, 1862.

The Congress adopted a flag, consisting of a red field with a white stripe, and a blue jack with a circle of white stars. Later the more popular flag was the red field with blue diagonal crossbars that held 13 white stars, for the 11 states in the Confederacy plus Kentucky and Missouri.

Lincoln's Address at Gettysburg, 1863

Fourscore and seven years ago our fathers brought forth on this continent a new nation, conceived in liberty and dedicated to the proposition that all men are created equal.

Now we are engaged in a great civil war, testing whether that nation or any nation so conceived and so dedicated can long endure. We are met on a great battle field of that war. We have come to dedicate a portion of that field, as a final resting-place for those who here gave their lives that that nation might live. It is altogether fitting and proper that we should do this.

But, in a larger sense, we can not dedicate—we can not consecrate—we can not hallow—this ground. The brave men, living and dead, who struggled here, have consecrated it, far above our poor power to add or detract. The world will little note, nor long remember, what we say here, but it can never forget what they did here. It is for us the living, rather, to be dedicated here to the unfinished work which they who fought here have thus far so nobly advanced. It is rather for us to be here dedicated to the great task remaining before us—that from these honored dead we take increased devotion to that cause for which they gave the last full measure of devotion—that we here highly resolve that these dead shall not have died in vain—that this nation, under God, shall have a new birth of freedom—and that government of the people, by the people, for the people, shall not perish from the earth.

Selected Landmark Decisions of the U.S. Supreme Court, 1803-2004

See also Year in Review: Notable Supreme Court Decisions, 2004-05.

1803: Marbury v. Madison. The Court ruled that Congress exceeded its power in the Judiciary Act of 1789; the Court thus established its power to review acts of Congress and declare invalid those it found in conflict with the Constitution.

1819: McCulloch v. Maryland. The Court ruled that Congress had the authority to charter a national bank, under the Constitution's granting of the power to enact all laws "necessary and proper" to responsibilities of government.

1819: Trustees of Dartmouth College v. Woodward. The Court ruled that a state could not arbitrarily alter the terms of a college's contract. (The Court later used a similar principle to limit the states' ability to interfere with business contracts.)

1857: Dred Scott v. Sanford. The Court declared unconstitutional the already-repealed Missouri Compromise of 1820 because it deprived a person of his or her property—a slave—without due process of law. The Court also ruled that slaves were not citizens of any state nor of the U.S. (The latter part of the decision was overturned by ratification of the 14th Amendment in 1868.)

1896: Plessy v. Ferguson. The Court ruled that a state law requiring federal railroad trains to provide separate but equal facilities for black and white passengers neither infringed upon federal authority to regulate interstate commerce nor violated the 13th and 14th Amendments. (The "separate but equal" doctrine remained effective until the 1954 **Brown v. Board of Education** decision.)

1904: Northern Securities Co. v. U.S. The Court ruled that a holding company formed solely to eliminate competition between two railroad lines was a combination in restraint of trade, violating the federal antitrust act.

1908: Muller v. Oregon. The Court upheld a state law limiting the working hours of women. (Louis D. Brandeis, counsel for the state, cited evidence from social workers, physicians, and factory inspectors that the number of hours women worked affected their health and morals.)

1911: Standard Oil Co. of New Jersey et al. v. U.S. The Court ruled that the Standard Oil Trust must be dissolved because of its unreasonable restraint of trade.

1919: Schenck v. U.S. The Court sustained the Espionage Act of 1917, maintaining that freedom of speech and press could be constrained if "the words used . . . create a clear and present danger. . ."

1925: Gitlow v. New York. The Court ruled that the First Amendment prohibition against government abridgment of the freedom of speech applied to the states as well as to the federal government. The decision was the first of a number of rulings holding that the 14th Amendment extended the guarantees of the Bill of Rights to state action.

1935: Schechter Poultry Corp. v. U.S. The Court ruled that Congress exceeded its authority to delegate legislative powers and to regulate interstate commerce when it enacted the National Industrial Recovery Act, which afforded the U.S. president too much discretionary power.

1951: Dennis et al. v. U.S. The Court upheld convictions under the Smith Act of 1940 for invoking Communist theory advocating the forcible overthrow of the government. (In the **1957 Yates v. U.S.** decision, the Court moderated this ruling by allowing such advocacy in the abstract, if not connected to action to achieve the goal.)

1954: Brown v. Board of Education of Topeka. The Court ruled that separate public schools for black and white students were inherently unequal, so that state-sanctioned segregation in public schools violated the equal protection guarantee of the 14th Amendment. And in **Bolling v. Sharpe** the Court ruled that the congressionally mandated segregated public school system in the District of Columbia violated the 5th Amendment's due process guarantee of personal liberty. (The Brown ruling also led to abolition of state-sponsored segregation in other public facilities.)

1957: Roth v. U.S., Alberts v. California. The Court ruled obscene material was not protected by First Amendment guarantees of freedom of speech and press, defining obscene as "utterly without redeeming social value" and appealing to "prurient interests" in the view of the average person. This definition was modified in later decisions, and the "average person" standard was replaced by the "local community" standard in **Miller v. California (1973).**

1961: Mapp v. Ohio. The Court ruled that evidence obtained in violation of the 4th Amendment guarantee against unreasonable search and seizure must be excluded from use at state as well as federal trials.

1962: Engel v. Vitale. The Court held that public schools could not require pupils to recite a state-composed prayer, even if nondenominational and voluntary, because this would be an unconstitutional attempt to establish religion.

1962: Baker v. Carr. The Court held that the constitutional challenges to the unequal distribution of voters among legislative districts could be resolved by federal courts.

1963: Gideon v. Wainwright. The Court ruled that state and federal defendants charged with serious crimes must have access to an attorney, at state expense if necessary.

1964: New York Times Co. v. Sullivan. The Court ruled that the First Amendment protected the press from libel suits for defamatory reports about public officials unless an injured party could prove that a defamatory report was made out of malice or "reckless disregard" for the truth.

1965: Griswold v. Conn. The Court ruled that a state unconstitutionally interfered with personal privacy in the marriage relationship when it prohibited anyone, including married couples, from using contraceptives.

1966: Miranda v. Arizona. The Court ruled that, under the guarantee of due process, suspects in custody, before being questioned, must be informed that they have the right to remain silent, that anything they say may be used against them, and that they have the right to counsel.

1973: Roe v. Wade, Doe v. Bolton. The Court ruled that the fetus was not a "person" with constitutional rights and that a right to privacy inherent in the 14th Amendment's due process guarantee of personal liberty protected a woman's decision to have an abortion. During the first trimester of pregnancy, the Court maintained, the decision should be left entirely to a woman and her physician. Some regulation of abortion procedures was allowed in the 2nd trimester, and some restriction of abortion in the 3rd.

1974: U.S. v. Nixon. The Court ruled that neither the separation of powers nor the need to preserve the confidentiality of presidential communications could alone justify an absolute executive privilege of immunity from judicial demands for evidence to be used in a criminal trial.

1976: Gregg v. Georgia, Profitt v. Fla., Jurek v. Texas. The Court held that death, as a punishment for persons convicted of first degree murder, was not in and of itself cruel and unusual punishment in violation of the 8th Amendment. But the Court ruled that the sentencing judge and jury must consider the individual character of the offender and the circumstances of the particular crime.

1978: Regents of Univ. of Calif. v. Bakke. The Court ruled that a special admissions program for a state medical school, under which a set number of places were reserved for minorities, violated the 1964 Civil Rights Act, which forbids excluding anyone, because of race, from a federally funded program. However, the Court ruled that race could be considered as one of a complex of factors.

1986: Bowers v. Hardwick. The Court refused to extend any constitutional right of privacy to homosexual activity, upholding a Georgia antisodomy law that in effect made such activity a crime. However, the law was struck down by the state supreme court in 1998, and in **Lawrence v. Texas (2003),** the U.S. Supreme Court struck down all state antisodomy laws, as violations of liberty prohibited in the 14th Amendment's due process clause. Also, in **Romer v. Evans (1996),** the Court struck down a Colorado constitutional provision that barred legislation protecting homosexuals from discrimination.

1990: Cruzan v. Missouri. The Court ruled that a person had the right to refuse life-sustaining medical treatment. However, the Court also ruled that, before treatment could be withheld from a comatose patient, a state could require "clear and convincing evidence" that the patient would not have wanted to live. And in 2 **1997** rulings, **Washington v. Glucksberg** and **Vacco v. Quill,** the Court ruled that states could ban doctor-assisted suicide.

1995: Adarand Constructors v. Peña. The Court held that federal programs that classify people by race, unless "narrowly tailored" to accomplish a "compelling governmental interest," may violate the right to equal protection.

1995: U.S. Term Limits Inc. v. Thornton. The Court ruled that neither states nor Congress could limit terms of members of Congress, since the Constitution reserves to the people the right to choose federal lawmakers.

1997: Clinton v. Jones. Rejecting an appeal by Pres. Clinton in a sexual harassment suit, the Court ruled that a sitting president did not have temporary immunity from a lawsuit for actions outside the realm of official duties.

1997: City of Boerne v. Flores. The Court overturned a 1993 law banning enforcement of laws that "substantially burden" religious practice unless there is a "compelling need" to do so. The Court held that the act was an unwarranted intrusion by Congress on states' prerogatives and an infringement of the judiciary's role.

1997: Reno v. ACLU. Citing the right to free expression, the Court overturned a provision making it a crime to display or distribute "indecent" or "patently offensive" material on the Internet. In **1998**, however, the Court ruled in **NEA v. Finley** that "general standards of decency" may be used as a criterion in federal arts funding.

1998: Clinton v. City of New York. The Court struck down the Line-Item Veto Act (1996), holding that it unconstitutionally gave the president "the unilateral power to change the text of duly enacted statutes."

1998: Faragher v. City of Boca Raton, Burlington Industries, Inc. v. Ellerth. The Court issued new guidelines for workplace sexual harassment suits, holding employers responsible for misconduct by supervisory employees. And in **Oncale v. Sundowner Offshore Services,** the Court ruled that the law against sexual harassment applies regardless of whether harasser and victim are the same sex.

1999: Dept. of Commerce v. U.S. House. Upholding a challenge to plans for the 2000 census, the Court required an actual head count for apportioning the U.S. House of Representatives, but allowed statistical sampling for other purposes, such as the allocation of federal funds.

1999: Alden v. Maine, Florida Prepaid v. College Savings Bank, College Savings Bank v. Florida. In a series of rulings, the Court applied the principle of "sovereign immunity" to shield states in large part from being sued under federal law.

2000: Troxel v. Granville. The justices found that a Washington state law allowing grandparents visitation rights, as broadly applied, interfered with parents' right to determine the best care for their children.

2000: Boy Scouts of America v. Dale. The Court ruled that the Boy Scouts could dismiss a troop leader after learning he was gay, holding that the right to freedom of association outweighed a New Jersey anti-discrimination statute.

2000: Stenberg v. Carhart. The Court struck down a Nebraska law that banned so-called partial-birth abortion. It argued that the law could be interpreted as banning other abortion procedures and that it should have made exception for reasons of health. (See 1973: *Roe* v. *Wade*.)

2000: Bush v. Gore. The Court ruled that manual recounts of presidential ballots in the Nov. 2000 election could not proceed because inconsistent evaluation standards in different counties violated the equal protection clause. In effect, the ruling meant existing official results leaving George W. Bush as narrow winner of the election would prevail.

2001: Easley v. Cromartie. The Court ruled that North Carolina's 12th Congressional District, whose irregular shape had been challenged as an unconstitutional racial gerrymander, was the permissible result of attempts to create a majority-Democrat district.

2001: Good News Club v. Milford Central School. The justices found that religious and secular organizations were entitled to equal access to public elementary school grounds for after-school meetings.

2002: Atkins v. Virginia. The Court ruled that the execution of mentally retarded felons violated the 8th Amendment ban on "cruel and unusual punishment."

2002: Ring v. Arizona. The Court found that only a jury, not a judge, could decide to impose the death penalty.

2002: Zelman v. Simmons-Harris. The Court ruled that publicly funded tuition vouchers could be used at religious schools without violating the separation of church and state.

2002: Federal Maritime Commission v. South Carolina State Ports Authority. The Court ruled that the 11th Amendment gave states immunity from private lawsuits involving federal agencies.

2003: Grotter v. Bollinger, Gratz v. Bollinger. The Court upheld affirmative action in admission policies at the University of Michigan Law School. However, in a second decision, the Court ruled against a strict point system based on racial and ethnic backgrounds, as used in the university's undergraduate admissions process.

2004: Rasul v. Bush, Al Odah v. United States. The Court ruled that terrorism detainees held at the U.S. naval base at Guantanamo Bay, Cuba, could challenge their detentions in U.S. courts.

2004: Tennessee v. Lane. The Court ruled that disabled individuals could sue states under the Americans With Disabilities Act for failing to provide adequate access to state courthouses, despite states' usual immunity from private lawsuits in federal court.

2004: Locke v. Davey. The justices decided that a scholarship program provided by the state of Washington did not violate the right to free exercise of religion in denying aid to students preparing for the clergy.

2004: Ashcroft v. American Civil Liberties Union, et al. The Court struck down the Child Online Protection Act (COPA), passed by Congress in 1998 to restrict access to online pornography by minors, on the basis that the law, as written, violated the 1st Amendment right of free speech.

IT'S A FACT: The U.S. Constitution was written on four parchment pages and contains 4,543 words, including the signatures. It is the world's oldest and shortest constitution of government still in use.

Presidential Oath of Office

The Constitution (Article II) directs that the president-elect shall take the following oath or affirmation to be inaugurated as president: "I do solemnly swear [affirm] that I will faithfully execute the office of President of the United States, and will, to the best of my ability, preserve, protect, and defend the Constitution of the United States." (Custom decrees the addition of the words "So help me God" at the end of the oath when taken by the president-elect, with the left hand on the Bible for the duration of the oath, and the right hand slightly raised.)

Law on Succession to the Presidency

If by reason of death, resignation, removal from office, inability, or failure to qualify there is neither a president nor vice president to discharge the powers and duties of the office of president, then the speaker of the House of Representatives shall upon his resignation as speaker and as representative, act as president. The same rule shall apply in the case of the death, resignation, removal from office, or inability of an individual acting as president.

If at the time when a speaker is to begin the discharge of the powers and duties of the office of president there is no speaker, or the speaker fails to qualify as acting president, then the president pro tempore of the Senate, upon his resignation as president pro tempore and as senator, shall act as president.

An individual acting as president shall continue to act until the expiration of the then current presidential term, except that (1) if his discharge of the powers and duties of the office is founded in whole or in part in the failure of both the president-elect and the vice president-elect to qualify, then he shall act only until a president or vice president qualifies, and (2) if his discharge of the powers and duties of the office is founded in whole or in part on the inability of the president or vice president, then he shall act only until the removal of the disability of one of such individuals.

If, by reason of death, resignation, removal from office, or failure to qualify, there is no president pro tempore to act as president, then the officer of the United States who is highest on the following list, and who is not under any disability to discharge the powers and duties of president shall act as president; the secretaries of state, treasury, defense, attorney general; secretaries of interior, agriculture, commerce, labor, health and human services, housing and urban development, transportation, energy, education, veterans affairs.

(Legislation approved July 18, 1947; amended Sept. 9, 1965, Oct. 15, 1966, Aug. 4, 1977, and Sept. 27, 1979. See also Constitutional Amendment XXV.)

Origin of the United States National Motto

In God We Trust, designated as the U.S. National Motto by Congress in 1956, originated during the Civil War as an inscription for U. S. coins, although it was used by Francis Scott Key in a slightly different form when he wrote "The Star-Spangled Banner" in 1814. On Nov. 13, 1861, when Union morale had been shaken by battlefield defeats, the Rev. M. R. Watkinson, of Ridleyville, PA, wrote to Secy. of the Treasury Salmon P. Chase. "From my heart I have felt our national shame in disowning God as not the least of our present national disasters," the minister wrote, suggesting "recognition of the Almighty God in some form on our coins." Secy. Chase ordered designs prepared with the inscription *In God We Trust* and backed coinage legislation that authorized use of this slogan. The motto first appeared on some U.S. coins in 1864, and disappeared and reappeared on various coins until 1955, when Congress ordered it placed on all paper money and all coins.

The Great Seal of the U.S.

On July 4, 1776, the Continental Congress appointed a committee consisting of Benjamin Franklin, John Adams, and Thomas Jefferson "to bring in a device for a seal of the United States of America." The designs submitted by this and a subsequent committee were considered unacceptable. After many delays, a third committee, appointed early in 1782, presented a design prepared by William Barton. Charles Thomson, the secretary of Congress, suggested certain changes, and Congress finally approved the design on June 20, 1782. The obverse side of the seal shows an American bald eagle. In its mouth is a ribbon bearing the motto *e pluribus unum* (one out of many). In the eagle's talons are the arrows of war and an olive branch of peace. The reverse side shows an unfinished pyramid with an eye (the eye of Providence) above it.

The Flag of the U.S.—The Stars and Stripes

The 50-star flag of the United States was raised for the first time officially at 12:01 AM on July 4, 1960, at Fort McHenry National Monument in Baltimore, MD. The 50th star had been added for Hawaii; a year earlier the 49th, for Alaska. Before that, no star had been added since 1912, when New Mexico and Arizona were admitted to the Union.

The true history of the Stars and Stripes has become so cluttered by myth and tradition that the facts are difficult, and in some cases impossible, to establish. For example, it is not certain who designed the Stars and Stripes, who made the first such flag, or even whether it ever flew in any sea fight or land battle of the American Revolution.

All agree, however, that the Stars and Stripes originated as the result of a resolution offered by the Marine Committee of the Second Continental Congress at Philadelphia and adopted on June 14, 1777. It read:

Resolved: that the flag of the United States be thirteen stripes, alternate red and white; that the union be thirteen stars, white in a blue field, representing a new constellation.

Congress gave no hint as to the designer of the flag, no instructions as to the arrangement of the stars, and no information on its appropriate uses. Historians have been unable to find the original flag law.

The resolution establishing the flag was not even published until Sept. 2, 1777. Despite repeated requests, Washington did not get the flags until 1783, after the American Revolution was over. And there is no certainty that they were the Stars and Stripes.

Early Flags

Many historians consider the first flag of the U.S. to have been the Grand Union (sometimes called Great Union) flag, although the Continental Congress never officially adopted it. This flag was a modification of the British Meteor flag, which had the red cross of St. George and the white cross of St. Andrew combined in the blue canton. For the Grand Union flag, 6 horizontal stripes were imposed on the red field, dividing it into 13 alternating red and white stripes. On Jan. 1, 1776, when the Continental Army came into formal existence, this flag was unfurled on Prospect Hill, Somerville, MA. Washington wrote that "we hoisted the Union Flag in compliment to the United Colonies."

One of several flags about which controversy has raged for years is at Easton, PA. Containing the devices of the national flag in reversed order, this flag has been in the public library at Easton for more than 150 years. Some contend that this flag was actually the first Stars and Stripes, first displayed on July 8, 1776. This flag has 13 red and white stripes in the canton, 13 white stars centered in a blue field.

A flag was hastily improvised from garments by the defenders of Fort Schuyler at Rome, NY, Aug. 3-22, 1777. Historians believe it was the Grand Union Flag.

The Sons of Liberty had a flag of 9 red and white stripes, to signify 9 colonies, when they met in New York in 1765 to oppose the Stamp Tax. By 1775, the flag had grown to 13 red and white stripes, with a rattlesnake on it.

At Concord, Apr. 19, 1775, the minutemen from Bedford, MA, are said to have carried a flag having a silver arm with sword on a red field. At Cambridge, MA, the Sons of Liberty used a plain red flag with a green pine tree on it.

In June 1775, Washington went from Philadelphia to Boston to take command of the army, escorted to New York by the Philadelphia Light Horse Troop. It carried a yellow flag that had an elaborate coat of arms—the shield charged with 13 knots, the motto "For These We Strive"—and a canton of 13 blue and silver stripes.

In Feb. 1776, Col. Christopher Gadsden, a member of the Continental Congress, gave the South Carolina Provincial Congress a flag "such as is to be used by the commander-in-chief of the American Navy." It had a yellow field, with a rattlesnake about to strike and the words "Don't Tread on Me."

At the Battle of Bennington, Aug. 16, 1777, patriots used a flag of 7 white and 6 red stripes with a blue canton extending down 9 stripes and showing an arch of 11 white stars over the figure 76 and a star in each of the upper corners. The stars are 7-pointed. This flag is preserved in the Historical Museum at Bennington, VT.

At the Battle of Cowpens, Jan. 17, 1781, the 3d Maryland Regiment is said to have carried a flag of 13 red and white stripes, with a blue canton containing 12 stars in a circle around one star.

Who Designed the Flag? No one knows for certain. Francis Hopkinson, designer of a naval flag, declared he also had designed the flag and in 1781 asked Congress to reimburse him for his services. Congress did not do so. Dumas Malone of Columbia University wrote: "This talented man . . . designed the American flag."

Who Called the Flag "Old Glory"? The flag is said to have been named Old Glory by William Driver, a sea captain of Salem, MA. One legend has it that when he raised the flag on his brig, the *Charles Doggett*, in 1824, he said: "I name thee Old Glory." But his daughter, who presented the flag to the Smithsonian Institution, said he named it at his 21st birthday celebration on Mar. 17, 1824, when his mother presented the homemade flag to him.

The Betsy Ross Legend. The widely publicized legend that Mrs. Betsy Ross made the first Stars and Stripes in June 1776, at the request of a committee composed of George Washington, Robert Morris, and George Ross, an uncle, was first made public in 1870, by a grandson of Mrs. Ross. Historians have been unable to find a historical record of such a meeting or committee.

Adding New Stars

The flag of 1777 was used until 1795. Then, on the admission of Vermont and Kentucky to the Union, Congress passed and Pres. Washington signed an act that after May 1, 1795, the flag should have 15 stripes, alternating red and white, and 15 white stars on a blue field.

When new states were admitted, it became evident that the flag would become burdened with stripes. Congress thereupon ordered that after July 4, 1818, the flag should have 13 stripes, symbolizing the 13 original states; that the union have 20 stars, and that whenever a new state was admitted a new star should be added on the July 4 following admission.

No law designates the permanent arrangement of the stars. However, since 1912, when a new state has been admitted, the new design has been announced by executive order. No star is specifically identified with any state.

Code of Etiquette for Display and Use of the U.S. Flag

Reviewed by National Flag Foundation

Although the Stars and Stripes originated in 1777, it was not until 146 years later that there was a serious attempt to establish a uniform code of etiquette for the U.S. flag. On Feb. 15, 1923, the War Department issued a circular on the rules of flag usage. These rules were adopted almost in their entirety June 14, 1923, by a conference of 68 patriotic organizations in Washington, D.C. Finally, on June 22, 1942, a joint resolution of Congress, amended by Public Law 94-344, July 7, 1976, codified "existing rules and customs pertaining to the display and use of the flag . . ."

When to Display the Flag—The flag should be displayed on all days, especially on legal holidays and other special occasions, on official buildings when in use, in or near polling places on election days, and in or near schools when in session. Citizens may fly the flag at any time. It is customary to display it only from sunrise to sunset on buildings and on stationary flagstaffs in the open. It may be displayed at night, however, on special occasions, preferably lighted. The flag now flies over the White House both day and night. It flies over the Senate wing of the Capitol when the Senate is in session and over the House wing when that body is in session. It flies day and night over the east and west fronts of the Capitol, without floodlights at night but receiving illumination from the Capitol Dome. It flies 24 hours a day at several other places, including the Fort McHenry National Monument in Baltimore, where it inspired Francis Scott Key to write "The Star Spangled Banner." The flag also flies 24 hours a day, properly illuminated, at U.S. Customs ports of entry.

Flying the Flag at Half-Staff—Flying the flag at half-staff, that is, halfway up the staff, is a signal of mourning. The flag should be hoisted to the top of the staff for an instant before being lowered to half-staff. It should be hoisted to the peak again before being lowered for the day or night.

As provided by presidential proclamation, the flag should fly at half-staff for 30 days from the day of death of a president or former president; for 10 days from the day of death of a vice president, chief justice or retired chief justice of the U.S., or speaker of the House of Representatives; from day of death until burial of an associate justice of the Supreme Court, cabinet member, former vice president, Senate president pro tempore, or majority or minority Senate or House leader; for a U.S. senator, representative, territorial delegate, or the resident commissioner of Puerto Rico, on day of death and the following day within the metropolitan area of the District of Columbia and from day of death until burial within the decedent's state, congressional district, territory or commonwealth; and for the death of the governor of a state, territory, or possession of the U.S., from day of death until burial.

On Memorial Day, the flag should fly at half-staff until noon and then be raised to the peak. The flag should also fly at half-staff on Korean War Veterans Armistice Day (July 27), National Pearl Harbor Remembrance Day (Dec. 7), and Peace Officers Memorial Day (May 15).

How to Fly the Flag—The flag should be hoisted briskly and lowered ceremoniously and should never be allowed to touch the ground or the floor. When the flag is hung over a sidewalk from a rope extending from a building to a pole, the union should be away from the building. When the flag is hung over the center of a street the union should be to the north in an east-west street and to the east in a north-south street. No other flag may be flown above or, if on the same level, to the right of the U.S. flag, except that at the United Nations Headquarters the UN flag may be placed above flags of all member nations and other national flags may be flown with equal prominence or honor with the flag of the U.S. At services by Navy chaplains at sea, the church pennant may be flown above the flag.

When 2 flags are placed against a wall with crossed staffs, the U.S. flag should be at right—its own right, and its staff should be in front of the staff of the other flag; when a number of flags are grouped and displayed from staffs, it should be at the center and highest point of the group.

Church and Platform Use—In an auditorium, the flag may be displayed flat, above and behind the speaker. When displayed from a staff in a church or in a public auditorium, the flag should hold the position of superior prominence, in advance of the audience, and in the position of honor at the speaker's right as she or he faces the audience. Any other flag so displayed should be placed on the left of the speaker or to the right of the audience.

When the flag is displayed horizontally or vertically against a wall, the stars should be uppermost and at the observer's left.

When used to cover a casket, the flag should be placed so that the union is at the head and over the left shoulder. It should not be lowered into the grave nor touch the ground.

How to Dispose of Worn Flags—When the flag is in such condition that it is no longer a fitting emblem for display, it should be destroyed in a dignified way, preferably by burning.

When to Salute the Flag—All persons present should face the flag, stand at attention, and salute on the following occasions: (1) when the flag is passing in a parade or in a review, (2) during the ceremony of hoisting or lowering, (3) when the national anthem is played, and (4) during the Pledge of Allegiance. Those present in uniform should render the military salute. Those not in uniform should place the right hand over the heart. A man wearing a hat should remove it with his right hand and hold it to his left shoulder during the salute.

Prohibited Uses of the Flag—The flag should not be dipped to any person or thing. (An exception—customarily, ships salute by dipping their colors.) It should never be displayed with the union down save as a distress signal. It should never be carried flat or horizontally, but always aloft and free.

It should not be displayed on a float, an automobile, or a boat except from a staff. It should never be used as a covering for a ceiling, nor have placed on it any word, design, or drawing. It should never be used as a receptacle for carrying anything. It should not be used to cover a statue or a monument.

The flag should never be used for advertising purposes, nor be embroidered on such articles as cushions or handkerchiefs, printed or otherwise impressed on boxes or anything that is designed for temporary use and discard; or used as a costume or athletic uniform. Advertising signs should not be fastened to its staff or halyard.

The flag should never be used as drapery of any sort, never festooned, drawn back, nor up, in folds, but always allowed to fall free. Bunting of blue, white, and red, always arranged with the blue above and the white in the middle, should be used for covering a speaker's desk, draping the front of a platform, and for decoration in general.

An act of Congress approved on Feb. 8, 1917, provided certain penalties for the desecration, mutilation, or improper use of the flag within the District of Columbia. A 1968 federal law provided penalties of as much as a year's imprisonment or a $1,000 fine or both for publicly burning or otherwise desecrating any U.S. flag. In addition, many states have laws against flag desecration. In 1989, the Supreme Court ruled that no laws could prohibit political protesters from burning the flag. The decision had the effect of declaring unconstitutional the flag desecration laws of 48 states, as well as a similar federal statute, in cases of peaceful political expression.

The Supreme Court, in June 1990, declared that a new federal law making it a crime to burn or deface the American flag violated the free-speech guarantee of the First Amendment. The 5-4 Court decision led to renewed calls in Congress for a constitutional amendment to make it possible to prosecute flag burners.

Pledge of Allegiance to the Flag

I pledge allegiance to the flag of the United States of America and to the republic for which it stands, one nation under God, indivisible, with liberty and justice for all.

This, the current official version of the Pledge of Allegiance, has developed from the original pledge, which was first published in the Sept. 8, 1892, issue of *Youth's Companion*, a weekly magazine then published in Boston. The original pledge contained the phrase "my flag," which was changed more than 30 years later to "flag of the United States of America." A 1954 act of Congress added the words "under God." (In June 2002 a 3-judge panel of the 9th Circuit U.S. Court of Appeals ruled, 2-1, that recitation of the pledge in public schools could not include that phrase; the decision was being appealed.)

The authorship of the pledge was in dispute for many years. The *Youth's Companion* stated in 1917 that the original draft was written by James B. Upham, an executive of the magazine who died in 1910. A leaflet circulated by the magazine later named Upham as the originator of the draft "afterwards condensed and perfected by him and his associates of the Companion force."

Francis Bellamy, a former member of *Youth's Companion* editorial staff, publicly claimed authorship of the pledge in 1923. In 1939, the United States Flag Association, acting on the advice of a committee named to study the controversy, upheld the claim of Bellamy, who had died 8 years earlier. In 1957 the Library of Congress issued a report attributing the authorship to Bellamy.

The History of the National Anthem

"The Star-Spangled Banner" was ordered played by the military and naval services by Pres. Woodrow Wilson in 1916. It was designated the national anthem by Act of Congress, Mar. 3, 1931. The words were written by Francis Scott Key, of Georgetown, MD, during the bombardment of Fort McHenry, Baltimore, Sept. 13-14, 1814. Key was a lawyer, a graduate of St. John's College, Annapolis, and a volunteer in a light artillery company. When a friend, Dr. Beanes, a Maryland physician, was taken aboard Admiral Cockburn's British squadron for interfering with ground troops, Key and J. S. Skinner, carrying a note from Pres. Madison, went to the fleet under a flag of truce on a cartel ship to ask Beanes's release. Cockburn consented, but as the fleet was about to sail up the Patapsco to bombard Fort McHenry, he detained them, first on HMS *Surprise* and then on a supply ship.

Key witnessed the bombardment from his own vessel. It began at 7 AM, Sept. 13, 1814, and lasted, with intermissions, for 25 hr. The British fired more than 1,500 shells, each weighing as much as 220 lb. They were unable to approach closely because the U.S. had sunk 22 vessels. Only 4 Americans were killed and 24 wounded. A British bomb-ship was disabled.

During the event, Key wrote a stanza on the back of an envelope. Next day at Indian Queen Inn, Baltimore, he wrote out the poem and gave it to his brother-in-law, Judge J. H. Nicholson. Nicholson suggested use of the tune, "Anacreon in Heaven" (attributed to a British composer named John Stafford Smith), and had the poem printed on broadsides, of which 2 survive. On Sept. 20 it appeared in the *Baltimore American*. Later Key made 3 copies; one is in the Library of Congress, and one in the Pennsylvania Historical Society. The copy Key wrote on Sept. 14 remained in the Nicholson family for 93 years. In 1907 it was sold to Henry Walters of Baltimore. In 1934 it was bought at auction by the Walters Art Gallery, Baltimore, for $26,400. In 1953 it was sold to the Maryland Historical Society for the same price.

The flag that Key saw during the bombardment is preserved in the Smithsonian Institution, Washington, DC. It measures 30 by 42 ft and has 15 alternating red and white stripes and 15 stars, for the original 13 states plus Kentucky and Vermont. It was made by Mary Young Pickersgill. The Baltimore Flag House, a museum, occupies her premises, which were restored in 1953.

The Star-Spangled Banner

Note: The 2nd and 3rd stanzas are commonly omitted as a courtesy to the British.

I

Oh, say can you see by the dawn's early light
What so proudly we hailed at the twilight's last gleaming?
Whose broad stripes and bright stars thru the perilous fight,
O'er the ramparts we watched were so gallantly streaming?
And the rocket's red glare, the bombs bursting in air,
Gave proof through the night that our flag was still there.
Oh, say does that star-spangled banner yet wave
O'er the land of the free and the home of the brave?

II

On the shore, dimly seen through the mists of the deep,
Where the foe's haughty host in dread silence reposes,
What is that which the breeze, o'er the towering steep,
As it fitfully blows, half conceals, half discloses?
Now it catches the gleam of the morning's first beam,
In full glory reflected now shines in the stream:
'Tis the star-spangled banner! Oh long may it wave
O'er the land of the free and the home of the brave!

III

And where is that band who so vauntingly swore
That the havoc of war and the battle's confusion,
A home and a country should leave us no more!
Their blood has washed out their foul footsteps' pollution.
No refuge could save the hireling and slave
From the terror of flight, or the gloom of the grave:
And the star-spangled banner in triumph doth wave
O'er the land of the free and the home of the brave!

IV

Oh! thus be it ever, when freemen shall stand
Between their loved home and the war's desolation!
Blest with victory and peace, may the heav'n rescued land
Praise the Power that hath made and preserved us a nation.
Then conquer we must, when our cause it is just,
And this be our motto: "In God is our trust."
And the star-spangled banner in triumph shall wave
O'er the land of the free and the home of the brave!

America (My Country 'Tis of Thee)

First sung in public on July 4, 1831, at a service in the Park Street Church, Boston, the words were written by Rev. Samuel Francis Smith, a Baptist clergyman, who set them to a melody he found in a German songbook, unaware that it was the tune for the British anthem, "God Save the King/Queen."

My country, 'tis of thee,
Sweet land of liberty,
Of thee I sing.
Land where my fathers died!
Land of the Pilgrims' pride!
From ev'ry mountainside,
Let freedom ring!

My native country, thee,
Land of the noble free,
Thy name I love.
I love thy rocks and rills,
Thy woods and templed hills;
My heart with rapture thrills
Like that above.

Let music swell the breeze,
And ring from all the trees
Sweet freedom's song.
Let mortal tongues awake;
Let all that breathe partake;
Let rocks their silence break,
The sound prolong.

Our fathers' God, to Thee,
Author of liberty,
To Thee we sing.
Long may our land be bright
With freedom's holy light;
Protect us by Thy might,
Great God, our King!

America, the Beautiful

Words composed by Katharine Lee Bates, a Massachusetts educator and author, in 1893, inspired by the view she experienced atop Pikes Peak. The final form was established in 1911, and it is set to the music of Samuel A. Ward's "Materna."

O beautiful for spacious skies.
For amber waves of grain,
For purple mountain majesties
Above the fruited plain.
America! America!
God shed His grace on thee,
And crown thy good with brotherhood
From sea to shining sea.

O beautiful for pilgrim feet
Whose stern impassion'd stress
A thorough-fare for freedom beat
Across the wilderness.
America! America!
God mend thine ev'ry flaw,
Confirm thy soul in self control,
Thy liberty in law.

O beautiful for heroes prov'd
In liberating strife,
Who more than self their country lov'd
And mercy more than life.
America! America!
May God thy gold refine
Till all success be nobleness,
And ev'ry gain divine.

O beautiful for patriot dream
That sees beyond the years,
Thine alabaster cities gleam,
Undimmed by human tears.
America! America!
God shed His grace on thee,
And crown thy good with brotherhood
From sea to shining sea.

The Liberty Bell: Its History and Significance

The Liberty Bell is housed in Independence National Historical Park, Philadelphia.

The original bell was ordered by Assembly Speaker and Chairman of the State House Superintendents Isaac Norris and was ordered from Thomas Lester, Whitechapel Foundry, London. It reached Philadelphia at the end of August 1752. It bore an inscription from Leviticus 25:10: "PROCLAIM LIBERTY THROUGHOUT ALL THE LAND UNTO ALL THE INHABITANTS THEREOF."

The bell was cracked by a stroke of its clapper in Sept. 1752 while it hung on a truss in the State House yard for testing. Pass & Stow, Philadelphia founders, recast the bell, adding 1 ½ ounces of copper to a pound of the original "Whitechapel" metal to reduce its high tone and brittleness. It was found that the bell contained too much copper, injuring its tone, so Pass & Stow recast it again, this time successfully.

In June 1753 the bell was hung in the old wooden steeple of the State House. In use while the Continental Congress was in session in the State House, it rang out in defiance of British tax and trade restrictions, and it proclaimed the Boston Tea Party and, on July 8, 1776, the first public reading of the Declaration of Independence.

On Sept. 18, 1777, when the British Army was about to occupy Philadelphia, the Liberty Bell was moved in a baggage train of the American Army to Allentown, PA, where it was hidden until June 27, 1778. The bell was moved back to Philadelphia after the British left the city.

In July 1781 the wooden steeple became insecure and had to be taken down. The bell was lowered into the brick section of the tower, where it remained until 1828. Between 1828 and 1844 the old State House bell continued to ring during special occasions. According to tradition, it cracked in 1835 as it tolled the death of Chief Justice John Marshall. It rang for the last time on Feb. 23, 1846. In 1852 it was placed on exhibition in the Declaration Chamber of Independence Hall.

In 1876, when thousands of Americans visited Philadelphia for the Centennial Exposition, the bell was placed in its old wooden support in the tower hallway. In 1877 it was hung from the ceiling of the tower by a chain of 13 links. It was returned again to the Declaration Chamber and in 1896 taken back to the tower hall, where it occupied a glass case. In 1915 the case was removed so that the public might touch it. On Jan. 1, 1976, just after midnight to mark the opening of the Bicentennial Year, the bell was moved to a new glass and steel pavilion behind Independence Hall for easier viewing.

The measurements of the bell are: circumference around the lip, 12 ft ½ in; circumference around the crown, 6 ft 11 ¼ in; lip to the crown, 3 ft; height over the crown, 2 ft 3 in; thickness at lip, 3 in; thickness at crown, 1 ¼ in; weight, 2,080 lb; length of clapper, 3 ft 2 in.

Statue of Liberty National Monument

Since 1886, the Statue of Liberty, formally known as "Liberty Enlightening the World," has stood as a symbol of freedom in New York harbor. It also commemorates French-American friendship, for it was given by the people of France and designed by French sculptor Frederic Auguste Bartholdi (1834-1904).

On Washington's Birthday, Feb. 22, 1877, Congress approved the use of a site on Bedloe's Island suggested by Bartholdi. This island of 12 acres had been owned in the 17th century by a Walloon named Isaac Bedloe. It was called Bedloe's until Aug. 3, 1956, when Pres. Dwight Eisenhower approved a measure changing the name to Liberty Island.

The statue was finished on May 21, 1884, and presented to the U.S. minister to France, Levi Parsons Morton, July 4, 1884, by Ferdinand de Lesseps, head of the Franco-American Union, promoter of the Panama Canal, and builder of the Suez Canal.

On Aug. 5, 1884, the Americans laid the cornerstone for the pedestal, to be built on the foundations of Fort Wood, erected by the government in 1811. The American committee had raised $125,000, but this was inadequate. Joseph Pulitzer, owner of the *New York World,* appealed on Mar. 16, 1885, for general donations. By Aug. 11, 1885, he had raised $100,000. The statue itself arrived dismantled, in 214 packing cases, from Rouen, France, in June 1885. The last rivet of the statue was driven on Oct. 28, 1886, when Pres. Grover Cleveland dedicated the monument.

The Statue of Liberty National Monument was designated as such in 1924. It is administered by the National Park Service. A $2.5 million building housing the American Museum of Immigration was opened by Pres. Richard Nixon on Sept. 26, 1972, at the base of the statue. It houses a permanent exhibition tracing the history of American immigration.

Four years of restoration work funded and led by the Statue of Liberty-Ellis Island Foundation were completed before the statue's 1986 centennial. Among other repairs, the $87 million project included replacing the 1,600 wrought iron bands that hold the statue's copper skin to its frame, replacing its torch, and installing an elevator. A 4-day "Liberty Weekend" extravaganza of concerts, tall ships, ethnic festivals, and fireworks, July 3-6, 1986, celebrated the 100th anniversary. Chief Justice Warren E. Burger swore in 5,000 new citizens on Ellis Island, while 20,000 others across the country were sworn in through a satellite telecast. Other ceremonies followed on Oct. 28, 1986, the statue's exact 100th birthday.

Following the Sept. 11 terrorist attacks, Liberty Island was closed to visitors. On Dec. 20, 2001, the secretary of the interior reopened the island after installing airport-type screening facilities at passenger embarkation areas at Battery Park in Manhattan and Liberty State Park in New Jersey.

To open the statue, the federal government needed to increase security throughout the park. In addition to federally funded security upgrades, significant safety improvements were made to meet building codes. The National Park Service turned to the Statue of Liberty-Ellis Island Foundation, which began a fund-raising campaign to help finance safety renovations inside the statue, additional exits, improved handicapped access, and upgraded fire suppression and emergency warning systems. The federal investment in upgrades amounted to about $30 million, with the private sector contributing an additional $7 million. Access to the statue was finally restored on Aug. 3, 2004.

Two tours are now available (they must be reserved in advance). Reservations are available by visiting www.statuereservations.com or by calling 1-866-STATUE4. A limited number of "walk up" reservations are also available at ferry embarkation areas. The "Observatory Tour" goes up the pedestal by elevator to a panoramic observation deck; also on that level is a view of the statue's interior. The "Promenade Tour" goes along the promenade above the fort on which the statue and pedestal were built. Both tours are ranger-guided and include a visit to the original torch, taken down during renovation in the 1980s, and the museum. The entire statue above the pedestal, including the crown, remains closed. (For more information, visit www.nps.gov/stli and www.statueofliberty.org)

Statue Statistics

The statue weighs 450,000 lb, or 225 tons. The copper sheeting weighs 200,000 lb. There are 167 steps from the land level to the top of the pedestal, 168 steps inside the statue to the head, and 54 rungs on the ladder leading to the arm that holds the torch.

	Ft.	In		Ft.	In.		Ft.	In.
Height from base to torch	151	1	Size of finger nail, 13x10 in.			Right arm, max. thickness	12	0
Foundation of pedestal to torch	305	1	Head from chin to cranium	17	3	Thickness of waist	35	0
Heel to top of head	111	1	Head thickness, ear to ear	10	0	Width of mouth	3	0
Length of hand	16	5	Length of nose	4	6	Tablet, length	23	7
Index finger	8	0	Right arm, length	42	0	Tablet, width	13	7

Emma Lazarus's Famous Poem

Engraved on pedestal below the statue.

The New Colossus

Not like the brazen giant of Greek fame,
With conquering limbs astride from land to land;
Here at our sea-washed, sunset gates shall stand
A mighty woman with a torch, whose flame
Is the imprisoned lightning, and her name
Mother of Exiles. From her beacon-hand
Glows world-wide welcome; her mild eyes command
The air-bridged harbor that twin cities frame.
"Keep ancient lands, your storied pomp!" cries she
With silent lips. "Give me your tired, your poor,
Your huddled masses yearning to breathe free,
The wretched refuse of your teeming shore.
Send these, the homeless, tempest-tost to me,
I lift my lamp beside the golden door!"

Ellis Island

Ellis Island was the gateway to America for over 12 million immigrants between 1892 and 1924. In the late 18th century, Samuel Ellis, a New York City merchant, purchased the island and gave it his name. From Ellis, it passed to New York State, and the U.S. government bought it in 1808. On Jan. 1, 1892, the government opened the first federal immigration center in the U.S. there. The 27½-acre site eventually supported more than 35 buildings, including the Main Building with its Great Hall, in which as many as 5,000 people a day were processed.

Closed as an immigration station in 1954, Ellis Island was proclaimed part of the Statue of Liberty National Monument in 1965 by Pres. Lyndon B. Johnson. After a 6-year, $170 million restoration project funded by the Statue of Liberty-Ellis Island Foundation, Ellis Island was reopened as a museum in 1990. Artifacts, historic photographs and documents, oral histories, and ethnic music depicting 400 years of American immigration are housed in the museum. The museum also includes The American Immigrant Wall of Honor® (www.wallofhonor.com), which is inscribed with more than 600,000 names that have been placed in tribute. Registrations are still being accepted for inclusion in the memorial.

The American Family Immigration History Center® opened in April 2001. It contains an electronic database of ship passenger arrival information through the Port of New York and Ellis Island from 1892 to 1924. Data on over 25 million individuals are available, as well as an interactive database which features a Living Family Archive, multimedia presentations on various immigration groups and patterns, reproductions of original ships' passenger manifests, and pictures of over 800 immigrant ships (www.ellisisland.org).

In 1998, the Supreme Court ruled that nearly 90% of the island (the 24.2 acres which are landfill) lies in New Jersey, while the original 3.3 acres, on which the museum is located, are in New York.

PRESIDENTS OF THE UNITED STATES

U.S. Presidents

No.	Name	Politics	Born	in	Inaug.	at age	Died	at age
1.	George Washington	Fed.	1732, Feb. 22	VA	1789	57	1799, Dec. 14	67
2.	John Adams	Fed.	1735, Oct. 30	MA	1797	61	1826, July 4	90
3.	Thomas Jefferson	Dem.-Rep.	1743, Apr. 13	VA	1801	57	1826, July 4	83
4.	James Madison	Dem.-Rep.	1751, Mar. 16	VA	1809	57	1836, June 28	85
5.	James Monroe	Dem.-Rep.	1758, Apr. 28	VA	1817	58	1831, July 4	73
6.	John Quincy Adams	Dem.-Rep.	1767, July 11	MA	1825	57	1848, Feb. 23	80
7.	Andrew Jackson	Dem.	1767, Mar. 15	SC	1829	61	1845, June 8	78
8.	Martin Van Buren	Dem.	1782, Dec. 5	NY	1837	54	1862, July 24	79
9.	William Henry Harrison	Whig	1773, Feb. 9	VA	1841	68	1841, Apr. 4	68
10.	John Tyler	Whig	1790, Mar. 29	VA	1841	51	1862, Jan. 18	71
11.	James Knox Polk	Dem.	1795, Nov. 2	NC	1845	49	1849, June 15	53
12.	Zachary Taylor	Whig	1784, Nov. 24	VA	1849	64	1850, July 9	65
13.	Millard Fillmore	Whig	1800, Jan. 7	NY	1850	50	1874, Mar. 8	74
14.	Franklin Pierce	Dem.	1804, Nov. 23	NH	1853	48	1869, Oct. 8	64
15.	James Buchanan	Dem.	1791, Apr. 23	PA	1857	65	1868, June 1	77
16.	Abraham Lincoln	Rep.	1809, Feb. 12	KY	1861	52	1865, Apr. 15	56
17.	Andrew Johnson	(1)	1808, Dec. 29	NC	1865	56	1875, July 31	66
18.	Ulysses Simpson Grant	Rep.	1822, Apr. 27	OH	1869	46	1885, July 23	63
19.	Rutherford Birchard Hayes	Rep.	1822, Oct. 4	OH	1877	54	1893, Jan. 17	70
20.	James Abram Garfield	Rep.	1831, Nov. 19	OH	1881	49	1881, Sept. 19	49
21.	Chester Alan Arthur	Rep.	1829, Oct. 5	VT	1881	50	1886, Nov. 18	57
22.	Grover Cleveland	Dem.	1837, Mar. 18	NJ	1885	47	1908, June 24	71
23.	Benjamin Harrison	Rep.	1833, Aug. 20	OH	1889	55	1901, Mar. 13	67
24.	Grover Cleveland	Dem.	1837, Mar. 18	NJ	1893	55	1908, June 24	71
25.	William McKinley	Rep.	1843, Jan. 29	OH	1897	54	1901, Sept. 14	58
26.	Theodore Roosevelt	Rep.	1858, Oct. 27	NY	1901	42	1919, Jan. 6	60
27.	William Howard Taft	Rep.	1857, Sept. 15	OH	1909	51	1930, Mar. 8	72
28.	Woodrow Wilson	Dem.	1856, Dec. 28	VA	1913	56	1924, Feb. 3	67
29.	Warren Gamaliel Harding	Rep.	1865, Nov. 2	OH	1921	55	1923, Aug. 2	57
30.	Calvin Coolidge	Rep.	1872, July 4	VT	1923	51	1933, Jan. 5	60
31.	Herbert Clark Hoover	Rep.	1874, Aug. 10	IA	1929	54	1964, Oct. 20	90
32.	Franklin Delano Roosevelt	Dem.	1882, Jan. 30	NY	1933	51	1945, Apr. 12	63
33.	Harry S. Truman	Dem.	1884, May 8	MO	1945	60	1972, Dec. 26	88
34.	Dwight David Eisenhower	Rep.	1890, Oct. 14	TX	1953	62	1969, Mar. 28	78
35.	John Fitzgerald Kennedy	Dem.	1917, May 29	MA	1961	43	1963, Nov. 22	46
36.	Lyndon Baines Johnson	Dem.	1908, Aug. 27	TX	1963	55	1973, Jan. 22	64
37.	Richard Milhous Nixon (2)	Rep.	1913, Jan. 9	CA	1969	56	1994, Apr. 22	81
38.	Gerald Rudolph Ford	Rep.	1913, July 14	NE	1974	61		
39.	Jimmy (James Earl) Carter	Dem.	1924, Oct. 1	GA	1977	52		
40.	Ronald Reagan	Rep.	1911, Feb. 6	IL	1981	69	2004, June 5	93
41.	George H. W. Bush	Rep.	1924, June 12	MA	1989	64		
42.	Bill (Wm. Jefferson) Clinton	Dem.	1946, Aug. 19	AR	1993	46		
43.	George W. Bush	Rep.	1946, July 6	CT	2001	54		

(1) Andrew Johnson was a Democrat nominated vice president by Republicans and elected with Lincoln on National Union ticket.
(2) Resigned Aug. 9, 1974.

U.S. Presidents, Vice Presidents, Congresses

President	Service	Vice President	Congresses
1. George Washington	Apr. 30, 1789—Mar. 3, 1797	1. John Adams	1, 2, 3, 4
2. John Adams	Mar. 4, 1797—Mar. 3, 1801	2. Thomas Jefferson	5, 6
3. Thomas Jefferson	Mar. 4, 1801—Mar. 3, 1805	3. Aaron Burr	7, 8
	Mar. 4, 1805—Mar. 3, 1809	George Clinton	9, 10
4. James Madison	Mar. 4, 1809—Mar. 3, 1813	4. (1)	11, 12
	Mar. 4, 1813—Mar. 3, 1817	5. Elbridge Gerry (2)	13, 14
5. James Monroe	Mar. 4, 1817—Mar. 3, 1825	6. Daniel D. Tompkins	15, 16, 17, 18
6. John Quincy Adams	Mar. 4, 1825—Mar. 3, 1829	John C. Calhoun	19, 20
7. Andrew Jackson	Mar. 4, 1829—Mar. 3, 1833	7. (3)	21, 22
	Mar. 4, 1833—Mar. 3, 1837	8. Martin Van Buren	23, 24
8. Martin Van Buren	Mar. 4, 1837—Mar. 3, 1841	9. Richard M. Johnson	25, 26
9. William Henry Harrison (4)	Mar. 4, 1841—Apr. 4, 1841	10. John Tyler	27
10. John Tyler	Apr. 6, 1841—Mar. 3, 1845		27, 28
11. James K. Polk	Mar. 4, 1845—Mar. 3, 1849	11. George M. Dallas	29, 30
12. Zachary Taylor (4)	Mar. 5, 1849—July 9, 1850		31
13. Millard Fillmore	July 10, 1850—Mar. 3, 1853	12. Millard Fillmore	31, 32
14. Franklin Pierce	Mar. 4, 1853—Mar. 3, 1857	13. William R. King (5)	33, 34
15. James Buchanan	Mar. 4, 1857—Mar. 3, 1861	14. John C. Breckinridge	35, 36
16. Abraham Lincoln	Mar. 4, 1861—Mar. 3, 1865	15. Hannibal Hamlin	37, 38
(4)	Mar. 4, 1865—Apr. 15, 1865		39
17. Andrew Johnson	Apr. 15, 1865—Mar. 3, 1869	16. Andrew Johnson	39, 40
18. Ulysses S. Grant	Mar. 4, 1869—Mar. 3, 1873	17. Schuyler Colfax	41, 42
	Mar. 4, 1873—Mar. 3, 1877	18. Henry Wilson (6)	43, 44
19. Rutherford B. Hayes	Mar. 4, 1877—Mar. 3, 1881	19. William A. Wheeler	45, 46
20. James A. Garfield (4)	Mar. 4, 1881—Sept. 19, 1881	20. Chester A. Arthur	47
21. Chester A. Arthur	Sept. 20, 1881—Mar. 3, 1885		47, 48
22. Grover Cleveland (7)	Mar. 4, 1885—Mar. 3, 1889	21. Thomas A. Hendricks (8)	49, 50
23. Benjamin Harrison	Mar. 4, 1889—Mar. 3, 1893	22. Levi P. Morton	51, 52
24. Grover Cleveland (7)	Mar. 4, 1893—Mar. 3, 1897	23. Adlai E. Stevenson	53, 54
25. William McKinley	Mar. 4, 1897—Mar. 3, 1901	24. Garret A. Hobart (9)	55, 56
(4)	Mar. 4, 1901—Sept. 14, 1901		57
26. Theodore Roosevelt	Sept. 14, 1901—Mar. 3, 1905	25. Theodore Roosevelt	57, 58
	Mar. 4, 1905—Mar. 3, 1909	26. Charles W. Fairbanks	59, 60
27. William H. Taft	Mar. 4, 1909—Mar. 3, 1913	27. James S. Sherman (10)	61, 62

	President	Service		Vice President	Congresses
28.	Woodrow Wilson	Mar. 4, 1913—Mar. 3, 1921	28.	Thomas R. Marshall	63, 64, 65, 66
29.	Warren G. Harding (4)	Mar. 4, 1921—Aug. 2, 1923	29.	Calvin Coolidge	67
30.	Calvin Coolidge	Aug. 3, 1923—Mar. 3, 1925			68
		Mar. 4, 1925—Mar. 3, 1929	30.	Charles G. Dawes	69, 70
31.	Herbert C. Hoover	Mar. 4, 1929—Mar. 3, 1933	31.	Charles Curtis	71, 72
32.	Franklin D. Roosevelt (11)	Mar. 4, 1933—Jan. 20, 1941	32.	John N. Garner	73, 74, 75, 76
		Jan. 20, 1941—Jan. 20, 1945	33.	Henry A. Wallace	77, 78
	(4)	Jan. 20, 1945—Apr. 12, 1945			79
33.	Harry S. Truman	Apr. 12, 1945—Jan. 20, 1949	34.	Harry S. Truman	79, 80
		Jan. 20, 1949—Jan. 20, 1953	35.	Alben W. Barkley	81, 82
34.	Dwight D. Eisenhower	Jan. 20, 1953—Jan. 20, 1961	36.	Richard M. Nixon	83, 84, 85, 86
35.	John F. Kennedy (4)	Jan. 20, 1961—Nov. 22, 1963	37.	Lyndon B. Johnson	87, 88
36.	Lyndon B. Johnson	Nov. 22, 1963—Jan. 20, 1965			88
		Jan. 20, 1965—Jan. 20, 1969	38.	Hubert H. Humphrey	89, 90
37.	Richard M. Nixon	Jan. 20, 1969—Jan. 20, 1973	39.	Spiro T. Agnew (12)	91, 92, 93
	(13)	Jan. 20, 1973—Aug. 9, 1974	40.	Gerald R. Ford (14)	93
38.	Gerald R. Ford (15)	Aug. 9, 1974—Jan. 20, 1977	41.	Nelson A. Rockefeller (16)	93, 94
39.	Jimmy (James Earl) Carter	Jan. 20, 1977—Jan. 20, 1981	42.	Walter F. Mondale	95, 96
40.	Ronald Reagan	Jan. 20, 1981—Jan. 20, 1989	43.	George H. W. Bush	97, 98, 99, 100
41.	George H. W. Bush	Jan. 20, 1989—Jan. 20, 1993	44.	Dan Quayle	101, 102
42.	Bill (Wm. Jefferson) Clinton	Jan. 20, 1993—Jan. 20, 2001	45.	Al Gore	103, 104, 105, 106
43.	George W. Bush	Jan. 20, 2001—	46.	Richard Cheney	107, 108, 109

(1) Died Apr. 20, 1812. (2) Died Nov. 23, 1814. (3) Resigned Dec. 28, 1832, to become U.S. senator. (4) Died in office. (5) Died Apr. 18, 1853. (6) Died Nov. 22, 1875. (7) Terms not consecutive. (8) Died Nov. 25, 1885. (9) Died Nov. 21, 1899. (10) Died Oct. 30, 1912. (11) First president to be inaugurated under 20th Amendment, Jan. 20, 1937. (12) Resigned Oct. 10, 1973. (13) Resigned Aug. 9, 1974. (14) First nonelected vice president, chosen under 25th Amendment procedure. (15) First president never elected president or vice president. (16) Second nonelected vice president, chosen under 25th Amendment.

Vice Presidents of the U.S.

The numerals given vice presidents do not coincide with those given presidents, because some presidents had none and some had more than one.

	Name	Birthplace	Year	Home	Inaug.	Politics	Place of death	Year	Age
1.	John Adams	Quincy, MA	1735	MA	1789	Fed.	Quincy, MA	1826	90
2.	Thomas Jefferson	Shadwell, VA	1743	VA	1797	Dem.-Rep.	Monticello, VA	1826	83
3.	Aaron Burr	Newark, NJ	1756	NY	1801	Dem.-Rep.	Staten Island, NY	1836	80
4.	George Clinton	Ulster Co., NY	1739	NY	1805	Dem.-Rep.	Washington, DC	1812	73
5.	Elbridge Gerry	Marblehead, MA	1744	MA	1813	Dem.-Rep.	Washington, DC	1814	70
6.	Daniel D. Tompkins	Scarsdale, NY	1774	NY	1817	Dem.-Rep.	Staten Island, NY	1825	51
7.	John C. Calhoun (1)	Abbeville, SC	1782	SC	1825	Dem.-Rep.	Washington, DC	1850	68
8.	Martin Van Buren	Kinderhook, NY	1782	NY	1833	Dem.	Kinderhook, NY	1862	79
9.	Richard M. Johnson (2)	Louisville, KY	1780	KY	1837	Dem.	Frankfort, KY	1850	70
10.	John Tyler	Greenway, VA	1790	VA	1841	Whig	Richmond, VA	1862	71
11.	George M. Dallas	Philadelphia, PA	1792	PA	1845	Dem.	Philadelphia, PA	1864	72
12.	Millard Fillmore	Summerhill, NY	1800	NY	1849	Whig	Buffalo, NY	1874	74
13.	William R. King	Sampson Co., NC	1786	AL	1853	Dem.	Dallas Co., AL	1853	67
14.	John C. Breckinridge	Lexington, KY	1821	KY	1857	Dem.	Lexington, KY	1875	54
15.	Hannibal Hamlin	Paris, ME	1809	ME	1861	Rep.	Bangor, ME	1891	81
16.	Andrew Johnson	Raleigh, NC	1808	TN	1865	(3)	Carter Co., TN	1875	66
17.	Schuyler Colfax	New York, NY	1823	IN	1869	Rep.	Mankato, MN	1885	62
18.	Henry Wilson	Farmington, NH	1812	MA	1873	Rep.	Washington, DC	1875	63
19.	William A. Wheeler	Malone, NY	1819	NY	1877	Rep.	Malone, NY	1887	68
20.	Chester A. Arthur	Fairfield, VT	1829	NY	1881	Rep.	New York, NY	1886	57
21.	Thomas A. Hendricks	Muskingum Co., OH	1819	IN	1885	Dem.	Indianapolis, IN	1885	66
22.	Levi P. Morton	Shoreham, VT	1824	NY	1889	Rep.	Rhinebeck, NY	1920	96
23.	Adlai E. Stevenson (4)	Christian Co., KY	1835	IL	1893	Dem.	Chicago, IL	1914	78
24.	Garret A. Hobart	Long Branch, NJ	1844	NJ	1897	Rep.	Paterson, NJ	1899	55
25.	Theodore Roosevelt	New York, NY	1858	NY	1901	Rep.	Oyster Bay, NY	1919	60
26.	Charles W. Fairbanks	Unionville Centre, OH	1852	IN	1905	Rep.	Indianapolis, IN	1918	66
27.	James S. Sherman	Utica, NY	1855	NY	1909	Rep.	Utica, NY	1912	57
28.	Thomas R. Marshall	N. Manchester, IN	1854	IN	1913	Dem.	Washington, DC	1925	71
29.	Calvin Coolidge	Plymouth, VT	1872	MA	1921	Rep.	Northampton, MA	1933	60
30.	Charles G. Dawes	Marietta, OH	1865	IL	1925	Rep.	Evanston, IL	1951	85
31.	Charles Curtis	Topeka, KS	1860	KS	1929	Rep.	Washington, DC	1936	76
32.	John Nance Garner	Red River Co., TX	1868	TX	1933	Dem.	Uvalde, TX	1967	98
33.	Henry Agard Wallace	Adair County, IA	1888	IA	1941	Dem.	Danbury, CT	1965	77
34.	Harry S. Truman	Lamar, MO	1884	MO	1945	Dem.	Kansas City, MO	1972	88
35.	Alben W. Barkley	Graves County, KY	1877	KY	1949	Dem.	Lexington, VA	1956	78
36.	Richard M. Nixon	Yorba Linda, CA	1913	CA	1953	Rep.	New York, NY	1994	81
37.	Lyndon B. Johnson	Johnson City, TX	1908	TX	1961	Dem.	San Antonio, TX	1973	64
38.	Hubert H. Humphrey	Wallace, SD	1911	MN	1965	Dem.	Waverly, MN	1978	66
39.	Spiro T. Agnew (5)	Baltimore, MD	1918	MD	1969	Rep.	Berlin, MD	1996	77
40.	Gerald R. Ford (6)	Omaha, NE	1913	MI	1973	Rep.			
41.	Nelson A. Rockefeller (7)	Bar Harbor, ME	1908	NY	1974	Rep.	New York, NY	1979	70
42.	Walter F. Mondale	Ceylon, MN	1928	MN	1977	Dem.			
43.	George H. W. Bush	Milton, MA	1924	TX	1981	Rep.			
44.	Dan Quayle	Indianapolis, IN	1947	IN	1989	Rep.			
45.	Al Gore	Washington, DC	1948	TN	1993	Dem.			
46.	Richard Cheney	Lincoln, NE	1941	WY	2001	Rep.			

(1) John C. Calhoun resigned Dec. 28, 1832, having been elected to the Senate to fill a vacancy. (2) Richard M. Johnson was the only vice president to be chosen by the Senate because of a tied vote in the Electoral College. (3) Andrew Johnson was a Democrat, nominated vice president by Republicans, and elected with Lincoln on the National Union Ticket. (4) Adlai E. Stevenson, 23rd vice president, was grandfather of Democratic candidate for president in 1952 and 1956. (5) Resigned Oct. 10, 1973. (6) First nonelected vice president, chosen under 25th Amendment procedure. (7) Second nonelected vice president, chosen under 25th Amendment.

Biographies of the Presidents

GEORGE WASHINGTON (1789-97), 1st president, Federalist, was born on Feb. 22, 1732, in Wakefield on Pope's Creek, Westmoreland Co., VA, the son of Augustine and Mary Ball Washington. He spent his early childhood on a farm near Fredericksburg. His father died when George was 11. He studied mathematics and surveying, and at 16, he went to live with his elder half brother, Lawrence, who built and named Mount Vernon. George surveyed the lands of Thomas Fairfax in the Shenandoah Valley, keeping a diary. He accompanied Lawrence to Barbados, West Indies, where he contracted smallpox and was deeply scarred. Lawrence died in 1752, and George inherited his property. He valued land, and when he died, he owned 70,000 acres in Virginia and 40,000 acres in what is now West Virginia.

Washington's military service began in 1753, when Lt. Gov. Robert Dinwiddie of Virginia sent him on missions deep into Ohio country. He clashed with the French and had to surrender Fort Necessity on July 3, 1754. He was an aide to the British general Edward Braddock and was at his side when the army was ambushed and defeated (July 9, 1755) on a march to Fort Duquesne. He helped take Fort Duquesne from the French in 1758.

After Washington's marriage to Martha Dandridge Custis, a widow, in 1759, he managed his family estate at Mount Vernon. Although not at first for independence, he opposed the repressive measures of the British crown and took charge of the Virginia troops before war broke out. He was made commander of the newly created Continental Army by the Continental Congress on June 15, 1775.

The American victory was due largely to Washington's leadership. He was resourceful, a stern disciplinarian, and the one strong, dependable force for unity. Washington favored a federal government. He became chairman of the Constitutional Convention of 1787 and helped get the Constitution ratified. Unanimously elected president by the Electoral College, he was inaugurated Apr. 30, 1789, on the balcony of New York's Federal Hall. He was reelected in 1792. Washington made an effort to avoid partisan politics as president.

Refusing to consider a 3rd term, Washington retired to Mount Vernon in March 1797. He suffered acute laryngitis after a ride in snow and rain around his estate, was bled profusely, and died Dec. 14, 1799.

JOHN ADAMS (1797-1801) 2nd president, Federalist, was born on Oct. 30, 1735, in Braintree (now Quincy), MA, the son of John and Susanna Boylston Adams. He was a great-grandson of Henry Adams, who came from England in 1636. He graduated from Harvard in 1755 and then taught school and studied law. He married Abigail Smith in 1764. In 1765 he argued against taxation without representation before the royal governor. In 1770 he successfully defended in court the British soldiers who fired on civilians in the Boston Massacre. He was a delegate to the Continental Congress and a signer of the Declaration of Independence. In 1778, Congress sent Adams and John Jay to join Benjamin Franklin as diplomatic representatives in Europe. Because he ran second to Washington in Electoral College balloting in February 1789, Adams became the nation's first vice president, a post he characterized as highly insignificant; he was reelected in 1792.

In 1796 Adams was chosen president by the electors. His administration was marked by growing conflict with fellow Federalist Alexander Hamilton and with others in his own cabinet who supported Hamilton's strongly anti-French position. Adams avoided full-scale war with France, but became unpopular, especially after securing passage of the Alien and Sedition Acts in 1798. His foreign policy contributed significantly to the election of Thomas Jefferson in 1800.

Adams lived for a quarter century after he left office, during which time he wrote extensively. He died July 4, 1826, on the same day as his rival Thomas Jefferson (the 50th anniversary of the Declaration of Independence).

THOMAS JEFFERSON (1801-9), 3rd president, Democratic-Republican, was born on Apr. 13, 1743, in Shadwell in Goochland (now Albemarle) Co., VA, the son of Peter and Jane Randolph Jefferson. Peter died when Thomas was 14, leaving him 2,750 acres and his slaves. Jefferson attended (1760-62) the College of William and Mary, read Greek and Latin classics, and played the violin. In 1769 he was elected to the Virginia House of Burgesses. In 1770 he began building his home, Monticello, and in 1772 he married Martha Wayles Skelton, a wealthy widow. Jefferson helped establish the Virginia Committee of Correspondence. As a member of the Second Continental Congress he drafted the Declaration of Independence. He also was a member of the Virginia House of Delegates (1776-79) and was elected governor of Virginia in 1779, succeeding Patrick Henry. He was reelected in 1780 but resigned in 1781 after British troops invaded Virginia. During his term he wrote the statute on religious freedom. After his wife's death in 1782, Jefferson again became a delegate to the Congress, and in 1784 he drafted the report that was the basis for the Ordinances of 1784, 1785, and 1787. He was minister to France from 1785 to 1789, when George Washington appointed him secretary of state.

Jefferson's strong faith in the consent of the governed conflicted with the emphasis on executive control, favored by Alexander Hamilton, secretary of the Treasury, and Jefferson resigned on Dec. 31, 1793. In the 1796 election Jefferson was the Democratic-Republican candidate for president; John Adams won the election, and Jefferson became vice president. In 1800, Jefferson and Aaron Burr received equal Electoral College votes; the House of Representatives elected Jefferson president. Jefferson was a strong advocate of westward expansion; major events of his first term were the Louisiana Purchase (1803) and the Lewis and Clark Expedition. An important development during his second term was passage of the Embargo Act, barring U.S. ships from setting sail to foreign ports. Jefferson established the University of Virginia and designed its buildings. He died July 4, 1826, on the same day as John Adams (the 50th anniversary of the Declaration of Independence).

Following analysis of DNA taken from descendants of Jefferson and Sally Hemings, one of his slaves, it has been widely acknowledged that Jefferson fathered at least one, perhaps all, of her six known children.

JAMES MADISON (1809-17), 4th president Democratic-Republican, was born on Mar. 16, 1751, in Port Conway, King George Co., VA, the son of James and Eleanor Rose Conway Madison. Madison graduated from Princeton in 1771. He served in the Virginia Constitutional Convention (1776), and, in 1780, became a delegate to the Second Continental Congress. He was chief recorder at the Constitutional Convention in 1787 and supported ratification in the *Federalist Papers*, written with Alexander Hamilton and John Jay. In 1789, Madison was elected to the House of Representatives, where he helped frame the Bill of Rights and fought against passage of the Alien and Sedition Acts. In the 1790s, he helped found the Democratic-Republican Party, which ultimately became the Democratic Party. He became Jefferson's secretary of state in 1801.

Madison was elected president in 1808. His first term was marked by tensions with Great Britain, and his conduct of foreign policy was criticized by the Federalists and by his own party. Nevertheless, he was reelected in 1812, the year war was declared on Great Britain. The war that many considered a second American revolution ended with a treaty that settled none of the issues. Madison's most important action after the war was demilitarizing the U.S.-Canadian border.

In 1817, Madison retired to his estate, Montpelier, where he served as an elder statesman. He edited his famous papers on the Constitutional Convention and helped found the University of Virginia, of which he became rector in 1826. He died June 28, 1836.

> ***IT'S A FACT:*** The first assassination attempt on a U.S. president took place on Jan. 30, 1835. A mentally ill man named Richard Lawrence attempted to fire two pistols at Andrew Jackson, who was attending a funeral at the U.S. Capitol. Both pistols misfired, and Jackson was not hurt.

JAMES MONROE (1817-25), 5th president, Democratic-Republican, was born on Apr. 28, 1758, in Westmoreland Co., VA, the son of Spence and Eliza Jones Monroe. He entered the College of William and Mary in 1774 but left to serve in the 3rd Virginia Regiment during the American Revolution. After the war, he studied law with Thomas Jefferson. In 1782 he was elected to the Virginia House of Delegates, and he served (1783-86) as a delegate to the Continental Congress. He opposed ratification of the Constitution because it lacked a bill of rights. Monroe was elected to the U.S. Senate in 1790. In 1794 President George Washington appointed Monroe minister to France. He served twice as governor of Virginia (1799-1802, 1811). President Jefferson also sent him to France as minister (1803), and from 1803 to 1807 he served as minister to Great Britain.

In 1816 Monroe was elected president; he was reelected in 1820 with all but one Electoral College vote. His administration became known as the Era of Good Feeling. He obtained Florida from Spain, settled boundary disputes with Britain over Canada, and eliminated border forts. He supported the antislavery position that led to the Missouri Compromise. His most significant contribution was the Monroe Doctrine, which opposed European intervention in the Western Hemisphere and became a cornerstone of U.S. foreign policy.

Although Monroe retired to Oak Hill, VA, financial problems forced him to sell his property and move to New York City. He died there on July 4, 1831.

JOHN QUINCY ADAMS (1825-29), 6th president, independent Federalist, later Democratic-Republican, was born on July 11, 1767, in Braintree (now Quincy), MA, the son of John and Abigail Adams. His father was the 2nd president. He studied abroad and at Harvard University, from which he graduated in 1787. In 1803, he was elected to the U.S. Senate. President Monroe chose him as his secretary of state in 1817. In this capacity he negotiated the cession of Florida from Spain, supported exclusion of slavery in the Missouri Compromise, and helped formulate the Monroe Doctrine. In 1824 Adams was elected president by the House of Representatives after he failed to win an Electoral College majority. His expansion of executive powers was strongly opposed, and in the 1828 election he lost to Andrew Jackson. In 1831 he entered the House of Representatives and served 17 years with distinction. He opposed slavery, the annexation of Texas, and the Mexican War. He helped establish the Smithsonian Institution.

Adams suffered a stroke in the House and died in the Speaker's Room on Feb. 23, 1848.

ANDREW JACKSON (1829-37), 7th president, Democratic-Republican, later a Democrat, was born on Mar. 15, 1767, in the Waxhaw district, on the border of North Carolina and South Carolina, the son of Andrew and Elizabeth Hutchinson Jackson. At the age of 13, he joined the militia to fight in the American Revolution and was captured. Orphaned at the age of 14, Jackson was brought up by a well-to-do uncle. By age 20, he was practicing law, and he later served as prosecuting attorney in Nashville, TN. In 1796 he helped draft the constitution of Tennessee, and for a year he occupied its one seat in the House of Representatives. The next year Jackson served in the U.S. Senate.

In the War of 1812, Jackson crushed (1814) the Creek Indians at Horseshoe Bend, AL, and, with a greatly outnumbered army consisting chiefly of backwoodsmen, defeated (1815) General Edward Pakenham's British troops at the Battle of New Orleans. Nicknamed "Old Hickory" for his toughness, he emerged a national hero.

In 1818 Jackson briefly invaded Spanish Florida to quell Seminoles and outlaws who harassed frontier settlements. He ran for president against John Quincy Adams in 1824, but. although he won the most popular and electoral votes, he did not have a majority. The House of Representatives decided the election and chose Adams. In the 1828 election, however, Jackson defeated Adams, carrying the West and the South.

As president, Jackson introduced what became known as the spoils system—rewarding party members with government posts. Perhaps his most controversial act, however, was depositing federal funds in so-called pet banks, those directed by Democratic bankers, rather than in the Bank of the United States. "Let the people rule" was his slogan. In 1832, Jackson killed the congressional caucus for nominating presidential candidates and substituted the national convention. When South Carolina refused to collect imports under his protective tariff, he ordered army and naval forces to Charleston. After leaving office in 1837, he retired to the Hermitage, outside Nashville, where he died on June 8, 1845.

MARTIN VAN BUREN (1837-41), 8th president, Democrat, was born on Dec. 5, 1782, in Kinderhook, NY, the son of Abraham and Maria Hoes Van Buren. After attending local schools, he studied law and became a lawyer at the age of 20. A consummate politician, Van Buren began his career in the New York state senate and then served as state attorney general from 1816 to 1819. He was elected to the U.S. Senate in 1821. He helped swing eastern support to Andrew Jackson in the 1828 election and then served as Jackson's secretary of state from 1829 to 1831. In 1832 he was elected vice president. Known as the "Little Magician," Van Buren was extremely influential in Jackson's administration.

In 1836, Van Buren defeated William Henry Harrison for president and took office as the financial panic of 1837 initiated a nationwide depression. Although he instituted the independent treasury system, his refusal to spend land revenues led to his defeat by William Henry Harrison in 1840. In 1844 he lost the Democratic nomination to James Knox Polk. In 1848 he again ran for president on the Free Soil ticket but lost. He died in Kinderhook on July 24, 1862.

WILLIAM HENRY HARRISON (1841), 9th president, Whig, who served only 31 days, was born on Feb. 9, 1773, in Berkeley, Charles City Co., VA, the son of Benjamin Harrison, a signer of the Declaration of Independence, and of Elizabeth Bassett Harrison. He attended Hampden-Sydney College. Harrison served as secretary of the Northwest Territory in 1798 and was its delegate to the House of Representatives in 1799. He was the first governor of the Indiana Territory and served as superintendent of Indian affairs. With 900 men he put down a Shawnee uprising at Tippecanoe, IN, on Nov. 7, 1811. A generation later, in 1840, he waged a rousing presidential campaign, using the slogan "Tippecanoe and Tyler too." The Tyler of the slogan was his running mate, John Tyler.

Although born to one of the wealthiest, most prestigious, and most influential families in Virginia, Harrison was elected president with a "log cabin and hard cider" slogan. He caught pneumonia during the inauguration and died Apr. 4, 1841, after only one month in office.

JOHN TYLER (1841-45), 10th president, independent Whig, was born on Mar. 29, 1790, in Greenway, Charles City Co., VA, the son of John and Mary Armistead Tyler. His father was governor of Virginia (1808-11). Tyler graduated from the College of William and Mary in 1807 and in 1811 was elected to the Virginia legislature. In 1816 he was chosen for the U.S. House of Representatives. He served in the

Virginia legislature again from 1823 to 1825, when he was elected governor of Virginia. After a stint in the U.S. Senate (1827-36), he was elected vice president (1840).

When William Henry Harrison died only a month after taking office, Tyler succeeded him. Because he was the first person to occupy the presidency without having been elected to that office, he was referred to as "His Accidency." He gained passage of the Preemption Act of 1841, which gave squatters on government land the right to buy 160 acres at the minimum auction price. His last act as president was to sign a resolution annexing Texas. Tyler accepted renomination in 1844 from some Democrats but withdrew in favor of the official party candidate, James K. Polk. He died in Richmond, VA, on Jan. 18, 1862.

JAMES KNOX POLK (1845-49), 11th president, Democrat, was born on Nov. 2, 1795, in Mecklenburg Co., NC, the son of Samuel and Jane Knox Polk. He graduated from the University of North Carolina in 1818 and served in the Tennessee state legislature from 1823 to 1825. He served in the U.S. House of Representatives from 1825 to 1839, the last 4 years as Speaker. He was governor of Tennessee from 1839 to 1841. In 1844, after the Democratic National Convention became deadlocked, it nominated Polk, who became the first "dark horse" candidate for president. He was nominated primarily because he favored annexation of Texas.

As president, Polk reestablished the independent treasury system originated by Van Buren. He was so intent on acquiring California from Mexico that he sent troops to the Mexican border and, when Mexicans attacked, declared that a state of war existed. The Mexican War ended with the annexation of California and much of the Southwest as part of America's "manifest destiny." Polk compromised on the Oregon boundary ("54-40 or fight!") by accepting the 49th parallel and yielding Vancouver Island to the British. A few months after leaving office, Polk died in Nashville, TN, on June 15, 1849.

ZACHARY TAYLOR (1849-50), 12th president, Whig, who served only 16 months, was born on Nov. 24, 1784, in Orange Co., VA, the son of Richard and Sarah Strother Taylor. He grew up on his father's plantation near Louisville, KY, where he was educated by private tutors. In 1808 Taylor joined the regular army and was commissioned first lieutenant. He fought in the War of 1812, the Black Hawk War (1832), and the second Seminole War (beginning in 1837). He was called "Old Rough and Ready." In 1846 President Polk sent him with an army to the Rio Grande. When the Mexicans attacked him, Polk declared war. Outnumbered 4-1, Taylor defeated (1847) Santa Anna at Buena Vista.

A national hero, Taylor received the Whig nomination in 1848 and was elected president, even though he had never bothered to vote. He resumed the spoils system and, though a slaveholder, worked to admit California as a free state. He fell ill and died in office on July 9, 1850.

MILLARD FILLMORE (1850-53), 13th president, Whig, was born on Jan. 7, 1800, in Cayuga Co., NY, the son of Nathaniel and Phoebe Millard Fillmore. Although he had little schooling, he became a law clerk at the age of 22 and a year later was admitted to the bar. He was elected to the New York state assembly in 1828 and served until 1831. From 1833 until 1835 and again from 1837 to 1843, he represented his district in the U.S. House of Representatives. He opposed the entrance of Texas as a slave state and voted for a protective tariff. In 1844 he was defeated for governor of New York.

In 1848 he was elected vice president, and he succeeded as president after Taylor's death. Fillmore favored the Compromise of 1850 and signed the Fugitive Slave Law. His policies pleased neither expansionists nor slaveholders, and he was not renominated in 1852. In 1856 he was nominated by the American (Know-Nothing) Party, but despite the support of the Whigs, he was defeated by James Buchanan. He died in Buffalo, NY, on Mar. 8, 1874.

FRANKLIN PIERCE (1853-57), 14th president, Democrat, was born on Nov. 23, 1804, in Hillsboro, NH, the son of Benjamin Pierce, Revolutionary War general and governor of New Hampshire, and Anna Kendrick. He graduated from Bowdoin College in 1824 and was admitted to the bar in 1827. He was elected to the New Hampshire state legislature in 1829 and was chosen Speaker in 1831. He went to the U.S. House in 1833 and was elected a U.S. senator in 1837. He enlisted in the Mexican War and became brigadier general under Gen. Winfield Scott.

In 1852 Pierce was nominated as the Democratic presidential candidate on the 49th ballot. He decisively defeated Gen. Scott, his Whig opponent, in the election. Although against slavery, Pierce was influenced by pro-slavery Southerners. He supported the controversial Kansas-Nebraska Act, which left the question of slavery in the new territories of Kansas and Nebraska to popular vote. Pierce signed a reciprocity treaty with Canada and approved the Gadsden Purchase of a border area on a proposed railroad route, from Mexico. Denied renomination, he spent most of his remaining years in Concord, NH, where he died on Oct. 8, 1869.

JAMES BUCHANAN (1857-61), 15th president, Federalist, later Democrat, was born on Apr. 23, 1791, near Mercersburg, PA, the son of James and Elizabeth Speer Buchanan. He graduated from Dickinson College in 1809 and was admitted to the bar in 1812. He fought in the War of 1812 as a volunteer. He was twice elected to the Pennsylvania general assembly, and in 1821 he entered the U.S. House of Representatives. After briefly serving (1832-33) as minister to Russia, he was elected U.S. senator from Pennsylvania. As Polk's secretary of state (1845-49), he ended the Oregon dispute with Britain and supported the Mexican War and annexation of Texas. As minister to Great Britain, he signed the Ostend Manifesto (1854), declaring a U.S. right to take Cuba by force should efforts to purchase it fail.

Nominated by Democrats, Buchanan was elected president in 1856. On slavery he favored popular sovereignty and choice by state constitutions but did not consistently uphold this position. He denied the right of states to secede but opposed coercion and attempted to keep peace by not provoking secessionists. Buchanan left office having failed to deal decisively with the situation. He died at Wheatland, his estate, near Lancaster, PA, on June 1, 1868.

ABRAHAM LINCOLN (1861-65), 16th president, Republican, was born on Feb. 12, 1809, in a log cabin on a farm then in Hardin Co., KY, now in Larue, the son of Thomas and Nancy Hanks Lincoln. The Lincolns moved to Spencer Co., IN, near Gentryville, when Abe was 7. After Abe's mother died, his father married (1819) Mrs. Sarah Bush Johnston. In 1830 the family moved to Macon Co., IL.

Defeated in 1832 in a race for the state legislature, Lincoln was elected on the Whig ticket 2 years later and served in the lower house from 1834 to 1842. In 1837 Lincoln was admitted to the bar and became partner in a Springfield, IL, law office. He soon won recognition as an effective and resourceful attorney. In 1846, he was elected to the House of Representatives, where he attracted attention during a single term for his opposition to the Mexican War and his position on slavery. In 1856 he campaigned for the newly founded Republican Party, and in 1858 he became its senatorial candidate against Stephen A. Douglas. Although he lost the election, Lincoln gained national recognition from his debates with Douglas.

In 1860, Lincoln was nominated for president by the Republican Party on a platform of restricting slavery. He ran against Douglas, a northern Democrat; John C. Breckinridge, a Southern proslavery Democrat; and John Bell, of the

Constitutional Union Party. As a result of Lincoln's winning the election, South Carolina seceded from the Union on Dec. 20, 1860, followed in 1861 by 10 other Southern states.

The Civil War erupted when Fort Sumter, which Lincoln decided to resupply, was attacked by Confederate forces on Apr. 12, 1861. Lincoln called successfully for recruits from the North. On Sept. 22, 1862, 5 days after the Battle of Antietam, Lincoln announced that slaves in territory then in rebellion would be free Jan. 1, 1863, the date of the Emancipation Proclamation. His speeches, including his Gettysburg and Inaugural addresses, are remembered for their eloquence.

Lincoln was reelected, in 1864, over Gen. George B. McClellan, Democrat. General Robert E. Lee surrendered on Apr. 9, 1865. On Apr. 14, Lincoln was shot by actor John Wilkes Booth in Ford's Theater, in Washington, DC. He died the next day.

ANDREW JOHNSON (1865-69), 17th president, Democrat, was born on Dec. 29, 1808, in Raleigh, NC, the son of Jacob and Mary McDonough Johnson. He was apprenticed to a tailor as a youth, but ran away after two years and eventually settled in Greeneville, TN. He became popular with the townspeople and in 1829 was elected councilman and later mayor. In 1835 he was sent to the state general assembly. In 1843 he was elected to the U.S. House of Representatives, where he served for 10 years. Johnson was governor of Tennessee from 1853 to 1857, when he was elected to the U.S. Senate. He supported John C. Breckinridge against Lincoln in the 1860 election. Although Johnson had held slaves, he opposed secession and tried to prevent Tennessee from seceding. In Mar. 1862, Lincoln appointed him military governor of occupied Tennessee.

In 1864, in order to balance Lincoln's ticket with a Southern Democrat, the Republicans nominated Johnson for vice president. He was elected vice president with Lincoln and then succeeded to the presidency upon Lincoln's death. Soon afterward, in a controversy with Congress over the president's power over the South, he proclaimed an amnesty to all Confederates, except certain leaders, if they would ratify the 13th Amendment abolishing slavery. States doing so added anti-Negro provisions that enraged Congress, which restored military control over the South. When Johnson removed Edwin M. Stanton, secretary of war, without notifying the Senate, the House, in Feb. 1868, impeached him. Charging him with thereby having violated the Tenure of Office Act, the House was actually responding to his opposition to harsh congressional Reconstruction, expressed in repeated vetoes. He was tried by the Senate, and in May, in two separate votes on different counts, was acquitted, both times by only one vote.

Johnson was denied renomination but remained politically active. He was reelected to the Senate in 1874. Johnson died July 31, 1875, at Carter Station, TN.

ULYSSES SIMPSON GRANT (1869-77), 18th president, Republican, was born on Apr. 27, 1822, in Point Pleasant, OH, the son of Jesse R. and Hannah Simpson Grant. The next year the family moved to Georgetown, OH. Grant was named Hiram Ulysses, but on entering West Point in 1839, his name was put down as Ulysses Simpson, and he adopted it. He graduated in 1843. During the Mexican War, Grant served under both Gen. Zachary Taylor and Gen. Winfield Scott. In 1854, he resigned his commission because of loneliness and drinking problems, and in the following years he engaged in generally unsuccessful farming and business ventures. With the start of the Civil War, he was named colonel and then brigadier general of the Illinois Volunteers. He took Forts Henry and Donelson and fought at Shiloh. His brilliant campaign against Vicksburg and his victory at Chattanooga made him so prominent that Lincoln placed him in command of all Union armies. Grant accepted Lee's surrender at Appomattox Court House on Apr. 9, 1865. President Johnson appointed Grant secretary of war when he suspended Stanton, but Grant was not confirmed.

Grant was nominated for president by the Republicans in 1868 and elected over Horatio Seymour, Democrat. The 15th Amendment, the amnesty bill, and peaceful settlement of disputes with Great Britain were events of his administration. The Liberal Republicans and Democrats opposed him with Horace Greeley in the 1872 election, but Grant was reelected. His second administration was marked by scandals, including widespread corruption in the Treasury Department and the Indian Service. An attempt by the Stalwarts (Old Guard Republicans) to nominate him in 1880 failed. In 1884 the collapse of an investment firm in which he was a partner left Grant penniless. He wrote his personal memoirs while ill with cancer and completed them shortly before his death at Mt. McGregor, NY, on July 23, 1885.

RUTHERFORD BIRCHARD HAYES (1877-81), 19th president, Republican, was born on Oct. 4, 1822, in Delaware, OH, the son of Rutherford and Sophia Birchard Hayes. He was reared by his uncle, Sardis Birchard. Hayes graduated from Kenyon College in 1842 and from Harvard Law School in 1845. He practiced law in Lower Sandusky (now Fremont), OH, and was city solicitor of Cincinnati from 1858 to 1861. During the Civil War, he was major of the 23rd Ohio Volunteers. He was wounded several times, and by the end of the war he had risen to the rank of brevet major general. While serving (1865-67) in the U.S. House of Representatives, Hayes supported Reconstruction and Johnson's impeachment. He was twice elected governor of Ohio (1867, 1869). After losing a race for the U.S. House in 1872, he was reelected governor of Ohio in 1875.

In 1876, Hayes was nominated for president and believed he had lost the election to Samuel J. Tilden, Democrat. But a few Southern states submitted 2 sets of electoral votes, and the result was in dispute. An electoral commission, consisting of 8 Republicans and 7 Democrats, awarded all disputed votes to Hayes, allowing him to become president by one electoral vote. Hayes, keeping a promise to southerners, withdrew troops from areas still occupied in the South, ending the era of Reconstruction. He proposed civil service reforms, alienating those favoring the spoils system, and advocated repeal of the Tenure of Office Act restricting presidential power to dismiss officials. He supported sound money and specie payments.

Hayes died in Fremont, OH, on Jan. 17, 1893.

JAMES ABRAM GARFIELD (1881), 20th president, Republican, was born on Nov. 19, 1831, in Orange, Cuyahoga Co., OH, the son of Abram and Eliza Ballou Garfield. His father died in 1833, and he was reared in poverty by his mother. He worked as a canal bargeman, a farmer, and a carpenter and managed to secure a college education. He taught at Hiram College and later became principal. In 1859 he was elected to the Ohio legislature. Antislavery and antisecession, he volunteered for military service in the Civil War, becoming colonel of the 42nd Ohio Infantry and brigadier in 1862. He fought at Shiloh, was chief of staff for Gen. William Starke Rosecrans, and was made major general for gallantry at Chickamauga. He entered Congress as a radical Republican in 1863, calling for execution or exile of Confederate leaders, but he moderated his views after the Civil War. On the electoral commission in 1877 he voted for Hayes against Tilden on strict party lines.

Garfield was a senator-elect in 1880 when he became the Republican nominee for president. He was chosen as a compromise over Gen. Grant, James G. Blaine, and John Sherman, and won election despite some bitterness among Grant's supporters. Much of his brief tenure as president was concerned with a fight with New York Sen. Roscoe Conkling, who opposed two major appointments made by Garfield. On July 2, 1881, Garfield was shot and seriously wounded by a mentally disturbed office-seeker, Charles J. Guiteau, while entering a railroad station in Washington, DC. He died on Sept. 19, 1881, in Elberon, NJ.

CHESTER ALAN ARTHUR (1881-85), 21st president, Republican, was born on Oct. 5, 1829, in Fairfield, VT, to William and Malvina Stone Arthur. He graduated from Union College in 1848, taught school in Vermont, then studied law and practiced in New York City. In 1853 he argued in a fugitive slave case that slaves transported through New York state were thereby freed. In 1871, he was appointed collector of the Port of New York. President Hayes, an opponent of the spoils system, forced him to resign in 1878. This made the New York machine enemies of Hayes. Arthur and the Stalwarts (Old Guard Republicans) tried to nominate Grant for a 3rd term as president in 1880. When Garfield was nominated, Arthur was nominated for vice president in the interests of harmony.

Upon Garfield's assassination, Arthur became president. Despite his past connections, he signed major civil service reform legislation. Arthur tried to dissuade Congress from enacting the high protective tariff of 1883. He was defeated for renomination in 1884 by James G. Blaine. He died in New York City on Nov. 18, 1886.

GROVER CLEVELAND (1885-89; 1893-97) *(According to a ruling of the State Dept., Grover Cleveland should be counted as both the 22nd and the 24th president, because his 2 terms were not consecutive.)* Democrat, was born Stephen Grover Cleveland on Mar. 18, 1837, in Caldwell, NJ, the son of Richard F. and Ann Neal Cleveland. When he was a small boy, his family moved to New York. Prevented by his father's death from attending college, he studied by himself and was admitted to the bar in Buffalo, NY, in 1859. In succession he became assistant district attorney (1863), sheriff (1871), mayor (1881), and governor of New York (1882). He was an independent, honest administrator who hated corruption. Cleveland was nominated for president over Tammany Hall opposition in 1884 and defeated Republican James G. Blaine.

As president, he enlarged the civil service and vetoed many pension raids on the Treasury. In the 1888 election he was defeated by Benjamin Harrison, although his popular vote was larger. Reelected over Harrison in 1892, he faced a money crisis brought about by a lowered gold reserve, circulation of paper, and exorbitant silver purchases under the Sherman Silver Purchase Act. He obtained a repeal of the Sherman Act, but was unable to secure effective tariff reform. A severe economic depression and labor troubles racked his administration, but he refused to interfere in business matters and rejected Jacob Coxey's demand for unemployment relief. In 1894, he broke the Pullman strike. Cleveland was not renominated in 1896.

He died in Princeton, NJ, on June 24, 1908.

BENJAMIN HARRISON (1889-93), 23rd president, Republican, was born on Aug. 20, 1833, in North Bend, OH, the son of John Scott and Elizabeth Irwin Harrison. His great-grandfather, Benjamin Harrison, was a signer of the Declaration of Independence; his grandfather, William Henry Harrison, was 9th president; his father was a member of Congress. He attended school on his father's farm and graduated from Miami University in Oxford, OH, in 1852. He was admitted to the bar in 1854 and practiced in Indianapolis. During the Civil War, he rose to the rank of brevet brigadier general and fought at Kennesaw Mountain, at Peachtree Creek, at Nashville, and in the Atlanta campaign. He lost the 1876 gubernatorial election in Indiana but succeeded in becoming a U.S. senator in 1881.

In 1888 he defeated Cleveland for president despite receiving fewer popular votes. As president, he expanded the pension list and signed the McKinley high tariff bill, the Sherman Antitrust Act, and the Sherman Silver Purchase Act. During his administration, 6 states were admitted to the Union. He was defeated for reelection in 1892. He died in Indianapolis on Mar. 13, 1901.

WILLIAM MCKINLEY (1897-1901), 25th president, Republican, was born on Jan. 29, 1843, in Niles, OH, the son of William and Nancy Allison McKinley. McKinley briefly attended Allegheny College. When the Civil War broke out in 1861, he enlisted and served for the duration. He rose to captain and in 1865 was made brevet major. After studying law in Albany, NY, he opened (1867) a law office in Canton, OH. He served twice in the U.S. House (1877-83; 1885-91) and led the fight there for the McKinley Tariff, passed in 1890; he was not reelected to the House as a result. He served two terms (1892-96) as governor of Ohio.

In 1896 he was elected president as a proponent of a protective tariff and sound money (gold standard), over William Jennings Bryan, the Democrat and a proponent of free silver. McKinley was reluctant to intervene in Cuba, but the loss of the battleship *Maine* at Havana crystallized opinion. He demanded Spain's withdrawal from Cuba; Spain made some concessions, but Congress announced a state of war as of Apr. 21, 1898. He was reelected in the 1900 campaign, defeating Bryan's anti-imperialist arguments with the promise of a "full dinner pail." McKinley was respected for his conciliatory nature and for his conservative stance on business issues. On Sept. 6, 1901, while welcoming citizens at the Pan-American Exposition, in Buffalo, NY, he was shot by Leon Czolgosz, an anarchist. He died Sept. 14.

THEODORE ROOSEVELT (1901-9), 26th president, Republican, was born on Oct. 27, 1858, in New York City, the son of Theodore and Martha Bulloch Roosevelt. He was a 5th cousin of Franklin D. Roosevelt and an uncle of Eleanor Roosevelt. Roosevelt graduated from Harvard University in 1880. He attended Columbia Law School briefly but abandoned law to enter politics. He was elected to the New York state assembly in 1881 and served until 1884. He spent the next 2 years ranching and hunting in the Dakota Territory. In 1886, he ran unsuccessfully for mayor of New York City. He was Civil Service commissioner in Washington, DC, from 1889 to 1895. From 1895 to 1897, he served as New York City's police commissioner. He was assistant secretary of the navy under McKinley. The Spanish-American War made him nationally known. He organized the 1st U.S. Volunteer Cavalry (Rough Riders) and, as lieutenant colonel, led the charge up Kettle Hill in San Juan. Elected New York governor in 1898, he fought the spoils system and achieved taxation of corporation franchises.

Nominated for vice president in 1900, he became the nation's youngest president when McKinley was assassinated. He was reelected in 1904. As president he fought corruption of politics by big business, dissolved the Northern Securities Co. and others for violating antitrust laws, intervened in the 1902 coal strike on behalf of the public, obtained the Elkins Law (1903) forbidding rebates to favored corporations, and helped pass the Hepburn Railway Rate Act of 1906 (extending jurisdiction of the Interstate Commerce Commission). He helped obtain passage of the Pure Food and Drug Act (1906), and of employers' liability laws. Roosevelt vigorously organized conservation efforts. He mediated (1905) the peace between Japan and Russia, for which he won the Nobel Peace Prize. He abetted the 1903 revolution in Panama that led to U.S. acquisition of territory for the Panama Canal.

In 1908 Roosevelt obtained the nomination of William H. Taft, who was elected. Feeling that Taft had abandoned his policies, he unsuccessfully sought the nomination in 1912. He then ran on the Progressive "Bull Moose" ticket against Taft and Woodrow Wilson, splitting the Republicans and ensuring Wilson's election. He was shot during the campaign but recovered. In 1916, after unsuccessfully seeking the presidential nomination, he supported the Republican candidate, Charles E. Hughes. A strong friend of Britain, he fought for U.S. intervention in World War I.

Roosevelt was a voracious reader and wrote some 40 books, of which *The Winning of the West* is perhaps best known. He died Jan. 6, 1919, at Sagamore Hill, Oyster Bay, NY.

WILLIAM HOWARD TAFT (1909-13), 27th president, Republican, and 10th chief justice of the U.S., was born on Sept. 15, 1857, in Cincinnati, OH, the son of Alphonso and Louisa Maria Torrey Taft. His father was secretary of war and attorney general in Grant's cabinet and minister to Austria and Russia under Arthur. Taft graduated from Yale in 1878 and from Cincinnati Law School in 1880. After working as a law reporter for Cincinnati newspapers, he served as assistant prosecuting attorney (1881-82), assistant county solicitor (1885), judge, superior court (1887), U.S. solicitor-general (1890), and federal circuit judge (1892). In 1900 he became head of the U.S. Philippines Commission and was the first civil governor of the Philippines (1901-4). In 1904 he served as secretary of war, and in 1906 he was sent to Cuba to help avert a threatened revolution.

Taft was groomed for the presidency by Theodore Roosevelt and elected over William Jennings Bryan in 1908. Taft vigorously continued Roosevelt's trust-busting, instituted the Department of Labor, and drafted the amendments calling for direct election of senators and the income tax. However, his tariff and conservation policies angered progressives. Although renominated in 1912, he was opposed by Roosevelt, who ran on the Progressive Party ticket; the result was Democrat Woodrow Wilson's election.

Taft, with some reservations, supported the League of Nations. After leaving office, he was professor of constitutional law at Yale (1913-21) and chief justice of the U.S. (1921-30). Taft was the only person in U.S. history to have been both president and chief justice. He died in Washington, DC, on Mar. 8, 1930.

(THOMAS) WOODROW WILSON (1913-21), 28th president, Democrat, was born on Dec. 28, 1856, in Staunton, VA, the son of Joseph Ruggles and Janet (Jessie) Woodrow Wilson. He grew up in Georgia and South Carolina. He attended Davidson College in North Carolina before graduating from Princeton University in 1879. He studied law at the University of Virginia and political science at Johns Hopkins University, where he received his PhD in 1886. He taught at Bryn Mawr (1885-88) and then at Wesleyan (1888-90) before joining the faculty at Princeton. He was president of Princeton from 1902 until 1910, when he was elected governor of New Jersey. In 1912 he was nominated for president with the aid of William Jennings Bryan, who sought to block James "Champ" Clark and Tammany Hall. Wilson won because the Republican vote for Taft was split by the Progressives.

As president, Wilson protected American interests in revolutionary Mexico and fought for American rights on the high seas. He oversaw the creation of the Federal Reserve system, cut the tariff, and developed a reputation as a reformer. His sharp warnings to Germany led to the resignation of his secretary of state, Bryan, a pacifist. In 1916 he was reelected by a slim margin with the slogan, "He kept us out of war," although his attempts to mediate in the war failed. After several American ships had been sunk by the Germans, he secured a declaration of war against Germany on Apr. 6, 1917.

Wilson outlined his peace program on Jan. 8, 1918, in the Fourteen Points, a state paper that had worldwide influence. He enunciated a doctrine of self-determination for the settlement of territorial disputes. The Germans accepted his terms and an armistice on Nov. 11, 1918.

Wilson went to Paris to help negotiate the peace treaty, the crux of which he considered the League of Nations. The Senate demanded reservations that would not make the U.S. subordinate to the votes of other nations in case of war. Wilson refused and toured the country to get support. He suffered a stroke in Oct. 1919. An invalid, he clung to his office while his wife and doctors effectively functioned as president.

Wilson was awarded the 1919 Nobel Peace Prize, but the treaty embodying the League of Nations was ultimately rejected by the Senate in 1920. He left the White House in Mar. 1921. He died in Washington, DC, on Feb. 3, 1924.

WARREN GAMALIEL HARDING (1921-23), 29th president, Republican, was born on Nov. 2, 1865, near Corsica (now Blooming Grove), OH, the son of George Tyron and Phoebe Elizabeth Dickerson Harding. He attended Ohio Central College, studied law, and became editor and publisher of a county newspaper. He entered the political arena as state senator (1901-4) and then served as lieutenant governor (1904-6). In 1910 he ran unsuccessfully for governor of Ohio; then in 1914 he was elected to the U.S. Senate. In the Senate he voted for antistrike legislation, woman suffrage, and the Volstead Prohibition Enforcement Act over President Wilson's veto. He opposed the League of Nations.

In 1920 he was nominated for president and defeated James M. Cox in the election. The Republicans capitalized on war weariness and fear that Wilson's League of Nations would curtail U.S. sovereignty. Harding stressed a return to "normalcy" and worked for tariff revision and the repeal of excess profits law and high income taxes. His secretary of interior, Albert B. Fall, became involved in the Teapot Dome scandal.

As rumors began to circulate about the corruption in his administration, Harding became ill while returning from a trip to Alaska, and he died in San Francisco on Aug. 2, 1923.

(JOHN) CALVIN COOLIDGE (1923-29), 30th president, Republican, was born on July 4, 1872, in Plymouth, VT, the son of John Calvin and Victoria J. Moor Coolidge. Coolidge graduated from Amherst College in 1895. He entered Republican state politics and served as mayor of Northampton, MA, as state senator, as lieutenant governor, and, in 1919, as governor. In Sept. 1919, Coolidge attained national prominence by calling out the state guard in the Boston police strike. He declared: "There is no right to strike against the public safety by anybody, anywhere, anytime." This brought his name before the Republican convention of 1920, where he was nominated for vice president.

Coolige succeeded to the presidency on Harding's death. As president, he opposed the League of Nations and the soldiers' bonus bill, which was passed over his veto. In 1924 he was elected to the presidency by a huge majority. He substantially reduced the national debt. He twice vetoed the McNary-Haugen farm bill, which would have provided relief to financially hard-pressed farmers.

With Republicans eager to renominate him, Coolidge simply announced, Aug. 2, 1927: "I do not choose to run for president in 1928." He died in Northampton, MA, on Jan. 5, 1933.

HERBERT CLARK HOOVER (1929-33), 31st president, Republican, was born on Aug. 10, 1874, in West Branch, IA, the son of Jesse Clark and Hulda Randall Minthorn Hoover. Hoover grew up in Indian Territory (now Oklahoma) and Oregon and graduated from Stanford University with a degree in geology in 1895. He worked briefly with the U.S. Geological Survey and then managed mines in Australia, Asia, Europe, and Africa. While chief engineer of imperial mines in China, he directed food relief for victims of the Boxer Rebellion. He gained a reputation not only as an engineer but as a humanitarian as he directed the American Relief Committee, London (1914-15) and the U.S. Commission for Relief in Belgium (1915-19). He was U.S. Food Administrator (1917-19), American Relief Administrator (1918-23), and in charge of Russian Relief (1918-23). He served as secretary of commerce under both Harding and Coolidge. Some historians believe that he was the most effective secretary of commerce ever to hold that office.

In 1928 Hoover was elected president over Alfred E. Smith. In 1929 the stock market crashed, and the economy collapsed. During the Great Depression, Hoover inaugurated some government assistance programs, but he was opposed to administration of aid through a federal bureaucracy. As the effects of the depression continued, he was defeated in the 1932 election by Franklin D. Roosevelt. Hoover remained active after leaving office. President Truman named him coordinator of the European Food Program (1946) and chairman of the Commission on Organization of the Executive Branch (1947-49; 1953-55).

Hoover died in New York City on Oct. 20, 1964.

FRANKLIN DELANO ROOSEVELT (1933-45), 32nd president, Democrat, was born on Jan. 30, 1882, in Hyde Park, NY, the son of James and Sara Delano Roosevelt. He graduated from Harvard University in 1903. He attended Columbia University Law School without taking a degree and was admitted to the New York state bar in 1907. His political career began when he was elected to the New York state senate in 1910. In 1913 President Wilson appointed him assistant secretary of the navy, a post he held during World War I.

In 1920 Roosevelt ran for vice president with James Cox and was defeated. From 1921 to 1928 he worked in his New York law office and was also vice president of a bank. In Aug. 1921, he was stricken with poliomyelitis, which left his legs paralyzed. As a result of therapy he was able to stand, or walk a few steps, with the aid of leg braces.

Roosevelt served 2 terms as governor of New York (1929-33). In 1932, W. G. McAdoo, pledged to John N. Garner, threw his votes to Roosevelt, who was nominated for president. The Depression and the promise to repeal Prohibition ensured his election. He asked for emergency powers, proclaimed the New Deal, and put into effect a vast number of administrative changes. Foremost was the use of public funds for relief and public works, resulting in deficit financing. He greatly expanded the federal government's regulation of business and by an excess profits tax and progressive income taxes produced a redistribution of earnings on an unprecedented scale. He also promoted legislation establishing the Social Security system. He was the last president inaugurated on Mar. 4 (1933) and the first inaugurated on Jan. 20 (1937).

Roosevelt was the first president to use radio for "fireside chats." When the Supreme Court nullified some New Deal laws, he sought power to "pack" the Court with additional justices, but Congress refused to give him the authority. He was the first president to break the "no 3rd term" tradition (1940) and was elected to a 4th term in 1944, despite failing health.

Roosevelt was openly hostile to fascist governments before World War II and launched a lend-lease program on behalf of the Allies. With British Prime Min. Winston Churchill he wrote a declaration of principles to be followed after Nazi defeat (the Atlantic Charter of Aug. 14, 1941) and urged the Four Freedoms (freedom of speech, of worship, from want, from fear) Jan. 6, 1941. When Japan attacked Pearl Harbor on Dec. 7, 1941, the U.S. entered the war. Roosevelt guided the nation through the war and conferred with allied heads of state at Casablanca (Jan. 1943), Quebec (Aug. 1943), Tehran (Nov.-Dec. 1943), Cairo (Nov. and Dec. 1943), and Yalta (Feb. 1945).

Roosevelt did not, however, live to see the end of the war. He died of a cerebral hemorrhage in Warm Springs, GA, on Apr. 12, 1945.

HARRY S. TRUMAN (1945-53), 33rd president, Democrat, was born on May 8, 1884, in Lamar, MO, the son of John Anderson and Martha Ellen Young Truman. A family disagreement on whether his middle name should be Shipp or Solomon, after names of 2 grandfathers, resulted in his using only the middle initial S. After graduating from high school in Independence, MO, he worked (1901) for the *Kansas City Star,* as a railroad timekeeper, and as a clerk in Kansas City banks until about 1905. He ran his family's farm from 1906 to 1917. He served in France during World War I. After the war he opened a haberdashery shop, was a judge on the Jackson Co. Court (1922-24), and attended Kansas City School of Law (1923-25).

Truman was elected to the U.S. Senate in 1934 and reelected in 1940. In 1944, with Roosevelt's backing, he was nominated for vice president and elected. On Roosevelt's death in 1945, Truman became president. In 1948, in a famous upset victory, he defeated Republican Thomas E. Dewey to win election to a new term.

Truman authorized the first uses of the atomic bomb (Hiroshima and Nagasaki, Aug. 6 and 9, 1945), bringing World War II to a rapid end. He was responsible for what came to be called the Truman Doctrine (to aid nations such as Greece and Turkey, threatened by Communist takeover), and his strong commitment to NATO and to the Marshall Plan helped bring them about. In 1948-49, he broke a Soviet blockade of West Berlin with a massive airlift. When Communist North Korea invaded South Korea (June 1950), he won UN approval for a "police action" and, boldly without prior congressional consent, sent in forces under Gen. Douglas MacArthur. When MacArthur opposed his policy of limited objectives, Truman removed him.

He died in Kansas City, MO, on Dec. 26, 1972.

DWIGHT DAVID EISENHOWER (1953-61), 34th president, Republican, was born on Oct. 14, 1890, in Denison, TX, the son of David Jacob and Ida Elizabeth Stover Eisenhower. He grew up on a small farm in Abilene, KS, and graduated from West Point in 1915. He was on the staff of Gen. Douglas MacArthur in the Philippines from 1935 to 1939. In 1942, he was made commander of Allied forces landing in North Africa; the next year he was made full general. He became supreme Allied commander in Europe that same year and as such led the Normandy invasion (June 6, 1944). He was given the rank of general of the army on Dec. 20, 1944, which was made permanent in 1946.

On May 7, 1945, Eisenhower received the surrender of Germany at Rheims. He returned to the U.S. to serve as chief of staff (1945-48). His war memoir, *Crusade in Europe* (1948), was a best-seller. In 1948 he became president of Columbia University; in 1950 he became Commander of NATO forces.

Eisenhower resigned from the army and was nominated for president by the Republicans in 1952. He defeated Adlai E. Stevenson in the 1952 election and again in 1956. Eisenhower called himself a moderate, favored the "free market system" vs. government price and wage controls, kept government out of labor disputes, reorganized the defense establishment, and promoted missile programs. He continued foreign aid, sped the end of the Korean War, endorsed Taiwan and SE Asia defense treaties, backed the UN in condemning the Anglo-French raid on Egypt, and advocated the "open skies" policy of mutual inspection with the USSR. He sent U.S. troops into Little Rock, AR, in Sept. 1957, during the segregation crisis.

Eisenhower died on Mar. 28, 1969, in Washington, DC.

JOHN FITZGERALD KENNEDY (1961-63), 35th president, Democrat, was born on May 29, 1917, in Brookline, MA, the son of Joseph P. and Rose Fitzgerald Kennedy. He graduated from Harvard University in 1940. While serving in the navy (1941-45), he commanded a PT boat in the Solomons and won the Navy and Marine Corps Medal. In 1956, while recovering from spinal surgery, he wrote *Profiles in Courage,* which won a Pulitzer Prize in 1957. He served in the House of Representatives from 1947 to 1953 and was elected to the Senate in 1952 and 1958. In 1960, he won the Democratic nomination for president and narrowly defeated Republican Vice Pres. Richard M. Nixon. Kennedy was the youngest president ever elected to the office and the first Catholic.

Despite the image of youth and vigor he conveyed to the public, Kennedy suffered from serious medical problems, including Addison's disease and severe chronic back pain that required him to wear a back brace. The public was not aware of the extent of these problems, or of his extensive womanizing, including an affair with a young White House press aide that only became known in 2003. However, scholars have not generally claimed that these aspects of his life affected his performance in office.

In Apr. 1961, the new Kennedy administration suffered a severe setback when an invasion force of anti-Castro Cubans, trained and directed by the CIA, failed to establish a beachhead at the Bay of Pigs in Cuba. By the same token, one of Kennedy's most important acts as president was his successful demand on Oct. 22, 1962, that the Soviet Union dismantle its missile bases in Cuba. Kennedy also defied Soviet attempts to force the Allies out of Berlin. He started the Peace Corps, and he backed civil rights and expanded medical care for the aged. Space exploration was greatly developed during his administration.

On Nov. 22, 1963, President Kennedy was assassinated while riding in a motorcade in Dallas, TX. A commission chaired by Chief Justice Earl Warren concluded in Sept. 1964 that the sole assassin had been Lee Harvey Oswald, a former U.S. Marine and, at the time of the shooting, an ardent Marxist. Oswald was captured a short time after the assassination and charged with the crime, but was shot dead by nightclub owner Jack Ruby two days later while being moved to a county jail, before he could go to trial.

LYNDON BAINES JOHNSON (1963-69), 36th president, Democrat, was born on Aug. 27, 1908, near Stonewall, TX, the son of Sam Ealy and Rebekah Baines Johnson. He graduated from Southwest Texas State Teachers College in 1930 and attended Georgetown University Law School. He taught public speaking in Houston (1930-31) and then served as secretary to Rep. R. M. Kleberg (1931-35). In 1937 Johnson won an election to fill the vacancy caused by the death of a U.S. representative and in 1938 was elected to the full term, after which he returned for 4 terms. During 1941 and 1942 he also served in the Navy in the Pacific, earning a Silver Star for bravery. He was elected U.S. senator in 1948 and reelected in 1954. He became Democratic leader of the Senate in 1953. Johnson had strong support for the Democratic presidential nomination at the 1960 convention, where the nominee, John F. Kennedy, asked him to run for vice president. His campaigning helped overcome religious bias against Kennedy in the South.

Johnson became president when Kennedy was assassinated. He was elected to a full term in 1964. Johnson's domestic program was of considerable importance. He won passage of major civil rights, anti-poverty, aid to education, and health-care (Medicare, Medicaid) legislation—the "Great Society" program. However, his escalation of the war in Vietnam came to overshadow the achievements of his administration. In the face of increasing division in the nation and in his own party over his handling of the war, Johnson declined to seek another term.

Johnson died on Jan. 22, 1973, in San Antonio, TX.

RICHARD MILHOUS NIXON (1969-74), 37th president, Republican, was born on Jan. 9, 1913, in Yorba Linda, CA, the son of Francis Anthony and Hannah Milhous Nixon. He graduated from Whittier College in 1934 and from Duke University Law School in 1937. After practicing law in Whittier and serving briefly in the Office of Price Administration in 1942, he entered the Navy and served in the South Pacific. Nixon was elected to the House of Representatives in 1946 and 1948. He achieved prominence as the House Un-American Activities Committee member who forced the showdown leading to the Alger Hiss perjury conviction. In 1950 he was elected to the Senate.

Nixon was elected vice president in the Eisenhower landslides of 1952 and 1956. He won the Republican nomination for president in 1960 but was narrowly defeated by John F. Kennedy. He ran unsuccessfully for governor of California in 1962. In 1968 he again won the GOP presidential nomination, then defeated Hubert Humphrey for the presidency.

As president, Nixon appointed 4 Supreme Court justices, including the chief justice, moving the court to the right, and as a "new federalist" sought to shift responsibility to state and local governments. He dramatically altered relations with China, which he visited in 1972—the first president to do so. With foreign affairs adviser Henry Kissinger he pursued détente with the Soviet Union, signing major arms limitation and other treaties and increasing trade. He began a gradual withdrawal from Vietnam, but U.S. troops remained there through his first term. He ordered an incursion into Cambodia (1970) and the bombing of Hanoi and mining of Haiphong Harbor (1972). Reelected by a large majority in Nov. 1972, he secured a Vietnam cease-fire in Jan. 1973.

Nixon's 2nd term was cut short by scandal, after disclosures relating to a June 1972 burglary of Democratic Party headquarters in the Watergate office complex. The courts and Congress sought tapes of Nixon's office conversations and calls for criminal proceedings against former White House aides and for a House inquiry into possible impeachment. Nixon claimed executive privilege, but the Supreme Court ruled against him. In July the House Judiciary Committee recommended adoption of 3 impeachment articles charging him with obstruction of justice, abuse of power, and contempt of Congress. On Aug. 5, he released transcripts of conversations that linked him to cover-up activities. He resigned on Aug. 9, becoming the first president ever to do so.

In later years, Nixon emerged as an elder statesman. He died Apr. 22, 1994, in New York City.

GERALD RUDOLPH FORD (1974-77), 38th president, Republican, was born on July 14, 1913, in Omaha, NE, the son of Leslie and Dorothy Gardner King, and was named Leslie Jr. When he was 2, his parents were divorced, and his mother moved with the boy to Grand Rapids, MI. There she met and married Gerald R. Ford, who formally adopted him and gave him his own name. Ford graduated from the University of Michigan in 1935 and from Yale Law School in 1941. He began practicing law in Grand Rapids, but in 1942 joined the navy and served in the Pacific, leaving the service in 1946 as a lieutenant commander. He entered the House of Representatives in 1949 and spent 25 years in the House, 8 of them as Republican leader.

On Oct. 12, 1973, after Vice President Spiro T. Agnew resigned, Ford was nominated by President Nixon to replace him. It was the first use of the procedures set out in the 25th Amendment. When Nixon resigned, Aug. 9, 1974, because of the Watergate scandal, Ford became president; he was the only president who was never elected either to the presidency or to the vice presidency.

President Ford was widely credited with having contributed to rebuilding morale after the Nixon presidency. But he was also criticized by many when, in a controversial move, he pardoned Nixon for any federal crimes he might have committed as president. Ford vetoed 48 bills in his first 21 months in office, mostly in the interest of fighting high inflation; he was less successful in curbing high unemployment. In foreign policy, Ford continued to pursue détente.

Ford was narrowly defeated in the 1976 election.

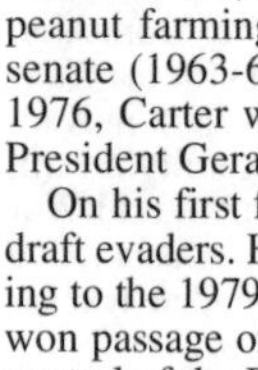

JIMMY (JAMES EARL) CARTER (1977-81), 39th president, Democrat, was the first president from the Deep South since before the Civil War. He was born on Oct. 1, 1924, in Plains, GA, the son of James and Lillian Gordy Carter. Carter graduated from the U.S. Naval Academy in 1946 and in 1952 entered the navy's nuclear submarine program as an aide to Capt. (later Adm.) Hyman Rickover. He studied nuclear physics at Union College. Carter's father died in 1953, and he left the navy to take over the family peanut farming businesses. He served in the Georgia state senate (1963-67) and as governor of Georgia (1971-75). In 1976, Carter won the Democratic nomination and defeated President Gerald R. Ford.

On his first full day in office, Carter pardoned all Vietnam draft evaders. He played a major role in the negotiations leading to the 1979 peace treaty between Israel and Egypt, and he won passage of new treaties with Panama providing for U.S. control of the Panama Canal to end in 2000. However, Carter was widely criticized for the poor state of the economy and was viewed by some as weak in his handling of foreign policy. In Nov. 1979, Iranian student militants attacked the U.S.

embassy in Tehran and held members of the embassy staff hostage. Efforts to obtain release of the hostages were a major preoccupation during the rest of his term. He reacted to the Soviet invasion of Afghanistan by imposing a grain embargo and boycotting the Moscow Olympic Games.

Carter was defeated by Ronald Reagan in the 1980 election. The American hostages were finally released on Inauguration Day, 1981, just after Reagan officially became president. After leaving office, Carter was active in humanitarian efforts and in seeking to mediate international disputes. In large part for his diplomatic efforts in office and subsequently, he was awarded the Nobel Peace Prize in 2002.

RONALD WILSON REAGAN (1981-89), 40th president, Republican, was born on Feb. 6, 1911, in Tampico, IL, the son of John Edward and Nellie Wilson Reagan. Reagan graduated from Eureka College in 1932, after which he worked as a sports announcer in Des Moines, IA. He began a successful career as an actor in 1937, starring in numerous movies, and later in television, until the 1960s. During World War II Reagan served in the Army Air Force, making training films. He was president of the Screen Actors Guild from 1947 to 1952 and in 1959-60. Reagan was elected governor of California in 1966 and reelected in 1970.

In 1980, Reagan gained the Republican presidential nomination and won a landslide victory over Jimmy Carter. He was easily reelected in 1984. Reagan successfully forged a bipartisan coalition in Congress, which led to enactment of his program of large-scale tax cuts, cutbacks in many government programs, and a major defense buildup. He signed a Social Security reform bill designed to provide for the long-term solvency of the system. In 1986, he signed into law a major tax-reform bill. He was shot and seriously wounded in an assassination attempt in 1981.

In 1982, the U.S. joined France and Italy in maintaining a peacekeeping force in Beirut, Lebanon, and the next year Reagan sent a task force to invade the island of Grenada after 2 Marxist coups there. Reagan's opposition to international terrorism led to the U.S. bombing of Libyan military installations in 1986. He strongly supported El Salvador, the Nicaraguan contras, and other anti-communist governments and forces throughout the world. He also held 4 summit meetings with Soviet leader Mikhail Gorbachev. At the 1987 meeting in Washington, DC, a historic treaty eliminating short- and medium-range missiles from Europe was signed.

Reagan faced a crisis in 1986-87, when it was revealed that the U.S. had sold weapons through Israeli brokers to Iran in exchange for release of U.S. hostages being held in Lebanon and that subsequently some of the money was diverted to the Nicaraguan contras (Congress had barred U.S. aid to the contras). The scandal led to the resignation of leading White House aides. As Reagan left office in Jan. 1989, the nation was experiencing its 6th consecutive year of economic prosperity. Over the same period, however, the federal government recorded large budget deficits.

In 1994, in a letter to the American people, Reagan revealed that he was suffering from Alzheimer's disease. He died on June 5, 2004, in Los Angeles, CA, from complications of the disease.

GEORGE HERBERT WALKER BUSH (1989-93), 41st president, Republican, was born on June 12, 1924, in Milton, MA, the son of Prescott and Dorothy Walker Bush. He served as a U.S. Navy pilot in World War II. After graduating from Yale University in 1948, he settled in Texas, where, in 1953, he helped found an oil company. After losing a bid for a U.S. Senate seat in Texas in 1964, he was elected to the House of Representatives in 1966 and 1968. He lost a 2nd U.S. Senate race in 1970. Subsequently he served as U.S. ambassador to the United Nations (1971-73), headed the U.S. Liaison Office in Beijing (1974-75), and was director of central intelligence (1976-77).

Following an unsuccessful bid for the 1980 Republican presidential nomination, Bush was chosen by Ronald Reagan as his vice presidential running mate. He served as U.S. vice president from 1981 to 1989.

In 1988, Bush gained the GOP presidential nomination and defeated Michael Dukakis in the November election. Bush took office faced with U.S. budget and trade deficits as well as the rescue of insolvent U.S. savings and loan institutions. He faced a severe budget deficit annually, struggled with military cutbacks in light of reduced cold war tensions, and vetoed abortion-rights legislation. In 1990 he agreed to a budget deficit-reduction plan that included tax hikes.

Bush supported Soviet reforms, Eastern Europe democratization, and good relations with Beijing. In Dec. 1989, Bush sent troops to Panama; they overthrew the government and captured strongman Gen. Manuel Noriega.

Bush reacted to Iraq's Aug. 1990 invasion of Kuwait by sending U.S. forces to the Persian Gulf area and assembling a UN-backed coalition, including NATO and Arab League members. After a month-long air war, in Feb. 1991, Allied forces retook Kuwait in a 4-day ground assault. The quick victory, with extremely light casualties on the U.S. side, gave Bush at the time one of the highest presidential approval ratings in history. His popularity plummeted by the end of 1991, however, as the economy slipped into recession. He was defeated by Bill Clinton in the 1992 election. His son George W. Bush became the 43rd president.

BILL (WILLIAM JEFFERSON) CLINTON (1993-2001), 42nd president, Democrat, was born on Aug. 19, 1946, in Hope, AR, son of William Blythe and Virginia Cassidy Blythe, and was named William Jefferson Blythe IV. Blythe died in an automobile accident before his son was born. His widow married Roger Clinton, and at the age of 16, William Jefferson Blythe IV changed his last name to Clinton.

Clinton became interested in politics in high school and went on to Georgetown University in Washington, DC, where he graduated with high honors in 1968. He then attended Oxford University for 2 years as a Rhodes scholar. During that time he legally avoided the draft and possible service in Vietnam, according to some critics by misleading his draft board. He went on to earn a degree from Yale Law School in 1973.

Clinton worked on George McGovern's 1972 presidential campaign. He taught at the University of Arkansas from 1973 to 1976, when he was elected state attorney general. In 1978, he was elected governor, becoming the nation's youngest. Defeated for reelection in 1980, he was returned to office several times thereafter. He married Hillary Rodham in 1975.

Despite some issues raised about his character, Clinton won most of the 1992 presidential primaries, moving his party toward the center as he tried to broaden his appeal; as the party's presidential nominee he defeated Pres. George H.W. Bush and Reform Party candidate Ross Perot in the November election. In 1993, Clinton won passage of a measure to reduce the federal budget deficit and won congressional approval of the North American Free Trade Agreement. His administration's plan for major health-care reform legislation died in Congress. After 1994 midterm elections, Clinton faced Republican majorities in both

IT'S A FACT: Former U.S. presidents George H. W. Bush and Bill Clinton, who faced each other as opponents in the 1992 presidential election, teamed up in Jan. 2005 to create a private fund for the countries hit by the devastating Indian Ocean tsunamis of Dec. 2004. The two toured the affected region in February and by May had raised $10 mil in aid money. Clinton was also appointed UN envoy Feb. 1 to head reconstruction efforts in the region. He was the most senior former U.S. official ever appointed as a UN envoy.

houses of Congress. He followed a centrist course at home, sent troops to Bosnia to help implement a peace settlement, and cultivated relations with Russia and China.

Though accused of improprieties in his involvement in an Arkansas real estate venture (Whitewater), Clinton easily won reelection in 1996, and an independent prosecutor found insufficient evidence of any criminality by Clinton or his wife. In 1997 he reached agreement with Congress on legislation to balance the federal budget by 2002. In 1998, Clinton became the 2nd U.S. president ever to be impeached by the House of Representatives. Charged with perjury and obstruction of justice in connection with an attempted cover-up of a sexual relationship with a former White House intern, Monica Lewinsky, he was acquitted by the Senate in 1999. He retained wide popularity, aided by a strong economy.

In 1999, the United States, under Clinton, joined other NATO nations in an aerial bombing campaign that induced Serbia to withdraw troops from the Kosovo region, where they had been terrorizing ethnic Albanians. In 2000 Clinton became the 1st president since the Vietnam war to visit Vietnam.

After leaving office, Clinton remained active in political affairs and encouraged the career of his wife, who was elected in 2000 to the U.S. Senate from New York. His memoirs, *My Life*, published in 2004, immediately went to the top of the best-seller list. He had quadruple heart bypass surgery, Sept. 6, 2004.

GEORGE WALKER BUSH (2001-), 43rd president, Republican, was born on July 6, 1946, in New Haven, CT. He was the first of six children born to George Herbert Walker Bush and his wife, the former Barbara Pierce, a descendant of Pres. Franklin Pierce. (His brother Jeb won the Florida governorship in 1998.) Bush was the first son of a former president to win the White House since John Quincy Adams took office in 1825.

Fun-loving, athletic, and popular, the young George Bush grew up in Midland and Houston, TX. In 1961 he was sent to the Phillips Academy in Andover, MA, the same prep school his father had attended. In 1964 he entered Yale University, his father's alma mater, where he majored in history. Eligible for the draft upon graduation during the Vietnam War, he signed on with the Texas Air National Guard. Bush received an honorable discharge but critics have questioned whether he fulfilled completely his guard service. After earning a master's degree from the Harvard Business School, he returned to Midland in 1975 and went into the oil business. Two years later he married Laura Welch, a schoolteacher and librarian; in 1981 she gave birth to twin daughters.

Bush, who had lost a race for Congress in 1978, returned to the oil business, but success proved elusive. Realizing that he had a drinking problem, he swore off alcohol and renewed commitment to Christian faith. After aiding in his father's successful 1988 presidential campaign, he joined a group of investors to buy the Texas Rangers baseball club and took a hands-on role as managing partner. Bush ran for governor in 1994, defeating a popular incumbent, Ann Richards. He won reelection by a landslide in 1998. As governor, he concentrated on building personal bonds with Democratic leaders and backed education reforms.

After defeating Sen. John McCain of Arizona and other rivals in the Republican party primaries, Bush chose Dick Cheney, a former U.S. representative and defense secretary, as his running mate. The Nov. 2000 presidential election was one of the closest in history. While Bush came out behind in the popular vote, by about 540,000 out of more than 100 million cast, the electoral vote total hinged on the outcome in Florida, where official totals, challenged by Democrats, gave him a razor-thin lead. In December the Supreme Court in effect ended a Democratic-backed effort to recount the vote there, and Florida's 25 electoral votes decided the election in Bush's favor. Among the issues Bush had campaigned on was that of lowering federal taxes, and in May 2001 he won approval from Congress for a large tax cut package.

On Sept. 11, 2001, Bush was faced with a crisis that would redefine his presidency. In a terrorist attack, 2 hijacked jetliners crashed into the twin towers of the World Trade Center in New York City, which were destroyed; another jet struck the Pentagon near Washington, DC, with a 4th crashing in rural Pennsylvania. Some 3,000 people were killed in the attack. The president vowed to punish those responsible, and in a "war against terrorism," the U.S. military attacked and deposed the Taliban regime in Afghanistan's capital, which was sheltering elements of the al-Qaeda terrorist network, held responsible for the attacks. However, Taliban and al-Qaeda continued to function in parts of Afghanistan, and al-Qaeda was blamed for continuing terrorist acts in a number of countries. In 2002 Bush won congressional approval to create a cabinet-level department for homeland security.

Bush met in May 2002 with Russian Pres. Vladimir Putin in Moscow, where they signed a pact cutting nuclear armaments in each country. In July, with corporate scandals and a slumping stock market fueling demands for tighter regulation of business, Bush signed legislation aimed at curbing financial abuses.

In March 2003, the United States, aided mainly by forces from Great Britain, launched an air and ground war against Iraq and deposed the dictatorial regime of Pres. Saddam Hussein. The regime was accused of harboring weapons of mass destruction and other violations of UN resolutions. Despite Hussein's capture in Iraq, Dec. 13, 2003, and the formation of a new Iraqi government in June 2004, insurgent violence continued into 2005. U.S. troops (some 140,000 as of Sept. 2005) remained in Iraq, sustaining further casualties. A Senate Intelligence Committee report issued in July 2004 concluded that pre-war intelligence on illicit weapons in Iraq had been seriously flawed. U.S. intelligence agencies were also criticized by a special 9-11 Commission for having failed to heed possible warnings of terrorism prior to the Sept. 11 attacks. The president argued that the removal of Saddam Hussein had been a necessity to help safeguard the U.S., as well as a benefit in itself; the administration's Iraq policy and conduct of the war and reconstruction efforts, along with domestic security, were major issues in the fall presidential campaign.

Bush was elected to a 2nd term as president in Nov. 2004, winning about 59 million popular votes, or 3 million more than Sen. John Kerry (D, MA). Bush continued the campaigns in Afghanistan and Iraq.

The economy expanded at a moderate pace in 2005. Bush proposed introducing private accounts into the Social Security system, a plan that met with strong resistance from Democrats.

In late Aug. 2005, Hurricane Katrina devastated the Gulf Coast. There were heavy casualties, hundreds of thousands of people were left homeless, and the flooded city of New Orleans was evacuated and shut down. The Federal Emergency Management Administration (FEMA) was severely criticized, and director Michael Brown stepped down. Also, with oil production in the Gulf of Mexico shut down, U.S. gas prices shot up over $3 a gallon. Bush and Congress quickly approved a $62 bil "down payment" on disaster relief efforts in the Gulf Coast region.

In July, Justice Sandra Day O'Connor resigned, creating the first Supreme Court vacancy in more than 11 years. Bush nominated federal appeals court judge John G. Roberts to replace her. Then, after the Sept. death of Chief Justice William H. Rehnquist, Bush re-nominated Roberts for chief justice.

WORLD ALMANAC QUICK QUIZ

Who was the first president born in a log cabin?

(a) George Washington (b) John Adams (c) Andrew Jackson (d) Abraham Lincoln

For the answer look in this chapter, or see page 1008.

IT'S A FACT: Hillary Rodham Clinton and Laura Bush are the only two First Ladies in U.S. history to have earned post-graduate degrees. Clinton received a law degree, and Bush received a masters in library science, both in 1973.

Wives and Children of the Presidents

Name (Born–died; married)	State	Sons/ Daughters
Martha Dandridge Custis Washington (1731-1802; 1759)	VA	None
Abigail Smith Adams (1744-1818; 1764)	MA	3/2
Martha Wayles Skelton Jefferson (1748-82; 1772)	VA	1/5
Dorothea "Dolley" Payne Todd Madison (1768-1849; 1794)	NC	None
Elizabeth Kortright Monroe (1768-1830; 1786)	NY	0/2 (A)
Louisa Catherine Johnson Adams (1775-1852; 1797)	MD (B)	3/1
Rachel Donelson Robards Jackson (1767-1828; 1791)	VA	None
Hannah Hoes Van Buren (1783-1819; 1807)	NY	4/0
Anna Tuthill Symmes Harrison (1775-1864; 1795)	NJ	6/4
Letitia Christian Tyler (1790-1842; 1813)	VA	3/4(A)
Julia Gardiner Tyler (1820-89; 1844)	NY	5/2
Sarah Childress Polk (1803-91; 1824)	TN	None
Margaret Mackall Smith Taylor (1788-1852; 1810)	MD	1/5
Abigail Powers Fillmore (1798-1853; 1826)	NY	1/1
Caroline Carmichael McIntosh Fillmore (1813-81; 1858)	NJ	None
Jane Means Appleton Pierce (1806-63; 1834)	NH	3/0
Mary Todd Lincoln (1818-82; 1842)	KY	4/0
Eliza McCardle Johnson (1810-76; 1827)	TN	3/2
Julia Boggs Dent Grant (1826-1902; 1848)	MO	3/1
Lucy Ware Webb Hayes (1831-89; 1852)	OH	7/1
Lucretia Randolph Garfield (1832-1918; 1858)	OH	4/1
Ellen Lewis Herndon Arthur (1837-80; 1859)	VA	2/1
Frances Folsom Cleveland (1864-1947; 1886)	NY	2/3
Caroline Lavinia Scott Harrison (1832-92; 1853)	OH	1/1
Mary Scott Lord Dimmick Harrison (1858-1948; 1896)	PA	0/1
Ida Saxton McKinley (1847-1907; 1871)	OH	0/2
Alice Hathaway Lee Roosevelt (1861-84; 1880)	MA	0/1
Edith Kermit Carow Roosevelt (1861-1948; 1886)	CT	4/1
Helen Herron Taft (1861-1943; 1886)	OH	2/1
Ellen Louise Axson Wilson (1860-1914; 1885)	GA	0/3
Edith Bolling Galt Wilson (1872-1961; 1915)	VA	None
Florence Kling De Wolfe Harding (1860-1924; 1891)	OH	None
Grace Anna Goodhue Coolidge (1879-1957; 1905)	VT	2/0
Lou Henry Hoover (1875-1944; 1899)	IA	2/0
Anna Eleanor Roosevelt Roosevelt (1884-1962; 1905)	NY	4/1(A)
Elizabeth Virginia "Bess" Wallace Truman (1885-1982; 1919)	MO	0/1
Mamie Geneva Doud Eisenhower (1896-1979; 1916)	IA	1/0(A)
Jacqueline Lee Bouvier Kennedy (1929-94; 1953)	NY	1/1(A)
Claudia "Lady Bird" Alta Taylor Johnson (1912; 1934)	TX	0/2
Thelma Catherine Patricia Ryan Nixon (1912-1993; 1940)	NV	0/2
Elizabeth Bloomer Warren Ford (1918; 1948)	IL	3/1
Rosalynn Smith Carter (1927; 1946)	GA	3/1
Anne Frances "Nancy" Robbins Davis Reagan (1921; 1952)	NY	1/1(C)
Barbara Pierce Bush (1925; 1945)	NY	4/2
Hillary Rodham Clinton (1947; 1975)	IL	0/1
Laura Welch Bush (1946; 1977)	TX	0/2

NOTE: Pres. Buchanan was unmarried. (A) plus 1 infant, deceased. (B) Born in London, father a MD citizen. (C) Pres. Reagan married and divorced Jane Wyman; they had a daughter who died in infancy, and a son and daughter who lived past infancy.

First Lady Laura Welch Bush

Laura Welch Bush was born in Midland, TX, Nov. 4, 1946. She graduated from Southern Methodist University, earned a master's in library science at the Univ. of Texas at Austin, and became a librarian and teacher in Texas public schools. She and George W. Bush were married in 1977; in 1981, their twin daughters, Jenna and Barbara, were born.

As First Lady of Texas from 1995 to 2001, Laura Bush worked for educational reform and stressed literacy programs. She launched an early childhood development initiative and also worked to promote breast cancer awareness.

Laura Bush's first solo appearance as First Lady came at the launch of D.C. Teaching Fellows, a program encouraging professionals to become teachers. In Nov. 2001 she became the first First Lady to give a speech of her own in place of the president's weekly radio address. In May 2005 she toured the Middle East seeking to promote women's rights and democracy in the region. She also continued to be involved in such interests as early childhood education, promotion of literacy and reading, and women's health.

Burial Places of the Presidents

President	Burial Place
Washington	Mt. Vernon, VA
J. Adams	Quincy, MA
Jefferson	Charlottesville, VA
Madison	Montpelier Station, VA
Monroe	Richmond, VA
J. Q. Adams	Quincy, MA
Jackson	Nashville, TN
Van Buren	Kinderhook, NY
W. H. Harrison	North Bend, OH
Tyler	Richmond, VA
Polk	Nashville, TN
Taylor	Louisville, KY
Fillmore	Buffalo, NY
Pierce	Concord, NH
Buchanan	Lancaster, PA
Lincoln	Springfield, IL
A. Johnson	Greeneville, TN
Grant	New York, NY
Hayes	Fremont, OH
Garfield	Cleveland, OH
Arthur	Albany, NY
Cleveland	Princeton, NJ
B. Harrison	Indianapolis, IN
McKinley	Canton, OH
T. Roosevelt	Oyster Bay, NY
Taft	Arlington Natl. Cemetery
Wilson	Wash. Natl. Cathedral
Harding	Marion, OH
Coolidge	Plymouth, VT
Hoover	West Branch, IA
F. Roosevelt	Hyde Park, NY
Truman	Independence, MO
Eisenhower	Abilene, KS
Kennedy	Arlington Natl. Cemetery
L. B. Johnson	Johnson City, TX
Nixon	Yorba Linda, CA
Reagan	Simi Valley, CA

Presidential Facts

Oldest president: Ronald Reagan, who was 77 when he left office
Youngest president: Theodore Roosevelt, who was 42 when sworn in after McKinley's death
Youngest person elected president: John F. Kennedy, who was 43 when elected in Nov. 1960
Tallest president: Abraham Lincoln, who was 6 feet, 4 inches
Shortest president: James Madison, who was 5 feet, 4 inches
First president to live in the White House: John Adams, who moved there in 1800
First president inaugurated in Washington, DC: Thomas Jefferson, in 1801
First president defeated for reelection: John Adams, in 1800
First president who did not seek reelection: James Knox Polk, in 1848
First president born in a log cabin: Andrew Jackson, in 1767
First president born a U.S. citizen: Martin Van Buren, in Kinderhook, NY; 1782
First president born outside the original colonies: Abraham Lincoln, in Kentucky, 1809
First president born west of the Mississippi River: Herbert Hoover, in 1874
Only president born in California: Richard M. Nixon, in 1913
First president of all 50 states: Dwight D. Eisenhower, first inaugurated in 1953
First president born from the "Baby Boom" generation: Bill Clinton, in 1946
First president born in the 20th century: John F. Kennedy, in 1917
First president to be photographed while in office: James Polk, in 1849
First president to have a telephone in the White House: Rutherford B. Hayes in 1879
First president to leave the continental U.S. while in office: Theodore Roosevelt, in 1906, on a visit to inspect construction work on the Panama Canal
First president to cross the Atlantic Ocean: Woodrow Wilson
First president to address the nation on radio: Warren G. Harding, in 1922
First president to appear on TV: Franklin D. Roosevelt, at opening ceremonies for the 1939 World's Fair
First president to give a live, televised news conference: John F. Kennedy, in 1961
Only president elected unanimously: George Washington, by 63 electoral votes
Only presidents who lost the popular vote while winning election: John Quincy Adams, in 1824 (elected by the House after general election failed to produce a majority); Rutherford B. Hayes, in 1876; Benjamin Harrison, in 1888; George W. Bush, in 2000. Popular vote totals before 1824 are unknown.
Only presidents chosen by the House of Representatives: Thomas Jefferson (1st term) and John Quincy Adams
Only presidents to graduate from West Point: Ulysses S. Grant and Dwight D. Eisenhower
Only president to graduate from Annapolis: Jimmy Carter
Only president with a Ph.D.: Woodrow Wilson; received a doctorate in political science from Johns Hopkins Univ. in 1886
Only left-handed presidents: James Garfield, Herbert Hoover, Harry Truman, Gerald Ford, Ronald Reagan, George H. W. Bush, and Bill Clinton
Only president to head a labor union: Ronald Reagan was president of the Screen Actors Guild, 1947-52, 1959-60
Only bachelor presidents: James Buchanan, who never married, and Grover Cleveland, who married Frances Folsom in the White House in 1886
Only divorced president: Ronald Reagan; divorced from actress Jane Wyman in 1948, married Nancy Davis in 1952
Only presidents to serve in Congress after leaving office: Andrew Johnson (Senate), John Quincy Adams (House)
Only president to also serve as chief justice of the U.S.: William Howard Taft
Presidents who died on July 4: John Adams and Thomas Jefferson (both 1826) and James Monroe (1831)
Only president buried in Washington, DC: Woodrow Wilson, who was interred at the Washington National Cathedral
Only presidents buried at Arlington National Cemetery: William H. Taft, in 1930, and John F. Kennedy, in 1963

Presidential Libraries

The libraries listed here, except for that of Richard Nixon (which is private), are coordinated by the National Archives and Records Administration (Website: www.archives.gov/presidential_libraries/index.html). NARA also has custody of the Nixon presidential historical materials and those of Bill Clinton. The William J. Clinton Library opened in Nov. 2004. NARA will release Clinton presidential records to the public at the Clinton Library beginning Jan. 20, 2006. Materials for presidents before Herbert Hoover are held by private institutions.

Herbert Hoover Library and Museum
210 Parkside Dr.
West Branch, IA 52358
PHONE: 319-643-5301
E-MAIL: hoover.library@nara.gov
WEBSITE: www.hoover.archives.gov

Franklin D. Roosevelt Library and Museum
4079 Albany Post Rd.
Hyde Park, NY 12538-1990
PHONE: 845-486-7770; 1-800-FDR-VISIT
E-MAIL: roosevelt.library@nara.gov
WEBSITE: www.fdrlibrary.marist.edu

Harry S. Truman Library and Museum
500 West U.S. Hwy. 24
Independence, MO 64050-2481
PHONE: 816-268-8200; 1-800-833-1225
E-MAIL: truman.library@nara.gov
WEBSITE: www.trumanlibrary.org

Dwight D. Eisenhower Library
200 S.E. 4th St.
Abilene, KS 67410-2900
PHONE: 785-263-6700; 1-877-RING-IKE
E-MAIL: eisenhower.library@nara.gov
WEBSITE: www.eisenhower.archives.gov

John Fitzgerald Kennedy Library
Columbia Pt.
Boston, MA 02125-3398
PHONE: 617-514-1600; 1-866-JFK-1960
E-MAIL: kennedy.library@nara.gov
WEBSITE: www.jfklibrary.org

Lyndon Baines Johnson Library and Museum
2313 Red River St.
Austin, TX 78705-5702
PHONE: 512-721-0200
E-MAIL: johnson.library@nara.gov
WEBSITE: www.lbjlib.utexas.edu

Richard Nixon Library & Birthplace
18001 Yorba Linda Blvd.
Yorba Linda, CA 92886
PHONE: 714-993-5075
E-MAIL: archives@nixonlibrary.org
WEBSITE: www.nixonfoundation.org

Gerald R. Ford Library
1000 Beal Ave.
Ann Arbor, MI 48109-2114
PHONE: 734-205-0555
E-MAIL: ford.library@nara.gov
WEBSITE: www.fordlibrarymuseum.gov

Jimmy Carter Library
441 Freedom Pkwy.
Atlanta, GA 30307-1498
PHONE: 404-865-7100
E-MAIL: carter.library@nara.gov
WEBSITE: www.jimmycarterlibrary.org

Ronald Reagan Library
40 Presidential Dr.
Simi Valley, CA 93065-0600
PHONE: 800-410-8354
E-MAIL: reagan.library@nara.gov
WEBSITE: www.reagan.utexas.edu

George H. W. Bush Library
1000 George Bush Dr. West
College Station, TX 77845
PHONE: 979-691-4000
E-MAIL: bush.library@nara.gov
WEBSITE: bush.library.tamu.edu

William J. Clinton Library and Museum
1200 President Clinton Ave.
Little Rock, AR 72201
PHONE: 501-374-4242
E-MAIL: clinton.library@nara.gov
WEBSITE: www.clintonlibrary.gov

Impeachment in U.S. History

The U.S. Constitution provides for impeachment and removal from office of federal officials on grounds of "Treason, Bribery, or other high Crimes and Misdemeanors" (Article II, Sect. 4). Impeachment is the bringing of charges by the House of Representatives. It is followed by a Senate trial; a two-thirds Senate vote is needed for conviction and removal from office.

In 1868, **Andrew Johnson** became the first president impeached by the House; he was tried but not convicted by the Senate. In 1974, impeachment articles against Pres. **Richard Nixon**, in connection with the Watergate scandal, were voted by the House Judiciary Committee; he resigned Aug. 9, before the full House could vote on impeaching him. In 1998, Pres. **Bill Clinton** was impeached by the House in connection with covering up a relationship with a former White House intern Monica Lewinsky; he was tried in the Senate in 1999 and acquitted.

PRESIDENTIAL ELECTIONS

Electoral and Popular Vote, 2004 and 2000[1]

Source: Associated Press (2004); Voter News Service (2000).

	2004					
	Electoral Vote			Democrat	Republican	Indep.[2]
State	Kerry	Bush	Nader	Kerry	Bush	Nader
AL	0	9	0	693,933	1,176,394	6,701
AK	0	3	0	111,025	190,889	5,069
AZ	0	10	—	893,524	1,104,294	—
AR	0	6	0	469,953	572,898	6,171
CA	55	0	—	6,745,485	5,509,826	—
CO	0	9	0	1,001,732	1,101,255	12,718
CT	7	0	0	857,488	693,826	12,969
DE	3	0	0	200,152	171,660	2,153
DC	3	0	0	202,970	21,256	1,485
FL	0	27	0	3,583,544	3,964,522	32,971
GA	0	15	—	1,366,149	1,914,254	—
HI	4	0	—	231,708	194,191	—
ID	0	4	—	181,098	409,235	—
IL	21	0	—	2,891,550	2,345,946	—
IN	0	11	—	969,011	1,479,438	—
IA	0	7	0	741,898	751,957	5,973
KS	0	6	0	434,993	736,456	9,348
KY	0	8	0	712,733	1,069,439	8,856
LA	0	9	0	820,299	1,102,169	7,032
ME	4	0	0	396,842	330,201	8,069
MD	10	0	0	1,334,493	1,024,703	11,854
MA	12	0	—	1,803,800	1,071,109	—
MI	17	0	0	2,479,183	2,313,746	24,035
MN	9[4]	0	0	1,445,014	1,346,695	18,683
MS	0	6	0	457,766	684,981	3,175
MO	0	11	—	1,259,171	1,455,713	—
MT	0	3	0	173,710	266,063	6,168
NE	0	5	0	254,328	512,814	5,698
NV	0	5	0	397,190	418,690	4,838
NH	4	0	0	340,511	331,237	4,479
NJ	15	0	0	1,911,430	1,670,003	19,418
NM	0	5	0	370,942	376,930	4,053
NY	31	0	0	4,314,280	2,962,567	99,873
NC	0	15	—	1,525,849	1,961,166	—
ND	0	3	0	111,052	196,651	3,756
OH	0	20	—	2,741,165	2,859,764	—
OK	0	7	—	503,966	959,792	—
OR	7	0	—	943,163	866,831	—
PA	21	0	—	2,938,095	2,793,847	—
RI	4	0	0	259,760	169,046	4,651
SC	0	8	0	661,699	937,974	5,520
SD	0	3	0	149,244	232,584	4,320
TN	0	11	0	1,036,477	1,384,375	8,992
TX	0	34	—	2,832,704	4,526,917	
UT	0	5	0	241,199	663,742	11,305
VT	3	0	0	184,067	121,180	4,494
VA	0	13	—	1,454,742	1,716,959	—
WA	11	0	0	1,510,201	1,304,894	23,283
WV	0	5	0	326,541	423,778	4,063
WI	10	0	0	1,489,504	1,478,120	16,390
WY	0	3	0	70,776	167,629	2,741
Total	**251**	**286**	**0**	**59,028,109**	**62,040,606**	**411,304**

	2000							
	Electoral Vote				Democrat	Republican	Green[2]	Reform[2]
State	Gore	Bush	Nader	Buchanan	Gore	Bush	Nader	Buchanan
AL	0	9	0	0	692,611	941,173	18,323	6,303
AK	0	3	0	0	79,004	167,398	28,747	4,194
AZ	0	8	0	0	685,341	781,652	45,645	10,903
AR	0	6	0	0	422,768	472,940	13,421	10,936
CA	54	0	0	0	5,861,203	4,567,429	418,707	39,897
CO	0	8	0	0	738,227	883,748	91,434	10,282
CT	8	0	0	0	816,015	561,094	64,452	4,382
DE	3	0	0	0	180,068	137,288	8,307	775
DC	2[3]	0	0	0	171,923	18,073	10,576	—
FL	0	25	0	—	2,912,253	2,912,790	97,488	17,356
GA	0	13	—	0	1,116,230	1,419,720	—	10,868
HI	4	0	0	0	205,286	137,845	21,623	1,071
ID	0	4	—	0	138,637	336,937	—	7,687
IL	22	0	0	0	2,589,026	2,019,421	103,759	16,060
IN	0	12	0	0	901,980	1,245,836	—	17,173
IA	7	0	0	0	638,517	634,373	29,374	6,942
KS	0	6	0	0	399,276	622,332	36,086	7,239
KY	0	8	0	0	638,923	872,520	23,118	4,181
LA	0	9	0	0	792,344	927,871	20,473	14,478
ME	4	0	0	0	319,951	286,616	37,127	4,315
MD	10	0	0	0	1,144,008	813,827	53,768	4,067
MA	12	0	0	0	1,616,487	878,502	173,564	11,086
MI	18	0	0	—	2,170,418	1,953,139	84,165	—
MN	10	0	0	0	1,168,266	1,109,659	126,696	22,256
MS	0	7	0	0	404,614	572,844	8,122	2,233
MO	0	11	0	0	1,111,138	1,189,924	38,515	9,806
MT	0	3	0	0	137,126	240,178	24,437	5,735
NE	0	5	0	0	231,780	433,862	24,540	3,431
NV	0	4	0	0	279,978	301,575	15,008	4,747
NH	0	4	0	0	266,348	273,559	22,198	2,603
NJ	15	0	0	0	1,788,850	1,284,173	94,554	6,868
NM	5	0	0	0	286,783	286,417	21,251	1,279
NY	33	0	0	0	4,112,965	2,405,570	244,360	33,202
NC	0	14	—	0	1,257,692	1,631,163	—	8,971
ND	0	3	0	0	95,284	174,852	9,486	7,330
OH	0	21	0	0	2,186,190	2,351,209	117,857	25,980
OK	0	8	—	0	474,276	744,337	—	9,014
OR	7	0	0	0	720,342	713,577	77,357	5,706
PA	23	0	0	0	2,485,967	2,281,127	103,392	16,879
RI	4	0	0	0	249,508	130,555	25,052	2,250
SC	0	8	0	0	566,039	786,892	20,279	3,540
SD	0	3	—	0	118,804	190,700	—	3,314
TN	0	11	0	0	981,720	1,061,949	19,781	4,218
TX	0	32	0	0	2,433,746	3,799,639	137,994	12,423
UT	0	5	0	0	203,053	515,096	35,850	9,277
VT	3	0	0	0	149,022	119,775	20,374	2,182
VA	0	13	0	0	1,217,290	1,437,490	59,398	5,578
WA	11	0	0	0	1,247,652	1,108,864	103,002	4,953
WV	0	5	0	0	295,497	336,475	10,680	3,101
WI	11	0	0	0	1,242,987	1,237,279	94,070	11,206
WY	0	3	—	0	60,481	147,947	—	2,724
Total	**266**	**271**	**0**	**0**	**51,003,894**	**50,459,211**	**2,834,410**	**441,001**

(—) = Not listed on state's ballot. (2) Listed on the ballot in some states as particular party. (3) One Washington, DC, elector abstained. (4) One Minnesota elector voted for Democratic vice-presidential candidate Sen. John Edwards (NC) for both president and vice president.

2004 Official Presidential General Election Results

Source: Federal Election Commission; Associated Press

Candidate (Party)	Popular Vote	Percent of Pop. Vote
George W. Bush (Republican)	62,040,606	50.76
John Kerry (Democrat)	59,028,109	48.29
Ralph Nader (Independent)	411,304	0.34
Michael Badnarik (Independent)	396,859	0.32
Michael Anthony Peroutka (Independent)	140,524	0.11
David Cobb (Green)	117,477	0.10
Leonard Peltier (Peace and Freedom)	27,607	0.02
Walter F. Brown (Socialist)	10,303	0.01
James Harris(Socialist Workers)	7,411	0.01
Róger Calero (Socialist Workers)	3,677	0.00
Thomas J. Harens (Christian Freedom)	2,387	0.00
Gene Amondson (Concerns of People)	1,944	0.00
Bill Van Auken (Socialist Equality)	1,850	0.00
John Parker (Workers World)	1,595	0.00
Charles Jay (Personal Choice)	946	0.00
Stanford E. Andress (Unaffiliated)	804	0.00
Earl F. Dodge (Prohibition Party)	140	0.00
Write-in	37,190	0.03
None of These Candidates	3,688	0.00
Total	**122,197,231**	**100.00**

Note: Party designations may vary from one state to another. Percents do not add because of rounding.

PRESIDENTIAL ELECTION RESULTS BY STATE AND COUNTY

All results are official. Results for New England states are for selected cities or towns. All totals statewide.

Source: Alaska results: Alaska Div. of Elections. Other 2004 results: ©Associated Press; all rights reserved; this material may not be published, broadcast, rewritten, or redistributed. 2000 results: Voter News Service; Fed. Election Commission. Not all write-ins are included.

Alabama

County	2004 Kerry (D)	2004 Bush (R)	2000 Gore (D)	2000 Bush (R)
Autauga	4,758	15,196	4,942	11,993
Baldwin	15,599	52,971	13,997	40,872
Barbour	4,832	5,899	2,197	1,860
Bibb	2,089	5,472	2,710	4,273
Blount	3,938	17,386	4,977	12,667
Bullock	3,210	1,494	3,395	1,433
Butler	3,413	4,979	3,606	4,127
Calhoun	15,083	29,814	15,781	22,306
Chambers	5,347	7,622	5,616	6,037
Cherokee	3,040	5,923	3,497	4,154
Chilton	3,778	12,829	4,806	10,066
Choctaw	3,303	3,897	3,707	3,600
Clarke	4,627	6,730	4,679	5,988
Clay	1,893	4,624	2,045	3,719
Cleburne	1,391	4,370	1,664	3,333
Coffee	4,480	13,019	5,220	9,938
Colbert	10,598	13,188	10,543	10,518
Conecuh	2,719	3,271	2,783	2,699
Coosa	2,055	2,905	2,104	2,382
Covington	3,423	11,119	4,440	8,961
Crenshaw	1,698	3,777	1,934	2,793
Cullman	8,045	26,818	9,758	19,157
Dale	4,484	13,621	4,906	10,593
Dallas	11,175	7,335	10,967	7,360
DeKalb	7,092	16,904	7,056	12,827
Elmore	6,471	22,056	6,652	16,777
Escambia	3,814	8,513	4,523	6,975
Etowah	15,328	26,999	17,433	21,087
Fayette	2,408	5,534	3,064	4,582
Franklin	4,514	7,690	4,793	6,119
Geneva	2,113	8,342	2,769	6,588
Greene	3,764	958	3,504	850
Hale	4,631	3,281	4,652	2,984
Henry	2,452	4,881	2,782	4,054
Houston	9,144	26,874	9,412	22,150
Jackson	8,635	11,534	9,066	8,475
Jefferson	132,286	158,680	129,889	138,491
Lamar	1,956	4,894	2,653	4,470
Lauderdale	14,628	22,161	13,875	17,478
Lawrence	6,155	7,730	6,296	5,671
Lee	16,227	27,972	14,574	22,433
Limestone	9,126	19,702	8,992	14,204
Lowndes	4,233	1,786	4,557	1,638
Macon	7,800	1,570	7,665	1,091
Madison	52,644	77,173	48,199	62,151
Marengo	5,037	5,255	4,841	4,690
Marion	3,808	8,983	4,600	6,910
Marshall	8,452	22,783	10,381	17,084
Mobile	63,732	92,014	58,640	78,162
Monroe	3,666	5,831	3,741	5,153
Montgomery	45,160	44,097	40,371	38,827
Morgan	14,131	32,477	16,060	25,774
Perry	3,767	1,738	4,020	1,732
Pickens	3,915	5,170	4,143	4,306
Pike	4,334	7,483	4,357	6,058
Randolph	2,817	6,127	3,094	4,666
Russell	8,375	8,337	8,396	6,198
St. Clair	5,456	23,500	6,485	17,117
Shelby	14,850	63,435	13,183	47,651
Sumter	4,527	1,880	4,415	1,629
Talladega	11,374	18,331	11,264	13,807
Tallapoosa	5,451	12,392	6,183	9,805
Tuscaloosa	26,447	42,877	24,614	34,003
Walker	9,016	19,167	11,621	13,486
Washington	3,145	5,060	3,386	4,117
Wilcox	3,838	1,834	3,444	1,661
Winston	2,236	8,130	2,692	6,413
Totals	**693,933**	**1,176,394**	**692,611**	**941,173**

Alabama Vote Since 1948

1948: Thurmond, States' Rights, 171,443; Dewey, R., 40,930; Wallace, Prog., 1,522; Watson, Proh., 1,085.

1952: Stevenson, D., 275,075; Eisenhower, R., 149,231; Hamblen, Proh., 1,814.

1956: Stevenson, D., 290,844; Eisenhower, R., 195,694; Ind. electors, 20,323.

1960: Kennedy, D., 324,050; Nixon, R., 237,981; Faubus, States' Rights, 4,367; Decker, Proh., 2,106; King, Afro-Americans, 1,485; scattered, 236.

1964: Goldwater, R., 479,085; Dem. (electors unpledged), 209,848; scattered, 105.

1968: Wallace, 3rd Party, 691,425; Humphrey, D., 196,579; Nixon, R., 146,923; Munn, Proh., 4,022.

1972: Nixon, R., 728,701; McGovern, D., 219,108 plus 37,815 Natl. Dem. Party of Alabama; Schmitz, Conservative, 11,918; Munn., Proh., 8,551.

1976: Carter, D., 659,170; Ford, R., 504,070; Maddox, Amer. Ind., 9,198; Bubar, Proh., 6,669; Hall, Com., 1,954; MacBride, Libertarian, 1,481.

1980: Reagan, R., 654,192; Carter, D., 636,730; Anderson, Independent, 16,481; Rarick, Amer. Ind., 15,010; Clark, Libertarian, 13,318; Bubar, Statesman, 1,743; Hall, Com., 1,629; DeBerry, Soc. Workers, 1,303; McReynolds, Socialist, 1,006; Commoner, Citizens, 517.

1984: Reagan, R., 872,849; Mondale, D., 551,899; Bergland, Libertarian, 9,504.

1988: Bush, R., 815,576; Dukakis, D., 549,506; Paul, Lib., 8,460; Fulani, Ind., 3,311.

1992: Bush, R., 804,283; Clinton, D., 690,080; Perot, Ind., 183,109; Marrou, Libertarian, 5,737; Fulani, New Alliance, 2,161.

1996: Dole, R., 769,044; Clinton, D., 662,165; Perot, Ind. (Ref.), 92,149; Browne, Libertarian, 5,290; Phillips, Ind., 2,365; Hagelin, Natural Law, 1,697; Harris, Ind., 516.

2000: Bush, R., 941,173; Gore, D., 692,611; Nader, Ind., 18,323; Buchanan, Ind., 6,351; Browne, Libertarian, 5,893; Phillips, Ind., 775 Hagelin, Ind., 447.

2004: Bush, R., 1,176,394; Kerry, D., 693,933; Nader, Ind., 6,701; Badnarik, Ind., 3,495; Peroutka, Ind., 1,994.

Alaska[1]

Election District[2]	2004 Kerry (D)	2004 Bush (R)	2000 Gore (D)	2000 Bush (R)
No. 1	1,949	4,522	1,284	4,681
No. 2	3,248	4,162	2,081	4,235
No. 3	4,808	3,031	3,693	3,135
No. 4	3,063	4,043	2,715	4,127
No. 5	2,974	3,674	1,931	3,545
No. 6	2,105	3,746	1,542	3,862
No. 7	3,259	5,272	1,893	4,868
No. 8	4,009	4,194	1,498	5,371
No. 9	2,232	3,909	1,203	4,789
No. 10	1,725	3,720	2,194	5,673
No. 11	1,523	6,416	2,043	3,960
No. 12	1,766	5,679	2,051	4,626
No. 13	2,325	6,489	2,661	3,853
No. 14	1,909	6,504	1,626	3,750
No. 15	2,331	6,030	2,106	2,453
No. 16	2,356	6,559	1,969	1,980
No. 17	2,190	6,366	2,230	4,564
No. 18	1,632	4,400	2,739	5,421
No. 19	2,521	4,087	2,350	4,619
No. 20	1,925	2,705	2,259	3,648
No. 21	2,917	4,836	2,309	3,263
No. 22	2,855	3,225	2,656	4,910
No. 23	3,449	2,789	1,282	2,961
No. 24	2,684	3,835	1,985	5,063
No. 25	2,837	3,062	1,697	5,489
No. 26	3,878	3,946	1,608	5,869
No. 27	2,670	4,713	2,199	6,714
No. 28	2,679	5,271	2,116	7,113
No. 29	2,058	3,874	2,806	4,054
No. 30	2,693	4,864	1,698	3,622
No. 31	2,853	5,803	1,831	3,326
No. 32	4,118	5,981	1,389	4,178
No. 33	1,879	5,523	1,765	5,804
No. 34	1,720	6,065	1,300	5,243
No. 35	3,780	4,442	1,208	4,278
No. 36	1,985	4,080	1,945	3,007
No. 37	1,587	2,591	1,821	2,725
No. 38	1,983	2,004	2.015	2,467
No. 39	1,963	2,407	2,282	2,321
No. 40	1,926	2,743	1,024	1,831
Totals	**111,025**	**190,889**	**79,004**	**167,398**

(1) In 2002, election district boundaries were redrawn. (2) Totals include some regional votes.

Alaska Vote Since 1960

1960: Nixon, R., 30,953; Kennedy, D., 29,809.

1964: Johnson, D., 44,329; Goldwater, R., 22,930.

1968: Nixon, R., 37,600; Humphrey, D., 35,411; Wallace, 3rd Party, 10,024.

1972: Nixon, R., 55,349; McGovern, D., 32,967; Schmitz, Amer., 6,903.

1976: Ford, R., 71,555; Carter, D., 44,058; MacBride, Libertarian, 6,785.

1980: Reagan, R., 86,112; Carter, D., 41,842; Clark, Libertarian, 18,479; Anderson, Ind., 11,155; write-in, 857.

1984: Reagan, R., 138,377; Mondale, D., 62,007; Bergland, Libertarian, 6,378.

1988: Bush, R., 119,251; Dukakis, D., 72,584; Paul, Lib., 5,484; Fulani, New Alliance, 1,024.

1992: Bush, R., 102,000; Clinton, D., 78,294; Perot, Ind., 73,481; Gritz, Populist/America First, 1,379; Marrou, Libertarian, 1,378.

1996: Dole, R., 122,746; Clinton, D., 80,380; Perot, Ref., 26,333; Nader, Green, 7,597; Browne, Libertarian, 2,276; Phillips, Taxpayers, 925; Hagelin, Natural Law, 729.
2000: Bush, R., 167,398; Gore, D., 79,004; Nader, Green, 28,747; Buchanan, Reform, 5,192; Browne, Libertarian, 2,636; Hagelin, Natural Law, 919; Phillips, Constitution, 596.
2004: Bush, R., 190,889; Kerry, D., 111,025; Nader, Populist, 5,069; Peroutka, AK Ind., 2,092; Badnarik, Libertarian, 1,675; Cobb, Green, 1,058.

Arizona

	2004		2000	
County	**Kerry (D)**	**Bush (R)**	**Gore (D)**	**Bush (R)**
Apache	15,658	8,384	13,025	5,947
Cochise	17,514	26,556	13,360	18,180
Coconino	29,243	22,526	20,280	17,562
Gila	8,314	12,343	7,700	9,158
Graham	3,185	7,467	3,355	6,007
Greenlee	1,146	1,899	1,216	1,619
La Paz	1,849	3,158	1,769	2,543
Maricopa	504,849	679,455	386,683	479,967
Mohave	20,503	36,794	17,470	24,386
Navajo	14,815	17,277	11,794	12,386
Pima	193,128	171,109	147,688	124,579
Pinal	27,252	37,006	19,650	20,122
Santa Cruz	6,909	4,668	5,233	3,344
Yavapai	33,127	53,468	24,063	40,144
Yuma	16,032	22,184	12,055	15,708
Totals	**893,524**	**1,104,294**	**685,341**	**781,652**

Arizona Vote Since 1948

1948: Truman, D., 95,251; Dewey, R., 77,597; Wallace, Prog., 3,310; Watson, Proh., 786; Teichert, Soc. Labor, 121.
1952: Eisenhower, R., 152,042; Stevenson, D., 108,528.
1956: Eisenhower, R., 176,990; Stevenson, D., 112,880; Andrews, Ind. 303.
1960: Nixon, R., 221,241; Kennedy, D., 176,781; Hass, Soc. Labor, 469.
1964: Goldwater, R., 242,535; Johnson, D., 237,753; Hass, Soc. Labor, 482.
1968: Nixon, R., 266,721; Humphrey, D., 170,514; Wallace, 3rd Party, 46,573; McCarthy, New Party, 2,751; Cleaver, Peace and Freedom, 217; Halstead, Soc. Workers, 85; Blomen, Soc. Labor, 75.
1972: Nixon, R., 402,812; McGovern, D., 198,540; Soc. Workers, 30,945; Schmitz, Amer., 21,208.
1976: Ford, R., 418,642; Carter, D., 295,602; McCarthy, Ind., 19,229; MacBride, Libertarian, 7,647; Camejo, Soc. Workers, 928; Anderson, Amer., 564; Maddox, Amer. Ind., 85.
1980: Reagan, R., 529,688; Carter, D., 246,843; Anderson, Ind., 76,952; Clark, Libertarian, 18,784; De Berry, Soc. Workers, 1,100; Commoner, Citizens, 551; Hall, Com., 25; Griswold, Workers World, 2.
1984: Reagan, R., 681,416; Mondale, D., 333,854; Bergland, Libertarian, 10,585.
1988: Bush, R., 702,541; Dukakis, D., 454,029; Paul, Lib., 13,351; Fulani, New Alliance, 1,662.
1992: Bush, R., 572,086; Clinton, D., 543,050; Perot, Ind., 353,741; Gritz, Populist/America First, 8,141; Marrou, Libertarian, 6,759; Hagelin, Natural Law, 2,267.
1996: Clinton, D., 653,288; Dole, R., 622,073; Perot, Ref., 112,072; Browne, Libertarian, 14,358.
2000: Bush, R., 781,652; Gore, D., 685,341; Nader, Green, 45,645; Buchanan, R., 12,373; Smith, Libertarian, 5,775; Hagelin, Natural Law, 1,120.
2004: Bush, R., 1,104,294; Kerry, D., 893,524; Badnarik, Libertarian, 11,856.

Arkansas

	2004		2000	
County	**Kerry (D)**	**Bush (R)**	**Gore (D)**	**Bush (R)**
Arkansas	3,110	3,789	2,877	3,353
Ashley	3,881	4,567	4,253	3,876
Baxter	7,129	11,128	6,516	9,538
Benton	20,756	46,571	17,277	34,838
Boone	4,640	9,793	4,493	8,569
Bradley	2,206	2,011	2,122	1,793
Calhoun	939	1,340	1,017	1,128
Carroll	4,161	6,184	3,595	5,556
Chicot	2,993	1,725	2,820	1,564
Clark	4,990	4,144	4,661	3,776
Clay	3,264	2,759	3,527	2,254
Cleburne	4,517	7,107	4,120	5,730
Cleveland	1,450	2,009	1,414	1,678
Columbia	4,108	5,729	4,003	5,018
Conway	3,982	4,009	3,496	3,545
Craighead	13,665	15,818	12,376	12,158
Crawford	6,764	13,391	6,288	10,804
Crittenden	8,277	6,930	7,224	5,857
Cross	3,135	3,864	3,096	3,033
Dallas	1,671	1,700	1,710	1,571
Desha	2,851	1,729	2,776	1,603
Drew	2,952	3,262	3,060	2,756
Faulkner	14,538	21,514	11,950	16,055
Franklin	3,008	4,181	2,674	3,277
Fulton	2,370	2,522	1,976	2,036
Garland	18,040	21,734	15,840	19,098
Grant	2,524	4,205	2,535	3,285
Greene	6,564	7,237	6,319	5,831
Hempstead	3,817	3,580	3,937	3,257
Hot Springs	5,901	5,960	5,527	5,042
Howard	2,166	2,736	2,063	2,326
Independence	5,443	7,430	5,146	6,145
Izard	2,586	2,833	2,587	2,301
Jackson	3,515	2,624	3,651	2,280
Jefferson	19,675	10,218	17,716	8,765
Johnson	3,622	4,311	3,270	3,657
Lafayette	1,567	1,604	1,806	1,538
Lawrence	3,544	2,951	3,255	2,626
Lee	2,548	1,492	2,727	1,351
Lincoln	2,149	1,921	1,957	1,526
Little River	2,677	2,575	2,883	2,283
Logan	3,361	5,076	3,283	4,487
Lonoke	7,454	14,398	6,851	10,606
Madison	2,421	3,873	2,055	3,387
Marion	2,602	4,127	2,233	3,402
Miller	6,139	8,448	6,278	7,276
Mississippi	7,593	6,121	7,107	5,199
Monroe	2,049	1,586	1,910	1,329
Montgomery	1,524	2,367	1,438	2,128
Nevada	1,694	1,752	1,867	1,796
Newton	1,506	2,779	1,205	2,529
Ouachita	5,188	5,345	5,464	4,739
Perry	1,921	2,435	1,648	2,114
Phillips	5,642	3,161	6,018	3,154
Pike	1,310	2,013	1,604	2,275
Poinsett	4,069	3,555	4,102	2,988
Polk	2,473	5,192	2,315	4,600
Pope	7,100	13,614	6,669	11,244
Prairie	1,562	2,030	1,563	1,862
Pulaski	84,532	67,903	68,320	55,866
Randolph	3,412	3,158	3,019	2,673
St. Francis	5,684	3,815	4,986	3,414
Saline	14,153	24,864	12,700	18,617
Scott	1,473	2,514	1,444	2,399
Searcy	1,370	2,565	1,229	2,610
Sebastian	16,479	27,303	15,555	23,483
Sevier	2,035	2,516	2,095	2,111
Sharp	3,265	4,097	3,236	3,698
Stone	2,255	3,188	2,043	2,623
Union	7,071	10,502	6,261	8,647
Van Buren	3,310	3,988	3,202	3,485
Washington	27,597	35,726	21,425	28,231
White	9,129	17,001	8,342	13,170
Woodruff	1,972	1,021	1,699	898
Yell	2,913	3,678	3,062	3,223
Totals	**469,953**	**572,898**	**422,768**	**472,940**

Arkansas Vote Since 1948

1948: Truman, D., 149,659; Dewey, R., 50,959; Thurmond, States' Rights, 40,068; Thomas, Soc., 1,037; Wallace, Prog., 751; Watson, Proh., 1.
1952: Stevenson, D., 226,300; Eisenhower, R., 177,155; Hamblen, Proh., 886; MacArthur, Christian Nat., 458; Hass, Soc. Labor, 1.
1956: Stevenson, D., 213,277; Eisenhower, R., 186,287; Andrews, Ind., 7,008.
1960: Kennedy, D., 215,049; Nixon, R., 184,508; Natl. States' Rights, 28,952.
1964: Johnson, D., 314,197; Goldwater, R., 243,264; Kasper, Natl. States' Rights, 2,965.
1968: Wallace, 3rd Party, 235,627; Nixon, R., 189,062; Humphrey, D., 184,901.
1972: Nixon, R., 445,751; McGovern, D., 198,899; Schmitz, Amer., 3,016.
1976: Carter, D., 498,604; Ford, R., 267,903; McCarthy, Ind., 639; Anderson, Amer., 389.
1980: Reagan, R., 403,164; Carter, D., 398,041; Anderson, Ind., 22,468; Clark, Libertarian, 8,970; Commoner, Citizens, 2,345; Bubar, Statesman, 1,350; Hall, Com., 1,244.
1984: Reagan, R., 534,774; Mondale, D., 338,646; Bergland, Libertarian, 2,220.
1988: Bush, R., 466,578; Dukakis, D., 349,237; Duke, Chr. Pop., 5,146; Paul, Lib., 3,297.
1992: Clinton, D., 505,823; Bush, R., 337,324; Perot, Ind., 99,132; Phillips, U.S. Taxpayers, 1,437; Marrou, Libertarian, 1,261; Fulani, New Alliance, 1,022.
1996: Clinton, D., 475,171; Dole, R., 325,416; Perot, Ref., 69,884; Nader, Ind., 3,649; Browne, Ind., 3,076; Phillips, Ind., 2,065; Forbes, Ind., 932; Collins, Ind., 823; Masters, Ind., 749; Moorehead, Ind., 747; Hagelin, Ind., 729; Hollis, Ind., 538; Dodge, Ind., 483.
2000: Bush, R., 472,940; Gore, D., 422,768; Nader, Green, 13,421; Buchanan, Reform, 7,358; Browne, Libertarian, 2,781; Phillips, Constitution, 1,415; Hagelin, Natural Law, 1,098.
2004: Bush, R., 572,898; Kerry, D., 469,953; Nader, Populist, 6,171; Badnarik, Libertarian, 2,352; Peroutka, Constitution, 2,083; Cobb, Green, 1,488.

California

County	2004 Kerry (D)	2004 Bush (R)	2000 Gore (D)	2000 Bush (R)
Alameda	422,585	130,911	342,889	119,279
Alpine	373	311	265	281
Amador	6,541	11,107	5,906	8,766
Butte	42,448	51,662	31,338	45,584
Calaveras	8,286	13,601	7,093	10,599
Colusa	1,947	4,142	1,745	3,629
Contra Costa	257,254	150,608	224,338	141,373
Del Norte	3,892	5,356	3,117	4,526
El Dorado	32,242	52,878	26,220	42,045
Fresno	103,154	141,988	95,059	117,342
Glenn	2,995	6,308	2,498	5,795
Humboldt	37,988	25,714	24,851	23,219
Imperial	17,964	15,890	15,489	12,524
Inyo	3,350	5,091	2,652	4,713
Kern	68,603	140,417	66,003	110,663
Kings	10,833	21,003	11,041	16,377
Lake	13,141	11,093	10,717	8,699
Lassen	3,158	8,126	2,982	7,080
Los Angeles	1,907,736	1,076,225	1,710,505	871,930
Madera	13,481	24,871	11,650	20,283
Marin	99,070	34,378	79,135	34,872
Mariposa	3,251	5,215	2,816	4,727
Mendocino	24,385	12,955	16,634	12,272
Merced	24,491	32,773	22,726	26,102
Modoc	1,149	3,235	945	2,969
Mono	2,628	2,621	1,788	2,296
Monterey	75,241	47,838	67,618	43,761
Napa	33,666	22,059	28,097	20,633
Nevada	24,220	28,790	17,670	25,998
Orange	419,239	641,832	391,819	541,299
Placer	55,573	95,969	42,449	69,835
Plumas	4,129	6,905	3,458	6,343
Riverside	228,806	322,473	202,576	231,955
Sacramento	236,657	235,539	212,792	195,619
San Benito	9,851	8,698	9,131	7,015
San Bernardino	227,789	289,306	214,749	221,757
San Diego	526,437	596,033	437,666	475,736
San Francisco	296,772	54,355	241,578	51,496
San Joaquin	87,012	100,978	79,776	81,773
San Luis Obispo	58,742	67,995	44,526	56,859
San Mateo	197,922	83,315	166,757	80,296
Santa Barbara	90,314	76,806	73,411	71,493
Santa Clara	386,100	209,094	332,490	188,750
Santa Cruz	89,102	30,354	66,618	29,627
Shasta	24,339	52,249	20,127	43,278
Sierra	646	1,249	540	1,172
Siskiyou	7,880	12,673	6,323	12,198
Solano	85,096	62,301	75,116	51,604
Sonoma	148,261	68,204	117,295	63,529
Stanislaus	58,829	85,407	56,448	67,188
Sutter	9,602	20,254	8,416	17,350
Tehama	7,504	15,572	6,507	13,270
Trinity	2,782	3,560	1,932	3,340
Tulare	32,494	65,399	33,006	54,070
Tuolumne	10,104	15,745	9,359	13,172
Ventura	148,859	160,314	133,258	136,173
Yolo	42,885	28,005	33,747	23,057
Yuba	5,687	12,076	5,546	9,838
Totals	**6,745,485**	**5,509,826**	**5,861,203**	**4,567,429**

California Vote Since 1948

1948: Truman, D., 1,913,134; Dewey, R., 1,895,269; Wallace, Prog., 190,381; Watson, Proh., 16,926; Thomas, Soc., 3,459; Thurmond, States' Rights, 1,228; Teichert, Soc. Labor, 195; Dobbs, Soc. Workers, 133.

1952: Eisenhower, R., 2,897,310; Stevenson, D., 2,197,548; Hallinan, Prog., 24,106; Hamblen, Proh., 15,653; MacArthur, (Tenny Ticket), 3,326; Hass, Soc. Labor, 273; Hoopes, Soc., 206; (Kellems Ticket) 178; scattered, 3,249.

1956: Eisenhower, R., 3,027,668; Stevenson, D., 2,420,136; Holtwick, Proh., 11,119; Andrews, Constitution, 6,087; Hass, Soc. Labor, 300; Hoopes, Soc., 123; Dobbs, Soc. Workers, 96; Smith, Christian Natl., 8.

1960: Nixon, R., 3,259,722; Kennedy, D., 3,224,099; Decker, Proh., 21,706; Hass, Soc. Labor, 1,051.

1964: Johnson, D., 4,171,877; Goldwater, R., 2,879,108; Hass, Soc. Labor, 489; DeBerry, Soc. Workers, 378; Munn, Proh., 305; Hensley, Universal, 19.

1968: Nixon, R., 3,467,664; Humphrey, D., 3,244,318; Wallace, 3rd Party, 487,270; Peace and Freedom, 27,707; McCarthy, Alternative, 20,721; Gregory, write-in, 3,230; Blomen, Soc. Labor, 341; Mitchell, Com., 260; Munn, Proh., 59; Soeters, Defense, 17.

1972: Nixon, R., 4,602,096; McGovern, D., 3,475,847; Schmitz, Amer., 232,554; Spock, Peace and Freedom, 55,167; Hospers, Libertarian, 980; Jenness, Soc. Workers, 574; Hall, Com., 373; Fisher, Soc. Labor, 197; Munn, Proh., 53; Green, Universal, 21.

1976: Ford, R., 3,882,244; Carter, D., 3,742,284; write-in, McCarthy, 58,412; MacBride, Libertarian, 56,388; Maddox, Amer. Ind., 51,098; Wright, People's, 41,731; Camejo, Soc. Workers, 17,259; Hall, Com., 12,766; write-in, 4,935.

1980: Reagan, Rep. 4,524,858; Carter, Dem., 3,083,661; Anderson, Ind., 739,833; Clark, Libertarian, 148,434; Commoner, Ind., 61,063; Smith, Peace and Freedom, 18,116; Rarick, Amer. Ind., 9,856.

1984: Reagan, Rep. 5,305,410; Mondale, D., 3,815,947; Bergland, Libertarian, 48,400.

1988: Bush, R., 5,054,917; Dukakis, D., 4,702,233; Paul, Lib., 70,105; Fulani, Ind., 31,181.

1992: Clinton, D., 5,121,325; Bush, R., 3,630,575; Perot, Ind., 2,296,006; Marrou, Libertarian, 48,139; Daniels, Ind., 18,597; Phillips, U.S. Taxpayers, 12,711.

1996: Clinton, D., 5,119,835; Dole, R., 3,828,380; Perot, Ref., 697,847; Nader, Green, 237,016; Browne, Libertarian, 73,600; Feinland, Peace & Freedom, 25,332; Phillips, Amer. Ind., 21,202; Hagelin, Natural Law, 15,403.

2000: Gore, D., 5,861,203; Bush, R., 4,567,429; Nader, Green, 418,707; Browne, Libertarian, 45,520; Buchanan, Reform, 44,987; Phillips, Amer. Ind., 17,042; Hagelin, Natural Law, 10,934.

2004: Kerry, D., 6,745,485; Bush, R., 5,509,826; Badnarik, Libertarian, 50,165; Cobb, Green, 40,771; Peltier, Peace & Freedom, 27,607; Peroutka, Amer. Ind., 26,645.

Colorado

County	2004 Kerry (D)	2004 Bush (R)	2000 Gore (D)	2000 Bush (R)
Adams	69,122	65,912	54,132	47,561
Alamosa	3,017	3,179	2,455	2,857
Arapahoe	110,262	119,475	82,614	97,768
Archuleta	2,141	3,601	1,432	2,988
Baca	483	1,680	531	1,663
Bent	785	1,338	783	1,096
Boulder	105,564	51,586	69,983	50,873
Broomfield[1]	10,935	12,007	NA	NA
Chaffee	3,766	4,875	2,768	4,300
Cheyenne	198	923	209	957
Clear Creek	2,989	2,522	2,188	2,247
Conejos	1,894	1,864	1,749	1,772
Costilla	1,170	566	1,054	504
Crowley	478	1,006	511	855
Custer	739	1,657	507	1,451
Delta	4,224	9,722	3,264	8,372
Denver	166,135	69,903	122,693	61,224
Dolores	333	785	293	741
Douglas	39,661	80,651	27,076	56,007
Eagle	9,744	8,533	6,772	7,165
Elbert	2,834	8,389	2,326	6,151
El Paso	77,648	161,361	61,799	128,294
Fremont	5,933	12,313	5,293	9,914
Garfield	9,228	11,123	6,087	9,103
Gilpin	1,807	1,329	1,099	1,006
Grand	3,243	4,260	2,308	3,570
Gunnison	4,782	3,479	3,059	3,128
Hinsdale	236	355	188	316
Huerfano	1,663	1,700	1,495	1,466
Jackson	210	710	173	682
Jefferson	126,558	140,644	100,970	120,138
Kiowa	172	712	211	728
Kit Carson	729	2,721	809	2,542
Lake	1,623	1,261	1,296	1,056
La Plata	13,409	11,704	7,864	9,993
Larimer	68,266	75,884	46,055	62,429
Las Animas	3,300	3,196	3,243	2,569
Lincoln	503	1,819	510	1,630
Logan	2,491	6,168	2,296	5,531
Mesa	19,564	41,539	15,465	32,396
Mineral	227	383	168	294
Moffat	1,355	4,247	1,223	3,840
Montezuma	3,867	6,988	2,556	6,158
Montrose	4,776	11,218	4,041	9,266
Morgan	3,039	6,787	2,885	5,722
Otero	3,164	4,947	2,963	4,082
Ouray	1,278	1,402	705	1,279
Park	3,445	4,781	2,393	3,677
Phillips	582	1,717	564	1,576
Pitkin	6,335	2,784	4,137	2,565
Prowers	1,308	3,392	1,361	3,026
Pueblo	35,369	31,117	28,888	22,827
Rio Blanco	566	2,403	543	2,185
Rio Grande	2,006	3,448	1,707	3,111
Routt	6,392	5,199	4,208	4,472
Saguache	1,594	1,163	1,145	1,078
San Juan	253	216	149	210
San Miguel	2,876	1,079	1,598	1,043
Sedgwick	374	971	384	877
Summit	8,144	5,370	5,304	4,497
Teller	3,556	8,094	2,750	6,477
Washington	455	2,050	477	1,878
Weld	31,868	55,591	23,436	37,409
Yuma	1,064	3,456	1,082	3,156
Totals	**1,001,732**	**1,101,255**	**738,227**	**883,748**

(1) City of Broomfield organized as a county in 2001; before that, the city fell across portions of 4 counties.

Colorado Vote Since 1948

1948: Truman, D., 267,288; Dewey, R., 239,714; Wallace, Prog., 6,115; Thomas, Soc., 1,678; Dobbs, Soc. Workers, 228; Teichert, Soc. Labor, 214.
1952: Eisenhower, R., 379,782; Stevenson, D., 245,504; MacArthur, Constitution, 2,181; Hallinan, Prog., 1,919; Hoopes, Soc., 365; Hass, Soc. Labor, 352.
1956: Eisenhower, R., 394,479; Stevenson, D., 263,997; Hass, Soc. Lab., 3,308; Andrews, Ind., 759; Hoopes, Soc., 531.
1960: Nixon, R., 402,242; Kennedy, D., 330,629; Hass, Soc. Labor, 2,803; Dobbs, Soc. Workers, 572.
1964: Johnson, D., 476,024; Goldwater, R., 296,767; DeBerry, Soc. Workers, 2,537; Munn, Proh., 1,356; Hass, Soc. Labor, 302.
1968: Nixon, R., 409,345; Humphrey, D., 335,174; Wallace, 3rd Party, 60,813; Blomen, Soc. Labor, 3,016; Gregory, New-party, 1,393; Munn, Proh., 275; Halstead, Soc. Workers, 235.
1972: Nixon, R., 597,189; McGovern, D., 329,980; Schmitz, Amer., 17,269; Fisher, Soc. Labor, 4,361; Spock, Peoples, 2,403; Hospers, Libertarian, 1,111; Jenness, Soc. Workers, 555; Munn, Proh., 467; Hall, Com., 432.
1976: Ford, R., 584,367; Carter, D., 460,353; McCarthy, Ind., 26,107; MacBride, Libertarian, 5,330; Bubar, Proh., 2,882.
1980: Reagan, R., 652,264; Carter, D., 367,973; Anderson, Ind., 130,633; Clark, Libertarian, 25,744; Commoner, Citizens, 5,614; Bubar, Statesman, 1,180; Pulley, Socialist, 520; Hall, Com., 487.
1984: Reagan, R., 821,817; Mondale, D., 454,975; Bergland, Libertarian, 11,257.
1988: Bush, R., 728,177; Dukakis, D., 621,453; Paul, Lib., 15,482; Dodge, Proh., 4,604.
1992: Clinton, D., 629,681; Bush, R., 562,850; Perot, Ind., 366,010; Marrou, Libertarian, 8,669; Fulani, New Alliance, 1,608.
1996: Dole, R., 691,848; Clinton, D., 671,152; Perot, Ref., 99,629; Nader, Green, 25,070; Browne, Libertarian, 12,392; Phillips, Amer. Constitution, 2,813; Collins, Ind., 2,809; Hagelin, Natural Law, 2,547; Hollis, Soc., 669; Moorehead, Workers World, 599; Templin, Amer., 557; Dodge, Proh., 375; Harris, Soc. Workers, 244.
2000: Bush, R., 883,748; Gore, Dem, 738,227; Nader, Green, 91,434; Browne, Libertarian, 12,799; Buchanan, Reform, 10,465; Hagelin, Reform, 2,240; Phillips, Amer. Constitution, 1,319; McReynolds, Soc., 712; Harris, Soc. Workers, 216; Dodge, Proh., 208.
2004: Bush, R., 1,101,255; Kerry, D., 1,001,732; Nader, Ref., 12,718; Badnarik, Libertarian, 7,664; Peroutka, Amer. Const., 2,562; Cobb, Green, 1,591; Andress, Ind., 804; Amondson, Concerns of People, 378; Van Auken, Soc. Equal., 329; Harris, Soc. Wkrs., 241; Brown, Soc., 216; Dodge, Prohib., 140.

Connecticut

	2004		2000	
City	**Kerry (D)**	**Bush (R)**	**Gore (D)**	**Bush (R)**
Bridgeport	26,280	10,326	24,303	7,406
Bristol	14,201	10,619	14,665	7,948
Danbury	13,477	12,399	12,987	9,371
Fairfield	15,068	14,706	14,210	13,042
Greenwich	14,334	15,830	12,780	14,905
Hartford	22,595	4,623	21,445	3,095
New Britain	14,122	6,560	13,913	5,059
New Haven	30,979	7,175	28,145	5,160
Norwalk	20,615	14,201	19,293	11,519
Stamford	27,588	18,866	27,430	15,159
Waterbury	16,122	15,961	18,069	12,415
West Hartford	21,612	11,641	21,069	10,447
Other	620,495	550,919	587,706	445,568
Totals	**857,488**	**693,826**	**816,015**	**561,094**

Connecticut Vote Since 1948

1948: Dewey, R., 437,754; Truman, D., 423,297; Wallace, Prog., 13,713; Thomas, Soc., 6,964; Teichert, Soc. Labor, 1,184; Dobbs, Soc. Workers, 606.
1952: Eisenhower, R., 611,012; Stevenson, D., 481,649; Hoopes, Soc., 2,244; Hallinan, Peoples, 1,466; Hass, Soc. Labor, 535; write-in, 5.
1956: Eisenhower, R., 711,837; Stevenson, D., 405,079; scattered, 205.
1960: Kennedy, D., 657,055; Nixon, R., 565,813.
1964: Johnson, D., 826,269; Goldwater, R., 390,996; scattered, 1,313.
1968: Humphrey, D., 621,561; Nixon, R., 556,721; Wallace, 3rd Party, 76,650; scattered, 1,300.
1972: Nixon, R., 810,763; McGovern, D., 555,498; Schmitz, Amer., 17,239; scattered, 777.
1976: Ford, R., 719,261; Carter, D., 647,895; Maddox, George Wallace Party, 7,101; LaRouche, U.S. Labor, 1,789.
1980: Reagan, R., 677,210; Carter, D., 541,732; Anderson, Ind., 171,807; Clark, Libertarian, 8,570; Commoner, Citizens, 6,130; scattered, 836.
1984: Reagan, R., 890,877; Mondale, D., 569,597.
1988: Bush, R., 750,241; Dukakis, D., 676,584; Paul, Lib., 14,071; Fulani, New Alliance, 2,491.
1992: Clinton, D., 682,318; Bush, R., 578,313; Perot, Ind., 348,771; Marrou, Libertarian, 5,391; Fulani, New Alliance, 1,363.
1996: Clinton, D., 735,740; Dole, R., 483,109; Perot, Ref., 139,523; Nader, Green, 24,321; Browne, Libertarian, 5,788; Phillips, Concerned Citizens, 2,425; Hagelin, Natural Law, 1,703.
2000: Gore, D., 816,015; Bush, R., 561,094; Nader, Green, 64,452; Phillips, Concerned Citizens, 9,695; Buchanan, Reform, 4,731; Browne, Libertarian, 3,484.
2004: Kerry, D., 857,488; Bush, R., 693,826; Nader, Petitioning Cand., 12,969; Cobb, Green, 9,564; Badnarik, Libertarian, 3,367; Peroutka, Concerned Citizens, 1,543.

Delaware

	2004		2000	
County	**Kerry (D)**	**Bush (R)**	**Gore (D)**	**Bush (R)**
Kent	23,875	31,578	22,790	24,081
New Castle	146,179	93,079	127,539	78,587
Sussex	30,098	47,003	29,739	34,620
Totals	**200,152**	**171,660**	**180,068**	**137,288**

Delaware Vote Since 1948

1948: Dewey, R., 69,688; Truman, D., 67,813; Wallace, Prog., 1,050; Watson, Proh., 343; Thomas, Soc., 250; Teichert, Soc. Labor, 29.
1952: Eisenhower, R., 90,059; Stevenson, D., 83,315; Hass, Soc. Lab., 242; Hamblen, Proh., 234; Hallinan, Prog., 155; Hoopes, Soc., 20.
1956: Eisenhower, R., 98,057; Stevenson, D., 79,421; Oltwick, Proh., 400; Hass, Soc. Labor, 110.
1960: Kennedy, D., 99,590; Nixon, R., 96,373; Faubus, States' Rights, 354; Decker, Proh., 284; Hass, Soc. Labor, 82.
1964: Johnson, D., 122,704; Goldwater, R., 78,078; Munn, Proh., 425; Hass, Soc. Labor, 113.
1968: Nixon, R., 96,714; Humphrey, D., 89,194; Wallace, 3rd Party, 28,459.
1972: Nixon, R., 140,357; McGovern, D., 92,283; Schmitz, Amer., 2,638; Munn, Proh., 238.
1976: Carter, D., 122,596; Ford, R., 109,831; McCarthy, non-partisan, 2,437; Anderson, Amer., 645; LaRouche, U.S. Labor, 136; Bubar, Proh., 103; Levin, Soc. Labor, 86.
1980: Reagan, R., 111,252; Carter, D., 105,754; Anderson, Ind., 16,288; Clark, Libertarian, 1,974; Greaves, Amer., 400.
1984: Reagan, R., 152,190; Mondale, D., 101,656; Bergland, Libertarian, 268.
1988: Bush, R., 139,639; Dukakis, D., 108,647; Paul, Lib., 1,162; Fulani, New Alliance, 443.
1992: Clinton, D., 126,054; Bush, R., 102,313; Perot, Ind., 59,213; Fulani, New Alliance, 1,105.
1996: Clinton, D., 140,355; Dole, R., 99,062; Perot, Ind. (Ref.), 28,719; Browne, Libertarian, 2,052; Phillips, Taxpayers, 348; Hagelin, Natural Law, 274.
2000: Gore, D., 180,068; Bush, R., 137,288; Nader, Green, 8,307; Buchanan, Reform, 777; Browne, Libertarian, 774; Phillips, Constitution, 208; Hagelin, Natural Law, 107.
2004: Kerry, D., 200,152; Bush, R., 171,660; Nader, Ind., 2,153; Badnarik, Libertarian, 586; Peroutka, Constitution, 289; Cobb, Green, 250; Brown, Nat. Law, 100.

District of Columbia

	2004		2000	
	Kerry (D)	**Bush (R)**	**Gore (D)**	**Bush (R)**
Totals	**202,970**	**21,256**	**171,923**	**18,073**

District of Columbia Vote Since 1964

1964: Johnson, D., 169,796; Goldwater, R., 28,801.
1968: Humphrey, D., 139, 566; Nixon, R., 31,012.
1972: McGovern, D., 127,627; Nixon, R., 35,226; Reed, Soc. Workers, 316; Hall, Com., 252.
1976: Carter, D., 137,818; Ford, R., 27,873; Camejo, Soc. Workers, 545; MacBride, Libertarian, 274; Hall, Com., 219; LaRouche, U.S. Labor, 157.
1980: Carter, D., 130,231; Reagan, R., 23,313; Anderson, Ind., 16,131; Commoner, Citizens, 1,826; Clark, Libertarian, 1,104; Hall, Com., 369; DeBerry, Soc. Workers, 173; Griswold, Workers World, 52; write-in, 690.
1984: Mondale, D., 180,408; Reagan, R., 29,009; Bergland, Libertarian, 279.
1988: Dukakis, D., 159,407; Bush, R., 27,590; Fulani, New Alliance, 2,901; Paul, Lib., 554.
1992: Clinton, D., 192,619; Bush, R., 20,698; Perot, Ind., 9,681; Fulani, New Alliance, 1,459; Daniels, Ind., 1,186.
1996: Clinton, D., 158,220; Dole, R., 17,339; Nader, Green, 4,780; Perot, Ref., 3,611; Browne, Libertarian, 588; Hagelin, Natural Law, 283; Harris, Soc. Workers, 257.
2000: Gore, D., 171,923; Bush, R., 18,073; Nader, Green, 10,576; Browne, Libertarian, 669; Harris, Soc. Workers, 114.
2004: Kerry, D., 202,970; Bush, R., 21,256; Nader, Ind., 1,485; Cobb, DC Statehd Green Pty., 737; Badnarik, Libertarian, 502; Harris, Soc. Wkrs., 130.

Florida

	2004		2000	
County	**Kerry (D)**	**Bush (R)**	**Gore (D)**	**Bush (R)**
Alachua	62,504	47,762	47,380	34,135
Baker	2,180	7,738	2,392	5,611
Bay	21,068	53,404	18,873	38,682
Bradford	3,244	7,557	3,075	5,416
Brevard	110,309	153,068	97,341	115,253
Broward	453,873	244,674	387,760	177,939
Calhoun	2,116	3,782	2,156	2,873
Charlotte	34,256	44,428	29,646	35,428
Citrus	29,277	39,500	25,531	29,801
Clay	18,971	62,078	14,668	41,903
Collier	43,892	83,631	29,939	60,467
Columbia	8,031	16,758	7,049	10,968
De Soto	3,913	5,524	3,321	4,256
Dixie	1,960	4,434	1,827	2,697
Duval	158,610	220,190	108,039	152,460

County	2004 Kerry (D)	2004 Bush (R)	2000 Gore (D)	2000 Bush (R)
Escambia	48,329	93,566	40,990	73,171
Flagler	18,578	19,633	13,897	12,618
Franklin	2,401	3,472	2,047	2,454
Gadsden	14,629	6,253	9,736	4,770
Gilchrist	2,017	4,936	1,910	3,300
Glades	1,718	2,443	1,442	1,841
Gulf	2,407	4,805	2,398	3,553
Hamilton	2,260	2,792	1,723	2,147
Hardee	2,149	5,049	2,342	3,765
Hendry	3,960	5,757	3,240	4,747
Hernando	37,187	42,635	32,648	30,658
Highlands	15,347	25,878	14,169	20,207
Hillsborough	214,132	245,576	169,576	180,794
Holmes	1,810	6,412	2,177	5,012
Indian River	23,956	36,938	19,769	28,639
Jackson	7,555	12,122	6,870	9,139
Jefferson	4,135	3,298	3,041	2,478
Lafayette	845	2,460	789	1,670
Lake	48,221	74,389	36,571	50,010
Lee	93,860	144,176	73,571	106,151
Leon	83,873	51,615	61,444	39,073
Levy	6,074	10,410	5,398	6,863
Liberty	1,070	1,927	1,017	1,317
Madison	4,050	4,191	3,015	3,038
Manatee	61,262	81,318	49,226	58,023
Marion	57,271	81,283	44,674	55,146
Martin	30,208	41,362	26,621	33,972
Miami-Dade	409,732	361,095	328,867	289,574
Monroe	19,654	19,467	16,487	16,063
Nassau	8,573	23,783	6,955	16,408
Okaloosa	19,368	69,693	16,989	52,186
Okeechobee	5,153	6,978	4,589	5,057
Orange	193,354	192,539	140,236	134,531
Osceola	38,633	43,117	28,187	26,237
Palm Beach	328,687	212,688	269,754	152,964
Pasco	84,749	103,230	69,576	68,607
Pinellas	225,460	225,686	200,657	184,849
Polk	86,009	123,559	75,207	90,310
Putnam	12,412	18,311	12,107	13,457
St. Johns	26,399	59,196	19,509	39,564
St. Lucie	51,835	47,592	41,560	34,705
Santa Rosa	14,659	52,059	12,818	36,339
Sarasota	88,442	104,692	72,869	83,117
Seminole	76,971	108,172	59,227	75,790
Sumter	11,584	19,800	9,637	12,127
Suwannee	4,522	11,153	4,076	8,009
Taylor	3,049	5,467	2,649	4,058
Union	1,251	3,396	1,407	2,332
Volusia	115,519	111,924	97,313	82,368
Wakulla	4,896	6,777	3,838	4,512
Walton	6,213	17,555	5,643	12,186
Washington	2,912	7,369	2,798	4,995
Totals	**3,583,544**	**3,964,522**	**2,912,253**	**2,912,790**

Florida Vote Since 1948

1948: Truman, D., 281,988; Dewey, R., 194,280; Thurmond, States' Rights, 89,755; Wallace, Prog., 11,620.

1952: Eisenhower, R., 544,036; Stevenson, D., 444,950; scattered, 351.

1956: Eisenhower, R., 643,849; Stevenson, D., 480,371.

1960: Nixon, R., 795,476; Kennedy, D., 748,700.

1964: Johnson, D., 948,540; Goldwater, R., 905,941.

1968: Nixon, R., 886,804; Humphrey, D., 676,794; Wallace, 3rd Party, 624,207.

1972: Nixon, R., 1,857,759; McGovern, D., 718,117; scattered, 7,407.

1976: Carter, D., 1,636,000; Ford, R., 1,469,531; McCarthy, Ind., 23,643; Anderson, Amer., 21,325.

1980: Reagan, R., 2,046,951; Carter, D., 1,419,475; Anderson, Ind., 189,692; Clark, Libertarian, 30,524; write-in, 285.

1984: Reagan, R., 2,728,775; Mondale, D., 1,448,344.

1988: Bush, R., 2,616,597; Dukakis, D., 1,655,851; Paul, Lib., 19,796, Fulani, New Alliance, 6,655.

1992: Bush, R., 2,171,781; Clinton, D., 2,071,651; Perot, Ind., 1,052,481; Marrou, Libertarian, 15,068.

1996: Clinton, D., 2,545,968; Dole, R., 2,243,324; Perot, Ref., 483,776; Browne, Libertarian, 23,312.

2000: Bush, R., 2,912,790; Gore, D., 2,912,253; Nader, Green, 97,488; Buchanan, Reform, 17,484; Browne, Libertarian, 16,415; Hagelin, Nat. Law, 2,281; Moorehead, Wkrs. World, 1,804; Phillips, Constit., 1,371; McReynolds, Soc., 622; Harris, Soc. Wkrs., 562.

2004: Bush, R., 3,964,522; Kerry, D., 3,583,544; Nader, Ref., 32,971; Badnarik, Libertarian, 11,996; Peroutka, Constitution, 6,626; Cobb, Green, 3,917; Brown, Soc., 3,502; Harris, Soc. Wkrs., 2,732.

Georgia

County	2004 Kerry (D)	2004 Bush (R)	2000 Gore (D)	2000 Bush (R)
Appling	1,848	4,494	2,093	3,940
Atkinson	799	1,666	821	1,228
Bacon	930	2,853	956	2,010
Baker	936	821	893	615
Baldwin	6,775	7,709	5,893	6,041
Banks	1,149	4,410	1,220	3,202
Barrow	4,095	13,520	3,657	7,925
Bartow	7,741	22,311	7,508	14,720
Ben Hill	2,180	3,331	2,234	2,381
Berrien	1,638	3,917	1,640	2,718
Bibb	29,322	28,107	24,996	24,071
Bleckley	1,281	3,167	1,273	2,436
Brantley	1,258	4,333	1,372	3,118
Brooks	2,193	2,912	2,096	2,406
Bryan	2,590	7,363	2,172	4,835
Bulloch	6,840	12,252	5,561	8,990
Burke	4,213	4,232	3,720	3,381
Butts	2,572	5,119	2,281	3,198
Calhoun	1,119	890	1,107	768
Camden	4,637	9,488	3,636	6,371
Candler	1,096	2,048	1,053	1,643
Carroll	10,224	24,837	8,752	16,326
Catoosa	5,807	16,406	5,470	12,033
Charlton	1,064	2,311	1,015	1,770
Chatham	45,630	45,484	37,590	37,847
Chattahoo-chee	773	905	600	590
Chattooga	2,809	4,992	2,729	3,640
Cherokee	14,824	58,238	12,295	38,033
Clarke	21,718	15,052	15,167	11,850
Clay	798	509	821	448
Clayton	56,113	23,106	40,042	19,966
Clinch	750	1,501	816	1,091
Cobb	103,955	173,467	86,676	140,494
Coffee	3,979	8,306	3,593	5,756
Colquitt	3,378	8,296	3,297	6,589
Columbia	11,442	35,549	8,969	26,660
Cook	1,733	3,065	1,639	2,279
Coweta	10,647	31,682	9,056	21,327
Crawford	1,552	2,830	1,513	1,987
Crisp	2,357	3,865	2,268	3,285
Dade	1,823	4,368	1,628	3,333
Dawson	1,407	6,649	1,458	4,210
Decatur	3,577	5,348	3,398	4,187
De Kalb	200,787	73,570	154,509	58,807
Dodge	2,384	4,584	2,326	3,472
Dooly	1,973	1,853	1,901	1,588
Dougherty	19,805	13,711	16,650	12,248
Douglas	15,997	25,846	11,162	18,893
Early	1,701	2,495	1,622	1,938
Echols	231	757	272	614
Effingham	3,613	12,503	3,232	7,326
Elbert	2,984	4,626	2,527	3,262
Emanuel	2,774	4,666	2,835	3,343
Evans	1,213	2,291	1,217	1,841
Fannin	2,727	6,862	2,736	5,463
Fayette	14,887	37,346	11,912	29,338
Floyd	10,038	21,400	10,282	16,194
Forsyth	9,201	47,267	6,694	27,769
Franklin	2,245	5,218	2,040	3,659
Fulton	199,436	134,372	152,039	104,870
Gilmer	2,510	7,414	2,230	4,941
Glascock	250	1,016	249	763
Glynn	8,962	18,608	7,778	14,346
Gordon	4,028	11,671	4,032	7,944
Grady	3,092	5,068	2,721	3,894
Greene	2,774	4,069	2,137	2,980
Gwinnett	81,708	160,445	61,434	121,756
Habersham	2,750	10,434	2,530	6,964
Hall	10,514	38,883	10,259	26,841
Hancock	2,715	822	2,414	662
Haralson	2,434	7,703	2,869	5,153
Harris	3,400	8,878	2,912	5,554
Hart	3,479	5,500	3,192	4,242
Heard	1,148	2,788	1,178	1,947
Henry	21,096	42,759	11,971	25,815
Houston	15,054	29,862	13,301	23,174
Irwin	1,051	2,347	1,105	1,720
Jackson	3,468	12,611	3,420	7,878
Jasper	1,558	3,157	1,558	2,298
Jeff Davis	1,277	3,549	1,379	2,797
Jefferson	3,447	3,066	2,973	2,559
Jenkins	1,494	1,898	1,250	1,317
Johnson	1,263	2,279	1,065	1,797
Jones	3,855	6,939	3,102	4,850
Lamar	2,432	4,027	2,194	2,912
Lanier	931	1,641	832	1,048
Laurens	6,281	10,883	5,724	8,133
Lee	2,182	8,201	1,936	5,872

County	2004 Kerry (D)	2004 Bush (R)	2000 Gore (D)	2000 Bush (R)
Liberty	6,619	6,131	5,347	4,455
Lincoln	1,337	2,309	1,275	1,807
Long	1,033	1,994	975	1,320
Lowndes	12,516	18,981	10,616	14,462
Lumpkin	2,091	6,690	2,121	4,427
Macon	2,906	1,851	2,757	1,566
Madison	2,527	7,254	2,285	5,529
Marion	1,275	1,670	982	1,187
McDuffie	2,899	4,846	2,580	3,926
McIntosh	2,523	2,837	2,047	1,766
Meriwether	3,709	4,402	3,441	3,162
Miller	736	1,694	783	1,349
Mitchell	3,360	3,885	2,971	2,790
Monroe	3,216	6,522	2,839	4,561
Montgomery	1,007	2,150	1,013	1,465
Morgan	2,304	4,902	2,238	3,524
Murray	2,899	7,745	2,684	5,539
Muscogee	32,867	30,850	28,193	23,479
Newton	10,939	18,095	6,703	11,127
Oconee	3,789	10,276	3,184	7,611
Oglethorpe	1,899	3,688	1,519	2,706
Paulding	9,420	30,843	6,743	16,881
Peach	3,961	4,554	3,540	3,525
Pickens	2,444	8,115	2,489	5,488
Pierce	1,234	4,680	1,300	3,348
Pike	1,506	5,193	1,413	3,358
Polk	3,868	8,467	4,112	5,841
Pulaski	1,294	2,202	1,390	1,922
Putnam	2,880	5,188	2,612	3,596
Quitman	543	409	542	348
Rabun	1,918	4,650	1,776	3,451
Randolph	1,612	1,418	1,381	1,174
Richmond	39,262	29,764	31,413	25,485
Rockdale	12,136	18,856	8,295	15,440
Schley	464	1,063	460	706
Screven	2,534	3,360	2,233	2,461
Seminole	1,278	1,977	1,313	1,537
Spalding	7,460	13,461	5,831	9,271
Stephens	2,714	6,904	2,869	5,370
Stewart	1,220	797	1,267	675
Sumter	5,562	5,688	4,748	4,847
Talbot	1,830	1,103	1,662	844
Taliaferro	612	335	556	271
Tattnall	1,787	4,657	1,963	3,597
Taylor	1,458	1,912	1,340	1,412
Telfair	1,590	2,171	1,777	1,693
Terrell	1,951	1,859	1,584	1,504
Thomas	5,997	9,659	4,862	7,093
Tift	3,864	8,619	3,547	6,678
Toombs	2,567	6,196	2,643	4,487
Towns	1,430	3,823	1,495	2,902
Treutlen	1,052	1,691	879	1,062
Troup	7,630	14,183	6,379	11,198
Turner	1,135	1,815	1,169	1,258
Twiggs	2,220	2,112	1,977	1,570
Union	2,327	6,847	2,230	4,567
Upson	3,424	6,634	3,158	5,019
Walker	5,986	15,340	6,341	12,326
Walton	5,887	21,594	5,484	12,966
Ware	3,449	7,790	3,480	6,099
Warren	1,360	1,121	1,196	933
Washington	3,733	4,081	3,476	3,162
Wayne	2,683	6,819	2,736	5,219
Webster	515	485	541	359
Wheeler	847	1,192	752	813
White	2,016	7,403	2,014	4,857
Whitfield	6,933	19,297	7,034	15,852
Wilcox	902	1,705	962	1,381
Wilkes	2,028	2,490	1,940	2,044
Wilkinson	2,235	2,261	1,884	1,800
Worth	2,219	5,105	2,214	3,792
Totals	**1,366,149**	**1,914,254**	**1,116,230**	**1,419,720**

Georgia Vote Since 1948

1948: Truman, D., 254,646; Thurmond, States' Rights, 85,055; Dewey, R., 76,691; Wallace, Prog., 1,636; Watson, Proh., 732.

1952: Stevenson, D., 456,823; Eisenhower, R., 198,979; Liberty Party, 1.

1956: Stevenson, D., 444,388; Eisenhower, R., 222,778; Andrews, Ind., write-in, 1,754.

1960: Kennedy, D., 458,638; Nixon, R., 274,472; write-in, 239.

1964: Goldwater, R., 616,600; Johnson, D., 522,557.

1968: Wallace, 3rd Party, 535,550; Nixon, R., 380,111; Humphrey, D., 334,440; write-in, 162.

1972: Nixon, R., 881,496; McGovern, D., 289,529; Schmitz, Amer., 812; scattered, 2,935.

1976: Carter, D., 979,409; Ford, R., 483,743; write-in, 4,306.

1980: Carter, D., 890,955; Reagan, R., 654,168; Anderson, Ind., 36,055; Clark, Libertarian, 15,627.

1984: Reagan, R., 1,068,722; Mondale, D., 706,628.

1988: Bush, R., 1,081,331; Dukakis, D., 714,792; Paul, Lib., 8,435; Fulani, New Alliance, 5,099.

1992: Clinton, D., 1,008,966; Bush, R., 995,252; Perot, Ind., 309,657; Marrou, Libertarian, 7,110.

1996: Dole, R., 1,080,843; Clinton, D., 1,053,849; Perot, Ref., 146,337; Browne, Libertarian, 17,870.

2000: Bush, R., 1,419,720; Gore, D., 1,116,230; Browne, Libertarian, 36,332; Buchanan, Independent, 10,926.

2004: Bush, R., 1,914,254; Kerry, D., 1,366,149; Badnarik, Libertarian, 18,387.

Hawaii

County	2004 Kerry (D)	2004 Bush (R)	2000 Gore (D)	2000 Bush (R)
Hawaii	35,116	22,032	28,670	17,050
Honolulu	152,873	144,232	139,662	101,336
Kauai	14,916	9,740	13,470	6,583
Maui	28,803	18,187	23,484	12,876
Totals	**231,708**	**194,191**	**205,286**	**137,845**

Hawaii Vote Since 1960

1960: Kennedy, D., 92,410; Nixon, R., 92,295.

1964: Johnson, D., 163,249; Goldwater, R., 44,022.

1968: Humphrey, D., 141,324; Nixon, R., 91,425; Wallace, 3rd Party, 3,469.

1972: Nixon, R., 168,865; McGovern, D., 101,409.

1976: Carter, D., 147,375; Ford, R., 140,003; MacBride, Libertarian, 3,923.

1980: Carter, D., 135,879; Reagan, R., 130,112; Anderson, Ind., 32,021; Clark, Libertarian, 3,269; Commoner, Citizens, 1,548; Hall, Com., 458.

1984: Reagan, R., 184,934; Mondale, D., 147,098; Bergland, Libertarian, 2,167.

1988: Dukakis, D., 192,364; Bush, R., 158,625; Paul, Lib., 1,999; Fulani, New Alliance, 1,003.

1992: Clinton, D., 179,310; Bush, R., 136,822; Perot, Ind., 53,003; Gritz, Populist/America First, 1,452; Marrou, Libertarian, 1,119.

1996: Clinton, D., 205,012; Dole, R., 113,943; Perot, Ref., 27,358; Nader, Green, 10,386; Browne, Libertarian, 2,493; Hagelin, Natural Law, 570; Phillips, Taxpayers, 358.

2000: Gore, D., 205,286; Bush, R., 137,845; Nader, Green, 21,623; Browne, Libertarian, 1,477; Buchanan, Reform, 1,071; Phillips, Constitution, 343; Hagelin, Natural Law, 306.

2004: Kerry, D., 231,708; Bush, R., 194,191; Cobb, Green, 1,737; Badnarik, Libertarian, 1,377.

Idaho

County	2004 Kerry (D)	2004 Bush (R)	2000 Gore (D)	2000 Bush (R)
Ada	58,523	94,641	40,650	75,050
Adams	555	1,468	336	1,476
Bannock	12,903	21,479	10,892	18,223
Bear Lake	494	2,506	517	2,296
Benewah	1,148	2,823	895	2,606
Bingham	3,605	12,734	3,310	10,628
Blaine	5,992	4,034	3,748	3,528
Boise	970	2,501	745	2,019
Bonner	6,649	10,697	4,318	8,945
Bonneville	8,356	30,048	7,235	24,988
Boundary	1,268	3,012	832	2,797
Butte	321	1,077	354	1,054
Camas	139	450	113	359
Canyon	13,415	41,599	10,588	30,560
Caribou	491	2,753	475	2,601
Cassia	1,153	6,562	1,087	5,983
Clark	46	302	63	311
Clearwater	1,117	2,839	841	2,885
Custer	559	1,762	416	1,794
Elmore	1,959	6,011	1,840	4,891
Franklin	456	4,527	513	3,594
Fremont	741	4,965	699	4,242
Gem	1,628	5,416	1,346	4,376
Gooding	1,278	3,973	1,282	3,502
Idaho	1,689	6,017	1,187	5,806
Jefferson	1,084	7,703	1,100	6,480
Jerome	1,344	5,177	1,360	4,418
Kootenai	17,584	36,173	13,488	28,162
Latah	8,430	8,686	5,661	8,161
Lemhi	915	3,079	660	2,859
Lewis	440	1,359	335	1,295
Lincoln	466	1,388	437	1,049
Madison	826	10,693	816	7,941
Minidoka	1,331	5,797	1,344	4,907
Nez Perce	6,476	11,009	4,995	10,577
Oneida	304	1,789	307	1,426
Owyhee	685	2,859	623	2,450
Payette	1,848	6,256	1,643	4,961
Power	829	2,105	755	1,872
Shoshone	2,331	2,922	2,225	2,879
Teton	1,416	2,235	720	1,745
Twin Falls	6,458	19,672	5,777	15,794
Valley	1,843	2,863	1,129	2,548
Washington	1,033	3,274	980	2,899
Totals	**181,098**	**409,235**	**138,637**	**336,937**

Idaho Vote Since 1948

1948: Truman, D., 107,370; Dewey, R., 101,514; Wallace, Prog., 4,972; Watson, Proh., 628; Thomas, Soc., 332.
1952: Eisenhower, R., 180,707; Stevenson, D., 95,081; Hallinan, Prog., 443; write-in, 23.
1956: Eisenhower, R., 166,979; Stevenson, D., 105,868; Andrews, Ind., 126; write-in, 16.
1960: Nixon, R., 161,597; Kennedy, D., 138,853.
1964: Johnson, D., 148,920; Goldwater, Rep., 143,557.
1968: Nixon, R., 165,369; Humphrey, D., 89,273; Wallace, 3rd Party, 36,541.
1972: Nixon, R., 199,384; McGovern, D., 80,826; Schmitz, Amer., 28,869; Spock, Peoples, 903.
1976: Ford, R., 204,151; Carter, D., 126,549; Maddox, Amer., 5,935; MacBride, Libertarian, 3,558; LaRouche, U.S. Labor, 739.
1980: Reagan, R., 290,699; Carter, D., 110,192; Anderson, Ind., 27,058; Clark, Libertarian, 8,425; Rarick, Amer., 1,057.
1984: Reagan, R., 297,523; Mondale, D., 108,510; Bergland, Libertarian, 2,823.
1988: Bush, R., 253,881; Dukakis, D., 147,272; Paul, Lib., 5,313; Fulani, Ind., 2,502.
1992: Bush, R., 202,645; Clinton, D., 137,013; Perot, Ind., 130,395; Gritz, Populist/America First, 10,281; Marrou, Libertarian, 1,167.
1996: Dole, R., 256,595; Clinton, D., 165,443; Perot, Ref., 62,518; Browne, Libertarian, 3,325; Phillips, Taxpayers, 2,230; Hagelin, Natural Law, 1,600.
2000: Bush, R., 336,937; Gore, D., 138,637; Buchanan, Reform, 7,615; Browne, Libertarian, 3,488; Phillips, Constitution, 1,469; Hagelin, Natural Law, 1,177.
2004: Bush, R., 409,235; Kerry, D., 181,098; Badnarik, Libertarian, 3,844; Peroutka, Constitution, 3,084.

Illinois

	2004		2000	
County	**Kerry (D)**	**Bush (R)**	**Gore (D)**	**Bush (R)**
Adams	10,511	20,834	12,197	17,331
Alexander	2,016	1,831	2,357	1,588
Bond	3,228	4,068	3,060	3,804
Boone	8,286	11,132	6,481	8,617
Brown	895	1,679	1,077	1,529
Bureau	7,961	9,822	7,754	8,526
Calhoun	1,367	1,317	1,310	1,229
Carroll	3,537	4,534	3,113	3,835
Cass	2,492	3,163	2,789	2,968
Champaign	41,524	39,896	35,515	34,645
Christian	6,112	9,044	6,799	7,537
Clark	2,877	5,082	2,932	4,398
Clay	2,101	4,416	2,212	3,789
Clinton	6,797	10,219	6,436	8,588
Coles	9,566	13,015	8,904	10,495
Cook	1,439,724	597,405	1,280,547	534,542
Crawford	3,194	6,083	3,333	4,974
Cumberland	1,862	3,497	1,870	2,964
De Kalb	19,263	21,095	14,798	17,139
De Witt	2,836	4,920	2,870	3,968
Douglas	2,767	5,702	3,215	4,734
DuPage	180,097	218,902	152,550	201,037
Edgar	3,093	5,258	3,216	4,833
Edwards	930	2,412	978	2,212
Effingham	4,388	11,774	4,225	9,855
Fayette	3,571	5,880	3,886	5,200
Ford	1,912	4,511	2,090	3,889
Franklin	8,816	10,388	10,201	8,490
Fulton	9,080	7,818	8,940	6,936
Gallatin	1,573	1,619	1,878	1,591
Greene	2,457	3,559	2,490	3,129
Grundy	8,463	11,198	7,516	8,709
Hamilton	1,814	2,653	1,943	2,519
Hancock	3,975	5,837	4,256	5,134
Hardin	923	1,501	1,184	1,366
Henderson	2,269	1,857	2,030	1,708
Henry	11,877	13,212	11,921	10,896
Iroquois	3,832	9,914	4,397	8,685
Jackson	14,300	11,190	11,773	9,823
Jasper	1,781	3,529	1,815	3,119
Jefferson	6,713	10,160	6,685	8,362
Jersey	4,597	5,435	4,355	4,699
Jo Daviess	5,311	6,174	4,585	5,304
Johnson	1,813	3,997	1,928	3,285
Kane	73,813	92,065	60,127	76,996
Kankakee	20,003	24,739	19,180	20,049
Kendall	12,497	19,776	8,444	13,688
Knox	13,403	11,111	12,572	9,912
Lake	134,352	139,081	115,058	120,988
LaSalle	24,263	26,101	23,355	21,276
Lawrence	2,518	4,162	2,822	3,594
Lee	6,416	9,307	6,111	8,069
Livingston	5,632	10,316	5,829	9,187
Logan	4,273	9,112	4,600	8,141
Macon	23,341	28,118	24,262	23,830
Macoupin	11,193	11,413	11,015	9,749
Madison	63,399	59,384	59,077	48,821
Marion	7,694	9,413	8,068	8,240
Marshall	2,806	3,734	2,570	3,145
Mason	3,215	3,907	3,192	3,411
Massac	2,805	4,578	2,912	3,676
McDonough	7,119	7,656	6,080	6,465
McHenry	50,330	76,412	40,698	62,112
McLean	29,877	41,276	24,936	34,008
Menard	2,137	4,408	2,164	3,862
Mercer	4,512	4,405	4,400	3,688
Monroe	6,788	9,468	5,797	7,632
Montgomery	5,979	6,851	6,542	6,226
Morgan	5,650	9,392	5,899	8,058
Moultrie	2,388	4,028	2,529	3,058
Ogle	9,018	14,918	7,673	12,325
Peoria	41,121	41,051	38,604	36,398
Perry	4,770	5,589	4,862	4,802
Piatt	3,124	5,392	3,488	4,619
Pike	2,849	5,032	3,198	4,706
Pope	918	1,500	927	1,346
Pulaski	1,372	1,720	1,518	1,430
Putnam	1,704	1,623	1,657	1,437
Randolph	6,771	8,076	6,794	7,127
Richland	2,529	5,153	2,491	4,718
Rock Island	39,880	29,663	37,957	25,194
St. Clair	62,410	50,203	55,961	42,299
Saline	4,697	7,057	5,427	5,933
Sangamon	38,630	55,904	38,414	50,374
Schuyler	1,594	2,403	1,587	2,077
Scott	927	1,696	954	1,458
Shelby	3,744	6,753	4,018	5,851
Stark	1,189	1,841	1,211	1,694
Stephenson	8,913	12,212	8,062	10,715
Tazewell	25,814	36,058	25,379	31,537
Union	3,735	5,333	3,982	4,397
Vermilion	14,726	18,731	15,406	15,783
Wabash	1,752	4,212	1,987	3,406
Warren	3,938	4,474	3,524	3,899
Washington	2,986	5,072	2,638	4,353
Wayne	2,139	6,102	2,209	5,347
White	3,071	5,180	2,958	4,521
Whiteside	13,723	12,959	12,886	11,252
Will	117,172	130,728	90,902	95,828
Williamson	11,685	18,086	12,192	14,012
Winnebago	59,740	60,782	51,981	53,816
Woodford	6,005	12,698	5,529	10,905
Totals	**2,891,550**	**2,345,946**	**2,589,026**	**2,019,421**

Illinois Vote Since 1948

1948: Truman, D., 1,994,715; Dewey, R., 1,961,103; Watson, Proh., 11,959; Thomas, Soc., 11,522; Teichert, Soc. Labor, 3,118.
1952: Eisenhower, R., 2,457,327; Stevenson, D., 2,013,920; Hass, Soc. Labor, 9,363; write-in, 448.
1956: Eisenhower, R., 2,623,327; Stevenson, D., 1,775,682; Hass, Soc. Labor, 8,342; write-in, 56.
1960: Kennedy, D., 2,377,846; Nixon, R., 2,368,988; Hass, Soc. Labor, 10,560; write-in, 15.
1964: Johnson, D., 2,796,833; Goldwater, R., 1,905,946; write-in, 62.
1968: Nixon, R., 2,174,774; Humphrey, D., 2,039,814; Wallace, 3rd Party, 390,958; Blomen, Soc. Labor, 13,878; write-in, 325.
1972: Nixon, Rep. 2,788,179; McGovern, D., 1,913,472; Fisher, Soc. Labor, 12,344; Hall, Com., 4,541; Schmitz, Amer., 2,471; others, 2,229.
1976: Ford, R., 2,364,269; Carter, D., 2,271,295; McCarthy, Ind., 55,939; Hall, Com., 9,250; MacBride, Libertarian, 8,057; Camejo, Soc. Workers, 3,615; Levin, Soc. Labor, 2,422; LaRouche, U.S. Labor, 2,018; write-in, 1,968.
1980: Reagan, R., 2,358,049; Carter, D., 1,981,413; Anderson, Ind., 346,754; Clark, Libertarian, 38,939; Commoner, Citizens, 10,692; Hall, Com., 9,711; Griswold, Workers World, 2,257; DeBerry, Soc. Workers, 1,302; write-in, 604.
1984: Reagan, R., 2,707,103; Mondale, D., 2,086,499; Bergland, Libertarian, 10,086.
1988: Bush, R., 2,310,939; Dukakis, D., 2,215,940; Paul, Lib., 14,944; Fulani, Solid., 10,276.
1992: Clinton, D., 2,453,350; Bush, R., 1,734,096; Perot, Ind., 840,515; Marrou, Libertarian, 9,218; Fulani, New Alliance, 5,267; Gritz, Populist/America First, 3,577; Hagelin, Natural Law, 2,751; Warren, Soc. Workers, 1,361.
1996: Clinton, D., 2,341,744; Dole, R., 1,587,021; Perot, Ref., 346,408; Browne, Libertarian, 22,548; Phillips, Taxpayers, 7,606; Hagelin, Natural Law, 4,606.
2000: Gore, D., 2,589,026; Bush, R., 2,019,421; Nader, Green, 103,759; Buchanan, Ind., 16,106; Browne, Libertarian, 11,623; Hagelin, Reform, 2,127.
2004: Kerry, D., 2,891,550; Bush, R., 2,345,946; Badnarik, Libertarian, 32,442.

Indiana

	2004		2000	
County	**Kerry (D)**	**Bush (R)**	**Gore (D)**	**Bush (R)**
Adams	3,512	9,734	3,775	8,555
Allen	46,710	82,013	41,636	70,426
Bartholomew	9,191	19,093	9,015	16,200
Benton	1,135	2,797	1,328	2,441
Blackford	1,903	3,447	2,103	2,699
Boone	5,636	17,055	4,763	13,161

County	2004 Kerry (D)	2004 Bush (R)	2000 Gore (D)	2000 Bush (R)
Brown	2,730	4,512	2,608	3,871
Carroll	2,689	5,868	2,965	5,102
Cass	4,315	9,480	5,412	9,305
Clark	17,648	24,495	17,360	19,417
Clay	3,333	7,361	3,605	6,393
Clinton	3,335	8,471	3,643	7,141
Crawford	1,932	2,609	1,817	2,327
Daviess	2,573	7,936	2,697	6,872
Dearborn	6,596	14,231	6,020	11,452
Decatur	2,621	7,499	2,889	6,115
Dekalb	4,810	10,468	4,776	8,701
Delaware	20,436	27,064	20,876	22,105
Dubois	5,210	11,726	5,090	10,134
Elkhart	17,966	42,967	16,402	36,756
Fayette	3,626	5,761	3,415	5,060
Floyd	13,857	19,877	13,209	16,486
Fountain	2,477	5,260	2,717	4,408
Franklin	2,925	6,977	2,591	5,587
Fulton	2,607	6,027	2,960	5,218
Gibson	5,378	9,133	5,802	7,734
Grant	8,509	18,769	9,712	16,153
Greene	4,606	8,609	4,898	7,452
Hamilton	26,388	77,887	18,002	56,372
Hancock	6,912	20,771	6,503	15,943
Harrison	6,171	11,015	5,870	8,711
Hendricks	13,548	38,430	10,786	28,651
Henry	7,176	13,137	7,647	10,321
Howard	12,998	23,714	12,899	20,331
Huntington	3,877	11,617	4,119	10,113
Jackson	5,092	11,083	5,330	9,054
Jasper	3,678	8,056	3,744	7,212
Jay	2,740	5,427	3,167	4,687
Jefferson	5,117	7,763	5,117	6,582
Jennings	3,538	6,864	3,549	5,732
Johnson	13,109	37,765	11,952	29,404
Knox	5,649	9,990	6,300	8,485
Kosciusko	5,977	22,136	5,785	19,040
LaGrange	21,114	20,916	2,733	5,437
Lake	114,743	71,903	109,078	63,389
LaPorte	21,114	20,916	19,736	18,994
Lawrence	5,346	12,207	5,071	10,677
Madison	21,882	32,526	23,403	27,956
Marion	162,249	156,072	134,189	137,810
Marshall	5,593	12,074	5,541	10,266
Martin	1,522	3,414	1,518	3,008
Miami	3,886	9,600	4,155	8,401
Monroe	26,965	22,834	17,523	19,147
Montgomery	3,536	10,901	3,899	8,891
Morgan	6,650	19,197	6,228	15,286
Newton	2,032	3,757	2,101	3,250
Noble	4,703	10,859	4,822	9,103
Ohio	1,139	1,796	951	1,515
Orange	2,885	5,683	2,601	4,687
Owen	2,536	5,000	2,253	4,019
Parke	2,362	4,550	2,481	3,841
Perry	4,131	4,137	3,823	3,461
Pike	2,418	3,745	2,605	3,566
Porter	29,388	34,794	26,790	31,157
Posey	4,085	7,833	4,430	6,498
Pulaski	1,750	3,797	1,919	3,497
Putnam	4,103	8,908	4,123	7,352
Randolph	3,812	7,172	3,906	6,020
Ripley	3,510	8,224	3,498	6,988
Rush	2,000	5,363	2,370	4,749
St. Joseph	52,637	55,254	47,703	47,581
Scott	3,822	4,793	3,915	3,761
Shelby	4,519	11,397	5,374	9,590
Spencer	3,920	5,934	3,752	5,096
Starke	3,987	4,846	4,136	4,349
Steuben	4,345	8,433	4,103	6,953
Sullivan	3,341	4,999	3,833	4,319
Switzerland	1,479	2,161	1,336	1,831
Tippecanoe	20,818	30,897	18,220	26,106
Tipton	2,203	5,628	2,392	4,784
Union	1,045	2,266	927	1,838
Vanderburgh	28,767	41,463	29,222	35,846
Vermillion	3,424	3,536	3,370	3,130
Vigo	18,426	20,988	17,570	18,021
Wabash	3,920	9,607	4,277	8,321
Warren	1,356	2,565	1,471	2,218
Warrick	8,980	16,930	8,749	13,205
Washington	3,879	6,915	3,675	5,868
Wayne	10,775	16,586	10,273	14,273
Wells	3,112	9,168	3,319	7,755
White	3,277	6,974	3,655	6,037
Whitley	3,880	9,512	4,107	8,080
Totals	**969,011**	**1,479,438**	**901,980**	**1,245,836**

Indiana Vote Since 1948

1948: Dewey, R., 821,079; Truman, D., 807,833; Watson, Proh., 14,711; Wallace, Prog., 9,649; Thomas, Soc., 2,179; Teichert, Soc. Labor, 763.

1952: Eisenhower, R., 1,136,259; Stevenson, D., 801,530; Hamblen, Proh., 15,335; Hallinan, Prog., 1,222; Hass, Soc. Labor, 979.

1956: Eisenhower, R., 1,182,811; Stevenson, D., 783,908; Holtwick, Proh., 6,554; Hass, Soc. Labor, 1,334.

1960: Nixon, R., 1,175,120; Kennedy, D., 952,358; Decker, Proh., 6,746; Hass, Soc. Labor, 1,136.

1964: Johnson, D., 1,170,848; Goldwater, R., 911,118; Munn, Proh., 8,266; Hass, Soc. Labor, 1,374.

1968: Nixon, R., 1,067,885; Humphrey, D., 806,659; Wallace, 3rd Party, 243,108; Munn, Proh., 4,616; Halstead, Soc. Workers, 1,293; Gregory, write-in, 36.

1972: Nixon, R., 1,405,154; McGovern, D., 708,568; Reed, Soc. Workers, 5,575; Spock, Peace and Freedom, 4,544; Fisher, Soc. Labor, 1,688.

1976: Ford, R., 1,185,958; Carter, D., 1,014,714; Anderson, Amer., 14,048; Camejo, Soc. Workers, 5,695; LaRouche, U.S. Labor, 1,947.

1980: Reagan, R., 1,255,656; Carter, D., 844,197; Anderson, Ind., 111,639; Clark, Libertarian, 19,627; Commoner, Citizens, 4,852; Greaves, Amer., 4,750; Hall, Com., 702; DeBerry, Soc., 610.

1984: Reagan, R., 1,377,230; Mondale, D., 841,481; Bergland, Libertarian, 6,741.

1988: Bush, R., 1,297,763; Dukakis, D., 860,643; Fulani, New Alliance, 10,215.

1992: Bush, R., 989,375; Clinton, D., 848,420; Perot, Ind., 455,934; Marrou, Libertarian, 7,936; Fulani, New Alliance, 2,583.

1996: Dole, R., 1,006,693; Clinton, D., 887,424; Perot, Ref., 224,299; Browne, Libertarian, 15,632.

2000: Bush, R., 1,245,836; Gore, D., 901,980; Buchanan, Ind., 16,959; Browne, Libertarian, 15,530.

2004: Bush, R., 1,479,438; Kerry, D., 969,011; Badnarik, Libertarian, 18,058.

Iowa

County	2004 Kerry (D)	2004 Bush (R)	2000 Gore (D)	2000 Bush (R)
Adair	1,844	2,402	1,753	2,275
Adams	977	1,317	897	1,170
Allamakee	3,449	3,530	2,883	3,277
Appanoose	3,063	3,340	2,560	2,992
Audubon	1,608	1,958	1,780	1,909
Benton	6,747	6,658	5,915	5,468
Black Hawk	35,392	28,046	30,112	23,468
Boone	7,027	6,870	6,270	5,625
Bremer	6,025	6,665	5,169	5,675
Buchanan	5,608	4,797	5,045	4,092
Buena Vista	3,520	4,887	3,297	4,354
Butler	3,001	4,417	2,735	3,837
Calhoun	2,243	3,255	2,132	2,776
Carroll	4,689	5,762	4,463	4,879
Cass	2,679	4,796	2,481	4,206
Cedar	4,747	4,869	4,033	4,031
Cerro Gordo	13,372	10,960	12,185	9,397
Cherokee	2,988	3,758	2,845	3,463
Chickasaw	3,708	3,040	3,435	2,936
Clarke	2,323	2,200	2,081	1,984
Clay	3,547	4,898	3,294	3,992
Clayton	4,736	4,312	4,238	4,034
Clinton	13,813	10,666	12,276	9,229
Crawford	3,220	3,955	2,838	3,482
Dallas	10,917	15,183	8,561	10,306
Davis	1,731	2,148	1,691	1,956
Decatur	1,859	2,088	1,674	1,903
Delaware	4,227	4,908	3,808	4,273
Des Moines	12,456	8,221	11,351	7,385
Dickinson	4,140	5,337	3,660	4,225
Dubuque	26,561	20,100	22,341	16,462
Emmet	2,405	2,697	2,165	2,331
Fayette	5,185	5,128	4,640	4,747
Floyd	4,349	3,745	3,830	3,191
Franklin	2,340	3,128	2,122	2,657
Fremont	1,510	2,362	1,459	2,069
Greene	2,459	2,618	2,301	2,282
Grundy	2,386	4,429	2,139	3,851
Guthrie	2,614	3,325	2,493	2,840
Hamilton	3,895	4,367	3,407	3,968
Hancock	2,484	3,368	2,281	2,988
Hardin	4,015	4,875	3,734	4,486
Harrison	2,906	4,680	2,551	3,802
Henry	4,127	5,220	3,907	4,476
Howard	2,614	2,028	2,426	1,922
Humboldt	2,146	3,162	1,949	2,846
Ida	1,415	2,342	1,411	1,968
Iowa	3,841	4,544	3,230	3,894
Jackson	5,656	4,242	4,945	3,769
Jasper	10,430	9,462	8,699	8,729
Jefferson	4,490	3,648	2,863	3,248
Johnson	41,847	22,715	31,174	17,899
Jones	5,054	4,834	4,690	4,201
Keokuk	2,294	3,119	2,181	2,571

County	2004 Kerry (D)	2004 Bush (R)	2000 Gore (D)	2000 Bush (R)
Kossuth	4,132	5,042	3,960	4,612
Lee	10,152	7,472	9,632	6,339
Linn	60,442	49,442	48,897	40,417
Louisa	2,297	2,572	2,294	2,207
Lucas	1,987	2,543	1,934	2,262
Lyon	1,303	4,751	1,313	3,918
Madison	3,380	4,538	3,093	3,662
Mahaska	3,790	6,858	3,370	5,971
Marion	6,574	9,990	5,741	8,358
Marshall	9,443	9,557	8,322	8,785
Mills	2,308	4,556	2,039	3,684
Mitchell	2,785	2,646	2,650	2,388
Monona	2,397	2,575	2,086	2,304
Monroe	1,855	2,067	1,699	1,858
Montgomery	1,899	3,601	1,838	3,417
Muscatine	9,542	9,020	8,058	7,483
O'Brien	2,330	5,328	2,170	4,674
Osceola	934	2,295	913	2,064
Page	2,211	5,243	2,293	4,588
Palo Alto	2,482	2,674	2,326	2,341
Plymouth	4,278	7,810	3,499	6,189
Pocahontas	1,822	2,441	1,736	2,242
Polk	105,218	95,828	89,715	79,927
Pottawattamie	16,906	24,558	14,726	18,783
Poweshiek	5,043	4,965	4,222	4,396
Ringgold	1,286	1,466	1,246	1,369
Sac	2,215	3,128	2,099	2,776
Scott	42,122	39,958	35,857	32,801
Shelby	2,355	4,256	2,179	3,655
Sioux	2,259	14,229	2,148	12,241
Story	23,296	20,819	17,478	16,228
Tama	4,487	4,456	4,045	4,034
Taylor	1,252	1,908	1,247	1,770
Union	2,747	3,165	2,540	3,003
Van Buren	1,568	2,211	1,440	2,016
Wapello	9,125	7,403	8,355	6,313
Warren	10,730	12,160	9,521	9,621
Washington	4,595	5,977	3,932	4,827
Wayne	1,379	1,733	1,300	1,666
Webster	9,561	8,959	8,479	8,172
Winnebago	2,707	3,175	2,691	2,662
Winneshiek	5,354	5,324	4,339	4,647
Woodbury	21,455	22,451	17,691	18,864
Worth	2,286	1,795	2,208	1,659
Wright	2,930	3,631	2,796	3,384
Totals	**741,898**	**751,957**	**638,517**	**634,373**

Iowa Vote Since 1948

1948: Truman, D., 522,380; Dewey, R., 494,018; Wallace, Prog., 12,125; Teichert, Soc. Labor, 4,274; Watson, Proh., 3,382; Thomas, Soc., 1,829; Dobbs, Soc. Workers, 26.

1952: Eisenhower, R., 808,906; Stevenson, D., 451,513; Hallinan, Prog., 5,085; Hamblen, Proh., 2,882; Hoopes, Soc., 219; Hass, Soc. Labor, 139; scattered, 29.

1956: Eisenhower, R., 729,187; Stevenson, D., 501,858; Andrews (A.C.P. of Iowa), 3,202; Hoopes, Soc., 192; Hass, Soc. Labor, 125.

1960: Nixon, R., 722,381; Kennedy, D., 550,565; Hass, Soc. Labor, 230; write-in, 634.

1964: Johnson, D., 733,030; Goldwater, R., 449,148; Munn, Proh., 1,902; Hass, Soc. Labor, 182; DeBerry, Soc. Workers, 159.

1968: Nixon, R., 619,106; Humphrey, D., 476,699; Wallace, 3rd Party, 66,422; Halstead, Soc. Workers, 3,377; Cleaver, Peace and Freedom, 1,332; Munn, Proh., 362; Blomen, Soc. Labor, 241.

1972: Nixon, R., 706,207; McGovern, D., 496,206; Schmitz, Amer., 22,056; Jenness, Soc. Workers, 488; Hall, Com., 272; Green, Universal, 199; Fisher, Soc. Labor, 195; scattered, 321.

1976: Ford, R., 632,863; Carter, D., 619,931; McCarthy, Ind., 20,051; Anderson, Amer., 3,040; MacBride, Libertarian, 1,452.

1980: Reagan, R., 676,026; Carter, D., 508,672; Anderson, Ind., 115,633; Clark, Libertarian, 13,123; Commoner, Citizens, 2,273; McReynolds, Socialist, 534; Hall, Com., 298; DeBerry, Soc. Wrkrs., 244; Greaves, Amer., 189; Bubar, Statesman, 150; scattered, 519.

1984: Reagan, R., 703,088; Mondale, D., 605,620; Bergland, Libertarian, 1,844.

1988: Dukakis, D., 670,557; Bush, R., 545,355; LaRouche, Ind., 3,526; Paul, Lib., 2,494.

1992: Clinton, D., 586,353; Bush, R., 504,891; Perot, Ind., 253,468; Hagelin, Natural Law, 3,079; Gritz, Populist/America First, 1,177; Marrou, Libertarian, 1,076.

1996: Clinton, D., 620,258; Dole, R., 492,644; Perot, Ref., 105,159; Nader, Green, 6,550; Hagelin, Natural Law, 3,349; Browne, Libertarian, 2,315; Phillips, Taxpayers, 2,229; Harris, Soc. Workers, 331.

2000: Gore, D., 638,517; Bush, R., 634,373; Nader, Green, 29,374; Buchanan, Reform, 5,731; Browne, Libertarian, 3,209; Hagelin, Ind., 2,281; Phillips, Constitution, 613; Harris, Soc. Workers, 190; McReynolds, Soc., 107.

2004: Bush, R., 751,957; Kerry, D., 741,898; Nader, Petitioning Cand., 5,973; Badnarik, Libertarian, 2,992; Peroutka, Constitution, 1,304; Cobb, Green, 1,141; Harris, Soc. Wkrs., 373; Van Auken, Petitioning Cand., 176.

Kansas

County	2004 Kerry (D)	2004 Bush (R)	2000 Gore (D)	2000 Bush (R)
Allen	1,922	3,867	2,132	3,379
Anderson	1,295	2,500	1,327	1,984
Atchison	3,120	3,880	3,171	3,378
Barber	588	1,782	637	1,755
Barton	2,874	8,666	3,238	7,302
Bourbon	2,216	4,372	2,211	3,852
Brown	1,268	3,092	1,512	2,985
Butler	7,495	18,438	6,755	13,377
Chase	418	1,055	391	848
Chautauqua	404	1,529	443	1,347
Cherokee	3,726	6,083	3,783	5,014
Cheyenne	320	1,353	350	1,312
Clark	257	1,014	292	926
Clay	793	3,174	951	2,998
Cloud	1,210	3,221	1,314	2,918
Coffey	1,093	3,259	1,196	2,700
Comanche	200	770	211	760
Cowley	4,818	9,407	5,535	8,080
Crawford	7,617	8,626	7,076	7,160
Decatur	355	1,355	424	1,255
Dickinson	2,364	6,295	2,413	5,243
Doniphan	1,065	2,491	1,134	2,350
Douglas	28,634	20,544	18,249	17,062
Edwards	386	1,084	447	1,062
Elk	369	1,119	402	1,080
Ellis	4,033	7,891	3,926	6,516
Ellsworth	801	2,259	825	1,845
Finney	2,351	7,479	2,431	6,442
Ford	2,286	6,632	2,566	6,050
Franklin	3,921	7,391	3,321	5,925
Geary	2,531	4,703	2,660	3,977
Gove	247	1,196	296	1,122
Graham	334	1,082	346	1,058
Grant	561	2,169	683	2,126
Gray	408	1,816	482	1,631
Greeley	138	584	143	628
Greenwood	911	2,282	1,027	2,392
Hamilton	229	888	264	901
Harper	727	2,154	869	2,076
Harvey	5,331	9,534	4,591	8,271
Haskell	227	1,356	263	1,323
Hodgeman	223	953	217	835
Jackson	2,064	3,730	1,990	3,001
Jefferson	3,253	5,408	3,000	4,423
Jewell	385	1,495	380	1,400
Johnson	97,866	158,103	79,118	129,965
Kearny	272	1,177	320	1,084
Kingman	904	2,801	991	2,672
Kiowa	256	1,275	294	1,262
Labette	3,615	5,400	3,745	4,475
Lane	181	823	252	846
Leavenworth	11,039	15,949	9,733	12,583
Lincoln	391	1,368	469	1,295
Linn	1,631	3,048	1,587	2,513
Logan	248	1,255	231	1,088
Lyon	5,234	7,951	5,190	6,652
Marion	1,536	4,516	1,475	4,156
Marshall	1,789	3,261	1,831	3,066
McPherson	3,589	9,595	3,272	8,501
Meade	356	1,748	400	1,604
Miami	4,838	9,013	4,554	6,611
Mitchell	693	2,609	751	2,350
Montgomery	4,338	9,598	4,770	8,496
Morris	931	1,961	882	1,599
Morton	276	1,287	321	1,203
Nemaha	1,355	4,027	1,494	3,578
Neosho	2,424	4,705	2,588	4,014
Ness	382	1,407	383	1,420
Norton	473	2,092	598	1,744
Osage	2,537	4,800	2,530	3,770
Osborne	454	1,587	484	1,432
Ottawa	595	2,333	631	1,977
Pawnee	773	2,172	968	1,850
Phillips	557	2,256	611	2,057
Pottawatomie	2,176	6,326	2,037	4,985
Pratt	1,200	3,121	1,314	2,885
Rawlins	289	1,414	306	1,349
Reno	9,114	17,748	9,025	15,179
Republic	607	2,238	604	2,239
Rice	1,130	3,182	1,422	2,903
Riley	7,908	12,672	6,188	10,672
Rooks	534	2,121	597	2,016
Rush	517	1,226	505	1,235
Russell	810	2,671	886	2,434
Saline	7,524	15,111	7,487	12,412

County	2004 Kerry (D)	2004 Bush (R)	2000 Gore (D)	2000 Bush (R)
Scott	347	1,924	418	1,811
Sedgwick	64,839	110,381	62,561	93,724
Seward	1,122	4,272	1,126	3,869
Shawnee	36,264	44,188	34,818	35,894
Sheridan	239	1,144	281	1,132
Sherman	632	2,088	681	1,894
Smith	540	1,803	534	1,534
Stafford	506	1,649	567	1,546
Stanton	165	796	215	785
Stevens	310	1,936	345	1,714
Sumner	3,217	7,092	3,549	6,176
Thomas	816	3,007	807	2,822
Trego	434	1,225	516	1,220
Wabaunsee	1,001	2,531	1,025	2,182
Wallace	112	742	103	737
Washington	643	2,498	687	2,446
Wichita	183	869	207	859
Wilson	1,060	3,263	1,186	2,748
Woodson	530	1,204	521	974
Wyandotte	34,923	17,919	32,411	14,024
Totals	**434,993**	**736,456**	**399,276**	**622,332**

Kansas Vote Since 1948

1948: Dewey, R., 423,039; Truman, D., 351,902; Watson, Proh., 6,468; Wallace, Prog., 4,603; Thomas, Soc., 2,807.

1952: Eisenhower, R., 616,302; Stevenson, D., 273,296; Hamblen, Proh., 6,038; Hoopes, Soc., 530.

1956: Eisenhower, R., 566,878; Stevenson, D., 296,317; Holtwick, Proh., 3,048.

1960: Nixon, R., 561,474; Kennedy, D., 363,213; Decker, Proh., 4,138.

1964: Johnson, D., 464,028; Goldwater, R., 386,579; Munn, Proh., 5,393; Hass, Soc. Labor, 1,901.

1968: Nixon, R., 478,674; Humphrey, D., 302,996; Wallace, 3rd Party, 88,921; Munn, Proh., 2,192.

1972: Nixon, R., 619,812; McGovern, D., 270,287; Schmitz, Conservative, 21,808; Munn, Proh., 4,188.

1976: Ford, R., 502,752; Carter, D., 430,421; McCarthy, Ind., 13,185; Anderson, Amer., 4,724; MacBride, Libertarian, 3,242; Maddox, Conservative, 2,118; Bubar, Proh., 1,403.

1980: Reagan, R., 566,812; Carter, D., 326,150; Anderson, Ind., 68,231; Clark, Libertarian, 14,470; Shelton, Amer., 1,555; Hall, Com., 967; Bubar, Statesman, 821; Rarick, Conservative, 789.

1984: Reagan, R., 674,646; Mondale, D., 332,471; Bergland, Libertarian, 3,585.

1988: Bush, R., 554,049; Dukakis, D., 422,636; Paul, Ind.,12,553; Fulani, Ind., 3,806.

1992: Bush, R., 449,951; Clinton, D., 390,434; Perot, Ind., 312,358; Marrou, Libertarian, 4,314.

1996: Dole, R., 583,245; Clinton, D., 387,659; Perot, Ref., 92,639; Browne, Libertarian, 4,557; Phillips, Ind., 3,519; Hagelin, Ind., 1,655.

2000: Bush, R., 622,332; Gore, D., 399,276; Nader, Ind., 36,086; Buchanan, Reform, 7,370; Browne, Libertarian, 4,525; Hagelin, Ind., 1,373; Phillips, Constitution, 1,254.

2004: Bush, R., 736,456; Kerry, D., 434,993; Nader, Ref., 9,348; Badnarik, Libertarian, 4,013; Peroutka, Ind., 2,899.

Kentucky

County	2004 Kerry (D)	2004 Bush (R)	2000 Gore (D)	2000 Bush (R)
Adair	1,764	5,628	1,779	5,460
Allen	1,923	5,202	1,950	4,415
Anderson	3,141	6,363	2,902	4,909
Ballard	1,759	2,389	1,880	1,824
Barren	5,216	10,822	4,930	8,741
Bath	2,608	2,269	2,087	2,303
Bell	4,210	6,722	4,787	5,585
Boone	12,391	32,329	9,248	22,016
Bourbon	3,198	4,953	3,048	3,881
Boyd	10,132	11,501	9,541	9,247
Boyle	4,646	7,764	3,963	6,126
Bracken	1,213	2,363	888	2,065
Breathitt	3,327	2,542	2,902	2,084
Breckinridge	2,884	5,580	2,595	4,763
Bullitt	9,043	19,433	8,195	14,054
Butler	1,436	4,109	1,299	3,654
Caldwell	2,245	4,066	2,223	3,161
Calloway	5,728	9,293	5,635	7,705
Campbell	14,253	25,540	12,040	20,789
Carlisle	1,102	1,734	1,149	1,405
Carroll	1,688	2,175	1,601	1,818
Carter	5,577	5,422	4,182	4,617
Casey	1,174	5,109	1,122	4,284
Christian	6,970	13,935	6,778	10,787
Clark	5,661	9,540	4,918	7,297
Clay	1,901	5,726	1,723	4,926
Clinton	952	3,369	1,032	3,224
Crittenden	1,438	2,726	1,610	2,469
Cumberland	848	2,356	736	2,220
Daviess	15,788	25,372	14,126	21,361
Edmonson	1,856	3,595	1,710	3,250
Elliott	2,064	871	1,525	827
Estill	1,907	3,633	1,591	3,033
Fayette	57,994	66,406	47,277	54,495
Fleming	2,406	3,749	1,813	3,282
Floyd	11,132	6,612	10,088	5,068
Franklin	11,620	12,281	10,853	10,209
Fulton	1,340	1,527	1,452	1,293
Gallatin	1,188	1,869	1,049	1,345
Garrard	1,841	4,784	1,713	4,043
Grant	2,818	5,951	2,568	4,405
Graves	6,206	9,903	6,097	7,849
Grayson	2,905	7,170	2,604	5,843
Green	1,312	3,866	1,085	3,615
Greenup	7,630	8,696	7,164	7,233
Hancock	1,709	2,286	1,508	2,032
Hardin	11,507	24,627	11,095	18,964
Harlan	4,332	6,659	5,365	4,980
Harrison	2,807	4,855	2,658	3,793
Hart	2,470	4,269	2,201	3,725
Henderson	8,101	10,467	8,054	7,698
Henry	2,366	4,094	2,117	3,244
Hickman	926	1,395	940	1,151
Hopkins	6,420	12,314	6,734	9,490
Jackson	769	4,369	701	4,079
Jefferson	170,158	164,566	149,901	145,052
Jessamine	5,476	12,972	4,633	10,074
Johnson	3,288	5,940	3,276	4,811
Kenton	22,834	43,664	19,100	35,363
Knott	4,685	2,648	4,349	2,029
Knox	3,822	8,108	3,690	6,058
Larue	1,823	4,111	1,727	3,384
Laurel	5,297	16,819	4,856	13,029
Lawrence	2,705	3,755	2,258	2,969
Lee	878	2,018	836	1,893
Leslie	1,266	3,661	1,210	3,159
Letcher	4,192	4,801	4,698	4,092
Lewis	1,667	3,778	1,293	3,217
Lincoln	2,796	5,996	2,678	4,795
Livingston	2,007	2,675	2,022	2,118
Logan	3,768	6,815	3,885	5,344
Lyon	1,769	2,132	1,680	1,688
Madison	11,525	18,922	9,309	13,682
Magoffin	2,843	2,836	2,603	2,785
Marion	3,399	3,905	2,778	3,259
Marshall	6,383	9,049	6,203	7,294
Martin	1,504	2,996	1,714	2,667
Mason	2,644	4,381	2,178	3,572
McCracken	11,361	18,218	11,412	14,745
McCreary	1,530	4,121	1,418	3,321
McLean	1,823	2,584	1,747	2,219
Meade	3,724	7,152	3,596	5,319
Menifee	1,284	1,215	1,038	1,170
Mercer	3,224	6,745	3,092	5,362
Metcalfe	1,472	2,645	1,318	2,476
Monroe	1,158	4,657	1,158	4,377
Montgomery	4,506	5,647	3,833	4,534
Morgan	2,532	2,682	1,875	2,295
Muhlenberg	6,636	6,749	6,295	5,518
Nelson	6,524	10,161	5,481	7,714
Nicholas	1,332	1,700	994	1,613
Ohio	3,627	6,311	3,303	5,413
Oldham	8,080	18,801	6,236	13,580
Owen	1,615	3,084	1,394	2,582
Owsley	430	1,558	339	1,466
Pendleton	1,940	4,045	1,670	3,044
Perry	5,400	6,187	5,514	5,300
Pike	14,002	12,611	13,611	11,005
Powell	2,249	2,687	2,008	2,258
Pulaski	5,829	19,535	5,415	15,845
Robertson	413	670	341	630
Rockcastle	1,320	4,804	1,174	3,992
Rowan	4,556	4,063	3,505	3,546
Russell	1,772	6,009	1,710	5,268
Scott	6,325	10,600	5,472	7,952
Shelby	5,277	10,909	4,435	8,068
Simpson	2,730	4,273	2,583	3,169
Spencer	1,970	4,816	1,554	3,150
Taylor	2,979	7,247	2,790	6,151
Todd	1,491	3,242	1,496	2,646
Trigg	2,046	4,023	2,110	3,130
Trimble	1,428	2,332	1,181	1,837
Union	2,398	3,534	2,547	2,749
Warren	14,326	25,100	12,180	20,235
Washington	1,724	3,479	1,458	3,044
Wayne	2,616	5,027	2,312	4,069
Webster	2,304	3,207	2,388	2,599
Whitley	3,985	9,559	4,101	7,502
Wolfe	1,744	1,385	1,136	1,267
Woodford	4,480	6,937	3,995	5,890
Totals	**712,733**	**1,069,439**	**638,923**	**872,520**

Kentucky Vote Since 1948

1948: Truman, D., 466,756; Dewey, R., 341,210; Thurmond, States' Rights, 10,411; Wallace, Prog., 1,567; Thomas, Soc., 1,284; Watson, Proh., 1,245; Teichert, Soc. Labor, 185.
1952: Stevenson, D., 495,729; Eisenhower, R., 495,029; Hamblen, Proh., 1,161; Hass, Soc. Labor, 893; Hallinan, Proh., 336.
1956: Eisenhower, R., 572,192; Stevenson, D., 476,453; Byrd, States' Rights, 2,657; Holtwick, Proh., 2,145; Hass, Soc. Labor, 358.
1960: Nixon, R., 602,607; Kennedy, D., 521,855.
1964: Johnson, D., 669,659; Goldwater, R., 372,977; Kasper, Natl. States Rights, 3,469.
1968: Nixon, R., 462,411; Humphrey, D., 397,547; Wallace, 3rd Party, 193,098; Halstead, Soc. Workers, 2,843.
1972: Nixon, R., 676,446; McGovern, D., 371,159; Schmitz, Amer., 17,627; Spock, Peoples, 1,118; Jenness, Soc. Workers, 685; Hall, Com., 464.
1976: Carter, D., 615,717; Ford, R., 531,852; Anderson, Amer., 8,308; McCarthy, Ind., 6,837; Maddox, Amer. Ind., 2,328; MacBride, Libertarian, 814.
1980: Reagan, R., 635,274; Carter, D., 616,417; Anderson, Ind., 31,127; Clark, Libertarian, 5,531; McCormack, Respect For Life, 4,233; Commoner, Citizens, 1,304; Pulley, Socialist, 393; Hall, Com., 348.
1984: Reagan, R., 815,345; Mondale, D., 536,756.
1988: Bush, R., 734,281; Dukakis, D., 580,368; Duke, Pop., 4,494; Paul, Lib., 2,118.
1992: Clinton, D., 665,104; Bush, R., 617,178; Perot, Ind., 203,944; Marrou, Libertarian, 4,513.
1996: Clinton, D., 636,614; Dole, R., 623,283; Perot, Ref., 120,396; Browne, Libertarian, 4,009; Phillips, Taxpayers, 2,204; Hagelin, Natural Law, 1,493.
2000: Bush, R., 872,520; Gore, D., 638,923; Nader, Green, 23,118; Buchanan, Reform, 4,152; Browne, Libertarian, 2,885; Hagelin, Natural Law, 1,513; Phillips, Constitution, 915.
2004: Bush, R., 1,069,439; Kerry, D., 712,733; Nader, Ind., 8,856; Badnarik, Libertarian, 2,619; Peroutka, Constitution, 2,213.

Louisiana

	2004		2000	
Parish	**Kerry (D)**	**Bush (R)**	**Gore (D)**	**Bush (R)**
Acadia	8,937	16,083	8,892	13,814
Allen	3,791	5,140	3,914	4,035
Ascension	13,955	24,661	13,385	16,818
Assumption	5,585	4,966	5,222	4,388
Avoyelles	6,976	8,302	6,701	7,329
Beauregard	3,666	9,470	3,958	7,862
Bienville	3,399	3,612	3,413	3,269
Bossier	12,317	30,040	11,933	23,224
Caddo	51,739	54,292	47,530	46,807
Calcasieu	32,864	46,075	33,919	38,086
Caldwell	1,384	3,308	1,359	2,817
Cameron	1,367	3,190	1,435	2,593
Catahoula	1,673	3,219	1,718	2,912
Claiborne	2,854	3,704	2,721	3,384
Concordia	3,446	5,427	3,569	4,627
DeSoto	5,026	6,211	5,036	5,260
E. Baton Rouge	82,298	99,943	76,516	89,128
East Carroll	1,980	1,357	1,876	1,280
East Feliciana	4,091	5,021	3,870	4,051
Evangeline	5,757	7,949	5,763	7,290
Franklin	2,828	6,141	2,792	5,363
Grant	1,977	5,911	2,099	4,784
Iberia	12,426	19,420	11,762	17,236
Iberville	8,259	6,333	8,355	5,573
Jackson	2,525	5,038	2,582	4,347
Jefferson	72,136	117,882	70,411	105,003
Jefferson Davis	4,745	8,055	5,162	6,945
Lafayette	31,210	57,732	27,190	48,491
Lafourche	14,417	22,734	14,627	18,575
LaSalle	1,155	5,015	1,397	4,564
Lincoln	7,242	10,791	6,851	9,246
Livingston	9,895	33,976	11,008	24,889
Madison	2,334	2,291	2,489	2,127
Morehouse	5,336	7,471	5,289	6,641
Natchitoches	7,398	9,261	6,924	7,332
Orleans	152,610	42,847	137,630	39,404
Ouachita	22,016	41,750	21,457	35,107
Plaquemines	4,181	7,866	4,425	6,302
Pointe Coupee	5,712	5,429	5,813	4,710
Rapides	18,904	34,492	18,898	28,831
Red River	2,140	2,507	2,177	2,200
Richland	3,082	5,471	3,282	4,895
Sabine	2,743	6,711	2,846	5,754
St. Bernard	9,956	19,597	11,682	16,255
St. Charles	8,856	14,747	8,918	11,981
St. Helena	3,173	2,235	3,059	1,965
St. James	6,407	4,545	6,523	3,813
St. John the Baptist	10,305	9,039	9,745	7,423
St. Landry	18,166	18,315	18,067	15,449
St. Martin	10,321	12,095	9,853	9,961
St. Mary	9,547	12,877	9,851	11,325
St. Tammany	24,665	75,139	22,722	59,193
Tangipahoa	15,345	26,181	15,843	20,421
Tensas	1,469	1,453	1,580	1,330
Terrebonne	13,684	26,358	14,414	21,314
Union	3,089	7,457	3,205	5,772
Vermilion	9,085	15,069	8,704	12,495
Vernon	4,035	11,032	4,655	8,794
Washington	6,554	11,006	7,399	8,983
Webster	6,833	11,070	7,197	9,420
W. Baton Rouge	4,932	5,822	5,058	4,924
West Carroll	1,231	3,740	1,319	3,220
W. Feliciana	2,214	2,932	2,187	2,512
Winn	2,056	4,366	2,167	4,028
Totals	**820,299**	**1,102,169**	**792,344**	**927,871**

Louisiana Vote Since 1948

1948: Thurmond, States' Rights, 204,290; Truman, D., 136,344; Dewey, R., 72,657; Wallace, Prog., 3,035.
1952: Stevenson, D., 345,027; Eisenhower, R., 306,925.
1956: Eisenhower, R., 329,047; Stevenson, D., 243,977; Andrews, States' Rights, 44,520.
1960: Kennedy, D., 407,339; Nixon, R., 230,890; States' Rights (unpledged), 169,572.
1964: Goldwater, R., 509,225; Johnson, D., 387,068.
1968: Wallace, 3rd Party, 530,300; Humphrey, D., 309,615; Nixon, R., 257,535.
1972: Nixon, R., 686,852; McGovern, D., 298,142; Schmitz, Amer., 52,099; Jenness, Soc. Workers, 14,398.
1976: Carter, D., 661,365; Ford, R., 587,446; Maddox, Amer., 10,058; Hall, Com., 7,417; McCarthy, Ind., 6,588; MacBride, Libertarian, 3,325.
1980: Reagan, R., 792,853; Carter, D., 708,453; Anderson, Ind., 26,345; Rarick, Amer. Ind., 10,333; Clark, Libertarian, 8,240; Commoner, Citizens, 1,584; DeBerry, Soc. Work., 783.
1984: Reagan, R., 1,037,299; Mondale, D., 651,586; Bergland, Libertarian, 1,876.
1988: Bush, R., 883,702; Dukakis, D., 717,460; Duke, Pop., 18,612; Paul, Lib., 4,115.
1992: Clinton, D., 815,971; Bush, R., 733,386; Perot, Ind., 211,478; Gritz, Populist/America First, 18,545; Marrou, Libertarian, 3,155; Daniels, Ind., 1,663; Phillips, U.S. Taxpayers, 1,552; Fulani, New Alliance, 1,434; LaRouche, Ind., 1,136.
1996: Clinton, D., 927,837; Dole, R., 712,586; Perot, Ref., 123,293; Browne, Libertarian, 7,499; Nader, Liberty, Ecology, Community, 4,719; Phillips, Taxpayers, 3,366; Hagelin, Natural Law, 2,981; Moorehead, Workers World, 1,678.
2000: Bush, R., 927,871; Gore, D., 792,344; Nader, Green, 20,473; Buchanan, Reform, 14,356; Phillips, Constitution, 5,483; Browne, Libertarian, 2,951; Harris, Soc. Workers, 1,103; Hagelin, Natural Law, 1,075.
2004: Bush, R., 1,102,169; Kerry, D., 820,299; Nader, Better Life, 7,032; Peroutka, Constitution, 5,203; Badnarik, Libertarian, 2,781; Brown, Protect Wking Fam., 1,795; Amondson, Prohib., 1,566; Cobb, Green, 1,276; Harris, Soc. Wkrs., 985.

Maine

	2004		2000	
City	**Kerry (D)**	**Bush (R)**	**Gore (D)**	**Bush (R)**
Auburn	6,869	5,219	6,014	4,568
Augusta	5,543	4,149	5,116	3,344
Bangor	9,162	7,135	7,311	6,131
Biddeford	6,520	3,756	5,383	3,126
Brunswick	7,288	4,248	5,547	3,767
Gorham	4,393	4,133	3,394	3,353
Lewiston	11,021	6,523	9,663	5,255
Orono	3,649	1,578	2,701	1,506
Portland	26,800	9,455	20,506	8,838
Presque Isle	2,309	2,268	2,004	2,231
Saco	5,892	3,948	4,783	3,402
Sanford	5,582	4,634	4,653	3,871
Scarborough	5,651	5,569	4,278	4,964
S. Portland	8,965	4,882	7,267	4,390
Waterville	5,056	2,413	4,279	2,115
Westbrook	5,047	3,744	4,316	3,258
Windham	4,400	4,553	3,550	3,754
Other	272,695	251,994	219,478	218,743
Totals	**396,842**	**330,201**	**319,951**	**286,616**

Maine Vote Since 1948

1948: Dewey, R., 150,234; Truman, D., 111,916; Wallace, Prog., 1,884; Thomas, Soc., 547; Teichert, Soc. Labor, 206.
1952: Eisenhower, R., 232,353; Stevenson, D., 118,806; Hallinan, Prog., 332; Hass, Soc. Labor, 156; Hoopes, Soc., 138; scattered, 1.
1956: Eisenhower, R., 249,238; Stevenson, D., 102,468.
1960: Nixon, R., 240,608; Kennedy, D., 181,159.
1964: Johnson, D., 262,264; Goldwater, R., 118,701.
1968: Humphrey, D., 217,312; Nixon, R., 169,254; Wallace, 3rd Party, 6,370.
1972: Nixon, R., 256,458; McGovern, D., 160,584; scattered, 229.
1976: Ford, R., 236,320; Carter, D., 232,279; McCarthy, Ind., 10,874; Bubar, Proh., 3,495.
1980: Reagan, R., 238,522; Carter, D., 220,974; Anderson, Ind., 53,327; Clark, Libertarian, 5,119; Commoner, Citizens, 4,394; Hall, Com., 591; write-in, 84.
1984: Reagan, R., 336,500; Mondale, D., 214,515.
1988: Bush, R., 307,131; Dukakis, D., 243,569; Paul, Lib., 2,700; Fulani, New Alliance, 1,405.
1992: Clinton, D., 263,420; Perot, Ind., 206,820; Bush, R., 206,504; Marrou, Libertarian, 1,681.

1996: Clinton, D., 312,788; Dole, R., 186,378; Perot, Ref., 85,970; Nader, Green, 15,279; Browne, Libertarian, 2,996; Phillips, Taxpayers, 1,517; Hagelin, Natural Law, 825.
2000: Gore, D., 319,951; Bush, R., 286,616; Nader, Green, 37,127; Buchanan, Reform, 4,443; Browne, Libertarian, 3,074; Phillips, Constitution, 579.
2004: Kerry, D., 396,842; Bush, R., 330,201; Nader, Better Life, 8,069; Cobb, Green, 2,936; Badnarik, Libertarian, 1,965; Peroutka, Constitution, 735.

Maryland

	2004		2000	
County	**Kerry (D)**	**Bush (R)**	**Gore (D)**	**Bush (R)**
Allegany	10,576	18,980	10,894	14,656
Anne Arundel	103,324	133,231	89,624	104,209
Baltimore	182,474	166,051	160,635	133,033
Calvert	15,967	23,017	12,986	16,004
Caroline	3,810	7,396	3,396	5,300
Carroll	22,974	55,275	20,146	41,742
Cecil	14,680	22,556	12,327	15,494
Charles	29,354	28,442	21,873	21,768
Dorchester	5,411	7,801	5,232	5,847
Frederick	39,503	59,934	30,725	45,350
Garrett	3,291	9,085	2,872	7,514
Harford	39,685	71,565	35,665	52,862
Howard	72,257	59,724	58,556	49,809
Kent	4,278	4,900	3,627	4,155
Montgomery	273,936	136,334	232,453	124,580
Prince George's	260,532	55,532	214,345	50,017
Queen Anne's	7,070	14,489	6,257	9,970
St. Mary's	13,776	23,725	11,912	16,856
Somerset	4,034	4,884	3,785	3,609
Talbot	7,367	11,288	5,854	8,874
Washington	20,387	36,917	18,221	27,948
Wicomico	15,137	21,998	14,469	16,338
Worcester	9,648	15,349	9,389	10,742
CITY				
Baltimore	175,022	36,230	158,765	27,150
Totals	**1,334,493**	**1,024,703**	**1,144,008**	**813,827**

Maryland Vote Since 1948

1948: Dewey, R., 294,814; Truman, D., 286,521; Wallace, Prog., 9,983; Thomas, Soc., 2,941; Thurmond, States' Rights, 2,476; Wright, write-in, 2,294.
1952: Eisenhower, R., 499,424; Stevenson, D., 395,337; Hallinan, Prog., 7,313.
1956: Eisenhower, R., 559,738; Stevenson, D., 372,613.
1960: Kennedy, D., 565,800; Nixon, R., 489,538.
1964: Johnson, D., 730,912; Goldwater, R., 385,495; write-in, 50.
1968: Humphrey, D., 538,310; Nixon, R., 517,995; Wallace, 3rd Party, 178,734.
1972: Nixon, R., 829,305; McGovern, D., 505,781; Schmitz, Amer., 18,726.
1976: Carter, D., 759,612; Ford, R., 672,661.
1980: Carter, D., 726,161; Reagan, R., 680,606; Anderson, Ind., 119,537; Clark, Libertarian, 14,192.
1984: Reagan, R., 879,918; Mondale, D., 787,935; Bergland, Libertarian, 5,721.
1988: Bush, R., 876,167; Dukakis, D., 826,304; Paul, Lib., 6,748; Fulani, New Alliance, 5,115.
1992: Clinton, D., 988,571; Bush, R., 707,094; Perot, Ind., 281,414; Marrou, Libertarian, 4,715; Fulani, New Alliance, 2,786.
1996: Clinton, D., 966,207; Dole, R., 681,530; Perot, Ref., 115,812; Browne, Libertarian, 8,765; Phillips, Taxpayers, 3,402; Hagelin, Natural Law, 2,517.
2000: Gore, D., 1,144,008; Bush, R., 813,827; Nader, Green, 53,768; Browne, Libertarian, 5,310; Buchanan, Reform., 4,248; Phillips, Constitution, 918.
2004: Kerry, D., 1,334,493; Bush, R., 1,024,703; Nader, Populist, 11,854; Badnarik, Libertarian, 6,094; Cobb, Green, 3,632; Peroutka, Constitution, 3,421.

Massachusetts

	2004		2000	
City	**Kerry (D)**	**Bush (R)**	**Gore (D)**	**Bush (R)**
Boston	160,884	44,518	132,393	36,389
Brockton	20,091	10,058	18,563	8,288
Brookline	21,256	5,269	19,384	4,350
Cambridge	35,886	5,338	28,846	5,166
Chicopee	14,642	7,957	13,236	6,512
Fall River	23,859	7,369	22,051	5,621
Framingham	17,239	8,448	17,308	7,347
Lawrence	11,547	4,796	10,048	3,700
Lowell	18,195	10,554	17,554	7,790
Lynn	19,372	8,373	18,836	6,776
Medford	17,737	7,932	16,776	6,353
New Bedford	25,551	7,328	23,880	5,473
Newton	32,061	10,025	29,918	8,132
Quincy	24,173	13,373	23,117	11,282
Somerville	24,300	5,232	19,984	4,468
Springfield	33,583	13,028	29,728	10,288
Waltham	14,517	8,228	13,736	6,700
Weymouth	15,367	10,912	15,570	8,884
Worcester	38,264	17,648	35,231	14,402
Other	1,227,624	858,194	1,110,328	710,581
Totals	**1,803,800**	**1,071,109**	**1,616,487**	**878,502**

Massachusetts Vote Since 1948

1948: Truman, D., 1,151,788; Dewey, R., 909,370; Wallace, Prog., 38,157; Teichert, Soc. Labor, 5,535; Watson, Proh., 1,663.
1952: Eisenhower, R., 1,292,325; Stevenson, D., 1,083,525; Hallinan, Prog., 4,636; Hass, Soc. Labor, 1,957; Hamblen, Proh., 886; scattered, 69; blanks, 41,150.
1956: Eisenhower, R., 1,393,197; Stevenson, D., 948,190; Hass, Soc. Labor, 5,573; Holtwick, Proh., 1,205; others, 341.
1960: Kennedy, D., 1,487,174; Nixon, R., 976,750; Hass, Soc. Labor, 3,892; Decker, Proh., 1,633; others, 31; blank and void, 26,024.
1964: Johnson, D., 1,786,422; Goldwater, R., 549,727; Hass, Soc. Labor, 4,755; Munn, Proh., 3,735; scattered, 159; blank, 48,104.
1968: Humphrey, D., 1,469,218; Nixon, R., 766,844; Wallace, 3rd Party, 87,088; Blomen, Soc. Labor, 6,180; Munn, Proh., 2,369; scattered, 53; blanks, 25,394.
1972: McGovern, D., 1,332,540; Nixon, R., 1,112,078; Jenness, Soc. Workers, 10,600; Schmitz, Amer., 2,877; Fisher, Soc. Labor, 129; Spock, Peoples, 101; Hall, Com., 46; Hospers, Libertarian, 43; scattered, 342.
1976: Carter, D., 1,429,475; Ford, R., 1,030,276; McCarthy, Ind., 65,637; Camejo, Soc. Workers, 8,138; Anderson, Amer., 7,555; La Rouche, U.S. Labor, 4,922; MacBride, Libertarian, 135.
1980: Reagan, R., 1,057,631; Carter, D., 1,053,802; Anderson, Ind., 382,539; Clark, Libertarian, 22,038; DeBerry, Soc. Workers, 3,735; Commoner, Citizens, 2,056; McReynolds, Soc., 62; Bubar, Statesman, 34; Griswold, Workers World, 19; scattered, 2,382.
1984: Reagan, R., 1,310,936; Mondale, D., 1,239,606.
1988: Dukakis, D., 1,401,415; Bush, R., 1,194,635; Paul, Lib., 24,251; Fulani, New Alliance, 9,561.
1992: Clinton, D., 1,318,639; Bush, R., 805,039; Perot, Ind., 630,731; Marrou, Libertarian, 9,021; Fulani, New Alliance, 3,172; Phillips, U.S. Taxpayers, 2,218; Hagelin, Natural Law, 1,812; LaRouche, Ind., 1,027.
1996: Clinton, D., 1,571,509; Dole, R., 718,058; Perot, Ref., 227,206; Browne, Libertarian, 20,424; Hagelin, Natural Law, 5,183; Moorehead, Workers World, 3,276.
2000: Gore, D., 1,616,487; Bush, R., 878,502; Nader, Green, 173,564; Browne, Libertarian, 16,366; Buchanan, Reform, 11,149; Hagelin, Natural Law, 2,884.
2004: Kerry, D., 1,803,800; Bush, R., 1,071,109; Badnarik, Libertarian, 15,022; Cobb, Green, 10,623.

Michigan

	2004		2000	
County	**Kerry (D)**	**Bush (R)**	**Gore (D)**	**Bush (R)**
Alcona	2,871	3,592	2,696	3,152
Alger	2,395	2,318	2,071	2,142
Allegan	19,355	34,022	15,495	28,197
Alpena	7,407	7,665	7,053	6,769
Antrim	5,072	8,379	4,329	6,780
Arenac	4,076	4,071	3,685	3,421
Baraga	1,660	1,977	1,400	1,836
Barry	11,312	18,638	9,769	15,716
Bay	31,049	25,448	28,251	22,150
Benzie	4,383	5,284	3,546	4,172
Berrien	32,846	41,076	28,152	35,689
Branch	7,004	10,784	6,691	8,743
Calhoun	29,891	32,093	27,312	26,291
Cass	9,537	12,964	8,808	10,545
Charlevoix	5,729	8,214	4,958	7,018
Cheboygan	5,941	7,798	5,484	6,815
Chippewa	7,203	9,122	6,370	7,526
Clare	6,984	7,088	6,287	5,937
Clinton	15,483	21,989	13,394	18,054
Crawford	3,126	4,017	2,790	3,345
Delta	9,381	9,680	7,970	8,871
Dickinson	5,650	7,734	5,533	6,932
Eaton	25,411	29,781	23,211	24,803
Emmet	6,846	10,332	5,451	8,602
Genesee	128,334	83,870	119,833	66,641
Gladwin	6,343	6,770	5,573	5,743
Gogebic	4,421	3,935	4,066	3,929
Grand Traverse	18,256	27,446	14,371	22,358
Gratiot	7,377	9,834	6,538	8,312
Hillsdale	7,123	12,804	6,495	10,483
Houghton	6,731	8,889	5,688	7,895
Huron	7,629	9,671	6,899	8,911
Ingham	76,877	54,734	69,231	47,314
Ionia	10,647	16,621	9,481	13,915
Iosco	6,557	7,301	6,505	6,345
Iron	3,215	3,224	3,014	2,967
Isabella	12,334	11,754	10,228	10,053
Jackson	31,025	40,029	28,160	32,066
Kalamazoo	61,462	57,147	48,807	48,254
Kalkaska	3,189	5,084	2,774	3,842
Kent	116,909	171,201	95,442	148,602
Keweenaw	630	781	540	740
Lake	2,675	2,503	2,584	1,961
Lapeer	18,086	25,556	15,749	20,351
Leelanau	6,048	7,733	4,635	6,840
Lenawee	20,787	25,675	18,365	20,681
Livingston	33,991	58,860	28,780	44,637
Luce	1,045	1,749	956	1,480
Mackinac	2,819	3,706	2,533	3,272
Macomb	196,160	202,166	172,625	164,265
Manistee	6,272	6,295	5,639	5,401

County	2004 Kerry (D)	2004 Bush (R)	2000 Gore (D)	2000 Bush (R)
Marquette	17,412	14,690	15,503	12,577
Mason	6,333	8,124	5,579	7,066
Mecosta	7,730	9,710	6,300	8,072
Menominee	5,326	5,942	4,597	5,529
Midland	18,355	24,369	15,959	21,887
Missaukee	2,319	5,055	2,062	4,274
Monroe	36,089	37,470	31,555	28,940
Montcalm	11,471	14,968	9,627	12,696
Montmorency	2,196	3,300	2,139	2,750
Muskegon	44,282	35,302	37,865	30,028
Newaygo	9,057	13,608	7,677	11,399
Oakland	319,387	316,633	281,201	274,319
Oceana	5,441	6,677	4,597	5,913
Ogemaw	5,215	5,454	4,896	4,706
Ontonagon	1,863	2,262	1,514	2,472
Osceola	4,467	6,599	4,006	5,680
Oscoda	1,792	2,570	1,677	2,207
Otsego	4,674	7,470	4,034	6,108
Ottawa	35,552	92,048	29,600	78,703
Presque Isle	3,432	3,982	3,242	3,660
Roscommon	6,810	7,364	6,433	6,190
Saginaw	54,887	47,165	50,825	41,152
Sanilac	7,883	12,632	7,153	10,966
Schoolcraft	2,137	2,267	2,036	2,088
Shiawassee	16,881	19,407	15,520	15,816
St. Clair	36,174	42,740	33,002	33,571
St. Joseph	9,648	15,340	8,574	12,906
Tuscola	12,631	15,389	10,845	13,213
Van Buren	16,151	17,634	13,796	14,792
Washtenaw	109,953	61,455	86,647	52,459
Wayne	600,047	257,750	530,414	223,021
Wexford	6,034	8,966	5,326	7,215
Totals	**2,479,183**	**2,313,746**	**2,170,418**	**1,953,139**

Michigan Vote Since 1948

1948: Dewey, R., 1,038,595; Truman, D., 1,003,448; Wallace, Prog., 46,515; Watson, Proh., 13,052; Thomas, Soc., 6,063; Teichert, Soc. Labor, 1,263; Dobbs, Soc. Workers, 672.
1952: Eisenhower, R., 1,551,529; Stevenson, D., 1,230,657; Hamblen, Proh., 10,331; Hallinan, Prog., 3,922; Hass, Soc. Labor, 1,495; Dobbs, Soc. Workers, 655; scattered, 3.
1956: Eisenhower, R., 1,713,647; Stevenson, D., 1,359,898; Holtwick, Proh., 6,923.
1960: Kennedy, D., 1,687,269; Nixon, R., 1,620,428; Dobbs, Soc. Workers, 4,347; Decker, Proh., 2,029; Daly, Tax Cut, 1,767; Hass, Soc. Labor, 1,718; Ind. Amer., 539.
1964: Johnson, D., 2,136,615; Goldwater, R., 1,060,152; DeBerry, Soc. Workers, 3,817; Hass, Soc. Labor, 1,704; Proh. (no candidate listed), 699; scattered, 145.
1968: Humphrey, D., 1,593,082; Nixon, R., 1,370,665; Wallace, 3rd Party, 331,968; Halstead, Soc. Workers, 4,099; Blomen, Soc. Labor, 1,762; Cleaver, New Politics, 4,585; Munn, Proh., 60; scattered, 29.
1972: Nixon, R., 1,961,721; McGovern, D., 1,459,435; Schmitz, Amer., 63,321; Fisher, Soc. Labor, 2,437; Jenness, Soc. Workers, 1,603; Hall, Com., 1,210.
1976: Ford, R., 1,893,742; Carter, D., 1,696,714; McCarthy, Ind., 47,905; MacBride, Libertarian, 5,406; Wright, People's, 3,504; Camejo, Soc. Workers, 1,804; LaRouche, U.S. Labor, 1,366; Levin, Soc. Labor, 1,148; scattered, 2,160.
1980: Reagan, R., 1,915,225; Carter, D., 1,661,532; Anderson, Ind., 275,223; Clark, Libertarian, 41,597; Commoner, Citizens, 11,930; Hall, Com., 3,262; Griswold, Workers World, 30; Greaves, Amer., 21; Bubar, Statesman, 9.
1984: Reagan, R., 2,251,571; Mondale, D., 1,529,638; Bergland, Libertarian, 10,055.
1988: Bush, R., 1,965,486; Dukakis, D., 1,675,783; Paul, Lib., 18,336; Fulani, Ind., 2,513.
1992: Clinton, D., 1,871,182; Bush, R., 1,554,940; Perot, Ind., 824,813; Marrou, Libertarian, 10,175; Phillips, U.S. Taxpayers, 8,263; Hagelin, Natural Law, 2,954.
1996: Clinton, D., 1,989,653; Dole, R., 1,481,212; Perot, Ref., 336,670; Browne, Libertarian, 27,670; Hagelin, Natural Law, 4,254; Moorehead, Workers World, 3,153; White, Soc. Equality, 1,554.
2000: Gore, D., 2,170,418; Bush, R., 1,953,139; Nader, Green, 84,165; Browne, Libertarian, 16,711; Phillips, U.S. Taxpayers, 3,791; Hagelin, Natural Law, 2,426.
2004: Kerry, D., 2,479,183; Bush, R., 2,313,746; Nader, Ind., 24,035; Badnarik, Libertarian, 10,552; Cobb, Green, 5,325; Peroutka, U.S. Taxpayers, 4,980; Brown, Nat. Law, 1,431.

Minnesota

County	2004 Kerry (D)	2004 Bush (R)	2000 Gore (D)	2000 Bush (R)
Aitkin	4,539	4,768	3,830	3,755
Anoka	80,226	91,853	68,008	69,256
Becker	6,756	9,795	5,253	8,152
Beltrami	10,592	10,237	7,301	8,346
Benton	8,059	10,043	6,009	7,663
Big Stone	1,536	1,483	1,430	1,370
Blue Earth	16,865	15,737	12,329	12,942
Brown	5,158	8,395	4,650	7,370
Carlton	11,462	6,642	8,620	5,578
Carver	16,456	28,510	12,462	20,790
Cass	6,835	8,875	5,534	7,134
Chippewa	3,424	3,089	2,952	2,977
Chisago	12,219	15,705	9,593	10,937
Clay	12,989	14,365	10,128	11,712
Clearwater	1,871	2,438	1,466	2,137
Cook	1,733	1,489	1,171	1,295
Cottonwood	2,726	3,557	2,503	3,369
Crow Wing	14,005	19,106	11,255	15,035
Dakota	104,635	108,959	85,446	87,250
Dodge	4,117	5,593	3,370	4,213
Douglas	8,219	11,793	6,352	9,811
Faribault	3,767	4,794	3,624	4,336
Fillmore	5,825	5,694	5,020	4,646
Freeborn	9,733	7,681	8,514	6,843
Goodhue	12,103	13,134	9,981	10,852
Grant	1,856	1,893	1,507	1,804
Hennepin	383,841	255,133	307,599	225,657
Houston	5,276	5,631	4,502	5,077
Hubbard	4,741	6,444	3,632	5,307
Isanti	7,883	11,190	6,247	7,668
Itasca	13,290	10,705	10,583	9,545
Jackson	2,652	3,024	2,364	2,773
Kanabec	3,592	4,527	2,831	3,480
Kandiyohi	9,337	11,704	8,220	10,026
Kittson	1,333	1,307	1,107	1,353
Koochiching	3,662	3,539	2,903	3,523
Lac Qui Parle	2,390	2,093	2,244	1,941
Lake	4,212	2,769	3,579	2,465
Lake of the Woods	921	1,428	848	1,216
Le Sueur	6,466	7,746	5,361	6,138
Lincoln	1,558	1,736	1,590	1,513
Lyon	5,292	7,203	4,737	6,087
Mahnomen	1,339	1,132	921	1,122
Marshall	2,308	3,187	1,910	2,912
Martin	4,590	6,311	4,166	5,686
McLeod	6,712	11,407	5,609	8,782
Meeker	5,292	6,854	4,402	5,520
Mille Lacs	5,677	7,194	4,376	5,223
Morrison	6,794	9,698	5,274	8,197
Mower	12,334	7,591	10,693	6,873
Murray	2,218	2,719	2,093	2,407
Nicollet	8,797	8,689	7,041	7,221
Nobles	3,898	5,159	3,760	4,766
Norman	1,954	1,794	1,575	1,808
Olmsted	33,285	37,371	25,822	30,641
Otter Tail	12,038	19,734	9,844	16,963
Pennington	3,117	3,767	2,458	3,380
Pine	7,228	7,033	6,148	5,854
Pipestone	1,900	3,066	1,970	2,693
Polk	6,729	8,724	5,764	7,609
Pope	3,301	3,303	2,771	2,808
Ramsey	171,846	97,096	138,470	87,669
Red Lake	963	1,164	830	1,090
Redwood	3,104	4,898	2,681	4,589
Renville	3,787	4,430	3,533	4,036
Rice	16,425	13,881	13,140	10,876
Rock	2,000	3,111	2,081	2,772
Roseau	2,442	5,355	2,128	4,695
Scott	23,958	36,055	17,503	23,954
Sherburne	15,816	25,182	12,109	16,813
Sibley	3,109	4,669	2,687	4,087
St. Louis	77,958	40,112	64,237	35,420
Stearns	32,659	41,726	24,800	32,402
Steele	7,994	10,389	6,900	8,223
Stevens	2,821	3,030	2,434	2,831
Swift	3,165	2,481	2,698	2,376
Todd	5,034	6,945	4,132	6,031
Traverse	1,026	1,076	884	1,074
Wabasha	5,548	6,120	4,522	5,245
Wadena	2,791	4,214	2,251	3,733
Waseca	4,179	5,457	3,694	4,608
Washington	61,395	65,751	49,637	51,502
Watonwan	2,514	2,970	2,258	2,562
Wilkin	1,169	2,303	1,046	2,032
Winona	14,231	12,686	11,069	10,773
Wright	22,618	36,176	16,762	23,861
Yellow Medicine	2,799	2,878	2,528	2,598
Totals	**1,445,014**	**1,346,695**	**1,168,266**	**1,109,659**

Minnesota Vote Since 1948

1948: Truman, D., 692,966; Dewey, R., 483,617; Wallace, Prog., 27,866; Thomas, Soc., 4,646; Teichert, Soc. Labor, 2,525; Dobbs, Soc. Workers, 606.
1952: Eisenhower, R., 763,211; Stevenson, D., 608,458; Hallinan, Prog., 2,666; Hass, Soc. Labor, 2,383; Hamblen, Proh., 2,147; Dobbs, Soc. Workers, 618.
1956: Eisenhower, R., 719,302; Stevenson, D., 617,525; Hass, Soc. Labor (Ind. Gov.), 2,080; Dobbs, Soc. Workers, 1,098.
1960: Kennedy, D., 779,933; Nixon, R., 757,915; Dobbs, Soc. Workers, 3,077; Industrial Gov., 962.
1964: Johnson, D., 991,117; Goldwater, R., 559,624; Hass, Industrial Gov., 2,544; DeBerry, Soc. Workers, 1,177.
1968: Humphrey, D., 857,738; Nixon, R., 658,643; Wallace, 3rd Party, 68,931; Cleaver, Peace, 935; Halstead, Soc. Workers, 808; McCarthy, write-in, 585; Mitchell, Com., 415; Blomen, Ind. Gov't., 285; scattered, 2,613.
1972: Nixon, R., 898,269; McGovern, D., 802,346; Schmitz, Amer., 31,407; Fisher, Soc. Labor, 4,261; Spock, Peoples, 2,805; Jenness, Soc. Workers, 940; Hall, Com., 662; scattered, 962.
1976: Carter, D., 1,070,440; Ford, R., 819,395; McCarthy, Ind., 35,490; Anderson, Amer., 13,592; Camejo, Soc. Workers, 4,149; MacBride, Libertarian, 3,529; Hall, Com., 1,092.
1980: Carter, D., 954,173; Reagan, R., 873,268; Anderson, Ind., 174,997; Clark, Libertarian, 31,593; Commoner, Citizens, 8,406; Hall, Com., 1,117; DeBerry, Soc. Workers, 711; Griswold, Workers World, 698; McReynolds, Soc., 536; write-in, 281.
1984: Mondale, D., 1,036,364; Reagan, R., 1,032,603; Bergland, Libertarian, 2,996.
1988: Dukakis, D., 1,109,471; Bush, R., 962,337; McCarthy, Minn. Prog., 5,403; Paul, Lib., 5,109.
1992: Clinton, D., 1,020,997; Bush, R., 747,841; Perot, Ind., 562,506; Marrou, Libertarian, 3,373; Gritz, Populist/America First, 3,363; Hagelin, Natural Law, 1,406.
1996: Clinton, D., 1,120,438; Dole, R., 766,476; Perot, Ref., 257,704; Nader, Green, 24,908; Browne, Libertarian, 8,271; Peron, Grass Roots, 4,898; Phillips, Taxpayers, 3,416; Hagelin, Natural Law, 1,808; Birrenbach, Ind. Grass Roots, 787; Harris, Soc. Workers, 684; White, Soc. Equality, 347.
2000: Gore, D., 1,168,266; Bush, R., 1,109,659; Nader, Green, 126,696; Buchanan, Reform Minnesota, 22,166; Browne, Libertarian, 5,282; Phillips, Constitution, 3,272; Hagelin, Reform, 2,294; Harris, Soc. Workers, 1,022.
2004: Kerry, D., 1,445,014; Bush, R., 1,346,695; Nader, Better Life, 18,683; Badnarik, Libertarian, 4,639; Cobb, Green, 4,408; Peroutka, Constitution, 3,074; Harens, other, 2,387; Van Auken, Soc. Equal., 539; Calero, Soc. Wkrs., 416.

Mississippi

	2004		2000	
County	**Kerry (D)**	**Bush (R)**	**Gore (D)**	**Bush (R)**
Adams	8,423	6,996	8,065	6,691
Alcorn	5,454	8,634	5,059	7,254
Amite	3,012	4,147	2,673	3,677
Attala	3,145	5,014	2,922	4,206
Benton	2,245	1,969	1,886	1,561
Bolivar	9,631	5,535	8,436	4,847
Calhoun	2,234	4,131	2,251	3,448
Carroll	1,900	3,664	1,726	3,165
Chickasaw	4,078	4,193	3,519	3,549
Choctaw	1,366	2,694	1,278	2,398
Claiborne	4,362	950	3,670	883
Clarke	2,402	5,068	2,368	4,503
Clay	4,753	4,342	4,515	3,570
Coahoma	6,805	3,676	5,662	3,695
Copiah	4,961	6,374	4,845	5,643
Covington	3,158	5,044	2,623	4,180
DeSoto	13,255	36,306	9,586	24,879
Forrest	10,220	16,318	8,500	13,281
Franklin	1,574	2,893	1,486	2,427
George	1,724	6,223	1,977	5,143
Greene	1,421	3,850	1,317	3,082
Grenada	4,180	5,872	3,813	4,743
Hancock	5,107	12,581	4,801	9,326
Harrison	23,076	39,703	19,142	32,256
Hinds	54,845	36,975	46,789	37,753
Holmes	6,366	1,961	5,447	1,937
Humphreys	3,168	1,679	2,288	1,628
Issaquena	516	439	555	366
Itawamba	2,802	6,833	2,994	5,424
Jackson	15,572	35,134	14,193	30,068
Jasper	4,117	3,855	3,104	3,294
Jefferson	2,821	630	2,786	600
Jefferson Davis	2,959	2,668	2,835	2,437
Jones	7,398	19,125	7,713	16,341
Kemper	2,465	2,109	2,311	1,915
Lafayette	6,218	9,004	5,139	7,081
Lamar	3,923	16,410	3,478	12,795
Lauderdale	10,292	19,736	8,412	17,315
Lawrence	2,308	3,956	2,841	3,674
Leake	3,212	4,962	2,793	4,114
Lee	10,127	20,254	9,142	15,551
Leflore	7,566	4,635	6,401	4,626
Lincoln	4,418	10,008	4,358	8,540
Lowndes	10,408	13,690	7,537	11,404
Madison	13,268	24,257	10,416	19,109
Marion	3,888	7,999	4,114	6,796
Marshall	8,591	5,975	7,735	4,723
Monroe	6,237	9,308	5,783	7,397
Montgomery	2,473	3,002	2,187	2,630
Neshoba	2,600	7,780	2,563	6,409
Newton	2,280	6,165	2,147	5,540
Noxubee	4,346	1,723	3,383	1,530
Oktibbeha	7,015	9,068	6,443	7,959
Panola	6,615	6,769	5,880	5,424
Pearl River	4,472	14,896	4,611	11,575
Perry	1,261	3,747	1,285	3,026
Pike	7,881	8,660	6,544	7,464
Pontotoc	2,660	8,480	2,771	6,601
Prentiss	3,327	6,538	3,287	5,101
Quitman	2,032	1,360	2,103	1,280
Rankin	11,005	43,054	8,050	32,983
Scott	3,802	6,395	3,548	5,601
Sharkey	1,560	1,120	1,706	1,074
Simpson	3,272	7,138	3,227	6,254
Smith	1,496	5,577	1,620	4,838
Stone	1,528	4,146	1,677	3,702
Sunflower	6,359	3,534	4,981	3,369
Tallahatchie	3,420	2,737	3,041	2,428
Tate	4,347	6,760	3,441	5,148
Tippah	3,016	6,174	2,908	5,381
Tishomingo	2,846	5,379	2,747	4,122
Tunica	2,140	950	1,539	792
Union	2,839	7,906	3,094	6,087
Walthall	2,435	3,888	2,356	3,476
Warren	8,224	11,356	7,485	10,892
Washington	11,569	7,731	10,405	7,367
Wayne	3,193	5,562	2,981	4,635
Webster	1,341	3,708	1,426	3,069
Wilkinson	2,794	1,563	2,551	1,423
Winston	3,978	5,386	3,672	4,645
Yalobusha	2,656	3,278	2,674	2,470
Yazoo	5,013	5,672	4,997	5,254
Totals	**457,766**	**684,981**	**404,614**	**572,844**

Mississippi Vote Since 1948

1948: Thurmond, States' Rights, 167,538; Truman, D., 19,384; Dewey, R., 5,043; Wallace, Prog., 225.
1952: Stevenson, D., 172,566; Eisenhower, Ind. vote pledged to Rep. candidate, 112,966.
1956: Stevenson, D., 144,498; Eisenhower, R., 56,372; Black and Tan Grand Old Party, 4,313; total, 60,685; Byrd, Ind., 42,966.
1960: Democratic unpledged electors, 116,248; Kennedy, D., 108,362; Nixon, R., 73,561. Mississippi's victorious slate of 8 unpledged Democratic electors cast their votes for Sen. Harry F. Byrd (D, VA).
1964: Goldwater, R., 356,528; Johnson, D., 52,618.
1968: Wallace, 3rd Party, 415,349; Humphrey, D., 150,644; Nixon, R., 88,516.
1972: Nixon, R., 505,125; McGovern, D., 126,782; Schmitz, Amer., 11,598; Jenness, Soc. Workers, 2,458.
1976: Carter, D., 381,309; Ford, R., 366,846; Anderson, Amer., 6,678; McCarthy, Ind., 4,074; Maddox, Ind., 4,049; Camejo, Soc. Workers, 2,805; MacBride, Libertarian, 2,609.
1980: Reagan, R., 441,089; Carter, D., 429,281; Anderson, Ind., 12,036; Clark, Libertarian, 5,465; Griswold, Workers World, 2,402; Pulley, Soc. Workers, 2,347.
1984: Reagan, R., 582,377; Mondale, D., 352,192; Bergland, Libertarian, 2,336.
1988: Bush, R., 557,890; Dukakis, D., 363,921; Duke, Ind., 4,232; Paul, Lib., 3,329.
1992: Bush, R., 487,793; Clinton, D., 400,258; Perot, Ind., 85,626; Fulani, New Alliance, 2,625; Marrou, Libertarian, 2,154; Phillips, U.S. Taxpayers, 1,652; Hagelin, Natural Law, 1,140.
1996: Dole, R., 439,838; Clinton, D., 394,022; Perot, Ind. (Ref.), 52,222; Browne, Libertarian, 2,809; Phillips, Taxpayers, 2,314; Hagelin, Natural Law, 1,447; Collins, Ind., 1,205.
2000: Bush, R., 572,844; Gore, D., 404,614; Nader, Ind., 8,122; Phillips, Constitution, 3,267; Buchanan, Reform, 2,265; Browne, Libertarian, 2,009; Harris, Ind., 613; Hagelin, Natural Law, 450.
2004: Bush, R., 684,981; Kerry, D., 457,766; Nader, Ref., 3,175; Badnarik, Libertarian, 1,793; Peroutka, Constitution, 1,758; Harris, Ind., 1,599; Cobb, Green, 1,073.

Missouri

County	2004 Kerry (D)	2004 Bush (R)	2000 Gore (D)	2000 Bush (R)
Adair	4,938	6,367	4,101	6,050
Andrew	3,069	5,135	2,795	4,257
Atchison	1,005	2,137	1,013	1,798
Audrain	4,318	6,294	4,551	5,256
Barry	4,223	9,599	4,135	7,885
Barton	1,373	4,572	1,424	3,836
Bates	3,398	5,004	3,386	4,245
Benton	3,381	5,575	3,150	4,218
Bollinger	1,754	4,102	1,692	3,487
Boone	37,643	37,801	28,811	28,426
Buchanan	17,799	19,812	17,085	16,423
Butler	4,666	11,696	4,996	9,111
Caldwell	1,645	2,593	1,488	2,220
Callaway	6,559	11,108	6,708	8,238
Camden	6,296	13,122	6,323	10,358
Cape Girardeau	10,568	23,814	9,334	19,832
Carroll	1,568	3,155	1,620	2,880
Carter	964	1,797	997	1,730
Cass	16,681	27,253	14,921	20,113
Cedar	1,910	4,238	1,979	3,530
Chariton	1,892	2,421	1,792	2,300
Christian	9,059	22,102	7,896	14,824
Clark	1,794	1,899	1,812	1,899
Clay	44,670	51,193	39,084	39,083
Clinton	4,165	5,287	3,994	4,323
Cole	11,753	24,752	12,056	20,167
Cooper	2,400	5,058	2,567	4,072
Crawford	3,632	5,686	3,350	4,754
Dade	1,104	2,963	1,193	2,468
Dallas	2,407	4,788	2,311	3,723
Daviess	1,402	2,351	1,367	2,011
DeKalb	1,707	2,941	1,562	2,363
Dent	1,865	4,369	1,839	3,996
Douglas	1,741	4,498	1,546	3,599
Dunklin	4,901	6,720	4,947	5,426
Franklin	18,556	26,429	16,172	21,863
Gasconade	2,355	4,753	2,257	4,190
Gentry	1,201	2,085	1,271	1,771
Greene	46,657	77,885	41,091	59,178
Grundy	1,561	3,172	1,563	2,976
Harrison	1,279	2,729	1,328	2,552
Henry	4,461	6,361	4,459	5,120
Hickory	2,043	2,791	1,961	2,172
Holt	811	1,864	871	1,738
Howard	1,972	2,915	1,944	2,414
Howell	5,118	11,097	4,641	9,018
Iron	2,157	2,477	2,044	2,237
Jackson	183,654	130,500	160,419	104,418
Jasper	13,002	31,846	11,737	24,899
Jefferson	46,057	46,624	38,616	36,766
Johnson	7,790	12,257	6,926	9,339
Knox	761	1,207	787	1,226
Laclede	4,213	10,578	4,183	8,556
Lafayette	6,412	9,656	6,343	7,849
Lawrence	4,506	11,194	4,235	8,305
Lewis	1,754	2,862	2,023	2,388
Lincoln	8,368	11,316	6,961	8,549
Linn	2,440	3,422	2,646	3,246
Livingston	2,278	4,029	2,425	3,709
Macon	2,856	4,673	2,817	4,232
Madison	1,972	2,905	1,828	2,460
Maries	1,563	2,825	1,554	2,216
Marion	4,568	7,815	4,993	6,550
McDonald	2,215	5,443	1,866	4,460
Mercer	582	1,207	555	1,250
Miller	2,959	7,797	3,217	5,945
Mississippi	2,374	2,903	2,756	2,395
Moniteau	1,913	4,743	2,176	3,764
Monroe	1,647	2,632	1,860	2,175
Montgomery	2,147	3,563	2,092	3,106
Morgan	3,053	5,657	3,235	4,460
New Madrid	3,716	4,154	3,738	3,416
Newton	6,564	17,187	6,447	14,232
Nodaway	3,830	6,226	3,553	5,161
Oregon	1,823	2,769	1,568	2,521
Osage	1,673	4,975	1,938	4,154
Ozark	1,561	3,083	1,432	2,663
Pemiscot	3,381	3,398	3,245	2,750
Perry	2,621	5,583	2,085	4,667
Pettis	5,801	11,603	5,855	9,533
Phelps	6,666	11,874	6,262	9,444
Pike	3,670	4,314	3,557	3,648
Platte	18,412	23,302	15,325	17,785
Polk	3,775	8,586	3,606	6,430
Pulaski	3,551	8,618	3,800	6,531
Putnam	772	1,660	708	1,593
Ralls	2,031	2,986	2,033	2,446
Randolph	3,586	6,551	4,116	4,844
Ray	5,034	5,673	4,970	4,517
Reynolds	1,449	1,896	1,298	1,762
Ripley	1,907	3,693	1,820	3,121
Saline	4,479	5,389	4,585	4,572
Schuyler	894	1,124	808	1,159
Scotland	828	1,352	790	1,335
Scott	6,057	11,330	6,452	8,999
Shannon	1,618	2,511	1,430	2,245
Shelby	1,201	2,280	1,262	1,936
St. Charles	66,855	95,826	53,806	72,114
St. Clair	1,841	3,098	1,866	2,731
St. Francois	10,748	12,087	9,075	9,327
St. Louis	295,284	244,969	250,631	224,689
Ste. Genevieve	4,281	3,791	3,600	3,505
Stoddard	3,946	9,242	4,476	7,727
Stone	4,578	10,534	4,055	7,793
Sullivan	1,178	1,880	1,127	1,877
Taney	5,601	13,578	5,092	9,647
Texas	3,664	7,234	3,486	6,136
Vernon	3,206	5,732	3,156	4,985
Warren	5,461	7,883	4,524	5,979
Washington	4,459	4,641	4,047	4,020
Wayne	2,250	3,919	2,387	3,346
Webster	4,657	10,194	4,174	7,350
Worth	436	691	469	651
Wright	2,188	6,090	2,250	5,391
CITY				
St. Louis	116,133	27,793	96,557	24,799
Totals	**1,259,171**	**1,455,713**	**1,111,138**	**1,189,924**

Missouri Vote Since 1948

1948: Truman, D., 917,315; Dewey, R., 655,039; Wallace, Prog., 3,998; Thomas, Soc., 2,222.

1952: Eisenhower, R., 959,429; Stevenson, D., 929,830; Hallinan, Prog., 987; Hamblen, Proh., 885; MacArthur, Christian Nationalist, 302; America First, 233; Hoopes, Soc., 227; Hass, Soc. Labor, 169.

1956: Stevenson, D., 918,273; Eisenhower, R., 914,299.

1960: Kennedy, D., 972,201; Nixon, R., 962,221.

1964: Johnson, D., 1,164,344; Goldwater, R., 653,535.

1968: Nixon, R., 811,932; Humphrey, D., 791,444; Wallace, 3rd Party, 206,126.

1972: Nixon, R., 1,154,058; McGovern, D., 698,531.

1976: Carter, D., 999,163; Ford, R., 928,808; McCarthy, Ind., 24,329.

1980: Reagan, R., 1,074,181; Carter, D., 931,182; Anderson, Ind., 77,920; Clark, Libertarian, 14,422; DeBerry, Soc. Workers, 1,515; Commoner, Citizens, 573; write-in, 31.

1984: Reagan, R., 1,274,188; Mondale, D., 848,583.

1988: Bush, R., 1,084,953; Dukakis, D., 1,001,619; Fulani, New Alliance, 6,656; Paul, write-in, 434.

1992: Clinton, D., 1,053,873; Bush, R., 811,159; Perot, Ind., 518,741; Marrou, Libertarian, 7,497.

1996: Clinton, D., 1,025,935; Dole, R., 890,016; Perot, Ref., 217,188; Phillips, Taxpayers, 11,521; Browne, Libertarian, 10,522; Hagelin, Natural Law, 2,287.

2000: Bush, R., 1,189,924; Gore, D., 1,111,138; Nader, Green, 38,515; Buchanan, Reform, 9,818; Browne, Libertarian, 7,436; Phillips, Constitution, 1,957; Hagelin, Natural Law, 1,104.

2004: Bush, R., 1,455,713; Kerry, D., 1,259,171; Badnarik, Libertarian, 9,831; Peroutka, Constitution, 5,355.

Montana

County	2004 Kerry (D)	2004 Bush (R)	2000 Gore (D)	2000 Bush (R)
Beaverhead	1,103	3,067	799	3,113
Big Horn	2,215	2,028	2,345	1,651
Blaine	1,300	1,424	1,246	1,410
Broadwater	533	1,778	462	1,488
Carbon	1,847	3,342	1,434	3,008
Carter	76	623	53	573
Cascade	13,701	19,028	13,137	18,164
Chouteau	946	1,913	686	2,039
Custer	1,630	3,297	1,501	3,156
Daniels	326	764	303	750
Dawson	1,494	2,884	1,364	2,723
Deer Lodge	2,700	1,725	2,672	1,493
Fallon	289	1,178	256	1,061
Fergus	1,582	4,425	1,352	4,353
Flathead	11,587	26,019	8,329	22,519
Gallatin	16,405	22,392	10,009	18,833
Garfield	52	590	61	651
Glacier	2,641	1,828	2,211	1,709
Golden Valley	119	396	88	405
Granite	404	1,144	295	1,181
Hill	2,997	3,505	2,760	3,392
Jefferson	1,881	3,844	1,513	3,308
Judith Basin	322	944	278	1,057
Lake	4,960	7,245	3,884	6,441
Lewis & Clark	12,717	16,494	9,982	15,091
Liberty	281	734	243	752
Lincoln	2,320	5,889	1,629	5,578
Madison	983	2,868	758	2,656
McCone	320	791	267	827
Meagher	247	698	176	698
Mineral	542	1,242	382	1,078

	2004		2000	
County	Kerry (D)	Bush (R)	Gore (D)	Bush (R)
Missoula	26,983	23,989	17,241	21,474
Musselshell	538	1,663	512	1,582
Park	3,199	4,771	2,154	4,523
Petroleum	55	228	36	254
Phillips	456	1,677	423	1,727
Pondera	956	1,853	792	1,948
Powder River	154	856	115	860
Powell	761	1,993	638	1,971
Prairie	181	546	164	541
Ravalli	6,144	13,279	4,451	11,241
Richland	1,120	3,110	1,018	2,858
Roosevelt	2,195	1,762	2,059	1,605
Rosebud	1,520	1,982	1,394	1,826
Sanders	1,502	3,461	1,165	3,144
Sheridan	846	1,159	702	1,176
Silver Bow	9,307	6,381	8,967	6,299
Stillwater	1,025	3,090	925	2,765
Sweet Grass	445	1,509	305	1,450
Teton	1,047	2,232	847	2,294
Toole	690	1,583	630	1,639
Treasure	121	348	106	344
Valley	1,431	2,476	1,273	2,500
Wheatland	250	706	243	708
Wibaux	144	407	121	369
Yellowstone	24,120	40,903	20,370	33,922
Totals	**173,710**	**266,063**	**137,126**	**240,178**

Montana Vote Since 1948

1948: Truman, D., 119,071; Dewey, R., 96,770; Wallace, Prog., 7,313; Thomas, Soc., 695; Watson, Proh., 429.
1952: Eisenhower, R., 157,394; Stevenson, D., 106,213; Hallinan, Prog., 723; Hamblen, Proh., 548; Hoopes, Soc., 159.
1956: Eisenhower, R., 154,933; Stevenson, D., 116,238.
1960: Nixon, R., 141,841; Kennedy, D., 134,891; Decker, Proh., 456; Dobbs, Soc. Workers, 391.
1964: Johnson, D., 164,246; Goldwater, R., 113,032; Kasper, Natl. States' Rights, 519; Munn, Proh., 499; DeBerry, Soc. Workers, 332.
1968: Nixon, R., 138,835; Humphrey, D., 114,117; Wallace, 3rd Party, 20,015; Munn, Proh., 510; Caton, New Reform, 470; Halstead, Soc. Workers, 457.
1972: Nixon, R., 183,976; McGovern, D., 120,197; Schmitz, Amer., 13,430.
1976: Ford, R., 173,703; Carter, D., 149,259; Anderson, Amer., 5,772.
1980: Reagan, R., 206,814; Carter, D., 118,032; Anderson, Ind., 29,281; Clark, Libertarian, 9,825.
1984: Reagan, R., 232,450; Mondale, D., 146,742; Bergland, Libertarian, 5,185.
1988: Bush, R., 190,412; Dukakis, D., 168,936; Paul, Lib., 5,047; Fulani, New Alliance, 1,279.
1992: Clinton, D., 154,507; Bush, R., 144,207; Perot, Ind., 107,225; Gritz, Populist/America First, 3,658.
1996: Dole, R., 179,652; Clinton, D., 167,922; Perot, Ref., 55,229; Browne, Libertarian, 2,526; Hagelin, Natural Law, 1,754.
2000: Bush, Rep, 240,178; Gore, D., 137,126; Nader, Green, 24,437; Buchanan, Reform, 5,697; Browne, Libertarian, 1,718; Phillips, Constitution, 1,155; Hagelin, Natural Law, 675.
2004: Bush, R., 266,063; Kerry, D., 173,710; Nader, Ind., 6,168; Peroutka, Constitution, 1,764; Badnarik, Libertarian, 1,733; Cobb, Green, 996.

Nebraska

	2004		2000	
County	Kerry (D)	Bush (R)	Gore (D)	Bush (R)
Adams	3,791	9,233	3,686	8,162
Antelope	613	2,761	678	2,562
Arthur	24	240	26	235
Banner	56	379	65	390
Blaine	38	301	43	299
Boone	546	2,309	575	2,196
Box Butte	1,657	3,396	1,614	3,208
Boyd	228	911	265	931
Brown	268	1,426	250	1,375
Buffalo	4,100	14,222	3,927	11,931
Burt	1,272	2,349	1,223	2,056
Butler	1,068	3,016	1,028	2,638
Cass	3,619	7,763	3,656	6,144
Cedar	1,083	3,387	1,062	2,989
Chase	302	1,652	306	1,505
Cherry	483	2,509	446	2,322
Cheyenne	893	3,791	844	3,207
Clay	743	2,543	774	2,326
Colfax	990	2,589	863	2,338
Cuming	966	3,330	857	3,232
Custer	1,040	4,518	976	4,245
Dakota	3,027	3,526	2,695	3,119
Dawes	1,119	2,809	823	2,549
Dawson	1,728	6,149	1,740	5,511
Deuel	222	820	213	783
Dixon	938	2,028	820	1,834
Dodge	5,250	10,716	5,021	8,871
Douglas	83,330	120,813	73,347	101,025
Dundy	186	858	179	801
Fillmore	828	2,314	848	2,024
Franklin	412	1,277	420	1,196
Frontier	275	1,160	244	1,102
Furnas	492	1,950	534	1,849
Gage	3,655	6,575	3,516	5,538
Garden	201	970	203	963
Garfield	196	806	202	718
Gosper	222	890	228	757
Grant	41	352	49	324
Greeley	361	865	416	839
Hall	6,228	14,592	5,952	11,803
Hamilton	1,012	3,785	1,066	3,251
Harlan	398	1,467	438	1,358
Hayes	66	524	66	486
Hitchcock	296	1,171	312	1,126
Holt	894	4,217	846	3,954
Hooker	64	392	74	317
Howard	900	2,020	955	1,760
Jefferson	1,352	2,600	1,361	2,351
Johnson	885	1,470	794	1,210
Kearney	707	2,621	680	2,333
Keith	743	3,356	778	2,953
Keya Paha	98	442	78	422
Kimball	366	1,491	379	1,379
Knox	1,086	3,062	1,037	2,784
Lancaster	52,747	69,764	44,650	55,514
Lincoln	4,905	11,056	5,205	9,220
Logan	67	357	60	336
Loup	68	314	84	284
Madison	2,934	10,981	2,772	9,636
McPherson	49	259	48	244
Merrick	833	2,771	848	2,380
Morrill	495	1,755	460	1,597
Nance	459	1,237	497	1,105
Nemaha	1,066	2,595	1,063	2,177
Nuckolls	541	1,884	644	1,701
Otoe	2,275	5,018	2,208	4,178
Pawnee	481	986	522	937
Perkins	262	1,285	243	1,170
Phelps	830	3,872	934	3,575
Pierce	546	2,824	570	2,534
Platte	2,657	11,130	2,612	9,861
Polk	549	2,146	610	1,925
Red Willow	1,055	4,129	1,188	3,680
Richardson	1,297	2,924	1,382	2,623
Rock	130	740	141	725
Saline	2,420	3,071	2,321	2,581
Sarpy	17,455	40,163	14,637	28,979
Saunders	2,884	6,441	2,852	5,688
Scotts Bluff	3,843	10,378	3,937	9,397
Seward	2,114	5,353	2,250	4,457
Sheridan	430	2,136	392	2,105
Sherman	541	1,072	564	1,072
Sioux	123	677	98	629
Stanton	559	2,159	500	1,895
Thayer	764	2,075	821	2,096
Thomas	60	378	55	329
Thurston	1,212	1,154	924	1,040
Valley	564	1,801	583	1,610
Washington	2,754	7,083	2,550	5,758
Wayne	1,059	2,971	1,001	2,774
Webster	557	1,403	584	1,302
Wheeler	81	366	85	351
York	1,304	5,393	1,407	4,816
Totals	**254,328**	**512,814**	**231,780**	**433,862**

Nebraska Vote Since 1948

1948: Dewey, R., 264,774; Truman, D., 224,165.
1952: Eisenhower, R., 421,603; Stevenson, D., 188,057.
1956: Eisenhower, R., 378,108; Stevenson, D., 199,029.
1960: Nixon, R., 380,553; Kennedy, D., 232,542.
1964: Johnson, D., 307,307; Goldwater, R., 276,847.
1968: Nixon, R., 321,163; Humphrey, D., 170,784; Wallace, 3rd Party, 44,904.
1972: Nixon, R., 406,298; McGovern, D., 169,991; scattered, 817.
1976: Ford, R., 359,219; Carter, D., 233,287; McCarthy, Ind., 9,383; Maddox, Amer. Ind., 3,378; MacBride, Libertarian, 1,476.
1980: Reagan, R., 419,214; Carter, D., 166,424; Anderson, Ind., 44,854; Clark, Libertarian, 9,041.
1984: Reagan, R., 459,135; Mondale, D., 187,475; Bergland, Libertarian, 2,075.
1988: Bush, R., 397,956; Dukakis, D., 259,235; Paul, Lib., 2,534; Fulani, New Alliance, 1,740.
1992: Bush, R., 343,678; Clinton, D., 216,864; Perot, Ind., 174,104; Marrou, Libertarian, 1,340.
1996: Dole, R., 363,467; Clinton, D., 236,761; Perot, Ref., 71,278; Browne, Libertarian, 2,792; Phillips, Ind., 1,928; Hagelin, Natural Law, 1,189.
2000: Bush, R., 433,862; Gore, D., 231,780; Nader, Green, 24,540; Buchanan, Ind., 3,646; Browne, Libertarian, 2,245; Hagelin, Natural Law, 478; Phillips, Ind., 468.
2004: Bush, R., 512,814; Kerry, D., 254,328; Nader, Petitioning Cand., 5,698; Badnarik, Libertarian, 2,041; Peroutka, Nebraska, 1,314; Cobb, Green, 978; Calero, Petitioning Cand., 82.

Nevada

	2004		2000	
County	Kerry (D)	Bush (R)	Gore (D)	Bush (R)
Churchill	2,705	7,335	2,191	6,237
Clark	281,767	255,337	196,100	170,932
Douglas	8,275	15,192	5,837	11,193
Elko	3,050	11,938	2,542	11,025
Esmeralda	99	367	116	333
Eureka	144	571	150	632
Humboldt	1,361	3,896	1,128	3,638
Lander	414	1,602	395	1,619
Lincoln	418	1,579	461	1,372
Lyon	5,637	11,136	3,955	7,270
Mineral	931	1,336	916	1,227
Nye	5,616	8,487	4,525	6,904
Pershing	538	1,341	476	1,221
Storey	871	1,253	666	1,014
Washoe	74,841	81,545	52,097	63,640
White Pine	1,082	2,604	1,069	2,234
CITY				
Carson City	9,441	13,171	7,354	11,084
Totals	**397,190**	**418,690**	**279,978**	**301,575**

Nevada Vote Since 1948

1948: Truman, D., 31,291; Dewey, R., 29,357; Wallace, Prog., 1,469.
1952: Eisenhower, R., 50,502; Stevenson, D., 31,688.
1956: Eisenhower, R., 56,049; Stevenson, D., 40,640.
1960: Kennedy, D., 54,880; Nixon, R., 52,387.
1964: Johnson, D., 79,339; Goldwater, R., 56,094.
1968: Nixon, R., 73,188; Humphrey, D., 60,598; Wallace, 3rd Party, 20,432.
1972: Nixon, R., 115,750; McGovern, D., 66,016.
1976: Ford, R., 101,273; Carter, D., 92,479; MacBride, Libertarian, 1,519; Maddox, Amer. Ind., 1,497; scattered, 5,108.
1980: Reagan, R., 155,017; Carter, D., 66,666; Anderson, Ind., 17,651; Clark, Libertarian, 4,358.
1984: Reagan, R., 188,770; Mondale, D., 91,655; Bergland, Libertarian, 2,292.
1988: Bush, R., 206,040; Dukakis, D., 132,738; Paul, Lib., 3,520; Fulani, New Alliance, 835.
1992: Clinton, D., 189,148; Bush, R., 175,828; Perot, Ind., 132,580; Gritz, Populist/America First, 2,892; Marrou, Libertarian, 1,835.
1996: Clinton, D., 203,974; Dole, R., 199,244; Perot, Ref., 43,986; "None of These Candidates," 5,608; Nader, Green, 4,730; Browne, Libertarian, 4,460; Phillips, Ind. Amer., 1,732; Hagelin, Natural Law, 545.
2000: Bush, R., 301,575; Gore, D., 279,978; Nader, Green, 15,008; Buchanan, Citizens First, 4,747; "None of These Candidates," 3,315; Browne, Libertarian, 3,311; Phillips, Ind. Amer., 621; Hagelin, Natural Law, 415.
2004: Bush, R., 418,690; Kerry, D., 397,190; Nader, Ind., 4,838; "None of These Candidates," Ind., 3,688; Badnarik, Libertarian, 3,176; Peroutka, Indep. Amer., 1,152; Cobb, Green, 853.

New Hampshire

	2004		2000	
City	Kerry (D)	Bush (R)	Gore (D)	Bush (R)
Concord	12,675	8,210	10,025	6,981
Derry	6,760	8,038	5,530	6,093
Dover	9,225	6,206	6,812	5,008
Hudson	5,390	6,172	4,573	4,527
Keene	8,378	4,004	5,856	3,704
Laconia	3,511	4,286	3,015	3,814
Londonderry	5,222	6,888	4,348	5,463
Manchester	23,116	23,286	19,991	19,152
Merrimack	6,682	7,927	5,571	6,239
Nashua	21,587	18,016	18,398	14,803
Portsmouth	8,436	4,185	6,862	3,896
Rochester	6,672	6,658	5,401	5,522
Salem	6,472	7,797	5,711	5,713
Other	216,385	219,564	164,255	182,644
Totals	**340,511**	**331,237**	**266,318**	**273,559**

New Hampshire Vote Since 1948

1948: Dewey, R., 121,299; Truman, D., 107,995; Wallace, Prog., 1,970; Thomas, Soc., 86; Teichert, Soc. Labor, 83; Thurmond, States' Rights, 7.
1952: Eisenhower, R., 166,287; Stevenson, D., 106,663.
1956: Eisenhower, R., 176,519; Stevenson, D., 90,364; Andrews, Const., 111.
1960: Nixon, R., 157,989; Kennedy, D., 137,772.
1964: Johnson, D., 182,065; Goldwater, R., 104,029.
1968: Nixon, R., 154,903; Humphrey, D., 130,589; Wallace, 3rd Party, 11,173; New Party, 421; Halstead, Soc. Workers, 104.
1972: Nixon, R., 213,724; McGovern, D., 116,435; Schmitz, Amer., 3,386; Jenness, Soc. Workers, 368; scattered, 142.
1976: Ford, R., 185,935; Carter, D., 147,645; McCarthy, Ind., 4,095; MacBride, Libertarian, 936; Reagan, write-in, 388; La Rouche, U.S. Labor, 186; Camejo, Soc. Workers, 161; Levin, Soc. Labor, 66; scattered, 215.
1980: Reagan, R., 221,705; Carter, D., 108,864; Anderson, Ind., 49,693; Clark, Libertarian, 2,067; Commoner, Citizens, 1,325; Hall, Com., 129; Griswold, Workers World, 76; DeBerry, Soc. Workers, 72; scattered, 68.
1984: Reagan, R., 267,051; Mondale, D., 120,377; Bergland, Libertarian, 735.
1988: Bush, R., 281,537; Dukakis, D., 163,696; Paul, Lib., 4,502; Fulani, New Alliance, 790.
1992: Clinton, D., 209,040; Bush, R., 202,484; Perot, Ind., 121,337; Marrou, Libertarian, 3,548.
1996: Clinton, D., 246,166; Dole, R., 196,486; Perot, Ref., 48,387; Browne, Libertarian, 4,214; Phillips, Taxpayers, 1,344.
2000: Bush, R., 273,559; Gore, D., 266,348; Nader, Green, 22,198; Browne, Libertarian, 2,757; Buchanan, Independence, 2,615; Phillips, Constitution, 328.
2004: Kerry, D., 340,511; Bush, R., 331,237; Nader, Ind., 4,479.

New Jersey

	2004		2000	
County	Kerry (D)	Bush (R)	Gore (D)	Bush (R)
Atlantic	55,746	49,487	52,880	35,593
Bergen	207,666	189,833	202,682	152,731
Burlington	110,411	95,936	99,506	72,254
Camden	137,765	81,427	127,166	62,464
Cape May	21,475	28,832	22,189	23,794
Cumberland	27,875	24,362	28,188	18,882
Essex	203,681	83,374	185,505	66,842
Gloucester	66,835	60,033	61,095	42,315
Hudson	127,447	60,646	118,206	43,804
Hunterdon	26,050	39,888	21,387	32,210
Mercer	91,580	56,604	83,256	46,670
Middlesex	166,628	126,492	154,998	93,545
Monmouth	133,773	163,650	131,476	119,291
Morris	98,066	135,241	88,039	111,066
Ocean	99,839	154,204	102,104	105,684
Passaic	94,962	75,200	90,324	61,043
Salem	13,749	15,721	13,718	12,257
Somerset	66,476	72,508	56,232	59,725
Sussex	23,990	44,506	21,353	33,277
Union	119,372	82,517	112,003	68,554
Warren	18,044	29,542	16,543	22,172
Totals	**1,911,430**	**1,670,003**	**1,788,850**	**1,284,173**

New Jersey Vote Since 1948

1948: Dewey, R., 981,124; Truman, D., 895,455; Wallace, Prog., 42,683; Watson, Proh., 10,593; Thomas, Soc., 10,521; Dobbs, Soc. Workers, 5,825; Teichert, Soc. Labor, 3,354.
1952: Eisenhower, R., 1,373,613; Stevenson, D., 1,015,902; Hoopes, Soc., 8,593; Hass, Soc. Labor, 5,815; Hallinan, Prog., 5,589; Krajewski, Poor Man's, 4,203; Dobbs, Soc. Workers, 3,850; Hamblen, Proh., 989.
1956: Eisenhower, R., 1,606,942; Stevenson D., 850,337; Holtwick, Proh., 9,147; Hass, Soc. Labor, 6,736; Andrews, Cons., 5,317; Dobbs, Soc. Workers, 4,004; Krajewski, Amer. Third Party, 1,829.
1960: Kennedy, D., 1,385,415; Nixon, R., 1,363,324; Dobbs, Soc. Workers, 11,402; Lee, Cons., 8,708; Hass, Soc. Labor, 4,262.
1964: Johnson, D., 1,867,671; Goldwater, R., 963,843; DeBerry, Soc. Workers, 8,181; Hass, Soc. Labor, 7,075.
1968: Nixon, R., 1,325,467; Humphrey, D., 1,264,206; Wallace, 3rd Party, 262,187; Halstead, Soc. Workers, 8,667; Gregory, Peace and Freedom, 8,084; Blomen, Soc. Labor, 6,784.
1972: Nixon, R., 1,845,502; McGovern, D., 1,102,211; Schmitz, Amer., 34,378; Spock, Peoples, 5,355; Fisher, Soc. Labor, 4,544; Jenness, Soc. Workers, 2,233; Mahalchik, Amer. First, 1,743; Hall, Com., 1,263.
1976: Ford, R., 1,509,688; Carter, D., 1,444,653; McCarthy, Ind., 32,717; MacBride, Libertarian, 9,449; Maddox, Amer., 7,716; Levin, Soc. Labor, 3,686; Hall, Com., 1,662; LaRouche, U.S. Labor, 1,650; Camejo, Soc. Workers, 1,184; Wright, People's, 1,044; Bubar, Proh., 554; Zeidler, Soc., 469.
1980: Reagan, R., 1,546,557; Carter, D., 1,147,364; Anderson, Ind., 234,632; Clark, Libertarian, 20,652; Commoner, Citizens, 8,203; McCormack, Right to Life, 3,927; Lynen, Middle Class, 3,694; Hall, Com., 2,555; Pulley, Soc. Workers, 2,198; McReynolds, Soc., 1,973; Gahres, Down With Lawyers, 1,718; Griswold, Workers World, 1,288; Wendelken, Ind., 923.
1984: Reagan, R., 1,933,630; Mondale, D., 1,261,323; Bergland, Libertarian, 6,416.
1988: Bush, R., 1,740,604; Dukakis, D., 1,317,541; Lewin, Peace and Freedom, 9,953; Paul, Lib., 8,421.
1992: Clinton, D., 1,436,206; Bush, R., 1,356,865; Perot, Ind., 521,829; Marrou, Libertarian, 6,822; Fulani, New Alliance, 3,513; Phillips, U.S. Taxpayers, 2,670; LaRouche, Ind., 2,095; Warren, Soc. Workers, 2,011; Daniels, Ind., 1,996; Gritz, Populist/America First, 1,867; Hagelin, Natural Law, 1,353.
1996: Clinton, D., 1,652,361; Dole, R., 1,103,099; Perot, Ref., 262,134; Nader, Green, 32,465; Browne, Libertarian, 14,763; Hagelin, Natural Law, 3,887; Phillips, Taxpayers, 3,440; Harris, Soc. Workers, 1,837; Moorehead, Workers World, 1,337; White, Soc. Equality, 537.
2000: Gore, D., 1,788,850; Bush, R., 1,284,173; Nader, Ind., 94,554; Buchanan, Ind., 6,989; Browne, Ind., 6,312; Hagelin, Ind., 2,215; McReynolds, Ind., 1,880; Phillips, Ind., 1,409; Harris, Ind., 844.
2004: Kerry, D., 1,911,430; Bush, R., 1,670,003; Nader, Ind., 19,418; Badnarik, Ind., 4,514; Peroutka, Ind., 2,750; Cobb, Ind., 1,807; Brown, Ind., 664; Van Auken, Ind., 575; Calero, Ind., 530.

New Mexico

	2004		2000	
County	Kerry (D)	Bush (R)	Gore (D)	Bush (R)
Bernalillo	132,252	121,454	99,461	95,249
Catron	551	1,427	353	1,273
Chaves	6,726	14,773	6,340	11,378
Cibola	3,913	3,477	4,127	2,752
Colfax	2,824	3,082	2,653	2,600
Curry	3,541	10,649	3,471	8,301
De Baca	281	706	349	612
Dona Ana	31,762	29,548	23,912	21,263
Eddy	6,880	13,268	7,108	10,335
Grant	7,095	6,135	5,673	4,961
Guadalupe	1,340	914	1,076	548
Harding	259	380	214	366
Hidalgo	861	1,081	839	954
Lea	3,646	14,430	3,855	10,157
Lincoln	2,822	6,070	2,027	4,458
Los Alamos	5,206	5,810	4,149	5,623
Luna	3,340	4,164	2,975	3,395
McKinley	13,051	7,351	10,281	5,070
Mora	1,876	928	1,456	668
Otero	6,433	14,066	5,465	10,258
Quay	1,422	2,661	1,471	2,292
Rio Arriba	9,753	5,149	8,169	3,495
Roosevelt	2,082	4,997	1,762	3,762
Sandoval	21,421	22,628	14,899	15,423
San Juan	14,843	29,525	11,980	21,434
San Miguel	8,683	3,313	6,540	2,215
Santa Fe	47,074	18,466	32,017	13,974
Sierra	1,926	3,162	1,689	2,721
Socorro	4,025	3,696	3,294	3,173
Taos	10,987	3,666	7,039	2,744
Torrance	2,386	4,026	1,868	2,891
Union	411	1,454	452	1,269
Valencia	11,270	14,474	9,819	10,803
Totals	**370,942**	**376,930**	**286,783**	**286,417**

New Mexico Vote Since 1948

1948: Truman, D., 105,464; Dewey, R., 80,303; Wallace, Prog., 1,037; Watson, Proh., 127; Thomas, Soc., 83; Teichert, Soc. Lab., 49.

1952: Eisenhower, R., 132,170; Stevenson, D., 105,661; Hamblen, Proh., 297; Hallinan, Ind. Prog., 225; MacArthur, Christian National, 220; Hass, Soc. Labor, 35.

1956: Eisenhower, R., 146,788; Stevenson, D., 106,098; Holtwick, Proh., 607; Andrews, Ind., 364; Hass, Soc. Labor, 69.

1960: Kennedy, D., 156,027; Nixon, R., 153,733; Decker, Proh., 777; Hass, Soc. Labor, 570.

1964: Johnson, D., 194,017; Goldwater, R., 131,838; Hass, Soc. Labor, 1,217; Munn, Proh., 543.

1968: Nixon, R., 169,692; Humphrey, D., 130,081; Wallace, 3rd Party, 25,737; Chavez, 1,519; Halstead, Soc. Workers, 252.

1972: Nixon, R., 235,606; McGovern, D., 141,084; Schmitz, Amer., 8,767; Jenness, Soc. Workers, 474.

1976: Ford, R., 211,419; Carter, D., 201,148; Camejo, Soc. Wkrs., 2,462; MacBride, Libert., 1,110; Zeidler, Soc., 240; Bubar, Proh., 211.

1980: Reagan, R., 250,779; Carter, D., 167,826; Anderson, Ind., 29,459; Clark, Libertarian, 4,365; Commoner, Citizens, 2,202; Bubar, Statesman, 1,281; Pulley, Soc. Workers, 325.

1984: Reagan, R., 307,101; Mondale, D., 201,769; Bergland, Libertarian, 4,459.

1988: Bush, R., 270,341; Dukakis, D., 244,497; Paul, Lib., 3,268; Fulani, New Alliance, 2,237.

1992: Clinton, D., 261,617; Bush, R., 212,824; Perot, Ind., 91,895; Marrou, Libertarian, 1,615.

1996: Clinton, D., 273,495; Dole, R., 232,751; Perot, Ref., 32,257; Nader, Green, 13,218; Browne, Libertarian, 2,996; Phillips, Taxpayers, 713; Hagelin, Natural Law, 644.

2000: Gore, D., 286,783; Bush, R., 286,417; Nader, Green, 21,251; Browne, Libertarian, 2,058; Buchanan, Reform, 1,392; Hagelin, Natural Law, 361; Phillips, Constitution, 343.

2004: Bush, R., 376,930; Kerry, D., 370,942; Nader, Ind., 4,053; Badnarik, Libert., 2,382; Cobb, Green, 1,226; Peroutka, Constitution, 771.

New York

	2004		2000	
County	Kerry (D)	Bush (R)	Gore (D)	Bush (R)
Albany	89,323	54,872	85,617	47,624
Allegany	6,566	12,310	6,336	11,436
Bronx	283,994	56,701	265,801	36,245
Brooklyn	514,973	167,149	497,513	96,609
Broome	46,281	43,568	45,381	36,946
Cattaraugus	13,514	20,051	13,697	18,382
Cayuga	17,534	17,743	17,031	14,988
Chautauqua	27,257	32,434	27,016	29,064
Chemung	17,080	21,321	17,424	18,779
Chenango	9,277	11,582	9,112	10,033
Clinton	17,624	15,330	15,542	13,274
Columbia	15,929	14,457	13,489	13,153
Cortland	10,670	11,613	9,691	9,857
Delaware	8,724	11,958	8,450	10,662
Dutchess	58,232	63,372	52,390	52,669
Erie	251,090	184,423	240,174	160,176
Essex	8,768	9,869	7,927	8,822
Franklin	9,543	8,383	8,870	7,643
Fulton	9,202	12,570	9,314	11,434
Genesee	10,331	16,725	10,191	14,459
Greene	8,933	12,996	8,480	11,332
Hamilton	1,145	2,475	1,114	2,388
Herkimer	11,675	16,024	12,224	14,147
Jefferson	16,860	21,231	16,799	18,192
Lewis	4,546	6,624	4,333	6,103
Livingston	11,504	17,729	10,476	15,244
Madison	13,121	16,537	12,017	14,879
Manhattan	526,765	107,405	454,523	82,113
Monroe	173,497	163,545	161,743	141,266
Montgomery	9,449	11,338	10,249	9,765
Nassau	323,070	288,355	341,610	226,954
Niagara	47,602	47,111	47,781	40,952
Oneida	40,792	52,392	43,933	47,603
Onondaga	116,381	94,006	109,896	83,678
Ontario	21,166	27,999	19,761	23,885
Orange	63,394	79,089	58,170	62,852
Orleans	5,959	10,317	5,991	9,202
Oswego	24,133	26,325	22,857	23,249
Otsego	12,723	13,342	11,460	12,219
Putnam	19,575	26,356	18,525	21,853
Queens	433,835	165,954	416,967	122,052
Rensselaer	36,075	34,734	34,808	29,562
Rockland	64,191	65,130	69,530	48,441
St. Lawrence	22,857	18,029	21,386	16,449
Saratoga	48,730	56,158	43,359	46,623
Schenectady	35,971	32,066	35,534	27,961
Schoharie	5,630	8,591	5,390	7,459
Schuyler	3,445	4,960	3,301	4,381
Seneca	6,979	7,981	6,841	6,734
Staten Island	68,448	90,325	73,828	63,903
Steuben	14,523	26,980	14,600	24,200
Suffolk	315,909	309,949	306,306	240,992
Sullivan	15,034	15,319	14,348	12,703
Tioga	9,694	13,762	9,170	12,239
Tompkins	27,229	13,994	21,807	13,351
Ulster	47,602	37,821	38,162	33,447
Warren	13,405	16,969	12,193	14,993
Washington	10,624	13,827	9,641	12,596
Wayne	15,709	24,709	14,977	21,701
Westchester	229,849	159,628	218,010	139,278
Wyoming	6,134	11,745	5,935	10,809
Yates	4,205	6,309	3,962	5,565
Totals	**4,314,280**	**2,962,567**	**4,112,963**	**2,405,570**

New York Vote Since 1948

1948: Dewey, R., 2,841,163; Truman, D., 2,557,642; Liberal, 222,562; total, 2,780,204; Wallace, Amer. Lab., 509,559; Thomas, Soc., 40,879; Teichert, Ind. Gov't., 2,729; Dobbs, Soc. Wkrs., 2,675.

1952: Eisenhower, R., 3,952,815; Stevenson, D., 2,687,890; Liberal, 416,711; total, 3,104,601; Hallinan, Amer. Lab., 64,211; Hoopes, Soc., 2,664; Dobbs, Soc. Workers, 2,212; Hass, Ind. Gov't., 1,560; scattered, 178; blank and void, 87,813.

1956: Eisenhower, R., 4,340,340; Stevenson, D., 2,458,212, Liberal, 292,557, total, 2,750,769; write-in votes for Andrews, 1,027; Werdel, 492; Hass, 150; Hoopes, 82; others, 476.

1960: Kennedy, D., 3,423,909; Liberal, 406,176; total, 3,830,085; Nixon, R., 3,446,419; Dobbs, Soc. Workers, 14,319; scattered, 256; blank and void, 88,896.

1964: Johnson, D., 4,913,156; Goldwater, R., 2,243,559; Hass, Soc. Labor, 6,085; DeBerry, Soc. Workers, 3,215; scattered, 188; blank and void, 151,383.

1968: Humphrey, D., 3,378,470; Nixon, R., 3,007,932; Wallace, 3rd Party, 358,864; Gregory, Freedom and Peace, 24,517; Halstead, Soc. Workers, 11,851; Blomen, Soc. Labor, 8,432; blank, void, and scattered, 171,624.

1972: Nixon, R., 3,824,642; McGovern, D., 2,767,956; Lib., 183,128; total, 2,951,084; Reed, Cons., 368,136; Soc. Wkrs., 7,797; Fisher, Soc. Labor, 4,530; Hall, Com., 5,641; blank, void, or scattered, 161,641.

1976: Carter, D., 3,389,558; Ford, R., 3,100,791; MacBride, Libertarian, 12,197; Hall, Com., 10,270; Camejo, Soc. Workers, 6,996; LaRouche, U.S. Labor, 5,413; blank, void, or scattered, 143,037.

1980: Reagan, R., 2,893,831; Carter, D., 2,728,372; Anderson, Ind., 467,801; Clark, Libertarian, 52,648; McCormack, Right To Life, 24,159; Commoner, Citizens, 23,186; Hall, Com., 7,414; DeBerry, Soc. Wkrs., 2,068; Griswold, Wkrs. World, 1,416; scattered, 1,064.

1984: Reagan, R., 3,664,763; Mondale, D., 3,119,609; Bergland, Libertarian, 11,949.

1988: Dukakis, D., 3,347,882; Bush, R., 3,081,871; Marra, Right to Life, 20,497; Fulani, New Alliance, 15,845.

1992: Clinton, D., 3,444,450; Bush, R., 2,346,649; Perot, Ind., 1,090,721; Warren, Soc. Workers, 15,472; Marrou, Libertarian, 13,451; Fulani, New Alliance, 11,318; Hagelin, Natural Law, 4,420.

1996: Clinton, D., 3,756,177; Dole, R., 1,933,492; Perot, Ind. (Ref.), 503,458; Nader, Green, 75,956; Phillips, Right to Life, 23,580; Browne, Libertarian, 12,220; Hagelin, Natural Law, 5,011; Moorehead, Workers World, 3,473; Harris, Soc. Workers, 2,762.

2000: Gore, D., 4,112,965; Bush, R., 2,405,570; Nader, Green, 244,360; Buchanan, Reform, 31,554; Hagelin, Independence, 24,369; Browne, Libertarian, 7,664; Harris, Soc. Workers, 1,790; Phillips, Constitution, 1,503.

2004: Kerry, D., 4,314,280; Bush, R., 2,962,567; Nader, Ind., 99,873; Badnarik, Libertarian, 11,607; Calero, Soc. Wkrs., 2,405.

North Carolina

County	2004 Kerry (D)	2004 Bush (R)	2000 Gore (D)	2000 Bush (R)
Alamance	20,686	33,302	17,459	29,305
Alexander	4,618	10,928	4,166	9,242
Alleghany	1,922	2,883	1,715	2,531
Anson	5,413	3,796	4,792	3,161
Ashe	4,477	7,292	4,011	6,226
Avery	1,805	5,678	1,686	4,956
Beaufort	7,025	12,432	6,634	10,531
Bertie	4,938	3,057	4,660	2,488
Bladen	6,109	6,174	5,889	4,977
Brunswick	14,903	22,925	13,118	15,427
Buncombe	51,868	52,491	38,545	46,101
Burke	11,728	18,922	11,924	18,466
Cabarrus	19,803	40,780	16,284	32,704
Caldwell	9,999	21,186	8,588	17,337
Camden	1,339	2,480	1,187	1,628
Carteret	7,732	17,716	8,839	17,381
Caswell	4,539	4,868	4,091	4,270
Catawba	18,858	39,602	16,246	34,244
Chatham	12,897	12,892	10,461	10,248
Cherokee	3,635	7,517	3,239	6,305
Chowan	2,406	2,967	2,430	2,415
Clay	1,628	3,209	1,361	2,416
Cleveland	14,215	22,750	13,455	19,064
Columbus	10,343	10,773	9,986	8,342
Craven	14,019	23,575	12,213	19,494
Cumberland	45,788	49,139	38,626	38,129
Currituck	2,909	6,013	2,595	4,095
Dare	6,136	9,345	5,589	7,301
Davidson	17,191	42,075	16,199	35,387
Davie	4,233	12,372	3,651	10,184
Duplin	6,923	9,611	6,475	7,840
Durham	74,524	34,614	53,907	30,150
Edgecombe	12,877	8,163	11,315	6,836
Forsyth	63,340	75,294	52,457	67,700
Franklin	9,286	11,540	7,454	8,501
Gaston	20,254	43,252	19,281	39,453
Gates	2,121	1,924	1,944	1,480
Graham	1,272	2,693	1,006	2,304
Granville	9,057	9,491	7,733	7,364
Greene	2,665	3,800	2,478	3,353
Guilford	100,042	98,254	80,787	84,394
Halifax	11,528	8,088	10,222	6,698
Harnett	11,563	20,922	9,155	14,762
Haywood	11,237	14,545	9,793	12,118
Henderson	15,003	28,025	12,562	25,688
Hertford	5,141	2,942	5,484	2,382
Hoke	5,794	5,257	5,017	3,439
Hyde	1,048	1,235	1,088	1,132
Iredell	18,065	38,675	15,434	29,853
Jackson	6,737	7,351	5,722	6,237
Johnston	17,266	36,903	13,704	27,212
Jones	1,893	2,607	1,822	2,114
Lee	7,657	11,834	6,785	9,406
Lenoir	10,207	12,939	9,527	11,512
Lincoln	9,434	20,052	8,412	15,951
Macon	5,489	9,448	4,683	8,406
Madison	4,234	5,175	3,505	4,676
Martin	5,102	5,334	4,929	4,420
McDowell	5,330	10,590	4,747	9,109
Mecklenburg	166,828	155,084	126,911	134,068
Mitchell	2,080	5,686	1,535	4,984
Montgomery	4,313	5,745	3,979	4,946
Moore	13,555	24,714	11,232	19,882
Nash	15,693	21,902	12,376	17,995
New Hanover	35,572	45,351	29,292	36,503
Northampton	5,584	3,176	5,513	2,667
Onslow	11,250	25,890	10,269	19,657
Orange	42,910	20,771	30,921	17,930
Pamlico	2,335	3,679	2,188	2,999
Pasquotank	6,984	6,609	5,874	4,943
Pender	6,999	10,037	6,415	7,661
Perquimans	1,971	2,965	2,033	2,230
Person	6,198	8,973	5,042	6,722
Pitt	24,924	28,590	19,685	23,192
Polk	3,787	5,140	3,114	5,074
Randolph	12,966	37,771	11,366	30,959
Richmond	8,383	7,709	7,935	6,263
Robeson	17,868	15,909	17,834	11,721
Rockingham	14,430	22,840	13,260	18,979
Rowan	16,735	34,915	14,891	28,922
Rutherford	8,184	16,343	7,697	13,755
Sampson	9,649	12,600	8,768	10,410
Scotland	6,386	5,141	5,627	3,740
Stanly	7,650	17,814	7,066	15,548
Stokes	5,767	13,583	5,030	12,028
Surry	8,304	17,587	7,757	15,401
Swain	2,419	2,593	2,097	2,224
Transylvania	6,097	9,386	5,044	9,011
Tyrrell	731	855	849	706
Union	17,974	42,820	14,890	31,876
Vance	8,762	6,884	7,092	5,564
Wake	169,909	177,324	123,466	142,494
Warren	5,171	2,840	4,576	2,202
Washington	2,969	2,484	2,704	2,169
Watauga	11,232	12,659	7,959	10,438
Wayne	15,076	24,883	13,005	20,758
Wilkes	7,862	19,197	7,226	16,826
Wilson	14,206	16,264	11,266	13,466
Yadkin	3,451	11,816	3,127	10,435
Yancey	4,434	4,940	3,714	4,970
Totals	**1,525,849**	**1,961,166**	**1,257,692**	**1,631,163**

North Carolina Vote Since 1948

1948: Truman, D., 459,070; Dewey, R., 258,572; Thurmond, States' Rights, 69,652; Wallace, Prog., 3,915.

1952: Stevenson, D., 652,803; Eisenhower, R., 558,107.

1956: Stevenson, D., 590,530; Eisenhower, R., 575,062.

1960: Kennedy, D., 713,136; Nixon, R., 655,420.

1964: Johnson, D., 800,139; Goldwater, R., 624,844.

1968: Nixon, R., 627,192; Wallace, 3rd Party, 496,188; Humphrey, D., 464,113.

1972: Nixon, R., 1,054,889; McGovern, D., 438,705; Schmitz, Amer., 25,018.

1976: Carter, D., 927,365; Ford, R., 741,960; Anderson, Amer., 5,607; MacBride, Libertarian, 2,219; LaRouche, U.S. Labor, 755.

1980: Reagan, R., 915,018; Carter, D., 875,635; Anderson, Ind., 52,800; Clark, Libertarian, 9,677; Commoner, Citizens, 2,287; DeBerry, Soc. Workers, 416.

1984: Reagan, R., 1,346,481; Mondale, D., 824,287; Bergland, Libertarian, 3,794.

1988: Bush, R., 1,237,258; Dukakis, D., 890,167; Fulani, New Alliance, 5,682; Paul, write-in, 1,263.

1992: Bush, R., 1,134,661; Clinton, D., 1,114,042; Perot, Ind., 357,864; Marrou, Libertarian, 5,171.

1996: Dole, R., 1,225,938; Clinton, D., 1,107,849; Perot, Ref., 168,059; Browne, Libertarian, 8,740; Hagelin, Natural Law, 2,771.

2000: Bush, R., 1,631,163; Gore, D., 1,257,692; Browne, Libertarian, 13,891; Buchanan, Reform, 8,874.

2004: Bush, R., 1,961,166; Kerry, D., 1,525,849; Badnarik, Libertarian, 11,731.

North Dakota

County	2004 Kerry (D)	2004 Bush (R)	2000 Gore (D)	2000 Bush (R)
Adams	353	915	286	826
Barnes	2,186	3,541	1,933	3,452
Benson	1,196	1,002	952	1,055
Billings	99	449	82	394
Bottineau	1,168	2,468	1,173	2,349
Bowman	397	1,280	330	1,080
Burke	336	808	296	698
Burleigh	11,621	26,577	9,842	22,467
Cass	26,010	39,619	21,451	33,536
Cavalier	887	1,522	618	1,513
Dickey	883	1,890	806	1,853
Divide	487	751	306	443
Dunn	571	1,178	474	1,124
Eddy	534	655	458	703
Emmons	611	1,449	405	1,430
Foster	518	1,219	474	1,172
Golden Valley	195	719	156	611
Grand Forks	12,646	17,298	10,593	15,875
Grant	264	952	235	1,077
Griggs	505	907	484	920
Hettinger	405	1,044	353	1,057
Kidder	433	902	283	837
La Moure	712	1,592	689	1,590
Logan	265	844	223	812
McHenry	1,030	1,744	888	1,682
McIntosh	436	1,254	350	1,178
McKenzie	847	1,897	653	1,634
McLean	1,664	3,014	1,465	2,891
Mercer	1,245	3,285	1,011	2,984
Morton	4,073	8,325	3,439	6,993
Mountrail	1,465	1,527	1,256	1,466
Nelson	778	1,107	687	1,031
Oliver	310	790	244	709
Pembina	1,321	2,466	1,093	2,430
Pierce	686	1,475	500	1,348
Ramsey	1,885	2,943	1,658	3,005
Ransom	1,199	1,352	1,080	1,488
Renville	497	953	443	820
Richland	2,821	5,264	2,490	4,999
Rolette	2,564	1,392	2,681	1,416
Sargent	1,021	1,147	959	1,103
Sheridan	200	727	161	707
Sioux	804	319	724	269
Slope	89	335	85	316
Stark	3,013	7,220	2,784	6,387
Steele	616	586	475	655
Stutsman	3,438	6,517	3,067	5,488
Towner	606	754	410	694

County	2004 Kerry (D)	2004 Bush (R)	2000 Gore (D)	2000 Bush (R)
Traill	1,651	2,543	1,512	2,392
Walsh	1,905	3,194	1,743	3,099
Ward	8,236	17,008	7,533	13,997
Wells	858	1,654	661	1,610
Williams	2,512	6,278	2,330	5,187
Totals	**111,052**	**196,651**	**95,284**	**174,852**

North Dakota Vote Since 1948

1948: Dewey, R., 115,139; Truman, D., 95,812; Wallace, Prog., 8,391; Thomas, Soc., 1,000; Thurmond, States' Rights, 374.
1952: Eisenhower, R., 191,712; Stevenson, D., 76,694; MacArthur, Christian Nationalist, 1,075; Hallinan, Prog., 344; Hamblen, Proh., 302.
1956: Eisenhower, R., 156,766; Stevenson, D., 96,742; Andrews, Amer., 483.
1960: Nixon, R., 154,310; Kennedy, D., 123,963; Dobbs, Soc. Workers, 158.
1964: Johnson, D., 149,784; Goldwater, R., 108,207; DeBerry, Soc. Workers, 224; Munn, Proh., 174.
1968: Nixon, R., 138,669; Humphrey, D., 94,769; Wallace, 3rd Party, 14,244; Halstead, Soc. Workers, 128; Munn, Prohibition, 38; Troxell, Ind., 34.
1972: Nixon, R., 174,109; McGovern, D., 100,384; Schmitz, Amer., 5,646; Jenness, Soc. Workers, 288; Hall, Com., 87.
1976: Ford, R., 153,470; Carter, D., 136,078; Anderson, Amer., 3,698; McCarthy, Ind., 2,952; Maddox, Amer. Ind., 269; MacBride, Libertarian, 256; scattered, 371.
1980: Reagan, R., 193,695; Carter, D., 79,189; Anderson, Ind., 23,640; Clark, Libertarian, 3,743; Commoner, Libertarian, 429; McLain, Natl. People's League, 296; Greaves, Amer., 235; Hall, Com., 93; DeBerry, Soc. Workers, 89; McReynolds, Soc., 82; Bubar, Statesman, 54.
1984: Reagan, R., 200,336; Mondale, D., 104,429; Bergland, Libertarian, 703.
1988: Bush, R., 166,559; Dukakis, D., 127,739; Paul, Lib., 1,315; LaRouche, Natl. Econ. Recovery, 905.
1992: Bush, R., 136,244; Clinton, D., 99,168; Perot, Ind., 71,084.
1996: Dole, R., 125,050; Clinton, D., 106,905; Perot, Ref., 32,515; Browne, Libertarian, 847; Phillips, Ind., 745; Hagelin, Natural Law, 349.
2000: Bush, R., 174,852; Gore, D., 95,284; Nader, Ind., 9,486; Buchanan, Reform, 7,288; Browne, Ind., 660; Phillips, Constitution, 373; Hagelin, Ind., 313.
2004: Bush, R., 196,651; Kerry, D., 111,052; Nader, Ind., 3,756; Badnarik, Libertarian, 851; Peroutka, Constitution, 514.

Ohio

County	2004 Kerry (D)	2004 Bush (R)	2000 Gore (D)	2000 Bush (R)
Adams	4,281	7,653	3,581	6,380
Allen	16,470	32,580	13,996	28,647
Ashland	8,576	16,209	6,685	13,533
Ashtabula	24,060	21,038	19,831	17,940
Athens	18,998	10,847	13,158	9,703
Auglaize	5,903	17,016	5,564	13,770
Belmont	17,576	15,589	15,980	12,625
Brown	7,140	12,647	5,972	10,027
Butler	56,243	109,872	46,390	86,587
Carroll	6,300	7,695	4,960	6,732
Champaign	6,968	11,718	5,955	9,220
Clark	33,535	34,941	27,984	27,660
Clermont	25,887	62,949	20,927	47,129
Clinton	5,417	12,938	4,791	9,824
Columbiana	23,429	25,753	20,657	21,804
Coshocton	7,378	9,839	5,594	8,243
Crawford	7,773	13,885	6,721	11,666
Cuyahoga	448,503	221,600	359,913	192,099
Darke	7,846	18,306	7,741	14,817
Defiance	6,975	11,397	6,175	9,540
Delaware	27,048	53,143	17,134	36,639
Erie	21,421	18,597	17,732	16,105
Fairfield	24,783	42,715	19,065	33,523
Fayette	4,334	7,376	3,363	5,685
Franklin	285,801	237,253	202,018	197,862
Fulton	8,224	13,640	6,805	11,546
Gallia	5,366	8,576	4,872	7,511
Geauga	19,850	30,370	15,327	25,417
Greene	30,531	48,388	25,059	37,946
Guernsey	7,768	9,962	6,643	8,181
Hamilton	199,679	222,616	161,578	204,175
Hancock	10,352	25,105	8,798	20,985
Hardin	4,891	8,441	4,557	7,124
Harrison	3,780	4,274	3,351	3,417
Henry	5,111	9,902	4,367	8,530
Highland	6,194	12,211	5,328	9,728
Hocking	6,175	6,936	4,474	5,702
Holmes	2,697	8,468	2,066	6,754
Huron	10,568	14,817	8,183	12,286
Jackson	5,700	8,585	5,131	6,958
Jefferson	19,024	17,185	17,488	15,038
Knox	9,820	17,068	7,133	13,393
Lake	59,049	62,193	46,497	51,747
Lawrence	12,118	15,454	11,307	12,531
Licking	30,053	49,016	23,196	37,180
Logan	6,825	14,471	5,945	11,849
Lorain	78,970	61,203	59,809	47,957
Lucas	132,715	87,160	108,344	73,342
Madison	6,203	11,117	5,287	8,892
Mahoning	83,194	48,761	69,212	40,460
Marion	11,930	17,171	10,370	13,617
Medina	36,272	48,196	26,635	37,349
Meigs	4,438	6,272	3,674	5,750
Mercer	5,118	15,650	5,212	12,485
Miami	17,606	33,992	15,584	26,037
Monroe	4,243	3,424	3,605	3,145
Montgomery	142,997	138,371	114,597	109,792
Morgan	2,875	3,758	2,261	3,451
Morrow	5,775	10,474	4,529	7,842
Muskingum	16,421	22,254	13,415	17,995
Noble	2,654	3,841	2,296	3,435
Ottawa	11,118	12,073	9,485	9,917
Paulding	3,610	6,206	3,384	5,210
Perry	7,257	7,856	5,895	6,440
Pickaway	8,579	14,161	6,598	10,717
Pike	5,989	6,520	4,923	5,333
Portage	40,675	35,583	31,446	28,271
Preble	7,274	13,734	6,375	11,176
Putnam	4,392	14,370	4,063	12,837
Richland	24,638	36,872	20,572	30,138
Ross	13,978	17,231	11,662	13,706
Sandusky	12,686	16,221	11,146	13,699
Scioto	16,827	18,259	13,997	15,022
Seneca	10,957	15,886	9,512	13,863
Shelby	6,535	16,204	6,593	12,476
Stark	95,337	92,215	75,308	78,153
Summit	156,587	118,558	119,759	96,721
Trumbull	66,673	40,977	57,643	34,654
Tuscarawas	18,853	23,829	15,879	19,549
Union	6,665	15,870	5,040	11,502
Van Wert	4,095	10,678	4,209	8,679
Vinton	2,651	3,249	2,037	2,720
Warren	26,044	68,037	19,142	48,318
Washington	12,538	17,532	10,383	15,342
Wayne	19,786	31,879	14,779	25,901
Williams	6,481	12,040	5,454	9,941
Wood	29,401	33,592	22,687	27,504
Wyandot	3,708	7,254	3,397	6,113
Totals	**2,741,165**	**2,859,764**	**2,186,190**	**2,351,209**

Ohio Vote Since 1948

1948: Truman, D., 1,452,791; Dewey, R., 1,445,684; Wallace, Prog., 37,596.
1952: Eisenhower, R., 2,100,391; Stevenson, D., 1,600,367.
1956: Eisenhower, R., 2,262,610; Stevenson, D., 1,439,655.
1960: Nixon, R., 2,217,611; Kennedy, D., 1,944,248.
1964: Johnson, D., 2,498,331; Goldwater, R., 1,470,865.
1968: Nixon, R., 1,791,014; Humphrey, D., 1,700,586; Wallace, 3rd Party, 467,495; Gregory, 372; Blomen, Soc. Labor, 120; Halstead, Soc. Workers, 69; Mitchell, Com., 23; Munn, Proh., 19.
1972: Nixon, R., 2,441,827; McGovern, D., 1,558,889; Schmitz, Amer., 80,067; Fisher, Soc. Labor, 7,107; Hall, Com., 6,437; Wallace, Ind., 460.
1976: Carter, D., 2,011,621; Ford, R., 2,000,505; McCarthy, Ind., 58,258; Maddox, Amer. Ind., 15,529; MacBride, Libertarian, 8,961; Hall, Com., 7,817; Camejo, Soc. Workers, 4,717; LaRouche, U.S. Labor, 4,335; scattered, 130.
1980: Reagan, R., 2,206,545; Carter, D., 1,752,414; Anderson, Ind., 254,472; Clark, Libertarian, 49,033; Commoner, Citizens, 8,564; Hall, Com., 4,729; Congress, Ind., 4,029; Griswold, Workers World, 3,790; Bubar, Statesman, 27.
1984: Reagan, R., 2,678,559; Mondale, D., 1,825,440; Bergland, Libertarian, 5,886.
1988: Bush, R., 2,416,549; Dukakis, D., 1,939,629; Fulani, Ind., 12,017; Paul, Ind., 11,926.
1992: Clinton, D., 1,984,942; Bush, R., 1,894,310; Perot, Ind., 1,036,426; Marrou, Libertarian, 7,252; Fulani, New Alliance, 6,413; Gritz, Populist/America First, 4,699; Hagelin, Natural Law, 3,437; LaRouche, Ind., 2,446.
1996: Clinton, D., 2,148,222; Dole, R., 1,859,883; Perot, Ref., 483,207; Browne, Ind., 12,851; Moorehead, Ind., 10,813; Hagelin, Natural Law, 9,120; Phillips, Ind., 7,361.
2000: Bush, R., 2,351,209; Gore, D., 2,186,190; Nader, Ind., 117,857; Buchanan, Ind., 26,724; Browne, Libertarian, 13,475; Hagelin, Natural Law, 6,169; Phillips, Ind., 3,823.
2004: Bush, R., 2,859,764; Kerry, D., 2,741,165; Badnarik, nonpartisan, 14,676; Peroutka, nonpartisan, 11,940.

Oklahoma

	2004		2000	
County	**Kerry (D)**	**Bush (R)**	**Gore (D)**	**Bush (R)**
Adair	2,562	4,971	2,361	3,503
Alfalfa	470	2,201	583	1,886
Atoka	1,946	3,142	1,906	2,375
Beaver	297	2,272	339	2,092
Beckham	1,931	5,454	2,408	4,067
Blaine	1,222	3,199	1,402	2,633
Bryan	5,745	8,615	5,554	6,084
Caddo	3,916	6,491	4,272	4,835
Canadian	9,712	33,297	8,367	22,679
Carter	6,466	12,178	6,659	9,667
Cherokee	8,623	9,569	7,256	6,918
Choctaw	2,639	3,168	2,799	2,461
Cimarron	184	1,242	227	1,230
Cleveland	34,007	65,720	27,792	47,393
Coal	1,203	1,396	1,148	1,196
Comanche	12,022	21,170	11,971	17,103
Cotton	898	1,742	1,068	1,388
Craig	2,504	3,894	2,568	2,815
Creek	9,929	18,848	9,753	13,580
Custer	2,801	7,839	3,115	6,527
Delaware	5,591	10,017	5,514	7,618
Dewey	408	1,843	599	1,607
Ellis	395	1,685	468	1,513
Garfield	5,586	17,685	6,543	14,902
Garvin	3,707	7,610	4,189	5,536
Grady	5,970	14,136	6,037	10,040
Grant	571	1,950	709	1,762
Greer	719	1,529	839	1,287
Harmon	354	838	507	692
Harper	268	1,397	374	1,296
Haskell	2,378	2,946	2,510	2,039
Hughes	2,283	3,066	2,334	2,196
Jackson	2,232	7,024	2,515	5,591
Jefferson	1,057	1,546	1,245	1,320
Johnston	1,713	2,635	1,809	2,072
Kay	5,957	14,121	6,122	11,768
Kingfisher	1,022	5,630	1,304	4,693
Kiowa	1,413	2,610	1,544	2,173
Latimer	1,945	2,535	1,865	1,739
Le Flore	6,741	10,683	6,536	8,215
Lincoln	4,041	10,149	4,140	7,387
Logan	4,869	11,474	4,510	8,187
Love	1,538	2,295	1,530	1,807
Major	537	3,122	635	2,672
Marshall	2,088	3,363	2,210	2,641
Mayes	6,933	9,946	6,618	7,132
McClain	3,742	10,041	3,679	6,750
McCurtain	3,684	7,472	3,752	6,601
McIntosh	4,488	4,692	4,206	3,444
Murray	2,130	3,665	2,263	2,609
Muskogee	12,585	15,124	12,520	11,820
Noble	1,335	3,993	1,416	3,230
Nowata	1,660	2,805	1,703	2,069
Okfuskee	1,743	2,542	1,814	1,910
Oklahoma	97,298	174,741	81,590	139,078
Okmulgee	7,367	8,363	7,186	5,797
Osage	8,068	11,467	7,540	8,138
Ottawa	5,086	7,443	5,647	5,625
Pawnee	2,564	4,412	2,435	3,386
Payne	10,101	19,560	9,319	15,256
Pittsburg	7,452	11,134	7,627	8,514
Pontotoc	5,165	9,647	5,387	7,299
Pottawatomie	8,638	17,215	8,763	13,235
Pushmataha	1,934	2,863	1,969	2,331
Roger Mills	382	1,388	441	1,234
Rogers	11,918	24,976	10,813	17,713
Seminole	3,648	5,624	3,783	4,011
Sequoyah	5,910	8,865	5,425	6,614
Stephens	5,515	13,646	6,467	10,860
Texas	1,016	5,450	1,084	4,964
Tillman	1,175	2,273	1,400	1,920
Tulsa	90,220	163,452	81,656	134,152
Wagoner	9,157	19,081	8,244	12,981
Washington	6,862	16,551	6,644	13,788
Washita	1,340	3,705	1,564	2,850
Woods	932	3,166	1,235	2,774
Woodward	1,458	6,193	1,950	5,067
Totals	**503,966**	**959,792**	**474,276**	**744,337**

Oklahoma Vote Since 1948

1948: Truman, D., 452,782; Dewey, R., 268,817.
1952: Eisenhower, R., 518,045; Stevenson, D., 430,939.
1956: Eisenhower, R., 473,769; Stevenson, D., 385,581.
1960: Nixon, R., 533,039; Kennedy, D., 370,111.
1964: Johnson, D., 519,834; Goldwater, R., 412,665.
1968: Nixon, R., 449,697; Humphrey, D., 301,658; Wallace, 3rd Party, 191,731.
1972: Nixon, R., 759,025; McGovern, D., 247,147; Schmitz, Amer., 23,728.
1976: Ford, R., 545,708; Carter, D., 532,442; McCarthy, Ind., 14,101.
1980: Reagan, R., 695,570; Carter, D., 402,026; Anderson, Ind., 38,284; Clark, Libertarian, 13,828.
1984: Reagan, R., 861,530; Mondale, D., 385,080; Bergland, Libertarian, 9,066.
1988: Bush, R., 678,367; Dukakis, D., 483,423; Paul, Lib., 6,261; Fulani, New Alliance, 2,985.
1992: Bush, R., 592,929; Clinton, D., 473,066; Perot, Ind., 319,878; Marrou, Libertarian, 4,486.
1996: Dole, R., 582,315; Clinton, D., 488,105; Perot, Ref., 130,788; Browne, Libertarian, 5,505.
2000: Bush, R., 744,337; Gore, D., 474,276; Buchanan, Reform, 9,014; Browne, Libertarian, 6,602.
2004: Bush, R., 959,792; Kerry, D., 503,966.

Oregon

	2004		2000	
County	**Kerry (D)**	**Bush (R)**	**Gore (D)**	**Bush (R)**
Baker	2,616	6,253	2,195	5,618
Benton	26,515	18,460	19,444	15,825
Clackamas	95,129	97,691	76,421	77,539
Clatsop	10,461	8,503	8,296	6,950
Columbia	12,563	11,868	10,331	9,369
Coos	14,393	18,291	11,610	15,626
Crook	3,024	6,830	2,474	5,363
Curry	5,220	7,332	4,090	6,551
Deschutes	31,179	41,757	22,061	32,132
Douglas	18,089	35,956	14,193	30,294
Gilliam	370	755	359	679
Grant	780	3,204	589	3,078
Harney	839	2,815	766	2,799
Hood River	5,587	4,124	4,072	3,721
Jackson	44,366	56,519	33,153	46,052
Jefferson	3,243	4,762	2,681	3,838
Josephine	15,214	26,241	11,864	22,186
Klamath	8,264	22,733	7,541	18,855
Lake	802	3,039	707	2,830
Lane	107,769	75,007	78,583	61,578
Lincoln	13,753	10,160	10,861	8,446
Linn	19,940	31,260	16,682	25,359
Malheur	2,577	8,123	2,336	7,624
Marion	57,671	69,900	49,430	57,443
Morrow	1,361	2,732	1,197	2,224
Multnomah	259,585	98,439	188,441	83,677
Polk	15,484	19,508	11,921	14,988
Sherman	390	694	326	679
Tillamook	6,750	7,003	5,762	5,775
Umatilla	8,884	17,068	7,809	14,140
Union	4,428	8,879	3,577	7,836
Wallowa	1,269	3,132	836	3,279
Wasco	5,691	6,119	4,616	5,356
Washington	121,140	107,223	90,662	86,091
Wheeler	245	612	202	584
Yamhill	17,572	23,839	14,254	19,193
Totals	**943,163**	**866,831**	**720,342**	**713,577**

Oregon Vote Since 1948

1948: Dewey, R., 260,904; Truman, D., 243,147; Wallace, Prog., 14,978; Thomas, Soc., 5,051.
1952: Eisenhower, R., 420,815; Stevenson, D., 270,579; Hallinan, Ind., 3,665.
1956: Eisenhower, R., 406,393; Stevenson, D., 329,204.
1960: Nixon, R., 408,060; Kennedy, D., 367,402.
1964: Johnson, D., 501,017; Goldwater, R., 282,779; write-in, 2,509.
1968: Nixon, R., 408,433; Humphrey, D., 358,866; Wallace, 3rd Party, 49,683; write-in, McCarthy, 1,496; N. Rockefeller, 69; others, 1,075.
1972: Nixon, R., 486,686; McGovern, D., 392,760; Schmitz, Amer., 46,211; write-in, 2,289.
1976: Ford, R., 492,120; Carter, D., 490,407; McCarthy, Ind., 40,207; write-in, 7,142.
1980: Reagan, R., 571,044; Carter, D., 456,890; Anderson, Ind., 112,389; Clark, Libertarian, 25,838; Commoner, Citizens, 13,642; scattered, 1,713.
1984: Reagan, R., 658,700; Mondale, D., 536,479.
1988: Dukakis, D., 616,206; Bush, R., 560,126; Paul, Lib., 14,811; Fulani, Ind., 6,487.
1992: Clinton, D., 621,314; Bush, R., 475,757; Perot, Ind., 354,091; Marrou, Libertarian, 4,277; Fulani, New Alliance, 3,030.
1996: Clinton, D., 649,641; Dole, R., 538,152; Perot, Ref., 121,221; Nader, Pacific, 49,415; Browne, Libertarian, 8,903; Phillips, Taxpayers, 3,379; Hagelin, Natural Law, 2,798; Hollis, Soc., 1,922.
2000: Gore, D., 720,342; Bush, R., 713,577; Nader, Green, 77,357; Browne, Libertarian, 7,447; Buchanan, Ind., 7,063; Hagelin, Reform, 2,574; Phillips, Constitution, 2,189.
2004: Kerry, D., 943,163; Bush, R., 866,831; Badnarik, Libertarian, 7,260; Cobb, Pac. Green, 5,315; Peroutka, Constitution, 5,257.

Pennsylvania

County	2004 Kerry (D)	2004 Bush (R)	2000 Gore (D)	2000 Bush (R)
Adams	13,764	28,247	11,682	20,848
Allegheny	368,912	271,925	329,963	235,361
Armstrong	12,025	18,925	11,127	15,508
Beaver	42,146	39,916	38,925	32,491
Bedford	6,016	16,606	5,474	13,598
Berks	76,309	87,122	59,150	71,273
Blair	18,105	35,751	15,774	28,376
Bradford	8,590	16,942	7,911	14,660
Bucks	163,438	154,469	132,914	121,927
Butler	30,090	54,959	25,037	44,009
Cambria	32,591	34,048	30,308	28,001
Cameron	794	1,599	779	1,383
Carbon	12,223	12,519	10,668	9,717
Centre	30,733	33,133	21,409	26,172
Chester	109,708	120,036	82,047	100,080
Clarion	6,049	11,063	5,605	9,796
Clearfield	13,518	20,533	11,718	18,019
Clinton	5,823	8,035	5,521	6,064
Columbia	10,679	16,052	8,975	12,095
Crawford	16,013	21,965	13,250	18,858
Cumberland	37,928	67,648	31,053	54,802
Dauphin	55,299	65,296	44,390	53,631
Delaware	162,601	120,425	134,861	105,836
Elk	6,602	7,872	5,754	7,347
Erie	67,921	57,372	59,399	49,027
Fayette	29,120	25,045	28,152	20,013
Forest	989	1,571	843	1,371
Franklin	16,562	41,817	14,922	33,042
Fulton	1,475	4,772	1,425	3,753
Greene	7,674	7,786	7,230	5,890
Huntingdon	5,879	12,126	5,073	10,408
Indiana	15,831	20,254	13,667	16,799
Jefferson	6,073	13,371	5,566	11,473
Juniata	2,797	7,144	2,656	5,795
Lackawanna	59,573	44,766	57,471	35,096
Lancaster	74,328	145,591	54,968	115,900
Lawrence	21,387	21,938	20,593	18,060
Lebanon	18,109	37,089	16,093	28,534
Lehigh	73,940	70,160	56,667	55,492
Luzerne	69,573	64,953	62,199	52,328
Lycoming	15,681	33,961	14,663	27,137
McKean	6,294	10,941	5,510	9,661
Mercer	24,831	26,311	23,817	23,132
Mifflin	4,889	11,726	4,835	9,400
Monroe	27,967	27,971	21,939	23,265
Montgomery	222,048	175,741	177,990	145,623
Montour	2,666	4,903	2,356	3,960
Northampton	63,446	62,102	53,097	47,396
Northumberland	14,602	22,262	13,670	18,142
Perry	5,423	13,919	4,459	11,184
Philadelphia	542,205	130,099	449,182	100,959
Pike	8,656	12,444	7,330	9,339
Potter	2,268	5,640	2,037	4,858
Schuylkill	29,231	35,640	26,215	29,841
Snyder	4,348	10,566	3,536	8,963
Somerset	12,842	23,802	12,028	20,218
Sullivan	1,213	2,056	1,066	1,928
Susquehanna	7,351	11,573	6,481	10,226
Tioga	5,437	12,019	4,617	9,635
Union	5,700	10,334	4,209	8,523
Venango	9,024	14,472	8,196	11,642
Warren	8,044	10,999	7,537	9,290
Washington	48,225	47,673	44,961	37,339
Wayne	8,060	13,713	6,904	11,201
Westmoreland	77,774	100,087	71,792	80,858
Wyoming	4,982	7,782	4,363	6,922
York	63,701	114,270	51,958	87,652
Totals	**2,938,095**	**2,793,847**	**2,485,967**	**2,281,127**

Pennsylvania Vote Since 1948

1948: Dewey, R., 1,902,197; Truman, D., 1,752,426; Wallace, Prog., 55,161; Thomas, Soc., 11,325; Watson, Proh., 10,338; Dobbs, Militant Workers, 2,133; Teichert, Ind. Gov., 1,461.
1952: Eisenhower, R., 2,415,789; Stevenson, D., 2,146,269; Hamblen, Proh., 8,771; Hallinan, Prog., 4,200; Hoopes, Soc., 2,684; Dobbs, Militant Workers, 1,502; Hass, Ind. Gov., 1,347; scattered, 155.
1956: Eisenhower, R., 2,585,252; Stevenson, D., 1,981,769; Hass, Soc. Labor, 7,447; Dobbs, Militant Workers, 2,035.
1960: Kennedy, D., 2,556,282; Nixon, R., 2,439,956; Hass, Soc. Labor, 7,185; Dobbs, Soc. Workers, 2,678; scattered, 440.
1964: Johnson, D., 3,130,954; Goldwater, R., 1,673,657; DeBerry, Soc. Workers, 10,456; Hass, Soc. Labor, 5,092; scattered, 2,531.
1968: Humphrey, D., 2,259,405; Nixon, R., 2,090,017; Wallace, 3rd Party, 378,582; Gregory, Peace and Freedom, 7,821; Blomen, Soc. Labor, 4,977; Halstead, Soc. Workers, 4,862; others, 2,264.
1972: Nixon, R., 2,714,521; McGovern, D., 1,796,951; Schmitz, Amer., 70,593; Jenness, Soc. Workers, 4,639; Hall, Com., 2,686; others, 2,715.
1976: Carter, D., 2,328,677; Ford, R., 2,205,604; McCarthy, Ind., 50,584; Maddox, Const., 25,344; Camejo, Soc. Workers, 3,009; LaRouche, U.S. Labor, 2,744; Hall, Com., 1,891; others, 2,934.
1980: Reagan, R., 2,261,872; Carter, D., 1,937,540; Anderson, Ind., 292,921; Clark, Libertarian, 33,263; DeBerry, Soc. Workers, 20,291; Commoner, Consumer, 10,430; Hall, Com., 5,184.
1984: Reagan, R., 2,584,323; Mondale, D., 2,228,131; Bergland, Libertarian, 6,982.
1988: Bush, R., 2,300,087; Dukakis, D., 2,194,944; McCarthy, Consumer, 19,158; Paul, Lib., 12,051.
1992: Clinton, D., 2,239,164; Bush, R., 1,791,841; Perot, Ind., 902,667; Marrou, Libertarian, 21,477; Fulani, New Alliance, 4,661.
1996: Clinton, D., 2,215,819; Dole, R., 1,801,169; Perot, Ref., 430,984; Browne, Libertarian, 28,000; Phillips, Constitutional, 19,552; Hagelin, Natural Law, 5,783.
2000: Gore, D., 2,485,967; Bush, R., 2,281,127; Nader, Green, 103,392; Buchanan, Reform, 16,023; Phillips, Constitution, 14,428; Browne, Libertarian, 11,248.
2004: Kerry, D., 2,938,095; Bush, R., 2,793,847; Badnarik, Libertarian, 21,185; Cobb, Green, 6,319; Peroutka, Constitution, 6,318.

Rhode Island

City	2004 Kerry (D)	2004 Bush (R)	2000 Gore (D)	2000 Bush (R)
Cranston	20,331	14,471	21,204	10,420
East Providence	13,655	6,359	13,033	5,072
Pawtucket	15,567	6,394	15,429	4,598
Providence	35,917	9,787	31,979	7,669
Warwick	23,164	16,640	23,948	12,741
Other	151,126	115,395	143,915	90,055
Totals	**259,760**	**169,046**	**249,508**	**130,555**

Rhode Island Vote Since 1948

1948: Truman, D., 188,736; Dewey, R., 135,787; Wallace, Prog., 2,619; Thomas, Soc., 429; Teichert, Soc. Labor, 131.
1952: Eisenhower, R., 210,935; Stevenson, D., 203,293; Hallinan, Prog., 187; Hass, Soc. Labor, 83.
1956: Eisenhower, R., 225,819; Stevenson, D., 161,790.
1960: Kennedy, D., 258,032; Nixon, R., 147,502.
1964: Johnson, D., 315,463; Goldwater, R., 74,615.
1968: Humphrey, D., 246,518; Nixon, R., 122,359; Wallace, 3rd Party, 15,678; Halstead, Soc. Workers, 383.
1972: Nixon, R., 220,383; McGovern, D., 194,645; Jenness, Soc. Workers, 729.
1976: Carter, D., 227,636; Ford, R., 181,249; MacBride, Libertarian, 715; Camejo, Soc. Workers, 462; Hall, Com., 334; Levin, Soc. Labor, 188.
1980: Carter, D., 198,342; Reagan, R., 154,793; Anderson, Ind., 59,819; Clark, Libertarian, 2,458; Hall, Com., 218; McReynolds, Soc., 170; DeBerry, Soc. Workers, 90; Griswold, Workers World, 77.
1984: Reagan, R., 212,080; Mondale, D., 197,106; Bergland, Libertarian, 277.
1988: Dukakis, D., 225,123; Bush, R., 177,761; Paul, Lib., 825; Fulani, New Alliance, 280.
1992: Clinton, D., 213,299; Bush, R., 131,601; Perot, Ind., 105,045; Fulani, New Alliance, 1,878.
1996: Clinton, D., 233,050; Dole, R., 104,683; Perot, Ref., 43,723; Nader, Green, 6,040; Browne, Libertarian, 1,109; Phillips, Taxpayers, 1,021; Hagelin, Natural Law, 435; Moorehead, Workers World, 186.
2000: Gore, D., 249,508; Bush, R., 130,555; Nader, Ind., 25,052; Buchanan, Reform, 2,273; Browne, Ind., 742; Hagelin, Ind., 271; Moorehead, Ind., 199; Phillips, Ind., 97; McReynolds, Ind., 52; Harris, Ind., 34.
2004: Kerry, D., 259,760; Bush, R., 169,046; Nader, Ref., 4,651; Cobb, Green, 1,333; Badnarik, Libertarian, 907; Peroutka, Constitution, 339; Parker, Workers World, 253.

South Carolina

County	2004 Kerry (D)	2004 Bush (R)	2000 Gore (D)	2000 Bush (R)
Abbeville	4,389	5,436	3,766	4,450
Aiken	19,799	39,077	16,409	33,203
Allendale	2,565	985	2,338	967
Anderson	20,697	43,355	19,606	35,827
Bamberg	3,841	2,138	3,451	2,047
Barnwell	3,982	4,606	3,661	4,521
Beaufort	21,505	33,331	17,487	25,561
Berkeley	20,142	32,104	17,707	24,796
Calhoun	3,393	3,448	3,063	3,216
Charleston	63,758	70,297	49,520	58,229
Cherokee	6,466	12,090	6,138	9,900
Chester	5,790	5,798	5,242	4,986
Chesterfield	6,729	7,252	6,111	6,266
Clarendon	7,087	6,061	5,999	5,186
Colleton	6,699	7,264	6,449	6,767
Darlington	11,829	13,416	10,253	11,290
Dillon	4,832	4,301	4,930	3,975
Dorchester	14,733	26,006	12,168	20,734
Edgefield	4,051	5,611	3,950	4,760
Fairfield	5,764	3,531	5,263	3,011
Florence	21,442	27,689	17,157	23,678
Georgetown	10,602	12,606	9,445	10,535
Greenville	55,347	111,481	43,810	92,714
Greenwood	8,954	14,264	8,139	12,193
Hampton	4,832	3,097	4,896	2,798
Horry	29,547	50,447	29,113	40,300

County	2004 Kerry (D)	2004 Bush (R)	2000 Gore (D)	2000 Bush (R)
Jasper	3,840	2,933	3,646	2,414
Kershaw	8,515	14,160	7,428	11,911
Lancaster	7,631	12,916	8,782	11,676
Laurens	9,205	14,466	7,920	12,102
Lee	4,960	2,901	3,899	2,675
Lexington	25,393	67,132	22,830	58,095
Marion	7,767	5,589	7,358	4,687
Marlboro	4,984	3,423	5,060	2,699
McCormick	2,648	2,396	1,896	1,704
Newberry	4,483	7,654	4,428	7,492
Oconee	8,395	18,811	7,571	15,364
Orangeburg	24,698	12,695	19,802	12,657
Pickens	10,287	29,759	8,927	24,681
Richland	76,283	56,212	63,179	50,164
Saluda	3,001	4,537	2,682	4,098
Spartanburg	33,633	62,004	29,559	52,114
Sumter	18,695	18,074	14,365	15,915
Union	5,236	6,592	4,662	6,234
Williamsburg	9,044	4,795	6,723	4,524
York	24,226	45,234	19,251	33,776
Totals	**661,699**	**937,974**	**566,039**	**786,892**

South Carolina Vote Since 1948

1948: Thurmond, States' Rights, 102,607; Truman, D., 34,423; Dewey, R., 5,386; Wallace, Prog., 154; Thomas, Soc., 1.
1952: Stevenson, D., 173,004. Under state law votes cast for 2 Eisenhower slates of electors could not be combined. Eisenhower, Ind., 158,289; R., 9,793; total, 168,082. Hamblen, Proh., 1.
1956: Stevenson, D., 136,372; Byrd, Ind., 88,509; Eisenhower, R., 75,700; Andrews, Ind., 2.
1960: Kennedy, D., 198,129; Nixon, R., 188,558; write-in, 1.
1964: Goldwater, R., 309,048; Johnson, D., 215,700; write-in: Wallace, 5; Nixon, 1; Powell, 1; Thurmond, 1.
1968: Nixon, R., 254,062; Wallace, 3rd Party, 215,430; Humphrey, D., 197,486.
1972: Nixon, R., 477,044; McGovern, D., 184,559; Schmitz, Amer., 10,075; United Citizens, 2,265; write-in, 17.
1976: Carter, D., 450,807; Ford, R., 346,149; Anderson, Amer., 2,996; Maddox, Amer. Ind., 1,950; write-in, 681.
1980: Reagan, R., 439,277; Carter, D., 428,220; Anderson, Ind., 13,868; Clark, Libertarian, 4,807; Rarick, Amer. Ind., 2,086.
1984: Reagan, R., 615,539; Mondale, D., 344,459; Bergland, Libertarian, 4,359.
1988: Bush, R., 606,443; Dukakis, D., 370,554; Paul, Lib., 4,935; Fulani, United Citizens, 4,077.
1992: Bush, R., 577,507; Clinton, D., 479,514; Perot, Ind., 138,872; Marrou, Libertarian, 2,719; Phillips, U.S. Taxpayers, 2,680; Fulani, New Alliance, 1,235.
1996: Dole, R., 573,458; Clinton, D., 506,283; Perot, Ref./Patriot, 64,386; Browne, Libertarian, 4,271; Phillips, Taxpayers, 2,043; Hagelin, Natural Law, 1,248.
2000: Bush, R., 786,892; Gore, D., 566,039; Nader, United Citizens, 20,279; Browne, Libertarian, 4,898; Buchanan, Reform, 3,309; Phillips, Constitution, 1,682; Hagelin, Natural Law, 943.
2004: Bush, R., 937,974; Kerry, D., 661,699; Nader, Ind., 5,520; Peroutka, Constitution, 5,317; Badnarik, Libertarian, 3,608; Brown, United Citizen, 2,124; Cobb, Green, 1,488.

South Dakota

County	2004 Kerry (D)	2004 Bush (R)	2000 Gore (D)	2000 Bush (R)
Aurora	620	1,009	513	847
Beadle	3,443	4,917	3,216	4,347
Bennett	759	833	377	712
Bon Homme	1,293	2,063	1,162	1,901
Brookings	5,443	7,662	4,546	6,212
Brown	7,943	10,386	7,173	9,060
Brule	1,040	1,544	818	1,268
Buffalo	603	223	256	140
Butte	1,009	3,166	840	2,760
Campbell	239	708	147	739
Charles Mix	2,155	2,556	1,300	2,205
Clark	875	1,435	791	1,272
Clay	3,315	2,692	2,638	2,363
Codington	4,803	7,778	4,192	6,718
Corson	972	720	549	629
Custer	1,272	2,922	955	2,495
Davison	3,263	5,561	2,936	4,445
Day	1,817	1,671	1,492	1,623
Deuel	961	1,406	926	1,245
Dewey	1,606	921	880	761
Douglas	393	1,596	363	1,311
Edmunds	765	1,434	676	1,257
Fall River	1,326	2,413	1,133	2,185
Faulk	418	945	388	904
Grant	1,633	2,392	1,475	2,235
Gregory	813	1,685	718	1,487
Haakon	219	1,007	164	938
Hamlin	1,015	1,946	923	1,731
Hand	668	1,482	565	1,419
Hanson	745	1,379	457	944
Harding	94	704	64	650
Hughes	2,697	6,017	2,212	5,188
Hutchinson	1,177	2,899	1,052	2,497
Hyde	259	631	218	592
Jackson/ Washabaugh	508	726	319	687
Jerauld	482	736	468	624
Jones	134	565	137	509
Kingsbury	1,163	1,804	1,049	1,612
Lake	2,509	3,359	2,331	2,724
Lawrence	3,857	7,489	2,797	6,327
Lincoln	5,703	11,161	3,844	6,546
Lyman	872	1,029	482	875
Marshall	1,099	1,242	939	1,097
McCook	1,201	2,017	965	1,610
McPherson	369	1,180	295	1,073
Meade	2,941	8,347	2,267	6,870
Mellette	361	553	222	495
Miner	641	810	523	724
Minnehaha	32,314	44,189	27,042	33,428
Moody	1,609	1,790	1,318	1,361
Pennington	14,213	29,976	11,123	24,696
Perkins	418	1,329	297	1,237
Potter	463	1,143	356	1,112
Roberts	2,527	2,396	1,700	2,237
Sanborn	581	817	468	767
Shannon	3,566	526	1,667	252
Spink	1,478	2,259	1,274	1,957
Stanley	464	1,129	402	955
Sully	201	702	209	633
Todd	2,543	889	993	478
Tripp	972	2,230	799	1,909
Turner	1,646	3,084	1,414	2,514
Union	3,000	3,987	2,358	3,265
Walworth	878	1,967	721	1,758
Yankton	4,237	6,003	3,596	4,904
Ziebach	641	447	314	384
Totals	**149,244**	**232,584**	**118,804**	**190,700**

South Dakota Vote Since 1948

1948: Dewey, R., 129,651; Truman, D., 117,653; Wallace, Prog., 2,801.
1952: Eisenhower, R., 203,857; Stevenson, D., 90,426.
1956: Eisenhower, R., 171,569; Stevenson, D., 122,288.
1960: Nixon, R., 178,417; Kennedy, D., 128,070.
1964: Johnson, D., 163,010; Goldwater, R., 130,108.
1968: Nixon, R., 149,841; Humphrey, D., 118,023; Wallace, 3rd Party, 13,400.
1972: Nixon, R., 166,476; McGovern, D., 139,945; Jenness, Soc. Workers, 994.
1976: Ford, R., 151,505; Carter, D., 147,068; MacBride, Libertarian, 1,619; Hall, Com., 318; Camejo, Soc. Workers, 168.
1980: Reagan, R., 198,343; Carter, D., 103,855; Anderson, Ind., 21,431; Clark, Libertarian, 3,824; Pulley, Soc. Workers, 250.
1984: Reagan, R., 200,267; Mondale, D., 116,113.
1988: Bush, R., 165,415; Dukakis, D., 145,560; Paul, Lib., 1,060; Fulani, New Alliance, 730.
1992: Bush, R., 136,718; Clinton, D., 124,888; Perot, Ind., 73,295.
1996: Dole, R., 150,543; Clinton, D., 139,333; Perot, Ref., 31,250; Browne, Libertarian, 1,472; Phillips, Taxpayers, 912; Hagelin, Natural Law, 316.
2000: Bush, R., 190,700; Gore, D., 118,804; Buchanan, Reform, 3,322; Phillips, Ind., 1,781; Browne, Libertarian, 1,662.
2004: Bush, R., 232,584; Kerry, D., 149,244; Nader, Ind., 4,320; Peroutka, Constitution, 1,103; Badnarik, Libertarian, 964.

Tennessee

County	2004 Kerry (D)	2004 Bush (R)	2000 Gore (D)	2000 Bush (R)
Anderson	12,896	18,510	13,556	14,688
Bedford	5,268	8,351	6,136	5,911
Benton	3,869	3,161	3,700	2,484
Bledsoe	1,927	2,849	1,756	2,380
Blount	15,047	33,241	14,688	25,273
Bradley	9,431	25,951	8,768	20,167
Campbell	6,163	7,859	6,492	5,784
Cannon	2,515	2,931	2,697	1,924
Carroll	5,070	6,605	5,239	5,465
Carter	6,395	15,768	6,724	12,111
Cheatham	5,918	9,676	6,062	6,356
Chester	2,242	4,086	2,192	3,487
Claiborne	4,034	6,448	3,841	5,023
Clay	1,675	1,650	1,931	1,468
Cocke	3,935	8,297	3,872	6,185
Coffee	8,243	11,793	8,741	8,788
Crockett	2,459	3,242	2,705	2,676
Cumberland	8,327	15,144	7,644	10,994
Davidson	132,737	107,839	120,508	84,117
Decatur	2,268	2,566	2,278	2,046
DeKalb	3,445	3,685	3,765	2,411
Dickson	8,597	10,567	8,332	7,016
Dyer	5,287	8,447	5,425	6,282
Fayette	5,696	8,962	5,037	6,402

County	2004 Kerry (D)	2004 Bush (R)	2000 Gore (D)	2000 Bush (R)
Fentress	2,371	4,293	2,529	3,417
Franklin	7,800	9,129	7,828	6,560
Gibson	8,511	10,596	8,663	8,286
Giles	5,273	6,163	5,527	4,377
Grainger	2,569	4,907	2,361	3,746
Greene	7,635	16,382	7,909	12,540
Grundy	2,789	2,107	2,970	1,553
Hamblen	7,433	14,742	7,564	11,824
Hamilton	57,302	78,547	51,708	66,605
Hancock	777	1,756	690	1,343
Hardeman	5,685	4,704	4,953	3,729
Hardin	3,834	6,087	3,735	4,951
Hawkins	6,684	13,447	6,753	10,071
Haywood	4,359	3,140	3,887	2,554
Henderson	3,448	6,585	3,166	5,153
Henry	5,732	7,340	6,093	5,944
Hickman	4,263	4,359	4,239	2,914
Houston	2,126	1,440	2,081	993
Humphreys	4,485	3,261	4,205	2,387
Jackson	2,998	2,026	3,304	1,384
Jefferson	5,469	11,625	5,226	8,657
Johnson	1,812	4,634	1,813	3,740
Knox	66,013	110,803	60,969	86,851
Lake	2,634	2,078	1,419	781
Lauderdale	4,474	4,164	4,224	3,329
Lawrence	6,592	9,959	6,643	7,613
Lewis	2,192	2,819	2,281	2,037
Lincoln	4,546	7,829	5,060	5,435
Loudon	5,708	14,041	5,905	10,266
Macon	2,738	4,670	3,059	3,366
Madison	16,840	21,679	15,781	17,862
Marion	5,548	5,862	5,441	4,651
Marshall	4,722	5,825	5,107	4,105
Maury	12,379	17,505	11,127	11,930
McMinn	5,891	11,980	6,142	10,155
McNairy	4,101	5,787	4,003	4,897
Meigs	1,595	2,500	1,555	1,797
Monroe	5,354	10,123	5,327	7,514
Montgomery	20,070	28,627	18,818	19,644
Moore	1,084	1,668	1,107	1,145
Morgan	2,924	4,401	2,921	3,144
Obion	5,549	7,859	6,056	6,168
Overton	4,518	3,941	4,507	2,875
Perry	1,579	1,522	1,650	1,165
Pickett	1,033	1,600	939	1,281
Polk	2,724	3,924	2,574	2,907
Putnam	10,566	15,637	10,785	11,248
Rhea	3,665	7,301	3,722	5,900
Roane	8,706	14,467	9,575	11,345
Robertson	9,865	15,331	10,249	9,675
Rutherford	31,647	52,200	27,360	33,445
Scott	3,086	4,509	2,967	3,579
Sequatchie	1,986	2,951	1,648	2,169
Sevier	8,621	22,143	8,208	16,734
Shelby	216,945	158,137	190,404	141,756
Smith	4,044	3,739	4,884	2,384
Stewart	2,860	2,675	2,870	1,826
Sullivan	19,637	42,555	21,354	33,482
Sumner	21,458	40,181	22,118	27,601
Tipton	7,379	14,178	6,300	10,070
Trousdale	1,851	1,314	1,966	950
Unicoi	2,374	5,030	2,566	3,780
Union	2,524	4,145	2,564	3,199
Van Buren	1,209	1,120	1,255	845
Warren	6,808	7,503	7,378	5,552
Washington	14,944	29,735	14,769	22,579
Wayne	1,951	3,999	1,859	3,370
Weakley	5,588	7,817	5,570	6,106
White	4,147	5,269	4,135	3,525
Williamson	21,732	57,451	18,745	38,901
Wilson	15,277	28,924	16,561	18,844
Totals	**1,036,477**	**1,384,375**	**981,720**	**1,061,949**

Tennessee Vote Since 1948

1948: Truman, D., 270,402; Dewey, R., 202,914; Thurmond, States' Rights, 73,815; Wallace, Prog., 1,864; Thomas, Soc., 1,288.

1952: Eisenhower, R., 446,147; Stevenson, D., 443,710; Hamblen, Proh., 1,432; Hallinan, Prog., 885; MacArthur, Christian Nationalist, 379.

1956: Eisenhower, R., 462,288; Stevenson, D., 456,507; Andrews, Ind., 19,820; Holtwick, Proh., 789.

1960: Nixon, R., 556,577; Kennedy, D., 481,453; Faubus, States' Rights, 11,304; Decker, Proh., 2,458.

1964: Johnson, D., 635,047; Goldwater, R., 508,965; write-in, 34.

1968: Nixon, R., 472,592; Wallace, 3rd Party, 424,792; Humphrey, D., 351,233.

1972: Nixon, R., 813,147; McGovern, D., 357,293; Schmitz, Amer., 30,373; write-in, 369.

1976: Carter, D., 825,879; Ford, R., 633,969; Anderson, Amer., 5,769; McCarthy, Ind., 5,004; Maddox, Amer. Ind., 2,303; MacBride, Libertarian, 1,375; Hall, Com., 547; LaRouche, U.S. Labor, 512; Bubar, Proh., 442; Miller, Ind., 316; write-in, 230.

1980: Reagan, R., 787,761; Carter, D., 783,051; Anderson, Ind., 35,991; Clark, Libertarian, 7,116; Commoner, Citizens, 1,112; Bubar, Statesman, 521; McReynolds, Soc., 519; Hall, Com., 503; DeBerry, Soc. Workers, 490; Griswold, Workers World, 400; write-in, 152.

1984: Reagan, R., 990,212; Mondale, D., 711,714; Bergland, Libertarian, 3,072.

1988: Bush, R., 947,233; Dukakis, D., 679,794; Paul, Ind., 2,041; Duke, Ind., 1,807.

1992: Clinton, D., 933,521; Bush, R., 841,300; Perot, Ind., 199,968; Marrou, Libertarian, 1,847.

1996: Clinton, D., 909,146; Dole, R., 863,530; Perot, Ind. (Ref.), 105,918; Nader, Ind., 6,427; Browne, Ind., 5,020; Phillips, Ind., 1,818; Collins, Ind., 688; Hagelin, Ind., 636; Michael, Ind., 408; Dodge, Ind., 324.

2000: Bush, R., 1,061,949; Gore, D., 981,720; Nader, Green, 19,781; Browne, Libertarian, 4,284; Buchanan, Reform, 4,250; Brown, Ind., 1,606; Phillips, Ind., 1,015; Hagelin, Reform, 613; Venson, Ind., 535.

2004: Bush, R., 1,384,375; Kerry, D., 1,036,477; Nader, Ind., 8,992; Badnarik, Ind., 4,866; Peroutka, Ind., 2,570.

Texas

County	2004 Kerry (D)	2004 Bush (R)	2000 Gore (D)	2000 Bush (R)
Anderson	4,678	11,525	5,041	9,835
Andrews	677	3,837	876	3,091
Angelina	9,302	18,932	9,957	16,648
Aransas	2,640	6,569	2,637	5,390
Archer	878	3,556	993	2,951
Armstrong	170	830	150	772
Atascosa	4,421	7,635	4,322	6,231
Austin	2,582	8,072	2,407	6,661
Bailey	525	1,882	488	1,589
Bandera	1,738	6,933	1,426	5,613
Bastrop	9,794	13,290	6,973	10,310
Baylor	467	1,169	663	1,285
Bee	4,045	5,428	3,795	4,429
Bell	27,165	52,135	21,011	41,208
Bexar	210,976	260,698	185,158	215,613
Blanco	1,267	3,277	811	2,777
Borden	55	303	62	283
Bosque	1,815	5,737	1,930	4,745
Bowie	11,880	21,791	11,662	18,325
Brazoria	28,904	63,662	24,883	53,445
Brazos	16,128	37,594	12,359	32,864
Brewster	1,729	1,980	1,349	1,867
Briscoe	191	620	224	544
Brooks	1,823	845	1,854	556
Brown	2,523	11,640	3,138	9,609
Burleson	2,276	4,405	2,235	3,542
Burnet	4,147	11,456	3,557	9,286
Caldwell	5,052	6,436	3,872	5,216
Calhoun	2,561	4,348	2,766	3,724
Callahan	1,073	4,542	1,174	3,656
Cameron	33,998	34,801	33,214	27,800
Camp	1,778	2,638	1,625	2,121
Carson	485	2,450	480	2,216
Cass	4,630	7,383	4,618	6,295
Castro	631	1,794	727	1,607
Chambers	2,953	8,618	2,888	6,769
Cherokee	4,439	11,329	4,755	9,599
Childress	511	1,629	602	1,506
Clay	1,299	3,971	1,460	3,112
Cochran	249	856	344	807
Coke	266	1,338	355	1,137
Coleman	778	3,035	853	2,687
Collin	68,935	174,435	42,884	128,179
Collingsworth	346	1,051	429	974
Colorado	2,161	5,488	2,229	4,913
Comal	9,153	31,574	7,131	24,599
Comanche	1,431	3,813	1,636	3,334
Concho	270	911	268	818
Cooke	3,142	11,908	3,153	10,128
Coryell	5,122	12,421	4,493	10,321
Cottle	214	549	241	502
Crane	254	1,314	387	1,246
Crockett	473	1,248	467	924
Crosby	622	1,647	705	1,270
Culberson	375	407	577	413
Dallam	305	1,473	341	1,385
Dallas	336,641	346,246	275,308	322,345
Dawson	1,114	3,419	1,463	3,337
De Witt	1,610	5,100	1,570	4,541
Deaf Smith	1,133	4,139	1,240	3,687
Delta	627	1,447	726	1,143
Denton	59,346	140,891	40,144	102,171
Dickens	245	815	284	589
Dimmit	2,365	1,188	2,678	1,032
Donley	349	1,429	360	1,333
Duval	2,916	1,160	3,990	1,010

County	2004		2000	
	Kerry (D)	Bush (R)	Gore (D)	Bush (R)
Eastland	1,582	5,249	1,774	4,531
Ector	8,579	27,502	9,425	22,893
Edwards	217	745	261	663
El Paso	95,142	73,261	83,848	57,574
Ellis	11,640	34,602	10,629	26,091
Erath	2,710	9,506	2,804	8,126
Falls	2,427	3,454	2,417	3,239
Fannin	4,001	7,893	4,102	6,074
Fayette	2,803	7,527	2,542	6,658
Fisher	758	1,161	884	968
Floyd	545	2,032	580	1,830
Foard	235	347	263	286
Fort Bend	68,722	93,625	47,569	73,567
Franklin	1,011	3,185	1,018	2,420
Freestone	2,070	5,057	2,316	4,247
Frio	1,931	1,991	2,317	1,774
Gaines	608	3,540	723	2,691
Galveston	43,919	61,290	40,020	50,397
Garza	326	1,480	454	1,302
Gillespie	2,104	9,297	1,511	8,096
Glasscock	44	488	39	528
Goliad	1,219	2,267	1,233	2,108
Gonzales	1,709	4,291	1,877	4,092
Gray	1,289	7,260	1,376	6,732
Grayson	13,452	30,777	13,647	25,596
Gregg	12,306	29,939	11,244	26,739
Grimes	2,713	5,263	2,450	4,197
Guadalupe	10,290	28,208	8,311	21,499
Hale	2,078	8,025	2,158	6,868
Hall	413	860	472	966
Hamilton	845	2,856	878	2,447
Hansford	240	1,903	198	1,874
Hardeman	480	1,214	566	976
Hardin	5,608	15,030	5,595	11,962
Harris	475,865	584,723	418,267	529,159
Harrison	9,642	16,473	8,878	13,834
Hartley	315	1,736	359	1,645
Haskell	867	1,539	1,401	1,488
Hays	20,110	27,021	11,387	20,170
Hemphill	257	1,380	251	1,203
Henderson	8,505	20,210	8,704	16,607
Hidalgo	62,369	50,931	61,390	38,301
Hill	3,751	9,225	3,524	7,054
Hockley	1,385	6,160	1,419	5,250
Hood	4,865	16,280	4,704	12,429
Hopkins	3,443	8,582	3,692	7,076
Houston	2,921	5,848	2,833	5,308
Howard	2,663	7,480	2,744	6,668
Hudspeth	302	577	380	514
Hunt	7,971	20,065	7,857	16,177
Hutchinson	1,503	7,839	1,796	7,443
Irion	141	684	162	624
Jack	643	2,470	822	2,107
Jackson	1,296	3,766	1,446	3,365
Jasper	4,471	8,347	4,533	7,071
Jeff Davis	378	764	283	708
Jefferson	47,066	44,423	45,409	40,320
Jim Hogg	1,344	712	1,512	623
Jim Wells	6,824	5,817	7,418	4,498
Johnson	12,325	34,818	11,778	26,202
Jones	1,658	4,254	1,899	4,080
Karnes	1,543	3,114	1,617	2,638
Kaufman	8,947	21,304	7,455	15,290
Kendall	2,532	11,434	1,901	8,788
Kenedy	85	82	119	106
Kent	138	382	185	346
Kerr	4,557	16,538	4,002	14,637
Kimble	324	1,482	328	1,313
King	18	137	14	120
Kinney	542	1,051	486	932
Kleberg	4,550	5,366	4,481	4,526
Knox	464	1,081	617	947
La Salle	1,229	989	1,266	731
La Vaca	2,152	5,974	1,569	4,526
Lamar	5,338	12,054	5,553	9,775
Lamb	857	3,410	1,114	3,451
Lampasas	1,593	5,422	2,171	5,288
Lee	1,899	4,160	1,733	3,699
Leon	1,754	5,023	1,893	4,362
Liberty	6,780	14,821	7,311	12,458
Limestone	2,752	5,028	2,768	4,212
Lipscomb	184	1,147	206	1,072
Live Oak	1,036	3,147	1,114	2,828
Llano	2,257	7,241	2,143	6,295
Loving	12	65	29	124
Lubbock	22,472	70,135	18,469	56,054
Lynn	490	1,776	562	1,507
Madison	1,235	2,837	1,241	2,333
Marion	1,884	2,441	1,852	2,039
Martin	288	1,514	415	1,520
Mason	459	1,600	417	1,352
Matagorda	4,355	8,119	4,696	7,584
Maverick	5,948	4,025	5,995	3,143
McCulloch	745	2,465	794	2,084
McLennan	26,760	52,090	23,462	43,955
McMullen	95	467	77	358
Medina	4,322	10,389	4,025	8,590
Menard	331	761	334	642
Midland	8,005	36,585	7,534	31,514
Milam	3,445	5,291	3,429	4,706
Mills	416	1,794	548	1,738
Mitchell	639	1,912	837	1,708
Montague	1,946	5,910	2,256	4,951
Montgomery	28,628	104,654	23,286	80,600
Moore	1,009	4,601	1,040	4,201
Morris	2,437	2,818	2,455	2,381
Motley	113	564	118	514
Nacogdoches	7,152	14,160	6,204	13,145
Navarro	5,259	10,715	5,366	8,358
Newton	2,513	3,159	2,503	2,423
Nolan	1,541	3,722	1,874	3,337
Nueces	44,439	59,359	45,349	49,906
Ochiltree	251	2,922	251	2,687
Oldham	108	733	108	659
Orange	11,476	20,292	11,887	17,325
Palo Pinto	2,816	7,137	3,263	5,690
Panola	2,958	7,021	3,011	5,975
Parker	8,966	31,795	8,878	23,651
Parmer	389	2,375	447	2,274
Pecos	1,242	3,167	1,539	2,700
Polk	6,964	13,778	6,877	11,746
Potter	7,489	21,401	7,242	17,629
Presidio	1,159	715	1,064	618
Rains	1,213	2,998	1,225	2,049
Randall	7,849	40,520	7,209	33,921
Reagan	184	956	282	959
Real	325	1,314	316	1,146
Red River	2,097	3,379	2,219	2,941
Reeves	1,600	1,777	1,872	1,273
Refugio	1,232	2,212	1,172	1,721
Roberts	46	461	72	472
Robertson	2,979	3,792	3,283	3,007
Rockwall	5,320	20,120	3,642	13,666
Runnels	792	3,239	969	3,020
Rusk	4,899	13,390	4,841	11,611
Sabine	1,476	3,138	1,753	2,764
San Augustine	1,506	2,235	1,636	2,116
San Jacinto	2,688	5,394	2,946	4,623
San Patricio	7,764	13,474	7,840	10,599
San Saba	529	1,894	618	1,691
Schleicher	312	1,012	338	826
Scurry	981	4,576	1,193	4,060
Shackelford	229	1,292	264	1,066
Shelby	2,951	6,295	3,227	5,692
Sherman	124	942	144	998
Smith	19,970	53,392	16,470	43,320
Somervell	831	2,701	752	2,120
Starr	7,199	2,552	6,505	1,911
Stephens	703	2,803	811	2,425
Sterling	71	544	132	520
Stonewall	250	499	294	496
Sutton	280	1,173	468	1,063
Swisher	626	1,487	856	1,612
Tarrant	207,286	349,462	173,758	286,921
Taylor	10,648	37,197	10,504	31,701
Terrell	159	306	219	243
Terry	794	3,166	1,108	2,910
Throckmorton	202	656	228	608
Titus	3,173	5,709	3,008	4,995
Tom Green	9,007	28,185	9,288	24,733
Travis	197,235	147,885	125,526	141,235
Trinity	2,204	3,985	2,142	3,093
Tyler	2,659	5,043	2,775	4,236
Upshur	4,225	10,232	4,180	8,448
Upton	185	1,009	266	982
Uvalde	3,298	5,148	3,436	4,855
Val Verde	4,757	6,968	5,056	6,223
Van Zandt	4,822	14,976	5,245	12,383
Victoria	8,553	20,875	8,176	18,787
Walker	5,977	11,710	4,943	9,076

	2004		2000	
County	**Kerry (D)**	**Bush (R)**	**Gore (D)**	**Bush (R)**
Waller	6,145	7,679	5,046	5,686
Ward	901	2,856	1,256	2,534
Washington	3,389	9,597	2,996	8,645
Webb	23,654	17,753	18,120	13,076
Wharton	4,702	9,288	4,838	8,455
Wheeler	420	1,960	579	1,787
Wichita	12,819	32,472	14,108	27,802
Wilbarger	1,284	3,685	1,356	3,138
Willacy	2,734	2,209	3,218	1,789
Williamson	43,117	83,284	26,591	65,041
Wilson	4,409	10,400	3,997	7,509
Winkler	391	1,604	556	1,468
Wise	4,783	15,177	4,830	11,234
Wood	4,034	12,831	3,893	9,810
Yoakum	376	2,228	531	1,911
Young	1,511	5,874	1,843	5,022
Zapata	1,662	1,228	1,638	953
Zavala	2,332	777	2,616	751
Totals	**2,832,704**	**4,526,917**	**2,433,746**	**3,799,639**

Texas Vote Since 1948

1948: Truman, D., 750,700; Dewey, R., 282,240; Thurmond, States' Rights, 106,909; Wallace, Prog., 3,764; Watson, Proh., 2,758; Thomas, Soc., 874.
1952: Eisenhower, R., 1,102,878; Stevenson, D., 969,228; Hamblen, Proh., 1,983; MacArthur, Christian Nationalist, 833; MacArthur, Constitution, 730; Hallinan, Prog., 294.
1956: Eisenhower, R., 1,080,619; Stevenson, D., 859,958; Andrews, Ind., 14,591.
1960: Kennedy, D., 1,167,932; Nixon, R., 1,121,699; Sullivan, Constitution, 18,169; Decker, Proh., 3,870; write-in, 15.
1964: Johnson, D., 1,663,185; Goldwater, R., 958,566; Lightburn, Constitution, 5,060.
1968: Humphrey, D., 1,266,804; Nixon, R., 1,227,844; Wallace, 3rd Party, 584,269; write-in, 489.
1972: Nixon, R., 2,298,896; McGovern, D., 1,154,289; Jenness, Soc. Workers, 8,664; Schmitz, Amer., 6,039; others, 3,393.
1976: Carter, D., 2,082,319; Ford, R., 1,953,300; McCarthy, Ind., 20,118; Anderson, Amer., 11,442; Camejo, Soc. Workers, 1,723; write-in, 2,982.
1980: Reagan, R., 2,510,705; Carter, D., 1,881,147; Anderson, Ind., 111,613; Clark, Libertarian, 37,643; write-in, 528.
1984: Reagan, R., 3,433,428; Mondale, D., 1,949,276.
1988: Bush, R., 3,036,829; Dukakis, D., 2,352,748; Paul, Lib., 30,355; Fulani, New Alliance, 7,208.
1992: Bush, R., 2,496,071; Clinton, D., 2,281,815; Perot, Ind., 1,354,781; Marrou, Libertarian, 19,699.
1996: Dole, R., 2,736,167; Clinton, D., 2,459,683; Perot, Ind. (Ref.), 378,537; Browne, Libertarian, 20,256; Phillips, Taxpayers, 7,472; Hagelin, Natural Law, 4,422.
2000: Bush, R., 3,799,639; Gore, D., 2,433,746; Nader, Green, 137,994; Browne, Libertarian, 23,160; Buchanan, Ind., 12,394.
2004: Bush, R., 4,526,917; Kerry, D., 2,832,704; Badnarik, Libertarian, 38,787.

Utah

	2004		2000	
County	**Kerry (D)**	**Bush (R)**	**Gore (D)**	**Bush (R)**
Beaver	493	2,023	541	1,653
Box Elder	2,244	15,751	2,555	12,288
Cache	6,375	32,486	5,170	25,920
Carbon	3,415	4,950	3,298	3,758
Daggett	108	380	104	317
Davis	20,893	86,187	18,845	64,375
Duchesne	738	4,742	779	3,622
Emery	831	3,781	958	3,243
Garfield	264	1,848	178	1,719
Grand	1,858	2,130	1,158	1,822
Iron	2,267	12,815	1,789	10,106
Juab	605	2,681	619	2,023
Kane	576	2,414	387	2,254
Millard	626	4,084	696	3,850
Morgan	472	3,301	553	2,464
Piute	123	646	133	626
Rich	109	922	152	736
Salt Lake	135,949	215,728	107,576	171,585
San Juan	1,906	2,971	1,838	2,721
Sanpete	1,189	7,004	1,211	5,781
Sevier	920	6,597	1,046	5,763
Summit	6,977	7,936	4,601	6,168
Tooele	4,130	12,181	4,001	7,807
Uintah	1,266	8,518	1,387	6,733
Utah	17,357	128,269	16,445	98,255
Wasatch	1,854	5,503	1,476	3,819
Washington	7,513	35,633	5,465	25,481
Wayne	279	1,062	202	953
Weber	19,862	51,199	19,890	39,254
Totals	**241,199**	**663,742**	**203,053**	**515,096**

Utah Vote Since 1948

1948: Truman, D., 149,151; Dewey, R., 124,402; Wallace, Prog., 2,679; Dobbs, Soc. Workers, 73.
1952: Eisenhower, R., 194,190; Stevenson, D., 135,364.
1956: Eisenhower, R., 215,631; Stevenson, D., 118,364.
1960: Nixon, R., 205,361; Kennedy, D., 169,248; Dobbs, Soc. Workers, 100.
1964: Johnson, D., 219,628; Goldwater, R., 181,785.
1968: Nixon, R., 238,728; Humphrey, D., 156,665; Wallace, 3rd Party, 26,906; Peace and Freedom, 180; Halstead, Soc. Workers, 89.
1972: Nixon, R., 323,643; McGovern, D., 126,284; Schmitz, Amer., 28,549.
1976: Ford, R., 337,908; Carter, D., 182,110; Anderson, Amer., 13,304; McCarthy, Ind., 3,907; MacBride, Libertarian, 2,438; Maddox, Amer. Ind., 1,162; Camejo, Soc. Workers, 268; Hall, Com., 121.
1980: Reagan, R., 439,687; Carter, D., 124,266; Anderson, Ind., 30,284; Clark, Libertarian, 7,226; Commoner, Citizens, 1,009; Greaves, Amer., 965; Rarick, Amer. Ind., 522; Hall, Com., 139; DeBerry, Soc. Workers, 124.
1984: Reagan, R., 469,105; Mondale, D., 155,369; Bergland, Libertarian, 2,447.
1988: Bush, R., 428,442; Dukakis, D., 207,352; Paul, Lib., 7,473; Dennis, Amer., 2,158.
1992: Bush, R., 322,632; Perot, Ind., 203,400; Clinton, D., 183,429; Gritz, Populist/America First, 28,602; Marrou, Libertarian, 1,900; Hagelin, Natural Law, 1,319; LaRouche, Ind., 1,089.
1996: Dole, R., 361,911; Clinton, D., 221,633; Perot, Ref., 66,461; Nader, Green, 4,615; Browne, Libertarian, 4,129; Phillips, Taxpayers, 2,601; Templin, Ind. Amer., 1,290; Crane, Ind., 1,101; Hagelin, Natural Law, 1,085; Moorehead, Workers World, 298; Harris, Soc. Workers, 235; Dodge, Proh., 111.
2000: Bush, R., 515,096; Gore, D., 203,053; Nader, Green, 35,850; Buchanan, Reform, 9,319; Browne, Libertarian, 3,616; Phillips, Ind. Amer., 2,709; Hagelin, Natural Law, 763; Harris, Soc. Workers, 186; Youngkeit, Ind., 161.
2004: Bush, R., 663,742; Kerry, D., 241,199; Nader, Ind., 11,305; Peroutka, Constitution, 6,841; Badnarik, Libertarian, 3,375; Jay, Pers. Choice, 946; Harris, Soc. Wkrs., 393.

Vermont

	2004		2000	
City	**Kerry (D)**	**Bush (R)**	**Gore (D)**	**Bush (R)**
Barre City	2,037	1,703	1,895	1,676
Bennington	4,252	2,471	3,745	2,384
Brattleboro	4,500	1,408	3,128	1,486
Burlington	14,468	4,035	10,961	4,273
Colchester	4,406	3,126	3,876	2,989
Essex	5,760	4,349	4,632	4,344
Hartford	2,914	1,896	2,462	1,957
Montpelier	3,536	1,048	2,576	1,265
Rutland City	4,142	3,293	3,916	3,003
S. Burlington	5,609	3,229	4,393	2,995
Springfield	2,562	1,823	2,386	1,720
Other	129,881	92,799	105,052	191,683
Totals	**184,067**	**121,180**	**149,022**	**119,775**

Vermont Vote Since 1948

1948: Dewey, R., 75,926; Truman, D., 45,557; Wallace, Prog., 1,279; Thomas, Soc., 585.
1952: Eisenhower, R., 109,717; Stevenson, D., 43,355; Hallinan, Prog., 282; Hoopes, Soc., 185.
1956: Eisenhower, R., 110,390; Stevenson, D., 42,549; scattered, 39.
1960: Nixon, R., 98,131; Kennedy, D., 69,186.
1964: Johnson, D., 107,674; Goldwater, R., 54,868.
1968: Nixon, R., 85,142; Humphrey, D., 70,255; Wallace, 3rd Party, 5,104; Gregory, New Party, 579; Halstead, Soc. Workers, 295.
1972: Nixon, R., 117,149; McGovern, D., 68,174; Spock, Liberty Union, 1,010; Jenness, Soc. Workers, 296; scattered, 318.
1976: Ford, R., 100,387; Carter, D., 77,798; Carter, Ind. Vermonter, 991; total, 79,789; McCarthy, Ind., 4,001; Camejo, Soc. Workers, 430; LaRouche, U.S. Labor, 196; scattered, 99.
1980: Reagan, R., 94,598; Carter, D., 81,891; Anderson, Ind., 31,760; Commoner, Citizens, 2,316; Clark, Libertarian, 1,900; McReynolds, Liberty Union, 136; Hall, Com., 118; DeBerry, Soc. Workers, 75; scattered, 413.
1984: Reagan, R., 135,865; Mondale, D., 95,730; Bergland, Libertarian, 1,002.
1988: Bush, R., 124,331; Dukakis, D., 115,775; Paul, Lib., 1,000; LaRouche, Ind., 275.
1992: Clinton, D., 133,590; Bush, R., 88,122; Perot, Ind., 65,985.
1996: Clinton, D., 137,894; Dole, R., 80,352; Perot, Ref., 31,024; Nader, Green, 5,585; Browne, Libertarian, 1,183; Hagelin, Natural Law, 498; Peron, Grass Roots, 480; Phillips, Taxpayers, 382; Hollis, Liberty Union, 292; Harris, Soc. Workers, 199.
2000: Gore, D., 149,022; Bush, R., 119,775; Nader, Green, 20,374; Buchanan, Reform, 2,192; Lane, Grass Roots, 1,044; Browne, Libertarian, 784; Hagelin, Natural Law, 219; McReynolds, Liberty Union, 161; Phillips, Constitution, 153; Harris, Soc. Workers, 70.
2004: Kerry, D., 184,067; Bush, R., 121,180; Nader, Ind., 4,494; Badnarik, Libertarian, 1,102; Parker, Liberty Union, 265; Calero, Soc. Wkrs., 244.

Virginia

	2004		2000	
County	**Kerry (D)**	**Bush (R)**	**Gore (D)**	**Bush (R)**
Accomack	5,518	7,726	5,092	6,352
Albemarle	22,088	21,189	16,255	18,291
Alleghany	3,203	3,962	2,214	2,808
Amelia	1,862	3,499	1,754	2,947
Amherst	4,866	7,758	4,812	6,660
Appomattox	2,191	4,366	2,132	3,654
Arlington	63,987	29,635	50,260	28,555
Augusta	7,019	22,100	6,643	17,744
Bath	828	1,432	822	1,311
Bedford	9,102	21,925	8,160	17,224
Bland	846	1,962	851	1,759
Botetourt	4,801	10,865	4,627	8,867
Brunswick	4,062	2,852	3,387	2,561
Buchanan	5,275	4,507	5,745	3,867
Buckingham	2,789	3,185	2,561	2,738
Campbell	6,862	15,891	6,659	13,162
Caroline	4,878	4,999	4,314	3,873
Carroll	3,888	8,173	3,638	7,142
Charles City	2,155	1,254	1,981	1,023
Charlotte	2,223	3,166	2,017	2,855
Chesterfield	49,346	83,745	38,638	69,924
Clarke	2,699	3,741	2,166	2,883
Craig	901	1,706	851	1,580
Culpeper	5,476	10,026	4,364	7,440
Cumberland	1,721	2,377	1,405	1,974
Dickenson	3,761	3,591	3,951	3,122
Dinwiddie	4,569	6,193	4,001	4,959
Essex	2,007	2,304	1,750	1,995
Fairfax	245,671	211,980	196,501	202,181
Fauquier	10,712	19,011	8,296	14,456
Floyd	2,488	4,162	1,957	3,423
Fluvanna	4,415	6,458	3,431	4,962
Franklin	8,002	14,048	7,145	11,225
Frederick	8,853	19,386	7,158	14,574
Giles	3,047	4,320	3,004	3,574
Gloucester	5,105	11,084	4,553	8,718
Goochland	3,583	6,668	3,197	5,378
Grayson	2,430	4,655	2,467	4,236
Greene	2,240	4,570	1,774	3,375
Greensville	2,514	1,732	2,314	1,565
Halifax	6,220	8,363	5,963	7,732
Hanover	13,941	35,404	12,044	28,614
Henrico	60,864	71,809	48,645	62,887
Henry	9,851	13,358	8,898	11,870
Highland	522	982	453	942
Isle of Wight	5,871	9,929	5,162	7,587
James City	11,934	18,949	9,090	14,628
King and Queen	1,506	1,737	1,387	1,423
King George	2,739	5,124	2,070	3,590
King William	2,436	4,397	2,125	3,547
Lancaster	2,477	3,724	1,937	3,411
Lee	4,005	5,664	4,031	4,551
Loudoun	47,271	60,382	30,938	42,453
Louisa	4,844	7,083	4,309	5,461
Lunenburg	2,362	2,858	2,026	2,510
Madison	2,176	3,556	1,844	2,940
Mathews	1,589	3,497	1,499	2,951
Mecklenburg	5,293	7,319	4,797	6,600
Middlesex	1,914	3,336	1,671	2,844
Montgomery	14,128	17,070	11,720	13,991
Nelson	3,543	3,539	2,907	2,913
New Kent	2,443	5,414	2,055	3,934
Northampton	2,775	2,669	2,340	2,299
Northumberland	2,548	3,832	2,118	3,362
Nottoway	2,635	3,303	2,460	2,870
Orange	5,015	7,749	4,126	5,991
Page	3,324	6,221	2,726	5,089
Patrick	2,572	5,507	2,254	4,901
Pittsylvania	9,274	17,673	7,834	15,760
Powhatan	3,112	8,955	2,708	6,820
Prince Edward	3,632	3,571	2,922	3,214
Prince George	5,066	8,131	4,182	6,579
Prince William	61,271	69,776	44,745	52,788
Pulaski	5,310	8,769	5,255	7,089
Rappahannock	1,837	2,172	1,462	1,850
Richmond	1,243	2,082	1,076	1,784
Roanoke	16,082	30,596	16,141	25,740
Rockbridge	3,627	5,412	2,953	4,522
Rockingham	7,273	21,737	5,834	17,482
Russell	5,167	6,077	5,442	5,065
Scott	3,324	6,479	3,552	5,535
Shenandoah	5,186	11,820	4,420	9,636
Smyth	4,143	7,906	4,836	6,580
Southampton	3,431	4,018	3,359	3,293
Spotsylvania	16,623	28,527	13,455	20,739
Stafford	17,208	28,500	12,596	20,731
Surry	1,954	1,543	1,845	1,313
Sussex	2,420	1,890	2,006	1,745
Tazewell	7,184	10,039	7,227	8,655
Warren	5,241	8,600	4,313	6,335
Washington	7,339	14,749	7,549	12,064
Westmoreland	3,370	3,433	2,922	2,932
Wise	5,802	8,330	6,412	6,504
Wythe	3,581	7,911	3,462	6,539
York	10,276	19,396	8,622	15,312
CITIES				
Alexandria	41,116	19,844	33,633	19,043
Bedford	1,042	1,472	1,078	1,269
Bristol	2,400	4,275	2,646	3,495
Buena Vista	936	1,417	941	980
Charlottesville	11,088	4,172	7,762	4,034
Chesapeake	38,744	52,283	33,578	39,684
Clifton Forge[1]	NA	NA	868	613
Colonial Heights	2,061	6,129	2,100	5,519
Covington	1,179	1,104	1,168	966
Danville	9,436	9,399	8,221	9,427
Emporia	1,247	970	1,116	938
Fairfax	5,395	5,045	4,361	4,762
Falls Church	3,944	2,074	3,109	2,131
Franklin	1,910	1,613	1,763	1,393
Fredericksburg	4,085	3,390	3,360	2,935
Galax	987	1,336	996	1,160
Hampton	32,016	23,399	27,490	19,561
Harrisonburg	4,726	6,165	3,482	5,741
Hopewell	3,573	4,251	3,024	3,749
Lexington	1,340	982	1,048	957
Lynchburg	11,727	14,400	10,374	12,518
Manassas	5,562	7,257	5,262	6,752
Manassas Park	1,498	1,807	1,048	1,460
Martinsville	3,036	2,538	3,048	2,560
Newport News	35,319	32,208	29,779	27,006
Norfolk	43,518	26,401	38,221	21,920
Norton	725	768	867	639
Petersburg	9,682	2,238	8,751	2,109
Poquoson	1,424	5,004	1,448	4,271
Portsmouth	24,112	15,212	22,286	12,628
Radford	2,244	2,564	2,063	2,190
Richmond	52,167	21,637	42,717	20,265
Roanoke	18,862	16,661	17,920	14,630
Salem	4,254	7,115	4,348	6,188
Staunton	3,756	5,805	3,324	4,878
Suffolk	15,233	16,763	12,471	11,836
Virginia Beach	70,666	103,752	62,268	83,674
Waynesboro	2,792	5,092	2,737	4,084
Williamsburg	2,216	2,064	1,724	1,777
Winchester	3,967	5,283	3,318	4,314
Totals	**1,454,742**	**1,716,959**	**1,217,290**	**1,437,490**

(1) No longer a county-equivalent; for 2004 election included in Alleghany County results.

Virginia Vote Since 1948

1948: Truman, D., 200,786; Dewey, R., 172,070; Thurmond, States' Rights, 43,393; Wallace, Prog., 2,047; Thomas, Soc., 726; Teichert, Soc. Labor, 234.

1952: Eisenhower, R., 349,037; Stevenson, D., 268,677; Hass, Soc. Labor, 1,160; Hoopes, Soc. D., 504; Hallinan, Prog., 311.

1956: Eisenhower, R., 386,459; Stevenson, D., 267,760; Andrews, States' Rights, 42,964; Hoopes, Soc. D., 444; Hass, Soc. Labor, 351.

1960: Nixon, R., 404,521; Kennedy, D., 362,327; Coiner, Cons., 4,204; Hass, Soc. Labor, 397.

1964: Johnson, D., 558,038; Goldwater, R., 481,334; Hass, Soc. Labor, 2,895.

1968: Nixon, R., 590,319; Humphrey, D., 442,387; Wallace, 3rd Party, *320,272; Blomen, Soc. Labor, 4,671; Gregory, Peace and Freedom, 1,680; Munn, Proh., 601. *10,561 votes for Wallace were omitted in the count.

1972: Nixon, R., 988,493; McGovern, D., 438,887; Schmitz, Amer., 19,721; Fisher, Soc. Labor, 9,918.

1976: Ford, R., 836,554; Carter, D., 813,896; Camejo, Soc. Workers, 17,802; Anderson, Amer., 16,686; LaRouche, U.S. Labor, 7,508; MacBride, Libertarian, 4,648.

1980: Reagan, R., 989,609; Carter, D., 752,174; Anderson, Ind., 95,418; Commoner, Citizens, 14,024; Clark, Libertarian, 12,821; DeBerry, Soc. Workers, 1,986.

1984: Reagan, R., 1,337,078; Mondale, D., 796,250.

1988: Bush, R., 1,309,162; Dukakis, D., 859,799; Fulani, Ind., 14,312; Paul, Lib., 8,336.

1992: Bush, R., 1,150,517; Clinton, D., 1,038,650; Perot, Ind., 348,639; LaRouche, Ind., 11,937; Marrou, Libertarian, 5,730; Fulani, New Alliance, 3,192.

1996: Dole, R., 1,138,350; Clinton, D., 1,091,060; Perot, Ref., 159,861; Phillips, Taxpayers, 13,687; Browne, Libertarian, 9,174; Hagelin, Natural Law, 4,510.

2000: Bush, R., 1,437,490; Gore, D., 1,217,290; Nader, Green, 59,398; Browne, Libertarian, 15,198; Buchanan, Reform, 5,455; Phillips, Constitution, 1,809.

2004: Bush, R., 1,716,959; Kerry, D., 1,454,742; Badnarik, Libertarian, 11,032; Peroutka, Constitution, 10,161.

Washington

County	2004 Kerry (D)	2004 Bush (R)	2000 Gore (D)	2000 Bush (R)
Adams	1,315	3,751	1,406	3,440
Asotin	3,319	5,320	2,736	4,909
Benton	21,549	44,350	19,512	38,367
Chelan	10,471	18,482	8,412	16,980
Clallam	17,049	18,871	13,779	16,251
Clark	79,538	88,646	61,767	67,219
Columbia	605	1,470	515	1,523
Cowlitz	21,589	20,217	18,233	16,873
Douglas	4,306	8,900	3,822	8,512
Ferry	1,201	2,019	932	1,896
Franklin	5,188	10,757	4,653	8,594
Garfield	365	935	300	982
Grant	7,779	17,799	7,073	15,830
Grays Harbor	14,583	12,871	13,304	11,225
Island	18,216	19,754	14,778	16,408
Jefferson	11,610	6,650	8,281	6,095
King	580,378	301,043	476,700	273,171
Kitsap	60,796	55,608	50,302	46,427
Kittitas	6,731	9,052	5,516	7,727
Klickitat	4,036	5,016	3,062	4,557
Lewis	10,726	21,042	9,891	18,565
Lincoln	1,706	4,015	1,417	3,546
Mason	12,894	11,987	10,876	10,257
Okanogan	6,309	9,636	4,335	9,384
Pacific	5,570	4,634	4,895	4,042
Pend Oreille	2,310	3,693	1,973	3,076
Pierce	158,231	150,783	138,249	118,431
San Juan	6,589	3,290	4,426	3,005
Skagit	25,131	26,139	20,432	22,163
Skamania	2,374	2,695	1,753	2,151
Snohomish	156,468	134,317	129,612	109,615
Spokane	87,490	111,606	74,604	89,299
Stevens	6,822	13,015	5,560	11,299
Thurston	62,650	47,992	50,467	39,924
Wahkiakum	1,021	1,171	803	1,033
Walla Walla	8,257	14,323	7,188	13,304
Whatcom	48,268	40,296	34,033	34,287
Whitman	8,287	9,397	6,509	9,003
Yakima	28,474	43,352	25,546	39,494
Totals	**1,510,201**	**1,304,894**	**1,247,652**	**1,108,864**

Washington Vote Since 1948

1948: Truman, D., 476,165; Dewey, R., 386,315; Wallace, Prog., 31,692; Watson, Proh., 6,117; Thomas, Soc., 3,534; Teichert, Soc. Labor, 1,133; Dobbs, Soc. Workers, 103.

1952: Eisenhower, R., 599,107; Stevenson, D., 492,845; MacArthur, Christian Nationalist, 7,290; Hallinan, Prog., 2,460; Hass, Soc. Labor, 633; Hoopes, Soc., 254; Dobbs, Soc. Workers, 119.

1956: Eisenhower, R., 620,430; Stevenson, D., 523,002; Hass, Soc. Labor, 7,457.

1960: Nixon, R., 629,273; Kennedy, D., 599,298; Hass, Soc. Labor, 10,895; Curtis, Constitution, 1,401; Dobbs, Soc. Workers, 705.

1964: Johnson, D., 779,699; Goldwater, R., 470,366; Hass, Soc. Labor, 7,772; DeBerry, Freedom Soc., 537.

1968: Humphrey, D., 616,037; Nixon, R., 588,510; Wallace, 3rd Party, 96,990; Cleaver, Peace and Freedom, 1,609; Blomen, Soc. Labor, 488; Mitchell, Free Ballot, 377; Halstead, Soc. Workers, 270.

1972: Nixon, R., 837,135; McGovern, D., 568,334; Schmitz, Amer., 58,906; Spock, Ind., 2,644; Hospers, Libertarian, 1,537; Fisher, Soc. Labor, 1,102; Jenness, Soc. Workers, 623; Hall, Com., 566.

1976: Ford, R., 777,732; Carter, D., 717,323; McCarthy, Ind., 36,986; Maddox, Amer. Ind., 8,585; Anderson, Amer., 5,046; MacBride, Libertarian, 5,042; Wright, People's, 1,124; Camejo, Soc. Workers, 905; LaRouche, U.S. Labor, 903; Hall, Com., 817; Levin, Soc. Labor, 713; Zeidler, Soc., 358.

1980: Reagan, R., 865,244; Carter, D., 650,193; Anderson, Ind., 185,073; Clark, Libertarian, 29,213; Commoner, Citizens, 9,403; DeBerry, Soc. Workers, 1,137; McReynolds, Soc., 956; Hall, Com., 834; Griswold, Workers World, 341.

1984: Reagan, R., 1,051,670; Mondale, D., 798,352; Bergland, Libertarian, 8,844.

1988: Dukakis, D., 933,516; Bush, R., 903,835; Paul, Lib., 17,240; LaRouche, Ind., 4,412.

1992: Clinton, D., 993,037; Bush, R., 731,234; Perot, Ind., 541,780; Marrou, Libertarian, 7,533; Gritz, Populist/America First, 4,854; Hagelin, Natural Law, 2,456; Phillips, U.S. Taxpayers, 2,354; Fulani, New Alliance, 1,776; Daniels, Ind., 1,171.

1996: Clinton, D., 1,123,323; Dole, R., 840,712; Perot, Ref., 201,003; Nader, Ind., 60,322; Browne, Libertarian, 12,522; Hagelin, Natural Law, 6,076; Phillips, Taxpayers, 4,578; Collins, Ind., 2,374; Moorehead, Workers World, 2,189; Harris, Soc. Workers, 738.

2000: Gore, D., 1,247,652; Bush, R., 1,108,864; Nader, Green, 103,002; Browne, Libertarian, 13,135; Buchanan, Freedom, 7,171; Hagelin, Natural Law, 2,927; ; Phillips, Constitution, 1,989; Moorehead, Wkrs. World, 1,729; McReynolds, Soc., 660; Harris, Soc. Wkrs., 304.

2004: Kerry, D., 1,510,201; Bush, R., 1,304,894; Nader, Ind., 23,283; Badnarik, Libertarian, 11,955; Peroutka, Constitution, 3,922; Cobb, Green, 2,974; Parker, Workers World, 1,077; Harris, Soc. Wkrs., 547; Van Auken, Soc. Equal., 231.

West Virginia

County	2004 Kerry (D)	2004 Bush (R)	2000 Gore (D)	2000 Bush (R)
Barbour	2,610	4,004	2,503	3,411
Berkeley	12,244	21,293	8,797	13,619
Boone	5,933	4,207	5,656	3,353
Braxton	3,035	2,986	2,719	2,529
Brooke	5,493	5,189	4,678	4,195
Cabell	16,583	21,035	14,896	16,440
Calhoun	1,266	1,588	1,112	1,425
Clay	1,835	2,198	1,617	1,887
Doddridge	800	2,362	773	1,955
Fayette	8,971	7,881	8,371	5,897
Gilmer	1,159	1,665	1,092	1,560
Grant	963	4,063	891	3,571
Greenbrier	6,084	8,358	5,627	6,866
Hampshire	2,455	5,489	2,069	3,879
Hancock	6,906	7,298	6,249	6,458
Hardy	1,617	3,635	1,621	2,816
Harrison	13,238	17,111	13,009	12,948
Jackson	5,384	7,686	4,937	6,341
Jefferson	9,301	10,539	6,860	7,045
Kanawha	43,010	44,430	38,524	36,809
Lewis	2,475	4,445	2,355	3,606
Lincoln	4,048	4,102	3,939	3,389
Logan	7,877	7,047	8,927	5,334
Marion	12,771	12,150	12,315	9,972
Marshall	6,435	8,516	6,000	6,859
Mason	5,408	6,487	4,963	5,972
McDowell	4,501	2,762	4,845	2,348
Mercer	9,178	13,057	8,347	10,206
Mineral	3,518	7,854	3,341	6,180
Mingo	5,983	4,612	6,049	3,866
Monongalia	16,313	17,670	12,603	13,595
Monroe	2,311	3,590	2,094	2,940
Morgan	2,272	4,511	1,939	3,639
Nicholas	4,788	5,485	4,059	4,359
Ohio	8,543	11,694	7,653	9,607
Pendleton	1,381	2,146	1,172	1,996
Pleasants	1,349	2,061	1,267	1,884
Pocahontas	1,573	2,295	1,392	1,970
Preston	3,963	7,855	3,515	6,607
Putnam	9,301	15,716	7,891	12,173
Raleigh	11,815	18,519	11,047	12,587
Randolph	4,892	6,512	4,028	5,248
Ritchie	1,070	3,086	1,024	2,717
Roane	2,612	3,440	2,332	3,172
Summers	2,504	2,978	2,299	2,304
Taylor	2,617	3,893	2,473	3,124
Tucker	1,400	2,179	1,319	1,935
Tyler	1,401	2,798	1,214	2,582
Upshur	3,034	6,191	2,770	5,165
Wayne	8,411	10,070	7,940	7,993
Webster	1,965	1,724	1,764	1,484
Wetzel	3,330	3,656	2,849	3,239
Wirt	896	1,727	818	1,518
Wood	14,025	24,948	12,664	20,428
Wyoming	3,694	4,985	4,289	3,473
Totals	**326,541**	**423,778**	**295,497**	**336,475**

West Virginia Vote Since 1948

1948: Truman, D., 429,188; Dewey, R., 316,251; Wallace, Prog., 3,311.

1952: Stevenson, D., 453,578; Eisenhower, R., 419,970.

1956: Eisenhower, R., 449,297; Stevenson, D., 381,534.

1960: Kennedy, D., 441,786; Nixon, R., 395,995.

1964: Johnson, D., 538,087; Goldwater, R., 253,953.

1968: Humphrey, D., 374,091; Nixon, R., 307,555; Wallace, 3rd Party, 72,560.

1972: Nixon, R., 484,964; McGovern, D., 277,435.

1976: Carter, D., 435,864; Ford, R., 314,726.

1980: Carter, D., 367,462; Reagan, R., 334,206; Anderson, Ind., 31,691; Clark, Libertarian, 4,356.

1984: Reagan, R., 405,483; Mondale, D., 328,125.

1988: Dukakis, D., 341,016; Bush, R., 310,065; Fulani, New Alliance, 2,230.

1992: Clinton, D., 331,001; Bush, R., 241,974; Perot, Ind., 108,829; Marrou, Libertarian, 1,873.

1996: Clinton, D., 327,812; Dole, R., 233,946; Perot, Ref., 71,639; Browne, Libertarian, 3,062.

2000: Bush, R., 336,475; Gore, D., 295,497; Nader, Green, 10,680; Buchanan, Reform, 3,169; Browne, Libertarian, 1,912; Hagelin, Natural Law, 367.

2004: Bush, R., 423,778; Kerry, D., 326,541; Nader, Ind., 4,063; Badnarik, Libertarian, 1,405.

Wisconsin

County	2004 Kerry (D)	2004 Bush (R)	2000 Gore (D)	2000 Bush (R)
Adams	5,447	4,890	4,826	3,920
Ashland	5,805	3,313	4,356	3,038
Barron	11,696	12,030	8,928	9,848
Bayfield	5,845	3,754	4,427	3,266
Brown	54,935	67,173	49,096	54,258

County	2004 Kerry (D)	2004 Bush (R)	2000 Gore (D)	2000 Bush (R)
Buffalo	3,998	3,502	3,237	3,038
Burnett	4,499	4,743	3,626	3,967
Calumet	10,290	14,721	8,202	10,837
Chippewa	14,751	15,450	12,102	12,835
Clark	6,966	7,966	5,931	7,461
Columbia	14,300	14,956	12,636	11,987
Crawford	4,656	3,680	4,005	3,024
Dane	181,052	90,369	142,317	75,790
Dodge	16,690	27,201	14,580	21,684
Door	8,367	8,910	6,560	7,810
Douglas	16,537	8,448	13,593	6,930
Dunn	12,039	10,879	9,172	8,911
Eau Claire	30,068	24,653	24,078	20,921
Florence	993	1,703	816	1,528
Fond du Lac	19,216	33,291	18,181	26,548
Forest	2,509	2,608	2,158	2,404
Grant	12,864	12,208	10,691	10,240
Green	9,575	8,497	7,863	6,790
Green Lake	3,605	6,472	3,301	5,451
Iowa	7,122	5,348	5,842	4,221
Iron	1,956	1,884	1,620	1,734
Jackson	5,249	4,387	4,380	3,670
Jefferson	17,925	23,776	15,203	19,204
Juneau	5,734	6,473	4,813	4,910
Kenosha	40,107	35,587	32,429	28,891
Kewaunee	5,175	5,970	4,670	4,883
La Crosse	33,170	28,289	28,455	24,327
La Fayette	4,402	3,929	3,710	3,336
Langlade	4,751	6,235	4,199	5,125
Lincoln	7,484	8,024	6,664	6,727
Manitowoc	20,652	23,027	17,667	19,358
Marathon	30,899	36,394	26,546	28,883
Marinette	10,190	11,866	8,676	10,535
Marquette	3,785	4,604	3,437	3,522
Menominee	1,412	288	949	225
Milwaukee	297,653	180,287	252,329	163,491
Monroe	8,973	10,375	7,460	8,217
Oconto	8,534	11,043	7,260	8,706
Oneida	10,464	11,351	8,339	9,512
Outagamie	40,169	48,903	32,735	39,460
Ozaukee	17,714	34,904	15,030	31,155
Pepin	2,181	1,853	1,854	1,631
Pierce	11,176	10,437	8,559	8,169
Polk	11,173	12,095	8,961	9,557
Portage	21,861	16,546	17,942	13,214
Price	4,349	4,312	3,413	4,136
Racine	48,229	52,456	41,563	44,014
Richland	4,501	4,836	3,837	3,994
Rock	46,598	33,151	40,472	27,467
Rusk	3,820	3,985	3,161	3,758
Sauk	15,708	14,415	13,035	11,586
Sawyer	4,411	4,951	3,333	3,972
Shawano	8,657	12,150	7,335	9,548
Sheboygan	27,608	34,458	23,569	29,648
St. Croix	18,784	22,679	13,077	15,240
Taylor	3,829	5,582	3,254	5,278
Trempealeau	8,075	5,878	6,678	5,002
Vernon	7,924	6,774	6,577	5,684
Vilas	5,713	8,155	4,706	6,958
Walworth	19,177	28,754	15,492	22,982
Washburn	4,705	4,762	3,695	3,912
Washington	21,234	50,641	18,115	41,162
Waukesha	73,626	154,926	64,319	133,105
Waupaca	10,792	15,941	8,787	12,980
Waushara	5,257	6,888	4,239	5,571
Winnebago	40,943	46,542	33,983	38,330
Wood	18,950	20,592	15,936	17,803
Totals	**1,489,504**	**1,478,120**	**1,242,987**	**1,237,279**

Wisconsin Vote Since 1948

1948: Truman, D., 647,310; Dewey, R., 590,959; Wallace, Prog., 25,282; Thomas, Soc., 12,547; Teichert, Soc. Labor, 399; Dobbs, Soc. Workers, 303.

1952: Eisenhower, R., 979,744; Stevenson, D., 622,175; Hallinan, Ind., 2,174; Dobbs, Ind., 1,350; Hoopes, Ind., 1,157; Hass, Ind., 770.

1956: Eisenhower, R., 954,844; Stevenson, D., 586,768; Andrews, Ind., 6,918; Hoopes, Soc., 754; Hass, Soc. Labor, 710; Dobbs, Soc. Workers, 564.

1960: Nixon, R., 895,175; Kennedy, D., 830,805; Dobbs, Soc. Workers, 1,792; Hass, Soc. Labor, 1,310.

1964: Johnson, D., 1,050,424; Goldwater, R., 638,495; DeBerry, Soc. Workers, 1,692; Hass, Soc. Labor, 1,204.

1968: Nixon, R., 809,997; Humphrey, D., 748,804; Wallace, 3rd Party, 127,835; Blomen, Soc. Labor, 1,338; Halstead, Soc. Workers, 1,222; scattered, 2,342.

1972: Nixon, R., 989,430; McGovern, D., 810,174; Schmitz, Amer., 47,525; Spock, Ind., 2,701; Fisher, Soc. Labor, 998; Hall, Com., 663; Reed, Ind., 506; scattered, 893.

1976: Carter, D., 1,040,232; Ford, R., 1,004,987; McCarthy, Ind., 34,943; Maddox, Amer. Ind., 8,552; Zeidler, Soc., 4,298; MacBride, Libertarian, 3,814; Camejo, Soc. Workers, 1,691; Wright, People's, 943; Hall, Com., 749; LaRouche, U.S. Lab., 738; Levin, Soc. Labor, 389; scattered, 2,839.

1980: Reagan, R., 1,088,845; Carter, D., 981,584; Anderson, Ind., 160,657; Clark, Libertarian, 29,135; Commoner, Citizens, 7,767; Rarick, Constitution, 1,519; McReynolds, Soc., 808; Hall, Com., 772; Griswold, Workers World, 414; DeBerry, Soc. Workers, 383; scattered, 1,337.

1984: Reagan, R., 1,198,584; Mondale, D., 995,740; Bergland, Libertarian, 4,883.

1988: Dukakis, D., 1,126,794; Bush, R., 1,047,499; Paul, Lib., 5,157; Duke, Pop., 3,056.

1992: Clinton, D., 1,041,066; Bush, R., 930,855; Perot, Ind., 544,479; Marrou, Libertarian, 2,877; Gritz, Populist/America First, 2,311; Daniels, Ind., 1,883; Phillips, U.S. Taxpayers, 1,772; Hagelin, Natural Law, 1,070.

1996: Clinton, D., 1,071,971; Dole, R., 845,029; Perot, Ref., 227,339; Nader, Green, 28,723; Phillips, Taxpayers, 8,811; Browne, Libertarian, 7,929; Hagelin, Natural Law, 1,379; Moorehead, Workers World, 1,333; Hollis, Soc., 848; Harris, Soc. Workers, 483.

2000: Gore, D., 1,242,987; Bush, R., 1,237,279; Nader, Green, 94,070; Buchanan, Reform, 11,446; Browne, Libertarian, 6,640; Phillips, Constitution, 2,042; Moorehead, Workers World, 1,063; Hagelin, Reform, 878; Harris, Soc. Workers, 306.

2004: Kerry, D., 1,489,504; Bush, R., 1,478,120; Nader, Ind., 16,390; Badnarik, Libertarian, 6,464; Cobb, Green, 2,661; Brown, Ind., 471; Harris, Ind., 411.

Wyoming

County	2004 Kerry (D)	2004 Bush (R)	2000 Gore (D)	2000 Bush (R)
Albany	7,117	9,006	5,069	7,814
Big Horn	960	4,232	1,004	3,720
Campbell	2,464	12,415	1,967	10,203
Carbon	2,158	4,758	2,206	4,498
Converse	1,184	4,447	1,076	3,919
Crook	501	2,836	361	2,289
Fremont	5,338	11,429	4,172	10,560
Goshen	1,566	4,114	1,439	3,922
Hot Springs	623	1,812	544	1,733
Johnson	676	3,231	555	2,886
Laramie	13,171	25,951	12,162	21,797
Lincoln	1,364	6,423	1,184	5,415
Natrona	9,863	21,512	8,646	18,439
Niobrara	230	1,064	190	888
Park	3,007	10,917	2,424	9,884
Platte	1,328	3,149	1,249	2,925
Sheridan	4,066	9,689	3,330	8,424
Sublette	730	2,847	458	2,624
Sweetwater	5,208	10,653	5,521	9,425
Teton	5,972	5,124	4,019	5,454
Uinta	1,815	6,081	1,650	5,469
Washakie	855	3,200	806	3,138
Weston	580	2,739	449	2,521
Totals	**70,776**	**167,629**	**60,481**	**147,947**

Wyoming Vote Since 1948

1948: Truman, D., 52,354; Dewey, R., 47,947; Wallace, Prog., 931; Thomas, Soc., 137; Teichert, Soc. Labor, 56.

1952: Eisenhower, R., 81,047; Stevenson, D., 47,934; Hamblen, Proh., 194; Hoopes, Soc., 40; Haas, Soc. Labor, 36.

1956: Eisenhower, R., 74,573; Stevenson, D., 49,554.

1960: Nixon, R., 77,451; Kennedy, D., 63,331.

1964: Johnson, D., 80,718; Goldwater, R., 61,998.

1968: Nixon, R., 70,927; Humphrey, D., 45,173; Wallace, 3rd Party, 11,105.

1972: Nixon, R., 100,464; McGovern, D., 44,358; Schmitz, Amer., 748.

1976: Ford, R., 92,717; Carter, D., 62,239; McCarthy, Ind., 624; Reagan, Ind., 307; Anderson, Amer., 290; MacBride, Libertarian, 89; Brown, Ind., 47; Maddox, Amer. Ind., 30.

1980: Reagan, R., 110,700; Carter, D., 49,427; Anderson, Ind., 12,072; Clark, Libertarian, 4,514.

1984: Reagan, R., 133,241; Mondale, D., 53,370; Bergland, Libertarian, 2,357.

1988: Bush, R., 106,867; Dukakis, D., 67,113; Paul, Lib., 2,026; Fulani, New Alliance, 545.

1992: Bush, R., 79,347; Clinton, D., 68,160; Perot, Ind., 51,263.

1996: Dole, R., 105,388; Clinton, D., 77,934; Perot, Ind. (Ref.), 25,928; Browne, Libertarian, 1,739; Hagelin, Natural Law, 582.

2000: Bush, R., 147,947; Gore, D., 60,481; Buchanan, Reform, 2,724; Browne, Libertarian, 1,443; Phillips, Ind., 720; Hagelin, Natural Law, 411.

2004: Bush, R., 167,629; Kerry, D., 70,776; Nader, Ind., 2,741; Badnarik, Libertarian, 1,171; Peroutka, Ind., 631.

The Electoral College

The president and the vice president are the only elective federal officials not chosen by direct vote of the people. They are elected by the members of the Electoral College, an institution provided for in the U.S. Constitution.

On presidential election day, the first Tuesday after the first Monday in November of every 4th year, each state chooses as many electors as it has senators and representatives in Congress. In 1964, for the first time, as provided by the 23rd Amendment to the Constitution, the District of Columbia voted for 3 electors. Thus, with 100 senators and 435 representatives, there are 538 members of the Electoral College, with a majority of 270 electoral votes needed to elect the president and vice president.

Although political parties were not part of the original plan created by the Founding Fathers, today political parties customarily nominate their lists of electors at their respective state conventions. Some states print names of the candidates for president and vice president at the top of the Nov. ballot; others list only the electors' names. In either case, the electors of the party receiving the highest vote are elected. Two states, Maine and Nebraska, allow for proportional allocation.

The electors meet on the first Monday after the 2nd Wednesday in December in their respective state capitals or in some other place prescribed by state legislatures. By long-established custom, they vote for their party nominees, although this is not required by federal law; some states do require it.

The Constitution requires electors to cast a ballot for at least one person who is not an inhabitant of that elector's home state. This ensures that presidential and vice presidential candidates from the same party will not be from the same state. (In 2000, Republican vice presidential nominee Dick Cheney changed his voter registration to Wyoming from Gov. George W. Bush's home state of Texas.) Also, an elector cannot be a member of Congress or hold federal office.

Certified and sealed lists of the votes of the electors in each state are sent to the president of the U.S. Senate, who then opens them in the presence of the members of the Senate and House of Representatives in a joint session held in early Jan., and the electoral votes of all the states are then officially counted.

If no candidate for president has a majority, the House of Representatives chooses a president from the top 3 candidates, with all representatives from each state combining to cast one vote for that state. The House decided the outcome of the 1800 and 1824 presidential elections. If no candidate for vice president has a majority, the Senate chooses from the top 2, with the senators voting as individuals. The Senate chose the vice president following the 1836 election.

Under the electoral college system, a candidate who fails to be the top vote getter in the popular vote still may win a majority of electoral votes. This happened in the elections of 1876, 1888, and 2000.

Electoral Votes for President

Electoral votes based on the 2000 Census were in force beginning with the 2004 elections.

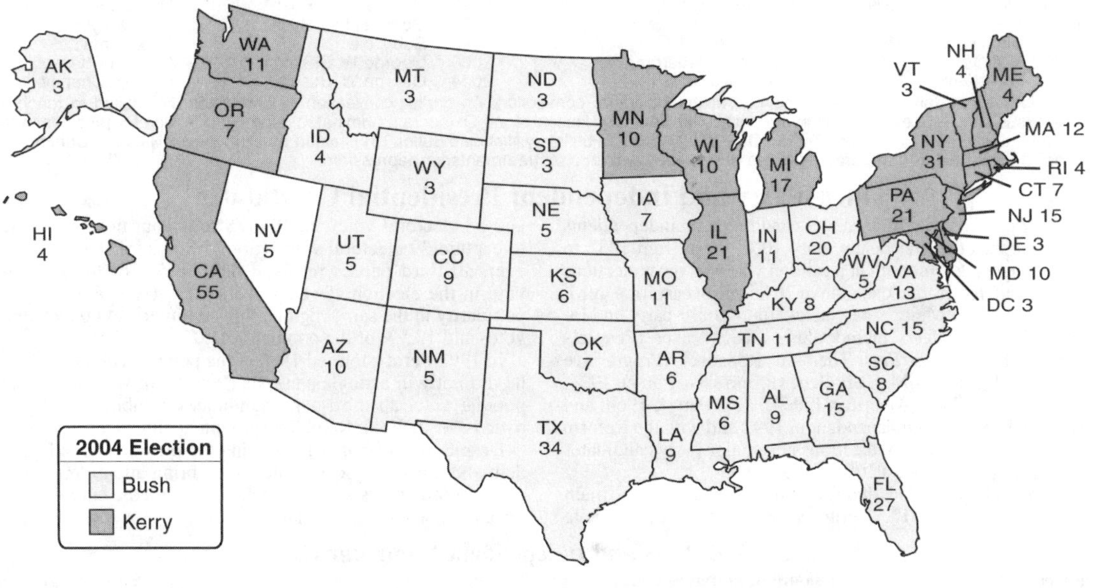

Voter Turnout in Presidential Elections, 1932-2004

Source: Federal Election Commission; Commission for Study of American Electorate; *Congressional Quarterly*

	Candidates	Voter Participation (% of voting-age population)
1932	Roosevelt-Hoover	52.4
1936	Roosevelt-Landon	56.0
1940	Roosevelt-Willkie	58.9
1944	Roosevelt-Dewey	56.0
1948	Truman-Dewey	51.1
1952	Eisenhower-Stevenson	61.6
1956	Eisenhower-Stevenson	59.3
1960	Kennedy-Nixon	62.8
1964	Johnson-Goldwater	61.9
1968	Nixon-Humphrey	60.9
1972	Nixon-McGovern	55.2[1]
1976	Carter-Ford	53.5
1980	Reagan-Carter	54.0
1984	Reagan-Mondale	53.1
1988	Bush-Dukakis	50.2
1992	Clinton-Bush-Perot	55.9
1996	Clinton-Dole-Perot	49.0
2000	Bush-Gore	51.3
2004	Bush-Kerry	60.7

(1) The sharp drop in 1972 followed the expansion of eligibility with the enfranchisement of 18- to 20-year-olds.

Major-Party Nominees for President and Vice President, 1856-2004

Asterisk (*) denotes winning ticket

Democratic			Republican		
Year	**President**	**Vice President**	**Year**	**President**	**Vice President**
1856	James Buchanan*	John Breckinridge	1856	John Frémont	William Dayton
1860	Stephen A. Douglas (1)	Herschel V. Johnson	1860	Abraham Lincoln*	Hannibal Hamlin
1864	George McClellan	G.H. Pendleton	1864	Abraham Lincoln*	Andrew Johnson
1868	Horatio Seymour	Francis Blair	1868	Ulysses S. Grant*	Schuyler Colfax
1872	Horace Greeley	B. Gratz Brown	1872	Ulysses S. Grant*	Henry Wilson
1876	Samuel J. Tilden	Thomas Hendricks	1876	Rutherford B. Hayes*	William Wheeler
1880	Winfield Hancock	William English	1880	James A. Garfield*	Chester A. Arthur
1884	Grover Cleveland*	Thomas Hendricks	1884	James Blaine	John Logan
1888	Grover Cleveland	A.G. Thurman	1888	Benjamin Harrison*	Levi Morton
1892	Grover Cleveland*	Adlai Stevenson	1892	Benjamin Harrison	Whitelaw Reid
1896	William J. Bryan	Arthur Sewall	1896	William McKinley*	Garret Hobart
1900	William J. Bryan	Adlai Stevenson	1900	William McKinley*	Theodore Roosevelt
1904	Alton Parker	Henry Davis	1904	Theodore Roosevelt*	Charles Fairbanks
1908	William J. Bryan	John Kern	1908	William H. Taft*	James Sherman
1912	Woodrow Wilson*	Thomas Marshall	1912	William H. Taft	James Sherman (2)
1916	Woodrow Wilson*	Thomas Marshall	1916	Charles Hughes	Charles Fairbanks
1920	James M. Cox	Franklin D. Roosevelt	1920	Warren G. Harding*	Calvin Coolidge
1924	John W. Davis	Charles W. Bryan	1924	Calvin Coolidge*	Charles G. Dawes
1928	Alfred E. Smith	Joseph T. Robinson	1928	Herbert Hoover*	Charles Curtis
1932	Franklin D. Roosevelt*	John N. Garner	1932	Herbert Hoover	Charles Curtis
1936	Franklin D. Roosevelt*	John N. Garner	1936	Alfred M. Landon	Frank Knox
1940	Franklin D. Roosevelt*	Henry A. Wallace	1940	Wendell L. Willkie	Charles McNary
1944	Franklin D. Roosevelt*	Harry S. Truman	1944	Thomas E. Dewey	John W. Bricker
1948	Harry S. Truman*	Alben W. Barkley	1948	Thomas E. Dewey	Earl Warren
1952	Adlai E. Stevenson	John J. Sparkman	1952	Dwight D. Eisenhower*	Richard M. Nixon
1956	Adlai E. Stevenson	Estes Kefauver	1956	Dwight D. Eisenhower*	Richard M. Nixon
1960	John F. Kennedy*	Lyndon B. Johnson	1960	Richard M. Nixon	Henry Cabot Lodge
1964	Lyndon B. Johnson*	Hubert H. Humphrey	1964	Barry M. Goldwater	William E. Miller
1968	Hubert H. Humphrey	Edmund S. Muskie	1968	Richard M. Nixon*	Spiro T. Agnew
1972	George S. McGovern	R. Sargent Shriver Jr. (3)	1972	Richard M. Nixon*	Spiro T. Agnew
1976	Jimmy Carter*	Walter F. Mondale	1976	Gerald R. Ford	Bob Dole
1980	Jimmy Carter	Walter F. Mondale	1980	Ronald Reagan*	George H. W. Bush
1984	Walter F. Mondale	Geraldine Ferraro	1984	Ronald Reagan*	George H. W. Bush
1988	Michael S. Dukakis	Lloyd Bentsen	1988	George H.W. Bush*	Dan Quayle
1992	Bill Clinton*	Al Gore	1992	George H.W. Bush	Dan Quayle
1996	Bill Clinton*	Al Gore	1996	Bob Dole	Jack Kemp
2000	Al Gore	Joseph Lieberman	2000	George W. Bush*	Richard Cheney
2004	John Kerry	John Edwards	2004	George W. Bush*	Richard Cheney

(1) Douglas and Johnson were nominated at the Baltimore convention. An earlier convention in Charleston, SC, failed to reach a consensus and resulted in a split in the party. The Southern faction of the Democrats nominated John Breckinridge for president and Joseph Lane for vice president. (2) Died Oct. 30; replaced on ballot by Nicholas Butler. (3) Chosen by Democratic National Committee after Thomas Eagleton withdrew because of controversy over past treatments for depression.

Third-Party and Independent Presidential Candidates

Although many "third party" candidates or independents have pursued the presidency, only 10 of these from 1832 to 2000 have polled more than a million votes. In most elections since 1860, fewer than one vote in 20 has been cast for a third-party candidate. Major vote getters among third-party and independent candidates include James B. Weaver (People's Party), 1892; former Pres. Theodore Roosevelt (Progressive Party), 1912; Robert M. La Follette (Progressive Party), 1924; George C. Wallace (American Independent Party), 1968; and H. Ross Perot, as an independent in 1992 and with the Reform Party in 1996. In these 6 elections non-major-party candidates combined polled at least 10% of the vote.

Roosevelt outpolled the Republican candidate, William Howard Taft, in 1912, capturing 28% of the popular vote and 88 electoral votes. In 1948, Strom Thurmond was able to capture 39 electoral votes (from 5 Southern states); however, all third parties received only 5.75% of the popular vote in the election. Twenty years later, George Wallace's popularity in the same region allowed him to get 46 electoral votes and 13.5% of the popular vote.

In 1992 Perot captured 19% of the popular vote; however, he did not win a single state. In 1996, Perot won 8% of the popular vote; all third-party candidates combined won just over 10%. In 2000, Ralph Nader won about 3% of the vote.

Despite the difficulty in winning the presidency, independent and third-party candidates often bring attention to their most prominent issues. They can also affect the outcome between major-party candidates.

Notable Third Party and Independent Campaigns by Year

Party	Presidential nominee	Year	Issues	Strength in . . .
Anti-Masonic	William Wirt	1832	Against secret societies and oaths	PA, VT
Liberty	James G. Birney	1844	Anti-slavery	North
Free Soil	Martin Van Buren	1848	Anti-slavery	NY, OH
American (Know-Nothing)	Millard Fillmore	1856	Anti-immigrant	Northeast, South
Greenback	Peter Cooper	1876	For "cheap money," labor rights	National
Greenback	James B. Weaver	1880	For "cheap money," labor rights	National
Prohibition	John P. St. John	1884	Anti-liquor	National
People's (Populists)	James B. Weaver	1892	For "cheap money," end of national banks	South, West
Socialist	Eugene V. Debs	1900-12; 1920	For public ownership	National
Progressive (Bull Moose)	Theodore Roosevelt	1912	Against high tariffs	Midwest, West
Progressive	Robert M. La Follette	1924	Farmer and labor rights	Midwest, West
Socialist	Norman Thomas	1928-48	Liberal reforms	National
Union	William Lemke	1936	Anti-New Deal	National
States' Rights (Dixiecrats)	Strom Thurmond	1948	For states' rights	South
Progressive	Henry A. Wallace	1948	Anti-Cold War	NY, CA
American Independent	George C. Wallace	1968	For states' rights	South
American	John G. Schmitz	1972	For "law and order"	Far West, OH, LA
None (Independent)	John B. Anderson	1980	A 3rd choice	National
None (Independent)	H. Ross Perot	1992	Federal budget deficit	National
Reform	H. Ross Perot	1996	Deficit; campaign finance	National
Green, Independent	Ralph Nader	2000, 2004	Corporate power; domestic priorities	National

Popular and Electoral Vote for President, 1789-2004

(D) Democrat; (DR) Democratic Republican; (F) Federalist; (LR) Liberal Republican; (NR) National Republican; (P) People's; (PR) Progressive; (R) Republican; (RF) Reform; (SR) States' Rights; (W) Whig; Asterisk (*)–See notes at bottom.

Year	President elected	Popular	Elec.	Major losing candidate(s)	Popular	Elec.
1789	George Washington (F)	Unknown	69	No opposition	—	—
1792	George Washington (F)	Unknown	132	No opposition	—	—
1796	John Adams (F)	Unknown	71	Thomas Jefferson (DR)	Unknown	68
1800*	Thomas Jefferson (DR)	Unknown	73	Aaron Burr (DR)	Unknown	73
1804	Thomas Jefferson (DR)	Unknown	162	Charles Pinckney (F)	Unknown	14
1808	James Madison (DR)	Unknown	122	Charles Pinckney (F)	Unknown	47
1812	James Madison (DR)	Unknown	128	DeWitt Clinton (F)	Unknown	89
1816	James Monroe (DR)	Unknown	183	Rufus King (F)	Unknown	34
1820	James Monroe (DR)	Unknown	231	John Quincy Adams (DR)	Unknown	1
1824*	John Quincy Adams (DR)	113,122	84	Andrew Jackson (DR)	151,271	99
				Henry Clay (DR)	46,587	37
				William H. Crawford (DR)	44,282	41
1828	Andrew Jackson (D)	642,553	178	John Quincy Adams (NR)	500,897	83
1832	Andrew Jackson (D)	701,780	219	Henry Clay (NR)	484,205	49
1836	Martin Van Buren (D)	764,176	170	William H. Harrison (W)	550,816	73
1840	William H. Harrison (W)	1,275,390	234	Martin Van Buren (D)	1,128,854	60
1844	James K. Polk (D)	1,339,494	170	Henry Clay (W)	1,300,004	105
1848	Zachary Taylor (W)	1,361,393	163	Lewis Cass (D)	1,223,460	127
				Martin Van Buren (Free Soil)	291,501	—
1852	Franklin Pierce (D)	1,607,510	254	Winfield Scott (W)	1,386,942	42
1856	James Buchanan (D)	1,836,072	174	John C. Fremont (R)	1,342,345	114
				Millard Fillmore (American)	873,053	8
1860	Abraham Lincoln (R)	1,865,908	180	Stephen A. Douglas (D)	848,019	12
				John C. Breckinridge (D)	845,763	72
				John Bell (Const. Union)	589,581	39
1864	Abraham Lincoln (R)	2,218,388	212	George McClellan (D)	1,812,807	21
1868	Ulysses S. Grant (R)	3,013,650	214	Horatio Seymour (D)	2,708,744	80
1872*	Ulysses S. Grant (R)	3,598,235	286	Horace Greeley (D-LR)*	2,834,671	—
1876*	Rutherford B. Hayes (R)	4,034,311	185	Samuel J. Tilden (D)	4,288,546	184
1880	James A. Garfield (R)	4,446,158	214	Winfield S. Hancock (D)	4,444,260	155
1884	Grover Cleveland (D)	4,874,621	219	James G. Blaine (R)	4,848,936	182
1888	Benjamin Harrison (R)	5,443,892	233	Grover Cleveland (D)	5,534,488	168
1892	Grover Cleveland (D)	5,551,883	277	Benjamin Harrison (R)	5,179,244	145
				James Weaver (P)	1,027,329	22
1896	William McKinley (R)	7,108,480	271	William J. Bryan (D-P)	6,511,495	176
1900	William McKinley (R)	7,218,039	292	William J. Bryan (D)	6,358,345	155
1904	Theodore Roosevelt (R)	7,626,593	336	Alton B. Parker (D)	5,082,898	140
1908	William H. Taft (R)	7,676,258	321	William J. Bryan (D)	6,406,801	162
1912	Woodrow Wilson (D)	6,293,152	435	Theodore Roosevelt (PR)	4,119,207	88
				William H. Taft (R)	3,483,922	8
1916	Woodrow Wilson (D)	9,126,300	277	Charles E. Hughes (R)	8,546,789	254
1920	Warren G. Harding (R)	16,153,115	404	James M. Cox (D)	9,133,092	127
1924	Calvin Coolidge (R)	15,719,921	382	John W. Davis (D)	8,386,704	136
				Robert M. La Follette (PR)	4,822,856	13
1928	Herbert Hoover (R)	21,437,277	444	Alfred E. Smith (D)	15,007,698	87
1932	Franklin D. Roosevelt (D)	22,829,501	472	Herbert Hoover (R)	15,760,684	59
1936	Franklin D. Roosevelt (D)	27,757,333	523	Alfred Landon (R)	16,684,231	8
1940	Franklin D. Roosevelt (D)	27,313,041	449	Wendell Willkie (R)	22,348,480	82
1944	Franklin D. Roosevelt (D)	25,612,610	432	Thomas E. Dewey (R)	22,117,617	99
1948	Harry S. Truman (D)	24,179,345	303	Thomas E. Dewey (R)	21,991,291	189
				Strom Thurmond (SR)	1,169,021	39
				Henry A. Wallace (PR)	1,157,172	—
1952	Dwight D. Eisenhower (R)	33,936,234	442	Adlai E. Stevenson (D)	27,314,992	89
1956*	Dwight D. Eisenhower (R)	35,590,472	457	Adlai E. Stevenson (D)	26,022,752	73
1960*	John F. Kennedy (D)	34,226,731	303	Richard M. Nixon (R)	34,108,157	219
1964	Lyndon B. Johnson (D)	43,129,566	486	Barry M. Goldwater (R)	27,178,188	52
1968	Richard M. Nixon (R)	31,785,480	301	Hubert H. Humphrey (D)	31,275,166	191
				George C. Wallace (3rd party)	9,906,473	46
1972*	Richard M. Nixon (R)	47,169,911	520	George S. McGovern (D)	29,170,383	17
1976*	Jimmy Carter (D)	40,830,763	297	Gerald R. Ford (R)	39,147,793	240
1980	Ronald Reagan (R)	43,904,153	489	Jimmy Carter (D)	35,483,883	49
				John B. Anderson (independent)	5,719,437	—
1984	Ronald Reagan (R)	54,455,075	525	Walter F. Mondale (D)	37,577,185	13
1988*	George H. W. Bush (R)	48,886,097	426	Michael S. Dukakis (D)	41,809,074	111
1992	Bill Clinton (D)	44,908,254	370	George H. W. Bush (R)	39,102,343	168
				H. Ross Perot (independent)	19,741,065	—
1996	Bill Clinton (D)	45,590,703	379	Bob Dole (R)	37,816,307	159
				H. Ross Perot (RF)	7,866,284	—
2000*	George W. Bush (R)	50,459,211	271	Al Gore (D)	51,003,894	266
				Ralph Nader (Green)	2,834,410	—
2004*	George W. Bush (R)	62,040,606	286	John Kerry (D)	59,028,109	251
				Ralph Nader (Independent)	411,304	—

***1800**—Elected by House of Representatives because of tied electoral vote. **1824**—Elected by House of Representatives because no candidate had polled a majority. By 1824, the Democratic Republicans had become a loose coalition of competing political groups. By 1828, the supporters of Jackson were known as Democrats, and the John Q. Adams and Henry Clay supporters as National Republicans. **1872**—Greeley died Nov. 29, 1872. His electoral votes were split among 4 individuals. **1876**—FL, LA, OR, and SC election returns were disputed. Congress in joint session (Mar. 2, 1877) declared Hayes and Wheeler elected president and vice president. **1956**—Democrats elected 74 electors, but one from Alabama refused to vote for Stevenson. **1960**—Sen. Harry F. Byrd (D, VA) received 15 electoral votes. **1972**—John Hospers of California received one vote from an elector of Virginia. **1976**—Ronald Reagan of CA received one vote from an elector of Washington. **1988**—Sen. Lloyd Bentsen (D, TX) received 1 vote from an elector of West Virginia. **2000**—One Gore elector from Washington, DC, abstained. Nader was listed as "Independent" on the ballot in some states, and was not on the ballot in all states. **2004**—One Minnesota elector voted for VP candidate John Edwards for both president and vice president.

EDUCATION

U.S. Public Schools: Students, Staff, Spending, 1899-2003

Source: National Center for Education Statistics, U.S. Dept. of Education

	1899-1900	1919-20	1939-40	1959-60	1969-70	1979-80	1989-90	1999-2000	2002-03
Population statistics (thousands)									
Total U.S. population[1]	75,995	104,514	131,028	177,830	201,385	224,567	246,819	279,040	287,941
Population 5-17 years of age	21,573	27,571	30,151	43,881	52,386	48,041	44,947	52,811	53,316
Percentage 5-17 years of age	28.4	26.4	23.0	24.7	26.0	21.4	18.2	18.9	18.5
Enrollment (thousands)									
Elementary and secondary[2]	15,503	21,578	25,434	36,087	45,550	41,651	40,543	46,857	48,183
Kindergarten & grades 1-8	14,984	19,378	18,833	27,602	32,513	28,034	29,152	33,488	34,116
Grades 9-12	519	2,200	6,601	8,485	13,037	13,616	11,390	13,369	14,067
Percentage pop. 5-17 enrolled	71.9	78.3	84.4	82.2	87.0	86.7	90.2	88.7	90.4
Percentage in high schools	3.3	10.2	26.0	23.5	28.6	32.7	28.1	28.5	29.2
High school graduates (thousands)	62	231	1,143	1,627	2,589	2,748	2,320	2,554	NA
School term; staff									
Average school term (in days)	144.3	161.9	175.0	178.0	178.9	178.5	*	*	*
Total instructional staff (thousands)	*	678	912	1,457	2,286	2,406	2,986	3,820	4,017
Teachers, librarians, and other non-supervisory instructional staff (thousands)	423	657	875	1,393	2,195	2,300	2,860	3,683	3,853
Revenue and expenditures (millions)									
Total revenue	$220	$970	$2,261	$14,747	$40,267	$96,881	$208,548	$372,944	$440,157
Total expenditures	215	1,036	2,344	15,613	40,683	95,962	212,770	381,838	454,906
Current expenditures[3]	180	861	1,942	12,329[5]	34,218[5]	86,984[5]	188,229[5]	323,889[5]	387,592[5]
Capital outlay	35	154	258	2,662	4,659	6,506	17,781	43,357	48,940
Interest on school debt	*	18	131	490	1,171	1,874	3,776	9,135	11,499
Others	*	3	13	133	636	598	2,983	5,457	6,874
Salaries and pupil cost									
Avg. annual salary of instruct. staff[4]	$325	$871	$1,441	$3,010	$8,626	$15,970	$31,367	$41,827	$45,822
Expenditure per capita total pop.	2.83	9.91	17.89	88	202	427	862	1,368	1,580
Current expenditure[5] per pupil ADA[6]	16.67	53.32	88.09	375	816	2,272	4,980	7,394	8,600

NOTE: Because of rounding, details may not add to totals. * = Data not collected. Prior to 1959-60, data do not include Alaska and Hawaii. (1) Population data for 1899-1900 are based on total population from the decennial census. From 1919-20 to 1959-60, population data are total population, including armed forces overseas, as of July 1 preceding the school year. Data for later years are for resident population that excludes armed forces overseas. (2) Data for 1899 through 1960 are school year enrollment; data for later years are fall enrollment. (3) In 1899-1900, includes interest on school debt. (4) Data prior to 1959-60 includes supervisors, principals, teachers, and nonsupervisory instructional staff. (5) Because of changes in the definition of "current expenditures," data for 1959-60 and later years are not entirely comparable with prior years. (6) ADA means average daily attendance.

Programs for the Disabled, 1992-2003

Source: Office of Special Education Programs, U.S. Dept. of Education

(Number of children from 6 to 21 years old served annually in educational programs for the disabled; in thousands)

Type of Disability	1992-93	1993-94	1994-95	1995-96	1996-97	1997-98	1998-99	1999-2000	2000-01	2001-02	2002-03
Learning disabilities	2,366	2,428	2,510	2,602	2,674	2,754	2,817	2,834	2,848	2,846	2,834
Speech impairments	998	1,018	1,020	1,027	1,049	1,064	1,075	1,081	1,085	1,084	1,102
Mental retardation	532	554	571	586	594	603	611	600	599	592	580
Emotional disturbance	402	415	428	439	446	454	463	469	472	476	480
Multiple disabilities	103	110	90	95	99	107	108	111	121	127	130
Hearing impairments	61	65	65	68	69	70	71	71	70	70	71
Orthopedic impairments	53	57	60	63	66	67	69	71	73	73	74
Other health impairments	66	83	107	134	161	191	221	253	290	337	390
Visual impairments	24	25	25	25	26	26	26	65	25	25	25
Autism	16	19	23	29	34	43	54	65	78	97	118
Deaf-blindness	1	1	1	1	1	1	2	2	1	2	2
Traumatic brain injury	4	5	7	10	10	12	13	14	15	21	21
Developmental delay*	—	—	—	—	—	—	—	—	—	45	58
ALL DISABILITIES	**4,626**	**4,779**	**4,908**	**5,079**	**5,231**	**5,397**	**5,541**	**5,614**	**5,705**	**5,795**	**5,885**

NOTE: Counts based on reports from states and District of Columbia. Details may not add to totals because of rounding and/or incomplete enumeration. — = not available or not reliable data. * Applicable only to ages 3-9.

Technology in U.S. Public Schools*

Source: Quality Education Data, Inc., Denver, CO

(Number and percentage of schools in each category that have the technology indicated.)

	Total		Elementary[1]		Middle/ Jr. High[2]		Senior High[3]		K-12[4]		Special Ed./ Adult Ed.	
TOTAL SCHOOLS	**93,189**	**100%**	**56,232**	**100%**	**14,475**	**100%**	**20,161**	**100%**	**2,530**	**100%**	**2,310**	**100%**
Schools with computers	**83,057**	**89**	**51,418**	**91**	**12,911**	**89**	**17,100**	**85**	**2,026**	**80**	**1,625**	**70**
By number of computers:												
1-10	3,170	3	1,990	4	194	1	597	3	59	2	389	17
11-20	4,590	5	3,123	6	345	2	829	4	129	5	293	13
21-50	16,741	18	11,934	21	1,728	12	2,628	13	493	19	449	19
51-100	23,753	25	16,940	30	3,372	23	3,178	16	607	24	262	11
100+	34,803	37	17,431	31	7,272	50	9,868	49	738	29	232	10
Schools with LANs[5]	**61,104**	**66**	**36,791**	**66**	**10,652**	**74**	**14,030**	**72**	**1,614**	**65**	**707**	**30**
By enrollment:												
100-299	13,607	15	8,610	15	1,212	8	3,309	17	774	31	476	20
300-499	18,256	20	13,802	25	2,098	15	2,294	12	403	16	62	3
500+	29,241	32	14,379	26	7,342	51	8,427	43	437	18	169	7
Schools with WANs[6]	**45,933**	**50**	**27,549**	**49**	**8,011**	**56**	**9,932**	**51**	**996**	**40**	**441**	**19**
By enrollment:												
100-299	8,816	10	5,701	10	769	5	2,032	10	434	18	314	13
300-499	14,574	16	11,100	20	1,735	12	1,707	9	289	12	32	1
500+	22,543	24	10,748	19	5,507	38	6,193	32	273	11	95	4

*Data for schools with computers as of 2005. All other data from 2004 (1) Includes preschool and schools with grade spans of Preschool-3, K-6, K-8, and K-12. (2) Includes schools with grade spans of 4-8, 7-8, and 7-9. (3) Includes vocational, technical, and alternative high schools and schools with grade spans of 7-12, 9-12, and 10-12. (4) K-12 also included under Elementary schools. (5) LAN=Local area computer network. (6) WAN=Wide area computer network.

Students Per Computer in U.S. Public Schools, 1983-2004

Source: Quality Education Data, Inc., Denver, CO

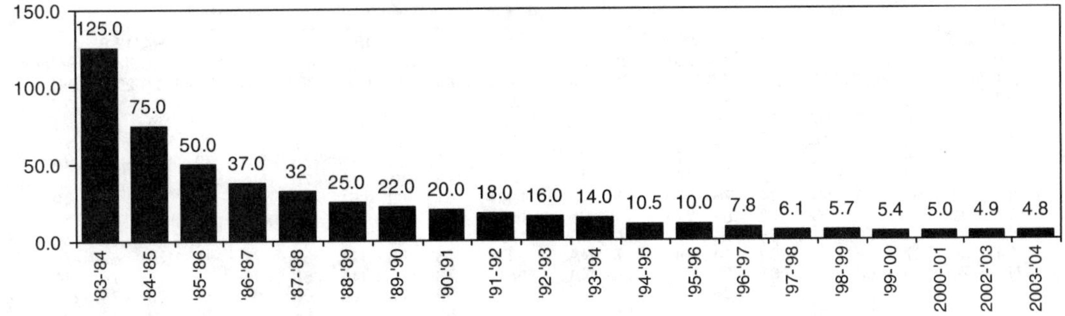

Overview of U.S. Public Schools, Fall 2003*

Source: National Center for Education Statistics, U.S. Dept. of Education; National Education Association

	Local school districts	Elementary schools[1]	Secondary schools[2]	Classroom teachers	Total enrollment	Pupils per teacher	Teacher's avg. pay[3]	Expend. per pupil[4]
Alabama	130	938	403	58,070	731,220	12.6	$38,246	$6,300
Alaska	53	194	85	7,808	133,933	17.2	49,685	$9,870
Arizona	313	1,261	560	47,507	1,012,068	21.3	40,894	$6,282
Arkansas	309	711	424	30,876	454,523	14.7	37,753	$6,482
California	989	6,579	2,187	304,311	6,413,862	21.1	56,283	$7,552
Colorado	178	1,196	401	44,904	757,693	16.9	41,275	$7,384
Connecticut	166	824	240	42,370	577,203	13.6	54,362	$11,057
Delaware	19	137	44	7,749	117,668	15.2	50,772	$9,693
Dist. of Columbia	1	139	43	5,676	78,057	13.8	50,763	$11,847
Florida	67	2,350	481	144,955	2,587,628	17.9	39,465	$6,439
Georgia	180	1,637	356	97,150	1,522,611	15.7	45,533	$7,774
Hawaii	1	208	54	11,129	183,609	16.5	44,464	$8,100
Idaho	114	417	223	14,049	252,120	17.9	40,148	$6,081
Illinois	887	3,189	1,005	127,669	2,100,961	16.5	51,289	$8,287
Indiana	294	1,420	448	59,924	1,011,130	16.9	45,097	$8,057
Iowa	370	1,023	424	34,791	481,226	13.8	38,921	$7,574
Kansas	302	977	423	32,589	470,490	14.4	38,123	$7,454
Kentucky	176	1,007	337	41,201	663,885	16.1	38,981	$6,661
Louisiana	68	1,037	312	50,495	727,709	14.4	36,878	$6,922
Maine	283	518	156	17,621	202,084	11.5	38,121	$9,344
Maryland	24	1,085	269	55,140	869,113	15.8	49,677	$9,153
Massachusetts	350	1,464	334	72,062	980,459	13.6	52,043	$10,460
Michigan	553	2,698	843	97,014	1,757,604	18.1	54,071	$8,781
Minnesota	348	1,256	836	51,611	842,854	16.3	42,833	$8,109
Mississippi	152	599	327	32,591	493,540	15.1	34,555	$5,792
Missouri	524	1,560	650	65,169	905,941	13.9	38,826	$7,495
Montana	438	497	362	10,301	148,356	14.4	35,754	$7,496
Nebraska	518	885	333	20,921	285,542	13.6	37,896	$8,074
Nevada	17	406	127	20,234	385,401	19.0	41,795	$6,092
New Hampshire	178	375	97	15,112	207,417	13.7	40,519	$8,579
New Jersey	598	1,911	462	109,077	1,380,753	12.7	54,166	$12,568
New Mexico	89	575	205	21,569	323,066	15.0	36,687	$7,125
New York	726	3,187	995	216,116	2,864,775	13.3	52,600	$11,961
North Carolina	117	1,770	390	89,988	1,360,209	15.1	43,076	$6,562
North Dakota	213	322	200	8,037	102,233	12.7	33,210	$6,870
Ohio	613	2,738	1,003	121,735	1,845,428	15.2	45,452	$8,632
Oklahoma	541	1,198	583	39,253	626,160	16.0	34,854	$6,092
Oregon	199	913	274	26,732	551,273	20.6	47,600	$7,491
Pennsylvania	501	2,375	802	119,889	1,821,146	15.2	51,800	$8,997
Rhode Island	38	268	68	11,918	159,375	13.4	51,076	$10,349
South Carolina	89	849	285	45,830	699,198	15.3	41,279	$7,040
South Dakota	172	441	281	9,245	125,537	13.6	32,416	$6,547
Tennessee	136	1,259	354	59,584	936,681	15.7	39,677	$6,118
Texas	1,040	5,241	1,835	289,481	4,331,751	15.0	40,001	$7,136
Utah	40	546	309	22,147	495,981	22.4	38,413	$4,838
Vermont	299	276	69	8,749	99,103	11.3	41,603	$10,454
Virginia	134	1,482	412	90,573	1,192,092	13.2	43,152	$7,822
Washington	296	1,425	592	52,824	1,021,349	19.3	44,949	$7,252
West Virginia	55	588	178	20,020	281,215	14.0	38,508	$8,319
Wisconsin	437	1,552	593	58,216	880,031	15.1	42,871	$9,004
Wyoming	48	255	108	6,567	87,462	13.3	37,876	$8,985
TOTAL U.S.	**14,383**	**65,758**	**22,782**	**3,048,549**	**48,540,725**	**15.9**	**$45,822**	**$8,044**

*Full-time elementary and secondary day schools only. (1) Includes schools below grade 9. (2) Includes schools with no grade lower than 7. (3) National Education Association estimate, Fall 2002. (4) Fall 2002, per total number of pupils.

WORLD ALMANAC QUICK QUIZ

Rank the following libraries from biggest to smallest in terms of volumes held.

(a) New York Public Library (b) Library of Congress
(c) Boston Public Library (d) Harvard University Library

For the answer look in this chapter, or see page 1008.

Mathematics, Reading, and Science Achievement of U.S. Students

Source: National Assessment of Educational Progress, National Center for Education Statistics, U.S. Dept. of Education

Percent of public school students who scored at or above basic level in national tests.*

	GRADE 4				GRADE 8					
	Math		Reading		Math		Reading		Science	
State	2000	2003	1998	2003	2000	2003	1998	2003	1996	2000
AL	57	65	56	53	52	53	67	65	47	51
AK	NA	76	NA	58	NA	70	NA	67	65	NA
AZ	58	70	51	54	62	62	72	66	55	57
AR	56	71	54	60	52	57	68	70	55	54
CA	52	67	48	49	52	55	63	61	47	40
CO	NA	77	69	70	NA	74	76	78	68	NA
CT	77	82	76	74	72	73	81	77	68	65
DE	NA	81	53	71	NA	68	64	77	51	NA
DC	24	36	27	32	23	29	44	47	19	NA
FL	NA	76	53	63	NA	61	67	67	51	NA
GA	58	71	54	58	55	59	68	70	49	52
HI	55	69	45	53	52	55	59	61	42	40
ID	71	79	NA	64	71	72	NA	76	NA	73
IL	66	73	NA	61	68	66	NA	76	NA	62
IN	78	82	NA	66	76	73	NA	77	65	68
IA	78	83	67	71	NA	76	NA	80	71	NA
KS	76	86	70	66	77	76	81	77	NA	NA
KY	60	72	62	65	63	66	74	78	58	62
LA	57	68	44	49	48	57	63	64	40	45
ME	74	83	72	71	76	74	83	79	78	75
MD	61	72	58	62	65	67	70	71	55	59
MA	79	84	70	73	76	76	79	81	69	74
MI	72	78	62	64	70	68	NA	76	65	69
MN	78	84	69	69	80	82	81	78	72	73
MS	45	62	47	48	41	47	62	66	39	42
MO	72	79	61	68	67	71	75	80	64	68
MT	73	81	72	69	80	79	83	82	77	80
NE	67	79	NA	66	74	74	NA	77	71	70
NV	60	69	51	52	58	60	70	63	NA	54
NH	NA	88	75	75	NA	79	NA	81	NA	NA
NJ	NA	81	NA	70	NA	71	NA	78	NA	NA
NM	51	63	51	48	50	52	71	62	49	48
NY	67	79	62	67	68	71	76	75	57	61
NC	76	85	58	65	70	71	74	72	56	56
ND	75	83	NA	69	77	81	NA	82	78	74
OH	73	81	NA	68	75	73	NA	78	NA	73
OK	69	73	66	60	64	64	80	74	NA	62
OR	65	79	58	64	71	70	78	74	68	67
PA	NA	78	NA	65	NA	69	NA	76	NA	NA
RI	67	71	64	63	64	63	76	71	59	61
SC	60	79	53	59	55	67	66	69	45	50
SD	NA	82	NA	68	NA	78	NA	82	NA	NA
TN	60	69	57	57	53	59	71	69	53	57
TX	77	82	59	60	68	69	74	71	55	53
UT	70	79	62	66	68	72	77	76	70	68
VT	73	84	NA	74	75	77	NA	82	70	74
VA	73	83	62	69	67	72	78	78	59	63
WA	NA	81	64	67	NA	72	76	76	61	NA
WV	68	75	60	65	62	63	75	72	56	61
WI	NA	79	72	68	NA	75	79	78	73	NA
WY	73	87	64	68	70	76	76	79	71	71
U.S.	**67**	**77**	**58**	**62**	**65**	**66**	**71**	**72**	**60**	**59**

NA = Not administered. * "Basic level" denotes a partial mastery of prerequisite knowledge and skills fundamental for proficient work at each grade.

Revenues[1] for Public Elementary and Secondary Schools, by State, 2004-2005

Source: National Education Association; in thousands

		Federal		State		Local and intermediate	
STATE	Total	Amount	%	Amount	%	Amount	%
Alabama	$5,550,659	$631,427	11.4	$3,168,321	57.1	$1,750,911	31.5
Alaska	1,305,183*	163,525*	12.5*	829,259*	63.5*	312,399*	23.9*
Arizona	7,521,813*	582,344*	7.7*	3,854,582*	51.2*	3,084,887*	41.0*
Arkansas	3,703,559*	418,455*	11.3*	1,920,276*	51.8*	1,364,828*	36.9*
California	63,853,237	6,891,800	10.8	40,702,047	63.7	16,259,390	25.5
Colorado	6,625,435	434,443	6.6	2,855,490	43.1	3,335,502	50.3
Connecticut	7,664,500	460,000	6.0	3,008,000	39.2	4,196,500	54.8
Delaware	1,313,545*	87,679*	6.7*	842,341*	64.1*	383,525*	29.2*
District of Columbia	875,869*	129,447*	14.8*	0*	0.0*	746,422*	85.2*
Florida	22,927,896	2,465,995	10.8	9,784,197	42.7	10,677,704	46.6
Georgia	14,958,471*	1,314,698*	8.8*	6,753,646*	45.1*	6,890,127*	46.1*
Hawaii	2,137,479	175,526	8.2	1,929,936	90.3	32,017	1.5
Idaho	1,671,550*	160,050*	9.6*	1,004,000*	60.1*	507,500*	30.4*
Illinois	18,588,349	1,440,850	7.8	5,640,346	30.3	11,507,153	61.9
Indiana	10,184,727*	687,708*	6.8*	5,125,130*	50.3*	4,371,889*	42.9*
Iowa	4,339,853	318,811	7.3	2,005,990	46.2	2,015,052	46.4
Kansas	4,358,900	351,592	8.1	2,300,000	52.8	1,707,308	39.2
Kentucky	5,356,238	638,470	11.9	3,126,048	58.4	1,591,720	29.7
Louisiana	5,980,918	809,520	13.5	2,909,554	48.6	2,261,844	37.8
Maine	2,225,908	210,351	9.5	930,786	41.8	1,084,771	48.7
Maryland	9,487,269*	686,600*	7.2*	3,537,308*	37.3*	5,263,361*	55.5*
Massachusetts	12,804,417	846,351	6.6	4,923,947	38.5	7,034,119	54.9
Michigan	17,371,493*	985,343*	5.7*	11,619,892*	66.9*	4,766,258*	27.4*
Minnesota	8,724,560	592,019	6.8	6,067,078	69.5	2,065,463	23.7
Mississippi	3,599,875*	541,857*	15.1*	1,951,277*	54.2*	1,106,741*	30.7*
Missouri	8,312,309*	760,401*	9.1*	2,689,718*	32.4*	4,862,190*	58.5*
Montana	1,291,163*	157,041*	12.2*	608,383*	47.1*	525,739*	40.7*
Nebraska	2,291,379	163,052	7.1	925,648	40.4	1,202,679	52.5
Nevada	3,309,193	250,161	7.6	1,045,996	31.6	2,013,036	60.8
New Hampshire	2,163,230*	130,641*	6.0*	1,132,650*	52.4*	899,939*	41.6*
New Jersey	18,972,353*	526,068*	2.8*	7,266,110*	38.3*	11,180,175*	58.9*
New Mexico	2,852,262	440,125	15.4	2,068,787	72.5	343,350	12.0
New York	39,500,000	2,600,000	6.6	17,900,000	45.3	19,000,000	48.1
North Carolina	9,892,919	1,197,719	12.1	6,276,896	63.4	2,418,304	24.4
North Dakota	854,434	121,701	14.2	305,383	35.7	427,350	50.0
Ohio	19,712,163*	1,235,889*	6.3*	9,063,054*	46.0*	9,413,220*	47.8*
Oklahoma	4,548,154*	597,564*	13.1*	2,438,842*	53.6*	1,511,748*	33.2*
Oregon	4,607,424*	506,159*	11.0*	2,483,055*	53.9*	1,618,210*	35.1*
Pennsylvania	20,024,552*	1,659,858*	8.3*	7,126,038*	35.6*	11,238,656*	56.1*
Rhode Island	1,535,220*	52,905*	3.4*	563,222*	36.7*	919,094*	59.9*
South Carolina	6,367,184	733,208	11.5	2,851,967	44.8	2,782,009	43.7
South Dakota	1,043,458*	171,396*	16.4*	358,856*	34.4*	513,206*	49.2*
Tennessee	6,442,030	767,972	11.9	2,919,001	45.3	2,755,057	42.8
Texas	35,841,377	4,159,173	11.6	13,354,756	37.3	18,327,448	51.1
Utah	3,168,699*	299,909*	9.5*	1,827,701*	57.7*	1,041,089*	32.9*
Vermont	1,241,188	99,269	8.0	1,066,196	85.9	75,723	6.1
Virginia	12,169,967*	829,408*	6.8*	5,045,794*	41.5*	6,294,765*	51.7*

STATE	Total	Federal Amount	%	State Amount	%	Local and intermediate Amount	%
Washington	$9,097,103	$937,612	10.3	$5,603,089	61.6	$2,556,402	28.1
West Virginia	2,815,286	335,472	11.9	1,669,077	59.3	810,737	28.8
Wisconsin	9,822,445*	562,055*	5.7*	5,329,555*	54.3*	3,930,835*	40.0*
Wyoming	1,008,310	96,100	9.5	518,700	51.4	393,510	39.0
50 States and DC	472,015,505	41,415,719	8.8	229,227,924	48.6	201,371,862	42.7

*Indicates NEA estimate. (1) Included as revenue receipts are all appropriations from general funds of federal, state, county, and local governments; receipts from taxes levied for school purposes; income from permanent school funds and endowments; and income from leases of school lands and miscellaneous sources (interest on bank deposits, tuition, gifts, school lunch charges, etc.).

Enrollment in U.S. Public and Private Schools, 1899-2014

Source: National Center for Education Statistics, U.S. Dept. of Education

School year[1]	Public school[2]	Private school[2]	% Private
1899-1900	15,503	1,352	8.7
1909-10	17,814	1,558	8.7
1919-20	21,578	1,699	7.9
1929-30	25,678	2,651	10.3
1939-40	25,434	2,611	10.3
1949-50	25,111	3,380	13.5
1959-60	35,182	5,675	16.1
1969-70	45,550	5,500[3]	12.1
1979-80	41,651	5,000[3]	12.0
1989-90	40,543	5,198	11.4
1999-2000	46,857	6,018	11.4
2000-2001	47,204	6,162	11.5
2004-2005[4]	48,175	6,279	11.5
2005-2006[4]	48,304	6,311	11.6
2006-2007[4]	48,524	6,383	11.6
2013-2014[4]	49,737	6,627	11.8

*Private includes all nonpublic schools. (1) Fall enrollment. (2) In thousands. (3) Estimated. (4) Projected.

Homeschooled Students

A total of 1,096,000 U.S. students in grades K-12 were being homeschooled in 2003, 82% of them full-time, according to the latest available statistics from the U.S. Dept. of Education.

In a 2003 U.S. Dept. of Education survey of parents who homeschool their children the reasons given as *most important* included concern over the school environment, including such factors as safety, drugs, or negative peer pressure (31.2%); desire to provide religious or moral instruction (29.8%); dissatisfaction with academic instruction in schools (16.5%); and a physical or mental health problem or other special need (13.7%). In all, 85.4% cited concern over school environment as one of their reasons, while 72.3% cited religious or moral instruction and 68.2% cited dissatisfaction with academic instruction.

Below is a breakdown of homeschooled students by categories for 2003 and 1999.

Characteristic	1999 Number	1999 Percentage distribution	1999 Home-schooling rate[1]	2003 Number	2003 Percentage distribution	2003 Home-schooling rate[1]
Total	850,000	100.0	1.7	1,096,000	100.0	2.2
Homeschooled entirely	697,000	82.0	—	898,000	82.0	—
Homeschooled and enrolled in school part time	153,000	18.0	—	198,000	18.0	—
Race/ethnicity[2]						
Black	84,000	9.9	1.0	103,000	9.4	1.3
White	640,000	75.3	2.0	843,000	77.0	2.7
Other	49,000	5.8	1.9	91,000	8.3	3.0
Hispanic	77,000	9.1	1.1	59,000	5.3	0.7
Number of children in the household						
One child	120,000	14.1	1.5	110,000	10.1	1.4
Two children	207,000	24.4	1.0	306,000	28.0	1.5
Three or more children	523,000	61.6	2.4	679,000	62.0	3.1
Household income						
$25,000 or less	262,000	30.9	1.6	283,000	25.8	2.3
$25,001–50,000	278,000	32.7	1.8	311,000	28.4	2.4
$50,001–75,000	162,000	19.1	1.9	264,000	24.1	2.4
$75,001 or more	148,000	17.4	1.5	238,000	21.7	1.7
Parents' education						
High school diploma or less	160,000	18.9	0.9	269,000	24.5	1.7
Some college or vocational/technical	287,000	33.7	1.9	338,000	30.8	2.1
Bachelor's degree	213,000	25.1	2.6	274,000	25.0	2.8
Graduate/professional degree	190,000	22.3	2.3	215,000	19.6	2.5

(1) The homeschooling rate is the percentage of the total group or subgroup that is homeschooled. For example, in 2003, 0.7% of all Hispanic students K-12 were homeschooled. (2) Race categories exclude Hispanic.

U.S. Public High School Graduation Rates, 2001-2002

Source: National Center for Education Statistics, U.S. Dept. of Education

	Rate (%)[1]	Rank
Alabama	57.2	47
Alaska	60.7	43
Arizona	69.9	32
Arkansas	74.2	17
California	69.6	33
Colorado	70.0	31
Connecticut	74.9	16
Delaware	62.0	41
District of Columbia	70.4	29
Florida	55.7	49
Georgia	53.6	50
Hawaii	64.8	38
Idaho	77.2	11
Illinois	72.2	25
Indiana	68.6	35
Iowa	82.9	3
Kansas	75.2	14
Kentucky	64.9	37
Louisiana	59.2	45
Maine	75.7	13
Maryland	74.1	18
Massachusetts	74.0	19
Michigan	71.5	27
Minnesota	82.3	5
Mississippi	59.1	46
Missouri	73.6	21
Montana	77.3	10
Nebraska	80.0	6
Nevada	70.2	30
New Hampshire	75.2	15
New Jersey	89.8	1
New Mexico	61.5	42
New York	62.1	40
North Carolina	60.6	44
North Dakota	83.7	2
Ohio	72.3	24
Oklahoma	73.2	22
Oregon	68.8	34
Pennsylvania	77.1	12
Rhode Island	72.0	26
South Carolina	49.2	51
South Dakota	77.8	9
Tennessee	56.7	48
Texas	64.2	39
Utah	82.5	4
Vermont	78.6	8
Virginia	73.7	20
Washington	68.5	36
West Virginia	71.2	28
Wisconsin	79.0	7
Wyoming	72.7	23
TOTAL U.S.	**68.5**	

NOTE: Data exclude ungraded pupils and have not been adjusted for interstate migration. (1) Graduates as percentage of fall 1998 9th-grade enrollment.

Teachers' Salaries in Upper Secondary Education, Selected Countries, 2002

Source: Organization for Economic Cooperation and Development

Annual statutory teachers' salaries in public institutions in upper secondary (senior high school) education, general programs, in equivalent U.S. dollars converted using PPPs[1]; ranked by starting salaries.

	Starting salary	Salary with 15 years' experience	Salary at top of scale
Switzerland	$48,704	$63,200	$74,689
Germany	41,441	50,805	53,085
Spain	32,679	38,067	47,323
Finland	32,136	40,482	42,652
Belgium (Fl.)	31,924	46,076	55,383
Belgium (Fr.)	30,793	44,854	54,100
Denmark	30,384	43,063	46,096
United States	**29,641**	**42,918**	**51,308**
Netherlands	29,326	51,444	58,913
Scotland	27,789	40,619	40,619
Australia	27,394	40,479	40,479
Korea	26,852	46,269	74,541
Norway	26,637	30,533	32,695
France	25,563	33,394	48,070
England	25,403	39,350	39,350
Austria	24,846	34,444	52,294
Italy	24,710	31,073	38,604
Sweden	24,544	29,315	31,711
Ireland	23,767	38,066	43,137
Japan	23,493	44,372	58,286
Iceland	22,017	27,941	30,551
Greece	20,906	25,563	31,013
Tunisia	$19,878	$20,065	$26,167
Portugal	19,445	31,876	51,829
India[2]	18,247	26,831	26,831
New Zealand	18,109	35,034	35,034
Czech Republic	15,476	18,898	23,452
Paraguay[2,3]	15,269	15,269	15,269
Brazil[2]	13,853	16,397	NA
Malaysia[2]	13,647	23,315	23,315
Argentina[2]	12,076	17,007	17,007
Chile	11,033	13,454	13,926
Jamaica	10,955	12,686	12,686
Turkey	10,272	11,759	13,342
Philippines	9,857	10,880	10,880
Hungary	8,790	12,851	16,797
Jordan	7,976	10,414	868
Uruguay[2,3]	5,873	6,944	NA
Thailand	5,862	14,406	14,406
Slovak Republic	5,134	6,611	9,786
Peru[2,3]	4,577	4,577	5,273
Sri Lanka	3,574	4,596	3,319
Indonesia	1,014	1,858	1,990

NA = Not available. (1) Purchasing power parities (PPPs) are the rates of currency conversion that equalize the purchasing power of different currencies by eliminating the differences in price levels between countries. (2) Year of reference 2001. (3) Salaries are for a position of 20 hours per week. Most teachers hold two positions.

Percent of Population with Upper Secondary Education, Selected Countries, 2002

Source: Organization for Economic Cooperation and Development

Percentage of the population ages 25-64 that have received at least some upper secondary (senior high school) education

Czech Republic	88
United States	**87**
Norway	86
Slovak Republic	86
Japan	84
Canada	83
Germany	83
Switzerland	82
Sweden	82
Denmark	80
Israel	80
Austria	78
New Zealand	76
Finland	75
Hungary	71
Korea	71
Netherlands	66
France	65
United Kingdom	64
Australia	61
Belgium	61
Ireland	60
Iceland	59
Luxembourg	57
Greece	50
Chile	47
Poland	47
Italy	44
Peru[1]	44
Philippines	43
Argentina[1]	42
Malaysia[1]	41
Spain	41
Jordan	39
Uruguay[1]	33
Brazil[1]	27
Turkey	25
Indonesia	22
Paraguay[1]	22
Portugal	20
Thailand	19
Mexico	13

(1) Year of reference 2001.

Charges at U.S. Institutions of Higher Education, 1969-70 to 2002-2003

Source: National Center for Education Statistics, U.S. Dept. of Education

Figures for 1969-70 are average charges for full-time resident degree-credit students; figures for later years are average charges per full-time equivalent student. Room and board are based on full-time students. These figures are enrollment-weighted, according to the number of full-time-equivalent undergraduates, and thus may vary from averages given elsewhere.

	TUITION AND FEES			BOARD RATES			DORMITORY CHARGES		
	All institutions	2-yr	4-yr	All institutions	2-yr	4-yr	All institutions	2-yr	4-yr
PUBLIC (in-state)									
1969-70	$323	$178	$427	$511	$465	$540	$369	$308	$395
1979-80	583	355	840	867	894	898	715	572	749
1989-90	1,356	756	2,035	1,635	1,581	1,728	1,513	962	1,561
1990-91	1,454	824	2,159	1,691	1,594	1,767	1,612	1,050	1,658
1995-96	2,179	1,239	2,848	2,020	1,681	2,045	2,057	1,297	2,121
1996-97	2,271	1,276	2,987	2,111	1,789	2,133	2,148	1,339	2,214
1997-98	2,360	1,314	3,110	2,228	1,795	2,263	2,225	1,401	2,301
1998-99	2,430	1,327	3,229	2,347	1,828	2,389	2,330	1,450	2,409
1999-2000	2,506	1,338	3,349	2,364	1,834	2,406	2,440	1,549	2,519
2000-2001	2,562	1,333	3,501	2,455	1,906	2,499	2,569	1,600	2,654
2001-2002	2,700	1,380	3,735	2,598	2,036	2,645	2,723	1,722	2,816
2002-2003[1]	2,928	1,479	4,059	2,702	2,174	2,747	2,925	1,943	3,022
PRIVATE									
1969-70	1,533	1,034	1,809	561	546	608	436	413	503
1979-80	3,130	2,062	3,811	955	924	1,078	827	769	999
1989-90	8,147	5,196	10,348	1,948	1,811	2,339	1,923	1,663	2,411
1990-91	8,772	5,570	11,379	2,074	1,989	2,470	2,063	1,744	2,654
1995-96	11,864	7,094	12,243	2,606	2,098	2,617	2,738	2,371	2,751
1996-97	12,498	7,236	12,881	2,663	2,181	2,672	2,878	2,537	2,889
1997-98	12,801	7,464	13,344	2,762	2,785	2,761	2,954	2,672	2,964
1998-99	13,428	7,854	13,973	2,865	2,884	2,865	3,075	2,581	3,091
1999-2000	14,081	8,235	14,588	2,882	2,922	2,881	3,224	2,808	3,237
2000-2001	15,000	9,067	15,470	2,993	3,000	2,993	3,374	2,722	3,392
2001-2002	15,742	10,076	16,211	3,104	2,633	3,109	3,567	3,116	3,576
2002-2003[1]	16,517	10,755	16,948	3,236	3,821	3,229	3,750	3,184	3,762

(1) Preliminary.

IT'S A FACT: About 63% of all undergraduates enrolled in U.S. colleges and universities in 2003-04 received some type of financial aid. About 51% of undergraduates received grants and about 35% took out student loans. The average amount of grants received was $4,000, and the average amount borrowed was $5,800.

Top 20 Colleges and Universities in Endowment Assets, 2004[1]

Source: *2004 NACUBO Endowment Study*, National Association of College and University Business Officers (NACUBO)

	College/University	Endowment assets[2]
1.	Harvard University	$22,143,649
2.	Yale University	12,747,150
3.	University of Texas System	10,336,687
4.	Princeton University	9,928,200
5.	Stanford University	9,922,000
6.	Massachusetts Institute of Technology	5,865,212
7.	University of California	4,767,466
8.	Emory University	4,535,587
9.	Columbia University	4,493,085
10.	The Texas A&M University System and Foundations	4,373,047
11.	University of Michigan	$4,163,382
12.	University of Pennsylvania	4,018,660
13.	Washington University	4,000,823
14.	Northwestern University	3,668,405
15.	University of Chicago	3,620,728
16.	Duke University	3,313,859
17.	Rice University	3,302,455
18.	Cornell University	3,238,350
19.	University of Notre Dame	3,095,703
20.	University of Virginia	2,793,225

NOTE: Market value of endowment assets, excluding pledges and working capital. (1) As of June 30, 2004. (2) In thousands.

U.S. Higher Education Trends: Bachelor's Degrees Conferred

Source: National Center for Education Statistics, U.S. Dept. of Education

Figures for 2002-2003 and 2009-2010 are projected.

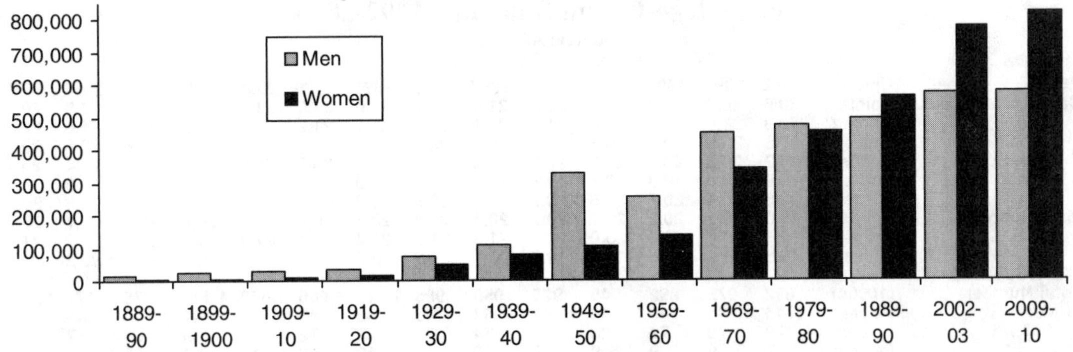

Financial Aid for College and Other Postsecondary Education

Reviewed by National Assoc. of Student Financial Aid Administrators

The cost of postsecondary education in the U.S. has increased in recent years, but financial aid, which may be in the form of **grants** (no repayment needed), **loans**, and/or **work-study** programs, is widely available to help families meet these expenses. Most aid is limited to family financial need as determined by standard formulas. Students interested in receiving aid are advised to apply, without making prior assumptions. Financial aid personnel at each school can provide information about programs available to students, steps to apply for them, and deadlines, all of which may vary.

All applicants for federal aid must file a Free Application for Federal Student Aid **(FAFSA)**, generally as soon as possible after Jan. 1 for the academic year starting the following September. Figures provided should agree with federal income tax forms filed for the previous year. Other possible sources of aid include state governments, employers and unions, civic organizations, and the institutions themselves. There are also special federal programs that pay for postsecondary education in return for service: AmeriCorps (phone: 1-800-942-2677) and ROTC (phone: 1-800-USA-ROTC). Additional forms and certain fees may be required if a student is to be considered for institutional aid. Aid must be reapplied for annually.

A **federal formula**, based on information provided on the FAFSA, takes into account such factors as family income in the preceding calendar year, parental and student assets (excluding the parents' home or farm), length of time to parents' retirement, and unusual expenses (such as very high medical expenses).

The resulting **Expected Family Contribution**, or EFC (which is divided among the family members—excluding parents—in college), is subtracted from the total cost of attendance for each person (including tuition and fee charges, room and board or allowance for living costs, books and supplies, transportation to and from school, and other miscellaneous costs) to determine financial need, and thus the maximum federal aid for which the family may be eligible. (Some institutions use a separate formula for need-based institutional aid.) Some schools guarantee to meet the full financial need of each admitted student; however, most others try to do so but may fall short, depending on the availability of funds. Outside scholarships (even if non-need-based) are taken into account in determining the amount of aid eligibility for federal, institutional, and state financial aid programs.

The **aid package** offered by each school may include one or more of the following resources: Federal Pell Grants, for those with greatest financial need; Federal Supplemental Educational Opportunity Grants, for those with great financial need who are also eligible for Pell Grants; grants from the school; Federal Work-Study or other work programs; low-interest Perkins loans; and subsidized and unsubsidized Stafford loans. Parents of undergraduates may also apply for a Federal PLUS loan. For unsubsidized Stafford loans and all PLUS loans to parents, need is not a requirement, but students and parents must still complete the FAFSA before eligibility for unsubsidized Stafford loans is determined.

Loans have varying interest rates and other requirements. Repayment of Perkins and Stafford loans does not begin until after graduation; deferments are available under certain circumstances. For PLUS loans, parents must pass a credit check and begin repayment of both principal and interest while the student is still in school.

Certain federal income **tax credits**—dollar for dollar reductions of the amount of tax due—are available to families who meet income and other requirements; see the chapter on Taxes.

Rules for financial aid are complex and changeable. *The Student Guide*, a comprehensive resource on financial aid from the U.S. Dept. of Education, can be found at the website www.studentaid.ed.gov/students/publications/student_guide/index.html

Further information and FAFSA forms are available from the school or from the Federal Student Aid Information Center, PO Box 84, Washington, DC 20044; phone: 1-800-4-FED-AID, Mon.-Fri., 8 AM - 12 midnight Eastern Time. The Information Center also has a free booklet called *The EFC Formula Book*. FAFSA forms can be obtained online at www.fafsa.ed.gov

Average Salaries of U.S. College Professors, 2004-2005

Source: American Association of University Professors

TEACHING LEVEL		MEN Type of institution Public	MEN Private/ Independent	MEN Church-related	WOMEN Type of institution Public	WOMEN Private/ Independent	WOMEN Church-related
Doctoral level	Professor	$99,685	$129,237	$108,589	$90,330	$118,237	$99,372
	Associate	70,400	84,298	75,584	65,279	78,852	70,878
	Assistant	60,631	73,571	63,245	55,234	66,283	58,974
Master's level	Professor	77,514	85,742	79,296	74,424	79,275	72,828
	Associate	62,034	65,682	62,060	59,437	62,381	58,920
	Assistant	52,290	54,036	51,327	50,123	51,876	48,664
General 4-year	Professor	72,729	86,716	64,652	67,673	82,788	61,668
	Associate	58,849	63,258	53,000	56,249	61,653	51,392
	Assistant	49,440	51,947	45,215	46,807	50,586	44,060
2-year	Professor	68,036	57,484	NA	64,447	56,403	NA
	Associate	54,912	50,015	NA	52,873	50,518	NA
	Assistant	48,366	42,455	NA	47,015	41,375	NA

NA = Not available.

ACT (formerly American College Testing) Mean Scores and Characteristics of College-Bound Students, 1992-2005

Source: ACT, Inc.
(for school year ending in year shown)

SCORES[1]	Unit[1]	1992	1993	1994	1995	1996	1997	1998	1999	2000	2001	2002	2003	2004	2005
Composite Scores	**Points**	**20.6**	**20.7**	**20.8**	**20.8**	**20.9**	**21.0**	**21.0**	**21.0**	**21.0**	**21.0**	**20.8**	**20.8**	**20.9**	**20.9**
Male	Points	20.9	21.0	20.9	21.0	21.0	21.1	21.2	21.1	21.2	21.1	20.9	21.0	21.0	21.1
Female	Points	20.5	20.5	20.7	20.7	20.8	20.8	20.9	20.9	20.9	20.9	20.7	20.8	20.9	20.9
English Score	**Points**	**20.2**	**20.3**	**20.3**	**20.2**	**20.3**	**20.3**	**20.4**	**20.5**	**20.5**	**20.5**	**20.2**	**20.3**	**20.4**	**20.4**
Male	Points	19.8	19.8	19.8	19.8	19.8	19.9	19.9	20.0	20.0	20.0	19.7	19.8	19.9	20.0
Female	Points	20.6	20.6	20.7	20.6	20.7	20.7	20.8	20.9	20.9	20.8	20.6	20.7	20.8	20.8
Math Score	**Points**	**20.0**	**20.1**	**20.2**	**20.2**	**20.2**	**20.6**	**20.8**	**20.7**	**20.7**	**20.7**	**20.6**	**20.6**	**20.7**	**20.7**
Male	Points	20.7	20.8	20.8	20.9	20.9	21.3	21.5	21.4	21.4	21.4	21.2	21.2	21.3	21.3
Female	Points	19.5	19.6	19.6	19.7	19.7	20.1	20.2	20.2	20.2	20.2	20.1	20.1	20.2	20.2
PARTICIPANTS															
Total Number	**(1000s)**	**832**	**875**	**892**	**945**	**925**	**959**	**995**	**1,019**	**1,065**	**1,070**	**1,116**	**1,175**	**1,171**	**1,186**
Male	Percent	45	45	45	44	44	44	43	43	43	43	44	44	43	44
White	Percent	79	79	79	80	79	74	76	72	72	71	69	68	67	66
Black	Percent	9	9	9	9	9	10	11	10	10	11	11	11	11	12
Hispanic	Percent	5	5	5	5	5	5	5	5	5	6	6	6	7	7
Composite Scores															
27 or above	Percent	12	12	13	13	13	14	14	14	14	14	13	14	14	14
18 or below	Percent	35	35	34	34	34	33	33	33	32	33	35	35	34	34

(1) Minimum point score, 1; maximum score, 36. Test scores and characteristics of college-bound students are based on the performance of all ACT-tested students who graduated in the spring of a given school year and took the ACT Assessment during junior or senior year of high school.

ACT Average Composite Scores by State, 2004-2005

Source: ACT, Inc.

STATE	Avg. Comp. Score	% Grads Taking ACT[1]	STATE	Avg. Comp. Score	% Grads Taking ACT[1]	STATE	Avg. Comp. Score	% Grads Taking ACT[1]
Alabama	20.2	77	Louisiana	19.8	85	Oklahoma	20.4	69
Alaska	21.3	26	Maine	22.4	10	Oregon	22.6	12
Arizona	21.5	19	Maryland	21.0	12	Pennsylvania	21.7	9
Arkansas	20.3	76	Masschusetts	22.8	12	Rhode Island	21.9	8
California	21.6	14	Michigan	21.4	69	South Carolina	19.4	38
Colorado	20.2	100	Minnesota	22.3	68	South Dakota	21.5	76
Connecticut	22.8	10	Mississippi	18.7	94	Tennessee	20.5	92
Delaware	20.8	4	Missouri	21.6	70	Texas	20.2	29
District of Columbia	18.0	29	Montana	21.8	57	Utah	21.5	68
Florida	20.4	41	Nebraska	21.8	76	Vermont	22.6	16
Georgia	20.0	29	Nevada	21.5	28	Virginia	20.8	14
Hawaii	21.9	16	New Hampshire	22.3	10	Washington	22.7	16
Idaho	21.3	58	New Jersey	21.3	6	West Virginia	20.4	65
Illinois	20.3	100	New Mexico	20.0	61	Wisconsin	22.2	69
Indiana	21.7	21	New York	22.4	17	Wyoming	21.4	69
Iowa	22.0	66	North Carolina	20.2	15			
Kansas	21.7	76	North Dakota	21.3	82			
Kentucky	20.4	76	Ohio	21.4	66	**U.S. AVG.**	**20.9**	**40**

(1) Based on number of high school graduates in 2005, as projected by the Western Interstate Commission for Higher Education, and number of students in the class of 2005 who took the ACT.

SAT Mean Verbal and Math Scores of College-Bound Seniors, 1975-2005

Source: The College Board
(recentered scale; for school year ending in year shown)

	1975	1980	1985	1990	1995	1998	1999	2000	2001	2002	2003	2004	2005
Verbal Scores	**512**	**502**	**509**	**500**	**504**	**505**	**505**	**505**	**506**	**504**	**507**	**508**	**508**
Male	515	506	514	505	505	509	509	507	509	507	512	512	513
Female	509	498	503	496	502	502	502	504	502	502	503	504	505
Math Scores	**498**	**492**	**500**	**501**	**506**	**512**	**511**	**514**	**514**	**516**	**519**	**518**	**520**
Male	518	515	522	521	525	531	531	533	533	534	537	537	538
Female	479	473	480	483	490	496	495	498	498	500	503	501	504

NOTE: In 1995, the College Board recentered the scoring scale for the SAT by reestablishing the original mean score of 500 on the 200-800 scale. Earlier scores have been adjusted to account for this recentering.

SAT Mean Scores by State, 1990 and 2000-2005

Source: The College Board

(recentered scale; for school year ending in year shown)

	1990		2000		2001		2002		2003		2004		2005		% Grads Taking
STATE	V	M	V	M	V	M	V	M	V	M	V	M	V	M	SAT[1]
Alabama	545	534	559	555	559	554	560	559	559	552	560	553	567	559	10%
Alaska	514	501	519	515	514	510	516	519	518	518	518	514	523	519	52%
Arizona	521	520	521	523	523	525	520	523	524	525	523	524	526	530	33%
Arkansas	545	532	563	554	562	550	560	556	564	554	569	555	563	552	6%
California	494	508	497	518	498	517	496	517	499	519	501	519	504	522	50%
Colorado	533	534	534	537	539	542	543	548	551	553	554	553	560	560	26%
Connecticut	506	496	508	509	509	510	509	509	512	514	515	515	517	517	86%
Delaware	510	496	502	496	501	499	502	500	501	501	500	499	503	502	74%
District of Columbia	483	467	494	486	482	474	480	473	484	474	489	476	490	478	79%
Florida	495	493	498	500	498	499	496	499	498	498	499	499	498	498	65%
Georgia	478	473	488	486	491	489	489	491	493	491	494	493	497	496	75%
Hawaii	480	505	488	519	486	515	488	520	486	516	487	514	490	516	61%
Idaho	542	524	540	541	543	542	539	541	540	540	540	539	544	542	21%
Illinois	542	547	568	586	576	589	578	596	583	596	585	597	594	606	10%
Indiana	486	486	498	501	499	501	498	503	500	504	501	506	504	508	66%
Iowa	584	588	589	600	593	603	591	602	586	597	593	602	596	608	5%
Kansas	566	563	574	580	577	580	578	580	578	582	584	585	585	588	9%
Kentucky	548	541	548	550	550	550	550	552	554	552	559	557	561	559	12%
Louisiana	551	537	562	558	564	562	561	559	563	559	564	561	565	562	8%
Maine	501	490	504	500	506	500	503	502	503	501	505	501	509	505	75%
Maryland	506	502	507	509	508	510	507	513	509	515	511	515	511	515	71%
Massachusetts	503	498	511	513	511	515	512	516	516	522	518	523	520	527	86%
Michigan	529	534	557	569	561	572	558	572	564	576	563	573	568	579	10%
Minnesota	552	558	581	594	580	589	581	591	582	591	587	593	592	597	11%
Mississippi	552	538	562	549	566	551	559	547	565	551	562	547	564	554	4%
Missouri	548	541	572	577	577	577	574	580	582	583	587	585	588	588	7%
Montana	540	542	543	546	539	539	541	547	538	543	537	539	540	540	31%
Nebraska	559	562	560	571	562	568	561	570	573	578	569	576	574	579	8%
Nevada	511	511	510	517	509	515	509	518	510	517	507	514	508	513	39%
New Hampshire	518	510	520	519	520	516	519	519	522	521	522	521	525	525	81%
New Jersey	495	498	498	513	499	513	498	513	501	515	501	514	503	517	86%
New Mexico	554	546	549	543	551	542	551	543	548	540	554	543	558	547	13%
New York	489	496	494	506	495	505	494	506	496	510	497	510	497	511	92%
North Carolina	478	470	492	496	493	499	493	505	495	506	499	507	499	511	74%
North Dakota	579	578	588	609	592	599	597	610	602	613	582	601	590	605	4%
Ohio	526	522	533	539	534	539	533	540	536	541	538	542	539	543	29%
Oklahoma	553	542	563	560	567	561	565	562	569	562	569	566	570	563	7%
Oregon	515	509	527	527	526	526	524	528	526	527	527	528	526	528	59%
Pennsylvania	497	490	498	497	500	499	498	500	500	502	501	502	501	503	75%
Rhode Island	498	488	505	500	501	499	504	503	502	504	503	502	503	505	72%
South Carolina	475	467	484	482	486	488	488	493	493	496	491	495	494	499	64%
South Dakota	580	570	587	588	577	582	576	586	588	588	594	597	589	589	5%
Tennessee	558	544	563	553	562	553	562	555	568	560	567	557	572	563	16%
Texas	490	489	493	500	493	499	491	500	500	491	493	499	493	502	54%
Utah	566	555	570	569	575	570	563	559	566	559	565	556	566	557	7%
Vermont	507	493	513	508	511	506	512	510	515	512	516	512	521	517	67%
Virginia	501	496	509	500	510	501	510	506	514	510	515	509	516	514	73%
Washington	513	511	526	528	527	527	525	529	530	532	528	531	532	534	55%
West Virginia	520	514	526	511	527	512	525	515	522	510	524	514	523	511	20%
Wisconsin	552	559	584	597	584	596	583	599	585	594	587	596	592	599	6%
Wyoming	534	538	545	545	547	545	531	537	548	549	551	546	544	543	12%
NATIONAL AVG.	**500**	**501**	**505**	**514**	**506**	**514**	**504**	**516**	**507**	**519**	**508**	**518**	**508**	**520**	**49%**

NOTE: In 1995, the College Board recentered the scoring scale for the SAT by reestablishing the original mean score of 500 on the 200-800 scale. The College Board states that comparing states or ranking them on the basis of SAT scores alone is invalid, and the College Board discourages doing so. (1) Based on number of high school graduates in 2005, as projected by the Western Interstate Commission for Higher Education, and number of students in the class of 2005 who took the SAT.

Average SAT Scores by Parental Education, 2005

Source: The College Board

(Deviation in points from mean score shown by highest level of educational attainment of test taker's parent. Mean 2005 verbal score was 508. Mean 2005 math score was 520.)

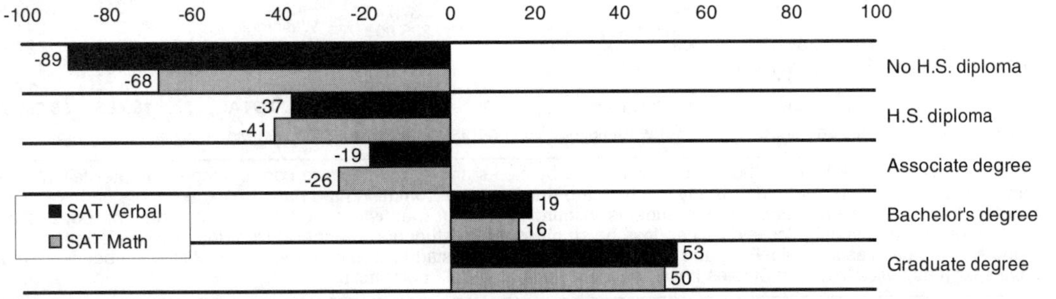

Top 100 Libraries in U.S. by Volumes Held, 2003

Source: American Library Association, *ALA Library Fact Sheet 22*, August 2005

	Institution	Volumes Held*
1.	Library of Congress	29,550,914
2.	Harvard University	15,181,349
3.	Boston Public Library	14,933,349
4.	Yale University	11,114,308
5.	Chicago Public Library	10,745,608
6.	University of Illinois - Urbana-Champaign	10,015,321
7.	Public Library of Cincinnati & Hamilton County	9,885,359
8.	Queens Borough Public Library	9,691,126
9.	University of California - Berkeley	9,572,462
10.	County of Los Angeles Public Library	9,185,321
11.	University of Texas - Austin	8,322,944
12.	Stanford University	8,000,000
13.	University of Michigan	7,800,389
14.	Columbia University	7,697,488
15.	University of California - Los Angeles	7,576,790
16.	Detroit Public Library	7,265,306
17.	University of Wisconsin - Madison	7,232,850
18.	Cornell University	7,120,301
19.	University of Chicago	6,977,186
20.	New York Public Library	6,777,587
21.	Indiana University	6,647,355
22.	University of Washington	6,436,960
23.	Free Library of Philadelphia	6,388,077
24.	Princeton University	6,224,270
25.	University of Minnesota	6,200,669
26.	Dallas Public Library	5,916,549
27.	Brooklyn Public Library	5,845,212
28.	Ohio State University	5,674,784
29.	Los Angeles Public Library	5,554,904
30.	University of North Carolina - Chapel Hill	5,492,451
31.	Duke University	5,360,303
32.	University of Pennsylvania	5,273,887
33.	University of Arizona	5,040,584
34.	University of Virginia	4,921,442
35.	Pennsylvania State University Libraries	4,779,165
36.	Michigan State University	4,582,004
37.	University of Oklahoma	4,427,670
38.	University of Pittsburgh	4,420,970
39.	University of Iowa	4,380,734
40.	Houston Public Library	4,339,128
41.	Northwestern University Library	4,315,314
42.	King County Library System	4,213,810
43.	New York University	4,176,065
44.	Rutgers University	4,050,009
45.	University of Florida	4,021,629
46.	Cleveland Public Library	3,999,771
47.	Miami-Dade Public Library System	3,998,192
48.	University of Kansas	3,980,589
49.	University of Georgia	3,955,004
50.	Arizona State University Libraries	3,856,561
51.	University of Southern California	3,800,702
52.	Washington University - St. Louis	3,608,538
53.	Johns Hopkins University	3,572,375
54.	Buffalo & Erie County Public Library	3,539,038
55.	Cuyahoga County Public Library	3,465,469
56.	University of South Carolina	3,374,496
57.	Brigham Young University	3,373,793
58.	University of California - Davis	3,365,689
59.	St. Louis Public Library	3,360,942
60.	State University of New York - Buffalo	3,330,476
61.	Wayne State University	3,323,580
62.	University of Colorado	3,314,432
63.	University of Hawaii	3,294,184
64.	Hawaii State Public Library System	3,281,117
65.	Brown University	3,257,242
66.	North Carolina State University	3,236,096
67.	Louisiana State University	3,213,314
68.	University of Rochester	3,185,231
69.	San Diego Public Library	3,169,565
70.	University of Connecticut	3,168,617
71.	University of Missouri - Columbia	3,149,211
72.	University of Massachusetts	3,132,418
73.	University of Utah	3,128,547
74.	Mid-Continent Public Library	3,120,544
75.	University of Notre Dame	3,054,075
76.	University of Kentucky	3,053,726
77.	University of Maryland	3,016,940
78.	Texas A&M University Libraries	3,016,358
79.	Milwaukee Public Library	2,989,081
80.	University of Cincinnati Libraries	2,977,475
81.	Montgomery County Dept. of Public Libraries	2,959,184
82.	Columbus Metropolitan Library	2,955,569
83.	University of California - San Diego	2,953,024
84.	Enoch Pratt Free Library	2,906,821
85.	Temple University	2,900,832
86.	Syracuse University	2,900,448
87.	Vanderbilt University	2,882,057
88.	University of Tennessee - Knoxville	2,880,949
89.	Broward County Libraries Division	2,825,077
90.	Orange County Public Library	2,794,942
91.	Southern Illinois University - Carbondale	2,791,775
92.	St. Louis County Library District	2,781,301
93.	University of Nebraska - Lincoln	2,767,320
94.	University of California - Santa Barbara	2,765,756
95.	Emory University	2,755,929
96.	Auburn University	2,724,011
97.	Fairfax County Public Library	2,712,212
98.	Massachusetts Institute of Technology	2,707,849
99.	Toledo-Lucas County Public Library	2,689,922
100.	Kent State University Libraries	2,634,374

*Figures for public libraries include holdings by branches and include circulating books only.

Number of Public Libraries and Operating Income, by State, 2002

Source: Public Libraries Survey, National Center for Education Statistics, U.S. Dept. of Education
(data for fiscal year 2002; operating income in thousands)

STATE	No. of libraries(1)	Operating income(2)
Alabama	282	$71,059
Alaska	102	24,139
Arizona	176	122,036
Arkansas	210	40,042
California	1,074	959,701
Colorado	243	181,292
Connecticut	242	151,858
Delaware	33	17,553
District of Columbia	27	28,413
Florida	478	422,470
Georgia	366	155,492
Hawaii	50	25,414
Idaho	142	27,048
Illinois	788	581,222
Indiana	432	258,505
Iowa	562	77,008
Kansas	376	83,344
Kentucky	189	$87,316
Louisiana	329	122,029
Maine	281	29,586
Maryland	176	192,316
Massachusetts	489	238,952
Michigan	659	335,297
Minnesota	359	161,240
Mississippi	240	37,985
Missouri	365	159,964
Montana	108	18,831
Nebraska	291	39,232
Nevada	86	62,644
New Hampshire	237	37,743
New Jersey	457	335,803
New Mexico	113	29,070
New York	1,088	884,665
North Carolina	381	155,205
North Dakota	90	9,173
Ohio	717	$645,383
Oklahoma	205	66,313
Oregon	209	120,079
Pennsylvania	628	292,397
Rhode Island	72	39,904
South Carolina	184	79,675
South Dakota	144	17,194
Tennessee	287	81,765
Texas	848	337,926
Utah	108	62,314
Vermont	192	13,702
Virginia	341	203,157
Washington	325	241,379
West Virginia	176	27,259
Wisconsin	455	176,262
Wyoming	74	17,279
U.S. TOTAL	**16,486**	**$8,585,738**

(1) Includes central libraries and branches. (2) Some totals may be underestimated because of nonresponse.

IT'S A FACT: Back in the 1700s red ink was used by clerks and accountants to correct ledgers. It later fell into the hands of schoolteachers. But today, many teachers are moving away from using red pens to grade papers on the ground that red is too negative and stressful for students. According to color theorists, purple has the authority of red, and the serenity of blue and should convey a nicer, less harsh message to students. Teacher-driven demand has led major pen manufacturers such as Bic, Pilot Pen, and Sanford to make purple a standard color in their product lines. In addition, retail chains such as Office Max and Staples have begun stocking all-purple-pen packs.

Four-Year Colleges and Universities

General Information for the 2004-2005 Academic Year

Note: These listings **include only accredited degree-granting institutions** in the U.S. and the U.S. territories **with a total enrollment of 1,000 or more**. Only **four-year** colleges and universities (which award a bachelor's degree as their highest undergraduate degree) are included. Data reported **only for institutions that provided updated information** on Peterson's Annual Survey of Undergraduate Institutions for the 2004-2005 academic year.

All institutions are coeducational except those where the ZIP code is followed directly by a number in parentheses. (1) = men only, (2) = primarily men, (3) = women only, (4) = primarily women.

The **Tuition & Fees** column shows the annual tuition and required fees for full-time students, or, where indicated, the tuition and standard fees per unit for part-time students. Where tuition varies according to residence, the figure is given for the most local resident and is coded: (A) = area residents, (S) = state residents; all other figures apply to all students regardless of residence. Where annual expenses are expressed as a lump sum (including full-time tuition, mandatory fees, and room and board), the figure is entered under Tuition & Fees and coded: (C) = comprehensive fee. **Rm. & Board** is the average cost for one academic year. * indicates fee only.

Control: 1 = independent (nonprofit), 2 = independent-religious, 3 = proprietary (profit-making), 4 = federal, 5 = state, 6 = commonwealth (Puerto Rico), 7 = territory (U.S. territories), 8 = county, 9 = district, 10 = city, 11 = state and local, 12 = state-related, 13 = private (unspecified). **Degree** means the highest degree offered (B = bachelor's, M = master's, F = first professional, D = doctorate).

Enrollment is the total number of matriculated undergraduate and (if applicable) graduate students.

Faculty is the total number of faculty members teaching undergraduate courses and (if available) graduate courses.

NA or a **dash** indicates category is inapplicable or data not available. **NR** indicates data not reported.

Name, address	Year Founded	Tuition & Fees	Rm. & Board	Control, Degree	Enroll-ment	Faculty
Abilene Christian Univ, Abilene, TX 79699-9100	1906	$14,200	$5,270	2-D	4,761	347
Acad of Art Univ, San Francisco, CA 94105-3410	1929	$13,280	$12,000	3-M	6,706	651
Adams State Coll, Alamosa, CO 81102	1921	$2,603 (S)	$9,240	5-M	6,111	211
Adelphi Univ, Garden City, NY 11530	1896	$18,700	$8,500	1-D	7,592	751
Adrian Coll, Adrian, MI 49221-2575	1859	$17,600	$5,770	2-B	1,013	104
Agnes Scott Coll, Decatur, GA 30030-3797 (3)	1889	$22,210	$8,200	2-M	1,002	103
Alabama Agr & Mech Univ, Huntsville, AL 35811	1875	$4,420 (S)	$3,498	5-D	6,323	384
Alabama State Univ, Montgomery, AL 36101-0271	1867	$4,008 (S)	$3,700	5-D	5,653	396
Albany State Univ, Albany, GA 31705-2717	1903	$2,896 (S)	$3,690	5-M	3,668	211
Albertus Magnus Coll, New Haven, CT 06511-1189	1925	$16,858	$7,550	2-M	2,361	201
Albion Coll, Albion, MI 49224-1831	1835	$22,918	$6,536	2-B	1,867	169
Albright Coll, Reading, PA 19612-5234	1856	$24,580	$7,510	2-M	2,243	156
Alcorn State Univ, Alcorn State, MS 39096-7500	1871	$4,465 (S)	$4,012	5-M	3,443	224
Alfred Univ, Alfred, NY 14802-1205	1836	$20,060	$9,374	1-D	2,355	212
Allegheny Coll, Meadville, PA 16335	1815	$26,950	$6,550	1-B	1,955	165
Alliant Intl Univ, San Diego, CA 92131-1799	1952	$19,360	$7,430	1-D	3,556	589
Alma Coll, Alma, MI 48801-1599	1886	$19,986	$7,032	2-B	1,268	125
Alvernia Coll, Reading, PA 19607-1799	1958	$17,675	$7,330	2-M	2,380	133
Alverno Coll, Milwaukee, WI 53234-3922 (3)	1887	$14,410	$5,400	2-M	2,241	218
Amberton Univ, Garland, TX 75041-5595	1971	$6,000	NA	2-M	1,648	39
Amer Coll of Comp & Info Sci, Birmingham, AL 35205 (2)	1988	$155/cr. hr.	NA	3-M	15,722	37
Amer InterContinental Univ, Los Angeles, CA 90066	1982	$16,190	$5,500	3-M	1,405	133
Amer InterContinental Univ, Weston, FL 33326	NA	$58,500	NA	3-M	1,939	92
Amer InterContinental Univ, Atlanta, GA 30326-1016	1977	$15,525	$4,500	3-M	1,732	111
Amer InterContinental Univ, Atlanta, GA 30328	1970	$17,945	NA	3-M	1,150	119
Amer Intl Coll, Springfield, MA 01109-3189	1885	$18,000	$8,500	1-D	1,625	163
Amer Publ Univ Syst, Charles Town, WV 25414	1991	$6,000	NA	3-M	9,716	342
Amer Univ, Washington, DC 20016-8001	1893	$26,307	$10,260	2-D	11,185	914
Amer Univ of Puerto Rico, Bayamón, PR 00960-2037	1963	$4,590	NA	1-B	3,691	221
Amherst Coll, Amherst, MA 01002-5000	1821	$31,364	$8,160	1-B	1,638	218
Anderson Coll, Anderson, SC 29621-4035	1911	$15,200	$6,050	2-B	1,666	151
Anderson Univ, Anderson, IN 46012-3495	1917	$18,900	$6,150	2-D	2,677	208
Andrews Univ, Berrien Springs, MI 49104	1874	$16,506	$5,280	2-D	3,017	301
Angelo State Univ, San Angelo, TX 76909	1928	$3,126 (S)	$4,696	5-M	6,137	337
Anna Maria Coll, Paxton, MA 01612	1946	$20,135	$7,415	2-M	1,108	156
Appalachian State Univ, Boone, NC 28608	1899	$3,351 (S)	$5,270	5-D	14,653	946
Aquinas Coll, Grand Rapids, MI 49506-1799	1886	$16,992	$5,600	2-M	2,235	221
Arcadia Univ, Glenside, PA 19038-3295	1853	$24,270	$9,300	2-D	3,391	347
Argosy Univ/Schaumburg, Schaumburg, IL 60173	1979	$360/cr. hr.	NA	3-D	NA	NA
Argosy Univ/Twin Cities, Eagan, MN 55121	1961	$12,220	NA	3-D	1,580	140
Argosy Univ/Twin Cities, Eagan, MN 55121 (4)	1987	$11,600	NA	3-D	1,334	140
Arizona State Univ, Tempe, AZ 85287	1885	$4,064 (S)	$6,574	5-D	49,171	2,184
Arizona State Univ East, Mesa, AZ 85212	1995	$4,015 (S)	$5,155	5-M	3,983	121
Arizona State Univ West, Phoenix, AZ 85069-7100	1984	$4,064 (S)	$4,455	5-M	7,348	356
Arkansas State Univ, State University, AR 72467	1909	$5,155 (S)	$4,000	5-D	10,508	621
Arkansas Tech Univ, Russellville, AR 72801	1909	$4,468 (S)	$3,841	5-M	6,483	367
Armstrong Atlantic State Univ, Savannah, GA 31419-1997	1935	$2,734 (S)	$4,500	5-M	6,653	408
Art Ctr Coll of Design, Pasadena, CA 91103-1999	1930	$25,044	NA	1-M	1,519	407
Art Inst of Atlanta, Atlanta, GA 30328	1949	$17,040	$7,311	3-B	2,651	165
Art Inst of Boston at Lesley Univ, Boston, MA 02215-2598	1912	$19,600	$9,950	1-M	6,521	185
Art Inst of California-Los Angeles, Santa Monica, CA 90405-3035	NA	$18,336	$8,379	3-B	2,106	142
Art Inst of California-Orange Cty, Santa Ana, CA 92704-9888	2000	$388/qtr hr.	$9,920	3-B	1,833	126
Art Inst of California-San Diego, San Diego, CA 92121	1981	$18,936	$9,200	3-B	1,708	113
Art Inst of California-San Francisco, San Francisco, CA 94102-4908	1939	$18,486	NA	3-B	1,347	108
Art Inst of Colorado, Denver, CO 80203	1952	$23,040	$5,985	3-B	2,226	135
Art Inst of Dallas, Dallas, TX 75231-9959	1978	$16,855	NA	3-B	1,418	75
Art Inst of Fort Lauderdale, Fort Lauderdale, FL 33316-3000	1968	$16,425	$4,785	3-B	3,500	148
Art Inst of Houston, Houston, TX 77056-4115	1978	$16,740	$4,545	3-B	1,647	95
Art Inst of Phoenix, Phoenix, AZ 85021-2859	1995	$16,752	$6,620	3-B	1,297	86
Art Inst of Pittsburgh, Pittsburgh, PA 15219	1921	$21,965	$6,900	3-B	4,872	136
Art Inst of Portland, Portland, OR 97209	1963	$16,610	$5,355	3-B	1,543	131
Art Inst of Seattle, Seattle, WA 98121-1642	1982	$16,020	$8,355	3-B	2,492	162
Art Inst of Washington, Arlington, VA 22209	2000	$17,472	$8,160	3-B	1,000	64
Art Institutes Intl Minnesota, Minneapolis, MN 55402-3137	1964	$16,944	$6,864	3-B	1,391	76

Name, address	Year Founded	Tuition & Fees	Rm. & Board	Control, Degree	Enroll-ment	Faculty
Asbury Coll, Wilmore, KY 40390-1198	1890	$17,808	$4,498	2-M	1,278	154
Ashland Univ, Ashland, OH 44805-3702	1878	$19,778	$7,314	2-D	6,922	590
Assumption Coll, Worcester, MA 01609-1296	1904	$22,655	$5,395	2-M	2,452	217
Athens State Univ, Athens, AL 35611-1902	1822	$3,870 (S)	$900	5-B	2,577	172
Auburn Univ, Auburn University, AL 36849	1856	$4,828 (S)	$6,686	5-D	22,928	1,320
Auburn Univ Montgomery, Montgomery, AL 36124-4023	1967	$4,460 (S)	$5,780	5-D	5,123	327
Augsburg Coll, Minneapolis, MN 55454-1351	1869	$20,758	$6,080	2-M	3,375	315
Augustana Coll, Rock Island, IL 61201-2296	1860	$22,131	$6,042	2-B	2,309	223
Augustana Coll, Sioux Falls, SD 57197	1860	$18,860	$5,334	2-M	1,799	176
Augusta State Univ, Augusta, GA 30904-2200	1925	$2,702 (S)	NA	5-M	6,353	322
Aurora Univ, Aurora, IL 60506-4892	1893	$15,600	$6,840	1-D	3,326	287
Austin Coll, Sherman, TX 75090-4400	1849	$20,495	$7,376	2-M	1,323	132
Austin Peay State Univ, Clarksville, TN 37044-0001	1927	$4,224 (S)	$4,296	5-M	8,650	462
Averett Univ, Danville, VA 24541-3692	1859	$18,430	$6,330	2-M	2,719	270
Avila Univ, Kansas City, MO 64145-1698	1916	$15,870	$5,400	2-M	2,104	224
Azusa Pacific Univ, Azusa, CA 91702-7000	1899	$20,666	$6,132	2-D	8,162	356
Babson Coll, Babson Park, MA 02457-0310	1919	$28,832	$10,376	1-M	3,288	232
Baker Coll of Allen Park, Allen Park, MI 48101 (4)	2003	$6,120	NA	1-B	1,033	88
Baker Coll of Auburn Hills, Auburn Hills, MI 48326-1586	1911	$6,120	NA	1-B	3,488	155
Baker Coll of Cadillac, Cadillac, MI 49601	1986	$6,120	NA	1-B	1,546	105
Baker Coll of Clinton Township, Clinton Township, MI 48035-4701	1990	$6,120	NA	1-B	4,823	208
Baker Coll of Flint, Flint, MI 48507-5508	1911	$6,120	$2,600	1-B	6,034	315
Baker Coll of Jackson, Jackson, MI 49202	1994	$6,120	NA	1-B	1,603	85
Baker Coll of Muskegon, Muskegon, MI 49442-3497	1888	$6,120	$2,400	1-B	4,433	177
Baker Coll of Owosso, Owosso, MI 48867-4400	1984	$6,120	$2,400	1-B	2,716	144
Baker Coll of Port Huron, Port Huron, MI 48060-2597	1990	$6,120	NA	1-B	1,505	126
Baldwin-Wallace Coll, Berea, OH 44017-2088	1845	$19,494	$6,418	2-M	4,600	399
Ball State Univ, Muncie, IN 47306-1099	1918	$6,260 (S)	$6,228	5-D	20,544	1,169
Bard Coll, Annandale-on-Hudson, NY 12504	1860	$30,742	$9,418	1-D	1,726	208
Barnard Coll, New York, NY 10027-6598 (3)	1889	$28,340	$10,800	1-B	2,287	296
Barry Univ, Miami Shores, FL 33161-6695	1940	$22,430	$7,620	2-D	9,207	910
Barton Coll, Wilson, NC 27893-7000	1902	$16,670	$5,800	2-B	1,231	109
Bates Coll, Lewiston, ME 04240-6028	1855	$39,900 (C)	NA	1-B	1,743	189
Bayamón Central Univ, Bayamón, PR 00960-1725	1970	$4,440	NA	2-M	3,311	218
Baylor Univ, Waco, TX 76798	1845	$21,070	$6,485	2-D	13,799	883
Bay Path Coll, Longmeadow, MA 01106-2292 (3)	1897	$19,440	$8,260	1-M	1,417	127
Becker Coll, Worcester, MA 01609	1784	$17,590	$8,000	1-B	1,660	103
Belhaven Coll, Jackson, MS 39202-1789	1883	$14,050	$5,430	2-M	2,505	263
Bellarmine Univ, Louisville, KY 40205-0671	1950	$21,530	$6,380	2-D	3,134	251
Bellevue Univ, Bellevue, NE 68005-3098	1965	$4,740	NA	1-M	5,524	351
Belmont Univ, Nashville, TN 37212-3757	1951	$16,220	$6,156	2-D	3,941	437
Beloit Coll, Beloit, WI 53511-5596	1846	$25,736	$5,696	1-B	1,389	126
Bemidji State Univ, Bemidji, MN 56601-2699	1919	$6,404 (S)	$5,012	5-M	4,971	362
Benedict Coll, Columbia, SC 29204	1870	$11,586	$5,434	2-B	3,005	168
Benedictine Coll, Atchison, KS 66002-1499	1859	$15,126	$6,128	2-M	1,441	99
Benedictine Univ, Lisle, IL 60532-0900	1887	$18,310	$6,290	2-D	3,232	368
Bentley Coll, Waltham, MA 02452-4705	1917	$27,244	$9,860	1-M	5,601	453
Berea Coll, Berea, KY 40404	1855	$516	$4,748	1-B	1,556	160
Bernard M. Baruch Coll of the City Univ of New York, New York, NY 10010-5585	1919	$4,300 (S)	NA	11-D	15,537	921
Berry Coll, Mount Berry, GA 30149-0159	1902	$16,240	$6,450	2-M	2,008	167
Bethel Coll, Mishawaka, IN 46545-5591	1947	$15,360	$4,880	2-M	1,847	143
Bethel Coll, McKenzie, TN 38201	1842	$9,630	$5,384	2-F	1,297	74
Bethel Univ, St. Paul, MN 55112-6999	1871	$21,300	$6,800	2-M	3,605	284
Bethune-Cookman Coll, Daytona Beach, FL 32114-3099	1904	$10,610	$6,374	2-B	2,895	194
Biola Univ, La Mirada, CA 90639-0001	1908	$22,702	$7,100	2-D	5,370	378
Birmingham-Southern Coll, Birmingham, AL 35254	1856	$21,055	$7,080	2-M	1,453	124
Black Hills State Univ, Spearfish, SD 57799	1883	$4,820 (S)	$3,449	5-M	3,846	194
Bloomfield Coll, Bloomfield, NJ 07003-9981	1868	$15,100	$7,400	2-B	2,166	202
Bloomsburg Univ of Pennsylvania, Bloomsburg, PA 17815-1301	1839	$6,089 (S)	$5,200	5-D	8,304	395
Bluefield State Coll, Bluefield, WV 24701-2198	1895	$3,114 (S)	NA	5-B	3,506	266
Bluffton Univ, Bluffton, OH 45817	1899	$18,350	$6,304	2-M	1,191	115
Boise State Univ, Boise, ID 83725-0399	1932	$3,520 (S)	$5,384	5-D	18,332	1,138
Boricua Coll, New York, NY 10032-1560	1974	$7,300	NA	1-M	1,520	116
Boston Coll, Chestnut Hill, MA 02467-3800	1863	$29,396	$9,620	2-D	13,814	1,201
Boston Univ, Boston, MA 02215	1839	$30,402	$9,680	1-D	29,596	3,514
Bowdoin Coll, Brunswick, ME 04011	1794	$31,626	$8,054	1-B	1,677	183
Bowie State Univ, Bowie, MD 20715-9465	1865	$6,846 (S)	$8,674	5-D	5,415	351
Bowling Green State Univ, Bowling Green, OH 43403	1910	$8,072 (S)	$6,588	5-D	18,989	1,050
Bradley Univ, Peoria, IL 61625-0002	1897	$17,730	$6,150	1-M	6,069	532
Brandeis Univ, Waltham, MA 02454-9110	1948	$31,072	$8,656	1-D	5,072	441
Brewton-Parker Coll, Mt. Vernon, GA 30445-0197	1904	$12,600	$5,200	2-B	1,136	117
Briarcliffe Coll, Bethpage, NY 11714	1966	$15,008	$7,350	3-B	3,227	191
Briar Cliff Univ, Sioux City, IA 51104-0100	1930	$16,995	$5,433	2-M	1,116	59
Bridgewater Coll, Bridgewater, VA 22812-1599	1880	$18,990	$8,800	2-B	1,532	124
Bridgewater State Coll, Bridgewater, MA 02325-0001	1840	$5,296 (S)	$6,512	5-M	9,626	494
Brigham Young Univ-Hawaii, Laie, HI 96762-1294	1955	$2,660	$4,800	2-B	2,486	224
Brigham Young Univ, Provo, UT 84602-1001	1875	$4,920	$5,570	2-D	34,609	1,744
Brooklyn Coll of the City Univ of New York, Brooklyn, NY 11210-2889	1930	$4,353 (S)	NA	11-M	15,384	1,066
Brooks Inst of Photog, Santa Barbara, CA 93108-2399	1945	$20,250	NA	3-M	1,507	39
Brown Univ, Providence, RI 02912	1764	$31,573	$8,474	1-D	8,004	796
Bryant Univ, Smithfield, RI 02917-1284	1863	$24,762	$9,568	1-M	3,518	256
Bryn Mawr Coll, Bryn Mawr, PA 19010-2899 (3)	1885	$28,630	$9,700	1-D	1,772	196
Bucknell Univ, Lewisburg, PA 17837	1846	$32,788	$6,872	1-M	3,609	322
Buena Vista Univ, Storm Lake, IA 50588	1891	$20,854	$5,822	2-M	1,316	121
Buffalo State Coll, State Univ of New York, Buffalo, NY 14222-1095	1867	$5,137 (S)	$6,200	5-M	11,072	715
Butler Univ, Indianapolis, IN 46208-3485	1855	$22,484	$7,780	1-F	4,415	435
Cabrini Coll, Radnor, PA 19087-3698	1957	$22,250	$8,980	2-M	2,176	216
Caldwell Coll, Caldwell, NJ 07006-6195	1939	$18,950	$7,500	2-M	2,175	184
California Baptist Univ, Riverside, CA 92504-3206	1950	$15,940	$6,310	2-M	2,905	207
California Coll for Health Sci, Salt Lake City, UT 84107	1978	$13,975	NA	3-M	5,458	34
California Coll of the Arts, San Francisco, CA 94107	1907	$24,640	$8,230	1-M	1,587	339
California Inst of Tech, Pasadena, CA 91125-0001	1891	$25,551	$8,013	1-D	2,172	324

Name, address	Year Founded	Tuition & Fees	Rm. & Board	Control, Degree	Enroll-ment	Faculty
California Inst of the Arts, Valencia, CA 91355-2340	1961	$27,260	$7,697	1-M	1,325	274
California Lutheran Univ, Thousand Oaks, CA 91360-2787	1959	$22,285	$7,570	2-D	3,019	256
California Polytechnic State Univ, San Luis Obispo, San Luis Obispo, CA 93407	1901	$3,972 (S)	$8,146	5-M	17,582	1,182
California State Polytechnic Univ, Pomona, Pomona, CA 91768-2557	1938	$2,832 (S)	$7,212	5-M	19,002	1,012
California State Univ, Bakersfield, Bakersfield, CA 93311-1022	1970	$2,959 (S)	$5,946	5-M	7,924	515
California State Univ, Chico, Chico, CA 95929-0722	1887	$3,154 (S)	$7,493	5-M	15,734	857
California State Univ, Dominguez Hills, Carson, CA 90747-0001	1960	$2,478 (S)	$5,022	5-M	12,613	678
California State Univ, East Bay, Hayward, CA 94542-3000	1957	$2,706 (S)	$3,705	5-M	13,061	741
California State Univ, Fresno, Fresno, CA 93740-8027	1911	$2,704 (S)	$7,073	5-D	19,781	1,113
California State Univ, Fullerton, Fullerton, CA 92834-9480	1957	$2,804 (S)	$4,356	5-M	32,744	1,856
California State Univ, Long Beach, Long Beach, CA 90840	1949	$2,864 (S)	$6,530	5-M	33,479	1,846
California State Univ, Los Angeles, Los Angeles, CA 90032-8530	1947	$3,034 (S)	$3,338	5-D	20,637	1,062
California State Univ, Monterey Bay, Seaside, CA 93955-8001	1994	$2,947 (S)	$6,900	5-M	3,020	280
California State Univ, Northridge, Northridge, CA 91330	1958	$2,778 (S)	$8,216	5-M	31,448	1,746
California State Univ, Sacramento, Sacramento, CA 95819-6048	1947	$3,010 (S)	$6,574	5-D	27,972	1,433
California State Univ, San Bernardino, San Bernardino, CA 92407-2397	1965	$3,398 (S)	$5,886	5-M	16,195	587
California State Univ, San Marcos, San Marcos, CA 92096-0001	1990	$2,786 (S)	$7,470	5-M	6,728	402
California State Univ, Stanislaus, Turlock, CA 95382	1957	$2,807 (S)	$6,522	5-M	7,858	457
California Univ of Pennsylvania, California, PA 15419-1394	1852	$6,251 (S)	$7,280	5-M	6,640	364
Calumet Coll of St Joseph, Whiting, IN 46394-2195	1951	$9,450	NA	2-M	1,327	123
Calvin Coll, Grand Rapids, MI 49546-4388	1876	$17,770	$6,185	2-M	4,180	397
Cambridge Coll, Cambridge, MA 02138-5304	1971	$10,050	NA	1-M	3,795	518
Cameron Univ, Lawton, OK 73505-6377	1908	$3,000 (S)	$3,126	5-M	5,933	289
Campbellsville Univ, Campbellsville, KY 42718-2799	1906	$13,952	$5,440	2-M	2,187	210
Campbell Univ, Buies Creek, NC 27506	1887	$14,386	$5,100	2-D	4,256	336
Canisius Coll, Buffalo, NY 14208-1098	1870	$21,811	$8,395	2-M	5,018	452
Capella Univ, Minneapolis, MN 55402	1993	NA	NA	3-D	12,000	372
Capital Univ, Columbus, OH 43209-2394	1830	$22,540	$6,160	2-F	3,894	436
Cardinal Stritch Univ, Milwaukee, WI 53217-3985	1937	$15,660	$5,280	2-D	6,785	880
Carleton Coll, Northfield, MN 55057-4001	1866	$30,666	$6,309	1-B	1,951	206
Carlos Albizu Univ, Miami Cmps, Miami, FL 33172-2209 (4)	1980	$9,369	NA	1-D	1,007	48
Carlow Univ, Pittsburgh, PA 15213-3165 (4)	1929	$16,460	$6,538	2-M	2,088	239
Carnegie Mellon Univ, Pittsburgh, PA 15213-3891	1900	$31,036	$8,244	1-D	9,803	989
Carroll Coll, Helena, MT 59625-0002	1909	$16,978	$6,246	2-B	1,461	142
Carroll Coll, Waukesha, WI 53186-5593	1846	$19,050	$5,810	2-M	3,014	247
Carson-Newman Coll, Jefferson City, TN 37760	1851	$14,420	$4,930	2-M	2,053	198
Carthage Coll, Kenosha, WI 53140-1994	1847	$22,500	$6,500	2-M	2,679	183
Case Western Reserve Univ, Cleveland, OH 44106	1826	$27,062	$8,202	1-D	9,095	592
Castleton State Coll, Castleton, VT 05735	1787	$6,484 (S)	$6,674	5-M	1,971	180
Catawba Coll, Salisbury, NC 28144-2488	1851	$17,600	$5,900	2-M	1,395	109
Catholic Univ of America, Washington, DC 20064	1887	$26,000	$9,838	2-D	5,981	704
Cazenovia Coll, Cazenovia, NY 13035-1084	1824	$18,940	$7,590	1-B	1,180	138
Cedar Crest Coll, Allentown, PA 18104-6196 (3)	1867	$23,012	$7,953	2-M	1,856	145
Cedarville Univ, Cedarville, OH 45314-0601	1887	$16,032	$5,010	2-M	3,070	258
Centenary Coll, Hackettstown, NJ 07840-2100	1867	$19,360	$7,500	2-M	2,600	217
Centenary Coll of Louisiana, Shreveport, LA 71104	1825	$17,360	$6,070	2-M	1,040	115
Central Coll, Pella, IA 50219-1999	1853	$18,892	$6,486	2-B	1,750	153
Central Connecticut State Univ, New Britain, CT 06050-4010	1849	$5,902 (S)	$7,036	5-D	12,320	884
Central Michigan Univ, Mount Pleasant, MI 48859	1892	$5,365 (S)	$6,160	5-D	27,683	1,062
Central Missouri State Univ, Warrensburg, MO 64093	1871	$5,970 (S)	$5,180	5-M	10,051	573
Central State Univ, Wilberforce, OH 45384	1887	$4,710 (S)	$6,432	5-M	1,621	143
Central Washington Univ, Ellensburg, WA 98926	1891	$4,647 (S)	$6,402	5-M	9,985	535
Centre Coll, Danville, KY 40422-1394	1819	$21,800	$7,300	2-B	1,069	108
Chadron State Coll, Chadron, NE 69337	1911	$3,495 (S)	$3,986	5-M	2,569	116
Chaminade Univ of Honolulu, Honolulu, HI 96816-1578	1955	$14,330	$8,870	2-M	1,783	136
Champlain Coll, Burlington, VT 05402-0670	1878	$14,910	$9,695	1-M	2,555	256
Chapman Univ, Orange, CA 92866	1861	$26,150	$10,000	2-F	5,565	521
Charleston Southern Univ, Charleston, SC 29423-8087	1964	$15,332	$5,878	2-M	2,875	179
Charter Oak State Coll, New Britain, CT 06053-2142	1973	$160/credit (S)	NA	5-B	1,495	71
Chatham Coll, Pittsburgh, PA 15232-2826 (3)	1869	$21,996	$7,050	1-D	1,249	75
Chestnut Hill Coll, Philadelphia, PA 19118-2693 (4)	1924	$20,380	$7,500	2-D	1,679	230
Cheyney Univ of Pennsylvania, Cheyney, PA 19319-0200	1837	$5,565 (S)	$5,524	5-M	1,545	108
Chicago State Univ, Chicago, IL 60628	1867	$6,143 (S)	$6,032	5-M	6,835	431
Christian Brothers Univ, Memphis, TN 38104-5581	1871	$18,230	$5,300	2-M	1,907	176
Christopher Newport Univ, Newport News, VA 23606-2998	1960	$5,314 (S)	$7,200	5-M	4,681	318
Citadel, The Military Coll of South Carolina, Charleston, SC 29409 (2)	1842	$6,828 (S)	$4,684	5-M	3,351	230
City Coll of the City Univ of New York, New York, NY 10031-9198	1847	$4,339 (S)	NA	11-F	12,108	1,109
City Univ, Bellevue, WA 98005	1973	$9,440	NA	1-M	4,254	1,041
Claflin Univ, Orangeburg, SC 29115	1869	$12,584	$5,908	2-M	1,814	121
Claremont McKenna Coll, Claremont, CA 91711	1946	$29,210	$9,780	1-B	1,066	135
Clarion Univ of Pennsylvania, Clarion, PA 16214	1867	$4,810 (S)	$4,816	5-M	6,497	313
Clark Atlanta Univ, Atlanta, GA 30314	1865	$13,486	$6,816	2-D	4,598	264
Clarke Coll, Dubuque, IA 52001-3198	1843	$17,960	$6,289	2-M	1,180	92
Clarkson Univ, Potsdam, NY 13699	1896	$25,585	$9,345	1-D	3,123	189
Clark Univ, Worcester, MA 01610-1477	1887	$28,265	$5,400	1-D	3,115	276
Clayton State Univ, Morrow, GA 30260-0285	1969	$2,802 (S)	NA	5-B	5,954	299
Clemson Univ, Clemson, SC 29634	1889	$8,074 (S)	$5,292	5-D	17,110	1,105
Cleveland State Univ, Cleveland, OH 44115	1964	$6,792 (S)	$6,610	5-D	15,673	957
Coastal Carolina Univ, Conway, SC 29528-6054	1954	$6,100 (S)	$5,970	5-M	7,021	400
Coe Coll, Cedar Rapids, IA 52402-5092	1851	$22,650	$5,950	2-M	1,354	121
Colby Coll, Waterville, ME 04901-8840	1813	$39,800 (C)	NA	1-B	1,821	224
Colgate Univ, Hamilton, NY 13346-1386	1819	$31,440	$7,620	1-M	2,830	300
Coll for Creative Stds, Detroit, MI 48202-4034	1926	$23,116	$3,900	1-B	1,265	204
Coll Misericordia, Dallas, PA 18612-1098	1924	$18,800	$7,850	2-M	2,271	261
Coll of Biblical Stds-Houston, Houston, TX 77036	1979	$4,180	NA	2-B	1,492	50
Coll of Charleston, Charleston, SC 29424-0001	1770	$6,202 (S)	$6,506	5-M	11,607	836
Coll of Mount St Joseph, Cincinnati, OH 45233-1670	1920	$18,790	$6,070	2-M	2,158	225
Coll of Mount St Vincent, Riverdale, NY 10471-1093	1911	$19,900	$8,250	1-M	1,685	150
Coll of New Jersey, Ewing, NJ 08628	1855	$8,988 (S)	$8,093	5-M	6,812	685
Coll of New Rochelle, New Rochelle, NY 10805-2308 (4)	1904	$20,596	$7,880	1-M	2,564	162
Coll of Notre Dame of Maryland, Baltimore, MD 21210-2476 (3)	1873	$21,600	$8,000	2-D	3,307	88
Coll of St Benedict, Saint Joseph, MN 56374-2091 (4)	1887	$22,148	$6,208	2-B	2,033	174
Coll of St Catherine-Minneapolis, Minneapolis, MN 55454-1494 (4)	1964	$14,270	$5,808	2-M	4,807	519

Name, address	Year Founded	Tuition & Fees	Rm. & Board	Control, Degree	Enroll-ment	Faculty
Coll of St Catherine, St. Paul, MN 55105-1789 (3)	1905	$18,550	$5,460	2-D	4,809	528
Coll of St Elizabeth, Morristown, NJ 07960-6989 (3)	1899	$18,437	$8,618	2-M	1,976	196
Coll of St Rose, Albany, NY 12203-1419	1920	$16,780	$7,472	1-M	4,971	452
Coll of St Scholastica, Duluth, MN 55811-4199	1912	$20,760	$5,916	2-F	3,012	222
Coll of Santa Fe, Santa Fe, NM 87505-7634	1947	$20,840	$6,250	1-M	1,769	268
Coll of Staten Island of the City Univ of New York, Staten Island, NY 10314-6600	1955	$4,308 (S)	NA	11-M	12,442	823
Coll of the Holy Cross, Worcester, MA 01610-2395	1843	$29,686	$8,860	2-B	2,745	295
Coll of the Ozarks, Point Lookout, MO 65726	1906	$280	$3,850	2-B	1,723	115
Coll of William & Mary, Williamsburg, VA 23187-8795	1693	$7,096 (S)	$6,066	5-D	7,575	737
Coll of Wooster, Wooster, OH 44691-2363	1866	$26,560	$6,640	2-B	1,827	184
Colorado Christian Univ, Lakewood, CO 80226	1914	$16,060	$6,500	2-M	1,583	334
Colorado Coll, Colorado Springs, CO 80903-3294	1874	$28,644	$7,216	1-M	2,044	208
Colorado Sch of Mines, Golden, CO 80401-1887	1874	$7,224 (S)	$6,600	5-D	3,666	299
Colorado State Univ, Fort Collins, CO 80523-0015	1870	$3,790 (S)	$5,766	5-D	26,801	896
Colorado State Univ-Pueblo, Pueblo, CO 81001-4901	1933	$3,220 (S)	$5,912	5-M	5,835	312
Colorado Tech Univ, Colorado Springs, CO 80907-3896	1965	$9,438	NA	3-D	1,684	137
Colorado Tech Univ Sioux Falls Cmps, Sioux Falls, SD 57108	1965	$12,840	NA	3-M	1,036	61
Columbia Coll, Columbia, MO 65216-0002	1851	$11,995	$5,011	2-M	1,108	94
Columbia Coll, New York, NY 10027	1754	$31,472	$9,066	1-B	4,115	NA
Columbia Coll, Columbia, SC 29203-5998 (3)	1854	$18,040	$5,620	2-M	1,453	168
Columbia Coll Chicago, Chicago, IL 60605-1996	1890	$15,998	$9,300	1-M	10,354	1,616
Columbia Intl Univ, Columbia, SC 29230-3122	1923	$12,845	$5,380	2-D	1,016	43
Columbia Southern Univ, Orange Beach, AL 36561	NA	$375/course	NA	3-M	2,200	45
Columbia Union Coll, Takoma Park, MD 20912-7796	1904	$16,433	$5,560	2-M	1,115	57
Columbia Univ, Sch of Genl Stds, New York, NY 10027-6939	1754	$30,900	NA	1-B	1,571	632
Columbia Univ, The Fu Foundation Sch of Engr & Appl Sci, New York, NY 10027	1864	$31,472	$9,066	1-D	1,387	NA
Columbus Coll of Art & Design, Columbus, OH 43215-1758	1879	$19,330	$6,400	1-B	1,562	185
Columbus State Univ, Columbus, GA 31907-5645	1958	$2,808 (S)	$5,550	5-M	7,224	390
Concordia Coll, Moorhead, MN 56562	1891	$17,920	$4,690	2-M	2,814	260
Concordia Univ, Irvine, CA 92612-3299	1972	$19,930	$7,050	2-M	1,834	180
Concordia Univ, River Forest, IL 60305-1499	1864	$19,000	$5,900	2-D	2,056	209
Concordia Univ, Seward, NE 68434-1599	1894	$16,880	$4,580	2-M	1,317	120
Concordia Univ, Portland, OR 97211-6099	1905	$18,390	$5,780	2-M	1,404	103
Concordia Univ at Austin, Austin, TX 78705-2799	1926	$16,160	$6,570	2-M	1,155	85
Concordia Univ, St Paul, St. Paul, MN 55104-5494	1893	$21,312	$6,464	2-M	2,217	383
Concordia Univ Wisconsin, Mequon, WI 53097-2402	1881	$16,430	$6,230	2-D	5,395	192
Concord Univ, Athens, WV 24712-1000	1872	$3,588 (S)	$5,600	5-M	2,937	193
Connecticut Coll, New London, CT 06320-4196	1911	$39,975 (C)	NA	1-M	1,905	214
Converse Coll, Spartanburg, SC 29302-0006 (3)	1889	$19,960	$6,110	1-M	1,419	165
Coppin State Univ, Baltimore, MD 21216-3698	1900	$4,879 (S)	$6,239	5-M	4,003	202
Cornell Coll, Mount Vernon, IA 52314-1098	1853	$22,650	$6,240	2-B	1,155	102
Cornell Univ, Ithaca, NY 14853-0001	1865	$30,167	$9,882	1-D	19,518	1,826
Cornerstone Univ, Grand Rapids, MI 49525-5897	1941	$14,700	$5,520	2-F	2,414	124
Creighton Univ, Omaha, NE 68178-0001	1878	$21,118	$7,200	2-D	6,723	783
Crown Coll, St. Bonifacius, MN 55375-9001	1916	$15,646	$6,572	2-M	1,106	81
Culinary Inst of America, Hyde Park, NY 12538-1499	1946	$18,795	$6,510	1-B	2,409	139
Cumberland Univ, Lebanon, TN 37087-3408	1842	$13,744	$4,820	1-M	1,475	98
Curry Coll, Milton, MA 02186-9984	1879	$21,670	$8,180	1-M	2,877	350
Daemen Coll, Amherst, NY 14226-3592	1947	$16,020	$7,370	1-F	2,186	215
Dakota State Univ, Madison, SD 57042-1799	1881	$4,614 (S)	$3,193	5-M	2,282	102
Dallas Baptist Univ, Dallas, TX 75211-9299	1965	$11,610	$4,644	2-M	4,714	413
Dalton State Coll, Dalton, GA 30720-3797	1963	$1,592 (S)	NA	5-B	4,252	150
Daniel Webster Coll, Nashua, NH 03063-1300	1965	$21,630	$8,170	1-B	1,109	61
Dartmouth Coll, Hanover, NH 03755	1769	$30,575	$9,124	1-D	5,704	623
David N. Myers Univ, Cleveland, OH 44115-1096	1848	$11,170	NA	1-M	1,177	165
Davidson Coll, Davidson, NC 28035	1837	$27,171	$7,732	2-B	1,714	170
Defiance Coll, Defiance, OH 43512-1610	1850	$18,230	$5,590	2-M	1,035	87
Delaware State Univ, Dover, DE 19901-2277	1891	$4,976 (S)	$6,816	5-D	3,178	264
Delaware Valley Coll, Doylestown, PA 18901-2697	1896	$20,888	$7,742	1-M	1,965	192
Delta State Univ, Cleveland, MS 38733-0001	1924	$4,072 (S)	$3,734	5-D	3,853	281
Denison Univ, Granville, OH 43023	1831	$27,310	$7,670	1-B	2,229	196
DePaul Univ, Chicago, IL 60604-2287	1898	$19,765	$9,307	2-D	23,531	1,546
DePauw Univ, Greencastle, IN 46135-0037	1837	$25,500	$7,300	2-B	2,391	254
DeSales Univ, Center Valley, PA 18034-9568	1964	$19,390	$7,590	2-M	2,927	151
DeVry Inst of Tech, Long Island City, NY 11101	1998	$12,710	NA	3-M	1,453	83
DeVry Univ, Phoenix, AZ 85021-2995	1967	$11,490	NA	3-M	1,446	81
DeVry Univ, Fremont, CA 94555	1998	$12,720	NA	3-M	1,462	71
DeVry Univ, Long Beach, CA 90806	1984	$12,130	NA	3-M	1,459	88
DeVry Univ, Pomona, CA 91768-2642	1983	$12,130	NA	3-M	2,118	86
DeVry Univ, Miramar, FL 33027-4150	2002	$12,130	NA	3-M	1,024	27
DeVry Univ, Orlando, FL 32839	2000	$12,130	NA	3-M	1,250	57
DeVry Univ, Decatur, GA 30030-2198	1969	$11,450	NA	3-M	2,248	121
DeVry Univ, Addison, IL 60101-6106	1982	$11,580	NA	3-B	1,853	116
DeVry Univ, Chicago, IL 60618-5994	1931	$11,580	NA	3-B	2,477	112
DeVry Univ, Tinley Park, IL 60477	2000	$11,580	NA	3-M	1,238	91
DeVry Univ, Kansas City, MO 64131-3698	1931	$11,450	NA	3-M	1,380	95
DeVry Univ, North Brunswick, NJ 08902-3362	1969	$11,580	NA	3-B	1,886	135
DeVry Univ, Columbus, OH 43209-2705	1952	$11,450	NA	3-M	2,778	103
DeVry Univ, Irving, TX 75063-2439	1969	$11,430	NA	3-M	1,928	120
DeVry Univ, Federal Way, WA 98001	2001	$12,710	NA	3-B	1,005	35
Dickinson Coll, Carlisle, PA 17013-2896	1773	$32,120	$8,050	1-B	2,321	210
Dickinson State Univ, Dickinson, ND 58601-4896	1918	$4,559 (S)	NA	5-B	2,479	205
Dillard Univ, New Orleans, LA 70122-3097	1869	$11,550	$6,840	2-B	2,155	201
Doane Coll, Crete, NE 68333-2430	1872	$15,970	$4,720	2-M	2,429	127
Dominican Coll, Orangeburg, NY 10962-1210	1952	$17,250	$8,470	1-M	1,639	173
Dominican Univ, River Forest, IL 60305-1099	1901	$19,000	$5,890	2-M	3,188	312
Dominican Univ of California, San Rafael, CA 94901-2298	1890	$24,454	$10,270	2-M	1,910	250
Dordt Coll, Sioux Center, IA 51250-1697	1955	$16,670	$4,650	2-M	1,346	110
Dowling Coll, Oakdale, NY 11769-1999	1955	$16,050	$5,512	1-D	6,092	416
Drake Univ, Des Moines, IA 50311-4516	1881	$20,550	$5,920	1-D	5,221	374
Drew Univ, Madison, NJ 07940-1493	1867	$29,546	$8,018	2-D	2,675	166
Drexel Univ, Philadelphia, PA 19104-2875	1891	$22,020	$10,050	1-D	17,656	1,308
Drury Univ, Springfield, MO 65802-3791	1873	$14,669	$5,280	1-M	1,894	165

Name, address	Year Founded	Tuition & Fees	Rm. & Board	Control, Degree	Enroll-ment	Faculty
Duke Univ, Durham, NC 27708-0586	1838	$30,720	$8,520	2-D	12,770	NA
Duquesne Univ, Pittsburgh, PA 15282-0001	1878	$20,360	$7,820	2-D	9,722	874
D'Youville Coll, Buffalo, NY 14201-1084	1908	$14,890	$7,340	1-D	2,729	207
Earlham Coll, Richmond, IN 47374-4095	1847	$26,042	$5,740	2-F	1,275	114
East Carolina Univ, Greenville, NC 27858-4353	1907	$3,454 (S)	$6,640	5-D	22,767	1,284
East Central Univ, Ada, OK 74820-6899	1909	$3,952 (S)	$2,910	5-M	4,691	203
Eastern Connecticut State Univ, Willimantic, CT 06226-2295	1889	$6,472 (S)	$7,580	5-M	5,156	374
Eastern Illinois Univ, Charleston, IL 61920-3099	1895	$5,782 (S)	$7,150	5-M	11,651	730
Eastern Kentucky Univ, Richmond, KY 40475-3102	1906	$3,792 (S)	$4,658	5-M	16,183	956
Eastern Mennonite Univ, Harrisonburg, VA 22802-2462	1917	$19,500	$5,950	2-F	1,297	159
Eastern Michigan Univ, Ypsilanti, MI 48197	1849	$5,762 (S)	$6,082	5-D	23,593	1,111
Eastern Nazarene Coll, Quincy, MA 02170-2999	1918	$17,434	$5,920	2-M	1,212	48
Eastern New Mexico Univ, Portales, NM 88130	1934	$2,616 (S)	$4,340	5-M	3,939	238
Eastern Oregon Univ, La Grande, OR 97850-2899	1929	$5,517 (S)	$6,099	5-M	3,338	110
Eastern Univ, St. Davids, PA 19087-3696	1952	$18,830	$7,840	2-M	3,253	343
Eastern Washington Univ, Cheney, WA 99004-2431	1882	$4,056 (S)	$5,460	5-D	10,707	561
East Stroudsburg Univ of Pennsylvania, East Stroudsburg, PA 18301-2999	1893	$6,224 (S)	$4,506	5-M	6,553	308
East Tennessee State Univ, Johnson City, TN 37614	1911	$4,059 (S)	$4,858	5-D	11,869	760
East Texas Baptist Univ, Marshall, TX 75670-1498	1912	$12,000	$3,873	2-B	1,412	108
East-West Univ, Chicago, IL 60605-2103	1978	$10,840	NA	1-B	1,040	70
Eckerd Coll, St. Petersburg, FL 33711	1958	$24,362	$6,326	2-B	1,688	152
Edgewood Coll, Madison, WI 53711-1997	1927	$16,050	$5,691	2-M	2,454	259
Edinboro Univ of Pennsylvania, Edinboro, PA 16444	1857	$6,089 (S)	$5,338	5-M	7,773	405
Elizabeth City State Univ, Elizabeth City, NC 27909-7806	1891	$3,223 (S)	$4,608	5-M	2,470	216
Elizabethtown Coll, Elizabethtown, PA 17022-2298	1899	$23,710	$6,600	2-M	2,136	215
Elmhurst Coll, Elmhurst, IL 60126-3296	1871	$20,090	$6,304	2-M	2,670	278
Elmira Coll, Elmira, NY 14901	1855	$27,030	$8,330	1-M	1,853	97
Elon Univ, Elon, NC 27244-2010	1889	$17,555	$6,010	2-D	4,796	338
Embry-Riddle Aeron Univ, Prescott, AZ 86301-3720 (2)	1978	$23,490	$6,516	1-M	1,668	106
Embry-Riddle Aeron Univ, Daytona Beach, FL 32114-3900 (2)	1926	$23,500	$6,936	1-M	4,788	310
Embry-Riddle Aeron Univ, Extended Cmps, Daytona Beach, FL 32114-3900 (2)	1970	$4,224	NA	1-M	11,004	3,872
Emerson Coll, Boston, MA 02116-4624	1880	$718/cr. hr.	NA	1-D	4,398	340
Emmanuel Coll, Boston, MA 02115	1919	$20,500	$9,000	2-M	2,165	183
Emory & Henry Coll, Emory, VA 24327-0947	1836	$16,690	$6,250	2-M	1,028	88
Emory Univ, Atlanta, GA 30322-1100	1836	$29,322	$9,650	2-D	11,781	2,662
Emporia State Univ, Emporia, KS 66801-5087	1863	$3,036 (S)	$4,474	5-D	6,194	273
Endicott Coll, Beverly, MA 01915-2096	1939	$19,432	$9,300	1-M	3,285	131
Evangel Univ, Springfield, MO 65802-2191	1955	$12,750	$4,620	2-M	1,801	158
Evergreen State Coll, Olympia, WA 98505	1967	$4,056 (S)	$5,784	5-M	4,410	224
Excelsior Coll, Albany, NY 12203-5159	1970	$240/credit	NA	1-M	26,395	NA
Fairfield Univ, Fairfield, CT 06824-5195	1942	$28,415	$9,270	2-M	5,060	426
Fairleigh Dickinson Univ, Coll at Florham, Madison, NJ 07940-1099	1942	$23,386	$8,608	1-M	3,684	331
Fairleigh Dickinson Univ, Metropolitan Cmps, Teaneck, NJ 07666-1914	1942	$21,734	$9,056	1-D	7,634	549
Fairmont State Univ, Fairmont, WV 26554	1865	$4,112 (S)	$6,052	5-M	7,519	527
Farmingdale State Univ of New York, Farmingdale, NY 11735	1912	$5,211 (S)	$7,680	5-B	6,250	452
Fashion Inst of Tech, New York, NY 10001-5992 (4)	1944	$4,720 (S)	$7,066	11-M	10,513	939
Faulkner Univ, Montgomery, AL 36109-3398	1942	$10,425	$5,200	2-F	2,583	138
Fayetteville State Univ, Fayetteville, NC 28301-4298	1867	$2,832 (S)	$4,120	5-D	5,441	237
Felician Coll, Lodi, NJ 07644-2117	1942	$17,100	$7,500	2-M	1,665	162
Ferris State Univ, Big Rapids, MI 49307	1884	$6,332 (S)	$6,522	5-F	11,803	818
Fitchburg State Coll, Fitchburg, MA 01420-2697	1894	$4,588 (S)	$5,882	5-M	5,201	238
Five Towns Coll, Dix Hills, NY 11746-6055	1972	$14,100	$10,250	1-D	1,162	123
Flagler Coll, St. Augustine, FL 32085-1027	1968	$8,600	$5,190	1-B	2,106	210
Florida Agr & Mech Univ, Tallahassee, FL 32307-3200	1887	$3,318 (S)	$5,766	5-D	13,064	621
Florida Atlantic Univ, Boca Raton, FL 33431-0991	1961	$3,092 (S)	$7,100	5-D	25,383	1,304
Florida Gulf Coast Univ, Fort Myers, FL 33965-6565	1991	$3,151 (S)	$8,500	5-M	5,955	411
Florida Inst of Tech, Melbourne, FL 32901-6975	1958	$23,730	$6,220	1-D	4,683	261
Florida Intl Univ, Miami, FL 33199	1965	$3,158 (S)	$8,860	5-D	34,865	1,459
Florida Metropolitan Univ-Brandon Cmps, Tampa, FL 33619	1890	$13,200	NA	3-M	1,332	65
Florida Metropolitan Univ-North Orlando Cmps, Orlando, FL 32810-5674	1953	$9,900	NA	3-M	1,498	96
Florida Metropolitan Univ-Pinellas Cmps, Clearwater, FL 33759	1890	$11,430	NA	3-M	1,201	44
Florida Metropolitan Univ-Pompano Beach Cmps, Pompano Beach, FL 33062	1940	$9,150	NA	3-M	1,612	70
Florida Metropolitan Univ-South Orlando Cmps, Orlando, FL 32819	NA	$8,640	NA	3-M	1,964	77
Florida Metropolitan Univ-Tampa Cmps, Tampa, FL 33614-5899	1890	$9,900	NA	3-M	1,390	83
Florida Southern Coll, Lakeland, FL 33801-5698	1885	$18,240	$6,410	2-M	1,990	178
Florida State Univ, Tallahassee, FL 32306	1851	$3,038 (S)	$7,208	5-D	38,431	1,486
Fontbonne Univ, St. Louis, MO 63105-3098	1917	$15,420	$6,988	2-M	2,827	335
Fordham Univ, New York, NY 10458	1841	$27,047	$10,248	2-D	14,861	1,326
Fort Hays State Univ, Hays, KS 67601-4099	1902	$3,217 (S)	$5,061	5-M	7,373	291
Fort Lewis Coll, Durango, CO 81301-3999	1911	$3,060 (S)	$5,894	5-B	4,190	242
Fort Valley State Univ, Fort Valley, GA 31030-4313	1895	$3,510 (S)	$4,386	5-D	2,558	121
Framingham State Coll, Framingham, MA 01701-9101	1839	$4,740 (S)	$5,539	5-M	6,015	296
Franciscan Univ of Steubenville, Steubenville, OH 43952-1763	1946	$15,700	$5,350	2-M	2,374	NA
Francis Marion Univ, Florence, SC 29501-0547	1970	$5,540 (S)	$4,656	5-M	3,698	213
Franklin & Marshall Coll, Lancaster, PA 17604-3003	1787	$30,440	$7,540	1-B	1,972	207
Franklin Pierce Coll, Rindge, NH 03461-0060	1962	$23,710	$7,990	1-B	1,608	154
Franklin Univ, Columbus, OH 43215-5399	1902	$6,990	NA	1-M	6,823	599
Freed-Hardeman Univ, Henderson, TN 38340-2399	1869	$12,440	$6,200	2-M	1,942	135
Fresno Pacific Univ, Fresno, CA 93702-4709	1944	$18,728	$5,600	2-M	2,255	NA
Friends Univ, Wichita, KS 67213	1898	$14,600	NA	1-M	3,190	225
Frostburg State Univ, Frostburg, MD 21532-1099	1898	$6,230 (S)	$6,148	5-M	5,327	346
Furman Univ, Greenville, SC 29613	1826	$24,408	$6,272	1-M	3,359	257
Gallaudet Univ, Washington, DC 20002-3625	1864	$11,255	$8,420	1-D	1,834	230
Gannon Univ, Erie, PA 16541-0001	1925	$17,500	$6,990	2-D	3,441	298
Gardner-Webb Univ, Boiling Springs, NC 28017	1905	$15,150	$5,340	2-D	3,724	126
Geneva Coll, Beaver Falls, PA 15010-3599	1848	$16,590	$6,600	2-M	2,141	158
George Fox Univ, Newberg, OR 97132-2697	1891	$20,590	$6,550	2-D	2,981	361
George Mason Univ, Fairfax, VA 22030	1957	$5,448 (S)	$6,240	5-D	28,874	1,846
Georgetown Coll, Georgetown, KY 40324-1696	1829	$19,170	$5,780	2-M	1,845	160
Georgetown Univ, Washington, DC 20057	1789	$30,163	$10,554	2-D	13,233	1,068
George Washington Univ, Washington, DC 20052	1821	$34,030	$10,210	1-D	23,092	1,922
Georgia Coll & State Univ, Milledgeville, GA 31061	1889	$3,862 (S)	$6,482	5-M	5,531	407
Georgia Inst of Tech, Atlanta, GA 30332-0001	1885	$4,278 (S)	$6,526	5-D	16,841	813

Name, address	Year Founded	Tuition & Fees	Rm. & Board	Control, Degree	Enroll-ment	Faculty
Georgian Court Univ, Lakewood, NJ 08701-2697 (3)	1908	$17,924	$7,200	2-M	3,065	282
Georgia Southern Univ, Statesboro, GA 30460	1906	$3,062 (S)	$6,000	5-D	16,100	708
Georgia Southwestern State Univ, Americus, GA 31709-4693	1906	$2,892 (S)	$4,506	5-M	2,323	136
Georgia State Univ, Atlanta, GA 30303-3083	1913	$4,464 (S)	$7,368	5-D	27,267	1,428
Gettysburg Coll, Gettysburg, PA 17325-1483	1832	$30,240	$7,354	2-B	2,471	276
Glenville State Coll, Glenville, WV 26351-1200	1872	$3,276 (S)	$5,060	5-B	1,319	92
Global Univ of the Assemblies of God, Springfield, MO 65804	1948	$2,160	NA	2-F	6,735	590
Globe Inst of Tech, New York, NY 10007	NA	$9,086	$3,500	3-B	1,229	122
Golden Gate Univ, San Francisco, CA 94105-2968	1853	$10,320	NA	1-D	4,069	662
Goldey-Beacom Coll, Wilmington, DE 19808-1999	1886	$13,736	$4,240	1-M	1,324	49
Gonzaga Univ, Spokane, WA 99258	1887	$22,118	$6,650	2-D	6,016	266
Gordon Coll, Wenham, MA 01984-1899	1889	$21,448	$6,092	2-M	1,672	161
Goucher Coll, Baltimore, MD 21204-2794	1885	$26,150	$8,575	1-M	2,349	182
Governors State Univ, University Park, IL 60466-0975	1969	$3,704 (S)	NA	5-M	5,652	212
Grace Coll, Winona Lake, IN 46590-1294	1948	$15,030	$6,150	2-M	1,258	117
Graceland Univ, Lamoni, IA 50140	1895	$16,150	$5,400	2-M	2,351	114
Grambling State Univ, Grambling, LA 71245	1901	$3,506 (S)	$4,034	5-D	5,039	247
Grand Canyon Univ, Phoenix, AZ 85017-1097	1949	$14,500	$7,130	2-M	4,113	274
Grand Valley State Univ, Allendale, MI 49401-9403	1960	$5,782 (S)	$6,160	5-M	22,063	1,321
Grand View Coll, Des Moines, IA 50316-1599	1896	$15,392	$5,436	2-B	1,759	167
Granite State Coll, Concord, NH 03301	1972	$4,563 (S)	NA	11-B	1,827	223
Greensboro Coll, Greensboro, NC 27401-1875	1838	$16,820	$6,460	2-M	1,226	125
Greenville Coll, Greenville, IL 62246-0159	1892	$16,824	$5,760	2-M	1,305	133
Grinnell Coll, Grinnell, IA 50112-1690	1846	$25,820	$6,870	1-B	1,556	190
Grove City Coll, Grove City, PA 16127-2104	1876	$10,107	$5,092	2-B	2,318	182
Guilford Coll, Greensboro, NC 27410-4173	1837	$21,640	$6,530	2-B	2,511	173
Gustavus Adolphus Coll, St. Peter, MN 56082-1498	1862	$22,955	$5,810	2-B	2,577	249
Gwynedd-Mercy Coll, Gwynedd Valley, PA 19437-0901	1948	$17,400	$7,500	2-M	2,751	280
Hamilton Coll, Clinton, NY 13323-1296	1812	$31,700	$7,825	1-B	1,792	205
Hamline Univ, St. Paul, MN 55104-1284	1854	$22,070	$6,536	2-D	4,490	433
Hampden-Sydney Coll, Hampden-Sydney, VA 23943 (1)	1776	$22,946	$7,370	2-B	1,082	106
Hampshire Coll, Amherst, MA 01002	1965	$30,978	$8,113	1-B	1,352	141
Hampton Univ, Hampton, VA 23668	1868	$14,996	$6,424	1-D	6,156	463
Hannibal-LaGrange Coll, Hannibal, MO 63401-1999	1858	$10,876	$4,050	2-B	1,067	94
Hanover Coll, Hanover, IN 47243-0108	1827	$20,600	$6,200	2-B	1,062	97
Harding Univ, Searcy, AR 72149-0001	1924	$10,780	$5,182	2-M	5,348	316
Hardin-Simmons Univ, Abilene, TX 79698-0001	1891	$13,376	$3,922	2-D	2,392	179
Harrington Coll of Design, Chicago, IL 60606 (4)	1931	$17,050	$5,000	3-B	1,555	137
Harris-Stowe State Coll, St. Louis, MO 63103-2136	1857	$4,255 (S)	NA	5-B	1,605	133
Hartwick Coll, Oneonta, NY 13820-4020	1797	$26,480	$7,480	1-B	1,479	154
Harvard Univ, Cambridge, MA 02138	1636	$30,620	$9,260	1-D	20,130	760
Haskell Indian Nations Univ, Lawrence, KS 66046-4800	1884	$420 (S)	NA	4-B	1,028	48
Hastings Coll, Hastings, NE 68901-7696	1882	$16,290	$4,760	2-M	1,153	115
Haverford Coll, Haverford, PA 19041-1392	1833	$30,270	$9,420	1-B	1,172	117
Hawai`i Pacific Univ, Honolulu, HI 96813-2785	1965	$11,002	$9,020	1-M	7,800	587
Heidelberg Coll, Tiffin, OH 44883-2462	1850	$14,900	$6,710	2-M	1,398	NA
Henderson State Univ, Arkadelphia, AR 71999-0001	1890	$4,110 (S)	$3,738	5-M	3,461	218
Hendrix Coll, Conway, AR 72032-3080	1876	$21,636	$6,010	2-M	1,049	100
Heritage Univ, Toppenish, WA 98948-9599	1982	$7,120	NA	1-M	1,355	143
High Point Univ, High Point, NC 27262-3598	1924	$16,760	$6,950	2-M	2,842	245
Hilbert Coll, Hamburg, NY 14075-1597	1957	$14,300	$5,380	1-B	1,108	101
Hillsdale Coll, Hillsdale, MI 49242-1298	1844	$16,900	$6,600	1-B	1,273	136
Hiram Coll, Hiram, OH 44234-0067	1850	$22,595	$7,505	2-M	1,125	119
Hobart & William Smith Colls, Geneva, NY 14456-3397	1822	$30,643	$7,987	1-B	1,847	185
Hofstra Univ, Hempstead, NY 11549	1935	$20,012	$9,000	1-D	12,999	1,256
Hollins Univ, Roanoke, VA 24020-1603 (3)	1842	$21,675	$7,700	1-M	1,057	111
Holy Family Univ, Philadelphia, PA 19114-2094	1954	$16,490	NA	2-M	2,670	258
Hood Coll, Frederick, MD 21701-8575	1893	$22,335	$7,750	1-M	1,948	190
Hope Coll, Holland, MI 49422-9000	1866	$20,420	$6,318	2-B	3,112	307
Hope Intl Univ, Fullerton, CA 92831-3138	1928	$16,400	$5,400	2-M	1,275	155
Houghton Coll, Houghton, NY 14744	1883	$18,660	$6,320	2-M	1,480	101
Houston Baptist Univ, Houston, TX 77074-3298	1960	$12,915	$4,566	2-M	2,227	181
Howard Payne Univ, Brownwood, TX 76801-2715	1889	$12,000	$4,242	2-B	1,319	125
Howard Univ, Washington, DC 20059-0002	1867	$11,645	$5,870	1-D	10,623	1,576
Humboldt State Univ, Arcata, CA 95521-8299	1913	$2,866 (S)	$7,281	5-M	7,550	490
Hunter Coll of the City Univ of New York, New York, NY 10021-5085	1870	$4,329 (S)	$2,600	11-M	20,243	1,358
Husson Coll, Bangor, ME 04401-2999	1898	$11,050	$5,850	1-M	2,039	53
Idaho State Univ, Pocatello, ID 83209	1901	$3,700 (A)	$4,850	5-D	13,802	753
Illinois Coll, Jacksonville, IL 62650-2299	1829	$14,600	$6,200	2-B	1,037	98
Illinois Inst of Art, Chicago, IL 60654	1916	$18,540	$7,434	3-B	2,400	110
Illinois Inst of Art-Schaumburg, Schaumburg, IL 60173	NA	$16,605	NA	3-B	1,187	73
Illinois Inst of Tech, Chicago, IL 60616-3793	1890	$22,982	NA	1-D	6,378	580
Illinois State Univ, Normal, IL 61790-2200	1857	$6,328 (S)	$5,576	5-D	20,757	1,088
Illinois Wesleyan Univ, Bloomington, IL 61702-2900	1850	$27,624	$6,426	1-B	2,118	223
Immaculata Univ, Immaculata, PA 19345 (4)	1920	$19,625	$8,850	2-D	3,811	258
Indiana Inst of Tech, Fort Wayne, IN 46803-1297	1930	$17,600	$6,750	1-M	3,425	280
Indiana State Univ, Terre Haute, IN 47809-1401	1865	$5,640 (S)	$5,615	5-D	11,200	691
Indiana Univ-Purdue Univ Fort Wayne, Fort Wayne, IN 46805-1499	1917	$5,312 (S)	NA	5-M	11,810	734
Indiana Univ-Purdue Univ Indianapolis, Indianapolis, IN 46202-2896	1969	$5,930 (S)	$2,656	5-D	29,953	3,107
Indiana Univ Bloomington, Bloomington, IN 47405-7000	1820	$6,777 (S)	$6,006	5-D	37,821	2,251
Indiana Univ East, Richmond, IN 47374-1289	1971	$4,601 (S)	NA	5-B	2,516	202
Indiana Univ Kokomo, Kokomo, IN 46904-9003	1945	$4,632 (S)	NA	5-M	2,903	184
Indiana Univ Northwest, Gary, IN 46408-1197	1959	$4,707 (S)	NA	5-M	5,138	393
Indiana Univ of Pennsylvania, Indiana, PA 15705-1087	1875	$6,085 (S)	$4,868	5-D	13,998	689
Indiana Univ South Bend, South Bend, IN 46634-7111	1922	$4,755 (S)	NA	5-M	7,501	551
Indiana Univ Southeast, New Albany, IN 47150-6405	1941	$4,673 (S)	NA	5-M	6,238	425
Indiana Wesleyan Univ, Marion, IN 46953-4974	1920	$16,184	$5,890	2-D	11,020	148
Inter Amer Univ of Puerto Rico, Aguadilla Cmps, Aguadilla, PR 00605	1957	$3,784	NA	1-M	4,266	254
Inter Amer Univ of Puerto Rico, Arecibo Cmps, Arecibo, PR 00614-4050	1957	$3,240	NA	1-M	3,926	234
Inter Amer Univ of Puerto Rico, Barranquitas Cmps, Barranquitas, PR 00794	1957	$4,310	NA	1-B	2,271	105
Inter Amer Univ of Puerto Rico, Bayamón Cmps, Bayamón, PR 00957	1912	$3,760	NA	1-M	5,245	298
Inter Amer Univ of Puerto Rico, Fajardo Cmps, Fajardo, PR 00738-7003	1965	$3,296	NA	1-B	1,710	118
Inter Amer Univ of Puerto Rico, Guayama Cmps, Guayama, PR 00785	1958	$1,682	NA	1-B	1,246	139

Name, address	Year Founded	Tuition & Fees	Rm. & Board	Control, Degree	Enroll-ment	Faculty
Inter Amer Univ of Puerto Rico, Metropolitan Cmps, San Juan, PR 00919-1293	1960	$3,536	NA	1-D	10,675	599
Inter Amer Univ of Puerto Rico, Ponce Cmps, Mercedita, PR 00715-1602	1962	$4,296	NA	1-M	5,265	249
Inter Amer Univ of Puerto Rico, San Germán Cmps, San Germán, PR 00683-5008	1912	$4,616	$2,400	1-D	6,217	355
Intl Acad of Design & Tech, Tampa, FL 33634-7350	1984	$17,820	$6,609	3-B	2,405	171
Intl Acad of Design & Tech, Chicago, IL 60602-9736	1977	$20,000	NA	3-B	2,905	184
Intl Coll, Naples, FL 34119	1990	$9,020	NA	1-M	1,544	109
Iona Coll, New Rochelle, NY 10801-1890	1940	$19,530	$9,698	2-M	4,329	370
Iowa State Univ of Sci & Tech, Ames, IA 50011	1858	$5,426 (S)	$5,958	5-D	26,380	1,610
Ithaca Coll, Ithaca, NY 14850-7020	1892	$23,690	$9,704	1-M	6,337	616
Jackson State Univ, Jackson, MS 39217	1877	$3,842 (S)	$4,974	5-D	8,351	465
Jacksonville State Univ, Jacksonville, AL 36265-1602	1883	$4,040 (S)	$3,312	5-M	8,930	412
Jacksonville Univ, Jacksonville, FL 32211-3394	1934	$19,970	$6,460	1-M	2,948	162
James Madison Univ, Harrisonburg, VA 22807	1908	$5,476 (S)	$6,116	5-D	16,108	1,110
Jamestown Coll, Jamestown, ND 58405	1883	$10,000	$4,130	2-B	1,064	67
John Brown Univ, Siloam Springs, AR 72761-2121	1919	$14,434	$5,324	2-M	1,928	143
John Carroll Univ, University Heights, OH 44118-4581	1886	$23,630	$7,526	2-M	4,101	409
John F. Kennedy Univ, Pleasant Hill, CA 94523-4817	1964	$14,436	NA	1-D	1,653	728
John Jay Coll of Criminal Justice of the City Univ of New York, New York, NY 10019-1093	1964	$4,259 (S)	NA	11-D	12,984	913
Johns Hopkins Univ, Baltimore, MD 21218-2699	1876	$30,140	$9,516	1-D	5,898	484
Johnson & Wales Univ, Denver, CO 80220	1993	$20,100	$8,490	1-B	1,512	65
Johnson & Wales Univ, North Miami, FL 33181	1992	$20,100	$9,327	1-B	2,389	82
Johnson & Wales Univ, Providence, RI 02903-3703	1914	$20,100	$7,545	1-D	9,982	398
Johnson C. Smith Univ, Charlotte, NC 28216-5398	1867	$13,712	$5,298	1-B	1,415	120
Johnson State Coll, Johnson, VT 05656-9405	1828	$6,580 (S)	$6,454	5-M	1,759	203
Judson Coll, Elgin, IL 60123-1498	1963	$17,150	$6,200	2-M	1,222	114
Juniata Coll, Huntingdon, PA 16652-2119	1876	$25,890	$7,240	2-B	1,427	127
Kalamazoo Coll, Kalamazoo, MI 49006-3295	1833	$24,351	$6,609	2-B	1,234	114
Kansas State Univ, Manhattan, KS 66506	1863	$4,665 (S)	$5,738	5-D	23,151	1,048
Kean Univ, Union, NJ 07083	1855	$7,151 (S)	$8,093	5-M	12,897	1,098
Keene State Coll, Keene, NH 03435	1909	$6,900 (S)	$5,966	5-M	4,937	386
Kennesaw State Univ, Kennesaw, GA 30144-5591	1963	$2,758 (S)	$5,376	5-M	17,955	858
Kent State Univ, Kent, OH 44242-0001	1910	$7,504 (S)	$6,410	5-D	24,347	1,395
Kentucky State Univ, Frankfort, KY 40601	1886	$3,780 (S)	$5,658	12-M	2,335	162
Kenyon Coll, Gambier, OH 43022-9623	1824	$32,170	$5,270	1-B	1,634	176
Kettering Univ, Flint, MI 48504-4898	1919	$23,360	NA	1-M	2,992	151
Keuka Coll, Keuka Park, NY 14478-0098	1890	$17,080	$7,790	2-M	1,154	99
King's Coll, Wilkes-Barre, PA 18711-0801	1946	$20,110	$8,250	2-M	2,223	180
Knox Coll, Galesburg, IL 61401	1837	$25,236	$6,102	1-B	1,205	116
Kutztown Univ of Pennsylvania, Kutztown, PA 19530-0730	1866	$6,256 (S)	$5,274	5-M	9,584	432
Lafayette Coll, Easton, PA 18042-1798	1826	$29,982	$9,285	2-B	2,303	224
LaGrange Coll, LaGrange, GA 30240-2999	1831	$15,206	$6,318	2-M	1,044	103
Lake Forest Coll, Lake Forest, IL 60045-2399	1857	$25,828	$6,222	1-M	1,407	170
Lakeland Coll, Sheboygan, WI 53082-0359	1862	$15,770	$5,635	2-M	4,013	67
Lake Superior State Univ, Sault Sainte Marie, MI 49783-1626	1946	$6,372 (S)	$6,165	5-M	2,889	211
Lamar Univ, Beaumont, TX 77710	1923	$3,156 (S)	$5,706	5-D	10,804	525
Lander Univ, Greenwood, SC 29649-2099	1872	$6,016 (S)	$5,176	5-M	2,918	183
Lane Coll, Jackson, TN 38301-4598	1882	$7,176	$4,534	2-B	1,045	52
La Roche Coll, Pittsburgh, PA 15237-5898	1963	$16,582	$6,862	2-M	1,681	223
La Salle Univ, Philadelphia, PA 19141-1199	1863	$26,190	$9,410	2-D	6,217	492
Lasell Coll, Newton, MA 02466-2709	1851	$19,700	$8,800	1-M	1,181	150
La Sierra Univ, Riverside, CA 92515	1922	$19,083	$5,244	2-D	1,924	186
Lawrence Tech Univ, Southfield, MI 48075-1058	1932	$17,210	$7,035	1-D	4,148	410
Lawrence Univ, Appleton, WI 54912-0599	1847	$27,924	$5,900	1-B	1,380	162
Lebanon Valley Coll, Annville, PA 17003-1400	1866	$23,600	$6,590	2-F	1,882	186
Lee Univ, Cleveland, TN 37320-3450	1918	$9,075	$4,560	2-M	3,849	300
Lehigh Univ, Bethlehem, PA 18015-3094	1865	$29,340	$8,230	1-D	6,641	597
Lehman Coll of the City Univ of New York, Bronx, NY 10468-1589	1931	$4,270 (A)	NA	11-M	10,281	780
Le Moyne Coll, Syracuse, NY 13214-1399	1946	$20,150	$7,890	2-M	3,487	300
Lenoir-Rhyne Coll, Hickory, NC 28603	1891	$18,920	$6,680	2-M	1,579	146
Lesley Univ, Cambridge, MA 02138-2790	1909	$22,750	$9,950	1-D	6,526	185
LeTourneau Univ, Longview, TX 75607-7001	1946	$15,890	$6,286	2-M	3,758	301
Lewis & Clark Coll, Portland, OR 97219-7899	1867	$26,154	$7,330	1-D	3,259	380
Lewis-Clark State Coll, Lewiston, ID 83501-2698	1893	$3,392 (S)	$3,995	5-B	3,325	187
Lewis Univ, Romeoville, IL 60446	1932	$17,990	$7,500	2-D	4,826	459
Liberty Univ, Lynchburg, VA 24502	1971	$14,550	$5,400	2-D	13,464	396
Life Univ, Marietta, GA 30060-2903	1974	$5,496	NA	1-F	1,233	32
Lincoln Memorial Univ, Harrogate, TN 37752-1901	1897	$12,600	$4,910	1-M	2,442	152
Lincoln Univ, Jefferson City, MO 65102	1866	$4,952 (S)	$3,790	5-M	3,275	134
Lincoln Univ, Lincoln University, PA 19352	1854	$7,268 (S)	$6,560	12-M	2,012	158
Lindenwood Univ, St. Charles, MO 63301-1695	1827	$11,720	$5,600	2-M	8,615	516
Lindsey Wilson Coll, Columbia, KY 42728-1298	1903	$13,814	$5,926	2-M	1,846	123
Linfield Coll, McMinnville, OR 97128-6894	1849	$22,022	$6,370	2-B	1,656	179
Lipscomb Univ, Nashville, TN 37204-3951	1891	$13,486	$6,090	2-F	2,537	201
Livingstone Coll, Salisbury, NC 28144-5298	1879	$13,527	$5,919	2-B	1,016	67
Lock Haven Univ of Pennsylvania, Lock Haven, PA 17745-2390	1870	$6,100 (S)	$5,516	5-M	5,126	259
Logan Univ-Coll of Chiropractic, Chesterfield, MO 63006-1065	1935	$3,750	NA	1-F	1,045	93
Loma Linda Univ, Loma Linda, CA 92350	1905	$22,320	$2,835	2-D	4,010	187
Long Island Univ, Brentwood Cmps, Brentwood, NY 11717	1959	$21,800	NA	1-M	1,115	110
Long Island Univ, Brooklyn Cmps, Brooklyn, NY 11201-8423	1926	$21,922	$7,350	1-D	8,003	NA
Long Island Univ, C.W. Post Cmps, Brookville, NY 11548-1300	1954	$21,960	$8,240	1-D	8,421	1,018
Longwood Univ, Farmville, VA 23909-1800	1839	$6,441 (S)	$5,424	5-M	4,289	242
Loras Coll, Dubuque, IA 52004-0178	1839	$19,678	$5,845	2-M	1,743	143
Louisiana Coll, Pineville, LA 71359-0001	1906	$10,300	$3,886	2-B	1,085	92
Louisiana State Univ & Agr & Mech Coll, Baton Rouge, LA 70803	1860	$4,226 (S)	$5,882	5-D	32,241	1,475
Louisiana State Univ Health Sci Ctr, New Orleans, LA 70112-2223	1931	$4,392 (S)	$2,916	5-D	2,240	1,380
Louisiana State Univ in Shreveport, Shreveport, LA 71115-2399	1965	$3,815 (S)	$2,196	5-M	4,401	254
Louisiana Tech Univ, Ruston, LA 71272	1894	$4,375 (S)	$4,035	5-D	11,691	499
Lourdes Coll, Sylvania, OH 43560-2898	1958	$12,270	NA	2-M	1,460	150
Loyola Coll in Maryland, Baltimore, MD 21210-2699	1852	$28,170	$8,959	2-D	6,156	541
Loyola Marymount Univ, Los Angeles, CA 90045-2659	1911	$25,756	$9,456	2-D	8,855	868
Loyola Univ Chicago, Chicago, IL 60611-2196	1870	$23,836	$9,060	2-D	13,909	991

Name, address	Year Founded	Tuition & Fees	Rm. & Board	Control, Degree	Enroll-ment	Faculty
Loyola Univ New Orleans, New Orleans, LA 70118-6195	1912	$25,246	$8,312	2-F	5,423	483
Lubbock Christian Univ, Lubbock, TX 79407-2099	1957	$11,994	$4,130	2-M	1,974	155
Luther Coll, Decorah, IA 52101-1045	1861	$23,070	$4,170	2-B	2,573	234
Luther Rice Bible Coll & Sem, Lithonia, GA 30038-2454	1962	$3,964	NA	2-D	1,600	33
Lycoming Coll, Williamsport, PA 17701-5192	1812	$22,886	$6,242	2-B	1,536	103
Lynchburg Coll, Lynchburg, VA 24501-3199	1903	$22,885	$5,000	2-M	2,248	209
Lyndon State Coll, Lyndonville, VT 05851-0919	1911	$6,146 (S)	$6,454	5-M	1,349	163
Lynn Univ, Boca Raton, FL 33431-5598	1962	$25,850	$9,100	1-D	2,510	171
Macalester Coll, St. Paul, MN 55105-1899	1874	$28,810	$7,858	2-B	1,900	216
Macon State Coll, Macon, GA 31206	1968	$1,784 (S)	NA	5-B	5,733	248
Madonna Univ, Livonia, MI 48150-1173	1947	$9,800	$5,612	2-M	4,349	312
Malone Coll, Canton, OH 44709-3897	1892	$15,880	$6,120	2-M	2,250	195
Manchester Coll, North Manchester, IN 46962-1225	1889	$19,360	$6,910	2-M	1,068	73
Manhattan Coll, Riverdale, NY 10471	1853	$20,600	$9,025	2-M	3,301	282
Manhattanville Coll, Purchase, NY 10577-2132	1841	$24,570	$10,130	1-M	2,608	343
Mansfield Univ of Pennsylvania, Mansfield, PA 16933	1857	$6,230 (S)	$5,456	5-M	3,556	208
Marian Coll, Indianapolis, IN 46222-1997	1851	$19,060	$6,400	2-M	1,685	145
Marian Coll of Fond du Lac, Fond du Lac, WI 54935-4699	1936	$15,825	$5,240	2-M	2,918	232
Marietta Coll, Marietta, OH 45750-4000	1835	$21,730	$6,186	1-M	1,480	116
Marist Coll, Poughkeepsie, NY 12601-1387	1929	$21,015	$9,218	1-M	5,646	596
Marquette Univ, Milwaukee, WI 53201-1881	1881	$21,932	$7,890	2-D	11,510	1,001
Marshall Univ, Huntington, WV 25755	1837	$4,296 (S)	$6,060	5-D	13,920	711
Mars Hill Coll, Mars Hill, NC 28754	1856	$16,598	$6,136	2-B	1,378	144
Mary Baldwin Coll, Staunton, VA 24401-3610	1842	$19,991	$5,689	1-M	1,718	134
Marygrove Coll, Detroit, MI 48221-2599 (4)	1905	$12,440	$6,000	2-M	4,610	72
Maryland Inst Coll of Art, Baltimore, MD 21217	1826	$25,204	$7,080	1-M	1,608	241
Marylhurst Univ, Marylhurst, OR 97036-0261	1893	$14,220	NA	2-M	1,245	197
Marymount Coll of Fordham Univ, Tarrytown, NY 10591-3796 (3)	1907	$19,702	$9,760	1-B	1,036	170
Marymount Manhattan Coll, New York, NY 10021-4597	1936	$17,352	$12,366	1-B	2,077	316
Marymount Univ, Arlington, VA 22207-4299	1950	$17,090	$7,520	2-D	3,717	387
Maryville Coll, Maryville, TN 37804-5907	1819	$21,065	$6,500	2-B	1,080	112
Maryville Univ of St Louis, St. Louis, MO 63141-7299	1872	$16,300	$7,000	1-M	3,140	342
Marywood Univ, Scranton, PA 18509-1598	1915	$21,640	$9,100	2-D	3,127	313
Massachusetts Coll of Art, Boston, MA 02115-5882	1873	$6,400 (S)	$9,737	5-M	2,049	216
Massachusetts Coll of Lib Arts, North Adams, MA 01247-4100	1894	$5,397 (S)	$5,620	5-M	1,811	122
Massachusetts Coll of Pharm & Health Sci, Boston, MA 02115-5896	1823	$20,220	$10,570	1-D	2,587	150
Massachusetts Inst of Tech, Cambridge, MA 02139-4307	1861	$30,800	$9,100	1-D	10,320	1,669
Master's Coll & Sem, Santa Clarita, CA 91321-1200	1927	$18,170	$6,370	2-D	1,523	159
McDaniel Coll, Westminster, MD 21157-4390	1867	$24,800	$5,600	1-M	3,304	190
McKendree Coll, Lebanon, IL 62254-1299	1828	$16,600	$6,360	2-M	2,257	225
McMurry Univ, Abilene, TX 79697	1923	$14,350	$5,500	2-B	1,386	135
McNeese State Univ, Lake Charles, LA 70609	1939	$3,159 (S)	$4,637	5-M	8,785	413
Medaille Coll, Buffalo, NY 14214-2695	1875	$14,320	$6,800	1-M	2,526	297
Medgar Evers Coll of the City Univ of New York, Brooklyn, NY 11225-2298	1969	$4,230 (S)	NA	11-B	5,098	339
Med Coll of Georgia, Augusta, GA 30912	1828	$3,954 (S)	$2,334	5-D	2,115	764
Med Univ of South Carolina, Charleston, SC 29425-0002	1824	$9,446 (S)	NA	5-D	2,428	1,281
Mercer Univ, Macon, GA 31207-0003	1833	$22,050	$7,060	2-D	7,180	577
Mercy Coll, Dobbs Ferry, NY 10522-1189	1951	$11,374	$8,426	1-M	10,395	989
Mercyhurst Coll, Erie, PA 16546	1926	$19,113	$7,074	2-M	4,035	237
Meredith Coll, Raleigh, NC 27607-5298 (3)	1891	$19,950	$5,600	1-M	2,168	262
Merrimack Coll, North Andover, MA 01845-5800	1947	$22,100	$9,200	2-M	2,326	244
Mesa State Coll, Grand Junction, CO 81501-3122	1925	$2,724 (S)	$6,501	5-M	6,235	361
Messiah Coll, Grantham, PA 17027	1909	$20,790	$6,560	2-B	2,917	310
Methodist Coll, Fayetteville, NC 28311-1498	1956	$17,850	$6,770	2-M	2,257	198
Metropolitan Coll of New York, New York, NY 10013-1919 (4)	1964	$14,124	NA	1-M	1,591	277
Metropolitan State Coll of Denver, Denver, CO 80217-3362	1963	$2,859 (S)	NA	5-B	20,761	1,141
Metropolitan State Univ, St. Paul, MN 55106-5000	1971	$4,392 (S)	NA	5-M	6,516	422
Miami Intl Univ of Art & Design, Miami, FL 33132-1418	1965	$17,952	$4,880	3-M	1,406	105
Miami Univ, Oxford, OH 45056	1809	$9,642 (S)	$7,010	12-D	17,151	1,161
Michigan State Univ, East Lansing, MI 48824	1855	$7,000 (S)	$5,458	5-D	44,836	2,671
Michigan Tech Univ, Houghton, MI 49931-1295	1885	$7,610 (S)	$6,096	5-D	6,540	405
MidAmerica Nazarene Univ, Olathe, KS 66062-1899	1966	$14,780	$5,790	2-M	1,985	172
Middlebury Coll, Middlebury, VT 05753-6002	1800	$40,400 (C)	NA	1-D	2,357	242
Middle Tennessee State Univ, Murfreesboro, TN 37132	1911	$4,230 (S)	$4,814	5-D	22,322	1,054
Midway Coll, Midway, KY 40347-1120 (3)	1847	$12,750	$5,800	2-B	1,271	179
Midwestern State Univ, Wichita Falls, TX 76308	1922	$3,740 (S)	$4,844	5-M	6,348	315
Miles Coll, Birmingham, AL 35208	1905	$5,660	$5,074	2-B	1,716	129
Millersville Univ of Pennsylvania, Millersville, PA 17551-0302	1855	$6,081 (S)	$5,642	5-M	7,998	468
Millikin Univ, Decatur, IL 62522-2084	1901	$20,300	$6,510	2-M	2,672	287
Millsaps Coll, Jackson, MS 39210-0001	1890	$20,690	$7,566	2-M	1,146	97
Mills Coll, Oakland, CA 94613-1000 (3)	1852	$27,085	$9,400	1-D	1,256	154
Milwaukee Sch of Engr, Milwaukee, WI 53202-3109	1903	$23,955	$5,892	1-M	2,363	209
Minnesota State Univ Mankato, Mankato, MN 56001	1868	$5,088 (S)	$4,716	5-M	14,153	696
Minnesota State Univ Moorhead, Moorhead, MN 56563-0002	1885	$4,894 (S)	$4,530	5-M	7,642	302
Minot State Univ, Minot, ND 58707-0002	1913	$3,712 (S)	$3,592	5-M	3,851	238
Mississippi Coll, Clinton, MS 39058	1826	$12,058	$5,694	2-F	3,588	283
Mississippi State Univ, Mississippi State, MS 39762	1878	$4,106 (S)	$5,994	5-D	15,934	1,139
Mississippi Univ for Women, Columbus, MS 39701-9998 (4)	1884	$3,495 (S)	$3,778	5-M	2,328	214
Mississippi Valley State Univ, Itta Bena, MS 38941-1400	1946	$3,832 (S)	$3,506	5-M	3,621	173
Missouri Baptist Univ, St. Louis, MO 63141-8660	1964	$13,030	$5,800	2-M	4,058	184
Missouri Southern State Univ, Joplin, MO 64801-1595	1937	$3,976 (S)	$4,770	5-M	5,256	284
Missouri State Univ, Springfield, MO 65804-0094	1905	$5,128 (S)	$4,660	5-D	19,114	978
Missouri Valley Coll, Marshall, MO 65340-3197	1889	$13,500	$5,200	2-B	1,623	113
Missouri Western State Coll, St. Joseph, MO 64507-2294	1915	$4,778 (S)	$4,396	5-B	5,065	313
Molloy Coll, Rockville Centre, NY 11571-5002	1955	$15,850	NA	1-M	3,352	357
Monmouth Coll, Monmouth, IL 61462-1998	1853	$19,350	$5,450	2-B	1,253	105
Monmouth Univ, West Long Branch, NJ 07764-1898	1933	$19,704	$7,911	1-M	6,329	534
Montana State Univ-Billings, Billings, MT 59101-0298	1927	$4,550 (S)	$4,500	5-M	4,702	279
Montana State Univ-Northern, Havre, MT 59501-7751	1929	$4,519 (S)	$5,190	5-M	1,589	103
Montana State Univ, Bozeman, MT 59717	1893	$4,577 (S)	$5,500	5-D	12,003	816
Montana Tech of The Univ of Montana, Butte, MT 59701-8997	1895	$404/credit (S)	$5,128	5-M	2,188	149
Montclair State Univ, Upper Montclair, NJ 07043-1624	1908	$7,026 (S)	$8,212	5-D	15,637	1,092
Montreat Coll, Montreat, NC 28757-1267	1916	$15,560	$5,008	2-M	1,035	120

Name, address	Year Founded	Tuition & Fees	Rm. & Board	Control, Degree	Enroll-ment	Faculty
Moody Bible Inst, Chicago, IL 60610-3284	1886	$1,400	$12,480	2-F	2,687	100
Moravian Coll, Bethlehem, PA 18018-6650	1742	$23,574	$7,310	2-F	2,078	193
Morehead State Univ, Morehead, KY 40351	1922	$3,840 (S)	$4,410	5-M	9,293	488
Morehouse Coll, Atlanta, GA 30314 (1)	1867	$15,740	$8,748	1-B	2,891	225
Morgan State Univ, Baltimore, MD 21251	1867	$5,718 (S)	$6,780	5-D	6,621	458
Morningside Coll, Sioux City, IA 51106-1751	1894	$17,170	$5,400	2-M	1,204	109
Mountain State Univ, Beckley, WV 25802-9003	1933	$5,400	$5,440	1-M	4,107	216
Mount Aloysius Coll, Cresson, PA 16630-1999	1939	$14,530	$5,960	2-M	1,500	160
Mount Holyoke Coll, South Hadley, MA 01075 (3)	1837	$30,938	$9,060	1-M	2,073	249
Mount Ida Coll, Newton, MA 02459-3310	1899	$19,096	$9,830	1-B	1,297	214
Mount Marty Coll, Yankton, SD 57078-3724	1936	$14,936	$4,764	2-M	1,163	133
Mount Mary Coll, Milwaukee, WI 53222-4597 (3)	1913	$16,155	$5,350	2-M	1,632	195
Mount Mercy Coll, Cedar Rapids, IA 52402-4797	1928	$18,840	$5,680	2-B	1,486	142
Mount Olive Coll, Mount Olive, NC 28365	1951	$11,800	$4,800	2-B	2,582	191
Mount St Mary Coll, Newburgh, NY 12550-3494	1960	$15,690	$7,640	1-M	2,621	249
Mount St Mary's Coll, Los Angeles, CA 90049-1599 (4)	1925	$21,782	$8,635	2-M	2,257	287
Mount St Mary's Univ, Emmitsburg, MD 21727-7799	1808	$22,900	$8,030	2-F	2,125	152
Mt. Sierra Coll, Monrovia, CA 91016	1990	$16,200	NA	3-B	1,100	50
Mount Union Coll, Alliance, OH 44601-3993	1846	$18,810	$5,630	2-B	2,333	215
Mount Vernon Nazarene Univ, Mount Vernon, OH 43050-9500	1964	$14,976	$4,734	2-M	2,455	230
Muhlenberg Coll, Allentown, PA 18104-5586	1848	$26,800	$7,025	2-B	2,446	255
Murray State Univ, Murray, KY 42071-0009	1922	$3,984 (S)	$4,510	5-M	10,120	539
Muskingum Coll, New Concord, OH 43762	1837	$15,630	$6,200	2-M	2,142	129
Naropa Univ, Boulder, CO 80302-6697	1974	$16,548	$7,236	1-F	1,219	298
Natl-Louis Univ, Chicago, IL 60603	1886	$16,320	$6,213	1-D	7,665	284
Natl Univ, La Jolla, CA 92037-1011	1971	$9,500	NA	1-M	25,684	2,204
Nazareth Coll of Rochester, Rochester, NY 14618-3790	1924	$18,776	$7,840	1-M	3,140	294
Nebraska Wesleyan Univ, Lincoln, NE 68504-2796	1887	$17,390	$4,630	2-M	1,953	190
Neumann Coll, Aston, PA 19014-1298	1965	$17,190	$7,740	2-M	2,682	218
Newbury Coll, Brookline, MA 02445	1962	$16,100	$8,250	1-B	1,161	93
New Coll of California, San Francisco, CA 94102-5206	1971	$12,223	NA	1-M	1,133	192
New England Coll, Henniker, NH 03242-3293	1946	$23,010	$8,456	1-M	1,329	130
New England Inst of Art, Brookline, MA 02445	NA	$17,225	$9,450	3-B	1,235	100
New Jersey City Univ, Jersey City, NJ 07305-1597	1927	$6,550 (S)	$6,958	5-M	8,799	636
New Jersey Inst of Tech, Newark, NJ 07102	1881	$9,180 (S)	$8,242	5-D	8,249	643
Newman Univ, Wichita, KS 67213-2097	1933	$16,002	$6,586	2-M	2,179	180
New Mexico Highlands Univ, Las Vegas, NM 87701	1893	$2,300 (S)	$4,274	5-M	3,671	246
New Mexico Inst of Mining & Tech, Socorro, NM 87801	1889	$3,280 (S)	$4,670	5-D	1,806	151
New Mexico State Univ, Las Cruces, NM 88003-8001	1888	$3,666 (S)	$5,046	5-D	16,428	982
New Orleans Baptist Theol Sem, New Orleans, LA 70126-4858 (2)	1917	$3,770	NA	2-D	2,712	84
New Sch Bach's Prog, New Sch Univ, New York, NY 10011-8603	1919	$16,254	$10,810	1-D	1,809	515
New York Inst of Tech, Old Westbury, NY 11568-8000	1955	$18,190	$7,780	1-D	9,387	866
New York Univ, New York, NY 10012-1019	1831	$30,094	$11,390	1-D	39,408	4,167
Niagara Univ, Niagara University, NY 14109	1856	$18,420	$8,050	2-M	3,807	327
Nicholls State Univ, Thibodaux, LA 70310	1948	$3,240 (S)	$3,534	5-M	7,473	281
Nichols Coll, Dudley, MA 01571-5000	1815	$20,810	$8,052	1-M	1,792	65
Norfolk State Univ, Norfolk, VA 23504	1935	$4,295 (S)	$6,236	5-D	6,846	446
North Carolina Agr & Tech State Univ, Greensboro, NC 27411	1891	$3,066 (S)	$5,070	5-D	9,115	458
North Carolina Central Univ, Durham, NC 27707-3129	1910	$3,042 (S)	$4,311	5-F	7,727	471
North Carolina State Univ, Raleigh, NC 27695	1887	$4,667 (S)	$6,851	5-D	29,957	1,825
North Carolina Wesleyan Coll, Rocky Mount, NC 27804-8677	1956	$14,814	$6,555	2-B	1,776	177
North Central Coll, Naperville, IL 60566-7063	1861	$20,400	$6,747	2-M	2,377	209
Northcentral Univ, Prescott, AZ 86301-1747	NA	$9,000	NA	3-D	1,401	138
North Central Univ, Minneapolis, MN 55404-1322	1930	$11,284	$4,350	2-B	1,241	80
North Dakota State Univ, Fargo, ND 58105	1890	$4,775 (A)	$4,727	5-D	12,026	609
Northeastern Illinois Univ, Chicago, IL 60625-4699	1961	$4,235 (S)	NA	5-M	12,164	664
Northeastern State Univ, Tahlequah, OK 74464-2399	1846	$3,000 (S)	$3,080	5-F	9,562	480
Northeastern Univ, Boston, MA 02115-5096	1898	$27,080	$10,180	1-D	18,979	1,174
Northern Arizona Univ, Flagstaff, AZ 86011	1899	$4,073 (S)	$5,785	5-D	19,147	1,316
Northern Illinois Univ, De Kalb, IL 60115-2854	1895	$5,760 (S)	$5,740	5-D	24,818	1,152
Northern Kentucky Univ, Highland Heights, KY 41099	1968	$4,368 (S)	$4,660	5-F	13,908	788
Northern Michigan Univ, Marquette, MI 49855-5301	1899	$5,434 (S)	$6,182	5-M	9,846	428
Northern State Univ, Aberdeen, SD 57401-7198	1901	$4,448 (S)	$3,733	5-M	2,346	100
North Georgia Coll & State Univ, Dahlonega, GA 30597	1873	$2,944 (S)	$4,408	5-M	4,552	315
North Greenville Coll, Tigerville, SC 29688-1892	1892	$10,350	$5,950	2-B	1,766	132
North Park Univ, Chicago, IL 60625-4895	1891	$20,410	$6,980	2-D	2,181	121
Northwestern Coll, Orange City, IA 51041-1996	1882	$16,360	$4,656	2-B	1,284	130
Northwestern Coll, St. Paul, MN 55113-1598	1902	$18,370	$6,020	2-B	2,734	167
Northwestern Oklahoma State Univ, Alva, OK 73717-2799	1897	$3,000 (S)	$2,920	5-M	2,129	145
Northwestern State Univ of Louisiana, Natchitoches, LA 71497	1884	$3,241 (S)	$3,426	5-M	10,546	578
Northwestern Univ, Evanston, IL 60208	1851	$31,789	$9,873	1-D	16,663	1,135
Northwest Missouri State Univ, Maryville, MO 64468-6001	1905	$5,505 (S)	$5,080	5-M	6,230	259
Northwest Nazarene Univ, Nampa, ID 83686-5897	1913	$17,730	$4,860	2-M	1,578	96
Northwest Univ, Kirkland, WA 98033	1934	$15,944	$6,450	2-M	1,180	93
Northwood Univ, Midland, MI 48640-2398	1959	$15,183	$6,696	1-M	3,748	84
Northwood Univ, Texas Cmps, Cedar Hill, TX 75104-1204	1966	$15,183	$6,849	1-B	1,139	34
Norwich Univ, Northfield, VT 05663	1819	$19,650	$7,090	1-M	2,707	272
Notre Dame Coll, South Euclid, OH 44121-4293	1922	$18,350	$6,460	2-M	1,299	87
Notre Dame de Namur Univ, Belmont, CA 94002-1908	1851	$22,770	$10,070	2-M	1,652	184
Nova Southeastern Univ, Fort Lauderdale, FL 33314-7796	1964	$15,820	$8,126	1-D	25,430	1,531
Nyack Coll, Nyack, NY 10960-3698	1882	$15,550	$7,600	2-F	2,908	288
Oakland City Univ, Oakland City, IN 47660-1099	1885	$13,560	$5,030	2-D	1,928	191
Oakland Univ, Rochester, MI 48309-4401	1957	$5,354 (S)	$5,820	5-D	16,901	839
Oakwood Coll, Huntsville, AL 35896	1896	$11,298	$6,374	2-B	1,778	161
Oberlin Coll, Oberlin, OH 44074	1833	$31,163	$7,643	1-M	2,827	286
Occidental Coll, Los Angeles, CA 90041-3314	1887	$31,314	$8,672	1-M	1,887	203
Oglethorpe Univ, Atlanta, GA 30319-2797	1835	$22,300	$8,000	1-M	1,053	136
Ohio Dominican Univ, Columbus, OH 43219-2099	1911	$18,050	$6,200	2-M	2,844	192
Ohio Northern Univ, Ada, OH 45810-1599	1871	$25,815	$6,360	2-F	3,495	316
Ohio State Univ-Mansfield Cmps, Mansfield, OH 44906-1599	1958	$4,977 (S)	$6,012	5-M	1,634	89
Ohio State Univ-Newark Cmps, Newark, OH 43055-1797	1957	$4,977 (S)	$6,012	5-M	2,143	125
Ohio State Univ, Columbus, OH 43210	1870	$7,479 (S)	$6,909	5-D	50,995	3,782
Ohio State Univ at Lima, Lima, OH 45804-3576	1960	$4,977 (S)	$6,012	5-M	1,281	82

Name, address	Year Founded	Tuition & Fees	Rm. & Board	Control, Degree	Enroll-ment	Faculty
Ohio State Univ at Marion, Marion, OH 43302-5695	1958	$4,977 (S)	$6,012	5-M	1,521	108
Ohio Univ-Chillicothe, Chillicothe, OH 45601-0629	1946	$4,008 (S)	NA	5-M	2,000	106
Ohio Univ-Eastern, St. Clairsville, OH 43950-9724	1957	$4,008 (S)	NA	5-B	1,118	114
Ohio Univ-Lancaster, Lancaster, OH 43130-1097	1968	$4,008 (S)	NA	5-M	1,744	104
Ohio Univ-Southern Cmps, Ironton, OH 45638-2214	1956	$4,026 (S)	NA	5-M	1,746	155
Ohio Univ-Zanesville, Zanesville, OH 43701-2695	1946	$4,263 (S)	NA	5-M	1,877	130
Ohio Univ, Athens, OH 45701-2979	1804	$7,770 (S)	$7,539	5-D	20,096	1,162
Ohio Wesleyan Univ, Delaware, OH 43015	1842	$26,820	$7,330	2-B	1,944	195
Oklahoma Baptist Univ, Shawnee, OK 74804	1910	$13,162	$3,800	2-M	1,883	119
Oklahoma Christian Univ, Oklahoma City, OK 73136-1100	1950	$13,749	$5,000	2-M	1,947	160
Oklahoma City Univ, Oklahoma City, OK 73106-1402	1904	$16,040	$5,950	2-F	3,695	285
Oklahoma Panhandle State Univ, Goodwell, OK 73939-0430	1909	$2,720 (S)	$2,810	5-B	1,237	89
Oklahoma State Univ, Stillwater, OK 74078	1890	$4,071 (S)	$5,602	5-D	23,626	1,184
Old Dominion Univ, Norfolk, VA 23529	1930	$5,268 (S)	$5,802	5-D	20,595	900
Olivet Coll, Olivet, MI 49076-9701	1844	$16,464	$5,480	2-M	1,069	67
Olivet Nazarene Univ, Bourbonnais, IL 60914-2271	1907	$16,490	$6,100	2-M	4,364	123
Oral Roberts Univ, Tulsa, OK 74171-0001	1963	$15,880	$6,530	2-D	3,828	267
Oregon Health & Sci Univ, Portland, OR 97239-3098	1974	$9,369 (S)	NA	12-D	1,849	836
Oregon Inst of Tech, Klamath Falls, OR 97601-8801	1947	$4,974 (S)	$5,935	5-M	3,373	130
Oregon State Univ, Corvallis, OR 97331	1868	$5,319 (S)	$6,786	5-D	19,162	808
Otis Coll of Art & Design, Los Angeles, CA 90045-9785	1918	$25,100	NA	1-M	1,043	235
Otterbein Coll, Westerville, OH 43081	1847	$21,342	$6,189	2-M	3,090	271
Ouachita Baptist Univ, Arkadelphia, AR 71998-0001	1886	$15,920	$5,000	2-B	1,511	142
Our Lady of Holy Cross Coll, New Orleans, LA 70131-7399	1916	$6,140	NA	2-M	1,446	123
Our Lady of the Lake Coll, Baton Rouge, LA 70808 (4)	1990	$7,280	NA	2-M	1,990	134
Our Lady of the Lake Univ of San Antonio, San Antonio, TX 78207-4689	1895	$16,430	$5,230	2-D	3,025	298
Pace Univ, New York, NY 10038	1906	$22,712	$8,400	1-D	13,670	1,219
Pacific Lutheran Univ, Tacoma, WA 98447	1890	$20,790	$6,410	2-M	3,643	259
Pacific Union Coll, Angwin, CA 94508-9707	1882	$18,054	$5,136	2-M	1,547	98
Pacific Univ, Forest Grove, OR 97116-1797	1849	$20,664	$5,764	1-D	2,521	278
Palm Beach Atlantic Univ, West Palm Beach, FL 33416-4708	1968	$17,342	$6,306	2-F	3,066	253
Palmer Coll of Chiropractic, Davenport, IA 52803-5287	1897	$5,895	NA	1-F	1,669	126
Park Univ, Parkville, MO 64152-3795	1875	$6,048	$5,180	1-M	12,548	889
Parsons Sch of Design, New Sch Univ, New York, NY 10011-8878	1896	$25,925	$10,810	1-M	2,958	759
Peirce Coll, Philadelphia, PA 19102-4699	1865	$12,310	NA	1-B	1,892	162
Pennsylvania Coll of Tech, Williamsport, PA 17701-5778	1965	$9,480 (S)	$5,132	12-B	6,358	469
Pennsylvania State Univ Abington Coll, Abington, PA 19001	1950	$9,614 (S)	NA	12-B	3,143	213
Pennsylvania State Univ Altoona Coll, Altoona, PA 16601-3760	1939	$10,026 (S)	$6,230	12-B	3,766	286
Pennsylvania State Univ at Erie, The Behrend Coll, Erie, PA 16563-0001	1948	$10,026 (S)	$6,230	12-M	3,593	267
Pennsylvania State Univ Berks Cmps of the Berks-Lehigh Valley Coll, Reading, PA 19610-6009	1924	$10,026 (S)	$6,810	12-B	2,416	178
Pennsylvania State Univ Harrisburg Cmps of the Capital Coll, Middletown, PA 17057-4898	1966	$10,016 (S)	$7,650	12-D	3,729	271
Pennsylvania State Univ Univ Park Cmps, University Park, PA 16802-1503	1855	$10,856 (S)	$6,230	12-D	41,289	2,543
Pepperdine Univ, Malibu, CA 90263	1937	$28,720	$8,640	2-D	7,919	743
Peru State Coll, Peru, NE 68421	1867	$3,534 (S)	$4,486	5-M	1,683	130
Pfeiffer Univ, Misenheimer, NC 28109-0960	1885	$14,570	$5,830	2-M	2,027	134
Philadelphia Biblical Univ, Langhorne, PA 19047-2990	1913	$14,500	$6,100	2-F	1,372	147
Philadelphia Univ, Philadelphia, PA 19144-5497	1884	$21,010	$7,782	1-D	3,212	428
Piedmont Coll, Demorest, GA 30535-0010	1897	$13,500	$4,700	2-M	2,222	176
Pikeville Coll, Pikeville, KY 41501	1889	$10,500	$5,000	2-F	1,066	70
Pittsburg State Univ, Pittsburg, KS 66762	1903	$3,294 (S)	$4,234	5-M	6,537	376
Plymouth State Univ, Plymouth, NH 03264-1595	1871	$6,618 (S)	$6,322	5-M	5,151	340
Point Loma Nazarene Univ, San Diego, CA 92106-2899	1902	$20,730	$7,150	2-M	3,209	295
Point Park Univ, Pittsburgh, PA 15222-1984	1960	$15,960	$7,000	1-M	3,292	343
Polytechnic Univ, Brooklyn Cmps, Brooklyn, NY 11201-2990	1854	$27,170	$8,000	1-D	2,819	277
Polytechnic Univ of Puerto Rico, Hato Rey, PR 00919	1966	$5,550	NA	1-M	5,674	354
Pomona Coll, Claremont, CA 91711	1887	$28,370	$10,380	1-B	1,562	221
Pontifical Catholic Univ of Puerto Rico, Ponce, PR 00717-0777	1948	$4,778	$3,140	2-D	7,548	234
Portland State Univ, Portland, OR 97207-0751	1946	$4,311 (S)	$8,310	5-D	23,444	1,199
Post Univ, Waterbury, CT 06723-2540	1890	$18,800	$7,950	1-B	1,198	127
Prairie View A&M Univ, Prairie View, TX 77446-0519	1878	$4,202 (S)	$6,068	5-D	8,350	467
Pratt Inst, Brooklyn, NY 11205-3899	1887	$27,580	$8,576	1-F	4,540	834
Presbyterian Coll, Clinton, SC 29325	1880	$21,622	$6,326	2-B	1,187	120
Prescott Coll, Prescott, AZ 86301	1966	$17,450	NA	1-M	1,036	70
Princeton Univ, Princeton, NJ 08544-1019	1746	$29,910	$8,387	1-D	6,836	1,052
Providence Coll, Providence, RI 02918	1917	$25,310	$9,270	2-M	5,366	355
Purchase Coll, State Univ of New York, Purchase, NY 10577-1400	1967	$5,823 (S)	$7,212	5-M	3,832	332
Purdue Univ, West Lafayette, IN 47907	1869	$6,335 (S)	$7,406	5-D	38,653	2,224
Purdue Univ Calumet, Hammond, IN 46323-2094	1951	$4,662 (S)	$3,990	5-M	9,222	291
Purdue Univ North Central, Westville, IN 46391-9542	1967	$4,712 (S)	NA	5-M	3,467	244
Queens Coll of the City Univ of New York, Flushing, NY 11367-1597	1937	$4,361 (S)	NA	11-M	17,395	1,180
Queens Univ of Charlotte, Charlotte, NC 28274-0002	1857	$18,028	$6,500	2-M	2,107	105
Quincy Univ, Quincy, IL 62301-2699	1860	$17,650	$5,725	2-M	1,294	131
Quinnipiac Univ, Hamden, CT 06518-1940	1929	$24,340	$10,300	1-D	7,220	741
Radford Univ, Radford, VA 24142	1910	$4,762 (S)	$5,886	5-M	9,329	533
Ramapo Coll of New Jersey, Mahwah, NJ 07430-1680	1969	$8,081 (S)	$8,208	5-M	5,617	388
Randolph-Macon Coll, Ashland, VA 23005-5505	1830	$22,625	$6,510	2-B	1,127	137
Reed Coll, Portland, OR 97202-8199	1908	$30,900	$8,070	1-M	1,341	130
Regent Univ, Virginia Beach, VA 23464-9800	1977	$11,362	NA	1-D	3,447	NA
Regis Coll, Weston, MA 02493 (3)	1927	$20,500	$9,360	2-M	1,271	117
Regis Univ, Denver, CO 80221-1099	1877	$22,400	$7,870	2-D	16,335	2,379
Reinhardt Coll, Waleska, GA 30183-2981	1883	$12,200	$5,762	2-B	1,096	112
Rensselaer Polytechnic Inst, Troy, NY 12180-3590	1824	$29,786	$9,083	1-D	7,521	492
Rhode Island Coll, Providence, RI 02908-1991	1854	$4,676 (S)	$7,010	5-D	8,881	NA
Rhode Island Sch of Design, Providence, RI 02903-2784	1877	$27,975	$7,722	1-F	2,282	482
Rhodes Coll, Memphis, TN 38112-1690	1848	$25,956	$6,904	2-M	1,633	175
Rice Univ, Houston, TX 77251-1892	1912	$21,206	$8,380	1-D	4,973	675
Richard Stockton Coll of New Jersey, Pomona, NJ 08240-0195	1969	$7,203 (S)	$7,252	5-M	7,004	461
Rider Univ, Lawrenceville, NJ 08648-3001	1865	$23,470	$8,840	1-M	5,502	512
Ringling Sch of Art & Design, Sarasota, FL 34234-5895	1931	$20,195	$8,811	1-B	1,008	121
Rivier Coll, Nashua, NH 03060-5086	1933	$19,875	$7,273	2-M	2,289	179
Roanoke Coll, Salem, VA 24153-3794	1842	$22,109	$6,912	2-B	1,850	168

Name, address	Year Founded	Tuition & Fees	Rm. & Board	Control, Degree	Enroll-ment	Faculty
Robert Morris Coll, Chicago, IL 60605	1913	$14,250	$6,390	1-B	5,520	389
Robert Morris Univ, Moon Township, PA 15108-1189	1921	$14,226	$7,286	1-D	4,971	383
Roberts Wesleyan Coll, Rochester, NY 14624-1997	1866	$19,324	$5,028	2-M	1,926	196
Rochester Coll, Rochester Hills, MI 48307-2764	1959	$11,456	$6,316	2-B	1,011	106
Rochester Inst of Tech, Rochester, NY 14623-5603	1829	$22,413	$8,136	1-D	14,552	1,218
Rockford Coll, Rockford, IL 61108-2393	1847	$22,460	$7,221	1-M	1,280	162
Rockhurst Univ, Kansas City, MO 64110-2561	1910	$18,560	$5,500	2-D	2,764	203
Rogers State Univ, Claremore, OK 74017-3252	1909	$2,430 (S)	$5,985	5-B	3,300	151
Roger Williams Univ, Bristol, RI 02809	1956	$22,866	$10,237	1-F	5,070	383
Rollins Coll, Winter Park, FL 32789-4499	1885	$27,700	$8,570	1-M	2,571	229
Roosevelt Univ, Chicago, IL 60605-1394	1945	$16,330	$8,400	1-D	7,385	662
Rose-Hulman Inst of Tech, Terre Haute, IN 47803-3999 (2)	1874	$26,136	$7,065	1-M	1,904	150
Rosemont Coll, Rosemont, PA 19010-1699 (3)	1921	$19,365	$8,400	2-M	1,083	166
Rowan Univ, Glassboro, NJ 08028-1701	1923	$7,970 (S)	$7,642	5-D	9,688	788
Rush Univ, Chicago, IL 60612-3832	1969	$16,848	$5,535	1-D	1,362	796
Rust Coll, Holly Springs, MS 38635-2328	1866	$6,060	$2,600	2-B	1,001	50
Rutgers, The State Univ of New Jersey, Camden, Camden, NJ 08102-1401	1927	$8,389 (S)	$7,862	5-F	5,563	419
Rutgers, The State Univ of New Jersey, Newark, Newark, NJ 07102	1892	$8,209 (S)	$8,570	5-D	10,293	638
Rutgers, The State Univ of New Jersey, New Brunswick/Piscataway, New Brunswick, NJ 08901-1281	1766	$8,564 (S)	$8,357	5-D	34,696	2,330
Sacred Heart Univ, Fairfield, CT 06825-1000	1963	$21,990	$9,280	2-D	5,454	446
Sage Coll of Albany, Albany, NY 12208-3425	1957	$16,020	$7,150	1-B	1,051	77
Saginaw Valley State Univ, University Center, MI 48710	1963	$4,913 (S)	$5,850	5-M	9,448	243
St Ambrose Univ, Davenport, IA 52803-2898	1882	$17,565	$6,635	2-D	3,534	315
St Anselm Coll, Manchester, NH 03102-1310	1889	$24,660	$9,070	2-B	1,987	176
St Augustine Coll, Chicago, IL 60640-3501	1980	$7,128	NA	1-B	1,582	135
St Augustine's Coll, Raleigh, NC 27604-2298	1867	$10,388	$5,312	2-B	1,395	97
St Bonaventure Univ, St. Bonaventure, NY 14778-2284	1858	$19,485	$6,910	2-M	2,806	229
St Cloud State Univ, St. Cloud, MN 56301-4498	1869	$5,176 (S)	$4,088	5-M	15,608	842
St Edward's Univ, Austin, TX 78704	1885	$17,320	NA	2-M	4,651	410
St Francis Coll, Brooklyn Heights, NY 11201-4398	1884	$11,785	$8,000	2-B	2,326	211
St Francis Univ, Loretto, PA 15940-0600	1847	$20,440	$7,420	2-M	1,846	164
St John Fisher Coll, Rochester, NY 14618-3597	1948	$18,450	$7,900	2-M	3,376	355
St John's Univ, Collegeville, MN 56321 (2)	1857	$22,148	$6,118	2-F	2,015	167
St John's Univ, Jamaica, NY 11439	1870	$23,280	$11,000	2-D	19,813	1,378
St Joseph Coll, West Hartford, CT 06117-2700 (3)	1932	$21,970	$9,225	2-M	1,792	85
St Joseph's Coll, Rensselaer, IN 47978	1889	$19,160	$6,300	2-M	1,010	92
St Joseph's Coll, New York, Brooklyn, NY 11205-3688	1916	$11,430	NA	1-M	1,313	137
St Joseph's Coll, Suffolk Cmps, Patchogue, NY 11772-2399	1916	$11,954	NA	1-M	4,005	386
St Joseph's Univ, Philadelphia, PA 19131-1395	1851	$25,905	$9,610	2-D	7,730	569
St Lawrence Univ, Canton, NY 13617-1455	1856	$30,480	$7,755	1-M	2,277	206
St Leo Univ, Saint Leo, FL 33574-6665	1889	$14,080	$7,260	2-M	1,825	122
St Louis Univ, St. Louis, MO 63103-2097	1818	$23,558	$7,780	2-D	11,422	1,002
St Martin's Coll, Lacey, WA 98503-1297	1895	$19,980	$6,200	2-M	1,512	75
St Mary-of-the-Woods Coll, Saint Mary-of-the-Woods, IN 47876 (3)	1840	$17,860	$6,560	2-M	1,703	68
St Mary's Coll, Notre Dame, IN 46556 (3)	1844	$24,358	$8,180	2-B	1,418	189
St Mary's Coll of California, Moraga, CA 94575	1863	$25,150	$9,530	2-D	4,536	564
St Mary's Coll of Maryland, St. Mary's City, MD 20686-3001	1840	$9,680 (S)	$7,400	5-B	1,935	199
St Mary's Univ of Minnesota, Winona, MN 55987-1399	1912	$17,925	$5,450	2-D	4,861	564
St Mary's Univ of San Antonio, San Antonio, TX 78228-8507	1852	$17,756	$6,498	2-D	4,110	327
St Michael's Coll, Colchester, VT 05439	1904	$25,535	$6,250	2-M	2,424	211
St Norbert Coll, De Pere, WI 54115-2099	1898	$21,510	$5,980	2-M	2,103	161
St Olaf Coll, Northfield, MN 55057-1098	1874	$26,500	$6,300	2-B	3,046	327
St Peter's Coll, Jersey City, NJ 07306-5997	1872	$19,750	$8,430	2-M	3,282	NA
St Thomas Aquinas Coll, Sparkill, NY 10976	1952	$16,600	$8,850	1-M	2,336	164
St Thomas Univ, Miami Gardens, FL 33054-6459	1961	$17,010	$10,720	2-F	2,630	302
St Vincent Coll, Latrobe, PA 15650-2690	1846	$20,822	$6,424	2-M	1,490	148
St Xavier Univ, Chicago, IL 60655-3105	1847	$17,330	$6,724	2-M	5,722	398
Salem Coll, Winston-Salem, NC 27108-0548 (3)	1772	$16,490	$8,870	2-M	1,114	92
Salem State Coll, Salem, MA 01970-5353	1854	$5,284 (S)	$7,350	5-M	9,347	562
Salisbury Univ, Salisbury, MD 21801-6837	1925	$5,976 (S)	$7,050	5-M	6,942	494
Salve Regina Univ, Newport, RI 02840-4192	1934	$22,200	$9,000	2-D	2,479	237
Samford Univ, Birmingham, AL 35229-0002	1841	$13,944	$5,506	2-D	4,416	406
Sam Houston State Univ, Huntsville, TX 77341	1879	$4,260 (S)	$4,336	5-D	14,371	584
Samuel Merritt Coll, Oakland, CA 94609-3108 (4)	1909	$23,928	$10,055	1-D	1,008	154
San Diego State Univ, San Diego, CA 92182	1897	$2,936 (S)	$9,391	5-D	32,936	1,618
San Francisco State Univ, San Francisco, CA 94132-1722	1899	$3,066 (S)	$8,870	5-D	28,804	1,632
San Jose State Univ, San Jose, CA 95192-0001	1857	NA	NA	5-M	29,044	1,661
Santa Clara Univ, Santa Clara, CA 95053	1851	$27,135	$9,693	2-D	7,908	710
Sarah Lawrence Coll, Bronxville, NY 10708-5999	1926	$32,416	$11,438	1-M	1,574	213
Savannah Coll of Art & Design, Savannah, GA 31402-3146	1978	$22,100	$8,700	1-M	6,776	368
Savannah State Univ, Savannah, GA 31404	1890	$2,940 (S)	$4,498	5-M	2,800	160
Sch of the Art Inst of Chicago, Chicago, IL 60603-3103	1866	$27,150	$8,200	1-M	2,660	472
Sch of Visual Arts, New York, NY 10010-3994	1947	$19,620	$11,250	3-M	3,442	848
Seattle Pacific Univ, Seattle, WA 98119-1997	1891	$20,466	$7,368	2-D	3,779	310
Seattle Univ, Seattle, WA 98122-1090	1891	$21,285	$7,038	2-D	6,810	565
Seton Hall Univ, South Orange, NJ 07079-2697	1856	$23,460	$10,162	2-D	9,824	908
Seton Hill Univ, Greensburg, PA 15601	1883	$20,630	$6,420	2-M	1,706	154
Shawnee State Univ, Portsmouth, OH 45662-4344	1986	$5,202 (S)	$6,510	5-B	3,798	290
Shaw Univ, Raleigh, NC 27601-2399	1865	$9,438	$6,050	2-F	2,709	265
Shenandoah Univ, Winchester, VA 22601-5195	1875	$19,240	$7,090	2-D	3,000	325
Shepherd Univ, Shepherdstown, WV 25443-3210	1871	$3,654 (S)	$5,574	5-M	5,206	310
Shippensburg Univ of Pennsylvania, Shippensburg, PA 17257-2299	1871	$5,986 (S)	$5,274	5-M	7,653	378
Siena Coll, Loudonville, NY 12211-1462	1937	$19,130	$7,575	2-B	3,338	323
Siena Heights Univ, Adrian, MI 49221-1796	1919	$15,520	$5,460	2-M	2,153	NA
Silver Lake Coll, Manitowoc, WI 54220-9319	1869	$16,000	$4,250	2-M	1,034	162
Simmons Coll, Boston, MA 02115 (3)	1899	$25,440	$10,200	1-D	4,549	456
Simpson Coll, Indianola, IA 50125-1297	1860	$19,635	$5,561	2-B	1,964	130
Simpson Univ, Redding, CA 96003-8606	1921	$17,000	$5,900	2-M	1,134	87
Skidmore Coll, Saratoga Springs, NY 12866-1632	1903	$31,108	$8,710	1-M	2,691	328
Slippery Rock Univ of Pennsylvania, Slippery Rock, PA 16057-1383	1889	$6,096 (S)	$4,714	5-D	7,928	379
Smith Coll, Northampton, MA 01063 (3)	1871	$29,156	$9,730	1-D	3,159	305
Sojourner-Douglass Coll, Baltimore, MD 21205-1814 (4)	1980	$6,190	NA	1-M	1,124	136

Name, address	Year Founded	Tuition & Fees	Rm. & Board	Control, Degree	Enroll-ment	Faculty
Sonoma State Univ, Rohnert Park, CA 94928-3609	1960	$3,408 (S)	$8,805	5-M	7,977	505
South Carolina State Univ, Orangeburg, SC 29117-0001	1896	$6,355 (S)	$5,776	5-D	4,294	267
South Dakota Sch of Mines & Tech, Rapid City, SD 57701-3995	1885	$4,534 (S)	$3,684	5-D	2,353	137
South Dakota State Univ, Brookings, SD 57007	1881	$4,732 (S)	$4,769	5-D	10,884	547
Southeastern Coll of the Assemblies of God, Lakeland, FL 33801-6099	1935	$10,140	$5,470	2-B	1,964	116
Southeastern Louisiana Univ, Hammond, LA 70402	1925	$3,191 (S)	$4,290	5-M	15,472	730
Southeastern Oklahoma State Univ, Durant, OK 74701-0609	1909	$3,123 (S)	$3,470	5-M	4,203	223
Southeast Missouri State Univ, Cape Girardeau, MO 63701-4799	1873	$4,875 (S)	$5,317	5-M	9,618	516
Southern Adventist Univ, Collegedale, TN 37315-0370	1892	$14,020	$4,480	2-M	2,391	194
Southern Arkansas Univ-Magnolia, Magnolia, AR 71753	1909	$3,858 (S)	$3,600	5-M	3,057	184
Southern Connecticut State Univ, New Haven, CT 06515-1355	1893	$5,814 (S)	$7,698	5-D	12,177	816
Southern Illinois Univ Carbondale, Carbondale, IL 62901-4701	1869	$6,341 (S)	$5,200	5-D	21,589	1,061
Southern Illinois Univ Edwardsville, Edwardsville, IL 62026-0001	1957	$5,179 (S)	$5,819	5-F	13,493	770
Southern Methodist Univ, Dallas, TX 75275	1911	$26,880	$9,208	2-D	10,901	888
Southern Nazarene Univ, Bethany, OK 73008	1899	$13,638	$5,266	2-M	2,177	213
Southern New Hampshire Univ, Manchester, NH 03106-1045	1932	$19,314	$7,866	1-D	3,887	389
Southern Oregon Univ, Ashland, OR 97520	1926	$4,863 (S)	$7,560	5-M	5,162	312
Southern Polytechnic State Univ, Marietta, GA 30060-2896	1948	$2,892 (S)	$4,946	5-M	3,801	226
Southern Univ & Agr & Mech Coll, Baton Rouge, LA 70813	1880	$3,440 (S)	$4,310	5-D	9,400	561
Southern Univ at New Orleans, New Orleans, LA 70126-1009	1959	$2,990 (S)	NA	5-M	5,000	NA
Southern Utah Univ, Cedar City, UT 84720-2498	1897	$3,054 (S)	$5,400	5-M	6,672	290
Southern Wesleyan Univ, Central, SC 29630-1020	1906	$14,750	$5,200	2-M	2,632	231
Southwest Baptist Univ, Bolivar, MO 65613-2597	1878	$13,250	$3,950	2-M	3,445	281
Southwestern Adventist Univ, Keene, TX 76059	1894	$11,858	$5,534	2-M	1,191	92
Southwestern Assemblies of God Univ, Waxahachie, TX 75165-2397	1927	$8,430	$4,470	2-M	1,676	95
Southwestern Coll, Winfield, KS 67156-2499	1885	$16,118	$2,334	2-M	1,410	167
Southwestern Oklahoma State Univ, Weatherford, OK 73096-3098	1901	$3,000 (S)	$3,090	5-F	4,841	NA
Southwestern Univ, Georgetown, TX 78626	1840	$20,220	$6,359	2-B	1,276	166
Southwest Minnesota State Univ, Marshall, MN 56258-1598	1963	$5,294 (S)	$4,806	5-M	5,636	159
Spalding Univ, Louisville, KY 40203-2188	1814	$14,100	$4,572	2-D	1,679	283
Spelman Coll, Atlanta, GA 30314-4399 (3)	1881	$15,945	$8,455	1-B	2,186	233
Spring Arbor Univ, Spring Arbor, MI 49283-9799	1873	$16,096	$5,610	2-M	3,511	143
Springfield Coll, Springfield, MA 01109-3797	1885	$21,360	$7,350	1-D	3,119	346
Spring Hill Coll, Mobile, AL 36608-1791	1830	$19,950	$7,192	2-M	1,427	131
Stanford Univ, Stanford, CA 94305-9991	1891	$29,847	$9,500	1-D	18,836	1,031
State Univ of New York at Binghamton, Binghamton, NY 13902-6000	1946	$5,756 (S)	$7,710	5-D	13,860	719
State Univ of New York at New Paltz, New Paltz, NY 12561	1828	$5,220 (S)	$6,860	5-M	7,603	686
State Univ of New York at Oswego, Oswego, NY 13126	1861	$5,238 (S)	$7,890	5-M	8,289	467
State Univ of New York at Plattsburgh, Plattsburgh, NY 12901-2681	1889	$5,268 (S)	$6,712	5-M	5,909	446
State Univ of New York Coll at Brockport, Brockport, NY 14420-2997	1867	$5,263 (S)	$7,226	5-M	8,595	565
State Univ of New York Coll at Cortland, Cortland, NY 13045	1868	$5,300 (S)	$7,290	5-M	7,331	512
State Univ of New York Coll at Geneseo, Geneseo, NY 14454-1401	1871	$5,435 (S)	$6,820	5-M	5,573	345
State Univ of New York Coll at Old Westbury, Old Westbury, NY 11568-0210	1965	$5,072 (S)	$7,914	5-M	3,359	233
State Univ of New York Coll at Oneonta, Oneonta, NY 13820-4015	1889	NA	$7,230	5-M	5,806	440
State Univ of New York Coll at Potsdam, Potsdam, NY 13676	1816	$5,250 (S)	$7,270	5-M	4,311	327
State Univ of New York Coll of Agr & Tech at Cobleskill, Cobleskill, NY 12043	1916	$5,345 (S)	$7,270	5-B	2,510	146
State Univ of New York Coll of Envir Sci & For, Syracuse, NY 13210-2779	1911	$4,991 (S)	$9,790	5-D	2,046	147
State Univ of New York Empire State Coll, Saratoga Springs, NY 12866-4391	1971	$4,555 (S)	NA	5-M	9,750	768
State Univ of New York, Fredonia, Fredonia, NY 14063-1136	1826	$5,391 (S)	$6,940	5-M	5,359	440
State Univ of New York Inst of Tech, Utica, NY 13504-3050	1966	$5,244 (S)	$7,160	5-M	2,432	178
State Univ of New York Maritime Coll, Throggs Neck, NY 10465-4198 (2)	1874	$5,850 (S)	$7,046	5-M	1,128	82
State Univ of New York Upstate Med Univ, Syracuse, NY 13210-2334	1950	$9,166 (S)	$3,586	5-D	1,180	695
Stephen F. Austin State Univ, Nacogdoches, TX 75962	1923	$4,298 (S)	$5,012	5-D	11,287	582
Stetson Univ, DeLand, FL 32723	1883	$24,135	$7,060	1-F	3,577	262
Stevens Inst of Tech, Hoboken, NJ 07030	1870	$29,760	$8,926	1-D	4,634	328
Stillman Coll, Tuscaloosa, AL 35403-9990	1876	$8,718	$4,200	2-B	1,458	86
Stonehill Coll, Easton, MA 02357-5510	1948	$23,008	$10,206	2-M	2,490	250
Stony Brook Univ, State Univ of New York, Stony Brook, NY 11794	1957	$5,389 (S)	$7,730	5-D	21,685	1,338
Strayer Univ, Washington, DC 20005-2603	1892	$10,368	NA	3-M	20,138	881
Suffolk Univ, Boston, MA 02108-2770	1906	$19,870	$11,411	1-D	8,188	684
Sullivan Univ, Louisville, KY 40205	1864	$12,655	$3,690	3-M	4,928	136
Sul Ross State Univ, Alpine, TX 79832	1920	$3,870 (S)	$4,050	5-M	1,954	133
Susquehanna Univ, Selinsgrove, PA 17870	1858	$24,810	$6,840	2-B	2,071	182
Swarthmore Coll, Swarthmore, PA 19081-1397	1864	$30,094	$9,314	1-B	1,474	203
Syracuse Univ, Syracuse, NY 13244-0003	1870	$26,734	$9,970	1-D	16,753	1,406
Tarleton State Univ, Stephenville, TX 76402	1899	$3,835 (S)	$5,900	5-D	8,985	523
Taylor Univ, Upland, IN 46989-1001	1846	$20,746	$5,630	2-M	1,866	187
Temple Univ, Philadelphia, PA 19122-6096	1884	$9,102 (S)	$7,522	12-D	33,552	2,361
Tennessee State Univ, Nashville, TN 37209-1561	1912	$4,038 (S)	$4,270	5-D	9,100	604
Tennessee Tech Univ, Cookeville, TN 38505	1915	$3,998 (S)	$5,270	5-D	9,217	556
Texas A&M Intl Univ, Laredo, TX 78041-1900	1969	$3,813 (S)	$5,240	5-D	4,078	252
Texas A&M Univ-Comm, Commerce, TX 75429-3011	1889	$4,178 (S)	$5,246	5-D	6,317	519
Texas A&M Univ-Corpus Christi, Corpus Christi, TX 78412-5503	1947	$4,279 (S)	$5,355	5-D	8,227	446
Texas A&M Univ-Kingsville, Kingsville, TX 78363	1925	$3,906 (S)	$4,214	5-D	7,126	438
Texas A&M Univ-Texarkana, Texarkana, TX 75505-5518	1971	$2,340 (S)	NA	5-M	1,559	91
Texas A&M Univ, College Station, TX 77843	1876	$5,955 (S)	$6,887	5-D	44,435	2,232
Texas A&M Univ at Galveston, Galveston, TX 77553-1675	1962	$4,682 (S)	$4,870	5-M	1,615	170
Texas Christian Univ, Fort Worth, TX 76129-0002	1873	$19,740	$5,880	2-D	8,632	748
Texas Lutheran Univ, Seguin, TX 78155-5999	1891	$16,600	$5,030	2-B	1,414	122
Texas Southern Univ, Houston, TX 77004-4584	1947	$3,732 (S)	$5,824	5-D	11,635	630
Texas State Univ-San Marcos, San Marcos, TX 78666	1899	$4,680 (S)	$5,456	5-D	26,783	1,077
Texas Tech Univ, Lubbock, TX 79409	1923	$5,848 (S)	$6,421	5-D	28,325	1,111
Texas Wesleyan Univ, Fort Worth, TX 76105-1536	1890	$13,000	$5,400	2-F	2,742	258
Texas Woman's Univ, Denton, TX 76201 (4)	1901	$3,395 (S)	$5,094	5-D	10,750	700
Thiel Coll, Greenville, PA 16125-2181	1866	$16,390	$6,584	2-B	1,245	120
Thomas Edison State Coll, Trenton, NJ 08608-1176	1972	$3,490/yr (S)	NA	5-M	11,000	NA
Thomas Jefferson Univ, Philadelphia, PA 19107	1824	$20,914	$7,983	1-D	2,457	260
Thomas More Coll, Crestview Hills, KY 41017-3495	1921	$18,320	$6,100	2-M	1,465	129
Tiffin Univ, Tiffin, OH 44883-2161	1888	$14,280	$6,150	1-M	1,407	147
Touro Coll, New York, NY 10010	1971	$10,400	$5,000	1-D	11,447	999
Touro Univ Intl, Cypress, CA 90630	NA	$8,000	NA	1-D	2,165	184
Towson Univ, Towson, MD 21252-0001	1866	$6,672 (S)	$6,468	5-D	17,667	1,259
Transylvania Univ, Lexington, KY 40508-1797	1780	$19,650	$6,590	2-B	1,114	92

Name, address	Year Founded	Tuition & Fees	Rm. & Board	Control, Degree	Enroll-ment	Faculty
Trevecca Nazarene Univ, Nashville, TN 37210-2877	1901	$12,792	$5,868	2-D	2,089	191
Trinity Christian Coll, Palos Heights, IL 60463-0929	1959	$16,400	$6,044	2-B	1,234	127
Trinity Coll, Hartford, CT 06106-3100	1823	$31,940	$8,260	1-M	2,371	237
Trinity Intl Univ, Deerfield, IL 60015-1284	1897	$18,150	$6,080	2-D	2,815	144
Trinity Univ, Washington, DC 20017-1094 (3)	1897	$17,360	$7,574	2-M	1,672	158
Trinity Univ, San Antonio, TX 78212-7200	1869	$20,010	$8,205	2-M	2,718	280
Tri-State Univ, Angola, IN 46703-1764	1884	$20,200	$6,000	1-M	1,232	95
Troy Univ, Troy, AL 36082	1887	$4,162 (S)	$4,812	5-M	8,847	425
Troy Univ Dothan, Dothan, AL 36303	1961	$4,162 (S)	NA	5-M	1,894	116
Troy Univ Montgomery, Montgomery, AL 36103-4419	1965	$3,920 (S)	NA	5-M	4,313	223
Truman State Univ, Kirksville, MO 63501-4221	1867	$5,482 (S)	$5,175	5-M	5,862	377
Tufts Univ, Medford, MA 02155	1852	$31,248	$9,030	1-D	9,693	1,036
Tulane Univ, New Orleans, LA 70118-5669	1834	$31,210	$7,925	1-D	12,691	1,371
Tusculum Coll, Greeneville, TN 37743-9997	1794	$15,110	$5,950	2-M	2,305	69
Tuskegee Univ, Tuskegee, AL 36088	1881	$11,590	$5,940	1-D	2,870	250
Union Coll, Barbourville, KY 40906-1499	1879	$13,750	$4,400	2-M	1,047	73
Union Coll, Schenectady, NY 12308-2311	1795	$38,703 (C)	NA	1-B	2,192	221
Union Inst & Univ, Cincinnati, OH 45206-1925	1969	$8,116	NA	1-D	2,910	240
Union Univ, Jackson, TN 38305-3697	1823	$15,370	$4,970	2-D	2,843	229
United States Air Force Acad, USAF Academy, CO 80840-5025 (2)	1954	$0 (C)	NA	4-B	4,157	531
United States Merchant Marine Acad, Kings Point, NY 11024-1699	1943	$0 (C)	NA	4-B	1,007	95
United States Military Acad, West Point, NY 10996 (2)	1802	$0 (C)	NA	4-B	4,183	589
United States Naval Acad, Annapolis, MD 21402-5000 (2)	1845	$0 (C)	NA	4-B	4,349	591
Universidad del Este, Carolina, PR 00984-2010	1949	$4,498	NA	1-B	7,077	439
Universidad del Turabo, Gurabo, PR 00778-3030	1972	$4,498	NA	1-M	8,065	410
Universidad Metropolitana, Río Piedras, PR 00928-1150	1980	$4,498	NA	1-M	5,857	358
Univ at Albany, State Univ of New York, Albany, NY 12222-0001	1844	$5,810 (S)	$7,540	5-D	16,293	1,121
Univ at Buffalo, The State Univ of New York, Buffalo, NY 14260	1846	$5,966 (S)	$7,226	5-D	27,276	1,746
Univ of Advancing Tech, Tempe, AZ 85283-1042	1983	$14,600	NA	3-M	1,004	43
Univ of Akron, Akron, OH 44325-0001	1870	$7,510 (S)	$6,660	5-D	23,282	1,580
Univ of Alabama, Tuscaloosa, AL 35487	1831	$4,630 (S)	$4,734	5-D	20,929	1,051
Univ of Alabama at Birmingham, Birmingham, AL 35294	1969	$4,662 (S)	$3,060	5-D	16,694	881
Univ of Alabama in Huntsville, Huntsville, AL 35899	1950	$4,516 (S)	$5,200	5-D	7,036	459
Univ of Alaska Anchorage, Anchorage, AK 99508-8060	1954	$3,465 (S)	$7,810	5-M	16,261	1,202
Univ of Alaska Fairbanks, Fairbanks, AK 99775-7520	1917	$4,762 (S)	$5,580	5-D	8,693	314
Univ of Alaska Southeast, Juneau, AK 99801	1972	$3,342 (S)	$5,370	5-M	3,379	228
Univ of Arizona, Tucson, AZ 85721	1885	$4,093 (S)	$7,108	5-D	36,932	1,416
Univ of Arkansas, Fayetteville, AR 72701-1201	1871	$5,135 (S)	$5,927	5-D	17,269	847
Univ of Arkansas at Fort Smith, Fort Smith, AR 72913-3649	1928	$2,280 (A)	NA	11-B	6,623	333
Univ of Arkansas at Little Rock, Little Rock, AR 72204-1099	1927	$4,955 (S)	$2,850	5-D	11,757	749
Univ of Arkansas at Monticello, Monticello, AR 71656	1909	$3,765 (S)	$3,150	5-M	2,875	247
Univ of Arkansas at Pine Bluff, Pine Bluff, AR 71601-2799	1873	$4,044 (S)	$5,436	5-M	3,303	236
Univ of Baltimore, Baltimore, MD 21201-5779	1925	$6,793 (S)	NA	5-D	4,987	331
Univ of Bridgeport, Bridgeport, CT 06604	1927	$19,525	$8,400	1-D	3,274	347
Univ of California, Berkeley, Berkeley, CA 94720-1500	1868	$6,730 (S)	$11,630	5-D	32,814	1,965
Univ of California, Davis, Davis, CA 95616	1905	$6,936 (S)	$10,234	5-D	30,229	1,950
Univ of California, Irvine, Irvine, CA 92697	1965	$6,313 (S)	$9,176	5-D	24,307	1,290
Univ of California, Los Angeles, Los Angeles, CA 90095	1919	$6,576 (S)	$11,187	5-D	24,946	2,466
Univ of California, Riverside, Riverside, CA 92521-0102	1954	$6,685 (S)	$9,800	5-D	17,104	795
Univ of California, San Diego, La Jolla, CA 92093	1959	$6,224 (S)	$8,996	5-D	24,105	1,206
Univ of California, Santa Barbara, Santa Barbara, CA 93106	1909	$6,495 (S)	$9,897	5-D	21,026	1,033
Univ of California, Santa Cruz, Santa Cruz, CA 95064	1965	$7,023 (S)	$10,947	5-D	15,036	729
Univ of Central Arkansas, Conway, AR 72035-0001	1907	$5,053 (S)	$3,920	5-D	10,071	556
Univ of Central Florida, Orlando, FL 32816	1963	$3,180 (S)	$7,232	5-D	42,568	1,628
Univ of Central Oklahoma, Edmond, OK 73034-5209	1890	$3,012 (S)	$4,206	5-M	15,584	802
Univ of Chicago, Chicago, IL 60637-1513	1891	$30,729	$9,623	1-D	13,885	2,710
Univ of Cincinnati, Cincinnati, OH 45221	1819	$8,379 (S)	$8,004	5-D	27,178	1,193
Univ of Colorado at Boulder, Boulder, CO 80309	1876	$4,341 (S)	$7,564	5-D	31,943	1,746
Univ of Colorado at Colorado Springs, Colorado Springs, CO 80918	1965	$4,106 (S)	$6,729	5-D	7,629	423
Univ of Colorado at Denver & Health Sci Ctr - Downtown Denver Cmps, Denver, CO 80217-3364	1912	$4,457 (S)	NA	5-D	15,596	944
Univ of Colorado at Denver & Health Sci Ctr - Health Sci Prog, Denver, CO 80262	1883	$6,560 (S)	NA	5-D	2,567	2,928
Univ of Connecticut, Storrs, CT 06269	1881	$7,912 (S)	$7,848	5-D	22,694	1,234
Univ of Dallas, Irving, TX 75062-4736	1955	$20,411	$7,026	2-D	3,005	208
Univ of Dayton, Dayton, OH 45469-1300	1850	$20,250	$6,300	2-D	10,495	823
Univ of Delaware, Newark, DE 19716	1743	$6,954 (S)	$6,458	12-D	20,713	1,379
Univ of Denver, Denver, CO 80208	1864	$26,610	$8,363	1-D	9,808	997
Univ of Detroit Mercy, Detroit, MI 48219-0900	1877	$22,470	$7,328	2-D	5,521	708
Univ of Dubuque, Dubuque, IA 52001-5099	1852	$16,845	$5,700	2-D	1,380	158
Univ of Evansville, Evansville, IN 47722-0002	1854	$20,515	$6,010	2-M	2,687	229
Univ of Findlay, Findlay, OH 45840-3653	1882	$20,914	$7,274	2-M	4,654	356
Univ of Florida, Gainesville, FL 32611	1853	$2,955 (S)	$6,040	5-D	47,858	1,654
Univ of Georgia, Athens, GA 30602	1785	$4,272 (S)	$6,006	5-D	33,405	2,080
Univ of Guam, Mangilao, GU 96923	1952	$4,084 (S)	$6,918	7-M	2,923	254
Univ of Hartford, West Hartford, CT 06117-1599	1877	$23,480	$8,996	1-D	7,246	744
Univ of Hawaii at Hilo, Hilo, HI 96720-4091	1970	$2,604 (S)	$5,374	5-M	3,288	264
Univ of Hawaii at Manoa, Honolulu, HI 96822	1907	$3,504 (S)	$5,942	5-D	20,549	1,215
Univ of Houston-Clear Lake, Houston, TX 77058-1098	1971	$4,190 (S)	NA	5-M	7,785	486
Univ of Houston-Downtown, Houston, TX 77002-1001	1974	$3,934 (S)	NA	5-M	11,408	553
Univ of Houston-Victoria, Victoria, TX 77901-4450	1973	$4,290 (S)	NA	5-M	2,418	122
Univ of Houston, Houston, TX 77204	1927	$4,973 (S)	$6,030	5-D	35,180	1,624
Univ of Idaho, Moscow, ID 83844-2282	1889	$3,632 (S)	$5,034	5-D	12,824	557
Univ of Illinois at Chicago, Chicago, IL 60607-7128	1946	$8,502 (S)	$7,160	5-D	24,810	1,456
Univ of Illinois at Springfield, Springfield, IL 62703-5407	1969	$4,962 (S)	$2,878	5-D	4,396	285
Univ of Illinois at Urbana-Champaign, Champaign, IL 61820	1867	$8,553 (S)	$6,710	5-D	40,694	2,559
Univ of Indianapolis, Indianapolis, IN 46227-3697	1902	$17,200	$6,150	2-D	4,188	358
Univ of Iowa, Iowa City, IA 52242-1316	1847	$5,612 (S)	$6,560	5-D	28,442	1,713
Univ of Kansas, Lawrence, KS 66045	1866	$4,737 (S)	$5,216	5-D	28,905	1,336
Univ of Kentucky, Lexington, KY 40506-0032	1865	$5,165 (S)	$4,735	5-D	25,686	1,695
Univ of La Verne, La Verne, CA 91750-4443	1891	$22,800	$9,110	1-D	4,021	389
Univ of Louisiana at Lafayette, Lafayette, LA 70504	1898	$3,228 (S)	$3,386	5-D	16,563	699
Univ of Louisiana at Monroe, Monroe, LA 71209-0001	1931	$3,076 (S)	$3,290	5-D	8,831	480

Name, address	Year Founded	Tuition & Fees	Rm. & Board	Control, Degree	Enroll-ment	Faculty
Univ of Louisville, Louisville, KY 40292-0001	1798	$5,532 (S)	$6,036	5-D	20,731	1,294
Univ of Maine, Orono, ME 04469	1865	$6,328 (S)	$6,412	5-D	11,358	740
Univ of Maine at Augusta, Augusta, ME 04330-9410	1965	$4,695 (S)	NA	5-B	5,538	288
Univ of Maine at Farmington, Farmington, ME 04938-1990	1863	$5,240 (S)	$5,700	5-B	2,349	159
Univ of Maine at Fort Kent, Fort Kent, ME 04743-1292	1878	$4,514 (S)	$5,600	5-B	1,076	72
Univ of Maine at Machias, Machias, ME 04654-1321	1909	$4,515 (S)	$5,408	5-B	1,191	92
Univ of Maine at Presque Isle, Presque Isle, ME 04769-2888	1903	$4,460 (S)	$5,114	5-B	1,652	115
Univ of Mary, Bismarck, ND 58504-9652	1959	$10,817	$4,110	2-D	2,757	269
Univ of Mary Hardin-Baylor, Belton, TX 76513	1845	$12,380	$4,000	2-M	2,713	221
Univ of Maryland, Baltimore Cty, Baltimore, MD 21250	1963	$8,020 (S)	$7,620	5-D	11,852	731
Univ of Maryland, Coll Park, College Park, MD 20742	1856	$7,410 (S)	$7,931	5-D	35,262	2,097
Univ of Maryland Eastern Shore, Princess Anne, MD 21853-1299	1886	$5,558 (S)	$5,880	5-D	3,762	234
Univ of Maryland Univ Coll, Adelphi, MD 20783	1947	$5,424 (S)	NA	5-D	28,374	1,341
Univ of Mary Washington, Fredericksburg, VA 22401-5358	1908	$5,128 (S)	$5,744	5-M	4,792	331
Univ of Massachusetts Amherst, Amherst, MA 01003	1863	$9,008 (S)	$6,189	5-D	24,646	1,316
Univ of Massachusetts Boston, Boston, MA 02125-3393	1964	$8,034 (S)	NA	5-D	11,682	821
Univ of Massachusetts Dartmouth, North Dartmouth, MA 02747-2300	1895	$7,802 (S)	$7,471	5-D	8,299	543
Univ of Massachusetts Lowell, Lowell, MA 01854-2881	1894	$7,891 (S)	$6,011	5-D	11,089	NA
Univ of Memphis, Memphis, TN 38152	1912	$4,480 (S)	$4,920	5-D	20,668	1,183
Univ of Miami, Coral Gables, FL 33124	1925	$27,840	$8,602	1-D	15,250	1,220
Univ of Michigan-Dearborn, Dearborn, MI 48128-1491	1959	$6,112 (S)	NA	5-M	8,631	517
Univ of Michigan-Flint, Flint, MI 48502-1950	1956	$6,018 (S)	NA	5-F	6,188	372
Univ of Michigan, Ann Arbor, MI 48109	1817	$8,201 (S)	$7,030	5-D	39,533	2,927
Univ of Minnesota, Crookston, Crookston, MN 56716-5001	1966	$7,608 (S)	$4,800	5-B	2,088	91
Univ of Minnesota, Duluth, Duluth, MN 55812-2496	1947	$8,291 (S)	$5,282	5-F	10,366	477
Univ of Minnesota, Morris, Morris, MN 56267-2134	1959	$9,056 (S)	$5,250	5-B	1,836	161
Univ of Minnesota, Twin Cities Cmps, Minneapolis, MN 55455-0213	1851	$8,030 (S)	$6,458	5-D	50,954	3,079
Univ of Mississippi, University, MS 38677	1844	$4,110 (S)	$5,610	5-D	14,497	NA
Univ of Mississippi Med Ctr, Jackson, MS 39216-4505	1955	$3,357 (S)	$3,192	5-D	2,003	2,317
Univ of Missouri-Columbia, Columbia, MO 65211	1839	$7,100 (S)	$6,220	5-D	28,257	1,364
Univ of Missouri-Kansas City, Kansas City, MO 64110-2499	1929	$7,250 (S)	$7,505	5-D	14,256	993
Univ of Missouri-Rolla, Rolla, MO 65409-0910	1870	$7,299 (S)	$3,436	5-D	5,407	392
Univ of Missouri-St Louis, St. Louis, MO 63121	1963	$7,378 (S)	$6,194	5-D	15,512	739
Univ of Mobile, Mobile, AL 36663-0220	1961	$10,505	$5,200	2-M	1,864	153
Univ of Montana-Missoula, Missoula, MT 59812-0002	1893	$4,699 (S)	$5,646	5-D	13,558	705
Univ of Montana-Western, Dillon, MT 59725-3598	1893	$3,530 (S)	$4,740	5-B	1,146	71
Univ of Montevallo, Montevallo, AL 35115	1896	$5,474 (S)	$3,850	5-M	3,061	208
Univ of Nebraska-Lincoln, Lincoln, NE 68588	1869	$5,268 (S)	$6,008	5-D	21,792	1,043
Univ of Nebraska at Kearney, Kearney, NE 68849-0001	1903	$4,260 (S)	$4,990	5-M	6,382	392
Univ of Nebraska at Omaha, Omaha, NE 68182	1908	$4,533 (S)	$5,960	5-D	13,824	812
Univ of Nebraska Med Ctr, Omaha, NE 68198	1869	$6,657 (S)	NA	5-D	2,904	909
Univ of Nevada, Las Vegas, Las Vegas, NV 89154-9900	1957	$3,532 (S)	$8,326	5-D	27,344	1,435
Univ of Nevada, Reno, Reno, NV 89557	1874	$3,010 (S)	$7,385	5-D	15,950	1,144
Univ of New England, Biddeford, ME 04005-9526	1831	$20,915	$8,155	1-F	3,327	271
Univ of New Hampshire, Durham, NH 03824	1866	$9,226 (S)	$6,612	5-D	14,405	689
Univ of New Hampshire at Manchester, Manchester, NH 03101-1113	1967	$6,593 (S)	NA	5-M	1,215	92
Univ of New Haven, West Haven, CT 06516-1916	1920	$22,982	$9,550	1-M	4,173	367
Univ of New Mexico, Albuquerque, NM 87131-2039	1889	$4,364 (S)	$6,180	5-D	25,686	1,400
Univ of New Orleans, New Orleans, LA 70148	1958	$3,492 (S)	$4,122	5-D	17,350	785
Univ of North Alabama, Florence, AL 35632-0001	1830	$4,096 (S)	$4,140	5-M	5,961	298
Univ of North Carolina at Asheville, Asheville, NC 28804-3299	1927	$3,392 (S)	$5,212	5-M	3,607	312
Univ of North Carolina at Chapel Hill, Chapel Hill, NC 27599	1789	$4,451 (S)	$6,245	5-D	26,878	1,440
Univ of North Carolina at Charlotte, Charlotte, NC 28223-0001	1946	$3,473 (S)	$5,304	5-D	19,846	1,164
Univ of North Carolina at Greensboro, Greensboro, NC 27412-5001	1891	$3,435 (S)	$5,000	5-D	14,328	947
Univ of North Carolina at Pembroke, Pembroke, NC 28372-1510	1887	$2,832 (S)	$4,560	5-M	5,027	355
Univ of North Carolina at Wilmington, Wilmington, NC 28403-3297	1947	$3,626 (S)	$5,800	5-D	11,327	686
Univ of North Dakota, Grand Forks, ND 58202	1883	$4,828 (S)	$4,455	5-D	13,187	818
Univ of Northern Colorado, Greeley, CO 80639	1890	$3,370 (S)	$5,954	5-D	13,204	581
Univ of Northern Iowa, Cedar Falls, IA 50614	1876	$5,387 (S)	$5,261	5-D	12,927	784
Univ of North Florida, Jacksonville, FL 32224-2645	1965	$3,101 (S)	$6,278	5-D	14,534	652
Univ of North Texas, Denton, TX 76203	1890	$5,561 (S)	$5,124	5-D	31,155	1,520
Univ of Notre Dame, Notre Dame, IN 46556	1842	$29,512	$7,418	2-D	11,479	NA
Univ of Oklahoma, Norman, OK 73019-0390	1890	$4,140 (S)	$5,814	5-D	24,551	1,204
Univ of Oklahoma Health Sci Ctr, Oklahoma City, OK 73190	1890	$4,082 (S)	NA	5-D	3,328	389
Univ of Oregon, Eugene, OR 97403	1872	$5,550 (S)	$7,331	5-D	20,295	1,116
Univ of Pennsylvania, Philadelphia, PA 19104	1740	$30,716	$8,918	1-D	18,642	1,958
Univ of Phoenix-Atlanta Cmps, Atlanta, GA 30350-4153	NA	$10,830	NA	3-B	2,031	143
Univ of Phoenix-Chicago Cmps, Schaumburg, IL 60173-4399	2002	$10,350	NA	3-M	1,399	122
Univ of Phoenix-Colorado Cmps, Lone Tree, CO 80124-5453	NA	$9,000	NA	3-M	3,364	225
Univ of Phoenix-Dallas Cmps, Dallas, TX 75251	2001	$11,010	NA	3-D	2,546	164
Univ of Phoenix-Fort Lauderdale Cmps, Fort Lauderdale, FL 33324-1393	NA	$10,170	NA	3-M	2,586	177
Univ of Phoenix-Hawaii Cmps, Honolulu, HI 96813-4317	NA	$10,650	NA	3-M	1,480	123
Univ of Phoenix-Houston Cmps, Houston, TX 77079-2004	2001	$11,010	NA	3-M	4,297	318
Univ of Phoenix-Jacksonville Cmps, Jacksonville, FL 32216-0959	1976	$10,170	NA	3-M	2,122	152
Univ of Phoenix-Kansas City Cmps, Kansas City, MO 64131-4517	2002	$10,350	NA	3-M	1,016	97
Univ of Phoenix-Louisiana Cmps, Metairie, LA 70001-2082	1976	$9,330	NA	3-M	2,585	220
Univ of Phoenix-Maryland Cmps, Columbia, MD 21045-5424	NA	$10,800	NA	3-M	2,132	111
Univ of Phoenix-Metro Detroit Cmps, Troy, MI 48098-2623	NA	$11,790	NA	3-M	3,948	222
Univ of Phoenix-Nashville Cmps, Nashville, TN 37214	2003	$10,410	NA	3-M	1,106	97
Univ of Phoenix-Nevada Cmps, Las Vegas, NV 89106-3797	1994	$9,300	NA	3-M	4,125	223
Univ of Phoenix-New Mexico Cmps, Albuquerque, NM 87109-4645	NA	$8,940	NA	3-M	4,812	298
Univ of Phoenix-Northern California Cmps, Pleasanton, CA 94588-3677	NA	$12,630	NA	3-M	5,707	536
Univ of Phoenix-Northern Virginia Cmps, Reston, VA 20190	NA	$10,800	NA	3-M	1,266	133
Univ of Phoenix-Oklahoma City Cmps, Oklahoma City, OK 73116-8244	1976	$8,910	NA	3-M	1,049	124
Univ of Phoenix-Oregon Cmps, Portland, OR 97223-8368	1976	$9,960	NA	3-M	2,130	195
Univ of Phoenix-Orlando Cmps, Maitland, FL 32751-7057	1996	$10,170	NA	3-M	2,142	149
Univ of Phoenix-Philadelphia Cmps, Wayne, PA 19087-2121	1999	$12,000	NA	3-M	1,704	151
Univ of Phoenix-Phoenix Cmps, Phoenix, AZ 85040-1958	1976	$9,090	NA	3-M	9,699	462
Univ of Phoenix-Puerto Rico Cmps, Guaynabo, PR 00970-3870	1995	$5,910	NA	3-M	2,326	65
Univ of Phoenix-Sacramento Cmps, Sacramento, CA 95833-3632	1993	$11,850	NA	3-M	4,365	337
Univ of Phoenix-San Diego Cmps, San Diego, CA 92130-2092	1988	$11,370	NA	3-M	4,761	320
Univ of Phoenix-Southern Arizona Cmps, Tucson, AZ 85712-2732	1979	$8,910	NA	3-M	3,660	230
Univ of Phoenix-Southern California Cmps, Costa Mesa, CA 92626	1980	$12,360	NA	3-M	15,913	936

Name, address	Year Founded	Tuition & Fees	Rm. & Board	Control, Degree	Enroll-ment	Faculty
Univ of Phoenix-Southern Colorado Cmps, Colorado Springs, CO 80919-2335	1999	$9,000	NA	3-M	1,410	103
Univ of Phoenix-Tampa Cmps, Tampa, FL 33637-1920	NA	$10,170	NA	3-M	2,570	127
Univ of Phoenix-Tulsa Cmps, Tulsa, OK 74146-3801	1998	$8,910	NA	3-M	1,202	109
Univ of Phoenix-Utah Cmps, Salt Lake City, UT 84123-4617	1984	$9,540	NA	3-M	4,057	253
Univ of Phoenix-Washington Cmps, Seattle, WA 98188-7500	1997	$10,290	NA	3-M	2,197	179
Univ of Phoenix-West Michigan Cmps, Grand Rapids, MI 49544-1683	2000	$11,520	NA	3-M	1,167	142
Univ of Phoenix-Wisconsin Cmps, Brookfield, WI 53045-6608	2001	$10,020	NA	3-M	1,296	125
Univ of Phoenix Online Cmps, Phoenix, AZ 85034-7209	1989	$13,200	NA	3-D	115,796	4,794
Univ of Pittsburgh, Pittsburgh, PA 15260	1787	$10,830 (S)	$7,090	12-D	26,731	NA
Univ of Pittsburgh at Bradford, Bradford, PA 16701-2812	1963	$9,980 (S)	$6,344	12-B	1,460	115
Univ of Pittsburgh at Greensburg, Greensburg, PA 15601-5860	1963	$9,960 (S)	$6,960	12-B	1,860	140
Univ of Pittsburgh at Johnstown, Johnstown, PA 15904-2990	1927	$9,972 (S)	$5,930	12-B	3,209	190
Univ of Portland, Portland, OR 97203-5798	1901	$23,520	$7,050	2-M	3,343	305
Univ of Puerto Rico at Humacao, Humacao, PR 00791	1962	$1,090 (S)	NA	6-B	4,507	284
Univ of Puerto Rico, Cayey Univ Coll, Cayey, PR 00736	1967	$1,245 (A)	NA	6-B	3,987	219
Univ of Puerto Rico, Mayagüez Cmps, Mayagüez, PR 00681-9000	1911	NA	NA	6-D	12,108	650
Univ of Puerto Rico, Río Piedras, San Juan, PR 00931	1903	$790 (S)	$4,940	6-D	21,666	1,793
Univ of Puget Sound, Tacoma, WA 98416	1888	$26,880	$6,730	1-F	2,892	258
Univ of Redlands, Redlands, CA 92373-0999	1907	$25,524	$8,696	1-M	2,451	325
Univ of Rhode Island, Kingston, RI 02881	1892	$6,752 (S)	$7,810	5-D	14,749	706
Univ of Richmond, University of Richmond, VA 23173	1830	$27,850	$5,660	1-F	3,637	326
Univ of Rio Grande, Rio Grande, OH 45674	1876	$12,345 (A)	$6,024	1-M	2,522	147
Univ of Rochester, Rochester, NY 14627-0250	1850	$28,982	$9,565	1-D	8,365	623
Univ of St Francis, Joliet, IL 60435-6169	1920	$17,670	$6,180	2-M	2,110	208
Univ of St Francis, Fort Wayne, IN 46808-3994	1890	$16,460	$5,450	2-M	1,883	227
Univ of St Thomas, St. Paul, MN 55105-1096	1885	$21,828	$6,542	2-D	10,474	817
Univ of St Thomas, Houston, TX 77006-4696	1947	$16,312	$7,300	2-D	3,648	260
Univ of San Diego, San Diego, CA 92110-2492	1949	$26,856	$10,190	2-D	7,486	706
Univ of San Francisco, San Francisco, CA 94117-1080	1855	$26,840	$10,240	2-D	8,271	820
Univ of Sci & Arts of Oklahoma, Chickasha, OK 73018	1908	$3,180 (S)	$3,990	5-B	1,414	88
Univ of Scranton, Scranton, PA 18510	1888	$22,474	$9,524	2-D	4,795	391
Univ of Sioux Falls, Sioux Falls, SD 57105-1699	1883	$14,900	$4,350	2-D	1,586	131
Univ of South Alabama, Mobile, AL 36688-0002	1963	$4,290 (S)	$4,222	5-D	13,340	978
Univ of South Carolina, Columbia, SC 29208	1801	$5,778 (S)	$5,590	5-D	25,597	1,520
Univ of South Carolina Aiken, Aiken, SC 29801-6309	1961	$5,642 (S)	$4,250	5-M	3,382	238
Univ of South Carolina Beaufort, Beaufort, SC 29902-4601	1959	$4,790 (S)	NA	5-B	1,277	106
Univ of South Carolina Upstate, Spartanburg, SC 29303-4999	1967	$6,186 (S)	$5,140	5-M	4,376	310
Univ of South Dakota, Vermillion, SD 57069-2390	1862	$4,749 (S)	$3,741	5-D	8,120	345
Univ of Southern California, Los Angeles, CA 90089	1880	$30,512	$8,988	1-D	32,160	2,408
Univ of Southern Indiana, Evansville, IN 47712-3590	1965	$4,077 (S)	$5,480	5-M	10,050	576
Univ of Southern Maine, Portland, ME 04104-9300	1878	$5,510 (S)	$6,908	5-D	11,089	597
Univ of Southern Mississippi, Hattiesburg, MS 39406-0001	1910	$4,106 (S)	$5,010	5-D	15,253	808
Univ of South Florida, Tampa, FL 33620-9951	1956	$3,164 (S)	$6,730	5-D	42,238	1,802
Univ of Tampa, Tampa, FL 33606-1490	1931	$18,172	$6,666	1-M	4,879	408
Univ of Tennessee, Knoxville, TN 37996	1794	$5,376 (S)	$5,398	5-D	27,764	1,557
Univ of Tennessee at Chattanooga, Chattanooga, TN 37403-2598	1886	$4,928 (S)	$5,808	5-D	8,844	668
Univ of Tennessee at Martin, Martin, TN 38238-1000	1900	$4,134 (S)	$4,100	5-M	6,104	387
Univ of Texas-Pan Amer, Edinburg, TX 78541-2999	1927	$3,152 (S)	$4,233	5-D	17,030	730
Univ of Texas at Arlington, Arlington, TX 76019	1895	$5,300 (S)	$5,212	5-D	25,297	1,081
Univ of Texas at Austin, Austin, TX 78712-1111	1883	$5,735 (S)	$6,184	5-D	50,377	2,721
Univ of Texas at Brownsville, Brownsville, TX 78520-4991	1973	$2,805 (S)	$2,300	5-M	11,560	633
Univ of Texas at Dallas, Richardson, TX 75083-0688	1969	$6,363 (S)	$6,244	5-D	14,092	627
Univ of Texas at El Paso, El Paso, TX 79968-0001	1913	$5,064 (S)	$4,095	5-D	18,918	949
Univ of Texas at San Antonio, San Antonio, TX 78249-0617	1969	$5,272 (S)	$5,306	5-D	26,175	1,089
Univ of Texas at Tyler, Tyler, TX 75799-0001	1971	$4,046 (S)	$5,373	5-M	5,303	324
Univ of Texas Health Sci Ctr at Houston, Houston, TX 77225-0036	1972	$5,602 (S)	NA	5-D	3,399	1,247
Univ of Texas Health Sci Ctr at San Antonio, San Antonio, TX 78229-3900	1976	$3,797 (S)	NA	5-D	2,754	1,372
Univ of Texas Med Branch, Galveston, TX 77555	1891	$3,210 (S)	$2,160	5-D	2,121	102
Univ of Texas of the Permian Basin, Odessa, TX 79762-0001	1969	$3,900 (S)	$4,176	5-M	2,695	158
Univ of Texas Southwestern Med Ctr at Dallas, Dallas, TX 75390	1943	$2,820 (S)	NA	5-D	2,267	111
Univ of the Arts, Philadelphia, PA 19102-4944	1870	$23,010	$5,800	1-M	2,142	434
Univ of the Cumberlands, Williamsburg, KY 40769-1372	1889	$12,658	$5,526	2-M	1,744	102
Univ of the District of Columbia, Washington, DC 20008-1175	1976	$2,070 (S)	NA	9-M	5,165	335
Univ of the Incarnate Word, San Antonio, TX 78209-6397	1881	$17,072	$6,234	2-D	4,800	389
Univ of the Pacific, Stockton, CA 95211-0197	1851	$24,750	$7,858	1-D	6,268	656
Univ of the Sacred Heart, San Juan, PR 00914-0383	1935	$4,810	$2,000	2-M	5,206	343
Univ of the Sci in Philadelphia, Philadelphia, PA 19104-4495	1821	$22,648	$8,932	1-D	2,824	250
Univ of the South, Sewanee, TN 37383-1000	1857	$25,580	$7,120	2-D	1,492	175
Univ of the Virgin Islands, Saint Thomas, VI 00802-9990	1962	$3,796 (S)	$7,740	7-M	2,565	270
Univ of Toledo, Toledo, OH 43606-3390	1872	$7,054 (S)	$7,488	5-D	19,480	1,281
Univ of Tulsa, Tulsa, OK 74104-3189	1894	$17,630	$5,926	2-D	4,174	427
Univ of Utah, Salt Lake City, UT 84112-1107	1850	$4,000 (S)	$5,726	5-D	28,933	1,682
Univ of Vermont, Burlington, VT 05405	1791	$10,226 (S)	$7,016	5-D	10,940	691
Univ of Virginia, Charlottesville, VA 22903	1819	$6,790 (S)	$5,960	5-D	23,341	1,322
Univ of Virginia's Coll at Wise, Wise, VA 24293	1954	$5,081 (S)	$6,200	5-B	1,836	136
Univ of Washington, Seattle, WA 98195	1861	$5,286 (S)	$7,017	5-D	39,246	3,383
Univ of Washington, Bothell, Bothell, WA 98011-8246	NA	$5,157 (S)	$7,017	5-M	1,620	103
Univ of Washington, Tacoma, Tacoma, WA 98402-3100	1990	$5,190 (S)	NA	5-M	2,052	131
Univ of West Alabama, Livingston, AL 35470	1835	$4,196 (S)	$3,119	5-M	2,667	92
Univ of West Florida, Pensacola, FL 32514-5750	1963	$3,039 (S)	$6,294	5-D	9,518	547
Univ of West Georgia, Carrollton, GA 30118	1933	$2,906 (S)	$4,550	5-D	10,216	511
Univ of Wisconsin-Eau Claire, Eau Claire, WI 54702-4004	1916	$4,864 (S)	$4,310	5-M	10,540	506
Univ of Wisconsin-Green Bay, Green Bay, WI 54311-7001	1968	$5,154 (S)	$4,716	5-M	5,706	282
Univ of Wisconsin-La Crosse, La Crosse, WI 54601-3742	1909	$4,895 (S)	$4,570	5-M	8,511	447
Univ of Wisconsin-Madison, Madison, WI 53706-1380	1848	$5,860 (S)	$6,250	5-D	41,169	2,984
Univ of Wisconsin-Milwaukee, Milwaukee, WI 53201-0413	1956	$5,835 (S)	$4,505	5-D	26,832	NA
Univ of Wisconsin-Oshkosh, Oshkosh, WI 54901	1871	$4,616 (S)	$4,630	5-M	11,039	566
Univ of Wisconsin-Parkside, Kenosha, WI 53141-2000	1968	$4,652 (S)	$5,415	5-M	5,072	294
Univ of Wisconsin-Platteville, Platteville, WI 53818-3099	1866	$4,812 (S)	$4,412	5-M	6,158	320
Univ of Wisconsin-River Falls, River Falls, WI 54022-5001	1874	$4,968 (S)	NA	5-M	5,950	337
Univ of Wisconsin-Stevens Point, Stevens Point, WI 54481-3897	1894	$4,704 (S)	$4,094	5-M	9,023	422
Univ of Wisconsin-Stout, Menomonie, WI 54751	1891	$6,262 (S)	$4,334	5-M	7,547	397
Univ of Wisconsin-Superior, Superior, WI 54880-4500	1893	$4,808 (S)	$4,342	5-F	2,804	189

Name, address	Year Founded	Tuition & Fees	Rm. & Board	Control, Degree	Enroll-ment	Faculty
Univ of Wisconsin-Whitewater, Whitewater, WI 53190-1790	1868	$5,080 (S)	$4,210	5-M	10,938	503
Univ of Wyoming, Laramie, WY 82070	1886	$3,243 (S)	$5,953	5-D	13,207	692
Urbana Univ, Urbana, OH 43078-2091	1850	$14,220	$5,680	1-M	1,531	118
Ursinus Coll, Collegeville, PA 19426-1000	1869	$31,450	$7,350	1-B	1,499	161
Ursuline Coll, Pepper Pike, OH 44124-4398 (3)	1871	$18,150	$5,896	2-M	1,462	195
Utah State Univ, Logan, UT 84322	1888	$3,374 (S)	$4,230	5-D	16,130	764
Utah Valley State Coll, Orem, UT 84058-5999	1941	$2,788 (S)	NA	5-B	24,149	1,172
Utica Coll, Utica, NY 13502-4892	1946	$21,270	$8,600	1-F	2,652	243
Valdosta State Univ, Valdosta, GA 31698	1906	$2,992 (S)	$5,208	5-D	10,400	491
Valley City State Univ, Valley City, ND 58072	1890	$3,130 (S)	$4,074	5-B	1,033	88
Valparaiso Univ, Valparaiso, IN 46383	1859	$21,700	$5,840	2-F	3,969	362
Vanderbilt Univ, Nashville, TN 37240-1001	1873	$29,990	$9,736	1-D	11,294	NA
Vanguard Univ of Southern California, Costa Mesa, CA 92626-9601	1920	$20,330	$6,756	2-M	2,195	146
Vassar Coll, Poughkeepsie, NY 12604	1861	$31,350	$7,680	1-M	2,475	315
Vaughn Coll of Aeronautics & Tech, Flushing, NY 11369-1037 (2)	1932	$13,780	NA	1-B	1,244	60
Vermont Tech Coll, Randolph Center, VT 05061-0500	1866	$7,502 (S)	$6,454	5-B	1,332	125
Villa Julie Coll, Stevenson, MD 21153	1952	$14,653	$6,600	1-M	2,740	290
Villanova Univ, Villanova, PA 19085-1699	1842	$27,850	$9,067	2-D	10,626	892
Virginia Coll at Birmingham, Birmingham, AL 35209	1989	$8,820	NA	3-B	2,407	201
Virginia Commonwealth Univ, Richmond, VA 23284-9005	1838	$5,385 (S)	$7,042	5-D	28,462	2,147
Virginia Intermont Coll, Bristol, VA 24201-4298	1884	$15,200	$5,650	2-B	1,152	96
Virginia Military Inst, Lexington, VA 24450 (2)	1839	$6,529 (S)	$5,474	5-B	1,362	151
Virginia Polytechnic Inst & State Univ, Blacksburg, VA 24061	1872	$5,836 (S)	$4,288	5-D	25,619	1,490
Virginia State Univ, Petersburg, VA 23806-0001	1882	$4,602 (S)	$6,260	5-D	4,859	317
Virginia Union Univ, Richmond, VA 23220-1170	1865	$12,260	$5,436	2-D	1,777	140
Virginia Wesleyan Coll, Norfolk, VA 23502-5599	1961	$20,448	$6,600	2-B	1,442	126
Viterbo Univ, La Crosse, WI 54601-4797	1890	$16,660	$5,430	2-M	2,690	199
Wagner Coll, Staten Island, NY 10301-4495	1883	$23,900	$7,500	1-M	2,259	209
Wake Forest Univ, Winston-Salem, NC 27109	1834	$30,210	$8,500	1-D	6,504	531
Walden Univ, Minneapolis, MN 55401	1970	$8,280	NA	3-D	13,553	616
Walla Walla Coll, College Place, WA 99324-1198	1892	$17,829	$3,684	2-M	1,968	199
Walsh Coll of Accountancy & Bus Admin, Troy, MI 48007-7006	1922	$7,550	NA	1-M	3,105	128
Walsh Univ, North Canton, OH 44720-3396	1958	$15,610	$7,700	2-M	1,951	172
Warner Southern Coll, Lake Wales, FL 33859	1968	$11,990	$5,160	2-M	1,024	131
Wartburg Coll, Waverly, IA 50677-0903	1852	$19,700	$5,515	2-B	1,804	165
Washburn Univ, Topeka, KS 66621	1865	$4,562 (S)	$4,972	10-F	7,002	497
Washington & Jefferson Coll, Washington, PA 15301-4801	1781	$24,620	$6,710	1-B	1,355	128
Washington & Lee Univ, Lexington, VA 24450-0303	1749	$25,760	$6,790	1-F	2,166	209
Washington Coll, Chestertown, MD 21620-1197	1782	$26,550	$6,000	1-M	1,426	142
Washington State Univ, Pullman, WA 99164	1890	$5,358 (S)	$6,450	5-D	23,240	1,297
Washington Univ in St Louis, St. Louis, MO 63130-4899	1853	$32,042	$10,064	1-D	13,380	1,100
Wayland Baptist Univ, Plainview, TX 79072-6998	1908	$9,250	$3,420	2-M	1,067	96
Waynesburg Coll, Waynesburg, PA 15370-1222	1849	$14,540	$5,800	2-M	2,102	124
Wayne State Coll, Wayne, NE 68787	1910	$3,672 (S)	$4,120	5-M	3,398	205
Wayne State Univ, Detroit, MI 48202	1868	$5,399 (S)	$6,700	5-D	33,314	1,925
Weber State Univ, Ogden, UT 84408-1001	1889	$2,876 (S)	$6,400	5-M	18,517	454
Webster Univ, St. Louis, MO 63119-3194	1915	$16,250	$6,610	1-D	7,424	806
Wellesley Coll, Wellesley, MA 02481 (3)	1870	$29,796	$9,202	1-B	2,289	310
Wentworth Inst of Tech, Boston, MA 02115-5998	1904	$18,500	$9,000	1-B	3,597	239
Wesleyan Univ, Middletown, CT 06459-0260	1831	$31,670	$8,474	1-D	3,217	364
Wesley Coll, Dover, DE 19901-3875	1873	$15,379	$6,960	2-M	2,037	135
West Chester Univ of Pennsylvania, West Chester, PA 19383	1871	$6,006 (S)	$5,782	5-M	12,822	787
Western Carolina Univ, Cullowhee, NC 28723	1889	$3,449 (S)	$4,028	5-D	8,396	608
Western Connecticut State Univ, Danbury, CT 06810-6885	1903	$5,661 (S)	$6,582	5-D	5,884	443
Western Governors Univ, Salt Lake City, UT 84107	1998	$5,245	NA	1-M	2,821	51
Western Illinois Univ, Macomb, IL 61455-1390	1899	$6,183 (S)	$5,768	5-M	13,558	704
Western Intl Univ, Phoenix, AZ 85021-2718	1978	$9,760	NA	3-M	3,751	243
Western Kentucky Univ, Bowling Green, KY 42101-3576	1906	$5,391 (S)	$4,778	5-M	18,485	1,143
Western Michigan Univ, Kalamazoo, MI 49008-5202	1903	$5,668 (S)	$6,496	5-D	27,829	1,488
Western New England Coll, Springfield, MA 01119	1919	$21,986	$8,524	1-F	4,025	332
Western New Mexico Univ, Silver City, NM 88062-0680	1893	$2,451 (S)	$4,280	5-M	3,074	145
Western Oregon Univ, Monmouth, OR 97361-1394	1856	$4,332 (S)	$6,276	5-M	4,772	289
Western State Coll of Colorado, Gunnison, CO 81231	1901	$2,761 (S)	$6,705	5-B	2,270	135
Western Washington Univ, Bellingham, WA 98225-5996	1893	$4,452 (S)	$6,242	5-M	14,190	616
Westfield State Coll, Westfield, MA 01086	1838	$4,857 (S)	$5,742	5-M	4,906	293
West Liberty State Coll, West Liberty, WV 26074	1837	$3,380 (S)	$5,006	5-B	2,374	156
Westminster Coll, New Wilmington, PA 16172-0001	1852	$22,680	$6,700	2-M	1,626	147
Westminster Coll, Salt Lake City, UT 84105-3697	1875	$18,476	$5,636	1-M	2,417	281
Westmont Coll, Santa Barbara, CA 93108-1099	1937	$26,240	$8,610	2-B	1,376	145
West Texas A&M Univ, Canyon, TX 79016-0001	1909	$3,472 (S)	$4,592	5-D	7,299	377
West Virginia State Univ, Institute, WV 25112-1000	1891	$3,222 (S)	$4,720	5-M	3,344	197

WORLD ALMANAC EDITORS' PICKS

The Unferocious Conference

The editors of The World Almanac have chosen the following team names as the least ferocious among American colleges.

EASTERN CONFERENCE

Violets (New York University)

Quakers (University of Pennsylvania)

Squirrels (Mary Baldwin College)

Koalas (Columbia College, SC)

Sailfish (Palm Beach Atlantic Univ.)

Zips (University of Akron)

WESTERN CONFERENCE

Banana Slugs (University of California-Santa Cruz)

Goeyducks (Evergreen State University)

Rainbows (University of Hawaii)

Peacocks (Upper Iowa University)

Poets (Whittier College)

Anteaters (University of California-Irvine)

WORLD HISTORY

Chronology of World History

Prehistory: Our Ancestors Emerge

Revised by Susan Skomal, Ph.D.

Evidence of the origins of *Homo sapiens sapiens,* the species to which all humans belong, comes from a small, but increasing, number of fossils, from genetic and anatomical studies, and from interpretation of the geological record. The latest evidence suggests that humans evolved from apelike primate ancestors that lived in central Africa 6-7 mil years ago (MYA). Although all humans living today are members of a single subspecies, the fossil record confirms that our ancestors coexisted with a number of similar species throughout evolution. Current theories trace the first hominid (upright walking, humanlike primate) to Africa, where several distinct species appeared 5-7 mil years ago. These species lived in a variety of environments throughout the continent, including swampy forests, woodlands, and open savannas. In addition to *Australopithecus*—best known from "Lucy," a 3.2-MYA-Ethiopian specimen found in 1974—these early hominid species include such recent discoveries as *Sahelanthropus*, *Ardipithecus*, *Kenyanthropus*, and *Orrorin*.

Our own human ancestry arose 2-3 MYA, when hominid species began to produce elaborate stone tools. The oldest tools are dated to 2.5-2.6 MYA from Ethiopia, and were made by systematically removing sharp flakes from a core. This produced tools for scraping meat and sinew, as well as a sharp chopping implement useful for obtaining marrow from long bones. Although we cannot determine whether these early hominids had the ability to speak, they were social animals, lived in semi-permanent camps, and had a food-gathering economy. A closer ancestor, *Homo erectus,* appeared in Africa 1.9 MYA and was the first to leave the continent, spreading into Asia by 1.3 MYA, and Europe shortly thereafter. These individuals had skeletal structures similar to modern humans, hunted, learned to control fire, and may have had primitive language skills.

Europe has provided a particularly rich set of fossil evidence. Human-like in many important respects, Neanderthal appeared c. 200,000 BP (years before the present), had sophisticated tools and a developed social culture, and was well adapted to the harsh climate of Ice Age Europe. Recent genetic evidence supports the theory that Neanderthal was a distinct species that in some places coexisted with, but did not interbreed with, early modern humans (also called Cro-Magnons). A similar situation may have occurred in Asia, where more primitive species of *Homo* coexisted with early modern humans 100,000-150,000 BP. Further study of *Homo antecessor,* a new species identified in Spain, may clarify the relationship between anatomically modern *Homo sapiens* and Neanderthals in Europe.

The 1st *Homo sapiens sapiens* originated in E Africa 100,000-200,000 BP. The oldest modern human fossils are dated to 195,000 BP, and were found at the Ethiopian site of Omo. Our species quickly spread. Humans were living in Israel by 100,000 BP, and in Romania by 35,000 BP. Migration from Asia to Australia via the Timor Straits took place as early as 100,000 BP. First confirmation for the crossing from Asia to the Americas by land bridge dates to the end of the last Ice Age, at 14,000 BP; however, genetic data suggest that small, isolated groups of people arrived in the Americas 18,000 to 14,000 years ago, settling in both continents.

A variety of cultural modes—in toolmaking, diet, shelter, social arrangements, and spiritual expression—arose as humans adapted to different geographic and climatic zones and the knowledge base grew. Sites from all over the world show seasonal migration patterns and efficient exploitation of a wide range of plant and animal foods.

Fire-making probably began 1 MYA in Africa and spread to Asia and Europe. Hearths were used in N Israel by c. 750,000 BP, and by 465,000 BP in W France. Fire-hardened wooden spears, weighted and set with small stone blades, were fashioned by big-game hunters 400,000 BP in Germany. Scraping tools, dated 30,000-200,000 BP in Europe, N Africa, the Middle East, and Central Asia, suggest the treatment of skins for clothing. Impressions in clay artifacts from the Czech Republic document the ability to weave cloth baskets and nets by 28,000 BP. By the time Australia was settled, human ancestors had learned to navigate in boats over open water. The earliest bone tools found so far were developed 80,000 BP in the Congo basin by fishermen, who created sophisticated fishing tackle to catch giant catfish.

About 60,000 BP the earliest immigrants to Australia carved and painted designs on rocks. Painting and decoration flourished, along with stone and ivory sculpture, from 35,000 BP in Europe, where more than 200 caves show remarkable examples of naturalistic wall painting. A variety of musical instruments, including bone flutes with precisely bored holes, have been found in sites dated to 40,000-80,000 BP. Around 30,000 BP, the number of people surviving long enough to become grandparents dramatically increased. There were now 2 adults over 30 for every adult under 30. With more adults available to provide child care, humans began to develop more complex social systems.

Shortly after 10,000 BC, among widely separated communities, a series of dramatic technological and social changes occurred, marking the Neolithic, or New Stone, Age. As the world climate became drier and warmer, humans learned to cultivate plants and domesticate animals. This encouraged growth of permanent settlements. Manufacture of pottery and cloth began at this time. These techniques precipitated a dramatic increase in world population and social complexity.

Sites in the Americas, SE Europe, and the Middle East show roughly contemporaneous (8000-10,000 BC) evidence of Neolithic traits. Dates near 5000-8000 BC have been given for E and S Asian, W European, and sub-Saharan African Neolithic remains. Farming spread rapidly throughout the Mediterranean, perhaps in 100-200 years. The variety of crops—field grains, rice, maize, squash, and roots—and a mix of other characteristics suggest that this adaptation occurred independently in each region. Evidence for fermented beverages likewise coincides with the early Neolithic settled farming lifestyle. Northern Chinese farmers concocted a wine-like drink from rice, honey, and fruit between 6000 and 7000 BC; in the Middle East, Iranian vintners were fermenting grapes by 5400 BC.

History Begins: 4000-1000 BC

Near Eastern cradle. If history began with writing, the first chapter opened in Mesopotamia, the Tigris-Euphrates river valley. The Sumerians used clay tablets with pictographs to keep records after 4000 BC. A **cuneiform** (wedge-shaped) script evolved by 3000 BC as a full syllabic alphabet. Neighboring peoples adapted the script for their own use.

Sumerian life centered, from 4000 BC, on large cities (Eridu, Ur, Uruk, Nippur, Kish, and Lagash) organized around temples and priestly bureaucracies, with surrounding plains watered by vast irrigation works and worked with traction plows. Sailboats, wheeled vehicles, potter's wheels, and kilns were used. Copper was smelted and tempered from c. 4000 BC; bronze was produced not long after. Ores, as well as precious stones and metals, were obtained through long-distance ship and caravan trade. Iron was used from c. 2000 BC. Improved ironworking, developed partly by the Hittites, became widespread by 1200 BC.

Sumerian political primacy passed among cities and their kingly dynasties. Semitic-speaking peoples, with cultures derived from the Sumerian, founded a succession of dynasties that ruled in Mesopotamia and neighboring areas for most of 1,800 years; among them were the **Akkadians** (first under Sargon I, c. 2350 BC), the Amorites (whose laws, codified by **Hammurabi,** c. 1792-1750 BC, have biblical parallels), and the Assyrians, with interludes of rule by the Hittites, Kassites, and Mitanni.

Major Gods & Goddesses of Ancient Egypt

Name	Relations	Sphere or Position	Emblem/Attribute
Ra (Re)/Atum/Amon	Self-created	The sun, creation	Hawk
Thoth (Djeheuty)	Son of Ra	The moon, wisdom, writing	Ibis/baboon
Ptah	Creator of Atum	Creation, craftsmen	----
Osiris	Brother of Set(h) & Isis	The underworld (dead), fertility, resurrection, vegetation	Bull
Isis	Sister/consort of Osiris	The underworld (dead)	----
Set(h)	Brother of Osiris	Evil, trickery, chaos	Boar, pig
Horus	Son of Osiris & Isis/ Ra & Hathor	The earth	Falcon
Hathor	Consort of Ra	Motherhood, love	Cow
Anubis	Son of Osiris	Embalmer & judge of the dead	Jackal/dog

Mesopotamian learning, maintained by scribes and preserved in vast libraries, was practically oriented. Lists of astronomical phenomena, plants, animals, and stones were maintained; medical texts listed ailments and herbal cures. The Sumerians worshiped anthropomorphic gods representing natural forces. Sacrifices were made at **ziggurats**—huge stepped temples.

The Syria-Palestine area, site of some of the earliest urban remains (Jericho, 7000 BC), and of the recently uncovered **Ebla** civilization (fl. 2500 BC), experienced Egyptian cultural and political influence along with Mesopotamian. The **Phoenician** coast was an active commercial center. A phonetic alphabet was invented here before 1600 BC. It became the ancestor of many other alphabets.

Egyptian hieroglyphics

Egypt. Agricultural villages along the Nile River were united by around 3300 BC into 2 kingdoms, Upper and Lower Egypt, unified (c. 3100 BC) under the pharaoh Menes. A bureaucracy supervised construction of canals and monuments (pyramids starting 2700 BC). Control over Nubia to the S was asserted from 2600 BC. Brilliant **Old Kingdom** Period achievements in architecture, sculpture, and painting reached their height during the 3rd and 4th Dynasties. Hieroglyphic writing appeared by 3200 BC, recording a sophisticated literature that included religious writings, philosophy, history, and science. An ordered hierarchy of gods, including totemistic animal elements, was served by a powerful priesthood in Memphis. The pharaoh was identified with the falcon god Horus. Other trends included belief in an afterlife and short-lived quasi-monotheistic reforms introduced by the pharaoh Akhenaton (c. 1379-1362 BC).

After a period of dominance by Semitic Hyksos from Asia (c. 1700-1550 BC), the **New Kingdom** established an empire in Syria. Egypt became increasingly embroiled in Asiatic wars and diplomacy. Conquered by Persia in 525 BC, it eventually faded away as an independent culture.

India. An urban civilization with a so-far-undeciphered writing system stretched across the Indus Valley and along the Arabian Sea c. 3000-1500 BC. Major sites are Harappa and **Mohenjo-Daro** in Pakistan, well-planned geometric cities with underground sewers and vast granaries. The entire region may have been ruled as a single state. Bronze was used, and arts and crafts were well developed. Religious life apparently took the form of fertility cults. Indus civilization was probably in decline when it was destroyed by **Aryans** who arrived from the NW, speaking an Indo-European language. Led by a warrior aristocracy whose legendary deeds are in the **Rig Veda**, the Aryans spread E and S, bringing their sky gods, priestly (Brahman) ritual, and the beginnings of the caste system; local customs and beliefs were assimilated by the conquerors.

Europe. On Crete, the Bronze Age **Minoan civilization** emerged c. 2500 BC. A prosperous economy and richly decorative art was supported by seaborne commerce. Mycenae and other cities in mainland Greece and Asia Minor (e.g., **Troy**) preserved elements of the culture until c. 1200 BC. Cretan Linear A script (c. 2000-1700 BC) remains undeciphered; Linear B script (c. 1300-1200 BC) records an early Greek dialect. The possible connection between Mycenaean monumental stonework and the megalithic monuments of W Europe, Iberia, and Malta (c. 4000-1500 BC) is unclear.

China. Proto-Chinese neolithic cultures had long covered N and SE China when the first large political state was organized in the N by the **Shang dynasty** (c. 1523 BC). Shang kings called themselves Sons of Heaven, and they presided over a cult of human and animal sacrifice to ancestors and nature gods. The Chou dynasty, starting c. 1027 BC, expanded the area of the Son of Heaven's dominion, but feudal states exercised most temporal power. A writing system with 2,000 characters was already in use under the Shang, with **pictographs** later supplemented by phonetic characters. Many of its principles and symbols, despite changes in spoken Chinese, were preserved in later writing systems. Technical advances allowed urban specialists to create fine ceramic and jade products, and bronze casting after 1500 BC was the most advanced in the world. Bronze artifacts discovered in N Thailand date from 3600 BC, hundreds of years before similar Middle Eastern finds.

Americas. Olmecs settled (1500 BC) on the Gulf coast of Mexico and developed the first known civilization in the western hemisphere. Temple cities and huge stone sculpture date from 1200 BC. A rudimentary calendar and writing system existed. Olmec religion, centering on a jaguar god, and Olmec art forms influenced later Meso-American cultures.

Classical Era of Old World Civilizations: 1000 BC-400 BC

Greece. After a period of decline during the Dorian Greek invasions (1200-1000 BC), the Aegean area developed a unique civilization. Drawing on Mycenaean traditions, Mesopotamian learning (weights and measures, lunisolar calendar, astronomy, musical scales), the Phoenician alphabet (modified for Greek), and Egyptian art, **Greek city-states** saw a rich elaboration of intellectual life. The two great epic poems attributed to **Homer**, the *Iliad* and the *Odyssey,* were probably composed around the 8th cent. BC. Long-range commerce was aided by metal coinage (introduced by the Lydians in Asia Minor before 700 BC); colonies were founded around the Mediterranean (Cumae in Italy in 760 BC; Massalia in France c. 600 BC) and Black Sea shores.

Philosophy, starting with Ionian speculation on the nature of matter (Thales, c. 634-546 BC), continued by other "Pre-Socratics" (e.g., Heraclitus, c. 535-415 BC; Parmenides, b. c. 515 BC), reached a high point in Athens in the rationalist idealism of **Plato** (c. 428-347 BC), a disciple of **Socrates** (c. 469-399 BC; executed for alleged impiety), and in **Aristotle** (384-322 BC), a pioneer in many fields, from natural sciences to logic, ethics, and metaphysics. The **arts** were highly valued. Architecture culminated in the **Parthenon** (438 BC) by Phidias (fl. 490-430 BC). Poetry (Sappho, c. 610-580 BC; Pindar, c. 518-438 BC) and **drama** (Aeschylus, 525-456 BC; Sophocles, c. 496-406 BC; Euripides, c. 484-406 BC) thrived. Male beauty and strength, a chief artistic theme, were celebrated at the national games at Olympia.

Ruled by local tyrants or **oligarchies**, the Greeks were not politically united, but managed to resist inclusion in the Persian Empire—Persian king Darius was defeated at Marathon (490 BC), his son Xerxes at Salamis (480 BC), and the Persian army at Plataea (479 BC). Local warfare was common; the **Peloponnesian Wars** (431-404 BC) ended in Sparta's victory over Athens. Greek political power subsequently waned, but Greek cultural forms spread far and wide.

IT'S A FACT: Tutankhamen became a pharaoh in 1343 BC at the age of 9, and ruled until his death at about age 18. Despite his short life, he lives on more than most Egyptian pharoahs because his underground tomb, discovered in 1922 by archaeologist Howard Carter, is the only pharoah's tomb to have survived into modern times virtually untouched. Treasures from King Tut's tomb went on tour in the U.S. in 1976-79, and a new 27-month tour was launched in Los Angeles in June 2005. Items on display include his royal diadem, a sculpture of the boy king in alabaster, and a jeweled container that holds his mummified organs.

Hebrews. Nomadic Hebrew tribes entered Canaan before 1200 BC, settling among other Semitic peoples speaking the same language. They brought from the desert a **monotheistic** faith said to have been revealed to Abraham in Canaan c. 1800 BC and Moses at Mt. Sinai c. 1250 BC, after the Hebrews' escape from bondage in Egypt. David (r. 1000-961 BC) and Solomon (r. 961-922 BC) united them in a kingdom that briefly dominated the area. **Phoenicians** to the N founded Mediterranean colonies (Carthage, c. 814 BC) and sailed into the Atlantic.

A temple in Jerusalem became the national religious center, with sacrifices performed by a hereditary priesthood. Polytheistic influences, especially of the fertility cult of Baal, were opposed by **prophets** (Elijah, Amos, Isaiah).

Divided into **two kingdoms** after Solomon, the Hebrews were unable to resist the revived Assyrian empire, which conquered Israel, the N kingdom, in 722 BC. Judah, the S kingdom, was conquered in 586 BC by the Babylonians under Nebuchadnezzar II. With the fixing of most of the biblical canon by the mid-4th cent. BC and the emergence of rabbis, Judaism successfully survived the loss of Hebrew autonomy. A Jewish kingdom was revived under the Hasmoneans (168-42 BC).

China. During the **Eastern Chou** dynasty (770-256 BC), Chinese culture spread E to the sea and S to the Yangtze R. Large feudal states on the periphery of the empire contended for preeminence, but continued to recognize the Son of Heaven (king), who retained a purely ritual role enriched with courtly music and dance. In the Age of Warring States (403-221 BC), when the first sections of the **Great Wall** were built, the Ch'in state in the W gained supremacy and finally united all of China.

Iron tools entered China c. 500 BC, and casting techniques were advanced, aiding agriculture. Peasants owned their land and owed civil and military service to nobles. China's cities grew in number and size; barter remained the chief trade medium.

Intellectual ferment among noble scribes and officials produced the Classical Age of Chinese literature and philosophy. **Confucius** (551-479 BC) urged a restoration of a supposedly harmonious social order of the past through proper conduct in accordance with one's station and through filial and ceremonial piety. The *Analects* attributed to him are revered throughout E Asia.

Among other thinkers, **Mencius** (d. 289 BC) added the view that the Mandate of Heaven can be removed from an unjust dynasty. The Legalists sought to curb the supposed natural wickedness of people through new institutions and harsh laws. The Naturalists emphasized the balance of opposites—yin, yang—in the world. **Taoists** sought mystical knowledge through meditation and disengagement.

India. The political and cultural center of India shifted from the Indus to the Ganges River Valley. Buddhism, Jainism, and mystical revisions of orthodox Vedism all developed c. 500-300 BC. The *Upanishads,* last part of the *Veda*, urged escape from the physical world. Vedism remained the preserve of the Brahman caste.

Buddha

In contrast, **Buddhism**, founded by Siddhartha Gautama (c. 563-c. 483 BC)—Buddha ("Enlightened One")—appealed to merchants in the urban centers and took hold at first (and most lastingly) on the geographic fringes of Indian civilization. The classic Indian epics were composed in this era: the **Ramayana** perhaps c. 300 BC, the **Mahabharata** over a period starting around 400 BC.

N India was divided into a large number of monarchies and aristocratic republics, probably derived from tribal groupings, when the Magadha kingdom was formed in Bihar c. 542 BC. It soon became the dominant power. The **Maurya dynasty**, founded by Chandragupta c. 321 BC, expanded the kingdom, uniting most of N India in a centralized bureaucratic empire. The third Mauryan king, **Asoka** (reigned c. 274-236 BC), conquered most of the subcontinent. He converted to Buddhism and inscribed its tenets on pillars throughout India. He downplayed the caste system.

Before its final decline in India, Buddhism developed into a popular worship of heavenly Bodhisattvas ("enlightened beings"), and it produced a refined architecture (the Great Stupa [shrine] at Sanchi, AD 100) and sculpture (Gandhara reliefs, AD 1-400).

Persia. Aryan peoples (Persians, Medes) dominated the area of present Iran by the beginning of the 1st millennium BC. The prophet **Zoroaster** (born c. 628 BC) introduced a dualistic religion in which the forces of good (Ahura Mazda, "Lord of Wisdom") and evil (Ahriam) battle for dominance; individuals are judged by their actions and earn damnation or salvation. Zoroaster's hymns (*Gathas*) are included in the *Avesta*, the Zoroastrian scriptures. A version of this faith became the established religion of the Persian Empire.

Africa. Nubia, periodically occupied by Egypt since about 2600 BC, ruled Egypt c. 750-661 BC and survived as an independent Egyptianized kingdom (**Kush;** capital Meroe) for 1,000 years. The Iron Age Nok culture flourished c. 500 BC- AD 200 on the Benue Plateau of **Nigeria.**

Americas. The Chavin culture controlled N Peru c. 900 BC to 200 BC. Its ceremonial centers, featuring the jaguar god, survived long after. Its architecture, ceramics, and textiles had influenced other Peruvian cultures. **Mayan civilization** began to develop in Central America as early as 1500 BC.

Great Empires Unite the Civilized World: 400 BC-AD 400

Alexander the Great

Persia and Alexander the Great. Cyrus, ruler of a small kingdom in Persia from 559 BC, united the Persians and Medes within 10 years and conquered Asia Minor and Babylonia in another 10. His son Cambyses, followed by **Darius** (r. 522-486 BC), added vast lands to the E and N as far as the Indus Valley and Central Asia, as well as Egypt and Thrace. The whole empire was ruled by an international bureaucracy and army, with Persians holding the chief positions. The resources and styles of all the subject civilizations were exploited to create a rich syncretic art.

The kingdom of Macedon, which under Philip II dominated the Greek world and Egypt, was passed on to his son **Alexander** in 336 BC. Within 13 years, Alexander had conquered all the Persian dominions. Imbued by his tutor Aristotle with Greek ideals, Alexander encouraged colonization, and Greek-style cities were founded. After his death in 323 BC, wars of succession divided the empire into 3 parts—**Macedon,** Egypt (ruled by the **Ptolemies**), and the **Seleucid** Empire. In the ensuing 300 years (the **Hellenistic Era**), a cosmopolitan Greek-oriented culture permeated the ancient world from W Europe to the borders of India, absorbing native elites everywhere.

Hellenistic philosophy stressed the private individual's search for happiness. The Cynics followed Diogenes (c. 372-287 BC), who stressed self-sufficiency and restriction of desires and expressed contempt for luxury and social convention. Zeno (c. 335-c.263 BC) and the **Stoics** exalted reason, identified it with virtue, and counseled an ascetic disregard for misfortune. The **Epicureans** tried to build lives of moderate pleasure without political or emotional involvement. Hellenistic arts imitated life realistically, especially in sculpture and literature (comedies of Menander, 342-292 BC).

The Seven Wonders of the Ancient World

These ancient works of art and architecture were considered awe-inspiring by the Greek and Roman world of the first few centuries BC. Later classical writers disagreed as to which works belonged, but the following were usually included:

The Pyramids of Egypt: The only surviving ancient Wonder, these monumental structures of masonry, located at Giza on the W bank of the Nile R above Cairo, were built from c. 2700 to 2500 BC as royal tombs. Three—Khufu (Cheops), Khafra (Chephren), and Menkaura (Mycerimus)—were often grouped as the first Wonder of the World. The largest, the Great Pyramid of Khufu covers 13 acres. It is estimated to contain 2.3 million blocks of stone, the stones themselves averaging 2½ tons and some weighing 30 tons. Its construction reputedly took 100,000 laborers 20 years.

The Hanging Gardens of Babylon: These gardens were laid out on a brick terrace 400 ft square and 75 ft above the ground. To irrigate the plants, screws were turned to lift water from the Euphrates R. The gardens were probably built by King Nebuchadnezzar II about 600 BC. The Walls of Babylon, long, thick, and made of colorfully glazed brick, were also considered by some among the Seven Wonders.

The Pharos (Lighthouse) of Alexandria: This structure was designed about 270 BC, during the reign of Ptolemy II, by the Greek architect Sostratos. Estimates of its height range from 200 to 600 ft.

The Colossus of Rhodes: A bronze statue of the sun god Helios, the Colossus was worked on for 12 years in the third cent. BC by the sculptor Chares. It was probably 120 ft high. A symbol of the city of Rhodes at its height, the statue stood on a promontory overlooking the harbor.

The Temple of Artemis (Diana) at Ephesus: This largest and most complex temple of ancient times was built about 550 BC and was made of marble except for its tile-covered wooden roof. It was begun in honor of a non-Hellenic goddess who later became identified with the Greek goddess of the same name. Ephesus was one of the greatest of the Ionian cities.

The Mausoleum at Halicarnassus: The source of our word *mausoleum*, this marble tomb was built in what is now SE Turkey by Artemisia for her husband Mausolus, king of Caria in Asia Minor, who died in 353 BC. About 135 ft high, the tomb was adorned with the works of 4 sculptors.

The Statue of Zeus (Jupiter) at Olympia: This statue showed Zeus seated on a throne. His flesh was made of ivory, his robe and ornaments of gold. Reputedly 40 ft high, the statue was made by Phidias and was placed in the great temple of Zeus in the sacred grove of Olympia about 457 BC.

The sciences thrived, especially at Alexandria, where the Ptolemies financed a great library and museum. Fields of study included mathematics (**Euclid's** geometry, c. 300 BC); astronomy (heliocentric theory of Aristarchus, 310-230 BC; Julian calendar, 45 BC; **Ptolemy**'s *Almagest*, c. AD 150); geography (world map of Eratosthenes, 276-194 BC); hydraulics (**Archimedes,** 287-212 BC); medicine (Galen, AD 130-200); and chemistry. Inventors refined uses for siphons, valves, gears, springs, screws, levers, cams, and pulleys.

A restored Persian empire under the **Parthians** (northern Iranian tribesmen) controlled the eastern Hellenistic world from 250 BC to AD 229. The Parthians and the succeeding Sassanian dynasty (c. AD 224-651) fought with Rome periodically. The **Sassanians** revived Zoroastrianism as a state religion and patronized a nationalistic artistic and scholarly renaissance.

Rome. The city of Rome was founded, according to legend, by Romulus in 753 BC. Through military expansion and colonization, and by granting citizenship to conquered tribes, the city annexed all of Italy S of the Po in the 100-year period before 268 BC. The Latin and other Italic tribes were annexed first, followed by the **Etruscans** (founders of a great civilization, N of Rome) and the Greek colonies in the S. With a large standing army and reserve forces of several hundred thousand, Rome was able to defeat **Carthage** in the 3 **Punic Wars** (264-241, 218-201, 149-146 BC), despite the invasion of Italy by **Hannibal (218 BC)**, thus gaining Sicily and territory in Spain and N Africa.

Rome exploited local disputes to conquer Greece and Asia Minor in the 2nd cent. BC, and Egypt in the 1st (after the defeat and suicide of **Antony and Cleopatra**, 30 BC). The Mediterranean civilized world, up to the disputed Parthian border, was now Roman and remained so for 500 years. Less civilized regions were added to the Empire: Gaul (conquered by **Julius Caesar**, 58-51 BC), Britain (AD 43), and Dacia NE of the Danube (AD 107).

The original aristocratic republican government, with democratic features added in the 5th and 4th cent. BC, deteriorated under the pressures of empire and class conflict (**Gracchus** brothers, social reformers, murdered in 133 BC and 121 BC; slave revolts in 135 BC and 73 BC). After a series of civil wars (Marius vs. Sulla 88-82 BC, Caesar vs. **Pompey** 49-45 BC, triumvirate vs. Caesar's assassins 44-43 BC, Antony vs. Octavian 32-30 BC), the empire came under the rule of a deified monarch (first emperor, **Augustus**, 27 BC-AD 14).

Provincials (nearly all granted citizenship by Caracalla, AD 212) came to dominate the army and civil service. Traditional **Roman law,** systematized and interpreted by independent jurists, and local self-rule in provincial cities were supplanted by a vast tax-collecting bureaucracy in the 3rd and 4th cent. The legal rights of women, children, and slaves were strengthened.

Roman innovations in **civil engineering** included water mills, windmills, and rotary mills and use of cement that hardened under water. Monumental architecture (baths, theaters, temples) relied on the arch and the dome. The network of roads (some still standing) stretched 53,000 mi, passing through mountain tunnels as long as 3.5 mi. Aqueducts brought water to cities; underground sewers removed waste.

Roman art and literature were to a large extent derivative of Greek models. Innovations were made in sculpture (naturalistic busts, equestrian statues), decorative wall painting (as at Pompeii), satire (**Juvenal,** AD 60-127), history (**Tacitus,** AD 56-120), prose romance (Petronius, d. AD 66). Gladiatorial contests dominated public amusements, which were supported by the state.

India. The **Gupta** monarchs reunited N India c. AD 320. Their peaceful and prosperous reign saw a revival of Hindu religious thought and Brahman power. The old Vedic traditions were combined with devotion to many indigenous deities (who were seen as manifestations of Vedic gods). Caste lines were reinforced, and Buddhist practices gradually disappeared or were integrated with Hindu traditions. The art (often erotic), architecture, and literature of the period, patronized by the Gupta court, are considered among India's finest achievements (Kalidasa, poet and dramatist, fl. c. AD 400). Mathematical innovations included use of the zero and decimal numbers. Invasions by White Huns from the NW destroyed the empire c. 550.

Rich cultures also developed in S India during this period. Emotional Tamil religious poetry contributed to the Hindu revival. The Pallava kingdom controlled much of S India c. 350-880 and helped to spread Indian civilization to SE Asia.

China. The Ch'in ruler Shih Huang Ti (r. 221-210 BC), known as the First Emperor, centralized political authority. standardized the written language, laws, weights, measures, and coinage, and conducted a census, but tried to destroy most philosophical texts. The **Han dynasty** (202 BC-AD 220) instituted the Mandarin bureaucracy, which lasted 2,000 years. Local officials were selected by examination in Confucian classics and trained at the imperial university and provincial schools.

The invention of **paper** facilitated this bureaucratic system. Agriculture was promoted, but peasants bore most of the tax burden. Irrigation was improved, water clocks and sundials were used, astronomy and mathematics thrived, and landscape painting was perfected.

With the expansion S and W (to nearly the present borders of today's China), trade was opened with India, SE Asia, and the Middle East, over sea and caravan routes. Indian missionaries brought Mahayana Buddhism to China by the 1st cent. AD and spawned a variety of sects. Taoism was revived and merged with popular superstitions. **Taoist and Buddhist monasteries** and convents multiplied in the turbulent centuries after the collapse of the Han dynasty.

Major Gods & Goddesses of the Classical World

Greek	Roman	Relations	Sphere or Position
Aphrodite	Venus	Daughter of Zeus & Dione	Love
Apollo	——	Son of Zeus & Leto	Healing, poetry, light
Ares	Mars	Son of Zeus & Hera	War
Artemis	Diana	Daughter of Zeus & Leto	Hunting, chastity
Athena	Minerva	Daughter of Zeus & Metis	Wisdom, crafts, war
Cronus	Saturn	Father of Zeus	Titans' ruler
Demeter	Ceres	Sister of Zeus	Agriculture, fertility
Dionysus	Bacchus	Son of Zeus & Semele	Wine, fertility, ecstasy
Eros	Cupid	Son of Ares & Aphrodite	Love
Hades	Pluto	Brother of Zeus	The underworld, death
Hephaestus	Vulcan	Son of Zeus & Hera	Fire
Hera	Juno	Wife & sister of Zeus	Earth
Hermes	Mercury	Son of Zeus & Maia	Travel, commerce, gods' messenger
Hestia	Vesta	Sister of Zeus	The hearth
Pan	——	Son of Hermes & a wood nymph	Forests, flocks, shepherds
Persephone	Proserpina	Daughter of Zeus & Demeter	Grain
Poseidon	Neptune	Brother of Zeus	The sea
Rhea	Ops	Mother of Zeus	The earth
Uranus	Uranus	Father of Titans (elder gods)	The heavens
Zeus	Jupiter	Son of Cronus & Rhea	Ruler of the gods

Monotheism Spreads: AD 1-750

Roman Empire. Polytheism was practiced in the Roman Empire, and religions indigenous to particular Middle Eastern nations became international. Roman citizens worshiped **Isis** of Egypt, **Mithras** of Persia, **Demeter** of Greece, and the great mother **Cybele** of Phrygia. Their cults centered on mysteries (secret ceremonies) and the promise of an afterlife, symbolized by the death and rebirth of the god. The Jews of the empire preserved their monotheistic religion, Judaism, the world's oldest (c. 1300 BC) continuous religion. Its teachings are contained in the Bible (the Old Testament). 1st-cent. Judaism embraced several sects, including the **Sadducees**, mostly drawn from the Temple priesthood, who were culturally Hellenized; the **Pharisees**, who upheld the full range of traditional customs and practices as of equal weight to literal scriptural law and elaborated synagogue worship; and the **Essenes**, an ascetic, millennarian sect. Messianic fervor led to repeated, unsuccessful rebellions against Rome (66-70, 135). As a result, the Temple in Jerusalem was destroyed and the population decimated; this event marked the beginning of the Diaspora (living in exile). To preserve the faith, a program of codification of law was begun at the academy of Yavneh. The work continued for some 500 years in Palestine and in Babylonia, ending in the final redaction (c. 600) of the **Talmud**, a huge collection of legal and moral debates, rulings, liturgy, biblical exegesis, and legendary materials.

Christianity, which emerged as a distinct sect by the 2nd half of the 1st cent., is based on the teachings of **Jesus**, whom believers considered the Savior (Messiah or Christ) and son of God. Missionary activities of the Apostles and such early leaders as **Paul of Tarsus** spread the faith. Intermittent persecution, as in Rome under Nero in AD 64, on grounds of suspected disloyalty, failed to disrupt the Christian communities. Each congregation, generally urban and of plebeian character, was tightly organized under a leader (bishop), elders (presbyters or priests), and assistants (deacons). The four **Gospels** (accounts of the life and teachings of Jesus) and the Acts of the Apostles were written down in the late 1st and early 2nd cent. and circulated along with letters of Paul and other Christian leaders. An authoritative canon of these writings was not fixed until the 4th cent.

A school for priests was established at Alexandria in the 2nd cent. Its teachers (**Origen** c. 182-251) helped define doctrine and promote the faith in Greek-style philosophical works. Neoplatonism underwent Christian coloration in the writings of Church Fathers such as **Augustine** (354-430). Christian hermits began to associate in monasteries, first in Egypt (St. Pachomius c. 290-345), then in other eastern lands, then in the W (**St. Benedict's rule**, 529). Devotion to saints, especially Mary, mother of Jesus, spread. Under **Constantine** (r. 306-37), Christianity became in effect the established religion of the Empire. Pagan temples were expropriated, state funds were used to build churches and support the hierarchy, and laws were adjusted in accordance with Christian ideas. Pagan worship was banned by the end of the 4th cent., and severe restrictions were placed on Judaism.

The newly established church was rocked by doctrinal disputes, often exacerbated by regional rivalries. Chief heresies (as defined by church councils, backed by imperial authority) were **Arianism**, which denied the divinity of Jesus; **Monophysitism,** denying the human nature of Christ; **Donatism**, which regarded as invalid any sacraments administered by sinful clergy; and **Pelagianism,** which denied the necessity of unmerited divine aid (grace) for salvation.

Islam. The earliest Arab civilization emerged by the end of the 2nd millennium BC in the watered highlands of Yemen. Seaborne and caravan trade in frankincense and myrrh connected the area with the Nile and Fertile Crescent. The Minaean, Sabean (Sheba), and Himyarite states successively held sway. By Muhammad's time (7th cent. AD), the region was a province of Sassanian Persia. In the N, the Nabataean kingdom at Petra and the kingdom of Palmyra were Aramaicized, Romanized, and finally absorbed, as neighboring Judea had been, into the Roman Empire. Nomads shared the central region with a few trading towns and oases. Wars between tribes and raids on communities were common and were celebrated in a poetic tradition that by the 6th cent. helped establish a classic literary Arabic.

About 610, **Muhammad**, a 40-year-old Arab of Mecca, emerged as a prophet. He proclaimed a revelation from the one true God, calling on contemporaries to abandon idolatry and restore the faith of Abraham. He introduced his religion as "**Islam**," meaning "submission" to the one God, Allah, as a continuation of the biblical faith of Abraham, Moses, and Jesus, all respected as prophets in this system. His teachings, recorded in the **Koran** (*al-Qur'an* in Arabic), in many ways were inclusive of Abrahamic monotheistic ideas known to the Jews and Christians in Arabia. A key aspect of the Abrahamic connection was insistence on justice in society, which led to severe opposition among the aristocrats in Mecca. As conditions worsened for Muhammad and his followers, he decided in 622 to make a ***hijra*** (emigration) to Medina, 200 mi to the N. This event marks the beginning of the Muslim lunar calendar. Hostilities between Mecca and Medina increased, and in 629 Muhammad conquered Mecca. By the time he died in 632, nearly all the Arabian peninsula accepted his political and religious leadership.

After his death the majority of Muslims recognized the leadership of the **caliph** ("successor") Abu Bakr (632-34), followed by Umar (634-44), Uthman (644-56), and Ali (656-60). A minority, the **Shiites**, insisted instead on the leadership of Ali, Muhammad's cousin and son-in-law. By 644, **Muslim rule** over Arabia was confirmed. Muslim armies had threatened the Byzantine and Persian empires, which were weakened by wars and disaffection among subject peoples (including Coptic and Syriac Christians opposed to the Byzantine Orthodox establishment). Syria,

Palestine, Egypt, Iraq, and Persia fell to Muslim armies. The new administration assimilated existing systems in the region; hence the conquered peoples participated in running of the empire. The Koran recognized the so-called Peoples of the Book, i.e., Christians, Jews, and Zoroastrians, as tolerated monotheists, and Muslim policy was relatively tolerant to minorities living as "protected" peoples. An expanded tax system, based on conquests of the Persian and Byzantine empires, provided revenue to organize campaigns against neighboring non-Muslim regions.

Under the **Umayyads** (661-750) and **Abbasids** (750-1256), territorial expansion led Muslim armies across N Africa and into Spain (711). Muslim armies in the W were stopped at Tours (France) in 732 by the Frankish ruler **Charles Martel**. Asia Minor, the Indus Valley, and Transoxiana were conquered in the E. The conversion of conquered peoples to Islam was gradual. In many places the official Arabic language supplanted the local tongues. But in the eastern regions the Arab rulers and their armies adopted Persian cultures and language as part of their Muslim identity.

Disputes over succession, and pious opposition to injustices in society, led to a number of oppositional movements, which also led to the factionalization of Muslim community. The **Shiites** supported leadership candidates descended from Muhammad, believing them to be carriers of some kind of divine authority. The **Kharijites** supported an egalitarian system derived from the Koran, opposing and even engaging in battle against those who did not agree with them.

New Peoples Enter World History: 400-900

Barbarian invasions. Germanic tribes infiltrated S and E from their Baltic homeland during the 1st millennium BC, reaching S Germany by 100 BC and the Black Sea by AD 214. Organized into large federated tribes under elected kings, most resisted Roman domination and raided the empire in time of civil war (Goths took Dacia in 214, raided Thrace in 251-69). Germanic troops and commanders dominated the Roman armies by the end of the 4th cent. **Huns**, invaders from Asia, entered Europe in 372, driving more Germans into the W empire. Emperor Valens allowed Visigoths to cross the Danube in 376. Huns under Attila (d. 453) raided Gaul, Italy, and the Balkans.

The W empire, weakened by overtaxation and social stagnation, was overrun in the 5th cent. Gaul was effectively lost in 406-7, Spain in 409, Britain in 410, Africa in 429-39. Rome was sacked in 410 by Visigoths under Alaric and in 455 by Vandals. **The last western emperor**, Romulus Augustulus, was deposed in 476 by the Germanic chief Odovacar.

Celts. Celtic cultures, which in pre-Roman times covered most of W Europe, were confined almost entirely to the British Isles after the Germanic invasions. **St. Patrick** completed (c. 457-92) the conversion of Ireland and a strong monastic tradition took hold. Irish monastic missionaries in Scotland, England, and the continent (Columba c. 521-97; Columban c. 543-615) helped restore Christianity after the Germanic invasions. **Monasteries** became centers of classic and Christian learning and presided over the recording of a Christianized Celtic mythology, elaborated by secular writers and bards. An intricate decorative art style developed, especially in book illumination (Lindisfarne Gospels, c. 700; Book of Kells, 8th cent.).

Successor states. The Visigothic kingdom in Spain (from 419) and much of France (to 507) saw continuation of Roman administration, language, and law (Breviary of Alaric, 506) until its destruction by the Muslims (711). The Vandal kingdom in Africa (from 429) was conquered by the Byzantines in 533. Italy was ruled successively by an Ostrogothic kingdom under Byzantine suzerainty (489-554), direct Byzantine government, and German Lombards (568-774). The Lombards divided the peninsula with the Byzantines and papacy under the dynamic reformer **Pope Gregory the Great** (590-604) and successors.

King Clovis (r. 481-511) united the Franks on both sides of the Rhine and, after his conversion to Christianity, defeated the Arian heretics, Burgundians (after 500), and Visigoths (507) with the support of native clergy and the papacy. Under the **Merovingian** kings, a feudal system emerged: Power was fragmented among hierarchies of military landowners. Social stratification, which in late Roman times had acquired legal, hereditary sanction, was reinforced. The Carolingians (747-987) expanded the kingdom and restored central power. **Charlemagne** (r. 768-814) conquered nearly all the Germanic lands, including Lombard Italy, and was crowned Emperor by Pope Leo III in Rome in 800. A centuries-long decline in commerce and arts was reversed under Charlemagne's patronage. He welcomed Jews to his kingdom, which became a center of Jewish learning (Rashi, 1040-1105). He sponsored the Carolingian Renaissance of learning under the Anglo-Latin scholar Alcuin (c. 732-804), who reformed church liturgy.

Byzantine Empire. Under **Diocletian** (r. 284-305) the empire had been divided into 2 parts to facilitate administration and defense. **Constantine** founded (330) **Constantinople** (at old Byzantium) as a fully Christian city. Commerce and taxation financed a sumptuous, orientalized court, a class of hereditary bureaucratic families, and magnificent urban construction (Hagia Sophia, 532-37). The city's fortifications and naval innovations repelled assaults by Goths, Huns, Slavs, Bulgars, Avars, Arabs, and Scandinavians. Greek replaced Latin as the official language by c. 700. **Byzantine art**, a solemn, sacral, and stylized variation of late classical styles (mosaics at the Church of San Vitale, Ravenna, Italy 526-48), was a starting point for medieval art in E and W Europe.

Justinian (r. 527-65) reconquered parts of Spain, N Africa, and Italy, codified **Roman law** (Codex Justinianus [529] was medieval Europe's chief legal text), closed the Platonic Academy at Athens, and ordered all pagans to convert. Lombards in Italy and Arabs in Africa retook most of his conquests. The Isaurian dynasty from Anatolia (from 717) and the Macedonian dynasty (867-1054) restored military and commercial power. The Iconoclast controversy (726-843) over the permissibility of images helped alienate the Eastern Church from the papacy.

Major Norse Gods & Goddesses

Name	Relations	Sphere or Position	Emblem/Attribute
Odin	Father of the Aesir (gods)	War and death, poetry, wisdom, magic	Spear, mead, ring/One-eyed
Thor	Son of Odin	Thunder, lightning, rain; champion of the gods	Hammer, belt
Njord	Father of Freyja & Freyr	Wind and sea, wealth and prosperity	----
Frigg	Wife of Odin	Marriage and motherhood, home	----
Freyja (Freya)	Daughter of Njord	Fertility, birth, crops	Necklace
Freyr	Son of Njord	Agriculture, sun, rain	Magic ship, golden boar
Tyr	Son of Odin ?	Justice, war	Spear/One-handed
Heimdall	Son of nine giantesses	Watchman of the gods; keen sight & hearing	Horn
Balder (Baldur)	Son of Odin	Light, purity	----
Loki	Son of giants; father of Hel (goddess of death), Jormungand (serpent encompassing the world), Fenrir (the wolf).	Malicious trickster	----

Abbasid Empire. Baghdad (est. 762), became seat of the **Abbasid dynasty** (est. 750), while Ummayads continued to rule in Spain. A brilliant cosmopolitan civilization emerged, inaugurating a Muslim-Arab golden age. Arabic was the lingua franca of the empire; intellectual sources from Persian, Sanskrit, Greek, and Syriac were rendered into Arabic. Christians and Jews equally participated in this translation movement, which also involved interaction between Jewish legal thought and Islamic law, as much as between Christian theology and Muslim scholasticism. Persian-style court life, with art and music, flourished at the court of **Harun al-Rashid** (786-809), celebrated in the masterpiece known to English readers as *The Arabian Nights*. The sciences, medicine, and mathematics were pursued at Baghdad, Cordova, and Cairo (est. 969). The culmination of this intellectual synthesis in Islamic civilization came with the scientific and philosophical works of **Avicenna** (Ibn Sina, 980-1037), **Averroes** (Ibn Rushd, 1126-98), and **Maimonides** (1135-1204), a Jew who wrote in Arabic. This intellectual tradition was translated into Latin and opened a new period in Christian thought.

The decentralization of the **Abbasid** empire, from 874, led to establishment of various Muslim dynasties under different ethnic groups. Persians, Berbers, and Turks ruled different regions, retaining connection with the Abbasid caliph at the religious level. The Abbasid period also saw various religious movements against the orthodox position held by governing authorities. This situation in Muslim religion led to the establishment of different legal, theological, and mystical schools of thought. The most influential mass movement was **Sufism**, which aimed at the reaching out of the average individual in quest of a spiritual path. Al-Ghazali (1058-1111) is credited with reconciling personal Sufism with orthodox Sunni tradition.

Africa. Immigrants from Saba in S Arabia helped set up the **Axum** kingdom in Ethiopia in the 1st cent. (their language, Ge'ez, is preserved by the Ethiopian Church). In the 3rd cent., when the kingdom became Christianized, it defeated Kushite Meroe and expanded its influence into Yemen. Axum was the center of a vast ivory trade and controlled the Red Sea coast until c. 1100. Arab conquest in Egypt cut Axum's political and economic ties with Byzantium.

The Iron Age entered W Africa by the end of the 1st millennium BC. **Ghana**, the first known sub-Saharan state, ruled in the upper Senegal-Niger region c. 400-1240, controlling the trade of gold from mines in the S to trans-Sahara caravan routes to the N. The **Bantu** peoples, probably of W African origin, began to spread E and S perhaps 2,000 years ago, displacing the Pygmies and Bushmen of central and S Africa during a 1,500-year period.

Japan. The advanced Neolithic Yayoi period, when irrigation, rice farming, and iron and bronze casting techniques were introduced from China or Korea, persisted to c. AD 400. The myriad Japanese states were then united by the **Yamato** clan, under an emperor who acted as chief priest of the animistic Shinto cult. Japanese political and military intervention by the 6th cent. in Korea, then under strong Chinese influence, quickened a Chinese cultural invasion of Japan, bringing Buddhism, the Chinese language (which long remained a literary and governmental medium), Chinese ideographs, and Buddhist styles in painting, sculpture, literature, and architecture (7th cent., Horyu-ji temple at Nara). The Taika Reforms (646) tried unsuccessfully to centralize Japan according to Chinese bureaucratic and Buddhist philosophical values.

A nativist reaction against the Buddhist **Nara period** (710-94) ushered in the **Heian period** (794-1185) centered at the new capital, Kyoto. Japanese elegance and simplicity modified Chinese styles in architecture, scroll painting, and literature; the writing system was also simplified. The courtly novel *Tale of Genji* (1010-20) testifies to the enhanced role of women.

Southeast Asia. The historic peoples of SE Asia began arriving some 2,500 years ago from China and Tibet, displacing scattered aborigines. Their agriculture relied on rice and yams. Indian cultural influences were strongest; literacy and Hindu and Buddhist ideas followed the S India-China trade route. From the S tip of Indochina, the kingdom of **Funan** (1st-7th cent.) traded as far W as Persia. It was absorbed by Chenla, itself conquered by the **Khmer Empire** (600-1300). The Khmers, under Hindu god-kings (Suryavarman II, 1113-c. 1150), built the monumental Angkor Wat temple center for the royal phallic cult. The **Nam-Viet** kingdom in Annam, dominated by China and Chinese culture for 1,000 years, emerged in the 10th cent., growing at the expense of the Khmers, who also lost ground in the NW to the new, highly organized **Thai** kingdom. On Sumatra, the **Srivijaya** Empire controlled vital sea lanes (7th to 10th cent.). A Buddhist dynasty, the Sailendras, ruled central **Java** (8th-9th cent.), building at Borobudur one of the largest stupas in the world.

China. The Sui dynasty (581-618) ushered in a period of commercial, artistic, and scientific achievement in China, continuing under the **Tang** dynasty (618-906). Inventions like the magnetic compass, gunpowder, the abacus, and printing were introduced or perfected. Medical innovations included cataract surgery. The state, from its cosmopolitan capital, Chang-an, supervised foreign trade, which exchanged Chinese silks, porcelains, and art for spices, ivory, etc., over Central Asian caravan routes and sea routes reaching Africa. A golden age of poetry bequeathed valuable works to later generations (Tu Fu, 712-70; Li Po, 701-62). Landscape painting flourished.

Commercial and industrial expansion continued under the **Northern Sung** dynasty (960-1126), facilitated by paper money and credit notes. But commerce never achieved respectability; government monopolies expropriated successful merchants. The population, long stable at 50 million, doubled in 200 years with the introduction of early-ripening rice and the double harvest. In art, native Chinese styles were revived.

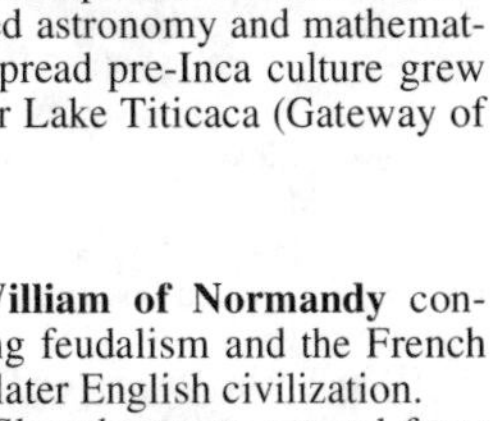
Mayan temple

Americas. From 300 to 600 a Native American empire stretched from the Valley of Mexico to Guatemala, centering on the huge city **Teotihuacán** (founded 100 BC). To the S, in Guatemala, a high **Mayan** civilization developed (150-900) around hundreds of rural ceremonial centers. The Mayans improved on Olmec writing and the calendar and pursued astronomy and mathematics. In South America, a widespread pre-Inca culture grew from **Tiahuanacu,** Bolivia, near Lake Titicaca (Gateway of the Sun, c. 700).

Christian Europe Regroups and Expands: 900-1300

Scandinavians. Pagan Danish and Norse (Viking) adventurers, traders, and pirates raided the coasts of the British Isles (Dublin, est. c. 831), France, and even the Mediterranean for over 200 years beginning in the late 8th cent. Inland settlement in the W was limited to Great Britain (King Canute, 994-1035) and Normandy, settled (911) under Rollo, as a fief of France. Vikings also reached Iceland (874), Greenland (c. 986), and North America (**Leif Ericson** and others, c. 1000). Norse traders (**Varangians**) developed Russian river commerce from the 8th to the 11th cent. and helped set up a state at Kiev in the late 9th cent. Conversion to Christianity occurred in the 10th cent., reaching Sweden 100 years later. In the 11th cent. Norman bands conquered S Italy and Sicily, and Duke **William of Normandy** conquered (1066) England, bringing feudalism and the French language, essential elements in later English civilization.

Central and East Europe. Slavs began to expand from about AD 150 in all directions in Europe, and by the 7th cent. they reached as far S as the Adriatic and Aegean seas. In the Balkan Peninsula they dislocated Romanized local populations or assimilated newcomers (Bulgarians, a Turkic people). The first **Slavic states** were Moravia (628) in Central Europe and the Bulgarian state (680) in the Balkans. Missions of St. Methodius and Cyril (whose Greek-based cyrillic alphabet is still used by some S and E Slavs) converted (863) Moravia.

IT'S A FACT: In 13th-century Europe salt was cheap but pepper was expensive (an ounce cost the same as a whole chicken). Knives and spoons were used at table, but there were no forks. People of means could enjoy fish, meats, vegetables, eggs, cheese, soup, and wine, but there was no coffee, tea, potatoes, pasta, corn, tomatoes, or chocolate.

The Eastern Slavs, part-civilized under the overlordship of the Turkish-Jewish **Khazar** trading empire (7th-10th cent.), gravitated toward Constantinople by the 9th cent. The **Kievan state** adopted (989) Eastern Christianity under Prince Vladimir. King Boleslav I (992-1025) began **Poland's** long history of eastern conquest. The Magyars (**Hungarians**), in present-day Hungary since 896, accepted (1001) Latin Christianity.

Germany. The German kingdom that emerged after the breakup of Charlemagne's W Empire remained a confederation of largely autonomous states. Otto I, a Saxon who was king from 936, established the **Holy Roman Empire**—a union of Germany and N Italy—in alliance with Pope John XII, who crowned (962) him emperor; he defeated (955) the Magyars. Imperial power was greatest under the **Hohenstaufens** (1138-1254), despite the growing opposition of the papacy, which ruled central Italy, and the Lombard League cities. Frederick II (1194-1250) improved administration and patronized the arts; after his death, German influence was removed from Italy.

Christian Spain. From its N mountain redoubts, Christian rule slowly migrated S through the 11th cent., when Muslim unity collapsed. After the capture (1085) of **Toledo**, the kingdoms of Portugal, Castile, and Aragon undertook repeated crusades of reconquest, finally completed in 1492. Elements of Islamic civilization persisted in recaptured areas, influencing all Western Europe.

Crusades. Pope Urban II called (1095) for a crusade to restore Asia Minor to Byzantium and to regain the Holy Land from the Turks. Some ten crusades (lasting until 1291) succeeded only in founding four temporary Frankish states in the Levant. The 4th crusade sacked (1204) Constantinople. In Rhineland (1096), England (1290), and France (1306), Jews were massacred or expelled, and wars were launched against Christian heretics (**Albigensian** crusade in France, 1229). Trade in eastern luxuries expanded, led by the Venetian naval empire.

Economy. The agricultural base of European life benefited from improvements in **plow design** (c. 1000) and by draining of lowlands and clearing of forests, leading to a rural population increase. Towns grew in N Italy, Flanders, and N Germany (Hanseatic League). Improvements in **loom design** permitted factory textile production. **Guilds** dominated urban trades from the 12th cent. Banking (centered in Italy, 12th-15th cent.) facilitated long-distance trade.

The Church. The split between the Eastern and Western churches was formalized in 1054. Western and Central Europe was divided into 500 bishoprics under one united hierarchy, but conflicts between secular and church authorities were frequent (German **Investiture Controversy**, 1075-1122). Clerical power was first strengthened through the international monastic reform begun at Cluny in 910. Popular religious enthusiasm often expressed itself in heretical movements (Waldensians from 1173), but was channeled by the **Dominican** (1215) and **Franciscan** (1223) friars into the religious mainstream.

Chartres Cathedral

Arts. Romanesque architecture (11th-12th cent.) expanded on late Roman models, using the rounded arch and massed stone to support enlarged basilicas. Painting and sculpture followed Byzantine models. The literature of **chivalry** was exemplified by the epic (*Chanson de Roland*, c. 1100) and by courtly love poems of the troubadours of Provence and minnesingers of Germany. **Gothic** architecture emerged in France (choir of St. Denis, c. 1040) and spread along with French cultural influence. Rib vaulting and pointed arches were used to combine soaring heights with delicacy, and they freed walls for display of stained glass. Exteriors were covered with painted relief sculpture and embellished with elaborate architectural detail.

Learning. Law, medicine, and philosophy were advanced at independent **universities** (Bologna, late 11th cent.), originally corporations of students and masters. Twelfth-cent. translations of Greek classics, especially Aristotle, encouraged an analytic approach. Scholastic philosophy, from Anselm (1033-1109) to **Aquinas** (1225-74), attempted to understand revelation through reason.

Apogee of Central Asian Power; Islam Grows: 1250-1500

Turks. Turkic peoples, of Central Asian ancestry, were a military threat to the Byzantine and Persian Empires from the 6th cent. After several waves of invasions, during which most of the Turks adopted Islam, the **Seljuk Turks** took (1055) Baghdad. They ruled Persia, Iraq and, after 1071, Asia Minor, where massive numbers of Turks settled. The empire was divided in the 12th cent. into smaller states ruled by Seljuks, Kurds (**Saladin,** c. 1137-93), and Mamluks (a military caste of former Turk, Kurd, and Circassian slaves), which governed Egypt and the Middle East until the Ottoman era (c. 1290-1922).

Osman I (r. c. 1290-1326) and succeeding sultans united Anatolian Turkish warriors in a militaristic state that waged holy war against Byzantium and Balkan Christians. Most of the Balkans had been subdued, and Anatolia united, when Constantinople fell (1453). By the mid-16th cent., Hungary, the Middle East, and N Africa had been conquered. The Turkish advance was stopped at Vienna (1529) and at the naval battle of Lepanto (1571) by Spain, Venice, and the papacy.

The Ottoman state was governed in accordance with orthodox Muslim law. Greek, Armenian, and Jewish communities were segregated and were ruled by religious leaders responsible for taxation; they dominated trade. State offices and most army ranks were filled by slaves through a system of child conscription among Christians.

India. Mahmud of Ghazni (971-1030) led repeated Turkish raids into N India. Turkish power was consolidated in 1206 with the start of the **Sultanate at Delhi**. Centralization of state power under the early Delhi sultans went far beyond traditional Indian practice. Muslim rule of most of the subcontinent lasted until the British conquest 600 years later.

Mongols. Genghis Khan (c. 1167-1227) first united the feuding Mongol tribes, and built their armies into an effective offensive force around a core of highly mobile cavalry. He and his immediate successors created the largest land empire in history; by 1279 it stretched from the E coast of Asia to the Danube, from the Siberian steppes to the Arabian Sea. East-West trade and contacts were facilitated (Marco Polo, c. 1254-1324).

The western Mongols were Islamized by 1295; successor states soon lost their Mongol character by assimilation. They were briefly reunited under the Turk Tamerlane (1336-1405).

Kublai Khan ruled China from his new capital Beijing (est. c. 1264). Naval campaigns against Japan (1274, 1281) and Java (1293) were defeated, the latter by the Hindu-Buddhist maritime kingdom of Majapahit. The **Yuan** dynasty used Mongols and other foreigners (including Europeans) in official posts and tolerated the return of Nestorian Christianity (suppressed 841-45) and the spread of Islam in the S and W. A native reaction expelled the Mongols in 1367-68.

Russia. The Kievan state in Russia, weakened by the decline of Byzantium and the rise of the Catholic Polish-Lithuanian state, was overrun (1238-40) by the Mongols. Only the northern trading republic of Novgorod remained independent. The grand dukes of Moscow emerged as leaders of a coalition of princes that eventually (by 1481) defeated the Mongols. After the fall of Constantinople in 1453, the **Tsars** (Caesars) at Moscow (from Ivan III, r. 1462-1505) set up an independent Russian Orthodox Church. Commerce failed to revive. The isolated Russian state remained agrarian, with the peasant class falling into serfdom.

Persia. A revival of Persian literature, making use of the Arab alphabet and literary forms, began in the 10th cent. (epic of Firdausi, 935-1020). An art revival, influenced by Chinese styles introduced after the Mongols came to power in Iran, began in the 13th cent. Persian cultural and political forms, and often the Persian language, were used for centuries by Turkish and Mongol elites from the Balkans to India. Persian mystics from Rumi (1207-73) to Jami (1414-92) promoted **Sufism** in their poetry.

Africa. Two militant Islamic Berber dynasties emerged from the Sahara to carve out empires from the Sahel to central Spain—the **Almoravids** (c. 1050-1140) and the fanatical **Almohads** (c. 1125-1269). The Ghanaian empire was replaced in the upper Niger by Mali (c. 1230-1340), whose Muslim rulers imported Egyptians to help make **Timbuktu** a center of commerce (in gold, leather, and slaves) and learning. The Songhay empire (to 1590) replaced Mali. To the S, forest kingdoms produced refined artworks (Ife terra cotta, **Benin** bronzes).

Other **Muslim states** in Nigeria (Hausas) and Chad originated in the 11th cent. and continued in some form until the 19th-cent. European conquest. Less-developed Bantu kingdoms existed across central Africa.

Some 40 Muslim Arab-Persian trading colonies and city-states were established all along the E African coast from the 10th cent. (Kilwa, Mogadishu). The interchange with Bantu peoples produced the **Swahili** language and culture. Gold, palm oil, and slaves were brought from the interior, stimulating the growth of the Monamatapa kingdom of the Zambezi (15th cent.). The Christian Ethiopian empire (from 13th cent.) continued the traditions of Axum.

Southeast Asia. Islam was introduced into Malaya and the Indonesian islands by Arab, Persian, and Indian traders. Coastal Muslim cities and states (starting before 1300) soon dominated the interior. Chief among these was the **Malacca** state (c. 1400-1511), on the Malay peninsula.

Arts and Statecraft Thrive in Europe: 1350-1600

Italian Renaissance and Humanism. Distinctive Italian achievements in the arts in the late Middle Ages (**Dante,** 1265-1321; Giotto, 1276-1337) led to the vigorous new styles of the Renaissance (14th-16th cent.). Patronized by the rulers of the quarreling petty states of Italy (**Medicis** in Florence and the papacy, c. 1400-1737), the plastic arts perfected realistic techniques, including **perspective** (Masaccio, 1401-28, **Leonardo,** 1452-1519). Classical motifs were used in architecture, and increased talent and expense were put into secular buildings. The Florentine dialect was refined as a national literary language (**Petrarch,** 1304-74). Greek refugees from the E strengthened the respect of humanist scholars for the classic sources. Soon an international movement aided by the spread of **printing** (Gutenberg, c. 1397(?)-1468), **humanism** was optimistic about the power of human reason (Erasmus of Rotterdam, 1466-1536, **More's** *Utopia*, 1516) and valued individual effort in the arts and in politics (**Machiavelli,** 1469-1527).

France. The French monarchy, strengthened in its repeated struggles with powerful nobles (Burgundy, Flanders, Aquitaine) by alliances with the growing commercial towns, consolidated bureaucratic control under Philip IV (r. 1285-1314) and extended French influence into Germany and Italy (popes at Avignon, France, 1309-1417). The **Hundred Years War** (1337-1453) ended English dynastic claims in France (battles of Crécy, 1346, and Poitiers, 1356; Joan of Arc executed, 1431). A French Renaissance, dating from royal invasions (1494, 1499) of Italy, was encouraged at the court of Francis I (r. 1515-47), who centralized taxation and law. French vernacular literature consciously asserted its independence (La Pléiade, 1549).

Henry VIII

England. The evolution of England's unique political institutions began with the **Magna Carta** (1215), by which King John guaranteed the privileges of nobles and church against the monarchy and assured jury trial. After the **Wars of the Roses** (1455-85), the **Tudor dynasty** reasserted royal prerogatives (Henry VIII, r. 1509-47), but the trend toward independent departments and ministerial government also continued. English trade (wool exports from c. 1340) was protected by the nation's growing maritime power (**Spanish Armada** destroyed, 1588).

English replaced French and Latin in the late 14th cent. in law and literature (**Chaucer,** c. 1340-1400) and English translation of the Bible began (Wycliffe, 1380s). **Elizabeth I** (r. 1558-1603) presided over a confident flowering of poetry (Spenser, 1552-99), drama (**Shakespeare**, 1564-1616), and music.

German Empire. From among a welter of minor feudal states, church lands, and independent cities, the **Habsburgs** assembled a far-flung territorial domain, based in Austria from 1276. Family members held the title of Holy Roman Emperor from 1438 to the Empire's dissolution in 1806, but failed to centralize its domains, leaving Germany disunited for centuries. Resistance to Turkish expansion brought Hungary under Austrian control from the 16th cent. The Netherlands, Luxembourg, and Burgundy were added in 1477, curbing French expansion.

The Flemish painting tradition of naturalism, technical proficiency, and bourgeois subject matter began in the 15th cent. (**Jan Van Eyck,** c. 1390-1441), the earliest northern manifestation of the Renaissance. Albrecht **Dürer** (1471-1528) typified the merging of late Gothic and Italian trends in 16th-cent. German art. Imposing civic architecture flourished in the prosperous commercial cities.

Spain. Despite the unification of Castile and Aragon in 1479, the 2 countries retained separate governments, and the nobility, especially in Aragon and Catalonia, retained many privileges. Spanish lands in Italy (Naples, Sicily) and the Netherlands entangled the country in European wars through the mid-17th cent., while explorers, traders, and conquerors built up a Spanish empire in the Americas and the Philippines.

From the late 15th cent., a **golden age** of literature and art produced works of social satire (plays of Lope de Vega, 1562-1635; **Cervantes,** 1547-1616), as well as spiritual intensity (**El Greco,** 1541-1614; **Velazquez,** 1599-1660).

Black Death. The bubonic plague reached Europe from the E in 1348, killing up to half the population by 1350. Labor scarcity forced wages to rise and brought greater freedom to the peasantry, making possible **peasant uprisings** (Jacquerie in France, 1358; Wat Tyler's rebellion in England, 1381).

Explorations. Organized European maritime exploration began, seeking to evade the Venice-Ottoman monopoly of E trade and to promote Christianity. Beginning in 1418, expeditions from Portugal explored the W coast of Africa, until Vasco da Gama rounded the Cape of Good Hope in 1497 and reached India. A Portuguese trading empire was consolidated by the seizure of Goa (1510) and Malacca (1551). Japan was reached in 1542. The voyages of Christopher **Columbus** (1492-1504) uncovered a world new to Europeans, which Spain hastened to subdue. Navigation schools in Spain and Portugal, the development of large sailing ships (carracks), and the invention (c. 1475) of the rifle aided European penetration.

Christopher Columbus

Mughals and Safavids. E of the Ottoman Empire, 2 Muslim dynasties ruled unchallenged in the 16th and 17th cent. The Mughal dynasty of India, founded by Persianized Turkish invaders from the NW under Babur, dates from their 1526 conquest of the Delhi Sultanate. The dynasty ruled

Taj Mahal

most of India for more than 200 years, surviving nominally until 1857. **Akbar** (r. 1556-1605) consolidated administration at his glorious court, where the Urdu language (Persian-influenced Hindi) developed. Trade relations with Europe increased. Under Shah Jahan (1629-58), a secularized art fusing Hindu and Muslim elements flourished in miniature painting and in architecture (**Taj Mahal**). **Sikhism** (founded c. 1519) combined elements of both faiths. Suppression of Hindus and Shi'ite Muslims in S India in the late 17th cent. weakened the empire.

Fanatical devotion to the Shi'ite sect characterized the Safavids (1502-1736) of Persia and led to hostilities with the Sunni Ottomans for more than a century. The prosperity and the strength of the empire are evidenced by the mosques at its capital city, **Isfahan**. The Safavids enhanced Iranian national consciousness.

China. The **Ming** emperors (1368-1644), the last native dynasty in China, wielded unprecedented personal power, while the Confucian bureaucracy began to suffer from inertia. European trade (Portuguese monopoly through **Macao** from 1557) was strictly controlled. Jesuit scholars and scientists (Matteo Ricci, 1552-1610) introduced some Western science; their writings familiarized the West with China. Chinese technological inventiveness declined from this era, but the arts thrived, especially in the areas of painting and ceramics.

Japan. After the decline of the first hereditary shogunate (chief generalship) at **Kamakura** (1185-1333), fragmentation of power accelerated, as did the consequent social mobility. Under Kamakura and the Ashikaga shogunate (1338-1573), the daimyos (lords) and samurai (warriors) grew more powerful and promoted a martial ideology. Japanese pirates and traders plied the China coast. Popular Buddhist movements included the nationalist Nichiren sect (from c. 1250) and **Zen** (brought from China, 1191), which stressed meditation and a disciplined esthetic (tea ceremony, gardening, martial arts, *No* drama).

Reformed Europe Expands Overseas: 1500-1700

Reformation. Theological debate and protests against real and perceived clerical corruption existed in the medieval Christian world, expressed by such dissenters as John **Wycliffe** (c. 1320-84) and his followers (the Lollards) in England, and **Huss** (burned as a heretic, 1415) in Bohemia.

Martin **Luther** (1483-1546) preached that faith alone leads to salvation, without the mediation of clergy or good works. He attacked the authority of the pope, rejected priestly celibacy, and recommended individual study of the Bible (which he translated c. 1525). His 95 Theses (1517) led to his excommunication (1521). John **Calvin** (1509-64) said that God's elect were predestined for salvation and that good conduct and success were signs of election. Calvin in Geneva and John **Knox** (1505-72) in Scotland established theocratic states.

Martin Luther

Henry VIII asserted English national authority and secular power by breaking away (1534) from the Catholic Church. Monastic property was confiscated, and some Protestant doctrines given official sanction.

Religious wars. A century and a half of religious wars began with a S German peasant uprising (1524), repressed with Luther's support. Radical sects—democratic, pacifist, millennarian—arose (Anabaptists ruled Münster in 1534-35) and were suppressed violently. Civil war in France from 1562 between **Huguenots** (Protestant nobles and merchants) and Catholics ended with the 1598 **Edict of Nantes,** tolerating Protestants (revoked 1685). Habsburg attempts to restore Catholicism in Germany were resisted in 25 years of fighting; the 1555 Peace of Augsburg guarantee of religious independence to local princes and cities was confirmed only after the **Thirty Years War** (1618-48), when much of Germany was devastated by local and foreign armies (Sweden, France).

A Catholic Reformation, or **Counter Reformation**, met the Protestant challenge, defining an official theology at the Council of Trent (1545-63). The **Jesuit** order (Society of Jesus), founded in 1534 by Ignatius Loyola (1491-1556), helped reconvert large areas of Poland, Hungary, and S Germany and sent missionaries to the New World, India, and China, while the **Inquisition** suppressed heresy in Catholic countries. A revival of religious fervor appeared in the devotional literature (Teresa of Avila, 1515-82) and in grandiose **Baroque** art (Bernini, 1598-1680).

Scientific Revolution. The late nominalist thinkers (Ockham, c. 1300-49) of Paris and Oxford challenged Aristotelian orthodoxy, allowing for a freer scientific approach. At the same time, metaphysical values, such as the Neoplatonic faith in an orderly, mathematical cosmos, still motivated and directed inquiry. Nicolaus **Copernicus** (1473-1543) promoted the heliocentric theory, which was confirmed when Johannes **Kepler** (1571-1630) discovered the mathematical laws describing the orbits of the planets. The traditional Christian-Aristotelian belief that the heavens and the earth were fundamentally different collapsed when **Galileo** (1564-1642) discovered moving sunspots, irregular moon topography, and moons around Jupiter, though he did face religious opposition (Galileo's retraction, 1633). He and Sir Isaac **Newton** (1642-1727) developed a mechanics that unified cosmic and earthly phenomena. Newton and Gottfried von **Leibniz** (1646-1716) invented calculus. René **Descartes** (1596-1650), best known for his influential philosophy, also invented analytic geometry.

Copernicus

An explosion of **observational science** included the discovery of blood circulation (Harvey, 1578-1657) and microscopic life (Leeuwenhoek, 1632-1723) and advances in anatomy (Vesalius, 1514-64, dissected corpses) and chemistry (Boyle, 1627-91). Scientific research institutes were founded: Florence (1657), London (**Royal Society**, 1660), Paris (1666). Inventions proliferated (Savery's steam engine, 1696).

Arts. Mannerist trends of the High Renaissance (**Michelangelo**, 1475-1564) exploited virtuosity, grace, novelty, and exotic subjects and poses. The notion of artistic genius was promoted. Private connoisseurs entered the art market. These trends were elaborated in the 17th cent. **Baroque** era on a grander scale. Dynamic movement in painting and sculpture was emphasized by sharp lighting effects, rich materials (colored marble, gilt), and realistic details. Curved facades, broken lines, rich detail, and ceiling decoration characterized Baroque architecture. Monarchs, princes, and prelates, usually Catholic, used Baroque art to enhance and embellish their authority, as in royal portraits (Velazquez, 1599-1660; Van Dyck, 1599-1641).

National styles emerged. In France, a taste for rectilinear order and serenity (Poussin, 1594-1665), linked to the new rational philosophy, was expressed in classical forms. The influence of **classical values** in French literature (tragedies of **Racine**, 1639-99) gave rise to the "battle of the Ancients and Moderns." New forms included the essay (**Montaigne**, 1533-92) and novel (*Princesse de Cleves*, La Fayette, 1678).

Dutch painting of the 17th cent. was unique in its wide social distribution. The Flemish tradition of undemonstrative realism reached its peak in **Rembrandt** (1606-69) and Jan Vermeer (1632-75).

Economy. European economic expansion was stimulated by the new trade with the East, by New World gold and silver, and by a doubling of population (50 million in 1450, 100 million in 1600). **New business and financial techniques** were developed and refined, such as joint-stock companies, insurance, and letters of credit and exchange. The Bank of Amsterdam (1609) and the Bank of England (1694) broke the old monopoly of private banking families. The rise of a business mentality was typified by the spread of clock towers in cities in the 14th cent. By the mid-15th cent., portable clocks were available; the first watch was invented in 1502.

By 1650, most governments had adopted the **mercantile system**, in which they sought to amass metallic wealth by protecting merchants' foreign and colonial trade monopolies. The rise in prices and the new coin-based economy undermined craft guild and feudal manorial systems. Expanding industries (clothweaving, mining) benefited from technical advances. Coal replaced wood as the chief fuel; it was used to fuel new 16th-cent. blast furnaces making cast iron.

New World. The **Aztecs** united much of the Meso-American area in a militarist empire by 1519, from their capital, Tenochtitlán (pop. 300,000), which was the center of a cult requiring ritual human sacrifice. Most of the civilized areas of South America were ruled by the centralized Inca Empire (1476-1534), stretching 2,000 mi from Ecuador to NW Argentina. Lavish and sophisticated traditions in pottery, weaving, sculpture, and architecture were maintained in both regions.

These empires, beset by revolts, fell in 2 short campaigns to gold-seeking Spanish forces based in the Antilles and Panama. Hernan **Cortes** took Mexico (1519-21); Francisco **Pizarro,** Peru (1532-35). From these centers, land and sea expeditions claimed most of North and South America for Spain. The indigenous high cultures did not survive the impact of **Christian missionaries** and the new upper class of whites and mestizos. Although the Spanish administration intermittently concerned itself with their welfare, the population was reduced by European diseases and remained impoverished at most levels. New World silver and such native products as potatoes, tobacco, corn, peanuts, chocolate, and rubber exercised a major economic influence on Europe.

Brazil, which the Portuguese reached in 1500 and settled after 1530, and the Caribbean colonies of several European nations developed a plantation economy where sugarcane, tobacco, cotton, coffee, rice, indigo, and lumber were grown by slaves. From the early 16th to late 19th cent., 10 million Africans were transported to **slavery** in the New World.

Netherlands. The urban, Calvinist N provinces of the Netherlands rebelled (1568) against Habsburg Spain and founded an oligarchic mercantile republic. Their control of the Baltic grain market enabled them to exploit Mediterranean food shortages. Religious refugees—French and Belgian Protestants, Iberian Jews—added to the commercial talent pool. After Spain absorbed Portugal (1580), the Dutch seized Portuguese possessions and created a vast but short-lived commercial empire in Brazil, the Antilles, Africa, India, Ceylon, Malacca, Indonesia, and Taiwan. The Dutch also challenged or supplanted Portuguese traders in China and Japan. Revolution in 1640 restored Portuguese independence.

England. Anglicanism became firmly established under **Elizabeth I** after a brief Catholic interlude under "Bloody Mary" (1553-58). But religious and political conflicts led to a rebellion (1642) by Parliament. Forces of the Roundheads (Puritans) defeated the Cavaliers (Royalists); Charles I was beheaded (1649). The new Commonwealth was ruled as a military dictatorship by Oliver **Cromwell**, who also brutally crushed (1649-51) an Irish rebellion. Conflicts within the Puritan camp (democratic Levelers defeated, 1649) aided the Stuart restoration (1660), but Parliament was strengthened and the peaceful **"Glorious Revolution"** (1688) advanced political and religious liberties (writings of **Locke,** 1632-1704). British privateers (Drake, 1540-96) challenged Spanish control of the New World and penetrated Asian trade routes (Madras taken, 1639). North American colonies (Jamestown, 1607; Plymouth, 1620) provided an outlet for religious dissenters from Europe.

Elizabeth I

France. Emerging from the religious civil wars in 1628, France regained military and commercial great power status (under the ministries of **Richelieu**, Mazarin, and Colbert). Under **Louis XIV** (reigned 1643-1715), royal absolutism triumphed over nobles and local *parlements* (defeat of Fronde, 1648-53). Permanent colonies were founded in Canada (1608), the Caribbean (1626), and India (1674).

Sweden. Sweden seceded from the Scandinavian Union in 1523. The thinly populated agrarian state (with copper, iron, and timber exports) was united by the Vasa kings, whose conquests by the mid-17th cent. made Sweden the dominant Baltic power. The empire collapsed in the Great Northern War (1700-21).

Poland. After the union with Lithuania in 1447, Poland ruled vast territories from the Baltic to the Black Sea, resisting German and Turkish incursions. Catholic nobles failed to gain the loyalty of their Orthodox Christian subjects in the E; commerce and trades were practiced by German and Jewish immigrants. The bloody 1648-49 Cossack uprising began the kingdom's dismemberment.

China. A new dynasty, the **Manchus,** invaded from the NE, seized power in 1644, and expanded Chinese control to its greatest extent in Central and SE Asia. Trade and diplomatic contact with Europe grew, carefully controlled by China. New crops (sweet potato, maize, peanut) allowed an economic and population growth (pop. 300 million, in 1800). Traditional arts and literature were pursued with increased sophistication (*Dream of the Red Chamber*, novel, mid-18th cent.).

Japan. Tokugawa Ieyasu, shogun from 1603, finally unified and pacified feudal Japan. Hereditary daimyos and samurai monopolized government office and the professions. An urban merchant class grew, literacy spread, and a cultural renaissance occurred (**haiku,** a verse innovation of the poet Basho, 1644-94). Fear of European domination led to persecution of Christian converts from 1597 and to stringent isolation from outside contact from 1640.

Philosophy, Industry, and Revolution: 1700-1800

Science and Reason. Greater faith in reason and empirical observation, espoused since the Renaissance (Francis Bacon, 1561-1626), was bolstered by scientific discoveries . René **Descartes** (1596-1650) used a rationalistic approach modeled on geometry and introspection to discover "self-evident" truths as a foundation of knowledge. Sir Isaac **Newton** emphasized induction from experimental observation. Baruch de **Spinoza** (1632-77), who called for political and intellectual freedom, developed a systematic rationalistic philosophy in his classic work *Ethics.*

French philosophers assumed leadership of the **Enlightenment** in the 18th cent. Montesquieu (1689-1755) used British history to support his notions of limited government. **Voltaire's** (1694-1778) diaries and novels of exotic travel illustrated the intellectual trends toward secular ethics and relativism. Jean-Jacques **Rousseau's** (1712-1778) radical concepts of the **social contract** and of the inherent goodness of the common man gave impetus to antimonarchical republicanism. The *Encyclopedia* (1751-72, edited by Diderot and d'Alembert), designed as a monument to reason, was largely devoted to practical technology.

In England, ideals of liberty were connected with empiricist philosophy and science in the followers of John **Locke**. But British empiricism, especially as developed by the skeptical David **Hume** (1711-76), radically reduced the role of reason in philosophy, as did the evolutionary approach to law and politics of Edmund Burke (1729-97) and the utilitarian ethics of Jeremy Bentham (1748-1832). Adam Smith

(1723-90) and other **physiocrats** called for a rationalization of economic activity by removing artificial barriers to a supposedly natural free exchange of goods.

German writers participated in the new philosophical trends popularized by Christian von Wolff (1679-1754). Immanuel **Kant's** (1724-1804) transcendental idealism, unifying an empirical epistemology with a priori moral and logical concepts, directed German thought away from skepticism. Italian contributions included work on electricity (Galvani, 1737-98; Volta, 1745-1827), the pioneer historiography of Vico (1668-1744), and writings on penal reform (Beccaria, 1738-94). Benjamin Franklin (1706-90) was celebrated in Europe for his varied achievements.

The growth of the **press** (*Spectator*, 1711-12) and the wide distribution of realistic but sentimental **novels** attested to the increase of a large bourgeois public.

Arts. Rococo art, characterized by extravagant decorative effects, asymmetries copied from organic models, and artificial pastoral subjects, was favored by the continental aristocracy for most of the cent. (Watteau, 1684-1721) and had musical analogies in the ornamentalized polyphony of late Baroque. The **Neoclassical** art after 1750, associated with the new scientific archaeology, was more streamlined and was infused with the supposed moral and geometric rectitude of the Roman Republic (David, 1748-1825). In England, **town planning** on a grand scale began.

Industrial Revolution in England. Agricultural improvements, such as the sowing drill (1701) and livestock breeding, were implemented on the large fields provided by enclosure of common lands by private owners. Profits from agriculture and from colonial and foreign trade (1800 volume, £54 million) were channeled through hundreds of banks and the **Stock Exchange** (est. 1773) into new industrial processes.

The Newcomen steam pump (1712) aided coal mining. Coal fueled the new efficient steam engines patented by James Watt in 1769, and coke-smelting produced cheap, sturdy iron for machinery by the 1730s. The **flying shuttle** (1733) and **spinning jenny** (c. 1764) were used in the large new cotton textile factories, where women and children were much of the work force. Goods were transported cheaply over **canals** (2,000 mi; built 1760-1800).

American Revolution. The British colonies in North America attracted a mass immigration of religious dissenters and poor people throughout the 17th and 18th cent., coming from the British Isles, Germany, the Netherlands, and other countries. The population reached 3 million non-natives by the 1770s. The small native population was greatly reduced by European diseases and by wars with the various colonies. British attempts to control colonial trade and to tax the colonists to pay for the costs of colonial administration and defense clashed with notions of local self-government and eventually provoked the colonies to rebellion.

Central and East Europe. The monarchs of the three states that dominated E Europe—Austria, Prussia, and Russia—accepted the advice and legitimation of philosophes in creating modern, centralized institutions in their kingdoms, which were enlarged by the division (1772-95) of Poland.

Under **Frederick II** (called the Great) (r. 1740-86) Prussia, with its efficient modern army, doubled in size. State monopolies and tariff protection fostered industry, and some legal reforms were introduced. Austria's heterogeneous realms were unified under **Maria Theresa** (r. 1740-80) and **Joseph II** (r. 1780-90). Reforms in education, law, and religion were enacted, and the Austrian serfs were freed (1781). With its defeat in the Seven Years' War in 1763, Austria failed to regain Silesia, which had been seized by Prussia, but it was compensated by expansion to the E and S (Hungary, Slavonia, 1699; Galicia, 1772).

Russia, whose borders continued to expand, adopted some Western bureaucratic and economic policies under **Peter I** (r. 1682-1725) and **Catherine II** (r. 1762-96). Trade and cultural contacts with the West multiplied from the new Baltic Sea capital, **St. Petersburg** (est. 1703).

French Revolution. The growing French middle class lacked political power and resented aristocratic tax privileges, especially in light of the successful American Revolution. Peasants lacked adequate land and were burdened with feudal obligations to nobles. War with Britain led to the loss of French Canada and drained the treasury, finally forcing the king to call the **Estates-General** in 1789 (first time since 1614), in an atmosphere of food riots (poor crop in 1788).

Aristocratic resistance to absolutism was soon overshadowed by the reformist Third Estate (middle class), which proclaimed itself the **National Constituent Assembly** June 17 and took the "Tennis Court oath" on June 20 to secure a constitution. The storming of the **Bastille** on July 14, 1789, by Parisian artisans was followed by looting and seizure of aristocratic property throughout France. Assembly reforms included abolition of class and regional privileges, a Declaration of Rights, suffrage by taxpayers (75% of males), and the **Civil Constitution of the Clergy** providing for election and loyalty oaths for priests. A republic was declared Sept. 22, 1792, in spite of royalist pressure from Austria and Prussia, which had declared war in April (joined by Britain the next year). Louis XVI was beheaded Jan. 21, 1793, and Queen Marie Antoinette was beheaded Oct. 16, 1793.

Royalist uprisings in La Vendée and military reverses led to institution of a **reign of terror** in which tens of thousands of opponents of the Revolution and criminals were executed. Radical reforms in the **Convention** period (Sept. 1793-Oct. 1795) included the abolition of colonial slavery, economic measures to aid the poor, support of public education, and a short-lived de-Christianization.

Division among radicals (execution of Hebert, Danton, and Robespierre, 1794) aided the ascendancy of a moderate **Directory**, which consolidated military victories. **Napoleon Bonaparte** (1769-1821), a popular young general, exploited political divisions and participated in a coup Nov. 9, 1799, making himself first consul (dictator).

Napoleon Bonaparte

India. Sikh and Hindu rebels (Rajputs, Marathas) and Afghans destroyed the power of the Mughals during the 18th cent. After France's defeat (1763) in the Seven Years' War, Britain was the primary European trade power in India. Its control of inland **Bengal and Bihar** was recognized (1765) by the Mughal shah, who granted the **British East India Co.** (under Clive, 1725-74) the right to collect land revenue there. Despite objections from Parliament (1784 India Act), the company's involvement in local wars and politics led to repeated acquisitions of new territory. The company exported Indian textiles, sugar, and indigo.

Change Gathers Steam: 1800-40

French ideals and empire spread. Inspired by the ideals of the French Revolution, and supported by the expanding French armies, new republican regimes arose near France: the **Batavian** Republic in the Netherlands (1795-1806), the **Helvetic** Republic in Switzerland (1798-1803), the **Cisalpine** Republic in N Italy (1797-1805), the **Ligurian** Republic in Genoa (1797-1805), and the **Parthenopean** Republic in S Italy (1799). A Roman Republic existed briefly in 1798 after Pope Pius VI was arrested by French troops. In Italy and Germany, new nationalist sentiments were stimulated both in imitation of and in reaction to developments in France (anti-French and anti-Jacobin peasant uprisings in Italy, 1796-99).

From 1804, when Napoleon declared himself emperor, to 1812, a succession of military victories (Austerlitz, 1805; Jena, 1806) extended his control over most of Europe, through puppet states (**Confederation of the Rhine** united W German states for the first time and **Grand Duchy of Warsaw** revived Polish national hopes), expansion of the empire, and alliances.

Among the lasting reforms initiated under Napoleon's absolutist reign were: establishment of the Bank of France, centralization of tax collection, codification of law along Roman models (Code Napoléon), and reform and extension of secondary and university education. In an 1801 concordat, the papacy recognized the effective autonomy of the French Catholic Church.

Napoleon's continental successes were offset by British victory under Adm. Horatio Nelson in the **Battle of Trafalgar** (1805).

In all, some 400,000 French soldiers were killed in the Napoleonic Wars, along with about 600,000 foreign troops.

Last gasp of old regime. The disastrous 1812 invasion of Russia exposed Napoleon's overextension. After Napoleon's 1814 exile at Elba, his armies were defeated (1815) at **Waterloo**, by British and Prussian troops.

At the **Congress of Vienna**, the monarchs and princes of Europe redrew their boundaries, to the advantage of Prussia (in Saxony and the Ruhr), Austria (in Illyria and Venetia), and Russia (in Poland and Finland). British conquest of Dutch and French colonies (S Africa, Ceylon, Mauritius) was recognized, and France, under the restored Bourbons, retained its expanded 1792 borders. The settlement brought 50 years of international peace to Europe.

But the Congress was unable to check the advance of liberal ideals and of nationalism among the smaller European nations. The 1825 **Decembrist uprising** by liberal officers in Russia was easily suppressed. But an independence movement in **Greece**, stirred by commercial prosperity and a cultural revival, succeeded in expelling Ottoman rule by 1831, with the aid of Britain, France, and Russia.

A constitutional monarchy was secured in France by the **1830 Revolution**; Louis Philippe became king. The revolutionary contagion spread to **Belgium**, which gained its independence (1830) from the Dutch monarchy, to **Poland**, whose rebellion was defeated (1830-31) by Russia, and to Germany.

Romanticism. A new style in intellectual and artistic life replaced Neoclassicism and Rococo after the mid-18th cent. By the early 19th cent., Romanticism prevailed in Europe.

Rousseau had begun the reaction against rationalism; in education (*Émile*, 1762) he stressed subjective spontaneity over regularized instruction. German writers (Lessing, 1729-81; Herder, 1744-1803) favorably compared the German folk song to classical forms and began a cult of Shakespeare, whose passion and "natural" wisdom was a model for the romantic *Sturm und Drang* (Storm and Stress) movement. **Goethe's** *Sorrows of Young Werther* (1774) set the model for the tragic, passionate genius.

A new interest in **Gothic architecture** in England after 1760 (Walpole, 1717-97) spread through Europe, associated with an aesthetic Christian and mystic revival (**Blake,** 1757-1827). Celtic, Norse, and German mythology and folk tales were revived or imitated (Macpherson's Ossian translation, 1762; Grimm's Fairy Tales, 1812-22). The medieval revival (Scott's *Ivanhoe*, 1819) led to a new interest in history, stressing national differences and organic growth (**Carlyle,** 1795-1881; Michelet, 1798-1874), corresponding to theories of natural evolution (Lamarck's *Philosophie Zoologique*, 1809; Lyell's *Geology*, 1830-33). A reaction against classicism characterized the English **romantic poets** (beginning with **Wordsworth,** 1770-1850). Revolution and war fed an emphasis on freedom and conflict, expressed by both poets (**Byron**, 1788-1824; **Hugo**, 1802-85) and philosophers (**Hegel**, 1770-1831).

Wild gardens replaced the formal French variety, and painters favored rural, stormy, and mountainous landscapes (**Turner**, 1775-1851; **Constable**, 1776-1837). Clothing became freer, with wigs, hoops, and ruffles discarded. Originality and genius were expected in the life as well as the work of inspired artists (Murger's *Scenes from Bohemian Life*, 1847-49). Exotic locales and themes (as in Gothic horror stories) were used in art and literature (Delacroix, 1798-1863; **Poe**, 1809-49).

Music exhibited the new dramatic style and a breakdown of classical forms (**Beethoven,** 1770-1827). The use of folk melodies and modes aided the growth of distinct national traditions (Glinka in Russia, 1804-57).

Latin America. Francois **Toussaint L'Ouverture** led a successful slave revolt in Haiti, which subsequently became the first Latin American state to achieve independence (1804). The mainland Spanish colonies won their independence (1810-24), under such leaders as Simon **Bolivar** (1783-1830). Brazil became an independent empire (1822) under the Portuguese prince regent. A new class of military officers divided power with large landholders and the church.

Francois Toussaint L'Ouverture

United States. Territory under U.S. control nearly doubled in size with the **Louisiana Purchase** (1803). Heavy immigration and exploitation of ample natural resources fueled rapid economic growth. The spread of the franchise, public education, and antislavery sentiment were signs of a widespread democratic ethic.

China. Failure to keep pace with Western arms technology exposed China to greater European influence and hampered efforts to bar imports of opium, which had damaged Chinese society and drained wealth overseas. In the **Opium War** (1839-42), Britain forced China to expand trade opportunities and to cede Hong Kong.

Triumph of Progress: 1840-80

Charles Darwin

Idea of Progress. As a result of the cumulative scientific, economic, and political changes of the preceding eras, the idea took hold among literate people in the West that continuing growth and improvement was the usual state of human and natural life.

Charles **Darwin's** statement of the **theory of evolution** and survival of the fittest (*Origin of Species*, 1859), defended by intellectuals and scientists against theological objections, was taken as confirmation that progress was the natural direction of life. The controversy helped define popular ideas of the dedicated scientist and of science's increasing control over the world (Foucault's demonstration of earth's rotation, 1851; **Pasteur's** germ theory, 1861).

Liberals following Ricardo (1772-1823) in their faith that unrestrained competition would bring continuous economic expansion sought to adjust political life to new social realities and believed that unregulated competition of ideas would yield truth (**Mill,** 1806-73). In England, successive reform bills (1832, 1867, 1884) gave representation to the new industrial towns and extended the franchise to the middle and lower classes and to Catholics, Dissenters, and Jews. On both sides of the Atlantic, reformists tried to improve conditions for the mentally ill (**Dix,** 1802-87), women (Anthony, 1820-1906), and prisoners. Slavery was barred in the British Empire (1833), the U.S. (1865), and Brazil (1888).

Socialist theories based on ideas of human perfectibility or progress were widely disseminated. Utopian socialists such as Saint-Simon (1760-1825) envisaged an orderly, just society directed by a technocratic elite. A model factory town, New Lanark, Scotland, was set up by utopian Robert Owen (1771-1858), and communal experiments were tried in the U.S. (Brook Farm, Mass., 1841-47). Bakunin's (1814-76) anarchism represented the opposite extreme of total freedom. Karl **Marx** (1818-83) posited the inevitable triumph of socialism in industrial countries through a dialectical process of class conflict.

Spread of industry. The technical processes and managerial innovations of the English industrial revolution spread to Europe (especially Germany) and the U.S., causing an explosion of industrial production, demand for raw materials, and competition for markets. Inventors, both trained and self-taught, provided means for larger-scale production (Bessemer steel, 1856; sewing machine, 1846). Many inventions were shown at the universal prosperity-themed 1851 London Great Exhibition at the **Crystal Palace**.

Local specialization and long-distance trade were aided by a revolution in transportation and communication. Railroads were first introduced in the 1820s in England and the U.S. Over 150,000 mi of track had been laid worldwide by 1880, with another 100,000 mi laid in the next decade. Steamships were improved (*Savannah* crossed Atlantic, 1819). The **telegraph**, perfected by 1844 (Morse), connected the Old and New Worlds by cable in 1866 and quickened the pace of international commerce and politics. The first commercial **telephone** exchange went into operation in the U.S. in 1878.

The new class of industrial workers, uprooted from their rural homes, lacked job security and suffered from dangerous overcrowding at work and at home. Many responded by organizing **trade unions** (legalized in England, 1824; France, 1884). The U.S. Knights of Labor had 700,000 members by 1886. The First International (1864-76) tried to unite workers worldwide around a Marxist program. The quasi-Socialist Paris Commune uprising (1871) was violently suppressed. Acts to reduce child labor and regulate conditions were passed (1833-50 in England). Social security measures were introduced by the Bismarck regime (1883-89) in Germany.

Revolutions of 1848. Among the causes of the continent-wide revolutions were an international collapse of credit and resulting unemployment, bad harvests in 1845-47, and a cholera epidemic. The new urban proletariat and expanding bourgeoisie demanded greater political roles. Republics were proclaimed in France, Rome, and Venice. Nationalist feelings reached fever pitch in the Habsburg empire, as Hungary declared independence under Kossuth, as a Slav Congress demanded equality, and as Piedmont tried to drive Austria from Lombardy. A national liberal assembly at Frankfurt called for German unification.

Karl Marx

But riots fueled bourgeois fear of socialism (**Marx and Engels**, *Communist Manifesto*, 1848), and peasants remained conservative. The old establishment—the Papacy, the Habsburgs with the help of the Czarist Russian army —was able to rout the revolutionaries by 1849. The French Republic succumbed to a renewed monarchy by 1852 (Emperor Napoleon III).

Great nations unified. Using the "blood and iron" tactics of Bismarck from 1862, Prussia controlled N Germany by 1867 (war with Denmark, 1864; Austria, 1866). After defeating France in 1870 (annexation of Alsace-Lorraine), it won the allegiance of S German states. A new **German Empire** was proclaimed (1871). **Italy**, inspired by Giuseppe Mazzini (1805-72) and Giuseppe Garibaldi (1807-82), was unified by the reformed Piedmont kingdom through uprisings, plebiscites, and war.

The **U.S.**, its area expanded after the 1846-48 Mexican War, defeated (1861-65) a secession attempt by southern states in the **Civil War**. Canadian provinces were united in an autonomous **Dominion of Canada** (1867). Control in **India** was removed from the East India Co. and centralized under British administration after the 1857-58 Sepoy rebellion, laying the groundwork for the modern Indian State. Queen Victoria was named Empress of India (1876).

Europe dominates Asia. The Ottoman Empire began to collapse in the face of Balkan nationalisms and European imperial incursions in N Africa (**Suez Canal**, 1869). The Turks had lost control of most of both regions by 1882. Russia completed its expansion S by 1884 (despite the temporary setback of the **Crimean War** with Turkey, Britain, and France, 1853-56), taking Turkestan, all the Caucasus, and Chinese areas in the E and sponsoring Balkan Slavs against the Turks. A succession of reformist and reactionary regimes presided over a slow modernization (serfs freed, 1861). Persian independence suffered as Russia and British India competed for influence.

China was forced to sign a series of unequal treaties with European powers and Japan. Overpopulation and an inefficient dynasty brought misery and caused rebellions (Taiping, Muslims) leaving tens of millions dead. **Japan** was forced by the U.S. (Commodore Perry's visits, 1853-54) and Europe to end its isolation. The Meiji restoration (1868) gave power to a Westernizing oligarchy. Intensified empire-building gave Burma to Britain (1824-85) and Indochina to France (1862-95). Christian missionary activity followed imperial and trade expansion in Asia.

Respectability. Fine arts were expected to reflect and encourage the good morals and manners among the Victorians. Prudery, exaggerated delicacy, and familial piety were heralded by **Bowdler's** expurgated Shakespeare edition (1818). Government-supported mass education sought to inculcate a work ethic as a means to escape poverty (**Horatio Alger,** 1832-99).

The official **Beaux Arts** school in Paris set an international style of imposing public buildings (Paris Opera, 1861-74; Vienna Opera, 1861-69) and uplifting statues (Bartholdi's Statue of Liberty, 1884). Realist painting, influenced by photography (Daguerre, 1837), appealed to a new mass audience with social or historical narrative (Wilkie, 1785-1841; Poynter, 1836-1919) or with serious religious, moral, or social messages (pre-Raphaelites, Millet's *Angelus*, 1858) often drawn from ordinary life. The **Impressionists** (Monet, 1840-1926; Pissarro, 1830-1903; Renoir, 1841-1919) rejected the formalism, sentimentality, and precise techniques of academic art in favor of a spontaneous, undetailed rendering of the world through careful representation of the effect of natural light on objects.

Realistic **novelists** presented the full panorama of social classes and personalities, but retained sentimentality and moral judgment (**Dickens,** 1812-70; **Eliot,** 1819-80; **Tolstoy,** 1828-1910; **Balzac,** 1799-1850).

Veneer of Stability: 1880-1900

Imperialism triumphant. The vast **African** interior, visited by European explorers (Barth, 1821-65; Livingstone, 1813-73), was conquered by the European powers in rapid, competitive thrusts from their coastal bases after 1880, mostly for domestic political and international strategic reasons. W African Muslim kingdoms (Fulani), Arab slave traders (Zanzibar), and Bantu military confederations (Zulu) were alike subdued. Only Christian Ethiopia (defeat of Italy, 1896) and Liberia resisted successfully. France (W Africa) and Britain ("Cape to Cairo," **Boer War,** 1899-1902) were the major beneficiaries. The ideology of "the white man's burden" (Kipling, *Barrack Room Ballads*, 1892) or of a "civilizing mission" (France) justified the conquests.

W European foreign capital investment soared to nearly $40 billion by 1914, but most was in E Europe (France, Germany), the Americas (Britain), and Europe's colonies. The foundation of the modern interdependent world economy was laid, with cartels dominating raw material trade.

An industrious world. Industrial and technological proficiency characterized the 2 new great powers—Germany and the U.S. Coal and iron deposits enabled Germany to reach 2nd or 3rd place status in iron, steel, and shipbuilding by the 1900s. German electrical and chemical industries were world leaders. The U.S. post-Civil War boom (interrupted by "panics"—1884, 1893, 1896) was shaped by massive immigration from S and E Europe from 1880, government subsidy of railroads, and huge private monopolies (Standard Oil, 1870; U.S. Steel, 1901). The **Spanish-American War**, 1898 (Philippine Insurrection, 1899-1902), and the **Open Door policy** in China (1899) made the U.S. a world power.

Hyde Park, London

England led in **urbanization**, with **London** the world capital of finance, insurance, and shipping. Sewer systems (Paris, 1850s), electric subways (London, 1890), parks, and bargain department stores helped improve living standards for most of the urban population of the industrial world.

Westernization of Asia. Asian reaction to European economic, military, and religious incursions took the form of imitation of Western techniques and adoption of Western ideas of progress and freedom. The Chinese "self-strengthening" movement of the 1860s and 1870s included rail, port, and arsenal improvements and metal and textile mills. Reformers such as **K'ang Yu-wei** (1858-1927) won liberalizing reforms in 1898, right after the European and Japanese "scramble for concessions."

A universal education system in Japan and importation of foreign industrial, scientific, and military experts aided Japan's rapid modernization after 1868, under the authoritarian Meiji regime. Japan's victory in the **Sino-Japanese War** (1894-95) put Formosa and Korea in its power.

In India, the British alliance with the remaining princely states masked reform sentiment among the Westernized urban elite; higher education had been conducted largely in English for 50 years. The **Indian National Congress**, founded in 1885, demanded a larger government role for Indians.

***Fin-de-siècle* sophistication. Naturalist** writers pushed realism to its extreme limits, adopting a quasi-scientific attitude and writing about formerly taboo subjects such as sex, crime, extreme poverty, and corruption (Flaubert, 1821-80; Zola, 1840-1902; Hardy, 1840-1928). Unseen or repressed psychological motivations were explored in the clinical and theoretical works of Sigmund **Freud** (1856-1939) and in works of fiction (**Dostoyevsky,** 1821-81; James, 1843-1916; Schnitzler, 1862-1931; others).

A contempt for bourgeois life or a desire to shock a complacent audience was shared by the French **symbolist** poets (Verlaine, 1844-96; Rimbaud, 1854-91), by neopagan English writers (Swinburne, 1837-1909), by continental dramatists (**Ibsen,** 1828-1906), and by satirists (**Wilde,** 1854-1900). The German philosopher Friedrich **Nietzsche** (1844-1900) was influential in his elitism and pessimism.

Postimpressionist art neglected long-cherished conventions of representation (Cézanne, 1839-1906) and showed a willingness to learn from primitive and non-European art (Gauguin, 1848-1903; Japanese prints).

Racism. Gobineau (1816-82) gave a pseudobiological foundation to modern racist theories, which spread in Europe in the latter 19th cent., along with **Social Darwinism**, the belief that societies are and should be organized as a struggle for survival of the fittest. The medieval period was interpreted as an era of natural Germanic rule (Chamberlain, 1855-1927), and notions of racial superiority were associated with German national aspirations (Treitschke, 1834-96). **Anti-Semitism**, with a new racist rationale, became a significant political force in Germany (Anti-Semitic Petition, 1880), Austria (Lueger, 1844-1910), and France (**Dreyfus affair**, 1894-1906).

Last Respite: 1900-9

Alliances. While the peace of Europe (and its dependencies) continued to hold (1907 **Hague Conference** extended the rules of war and international arbitration procedures), imperial rivalries, protectionist trade practices (in Germany and France), and the escalating arms race (British *Dreadnought* battleship launched; Germany widens Kiel canal, 1906) exacerbated minor disputes (German-French Moroccan "crises," 1905, 1911).

Security was sought through alliances: **Triple Alliance** (Germany, Austria-Hungary, Italy; renewed in 1902 and 1907); Anglo-Japanese Alliance (1902), Franco-Russian Alliance (1899), **Entente Cordiale** (Britain, France, 1904), Anglo-Russian Treaty (1907), German-Ottoman friendship.

Ottomans decline. The inefficient, corrupt Ottoman government was unable to resist further loss of territory. Nearly all European lands were lost in 1912 to Serbia, Greece, Montenegro, and Bulgaria. Italy took Libya and the Dodecanese islands the same year, and Britain took Kuwait (1899) and the Sinai (1906). The **Young Turk** revolution in 1908 forced the sultan to restore a constitution, and it introduced some social reform, industrialization, and secularization.

British Empire. British trade and cultural influence remained dominant in the empire, but constitutional reforms presaged its eventual dissolution: The colonies of **Australia** were united in 1901 under a self-governing commonwealth. **New Zealand** acquired dominion status in 1907. The old Boer republics joined Cape Colony and Natal in the self-governing **Union of South Africa** in 1910.

The 1909 Indian Councils Act enhanced the role of elected province legislatures in **India**. The Muslim League (founded 1906) sought separate communal representation.

East Asia. Japan exploited its growing industrial power to expand its empire. Victory in the 1904-5 war against Russia (naval battle of Tsushima, 1905) assured Japan's domination of **Korea** (annexed 1910) and Manchuria (Port Arthur taken, 1905).

In China, central authority began to crumble (empress died, 1908). Reforms (Confucian exam system ended 1905, modernization of the army, building of railroads) were inadequate, and secret societies of reformers and nationalists, inspired by the Westernized **Sun Yat-sen** (1866-1925) fomented periodic uprisings in the S.

Sun Yat-sen

Siam, whose independence had been guaranteed by Britain and France in 1896, was split into spheres of influence by those countries in 1907.

Russia. The population of the Russian Empire approached 150 million in 1900. Reforms in education, in law, and in local institutions (*zemstvos*) and an industrial boom starting in the 1880s (oil, railroads) created the beginnings of a modern state, despite the autocratic tsarist regime. Liberals (1903 Union of Liberation), Socialists (Social Democrats founded 1898, Bolsheviks split off 1903), and populists (Social Revolutionaries founded 1901) were periodically repressed, and national minorities were persecuted (anti-Jewish pogroms, 1903, 1905-6).

An industrial crisis after 1900 and harvest failures aggravated poverty among urban workers, and the 1904-5 defeat by Japan (which checked Russia's Asian expansion) sparked **the Revolution of 1905-6.** A **Duma** (parliament) was created, and an agricultural reform (under Stolypin, prime minister 1906-11) created a large class of land-owning peasants (kulaks).

The world shrinks. Developments in transportation and communication and mass population movements helped create an awareness of an interdependent world. Early **automobiles** (Daimler, Benz, 1885) were experimental or were designed as luxuries. Assembly-line mass production (Ford Motor Co., 1903) made the invention practicable, and by 1910 nearly 500,000 motor vehicles were registered in the U.S. alone. **Heavier-than-air flights** began in 1903 in the U.S. (Wright brothers' *Flyer*), preceded by glider, balloon, and model plane advances in several countries. Trade was advanced by improvements in **ship design** (gyrocompass, 1910), speed (*Lusitania* crossed Atlantic in 5 days, 1907), and reach (Panama Canal begun, 1904).

The first transatlantic **radio** telegraphic transmission occurred in 1901, 6 years after Marconi discovered radio. Radio transmission of human speech had been made in 1900. Telegraphic transmission of photos was achieved in 1904, lending immediacy to news reports. **Phonographs**, popularized by Caruso's recordings (starting 1902), made for quick international spread of musical styles (ragtime). **Motion pictures**, perfected in the 1890s (Dickson, Lumière brothers), became a popular and artistic medium after 1900; newsreels appeared in 1909.

Emigration from crowded European centers soared in the decade: 9 million migrated to the U.S., and millions more went to Siberia, Canada, Argentina, Australia, South Africa, and Algeria. Some 70 million Europeans emigrated in the cent. before 1914. Several million Chinese, Indians, and Japanese migrated to SE Asia, where their urban skills often enabled them to take a predominant economic role.

Social reform. The social and economic problems of the poor were kept in the public eye by realist fiction writers (Dreiser's *Sister Carrie*, 1900; Gorky's *Lower Depths*, 1902; Sinclair's *The Jungle*, 1906), journalists (U.S. **muckrakers**—Steffens, Tarbell), and artists (Ashcan school). Frequent labor strikes and occasional assassinations by anarchists or radicals (Empress Elizabeth of Austria, 1898; King Umberto I of Italy, 1900; U.S. Pres. McKinley, 1901; Russian Interior Minister Plehve, 1904; Portugal's King Carlos, 1908) added to social tension and fear of revolution.

But democratic reformism prevailed. In Germany, Bernstein's (1850-1932) **revisionist Marxism**, downgrading revolution, was accepted by the powerful Social Democrats and trade unions. The British Fabian Society (the Webbs, Shaw) and the Labour Party (founded 1906) worked for reforms such as Social Security and union rights (1906), while woman suffragists grew more militant. U.S. **progressives** fought big business (Pure Food and Drug Act, 1906). In France, the 10-hour work day (1904) and separation of church and state (1905) were reform victories, as was universal suffrage in Austria (1907).

Arts. An unprecedented period of experimentation, centered in France, produced several new **painting** styles: Fauvism exploited bold color areas (Matisse, *Woman With Hat*, 1905); expressionism reflected powerful inner emotions (the Brücke group, 1905); cubism combined several views of an object on one flat surface (Picasso's *Demoiselles*, 1906-7); futurism tried to depict speed and motion (Italian Futurist Manifesto, 1910). **Architects** explored new uses of steel structures, with facades either neoclassical (Adler and Sullivan in U.S.); curvilinear Art Nouveau (Gaudi's Casa Mila, 1905-10); or functionally streamlined (Wright's Robie House, 1909).

Music and dance shared the experimental spirit. Ruth St. Denis (1877-1968) and Isadora Duncan (1878-1927) pioneered modern dance, while Sergei Diaghilev in Paris revitalized classic ballet from 1909. Composers explored atonal music (Debussy, 1862-1918) and dissonance (Schoenberg, 1874-1951) or revolutionized classical forms (Stravinsky, 1882-1971), often showing jazz or folk music influences.

War and Revolution: 1910-19

War threatens. Germany under Wilhelm II sought a political and imperial role consonant with its industrial strength, challenging Britain's world supremacy and threatening France, which was still resenting the loss (1871) of Alsace-Lorraine. Austria wanted to curb an expanded Serbia (after 1912) and the threat it posed to its own Slav lands. Russia feared Austrian and German political and economic aims in the Balkans and Turkey.

An accelerated arms race resulted from these circumstances. The German standing army rose to more than 2 million men by 1914. Russia and France had more than a million each, and Austria and the British Empire nearly a million each. Dozens of enormous battleships were built by the powers after 1906.

The **assassination of Austrian Archduke Franz Ferdinand** by a Serbian, June 28, 1914, was the pretext for war. The system of alliances made the conflict Europe-wide; Germany's invasion of Belgium to outflank France forced Britain to enter the war. Patriotic fervor was nearly unanimous among all classes in most countries.

World War I. German forces were stopped in France in one month. The rival armies dug **trench networks**. Artillery and improved machine guns prevented either side from any lasting advance despite repeated assaults (600,000 dead at **Verdun**, Feb.-July 1916). Poison gas, used by Germany in 1915, proved ineffective. The entrance of more than 1 million U.S. troops tipped the balance after mid-1917, forcing Germany to sue for peace the next year. The formal armistice was signed on Nov. 11, 1918.

In the E, the Russian armies were thrown back (battle of **Tannenberg**, Aug. 20, 1914), and the war grew unpopular in Russia. An allied attempt to relieve Russia through Turkey failed (**Gallipoli,** 1915). The **Russian Revolution** (1917) abolished the monarchy. The new Bolshevik regime signed the capitulatory Brest-Litovsk peace in March 1918. Italy entered the war on the allied side in May 1915 but was pushed back by Oct. 1917. A renewed offensive with Allied aid in Oct.-Nov. 1918 forced Austria to surrender.

The British Navy successfully blockaded Germany, which responded with submarine U-boat attacks; **unrestricted submarine warfare** against neutrals after Jan. 1917 helped bring the U.S. into the war. Other battlefields included Palestine and Mesopotamia, both of which Britain wrested from the Turks in 1917, and the African and Pacific colonies of Germany, most of which fell to Britain, France, Australia, Japan, and South Africa.

Settlement. At the **Paris Peace Conference** (Jan.-June 1919), concluded by the **Treaty of Versailles**, and in subsequent negotiations and local wars (Russian-Polish War, 1920), the **map of Europe** was **redrawn** with a nod to U.S. Pres. Woodrow Wilson's principle of self-determination. Austria and Hungary were separated, and much of their land was given to Yugoslavia (formerly Serbia), Romania, Italy, and the newly independent Poland and Czechoslovakia. Germany lost territory in the W, N, and E, while Finland and the Baltic states were detached from Russia. Turkey lost nearly all its Arab lands to British-sponsored Arab states or to direct French and British rule. Belgium's sovereignty was recognized.

From 1916, the civilian populations and economies of both sides were mobilized to an unprecedented degree. Hardships intensified among fighting nations in 1917 (French mutiny crushed in May). More than 10 million soldiers died in the war.

A huge **reparations** burden and partial demilitarization were imposed on Germany. Pres. Wilson obtained approval for a League of Nations, but the U.S. Senate refused to allow the U.S. to join.

Russian revolution. Military defeats and high casualties caused a contagious lack of confidence in Tsar Nicholas, who was forced to abdicate Mar. 1917. A liberal provisional government failed to end the war, and massive desertions, riots, and fighting between factions followed. A moderate socialist government under Aleksandr Kerensky was overthrown (Nov. 1917) in a violent coup by the **Bolsheviks** in Petrograd under **Lenin,** who later disbanded the elected Constituent Assembly.

The Bolsheviks brutally suppressed all opposition and ended the war with Germany in Mar. 1918. **Civil war** broke out in the summer between the Red Army (the Bolsheviks and their supporters), and monarchists, anarchists, nationalities (Ukrainians, Georgians, Poles), and others. Small U.S., British, French, and Japanese units also opposed the Bolsheviks (1918-19; Japan in Vladivostok to 1922). The civil war, anarchy, and pogroms devastated the country until the 1920 Red Army victory. The **Communist Party** leadership retained absolute power.

Other European revolutions. An unpopular monarchy in **Portugal** was overthrown in 1910. The new republic took severe anticlerical measures in 1911.

After a century of Home Rule agitation, during which **Ireland** was devastated by famine (1 million dead, 1846-47) and emigration, republican militants staged an unsuccessful uprising in Dublin during **Easter 1916**. The execution of the leaders and mass arrests by the British won popular support for the rebels. The **Irish Free State,** comprising all but the 6 N counties, achieved dominion status in 1922.

In the aftermath of the world war, radical revolutions were attempted in Germany (**Spartacist** uprising, Jan. 1919), **Hungary** (Kun regime, 1919), and elsewhere. All were suppressed or failed for lack of support.

Chinese revolution. The Manchu Dynasty was overthrown and a republic proclaimed in Oct. 1911. First Pres. Sun Yat-sen resigned in favor of strongman Yuan Shih-k'ai. Sun organized the parliamentarian **Kuomintang** party.

Students launched protests on May 4, 1919, against League of Nations concessions in China to Japan. Nationalist, liberal, and socialist ideas and political groups spread. The **Communist Party** was founded in 1921. A Communist regime took power in Mongolia with Soviet support in 1921.

India restive. Indian objections to British rule erupted in nationalist riots as well as in the nonviolent tactics of Mahatma **Gandhi** (1869-1948). Nearly 400 unarmed demonstrators were shot at **Amritsar** in Apr. 1919. Britain approved limited self-rule that year.

Mexican revolution. Under the long Diaz dictatorship (1877-1911) the economy advanced, but Indian and mestizo lands were confiscated, and concessions to foreigners (mostly U.S.) damaged the middle class. A **revolution in 1910** led to civil wars and U.S. intervention (1914, 1916-17). Land reform and a more democratic constitution (1917) were achieved.

The Aftermath of War: 1920-29

New York City

U.S. Easy credit, technological ingenuity, and war-related industrial decline in Europe caused a long economic boom, in which ownership of the new products—autos, phones, radios—became more democratized. **Prosperity,** an increase in women workers, women's suffrage (1920), and drastic change in fashion (flappers, mannish bob for women, clean-shaven men) created a wide perception of social change, despite prohibition of alcoholic beverages (1919-33). Union membership and strikes increased. Fear of radicals led to Palmer raids (1919-20) and the Sacco/Vanzetti case (1921-27).

Europe sorts itself out. Germany's liberal **Weimar constitution** (1919) could not guarantee a stable government in the face of rightist violence (Rathenau assassinated, 1922) and Communist refusal to cooperate with Socialists. Reparations and Allied occupation of the Rhineland caused staggering inflation that destroyed middle-class savings, but economic expansion resumed after mid-decade, aided by U.S. loans. A sophisticated, **innovative culture** developed in architecture and design (Bauhaus, 1919-28), film (Lang, *M*, 1931), painting (Grosz), music (Weill, *Threepenny Opera*, 1928), theater (Brecht, *A Man's a Man*, 1926), criticism (Benjamin), philosophy (Jung), and fashion. This culture was considered decadent and socially disruptive by rightists.

England elected its first Labour governments (Jan. 1924, June 1929). A 10-day general strike in support of coal miners failed in May 1926. In **Italy**, strikes, political chaos, and violence by small Fascist bands culminated in the Oct. 1922 Fascist March on Rome, which established **Mussolini's** dictatorship. Strikes were outlawed (1926), and Italian influence was pressed in the Balkans (Albania a protectorate, 1926). A conservative dictatorship was also established in **Portugal** in a 1926 military coup.

Czechoslovakia, the only stable democracy to emerge from the war in Central or E Europe, faced opposition from Germans (in the Sudetenland), Ruthenians, and some Slovaks. As the industrial heartland of the old Habsburg empire, it remained fairly prosperous. With French backing, it formed the Little Entente with Yugoslavia (1920) and **Romania** (1921) to block Austrian or Hungarian irredentism. Croats and Slovenes in **Yugoslavia** demanded a federal state until King Alexander I proclaimed (1929) a royal dictatorship. Poland faced nationality problems as well (Germans, Ukrainians, Jews); Pilsudski ruled as dictator from 1926. The Baltic states were threatened by traditionally dominant ethnic Germans and by Soviet-supported Communists.

An economic collapse and famine in **Russia** (1921-22) claimed 5 million lives. The New Economic Policy (1921) allowed land ownership by peasants and some private commerce and industry. **Stalin** was absolute ruler within 4 years of Lenin's death (1924). He inaugurated a brutal collectivization program (1929-32) and used foreign Communist parties for Soviet state advantage.

Internationalism. Revulsion against World War I led to pacifist agitation, to the Kellogg-Briand Pact renouncing aggressive war (1928), and to **naval disarmament** pacts (Washington, 1922; London, 1930). But the League of Nations was able to arbitrate only minor disputes (Greece-Bulgaria, 1925).

Middle East. Mustafa Kemal (**Ataturk**) led **Turkish** nationalists in resisting Italian, French, and Greek military advances (1919-23). The sultanate was abolished (1922), and elaborate reforms were passed, including secularization of law and adoption of the Latin alphabet. Ethnic conflict led to persecution of **Armenians** (more than 1 million dead in 1915, 1 million expelled), Greeks (forced Greek-Turk population exchange, 1923), and Kurds (1925 uprising).

With evacuation of the Turks from **Arab** lands, the puritanical Wahabi dynasty of E Arabia conquered (1919-25) what is now Saudi Arabia. British, French, and Arab dynastic and nationalist maneuvering resulted in the creation of 2 more Arab monarchies in 1921—Iraq and Transjordan (both under British control)—and 2 French mandates—Syria and Lebanon. Jewish immigration into British-mandated **Palestine**, inspired by the Zionist movement, was resisted by Arabs, at times violently (1921, 1929 massacres).

Reza Khan ruled **Persia** after his 1921 coup (shah from 1925), centralized control, and created the trappings of a modern secular state.

In 1922, English archaeologist Howard Carter discovered the **tomb** of the boy pharaoh **Tutankhamen** in the Valley of the Kings in Egypt.

China. The Kuomintang under **Chiang Kai-shek** (1887-1975) subdued the warlords by 1928. The Communists were brutally suppressed after their alliance with the Kuomintang was broken in 1927. Relative peace thereafter allowed for industrial and financial improvements, with some Russian, British, and U.S. cooperation.

Arts. Nearly all bounds of subject matter, style, and attitude were broken in the arts of the period. **Abstract** art first took inspiration from natural forms or narrative themes (Kandinsky from 1911) and then worked free of any representational aims (Malevich's suprematism, 1915-19; Mondrian's geometric style from 1917). The **Dada** movement (from 1916) mocked artistic pretension with absurd collages and constructions. Paradox, illusion, and psychological taboos were exploited by **surrealists** by the late 1920s (Dali, Magritte). Architectural schools celebrated industrial values, whether vigorous abstract constructivism (Tatlin, *Monument to 3rd International*, 1919) or the machined, streamlined **Bauhaus** style, which was extended to many design fields (Helvetica typeface).

Prose writers explored revolutionary narrative modes related to dreams (Kafka's *Trial*, 1925), internal monologue (Joyce's ***Ulysses***, 1922), and word play (Stein's *Making of Americans*, 1925). Poets and novelists wrote of modern alienation (Eliot's ***Waste Land*,** 1922) and aimlessness (Lost Generation).

Albert Einstein

Sciences. Scientific specialization prevailed by the 20th cent. Advances in knowledge and technological aptitude increased with the geometric rise in the number of practitioners. Physicists challenged commonsense views of causality, observation, and a mechanistic universe, putting science further beyond popular grasp (**Einstein's** general theory of relativity, 1916; Bohr's quantum mechanics, 1913; Heisenberg's uncertainty principle, 1927).

Rise of Totalitarians: 1930-39

Mussolini & Hitler

Depression. A worldwide financial panic and economic depression began with the Oct. 1929 U.S. stock market crash and the May 1931 failure of the Austrian Credit-Anstalt. A credit crunch caused international bankruptcies and **unemployment**: 12 million jobless by 1932 in the U.S., 5.6 million in Germany, 2.7 million in England. Governments responded with **tariff restrictions** (Smoot-Hawley Act, 1930; Ottawa Imperial Conference, 1932), which dried up world trade. Government public works programs were vitiated by deflationary budget balancing.

Germany. Years of agitation by violent extremists were brought to a head by the Depression. Nazi leader Adolf Hitler was named chancellor in Jan. 1933 and given dictatorial power by the Reichstag in March. Opposition parties were disbanded, strikes banned, and all aspects of economic, cultural, and religious life were brought under central government and Nazi party control and manipulated by sophisticated propaganda. Severe persecution of Jews began (**Nuremberg Laws,** Sept. 1935). Many Jews, political opponents, and others were sent to concentration camps (Dachau, 1933), where thousands died or were killed. Public works, renewed conscription (1935), arms production, and a 4-year plan (1936) all but ended unemployment.

Hitler's expansionism started with reincorporation of the Saar (1935), occupation of the **Rhineland** (Mar. 1936), and annexation of Austria (Mar. 1938). At **Munich** (Sept. 1938) an indecisive Britain and France sanctioned German dismemberment of Czechoslovakia.

Russia. Rapid industrialization was achieved through successive **5-year plans** starting in 1928, using severe labor discipline and mass forced labor. Industry was financed by a decline in living standards and exploitation of agriculture, which was almost totally collectivized by the early 1930s (*kolkhoz*, collective farm; *sovkhoz*, state farm, often in newly worked lands). Successive **purges** increased the role of professionals and management at the expense of workers. Millions perished in a series of manufactured disasters: extermination (1929-34) of kulaks (peasant landowners), severe famine (1932-33), party purges and show trials (Great Purge, 1936-38), suppression of nationalities, and poor conditions in labor camps.

Spain. An industrial revolution during World War I created an urban proletariat, which was attracted to socialism and anarchism; Catalan nationalists challenged central authority. The 5 years after King Alfonso left Spain in Apr. 1931 were dominated by tension between intermittent leftist and anticlerical governments and clericals, monarchists, and other rightists. Anarchist and Communist rebellions were crushed, but a July 1936 extreme right rebellion led by Gen. Francisco **Franco** and aided by Nazi Germany and Fascist Italy succeeded, after a 3-year **civil war** (more than 1 million dead in battles and atrocities). The war polarized international public opinion.

Italy. Despite propaganda for the ideal of the Corporate State, few domestic reforms were attempted. An entente with Hungary and Austria (Mar. 1934), a pact with Germany and Japan (Nov. 1937), and intervention by 50,000-75,000 troops in Spain (1936-39) sealed Italy's identification with the fascist bloc (anti-Semitic laws after Mar. 1938). Ethiopia was conquered (1935-36), and Albania annexed (Jan. 1939) in conscious imitation of ancient Rome.

East Europe. Repressive regimes fought for power against an active opposition (liberals, socialists, Communists, peasants, Nazis). Minority groups and Jews were restricted within national boundaries that did not coincide with ethnic population patterns. In the destruction of **Czechoslovakia**, Hungary occupied S Slovakia (Nov. 1938) and Ruthenia (Mar. 1939), and a pro-Nazi regime took power in the rest of Slovakia. Other boundary disputes (e.g., Poland-Lithuania, Yugoslavia-Bulgaria, and Romania-Hungary) doomed attempts to build joint fronts against Germany or Russia. Economic depression was severe.

East Asia. After a period of liberalism in **Japan**, nativist militarists dominated the government with peasant support. Manchuria was seized (Sept. 1931-Feb. 1932), and a puppet state was set up (Manchukuo). Adjacent Jehol (Inner Mongolia) was occupied in 1933. China proper was invaded in July 1937; large areas were conquered by Oct. 1938. Hundreds of thousands of rapes, murders, and other atrocities were attributed to the Japanese.

In **China** Communist forces left Kuomintang-besieged strongholds in the S in a Long March (1934-35) to the N. The Kuomintang-Communist civil war was suspended in Jan. 1937 in the face of threatening Japan.

The democracies. The Roosevelt Administration, in office Mar. 1933, embarked on an extensive program of **New Deal** social reform and economic stimulation, including protection for labor unions (heavy industries organized), Social Security, public works, wage-and-hour laws, and assistance to farmers. Isolationist sentiment (1937 Neutrality Act) prevented U.S. intervention in Europe, but military expenditures were increased in 1939.

French political instability and polarization prevented resolution of economic and international security questions. The **Popular Front** government under Leon Blum (June 1936-Apr. 1938) passed social reforms (40-hr week) and raised arms spending. National coalition governments, which ruled Britain from Aug. 1931, brought economic recovery but failed to define a consistent international policy until Chamberlain's government (from May 1937), which practiced **appeasement** of Germany and Italy.

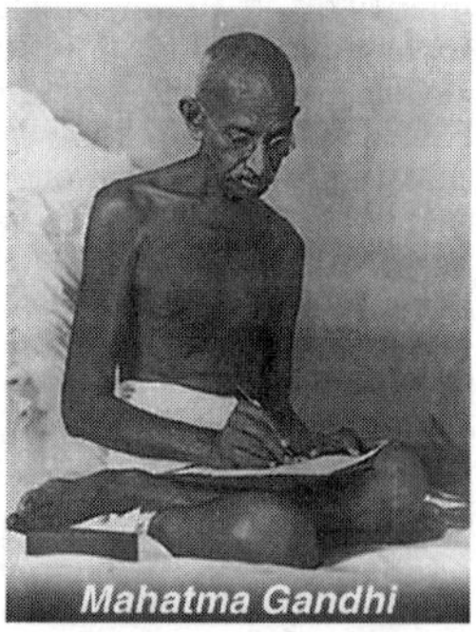
Mahatma Gandhi

India. Twenty years of agitation for autonomy and then for independence (Gandhi's **salt march**, 1930) achieved some constitutional reform (extended provincial powers, 1935) despite Muslim-Hindu strife. Social issues assumed prominence with peasant uprisings (1921), strikes (1928), Gandhi's efforts for untouchables (1932 "fast unto death"), and social and agrarian reform by the provinces after 1937.

War, Hot and Cold: 1940-49

Arts. The streamlined, geometric design motifs of Art Deco (from 1925) prevailed through the 1930s. **Abstract art** flourished (Moore sculptures from 1931) alongside a new **realism** related to social and political concerns (Socialist Realism, the official Soviet style from 1934; Mexican muralist Rivera, 1886-1957; and Orozco, 1883-1949), which were also expressed in fiction and poetry (Steinbeck's *Grapes of Wrath*, 1939; Sandburg's *The People, Yes*, 1936). Modern architecture (International Style, 1932) was unchallenged in its use of artificial materials (concrete, glass), lack of decoration, and monumentality (Rockefeller Center, 1929-40). Larger-than-life U.S.-made films captured a worldwide audience *(Gone With the Wind, The Wizard of Oz,* both 1939).

War in Asia-Pacific. Japan occupied Indochina in Sept. 1940, dominated Thailand in Dec. 1941, and attacked Hawaii (**Pearl Harbor**), the Philippines, Hong Kong, and Malaya on Dec. 7, 1941 (precipitating U.S. entrance into the war). Indonesia was attacked in Jan. 1942, and Burma was conquered in Mar. 1942. The Battle of **Midway** (June 1942) turned back the Japanese advance. "Island-hopping" battles (**Guadalcanal,** Aug. 1942-Jan. 1943; **Leyte Gulf,** Oct. 1944; **Iwo Jima,** Feb.-Mar. 1945; **Okinawa,** Apr. 1945) and

Pearl Harbor

massive bombing raids on Japan from June 1944 wore out Japanese defenses. U.S. atom bombs, dropped Aug. 6 and 9 on **Hiroshima** and Nagasaki, forced Japan to agree, on Aug. 14, to surrender; formal surrender was on Sept. 2, 1945.

War in Europe. The Nazi-Soviet nonaggression pact (Aug. 1939) freed Germany to attack Poland (Sept.). Britain and France, which had guaranteed Polish independence, declared war on Germany. Russia seized E Poland (Sept.), attacked Finland (Nov.), and took the Baltic states (July 1940). Mobile German forces staged *blitzkrieg* attacks during Apr.-June 1940, conquering neutral Denmark, Norway, and the Low Countries and defeating France; 350,000 British and French troops were evacuated at **Dunkirk** (May). The **Battle of Britain** (June-Dec. 1940) denied Germany air superiority. German-Italian campaigns won the Balkans by Apr. 1941. Three million Axis troops **invaded Russia** in June 1941, marching through Ukraine to the Caucasus, and through White Russia and the Baltic republics to Moscow and Leningrad.

Russian winter counterthrusts (1941-42 and 1942-43) stopped the German advance (**Stalingrad,** Sept. 1942-Feb. 1943). Sustaining great casualties, the Russians drove the Axis from all E Europe and the Balkans in the next 2 years.

Stalin, Roosevelt & Churchill

Invasions of N Africa (Nov. 1942), Italy (Sept. 1943), and **Normandy** (launched on D-Day, June 6, 1944) brought U.S., British, Free French, and allied troops to Germany by spring 1945. In Feb. 1945, the 3 Allied leaders, Winston **Churchill** (Britain), Joseph **Stalin** (USSR), and Franklin D. Roosevelt (U.S.), met in Yalta to discuss strategy and resolve political issues, including the postwar Allied occupation of Germany. Germany surrendered May 7, 1945.

Atrocities. The war brought 20th-cent. cruelty to its peak. The Nazi regime systematically killed an estimated 5-6 million Jews, including some 3 million who died in death camps (e.g., **Auschwitz**). Gypsies, political opponents, sick and retarded people, and others deemed undesirable were also murdered by the Nazis, as were vast numbers of Slavs.

Civilian deaths. German bombs killed 70,000 British civilians. More than 100,000 Chinese civilians were killed by Japanese forces in the capture and occupation of Nanking. Severe retaliation by the Soviet army, E European partisans, Free French, and others took a heavy toll. U.S. and British bombing of Germany killed hundreds of thousands, as did U.S. bombing of Japan (80,000-200,000 at Hiroshima alone). Some 45 million people lost their lives in the war.

Settlement. The **United Nations** charter was signed in San Francisco on June 26, 1945, by 50 nations. The International Tribunal at **Nuremberg** convicted 22 German leaders for war crimes in Sept. 1946; 23 Japanese leaders were convicted in Nov. 1948. Postwar border changes included large gains in territory for the USSR, losses for Germany, a shift to the W in Polish borders, and minor losses for Italy. Communist regimes, supported by Soviet troops, took power in most of E Europe, including Soviet-occupied Germany (GDR proclaimed Oct. 1949). Japan lost all overseas lands.

Recovery. Basic political and social changes were imposed on Japan and W Germany by the western allies (Japan constitution adopted, Nov. 1946; W German basic law, May 1949). U.S. **Marshall Plan** aid ($12 billion, 1947-51) spurred W European economic recovery after a period of severe inflation and strikes in Europe and the U.S. The British Labour Party introduced a national health service and nationalized basic industries in 1946.

Cold War. Western fears of further Soviet advances (Cominform formed in Oct. 1947; Czechoslovakia coup, Feb. 1948; Berlin blockade, Apr. 1948-Sept. 1949) led to the formation of **NATO**. Civil War in Greece and Soviet pressure on Turkey led to U.S. aid under the **Truman Doctrine** (Mar. 1947). Other anti-Communist security pacts were the Organization of American States (Apr. 1948) and the SE Asia Treaty Organization (Sept. 1954). A new wave of **Soviet purges** and repression intensified in the last years of Stalin's rule, extending to E Europe (Slansky trial in Czechoslovakia, 1951). Only Yugoslavia resisted Soviet control (expelled by Cominform, June 1948; U.S. aid, June 1949).

China, Korea. Communist forces emerged from World War II strengthened by the Soviet takeover of industrial Manchuria. In 4 years of fighting, the Kuomintang was driven from the mainland; the People's Republic was proclaimed Oct. 1, 1949. Korea was divided by USSR and U.S. occupation forces. Separate republics were proclaimed in the 2 zones in Aug.-Sept. 1948.

India. India and Pakistan became independent dominions on Aug. 15, 1947. Millions of Hindu and Muslim refugees were created by the partition; riots (1946-47) took hundreds of thousands of lives; Mahatma **Gandhi** was assassinated in Jan. 1948. Burma became completely independent in Jan. 1948; Ceylon took dominion status in Feb.

Middle East. The UN approved partition of Palestine into Jewish and Arab states. **Israel** was proclaimed a state, May 14, 1948. Arabs rejected partition, but failed to defeat Israel in war (May 1948-July 1949). Immigration from Europe and the Middle East swelled Israel's Jewish population. British and French forces left Lebanon and Syria in 1946. Transjordan occupied most of Arab Palestine.

Southeast Asia. Communists and others fought against restoration of French rule in **Indochina** from 1946; a non-Communist government was recognized by France in Mar. 1949, but fighting continued. Both Indonesia and the Philippines became independent; the former in 1949 after 4 years of war with Netherlands, the latter in 1946. Philippine economic and military ties with the U.S. remained strong; a Communist-led peasant rising was checked in 1948.

Arts. New York became the center of the world art market; **abstract expressionism** was the chief mode (Pollock from 1943, de Kooning from 1947). Literature and philosophy explored **existentialism** (Camus's *The Stranger*, 1942; Sartre's *Being and Nothingness*, 1943). Non-Western attempts to revive or create regional styles (Senghor's Négritude, Mishima's novels) only confirmed the emergence of a universal culture. Radio and phonograph records spread American popular music (swing, bebop) around the world.

The American Decade: 1950-59

Polite decolonization. The peaceful decline of European political and military power in Asia and Africa accelerated in the 1950s. Nearly all of **N Africa** was freed by 1956, but France fought a bitter war to retain Algeria, with its large European minority, until 1962. **Ghana**, independent in 1957, led a parade of new black African nations (more than 2 dozen by 1962), which altered the political character of the UN. Ethnic disputes often exploded in the new nations after decolonization (UN troops in Cyprus, 1964; **Nigerian civil war**, 1967-70). Leaders of the new states, mostly sharing socialist ideologies, tried to create an Afro-Asian bloc (Bandung Conference, 1955), but Western economic influence and U.S. political ties remained strong (Baghdad Pact, 1955).

Trade. World trade volume soared, in an atmosphere of monetary stability assured by international accords (**Bretton Woods,** 1944). In Europe, economic integration advanced (**European Economic Community,** 1957; European Free Trade Association, 1960). Comecon (1949) coordinated the economies of Soviet-bloc countries.

U.S. Economic growth produced an abundance of consumer goods (9.3 million motor vehicles sold, 1955). Suburban housing changed life patterns for middle and working classes (Levittown, 1947-51). Pres. Dwight **Eisenhower's** landslide election victories (1952, 1956) reflected consensus politics. A system of alliances and military bases bolstered U.S. influence on all continents. Trade and payments surpluses were balanced by overseas investments and foreign aid ($50 billion, 1950-59).

USSR. In the "thaw" after Stalin's death in 1953, relations with the West improved (evacuation of Vienna, Geneva summit conference, both 1955). Repression of scientific and cultural life eased, and many prisoners were freed culminating in **de-Stalinization** (1956). **Nikita Khrushchev's** leadership aimed at consumer sector growth, but farm production lagged, despite the virgin lands program (from 1954). Soviet crushing of the 1956 Hungarian revolution, the 1960 U-2 spy plane episode, and other incidents renewed East-West tension and domestic curbs.

Eastern Europe. Resentment of Russian domination and Stalinist repression combined with nationalist, economic, and religious factors to produce periodic violence. E Berlin workers rioted (1953), Polish workers rioted in Poznan (June 1956), and a broad-based **revolution** broke out in **Hungary** (Oct. 1956). All were suppressed by Soviet force or threats (at least 7,000 dead in Hungary), but Poland was allowed to restore private ownership of farms, and a degree of personal and economic freedom returned to Hungary. Yugoslavia experimented with worker self-management and a market economy.

Korea. The 1945 division of Korea along the 38th parallel left industry in the N, which was organized into a militant regime and armed by the USSR. The S was politically disunited. More than 60,000 N Korean troops invaded the S on June 25, 1950. The U.S., backed by the UN Security Council, sent troops. **UN troops** reached the Chinese border in Nov. Some 200,000 Chinese troops crossed the Yalu R. and drove back UN forces. By spring 1951 battle lines had become stabilized near the original 38th parallel border, but heavy fighting continued. Finally, an armistice was signed on July 27, 1953. U.S. troops remained in the S, and U.S. economic and military aid continued. The war stimulated rapid economic recovery in Japan.

China. Starting in 1952, industry, agriculture, and social institutions were forcibly collectivized. In a massive purge, as many as several million people were executed as Kuomintang supporters or as class and political enemies. The **Great Leap Forward** (1958-60) unsuccessfully tried to force the pace of development by substituting labor for investment.

Indochina. Ho Chi Minh's forces, aided by the USSR and the new Chinese Communist government, fought French and pro-French Vietnamese forces to a standstill and captured the strategic **Dienbienphu** camp in May 1954. The Geneva Agreements divided Vietnam in half pending elections (never held) and recognized Laos and Cambodia as independent. The U.S. aided the anti-Communist Republic of Vietnam in the S.

Middle East. Arab revolutions placed leftist, militantly nationalist regimes in power in Egypt (1952) and Iraq (1958). But Arab unity attempts failed (United Arab Republic joined Egypt, Syria, Yemen, 1958-61). Arab refusal to recognize Israel (Arab League economic blockade began Sept. 1951) led to a permanent **state of war**, with repeated incidents (Gaza, 1955). Israel occupied Sinai, and Britain and France took (Oct. 1956) the Suez Canal, but were replaced by the UN Emergency Force. The Mossadegh government in Iran nationalized (May 1951) the British-owned oil industry in May, but was overthrown (Aug. 1953) in a U.S.-aided coup.

Latin America. Argentinian dictator Juan **Perón,** in office 1946, crushed opposition and enforced land reform, some nationalization, welfare state measures, and curbs on the Roman Catholic Church. A Sept. 1955 coup deposed Perón. The 1952 revolution in Bolivia brought land reform, nationalization of tin mines, and improvement in the status of Native Americans, who nevertheless remained poor. The Batista regime in Cuba was overthrown (Jan. 1959) by Fidel **Castro,** who imposed a Communist dictatorship, aligned Cuba with the USSR, but improved education and health care. A U.S.-backed anti-Castro invasion (**Bay of Pigs**, Apr. 1961) was crushed. Self-government advanced in the British Caribbean.

Technology. Large outlays on research and development in the U.S. and the USSR focused on military applications (H-bomb in U.S., 1952; USSR, 1953; Britain, 1957; intercontinental missiles, late 1950s). Soviet launching of the **Sputnik** satellite (Oct. 4, 1957) spurred increases in U.S. science education funds (National Defense Education Act).

Literature and film. Alienation from social and literary conventions reached an extreme in the theater of the absurd (Beckett's *Waiting for Godot,* 1952), the "new novel" (Robbe-Grillet's *Voyeur,* 1955), and avant-garde film (Antonioni's *L'Avventura,* 1960). U.S. beatniks (Kerouac's *On the Road,* 1957) and others rejected the supposed conformism of Americans (Riesman's *The Lonely Crowd,* 1950).

Rising Expectations: 1960-69

Economic boom. The longest sustained economic boom on record spanned almost the entire decade in the capitalist world; the closely watched GNP figure doubled (1960-70) in the U.S., fueled by Vietnam War-related budget deficits. The **General Agreement on Tariffs and Trade** (1967) stimulated W European prosperity, which spread to peripheral areas (Spain, Italy, E Germany). Japan became a top economic power. Foreign investment aided the industrialization of Brazil. There were limited Soviet economic reform attempts.

Reform and radicalization. Pres. John F. **Kennedy**, inaugurated 1961, emphasized youthful idealism and vigor; his assassination Nov. 22, 1963, was a national trauma. A series of political and social reform movements took root in the U.S. and other countries. Blacks demonstrated nonviolently and with partial success against segregation and poverty (1963 March on Washington; 1964 **Civil Rights Act**), but some urban areas erupted in extensive riots (Watts, 1965; Detroit, 1967; **Martin Luther King** assassination, Apr. 4, 1968). New concern for the poor (Harrington's *Other America*, 1963) helped lead to Pres. Lyndon Johnson's **"Great Society"** programs (Medicare, Water Quality Act, Higher Education Act, all 1965). Concern for the **environment** surged (Carson's *Silent Spring*, 1962).

Feminism revived as a cultural and political movement (Friedan's *Feminine Mystique*, 1963; National Organization for Women founded 1966), and a movement for homosexual rights emerged (Stonewall riot in NYC, 1969). Pope John XXIII called the **Second Vatican Council** (1962-65), which liberalized Roman Catholic liturgy and some other aspects of Catholicism.

Opposition to U.S. involvement in Vietnam, especially among university students (**Moratorium** protest, Nov. 1969), turned violent (Weatherman Chicago riots, Oct. 1969). **New Left** and Marxist theories became popular, and membership in radical groups (Students for a Democratic Society, Black Panthers) increased. Maoist groups, especially in Europe, called for total transformation of society. In France, students sparked a nationwide strike affecting 10 million workers in May-June 1968, but an electoral reaction barred revolutionary change.

China. China's revolutionary militancy under **Mao** Zedong caused disputes with the USSR under "revisionist" Khrushchev, starting in 1960. The 2 powers exchanged fire in 1969 border disputes. China used force to capture (1962) areas disputed with India. The **"Great Proletarian Cultural Revolution"** tried to impose a utopian egalitarian program in China and spread revolution abroad; political struggle, often violent, convulsed China in 1965-68.

Indochina. Communist-led guerrillas aided by N Vietnam fought from 1960 against the S Vietnam government of Ngo Dinh Diem (killed 1963). The U.S. military role in-

Mao Zedong

creased after the 1964 **Tonkin Gulf** incident. U.S. forces peaked at 543,400 in Apr. 1969. Massive numbers of N Vietnamese troops also fought. Laotian and Cambodian neutrality were threatened by Communist insurgencies, with N Vietnamese aid, and U.S. intrigues.

Developing World. A bloc of authoritarian leftist regimes among the newly independent nations emerged in political opposition to the U.S.-led Western alliance and came to dominate the conference of nonaligned nations (Belgrade, 1961; Cairo, 1964; Lusaka, 1970). Soviet political ties and military bases were established in Cuba, Egypt, Algeria, Guinea, and other countries whose leaders were regarded as revolutionary heroes by opposition groups in pro-Western or colonial countries. Some leaders were ousted in coups by pro-Western groups—Zaire's Patrice Lumumba (killed 1961), Ghana's Kwame Nkrumah (exiled 1966), and Indonesia's Sukarno (effectively ousted in 1965 after a Communist coup failed).

Middle East. Arab-Israeli tension erupted into a brief war June 1967. Israel emerged from the war as a major regional power. Military shipments before and after the war brought much of the Arab world into the Soviet political sphere. Most Arab states broke U.S. diplomatic ties, while Communist countries cut their ties to Israel. Intra-Arab disputes continued: Egypt and Saudi Arabia supported rival factions in a bloody Yemen civil war 1962-70; Lebanese troops fought Palestinian commandos 1969.

East Europe. To stop the large-scale exodus of citizens, E German authorities built (Aug. 1961) a **fortified wall across Berlin.** Soviet sway in the Balkans was weakened by Albania's support of China (USSR broke ties in Dec. 1961) and Romania's assertion (1964) of industrial and foreign policy autonomy. Liberalization (spring 1968) in Czechoslovakia was crushed with massive force by troops of 5 Warsaw Pact countries. W German treaties (1970) with the USSR and Poland facilitated the transfer of German technology and confirmed postwar boundaries.

Arts and styles. The boundary between fine and popular arts was blurred to some extent by Pop Art (Warhol) and rock musicals (*Hair*, 1968). Informality and exaggeration prevailed in fashion (beards, miniskirts). A nonpolitical "counterculture" developed, rejecting traditional bourgeois life goals and personal habits, and use of marijuana and hallucinogens spread (**Woodstock** festival, Aug. 1969). Indian influence was felt in religion (Ram Dass) and fashion, and The **Beatles,** who brought unprecedented sophistication to rock music, became for many a symbol of the decade.

Buzz Aldrin on Moon, 1969

Science. Achievements in space (**humans on the moon,** July 1969) and electronics (lasers, integrated circuits) encouraged a faith in scientific solutions to problems in agriculture ("green revolution"), medicine (heart transplants, 1967), and other areas. Harmful technology, it was believed, could be controlled (1963 nuclear weapon test ban treaty, 1968 nonproliferation treaty).

Disillusionment: 1970-79

U.S.: Caution and neoconservatism. A relatively sluggish economy, energy shortages, and environmental problems contributed to a **"limits of growth"** philosophy. Suspicion of science and technology killed or delayed major projects (supersonic transport dropped, 1971; Seabrook nuclear power plant protests, 1977-78) and was fed by the Three Mile Island nuclear reactor accident (Mar. 1979).

There were signs of growing mistrust of big government and less support for new social policies. School busing and racial quotas were opposed (Bakke decision, June 1978); the proposed Equal Rights Amendment for women languished; civil rights legislation aimed at protecting homosexuals was opposed (Dade County referendum, June 1977).

Completion of Communist forces' takeover of **South Vietnam** (evacuation of U.S. civilians, Apr. 1975), revelations of Central Intelligence Agency misdeeds (Rockefeller Commission report, June 1975), and **Watergate** scandals (Nixon resigned in Aug. 1974) reduced faith in U.S. moral and material capacity to influence world affairs. Revelations of Soviet crimes (Solzhenitsyn's *Gulag Archipelago,* 1974) and Soviet intervention in Africa helped foster a revival of anti-Communist sentiment.

Economy sluggish. The 1960s boom faltered in the 1970s; a severe recession in the U.S. and Europe (1974-75) followed a huge oil price hike (Dec. 1973). Monetary instability (U.S. cut ties to gold in Aug. 1971), the decline of the dollar, and protectionist moves by industrial countries (1977-78) threatened trade. Business investment and spending for research declined. Severe inflation plagued many countries (25% in Britain, 1975; 18% in U.S., 1979).

China picks up pieces. After the 1976 deaths of Mao Zedong and Zhou Enlai, struggle for the leadership succession was won by pragmatists. A nationwide purge of orthodox Maoists was carried out, and the **Gang of Four,** led by Mao's widow, Chiang Ching, arrested. The new leaders freed more than 100,000 political prisoners and reduced public adulation of Mao. Political and trade ties were expanded with Japan, Europe, and the U.S. in the late 1970s, as relations worsened with the USSR, Cuba, and Vietnam (4-week invasion by China, 1979). Ideological guidelines in industry, science, education, and the armed forces, which the ruling faction said had caused chaos and decline, were reversed (bonuses to workers, Dec. 1977; exams for college entrance, Oct. 1977). Severe restrictions on cultural expression were eased.

Europe. European unity moves (EEC-EFTA trade accord, 1972) faltered as economic problems appeared (Britain floated pound, 1972; France floated franc, 1974). Germany and Switzerland curbed guest workers from southern Europe. Greece and Turkey quarreled over Cyprus and Aegean oil rights.

All non-Communist Europe was under democratic rule after free elections were held (June 1976) in **Spain** 7 months after the death of Franco. The conservative, colonialist regime in **Portugal** was overthrown in Apr. 1974. In **Greece** the 7-year-old military dictatorship yielded power in 1974. Northern Europe, though ruled mostly by Socialists (**Swedish** Socialists unseated in 1976 after 44 years in power), turned more conservative. The **British** Labour government imposed (1975) wage curbs and suspended nationalization schemes. Terrorism in **Germany** (1972 Munich Olympics killings) led to laws curbing some civil liberties. **French** "new philosophers" rejected leftist ideologies, and the shaky Socialist-Communist coalition lost a 1978 election bid.

Religion and politics. The improvement in **Muslim** countries' political fortunes by the 1950s (with the exception of Central Asia under Soviet and Chinese rule) and the growth of Arab oil wealth were followed by a resurgence of traditional religious fervor. Libyan dictator Muammar al-Qaddafi mixed Islamic laws with socialism and called for Muslim return to Spain and Sicily. The illegal Muslim Brotherhood in **Egypt** was accused of violence, while extreme groups bombed (1977) theaters to protest Western and secular values.

In **Turkey**, the National Salvation Party was the first Islamic group to share (1974) power since secularization in the 1920s. In **Iran, Ayatollah Ruhollah Khomeini,** led a revolution that deposed the secular shah (Jan. 1979) and created an Islamic republic there. Religiously motivated Muslims took part in an insurrection in Saudi Arabia that briefly seized (1979) the Grand Mosque in Mecca. Muslim puritan opposition to **Pakistan** Pres. Zulfikar Ali-Bhutto helped lead to his overthrow in July 1977. Muslim solidarity, however, could not prevent Pakistan's eastern province (**Bangladesh**) from declaring (Dec. 1971) independence after a bloody civil war.

Muslim and Hindu resentment of coerced sterilization in **India** helped defeat the Gandhi government, which was replaced (Mar. 1977) by a coalition including religious Hindu parties. Muslims in the S **Philippines**, aided by Libya, rebelled against central rule from 1973.

The Buddhist Soka Gakkai movement launched (1964) the Komeito party in **Japan,** which became a major opposition party in 1972 and 1976 elections.

Evangelical Protestant groups grew in the U.S. A revival of interest in Orthodox Christianity occurred among **Russian** intellectuals (Solzhenitsyn). The secularist **Israeli** Labor party, after decades of rule, was ousted in 1977 by conservatives led by Menachem Begin; religious militants founded settlements on the disputed West Bank, part of biblically promised Israel. U.S. Reform Judaism revived many previously discarded traditional practices.

Old-fashioned religious wars raged intermittently in **Northern Ireland** (Catholic vs. Protestant, 1969-) and **Lebanon** (Christian vs. Muslim, 1975-), while religious militancy complicated the Israel-Arab dispute (1973 Israel-Arab war). The Camp David Accords in 1978, negotiated by Egyptian Pres. Anwar al-Sadat, Israeli Prime Min. Menachem Begin, and U.S. Pres. Jimmy Carter, facilitated the landmark 1979 **Egypt-Israel peace treaty**, but increased militancy on the West Bank impeded further progress.

Sadat, Carter, Begin

Latin America. Repressive conservative regimes strengthened their hold on most of the continent, with a violent coup against the elected (Sept. 1973) Allende government in **Chile**, a 1976 military coup in **Argentina**, and coups against reformist regimes in **Bolivia** (1971, 1979) and **Peru** (1976). In Central America increasing liberal and leftist militancy led to the ouster (1979) of the Somoza regime of **Nicaragua** and to civil conflict in **El Salvador**.

Indochina. Communist victories in Vietnam, Cambodia, and Laos by May 1975 led to new turmoil. The **Pol Pot regime** ordered millions of city-dwellers to resettle in rural areas, in a program of forced labor, combined with terrorism, that cost more than 1 million lives (1975-79) and caused hundreds of thousands of ethnic Chinese and others to flee Vietnam ("boat people," 1979). The Vietnamese invasion of Cambodia swelled the refugee population and contributed to widespread starvation in that devastated country.

Russian expansion. Soviet influence, checked in some countries (troops ousted by Egypt, 1972), was projected farther afield, often with the use of Cuban troops (Angola, 1975-89; Ethiopia, 1977-88) and aided by a growing navy, a merchant fleet, and international banking ability. **Détente** with the West—1972 Berlin pact, 1972 strategic arms pact (**SALT**)—gave way to a more antagonistic relationship in the late 1970s, exacerbated by the Soviet invasion (1979) of **Afghanistan.**

Africa. The last remaining European colonies were granted independence (**Spanish Sahara**, 1976; **Djibouti,** 1977) and, after 10 years of civil war and many negotiation sessions, a black government took over (1979) in Zimbabwe (Rhodesia); white domination remained in **South Africa**. Great power involvement in local wars (Russia in **Angola, Ethiopia**; France in **Chad, Zaire, Mauritania**) and the use of tens of thousands of Cuban troops were denounced by some African leaders. Ethnic or tribal clashes made Africa a locus of sustained warfare during the late 1970s.

Arts. Traditional modes of painting, architecture, and music received increased popular and critical attention in the 1970s. These more conservative styles coexisted with modernist works in an atmosphere of increased variety and tolerance.

Revitalization of Capitalism, Demand for Democracy: 1980-89

USSR, Eastern Europe. A troublesome 1980-85 for the USSR was followed by 5 years of astonishing change: the surrender of the Communist monopoly, the remaking of the Soviet state, and the beginning of the disintegration of the Soviet empire. After the deaths of Leonid **Brezhnev** (1982) and 2 successors (Andropov in 1984 and Chernenko in 1985), the harsh treatment of dissent and restriction of emigration, and the Soviet invasion (Dec. 1979) of Afghanistan, Gen. Sec. Mikhail **Gorbachev** (in office 1985-1991) promoted *glasnost* and *perestroika*—economic, political, and social reform. Supported by the Communist Party (July 1988), he signed (Dec. 1987) the INF disarmament treaty, and he pledged (1988) to cut the military budget. Military withdrawal from Afghanistan was completed in Feb. 1989, the process of democratization went ahead unhindered in Poland and Hungary, and the Soviet people chose (Mar. 1989) part of the new Congress of People's Deputies from competing candidates. By decade's end the **Cold War** appeared to be fading away.

Reagan and Gorbachev

In **Poland, Solidarity**, the labor union founded (1980) by Lech **Walesa**, was outlawed in 1982 and then legalized in 1988, after years of unrest. Poland's first free election since the Communist takeover brought Solidarity victory (June 1989); Tadeusz Mazowiecki, a Walesa adviser, became (Aug. 1989) prime minister in a government with the Communists. In the fall of 1989 the failure of Marxist economies in **Hungary**, **East Germany**, **Czechoslovakia, Bulgaria,** and **Romania** brought the collapse of the Communist monopoly and a demand for democracy. In a historic step, the **Berlin Wall** was opened in Nov. 1989.

U.S. "The Reagan Years" (1981-88) brought the **longest economic boom** yet in U.S. history via budget and tax cuts, deregulation, "junk bond" financing, leveraged buyouts, and mergers and takeovers. However, there was a stock market crash (Oct. 1987), and federal budget deficits and the trade deficit increased. Foreign policy showed a **strong anti-Communist stance**, via increased defense spending, aid to anti-Communists in Central America, invasion of Cuba-threatened Grenada, and championing of the MX missile system and "Star Wars" missile defense program. Four Reagan-Gorbachev summits (1985-88) climaxed in the INF treaty (1987), as the Cold War began to wind down. The Iran-contra affair (North's TV testimony, July 1987) was a major political scandal. Homelessness and drug abuse (especially "crack" cocaine) were growing social problems. In 1988, Vice Pres. George Bush was elected to succeed Ronald Reagan as president.

Middle East. The Middle East remained militarily unstable, with sharp divisions along economic, political, racial, and religious lines. In **Iran**, the Islamic revolution of 1979 created a strong anti-U.S. stance (hostage crisis, Nov. 1979-Jan. 1981). In Sept. 1980, **Iraq** repudiated its border agreement with Iran and began major hostilities that led to an 8-year war in which millions were killed.

Libya's support for international terrorism induced the U.S. to close (May 1981) its diplomatic mission there and embargo (Mar. 1982) Libyan oil. The U.S. accused Libyan leader Muammar al-Qaddafi of aiding (Dec. 1985) terrorists in Rome and of Vienna airport attacks, and retaliated by bombing Libya (Apr. 1986).

Israel affirmed (July 1980) all Jerusalem as its capital, destroyed (1981) an Iraqi atomic reactor, and invaded (1982) Lebanon, forcing the PLO to agree to withdraw. A **Palestinian uprising**, including women and children hurling rocks and bottles at troops, began (Dec. 1987) in Israeli-occupied Gaza and spread to the West Bank; troops responded with force, killing 300 by the end of 1988, with 6,000 more in detention camps.

Israeli withdrawal from **Lebanon** began in Feb. 1985 and ended in June 1985, as Lebanon continued torn by military and political conflict. Artillery duels (Mar.-Apr. 1989) between Christian East Beirut and Muslim West Beirut left 200 dead and 700 wounded. At decade's end, violence still dominated.

Latin America. In **Nicaragua**, the leftist Sandinista National Liberation Front, in power after the 1979 civil war, faced problems as a result of Nicaragua's military aid to leftist guerrillas in El Salvador and U.S. backing of antigovernment contras. The U.S. CIA admitted (1984) having directed the mining of Nicaraguan ports, and the U.S. sent humanitarian (1985) and military (1986) aid. Profits from secret arms sales to Iran were found (1987) diverted to contras. Cease-fire talks between the Sandinista government and contras came in 1988, and elections were held in Nicaragua in Feb. 1990.

In **El Salvador**, a military coup (Oct. 1979) failed to halt extreme right-wing violence and left-wing terrorism. Archbishop Oscar Romero was assassinated in Mar. 1980; from Jan. to June some 4,000 civilians were killed in the civil unrest. In 1984, newly elected Pres. José Napoleon Duarte worked to stem human rights abuses, but violence continued.

In **Chile**, Gen. Augusto Pinochet yielded the presidency after a democratic election (Dec. 1989), but remained as head of the army. He had ruled the country since 1973, imposing harsh measures against leftists and dissidents; at the same time he introduced economic programs that restored prosperity to Chile.

Africa. 1980-85 marked a rapid decline in the economies of virtually all African countries, a result of accelerating desertification, the world economic recession, heavy indebtedness to overseas creditors, rapid population growth, and political instability. Some 60 million Africans faced prolonged hunger in 1981; much of Africa had one of the worst droughts ever in 1983, and by year's end **150 million faced near-famine**. "Live Aid," a marathon rock concert, was presented in July 1985, and the U.S. and Western nations sent aid in Sept. 1985. Economic hardship fueled political unrest and coups. Wars in Ethiopia and Sudan and military strife in several other nations continued. AIDS took a heavy toll.

South Africa. Anti-apartheid sentiment gathered force in South Africa as demonstrations and violent police response grew. White voters approved (Nov. 1983) the first constitution to give Coloureds and Asians a voice, while still excluding blacks (70% of the population). The U.S. imposed economic sanctions in Aug. 1985, and 11 Western nations followed in September. P. W. **Botha**, 1980s president, was succeeded by F. W. **de Klerk**, in Sept. 1989, who promised "evolutionary" change via negotiation with the black population.

China. During the 1980s the Communist government and paramount leader **Deng Xiaoping** pursued **far-reaching changes**, expanding commercial and technical ties to the industrialized world and increasing the role of market forces in stimulating urban development. Apr. 1989 brought new demands for political reforms; student demonstrators camped out in Tiananmen Square, Beijing, in a massive peaceful protest. Some 100,000 students and workers marched, and at least 20 other cities saw protests. In response, martial law was imposed; army troops crushed the demonstration in and around Tiananmen Square on June 3-4, with death toll estimates at 500-7,000, up to 10,000 dissidents arrested, 31 people tried and executed. The conciliatory Communist Party chief was ousted; the Politburo adopted (July) reforms against official corruption.

Japan. Japan's relations with other nations, especially the U.S., were dominated by **trade imbalances favoring Japan**. In 1985 the U.S. trade deficit with Japan was $49.7 billion, one-third of the total U.S. trade deficit. After Japan was found (Apr. 1986) to sell semiconductors and computer memory chips below cost, the U.S. was assured a "fair share" of the market, but charged (Mar. 1987) Japan with failing to live up to the agreement.

Margaret Thatcher

European Community. With the addition of Greece, Portugal, and Spain, the EC became a common market of more than **300 million people**, the West's largest trading entity. Margaret **Thatcher** became the first British prime minister in the 20th century to win a 3rd consecutive term (1987). France elected (1981) its first socialist president, François **Mitterrand**, who was reelected in 1988. Italy elected (1983) its first socialist premier, Bettino **Craxi**.

International terrorism. With the 1979 overthrow of the shah of Iran, terrorism became a prominent tactic. It increased through the 1980s, but with fewer high-profile attacks after 1985. In 1979-81, Iranian militants held 52 U.S. hostages in Iran for 444 days; in 1983 a TNT-laden suicide terrorist blew up U.S. Marine headquarters in Beirut, killing 241 Americans, and a truck bomb blew up a French paratroop barracks, killing 58. The *Achille Lauro* cruise ship was hijacked in 1986, and an American passenger killed; the U.S. subsequently intercepted the Egyptian plane flying the terrorists to safety. Incidents rose to 700 in 1985, and to 1,000 in 1988. **Assassinated leaders** included Egypt's Pres. Anwar al-**Sadat** (1981), India's Prime Min. Indira **Gandhi** (1984), and Lebanese Premier Rashid **Karami** (1987).

Post–Cold War World: 1990-99

Soviet Empire breakup. The world community witnessed the extraordinary disintegration of the **Soviet Union** into 15 independent states. The 1980s had already seen internal reforms and a decline of Communist power both within the Soviet Union and in Eastern Europe. The Soviet breakup began in earnest with the declarations of independence adopted by the Baltic republics of **Lithuania, Latvia,** and **Estonia** during an abortive coup against reformist leader Mikhail **Gorbachev** (Aug. 1991). The other republics soon took the same step. In Dec. 1991, **Russia, Ukraine**, and **Belarus** declared the Soviet Union dead; Gorbachev resigned, and the Soviet Parliament went out of existence. The Warsaw Pact and the Council for Mutual Economic Assistance (Comecon) were disbanded. Most of the former Soviet republics joined in a loose confederation called the **Commonwealth of Independent States**. **Russia** remained the predominant country after the breakup, but its people soon suffered severe economic hardship as the nation, under Pres. Boris **Yeltsin,** moved to revamp the economy and adopt a free market system. In Oct. 1993, **anti-Yeltsin forces** occupied the Parliament building and were ousted by the army; about 140 people died in the fighting.

The Muslim republic of **Chechnya** declared independence from the rest of Russia, but this was met with an invasion by Russian troops (Dec. 1994). After almost 21 months of vicious fighting, a cease-fire took hold in 1996, and the Russians withdrew. In 1999 Russia forcibly suppressed Muslim insurgents in Dagestan and entered neighboring Chechnya, again fighting to gain control over separatist rebels there. Yeltsin resigned office Dec. 31, 1999, to be replaced by Vladimir **Putin** (elected in his own right, Mar. 2000).

Europe. Yugoslavia broke apart, and hostilities ensued among the republics along ethnic and religious lines. **Croatia, Slovenia**, and **Macedonia** declared independence (1991), followed by **Bosnia-Herzegovina** (1992). **Serbia** and **Montenegro** remained as the republic of Yugoslavia. Bitter fighting followed, especially in Bosnia, where Serbs reportedly engaged in **"ethnic cleansing"** of the Muslim population; a peace plan (Dayton accord), brokered by the United States, was signed by **Bosnia, Serbia**, and **Croatia** (Dec. 1995), with **NATO** responsible for policing its implementation. In spring 1999, NATO conducted a bombing campaign aimed at stopping Yugoslavia from its campaign to drive out ethnic Albanians from the Kosovo region; a peace accord was reached in June under which NATO peacekeeping troops entered Kosovo.

The two **Germanys** were reunited after 45 years (Oct. 1990). The union was greeted with jubilation, but stresses became apparent when free market principles were applied to the aging East German industries, resulting in many plant closings and rising unemployment. West German chancellor Helmut **Kohl**, a Christian Democrat, lost power after 16 years, in Sept. 1998 elections; Gerhard **Schroeder**, a Social Democrat, took over. Czechoslovakia broke apart peacefully (Jan. 1993), becoming the **Czech Republic** and **Slovakia.** In **Poland**, Lech **Walesa** was elected president (Dec. 1991) but was defeated in his bid for a 2nd term (Nov. 1995).

NATO approved the **Partnership for Peace** Program (Jan. 1994) coordinating the defense of **Eastern** and **Central European** countries; Russia joined the program later that year. NATO signed a pact with **Russia** (1997) providing for NATO expansion into the former Soviet-bloc countries; a similar treaty was set up with **Ukraine**. The **Czech Republic**, **Hungary**, and **Poland** became members in Jan. 1999; in that year **NATO** celebrated its 50th anniversary. Efforts toward European unity continued with adoption of a single market (Jan. 1993) and conversion of the European Community to the **European Union** as the Maestricht Treaty took effect (Nov. 1993). Agreement was reached for 11 EU members to participate in Economic and Monetary Union, adopting a common currency **(euro)** for some purposes in Jan. 1999.

An intraparty revolt forced Margaret **Thatcher** out as prime minister of **Great Britain**, to be succeeded by John **Major** (Nov. 1990); 7 years later, Major suffered an overwhelming defeat at the hands of the new Labour Party leader, Tony **Blair** (May 1997). The divorce of Prince **Charles and** Princess **Diana**, followed by the death of Diana in a car accident (Aug. 1997), made headlines around the world. Talks on **peace** in **Northern Ireland** that included participation of Sinn Fein, political arm of the IRA, led to a ground-breaking peace plan, approved in an all-Ireland vote (May 1998). In Dec. 1999, Northern Ireland was granted home rule under a power-sharing cabinet. In **Scotland** voters overwhelmingly approved establishment of a regional legislature (1997), and in **Wales** voters narrowly approved establishment of a local assembly (1997). In a historic innovation, the Church of England **ordained 32 women** as priests (Mar. 1994).

Middle East. In Aug. 1990, **Iraq's Saddam Hussein** ordered his troops to invade **Kuwait.** The UN approved military action in response (Nov. 1990), and an international military force, led by the U.S., bombed Iraq (Jan. 1991) and launched a land attack, crushing the invasion (Feb. 1991). After Iraq accepted a cease-fire (Apr. 1991), U.S. troops withdrew, but "no-fly" zones were set up over northern Iraq to protect the Kurds and over southern Iraq to protect Shiite Muslims. The **UN** imposed **sanctions** on Iraq for failure to abide by the cease-fire. Iraq's reported failure to cooperate with UN arms inspectors seeking to eliminate "weapons of mass destruction" led to repeated air strikes by the U.S. and Britain.

The last Western hostages were freed in **Lebanon,** June 1992. **Israel** and the **Palestine Liberation Organization** signed a peace accord (Sept. 1993) providing for Palestinian self-government in the West Bank and Gaza Strip. Prime Min. Yitzhak **Rabin** and Foreign Min. Shimon **Peres** of Israel and Yasir **Arafat** of the PLO received the Nobel Peace Prize for their efforts (1994). Six Arab nations relaxed their boycott against Israel (1994), and Israel and **Jordan** signed a peace treaty (Oct. 1994). **Rabin was assassinated** (Nov. 1995) by an Israeli opponent of the peace process. After new elections (May 1996), Benjamin Netanyahu as prime minister adopted a harder line in peace negotiations. **Arafat** was elected to the presidency of the Palestinian Authority (Jan. 1996). A long-delayed interim agreement (the Wye Memorandum) on Israel military withdrawal from part of the West Bank was reached Oct. 1998. A Labour government under Ehud **Barak** took power after May 1999 elections, but further progress in peace negotiations proved elusive.

King **Hussein** of Jordan died (Feb. 1999), to be succeeded by his son Abdullah.

Asia and the Pacific. Hong Kong was returned to **China** (July 1997) after 156 years as a British colony, and **Macao** reverted to Chinese sovereignty (Dec. 1999) after over 400 years of Portuguese rule. Both were to retain their legal and capitalist economic systems for 50 years. **Jiang Zemin**, general secretary of the Chinese Communist Party, assumed the additional post of president of China (Mar. 1993) and emerged as the key leader after the death of leader **Deng Xiaoping** (Feb. 1997). China released from prison—and exiled—some well-known dissidents but continued to be criticized for detentions and other alleged widespread **human rights abuses**. In Nov. 1999 the U.S. and China signed a landmark pact normalizing trade relations.

After years of prosperity, **Thailand, Indonesia**, and **South Korea** in 1997 began to suffer economic reverses that had a worldwide ripple effect. These countries received billion-dollar IMF bailout packages. In **Indonesia**, protests over mismanagement led to the resignation of Pres. **Suharto** (May 1998) after 32 years of nearly autocratic rule. Abdurraham Wahid was elected (Oct. 1999) in the country's first fully democratic elections. In a referendum (Aug. 1999), **East Timor** voted overwhelmingly for independence from Indonesia; pro-Indonesian militias then rampaged through the territory, but a multinational peacekeeping force was allowed in (Sept. 1999) to help restore order. In **South Korea**, former dissident **Kim Dae Jung** was elected president (Dec. 1997). Two previous presidents, Roh Tae Woo and Chun Doo Hwan, were convicted of crimes committed in office but were given amnesty by the new president.

In **Japan** members of a religious cult, released the nerve gas sarin on 5 Tokyo subway cars, killing 12 people and injuring more than 5,500 (Mar. 1995). Tamil rebels continued their armed conflict in **Sri Lanka**. In **Afghanistan** the **Taliban**, an extreme Islamic fundamentalist group, gained control of Kabul (Sept. 1996) and, eventually, most of the country. In **North Korea**, longtime dictator **Kim Il Sung** died (July 1994), to be succeeded by his son, **Kim Jong Il**. In the same year the country signed an agreement with the U.S. setting a timetable for North Korea to eliminate its nuclear program. The country also suffered a severe drought, and widespread starvation was feared.

India was beset by riots following destruction of a mosque by Hindu militants (Dec. 1992); Indian army troops repeatedly clashed with pro-independence demonstrators in the disputed Muslim region of **Kashmir**, exacerbating relations with **Pakistan**. Uneasy relations between India and Pakistan reached a new level when both nations conducted nuclear tests in 1998. Conflict in Pakistan between government and the military led to a bloodless coup (Oct. 1999).

Africa. South Africa was transformed as the white-dominated government abandoned **apartheid** and the country made the transition to a nonracial democratic government. Pres. F. W. **de Klerk** released Nelson **Mandela** from prison (Feb. 1990), after he had been held by the government for 27 years, and lifted a ban on the African National Congress. The white government repealed its apartheid laws (1990, 1991). **Mandela** was elected **president** (Apr. 1994), and a new constitution became law (Dec. 1996). Thabo **Mbeki**, the ANC's candidate to succeed Mandela, was overwhelmingly elected president in June 1999.

In **Nigeria**, Gen. Olusegun **Obasanjo** was elected president (Feb. 1999), to become the country's first civilian leader in 15 years.

The decades-long rule of **Mobutu** Sese Seko in **Zaire** came to an end (May 1997) at the hands of rebel forces led by Laurent **Kabila**; an ailing Mobutu fled the country and soon after died. Kabila changed the country's name back to **Democratic Republic of the Congo**; conditions remained unstable.

After the presidents of **Burundi** and **Rwanda** were killed in an airplane crash (Apr. 1994), violence erupted in Rwanda between Hutu and Tutsi factions; hundreds of thousands were slain. The conflict spread to refugee camps in neighboring Zaire and Burundi. Factional fighting also erupted in **Somalia** after Pres. Muhammad Siad Barre was ousted (Jan. 1991). The UN sent a U.S.-led **peacekeeping force**, but it was unsuccessful in restoring order. Some soldiers of the peacekeeping force were killed, including 23 Pakistanis (June 1993) and 18 U.S. Rangers (Oct. 1993). The UN ended its mission (Mar. 1995) with no durable government in place. **Liberia** endured factional fighting that lasted almost 5 years and claimed over 150,000 lives; a cease-fire was concluded in Aug. 1995. The World Health Organization reported (1995) that Africa accounted for 70% of **AIDS** cases worldwide.

A 16-year civil war appeared to end in **Angola** (May 1991) when the government signed a peace accord with the rebel UNITA faction. But despite the inauguration of a national unity government (Apr. 1997), insurgents continued to fight and gain territory. **Namibia** officially became independent in Mar. 1990. Claimed by South Africa since 1919 and placed under UN authority in 1971, it had long been a focus of colonial rivalries. In **Algeria,** the army cancelled a 2nd round of parliamentary elections (Jan. 1992) after the Islamic party won a first round. Islamic fundamentalists then began a terrorist campaign that, along with killings by pro-government squads, eventually claimed thousands of lives. A peace plan was worked out with the militants in 1999.

North America. The **North American Free Trade Agreement** (NAFTA), liberalizing trade between the United States, Canada, and Mexico, went into effect Jan. 1, 1994. In **Canada**, the Progressive Conservative Party suffered a crushing defeat in general elections (Oct. 1993), and liberal Jean **Chrétien** became prime minister. The map of Canada was altered in Apr. 1999 to create a new territory, **Nunavut,** out of an area that had been part of Northwest Territories.

In the **United States**' 1992 presidential election, Democrat Bill **Clinton** defeated Pres. George Bush, but in 1994 congressional elections Republicans gained control of Congress. Clinton reached agreement with Congress on measures to eliminate the federal budget deficit. Clinton won reelection in 1996; the new administration was plagued by scandals but remained popular amid continued economic prosperity. In Dec. 1998 **Clinton** was **impeached** by the U.S. House on charges related to the Monica Lewinsky scandal; he was **acquitted** by the Senate in Feb. 1999.

The U.S. Army and Navy were torn by sexual scandals involving abuse of women personnel. The **United States** suffered embarrassment with the discovery of espionage by CIA agents (Aldrich Ames, Harold Nicholson).

In **Mexico,** Ernesto **Zedillo** of the ruling PRI party was elected president (July 1994) after the party's first candidate was assassinated. The country soon faced a crisis affecting the value of the peso, but recovered with the help of a bailout package from the U.S. A peasant revolt spearheaded by the **Zapatista National Liberation Army** erupted in the state of Chiapas (Jan. 1994) and was suppressed.

Central America and the Caribbean. In **Haiti**, Jean-Bertrand **Aristide** was elected president (Dec. 1990) but was ousted in a military coup after 9 months in office. The UN approved a U.S.-led invasion to restore the elected leader; shortly before troops arrived, a delegation headed by former U.S. Pres. Jimmy Carter arranged (Sept. 1994) for the junta to step aside for Aristide, who served until 1996. In **Nicaragua**, Violetta Chamarro defeated Daniel **Ortega** in the presidential election (Feb. 1990), thus ousting the Sandinistas. In **Panama**, U.S. troops invaded and overthrew the government of Manuel **Noriega** (Dec. 1989), who was wanted on drug charges; Noriega was captured Jan. 1990. On Dec. 31, 1999, Panama assumed full control of the **Panama Canal**, in accord with a treaty with the U.S. In **El Salvador** (1992) and **Guatemala** (1996) the governments signed agreements with rebel factions aimed at ending long-running civil conflicts.

South America. Alberto **Fujimori** was elected president of **Peru** in June 1990 and, despite his suppression of the constitution (1992), was reelected in 1995. Peru succeeded in capturing (Sept. 1992) the leader of the **Shining Path** guerrilla movement. Leftist guerrillas took hostages at an ambassador's residence in Lima (Dec. 1996); one hostage was killed during a government assault rescuing the rest (Apr. 1997). Peronist Pres. Carlos Saúl **Menem** served as **Argentina**'s president for much of the decade (elected 1989, reelected 1995), imposing stringent economic measures; he was succeeded in 1999 by Fernando de la **Rúa**.

Former Chilean Pres. Gen. Augusto **Pinochet** continued to head the army until Mar. 1998; he was arrested in London (Oct. 1998) on human rights charges but was judged medically unfit for trial and returned to Chile (Mar. 2000).

In **Brazil**, Fernando Henrique **Cardoso** was elected president (Oct. 1994) and reelected in 1998 amid a growing economic slump; the IMF announced a $42 billion aid package (Nov. 1998). The first UN Conference on Environment and Development, or **Earth Summit**, was held (June 1992) in **Rio de Janeiro,** with delegates from 178 nations.

Terrorism and Crime. Terrorism, often linked to Mideastern sources and with the U.S. as object, continued. A terrorist bomb exploded in a garage beneath New York City's **World Trade Center**, killing 6 people (Feb. 1993). Bombings of a U.S. military training center (Nov. 1995) and a barracks holding U.S. airmen (June 1996), both in **Saudi Arabia,** killed 7 and 19, respectively. Bombs exploded outside **U.S. embassies** in Kenya and Tanzania, Aug. 1998, killing over 220 people; the U.S. retaliated with missiles fired at alleged terrorist-linked sites in Afghanistan and Sudan. The Alfred P. Murrah Federal Building in **Oklahoma City**, OK, was destroyed by a bomb that killed 168 people (Apr. 1995).

Science. The powerful **Hubble Space Telescope** was launched in Apr. 1990; flaws in its mirrors and solar panels were repaired by space-walking astronauts (Dec. 1993). U.S. space shuttle ***Atlantis*** docked with the orbiting Russian space station ***Mir*** (June 1995) in first of several joint missions in a spirit of post-Cold-War cooperation. In Nov. 1998 first component for a new **International Space Station** was launched into space from Kazakhstan.

Mir *and Shuttle* Atlantis

Scottish scientist Ian Wilmut announced (Feb. 1997) the **cloning** of a sheep, nicknamed Dolly—the first mammal successfully cloned from a cell from an adult animal.

Opening a New Century: 2000-2004

Terrorism. In Oct. 2000, 17 American sailors were killed aboard the **USS *Cole*** in Aden, **Yemen**, when a small boat exploded alongside it in a terrorist attack. On **Sept. 11, 2001**, hijackers crashed 2 jetliners into the twin towers of the **World Trade Center** in New York City and another into the **Pentagon** outside Washington, DC; a 4th crashed in a field in **Pennsylvania**. The attacks, which destroyed both towers and damaged the Pentagon, killed about 3,000 people, including all 265 aboard the planes. Saudi exile Osama bin Laden and his **al-Qaeda terrorist network**, based in **Afghanistan** and backed by the Taliban government there, emerged as responsible for the attacks. A U.S.-led military campaign launched in Oct. 2001 **ousted the Taliban**, and a transitional government was installed (Dec. 2001), although al-Qaeda remained active in some areas of Afghanistan and elsewhere, and Bin Laden remained at large.

Among incidents elsewhere, a bomb exploded in a truck outside a synagogue in **Tunisia** (Apr. 2002), killing 17 (including the driver). A car bomb on the Indonesian island of **Bali** (Oct. 2002) killed about 200, mostly foreign tourists; Muslim extremists were arrested. Chechen guerrillas seized a **Moscow movie theater** (Oct. 2002); more than 100 hostages were killed in a subsequent raid by Russian troops. A terrorist explosion in **Moscow subways** killed 39 (Feb. 2004), and 89 died when 2 Russian planes were destroyed apparently by bombs (Aug. 2004). Chechen guerrillas took over a **Beslan, Russia, school**; 330 hostages, many students, and 31 guerrillas were killed in the standoff (Sept. 2004). The bombing of an Israeli-owned **hotel in Kenya** (Nov. 2002) killed 13 (including the 3 bombers). Suicide attacks against Western targets in **Riyadh**, Saudi Arabia (May 2003), killed 34 people (including 9 attackers). Suicide bombings in **Istanbul**, Turkey (Nov. 2003), hit two Jewish synagogues and British targets, killing about 60 people in all. Four **commuter trains were bombed** in Madrid, Spain, killing 202 (Mar. 2004); elections held a week later ousted Spain's premier.

War in Iraq. The U.S., with Great Britain, launched an **invasion of Iraq** (Mar. 2003), aimed at ousting the dictatorial regime of **Saddam Hussein**. Troops took control of Baghdad and other cities, and Pres. Bush declared major combat ended, May 1, but **insurgents** caused continuing casualties among troops and civilians. Searches for **weapons of mass destruction**, cited as major grounds for the invasion, yielded no evidence. **Saddam Hussein** was eventually **captured** (Dec. 2003), as well as other regime leaders, to be put on trial by Iraqis. An interim gov't was installed (June 2004). Evidence that U.S. soldiers at **Abu Ghraib** prison in Iraq abused detainees arose in Apr. 2004. U.S. military deaths topped 1,000 (Sept. 2004) as attacks by insurgents continued; despite threats by insurgents, Iraqis turned out in large numbers to vote in national elections (Jan. 2005).

Middle East. Violence between Israelis and Palestinians escalated, with **suicide bombings** by Palestinians and retaliation by Israeli armed forces, the peace process languished. Likud leader Ariel **Sharon** was **elected** prime minister of Israel (Feb. 2001). In reponse to Palestinian suicide attacks that killed 26, Israeli forces stormed the compound of Palestinian leader Yasir Arafat (Mar. 2002), keeping him confined there until early May. **Arafat died** in a Paris hospital (Nov. 2004) and was succeeded by Mahmoud Abbas following elections. The U.S., Russia, UN, and European Union formally initiated (Apr. 2003) a "**road map**" plan for Israeli-Palestinian **peace negotiations**, but little progress was made. Syrian Pres. Hafez al-**Assad died** (June 2000); succeeded by his son. Iran was censured (Dec. 2003) by the UN Intl. Atomic Energy Agency for covering up aspects of its nuclear weapons program.

Europe. In Oct. 2000, Yugoslav strongman Slobodan **Milosevic yielded** power to Vojislav Kostunica, who had declared himself president in the face of anti-Milosevic protests after a disputed election. Milosevic surrendered to Serbian authorities; in Feb. 2002 he went on trial for **war crimes** allegedly committed during 1990s ethnic conflicts in the Balkans. The first-ever **Concorde jet crash**, near Paris, killed 113 people (July 2000). The Russian nuclear sub ***Kursk* sank** in the Barents Sea, killing 118 crew members.

By early 2002 the **euro** was the common currency in 12 European Union nations. The EU admitted 10 Eastern European nations (May 2004). Some 35,000 people across Europe, including over 11,000 in France, reportedly died in 2003 **summer heat waves**.

Russia. The Russian nuclear sub ***Kursk* sank** in the Barents Sea (Aug. 2000) killing 118 crew members. Vladimir Putin, reelected in Mar. 2004, signed legislation ending popular election of governors (Dec. 2004).

Asia. South Korean Pres. **Kim Dae Jung** and **North Korean** ruler **Kim Jong Il** held a **summit** meeting and agreed to seek peace and reunification (June 2000), but tensions rose after North Korea admitted conducting a covert nuclear weapons development program (Oct. 2002). **Nepal**'s King **Birendra** and other Nepal royals were shot to death inside the palace, apparently by Crown Prince Dipendra, who then killed himself (June 2001). **Chinese** Pres. Jiang Zemin and **Russian** Pres. Vladimir Putin signed a **friendship treaty** (July 2001). With Jiang's retirement **Hu Jintao** was named as China's new Communist party chief (Nov. 2002) and president (Mar. 2003).

North Korea **withdrew** (Jan. 2003) from the Nuclear Nonproliferation Treaty; multi-nation talks were held in Beijing (Aug. 2003) about the status of its **nuclear program**. Pakistan and India **restored diplomatic ties** (May 2003) and declared a **cease-fire** in disputed territory (Nov. 2003). Pakistani Pres. Gen. Pervez Musharraf twice **escaped assassination** by Islamic militants (Dec. 2003). Afghanistan held its first presidential elections and selected Hamid Karzai (Oct.-Nov 2004). A massive **tsunami** in the Indian Ocean (Dec. 2004) devastated parts of Indonesia, Thailand, India, Sri Lanka, and other Asian and African nations and left some 200,000 dead.

Africa. The 13th International **AIDS Conference**, held in Durban, South Africa (July 2000), focused on ways of controlling surging AIDS rates in developing countries. **Ethiopia** and **Eritrea** signed a **peace treaty** (Dec. 2000). Laurent **Kabila**, president of the Democratic Republic of the **Congo**, was **shot to death** by a bodyguard (Jan. 2001). Liberian Pres. Charles Taylor went into voluntary exile (Aug. 2003) as part of a deal to end a 14-year-old civil war; other accords were reached aimed at **ending civil wars** in Angola (Apr. 2002) and Côte d'Ivoire (Jan. 2003).

A peace agreement in the Dem. Rep. of **Congo** (Apr. 2003) did not end violence there. Civil war between the Muslim-led government and rebels from Christian areas in **Sudan** continued, with massive casualties. Sudanese government-backed militias (janjaweed) in the Darfur region were accused of displacing 2 mil. people in acts bordering on genocide. Zimbabwean Pres. Robert Mugabe pulled his country out of the **Commonwealth** (Dec. 2003) after the group reaffirmed suspension of **Zimbabwe** for alleged fraud in the 2002 election. **Libya** agreed (Dec. 2003) to abandon programs pursuing weapons of mass destruction.

Americas and the Caribbean. Vicente **Fox** of the center-right National Action Party (PAN) was elected **president of Mexico** (July 2000), in a historic defeat for the long-supreme Institutional Revolutionary Party (PRI). Peruvian Pres. Alberto **Fujimori stepped down** during his 3rd term (Nov. 2000), amid scandal, and did not seek reelection. In Jan. 2001, George W. **Bush** was inaugurated as U.S. president, after one of the tightest and most controversial elections in U.S. history; he was reelected in Nov. 2004. Venezuelan Pres. Hugo Chavez regained power after 48-hr. coup (Dec. 2002). Argentina's **record default** on International Monetary Fund loans resulted (Sept. 2003) in a **$12.5 billion debt-refinancing** agreement. **Haiti** was wracked by anti-govenment protests (leading to the resignation of Jean-Bertrand **Aristide** in Feb. 2004).

Paul Martin succeeded Jean Chrétien as **Canadian prime minister** (Dec. 2003) after he was elected to lead the ruling Liberal Party. He lost his majority in June 2004 but remained prime minister of the minority government.

Space. The U.S. space shuttle ***Columbia*** broke up on reentering Earth's atmosphere Feb. 1, 2003, killing all 7 crew members.

International. Negotiators from 178 countries agreed to adopt the **Kyoto Protocol**, calling for a reduction of greenhouse gases in developed nations (July 2001).

WORLD ALMANAC QUICK QUIZ

How long ago is it believed that the first humans came to the Americas across a land bridge from Asia?

(a) 900-1,200 years ago (b) 14,000-18,000 years ago
(c) about 200,000 years ago (d) they actually came from Scandinavia

For the answer look in this chapter, or see page 1008.

HISTORICAL FIGURES

Ancient Greeks and Romans

Greeks

Aeschines, orator, 389-314 BC
Aeschylus, dramatist, 525-456 BC
Aesop, fableist, c620-c560 BC
Alcibiades, politician, 450-404 BC
Anacreon, poet, c582-c485 BC
Anaxagoras, philosopher, c500-428 BC
Anaximander, philosopher, 611-546 BC
Anaximenes, philosopher, c570-500 BC
Antiphon, speechwriter, c480-411 BC
Apollonius, mathematician, c265-170 BC
Archimedes, math., 287-212 BC
Aristophanes, dramatist, c448-380 BC
Aristotle, philosopher, 384-322 BC
Athenaeus, scholar, fl. c200
Callicrates, architect, fl. 5th cent. BC
Callimachus, poet, c305-240 BC
Cratinus, comic dramatist, 520-421 BC
Democritus, philosopher, c460-370 BC
Demosthenes, orator, 384-322 BC
Diodorus, historian, fl. 20 BC
Diogenes, philosopher, 372-c287 BC
Dionysius, historian, d. c7 BC
Empedocles, philosopher, c490-430 BC
Epicharmus, dramatist, c530-440 BC
Epictetus, philosopher, c55-c135
Epicurus, philosopher, 341-270 BC
Eratosthenes, scientist, 276-194 BC
Euclid, mathematician, fl. c300 BC
Euripides, dramatist, c484-406 BC
Galen, physician, 130-200
Heraclitus, philosopher, c540-c475 BC
Herodotus, historian, c484-420 BC
Hesiod, poet, 8th cent. BC
Hippocrates, physician, c460-377 BC
Homer, poet, fl. c700 BC(?)
Isocrates, orator, 436-338 BC
Menander, dramatist, 342-292 BC
Parmenides, philosopher, b. c515 BC
Pericles, statesman, c495-429 BC
Phidias, sculptor, c500-435 BC
Pindar, poet, c518-c438 BC
Plato, philosopher, c428-347 BC
Plutarch, biographer, c46-120
Polybius, historian, c200-c118 BC
Praxiteles, sculptor, 400-330 BC
Pythagoras, phil., math., c580-c500 BC
Sappho, poet, c610-c580 BC
Simonides, poet, 556-c468 BC
Socrates, philosopher, 469-399 BC
Solon, statesman, 640-560 BC
Sophocles, dramatist, c496-406 BC
Strabo, geographer, c63 BC-AD 24
Thales, philosopher, c634-546 BC
Themistocles, politician, c524-c460 BC
Theocritus, poet, c310-250 BC
Theophrastus, phil., c372-c287 BC
Thucydides, historian, fl. 5th cent. BC
Timon, philosopher, c320-c230 BC
Xenophon, historian, c434-c355 BC
Zeno, philosopher, c335-c263 BC

Romans

Ammianus, historian, c330-395
Apuleius, satirist, c124-c170
Boethius, scholar, c480-524
Caesar, Julius, leader, 100-44 BC
Catiline, politician, c108-62 BC
Cato (Elder), statesman, 234-149 BC
Catullus, poet, c84-54 BC
Cicero, orator, 106-43 BC
Claudian, poet, c370-c404
Ennius, poet, 239-170 BC
Gellius, author, c130-c165
Horace, poet, 65-8 BC
Juvenal, satirist, 60-127
Livy, historian, 59 BC-AD 17
Lucan, poet, 39-65
Lucilius, poet, c180-c102 BC
Lucretius, poet, c99-c55 BC
Martial, epigrammatist, c38-c103
Nepos, historian, c100-c25 BC
Ovid, poet, 43 BC-AD 17
Persius, satirist, 34-62
Plautus, dramatist, c254-c184 BC
Pliny the Elder, scholar, 23-79
Pliny the Younger, author, 62-113
Quintilian, rhetorician, c35-c97
Sallust, historian, 86-34 BC
Seneca, philosopher, 4 BC-AD 65
Silius, poet, c25-101
Statius, poet, c45-c96
Suetonius, biographer, c69-c122
Tacitus, historian, 56-120
Terence, dramatist, 185-c159 BC
Tibullus, poet, c55-c19 BC
Vergil, poet, 70-19 BC
Vitruvius, architect, fl. 1st cent. BC

Rulers of England and Great Britain

ENGLAND

Name		Reign Began	Died	Death Age	Years Reigned
	Saxons and Danes				
Egbert	King of Wessex, won allegiance of all English	**829**	**839**	—	10
Ethelwulf	Son, King of Wessex, Sussex, Kent, Essex	**839**	**858**	—	19
Ethelbald	Son of Ethelwulf, displaced father in Wessex	**858**	**860**	—	2
Ethelbert	2nd son of Ethelwulf, united Kent and Wessex	**860**	**866**	—	6
Ethelred I	3rd son, King of Wessex, fought Danes	**866**	**871**	—	5
Alfred	The Great, 4th son, defeated Danes, fortified London	**871**	**899**	52	28
Edward	The Elder, Alfred's son, united English, claimed Scotland	**899**	**924**	55	25
Athelstan	The Glorious, Edward's son, King of Mercia, Wessex	**924**	**940**	45	16
Edmund	3rd son of Edward, King of Wessex, Mercia	**940**	**946**	25	6
Edred	4th son of Edward	**946**	**955**	32	9
Edwy	The Fair, eldest son of Edmund, King of Wessex	**955**	**959**	18	3
Edgar	The Peaceful, 2nd son of Edmund, ruled all English	**959**	**975**	32	17
Edward	The Martyr, eldest son of Edgar, murdered by stepmother	**975**	**978**	17	4
Ethelred II	The Unready, 2nd son of Edgar, married Emma of Normandy	**978**	**1016**	48	37
Edmund II	Ironside, son of Ethelred II, King of London	**1016**	**1016**	27	0
Canute	The Dane, gave Wessex to Edmund, married Emma	**1016**	**1035**	40	19
Harold I	Harefoot, natural son of Canute	**1035**	**1040**	—	5
Hardecanute	Son of Canute by Emma, Danish King	**1040**	**1042**	24	2
Edward	The Confessor, son of Ethelred II (canonized 1161)	**1042**	**1066**	62	24
Harold II	Edward's brother-in-law, last Saxon King	**1066**	**1066**	44	0
	House of Normandy				
William I	The Conqueror, defeated Harold at Hastings	**1066**	**1087**	60	21
William II	Rufus, 3rd son of William I, killed by arrow	**1087**	**1100**	43	13
Henry I	Beauclerc, youngest son of William I	**1100**	**1135**	67	35
	House of Blois				
Stephen	Son of Adela, daughter of William I, and Count of Blois	**1135**	**1154**	50	19
	House of Plantagenet				
Henry II	Son of Geoffrey Plantagenet (Angevin) by Matilda, daughter of Henry I	**1154**	**1189**	56	35
Richard I	Coeur de Lion, son of Henry II, crusader	**1189**	**1199**	42	10
John	Lackland, son of Henry II, approved Magna Carta, 1215	**1199**	**1216**	50	17
Henry III	Son of John, acceded at 9, under regency until 1227	**1216**	**1272**	65	56
Edward I	Son of Henry III	**1272**	**1307**	68	35
Edward II	Son of Edward I, deposed by Parliament, 1327	**1307**	**1327**	43	20
Edward III	Of Windsor, son of Edward II	**1327**	**1377**	65	50
Richard II	Grandson of Edward III, minor until 1389, deposed 1399	**1377**	**1400**	33	22

IT'S A FACT: England's series of civil wars between ruling families (1455-85) was later dubbed the "War of the Roses," after the white rose insignias worn by those supporting the House of Lancaster and the red rose insignias worn by armies of the House of York.

Name	House of Lancaster	Reign Began	Died	Death Age	Years Reigned
Henry IV	Son of John of Gaunt, Duke of Lancaster, son of Edward III	**1399**	**1413**	47	13
Henry V	Son of Henry IV, victor of Agincourt	**1413**	**1422**	34	9
Henry VI	Son of Henry V, deposed 1461, died in Tower	**1422**	**1471**	49	39
	House of York				
Edward IV	Great-great-grandson of Edward III, son of Duke of York	**1461**	**1483**	40	22
Edward V	Son of Edward IV, murdered in Tower of London	**1483**	**1483**	13	0
Richard III	Brother of Edward IV, fell at Bosworth Field	**1483**	**1485**	32	2
	House of Tudor				
Henry VII	Son of Edmund Tudor, Earl of Richmond, whose father had married the widow of Henry V; descended from Edward III through his mother, Margaret Beaufort, via John of Gaunt. By marrying daughter of Edward IV united Lancaster and York	**1485**	**1509**	53	24
Henry VIII	Son of Henry VII, by Elizabeth, daughter of Edward IV	**1509**	**1547**	56	38
Edward VI	Son of Henry VIII, by Jane Seymour, his 3rd queen. Ruled under regents. Was forced to name Lady Jane Grey his successor. Council of State proclaimed her queen July 10, 1553. Mary Tudor won Council, was proclaimed queen July 19, 1553. Mary had Lady Jane Grey beheaded for treason, Feb. 1554	**1547**	**1553**	16	6
Mary I	Daughter of Henry VIII, by Catherine of Aragon	**1553**	**1558**	43	5
Elizabeth I	Daughter of Henry VIII, by Anne Boleyn	**1558**	**1603**	69	44
	GREAT BRITAIN				
	House of Stuart				
James I	James VI of Scotland, son of Mary, Queen of Scots. *First to call himself King of Great Britain. This became official with the Act of Union, 1707*	**1603**	**1625**	59	22
Charles I	Only surviving son of James I; beheaded Jan. 30, 1649	**1625**	**1649**	48	24
	Commonwealth, 1649–1660				
	Council of State, 1649; Protectorate, 1653[1]				
The Cromwells	Oliver Cromwell, Lord Protector	**1653**	**1658**	59	5
	Richard Cromwell, son, Lord Protector, resigned May 25, 1659	**1658**	**1712**	86	1
	House of Stuart (Restored)				
Charles II	Eldest son of Charles I, died without issue	**1660**	**1685**	55	25
James II	2nd son of Charles I. Deposed 1688. Interregnum 1688-1689	**1685**	**1701**	68	3
William III	Son of William, Prince of Orange, by Mary, daughter of Charles I	**1689**	**1702**	51	13
and Mary II	Eldest daughter of James II and wife of William III	**1689**	**1694**	33	6
Anne	2nd daughter of James II	**1702**	**1714**	49	12
	House of Hanover				
George I	Son of Elector of Hanover, by Sophia, granddaughter of James I	**1714**	**1727**	67	13
George II	Only son of George I, married Caroline of Brandenburg	**1727**	**1760**	77	33
George III	Grandson of George II, married Charlotte of Mecklenburg	**1760**	**1820**	81	59
George IV	Eldest son of George III, Prince Regent, from Feb. 1811	**1820**	**1830**	67	10
William IV	3rd son of George III, married Adelaide of Saxe-Meiningen	**1830**	**1837**	71	7
Victoria	Daughter of Edward, 4th son of George III; married (1840) Prince Albert of Saxe-Coburg and Gotha, who became Prince Consort	**1837**	**1901**	81	63
	House of Saxe-Coburg and Gotha				
Edward VII	Eldest son of Victoria, married Alexandra, Princess of Denmark	**1901**	**1910**	68	9
	House of Windsor[2]				
George V	2nd son of Edward VII, married Princess Mary of Teck	**1910**	**1936**	70	25
Edward VIII	Eldest son of George V; acceded Jan. 20, 1936, abdicated Dec. 11, 1936	**1936**	**1972**	77	1
George VI	2nd son of George V; married Lady Elizabeth Bowes-Lyon	**1936**	**1952**	56	15
Elizabeth II	Elder daughter of George VI, acceded Feb. 6, 1952	**1952**			

— = age/birth date not certain. (1) The Cromwells ruled Britain following overthow of the monarchy in 1649. (2) Name adopted by proclamation of George V, July 17, 1917.

Rulers of Scotland

Kenneth I MacAlpin was the first Scot to rule both Scots and Picts, AD 846.

Duncan I was the first general ruler, 1034. Macbeth seized the kingdom 1040, was slain by Duncan's son, Malcolm III MacDuncan (Canmore), 1057.

Malcolm married Margaret, Saxon princess who had fled from the Normans. Queen Margaret introduced English language and monastic customs. She was canonized, 1250. Her son Edgar, 1097, moved the court to Edinburgh. His brothers Alexander I and David I succeeded. Malcolm IV, the Maiden, 1153, grandson of David I, was followed by his brother, William the Lion, 1165, whose son was Alexander II, 1214. The latter's son, Alexander III, 1249, defeated the Norse and regained the Hebrides. When he died, 1286, his granddaughter, Margaret, child of Eric of Norway and grandniece of Edward I of England, known as the Maid of Norway, was chosen ruler, but died 1290, aged 8.

John Baliol, 1292-1296. (Interregnum, 10 years.)

Robert Bruce (The Bruce), 1306-1329, victor at Bannockburn, 1314. David II, his only son, 1329-1371.

Robert II, 1371-1390, grandson of Robert Bruce, son of Walter, the Steward of Scotland, was called The Steward, first of the so-called Stuart line.

Robert III, son of Robert II, 1390-1406.

James I, son of Robert III, 1406-1437.

James II, son of James I, 1437-1460.

James III, eldest son of James II, 1460-1488.

James IV, eldest son of James III, 1488-1513.

James V, eldest son of James IV, 1513-1542.

Mary, daughter of James V, b. 1542, became queen at 1 week old; crowned 1543. Married, 1558, Francis, son of Henry II of France, who became king 1559, d. 1560. Mary ruled Scots 1561 until abdication, 1567. She also married Henry Stewart, Lord Darnley (1565), and James, Earl of Bothwell (1567). Imprisoned by Elizabeth I; beheaded 1587.

James VI, 1566-1625, son of Mary and Lord Darnley, became King of England on death of Elizabeth in 1603. Although the thrones were thus united, the legislative union of Scotland and England was not effected until the Act of Union, May 1, 1707.

WORLD ALMANAC QUICK QUIZ

Which French monarch was known as the "citizen king"?

(a) Henry IV (c) Louis-Philippe

(b) Louis XIV (d) Napoleon III

For the answer look in this chapter, or see page 1008.

Prime Ministers of Great Britain

Designations in parentheses describe each government;
W=Whig; T=Tory; Cl=Coalition; P=Peelite; Li=Liberal; C=Conservative[1]; La=Labour.

Sir Robert Walpole (W)[2]	1721-1742
Earl of Wilmington (W)	1742-1743
Henry Pelham (W)	1743-1754
Duke of Newcastle (W)	1754-1756
Duke of Devonshire (W)	1756-1757
Duke of Newcastle (W)	1757-1762
Earl of Bute (T)	1762-1763
George Grenville (W)	1763-1765
Marquess of Rockingham (W)	1765-1766
William Pitt the Elder (Earl of Chatham) (W)	1766-1768
Duke of Grafton (W)	1768-1770
Frederick North (Lord North) (T)	1770-1782
Marquess of Rockingham (W)	1782
Earl of Shelburne (W)	1782-1783
Duke of Portland (Cl)	1783
William Pitt the Younger (T)	1783-1801
Henry Addington (T)	1801-1804
William Pitt the Younger (T)	1804-1806
William Wyndham Grenville, Baron Grenville (W)	1806-1807
Duke of Portland (T)	1807-1809
Spencer Perceval (T)	1809-1812
Earl of Liverpool (T)	1812-1827
George Canning (T)	1827
Viscount Goderich (T)	1827-1828
Duke of Wellington (T)	1828-1830
Earl Grey (W)	1830-1834
Viscount Melbourne (W)	1834
Sir Robert Peel (C)	1834-1835
Viscount Melbourne (W)	1835-1841
Sir Robert Peel (C)	1841-1846
Lord (later Earl) John Russell (W)	1846-1852
Earl of Derby (C)	1852
Earl of Aberdeen (P)	1852-1855
Viscount Palmerston (Li)	1855-1858
Earl of Derby (C)	1858-1859
Viscount Palmerston (Li)	1859-1865
Earl Russell (Li)	1865-1866
Earl of Derby (C)	1866-1868
Benjamin Disraeli (C)	1868
William E. Gladstone (Li)	1868-1874
Benjamin Disraeli (C)	1874-1880
William E. Gladstone (Li)	1880-1885
Marquess of Salisbury (C)	1885-1886
William E. Gladstone (Li)	1886
Marquess of Salisbury (C)	1886-1892
William E. Gladstone (Li)	1892-1894
Earl of Rosebery (Li)	1894-1895
Marquess of Salisbury (C)	1895-1902
Arthur J. Balfour (C)	1902-1905
Sir Henry Campbell Bannerman (Li)	1905-1908
Herbert H. Asquith (Li)	1908-1915
Herbert H. Asquith (Cl)	1915-1916
David Lloyd George (Cl)	1916-1922
Andrew Bonar Law (C)	1922-1923
Stanley Baldwin (C)	1923-1924
James Ramsay MacDonald (La)	1924
Stanley Baldwin (C)	1924-1929
James Ramsay MacDonald (La)	1929-1931
James Ramsay MacDonald (Cl)	1931-1935
Stanley Baldwin (Cl)	1935-1937
Neville Chamberlain (Cl)	1937-1940
Winston Churchill (Cl)	1940-1945
Winston Churchill (C)	1945
Clement Attlee (La)	1945-1951
Sir Winston Churchill (C)	1951-1955
Sir Anthony Eden (C)	1955-1957
Harold Macmillan (C)	1957-1963
Sir Alec Douglas-Home (C)	1963-1964
Harold Wilson (La)	1964-1970
Edward Heath (C)	1970-1974
Harold Wilson (La)	1974-1976
James Callaghan (La)	1976-1979
Margaret Thatcher (C)	1979-1990
John Major (C)	1990-1997
Tony Blair (La)	1997-

(1) The Conservative Party was formed in 1834, an outgrowthof the Tory party. (2) Walpole is commonly regarded as the first prime minister of Britain, though the title was not commonly used then and did not become official until 1905.

Rulers of France: Kings, Queens, Presidents

Caesar to Charlemagne

Julius Caesar subdued the Gauls, native tribes of Gaul (France), 58 to 51 BC. The Romans ruled 500 years. The Franks, a Teutonic tribe, reached the Somme from the East c. AD 250. By the 5th century the Merovingian Franks ousted the Romans. In 451, with the help of Visigoths, Burgundians, and others, they defeated Attila and the Huns at Chalons-sur-Marne.

Childeric I became leader of the Merovingians 458. His son Clovis I (Chlodwig, Ludwig, Louis), crowned 481, founded the dynasty. After defeating the Alemanni (Germans) 496, he was baptized a Christian and made Paris his capital. His line ruled until Childeric III was deposed, 751.

The West Merovingians were called Neustrians, the eastern Austrasians. Pepin of Herstal (687-714), major domus, or head of the palace, of Austrasia, took over Neustria as dux (leader) of the Franks. Pepin's son, Charles, called Martel (the Hammer), defeated the Saracens at Tours-Poitiers, 732; was succeeded by his son, Pepin the Short, 741, who deposed Childeric III and ruled as king until 768.

His son, Charlemagne, or Charles the Great (742-814), became king of the Franks, 768, with his brother Carloman, who died 771. Charlemagne ruled France, Germany, parts of Italy, Spain, and Austria, and enforced Christianity. Crowned Emperor of the Romans by Pope Leo III in St. Peter's, Rome, Dec. 25, 800. Succeeded by son, Louis I the Pious, 814. At death, 840, Louis left empire to sons, Lothair (Roman emperor); Pepin I (king of Aquitaine); Louis II (of Germany); Charles the Bald (France). They quarreled and, by the peace of Verdun, 843, divided the empire.

The date preceding each entry is year of accession.

The Carolingians

843 Charles I (the Bald); Roman Emperor, 875
877 Louis II (the Stammerer), son
879 Louis III (died 882) and Carloman, brothers
885 Charles II (the Fat); Roman Emperor, 881
888 Eudes (Odo), elected by nobles
898 Charles III (the Simple), son of Louis II, defeated by
922 Robert, brother of Eudes, killed in war
923 Rudolph (Raoul), Duke of Burgundy
936 Louis IV, son of Charles III
954 Lothair, son, aged 13, defeated by Capet
986 Louis V (the Sluggard), left no heirs

The Capets

987 Hugh Capet, son of Hugh the Great
996 Robert II (the Wise), his son
1031 Henry I, son
1060 Philip I (the Fair), son
1108 Louis VI (the Fat), son
1137 Louis VII (the Younger), son
1180 Philip II (Augustus), son, crowned at Reims
1223 Louis VIII (the Lion), son
1226 Louis IX, son, crusader; Louis IX (1214-1270) reigned 44 years, arbitrated disputes with English King Henry III; led crusades, 1248 (captured in Egypt 1250) and 1270, when he died of plague in Tunis. Canonized 1297 as St. Louis.
1270 Philip III (the Hardy), son
1285 Philip IV (the Fair), son, king at 17
1314 Louis X (the Headstrong), son. His posthumous son, John I, lived only 7 days
1316 Philip V (the Tall), brother of Louis X
1322 Charles IV (the Fair), brother of Louis X

House of Valois

1328 Philip VI (of Valois), grandson of Philip III
1350 John II (the Good), his son, retired to England
1364 Charles V (the Wise), son
1380 Charles VI (the Beloved), son
1422 Charles VII (the Victorious), son. In 1429 Joan of Arc (Jeanne d'Arc) promised Charles to oust the English, who occupied northern France. Joan won at Orleans and Patay and had Charles crowned at Reims, July 17, 1429. Joan was captured May 24, 1430, and executed May 30, 1431, at Rouen for heresy. Charles ordered her rehabilitation, effected 1455.
1461 Louis XI (the Cruel), son, civil reformer
1483 Charles VIII (the Affable), son

IT'S A FACT: Louis XVII, son of Louis XVI and Marie Antoinette, was imprisoned in Paris with his family during the French Revolution. After his father was beheaded in 1793, he was proclaimed king by royalists, but he remained in prison, where he died in 1795 at the age of 10. There was a legend he had escaped and survived, and more than 30 people later claimed to be "the lost dauphin." However, DNA tests conducted in 2000 on a preserved heart believed to be his and on hair samples from his mother confirmed that the child who died in prison was Louis XVII.

1498 Louis XII, great-grandson of Charles V

1515 Francis I, of Angouleme, nephew, son-in-law. Francis I (1494-1547) reigned 32 years, fought 4 big wars, was patron of the arts, aided Cellini, del Sarto, Leonardo da Vinci, Rabelais, embellished Fontainebleau.

1547 Henry II, son, killed at a joust in a tournament. He was the husband of Catherine de Medicis (1519-1589) and the lover of Diane de Poitiers (1499-1566). Catherine was born in Florence, daughter of Lorenzo de Medici. By her marriage to Henry II she became the mother of Francis II, Charles IX, Henry III, and Queen Margaret (Reine Margot), wife of Henry IV. She persuaded Charles IX to order the massacre of Huguenots on the Feast of St. Bartholomew, Aug. 24, 1572, six days after her daughter was married to Henry of Navarre.

1559 Francis II, son. In 1548, Mary, Queen of Scots since infancy, was betrothed when 6 to Francis, aged 4. They were married 1558. Francis died 1560, aged 16; Mary ruled Scotland, abdicated 1567.

1560 Charles IX, brother

1574 Henry III, brother, assassinated

House of Bourbon

1589 Henry IV, of Navarre, assassinated. Henry IV made enemies when he gave tolerance to Protestants by Edict of Nantes, 1598. He was grandson of Queen Margaret of Navarre, literary patron. He married Margaret of Valois, daughter of Henry II and Catherine de Medicis; was divorced; in 1600 married Marie de Medicis, who became Regent of France, 1610-1617, for her son, Louis XIII, but was exiled by Richelieu, 1631.

1610 Louis XIII (the Just), son. Louis XIII (1601-1643) married Anne of Austria. He came to be dominated by his chief minister (1622-42), Cardinal Richelieu.

1643 Louis XIV ("the Sun King"), son. Louis XIV was king 72 years. Until 1661, Anne of Austria was regent, with Cardinal Mazarin as chief minister; after that, Louis ruled absolutely. Known for his lavish court and patronage of the arts, he exhausted a prosperous country in wars for thrones and territory.

1715 Louis XV, great-grandson. Louis XV married a Polish princess; lost Canada to the English. His favorites, Mme. Pompadour and Mme. Du Barry, influenced policies. Noted for saying "After me, the deluge."

1774 Louis XVI, grandson; married Marie Antoinette, daughter of Empress Maria Therese of Austria. King and queen beheaded by Revolution, 1793. Their son, called Louis XVII, died in prison, never ruled.

First Republic

1792 National Convention of the French Revolution

1795 Directory, under Barras and others

1799 Consulate, Napoleon Bonaparte, first consul. Elected consul for life, 1802.

First Empire

1804 Napoleon I (Napoleon Bonaparte), emperor. Josephine (de Beauharnais), empress, 1804-1809; Marie Louise, empress, 1810-1814. Her son, Francois (1811-1832), titular King of Rome, later Duke de Reichstadt and "Napoleon II," never ruled. Napoleon abdicated 1814, died 1821.

Bourbons Restored

1814 Louis XVIII, king; brother of Louis XVI

1824 Charles X, brother; reactionary; deposed by the July Revolution, 1830

House of Orleans

1830 Louis-Philippe, the "citizen king"

Second Republic

1848 Louis Napoleon Bonaparte, president, nephew of Napoleon I.

Second Empire

1852 Napoleon III (Louis Napoleon Bonaparte), emperor; Eugenie (de Montijo), empress. Lost Franco-Prussian war, deposed 1870. Son, Prince Imperial (1856-1879), died in Zulu War. Eugenie died 1920.

Third Republic—Presidents

1871 Thiers, Louis Adolphe (1797-1877)
1873 MacMahon, Marshal Patrice M. de (1808-1893)
1879 Grevy, Paul J. (1807-1891)
1887 Sadi-Carnot, M. (1837-1894), assassinated
1894 Casimir-Perier, Jean P. P. (1847-1907)
1895 Faure, François Felix (1841-1899)
1899 Loubet, Emile (1838-1929)
1906 Fallieres, C. Armand (1841-1931)
1913 Poincare, Raymond (1860-1934)
1920 Deschanel, Paul (1856-1922)
1920 Millerand, Alexandre (1859-1943)
1924 Doumergue, Gaston (1863-1937)
1931 Doumer, Paul (1857-1932), assassinated
1932 Lebrun, Albert (1871-1950), resigned 1940
1940 Vichy govt. under German armistice: Henri Philippe Petain (1856-1951), Chief of State, 1940-1944.

Provisional govt. after liberation: Charles de Gaulle (1890-1970), Oct. 1944-Jan. 21, 1946; Felix Gouin (1884-1977), Jan. 23, 1946; Georges Bidault (1899-1983), June 24, 1946.

Fourth Republic—Presidents

1947 Auriol, Vincent (1884-1966)
1954 Coty, Rene (1882-1962)

Fifth Republic—Presidents

1959 De Gaulle, Charles Andre J. M. (1890-1970)
1969 Pompidou, Georges (1911-1974)
1974 Giscard d'Estaing, Valery (1926-)
1981 Mitterrand, François (1916-1996)
1995 Chirac, Jacques (1932-)

Rulers of Middle Europe; Rise and Fall of Dynasties; Rulers of Germany

Carolingian Dynasty

Charles the Great, or Charlemagne, ruled France, Italy, and Middle Europe; established Ostmark (later Austria); crowned Roman emperor by pope in Rome, AD 800; died 814.

Louis I (Ludwig) the Pious, son; crowned by Charlemagne 814; died 840.

Louis II, the German, son; succeeded to East Francia (Germany) 843-876.

Charles the Fat, son; inherited East Francia and West Francia (France) 876, reunited empire, crowned emperor by pope 881, deposed 887.

Arnulf, nephew, 887-899. Partition of empire.

Louis the Child, 899-911, last direct descendant of Charlemagne.

Conrad I, duke of Franconia, first elected German king, 911-918, founded House of Franconia.

Saxon Dynasty; First Reich

Henry I, the Fowler, duke of Saxony, 919-936.

Otto I, the Great, 936-973, son; crowned Holy Roman Emperor by pope, 962.

Otto II, 973-983, son; failed to oust Greeks and Arabs from Sicily.

Otto III, 983-1002, son; crowned emperor at 16.

Henry II, the Saint, duke of Bavaria, 1002-1024, great-grandson of Otto the Great.

House of Franconia

Conrad II, 1024-1039, elected king of Germany.

Henry III, the Black, 1039-1056, son; deposed 3 popes; annexed Burgundy.

Henry IV, 1056-1106, son; regency by his mother, Agnes of Poitou. Banned by Pope Gregory VII, he did penance at Canossa.

Henry V, 1106-1125, son; last of Salic House.

Lothair, duke of Saxony, 1125-1137. Crowned emperor in Rome, 1134.

House of Hohenstaufen

Conrad III, duke of Swabia, 1138-1152. In 2nd Crusade.

Frederick I, Barbarossa, 1152-1190; Conrad's nephew.

Henry VI, 1190-1196, took lower Italy from Normans. Son became king of Sicily.

Philip of Swabia, 1197-1208, brother.

Otto IV, of House of Welf, 1198-1215; deposed.

Frederick II, 1215-1250, son of Henry VI; king of Sicily; crowned king of Jerusalem in 5th Crusade.

Conrad IV, 1250-1254, son; lost lower Italy to Charles of Anjou.

Conradin, 1252-1268, son, king of Jerusalem and Sicily, beheaded. Last Hohenstaufen.

Interregnum, 1254-1273, Rise of the Electors.

Transition

Rudolph I of Hapsburg, 1273-1291, defeated King Ottocar II of Bohemia. Bequeathed duchy of Austria to eldest son, Albert.

Adolph of Nassau, 1292-1298, killed in war with Albert of Austria.

Albert I, king of Germany, 1298-1308, son of Rudolph.

Henry VII, of Luxemburg, 1308-1313, crowned emperor in Rome. Seized Bohemia, 1310.

Louis IV of Bavaria (Wittelsbach), 1314-1347. Also elected was Frederick of Austria, 1314-1330 (Hapsburg). Abolition of papal sanction for election of Holy Roman Emperor.

Charles IV, of Luxemburg, 1347-1378, grandson of Henry VII, German emperor and king of Bohemia, Lombardy, Burgundy; took Mark of Brandenburg.

Wenceslaus, 1378-1400, deposed.

Rupert, Duke of Palatine, 1400-1410.

Sigismund, 1411-1437.

Hungary

Stephen I, house of Arpad, 997-1038. Crowned king 1000; converted Magyars; canonized 1083. After several centuries of feuds Charles Robert of Anjou became Charles I, 1308-1342.

Louis I, the Great, son, 1342-1382; joint ruler of Poland with Casimir III, 1370. Defeated Turks.

Mary, daughter, 1382-1395, ruled with husband. Sigismund of Luxemburg, 1387-1437, also king of Bohemia. As brother of Wenceslaus he succeeded Rupert as Holy Roman Emperor, 1410.

Albert, 1438-1439, son-in-law of Sigismund; also Roman emperor as Albert II *(see under Hapsburg).*

Ulaszlo I of Poland, 1440-1444.

Ladislaus V, posthumous son of Albert II, 1444-1457. John Hunyadi (Hunyadi Janos), governor (1446-1452), fought Turks, Czechs; died 1456.

Matthias I (Corvinus), son of Hunyadi, 1458-1490. Shared rule of Bohemia, captured Vienna, 1485, annexed Austria, Styria, Carinthia.

Ulaszlo II (king of Bohemia), 1490-1516.

Louis II, son, aged 10, 1516-1526. Wars with Suleiman, Turk. In 1527 Hungary split between Ferdinand I, Archduke of Austria, bro.-in-law of Louis II, and John Zapolya of Transylvania. After Turkish invasion, 1547, Hungary split between Ferdinand, Prince John Sigismund (Transylvania), and the Turks.

House of Hapsburg

Albert V of Austria, Hapsburg, crowned king of Hungary, Jan. 1438, Roman emperor, March 1438, as Albert II; died 1439.

Frederick III, cousin, 1440-1493. Fought Turks.

Maximilian I, son, 1493-1519. Assumed title of Holy Roman Emperor (German), 1493.

Charles V, grandson, 1519-1556. King of Spain with mother co-regent; crowned Roman emperor at Aix, 1520. Confronted Luther at Worms; attempted church reform and religious conciliation; abdicated 1556.

Ferdinand I, king of Bohemia, 1526, of Hungary, 1527; disputed. German king, 1531. Crowned Roman emperor on abdication of brother Charles V, 1556.

Maximilian II, son, 1564-1576.

Rudolph II, son, 1576-1612.

Matthias, brother, 1612-1619, king of Bohemia and Hungary.

Ferdinand II of Styria, king of Bohemia, 1617, of Hungary, 1618, Roman emperor, 1619. Bohemian Protestants deposed him, elected Frederick V of Palatine, starting Thirty Years War.

Ferdinand III, son, king of Hungary, 1625, Bohemia, 1627, Roman emperor, 1637. Peace of Westphalia, 1648, ended war. Leopold I, 1658-1705; Joseph I, 1705-1711; Charles VI, 1711-1740.

Maria Theresa, daughter, 1740-1780, Archduchess of Austria, queen of Hungary; ousted pretender, Charles VII, crowned 1742; in 1745 obtained election of her husband Francis I as Roman emperor and co-regent (d. 1765). Fought Seven Years' War with Frederick II of Prussia. Mother of Marie Antoinette.

Joseph II, son, 1765-1790, Roman emperor, reformer; powers restricted by Empress Maria Theresa until her death, 1780. First partition of Poland. Leopold II, 1790-1792.

Francis II, son, 1792-1835. Fought Napoleon. Proclaimed first hereditary emperor of Austria, 1804. Forced to abdicate as Roman emperor, 1806; last use of title. Ferdinand I, son, 1835-1848, abdicated during revolution.

Austro-Hungarian Monarchy

Francis Joseph I, nephew, 1848-1916, emperor of Austria, king of Hungary. Dual monarchy of Austria-Hungary formed, 1867. After assassination of heir, Archduke Francis Ferdinand, June 28, 1914, Austrian diplomacy precipitated World War I.

Charles I, grand-nephew, 1916-1918, last emperor of Austria and king of Hungary. Abdicated Nov. 11-13, 1918, died 1922.

Rulers of Prussia

Nucleus of Prussia was the Mark of Brandenburg. First margrave Albert the Bear (Albrecht), 1134-1170. First Hohenzollern margrave was Frederick, burgrave of Nuremberg, 1417-1440.

Frederick William, 1640-1688, the Great Elector. Son, Frederick III, 1688-1713, crowned King Frederick of Prussia, 1701.

Frederick William I, son, 1713-1740.

Frederick II, the Great, son, 1740-1786, annexed Silesia, part of Austria.

Frederick William II, nephew, 1786-1797.

Frederick William III, son, 1797-1840. Napoleonic wars.

Frederick William IV, son, 1840-1861. Uprising of 1848 and first parliament and constitution.

Second and Third Reich

William I, 1861-1888, brother. Annexation of Schleswig and Hanover; Franco-Prussian war, 1870-1871, proclamation of German Reich, Jan. 18, 1871, at Versailles; William, German emperor (Deutscher Kaiser), Bismarck, chancellor.

Frederick III, son, 1888.

William II, son, 1888-1918. Led Germany in World War I, abdicated as German emperor and king of Prussia, Nov. 9, 1918. Died in exile in Netherlands, June 4, 1941. Minor rulers of Bavaria, Saxony, Wurttemberg also abdicated.

Germany proclaimed republic at Weimar, July 1, 1919. Presidents included: Frederick Ebert, 1919-1925; Paul von Hindenburg-Beneckendorff, 1925, reelected 1932, d. Aug. 2, 1934. Adolf Hitler, chancellor, chosen successor as Leader-Chancellor (Fuehrer-Reichskanzler) of Third Reich. Annexed Austria, Mar. 1938. Precipitated World War II, 1939-1945. Suicide Apr. 30, 1945.

Germany After 1945

Following World War II, Germany was split between democratic West and Soviet-dominated East. West German chancellors: Konrad Adenauer, 1949-1963; Ludwig Erhard, 1963-1966; Kurt Georg Kiesinger, 1966-1969; Willy Brandt, 1969-1974; Helmut Schmidt, 1974-1982; Helmut Kohl, 1982-1990. East German Communist party leaders: Walter Ulbricht, 1946-1971; Erich Honecker, 1971-1989; Egon Krenz, 1989-1990.

Germany reunited Oct. 3, 1990. Post-reunification chancellors: Helmut Kohl, 1990-1998; Gerhard Schröder, 1998- .

Rulers of Poland

House of Piasts

Miesko I, 962?-992; Poland Christianized 966. Expansion under 3 Boleslavs: I, 992-1025, son, crowned king 1024; II, 1058-1079, great-grandson, exiled after killing bishop Stanislav who became chief patron saint of Poland; III, 1106-1138, nephew, divided Poland among 4 sons, eldest suzerain.

1138-1306, feudal division. 1226 founding in Prussia of military order Teutonic Knights. 1226 invasion by Tartars/Mongols.

Vladislav I, 1306-1333, reunited most Polish territories, crowned king 1320. Casimir III the Great, 1333-1370, son, developed economic, cultural life, foreign policy.

House of Anjou

Louis I, 1370-1382, nephew/was also Louis I of Hungary.

Jadwiga, 1384-1399, daughter, married 1386 Jagiello, Grand Duke of Lithuania.

House of Jagiellonians

Vladislav II, 1386-1434, Christianized Lithuania, founded personal union between Poland and Lithuania. Defeated 1410 Teutonic Knights at Grunwald.

Vladislav III, 1434-1444, son, simultaneously king of Hungary. Fought Turks, killed 1444 in battle of Varna.

Casimir IV, 1446-1492, brother, competed with Hapsburgs, put son Vladislav on throne of Bohemia, later also of Hungary (Ulaszlo II).

Sigismund I, 1506-1548, son, patronized science and arts, his and son's reign "Golden Age."

Sigismund II, 1548-1572, son, established 1569 real union of Poland and Lithuania (lasted until 1795).

Elective Kings

Polish nobles in 1572 proclaimed Poland a republic headed by king to be elected by whole nobility.

Stephen Batory, 1576-1586, duke of Transylvania, married Ann, sister of Sigismund II August. Fought Russians.

Sigismund III Vasa, 1587-1632, nephew of Sigismund II. 1592-1598 also king of Sweden. His generals fought Russians, Turks.

Vladislav II Vasa, 1632-1648, son. Fought Russians.

John II Casimir Vasa, 1648-1668, brother. Fought Cossacks, Swedes, Russians, Turks, Tatars (the "Deluge"). Abdicated 1668.

John III Sobieski, 1674-1696. Won Vienna from besieging Turks, 1683.

Stanislav II, 1764-1795, last king. Encouraged reforms; 1791 1st modern Constitution in Europe. 1772, 1793, 1795 Poland partitioned among Russia, Prussia, Austria. Unsuccessful insurrection against foreign invasion 1794 under Kosciusko, American-Polish general.

1795-1918: Poland Under Foreign Rule

1807-1815 Grand Duchy of Warsaw created by Napoleon I, Frederick August of Saxony grand duke.

1815 Congress of Vienna proclaimed part of Poland "Kingdom" in personal union with Russia.

Polish uprisings: 1830 against Russia; 1846, 1848 against Austria; 1863 against Russia—all repressed.

1918-1939: Second Republic

1918-1922 Head of State Jozef Pilsudski. Presidents: Gabriel Narutowicz 1922, assassinated; Stanislav Wojciechowski 1922-1926, had to abdicate after Pilsudski's coup d'état; Ignacy Moscicki, 1926-1939, ruled (with Pilsudski until his death, 1935) as virtual dictator.

1939-1945: Poland Under Foreign Occupation

Nazi and Soviet invasion Sept. 1939. Polish government-in-exile, first in France, then in England. Vladislav Raczkiewicz president; Gen. Vladislav Sikorski, then Stanislav Mikolajczyk, prime ministers. Soviet-sponsored Polish Committee of National Liberation proclaimed at Lublin July 1944, transformed into government Jan. 1, 1945.

Poland After 1945

In the late 1940s, Poland came increasingly under Soviet control. Communist party ruled in Poland until Aug. 1989, when democratic Solidarity party, led by Lech Walesa, gained control of government. Walesa was elected president in 1990, but lost the office to former communist Aleksander Kwasniewski in 1995. The government remained democratic, and Kwasniewski was re-elected in Oct. 2000.

Rulers of Denmark, Sweden, Norway

Denmark

Earliest rulers invaded Britain; King Canute, who ruled in London 1016-1035, was most famous. The Valdemars furnished kings until the 15th century. In 1282 the Danes won the first national assembly, Danehof, from King Erik V.

Most redoubtable medieval character was Margaret, daughter of Valdemar IV, born 1353, married at 10 to King Haakon VI of Norway. In 1376 she had her first infant son Olaf made king of Denmark. After his death, 1387, she was regent of Denmark and Norway. In 1388 Sweden accepted her as sovereign. In 1389 she made her grand-nephew, Duke Erik of Pomerania, titular king of Denmark, Sweden, and Norway, with herself as regent. In 1397 she effected the Union of Kalmar of the three kingdoms and had Erik VII crowned. In 1439 the three kingdoms deposed him and elected, 1440, Christopher of Bavaria king (Christopher III). On his death, 1448, the union broke up.

Succeeding rulers were unable to enforce their claims as rulers of Sweden until 1520, when Christian II conquered Sweden. He was thrown out 1522, and in 1523 Gustavus Vasa united Sweden. Denmark continued to dominate Norway until the Napoleonic wars, when Frederick VI, 1808-1839, joined the Napoleonic cause after Britain had destroyed the Danish fleet, 1807. In 1814 he was forced to cede Norway to Sweden and Helgoland to Britain, receiving Lauenburg. Successors Christian VIII, 1839; Frederick VII, 1848; Christian IX, 1863; Frederick VIII, 1906; Christian X, 1912; Frederick IX, 1947; Margrethe II, 1972.

Sweden

Early kings ruled at Uppsala, but did not dominate the country. Sverker, c1130-c1156, united the Swedes and Goths. In 1435 Sweden obtained the Riksdag, or parliament. After the Union of Kalmar, 1397, the Danes either ruled or harried the country until Christian II of Denmark conquered it anew, 1520. This led to a rising under Gustavus Vasa, who ruled Sweden 1523-1560, and established an independent kingdom. Charles IX, 1599-1611, crowned 1604, conquered Moscow. Gustavus II Adolphus, 1611-1632, was called the Lion of the North. Later rulers: Christina, 1632; Charles X Gustavus, 1654; Charles XI, 1660; Charles XII (invader of Russia and Poland, defeated at Poltava, June 28, 1709), 1697; Ulrika Eleanora, sister, elected queen 1718; Frederick I (of Hesse), her husband, 1720; Adolphus Frederick, 1751; Gustavus III, 1771; Gustavus IV Adolphus, 1792; Charles XIII, 1809. (Union with Norway began 1814.) Charles XIV John, 1818 (he was Jean Bernadotte, Napoleon's Prince of Ponte Corvo, elected 1810 to succeed Charles XIII); he founded the present dynasty: Oscar I, 1844; Charles XV, 1859; Oscar II, 1872; Gustavus V, 1907; Gustav VI Adolf, 1950; Carl XVI Gustaf, 1973.

Norway

Overcoming many rivals, Harald Haarfager, 872-930, conquered Norway, Orkneys, and Shetlands; Olaf I, great-grandson, 995-1000, brought Christianity into Norway, Iceland, and Greenland. In 1035 Magnus the Good also became king of Denmark. Haakon V, 1299-1319, had married his daughter to Erik of Sweden. Their son, Magnus, became ruler of Norway and Sweden at 6. His son, Haakon VI, married Margaret of Denmark; their son Olaf IV became king of Norway and Denmark, followed by Margaret's regency and the Union of Kalmar, 1397.

In 1450 Norway became subservient to Denmark. Christian IV, 1588-1648, founded Christiania, now Oslo. After Napoleonic wars, when Denmark ceded Norway to Sweden, a strong nationalist movement forced recognition of Norway as an independent kingdom united with Sweden under the Swedish kings, 1814-1905. In 1905 the union was dissolved and Prince Charles of Denmark became Haakon VII. He died Sept. 21, 1957; succeeded by son, Olav V. Olav V died Jan. 17, 1991; succeeded by son, Harald V.

Rulers of the Netherlands and Belgium

The Netherlands (Holland)

William Frederick, Prince of Orange, led a revolt against French rule, 1813; crowned king, 1815. Belgium seceded Oct. 4, 1830, after a revolt. The secession was ratified by the two kingdoms by treaty, Apr. 19, 1839.

Succession: William II, son, 1840; William III, son, 1849; Wilhelmina, daughter of William III and his 2nd wife Princess Emma of Waldeck, 1890; Wilhelmina abdicated, Sept. 4, 1948, in favor of daughter, Juliana. Juliana abdicated, Apr. 30, 1980, in favor of daughter, Beatrix.

Belgium

A national congress elected Prince Leopold of Saxe-Coburg as king; he took the throne July 21, 1831, as Leopold I.

Succession: Leopold II, son, 1865; Albert I, nephew of Leopold II, 1909; Leopold III, son of Albert, 1934; Prince Charles, Regent 1944; Leopold returned 1950, yielded powers to son Baudouin, Prince Royal, Aug. 6, 1950, abdicated July 16, 1951. Baudouin I took throne July 17, 1951, died July 31, 1993; succeeded by brother, Albert II.

Roman Rulers

From Romulus to the end of the Empire in the West. Rulers in the East sat in Constantinople and, for a brief period, in Nicaea, until the capture of Constantinople by the Turks in 1453, when Byzantium was succeeded by the Ottoman Empire.

The Kingdom

BC
753 Romulus (Quirinus)
716 Numa Pompilius
673 Tullus Hostilius
640 Ancus Marcius
616 L. Tarquinius Priscus
578 Servius Tullius
534 L. Tarquinius Superbus

The Republic

509 Consulate established
509 Quaestorship instituted
498 Dictatorship introduced
494 Plebeian Tribunate created
494 Plebeian Aedileship created
444 Consular Tribunate organized
435 Censorship instituted
366 Praetorship established
366 Curule Aedileship created
362 Military Tribunate elected
326 Proconsulate introduced
311 Naval Duumvirate elected
217 Dictatorship of Fabius Maximus
133 Tribunate of Tiberius Gracchus
123 Tribunate of Gaius Gracchus
82 Dictatorship of Sulla
60 First Triumvirate formed (Caesar, Pompeius, Crassus)
46 Dictatorship of Caesar
43 Second Triumvirate formed (Octavianus, Antonius, Lepidus)

The Empire

27 Augustus (Octavian)
AD
14 Tiberius I
37 Caligula
41 Claudius I
54 Nero
68 Galba
69 Galba; Otho, Vitellius
69 Vespasianus
79 Titus
81 Domitianus
96 Nerva
98 Trajanus
117 Hadrianus
138 Antoninus Pius

161 Marcus Aurelius and Lucius Verus
169 Marcus Aurelius (alone)
180 Commodus
193 Pertinax; Julianus I
193 Septimius Severus
211 Caracalla and Geta
212 Caracalla (alone)
217 Macrinus
218 Elagabalus (Heliogabalus)
222 Alexander Severus
235 Maximinus I (the Thracian)
238 Gordianus I and Gordianus II; Pupienus and Balbinus
238 Gordianus III
244 Philippus (the Arabian)
249 Decius
251 Gallus and Volusianus
253 Aemilianus
253 Valerianus and Gallienus
258 Gallienus (alone)
268 Claudius Gothicus
270 Quintillus
270 Aurelianus
275 Tacitus
276 Florianus
276 Probus
282 Carus
283 Carinus and Numerianus
286 Diocletianus and Maximianus
305 Galerius and Constantius I
306 Galerius, Maximinus II, Severus I
307 Galerius, Maximinus II, Constantinus I, Licinius, Maxentius
311 Maximinus II, Constantinus I, Licinius, Maxentius
314 Maximinus II, Constantinus I, Licinius
314 Constantinus I and Licinius
324 Constantinus I (the Great)
337 Constantinus II, Constans I, Constantius II
340 Constantius II and Constans I
350 Constantius II
361 Julianus II (the Apostate)
363 Jovianus

West (Rome) and East (Constantinople)

364 Valentinianus I (West) and Valens (East)
367 Valentinianus I with Gratianus (West) and Valens (East)
375 Gratianus with Valentinianus II (West) and Valens (East)
378 Gratianus with Valentinianus II (West),Theodosius I (East)
383 Valentinianus II (West) and Theodosius I (East)
394 Theodosius I (the Great)
395 Honorius (West) and Arcadius (East)
408 Honorius (West) and Theodosius II (East)
423 Valentinianus III (West) and Theodosius II (East)
450 Valentinianus III (West) and Marcianus (East)
455 Maximus (West), Avitus (West); Marcianus (East)
456 Avitus (West), Marcianus (East)
457 Majorianus (West), Leo I (East)
461 Severus II (West), Leo I (East)
467 Anthemius (West), Leo I (East)
472 Olybrius (West), Leo I (East)
473 Glycerius (West), Leo I (East)
474 Julius Nepos (West), Leo II (East)
475 Romulus Augustulus (West) and Zeno (East)
476 End of Empire in West; Odovacar, King, drops title of Emperor; murdered by King Theodoric of Ostrogoths, 493

Rulers of Modern Italy

After the fall of Napoleon in 1814, the Congress of Vienna, 1815, restored Italy as a political patchwork, comprising the Kingdom of Naples and Sicily, the Papal States, and smaller units. Piedmont and Genoa were awarded to Sardinia, ruled by King Victor Emmanuel I of Savoy.

United Italy emerged under the leadership of Camillo, Count di Cavour (1810-1861), Sardinian prime minister. Agitation was led by Giuseppe Mazzini (1805-1872) and Giuseppe Garibaldi (1807-1882), soldier; Victor Emmanuel I abdicated 1821. After a brief regency for a brother, Charles Albert was king 1831-1849, abdicating when defeated by the Austrians at Novara. Succeeded by Victor Emmanuel II, 1849-1861.

In 1859 France forced Austria to cede Lombardy to Sardinia, which gave rights to Savoy and Nice to France. In 1860 Garibaldi led 1,000 volunteers in a spectacular campaign, took Sicily and expelled the King of Naples. In 1860 the House of Savoy annexed Tuscany, Parma, Modena, Romagna, the Two Sicilys, the Marches, and Umbria. Victor Emmanuel assumed the title of King of Italy at Turin Mar. 17, 1861.

In 1866, Victor Emmanuel allied with Prussia in the Austro-Prussian War, and with Prussia's victory received Venetia. On Sept. 20, 1870, his troops under Gen. Raffaele Cadorna entered Rome and took over the Papal States, ending the temporal power of the Roman Catholic Church.

Succession: Umberto I, 1878, assassinated 1900; Victor Emmanuel III, 1900, abdicated 1946, died 1947; Humbert II, 1946, ruled a month. In 1921 Benito Mussolini (1883-1945) formed the Fascist party; he became prime minister Oct. 31, 1922. He entered World War II as an ally of Hitler. He was deposed July 25, 1943.

At a plebiscite June 2, 1946, Italy voted for a republic; Premier Alcide de Gasperi became chief of state June 13, 1946. On June 28, 1946, the Constituent Assembly elected Enrico de Nicola, Liberal, provisional president. Successive presidents: Luigi Einaudi, elected May 11, 1948; Giovanni Gronchi, Apr. 29, 1955; Antonio Segni, May 6, 1962; Giuseppe Saragat, Dec. 28, 1964; Giovanni Leone, Dec. 29, 1971; Alessandro Pertini, July 9, 1978; Francesco Cossiga, July 9, 1985; Oscar Luigi Scalfaro, May 28, 1992; Carlo Azeglio Ciampi, May 18, 1999.

Rulers of Spain

From 8th to 11th centuries Spain was dominated by the Moors (Arabs and Berbers). The Christian reconquest established small kingdoms (Asturias, Aragon, Castile, Catalonia, Leon, Navarre, and Valencia). In 1474 Isabella, b. 1451, became Queen of Castile & Leon. Her husband, Ferdinand, b. 1452, inherited Aragon 1479, with Catalonia, Valencia, and the Balearic Islands, became Ferdinand V of Castile. By Isabella's request Pope Sixtus IV established the Inquisition, 1478. Last Moorish kingdom, Granada, fell 1492. Columbus opened New World of colonies, 1492. Isabella died 1504, succeeded by her daughter, Juana "the Mad," but Ferdinand ruled until his death 1516.

Charles I, b. 1500, son of Juana, grandson of Ferdinand and Isabella, and of Maximilian I of Hapsburg; succeeded later as Holy Roman Emperor, Charles V, 1520; abdicated 1556. Philip II, son, 1556-1598, inherited only Spanish throne; conquered Portugal, fought Turks, sent Armada vs. England. Married to Mary I of England, 1554-1558. Succession: Philip III, 1598-1621; Philip IV, 1621-1665; Charles II, 1665-1700, left Spain to Philip of Anjou, grandson of Louis XIV, who as Philip V, 1700-1746, founded Bourbon dynasty; Ferdinand VI, 1746-1759; Charles III, 1759-1788; Charles IV, 1788-1808, abdicated.

Napoleon now dominated politics and made his brother Joseph King of Spain 1808, but the Spanish ousted him in 1813. Ferdinand VII, 1808, 1814-1833, lost American colonies; succeeded by daughter Isabella II, aged 3, with wife Maria Christina of Naples regent until 1843. Isabella deposed by revolution 1868. Elected king by the Cortes, Amadeo of Savoy, 1870; abdicated 1873. First republic, 1873-74. Alfonso XII, son of Isabella, 1875-85. His posthumous son was Alfonso XIII, with his mother, Queen Maria Christina regent; Spanish-American war, Spain lost Cuba, gave up Puerto Rico, Philippines, Sulu Is., Marianas. Alfonso took throne 1902, aged 16, married British Princess Victoria Eugenia of Battenberg. Dictatorship of Primo de Rivera, 1923-30, precipitated revolution of 1931. Alfonso agreed to leave without formal abdication. Monarchy abolished; the second republic established, with socialist backing. Niceto Alcala Zamora was president until 1936, when Manuel Azaña was chosen.

In July 1936, the army in Morocco revolted against the government and General Francisco Franco led the troops into Spain. The revolution succeeded by Feb. 1939, when Azaña resigned. Franco became chief of state, with provisions that if he was incapacitated, the Regency Council by two-thirds vote could propose a king to the Cortes, which needed to have a two-thirds majority to elect him.

Alfonso XIII died in Rome Feb. 28, 1941, aged 54. His property and citizenship had been restored.

A law restoring the monarchy was approved in a 1947 referendum. Prince Juan Carlos, b. 1938, grandson of Alfonso XIII, was designated by Franco and the Cortes (Parliament) in 1969 as future king and chief of state. Franco died in office, Nov. 20, 1975; Juan Carlos proclaimed king, Nov. 22.

Rulers of Russia; Leaders of the USSR and Russian Federation

First ruler to consolidate Slavic tribes was Rurik, leader of the Russians who established himself at Novgorod, AD 862. He and his immediate successors had Scandinavian affiliations. They moved to Kiev after 972 and ruled as Dukes of Kiev. In 988 Vladimir was converted and adopted the Byzantine Greek Orthodox service, later modified by Slav influences. Important as organizer and lawgiver was Yaroslav, 1019-1054, whose daughters married kings of Norway, Hungary, and France. His grandson, Vladimir II (Monomakh), 1113-1125, was progenitor of several rulers, but in 1169 Andrew Bogolubski overthrew Kiev and began the line known as Grand Dukes of Vladimir.

Of the Grand Dukes of Vladimir, Alexander Nevsky, 1246-1263, had a son, Daniel, first to be called Duke of Muscovy (Moscow), who ruled 1263-1303. His successors became Grand Dukes of Muscovy. After Dmitri III Donskoi defeated the Tatars in 1380, they also became Grand Dukes of all Russia. Tatar independence and considerable territorial expansion were achieved under Ivan III, 1462-1505.

Tsars of Muscovy—Ivan III was referred to in church ritual as Tsar. He married Sofia, niece of the last Byzantine emperor. His successor, Basil III, died in 1533 when Basil's son Ivan was only 3. He became Ivan IV, "the Terrible"; crowned 1547 as Tsar of all the Russias, ruled until 1584. Under the weak rule of his son, Feodor I, 1584-1598, Boris Godunov had control. The dynasty died, and after years of tribal strife and intervention by Polish and Swedish armies, the Russians united under 17-year-old Michael Romanov, distantly related to the first wife of Ivan IV. He ruled 1613-1645 and established the Romanov line. Fourth ruler after Michael was Peter I.

Tsars, or Emperors, of Russia (Romanovs)—Peter I, 1682-1725, known as Peter the Great, took title of Emperor in 1721. His successors and dates of accession were: Catherine, his widow, 1725; Peter II, his grandson, 1727; Anne, Duchess of Courland, 1730, daughter of Peter the Great's brother, Tsar Ivan V; Ivan VI, 1740, great-grandson of Ivan V, child, kept in prison and murdered 1764; Elizabeth, daughter of Peter I, 1741; Peter III, grandson of Peter I, 1761, deposed 1762 for his consort, Catherine II, former princess of Anhalt Zerbst (Germany) who is known as Catherine the Great; Paul I, her son, 1796, killed 1801; Alexander I, son of Paul, 1801, defeated Napoleon; Nicholas I, his brother, 1825; Alexander II, son of Nicholas, 1855, assassinated 1881 by terrorists; Alexander III, son, 1881. Nicholas II, son, 1894-1917, last Tsar of Russia, was forced to abdicate by the March 1917 Revolution that followed losses to Germany in WWI. The Tsar, Empress, Tsarevich (Crown Prince), and Tsar's 4 daughters were murdered by the Bolsheviks in Yekaterinburg, July 16, 1918.

Provisional Government—premiers, Prince Georgi Lvov, followed by Alexander Kerensky, 1917.

Union of Soviet Socialist Republics

Bolshevik Revolution, Nov. 7, 1917, removed Kerensky from power; council of People's Commissars formed, Lenin (Vladimir Ilyich Ulyanov) became premier. Lenin died Jan. 21, 1924. Aleksei Rykov (executed 1938) and V. M. Molotov held the office, but actual ruler was Joseph Stalin (Joseph Vissarionovich Djugashvili), general secretary of the Central Committee of the Communist Party. Stalin became president of the Council of Ministers (premier) May 7, 1941, died Mar. 5, 1953. Succeeded by Georgi M. Malenkov, as head of the Council and premier, and Nikita S. Khrushchev, first secretary of the Central Committee. Malenkov resigned Feb. 8, 1955, became deputy premier, was dropped July 3, 1957. Marshal Nikolai A. Bulganin became premier Feb. 8, 1955; was demoted and Khrushchev became premier Mar. 27, 1958.

Khrushchev was ousted Oct. 14-15, 1964, replaced by Leonid I. Brezhnev as first secretary of the party and by Aleksei N. Kosygin as premier. On June 16, 1977, Brezhnev also took office as president. He died Nov. 10, 1982; 2 days later the Central Committee elected former KGB head Yuri V. Andropov president. Andropov died Feb. 9, 1984; on Feb. 13, Konstantin U. Chernenko chosen by Central Committee as its general secretary. Chernenko died Mar. 10, 1985; on Mar. 11, he was succeeded as general secretary by Mikhail Gorbachev, who replaced Andrei Gromyko as president on Oct. 1, 1988. Gorbachev resigned Dec. 25, 1991, and the Soviet Union officially disbanded the next day. Each of the 15 former Soviet constituent republics became independent.

Post-Soviet Russia

After adopting a degree of sovereignty, the Russian Republic had held elections in June 1991. Boris Yeltsin was sworn in July 10, 1991, as Russia's first elected president. With the Dec. 1991 dissolution of the Soviet Union, Russia (officially Russian Federation) became a founding member of the Commonwealth of Independent States. On Dec. 31, 1999, Yeltsin stepped down as president; he named Vladimir Putin his interim successor. Putin won a presidential election Mar. 26, 2000, and was reelected Mar. 14, 2004.

Leaders in the South American Wars of Liberation

Simon Bolivar (1783-1830), Jose Francisco de San Martin (1778-1850), and Francisco Antonio Gabriel Miranda (1750-1816) are among the heroes of the early 19th-century struggles of South American nations to free themselves from Spain. All three, and their contemporaries, operated in periods of factional strife, during which soldiers and civilians suffered.

Miranda, a Venezuelan, who had served with the French in the American Revolution and commanded parts of the French Revolutionary armies in the Netherlands, attempted to start a revolt in Venezuela in 1806 and failed. In 1810, with British and American backing, he returned and was briefly a dictator, until the British withdrew their support. In 1812 he was overcome by the royalists in Venezuela and taken prisoner, dying in a Spanish prison in 1816.

San Martin was born in Argentina and during 1789-1811 served in campaigns of the Spanish armies in Europe and Africa. He first joined the independence movement in Argentina in 1812 and in 1817 invaded Chile with 4,000 men over the mountain passes. Here he and Gen. Bernardo O'Higgins (1778-1842) defeated the Spaniards at Chacabuco, 1817; O'Higgins was named Liberator and became first director of Chile, 1817-23. In 1821 San Martin occupied Lima and Callao, Peru, and became protector of Peru.

Bolivar, the greatest leader of South American liberation from Spain, was born in Venezuela, the son of an aristocratic family. He first served under Miranda in 1812 and in 1813 captured Caracas, where he was named Liberator. Forced out next year by civil strife, he led a campaign that captured Bogota in 1814. In 1817 he was again in control of Venezuela and was named dictator. He organized Nueva Granada with the help of General Francisco de Paula Santander (1792-1840). By joining Nueva Granada, Venezuela, and the area that is now Panama and Ecuador, the republic of Colombia was formed, with Bolivar president. After numerous setbacks he decisively defeated the Spaniards in the second battle of Carabobo, Venezuela, June 24, 1821.

In May 1822, Gen. Antonio Jose de Sucre, Bolivar's lieutenant, took Quito. Bolivar went to Guayaquil to confer with San Martin, who resigned as protector of Peru and withdrew from politics. With a new army of Colombians and Peruvians Bolivar defeated the Spaniards in a battle at Junin in 1824 and cleared Peru.

De Sucre organized Charcas (Upper Peru) as Republica Bolivar (now Bolivia) and acted as president in place of Bolivar, who wrote its constitution. De Sucre defeated the Spanish faction of Peru at Ayacucho, Dec. 19, 1824.

Continued civil strife finally caused the Colombian federation to break apart. Santander turned against Bolivar, but the latter defeated him and banished him. In 1828 Bolivar gave up the presidency he had held precariously for 14 years. He became ill from tuberculosis and died Dec. 17, 1830. He is buried in the national pantheon in Caracas.

WORLD ALMANAC QUICK QUIZ

Which English King changed his dynasty's name from Saxe-Coburg-Gotha to Windsor, in order to downplay his German origins?
(a) Henry IV (b) James II (c) George III (d) George V

For the answer look in this chapter, or see page 1008.

Governments of China

(Until 221 BC and frequently thereafter, China was not a unified state. Where dynastic dates overlap, the rulers or events referred to appeared in different areas of China.)

Hsia	1994 BC – c1523 BC
Shang	c1523 BC – c1028 BC
Western Chou	c1027 BC – 770 BC
Eastern Chou	770 BC – 256 BC
Warring States	403 BC – 222 BC
Ch'in (first unified empire)	221 BC – 206 BC
Han	202 BC – AD 220
Western Han (expanded Chinese state beyond the Yellow and Yangtze River valleys)	202 BC – AD 9
Hsin (Wang Mang, usurper)	AD 9 – 23
Eastern Han (expanded Chinese state into Indochina and Turkestan)	25 – 220
Three Kingdoms (Wei, Shu, Wu)	220 – 265
Chin (western)	265 – 317
(eastern)	317 – 420
Northern Dynasties (followed several short-lived governments by Turks, Mongols, etc.)	386 – 581
Southern Dynasties (capital: Nanjing)	420 – 589
Sui (reunified China)	581 – 618
Tang (a golden age of Chinese culture; capital: Xian)	618 – 906
Five Dynasties (Yellow River basin)	902 – 960
Ten Kingdoms (southern China)	907 – 979
Liao (Khitan Mongols; capital at site of Beijing)	947 – 1125
Sung	960 – 1279
Northern Sung (reunified central and southern China)	960 – 1126
Western Hsai (non-Chinese rulers in northwest)	990 – 1227
Chin (Tatars; drove Sung out of central China)	1115 – 1234
Yuan (Mongols; Kublai Khan est. capital at site of Beijing, c. 1264)	1271 – 1368
Ming (China reunified under Chinese rule; capital: Nanjing, then Beijing in 1420)	1368 – 1644
Ch'ing (Manchus, descendents of Tatars)	1644 – 1912
Republic (disunity; provincial rulers, warlords)	1912 – 1949
People's Republic of China	1949 –

Leaders of China Since 1949

Mao Zedong	Chairman, Central People's Administrative Council, Communist Party (CPC), 1949-1976
Zhou Enlai	Premier, foreign minister, 1949-1976
Deng Xiaoping	Vice Premier, 1952-1966, 1973-1976, 1977-1980; "paramount leader," 1978-1997
Liu Shaoqi	President, 1959-1969
Hua Guofeng	Premier, 1976-1980; CPC Chairman, 1976-1981
Zhao Ziyang	Premier, 1980-1988; CPC General Secretary, 1987-1989
Hu Yaobang	CPC Chairman, 1981-1982; CPC General Secretary, 1982-1987
Li Xiannian	President, 1983-1988
Yang Shangkun	President, 1988-1993
Li Peng	Premier, 1988-98
Jiang Zemin	CPC General Secretary, 1989-2002; President, 1993-2003
Zhu Rongji	Premier, 1998-2003
Hu Jintao	CPC General Secretary, 2002-; President, 2003-
Wen Jiabao	Premier, 2003-

Historical Periods of Japan

Yamato	c. 300 – 592	Conquest of Yamato plain c. AD 300.
Asuka	592 – 710	Accession of Empress Suiko, 592.
Nara	710 – 794	Completion of Heijo (Nara), 710; the capital moves to Nagaoka, 784.
Heian	794 – 1185	Completion of Heian (Kyoto), 794.
Fujiwara	858 – 1160	Fujiwara-no-Yoshifusa becomes regent, 858.
Taira	1160 – 1185	Taira-no-Kiyomori assumes control, 1160; Minamoto-no-Yoritomo victor over Taira, 1185.
Kamakura	1192 – 1333	Yoritomo becomes shogun, 1192.
Namboku	1334 – 1392	Restoration of Emperor Godaigo, 1334; Southern Court established by Godaigo at Yoshino, 1336.
Ashikaga	1338 – 1573	Ashikaga Takauji becomes shogun, 1338.
Muromachi	1392 – 1573	Unification of Southern and Northern Courts, 1392.
Sengoku	1467 – 1600	Beginning of the Onin war, 1467.
Momoyama	1573 – 1603	Oda Nobunaga enters Kyoto, 1568; Nobunaga deposes last Ashikaga shogun, 1573; Tokugawa Ieyasu victor at Sekigahara, 1600.
Edo	1603 – 1867	Ieyasu becomes shogun, 1603.
Meiji	1868 – 1912	Enthronement of Emperor Mutsuhito (Meiji), 1867; Meiji Restoration and Charter Oath, 1868.
Taisho	1912 – 1926	Accession of Emperor Yoshihito, 1912.
Showa	1926 – 1989	Accession of Emperor Hirohito, 1926.
Heisei	1989–	Accession of Emperor Akihito, 1989.

IT'S A FACT: Hirohito was the longest-serving emperor in Japanese history, reigning from 1926 to his death in 1989 at age 88. He defied the ancient tradition of public imperial silence when he broadcast Japan's surrender in World War II by radio on Aug. 15, 1945. After the war, in Jan. 1946, he repudiated the idea of imperial divinity. He was the first emperor to travel abroad, when he visited Europe in 1971.

WORLD EXPLORATION AND GEOGRAPHY

Early Explorers of the Western Hemisphere

Reviewed by Susan Skomal, PhD

In the light of recent discoveries, theories about how and when the first people arrived in the western hemisphere are being reconsidered. Genetic evidence suggests that beginning 14,000 years before the present (BP), the earliest immigrants crossed a "land bridge" from Siberia to Alaska in small groups and spread south through the Americas. Kennewick Man, found in Washington state (9,200-9,600 BP), and "Luzia" from Brazil (11,500 BP) are examples of these early arrivals. Modern Native Americans, who exhibit markedly different physical characteristics from Kennewick and Luzia, appear to be descended from peoples from N and Central Asia who arrived in subsequent waves of migration. A growing body of genetic, skeletal, and linguistic evidence documents their migration throughout the Americas.

Archaeologists have confirmed evidence of habitation by at least 12,900 BP at sites located on the shores of ancient lakes 2 miles high in the Atacama Desert of Chile. There is also growing support for the settlement of the lowland jungles of Chile 2,000 years earlier. Because a glacier covered most of N America from 20,000 to 13,000 years ago, those who settled in S America may have traveled in vessels along the west coast, sailed directly from Australia or S Asia, or spread from N to S America before the ice came. Evidence from a burial site at Santana do Riacho 1 in Brazil (8,000-11,000 BP) suggests that some of the early immigrants who came via the land bridge from Siberia may have originated in Africa. Long before Europeans arrived, the Americas were densely populated by complex societies. The earliest known civilization occupied a 700-square-mile area in 4 river valleys of coastal Peru between 500 and 3500 BP; agriculture based civilizations developed by 4200 BP at Los Ajos in SW Uruguay.

Norsemen (Norwegian Vikings sailing out of Iceland and Greenland), led by Leif Ericson, are credited with having been the first Europeans to reach America, with at least 5 voyages occurring about AD 1000 to areas they called Helluland, Markland, and Vinland—possibly what are known today as Labrador, Nova Scotia or Newfoundland, and New England. L'Anse aux Meadows, on the N tip of Newfoundland, is the only documented settlement.

Sustained contact between the hemispheres began with the first voyage of Christopher Columbus (born Cristoforo Colombo, c. 1451, near Genoa, Italy). Columbus made trips to the New World while sailing for the Spanish. He left Palos, Spain, Aug. 3, 1492, with 88 men and landed at San Salvador (Watling Islands, Bahamas), Oct. 12, 1492. His fleet included 3 vessels, the *Niña*, *Pinta*, and *Santa María*, and also stopped on Cuba and Hispaniola. A 2nd expedition left Cadiz, Spain, Sept. 25, 1493, with 17 ships and 1,500 men, reaching the Lesser Antilles Nov. 3. His 3rd voyage brought him from Sanlucar, Spain (May 30, 1498, with 6 ships), to the N coast of S America. A 4th voyage reached the mainland of Central America, after leaving Cadiz, Spain, May 9, 1502. Columbus died in 1506 convinced he had reached Asia by sailing west.

In N America, John and Sebastian Cabot, Italian explorers sailing for the English, reached Newfoundland and possibly Nova Scotia in 1497. John's 2nd voyage (1498), seeking a new trade route to Asia, resulted in the loss of his entire fleet. During this period exploration was dominated by Spain and Portugal.

In 1497 and 1499 Amerigo Vespucci (for whom the Americas are named), an Italian explorer sailing for Spain, passed along the N and E coasts of S America. He was the first to argue that the newly discovered lands were a continent other than Asia.

Other early explorations are listed below.

Year	Explorer	Nationality (sponsor, if different)	Area reached or explored
1497-98	Vasco da Gama	Portuguese	Cape of Good Hope (Africa), India
1499	Alonso de Ojeda	Spanish	N South American coast, Venezuela
1500, Feb.	Vicente Yañez Pinzon	Spanish	S. American coast, Amazon R.
1500, Apr.	Pedro Álvarez Cabral	Portuguese	Brazil
1501	Rodrigo de Bastidas	Spanish	Central America
1513	Vasco Núñez de Balboa	Spanish	Panama, Pacific Ocean
1513	Juan Ponce de León	Spanish	Florida, Yucatán Peninsula
1515	Juan de Solis	Spanish	Río de la Plata
1519	Alonso de Pineda	Spanish	Mouth of Mississippi R.
1519	Hernando Cortes	Spanish	Mexico
1519-20	Ferdinand Magellan	Portuguese (Spanish)	Straits of Magellan, Tierra del Fuego
1524	Giovanni da Verrazano	Italian (French)	Atlantic coast, incl. New York harbor
1528	Cabeza de Vaca	Spanish	Texas coast and interior
1532	Francisco Pizarro	Spanish	Peru
1534	Jacques Cartier	French	Canada, Gulf of St. Lawrence
1536	Pedro de Mendoza	Spanish	Buenos Aires
1539	Francisco de Ulloa	Spanish	California coast
1539-41	Hernando de Soto	Spanish	Mississippi R., near Memphis
1539	Marcos de Niza	Italian (Spanish)	SW United States
1540	Francisco de Coronado	Spanish	SW United States
1540	Hernando Alarcon	Spanish	Colorado R.
1540	Garcia de Lopez Cardenas	Spanish	Colorado, Grand Canyon
1541	Francisco de Orellana	Spanish	Amazon R.
1542	Juan Rodriguez Cabrillo	Portuguese (Spanish)	W Mexico, San Diego harbor
1565	Pedro Menéndez de Aviles	Spanish	St. Augustine, FL
1576	Sir Martin Frobisher	English	Frobisher Bay, Canada
1577-80	Sir Francis Drake	English	California coast
1582	Antonio de Espejo	Spanish	Southwest U.S. (New Mexico)
1584	Amadas & Barlow (for Raleigh)	English	Virginia
1585-87	Sir Walter Raleigh's men	English	Roanoke Isl., NC
1595	Sir Walter Raleigh	English	Orinoco R.
1603-09	Samuel de Champlain	French	Canadian interior, Lake Champlain
1607	Capt. John Smith	English	Atlantic coast
1609-10	Henry Hudson	English (Dutch)	Hudson R., Hudson Bay
1634	Jean Nicolet	French	Lake Michigan, Wisconsin
1673	Jacques Marquette, Louis Jolliet	French	Mississippi R., S to Arkansas
1682	Robert Cavelier, sieur de La Salle	French	Mississippi R., S to Gulf of Mexico
1727-29	Vitus Bering	Danish (Russian)	Bering Strait and Alaska
1789	Sir Alexander Mackenzie	Canadian	NW Canada
1804-06	Meriwether Lewis and William Clark	American	Missouri R., Rocky Mts., Columbia R.

Arctic Exploration

Early Explorers

1587 — John Davis (Eng.). Davis Strait to Sanderson's Hope, 72°12´N.

1596 — Willem Barents and Jacob van Heemskerck (Holland). Discovered Bear Isl., touched NW tip of Spitsbergen, 79°49´ N, rounded Novaya Zemlya, wintered at Ice Haven.

1607 — Henry Hudson (Eng.). North along Greenland's E coast to Cape Hold-with-Hope, 73°30´, then N of Spitsbergen to 80°23´. Explored Hudson's Touches (Jan Mayen).

1616 — William Baffin and Robert Bylot (Eng.). Baffin Bay to Smith Sound.

1728 — Vitus Bering (Russ.). Sailed through strait (Bering) proving Asia and America are separate.

1733-40 — Great Northern Expedition (Russ.). Surveyed Siberian Arctic coast.

1741 — Vitus Bering (Russ.). Sighted Alaska, named Mount St. Elias. His lieutenant, Chirikof, explored coast.

1771 — Samuel Hearne (Hudson's Bay Co.). Overland from Prince of Wales Fort (Churchill) on Hudson Bay to mouth of Coppermine R.

1778 — James Cook (Brit.). Through Bering Strait to Icy Cape, AK, and North Cape, Siberia.

1789 — Alexander Mackenzie (North West Co., Brit.). Montreal to mouth of Mackenzie River.

1806 — William Scoresby (Brit.). N of Spitsbergen to 8°30´.

1820-23 — Ferdinand von Wrangel (Russ.). Surveyed Siberian Arctic coast. His exploration joined James Cook's at North Cape, confirming separation of the continents.

1878-79 — (Nils) Adolf Erik Nordenskjöld (Swed.). The 1st to navigate the Northeast Passage—an ocean route connecting Europe's North Sea, along the Arctic coast of Asia and through the Bering Sea, to the Pacific Ocean.

1881 — The U.S. steamer *Jeannette*, led by Lt. Cmdr. George W. DeLong, was trapped in ice and crushed, June 1881. DeLong and 11 others died; 12 survived.

1888 — Fridtjof Nansen (Nor.) crossed Greenland icecap.

1893-96 — Nansen in *Fram* drifted from New Siberian Isls. to Spitsbergen; tried polar dash in 1895, reached Franz Josef Land, 86°14´N.

1897 — Salomon A. Andrée (Sweden) and 2 others started in balloon from Spitsbergen, July 11, to drift across pole to U.S., and disappeared. Aug. 6, 1930, their bodies were found on White Isl., 82°57´N, 29°52´E.

1903-6 — Roald Amundsen (Nor.) 1st sailed the Northwest Passage—an ocean route linking the Atlantic Ocean to the Pacific via Canada's marine waterways.

North Pole Exploration

Robert E. Peary explored Greenland's coast, 1891-92; tried for North Pole, 1893. In 1900 he reached N limit of Greenland and 83°50´N; in 1902 he reached 84°17´N; in 1906 he went from Ellesmere Isl. to 87° 06´N. He sailed in the *Roosevelt*, July 1908, to winter off Cape Sheridan, Grant Land. The dash for the North Pole began Mar. 1 from Cape Columbia, Ellesmere Isl. Peary reportedly reached the pole, 90°N, Apr. 6, **1909**; however, later research suggests he may have fallen short of his goal by c. 30-60 mi. The first surface expedition independently confirmed to have reached the N Pole was that of Ralph Plaisted in 1968 (see below).

Peary had several support groups carrying supplies until the last group turned back at 87°47´ N. Peary, Matthew Henson, and 4 Eskimos proceeded with dog teams and sleds. They were said to have crossed the pole several times, then built an igloo there and remained 36 hours. Started south, Apr. 7 at 4 PM, for Cape Columbia.

1914 — Donald MacMillan (U.S.). Northwest, 200 mi, from Axel Heiberg Isl. to seek Peary's Crocker Land.

1915-17 — Vihjalmur Stefansson (Can.). Discovered Borden, Brock, Meighen, and Lougheed Isls.

1918-20 — Roald Amundsen (Nor.) sailed the Northeast Passage.

1925 — Amundsen and Lincoln Ellsworth (U.S.) reached 87°44´N in attempt to fly to N Pole from Spitsbergen.

1926 — Richard E. Byrd and Floyd Bennett (U.S.) reputedly flew over North Pole, May 9. (Claim to have reached the pole is in dispute, however.)

1926 — Amundsen, Ellsworth, and Umberto Nobile (It.) flew from Spitsbergen over N Pole May 12, to Teller, AK, in dirigible *Norge*.

1928 — Nobile crossed N Pole in airship, May 24; crashed, May 25. Amundsen died attempting a rescue.

North Pole Exploration Records

On Aug. 3, 1958, submarine *Nautilus*, under Comdr. William R. Anderson, crossed the N Pole beneath the ice.

In Aug. 1960, the nuclear-powered U.S. submarine *Seadragon* (Comdr. George P. Steele 2nd) made the 1st E-W underwater transit through the Northwest Passage. Traveling submerged for the most part, it took 6 days to make the 850-mi trek from Baffin Bay to the Beaufort Sea.

On Apr. 19, 1968, Ralph Plaisted (U.S.) and 3 amateur explorers on snowmobiles became the first independently confirmed surface expedition to reach the N. Pole.

On Aug. 16, 1977, the Soviet nuclear icebreaker *Arktika* became the 1st surface ship to reach the N Pole.

On Apr. 30, 1978, Naomi Uemura (Jap.) became the 1st person to reach the N Pole alone, traveling by dog sled in a 54-day, 600-mi trek over the frozen Arctic.

In Apr. 1982, Sir Ranulph Fiennes and Charles Burton, Brit. explorers, reached the N Pole and became the 1st to circle the earth from pole to pole. They had reached the S Pole 16 months earlier. The 52,000-mi trek took 3 years, involved 23 people, and cost an estimated $18 mil.

On May 2, 1986, 6 explorers reached the N Pole assisted only by dogs. They became the 1st to reach the pole without aerial logistics support since at least 1909. The explorers, Amer. Will Steger, Paul Schurke, Ann Bancroft, and Geoff Carroll, and Can. Brent Boddy and Richard Weber, completed the 500-mi journey in 56 days.

On June 15, 1995, Weber and Russ. Mikhail Malakhov became the 1st pair to make it to the pole and back without any mechanical assistance. The 940-mi trip, made entirely on skis, took 121 days.

On May 20, 2003, Pen Hadow (U.K.) became the 1st to reach the pole from Canada, solo and without resupply. The 377-mile journey across the ice took 64 days.

Antarctic Exploration

Antarctica has been approached since 1773-75, when Capt. James Cook (Brit.) reached 71°10´S. Many sea and landmarks bear names of early explorers. Fabian von Bellingshausen (Russ.) discovered Peter I and Alexander I Isls., 1819-21. Nathaniel Palmer (U.S.) traveled throughout Palmer Peninsula, 60°W, 1820, without realizing that this was a continent. Capt. John Davis (U.S.) made the 1st known landing on the continent on Feb. 7, 1821. Later, in 1823, James Weddell (Brit.) found Weddell Sea, 74°15´S, the southernmost point that had been reached.

First to announce existence of the continent of Antarctica was Charles Wilkes (U.S.), who followed the coast for 1,500 mi, 1840. Adelie Coast, 140° E, was found by Dumont d'Urville (Fr.), 1840. Ross Ice Shelf was found by James Clark Ross (Brit.), 1841-42.

1895 — Leonard Kristensen (Nor.) landed a party on the coast of Victoria Land. They were the 1st ashore on the main continental mass. C. E. Borchgrevink, a member of that party, returned in 1899 with a Brit. expedition, 1st to winter on Antarctica.

1902-4 — Robert Falcon Scott (Brit.) explored Edward VII Peninsula to 82°17´S, 146°33´E from McMurdo Sound.

1908-9 — Ernest Shackleton (Brit.) 1st to use Manchurian ponies in Antarctic sledging. He reached 88°23´S, discovering a route on to the plateau by way of the Beardmore Glacier and pioneering the way to the pole.

1911 — Roald Amundsen (Nor.) with 4 men and dog teams reached the S Pole, Dec. 14.

1912 — Scott reached the pole from Ross Isl., Jan. 18, with 4 companions. None of Scott's party survived. Their bodies and expedition notes were found, Nov. 12.

1928 — 1st person to use an airplane over Antarctica was Sir George Hubert Wilkins (Austral.).

1929 — Richard E. Byrd (U.S.) established Little America on Bay of Whales. On 1,600-mi airplane flight begun Nov. 28, he crossed S Pole, Nov. 29, with 3 others.

1934-35 — Byrd led 2nd expedition to Little America, explored 450,000 sq mi, wintered alone at 80°08´S.

WORLD ALMANAC QUICK QUIZ

Excluding Asian peaks, where is the highest mountain in the world?

(a) South America (Aconcagua) (b) North America (McKinley)

(c) Africa (Kilimanjaro) (d) Antarctica (Vinson Massif)

For the answer look in this chapter, or see page 1008.

1934-37 — John Rymill led British Graham Land expedition; discovered Palmer Penin. is part of mainland.

1935 — Lincoln Ellsworth (U.S.) flew S along E Coast of Palmer Penin., then crossed continent to Little America, making 4 landings.

1939-41 — U.S. Navy plane flights discovered about 150,000 sq mi of new land.

1940 — Byrd charted most of coast between Ross Sea and Palmer Penin.

1946-47 — U.S. Navy undertook Operation Highjump, commanded by Byrd, included 13 ships and 4,000 men. Airplanes photomapped coastline and penetrated beyond pole.

1946-48 — Ronne Antarctic Research Expedition Comdr., Finn Ronne, USNR, determined the Antarctic to be only one continent with no strait between Weddell Sea and Ross Sea; explored 250,000 sq mi of land by flights to 79ºS.

1955-57 — U.S. Navy's Operation Deep Freeze led by Adm. Byrd. Supporting U.S. scientific efforts for the International Geophysical Year (IGY), the operation established 5 coastal stations fronting the Indian, Pacific, and Atlantic oceans and also 3 interior stations; explored more than 1,000,000 sq mi in Wilkes Land.

1957-58 — During the IGY, July 1957 through Dec. 1958, scientists from 12 countries conducted Antarctic research at a network of some 60 stations on Antarctica.

Dr. Vivian E. Fuchs led a 12-person Trans-Antarctic Expedition on the 1st land crossing of Antarctica. Starting from the Weddell Sea, they reached Scott Station, Mar. 2, 1958, after traveling 2,158 mi in 98 days.

1958 — A group of 5 U.S. scientists led by Edward C. Thiel, seismologist, moving by tractor from Ellsworth Station on Weddell Sea, identified a huge mountain range, 5,000 ft above the ice sheet and 9,000 ft above sea level. The range, originally seen by a Navy plane, was named the Dufek Massif, for Rear Adm. George Dufek.

1959 — Argentina, Australia, Belgium, Chile, France, Japan, New Zealand, Norway, South Africa, USSR, U.K., and U.S. signed a treaty suspending territorial claims for 30 yrs. and reserving the continent, S of 60°S, for research.

1961-62 — Scientists discovered the Bentley Trench, running from Ross Ice Shelf into Marie Byrd Land, near the end of the Ellsworth Mts., toward the Weddell Sea.

1962 — Nuclear power plant online at McMurdo Sound.

1963 — On Feb. 22, a U.S. plane made the region's longest nonstop flight from McMurdo Station S past the pole to Shackleton Mts., SE to the "Area of Inaccessibility," and back to McMurdo Station covering 3,600 mi in 10 hrs.

1964 — New Zealanders mapped the mountain area from from Cape Adare W some 400 mi to Pennell Glacier.

1985 — Igor A. Zotikov, a Russian researcher, discovered sediments in the Ross Ice Shelf that seem to support the continental drift theory. Ocean Drilling Project finds that the ice sheets of E Antarctica are 37 million yrs. old.

1989 — Victoria Murden and Shirley Metz became both the 1st women and the 1st Americans to reach the S Pole overland when they arrived with 9 others on Jan. 17, 1989.

1991 — 24 nations approved a protocol to the 1959 Antarctica Treaty, Oct. 4. New conservation provisions, including banning oil and other mineral exploration for 50 yrs.

1994 — On Dec. 25, after 50-day trek, Liv Arnesen (Nor.) became 1st woman to ski alone and unaided to the S Pole.

1995 — On Dec. 22, a Norwegian, Borge Ousland, reached the S Pole in the fastest time on skis: 44 days.

1996-97 — Ousland became 1st person to traverse Antarctica alone; reached S Pole Dec. 19, 1996; traveled 1,675 mi in 64 days, ending Jan. 18, 1997.

2000-2001 — On Feb. 11, Ann Bancroft and Liv Arnesen (Nor.) became 1st women to ski unaided across Antarctica. The 1,717-mile journey took 94 days.

Volcanoes

Sources: *Volcanoes of the World*, Geoscience Press; Global Volcanism Network, Smithsonian Institution

Roughly 540 volcanoes are known to have erupted during historical times. Nearly 75% of these historically active volcanoes lie along the so-called **Ring of Fire**, running along the W coast of the Americas from the southern tip of Chile to Alaska, down the E coast of Asia from Kamchatka to Indonesia, and continuing from New Guinea to New Zealand. The Ring of Fire marks the boundary between the mobile tectonic plates underlying the Pacific Ocean and those of the surrounding continents. Other active regions occur along rift zones, where plates pull apart, as in Iceland, or where molten material moves up from the mantle over local "hot spots," as in Hawaii. The vast majority of the earth's volcanism occurs at submarine rift zones. For more information on volcanoes, see the website at www.volcano.si.edu/gvp

Notable Volcanic Eruptions

Approximately 7,000 years ago, Mazama, a 9,900-ft volcano in southern Oregon, erupted violently, ejecting large amounts of ash and pumice and voluminous pyroclastic flows. The ash spread over the entire northwestern U.S. and as far away as Saskatchewan, Can. During the eruption, the top of the mountain collapsed, leaving a caldera 6 mi across and about a half mile deep, which filled with rainwater to form what is now called Crater Lake.

In AD 79, Vesuvio, or Vesuvius, a 4,190-ft volcano overlooking Naples Bay, became active after several centuries of apparent inactivity. On Aug. 24 of that year, a heated mud and ash flow swept down the mountain, engulfing the cities of Pompeii, Herculaneum, and Stabiae with debris more than 60 ft deep. About 10% of the population of the 3 towns were killed.

In 1883, an eruption similar to the Mazama eruption occurred on the island of Krakatau. At least 2,000 people died in pyroclastic flows on Aug. 26. The next day, the 2,640-ft peak of the volcano collapsed to 1,000 ft below sea level, sinking most of the island and killing over 3,000. A tsunami (tidal wave) generated by the collapse killed more than 31,000 people in Java and Sumatra, and eventually reached England. Ash from the eruption colored sunsets around the world for 2 years. A similar, even more powerful eruption had taken place 68 years earlier at Mt. Tambora on the Indonesian island of Sumbawa.

Date	Volcano	Deaths (est.)
Aug. 24, AD 79	Mt. Vesuvius, Italy	16,000
1586	Kelut, Java, Indon.	10,000
Dec. 15, 1631	Mt. Vesuvius, Italy	4,000
Aug. 12, 1772	Mt. Papandayan, Java, Indon.	3,000
June 8, 1783	Laki, Iceland	9,350
May 21, 1792	Mt. Unzen, Japan	14,500
Apr. 10-12, 1815	Mt. Tambora, Sumbawa, Indon.	92,000 (1)
Aug. 26-28, 1883	Krakatau, Indon.	36,000
Apr. 24, 1902	Santa María, Guatemala	1,000 (2)
May 8, 1902	Mt. Pelée, Martinique	28,000
Jan. 30, 1911	Mt. Taal, Phil.	1,400
May 19, 1919	Mt. Kelut, Java, Indon.	5,000
Jan. 17-21, 1951	Mt. Lamington, New Guinea	3,000
May 18, 1980	Mt. St. Helens, U.S.	57
Mar. 28, 1982	El Chichon, Mex.	1,880
Nov. 13, 1985	Nevado del Ruiz, Colombia	23,000
Aug. 21, 1986	Lake Nyos, Cameroon	1,700
June 15, 1991	Mt. Pinatubo, Luzon, Phil.	800

(1) Of these, 10,000 were directly related to the eruption; an additional 82,000 were the result of starvation and disease brought on by the event. (2) An additional 3,000 deaths due to a malaria outbreak are sometimes attributed to the eruption.

Notable Active Volcanoes

Active volcanoes display a wide range of activity. In this table, years are given for last display of eruptive activity, as of mid-2005; the list does not include submarine volcanoes. An eruption may involve explosive ejection of new or old fragmental material, escape of liquid lava, or both. Volcanoes are listed by height, which does not reflect eruptive magnitude.

Name (latest eruption)	Location	Height (ft)
Africa		
Mt. Cameroon (2000)	Cameroon	13,435
Nyiragongo (2005)	Congo	11,384
Nyamuragira (2004)	Congo	10,033
Mt. Oku [Lake Nyos] (1986)	Cameroon	9,878
Ol Doinyo Lengai (2004)	Tanzania	9,711
Fogo (1995)	Cape Verde Isls.	9,281
Piton de la Fournaise (2004)	Réunion Isl., Indian O.	8,632
Karthala (1991)	Comoros	7,746
Erta Ale (2004)	Ethiopia	2,011
Antarctica		
Erebus (2005)	Ross Isl	12,447
Deception Island (1970)	S. Shetland Isl.	1,890
Asia-Oceania		
Kliuchevskoi (2004)	Kamchatka, Russia	15,863
Kerinci (2004)	Sumatra, Indon.	12,467
Fuji (1708)	Honshu, Japan	12,388
Tolbachik (1976)	Kamchatka, Russia	12,080
Semeru (2005)	Java, Indon.	12,060
Slamet (1999)	Java, Indon.	11,247
Raung (2002)	Java, Indon.	10,932
Shiveluch (2005)	Kamchatka, Russia	10,771
On-take (1980)	Honshu, Japan	10,049
Merapi (2002)	Java, Indon.	9,737
Bezymianny (2005)	Kamchatka, Russia	9,455
Peuet Sague (2000)	Sumatra, Indon.	9,190
Ruapehu (1997)	New Zealand	9,176
Heard (2004)	Indian Ocean	9,006
Baitoushan (1702)	China/Korea	9,003
Asama (2004)	Honshu, Japan	8,425
Mayon (2004)	Luzon, Phil.	8,077
Canlaon (2003)	Negros Isls., Phil.	7,989
Niigata Yake-yama (1998)	Honshu, Japan	7,874
Alaid (1996)	Kuril Isl., Russia	7,674
Ulawun (2003)	Papua New Guinea	7,657
Chokai (1974)	Honshu, Japan	7,326
Galunggung (1984)	Java, Indon.	7,113
Azuma (1977)	Honshu, Japan	6,676
Tongariro (Ngauruhoe) (1977)	New Zealand	6,489
Sangeang Api (1988)	Lesser Sunda Isl., Indon.	6,394
Nasu (1963)	Honshu, Japan	6,283
Karkar (1979)	Papua New Guinea	6,033
Tiatia (1981)	Kuril Isl., Russia	5,968
Bandai (1888)	Honshu, Japan	5,968
Manam (2005)	Papua New Guinea	5,928
Kuju (1996)	Kyushu, Japan	5,876
Karangetang (Api Siau) (2005)	Sangihe Isls., Indon.	5,853
Soputan (2004)	Sulawesi, Indon.	5,853
Bagana (2005)	Papua New Guinea	5,741
Kelut (1990)	Java, Indon.	5,679
Adatara (1996)	Honshu, Japan	5,636
Gamalama (2003)	Halmahera, Indon.	5,627
Kirishima (1992)	Kyushu, Japan	5,577
Gamkonora (1987)	Halmahera, Indon.	5,364
Aso (2004)	Kyushu, Japan	5,223
Lokon-Empung (2003)	Sulawesi, Indon.	5,184
Bulusan (1995)	Luzon, Phil.	5,134
Karymsky (2005)	Kamchatka, Russia	5,039
Unzen (1996)	Kyushu, Japan	4,921
Akan (1998)	Hokkaido, Japan	4,918
Sarychev Peak (1989)	Kuril Isl., Russia	4,908
Pinatubo (1993)	Luzon, Phil.	4,875
Lopevi (2005)	Vanuatu	4,636
Akita-Yake-yama (1997)	Honshu, Japan	4,482
Ambrym (2005)	Vanuatu	4,377
Langila (2004)	Papua New Guinea	4,363
Awu (2004)	Sangihe Isl., Indon.	4,331
Dukono (2005)	Halmahera, Indon.	3,888
Akademia Nauk (1996)	Kamchatka, Russia	3,871
Komaga-take (2000)	Hokkaido, Japan	3,711
Sakura-jima (2005)	Kyushu, Japan	3,665
Miyake-jima (2004)	Izu Isls., Japan	2,674
Krakatau (2001)	Indonesia	2,667
Suwanose-jima (2005)	Ryukyu Isls., Japan	2,621
Gaua (1982)	Vanuatu	2,615
Oshima (1990)	Izu Isls., Japan	2,507
Usu (2001)	Hokkaido, Japan	2,418
Rabaul (2004)	Papua New Guinea	2,257
Pagan (1993)	N. Mariana Isl.	1,870
Taal (1977)	Luzon, Phil.	1,312
Yasur (2005)	Tanna Island, Vanuatu	1,184
White Island (2001)	Bay of Plenty, New Zealand	1,053
McDonald Islands (2001)	Indian Ocn., Australia	755
Central America—Caribbean		
Tacaná (1986)	Guatemala	13,320
Acatenango (1972)	Guatemala	13,044
Santa María (2004)	Guatemala	12,375
Fuego (2005)	Guatemala	12,346
Irazú (1994)	Costa Rica	11,260
Turrialba (1866)	Costa Rica	10,958
Póas (1996)	Costa Rica	8,884
Pacaya (2002)	Guatemala	8,373
San Miguel (2002)	El Salvador	6,988
Rincón de la Vieja (1998)	Costa Rica	6,286
San Cristobal (2004)	Nicaragua	5,725
Concepción (2005)	Nicaragua	5,577
Arenal (2005)	Costa Rica	5,436
Soufrière Guadeloupe (1977)	Guadeloupe	4,813
Pelée (1932)	Martinique	4,583
Momotombo (1905)	Nicaragua	4,255
Soufrière St. Vincent (1979)	St. Vincent	4,003
Soufrière Hills (2004)	Montserrat	3,002
Masaya (2003)	Nicaragua	2,083
South America		
Llullaillaco (1877)	Argentina-Chile	22,109
Guallatiri (1960)	Chile	19,918
Tupungatito (1987)	Chile	19,685
Cotopaxi (1940)	Ecuador	19,393
El Misti (1784)	Peru	19,101
Láscar (2002)	Chile	18,346
Nevado del Ruiz (1991)	Colombia	17,457
Sangay (2005)	Ecuador	17,159
Irruputuncu (1995)	Chile	16,939
Tungurahua (2005)	Ecuador	16,479
Guagua Pichincha (2004)	Ecuador	15,695
Puracé (1977)	Colombia	15,256
Galeras (2005)	Colombia	14,029
Llaima (2003)	Chile	10,253
Villarrica (2005)	Chile	9,340
Cerro Hudson (1991)	Chile	6,250
Fernandina (1995)	Galapagos Isls., Ecuad.	4,842
Mid-Pacific		
Mauna Loa (1984)	Hawaii, HI	13,681
Kilauea (2005)	Hawaii, HI	4,009
Mid-Atlantic Ridge		
Jan Mayen (1985)	N. Atlantic Ocn., Norway	7,470
Grímsvötn (2004)	Iceland	5,659
Hekla (2000)	Iceland	4,892
Krafla (1984)	Iceland	2,133
Europe		
Etna (2005)	Italy	10,991
Vesuvius (1944)	Italy	4,203
Stromboli (2005)	Italy	3,038
Santorini (1950)	Greece	1,204
North America		
Pico de Orizaba (1846)	Mexico	18,619
Popocatépetl (2004)	Mexico	17,802
Rainier (1825?)	Washington	14,409
Wrangell (1999)	Alaska	14,163
Shasta (1786)	California	14,163
Colima (2005)	Mexico	12,631
Lassen Peak (1917)	California	10,456
Redoubt (1990)	Alaska	10,197
Iliamna (1876)	Alaska	10,016
Shishaldin (2004)	Aleutian Isl., AK	9,373
St. Helens (2005)	Washington	8,363
Pavlof (1997)	Alaska	8,264
Veniaminof (2004)	Alaska	8,225
Katmai [Novarupta] (1912)	Alaska	6,716
Makushin (1995)	Aleutian Isl., AK	5,905
Great Sitkin (1974)	Aleutian Isl., AK	5,709
Cleveland (2001)	Aleutian Isl., AK	5,676
Gareloi (1989)	Aleutian Isl., AK	5,161
Korovin [Atka complex] (1998)	Aleutian Isl., AK	5,029
Akutan (1992)	Aleutian Isl., AK	4,275
Augustine (1986)	Alaska	4,108
Kiska (1990)	Aleutian Isl., AK	4,003
El Chichón (1982)	Mexico	3,773
Okmok (1997)	Aleutian Isl., AK	3,520
Seguam (1993)	Aleutian Isl., AK	3,458

IT'S A FACT: Everest climbers Moni Mulepati and Pem Dorjee surprised friends and family members in the spring of 2005 by marrying in a simple ceremony at the summit of the Himalayan peak, an Everest first. The Nepalese couple temporarily removed their oxygen masks to apply traditional red powder to the bride's forehead and exchange vows.

Mountains

Height of Mount Everest

Mt. Everest, the world's highest mountain, was considered 29,002 ft when Edmund Hillary and Tenzing Norgay became the 1st climbers to scale it, in 1953. This triangulation figure had been accepted since 1850. In 1954 the Surveyor General of the Republic of India set the height at 29,028 ft, plus or minus 10 ft because of snow; this figure was also accepted by the National Geographic Society.

In 1999, a team of climbers sponsored by Boston's Museum of Science and the National Geographic Society measured the height at the summit using sophisticated satellite-based technology. This new measurement, of 29,035 ft, was accepted by the National Geographic Society and other authorities, including the U.S. National Imagery and Mapping Agency.

By May 31, 2005, over 50 years after the 1st climbers had reached the summit, some 1,400 more had followed, and about 180 had died in the attempt.

United States, Canada, Mexico

Peak, place	Height (ft)	Peak, place	Height (ft)	Peak, place	Height (ft)
McKinley, AK	20,320	Alverstone, AK-Yukon	14,565	Shavano, CO.	14,229
Logan, Yukon	19,551	Browne Tower, AK.	14,530	Belford, CO	14,197
Pico de Orizaba, Mexico	18,555	Whitney, CA.	14,494	Princeton,	14,197
St. Elias, AK-Yukon	18,008	Elbert, CO	14,433	Crestone Needle, CO	14,197
Popocatépetl, Mexico.	17,930	Massive, CO	14,421	Yale, CO	14,196
Foraker, AK	17,400	Harvard, CO	14,420	Bross, CO	14,172
Iztaccihuatl, Mexico	17,343	Rainier, WA	14,410	Kit Carson, CO	14,165
Lucania, Yukon	17,147	University Peak, AK.	14,410	Wrangell, AK.	14,163
King, Yukon	16,971	Williamson, CA	14,375	Shasta, CA	14,162
Steele, Yukon.	16,644	La Plata Peak, CO.	14,361	El Diente Peak, CO.	14,159
Bona, AK	16,550	Blanca Peak, CO.	14,345	Point Success, WA	14,158
Blackburn, AK	16,390	Uncompahgre Peak, CO	14,309	Maroon Peak, CO	14,156
Kennedy, AK	16,286	Crestone Peak, CO	14,294	Tabeguache, CO.	14,155
Sanford, AK	16,237	Lincoln, CO	14,286	Oxford, CO	14,153
Vancouver, AK-Yukon	15,979	Grays Peak, CO	14,270	Sill, CA	14,153
South Buttress, AK.	15,885	Antero, CO.	14,269	Sneffels, CO	14,150
Wood, Yukon	15,885	Torreys Peak, CO	14,267	Democrat, CO.	14,148
Churchill, AK	15,638	Castle Peak, CO	14,265	Capitol Peak,CO	14,130
Fairweather, AK-BC	15,300	Quandary Peak, CO	14,265	Liberty Cap, WA	14,112
Zinantecatl (Toluca), Mexico	15,016	Evans, CO.	14,264	Pikes Peak, CO.	14,110
Hubbard, AK-Yukon	15,015	Longs Peak, CO	14,255	Snowmass, CO.	14,092
Bear, AK.	14,831	McArthur, Yukon	14,253	Russell, CA	14,088
Walsh, Yukon	14,780	Wilson, CO	14,246	Eolus, CO	14,083
East Buttress, AK.	14,730	White Mt. Peak, CA	14,246	Windom,CO.	14,082
Matlalcueyetl, Mexico.	14,636	North Palisade, CA	14,242	Columbia,CO.	14,073
Hunter, AK	14,753	Cameron, CO	14,238	Augusta, AK	14,070

South America

Peak, country	Height (ft)	Peak, country	Height (ft)	Peak, country	Height (ft)
Aconcagua, Argentina	22,834	Coropuna, Peru	21,083	Solo, Argentina	20,492
Ojos del Salado, Arg.-Chile	22,572	Laudo, Argentina	20,997	Polleras, Argentina	20,456
Bonete, Argentina	22,546	Ancohuma, Bolivia.	20,958	Pular, Chile	20,423
Tupungato, Argentina-Chile	22,310	Ausangate, Peru	20,945	Chani, Argentina	20,341
Pissis, Argentina	22,241	Toro, Argentina-Chile	20,932	Aucanquilcha, Chile	20,295
Mercedario, Argentina	22,211	Illampu, Bolivia	20,873	Juncal, Argentina-Chile.	20,276
Huascaran, Peru	22,205	Tres Cruces, Argentina-Chile	20,853	Negro, Argentina.	20,184
Llullaillaco, Argentina-Chile	22,109	Huandoy, Peru.	20,852	Quela, Argentina	20,128
El Libertador, Argentina	22,047	Parinacota, Bolivia-Chile	20,768	Condoriri, Bolivia.	20,095
Cachi, Argentina.	22,047	Tortolas, Argentina-Chile.	20,745	Palermo, Argentina	20,079
Incahuasi, Argentina-Chile	21,720	Ampato, Peru.	20,702	Solimana, Peru	20,068
Yerupaja, Peru	21,709	El Condor, Argentina	20,669	San Juan, Argentina-Chile	20,049
Galan, Argentina	21,654	Salcantay, Peru	20,574	Sierra Nevada, Arg.-Chile	20,023
El Muerto, Argentina-Chile	21,457	Chimborazo, Ecuador	20,561	Antofalla, Argentina.	20,013
Sajama, Bolivia	21,391	Huancarhuas, Peru	20,531	Marmolejo, Argentina-Chile.	20,013
Nacimiento, Argentina	21,302	Famatina, Argentina	20,505	Chachani, Peru	19,931
Illimani, Bolivia	21,201	Pumasillo, Peru	20,492		

The highest point in the West Indies is in the Dominican Republic, Pico Duarte (10,417 ft).

Africa

Peak, country	Height (ft)	Peak, country	Height (ft)	Peak, country	Height (ft)
Kilimanjaro, Tanzania.	19,340	Meru, Tanzania	14,979	Guna, Ethiopia	13,881
Kenya, Kenya.	17,058	Karisimbi, Congo-Rwanda	14,787	Gughe, Ethiopia	13,780
Margherita Pk., Uganda-Congo	16,763	Elgon, Kenya-Uganda	14,178	Toubkal, Morocco	13,661
Ras Dashan, Ethiopia	15,158	Batu, Ethiopia	14,131	Cameroon, Cameroon.	13,435

Australia, New Zealand, SE Asian Islands

Peak, country	Height (ft)	Peak, country	Height (ft)	Peak, country	Height (ft)
Jaya, New Guinea	16,500	Wilhelm, New Guinea	14,793	Cook, New Zealand.	12,349
Trikora, New Guinea	15,585	Kinabalu, Malaysia	13,455	Semeru, Java, Indon.	12,060
Mandala, New Guinea	15,420	Kerinci, Sumatra, Indon.	12,467	Kosciusko, Australia	7,310

Europe

Peak, country	Height (ft)
Alps	
Mont Blanc, Fr.-It.	15,771
Monte Rosa (highest peak of group), Switz.	15,203
Dom, Switz.	14,911
Liskamm, It., Switz.	14,852
Weisshorn, Switz.	14,780
Taschhorn, Switz.	14,733
Matterhorn, It., Switz.	14,690
Dent Blanche, Switz.	14,293
Nadelhorn, Switz.	14,196
Grand Combin, Switz.	14,154
Lenzpitze, Switz.	14,088
Finsteraarhorn, Switz.	14,022
Castor, Switz.	13,865
Zinalrothorn, Switz.	13,849
Hohberghom, Switz.	13,842
Alphubel, Switz.	13,799
Rimpfischhom, Switz.	13,776
Aletschorn, Switz.	13,763
Strahlhorn, Switz.	13,747
Dent D'Herens, Switz.	13,686
Breithorn, It., Switz.	13,665
Bishorn, Switz.	13,645
Jungfrau, Switz.	13,642
Ecrins, Fr.	13,461
Monch, Switz.	13,448
Pollux, Switz.	13,422
Schreckhorn, Switz.	13,379
Ober Gabelhorn, Switz.	13,330
Gran Paradiso, It.	13,323
Bernina, It., Switz.	13,284
Fiescherhorn, Switz.	13,283
Grunhorn, Switz.	13,266
Lauteraarhorn, Switz.	13,261
Durrenhorn, Switz.	13,238
Allalinhorn, Switz.	13,213
Weissmies, Switz.	13,199
Lagginhorn, Switz.	13,156
Zupo, Switz.	13,120
Fletschhorn, Switz.	13,110
Adlerhorn, Switz.	13,081
Gletscherhorn, Switz.	13,068
Schalihorn, Switz.	13,040
Scerscen, Switz.	13,028
Eiger, Switz.	13,025
Jagerhorn, Switz.	13,024
Rottalhorn, Switz.	13,022
Pyrenees	
Aneto, Sp.	11,168
Posets, Sp.	11,073
Perdido, Sp.	11,007
Vignemale, Fr.-Sp.	10,820
Long, Sp.	10,479
Estats, Sp.	10,304
Montcalm, Sp.	10,105
Caucasus (Europe-Asia)	
Elbrus, Russia	18,510
Shkhara, Georgia	17,064
Dykh Tau, Russia	17,054
Kashtan Tau, Russia	16,877
Janqi, Georgia	16,565
Kazbek, Georgia	16,558

Asia (Mainland)

Peak, place	Height (ft)
Everest, Nepal-Tibet	29,035
K2 (Godwin Austen), Kashmir	28,250
Kanchenjunga, India-Nepal	28,208
Lhotse I (Everest), Nepal-Tibet	27,923
Makalu I, Nepal-Tibet	27,824
Lhotse II (Everest), Nepal-Tibet	27,560
Dhaulagiri, Nepal	26,810
Manaslu I, Nepal	26,760
Cho Oyu, Nepal-Tibet	26,750
Nanga Parbat, Kashmir	26,660
Annapurna I, Nepal	26,504
Gasherbrum, Kashmir	26,470
Broad, Kashmir	26,400
Gosainthan Nepal-Tibet	26,287
Annapurna II, Nepal	26,041
Gyachung Kang, Nepal-Tibet	25,910
Disteghil Sar, Kashmir	25,868
Himalchuli, Nepal	25,801
Nuptse (Everest), Nepal-Tibet	25,726
Masherbrum, Kashmir	25,660
Nanda Devi, India	25,645
Rakaposhi, Kashmir	25,550
Kamet, India-Tibet	25,447
Namcha Barwa, Tibet	25,445
Gurla Mandhata, Tibet	25,355
Ulugh Muz Tagh, Xinjiang-Tibet	25,340
Kungur, Xinjiang	25,325
Tirich Mir, Pakistan	25,230
Makalu II, Nepal-Tibet	25,120
Minya Konka, China	24,900
Kula Gangri, Bhutan-Tibet	24,784
Changtzu (Everest), Nepal-Tibet	24,780
Muz Tagh Ata, Xinjiang	24,757
Skyang Kangri, Kashmir	24,750
Ismail Semani Peak,Tajikistan	24,590
Jongsang Peak, India-Nepal	24,472
Jengish Chokusu, Xinjiang-Kyrgyzstan	24,406
Sia Kangri, Kashmir	24,350
Haramosh Peak, Pakistan	24,270
Istoro Nal, Pakistan	24,240
Tent Peak, India-Nepal	24,165
Chomo Lhari, Bhutan-Tibet	24,040
Chamlang, Nepal	24,012
Kabru, India-Nepal	24,002
Alung Gangri, Tibet	24,000
Baltoro Kangri, Kashmir	23,990
Mussu Shan, Xinjiang	23,890
Mana, India	23,860
Baruntse, Nepal	23,688
Nepal Peak, India-Nepal	23,500
Amne Machin, China	23,490
Gauri Sankar, Nepal-Tibet	23,440
Badrinath, India	23,420
Nunkun, Kashmir	23,410
Lenin Peak, Tajikistan	23,405
Pyramid, India-Nepal	23,400
Api, Nepal	23,399
Pauhunri, India-Tibet	23,385
Trisul, India	23,360
Kangto, India-Tibet	23,260
Nyenchhe Thanglha, Tibet	23,255
Trisuli, India	23,210
Pumori, Nepal-Tibet	23,190
Dunagiri, India	23,184
Lombo Kangra, Tibet	23,165
Saipal, Nepal	23,100
Macha Pucchare, Nepal	22,958
Numbar, Nepal	22,817
Kanjiroba, Nepal	22,580
Ama Dablam, Nepal	22,350
Cho Polu, Nepal	22,093
Lingtren, Nepal-Tibet	21,972
Khumbutse, Nepal-Tibet	21,785
Hlako Gangri, Tibet	21,266
Mt. Grosvenor, China	21,190
Thagchhab Gangri, Tibet	20,970
Damavand, Iran	18,606
Ararat, Turkey	16,804

Antarctica

Peak	Height (ft)
Vinson Massif	16,864
Tyree	16,290
Shinn	15,750
Gardner	15,375
Epperly	15,100
Kirkpatrick	14,855
Elizabeth	14,698
Markham	14,290
Bell	14,117
Mackellar	14,098
Anderson	13,957
Bentley	13,934
Kaplan	13,878
Andrew Jackson	13,750
Sidley	13,720
Ostenso	13,710
Minto	13,668
Miller	13,650
Long Gables	13,620
Dickerson	13,517
Giovinetto	13,412
Wade	13,400
Fisher	13,386
Fridtjof Nansen	13,350
Wexler	13,202
Lister	13,200
Shear	13,100
Odishaw	13,008
Donaldson	12,894
Ray	12,808
Sellery	12,779
Waterman	12,730
Anne	12,703
Press	12,566
Falla	12,549
Rucker	12,520
Goldthwait	12,510
Morris	12,500
Erebus	12,450
Campbell	12,434
Don Pedro Christophersen	12,355
Lysaght	12,326
Huggins	12,247
Sabine	12,200
Astor	12,175
Mohl	12,172
Frankes	12,064
Jones	12,040
Gjelsvik	12,008
Coman	12,000

Some Notable U.S. Mountains

Peak, place	Height (ft)
Gannett Peak, WY	13,804
Grand Teton, WY	13,766
Kings, UT	13,528
Cloud, WY	13,175
Wheeler, NM	13,161
Boundary, NV	13,140
Granite, MT	12,799
Borah, ID	12,662
Humphreys, AZ	12,633
Adams, WA	12,277
San Gorgonio, CA	11,502
Hood, OR	11,239
Lassen, CA	10,457
Granite, CA	10,321
Guadalupe, TX	8,749
Olympus, WA	7,965
Harney, SD	7,242
Mitchell, NC	6,684
Clingmans Dome, NC-TN	6,643
Washington, NH	6,288
Rogers, VA	5,729
Marcy, NY	5,344
Katahdin, ME	5,268
Spruce Knob, WV	4,861
Mansfield, VT	4,393
Black Mountain, KY	4,145

Important Islands and Their Areas

Figures are for total areas in square miles. Boldface figure in parentheses shows rank among the world's 10 largest individual islands. Because some islands have not been surveyed accurately, some areas shown are estimates. Some "islands" listed are island groups. Only the largest islands in a group are listed individually. Only islands over 10 sq. miles in area are listed.

Antarctica

Adelaide	1,400
Alexander	16,700
Berkner	18,500
Roosevelt	2,900

Arctic Ocean

Akimiski, Nunavut	1,159
Amund Ringnes, Nun.	2,029
Axel Heiberg, Nun.	16,671
Baffin, Nun. **(5)**	195,928
Banks, Northwest Territories	27,038
Bathurst, Nun.	6,194
Bolshevik, Russia	4,368
Bolshoy Lyakhovsky, Russia	1,776
Borden, NWT., Nun.	1,079
Bylot, Nun.	4,273
Coats, Nun.	2,123
Cornwallis, Nun.	2,701
Devon, Nun.	21,331
Disko, Greenland	3,312
Ellef Ringnes, Nun.	4,361
Ellesmere, Nun. **(10)**	75,767
Faddayevskiy, Russia	1,930
Franz Josef Land, Russia	8,000
Iturup (Etorofu), Russia	2,596
King William, Nun.	5,062
Komsomolets, Russia	3,477
Mackenzie King, NWT	1,949
Mansel, Nun.	1,228
Melville, NWT, Nun.	16,274
Milne Land, Greenland	1,400
New Siberian Islands, Russia	14,500
Kotelnyy, Russia	4,504
Novaya Zemlya, Russia (2 isls.)	31,730
Oktyabrskoy, Russia	5,471
Prince Charles, NWT	3,676
Prince of Wales, Nun.	12,872
Prince Patrick, NWT	6,119
Somerset, Nun.	9,570
Southampton, Nun.	15,913
Svalbard (tot. group)	23,957
Nordaustlandet	5,410
Spitsbergen	15,060
Traill, Greenland	1,300
Victoria, NWT, Nun. **(9)**	83,897
Wrangel, Russia	2,800

Atlantic Ocean

Anticosti, Canada	3,068
Ascension, UK	34
Azores, Portugal (tot. group)	868
Faial	67
San Miguel	291
Bahama Isls. (tot. group)	5,382
Andros, Bahamas	2,300
Bermuda Islands, UK	20
Bioko Isl., Equatorial Guinea	785
Block Islands, RI, US	21
Canary Islands, Spain (tot. group)	2,807
Fuerteventura	688
Gran Canaria	592
Tenerife	795
Cape Breton, Canada	3,981
Cape Verde Islands	1,557
Caviana, Para, Brazil	1,918
Channel Islands, UK (tot. group)	75
Guernsey	24
Jersey	45
Faroe Islands, Denmark	540
Falkland Islands, UK (tot. group)	4,700
East Falkland	2,550
West Falkland	1,750
Great Britain, UK **(8)**	84,200
Greenland, Denmark **(1)**	840,000
Gurupa, Para, Brazil	1,878
Hebrides, Scotland	2,744
Iceland	39,699
Ireland (tot. group)	32,589
Irish Republic	27,137
Northern Ireland (UK)	5,452
Isle of Man, UK	227
Isle of Wight, England	147
Long Island, NY, US	1,320
Madeira Islands, Portugal	306
Marajo, Brazil	15,444
Martha's Vineyard, MA, US	89
Mount Desert, ME, US	104
Nantucket, MA, US	45
Newfoundland, Canada	42,031
Orkney Islands, Scotland	390
Prince Edward, Canada	2,185
St. Helena, UK	47
Shetland Islands, Scotland	587
Skye, Scotland	670
South Georgia, UK	1,450
Tierra del Fuego, Chile, Arg.	18,800
Tristan da Cunha, UK	40

Baltic Sea

Aland Islands, Finland	590
Bornholm, Denmark	227
Gotland, Sweden	1,159

Caribbean Sea

Antigua	108
Aruba, Netherlands	75
Barbados	166
Cuba	42,804
Isle of Youth	926
Cayman Islands	100
Curacao, Netherlands	171
Dominica	290
Guadeloupe, France	687
Hispaniola (Haiti and Dominican Rep)	29,389
Jamaica	4,244
Martinique, France	436
Puerto Rico, US	3,339
Tobago	116
Trinidad	1,864
Virgin Islands, UK	59
Virgin Islands, US	134

East Indies

Bali, Indonesia	2,171
Bangka, Indonesia	4,375
Borneo, Indonesia-Malaysia-Brunei **(3)**	280,100
Bougainville, Papua New Guinea	3,880
Buru, Indonesia	3,670
Celebes, Indonesia	69,000
Flores, Indonesia	5,500
Halmahera, Indonesia	6,865
Java (Jawa), Indonesia	48,900
Madura, Indonesia	2,113
Moluccas, Indonesia	32,307
New Britain, Papua New Guinea	14,093
New Guinea, Indon.-PNG **(2)**	306,000
New Ireland, PNG	3,707
Seram, Indonesia	6,621
Sumba, Indonesia	4,306
Sumbawa, Indonesia	5,965
Sumatra, Indonesia **(6)**	165,000
Timor, Indonesia	13,094
Yos Sudarsa, Indonesia	4,500

Indian Ocean

Andaman Isls., India	2,500
Kerguelen	2,247
Madagascar **(4)**	226,658
Mauritius	720
Pemba, Tanzania	380
Reunion, France	970
Seychelles	176
Sri Lanka	25,332
Zanzibar, Tanzania	640

Mediterranean Sea

Balearic Isls., Spain	1,927
Corfu, Greece	229
Corsica, France	3,369
Crete, Greece	3,189
Cyprus	3,572
Elba, Italy	86
Euboea, Greece	1,411
Malta	95
Rhodes, Greece	540
Sardinia, Italy	9,301
Sicily, Italy	9,926

Pacific Ocean

Admiralty, AK, US	1,709
Aleutian Isls., AK, US (tot. group)	6,912
Adak	275
Amchitka	116
Attu	350
Kanaga	142
Kiska	106
Tanaga	195
Umnak	686
Unalaska	1,051
Unimak	1,571
Baranof, AK, US	1,636
Chichagof, AK, US	2,062
Chiloe, Chile	3,241
Christmas, Kiribati	94
Diomede, Big, Russia	11
Easter Isl., Chile	69
Fiji (tot. group)	7,056
Vanua Levu	2,242
Viti Levu	4,109
Galapagos Isls., Ecuador	3,043
Graham Isl., British Columbia	2,456
Guadalcanal, Solomon Isls.	2,180
Guam, US	210
Hainan, China	13,000
Hawaiian Isls., HI, US (tot. group)	6,428
Hawaii	4,028
Oahu	600
Hong Kong, China	31
Hoste, Chile	1,590
Japan (tot. group)	145,850
Hokkaido	30,144
Honshu **(7)**	87,805
Kyushu	14,114
Okinawa	459
Shikoku	7,049
Kangaroo, South Australia	1,680
Kodiak, AK, US	3,485
Kupreanof, AK, US	1,084
Marquesas Isls., France	492
Marshall Isls.	70
Melville, N Terr., Austral	2,240
Micronesia	271
New Caledonia, France	6,530
New Zealand (tot. group)	104,454
Chatham Isls.	372
North	44,204
South	58,384
Stewart	674
North Mariana Isls., US	179
Nunivak, AK, US	1,600
Palau	188
Philippines (tot. group)	115,860
Leyte	2,787
Luzon	40,680
Mindanao	36,775
Mindoro	3,690
Negros	4,907
Palawan	4,554
Panay	4,446
Samar	5,050
Prince of Wales, AK, US	2,770
Revillagigedo, AK, US	1,134
Riesco, Chile	1,973
St. Lawrence, AK, US	1,780
Sakhalin, Russia	29,500
Samoa Isls. (tot. group)	1,177
American Samoa, US	77
Tutuila, US	55
Savail, Samoa	659
Upolu, Samoa	432
Santa Catalina, CA, US	75
Santa Ines, Chile	1,407
Tahiti, France	402
Taiwan, China (tot. group)	13,969
Jinmen Dao (Quemoy)	56
Tasmania, Australia	26,178
Tonga Isls.	290
Vancouver Isl., Brit. Columbia	12,079
Vanuatu	4,707
Wellington, Chile	2,549

Persian Gulf

Bahrain	217

WORLD ALMANAC QUICK QUIZ

How many of the 50 highest mountains in the world are in Asia?

(a) 32 (b) 40 (c) 46 (d) 50

For the answer look in this chapter, or see page 1008.

Areas and Average Depths of Oceans, Seas, and Gulfs[1]

Geographers and mapmakers recognize at least 4 major bodies of water: the Pacific, the Atlantic, the Indian, and the Arctic oceans. The Atlantic and Pacific oceans are considered divided at the equator into the N and S Atlantic and the N and S Pacific. The Arctic Ocean is the name for waters N of the continental landmasses in the region of the Arctic Circle.

	Area (sq mi)	Avg. depth (ft)
Pacific Ocean	64,186,300	12,925
Atlantic Ocean	33,420,000	11,730
Indian Ocean	28,350,500	12,598
Arctic Ocean	5,105,700	3,407
South China Sea	1,148,500	4,802
Caribbean Sea	971,400	8,448
Mediterranean Sea	969,100	4,926
Bering Sea	873,000	4,893
Gulf of Mexico	582,100	5,297
Sea of Okhotsk	537,500	3,192
Sea of Japan	391,100	5,468
Hudson Bay	281,900	305
East China Sea	256,600	620
Andaman Sea	218,100	3,667
Black Sea	196,100	3,906
Red Sea	174,900	1,764
North Sea	164,900	308
Baltic Sea	147,500	180
Yellow Sea	113,500	121
Persian Gulf	88,800	328
Gulf of California	59,100	2,375

(1) The International Hydrographic Organization delimited a fifth world ocean in 2000. The Southern Ocean as defined extends from the coast of Antarctica north to 60° south latitude, covering portions of the Atlantic, Indian, and Pacific oceans, an area of 7,848,400 square miles.

Principal Ocean Depths

Source: National Imagery and Mapping Agency, U.S. Dept. of Defense

Name of area	Location (lat.)	Location (long.)	Depth (meters)	Depth (fathoms)	Depth (ft)
Pacific Ocean					
Marianas Trench	11°22´ N	142°36´E	10,924	5,973	35,840
Tonga Trench	23°16´ S	174°44´W	10,800	5,906	35,433
Philippine Trench	10°38´ N	126°36´ E	10,057	5,499	32,995
Kermadec Trench	31°53´ S	177°21´W	10,047	5,494	32,963
Bonin Trench	24°30´ N	143°24´E	9,994	5,464	32,788
Kuril Trench	44°15´ N	150°34´E	9,750	5,331	31,988
Izu Trench	31°05´ N	142°10´E	9,695	5,301	31,808
New Britain Trench	06°19´ S	153°45´E	8,940	4,888	29,331
Yap Trench	08°33´ N	138°02´E	8,527	4,663	27,976
Japan Trench	36°08´ N	142°43´E	8,412	4,600	27,599
Peru-Chile Trench	23° 18´ S	71°14´W	8,064	4,409	26,457
Palau Trench	07° 52´ N	134° 56´E	8,054	4,404	26,424
Aleutian Trench	50°51´ N	177°11´E	7,679	4,199	25,194
New Hebrides Trench	20°36´ S	168° 37´E	7,570	4,139	24,836
North Ryukyu Trench	24°00´ N	126°48´E	7,181	3,927	23,560
Mid. America Trench	14°02´ N	93°39´W	6,662	3,643	21,857
Atlantic Ocean					
Puerto Rico Trench	19°55´ N	65°27´ W	8,605	4,705	28,232
S Sandwich Trench	55°42´ S	25°56´ W	8,325	4,552	27,313
Romanche Gap	0°13´ S	18°26´ W	7,728	4,226	25,354
Cayman Trench	19°12´ N	80°00´ W	7,535	4,120	24,721
Brazil Basin	09°10´ S	23°02´ W	6,119	3,346	20,076
Indian Ocean					
Java Trench	10°19´ S	109°58´E	7,125	3,896	23,376
Ob' Trench	09° 45´ S	67°18´E	6,874	3,759	22,553
Diamantina Trench	35° 50´ S	105°14´E	6,602	3,610	21,660
Vema Trench	09°08´ S	67°15´E	6,402	3,501	21,004
Agulhas Basin	45°20´ S	26°50´E	6,195	3,387	20,325
Arctic Ocean					
Eurasia Basin	82°23´ N	19°31´E	5,450	2,980	17,881
Mediterranean Sea					
Ionian Basin	36°32´ N	21°06´E	5,150	2,816	16,896

Note: Greater depths have been reported in some areas but are not officially confirmed by research vessels.

Latitude and Longitude of World Cities

Source: National Imagery Mapping Agency, U.S. Dept. of Defense

City	Lat. ° ´	Long. ° ´
Athens, Greece	37 59 N	23 44 E
Bangkok, Thailand	13 45 N	100 31 E
Beijing, China	39 56 N	116 24 E
Berlin, Germany	52 31 N	13 25 E
Bogotá, Colombia	04 36 N	74 05 W
Bombay (Mumbai), India	18 58 N	72 50 E
Buenos Aires, Argentina	34 36 S	58 28 W
Cairo, Egypt	30 03 N	31 15 E
Jakarta, Indonesia	06 10 S	106 48 E
Jerusalem, Israel	31 46 N	35 14 E
Johannesburg, South Africa	26 12 S	28 05 E
Kathmandu, Nepal	27 43 N	85 19 E
Kiev, Ukraine	50 26 N	30 31 E
London, UK (Greenwich)	51 30 N	00 00
Manila, Philippines	14 35 N	121 00 E
Mexico City, Mexico	19 24 N	99 09 W
Moscow, Russia	55 45 N	37 35 E
New Delhi, India	28 36 N	77 12 E
Panama City, Panama	08 58 N	79 32 W
Paris, France	48 52 N	02 20 E
Quito, Ecuador	00 13 S	78 30 W
Rio de Janeiro, Brazil	22 43 S	43 13 W
Rome, Italy	41 53 N	12 30 E
Santiago, Chile	33 27 S	70 40 W
Seoul, South Korea	37 34 N	127 00 E
Sydney, Australia	33 53 S	151 12 E
Tehran, Iran	35 40 N	51 26 E
Tokyo, Japan	35 42 N	139 46 E
Warsaw, Poland	52 15 N	21 00 E
Wellington, New Zealand	41 18 S	174 47 E

Latitude, Longitude, and Altitude of U.S. and Canadian Cities

Source: U.S. geographic positions, U.S. altitudes provided by Geological Survey, U.S. Dept. of the Interior. Canadian geographic positions and altitudes provided by Natural Resources Canada.

City	Lat. N °	′	″	Long. W °	′	″	Elev. (ft)
Abilene, TX	32	26	55	99	43	58	1,718
Akron, OH	41	4	53	81	31	9	1,050
Albany, NY	42	39	9	73	45	24	20
Albuquerque, NM	35	5	4	106	39	2	4,955
Alert, N.W.T.	82	30	0	62	22	0	100
Allentown, PA	40	36	30	75	29	26	350
Amarillo, TX	35	13	19	101	49	51	3,685
Anchorage, AK	61	13	5	149	54	1	101
Ann Arbor, MI	42	16	15	83	43	35	880
Asheville, NC	35	36	3	82	33	15	2,134
Ashland, KY	38	28	42	82	38	17	558
Atlanta, GA	33	44	56	84	23	17	1,050
Atlantic City, NJ	39	21	51	74	25	24	8
Augusta, GA	33	28	15	81	58	30	414
Augusta, ME	44	18	38	69	46	48	45
Austin, TX	30	16	1	97	44	34	501
Bakersfield, CA	35	22	24	119	1	4	408
Baltimore, MD	39	17	25	76	36	45	100
Bangor, ME	44	48	4	68	46	42	158
Baton Rouge, LA	30	27	2	91	9	16	53
Battle Creek, MI	42	19	16	85	10	47	820
Bay City, MI	43	35	40	83	53	20	595
Beaumont, TX	30	5	9	94	6	6	20
Belleville, Ont.	44	14	0	77	21	0	320
Bellingham, WA	48	45	35	122	29	13	100
Berkeley, CA	37	52	18	122	16	18	150
Billings, MT	45	47	0	108	30	0	3,124
Biloxi, MS	30	23	45	88	53	7	25
Binghamton, NY	42	5	55	75	55	6	865
Birmingham, AL	33	31	14	86	48	9	600
Bismarck, ND	46	48	30	100	47	0	1,700
Bloomington, IL	40	29	3	88	59	37	829
Boise, ID	43	36	49	116	12	9	2,730
Boston, MA	42	21	30	71	3	37	20
Bowling Green, KY	36	59	25	86	26	37	510
Brandon, Man.	49	54	35	99	57	03	1,343
Brantford, Ont.	43	08	0	80	16	0	815
Brattleboro, VT	42	51	3	72	33	30	240
Bridgeport, CT	41	10	1	73	12	19	10
Brockton, MA	42	5	0	71	1	8	112
Buffalo, NY	42	53	11	78	52	43	585
Burlington, Ont.	43	23	10	79	50	15	640
Burlington, VT	44	28	33	73	12	45	113
Butte, MT	46	0	14	112	32	2	5,549
Calgary, Alta.	51	03	0	114	05	0	3,557
Cambridge, MA	42	22	30	71	6	22	30
Canton, OH	40	47	56	81	22	43	1,100
Carson City, NV	39	9	50	119	45	59	4,730
Cedar Rapids, IA	42	0	30	91	38	38	730
Central Islip, NY	40	47	26	73	12	8	88
Champaign, IL	40	6	59	88	14	36	740
Charleston, SC	32	46	35	79	55	52	118
Charleston, WV	38	20	59	81	37	58	606
Charlotte, NC	35	13	37	80	50	36	850
Charlottetown, P.E.I.	46	14	25	63	08	05	160
Chattanooga, TN	35	2	44	85	18	35	685
Cheyenne, WY	41	8	24	104	49	11	6,067
Chicago, IL	41	51	0	87	39	0	596
Churchill, Man.	58	43	30	94	07	0	94
Cincinnati, OH	39	9	43	84	27	25	683
Cleveland, OH	41	29	58	81	41	44	690
Colorado Springs, CO	38	50	2	104	49	15	6,008
Columbia, MO	38	57	6	92	20	2	758
Columbia, SC	34	0	2	81	2	6	314
Columbus, GA	32	27	39	84	59	16	300
Columbus, OH	39	57	40	82	59	56	800
Concord, NH	43	12	29	71	32	17	288
Corpus Christi, TX	27	48	1	97	23	46	35
Dallas, TX	32	47	0	96	48	0	463
Dawson, Yukon	64	03	45	139	25	50	1,214
Dayton, OH	39	45	32	84	11	30	750
Daytona Beach, FL	29	12	38	81	1	23	10
Decatur, IL	39	50	25	88	57	17	670
Denver, CO	39	44	21	104	59	3	5,260
Des Moines, IA	41	36	2	93	36	32	803
Detroit, MI	42	19	53	83	2	45	585
Dodge City, KS	37	45	10	100	1	0	2,550
Dubuque, IA	42	30	2	90	39	52	620
Duluth, MN	46	47	0	92	6	23	610
Durham, NC	35	59	38	78	53	56	394
Eau Claire, WI	44	48	41	91	29	54	850
Edmonton, Alta.	53	33	0	113	28	0	2,200
Elizabeth, NJ	40	39	50	74	12	40	38
El Paso, TX	31	45	31	106	29	11	3,695
Enid, OK	36	23	44	97	52	41	1,246
Erie, PA	42	7	45	80	5	7	650
Eugene, OR	44	3	8	123	5	8	419
Eureka, CA	40	48	8	124	9	45	44
Evansville, IN	37	58	29	87	33	21	388
Fairbanks, AK	64	50	16	147	42	59	440
Fall River, MA	41	42	5	71	9	20	200
Fargo, ND	46	52	38	96	47	22	900
Flagstaff, AZ	35	11	53	111	39	2	6,900
Flint, MI	43	0	45	83	41	15	750
Ft. Smith, AR	35	23	9	94	23	54	446
Ft. Wayne, IN	41	7	50	85	7	44	781
Ft. Worth, TX	32	43	31	97	19	14	670
Fredericton, N.B.	45	56	43	66	40	0	67
Fresno, CA	36	44	52	119	46	17	296
Gadsden, AL	34	0	51	86	0	24	554
Gainesville, FL	29	39	5	82	19	30	183
Gallup, NM	35	31	41	108	44	31	6,508
Galveston, TX	29	18	4	94	47	51	10
Gary, IN	41	35	36	87	20	47	600
Grand Junction, CO	39	3	50	108	33	0	4,597
Grand Rapids, MI	42	57	48	85	40	5	610
Great Falls, MT	47	30	1	111	18	0	3,334
Green Bay, WI	44	31	9	88	1	11	594
Greensboro, NC	36	4	21	79	47	32	770
Greenville, SC	34	51	9	82	23	39	966
Guelph, Ont.	43	33	0	80	15	0	1,100
Gulfport, MS	30	22	2	89	5	34	25
Halifax, N.S.	44	52	0	63	43	0	477
Hamilton, OH	39	23	58	84	33	41	600
Hamilton, Ont.	43	14	0	79	57	0	780
Harrisburg, PA	40	16	25	76	53	5	320
Hartford, CT	41	45	49	72	41	8	40
Helena, MT	46	35	34	112	2	7	4,090
Hilo, HI	19	43	47	155	5	24	38
Honolulu, HI	21	18	25	157	51	30	18
Houston, TX	29	45	47	95	21	47	40
Huntsville, AL	34	43	49	86	35	10	641
Indianapolis, IN	39	46	6	86	9	29	717
Iowa City, IA	41	39	40	91	31	48	685
Jackson, MI	42	14	45	84	24	5	940
Jackson, MS	32	17	55	90	11	5	294
Jacksonville, FL	30	19	55	81	39	21	12
Jersey City, NJ	40	43	41	74	4	41	83
Johnstown, PA	40	19	36	78	55	20	1200
Joplin, MO	37	5	3	94	30	47	990
Juneau, AK	58	18	7	134	25	11	50
Kalamazoo, MI	42	17	30	85	35	14	755
Kansas City, KS	39	6	51	94	37	38	750
Kansas City, MO	39	5	59	94	34	42	740
Kenosha, WI	42	35	5	87	49	16	610
Key West, FL	24	33	19	81	46	58	8
Kingston, Ont.	44	18	0	76	28	0	305
Kitchener, Ont.	43	27	0	80	29	0	1,040
Knoxville, TN	35	57	38	83	55	15	889
Lafayette, IN	40	25	0	86	52	31	567
Lancaster, PA	40	2	16	76	18	21	368
Lansing, MI	42	43	57	84	33	20	830
Laredo, TX	27	30	22	99	30	26	414
Las Vegas, NV	36	10	30	115	8	11	2,000
Lawrence, MA	42	42	25	71	9	49	50
Lethbridge, Alta.	49	42	0	112	49	0	3,047
Lexington, KY	37	59	19	84	28	40	955
Lihue, HI	21	58	52	159	22	16	206
Lima, OH	40	44	33	84	6	19	875
Lincoln, NE	40	48	0	96	40	0	1,150
Little Rock, AR	34	44	47	92	17	22	350
London, Ont.	42	59	0	81	14	0	875
Los Angeles, CA	34	3	8	118	14	34	330
Louisville, KY	38	15	15	85	45	34	462
Lowell, MA	42	38	0	71	19	0	102
Lubbock, TX	33	34	40	101	51	17	3,195

City	Lat. N °	′	″	Long. W °	′	″	Elev. (ft)
Macon, GA	32	50	26	83	37	57	400
Madison, WI	43	4	23	89	24	4	863
Manchester, NH	42	59	44	71	27	19	175
Marshall, TX	32	32	41	94	22	2	410
Medicine Hat, Alta.	50	03	0	110	40	0	2,352
Memphis, TN	35	8	58	90	2	56	254
Meriden, CT	41	32	17	72	48	27	190
Miami, FL	25	46	26	80	11	38	11
Milwaukee, WI	43	2	20	87	54	23	634
Minneapolis, MN	44	58	48	93	15	49	815
Minot, ND	48	13	57	101	17	45	1,555
Mobile, AL	30	41	39	88	2	35	16
Moncton, N.B.	46	06	57	64	48	11	232
Montgomery, AL	32	22	0	86	18	0	250
Montpelier, VT	44	15	36	72	34	33	525
Montréal, Que.	45	31	0	73	39	0	221
Moose Jaw, Sask.	50	24	0	105	32	0	1,892
Muncie, IN	40	11	36	85	23	11	952
Nashville, TN	36	9	57	86	47	4	440
Natchez, MS	31	33	37	91	24	11	230
Newark, NJ	40	44	8	74	10	22	95
New Britain, CT	41	39	40	72	46	48	200
New Haven, CT	41	18	29	72	55	43	40
New Orleans, LA	29	57	16	90	4	30	11
New York, NY	40	42	51	74	0	23	55
Niagara Falls, Ont.	43	06	0	79	04	0	589
Nome, AK	64	30	4	165	24	23	25
Norfolk, VA	36	50	48	76	17	8	10
North Bay, Ont.	46	19	0	79	28	0	1,200
Oakland, CA	37	48	16	122	16	11	42
Ogden, UT	41	13	23	111	58	23	4,299
Oklahoma City, OK	35	28	3	97	30	58	1,195
Omaha, NE	41	15	31	95	56	15	1,040
Orlando, FL	28	32	17	81	22	46	106
Ottawa, Ont.	45	16	0	75	45	0	382
Paducah, KY	37	5	0	88	36	0	345
Pasadena, CA	34	8	52	118	8	37	865
Paterson, NJ	40	55	0	74	10	20	70
Pensacola, FL	30	25	16	87	13	1	32
Peoria, IL	40	41	37	89	35	20	470
Peterborough, Ont.	44	18	0	78	19	0	628
Philadelphia, PA	39	57	8	75	9	51	40
Phoenix, AZ	33	26	54	112	4	24	1,090
Pierre, SD	44	22	6	100	21	2	1,484
Pittsburgh, PA	40	26	26	79	59	46	770
Pittsfield, MA	42	27	0	73	14	45	1,039
Pocatello, ID	42	52	17	112	26	41	4,464
Pt. Arthur, TX	29	53	55	93	55	43	10
Portland, ME	43	39	41	70	15	21	25
Portland, OR	45	31	25	122	40	30	50
Portsmouth, NH	43	4	18	70	45	47	21
Portsmouth, VA	36	50	7	76	17	55	10
Prince Rupert, B.C.	54	19	0	130	19	0	116
Providence, RI	41	49	26	71	24	48	80
Provo, UT	40	14	2	111	39	28	4,549
Pueblo, CO	38	15	16	104	36	31	4,662
Québec City, Que.	46	49	0	71	13	0	244
Racine, WI	42	43	34	87	46	58	630
Raleigh, NC	35	46	19	78	38	20	350
Rapid City, SD	44	4	50	103	13	50	3,247
Reading, PA	40	20	8	75	55	38	266
Regina, Sask.	50	27	0	104	37	0	1,894
Reno, NV	39	31	47	119	48	46	4,498
Richmond, VA	37	33	13	77	27	38	190
Roanoke, VA	37	16	15	79	56	30	940
Rochester, MN	44	1	18	92	28	11	990
Rochester, NY	43	9	17	77	36	57	515
Rockford, IL	42	16	16	89	5	38	715
Sacramento, CA	38	34	54	121	29	36	20
Saginaw, MI	43	25	10	83	57	3	595
St. Catharines, Ont.	43	10	0	79	15	0	321
St. Cloud, MN	45	33	39	94	9	44	1,040
St. John, N.B.	45	15	33	66	02	20	357
St. John's, Nfld.	47	34	0	52	44	0	461
St. Joseph, MO	39	46	7	94	50	47	850
St. Louis, MO	38	37	38	90	11	52	455
St. Paul, MN	44	56	40	93	5	35	780
St. Petersburg, FL	27	46	14	82	40	46	44
Salem, OR	44	56	35	123	2	2	154
Salina, KS	38	50	25	97	36	40	1,225
Salt Lake City, UT	40	45	39	111	53	25	4,266
San Antonio, TX	29	25	26	98	29	36	650

City	Lat. N °	′	″	Long. W °	′	″	Elev. (ft)
San Bernardino, CA	34	6	30	117	17	20	1,200
San Diego, CA	32	42	55	117	9	23	40
San Francisco, CA	37	46	30	122	25	6	63
San Jose, CA	37	20	22	121	53	38	87
San Juan, P.R.	18	28	6	66	6	22	8
Santa Barbara, CA	34	25	15	119	41	50	50
Santa Cruz, CA	36	58	27	122	1	47	20
Santa Fe, NM	35	41	13	105	56	14	6,989
Sarasota, FL	27	20	10	82	31	51	27
Saskatoon, Sask.	52	07	0	106	38	0	1,653
Sault Ste. Marie, Ont.	46	31	0	84	20	0	630
Savannah, GA	32	5	0	81	6	0	42
Schenectady, NY	42	48	51	73	56	24	245
Seattle, WA	47	36	23	122	19	51	350
Sheboygan, WI	43	45	3	87	42	52	630
Sherbrooke, Que.	45	24	0	71	54	0	792
Sheridan, WY	44	47	50	106	57	20	3,742
Shreveport, LA	32	31	30	93	45	0	209
Sioux City, IA	42	30	0	96	24	0	1,117
Sioux Falls, SD	43	32	48	96	43	48	1,442
South Bend, IN	41	41	0	86	15	0	725
Spartanburg, SC	34	56	58	81	55	56	816
Spokane, WA	47	39	32	117	25	30	2,000
Springfield, IL	39	48	6	89	38	37	610
Springfield, MA	42	6	5	72	35	25	70
Springfield, MO	37	12	55	93	17	53	1,300
Springfield, OH	39	55	27	83	48	32	1,000
Stamford, CT	41	3	12	73	32	21	35
Steubenville, OH	40	22	11	80	38	3	1,060
Stockton, CA	37	57	28	121	17	23	15
Sudbury, Ont.	46	31	0	80	54	0	1,140
Superior, WI	46	43	15	92	6	14	642
Sydney, N.S.	46	09	0	60	11	0	203
Syracuse, NY	43	2	53	76	8	52	400
Tacoma, WA	47	15	11	122	26	35	380
Tallahassee, FL	30	26	17	84	16	51	188
Tampa, FL	27	56	50	82	27	31	48
Terre Haute, IN	39	28	0	87	24	50	501
Texarkana, TX	33	25	30	94	2	51	324
Thunder Bay, Ont.	48	24	0	89	19	0	653
Timmins, Ont.	48	28	0	81	20	0	967
Toledo, OH	41	39	50	83	33	19	615
Topeka, KS	39	2	54	95	40	40	1,000
Toronto, Ont.	43	37	39	79	23	46	251
Trenton, NJ	40	13	1	74	44	36	54
Trois-Rivières, Que.	46	21	0	72	33	0	198
Troy, NY	42	43	42	73	41	32	35
Tucson, AZ	32	13	18	110	55	33	2,390
Tulsa, OK	36	9	14	95	59	33	804
Urbana, IL	40	6	38	88	12	26	725
Utica, NY	43	6	3	75	13	59	415
Vancouver, B.C.	49	15	0	123	07	0	14
Victoria, B.C.	48	26	0	123	22	0	63
Waco, TX	31	32	57	97	8	47	405
Walla Walla, WA	46	3	53	118	20	31	1,000
Washington, DC	38	53	42	77	2	12	25
Waterloo, IA	42	29	34	92	20	34	850
West Palm Beach, FL	26	42	54	80	3	13	21
Wheeling, WV	40	3	50	80	43	16	672
Whitehorse, Yukon	60	43	0	135	03	0	2,305
White Plains, NY	41	2	2	73	45	48	220
Wichita, KS	37	41	32	97	20	14	1,305
Wilkes-Barre, PA	41	14	45	75	52	54	550
Wilmington, DE	39	44	45	75	32	49	100
Wilmington, NC	34	13	32	77	56	42	50
Windsor, Ont.	42	18	0	83	01	0	622
Winnipeg, Man.	49	54	39	97	14	36	783
Winston-Salem, NC	36	5	59	80	14	40	912
Worcester, MA	42	15	45	71	48	10	480
Yakima, WA	46	36	8	120	30	17	1,066
Yellowknife, N.W.T.	62	27	20	114	21	0	675
Youngstown, OH	41	5	59	80	38	59	861
Yuma, AZ	32	43	31	114	37	25	160
Zanesville, OH	39	56	25	82	0	48	710

WORLD ALMANAC QUICK QUIZ

How many miles downward would you travel to go from the surface to the deepest point on the Pacific Ocean floor?

(a) 1.2 miles (b) 4.5 miles
(c) 6.8 miles (d) less than a mile

For the answer look in this chapter, or see page 1008.

Principal World Rivers

For N American rivers, see separate table.

River	Outflow	Length (mi)
Africa		
Chari	Lake Chad	500
Congo	Atlantic Ocean	2,900
Gambia	Atlantic Ocean	700
Kasai	Congo River	1,000
Limpopo	Indian Ocean	1,100
Lualaba	Congo River	1,100
Niger	Gulf of Guinea	2,590
Nile	Mediterranean	4,160
Okavango	Okavango Delta	1,000
Orange	Atlantic Ocean	1,300
Senegal	Atlantic Ocean	1,020
Ubangi	Congo River	660
Zambezi	Indian Ocean	1,700
Asia		
Amu Darya	Aral Sea	1,550
Amur	Tatar Strait	1,780
Angara	Yenisey River	1,151
Brahmaputra	Bay of Bengal	1,800
Chang	East China Sea	3,964
Euphrates	Shatt al-Arab	1,700
Ganges	Bay of Bengal	1,560
Godavari	Bay of Bengal	900
Hsi (see Xi)		
Huang	Yellow Sea	3,395
Indus	Arabian Sea	1,800
Irrawaddy	Andaman Sea	1,337
Jordan	Dead Sea	200
Kolyma	Arctic Ocean	1,323
Krishna	Bay of Bengal	800
Kura	Caspian Sea	848
Lena	Laptev Sea	2,734
Mekong	South China Sea	2,700
Narbada (see Narmada)		
Narmada	Arabian Sea	800
Ob	Gulf of Ob	2,268
Ob-Irtysh	Gulf of Ob	3,362
Salween	Gulf of Martaban	1,500
Songhua	Amur River	1,150
Sungari	Amur River	1,197
Sutlej	Indus River	900
Syr	Aral Sea	1,370
Tarim	Lop Nor Basin	1,261
Tigris	Shatt al-Arab	1,180
Xi	South China Sea	1,200
Yamuna	Ganges River	855
Yangtze (see Chang)		
Yellow (see Huang)		
Yenisey	Kara Sea	2,543
Australia		
Murray-Darling	Indian Ocean	2,310
Murrumbidgee	Murray River	981
Europe		
Bug, Northern	Wisla	481
Bug, Southern	Dnieper River	532
Danube	Black Sea	1,776
Don	Sea of Azov	1,224
Dnieper	Black Sea	1,420
Dniester	Black Sea	877
Drava	Danube River	447
Dvina, North	White Sea	824
Dvina, West	Gulf of Riga	634
Ebro	Mediterranean	565
Elbe	North Sea	724
Garonne	Bay of Biscay	357
Kama	Volga River	1,122
Loire	Bay of Biscay	634
Mame	Seine River	326
Meuse	North Sea	580
Oder	Baltic Sea	567
Oka	Volga River	932
Pechora	Barents Sea	1,124
Po	Adriatic Sea	405
Rhine	North Sea	820
Rhone	Gulf of Lions	505
Seine	English Channel	496
Shannon	Atlantic Ocean	230
Tagus	Atlantic Ocean	626
Thames	North Sea	210
Tiber	Tyrrhenian Sea	252
Tisza	Danube River	600
Ural	Caspian Sea	1,575
Volga	Caspian Sea	2,290
Weser	North Sea	454
Wisla	Gulf of Gdansk	675
South America		
Amazon	Atlantic Ocean	4,000
Araguaia	Tocantins River	1,100
Iça (see Putumayo)		
Iguaça	Parana River	808
Japura	Amazon River	1,750
Madeira	Amazon River	2,013
Magdalena	Caribbean Sea	956
Negro	Amazon River	1,400
Orinoco	Atlantic Ocean	1,600
Paraguay	Parana River	1,584
Parana	Rio de la Plata	2,485
Pilcomayo	Paraguay River	1,000
Purus	Amazon River	2,100
Putumayo	Amazon River	1,000
Rio de la Plata	Atlantic Ocean	150
Rio Roosevelt	Aripuana	400
Sao Francisco	Atlantic Ocean	1,988
Tocantins	Para River	1,677
Ucayali	Marañón River	910
Uruguay	Rio de la Plata	1,000
Xingu	Amazon River	1,300

Major Rivers in North America

River	Source or upper limit of length	Outflow	Length (mi)
Alabama	Gilmer County, GA	Mobile River	729
Albany	Lake St. Joseph, Ontario	James Bay	610
Allegheny	Potter County, PA.	Ohio River	325
Altamaha-Ocmulgee	Junction of Yellow and South Rivers, Newton County, GA	Atlantic Ocean	392
Apalachicola-Chattahoochee	Towns County, GA	Gulf of Mexico	524
Arkansas	Lake County, CO	Mississippi River	1,459
Assiniboine	Eastern Saskatchewan	Red River	450
Attawapiskat	Attawapiskat, Ontario	James Bay	465
Back (NWT)	Contwoyto Lake	Chantrey Inlet, Arctic Ocean	605
Big Black (MS)	Webster County, MS	Mississippi River	330
Brazos	Junction of Salt and Double Mountain Forks, Stonewall County, TX	Gulf of Mexico	950
Canadian	Las Animas County, CO	Arkansas River	906
Cedar (IA)	Dodge County, MN	Iowa River	329
Cheyenne	Junction of Antelope Creek and Dry Fork, Converse County, WY	Missouri River	290
Churchill, Lab.	Lake Ashuanipi, Labrador	Atlantic Ocean	532
Churchill, Man.	Methy Lake, Saskatchewan	Hudson Bay	1,000
Cimarron	Colfax County, NM	Arkansas River	600
Colorado (AZ)	Rocky Mountain Natl. Park, CO (90 mi in Mexico)	Gulf of California	1,450
Colorado (TX)	West Texas	Matagorda Bay	862
Columbia	Columbia Lake, British Columbia	Pacific Ocean, bet. OR and WA	1,243
Columbia, Upper	Columbia Lake, British Columbia	To mouth of Snake River	890
Connecticut	Third Connecticut Lake, NH	Long Island Sound, CT	407
Coppermine (NWT)	Lac de Gras	Coronation Gulf, Arctic Ocean	525
Cumberland	Letcher County, KY	Ohio River	720
Delaware	Schoharie County, NY	Liston Point, Delaware Bay	390
Fraser	Near Mount Robson (on Continental Divide)	Strait of Georgia	850
Gila	Catron County, NM	Colorado River	649
Green (UT-WY)	Junction of Wells and Trail Creeks, Sublette County, WY	Colorado River	730
Hudson	Henderson Lake, Essex County, NY	Upper NY Bay	306
Illinois	St. Joseph County, IN	Mississippi River	420
James (ND-SD)	Wells County, ND	Missouri River	710
James (VA)	Junction of Jackson and Cowpasture Rivers, Botetourt County, VA	Hampton Roads	340
Kanawha-New	Junction of North and South Forks of New River, NC	Ohio River	352
Kentucky	Junction of North and Middle Forks, Lee County, KY	Ohio River	259
Klamath	Lake Ewauna, Klamath Falls, OR	Pacific Ocean	250
Kootenay	Kootenay Lake, British Columbia	Columbia River	485
Koyukuk	Endicott Mountains, AK	Yukon River	470
Kuskokwim	Alaska Range	Kuskokwim Bay	724
Liard	Southern Yukon, AK	Mackenzie River	693
Little Missouri	Crook County, WY	Missouri River	560

River	Source or upper limit of length	Outflow	Length (mi)
Mackenzie	Great Slave Lake, N.W.T.	Arctic Ocean	1,060
Milk	Junction of North and South Forks, Alberta	Missouri River	625
Minnesota	Big Stone Lake, MN	Mississippi River	332
Mississippi	Lake Itasca, MN	Gulf of Mexico	2,340
Mississippi-Missouri-Red Rock	Source of Red Rock, Beaverhead Co., MT	Gulf of Mexico	3,710
Missouri	Junction of Jefferson, Madison, and Gallatin Rivers, Gallatin County, MT	Mississippi River	2,315
Missouri-Red Rock	Source of Red Rock, Beaverhead Co., MT	Mississippi River	2,540
Mobile-Alabama-Coosa	Gilmer County, GA	Mobile Bay	774
Nelson (Man.)	Lake Winnipeg	Hudson Bay	410
Neosho	Morris County, KS	Arkansas River, OK	460
Niobrara	Niobrara County, WY	Missouri River, NE	431
North Canadian	Union County, NM	Canadian River, OK	800
North Platte	Junction of Grizzly and Little Grizzly Creeks, Jackson County, CO	Platte River, NE	618
Ohio	Junction of Allegheny and Monongahela Rivers, Pittsburgh, PA	Mississippi River	981
Ohio-Allegheny	Potter County, PA	Mississippi River	1,310
Osage	East-central Kansas	Missouri River	500
Ottawa	Lake Capimitchigama	St. Lawrence River	790
Ouachita	Polk County, AR	Black River	605
Peace	Stikine Mountains, B.C.	Slave River	1,210
Pearl	Neshoba County, MS	Gulf of Mexico	411
Pecos	Mora County, NM	Rio Grande	926
Pee Dee-Yadkin	Watauga County, NC	Winyah Bay	435
Pend Oreille-Clark Fork	Near Butte, MT	Columbia River	531
Platte	Junction of North and South Platte Rivers, NE	Missouri River	310
Porcupine	Ogilvie Mountains, AK	Yukon River, AK	569
Potomac	Garrett County, MD	Chesapeake Bay	383
Powder	Junction of South and Middle Forks, WY	Yellowstone River	375
Red (OK-TX-LA)	Curry County, NM	Mississippi River	1,290
Red River of the North	Junction of Otter Tail and Bois de Sioux Rivers, Wilkin County, MN	Lake Winnipeg	545
Republican	Junction of North Fork and Arikaree River, NE	Kansas River	445
Rio Grande	San Juan County, CO	Gulf of Mexico	1,900
Roanoke	Junction of N and S Forks, Montgomery Co., VA	Albemarle Sound	380
Rock (IL-WI)	Dodge County, WI	Mississippi River	300
Sabine	Junction of S and Caddo Forks, Hunt County, TX	Sabine Lake	380
Sacramento	Siskiyou County, CA	Suisun Bay	377
St. Francis	Iron County, MO	Mississippi River	425
St. John	Northwestern Maine	Bay of Fundy	418
St. Lawrence	Lake Ontario	Gulf of St. Lawrence, Atlantic Ocean	800
Saguenay	Lake St. John, Quebec	St. Lawrence River	434
Salmon (ID)	Custer County, ID	Snake River	420
San Joaquin	Junction of S and Middle Forks, Madera Co., CA	Suisun Bay	350
San Juan	Silver Lake, Archuleta County, CO	Colorado River	360
Santee-Wateree-Catawba	McDowell County, NC	Atlantic Ocean	538
Saskatchewan, North	Rocky Mountains	Saskatchewan R.	800
Saskatchewan, South	Rocky Mountains	Saskatchewan R.	865
Savannah	Junction of Seneca and Tugaloo Rivers, Anderson County, SC	Atlantic Ocean, GA-SC	314
Severn (Ont.)	Sandy Lake	Hudson Bay	610
Smoky Hill	Cheyenne County, CO	Kansas River, KS	540
Snake	Teton County, WY	Columbia River, WA	1,038
South Platte	Junction of S and Middle Forks, Park County, CO	Platte River	424
Susitna	Alaska Range	Cook Inlet	313
Susquehanna	Huyden Creek, Otsego County, NY	Chesapeake Bay	447
Tallahatchie	Tippah County, MS	Yazoo River	301
Tanana	Wrangell Mountains, AK	Yukon River	659
Tennessee	Junction of French Broad and Holston Rivers	Ohio River	652
Tennessee-French Broad	Courthouse Creek, Transylvania County, NC	Ohio River	886
Tombigbee	Prentiss County, MS	Mobile River	525
Trinity	North of Dallas, TX	Galveston Bay	360
Wabash	Darke County, OH	Ohio River	512
Washita	Hemphill County, TX	Red River, OK	500
White (AR-MO)	Madison County, AR	Mississippi River	722
Willamette	Douglas County, OR	Columbia River	309
Wind-Bighorn	Junction of Wind and Little Wind Rivers, Fremont Co., WY (Source of Wind R. is Togwotee Pass, Teton Co., WY)	Yellowstone River	338
Wisconsin	Lac Vieux Desert, Vilas County, WI	Mississippi River	430
Yellowstone	Park County, WY	Missouri River	682
Yukon	McNeil R., Yukon Territory	Bering Sea	1,979

Highest and Lowest Continental Altitudes

Source: National Geographic Society

Continent	Highest point	Elev. (ft)	Lowest point	ft below sea level
Asia	Mount Everest, Nepal-Tibet	29,035	Dead Sea, Israel-Jordan	1,348
South America	Mount Aconcagua, Argentina	22,834	Valdes Peninsula, Argentina	131
North America	Mount McKinley, Alaska	20,320	Death Valley, California	282
Africa	Kilimanjaro, Tanzania	19,340	Lake Assal, Djibouti	512
Europe	Mount Elbrus, Russia	18,510	Caspian Sea, Russia, Azerbaijan	92
Antarctica	Vinson Massif	16,864	Bentley Subglacial Trench	8,327[1]
Australia	Mount Kosciusko, New South Wales	7,310	Lake Eyre, South Australia	52

(1) Estimated level of the continental floor. Lower points that have yet to be discovered may exist further beneath the ice.

Major Natural Lakes of the World

Source: Geological Survey, U.S. Dept. of the Interior; GeoAccess Division, Natural Resources Canada

A lake is generally defined as a body of water surrounded by land. By this definition some bodies of water that are called seas, such as the Caspian Sea and the Aral Sea, are really lakes. In the following table, the word *lake* is omitted when it is part of the name.

Name	Continent	Area (sq mi)	Length (mi)	Maximum depth (ft)	Elevation (ft)
Caspian Sea[1]	Asia-Europe	143,244	760	3,363	–92
Superior	North America	31,700	350	1,330	600
Victoria	Africa	26,828	250	270	3,720
Huron	North America	23,000	206	750	579
Michigan	North America	22,300	307	923	579
Aral Sea[1]	Asia	13,000[2]	260	220	125
Tanganyika	Africa	12,700	420	4,823	2,534
Baykal	Asia	12,162	395	5,315	1,493
Great Bear	North America	12,096	192	1,463	512
Nyasa (Malawi)	Africa	11,150	360	2,280	1,550
Great Slave	North America	11,031	298	2,015	513
Erie	North America	9,910	241	210	570
Winnipeg	North America	9,417	266	200	713
Ontario	North America	7,340	193	802	245
Balkhash[1]	Asia	7,115	376	85	1,115
Ladoga	Europe	6,835	124	738	13
Maracaibo	South America	5,217	133	115	sea level
Onega	Europe	3,710	145	328	108
Eyre[1]	Australia	3,600[3]	90	4	–52
Titicaca	South America	3,200	122	922	12,500
Nicaragua	North America	3,100	102	230	102
Athabasca	North America	3,064	208	407	700
Reindeer	North America	2,568	143	720	1,106
Tonle Sap	Asia	2,500[3]	...	45	...
Turkana (Rudolf)	Africa	2,473	154	240	1,230
Issyk Kul[1]	Asia	2,355	115	2,303	5,279
Torrens[1]	Australia	2,230[3]	130	...	92
Vanern	Europe	2,156	91	328	144
Nettilling	North America	2,140	67	...	95
Winnipegosis	North America	2,075	141	38	830
Albert	Africa	2,075	100	168	2,030
Nipigon	North America	1,872	72	540	1,050
Gairdner[1]	Australia	1,840[3]	90	...	112
Urmia[1]	Asia	1,815	90	49	4,180
Manitoba	North America	1,799	140	21	813
Chad	Africa	839[4]	175	24	787

(1) Salt lake. (2) Approximate figure, could be less. The diversion of feeder rivers since the 1960s has devastated the Aral—once the world's 4th-largest lake (26,000 sq. miles). By 2000, the Aral had effectively become three lakes, with the total area shown. (3) Approximate figure, subject to great seasonal variation. (4) Once 4th-largest lake in Africa (about 10,000 sq. mi in the 1960s), Chad had shrunk more than 90% by 2001 as a result of irrigation and long-term drought.

The Great Lakes

Source: National Ocean Service, U.S. Dept. of Commerce

The Great Lakes form the world's **largest body of fresh water** (in surface area), and with their connecting waterways are the largest inland water transportation unit. Draining the great North Central basin of the U.S., they enable shipping to reach the Atlantic via their outlet, the St. Lawrence R., and to reach the Gulf of Mexico via the Illinois Waterway, from Lake Michigan to the Mississippi R. A 3rd outlet connects with the Hudson R. and then the Atlantic via the New York State Barge Canal System. Traffic on the Illinois Waterway and the N.Y. State Barge Canal System is limited to recreational boating and small shipping vessels.

Only one of the lakes, Lake Michigan, is wholly in the U.S.; the others are shared with Canada. Ships move from the shores of Lake Superior to Whitefish Bay at the E end of the lake, then through the Soo (Sault Ste. Marie) locks, through the St. Mary's R. and into Lake Huron. To reach Gary and the Port of Indiana and South Chicago, IL, ships move W from Lake Huron to Lake Michigan through the Straits of Mackinac. Lake Superior is 601 ft above low water datum at Rimouski, Quebec, on the International Great Lakes Datum (1985). From Duluth, MN, to the E end of Lake Ontario is 1,156 mi.

	Superior	Michigan	Huron	Erie	Ontario
Length in mi	350	307	206	241	193
Breadth in mi	160	118	183	57	53
Deepest soundings in ft	1,333	923	750	210	802
Volume of water in cu mi	2,935	1,180	850	116	393
Area (sq mi) water surface—U.S.	20,600	22,300	9,100	4,980	3,460
Canada	11,100	.....	13,900	4,930	3,880
Area (sq mi) entire drainage basin—U.S.	16,900	45,600	16,200	18,000	15,200
Canada	32,400	.....	35,500	4,720	12,100
TOTAL AREA (sq mi) U.S. and Canada	**81,000**	**67,900**	**74,700**	**32,630**	**34,850**
Low water datum above mean water level at Rimouski, Quebec, avg. level in ft (1985)	601.10	577.50	577.50	569.20	243.30
Latitude, N	46° 25′	41° 37′	43v 00′	41° 23′	43°11′
	49° 00′	46° 06′	46v 17′	42° 52′	44°15′
Longitude, W	84° 22′	84° 45′	79° 43′	78° 51′	76° 03′
	92° 06′	88° 02′	84° 45′	83° 29′	79°53′
National boundary line in mi	282.8	None	260.8	251.5	174.6
United States shoreline (mainland only) mi	863	1,400	580	431	300

Famous Waterfalls

Source: National Geographic Society

The earth has thousands of waterfalls, some of considerable magnitude. Their magnitude is determined not only by height but also by volume of flow, steadiness of flow, crest width, whether the water drops sheerly or over a sloping surface, and whether it descends in one leap or in a succession of leaps. A series of low falls flowing over a considerable distance is known as a **cascade**.

Estimated mean annual flow, in cubic feet per second, of major waterfalls is as follows: Niagara, 212,200; Paulo Afonso, 100,000; Urubupunga, 97,000; Iguazu, 61,000; Patos-Maribondo, 53,000; Victoria, 35,400; and Kaieteur, 23,400.

Height = total drop in feet in one or more leaps. # = falls of more than one leap; * = falls that diminish greatly seasonally; ** = falls that reduce to a trickle or are dry for part of each year. If the river names are not shown, they are same as the falls. R. = river; (C) = cascade.

Name and location	Height (ft)
Africa	
Angola	
Ruacana, Cunene R.	406
Ethiopia	
Fincha	508
Lesotho	
Maletsunyane*	630
Zimbabwe-Zambia	
Victoria, Zambezi R.*	343
South Africa	
Augrabies, Orange R.*	480
Tugela#	2,014
Tanzania-Zambia	
Kalambo*	726
Asia	
India	
Cauvery*	330
Jog (Gersoppa), Sharavathi R.*	830
Japan	
Kegon, Daiya R.*	330
Australia	
New South Wales	
Wentworth	614
Wollomombi	1,100
Queensland	
Tully	885
Wallaman, Stony Cr.#	1,137
New Zealand	
Helena	890
Sutherland, Arthur R.#	1,904
Europe	
Austria	
Gastein#	492
Krimml#	1,312
France	
Gavarnie*	1,385
Great Britain	
Scotland	
Glomach	370
Wales	
Rhaiadr	240
Italy	
Frua, Toce R. (C)	470
Norway	
Mardalsfossen (Northern)	1,535
Mardalsfossen (Southern)#	2,149
Skjeggedal, Nybuai R.#**	1,378
Skykje**	984
Vetti, Morka-Koldedola R.	900
Sweden	
Handol#	427
Switzerland	
Giessbach (C)	984
Reichenbach#	656
Simmen#	459
Staubbach	984
Trummelbach#	1,312
North America	
Canada	
Alberta	
Panther, Nigel Cr.	600
British Columbia	
Della#	1,443
Takakkaw, Daly Glacier#	1,200
Quebec	
Montmorency	274
Canada—United States	
Niagara: American	182
Horseshoe	173
United States	
California	
Feather, Fall R.*	640
Yosemite National Park	
Bridalveil*	620
Illilouette*	370
Nevada, Merced R.*	594
Ribbon**	1,612
Silver Strand, Meadow Br.**	1,170
Vernal, Merced R. *	317
Yosemite#**	2,425
Colorado	
Seven, South Cheyenne Cr.#	300
Hawaii	
Akaka, Kolekole Str.	442
Idaho	
Shoshone, Snake R.**	212
Kentucky	
Cumberland	68
Maryland	
Great, Potomac R. (C) *	71
Minnesota	
Minnehaha**	53
New Jersey	
Passaic	70
New York	
Taughannock*	215
Oregon	
Multnomah#	620
Tennessee	
Fall Creek	256
Washington	
Mt. Rainier Natl. Park	
Sluiskin, Paradise R.	300
Snoquvalmie**	268
Wisconsin	
Big Manitou, Black R. (C)*	165
Wyoming	
Yellowstone Natl. Pk. Tower	132
Yellowstone (upper)*	109
Yellowstone (lower)*	308
Mexico	
El Salo	218
South America	
Argentina-Brazil	
Iguazu	230
Brazil	
Glass	1,325
Patos-Maribondo, Grande R.	115
Paulo Afonso, Sao Francisco R.	275
Urubupunga, Parana R.	39
Colombia	
Catarvata de Candelas, Cusiana R.	984
Tequendama, Bogota R.*	427
Ecuador	
Agoyan, Pastaza R.*	200
Guyana	
Kaieteur, Potaro R.	741
Great, Kamarang R.	1,600
Marina, Ipobe R.#	500
Venezuela	
Angel#*	3,212
Cuquenan	2,000

Notable Deserts of the World

Deserts are defined as regions of the Earth receiving less than 10 in. of precipitation annually, usually in combination with an evaporation rate exceeding precipitation.

In addition to areas listed below, the continent of Antarctica, with an area of about 5.4 mil square miles (roughly doubled by ice in winter), is generally considered a desert. Annual precipitation averages 8 in. along the coast and far less in the deep interior; however, there is little evaporation.

Arabian (Eastern), 70,000 sq mi in Egypt between the Nile R. and Red Sea, extending southward into Sudan
Atacama, 600-mi-long area rich in nitrate and copper deposits in N Chile
Chihuahuan, 140,000 sq mi in TX, NM, AZ, and Mexico
Dasht-e Kauir, approx. 300 mi long by approx. 100 mi wide in N central Iran
Dasht-e Lut, 20,000 sq mi in E Iran
Death Valley, 3,300 sq mi in CA and NV
Gibson, 120,000 sq mi in the interior of W Australia
Gobi, 500,000 sq mi in Mongolia and China
Great Sandy, 150,000 sq mi in W Australia
Great Victoria, 150,000 sq mi in SW Australia
Kalahari, 225,000 sq mi in S Africa
Kara Kum, 120,000 sq mi in Turkmenistan
Kyzyl Kum, 100,000 sq mi in Kazakhstan and Uzbekistan
Libyan, 450,000 sq mi in the Sahara, extending from Libya through SW Egypt into Sudan
Mojave, 15,000 sq mi in southern CA
Namib, long narrow area (varies from 30-100 mi wide) extending 800 mi along SW coast of Africa
Nubian, 100,000 sq mi in the Sahara in NE Sudan
Painted Desert, section of high plateau in northern AZ extending 150 mi
Patagonia, 300,000 sq mi in S Argentina
Rub al-Khali (Empty Quarter), 250,000 sq mi in the S Arabian Peninsula
Sahara, 3,500,000 sq mi in N Africa, extending westward to the Atlantic. Largest desert in the world
Sonoran, 70,000 sq mi in southwestern AZ and southeastern CA extending into NW Mexico
Syrian, 100,000-sq-mi arid wasteland extending over much of N Saudi Arabia, E Jordan, S Syria, and W Iraq
Taklimakan, 140,000 sq mi in Xinjiang Prov., China
Thar (Great Indian), 100,000-sq-mi arid area extending 400 mi along India-Pakistan border

RELIGION

Membership of Religious Groups in the U.S.

Sources: *2005 Yearbook of American & Canadian Churches*, © National Council of the Churches of Christ in the USA; World Christian Database; *World Almanac* research

These membership figures are the latest available and generally are based on reports made by officials of each group, and not on any religious census. Figures from other sources may vary. Many groups keep careful records; others only estimate. Not all groups report annually. Church membership figures vary from one denomination to another, but generally the figures reported in this table are inclusive and do not refer simply to full communicants or confirmed members.

The number of houses of worship appears in parentheses. * Indicates that the group declines to make membership figures public. Groups reporting fewer than 5,000 members are not included; where membership numbers are not available, only those groups with 50 or more houses of worship are listed.

Religious Group	Members
Adventist churches:	
Advent Christian Ch. (303)	25,277
Seventh-day Adventist Ch. (4,619)	935,428
American Catholic Church (100)	**25,000**
Apostolic Christian Churches of America (86)	**12,780**
Apostolic Episcopal Church (250)	**18,000**
Bahá'í Faith (1,127 assemblies)	**151,771**
Baptist churches:	
American Baptist Assn. (1,760)	275,000
American Baptist Chs. in the U.S.A. (5,836)	1,433,075
Baptist Bible Fellowship Intl. (4,500)	1,200,000
Baptist General Conference (902)	145,148
Baptist Missionary Assn. of America (1,334)	234,732
Conservative Baptist Assn. of America (1,200)	200,000
Free Will Baptists, Natl. Assn. of (2,470)	198,795
General Assn. of General Baptists (713)	85,924
General Assn. of Regular Baptist Chs. (1,415)	129,407
Natl. Baptist Convention, U.S.A., Inc. (9,000)	5,000,000
Natl. Missionary Baptist Convention of America	2,500,000
North American Baptist Conference (270)	47,692
Progressive National Baptist Convention (2,000)	2,500,000
Separate Baptists in Christ (100)	8,000
Southern Baptist Convention (42,775)	16,439,603
Brethren in Christ (232)	**20,739**
Brethren (German Baptists):	
Brethren Ch. (Ashland, OH) (117)	10,240
Church of the Brethren (1,069)	132,481
Grace Brethren Chs., Fellowship of (260)	30,371
Old German Baptist Brethren (55)	6,285
Buddhists	**2,721,000[1]**
Christian Brethren (Plymouth Brethren) (1,165)	**86,000**
Christian Church (Disciples of Christ) (3,691)	**770,793**
Christian Congregation, Inc. (1,439)	**120,972**
Christian and Missionary Alliance (1,963)	**400,409**
Christian Union (111)	6,163
Christian Union, Churches of Christ in (233)	**11,504**
Church of Christ (Holiness) U.S.A. (159)	**10,321**
Church of Christ, Scientist (2,000)	**862,000[1]**
Chs. of God, General Conference (Oregon, IL, and Morrow, GA) (89)	**5,018**
Church of the United Brethren in Christ (217)	**22,740**
Churches of Christ (15,000)	**1,500,000**
Churches of God:	
Chs. of God, General Conference (337)	32,961
Ch. of God (Anderson, IN) (2,290)	247,007
Ch. of God (Seventh Day), Denver, CO (200)	11,000
Ch. of God by Faith, Inc. (148)	30,000
Ch. of God, Mountain Assembly, Inc.(118)	8,000
Church of the Nazarene (4,983)	**621,048**
Community Churches, Intl. Council of (192)	**115,812**
Congreg. Christian Chs., Nat'l Assoc. of (432)	**65,392**
Conservative Congregational Christian Conference (259)	**40,041**
Eastern Catholic Churches:	
Armenian Catholic Church (U.S. and Canada) (9)	36,000
Chaldean Catholic Church (14)	112,000
Maronite Catholic Church (65)	57,500
Melkite Greek Catholic Church (35)	29,024
Romanian Greek Catholic Church (15)	5,000
Ruthenian Byzantine Catholic Church (205)	99,381
Syrian Catholic Church (11)	13,140
Syro-Malabar Catholic Church (5)	100,000
Ukranian Greek Catholic Church (202)	105,558
Eastern Orthodox churches:	
American Carpatho-Russian Orthodox Greek Catholic Ch. (80)	13,377
Antiochian Orthodox Christian Archdiocese of N.A. (225)	390,000
Apostolic Catholic Assyrian Ch. of the East, N.A. Dioceses (22)	120,000
Armenian Apostolic Ch. of America (34)	360,000
Armenian Apostolic Church, Dioceses of America (72)	414,000
Coptic Orthodox Ch. (100)	300,000
Greek Orthodox Archdiocese of America (510)	1,500,000
Mar Thoma Syrian Church of India (68)	35,000

Religious Group	Members
Orthodox Ch. in America (725)	1,000,000
Patriarchal Parishes of the Russian Orthodox Ch. in the USA (31)	7,000
Russian Orthodox Church Outside of Russia (177)	480,000
Serbian Orthodox Ch. of the U.S. and Can. (68)	67,000
Syrian Orthodox Ch. of Antioch (25)	32,500
Ukrainian Orthodox Ch. of the USA (115)	13,000
Episcopal Church (7,344)	**2,320,221**
Evangelical Church (133)	**12,475**
Evangelical Congregational Church (150)	**20,743**
Evangelical Covenant Church (718)	**105,956**
Evangelical Free Church of America (1,224)	**350,000**
Friends:	
Evangelical Friends Intl.-N.A. Region (278)	39,913
Friends General Conference (650)	34,000
Friends United Meeting (427)	42,680
Religious Society of Friends (Conservative) (1,200)	104,000
Full Gospel Fellowship of Churches and Ministers Intl. (902)	**346,800**
General Church of the New Jerusalem (35)	**6,522**
Grace Gospel Fellowship (128)	**60,000**
Hindus	**1,144,000[1]**
Independent Fundamental Churches of America Int'l., Inc. (IFCA) (659)	**61,655**
Jehovah's Witnesses (11,876)	**1,041,030**
Jews	**5,290,000[2]**
Jewish organizations:[3]	
Union for Reform Judaism (900+)	1,500,000
Union of Orthodox Jewish Congregations of America (1,000)	*
United Synagogue of Conservative Judaism, The (760)	1,500,000+
Jewish Reconstructionist Federation (103)	180,000
Latter-day Saints:	
Ch. of Jesus Christ of Latter-day Saints (Mormon) (11,879)	4,935,548
Reorganized Ch. of Jesus Christ of Latter-day Saints (Community of Christ) (951)	142,106
Liberal Catholic Church—Province of the U.S.A. (24)	5,800
Lutheran churches:	
Apostolic Lutheran Ch. of America (58)	*
Ch. of the Lutheran Brethren of America (108)	13,702
Ch. of the Lutheran Confession (77)	8,390
Evangelical Lutheran Ch. in America (10,721)	4,984,925
Evangelical Lutheran Synod (138)	39,913
Free Lutheran Congregations, Assn. of (252)	39,409
Latvian Evangelical Lutheran Church in America (68)	13,584
Lutheran Ch.—Missouri Synod (6,142)	2,488,936
Lutheran Chs., American Assn. of (101)	18,252
Wisconsin Evangelical Lutheran Synod (1,250)	400,622
Mennonite churches:	
Beachy Amish Mennonite Chs. (153)	10,773
Church of God in Christ (Mennonite) (115)	132,481
Hutterian Brethren (444)	43,000
Mennonite Brethren Chs., Gen. Conf. (368)	82,130
Mennonite Church USA (964)	112,688
Old Order Amish Ch. (898)	80,820
Methodist churches:	
African Methodist Episcopal Ch.	2,500,000
African Methodist Episcopal Zion Ch. (3,226)	1,432,795
Evangelical Methodist Ch. (123)	8,615
Free Methodist Ch. of North America (978)	71,459
Southern Methodist Ch. (108)	6,493
United Methodist Ch. (35,102)	8,251,175
The Wesleyan Church (1,628)	124,550
Messianic Jews	**c. 75,000**
Metropolitan Community Churches, Universal Fellowship of (300)	**44,000**
Missionary Church (386)	**36,162**
Moravian Ch. in America, Northern Province (93)	**24,650**
Muslims	**4,657,000[1]**
Natl. Organization of the New Apostolic Ch. of North America (340)	**37,382**

Religious Group	Members
Pentecostal churches:	
Apostolic Faith Mission Ch. of God (23)	10,330
Assemblies of God (12,133)	2,729,562
Bible Church of Christ, Inc. (6)	6,850
Bible Fellowship Church (57)	7,427
Church of God (Cleveland, TN) (6,623)	961,390
Church of God in Christ (15,300)	5,499,875
Church of God of Prophecy (1,841)	105,976
Elim Fellowship (100)	*
Intl. Ch. of the Foursquare Gospel (1,847)	326,614
Intl. Pentecostal Church of Christ (67)	4,961
Intl. Pentecostal Holiness Church (1,905)	276,916
Open Bible Standard Chs. (314)	38,000
Pentecostal Assemblies of the World Inc. (1,750)	1,500,000
Pentecostal Church of God (1,197)	104,000
Pentecostal Free Will Baptist Ch. (150)	28,000
United Pentecostal Ch. Intl. (4,100)	*
Presbyterian churches:	
Associate Reformed Presbyterian Ch. (General Synod) (264)	40,703
Cumberland Presbyterian Ch. (780)	83,742
Cumberland Presbyterian Ch. in America (152)	15,142
Evangelical Presbyterian Ch. (190)	71,755
Genl. Assembly of the Korean Presbyterian Church in America (305)	55,000
Orthodox Presbyterian Ch. (237)	27,582
Presbyterian Ch. in America (1,499)	315,981
Presbyterian Ch. (U.S.A.) (11,097)	3,241,309
Reformed Presbyterian Ch. of N. America (86)	6,259
Reformed churches:	
Christian Reformed Ch. in N. America (762)	190,587
Hungarian Reformed Ch. in America (27)	6,000
Netherlands Reformed Congregations (27)	9,524
Protestant Reformed Churches in America (27)	7,080
Reformed Ch. in America (901)	278,739
United Church of Christ (5,850)	1,296,652
Reformed Episcopal Church (137)	**11,281**
Roman Catholic Church (19,484)	**67,259,768**
Salvation Army (1,369)	**564,885**
Sikhs	**270,000[1]**
Unitarian Universalist Assn. of Congregations (1,010)	**214,738**

(1) Source: World Christian Database. (2) From American Jewish Committee. (3) As reported by organizations.

Headquarters of Selected Religious Groups in the U.S.

Sources: *2005 Yearbook of American & Canadian Churches*, © National Council of the Churches of Christ in the USA; *World Almanac* research
(Year organized in parentheses)

African Methodist Episcopal Church (1787), 3801 Market St., Suite 300, Philadelphia, PA 29204; Senior Bishop, Bishop Philip Robert Cousin

African Methodist Episcopal Zion Church (1796), 3225 West Sugar Creek Rd., Charlotte, NC 28269; Pres. Warren M. Brown (Note: Presidency rotates every 6 mos. according to seniority.)

American Baptist Churches in the U.S.A. (1907), PO Box 851, Valley Forge, PA 19482; www.abc-usa.org; Pres., Margaret Johnson

American Rescue Workers (1890), 25 Ross St., Williamsport, PA 17701; www.arwus.com; Commander-in-Chief & Pres., Gen. Claude S. Astin Jr., Rev.

Antiochian Orthodox Christian Archdiocese of North America (1895), 358 Mountain Rd., Englewood, NJ 07631; www.antiochian.org; Primate, Metropolitan Philip Saliba

Armenian Apostolic Church of America (1887), **Eastern Prelacy**: 138 E. 39th St., New York, NY 10016; www.armprelacy.org; Prelate, Archbishop Oshagan Choloyan; **Western Prelacy**: 6252 Honolulu Ave., La Crecsenta, CA 91214; Prelate, Bishop Moushegh Mardirossian

Assemblies of God (1914), 1445 N. Boonville Ave., Springfield, MO 65802; www.ag.org; Gen. Supt., Thomas E. Trask

Bahá'í Faith, National Spiritual Assembly of the Bahá'í's of the U.S., 1233 Central St., Evanston, IL 60201; www.us.bahai.org; Secy. Gen., Dr. Robert C. Henderson

Baptist Bible Fellowship Intl. (1950), Baptist Bible Fellowship Missions Bldg., 720 E. Kearney St., Springfield, MO 65803; www.bbfi.org; Pres., Rev. Bill Monroe

Baptist Convention, Southern (1845), 901 Commerce St., Nashville, TN 37203; www.sbc.net; Pres. Bobby Welch,

Baptist Convention, U.S.A., Inc., National (1895), 1700 Baptist World Center Dr., Nashville, TN 37207; www.nationalbaptist.com; Pres., Dr. William J. Shaw

Baptist Convention of America, Inc., National (1880), 777 S. R.L. Thornton Freeway, Ste. 205, Dallas, TX 75203; Pres., Dr. E. Edward Jones

Baptist Convention of America, Natl. Missionary (1988), 1404 E. Firestone, Los Angeles, CA 90001; www.nmbca.com; Pres., Dr. W. T. Snead Sr.

Baptist General Conference (1852), 2002 S. Arlington Heights Rd., Arlington Heights, IL 60005; www.bgcworld.org; Pres. and CEO, Dr. Gerald Sheveland

Brethren in Christ Church (1778), PO Box A, Grantham, PA 17027; www.bic-church.org/index.htm; Moderator, Dr. Warren L. Hoffman

Buddhist Churches of America (1899), 1710 Octavia St., San Francisco, CA 94109; www.buddhistchurchesofamerica.com; Presiding Bishop, Hakubun Watanabe

Christian and Missionary Alliance (1897), PO Box 35000, Colorado Springs, CO 80935; www.cmalliance.org; Pres., Rev. Peter N. Nanfelt, D.D.

Christian Church (Disciples of Christ) (1832), Disciples Center, 130 E. Washington St., PO Box 1986, Indianapolis, IN 46206; www.disciples.org; Gen. Minister and Pres., William Chris Hobgood

Christian Churches and Churches of Christ, 4210 Bridgetown Rd., Box 11326, Cincinnati, OH 45211; www.cwv.net/christ'n

Christian Congregation, Inc., The (1787), 812 W. Hemlock St., LaFollette, TN 37766; www.netministries.org/see/churches.exe/ch10619; Gen. Supt., Rev. Ora W. Eads, D.D.

Christian Methodist Episcopal Church (1870), 4466 Elvis Presley Blvd., Memphis, TN 38116; Executive Secretary, Attorney Juanita Bryant

Christian Reformed Church in North America (1857), 2850 Kalamazoo Ave. SE, Grand Rapids, MI 49560; www.crcna.org; Gen. Secy., Dr. David H. Engelhard

Church of the Brethren (1708), General Offices, 1451 Dundee Ave., Elgin, IL 60120; www.brethren.org; Moderator, Christopher D. Bowman

Church of Christ (1830), Temple Lot, 200 S. River St., PO Box 472, Independence, MO 64051; http://church-of-christ.com; Council of Apostles, Secy., Apostle Smith N. Brickhouse

Church of Christ, Scientist, *see* First Church of Christ, Scientist.

Church of God (Anderson, IN) (1881), Box 2420, Anderson, IN 46018; www.chog.org; Gen. Dir., Pres. J. Perry Grubbs

Church of God (Cleveland, TN) (1886), 2490 Keith St. NW, Cleveland, TN 37320; www.churchofgod.cc/default_nav40.asp; Gen. Overseer, R. Lamar Vest

Church of God in Christ (1907), Mason Temple, 938 Mason St., Memphis, TN 38126; www.netministries.org/see/churches/ch00833; Presiding Bishop, Bishop Chandler D. Owens

Church of Jesus Christ (Bickertonites) (1862), 6th & Lincoln Sts., Monongahela, PA 15063; Pres., Dominic Thomas

Church of Jesus Christ of Latter-day Saints (Mormon), The (1830), 47 E. South Temple St., Salt Lake City, UT 84150; www.lds.org; Pres., Gordon B. Hinckley

Church of the Nazarene (1907), 6401 The Paseo, Kansas City, MO 64131; www.nazarene.org; Gen. Secy., Dr. Jack Stone

Community of Christ (Reorganized Church of Jesus Christ of Latter-Day Saints) (1830), Int'l. Headquarters, 1001 W. Walnut, Independence, MO 54050; www.CofChrist.org; Pres. W. Grant McMurray

Community Churches, International Council of (1950), 21116 Washington Pkwy., Frankfort, IL 60423; Pres., Grace O'Neal

Conservative Judaism, United Synagogue of, 155 5th Ave., New York, NY 10010; www.uscj.org; Pres., Judy Yudof

Coptic Orthodox Church, 5 Woodstone Dr., Cedar Grove, NJ 07009; www.coptic.org; Fr. Isaac Boulos Azmy

Cumberland Presbyterian Church (1810), 1978 Union Ave., Memphis, TN 38104; www.cumberland.org; Moderator, Rev. E. G. Sims

Episcopal Church (1789), 815 Second Ave., New York, NY 10017; www.ecusa.anglican.org; Presiding Bishop and Primate, Most Rev. Frank Tracy Griswold

Evangelical Free Church of America (1884), 901 E. 78th St., Minneapolis, MN 55420; www.efca.org; Acting Pres., Rev. William Hamel

Evangelical Lutheran Church in America (1987), 8765 W. Higgins Rd., Chicago, IL 60631; www.elca.org; Presiding Bishop, Rev. Mark S. Hanson

Fellowship of Grace Brethren Churches (1882), PO Box 386, Winona Lake, IN 46590; www.fgbc.org; Moderator, Dr. Galen Wiley

First Church of Christ, Scientist, The (1879), Christian Science Plaza, 175 Huntington Ave., Boston, MA 02115; www.spirituality.com; Pres., Cynthia Neely

Free Methodist Church of North America (1860), World Ministries Center, 770 N. High School Rd., Indianapolis, IN 46214; www.freemethodistchurch.org

Friends General Conference (1900), 1216 Arch St., 2B, Philadelphia, PA 19107; www.fgcquaker.org; Gen. Secy., Bruce Birchard

Full Gospel Fellowship of Churches and Ministers Int'l. (1962), 1000 N. Belt Line Rd., Irving, TX 75061; www.fgfcmi.org Pres., Dr. Don Arnold

Greek Orthodox Archdiocese of America (1922), 8-10 E. 79th St., New York, NY 10021; www.goarch.org; Primate, Archbishop Demetrios

International Church of the Foursquare Gospel (1927), 1910 W. Sunset Blvd., Ste. 200, PO Box 26902, Los Angeles, CA 90026; www.foursquare.org; Pres., Dr. Paul C. Risser

Islamic Society of North America, P.O. Box 38, Plainfield, IN 46168; www.isna.net; Genl. Secy., Dr. Sayyid M. Syeed

Jehovah's Witnesses (1884), 25 Columbia Heights, Brooklyn, NY 11201; www.watchtower.org; Pres., Don Adams

Jewish Reconstructionist Federation (1935), Beit Devora, 7804 Montgomery Ave., Suite 9, Elkins Park, PA 19027; www.jrf.org; Dir., Chayim Herzig-Moss

Lutheran Church—Missouri Synod (1847), 1333 S. Kirkwood Rd., St. Louis, MO 63122; www.lcms.org; Pres., Dr. Gerald B. Kieschnick

Mennonite Brethren Churches, General Conference of (1860), 4812 E. Butler Ave., Fresno CA 93727; Moderator, Ed Boschman

Mennonite Church USA (2001), 722 Main St., PO Box 347, Newton, KS 67114. www.MennoniteChurchUSA.org; Moderator, Duane Oswald

Moravian Church in America (1735), **Northern Prov.:** 1021 Center St., PO Box 1245, Bethlehem, PA 18016; www.moravian. org; Pres., David L. Wickmann; **Southern Prov.:** 459 S. Church St., Winston-Salem, NC 27101; Pres., Rev. Dr. Robert E. Sawyer; **Alaska Prov.:** PO Box 545, 361 3rd Ave., Bethel, AK 99559; Pres., Rev. Peter Green

North American Shi'a Muslim Communities Organization (NASIMCO), P.O. Box 29691, Minneapolis, MN 55429; www.nasimco.org; Pres., Hussein Walji

Orthodox Church in America (1794), PO Box 675, Syosset, NY 11791; www.oca.org; Primate, Most Blessed Herman

Orthodox Jewish Congregations in America, Union of (1898), 11 Broadway, New York, NY 10004; www.ou.org; Pres., Harvey Blitz

Pentecostal Assemblies of the World, Inc., 3939 Meadows Dr., Indianapolis, IN 46205; Presiding Bishop, Norman L. Wagner

Presbyterian Church (U.S.A.), (1983), 100 Witherspoon St., Louisville, KY 40202; www.pcusa.org; Moderator, Rich Ufford-Chase

Presbyterian Church in America (1973), 1700 N. Brown Rd., Lawrenceville, GA 30043 www.pcanet.org; Moderator, Dr. Skip Ryan

Progressive National Baptist Convention, Inc. (1961), 601 50th St., NE, Washington, DC 20019; www.pribc.org; Pres., Dr. Bennett W. Smith Sr.

Reformed Church in America (1628), 475 Riverside Dr., New York, NY 10115; www.rca.org; Pres., Rev. Steven Vander Molen

Reform Judaism, Union for, 633 3rd Ave., New York, NY 10017; www.urj.org; Pres., Rabbi Eric Yoffie

Roman Catholic Church (1634), U.S. Conference of Catholic Bishops, 3211 Fourth St. NE, Washington, DC 20017; www.usccb.org; Pres., Bishop William S. Skylstad

Romanian Orthodox Episcopate of America (1929), 2525 Grey Tower Rd., Jackson, MI 49201; www.roea.org; Ruling Bishop, Most Rev. Archbishop Nathaniel Popp

Salvation Army (1865), 615 Slaters Lane, Alexandria, VA 22313; www.salvationarmy.org; National Comdr., Commissioner W. Todd Bassett

Seventh-day Adventist Church (1863), 12501 Old Columbia Pike, Silver Spring, MD 20904; Pres., Jan Paulsen

Swedenborgian Church (1792), 11 Highland Ave., Newtonville, MA 02460; www.swedenborg.org; Pres., Rev. Christine Laitner

Unitarian Universalist Association of Congregations (1961), 25 Beacon St., Boston, MA 02108; www.uua.org; Pres., The Rev. William Sinkford

United Church of Christ (1957), 700 Prospect Ave., Cleveland, OH 44115; www.ucc.org; Pres., Rev. John H. Thomas

United Methodist Church (1968), www.umc.org; Pres. Council of Bishops, Bishop Sharon Brown Christopher

United Pentecostal Church Intl. (1925), 8855 Dunn Rd., Hazelwood, MO 63042; www.upci.org; Gen. Supt., Rev. Kenneth F. Haney

Volunteers of America (1896), 1660 Duke St., Alexandria, VA 22314; www.voa.org; Chairperson, Frances Hesselbein

Wesleyan Church (1968), PO Box 50434, Indianapolis, IN 46250; www.wesleyan.org; Gen. Supts., Dr. Earle L. Wilson, Dr. David H. Holdren, Dr. Thomas E. Armiger

Episcopal Church Liturgical Colors and Calendar

Source: The Rt. Rev. Barry E. Yingling, Editor, the *Churchman's Ordo Kalendar*

The most common liturgical colors in the Episcopal Church are: **White**—Christmas Day through First Sunday after Epiphany; Maundy Thursday (as an alternative to crimson at the Eucharist); from the Vigil of Easter to the Day of Pentecost (Whitsunday); Trinity Sunday; Feasts of the Lord (except Holy Cross Day); the Confession of St. Peter; the Conversion of St. Paul; St. Joseph; St. Mary Magdalene; St. Mary the Virgin; St. Michael and All Angels; All Saints' Day; St. John the Evangelist; memorials of other saints who were not martyred; Independence Day and Thanksgiving Day; weddings and funerals. **Red**—the Day of Pentecost; Holy Cross Day; feasts of apostles and evangelists (except those listed above); feasts and memorials of martyrs (including Holy Innocents' Day). **Violet**—Advent and Lent. **Crimson** or oxblood (dark red)—Holy Week. **Green**—the seasons after Epiphany and after Pentecost. **Black**—optional alternative for funerals and Good Friday.

The days of fasting are Ash Wednesday and Good Friday. Other days of special devotion (penitence) include the 40 days of Lent. Ember Days are days of prayer for the church's ministry. They fall on the Wednesday, Friday, and Saturday after the first Sunday in Lent, the Day of Pentecost, Holy Cross Day, and December 13. Rogation Days, the 3 days before Ascension Day, are days of prayer for God's blessing on the crops, on commerce and industry, and for conservation of the earth's resources.

Days, etc.	2005	2006	2007	2008	2009
Golden Number	11	12	13	14	15
Sunday Letter	B	A	G	F	D
Sundays after Epiphany	5	8	7	4	7
Ash Wednesday	Feb. 9	Mar. 1	Feb. 21	Feb. 6	Feb. 25
First Sunday in Lent	Feb. 13	Mar. 5	Feb. 25	Feb. 10	Mar. 1
Passion/Palm Sunday	Mar. 20	Apr. 9	Apr. 1	Mar. 16	Apr. 5
Good Friday	Mar. 25	Apr. 14	Apr. 6	Mar. 21	Apr. 10
Easter Day	Mar. 27	Apr. 16	Apr. 8	Mar. 23	Apr. 12
Ascension Day	May 5	May 25	May 17	May 1	May 21
The Day of Pentecost	May 15	June 4	May 27	May 11	May 31
Trinity Sunday	May 22	June 11	June 3	May 18	June 7
Numbered Proper of 2 Pentecost	#4	#6	#5	#3	#6
First Sunday of Advent	Nov. 27	Dec. 3	Dec. 2	Nov. 30	Nov. 29

WORLD ALMANAC QUICK QUIZ

When was the last time before 2005 that a pope was elected from what is now Germany?

(a) 1055 (b) 1473 (c)1790 (d) there had never been a German pope

For the answer look in this chapter, or see page 1008

Greek Orthodox Movable Ecclesiastical Dates, 2005-2009

Feast days and fasting days are determined annually on the basis of the date of Holy Pascha (Easter). This ecclesiastical cycle begins with the first day of the Triodion and ends with the Sunday of All Saints, a total of 18 weeks.

	2005	2006	2007	2008	2009
Triodion begins	Feb. 20	Feb. 12	Jan. 28	Feb. 17	Feb. 8
1st Sat. of Souls	Mar. 5	Feb. 25	Feb. 10	Mar. 1	Feb. 21
Meat Fare	Mar. 6	Feb. 26	Feb. 11	Mar. 2	Feb. 22
2nd Sat. of Souls	Mar. 12	Mar. 4	Feb. 17	Mar. 8	Feb. 28
Lent Begins	Mar. 14	Mar. 6	Feb. 19	Mar. 10	March 2
St. Theodore—3rd Sat. of Souls	Mar. 19	Mar. 11	Feb. 24	Mar. 15	March 7
Sunday of Orthodoxy	Mar. 20	Mar. 12	Feb. 25	Mar. 16	March 8
Sat. of Lazarus	Apr. 23	Apr. 15	Mar. 31	Apr. 19	April 11
Palm Sunday	Apr. 24	Apr. 16	Apr. 1	Apr. 20	April 12
Holy (Good) Friday	Apr. 29	Apr. 21	Apr. 6	Apr. 25	April 17
Western Easter	Mar. 27	Apr. 16	Apr. 8	Mar. 23	April 12
Orthodox Easter	May 1	Apr. 23	Apr. 8	Apr. 27	April 19
Ascension	June 9	June 1	May 17	June 5	May 28
Sat. of Souls	June 18	June 10	May 26	June 14	June 6
Pentecost	June 19	June 11	May 27	June 15	June 7
All Saints	June 26	June 18	June 3	June 22	June 14
Fast of Holy Apostles (First day)	June 27	June 19	June 4	June 23	June 15

Important Islamic Dates, 1426-1430 AH (2005-2009)

Source: Imad-ad-Dean, Inc., Bethesda, MD 20814

The Islamic calendar is a strict lunar calendar reckoned from the year of the Hijra (Anno Hegirae, or AH)—Muhammad's flight from Mecca to Medina, in 622 AD. Each year consists of 12 lunar months of 29 or 30 days beginning and ending with each new moon's visible crescent. Common years have 354 days; leap years have 355 days. Some Muslim countries employ a conventionalized calendar with the leap day added to the last month, Dhûl Hijah, but for religious purposes the leap date is taken into account by tracking each new moon sighting. The dates given below are based on the convention that the first new moon must be seen before the following dawn on the East Coast of the Americas. Actual (local) Western Hemisphere sightings may occur a day later, but never a day earlier, than these dates reflect. Holy days begin at sunset on the previous day.

	(1426) 2005-06	(1427) 2006	(1428) 2007	(1429) 2008	(1430) 2008-09
New Year's Day (Muharram 1)	Feb. 10, 2005	Jan. 30, 2006	Jan. 20, 2007	Jan. 9, 2008	Dec. 28, 2008
Ashura (Muharram 10)	Feb. 19, 2005	Feb. 8, 2006	Jan. 29, 2007	Jan. 18, 2008	Jan. 6, 2009
Mawlid (Rabi'l 12)	April 21, 2005	Apr. 10, 2006	Mar. 31, 2007	Mar. 20, 2008	Mar. 9, 2009
Ramadan 1	Oct. 4, 2005	Sept. 23, 2006	Sept. 12, 2007	Sept. 1, 2008	Aug. 21, 2009
Eid al-Fitr (Shawwal 1)	Nov. 3, 2005	Oct. 23, 2006	Oct. 12, 2007	Sept. 30, 2008	Sept. 20, 2009
Eid al-Adha (Dhûl-Hijjah 10)	Jan. 10, 2006	Dec. 30, 2006	Dec. 20, 2007	Dec. 8, 2008	Nov. 27, 2009

Jewish Holy Days, Festivals, and Fasts, 5766-5770 (2005-2010)

The Jewish calendar consists of 12 lunar months, alternating between 29 and 30 days. It is lunisolar, and adjusts for the solar cycle by adding an extra month (Adar II) in the 3rd, 6th, 8th, 11th, 14th, 17th, and 19th years of a 19-year cycle. The calendar started on the day of Creation, reckoned in the 2nd-3rd cent. BC as Tishrei 1, 3,761 years before the common era.

The religious calendar begins with the month Nisan, from which all other months are counted, and the civil calendar with Tishrei. The months are 1) Nisan; 2) Iyar; 3) Sivan; 4) Tammuz; 5) Av (also Abh); 6) Elul; 7) Tishrei; 8) Cheshvan (also Marcheshvan); 9) Kislev; 10) Tevet (also Tebeth); 11) Shevat (also Shebhat); 12) Adar; 12a) Adar Sheni (II), added in leap years. The names are Aramaic versions of the Babylonian months, adopted during the Jews' exile in Babylon in the 4th century bc. Rosh Hashanah, the New Year, begins on Tishrei 1 (Sept.-Oct.). Yom Kippur is the holiest day of the year. All holidays listed below begin at sunset on the previous day, except where noted.

Holiday	Date on Jewish Cal.	(5766) 2005-06		(5767) 2006-07		(5768) 2007-08		(5769) 2008-09		(5770) 2009-10	
Rosh Hashanah (New Year)	Tishrei 1-2	Oct. 4	Tue.	Sept. 23	Sat.	Sept. 13	Thu.	Sept. 30	Tue.	Sept. 19	Sat.
		Oct. 5	Wed.	Sept. 24	Sun.	Sept. 14	Fri.	Oct. 1	Wed.	Sept. 20	Sun.
Fast of Gedalya[1]	Tishrei 3	Oct. 6	Thu.	Sept. 25	Mon.	Sept. 16	Sun.*	Oct. 2	Thu.	Sept. 21	Mon.
Yom Kippur (Day of Atonement)	Tishrei 10	Oct. 13	Thu.	Oct. 2	Mon.	Sept. 22	Sat.	Oct. 9	Thu.	Sept. 28	Mon.
Sukkot	Tishrei 15-21	Oct. 18	Tue.	Oct. 7	Sat.	Sept. 27	Thu.	Oct. 14	Tue.	Oct. 3	Sat.
		Oct. 24	Mon.	Oct. 13	Fri.	Oct. 3	Wed.	Oct. 20	Mon.	Oct. 9	Fri.
Shemini Atzeret	Tishrei 22	Oct. 25	Tue.	Oct. 14	Sat.	Oct. 4	Thu.	Oct. 21	Tue.	Oct. 10	Sat.
Simchat Torah	Tishrei 23	Oct. 26	Wed.	Oct. 15	Sun.	Oct. 5	Fri.	Oct. 22	Wed.	Oct. 11	Sun.
Hanukkah	Kislev 25-Tevet 2	Dec. 26	Mon.	Dec. 16	Sat.	Dec. 5	Wed.	Dec. 22	Mon.	Dec. 11	Sat.
		2006 Jan. 2	Mon.	Dec. 23	Sat.	Dec. 12	Wed.	Dec. 29	Mon.	Dec. 19	Sat.
Fast of the 10th of Tevet[1]	Tevet 10	Jan. 10	Tue.	Dec. 31	Sun.	Dec. 19	Wed.	**2009** Jan. 6,	Tue.	Dec. 27	Sun
Tu B'Shevat	Shevat 15	Feb. 13,	Mon.	**2007** Feb. 3	Sat.	**2008** Jan. 22	Tue.	Feb. 9	Mon.	**2010** Jan. 30,	Sat.
Ta'anis Esther (Fast of Esther)[1]	Adar 13	Mar. 13	Mon.	Mar. 1	Thu.*	Mar. 20	Thu.	Mar. 9	Mon.	Feb. 25	Thu.
Purim	Adar 14	Mar. 14	Tue.	Mar. 4	Sun.	Mar. 21	Fri.	Mar. 10	Tue.	Feb. 28	Sun.
Pesach (Passover)	Nisan 15-22	Apr. 13	Thu.	Apr. 3	Tue.	Apr. 20	Sun.	Apr. 9	Thu.	Mar. 30	Tue.
		Apr. 20	Thu.	Apr. 10	Tue.	Apr. 27	Sun.	Apr. 16	Thu.	Apr. 6	Tue.
Lag B'Omer	Iyar 18	May 16	Tue.	May 6	Sun.	May 23	Fri.	May 12	Tue.	May 2	Sun.
Shavuot (Pentecost)	Sivan 6-7	June 2	Fri.	May 23	Wed.	June 9	Mon.	May 29	Fri.	May 19	Wed
		June 3	Sat.	May 24	Thu.	June 10	Tue.	May 30	Sat.	May 20	Thu.
Fast of the 17th Day of Tammuz[1]	Tammuz 17	July 13	Thu.	July 3	Tue.	July 20	Sun.	July 9	Thu.	June 29	Tue.
Fast of the 9th Day of Av	Av 9	Aug. 3	Thu.	July 24	Tue.	Aug.10	Sun.	July 30	Thu.	July 20	Tue.

*Date changed to avoid Sabbath. (1) "Minor fasts" begin at sunrise.

Ash Wednesday and Easter Sunday (Western churches), 1901-2100

Year	Ash Wed.	Easter Sunday	Year	Ash Wed.	Easter Sunday	Year	Ash Wed.	Easter Sunday	Year	Ash Wed.	Easter Sunday	Year	Ash Wed.	Easter Sunday
1901	Feb. 20	Apr. 7	1941	Feb. 26	Apr. 13	1981	Mar. 4	Apr. 19	2021	Feb. 17	Apr. 4	2061	Feb. 23	Apr. 10
1902	Feb. 12	Mar. 30	1942	Feb. 18	Apr. 5	1982	Feb. 24	Apr. 11	2022	Mar. 2	Apr. 17	2062	Feb. 8	Mar. 26
1903	Feb. 25	Apr. 12	1943	Mar. 10	Apr. 25	1983	Feb. 16	Apr. 3	2023	Feb. 22	Apr. 9	2063	Feb. 28	Apr. 15
1904	Feb. 17	Apr. 3	1944	Feb. 23	Apr. 9	1984	Mar. 7	Apr. 22	2024	Feb. 14	Mar. 31	2064	Feb. 20	Apr. 6
1905	Mar. 8	Apr. 23	1945	Feb. 14	Apr. 1	1985	Feb. 20	Apr. 7	2025	Mar. 5	Apr. 20	2065	Feb. 11	Mar. 29
1906	Feb. 28	Apr. 15	1946	Mar. 6	Apr. 21	1986	Feb. 12	Mar. 30	2026	Feb. 18	Apr. 5	2066	Feb. 24	Apr. 11
1907	Feb. 13	Mar. 31	1947	Feb. 19	Apr. 6	1987	Mar. 4	Apr. 19	2027	Feb. 10	Mar. 28	2067	Feb. 16	Apr. 3
1908	Mar. 4	Apr. 19	1948	Feb. 11	Mar. 28	1988	Feb. 17	Apr. 3	2028	Mar. 1	Apr. 16	2068	Mar. 7	Apr. 22
1909	Feb. 24	Apr. 11	1949	Mar. 2	Apr. 17	1989	Feb. 8	Mar. 26	2029	Feb. 14	Apr. 1	2069	Feb. 27	Apr. 14
1910	Feb. 9	Mar. 27	1950	Feb. 22	Apr. 9	1990	Feb. 28	Apr. 15	2030	Mar. 6	Apr. 21	2070	Feb. 12	Mar. 30
1911	Mar. 1	Apr. 16	1951	Feb. 7	Mar. 25	1991	Feb. 13	Mar. 31	2031	Feb. 26	Apr. 13	2071	Mar. 4	Apr. 19
1912	Feb. 21	Apr. 7	1952	Feb. 27	Apr. 13	1992	Mar. 4	Apr. 19	2032	Feb. 11	Mar. 28	2072	Feb. 24	Apr. 10
1913	Feb. 5	Mar. 23	1953	Feb. 18	Apr. 5	1993	Feb. 24	Apr. 11	2033	Mar. 2	Apr. 17	2073	Feb. 8	Mar. 26
1914	Feb. 25	Apr. 12	1954	Mar. 3	Apr. 18	1994	Feb. 16	Apr. 3	2034	Feb. 22	Apr. 9	2074	Feb. 28	Apr. 15
1915	Feb. 17	Apr. 4	1955	Feb. 23	Apr. 10	1995	Mar. 1	Apr. 16	2035	Feb. 7	Mar. 25	2075	Feb. 20	Apr. 7
1916	Mar. 8	Apr. 23	1956	Feb. 15	Apr. 1	1996	Feb. 21	Apr. 7	2036	Feb. 27	Apr. 13	2076	Mar. 4	Apr. 19
1917	Feb. 21	Apr. 8	1957	Mar. 6	Apr. 21	1997	Feb. 12	Mar. 30	2037	Feb. 18	Apr. 5	2077	Feb. 24	Apr. 11
1918	Feb. 13	Mar. 31	1958	Feb. 19	Apr. 6	1998	Feb. 25	Apr. 12	2038	Mar. 10	Apr. 25	2078	Feb. 16	Apr. 3
1919	Mar. 5	Apr. 20	1959	Feb. 11	Mar. 29	1999	Feb. 17	Apr. 4	2039	Feb. 23	Apr. 10	2079	Mar. 8	Apr. 23
1920	Feb. 18	Apr. 4	1960	Mar. 2	Apr. 17	2000	Mar. 8	Apr. 23	2040	Feb. 15	Apr. 1	2080	Feb. 21	Apr. 7
1921	Feb. 9	Mar. 27	1961	Feb. 15	Apr. 2	2001	Feb. 28	Apr. 15	2041	Mar. 6	Apr. 21	2081	Feb. 12	Mar. 30
1922	Mar. 1	Apr. 16	1962	Mar. 7	Apr. 22	2002	Feb. 13	Mar. 31	2042	Feb. 19	Apr. 6	2082	Mar. 4	Apr. 19
1923	Feb. 14	Apr. 1	1963	Feb. 27	Apr. 14	2003	Mar. 5	Apr. 20	2043	Feb. 11	Mar. 29	2083	Feb. 17	Apr. 4
1924	Mar. 5	Apr. 20	1964	Feb. 12	Mar. 29	2004	Feb. 25	Apr. 11	2044	Mar. 2	Apr. 17	2084	Feb. 9	Mar. 26
1925	Feb. 25	Apr. 12	1965	Mar. 3	Apr. 18	2005	Feb. 9	Mar. 27	2045	Feb. 22	Apr. 9	2085	Feb. 28	Apr. 15
1926	Feb. 17	Apr. 4	1966	Feb. 23	Apr. 10	2006	Mar. 1	Apr. 16	2046	Feb. 7	Mar. 25	2086	Feb. 13	Mar. 31
1927	Mar. 2	Apr. 17	1967	Feb. 8	Mar. 26	2007	Feb. 21	Apr. 8	2047	Feb. 27	Apr. 14	2087	Mar. 5	Apr. 20
1928	Feb. 22	Apr. 8	1968	Feb. 28	Apr. 14	2008	Feb. 6	Mar. 23	2048	Feb. 19	Apr. 5	2088	Feb. 25	Apr. 11
1929	Feb. 13	Mar. 31	1969	Feb. 19	Apr. 6	2009	Feb. 25	Apr. 12	2049	Mar. 3	Apr. 18	2089	Feb. 16	Apr. 3
1930	Mar. 5	Apr. 20	1970	Feb. 11	Mar. 29	2010	Feb. 17	Apr. 4	2050	Feb. 23	Apr. 10	2090	Mar. 1	Apr. 16
1931	Feb. 18	Apr. 5	1971	Feb. 24	Apr. 11	2011	Mar. 9	Apr. 24	2051	Feb. 15	Apr. 2	2091	Feb. 21	Apr. 8
1932	Feb. 10	Mar. 27	1972	Feb. 16	Apr. 2	2012	Feb. 22	Apr. 8	2052	Mar. 6	Apr. 21	2092	Feb. 13	Mar. 30
1933	Mar. 1	Apr. 16	1973	Mar. 7	Apr. 22	2013	Feb. 13	Mar. 31	2053	Feb. 19	Apr. 6	2093	Feb. 25	Apr. 12
1934	Feb. 14	Apr. 1	1974	Feb. 27	Apr. 14	2014	Mar. 5	Apr. 20	2054	Feb. 11	Mar. 29	2094	Feb. 17	Apr. 4
1935	Mar. 6	Apr. 21	1975	Feb. 12	Mar. 30	2015	Feb. 18	Apr. 5	2055	Mar. 3	Apr. 18	2095	Mar. 9	Apr. 24
1936	Feb. 26	Apr. 12	1976	Mar. 3	Apr. 18	2016	Feb. 10	Mar. 27	2056	Feb. 16	Apr. 2	2096	Feb. 29	Apr. 15
1937	Feb. 10	Mar. 28	1977	Feb. 23	Apr. 10	2017	Mar. 1	Apr. 16	2057	Mar. 7	Apr. 22	2097	Feb. 13	Mar. 31
1938	Mar. 2	Apr. 17	1978	Feb. 8	Mar. 26	2018	Feb. 14	Apr. 1	2058	Feb. 27	Apr. 14	2098	Mar. 5	Apr. 20
1939	Feb. 22	Apr. 9	1979	Feb. 28	Apr. 15	2019	Mar. 6	Apr. 21	2059	Feb. 12	Mar. 30	2099	Feb. 25	Apr. 12
1940	Feb. 7	Mar. 24	1980	Feb. 20	Apr. 6	2020	Feb. 26	Apr. 12	2060	Mar. 3	Apr. 18	2100	Feb. 10	Mar. 28

Popes of the Roman Catholic Church

Source: Annuario Pontificio. Table lists year of accession of each pope.

The Roman Catholic Church named the Apostle Peter as founder of the church in Rome and the first pope. He arrived there c 42, was martyred there c 67, and was ultimately canonized as a saint. **The pope's temporal title is:** Sovereign of the State of Vatican City. **The pope's spiritual titles are:** Bishop of Rome, Vicar of Jesus Christ, Successor of St. Peter, Prince of the Apostles, Supreme Pontiff of the Universal Church, Patriarch of the West, Primate of Italy, Archbishop and Metropolitan of the Roman Province.

The names of antipopes are *in italics* and followed by an *. Antipopes were illegitimate claimants to the papal throne.

Year	Pope
	St. Peter
67	St. Linus
76	St. Anacletus or Cletus
88	St. Clement I
97	St. Evaristus
105	St. Alexander I
115	St. Sixtus I
125	St. Telesphorus
136	St. Hyginus
140	St. Pius I
155	St. Anicetus
166	St. Soter
175	St. Eleutherius
189	St. Victor I
199	St. Zephyrinus
217	St. Callistus I
217	*St. Hippolytus**
222	St. Urban I
230	St. Pontian
235	St. Anterus
236	St. Fabian
251	St. Cornelius
251	*Novatian**
253	St. Lucius I
254	St. Stephen I
257	St. Sixtus II
259	St. Dionysius
269	St. Felix I
275	St. Eutychian
283	St. Caius
296	St. Marcellinus
308	St. Marcellus I
309	St. Eusebius
311	St. Melchiades
314	St. Sylvester I
336	St. Marcus
337	St. Julius I
352	Liberius
355	*Felix II**
366	St. Damasus I
366	*Ursinus**
384	St. Siricius
399	St. Anastasius I
401	St. Innocent I
417	St. Zosimus
418	St. Boniface I
418	*Eulalius**
422	St. Celestine I
432	St. Sixtus III
440	St. Leo I
461	St. Hilary
468	St. Simplicius
483	St. Felix III (II)
492	St. Gelasius I
496	Anastasius II
498	St. Symmachus
498	*Lawrence** (501-505)
514	St. Hormisdas
523	St. John I, Martyr
526	St. Felix IV (III)
530	Boniface II
530	*Dioscorus**
533	John II
535	St. Agapitus I
536	St. Silverius, Martyr
537	Vigilius
556	Pelagius I
561	John III
575	Benedict I
579	Pelagius II
590	St. Gregory I
604	Sabinian
607	Boniface III
608	St. Boniface IV
615	St. Deusdedit or Adeodatus
619	Boniface V
625	Honorius I
640	Severinus
640	John IV
642	Theodore I
649	St. Martin I, Martyr
654	St. Eugene I
657	St. Vitalian
672	Adeodatus II
676	Donus
678	St. Agatho
682	St. Leo II
684	St. Benedict II
685	John V
686	Conon
687	*Theodore**
687	*Paschal**
687	St. Sergius I
701	John VI
705	John VII
708	Sisinnius
708	Constantine
715	St. Gregory II
731	St. Gregory III
741	St. Zachary
752	Stephen II (III)[1]
757	St. Paul I
767	*Constantine**
768	*Philip**
768	Stephen III (IV)
772	Adrian I
795	St. Leo III
816	Stephen IV (V)
817	St. Paschal I
824	Eugene II
827	Valentine
827	Gregory IV
844	*John**
844	Sergius II
847	St. Leo IV
855	Benedict III
855	*Anastasius**
858	St. Nicholas I
867	Adrian II
872	John VIII
882	Marinus I
884	St. Adrian III
885	Stephen V (VI)
891	Formosus
896	Boniface VI
896	Stephen VI (VII)
897	Romanus
897	Theodore II
898	John IX
900	Benedict IV
903	Leo V
903	*Christopher**
904	Sergius III
911	Anastasius III
913	Landus
914	John X
928	Leo VI
928	Stephen VII(VIII)
931	John XI
936	Leo VII
939	Stephen VIII(IX)
942	Marinus II
946	Agapitus II
955	John XII
963	Leo VIII
964	Benedict V
965	John XIII
973	Benedict VI
974	*Boniface VII**
974	Benedict VII
983	John XIV
985	John XV
996	Gregory V
997	*John XVI**
999	Sylvester II
1003	John XVII
1004	John XVIII
1009	Sergius IV
1012	Benedict VIII
1012	*Gregory**
1024	John XIX
1032	Benedict IX
1045	Sylvester III
1045	Benedict IX
1045	Gregory VI
1046	Clement II
1047	Benedict IX
1048	Damasus II
1049	St. Leo IX
1055	Victor II
1057	Stephen IX (X)
1058	*Benedict X**
1059	Nicholas II

POPE BENEDICT XVI

Cardinal Joseph Ratzinger, was elected pope by the College of Cardinals on April 19, 2005, the 2nd day of the conclave that met following the death, April 2, of Pope John Paul II (see Obituaries). He was the first pope elected from what is now Germany since Victor II in 1055. He took the name Benedict XVI in honor of Europe's patron saint and of Benedict XV, who became pope in 1914 and sought to promote a peace settlement to end World War I.

Joseph Ratzinger was born in Marktl am Inn, in Bavaria, Germany, on April 16, 1927. Required to join Hitler Youth, for a time, he was then exempted because of his intention to pursue seminary studies. During World War II he was drafted into an anti-aircraft unit and then into the German army. In early 1945, he deserted, and spent a brief time in a U.S. prisoner-of-war camp. Ratzinger was ordained a priest on June 29, 1951, and received a doctorate in theology 2 years later. He attended the Second Vatican Council as an expert (1962-65). He also taught at several German universities in the 1960s, and eventually became known as a theological conservative. Named archbishop of Munich and Freising in March 1977, he was elevated to cardinal 3 months later. In 1981, he was appointed prefect of the Congregation for the Doctrine of the Faith, a Vatican body that maintains the church's doctrine on faith and morals. A close associate of the former pope, he was confirmed as dean of the College of Cardinals on Nov. 30, 2002.

Year	Pope
1061	Alexander II
1061	*Honorius II**
1073	St. Gregory VII
1080	*Clement III**
1086	Bl. Victor III
1088	Bl. Urban II
1099	Paschal II
1100	*Theodoric**
1102	*Albert**
1105	*Sylvester IV**
1118	Gelasius II
1118	*Gregory VIII**
1119	Callistus II
1124	Honorius II
1124	*Celestine II**
1130	Innocent II
1130	*Anacletus II**
1138	*Victor IV**
1143	Celestine II
1144	Lucius II
1145	Bl. Eugene III
1153	Anastasius IV
1154	Adrian IV
1159	Alexander III
1159	*Victor IV**
1164	*Paschal III**
1168	*Callistus III**
1179	*Innocent III**
1181	Lucius III
1185	Urban III
1187	Clement III
1187	Gregory VIII
1191	Celestine III
1198	Innocent III
1216	Honorius III
1227	Gregory IX
1241	Celestine IV
1243	Innocent IV
1254	Alexander IV
1261	Urban IV
1265	Clement IV
1271	Bl. Gregory X
1276	Bl. Innocent V
1276	Adrian V
1276	John XXI
1277	Nicholas III
1281	Martin IV
1285	Honorius IV
1288	Nicholas IV
1294	St. Celestine V
1294	Boniface VIII
1303	Bl. Benedict XI
1305	Clement V
1316	John XXII
1328	*Nicholas V**
1334	Benedict XII
1342	Clement VI
1352	Innocent VI
1362	Bl. Urban V
1370	Gregory XI
1378	Urban VI
1378	*Clement VII**
1389	Boniface IX
1394	*Benedict XIII**
1404	Innocent VII
1406	Gregory XII
1409	*Alexander V**
1410	*John XXIII**
1417	Martin V
1431	Eugene IV
1439	*Felix V**
1447	Nicholas V
1455	Callistus III
1458	Pius II
1464	Paul II
1471	Sixtus IV
1484	Innocent VIII
1492	Alexander VI
1503	Pius III
1503	Julius II
1513	Leo X
1522	Adrian VI
1523	Clement VII
1534	Paul III
1550	Julius III
1555	Marcellus II
1555	Paul IV
1559	Pius IV
1566	St. Pius V
1572	Gregory XIII
1585	Sixtus V
1590	Urban VII
1590	Gregory XIV
1591	Innocent IX
1592	Clement VIII
1605	Leo XI
1605	Paul V
1621	Gregory XV
1623	Urban VIII
1644	Innocent X
1655	Alexander VII
1667	Clement IX
1670	Clement X
1676	Bl. Innocent XI
1689	Alexander VIII
1691	Innocent XII
1700	Clement XI
1721	Innocent XIII
1724	Benedict XIII
1730	Clement XII
1740	Benedict XIV
1758	Clement XIII
1769	Clement XIV
1775	Pius VI
1800	Pius VII
1823	Leo XII
1829	Pius VIII
1831	Gregory XVI
1846	Pius IX
1878	Leo XIII
1903	St. Pius X
1914	Benedict XV
1922	Pius XI
1939	Pius XII
1958	John XXIII
1963	Paul VI
1978	John Paul I
1978	John Paul II
2005	Benedict XVI

(1) After St. Zachary, a Roman priest named Stephen was elected, but died before assuming the papacy. Another Stephen was then elected to succeed Zachary as Stephen II. He is sometimes listed as Stephen III.

College of Cardinals

Source: U.S. Catholic Conference

Members of the Sacred College of Cardinals are chosen by the pope to be his chief assistants and advisers in the administration of the church. Among their duties is the election of the pope.

In its present form, the College of Cardinals dates from the 12th century. The first cardinals, from about the 6th century, were deacons and priests of the leading churches of Rome and were bishops of neighboring dioceses. The title of cardinal was limited to members of the college in 1567. The number of cardinals was set at 70 in 1586 by Pope Sixtus V. From 1959 Pope John XXIII began to increase the number; however, the number eligible to participate in papal elections was limited to 120. Previous limitations were set aside by Pope John Paul II when he created new cardinals. In 1918 the Code of Canon Law specified that all cardinals must be priests. Pope John XXIII in 1962 established that all cardinals must be bishops, but this can be dispensed with, as in the case of Cardinal Avery Dulles. In 1971, Pope Paul VI decreed that at age 80 cardinals must retire from curial departments and offices and from participation in papal elections.

As of Sept. 2005, there were 182 members of the College, of whom 113 remained eligible to vote.

North American Cardinals

Name	Office	Born	Named Cardinal
Aloysius M. Ambrozic	Archbishop of Toronto	1930	1998
William W. Baum	Archbishop emeritus of Washington, DC	1926	1976
Anthony J. Bevilacqua[1]	Archbishop emeritus of Philadelphia	1923	1991
Ernesto Corripio Ahumada[1]	Archbishop emeritus of Mexico City	1919	1979
Avery Robert Dulles[1]	Professor, Fordham University, NYC	1918	2001
Edward M. Egan	Archbishop of New York	1932	2001
Edouard Gagnon[1]	Pres. emeritus of the Commission of Intl. Eucharistic Congresses	1918	1985
Francis E. George	Archbishop of Chicago	1937	1998
William Henry Keeler	Archbishop of Baltimore	1931	1994
Bernard F. Law	Archbishop emeritus of Boston	1931	1985
Roger Mahony	Archbishop of Los Angeles	1936	1991
Javier Lozano Barragan	Pres. Pontifical Council for Health Care Workers, Mexico	1933	2003
Adam Joseph Maida	Archbishop of Detroit	1930	1994
Luis Aponte Martinez[1]	Archibishop emeritus of San Juan	1922	1973
Theodore E. McCarrick	Archbishop of Washington, DC	1930	2001
Marc Ouellet	Archbishop of Quebec	1944	2003
Justin F. Rigali	Archbishop of Philadelphia	1935	2003
Norberto Rivera Carrera	Archbishop of Mexico City	1942	1998
Juan Sandoval Iniguez	Archbishop of Guadalajara	1933	1994
James F. Stafford	President of the Pontifical Council for the Laity	1932	1998
Adolfo Antonio Suarez Rivera	Archbishop emeritus of Monterrey	1927	1994
Edmund C. Szoka	Pres. Governorate of Vatican City State	1927	1988
Jean-Claude Turcotte	Archbishop of Montreal	1936	1994
Louis-Albert Vachon[1]	Archbishop emeritus of Quebec	1912	1985

(1) Ineligible to take part in papal elections (as of Sept. 2005).

The Ten Commandments

In the Hebrew Bible (Old Testament) the Ten Commandments (also called the Decalogue, from the Greek meaning "ten words") were revealed by God to Moses on Mt. Sinai. They form the covenant between God and the Israelites and the moral code that is the basis for the Jewish and Christian religions. The Ten Commandments appear in 2 places in the Old Testament—Exodus 20:1-17 and Deuteronomy 5:6-21.

Most Protestant, Anglican, and Orthodox Christians follow Jewish tradition, as here, which considers the introduction ("I am the Lord . . .") the first commandment and makes the prohibition against idolatry the second. Roman Catholic and Lutheran traditions combine I and II and split the last commandment into 2 that separately prohibit coveting of a neighbor's wife and a neighbor's goods. This arrangement alters the numbering of the other commandments by one.

Following is the text of the Ten Commandments as it appears in Exodus 20:1-17, in the King James version of the Bible [Roman numerals added]:

And God spake all these words, saying,

I. I *am* the LORD thy God, which have brought thee out of the land of Egypt, out of the house of bondage. Thou shalt have no other gods before me.

II. Thou shalt not make unto thee any graven image, or any likeness of *any thing* that *is* in heaven above, or that *is* in the earth beneath, or that *is* in the water under the earth. Thou shalt not bow down thyself to them, nor serve them: for I the LORD thy God *am* a jealous God, visiting the iniquity of the fathers upon the children unto the third and fourth *generation* of them that hate me; and shewing mercy unto thousands of them that love me, and keep my commandments.

III. Thou shalt not take the name of the LORD thy God in vain: for the LORD will not hold him guiltless that taketh his name in vain.

IV. Remember the sabbath day, to keep it holy. Six days shalt thou labour, and do all thy work: but the seventh day *is* the sabbath of the LORD thy God: *in it* thou shalt not do any work, thou, nor thy son, nor thy daughter, thy manservant, nor thy maidservant, nor thy cattle, nor thy stranger that *is* within thy gates: for *in* six days the LORD made heaven and earth, the sea, and all that in them *is*, and rested the seventh day: wherefore the LORD blessed the sabbath day, and hallowed it.

V. Honour thy father and thy mother: that thy days may be long upon the land which the LORD thy God giveth thee.

VI. Thou shalt not kill.

VII. Thou shalt not commit adultery.

VIII. Thou shalt not steal.

IX. Thou shalt not bear false witness against thy neighbour.

X. Thou shalt not covet thy neighbour's house, thou shalt not covet thy neighbour's wife, nor his manservant, nor his maidservant, nor his ox, nor his ass, nor any thing that *is* thy neighbour's.

Books of the Bible

Old Testament—Standard Protestant List

Genesis	I Kings	Ecclesiastes	Obadiah
Exodus	II Kings	Song of Solomon	Jonah
Leviticus	I Chronicles	Isaiah	Micah
Numbers	II Chronicles	Jeremiah	Nahum
Deuteronomy	Ezra	Lamentations	Habakkuk
Joshua	Nehemiah	Ezekiel	Zephaniah
Judges	Esther	Daniel	Haggai
Ruth	Job	Hosea	Zechariah
I Samuel	Psalms	Joel	Malachi
II Samuel	Proverbs	Amos	

New Testament List

Matthew	Ephesians	Hebrews
Mark	Phillippians	James
Luke	Colossians	I Peter
John	I Thessalonians	II Peter
Acts	II Thessalonians	I John
Romans	I Timothy	II John
I Corinthians	II Timothy	III John
II Corinthians	Titus	Jude
Galatians	Philemon	Revelation

The standard Protestant Old Testament consists of the same 39 books as in the Bible of Judaism, but the latter is organized differently. The Old Testament used by Roman Catholics has 7 additional "deuterocanonical" books, plus some additional parts of books. The 7 are: **Tobit, Judith, Wisdom, Sirach (Ecclesiasticus), Baruch, I Maccabees,** and **II Maccabees**. Both Catholic and Protestant versions of the New Testament have 27 books, with the same names.

Figures in the Hebrew Bible (Old Testament)

Aaron: First of Hebrew high priests; brother of Moses and Miriam.
Abel: Second son of Adam and Eve; slain by Cain.
Abraham: Founder of monotheism; patriarch; also called Abram.
Adam: First human according to Genesis.
Amos: Herdsman; prophesized against social injustice and oppression of the poor.
Bathsheba: Seduced by King David; mother of King Solomon.
Cain: Tiller of the soil; son of Adam and Eve; killed his brother Abel.
Cyrus: Persian ruler; sent Jews home from exile.
Daniel: Cast into lion's den by Nebuchadnezzer; saved.
David: Israel's greatest king; shepherd, warrior, musician, psalmist.
Deborah: Prophet and judge; ruled over Israel.
Elijah: Great prophet; was victorious over the priests of the Phoenician god, Baal.
Elisha: Prophet; successor to Elijah.
Esther: Jewish wife of the king of Persia; saved Jews from annihilation.
Eve: First woman according to Genesis.
Ezekiel: Visionary; prophesized hope to exiled Jews in Babylon.
Ezra: Great Jewish leader; rededicated worship and Torah law after exile.
Goliath: Giant Philistine warrior; slain by David.
Hannah: Childless; promised child to God; mother to the prophet Samuel.
Hosea: Enacted prophecy; asked God's forgiveness for Israel's unfaithfulness.
Isaac: Son of Abraham and Sarah; saved from sacrificial altar.
Isaiah: Highly educated prophet; avoided war with Assyria. Israel destroyed. Jerusalem survived.
Jacob: Son of Isaac; father of the Twelve Tribes; renamed "Israel" by angel.
Jeremiah: Confronted leaders; urged surrender to Babylon.
Jezebel: Phoenician queen of King Ahab; had Israelite prophets killed.
Job: "Blameless" man; lost family and possessions but not his faith.
Jonah: Swallowed by a great fish; prophesized repentance in Nineveh.
Jonathan: Son of King Saul; friend of David.
Joseph: Favorite of Jacob; interprets Pharaoh's dreams; brings Hebrews to Egypt.
Josiah: Reformist king; repaired Temple; restored worship; reintroduced Passover.
Joshua: Successor of Moses; led Hebrews into land of Israel.
Leah: Matriarch; older sister of Rachel; Jacob's wife and Joseph's mother.
Micah: Prophet; predicted the end of war and beginning of peace.
Miriam: Prophet and great leader of the Hebrews; sister to Moses and Aaron.
Moses: Most important Hebrew prophet; leader of the Israelites; received the Torah.
Nathan: Prophet; confronted King David over his seduction of Bathsheba.
Nebuchadnezzer: Babylonian king; destroyed Jerusalem.
Nehemiah: Led Jews back to Jerusalem from Babylonian exile.
Noah: A man of great faith who, according to *Genesis*, saved the world from a great flood.
Rachel: Matriarch; younger sister of Leah; Jacob's wife; Joseph's mother.
Rebecca: Matriarch; wife of Isaac; mother of Jacob.
Ruth: Moabite convert; ancestor of David and all the kings of Israel.
Samuel: Prophet; anointed Saul king of Israel and later anointed David to succeed him.
Samson: Judge and military leader of Israel, possessed super-human strength .
Sarah: First matriarch of Israel; wife of Abraham; mother of Isaac.
Saul: First king of Israel; father of Jonathan.
Solomon: King of Israel at its zenith; known for great wisdom.
Zachariah: Prophet; encouraged rebuilding of Temple destroyed by Babylonians.

Figures in the New Testament

Andrew: One of the Twelve Apostles; brother of Peter and former fisherman; one of the earlier disciples.
Barabbas: Imprisoned with Jesus; set free by Pilate on Passover.
Barnabas: Disciple of Jesus; closely connected with Paul.
Bartholomew: A lesser known member of the Twelve Apostles; cheerful and prayed often.
Cornelius: A Roman convert defended by Peter, allowing Gentiles to become Christians.
Elizabeth: Mother of John the Baptist; relation of the Virgin Mary.
Gabriel: Archangel; appeared to the Virgin Mary to announce that she was to give birth to the messiah.
Herod: Two Herods appear in the New Testament: Herod the Great ordered the death of children around the time of Jesus's birth; his son, Herod, imprisoned John the Baptist, leading to his beheading.
James: One of the Twelve; brother of John the apostle.
Jesus: Central figure of the Gospels; believed to be the messiah and son of God; crucified by the Romans.
John (Baptist): Known as "John the Baptist"; important prophet and forerunner to Jesus; relation of the Virgin Mary.
John (Apostle): Beloved disciple of Jesus; one of the Twelve; possible author of 4th Gospel; brother of James.
Joseph: Husband of the Virgin Mary; descendant of King David.
Judas Iscariot: Betrayer of Jesus; prominent member of the apostles; committed suicide.
Judas Thaddeus: One of the Twelve; also called "Jude" to distinguish him from Judas Iscariot.
Lazarus: Brother of the disciples Martha and Mary of Bethany; raised from the dead at their request; possibly the same Lazarus who appears in Jesus's parable of the rich man.
Luke: Traditional author of the Gospel of Luke; possibly a follower of Paul.
Mark: Traditional author of the Gospel of Mark; possibly the same Mark who is a companion of Peter.
Matthew: One of the Twelve; possible author of the Gospel of Matthew; a former tax collector.
Mary Magdalene: Important female disciple of Jesus; witness to his death and resurrection.
Mary, the mother of Jesus: traditionally believed to be a virgin and conceived without sin; wife of Joseph.
Matthias: Often included on lists of the Twelve Apostles as the apostle who replaced Judas Iscariot after his betrayal.
Paul (Saul): Writer of nearly a quarter of the New Testament; a former persecutor of Christians, converted after a vision; played a significant role in spreading Christianity.
Peter: Considered to be the foremost of the Twelve Apostles; traditionally the first pope and "rock" of the Christian church; author of epistles; also called Simon and Simon Peter.
Philip: One of the Twelve; considered pragmatic and sensible.
Pilate, Pontius: A Roman prefect; played large role in the trial and crucifixion of Jesus.
Simon: One of the Twelve; known as "the Zealot" to distinguish from Simon Peter.
Stephen: Fervently preached that Jesus was the Messiah; stoned to death by angry mob, including Saul; important figure in Saul's conversion.
Thomas: One of the Twelve; known as "Doubting Thomas" because he did not believe Jesus was risen until he could touch him.
Timothy: A disciple closely connected with Paul; author of epistles.
Zechariah: Father of John the Baptist; husband of Elizabeth; struck dumb when he doubted his barren wife could become pregnant.

Adherents of All Religions by Six Continental Areas[1], Mid-2004

Source: *2005 Encyclopædia Britannica Book of the Year; figures rounded*

	Africa	Asia	Europe	Latin America	Northern America	Oceania	World
Baha'is	1,929,000	3,639,000	146,000	813,000	847,000	122,000	7,496,000
Buddhists	148,000	369,394,000	1,634,000	699,000	3,063,000	493,000	375,440,000
Chinese Universists	35,400	400,718,000	266,000	200,000	713,000	133,000	402,065,000
Christians	401,717,000	341,337,000	553,689,000	510,131,000	273,941,000	26,147,000	2,106,962,000
Roman Catholics	143,065,000	121,618,000	276,739,000	476,699,000	79,217,000	8,470,000	1,105,808,000
Protestants	115,276,000	56,512,000	70,908,000	53,572,000	65,881,000	7,699,000	369,848,000
Orthodox	37,989,000	13,240,000	158,974,000	848,000	6,620,000	756,000	218,427,000
Anglicans	43,404,000	733,000	25,727,000	909,000	2,986,000	4,986,000	78,745,000
Independents	87,913,000	176,516,000	24,445,000	44,810,000	81,138,000	1,719,000	416,541,000
Confucianists	300	6,379,000	16,600	800	0	50,600	6,447,000
Ethnic religionists	105,251,000	141,589,000	1,238,000	3,109,000	1,263,000	319,000	252,769,000
Hindus	2,604,000	844,593,000	1,467,000	766,000	1,444,000	417,000	851,291,000
Jains	74,900	4,436,000	0	0	7,500	700	4,519,000
Jews	224,000	5,317,000	1,985,000	1,206,000	6,154,000	104,000	14,990,000
Muslims	350,453,000	892,440,000	33,290,000	1,724,000	5,109,000	408,000	1,283,424,000
New-Religionists	112,000	104,352,000	381,000	764,000	1,561,000	84,800	107,255,000
Shintoists	0	2,717,000	0	7,200	60,000	0	2,784,000
Sikhs	58,400	24,085,000	238,000	0	583,000	24,800	24,989,000
Spiritists	3,100	2,000	135,000	12,575,000	160,000	7,300	12,882,000
Taoists	0	2,702,000	0	0	11,900	0	2,714,000
Zoroastrians	900	2,429,000	89,900	0	81,600	3,200	2,605,000
Other religionists	75,000	68,000	257,500	105,000	650,000	10,000	1,166,000
Nonreligious	5,912,000	601,478,000	108,674,000	15,939,000	31,286,000	3,894,600	767,184,000
Atheists	585,000	122,870,000	22,048,000	2,756,000	1,997,000	400,000	150,656,000

(1) **Continental Areas.** Following current UN demographic terminology, which divides the world into the 6 major areas shown above. Note that "Asia" includes the former Soviet Central Asian states and "Europe" includes all of Russia, extending eastward to Vladivostok, the East Sea/Sea of Japan, and the Bering Strait.
Adherents. As defined in the 1948 Universal Declaration of Human Rights, a person's religion is what he or she says it is. Totals are enumerated following the methodology of the *World Christian Encyclopedia*, 2nd ed. (2001) and *World Christian Trends* (2001), using recent censuses, polls, literature, and other data. Totals may conflict with some estimates for total populations.
Buddhists. 56% Mahayana, 38% Theravada (Hinayana), 6% Tantrayana (Lamaism). **Chinese Universists (folk religionists).** Followers of traditional Chinese religion (local deities, ancestor veneration, Confucian ethics, universism, divination, some Buddhist elements). **Christians.** Total Christians include those affiliated with churches not shown, plus other persons professing in censuses or polls to be Christians but not affiliated with any church. Figures for the subgroups of Christians do not add up to the totals because all subgroups are not shown and some Christians adhere to more than one denomination. **Confucianists.** Non-Chinese followers of Confucius and Confucianism, mostly Koreans in Korea. **Ethnic religionists.** Followers of local, tribal, animistic, or shamanistic religions, with members restricted to one ethnic group. **Hindus.** 70% Vaishnavites, 25% Shaivites, 2% neo-Hindus and reform Hindus. **Independents.** Members of churches and networks that regard themselves as postdenominationalist and neo-apostolic and thus independent of historic, organized, institutionalized denominationalist Christianity. **Jews.** Adherents of Judaism. **Muslims.** 83% Sunni Muslims, 16% Shia Muslims (Shi'ites), 1% other schools. **New-Religionists.** Followers of Asian 20th-cent. New Religions, New Religious movements, radical new crisis religions, and non-Christian syncretistic mass religions, all founded since 1800 and most since 1945. **Other religionists.** Including a handful of religions, quasi-religions, pseudoreligions, parareligions, religious or mystic systems, and religious and semireligious brotherhoods of numerous varieties. **Nonreligious.** Persons professing no religion, nonbelievers, agnostics, freethinkers, uninterested, dereligionized secularists indifferent to all religion. **Atheists.** Persons professing atheism, skepticism, disbelief, or irreligion, including antireligious (opposed to all religion).

Major Christian Denominations:

Brackets indicate some features that tend to

Denom-ination	Origins	Organization	Authority	Special rites
Baptists	In radical Reformation, objections to infant baptism, demands for church and state separation; John Smyth, English Separatist, in 1609; Roger Williams, 1638, Providence, RI.	Congregational; each local church is autonomous.	Scripture; some Baptists, particularly in the South, interpret the Bible literally.	*[Baptism, usually early teen years and after, by total immersion;]* Lord's Supper.
Church of Christ (Disciples)	Among evangelical Presbyterians in KY (1804) and PA (1809), in distress over Protestant factionalism and decline of fervor; organized in 1832.	Congregational.	*["Where the Scriptures speak, we speak; where the Scriptures are silent, we are silent."]*	Adult baptism; Lord's Supper (weekly).
Episcopalians	Henry VIII separated English Catholic Church from Rome, 1534, for political reasons; Protestant Episcopal Church in U.S. founded in 1789.	*[Diocesan bishops, in apostolic succession, are elected by parish representatives; the national Church is headed by General Convention and Presiding Bishop; part of the Anglican Communion.]*	Scripture as interpreted by tradition, especially *39 Articles* (1563); tri-annual convention of bishops, priests, and lay people.	Infant baptism, Eucharist, and other sacraments; sacrament taken to be symbolic, but as having real spiritual effect.
Jehovah's Witnesses	Founded in 1870 in PA by Charles Taze Russell; incorporated as Watch Tower Bible and Tract Society of PA, 1884; name Jehovah's Witnesses adopted in 1931.	A governing body located in NY coordinates worldwide activities; each congregation cared for by a body of elders; each Witness considered a minister.	The Bible.	Baptism by immersion; annual Lord's Meal ceremony.
Latter-day Saints (Mormons)	In a vision of the Father and the Son reported by Joseph Smith (1820s) in NY. Smith also reported receiving new scripture on golden tablets: The Book of Mormon.	Theocratic; 1st Presidency (church president, 2 counselors), 12 Apostles preside over international church. Local congregations headed by lay priesthood leaders.	Revelation to living prophet (church president). The Bible, Book of Mormon, and other revelations to Smith and his successors.	Baptism, at age 8; laying on of hands (which confers the gift of the Holy Ghost); Lord's Supper; temple rites: baptism for the dead, marriage for eternity, others.
Lutherans	Begun by Martin Luther in Wittenberg, Germany, in 1517; objection to Catholic doctrine of salvation and sale of indulgences; break complete, 1519.	Varies from congregational to episcopal; in U.S., a combination of regional synods and congregational polities is most common.	Scripture alone. *The Book of Concord* (1580), which includes the three Ecumenical Creeds, is subscribed to as a correct exposition of Scripture.	Infant baptism; Lord's Supper; Christ's true body and blood present "in, with, and under the bread and wine."
Methodists	Rev. John Wesley began movement in 1738, within Church of England; first U.S. denomination, Baltimore (1784).	Conference and superintendent system; *[in United Methodist Church, general superintendents are bishops—not a priestly order, only an office—who are elected for life.]*	Scripture as interpreted by tradition, reason, and experience.	Baptism of infants or adults; Lord's Supper commanded; other rites: marriage, ordination, solemnization of personal commitments.
Orthodox	Developed in original Christian proselytizing; broke with Rome in 1054, after centuries of doctrinal disputes and diverging traditions.	Synods of bishops in autonomous, usually national, churches elect a patriarch, archbishop, or metropolitan; these men, as a group, are the heads of the church.	Scripture, tradition, and the first 7 church councils up to Nicaea II in 787; bishops in council have authority in doctrine and policy.	Seven sacraments: infant baptism and anointing, Eucharist, ordination, penance, marriage, and anointing of the sick.
Pentecostal	In Topeka, KS (1901) and Los Angeles (1906), in reaction to perceived loss of evangelical fervor among Methodists and others.	Originally a movement, not a formal organization, Pentecostalism now has a variety of organized forms and continues also as a movement.	Scripture; individual charismatic leaders, the teachings of the Holy Spirit.	*[Spirit baptism, especially as shown in "speaking in tongues"; healing and sometimes exorcism;]* adult baptism; Lord's Supper.
Presbyterians	In 16th-cent. Calvinist reformation; differed with Lutherans over sacraments, church government; John Knox founded Scotch Presbyerian church about 1560.	*[Highly structured representational system of ministers and lay persons (presbyters) in local, regional, and national bodies (synods).]*	Scripture.	Infant baptism; Lord's Supper; bread and wine symbolize Christ's spiritual presence.
Roman Catholics	Traditionally, founded by Jesus who named St. Peter the 1st vicar; developed in early Christian proselytizing, especially after the conversion of imperial Rome in the 4th cent.	*[Hierarchy with supreme power vested in pope elected by cardinals;]* councils of bishops advise on matters of doctrine and policy.	*[The pope, when speaking for the whole church in matters of faith and morals; and tradition (which is expressed in church councils and in part contained in Scripture).]*	Mass; 7 sacraments: baptism, reconciliation, Eucharist, confirmation, marriage, ordination, and anointing of the sick (unction).
United Church of Christ	*[By ecumenical union, in 1957, of Congregationalists and Evangelical & Reformed, representing both Calvinist and Lutheran traditions.]*	Congregational; a General Synod, representative of all congregations, sets general policy.	Scripture.	Infant baptism; Lord's Supper.

How Do They Differ?

distinguish a denomination sharply from others.

Practice	Ethics	Doctrine	Other	Denom-ination
Worship style varies from staid to evangelistic; extensive missionary activity.	Usually opposed to alcohol and tobacco; some tendency toward a perfectionist ethical standard.	*[No creed; true church is of believers only, who are all equal.]*	Believing no authority can stand between the believer and God, the Baptists are strong supporters of church and state separation.	**Baptists**
Tries to avoid any rite not considered part of the 1st-century church; some congregations may reject instrumental music.	Some tendency toward perfectionism; increasing interest in social action programs.	Simple New Testament faith; avoids any elaboration not firmly based on Scripture.	Highly tolerant in doctrinal and religious matters; strongly supportive of scholarly education.	**Church of Christ (Disciples)**
Formal, based on "Book of Common Prayer," updated 1979; services range from austerely simple to highly liturgical.	Tolerant, sometimes permissive; some social action programs.	Scripture; the "historic creeds," which include the Apostles, Nicene, and Athanasian, and the "Book of Common Prayer"; ranges from Anglo-Catholic to low church, with Calvinist influences.	Strongly ecumenical, holding talks with many branches of Christendom.	**Episco-palians**
Meetings are held in Kingdom Halls and members' homes for study and worship; *[extensive door-to-door visitations.]*	High moral code; stress on marital fidelity and family values; avoidance of tobacco and blood transfusions.	*[God, by his first creation, Christ, will soon destroy all wickedness; 144,000 faithful ones will rule in heaven with Christ over others on a paradise earth.]*	Total allegiance proclaimed only to God's kingdom or heavenly government by Christ; main periodical, *The Watchtower,* is printed in 115 languages.	**Jehovah's Witnesses**
Simple service with prayers, hymns, sermon; private temple ceremonies may be more elaborate.	Temperance; strict moral code; *[tithing]*; a strong work ethic with communal self-reliance; *[strong missionary activity]*; family emphasis.	Jesus Christ is the Son of God, the Eternal Father. Jesus' atonement saves all humans; those who are obedient to God's laws may become joint-heirs with Christ in God's kingdom.	Mormons believe theirs is the true church of Jesus Christ, restored by God through Joseph Smith. Official name: The Church of Jesus Christ of Latter-day Saints.	**Latter-day Saints (Mormons)**
Relatively simple, formal liturgy with emphasis on the sermon.	Generally conservative in personal and social ethics; doctrine of "2 kingdoms" (worldly and holy) supports conservatism in secular affairs.	Salvation by grace alone through faith; Lutheranism has made major contributions to Protestant theology.	Though still somewhat divided along ethnic lines (German, Swedish, etc.), main divisions are between fundamentalists and liberals.	**Lutherans**
Worship style varies widely by denomination, local church, geography.	Originally pietist and perfectionist; always strong social activist elements.	No distinctive theological development; 25 Articles abridged from Church of England's 39, not binding.	In 1968, The United Methodist Church was formed by the union of The Methodist Church and The Evangelical United Brethren Church.	**Methodists**
[Elaborate liturgy, usually in the vernacular, though extremely traditional; the liturgy is the essence of Orthodoxy; veneration of icons.]	Tolerant; little stress on social action; divorce, remarriage permitted in some cases; bishops are celibate; priests need not be.	Emphasis on Christ's resurrection, rather than crucifixion; the Holy Spirit proceeds from God the Father only.	Orthodox Church in America originally under Patriarch of Moscow, was granted autonomy in 1970; Greek Orthodox do not recognize this autonomy.	**Orthodox**
Loosely structured service with rousing hymns and sermons, culminating in spirit baptism.	Usually, emphasis on perfectionism, with varying degrees of tolerance.	Simple traditional beliefs, usually Protestant, with emphasis on the immediate presence of God in the Holy Spirit.	Once confined to lower-class "holy rollers," Pentecostalism now appears in mainline churches and has established middle-class congregations.	**Pentecostal**
A simple, sober service in which the sermon is central.	Traditionally, a tendency toward strictness, with firm church- and self-discipline; otherwise tolerant.	Emphasizes the sovereignty and justice of God; no longer dogmatic.	Although traces of belief in predestination (that God has foreordained salvation for the "elect") remain, this idea is no longer a central element in Presbyterianism.	**Presby-terians**
Relatively elaborate ritual centered on the Mass; also rosary recitation, novenas, etc.	Traditionally strict, but increasingly tolerant in practice; divorce and remarriage not accepted, but annulments sometimes granted; celibate clergy, except in Eastern rite.	Highly elaborated; salvation by merit gained through grace; dogmatic; special veneration of Mary, the mother of Jesus.	Relatively rapid change followed Vatican Council II; Mass now in vernacular; more stress on social action, tolerance, ecumenism.	**Roman Catholics**
Usually simple services with emphasis on the sermon.	Tolerant; some social action emphasis.	Standard Protestant; "Statement of Faith" (1959) is not binding.	The 2 main churches in the 1957 union represented earlier unions with small groups of almost every Protestant denomination.	**United Church of Christ**

Major Non-Christian World Religions

Sources: Reviewed by Anthony Padovano, PhD, STD, prof. of literature & relig. studies, Ramapo College, NJ, adj. prof. of theol., Fordham U., NYC; Islam reviewed by Abdulaziz Sachedina, PhD, prof. of Islamic studies, Univ. of Virginia

Buddhism

Founded: About 525 BC, reportedly near Benares, India.

Founder: Gautama Siddhartha (c 563-483 BC), the Buddha, who achieved enlightenment through intense meditation.

Sacred Texts: The *Tripitaka*, a collection of the Buddha's teachings, rules of monastic life, and philosophical commentaries on the teachings; also a vast body of Buddhist teachings and commentaries, many of which are called *sutras.*

Organization: The basic institution is the *sangha*, or monastic order, through which the traditions are passed from generation to generation. Monastic life tends to be democratic and anti-authoritarian. Large lay organizations have developed in some sects.

Practice: Varies widely according to the sect, and ranges from austere meditation to magical chanting and elaborate temple rites. Many practices, such as exorcism of devils, reflect pre-Buddhist beliefs.

Divisions: A variety of sects grouped into 3 primary branches: Theravada (sole survivor of the ancient Hinayana schools), which emphasizes the importance of pure thought and deed; Mahayana (includes Zen and Soka-gakkai), which ranges from philosophical schools to belief in the saving grace of higher beings or ritual practices and to practical meditative disciplines; and Tantrism, a combination of belief in ritual magic and sophisticated philosophy.

Location: Throughout Asia, from Sri Lanka to Japan. Zen and Soka-gakkai have some 15,000 adherents in the U.S.

Beliefs: Life is misery and decay, and there is no ultimate reality in it or behind it. The cycle of endless birth and rebirth continues because of desire and attachment to the unreal "self." Right meditation and deeds will end the cycle and achieve Nirvana, the Void, nothingness.

Hinduism

Founded: About 1500 BC by Aryans who migrated to India, where their Vedic religion intermixed with the practices and beliefs of the natives.

Sacred texts: The *Veda,* including the *Upanishads,* a collection of rituals and mythological and philosophical commentaries; a vast number of epic stories about gods, heroes, and saints, including the *Bhagavadgita,* a part of the *Mahabharata,* and the *Ramayana;* and a great variety of other literature.

Organization: None, strictly speaking. Generally, rituals should be performed or assisted by Brahmins, the priestly caste, but in practice, simpler rituals can be performed by anyone. Brahmins are the final judges of ritual purity, the vital element in Hindu life. Temples and religious organizations are usually presided over by Brahmins.

Practice: A variety of private rituals, primarily passage rites (e.g., initiation, marriage, death, etc.) and daily devotions, and a similar variety of public rites in temples. Of the public rites, the *puja,* a ceremonial dinner for a god, is the most common.

Divisions: There is no concept of orthodoxy in Hinduism, which presents a variety of sects, most of them devoted to the worship of one of the many gods. The 3 major living traditions are those devoted to the gods Vishnu and Shiva and to the goddess Shakti; each is divided into further subsects. Numerous folk beliefs and practices, often in amalgamation with the above groups, exist side by side with sophisticated philosophical schools and exotic cults.

Location: Mainly India, Nepal, Malaysia, Guyana, Suriname, and Sri Lanka.

Beliefs: There is only one divine principle; the many gods are only aspects of that unity. Life in all its forms is an aspect of the divine, but it appears as a separation from the divine, a meaningless cycle of birth and rebirth (*samsara*) determined by the purity or impurity of past deeds (*karma*). To improve one's *karma* or escape *samsara* by pure acts, thought, and/or devotion is the aim of every Hindu.

Islam

Founded: About AD 622 in Mecca, Arabian Peninsula.

Founder: Muhammad (c 570-632), the Prophet.

Sacred texts: The *Koran* (al-Qur'an), the Word of God; *Sunna*, collections of *Hadith*, describing what Muhammad said or did.

Organization: Since the founder was both a prophet and a statesman, Muslim leadership has combined the civil and moral function of a state. Within the larger community, there are cultural and national groups, held together by a common religious law, the *Shari'a*, enforced uniformly in matters of religion only. In social transactions the community has often departed from traditional formulations. Although Islam is basically egalitarian and suspicious of authoritarianism, Muslim culture tends to be dominated by the conservative spirit of its religious establishment, the *ulema*.

Practice: Besides the general moral guidance that determines everyday life, there are "Five Pillars of Islam": profession of faith (oneness of God and prophethood of Muhammad); prayer 5 times a day; alms *(zakat)* from one's savings and estate; dawn-to-dusk fasting in the month of Ramadan; and once in a lifetime, pilgrimage to Mecca, if possible.

Divisions: There are 2 major groups: the majority known as Sunni and the minority Shiites. Shiites believe in Twelve Imams (perfect teachers) after the Prophet, of whom the last Imam has lived an invisible existence since 874, continuing to guide his community. Sunni Muslims believe in God's overpowering will over their affairs and tend to be predestinarian; Shiites believe in free will and give a substantial role to human reason in daily life. Sufism (mystical dimension of Islam) is prevalent among both Sunni and Shiites. Sufis emphasize personal relation to God and obedience informed by love of God.

Location: W Africa to Philippines, across band including E Africa, Central Asia and W China, India, Malaysia, Indonesia. Islam has several million adherents in North America.

Beliefs: Strictly monotheistic. God is creator of the universe, omnipotent, omniscient, just, forgiving, and merciful. The human is God's highest creation, but weak and egocentric, prone to forget the goal of life, constantly tempted by the Satan, an evil being. God revealed the Koran to Muhammad to guide humanity to truth and justice. Those who repent and sincerely "submit" (literal meaning of "islam") to God attain salvation. The forgiven enter the Paradise, and the wicked burn in Hell.

Judaism

Founded: About 2000 BC.

Founder: Abraham is regarded as the founding patriarch, but the Torah of Moses is the basic source of the teachings.

Sacred Texts: The 5 books of Moses constitute the written Torah. Special sanctity is also assigned other writings of the Hebrew Bible—the teachings of oral Torah are recorded in the Talmud, in the Midrash, and in various commentaries.

Organization: Originally theocratic, Judaism has evolved a congregational polity. The basic institution is the local synagogue, operated by the congregation and led by a rabbi of their choice. Chief rabbis in France and Great Britain have authority only over those who accept it; in Israel, the 2 chief rabbis have civil authority in family law.

Practice: Among traditional practicioners, almost all areas of life are governed by strict religious discipline. Sabbath and holidays are marked by special observances, and attendance at public worship is considered especially important then. Chief annual observances are Passover, celebrating liberation of the Israelites from Egypt and marked by the Seder meal in homes, and the 10 days from Rosh Hashanah (New Year) to Yom Kippur (Day of Atonement), a period of fasting and penitence.

Divisions: Judaism is an unbroken spectrum from ultraconservative to ultraliberal, largely reflecting different points of view regarding the binding character of the prohibitions and duties—particularly the dietary and Sabbath observations—traditionally prescribed for the daily life of the Jew.

Location: Almost worldwide, with concentrations in Israel and the U.S.

Beliefs: Strictly monotheistic. God is the creator and absolute ruler of the universe. God established a particular relationship with the Hebrew people: by obeying a divine law God gave them, they would be a special witness to God's mercy and justice. Judaism stresses ethical behavior (and, among the traditional, careful ritual obedience) as true worship of God.

LANGUAGE

New Words in English

The following words and definitions were provided by Merriam-Webster Inc., publishers of *Merriam-Webster's Collegiate Dictionary, Eleventh Edition*, released in 2003. The words or meanings are among those that the Merriam-Webster editors decided had achieved enough currency in English to be added to this latest revision of the dictionary.

amuse-bouche a small complimentary appetizer offered at some restaurants
assisted living a system of housing and limited care that is designed for senior citizens who need some assistance with daily activities but do not require care in a nursing home
blog or **Weblog** a Web site that contains an online personal journal with reflections, comments, and often hyperlinks provided by the writer
Boston marriage a long-term loving relationship between two women
brain freeze a sudden shooting pain in the head caused by ingesting very cold food (as ice cream) or drink
burka or **burqa** a loose enveloping garment that covers the face and body and is worn in public by certain Muslim women
chai a beverage that is a blend of black tea, honey, spices, and milk
chick flick a motion picture intended to appeal especially to women
chin music 1: idle talk **2**: a usually high inside pitch intended to intimidate the batter
civil union the legal status that ensures to same-sex couples specified rights and responsibilities of married couples
cybrarian a person whose job is to find, collect, and manage information that is available on the World Wide Web
deathcare of, relating to, or providing products or services for the burial or cremation of the dead
digital subscriber line (DSL) a high-speed communications connection used for accessing the Internet and carrying short-range transmissions over ordinary telephone lines
dream catcher a circular framed net with a hole in the center that is used by some American Indian peoples to block bad dreams and catch good ones
hazmat a material that would be a danger to life or to the environment if released without precautions
hospitalist a physician who specializes in treating hospitalized patients of other physicians in order to minimize the number of hospital visits by other physicians
information technology the technology involving the development, maintenance, and use of computer systems, software, and networks for the processing and distribution of data
jihadist a Muslim who advocates or participates in a jihad
mai tai a cocktail made with rum, curaçao, orgeat, lime, and fruit juices
metadata data that provides information about other data
MPEG 1: any of a group of computer file formats for the compression and storage of digital video and audio data **2**: a computer file (as of a movie) in an MPEG format
MP3 1: a computer file format for the compression and storage of digital audio data **2**: a computer file (as of a song) in the MP3 format
nanostructure an arrangement, structure, or part of something of molecular dimensions
neo-pagan a person who practices a contemporary form of paganism (as Wicca)
scrunchie (or **scrunchy**) a fabric-covered elastic used for holding back hair (as in a ponytail)
skank a rhythmic dance performed by swinging the arms while bending the knees especially to reggae or ska; also: the music for this dance
sleep apnea apnea that recurs during sleep and is caused especially by obstruction of the airway or a disturbance in the brain's respiratory center
slurve a baseball pitch having the characteristics of both a slider and a curve
soundscape a mélange of musical and sometimes nonmusical sounds
steganography the art or practice of concealing a message, image, or file within another message, image, or file
streaming relating to or being the transfer of data (as audio or video material) in a continuous stream especially for immediate processing or playback
sticky note a slip of notepaper having an adhesive strip on the back that allows attachment to and removal from a surface
wushu Chinese martial arts

Words About Words

allegory: extended use of symbols, in the form of characters, animals, or events, that represent ideas or themes. Ex: John Bunyan, *Pilgrim's Progress*

alliteration: repetition of same, initial consonant sounds of two or more words in sequence or in short intervals. Ex: "I have *s*tood *s*till and *s*topped the *s*ound of feet." — Robert Frost

anagram: a word or phrase made by rearranging letters from another word or phrase. Ex: Clint Eastwood = Old West Action

antithesis: an expression in which contrasting ideas are intentionally juxtaposed, usually in parallel structure. Ex: "The world will little note, nor long remember, what we say here, but it can never forget what they did here." — Abraham Lincoln, "Gettysburg Address"

assonance: repetition of same or similar vowel sounds in words located near each other. Ex: "Green as a dream, and deep as death." — Rupert Brooke

cliché: a saying or expression that has been used so often it has lost its effect. Ex: work like a dog

eponym: a word derived from the name of a person. Ex: sandwich, from the Earl of Sandwich.

euphemism: a mild, indirect expression used instead of a plainer one that might be harsh, unpleasant, or offensive. Ex: restroom, pass away

hyperbole: exaggeration for emphasis or effect. Ex: "And fired the shot heard round the world." — Ralph Waldo Emerson, "Concord Hymn"

irony: an expression in which the intended meaning is contrary to its literal meaning; the words say one thing but mean another. Ex: "Yet Brutus says he was ambitious;/ And Brutus is an honorable man." — Shakespeare, *Julius Caesar*

litotes: intentional understatement made by negating the opposite of what is meant. Ex: This was no small matter.

metaphor: implied comparison of two dissimilar things, without using "as" or "like." Ex: "Dawn's rosy fingers" — Homer

metonymy: substitution of one word for another which it suggests. Ex: The pen is mightier than the sword.

onomatopoeia: words that imitate the sounds they describe. Ex: buzz, murmur

oxymoron: juxtaposition of contradictory words. Ex: deafening silence

palindrome: a type of anagram in which a word, phrase, or sentence reads the same backward and forward. Ex: Ma is a nun as I am.

paradox: a statement that is seemingly contradictory, odd, or opposed to common sense or expectation and yet is presented as true. Ex: "What a pity that youth must be wasted on the young." — George Bernard Shaw

personification: treating ideas or objects as though they were persons. Ex: "Because I could not stop for Death—/He kindly stopped for me." — Emily Dickinson

portmanteau: two words combined to form one word. Ex: smog (smoke + fog)

simile: a comparison between two dissimilar things using "like" or "as." Ex: "My love is like a red, red rose" — Robert Burns

synecdoche: (a form of metonymy) the use of a part for the whole, or the whole for the part. Ex: All hands on deck!

tautology: unnecessary repetition of an idea in different words, phrases, or sentences. Ex: close proximity

IT'S A FACT: The Oxford English Dictionary (OED) was first conceived in 1857 by the Philological Society of Great Britain, but work did not commence until 1879 when the society partnered with the Oxford University Press and appointed James A. H. Murray as editor. The dictionary was initially planned to take 10 years to complete, but after 5 years of work, only the section "A-Ant" was done. The rest of the OED was published in installments over the next 44 years. When the final section of the first edition was finished in 1928, the dictionary contained 12 volumes, 15,487 pages, and 414,825 entries.

National Spelling Bee

The Scripps Howard National Spelling Bee, conducted by Scripps Howard Newspapers and other leading newspapers since 1939, was instituted by the Louisville (KY) *Courier-Journal* in 1925. Children under 16 years old and not beyond 8th grade are eligible to compete for cash prizes at the finals, held annually in Washington, DC. (The experiences of 8 contestants in the 1999 spelling bee were highlighted in a popular 2002 film, *Spellbound.*) The 2005 winners were: 1st place, Anurag Kashyap, San Diego, CA; 2nd place (tie), Aliya Deri, San Francisco, CA; Samir Patel, Fort Worth, TX.

Here are the last words given, and spelled correctly, in each of the years 1981-2005 at the national spelling bee.

1981	sarcophagus	1986	odontalgia	1991	antipyretic	1996	vivisepulture	2001	succedaneum
1982	psoriasis	1987	staphylococci	1992	lyceum	1997	euonym	2002	prospicience
1983	purim	1988	elegiacal	1993	kamikaze	1998	chiaroscurist	2003	pococurante
1984	luge	1989	spoliator	1994	antediluvian	1999	logorrhea	2004	autochthonous
1985	milieu	1990	fibranne	1995	xanthosis	2000	demarche	2005	appoggiatura

Names of the Days

ENGLISH	RUSSIAN	HEBREW	FRENCH	ITALIAN	SPANISH	GERMAN	JAPANESE
Sunday	voskresenye	yom rishon	dimanche	domenica	domingo	Sonntag	nichiyoubi
Monday	ponedelnik	yom sheni	lundi	lunedì	lunes	Montag	getsuyoubi
Tuesday	vtornik	yom shlishi	mardi	martedì	martes	Dienstag	kayoubi
Wednesday	sreda	yom ravii	mercredi	mercoledì	miércoles	Mittwoch	suiyoubi
Thursday	chetverg	yom hamishi	jeudi	giovedì	jueves	Donnerstag	mokuyoubi
Friday	pyatnitsa	yom shishi	vendredi	venerdì	viernes	Freitag	kinyoubi
Saturday	subbota	shabbat	samedi	sabato	sábado	Samstag	doyoubi

Foreign Words and Phrases

(A=Arabic; F=French; Ger=German; Gk=Greek; I=Italian; L=Latin; S=Spanish; Y=Yiddish)

à bientôt (F; ah bee-en-TOE): so long; see you soon
ad hoc (L; ad HOK): for the end or purpose at hand; impromptu.
ad hominem (L; ad HOH-mee-nem): emotional rather than intellectual; in a dispute, using slander to obscure issues.
al fresco (I; ahl FRAYS-koh): outdoors
antebellum (L; AHN-teh-BEL-lum): pre-war
apercu(s) (F; ah-per-SOO): first perception or insight; outline
auf Wiedersehen (Ger; owf-VEE-duh-zehn): Good-bye
belles lettres (F; bel-LET-truh): writing aspiring to artistic merit
bête noire (F; BET NWAHR): a thing or person viewed with particular dislike or fear
bijou (F; BEE-zhoo) gem, jewel
Bildungsroman (Ger; BIL-doongs-roh-mahn): novel embodying coming-of-age story
bodega (S; boh-DAY-gah) grocery store
bonhomie (F; boh-noh-MEE): friendliness
bon vivant (F; bon-vee-VAHN) a person with refined tastes, especially for food and drink
bourgeois (F; boo-ZHWAH): middle-class; conventional; materialistic
carte blanche (F; kahrt BLANSH): full discretionary power
casus belli (L; KAH-soos BEL-lee): reason for going to war.
cause célèbre (F; kawz suh-LEB-ruh): a notorious incident
cognoscenti (I; koh-nyoh-SHEN-tee): experts; connoissuers
contretemps (F; kon-truh-tahm): awkward situation
coup de grâce (F; kooh duh GRAHS): the final blow
cum laude/magna cum laude/summa cum laude (L; kuhm LOUD-ay; MAGN-a ...; SOO-ma ...): with praise or honor/with great praise or honor/with the highest praise or honor
de facto (L; day FAK-toh): in fact, if not by law
de jure (L; dee JOOR-ee, day YOOR-ay): in accordance with right or law; officially
deo gratias (L; dey oh GROT-SEE-us): thanks be to God
de rigueur (F; duh ree-GUR): necessary according to convention or etiquette
détente (F; day-TAHNT): an easing of strained relations
deus ex machina (L; DAY-us eks MAH-keh-nah): a person/event that provides a solution unexpectedly or suddenly, espec. (in literature) a contrived solution to a plot
dictum (L; DIK-tahm) an official or formal pronouncment.
double entendre (F; DOO-blahn-TAHN-druh): expression with with double meaning, one meaning of which is often risqué
éminence grise (F; ay-meh-nahns-GREEZ): one who wields power behind the scenes
enfant terrible (F; ahn-FAHN te-REE-bluh): one who is noteworthy for embarrassing or unconventional behavior
ennui (F; ah-NOOEE); boredom; world-weariness; annoyance
e pluribus unum (L; eh-PLOO-ree-boos-OO-noom): out of many, one (U.S. motto)
ersatz (Ger; EHR-zats): artificial; being a (usually inferior) substitute
eureka (Gk; yoor-EE-kuh): I have found it!; hurrah!
ex post facto (L; eks pohst FAK-toh): retroactive(ly)
fait accompli (F; fayt uh-kom-PLEE): an accomplished fact
fatwa (A; FAHT-wah): in Islam, a legal or religious decree
faux pas (F; foh PAH): as false step; a social blunder or breach of etiquette
habeas corpus (L; HAY-bee-ahs KOR-pus): an order for an accused person to be brought to court
hoi polloi (Gk; hoy puh-LOY): the masses
impresario (I; im-prah-SAH-ri-oh): manager, promoter, or sponsor of a muscial or theatrical program or company
imprimatur (L; im-prah-MAH-toor): approval or official permission to print, espec. by the Roman Catholic church
in loco parentis (L; in LOH-koh puh-REN-tis): in place of parent
in medias res (L; in MAY-dee-oos rays): into the middle of things
in omnibus (L; in OHM-nee-bus): in all things; in all ways
je ne sais quoi (F; zhuh nuh say KWAH): I don't know what; the little something that eludes description
joie de vivre (F; zhwah duh VEEV-ruh): zest for life
leitmotif (Ger; lyt-moh-TEEF) the central theme or idea, particularly in art and literature
mano a mano (S; MAH-noh ah MAH-noh): hand to hand; in direct combat
mea culpa (L; MAY-uh CUL-puh): through my fault
mensch (Y; mentsh): an upright, noble, admirable person
modus operandi (L; MOH-duhs op-uh-RAN-dee): method of operation
mujahadeen (A; moo-jah-ha-DEEN): Islamic holy fighters
noblesse oblige (F; noh-BLES oh-BLEEZH): the obligation of nobility to help the less fortunate
nolo contendere (L; NOH-loh-kohn-TEN-deh-reh): "I will not contest," a plea of no defense, equivalent to a plea of guilty
non compos mentis (L; non KOM-puhs MEN-tis): not of sound mind
non sequitur (L; non SEH-kwi-tour): a conclusion that does not logically follow from what preceded it
nouveau riche (F; noo-voh REESH): a person newly rich, espec. one who spends money conspicuously
par excellence (F; par ek-seh-LANS): best of all; incomparable.
parvenu (F; par-vuh-NOO): upstart
persona non grata (L; per-SOH-nah non GRAH-tah): unwelcome person
pièce de résistance (F; pee-es duh ray-ZEES-tonz): the outstanding item in a series or group
pro bono (L; proh BOH-noh): (legal work) donated for the public good
qué será será (S; keh sair-AH sair-AH): what will be will be
quid pro quo (L; kwid proh KWOH): something given or received for something else
raison d'être (F; RAY-zohnn DET-ruh): reason for being
sans souci (F; SAHNN sooh-SEE): without worry
savoir faire (F; sav-wahr-FAIR): dexterity in social affairs
Schadenfreude (Ger; SHAH-d'n-froy-deh): joy at another's misfortune
schlemiel (Y; shleh-MEEL): an unlucky, bungling person
schlepp (Y; shlep): move slowly, tediously, drag oneself along
semper fidelis (L; SEM-puhr fee-DAY-lis): always faithful
sobriquet (F; soh-bree-KAY): nickname
terra firma (L; TER-uh FUR-muh): solid ground
vis-à-vis (F; vee-zuh-VEE): compared with; with regard to
voir dire (F; vwar-DEER): examination by lawyers or judge to determine the suitability of a witness or a prospective juror
zeitgeist (Ger; ZITE-gyste): the general intellectual, moral, and cultural climate of an era
wadi (A; WAH-dee): a stream bed or valley that fills with water only during seasonal rains; gully

Names for Animal Young

bunny: rabbit
calf: cattle, elephant, antelope, rhino, hippo, whale, others
cheeper: grouse, partridge, quail
chick, chicken: fowl
cockerel: rooster
codling, sprag: codfish
colt: horse (male)
cria: llama, alpaca
cub: lion, bear, shark, fox, others
cygnet: swan
duckling: duck
eaglet: eagle
elver: eel
eyas: hawk, others
fawn: deer
filly: horse (female)
fingerling: fish generally
flapper: wild fowl
fledgling: birds generally
foal: horse, zebra, others
fry: fish generally
gosling: goose
heifer: cow
joey: kangaroo, opossum, others
kid: goat
kit: fox, beaver, rabbit, cat
kitten, kitty, catling: cats, other small mammals
lamb, lambkin, cosset, hog: sheep
leveret: hare
nestling: birds generally
nymph: insects
owlet: owl
parr, smolt, grilse: salmon
peachick: peafowl
piglet, shoat, farrow, suckling: pig
polliwog, tadpole: frog
poult: turkey
pullet: hen
pup: dog, seal, sea lion, fox
puss, pussy: cat
spat: oyster
spike, blinker, tinker: mackerel
squab: pigeon
squeaker: pigeon, others
whelp: dog, tiger, beasts of prey
yearling: cattle, sheep, horse, others

Names for Animal Collectives

alligators: congregation
ants: army or colony
apes: shrewdness
badgers: cete
bats: colony
bears: sleuth
bees: grist or swarm
birds: flight or volery
boars/swine: sounder
buffalo sores: gang, obstinacy
butterflies: flutter
buzzards: wake
camels: train or caravan
cats: clowder or clutter
cattle: drove
cheetahs: coalition
chicks: brood or clutch
clams/oysters: bed
cockroaches: intrusion
cormorants: gulp
cranes: sedge or siege
crocodiles: bask
crows: murder
dolphins: pod
doves: dule or pitying
ducks: brace or team
eagles: convocation or aerie
elephants: herd
elks: gang
ferrets: business
finches: charm
fish: school or shoal
flamingos: stand
foxes: skulk
frogs: army
geese: flock, gaggle, or skein
gnats: cloud or horde
goats: tribe or trip
gorillas: band
grasshoppers: cloud
hares: down or husk
hawks: cast
hippopotami: bloat
horses: pair or team
hounds: cry, mute, or pack
hyenas: cackle
jellyfish: smack
kangaroos: mob or troop
kittens: kindle or kendle
larks: exaltation
leopards: leap
lions: pride
monkeys: troop
mules: span
nightingales: watch
owls: parliament
oxen: yoke
partridge/quail: covey
peacocks: muster
pheasants: nest or nide
pigs: litter
ponies: string
raccoons: gaze
ravens: unkindness
rhinoceroses: crash
seals: pod
sharks: shiver
sheep: flock, drove
snakes: nest
squirrels: dray or scurry
swans: bevy
swine: drift
tigers: streak
toads: knot
turkeys: gang or rafter
turtles: bale
vultures: committee
whales: gam, herd, pod
wolves: pack
woodchucks: fall
woodpeckers: descent

Some Common Abbreviations and Acronyms

Acronyms are pronounceable words formed from first letters (or syllables) of other words. Some **abbreviations** below (e.g., AIDS, RICE, NATO) are thus acronyms. Some acronyms are words coined as abbreviations and written in lower case (e.g., "sonar," "yuppie"). Acronyms do not have periods; usage for other abbreviations varies, but periods have become less common. Capitalization usage may vary from what is shown here. Italicized words preceding parenthetical definitions below are Latin unless otherwise noted. See also other chapters, including Computers and Telecommunications; Weights and Measures.

AA=Alcoholics Anonymous; Associate in Arts; administrative assistant
AAA=American Automobile Association
AARP=American Association of Retired Persons
ABA=American Bar Association
abr.=abridged
AC=alternating current
AD=*anno Domini* (in the year of the Lord)
AFL-CIO=American Federation of Labor and Congress of Industrial Organizations
AI=artificial intelligence
AIDS=acquired immune deficiency syndrome
AM=*ante meridiem* (before noon)
AMA=American Medical Association
anon=anonymous
APO=army post office
APR=annual percentage rate
ARM=adjustable rate mortgage
ASCAP=American Society of Composers, Authors, and Publishers
ASPCA=American Society for Prevention of Cruelty to Animals
ATM=automated teller machine
AWOL=absent without leave
BA=Bachelor of Arts
bbl=barrel(s)
BC=before Christ
BCE=before Common Era
bpd=barrels per day
BS=Bachelor of Science
Btu=British thermal unit(s)
bu=bushel(s)
byob=bring your own bottle
C= Celsius, centigrade
c=*circa* (about); copyright
CAFTA=Central American Free Trade Agreement
CAT=computerized axial tomography
CBD=Central Business District
CDC=Centers for Disease Control and Prevention, Community Development Corporation
CE=Common Era
CEO=chief executive officer
cf.=*confer* (compare)
CFO=chief financial officer
CIA=Central Intelligence Agency
CIF=cost, insurance, and freight
CIO=chief information officer
COD=cash (or collect) on delivery
Col.=Colonel
COLA=cost of living adjustment
COO=chief operating officer
CPA=certified public accountant
CPI=Consumer Price Index
Cpl.=Corporal
CPR=cardiopulmonary resuscitation
CPU=central processing unit
CST=Central StandardTime
DA=district attorney
DC=direct current
DD=Doctor of Divinity
DDS=Doctor of Dental Science (or Surgery)
DHS=Dept. of Homeland Security
DMD=Doctor of Dental Medicine
DMZ=demilitarized zone
DNA=deoxyribonucleic acid
DNR=do not resuscitate
DOA=dead on arrival
DOB=date of birth
dpi=dots per inch
DPT=diphtheria, pertussis, tetanus
DUI=driving under the influence
DVD=digital video disc
DVM=Doctor of Veterinary Medicine
DWI=driving while intoxicated
ed.=edited, edition, editor
EEG=electroencephalogram
e.g.=*exempli gratia* (for example)
EKG=electrocardiogram
EOE=equal opportunity employer
EPA=Environmental Protection Agency
ERA=Equal Rights Amendment; earned run average
ESL=English as a second language
ESP=extrasensory perception
Esq.=esquire
EST=Eastern standard time
et al.=*et alii* (and others)
etc.=*et cetera* (and so forth)
EU=European Union
EVA=extravehicular activity
F=Fahrenheit
FBI=Federal Bureau of Investigation
FDA=Food and Drug Administration
FDIC=Federal Deposit Insurance Corp.
FEMA=Federal Emergency Management Agency
ff.=and those following
FICA=Federal Insurance Contributions Act (Social Security)
fl.=*floruit* (flourished), used for hist. figures when life dates uncertain
FOB=free on board
fte=full-time equivalent
FY=fiscal year
FYI=for your information
GATT=General Agreement on Tariffs and Trade
GB=gigabyte(s)
GDP=gross domestic product
GED=general equivalency diploma (for high school)
GMT=Greenwich mean time
GOP=Grand Old Party (Republican Party)
GPS=Global Positioning System
Hazmat=hazardous material
HMS=His/Her Majesty's Ship (UK)
Hon.=the Honorable
HOV=high-occupancy vehicle

HRH=her (his) royal highness (UK)
HVAC=heating, ventilating, and air-conditioning
Hz=hertz
ibid=*ibidem* (in the same place)
i.e.=*id est* (that is)
IMF=International Monetary Fund
IOC=International Olympic Committee
IQ=intelligence quotient
IRA=individual retirement account; Irish Republican Army
IRS=Internal Revenue Service
ISBN=International Standard Book Number
JCS=Joint Chiefs of Staff
JD=*Juris Doctor* (doctor of laws)
K=Kelvin
k=karat
KCB=Knight Commander of the Bath (UK)
K of C=Knights of Columbus
kWh=kilowatt-hour(s)
laser=Light Amplification by Stimulated Emission of Radiation
Lieut. or Lt.=Lieutenant
LLB=*Legum Baccalaurens* (Bachelor of Laws)
LLP=limited licensed partners
loc. cit.=*loco citato* (in the place cited)
LSAT=Law School Admission Test
MA=Master of Arts
MBA=Master of Business Administration
MCAT=Medical College Admission Test
MV=megabyte(s)
MD=*Medicinae Doctor* (doctor of medicine)
MFN=most favored nation
MIA=missing in action
modem=MOdulator-DEModulator
MP=Member of Parliament (UK)
mph=miles per hour
MRI=magnetic resonance imaging
ms, mss=manuscript(s)
MS=Master of Science; multiple sclerosis
MSG=monosodium glutamate
MST=mountain standard time
MVP=most valuable player
NA=not applicable; not available
NAACP=National Association for the Advancement of Colored People
NAFTA=North American Free Trade Agreement
NASA=National Aeronautics and Space Administration
NATO=North Atlantic Treaty Org.
NB=*nota bene* (note carefully)
NCAA=National Collegiate Athletic Assn.
NIH=National Institutes of Health
NOW=National Organization for Women
NPR=National Public Radio
NRA=National Rifle Association
OE=Old English
OED=Oxford English Dictionary
op=*opus* (work)
OPEC=Organization of Petroleum Exporting Countries
OTC=over the counter
p, pp=page(s)
PA=Public Address
PC=personal computer; political correctness
pd.=paid, per diem
PAC=political action committee
PDA=Personal Digital Assistant
Ph.D.=*Philosophiae Doctor* (doctor of philosophy)
PIN=Personal Identification Number
pl=plate, plural
PM=*post meridiem* (afternoon)
PS=*post scriptum* (postscript)
PST=Pacific Standard Time
pt=part(s), pint(s), point(s)
Pvt.=Private
QC=queen's counsel (UK)
q.v.=*quod vide* (which see)
radar=radio detecting and ranging
RCMP=Royal Canadian Mounted Police
REM=rapid eye movement
Rev.=Reverend
rev.=revised
RFD=rural free delivery
RICE=rest, ice, compression, elevation
RIP=*requiescat in pace* (May he/she rest in peace)
RN=registered nurse
RNA=ribonucleic acid
ROTC=Reserve Officers' Training Corps
rpm=revolutions per minute
RSVP=*répondez s'il vous plaît* (Fr.) (Please reply)
SARS=severe acute respiratory syndrome
SASE=self-addressed stamped envelope
Sgt.=Sergeant
SIDS=suddent infant death syndrome
S.J.=Society of Jesus (Jesuits)
sonar=sound navigation and ranging
SOP=Standard Operating Procedure
SRO=standing room only
SSI=Supplementary Security Income
SUV=sport utility vehicle
TBA=to be announced
TBD=to be determined
TEFL=teaching English as a foreign language
TGIF=thank God it's Friday
UFO=unidentified flying object
UPC=Universal Product Code
URL=Univeral Resource Locator
USS=United States ship
UTC=coordinated univeral time
var.=variant
VCR=videocassette recorder
viz=*videlicet*, namely
W=watt(s)
WHO=World Health Organization
WMD=weapons of mass destruction
WPM=words per minute
YTD=year to date
yuppie=young urban professional
ZIP=zone improvement plan (U.S. Postal Service)

A **Spoonerism** is a play on words in which the initial sounds of two or more words are transposed, creating different phrases whose meanings, when compared, can be humorous. Spoonerisms are named for the English academic and cleric Rev. William A. Spooner (1844-1930), who reportedly made such "tips of the slongue" often. Here are a few examples:

a well-boiled icicle *instead* of a well-oiled bicycle
a blushing crow *instead* of a crushing blow
wave the sails *instead* of sail the waves
fighting a liar *instead* of lighting a fire

Eponyms

(words named for people)

Bloody Mary—a vodka and tomato juice drink; after the nickname of Mary I, Queen of England (1553-58), notorious for persecution of Protestants
bobbies—in Great Britain, police officers; after Sir Robert Peel, who organized the London police force in 1850
bowdlerize—to delete written matter considered indelicate; after Thomas Bowdler, English editor of an expurgated Shakespeare (1825)
boycott—to avoid trade or dealings with, as a protest; after Charles C. Boycott, an English land agent in County Mayo, Ireland, ostracized in 1880 for refusing to reduce rents
chauvinist—excessively patriotic; after Nicolas Chauvin, a character in a 19th-cent. play who is devoted to Napoleon
derby—a stiff felt hat with a dome-shaped crown and rather narrow rolled brim; after Edward Stanley, 12th earl of Derby, who in 1780 founded the Derby horse race, to which these hats are worn
diesel—a type of internal combustion engine; after Rudolf Diesel (1858-1913), who built the first successful diesel engine
draconian—harsh or severe; after Draco, a statesman who codified the laws in Athens in 621 BC
galvanize—to shock with an electric current, to energize or spur; from Luigi Galvano, Italian physicist who invented process to cover metals with electrons for protection against rust
gerrymander—to draw an election district in such a way as to favor a political party; after Elbridge Gerry, who created (1812) just such an election district (shaped like a salamander) during his governorship of Massachusetts
guillotine—a machine for beheading; after Joseph Guillotin, a French physician who proposed its use in 1789 as more humane than hanging
leotard—a close-fitting garment, worn by dancers, acrobats, and the like; after Julius Leotard, a 19th-cent. French aerial gymnast
Luddite—one who opposes new technology; from Ned Ludd, leader of a group of textile workers in England who destroyed machinery in the early 1800s
maudlin—excessively sentimental, from Mary Magdalene, a Scriptural figure whose portraits often showed her weeping
mesmerize—to hypnotize or enthrall; from Franz Mesmer, an 18th-century German physicist who developed therapy using magnetism that led to hypnosis
philippic—a tirade or heated denunciation; from 4th cent. BC Greek orator Demosthenes' speeches against the rise of Philip II of Macedonia
pollyanna—an overly optimistic person; based on the title character in a novel (1913) by American writer Eleanor Porter
sandwich—2 or more slices of bread with a filling in between; after John Montagu, 4th earl of Sandwich (1718-92), who supposedly ate these at the gaming table
shrapnel—originally, a projecticle with lead balls designed to inflict maximum damage in explosions, later pieces of shell casings; from Henry Shrapnel (1761-1842), British artillery officer who designed the projectile
silhouette—an outline image; from Étienne de Silhouette (1709-67), a close-fisted French finance minister

WORLD ALMANAC QUICK QUIZ

Which famous author was born Howard Allen O'Brien?
(a) O. Henry (b) Frank O'Connor (c) Anne Rice (d) Lewis Carroll
For the answer look in this chapter, or see page 1008.

IT'S A FACT: The top ten U.S. baby names in 2004, according to the Social Security Administration, were: **boys,** Jacob, Michael, Joshua, Matthew, Ethan, Andrew, Daniel, William, Joseph, Christopher; **girls,** Emily, Emma, Madison, Olivia, Hannah, Abigail, Isabella, Ashley, Samantha, Elizabeth. William and Isabella joined the top 10, displacing Anthony and Alexis.

Top 10 First Names of Americans by Decade of Birth

Source: Compiled by Dr. Cleveland Kent Evans, Bellevue University, Bellevue, NE; based on Social Security Administration records

BOYS:

1880-1889 ....John, William, Charles, George, James, Frank, Joseph, Harry, Henry, Edward
1890-1899 ....John, William, George, James, Charles, Joseph, Frank, Robert, Harry, Henry
1900-1909 ....John, William, James, George, Joseph, Charles, Robert, Frank, Edward, Henry
1910-1919 ....John, William, James, Robert, Joseph, Charles, George, Edward, Frank, Walter
1920-1929 ....John, Robert, James, William, Charles, George, Joseph, Richard, Edward, Donald
1930-1939 ....Robert, James, John, William, Richard, Charles, Donald, George, Thomas, Joseph
1940-1949 ....James, Robert, John, William, Richard, David, Charles, Thomas, Michael, Ronald
1950-1959 ....Michael, James, Robert, John, David, William, Steven, Richard, Thomas, Mark
1960-1969 ....Michael, John, David, James, Robert, Mark, Steven, William, Jeffrey, Richard
1970-1979 ....Michael, Christopher, Jason, David, James, John, Brian, Robert, Steven, William
1980-1989 ....Michael, Christopher, Matthew, Joshua, David, Daniel, James, John, Robert, Brian
1990-1999 ....Michael, Christopher, Matthew, Joshua, Nicholas, Jacob, Andrew, Daniel, Brandon, Tyler

GIRLS:

1880-1889 ....Mary, Anna, Elizabeth, Catherine, Margaret, Emma, Bertha, Minnie, Florence, Clara
1890-1899 ....Mary, Anna, Margaret, Helen, Catherine, Elizabeth, Florence, Ruth, Rose, Ethel
1900-1909 ....Mary, Helen, Margaret, Anna, Ruth, Catherine, Elizabeth, Dorothy, Marie, Mildred
1910-1919 ....Mary, Helen, Dorothy, Margaret, Ruth, Catherine, Mildred, Anna, Elizabeth, Frances
1920-1929 ....Mary, Dorothy, Betty, Helen, Margaret, Ruth, Virginia, Catherine, Doris, Frances
1930-1939 ....Mary, Betty, Barbara, Shirley, Patricia, Dorothy, Joan, Margaret, Carol, Nancy
1940-1949 ....Mary, Linda, Barbara, Patricia, Carol, Sandra, Nancy, Sharon, Judith, Susan
1950-1959 ....Deborah, Mary, Linda, Patricia, Susan, Barbara, Karen, Nancy, Donna, Catherine
1960-1969 ....Lisa, Deborah, Mary, Karen, Michelle, Susan, Kimberly, Lori, Teresa, Linda
1970-1979 ....Jennifer, Michelle, Amy, Melissa, Kimberly, Lisa, Angela, Heather, Kelly, Sarah
1980-1989 ....Jessica, Jennifer, Ashley, Sarah, Amanda, Stephanie, Nicole, Melissa, Katherine, Megan
1990-1999 ....Ashley, Jessica, Sarah, Brittany, Emily, Kaitlyn, Samantha, Megan, Brianna, Katherine

Origins of Popular American Given Names

Source: Dr. Cleveland Kent Evans, Bellevue University, Bellevue, NE

Boys

Andrew: Gr. *andreios*, "man, manly"
Anthony: Roman *Antonius*, pos. from Gr. *anthos*, "flower"
Brandon: Eng. place name, "gorse-covered hill"
Brian: Irish, perhaps Celtic *Brigonos*, "high, noble"
Charles: Ger. *ceorl*, "free man"
Christopher: Gr. *Khristophoros*, "bearing Christ [in one's heart]"
Daniel: Heb. "God is my judge"
David: Heb. *Dodavehu*, perhaps "darling"
Donald: Scots Gaelic *Domhnall*, "world rule"
Edward: Old Eng. *Eadweard*, "wealth-guard"
Ethan: Heb. "solid," "firm"
Frank: Ger. "Frenchman"
George: Gr. *georgos*, "soil tiller, farmer"
Harry: Middle Eng. form of Henry
Henry: Ger. *Haimric,* "home-power"
Jacob: Heb. *Yaakov,* "God protects" or "supplanter"
James: Late Lat. *lacomus*, form of Jacob
Jason: Gr. *Iason*, "healer"
Jeffrey: Norman Fr. , from Ger. *Gaufrid*, "land-peace," or *Gisfrid*, "pledge-peace"
John: Heb. *Yohanan*, "God is gracious"
Joseph: Heb. *Yosef*, "[God] shall add"
Joshua: Heb. *Yoshua*, "God saves"
Mark: Lat. *Marcus*, perhaps from Mars, the war god
Matthew: Heb. *Mattathia*, "gift of God"
Michael: Heb. "Who could ever be like God?"
Nicholas: Gr. *Nikolaos*, "victory-people"
Patrick: Lat. *Patricius,* "belonging to the noble class"
Richard: Ger. "power-hardy"
Robert: Ger. *Hrodberht*, "fame-bright"
Sean: Gaelic form of John
Steven: Gr. *stephanos*, "crown, garland"
Theodore: Gr. *Theodoros,* "gift of God"
Thomas: Aramaic "twin"
Tyler: Old Eng. *tigeler*, "tile layer"
Walter: Ger. *Waldheri*, "rule-army"
William: Ger. *Wilhelm*, "will-helmet"

Girls

Abigail: Heb. "My father is joy"
Alexis: Gr. "helper" or "defender"
Amanda: 17th-cent. invention from Lat., "lovable"
Amy: Old Fr. *Amee*, "beloved"
Angela: Gr. *angelos*, "messenger [of God]"
Ann (Eng. form), **Anne** (Eng., Fr., Ger. form) of Hannah
Anna: Lat. and Gr. form of Hannah
Ashley: Eng. place name, "ash grove"
Barbara: Gr. *barbarus*, "foreign"
Bertha: Ger. *behrt,* "bright"
Betty: 18th-cent. pet form of Elizabeth
Brianna: modern fem. form of Brian
Brittany: place name, Fr. province settled by Britons
Carol: form of Charles
Clara: Lat. *clarus,* "famous"
Deborah: Heb. "bee"
Donna: Ital. "lady"
Doris: Gr. "woman of the Dorian tribe," name of a sea nymph
Dorothy: Gr. *Dorothea*, "gift of God"
Elizabeth: Heb. *Elisheba*, perhaps "God is my oath" or "God is good fortune"
Emily: Roman *Aemilia*, possibly from Lat. *aemulus*, "rival"
Emma: Ger. *ermen,* "whole, entire"
Ethel: Old Eng. *aethel,* "noble"
Florence: Lat. *florens*, "flourishing"
Frances: fem. form of Francis, "a Frenchman"
Haley: Eng. place name, "hay clearing"
Hannah: Heb. "He has favored me"
Heather: Middle Eng. *hathir*, "heather"
Helen: Gr. *Helene,* possibly "sunbeam"
Isabella, Isabel: Lat., Sp. variant of Elizabeth
Jennifer: Cornish form of Welsh *Gwenhwyfar*, "fair-smooth"
Jessica: Shakesp. invention, prob. fem. form of Jesse, Heb. "God exists"
Joan: Middle Eng. fem. form of John
Judith: Heb. "Jewish woman"
Kaitlyn: American spelling of Caitlin, the Irish form of Katherine
Karen: Danish form of Katherine
Katherine: from *Aikaterine*, Egyptian name later modified to resemble Gr. *katharos*, "pure"
Kelly: Irish Gaelic *Ceallagh,* perhaps "churchgoer" or "bright-headed"
Kimberly: Eng. place name, "Cyneburgh's clearing"
Linda: Sp. "pretty" or Ger. "tender"
Lisa: pet form of Elizabeth
Lori: pet form of either Lorraine (French "land of Lothar's people") or Laura (Latin "laurel")
Madison: Middle Eng. surname, "son of Madeline or Maud"
Margaret: Gr. *margaron*, "pearl"
Maria: Lat. form of Mary
Marie: Fr. form of Mary
Mary: Eng. form of Heb. *Maryam,* perhaps "seeress" or "wished-for child"
Megan: Welsh form of Margaret
Melissa: Gr. "bee"
Michelle: Fr. fem. form of Michael
Mildred: Old Eng. *Mildthryth*, "mild-strength"
Minnie: Pet form of Wilhelmina, fem. form of William
Nancy: medieval Eng. pet form of Agnes, Gr. *hagnos*, "holy"; later also pet form for Ann
Nicole: Fr. fem. form of Nicholas
Olivia: Lat. oliva, "olive tree"
Patricia: Lat. fem. form of Patrick
Rose: Ger. *hros,* "horse," or Lat. *rosa,* "rose"
Ruth: Heb., perhaps "companion"
Samantha: colonial American invention, probably combining Sam from Samuel [Heb. "name of God"] with -antha from Gr. *anthos,* "flower"
Sandra: short form of Alessandra, Ital. fem. of Alexander, Gr. "defend-man"
Sarah: Heb., "princess"
Sharon: Biblical place name, Heb. "plain"
Shirley: Eng. place name, "bright clearing" or "shire meadow"
Stephanie: Fr. fem. form of Steven
Susan: Eng. form of Heb. *Shoshana*, "lily"
Teresa: Spanish, perhaps "woman from Therasia"
Virginia: Lat., "virgin-like"

30 Most Common Last Names in the U.S. Population

Source: U.S. Census Bureau, based on 1990 Census data

Rank	Name	Frequency[1] (%)	Rank	Name	Frequency[1] (%)	Rank	Name	Frequency[1] (%)
1.	Smith	1.006	11.	Anderson	0.311	21.	Clark	0.231
2.	Johnson	0.810	12.	Thomas	0.311	22.	Rodriguez	0.229
3.	Williams	0.699	13.	Jackson	0.310	23.	Lewis	0.226
4.	Jones	0.621	14.	White	0.279	24.	Lee	0.220
5.	Brown	0.621	15.	Harris	0.275	25.	Walker	0.219
6.	Davis	0.480	16.	Martin	0.273	26.	Hall	0.200
7.	Miller	0.424	17.	Thompson	0.269	27.	Allen	0.199
8.	Wilson	0.339	18.	Garcia	0.254	28.	Young	0.193
9.	Moore	0.312	19.	Martinez	0.234	29.	Hernandez	0.192
10.	Taylor	0.311	20.	Robinson	0.233	30.	King	0.190

(1) Percent of people in the population sample with the name shown.

Pen Names

Shalom Aleichem	Solomon J. Rabinowitz
Woody Allen	Allen Stewart Konigsberg
Maya Angelou	Marguerite Johnson
Nellie Bly	Elizabeth Jane Cochrane Seaman
John le Carré	David John Moore Cornwell
Lewis Carroll	Charles Lutwidge Dodgson
Colette	Sidonie Gabrielle Colette
Amanda Cross	Carolyn Heilbrun
Isak Dinesen	Karen Blixen
Elia	Charles Lamb
George Eliot	Mary Ann or Marian Evans
Maksim Gorky	Aleksey Maksimovich Peshkov
O. Henry	William Sydney Porter
James Herriot	James Alfred Wight
P. D. James	Phyllis Dorothy James White
Ann Landers	Esther Pauline Lederer
[John] Ross Macdonald	Kenneth Millar
André Maurois	Émile Herzog
Molière	Jean Baptiste Poquelin
Toni Morrison	Chloe Anthony Wofford
Frank O'Connor	Michael Donovan
George Orwell	Eric Arthur Blair
Ellery Queen	Frederic Danay and Manfred B. Lee
Mary Renault	Mary Challans
Anne Rice	Howard Allen O'Brien
Saki	Hector Hugh Munro
George Sand	Amandine Lucie Aurore Dupin
Dr. Seuss	Theodor Seuss Geisel
Lemony Snicket	Daniel Handler
Stendhal	Marie Henri Beyle
Mark Twain	Samuel Clemens
Voltaire	François Marie Arouet

Commonly Misspelled English Words

accidentally
accommodate
acknowledgment
acquainted
acquire
across
all right
already
amateur
appearance
appropriate
bellwether
bureau
business
calendar
canceled
Caribbean
cemetery
changeable
chrysanthemum
Cincinnati
collectible
commitment
committee
connoisseur
conscientious
conscious
convenience
corduroy
deceive
defendant
definitely
desirable
desperate
eligible
eliminate
embarrass
environment
existence
fascinating
February
fluorine
foreign
forty
gauge
government
grammar
grateful
harass
humorous
hurrying
incidentally
independent
indispensable
inoculate
irresistible
jewelry
judgment
laboratory
liaison
leisure
library
license
lieutenant
lightning
liquefy
maintenance
marriage
medieval
millennium
miniature
miscellaneous
Mississippi
misspelled
mnemonic
mysterious
necessary
noticeable
occasionally
occurrence
opportunity
optimistic
parallel
patience
performance
permanent
permissible
perseverance
personnel
possess
privilege
propaganda
questionnaire
receipt
receive
restaurant
rhythm
ridiculous
sacrilegious
sergeant
separate
seize
sheriff
sincerely
stubbornness
supersede
tangible
temperament
temperature
transferred
truly
twelfth
vaccinate
vacuum
Wednesday
weird
wholly

American Manual Alphabet

In the American Manual Alphabet, each letter of the alphabet is represented by a position of the fingers. This system was originally developed in France by Abbe Charles Michel De I'Epee in the late 1700s. It was brought to the United States by Laurent Clerce (1785-1869), a Frenchman who taught deaf or hearing-impaired people.

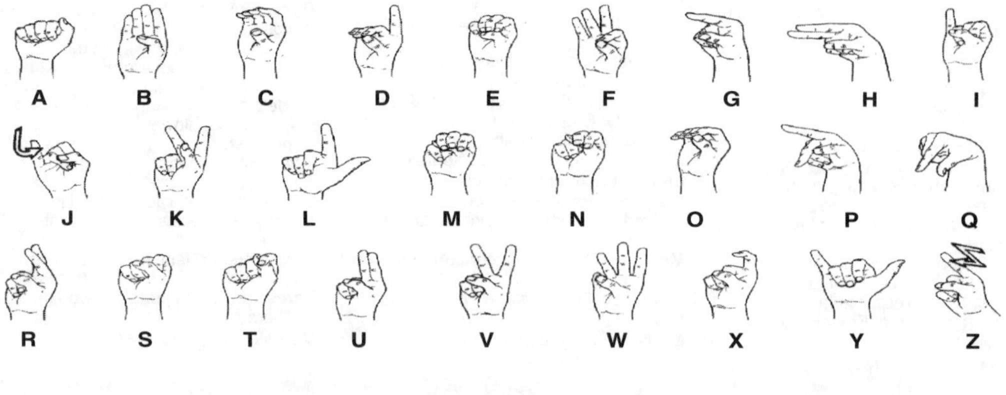

The Principal Languages of the World

Source: Database of *Ethnologue: Languages of the World,* 15th Edition, www.ethnologue.com. Raymond G. Gordon, Editor. Copyright © 2004, SIL International. Used by permission.

The following tables count only "first language" speakers. All figures are estimates.

Languages Spoken by the Most People

Speakers	(millions)
Chinese, Mandarin	873
Spanish	322
English	309
Hindi	180
Portuguese	177
Bengali	171
Russian	145
Japanese	122
German, standard	95
Chinese, Wu	77
Javanese	75
Telugu	69
Marathi	68
Vietnamese	67
Korean	67

Languages Spoken by at Least 2 Million People

A "Hub" country is the country of origin, not necessarily the country where the most speakers reside (e.g., Portugal is the "hub" country of Portuguese, although more Portuguese speakers live in Brazil).

Language	Hub	Countries	Speakers (millions)
Chinese, Mandarin	China	16	873
Spanish	Spain	43	322
English	United Kingdom	107	309
Hindi	India	17	180
Portuguese	Portugal	33	177
Bengali	Bangladesh	9	171
Russian	Russia	31	145
Japanese	Japan	25	122
German, standard	Germany	41	95
Chinese, Wu	China	1	77
Javanese	Indonesia	4	75
Telugu	India	7	69
Marathi	India	3	68
Vietnamese	Vietnam	20	67
Korean	Korea, South	31	67
Tamil	India	15	66
French	France	56	64
Italian	Italy	30	61
Panjabi, Western	Pakistan	7	60
Urdu	Pakistan	21	60
Chinese, Yue	China	20	54
Turkish	Turkey	35	50
Arabic, Egyptian spoken	Egypt	9	46
Chinese, Min Nan	China	9	46
Gujarati	India	17	46
Chinese, Jinyu	China	1	45
Polish	Poland	21	42
Ukrainian	Ukraine	25	39
Chinese, Xiang	China	1	36
Malayalam	India	9	35
Kannada	India	1	35
Burmese	Myanmar	5	32
Oriya	India	2	31
Chinese, Hakka	China	16	29
Panjabi, Eastern	India	11	27
Sunda	Indonesia	1	27
Bhojpuri	India	3	26
Maithili	India	2	24
Azerbaijani, South	Iran	8	24
Farsi, Western	Iran	26	24
Hausa	Nigeria	13	24
Romanian	Romania	17	23
Indonesian	Indonesia	6	23
Arabic, Algerian spoken	Algeria	5	21
Chinese, Gan	China	1	20
Awadhi	India	2	20
Thai	Thailand	4	20
Cebuano	Philippines	2	20
Sindhi	Pakistan	7	19
Arabic, Moroccan spoken	Morocco	8	19
Yoruba	Nigeria	5	19
Arabic, Sudanese spoken	Sudan	5	18
Arabic, Sa'idi spoken	Egypt	1	18
Uzbek, Northern	Uzbekistan	12	18
Igbo	Nigeria	1	18
Malay	Malaysia	8	17
Amharic	Ethiopia	4	17
Dutch	Netherlands	8	17
Nepali	Nepal	4	17
Tagalog	Philippines	7	15
Assamese	India	3	15
Arabic, Mesopotamian spoken	Iraq	5	15
Thai, Northeastern	Thailand	1	15
Arabic, North Levantine spoken	Syria	15	14
Chittagonian	Bangladesh	2	14
Seraiki	Pakistan	3	13
Madura	Indonesia	2	13
Hungarian	Hungary	11	13
Sinhala	Sri Lanka	6	13
Marwari	India	3	13
Haryanvi	India	1	13
Magahi	India	1	13
Somali	Somalia	12	12
Greek	Greece	35	12
Chhattisgarhi	India	1	11
Czech	Czech Republic	10	11
Serbian	Serbia and Montenegro	16	11
Deccan	India	1	10
Shona	Zimbabwe	4	10
Sylheti	Bangladesh	10	10
Chinese, Min Bei	China	2	10
Belarusan	Belarus	16	10
Zhuang, Northern	China	1	10
Arabic, Najdi spoken	Saudi Arabia	7	9
Pashto, Northern	Pakistan	5	9
Zulu	South Africa	6	9
Arabic, Tunisian spoken	Tunisia	4	9
Lombard	Italy	3	9
Kurdish, Northern	Turkey	31	9
Chinese, Min Dong	China	6	9
Dhundari	India	1	9
Bulgarian	Bulgaria	11	8
Oromo, West Central	Ethiopia	2	8
Swedish	Sweden	7	8
Akan	Ghana	1	8
Kazakh	Kazakhstan	13	8
Ilocano	Philippines	2	8
Pashto, Central	Pakistan	1	7
Uyghur	China	16	7
Farsi, Eastern	Afghanistan	3	7
Arabic, Sanaani spoken	Yemen	1	7
Bavarian	Austria	5	7
Haitian Creole French	Haiti	9	7
Rwanda	Rwanda	4	7
Xhosa	South Africa	3	7

Language	Hub	Countries	Speakers (millions)
Khmer, Central	Cambodia	7	7
Azerbaijani, North	Azerbaijan	9	7
Napoletano-Calabrese	Italy	1	7
Hiligaynon	Philippines	2	7
Arabic, Ta'izzi-Adeni spoken	Yemen	5	6
Catalan-Valencian-Balear	Spain	18	6
Armenian	Armenia	30	6
Minangkabau	Indonesia	1	6
Turkmen	Turkmenistan	13	6
Luba-Kasai	Democratic Republic of Congo	1	6
Arabic, North Mesopotamian spoken	Iraq	4	6
Croatian	Croatia	8	6
Santali	India	4	6
Arabic, South Levantine spoken	Jordan	8	6
Schwyzerdütsch	Switzerland	5	6
Thai, Northern	Thailand	2	6
Kanauji	India	1	6
Arabic, Hijazi spoken	Saudi Arabia	2	6
Afrikaans	South Africa	10	5
Malagasy, Plateau	Madagascar	3	5
Kurdish, Southern	Iran	2	5
Nyanja	Malawi	5	5
Gikuyu	Kenya	1	5
Danish	Denmark	8	5
Finnish	Finland	7	5
Tigrigna	Ethiopia	4	5
Hebrew	Israel	8	5
Mòoré	Burkina Faso	6	5
Slovak	Slovakia	8	5
Mewati	India	1	5
Sukuma	Tanzania	1	5
Thai, Southern	Thailand	1	5
Rundi	Burundi	4	4
Guaraní, Paraguayan	Paraguay	2	4
Sicilian	Italy	1	4
Kashmiri	India	3	4
Sotho, Southern	Lesotho	3	4
Oromo, Eastern	Ethiopia	1	4
Arabic, Libyan spoken	Libya	3	4
Tswana	Botswana	4	4
Tajiki	Tajikistan	8	4
Kituba	Democratic Republic of Congo	1	4
Georgian	Georgia	13	4
Umbundu	Angola	2	4
Bosnian	Bosnia and Herzegovina	1	4
Zhuang, Southern	China	1	4
Konkani	India	1	4
Oromo, Borana-Arsi-Guji	Ethiopia	3	3
Bali	Indonesia	1	3
Kurdish, Central	Iraq	2	3
Sotho, Northern	South Africa	2	3
Luyia	Kenya	2	3
Quechua, South Bolivian	Bolivia	2	3
Konkani, Goanese	India	3	3
Wolof	Senegal	6	3
Bugis	Indonesia	2	3
Kanuri, Central	Nigeria	6	3
Luo	Kenya	2	3
Balochi, Southern	Pakistan	4	3
Mongolian, Peripheral	China	2	3
Tsonga	South Africa	4	3
Gilaki	Iran	1	3
Mazanderani	Iran	1	3
Pulaar	Senegal	6	3
Lao	Laos	7	3
Galician	Spain	2	3
Jamaican Creole English	Jamaica	7	3
Malay, Balinese	Indonesia	1	3
Tamazight, Central Atlas	Morocco	3	3
Yiddish, Eastern	Israel	21	3
Kirghiz	Kyrgyzstan	7	3
Lithuanian	Lithuania	19	3
Kabyle	Algeria	3	3
Éwé	Ghana	2	3
Piemontese	Italy	3	3
Malay, Pattani	Thailand	1	3
Ganda	Uganda	1	3
Mbundu	Angola	1	3
Shekhawati	India	1	3
Aceh	Indonesia	1	3
Banjar	Indonesia	2	3
Tachelhit	Morocco	3	3
Rajbanshi	India	3	2
Albanian, Tosk	Albania	9	2
Shan	Myanmar	3	2
Garhwali	India	1	2
Pular	Guinea	6	2
Lambadi	India	1	2
Hassaniyya	Mauritania	6	2
Bamanankan	Mali	7	2
Albanian, Gheg	Serbia and Montenegro	7	2
Betawi	Indonesia	1	2
Ndau	Mozambique	2	2
Pashto, Southern	Pakistan	6	2
Chinese, Pu-Xian	China	3	2
Makhuwa	Mozambique	1	2
Bicolano, Central	Philippines	1	2
Kalenjin	Kenya	1	2
Kamba	Kenya	1	2
Waray-Waray	Philippines	1	2
Kumauni	India	2	2
Arabic, Gulf spoken	Iraq	9	2
Mongolian, Halh	Mongolia	4	2
Bemba	Zambia	4	2
Aymara, Central	Bolivia	4	2
Tiv	Nigeria	2	2
Brahui	Pakistan	4	2
Hazaragi	Afghanistan	4	2
Zarma	Niger	4	2
Venetian	Italy	3	2
Sadri	India	2	2
Lingala	Democratic Republic of Congo	3	2
Baoulé	Côte d'Ivoire	1	2
Dogri	India	1	2
Sasak	Indonesia	1	2
Bagri	India	2	2
Arakanese	Myanmar	3	2
Mundari	India	3	2
Kurux	India	2	2
Bouyei	China	4	2
Emiliano-Romagnolo	Italy	2	2
Maninkakan, Eastern	Guinea	3	2
Beti	Cameroon	1	2
Saxon, Upper	Germany	1	2
Batak Toba	Indonesia	1	2

WORLD ALMANAC QUICK QUIZ

Can you match the animal name with the word for a group of the animals?

1. foxes	(a) pod
2. seals	(b) smack
3. jellyfish	(c) skulk
4. vultures	(d) committee

For the answer look in this chapter, or see page 1008.

BUILDINGS, BRIDGES, AND TUNNELS

Tallest Buildings in the World

Source: Council on Tall Buildings and Urban Habitat, Illinois Inst. of Technology, www.ctbuh.com; Emporis.com, www.emporis.com

Structures under construction as of mid-2005 are denoted by asterisk *. Year is date of completion or projected completion.

Building	Ht. (ft.)	Stories
Taipei 101, Taipei, Taiwan (2004)	1,670	101
Petronas Tower I, Kuala Lumpur, Malaysia (1998)	1,483	88
Petronas Tower II, Kuala Lumpur, Malaysia (1998)	1,483	88
Sears Tower, Chicago, IL, U.S. (1974)	1,450	110
Jin Mao Bldg., Shanghai, China (1999)	1,380	88
Two International Finance Centre, Hong Kong, China (2003)	1,362	88
CITIC Plaza, Guangzhou, China (1996)	1,283	80
Shun Hing Square, Shenzhen, China (1996)	1,260	69
Empire State Building, New York, U.S. (1931)	1,250	102
Central Plaza, Hong Kong, China, (1992)	1,227	78
Bank of China, Hong Kong, China (1989)	1,209	72
Emirates Tower One, Dubai, U.A.E. (1999)	1,165	54
Tuntex Sky Tower, Kaohsiung, Taiwan (1997)	1,140	85
Aon Centre, Chicago, IL, U.S. (1973)	1,136	80
The Center, Hong Kong, China (1998)	1,135	73
John Hancock Center, Chicago, IL, U.S. (1969)	1,127	100
*Wuhan International Securities Bldg, Wuhan, China (2005)	1,087	68
*Shimao International Plaza, Shanghai, China (2005)	1,087	60
Ryugyong Hotel, Pyongyang, North Korea (1995)	1,083	105
*Q1, Gold Coast, Australia (2005)	1,059	78
Burj al Arab Hotel, Dubai, U.A.E. (1999)	1,053	60
*Nina Tower 1, Hong Kong, China (2005)	1,046	80
Chrysler Bldg., New York, U.S. (1930)	1,046	77
Bank of America Plaza, Atlanta, GA, U.S. (1993)	1,023	55
U.S. Bank Tower, Los Angeles, CA, U.S. (1990)	1,018	73
Menara Telekom Headquarters, Kuala Lumpur, Malaysia (1999)	1,017	55
Emirates Tower Two, Dubai, U.A.E. (2000)	1,014	56
AT&T Corporate Center, Chicago, IL, U.S. (1989)	1,007	60
JP Morgan Chase Tower, Houston, TX, U.S. (1982)	1,002	75
Baiyoke Tower II, Bangkok, Thailand (1997)	997	85
Two Prudential Plaza, Chicago, IL, U.S. (1990)	995	64
Kingdom Centre, Riyadh, Saudi Arabia (2002)	992	41
First Canadian Place, Toronto, Canada (1975)	978	72
*Eureka Tower, Melbourne, Australia (2006)	975	91
Wells Fargo Plaza, Houston, TX, U.S. (1983)	972	71
Landmark Tower, Yokohama, Japan (1993)	971	70
311 S. Wacker Drive, Chicago, IL, U.S. (1990)	961	65
SEG Plaza, Shenzhen, China (2000)	957	71
American International Bldg., New York, U.S. (1932)	952	67
Key Tower, Cleveland, OH, U.S. (1991)	947	57
Plaza 66, Shanghai, China (2001)	945	66
One Liberty Place, Philadelphia, PA, U.S. (1987)	945	61
Sunjoy Tomorrow Square, Shanghai, China (2003)	934	55
Bank of America Center, Seattle, WA, U.S. (1984)	933	76
Cheung Kong Centre, Hong Kong, China (1999)	929	63
*Chongqing World Trade Center, Chonqing, China (2005)	929	60
The Trump Bldg., New York, U.S. (1930)	927	71
Bank of America Plaza, Dallas, TX, U.S. (1985)	921	72
United Overseas Bank Plaza, Singapore (1992)	919	66
Republic Plaza, Singapore (1995)	919	66
Union Bank Centre, Singapore (1986)	919	63

World's 10 Tallest Free-Standing Towers

Name	City	Country	Ht. (ft.)	Year
*Indos at Telecom Tower	Jakarta	Indonesia	1,831	2009
CN Tower	Toronto	Canada	1,815	1976
Ostankino Tower	Moscow	Russia	1,772	1967
*Xi'an Broadcasting, Telephone and TV Tower	Xi'an	China	1,542	NA
Oriental Pearl TV Tower	Shanghai	China	1,535	1995
Milad Tower	Tehran	Iran	1,427	2005
Manara Kuala Lumpur	Kuala Lumpur	Malaysia	1,379	1996
Tianjin Radio & TV Tower	Tianjin	China	1,362	1991
Central TV Tower	Beijing	China	1,268	1992
TV Tower	Kiev	Ukraine	1,246	1974

Tall Buildings in Selected North American Cities

Source: Marshall Gerometta and Rick Bronson, Emporis.com, www.emporis.com;
Council on Tall Buildings and Urban Habitat, Illinois Inst. of Technology, www.ctbuh.org

Lists include freestanding towers and other structures that do not have stories and are not technically considered "buildings." Also included are some structures still under construction as of mid-2005 (denoted by asterisk *). Year in parentheses is date of completion or projected completion. Height is generally measured from sidewalk to roof, including penthouse and tower if enclosed as integral part of structure; stories generally counted from street level. NA = not available or not applicable.

Atlanta, GA

Building	Ht. (ft.)	Stories
Bank of America Plaza (incl. spire), 600 Peachtree NE (1992)	1,023	55
SunTrust Bank Tower, 303 Peachtree NE (1992)	871	60
One Atlantic Center, 1201 W. Peachtree (1987)	820	50
191 Peachtree Tower (1991)	770	50
Westin Peachtree Plaza, 210 Peachtree NW (1976)[1]	723	73
Georgia Pacific Tower, 133 Peachtree St. NE (1981)	697	51
Promenade II, 1230 Peachtree St. NE (1989)	691	40
Bellsouth, 675 W. Peachtree (1980)	677	47
*Symphony Center Tower, 1180 Peachtree St. NE (2005)	612	41
GLG Grand/Four Seasons Hotel, 75 14th St. NE (1992)	609	53
Wachovia Bank of Georgia, 2 Peachtree St. NW (1967)	556	44
Marriott Marquis, 265 Peachtree Center Ave. NE (1985)	554	52
Park Avenue Condominiums, 750 Park Ave. NE (2000)	486	42
Paramount at Buckhead, 3445 Stratford Rd. NE (2004)	478	40
*Terminus Tower, 3280 Peachtree NW (2007)	467	25
Centennial Tower, 101 Marietta St. (1976)	459	36
Equitable Bldg., 100 Peachtree St. (1967)	453	34
*Spire, 860 Peachtree St. (2005)	453	28
Buckhead Grand (2004)	451	38
One Park Tower, 34 Peachtree St. (1961)	439	32
1100 Peachtree St. NE (1990)	428	28
Atlanta Plaza I, 950 E. Paces Ferry Rd. (1986)	425	32
Park Place, 2660 Peachtree Rd. NW (1986)	420	40
2828 Peachtree Luxury Condominiums (2002)	420	33
Oakwood Apts., 1280 W. Peachtree St. NW (1989)	410	38
Peachtree Summit No. 1, 401 Peachtree NE (1975)	406	31
One Coca-Cola Plaza, 310 North Ave. NW (1979)	403	29
Tower Place 100, 3340 Peachtree Rd. NE (1974)	401	29

(1) 883 ft. with antenna.

Baltimore, MD

Building	Ht. (ft.)	Stories
Legg Mason Building, 100 Light Street (1973)	529	50
Bank of America, 10 Light Street (1924)	509	37
William DOnald Schaefer Tower, 6 St. Paul St. (1992)	493	29
Commerce Place, 1 South Street, (1992)	454	31
Marriott Baltimore Inner Harbor East, 700 Aliceanna St. (2001)	430	32
World Trade Center 401 E. Pratt St. (1977)	405	32

Bellevue, WA

Building	Ht. (ft.)	Stories
*Lincoln Tower One, 604 Bellevue Way (2006)	450	42
*Lincoln Tower Two, 770 Bellevue Way NE (2006)	412	27

Birmingham, AL

Building	Ht. (ft.)	Stories
Southtrust Tower, 420 N. 20th St. (1986)	454	34
AmSouth/Harbert Plaza, 1901 6th Ave. N (1989)	437	32

Boston, MA

Building	Ht. (ft.)	Stories
John Hancock Tower, 200 Clarendon St. (1976)	790	62
Prudential Tower, 800 Boylston St. (1964)[1]	750	52
Federal Reserve Bldg., 600 Atlantic Ave. (1978)	604	32
Boston Company Bldg., 1 Boston Place (1970)	601	41
One International Place, 100 Oliver St. (1987)	600	46
First National Bank of Boston, 100 Federal St. (1971)	591	37
One Financial Center, 10 Dewey Sq. (1984)	590	46
111 Huntington Ave. (2002)	564	36
Two International Place (1993)	538	35
One Post Office Square (1981)	525	40
1 Federal St. (1975)	520	38
Exchange Place, 53 State St. (1984)	510	39
Sixty State St. (1977)	509	38
1 Beacon St. (1972)	507	36
1 Lincoln Place (2003)	503	36
28 State Street (1970)	500	40
Mariott's Custom House, 3 McKinley Sq. (1915)	496	32
John Hancock Bldg., 175 Berkeley St. (1949)	495	26
33 Arch St. (2003)	489	31
State St. Bank, 225 Franklin St., (1966)	477	33
Millennium Place 1, Ritz Carlton Hotel (2001)	475	38
125 High St. (1990)	452	30
100 Summer St. (1975)	450	33
Millennium Place 2, 3 Avery St. (2001)	445	36
McCormack Bldg., 1 Ashburton Pl. (1975)	401	22
Harbor Towers I, 85 E. India (1971)	400	40
Keystone Building (1971)	400	32

(1) 836 ft. with antenna

Calgary, Alberta

Building	Ht. (ft.)	Stories
Petro Canada Centre West Tower, 150 6th Ave. SW (1984)	705	53
Bankers Hall East Tower, 855 2nd St. SW (1989)	645	50
Bankers Hall West Tower, 888 3rd St. SW (2000)	645	50
Calgary Tower, 101 9th Ave. SW (1967)	626	NA
TransCanada Tower, 450 1st St. SW (2000)	608	37
Canterra Tower, 400 3rd Ave. SW (2001)	581	38
First Canadian Centre, 350 7th Ave. SW (1983)	530	43
Canada Trust, Calgary Eatons Centre, 421 7th Ave. SW (1991)	530	40
Scotia Square, 700 2nd St. SW (1975)	525	42

Building	Ht. (ft.)	Stories
Western Canadian Place–N. Tower, 707 6th St. SW (1983)	507	41
Nexen Bldg., 801 7th Ave. SW (1982)	500	37
Petro-Canada Tower, E. Tower, 111 5th Ave. SW (1983)	469	33
Two Bow Valley Square, 205 5th Ave. SW (1974)	468	39
Dome Tower, 333 7th Ave. SW (1976)	463	34
5th & 5th Bldg., 605 5th Ave. SW (1980)	460	35
Shell Centre, 400 4th Ave. SW (1977)	460	34
T.D. Square North, 324 8th Ave. SW (1976)	449	33
Four Bow Valley Square, 250 6th Ave. SW (1982)	441	37
Fifth Avenue Place East Tower, 425 1st St. SW (1981)	435	35
Fifth Avenue Place West Tower, 237 4th Ave. SW (1981)	435	35
*Calgary Courts Centre (2007)	423	24
Western Canadian Place–S. Tower, 801 6th St. SW (1983)	420	32
Altius Centre, 500 4th Ave. SW (1972)	415	32
Encana Place, 150 9th Ave. SW (1982)	410	28
Hewlett Packard Tower, 715 5th Ave. SW (1975)	408	31
Alberta Stock Exchange, 300 5th Ave. (1979)	407	33

Charlotte, NC

Building	Ht. (ft.)	Stories
Bank of America Corporate Center, 100 N. Tryon St. (1992)	871	60
Hearst Tower, 214 N. Tryon St. (2002)	659	50
One Wachovia Center, 301 S. College St. (1988)	588	42
Bank of America Plaza, 101 S. Tryon St. (1974)	503	40
Interstate Tower, 121 W. Trade St. (1990)	462	32
IJL Financial Center, 201 N. Tryon St. (1997)	447	30
Three Wachovia Center, 401 S. Tryon St. (2000)	440	29
Two Wachovia Plaza, 301 S. Tryon St. (1971)	433	32
Wachovia Center, 400 S. Tryon St. (1974)	420	32

Chicago, IL

Building	Ht. (ft.)	Stories
Sears Tower, 233 S. Wacker Dr. (1974)[1]	1,450	108
*Trump International Hotel + Tower (Incl. spire), 401 N. Wabash Ave. (2008)	1,362	92
Aon Center, 200 E. Randolph St. (1973)	1,136	83
John Hancock Center, 875 N. Michigan Ave. (1969)[2]	1,127	100
AT&T Corporate Center (incl. spire), 227 W. Monroe St. (1989)	1,007	61
Two Prudential Plaza (incl. spire), 180 N. Stetson Ave. (1990)	995	64
311 S. Wacker Drive (1990)	961	65
900 N. Michigan Ave. (1989)	871	66
Water Tower Place, 845 N. Michigan Ave. (1976)	859	74
Bank One Plaza (1969)	850	60
Park Tower, 800 N. Michigan Ave. (2000)	844	67
3 First National Plaza, 70 W. Madison St. (1981)	767	57
Chicago Title & Trust Center, 161 N. Clark St. (1992)	756	50
Olympia Centre, 737 N. Michigan Ave. (1986)	725	63
IBM Bldg., 330 N. Wabash Ave. (1973)	695	52
Hyatt Center, 71 S. Wacker Drive (2005)	682	48
111 S. Wacker Drive (2005)	681	51
181 W. Madison St. (1990)	680	50
One Magnificent Mile, 980 N. Michigan Ave. (1983)	673	58
*340 on the Park, 340 Randolph St. (2007)	672	64
R.R. Donnelley Center, 77 W. Wacker Dr. (1992)	668	49
UBS Tower, 1 N. Wacker Dr. (2001)	652	50
Daley Center, 55 W. Washington St. (1965)	648	31
55 E. Erie St. (2003)	647	56
Lake Point Tower, 505 N. Lake Shore Dr. (1968)	645	70
River East Center, 350 E. Illinois St. (2001)	644	58
Grand Plaza I, 540 N. State St. (2003)	641	57
Leo Burnett Bldg., 35 W. Wacker Dr. (1989)	635	50
The Heritage at Millennium Park, 125 N. Wabash Ave. (2004)	631	57
NBC Tower (incl. spire), 445 N. Cityfront Plaza Dr. (1989)	627	37
Millennium Centre, 33 W. Ontario St. (2003)	610	59
Chicago Place, 700 N. Michigan Ave. (1991)	608	49
Board of Trade (incl. statue), 141 W. Jackson Blvd. (1930)	605	44
CNA Plaza, 325 S. Wabash St. (1972)	601	45
Prudential Bldg., 130 E. Randolph St. (1955)[3]	601	41
Heller International Tower, 500 W. Monroe St. (1992)	600	45
One Madison Plaza, 200 W. Madison St. (1982)	599	45
1000 Lake Shore Plaza. (1964)	590	55
Marina City Apts. 1, 300 N. State St. (1964)	588	61
Marina City Apts. 2, 300 N. State St. (1964)	588	61
Citicorp Center, 500 W. Madison St. (1985)	588	41
Mid Continental Plaza, 55 E. Monroe St. (1972)	582	50
North Pier Apt. Tower, 474 N. Lake Shore Dr. (1990)	581	61
Bank One Center, 131 S. Dearborn St. (2003)	580	37
Smurfit-Stone Bldg., 150 N. Michigan Ave. (1983)	575	41
The Fordham, 25 E. Superior St. (2003)	574	52
190 S. LaSalle St. (1987)	573	42
*One S. Dearborn (2005)	571	39
Onterie Center, 446 E. Ontario St. (1985)	570	57
Chicago Temple, 77 W. Washington St. (1924)	568	21
Palmolive Bldg., 919 N. Michigan Ave. (incl. beacon) (1929)	565	37
Huron Plaza Apts., 30 E. Huron St. (1983)	560	56
Boeing Int'l Headquarters, 100 N. Riverside Plaza (1990)	560	36
The Parkshore, 195 N. Harbor Dr. (1991)	556	56
North Harbor Tower, 175 N. Harbor Dr. (1988)	556	55
Civic Opera Bldg., 20 N. Wacker Dr. (1929)	555	45
Newberry Plaza, 1000 N. State St. (1974)	553	53
Michigan Plaza South, 205 N. Michigan Ave. (1985)	553	44
30 N. LaSalle St. (1975)	553	43
Pittsfield Bldg., 55 E. Washington St. (1927)	551	38
Harbor Point, 155 N. Harbor Dr. (1975)	550	54
One S. Wacker Dr. (1983)	550	42
Kluczynski Federal Bldg., 230 S. Dearborn St. (1975)	545	45
Park Millennium, 222 N. Columbus Dr. (2002)	544	53
USG Building, 125 S. Franklin St. (1992)	538	35
The Pinnacle, 21 E. Huron St. (2004)	535	48
LaSalle National Bank, 135 S. LaSalle St. (1934)	535	44
Park Place Tower, 655 W. Irving Park Rd. (1973)	531	56
One N. LaSalle St. (1930)	530	49
The Elysees, 111 E. Chestnut St. (1973)	529	56
River Plaza, 405 N. Wabash St. (1977)	524	56
35 E. Wacker Dr. (1926)	523	40
Unitrin Bldg., 1 E. Wacker Dr. (1962)	522	41
Mather Tower, 75 E. Wacker Dr. (1928)	521	41
Chicago Mercantile Exchange, 10 S. Wacker Dr. (1987)	520	40
Chicago Merc. Exchange, 30 S. Wacker Dr. (1983)	520	40
191 N. Wacker Dr. (2002)	516	37
401 E. Ontario St. (1990)	515	51
One Financial Place, 440 S. LaSalle St. (1985)	515	40
*345 E. Ohio St. (2006)	514	48
Park Tower Condos, 5415 N. Sheridan Rd. (1973)	513	54
LaSalle-Wacker, 221 N. LaSalle St. (1930)[4]	512	41
Harris Bank III, 115 S. LaSalle St. (1977)	510	35
321 N. Clark St. (1987)	510	35
400 E. Ohio St. (1982)	505	50
Carbide & Carbon Bldg. , 230 N. Michigan Ave. (1929)	503	37
1 Superior Place, 1 W. Superior St. (1999)	502	52
120 N. LaSalle St. (1991)	501	41
Chase Plaza, 10 S. LaSalle St. (1986)	501	37
200 S. Wacker Dr. (1981)	500	38
Ontario Place, 10 E. Ontario St. (1983)	495	49
Xerox Centre, 55 W. Monroe St. (1980)	495	40
1 N. Franklin St. (1990)	494	34
The Bristol, 57E. Delaware Pl. (2000)	488	42
333 W. Wacker Dr. (1983)	487	36
Northern Trust Bldg., 125 S. Wacker Dr. (1974)	487	31
AT&T, 10 S. Canal St. (1971)	485	32
Plaza 440, 440 N. Wabash Ave. (1991)	480	49
33 N. LaSalle St. (1930)	479	40
Bankers Bldg., 15 W. Adams St. (1927)	476	41
Cook County Administration Bldg., 69 W. Washington St. (1965)	475	37
Metropolitan Tower, 310 S. Michigan Ave. (1924)	475	37
American Furniture Mart, 680 N. Lake Shore Dr. (1926)	474	30
Intercontinental Hotel, 505 N. Michigan Ave. (1929)	471	42
City Place, 676 N. Michigan Ave. (1990)	470	40
Columbus Plaza, 233 E. Wacker Dr. (1980)	468	49
The Sterling, 345 N. LaSalle St. (2001)	466	50
*The Regatta, Lakeshore East (2006)	466	45
Randolph Tower, 188 W. Randolph St. (1925)	465	45
200 N. Dearborn St. (1989)	463	47
Tribune Tower, 435 N. Michigan Ave. (1925)	463	36
The New York, 3660 N. Lake Shore Dr. (1986)	461	50
Presidential Towers, 555 W. Madison St. (1985)	461	49
Presidential Towers, 575 W. Madison St. (1985)	461	49
Presidential Towers, 605 W. Madison St. (1985)	461	49
Presidential Towers, 625 W. Madison St. (1985)	461	49
Chicago Marriott, 540 N. Michigan Ave. (1978)	460	45
Grand Plaza II, 545 Dearborn St. (2003)	458	38
Swissotel, 323 E. Wacker Dr. (1989)	457	43
Equitable Bldg., 401 N. Michigan Ave. (1965)	457	35
400 N. LaSalle St. (2003)	454	45
ABN-AMRO Plaza I, 550 W. Madison St. (2003)	453	37
Roanoke Bldg., 11 S. LaSalle St. (1925)	452	37
Riverbend, 323 N. Canal St. (2002)	451	32
*The Shoreham, Lakeshore East (2005)	450	50
Eugenie Terrace on the Park, 1730 N. Clark St. (1987)	450	44
Gateway Center III, 222 S. Riverside Plaza (1972)	450	35

(1) 1,730 ft. with antenna. (2) 1,499 ft. with antenna. (3) 912 ft. with antenna. (4) 543 ft. with antenna.

Cincinnati, OH

Building	Ht. (ft.)	Stories
Carew Tower, 441 Vine St. (1931)	574	49
PNC Tower , 1 W. 4th St. (1913)	495	31
Scripps Center, 312 Walnut St. (1990)	468	36
Fifth Third Center, 511 Walnut St. (1969)	423	32
Chemed Center, 255 5th St. (1990)	410	32
Convergys Center, 600 Vine St. (1984)	402	29

Cleveland, OH

Building	Ht. (ft.)	Stories
Key Tower (incl. spire), 127 Public Square (1991)	947	57
Terminal Tower, 50 Public Square (1930)	708	52
BP America, 200 Public Square (1985)	658	46
100 Erieview, 1801 E. 9th St. (1964)	529	40
One Cleveland Center, 1375 E. 9th St. (1983)	450	31
Bank One Center, 600 Superior Ave. (1991)	446	28
Federal Courthouse, 801 W. Superior Ave. (2002)	430	24
Justice Center, 1250 Ontario St. (1976)	420	26
Federal Building, 240 E. 9th St. (1967)	419	32
National City Center, 1900 E. 9th St. (1980)	410	35

Columbus, OH

Building	Ht. (ft.)	Stories
James A. Rhodes State Office Tower, 30 E. Broad St. (1973)	624	41
Leveque-Lincoln Tower, 50 W. Broad St. (1927)	555	47
William Green Building, 30 W. Spring St. (1990)	530	33
Huntington Center, 41 S. High St. (1983)	512	37
Vern Riffe State Office Tower, 77 S. High St. (1988)	503	33
One Nationwide Plaza (1976)	485	40

Building	Ht. (ft.)	Stories
Franklin County Courthouse, 373 S. High St. (1991)	464	27
AEP Building, One Riverside Plaza (1983)	456	31
Borden Bldg., 180 E. Broad St. (1974)	438	34
Three Nationwide Plaza (1989)	408	27

Dallas, TX

Building	Ht. (ft.)	Stories
Bank of America Plaza, 901 Main St. (1985)	921	72
Renaissance Tower (incl. spire), 1201 Elm St. (1974)	886	56
Bank One Center, 1717 Main St. (1987)	787	60
Chase Texas Plaza, 2200 Ross Ave. (1987)	738	55
Fountain Place, 1445 Ross Ave. (1986)	720	58
Trammel Crow Tower, 2001 Ross Ave. (1984)	686	50
1700 Pacific Ave. (1983)	655	50
Thanksgiving Tower, 1600 Pacific Ave. (1982)	645	50
Energy Plaza, 1601 Bryan St. (1983)	629	49
Elm Place, 1401 Elm St. (1965)	625	52
Republic Center Tower I (incl. spire), 300 N. Ervay (1954)	602	36
Republic Center Tower II, 325 N. St. Paul (1964)	598	50
One Bell Plaza, 208 S. Akard St. (1984)	580	37
One Lincoln Plaza, 500 Akard St. (1984)	579	45
Cityplace Center East, 2711 N. Haskell Ave. (1989)	560	42
Reunion Tower, 300 Reunion Blvd. (1976)	560	NA
Adams Mark Hotel Center Tower, 400 Olive St. (1959)	550	42
Mercantile Bldg., 1700 Main St. (1943)	523	31
2001 Bryan St. (1973)	512	40
Harwood Center, 1999 Bryan St. (1982)	483	36
KMPG Centre, 717 N. Harwood St. (1980)	481	34
San Jacinto Tower, 2121 San Jacinto St. (1982)	456	33
Renaissance Hotel, 2222 Stemmons Fwy. (1983)	451	29
Adam's Mark Hotel North Tower (1980)	448	31
One Dallas Centre, 350 N. Paul St. (1979)	448	30
One Main Place, 1201 Main St. (1968)	445	34
*W Dallas Victory Hotel + Residences (2006)	439	32
1600 Pacific Bldg. (1964)	434	31
Magnolia Bldg., 108 Akard St. (1923)	430	27
Fidelity Union Tower, 1507 Pacific Ave. (1959)	400	33

Denver, CO

Building	Ht. (ft.)	Stories
Republic Plaza, 330 17th St. (1984)	714	56
1801 California St. (1982)	709	52
Wells Fargo Center, 1700 Lincoln Ave. (1983)	698	50
1999 Broadway (1985)	544	43
MCI Plaza/Marriott City Center, 707 17th St. (1981)	522	42
Qwest Tower, 555 17th St. (1978)	507	40
1670 Broadway (1980)	448	36
*Colorado Convention Center Hotel, 650 15th St. (2005)	439	37
17th St. Plaza, 1225 17th St. (1982)	438	32
First Interstate Tower North, 633 17th St. (1974)	434	32
Brooks Towers, 1020 15th St. (1968)	420	42
Denver Place South Tower, 999 18th St. (1981)	416	34
One Tabor Center, 1200 17th St. (1984)	408	32
Manville Plaza, 717 17th St. (1989)	404	29

Des Moines, IA

Building	Ht. (ft.)	Stories
801 Grand, 801 Grand Ave. (1991)	630	44
Ruan Center, 666 Grand Ave. (1974)	457	36

Detroit, MI

Building	Ht. (ft.)	Stories
Marriott Hotel, Renaissance Center I (1977)	727	73
Comerica Tower, 500 Woodward Ave. (1991)	619	45
Penobscot Bldg., 633 Griswold Ave. (1928)	566	46
Renaissance Center 100 Tower (1976)	508	39
Renaissance Center 200 Tower(1976)	508	39
Renaissance Center 300 Tower (1976)	508	39
Renaissance Center 400 Tower (1976)	508	39
Guardian Bldg., 500 Griswold Ave. (1929)	489	36
Book Tower, 1249 Washington Blvd. (1925)	472	35
Madden Bldg., 150 W. Jefferson Ave. (1988)	470	29
Fisher Bldg., 3011 W. Grand Blvd. (1928)	447	28
Cadillac Tower, 65 Cadillac Sq. (1928)	437	40
David Stott Bldg., 1150 Griswold St. (1928)	436	38
ANR Bldg., 1 Woodward Ave. (1962)	430	30

Edmonton, Alberta

Building	Ht. (ft.)	Stories
Manulife Place, 10170-101 St. (1983)	480	36
Telus Plaza South, 10020-100 St. (1971)	441	34
Bell Tower, 10104-103 Ave. (1982)	426	34
Commerce Place, 10155-102 St. (1990)	404	27

Fort Worth, TX

Building	Ht. (ft.)	Stories
Burnett Plaza, 801 Cherry St. (1983)	567	40
City Center Tower II, 301 Commerce St. (1984)	547	38
Carter Burgess Plaza, 777 Main St. (1982)	525	40
Block 82 Tower, 400 Throckmorton St. (1974)	488	36
Landmark Tower, 200 W. 7th St. (1957)	481	32
Chase Texas Tower, 201 Main St. (1982)	477	33

Hartford, CT

Building	Ht. (ft.)	Stories
City Place, 185 Asylum St. (1980)	535	38
Travelers Tower, 26 Grove St. (1919)	527	34
Goodwin Square, 225 Asylum St. (1990)	522	30
*Hartford 21 (2006)	440	36

Honolulu, HI

Building	Ht. (ft.)	Stories
First Hawaiian Bank Bldg., 999 Bishop St. (1996)	429	30
Nauru Tower, 1330 Ala Moana Blvd. (1991)	418	45
*Hokua Tower, 1288 Ala Moana Blvd. (2005)	418	41
Hawaiki Tower, 88 Pii Koi St. (1999)	400	45
*Ko'olani (2006)	400	45
One Waterfront Tower–Makai, 425 S. King St. (1990)	400	45
One Waterfront Tower–Mauka, 415 S. King St. (1990)	400	45
One Archer Lane, 801 S. King St.(1998)	400	41
Imperial Plaza, 725 Kapiolani Blvd. (1992)	400	40

Houston, TX

Building	Ht. (ft.)	Stories
JPMorgan Chase Tower, 600 Travis St. (1982)	1,002	75
Wells Fargo Plaza, 1000 Louisiana St. (1983)	972	71
Williams Tower, 2800 Post Oak Blvd. (1983)	901	64
Bank of America Center, 700 Louisiana St. (1983)	780	56
Texaco Heritage Plaza, 1111 Bagby St. (1987)	762	53
1100 Louisiana Bldg. (1980)	748	55
Reliant Energy Plaza, 1111 Louisiana St. (1974)	741	47
Continental Airlines Center, 1600 Smith St. (1984)	732	55
Chevron Tower, 1301 McKinney St. (1982)	725	52
One Shell Plaza, 900 Louisiana St. (1970)[1]	714	50
1400 Smith St. (1983)	691	50
3 Allen Center, 333 Clay St. (1980)	685	50
One Houston Center, 1221 McKinney St. (1978)	678	47
First City Tower, 1001 Fannin St. (1984)	662	47
San Felipe Plaza, 5847 San Felipe Blvd. (1984)	625	45
Exxon Bldg., 800 Bell Ave. (1962)	606	44
1500 Louisiana St. (2002)	600	40
America Tower, 2929 Allen Parkway (1983)	590	42
Two Houston Center, 909 Fannin St. (1974)	579	40
San Jacinto Column (monument) (1939)	570	NA
Marathon Oil Tower, 5555 San Felipe Blvd. (1983)	562	41
Wedge International Tower, 1415 Louisiana St. (1983)	550	44
Kellogg Tower, 601 Jefferson St. (1973)	550	40
Pennzoil Place 1, 700 Milam St. (1976)	523	36
Pennzoil Place 2, 700 Louisiana St. (1976)	523	36
Devon Energy Center, 1200 Smith St. (1978)	521	36
1000 Main Street (2003)	518	36
1201 Louisiana Bldg. (1971)	518	35
The Huntington, 2121 Kirby Dr. (1982)	503	34
El Paso Energy Bldg., 1010 Milam St. (1962)	502	33
*Orion Tower 1, 8 Asbury Pl (2007)	494	37
5 Greenway Plaza (1973)	465	31
Calpine Center, 717 Texas Ave. (2003)	453	34
One Allen Center, 500 Dallas St. (1974)	452	34
Four Leafs Towers I, 5100 San Felipe Blvd. (1982)	444	40
Four Leafs Towers II, 5110 San Felipe Blvd. (1982)	444	40
9 Greenway Plaza (1978)	441	31
11 Greenway Plaza (1979)	441	31
Phoenix Tower, 3200 Southwest Fwy. (1984)	434	34
*Memorial Hermann Medical Plaza (2007)	430	30
Chase Bank Bldg., 712 Main St. (1929)	428	37
The Spires, 2001 Holcomb Blvd. (1984)	426	41
Aon Tower, 4 Oaks Place, 1330 Post Oak Blvd. (1983)	420	30
One City Center, 1001 Main St. (1960)	410	32
Bob Lanier Public Works Bldg., 611 Walker Ave. (1968)	410	27
Neils Esperson Bldg., 802 Travis St. (1927)	410	31
Hyatt Regency, 1200 Lousiana St. (1972)	401	30
The Mercer West Tower, 3288 Sage Rd. (2003)	401	30

(1) 999 ft. with antenna.

Indianapolis, IN

Building	Ht. (ft.)	Stories
Bank One Tower (incl. spire), 111 Monument Circle (1990)	811	49
One America Tower, 200 N. Illinois St. (1982)	533	38
One Indiana Square, 200 N. Delaware St. (1970)	504	36
Market Tower, 10 W. Market St. (1988)	421	32
300 N. Meridian Bldg. (1988)	408	28
First Indiana Plaza, 135 N. Pennsylvania St. (1988)	401	29

Jacksonville, FL

Building	Ht. (ft.)	Stories
Bank of America Tower, 50 N. Laura St. (1990)	617	42
Modis Tower, 1 Independent Dr. (1975)	535	37
BellSouth Tower 424 N. Pearl St. (1983)	435	27
Riverplace Tower, 1301 Riverplace Blvd. (1967)	433	28

Jersey City, NJ

Building	Ht. (ft.)	Stories
30 Hudson St. (2004)	781	42
Merrill Lynch Building, 101 Hudson St. (1992)	548	42
Newport Tower, 525 Washington Blvd. (1990)	528	37
Exchange Place Centre, 10 Exchange Place (1990)	516	32
Newport Office Center VII (2002)	495	29
Harborside Financial Plaza 5 (2002)	480	34

Kansas City, MO

Building	Ht. (ft.)	Stories
One Kansas City Place, 1200 Main St. (1988)	632	42
Town Pavilion, 1111 Main St. (1986)	591	38
Hyatt Regency, 2345 McGee St. (1980)	504	45
Power & Light Bldg., 1330 Baltimore Ave. (1931)	481	32
Fidelity Bank & Trust Bldg. Apts, 909 Walnut St.[1]	454	35
City Hall, 414 E. 12th St. (1937)	443	29
1201 Walnut St. (1991)	427	30
Commerce Tower, 911 Main St. (1965)	407	32
City Center Square, 1100 Main St. (1977)	404	30

(1) Renovations expected to be completed in 2006

Las Vegas, NV

Building	Ht. (ft.)	Stories
Stratosphere Tower, 2000 S. Las Vegas Blvd. (1996)	1,149	NA
*Trump International Hotel Tower I (2007)	645	64
*The Palazzo (2007)	642	53
Wynn Las Vegas (2005)	614	50
Eiffel Tower, Paris Hotel and Casino, 3645 S. Las Vegas Blvd. (1998)	540	NA
New York, New York Hotel and Casino, 3790 S. Las Vegas Blvd. (1997)	529	48
*Sky Las Vegas, 2780 S. Las Vegas Blvd. 2006.	500	45
Bellagio Hotel and Casino, 3600 S. Las Vegas Blvd. (1998)	508	37
THEhotel, Mandalay Bay, 3950 S. Las Vegas Blvd. (1999)	485	43
Turnberry Place I, 2777 Paradise Road (2001)	477	38
Turnberry Place II, 2777 Paradise Road (2002)	477	38
Turnberry Place III, 2777 Paradise Road (2004)	477	38
*Turnberry IV, 2777 Paradise Rd (2006)	477	38

Building	Ht. (ft.)	Stories
*The Residences at MGM Grand I, Tower A, 155 E. Harmon Ave. (2005)	475	38
*The Residentces at MGM Grand II, 155 E. Harmon Ave. (2006)	475	38
Venetian Resort-Hotel–Casino 1, 3355 Las Vegas Blvd. W. (1999)	475	35
Caesars Palace Tower, 3570 S. Las Vegas Blvd. (1998)	470	29
*Palms Resort Tower II, 4321 W. Flamingo Rd (2007)	457	40
Paris Hotel and Casino, 3645 S. Las Vegas Blvd. (1999)	440	34
Rio Masquerade Tower, 3700 W. Flamingo Rd. (1997)	423	42
*Panorama Tower I, 4631 Industrial Blvd (2005)	420	32
*Panorama Tower II, 4631 Industrial Blvd (2006)	420	32
Palms Casino Hotel, 4321 W. Flamingo Rd. (2001)	413	42
Aladdin Hotel and Casino, 3667 S. Las Vegas Blvd. (2000)	408	39
*Hilton Grand Vacations Club II, 2650 S. Las Vegas Blvd. (2006)	405	41
Harrah's Carnaval Tower, 3475 S. Las Vegas Blvd. (1997)	400	35
Fitzgeralds Hotel & Casino, 301 Fremont St. (1980)	400	33

Little Rock, AR

Building	Ht. (ft.)	Stories
TCBY Tower, 425 W. Capitol Ave. (1986)	546	40
Regions Center, 400 W. Capitol Ave. (1975)	454	30

Los Angeles, CA

Building	Ht. (ft.)	Stories
US Bank Tower, 633 W. 5th St. (1990)	1,018	73
Aon Center, 707 Wilshire Blvd. (1974)	858	62
Two California Plaza, 350 S. Grand Ave. (1992)	750	52
Gas Company Tower, 555 W. 5th St. (1991)	749	52
BP Plaza, 333 South Hope St. (1975)	735	55
777 Tower, 777 S. Figueroa St. (1991)	725	53
Wells Fargo Center, 333 S. Grand Ave. (1983)	723	54
Figueroa at Wiltshire, 601 S. Figueroa St. (1989)	717	52
Paul Hastings Tower, 515 S. Flower St. (1971)	699	52
Bank of America Tower, 555 S. Flower St. (1971)	699	52
Citigroup Center, 444 S. Flower St. (1979)	625	48
611 Place, 611 W. 6th St. (1969)	620	42
One California Plaza, 300 S. Grand Ave. (1985)	578	42
Century Plaza Tower 1, 2029 Cent. Park E. (1973)	571	44
Century Plaza Tower 2, 2049 Cent. Park E. (1973)	571	44
KPMG Tower, 355 S. Grand Ave. (1984)	560	45
Ernst & Young, LLP Plaza, 725 S. Figueroa St. (1986)	534	41
SunAmerica Tower, 1999 Ave. of the Stars (1989)	533	39
TCW Tower, 865 S. Figueroa St. (1990)	517	37
Union Bank Plaza, 445 S. Figueroa St. (1968)	516	40
10 Universal City Plaza (1984)	506	36
1100 Wilshire (1987)	496	36
Fox Plaza, 2121 Ave. of the Stars (1987)	492	34
Constellation Place, 10250 Constellation Blvd. (2003)	491	34
1055 W. 7th St. (1988)	462	33
Equitable Life, 3435 Wilshire Blvd. (1969)	454	34
City Hall, 200 N. Spring St. (1927)	454	28
SBC Tower, 1150 Olive St. (1965)	452	32
Madison Complex/Pacific Bell Switching Station, 420 S. Grand Ave. (1961)	448	17
5900 Wilshire Blvd. (1971)	435	32
Warner Center Plaza III, 21650 Oxnard St., Woodland Hills (1991)	415	25
MCI Plaza, 700 S. Flower St. (1973)	414	33
MTA Gateway Tower (1997)	405	26

Louisville, KY

Building	Ht. (ft.)	Stories
AEGON Center, 400 W. Market St. (1992)	549	35
National City Tower, 101 S. 5th St. (1972)	512	40
PNC Bank Bldg., 5th and Jefferson St. (1971)	420	30
Humana Center, 500 W. Main St. (1985)	417	27

Mexico City, Mexico

Building	Ht. (ft.)	Stories
Torre Mayor, Paseo de la Reforma 505 (2003)	738	55
Torre de Pemex, Marina Macional 329 Col. Huasteca (1984)	702	52
Torre Altus, Paseo de los Laureles 416 (1999)	640	42
Torre Latino Americana (incl. spire) (1956)	597	45
World Trade Center, Montecito 38 Col. Napoles (1972)	565	50
Los Arcos Bosques I, Paeo de los Tamarindos 400 (1997)	529	34
*Santa Fe Flats, Av. Santa Fe 443 (2005)	492	37
Torre Las Lomas (1993)	453	36
Hotel Nikko Mexico, Campos Eliseos 24	446	38
Torre del Caballito, Paseo de la Reforma 10	443	34
Torre Mural, Insurgentes Sur 1605 (1995)	440	33
Edificio Mexicana de Aviacion (1984)	433	30
*Torre Reforme El Angel, Paseo de la Reforma 347 (2005)	430	30
Presidente Inter-Continental Hotel, Campos Eliseos 218 (1976)	427	42
*Torre Libertad, Paseo de la Reforma 439 (2004)	427	30
Torre Insignia (1962)	417	25
Corporativo Santa Fe 505 (2003)	410	30
*Punta Poniente (2005)	410	30
Torre Reforma, Andres Bello 45	410	28

Miami, FL

Building	Ht. (ft.)	Stories
Four Seasons Hotel and Tower, 1441 Brickell Ave. (2003)	789	64
Wachovia Financial Center, 200 S. Biscayne Blvd. (1983)	764	55
*900 Biscayne Bay, 900 Biscayne Blvd. (2006)	712	65
Bank of America Tower, 100 S. E. 2nd St. (1987)	625	47
*Marinablue, 888 Biscayne Blvd. (2006)	615	57
*Plaza on Brickell Tower I, 901 Brickell Ave. (2006)	610	56
*Ten Museum Park, 1040 Biscayne Blvd. (2006)	585	50
*50 Biscayne Blvd. (2007)	554	55
*Quantum on the Bay South Tower, 1900 N. Bayshore Dr. (2007)	554	55
*Ice 2, 620 NE 31st St (2007)	545	54
*Opera Tower, 1750 N. Bayshore Dr. (2006)	543	56
*Everglades on the South Bay Tower, 244 Biscayne Blvd. (2006)	538	49
*Quantum on the Bay North Tower, 1900 N. Bayshore Dr. (2006)	536	48
Jade at Brickell Bay, 1295 Brickell Bay Dr. (2004)	528	49
*Plaza on Brickell Tower 2, 901 Brickell Ave (2006)	525	48
Santa Maria, 1643 Brickell Ave. (1997)	520	51
*The Ivy, 90 SW 3rd St. (2006)	512	45
Stephen P. Clark Center, 111 NW 1st St. (1985)	510	28
One Biscayne Tower, 2 S. Biscayne Blvd. (1973)	492	39
Espirito Santo Plaza, 1301 Brickell Ave. (2003)	487	36
Citicorp Tower at Miami Centre, 201 S. Biscayne Blvd. (1986)	484	35
*Brickell on the River North, 27 SE 5th St. (2005)	482	42
Three Tequesta Point, 848 Brickell Key Dr. (2001)	480	46
*Latitude on the River, 615 SW 2nd Ave. (2007)	476	44
*One Miami E. Tower, 205 S. Brickell Ave. (2005)	460	44
701 Brickell Ave. (1986)	450	33
*One Miami W. Tower, 205 S. Brickell Ave. (2005)	449	45
*Met 1, 300 SE 3rd St. (2006)	440	40
*Park Place at Brickell I, 1440 Brickell Ave. (2005)	439	36
Mellon Financial Center, 1111 Brickell Ave. (2001)	435	31
*The Loft 2, 133 NE 2nd Ave. (2007)	433	35
*Blue on the Bay, 510 NE 36th St. (2005)	425	36
*1800 Club, 1800 N. Bayshore Dr. (2006)	423	42
*Brickell on the River South, 31 SE 5th St. (2006)	423	42
Vue at Brickell, 1200 S. Miami Ave. (2004)	423	37
Mark on Brickell, 1155 Brickell Bay Dr. (2001)	420	36
The Club at Brickell Bay, 1200 Brickell Ave.	411	42
Two Tequesta Point, 808 Brickell Key Dr. (1999)	410	40
Courthouse Center, 175 NW First Ave. (1986)	405	30
The Palace, 1541 Brickell Ave. (1982)	400	42

Miami Beach, FL

Building	Ht. (ft.)	Stories
Blue Diamond Tower, 4779 Collins Ave. (2000)	559	44
Green Diamond Tower, 4775 Collins Ave. (2000)	559	44
Akoya Condominiums, 6365 Collins Ave. (2004)	492	47
PortofinoTower, 300 S. Pointe Dr. (1997)	484	44
The Continuum on South Beach, South Tower, 1 S.Pointe Dr. (2002)	474	43
ICON at South Beach, 450 Alton Rd. (2004)	423	43
Murano Grande at Portofino, 400 Alton Rd. (2003)	407	37
Murano at Portofino, 1000 S. Pointe Dr. (2001)	402	38

Milwaukee, WI

Building	Ht. (ft.)	Stories
U.S. Bank Center, 777 E. Wisconsin Ave. (1973)	601	42
100 E. Wisconsin Ave (1989)	549	37
*University Club Tower, 825 N. Prospect Ave. (2005)	446	36
Milwaukee Center, 111 E. Kilbourn Ave. (1987)	426	29
411 Bldg., 411 E. Wisconsin Ave. (1983)	408	30

Minneapolis, MN

Building	Ht. (ft.)	Stories
IDS Center, 80 8th St. S. (1973)[1]	792	57
225 South Sixth (1992)	776	56
Wells Fargo Center, 90 7th St. S. (1988)	774	57
33 S. 6th St. (1983)	668	52
Campbell Mithun Tower, 222 9th St. S. (1984)	579	42
US Bank Plaza, 200 6th St. S. (1981)	561	41
Dain Rauscher Plaza, 60 6th St. S. 1992)	539	40
Fifth Street Towers II, 150 5th St. S. (1988)	503	36
American Express Finance Center, 707 2nd Ave. South (2000)	498	31
Target Plaza South, 1020 Nicollet Mall (2001)	492	33
Plaza VII, 45 7th St. S. (1987)	475	36
*The Carlyle, 220 2nd St. S. (2006)	473	39
US Bancorp Center, 800 Nicollet Mall (2000)	468	32
AT&T Tower, 901 Marquette Ave. (1991)	464	34
Accenture Tower, 333 7th St. S. (1987)	455	33
Foshay Tower, 821 Marquette Ave. (1929)	447	32
Qwest, 224 5th St. S. (1931)	416	26
50 South Sixth (2001)	404	30
Hennepin Co. Government Center, 300 6th St. S. (1977)	403	24

(1) 910 ft. with antenna.

Montreal, Quebec

Building	Ht. (ft.)	Stories
Marathon (IBM) (incl. spire), 1250 Blvd. René Lévesque (1992)	743	47
1000 Rue de la Gauchetière (1992)	673	51
Tour de la Bourse, 800 Place Victoria (1963)	624	47
1 Place Villa Marie (1962)	616	42
La Tour CIBC, 1155 Blvd. René Lévesque (1962)	604	43
Montreal Tower (1987)	574	NA
Tour McGill College, 1501 McGill College (1992)	519	38
Le Complexe Desjardins Sud (1975)	498	40
Les Cooperants, 600 Maisonneuve (1987)	479	34
Place Montreal Trust, 1800 McGill College (1988)	440	30
Tour TELUS, 630 Blvd. René Lévesque (1962)	429	32
Le Complexe Desjardins Est (1975)	428	32
La Tour Laurier	425	36
Port Royal Apts., 1455 Sherbrooke Quest (1964)	424	33
Marriott Hotel, 1 Place du Canada (1967)	420	38
Tour de la Banque Nationale, 600 Rue de la Gauchetiere (1983)	420	29
Tour Bell, 700 Rue de la Gauchetiere (1983)	420	28
Centre Mount Royal, 1000 Sherbrooke Quest (1976)	420	28
Tour Terminal, 800 René Lévesque Blvd. Quest (1966)	400	30

IT'S A FACT: While being constructed in 1929, the Chrysler Building and the Bank of Manhattan Building (now the Trump Building) in New York City were locked in a "race for the sky" to become the world's tallest building. The Bank of Manhattan Building was finished first, at 927 feet—just 2 feet taller than the announced height of its rival. However, Chrysler Building architect William Van Alen had concealed a 27-ton, 185-foot steel spire inside the structure. When it was raised into place, it brought the total height to 1,046 ft, more than 100 feet taller than the Bank of Manhattan Building.

Nashville, TN

Building	Ht. (ft.)	Stories
BellSouth Tower (incl. spire), 333 Commerce St. (1994)	617	33
Sun Trust Bank, 424 Church St. (1986)	490	31
William R. Snodgrass Tennessee Tower, 311 7th Avenue North (1970)	452	31
Nashville Life & Casualty Tower, 401 Church St. (1957)	409	30
City Center, 511 Union St. (1987)	402	27

Newark, NJ

Building	Ht. (ft.)	Stories
Midatlantic National Bank, 744 Broad St. (1931)	465	36
1180 Raymond Blvd. (1930)	448	34

New Orleans, LA

Building	Ht. (ft.)	Stories
One Shell Square, 701 Poydras St. (1972)	697	51
Bank One Center, 201 St. Charles Ave. (1985)	645	53
Plaza Tower, 1001 Howard Ave. (1969)	531	45
Energy Centre, 1100 Poydras St. (1984)	530	39
LL&E Tower, 901 Poydras St. (1987)	481	36
Sheraton Hotel, 500 Canal St. (1985)	478	47
Marriott Hotel, 555 Canal St. (1972)	450	42
Texaco Center, 400 Poydras St. (1983)	442	33
Canal Place One, 365 Canal St. (1979)	439	32
Bank of New Orleans, 1010 Common St. (1971)	438	31
World Trade Center, 2 Canal St. (1965)	407	33
CNG Tower, 1450 Poydras St. (1989)	406	26

New York, NY

Building	Ht. (ft.)	Stories
Empire State Bldg., 350 5th Ave. (1931)[1]	1,250	102
Chrysler Bldg. (incl. spire), 405 Lexington Ave. (1930)	1,046	77
*New York Times Tower (incl. spire), 405 Lexington Ave. (2007)	1,046	52
American International Bldg., 70 Pine St. (1932)	952	67
*Bank of America Tower (2008)	945	67
The Trump Bldg., 40 Wall St. (1930)	927	71
Citigroup Center, 153 E. 53rd St. (1977)	915	59
Trump World Tower, 845 UN Plaza (2001)	861	72
G. E. Bldg., 30 Rockefeller Center (1933)	850	70
Cityspire, 150 W. 56th St. (1989)	814	75
One Chase Manhattan Plaza (1960)	813	60
Condé Nast Bldg., 4 Times Square (1999)[2]	809	48
MetLife Bldg., 200 Park Ave. (1963)	808	59
Bloomberg Tower, 731 Lexington Ave. (2005)[3]	806	55
Woolworth Bldg., 233 Broadway (1913)	792	57
1 Worldwide Plaza, 935 8th Ave. (1989)	778	47
Carnegie Hall Tower, 152 W. 57th St. (1991)	757	60
Bear Stearns World Hdq., 383 Madison Ave. (2001)	755	47
AXA Center, 787 7th Ave. (1985)	752	51
One Penn Plaza, 250 W. 34th St. (1972)	750	57
Time Warner Center North Tower, 10 Columbus Circle (2004)	750	55
Time Warner Center South Tower, 10 Columbus Circle (2004)	750	55
1251 Ave. of Americas (1971)	750	54
J.P. Morgan Headquarters, 60 Wall St. (1989)	745	55
One Astor Plaza, 1515 Broadway (1970)	745	54
1 Liberty Plaza, 165 Broadway (1973)	743	54
20 Exchange Place (1931)	741	57
*7 World Trade Center (2005)	741	52
American Express Tower, Three World Financial Center, 200 Vesey St. (1986)	739	51
Times Square Tower (2004)	726	47
Metropolitan Tower, 142 W. 57th St. (1985)	716	68
JP Morgan Chase World Headquarters, 270 Park Ave. (1960)	707	52
General Motors Bldg., 767 5th Ave. (1968)	705	50
Metropolitan Life Tower, 1 Madison Ave. (1909)	700	50
500 5th Ave. (1931)	697	60
Americas Tower, 1177 Ave. of the Amer. (1992)	692	48
Solow Bldg., 9 W. 57th St. (1974)	689	49
HSBC Bank Bldg., 140 Broadway (1967)	688	52
55 Water St. (1972)	687	53
277 Park Ave. (1963)	687	50
1585 Broadway (1989)	685	42
Random House, Park Imperial, 1739 Bway (2003)	684	52
Four Seasons Hotel, 57 E. 57th St. (1993)	682	52
Bertelsmann Bldg., 1540 Broadway (1990)	676	42
McGraw Hill Bldg., 1221 Ave. of Amer. (1972)	674	51
Lincoln Bldg., 60 E. 42nd St. (1930)	673	53
Paramount Plaza, 1633 Broadway (1970)	670	48
Trump Tower, 725 5th Ave. (1982)	664	58
Citicorp, Queens (1990)	658	50
Bank of New York Bldg., 1 Wall St. (1932)	654	50
599 Lexington Ave. (1986)	653	51
712 5th Ave. (1990)	650	53
Chanin Bldg., 122 E. 42nd St. (1929)	649	56
245 Park Ave. (1967)	648	47
Sony Bldg., 550 Madison Ave. (1983)	647	37
Merrill Lynch, Two World Financial Center, 225 Liberty St. (1986)	645	44
RCA Victor Bldg., 570 Lexington Ave. (1930)	642	50
One New York Plaza, 1 Water St. (1969)	640	50
1 Dag Hammarskjold Plaza, 885 2nd Ave. (1972)	637	48
345 Park Ave. (1968)	634	44
10 E. 40th St. (1929)	632	48
Grace Plaza, 1114 Ave. of the Amer. (1972)	630	50
Home Insurance Co., 59 Maiden Lane (1966)	630	44
Verizon Tower, 1095 Ave. of the Amer. (1970)	630	40
101 Park Ave. (1982)	629	49
Central Park Place, 301 W. 57th St. (1988)	628	56
888 7th Ave. (1971)	628	45
Alliance Capital Bldg., 1345 Ave. of the Amer. (1969)	625	50
Waldorf-Astoria, 301 Park Ave. (1931)	625	47
Trump Palace, 200 E. 69th St. (1991)	623	55
Olympic Tower, 645 5th Ave. (1976)	620	51
425 Fifth Avenue (2003)	618	55
*125 W. 31st St. (2006)	615	58
919 Third Ave. (1970)	615	47
750 7th Ave. (incl. spire) (1989)	615	35
New York Life, 51 Madison Ave. (1928)	615	33
Tower 49, 12 E. 49th St. (1985)	614	44
Credit Lyonnais Bldg., 1301 Ave. of the Amer. (1964)	609	46
*The Orion, 350 W. 42nd St. (2006)	604	58
IBM Headquarters, 590 Madison Ave. (1983)	603	41
*Hearst Tower, 959 8th Avenue, (2006)	596	42
3 Lincoln Center, 160 W. 66th St. (1993)	595	60
Celanese Bldg., 1211 Ave. of the Amer. (1973)	592	45
Rihga Royal Hotel, 151 W. 54th St. (1990)	590	54
U.S. Court House, 505 Pearl St. (1927)	590	37
Millenium Hilton Hotel, 55 Church St. (1992)	588	58
*Sky House, 11 E 29th St.	588	54
Museum Tower Apts., 21 W. 53rd St. (1985)	588	52
Time-Life, 1271 Ave. of the Amer. (1959)	587	48
Jacob K. Javits Fed. Bldg., 26 Fed. Plaza (1967)	587	41
*10 Barclay St.	584	56
W Times Square, 1567 Broadway (2000)	584	53
Trump International Hotel & Tower, 15 Columbus Circle (1970)	583	44
Stevens Tower, 1185 Ave. of Amer. (1971)	580	42
Municipal Bldg., 1 Centre St. (1914)	580	34
520 Madison Ave. (1981)	577	43
Oppenheimer & Co., 1 World Financial Ctr., 200 Liberty St. (1985)	577	37
Merchandise Mart, 41 Madison Ave. (1973)	576	42
Park Ave. Plaza, 55 E. 52nd St. (1981)	575	44
Lehman Building, 745 7th Ave., (2001)	575	38
One Financial Square, 33 Old Slip (1987)	575	37
Marriott Marquis Times Square, 1531 Bway (1985)	574	50
Westavco Bldg., 299 Park Ave. (1967)	574	42
Ernst & Young Tower, 5 Times Sq., 590 7th Ave. (2002)	574	40
1166 Ave. of the Americas (1974)	572	44
Socony Mobil, 150 E. 42nd Street (1956)	572	42
Wang Bldg., 780 3rd Ave. (1983)	570	49
AXA Finance Center, 1290 Ave. of the Amer. (1963)	570	43
600 3rd Ave. (1971)	570	42
450 Lexington Ave. (1991)	568	38
Paramount Tower, 240 E. 39th St. (1998)	567	51
Helmsley Bldg., 230 Park Ave. (1928)	566	35
New York Palace Hotel, 455 Madison Ave. (1980)	563	51
30 Broad St. (1932)	562	48
Park Ave. Tower, 65 E. 55th St. (1986)	561	36
Nelson Tower, 450 7th Ave. (1931)	560	46
Sherry-Netherland, 781 5th Ave. (1927)	560	40
Swiss Bank Tower, 10 E. 50th St. (1990)	560	36
100 UN Plaza, 327 E. 48th St. (1986)	557	52
Continental Can, 633 3rd Ave. (1962)	557	39
3 Park Ave. (1975)	556	42
Continental Corp., 180 Maiden Lane (1983)	555	41
Sperry & Hutchinson, 330 Madison Ave. (1964)	555	41
Reuters Bldg., 3 Times Square (2001)[4]	555	30
Madison Belvedere, 14 E. 29th St. (1999)	554	48
Inmont Bldg., 1133 Ave. of the Amer. (1970)	552	45
Equitable Trust Co. Bldg., 15 Broad St. (1927)	551	42
Biltmore Tower, 267 W. 47th St. (2003)	550	51
Burroughs Bldg., 605 3rd Ave. (1963)	550	44
Two Grand Central Tower, 140 E. 45th St. (1982)	550	44
Bell Atlantic, 33 Thomas St. (1974)	550	29
Bankers Trust, 33 E. 48th St. (1971)	547	41
The Corinthian, 330 E. 38th St. (1988)	546	55
Transportation Bldg., 225 Broadway (1928)	546	44
Millennium Tower, 101 W. 67th St. (1995)	545	54
Equitable, 120 Broadway (1915)	545	36
Galleria, 117 E. 57th St. (1975)	544	56
2 Gold Street (2004)	543	51
220 Riverside Blvd. at Trump Place (2003)	542	49
17 State St. (1988)	542	41
Grand Central Plaza, 622 Third Ave. (1973)	542	38
New York Telephone, 375 Pearl St. (1976)	540	42
Paine Webber Bldg., 1285 Ave. of the Amer. (1959)	540	42
Ritz Tower, 109 E. 57th St. (1925)	540	41
Bankers Trust, 16 Wall St. (1912)	540	39
Tribeca Tower, 105 Duane St. (1990)	537	53
Lefcourt Colonial Bldg., 295 Madison Ave. (1929)	537	45
300 Madison Ave. (2003)	535	35
1700 Broadway (1969)	533	41
Westin Hotel New York, 43rd St. and 8th Ave. (2002)	532	45
515 Park. Ave. (1999)	532	43
The Metropolis, 150 E. 44th St. (2001)	528	50

Building	Ht. (ft.)	Stories
North American Plywood, 800 3rd Ave. (1972)	526	41
Hotel Pierre, 2 E. 61st St. (1928)	525	44
767 3rd Ave. (1980)	525	39
Citibank, 399 Park Ave. (1961)	524	41
High Point Condominium, 250 E. 40th St. (1988)	522	49
Random House, 825 3rd Ave. (1969)	522	51
Du Mont Bldg., 515 Madison Ave. (1931)	520	42
26 Broadway (1922)	520	31
Newsweek Bldg., 444 Madison Ave. (1931)	518	42
Downtown Athletic Club, 19 West St. (1930)	518	39
964 Third Ave. (1969)	518	39
House of Seagram, 375 Park Ave. (1958)	518	38
Deutsche Bank, 130 Liberty St. (1974)	517	39
South Park Tower, 124 W. 60th St. (1986)	516	51
High Point Condominiums, 250 E. 40th St. (1988)	516	49
Sterling Drug Bldg., 90 Park Ave. (1964)	515	41
Navarre, 512 7th Ave. (1930)[5]	513	44
Bank of New York, 48 Wall St. (1927)	513	31
The Belaire, 524 E. 72d St. (1988)	512	50
Republic National Bank, Brooklyn, 1 Hansen Place (1929)	512	42
1407 Broadway Realty Corp. (1950)	512	41
International, Rockefeller Center, 630 5th Ave. (1935)	512	41
ITT-American, 437 Madison Ave. (1967)	512	40
Continental Bldg, 1450 Broadway (1931)	511	42
1155 Ave. of the Americas (1984)	511	40
10 Liberty St. (2004)	510	45
810 7th Ave. (1970)	506	41
The Sheffield Apts., 325 W. 56th St. (1978)	505	50
United Nations Secretariat Bldg., 405 42nd St. (1950)	505	39
1 UN Plaza (1975), 2 UN Plaza (1981)	505	39
2 New York Plaza, 125 Broad St. (1970)	504	40
22 E. 40th St. (1931)	503	43
60 Broad St. (1962)	503	39
Lefcourt National Bldg., 521 5th Ave. (1928)	503	37
1325 Ave. of the Americas (1989)	502	35
Sheraton Centre, 811 7th Ave. (1962)	501	51
World Apparel Center, 1411 Broadway (1969)	501	39
Bristol Plaza, 200 E. 65th St. (1987)	500	50
Pennmark Towers, 315 W. 33rd St. (2001)	500	35
Dow Jones, 4 World Fin. Center, 250 Vesey (1988)	500	34

(1) 1,455 ft. with antenna. (2) 1,118 ft. with antenna. (3) 941 ft. with antenna. (4) 659 ft. with antenna. (5) Site of World Almanac offices.

Oklahoma City, OK

Building	Ht. (ft.)	Stories
Bank One Tower, 100 N. Broadway Ave. (1971)	500	36
First National Center, 120 N. Robinson St. (1931)	493	33
City Place, 204 N. Robinson St. (1931)	440	32
Oklahoma Tower, 210 Park Ave. (1982)	434	31

Omaha, NE

Building	Ht. (ft.)	Stories
The Tower at First National Center, 1601 Dodge St. (2002)	634	45
Woodmen Tower, 1700 Farnam St. (1969)	478	30

Orlando, FL

Building	Ht. (ft.)	Stories
SunTrust Center Tower, 200 S. Orange Ave. (1988)	441	31
*Vue at Lake Eola (2006)	426	35
Orange Co. Courthouse, 425 N. Orange Ave. (1997)	416	24
Bank of America Center, 390 N. Orange Ave. (1988)	409	28

Philadelphia, PA

Building	Ht. (ft.)	Stories
*Comcast Center, 1701 JFK Blvd. (2007)	975	57
One Liberty Place (incl. spire), 1650 Market St. (1987)	945	61
Two Liberty Place, 1601 Chestnut St. (1989)	848	58
Mellon Bank Center, 1735 Market St. (1990)	792	54
Bell–Atlantic Tower, 1717 Arch St. (1991)	725	53
Blue Cross Tower, 1901 Market St. (1990)	625	45
Commerce Square #1, 2005 Market St. (1990)	572	40
Commerce Square #2, 2001 Market St. (1992)	572	40
City Hall (incl. statue) (1901)	548	7
1818 Market St. (1974)	500	40
The St. James, 700 Walnut St. (2004)	498	45
Loews Philadelphia Hotel , 12 S. 12th St. (1932)	492	39
PNC, 1600 Market St. (1983)	491	40
Centre Square II, 1542 Market St. (1973)	490	38
5 Penn Center (1970)	488	36
1700 Market St. (1969)	482	32
1 South Broad St. (1930)	472	28
Cira Centre, Arch St. and 30th St. (2005)	436	28
Two Logan Square, 100 N. 18th St. (1988)	435	34
2000 Market St. (1973)	435	29
11 Penn Center, 1835 Market St. (1985)	430	29
Aramark Tower, 1101 Market St. (1984)	417	31
Centre Square I, 1500 Market St. (1973)	416	32
First Union Bank, 123 S. Broad St. (1927)	405	30
Ritz-Carlton Hotel, 28 S. Broad St. (1930)	404	30
Lewis Tower, 1419 Locust St. (1929)	400	33
One Logan Square, 130 N. 18th St. (1982)	400	32

Phoenix, AZ

Building	Ht. (ft.)	Stories
Bank One Center, 201 N. Central (1972)	486	40
101 N. Second Ave. (1976)	407	31
*44 Monroe (2007)	400	34

Pittsburgh, PA

Building	Ht. (ft.)	Stories
US Steel Tower, 600 Grant St. (1970)	841	64
One Mellon Bank Center, 500 Grant St. (1983)	725	54
One PPG Place (1984)	635	40
Fifth Ave. Place, 120 5th Ave. (1987)	616	32
One Oxford Centre, 301 Grant St. (1982)	615	46
Gulf Tower, 707 Grant St. (1932)	582	44
Univ. of Pittsburgh Cath. of Learning, 4200 5th Ave. (1936)	535	42
3 Mellon Bank Center, 525 Wm. Penn Way (1951)	520	41
Freemarket Center, 210 6th Ave. (1968)	511	40
Grant Bldg., 330 Grant St. (1928)	485	40
Koppers Bldg., 436 7th Ave. (1929)	475	34
2 PNC Plaza, 620 Liberty Ave. (1976)	445	34
Dominion Tower, 625 Liberty Ave. (1987)	430	32
One PNC Plaza, 249 5th Avenue (1972)	424	30
Regional Enterprise Tower, 425 6th Ave. (1953)	410	30

Portland, OR

Building	Ht. (ft.)	Stories
Wells Fargo Center, 1300 SW 5th Ave. (1973)	546	40
U.S. Bancorp Tower, 111 SW 5th Ave. (1983)	536	42
Koin Tower Plaza, 222 SW Columbia St. (1984)	509	31
Pacwest Center, 1211 SW 5th Ave. (1984)	418	30

Providence, RI

Building	Ht. (ft.)	Stories
Fleet Bank Bldg., 55 Exchange Pl. (1927)	428	26
FleetBoston Tower (1973)	410	28

Richmond, VA

Building	Ht. (ft.)	Stories
James Monroe Bldg., 101 N. 14th St. (1981)	449	29
SunTrust Plaza, 919 E. Main St. (1984)	400	24

St. Louis, MO

Building	Ht. (ft.)	Stories
Gateway Arch (1965)	630	NA
Metropolitan Square Tower, 211 N. Broadway (1988)	593	42
One Bell Center, 900 Pine St. (1984)	588	44
Thomas F. Eagleton Fed. Courthouse, 111 S. 10th St. (2000)	557	29
U.S. Bank Plaza, 505 N. 7th St. (1976)	484	35
Laclede Gas Bldg., 720 Olive St. (1969)	400	31

St. Paul, MN

Building	Ht. (ft.)	Stories
Minnesota World Trade Center, 30 E. 7th St. (1987)	471	36
Galtier Plaza Jackson Tower, 168 E. 6th St. (1986)	453	46
First National Bank, 332 Minnesota St. (1930)	417	32

Salt Lake City, UT

Building	Ht. (ft.)	Stories
Wells Fargo Center, 299 S. Main St. (1998)	422	24
L.D.S. Church Office Bldg., 50 E. North Temple St. (1972)	420	28

San Antonio, TX

Building	Ht. (ft.)	Stories
Tower of the Americas, 600 Hemisphere Way (1968)	622	NA
Marriott Rivercenter, 101 Bowie St. (1988)	546	38
*Hyatt Downtown Convention Center Hotel (2008)	525	43
Weston Centre, 112 Pecan St. (1988)	444	32
Tower Life, 310 S. St. Mary's St. (1929)	404	30

San Diego, CA

Building	Ht. (ft.)	Stories
One American Plaza, 600 W. Broadway (1991)	500	34
Symphony Tower, 759 B St. (1989)	499	34
Manchester Grand Hyatt, One Market Pl. (1992)	497	40
*Electra, 701 W. Broadway (2007)	475	43
*Pinnacle Museum Tower, 500 Front St. (2005)	450	36
Emerald Plaza, 400 W. Broadway (1990)	450	30
Manchester Grand Hyatt Tower 2, One Market Pl. (2003)	446	32
One and Two Harbor Drive (2 bldgs.), 100 Harbor Dr. (1992)	424	41
*The Grande North at Santa Fe Pl. (2005)	420	39
*The Grande South at Santa Fe Pl. (2004)	420	39
*Broadway 655 (2005)	412	23

Sandy Springs, GA

Building	Ht. (ft.)	Stories
Concourse Corp. Center V, 5 Concourse Pkwy. (1988)	570	34
Concourse Corp. Center VI, 6 Concourse Pkwy. (1991)	553	34

San Francisco, CA

Building	Ht. (ft.)	Stories
Sutro Tower (1972)	977	NA
Transamerica Pyramid, 600 Montgomery St. (1972)	853	48
Bank of America, 555 California St. (1969)	779	52
345 California Center (1986)	695	48
101 California St. (1986)	600	48
50 Fremont (1983)	600	43
575 Market Center (1975)	573	40
Four Embarcadero Center, 55 Clay St. (1984)	570	45
One Embarcadero Center, 355 Clay St. (1970)	569	45
Wells Fargo, 44 Montgomery St. (1967)	565	43
Spear Tower, 1 Market St. (1976)	565	42
Citicorp Center, 1 Sansome St. (1984)	550	39
Shaklee Terrace Bldg., 444 Market St. (1982)	537	38
One Post Plaza, 1 Post St. (1969)	529	38
525 Market St. (1972)	529	38
One Metro Plaza, 425 Market St. (1973)	524	38
Pacific Telesis Center, 1 Montgomery St. (1971)	500	38
333 Bush St. (1986)	495	43
Hilton Hotel, 201 Mason St. (1971)	493	46
Pacific Gas & Electric, 77 Beale St. (1971)	492	34
50 California St. (1972)	487	37
*St. Regis Museum Tower, 3rd and Mission (2005)	484	42
100 Pine Center (1972)	476	27
Bechtel Bldg., 45 Fremont St. (1979)	475	34
333 Market Bldg. (1979)	474	33
*Hartford Bldg., 650 California St. (1965)	465	33
*300 Spear 1 (2007)	450	41
100 First Plaza (1988)	447	37
One California St. (1969)	438	32
Marriott Hotel, 777 Market St. (1989)	436	39
Russ Bldg., 235 Montgomery St. (1927)	435	32
Pacific Bell Hdqtrs., 140 Montgomery St. (1925)	435	26

Building	Ht. (ft.)	Stories
JP Morgan Chase Bldg., 560 Mission St. (2002)	421	31
Paramount, 680 Mission St. (2002)	418	41
Providian Financial Bldg., 201 Mission St. (1983)	416	30
Two Embarcadero Center, 255 Clay St. (1974)	412	31
Three Embarcadero Center, 155 Clay St. (1976)	412	31
595 Market Bldg. (1977)	412	31
123 Mission Bldg. (1986)	406	29
Embarcadero Center West, 275 Battery St. (1988)	405	33
101 Montgomery St. (1983)	405	29

Seattle, WA

Building	Ht. (ft.)	Stories
Bank of America Center, 701 5th Ave. (1985)[1]	933	76
Washington Mutual Tower, 1201 3rd Ave. (1988)	772	55
Two Union Square, 601 Union St. (1989)	740	56
Seattle Municipal Tower, 700 5th Ave. (1990)	722	57
1001 Fourth Avenue Plaza (1969)	609	50
*Museum Plaza Tower, 1301 2nd Ave. (2006)	608	42
Space Needle, 203 6th Ave. (1962)	605	NA
U.S. Bank Centre, 1420 5th Ave. (1989)	580	44
Wells Fargo Center, 999 3rd Ave. (1983)	574	47
800 Fifth Avenue Plaza (1981)	543	42
Security Pacific Bank, 900 4th Ave. (1973)	536	41
Rainier Tower, 1301 5th Ave. (1977)	514	31
IDX Tower, 915 4th Ave. (2003)	512	40
1000 2nd Ave. (1986)	493	40
Henry M. Jackson Bldg., 915 2nd Ave. (1974)	487	37
Qwest Plaza, 1600 7th Ave. (1976)	466	33
Smith Tower, 506 2nd Ave. (1914)	465	38
One Union Square, 600 University Ave. (1981)	456	36
1111 3rd Ave. (1980)	454	34
Westin Hotel North Tower, 1900 5th Ave. (1982)	448	44
Westin Bldg., 2001 6th Ave. (1981)	409	34

(1) 997 ft. with antenna

Southfield, MI

Building	Ht. (ft.)	Stories
Prudential, 3000 Town Center (1975)	448	32
1000 Town Center (1988)	405	32

Sunny Isles Beach, FL

Building	Ht. (ft.)	Stories
Trump Palace, 18101 Collins Ave. (2005)	551	43
*Trump Royale, 18201 Collins Ave. (2007)	551	43
*Jade on the Beach Condominiums, 17001 Collins Ave. (2006)	550	53
Aqualina, 17875 Collins Ave. (2004)	550	51
The Pinnacle, 17555 Collins Ave. (1999)	476	40
Ocean Two Condominiums I and II (2 bldgs.), 19111 Collins Ave. (2001)	426	40
Ocean Three Condominiums, 18925 Collins Ave. (2003)	405	37

Tampa, FL

Building	Ht. (ft.)	Stories
AmSouth Bldg., 100 N. Tampa St. (1992)	579	42
Bank of America Plaza, 101 E. Kennedy Blvd. (1986)	577	42
One Tampa City Center, 201 N. Franklin St. (1981)	537	39
Suntrust Financial Center, 401 E. Jackson St. (1992)	525	36
Park Tower, 400 N. Tampa St. (1973)	458	36
400 N. Ashley Plaza, 400 N. Ashley Dr. (1988)	454	33

Toledo, OH

Building	Ht. (ft.)	Stories
One SeaGate (1982)	411	32
Hytower, Jefferson St. and St. Clair St. (1970)	400	30

Toronto, Ontario

Building	Ht. (ft.)	Stories
CN Tower, 310 Front St. W (1976)	1,815	NA
First Canadian Place, 100 King St. West (1975)[1]	978	72
Scotia Plaza, 40 King St. West (1989)	902	68
BCE Place, Canada Trust Tower, 161 Bay St. (1990)	856	53
Commerce Court West, 199 Bay St. (1973)[2]	784	57
TD Centre–Toronto Dominion Bank Tower, 66 Wellington St. West (1967)	731	56
BCE Place, Bay-Wellington Tower, 181 Bay St. (1991)	679	49
TD Centre–Royal Trust Tower, 77 King St. W. (1969)	600	46
*1 King West (2004)	578	51
Royal Bank Plaza–South Tower, 200 Bay St. (1976)	567	41
44 Charles St. West (1974)	545	51
*Residences @ College Park I, Bay St. and College St. (2005)	505	51
TD Centre–79 Wellington St. West (1985)	504	39
The 250, 250 Yonge St. (1991)	494	35
*Harbourview Estates Phase 2 (2005)	491	49
Two Bloor West (1974)	488	34
Simcoe Place, 200 Front St. (1995)	486	33
*West One (2005)	484	49
Exchange Tower, 130 King St. West (1983)	480	30
CIBC-Commerce Court North, 25 King St. West (1931)	476	34
Spire (2005)	476	45
Simpson Tower, 401 Bay St. (1968)	472	33
Cadillac-Fairview Tower, 20 Queen St. West (1982)	466	36
Pantages Tower (2002)	458	45
One Palace Pier Court, Etobicoke (1991)	455	46
Three Palace Pier Court, Etobicoke (1978)	453	46
Laurentian Bank Bldg., 130 Adelaide St. West (1980)	450	35
Sheraton Centre, 123 Queen St. West (1972)	443	43
Two Bloor East (1974)	439	35
Royal York Hotel, 200 Front Street (1929)	439	26
TD Centre–Ernst & Young Tower, 222 Bay St. (1990)	437	31
*Empire Tower, 17 Barberry Pl. (2005)	427	28
One Financial Place, 1 Adelaide St. E.(1991)	424	31
Leaside Towers (2 bldgs.), 95 Thorncliffe Park Dr. 1970)	423	44
TD Centre–Maritime Life Tower, 100 Wellington St. West (1974)	420	32
Metro Hall West, 55 John St. (1991)	420	27
Marriott Hotel/Plaza 2 Apts., 90 Bloor St. East (1973)	415	41
Sun Life Financial Centre East Tower, 150 King St. West (1981)	410	27
Young-Eglington Centre I, 2300 Younge St. (1974)	408	30

(1) 1,116 ft. with antenna. (2) 942 ft. with antenna.

Tulsa, OK

Building	Ht. (ft.)	Stories
Williams Center, 1 W. 2nd St. (1975)	667	52
Cityplex Central Tower, 2448 E. 81st St. (1981)	648	60
First National Bank, 15 E. 5th St. (1973)	516	41
Mid-Continent Tower, 401 S. Boston St. (1984)	513	36
Fourth National vBank, 15 W. 6th St. (1966)	412	33
National Bank of Tulsa, 320 S. Boston St. (1918)	400	24

Vancouver, British Columbia

Building	Ht. (ft.)	Stories
*Living Shangri-La, 1120 W. Georgia St. (2008)	642	60
One Wall Centre, 1000 Burrard St. (2001)	491	45
Shaw Tower, 298 Thurlow St. (2004)	489	40
200 Granville Square (1973)	466	32
*The Melville, 1189 Melville St. (2006)	464	43
Royal Bank Tower, 1055 W. Georgia St. (1973)	461	37
Park Place, 666 Burrard St. (1984)	459	35
Bentall IV Canada Trust, 1055 Dunsmir (1981)	454	36
Scotia Tower, 650 W. Georgia St. (1977)	452	36
Harbour Centre, 555 W. Hastings (1977)	426	28
TD Bank Tower, 700 W. Georgia St. (1970)	417	30
Bentall III, Bank of Montreal, 595 Burrard St. (1974)	400	31

Winnipeg, Manitoba

Building	Ht. (ft.)	Stories
CanWest Global Place, 201 Portage Ave. (1990)	420	33
Richardson Bldg., 1 Lombard Place (1969)	406	34

Winston-Salem, NC

Building	Ht. (ft.)	Stories
Wachovia Center, 100 N. Main St. (1995)	460	34
301 N. Main St. (1965)	410	26

Other Tall Buildings in North American Cities

Building		Ht. (ft.)	Stories
*RSA Battlehouse Tower (2006)	Mobile, AL	745	35
Dataflux Tower (2000)	Monterrey, Mexico	597	43
Erastus Corning II Tower (1973)	Albany, NY	589	44
Washington Monument (1884)	Washington, DC	555	NA
One HSBC Center (1970)	Buffalo, NY	529	40
Vehicle Assembly Bldg. (1965)	Cape Canaveral, FL	525	40
Frost Bank Tower (2004)	Austin, TX	516	33
Mohegan Sun Hotel (2002)	Uncasville, CT	487	34
Borgata Hotel and Casino (2003)	Atlantic City, NJ	480	40
State Capitol (1932)	Baton Rouge, LA	460	34
Tower Burbank, 3900 W. Alameda (1988)	Burbank, CA	460	32
Las Olas River House 1 (2004)	Ft. Lauderdale, FL	452	42
*One Lincoln Tower (2005)	Bellevue, WA	450	42
The Diplomat (2002)	Hollywood, FL	444	39
Ravinia #3 (1991)	Dunwoody, GA	444	33
Xerox Tower (1967)	Rochester, NY	443	30
One Summit Square (1981)	Fort Wayne, IN	442	27
Anadarko Tower (2002)	The Woodlands, TX	439	32
BBT/Two Hanover Square (1991)	Raleigh, NC	431	29
Union Planters Bank (1965)	Memphis, TN	430	38
Taj Mahal, 1000 Boardwalk (1990)	Atlantic City, NJ	429	43
Torre Commercial America (1994)	Monterrey, Mexico	427	35
AmSouth Bank Bldg. (1969)	Mobile, AL	424	33
Wells Fargo Center (1991)	Sacramento, CA	423	30
Century 21	Hamilton, Ont.	418	43
Hidden Bay 1 (2000)	Aventura, FL	417	40
Galaxie Apts. (3 bldgs.) (1976)	Guttenberg, NJ	415	44
Complexe G (1972)	Quebec City, Que.	415	33
AmSouth Bank Bldg. (1996)	Montgomery, AL	415	24
*Lincoln Tower 2, 770 Bellevue Way NE (2006)	Bellevue, WA	412	27
One Shoreline Plaza, South Tower (1988)	Corpus Christi, TX	411	28
Silver Legacy Hotel & Casino (1995)	Reno, NV	410	38
110 Tower (1988)	Ft. Lauderdale, FL	410	30
Lexington Financial Center (1987)	Lexington, KY	410	30
Plaza in Clayton (2002)	Clayton, MO	409	30
Kettering Tower (1970)	Dayton, OH	408	30
Ordway Bldg. (1985)	Oakland, CA	404	28
Morgan Keegan Tower	Memphis, TN	403	34
Three Lakeway Center (1987)	Metairie, LA	403	34
Clark Tower (1972)	Memphis, TN	400	34
Monarch Place (1987)	Springfield, MA	400	26
Bank of America (1990)	St. Petersburg, FL	400	26
Riverview Tower (1977)	Knoxville, TN	400	24
*Ocean Palms Phase I, 3101 S. Ocean Dr. (2006)	Hollywood, Fl	400	38

Notable Bridges in North America

Source: Federal Highway Administration, Bridge Division, U.S. Dept. of Transportation; World Almanac research

Asterisk (*) designates railroad bridge. Year is date of completion. Span of a bridge is the distance between its supports.

Suspension

Year	Bridge	Location	Main span (ft.)
1964	Verrazano-Narrows	New York, NY	4,205
1937	Golden Gate	San Fran. Bay, CA	4,200
1957	Mackinac Straits	Sts. of Mackinac, MI	3,800
1931	Geo. Washington	Hudson R., NY–NJ	3,500
2003	Carquinez (Al Zampa Memorial)	Solano, CA	3,478
1940	Tacoma Narrows	Tacoma, WA	2,800
1950	Tacoma Narrows II	Tacoma, WA	2,800
1936	San. Fran.-Oakland Bay[1]	San Fran. Bay, CA	2,310
1939	Bronx-Whitestone	East R., NY	2,300
1970	Pierre Laporte	Quebec, Canada	2,190
1951	Del. Memorial	Wilmington, DE	2,150
1957	Walt Whitman	Philadelphia, PA	2,000
1929	Ambassador	Detroit, MI–Can.	1,850
1961	Throgs Neck	Long Is. Sound, NY	1,780
1926	Benjamin Franklin	Philadelphia, PA	1,750
1924	Bear Mt.	Hudson R., NY	1,632
1903	Williamsburg	East R., NY	1,600
1952	Wm. Preston La. Mem.[2]	Sandy Point, MD	1,600
1969	Newport	Narragansett Bay, RI	1,600
1883	Brooklyn	East R., NY	1,596
1939	Lion's Gate	Burrard Inlet, BC	1,550
1963	Vincent Thomas	L. A. Harbor, CA	1,500
1930	Mid-Hudson	Poughkeepsie, NY	1,495
1909	Manhattan	East R., NY	1,470
1953	MacDonald Bridge	Halifax, Nova Scotia	1,447
1970	A. Murray Mackay	Halifax, Nova Scotia	1,400
1936	Triborough Br.,QB Mainline	East R., NY	1,380
1931	St. Johns	Portland, OR	1,207
1929	Mount Hope	RI	1,200
1960	Ogdensburg-Prescott	St. Lawrence R., NY	1,150
1965	Bidwell Bar Bridge	Oroville, CA	1,108
1964	Middle Fork Feather	Butte Co., CA	1,105
1939	Deer Isle	ME	1,080
1931	Simon Kenton Memorial	Ohio R., Maysville, KY	1,060
1936	Ile d'Orleans	St. Lawrence R., Quebec	1,059
1867	John A. Roebling	Ohio R., KY	1,057
1971	Dent	Clearwater Co., ID	1,050
1900	Miampimi	Mexico	1,030
1849	Wheeling	Ohio R., WV	1,010

Cantilever

Year	Bridge	Location	Main span (ft.)
1917	Québec Bridge	St. Lawrence R., Quebec	1,800
1988	Greater New Orleans Bridge	Mississippi R., New Orleans, LA	1,575
1936	East Bay	San Fran. Bay, CA	1,499
1995	Gramercy Bridge	Mississippi R., Gramercy, LA	1,460
1968	Baton Rouge Bridge	Mississippi R., Baton Rouge, LA	1,235
1953	Tappan Zee	Hudson R., NY	1,212
1930	Lewis and Clark	Longview, WA–OR	1,200
1909	Queensboro	East R., NY	1,182
1927	Carquinez Strait	San Fran. Bay, CA	1,100
1958	Parallel Span	San Fran. Bay, CA	1,100
1930	Jacques Cartier	Montreal, Quebec	1,097
1968	Isaiah D. Hart	Jacksonville, FL	1,088
1956	Richmond-San Rafael[3]	San Fran. Bay, CA	1,070
1929	Grace Memorial	Charleston, SC	1,050
1980	Newburgh-Beacon	Hudson R., NY	1,000
1949	Martin Luther King	St. Louis, MO	963
1975	Caruthersville	Mississippi R., MO–TN	920
1969	Silver Memorial	Pt. Pleasant, WV–OH	900
1977	Saint Marys	Saint Marys, WV–OH	900
1981	Ravenswood	WV	900
1987	Carl Perkins	Ohio R., KY	900
1941	Mississippi R.	Natchez, MS	875
1988	Mississippi R.	Natchez, MS	875
1938	Blue Water	Pt. Huron, MI	871
1972	Mississippi R.	Vicksburg, MS	870
1972	N. Fork American R.	Auburn, CA	862
1940	*Baton Rouge	Mississippi R., LA	848
1899	*Cornwall	St. Lawrence R., LA	843
1940	Rte. 82	Mississippi R., AR	840
1961	Mississippi R.	Greenville, MS	840
1963	Brent Spence	KY–OH	830
1940	Mississippi R.	Vicksburg, MS	825
1963	Mississippi R.	Donaldsonville, LA	825
1931	Mississippi R.	Vicksburg, MS	824
1929	Clark Memorial	Ohio R., KY	820
1961	Campbellton-Cross Pt.	New Brunswick, Can.	815
1932	Washington Mem.	Seattle, WA	800
1935	Rip Van Winkle	Catskill, NY	800
1938	Cairo	Ohio R., IL–KY	800
1936	McCullough	Coos Bay, OR	793
1949	Memphis	Mississippi R., TN	790
1935	Huey P. Long[4]	New Orleans, LA	790
1949	Rte. 55	Mississippi R., AR–TN	790
1910	*P&LE RR Bridge	Ohio R., PA	750
1930	Coal Grove Bridge	Ashland-Coal Grove Bridge, OH	739
1922	Ohio River, N&W RR	Ironton-Russell Bridge, OH	725
1932	Bi-State Vietnam Gold Star	Henderson, KY	720
1979	I-275	Ohio R., Fort Thomas, KY	720
1926	Columbia R.	Cascade Locks, OR	706
1964	John F. Kennedy (I-65)	Ohio R., Louisville, KY	700
1928	Ohio River, B&O RR, HV RR	Pomeroy-Mason, OH	657
1941	*Pit River	Redding, CA	630
1941	Columbia R.	Kettle Falls, WA	600
1954	Columbia R.	Umatilla, OR	600
1965	Bi-State Vietnam Gold Star	Henderson , KY	600
1954	Columbia R.	The Dalles, OR	576
1968	W. 17th St.	Huntington, WV	562

Simple Truss

Year	Bridge	Location	Main span (ft.)
1976	Chester	Chester, WV	745
1929	Irvin S. Cobb	Ohio R., IL–KY	716
1922	*Tanana R.	Nenana, AK	700
1967	I-77, Ohio R.	Williamstown, WV	650
1917	MacArthur[4]	St. Louis, IL–MO	647
1992	St. Charles	Missouri R, MO	625
1933	Atchafalaya	Morgan City, LA	608
1924	*Castleton	Hudson R., NY	598
1937	Delaware R.	Easton, PA	550
1930	Swindell Bridge	Pittsburgh, PA	545
1952	Allegheny R. Tpk.	Pittsburgh, PA	534
1951	Rankin	Pittsburgh, PA	525
1914	Old Brownsville	Brownsville, PA	520
1906	Donora-Webster	Donora-Webster, PA	515
1909	Hulton	Pittsburgh, PA	505
1967	Tanana R.	AK	500

Steel Truss

Year	Bridge	Location	Main span (ft.)
1988	Glade Creek	Raleigh Co., WV	784
1973	Atchafalaya R.	Krotz Springs, LA	780
1972	Piscataqua R.	NH–ME	756
1972	Atchafalaya R.	Simmesport, LA	720
1957	SR-3, Rappahannock R.	Middlesex Co., VA	648
1978	Atchafalaya R.	Morgan City, LA	607
1959	Summit	Summit, DE	600
1969	Reedy Point	Delaware City, DE	600
1937	US-22	Delaware R., NJ	550
1955	Interstate (I-5)	Columbia R., OR–WA	531
1910	McKinley, St. Louis[4]	Mississippi R., MO	517
1972	Mississippi R.	Muscatine, IA	512
1896	Newport	Ohio R., KY	511
1989	US 190, Atchafalaya R.	Krotz Springs, LA	506
1900	Norfolk Southern RR	Cincinnati, OH	500
1931	Lucy Jefferson Lewis	Cumberland R., KY	500
1958	Lake Oahe	Gettysburg, SD	500
1958	Lake Oahe	Mobridge, SD	500
1970	Lake Koocanusa	Lincoln Co., MT	500

Continuous Truss

Year	Bridge	Location	Main span (ft.)
1966	Columbia R. (Astoria)	OR–WA	1,232
1976	Francis Scott Key	Baltimore, MD	1,200
1981	Ravenswood/Ohio R.	Ravenswood, WV	902
1995	Central	Ohio R., KY–OH	850
1943	Dubuque	Mississippi R., IA	845
1966	Charles Braga	Fall River, MA	840
1956	Earl C. Clements[5]	Ohio R., IL–KY	825
1929	U.S. 31	Ohio R., IN–KY	820
1953	John E. Mathews	Jacksonville, FL	810
1950	Maurice J. Tobin	Boston, MA	801
1940	Gov. Nice Memorial	Potomac River, MD	800
1957	Kingston-Rhinecliff	Hudson R., NY	800
1992	Mark Clark Expy. I-526	Cooper R., Charleston, SC	800
1986	Rochester-Monaca	Rochester-Monaca, PA	780
1940	U.S. 231	Ohio R., IN	750
1974	Carroll L. Cropper (I-275)	Ohio R., IN–KY	750
1981	Sewickley	Sewickley, PA	750
1984	13th St. Bridge, Ohio R.	Ashland, KY	740
1959	Monaca-E. Rochester	Monaca-E. Rochester, PA	730
1976	Betsy Ross	Philadelphia, PA	729
1929	U.S. 421	Ohio R., IN–KY	727
1967	Matthew E. Welsh[6]	Mauckport, IN	725
1962	U.S. 41	Ohio R., IN–KY	720
1994	6th St.	Huntington, WV	720
1970	Vanport	Vanport, PA	715
1962	Champlain	Montreal, Que.	707
1962	John F. Kennedy (I-65)[7]	Ohio R., IN–KY	701
1973	Girard Point	Philadelphia, PA	700
1954	PA Tpk., Delaware R.	Philadelphia, PA	682
1938	Rainbow Br., Neches R.	Port Arthur-Orange, TX	680
1949	George Platt	Philadelphia, PA	680
1926	Cape Girardeau	Mississippi R., MO	677
1946	Chester	Mississippi R, IL	670
1994	Williamstown-Marietta	Williamstown, WV	650
1955	Jefferson City	Missouri R., MO	640
1930	Quincy Memorial Bridge	Mississippi R., IL	628
1959	US 181, over harbor	Corpus Christi, TX	620

Year	Bridge	Location	Main span (ft.)
1961	Shippingport	Shippingport, PA	620
1935	Bourne-Sagamore	Cape Cod Canal, MA	616
1965	Clarion R. (I-80)	Clarion, PA	612
1975	Donora-Monessen	Donora-Monessen, PA	608
1957	Blatnik	Duluth, MN	600
1965	Rio Grande Gorge	Taos, NM	600
1991	Hoffstadt Creek	Mt. St. Helens, WA	600
1991	Jefferson City	Missouri R., MO	596
1962	W. Branch Feather R.	Oroville, CA	576
1967	Glenwood	Pittsburgh, PA	567
1936	Mark Twain Mem.	Hannibal, MO	562
1932	Pulaski Skyway	Passaic R.-Hackensack R., NJ	550
1966	Emlenton	Emlenton, PA	540
1973	Gold Star Memorial	New London, CT	540
1936	Homestead High Level	Pittsburgh, PA	534
1962	Benicia Martinez	Benicia-Martinez, CA	528
1960	Brownsville High Level	Brownsville, PA	518
1971	Grandad	Elk River, ID	504
1945	Mansfield-Dravosburg	Pittsburgh, PA	500

Continuous Box and Plate Girder

Year	Bridge	Location	Main span (ft.)
1967	San Mateo-Hayward #2	San Fran. Bay, CA	750
1976	Intracoastal Canal	Forked Is., LA	750
1977	Intracoastal Canal	Gibbstown, LA	750
1969	San Diego-Coronado[8]	San Diego Bay, CA	660
1987	Umatilla, Columbia R.	OR–WA	660
1994	Acosta	Jacksonville, FL	630
1981	Douglas	Juneau, AK	620
1976	Wax L. Outlet	Calumet, LA	618
1963	Poplar St.	St. Louis, MO	600
1981	Glenn Jackson (I-205)	Columbia R., OR–WA	600
1976	Stanislaus River	Sonora, CA	550
1982	Illinois R.	Pekin, IL	550
1982	I-440	Arkansas R., AR	540
1980	US-64, Tennessee R.	Savannah, TN	525
1965	McDonald-Cartier	Ottawa, Ont.	520
1988	Mon City	Monongahela, PA	520
1984	Columbia R.	Richland, WA	450
1986	Veterans	Pittsburgh, PA	440
1987	SR 76, Cumberland R.	Dover, TN	440
1987	SR 20, Tennessee R.	Perryville, TN	440
1970	Willamette R., I-205	West Linn, OR	430
1974	I-430	Arkansas R., AR	430
1965	I-24, Tennessee R.	Marion Co., TN	420
1974	Dunbar-S. Charleston	S. Charleston, WV	420
1975	36th St.	Charleston, WV	420
1978	Snake R.	Clarkston, WA	420
1984	FAU 3456, TN R.	Chattanooga, TN	420

Continuous Plate

Year	Bridge	Location	Main span (ft.)
1973	Sidney Sherman Bridge, I-610	Houston, TX	630
1971	W. Atchafalaya	Henderson, LA	573
1992	State Route 76	Paris, TN	525
1997	SR 114, Clifton	Tennessee R., TN	525
1981	Illinois 23	Illinois R., IL	510
1968	IH-45 over Trinity R.	Dallas, TX	480
1978	San Joaquin R.	Antioch, CA	460
1977	Thomas Johnson Mem.	Solomons, MD	451
1967	Mississippi R.	La Crosse, WI	450
1975	I-129	Missouri R., IA–NE	450
1979	Lewis	St. Louis, MO	450
1992	Cuba Landing Bridge	Tennessee R., TN	450
1966	I-480	Missouri R., IA–NE	425
1972	Whiskey Bay Pilot	Ramah, LA	425
1972	I-80	Missouri R., IA–NE	425
1972	I-635, Kansas City	Missouri R., KS–MO	425
1983	US-36	Missouri R., KS–MO	425
1987	I-435	Missouri R., KS–MO	425
1978	I-24	Cumberland R., KY	420
1993	Bob Michel Bridge	Peoria, IL	360
1999	SR 53, Clear Fork River	Fentress/Morgan Co., TN	350

Cable-Stayed

Year	Bridge	Location	Main span (ft.)
2005	Arthur Ravenel Jr.	Cooper River, SC	1,546
1986	Annacis (Alex Fraser)	Vancouver, BC	1,526
1993	Quetzalapa Bridge	Quetzalapa, Mexico	1,391
1988	Dames Point	Jacksonville, FL	1,300
1995	Fred Hartlan Bridge, Houston Ship Channel	Baytown,TX	1,250
1983	Hale Boggs Memorial	Luling, LA	1,222
1987	Sunshine Skyway	Tampa Bay, FL	1,200
1988	Tampico/Panuco R.	Mexico	1,181
1988	ALRT Fraser River Bridge	Vancouver, BC	1,115
1990	Talmadge Mem.	Savannah, GA	1,100
1993	Mezcala	Mex. City/Acapulco Hwy.	1,024
1978	Pasco-Kennewick	Columbia R., WA	981
1984	Coatzacoalcos R.	Mexico	919
1985	E. Huntington	E. Huntington, WV	900
1987	Bayview Bridge	Quincy, IL	900
1970	Burton Bridge	New Brunswick, Canada	850
1990	Weirton-Steubenville	WV–OH	820
1969	Papineau-Leblanc	Montreal, Que.	790
1991	Cochrane	Mobile, AL	780
1994	Clark Bridge	Alton, IL	756
1995	Chesapeake & Delaware Canal Bridge	Dover-Wilmington, DE	750
2002	Leonard Zakim	Bunker Hill, Boston, MA	745
1966	Longs Creek	New Brunswick, Canada	713
1967	Hawkshaw	New Brunswick, Canada	713
1993	Quetzalapa Bridge	Quetzalapa, Mexico	699
1993	Burlington Bridge	Burlington, IA	660
1991	Veterans Memorial Br., Neches R.	Port Arthur-Orange,TX	640
1989	James River Bridge	Richmond, VA	630

I-Beam Girder

Year	Bridge	Location	Main span (ft.)
1980	Interstate 20	Shreveport, LA	438
2001	Moore Haven Bridge	Caloosahachee Canal, FL	320
1988	Route 18	Weston's Mill Pond, NJ	276

Steel Arch

Year	Bridge	Location	Main span (ft.)
1977	New River Gorge	Fayetteville, WV	1,700
1931	Bayonne (Kill Van Kull)	Bayonne, NJ	1,675
1973	Fremont	Portland, OR	1,255
1964	Port Mann	Vancouver, BC	1,200
1967	Laviolette	Trois-Rivières, Quebec	1,100
1992	Roosevelt Lake	Roosevelt Lake, AZ	1,080
1917	*Hell Gate	East R., N.Y	1,038
1959	Glen Canyon	Page, AZ	1,028
1962	Lewiston-Queenston	Niagara R., Ont.	1,000
1976	Perrine	Twin Falls, ID	993
1941	Rainbow Bridge	Niagara Falls, NY	984
1977	Moundsville	Ohio R., WV	912
1992	I-255, Miss. R.	St. Louis, MO	909
1972	I-40, Miss. R.[9]	AR–TN	900
1936	Henry Hudson	Harlem R., NY	840
1967	Lincoln Trail Bridge	Ohio R., IN–KY	825
1978	I-57, Miss. R.	Cairo , IL	821
1961	Sherman-Minton Bridge, I-64	IN	800
1980	I-65, Mobile R.	Mobile, AL	800
1930	West End	Pittsburgh, PA	780
1978	I-470 Bridge, Ohio R.	Wheeling, WV	780
1996	Navajo Bridge	Glen Canyon, AZ	726
1959	Kosciusko Twin	Mohawk R., NY	600
1917	Cuyohoga River	Cleveland, OH	591
2002	Paper Mill Ridge Road	Baltimore, MD	518

Concrete Arch

Year	Bridge	Location	Main span (ft.)
1995	Natchez Trace Pkwy.	Franklin, TN	582
1993	Lake Street Bridge	St. Paul, MN	556
1971	Selah Creek (twin)	Selah, WA	549
1968	Cowlitz R.	Mossyrock, WA	520
1931	Westinghouse	Pittsburgh, PA	460
1923	Cappelen	Minneapolis, MN	435
2000	Crooked River Gorge	Madras, OR	410
1930	Jack's Run	Pittsburgh, PA	400
1931	Rogue River	Gold Beach, OR	230

Segmental Concrete

Year	Bridge	Location	Main span (ft.)
1997	Confederation Bridge	Prince Edward Isl., NB	820
1978	Shubenacadie River	S. Maitland, Nova Scotia	790
1982	Jesse H, Jones Memorial	Houston, TX	750
1992	Narragansett Bay Crossing	Jamestown, RI	674
2002	SR-895, James R. & I-95	Richmond, VA	672
1986	WB I-82 (Columbia R.)	Umatilla, OR	660
1978	Stanislaus River	Parrets Ferry. CA	640
1992	Jamestown-Verrazano	Jamestown, RI	636
1981	Gastineau Channel Br.	Juneau, AK	620
1991	Veterans Memorial Centennial Bridge	Coeur d'Alene, ID	520
2001	Smart Highway	Blacksburg, VA	472
1974	Pine Valley Creek	Pine Valley, CA	450
1988	Zilwaukee Bridge (twin)	Zilwaukee, MI	392
1985	Red River Bridge	Boyce, LA	370

Twin Concrete Trestle[10]

Year	Bridge	Location	Main span (ft.)
1979	I-55/I-10	Manchac, LA	181,157
1969	L. Pontchartrain Cswy.	Mandeville, LA	126,720
1972	Atchafalaya Flwy.	Baton Rouge, LA	93,984
1963	L. Pontchartrain	Slidell, LA	28,547
1983	*Interstate 310	Kenner, LA	25,925

Concrete Slab Dam[10]

Year	Bridge	Location	Main span (ft.)
1927	Conowingo Dam	MD	4,611
1952	SR-4, Roanoke R.	Mecklenburg Co., VA	2,785
1936	Hoover Dam	Lake Mead, NV	1,324

Miscellaneous Bridges

Year	Bridge	Type	Loc.	Main span (ft.)
1962	International	Arch Truss	Sault Ste. Marie, MI	430
1997	Second Blue Water	Continuous Tied Arch	Pt. Huron, MI	922
1982	SR 193	Seg. Box Girder	Dauphin Is., AL	400
1958	Castleton	Through Truss	Hudson R., NY.	598
1939	US 43, Tenn. R.	Through Truss	Florence, AL	420
1958	SR 117, Tenn. R.	Through Truss	Stevenson, AL.	500
1936	Yaquina Bay	Steel Braced and Concrete Tied Arches	Newport, OR	600
1958	Tomibigbee R.	Steel Girder	Choctow Co., AL	400
1916	C&O RR	Steel Girder	Portsmouth, OH	775
1987	Powder Point[10]	Tropical Hardwood	Duxbury, MA	2,200
2002	Croatan Sound[10]	Continuous Postension Girder	Manteo, NC	5.2 mi

Drawbridges

Vertical Lift

Year	Bridge	Location	Main span (ft.)
1959	*Arthur Kill	NY–NJ	558
1965	Pennsylvania Railroad	Kirkwood-Mt. Pleas., DE	548
1935	*Cape Cod Canal	Cape Cod, MA	544
1961	*Delair	Delaware R., NJ	542
1931	Burlington-Bristol	Delaware R., NJ–PA	540
1937	Marine Parkway	Jamaica Bay, NY	540
1908	*Willamette R.	Portland, OR	521
1968	Second Narrows	Vancouver, B.C.	493
1912	*A-S-B Fratt	Kansas City, MO	428
1945	*Harry S Truman	Kansas City, MO	427
1955	Roosevelt Island	East R., NY	418
1980	US-17, James R.	Isle of Wight, Co., VA	415
1932	*M-K-T R.R.	Missouri R., MO	414
1969	Cape Fear Mem.	Wilmington, NC	408
1930	Aerial	Duluth, MN	386
1962	Burlington	Ontario, Can.	370
1941	Main Street	Jacksonville, FL	365
1967	SR-156, James R.	Prince George Co., VA	364
1950	Red R.	Moncla, LA	360
1957	Industrial Canal	New Orleans, LA	360
1936	Triborough	Harlem R., NY	344
1939	U.S. 1&9, Passaic R.	Newark, NJ	333
1930	*Martinez	Martinez, CA	328
1960	St. Andrews Bay	Panama City, FL	327
1929	*Penn-Lehigh	Newark Bay, PA	322
1987	Industrial Canal	New Orleans, LA	320
1920	*Chattanooga	Tennessee R., TN	310
1961	Broadway	Harlem R., NY	304
1910	Willamette R. Hawthorne	Portland, OR	244

Steel Suspension

Year	Bridge	Location	Main span (ft.)
1931	Maumee R.	Toledo, OH	785

Bascule

Year	Bridge	Location	Main span (ft.)
1917	SR-8, Tennessee R.	Chattanooga, TN	306
2003	*SW 2nd Avenue Br.	Miami, FL	302
1956	Duwamish R.	Seattle, WA.	300
1955	Chehalis R.	Aberdeen, WA	288
1968	Elizabeth R.	Chesapeake, VA.	280
1913	Broadway	Portland, OR.	278
1936	Siuslaw River	Florence, OR	154

Swing Bridges

Year	Bridge	Location	Main span (ft.)
1927	Fort Madison[4]	Mississippi R., IA	545
1991	SW. Spokane St.	Seattle, WA.	480
1930	Rigolets Pass	New Orleans, LA	400
1950	Douglass Memorial	Washington, DC	386
1945	Lord Delaware	Mattaponi R., VA	252

Swing Span

Year	Bridge	Location	Main span (ft.)
1897	*Duluth	St. Louis Bay, MN	486
1899	*C.M.&N.R.R.	Chicago, IL	474
1913	Rt. 82, Conn-R.	E. Haddam, CT	465
1914	*Coos Bay RR Xing	OR	458
1936	Umpqua River	Reedsport. OR	430

Floating Pontoon

Year	Bridge	Location	Main span (ft.)
1963	Evergreen Pt.	Seattle, WA.	7,578
1961	Hood Canal	Pt. Gamble, WA	6,521
1993	Lacey V. Murrow[11]	Seattle, WA.	6,620
1989	Third Lake Washington	Seattle, WA.	5,811

(1) Swing span bridge with 2 spans of 2,310 ft. each. (2) A second bridge in parallel was completed in 1978. (3) The Richmond Bridge has twin spans 1,070 ft. each. (4) Railroad and vehicular bridge. (5) Two spans each 825 ft. (6) Two spans each 707 ft. (7) Two spans each 700 ft. (8) Two spans each 660 ft. (9) Two spans each 900 ft. (10) Length listed is total length of bridge. (11) Replaces the original Lacey V. Murrow bridge, which opened in 1940 and sank in 1990.

Oldest U.S. Bridges in Continuous Use

Built in 1697, the stone-arch Frankford Ave. Bridge crosses Pennypack Creek in Philadelphia, PA. A 3-span bridge with a total length of 75 ft., it was constructed as part of the King's Road, which eventually connected Philadelphia to New York.

The oldest covered bridge, completed in 1827, is the double-span, 278-ft. Haverhill Bath Bridge, which spans the Ammonoosuc River, between the towns of Bath and Haverhill, NH.

Some Notable International Bridges

Span of bridge is the distance between its supports. Asterisk (*) designates under construction.

Suspension

Year	Bridge	Location	Main span (ft.)
1998	Akashi Kaikyo	Japan	6,570
NA	*Izmit Bay	Turkey	5,538
1998	Storebælt (East Bridge)	Denmark	5,328
2005	Runyang	China	4,888
1981	Humber	England	4,626
1999	Jiangyin Yangtze	China	4,544
1997	Tsing Ma[1]	China	4,518
1997	Hoga Kusten	Sweden	3,970
1988	Minami Bisan-Seto	Japan	3,609
1988	Bosphorus II	Turkey	3,576
1973	Bosphorus I	Turkey	3,524
1999	Kurushima III	Japan	3,379
1999	Kurushima II	Japan	3,346
1966	Tagus River[2]	Portugal	3,323
1964	Forth Road	Scotland	3,300
1988	Kita Bisan-Seto	Japan	3,248
1966	Severn	England	3,241
2001	Yichang	China	3,150
1988	Shimotsui Strait	Japan	3,084

Steel Arch

Year	Bridge	Location	Main span (ft.)
2003	Lupu Bridge	China	1,800
1932	Sydney Harbour	Australia	1,650
1967	Zdakov	Czech Republic	1,244
1962	Thatcher	Panama Canal Zone	1,128
1961	Runcorn-Widnes	England	1,082
1935	Birchenough	Zimbabwe	1,080

Concrete Arch

Year	Bridge	Location	Main span (ft.)
1997	Wanxian Bridge	China	1,378
1980	Krk I	Croatia	1,280
1964	Gladesville	Australia	1,000
1964	Amizade	Brazil	951
1963	Arrabida	Portugal	886
1943	Sando	Sweden	866

Cantilever

Year	Bridge	Location	Main span (ft.)
1917	Quebec Bridge	Canada	1,800
1890	Forth[3] (rail)	Scotland	1,710
1974	Nanko	Japan	1,673

Steel Plate and Box Girder

Year	Bridge	Location	Main span (ft.)
1974	President Costa e Silva	Brazil	984
1956	Sava I	Serbia & Montenegro	856
1966	Zoobrüke	Germany	850

Cable-Stayed

Year	Bridge	Location	Main span (ft.)
2005	Millau Viaduc	France	8,071
1999	Tatara	Japan	2,920
1995	Pont de Normandie	France	2,808
1996	Quingzhou Minjang	China	1,985
1993	Yangpu	China	1,975
1997	Xupu	China	1,936
1998	Meiko Chuo	Japan	1,936
1991	Skarnsundet	Norway	1,739
1999	Queshi	China	1,700
1995	Tsurumi Tsubasa	Japan	1,673
2000	Oresund	Denmark/Sweden	1,614
1991	Ikuchi	Japan	1,608
1994	Higashi Kobe	Japan	1,591
1998	Zhanjiang	China	1,575
1997	Ting Kau	China	1,558
1999	Seo Hae Grand	South Korea	1,542
1989	Yokohama Bay	Japan	1,509
1993	Second Hooghly River	India	1,499
1995	Second Severn Crossing	England/Wales	1,496

WORLD ALMANAC QUICK QUIZ

Which of these nations is home to 5 of the 10 tallest buildings in the world?

(a) United States (b) United Arab Emirates (c) China (d) Great Britain

For the answer look in this chapter, or see page 1008.

IT'S A FACT: The Pennsylvania Turnpike is home to 5 of the 15 longest land vehicular tunnels in the U.S. It was known as the "tunnel highway" when it opened in 1940, running through 7 former railroad tunnels along a 160-mile route. In the 1960s a campaign called "Peace, Love and the Pennsylvania Turnpike" promoted safe driving with signs such as "The road to success is always under construction" and "Spread the love, let someone merge."

World's Longest Railway Tunnels

Source: World Almanac research
(* = under construction)

Tunnel	Date	Miles	Operating railway	Country
Sei-kan	1988	33.5	Japan Railways	Japan
English Channel Tunnel	1994	33.5	Eurotunnel	UK-France
*Loetschberg	2007	21.5	BLS AlpsTransit	Switzerland
*Guadarrama	2007	17.6	NA	Spain
Iwate-ichinohe	2002	16.0	Japan Railways	Japan
Dai-shimizu	1982	13.8	Japan Railways	Japan
Simplon No. 1 and 2	1906, 1922	12.3	BLS Lötschberbahn AG	Switzerland-Italy
Vereina	1999	11.8	Rhätische Bahn	Switzerland
*Channel Tunnel Link	2007	11.8	CTRL	UK
Shin-Kanmon	1975	11.6	Japan Railways	Japan
Vaglia	2006	11.5	Italian state	Italy
Apennino	1934	11.5	Italian state	Italy
Qinling No. 1 and 2	2002	11.5	Chinese state	China
Rokko	1972	10.1	Japan Railways	Japan
Furka Base Tunnel	1982	9.6	Furka Oberalp Bahn	Switzerland
Haruna	1982	9.5	Japan Railways	Japan
Severomuyskiy	2001	9.5	Baikal-Amur (state-owned)	Russia
Gorigamine	1997	9.4	Japan Railways	Japan
Monte Santomarco	1987	9.3	Italian state	Italy

Underwater Vehicular Tunnels in North America

(more than 5,000 ft. in length; year in parentheses is year of completion)

Name	Location	Waterway	Feet
Brooklyn-Battery (1950) (twin)	New York, NY	East River	9,117
Holland Tunnel (1927) (twin)	New York, NY	Hudson River	8,557
Ted Williams Tunnel (1995)	Boston, MA	Boston Harbor	8,448
Lincoln Tunnel (1937, 1945, 1957) (3 tubes)	New York, NY	Hudson River	8,216
Thimble Shoal Channel (1964)	Northampton Co., VA	Chesapeake Bay	8,187
Chesapeake Channel (1964)	Northampton Co., VA	Chesapeake Bay	7,941
Fort McHenry Tunnel (1985) (twin)	Baltimore, MD	Baltimore Harbor	7,920
Hampton Roads (1957) (twin)	Hampton, VA	Hampton Roads	7,479
Baltimore Harbor Tunnel (1957) (twin)	Baltimore, MD	Patapsco River	7,392
Queens Midtown (1940) (twin)	New York, NY	East River	6,414
Sumner Tunnel (1934)	Boston, MA	Boston Harbor	5,653
Louis-Hippolyte Lafontaine Tunnel	Montreal, Que.	St. Lawrence River	5,280
Detroit-Windsor (1930)	Detroit, MI	Detroit River	5,160
Callahan Tunnel (1961)	Boston, MA	Boston Harbor	5,070

Land Vehicular Tunnels in the U.S.

Source: Federal Highway Administration
(more than 3,000 ft. in length)

Name	Location	Feet
Anton Anderson Mem. Tunnel[1]	Whittier, AK	13,300
E. Johnson Memorial	I-70, CO	8,959
Eisenhower Memorial	I-70, CO	8,941
Allegheny (twin)	PA Turnpike	6,072
Liberty Tubes	Pittsburgh, PA	5,920
Zion Natl. Park	Rte. 9, UT	5,766
East River Mt.	Mercer Co., WV/ Bland Co., VA	5,654
East River Mt. (twin)	VA–WV	5,412
Tuscarora (twin)	PA Turnpike	5,400
Tetsuo Harano (twin)	H-3, HI	5,165
Kittatinny (twin)	PA Turnpike	4,660
Cumberland Gap (twin)	KY–TN	4,600
Blue Mountain (twin)	PA Turnpike	4,435
Lehigh (twin)	PA Turnpike	4,379
Wawona	Yosemite Natl. Pk., CA	4,233
Big Walker Mt. (twin)	Bland Co., VA	4,229
Squirrel Hill	Pittsburgh, PA	4,225
Hanging Lake (twin)	Glenwood Canyon, CO	4,000
Caldecott (3 tubes)	Oakland, CA	3,616
Fort Pitt (twin)	Pittsburgh, PA	3,560
Mount Baker Ridge	Seattle, WA	3,456
Devil's Side Tunnel	U.S. 101 CA	3,400
Dingess Tunnel	Mingo Co., WV	3,400
Mall Tunnel	Dist. of Columbia	3,400
Cody No. 1	U.S. 14, 16, 20, WY	3,202

(1) Tunnel is used for vehicular and railroad traffic.

Major Dams of the World

Source: Intl. Commission on Large Dams, *World Register of Dams*

World's Highest Dams

Rank order	Name	Country	Height above lowest formation (m)
1.	Rogun*	Tajikistan	335
2.	Nurek*	Tajikistan	300
3.	Xiaowan (Yunnan Gorge)*	China	292
4.	Grand Dixence	Switzerland	285
5.	Inguri	Georgia	272
6.	Vajont	Italy	262
7.	Manuel M. Torres	Mexico	261
8.	Tehri*	India	261
9.	Alvaro Obregon	Mexico	260
10.	Mauvoisin	Switzerland	250
11.	Mica	Canada	243
12.	Alberto Lleras C	Colombia	243
13.	Sayano-Shushenskskaya	Russia	242
14.	Ertan*	China	240
15.	La Esmeralda	Colombia	237
16.	Kishau*	India	236
17.	Oroville	U.S.	235
18.	El Cajón	Honduras	234
19.	Chirkey	Russia	233
20.	Shuibuya*	China	233

*Under construction.

World's Largest-Volume Embankment Dams

Rank order	Name	Country	Volume cubic meters x 1000
1.	Tarbela	Pakistan	148,500
2.	Fort Peck Gorge	U.S.	96,050
3.	Tucurui	Brazil	85,200
4.	Ataturk	Turkey	85,000
5.	Yacyreta	Argentina	81,000
6.	Rogun*	Tajikistan	75,500
7.	Oahe	U.S.	70,339
8.	Guri	Venezuela	70,000
9.	Parambikulam	India	69,165
10.	High Island West	China	67,000
11.	Gardiner	Canada	65,000
12.	Afsluitdijk	Netherlands	63,400
13.	Mangla	Pakistan	63,379
14.	Oroville	U.S.	59,635
15.	San Luis	U.S.	59,559
16.	Nurek*	Tajikistan	58,000
17.	Tanda	Pakistan	57,250
18.	Garrison	U.S.	50,843
19.	Cochiti	U.S.	50,228
20.	Oosterschelde	Netherlands	50,000

Major U.S. Dams and Reservoirs

Source: Committee on Register of Dams, Corps of Engineers, U.S. Army, Sept. 2005

Highest U.S. Dams

Rank Order	Dam name	River	State	Type	Height Feet	Height Meters	Year completed
1.	Oroville	Feather	California	E	770	230	1968
2.	Hoover	Colorado	Nevada-Arizona	A	730	221	1936
3.	Dworshak	N. Fork Clearwater	Idaho	G	717	219	1973
4.	Glen Canyon	Colorado	Arizona	A	710	216	1964
5.	New Bullards Bar	North Yuba	California	A	645	194	1969
6.	Seven Oaks	Santa Ana	California	E	632	193	1999
7.	New Melones	Stanislaus	California	R	625	191	1979
8.	Mossyrock	Cowlitz	Washington	A	606	185	1968
9.	Shasta	Sacramento	California	G	602	183	1945
10.	Don Pedro	Tuolumne	California	G	585	178	1971

E = Embankment, Earthfill; R = Embankment, Rockfill; G = Gravity; A = Arch.

Largest U.S. Embankment Dams

Rank Order	Dam name	River	State	Type	Volume Cubic yards x 1000	Volume Cubic meters x 1000	Year completed
1.	Fort Peck	Missouri	Montana	E	125,624	96,050	1957
2.	Oahe	Missouri	South Dakota	E	91,996	70,339	1958
3.	Oroville	Feather	California	E	77,997	59,635	1968
4.	San Luis	San Luis Creek	California	E	77,897	59,559	1967
5.	Garrison	Missouri	North Dakota	E	66,498	50,843	1953
6.	Cochiti	Rio Grande	New Mexico	E	65,693	50,228	1975
7.	Fort Randall	Missouri	South Dakota	E	49,962	38,200	1952
8.	Castaic	Castaic Creek	California	E	43,998	33,640	1973
9.	Ludington P/S	Lake Michigan	Michigan	E	37,699	28,824	1973
10.	Kingsley	N. Platte	Nebraska	E	31,999	24,466	1941

E = Earthfill.

Largest U.S. Reservoirs

Rank Order	Dam name	Reservoir name	State	Reservoir capacity Cubic meters x 1000	Year completed
1.	Hoover	Lake Mead	Nevada	34,850,000	1936
2.	Glen Canyon	Lake Powell	Arizona	33,300,000	1964
3.	Garrison	Lake Sakakawea	North Dakota	27,920,000	1953
4.	Oahe	Lake Oahe	South Dakota	27,430,000	1966
5.	Fort Peck	Fort Peck Lake	Montana	22,120,000	1957
6.	Grand Coulee	F. D. Roosevelt Lake	Washington	11,790,000	1942
7.	Libby	Lake Koocanusa	Montana	7,170,000	1973
8.	Shasta	Lake Shasta	California	5,610,000	1945
9.	Toledo Bend	Toledo Bend Lake	Louisiana	5,520,000	1966
10.	Fort Randall	Lake Francis Case	South Dakota	5,700,000	1954

World's Largest-Capacity Reservoirs

Source: Intl. Commission on Large Dams, *World Register of Dams*

Rank Order	Name	Country	Capacity cubic meters x 1,000,000
1.	Kariba Gorges	Zimbabwe/Zambia	180,600
2.	Bratsk	Russia	169,000
3.	High Aswan	Egypt	162,000
4.	Akosombo	Ghana	147,960
5.	Daniel Johnson	Canada	141,851
6.	Guri	Venezuela	135,000
7.	W.A.C. Bennett	Canada	74,300
8.	Krasnoyarsk	Russia	73,300
9.	Zeya	Russia	68,400
10.	La Grande 2	Canada	61,715
11.	La Grande 3	Canada	60,020
12.	Ust-Ilim	Russia	59,300
13.	Boguchany	Russia	58,200
14.	Kuibyshev	Russia	58,000
15.	Serra da Mesa	Brazil	54,400

World's Largest-Capacity Hydro Plants

Source: Intl. Commission on Large Dams, *World Register of Dams*

Rank[1]	Name	Country	Rated capacity planned (MW)
1.	Sanxia (Three Gorges Dam)*	China	18,200
2.	Itaipu	Brazil	12,600
3.	Guri (Raúl Leoni)	Venezuela	10,000
4.	Tucuruí	Brazil	8,370
5.	Sayano-Shushenskaya*	Russia	6,400
6.	Itaipu	Paraguay	6,300
7.	Krasnoyarsk	Russia	6,000
8.	Bratsk	Russia	4,500
9.	Longtan (Guangxi, Tian'e)	China	4,200
10.	Xiaowan (Yunnan)	China	4,200
11.	Ust-Ilim	Russia	3,840
12.	Ilha Solteira	Brazil	3,230
13.	Ertan	China	3,300
14.	Yacyreta	Argentina/ Paraguay	3,100
15.	Xingo	Brazil	3,000
16.	Macagua II	Venzuela	2,940
17.	Gezhouba	China	2,715
18.	Minamiaiki	Japan	2,700
19.	Volgograd	Russia	2,541
20.	Chief Joseph Dam	U.S.	2,512

(1) Ranked by rated capacity planned. *Planned or under construction.

IT'S A FACT: The Loetschberg Tunnel, burrowing 21 miles though the Alps from Bern, Switzerland, to ski areas to the south, will be the world's longest overland tunnel, and the 3rd longest railroad tunnel of all, when it opens in 2007. Excavation of the tunnel was completed in April 2005, as the two halves were joined together and workmen waved Swiss flags to the accompaniment of a mountain melody.

TRAVEL AND TOURISM

Tourism Trends

After slumping by 1.2% in 2003, world tourist arrivals rebounded sharply, by 10.7% in 2004, according to the World Tourism Organization based in Madrid, Spain. Worldwide, there were 763 million international tourist arrivals in 2004, 74 million more than in 2003. Worldwide tourism receipts as measured in constant U.S. dollars and prices rose 10.3%. Tourism receipts also reached a record value of $622 billion in 2004 (compared to $525 billion in 2003), but roughly half that gain resulted from the depreciation of the U.S. dollar, causing receipts in other currencies to convert to higher amounts. Europe once again commanded the largest share of international arrivals, 54.4% of the world total, with 415.2 million international tourist arrivals, an increase of 4.9%. After a 9.3% decrease in 2003, largely due to the aftermath of the SARS outbreak, Asia and the Pacific tourism posted the 2nd-largest share of world tourism at 20.1%, with 152.9 million arrivals in 2004, an increase of 27.8% over 2003. Africa saw 33.2 million arrivals, up by 8.2%. The Middle East had 35.6 million arrivals, a 20.5% increase from 2003. With 125.7 million arrivals, the Americas experienced their first increase in tourism in 3 years, up by about 11.1% from 2003.

The upward trend continued in the first months of 2005, except in many areas affected by the Dec. 26, 2004, tsunami. The tourism industry in Maldives was hardest hit, with arrivals falling by 52.8% in the first 4 months of 2005 as compared to 2004; Indonesia also posted a slight decline, of 1.4%. On the other hand, several tsunami-affected countries, including Bali, Sri Lanka, and Thailand, were posting double-digit increases by Mar. 2005. Travel in all regions continued to climb, especially South America and the Middle East. The International Air Transport Assoc., which measures air passenger traffic in revenue passenger kilometers, reported an 8.7% increase in international passenger traffic in Jan.-Apr. 2005, compared with the same period in 2004. The Middle East and Latin America regions had the largest increases, at 13.6% and 13.7%, respectively. According to the Air Transport Assoc. of America, international air passenger traffic in the U.S. (measured in revenue passenger miles) rose by 12.3% in the first four months of 2005 compared with same period in 2004.

World Tourism Receipts, 1990-2004[1]

Source: World Tourism Organization

(in billions; figures rounded)

Year	Receipts	Year	Receipts	Year	Receipts	Year	Receipts	Year	Receipts
1990	$264	**1993**	$323	**1996**	$439	**1999**	$455	**2002**	$474
1991	278	**1994**	356	**1997**	443	**2000**	473	**2003**	525
1992	317	**1995**	405	**1998**	445	**2001**	459	**2004**	622

(1) Tourism receipts are the total of all expenditures made by or on behalf of visitors, for and during the trip and stay.

Top 10 Countries in Tourism Earnings, 2004

Source: World Tourism Organization

International tourism receipts (excluding transportation); in billions of dollars

Rank	Country	Receipts 2004	Receipts 2003	% change
1.	United States	$74.5	$64.3	15.7
2.	Spain	45.2	39.6	14.1
3.	France	40.8	36.6	11.6
4.	Italy	35.7	31.2	14.1
5.	Germany	27.7	23.1	19.7
6.	United Kingdom	$27.3	$22.7	20.5
7.	China[1]	25.7	17.4	47.9
8.	Turkey	15.9	13.2	20.3
9.	Austria	15.4	14.0	10.4
10.	Australia	13.0	10.3	25.5

(1) Excluding Hong Kong.

Average Number of Vacation Days per Year, Selected Countries

Source: World Tourism Organization

Country	Days	Country	Days	Country	Days
Italy	42	Brazil	34	Korea	25
France	37	United Kingdom	28	Japan	25
Germany	35	Canada	26	United States	13

World's Top 10 Tourist Destinations, 2004

Source: World Tourism Organization

(number of arrivals in millions; excluding same-day visitors)

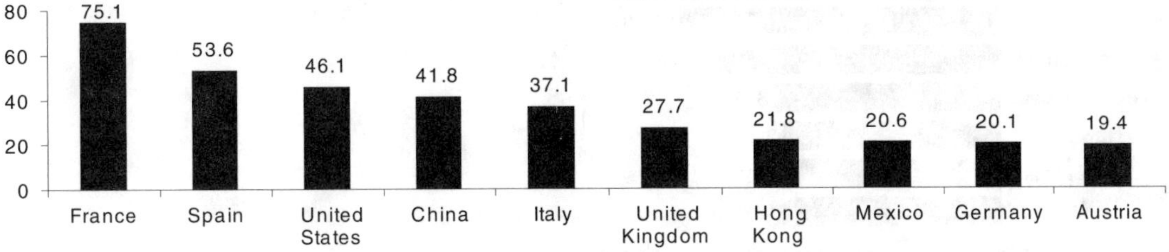

International Travel to the U.S., 1986-2004

Source: Office of Travel and Tourism Industries, Dept. of Commerce

(Visitors each year are in millions; some figures are revised and may differ from other sources.)

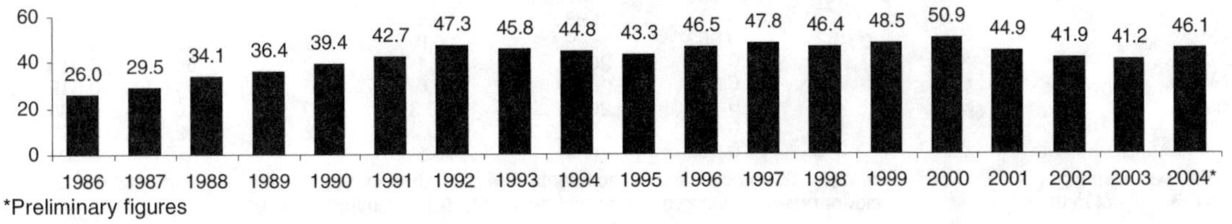

*Preliminary figures

International Visitors to the U.S., 2003[1]

Source: Office of Travel and Tourism Industries, Dept. of Commerce

Country of origin	Visitors (thousands)	Expenditures (millions)[2]	Expenditures per visitor	Country of origin	Visitors (thousands)	Expenditures (millions)[2]	Expenditures per visitor
Canada[3]	12,666	$6,844	$540	Brazil	349	$1,214	$3,479
Mexico[3]	10,526	5,861	557	Venezuela	284	964	3,394
United Kingdom	3,936	8,579	2,152	Spain	284	846	2,979
Japan	3,170	7,595	2,396	India	272	1,180	4,338
Germany	1,180	2,953	2,503	China	271	1,050	3,875
France	689	1,739	2,524	Israel	249	732	2,940
South Korea	618	2,151	3,481	Taiwan	239	659	2,757
Italy	409	1,130	2,763	Switzerland	230	624	2,713
Australia	406	1,502	3,700	Sweden	211	513	2,431
Netherlands	374	1,022	2,733	**All countries**	**41,218**	**64,500**	**1,565**

(1) Excludes cruise travel. (2) Excludes international passenger fare payments. (3) Does not include international traveler spending on U.S. carriers for transactions made outside the U.S.

Traveler Spending in the U.S., 1987-2003

Source: Office of Travel and Tourism Industries, Dept. of Commerce
(in billions)

	Domestic Travelers	International Travelers		Domestic Travelers	International Travelers		Domestic Travelers	International Travelers
1987	$235	$31	1993	$323	$58	1999	$458	$75
1988	258	38	1994	340	58	2000	488	82
1989	273	47	1995	360	63	2001	479	72
1990	291	43	1996	385	70	2002	474	67
1991	296	48	1997	406	73	2003	491*	65
1992	306	55	1998	425	71			

*Preliminary figure.

U.S. Domestic Leisure Travel Volume, 1994-2004[1]

Source: Travel Industry Assn. of America, TravelScope
(in millions of person-trips of 50 mi or more, one-way)

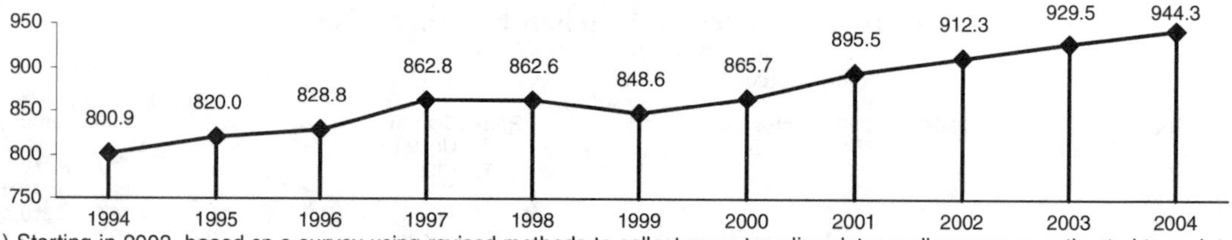

(1) Starting in 2003, based on a survey using revised methods to collect more traveling data; earlier years re-estimated to maintain comparability.

Top U.S. States by Domestic Traveler Spending

Source: Travel Industry Assn. of America
(billions of dollars; in 2003)

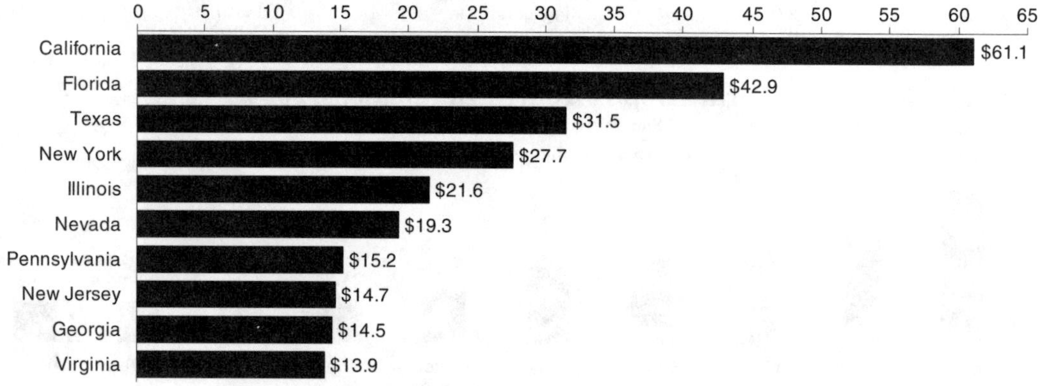

U.S. Airline Safety, Scheduled Commercial Carriers, 1985-2004

Source: Federal Aviation Administration

	Departures (millions)	Fatal accidents	Fatalities	Accident rate[1]		Departures (millions)	Fatal accidents	Fatalities	Accident rate[1]
1985	6.1	4	197	0.066	1997	9.9	3	3	0.030
1990	7.8	6	39	0.077	1998	10.5	1	1[3]	0.009
1991	7.5	4	62	0.053	1999	10.9	2	12	0.018
1992	7.5	4	33	0.053	2000	11.1	2	89	0.018
1993	7.7	1	1	0.013	2001[2]	10.6	6	531	0.019
1994[2]	7.8	4	239	0.051	2002	10.3	0	0	0.000
1995	8.1	1	160	0.012	2003	10.2	2	22	0.020
1996	7.9	3	342	0.038	2004[4]	10.5	1	13	0.009

(1) Fatal accidents per 100,000 departures. (2) Sabotage-caused accidents are included in the number of fatal accidents and fatalities, but not in the calculation of accident rates. (3) On-ground employee fatality. (4) Preliminary figures.

U.S. Scheduled Airline Traffic, 1990-2004

Source: Courtesy of Air Transport Association of America, Inc. Reprinted with permission.

(in thousands, except where otherwise noted)

	1990	1995	2000	2001*	2002*	2003*	2004
Revenue passengers enplaned	465,600	547,800	666,200	622,100	612,877	646,523	697,800
Revenue passenger miles	457,926,000	540,656,000	692,757,000	651,700,000	641,102,000	655,850,000	731,926,000
Available seat miles	733,375,000	807,078,000	956,950,000	930,511,000	892,554,000	893,902,000	968,976,000
% of seating utilized	62.4	67.0	72.4	70.0	71.8	73.4	75.5
Cargo traffic (ton miles)	12,549,000	16,921,000	23,888,000	22,003,000	23,243,000	24,608,000	27,978,000
Passenger revenue	$58,453,000	$69,594,000	$93,622,000	$80,947,000	$73,577,000	73,281,000	85,657,000
Net profit	–$3,921,000	$2,314,000	$2,486,000	–$8,275,000	–$11,312,415	–$3,624,682	–$9,071,000
Employees[1]	545,809	546,987	679,967	671,969	601,355	570,868	569,084

NA = Not available. (1) Not in thousands. *Revenues and profit measures include aid payments from the U.S. government after Sept. 2001 terrorist attacks.

Leading U.S. Passenger Airlines, 2004

Source: Courtesy of Air Transport Association of America, Inc. Reprinted with permission.

(in thousands)

Airline	Passengers
American	91,570
Delta	86,755
Southwest	81,066
United	70,786
Northwest	55,373
US Airways	42,400
Continental	40,551
America West	21,119
Alaska	16,280
American Eagle	14,869
ExpressJet	13,659
SkyWest	13,417
AirTran	13,170
Comair	12,632
JetBlue	11,731
Atlantic Southeast	10,420
ATA	10,024
Mesa	9,122
Independence	7,041
Air Wisconsin	6,954
Frontier	6,406
Pinnacle	6,362
Horizon	5,930
Hawaiian	5,585
Mesaba	5,427

Passenger Traffic at U.S. Airports, 2004

Source: Airports Council International-North America

Airport	Passenger Arrivals and Departures
Hartsfield Atlanta (ATL)	83,606,583
Chicago O'Hare (ORD)	75,533,822
Los Angeles (LAX)	60,688,609
Dallas/Ft. Worth (DFW)	59,412,217
Denver (DEN)	42,393,766
Las Vegas (LAS)	41,441,531
Phoenix Sky Harbor (PHX)	39,504,898
JFK-New York (JFK)	37,518,143
Minneapolis/St. Paul (MSP)	36,713,173
Houston (IAH)	36,506,116
Detroit (DTW)	35,187,517
San Francisco (SFO)	32,247,746
Newark (EWR)	31,947,266
Orlando (MCO)	31,143,388
Miami (MIA)	30,165,197
Seattle-Tacoma (SEA)	28,804,554
Philadelphia (PHL)	28,507,420
Boston Logan (BOS)	26,142,516
Charlotte (CLT)	25,534,374
La Guardia-New York (LGA)	24,435,661

Passenger Traffic at World Airports, 2004[1]

Source: Airports Council International

Airport Location (Name)	Passenger Arrivals and Departures
London, UK (Heathrow)	67,344,054
Tokyo, Japan (Haneda)	62,291,405
Paris, France (Charles de Gaulle)	51,260,363
Frankfurt On Main, Germany (Frankfurt Intl.)	51,098,271
Amsterdam, Netherlands (Schiphol)	42,541,180
Madrid, Spain (Barajas)	38,704,731
Bangkok, Thailand (Bangkok Intl.)	37,960,169
Hong Kong, China (Hong Kong Intl.)	36,711,920
Beijing, China (Beijing Capital Intl.)	34,883,190
London, UK (Gatwick)	31,461,454
Tokyo, Japan (Narita)	31,057,252
Singapore (Changi)	30,353,565
Toronto, Ontario, Canada (Toronto Pearson Intl.)	28,615,709
Rome, Italy (Fiumicino)	28,118,899
Sydney, Australia (Kingsford Smith)	26,983,107
Munich, Germany (Franz Josef Strauss)	26,814,505
Jakarta, Indonesia (Sukarno-Hatta Intl.)	26,083,267
Barcelona, Spain (Barcelona)	24,550,949
Seoul, South Korea (Inchon Intl.)	24,235,089
Paris, France (Orly)	24,053,215
Mexico City, Mexico (Benito Juarez Intl.)	22,994,043
Dubai, United Arab Emirates (Dubai)	21,711,522
Manchester, UK (Manchester Intl.)	21,544,199
Shanghai, China (Pudong)	21,124,233
Kuala Lumpur, Malaysia (KL Intl.)	21,058,572
London, UK (Stansted)	20,908,006
Palma de Mallorca, Spain (Palma de Mallorca)	20,411,024
Guangzhou, China (Baiyun Intl.)	20,354,400
Melbourne, Australia (Melbourne)	20,266,961
Taiwan (Chiang Kai-Shek Intl.)	20,083,555

(1) Excludes U.S. airports (see above), and airports not participating in Airports Council Intl. Airport Traffic Statistics collection.

Top 25 Travel Websites

Source: comScore Media Metrix

Rank	Visitors[1]
1. Expedia Travel	26,141,000
2. Trip Network Inc.	21,753,000
3. Orbitz.com	16,134,000
4. Travelocity	14,420,000
5. Hotels.com sites	12,103,000
6. Priceline.com	11,825,000
7. Yahoo! Travel	11,005,000
8. Southwest.com	10,452,000
9. Tripadvisor.com	7,772,000
10. Hotwire.com	6,867,000
11. Delta Airlines	6,771,000
12. AOL Travel	6,166,000
13. American Airlines	5,988,000
14. United Airlines	5,641,000
15. InterContinental Hotels Group	4,942,000
16. Marriott	4,833,000
17. Hilton Hotels	4,400,000
18. Travelzoo.com	4,231,000
19. Sidestep.com	3,692,000
20. Walt Disney Parks & Resorts Online	3,593,000
21. NWA.com	3,333,000
22. USAirways.com	3,279,000
23. JetBlue Airways	3,269,000
24. Continental Airlines Sites	3,117,000
25. About Travel	2,983,000

(1) Number of users who visited at least once in July 2005.

Travel Websites

The following websites are among those that may be of use in planning trips and making arrangements. Websites listed under "Maps" enable the user to plot a route to a destination. Inclusion here does not represent endorsement by *The World Almanac*.

AIRLINES

American Airlines
www.aa.com
America West Airlines
www.americawest.com
Continental Airlines
www.continental.com
Delta Air Lines
www.delta.com
Northwest Airlines
www.nwa.com
Southwest Airlines
www.southwest.com
United Airlines
www.ual.com
USAirways
www.usair.com

BUSES

Gray Line Worldwide
www.grayline.com
Greyhound Lines
www.greyhound.com
Peter Pan Bus Lines
www.peterpanbus.com

TRAINS

Amtrak
www.amtrak.com
BC Rail (Canada)
www.bcrail.com
Rail Europe
www.raileurope.com

CAR RENTALS

Alamo Rent A Car
www.alamo.com
Avis Rent-A-Car
www.avis.com
Budget Rent A Car
www.budget.com
Dollar Rent A Car
www.dollar.com
Enterprise Rent-A-Car
www.enterprise.com
Hertz
www.hertz.com
National Car Rental
www.nationalcar.com
Rent-A-Wreck
www.rentawreck.com
Thrifty Rent-A-Car
www.thrifty.com

CRUISE LINES

Carnival Cruise Lines
www.carnival.com
Celebrity Cruises
www.celebrity.com
Costa Cruise Lines
www.costacruises.com
Cunard Line
www.cunardline.com
Holland America Line
www.hollandamerica.com
Norwegian Cruise Line
www.ncl.com
Princess Cruises
www.princess.com
Royal Caribbean Int'l.
www.royalcaribbean.com
Windjammer Barefoot Cruises
www.windjammer.com

HOTELS/RESORTS

Best Western Int'l.
www.bestwestern.com
Choice Hotels Int'l., Clarion Hotels & Resorts, Comfort Inns, Econo Lodges, MainStay Suites, Quality Inns, Rodeway Inns, Sleep Inns
www.hotelchoice.com
Days Inn of America
www.daysinn.com
Doubletree Hotels
www.doubletree.com
Embassy Suites
www.embassysuites.com
Four Seasons Hotels
www.fourseasons.com
Hilton Hotels
www.hilton.com
Holiday Inn Worldwide
www.holidayinn.com
Hyatt Hotels and Resorts
www.hyatt.com
Hotels.com
www.hotels.com
Inter-Continental Hotels
www.interconti.com
Loews Hotels
www.loewshotels.com
Marriott Int'l.
www.marriott.com
Radisson Hotels Int'l.
www.radisson.com
Sheraton Hotels & Resorts
www.starwood.com/sheraton
Westin Hotels & Resorts
www.starwood.com/westin
Wyndham Hotels & Resorts
www.wyndham.com

TRAVEL PLANNING

www.bestfares.com
www.cheaptickets.com
www.expedia.com
www.fodors.com
www.frommers.com
www.itn.net (American Express)
www.libertytravel.com
www.lowestfare.com
www.orbitz.com
www.priceline.com
www.travelocity.com

MAPS

www.freetrip.com
maps.google.com
www.mapquest.com
www.mapsonus.com
maps.yahoo.com

Passports, Health Regulations, and Travel Warnings for Foreign Travel

Source: Bureau of Consular Affairs, U.S. Dept. of State; www.travel.state.gov

Passports, Visas

Passports are issued by the U.S. Department of State to citizens and nationals of the U.S. to provide documentation for foreign travel. It is important to apply well in advance of need; receiving a passport may take up to 6 weeks.

For U.S. citizens traveling on business or as tourists, especially in Europe, a U.S. passport is often sufficient to gain admission for a limited stay. For many countries, however, a **visa** must also be obtained before entering. It is the responsibility of the traveler to check in advance and obtain any required visas from the appropriate embassies or nearest consulates.

Each country has its own specific guidelines concerning length and purpose of visit, etc. Some may require visitors to display proof that they have (1) sufficient funds to stay for the intended time period, (2) onward/return tickets, and/or (3) at least 6-months remaining validity on their U.S. passports.

For up-to-date passport and international travel information, visit the Consular Affairs website (www.travel.state.gov), or call the National Passport Information Center at 1-877-487-2778 (TDD/TYY: 1-888-874-7793). Customer service representatives are available from 7 AM to midnight, Eastern Time, Mon.-Fri., excluding federal holidays.

Health Regulations

Under World Health Organization regulations, a country may require International Certificates of Vaccination against yellow fever. Cholera immunization may be required for travelers from infected areas. Check with health care providers or your records to see that other immunizations (e.g., for tetanus and polio) are up-to-date.

Other preventative measures, including prophylactic medication for malaria, are advisable for travel to some countries. No immunizations are needed to return to the U.S. Many countries have regulations regarding AIDS testing, particularly for longtime visitors.

Detailed information and recommendations are included in *Health Information for International Travel*, the "Yellow Book" published every 2 years by the Centers for Disease Control (CDC). It can be ordered from the Public Health Foundation for $29 by calling 1-800-545-2500 and asking for ISBN number 032303716X. Updates to the book are available online at www.cdc.gov/travel/yb/index.htm.

Information may also be obtained from your local health department or physician, or by calling the Centers for Disease Control and Prevention at 1-877-FYI-TRIP (1-877-394-8747). The more technical *International Travel and Health* is available from the World Health Organization for $22.50, with portions of the book accessible online, at www.who.int/ith

Travel Warnings

The State Dept. issues travel warnings when it decides, based on relevant information, to recommend that Americans avoid travel to certain countries; these are subject to change. As of Sept. 1, 2005, travel warnings were in effect for: Afghanistan, Algeria, Bosnia and Herzegovina, Burundi, Central African Rep., Colombia, Côte d'Ivoire, Dem. Rep. of the Congo, Haiti, Indonesia, Iran, Iraq, Israel (incl. West Bank and Gaza), Kenya, Lebanon, Liberia, Nepal, Nigeria, Pakistan, Philippines, Saudi Arabia, Somalia, Sudan, Uzbekistan, Yemen, and Zimbabwe. For the most current information, visit www.travel.state.gov

IT'S A FACT: The Depts. of State and Homeland Security announced in 2005 that they would be imposing new restrictions on travelers returning to the U.S. If new federal regulations go into effect as scheduled, by Dec. 31, 2006, all U.S. citizens returning to the U.S. or its territories after air or sea travel anywhere outside the country—including, for the first time, Mexico, Canada, and the Caribbean—will be required to have a passport to reenter. These stricter regulations were also expected to apply to land-border crossing after Dec. 31, 2007, but federal officials were considering possible alternatives to requiring passports for land travels.

Some Notable Roller Coasters

Source: American Coasters Network; as of Sept. 2005

Fastest Roller Coasters

Name	Speed	Location
Kingda Ka	128 mph	Six Flags Great Adventure; Jackson, NJ
Top Thrill Dragster	120 mph	Cedar Point; Sandusky, OH
Dodonpa	107 mph	Fujikyu Highland; Yamanashi, Japan
Tower of Terror	100 mph	Dreamworld; Coomera, Queensland, Australia
Superman: The Escape	100 mph	Six Flags Magic Mountain; Valencia, CA

Longest Roller Coasters

Name	Length	Location
Steel Dragon 2000	8,133 ft	Nagashima Spaland; Mie, Japan
Daidarasaurus	7,677 ft	Expoland; Osaka, Japan
The Ultimate	7,442 ft	Lightwater Valley; North Yorkshire, UK
Beast	7,400 ft	Paramount's Kings Island; Kings Mills, OH
Son of Beast	7,032 ft	Paramount's Kings Island; Kings Mills, OH

Tallest Roller Coasters

Name	Height	Location
Kingda Ka	456 ft	Six Flags Great Adventure; Jackson, NJ
Top Thrill Dragster	420 ft	Cedar Point; Sandusky, OH
Superman The Escape	415 ft	Six Flags Magic Mountain; Valencia, CA
Tower of Terror	377 ft	Dreamworld; Coomera, Queensland, Australia
Steel Dragon 2000	318 ft	Nagashima Spaland; Mie, Japan

Roller Coasters With Longest Drop

Name	Drop	Location
Kingda Ka	418 ft	Six Flags Great Adventure; Jackson, NJ
Top Thrill Dragster	400 ft	Cedar Point; Sandusky, OH
Superman: The Escape	328 ft	Six Flags Magic Mountain; Valencia, CA
Tower of Terror	328 ft	Dreamworld; Coomera, Queensland, Australia
Steel Dragon 2000	307 ft	Nagashima Spaland; Mie, Japan

Top 50 Amusement/Theme Parks Worldwide, Year-end 2004

(ranked by estimated attendance)

Source: Amusement Business

Rank	Park and Location	Country	Attendance
1.	Magic Kingdom at Walt Disney World, Lake Buena Vista, FL	United States	15,170,000
2.	Disneyland, Anaheim, CA	United States	13,360,000
3.	Tokyo Disneyland	Japan	13,200,000
4.	Tokyo Disney Sea	Japan	12,200,000
5.	Disneyland Paris, Marne-La-Vallee	France	10,200,000
6.	Universal Studios Japan, Osaka	Japan	9,900,000
7.	Epcot at Walt Disney World, Lake Buena Vista, FL	United States	9,400,000
8.	Disney-MGM Studios at Walt Disney World, Lake Buena Vista, FL	United States	8,260,000
9.	Lotte World, Seoul	South Korea	8,000,000
10.	Disney's Animal Kingdom at Walt Disney World, Lake Buena Vista, FL	United States	7,820,000
11.	Everland, Kyonggi-Do	South Korea	7,500,600
12.	Universal Studios at Universal Orlando, Orlando, FL	United States	6,700,000
13.	Islands of Adventure at Universal Orlando, Orlando, FL	United States	6,300,000
14.	Blackpool Pleasure Beach, Blackpool, England	United Kingdom	6,200,000
15.	Disney's California Adventure, Anaheim, CA	United States	5,630,000
16.	SeaWorld Florida, Orlando, FL	United States	5,600,000
17.	Yokohama Hakkeijima Sea Paradise, Yokohama	Japan	5,100,000
18.	Universal Studios Hollywood, Universal City, CA	United States	5,000,000
19.	Adventuredome at Circus Circus, Las Vegas, NV	United States	4,400,000
20.	Tivoli Gardens, Copenhagen	Denmark	4,240,000
21.	Busch Gardens, Tampa Bay, FL	United States	4,100,000
22.	SeaWorld California, San Diego, CA	United States	4,000,000
23.	Ocean Park, Hong Kong	China	3,800,000
	Nagashima Spa Land, Kuwana	Japan	3,800,000
25.	Knott's Berry Farm, Buena Park, CA	United States	3,580,000
26.	Paramount's Kings Island, Kings Island, OH	United States	3,510,000
27.	Paramount Canada's Wonderland, Maple, Ontario	Canada	3,420,000
28.	Europa-Park, Rust	Germany	3,300,000
29.	De Efteling, Kaatsheuvel	The Netherlands	3,200,000
30.	Cedar Point, Sandusky, OH	United States	3,170,000
31.	Morey's Piers, Wildwood, NJ	United States	3,100,000
	Port Aventuria, Salou	Spain	3,100,000
	Gardaland, Castelnuovo del Garda	Italy	3,100,000
34.	Liseburg, Gothenburg	Sweden	3,000,000
	Santa Cruz Beach Boardwalk, Santa Cruz, CA	United States	3,000,000
36.	Six Flags Great Adventure, Jackson, NJ	United States	2,800,000
37.	Huis Ten Bosch, Sasebo City	Japan	2,750,000
38.	HersheyPark, Hershey, PA	United States	2,710,000
39.	Six Flags Magic Mountain, Valencia, CA	United States	2,700,000
	La Feria de Chapultapec, Mexico City	Mexico	2,700,000
41.	Suzuka Circuit, Suzuka	Japan	2,600,000
42.	Camp Snoopy at Mall of America, Bloomington, MN	United States	2,590,000
43.	Bakken, Klampenborg	Denmark	2,500,000
44.	Alton Towers, Staffordshire, England	United Kingdom	2,400,000
	Busch Gardens (The Old Country), Williamsburg, VA	United States	2,400,000
46.	Six Flags Great America, Gurnee, IL	United States	2,300,000
47.	Seoul Land, Seoul	South Korea	2,250,000
48.	Walt Disney Studios Park, Marne-La-Vallee	France	2,200,000
	Six Flags Over Texas, Arlington, TX	United States	2,200,000
50.	Six Flags Mexico, Mexico City	Mexico	2,150,000

NATIONS OF THE WORLD

As of mid-2005, there were **193 nations** in the world. This number includes 2 nations that are not members of the United Nations—Taiwan and Vatican City (the Holy See). The 193 nations are profiled below, in alphabetical order. Certain regions and territories that are not independent nations can be found under the entry for the governing nation. Following the nation profiles are comparative statistics, information on international organizations, and other information about nations.

Sources: U.S. Census Bureau: Intl. Data Base; U.S. Central Intelligence Agency: *The World Factbook;* U.S. Dept. of Energy; U.S. Dept. of State. UN Education, Scientific, and Cultural Org. (UNESCO); UN Food and Agriculture Org.: FAO Statistical Database and Yearbook of Fishery Statistics; Intl. Monetary Fund; Intl. Telecommunication Union (for telephone and internet data); UN Population Division: *World Population Prospects and World Urbanization Prospects;* UN Statistics Division: *Statistical Yearbook*; World Tourism Organization; Intl. Institute for Strategic Studies: *The Military Balance.*

Note: Because of rounding or incomplete enumeration, some percentages may not add to 100%. **FY = fiscal year. National population and health** figures are mid-2005 estimates, unless otherwise noted. **Percentage of urban population** is for mid-2003. **City** populations, except capitals, are 2000 estimates for **urban agglomerations,** i.e., whole metropolitan areas. All **capital** populations are estimates for urban agglomerations in 2003. Where indicated, the latest available population of the city proper is also given. **GDP** estimates are based on purchasing power parity calculations, which involve use of intl. dollar price weights applied to quantities of goods and services produced. **Tourism** figures represent receipts from international tourism. **Budget** figures are for expenditures, unless otherwise noted. **Motor vehicle** and **civil aviation** statistics are latest available; comm. (commercial) vehicles include trucks and buses. Airport figures include total number with paved runways in 2002. **TV, radio,** and **daily newspapers** figures are latest available. **Telephone and Internet** data are for 2004, unless otherwise noted. **Life expectancy** is at birth for persons born in 2005. **AIDS rate** is the est. number of adults, aged 15-49, living with HIV at year-end 2003, divided by the total 2003 population aged 15-49. **Education** figures are for the 2002-2003 school year. **Literacy rates** given generally measure the percent of population able to read and write on a lower elementary school level, not the (smaller) percent able to read instructions necessary for a job or license. Figures for **gold reserves, international reserves less gold,** and changes in **consumer prices** are from 2003 to 2004, except where noted. **Embassy addresses** are for Wash., DC, area code (202), unless otherwise noted.

For further details and later information on developments around the world, see the Chronology of the Year's Events. See pages 457-472 for full-color maps and flags of all nations.

Afghanistan

Islamic Republic of Afghanistan

People: Population: 29,928,987. **Age distrib.** (%) <15: 44.7; 65+: 2.4. **Pop. density:** 120 per sq mi, 46 per sq km. **Urban:** 23.3%. **Ethnic groups:** Pashtun 44%, Tajik 25%, Hazara 10%, Uzbek 8%. **Principal languages:** Dari (Afghan Persian), Pashtu (both official); Turkic (incl. Uzbek, Turkmen); Balochi, Pashai, many others. **Chief religion:** Muslim (official; Sunni 80%, Shi'a 19%).

Geography: Total area: 250,001 sq mi, 647,500 sq km; **Land area:** 250,001 sq mi, 647,500 sq km. **Location:** In SW Asia, NW of the Indian subcontinent. **Neighbors:** Pakistan on E, S; Iran on W; Turkmenistan, Tajikistan, Uzbekistan on N. The NE tip touches China. **Topography:** The country is landlocked and mountainous, much of it over 4,000 ft. above sea level. The Hindu Kush Mts. tower 16,000 ft. above Kabul and reach a height of 25,000 ft. to the E. Trade with Pakistan flows through the 35-mile-long Khyber Pass. The climate is dry, with extreme temperatures, and there are large desert regions. **Capital:** Kabul, 2,956,000.

Government: Type: Islamic republic. **Head of state and gov.:** Pres. Hamid Karzai; b Dec. 24, 1957; in office: June 19, 2002. **Local divisions:** 32 provinces. **Defense budget** (2002): $250 mil. **Active troops:** 60,000–70,000.

Economy: Industries: textiles, soap, furniture, shoes. **Chief crops:** wheat, fruits, nuts, wool. **Natural resources:** nat. gas, oil, coal, copper, chromite, talc, barite, sulfur, lead, zinc, iron ore, salt, gems. **Arable land:** 12%. **Livestock** (2002): chickens: 6.50 mil; goats: 5 mil; sheep: 11 mil. **Fish catch** (2003): 900 metric tons. **Electricity prod.** (2003): 0.91 bil. kWh. **Labor force** (2004 est.): agriculture 80%, industry 10%, services 10%.

Finance: Monetary unit: Afghani (AFA) (Sept. 2005: 42.78 = $1 U.S.). **GDP** (2003 est.): $21.5 bil.; **per capita GDP:** $800; **GDP growth:** 7.5%. **Imports** (2004 est.): $3.759 bil.; partners (2004): Pakistan 25.2%, US 8.7%, South Korea 7.7%, India 7.6%, Germany 6.5%, Turkmenistan 4.5%, Turkey 4.1%. **Exports** (2004): $446.0 mil; partners (2004): India 23.1%, Pakistan 20.5%, US 12.9%, Germany 6%. **Tourism** (1998): $1 mil. **Budget** (2005): $609.0 mil.

Transport: Railroad: Length: 15 mi. **Motor vehicles:** 8,600 pass. cars, 4,500 comm. vehicles. **Civil aviation:** 88.9 mil. pass.-mi; 10 airports.

Communications: TV sets: 14 per 1,000 pop. **Radios:** 132 per 1,000 pop. **Telephone lines**: 29,000 main lines. **Daily newspaper circ.:** 5.6 per 1,000 pop.

Health: Life expect.: 42.7 male; 43.1 female. **Births** (per 1,000 pop.): 47.0. **Deaths** (per 1,000 pop.): 20.8. **Natural inc.:** 2.63%. **Infant mortality** (per 1,000 live births): 163.1.

Education: Compulsory: ages 7-12. **Literacy:** 36%.

Major Intl. Organizations: UN (FAO, IBRD, ILO, IMF, WHO).

Embassy: 2341 Wyoming Ave. NW 20008; 483.6410.

Website: www.embassyofafghanistan.org

Afghanistan, occupying a favored invasion route since antiquity, has been variously known as Ariana or Bactria (in ancient times) and Khorasan (in the Middle Ages). Foreign empires alternated rule with local emirs and kings until the 18th century, when a unified kingdom was established. In 1973, a military coup ushered in a republic.

Pro-Soviet leftists took power in a bloody 1978 coup and concluded an economic and military treaty with the USSR. In Dec. 1979 the USSR began a massive airlift into Kabul and backed a new coup, leading to installation of a more pro-Soviet leader. Soviet troops fanned out over Afghanistan and waged a protracted guerrilla war with Muslim rebels, in which some 15,000 Soviet troops reportedly died.

A UN-mediated agreement was signed Apr. 14, 1988, providing for withdrawal of Soviet troops, a neutral Afghan state, and repatriation of refugees. Afghan rebels rejected the pact. The Soviets completed their troop withdrawal Feb. 15, 1989; fighting between Afghan rebels and government forces ensued. Communist Pres. Najibullah resigned Apr. 16, 1992, as competing guerrilla forces advanced on Kabul. The rebels achieved power Apr. 28, ending 14 years of Soviet-backed regimes. More than 2 million Afghans had been killed and 6 million had left the country since 1979.

Following the rebel victory there were clashes between moderates and Islamic fundamentalist forces. Burhanuddin Rabbani, a guerrilla leader, became president June 28, 1992, but fierce fighting continued around Kabul and elsewhere. The Taliban, an insurgent Islamic radical faction, gained increasing control and in Sept. 1996 captured Kabul and set up a government. The Taliban executed former President Najibullah and empowered Islamic religious police to enforce codes of dress and behavior that were especially restrictive to women. Rabbani and other ousted leaders fled to the north.

Victories in the northern cities of Mazar-e Sharif, Aug. 8, 1998, and Taloqan, Aug. 8-11, 1998, gave the Taliban control over more than 90% of the country. On Aug. 20, U.S. cruise missiles struck SE of Kabul, hitting facilities the U.S. said were terrorist training camps run by a wealthy Saudi, Osama bin Laden. The UN imposed sanctions Nov. 14, 1999, when Afghanistan refused to turn over bin Laden to the U.S. for prosecution; a UN ban on all military aid to the Taliban took effect Jan. 19, 2001. By March, aid agencies reported that drought and continued warfare had put more than 1 million people at risk of famine. Meanwhile, the Taliban launched a campaign to destroy non-Islamic antiquities.

Ahmed Shah Massoud, leader of the anti-Taliban resistance, died of wounds sustained in a suicide bombing, Sept. 9, 2001, by assassins posing as journalists. After the Sept. 11 attacks on the World Trade Center and Pentagon, the U.S., blaming bin Laden, demanded that the Taliban surrender him and shut down his al-Qaeda terrorist network. When the Taliban refused, the U.S., with British assistance, began bombing Afghanistan Oct. 7. Supported by the U.S., the opposition Northern Alliance recaptured Mazar-e Sharif Nov. 9 and took Kabul 4 days later; the Taliban forces abandoned Kandahar, their last stronghold, to S tribesmen Dec. 7. A power-sharing agreement signed in Bonn, Germany, Dec. 5 by 4 anti-Taliban factions, including the Northern Alliance, provided for an interim government headed by Hamid Karzai, a Pashtun tribal leader; the UN authorized Dec. 20 a multinational security force. Meanwhile, U.S. and allied forces continued to hunt for bin Laden and other top al-Qaeda and Taliban officials.

At a conference in Tokyo, Jan. 21-22, 2002, donor countries and agencies pledged more than $4.5 bil in aid to Afghanistan over 5 years. In March 2002, the U.S. launched Operation Anaconda to hunt down Taliban in the mountains of the SE. Meeting June 13 in Kabul, a traditional council (*loya jirga*) chose Karzai to head a new transitional government. An errant U.S. air strike on the night of June 30-July 1 apparently killed 48 people at Kakarak, N of Kandahar. Gunmen July 6 assassinated Vice Pres. Haji Abdul Qadir, a Pashtun. A car bomb in Kabul killed 30 people Sept. 5; the same day Karzai, guarded by U.S. troops, survived an assassination attempt. Continued lawlessness allowed for a dramatic increase in opium production.

The U.S. announced the end of major combat operations in Afghanistan, May 1, 2003, but resistance continued. Attacks against aid workers forced the UN to suspend humanitarian operations Aug. 10 in many southern regions. NATO officially assumed control of peacekeeping forces (ISAF) Aug. 11.

A new constitution took effect Jan. 26, 2004. The aid group Doctors Without Borders suspended Afghan operations after 5 relief workers were killed in a Taliban ambush, June 2. In Kunduz, June 10, gunmen killed 11 Chinese road construction workers and an Afghan guard. Pres. Karzai won reelection Oct. 9 with 55.4% of the vote. During the campaign, insurgents attempted to kill Pres. Karzai, Sept. 16; Vice Pres. Nematullah Shahrani, Sept. 20; and Karzai's vice-pres. running mate, Ahmed Zia Massoud (brother of the slain anti-Taliban leader), Oct. 6. U.S. troops launched a new offensive, Dec. 11, but were unable to suppress the insurgency.

A prominent anti-Taliban Muslim cleric, Mawlavi Abdullah Fayaz, was assassinated in Kandahar, May 29, 2005; a suicide bomb at his funeral, June 1, killed at least 20 people in a Kandahar mosque, including the police chief of Kabul. Afghan authorities announced June 20 that they had foiled a plot to kill the U.S. ambassador. Violence continued to rise in the run-up to elections Sept. 18, 2005, for a 249-seat national assembly. Millions defied threats of violence to vote; at least 14 people were killed in more than 20 attacks by insurgents. The U.S.-led coalition had 20,000 troops in the country, and the NATO peacekeeping force had 11,000.

Albania

Republic of Albania

People: Population: 3,563,112. **Age distrib.** (%) <15: 25.6; 65+: 8.6. **Pop. density:** 321 per sq mi, 124 per sq km. **Urban:** 23.3%. **Ethnic groups:** Albanian 95%, Greek 3%. **Principal languages:** Albanian (Tosk is the official dialect), Greek. **Chief religions:** Muslim 70%, Albanian Orthodox 20%, Roman Catholic 10%.

Geography: Total area: 11,100 sq mi, 28,748 sq km; **Land area:** 10,578 sq mi, 27,398 sq km. **Location:** SE Europe, on SE coast of Adriatic Sea. **Neighbors:** Greece on S, Yugoslavia on N, Macedonia on E. **Topography:** Apart from a narrow coastal plain, Albania consists of hills and mountains covered with scrub forest, cut by small E-W rivers. **Capital:** Tirana, 367,000.

Government: Type: Republic. **Head of state:** Pres. Alfred Moisiu; b Dec. 1, 1929; in office: July 24, 2002. **Head of gov.:** Prime Min. Sali Berisha; b Oct. 15, 1944; in office: Sept. 11, 2005. **Local divisions:** 12 counties divided into 36 districts. **Defense budget** (2003): $65 mil. **Active troops:** 22,000.

Economy: Industries: food proc., textiles, clothing, lumber. **Chief crops:** wheat, corn, potatoes, sugar beets, grapes. **Natural resources:** oil, nat. gas, coal, chromium, copper, timber, nickel, hydropower. **Crude oil reserves** (2004): 165 mil bbls. **Arable land:** 21%. **Livestock** (2004): cattle: 700,000; chickens: 4.3 mil; goats: 1.0 mil; pigs: 109,000; sheep: 1.8 mil. **Fish catch** (2003): 3,560 metric tons. **Electricity prod.** (2003): 4.1 bil. kWh. **Labor force** (2004 est.): agriculture 57%, non-agricultural private sector 20%, public sector 23%.

Finance: Monetary unit: Lek (ALL) (Sept. 2005: 99.80 = $1 U.S.). **GDP** (2004 est.): $17.5 bil.; **per capita GDP:** $4,900; **GDP growth:** 5.6%. **Imports** (2004 est.): $2.076 bil.; partners (2004): Italy 36%, Greece 20.4%, Turkey 8.1%, Germany 5.5%. **Exports** (2004 est.): $552.4 mil; partners (2004): Italy 71.9%, Greece 6.3%, Canada 4.4%. **Tourism:** $522 mil. **Budget** (2004 est.): $2.5 bil. **Intl. reserves less gold:** $874 mil. **Gold:** 70,000 oz t. **Consumer prices:** 2.28%.

Transport: Railroad: Length: 278 mi. **Motor vehicles** 148,500 pass. cars, 73,000 comm. vehicles. **Civil aviation:** 57.8 mil. pass.-mi; 4 airports. **Chief ports:** Durres, Sarande, Vlore.

Communications: TV sets: 146 per 1,000 pop. **Radios:** 259 per 1,000 pop. **Telephone lines:** 255,000. **Daily newspaper circ.:** 36 per 1,000 pop. **Internet**: 30,000 users.

Health: Life expect.: 74.6 male; 80.2 female. **Births** (per 1,000 pop.): 15.1. **Deaths** (per 1,000 pop.): 5.1. **Natural inc.:** 1.00%. **Infant mortality** (per 1,000 live births): 21.5.

Major Intl. Organiz.: UN (IBRD, ILO, IMF, IMO, WHO), OSCE.

Education: Compulsory: ages 6-13. **Literacy:** 86.5%.

Embassy: 2100 S St. NW 20008; 223-4942.

Website: www.keshilliministrave.al/english/

Ancient Illyria was conquered by Romans, Slavs, and Turks (15th century); the latter Islamized the population. Independent Albania was proclaimed in 1912, republic was formed in 1920. King Zog I ruled 1925-39, until Italy invaded.

Communist partisans took over in 1944, allied Albania with USSR, then broke with USSR in 1960 over de-Stalinization. Strong political alliance with China followed, leading to several billion dollars in aid, which was curtailed after 1974. China cut off aid in 1978 when Albania attacked its policies after the death of Chinese ruler Mao Zedong. Large-scale purges of officials occurred during the 1970s.

Enver Hoxha, the nation's ruler for 4 decades, died Apr. 11, 1985. Eventually the new regime introduced some liberalization, including measures in 1990 providing for freedom to travel abroad. Efforts were begun to improve ties with the outside world. Mar. 1991 elections left the former Communists in power, but a general strike and urban opposition led to the formation of a coalition cabinet including non-Communists.

Albania's former Communists were routed in elections Mar. 1992, amid economic collapse and social unrest. Sali Berisha was elected as the first non-Communist president since World War II. Berisha's party claimed a landslide victory in disputed parliamentary elections, May 26 and June 2, 1996. Public protests over the collapse of fraudulent investment schemes in Jan. 1997 led to armed rebellion and anarchy. The UN Security Council, Mar. 28, authorized a 7,000-member force to restore order. Socialists and their allies won parliamentary elections, June 29 and July 6, and international peacekeepers completed their pullout by Aug. 11.

During NATO's air war against Yugoslavia, Mar.-June 1999, Albania hosted some 465,000 Kosovar refugees. Victory by a coalition backing Berisha in parliamentary voting, July 3, 2005, ended 8 years of Socialist rule.

Algeria

People's Democratic Republic of Algeria

People: Population: 32,531,853. **Age distrib.** (%) <15: 29.0; 65+: 4.7. **Pop. density:** 35 per sq mi, 14 per sq km. **Urban:** 58.8%. **Ethnic groups:** Arab-Berber 99%. **Principal languages:** Arabic (official), French, Berber dialects. **Chief religion:** Sunni Muslim (official) 99%.

Geography: Total area: 919,595 sq mi, 2,381,740 sq km; **Land area:** 919,595 sq mi, 2,381,740 sq km. **Location:** In NW Africa, from Mediterranean Sea into Sahara Desert. **Neighbors:** Morocco on W; Mauritania, Mali, Niger on S; Libya, Tunisia on E. **Topography:** The Tell, located on the coast, comprises fertile plains 50-100 miles wide, with a moderate climate and adequate rain. Two major chains of the Atlas Mts., running roughly E-W and reaching 7,000 ft., enclose a dry plateau region. Below lies the Sahara, mostly desert with major mineral resources. **Capital:** Algiers (El Djazair), 3,060,000.

Government: Type: Republic. **Head of state:** Pres. Abdelaziz Bouteflika; b Mar. 2, 1937; in office: Apr. 27, 1999. **Head of gov.:** Prime Min. Ahmed Ouyahia; b July 2, 1952; in office: May 5, 2003. **Local divisions:** 48 provinces. **Defense budget** (2004): $2.8 bil. **Active troops:** 127,500.

Economy: Industries: oil, nat. gas, light industries, mining, petrochemical, food proc. **Chief crops:** wheat, barley, oats, grapes, olives, citrus. **Natural resources:** oil, nat. gas, iron ore, phosphates, uranium, lead, zinc. **Crude oil reserves** (2004): 11.8 bil. bbls. **Arable land:** 3%. **Livestock** (2004): cattle: 1.6 mil; chickens: 125 mil; goats: 3.2 mil; pigs: 5,700; sheep: 18.7 mil. **Fish catch** (2003): 142,004 metric tons. **Electricity prod.** (2003): 27.0 bil. kWh. **Labor force** (2003 est.): agriculture 14%, industry 13.4%, construction and public works 10%, trade 14.6%, government 32%, other 16%.

Finance: Monetary unit: Dinar (DZD) (Sept. 2005: 71.65 = $1 U.S.). **GDP** (2004 est.): $212.3 bil.; **per capita GDP:** $6,600; **GDP growth:** 6.1%. **Imports** (2004 est.): $15.25 bil.; partners (2004): France 31.6%, Italy 8.5%, Germany 6.3%, Spain 5.6%, China 5.3%, US 4.9%, Turkey 4.5%. **Exports** (2004 est.): $32.2 bil.; partners (2004): US 22.5%, Italy 17.8%, France 11.8%, Spain 10.2%, Canada 7.8%, Belgium 4.8%. **Tourism:** $161 mil. **Budget** (2004 est.): $29.3 bil. **Intl. reserves less gold:** $27.85 bil. **Gold:** 5.58 mil. oz t. **Consumer prices:** 3.56%.

Transport: Railroad: Length: 2,469 mi. **Motor vehicles** 1.71 mil pass. cars, 1.0 mil. comm. vehicles. **Civil aviation:** 2.2 bil pass.-mi. **Chief ports:** Algiers, Annaba, Oran.

Communications: TV sets: 107 per 1,000 pop. **Radios:** 242 per 1,000 pop. **Telephone lines:** 2.2 mil. **Daily newspaper circ.:** 27.3 per 1,000 pop. **Internet** (2002): 500,000 users.

Health: Life expect.: 71.5 male; 74.6 female. **Births** (per 1,000 pop.): 17.1. **Deaths** (per 1,000 pop.): 4.6. **Natural inc.:** 1.25%. **Infant mortality** (per 1,000 live births): 31.0. **AIDS rate:** 0.1%

Education: Compulsory: ages 6-14. **Literacy:** 70%.

Major Intl. Organizations: UN (FAO, IBRD, ILO, IMF, IMO, WHO), AL, AU, OPEC.

Embassy: 2118 Kalorama Rd. NW 20008; 265-2800.

Website: www.algeria-us.org

Earliest known inhabitants were ancestors of Berbers, followed by Phoenicians, Romans, Vandals, and, finally, Arabs. Turkey ruled 1518 to 1830, when France took control.

Large-scale European immigration and French cultural inroads did not prevent an Arab nationalist movement from launching guerrilla war. Peace, and French withdrawal, was negotiated with French Pres. Charles de Gaulle. One million Europeans left. Independence came July 5, 1962. Ahmed Ben Bella was the victor of infighting and ruled until 1965, when an army coup installed Col. Houari Boumedienne. He ruled in 1978.

In 1967, Algeria declared war on Israel, broke ties with U.S., and moved toward eventual military and political ties with the USSR. Some 500 died in riots protesting economic hardship in 1988. In 1989, voters approved a new constitution, which cleared the way for a multiparty system.

The government canceled the Jan. 1992 elections that Islamic fundamentalists were expected to win, and banned all nonreligious activities at Algeria's 10,000 mosques. Pres. Mohammed Boudiaf was assassinated June 29, 1992. There were repeated attacks on high-ranking officials, security forces, foreigners, and others by militant Muslim fundamentalists over the next 7 years; pro-government death squads also were active.

Liamine Zeroual won the presidential election of Nov. 16, 1995. A new constitution banning Islamic political parties and increasing the president's powers passed in a referendum on Nov. 28, 1996. Abdelaziz Bouteflika, who became president after a flawed election on Apr. 15, 1999, made peace with rebels and won approval for an amnesty plan in a referendum on Sept. 16; by then, about 100,000 people had died in the civil war. Some 100 people died and thousands were injured in violent protests Apr.-June 2001, chiefly by Algeria's Berber minority. Bouteflika was reelected Apr. 8, 2004, in a landslide; opponents charged fraud.

An earthquake in N Algeria, May 21, 2003, claimed over 2,200 lives and left 200,000 people homeless. The army launched a campaign against the militant Islamic group GSPC after its members killed 12 soldiers in June. GSPC leader Nabil Sahraoui was killed by Algerian forces, June 20, 2004.

Andorra

Principality of Andorra

People: Population: 70,549. **Age distrib.** (%) <15: 14.8; 65+: 13.7. **Pop. density:** 390 per sq mi, 151 per sq km. **Urban:** 91.7%. **Ethnic groups:** Spanish 43%, Andorran 33%, Portuguese 11%, French 7%. **Principal languages:** Catalan (official), Castilian Spanish, French. **Chief religion:** Predominantly Roman Catholic.

Geography: Total area: 181 sq mi, 468 sq km; **Land area:** 181 sq mi, 468 sq km. **Location:** SW Europe, in Pyrenees Mts. **Neighbors:** Spain on S, France on N. **Topography:** High mountains and narrow valleys cover the country. **Capital:** Andorra la Vella, 21,000.

Government: Type: Parliamentary co-principality. **Heads of state:** President of France & Bishop of Urgel (Spain), as co-princes. **Head of gov.:** Albert Pintat Santolària; b June 23, 1943; in office: May 27, 2005. **Local divisions:** 7 parishes. **Defense budget:** Responsibility of France and Spain.

Economy: Industries: tourism, cattle raising, timber, tobacco, banking. **Chief crops:** tobacco, rye, wheat, barley, oats. **Natural resources:** hydropower, mineral water, timber, iron ore, lead. **Arable land:** 2%. **Labor force** (2000 est.): agriculture 1%, industry 21%, services 78%.

Finance: Monetary unit: Euro (EUR) (Sept. 2005: 0.80 = $1 U.S.). **GDP** (2003 est.): $1.9 bil.; **per capita GDP:** $26,800; **GDP growth:** 2%. **Imports** (1998): $1.1 bil.; partners (2000): Spain 48%, France 35%, U.S. 2.3%. **Exports** (1998): $58.0 mil; partners (2000): Spain 58%, France 34%. **Budget** (1997): $342.0 mil.

Transport: Motor vehicles: 35,358 pass. cars, 4,238 comm. vehicles.

Communications: TV sets: 440 per 1,000 pop. **Radios:** 229 per 1,000 pop. **Telephone lines:** 35,000. **Daily newspaper circ.:** 60 per 1,000 pop. **Internet:** 7,000 users.

Health: Life expect.: 80.6 male; 86.6 female. **Births** (per 1,000 pop.): 9.0. **Deaths** (per 1,000 pop.): 6.1. **Natural inc.:** 0.29%. **Infant mortality** (per 1,000 live births): 4.1.

Education: Compulsory: ages 6-16. **Literacy:** 100%.

Major Intl. Organizations: UN.

Embassy: 2 UN Plaza, 25th floor, New York, NY 10017; 750-8064.

Website: www.andorra.ad/ang/home/index.htm

Andorra was a co-principality, with joint sovereignty by France and the bishop of Urgel, from 1278 to 1993.

Tourism, especially skiing, is the economic mainstay. A free port, allowing for an active trading center, draws some 13 million tourists annually. Andorran voters chose to end a feudal system that had been in place for 715 years and adopt a parliamentary system of government Mar. 14, 1993.

Angola

Republic of Angola

People: Population: 11,827,315. **Age distrib.** (%) <15: 43.4; 65+: 2.8. **Pop. density:** 25 per sq mi, 9 per sq km. **Urban:** 35.7%. **Ethnic groups:** Ovimbundu 37%, Kimbundu 25%, Bakongo 13%. **Principal languages:** Portuguese (official), Bantu and other African languages. **Chief religions:** Roman Catholic 62%, other Christian 32%.

Geography: Total area: 481,354 sq mi, 1,246,700 sq km; **Land area:** 481,354 sq mi, 1,246,700 sq km. **Location:** In SW Africa on Atlantic coast. **Neighbors:** Namibia on S, Zambia on E, Congo-Kinshasa (formerly Zaire) on N; Cabinda, an enclave separated from rest of country by short Atlantic coast of Congo-Kinshasa, borders Congo-Brazzaville. **Topography:** Most of Angola consists of a plateau elevated 3,000 to 5,000 feet above sea level, rising from a narrow coastal strip. There is also a temperate highland area in the west-central region, a desert in the S, and a tropical rains forest covering Cabinda. **Capital:** Luanda, 2,623,000.

Government: Type: Republic. **Head of state:** Pres. José Eduardo dos Santos; b Aug. 28, 1942; in office: Sept. 20, 1979. **Head of gov.:** Prime Min. Fernando da Piedade Dias dos Santos; b Mar. 5, 1952; in office: Dec. 6, 2002. **Local divisions:** 18 provinces. **Defense budget** (2004): $958 mil. **Active troops:** 108,400.

Economy: Industries: oil, mining, cement, metals, fish & food proc. **Chief crops:** bananas, sugarcane, coffee, sisal. **Natural resources:** oil, diamonds, iron ore, phosphates, copper, feldspar, gold, bauxite, uranium. **Livestock** (2003): cattle: 4.15 mil; chickens: 6.8 mil; goats: 2.05 mil; pigs: 780,000; sheep: 340,000. **Crude oil reserves** (2004): 5.4 bil. bbls. **Arable land:** 2%. **Livestock** (2004): cattle: 4.2 mil; chickens: 6.8 mil. ; goats: 2.1 mil; pigs: 780,000; sheep: 340,000. **Fish catch** (2003): 211,539 metric tons. **Electricity prod.** (2003): 1.9 bil. kWh. **Labor force** (2003 est.): agriculture 85%, industry and services 15%.

Finance: Monetary unit: New Kwanza (AON) (Sept. 2004: 85.30 = $1 U.S.). **GDP** (2004 est.): $23.2 bil.; **per capita GDP:** $2,100; **GDP growth:** 11.7%. **Imports** (2004 est.): $4.896 bil.; partners (2004): Portugal 18.4%, US 13.1%, South Africa 10.7%, Japan 6.9%, France 6.3%, Brazil 5.6%, UK 4.9%, China 4.5%. **Exports** (2004 est.): $12.8 bil.; partners (2004): US 39.8%, China 30.3%, Taiwan 8.1%, France 7.1%. **Tourism:** $71 mil. **Budget** (2004 est.): $9.6 bil. **Intl. reserves less gold:** $879 mil. **Consumer prices:** 37.34%.

Transport: Railroad: Length: 1,716 mi. **Motor vehicles** 117,200 pass. cars, 118,300 comm. vehicles. **Civil aviation:** 288.9 mil. pass.-mi; 32 airports. **Chief ports:** Cabinda, Lobito, Luanda.

Communications: TV sets: 15 per 1,000 pop. **Radios:** 67 per 1,000 pop. **Telephone lines:** 96,300. **Daily newspaper circ.:** 11 per 1,000 pop. **Internet** (2002): 41,000 users.

Health: Life expect.: 37.3 male; 39.6 female. **Births** (per 1,000 pop.): 45.6. **Deaths** (per 1,000 pop.): 24.5. **Natural inc.:** 2.11%. **Infant mortality** (per 1,000 live births): 187.5. **AIDS rate:** 3.9%.

Education: Compulsory: ages 4-9. **Literacy:** 42%.

Major Intl. Organizations: UN (FAO, IBRD, ILO, IMF, IMO, WHO, WTrO), AU.

Embassy: 2100-2108 16th St. NW 20009; 785-1156.

Website: www.angola.org

From the early centuries AD to 1500, Bantu tribes penetrated most of the region. Portuguese came in 1583, allied with the Bakongo kingdom in the north, and developed the slave trade. Large-scale colonization did not begin until the 20th century, when 400,000 Portuguese immigrated.

A guerrilla war begun in 1961 lasted until 1975, when Portugal granted independence. Fighting then erupted between three rival rebel groups—the National Front, based in Zaire (now Congo), the Soviet-backed Popular Movement for the Liberation of Angola (MPLA), and the National Union for the Total Independence of Angola (UNITA), aided by the U.S. and South Africa.

Cuban troops and Soviet aid helped the MPLA win control of most of the country by 1976, although fighting continued through the 1980s. A peace accord between the MPLA government and UNITA was signed May 1, 1991.

Elections were held in Sept. 1992, but fighting again broke out, as UNITA rejected the results. UNITA signed a new peace treaty with the government, Nov. 20, 1994, but the rebels were slow to demobilize. The UN Security Council voted, Aug. 28, 1997, to impose sanctions on UNITA. In Aug. 1998, Angola sent thousands of troops into Congo-Kinshasa (formerly Zaire) to support Laurent Kabila's regime. The UN ended its mission in Angola in Mar. 1999, as the civil war continued.

As of 2001, the UN estimated that the war with UNITA had claimed some 1 million lives and left another 2.5 million people homeless. More than 250 died when UNITA rebels ambushed a train Aug. 10. Rebel leader Jonas Savimbi was killed by government troops Feb. 22, 2002. UNITA agreed to a truce Apr. 4 of that year, ending the 27-year-long civil war. Fighting continued, however, between government forces and separatist guerrillas in oil-rich Cabinda.

Mismanagement and corruption led to the diversion of up to $4.2 bil in oil revenues during 1997-2002, according to a Human Rights Watch report. In Apr. 2004, the govt. arrested nearly 3,000 illegal diamond diggers, many of them foreigners. An outbreak of Marburg hemorrhagic fever, caused by a rare Ebola-like virus, claimed more than 300 lives in 2005.

Antigua and Barbuda

People: Population: 68,722. **Age distrib.** (%) <15: 27.9; 65+: 4.1. **Pop. density:** 402 per sq mi, 155 per sq km. **Urban:** 37.7%. **Ethnic groups:** Black, British, Portuguese, Lebanese, Syrian. **Principal languages:** English (official), local dialects. **Chief religions:** Predominantly Protestant; some Roman Catholic.

Geography: Total area: 171 sq mi, 443 sq km; **Land area:** 171 sq mi, 443 sq km. **Location:** Eastern Caribbean. **Neighbors:** St. Kitts & Nevis to W, Guadeloupe (Fr.) to S. Topography: These are mostly low-lying and limestone coral islands. Antigua is mostly hilly with an indented coast; Barbuda is a flat island with a large lagoon on the W. **Capital:** Saint John's, (2001) 28,000.

Government: Type: Constitutional monarchy with British-style parliament. **Head of state:** Queen Elizabeth II; represented by Gov.-Gen. James Carlisle; b Aug. 5, 1937; in office: June 10, 1993. **Head of gov.:** Prime Min. Baldwin Spencer; b Oct. 8, 1948; in office: Mar. 24, 2004. **Local divisions:** 6 parishes, 2 dependencies. **Defense budget** (2004): $4 mil. **Active troops:** 170.

Economy: Industries: tourism, constr., light mfg. **Chief crops:** cotton, fruits, vegetables. **Arable land:** 18%. **Livestock** (2004): cattle: 14,300; chickens: 105,000; goats: 36,000; pigs: 5,700; sheep: 19,000. **Fish catch** (2003): 2,587 metric tons. **Electricity prod.** (2003): 0.10 bil. kWh. **Labor force** (1983): agriculture 7%, industry 11%, services 82%.

Finance: Monetary unit: East Caribbean Dollar (XCD) (Sept. 2005: 2.67 = $1 U.S.). **GDP** (2002 est.): $750.0 mil; **per capita GDP:** $11,000; **GDP growth:** 3%. **Imports** (2002 est.): $692 mil; partners (2004): US 21.8%, Singapore 18.8%, China 10.7%, Poland 6.7%, Trinidad and Tobago 4.6%, UK 4.4%. **Exports** (2002): $689.0 mil; partners (2004): Germany 49.5%, UK 29.7%, France 3.5%. **Tourism:** $301 mil. **Budget** (2000 est.): $145.9 mil. **Intl. reserves less gold:** $77 mil.

Transport: Railroad: Length: 48 mi. **Motor vehicles** 24,000 pass. cars, 4,800 comm. vehicles. **Civil aviation:** 188.9 mil. pass.-mi; 2 airports.

Communications: TV sets: 493 per 1,000 pop. **Radios:** 545 per 1,000 pop. **Telephone lines** (2002): 38,000. **Daily newspaper circ.:** 91 per 1,000 pop. **Internet** (2002): 10,000 users.

Health: Life expect.: 69.5 male; 74.4 female. **Births** (per 1,000 pop.): 17.3. **Deaths** (per 1,000 pop.): 5.4. **Natural inc.:** 1.18%. **Infant mortality** (per 1,000 live births): 19.5.

Education: Compulsory: ages 5-16. **Literacy:** 89%.

Major Intl. Organizations: UN (FAO, IBRD, ILO, IMF, IMO, WHO, WTrO), Caricom, the Commonwealth, OAS, OECS.

Embassy: 3216 New Mexico Ave. NW 20016; 362-5211.

Website: www.antigua-barbuda.com

Columbus landed on Antigua in 1493. The British colonized it in 1632.

The British associated state of Antigua achieved independence as Antigua and Barbuda on Nov. 1, 1981. The government maintains close relations with the U.S., United Kingdom, and Venezuela. The country was hit hard by Hurricane Luis, Sept. 1995. About 3,000 refugees from the nearby island of Montserrat settled in Antigua following volcanic eruptions there in 1995-97.

Argentina

Argentine Republic

People: Population: 39,537,943. **Age distrib.** (%) <15: 25.6; 65+: 10.6. **Pop. density:** 37 per sq mi, 14 per sq km **Urban:** 90.1%. **Ethnic groups:** European 97%, Amerindian 3%. **Principal languages:** Spanish (official), English, Italian, German, French. **Chief religion:** Roman Catholic 92% (official).

Geography: Total area: 1,068,302 sq mi, 2,766,890 sq km; **Land area:** 1,056,642 sq mi, 2,736,690 sq km. **Location:** Occupies most of southern South America. **Neighbors:** Chile on W; Bolivia, Paraguay on N; Brazil, Uruguay on NE. **Topography:** Mountains in the W are: the Andean, Central, Misiones, and Southern ranges. Aconcagua is the highest peak in the western hemisphere, alt. 22,834 ft. E of the Andes are heavily wooded plains, called the Gran Chaco in the N, and the fertile, treeless Pampas in the central region. Patagonia, in the S, is bleak and arid. Rio de la Plata, an estuary in the NE, 170 by 140 mi., is mostly fresh water, from 2,485-mi Parana and 1,000-mi Uruguay rivers. **Capital:** Buenos Aires, 13,047,000 (the Senate has approved moving the capital to the Patagonia Region). **Cities (urban aggr.):** Cordoba, 1,444,000; Rosario, 1,231,000.

Government: Type: Republic. **Head of state and gov.:** Pres. Néstor Kirchner; b Feb. 25, 1950; in office: May 25, 2003. **Local divisions:** 23 provinces, 1 federal district. **Defense budget** (2004): $1.6 bil. **Active troops:** 71,400.

Economy: Industries: food proc., vehicles, consumer durables, textiles, chemicals. **Chief crops:** sunflower seeds, lemons, soybeans, grapes, corn. **Natural resources:** lead, zinc, tin, copper, iron ore, mang., oil, uranium. **Crude oil reserves** (2004): 2.7 bil. bbls. **Arable land:** 9%. **Livestock** (2004): cattle: 50.8 mil; chickens: 95 mil; goats: 4.2 mil; pigs: 3.1 mil; sheep: 12.5 mil. **Fish catch** (2003): 916,246 metric tons. **Electricity prod.** (2003): 83.3 bil. kWh.

Finance: Monetary unit: Peso (ARS) (Sept. 2005: 2.87 = $1 U.S.). **GDP** (2004 est.): $483.5 bil.; **per capita GDP:** $12,400; **GDP growth:** 8.3%. **Imports** (2004 est.): $22.06 bil.; partners (2004): Brazil 27%, US 20%, Germany 6.6%, China 4.6%, France 4.2%, Italy 4.1%. **Exports** (2004 est.): $33.8 bil.; partners (2004): Brazil 16.5%, Chile 10.9%, US 10.2%, China 8.5%, Spain 4.5%. **Tourism:** $2,097 mil. **Budget** (2004 est.): $26.8 bil. **Intl. reserves less gold:** $12.16 bil. **Gold:** 1.77 mil. oz t. **Consumer prices:** 4.42%.

Transport: Railroad: Length: 21,183 mi. **Motor vehicles** 5.3867 mil pass. cars, 1.004 mil comm. vehicles. **Civil aviation:** 5.2 bil pass.-mi; 145 airports. **Chief ports:** Buenos Aires, Bahia Blanca, La Plata.

Communications: TV sets: 293 per 1,000 pop. **Radios:** 681 per 1,000 pop. **Telephone lines** (2002): 8.0 mil. **Daily newspaper circ.:** 37.3 per 1,000 pop. **Internet** (2002): 4.1 mil. users.

Health: Life expect.: 72.2 male; 79.9 female. **Births** (per 1,000 pop.): 16.9. **Deaths** (per 1,000 pop.): 7.6. **Natural inc.:** 0.93%. **Infant mortality** (per 1,000 live births): 15.2. **AIDS rate:** 0.7%

Education: Compulsory: ages 5-14. **Literacy:** 97.1%.

Major Intl. Organizations: UN (FAO, IBRD, ILO, IMF, IMO, WHO, WTrO), OAS.

Embassy: 1600 New Hampshire Ave. NW 20009; 238-6400.

Website: www.turismo.gov.ar/eng/menu.htm

Nomadic Indians roamed the Pampas when Spaniards arrived, 1515-16, led by Juan Diaz de Solis. Nearly all the Indians were killed by the late 19th century. The colonists won independence, 1816, and a long period of disorder ended in a strong centralized government.

Large-scale Italian, German, and Spanish immigration in the decades after 1880 spurred modernization. Social reforms were enacted in the 1920s, but military coups prevailed 1930-46, until the election of Gen. Juan Perón as president.

Perón, with his wife, Eva Duarte (d 1952), effected labor reforms, but also suppressed speech and press freedoms, closed religious schools, and ran the country into debt. A 1955 coup exiled Perón, who was followed by a series of military and civilian regimes. Perón returned in 1973, and was once more elected president. He died 10 months later, succeeded by his wife Isabel, who had been elected vice president, and who became the first woman head of state in the western hemisphere.

A military junta ousted Mrs. Perón in 1976 amid charges of corruption. Under a continuing state of siege, the army conducted a "dirty war" against guerrillas and leftists in which an estimated 30,000 people "disappeared." On Dec. 9, 1985, after a trial of 5 months and nearly 1,000 witnesses, 5 former junta members were found guilty of murder and human rights abuses.

Argentine troops seized control of the British-held Falkland Islands on Apr. 2, 1982. Both countries had claimed sovereignty over the islands, located 250 miles off the Argentine coast, since 1833. The British dispatched a task force and declared a total air and sea blockade around the Falklands. Fighting began May 1; several hundred lost their lives as the result of the destruction of a British destroyer and the sinking of an Argentine cruiser.

British troops landed on East Falkland Island May 21 and eventually surrounded Stanley, the capital city and Argentine stronghold. The Argentine troops surrendered, June 14; Argentine Pres. Leopoldo Galtieri resigned June 17.

Democratic rule returned in 1983 as Raul Alfonsín's Radical Civic Union party gained an absolute majority in the presidential electoral college and Congress. By 1989 the nation was plagued by severe financial and political problems, as hyperinflation sparked looting and rioting in several cities. The government of Peronist Pres. Carlos Saúl Menem, installed 1989, introduced harsh economic measures to curtail inflation, control government spending, and restructure the foreign debt.

About 85 people were killed and nearly 300 injured in the terrorist bombing of a Jewish cultural center in Buenos Aires, July 18, 1994. Following passage of a new constitution in Aug. 1994, Menem was reelected president on May 14, 1995.

Buenos Aires Mayor Fernando de la Rúa won the presidential election Oct. 24, 1999. A prolonged recession and a debt of more than $130 billion left Argentina facing an economic crisis in 2001, which austerity measures and IMF aid failed to remedy. After widespread rioting and looting Dec. 19, de la Rúa resigned.

A 2-week period of protests and political upheavals abated when Congress, Jan. 1, 2002, chose a Peronist, Eduardo Alberto Duhalde, to finish de la Rúa's term. Duhalde devalued the peso by cutting its ties with the U.S. dollar. Further economic decline and renewed protests led Duhalde July 2 to schedule an early presidential election for Mar. 2003; another Peronist, Néstor Kirchner, took office May 25, 2003, after Menem pulled out of a runoff election. Kirchner moved to end corruption and human rights abuses among the military and police. A new IMF aid deal, approved Sept. 10, 2003, rescued Argentina from default.

Fire at a Buenos Aires nightclub, Dec. 30, 2004, killed 194 people. The supreme court, June 14, 2005, overturned amnesty laws that had barred prosecution for "dirty war" crimes committed while the military ruled Argentina.

Armenia

Republic of Armenia

People: Population: 2,982,904. **Age distrib.** (%) <15: 21.6; 65+: 10.9. **Pop. density:** 259 per sq mi, 100 per sq km. **Urban:** 64.4%. **Ethnic groups:** Armenian 93%, Russian 2%. **Principal languages:** Armenian (official), Russian. **Chief religions:** Armenian Apostolic 95%, other Christian 4%, Yezidi 2%.

Geography: Total area: 11,506 sq mi, 29,800 sq km; **Land area:** 10,965 sq mi, 28,400 sq km. **Location:** SW Asia. **Neighbors:** Georgia on N, Azerbaijan on E, Iran on S, Turkey on W. **Topography:** Mountainous with many peaks above 10,000 ft. **Capital:** Yerevan, 1,079,000.

Government: Type: Republic. **Head of state:** Pres. Robert Kocharian; b Aug. 31, 1954; in office: Apr. 9, 1998. **Head of gov.:** Prime Min. Andranik Markarian; b June 12, 1951; in office: May 12, 2000. **Local divisions:** 10 provinces, 1 city. **Defense budget** (2004): $89 mil. **Active troops:** 44,874.

Economy: Industries: machine tools & machines, electric motors, tires, knitted wear. **Chief crops:** grapes, vegetables. **Natural resources:** gold, copper, molybd., zinc, alumina. **Arable land:** 17%. **Livestock** (2004): cattle: 565,844; chickens: 3.6 mil; goats: 48,297; pigs: 85,393; sheep: 580,178. **Fish catch** (2003): 1,633 metric tons. **Electricity prod.** (2003): 5.0 bil. kWh. **Labor force** (2002 est.): agriculture 45%, industry 25%, services 30%.

Finance: Monetary unit: Dram (AMD) (Sept. 2005: 439.50 = $1 U.S.). **GDP** (2004 est.): $13.7 bil.; **per capita GDP:** $4,600; **GDP growth:** 9%. **Imports** (2004 est.): $1.3 bil.; partners (2004): Belgium 10.3%, Iran 10.2%, Russia 9.8%, Israel 8.6%, US 7.7%, UAE 6.2%, Italy 5.4%, Germany 5%, France 4.6%, Ukraine 4.5%. **Exports** (2004 est.): $850.0 mil; partners (2004): Belgium 16.8%, Israel 14.3%, Russia 14.2%, Germany 11.4%, Iran 9.9%, US 7.8%, Netherlands 5.8%. **Tourism:** $73 mil. **Budget** (2004 est.): $491.2 mil. **Intl. reserves less gold:** $371 mil. **Consumer prices:** 6.93%.

Transport: Railroad: Length: 525 mi. **Civil aviation:** 438,688 pass.-mi; 8 airports.

Communications: TV sets: 241 per 1,000 pop. **Radios:** 239 per 1,000 pop. **Telephone lines:** 563,700. **Daily newspaper circ.:** 5.0 per 1,000 pop. **Internet**: 140,000 users.

Health: Life expect.: 72.2 male; 79.9 female. **Births** (per 1,000 pop.): 16.9. **Deaths** (per 1,000 pop.): 7.6. **Natural inc.:** 0.93%. **Infant mortality** (per 1,000 live births): 15.2. **AIDS rate:** 0.1%.

Education: Compulsory: ages 7-15. **Literacy:** 98.6%.

Major Intl. Organizations: UN (FAO, IBRD, ILO, IMF, WHO, WTrO), CIS, OSCE.

Embassy: 2225 R St. NW 20008; 319-1976.

Website: www.armeniaemb.org

Ancient Armenia extended into parts of what are now Turkey and Iran. Present-day Armenia was set up as a Soviet republic Apr.

2, 1921. It joined Georgian and Azerbaijan SSRs Mar. 12, 1922, to form the Transcaucasian SFSR, which became part of the USSR Dec. 30, 1922. Armenia became a constituent republic of the USSR Dec. 5, 1936. An earthquake struck Armenia Dec. 7, 1988; approximately 55,000 were killed and several cities and towns were left in ruins.

Armenia declared independence Sept. 23, 1991, and became an independent state when the USSR disbanded Dec. 26, 1991.

Fighting between mostly Christian Armenia and mostly Muslim Azerbaijan escalated in 1992. Each country claimed Nagorno-Karabakh, an enclave in Azerbaijan that has a majority population of ethnic Armenians. A temporary cease-fire was announced in May 1994, with Armenian forces in control of the enclave.

Voters approved, July 5, 1995, a new constitution increasing presidential powers. Pres. Levon Ter-Petrosian won reelection on Sept. 22, 1996, amid claims of fraud; he resigned Feb. 3, 1998, in a conflict over Nagorno-Karabakh. Robert Kocharian, a nationalist born in the disputed region, won the presidency on Mar. 30, 1998. Gunmen stormed Parliament Oct. 27, 1999, killing Prime Min. Vazgen Sarkissian and 7 others. Kocharian won a 2nd term Mar. 5, 2003, in a runoff vote viewed as flawed by opposition groups and Western observers.

Australia

Commonwealth of Australia

People: Population: 20,090,437. **Age distrib.** (%) <15: 19.8; 65+: 12.9. **Pop. density:** 7 per sq mi, 3 per sq km. **Urban:** 92.0%. **Ethnic groups:** White 92%, Asian 7%, Aborigine and other 1%. **Principal languages:** English (official), Aboriginal languages. **Chief religions:** Roman Catholic 26%, Anglican 21%, other Christian 21%.

Geography: Total area: 2,967,909 sq mi, 7,686,850 sq km; **Land area:** 2,941,299 sq mi, 7,617,930 sq km. **Location:** SE of Asia, Indian O. is W and S, Pacific O. (Coral, Tasman seas) is E; they meet N of Australia in Timor and Arafura seas. Tasmania lies 150 mi. S of Victoria state, across Bass Strait. **Neighbors:** Nearest are Indonesia, Papua New Guinea on N; Solomons, Fiji, and New Zealand on E. **Topography:** An island continent. The Great Dividing Range along the E coast has Mt. Kosciusko, 7,310 ft. The W plateau rises to 2,000 ft., with arid areas in the Great Sandy and Great Victoria deserts. The NW part of Western Australia and Northern Terr. are arid and hot. The NE has heavy rainfall and Cape York Peninsula has jungles. **Capital:** Canberra, 373,000. **Cities (urban aggr.):** Sydney, 4,099,000; Melbourne, 3,447,000; Brisbane, 1,626,000; Perth, 1,376,000; Adelaide, 1,104,000.

Government: Type: Democratic, federal state system. **Head of state:** Queen Elizabeth II, represented by Gov.-Gen. Michael Jeffery; b Dec. 12, 1937; in office: Aug. 11, 2003. **Head of gov.:** Prime Min. John Howard; b July 26, 1939; in office: Mar. 11, 1996. **Local divisions:** 6 states, 2 territories. **Defense budget** (2004): $11.7 bil. **Active troops:** 51,800.

Economy: Industries: mining, industrial & transp. equip., food proc., chemicals, steel. **Chief crops:** wheat, barley, sugarcane, fruits. **Natural resources:** bauxite, coal, iron ore, copper, tin, silver, uranium, nickel, tungsten, mineral sands, lead, zinc, diamonds, nat. gas, oil. **Crude oil reserves** (2004): 1.5 bil. bbls. **Other resources:** Wool (world's leading producer), beef. **Arable land:** 6%. **Livestock** (2004): cattle: 26.4 mil; chickens: 90 mil; goats: 400,000; pigs: 2.7 mil; sheep: 94.5 mil. **Fish catch** (2003): 248,949 metric tons. **Electricity prod.** (2003): 215.8 bil. kWh. **Labor force** (2004 est.): agriculture 3.6%, industry 26.4%, services 70%.

Finance: Monetary unit: Australian Dollar (AUD) (Sept. 2005: 1.31 = $1 U.S.). **GDP** (2004 est.): $611.7 bil.; **per capita GDP:** $30,700; **GDP growth:** 3.5%. **Imports** (2004 est.): $98.1 bil.; partners (2004): US 14.8%, China 12.7%, Japan 11.8%, Germany 5.8%, Singapore 4.4%, UK 4.1%. **Exports** (2004 est.): $86.9 bil.; partners (2004): Japan 18.6%, China 9.2%, US 8.1%, South Korea 7.7%, New Zealand 7.4%, India 4.6%, UK 4.2%. **Tourism:** $10,318 mil. **Budget** (2004 est.): $221.7 bil. **Intl. reserves less gold:** $23.05 bil. **Gold:** 2.56 mil. oz t.

Transport: Railroad: Length: 27,350 mi. **Motor vehicles** 9.84 mil pass. cars, 2.24 mil comm. vehicles. **Civil aviation:** 52.8 bil. pass.-mi; 294 airports. **Chief ports:** Sydney, Melbourne, Brisbane, Adelaide, Fremantle, Geelong.

Communications: TV sets: 716 per 1,000 pop. **Radios:** 1,391 per 1,000 pop. **Telephone lines:** 10.8 mil. **Daily newspaper circ.:** 293 per 1,000 pop. **Internet** 11.3 mil. users.

Health: Life expect.: 77.5 male; 83.4 female. **Births** (per 1,000 pop.): 12.3. **Deaths** (per 1,000 pop.): 7.4. **Natural inc.:** 0.48%. **Infant mortality** (per 1,000 live births): 4.7. **AIDS rate:** 0.1%.

Education: Compulsory: ages 5-15. **Literacy:** 100%.

Major Intl. Organizations: UN and all of its specialized agencies, APEC, the Commonwealth, OECD.

Embassy: 1601 Massachusetts Ave. NW 20036; 797-3000.

Website: www.australia.gov.au

Australia harbors many plant and animal species not found elsewhere, including kangaroos, koalas, platypuses, dingos (wild dogs), Tasmanian devils (raccoon-like marsupials), wombats (bear-like marsupials), and barking and frilled lizards.

Capt. James Cook explored the E coast in 1770, when the continent was inhabited by a variety of different tribes. The first settlers, beginning in 1788, were mostly convicts, soldiers, and government officials. By 1830, Britain had claimed the entire continent, and the immigration of free settlers began to accelerate. The Commonwealth was proclaimed Jan. 1, 1901. Northern Terr. was granted limited self-rule July 1, 1978.

State/Territory, Capital	Area (sq. mi.)	Population (2002 est.)
New South Wales, Sydney	309,500	6,257,351
Victoria, Melbourne	87,900	4,888,234
Queensland, Brisbane	666,990	3,729,028
Western Australia, Perth	975,100	1,934,494
South Australia, Adelaide	379,900	1,522,456
Tasmania, Hobart	26,200	473,365
Australian Capital Terr., Canberra	900	322,234
Northern Terr., Darwin	519,800	197,724

Racially discriminatory immigration policies were abandoned in 1973, after 3 million Europeans (half British) had entered since 1945. The 50,000 aborigines and 150,000 part-aborigines are mostly detribalized, but there are several preserves in the Northern Territory. They remain economically disadvantaged.

Australia's agricultural success makes the country among the top exporters of beef, lamb, wool, and wheat. Major mineral deposits have been developed, largely for export. Industrialization has been completed. The nation endured a deep recession 1990-93 but has rebounded strongly.

The Labor Party won a majority in Feb. 1983 general elections and was reelected in 1984, 1987, 1990, and 1993. After an election that focused mainly on economic issues, conservatives swept into power in elections Mar. 2, 1996.

Incumbent Prime Min. John Howard retained power, but with a reduced majority, in parliamentary elections Oct. 3, 1998. Australia led an international peacekeeping force into East Timor in Sept. 1999. In a referendum Nov. 6, voters rejected a proposal that would have made Australia a republic. Sydney hosted the Summer Olympics Sept. 15-Oct. 1, 2000. Howard won a 3rd term in the elections of Nov. 10, 2001.

Australian troops fought in U.S.-led military operations in Afghanistan (2001) and Iraq (2003). Some 2,000 Australian peacekeepers began arriving in the Solomon Is., July 24, 2003; nearly all had been withdrawn by mid-2005. Howard won a 4th term in Oct. 9, 2004, elections.

Australian External Territories

Norfolk Isl., area 13 sq. mi., pop. (2004 est.) 1,841, was taken over, 1914. The soil is very fertile, suitable for citrus, bananas, and coffee. Many of the inhabitants are descendants of the *Bounty* mutineers, moved to Norfolk 1856 from Pitcairn Isl. Australia offered the island limited home rule in 1978.

Coral Sea Isls. Territory, area 1 sq. mi., is administered from Norfolk Isl.

Territory of Ashmore and Cartier Isls., area 2 sq. mi., in the Indian O., came under Australian authority 1934 and are administered as part of Northern Territory. **Heard Isl. and McDonald Isls.,** area 159 sq. mi., are administered by the Dept. of Science.

Cocos (Keeling) Isls., 27 small coral islands in the Indian O. 1,750 mi. NW of Australia. Pop. (2004 est.) 629; area 5 sq. mi. The residents voted to become part of Australia, Apr. 1984.

Christmas Isl., area 52 sq. mi. (2004 est.) 396; 230 mi. S of Java, was transferred by Britain in 1958. It has phosphate deposits.

Australian Antarctic Territory was claimed by Australia in 1933, including 2,362,000 sq. mi. of territory S of 60th parallel S Lat. and between 160th-45th meridians E Long. It does not include Adelie Coast.

Austria

Republic of Austria

People: Population: 8,184,691. **Age distrib.** (%) <15: 15.6; 65+: 16.6. **Pop. density:** 253 per sq mi, 98 per sq km. **Urban:** 65.8%. **Ethnic groups:** German 88%. **Principal languages:** German (official), Serbo-Croatian, Slovenian. **Chief religions:** Roman Catholic 74%, Protestant 5%.

Geography: Total area: 32,382 sq mi, 83,870 sq km; **Land area:** 31,832 sq mi, 82,444 sq km. **Location:** In S Central Europe. **Neighbors:** Switzerland, Liechtenstein on W; Germany, Czech Rep. on N; Slovakia, Hungary on E; Slovenia, Italy on S. **Topography:** Austria is primarily mountainous, with the Alps and foothills covering the western and southern provinces. The eastern provinces and Vienna are located in the Danube River Basin. **Capital:** Vienna, 2,179,000.

Government: Type: Federal republic. **Head of state:** Pres. Heinz Fischer; b Oct. 9, 1938; in office: July 8, 2004. **Head of gov.:** Chancellor Wolfgang Schüssel; b June 7, 1945; in office: Feb. 4, 2000. **Local divisions:** 9 bundeslaender (states). **Defense budget** (2004): $2.7 bil. **Active troops:** 35,000.

Economy: Industries: constr., machinery, vehicles & parts, food, chemicals. **Chief crops:** grains, potatoes, sugar beets, grapes. **Natural resources:** iron ore, oil, timber, magnesite, lead, coal, lignite, copper, hydropower. **Crude oil reserves** (2004): 62 mil bbls. **Arable land:** 17%. **Livestock** (2004): cattle: 2.1 mil; chickens: 11.6 mil; goats: 58,000; pigs: 3.2 mil; sheep: 325,000. **Fish catch** (2003): 2,605 metric tons. **Electricity prod.** (2003): 55.8 bil. kWh. **Labor force** (2001 est.): agriculture and forestry 4%, industry and crafts 29%, services 67%.

Finance: Monetary unit: Euro (EUR) (Sept. 2005: 0.80 = $1 U.S.). **GDP** (2004 est.): $255.9 bil.; **per capita GDP:** $31,300; **GDP growth:** 1.9%. **Imports** (2004 est.): $101.2 bil.; partners

(2004): Germany 45.9%, Italy 6.7%, Switzerland 4.3%. **Exports** (2004 est.): $102.7 bil.; partners (2004): Germany 31.4%, Italy 9%, US 6%, Switzerland 4.8%, UK 4.4%, France 4.2%. **Tourism:** $14,068 mil. **Budget** (2004 est.): $146.4 bil. **Intl. reserves less gold:** $5.06 bil. **Gold:** 9.89 mil. oz t. **Consumer prices:** 2.05%.

Transport: Railroad: Length: 3,741 mi. **Motor vehicles:** 3.9871 mil pass. cars, 765,600 comm. vehicles. **Civil aviation:** 8.6 bil pass.-mi; 24 airports. **Chief ports:** Linz, Vienna, Enns, Krems.

Communications: TV sets: 526 per 1,000 pop. **Radios:** 751 per 1,000 pop. **Telephone lines:** 4.0 mil. **Daily newspaper circ.:** 296 per 1,000 pop. **Internet**: 3.7 mil. users.

Health: Life expect.: 76.0 male; 82.0 female. **Births** (per 1,000 pop.): 8.8. **Deaths** (per 1,000 pop.): 9.7. **Natural inc.:** –0.09%. **Infant mortality** (per 1,000 live births): 4.7. **AIDS rate:** 0.3%.

Education: Compulsory: ages 6-14. **Literacy:** 98%.

Major Intl. Organizations: UN and all of its specialized agencies, EU, OECD, OSCE.

Embassy: 3524 International Ct. NW 20008; 895-6700.

Website: www.austria.gv.at/DesktopDefault.aspx?alias=english

Rome conquered Austrian lands from Celtic tribes around 15 BC. In 788 the territory was incorporated into Charlemagne's empire. By 1300, the House of Hapsburg had gained control; they added vast territories in all parts of Europe to their realm in the next few hundred years.

Austrian dominance of Germany was undermined in the 18th century and ended by Prussia by 1866. But the Congress of Vienna, 1815, confirmed Austrian control of a large empire in southeast Europe consisting of Germans, Hungarians, Slavs, Italians, and others. The dual Austro-Hungarian monarchy was established in 1867, giving autonomy to Hungary and almost 50 years of peace.

World War I, started after the June 28, 1914, assassination of Archduke Franz Ferdinand, the Hapsburg heir, by a Serbian nationalist, destroyed the empire. By 1918 Austria was reduced to a small republic, with the borders it has today.

Nazi Germany invaded Austria Mar. 13, 1938. The republic was reestablished in 1945, under Allied occupation. Full independence and neutrality were restored in 1955. Austria joined the European Union Jan. 1, 1995.

The rise of the right-wing, anti-immigrant Austrian Freedom Party challenged the dominance of the Austrian Social Democratic Party in the late 1990s. When Freedom Party members joined the cabinet, Feb. 4, 2000, the EU imposed political sanctions on Austria, Feb. 4-Sept. 12, 2000. Party support plummeted in elections Nov. 24, 2002. Pres. Thomas Klestil died July 6, 2004, 2 days before his term expired; he was succeeded by recently elected Heinz Fischer, a Social Democrat.

Azerbaijan

Republic of Azerbaijan

People: Population: 7,911,974. **Age distrib.** (%) <15: 26.4; 65+: 7.8. **Pop. density:** 237 per sq mi, 91 per sq km. **Urban:** 50.0%. **Ethnic groups:** Azeri 90%, Dagestani 3%, Russian 3%, Armenian 2%. **Principal languages:** Azeri (official), Russian, Armenian. **Chief religions:** Muslim 93%, Russian Orthodox 3%, Armenian Orthodox 2%.

Geography: Total area: 33,436 sq mi, 86,600 sq km; **Land area:** 33,243 sq mi, 86,100 sq km. **Location:** SW Asia. **Neighbors:** Russia, Georgia on N; Iran on S; Armenia on W; Caspian Sea on E. Topography: The Great Caucasus Mts. in N, Karabakh Upland in W border the Kur-Abas lowland; climate is arid except in the subtropical SE. **Capital:** Baku, 1,816,000.

Government: Type: Republic. **Head of state:** Pres. Ilham Aliyev; b Dec. 24, 1961; in office: Oct. 31, 2003. **Head of gov.:** Prime Min. Artur Rasizade; b Feb. 26, 1935; in office: Nov. 4, 2003. **Local division:** 59 rayons, 11 cities, 1 autonomous republic. **Defense budget** (2004): $156 mil. **Active troops:** 66,490.

Economy: Industries: oil products, oil field equip., steel, iron ore, cement. **Chief crops:** cotton, grain, rice, grapes. **Natural resources:** oil, nat. gas, iron ore, nonferrous metals, alumina. **Crude oil reserves** (2004): 7.0 bil. bbls. **Arable land:** 18%. **Livestock** (2004): cattle: 1.9 mil; chickens: 16.8 mil; goats: 604,112; pigs: 20,442; sheep: 6.7 mil. **Fish catch** (2003): 6,937 metric tons. **Electricity prod.** (2003): 20.0 bil. kWh. **Labor force** (2001): agriculture and forestry 41%, industry 7%, services 52%.

Finance: Monetary unit: Manat (AZM) (Sept. 2005: 4,609.00 = $1 U.S.). **GDP** (2004 est.): $30.0 bil.; **per capita GDP:** $3,800; **GDP growth:** 9.8%. **Imports** (2004 est.): $3.622 bil.; partners (2004): UK 13.9%, Russia 13.1%, Turkey 11.5%, Germany 8%, Netherlands 5.3%, China 5%, US 4.7%, Italy 4.5%, Ukraine 4.3%. **Exports** (2004 est.): $3.2 bil.; partners (2004): Italy 31.1%, Czech Republic 14.5%, Germany 9.4%, Turkey 6.1%, Russia 6%, Georgia 5.3%, France 4.9%. **Tourism:** $58 mil. **Budget** (2004 est.): $2.8 bil. **Intl. reserves less gold:** $702 mil. **Consumer prices:** 6.71%.

Transport: Railroad: Length: 1,837 mi. **Motor vehicles** 350,600 pass. cars, 120,400 comm. vehicles. **Civil aviation:** 317.5 mil. pass.-mi; 27 airports. **Chief port:** Baku.

Communications: TV sets: 257 per 1,000 pop. **Radios:** 23 per 1,000 pop. **Telephone lines:** 941,400. **Daily newspaper circ.:** 27 per 1,000 pop. **Internet (2002):** 300,000 users.

Health: Life expect.: 59.2 male; 67.7 female. **Births** (per 1,000 pop.): 20.4. **Deaths** (per 1,000 pop.): 9.9. **Natural inc.:** 1.05%. **Infant mortality** (per 1,000 live births): 81.7. **AIDS rate:** <0.1%.

Education: Compulsory: ages 6-17. **Literacy:** 97%.

Major Intl. Organizations: UN (FAO, IBRD, ILO, IMF, IMO, WHO), CIS, OSCE.

Embassy: 2741 34th St NW 20008 337-3500.

Website: www.azembassy.com

Azerbaijan was the home of Scythian tribes and part of the Roman Empire. Overrun by Turks in the 11th century and conquered by Russia in 1806 and 1813, it joined the USSR Dec. 30, 1922, and became a constituent republic in 1936. Azerbaijan declared independence Aug. 30, 1991, and became an independent state when the Soviet Union disbanded Dec. 26, 1991.

Fighting between mostly Muslim Azerbaijan and mostly Christian Armenia escalated in 1992 and continued in 1993 and 1994. Each country claimed Nagorno-Karabakh, an enclave in Azerbaijan with a majority population of ethnic Armenians. A temporary cease-fire was announced in May 1994, with Armenian forces in control of the enclave.

A National Council ousted Communist Pres. Mutaibov and took power May 19, 1992. Abulfez Elchibey became the nation's first democratically elected president June 7, but was ousted from office by Surat Huseynov, commander of a private militia, June 30, 1993. Huseynov became prime minister, and Haydar Aliyev, a pro-Russian former Communist, became president. Huseynov fled the country after his supporters staged an unsuccessful coup attempt Oct. 1994. Voters approved a new constitution expanding presidential powers, Nov. 12, 1995. Pres. Aliyev was reelected Oct. 11, 1998, but international monitors called the election seriously flawed. In Dec. 2001, a presidential decree made Latin script obligatory for the Azerbaijaini language, replacing the Cyrillic alphabet used during Soviet rule.

The dying Pres. Aliyev named his son Ilham prime minister Aug. 4, 2003. The younger Aliyev won the presidential election of Oct. 15, in a vote considered fraudulent by international observers; he responded to violent protests Oct. 16 by arresting hundreds of opposition leaders and their supporters.

The Bahamas

Commonwealth of The Bahamas

People: Population: 301,790. **Age distrib.** (%) <15: 27.9; 65+: 6.2. **Pop. density:** 56 per sq mi, 22 per sqq km. **Urban:** 89.5%. **Ethnic groups:** Black 85%, White 12%. **Principal languages:** English, Creole (among Haitian immigrants). **Chief religions:** Baptist 35%, Anglican 15%, Roman Catholic 14%, other Christian 15%.

Geography: Total area: 5,382 sq mi, 13,940 sq km; **Land area:** 3,888 sq mi, 10,070 sq km. **Location:** In Atlantic O., E of Florida. **Neighbors:** Nearest are U.S. on W, Cuba on S. **Topography:** Nearly 700 islands (29 inhabited) and over 2,000 islets in the W Atlantic O. extend 760 mi. NW to SE. **Capital:** Nassau, 222,000. **Cities (urban aggr.):** (2001 est.) Grand Bahama, 40,898.

Government: Type: Independent commonwealth. **Head of state:** Queen Elizabeth II, represented by Gov.-Gen. Dame Ivy Dumont; b Oct. 2, 1930; in office: Nov. 13, 2001. **Head of gov.:** Prime Min. Perry Christie; b Aug. 21,1943; in office: May 3, 2002. **Local divisions:** 21 districts. **Defense budget** (2004): $30 mil. **Active troops:** 860.

Economy: Industries: tourism, banking, cement, oil refining & shipment, salt, rum. **Chief crops:** citrus, vegetables. **Natural resources:** salt, aragonite, timber. **Arable land:** 1%. **Livestock** (2004): cattle: 750; chickens: 3 mil; goats: 14,500; pigs: 5,000; sheep: 6,500. **Fish catch** (2003): 12,653 metric tons. **Electricity prod.** (2003): 1.8 bil. kWh. **Labor force** (1999 est.): agriculture 5%, industry 5%, tourism 50%, other services 40%.

Finance: Monetary unit: Bahamian Dollar (BSD) (Sept. 2005: 1.00 = $1 U.S.). **GDP** (2004 est.): $5.3 bil.; **per capita GDP:** $17,700; **GDP growth:** 3%. **Imports** (2003): $1.6 bil.; partners (2004): US 22.3%, South Korea 19%, Japan 8.2%, Brazil 8.2%, Italy 8.1%, Venezuela 6.8%. **Exports** (2003 est.): $636.0 mil; partners (2004): US 42.1%, Spain 10.3%, Poland 6.1%, Germany 6.1%, Switzerland 4.9%, Paraguay 4.8%, France 4.5%, Mexico 4.5%. **Tourism:** $1,782 mil. **Budget** (2004 est.): $1.0 bil. **Intl. reserves less gold:** $434 mil. **Consumer prices:** 0.87%.

Transport: Motor vehicles: 80,000 pass. cars, 25,000 comm. vehicles. **Civil aviation:** 242,956 pass.-mi; 30 airports. **Chief ports:** Nassau, Freeport.

Communications: TV sets: 243 per 1,000 pop. **Radios:** 739 per 1,000 pop. **Telephone lines:** 131,700. **Daily newspaper circ.:** 125 per 1,000 pop. **Internet**: 84,000 users.

Health: Life expect.: 62.1 male; 69.0 female. **Births** (per 1,000 pop.): 17.9. **Deaths** (per 1,000 pop.): 9.0. **Natural inc.:** 0.89%. **Infant mortality** (per 1,000 live births): 25.2. **AIDS rate:** 3%.

Education: Compulsory: ages 5-16. **Literacy:** 95.6%.

Major Intl. Organizations: UN (FAO, IBRD, ILO, IMF, IMO, WHO), Caricom, the Commonwealth, OAS.

Embassy: 2220 Massachusetts Ave. NW 20008; 319-2660.

Website: www.bahamas.gov.bs

Christopher Columbus first set foot in the New World on San Salvador (Watling Isl.) in 1492, when Arawak Indians inhabited the islands. British settlement began in 1647; the islands became a British colony in 1783. Internal self-government was granted in 1964; full independence within the Commonwealth was attained July 10, 1973. International banking and investment management have become major industries alongside tourism.

Bahrain

Kingdom of Bahrain

People: Population: 688,345. **Age distrib.** (%) <15: 27.8; 65+: 3.4. **Pop. density:** 2,678 per sq mi, 1,035 per sq km. **Urban:** 90.0%. **Ethnic groups:** Arab 73%, Asian 19%, Iranian 8%. **Principal languages:** Arabic (official), English, Farsi, Urdu. **Chief religion:** Muslim (Shi'a 70% and Sunni) 81%.

Geography: Total area: 257 sq mi, 665 sq km; **Land area:** 257 sq mi, 665 sq km. **Location:** SW Asia, in Persian Gulf. **Neighbors:** Nearest are Saudi Arabia on W, Qatar on E. **Topography:** Bahrain Island, and several adjacent, smaller islands, are flat, hot, and humid, with little rain. **Capital:** Manama, 139,000.

Government: Type: Constitutional monarchy. **Head of state:** King Hamad bin Isa al-Khalifa; b Jan. 28, 1950; in office: as emir Mar. 6, 1999; as king Feb. 14, 2002. **Head of gov.:** Prime Min. Khalifa bin Sulman al-Khalifa; b 1936; in office: Jan. 19, 1970. **Local divisions:** 12 municipalities. **Defense budget** (2004): $473 mil. **Active troops:** 11,200.

Economy: Industries: oil proc. & refining, aluminum smelting, offshore banking, ship repair. **Chief crops:** fruit, vegetables. **Natural resources:** oil, nat. gas, fish, pearls. **Crude oil reserves** (2004): 125 mil bbls. **Arable land:** 1%. **Livestock** (2004): cattle: 9,010; chickens: 470,000; goats: 25,000; sheep: 39,170. **Fish catch** (2003): 13,641 metric tons. **Electricity prod.** (2003): 7.3 bil. kWh. **Labor force** (1997 est.): agriculture 1%, industry, commerce, and services 79%, government 20%.

Finance: Monetary unit: Dinar (BHD) (Sept. 2005: 0.38 = $1 U.S.). **GDP** (2004 est.): $13.0 bil.; **per capita GDP:** $19,200; **GDP growth:** 5.6%. **Imports** (2004 est.): $5.9 bil.; partners (2004): Saudi Arabia 33.1%, Japan 7.6%, Germany 6.1%, US 5.7%, UK 5.6%, France 4.9%. **Exports** (2004 est.): $8.2 bil.; partners (2004): US 3.1%, South Korea 2.3%, Japan 2%. **Tourism:** $740 mil. **Budget** (2004 est.): $3.3 bil. **Intl. reserves less gold:** $1.25 bil. **Gold:** 150,000 oz t. **Consumer prices** (changed 2002): 1.2%

Transport: Motor vehicles187,000 pass. cars, 38,400 comm. vehicles. **Civil aviation:** 1.9 bil pass.-mi; 3 airports. **Chief ports:** Manama, Sitrah.

Communications: TV sets: 446 per 1,000 pop. **Radios:** 64 per 1,000 pop. **Telephone lines:** 185,800. **Daily newspaper circ.:** 117 per 1,000 pop. **Internet**: 150,000 users.

Health: Life expect.: 71.8 male; 76.8 female. **Births** (per 1,000 pop.): 18.1. **Deaths** (per 1,000 pop.): 4.1. **Natural inc.:** 1.40%. **Infant mortality** (per 1,000 live births): 17.3. **AIDS rate:** 0.2%.

Education: Free, compulsory: ages 6-17. **Literacy:** 89.1%.

Major Intl. Organizations: UN (FAO, IBRD, ILO, IMF, IMO, WHO, WTrO), AL.

Embassy: 3502 International Dr. NW 20008; 342-1111.

Website: www.bahrain.gov.bh/english/index.asp

Long ruled by the Khalifa family, Bahrain was a British protectorate from 1861 to Aug. 15, 1971, when it regained independence.

Pearls, shrimp, fruits, and vegetables were the mainstays of the economy until oil was discovered in 1932. By the 1970s, oil reserves were depleted; international banking thrived.

Bahrain took part in the 1973-74 Arab oil embargo against the U.S. and other nations. The government bought controlling interest in the oil industry in 1975. Shiite dissidents have clashed with the Sunni-led government since 1996.

Emir Hamad bin Isa al-Khalifa proclaimed himself king Feb. 14, 2002. Local elections in May marked the 1st time Bahraini women were allowed to vote and run for office.

Bangladesh

People's Republic of Bangladesh

People: Population: 144,319,628. **Age distrib.** (%) <15: 33.1; 65+: 3.4. **Pop. density:** 2,596 per sq mi, 1,002 per sq km. **Urban:** 24.2%.**Ethnic groups:** Bengali 98%. **Principal languages:** Bangla (official, also known as Bengali), English. **Chief religions:** Muslim 83% (official), Hindu 16%.

Geography: Total area: 55,599 sq mi, 144,000 sq km; **Land area:** 51,703 sq mi, 133,910 sq km. **Location:** In S Asia, on N bend of Bay of Bengal. **Neighbors:** India nearly surrounds country on W, N, E; Myanmar on SE. **Topography:** The country is mostly a low plain cut by the Ganges and Brahmaputra rivers and their delta. The land is alluvial and marshy along the coast, with hills only in the extreme SE and NE. A tropical monsoon climate prevails, among the rainiest in the world. **Capital:** Dhaka, 11,560,000. **Cities (urban aggr.):** Chittagong, 3,271,000; Khulna, 1,264,000.

Government: Type: Parliamentary democracy. **Head of state:** Pres. Iajuddin Ahmed; b Feb. 1,1931; in office: Sept. 6, 2002. **Head of gov.:** Prime Min. Khaleda Zia; b Aug. 15,1945; in office: Oct. 10, 2001. **Local divisions:** 6 divisions. **Defense budget** (2004): $657 mil. **Active troops:** 125,500.

Economy: Industries: cotton textiles, jute, garments, tea processing, newsprint, cement, chemical fertilizer, light engineering, sugar. **Chief crops:** rice, jute, tea, wheat, sugarcane, potatoes, tobacco. **Natural resources:** nat. gas, timber, coal. **Crude oil reserves** (2004): 56 mil bbls. **Arable land:** 73%. **Livestock** (2004): cattle: 24.5 mil; chickens: 140 mil; goats: 34.5 mil; sheep: 1.3 mil. **Fish catch** (2003): 1,998,197 metric tons. **Electricity prod.** (2003): 17.4 bil. kWh. **Labor force** (1996): agriculture 63%, industry 11%, services 26%.

Finance: Monetary unit: Taka (BDT) (Sept. 2005: 65.72 = $1 U.S.). **GDP** (2004 est.): $275.7 bil.; **per capita GDP:** $2,000; **GDP growth:** 4.9%. **Imports** (2004 est.): $10.0 bil.; partners (2004): India 14.6%, China 11.7%, Singapore 7.8%, Japan 5.8%, Hong Kong 4.8%. **Exports** (2004 est.): $7.5 bil.; partners (2004): US 22.7%, Germany 14.5%, UK 10.8%, France 6.7%. **Tourism:** $57 mil. **Budget** (2004 est.): $8.3 bil. **Intl. reserves less gold:** $2.04 bil. **Gold:** 110,000 oz t. **Consumer prices:** 4.6%.

Transport: Railroad: Length: 1,681 mi. **Motor vehicles:** 65,000 pass. cars, 145,900 comm. vehicles. **Civil aviation:** 2.7 bil pass.-mi; 15 airports. **Chief ports:** Chittagong, Dhaka, Mongla Port.

Communications: TV sets: 7 per 1,000 pop. **Radios:** 50 per 1,000 pop. **Telephone lines:** 742,000. **Daily newspaper circ.:** 53.4 per 1,000 pop. **Internet**: 243,000 users.

Health: Life expect.: 62.1 male; 62.0 female. **Births** (per 1,000 pop.): 30.0. **Deaths** (per 1,000 pop.): 8.4. **Natural inc.:** 2.16%. **Infant mortality** (per 1,000 live births): 62.6.

Education: Compulsory: ages 6-10. **Literacy:** 43.1%.

Major Intl. Organizations: UN (FAO, IBRD, ILO, IMF, IMO, WHO, WTrO), the Commonwealth.

Embassy: 3510 International Dr. NW 20007; 202-244-0183.

Website: www.bangladeshgov.org

Muslim invaders conquered the formerly Hindu area in the 12th century. British rule lasted from the 18th century to 1947, when East Bengal became part of Pakistan.

Charging West Pakistani domination, the Awami League, based in the East, won National Assembly control in 1971. Assembly sessions were postponed; riots broke out. Pakistani troops attacked Mar. 25; Bangladesh independence was proclaimed the next day. In the ensuing civil war, one million died and 10 million fled to India.

War between India and Pakistan broke out Dec. 3, 1971. Pakistan surrendered in the East on Dec. 16. Mujibur Rahman, known as Sheikh Mujib, became prime minister; he was killed in a coup Aug. 15, 1975. During the 1970s the country moved into the Indian and Soviet orbits in response to U.S. support of Pakistan, and much of the economy was nationalized.

On May 30, 1981, Pres. Ziaur Rahman was killed in an unsuccessful coup attempt by army rivals. Vice Pres. Abdus Sattar assumed the presidency but was ousted in a coup led by army chief of staff Gen. H. M. Ershad, Mar. 1982. Ershad declared Bangladesh an Islamic Republic in 1988; a parliamentary system of government was adopted in 1991.

Bangladesh is subject to devastating storms and floods that kill thousands. A cyclone struck Apr. 1991, killing over 131,000 people and causing $2.7 billion in damages. Chronic destitution in the densely crowded population has been worsened by the decline of jute as a world commodity. Pollution of surface water and naturally occurring contamination of groundwater by arsenic have caused widespread health problems.

Political turmoil led to the resignation, Mar. 30, 1996, of Prime Min. Khaleda Zia, the widow of Ziaur Rahman. Sheikh Mujib's daughter, Hasina

(known as Sheikh Hasina), led the country after the June 12, 1996 election. Bangladesh and India signed a treaty, Dec. 12, resolving their long-standing dispute over the use of water from the Ganges River. A cyclone in May 1997 left an estimated 800,000 people homeless. Floods in July-Sept. 1998 inundated most of the country, killed over 1,400 people (many through disease), and stranded at least 30 million.

Khaleda Zia returned to power following the parliamentary elections of Oct. 1, 2001. Floods July-Aug. 2004 caused at least 950 deaths and $7 bil. in property damage. Militant Islamists set off more than 400 small bombs in over 50 cities and towns, Aug. 17, 2005, killing 2 people and wounding at least 125.

Barbados

People: Population: 278,870. **Age distrib.** (%) <15: 20.6; 65+: 8.8. **Pop. density:** 1,680 per sq mi, 647 per sq km. **Urban:** 51.7%. **Ethnic groups:** Black 90%, White 4%. **Principal languages:** English. **Chief religions:** Protestant 67%, Roman Catholic 4%.

Geography: Total area: 166 sq mi, 431 sq km; **Land area:** 166 sq mi, 431 sq km. **Location:** In Atlantic O., farthest E of West Indies. **Neighbors:** Nearest are St. Lucia and St. Vincent & the Grenadines to the W. **Topography:** The island lies alone in the Atlantic almost completely surrounded by coral reefs. Highest point is Mt. Hillaby, 1,115 ft. **Capital:** Bridgetown, 140,000.

Government: Type: Parliamentary democracy. **Head of state:** Queen Elizabeth II, represented by Gov.-Gen. Sir Clifford Husbands; b Aug. 5, 1926; in office: June 1, 1996. **Head of gov.:** Prime Min. Owen Arthur; b Oct. 17, 1949; in office: Sept. 7, 1994. **Local divisions:** 11 parishes and Bridgetown. **Defense budget** (2004): $13 mil. **Active troops:** 610.

Economy: Industries: tourism, sugar, light mfg., component assembly. **Chief crops:** sugarcane, vegetables, cotton. **Natural resources:** oil, fish, nat. gas. **Crude oil reserves** (2004): 3 mil bbls. **Other resources:** Fish. **Arable land:** 37%. **Livestock** (2004): cattle: 9,000; chickens: 3.4 mil; goats: 5,100; pigs: 18,500; sheep: 13,500. **Fish catch** (2003): 2,500 metric tons. **Electricity prod.** (2003): 0.82 bil. kWh. **Labor force** (1996 est.): agriculture 10%, industry 15%, services 75%.

Finance: Monetary unit: Barbados Dollar (BBD) (Sept. 2005: 1.99 = $1 U.S.). **GDP** (2004 est.): $4.6 bil.; **per capita GDP:**

$16,400; **GDP growth:** 2.3%. **Imports** (2002): $1.0 bil.; partners (2004): US 31.6%, Trinidad and Tobago 21.6%, UK 7.9%, Japan 5.3%. **Exports** (2002): $206.0 mil; partners (2004): Trinidad and Tobago 14.2%, US 13.9%, UK 13%, Jamaica 7.7%, Saint Lucia 5.8%, Spain 5.8%, Saint Vincent and the Grenadines 4.6%. **Tourism:** $758 mil. **Budget** (2000 est.): $886.0 mil. **Intl. reserves less gold:** $373 mil. **Consumer prices:** 1.43%.

Transport: Motor vehicles: 62,100 pass. cars, 9,400 comm. vehicles. **Civil aviation:** 204.9 mil pass.-mi.; 1 airport. **Chief port:** Bridgetown.

Communications: TV sets: 290 per 1,000 pop. **Radios:** 651 per 1,000 pop. **Telephone lines:** 134,000. **Daily newspaper circ.:** 155 per 1,000 pop. **Internet**: 100,000 users.

Health: Life expect.: 70.6 male; 74.6 female. **Births** (per 1,000 pop.): 12.8. **Deaths** (per 1,000 pop.): 8.7. **Natural inc.:** 0.41%. **Infant mortality** (per 1,000 live births): 11.7. **AIDS rate:** 1.5%.

Education: Compulsory: ages 4-16. **Literacy:** 97.4%.

Major Intl. Organizations: UN (FAO, IBRD, ILO, IMF, IMO, WHO, WTrO), Caricom, the Commonwealth, OAS.

Embassy: 2144 Wyoming Ave. NW 20008; 939-9200.

Website: www.barbados.gov.bb

Barbados was probably named by Portuguese sailors in reference to bearded fig trees. An English ship visited in 1605, and British settlers arrived on the uninhabited island in 1627. Slaves worked the sugar plantations until slavery was abolished in 1834. Self-rule came gradually, with full independence proclaimed Nov. 30, 1966. British traditions have remained.

Belarus

Republic of Belarus

People: Population: 10,300,483. **Age distrib.** (%) <15: 16.0; 65+: 14.6. **Pop. density:** 129 per sq mi, 50 per sq km. **Urban:** 70.9%. **Ethnic groups:** Belarusian 81%, Russian 11%. **Principal languages:** Belarusian, Russian. **Chief religions:** Eastern Orthodox 80%, other 20%.

Geography: Total area: 80,155 sq mi, 207,600 sq km; **Land area:** 80,155 sq mi, 207,600 sq km. **Location:** E Europe. **Neighbors:** Poland on W; Latvia, Lithuania on N; Russia on E; Ukraine on S. Topography: Belarus is a landlocked country consisting mostly of hilly lowland with significant marsh areas in S. **Capital:** Minsk, 1,705,000.

Government: Type: Republic. **Head of state:** Pres. Aleksandr Lukashenko; b Aug. 30, 1954; in office: July 20,1994. **Head of gov.:** Prime Min. Syarhey Sidorski; b Mar. 13, 1954; in office: Dec. 19, 2003 (acting from July 10, 2003). **Local divisions:** 6 oblasts and 1 municipality. **Defense budget** (2004): $156 mil. **Active troops:** 72,940.

Economy: Industries: machine tools, tractors, trucks, earthmovers, motorcycles. **Chief crops:** grain, potatoes, vegetables, sugar beets, flax. **Natural resources:** timber, peat, oil, nat. gas, granite, dolomitic limestone, marl, chalk, sand, gravel, clay. **Crude oil reserves** (2004): 198 mil bbls. **Arable land:** 29%. **Livestock** (2004): cattle: 3.9 mil; chickens: 24 mil; goats: 63,000; pigs: 3.3 mil; sheep: 63,000. **Fish catch** (2003): 12,318 metric tons. **Electricity prod.** (2003): 25.1 bil. kWh. **Labor force** (2003 est.): agriculture 14%, industry 34.7%, services 51.3%.

Finance: Monetary unit: Ruble (BYR) (Sept. 2005: 2,136.17 = $1 U.S.). **GDP** (2004 est.): $70.5 bil.; **per capita GDP:** $6,800; **GDP growth:** 6.4%. **Imports** (2004 est.): $13.6 bil.; partners (2004): Russia 50%, Germany 13.3%, Ukraine 4.3%, Poland 4.2%. **Exports** (2004 est.): $11.5 bil.; partners (2004): Russia 38.7%, Poland 6.5%, Latvia 5.1%, Germany 5.1%, Ukraine 5.1%. **Tourism:** $267 mil. **Budget** (2004 est.): $3.6 bil. **Intl. reserves less gold:** $483 mil. **Consumer prices:** 18.11%.

Transport: Railroad: Length: 3,432 mi. **Motor vehicles** 1.55 mil pass. cars. **Civil aviation:** 210,645 pass.-mi. **Chief port:** Mazyr.

Communications: TV sets: 331 per 1,000 pop. **Radios:** 292 per 1,000 pop. **Telephone lines:** 3.1 mil. **Daily newspaper circ.:** 152 per 1,000 pop. **Internet**: 1.4 mil. users.

Health: Life expect.: 63.0 male; 74.7 female. **Births** (per 1,000 pop.): 10.8. **Deaths** (per 1,000 pop.): 14.2. **Natural inc.:** –0.33%. **Infant mortality** (per 1,000 live births): 13.4.

Education: Compulsory: ages 6-16. **Literacy:** 99.6%.

Major Intl. Organizations: UN (IBRD, ILO, IMF, WHO), CIS, OSCE.

Embassy: 1619 New Hampshire Ave. NW 20009; 986-1604.

Website: www.belarusembassy.org

The region was subject to Lithuanians and Poles in medieval times, and was a prize of war between Russia and Poland beginning in 1503. It became part of the USSR in 1922, although the western part of the region was controlled by Poland. Belarus was overrun by German armies in 1941; recovered by Soviet troops in 1944. Following World War II, Belarus increased in area through Soviet annexation of part of NE Poland. Belarus declared independence Aug. 25, 1991. It became an independent state when the Soviet Union disbanded Dec. 26, 1991.

A new constitution was adopted, Mar. 15, 1994, and a new president was chosen in elections concluding July 1. Russia and Belarus signed a pact Apr. 2, 1996, linking their political and economic systems. An authoritarian constitution enacted in Nov. gave Pres. Aleksandr Lukashenko vast new powers. Opponents charged harassment and fraud in the presidential election of Sept. 9, 2001, won by Lukashenko. In elections on Oct. 17, 2004, considered flawed by foreign observers, nearly all winning candidates were Lukashenko supporters, and a constitutional provision limiting the president to 2 terms was repealed.

Belgium

Kingdom of Belgium

People: Population: 10,364,388. **Age distrib.** (%) <15: 16.9; 65+: 17.4. **Pop. density:** 879 per sq mi, 340 per sq km. **Urban:** 97.2%. **Ethnic groups:** Fleming 58%, Walloon 31%. **Principal languages:** Dutch, French, German (all official); Flemish, Luxembourgish. **Chief religions:** Roman Catholic 75%, Protestant, other 25%.

Geography: Total area: 11,787 sq mi, 30,528 sq km; **Land area:** 11,690 sq mi, 30,278 sq km. **Location:** In W Europe, on North Sea. **Neighbors:** France on W and S, Luxembourg on SE, Germany on E, Netherlands on N. **Topography:** Mostly flat, the country is trisected by the Scheldt and Meuse, major commercial rivers. The land becomes hilly and forested in the SE (Ardennes) region. **Capital:** Brussels, 998,000.

Government: Type: Parliamentary democracy under a constitutional monarch. **Head of state:** King Albert II; b June 6, 1934; in office: Aug. 9, 1993. **Head of gov.:** Premier Guy Verhofstadt; b Apr. 11, 1953; in office: July 12, 1999. **Local divisions:** 10 provinces and Brussels. **Defense budget** (2004): $3.3 bil. **Active troops:** 40,800.

Economy: Industries: engineering & metal products, motor vehicle assembly, proc. food & beverages, chemicals, textiles, glass, oil, coal. **Chief crops:** sugar beets, vegetables, fruits, grain, tobacco. **Natural resources:** coal, nat. gas. **Arable land**: 24%. **Livestock** (2004): cattle: 2.7 mil; chickens: 36.5 mil; goats: 25,500; pigs: 6.4 mil; sheep: 151,000. **Fish catch** (2003): 27,841 metric tons. **Electricity prod.** (2003): 78.8 bil. kWh. **Labor force** (2003 est.): agriculture 1.3%, industry 24.5%, services 74.2%.

Finance: Monetary unit: Euro (EUR) (Sept. 2005: 0.80 = $1 U.S.). **GDP** (2004 est.): $316.2 bil.; **per capita GDP:** $30,600; **GDP growth:** 2.6%. **Imports** (2003 est.): $235.0 bil.; partners (2004): Germany 18.4%, Netherlands 17%, France 12.5%, UK 6.8%, Ireland 6.3%, US 5.5%. **Exports** (2003 est.): $255.7 bil.; partners (2004): Germany 19.9%, France 17.2%, Netherlands 11.8%, UK 8.6%, US 6.5%, Italy 5.2%. **Tourism:** $8,130 mil. **Budget** (2004 est.): $174.8 bil. **Intl. reserves less gold:** $6.67 bil. **Gold:** 8.29 mil. oz t. **Consumer prices:** 2.1%.

Transport: Railroad: Length: 2,186 mi. **Motor vehicles** 4.7841 mil pass. cars, 602,100 comm. vehicles. **Civil aviation:** 9.5 bil pass.-mii; 25 airports. **Chief ports:** Antwerp (one of the world's busiest), Zeebrugge, Ghent.

Communications: TV sets: 532 per 1,000 pop. **Radios:** 797 per 1,000 pop. **Telephone lines**: 5.1 mil. **Daily newspaper circ.:** 160 per 1,000 pop. **Internet**: 4.0 mil. users.

Health: Life expect.: 75.4 male; 81.9 female. **Births** (per 1,000 pop.): 10.5. **Deaths** (per 1,000 pop.): 10.2. **Natural inc.:** 0.03%. **Infant mortality** (per 1,000 live births): 4.7. **AIDS rate:** 0.2%.

Education: Compulsory: ages 6-18. **Literacy:** 98%.

Major Intl. Organizations: UN and all of its specialized agencies, EU, NATO, OECD, OSCE.

Embassy: 3330 Garfield St. NW 20008; 333-6900.

Website: belgium.fgov.be

Belgium derives its name from the Belgae, the first recorded inhabitants, probably Celts. The land was conquered by Julius Caesar, and was ruled for 1800 years by conquerors, including Rome, the Franks, Burgundy, Spain, Austria, and France. After 1815, Belgium was made a part of the Netherlands, but it became an independent constitutional monarchy in 1830.

Belgian neutrality was violated by Germany in both world wars. King Leopold III surrendered to Germany, May 28, 1940. After the war, he was forced by political pressure to abdicate in favor of his son, King Baudouin. Baudouin was succeeded by his brother, Albert II, Aug. 9, 1993.

The Flemings of northern Belgium speak Dutch, while French is the language of the Walloons in the south. The language difference has been a perennial source of controversy and led to antagonism between the 2 groups. Parliament has passed measures aimed at transferring power from the central government to 3 regions—Wallonia, Flanders, and Brussels. Constitutional changes in 1993 made Belgium a federal state. Sabena, the national airline, went bankrupt Nov. 6, 2001.

Belize

People: Population: 281,084. **Age distrib.** (%) <15: 40.1; 65+: 3.5. **Pop. density:** 32 per sq mi, 12 per sq km. **Urban:** 48.3%. **Ethnic groups:** Mestizo 49%, Creole 25%, Maya 11%, Garifuna 6%. **Principal languages:** English (official), Spanish, Mayan, Garifuna (Carib), Creole. **Chief religions:** Roman Catholic 50%, Protestant 27%.

Geography: Total area: 8,867 sq mi, 22,966 sq km; **Land area:** 8,805 sq mi, 22,806 sq km. **Location:** Eastern coast of Central America. **Neighbors:** Mexico on N, Guatemala on W and S. Topography: Belize has swampy lowlands in N, Maya Mts. in S, coral reefs and cays near coast. Climate is tropical. **Capital:** Belmopan, 9,000.

Government: Type: Parliamentary democracy. **Head of state:** Queen Elizabeth II, represented by Gov.-Gen. Sir Colville Young;

b Nov. 20, 1932; in office: Nov. 17, 1993. **Head of gov.:** Prime Min. Said Musa; b Mar. 19, 1944; in office: Aug. 28, 1998. **Local divisions:** 6 districts. **Defense budget** (2004): $19 mil. **Active troops:** 1,050.

Economy: Industries: clothing, food proc., tourism, constr. **Chief crops:** bananas, coca, citrus, sugarcane. **Natural resources:** timber, fish, hydropower. **Arable land:** 2%. **Livestock** (2004): cattle: 57,800; chickens: 1.6 mil; goats: 165; pigs: 21,224; sheep: 6,265. **Fish catch** (2003): 15,353 metric tons. **Electricity prod.** (2003): 0.12 bil. kWh. **Labor force** (2001 est.): agriculture 27%, industry 18%, services 55%.

Finance: Monetary unit: Belize Dollar (BZD) (Sept. 2005: 1.97 = $1 U.S.). **GDP** (2004 est.): $1.8 bil.; **per capita GDP:** $6,500; **GDP growth:** 3.5%. **Imports** (2004 est.): $579.9 mil; partners (2004): US 32.7%, Mexico 14.4%, Cuba 6.5%, Japan 4.7%. **Exports** (2004 est.): $401.4 mil; partners (2004): US 36.8%, UK 28.5%, Thailand 3.6%. **Tourism:** $156 mil. **Budget** (2004 est.): $300.0 mil. **Intl. reserves less gold:** $31 mil. **Consumer prices:** 2.6%.

Transport: Motor vehicles: 32,600 pass. cars, 7,800 comm. vehicles; 4 airports. **Chief ports:** Belize City, Big Creek.

Communications: TV sets: 183 per 1,000 pop. **Radios:** 594 per 1,000 pop. **Telephone lines:** 33,300. **Internet** (2002): 30,000 users.

Health: Life expect.: 66.5 male; 70.4 female. **Births** (per 1,000 pop.): 29.3. **Deaths** (per 1,000 pop.): 5.7. **Natural inc.:** 2.37%. **Infant mortality** (per 1,000 live births): 25.4. **AIDS rate:** 2.4%.

Education: Compulsory: ages 5-14. **Literacy:** 94.1%.

Major Intl. Organizations: UN (FAO, IBRD, ILO, IMF, IMO, WHO, WTrO), Caricom, the Commonwealth, OAS.

Embassy: 2535 Massachusetts Ave. NW 20008; 332-9636.

Website: www.belize.gov.bz

Belize (formerly British Honduras) was Britain's last colony on the American mainland; independence was achieved Sept. 21, 1981. Relations with neighboring Guatemala, initially tense, have improved in recent years. Belize has become a center for drug trafficking between Colombia and the U.S.

Benin

Republic of Benin

People: Population: 7,649,360. **Age distrib.** (%) <15: 46.5; 65+: 2.3. **Pop. density:** 176 per sq mi, 68 per sq km. **Urban:** 44.6%. **Ethnic groups:** 42 groups, incl. Fon, Adja, Yoruba, and Bariba. **Principal languages:** French (official), Fon, Yoruba, various tribal languages. **Chief religions:** Indigenous beliefs 50%, Christian 30%, Muslim 20%.

Geography: Total area: 43,483 sq mi, 112,620 sq km; **Land area:** 42,711 sq mi, 110,690 sq km. **Location:** In W Africa on Gulf of Guinea. **Neighbors:** Togo on W; Burkina Faso, Niger on N; Nigeria on E. **Topography:** Most of Benin is flat and covered with dense vegetation. The coast is hot, humid, and rainy. **Capitals:** Porto-Novo (constitutional), 238,000; Cotonou (administrative), 828,000.

Government: Type: Republic. **Head of state and gov.:** Pres. Mathieu Kerekou; b Sept. 2, 1933; in office: Apr. 4, 1996. **Local divisions:** 12 departments. **Defense budget** (2004): $67 mil. **Active troops:** 4,550.

Economy: Industries: textiles, food proc., chemical prod., constr. materials. **Chief crops:** cotton, corn, cassava, yams, beans. **Natural resources:** oil, limestone, marble, timber. **Crude oil reserves** (2004): 8.21 mil bbls. **Arable land:** 13%. **Livestock** (2004): cattle: 1.7 mil; chickens: 13 mil; goats: 1.4 mil; pigs: 308,899; sheep: 700,000. **Fish catch** (2003): 41,900 metric tons. **Electricity prod.** (2003): 0.07 bil. kWh.

Finance: Monetary unit: CFA Franc BCEAO (XOF) (Sept. 2005: 525.28 = $1 U.S.). **GDP** (2004 est.): $8.3 bil.; **per capita GDP:** $1,200; **GDP growth:** 5%. **Imports** (2004 est.): $934.5 mil; partners (2004): China 29.7%, France 13.8%, Thailand 7.2%, Côte d'Ivoire 4.6%. **Exports** (2004 est.): $720.9 mil; partners (2004): China 30.2%, India 15.6%, Thailand 6%, Ghana 5.9%, Niger 4.5%. **Tourism** (2001): $85 mil. **Budget** (2004 est.): $720.4 mil. **Intl. reserves less gold:** $285 mil. **Consumer prices:** 0.87%.

Transport: Railroad: Length: 359 mi. **Motor vehicles:** 7,300 pass. cars, 6,200 comm. vehicles. **Civil aviation:** 80,778 pass.-mi; 1 airport. **Chief port:** Cotonou.

Communications: TV sets: 44 per 1,000 pop. **Radios:** 448 per 1,000 pop. **Telephone lines:** 66,500. **Daily newspaper circ.:** 5.3 per 1,000 pop. **Internet:** 70,000 users.

Health: Life expect.: 51.5 male; 53.8 female. **Births** (per 1,000 pop.): 39.6. **Deaths** (per 1,000 pop.): 12.5. **Natural inc.:** 2.71%. **Infant mortality** (per 1,000 live births): 81.3. **AIDS rate:** 1.9%.

Education: Compulsory: ages 6-11. **Literacy:** 40.9%.

Major Intl. Organizations: UN (FAO, IBRD, ILO, IMF, IMO, WHO, WTrO), AU.

Embassy: 2124 Kalorama Rd. NW 20008; 232-6656.

Website: www.gouv.bj/en/index.php

The Kingdom of Abomey, rising to power in wars with neighboring kingdoms in the 17th century, came under French domination in the late 19th century and was incorporated into French West Africa by 1904.

Under the name Dahomey, the country gained independence Aug. 1, 1960; it became Benin in 1975. In the fifth coup since independence Col. Ahmed Kerekou took power in 1972; two years later he declared a socialist state with a "Marxist-Leninist" philosophy. In Dec. 1989, Kerekou announced Marxism-Leninism would no longer be the state ideology.

In Mar. 1991, Kerekou lost to Nicéphore Soglo in Benin's first free presidential election in 30 years. Kerekou defeated Soglo in Mar. 1996 to reclaim the presidency. He won reelection in a runoff Mar. 22, 2001. A plane bound for Beirut, Lebanon, crashed on takeoff from Cotonou, Dec. 25, 2003, killing 140 people.

Bhutan

Kingdom of Bhutan

People: Population: 2,232,291. **Age distrib.** (%) <15: 39.1; 65+: 4.0. **Pop. density:** 123 per sq mi, 47 per sq km. **Urban:** 8.5%. **Ethnic groups:** Bhote 50%, Nepalese 35%, indigenous tribes 15%. **Principal languages:** Dzongkha (official); Tibetan, Nepalese dialects. **Chief religions:** Lamaistic Buddhist 75% (official), Hindu 25%.

Geography: Total area: 18,147 sq mi, 47,000 sq km; **Land area:** 18,147 sq mi, 47,000 sq km. **Location:** S Asia, in eastern Himalayan Mts. **Neighbors:** India on W (Sikkim) and S, China on N. **Topography:** Bhutan is comprised of very high mountains in the N, fertile valleys in the center, and thick forests in the Duar Plain in the S. **Capital:** Thimphu, 35,000.

Government: Type: Monarchy. **Head of state:** King Jigme Singye Wangchuk; b Nov. 11, 1955; in office: July 21, 1972. **Head of gov.:** Prime Min. Lyonpo Sangay Ngedup; b July 1, 1953; in office Sept. 5, 2005. **Local divisions:** 18 districts. **Defense budget** (2002): $19 mil. **Active troops:** NA.

Economy: Industries: cement, wood products, proc. fruits, alcoholic beverages, calcium carbide. **Chief crops:** rice, corn, root crops, citrus, grains. **Natural resources:** timber, hydropower, gypsum, calcium carbide. **Arable land:** 2%. **Livestock** (2004): cattle: 372,000; chickens: 230,000; goats: 30,000; pigs: 41,000; sheep: 20,000. **Fish catch** (2003): 300 metric tons. **Electricity prod.** (2003): 1.9 bil. kWh. **Labor force:** agriculture 93%, industry and commerce 2%, services 5%.

Finance: Monetary unit: Ngultrum (BTN) (Sept. 2005: 43.95 = $1 U.S.). **GDP** (2003 est.): $2.9 bil.; **per capita GDP:** $1,400; **GDP growth:** 5.3%. **Imports** (2000 est.): $196.0 mil; partners (2004): India 71.3%, Japan 7.8%, Austria 3%. **Exports** (2000 est.): $154.0 mil; partners (2004): India 87.9%, Bangladesh 4.6%, Philippines 2%. **Tourism:** $8 mil. **Budget** : $152.0 mil. **Intl. reserves less gold:** $257 mil. **Consumer prices:** 3.66%

Transport: Civil aviation: 29,204 pass.-mi; 1 airport.

Communications: TV sets: 6 per 1,000 pop. **Radios:** 19 per 1,000 pop. **Telephone lines:** 25,200. **Internet:** 15,000 users.

Health: Life expect.: 54.7 male; 54.1 female. **Births** (per 1,000 pop.): 34.0. **Deaths** (per 1,000 pop.): 12.9. **Natural inc.:** 2.11%. **Infant mortality** (per 1,000 live births): 100.4.

Education: Compulsory: ages 6-16. **Literacy:** 42.2%.

Major Intl. Organizations: UN (FAO, IBRD, IMF, WHO).

Embassy: UN mission: 763 First Avenue, New York, NY 10017, (212) 682-2268

Website: tourism.gov.bt

The region came under Tibetan rule in the 16th century. British influence grew in the 19th century. A Buddhist monarchy was set up in 1907. According to a 1910 treaty, Britain guided Bhutan's external affairs, while the country remained internally self-governing. Upon independence, India assumed Britain's role in a 1949 revision of the treaty. Isolated for much of its history, Bhutan has taken steps toward modernization. The king proposed, Mar. 27, 2005, a constitution creating a multiparty system, with an elected parliament empowered to impeach the sovereign.

Bolivia

Republic of Bolivia

People: Population: 8,857,870. **Age distrib.** (%) <15: 35.7; 65+: 4.5. **Pop. density:** 21 per sq mi, 8 per sq km. **Urban:** 63.4%. **Ethnic groups:** Quechua 30%, Mestizo 30%, Aymara 25%, white 15%. **Principal languages:** Spanish, Quechua, Aymara (all official) **Chief religion:** Roman Catholic 95% (official).

Geography: Total area: 424,164 sq mi, 1,098,580 sq km; **Land area:** 418,685 sq mi, 1,084,390 sq km. **Location:** In W central South America, in the Andes Mts. (one of 2 landlocked countries in South America). **Neighbors:** Peru and Chile on W, Argentina and Paraguay on S, Brazil on E and N. **Topography:** The great central plateau, at an altitude of 12,000 ft., over 500 mi. long, lies between two great cordilleras having 3 of the highest peaks in South America. Lake Titicaca, on Peruvian border, is highest lake in world on which steamboats ply (12,506 ft.). The E central region has semitropical forests; the llanos, or Amazon-Chaco lowlands are in E. **Capitals:** La Paz (administrative), 1,477,000; Sucre (judicial), 212,000. **Cities (urban aggr.):** Santa Cruz, 1,061,000.

Government: Type: Republic. **Head of state and gov.:** Pres. Eduardo Rodríguez Veltzé; b Mar. 2, 1956; in office: June 9, 2005. **Local divisions:** 9 departments. **Defense budget** (2004): $126 mil. **Active troops:** 31,500.

Economy: Industries: mining, smelting, oil, food & beverages, tobacco, handicrafts, clothing. **Chief crops:** soybeans, coffee, coca, cotton, corn, sugarcane, rice, potatoes, timber. **Natural resources:** tin, nat. gas, oil, zinc, tungsten, antimony, silver, iron, lead, gold, timber, hydropower. **Crude oil reserves** (2004): 441 mil bbls. **Other resources:** Timber. **Arable land:** 2%. **Livestock**

(2004): cattle: 6.8 mil; chickens: 75 mil; goats: 1.5 mil; pigs: 3.0 mil; sheep: 8.6 mil. **Fish catch** (2003): 6,974 metric tons. **Electricity prod.** (2003): 4.3 bil. kWh.

Finance: Monetary unit: Boliviano (BOB) (Sept. 2005: 8.07 = $1 U.S.). **GDP** (2004 est.): $22.3 bil.; **per capita GDP:** $2,600; **GDP growth:** 3.7%. **Imports** (2004 est.): $1.6 bil.; partners (2004): Brazil 25.3%, Argentina 17%, US 13.1%, Chile 9.2%, Peru 7.2%. **Exports** (2004 est.): $2.0 bil.; partners (2004): Brazil 33.9%, US 12.7%, Colombia 11.8%, Venezuela 11.6%, Peru 5.1%, Japan 4.2%. **Tourism:** $111 mil. **Budget** (2004 est.): $2.8 bil. **Intl. reserves less gold:** $562 mil. **Gold:** 910,000 oz t. **Consumer prices:** 4.44%.

Transport: Railroad: Length: 2,187 mi. **Motor vehicles** 316,300 pass. cars, 155,500 comm. vehicles. **Civil aviation:** 973,689 pass.-mi; 12 airports.

Communications: TV sets: 118 per 1,000 pop. **Radios:** 675 per 1,000 pop. **Telephone lines:** 608,000. **Daily newspaper circ.:** 55 per 1,000 pop. **Internet** (2002): 270,000 users.

Health: Life expect.: 62.9 male; 68.3 female. **Births** (per 1,000 pop.): 23.8. **Deaths** (per 1,000 pop.): 7.6. **Natural inc.:** 1.61%. **Infant mortality** (per 1,000 live births): 53.1. **AIDS rate:** 0.1%.

Education: Compulsory: ages 6-13. **Literacy:** 87.2%.

Major Intl. Organizations: UN (FAO, IBRD, ILO, IMF, IMO, WHO, WTrO), OAS.

Embassy: 3014 Massachusetts Ave. NW 20008; 483-4410.

The Incas conquered the region from earlier Indian inhabitants in the 13th century. Spanish rule began in the 1530s and lasted until Aug. 6, 1825. The country is named after Simon Bolivar, independence fighter.

Website: megalink.com/usemblapaz/english/engindex.htm

In a series of wars, Bolivia lost its Pacific coast to Chile, the oil-bearing Chaco to Paraguay, and rubber-growing areas to Brazil, 1879-1935.

Economic unrest, especially among militant mine workers, has contributed to continuing political instability. A reformist government under Victor Paz Estenssoro, 1951-64, nationalized tin mines and attempted to improve conditions for Indian majority but was overthrown by a military junta. A long series of coups and countercoups continued until constitutional government was restored in 1982.

U.S. pressure on the government to reduce the country's coca output, the raw material for cocaine, has led to clashes between police and coca growers and increased anti-U.S. feeling among Bolivians. Gen. Hugo Banzer Suárez, who ruled as a dictator, 1971-78, became president in Aug. 1997. 105 people died in earthquakes near Aiquile May 22, 1998. Stricken with cancer, Banzer resigned and was succeeded Aug. 7, 2001, by Vice-Pres. Jorge Quiroga Ramírez.

After an inconclusive presidential election June 30, 2002, Congress Aug. 4 chose Gonzalo Sánchez de Lozada, a U.S.-educated mining executive, as head of state. He quit Oct. 17, 2003, after a month of antigovernment protests, led by Bolivian Indians, in which over 70 people died. His successor, Vice-Pres. Carlos D. Mesa Gisbert, a former historian and TV reporter, won a referendum July 18, 2004, on his plan to boost exports of Bolivia's huge natural gas reserves. Further protests, mainly over energy issues, forced Mesa to step down, June 9, 2005; he was succeeded by supreme court chief Eduardo Rodríguez Veltzé.

Bosnia and Herzegovina

People: Population: 4,430,494. **Age distrib.** (%) <15: 18.3; 65+: 10.9. **Pop. density:** 224 per sq mi, 87 per sq km. **Urban:** 44.3%. **Ethnic groups:** Bosniak 48%, Serbian 37%, Croatian 14%. **Principal languages:** Bosnian (official), Croatian, Serbian. **Chief religions:** Muslim 40%, Orthodox 31%, Roman Catholic 15%, other 14%.

Geography: Total area: 19,741 sq mi, 51,129 sq km; **Land area:** 19,741 sq mi, 51,129 sq km. **Location:** On Balkan Peninsula in SE Europe. **Neighbors:** Yugoslavia on E and SE, Croatia on N and W. **Topography:** Hilly with some mountains. About 36% of the land is forested. **Capital:** Sarajevo, 579,000.

Government: Type: Federal republic. **Heads of state:** Collective presidency with rotating leadership. **Head of gov.:** Chrm. of Council Ministers Adnan Terzic; b 1960; in office: Dec. 23, 2002. **Local divisions:** Muslim-Croat Federation, divided into 10 cantons; Serbian-led region (Republika Srpska); internationally supervised Brcko district. **Defense budget** (2004): $148 mil. **Active troops:** 24,600 (16,400 Muslim-Croat; 8,200 Serbian).

Economy: Industries: steel, mining, vehicle assembly, textiles, tobacco products, wooden furniture, tank & aircraft assembly, domestic appliances. **Chief crops:** wheat, corn, fruits, vegetables. **Natural resources:** coal, iron, bauxite, mang., timber, copper, chromium, lead, zinc, hydropower. **Arable land:** 14%. **Livestock** (2004): cattle: 440,000; chickens: 4.7 mil; pigs: 300,000; sheep: 670,000. **Fish catch** (2003): 8,635 metric tons. **Electricity prod.** (2003): 10.5 bil. kWh.

Finance: Monetary unit: Converted Marka (BAM) (Sept. 2005: 1.57 = $1 U.S.). **GDP** (2004 est.): $26.2 bil.; **per capita GDP:** $6,500; **GDP growth:** 5%. **Imports** (2004 est.): $5.2 bil.; partners (2004): Croatia 26.4%, Germany 14.9%, Slovenia 13.4%, Italy 12%, Austria 6.9%, Hungary 6.4%. **Exports** (2004 est.): $1.7 bil.; partners (2004): Italy 22.9%, Croatia 22.1%, Germany 20.3%, Austria 7.5%, Slovenia 6.9%, Hungary 4.9%. **Tourism:** $235 mil. **Budget** (2004 est.): $3.6 bil. **Intl. reserves less gold:** $1.2 bil.

Transport: Railroad: Length: 634 mi. **Chief port:** Bosanski Brod. **Civil aviation:** 27,340 pass.-mi; 14 airports.

Communications: TV sets: 112 per 1,000 pop. **Radios:** 245 per 1,000 pop. **Telephone lines:** 938,000. **Daily newspaper circ.:** 152 per 1,000 pop. **Internet** (2002): 100,000 users.

Health: Life expect.: 74.2 male; 81.7 female. **Births** (per 1,000 pop.): 8.8. **Deaths** (per 1,000 pop.): 8.1. **Natural inc.:** 0.07%. **Infant mortality** (per 1,000 live births): 10.1. **AIDS rate:** <0.1%.

Education: Free, compulsory: ages 7-15. **Literacy:** NA%.

Major Intl. Organizations: UN (FAO, IBRD, ILO, IMF, IMO, WHO), OSCE.

Embassy: 2109 E St. NW, 20037; 337-6473.

Website: www.bhembassy.org

Bosnia was ruled by Croatian kings c. AD 958, and by Hungary 1000-1200. It became organized c. 1200 and later took control of Herzegovina. The kingdom disintegrated from 1391, with the southern part becoming the independent duchy Herzegovina. It was conquered by Turks in 1463 and made a Turkish province. The area was placed under control of Austria-Hungary in 1878, and made part of the province of **Bosnia and Herzegovina,** which was formally annexed to Austria-Hungary 1908; Bosnia became a province of Yugoslavia in 1918. It was reunited with Herzegovina as a federated republic in the 1946 Yugoslavian constitution.

Bosnia and Herzegovina declared sovereignty Oct. 15, 1991. A referendum for independence was passed Feb. 29, 1992. Ethnic Serbs' opposition to the referendum spurred violent clashes and bombings. The U.S. and EU recognized the republic Apr. 7. Fierce three-way fighting continued between Bosnia's Serbs, Muslims, and Croats. Serb forces massacred thousands of Bosnian Muslims and engaged in "ethnic cleansing" (the expulsion of Muslims and other non-Serbs from areas under Bosnian Serb control). The capital, Sarajevo, was surrounded and besieged by Bosnian Serb forces. Muslims and Croats in Bosnia reached a cease fire Feb. 23, 1994, and signed an accord, Mar. 18, to create a Muslim-Croat confederation in Bosnia. However, by mid-1994, Bosnian Serbs controlled over 70% of the country.

As fighting continued in 1995, the balance of power began to shift toward the Muslim-Croat alliance. Massive NATO air strikes at Bosnian Serb targets beginning Aug. 30 triggered a new round of peace talks, and the siege of Sarajevo was lifted Sept. 15. The new talks produced an agreement in principle to create autonomous regions within Bosnia, with the Serb region (Republika Srpska) constituting 49% of the country. A Croat-Muslim offensive in Sept. recaptured significant territory, leaving Bosnian Serbs in control of approximately half that percentage.

A peace agreement initialed in Dayton, Ohio, Nov. 21, 1995, was signed in Paris, Dec. 14, by leaders of Bosnia, Croatia, and Serbia. Some 60,000 NATO troops (about 20,000 from the U.S.) moved in to police the accord. Meanwhile, a UN tribunal began bringing charges against suspected war criminals. Elections were held Sept. 14, 1996, for a 3-person collective presidency, for seats in a federal parliament, and for regional offices. In Dec. a revamped NATO "stabilization force" (SFOR) of over 30,000 members (more than 8,000 from the U.S.) received an 18-month mandate, which was later extended.

In a landmark verdict Aug. 2, 2001, the UN tribunal found Radislav Krstic, a Bosnian Serb general, guilty in connection with the genocide of thousands of Muslims at Srebrenica in 1995. A European Union peacekeeping force (EUFOR), with 7,000 members, assumed responsibility from SFOR, Dec. 2, 2004.

Botswana

Republic of Botswana

People: Population: 1,640,115. **Age distrib.** (%) <15: 38.8; 65+: 3.8. **Pop. density:** 7 per sq mi, 3 per sq km. **Urban:** 51.6%. **Ethnic groups:** Tswana 79%, Kalanga 11%, Basarwa 3%. **Principal languages:** English (official), Setswana. **Chief religions:** Christian 72%, none 20.6.

Geography: Total area: 231,804 sq mi, 600,370 sq km; **Land area:** 226,013 sq mi, 585,370 sq km. **Location:** In southern Africa. **Neighbors:** Namibia on N and W, South Africa on S, Zimbabwe on NE; Botswana claims border with Zambia on N. **Topography:** The Kalahari Desert, supporting nomadic Bushmen and wildlife, spreads over SW; there are swamplands and farming areas in N, and rolling plains in E where livestock are grazed. **Capital:** Gaborone, 199,000.

Government: Type: Parliamentary republic. **Head of state and gov.:** Pres. Festus Mogae; b Aug. 21, 1939; in office: Apr. 1, 1998. **Local divisions:** 10 districts, 4 town councils. **Defense budget** (2004): $348 mil. **Active troops:** 9,000.

Economy: Industries: diamonds, copper, nickel, salt, soda ash, potash, proc., textiles. **Chief crops:** sorghum, maize, millet, beans, sunflowers. **Natural resources:** diamonds, copper, nickel, salt, soda ash, potash, coal, iron ore, silver. **Arable land:** 1%. **Livestock** (2004): cattle: 1.7 mil; chickens: 4 mil; goats: 2.3 mil; pigs: 8,000; sheep: 400,000. **Fish catch** (2003): 122 metric tons. **Electricity prod.** (2003): 0.94 bil. kWh.

Finance: Monetary unit: Pula (BWP) (Sept. 2005: 5.36 = $1 U.S.). **GDP** (2004 est.): $15.1 bil.; **per capita GDP:** $9,200; **GDP growth:** 3.5%. **Imports** (2000 est.): $2.3 bil.; partners Southern African Customs Union (SACU) 74%, European Free Trade Assn. (EFTA) 17%, Zimbabwe 4%. **Exports** (2004 est.): $2.9 bil.; partners (2000): EFTA 87%, SACU 7%, Zimbabwe 4%. **Tourism:** $356 mil. **Budget** (2004 est.): $3.7 bil. **Intl. reserves less gold:** $3.65 bil. **Consumer prices:** 6.95%.

Transport: Railroad: Length: 552 mi. **Motor vehicles** 44,500 pass. cars, 67,900 comm. vehicles. **Civil aviation:** 47,846 pass.-mi; 10 airports.

Communications: TV sets: 21 per 1,000 pop. **Radios:** 154 per 1,000 pop. **Telephone lines**: 131,800. **Daily newspaper circ.:** 27 per 1,000 pop. **Internet** (2002): 60,000 users.

Health: Life expect.: 33.9 male; 33.8 female. **Births** (per 1,000 pop.): 23.3. **Deaths** (per 1,000 pop.): 29.4. **Natural inc.:** –0.60%. **Infant mortality** (per 1,000 live births): 54.6. **AIDS rate:** 37.3%.

Education: Compulsory: ages 6-15. **Literacy:** 79.8%.

Major Intl. Organizations: UN (FAO, IBRD, ILO, IMF, WHO, WTrO), the Commonwealth, AU.

Embassy: 1531-3 New Hampshire Ave. NW 20036; 244-4990.

Website: www.gov.bw

First inhabited by bushmen, then Bantus, the region became the British protectorate of Bechuanaland in 1886, halting encroachment by Boers and Germans from the south and southwest. The country became fully independent Sept. 30, 1966, as Botswana. Cattle raising and mining (diamonds, copper, nickel) have contributed to economic growth; economy is closely tied to South Africa. According to UN estimates, more than one-third of the adult population has HIV/AIDS.

Brazil

Federative Republic of Brazil

People: Population: 186,112,794. **Age distrib.** (%) <15: 26.1; 65+: 6.0. **Pop. density:** 57 per sq mi, 22 per sq km. **Urban:** 83.1%. **Ethnic groups:** European 55%, Creole 38%, African 6%. **Principal languages:** Portuguese (official), Spanish, English, French. **Chief religion:** Roman Catholic (nominal) 74%, Protestant 15%.

Geography: Total area: 3,286,488 sq mi, 8,511,965 sq km; **Land area:** 3,265,077 sq mi, 8,456,510 sq km. **Location:** Occupies E half of South America. **Neighbors:** French Guiana, Suriname, Guyana, Venezuela on N; Colombia, Peru, Bolivia, Paraguay, on W; Uruguay on S. **Topography:** Brazil's Atlantic coastline stretches 4,603 miles. In N is the heavily wooded Amazon basin covering half the country. Its network of rivers is navigable for 15,814 mi. The Amazon itself flows 2,093 miles in Brazil, all navigable. The NE region is semiarid scrubland, heavily settled and poor. The S central region, favored by climate and resources, has almost half of the population, produces 75% of farm goods and 80% of industrial output. The narrow coastal belt includes most of the major cities. Almost the entire country has a tropical or semitropical climate. **Capital:** Brasília, 3,099,000. **Cities (urban aggr.):** São Paulo, 17,099,000, (2001 city est.: 10.4 mil.); Rio de Janeiro, 10,803,000; Belo Horizonte, 4,659,000.

Government: Type: Federal republic. **Head of state and gov.:** Luiz Inacio Lula da Silva; b. Oct. 27, 1945; in office: Jan. 1, 2003. **Local divisions:** 26 states, 1 federal district (Brasília). **Defense budget** (2004): $9.2 bil. **Active troops:** 302,909.

Economy: Industries: textiles, shoes, chemicals, cement, lumber, iron ore, steel, aircraft, motor vehicles & parts. **Chief crops:** coffee, soybeans, wheat, rice, corn, sugarcane, cocoa, citrus. **Natural resources:** bauxite, gold, iron ore, mang., nickel, phosphates, platinum, tin, uranium, oil, hydropower, timber. **Crude oil reserves** (2004): 10.6 bil. bbls. **Arable land:** 5%. **Livestock** (2004): cattle: 192.0 mil; chickens: 1.1 bil.; goats: 9.1 mil; pigs: 33.0 mil; sheep: 14.2 mil. **Fish catch** (2003): 1,086,504 metric tons. **Electricity prod.** (2003): 359.2 bil. kWh. **Labor force** (2003 est.): agriculture 20%, industry 14%, services 66%.

Finance: Monetary unit: Real (BRL) (Sept. 2005: 2.36 = $1 U.S.). **GDP** (2004 est.): $1.5 tril.; **per capita GDP:** $8,100; **GDP growth:** 5.1%. **Imports** (2004 est.): $61.0 bil.; partners (2004): US 22.4%, Germany 9.2%, Argentina 8.1%, China 5.5%. **Exports** (2004 est.): $95.0 bil.; partners (2004): US 21.2%, China 7.8%, Argentina 6%, Germany 5.1%, Netherlands 4.8%. **Tourism:** $2,479 mil. **Budget** (2004): $172.4 bil. **Intl. reserves less gold:** $33.96 bil. **Gold:** 450,000 oz t. **Consumer prices:** 6.6%.

Transport: Railroad: Length: 18,276 mi. **Motor vehicles** 15.21 mil pass. cars, 4.2567 mil comm. vehicles. **Civil aviation:** 29.0 bil pass.-mi; 665 airports. **Chief ports:** Santos, Rio de Janeiro, Vitoria, Salvador, Rio Grande, Recife.

Communications: TV sets: 333 per 1,000 pop. **Radios:** 434 per 1,000 pop. **Telephone lines**: 39.2 mil. **Daily newspaper circ.:** 43.1 per 1,000 pop. **Internet** (2002): 14.3 mil. users.

Health: Life expect.: 67.7 male; 75.9 female. **Births** (per 1,000 pop.): 16.8. **Deaths** (per 1,000 pop.): 6.2. **Natural inc.:** 1.07%. **Infant mortality** (per 1,000 live births): 29.6. **AIDS rate:** 0.7%.

Education: Compulsory: ages 7-14. **Literacy:** 86.4%.

Major Intl. Organizations: UN and most of its specialized agencies, OAS.

Embassy: 3006 Massachusetts Ave. NW 20008; 238-2700.

Website: www.brasilemb.org

Pedro Alvares Cabral, a Portuguese navigator, is generally credited as the first European to reach Brazil, in 1500. The country was thinly settled by various Indian tribes. Only a few have survived to the present, mostly in the Amazon basin.

In the next centuries, Portuguese colonists gradually pushed inland, bringing along large numbers of African slaves. (Slavery was not abolished until 1888.) The King of Portugal, fleeing before Napoleon's army, moved the seat of government to Brazil in 1808. Brazil thereupon became a kingdom under Dom Joao VI. After his return to Portugal, his son Pedro proclaimed the independence of Brazil, Sept. 7, 1822, and was crowned emperor. The second emperor, Dom Pedro II, was deposed in 1889, and a republic proclaimed, called the United States of Brazil. In 1967 the country was renamed the Federative Republic of Brazil.

A military junta took control in 1930; dictatorial power was assumed by Getulio Vargas, until finally forced out by the military in 1945. A democratic regime prevailed 1945-64, during which time the capital was moved from Rio de Janeiro to Brasília. In 1964, Pres. Joao Belchoir Marques Goulart instituted economic policies that aggravated Brazil's inflation; he was overthrown by an army revolt. The next 5 presidents were all military leaders. Censorship was imposed, and much of the opposition was suppressed amid charges of torture.

Since 1930, successive governments have pursued industrial and agricultural growth and interior area development. Exploiting vast natural resources and a huge labor force, Brazil became the leading industrial power of Latin America by the 1970s, while agricultural output soared. By the 1990s, Brazil had one of the world's largest economies; income was poorly distributed, however, and more than one out of four Brazilians continued to survive on less than $1 a day. Despite protective environmental legislation, development has destroyed much of the Amazon ecosystem. Brazil hosted delegates from 178 countries at the Earth Summit, June 3-14, 1992.

Democratic presidential elections were held in 1985 as the nation returned to civilian rule. Fernando Collor de Mello was elected president in Dec. 1989. In Sept. 1992, Collor was impeached for corruption. He resigned on Dec. 29 as his trial was beginning, and Itamar Franco, who had been acting president, was sworn in as president. In elections held on Oct. 3, 1994, Fernando Henrique Cardoso was elected president. Reelected Oct. 4, 1998, he guided Brazil through a series of financial crises.

A new civil code guaranteeing legal equality for women was enacted Aug. 15, 2001. The IMF approved a $30 bil. loan to Brazil Aug. 7, 2002; by then, Brazil's debt already exceeded $260 bil. Luiz Inacio Lula da Silva, a union leader and reformer, won a presidential runoff Oct. 27 with 61% of the vote. Brazil's space program suffered a setback when a rocket exploded on its launchpad Aug. 22, 2003, killing 21 people; the country successfully launched its 1st rocket into space Oct. 23, 2004.

A top aide to Pres. Lula resigned June 16, 2005, amid allegations the ruling party bribed legislators in exchange for votes.

Brunei

State of Brunei Darussalam

People: Population: 372,361. **Age distrib.** (%) <15: 28.6; 65+: 3.0. **Pop. density:** 167 per sq mi, 65 per sq km. **Urban:** 76.2%. **Ethnic groups:** Malay 67%, Chinese 15%, indigenous 6%. **Principal languages:** Malay (official), English, Chinese. **Chief religions:** Muslim (official) 67%, Buddhist 13%, Christian 10%; indigenous beliefs, other 10%.

Geography: Total area: 2,228 sq mi, 5,770 sq km; **Land area:** 2,035 sq mi, 5,270 sq km. **Location:** In SE Asia, on the N coast of the island of Borneo; it is surrounded on its landward side by the Malaysian state of Sarawak. Topography: Brunei has a narrow coastal plain, with mountains in E, hilly lowlands in W. There are swamps in W and NE. Climate is tropical. **Capital:** Bandar Seri Begawan, 61,000.

Government: Type: Independent sultanate. **Head of state and gov.:** Sultan Sir Muda Hassanal Bolkiah Mu'izzadin Waddaulah; b July 15, 1946; in office: Jan. 1, 1984 (sultan since Oct. 5, 1967). **Local divisions:** 4 districts. **Defense budget** (2004): $277 mil. **Active troops:** 7,000.

Economy: Industries: oil, oil refining, nat. gas liquefaction, constr. **Chief crops:** rice, vegetables, fruits. **Natural resources:** oil, nat. gas, timber. **Crude oil reserves** (2004): 1.4 bil. bbls. **Arable land:** 1%. **Livestock** (2004): cattle: 1,211; chickens: 12.6 mil; goats: 2,353; pigs: 6,800; sheep: 2,500. **Fish catch** (2004): cattle: 1,211; chickens: 12,640; goats: 2,353; pigs: 6,800; sheep: 2,500. **Fish catch** (2003): 2,157 metric tons. **Electricity prod.** (2003): 2.7 bil. kWh. **Labor force** (1999 est.): agriculture, forestry, and fishing 10%, production of oil, natural gas, services, and construction 42%, government 48%.

Finance: Monetary unit: Dollar (BND) (Sept. 2005: 1.68 = $1 U.S.). **GDP** (2003 est.): $6.8 bil.; **per capita GDP:** $23,600; **GDP growth:** 3.2%. **Imports** (2003): $5.2 bil.; partners (2004): Singapore 33.1%, Malaysia 21.5%, Japan 7.3%, UK 6.8%. **Exports** (2003 est.): $7.7 bil.; partners (2004): Japan 37.8%, South Korea 13.6%, Australia 11.1%, US 9%, Thailand 7.9%, China 5.9%. **Tourism** (1998): $37 mil. **Budget** (2003 est.): $4.2 bil.

Transport: Railroad: Length: 8 mi. **Motor vehicles:** 200,100 pass. cars, 20,300 comm. vehicles. **Civil aviation:** 2.3 bil pass.-mi; 1 airport.

Communications: TV sets: 637 per 1,000 pop. **Radios:** 302 per 1,000 pop. **Telephone lines** (2002): 90,000. **Daily newspaper circ.:** 69 per 1,000 pop. **Internet** (2001): 35,000 users.

Health: Life expect.: 72.4 male; 77.4 female. **Births** (per 1,000 pop.): 19.0. **Deaths** (per 1,000 pop.): 3.4. **Natural inc.:** 1.56%. **Infant mortality** (per 1,000 live births): 12.6. **AIDS rate:** <0.1%.

Education: Compulsory: ages 5-16. **Literacy:** 93.9%.

Major Intl. Organizations: UN and some of its specialized agencies, APEC, ASEAN, the Commonwealth.

Embassy: 3520 International Court NW 20008; 237-1838.

Website: www.brunei.gov.bn/index.htm

The Sultanate of Brunei was a powerful state in the early 16th century, with authority over all of the island of Borneo as well as parts of the Sulu Islands and the Philippines. In 1888, a treaty placed the state under the protection of Great Britain.

Brunei became a fully sovereign and independent state on Jan. 1, 1984. Much of the country's oil wealth has been squandered in recent years by members of the royal family.

Bulgaria

Republic of Bulgaria

People: Population: 7,450,349. **Age distrib.** (%) <15: 14.1; 65+: 17.2. **Pop. density:** 174 per sq mi, 67 per sq km. **Urban:** 69.8%. **Ethnic groups:** Bulgarian 84%, Turk 10%, Roma 5%. **Principal languages:** Bulgarian (official), Turkish. **Chief religions:** Bulgarian Orthodox 83%, Muslim 12%.

Geography: Total area: 42,823 sq mi, 110,910 sq km; **Land area:** 42,684 sq mi, 110,550 sq km. **Location:** SE Europe, in E Balkan Peninsula on Black Sea. **Neighbors:** Romania on N; Yugoslavia, Macedonia on W; Greece, Turkey on S. **Topography:** The Stara Planina (Balkan) Mts. stretch E-W across the center of the country, with the Danubian plain on N, the Rhodope Mts. on SW, and Thracian Plain on SE. **Capital:** Sofia, 1,076,000.

Government: Type: Republic. **Head of state:** Pres. Georgi Parvanov; b June 28, 1957; in office: Jan. 22, 2002. **Head of gov.:** Prime Min. Sergei Stanishev; b May 5, 1966; in office: Aug. 16, 2005. **Local divisions:** 28 provinces. **Defense budget** (2003): $527 mil. **Active troops:** 51,000.

Economy: Industries: utilities, food, beverages, tobacco, machinery, metals, chemicals. **Chief crops:** vegetables, fruits, tobacco, wine, wheat, barley, sunflowers, sugar beets. **Natural resources:** bauxite, copper, lead, zinc, coal, timber. **Crude oil reserves** (2004): 15 mil bbls. **Arable land:** 37%. **Livestock** (2004): cattle: 668,311; chickens: 18 mil; goats: 725,308; pigs: 1.0 mil; sheep: 2.1 mil. **Fish catch** (2003): 16,498 metric tons. **Electricity prod.** (2003): 38.1 bil. kWh. **Labor force** (3rd quarter 2004 est.): agriculture 11%, industry 32.7%, services 56.3%.

Finance: Monetary unit: Lev (BGN) (Sept. 2005: 1.59 = $1 U.S.). **GDP** (2004 est.): $61.6 bil.; **per capita GDP:** $8,200; **GDP growth:** 5.3%. **Imports** (2004 est.): $12.2 bil.; partners (2004): Germany 15.7%, Italy 10.9%, Russia 9%, Greece 8%, Turkey 7.5%, France 4.7%, Austria 4%. **Exports** (2004 est.): $9.1 bil.; partners (2004): Italy 13.2%, Germany 11.5%, Turkey 9.7%, Belgium 6.4%, Greece 6.1%, US 5.6%, France 5.1%. **Tourism:** $1,658 mil. **Budget** (2004 est.): $9.6 bil. **Intl. reserves less gold:** $5.65 bil. **Gold:** 1.28 mil. oz t. **Consumer prices:** 6.35%.

Transport: Railroad: Length: 2,668 mi. **Motor vehicles:** 2.1741 mil pass. cars, 323,000 comm. vehicles. **Civil aviation:** 224,936 pass.-mi; 128 airports. **Chief ports:** Burgas, Varna.

Communications: TV sets: 429 per 1,000 pop. **Radios:** 537 per 1,000 pop. **Telephone lines:** 2.9 mil. **Daily newspaper circ.:** 116.4 per 1,000 pop. **Internet:** 1.5 mil. users.

Health: Life expect.: 68.4 male; 75.9 female. **Births** (per 1,000 pop.): 9.7. **Deaths** (per 1,000 pop.): 14.3. **Natural inc.:** –0.46%. **Infant mortality** (per 1,000 live births): 20.6. **AIDS rate:** <0.1%.

Education: Compulsory: ages 7-14. **Literacy:** 98.6%.

Major Intl. Organizations: UN (FAO, IBRD, ILO, IMF, IMO, WHO, WTrO), OSCE.

Embassy: 1621 22d St. NW 20008; 387-0174.

Website: www.government.bg/English

Bulgaria was settled by Slavs in the 6th century. Turkic Bulgars arrived in the 7th century, merged with the Slavs, became Christians by the 9th century, and set up powerful empires in the 10th and 12th centuries. The Ottomans prevailed in 1396 and remained for 500 years.

An 1876 revolt led to an independent kingdom in 1908. Bulgaria expanded after the first Balkan War but lost its Aegean coastline in World War I, when it sided with Germany. Bulgaria joined the Axis in World War II but withdrew in 1944. Communists took power with Soviet aid; monarchy was abolished Sept. 8, 1946.

On Nov. 10, 1989, Communist Party leader and head of state Todor Zhivkov, who had held power for 35 years, resigned. Zhivkov was imprisoned, Jan. 1990, and convicted, Sept. 1992, of corruption and abuse of power. In Jan. 1990, Parliament voted to revoke the constitutionally guaranteed dominant role of the Communist Party. A new constitution took effect July 13, 1991. An economic austerity program was launched in May 1996. Former Prime Min. Andrei Lukanov, a longtime Communist leader, was assassinated Oct. 2 in Sofia. Petar Stoyanov won a presidential runoff election Nov. 3.

Bulgaria's deteriorating economy provoked nationwide strikes and demonstrations in Jan. 1997. The Union of Democratic Forces, an anti-Communist group, won national elections on Apr. 19, 1997. The UDF lost the elections of June 17, 2001, to a party headed by the former king, Simeon II. Socialist opposition leader Georgi Parvanov won a presidential runoff vote Nov. 18.

Bulgaria became a full member of NATO, Apr. 2, 2004, and was expected to enter the European Union by 2007. Following parliamentary elections, June 25, 2005, Socialist leader Sergei Stanishev formed a broad coalition government.

Burkina Faso

People: Population: 13,491,736. **Age distrib.** (%) <15: 46.0; 65+: 2.8. **Pop. density:** 127 per sq mi, 49 per sq km. **Urban:** 17.8%. **Ethnic groups:** Mossi (approx. 40%), Gurunsi, Senufo, Lobi, Bobo, Mande, Fulani. **Principal languages:** French (official), Sudanic languages. **Chief religions:** Muslim 50%, indigenous beliefs 40%, Christian (mainly Roman Catholic) 10%.

Geography: Total area: 105,869 sq mi, 274,200 sq km; **Land area:** 105,715 sq mi, 273,800 km. **Location:** In W Africa, S of the Sahara. **Neighbors:** Mali on NW; Niger on NE; Benin, Togo, Ghana, Côte d'Ivoire on S. **Topography:** Landlocked Burkina Faso is in the savanna region of W Africa. The N is arid, hot, and thinly populated. **Capital:** Ouagadougou, 821,000.

Government: Type: Republic. **Head of state:** Pres. Blaise Compaoré; b Feb. 3, 1951; in office: Oct. 15, 1987. **Head of gov.:** Prime Min. Paramanga Ernest Yonli; b 1956; in office: Nov. 7, 2000. **Local divisions:** 45 provinces. **Defense budget** (2004): $62 mil. **Active troops:** 10,800.

Economy: Industries: cotton, beverages, agric. proc., soap, cigarettes, textiles, gold. **Chief crops:** peanuts, shea nuts, sesame, cotton, sorghum, millet. **Natural resources:** mang., limestone, marble, gold, antimony, copper, nickel, bauxite, lead, phosphates, zinc, silver. **Arable land:** 13%. **Livestock** (2004): cattle: 5.2 mil; chickens: 24 mil; goats: 10.6 mil; pigs: 674,000; sheep: 7.0 mil. **Fish catch** (2003): 9,005 metric tons. **Electricity prod.** (2003): 0.38 bil. kWh. **Labor force** (2000 est.): agriculture 90%.

Finance: Monetary unit: CFA Franc BCEAO (XOF) (Sept. 2005: 525.28 = $1 U.S.). **GDP** (2004 est.): $15.7 bil.; **per capita GDP:** $1,200; **GDP growth:** 4.8%. **Imports** (2004 est.): $866.3 mil; partners (2004): France 31.5%, Côte d'Ivoire 13.9%, Togo 8.5%. **Exports** (2004 est.): $418.6 mil; partners (2004): China 32.3%, Singapore 10.7%, Bangladesh 4.5%, Ghana 4.4%, Colombia 4.4%. **Tourism** (2001): $20 mil. **Budget** (2004 est.): $876.3 mil. **Intl. reserves less gold:** $277 mil. **Consumer prices:** –0.4%.

Transport: Railroad: Length: 386 mi. **Motor vehicles:** 26,500 pass. cars, 22,600 comm. vehicles. **Civil aviation:** 98,177 pass.-mi; 2 airports.

Communications: TV sets: 11 per 1,000 pop. **Radios:** 34 per 1,000 pop. **Telephone lines:** 65,400. **Daily newspaper circ.:** 1.3 per 1,000 pop. **Internet:** 48,000 users.

Health: Life expect.: 47.0 male; 50.0 female. **Births** (per 1,000 pop.): 46.0. **Deaths** (per 1,000 pop.): 15.9. **Natural inc.:** 3.00%. **Infant mortality** (per 1,000 live births): 92.9. **AIDS rate:** 4.2%

Education: Compulsory: ages 6-15. **Literacy:** 26.6%.

Major Intl. Organizations: UN and many of its specialized agencies, AU.

Embassy: 2340 Massachusetts Ave. NW 20008; 332-5577.

Website: www.burkinaembassy-usa.org

The Mossi tribe entered the area in the 11th to 13th centuries. Their kingdoms ruled until they were defeated by the Mali and Songhai empires.

French control came by 1896, but Upper Volta (renamed Burkina Faso on Aug. 4, 1984) was not established as a separate territory until 1947. Full independence came Aug. 5, 1960, and a pro-French government was elected. The military seized power in 1980. A 1987 coup established the current regime, which instituted a multiparty democracy in the early 1990s.

Several hundred thousand farm workers migrate each year to Côte d'Ivoire and Ghana. Burkina Faso is heavily dependent on foreign aid.

Burma

(See Myanmar)

Burundi

Republic of Burundi

People: Population: 7,795,426. **Age distrib.** (%) <15: 46.0; 65+: 2.6. **Pop. density:** 725 per sq mi, 280 per sq km. **Urban:** 9.9%. **Ethnic groups:** Hutu 85%, Tutsi 14%, Twa (Pygmy) 1%. **Principal languages:** Kirundi, French (both official); Swahili. **Chief religions:** Roman Catholic 62%, indigenous beliefs 23%, Muslim 10%, Protestant 5%.

Geography: Total area: 10,745 sq mi, 27,830 sq km; **Land area:** 9,904 sq mi, 25,650 sq km. **Location:** In central Africa. **Neighbors:** Rwanda on N, Dem. Rep. of the Congo (formerly Zaire) on W, Tanzania on E and S. **Topography:** Much of the country is grassy highland, with mountains reaching 8,900 ft. The southernmost source of the White Nile is located in Burundi. Lake Tanganyika is the second deepest lake in the world. **Capital:** Bujumbura, 378,000.

Government: Type: In transition. **Head of state and gov.:** Pres. Pierre Nkurunziza; b 1964; in office: Aug. 26, 2005. **Local divisions:** 16 provinces. **Defense budget** (2003): $39 mil. **Active troops:** 50,500.

Economy: Industries: light consumer goods, component assembly, constr., food proc. **Chief crops:** coffee, cotton, tea, corn, sorghum, sweet potatoes, bananas. **Natural resources:** nickel, uranium, rare earth oxides, peat, cobalt, copper, platinum, vanadium, hydropower. **Arable land:** 44%. **Livestock** (2004): cattle: 325,000; chickens: 4.3 mil; goats: 750,000; pigs: 70,000; sheep: 230,000. **Fish catch** (2003): 14,897 metric tons. **Electricity prod.** (2003): 0.14 bil. kWh. **Labor force** (2002 est.): agriculture 93.6%, industry 2.3%, services 4.1%.

Finance: Monetary unit: Franc (BIF) (Sept. 2005: 1,034.92 = $1 U.S.). **GDP** (2004 est.): $4.0 bil.; **per capita GDP:** $600; **GDP growth:** 3%. **Imports** (2004 est.): $138.2 mil; partners (2004): Kenya 11.7%, Tanzania 9.6%, US 9.1%, Belgium 9%, France 8.8%, Italy 5.4%, Japan 4.8%, Uganda 4.8%, Zambia 4.2%. **Exports** (2004 est.): $31.8 mil; partners (2004): Switzerland 25.8%, Germany 12.2%, Belgium 7.9%, US 5.5%, Thailand 5.3%, Rwanda 5.2%. **Tourism:** $1 mil. **Budget** (2004 est.): $187.7 mil. **Intl. reserves less gold:** $42 mil. **Consumer prices:** 13.04%.

Transport: Motor vehicles: 7,000 pass. cars, 9,300 comm. vehicles. **Civil aviation:** 4,971 pass.-mi; 1 airport. **Chief port:** Bujumbura.

Communications: TV sets: 15 per 1,000 pop. **Radios:** 152 per 1,000 pop. **Telephone lines:** 23,900. **Daily newspaper circ.:** 2.4 per 1,000 pop. **Internet:** 14,000 users.

Health: Life expect.: 49.6 male; 51.0 female. **Births** (per 1,000 pop.): 42.5. **Deaths** (per 1,000 pop.): 13.8. **Natural inc.:** 2.87%. **Infant mortality** (per 1,000 live births): 64.4. **AIDS rate:** 6.0%.

Education: Compulsory: ages 7-12. **Literacy:** 51.6%.

Major Intl. Organizations: UN (FAO, IBRD, ILO, IMF, WHO, WTrO), AU.

Embassy: 2233 Wisconsin Ave. NW, Suite 212, 20007; 342-2574.

Website: www.burundiembassy-usa.org

The pygmy Twa were the first inhabitants, followed by Bantu Hutus, who were conquered in the 16th century by the Tutsi (Watusi), probably from Ethiopia. Under German control in 1899, the area fell to Belgium in 1916, which exercised successively a League of Nations mandate and UN trusteeship over Ruanda-Urundi (now the two countries of Rwanda and Burundi). Burundi became independent July 1, 1962.

An unsuccessful Hutu rebellion in 1972-73 left 10,000 Tutsi and 150,000 Hutu dead. Over 100,000 Hutu fled to Tanzania and Zaire (now Congo). In the 1980s, Burundi's Tutsi-dominated regime pledged itself to ethnic reconciliation and democratic reform. In the nation's first democratic presidential election, in June 1993, a Hutu, Melchior Ndadaye, was elected. He was killed in an attempted coup, Oct. 21, 1993. At least 150,000 Burundians died as a result of ethnic conflict during the next three years. Pres. Cyprien Ntaryamira, elected Jan. 1994, was killed with the president of Rwanda in a mysterious plane crash, Apr. 6. The incident sparked massive carnage in Rwanda; violence in Burundi, initially far more limited, intensified in 1995. Ethnic strife continued after a military coup, July 25, 1996. Former South African Pres. Nelson Mandela mediated peace talks from Dec. 1999; most warring groups signed a draft peace treaty in Arusha, Tanzania, Aug. 28, 2000. Coup attempts were suppressed Apr. 18 and July 23, 2001. A power-sharing government headed by Buyoya was sworn in Nov. 1, but clashes with rebels continued.

Domitien Ndayizeye, a Hutu, became president Apr. 30, 2003. The UN Security Council authorized, May 21, 2004, a 5,650-member peacekeeping force for Burundi. Hutu rebels Aug. 13 attacked a UN camp for Congolese Tutsi refugees in W Burundi, killing more than 160 people, many of them women and children. Approval of a power-sharing constitution by referendum, Feb. 28, 2005, paved the way for local and parliamentary elections. Pierre Nkurunziza, the former leader of a Hutu rebel group, became president Aug. 26.

Cambodia

Kingdom of Cambodia

People: Population: 13,636,398. **Age distrib.** (%) <15: 37.3; 65+: 3.1. **Pop. density:** 195 per sq mi, 75 per sq km. **Urban:** 18.6%. **Ethnic groups:** Khmer 90%, Vietnamese 5%, Chinese 1%. **Principal languages:** Khmer (official), French, English. **Chief religion:** Theravada Buddhist 95% (official).

Geography: Total area: 69,900 sq mi, 181,040 sq km; **Land area:** 68,155 sq mi, 176,520 sq km. **Location:** SE Asia, on Indochina Peninsula. **Neighbors:** Thailand on W and N, Laos on NE, Vietnam on E. **Topography:** The central area, formed by the Mekong R. basin and Tonle Sap lake, is level. Hills and mountains are in SE, a long escarpment separates the country from Thailand on NW. 76% of the area is forested. **Capital:** Phnom Penh, 1,157,000.

Government: Type: Constitutional monarchy. **Head of state:** King Norodom Sihamoni; b May 14, 1953; in office: Oct. 14, 2004. **Head of gov.:** Prime Min. Samdech Hun Sen; b Aug. 5, 1952; in office: Nov. 30, 1998. **Local divisions:** 20 provinces and 4 municipalities. **Defense budget** (2004): $73 mil. **Active troops:** 124,300.

Economy: Industries: tourism, garments, rice milling, fishing, wood & wood products, rubber, cement, gem mining, textiles. **Chief crops:** rice, rubber, corn, vegetables. **Natural resources:** timber, gems, iron ore, mang., phosphates. **Arable land:** 13%. **Livestock** (2004): cattle: 3.0 mil; chickens: 14.5 mil; pigs: 2.2 mil. **Fish catch** (2003): 382,857 metric tons. **Electricity prod.** (2003): 0.12 bil. kWh. **Labor force** (2004 est.): agriculture 75%.

Finance: Monetary unit: Riel (KHR) (Sept. 2005: 4,146.65 = $1 U.S.). **GDP** (2004 est.): $27.0 bil.; **per capita GDP:** $2,000; **GDP growth:** 5.4%. **Imports** (2004 est.): $3.1 bil.; partners (2004): Thailand 23.9%, Hong Kong 15%, China 13.5%, Singapore 11.5%, Vietnam 7.6%, Taiwan 7.3%. **Exports** (2004 est.): $2.3 bil.; partners (2004): US 56.2%, Germany 11.5%, UK 7%, Canada 4.3%. **Tourism:** $389 mil. **Budget** (2004 est.): $836.7 mil. **Intl. reserves less gold:** $607 mil. **Gold:** 400,000 oz t.

Transport: Railroad: Length: 374 mi. **Motor vehicles:** 8,300 pass. cars, 3,100 comm. vehicles 5 airports. **Chief port:** Kampong Saom (Sihanoukville).

Communications: TV sets: 9 per 1,000 pop. **Radios:** 128 per 1,000 pop. **Telephone lines:** 36,400. **Daily newspaper circ.:** 1.7 per 1,000 pop. **Internet:** 35,000 users.

Health: Life expect.: 57.0 male; 61.0 female. **Births** (per 1,000 pop.): 26.9. **Deaths** (per 1,000 pop.): 9.2. **Natural inc.:** 1.78%. **Infant mortality** (per 1,000 live births): 70.9. **AIDS rate:** 2.6%.

Education: Compulsory: ages 6-12. **Literacy:** 69.4%.

Major Intl. Organizations: UN (FAO, IBRD, ILO, IMF, IMO, WHO, WTrO), ASEAN.

Embassy: 4530 16th St. NW 20011; 726-7742.

Website: www.cambodia.gov.kh

Early kingdoms dating from that of Funan in the 1st century AD culminated in the great Khmer empire that flourished from the 9th century to the 13th, encompassing present-day Thailand, Cambodia, Laos, and southern Vietnam. The peripheral areas were lost to invading Siamese and Vietnamese, and France established a protectorate in 1863. Independence came in 1953.

Prince Norodom Sihanouk, king 1941-1955 and head of state from 1960, tried to maintain neutrality. Relations with the U.S. were broken in 1965, after South Vietnam planes attacked Vietcong forces within Cambodia. Relations were restored in 1969, after Sihanouk charged Viet Communists with arming Cambodian insurgents.

In 1970, pro-U.S. Prem. Lon Nol seized power, demanding removal of 40,000 North Viet troops; the monarchy was abolished. Sihanouk formed a government-in-exile in Beijing, and open war began between the government and Communist Khmer Rouge guerrillas. The U.S. provided heavy military and economic aid.

Khmer Rouge forces captured Phnom Penh Apr. 17, 1975. The new government evacuated all cities and towns, and shuffled the rural population, sending virtually the entire population to clear jungle, forest, and scrub. An estimated 1.7 million people were killed in executions and enforced hardships.

Severe border fighting broke out with Vietnam in 1978 and developed into a full-fledged Vietnamese invasion. Formation of a Vietnamese-backed government was announced, Jan. 8, 1979, one day after the Vietnamese capture of Phnom Penh. Thousands of refugees flowed into Thailand, and widespread starvation was reported.

On Jan. 10, 1983, Vietnam launched an offensive against rebel forces in the west. They overran a refugee camp, Jan. 31, driving 30,000 residents into Thailand. In March, Vietnam launched a major offensive against camps on the Cambodian-Thailand border, engaged Khmer Rouge guerrillas, and crossed the border, instigating clashes with Thai troops. Vietnam withdrew nearly all its troops by Sept. 1989.

Following UN-sponsored elections in Cambodia that ended May 28, 1993, the 2 leading parties agreed to share power in an interim government until a new constitution was adopted. On Sept. 21, a constitution reestablishing a monarchy was adopted by the National Assembly. It took effect Sept. 24, with Sihanouk as king. The Khmer Rouge, which had boycotted the elections, opposed the new government, and armed violence continued in the mid-1990s. Ieng Sary, a Khmer Rouge leader, broke with the guerrillas, formed a rival group, and announced his support for the monarchy in Aug. 1996, as Khmer Rouge strength rapidly diminished.

Co-Prime Min. Hun Sen staged a coup July 5, 1997, ousting his rival, Prince Norodom Ranariddh. Pol Pot, the Khmer Rouge leader who held power during the late 1970s, was denounced by his former comrades at a show trial, July 25, and sentenced to house arrest; he died Apr. 15, 1998. Hun Sen's party won parliamentary elections on July 26. He retained power in elections July 27, 2003, but without a parliamentary majority. Sihanouk abdicated because of poor health and was succeeded, Oct. 14, 2004, by his son Norodom Sihamoni. Charged with defaming Hun Sen and other members of the ruling coalition, opposition leader Sam Rainsy fled Feb. 3, 2005, after he was stripped of legal immunity.

Cameroon

Republic of Cameroon

People: Population: 16,988,132. **Age distrib.** (%) <15: 41.7; 65+: 3.3. **Pop. density:** 93 per sq mi, 36 per sq km. **Urban:** 51.4%. **Ethnic groups:** Highlanders 31%, Equatorial Bantu 19%, Kirdi 11%, Fulani 10%, NW Bantu 8%, E Nigritic 7%. **Principal languages:** English, French (both official); 24 African language groups. **Chief religions:** Indigenous beliefs 40%, Christian 40%, Muslim 20%.

Geography: Total area: 183,568 sq mi, 475,440 sq km; **Land area:** 181,252 sq mi, 469,440 sq km. **Location:** Between W and central Africa. **Neighbors:** Nigeria on NW; Chad, Central African Republic on E; Congo, Gabon, Equatorial Guinea on S. **Topography:** A low coastal plain with rain forests is in S; plateaus in center lead to forested mountains in W, including Mt. Cameroon, 13,435 ft.; grasslands in N lead to marshes around Lake Chad. **Capital:** Yaoundé, 1,616,000. **Cities** (urban ag.): Douala, 1,663,000.

Government: Type: Republic. **Head of state:** Pres. Paul Biya; b Feb. 13, 1933; in office: Nov. 6, 1982. **Head of gov.:** Prime Min. Ephraïm Inoni; b Aug. 16, 1947; in office: Dec. 8, 2004. **Local divisions:** 10 provinces. **Defense budget** (2004): $197 mil. **Active troops:** 23,100.

Economy: Industries: oil prod. & refining, food proc., light consumer goods, textiles, lumber. **Chief crops:** coffee, cocoa, cotton, rubber, bananas, oilseed, grains. **Natural resources:** oil, bauxite, iron ore, timber, hydropower. **Crude oil reserves** (2004): 400 mil bbls. **Arable land:** 13%. **Livestock** (2004): cattle: 6.0 mil; chickens: 31 mil; goats: 4.4 mil; pigs: 1.4 mil; sheep: 3.8 mil. **Fish catch** (2003): 108,121 metric tons. **Electricity prod.** (2003): 3.0 bil. kWh. **Labor force**: agriculture 70%, industry and commerce 13%, other 17%.

Finance: Monetary unit: CFA Franc BEAC (XAF) (Sept. 2005: 525.18 = $1 U.S.). **GDP** (2004 est.): $30.2 bil.; **per capita GDP:** $1,900; **GDP growth:** 4.9%. **Imports** (2004 est.): $2.0 bil.; partners (2004): France 28.2%, Nigeria 9.4%, Belgium 7.6%, US 4.8%, Germany 4.6%, China 4.4%, Italy 4%. **Exports** (2004 est.): $2.4 bil.; partners (2004): Spain 16.2%, Italy 14.1%, France 10.2%, UK 9.9%, US 9.6%, Netherlands 5.1%. **Tourism** (1995): $36 mil. **Budget** (2004 est.): $2.2 bil. **Intl. reserves less gold:** $534 mil. **Gold:** 30,000 oz t. **Consumer prices** (2002): 2.8%.

Transport: Railroad: Length: 626 mi. **Motor vehicles:** 115,900 pass. cars, 47,400 comm. vehicles. **Civil aviation:** 303,851 pass.-mi; 11 airports. **Chief ports:** Douala, Kribi.

Communications: TV sets: 34 per 1,000 pop. **Radios:** 163 per 1,000 pop. **Telephone lines** (2002): 110,900. **Daily newspaper circ.:** 6.7 per 1,000 pop. **Internet** (2002): 60,000 users.

Health: Life expect.: 50.7 male; 51.1 female. **Births** (per 1,000 pop.): 34.3. **Deaths** (per 1,000 pop.): 13.6. **Natural inc.:** 2.07%. **Infant mortality** (per 1,000 live births): 64.9. **AIDS rate:** 6.9%.

Education: Compulsory: ages 6-11. **Literacy:** 79%.

Major Intl. Organizations: UN (FAO, IBRD, ILO, IMF, IMO, WHO, WTrO), the Commonwealth, AU.

Embassy: 2349 Massachusetts Ave. NW 20008; 265-8790.

Website: www.ambacam-usa.org/main.htm

Portuguese sailors were the first Europeans to reach Cameroon, in the 15th century. The European and American slave trade was very active in the area. German control lasted from 1884 to 1916, when France and Britain divided the territory, later receiving League of Nations mandates and UN trusteeships. French Cameroon became independent Jan. 1, 1960; one part of British Cameroon joined Nigeria in 1961, the other part joined Cameroon. Stability has allowed for development of roads, railways, agriculture, and petroleum production.

Pres. Paul Biya has retained power in a series of elections that were boycotted by opposition parties or disputed as fraudulent.

Canada

People: Population: 32,805,041. **Age distrib.** (%) <15: 17.9; 65+: 13.2. **Pop. density:** 9 per sq mi, 3 per sq km. **Urban:** 80.4%. **Ethnic groups:** British 28%, French 23%, other European 15%, Amerindian 2%. **Principal languages:** English, French (both official). **Chief religions:** Roman Catholic 43%, Protestant 23%, none 16%.

Geography: Total area: 3,855,103 sq mi, 9,984,670 sq km; **Land area:** 3,511,023 sq mi, 9,093,507 sq km. the largest country in land size in the western hemisphere. **Topography:** Canada stretches 3,426 miles from east to west and extends southward from the North Pole to the U.S. border. Its seacoast includes 36,356 miles of mainland and 115,133 miles of islands, including the Arctic islands almost from Greenland to near the Alaskan border. **Climate:** While generally temperate, varies from freezing winter cold to blistering summer heat. **Capital:** Ottawa, 1,093,000. **Cities (urban aggr.)**: Toronto, 4.6 mil; Montreal, 3.4 mil; Vancouver, 2.0 mil; Edmonton, 924,000; Calgary, 927,000.

Government: Type: Confederation with parliamentary democracy. **Head of state:** Queen Elizabeth II, represented by Gov.-Gen. Michaëlle Jean; b 1957; in office: Sept. 27, 2005. **Head of gov.:** Prime Min. Paul Martin; b Aug. 28, 1938; in office: Dec. 12, 2003. **Local divisions:** 10 provinces, 3 territories. **Defense budget** (2003): $9.1 bil. **Active troops:** 52,300.

Economy: Industries: transp. equipment, chemicals, minerals, food & fish products, wood & paper products, oil & natural gas. **Chief crops:** wheat, barley, oilseed, tobacco, fruits, vegetables. **Natural resources:** iron ore, nickel, zinc, copper, gold, lead, molybd., potash, silver, fish, timber, wildlife, coal, oil, nat. gas, hydropower. **Crude oil reserves** (2004): 178.8 bil. bbls. **Arable land:** 5%. **Livestock** (2004): cattle: 14.7 mil; chickens: 16 mil; goats: 30,000; pigs: 14.6 mil; sheep: 1.0 mil. **Fish catch** (2003): 1,229,925 metric tons. **Electricity prod.** (2003): 566.3 bil. kWh. **Labor force** (2000): agriculture 3%, manufacturing 15%, construction 5%, services 74%, other 3%.

Finance: Monetary unit: Dollar (CAD) (Sept. 2005: 1.18 = $1 U.S.). **GDP** (2004 est.): $1.0 tril.; **per capita GDP:** $31,500; **GDP growth:** 2.4%. **Imports** (2004 est.): $256.1 bil.; partners (2004): US 58.9%, China 6.8%, Mexico 3.8%. **Exports** (2004 est.): $315.6 bil.; partners (2004): US 85.2%, Japan 2.1%, UK 1.6%. **Tourism:** $10,579 mil. **Budget** (2004 est.): $144.0 bil. **Intl. reserves less gold:** $22.17 bil. **Gold:** 110,000 oz t. **Consumer prices:** 1.83%.

Transport: Railroad: Length: 45,547 mi. **Motor vehicles:** 17.55 mil pass. cars, 644,300 comm. vehicles. **Civil aviation:** 42.8 bil pass.-mi; 507 airports. **Chief ports:** Halifax, Montreal, Quebec, Saint John, Toronto, Vancouver.

Communications: TV sets: 709 per 1,000 pop. **Radios:** 1,038 per 1,000 pop. **Telephone lines:** 20.7 mil. **Daily newspaper circ.:** 159 per 1,000 pop. **Internet** (2002): 15.2 mil. users.

Health: Life expect.: 76.7 male; 83.6 female. **Births** (per 1,000 pop.): 10.8. **Deaths** (per 1,000 pop.): 7.7. **Natural inc.:** 0.31%. **Infant mortality** (per 1,000 live births): 4.8. **AIDS rate:** 0.3%.

Education: Compulsory: ages 6-16. **Literacy:** 97%.

Major Intl. Organizations: UN and all of its specialized agencies, APEC, the Commonwealth, NATO, OAS, OECD, OSCE.

Embassy: 501 Pennsylvania Ave. NW 20001; 682-1740.

Website: canada.gc.ca/main_e.html

French explorer Jacques Cartier, who reached the Gulf of St. Lawrence in 1534, is generally regarded as Canada's founder. But English seaman John Cabot sighted Newfoundland in 1497, and Vikings are believed to have reached the Atlantic coast centuries before either explorer.

Canadian settlement was pioneered by the French who established Quebec City (1608) and Montreal (1642) and declared New France a colony in 1663.

Britain acquired Acadia (later Nova Scotia) in 1717 and, through military victory over French forces in Canada, captured Quebec (1759) and obtained control of the rest of New France in 1763. The French, through the Quebec Act of 1774, retained the rights to their own language, religion, and civil law. The British presence in Canada increased during the American Revolution when many colonials, proudly calling themselves United Empire Loyalists, moved north to Canada. Fur traders and explorers led Canadians westward across the continent. Sir Alexander Mackenzie reached the Pacific in 1793 and scrawled on a rock by the ocean, "from Canada by land."

In Upper and Lower Canada (later called Ontario and Quebec) and in the Maritimes, legislative assemblies appeared in the 18th century and reformers called for responsible government. But the War of 1812 intervened. The war, a conflict between Great Britain and the United States fought mainly in Upper Canada, ended in a stalemate in 1814.

In 1837 political agitation for more democratic government culminated in rebellions in Upper and Lower Canada. Britain sent Lord Durham to investigate; in a famous report (1839), he recommended union of the 2 parts into one colony called Canada. The union lasted until Confederation, July 1, 1867, when proclamation of the British North America (BNA) Act (now known as the Constitution Act, 1867) launched the Dominion of Canada, consisting of Ontario, Quebec, and the former colonies of Nova Scotia and New Brunswick.

Since 1840 the Canadian colonies had held the right to internal self-government. The BNA Act, which was the basis for the country's written constitution, established a federal system of government on the model of a British parliament and cabinet structure under the crown. Canada was proclaimed a self-governing Dominion within the British Empire in 1931. With the ratification of the Constitution Act, 1982, Canada severed its last formal legislative link with Britain by obtaining the right to amend its constitution.

Canada's Provinces and Territories

Provinces/Territories	Joined Confed.	Area (sq. mi.)	Population (2004 est.)*	Capital	Premier	Party	In office
Alberta	1905	255,287	3,172,121	Edmonton	Ralph Klein	Prog. Cons.	1992
British Columbia	1871	365,948	4,168,123	Victoria	Gordon Campbell	Liberal	2001
Manitoba	1870	250,947	1,165,944	Winnipeg	Gary Doer	New Democratic	1999
New Brunswick	1867	28,355	750,096	Fredericton	Bernard Lord	Prog. Cons.	1999
Newfoundland & Labrador	1949	156,649	519,897	St. John's	Danny Williams	Prog. Cons.	2003
Nova Scotia	1867	21,425	936,892	Halifax	Dr. John Hamm	Prog. Cons.	1999
Ontario	1867	412,581	12,293,669	Toronto	Dalton McGuinty	Liberal	2003
Prince Edward Island	1873	2,185	138,102	Charlottetown	Pat Binns	Prog. Cons.	1996
Quebec	1867	594,860	7,509,928	Québec	Jean Charest	Liberal	2003
Saskatchewan	1905	251,866	994,845	Regina	Lorne Calvert	New Democratic	2001
Northwest Territories[1]	1871	503,951	42,321	Yellowknife	Joe Handley	non-partisan	2003
Nunavut[1]	(2)	818,959	29,496	Iqaluit	Paul Okalik	non-partisan	1999
Yukon Territory[1]	1898	186,661	31,408	Whitehorse	Dennis Fentie	Yukon	2002

*Excludes incompletely enumerated Indian reserves or settlements. (1) Territories also have federally appointed commissioners to represent federal interests. (2) Territory created in 1999 from eastern portion of Northwest Territories.

The so-called Meech Lake Agreement was signed (subject to provincial ratification) June 3, 1987. The accord would have assured constitutional protection for Quebec's efforts to preserve its French language and culture. Critics charged it did not make any provision for other minority groups and it gave Quebec too much power, which might enable Quebec to override the nation's 1982 Charter of Rights and Freedoms (an integral part of the constitution). The accord died June 22, 1990.

Its failure sparked a separatist revival in Quebec, which culminated in Aug. 1992 in the Charlottetown agreement. This called for changes to the constitution, such as recognition of Quebec as a "distinct society" within the Canadian confederation. It was defeated in a national referendum Oct. 26, 1992.

Canada became the first nation to ratify the North American Free Trade Agreement between Canada, Mexico, and the U.S. June 23, 1993. It went into effect Jan. 1, 1994.

On Feb. 24, 1993, Brian Mulroney resigned as prime minister after more than 8 years in office; he was succeeded by Kim Campbell. In elections Oct. 25, 1993, the ruling Conservatives were defeated in a landslide that left them only 2 of the 295 seats in the House of Commons. Jean Chrétien became prime minister. In a Quebec referendum held Oct. 30, 1995, proponents of secession lost by a razor-thin margin. The elections of June 2, 1997, left the Liberals with a slim majority.

On Jan. 7, 1998, the government apologized to native peoples for 150 years of mistreatment and pledged to set up a "healing fund." Canada's highest court ruled, Aug. 20, that Quebec cannot secede unilaterally, even if a majority of the province approves. Nunavut ("Our Land"), carved from Northwest Territories as a homeland for the Inuit, was established Apr. 1, 1999. Victory by the Liberals in national elections Nov. 27, 2000, made Chrétien the 1st Canadian prime minister in over 50 years to head a 3rd successive majority government.

Canada sent 5 warships in Oct. 2001, and 850 troops in Feb. 2002, to join U.S. counterterrorism operations in Afghanistan. Four Canadian soldiers conducting a training exercise near Kandahar were accidentally killed Apr. 17 by U.S. forces, Canada's first war casualties since its participation in the Korean War. Relations between Canada and the U.S. cooled after Prime Min. Chrétien refused to contribute troops to the U.S.-led invasion of Iraq in Mar. 2003.

A SARS outbreak killed more than 40 people in the Toronto area in 2003, and cost the city and national economy millions of dollars in lost revenues. Chrétien retired Dec. 12, and Paul Martin became prime minister.

Weakened by a scandal involving improper payments to Quebec firms for advertising and sponsorship of cultural and sporting events, the Liberals won only 135 of 308 seats in parliamentary elections June 28, 2004; the Conservatives finished 2nd with 99. Martin stayed in office as head of a minority government. Parliament gave final approval July 19, 2005, to a bill making same-sex marriage (already permitted in 8 of 10 provinces) legal throughout the country. Michaëlle Jean, a Haitian-born TV journalist, was installed Sept. 27 as Canada's 1st black governor general.

Prime Ministers of Canada

Canada is a constitutional monarchy with a parliamentary system of government. It is also a federal state. Canada's official head of state, Queen Elizabeth II, is represented by a resident Governor-General. However, in practice the nation is governed by the Prime Minister, leader of the party that commands the support of a majority of the House of Commons, dominant chamber of Canada's bicameral Parliament.

Name	Party	Term
Sir John A. Macdonald	Conservative	1867-1873
Alexander Mackenzie	Liberal	1873-1878
Sir John A. Macdonald	Conservative	1878-1891
Sir John J. C. Abbott	Conservative	1891-1892
Sir John S. D. Thompson	Conservative	1892-1894
Sir Mackenzie Bowell	Conservative	1894-1896
Sir Charles Tupper	Conservative	1896[1]
Sir Wilfrid Laurier	Liberal	1896-1911
Sir Robert Laird Borden	Cons./Union.[2]	1911-1920
Arthur Meighen	Unionist	1920-1921
W. L. Mackenzie King	Liberal	1921-1926
Arthur Meighen	Conservative	1926[3]
W. L. Mackenzie King	Liberal	1926-1930
Richard Bedford Bennett	Conservative	1930-1935
W. L. Mackenzie King	Liberal	1935-1948
Louis St. Laurent	Liberal	1948-1957
John G. Diefenbaker	Prog. Cons.	1957-1963
Lester Bowles Pearson	Liberal	1963-1968
Pierre Elliott Trudeau	Liberal	1968-1979
Joe Clark	Prog. Cons.	1979-1980
Pierre Elliott Trudeau	Liberal	1980-1984
John Napier Turner	Liberal	1984[4]
Brian Mulroney	Prog. Cons.	1984-1993
Kim Campbell	Prog. Cons.	1993[5]
Jean Chrétien	Liberal	1993-2003
Paul Martin	Liberal	2003-

(1) May-July. (2) Conservative 1911-1917, Unionist 1917-1920. (3) June-Sept. (4) June-Sept. (5) June-Oct.

Cape Verde

Republic of Cape Verde

People: Population: 418,224. **Age distrib.** (%) <15: 39.0; 65+: 6.8. **Pop. density:** 269 per sq mi, 104 per sq km. **Urban:** 55.9%. **Ethnic groups:** Creole 71%, African 28%, European 1%. **Principal languages:** Portuguese (official), Crioulo. **Chief religions:** Roman Catholic (infused with indigenous beliefs); Protestant (mostly Church of the Nazarene).

Geography: Total area: 1,557 sq mi, 4,033 sq km; **Land area:** 1,557 sq mi, 4,033 sq km. **Location:** In Atlantic O., off W tip of Africa. **Neighbors:** Nearest are Mauritania, Senegal to E. **Topography:** Cape Verde Islands are 15 in number, volcanic in origin (active crater on Fogo). The landscape is eroded and stark, with vegetation mostly in interior valleys. **Capital:** Praia, 107,000.

Government: Type: Republic. **Head of state:** Pres. Pedro Pires; b Apr. 29, 1934; in office: Mar. 22, 2001. **Head of gov.:** Prime Min. José Maria Neves; b Mar. 28, 1960; in office: Feb. 1, 2001. **Local divisions:** 17 districts. **Defense budget** (2004): $4 mil. **Active troops:** 1,200.

Economy: Industries: food & beverages, fish proc., shoes & garments, salt mining, ship repair. **Chief crops:** bananas, corn, beans, sweet potatoes, sugarcane, coffee, peanuts. **Natural resources:** salt, basalt rock, limestone, kaolin, fish. **Arable land:** 11%. **Livestock** (2004): cattle: 22,500; chickens: 450,000; goats: 112,500; pigs: 205,000; sheep: 9,500. **Fish catch** (2003): 8,721 metric tons. **Electricity prod.** (2003): 0.04 bil. kWh.

Finance: Monetary unit: Escudo (CVE) (Sept. 2005: 89.72 = $1 U.S.). **GDP** (2002 est.): $600.0 mil; **per capita GDP:** $1,400; **GDP growth:** 5%. **Imports** (2004 est.): $387.3 mil; partners (2004): Portugal 43.2%, US 12.5%, Netherlands 8.7%. **Exports** (2004 est.): $61.1 mil; partners (2004): Portugal 62.5%, US 15.8%, UK 11.3%. **Tourism:** $85 mil.

Transport: Motor vehicles (1999): 13,500 pass. cars, 3,100 comm. vehicles. **Civil aviation:** 171,498 pass.-mi; 6 airports. **Chief ports:** Mindelo, Praia.

Communications: TV sets: 5 per 1,000 pop. **Radios:** 183 per 1,000 pop. **Telephone lines:** 71,700. **Internet:** 20,000 users.

Health: Life expect.: 67.1 male; 73.9 female. **Births** (per 1,000 pop.): 25.3. **Deaths** (per 1,000 pop.): 6.6. **Natural inc.:** 1.87%. **Infant mortality** (per 1,000 live births): 47.8.

Education: Compulsory: ages 6-11. **Literacy:** 76.6%.

Major Intl. Organizations: UN (FAO, IBRD, ILO, IMF, IMO, WHO), AU.

Embassy: 3415 Massachusetts Ave. NW 20007; 965-6820.

Website: virtualcapeverde.net

The uninhabited Cape Verdes were discovered by the Portuguese in 1456 or 1460. The first Portuguese colonists landed in 1462; African slaves were brought soon after, and most Cape Verdeans descend from both groups. Cape Verde independence came July 5, 1975. Antonio Mascarenhas Monteiro won the nation's first free presidential election Feb. 17, 1991; he was reelected without opposition five years later. Pedro Pires won a presidential runoff election Feb. 25, 2001.

Central African Republic

People: Population: 4,237,703. **Age distrib.** (%) <15: 42.5; 65+: 3.4. **Pop. density:** 18 per sq mi, 7 per sq km. **Urban:** 42.7%. **Ethnic groups:** Baya 33%, Banda 27%, Mandjia 13%, Sara 10%, Mboum 7%, M'Baka 4%, Yakoma 4%. **Principal languages:** French (official), Sangho (national), tribal languages. **Chief religions:** Indigenous beliefs 35%, Protestant 25%, Roman Catholic 25%, Muslim 15%.

Geography: Total area: 240,535 sq mi, 622,984 sq km; **Land area:** 240,535 sq mi, 622,984 sq km. **Location:** In central Africa. **Neighbors:** Chad on N, Cameroon on W, Congo-Brazzaville and Congo-Kinshasa (formerly Zaire) on S, Sudan on E. **Topography:** Mostly rolling plateau, average altitude 2,000 ft., with rivers draining S to the Congo and N to Lake Chad. Open, well-watered savanna covers most of the area, with an arid area in NE, and tropical rain forest in SW. **Capital:** Bangui, 698,000.

Government: Type: Republic. **Head of state:** Pres. François Bozizé; b Oct. 14, 1946; in office: Mar. 15, 2003. **Head of gov.:** Prime Min. Élie Doté; in office: June 13, 2005. **Local divisions:** 14 prefectures, 2 economic prefectures, 1 commune. **Defense budget** (2004): $37 mil. **Active troops:** 2,550.

Economy: Industries: diamond mining, sawmills, breweries, textiles, footwear, bicycle & motorcycle assembly. **Chief crops:** cotton, coffee, tobacco, cassava, yams, millet, corn, bananas. **Natural resources:** diamonds, uranium, timber, gold, oil, hydropower. **Arable land:** 3%. **Livestock** (2004): cattle: 3.4 mil; chickens: 4.8 mil; goats: 3.1 mil; pigs: 805,000; sheep: 259,000. **Fish catch** (2003): 15,000 metric tons. **Electricity prod.** (2003): 0.11 bil. kWh.

Finance: Monetary unit: CFA Franc BEAC (XAF) (Sept. 2005: 525.18 = $1 U.S.). **GDP** (2004 est.): $4.2 bil.; **per capita GDP:** $1,100; **GDP growth:** 0.5%. **Imports** (2002 est.): $136.0 mil; partners (2004): France 19.4%, US 16.3%, Cameroon 8.3%, Belgium 5.6%. **Exports** (2002 est.): $172.0 mil; partners (2004): Belgium 41%, Italy 8.9%, Spain 8.5%, Indonesia 7.6%, France 6.3%, US 5.3%. **Tourism** (2002): $3 mil. **Intl. reserves less gold:** $96 mil. **Gold:** 10,000 oz t. **Consumer prices:** –1.66%.

Transport: Motor vehicles: 5,300 pass. cars, 6,300 comm. vehicles. **Civil aviation:** 80,778 pass.-mi; 3 airport. **Chief port:** Bangui.

Communications: TV sets: 6 per 1,000 pop. **Radios:** 83 per 1,000 pop. **Telephone lines** (2002): 9,000. **Daily newspaper circ.:** 1.8 per 1,000 pop. **Internet**: 6,000 users.

Health: Life expect.: 43.3 male; 43.5 female. **Births** (per 1,000 pop.): 34.3. **Deaths** (per 1,000 pop.): 18.8. **Natural inc.:** 1.55%. **Infant mortality** (per 1,000 live births): 87.3. **AIDS rate:** 13.5%.

Education: Compulsory: ages 6-15. **Literacy:** 51%.

Major Intl. Organizations: UN (FAO, IBRD, ILO, IMF, WHO, WTrO), AU.

Embassy: 1618 22d St. NW 20008; 483-7800.

Website: www.state.gov/p/af/ci/ct

Various Bantu tribes migrated through the region for centuries before French control was asserted in the late 19th century, when the region was named Ubangi-Shari. Complete independence was attained Aug. 13, 1960.

All political parties were dissolved in 1960, and the country became a center for Chinese political influence in Africa. Relations with China were severed after 1965. Pres. Jean-Bedel Bokassa, who seized power in a 1965 military coup, proclaimed himself constitutional emperor of the renamed Central African Empire Dec. 1976.

Bokassa's rule was characterized by ruthless authoritarianism and human rights violations. He was ousted in a bloodless coup aided by the French government, Sept. 20, 1979. In 1981, Gen. André Kolingba became head of state in another bloodless coup. Multiparty legislative and presidential elections were held in Oct. 1992 but were canceled by the government when Kolingba was losing. New elections, held in Aug. and Sept. 1993, led to the replacement of Kolingba with a civilian government under Pres. Ange-Félix Patassé.

France sent in troops to suppress army mutinies in 1996 and 1997. Patassé loyalists won a narrow majority in legislative elections on Nov. 22 and Dec. 13, 1998, and he was reelected to a 2nd 6-year term on Sept. 19, 1999. After thwarting several coup attempts, Patassé was ousted Mar. 15, 2003, by rebels under former army chief François Bozizé. Bozizé won a presidential runoff election May 8, 2005.

Chad

Republic of Chad

People: Population: 9,657,069. **Age distrib.** (%) <15: 47.9; 65+: 2.8. **Pop. density:** 19 per sq mi, 8 per sq km. **Urban:** 24.9%. **Ethnic groups:** About 200 groups; largest are Arabs in N and Sara in S. **Principal languages:** French, Arabic (both official), Sara, more than 120 different languages and dialects. **Chief religions:** Muslim 51%, Christian 35%, animist 7%, other 7%.

Geography: Total area: 495,755 sq mi, 1,284,000 sq km; **Land area:** 486,180 sq mi, 1,259,200 sq km. **Location:** In central N Africa. **Neighbors:** Libya on N; Niger, Nigeria, Cameroon on W; Central African Republic on S; Sudan on E. **Topography:** Wooded savanna, steppe, and desert in the S; part of the Sahara in the N. Southern rivers flow N to Lake Chad, surrounded by marshland. **Capital:** N'Djamena, 797,000.

Government: Type: Republic. **Head of state:** Pres. Idriss Déby; b 1952; in office: Dec. 4, 1990. **Head of gov.:** Prime Min. Pascal Yoadimnadji; in office: Feb. 3, 2005. **Local divisions:** 14 prefectures. **Defense budget** (2004): $39 mil. **Active troops:** 30,350.

Economy: Industries: cotton textiles, meatpacking, beer brewing, sodium carbonate, soap, cigarettes, constr. materials. **Chief crops:** cotton, sorghum, millet, peanuts, rice, potatoes, cassava. **Natural resources:** oil, uranium, natron, kaolin, fish. **Arable land:** 3%. **Livestock** (2004): cattle: 6.4 mil; chickens: 5.2 mil; goats: 5.7 mil; pigs: 25,000; sheep: 2.6 mil. **Fish catch** (2003): 70,000 metric tons. **Electricity prod.** (2003): 0.12 bil. kWh. **Labor force**: agriculture more than 80% (subsistence farming, herding, and fishing).

Finance: Monetary unit: CFA Franc BEAC (XAF) (Sept. 2005: 525.18 = $1 U.S.). **GDP** (2004 est.): $15.7 bil.; **per capita GDP:** $1,600; **GDP growth:** 38%. **Imports** (2004 est.): $500.7 mil; partners (2004): France 22.9%, Cameroon 13.7%, US 11.8%, Portugal 10.9%, Germany 7.7%, Belgium 4.8%. **Exports** (2003 est.): $365.0 mil; partners (2004): US 74.2%, China 14.8%, Portugal 5.2%. **Tourism** (2002): $25 mil. **Budget** (2004 est.): $957.7 mil. **Intl. reserves less gold:** $143 mil. **Gold:** 10,000 oz t. **Consumer prices** (2003): –1.9%.

Transport: Motor vehicles: 8,700 pass. cars, 12,400 comm. vehicles. **Civil aviation:** 80,778 pass.-mi; 7 airports.

Communications: TV sets: 1 per 1,000 pop. **Radios:** 236 per 1,000 pop. **Telephone lines** (2002): 11,800. **Daily newspaper circ.:** 0.2 per 1,000 pop. **Internet** (2002): 15,000 users.

Health: Life expect.: 45.6 male; 48.9 female. **Births** (per 1,000 pop.): 46.2. **Deaths** (per 1,000 pop.): 16.7. **Natural inc.:** 2.95%. **Infant mortality** (per 1,000 live births): 93.1. **AIDS rate:** 4.8%.

Education: Compulsory: ages 6-11. **Literacy:** 47.5%.

Major Intl. Organizations: UN (FAO, IBRD, ILO, IMF, WHO, WTrO), AU.

Embassy: 2002 R St. NW 20009; 462-4009.

Website: www.chadembassy.org/site/index.cfm?lang=1

Chad was the site of paleolithic and neolithic cultures before the Sahara Desert formed. A succession of kingdoms and Arab slave traders dominated Chad until France took control around 1900. Independence came Aug. 11, 1960.

Northern Muslim rebels have fought animist and Christian southern government and French troops from 1966, despite numerous cease-fires and peace pacts.

Libyan troops entered the country at the request of a pro-Libyan Chad government, Dec. 1980. The troops were withdrawn from Chad in Nov. 1981. Rebel forces, led by Hissène Habré, captured the capital and forced Pres. Goukouni Oueddei to flee the country in June 1982.

In 1983, France sent some 3,000 troops to Chad to assist Pres. Habré in opposing Libyan-backed rebels. France and Libya agreed to a simultaneous withdrawal of troops from Chad in Sept. 1984, but Libyan forces remained in the north until Mar. 1987, when Chad forces drove them from their last major stronghold. In Dec. 1990, Habré was overthrown by a Libyan-supported insurgent group, the Patriotic Salvation Movement.

On Feb. 3, 1994, the World Court dismissed a long-standing territorial claim by Libya to the mineral-rich Aozou Strip, on the Libyan border. Libyan troops reportedly withdrew at the end of May. Following approval of a new constitution in March 1996, Chad's first multiparty presidential election was held in June and July. The U.S. Peace Corps withdrew from Chad in Apr. 1998 because of continuing clashes between rebels and Chad government forces.

Pres. Idriss Déby won reelection May 20, 2001, to another 5-year term. Oil began flowing July 15, 2003, through a 665-mi pipeline that allows landlocked Chad to export via Cameroon.

Chile

Republic of Chile

People: Population: 15,980,912. **Age distrib.** (%) <15: 25.2; 65+: 8.0. **Pop. density:** 55 per sq mi, 21 per sq km. **Urban:** 87.0%. **Ethnic groups:** European and Mestizo 95%, Amerindian 3%. **Principal languages:** Spanish (official), Araucanian. **Chief religions:** Roman Catholic 89%, Protestant 11%.

Geography: Total area: 292,260 sq mi, 756,950 sq km; **Land area:** 289,113 sq mi, 748,800 sq km. **Location:** Occupies western coast of S South America. **Neighbors:** Peru on N, Bolivia on NE, on E. **Topography:** Andes Mts. on E border incl. some of the world's highest peaks; on W is 2,650-mile Pacific coast. Width varies between 100 and 250 miles. In N is Atacama Desert, in center are agricultural regions, in S, forests and grazing lands. **Capital:** Santiago, 5,478,000.

Government: Type: Republic. **Head of state and gov.:** Pres. Ricardo Lagos Escobar; b Mar. 2, 1938; in office: Mar. 11, 2000. **Local divisions:** 13 regions. **Defense budget** (2004): $1.4 bil. **Active troops:** 77,700.

Economy: Industries: copper, other minerals, foodstuffs, fish proc., iron, steel, wood & wood products, transp. equip., cement, textiles. **Chief crops:** wheat, corn, grapes, beans, sugar beets, potatoes, fruit. **Natural resources:** copper, timber, iron ore, nitrates, prec. metals, molybd., hydropower. **Crude oil reserves** (2004): 150 mil bbls. **Arable land:** 5%. **Livestock** (2004): cattle: 4.0 mil; chickens: 88 mil; goats: 725,000; pigs: 3.2 mil; sheep: 3.7 mil. **Fish catch** (2003): 4,185,188 metric tons. **Electricity prod.** (2003): 45.3 bil. kWh. **Labor force** (2003): agriculture 13.6%, industry 23.4%, services 63%.

Finance: Monetary unit: Peso (CLP) (Sept. 2005: 541.53 = $1 U.S.). **GDP** (2004 est.): $169.1 bil.; **per capita GDP:** $10,700; **GDP growth:** 5.8%. **Imports** (2004 est.): $22.5 bil.; partners (2004): Argentina 17%, US 14.1%, Brazil 11.1%, China 7.1%. **Exports** (2004 est.): $29.2 bil.; partners (2004): US 14%, Japan 11.4%, China 9.9%, South Korea 5.5%, Netherlands 5.1%, Brazil 4.3%, Italy 4.1%, Mexico 4%. **Tourism:** $860 mil. **Budget** (2004 est.): $20.0 bil. **Intl. reserves less gold:** $10.30 bil. **Gold:** 10,000 oz t. **Consumer prices:** 1.05%.

Transport: Railroad: Length: 4,092 mi. **Motor vehicles:** 1.37 mil pass. cars, 734,000 comm. vehicles. **Civil aviation:** 7.2 bil pass.-mi. **Chief ports:** Valparaiso, Arica, Antofagasta.

Communications: TV sets: 240 per 1,000 pop. **Radios:** 354 per 1,000 pop. **Telephone lines:** 3.3 mil. **Daily newspaper circ.:** 98 per 1,000 pop. **Internet:** 4.0 mil. users.

Health: Life expect.: 73.3 male; 80.0 female. **Births** (per 1,000 pop.): 15.4. **Deaths** (per 1,000 pop.): 5.8. **Natural inc.:** 0.97%. **Infant mortality** (per 1,000 live births): 8.8. **AIDS rate:** 0.3%.

Education: Compulsory: ages 6-13. **Literacy:** 96.2%.

Major Intl. Organizations: UN and all of its specialized agencies, APEC, OAS.

Embassy: 1732 Massachusetts Ave. NW 20036; 785-1746.

Website: www.chileangovernment.cl/

Northern Chile was under Inca rule before the Spanish conquest, 1536-40. The southern Araucanian Indians resisted until the late 19th century. Independence was gained 1810-18, under José de San Martin and Bernardo O'Higgins; the latter, as supreme director 1817-23, sought social and economic reforms until deposed. Chile defeated Peru and Bolivia in 1836-39 and 1879-84, gaining mineral-rich northern land.

In 1970, Salvador Allende Gossens, a Marxist, became president with a narrow plurality of the popular vote. His government improved conditions for the poor, but property seizures by left-wing extremists, poorly planned socialist economic programs, and a destabilization campaign backed by the U.S. led to political and financial chaos.

A military junta seized power Sept. 11, 1973. With the presidential palace under attack, Allende refused to surrender; police said he killed himself. The junta, headed by Gen. Augusto Pinochet Ugarte, named a mostly military cabinet and announced plans to "exterminate Marxism." Repression continued through most of the 1980s.

In Dec. 1989 voters elected a civilian president, although Pinochet continued to head the army until Mar. 10, 1998. In Mar. 1994 a Chilean human rights group estimated that human rights violations had claimed more than 3,100 lives during Pinochet's rule. Initial attempts to prosecute him failed when he was declared mentally unfit to stand trial by courts in Britain and Chile.

Ricardo Lagos Escobar, Chile's 1st Socialist president since the 1973 coup, took office Mar. 11, 2000. Chile and the U.S. signed a free trade accord June 6, 2003. In Aug. 2004, Chile's Supreme Court voted to strip Pinochet of immunity from prosecution, allowing for the possibility of a future trial.

Tierra del Fuego is the largest (18,800 sq. mi.) island in the archipelago of the same name at the southern tip of South America, an area of majestic mountains, tortuous channels, and high winds. It was visited 1520 by Magellan and named Land of Fire because of its many Indian bonfires. Part of the island is in Chile, part in Argentina. Punta Arenas, on a mainland peninsula, is a center of sheep raising and the world's southernmost city (pop. about 70,000); Puerto Williams is the southernmost settlement.

China

People's Republic of China

(Statistical data do not include Hong Kong or Macao.)

People: Population: 1,306,313,812. **Age distrib.** (%) <15: 21.4; 65+: 7.6. **Pop. density:** 353 per sq mi, 136 per sq km. **Urban:** 38.6%. **Ethnic groups:** 56 groups; Han 92%. Also Zhuang, Manchu, Hui, Miao, Uygur, Yi, Tujia, Tong, Tibetan, Mongol, et al. **Principal languages:** Mandarin (official), Yue (Cantonese), Wu (Shanghaiese), Minbei (Fuzhou), Minnan (Hokkien-Taiwanese), Xiang, Gan, Hakka, minority languages. **Chief religions:** Officially atheist; Buddhism, Taoism, some Muslims, Christians.

Geography: Total area: 3,705,407 sq mi, 9,596,960 sq km; **Land area:** 3,600,947 sq mi, 9,326,410 sq km. **Location:** Occupies most of the habitable mainland of E Asia. **Neighbors:** Mongolia on N; Russia on NE and NW; Afghanistan, Pakistan, Tajikistan, Kyrgystan, Kazakhstan on W; India, Nepal, Bhutan, Myanmar, Laos, Vietnam on S; North Korea on NE. **Topography:** Two-thirds of the vast territory is mountainous or desert; only one-tenth is cultivated. Rolling topography rises to high elevations in the N in the Daxinganlingshanmai separating Manchuria and Mongolia; the Tien Shan in Xinjiang; the Himalayan and Kunlunshanmai in the SW and in Tibet. Length is 1,860 mi. from N to S, width E to W is more than 2,000 mi. The eastern half of China is one of the world's best-watered lands. Three great river systems, the Chang (Yangtze), Huang (Yellow), and Xi, provide water for vast farmlands. **Capital:** Beijing,10,848,000. **Cities (urban aggr.):** Shanghai,12,887,000; Tianjin, 9,156,000; Chongqing, 4,635,000; Shenyang, 4,828,000; Guangzhou, 3,893,000.

Government: Type: Communist Party-led state. **Head of state:** Pres. Hu Jintao; b Dec. 1942; in office: Mar. 15, 2003 (also gen. secy of Communist Party since Nov. 15, 2002). **Head of gov.:** Premier Wen Jiabao; b. Sept. 1942; in office: Mar. 16, 2003. **Local divisions:** 22 provinces (not including Taiwan), 5 autonomous regions, and 4 municipalities, plus the special administrative regions of Hong Kong (as of July 1, 1997) and Macao (as of Dec. 20, 1999). **Defense budget** (2004): $25 bil. **Active troops:** 2,255,000.

Economy: Industries: iron, steel, coal, machine building, armaments, textiles & apparel, oil, cement, chemical fertilizers. **Chief crops:** rice, wheat, potatoes, sorghum, peanuts, tea. **Natural resources:** coal, iron ore, oil, nat. gas, mercury, tin, tungsten, antimony, mang., molybd., vanadium, magnetite, aluminum, lead, zinc, uranium, hydropower. **Crude oil reserves** (2004): 18.3 bil. bbls. **Arable land:** 10%. **Livestock** (2004): cattle: 106.5 mil; chickens: 4.2 bil; goats: 183.4 mil; pigs: 472.9 mil; sheep: 155.7 mil. **Fish catch** (2003): 45,647,658 metric tons. **Electricity prod.** (2003): 1806.8 bil. kWh. **Labor force** (2003 est.): agriculture 49%, industry 22%, services 29%.

Finance: Monetary unit: Yuan Renminbi (CNY) (Sept. 2005: 8.09 = $1 U.S.). **GDP** (2004 est.): $7.3 tril.; **per capita GDP:** $5,600; **GDP growth:** 9.1%. **Imports** (2004 est.): $552.4 bil.; partners (2004): Japan 16.1%, Taiwan 10.9%, South Korea 10.4%, US 7.7%, Hong Kong 7.4%, Germany 5.4%. **Exports** (2004 est.): $583.1 bil.; partners (2004): US 22.8%, Hong Kong 16.2%, Japan 12.4%, South Korea 4.4%, Germany 4%. **Tourism:** $17,406 mil. **Budget** (2004 est.): $348.9 bil. **Intl. reserves less gold: Gold** (2003): 19.29 mil. oz t. **Consumer prices** (2003): 1.2%.

Transport: Railroad: Length: 43,532 mi. **Motor vehicles** 6.55 mil pass. cars, 6.3 mil comm. vehicles. **Civil aviation:** 65.8 bil pass.-mi; 351 airports. **Chief ports:** Shanghai, Qinhuangdao, Dalian, Guangzhou (Canton).

Communications: TV sets: 291 per 1,000 pop. **Radios:** 342 per 1,000 pop. **Telephone lines:** 262.7 mil. **Daily newspaper circ.:** 376.5 per 1,000 pop. **Internet:** 79.5 mil. users.

Health: Life expect.: 70.7 male; 74.1 female. **Births** (per 1,000 pop.): 13.1. **Deaths** (per 1,000 pop.): 6.9. **Natural inc.:** 0.62%. **Infant mortality** (per 1,000 live births): 24.2. **AIDS rate:** 0.1%.

Education: Compulsory: ages 6-14. **Literacy:** 90.9%.

Major Intl. Organizations: UN (FAO, IBRD, ILO, IMF, IMO, WHO, WTrO), APEC.

Embassy: 2300 Conn. Ave. NW 20008; 328-2500.

Website: www1.cei.gov.cn/govinfo/english/default1e.shtml

Remains of various humanlike creatures who lived as early as several hundred thousand years ago have been found in many parts of China. Neolithic agricultural settlements dotted the Huang (Yellow) R. basin from about 5000 BC. Their language, religion, and art were the sources of later Chinese civilization.

Bronze metallurgy reached a peak and Chinese pictographic writing, similar to today's, was in use in the more developed culture of the Shang Dynasty (c. 1500 BC-c. 1000 BC), which ruled much of North China.

A succession of dynasties and interdynastic warring kingdoms ruled China for the next 3,000 years. They expanded Chinese political and cultural domination to the south and west, and developed a brilliant technologically and a culturally advanced society. Rule by foreigners (Mongols in the Yuan Dynasty, 1271-1368, and Manchus in the Ch'ing Dynasty, 1644-1911) did not alter the underlying culture.

A period of relative stagnation left China vulnerable to internal and external pressures in the 19th century. Rebellions left tens of millions dead, and Russia, Japan, Britain, and other powers exercised political and economic control in large parts of the country. China became a republic Jan. 1, 1912, following the Wuchang Uprising inspired by Dr. Sun Yat-sen, founder of the Kuomintang (Nationalist) party. By 1928, the Kuomintang, led by Chiang Kai-shek, succeeded in nominal reunification of China. About the same time, a bloody purge of Communists from the ranks of the Kuomintang fomented hostilities between the two groups that would continue for decades.

For over 50 years, 1894-1945, China was involved in conflicts with Japan. In 1895, China ceded Korea, Taiwan, and other areas. On Sept. 18, 1931, Japan seized the Northeastern Provinces (Manchuria) and set up a puppet state called Manchukuo. The border province of Jehol was cut off as a buffer state in 1933. Taking advantage of Chinese dissension, Japan invaded China proper July 7, 1937. On Nov. 20 the retreating Nationalist government moved its capital to Chongqing (Chungking) from Nanking (Nanjing), which Japanese troops then ravaged Dec. 13.

From 1939 the Sino-Japanese War (1937-45) became part of the broader world conflict. After its defeat in World War II, Japan gave up all seized land, and internal conflicts involving the Kuomintang, Communists, and other factions resumed. China came under the domination of Communist armies, 1949-1950. The Kuomintang government moved to Taiwan, Dec. 8, 1949.

The Chinese People's Political Consultative Conference convened Sept. 21, 1949; The People's Republic of China was proclaimed in Beijing (Peking) Oct. 1, 1949, under Mao Zedong. China and the USSR signed a 30-year treaty of "friendship, alliance and mutual assistance," Feb. 15, 1950. The U.S. refused recognition of the new regime. On Nov. 26, 1950, the People's Republic sent armies into Korea against U.S. troops and forced a stalemate in the Korean War.

After an initial period of consolidation, 1949-52, industry, agriculture, and social and economic institutions were forcibly molded according to Maoist ideals. However, frequent drastic changes in policy and violent factionalism interfered with economic development. In 1957, Mao admitted an estimated 800,000 people had been executed 1949-54; opponents claimed much higher figures.

The Great Leap Forward, 1958-60, tried to force the pace of economic development through intensive labor on huge new rural communes, and through emphasis on ideological purity. The program caused resistance and was largely abandoned.

By the 1960s, relations with the USSR deteriorated, with disagreements on borders, ideology, and leadership of world Communism. The USSR canceled aid accords, and China, with Albania, launched anti-Soviet propaganda drives.

The Great Proletarian Cultural Revolution, 1965, was an attempt to oppose pragmatism and bureaucratic power and instruct a new generation in revolutionary principles. Massive purges took place. A program of forcibly relocating millions of urban teenagers into the countryside was launched. By 1968 the movement had run its course; many purged officials returned to office in subsequent years, and reforms that had placed ideology above expertise were gradually weakened.

On Oct. 25, 1971, the UN General Assembly ousted the Taiwan government from the UN and seated the People's Republic in its place. The U.S. had supported the mainland's admission but opposed Taiwan's expulsion.

U.S. Pres. Richard Nixon visited China Feb. 21-28, 1972, on invitation from Premier Zhou Enlai, ending years of antipathy between the 2 nations. China and the U.S. opened liaison offices in each other's capitals, May-June 1973. The U.S., Dec. 15, 1978, formally recognized the People's Republic of China as the sole legal government of China; diplomatic relations between the 2 nations were established, Jan. 1, 1979.

Mao died Sept. 9, 1976. By 1978, Vice Premier Deng Xiaoping had consolidated his power, succeeding Mao as "paramount leader" of China. The new ruling group modified Maoist policies in education, culture, and industry, and sought better ties with non-Communist countries. During this "reassessment" of Mao's policies his widow, Jiang Qing, and other "Gang of Four" leftists were convicted of "committing crimes during the 'Cultural Revolution,' " Jan. 25, 1981.

By the mid-1980s, China had enacted far-reaching economic reforms, deemphasizing centralized planning and incorporating market-oriented incentives. Some 100,000 students and workers staged a march in Beijing to demand political reforms, May 4, 1989. As the unrest spread, martial law was imposed, May 20. Troops entered Beijing, June 3-4, and crushed the pro-democracy protests, as tanks and armored personnel carriers rolled through Tiananmen Square. It is estimated that 5,000 died, 10,000 were injured, and hundreds of students and workers were arrested.

Deng Xiaoping died Feb. 19, 1997, leaving Jiang Zemin in control as president. By agreement with the UK, Hong Kong reverted to Chinese sovereignty July 1 (see below). NATO bombs hit the Chinese embassy in Belgrade, Yugoslavia, on May 7, 1999, killing 3 people and wounding 27, for which the U.S. paid compensation. The government banned a popular religious sect, the Falun Gong, July 22, after it staged the largest unauthorized demonstrations in Beijing since 1989. The U.S. and China signed a major trade agreement Nov. 15. Portugal returned Macao to China Dec. 20, 1999.

Beijing was chosen, July 13, 2001, to host the 2008 Summer Olympics. Admission to the WTrO Dec. 11 marked an economic milestone, though protested by many human rights and labor organizations. Hu Jintao was named Communist Party general secretary at the 16th party congress, Nov. 15, 2002, and elected president by the 10th National People's Congress, Mar. 15, 2003. A SARS epidemic beginning in late 2002 killed 349 people in mainland China by mid-2003.

In Aug. 2003, China assumed an unprecedented diplomatic role when it hosted multinational talks regarding N. Korea's nuclear weapons program. With the successful launch and recovery, Oct. 15-16, of the *Shenzhou 5* spacecraft, China became the 3rd nation (after the U.S. and U.S.S.R.) to send a man into space. Floods in summer 2004 killed more than 1,000 people and caused $8 billion in damage. Pres. Hu Jintao expanded his power when he became China's military chief Sept. 19 after Jiang Zemin's resignation.

China's industries, exports, and demand for oil have all increased rapidly since the 1980s. More than 1 million adults have HIV/AIDS, a growing problem in China.

See also the feature article Waking to China.

Manchuria. Home of the Manchus, rulers of China 1644-1911, Manchuria has accommodated millions of Chinese settlers in the 20th century. Under Japanese rule 1931-45, the area became industrialized. The region is divided into the 3 NE provinces of Heilongjiang, Jilin, and Liaoning.

Autonomous Regions

Guangxi Zhuang is in SE China, bounded on N by Guizhou and Hunan provinces, E and S by Guangdong, on SW by Vietnam, and on W by Yunnan. It produces rice in the river valleys and has valuable forest products. Pop. (2000): 44.89 mil

Inner Mongolia was organized by the People's Republic in 1947. Its boundaries have undergone frequent changes, reaching its greatest extent in 1956 (and restored in 1979), with an area of 454,600 sq. mi., allegedly in order to dilute the minority Mongol population. Chinese settlers outnumber the Mongols more than 10 to 1. Pop. (2000): 23.76 mil. Capital: Hohhot.

Ningxia Hui, in N central China, is about 60,000 sq. mi., pop. (2000): 5.62 mil. Capital: Yinchuan. Situated mainly of the semiarid Inner Mongolian plateau region with desert areas in the N. The Huang He (Yellow R.) flows across the N furnishes water for irrigation. Coal is mined in the E. Modern industry is relatively undeveloped and only one railroad crosses the region. The majority of the population is Han, and the Hui (Chinese Muslims) constitute about one-third of the population. The region experienced a significant population boom from 1950-80, which has now stabilized.

Xinjiang Uygur, in Central Asia, is 635,900 sq. mi., pop. (2000): 19.25 mil (75% Uygurs, a Turkic Muslim group, with a heavy Chinese increase in recent years). Capital: Urumqi. It is China's richest region in strategic minerals. China has moved to crack down on Uygur separatists, whom Beijing regards as terrorists.

Tibet, 471,700 sq. mi., is a thinly populated region of high plateaus and massive mountains, the Himalayas on the S, the Kunluns on the N. High passes connect with India and Nepal; roads lead into China proper. Capital: Lhasa. Average altitude is 15,000 ft. Jiachan, 15,870 ft., is believed to be the highest inhabited town on earth. Agriculture is primitive. Pop. (2000): 2.62 mil (of whom about 500,000 are Chinese). Another 4 million Tibetans form the majority of the population of vast adjacent areas that have long been incorporated into China.

China ruled all of Tibet from the 18th century. Independence came in 1911, but China reasserted control in 1951, and a Communist government was installed in 1953, revising the theocratic Lamaist Buddhist rule. Serfdom was abolished, but all land remained collectivized.

A Tibetan uprising within China in 1956 spread to Tibet in 1959. The rebellion was crushed with Chinese troops, and Buddhism was almost totally suppressed. The Dalai Lama and 100,000 Tibetans fled to India.

Hong Kong

Hong Kong (Xianggang), located at the mouth of the Zhu Jiang (Pearl R.) in SE China, 90 mi. S of Canton (Guangzhou), was a British dependency from 1842 until July 1, 1997, when it became a Special Administrative Region of China. Its nucleus is Hong Kong Isl., 31 sq. mi., occupied by the British in 1841 and formally ceded to them in 1842, on which is located the seat of government. Opposite is Kowloon Peninsula, 3 sq. mi., and Stonecutters Isl., added to the territory in 1860. An additional 355 sq. mi. known as the New Territories, a mainland area and islands, were leased from China, 1898, for 99 years. Area 422 sq. mi. (total); 402 sq. mi. (land); pop. (2004 est.) 6,855,125, including fewer than 20,000 British.

Hong Kong is a major center for trade and banking. Per capita GDP, $25,400 (2000 est.), is among the highest in the world. Principal industries are textiles and apparel; also tourism ($7.21 bil expenditures in 1999), electronics, shipbuilding, iron and steel, fishing, cement, and small manufactures. Hong Kong's spinning mills are among the best in the world.

Hong Kong harbor was long an important British naval station and one of the world's great transshipment ports. The colony was often a place of refuge for exiles from mainland China. It was occupied by Japan during World War II.

From 1949 to 1962 Hong Kong absorbed more than a million refugees fleeing Communist China. Starting in the 1950s, cheap labor led to a boom in light manufacturing, while liberal tax policies attracted foreign investment; Hong Kong became one of the wealthiest, most productive areas in the Far East. Poor living and working conditions and low wages for many led to political unrest in the 1960s, but legislation and public works programs raised the standard of living by the 1970s.

With the end of the 99-year lease on the New Territories drawing near, Britain and China signed an agreement, Dec. 19, 1984, under which all of Hong Kong was to be returned to China in 1997; under this agreement Hong Kong was to be allowed to keep its capitalist system for 50 years. In Dec. 1996, an electoral college appointed by China chose a shipping magnate, Tung Chee-hwa, to be Hong Kong's chief executive when it reverted to Chinese control.

Following the transfer of government on July 1, Hong Kong retained its street names and its currency, the Hong Kong dollar (HK$7.80 = $1 U.S.), but without the queen's picture. Official languages remained Chinese (Cantonese dialect) and English. Pro-democracy candidates did well in May 24, 1998, elections, despite having been excluded from the provisional gov't. in 1997. A SARS outbreak in 2003 claimed almost 300 lives and damaged the economy.

Hundreds of thousands of Hong Kong residents turned out July 1, 2003, to protest a proposed anti-subversion law; the bill was withdrawn Sept. 5. Another mass march, July 1, 2004, protested Beijing's refusal to allow greater freedom. Pro-democracy candidates won a majority of the popular vote in elections, Sept. 12, but failed to gain control of the Legislative Council. After Tung Chee-hwa resigned Mar. 10, 2005, Donald Tsang was chosen to serve the remaining 2 years of Tung's term as chief executive.

Macao

Macao, area of 10 sq. mi., is an enclave, a peninsula and 2 small islands, at the mouth of the Xi (Pearl) R. in China. It was established as a Portuguese trading colony in 1557. In 1849, Portugal claimed sovereignty over the territory; this claim was accepted by China in an 1887 treaty. Portugal granted broad autonomy in 1976. Under a 1987 agreement, Macao reverted to China Dec. 20, 1999. As in the case of Hong Kong, the Chinese government guaranteed Macao it would not interfere in its way of life and capitalist system for a period of 50 years. Pop. (2004 est.): 445,286.

Colombia

Republic of Colombia

People: Population: 42,954,279. **Age distrib.** (%) <15: 30.7; 65+: 5.1. **Pop. density:** 98 per sq mi, 38 per sq km. **Urban:** 76.5%. **Ethnic groups:** Mestizo 58%, European 20%, Creole 14%, Black 4%, Black-Amerindian 1%, Amerindian 3%. **Principal languages:** Spanish (official). **Chief religion:** Roman Catholic 90%.

Geography: Total area: 439,736 sq mi, 1,138,910 sq km; **Land area:** 401,044 sq mi, 1,038,700 sq km. **Location:** At the NW corner of South America. **Neighbors:** Panama on NW, Ecuador and Peru on S, Brazil and Venezuela on E. **Topography:** Three ranges of Andes—Western, Central, and Eastern Cordilleras—run through the country from N to S. The eastern range consists mostly of high tablelands, densely populated. The Magdalena R. rises in the Andes, flows N to Caribbean, through a rich alluvial plain. Sparsely settled plains in E are drained by Orinoco and Amazon systems. **Capital:** Bogotá (Full name: Santa Fe de Bogotá.), 7,290,000. **Cities (urban aggr.):** Medellin, 2,866,000; Cali, 2,233,000; Barranquilla, 1,683,000.

Government: Type: Republic. **Head of state and gov.:** Pres. Álvaro Uribe Vélez; b July 4, 1952; in office: Aug. 7, 2002. **Local divisions:** 32 departments, capital district of Bogota. **Defense budget** (2004): $2.8 bil. **Active troops:** 207,000.

Economy: Industries: textiles, food proc., oil, clothing & footwear, beverages, chemicals, cement, mining. **Chief crops:** coffee, cut flowers, bananas, rice, tobacco, corn, sugarcane, cocoa. **Natural resources:** oil, nat. gas, coal, iron ore, nickel, gold, copper, emeralds, hydropower. **Crude oil reserves** (2004): 1.5 bil. bbls. **Arable land:** 4%. **Livestock** (2004): cattle: 25.0 mil; chickens: 120 mil; goats: 1.2 mil; pigs: 2.3 mil; sheep: 2.2 mil. **Fish catch** (2003): 218,689 metric tons. **Electricity prod.** (2003): 47.1 bil. kWh. **Labor force** (1990): agriculture 30%, industry 24%, services 46%.

Finance: Monetary unit: Peso (COP) (Sept. 2005: 2,302.78 = $1 U.S.) **GDP** (2004 est.): $281.1 bil.; **per capita GDP:** $6,600; **GDP growth:** 3.6%. **Imports** (2004 est.): $15.3 bil.; partners (2004): US 30.6%, Venezuela 5.8%, Brazil 5.2%, Japan 5.2%, Germany 5.1%, Mexico 5%, China 4.2%. **Exports** (2004 est.): $15.5 bil.; partners (2004): US 40.9%, Ecuador 5.8%, Venezuela 4.8%. **Tourism:** $816 mil. **Budget** (2004 est.): $21.0 bil. **Intl. reserves less gold:** $8.62 bil. **Gold:** 330,000 oz t. **Consumer prices:** 5.9%.

Transport: Railroad: Length: 2,053 mi. **Motor vehicles** 812,100 pass. cars, 402,900 comm. vehicles. **Civil aviation:** 5.4 bil pass.-mi; 96 airports. **Chief ports:** Buenaventura, Barranquilla, Cartagena.

Communications: TV sets: 279 per 1,000 pop. **Radios:** 539 per 1,000 pop. **Telephone lines:** 7.8 mil. **Daily newspaper circ.:** 46 per 1,000 pop. **Internet**: 2.3 mil. users.

Health: Life expect.: 67.9 male; 75.7 female. **Births** (per 1,000 pop.): 20.8. **Deaths** (per 1,000 pop.): 5.6. **Natural inc.:** 1.52%. **Infant mortality** (per 1,000 live births): 21.0. **AIDS rate:** 0.7%.

Education: Compulsory: ages 5-14. **Literacy:** 92.5%.

Major Intl. Organizations: UN (FAO, IBRD, ILO, IMF, IMO, WHO, WTrO), OAS.

Embassy: 2118 Leroy Pl. NW 20008; 387-8338.

Website: www.colombiaemb.org

Spain subdued the local Indian kingdoms (Funza, Tunja) by the 1530s and ruled Colombia and neighboring areas as New Granada for 300 years. Independence was won by 1819. Venezuela and Ecuador broke away in 1829-30, and Panama withdrew in 1903.

Colombia is plagued by rural and urban violence. "La Violencia" of 1948-58 claimed 200,000 lives; since 1989, political violence has killed an average of 3,500 people a year, most of them civilians. Attempts at land and social reform and progress in industrialization have not reduced massive social problems.

The government's increased activity against local drug traffickers sparked a series of retaliation killings. On Aug. 18, 1989, Luis Carlos Galán, the ruling party's presidential hopeful for the 1990 election, was assassinated. In 1990, 2 other presidential candidates were assassinated, as drug traffickers carried on a campaign of intimidation.

Right-wing paramilitaries launched a campaign Dec. 22, 2000, against suspected left-wing guerrillas. Legislation expanding the powers of the military was signed Aug. 13, 2001. The collapse of talks with the rebels in Feb. 2002 brought an upsurge of fighting. A hardliner, Álvaro Uribe Vélez, whose father had been killed by leftist rebels in 1983, won a presidential election May 26. A wave of guerrilla violence as he took office led Uribe to declare a "state of unrest" Aug. 12. Police powers were increased Sept. 10 as part of a new government offensive. The constitution was amended, Nov. 30, 2004, to allow the president to seek a 2nd consecutive term.

Colombia produces an estimated 90% of the cocaine reaching the U.S. Since 2000, the U.S. has provided more than $3.3 billion to Colombia, much of it to combat narco-terrorism.

Comoros

Union of Comoros

People: Population: 671,247. **Age distrib.** (%) <15: 42.8; 65+: 3.0. **Pop. density:** 801 per sq mi, 309 per sq km. **Urban:** 35.0%. **Ethnic groups:** Antalote, Cafre, Makoa, Oimatsaha, Sakalava (all are mostly an African-Arab mix). **Principal languages:** Arabic, French (both official), Shikomoro (a blend of Swahili and Arabic). **Chief religion:** Muslim 98% (official).

Geography: Total area: 838 sq mi, 2,170 sq km; **Land area:** 838 sq mi, 2,170 sq km. **Location:** 3 islands—Grande Comore (Njazidja), Anjouan (Nzwani), and Moheli (Mwali)—in the Mozambique Channel between NW Madagascar and SE Africa. **Neighbors:** Nearest are Mozambique on W, Madagascar on E. **Topography:** The islands are of volcanic origin, with an active volcano on Grande Comore. **Capital:** Moroni, 53,000.

Government: Type: In transition. **Head of state and gov.:** Pres. Azali Assoumani; b Jan. 1,1959; in office: May 26, 2002. **Local divisions:** 3 main islands with 4 municipalities.

Economy: Industries: tourism, perfume distillation. **Chief crops:** vanilla, cloves, perfume essences, copra, coconuts, bananas, cassava. **Arable land:** 35%. **Livestock** (2004): cattle: 45,000; chickens: 510; goats: 115,000; sheep: 21,000. **Fish catch** (2003): 14,115 metric tons. **Electricity prod.** (2003): 0.02 bil. kWh. **Labor force**: agriculture 80%.

Finance: Monetary unit: Franc (KMF) (Sept. 2004: 404.79 = $1 U.S.). **GDP** (2002 est.): $441.0 mil; **per capita GDP:** $700; **GDP growth:** 2%. **Imports** (2002 est.): $88.0 mil; partners (2004): France 24.4%, South Africa 11.5%, UAE 7.3%, Kenya 6.1%, Italy 5.1%, Mauritius 4.8%, Singapore 4.2%. **Exports** (2002 est.): $28.0 mil; partners (2004): US 42.2%, France 18%, Singapore 16%, Turkey 4.7%. **Tourism** (1995): $21 mil. **Budget** (2001 est.): $0.0 **Intl. reserves less gold:** $67 mil.

Transport: Civil aviation: 97,555 pass.-mi; 4 airports. **Chief ports:** Fomboni, Moroni, Moutsamoudou.

Communications: TV sets: 4 per 1,000 pop. **Radios:** 141 per 1,000 pop. **Telephone lines:** 13,200. **Internet**: 5,000 users.

Health: Life expect.: 59.7 male; 64.3 female. **Births** (per 1,000 pop.): 37.5. **Deaths** (per 1,000 pop.): 8.4. **Natural inc.:** 2.91%. **Infant mortality** (per 1,000 live births): 74.9.

Education: Compulsory: ages 6-13. **Literacy:** 56.5%.

Major Intl. Organizations: UN (FAO, IBRD, ILO, IMF, WHO), AL, AU.

Embassy: 336 E. 45th St., 2d floor, New York, NY 10017 212-750-1637.

Website: www.state.gov/p/af/ci/cn

The islands were controlled by Muslim sultans until the French acquired them 1841-1909. They became a French overseas territory in 1947. A 1974 referendum favored independence, with only the Christian island of Mayotte preferring association with France. The French National Assembly decided to allow each of the islands to decide its own fate. The Comore Chamber of Deputies declared independence July 6, 1975, with Ahmed Abdallah as president. In a referendum in 1976, Mayotte voted to remain French.

A leftist regime that seized power from Abdallah in 1975 was deposed in a pro-French 1978 coup in which he regained the presidency. In Nov. 1989, Pres. Abdallah was assassinated; soon after, a multiparty system was instituted. A Sept. 1995 military coup, assisted by French mercenaries, ousted Pres. Said Mohamed Djohar. French troops invaded, Oct. 4, and forced coup leaders to surrender. Djohar returned from exile in Jan. 1996, and in Mar. a new presidential election was held. A hijacked Ethiopian Airlines Boeing 767 crashed offshore on Nov. 23, killing 123 of the 175 people on board.

Attempts to work out a new constitutional relationship between Grande Comore, Anjouan, and Moheli have been ongoing since Anjouan and Moheli seceded from the Comoros in 1997. Unrest on Grande Comore culminated in a military coup, Apr. 30, 1999. Anjouans endorsed secession in a disputed vote Jan. 23, 2000. Irregularities marred the presidential runoff election of Apr. 14, 2002, won by Azali Assoumani, who led the 1999 coup; each of the 3 islands also elected its own president in 2002. Elections for national and island assemblies took place Mar.-Apr. 2004.

Congo (formerly Zaire)

Democratic Republic of the Congo

(Congo, officially Democratic Republic of the Congo, is also known as Congo-Kinshasa. It should not be confused with Republic of the Congo, commonly called Congo Republic, and also known as Congo-Brazzaville.)

People: Population: 60,764,490. **Age distrib.** (%) <15: 48.1, 65+: 2.5. **Pop. density:** 4 per sq mi, 2 per sq km. **Urban:** 53.5%. **Ethnic groups:** Over 200 groups. Four largest, the Mongo, Luba, Kongo (all Bantu), and Mangbetu-Azande (Hamitic), make up 45% of pop. **Principal languages:** French (official), Lingala, Kingswana (a swahili dialect), Tshiluba. **Chief religions:** Roman Catholic 50%, Protestant 20%, Kimbanguist 10%, Muslim 10%.

Geography: Total area: 905,568 sq mi, 2,345,410 sq km; **Land area:** 875,525 sq mi, 2,267,600 sq km. **Location:** In central Africa. **Neighbors:** Congo-Brazzaville on W; Central African Republic, Sudan on N; Uganda, Rwanda, Burundi, Tanzania on E; Zambia, Angola on S. **Topography:** Congo includes the bulk of the Congo R. basin. The vast central region is a low-lying plateau covered by rain forest. Mountainous terraces in the W, savannas in the S and SE, grasslands toward the N, and the high Ruwenzori Mts. on the E surround the central region. A short strip of territory borders the Atlantic O. **Capital:** Kinshasa, 5,277,000. **Cities (urban aggr.):** Lubumbashi, 906,000.

Government: Type: In transition. **Head of state and gov.:** Pres. Joseph Kabila; b June 24, 1971; in office: Jan. 26, 2001. **Local divisions:** 10 provinces, 1 city. **Defense budget** (2002): $400 mil. **Active troops:** 64,800.

Economy: Industries: mining, mineral proc., textiles, footwear, cigarettes, proc. foods & beverages, cement. **Chief crops:** coffee, sugar, rubber, tea, quinine, cassava, bananas, root crops, corn, fruits, wood products. **Natural resources:** cobalt, copper, cadmium, oil, diamonds, gold, silver, zinc, mang., tin, germanium, uranium, radium, bauxite, iron ore, coal, hydropower, timber. **Crude oil reserves** (2004): 187 mil bbls. **Arable land:** 3%. **Livestock** (2004): cattle: 765,000; chickens: 19.6 mil; goats: 4.0 mil; pigs: 953,000; sheep: 897,000. **Fish catch** (2003): 222,965 metric tons. **Electricity prod.** (2003): 6.0 bil. kWh.

Finance: Monetary unit: franc (CDF) (Sept. 2005: 477.00 = $1 U.S.). **GDP** (2004 est.): $42.7 bil.; **per capita GDP:** $700; **GDP growth:** 3.7%. **Imports** (2002 est.): $933.0 mil; partners (2004): South Africa 18.5%, Belgium 15.6%, France 10.9%, US 6.2%, Germany 5.9%, Kenya 4.9%. **Exports** (2002 est.): $1.4 bil.; partners (2004): Belgium 42.5%, Finland 17.8%, Zimbabwe 12.2%, US 9.2%, China 6.5%. **Tourism** (1990): $7 mil. **Budget** (1996 est.): $244.0 mil. **Consumer prices** (change 2001–02): 32%.

Transport: Railroad: Length: 2,965 mi. **Motor vehicles:** 172,600 pass. cars, 34,600 comm. vehicles; 24 airports. **Chief ports:** Matadi, Boma, Kinshasa.

Communications: TV sets: 2 per 1,000 pop. **Radios:** 376 per 1,000 pop. **Telephone lines** (2002): 10,000. **Daily newspaper circ.:** 2.7 per 1,000 pop. **Internet** (2002): 50,000 users.

Health: Life expect.: 49.7 male; 52.6 female. **Births** (per 1,000 pop.): 44.1. **Deaths** (per 1,000 pop.): 13.5. **Natural inc.:** 3.05%. **Infant mortality** (per 1,000 live births): 90.7. **AIDS rate:** 4.2%.

Education: Compulsory: ages 6-13. **Literacy:** 65.5%.

Major Intl. Organizations: UN and most of its specialized agencies, AU.

Embassy: 1800 New Hampshire Ave. NW 20009; 234-7690.

Website: www.un.int/drcongo

The earliest inhabitants of Congo may have been the pygmies, followed by Bantus from the E and Nilotic tribes from the N. The large Bantu Bakongo kingdom ruled much of Congo and Angola when Portuguese explorers visited in the 15th century.

Leopold II, king of the Belgians, formed an international group to exploit the Congo region in 1876. In 1877 Henry M. Stanley explored the Congo, and in 1878 the king's group sent him back to organize the region and win over the native chiefs. The Conference of Berlin, 1884-85, organized the Congo Free State with Leopold as king and chief owner. Exploitation of native laborers on the rubber plantations caused international criticism and led to granting of a colonial charter, 1908; the colony became known as the Belgian Congo. Millions of Congolese are believed to have died between 1880 and 1920 as a result of slave labor and other causes under European rule.

Belgian and Congolese leaders agreed Jan. 27, 1960, the Congo would become independent in June. In the first general elections, May 31, the National Congolese movement of Patrice Lumumba won a plurality in the National Assembly. He was appointed premier June 21, and formed a coalition cabinet. The Republic of the Congo was proclaimed June 30.

Widespread violence caused Europeans and others to flee. The UN Security Council, Aug. 9, 1960, called on Belgium to withdraw its troops and sent a UN contingent. Pres. Joseph Kasavubu removed Lumumba as premier in Sept.; Lumumba was murdered Jan. 17, 1961. The last UN troops left the Congo June 30, 1964, and Moise Tshombe became president.

On Sept. 7, 1964, leftist rebels set up a "People's Republic" in Stanleyville (now Kisangani). Tshombe hired foreign mercenaries and sought to rebuild the Congolese Army. In Nov. and Dec. 1964 rebels killed scores of white hostages and thousands of Congolese; Belgian paratroopers, dropped from U.S. transport planes, rescued hundreds. By July 1965 the rebels had lost their effectiveness.

In late 1965 Gen. Joseph D. Mobutu was named president. He later changed his name to Mobutu Sese Seko and ruled as a dictator. The country became the Democratic Republic of the Congo (1966) and the Republic of Zaire (1971).

Economic decline and government corruption plagued Zaire in the 1980s and worsened in the 1990s. In 1990, Pres. Mobutu announced an end to a 20-year ban on multiparty politics. He sought to retain power despite mounting international pressure and internal opposition.

During 1994, Zaire was inundated with refugees from the massive ethnic bloodshed in Rwanda. Ethnic violence spread to E Zaire in 1996. In Oct. militant Hutus, who dominated in the refugee camps, fought against rebels (mostly Tutsis) in Zaire, precipitating intervention by government troops. As a result of the fighting, Rwandan refugees abandoned the camps; hundreds of thousands returned to Rwanda, while hundreds of thousands more were dispersed throughout E Zaire. The rebels, led by Gen. Laurent Kabila—a former Marxist and longtime opponent of Mobutu—gained momentum and began to move W across Zaire. As turmoil engulfed his nation, Mobutu stayed in W Europe during the latter part of 1996.

With Mobutu out of the country, the Zairean army put up little resistance; rebels were aided by several of Mobutu's enemies, notably Rwanda and Uganda. Mobutu returned to Zaire in March 1997, but attempts to negotiate with Kabila were ineffectual. On May 17, Kabila's troops entered Kinshasa and Mobutu went into exile. The country again assumed the name Democratic Republic of the Congo. Mobutu died Sept. 7 in Rabat, Morocco.

Kabila, who ruled by decree, alienated UN officials, international aid donors, and former allies. Rebels assisted by Rwanda and Uganda threatened Kinshasa in Aug. 1998, but the assault was turned back with help from Angola, Namibia, and Zimbabwe. Rebel groups agreed to a cease-fire on Aug. 31, 1999, but the truce was widely violated. Kabila was assassinated Jan. 16, 2001, apparently by one of his bodyguards, and was succeeded by his son Joseph.

The overall death toll from the civil war and related causes was estimated at 3.3 million through Nov. 2002. By then the war had apparently begun to wind down, with agreements by Rwanda and Uganda to pull out their remaining troops. A power-sharing accord signed Apr. 2, 2003, led to the installation of a new Congolese government in July. An apparent coup attempt by presidential guard members was crushed June 11, 2004. A new constitution won legislative approval May 13, 2005. A UN peacekeeping force (MONUC), established in 1999, had more than 16,000 troops in the Congo as of mid-2005.

Congo Republic

Republic of the Congo

(Congo Republic, officially Republic of the Congo, is also known as Congo-Brazzaville. It should not be confused with Democratic Republic of the Congo [formerly Zaire], now commonly called Congo, and also known as Congo-Kinshasa.)

People: Population: 3,602,269. **Age distrib.** (%) <15: 37.3; 65+: 3.7. **Pop. density:** 460 per sq mi, 178 per sq km. **Urban:** 31.6%. **Ethnic groups:** Kongo 48%, Sangha 20%, M'Bochi 12%, Teke 17%. **Principal languages:** French (official), Lingala, Monokutuba, Kikongo, many local languages and dialects. **Chief religions:** Christian 50%, animist 48%, Muslim 2%.

Geography: Total area: 132,047 sq mi, 342,000 sq km; **Land area:** 131,854 sq mi, 341,500 sq km. **Location:** In W central Africa. **Neighbors:** Gabon and Cameroon on W, Central African Republic on N, Congo-Kinshasa (formerly Zaire) on E, Angola on SW. **Topography:** Much of the Congo is covered by thick forests. A coastal plain leads to the fertile Niari Valley. The center is a plateau; the Congo R. basin consists of flood plains in the lower and savanna in the upper portion. **Capital:** Brazzaville, 1,080,000.

Government: Type: Republic. **Head of state and gov.:** Pres. Denis Sassou-Nguesso; b 1943; in office: Oct. 25, 1997. **Local divisions:** 10 regions, 6 communes. **Defense budget** (2004): $131 mil. **Active troops:** 10,000.

Economy: Industries: oil, cement, lumber, brewing, sugar, palm oil. **Chief crops:** cassava, sugar, rice, corn, peanuts, vegetables, coffee, cocoa. **Natural resources:** oil, timber, potash, lead, zinc, uranium, copper, phosphates, nat. gas, hydropower. **Crude oil reserves** (2004): 1.5 bil bbls. **Livestock:** (2004): cattle: 100,000; chickens: 2.2 mil; goats: 294,200; pigs: 46,300; sheep: 98,000. **Fish catch** (2003): 52,400 metric tons. **Electricity prod.** (2003): 6.0 bil kWh.

Finance: Monetary unit: CFA Franc BEAC (XAF) (Sept. 2005: 525.18 = $1 U.S.). **GDP** (2004 est.): $42.7 bil.; **per capita GDP:** $800; **GDP growth:** 7.5%. **Imports** (2004 est.): $749.3 mil; partners (2004): France 20.2%, China 6.6%, Italy 6.5%, India 4.8%, Belgium 4.7%, US 4.6%. **Exports** (2004 est.): $2.2 bil.; partners (2004): China 30.8%, US 18.2%, Taiwan 16.8%, South Korea 11.2%, Trinidad and Tobago 5.6%. **Tourism:** $20 mil. **Budget** (2004 est.): $1.1 bil. **Intl. reserves less gold: Gold:** 10,000 oz t. **Consumer prices**: –0.85%.

Transport: Railroad: Length: 556 mi. **Motor vehicles:** 29,700 pass. cars, 23,100 comm. vehicles. **Civil aviation:** 97,555 pass.-mi; 4 airports. **Chief ports:** Pointe-Noire, Brazzaville.

Communications: TV sets: 13 per 1,000 pop. **Radios:** 126 per 1,000 pop. **Telephone lines**: 7,000. **Daily newspaper circ.:** 8 per 1,000 pop. **Internet:** 15,000 users.

Health: Life expect.: 51.2 male; 53.4 female. **Births** (per 1,000 pop.): 43.0. **Deaths** (per 1,000 pop.): 13.3. **Natural inc.:** 2.97%. **Infant mortality** (per 1,000 live births): 87.4. **AIDS rate:** 4.9%.

Education: Compulsory: ages 6-15. **Literacy:** 83.8%.

Major Intl. Organizations: UN (FAO, IBRD, ILO, IMF, IMO, WHO), AU.

Embassy: 4891 Colorado Ave. NW 20011; 726-5500.

Website: www.state.gov/p/af/ci/cf

The Loango Kingdom flourished in the 15th century, as did the Anzico Kingdom of the Batekes; by the late 17th century they had become weakened. By 1885, France established control of the region, then called the Middle Congo. Republic of the Congo gained independence Aug. 15, 1960.

After a 1963 coup sparked by trade unions, the country adopted a Marxist-Leninist stance, with the USSR and China vying for influence. France remained a dominant trade partner and source of technical assistance, however, and French-owned private enterprise retained a major economic role. In 1970, the country was renamed People's Republic of the Congo.

In 1990, Marxism was renounced and opposition parties were legalized. In 1991 the country's name was changed back to Republic of the Congo, and a new constitution was approved. A democratically elected government came into office in 1992. Factional fighting broke out in Brazzaville, June 5, 1997, and intensified during the summer, devastating the capital. Troops loyal to former Marxist dictator Denis Sassou-Nguesso took control of the city Oct. 15. He claimed a lopsided victory in the presidential election of Mar. 10, 2002. The government and "Ninja" rebels in the Pool Region agreed to a cease-fire Mar. 17, 2003.

Costa Rica

Republic of Costa Rica

People: Population: 4,016,173. **Age distrib.** (%) <15: 28.9; 65+: 5.6. **Pop. density:** 204 per sq mi, 79 per sq km. **Urban:** 60.6%. **Ethnic groups:** European and Mestizo 94%, black 3%, Amerindian 1%, Chinese 1%. **Principal languages:** Spanish (official), English spoken around Puerto Limon. **Chief religions:** Roman Catholic 76% (official), Protestant 14%.

Geography: Total area: 19,730 sq mi, 51,100 sq km; **Land area:** 19,560 sq mi, 50,660 sq km. **Location:** In Central America. **Neighbors:** Nicaragua on N, Panama on S. **Topography:** Lowlands by the Caribbean are tropical. The interior plateau, with an altitude of about 4,000 ft., is temperate. **Capital:** San José, 1,085,000.

Government: Type: Republic. **Head of state and gov.:** Pres. Abel Pacheco; b Dec. 22, 1933; in office: May 8, 2002. **Local divisions:** 7 provinces. **Defense budget (2003):** $100 mil. **Active troops:** N/A.

Economy: Industries: microprocessors, food proc., textiles and clothing, constr. materials, fertilizer, plastics. **Chief crops:** coffee, pineapples, bananas, sugar, corn, rice, beans, potatoes, timber. **Natural resources:** hydropower. **Arable land:** 6%. **Livestock** (2004): cattle: 1.1 mil; chickens: 19.5 mil; goats: 4,700; pigs: 550,000; sheep: 2,700. **Fish catch** (2003): 49,873 metric tons. **Electricity prod.** (2003): 7.7 bil. kWh. **Labor force** (1999 est.): agriculture 20%, industry 22%, services 58%.

Finance: Monetary unit: Colon (CRC) (Sept. 2005: 483.79 = $1 U.S.). **GDP** (2004 est.): $38.0 bil.; **per capita GDP:** $9,600; **GDP growth:** 3.9%. **Imports** (2004 est.): $7.8 bil.; partners (2004): US 35.5%, Japan 4.8%, Mexico 3.7%. **Exports** (2004 est.): $6.2 bil.; partners (2004): US 23.7%, Netherlands 7.7%, UK 6.6%. **Tourism:** $1,293 mil. **Budget** (2004 est.): $3.1 bil. **Intl. reserves less gold:** $1.24 bil. **Consumer prices:** 12.32%.

Transport: Railroad: Length: 590 mi. **Motor vehicles:** 367,800 pass. cars, 191,300 comm. vehicles. **Civil aviation:** 1.3 bil pass.-mi. **Chief ports:** Limon, Puntarenas, Golfito.

Communications: TV sets: 229 per 1,000 pop. **Radios:** 774 per 1,000 pop. **Telephone lines**: 1.2 mil. **Daily newspaper circ.:** 94 per 1,000 pop. **Internet:** 1.2 mil. users.

Health: Life expect.: 74.3 male; 79.6 female. **Births** (per 1,000 pop.): 18.6. **Deaths** (per 1,000 pop.): 4.3. **Natural inc.:** 1.43%. **Infant mortality** (per 1,000 live births): 10.0. **AIDS rate:** 0.6%.

Education: Compulsory: ages 6-15. **Literacy:** 96%.

Major Intl. Organizations: UN (FAO, IBRD, ILO, IMF, IMO, WHO, WTrO), OAS.

Embassy: 2114 S St. NW 20008; 234-2945.

Website: www.costarica-embassy.org

Guaymi Indians inhabited the area when Spaniards arrived, 1502. Independence came in 1821. Costa Rica seceded from the Central American Federation in 1838. Since the civil war of 1948-49, there has been little violent social conflict, and free political institutions have been preserved. During 1993 there was an unusual wave of kidnappings and hostage-taking, some of it related to the international cocaine trade.

Costa Rica, though still a largely agricultural country, has achieved a relatively high standard of living, and land ownership is widespread. Tourism is growing rapidly.

Côte d'Ivoire

Republic of Côte d'Ivoire

People: Population: 17,298,040. **Age distrib.** (%) <15: 41.0; 65+: 2.7. **Pop. density:** 139 per sq mi, 54 per sq km. **Urban:** 44.9%. **Ethnic groups:** Akan 42%, Voltaiques (Gur) 18%, N Mandes 17%, Krous 11%, S Mandes 10%. **Principal languages:** French (official), Dioula, many native dialects. **Chief religions:** Muslim 35-40%, Christian 20-30%, indigenous beliefs 25-40%.

Geography: Total area: 124,503 sq mi, 322,460 sq km; **Land area:** 122,780 sq mi, 318,000 sq km. **Location:** On S coast of W Africa. **Neighbors:** Liberia, Guinea on W; Mali, Burkina Faso on N; Ghana on E. **Topography:** Forests cover the W half of the country, and range from a coastal strip to halfway to the N on the E. A sparse inland plain leads to low mountains in NW. **Capital:** Yamoussoukro (official), 416,000; Abidjan (de facto), 3,337,000.

Government: Type: In transition. **Head of state:** Pres. Laurent Gbagbo; b May 31, 1945; in office: Oct. 26, 2000. **Head of gov.:** Prime Min. Seydou Diarra; b Nov. 23, 1933; in office: Feb. 10, 2003. **Local divisions:** 58 departments. **Defense budget** (2004): $150 mil. **Active troops:** 17,050.

Economy: Industries: foodstuffs, beverages, wood products, oil refining, truck & bus assembly, textiles, fertilizer, building materials, electricity. **Chief crops:** coffee, cocoa beans, bananas, palm kernels. **Natural resources:** oil, nat. gas, diamonds, mang., iron ore, cobalt, bauxite, copper, hydropower. **Crude oil reserves** (2004): 100 mil bbls. **Arable land:** 8%. **Livestock** (2004): cattle: 1.5 mil; chickens: 33 mil; goats: 1.2 mil; pigs: 342,720; sheep: 1.5 mil. **Fish catch** (2003): 69,769 metric tons. **Electricity prod.** (2003): 5.1 bil. kWh. **Labor force:** 51% agric.; 12% manuf. & mining.

Finance: Monetary unit: CFA Franc BCEAO (XAF) (Sept. 2005: 525.18 = $1 U.S.). **GDP** (2004 est.): $24.8 bil.; **per capita GDP:** $1,500; **GDP growth:** –1%. **Imports** (2004 est.): $3.4 bil.; partners (2004): France 24.7%, Nigeria 18.5%, Italy 4%. **Exports** (2004 est.): $5.1 bil.; partners (2004): US 11.3%, Netherlands 10.1%, France 9.4%, Italy 5.3%, Belgium 4.7%, Germany 4.3%. **Tourism:** $84 mil. **Budget** (2004 est.): $2.8 bil. **Consumer prices** (2003): 1.44%.

Transport: Railroad: Length: 410 mi. **Motor vehicles:** 113,900 pass. cars, 54,900 comm. vehicles. **Civil aviation:** 80,778 pass.-mi; 7 airports. **Chief ports:** Abidjan, Dabou, San-Pédro.

Communications: TV sets: 65 per 1,000 pop. **Radios:** 161 per 1,000 pop. **Telephone lines:** 238,000. **Daily newspaper circ.:** 17 per 1,000 pop. **Internet:** 240,000 users.

Health: Life expect.: 46.1 male; 51.3 female. **Births** (per 1,000 pop.): 35.5. **Deaths** (per 1,000 pop.): 14.9. **Natural inc.:** 2.06%. **Infant mortality** (per 1,000 live births): 90.8. **AIDS rate:** 7.0%.

Education: Compulsory: ages 6-15. **Literacy:** 50.9%.

Major Intl. Organizations: UN and all of its specialized agencies, AU.

Embassy: 2424 Massachusetts Ave. NW 20008; 797-0300.

Website: usembassy.state.gov/abidjan/

A French protectorate from 1842, Côte d'Ivoire became independent in 1960. It is the most prosperous of all the tropical African nations, as a result of diversification of agriculture for export, close ties to France, and encouragement of foreign investment. About 20% of the population are workers from neighboring countries. Côte d'Ivoire officially changed its name from Ivory Coast in Oct. 1985.

Students and workers protested, Feb. 1990, demanding the ouster of longtime Pres. Félix Houphouët-Boigny. Côte d'Ivoire held its first multiparty presidential election Oct. 1990, and Houphouët-Boigny retained his office. He died Dec. 7, 1993. The National Assembly named a successor, Henri Konan Bédié, who was reelected Oct. 22, 1995; he was ousted in a military coup Dec. 24, 1999. The coup leader, Robert Guéi, apparently lost a presidential vote Oct. 22, 2000, but claimed victory anyway. After mass protests, he fled, and Laurent Gbagbo became president.

Guéi was killed in Abidjan Sept. 19, 2002, after a mutiny broke out there and in Bouaké and Korhogo. French troops Sept. 25 rescued 160 students (100 from the U.S.) trapped in Bouaké. Fueled by the conflict in neighboring Liberia, fighting in Côte d'Ivoire continued for months, despite the presence of French troops.

Agreement on power sharing was reached in Mar. 2003, and Gbagbo and former rebel leaders held a ceremony July 5, declaring that the war was over. The country remained divided, however, with rebels holding the north and government forces controlling the south. In Feb. 2004, the UN approved a peacekeeping force (UNOCI); by mid-2005, the country had about 7,000 UNOCI and more than 4,000 French peacekeepers. In Nov. 2004 the government troops raided rebel positions, and 9 French troops were killed in an alleged attack. The French responded with attacks on the Ivorian air force and anti-French riots ensued.

Croatia

Republic of Croatia

People: Population: 4,495,904. **Age distrib.** (%) <15: 16.4; 65+: 16.6. **Pop. density:** 206 per sq mi, 80 per sq km. **Urban:** 59.0%. **Ethnic groups:** Croat 78%, Serb 12%, Bosniak 1%. **Principal languages:** Croatian (official), Serbian. **Chief religions:** Roman Catholic 88%, Orthodox 5%.

Geography: Total area: 21,831 sq mi, 56,542 sq km; **Land area:** 21,782 sq mi, 56,414 sq km. **Location:** SE Europe, on the Balkan Peninsula. **Neighbors:** Slovenia, Hungary on N; Bosnia and Herzegovina, Yugoslavia on E. **Topography:** Flat plains in NE; highlands, low mtns. along Adriatic coast. **Capital:** Zagreb, 688,000.

Government: Type: Parliamentary democracy. **Head of state:** Pres. Stipe Mesic; b Dec. 24, 1934; in office: Feb. 18, 2000. **Head of gov.:** Prime Min. Ivo Sanader; b June 8, 1953; in office: Dec. 23, 2003. **Local divisions:** 20 counties and Zagreb. **Defense budget** (2004): $599 mil. **Active troops:** 20,800.

Economy: Industries: chemicals, plastics, machine tools, fabricated metal, electronics. **Chief crops:** wheat, corn, sugar beets, sunflower seeds, barley. **Natural resources:** oil, coal, bauxite, iron ore, calcium, natural asphalt, silica, mica, clays, salt, hydropower. **Crude oil reserves** (2004): 75.3 mil bbls. **Arable land:** 21%. **Livestock** (2004): cattle: 466,000; chickens: 10.2 mil; goats: 93,000; pigs: 1.5 mil; sheep: 721,000. **Fish catch** (2003): 27,551 metric tons. **Electricity prod.** (2003): 11.2 bil. kWh. **Labor force** (2004): agriculture 2.7%, industry 32.8%, services 64.5%.

Finance: Monetary unit: Kuna (HRK) (Sept. 2005: 5.94 = $1 U.S.). **GDP** (2004 est.): $50.3 bil.; **per capita GDP:** $11,200; **GDP growth:** 3.7%. **Imports** (2004 est.): $16.7 bil.; partners (2004): Italy 17.3%, Germany 15.7%, Slovenia 7.1%, Austria 7.1%, Russia 7%, France 4.3%. **Exports** (2004 est.): $7.8 bil.; partners (2004): Italy 23.1%, Bosnia and Herzegovina 14.7%, Germany 11.5%, Austria 9.6%, Slovenia 7.7%. **Tourism:** $6,376 mil. **Budget** (2004 est.): $15.7 bil. **Intl. reserves less gold:** $5.64 bil. **Consumer prices:** 3.72%.

Transport: Railroad: Length: 1,427 mi. **Motor vehicles:** 1.2443 mil pass. cars, 143,500 comm. vehicles. **Civil aviation:** 457,329 pass.-mi. **Chief ports:** Rijeka, Split, Dubrovnik.

Communications: TV sets: 286 per 1,000 pop. **Radios:** 337 per 1,000 pop. **Telephone lines** (2002): 1.8 mil. **Daily newspaper circ.:** 115 per 1,000 pop. **Internet** : 1.0 mil. users.

Health: Life expect.: 70.8 male; 78.3 female. **Births** (per 1,000 pop.): 9.6. **Deaths** (per 1,000 pop.): 11.4. **Natural inc.:** –0.18%. **Infant mortality** (per 1,000 live births): 6.8. **AIDS rate:** <0.1%.

Education: Compulsory: ages 7-15. **Literacy:** 98.5%.

Major Intl. Organizations: UN (FAO, IBRD, ILO, IMF, IMO, WHO), OSCE.

Embassy: 2343 Massachusetts Ave. NW 20008; 588-5899.

Website: www.vlada.hr/default.asp?ru=2

From the 7th century the area was inhabited by Croats, a south Slavic people. It was formed into a kingdom under Tomislav in 924, and joined with Hungary in 1102. The Croats became westernized and separated from Slavs under Austro-Hungarian influence. The Croats retained autonomy under the Hungarian crown. Slavonia was taken by Turks in the 16th century; the northern part was restored by the Treaty of Karlowitz in 1699. Croatia helped Austria put down the Hungarian revolution 1848-49 and as a result was set up with Slavonia as the separate Austrian crownland of Croatia and Slavonia, which was reunited to Hungary as part of Ausgleich in 1867. It united with other Yugoslav areas to proclaim the Kingdom of Serbs, Croats, and Slovenes in 1918. At the reorganization of Yugoslavia in 1929, Croatia and Slavonia became Savska county, which in 1939 was united with Primorje county to form the county of Croatia. A nominally independent state between 1941 and 1945, it became a constituent republic in the 1946 constitution.

On June 25, 1991, Croatia declared independence from Yugoslavia. Fighting began between ethnic Serbs and Croats, with the former gaining control of about 30% of Croatian territory. A cease-fire was declared in Jan. 1992, but new hostilities broke out in 1993. A cease-fire with Serb rebels forming a self-declared republic of Krajina was agreed to Mar. 30, 1994. Croatian government troops recaptured most of the Serb-held territory Aug. 1995. Pres. Franjo Tudjman signed a peace accord with leaders of Bosnia and Serbia in Paris, Dec. 14. Tudjman won reelection June 15, 1997; international monitors called the vote "free but not fair." The last Serb-held enclave, E Slavonia, returned to Croatian control Jan. 15, 1998.

Tudjman died Dec. 10, 1999. Stipe Mesic, a moderate, won a presidential runoff election Feb. 7, 2000, and was reelected Jan. 16, 2005. EU membership talks, scheduled to start Mar. 17, 2005, were postponed because of Croatia's failure to hand over a suspected war criminal, Gen. Ante Gotovina.

Cuba

Republic of Cuba

People: Population: 11,346,670. **Age distrib.** (%) <15: 19.6; 65+: 10.4. **Pop. density:** 265 per sq mi, 102 per sq km. **Urban:** 75.6%. **Ethnic groups:** Creole 51%, White 37%, Black 11%, Chinese 1%. **Principal language:** Spanish (official). **Chief religions:** Roman Catholic, Santeria.

Geography: Total area: 42,803 sq mi, 110,860 sq km; **Land area:** 42,803 sq mi, 110,860 sq km. **Location:** In the Caribbean, westernmost of West Indies. **Neighbors:** Bahamas and U.S. to N, Mexico to W, Jamaica to S, Haiti to E. **Topography:** The coastline is about 2,500 miles. The N coast is steep and rocky, the S coast low and marshy. Low hills and fertile valleys cover more than half the country. Sierra Maestra, in the E, is the highest of 3 mountain ranges. **Capital:** Havana, 2,189,000.

Government: Type: Communist state. **Head of state and gov.:** Pres. Fidel Castro Ruz; b Aug. 13, 1926; in office: Dec. 3, 1976 (formerly prime min. since Feb. 16, 1959). **Local divisions:** 14 provinces, 1 special municipality. **Defense budget** (2001): $37.7 mil. **Active troops:** 49,000.

Economy: Industries: sugar, oil, tobacco, chemicals, constr., services. **Chief crops:** sugar, tobacco, citrus, coffee, rice. **Natural resources:** cobalt, nickel, iron ore, copper, mang., salt, timber, silica, oil. **Crude oil reserves** (2004): 750 mil bbls. **Arable land:** 24%. **Livestock** (2004): cattle: 4.1 mil; chickens: 18.4 mil; goats: 425,000; pigs: 1.7 mil; sheep: 3.2 mil. **Fish catch** (2003): 68,363 metric tons. **Electricity prod.** (2003): 15.7 bil. kWh. **Labor force** (1999): agriculture 24%, industry 25%, services 51%.

Finance: Monetary unit: Peso (CUP) (Sept. 2004: 24.50 = $1 U.S.). **GDP** (2004 est.): $33.9 bil.; **per capita GDP:** $3,000; **GDP growth:** 3%. **Imports** (2004 est.): $5.3 bil.; partners (2004): Spain 15.4%, Venezuela 13.7%, US 11.5%, China 8%, Canada 6.6%, Italy 6.5%, Mexico 4.9%, Germany 4.2%. **Exports** (2004 est.): $2.1 bil.; partners (2004): Netherlands 23.5%, Canada 21.9%, China 8.3%, Russia 7.8%, Spain 6.6%. **Tourism:** $1,846 mil. **Budget** (2004 est.): $19.1 bil.

Transport: Railroad: Length: 2,139 mi. **Motor vehicles:** 10,100 comm. vehicles. **Civil aviation:** 2.0 bil pass.-mi; 70 airports. **Chief ports:** Havana, Matanzas, Cienfuegos, Santiago de Cuba.

Communications: TV sets: 248 per 1,000 pop. **Radios:** 352 per 1,000 pop. **Telephone lines**: 724,300. **Daily newspaper circ.:** 53.6 per 1,000 pop. **Internet:** 98,000.

Health: Life expect.: 74.9 male; 79.7 female. **Births** (per 1,000 pop.): 12.0. **Deaths** (per 1,000 pop.): 7.2. **Natural inc.:** 0.48%. **Infant mortality** (per 1,000 live births): 6.3. **AIDS rate:** 0.1%.

Education: Compulsory: ages 6-14. **Literacy:** 97%

Major Intl. Organizations: UN (FAO, ILO, IMO, WHO, WTrO).

Cuba Interests Section: 2630 and 2639 16th St. NW 20009; 797-8518.

Website: www.cubagob.cu/ingles/default.htm

Some 50,000 Indians lived in Cuba when it was reached by Columbus in 1492. Its name derives from the Indian Cubanacan. Except for British occupation of Havana, 1762-63, Cuba remained Spanish until 1898. A slave-based sugar plantation economy developed from the 18th century, aided by early mechanization of milling. Sugar remains the chief product and chief export despite government attempts to diversify.

A ten-year uprising ended in 1878 with guarantees of rights by Spain, which Spain failed to carry out. A full-scale movement under Jose Marti began Feb. 24, 1895.

The U.S. declared war on Spain in Apr. 1898, after the sinking of the USS *Maine* in Havana harbor, and defeated it in the Spanish-American War. Spain gave up all claims to Cuba. U.S. troops withdrew in 1902, but under 1903 and 1934 agreements, the U.S. leases a site at Guantánamo Bay in the SE as a naval base. U.S. and other foreign investments acquired a dominant role in the economy. In 1952, former Pres. Fulgencio Batista seized control and established a dictatorship, which grew increasingly harsh and corrupt. Fidel Castro assembled a rebel band in 1956; guerrilla fighting intensified in 1958. Batista fled Jan. 1, 1959, and in the resulting political vacuum Castro took power, becoming premier Feb. 16.

The government began a program of sweeping economic and social changes, without restoring promised liberties. Opponents were imprisoned, and some were executed. Some 700,000 Cubans emigrated in the first years after the Castro takeover, mostly to the U.S.

Cattle and tobacco lands were nationalized, while a system of cooperatives was instituted. By 1960 all banks and industrial companies had been nationalized, including over $1 billion worth of U.S.-owned properties, mostly without compensation.

Poor sugar crops resulted in farm collectivization, tight labor controls, and rationing, despite continued aid from the USSR and other Communist nations. A U.S.-imposed export embargo in 1962 severely damaged the economy.

In 1961, some 1,400 Cubans, trained and backed by the U.S. Central Intelligence Agency, unsuccessfully tried to invade and overthrow the regime. In the fall of 1962, the U.S. learned the USSR had brought nuclear missiles to Cuba. After an Oct. 22 warning from Pres. John F. Kennedy, the missiles were removed.

In 1977, Cuba and the U.S. signed agreements to exchange diplomats, without restoring full ties, and to regulate offshore fishing. In 1978 and 1980, the U.S. agreed to accept political prisoners released by Cuba, some of whom were criminals and mental patients. A 1987 agreement provided for 20,000 Cubans to emigrate to the U.S. each year; Cuba agreed to take back some 2,500 jailed in the U.S. since 1980.

In 1975-78, Cuba sent troops to aid one faction in the Angola civil war; the last Cuban troops were withdrawn by May 1991. Cuba's involvement in Central America, Africa, and the Caribbean contributed to poor relations with the U.S.

Cuba's economy, dependent on aid from other Communist countries, was severely shaken by the collapse of the Communist bloc in the late 1980s. Stiffer trade sanctions enacted by the U.S. in 1992 made things worse. Antigovernment demonstrations in Aug. 1994 prompted Castro to loosen emigration restrictions. A new U.S.-Cuba accord in Sept. ended the exodus of "boat people" after more than 30,000 had left Cuba. In another policy shift, the U.S. announced May 2, 1995, it would admit 20,000 Cuban refugees held at the Guantánamo base but would send further boat people back to Cuba.

The U.S. imposed additional sanctions after Cuba, Feb. 24, 1996, shot down 2 aircraft operated by an anti-Castro exile group based in Miami. Cuba blamed exile groups for bombings at Havana tourist hotels, July-Sept. 1997. Pope John Paul II visited Cuba, Jan. 21-25, 1998; he called for an end to U.S. trade sanctions, while pressing Castro to release political prisoners and allow political and religious freedom. U.S. restrictions on contact with Cuba were eased in 1999. On June 28, 2000, Elián González was returned to Cuba to live with his father, ending a 7-month legal battle that began when the boy was rescued off Florida from a shipwreck in which his mother was killed; the boy's Miami relatives had sought to keep him in the U.S.

The U.S., Jan. 11, 2002, began using its naval base at Guantánamo Bay to detain prisoners captured in Afghanistan. The indefinite detention and aggressive interrogation of Afghan prisoners and others at Guantánamo were criticized by human rights groups.

Visiting Havana May 12-17, 2002, former U.S. Pres. Jimmy Carter called for democratic reforms and for lifting the U.S. trade embargo. In one of its largest crackdowns in recent years, Cuba arrested about 78 dissidents in Mar. 2003. On Apr. 11, the government executed 3 men who had hijacked a ferry in Havana bay in a failed attempt to escape to the U.S. Both the crackdown and executions were denounced worldwide. New U.S. sanctions in May 2004 limited Cuban exiles' visits and remittances to the island, provided funds for U.S. govt. TV and radio broadcasts via airplane, and set aside $36 million to support Cuban dissidents.

Cyprus

Republic of Cyprus

People: Population: 780,133. **Age distrib.** (%) <15: 20.9; 65+: 11.4. **Pop. density:** 218 per sq mi, 84 per sq km. **Urban:** 69.2%. **Ethnic groups:** Greek 85%, Turkish 12%. **Principal languages:** Greek, Turkish (both official), English. **Chief religions:** Greek Orthodox 78%, Muslim 18%.

Geography: Total area: 3,571 sq mi, 9,250 sq km; **Land area:** 3,568 sq mi, 9,240 sq km. **Location:** In eastern Mediterranean Sea, off Turkish coast. **Neighbors:** Nearest are Turkey on N, Syria and Lebanon on E. **Topography:** Two mountain ranges run E-W, separated by a wide, fertile plain. **Capital:** Nicosia, 205,000.

Government: Type: Republic. **Head of state and gov.:** Pres. Tassos Papadopoulos; b Jan. 7, 1934; in office: Feb. 28, 2003. **Local divisions:** 6 districts. **Defense budget** (2004): $148 mil. **Active troops:** 10,000.

Economy: Industries: food, beverages, textiles, chemicals, metal products, tourism. **Chief crops:** potatoes, citrus, vegetables, barley, grapes, olives. **Natural resources:** copper, pyrites, asbestos, gypsum, timber, salt, marble, clay earth pigment. **Arable land:** 12%. **Livestock** (2004): cattle: 58,500; chickens: 3.6 mil; goats: 460,000; pigs: 491,000; sheep: 295,000. **Fish catch** (2003): 3,612 metric tons. **Electricity prod.** (2003): 3.8 bil. kWh. **Labor force**: Republic of Cyprus: agriculture 4.9%, industry 19.4%, services 75.6%.

Finance: Monetary unit: Pound (CYP) (Sept. 2005: 0.46 = $1 U.S.). **GDP** (2002 est.): Greek area: $15.7 bil.; Turkish area: $4.5 bil.; **per capita GDP:** Greek area: $20,300; Turkish area: $7,135. **GDP growth:** Greek area: 3.2%, Turkish area: 2.6 %. **Imports** (2004 est.): $5.3 bil.; partners (2004): Russia 30.2%, Italy 8%, Greece 7.5%, Germany 6.4%, UK 6.1%, Japan 5.8%, France 4.2%. **Exports** (2004 est.): $1.1 bil.; partners (2004): UK 20.2%, Greece 13.1%, Israel 7.4%, Germany 7%, Belgium 4.6%. **Tourism:** $2,015 mil. **Intl. reserves less gold:** $2.52 bil. **Consumer prices:** 2.29%.

Transport: Motor vehicles 287,600 pass. cars, 123,300 comm. vehicles. **Civil aviation:** 1.9 bil pass.-mi; 13 airports. **Chief ports:** Famagusta, Limassol.

Communications: Television sets: 154 per 1000 pop. **Radios:** 406 per 1,000 pop. **Telephone lines**: 424,100. **Daily newspaper circ.**: 124.7 per 1,000 pop. **Internet**: 250,000 users.

Health: Life expect.: 75.3 male; 80.1 female. **Births** (per 1,000 pop.): 12.6. **Deaths** (per 1,000 pop.): 7.6. **Natural inc.:** 0.49%. **Infant mortality** (per 1,000 live births): 7.2.

Education: Compulsory: ages 6-14. **Literacy:** 97.6%.

Major Intl. Organizations: UN (FAO, IBRD, ILO, IMF, IMO, WHO, WTrO), the Commonwealth, EU, OSCE.

Embassy: 2211 R St. NW 20008; 462-5772.
Website: www.moi.gov.cy/moi/pio/pio.nsf/index_en/index_en

The Ottoman Empire held Cyprus, 1571-1878, until it yielded control over the island to Britain. Agitation for enosis (union) with Greece increased after World War II, with the Turkish minority opposed, and broke into violence in 1955-56. In 1959, Britain, Greece, Turkey, and Cypriot leaders approved a plan for an independent republic, with constitutional guarantees for the Turkish minority and permanent division of offices on an ethnic basis. Greek and Turkish Communal Chambers dealt with religion, education, and other matters.

Archbishop Makarios III, formerly the leader of the enosis movement, was elected president, and full independence became final Aug. 16, 1960. Further communal strife led the United Nations to send a peacekeeping force in 1964; its mandate has been repeatedly renewed.

The Cypriot National Guard, led by officers from the army of Greece, seized the government July 15, 1974. On July 20, Turkey invaded the island; Greece mobilized its forces but did not intervene. A cease-fire was arranged but collapsed. By Aug. 16, Turkish forces had occupied the NE 40% of the island, despite the presence of UN peacekeeping forces.

Face-to-face talks between the Greek and Turkish Cypriot leaders resumed Dec. 4, 2001, for the 1st time in 4 years. Turkish Cyprus opened its border with Greek Cyprus Apr. 23, 2003, for the 1st time since partition. In separate referendums Apr. 24, 2004, 65% of Turkish Cypriot voters accepted a UN-sponsored reunification plan, but 76% of Greek Cypriots rejected it. Still divided, Cyprus became a full member of the EU on May 1.

Turkish Republic of Northern Cyprus

A declaration of independence was announced by Turkish-Cypriot leader Rauf Denktash, Nov. 15, 1983. The state is not internationally recognized, although it does have trade relations with some countries. Area of TRNC: 1,295 sq mi.; pop. (2001 est.): 208,886, 99% Turkish. Capital: Lefkosa (Nicosia).

Czech Republic

People: Population: 10,241,138. **Age distrib.** (%) <15: 14.7; 65+: 14.2. **Pop. density:** 336 per sq mi, 130 per sq km. **Urban:** 74.3%. **Ethnic groups:** Czech 81%, Moravian 13%, Slovak 3%. **Principal languages:** Czech (official), German, Polish, Romani. **Chief religions:** Roman Catholic 27%, Unaffiliated 59%, Protestant 5%, Orthodox 3%.

Geography: Total area: 30,450 sq mi, 78,866 sq km; **Land area:** 29,836 sq mi, 77,276 sq km. **Location:** In E central Europe. **Neighbors:** Poland on N, Germany on N and W, Austria on S, Slovakia on E and SE. **Topography:** Bohemia, in W, is a plateau surrounded by mountains; Moravia is hilly. **Capital:** Prague, 1,170,000.

Government: Type: Republic. **Head of state:** Vaclav Klaus; b June 19, 1941; in office: Mar. 7, 2003. **Head of gov.:** Prime Min. Jiri Paroubek; b Aug. 21, 1952; in office: Apr. 25, 2005. **Local divisions:** 13 regions and Prague. **Defense budget** (2004): $1.9 bil. **Active troops:** 45,000.

Economy: Industries: metallurgy, machinery, motor vehicles, glass, armaments. **Chief crops:** wheat, potatoes, sugar beets, hops, fruit. **Natural resources:** coal, kaolin, clay, graphite, timber. **Arable land:** 41%. **Crude oil reserves** (2004): 15 mil bbls. **Livestock** (2004): cattle: 1.4 mil; chickens: 14 mil; goats: 11,912; pigs: 3.1 mil; sheep: 115,852. **Fish catch** (2003): 24,797 metric tons. **Electricity prod.** (2003): 78.2 bil. kWh. **Labor force** (2002 est.): agriculture 4%, industry 38%, services 58%.

Finance: Monetary unit: Koruna (CZK) (Sept. 2005: 23.46 = $1 U.S.). **GDP** (2004 est.): $172.2 bil.; **per capita GDP:** $16,800; **GDP growth:** 3.7%. **Imports** (2004 est.): $68.2 bil.; partners (2004): Germany 36.2%, Austria 5.6%, Italy 5.4%, France 4.8%, Netherlands 4.7%, Slovakia 4.7%. **Exports** (2004 est.): $66.5 bil.; partners (2004): Germany 36.2%, Slovakia 9.1%, Austria 6.1%, Poland 5.5%. **Tourism:** $3,556 mil. **Budget** (2004 est.): $45.8 bil. **Intl. reserves less gold:** $18.20 bil. **Gold:** 470,000 oz t. **Consumer prices:** 2.83%.

Transport: Railroad: Length: 5,879 mi. **Motor vehicles** 3.6471 mil pass. cars, 397,600 comm. vehicles. **Civil aviation:** 2.2 bil pass.-mi; 44 airports. **Chief ports:** Decin, Prague, Ustinad Labem.

Communications: TV sets: 487 per 1,000 pop. Radios: 803 per 1,000 pop. **Telephone lines:** 3.6 mil. **Daily newspaper circ.:** 254 per 1,000 pop. **Internet:** 3.1 mil. users.

Health: Life expect.: 72.7 male; 79.5 female. **Births** (per 1,000 pop.): 9.1. **Deaths** (per 1,000 pop.): 10.5. **Natural inc.:** –0.15%. **Infant mortality** (per 1,000 live births): 3.9. **AIDS rate:** 0.1%.

Education: Compulsory: ages 6-15. **Literacy:** 99.9%

Major Intl. Organizations: UN (FAO, IBRD, ILO, IMF, IMO, WHO, WTrO), NATO, OECD, OSCE.

Embassy: 3900 Spring of Freedom St. NW 20008; 274-9100.
Website: www.czech.cz

Bohemia and Moravia were part of the Great Moravian Empire in the 9th century and later became part of the Holy Roman Empire. Under the kings of Bohemia, Prague in the 14th century was the cultural center of Central Europe. Bohemia and Hungary became part of Austria-Hungary.

In 1914-18 Thomas G. Masaryk and Eduard Benes formed a provisional government with the support of Slovak leaders including Milan Stefanik. They proclaimed the Republic of Czechoslovakia Oct. 28, 1918.

Czechoslovakia

By 1938 Nazi Germany had worked up disaffection among German-speaking citizens in Sudetenland and demanded its cession. British Prime Min. Neville Chamberlain, with the acquiescence of France, signed with Hitler at Munich, Sept. 30, 1938, an agreement to the cession, with a guarantee of peace by Hitler and Mussolini. Germany occupied Sudetenland Oct. 1-2.

Hitler on Mar. 15, 1939, dissolved Czechoslovakia, made protectorates of Bohemia and Moravia, and supported the autonomy of Slovakia, proclaimed independent Mar. 14, 1939.

Soviet troops with some Czechoslovak contingents entered eastern Czechoslovakia in 1944 and reached Prague in May 1945; Benes returned as president. In May 1946 elections, the Communist Party won 38% of the votes, and Benes accepted Klement Gottwald, a Communist, as prime minister.

In Feb. 1948, the Communists seized power in advance of scheduled elections. In May 1948 a new constitution was approved. Benes refused to sign it. On May 30 the voters were offered a one-slate ballot and the Communists won full control. Benes resigned June 7 and Gottwald became president. The country was renamed the Czechoslovak Socialist Republic. A harsh Stalinist period followed, with complete and violent suppression of all opposition.

In Jan. 1968 a liberalization movement spread through Czechoslovakia. Antonin Novotny, long the Stalinist ruler, was deposed as party leader and succeeded by Alexander Dubcek, a Slovak, who supported democratic reforms. On Mar. 22 Novotny resigned as president and was succeeded by Gen. Ludvik Svoboda. On Apr. 6, Prem. Joseph Lenart resigned and was succeeded by Oldrich Cernik, a reformer.

In July 1968 the USSR and 4 Warsaw Pact nations demanded an end to liberalization. On Aug. 20, the Soviet, Polish, East German, Hungarian, and Bulgarian armies invaded Czechoslovakia. Despite demonstrations and riots by students and workers, press censorship was imposed, liberal leaders were ousted from office and promises of loyalty to Soviet policies were made by some old-line Communist Party leaders.

On Apr. 17, 1969, Dubcek resigned as leader of the Communist Party and was succeeded by Gustav Husak. In Jan. 1970, Cernik was ousted. Censorship was tightened, and the Communist Party expelled a third of its members. In 1973, amnesty was offered to some of the 40,000 who fled the country after the 1968 invasion, but repressive policies continued.

More than 700 leading Czechoslovak intellectuals and former party leaders signed a human rights manifesto in 1977, called Charter 77, prompting a renewed crackdown by the regime.

The police crushed the largest antigovernment protests since 1968, when tens of thousands of demonstrators took to the streets of Prague, Nov. 17, 1989. As protesters demanded free elections, the Communist Party leadership resigned Nov. 24; millions went on strike Nov. 27.

On Dec. 10, 1989, the first cabinet in 41 years without a Communist majority took power; Vaclav Havel, playwright and human rights campaigner, was chosen president, Dec. 29. In Mar. 1990 the country was officially renamed the Czech and Slovak Federal Republic. Havel failed to win reelection July 3, 1992; his bid was blocked by a Slovak-led coalition.

Slovakia declared sovereignty, July 17. Czech and Slovak leaders agreed, July 23, on a basic plan for a peaceful division of Czechoslovakia into 2 independent states.

Czech Republic

Czechoslovakia split into 2 separate states—the Czech Republic and Slovakia—on Jan. 1, 1993. Havel was elected president of the Czech Republic on Jan. 26. Record floods in July 1997 caused more than $1.7 billion in damage. The country became a full member of NATO on Mar. 12, 1999. Floods Aug. 2002 damaged cultural treasures in Prague.

Vaclav Klaus was chosen Feb. 28, 2003, to replace the retiring Havel. After Czech voters June 13-14, 2003, endorsed joining the EU, the nation became a full EU member May 1, 2004. When his Social Democratic Party fared poorly in EU elections June 11-12, Prime Min. Vladimir Spidla resigned; his successor, 34-year-old Stanislav Gross, was Europe's youngest head of government. A scandal surrounding his 1999 purchase of a luxury apartment in Prague forced Gross to resign Apr. 25, 2005. The Czech Republic in June 2005 was one of several EU members to postpone a referendum on approval of the EU constitution.

Denmark

Kingdom of Denmark

People: Population: 5,432,335. **Age distrib.** (%) <15: 18.8; 65+: 15.1. **Pop. density:** 326 per sq mi, 126 per sq km. **Urban:** 85.3%. **Ethnic groups:** Mainly Danish; German minority in S. **Principal languages:** Danish (official), Faroese, Greenlandic (an Inuit dialect), German. **Chief religion: Chief religions:** Evangelical Lutheran 95% (official), other Christian 3%, Muslim 2%.

Geography: Total area: 16,639 sq mi, 43,094 sq km; **Land area:** 16,368 sq mi, 42,394 sq km. **Location:** In N Europe, separating the North and Baltic seas. **Neighbors:** Germany on S, Norway on NW, Sweden on NE. **Topography:** Denmark consists of the Jutland Peninsula and about 500 islands, 100 inhabited. The land is flat or gently rolling and is almost all in productive use. **Capital:** Copenhagen, 1,066,000.

Government: Type: Constitutional monarchy. **Head of state:** Queen Margrethe II; b Apr. 16, 1940; in office: Jan. 14, 1972. **Head of gov.:** Prime Min. Anders Fogh Rasmussen; b Jan. 26, 1953; in office: Nov. 27, 2001. **Local divisions:** 14 counties, 2 kommunes. **Defense budget** (2004): $2.9 bil. **Active troops:** 21,180.

Economy: Industries: food proc., machinery, textiles & clothing, chemicals, electronics, constr., furniture. **Chief crops:** barley, wheat, potatoes, sugar beets. **Natural resources:** oil, nat. gas, fish, salt, limestone, stone, gravel, sand. **Crude oil reserves** (2004): 1.3 bil. bbls. **Arable land:** 60%. **Livestock** (2004): cattle: 1.6 mil; chickens: 16.1 mil; pigs: 13.2 mil; sheep: 140,950. **Fish catch** (2003): 1,068,094 metric tons. **Electricity prod.** (2003): 43.3 bil. kWh. **Labor force** (2002 est.): agriculture 4%, industry 17%, services 79%.

Finance: Monetary unit: Krone (DKK) (Sept. 2005: 5.97 = $1 U.S.). **GDP** (2004 est.): $174.4 bil.; **per capita GDP:** $32,200; **GDP growth:** 2.1%. **Imports** (2004 est.): $63.5 bil.; partners (2004): Germany 22.9%, Sweden 12.4%, Netherlands 7.6%, France 5.6%, UK 5.4%, Norway 5%, Italy 4.3%. **Exports** (2004 est.): $73.1 bil.; partners (2004): Germany 16.9%, Sweden 14%, UK 6.9%, US 5.4%, France 5.2%, Netherlands 5.1%, Norway 4.8%. **Tourism:** $5,265 mil. **Budget** (2004 est.): $133.4 bil. **Intl. reserves less gold:** $25.17 bil. **Gold:** 2.14 mil. oz t. **Consumer prices:** 1.16%.

Transport: Railroad: Length: 1,966 mi. **Motor vehicles** 1.89 mil pass. cars, 415,700 comm. vehicles. **Civil aviation:** 4.3 bil pass.-mi; 28 airports. **Chief ports:** Copenhagen, Alborg, Arhus, Odense.

Communications: TV sets: 776 per 1,000 pop. **Radios:** 1,325 per 1,000 pop. **Telephone lines:** 3.6 mil. **Daily newspaper circ.:** 283.3 per 1,000 pop. **Internet:** 2.9 mil. users.

Health: Life expect.: 75.3 male; 80.0 female. **Births** (per 1,000 pop.): 11.4. **Deaths** (per 1,000 pop.): 10.4. **Natural inc.:** 0.09%. **Infant mortality** (per 1,000 live births): 4.6. **AIDS rate:** 0.2%.

Education: Compulsory: ages 7-16. **Literacy:** 100%.

Major Intl. Organizations: UN and all of its specialized agencies, EU, NATO, OECD, OSCE.

Embassy: 3200 Whitehaven St. NW 20008; 234-4300.

Website: denmark.dk

The origin of Copenhagen dates back to ancient times, when the fishing and trading place named Havn (port) grew up on a cluster of islets, but Bishop Absalon (1128-1201) is regarded as the actual founder of the city.

Danes formed a large component of the Viking raiders in the early Middle Ages. The Danish kingdom was a major power until the 17th century, when it lost its land in southern Sweden. Norway was separated in 1815, and Schleswig-Holstein in 1864. Northern Schleswig was returned in 1920.

Voters ratified the Maastricht Treaty, the basic document of the European Union, in May 1993, after rejecting it in 1992. On Sept. 28, 2000, Danes voted not to join the euro currency zone.

The **Faroe Islands** in the North Atlantic, about 300 mi. NW of the Shetlands, and 850 mi. from Denmark proper, 18 inhabited, have an area of 540 sq. mi. and pop. (2004 est.) of 46,662. They are an administrative division of Denmark, self-governing in most matters. Torshavn is the capital. Fish is a primary export (571,255 metric tons in 2002).

Greenland (Kalaallit Nunaat)

Greenland, a huge island between the North Atlantic and the Polar Sea, is separated from the North American continent by Davis Strait and Baffin Bay. Its total area is 836,330 sq. mi., 84% of which is ice-capped. Most of the island is a lofty plateau 9,000 to 10,000 ft. in altitude. The average thickness of the cap is 1,000 ft. The population (2004 est.) is 56,384. Under the 1953 Danish constitution the colony became an integral part of the realm with representatives in the Folketing (Danish legislature). The Danish parliament, 1978, approved home rule for Greenland, effective May 1, 1979. With home rule, Greenlandic place names came into official use. The technically correct name for Greenland is now Kalaallit Nunaat; the official name for its capital is Nuuk, rather than Godthab. Fish is the principal export (158,485 metric tons in 2001).

Djibouti

Republic of Djibouti

People: Population: 476,703. **Age distrib.** (%) <15: 43.3; 65+: 3.2. **Pop. density:** 54 per sq mi, 21 per sq km. **Urban:** 83.7%. **Ethnic groups:** Somali 60%, Afar 35%. **Principal languages:** French, Arabic (both official); Somali, Afar. **Chief religions:** Muslim 94%, Christian 6%.

Geography: Total area: 8,880 sq mi, 23,000 sq km; **Land area:** 8,873 sq mi, 22,980 sq km. **Location:** On E coast of Africa, separated from Arabian Peninsula by the strategically vital strait of Bab el-Mandeb. **Neighbors:** Ethiopia on W and SW, Eritrea on NW, Somalia on SE. **Topography:** The territory, divided into a low coastal plain, mountains behind, and an interior plateau, is arid, sandy, and desolate. The climate is generally hot and dry. **Capital:** Djibouti, 502,000.

Government: Type: Republic. **Head of state:** Pres. Ismail Omar Guelleh; b Nov. 27, 1947; in office: May 8, 1999. **Head of gov.:** Prime Min. Dileita Mohamed Dileita; b Mar. 12, 1958; in office: Mar. 7, 2001. **Local divisions:** 5 districts. **Defense budget** (2004): $25 mil. **Active troops:** 9,850.

Economy: Industries: constr., agricult. proc. **Chief crops:** fruits, vegetables. **Natural resources:** geothermal areas. **Livestock** (2004): cattle: 297,000; goats: 512,000; sheep: 466,000. **Fish catch** (2003): 350 metric tons. **Electricity prod.** (2003): 0.24 bil. kWh.

Finance: Monetary unit: Franc (DJF) (Sept. 2005: 172.75 = $1 U.S.). **GDP** (2002 est.): $619.0 mil; **per capita GDP:** $1,300; **GDP growth:** 3.5%. **Imports** (2002 est.): $665.0 mil; partners (2004): Saudi Arabia 21%, Ethiopia 9.9%, India 8.2%, China 7.8%, US 6.1%, France 6%. **Exports** (2002 est.): $155.0 mil; partners (2004): Somalia 63.9%, Yemen 22.6%, Ethiopia 5%. **Tourism** (1995): $4 mil. **Budget** (1999 est.): $182.0 mil. **Intl. reserves less gold:** $60 mil.

Transport: Railroad: Length: 62 mi. **Motor vehicles:** 13,500 pass. cars, 3,000 comm. vehicles; 3 airports. **Chief port:** Djibouti.

Communications: TV sets: 48 per 1,000 pop. **Radios:** 86 per 1,000 pop. **Telephone lines:** 10,200. **Daily newspaper circ.:** 8 per 1,000 pop. **Internet:** 6,500 users.

Health: Life expect.: 41.8 male; 44.4 female. **Births** (per 1,000 pop.): 40.0. **Deaths** (per 1,000 pop.): 19.4. **Natural inc.:** 2.06%. **Infant mortality** (per 1,000 live births): 104.1. **AIDS rate:** 2.9%.

Education: Compulsory: ages 6-15. **Literacy:** 67.9%.

Major Intl. Organizations: UN (FAO, IBRD, ILO, IMF, IMO, WHO, WTrO), AL, AU.

Embassy: 1156 15th St. NW, Ste. 515, 20005; 331-0270.

Website: djibouti.usembassy.gov

France gained control of the territory in stages between 1862 and 1900. As French Somaliland it became an overseas territory of France in 1945; in 1967 it was renamed the French Territory of the Afars and the Issas.

Ethiopia and Somalia have renounced their claims to the area, but each has accused the other of trying to gain control. There were clashes between Afars (ethnically related to Ethiopians) and Issas (related to Somalis) in 1976. Immigrants from both countries continued to enter the country up to independence, which came June 27, 1977.

French aid is the mainstay of the economy, as well as assistance from Arab countries. A peace accord Dec. 1994 ended a 3-year-long uprising by Afar rebels. As of early 2005, some 2,700 French and 1,800 U.S. troops were based in Djibouti.

Dominica

Commonwealth of Dominica

People: Population: 69,029. **Age distrib.** (%) <15: 26.7; 65+: 7.9. **Pop. density:** 237 per sq mi, 92 per sq km. **Urban:** 72.0%. **Ethnic groups:** Black, Creole, White, Carib Amerindian. **Principal languages:** English (official), French patois. **Chief religions:** Roman Catholic 77%, Protestant 15%.

Geography: Total area: 291 sq mi, 754 sq km; **Land area:** 291 sq mi, 754 sq km. **Location:** In Eastern Caribbean, most northerly Windward Isl. **Neighbors:** Guadeloupe to N, Martinique to S. **Topography:** Mountainous, a central ridge running from N to S, terminating in cliffs; volcanic in origin, with numerous thermal springs; rich deep topsoil on leeward side, red tropical clay on windward coast. **Capital:** Roseau, 27,000.

Government: Type: Parliamentary democracy. **Head of state:** Pres. Nicholas Liverpool; b 1934; in office: Oct. 2, 2003. **Head of gov.:** Prime Min. Roosevelt Skerrit; b June 8, 1972; in office: Jan. 8, 2004. **Local divisions:** 10 parishes.

Economy: Industries: soap, coconut oil, tourism, copra, furniture, cement blocks, shoes. **Chief crops:** bananas, citrus, mangoes, coconuts, cocoa. **Natural resources:** timber, hydropower. **Arable land:** 9%. **Livestock** (2004): cattle: 13,400; chickens: 190,000; goats: 9,700; pigs: 5,000; sheep: 7,600. **Fish catch** (2003): 1,103 metric tons. **Electricity prod.** (2003): 0.07 bil. kWh. **Labor force:** agriculture 40%, industry and commerce 32%, services 28%.

Finance: Monetary unit: East Caribbean Dollar (XCD) (Sept. 2005: 2.67 = $1 U.S.). **GDP** (2003 est.): $384.0 mil; **per capita GDP:** $5,500; **GDP growth:** –1%. **Imports** (2003 est.): $98.2 mil; partners (2004): China 20.1%, US 18.7%, Trinidad and Tobago 10.2%, UK 7.2%, South Korea 5.3%, Japan 4.5%. **Exports** (2003 est.): $39.0 mil; partners (2004): UK 21.5%, Jamaica 20%, Antigua and Barbuda 8.3%, Guyana 7%, Japan 5.3%, US 4.6%, Trinidad and Tobago 4.5%, Poland 4%. **Tourism:** $51 mil. **Budget** (2001 est.): $84.4 mil. **Intl. reserves less gold:** $27 mil. **Consumer prices:** 2.27%.

Transport: Motor vehicles: 8,700 pass. cars, 3,400 comm. vehicles. **Civil Aviation:** 2 airports. **Chief port:** Roseau.

Communications: TV sets: 232 per 1,000 pop. **Radios:** 648 per 1,000 pop. **Telephone lines** (2002): 23,700. **Internet** (2002): 12,500 users.

Health: Life expect.: 71.7 male; 77.7 female. **Births** (per 1,000 pop.): 15.7. **Deaths** (per 1,000 pop.): 6.8. **Natural inc.:** 0.89%. **Infant mortality** (per 1,000 live births): 14.2.

Education: Compulsory: ages 5-16. **Literacy:** 94%.

Major Intl. Organizations: UN (FAO, IBRD, ILO, IMF, IMO, WHO, WTrO), Caricom, the Commonwealth, OAS, OECS.

Embassy: 3216 New Mexico Ave. NW 20016; 364-6781.

Website: www.dominica.dm

A British colony since 1805, Dominica was granted self-government in 1967. Independence was achieved Nov. 3, 1978.

Hurricane David struck, Aug. 30, 1979, devastating the island and destroying the banana plantations, Dominica's economic mainstay. Coups were attempted in 1980 and 1981.

Dominica participated in the 1983 U.S.-led invasion of nearby Grenada. Prime Min. Pierre Charles, 49, died of a heart attack Jan. 6, 2004, and was succeeded by Roosevelt Skerrit.

Dominican Republic

People: Population: 9,049,595. **Age distrib.** (%) <15: 32.9; 65+: 5.4. **Pop. density:** 481 per sq mi, 186 per sq. **Urban:** 59.3%. **Ethnic groups:** Creole 73%, White 16%, Black 11%. **Principal languages:** Spanish (official). **Chief religion:** Roman Catholic 95%.

Geography: Total area: 18,815 sq mi, 48,730 sq km; **Land area:** 18,680 sq mi, 48,380 sq km. **Location:** In West Indies, sharing isl. of Hispaniola with Haiti. **Neighbors:** Haiti on W, Puerto Rico (U.S.) to E. **Topography:** The Cordillera Central range crosses the center of the country, rising to over 10,000 ft., highest in the Caribbean. The Cibao Valley to the N is major agricultural area. **Capital:** Santo Domingo, 1,865,000. **Cities (urban aggr.):** Santiago de los Caballeros, 804,000.

Government: Type: Republic. **Head of state and gov.:** Pres. Leonel Fernández Reyna; b Dec. 26, 1953; in office: Aug. 16, 2004. **Local divisions:** 29 provinces and national district. **Defense budget** (2004): $122 mil. **Active troops:** 24,500.

Economy: Industries: tourism, sugar proc., mining, textiles, cement, tobacco. **Chief crops:** sugarcane, coffee, cotton, cocoa, tobacco, rice, beans. **Natural resources:** nickel, bauxite, gold, silver. **Arable land:** 21%. **Livestock** (2004): cattle: 2.2 mil; chickens: 47 mil; goats: 189,000; pigs: 578,000; sheep: 123,000. **Fish catch** (2003): 21,651 metric tons. **Electricity prod.** (2003): 12.6 bil. kWh. **Labor force** (1998 est.): agriculture 17%, industry 24.3%, services and government 58.7%.

Finance: Monetary unit: Peso (DOP) (Sept. 2005: 29.00 = $1 U.S.). **GDP** (2004 est.): $55.7 bil.; **per capita GDP:** $6,300; **GDP growth:** 1.7%. **Imports** (2004 est.): $8.1 bil.; partners (2004): US 49%, Venezuela 13.8%, Mexico 4.6%, Colombia 4.2%. **Exports** (2004 est.): $5.4 bil.; partners (2004): US 79.7%, Canada 1.8%, Haiti 1.7%. **Tourism:** $3,110 mil. **Budget** (2004 est.): $3.4 bil. **Intl. reserves less gold:** $514 mil. **Gold:** 20,000 oz t. **Consumer prices:** 51.46%.

Transport: Railroad: Length: 934 mi. **Motor vehicles** 561,300 pass. cars, 284,700 comm. vehicles. **Civil aviation:** 3,107 pass.-mi; 13 airports. **Chief ports:** Santo Domingo, San Pedro de Macoris, Puerto Plata.

Communications: TV sets: 96 per 1,000 pop. **Radios:** 178 per 1,000 pop. **Telephone lines:** 901,800. **Daily newspaper circ.:** 27.5 per 1,000 pop. **Internet**: 800,000 users.

Health: Life expect.: 69.9 male; 73.0 female. **Births** (per 1,000 pop.): 23.5. **Deaths** (per 1,000 pop.): 5.7. **Natural inc.:** 1.78%. **Infant mortality** (per 1,000 live births): 29.4. **AIDS rate:** 1.7%.

Education: Compulsory: ages 5-13. **Literacy:** 84.7%.

Major Intl. Organizations: UN (FAO, IBRD, ILO, IMF, IMO, WHO, WTrO), OAS.

Embassy: 1715 22d St. NW 20008; 332-6280.

Website: www.domrep.org

Carib and Arawak Indians inhabited the island of Hispaniola when Columbus landed in 1492. The city of Santo Domingo, founded 1496, is the oldest settlement by Europeans in the hemisphere and has the supposed ashes of Columbus in an elaborate tomb in its ancient cathedral.

The western third of the island was ceded to France in 1697. Santo Domingo itself was ceded to France in 1795. Haitian leader Toussaint L'Ouverture seized it, 1801. Spain returned intermittently 1803-21, as several native republics came and went. Haiti ruled again, 1822-44; Spanish occupation occurred 1861-63.

The country was occupied by U.S. Marines from 1916 to 1924, when a constitutionally elected government was installed.

In 1930, Gen. Rafael Leonidas Trujillo Molina was elected president. Trujillo ruled brutally until his assassination in 1961. Pres. Joaquín Balaguer, appointed by Trujillo in 1960, resigned under pressure in 1962.

Juan Bosch, elected president in the first free elections in 38 years, was overthrown in 1963. On Apr. 24, 1965, a revolt was launched by followers of Bosch and others, including a few Communists. Four days later U.S. Marines intervened against pro-Bosch forces. Token units were later sent by 5 South American countries as a peacekeeping force. A provisional government supervised a June 1966 election, in which Balaguer defeated Bosch. Balaguer remained in office for most of the next 28 years, but his May 1994 reelection was widely denounced as fraudulent. He cut short his term and on June 30, 1996, Leonel Fernández Reyna was elected.

Hurricane Georges struck Sept. 22, 1998, causing extensive property damage and claiming more than 200 lives. The leftist candidate, Hipólito Mejía, won a presidential vote May 16, 2000. With the nation reeling from a banking scandal and soaring inflation, Fernández defeated Mejía in the election of May 16, 2004. Floods and mudslides in late May killed about 395 people. A fight between rival prison gangs led to a fire, Mar. 7, 2005, in which 136 inmates died.

East Timor

(*See* Timor-Leste)

Ecuador

Republic of Ecuador

People: Population: 13,363,593. **Age distrib.** (%) <15: 33.5; 65+: 4.9. **Pop. density:** 122 per sq mi, 47 per sq km. **Urban:** 61.8%. **Ethnic groups:** Mestizo 65%, Amerindian 25%, Black 3%. **Principal languages:** Spanish (official), Amerindian languages (especially Quechua). **Chief religion:** Roman Catholic 95%.

Geography: Total area: 109,483 sq mi, 283,560 sq km; **Land area:** 106,889 sq mi, 276,840 sq km. **Location:** In NW South America, on Pacific coast, astride the Equator. **Neighbors:** Colombia on N, Peru on E and S. **Topography:** Two ranges of Andes run N and S, splitting the country into 3 zones: hot, humid lowlands on the coast; temperate highlands between the ranges; and rainy, tropical lowlands to the E. **Capital:** Quito, 1,451,000. **Cities (urban aggr.):** Guayaquil, 2,077,000.

Government: Type: Republic. **Head of state and gov.:** Pres. Alfredo Palacio González; b Jan. 22, 1939; in office: Apr. 20, 2005. **Local divisions:** 22 provinces. **Defense budget** (2004): $588 mil. **Active troops:** 46,500.

Economy: Industries: oil, food proc., textiles, metal work, paper & wood products. **Chief crops:** bananas, coffee, cocoa, rice, potatoes, cassava, plantains, sugarcane. **Natural resources:** oil, fish, timber, hydropower. **Crude oil reserves** (2004): 4.6 bil. bbls. **Arable land:** 6%. **Livestock** (2004): cattle: 5.1 mil; chickens: 147 mil; goats: 500,000; pigs: 3.1 mil; sheep: 2.9 mil. **Fish catch** (2003): 465,084 metric tons. **Electricity prod.** (2003): 11.3 bil. kWh. **Labor force** (2001): agriculture 8%, industry 24%, services 68%.

Finance: Monetary unit: U.S. dollar. **GDP** (2004 est.): $49.5 bil.; **per capita GDP:** $3,700; **GDP growth:** 5.8%. **Imports** (2004 est.): $7.7 bil.; partners (2004): US 24.5%, Colombia 12.7%, Venezuela 8.3%, Brazil 5.8%, Chile 4.9%, China 4.8%, Japan 4.3%. **Exports** (2004 est.): $7.6 bil.; partners (2004): US 48.3%, Colombia 5.5%, Germany 4.8%. **Tourism:** $406 mil. **Budget** (2004 est.): $7.3 bil. **Intl. reserves less gold:** $689 mil. **Gold:** 850,000 oz t. **Consumer prices:** 2.74%.

Transport: Railroad: Length: 600 mi. **Motor vehicles:** 326,200 pass. cars, 268,200 comm. vehicles. **Civil aviation:** 444,280 pass.-mi; 61 airports. **Chief ports:** Guayaquil, Manta, Esmeraldas, Puerto Bolivar.

Communications: TV sets: 213 per 1,000 pop. **Radios:** 406 per 1,000 pop. **Telephone lines:** 1.5 mil. **Daily newspaper circ.:** 96.5 per 1,000 pop. **Internet:** 581,600 users.

Health: Life expect.: 73.4 male; 79.2 female. **Births** (per 1,000 pop.): 22.7. **Deaths** (per 1,000 pop.): 4.2. **Natural inc.:** 1.84%. **Infant mortality** (per 1,000 live births): 23.7. **AIDS rate:** 0.3%.

Education: Compulsory: ages 5-14. **Literacy:** 92.5%.

Major Intl. Organizations: UN (FAO, IBRD, ILO, IMF, IMO, WHO, WTrO), OAS.

Embassy: 2535 15th St. NW 20009; 234-7200.

Website: www.ecuador.org/main.htm

The region, which was the northern Inca empire, was conquered by Spain in 1533. Liberation forces defeated the Spanish May 24, 1822, near Quito. Ecuador became part of the Great Colombia Republic but seceded, May 13, 1830.

Ecuadoran Indians staged protests in the 1990s to demand greater rights. A border war with Peru flared from Jan. 26, 1995, until a truce took effect Mar. 1. Vice-Pres. Alberto Dahik resigned and fled Ecuador, Oct. 11, 1995, to avoid arrest on corruption charges. Elected president in a runoff, July 7, 1996, Abdalá Bucaram—a populist known as El Loco, or "The Crazy One"—imposed stiff price increases and other austerity measures. His rising unpopularity and erratic behavior led the National Congress, Feb. 6, 1997, to dismiss him for "mental incapacity."

Jamil Mahuad Witt, mayor of Quito, won a presidential runoff election July 12, 1998. In Sept. 1998 and Mar. 1999 he imposed emergency measures to cope with a continuing economic crisis. Opposed by Indian groups and military leaders, he was ousted Jan. 21, 2000, and succeeded by Vice-Pres. Gustavo Noboa Bejarano. Noboa went ahead with a plan introduced by Mahuad to replace the sucre with the U.S. dollar as Ecuador's currency. Lucio Gutiérrez Borbúa, a leader in the 2000 coup, won a presidential runoff Nov. 24, 2002. Noboa, under investigation for financial mismanagement, went into exile Aug. 23, 2003.

Gutiérrez imposed economic austerity measures, purged opponents from the supreme court, Dec. 2004, and then dissolved the court, Apr. 15, 2005. With street protests rising, the military withdrew support of Gutiérrez. Congress ousted him Apr. 20, and Vice Pres. Alfredo Palacio González became president.

The **Galápagos Islands,** pop. (2001 est.) 16,000, about 600 mi. to the W, are the home of huge tortoises and other unusual animals. The oil tanker *Jessica* ran aground Jan. 16, 2001, off San Cristóbal Is., spilling some 185,000 gallons of fuel.

WORLD ALMANAC QUICK QUIZ

Can you rank these countries in order of per capita GDP, from highest to lowest?

(a) Saudi Arabia (b) Luxembourg
(c) Japan (d) United States

For the answer look in this chapter, or see page 1008.

Egypt

Arab Republic of Egypt

People: Population: 77,505,756. **Age distrib.** (%): <15: 33.0; 65+: 4.4. **Pop. density:** 200 per sq mi, 77 per sq km. **Urban:** 42.1%. **Ethnic groups:** Egyptian Arab 99%. **Principal languages:** Arabic (official); English, French. **Chief religions:** Muslim (official; mostly Sunni) 94%, Coptic Christian and other 6%.

Geography: Total area: 386,662 sq mi, 1,001,450 sq km; **Land area:** 384,345 sq mi, 995,450 sq km. **Location:** Northeast corner of Africa. **Neighbors:** Libya on W, Sudan on S, Israel and Gaza Strip on E. **Topography:** Almost entirely desolate and barren, with hills and mountains in E and along Nile. The Nile Valley, where most of the people live, stretches 550 miles. **Capital:** Cairo, 10,834,000. **Cities (urban aggr.):** Alexandria, 3,506,000.

Government: Type: Republic. **Head of state:** Pres. Hosni Mubarak; b May 4, 1928; in office: Oct. 14, 1981. **Head of gov.:** Prime Min. Ahmed Nazif; b July 8, 1952; in office: July 14, 2004. **Local divisions:** 26 governorates. **Defense budget** (2003): $1.7 bil. **Active troops:** 450,000.

Economy: Industries: textiles, food proc., tourism, chemicals, hydrocarbons, constr., cement, metals. **Chief crops:** cotton, rice, corn, wheat, beans, fruits, vegetables. **Natural resources:** oil, nat. gas, iron ore, phosphates, mang., limestone, gypsum, talc, asbestos, lead, zinc. **Crude oil reserves** (2004): 3.7 bil. bbls. **Arable land:** 2%. **Livestock** (2004): cattle: 3.9 mil; chickens: 95 mil; goats: 3.7 mil; pigs: 30,500; sheep: 5.1 mil. **Fish catch** (2003): 875,990 metric tons. **Electricity prod.** (2003): 84.3 bil. kWh. **Labor force** (2001 est.): agriculture 32%, industry 17%, services 51%.

Finance: Monetary unit: Pound (EGP) (Sept. 2005: 5.74 = $1 U.S.). **GDP** (2004 est.): $316.3 bil.; **per capita GDP:** $4,200; **GDP growth:** 4.5%. **Imports** (2004 est.): $19.2 bil.; partners (2004): US 13.2%, Germany 7.2%, Italy 7.1%, France 6.1%, China 5.5%, UK 4.9%, Saudi Arabia 4.4%. **Exports** (2004 est.): $11.0 bil.; partners (2004): Italy 13.1%, US 11.6%, UK 7.5%, Germany 5.1%, Spain 4.5%, France 4.2%. **Tourism:** $4,584 mil. **Budget** (2004 est.): $20.8 bil. **Intl. reserves less gold:** $9.19 bil. **Gold:** 2.43 mil. oz t. **Consumer prices:** 11.27%.

Transport: Railroad: Length: 3,172 mi. **Motor vehicles** 1.847 mil pass. cars, 650,000 comm. vehicles. **Civil aviation:** 5.5 bil pass.-mi; 71 airports. **Chief ports:** Alexandria, Port Said, Suez, Damietta.

Communications: TV sets: 170 per 1,000 pop. **Radios:** 317 per 1,000 pop. **Telephone lines:** 8.7 mil. **Daily newspaper circ.:** 31.2 per 1,000 pop. **Internet**: 3.0 mil. users.

Health: Life expect.: 68.5 male; 73.6 female. **Births** (per 1,000 pop.): 23.3. **Deaths** (per 1,000 pop.): 5.3. **Natural inc.:** 1.81%. **Infant mortality** (per 1,000 live births): 32.6. **AIDS rate:** <0.1%.

Education: Compulsory: ages 6-13. **Literacy:** 57.7%.

Major Intl. Organizations: UN (FAO, IBRD, ILO, IMF, IMO, WHO, WTrO), AL, AU.

Embassy: 3521 International Ct. NW 20008; 895-5400.

Website: www.sis.gov.eg

Archaeological records of ancient Egyptian civilization date back to 4000 BC. A unified kingdom arose around 3200 BC and extended its way south into Nubia and as far north as Syria. A high culture of rulers and priests was built on an economic base of serfdom, fertile soil, and annual flooding of the Nile.

Imperial decline facilitated conquest by Asian invaders (Hyksos, Assyrians). The last native dynasty fell in 341 BC to the Persians, who were in turn replaced by Greeks (Alexander and the Ptolemies), Romans, Byzantines, and Arabs, who introduced Islam and the Arabic language. The ancient Egyptian language is preserved only in Coptic Christian liturgy.

Egypt was ruled as part of larger Islamic empires for many centuries. Britain intervened in Egypt in 1882 and ruled the country as a protectorate, 1914-22. A 1936 treaty strengthened Egyptian autonomy, but Britain retained bases in Egypt and a condominium over the Sudan. When the state of Israel was proclaimed in 1948, Egypt joined other Arab nations invading Israel and was defeated. In 1951 Egypt abrogated the 1936 treaty; the Sudan became independent in 1956.

An uprising on July 23, 1952, overthrew King Farouk and established a republic. Lt. Col. Gamal Abdel Nasser rose to power, becoming premier in 1954 and president in 1956. Nasser emerged as the most influential leader in the Arab world at the time; within Egypt, he pushed construction of the Aswan High Dam, completed in 1970.

After guerrilla raids across its border, Israel invaded Egypt's Sinai Peninsula, Oct. 29, 1956. Egypt rejected a cease-fire demand by Britain and France; on Oct. 31 the 2 nations dropped bombs and on Nov. 5-6 landed forces. Egypt and Israel accepted a UN cease-fire; fighting ended Nov. 7. Subsequently, a UN Emergency Force guarded the border. Full-scale war with Israel broke out again, June 5, 1967; before it ended under a UN cease-fire June 10, Israel had captured Gaza and the Sinai Peninsula and taken control of the E bank of the Suez Canal.

Nasser died Sept. 28,1970, and was replaced by Vice Pres. Anwar Sadat. In a surprise attack Oct. 6, 1973, Egyptian forces crossed the Suez Canal into the Sinai. (At the same time, Syrian forces attacked Israelis on the Golan Heights.) Egypt was supplied by a USSR military airlift; the U.S. responded with an airlift to Israel. Israel counterattacked, crossed the canal, and surrounded Suez City. A UN cease-fire took effect Oct. 24. Under an agreement signed Jan. 18, 1974, Israeli forces withdrew from the canal's W bank; limited numbers of Egyptian forces occupied a strip along the E bank. A second accord was signed in 1975, with Israel yielding Sinai oil fields.

Pres. Sadat's surprise visit to Jerusalem, Nov. 1977, opened the prospect of peace with Israel. On Mar. 26, 1979, Egypt and Israel signed a formal peace treaty, ending 30 years of war, and establishing diplomatic relations. On Oct. 6, 1981, Pres. Sadat was assassinated by Muslim extremists within the army; he was succeeded by Hosni Mubarak. Israel returned control of the Sinai to Egypt in Apr. 1982.

Egypt saw a rising tide of Islamic fundamentalist violence in the 1990s. U.S. aid to Egypt, totaling more than $50 billion since 1975, helped to keep Mubarak in power. Egypt supported the U.S.-led coalition against Iraq in the Persian Gulf War, 1991. Egyptian security forces conducted raids against Islamic militants, some of whom were executed for terrorism. Naguib Mahfouz, winner of the 1988 Nobel Prize for literature, was stabbed by Islamic militants Oct. 14, 1994. Pres. Mubarak escaped assassination in Ethiopia, June 26, 1995; Egypt blamed Sudan for the attack. On Nov. 17, 1997, near Luxor, Muslim extremists killed 58 foreign tourists and 4 Egyptians.

Mubarak, who was grazed by a knife-wielding assailant Sept. 6, 1999, was confirmed by popular vote Sept. 26 for a 4th presidential term. An EgyptAir jetliner bound from New York to Cairo plunged into the Atlantic near Nantucket Is., Oct. 31, 1999, killing all 217 people on board. Fire on a train bound from Cairo to Luxor, Feb. 20, 2002, left more than 360 people dead. An Egyptian charter plane plunged into the Red Sea shortly after takeoff Jan. 3, 2004, killing 148 people, including 133 French tourists.

Terrorists stepped up their campaign against the economically important tourism industry. Bombs Oct. 7, 2004, in and near Taba (a Sinai tourist site popular with Israelis) killed at least 35 people. Another 88 people were killed in bombings July 23, 2005, at Sharm el Sheikh, a Red Sea resort city. Pressured by the U.S., Mubarak agreed to allow opposition candidates in the Sept. 7 presidential election, which he won with an 88.5% majority; turnout was only 23%.

The **Suez Canal,** 103 mi. long, links the Mediterranean and Red seas. It was built by a French corporation 1859-69, but Britain obtained controlling interest in 1875. The last British troops were removed June 13, 1956. On July 26, Egypt nationalized the canal.

El Salvador

Republic of El Salvador

People: Population: 6,704,932. **Age distrib.** (%): <15: 36.5; 65+: 5.1. **Pop. density:** 825 per sq mi, 319 per sq km. **Urban:** 59.6%. **Ethnic groups:** Mestizo 90%, White 9%, Amerindian 1%. **Principal languages:** Spanish (official), Nahua. **Chief religions:** Roman Catholic 83%, many Protestant groups.

Geography: Total area: 8,124 sq mi, 21,040 sq km; **Land area:** 8,000 sq mi, 20,720 sq km. **Location:** In Central America. **Neighbors:** Guatemala on W, Honduras on N. **Topography:** A hot Pacific coastal plain in the south rises to a cooler plateau and valley region, densely populated. The N is mountainous, including many volcanoes. **Capital:** San Salvador, 1,424,000.

Government: Type: Republic. **Head of state and gov.:** Pres. Antonio Elías Saca González; b Mar. 9, 1965; in office: June 1, 2004. **Local divisions:** 14 departments. **Defense budget** (2004): $106 mil. **Active troops:** 15,500.

Economy: Industries: food proc., beverages, oil, chemicals, fertilizer, textiles, furniture, light metals. **Chief crops:** coffee, sugar, corn, rice, beans, oilseed, cotton, sorghum. **Natural resources:** hydropower, geothermal power, oil. **Arable land:** 27%. **Livestock** (2004): cattle: 1.3 mil; chickens: 13.2 mil; goats: 10,750; pigs: 188,025; sheep: 5,100. **Fish catch** (2003): 36,541 metric tons. **Electricity prod.** (2003): 4.3 bil. kWh. **Labor force** (2003 est.): agriculture 17.1%, industry 17.1%, services 65.8%.

Finance: Monetary unit: Colon (SVC) (Sept. 2004: 8.75 = $1 U.S.). **GDP** (2004 est.): $32.4 bil.; **per capita GDP:** $4,900; **GDP growth:** 1.8%. **Imports** (2004 est.): $6.0 bil.; partners (2004): US 37.3%, Guatemala 9%, Mexico 6.1%. **Exports** (2004 est.): $3.2 bil.; partners (2004): US 57.9%, Guatemala 13.6%, Honduras 7%. **Tourism:** $226 mil. **Budget** (2004 est.): $2.8 bil. **Intl. reserves less gold:** $1.24 bil. **Gold:** 420,000 oz t. **Consumer prices:** 4.45%.

Transport: Railroad: Length: 176 mi. **Motor vehicles** 148,000 pass. cars, 250,800 comm. vehicles. **Civil aviation:** 1.8 bil pass.-mi; 4 airports. **Chief ports:** La Union, Acajutla, La Libertad.

Communications: TV sets: 191 per 1,000 pop. **Radios:** 478 per 1,000 pop. **Telephone lines:** 752,600. **Daily newspaper circ.:** 28.3 per 1,000 pop. **Internet**: 550,000 users.

Health: Life expect.: 67.6 male; 75.0 female. **Births** (per 1,000 pop.): 27.0. **Deaths** (per 1,000 pop.): 5.9. **Natural inc.:** 2.12%. **Infant mortality** (per 1,000 live births): 25.1. **AIDS rate:** 0.7%.

Education: Compulsory: ages 7-15. **Literacy:** 80.2%.

Major Intl. Organizations: UN (FAO, IBRD, ILO, IMF, IMO, WHO, WTrO), OAS.

Embassy: 2308 California St. NW 20008; 265-9671.

Website: www.elsalvador.org/home.nsf/home

El Salvador became independent of Spain in 1821, and of the Central American Federation in 1839.

A fight with Honduras in 1969 over the presence of 300,000 Salvadoran workers left 2,000 dead.

A military coup overthrew the government of Pres. Carlos Humberto Romero in 1979, but the ruling military-civilian junta failed to quell a rebellion by leftist insurgents, armed by Cuba and Nicaragua. Extreme right-wing death squads organized to eliminate suspected leftists were blamed for thousands of deaths in the 1980s. The Reagan administration staunchly supported the government with military aid. The 12-year civil war ended Jan. 16, 1992, as the government and leftist rebels signed a formal peace treaty. The civil war had taken the lives of some 75,000 people. The treaty provided for military and political reforms.

Nine soldiers, including 3 officers, were indicted Jan. 1990 in the Nov. 1989 slaying of 6 Jesuit priests in San Salvador. Two of the officers received maximum 30-year jail sentences. They were released Mar. 20, 1993, when the National Assembly passed a sweeping amnesty.

Francisco Flores, candidate of the right-wing ARENA party, won the presidential election of Mar. 7, 1999. Another ARENA nominee, Antonio Saca, a businessman and former sportscaster, won the presidential election of Mar. 21, 2004.

Equatorial Guinea

Republic of Equatorial Guinea

People: Population: 529,034. **Age distrib.** (%): <15: 41.7; 65+: 3.8. **Pop. density:** 49 per sq mi, 19 per sq km. **Urban:** 48.1%. **Ethnic groups:** Fang 83%, Bubi 10%. **Principal languages:** Spanish, French (both official), Fang, Bubi, pidgin English, Portuguese Creole, Ibo. **Chief religions:** nominally Christian and predominantly Roman Catholic, pagan practices.

Geography: Total area: 10,831 sq mi, 28,051 sq km; **Land area:** 10,831 sq mi, 28,051 sq km. **Location:** Bioko Isl. off W Africa coast in Gulf of Guinea, and Rio Muni, mainland enclave. **Neighbors:** Gabon on S, Cameroon on E and N. **Topography:** Bioko Isl. consists of 2 volcanic mountains and a connecting valley. Rio Muni, with over 90% of the area, has a coastal plain and low hills beyond. **Capital:** Malabo, 95,000.

Government: Type: Republic. **Head of state:** Pres. Teodoro Obiang Nguema Mbasogo; b June 5, 1942; in office: Oct. 10, 1979. **Head of gov.:** Prime Min. Miguel Abia Biteo Borico; b 1961; in office: June 14, 2004. **Local divisions:** 7 provinces. **Defense budget** (2004): $7 mil. **Active troops:** 1,320.

Economy: Industries: oil, fishing, sawmilling, nat. gas. **Chief crops:** coffee, cocoa, rice, yams, cassava, bananas. **Natural resources:** oil, timber, gold, mang., uranium. **Crude oil reserves** (2004): 12 mil bbls. **Arable land:** 5%. **Livestock** (2004): cattle: 5,050; chickens: 320,000; goats: 9,000; pigs: 6,100; sheep: 37,600. **Fish catch** (2003): 3,500 metric tons. **Electricity prod.** (2003): 0.03 bil. kWh.

Finance: Monetary unit: CFA Franc BEAC (XAF) (Sept. 2004: 525.18 = $1 U.S.). **GDP** (2002 est.): $1.3 bil.; **per capita GDP:** $2,700; **GDP growth:** 20%. **Imports** (2004 est.): $1.2 bil.; partners (2004): US 32.1%, Côte d'Ivoire 16.9%, Spain 13.7%, France 8.6%, UK 7.4%. **Exports** (2004 est.): $2.8 bil.; partners (2004): US 34%, China 23.7%, Spain 21.1%, Canada 8.6%. **Tourism** (2001): $14 mil. **Budget** (2004 est.): $375.3 mil. **Intl. reserves less gold:** $608 mil.

Transport: Motor vehicles: 4,000 pass. cars, 3,600 comm. vehicles. **Civil aviation:** 2,485 pass.-mi; 2 airports. **Chief ports:** Malabo, Bata.

Communications: TV sets: 116 per 1,000 pop. **Radios:** 429 per 1,000 pop. **Telephone lines:** 9,600. **Daily newspaper circ.:** 4.9 per 1,000 pop. **Internet** (2002): 1,800 users.

Health: Life expect.: 48.0 male; 51.4 female. **Births** (per 1,000 pop.): 36.0. **Deaths** (per 1,000 pop.): 15.0. **Natural inc.:** 2.1%. **Infant mortality** (per 1,000 live births): 91.2.

Education: Compulsory: ages 7-11. **Literacy:** 85.7%.

Major Intl. Organizations: UN (FAO, IBRD, ILO, IMF, IMO, WHO), AU.

Embassy: 2020 16th St. NW 20009; 202-518-5700.

Website: www.state.gov/p/af/ci/ek

Fernando Po (now Bioko) Island was reached by Portugal in the late 15th century and ceded to Spain in 1778. Independence came Oct. 12, 1968. Riots occurred in 1969 over disputes between the island and the more backward Rio Muni province on the mainland. Masie Nguema Biyogo, a mainlander, became pres. for life in 1972.

Masie's reign was one of the most brutal in Africa, resulting in a bankrupted nation; most of the nation's 7,000 Europeans emigrated. He was ousted in a military coup, Aug. 1979. Teodoro Obiang Nguema Mbasogo, leader of the coup, became president and installed his family members in key government posts. His regime eventually agreed to elections, held Nov. 21, 1993. These were nominally won by the ruling party, but boycotted by opposition parties that maintained the rules were rigged. Elections for president, Feb. 25, 1996, and Dec. 15, 2002, were similarly condemned.

Oil sales, especially to the U.S., have boomed in recent years. Authorities in Zimbabwe and Equatorial Guinea arrested 85 people in Mar. 2004 on charges of plotting to overthrow the Obiang regime. Mark Thatcher, son of the former British prime min., was arrested in South Africa Aug. 25 for alleged involvement; in a plea bargain Jan. 13, 2005, he agreed to pay a $500,000 fine.

Eritrea

State of Eritrea

People: Population: 4,669,638. **Age distrib.** (%): <15: 44.8; 65+: 3.3. **Pop. density:** 100 per sq mi, 38 per sqkm. **Urban:** 19.9%. **Ethnic groups:** Tigrinya 50%, Tigre and Kunama 40%, Afar 4%, Saho 3%. **Principal languages:** Arabic, Tigrinya (both official); Afar, Amharic, Tigre, Kunama, other Cushitic languages. **Chief religions:** Muslim, Coptic Christian, Roman Catholic, Protestant.

Geography: Total area: 46,842 sq mi, 121,320 sq km; **Land area:** 46,842 sq mi, 121,320 sq km. **Location:** In E Africa, on SW coast of Red Sea. **Neighbors:** Ethiopia on S, Djibouti on SE, Sudan on W. **Topography:** Includes many islands of the Dahlak Archipelago, low coastal plains in S, mountain range with peaks to 9,000 ft. in N. **Capital:** Asmara, 556,000.

Government: Type: In transition. **Head of state and gov.:** Isaias Afwerki; b Feb. 2, 1946; in office: May 24, 1993. **Local divisions:** 8 provinces. **Defense budget** (2004): $74 mil. **Active troops:** 201,750.

Economy: Industries: food proc., beverages, clothing, textiles. **Chief crops:** sorghum, lentils, vegetables, corn, cotton, tobacco, coffee, sisal. **Natural resources:** gold, potash, zinc, copper, salt, fish. **Arable land:** 12%. **Livestock** (2004): cattle: 1.9 mil; chickens: 1.4 mil; goats: 1.7 mil; sheep: 2.1 mil. **Fish catch** (2003): 6,689 metric tons. **Electricity prod.** (2003): 0.27 bil. kWh. **Labor force:** agriculture 80%, industry and services 20%.

Finance: Monetary unit: Nakfa (ERN) (Sept. 2005: 13.50 = $1 U.S.). **GDP** (2004 est.): $4.2 bil.; **per capita GDP:** $900; **GDP growth:** 2.5%. **Imports** (2004 est.): $622.0 mil; partners (2004): US 32.3%, Italy 15.5%, Turkey 5.5%, UK 4.6%, Russia 4.4%, Italy 6.4%. **Exports** (2004 est.): $64.4 mil; partners (2004): Malaysia 54.7%, Italy 8.8%, France 3.7%. **Tourism** (2002): $73 mil. **Budget** (2004 est.): $373.2 mil. **Intl. reserves less gold:** $22 mil.

Transport: Railroad: Length: 190 mi. **Civil aviation:** 4 airports. **Chief ports:** Mitsiwa, Aseb.

Communications: TV sets: 16 per 1,000 pop. **Radios:** 484 per 1,000 pop. **Telephone lines:** 38,100. **Internet**: 30,000 users.

Health: Life expect.: 57.0 male; 60.0 female. **Births** (per 1,000 pop.): 34.8. **Deaths** (per 1,000 pop.): 9.9. **Natural inc.:** 2.49%. **Infant mortality** (per 1,000 live births): 47.4. **AIDS rate:** 2.7%.

Education: Compulsory: ages 7-13. **Literacy:** 58.6%.

Major Intl. Organizations: UN (FAO, IBRD, ILO, IMF, IMO, WHO), AU.

Embassy: 1708 New Hampshire Ave. NW 20009; 319-1991.

Website: shabait.com

Eritrea was part of the Ethiopian kingdom of Aksum. It was an Italian colony from 1890 to 1941, when it was captured by the British. Following a period of British and UN supervision, Eritrea was awarded to Ethiopia as part of a federation in 1952. Ethiopia annexed Eritrea as a province in 1962. This led to a 31-year struggle for independence, which ended when Eritrea formally declared itself an independent nation May 24, 1993. A constitution was ratified in 1997 but not implemented.

A border war with Ethiopia which erupted in June 1998 intensified in May 2000, as Ethiopian troops plunged into W Eritrea; a cease-fire signed June 18 provided for a UN peacekeeping force (UNMEE) to patrol a buffer zone on Eritrean territory. A peace treaty was signed Dec. 12, 2000. An international tribunal adjudicated the boundary dispute in Apr. 2002; the ruling was rejected by Ethiopia, Sept. 2003, but accepted "in principle," Nov. 2004. UNMEE had over 3,100 troops in the region in mid-2005.

Estonia

Republic of Estonia

People: Population: 1,332,893. **Age distrib.** (%): <15: 15.5; 65+: 16.8. **Pop. density:** 76 per sq mi, 29 per sq km. **Urban:** 69.4%. **Ethnic groups:** Estonian 65%, Russian 28%. **Principal languages:** Estonian (official), Russian, Ukrainian, Finnish. **Chief religions:** Unaffiliated 34%, others 32%, Evangelical Lutheran 14%, Russian Orthodox 13%.

Geography: Total area: 17,462 sq mi, 45,226 sq km; **Land area:** 16,684 sq mi, 43,211 sq km. **Location:** E Europe, bordering the Baltic Sea and Gulf of Finland. **Neighbors:** Russia on E, Latvia on S. **Topography**: Estonia is a marshy lowland with numerous lakes and swamps; about 40% forested. Elongated hills show evidence of former glaciation. More than 800 islands on Baltic coast. **Capital:** Tallinn, 391,000.

Government: Type: Republic. **Head of state:** Pres. Arnold Rüütel; b May 10, 1928; in office: Oct. 8, 2001. **Head of gov.:** Prime Min. Andrus Ansip; b Oct. 1, 1956; in office: Apr. 13, 2005. **Local divisions:** 15 counties. **Defense budget** (2004): $203 mil. **Active troops:** 4,980.

Economy: Industries: engineering, electronics, timber, wood products, textiles, telecom. **Chief crops:** potatoes, vegetables. **Natural resources:** oil shale, peat, phosphorite, clay, limestone, sand, dolomite, sea mud. **Arable land:** 25%. **Livestock** (2004): cattle: 257,200; chickens: 1.9 mil; goats: 3,500; pigs: 344,600; sheep: 30,800. **Fish catch** (2003): 79,454 metric tons. **Electricity prod.** (2003): 9.0 bil. kWh. **Labor force** (1999 est.): agriculture 11%, industry 20%, services 69%.

Finance: Monetary unit: Kroon (EEK) (Sept. 2005: 12.52 = $1 U.S.). **GDP** (2004 est.): $19.2 bil.; **per capita GDP:** $14,300; **GDP**

growth: 6%. **Imports** (2004 est.): $7.3 bil.; partners (2004): Finland 19.9%, Russia 13.2%, Germany 11.6%, Sweden 7.9%. **Exports** (2004 est.): $5.7 bil.; partners (2004): Finland 16.6%, Sweden 11.1%, UK 8.6%, Latvia 7.4%, Germany 7.2%, Russia 6.9%, US 5.5%, Lithuania 4%. **Tourism:** $674 mil. **Budget** (2004 est.): $4.6 bil. **Intl. reserves less gold:** $1.15 bil. **Gold:** 440,000 oz t. **Consumer prices:** 3.05%.

Transport: Railroad: Length: 601 mi. **Motor vehicles:** 400,700 pass. cars, 80,200 comm. vehicles. **Civil aviation:** 152,857 pass.-mi; 14 airports. **Chief port:** Tallinn.

Communications: TV sets: 567 per 1,000 pop. **Radios:** 992 per 1,000 pop. **Telephone lines**: 461,000. **Daily newspaper circ.:** 174 per 1,000 pop. **Internet**: 600,000 users.

Health: Life expect.: 66.3 male; 77.6 female. **Births** (per 1,000 pop.): 9.9. **Deaths** (per 1,000 pop.): 13.2. **Natural inc.:** –0.33%. **Infant mortality** (per 1,000 live births): 7.9. **AIDS rate:** 1.1%.

Education: Compulsory: ages 7-15. **Literacy:** 99.8%

Major Intl. Organizations: UN (FAO, IBRD, ILO, IMF, IMO, WHO), EU, NATO, OSCE.

Embassy: 2131 Massachusetts Av., NW 20008 588 0101

Website: www.riik.ee/en

Estonia was a province of imperial Russia before World War I, and was independent between World Wars I and II. It was conquered by the USSR in 1940 and incorporated as the Estonian SSR. Estonia declared itself an "occupied territory," and proclaimed itself a free nation Mar. 1990. During an abortive Soviet coup, Estonia declared immediate full independence, Aug. 20, 1991; the Soviet Union recognized its independence in Sept. 1991. The first free elections in over 50 years were held Sept. 20, 1992. The last occupying Russian troops were withdrawn by Aug. 31, 1994. Estonia became a full member of the EU and NATO in 2004.

Ethiopia

Federal Democratic Republic of Ethiopia

People: Population: 73,053,286. **Age distrib.** (%): <15: 43.9; 65+: 2.7. **Pop. density:** 168 per sq mi, 65 per sq km. **Urban:** 15.6%. **Ethnic groups:** Oromo 40%, Amhara and Tigre 32%, Sidamo 9%, Shankella 6%, Somali 6%, Afar 4%, Gurage 2%. **Principal languages:** Amharic, Tigrinya, Oromigna, Guaragigna, Somali, Arabic, over 200 other languages. **Chief religions:** Muslim 45%-50%, Ethiopian Orthodox 35%-40%, animist 12%.

Geography: Total area: 435,186 sq mi, 1,127,127 sq km; **Land area:** 432,312 sq mi, 1,119,683 sq km. **Location:** In East Africa. **Neighbors:** Sudan on W, Kenya on S, Somalia and Djibouti on E, Eritrea on N. **Topography:** A high central plateau, between 6,000 and 10,000 ft. high, rises to higher mountains near the Great Rift Valley, cutting in from the SW. The Blue Nile and other rivers cross the plateau, which descends to plains on both W and SE. **Capital:** Addis Ababa, 2,723,000.

Government: Type: Federal republic. **Head of state:** Pres. Girma Wolde Giorgis; b Dec. 1924; in office: Oct. 8, 2001. **Head of gov.:** Prime Min. Meles Zenawi; b May 8, 1955; in office: Aug. 23, 1995. **Local divisions:** 9 states, 2 charted cities. **Defense budget** (2004): $290 mil. **Active troops:** 182,500.

Economy: Industries: food proc., beverages, textiles, chemicals, metals proc., cement. **Chief crops:** cereals, coffee, oilseed, sugarcane, potatoes. **Natural resources:** gold, platinum, copper, potash, nat. gas, hydropower. **Arable land:** 12%. **Crude oil reserves** (2004): 0.4 mil bbls. **Livestock** (2004): cattle: 38.1 mil; chickens: 35.7 mil; goats: 9.6 mil; pigs: 28,000; sheep: 16.6 mil. **Fish catch** (2003): 9,213 metric tons. **Electricity prod.** (2003): 2.1 bil. kWh. **Labor force** (1985): agriculture and animal husbandry 80%, industry and construction 8%, government and services 12%.

Finance: Monetary unit: Birr (ETB) (Sept. 2005: 8.71 = $1 U.S.). **GDP** (2004 est.): $54.9 bil.; **per capita GDP:** $800; **GDP growth:** 11.6%. **Imports** (2004 est.): $2.1 bil.; partners (2004): Saudi Arabia 25%, US 15.9%, China 6.7%. **Exports** (2004 est.): $562.8 mil; partners (2004): Djibouti 13.6%, Germany 9.7%, Japan 9%, Saudi Arabia 6.5%, US 5.4%, Italy 4.9%, UK 4.3%. **Tourism** (2002): $72 mil. **Budget** (2004 est.): $2.4 bil. **Intl. reserves less gold:** $964 mil. **Gold** (2002): 250,000 oz t. **Consumer prices**: 17.8%.

Transport: Railroad: Length: 423 mi. **Motor vehicles:** 71,000 pass. cars, 34,600 comm. vehicles. **Civil aviation:** 1.8 bil pass.-mi; 14 airports.

Communications: TV sets: 5 per 1,000 pop. **Radios:** 185 per 1,000 pop. **Telephone lines:** 435,000. **Daily newspaper circ.:** 0.4 per 1,000 pop. **Internet**: 75,000 users.

Health: Life expect.: 47.7 male; 50.0 female. **Births** (per 1,000 pop.): 38.6. **Deaths** (per 1,000 pop.): 15.1. **Natural inc.:** 2.36%. **Infant mortality** (per 1,000 live births): 95.3. **AIDS rate:** 4.4%.

Education: Compulsory: ages 7-12. **Literacy:** 42.7%

Major Intl. Organizations: UN (FAO, IBRD, ILO, IMF, IMO, WHO), AU.

Embassy: 3506 International Dr. NW 20008; 364-1200.

Website: www.moinfo.gov.et

Ethiopian culture was influenced by Egypt and Greece. The ancient monarchy was invaded by Italy in 1880 but maintained its independence until another Italian invasion in 1936. British forces freed the country in 1941.

The last emperor, Haile Selassie I, established a parliament and judiciary system in 1931 but barred all political parties.

A series of droughts in the 1970s killed hundreds of thousands. An army mutiny, strikes, and student demonstrations led to the dethronement of Selassie in 1974; he died Aug. 1975, while being held by the ruling junta. The junta pledged to form a one-party socialist state and instituted a successful land reform; opposition was violently suppressed. The influence of the Coptic Church, embraced in AD 330, was curbed, and the monarchy was abolished in 1975.

The regime, torn by bloody coups, faced uprisings by tribal and political groups in part aided by Sudan and Somalia. Ties with the U.S., once a major ally, deteriorated, while cooperation accords were signed with the USSR in 1977. In 1978, Soviet advisers and Cuban troops helped defeat Somalian forces. Ethiopia and Somalia signed a peace agreement in 1988.

A worldwide relief effort began in 1984, as an extended drought threatened the country with famine; up to a million people may have died as a result of starvation and disease.

The Ethiopian People's Revolutionary Democratic Front (EPRDF), an umbrella group of 6 rebel armies, launched a major push against government forces, Feb. 1991. In May, Pres. Mengistu Haile Mariam resigned and left the country. The EPRDF took over and set up a transitional government. Ethiopia's first multiparty general elections were held in 1995.

Eritrea, a province on the Red Sea, declared its independence May 24, 1993. Fighting along the border with Eritrea, which erupted in June 1998, intensified in May 2000, as Ethiopian forces plunged into Eritrean territory; a cease-fire was signed June 18 and a peace treaty Dec. 12. The war displaced 350,000 Ethiopians and is estimated to have cost the country nearly $3 billion. A collapse of crop prices in 2001, followed by drought in 2002-03, led to severe food shortages. Ethnic clashes Dec. 2003-Jan. 2004 in the state of Gambella, W Ethiopia, left more than 250 people dead; thousands fled to Sudan.

The ruling EPRDF won parliamentary elections May 15, 2005, but opposition parties made big gains. Police opened fire on anti-government protesters in Addis Ababa, June 8, killing at least 36; the government arrested some 3,000 dissidents.

Fiji

Republic of the Fiji Islands

People: Population: 893,354. **Age distrib.** (%): <15: 31.4; 65+: 4.1. **Pop. density:** 127 per sq mi, 49 per sq km. **Urban:** 51.7%. **Ethnic groups:** Fijian 51%, Indian 44%. **Principal languages:** English (official), Fijian, Hindustani. **Chief religions:** Christian 52%, Hindu 38%, Muslim 8%.

Geography: Total area: 7,054 sq mi, 18,270 sq km; **Land area:** 7,054 sq mi, 18,270 sq km. **Location:** In western South Pacific O. **Neighbors:** Nearest are Vanuatu to W, Tonga to E. **Topography:** 322 islands (106 inhabited), many mountainous, with tropical forests and large fertile areas. Viti Levu, the largest island, has over half the total land area. **Capital:** Suva, 210,000.

Government: Type: Republic. **Head of state:** Pres. Ratu Josefa Iloilo; b Dec. 29, 1920; in office: July 18, 2000. **Head of gov.:** Prime Min. Laisenia Qarase; b Feb. 4, 1941; in office: Mar. 16, 2001. **Local divisions:** 4 divisions comprising 14 provinces and 1 dependency. **Defense budget** (2004): $36 mil. **Active troops:** 3,500.

Economy: Industries: tourism, sugar, clothing, copra, gold & silver prod. **Chief crops:** sugarcane, coconuts, cassava, rice, sweet potatoes, bananas. **Natural resources:** timber, fish, gold, copper, oil, hydropower. **Arable land:** 10%. **Livestock** (2004): cattle: 310,000; chickens: 4.2 mil; goats: 250,000; pigs: 139,000; sheep: 5,000. **Fish catch** (2003): 34,829 metric tons. **Electricity prod.** (2003): 0.78 bil. kWh. **Labor force** (2001 est.): agriculture, including subsistence agriculture 70%.

Finance: Monetary unit: Fiji Dollar (FJD) (Sept. 2005: 1.70 = $1 U.S.). **GDP** (2004 est.): $5.2 bil.; **per capita GDP:** $5,900; **GDP growth:** 3.6%. **Imports** (2002): $835.0 mil; partners (2004): Australia 27.7%, Singapore 24.8%, New Zealand 17.8%, Japan 4.2%. **Exports** (2002): $609.0 mil; partners (2004): US 23.6%, Australia 19.2%, UK 12.8%, Samoa 6.2%, Japan 4.1%. **Tourism:** $349 mil. **Budget** (2000 est.): $531.4 mil. **Intl. reserves less gold:** $308 mil. **Consumer prices** (2003): 4.2%.

Transport: Railroad: Length: 371 mi. **Motor vehicles:** 51,700 pass. cars, 48,600 comm. vehicles. **Civil aviation:** 1.5 bil pass.-mi; 3 airports. **Chief ports:** Suva, Lautoka.

Communications: TV sets: 110 per 1,000 pop. **Radios:** 677 per 1,000 pop. **Telephone lines:** 102,000. **Daily newspaper circ.:** 46 per 1,000 pop. **Internet**: 55,000 users.

Health: Life expect.: 67.1 male; 72.1 female. **Births** (per 1,000 pop.): 22.7. **Deaths** (per 1,000 pop.): 5.7. **Natural inc.:** 1.71%. **Infant mortality** (per 1,000 live births): 12.6. **AIDS rate:** 0.1%.

Education: Compulsory: ages 6-15. **Literacy:** 93.7%.

Major Intl. Organizations: UN (FAO, IBRD, ILO, IMF, IMO, WHO, WTrO), the Commonwealth.

Embassy: 2233 Wisconsin Ave. NW, Suite 240, 20007; 337-8320.

Website: www.fiji.gov.fj

A British colony since 1874, Fiji became an independent parliamentary democracy Oct. 10, 1970. Cultural differences between the Indian community (descendants of contract laborers brought to the islands in the 19th century) and indigenous Fijians have led to political polarization.

In 1987, a military coup ousted the government; order was restored May 21 under a compromise granting Lt. Col. Sitiveni Rabuka, the coup's leader, increased power. Rabuka staged a second coup Sept. 25 and declared Fiji a republic. Civilian government was restored in Dec. A new constitution favoring indigenous Fijians was issued July 25, 1990; amendments enacted in July 1997 made the constitution more equitable.

Fiji's 1st Indian prime minister, Mahendra Chaudhry, took office May 19, 1999. He and other government officials were taken captive May 19, 2000, by indigenous Fijian gunmen led by George Speight. The hostage crisis led to a military takeover, May 29. Release of the last remaining hostages in July 2000 coincided with the installation of an interim military-backed government. Speight was charged with treason (sentenced to life in prison Feb. 18, 2002). The government was reconstituted in Mar. 2001 after an appellate court ruled it illegal. Voting ending Sept. 1, 2001, returned caretaker Prime Min. Laisenia Qarase to office. Fiji's High Court, Aug. 5, 2004, convicted Vice Pres. Jope Seniloli of aiding the 2000 coup plot; he resigned his office Nov. 29 after winning early release from prison for medical reasons.

Finland

Republic of Finland

People: Population: 5,223,442. **Age distrib.** (%): <15: 17.3; 65+: 15.9. **Pop. density:** 40 per sq mi, 15 per sq km. **Urban:** 60.9%. **Ethnic groups:** Finnish 93%, Swedish 6%. **Principal languages:** Finnish, Swedish (both official); Russian, Sami. **Chief religion:** Lutheran National Church 85%.

Geography: Total area: 130,559 sq mi, 338,145 sq km; **Land area:** 117,558 sq mi, 304,473 sq km. **Location:** In northern Europe. **Neighbors:** Norway on N, Sweden on W, Russia on E. **Topography:** South and central Finland are generally flat areas with low hills and many lakes. The N has mountainous areas, 3,000-4,000 ft. above sea level. **Capital:** Helsinki, 1,075,000.

Government: Type: Constitutional republic. **Head of state:** Pres. Tarja Halonen; b Dec. 24, 1943; in office: Mar. 1, 2000. **Head of gov.:** Prim Min. Matti Vanhanen, b Nov. 4, 1955; in office: June 24, 2003. **Local divisions:** 6 laanit (provinces). **Defense budget** (2004): $2.6 bil. **Active troops:** 27,000.

Economy: Industries: metal products, electronics, shipbuilding, paper, copper refining, foodstuffs, chemicals, textiles, clothing. **Chief crops:** barley, wheat, sugar beets, potatoes. **Natural resources:** timber, copper, zinc, iron ore, silver. **Arable land:** 8%. **Livestock** (2004): cattle: 977,000; chickens: 6 mil; goats: 4,800; pigs: 1.4 mil; sheep: 95,000. **Fish catch** (2003): 135,295 metric tons. **Electricity prod.** (2003): 79.6 bil. kWh. **Labor force**: agriculture and forestry 8%, industry 22%, construction 6%, commerce 14%, finance, insurance, and business services 10%, transport and communications 8%, public services 32%.

Finance: Monetary unit: Euro (EUR) (Sept. 2005: 0.80 = $1 U.S.). **GDP** (2004 est.): $151.2 bil.; **per capita GDP:** $29,000; **GDP growth:** 3%. **Imports** (2004 est.): $45.2 bil.; partners (2004): Germany 16.2%, Sweden 14.1%, Russia 12.8%, Netherlands 6.3%, Denmark 5.3%, UK 4.6%, France 4.3%. **Exports** (2004 est.): $61.0 bil.; partners (2004): Sweden 11%, Germany 10.6%, Russia 8.9%, UK 7%, US 6.4%, Netherlands 5.2%, China 4.1%. **Tourism:** $1,894 mil. **Budget** (2004 est.): $92.0 bil. **Intl. reserves less gold:** $7.93 bil. **Gold:** 1.58 mil oz t. **Consumer prices** (2003 est.): 0.9%.

Transport: Railroad: Length: 3,635 mi. **Motor vehicles:** 2.1947 mil pass. cars, 329,700 comm. vehicles. **Civil aviation:** 5.1 bil pass.-mi; 74 airports. **Chief ports:** Helsinki, Turku, Rauma, Kotka.

Communications: TV sets: 643 per 1,000 pop. **Radios:** 1,564 per 1,000 pop. **Telephone lines:** 2.6 mil. **Daily newspaper circ.:** 445.5 per 1,000 pop. **Internet**: 2.8 mil. users.

Health: Life expect.: 74.8 male; 82.0 female. **Births** (per 1,000 pop.): 10.5. **Deaths** (per 1,000 pop.): 9.8. **Natural inc.:** 0.07%. **Infant mortality** (per 1,000 live births): 3.6. **AIDS rate:** 0.1%.

Education: Compulsory: ages 7-16. **Literacy:** 100%

Major Intl. Organizations: UN (FAO, IBRD, ILO, IMF, IMO, WHO, WTrO), EU, OECD, OSCE.

Embassy: 3301 Massachusetts Ave. NW 20008; 944-6195.

Website: www.eduskunta.fi

The early Finns probably migrated from the Ural area at about the beginning of the Christian era. Swedish settlers brought the country into Sweden, 1154 to 1809, when Finland became an autonomous grand duchy of the Russian Empire. Russian exactions created a strong national spirit; on Dec. 6, 1917, Finland declared its independence and in 1919 became a republic.

On Nov. 30, 1939, the Soviet Union invaded, and the Finns were forced to cede 16,173 sq. mi. of territory. After World War II, further cessions were exacted. In 1948, Finland signed a treaty of mutual assistance with the USSR; Finland and Russia nullified this treaty with a new pact in Jan. 1992.

Following approval by Finnish voters in an advisory referendum Oct. 16, 1994, Finland joined the European Union effective Jan. 1, 1995.

Aland or **Ahvenanmaa,** constituting an autonomous province, is a group of small islands, 590 sq. mi., in the Gulf of Bothnia, 25 mi. from Sweden, 15 mi. from Finland. Mariehamn is the chief port.

France

French Republic

People: Population: 60,656,178. **Age distrib.** (%): <15: 18.4; 65+: 16.4. **Pop. density:** 287 per sq mi, 111 per sq km. **Urban:** 76.3%. **Ethnic groups:** French, with Slavic, N African, Indochinese, Basque minorities. **Principal languages:** French (official), Italian, Breton, Alsatian (German), Corsican, Gascon, Portuguese, Provençal, Dutch, Flemish, Catalan, Basque, Romani. **Chief religions:** Roman Catholic 83%-88%, Muslim 5%-10%.

Geography: Total area: 211,209 sq mi, 547,030 sq km; **Land area:** 210,669 sq mi, 545,630 sq km. **Location:** In western Europe, between Atlantic O. and Mediterranean Sea. **Neighbors:** Spain on S; Italy, Switzerland, Germany on E; Luxembourg, Belgium on N. **Topography:** A wide plain covers more than half of the country, in N and W, drained to W by Seine, Loire, Garonne rivers. The Massif Central is a mountainous plateau in center. In E are Alps (Mt. Blanc is tallest in W Europe, 15,771 ft.), the lower Jura range, and the forested Vosges. The Rhone flows from Lake Geneva to Mediterranean. Pyrenees are in SW, on border with Spain. **Capital:** Paris, 9,794,000. **Cities (urban aggr.):** Lyon, 1,362,000; Marseilles, 1,357,000; Lille, 1,007,000.

Government: Type: Republic. **Head of state:** Pres. Jacques Chirac; b Nov. 29, 1932; in office: May 17, 1995. **Head of gov.:** Prime Min. Dominique de Villepin; b Nov. 14, 1953; in office: May 31, 2005. **Local divisions:** 22 administrative regions containing 96 departments. **Defense budget** (2004): $40 bil. **Active troops:** 259,050.

Economy: Industries: machinery, chemicals, automobiles, metallurgy, aircraft, electronics, textiles, food proc. tourism. **Chief crops:** wheat, cereals, sugar beets, potatoes, wine grapes. **Natural resources:** coal, iron ore, bauxite, zinc, potash, timber, fish. **Crude oil reserves** (2004): 146 mil bbls. **Other resources:** Timber, dairy. **Arable land:** 33%. **Livestock** (2004): cattle: 19.3 mil; chickens: 200 mil; goats: 1.2 mil; pigs: 15 mil; sheep: 9.2 mil. **Fish catch** (2003): 877,958 metric tons. **Electricity prod.** (2003): 536.9 bil. kWh. **Labor force** (1999): agriculture 4.1%, industry 24.4%, services 71.5%.

Finance: Monetary unit: Euro (EUR) (Sept. 2005: 0.80 = $1 U.S.). **GDP** (2004 est.): $1.7 tril.; **per capita GDP:** $28,700; **GDP growth:** 2.1%. **Imports** (2004 est.): $419.7 bil.; partners (2004): Germany 19.2%, Belgium 9.8%, Italy 8.8%, Spain 7.3%, UK 7%, Netherlands 6.7%, US 5.1%. **Exports** (2004 est.): $419.0 bil.; partners (2004): Germany 15%, Spain 9.4%, UK 9.3%, Italy 9%, Belgium 7.2%, US 6.7%. **Tourism:** $37,038 mil. **Budget** (2004 est.): $1.1 tril. **Intl. reserves less gold:** $22.74 bil. **Gold:** 95.98 oz t. **Consumer prices**: 2.13%.

Transport: Railroad: Length: 20,308 mi. **Motor vehicles:** 29.16 mil pass. cars, 6.178 mil comm. vehicles. **Civil aviation:** 69.8 bil pass.-mi; 273 airports. **Chief ports:** Marseille, Le Havre, Bordeaux, Rouen.

Communications: TV sets: 620 per 1,000 pop. **Radios:** 946 per 1,000 pop. **Telephone lines:** 33.9 mil. **Daily newspaper circ.:** 218 per 1,000 pop. **Internet:** 21.9 mil. users.

Health: Life expect.: 76.0 male; 83.4 female. **Births** (per 1,000 pop.): 12.2. **Deaths** (per 1,000 pop.): 9.1. **Natural inc.:** 0.31%. **Infant mortality** (per 1,000 live births): 4.3. **AIDS rate:** 0.4%.

Education: Compulsory: ages 6-16. **Literacy:** 99%.

Major Intl. Organizations: UN and most of its specialized agencies, EU, NATO, OECD, OSCE.

Embassy: 4101 Reservoir Rd. NW 20007; 944-6000.

Website: www.diplomatie.gouv.fr/index.gb.html

Celtic Gaul was conquered by Julius Caesar 58-51 BC; Romans ruled for 500 years. Under Charlemagne, Frankish rule extended over much of Europe. After his death France emerged as one of the successor kingdoms.

The monarchy was overthrown by the French Revolution (1789-93) and succeeded by the First Republic; followed by the First Empire under Napoleon (1804-15), a monarchy (1814-48), the Second Republic (1848-52), the Second Empire (1852-70), the Third Republic (1871-1946), the Fourth Republic (1946-58), and the Fifth Republic (1958 to present).

France suffered severe losses in manpower and wealth in the First World War, when it was invaded by Germany. By the Treaty of Versailles, France exacted return of Alsace and Lorraine, provinces seized by Germany in 1871. Germany invaded France again in May 1940, and signed an armistice with a government based in Vichy. After France was liberated by the Allies in Sept. 1944, Gen. Charles de Gaulle became head of the provisional government, serving until 1946.

De Gaulle again became premier in 1958, during a crisis over Algeria, and obtained voter approval for a new constitution, ushering in the Fifth Republic. He became president Jan. 1959. Using strong executive powers, he promoted French economic and technological advances in the context of the European Economic Community and guarded French foreign policy independence.

France had withdrawn from Indochina in 1954, and from Morocco and Tunisia in 1956. Most of its remaining African territories, including Algeria, were freed 1958-62. In 1966, France withdrew all its troops from the integrated military command of NATO, though 60,000 remained stationed in Germany.

In May 1968 rebellious students in Paris and other centers rioted, battled police, and were joined by workers who launched nationwide strikes. The government awarded pay increases to the strikers May 26. De Gaulle resigned from office in Apr. 1969, after losing a nationwide referendum on constitutional reform. Georges Pompidou, who was elected to succeed him, continued De Gaulle's emphasis on French independence from the U.S. and Soviet Union. After Pompidou's death, in 1974, Valery Giscard d'Estaing was elected president; he continued the basically conservative policies of his predecessors.

On May 10, 1981, France elected François Mitterrand, a Socialist, president. Under Mitterrand the government nationalized 5 major industries and most private banks. After 1986, however, when rightists won a narrow victory in the National Assembly, Mitterrand chose conservative Jacques Chirac as premier. A 2-year period of "cohabitation" ensued, and France began to pursue a privatization program in which many state-owned companies were sold. After Mitterrand was elected to a 2nd 7-year term in 1988, he appointed a Socialist as premier. The center-right won a large majority in 1993 legislative elections, ushering in another period of "cohabitation" with a conservative premier.

In 1993, France set tighter rules for entry into the country and made it easier for the government to expel foreigners. In 1994, France sent troops to Rwanda in an effort to help protect civilians there from ongoing massacres. The international terrorist known as Carlos the Jackal (Ilich Ramirez Sánchez) was arrested in Sudan in Aug. 1994 and extradited to France, where he had been sentenced in absentia to life imprisonment.

Former conservative Prime Min. Jacques Chirac won the presidency in a runoff May 7, 1995. A series of terrorist bombings and bombing attempts began in summer 1995; Islamic extremists, opposed to France's support of the Algerian government and its struggle with Islamic fundamentalists, were believed responsible. In Sept. 1995, France stirred widespread protests by resuming nuclear tests in the South Pacific, after a 3-year moratorium; the tests ended Jan. 1996.

Chirac cut government spending to help the French economy meet the budgetary goals set for the introduction of a common European currency. With unemployment at nearly 13%, legislative elections completed June 1, 1997, produced a decisive victory for the leftist parties. The result was a new period of "cohabitation," this time between a conservative president and a Socialist prime minister, Lionel Jospin. France contributed 7,000 troops to the NATO-led security force (KFOR) that entered Kosovo in June 1999.

French voters, disaffected by government scandals, shocked the political establishment in the 1st round of presidential voting Apr. 21, 2002, by giving far-right leader Jean-Marie Le Pen, leader of the far-right National Front, a 2nd place finish with 16.9% of the vote; Chirac won only 19.9%, and Jospin was 3rd, with 16.2%. Chirac easily won the May 5 runoff, with 82%, and his center-right allies won parliamentary elections June 9 and 16.

In Mar. 2003, Parliament approved constitutional amendments strengthening regional governments. Parliament gave final approval Mar. 3, 2004, to a law barring the wearing of Islamic head scarves and other religious symbols in public schools. Despite threats from Islamic extremists who abducted 2 French journalists in Iraq, it went into effect Sept. 20.

Displeased with sluggish economic growth, high unemployment, and budget cuts in entitlement programs, voters boosted left-wing parties in elections for regional offices, Mar. 21 and 28, 2004, and for the European Parliament, June 13. Voters again showed their discontent in a referendum May 29, 2005, by rejecting a proposed EU constitution strongly supported by the Chirac government. Prime Min. Jean-Pierre Raffarin resigned May 31 and was replaced by Dominique de Villepin.

The island of **Corsica,** in the Mediterranean W of Italy and N of Sardinia, is a territorial collectivity and region of France comprising 2 departments. It elects a total of 2 senators and 3 deputies to the French Parliament. Area: 3,369 sq. mi.; pop. (2001 census): 260,149. The capital is Ajaccio, birthplace of Napoleon I. Violence by Corsican separatist groups has hurt tourism, a leading industry on the island. Corsicans rejected, 51-49%, a limited autonomy plan in a referendum July 6, 2003.

Overseas Departments

French Guiana is on the NE coast of South America with Suriname on the W and Brazil on the E and S. Its area is 35,135 sq. mi. (total); 34,421 sq. mi. (land).; pop. (2004 est.) 191,309. Guiana sends one senator and 2 deputies to the French Parliament. Guiana is administered by a prefect and has a Council General of 16 elected members; capital is Cayenne.

The famous penal colony, Devil's Island, was phased out between 1938 and 1951. The European Space Agency maintains a satellite-launching center (established by France in 1964) in the city of Kourou.

Immense forests of rich timber cover 88% of the land. Fishing (especially shrimp), forestry, and gold mining are the most important industries.

Guadeloupe, in the West Indies' Leeward Islands, consists of 2 large islands, Basse-Terre and Grande-Terre, separated by the Salt River, plus Marie Galante and the Saintes group to the S and, to the N, Desirade, St. Barthelemy, and over half of St. Martin (the Netherlands' portion is called St. Maarten). A French possession since 1635, the department is represented in the French Parliament by 2 senators and 4 deputies; administration consists of a prefect (governor) as well as an elected general and regional councils.

Area of the islands is 687 sq. mi. (total); 659 sq. mi. (land); pop. (2004 est.) 444,515, mainly descendants of slaves; capital is Basse-Terre on Basse-Terre Island. The land is fertile; sugar, rum, and bananas are exported. Tourism is an important industry.

Martinique, the northernmost of the Windward Islands, in the West Indies, has been a possession since 1635, and a department since Mar. 1946. It is represented in the French Parliament by 2 senators and 4 deputies. The island was the birthplace of Napoleon's Empress Josephine.

It has an area of 425 sq. mi. (total); 409 sq. mi. (land); pop. (2004 est.) 429,510, mostly descendants of slaves. The capital is Fort-de-France (pop. 1991: 101,000). It is a popular tourist stop. The chief exports are rum, bananas, and petroleum products.

Réunion is a volcanic island in the Indian O. about 420 mi. E of Madagascar, and has belonged to France since 1665. Area, 972 sq. mi. (total); 968 sq. mi. (land); pop. (2004 est.) 766,153, 30% of French extraction. Capital: Saint-Denis. The chief export is sugar. It elects 5 deputies, 3 senators to the French Parliament.

Overseas Territorial Collectivities

Mayotte, claimed by Comoros and administered by France, voted in 1976 to become a territorial collectivity of France. An island NW of Madagascar, area is 144 sq. mi., pop. (2004 est.) 186,026. The capital is Mamoutzou.

St. Pierre and Miquelon, formerly an overseas territory (1816-1976) and department (1976-85), made the transition to territorial collectivity in 1985. It consists of 2 groups of rocky islands near the SW coast of Newfoundland, inhabited by fishermen. The exports are chiefly fish products. The St. Pierre group has an area of 10 sq. mi.; Miquelon, 83 sq. mi. Total pop. (2004 est.) 6,995. The capital is St. Pierre.

Both Mayotte and St. Pierre and Miquelon elect a deputy and a senator to the French Parliament.

Overseas Territories

Territory of **French Polynesia** comprises 130 islands widely scattered among 5 archipelagos in the South Pacific; administered by a Council of Ministers (headed by a president). Territorial Assembly and the Council have headquarters at Papeete, on Tahiti, one of the **Society Islands** (which include the **Windward** and **Leeward** islands). Two deputies and a senator are elected to the French Parliament.

Other groups are the **Marquesas Islands,** the **Tuamotu Archipelago,** including the **Gambier Islands,** and the **Austral Islands.**

Total area of the islands administered from Tahiti is 1,609 sq. mi. (total); 1,413 sq. mi. (land); pop. (2004 est.) 266,339, more than half on Tahiti. Tahiti is picturesque and mountainous with a productive coastline bearing coconuts, citrus, pineapples, and vanilla. Cultured pearls are also produced.

Tahiti was visited by Capt. James Cook in 1769 and by Capt. Bligh in the *Bounty*, 1788-89. Its beauty impressed Herman Melville, Paul Gauguin, and Charles Darwin. A coalition favoring independence for French Polynesia within 20 years gained control of the territorial assembly after elections May 23, 2004.

Territory of the **French Southern and Antarctic Lands** comprises **Adelie Land,** on Antarctica, and 4 island groups in the Indian O. **Area:** 3,023 sq. mi. (total); 3,023 sq. mi. (land).

Adelie, reached 1,840, has a research station, a coastline of 185 mi., and tapers 1,240 mi. inland to the South Pole. The U.S. does not recognize national claims in Antarctica. There are 2 huge glaciers, Ninnis, 22 mi. wide, 99 mi. long, and Mentz, 11 mi. wide, 140 mi. long. The Indian O. groups are:

Kerguelen Archipelago, visited 1772, consists of one large and 300 small islands. The chief is 87 mi. long, 74 mi. wide, and has Mt. Ross, 6,429 ft. tall. Principal research station is Port-aux-Français. Seals often weigh 2 tons; there are blue whales, coal, peat, semiprecious stones. **Crozet Archipelago,** reached 1772, covers 195 sq. mi. Eastern Island rises to 6,560 ft. **Saint Paul,** in southern Indian O., has warm springs with earth at places heating to 120° to 390° F. **Amsterdam** is nearby; both produce cod and rock lobster.

Territory of **New Caledonia** and Dependencies is a group of islands in the Pacific O. about 1,115 mi. E of Australia and approx. the same distance NW of New Zealand. Dependencies are the **Loyalty Islands, Isle of Pines, Belep Archipelago,** and **Huon Islands.**

The largest island, New Caledonia, is 6,530 sq. mi. Total area of the territory is 7,359 sq. mi. (total); 7,172 sq. mi. (land); pop. (2004 est.) 213,679. The group was acquired by France in 1853.

The territory is administered by a High Commissioner. There is a popularly elected Territorial Congress. Two deputies and a senator are elected to the French Parliament. Capital: Noumea.

Mining is the chief industry. New Caledonia is one of the world's largest nickel producers. Other minerals found are chrome, iron, cobalt, manganese, silver, gold, lead, and copper. Agricultural products include yams, sweet potatoes, potatoes, manioc (cassava), corn, and coconuts.

In 1987, New Caledonian voters chose by referendum to remain within the French Republic. There were clashes between French and Melanesians (Kanaks) in 1988. An agreement Apr. 21, 1998, between France and rival New Caledonian factions specified a 15- to 20-year period of "shared sovereignty." The French constitution was amended, July 6, to allow the territory a gradual increase in autonomy, and New Caledonian voters approved the plan Nov. 8, 1998, by a 72% majority.

Territory of the **Wallis and Futuna Islands** comprises 2 island groups in the SW Pacific S of Tuvalu, N of Fiji, and W of Western Samoa; became an overseas territory July 29, 1961. The islands have a total area of 106 sq. mi. and population (2004 est.) of 15,880. **Alofi,** attached to Futuna, is uninhabited. Capital: Mata-Utu. Chief products are copra, yams, taro roots, bananas, and coconuts. A senator and a deputy are elected to the French Parliament.

Gabon

Gabonese Republic

People: Population: 1,394,307. **Age distrib.** (%): <15: 42.1; 65+: 4.1. **Pop. density:** 13 per sq mi, 5 per sq km. **Urban:** 83.8%. **Ethnic groups:** Fang, Bapounou, Nzebi, Obamba, European. **Principal languages:** French (official), Fang, Myene, Nzebi, Bapounou/Eschira, Bandjabi. **Chief religion:** Christian 55%-75%.

Geography: Total area: 103,347 sq mi, 267,667 sq km; **Land area:** 99,486 sq mi, 257,667 sq km. **Location:** On Atlantic coast of W central Africa. **Neighbors:** Equatorial Guinea and Cameroon on N, Congo on E and S. **Topography:** Heavily forested, the country consists of coastal lowlands; plateaus in N, E, and S; mountains in N, SE, and center. The Ogooue R. system covers most of Gabon. **Capital:** Libreville, 611,000.

Government: Type: Republic. **Head of state:** Pres. Omar Bongo Ondimba; b Dec. 30, 1935; in office: Dec. 2, 1967. **Head of gov.:** Prime Min. Jean-François Ntoutoume-Emane; b Oct. 6, 1939; in office: Jan. 23, 1999. **Local divisions:** 9 provinces. **Defense budget** (2004): $17 mil. **Active troops:** 4,700.

Economy: Industries: food & beverages, textiles, lumber, cement, oil, mining, chemicals, ship repair. **Chief crops:** cocoa, coffee, sugar, palm oil, rubber. **Natural resources:** oil, mang., uranium, gold, timber, iron, hydropower. **Crude oil reserves** (2004): 2.5 bil. bbls. **Arable land:** 1%. **Livestock** (2004): cattle: 35,000; chickens: 3.1 mil; goats: 90,000; pigs: 212,000; sheep: 195,000. **Fish catch** (2003): 44,855 metric tons. **Electricity prod.** (2003): 1.5 bil. kWh. **Labor force**: agriculture 60%, industry 15%, services 25%.

Finance: Monetary unit: CFA Franc BEAC (XAF) (Sept. 2005: 525.18 = $1 U.S.). **GDP** (2004 est.): $8.0 bil.; **per capita GDP:** $5,900; **GDP growth:** 1.9%. **Imports** (2003 est.): $1.2 bil.; partners (2004): France 46.1%, U.S. 6.8%, U.K. 6.0%. **Exports** (2004 est.): $1.2 bil.; partners (2004): France 46.1%, US 6.8%, UK 6%. **Exports** (2004 est.): $3.7 bil.; partners (2004): US 51.9%, China 9.1%, France 7.7%. **Tourism** (2001): $17 mil. **Budget** (2004 est.): $1.6 bil. **Intl. reserves less gold:** $286 mil. **Gold:** 10,000 oz t. **Consumer prices** (change 1999–2000): 0.5%.

Transport: Railroad: Length: 506 mi. **Motor vehicles** 23,000 pass. cars, 10,000 comm. vehicles. **Civil aviation:** 395,813 pass.-mi; 10 airports. **Chief ports:** Port-Gentil, Owendo, Libreville.

Communications: TV sets: 251 per 1,000 pop. **Radios:** 501 per 1,000 pop. **Telephone lines:** 38,400. **Daily newspaper circ.:** 29 per 1,000 pop. **Internet**: 35,000 users.

Health: Life expect.: 53.6 male; 56.5 female. **Births** (per 1,000 pop.): 36.3. **Deaths** (per 1,000 pop.): 12.0. **Natural inc.:** 2.43%. **Infant mortality** (per 1,000 live births): 55.4. **AIDS rate:** 8.1%.

Education: Compulsory: ages 6-16. **Literacy:** 63.2%.

Major Intl. Organizations: UN (FAO, IBRD, ILO, IMF, IMO, WHO, WTrO), AU.

Embassy: 2034 20th St. NW, Ste. 200, 20009; 797-1000.

Website: usembassy.state.gov/Libreville

France established control over the region in the second half of the 19th century. Gabon became independent Aug. 17, 1960. A multiparty political system was introduced in 1990, and a new constitution was enacted Mar. 14, 1991. However, the reelection of longtime Pres. Omar Bongo, on Dec. 5, 1993, prompted rioting and charges of vote fraud; another Bongo victory on Dec. 6, 1998, was likewise allegedly marred by irregularities.

Gabon is one of the most prosperous black African countries, thanks to abundant natural resources, foreign private investment, and government development programs.

The Gambia

Republic of The Gambia

People: Population: 1,595,086. **Age distrib.** (%): <15: 44.5; 65+: 2.7. **Pop. density:** 366 per sq mi, 141 per sq km. **Urban:** 26.1%. **Ethnic groups:** Mandinka 42%, Fula 18%, Wolof 16%, Jola 10%, Serahuli 9%. **Principal languages:** English (official), Mandinka, Wolof, Fula, other native dialects. **Chief religions:** Muslim 90%, Christian 9%.

Geography: Total area: 4,363 sq mi, 11,300 sq km; **Land area:** 3,861 sq mi, 10,000 sq km. **Location:** On Atlantic coast near W tip of Africa. **Neighbors:** Surrounded on 3 sides by Senegal. **Topography:** A narrow strip of land on each side of the lower Gambia R. **Capital:** Banjul, 372,000.

Government: Type: Republic. **Head of state and gov.:** Yahya Jammeh; b May 25, 1965; in office: July 23, 1994. **Local divisions:** 5 divisions, 1 city. **Defense budget** (2004): $2.2 mil. **Active troops:** 800.

Economy: Industries: peanuts, fish, hides, tourism, beverages, agric. machinery, woodworking, metalworking, clothing. **Chief crops:** peanuts, millet, sorghum, rice, corn, sesame, cassava, palm kernels. **Natural resources:** fish. **Livestock** (2004): cattle: 328,000; chickens: 620,000; goats: 265,000; pigs: 17,800; sheep: 147,000. **Fish catch** (2003): 36,864 metric tons. **Electricity prod.** (2003): 0.14 bil. kWh. **Labor force**: agriculture 75%, industry, commerce, and services 19%, government 6%.

Finance: Monetary unit: Dalasi (GMD) (Sept. 2005: 27.82 = $1 U.S.). **GDP** (2004 est.): $2.8 bil.; **per capita GDP:** $1,800; **GDP growth:** 6%. **Imports** (2004 est.): $180.9 mil; partners (2004): China 25.1%, Senegal 9.2%, UK 6.3%, Brazil 6%, Netherlands 4.9%, US 4.8%. **Exports** (2004 est.): $114.4 mil; partners (2004): Thailand 16.6%, UK 15.5%, France 14.2%, India 12.3%, Germany 9.2%, Italy 8.3%, Malaysia 4.1%. **Tourism** (1995): $28 mil. **Budget** (2004 est.): $59.9 mil. **Intl. reserves less gold:** $54 mil. **Consumer prices:** 14.2%.

Transport: Motor vehicles (1998): 6,400 pass. cars, 3,500 comm. vehicles. **Civil aviation:** 31.1 mil pass.-mi.; 1 airport. **Chief port:** Banjul.

Communications: TV Sets: 3 per 1,000 pop. Radios: 394 per 1,000 pop. **Telephone lines** (2002): 38,400. **Daily newspaper circ.:** 1.7 per 1,000 pop. **Internet** (2002): 25,000 users.

Health: Life expect.: 51.9 male; 55.6 female. **Births** (per 1,000 pop.): 39.9. **Deaths** (per 1,000 pop.): 12.5. **Natural inc.:** 2.74%. **Infant mortality** (per 1,000 live births): 73.1. **AIDS rate:** 1.2%.

Education: Free: ages 7-13. **Literacy:** 40.1%.

Major Intl. Organizations: UN (FAO, IBRD, ILO, IMF, IMO, WHO, WTrO), the Commonwealth, AU.

Embassy: 1155 15th St., NW, Ste. 1000, 20005S; 785-1399.

Website: www.statehouse.gm/index.html

The tribes of Gambia were at one time associated with the West African empires of Ghana, Mali, and Songhay. The area became Britain's first African possession in 1588.

Independence came Feb. 18, 1965; republic status within the Commonwealth was achieved in 1970. The country suffered from severe famine in the 1970s. After a coup attempt in 1981, The Gambia formed the confederation of Senegambia with Senegal that lasted until 1989.

On July 23, 1994, after 24 years in power, Pres. Dawda K. Jawara was deposed in a bloodless coup by a military officer, Yahya Jammeh. Jammeh barred political activity, detained potential opponents, and governed by decree. A new constitution was approved by referendum, Aug. 8, 1996. On Sept. 27 Jammeh won the presidential election. Parliamentary balloting on Jan. 2, 1997, completed the nominal return to civilian rule, but Jammeh retained a firm grip on power. He followed his reelection win on Oct. 18, 2001, with a new crackdown on dissidents.

Georgia

People: Population: 4,677,401. **Age distrib.** (%): <15: 18.0; 65+: 16.0. **Pop. density:** 174 per sq mi, 67 per sq km. **Urban:** 51.9%. **Ethnic groups:** Georgian 70%, Armenian 8%, Russian 6%, Azeri 6%. **Principal languages:** Georgian (official), Russian, Armenian, Azeri, Abkhaz (official in Abkhazia). **Chief religions:** Georgian Orthodox 84%, Muslim 10%.

Geography: Total area: 26,911 sq mi, 69,700 sq km; **Land area:** 26,911 sq mi, 69,700 sq km. **Location:** SW Asia, on E coast of Black Sea. **Neighbors:** Russia on N and NE, Turkey and Armenia on S, Azerbaijan on SE. **Topography:** Separated from Russia on NE by main range of the Caucasus Mts. **Capital:** Tbilisi, 1,064,000.

Government: Type: Republic. **Head of state:** Pres. Mikhail Saakashvili; b Dec. 21, 1967; in office: Jan. 25, 2004. **Head of gov.:** Prime Min. Zurab Noghaideli; b Oct. 22, 1964; in office: Feb. 17, 2005. **Local divisions:** 53 rayons, 9 cities, and 2 autonomous republics. **Defense budget** (2004): $39 mil. **Active troops:** 17,770.

Economy: Industries: steel, aircraft, machine tools, appliances, mining, chemicals. **Chief crops:** citrus, grapes, tea, vegetables, potatoes. **Natural resources:** timber, hydropower, mang., iron ore, copper, coal, oil. **Crude oil reserves** (2004): 35 mil bbls. **Arable land:** 9%. **Livestock** (2004): cattle: 1.2 mil; chickens: 8.5 mil; goats: 99,400; pigs: 473,800; sheep: 622,800. **Fish catch** (2003): 3,361 metric tons. **Electricity prod.** (2003): 8.6 bil. kWh. **Labor force** (1999 est.): agriculture 40%, industry 20%, services 40%.

Finance: Monetary unit: Lari (GEL) (Sept. 2005: 1.79 = $1 U.S.). **GDP** (2004 est.): $14.5 bil.; **per capita GDP:** $3,100; **GDP growth:** 9.5%. **Imports** (2004 est.): $1.8 bil.; partners (2004): US 14.8%, Turkey 13.6%, Russia 11%, Germany 7.5%, UK 6.5%, Azerbaijan 6.2%, Ukraine 5.3%, Italy 4.1%. **Exports** (2004 est.): $909.4 mil; partners (2004): Turkey 28.1%, Russia 9.7%, Spain 7.9%, Turkmenistan 7.5%, US 7.1%, Armenia 5.3%, Greece 5%. **Tourism:** $147 mil. **Budget** (2004 est.): $804.7 mil. **Intl. reserves less gold:** $247 mil. **Gold:** 10,000 oz t. **Consumer prices:** 5.66%.

Transport: Railroad: Length: 1,002 mi. **Motor vehicles:** 252,000 pass. cars, 69,600 comm. vehicles. **Civil aviation:** 146,022 pass.-mi; 22 airports. **Chief ports:** Batumi, Sukhumi.

Communications: TV sets: 516 per 1,000 pop. **Radios:** 590 per 1,000 pop. **Telephone lines:** 657,100. **Daily newspaper circ.:** 4.9 per 1,000 pop. **Internet:** 117,000 users.

Health: Life expect.: 72.6 male; 79.7 female. **Births** (per 1,000 pop.): 10.3. **Deaths** (per 1,000 pop.): 9.1. **Natural inc.:** 0.12%. **Infant mortality** (per 1,000 live births): 18.6. **AIDS rate:** 0.1%.

Education: Compulsory: ages 6-14. **Literacy:** 99%.

Major Intl. Organizations: UN (FAO, IBRD, ILO, IMF, IMO, WHO), CIS, OSCE.

Embassy: 1101 15th Street NW, Suite 602, 20005, (202) 387-4537.

Website: www.parliament.ge

The region, which contained the ancient kingdoms of Colchis and Iberia, was Christianized in the 4th century and conquered by Arabs in the 8th century. Annexed by Russia in 1801, Georgia was forcibly incorporated into the USSR in 1922.

Georgia declared independence Apr. 9, 1991. It became an independent state when the Soviet Union disbanded Dec. 26, 1991. There was fighting during 1991 between rebel forces and loyalists of Pres. Zviad Gamsakhurdia, who fled the capital Jan. 6, 1992. The ruling Military Council picked former Soviet Foreign Minister Eduard A. Shevardnadze to chair a newly created State Council. An attempted coup by forces loyal to Gamsakhurdia was crushed June 24, 1992. Shevardnadze was later elected president. Gamsakhurdia died Jan. 1994, reportedly by suicide.

Since the country gained independence, rebel movements have challenged the Tbilisi government. In Abkhazia, an autonomous republic within Georgia, ethnic Abkhazis, reportedly aided by Russia, launched a bloody military campaign and, by late 1993, had gained control of much of the region. A cease-fire providing for Russian peacekeepers was signed in Moscow May 14, 1994, but intermittent clashes continued. Georgian government troops also fought South Ossetia secessionists. Chechen rebels based in Pankisi Gorge, NE of Tbilisi, launched attacks against Russian troops in Chechnya, heightening tensions with Russia.

Shevardnadze was wounded by a car bomb Aug. 29, 1995, while on his way to Parliament to sign a new constitution. He was reelected president Nov. 5. Shevardnadze escaped another assassination attempt, Feb. 9, 1998, when gunmen ambushed his motorcade. A mutiny by more than 200 soldiers was crushed Oct. 19.

Shevardnadze won another 5-year presidential term Apr. 9, 2000. But parliamentary elections Nov. 2, 2003, denounced as fraudulent by opposition groups and international observers, sparked massive antigovernment protests, causing him to resign Nov. 23. Opposition leader Mikhail Saakashvili won the presidential election of Jan. 4, 2004. Prime Min. Zurab Zhvania died Feb. 3, 2005, apparently by carbon-monoxide poisoning from a faulty gas heater; he was succeeded by Zurab Noghaideli. While U.S. Pres. George W. Bush addressed a large crowd in Tbilisi May 10, a live grenade was thrown toward the stage but failed to detonate.

Germany

Federal Republic of Germany

People: Population: 82,431,390. **Age distrib.** (%): <15: 14.4; 65+: 18.9. **Pop. density:** 598 per sq mi, 231 per sq km. **Urban:** 88.1%. **Ethnic groups:** German 92%, Turkish 2%. **Principal languages:** German (official), Turkish, Italian, Greek, English, Danish, Dutch, Slavic languages. **Chief religions:** Protestant 34%, Roman Catholic 34%, Muslim 4%.

Geography: Total area: 137,847 sq mi, 357,021 sq km; **Land area:** 134,836 sq mi, 349,223 sq km. **Location:** In central Europe. **Neighbors:** Denmark on N; Netherlands, Belgium, Luxembourg, France on W; Switzerland, Austria on S; Czech Rep., Poland on E. **Topography:** Germany is flat in N, hilly in center and W, and mountainous in Bavaria in the S. Chief rivers are Elbe, Weser, Ems, Rhine, and Main, all flowing toward North Sea, and Danube, flowing toward Black Sea. **Capital:** Berlin, 3,327,000. **Cities (urban aggr.):** Rhein-Ruhr North (including Essen), 6.54 mil; Rhein Main (Frankfurt am Mein), 3.68 mil; Rhein-Ruhr Middle (Dusseldorf), 3.24 mil; Rhein-Ruhr South (Cologne), 3.06 mil; Stuttgart, 2.68 mil; **Cities (proper)**: Hamburg, 2.67 mil; Munich, 2.3 mil; Cologne, 963,200; Frankfurt am Mein, 644,700.

Government: Type: Federal republic. **Head of state:** Pres. Horst Köhler; b Feb. 22, 1943; in office: July 1, 2004. **Head of gov.:** Chan. Gerhard Schröder; b Apr. 7, 1944; in office: Oct. 27, 1998. **Local divisions:** 16 laender (states). **Defense budget** (2004): $29.7 bil. **Active troops:** 284,500.

Economy: Industries: iron, steel, coal, cement, chemicals, machinery, vehicles, machine tools, electronics, food & beverages, shipbuilding. **Chief crops:** potatoes, wheat, barley, sugar beets, fruit, cabbages. **Natural resources:** iron ore, coal, potash, timber, lignite, uranium, copper, nat. gas, salt, nickel. **Crude oil reserves** (2004): 394.4 mil bbls. **Arable land:** 33%. **Livestock** (2004): cattle: 13.4 mil; chickens: 110 mil; goats: 160,000; pigs: 26.5 mil; sheep: 2.2 mil. **Fish catch** (2003): 335,147 metric tons. **Electricity prod.** (2003): 558.1 bil. kWh. **Labor force** (1999): agriculture 2.8%, industry 33.4%, services 63.8%.

Finance: Monetary unit: Euro (EUR) (Sept. 2005: 0.80 = $1 U.S.). **GDP** (2004 est.): $2.4 tril.; **per capita GDP:** $28,700; **GDP growth:** 1.7%. **Imports** (2004 est.): $716.7 bil.; partners (2004): France 9.2%, Netherlands 8.7%, US 6.5%, Italy 6.1%, UK 5.8%, Belgium 5.8%, China 5.3%, Austria 4.3%. **Exports** (2004 est.): $893.3 bil.; partners (2004): France 10.2%, US 8.8%, UK 8.2%, Italy 7.2%, Netherlands 6.3%, Belgium 5.7%, Austria 5.4%, Spain 5%. **Tourism:** $22,984 mil. **Budget** (2004 est.): $1.3 tril. **Intl. reserves less gold:** $31.44 bil. **Gold:** 110.38 mil. oz t. **Consumer prices:** 1.67%.

Transport: Railroad: Length: 28,281 mi. **Motor vehicles**: 44.38 mil pass. cars, 3.46 mil comm. vehicles. **Civil aviation:** 69.2 bil pass.-mi; 328 airports. **Chief ports:** Hamburg, Bremen, Bremerhaven, Lubeck, Rostock.

Communications: TV sets: 581 per 1,000 pop. **Radios:** 948 per 1,000 pop. **Telephone lines:** 54.3 mil. **Daily newspaper circ.:** 304.8 per 1,000 pop. **Internet** : 39.0 mil. users.

Health: Life expect.: 75.7 male; 81.8 female. **Births** (per 1,000 pop.): 8.3. **Deaths** (per 1,000 pop.): 10.6. **Natural inc.:** –0.22%. **Infant mortality** (per 1,000 live births): 4.2. **AIDS rate:** 0.1%.

Education: Compulsory: ages 6-18. **Literacy:** 99%.

Major Intl. Organizations: UN and all of its specialized agencies, EU, NATO, OECD, OSCE.

Embassy: 4645 Reservoir Rd. NW 20007; 298-4000.

Website: www.germany-info.org

Germany is a central European nation originally composed of numerous states, with a common language and traditions, that were united in one country in 1871; Germany was split into 2 countries from the end of World War II until 1990, when it was reunified.

History and government. Germanic tribes were defeated by Julius Caesar, 55 and 53 BC, but Roman expansion N of the Rhine was stopped in AD 9. Charlemagne, ruler of the Franks, consolidated Saxon, Bavarian, Rhenish, Frankish, and other lands; after him the eastern part became the German Empire. The Thirty Years' War, 1618-1648, split Germany into small principalities and kingdoms. After Napoleon, Austria contended with Prussia for dominance, but lost the Seven Weeks' War to Prussia, 1866. Otto von Bismarck, Prussian chancellor, formed the North German Confederation, 1867.

In 1870 Bismarck maneuvered Napoleon III into declaring war. After the quick defeat of France, Bismarck formed the **German Empire** and on Jan. 18, 1871, in Versailles, proclaimed King Wilhelm I of Prussia German emperor (Deutscher kaiser).

The German Empire reached its peak before World War I in 1914, with 208,780 sq. mi., plus a colonial empire. After that war Germany ceded Alsace-Lorraine to France; West Prussia and Posen (Poznan) province to Poland; part of Schleswig to Denmark; lost all colonies and ports of Memel and Danzig.

Republic of Germany, 1919-1933, adopted the Weimar constitution; met reparation payments and elected Friedrich Ebert and Gen. Paul von Hindenburg presidents.

Third Reich, 1933-1945, Adolf Hitler led the National Socialist German Workers' (Nazi) party after World War I. In 1923 he attempted to unseat the Bavarian government and was imprisoned. Pres. von Hindenburg named Hitler chancellor Jan. 30, 1933; on Aug. 3, 1934, the day after Hindenburg's death, the cabinet joined the offices of president and chancellor and made Hitler fuehrer (leader). Hitler abolished freedom of speech and assembly, and began a long series of persecutions climaxed by the murder of millions of Jews and others.

He repudiated the Versailles treaty and reparations agreements, remilitarized the Rhineland (1936), and annexed Austria (Anschluss, 1938). At Munich he made an agreement with Neville Chamberlain, British prime minister, which permitted Germany to annex part of Czechoslovakia. He signed a nonaggression treaty with the USSR, 1939 and declared war on Poland Sept. 1, 1939, precipitating World War II. With total defeat near, Hitler committed suicide in Berlin Apr. 1945. The victorious Allies voided all acts and annexations of Hitler's Reich.

Division of Germany. Germany was sectioned into 4 zones of occupation, administered by the Allied Powers (U.S., USSR, U.K., and France). The USSR took control of many E German states. The territory E of the so-called Oder-Neisse line was assigned to, and later annexed by, Poland. Northern East Prussia (now Kaliningrad) was annexed by the USSR. Greater Berlin, within but not part of the Soviet zone, was administered by the 4 occupying powers under the Allied Command. In 1948 the USSR withdrew, established its single command in East Berlin, and cut off supplies. The Western Allies utilized a gigantic airlift to bring food to West Berlin, 1948-49.

In 1949, 2 separate German states were established; in May the zones administered by the Western Allies became West Germany; in Oct. the Soviet sector became East Germany. West Berlin was considered an enclave of West Germany, although its status was disputed by the Soviet bloc.

East Germany. The German Democratic Republic (East Germany) was proclaimed in the Soviet sector of Berlin Oct. 7, 1949. It was declared fully sovereign in 1954, but Soviet troops remained on grounds of security and the 4-power Potsdam agreement.

Coincident with the entrance of West Germany into the European defense community in 1952, the East German government decreed a prohibited zone 3 miles deep along its 600-mile border with West Germany and cut Berlin's telephone system in two. Berlin was further divided by erection of a fortified wall in 1961, after over 3 million East Germans had fled to the West.

East Germany suffered severe economic problems at least until the mid-1960s. Then a "new economic system" was introduced, easing central planning controls and allowing factories to make profits provided they were reinvested in operations or redistributed to workers as bonuses. By the early 1970s, the economy of East Germany was highly industrialized, and the nation was credited with the highest standard of living among Warsaw Pact countries. But growth slowed in the late 1970s, because of shortages of natural resources and labor, and a huge debt to lenders in the West. Comparison with the lifestyle in the West caused many young people to emigrate.

The government firmly resisted following the USSR's policy of *glasnost,* but by Oct. 1989, was faced with nationwide demonstrations demanding reform. Pres. Erich Honecker, in office since 1976, was forced to resign, Oct. 18. On Nov. 4, the border with Czechoslovakia was opened and permission granted for refugees to travel to the West. On Nov. 9, the East German government announced its decision to open the border with the West, signaling the end of the "Berlin Wall," which was the supreme emblem of the cold war. On Aug. 23, 1990, the East German parliament agreed to formal unification with West Germany; this occurred Oct. 3.

West Germany. The Federal Republic of Germany (West Germany) was proclaimed May 23, 1949, in Bonn, after a constitution had been drawn up by a consultative assembly formed by representatives of the 11 laender (states) in the French, British, and American zones. Later reorganized into 9 units, the laender numbered 10 with the addition of the Saar, 1957. Berlin also was granted land (state) status, but the 1945 occupation agreements placed restrictions on it.

The occupying powers, the U.S., Britain, and France, restored civil status, Sept. 21, 1949. The Western Allies ended the state of war with Germany in 1951 (the U.S. resumed diplomatic relations July 2), while the USSR did so in 1955. The powers lifted controls and the republic became fully independent May 5, 1955.

Dr. Konrad Adenauer, Christian Democrat, was made chancellor Sept. 15, 1949, reelected 1953, 1957, 1961. Willy Brandt, heading a coalition of Social Democrats and Free Democrats, became chancellor Oct. 21, 1969. Brandt resigned May 1974 because of a spy scandal.

In 1970 Brandt signed friendship treaties with the USSR and Poland. In 1971, the U.S., Britain, France, and the USSR signed an agreement on Western access to West Berlin. In 1972 East and West Germany signed their first formal treaty, implementing the agreement easing access to West Berlin. In 1973 a West Germany-Czechoslovakia pact normalized relations and nullified the 1938 "Munich Agreement."

West Germany experienced strong economic growth from the 1950s through the 1980s. The country led Europe in provisions for worker participation in the management of industry.

In 1989 the changes in the East German government and opening of the Berlin Wall sparked talk of reunification of the 2 Germanys. In 1990, under Chancellor Helmut Kohl's leadership, West Germany moved rapidly to reunite with East Germany.

A New Era. As Communism was being rejected in East Germany, talks began concerning German reunification. At a meeting in Ottawa, Feb. 1990, the foreign ministers of the World War II "Big Four" Allied nations and of East Germany and West Germany reached agreement on a format for high-level talks on German reunification.

In May 1990, NATO ministers adopted a package of proposals on reunification, including the inclusion of the united Germany as a full member of NATO and the barring of the new Germany from having its own nuclear, chemical, or biological weapons. In July, the USSR agreed to conditions that would allow Germany to become a member of NATO.

The 2 nations agreed to monetary unification under the West German mark beginning in July. The merger of the 2 Germanys took place Oct. 3, and the first all-German elections since 1932 were held Dec. 2. Eastern Germany received over $1 trillion in public and private funds from western Germany between 1990 and 1995. In 1991, Berlin again became the capital of Germany; the legislature, most administrative offices, and most foreign embassies had shifted from Bonn to Berlin by late 1999.

Germany's highest court ruled, July 12, 1994, that German troops could participate in international military missions abroad, when approved by Parliament. Ceremonies were held marking the final withdrawal of Russian troops from Germany, Aug. 31. Ceremonies were held the following week marking the final withdrawal of American, British, and French troops from Berlin. General elections Oct. 16 left Chancellor Helmut Kohl's governing coalition with a slim parliamentary majority. On Oct. 31, 1996, after more than 14 years in office, Kohl surpassed Adenauer as Germany's longest-serving chancellor in the 20th century.

Unemployment hit a postwar high of 12.6% in Jan. 1998. The Kohl era ended with the defeat of the Christian Democrats in parliamentary elections Sept. 27; Gerhard Schröder, of the Social Democratic Party, became chancellor. Germany contributed 8,500 troops to the NATO-led security force (KFOR) that entered Kosovo in June 1999. Kohl resigned as honorary party chairman Jan. 18, 2000, amid allegations of illegal fund-raising. Kohl reached an agreement with prosecutors Feb. 8, 2001, in which he acknowledged committing a "breach of trust" and agreed to pay a fine, but did not plead guilty to any criminal charges.

Despite a stagnant economy, Schröder's coalition of Social Democrats and Greens retained a slim majority in the elections of Sept. 22, 2002; the chancellor was apparently aided by his government's response to devastating summer floods and by his criticism of U.S. policy toward Iraq. In early 2003, Germany worked with France and Russia to block the UN Security Council from endorsing the U.S.-led invasion of Iraq. However, polls showed Schröder's support sharply falling. Schröder's coalition did poorly in elections for the European Parliament, June 13. When his party lost its stronghold of North Rhine-Westphalia in regional voting, May 22, 2005, Schröder called for early elections for Sept. 18. The Christian Democrats, led by Angela Merkel, won a razor-thin plurality; the process of determining who would lead Germany's next governing coalition was expected to take some time.

As of mid-2005, about 2,000 German troops were serving in Afghanistan as part of a NATO peacekeeping force.

Helgoland, an island of 130 acres in the North Sea, was taken from Denmark by a British Naval Force in 1807 and later ceded to Germany to become part of Schleswig-Holstein province in return for rights in East Africa. The heavily fortified island was surrendered to UK, May 23, 1945, demilitarized in 1947, and returned to West Germany, Mar. 1, 1952. It is a free port.

Ghana

Republic of Ghana

People: Population: 21,946,247. **Age distrib.** (%): <15: 37.1; 65+: 3.7. **Pop. density:** 237 per sq mi, 92 per sq km. **Urban:** 45.4%. **Ethnic groups:** Akan 44%, Moshi-Dagomba 16%, Ewe 13%, Ga 8%, Gurma 3%, Yoruba 1%. **Principal languages:** English (official); about 75 African languages incl. Akan, Moshi-Dagomba, Ewe, and Ga. **Chief religions:** Christian 63%, indigenous beliefs 21%, Muslim 16%.

Geography: Total area: 92,456 sq mi, 239,460 sq km; **Land area:** 89,166 sq mi, 230,940 sq km. **Location:** On southern coast of W Africa. **Neighbors:** Côte d'Ivoire on W, Burkina Faso on N, Togo on E. **Topography:** Most of Ghana consists of low fertile plains and scrubland, cut by rivers and by the artificial Lake Volta. **Capital:** Accra, 1,847,000.

Government: Type: Republic. **Head of state and gov.:** Pres. John Agyekum Kufuor; b Dec. 8, 1938; in office: Jan. 7, 2001. **Local divisions:** 10 regions. **Defense budget** (2004): $22 mil. **Active troops:** 7,000.

Economy: Industries: mining, lumbering, light mfg., aluminum smelting, food proc. **Chief crops:** cocoa, rice, coffee, cassava, peanuts, corn, shea nuts, bananas. **Natural resources:** gold, timber, diamonds, bauxite, mang., fish, rubber, hydropower. **Crude oil reserves** (2004): 17 mil bbls. **Arable land:** 12%. **Livestock** (2004): cattle: 1.4 mil; chickens: 29.5 mil; goats: 3.6 mil; pigs: 300,000; sheep: 3.1 mil. **Fish catch** (2003): 391,694 metric tons. **Electricity prod.** (2003): 5.4 bil. kWh. **Labor force** (1999 est.): agriculture 60%, industry 15%, services 25%.

Finance: Monetary unit: Cedi (GHC) (Sept. 2005: 9,045.00 = $1 U.S.). **GDP** (2004 est.): $48.3 bil.; **per capita GDP:** $2,300; **GDP growth:** 5.4%. **Imports** (2004 est.): $3.7 bil.; partners (2004): Nigeria 12.8%, China 10.1%, UK 7%, US 6.7%, France 5.3%, South Africa 4.2%, Netherlands 4.2%, Germany 4.1%. **Exports** (2004 est.): $3.0 bil.; partners (2004): Netherlands 11.1%, UK 10.9%, France 6.9%, US 6%, Belgium 4.8%, Germany 4.4%, Japan 4.3%. **Tourism:** $414 mil. **Budget** (2004 est.): $2.6 bil. **Intl. reserves less gold:** $1.05 bil. **Gold:** 280,000 oz t. **Consumer prices:** 12.62%.

Transport: Railroad: Length: 592 mi. **Motor vehicles:** 91,200 pass. cars, 123,500 comm. vehicles. **Civil aviation:** 766,151 pass.-mi; 7 airports. **Chief ports:** Tema, Takoradi.

Communications: TV sets: 115 per 1,000 pop. **Radios:** 680 per 1,000 pop. **Telephone lines**: 302,300. **Daily newspaper circ.:** 14 per 1,000 pop. **Internet** (2002): 170,000 users.

Health: Life expect.: 57.7 male; 59.3 female. **Births** (per 1,000 pop.): 31.1. **Deaths** (per 1,000 pop.): 9.9. **Natural inc.:** 2.12%. **Infant mortality** (per 1,000 live births): 56.4. **AIDS rate:** 3.1%.

Education: Compulsory: ages 6-14. **Literacy:** 74.8%.

Major Intl. Organizations: UN and all of its specialized agencies, the Commonwealth, AU.

Embassy: 3512 International Dr. NW 20008; 686-4520.

Website: www.ghana.gov.gh

Named for an African empire along the Niger River, AD 400-1240, Ghana was ruled by Britain for 113 years as the Gold Coast. The UN in 1956 approved merger with the British Togoland trust territory. Independence came Mar. 6, 1957, and republic status within the Commonwealth in 1960.

Pres. Kwame Nkrumah built hospitals and schools, promoted development projects like the Volta R. hydroelectric and aluminum plants but ran the country into debt, jailed opponents, and was accused of corruption. A 1964 referendum gave Nkrumah dictatorial powers and set up a one-party socialist state. Nkrumah was overthrown in 1966 by a police-army coup, which expelled Chinese and East German teachers and technicians. Elections were held in 1969, but 4 further coups occurred in 1972, 1978, 1979, and 1981. The 1979 and 1981 coups, led by Flight Lieut. Jerry Rawlings, were followed by suspension of the constitution and banning of political parties. A new constitution, allowing multiparty politics, was approved in April 1992.

In Feb. 1993 more than 1,000 people were killed in ethnic clashes in northern Ghana. Rawlings won the presidential election of Dec. 7, 1996. Kofi Annan, a career UN diplomat from Ghana, became UN secretary general on Jan. 1, 1997. Opposition leader John Agyekum Kufuor won a runoff vote Dec. 28, 2000, and was sworn in Jan. 7, 2001, marking Ghana's 1st peaceful transfer of power from one elected president to another. He was reelected Dec. 7, 2004.

Greece

Hellenic Republic

People: Population: 10,668,354. **Age distrib.** (%): <15: 14.4; 65+: 18.8. **Pop. density:** 209 per sq mi, 81 per sq km. **Urban:** 60.8%. **Ethnic groups:** Greek 98%. **Principal languages:** Greek (official), English, French. **Chief religions:** Greek Orthodox 98% (official), Muslim 1%.

Geography: Total area: 50,942 sq mi, 131,940 sq km; **Land area:** 50,502 sq mi, 130,800 sq km. **Location:** Occupies southern end of Balkan Peninsula in SE Europe. **Neighbors:** Albania, Macedonia, Bulgaria on N; Turkey on E. **Topography:** About three-quarters of Greece is nonarable, with mountains in all areas. Pindus Mts. run through the country N to S. The heavily indented coastline is 9,385 mi. long. Of over 2,000 islands, only 169 are inhabited, among them Crete, Rhodes, Milos, Kerkira (Corfu), Chios, Lesbos, Samos, Euboea, Delos, Mykonos. **Capital:** Athens, 3,215,000 (1999 city proper: 748,110).

Government: Type: Parliamentary republic. **Head of state:** Pres. Karolos Papoulias; b June 4, 1929; in office: Mar. 10, 2005. **Head of gov.:** Prime Min. Konstantinos (Costas) Karamanlis; b Sept. 14, 1956; in office: Mar. 10, 2004. **Local divisions:** 13 regions comprising 51 prefectures. **Defense budget** (2004): $3.7 bil. **Active troops:** 170,800.

Economy: Industries: tourism, food & tobacco proc., textiles, chemicals, metal products, mining, oil. **Chief crops:** wheat, corn, barley, sugar beets, olives, tomatoes, grapes. **Natural resources:** bauxite, lignite, magnesite, oil, marble, hydropower potential. **Crude oil reserves** (2004): 7 mil bbls. **Arable land:** 19%. **Livestock** (2004): cattle: 624,000; chickens: 28 mil; goats: 5.4 mil; pigs: 948,000; sheep: 9.0 mil. **Fish catch** (2003): 194,592 metric tons. **Electricity prod.** (2003): 54.6 bil. kWh. **Labor force** (2004 est.): agriculture 12%, industry 20%, services 68%.

Finance: Monetary unit: Euro (EUR) (Sept. 2005: 0.80 = $1 U.S.). **GDP** (2004 est.): $226.4 bil.; **per capita GDP:** $21,300; **GDP growth:** 3.7%. **Imports** (2004 est.): $54.3 bil.; partners (2004): Germany 13.3%, Italy 12.6%, France 6.6%, Russia 5.4%, Netherlands 5.4%, South Korea 4.6%, US 4.4%, UK 4.1%. **Exports** (2004 est.): $15.5 bil.; partners (2004): Germany 13.3%, Italy 10.2%, UK 7.6%, Bulgaria 6.5%, US 5.2%, Cyprus 4.6%, Turkey 4.6%, France 4.2%. **Tourism:** $10,701 mil. **Budget** (2004 est.): $64.4 bil. **Intl. reserves less gold:** $767 mil. **Gold:** 3.46 mil. oz t. **Consumer prices:** 2.9%.

Transport: Railroad: Length: 1,598 mi. **Motor vehicles:** 3.42 mil pass. cars, 1.11 mil comm. vehicles. **Civil aviation:** 6.1 bil pass.-mi; 66 airports. **Chief ports:** Piraeus, Thessaloníki, Patrai.

Communications: TV sets: 480 per 1,000 pop. **Radios:** 475 per 1,000 pop. **Telephone lines:** 5.2 mil. **Daily newspaper circ.:** 22.4 per 1,000 pop. **Internet:** 1.7 mil. users.

Health: Life expect.: 76.6 male; 81.8 female. **Births** (per 1,000 pop.): 9.7. **Deaths** (per 1,000 pop.): 10.2. **Natural inc.:** –0.04%. **Infant mortality** (per 1,000 live births): 5.5. **AIDS rate:** 0.2%.

Education: Compulsory: ages 6-14. **Literacy:** 97.5%.

Major Intl. Organizations: UN (FAO, IBRD, ILO, IMF, IMO, WHO, WTrO), EU, NATO, OECD, OSCE.

Embassy: 2221 Massachusetts Ave. NW 20008; 939-1300.

Website: www.primeminister.gr/gr/lang/en/primeminister.asp

The achievements of ancient Greece in art, architecture, science, mathematics, philosophy, drama, literature, and democracy became legacies for succeeding ages. Greece reached the height of its glory and power, particularly in the Athenian city-state, in the 5th century BC. Greece fell under Roman rule in the 2d and 1st centuries BC. In the 4th century AD it became part of the Byzantine Empire and, after the fall of Constantinople to the Turks in 1453, part of the Ottoman Empire.

Greece won its war of independence from Turkey 1821-1829, and became a kingdom. A republic was established 1924; the monarchy was restored, 1935, and George II, King of the Hellenes, resumed the throne. In Oct. 1940, Greece rejected an ultimatum from Italy. Nazi support resulted in its defeat and occupation by Germans, Italians, and Bulgarians. By the end of 1944 the invaders withdrew. Communist resistance forces were defeated by Royalist and British troops. A plebiscite again restored the monarchy.

Communists waged guerrilla war 1947-49 against the government but were defeated with the aid of the U.S. A period of reconstruction and rapid development followed, mainly with conservative governments under Premier Constantine Karamanlis. The Center Union, led by George Papandreou, won elections in 1963 and 1964, but King Constantine, who acceded in 1964, forced Papandreou to resign. A period of political maneuvers ended in the military takeover of April 21, 1967, by Col. George Papadopoulos. King Constantine tried to reverse the consolidation of the harsh dictatorship Dec. 13, 1967, but failed and fled to Italy. Papadopoulos was ousted Nov. 25, 1973.

Greek army officers serving in the National Guard of Cyprus staged a coup on the island July 15, 1974. Turkey invaded Cyprus a week later, precipitating the collapse of the Greek junta, which was implicated in the Cyprus coup. Democratic government returned (and in 1975 the monarchy was abolished).

The 1981 electoral victory of the Panhellenic Socialist Movement (Pasok) of Andreas Papandreou brought substantial changes in Greece's internal and external policies. A scandal centered on George Kostokas, a banker and publisher, led to the arrest or investigation of leading Socialists, implicated Papandreou, and contributed to the defeat of the Socialists at the polls in 1989. However, Papandreou, who was narrowly acquitted Jan. 1992 of corruption charges, led the Socialists to a comeback victory in general elections Oct. 10, 1993.

Tensions between Greece and the Former Yugoslav Republic of Macedonia eased when the 2 countries agreed to normalize relations Sept. 13, 1995. The ailing Papandreou was replaced as prime minister by Costas Simitis, Jan. 18, 1996. Simitis led the Socialists to victory in the election of Sept. 22.

An earthquake that shook Athens Sept. 7, 1999, killed at least 143 people and left over 60,000 homeless. The Socialists retained power by a narrow margin in the elections of Apr. 9, 2000. Police in 2002 cracked down on the November 17 terrorist movement, blamed for 23 killings since the mid-1970s.

The conservative New Democracy Party won parliamentary elections, Mar. 7, 2004, and Konstantinos (Costas) Karamanlis became prime minister. Athens hosted the Olympic Summer Games, Aug. 13-29. A Cypriot jetliner crashed near Athens, Aug. 14, 2005, killing all 121 people on board.

Grenada

People: Population: 89,502. **Age distrib.** (%): <15: 33.9; 65+: 3.4. **Pop. density:** 673 per sq mi, 260 per sq km. **Urban:** 40.7%. **Ethnic groups:** Black 82%, Creole 13%. **Principal languages:** English (official), French patois. **Chief religions:** Roman Catholic 53%, Anglican 14%, other Protestant 33%.

Geography: Total area: 133 sq mi, 344 sq km; **Land area:** 133 sq mi, 344 sq km. **Location:** In Caribbean, 90 mi. N of Venezuela. **Neighbors:** Venezuela, Trinidid & Tobago to S; St. Vincent & the Grenadines to N. **Topography:** Main island is mountainous; country includes Carriacou and Petit Martinique islands. **Capital:** Saint George's, 33,000.

Government: Type: Parliamentary democracy. **Head of state:** Queen Elizabeth II, represented by Gov.-Gen. Daniel Williams; b Nov. 4, 1935; in office: Aug. 8, 1996. **Head of gov.:** Prime Min. Keith Mitchell; b Nov. 12, 1946; in office: June 22, 1995. **Local divisions:** 6 parishes, 1 dependency.

Economy: Industries: food, beverages, textiles, light assembly operations, tourism, constr. **Chief crops:** bananas, cocoa, nutmeg, mace, citrus, avocados. **Natural resources:** timber. **Arable land:** 15%. **Livestock** (2004): cattle: 4,450; chickens: 268,000; goats: 7,200; pigs: 5,850; sheep: 13,200. **Fish catch** (2003): 2,544 metric tons. **Electricity prod.** (2003): 0.16 bil. kWh. **Labor force** (1999 est.): agriculture 24%, industry 14%, services 62%.

Finance: Monetary unit: East Caribbean Dollar (XCD) (Sept. 2005: 2.67 = $1 U.S.). **GDP** (2002 est.): $440.0 mil; **per capita GDP:** $5,000; **GDP growth:** 2.5%. **Imports** (2004): US 27.7%, Trinidad and Tobago 25.4%, UK 5.2%. **Exports** (2002 est.): $46.0 mil; partners (2004): Saint Lucia 11.8%, US 11.6%, Netherlands 8.1%, Antigua and Barbuda 8%, Germany 7.7%, Saint Kitts and Nevis 7.2%, Dominica 7.2%, France 4.5%. **Tourism:** $104 mil. **Budget** (1997): $102.1 mil. **Intl. reserves less gold:** $78 mil. **Consumer prices** (changed in 2002): 1.1%.

Transport: Motor vehicles: 15,800 pass. cars, 4,200 comm. vehicles. **Civil aviation:** 3 airports. **Chief ports:** Saint George's, Grenville.

Communications: TV sets: 376 per 1,000 pop. **Radios:** 613 per 1,000 pop. **Telephone lines:** 32,600. **Internet:** 19,000 users.

Health: Life expect.: 62.7 male; 66.3 female. **Births** (per 1,000 pop.): 22.3. **Deaths** (per 1,000 pop.): 7.2. **Natural inc.:** 1.51%. **Infant mortality** (per 1,000 live births): 14.6.

Education: Compulsory: ages 5-16. **Literacy:** 98%.

Major Intl. Organizations: UN (FAO, IBRD, ILO, IMF, WHO, WTrO), Caricom, the Commonwealth, OAS, OECS.

Embassy: 1701 New Hampshire Ave. NW 20009; 265-2561.

Website: www.gov.gd

Columbus sighted Grenada in 1498. First European settlers were French, 1650. The island was held alternately by France and England until final British occupation, 1784. Grenada became fully independent Feb. 7, 1974, during a general strike. It is the smallest independent nation in the western hemisphere.

On Oct. 14, 1983, a military coup ousted Prime Minister Maurice Bishop, who was put under house arrest, later freed by supporters, rearrested, and, finally, on Oct. 19, executed. U.S. forces, with a token force from 6 area nations, invaded Grenada, Oct. 25. Resistance from the Grenadian army and Cuban advisors was quickly overcome as most people welcomed the invading forces. U.S. troops left Grenada in June 1985. Hurricane Ivan slammed into Grenada, Sept. 7, 2004, killing 39 people and damaging an estimated 90% of the buildings on the island.

Guatemala

Republic of Guatemala

People: Population: 12,013,907. **Age distrib.** (%): <15: 42.4; 65+: 3.3. **Pop. density:** 286 per sq mi, 110 per sq km. **Urban:** 46.3%. **Ethnic groups:** Mestizo 55%, Amerindian 43%. **Principal languages:** Spanish (official); more than 20 Amerindian languages, incl. Quiche, Cakchiquel, Kekchi, Mam, Garifuna, and Xinca. **Chief religions:** Mostly Roman Catholic; some Protestant, indigenous Mayan beliefs.

Geography: Total area: 42,043 sq mi, 108,890 sq km; **Land area:** 41,865 sq mi, 108,430 sq km. **Location:** In Central America. **Neighbors:** Mexico on N and W, El Salvador on S, Honduras and Belize on E. **Topography:** The central highland and mountain areas are bordered by the narrow Pacific coast and the lowlands and fertile river valleys on the Caribbean. There are numerous volcanoes in S, more than half a dozen over 11,000 ft. **Capital:** Guatemala City, 951,000.

Government: Type: Republic. **Head of state and gov.:** Pres. Oscar Berger Perdomo; b Aug. 11, 1946; in office: Jan. 14, 2004. **Local divisions:** 22 departments. **Defense budget** (2004): $160 mil. **Active troops:** 29,200.

Economy: Industries: sugar, textiles, clothing, furniture, chemicals, oil, metals, rubber, tourism. **Chief crops:** sugarcane, corn, bananas, coffee, beans, cardamom. **Natural resources:** oil, nickel, rare woods, fish, chicle, hydropower. **Crude oil reserves**

(2004): 526 mil bbls. **Arable land:** 12%. **Livestock** (2004): cattle: 2.5 mil; chickens: 27 mil; goats: 112,000; pigs: 780,000; sheep: 260,000. **Fish catch** (2003): 30,480 metric tons. **Electricity prod.** (2003): 6.9 bil. kWh. **Labor force** (1999 est.): agriculture 50%, industry 15%, services 35%.

Finance: Monetary unit: Quetzal (GTQ) (Sept. 2004: 7.57 = $1 U.S.). **GDP** (2004 est.): $59.5 bil.; **per capita GDP:** $4,200; **GDP growth:** 2.6%. **Imports** (2004 est.): $7.8 bil.; partners (2004): US 33.3%, Mexico 8.5%, South Korea 7.5%, El Salvador 5.2%, China 5%, Venezuela 4%. **Exports** (2004 est.): $2.9 bil.; partners (2004): US 55.6%, El Salvador 9.7%, Mexico 3.5%. **Tourism:** $621 mil. **Budget** (2004 est.): $3.4 bil. **Intl. reserves less gold:** $2.21 bil. **Gold:** 220,000 oz t. **Consumer prices:** 7.39%.

Transport: Railroad: Length: 551 mi. **Motor vehicles:** 646,500 pass. cars, 21,200 comm. vehicles. **Civil aviation:** 212,509 pass.-mi; 11 airports. **Chief ports:** Puerto Barrios, San Jose.

Communications: TV sets: 61 per 1,000 pop. **Radios:** 79 per 1,000 pop. **Telephone lines** (2002): 846,000. **Daily newspaper circ.:** 33 per 1,000 pop. **Internet** (2002): 400,000 users.

Health: Life expect.: 67.4 male; 70.8 female. **Births** (per 1,000 pop.): 30.6. **Deaths** (per 1,000 pop.): 5.3. **Natural inc.:** 2.53%. **Infant mortality** (per 1,000 live births): 32.0. **AIDS rate:** 1.1%.

Education: Compulsory: ages 7-15. **Literacy:** 70.6%.

Major Intl. Organizations: UN (FAO, IBRD, ILO, IMF, IMO, WHO, WTrO), OAS.

Embassy: 2220 R St. NW 20008; 745-4952.

Website: www.guatemala-embassy.org

The old Mayan Indian empire flourished in what is today Guatemala for over 1,000 years before the Spanish.

Guatemala was a Spanish colony 1524-1821; briefly a part of Mexico and then of the U.S. of Central America, the republic was established in 1839.

Since 1945 when a liberal government was elected to replace the long-term dictatorship of Jorge Ubico, the country has seen a variety of military and civilian governments and periods of civil war. Dissident army officers seized power Mar. 23, 1982, denouncing a presidential election as fraudulent and pledging to restore "authentic democracy" to the nation. Political violence caused large numbers of Guatemalans to seek refuge in Mexico. Another military coup occurred Oct. 8, 1983. The nation returned to civilian rule in 1986.

The crisis-ridden government of Pres. Jorge Serrano Elías was ousted by the military June 1, 1993. Ramiro de León Carpio was elected president by Congress June 6. A conservative businessman, Alvaro Arzú Irigoyen, won the presidency, Jan. 7, 1996. On Sept. 19 the Guatemalan government and leftist rebels approved a peace accord; the final agreement was signed Dec. 29. During more than 35 years of armed conflict, some 200,000 people were killed or "disappeared" (and are presumed dead); most of these casualties were attributed to the government and its paramilitary allies.

Violent episodes in 1998 included the daylight ambush of a busload of U.S. college students, Jan. 16, resulting in the rape of five young women, and the murder of Bishop Juan José Gerardi, a human rights activist, Apr. 26. U.S. Pres. Bill Clinton, on a visit to Guatemala Mar. 10, 1999, apologized for aid the U.S. had given to forces which he said "engaged in violence and widespread repression." Candidates of the right-wing populist Guatemalan Republican Front won control of Congress, Nov. 7, 1999, and the presidency, Dec. 26.

Drought and weak export prices during 2001-02 worsened the plight of Guatemala's poor, who make up 80% of the population. Oscar Berger Perdomo, the conservative former mayor of Guatemala City, won a presidential runoff election Dec. 28, 2003.

Guinea

Republic of Guinea

People: Population: 9,452,670. **Age distrib.** (%): <15: 44.4; 65+: 3.2. **Pop. density:** 100 per sq mi, 38 per sq km. **Urban:** 34.9%. **Ethnic groups:** Peuhl 40%, Malinke 30%, Soussou 20%. **Principal languages:** French (official); many African languages. **Chief religions:** Muslim 85%, Christian 8%, indigenous beliefs 7%.

Geography: Total area: 94,926 sq mi, 245,857 sq km; **Land area:** 94,926 sq mi, 245,857 sq km. **Location:** On Atlantic coast of W Africa. **Neighbors:** Guinea-Bissau, Senegal, Mali on N; Côte d'Ivoire on E; Liberia on S. **Topography:** A narrow coastal belt leads to the mountainous middle region, the source of the Gambia, Senegal, and Niger rivers. Upper Guinea, farther inland, is a cooler upland. The SE is forested. **Capital:** Conakry, 1,366,000.

Government: Type: Republic. **Head of state:** Pres. Gen. Lansana Conté; b 1934; in office: Apr. 5, 1984. **Head of gov.:** Prime Min. Cellou Dalein Diallo; b Feb. 3, 1952; in office: Dec. 9, 2004. **Local divisions:** 33 prefectures, 1 special zone. **Defense budget** (2004): $70 mil. **Active troops:** 9,700.

Economy: Industries: bauxite, gold, diamonds, aluminum refining, light mfg., agric. proc. **Chief crops:** rice, coffee, pineapples, palm kernels, cassava, bananas, sweet potatoes. **Natural resources:** bauxite, iron ore, diamonds, gold, uranium, hydropower, fish. **Arable land:** 2%. **Livestock** (2004): cattle: 3.3 mil; chickens: 14 mil; goats: 1.3 mil; pigs: 65,000; sheep: 1.1 mil. **Fish catch** (2003): 118,845 metric tons. **Electricity prod.** (2003): 0.78 bil. kWh. **Labor force** (2000 est.): agriculture 80%, industry and services 20%.

Finance: Monetary unit: Franc (GNF) (Sept. 2005: 3,780.00 = $1 U.S.). **GDP** (2004 est.): $19.5 bil.; **per capita GDP:** $2,100; **GDP growth:** 1%. **Imports** (2004 est.): $641.5 mil; partners (2004): France 14.6%, China 9.6%, Netherlands 6.8%, Belgium 6%, US 5.9%, Italy 5%, South Africa 4.6%, Côte d'Ivoire 4.3%, India 4%. **Exports** (2004 est.): $709.2 mil; partners (2004): South Korea 15.6%, Russia 13.1%, Spain 12.3%, Ireland 9.1%, US 7.5%, Germany 6.2%, France 5.9%, Ukraine 5.6%, Belgium 5.2%. **Tourism** (2000): $2 mil. **Budget** (2004 est.): $711.4 mil.

Transport: Railroad: Length: 693 mi. **Motor vehicles:** 23,200 pass. cars, 13,000 comm. vehicles. **Civil aviation:** 58,409 pass.-mi; 5 airports. **Chief port:** Conakry.

Communications: TV sets: 47 per 1,000 pop. **Radios:** 52 per 1,000 pop. **Telephone lines:** 26,200. **Internet:** 40,000 users.

Health: Life expect.: 48.2 male; 50.6 female. **Births** (per 1,000 pop.): 42.0. **Deaths** (per 1,000 pop.): 15.6. **Natural inc.:** 2.64%. **Infant mortality** (per 1,000 live births): 91.5. **AIDS rate:** 3.2%.

Education: Compulsory: ages 7-16. **Literacy:** 35.9%.

Major Intl. Organizations: UN and most of its specialized agencies, AU.

Embassy: 2112 Leroy Pl. NW 20008; 483-9420.

Website: guinea.usembassy.gov

Sékou Touré, Guinea's 1st president (1958-84), turned to Communist nations for support and set up a one-party state. Thousands of opponents were jailed in the 1970s, after an unsuccessful Portuguese invasion. Many were tortured and killed.

The military took control in a bloodless coup after the March 1984 death of Touré. A new constitution was approved in 1991, but movement toward democracy was slow. When presidential elections were finally held, in Dec. 1993, the incumbent, Gen. Lansana Conté, was the official winner; outside monitors called the elections flawed. Parliamentary elections June 11, 1995, raised similar complaints. Conté suppressed an army mutiny in Conakry, Feb. 2-3, 1996, and won reelection in Dec. 1998.

Fighting in early 2001 along the border with Liberia and Sierra Leone created a refugee crisis; as of mid-2004 more than 130,000 refugees, mostly Liberians, remained in Guinea. Major opposition parties boycotted the presidential election Dec. 21, 2003, in which the ailing Conté won 95.6% of the vote. After 2 months in office, Prime Min. François Fall resigned, Apr. 30, 2004, charging Conté with thwarting reform efforts.

Guinea-Bissau

Republic of Guinea-Bissau

People: Population: 1,413,446. **Age distrib.** (%): <15: 41.5; 65+: 3.0. **Pop. density:** 101 per sq mi, 39 per sq km. **Urban:** 34.0%. **Ethnic groups:** Balanta 30%, Fula 20%, Manjaca 14%, Mandinga 13%, Papel 7%. **Principal languages:** Portuguese (official), Crioulo, African languages. **Chief religions:** Indigenous beliefs 50%, Muslim 45%, Christian 5%.

Geography: Total area: 13,946 sq mi, 36,120 sq km; **Land area:** 10,811 sq mi, 28,000 sq km. **Location:** On Atlantic coast of W Africa. **Neighbors:** Senegal on N, Guinea on E and S. **Topography:** A swampy coastal plain covers most of the country; to the east is a low savanna region. **Capital:** Bissau, 336,000.

Government: Type: In transition. **Head of state:** Pres. Henrique Rosa; b. 1946; in office: Sept. 28, 2003 (interim). **Head of gov.:** Carlos Gomes Júnior; b 1949; in office: May 10, 2004. **Local divisions:** 9 regions. **Defense budget** (2002): $4 mil. **Active troops:** 9,250.

Economy: Industries: agric. proc., beer, soft drinks. **Chief crops:** rice, corn, beans, cassava, cashew nuts, peanuts, palm kernels, cotton. **Natural resources:** fish, timber, phosphates, bauxite, oil. **Arable land:** 11%. **Livestock** (2004): cattle: 520,000; chickens: 1.6 mil; goats: 330,000; pigs: 360,000; sheep: 290,000. **Fish catch** (2003): 5,000 metric tons. **Electricity prod.** (2003): 0.06 bil. kWh. **Labor force** (2000 est.): agriculture 82%.

Finance: Monetary unit: CFA Franc BCEAO (XOF) (Sept. 2005: 525.28 = $1 U.S.) **GDP** (2004 est.): $1.0 bil.; **per capita GDP:** $700; **GDP growth:** 2.6% **Imports** (2002 est.): $104.0 mil; partners (2004): Senegal 23.4%, Portugal 20.4%, China 8.2%, Netherlands 5.8%. **Exports** (2002 est.): $54.0 mil; partners (2004): India 54.9%, US 24.2%, Nigeria 12.7%, Italy 4.1%. **Tourism** (2002): $2 mil. **Intl. reserves less gold:** $146 mil. **Consumer prices:** 0.86%.

Transport: Motor vehicles: 3,500 pass. cars, 2,500 comm. vehicles. **Civil aviation:** 6,214 pass.-mi; 3 airports. **Chief port:** Bissau.

Communications: Radios: 43 per 1,000 pop. **Telephone lines:** 10,600. **Daily newspaper circ.:** 5.4 per 1,000 pop. **Internet:** 19,000 users.

Health: Life expect.: 44.8 male; 48.5 female. **Births** (per 1,000 pop.): 37.6. **Deaths** (per 1,000 pop.): 16.7. **Natural inc.:** 2.09%. **Infant mortality** (per 1,000 live births): 107.2.

Education: Compulsory: ages 7-12. **Literacy:** 42.4%.

Major Intl. Organizations: UN (FAO, IBRD, ILO, IMF, IMO, WHO, WTrO), AU.

Embassy: 15929 Yukon Lane, Rockville, MD 20855; 301-947-3958.

Website: www.state.gov/p/af/ci/pu

Portuguese mariners explored the area in the mid-15th century; the slave trade flourished in the 17th and 18th centuries, and colonization began in the 19th.

Beginning in the 1960s, an independence movement waged a guerrilla war and formed a government in the interior that had international support. Independence came Sept. 10, 1974, after the Portuguese regime was overthrown.

A November 1980 coup gave army chief João Bernardo Vieira absolute power. Vieira eventually initiated political liberalization; multiparty elections were held July 3, 1994. An army uprising June 7, 1998, triggered a civil war, with Senegal and Guinea aiding the Vieira regime. After a peace accord signed on Nov. 2 broke down, rebel troops ousted Vieira on May 7, 1999. Elections Nov. 28-29, 1999, and Jan. 16, 2000, brought a return of civilian rule. Top military officers staged an apparently bloodless coup Sept. 14, 2003. A caretaker government was installed Sept. 28, and legislative elections were held Mar. 2004. The ruling party's refusal to accept the results of a July 24, 2005, presidential runoff vote, apparently won by Vieira, triggered a new crisis.

Guyana

Co-operative Republic of Guyana

People: Population: 765,283. **Age distrib.** (%): <15: 26.4; 65+: 5.1. **Pop. density:** 9 per sq mi, 4 per sq km. **Urban:** 37.6%. **Ethnic groups:** East Indian 50%, black 36%, Amerindian 7%. **Principal languages:** English (official), Amerindian dialects, Creole, Hindi, Urdu. **Chief religions:** Christian 50%, Hindu 35%, Muslim 10%.

Geography: Total area: 83,000 sq mi, 214,970 sq km; **Land area:** 76,004 sq mi, 196,850 sq km. **Location:** On N coast of South America. **Neighbors:** Venezuela on W, Brazil on S, Suriname on E. **Topography:** Dense tropical forests cover much of the land, although a flat coastal area up to 40 mi. wide, where 90% of the population lives, provides rich alluvial soil for agriculture. A grassy savanna divides the 2 zones. **Capital:** Georgetown, 231,000.

Government: Type: Republic. **Head of state:** Pres. Bharrat Jagdeo; b Jan. 23, 1964; in office: Aug. 11, 1999. **Head of gov.:** Prime Min. Samuel Hinds; b Dec. 27, 1943; in office: Dec. 22, 1997. **Local divisions:** 10 regions. **Defense budget** (2004): $5.8 mil. **Active troops:** 1,600.

Economy: Industries: bauxite, sugar, rice milling, timber, textiles, gold mining. **Chief crops:** sugar, rice, wheat, vegetable oils. **Natural resources:** bauxite, gold, diamonds, hardwood timber, shrimp, fish. **Arable land:** 2%. **Livestock** (2004): cattle: 110,000; chickens: 21.3 mil; goats: 79,000; pigs: 20,000; sheep: 130,000. **Fish catch** (2003): 60,304 metric tons. **Electricity prod.** (2003): 0.78 bil. kWh. .

Finance: Monetary unit: Dollar (GYD) (Sept. 2005: 180.01 = $1 U.S.). **GDP** (2004 est.): $2.9 bil.; **per capita GDP:** $3,800; **GDP growth:** 1.9%. **Imports** (2004 est.): $650.1 mil; partners (2004): US 26.2%, Trinidad and Tobago 21.6%, UK 6.4%, Cuba 5.9%, China 4.7%. **Exports** (2004 est.): $570.2 mil; partners (2004): Canada 22.8%, US 19%, UK 12.1%, Portugal 8.2%, Jamaica 6.6%, Belgium 6.3%. **Tourism:** $39 mil. **Budget** (2004 est.): $371.6 mil. **Intl. reserves less gold:** $149 mil. **Consumer prices:** 4.67%.

Transport: Railroad: Length: 116 mi. **Motor vehicles:** 61,300 pass. cars, 15,500 comm. vehicles. **Civil aviation:** 108,740 pass.-mi; 8 airports. **Chief port:** Georgetown.

Communications: TV sets: 70 per 1,000 pop. **Radios:** 468 per 1,000 pop. **Telephone lines** (2002): 80,400. **Daily newspaper circ.:** 74.6 per 1,000 pop. **Internet** (2002): 125,000 users.

Health: Life expect.: 62.9 male; 68.3 female. **Births** (per 1,000 pop.): 18.5. **Deaths** (per 1,000 pop.): 8.3. **Natural inc.:** 1.01%. **Infant mortality** (per 1,000 live births): 33.3. **AIDS rate:** 2.5%.

Education: Compulsory: ages 6-15. **Literacy:** 98.8%.

Major Intl. Organizations: UN (FAO, IBRD, ILO, IMF, IMO, WHO, WTrO), Caricom, the Commonwealth, OAS.

Embassy: 2490 Tracy Place NW 20008; 265-6900.

Website: www.op.gov.gy

Guyana became a Dutch possession in the 17th century, but sovereignty passed to Britain in 1815. Indentured servants from India soon outnumbered African slaves. Ethnic tension has affected political life.

Guyana became independent May 26, 1966. A Venezuelan claim to the western half of Guyana was suspended in 1970 but renewed in 1982; an agreement was reached in 1989. The Suriname border is disputed. The government has nationalized most of the economy, which has remained severely depressed.

The Port Kaituma ambush of U.S. Rep. Leo J. Ryan and others investigating mistreatment of American followers of the Rev. Jim Jones's People's Temple cult triggered a mass suicide-execution of 911 cultists at Jonestown in the jungle, Nov. 18, 1978.

The People's National Congress, the party in power since Guyana became independent, was voted out of office with the election of Cheddi Jagan in Oct. 1992. When Pres. Jagan died Mar. 6, 1997, Prime Min. Samuel Hinds succeeded him. Jagan's widow, Janet, became prime min. Mar. 17. She won the presidency in a disputed election Dec. 15. She resigned because of ill health Aug. 11, 1999, and was succeeded by Bharrat Jagdeo, then 35, who became the youngest head of state in the Americas. He was reelected Mar. 19, 2001. Floods from torrential rains, Jan. 2005, affected about 40% of the population.

Haiti

Republic of Haiti

People: Population: 8,121,622. **Age distrib.** (%): <15: 42.6; 65+: 3.4. **Pop. density:** 758 per sq mi, 293 per sq km. **Urban:** 37.5%. **Ethnic groups:** Black 95%, Creole and other 5%. **Principal languages:** French, Creole (both official). **Chief religions:** Roman Catholic 80%, Protestant 16%; Voodoo widely practiced.

Geography: Total area: 10,714 sq mi, 27,750 sq km; **Land area:** 10,641 sq mi, 27,560 sq km. **Location:** In Caribbean, occupies western third of Isl. of Hispaniola. **Neighbors:** Dominican Republic on E, Cuba to W. **Topography:** About two-thirds of Haiti is mountainous. Much of the rest is semiarid. Coastal areas are warm and moist. **Capital:** Port-au-Prince, 1,961,000.

Government: Type: In transition. **Head of state:** Pres. Boniface Alexandre; b July 31, 1936; in office Feb. 29, 2004 (interim). **Head of gov.:** Gérard Latortue; b June 19, 1934; in office: Mar. 12, 2004. **Local divisions:** 9 departments. **Defense budget:** NA. **Active troops:** NA.

Economy: Industries: sugar refining, flour milling, textiles, cement, light assembly. **Chief crops:** coffee, mangoes, sugarcane, rice, corn, sorghum. **Natural resources:** bauxite, copper, calcium carbonate, gold, marble, hydropower. **Arable land:** 20%. **Livestock** (2004): cattle: 1.5 mil; chickens: 5.5 mil; goats: 1.9 mil; pigs: 1 mil; sheep: 153,500. **Fish catch** (2003): 5,000 metric tons. **Electricity prod.** (2003): 0.55 bil. kWh. **Labor force**: agriculture 66%, industry 9%, services 25%.

Finance: Monetary unit: Gourde (HTG) (Sept. 2005: 41.87 = $1 U.S.). **GDP** (2004 est.): $12.1 bil.; **per capita GDP:** $1,500; **GDP growth:** –3.5%. **Imports** (2004 est.): $1.1 bil.; partners (2004): US 52.9%, Dominican Republic 6%, Japan 2.9%. **Exports** (2004 est.): $338.1 mil; partners (2004): US 81.8%, Dominican Republic 7.2%, Canada 4.2%. **Tourism:** $93 mil. **Budget** (2004 est.): $529.6 mil. **Intl. reserves less gold:** $74 mil. **Consumer prices:** 22.81%.

Transport: Railroad: Length: 25 mi. **Motor vehicles:** 93,000 pass. cars, 61,600 comm. vehicles. **Civil aviation:** 2 airports. **Chief ports:** Port-au-Prince, Les Cayes, Cap-Haitien.

Communications: TV sets: 5 per 1,000 pop. **Radios:** 53 per 1,000 pop. **Telephone lines:** 140,000. **Daily newspaper circ.:** 2.5 per 1,000 pop. **Internet**: 150,000 users.

Health: Life expect.: 51.6 male; 54.3 female. **Births** (per 1,000 pop.): 36.6. **Deaths** (per 1,000 pop.): 12.3. **Natural inc.:** 2.43%. **Infant mortality** (per 1,000 live births): 73.5. **AIDS rate:** 5.6%.

Education: Compulsory: ages 6-11. **Literacy:** 52.9%.

Major Intl. Organizations: UN and most of its specialized agencies, OAS.

Embassy: 2311 Massachusetts Ave. NW 20008; 332-4090.

Website: www.haiti.org

Haiti, visited by Columbus, 1492, and a French colony from 1697, attained its independence, 1804, following the rebellion led by former slave Toussaint L'Ouverture. After a period of political violence, the U.S. occupied the country 1915-34.

François Duvalier, known as Papa Doc, was elected president in Sept. 1957; in 1964 he was named president for life. Upon his death in 1971, he was succeeded by his son, Jean Claude Duvalier, known as Baby Doc. Following several weeks of unrest, Jean Claude fled Haiti aboard a U.S. Air Force jet Feb. 7, 1986, ending the 28-year dictatorship by the Duvalier family.

Father Jean-Bertrand Aristide was elected president Dec. 1990, but in Sept. 1991, he was arrested by the military and expelled from the country. Some 35,000 Haitian refugees were intercepted by the U.S. Coast Guard as they tried to enter the U.S., 1991-92. Most were returned to Haiti. There was a new upsurge of refugees starting in late 1993.

The UN Security Council authorized, July 31, 1994, an invasion of Haiti by a multinational force. With U.S. troops already en route, a full-scale invasion was averted, Sept. 18, when military leaders agreed to step down. Aristide returned to Haiti and was restored in office Oct. 15. A UN peacekeeping force exercised responsibility in Haiti from Mar. 31, 1995 to Nov. 30, 1997. Aristide transferred power to his elected successor, René Préval, on Feb. 7, 1996.

At least 140 people died and more than 160,000 became homeless when Hurricane Georges struck Haiti Sept. 22, 1998. Aristide won the presidency Nov. 26, 2000, in an election boycotted by opposition groups. An armed uprising in early 2004 and pressure from France and the U.S. toppled Aristide, who went into exile Feb. 29. A US-led contingent, sent in after the upheaval, yielded authority June 1 to a UN stabilization force (MINUSTAH); expanded June 22, 2005, in anticipation of Oct.-Dec. elections, MINUSTAH had some 7,500 troops and 1,900 police.

Poverty, political violence, and government corruption have plagued Haiti for decades. Health officials estimate that at least 30,000 Haitians die each year of AIDS-related illness. Flooding in late May 2004 killed more than 1,000 people, and more than 2,400 were killed in Tropical Storm Jeanne in Sept. 2004.

Honduras

Republic of Honduras

People: Population: 7,167,902. **Age distrib.** (%): <15: 40.8; 65+: 3.7. **Pop. density:** 166 per sq mi, 64 per sq km. **Urban:** 45.6%. **Ethnic groups:** Mestizo 90%, Amerindian 7%, Black 2%, White 1%. **Principal languages:** Spanish (official), Garífuna, Amerindian dialects. **Chief religion:** Roman Catholic 97%.

Geography: Total area: 43,278 sq mi, 112,090 sq km; **Land area:** 43,201 sq mi, 111,890 sq km. **Location:** In Central America. **Neighbors:** Guatemala on W, El Salvador and Nicaragua on S. **Topography:** The Caribbean coast is 500 mi. long. Pacific coast, on Gulf of Fonseca, is 40 mi. long. Honduras is mountainous, with wide fertile valleys and rich forests. **Capital:** Tegucigalpa, 1,007,000.

Government: Type: Republic. **Head of state:** Pres. Ricardo Maduro; b Apr. 20, 1946; in office: Jan. 27, 2002. **Local divisions:** 18 departments. **Defense budget** (2004): $52 mil. **Active troops:** 12,000.

Economy: Industries: sugar, coffee, textiles, clothing, wood products. **Chief crops:** bananas, coffee, citrus. **Natural resources:** timber, gold, silver, copper, lead, zinc, iron ore, antimony, coal, fish, hydropower. **Arable land:** 15%. **Livestock** (2004): cattle: 1.8 mil; chickens: 18.7 mil; goats: 32,200; pigs: 478,000; sheep: 12,500. **Fish catch** (2003): 30,835 metric tons. **Electricity prod.** (2003): 4.3 bil. kWh. **Labor force** (2001 est.): agriculture 34%, industry 21%, services 45%.

Finance: Monetary unit: Lempira (HNL) (Sept. 2005: 18.86 = $1 U.S.). **GDP** (2004 est.): $18.8 bil.; **per capita GDP:** $2,800; **GDP growth:** 4.2%. **Imports** (2004 est.): $3.3 bil.; partners (2004): US 51.3%, El Salvador 3.3%, Mexico 2.9%. **Exports** (2004 est.): $1.5 bil.; partners (2004): US 63.3%, El Salvador 2.8%, Guatemala 2.6%. **Tourism:** $337 mil. **Budget** (2004 est.): $1.7 bil. **Intl. reserves less gold:** $1.27 bil. **Gold:** 20,000 oz t. **Consumer prices:** 8.11%.

Transport: Railroad: Length: 434 mi. **Motor vehicles:** 46,000 pass. cars, 39,300 comm. vehicles. **Civil aviation:** 189.5 mil pass.-mi.; 12 airports. **Chief ports:** Puerto Cortes, La Ceiba.

Communications: TV sets: 95 per 1,000 pop. **Radios:** 410 per 1,000 pop. **Telephone lines**: 334,400. **Daily newspaper circ.:** 55 per 1,000 pop. **Internet**: 272,300 users.

Health: Life expect.: 67.7 male; 71.0 female. **Births** (per 1,000 pop.): 28.9. **Deaths** (per 1,000 pop.): 5.3. **Natural inc.:** 2.36%. **Infant mortality** (per 1,000 live births): 26.5. **AIDS rate:** 1.8%.

Education: Compulsory: ages 7-12. **Literacy:** 76.2%.

Major Intl. Organizations: UN, (FAO, IBRD, ILO, IMF, IMO, WHO, WTrO), OAS.

Embassy: 3007 Tilden St. NW, Suite 4M, 20008; 966-7702.

Website: www.hondurasemb.org

Mayan civilization flourished in Honduras in the 1st millennium AD. Columbus arrived in 1502. Honduras became independent after freeing itself from Spain, 1821, and from the Fed. of Central America, 1838.

Gen. Oswaldo Lopez Arellano, president for most of the period 1963-75 by virtue of one election and 2 coups, was ousted by the army in 1975 over charges of pervasive bribery by United Brands Co. of the U.S. An elected civilian government took power in 1982. Some 3,200 U.S. troops were sent to Honduras after the Honduran border was violated by Nicaraguan forces, Mar. 1988.

Already one of the poorest countries in the western hemisphere, Honduras was devastated in late Oct. 1998 by Hurricane Mitch, which killed at least 5,600 people and caused more than $850 million in damage to crops and livestock.

Ricardo Maduro, a businessman who pledged to crack down on crime, won the presidency Nov. 25, 2001. A fire May 17, 2004, killed 104 inmates at an overcrowded prison in San Pedro Sula. Gunmen in that city Dec. 23 killed 28 passengers on a bus.

Hungary

Republic of Hungary

People: Population: 10,006,835. **Age distrib.** (%): <15: 15.8; 65+: 15.1. **Pop. density:** 279 per sq mi, 108 per sq km. **Urban:** 65.1%. **Ethnic groups:** Hungarian 90%, Roma 4%, German 3%, Serb 2%. **Principal languages:** Hungarian (official), Romani, German, Slavic languages, Romanian. **Chief religions:** Roman Catholic 52%, Calvinist 16%.

Geography: Total area: 35,919 sq mi, 93,030 sq km; **Land area:** 35,653 sq mi, 92,340 sq km. **Location:** In E central Europe. **Neighbors:** Slovakia, Ukraine on N; Austria on W; Slovenia, Yugoslavia, Croatia on S; Romania on E. **Topography:** The Danube R. forms the Slovak border in the NW, then swings S to bisect the country. The eastern half of Hungary is mainly a great fertile plain, the Alfold; the W and N are hilly. **Capital:** Budapest, 1,708,000.

Government: Type: Parliamentary democracy. **Head of state:** Pres. László Sólyom; b Jan. 3, 1942; in office: Aug. 5, 2005. **Head of gov.:** Prime Min. Ferenc Gyurcsány; b June 4, 1961; in office: Sept. 29, 2004. **Local divisions:** 19 counties, 20 urban counties, 1 capital. **Defense budget** (2002): $1.08 bil. **Active troops:** 33,400.

Economy: Industries: mining, metallurgy, constr. materials, proc. foods, textiles, pharm., auto. **Chief crops:** wheat, corn, sunflower seed, potatoes, sugar beets. **Natural resources:** bauxite, coal, nat. gas, fertile soils. **Crude oil reserves** (2004): 102 mil bbls. **Arable land:** 51%. **Livestock** (2004): cattle: 739,000; chickens: 37.5 mil; goats: 140,000; pigs: 4.9 mil; sheep: 1.3 mil. **Fish catch** (2003): 18,406 metric tons. **Electricity prod.** (2003): 32.2 bil. kWh. **Labor force** (2002): agriculture 6.2%, industry 27.1%, services 66.7%.

Finance: Monetary unit: Forint (HUF) (Sept. 2005: 194.57 = $1 U.S.). **GDP** (2004 est.): $149.3 bil.; **per capita GDP:** $14,900; **GDP growth:** 3.9%. **Imports** (2004 est.): $58.7 bil.; partners (2004): Germany 29.2%, Austria 8.3%, Russia 5.7%, Italy 5.5%, Netherlands 4.9%, China 4.8%, France 4.7%. **Exports** (2004 est.): $54.6 bil.; partners (2004): Germany 31.4%, Austria 6.8%, France 5.7%, Italy 5.6%, UK 5.1%. **Tourism:** $3,440 mil. **Budget** (2004 est.): $51.4 bil. **Intl. reserves less gold:** $10.24 bil. **Gold:** 100,000 oz t. **Consumer prices:** 6.78%.

Transport: Railroad: Length: 4,893 mi. **Motor vehicles** 2.6295 mil pass. cars, 399,300 comm. vehicles. **Civil aviation:** 2.0 bil pass.-mi; 17 airport.

Communications: TV sets: 447 per 1,000 pop. **Radios:** 690 per 1,000 pop. **Telephone lines:** 3.6 mil. **Daily newspaper circ.:** 465.5 per 1,000 pop. **Internet**: 2.4 mil. users.

Health: Life expect.: 68.2 male; 76.9 female. **Births** (per 1,000 pop.): 9.8. **Deaths** (per 1,000 pop.): 13.2. **Natural inc.:** –0.34%. **Infant mortality** (per 1,000 live births): 8.6. **AIDS rate:** 0.1%.

Education: Compulsory: ages 7-16. **Literacy:** 99.4%.

Major Intl. Organizations: UN (FAO, IBRD, ILO, IMF, IMO, WHO, WTrO), EU, NATO, OECD, OSCE.

Embassy: 3910 Shoemaker St. NW 20008; 362-6730.

Website: www.hungary.hu

Earliest settlers, chiefly Slav and Germanic, were overrun by Magyars from the E. Stephen I (997-1038) was made king by Pope Sylvester II in AD 1000. The country suffered repeated Turkish invasions in the 15th-17th centuries. After the defeats of the Turks, 1686-1697, Austria dominated, but Hungary obtained concessions until it regained internal independence in 1867, with the emperor of Austria as king of Hungary in a dual monarchy with a single diplomatic service. Defeated with the Central Powers in 1918, Hungary lost Transylvania to Romania, Croatia and Bacska to Yugoslavia, Slovakia and Carpatho-Ruthenia to Czechoslovakia, all of which had large Hungarian minorities. A republic under Michael Karolyi and a bolshevist revolt under Bela Kun were followed by a vote for a monarchy in 1920 with Admiral Nicholas Horthy as regent.

Hungary joined Germany in World War II, and was allowed to annex most of its lost territories. Russian troops captured the country, 1944-1945. By terms of an armistice with the Allied powers Hungary agreed to give up territory acquired by the 1938 dismemberment of Czechoslovakia and to return to its borders of 1937.

A republic was declared Feb. 1, 1946; Zoltan Tildy was elected president. In 1947 the Communists forced Tildy out. Premier Imre Nagy, who had been in office since mid-1953, was ousted for his moderate policy of favoring agriculture and consumer production, April 18, 1955.

In 1956, popular demands to oust Erno Gero, Communist Party secretary, and for formation of a government by Nagy, resulted in the latter's appointment Oct. 23; demonstrations against Communist rule developed into open revolt. On Nov. 4 Soviet forces launched a massive attack against Budapest with 200,000 troops, 2,500 tanks and armored cars.

About 200,000 persons fled the country. Thousands were arrested and executed, including Nagy in June 1958. In spring 1963 the regime freed many captives from the 1956 revolt.

Hungarian troops participated in the 1968 Warsaw Pact invasion of Czechoslovakia. Major economic reforms were launched early in 1968, switching from a central planning system to one based on market forces and profit.

In 1989 Parliament legalized freedom of assembly and association as Hungary shifted away from Communism. In Oct. the Communist Party was formally dissolved. The last Soviet troops left Hungary June 19, 1991. Hungary became a full member of NATO Mar. 12, 1999, and of the European Union May 1, 2004.

Iceland

Republic of Iceland

People: Population: 296,737. **Age distrib.** (%): <15: 22.1; 65+: 11.7. **Pop. density:** 7 per sq mi, 3 per sq km. **Urban:** 92.8%. **Ethnic groups:** Icelandic 94%. **Principal languages:** Icelandic (official) **Chief religion:** Evangelical Lutheran 86% (official).

Geography: Total area: 39,769 sq mi, 103,000 sq km; **Land area:** 38,707 sq mi, 100,250 sq km. **Location:** Isl. at N end of Atlantic O. **Neighbors:** Nearest is Greenland (Den.), to W. **Topography:** Recent volcanic origin. Three-quarters of the surface is wasteland: glaciers, lakes, a lava desert. There are geysers and hot springs, and the climate is moderated by the Gulf Stream. **Capital:** Reykjavík, 184,000.

Government: Type: Constitutional republic. **Head of state:** Pres. Olafur Ragnar Grímsson; b May 14, 1943; in office: Aug. 1, 1996. **Head of gov.:** Prime Min. Halldór Ásgrímsson; b Sept. 8, 1947; in office: Sept. 15, 2004. **Local divisions:** 23 counties, 14 independent towns. **Defense budget:** Icelandic Defense Force provided by the U.S.

Economy: Industries: fish proc., aluminum smelting, ferrosilicon prod., tourism. **Chief crops:** potatoes, turnips. **Natural resources:** fish, hydropower, geothermal power, diatomite. **Livestock** (2004): cattle: 68,000; chickens: 210,000; goats: 361;

pigs: 44,000; sheep: 470,000. **Fish catch** (2003): 1,984,349 metric tons. **Electricity prod.** (2003): 8.4 bil. kWh. **Labor force** (2003): agriculture, fishing and fish processing 10.3%, industry 18.3%, services 71.4%.

Finance: Monetary unit: Krona (ISK) (Sept. 2005: 61.38 = $1 U.S.). **GDP** (2004 est.): $9.4 bil.; **per capita GDP:** $31,900; **GDP growth:** 1.8%. **Imports** (2004 est.): $3.3 bil.; partners (2004): Germany 12.3%, US 10%, Norway 9.8%, Denmark 7.6%, UK 6.9%, Sweden 6.4%, Netherlands 5.7%. **Exports** (2004 est.): $2.9 bil.; partners (2004): UK 19.1%, Germany 17.1%, Netherlands 11%, US 10.2%, Spain 6.9%, Denmark 4.6%. **Tourism:** $319 mil. **Budget** (2004 est.): $4.1 bil. **Intl. reserves less gold:** $674 mil. **Gold:** 60,000 oz t. **Consumer prices:** 2.8%.

Transport: Motor vehicles: 161,700 pass. cars, 21,900 comm. vehicles. **Civil aviation:** 2.3 bil pass.-mi; 13 airports. **Chief port:** Reykjavík.

Communications: TV sets: 505 per 1,000 pop. **Radios:** 1,075 per 1,000 pop. **Telephone lines:** 190,700. **Daily newspaper circ.:** 335.7per 1,000 pop. **Internet**: 195,000 users.

Health: Life expect.: 78.1 male; 82.3 female. **Births** (per 1,000 pop.): 13.7. **Deaths** (per 1,000 pop.): 6.7. **Natural inc.:** 0.71%. **Infant mortality** (per 1,000 live births): 3.3. **AIDS rate:** 0.2%.

Education: Compulsory: ages 6-16. **Literacy:** 99.9%.

Major Intl. Organizations: UN (FAO, IBRD, ILO, IMF, IMO, WHO, WTrO), EFTA, NATO, OECD, OSCE.

Embassy: 1156 15th St. NW, Ste. 1200, 20005; 265-6653.

Website: www.iceland.is

Iceland was an independent republic from 930 to 1262, when it joined with Norway. Its language has maintained its purity for 1,000 years. Danish rule lasted from 1380-1918; the last ties with the Danish crown were severed in 1941. The Althing, or assembly, is the world's oldest surviving parliament.

India

Republic of India

People: Population: 1,080,264,388. **Age distrib.** (%): <15: 31.2; 65+: 4.9. **Pop. density:** 851 per sq mi, 329 per sq km. **Urban:** 28.3%. **Ethnic groups:** Indo-Aryan 72%, Dravidian 25%. **Principal languages:** Hindi, English, Bengali, Telugu, Marathi, Tamil, Urdu, Gujarati, Malayalam, Kannada, Oriya, Punjabi, Assamese, Kashmiri, Sindhi, and Sanskrit (all official); Hindustani, a mix of Hindi and Urdu spoken in the north, is popular but not official. **Chief religions:** Hindu 81%, Muslim 13%, Christian 2%, Sikh 2%.

Geography: Total area: 1,269,346 sq mi, 3,287,590 sq km; **Land area:** 1,147,955 sq mi, 2,973,190 sq km. **Location:** Occupies most of the Indian subcontinent in S Asia. **Neighbors:** Pakistan on W; China, Nepal, Bhutan on N; Myanmar, Bangladesh on E. **Topography:** The Himalaya Mts., highest in world, stretch across India's northern borders. Below, the Ganges Plain is wide, fertile, and among the most densely populated regions of the world. The area below includes the Deccan Peninsula. Close to one quarter of the area is forested. The climate varies from tropical heat in S to near-Arctic cold in N. Rajasthan Desert is in NW; NE Assam Hills get 400 in. of rain a year. **Capital:** New Delhi (2001 city est.), 300,000. **Cities (urban aggr.):** Mumbai (Bombay), 16,086,000; Kolkata (Calcutta), 13,058,000; Delhi 12,441,000; Hyderabad, 5,445,000; Chennai (Madras), 6,353,000; Bangalore, 5,567,000.

Government: Type: Federal republic. **Head of state:** Pres. A. P. J. Abdul Kalam; b Oct. 15, 1931; in office: July 25, 2002. **Head of gov.:** Prime Min. Manmohan Singh; b Sept. 26, 1932; in office May 22, 2004. **Local divisions:** 28 states, 6 union territories, 1 national capital territory. **Defense budget** (2004): $19.1 bil. **Active troops:** 1,325,000.

Economy: Industries: textiles, chemicals, food proc., steel, transp. equip., cement, mining, oil, machinery, software. **Chief crops:** rice, wheat, oilseed, cotton, jute, tea, sugarcane, potatoes. **Natural resources:** coal, iron ore, mang., mica, bauxite, titanium ore, chromite, nat. gas, diamonds, oil, limestone. **Crude oil reserves** (2004): 5.4 bil. bbls. **Arable land:** 56%. **Livestock** (2004): cattle:185.5 mil; chickens: 425 mil; goats: 120 mil; pigs: 14.3 mil; sheep: 62.5 mil. **Fish catch** (2004): cattle: 185.5 mil; chickens: 425,000; goats: 120.0 mil; pigs: 14.3 mil; sheep: 62.5 mil. **Fish catch** (2003): 5,904,584 metric tons. **Electricity prod.** (2003): 556.8 bil. kWh. **Labor force** (1999): agriculture 60%, industry 17%, services 23%.

Finance: Monetary unit: Rupee (INR) (Sept. 2005: 43.97 = $1 U.S.). **GDP** (2004 est.): $3.3 tril.; **per capita GDP:** $3,100; **GDP growth:** 6.2%. **Imports** (2004 est.): $89.3 bil.; partners (2004): US 7%, Belgium 6.1%, China 5.9%, Singapore 4.8%, Australia 4.6%, UK 4.6%, Germany 4.5%. **Exports** (2004 est.): $69.2 bil.; partners (2004): US 18.4%, China 7.8%, UAE 6.7%, UK 4.8%, Hong Kong 4.3%, Germany 4%. **Tourism:** $3,522 mil. **Budget** (2004 est.): $104.0 bil. **Intl. reserves less gold:** $81.52 bil. **Gold:** 11.5 mil. oz t. **Consumer prices:** 3.77%.

Transport: Railroad: Length: 39,468 mi. **Motor vehicles:** 6.04 mil pass. cars, 8.44 mil comm. vehicles. **Civil aviation:** 16.0 bil pass.-mi; 232 airports. **Chief ports:** Kolkata (Calcutta), Mumbai (Bombay), Chennai (Madras), Vishakhapatnam, Kandla.

Communications: TV sets: 75 per 1,000 pop. **Radios:** 120 per 1,000 pop. **Telephone lines:** 48.9 mil. **Daily newspaper circ.:** 60.5 per 1,000 pop. **Internet**: 18.5 mil. users.

Health: Life expect.: 63.6 male; 65.2 female. **Births** (per 1,000 pop.): 22.3. **Deaths** (per 1,000 pop.): 8.3. **Natural inc.:** 1.40%. **Infant mortality** (per 1,000 live births): 56.3. **AIDS rate:** 0.9%.

Education: Compulsory: ages 6-14. **Literacy:** 59.5%.

Major Intl. Organizations: UN (FAO, IBRD, ILO, IMF, IMO, WHO, WTrO), the Commonwealth.

Embassy: 2107 Massachusetts Ave. NW 20008; 939-7000.

Website: indiaimage.nic.in

India has one of the oldest civilizations in the world. Excavations trace the Indus Valley civilization back for at least 5,000 years. Paintings in the mountain caves of Ajanta, richly carved temples, the Taj Mahal in Agra, and the Kutab Minar in Delhi are among relics of the past.

Aryan tribes, speaking Sanskrit, invaded from the NW around 1500 BC. Asoka ruled most of the Indian subcontinent in the 3d century BC, and established Buddhism. But Hinduism revived and eventually predominated. Under the Guptas, 4th-6th century AD, science, literature, and the arts enjoyed a "golden age."

Arab invaders established a Muslim foothold in the W in the 8th century, and Turkish Muslims gained control of North India by 1200. The Mogul emperors ruled 1526-1857.

Vasco da Gama established Portuguese trading posts 1498-1503. The Dutch followed. The British East India Co. sent Capt. William Hawkins, 1609, to get concessions from the Mogul emperor for spices and textiles. Operating as the East India Co. the British gained control of most of India. The British parliament assumed political direction; under Lord Bentinck, 1828-35, rule by rajahs was curbed. After the Sepoy troops mutinied, 1857-58, the British supported the native rulers.

Nationalism grew rapidly after World War I. The Indian National Congress and the Muslim League demanded constitutional reform. A leader emerged in Mohandas K. Gandhi (called Mahatma, or Great Soul), born Oct. 2, 1869, assassinated Jan. 30, 1948. He advocated self-rule, nonviolence, and removal of the caste system of untouchability. In 1930 he launched a program of civil disobedience, including a boycott of British goods and rejection of taxes without representation.

In 1935 Britain gave India a constitution providing a bicameral federal congress. Muhammad Ali Jinnah, head of the Muslim League, sought creation of a Muslim nation, Pakistan.

The British government partitioned British India into the dominions of India and Pakistan. India became a member of the UN in 1945, a self-governing member of the Commonwealth in 1947, and a democratic republic, Jan. 26, 1950. More than 12 million Hindu and Muslim refugees crossed the India-Pakistan borders in a mass transferal of some of the 2 peoples during 1947; about 200,000 were killed in communal fighting.

After Pakistan troops began attacks on Bengali separatists in East Pakistan, Mar. 25, 1971, some 10 million refugees fled into India. India and Pakistan went to war Dec. 3, 1971, on both the East and West fronts. Pakistan troops in the east surrendered Dec. 16; Pakistan agreed to a cease-fire in the west Dec. 17.

Indira Gandhi, India's prime minister since Jan. 1966, invoked emergency powers in June 1975. Thousands of opponents were arrested and press censorship imposed. These and other actions, including enforcement of coercive birth control measures in some areas, were widely resented. Opposition parties, united in the Janata coalition, turned Gandhi's New Congress Party from power in federal and state parliamentary elections in 1977.

Gandhi became prime minister for the second time, Jan. 14, 1980. She was assassinated by 2 of her Sikh bodyguards Oct. 31, 1984, in response to the government suppression of a Sikh uprising in Punjab in June 1984, which included an assault on the Golden Temple at Amritsar, the holiest Sikh shrine. Widespread rioting followed the assassination; thousands of Sikhs were killed and some 50,000 left homeless. Rajiv, Indira Gandhi's son, replaced her as prime minister. He was swept from office in 1989 amid charges of incompetence and corruption, and assassinated May 21, 1991, while campaigning to regain power.

A gas leak at a Union Carbide chemical plant in Bhopal, in Dec. 1984, eventually killed an estimated 14,000 people. A lawsuit settled in 1989 provided $470 mil. in compensation to victims; in 2002 an Indian High Court upheld a culpable homicide conviction against former UC chairman Warren Anderson.

Many died in religious, ethnic, and political conflicts during the 1980s and '90s. To suppress the Sikh insurgency in Punjab, Indian government troops attacked the Golden Temple again in 1988. Nationwide riots followed the destruction of a 16th-century mosque by Hindu militants in Dec. 1992. Ethnic clashes in Assam in NW India, killed thousands in Feb. 1993. In the biggest wave of criminal violence in Indian history, a series of bombs jolted Bombay and Calcutta, Mar. 12-19, 1993, killing over 300.

Mother Teresa of Calcutta, renowned for her work among the poor, died Sept. 5, 1997. India's 1st lowest-caste president, K. R. Narayanan, took office July 25. The Hindu nationalist Bharatiya Janata Party (BJP) won enough seats in parliamentary elections, Feb. 1998, to form a government. Atal Bihari Vajpayee was sworn in as prime minister Mar. 19. India conducted a series of nuclear tests in mid-May, drawing wide condemnation and raising tensions with Pakistan.

An alliance led by Vajpayee won a majority in legislative elections, Sept. 5-Oct. 3, 1999. A cyclone that hit the state of Orissa, E India, on Oct. 29, 1999, left some 10,000 people dead. A powerful earthquake in Gujarat state on Jan. 26, 2001, claimed more than

20,000 lives. India blamed Pakistani-sponsored terrorist groups for an Oct. 1 suicide attack on the state legislature in Jammu and Kashmir (see below), in which at least 40 people died, and a Dec. 13 assault on the Indian parliament in New Delhi Dec. 13, which left 13 people dead. Hindu-Muslim clashes in Gujarat Feb. 27-Mar. 11, 2002, claimed more than 700 lives. A. P. J. Abdul Kalam, a Muslim scientist who spearheaded India's nuclear weapons program, became president July 25.

Two bombs in Mumbai, Aug. 25, 2003, killed more than 50 people; Indian authorities blamed Muslim militants. Led by Rajiv Gandhi's Italian-born widow, Sonia, the Congress Party won the most seats in parliamentary elections Apr.-May 2004. When Hindu nationalists objected to her candidacy, she chose not to become prime minister, and Manmohan Singh, a Sikh economist, took office instead.

The Indian Ocean tsunami of Dec. 26, 2004, left more than 10,700 people dead, some 5,600 missing, and over 647,000 displaced. Meeting at the White House with Prime Min. Singh, July 18, 2005, U.S. Pres. George Bush agreed to seek removal of a ban on sales of civilian nuclear technology to India.

Despite robust economic growth since the 1990s, especially in high-technology industries, nearly 80% of India's population still earns less than $2 per day.

Sikkim, bordered by Tibet, Bhutan, and Nepal, formerly British protected, became a protectorate of India in 1950. Area, 2,740 sq. mi; pop. (2001 census) 540,493; capital: Gangtok. In Sept. 1974, India's parliament voted to make Sikkim an associate Indian state, absorbing it into India.

Kashmir is a predominantly Muslim region in the NW that borders India, Pakistan, Afghanistan, and China. Originally a Hindu kingdom, Muslim rule began in 1341; after almost 200 years under the Moguls, the area was incorporated into British India in 1846. Fighting broke out in the region between India and Pakistan in 1947 following independence from Britain. A cease-fire was negotiated by the UN Jan. 1, 1949; it gave Pakistan control of one-third of the area as Azad Kashmir, in the west and northwest, and India the remaining two-thirds, as the Indian state of Jammu and Kashmir. It is India's only Muslim-majority state. Area: 39,146 sq. mi.; pop. 10,000,000, 2001 cens.; capitals: Srinagar (summer) and Jammu (winter). Fighting returned to the area during the 1965 and 1971 wars with Pakistan. China occupied about 14,000 sq. miles in the Ladakh district after a war with India in 1962.

In the 1990s there were repeated clashes between Indian army troops and separatist fighters triggered by India's decision to impose central government rule. The clashes strained relations between India and Pakistan, which India charged was aiding the separatists; fighting was especially heavy in May-June 1999. As 2002 began, some 1 million Indian and Pakistani troops faced each other across the "line of control" that divides Kashmir. Tensions escalated when Muslin gunmen May 14 killed 34 people, many of them women and children, at an army base near Jammu, and Pakistan conducted missile tests May 25-28. U.S. mediation in June helped ease the crisis. Legislative elections were held Sept.-Oct. 2002.

A cease-fire between Indian and Pakistani troops along the line of control took effect Nov. 25, 2003, but clashes between Indian forces and Islamic militants continued. Estimates of conflict-related deaths since 1989 range from 40,000 to over 80,000.

France, 1952-54, peacefully yielded to India its 5 colonies, former French India, comprising Pondicherry, Karikal, Mahe, Yanaon (which became **Pondicherry Union Territory**, area 190 sq. mi; pop. (2001 census) 973,829 and Chandernagor (which was incorporated into the state of **West Bengal**).

Indonesia
Republic of Indonesia

People: Population: 241,973,879. **Age distrib.** (%): <15: 29.1; 65+: 5.2. **Pop. density:** 327 per sq mi, 126 per sq km. **Urban:** 45.6%. **Ethnic groups:** Javanese 45%, Sundanese 14%, Madurese 8%, Malay 8%. **Principal languages:** Bahasa Indonesia (official, modified form of Malay), English, Dutch, Javanese, other dialects. **Chief religions:** Muslim 88%, Protestant 5%, Roman Catholic 3%, Hindu 2%, Buddhist 1%.

Geography: Total area: 741,100 sq mi, 1,919,440 sq km; **Land area:** 705,192 sq mi, 1,826,440 sq km. **Location:** Archipelago SE of Asian mainland along the Equator. **Neighbors:** Malaysia on N, Papua New Guinea on E. **Topography:** Indonesia comprises over 13,500 islands (6,000 inhabited), including Java (one of the most densely populated areas in the world with over 2,000 persons per sq. mi.), Sumatra, Kalimantan (most of Borneo), Sulawesi (Celebes), and West Irian (Irian Jaya, the W half of New Guinea). Also: Bangka, Billiton, Madura, Bali, Timor. The mountains and plateaus on the major islands have a cooler climate than the tropical lowlands. **Capital:** Jakarta, 12,296,000. **Cities (urban aggr.):** Bandung, 3,409,000; Surabaja, 2,461,000.

Government: Type: Republic. **Head of state and gov.:** Susilo Bambang Yudhoyono; b Sept. 9, 1949; in office: Oct. 20, 2004. **Local divisions:** 30 provinces, 2 special regions, 1 capital district. **Defense budget** (2004): $2.3 bil. **Active troops:** 302,000.

Economy: Industries: oil & nat. gas, textiles, apparel & footwear, mining, cement, fertilizers, plywood, rubber. **Chief crops:** rice, cassava, peanuts, rubber, cocoa, coffee, palm oil, copra. **Natural resources:** oil, tin, nat. gas, nickel, timber, bauxite, copper, coal, gold, silver. **Crude oil reserves** (2004): 4.7 bil. bbls. **Arable land:** 10%. **Livestock** (2004): cattle: 11.1 mil; chickens: 1.2 bil.; goats: 13.4 mil; pigs: 6.6 mil; sheep: 8.2 mil. **Fish catch** (2003): 5,671,759 metric tons. **Electricity prod.** (2003): 109.5 bil. kWh. **Labor force** (1999 est.): agriculture 45%, industry 16%, services 39%.

Finance: Monetary unit: Rupiah (IDR) (Sept. 2005: 10,237.33 = $1 U.S.). **GDP** (2004 est.): $827.4 bil.; **per capita GDP:** $3,500; **GDP growth:** 4.9%. **Imports** (2004 est.): $45.1 bil.; partners (2004): Japan 19.3%, China 11%, Singapore 9.2%, Thailand 6.8%, Malaysia 6.5%, US 5.7%, Australia 5%, Germany 4.2%. **Exports** (2004 est.): $69.9 bil.; partners (2004): Japan 21.8%, US 13.5%, China 7.5%, Singapore 7.4%, South Korea 5.9%, Malaysia 4.9%. **Tourism:** $4,037 mil. **Budget** (2004 est.): $55.9 bil. **Intl. reserves less gold:** $22.51 bil. **Gold:** 3.1 mil. oz t. **Consumer prices:** 6.24%.

Transport: Railroad: Length: 4,013 mi. **Motor vehicles:** 3.40 mil pass. cars, 2.58 mil comm. vehicles. **Civil aviation:** 10.0 bil pass.-mi; 153 airports. **Chief ports:** Jakarta, Surabaya, Palembang, Semarang, Ujungpandang.

Communications: TV sets: 143 per 1,000 pop. **Radios:** 155 per 1,000 pop. **Telephone lines**: 8.5 mil. **Daily newspaper circ.:** 22.8 per 1,000 pop. **Internet**: 8.1 mil. users.

Health: Life expect.: 67.1 male; 72.1 female. **Births** (per 1,000 pop.): 20.7. **Deaths** (per 1,000 pop.): 6.3. **Natural inc.:** 1.45%. **Infant mortality** (per 1,000 live births): 35.6. **AIDS rate:** 0.1%.

Education: Compulsory: ages 7-15. **Literacy:** 87.9%.

Major Intl. Organizations: UN and all of its specialized agencies, APEC, ASEAN, OPEC.

Embassy: 2020 Massachusetts Ave. NW 20036; 775-5200.

Website: www.embassyofindonesia.org

Hindu and Buddhist civilization from India reached Indonesia nearly 2,000 years ago, taking root especially in Java. Islam spread along the maritime trade routes in the 15th century, and became predominant by the 16th century. The Dutch replaced the Portuguese as the area's most important European trade power in the 17th century, securing territorial control over Java by 1750. The outer islands were not finally subdued until the early 20th century, when the full area of present-day Indonesia was united under one rule for the first time.

Following Japanese occupation, 1942-45, nationalists led by Sukarno and Hatta declared independence. The Netherlands ceded sovereignty Dec. 27, 1949, after 4 years of fighting. A republic was declared, Aug. 17, 1950, with Sukarno as president. West Irian, on New Guinea, remained under Dutch control. After the Dutch in 1957 rejected proposals for new negotiations over West Irian, Indonesia stepped up the seizure of Dutch property. In 1963 the UN turned the area (later renamed Irian Jaya and now known as Papua) over to Indonesia, which promised a plebiscite. In 1969, voting by tribal chiefs favored staying with Indonesia, despite an uprising and widespread opposition.

Sukarno suspended Parliament in 1960, and was named president for life in 1963. He made close alliances with Communist governments. In Sept. 1965 an attempted coup in which several military officers were murdered was successfully put down, but Sukarno was forced to cede power to the army, led by Gen. Suharto, who became acting president in 1967 and ruled Indonesia for the next 31 years. The regime blamed the coup on the Communist Party; more than 300,000 alleged Communists were killed in army-initiated massacres.

Parliament reelected Suharto to a 7th consecutive 5-year term Mar. 10, 1998, as a severe economic downturn focused public anger on nepotism, cronyism, and corruption in the Suharto regime. Price increases in May sparked mass protests and then mob violence in Jakarta and other cities, claiming some 500 lives. Suharto resigned May 21 and was succeeded by his vice-president, Bacharuddin Jusuf Habibie. Abdurrahman Wahid, leader of Indonesia's largest Muslim organization, was elected president Oct. 20, 1999. In Aug. 2000, under pressure from the legislature, he agreed to share power with Vice-Pres. Megawati Sukarnoputri, the daughter of the late Pres. Sukarno. Charging Wahid with incompetence and corruption, the legislature ousted him July 23, 2001, and Megawati became Indonesia's 1st woman president.

Clashes between Muslims and Christians in the Maluku (Molucca) Is., 1999-2002, claimed about 5,000 lives. Ethnic violence in Kalimantan, Borneo, killed more than 400 in Feb. 2001. East Timor, a former Portuguese colony that Indonesia invaded in Dec. 1975 and controlled until Oct. 1999, became a fully independent country May 20, 2002, as Timor-Leste. Separatists in Aceh, NW Sumatra, fought repeatedly against government troops during the 1980s and 90s; peace accords were announced in Dec. 2002 and, after that deal unraveled, in July 2005.

Investigators blamed Islamic terrorists affiliated with al-Qaeda for bombings that killed 202 people, mostly foreign tourists, at nightclubs in Bali, Oct. 12, 2002, and 12 people at a Marriott hotel in Jakarta, Aug. 5, 2003. A car bomb attack outside the Australian embassy in Jakarta, Sept. 9, 2004, killed 9 people and injured more than 180. Susilo Bambang Yudhoyono, a retired general, defeated Megawati Sept. 20 in a direct presidential runoff vote.

A massive earthquake off NW Sumatra, Dec. 26, 2004, triggered tsunamis that wreaked havoc in the Indian Ocean region. The death toll in Indonesia alone exceeded 125,000, not counting almost 40,000 missing. Another large quake off NW Sumatra, Mar. 28, 2005, left hundreds dead.

Iran

Islamic Republic of Iran

People: Population: 68,017,860. **Age distrib.** (%): <15: 27.1; 65+: 4.9. **Pop. density:** 107 per sq mi, 41 per sq km. **Urban:** 66.7%. **Ethnic groups:** Persian 51%, Azeri 24%, Gilaki/Mazandarani 8%, Kurd 7%, Arab 3%, Lur 2%, Balochi 2%, Turkmen 2%. **Principal languages:** Farsi/Persian (official), Kurdish, Pashto, Luri, Balochi, Gilaki, Mazandarami; Azeri and Turkic languages; Arabic, Turkish. **Chief religion:** Muslim (official; Shi'a 89%, Sunni 10%).

Geography: Total area: 636,296 sq mi, 1,648,000 sq km; **Land area:** 631,663 sq mi, 1,636,000 sq km. **Location:** Between the Middle East and S Asia. **Neighbors:** Turkey, Iraq on W; Armenia, Azerbaijan, Turkmenistan on N; Afghanistan, Pakistan on E. **Topography:** Interior highlands and plains surrounded by high mountains, up to 18,000 ft. Large salt deserts cover much of area, but there are many oases and forest areas. Most of the population inhabits the N and NW. **Capital:** Tehran, 7,190,000. **Cities** (urban aggr.): Esfahan, 1,381,000; Mashhad, 1,990,000.

Government: Type: Islamic republic. **Religious head:** Ayatollah Sayyed Ali Khamenei; b 1939; in office: June 4, 1989. **Head of state and gov.:** Pres. Mahmoud Ahmadinejad; b 1956; in office: Aug. 3, 2005. **Local divisions:** 28 provinces. **Defense budget** (2004): $3.5 bil. **Active troops:** 540,000.

Economy: Industries: oil, petrochems., textiles, constr. materials, food proc., metal fabricating, armaments. **Chief crops:** wheat, rice, other grains, sugar beets, fruits, nuts, cotton. **Natural resources:** oil, nat. gas, coal, chromium, copper, iron ore, lead, mang., zinc, sulfur. **Crude oil reserves** (2004): 125.8 bil. bbls. **Arable land:** 10%. **Livestock** (2004): cattle: 9.2 mil; chickens: 290 mil; goats: 26.3 mil; sheep: 54.0 mil. **Fish catch** (2003): 440,835 metric tons. **Electricity prod.** (2003): 142.3 bil. kWh. **Labor force** (2001 est.): agriculture 30%, industry 25%, services 45%.

Finance: Monetary unit: Rial (IRR) (Sept. 2005: 9,008.05 = $1 U.S.). **GDP** (2004 est.): $516.7 bil.; **per capita GDP:** $7,700; **GDP growth:** 6.3%. **Imports** (2004 est.): $31.3 bil.; partners (2004): Germany 13%, France 8.9%, Italy 8%, China 7.7%, UAE 6.4%, South Korea 6.3%, Russia 4.9%. **Exports** (2004 est.): $38.8 bil.; partners (2004): Japan 20%, China 9.9%, Italy 6.3%, South Africa 6.3%, Taiwan 4.8%, Turkey 4.7%, South Korea 4.7%, France 4.3%, Netherlands 4.3%. **Tourism:** $1,777 mil. **Budget** (2004 est.): $47.7 bil. **Consumer prices:** 14.76%.

Transport: Railroad: Length: 4,474 mi. **Motor vehicles:** 1.35 mil pass. cars, 384,900 comm. vehicles. **Civil aviation:** 5.5 bil pass.-mi; 122 airports. **Chief port:** Bandar-e Abbas.

Communications: TV sets: 154 per 1,000 pop. **Radios:** 265 per 1,000 pop. **Telephone lines:** 14.6 mil. **Daily newspaper circ.:** 28 per 1,000 pop. **Internet**: 4.8 mil. users.

Health: Life expect.: 68.6 male; 71.4 female. **Births** (per 1,000 pop.): 16.8. **Deaths** (per 1,000 pop.): 5.6. **Natural inc.:** 1.13%. **Infant mortality** (per 1,000 live births): 41.6. **AIDS rate:** 0.1%.

Education: Compulsory: ages 6-10. **Literacy:** 79.4%.

Major Intl. Organizations: UN (FAO, IBRD, ILO, IMF, IMO, WHO), OPEC.

Iranian Interests Section: 2209 Wisconsin Ave. NW, 20007; 965-4990.

Website: www.spk-gov.ir/Index.asp

Iran was once called Persia. The Iranians, who supplanted an earlier agricultural civilization, came from the E during the 2nd millennium BC; they were an Indo-European group related to the Aryans of India.

In 549 BC Cyrus the Great united the Medes and Persians in the Persian Empire, conquered Babylonia in 538 BC, and restored Jerusalem to the Jews. Alexander the Great conquered Persia in 333 BC, but Persians regained independence in the next century under the Parthians, themselves succeeded by Sassanian Persians in AD 226. Arabs brought Islam to Persia in the 7th century, replacing the indigenous Zoroastrian faith. After Persian political and cultural autonomy was reasserted in the 9th century, arts and sciences flourished.

Turks and Mongols ruled Persia in turn from the 11th century to 1502, when Ismael I established the Iranian Safavid dynasty, and made Shiite Islam the offical religion. The dynasty lasted until 1722. The British and Russian empires vied for influence in the 19th century; Afghanistan was severed from Iran by Britain in 1857.

Reza Khan, a military officer, became prime min., 1923, and shah in 1925. He began modernization, curbed foreign influence, and officially changed the country's name from Persia to Iran in 1935. Fearing the shah's Axis sympathies, British and Soviet troops forced him to abdicate, 1941; succeeded by his son, Mohammad Reza Pahlavi. With U.S. backing, he brought economic and social change to Iran (the "White Revolution"), but repression, often severe, of opposition groups intensified. Violent protests in 1978 eventually forced the shah to depart, Jan. 16, 1979. He appointed Prime Min. Shahpur Bakhtiar to head a regency council in his absence. Shiite leader Ayatollah Ruhollah Khomeini, exiled by the shah in 1963, returned to Tehran, Feb. 1, and by Feb. 11 pro-Khomeini forces had defeated gov. troops. Khomeini then established an Islamic theocracy.

Iranian militants seized the U.S. embassy, Nov. 4, 1979, and took hostages including 62 Americans. Despite international condemnations and U.S. efforts, including an abortive Apr. 1980 rescue attempt, the crisis continued. The U.S. broke diplomatic relations with Iran, Apr. 7. The shah died in Egypt, July 27. The hostage drama ended Jan. 20, 1981, when an accord, involving the release of frozen Iranian assets, was reached.

A dispute over the Shatt al-Arab waterway situated between Iran and Iraq led to a long and costly war between the 2 countries, beginning Sept. 22, 1980. Iraqi troops occupied Iranian territory, including the port city of Khorramshahr in October. Iranian troops recaptured the city and drove Iraqi troops back across the border, May 1982. In Nov. 1986 it became known that the U.S., which had generally sided with Iraq during the war, had secretly shipped arms to Iran to gain that country's help in obtaining the release of U.S. hostages held by terrorists in Lebanon. The revelation sparked a major scandal in the Reagan administration.

A U.S. Navy warship shot down an Iranian commercial airliner, July 3, 1988, after mistaking it for an F-14 fighter jet; all 290 aboard the plane died. In Aug. 1988, Iran agreed to accept a UN resolution calling for a cease-fire with Iraq.

An earthquake struck northern Iran June 21, 1990, killing more than 45,000, injuring 100,000, and leaving 400,000 homeless. Some one million Kurdish refugees fled from Iraq to Iran following the Persian Gulf War of 1991. To curb Iran's alleged support for international terrorism, the U.S. in 1996 authorized sanctions on foreign companies that invest there.

Mohammad Khatami, a moderate Shiite Muslim cleric, was elected president on May 23, 1997, winning nearly 70% of the vote. During the next 3 years, hardline Islamists clashed repeatedly and sometimes violently with reformers, who won a majority in parliamentary elections Feb. 18 and May 5, 2000. Inviting rapprochement with Iran, the U.S. eased some sanctions Mar. 18. Khatami was reelected June 8, 2001, with a 77% majority, but continued to face resistance from religious conservatives.

The U.S.-led war in Iraq, beginning Mar. 2003, contributed to a new period of instability in Iran, which the U.S. suspected was developing nuclear weapons and harboring members of al-Qaeda. In June, armed Islamist vigilantes harassed students who were holding pro-democracy protests in Tehran and other cities. An earthquake Dec. 26 in Bam, SE Iran, killed about 26,000 people. After the Guardian Council, dominated by religious conservatives, disqualified some 2,400 reformist candidates, hardliners won control of parliament in elections Feb. 20, 2004.

The Guardian Council, May 22, 2005, selected 6 candidates out of 1,014 presidential aspirants. The mayor of Tehran, Mahmoud Ahmadinejad, a religious conservative who campaigned as an economic reformer, defeated former Pres. Hashemi Rafsanjani in a runoff election June 24.The International Atomic Energy Agency, in Sept. passed a resolution requiring that Iran be reported to the UN Security Council for failing to convince the international community that its ongoing nuclear program was for peaceful purposes.

Iraq

Republic of Iraq

People: Population: 26,074,906. **Age distrib.** (%): <15: 40.0; 65+: 3.0. **Pop. density:** 155 per sq mi, 60 per sq km. **Urban:** 67.2%. **Ethnic groups:** Arab 75%-80%, Kurdish 15%-20%. **Principal languages:** Arabic (official), Kurdish (official in Kurdish regions), Assyrian, Armenian. **Chief religion:** Muslim (official; Shi'a 60%-65%, Sunni 32%-37%)

Geography: Total area: 168,754 sq mi, 437,072 sq km; **Land area:** 166,859 sq mi, 432,162 sq km. **Location:** In the Middle East, occupying most of historic Mesopotamia. **Neighbors:** Jordan and Syria on W, Turkey on N, Iran on E, Kuwait and Saudi Arabia on S. **Topography:** Mostly an alluvial plain, including the Tigris and Euphrates rivers, descending from mountains in N to desert in SW. Persian Gulf region is marshland. **Capital:** Baghdad, 5,620,000. **Cities (urban aggr.):** Arbil, 2,369,000; Basra (city est.), 1,076,000; Mosul, 1,056,000.

Government: Type: In transition. **Head of state:** Pres. Jalal Talabani; b 1933; in office: Apr. 7, 2005. **Head of gov.:** Prime Min. Ibrahim al-Jaafari; b 1947; in office: May 3, 2005. **Local divisions:** 18 governorates (3 in Kurdish Autonomous Region). **Defense budget** (2003): NA. **Active troops:** NA.

Economy: Industries: oil, chemicals, textiles, constr. materials, food proc. **Chief crops:** wheat, barley, rice, vegetables, dates, cotton. **Natural resources:** oil, nat. gas, phosphates, sulfur. **Arable land:** 12%. **Crude oil reserves** (2004): 115.0 bil. bbls. **Fish catch** (2003): 23,100 metric tons. **Electricity prod.** (2003): 14.7 bil. kWh.

Finance: Monetary unit: Dinar (IQD) (Sept. 2005: 1,468.10 = $1 U.S.). **GDP** (2004 est.): $54.4 bil.; **per capita GDP:** $2,100; **GDP growth:** 52.3%. **Imports** (2004 est.): $9.9 bil.; partners (2004): Turkey 25%, US 11.1%, Jordan 10%, Vietnam 7.7%, Germany 5.6%, Australia 4.8%. **Exports** (2004 est.): $10.1 bil.; partners (2004): US 55.8%, Spain 8%, Japan 7.3%, Italy 6.5%, Canada 5.8%. **Tourism** (1998): $13 mil. **Budget** (2004 budget): $28.2 bil.

Transport: Railroad: Length: 1,220 mi. **Motor vehicles:** 754,130 pass. cars, 372,230 comm. vehicles; 77 airports. **Chief port:** Basra.

Communications: TV sets: 82 per 1,000 pop. **Radios:** 229 per 1,000 pop. **Daily newspaper circ.:** 19 per 1,000 pop.

Health: Life expect.: 67.5 male; 70.0 female. **Births** (per 1,000 pop.): 32.5. **Deaths** (per 1,000 pop.): 5.5. **Natural inc.:** 2.70%. **Infant mortality** (per 1,000 live births): 50.3. **AIDS rate:** <0.1%.

Education: Compulsory: ages 6-11. **Literacy:** 40.4%.

Major Intl. Organizations: UN (FAO, IBRD, ILO, IMF, IMO, WHO), AL, OPEC.

Iraqi Interests Section: 1801 P St., NW, 20036; 483-7500.

Website: www.iraqigovernment.org/index_en.htm

The Tigris-Euphrates valley, formerly called Mesopotamia, was the site of one of the earliest civilizations in the world. Mesopotamia ceased to be a separate entity after the Persian, Greek, and Arab conquests. The Arabs founded Baghdad, from where the caliph ruled a vast Islamic empire in the 8th and 9th centuries. Mongol and Turkish conquests led to a decline in the region's population, economy, cultural life, and irrigation system.

Britain secured a League of Nations mandate over Iraq after World War I. Independence under a king came in 1932. Rebellious army officers killed King Faisal II, July 14, 1958, and established a leftist, pan-Arab republic, which pursued close ties with the USSR. Successive regimes were increasingly dominated by the Baath Arab Socialist Party. In the 1973 Arab-Israeli war Iraq sent forces to aid Syria.

A Baath leader, Saddam Hussein, became president of Iraq, July 16, 1979. After purging his enemies, he ruled as a dictator for more than 2 decades, repressing Iraq's Kurds and Shiites and launching disastrous wars against 2 neighboring nations, Iran and Kuwait. Hussein was believed to be seeking to develop weapons of mass destruction; Israeli planes destroyed a nuclear reactor near Baghdad June 7, 1981, claiming it could be used to produce nuclear weapons.

After skirmishing intermittently for 10 months over the sovereignty of the disputed Shatt al-Arab waterway that divides the two countries, Iraq and Iran entered into open warfare on Sept. 22, 1980. Iran repulsed early Iraqi advances, producing a long and costly stalemate; hundreds of thousands of Iraqis lost their lives during the 8-year conflict. Hussein used poison gas against Iraqi Kurds in 1988, killing up to 5,000 people in Halabja, the 1st mass use of poison gas against civilians since the Holocaust.

Iraq attacked and overran Kuwait Aug. 2, 1990. Backed by the UN, a U.S.-led coalition launched air and missile attacks on Iraq, Jan. 16, 1991. The coalition began a ground attack to retake Kuwait Feb. 23. Iraqi forces showed little resistance and were soundly defeated in 4 days. Some 175,000 Iraqis were taken prisoner, and Iraqi casualties were estimated at over 85,000. As part of the cease-fire agreement, Iraq agreed to scrap all poison gas and germ weapons and allow UN observers to inspect the sites. UN trade sanctions would remain in effect until Iraq complied with all terms.

In Feb. 1991, Iraqi troops drove Kurdish insurgents and civilians to the borders of Iran and Turkey, causing a refugee crisis. The U.S. and allies established havens inside Iraq for the Kurds. The U.S. launched a missile attack aimed at Iraq's intelligence headquarters in Baghdad June 26, 1993, citing evidence that Iraq had sponsored a plot to kill former Pres. George Bush. Iraqi cooperation with UN weapons inspection teams was intermittent throughout the 1990s. On Dec. 9, 1996, the UN began a program that meant to allow Baghdad to sell limited amounts of oil for food and medicine. An independant panel, in a series of reports to the UN, later concluded that there was massive corruption in UN administration of the program allowing the Iraqi regime to reap huge profits (aside from the large profits through oil smuggling).

Iraqi resistance to UN access to suspected weapons sites touched off diplomatic crises during 1997-98, culminating in intensive U.S. and British aerial bombardment of Iraqi military targets, Dec. 16-19, 1998. After 2 years of sporadic activity, U.S. and British warplanes struck harder at sites near Baghdad on Feb. 16, 2001.

In a speech before the UN, Sept. 12, 2002, Pres. George W. Bush accused Iraq of repeatedly violating UN resolutions to eliminate weapons of mass destruction, refrain from supporting terrorism, and end repression. Under Security Council Resolution 1441, approved Nov. 8, Iraq allowed UN inspectors to search for banned weapons, while the U.S. and Britain built up troops in the Persian Gulf. Despite opposition from some countries, including France, Germany, and Russia, a U.S.-led coalition launched an invasion of Iraq on the evening of Mar. 19 (EST), 2003. By Apr. 6 the British controlled Basra and other areas in the S, and the U.S. entered Baghdad Apr. 7. Hussein had disappeared, the Iraqi government had collapsed, and most of Iraq's armed forces had dissolved into the civilian population. On May 1, Pres. Bush declared that major combat there was over. Continuing searches failed to uncover evidence of stockpiled chemical, biological, or nuclear weapons.

The U.S. initially governed Iraq through a Coalition Provisional Authority, headed by L. Paul Bremer. A 25-member Iraqi Governing Council was appointed and named a cabinet Sept. 1, 2003. Reconstruction efforts continued but were hampered by guerrilla attacks from Baath remnants, Islamic extremists, and others. Iraqi resistance activities widened with the bombings of the Jordanian embassy, Aug. 7, the UN headquarters in Baghdad, Aug. 19, killing UN special envoy Sergio Vieira de Mello and 21 others, and a blast in Najaf Aug. 29 that killed at least 83 people, including Ayatollah Mohammad Bakir al-Hakim, a Shiite leader. After a 2nd bombing at its Baghdad headquarters Sept. 22, the UN scaled back its presence in Iraq.

Coalition forces succeeded in neutralizing many leaders of the former regime. Two of Hussein's sons, Uday and Qusay, were killed July 22, 2003 by U.S. troops in Mosul. Saddam Hussein was captured in an underground hideout Dec. 13; he appeared before an Iraqi tribunal July 1, 2004, and was charged with crimes against humanity. His trial was scheduled to begin Oct. 19, 2005.

The insurgency continued to mount attacks that killed large numbers of Iraqi civilians as well as many foreign troops and civilians participating in reconstruction, under leaders such as radical Shiite cleric Moqtada al-Sadr and Jordanian militant Abu Musab al-Zarqawi; the U.S. believed Zarqawi was behind a series of kidnappings, beheadings, and suicide bombings. Fallujah remained a center of Sunni Muslim resistance. Among other atrocities, gunmen ambushed and killed 4 security contractors in Fallujah in March, 2004, and a mob dragged their bodies through the streets. Attacks on pipelines and other facilities cut Iraq's oil production.

Photographs released in Apr. 2004 graphically showed instances of physical abuse and sexual humiliation of Iraqi inmates by U.S. military personnel at Baghdad's Abu Ghraib prison in fall 2003. The images sparked widespread condemnation and U.S. criminal proceedings against some individuals.

On June 28, 2004, U.S. authorities officially transferred sovereignty to a transitional Iraqi government led by Prime Min. Iyad Allawi. Despite threats by insurgents, an estimated 8 million people in Iraq, mostly Shiites and Kurds, cast ballots Jan. 30, 2005, for a 275-member transitional national assembly. On Apr. 6, the assembly elected Jalal al-Talabani, a Kurd, as president; Ibrahim al-Jaafari, a Shiite, became prime minister. The insurgents launched new waves of attacks, killing hundreds of police and army recruits. A new constitution, favored by Kurds and Shiites but opposed by Sunnis, was adopted by the assembly Aug. 28, pending a referendum. Rumors of a suicide bomber set off a stampede by Shiite pilgrims in N Baghdad Aug. 31, killing close to 1,000 people.

About 135,000 U.S. troops remained in Iraq, along with 22,000 allied forces and thousands of foreign civilian advisers and contractors. By late Sept. 2005 more than 1,900 U.S. service members had been killed and more than 14,000 wounded during the war and occupation. Attacks against coalition troops remained near their highest levels since the war officially ended. British troop losses were put at nearly 100; Italy, Ukraine, Poland, and other countries had smaller losses. Many thousands of Iraqi troops and civilians were killed in the continuing violence; a nonprofit organization, Iraq Body Count, stated as of late Sept. that more than 26,000 civilians had died as a direct or indirect result of the war and occupation.

Ireland

People: Population: 4,015,676. **Age distrib.** (%): <15: 20.9; 65+: 11.5. **Pop. density:** 148 per sq mi, 57 per sq km. **Urban:** 59.9%. **Ethnic groups:** Celtic; English minority. **Principal languages:** English, Irish Gaelic (both official); Irish Gaelic spoken by small number in western areas. **Chief religions:** Roman Catholic 88%, Anglican 3%.

Geography: Total area: 27,135 sq mi, 70,280 sq km; **Land area:** 26,599 sq mi, 68,890 sq km. **Location:** In the Atlantic O. just W of Great Britain. **Neighbors:** United Kingdom (Northern Ireland) on E. **Topography:** Ireland consists of a central plateau surrounded by isolated groups of hills and mountains. The coastline is heavily indented by the Atlantic O. **Capital:** Dublin, 1,015,000.

Government: Type: Parliamentary republic. **Head of state:** Pres. Mary McAleese; b June 27, 1951; in office: Nov. 11, 1997. **Head of gov.:** Prime Min. Bertie Ahern; b Sept. 12, 1951; in office: June 26, 1997. **Local divisions:** 26 counties. **Defense budget** (2004): $859 mil. **Active troops:** 10,460.

Economy: Industries: food products, brewing, textiles, clothing, pharm., chemicals. **Chief crops:** turnips, barley, potatoes, sugar beets; wheat. **Natural resources:** zinc, lead, nat. gas, barite, copper, gypsum, limestone, dolomite, peat, silver. **Arable land:** 13%. **Livestock** (2004): cattle: 7.0 mil; chickens: 12.8 mil; goats: 7,700; pigs: 1.7 mil; sheep: 4.9 mil. **Fish catch** (2003): 328,751 metric tons. **Electricity prod.** (2003): 23.4 bil. kWh. **Labor force** (2002 est.): agriculture 8%, industry 29%, services 63%.

Finance: Monetary unit: Euro (EUR) (Sept. 2005: 0.80 = $1 U.S.). **GDP** (2004 est.): $126.4 bil.; **per capita GDP:** $31,900; **GDP growth:** 5.1% **Imports** (2004 est.): $60.7 bil.; partners (2004): UK 35.2%, US 13.5%, Germany 8.9%, France 4.3%, Netherlands 4.3%. **Exports** (2004 est.): $103.8 bil.; partners (2004): US 20.2%, UK 17.5%, Belgium 14.8%, Germany 7.5%, France 5.9%, Italy 4.5%, Netherlands 4.4%. **Tourism:** $3,875 mil. **Budget** (2004 est.): $63.5 bil. **Intl. reserves less gold:** $1.82 bil. **Gold:** 180,000 oz t. **Consumer prices:** 2.19%.

Transport: Railroad: Length: 2,058 mi. **Motor vehicles:** 1.40 mil pass. cars, 231,700 comm. vehicles. **Civil aviation:** 8.6 bil pass.-mi; 16 airports. **Chief ports:** Dublin, Cork.

Communications: TV sets: 406 per 1,000 pop. **Radios:** 697 per 1,000 pop. **Telephone lines:** 2.0 mil. **Daily newspaper circ.:** 335.7 per 1,000 pop. **Internet**: 1.3 mil. users.

IT'S A FACT: In 1973, when Ireland joined the European Union (then the European Economic Community), it was the poorest member nation, with a per capita GDP amounting to only 59% of the EU average. In 2004, the "Celtic Tiger" had a per capita GDP of $31,900—which was 19% above the EU average and was the 2nd highest in the EU, behind Luxembourg. Since 1990, the Irish government has cut income taxes, increased spending on public education, and promoted foreign investment.

Health: Life expect.: 75.0 male; 80.3 female. **Births** (per 1,000 pop.): 14.5. **Deaths** (per 1,000 pop.): 7.9. **Natural inc.:** 0.66%. **Infant mortality** (per 1,000 live births): 5.4. **AIDS rate:** 0.1%.

Education: Compulsory: ages 6-15. **Literacy:** 98%.

Major Intl. Organizations: UN (FAO, IBRD, ILO, IMF, IMO, WHO, WTrO), EU, OECD, OSCE.

Embassy: 2234 Massachusetts Ave. NW 20008; 462-3939.

Website: www.irlgov.ie

Celtic tribes invaded the islands about the 4th century BC; their Gaelic culture and literature flourished and spread to Scotland and elsewhere in the 5th century AD, the same century in which St. Patrick converted the Irish to Christianity. Invasions by Norsemen began in the 8th century, ended with defeat of the Danes by the Irish King Brian Boru in 1014. English invasions started in the 12th century; for over 700 years the Anglo-Irish struggle continued with bitter rebellions and savage repressions.

The Easter Monday Rebellion in 1916 failed but was followed by guerrilla warfare and harsh reprisals by British troops called the "Black and Tans." The Dail Eireann (Irish parliament) reaffirmed independence in Jan. 1919. The British offered dominion status to Ulster (6 counties) and southern Ireland (26 counties) Dec. 1921. The constitution of the Irish Free State, a British dominion, was adopted Dec. 11, 1922. Northern Ireland remained part of the United Kingdom.

A new constitution adopted by plebiscite came into operation Dec. 29, 1937. It declared the name of the state Eire in the Irish language (Ireland in the English) and declared it a sovereign democratic state. On Dec. 21, 1948, an Irish law declared the country a republic rather than a dominion and withdrew it from the Commonwealth. The British Parliament recognized both actions, 1949, but reasserted its claim to incorporate the 6 northeastern counties in the U.K.

Irish governments have favored peaceful unification of all Ireland and cooperated with Britain against terrorist group. After negotiators in Northern Ireland approved a peace settlement on Good Friday, April 10, 1998, voters in the Irish Republic endorsed the accord, on May 22; the agreement required the removal from the Irish constitution of territorial claims on the north. Irish voters rejected, June 7, 2001, then reversed themselves and approved, Oct. 19, 2002, a plan calling for EU expansion.

Ireland's first woman president, Mary Robinson, resigned Sept. 12, 1997, to become UN high commissioner for human rights. She was succeeded by Mary McAleese, a law professor from Northern Ireland and the first northerner to hold the office. Expansion of educational opportunities and foreign investment in high-tech industries have helped make Ireland one of Europe's most prosperous countries in recent years.

Israel

State of Israel

People: Population: 6,276,883. **Age distrib.** (%): <15: 26.5; 65+: 9.8. **Pop. density:** 783 per sq mi, 302 per sq km. **Urban:** 51.8%. **Ethnic groups:** Jewish 80%, Arab and other 20%. **Principal languages:** Hebrew, Arabic (both official), English. **Chief religions:** Jewish 77%, Muslim (mostly Sunni) 15%, Christian 2%.

Geography: Total area: 8,019 sq mi, 20,770 sq km; **Land area:** 7,849 sq mi, 20,330 sq km. **Location:** Middle East, on E end of Mediterranean Sea. **Neighbors:** Lebanon on N; Syria, West Bank, and Jordan on E; Gaza Strip and Egypt on W. **Topography:** The Mediterranean coastal plain is fertile and well-watered. In the center is the Judean Plateau. A triangular-shaped semi-desert region, the Negev, extends from south of Beersheba to an apex at the head of the Gulf of Aqaba. The E border drops sharply into the Jordan Rift Valley, including Lake Tiberias (Sea of Galilee) and the Dead Sea, which is c.1,300 ft. below sea level, lowest point on the earth's surface. **Capital:** Jerusalem (most countries maintain their embassies in Tel Aviv), 686,000. **Cities (urban aggr.):** Tel Aviv-Yafo, 2,752,000; Haifa, 865,000.

Government: Type: Republic. **Head of state:** Pres. Moshe Katsav; b 1945; in office: Aug. 1, 2000. **Head of gov.:** Prime Min. Ariel Sharon; b 1928; in office: Mar. 7, 2001. **Local divisions:** 6 districts. **Defense budget** (2004): $7.8 bil. **Active troops:** 168,000.

Economy: Industries: high-tech products, wood & paper products, potash & phosphates, food, beverages, tobacco. **Chief crops:** citrus, vegetables, cotton. **Natural resources:** timber, potash, copper ore, nat. gas, phosphate rock, magnesium bromide, clays, sand. **Crude oil reserves** (2004): 2 mil bbls. **Arable land:** 17%. **Livestock** (2004): cattle: 400,000; chickens: 40 mil; goats: 64,000; pigs: 195,000; sheep: 390,000. **Fish catch** (2003): 24,831 metric tons. **Electricity prod.** (2003): 44.2 bil. kWh. **Labor force** (1996): agriculture, forestry, and fishing 2.6%, manufacturing 20.2%, construction 7.5%, commerce 12.8%, transport, storage, and communications 6.2%, finance and business 13.1%, personal and other services 6.4%, public services 31.2%.

Finance: Monetary unit: New Shekel (ILS) (Sept. 2005: 4.50 = $1 U.S.). **GDP** (2004 est.): $129.0 bil.; **per capita GDP:** $20,800; **GDP growth:** 3.9%. **Imports** (2004 est.): $36.8 bil.; partners (2004): US 15%, Belgium 10.1%, Germany 7.5%, Switzerland 6.5%, UK 6.1%. **Exports** (2004 est.): $34.4 bil.; partners (2004): US 36.8%, Belgium 7.5%, Hong Kong 4.9%. **Tourism:** $2,039 mil. **Budget** (2004 est.): $52.1 bil. **Intl. reserves less gold:** $17.45 bil. **Consumer prices:** –0.4%.

Transport: Railroad: Length: 398 mi. **Motor vehicles:** 1.47 mil pass. cars, 350,200 comm. vehicles. **Civil aviation:** 8.4 bil pass.-mi; 28 airports. **Chief ports:** Haifa, Ashdod, Elat.

Communications: TV sets: 328 per 1,000 pop. **Radios:** 524 per 1,000 pop. **Telephone lines:** 3.1 mil. **Daily newspaper circ.:** 290 per 1,000 pop. **Internet** (2002): 2.0 mil. users.

Health: Life expect.: 77.2 male; 81.6 female. **Births** (per 1,000 pop.): 18.2. **Deaths** (per 1,000 pop.): 6.2. **Natural inc.:** 1.20%. **Infant mortality** (per 1,000 live births): 7.0. **AIDS rate:** 0.1%.

Education: Compulsory: ages 5-15. **Literacy:** 95.4%.

Major Intl. Organizations: UN (FAO, IBRD, ILO, IMF, IMO, WHO, WTrO).

Embassy: 3514 International Dr. NW 20008; 364-5500.

Website: www.info.gov.il/LAPAMEng

Occupying the SW corner of the ancient Fertile Crescent, Israel contains some of the oldest known evidence of agriculture and of primitive town life. The Hebrews probably arrived early in the 2nd millennium BC. Under King David and his successors (c.1000 BC-597 BC), Judaism was developed and secured. After conquest by Babylonians, Persians, and Greeks, an independent Jewish kingdom was revived, 168 BC, but Rome took effective control in the next century, suppressed Jewish revolts in AD 70 and AD 135, and renamed Judea Palestine, after the earlier coastal inhabitants, the Philistines.

Arab invaders conquered Palestine in 636. The Arabic language and Islam prevailed within a few centuries, but a Jewish minority remained. The land was ruled from the 11th century as a part of non-Arab empires by Seljuks, Mamluks, and Ottomans (with a crusader interval, 1098-1291).

After 4 centuries of Ottoman rule, the land was taken in 1917 by Britain, which pledged in the Balfour Declaration to support a Jewish national homeland there. In 1920 a British Palestine Mandate was recognized; in 1922 the land east of the Jordan was detached.

Jewish immigration, begun in the late 19th century, swelled in the 1930s with refugees from the Nazis; heavy Arab immigration from Syria and Lebanon also occurred. Arab opposition to Jewish immigration turned violent in 1920, 1921, 1929, and 1936. The UN General Assembly voted in 1947 to partition Palestine into an Arab and a Jewish state. Britain withdrew in May 1948.

Israel was declared an independent state May 14, 1948; the Arabs rejected partition. Egypt, Jordan, Syria, Lebanon, Iraq, and Saudi Arabia invaded, but failed to destroy the Jewish state, which gained territory. Separate armistices with the Arab nations were signed in 1949; Jordan occupied the West Bank, Egypt occupied Gaza; neither granted Palestinian autonomy.

After persistent terrorist raids, Israel invaded Egypt's Sinai, Oct. 29, 1956, aided briefly by British and French forces. A UN cease-fire was arranged Nov. 6.

An uneasy truce between Israel and the Arab countries lasted until 1967, when Egypt reoccupied the Gaza Strip and closed the Gulf of Aqaba to Israeli shipping. In a 6-day war that started June 5, the Israelis took the Gaza Strip, occupied the Sinai Peninsula to the Suez Canal, and captured East Jerusalem, Syria's Golan Heights, and Jordan's West Bank.

Egypt and Syria attacked Israel, Oct. 6, 1973 (on Yom Kippur, the most solemn day on the Jewish calendar). Israel counter-attacked, driving the Syrians back, and crossed the Suez Canal. A cease-fire took effect Oct. 24 and a UN peacekeeping force went to the area. Under a disengagement agreement signed Jan. 18, 1974, Israel withdrew from the canal's west bank.Israeli forces raided Entebbe, Uganda, July 3, 1976, and rescued 103 hostages who had been seized by Arab and German terrorists.

Israel's prime ministers, including David Ben-Gurion, Golda Meir, and Yitzhak Rabin, pursued a moderate socialist program, 1948-77. In 1977, the conservative opposition, led by Menachem Begin, was voted into office for the first time. Egypt's Pres. Anwar al-Sadat visited Jerusalem Nov. 1977, and on Mar. 26, 1979, Egypt and Israel signed a formal peace treaty, ending 30 years of war. Israel returned the Sinai to Egypt in 1982.

On June 7, 1981, Israeli jets destroyed an Iraqi atomic reactor near Baghdad that, Israel claimed, would have enabled Iraq to manufacture nuclear weapons. Israeli forces invaded Lebanon, June 6, 1982, to destroy Palestine Liberation Organization (PLO) strongholds there. After massive Israeli bombing of West Beirut, the PLO agreed to evacuate the city. Israeli troops entered West Beirut after newly elected Lebanese Pres. Bashir Gemayel was assassinated on Sept. 14. Israel drew widespread condemnation when Lebanese Christian forces, Sept. 16, entered two West Beirut refugee camps and slaughtered hundreds of Palestinians.

In 1989, violence escalated over the Israeli military occupation of the West Bank and Gaza Strip. In a series of uprisings known as the 1st intifada, Palestinian protesters defied Israeli troops, who forcibly retaliated. During the Persian Gulf War, 1991, Iraq fired Scud missiles at Israel. The Labor Party of Yitzhak Rabin won parliamentary elections, June 23, 1992.

Ongoing peace talks led to historic agreements between Israel and the PLO, Sept. 1993. The PLO recognized Israel's right to exist; Israel recognized the PLO as the Palestinians' representative; the two sides then signed, Sept. 13, an agreement for limited Palestinian self-rule in the West Bank and Gaza. Israel and Jordan signed, July 25, 1994, in Washington, DC, a declaration ending their 46-year state of war.

Arab and Jewish extremists repeatedly challenged the peace process. A Jewish gunman opened fire on Arab worshippers at a mosque in Hebron, Feb. 25, 1994, killing at least 29 before he himself was killed. On Nov. 4, 1995, an Orthodox Jewish Israeli assassinated Rabin as he left a peace rally in Tel Aviv. Support for Rabin's successor, Shimon Peres, was shaken by a series of suicide bombings and rocket attacks against Israel by Islamic militants. Emphasizing security issues, the candidate of the conservative Likud bloc, Benjamin Netanyahu, was elected prime minister on May 29, 1996.

Under an interim accord brokered by Pres. Bill Clinton and signed by Netanyahu and PLO leader Yasir Arafat at the White House, Oct. 23, 1998, Israel yielded more West Bank territory to the Palestinians, in exchange for new security guarantees. Negotiations bogged down, however, and full implementation did not begin until Sept. 1999. In the interim, Netanyahu lost by a landslide to the Labor party candidate, Ehud Barak, in the general election of May 17.

Israel pulled virtually all its troops out of S Lebanon by May 24, 2000. Marathon summit talks in the U.S. between Barak and Arafat, July 11-25, failed. A 2nd intifada began in late Sept. in Israel and the Palestinian territories. Barak called new elections for prime minister but lost Feb. 6, 2001, to Ariel Sharon, a hardliner. The bloodshed intensified during the summer, as Palestinian suicide bombers launched attacks on Israeli civilians and Israel struck at against Palestinian-controlled territory and carried out an assassination campaign against suspected terrorists.

Israel launched a major West Bank offensive Mar. 29, 2002, 2 days after a suicide bomber killed 26 Israeli Jews at a Passover celebration in Netanya. Fighting was particularly fierce at the Jenin refugee camp, where 23 Israeli troops and at least 50 Palestinians were killed. Israel withdrew in early May but, after another wave of suicide bombings, reoccupied much of the West Bank June 21-27. In June 2002 the Israeli government began building a controversial security barrier in the West Bank to restrict Palestinian access to Israel; in a nonbinding ruling, July 9, 2004, the World Court said the barrier violated international law.

A U.S.-sponsored "road map" to Middle East peace, unveiled Apr. 30, 2003, made little headway. Israel Sept. 1 vowed "all-out war" against Hamas terrorists. Israeli missile strikes in Gaza City killed Hamas founder and leader Sheikh Ahmed Yassin Mar. 22, 2004, and his successor, Abdel Aziz al-Rantisi, Apr. 17. Hamas suicide bombers Aug. 31 blew up 2 buses in Beersheba, killing 16 people.

The death of Palestinian Pres. Arafat, Nov. 11, 2004, and the election Jan. 9, 2005, of his successor, Mahmoud Abbas (also called Abu Mazen), opened new opportunities for Israeli-Palestinian peace. Defying right-wing critics, Sharon ordered an Israeli pullout from the Gaza Strip (see below).

Since Sept. 2000, the conflict has claimed the lives of more than 970 Israelis and at least 3,450 Palestinians.

Gaza Strip

The Gaza Strip, also known as Gaza, extends NE from the Sinai Peninsula for 40 km (25 mi), with the Mediterranean Sea to the W and Israel to the E. The Palestinian Authority is responsible for civil government. Nearly all the inhabitants are Palestinian Arabs, more than 35% of whom live in refugee camps. Population (2004 est) 1,324,991. Area: 139 sq. mi.

Israel captured Gaza from Egypt in the 1967 war. It remained under Israeli occupation until May 1994, when the Israel Defense Forces withdrew. Agreements between Israel and the PLO in 1993 and 1994 provided for interim self-rule in Gaza, but Israel retained control over security. Israel forcibly evacuated all 9,000 Jewish settlers from Gaza by Aug. 22, 2005, and the last remaining Israeli soldiers pulled out Sept. 12. Israel established a fortified barrier on its Gaza border to block Palestinian infiltrators.

West Bank

Located W of the Jordan R. and Dead Sea, the West Bank is bounded by Jordan on the E and by Israel on the N, W, and S. The Palestinian Authority administers several major cities, but Israel retains control over much land, including Jewish settlements. Population (2004 est) 2,311,204. Area: 2,263 sq. mi.

Israel captured the West Bank from Jordan in the 1967 war. A 1974 Arab summit conference designated the PLO as sole representative of West Bank Arabs. In 1988 Jordan cut legal and administrative ties with the territory. Jericho was returned to Palestinian control in May 1994. An accord between Israel and the PLO expanding Palestinian self-rule in the West Bank was signed Sept. 28, 1995. Later agreements gave Palestinians full or shared control of 40% of West Bank territory.

Italy

Italian Republic

People: Population: 58,103,033. **Age distrib.** (%): <15: 13.9; 65+: 19.4. **Pop. density:** 500 per sq mi, 193 per sq km. **Urban:** 91.6%. **Ethnic groups:** Mostly Italian; small minorities of German, Slovene, Albanian. **Principal languages:** Italian (official), German, French, Slovenian, Albanian. **Chief religion:** Predominately Roman Catholic.

Geography: Total area: 116,306 sq mi, 301,230 sq km; **Land area:** 113,522 sq mi, 294,020 sq km. **Location:** In S Europe, jutting into Mediterranean Sea. **Neighbors:** France on W, Switzerland and Austria on N, Slovenia on E. **Topography:** Occupies a long boot-shaped peninsula, extending SE from the Alps into the Mediterranean, with the islands of Sicily and Sardinia offshore. The alluvial Po Valley drains most of N. The rest of the country is rugged and mountainous, except for intermittent coastal plains, like the Campania, S of Rome. Apennine Mts. run down through center of peninsula. **Capital:** Rome, 2,665,000. **Cities (urban aggr.):** Milan, 4,183,000; Naples, 2,995,000; Turin, 1,247,000.

Government: Type: Republic. **Head of state:** Pres. Carlo Azeglio Ciampi; b Dec. 9, 1920; in office: May 18, 1999. **Head of gov.:** Prime Min. Silvio Berlusconi; b Sept. 29, 1936; in office: June 11, 2001. **Local divisions:** 20 regions divided into 103 provinces. **Defense budget** (2004): $17.5 bil. **Active troops:** 194,000.

Economy: Industries: tourism, machinery, iron & steel, chemicals, food proc., textiles, autos. **Chief crops:** fruits, vegetables, grapes, potatoes, sugar beets, soybeans, grain, olives. **Natural resources:** mercury, potash, marble, sulfur, nat. gas, oil, fish, coal. **Crude oil reserves** (2004): 622 mil bbls. **Arable land:** 31%. **Livestock** (2004): cattle: 6.7 mil; chickens: 100 mil; goats: 961,000; pigs: 9.2 mil; sheep: 8.0 mil. **Fish catch** (2003): 487,356 metric tons. **Electricity prod.** (2003): 270.1 bil. kWh. **Labor force** (2001): agriculture 5%, industry 32%, services 63%.

Finance: Monetary unit: Euro (EUR) (Sept. 2005: 0.80 = $1 U.S.). **GDP** (2004 est.): $1.6 tril.; **per capita GDP:** $27,700; **GDP growth:** 1.3%. **Imports** (2004 est.): $329.3 bil.; partners (2004): Germany 18.1%, France 10.7%, Netherlands 5.8%, Spain 4.7%, Belgium 4.4%, UK 4.3%, China 4.1%. **Exports** (2004 est.): $336.4 bil.; partners (2004): Germany 13.7%, France 12.1%, US 8%, Spain 7.3%, UK 6.9%, Switzerland 4.1%. **Tourism:** $31,222 mil. **Budget** (2004 est.): $820.1 bil. **Intl. reserves less gold:** $17.94 bil. **Gold:** 78.83 mil. oz t. **Consumer prices:** 2.21%.

Transport: Railroad: Length: 12,112 mi. **Motor vehicles:** 33.13 mil pass. cars, 3.75 mil comm. vehicles. **Civil aviation:** 25.4 bil pass.-mi; 96 airports. **Chief ports:** Genoa, Venice, Trieste, Palermo, Naples, La Spezia.

Communications: TV sets: 492 per 1,000 pop. **Radios:** 880 per 1,000 pop. **Telephone lines:** 26.6 mil. **Daily newspaper circ.:** 104 per 1,000 pop. **Internet**: 18.5 mil. users.

Health: Life expect.: 76.8 male; 82.8 female. **Births** (per 1,000 pop.): 8.9. **Deaths** (per 1,000 pop.): 10.3. **Natural inc.:** –0.14%. **Infant mortality** (per 1,000 live births): 5.9. **AIDS rate:** 0.5%.

Education: Compulsory: ages 6-14. **Literacy:** 98.6%.

Major Intl. Organizations: UN and all of its specialized agencies, EU, NATO, OECD, OSCE.

Embassy: 3000 Whitehaven St. NW 20008; 612-4400.

Website: www.italyemb.org

Rome emerged as the major power in Italy after 500 BC, dominating the Etruscans to the N and Greeks to the S. Under the Empire, which lasted until the 5th century AD, Rome ruled most of Western Europe, the Balkans, the Middle East, and N Africa.

After the Germanic invasions, lasting several centuries, a high civilization arose in the city-states of the N, culminating in the Renaissance. But German, French, Spanish, and Austrian intervention prevented the unification of the country. In 1859 Lombardy came under the crown of King Victor Emmanuel II of Sardinia. By plebiscite in 1860, Parma, Modena, Romagna, and Tuscany joined, followed by Sicily and Naples, and by the Marches and Umbria. The first Italian Parliament declared Victor Emmanuel king of Italy Mar. 17, 1861. Mantua and Venetia were added in 1866 as an outcome of the Austro-Prussian war. The Papal States were taken by Italian troops Sept. 20, 1870, on the withdrawal of the French garrison. The states were annexed to the kingdom by plebiscite. Italy recognized Vatican City as independent Feb. 11, 1929.

Fascism appeared in Italy Mar. 23, 1919, led by Benito Mussolini, who took over the government at the invitation of the king Oct. 28, 1922. Mussolini acquired dictatorial powers. He made war on Ethiopia and proclaimed Victor Emmanuel III emperor, defied the sanctions of the League of Nations, sent troops to fight for Franco against the Republic of Spain, and joined Germany in World War II.

After Fascism was overthrown in 1943, Italy declared war on Germany and Japan and contributed to the Allied victory. It surrendered conquered lands and lost its colonies. Mussolini was killed by partisans Apr. 28, 1945. Victor Emmanuel III abdicated May 9, 1946; his son Humbert II was king until June 10, when Italy became a republic after a referendum, June 2-3.

Since World War II, Italy has enjoyed growth in industrial output and living standards, in part a result of membership in the European Community (now European Union). Political stability has not kept pace with economic prosperity, and organized crime and corruption have been persistent problems.

Christian Democratic leader and former Prime Min. Aldo Moro was abducted and murdered in 1978 by Red Brigade terrorists. The wave of left-wing political violence, including other kidnappings and assassinations, continued into the 1980s.

In the early 1990s, scandals implicated some of Italy's most prominent politicians. In Mar. 1994 voting, under reformed election rules, right-wing parties won a majority, dislodging Italy's long-powerful Christian Democratic Party. After a series of short-lived governments, a coalition of center-left parties won the election of Apr. 21, 1996. Italy led a 7,000-member international peacekeeping force in Albania, Apr.-Aug. 1997, and contributed 2,000 troops to the NATO-led security force (KFOR) that entered Kosovo in June 1999.

Supporters of Silvio Berlusconi, a multibillionaire media magnate, won the parliamentary elections of May 13, 2001. In 2003, Berlusconi backed the U.S.-led war in Iraq, and Italian troops served in the coalition. On trial for bribing judges in the 1980s, he was helped when Parliament passed a bill in June immunizing top government leaders from prosecution while they held office. Over 4,100 elderly Italians died because of a severe summer heat wave.

Corruption charges against Berlusconi were dismissed Dec. 10, 2004. Public opposition to his Iraq policy intensified after U.S. troops at a Baghdad checkpoint fired on a car carrying a freed hostage, Mar. 4, 2005, wounding her and killing the Italian agent who was protecting her. Berlusconi weathered a cabinet crisis after his conservative coalition lost regional elections, Apr. 3-4. Turin has been chosen to host the Winter Olympics in 2006.

Sicily, 9,926 sq. mi., pop. (2001 est.) 4,866,200 is an island 180 by 120 mi., seat of a region that embraces the island of **Pantelleria,** 32 sq. mi., and the **Lipari** group, 44 sq. mi., including 2 active volcanoes: **Vulcano,** 1,637 ft., and **Stromboli,** 3,038 ft. From prehistoric times Sicily has been settled by various peoples; a Greek state had its capital at Syracuse. Rome took Sicily from Carthage 215 BC. **Mt. Etna,** an 11,053-ft. active volcano, is its tallest peak.

Sardinia, 9,301 sq. mi., pop. (2001 est.) 1,599,500, lies in the Mediterranean, 115 mi. W of Italy and 7$^1/_2$ mi. S of Corsica. It is 160 mi. long, 68 mi. wide, and mountainous, with mining of coal, zinc, lead, copper. In 1720 Sardinia was added to the possessions of the Dukes of Savoy in Piedmont and Savoy to form the Kingdom of Sardinia. Giuseppe Garibaldi is buried on the nearby isle of Caprera. **Elba,** 86 sq. mi., lies 6 mi. W of Tuscany. Napoleon I lived in exile on Elba 1814-1815.

Jamaica

People: Population: 2,735,520. **Age distrib.** (%): <15: 27.5; 65+: 6.9. **Pop. density:** 645 per sq mi, 249 per sq km. **Urban:** 67.4%. **Ethnic groups:** Black 91%, mixed 7%, East Indian and other 2%. **Principal languages:** English, patois English. **Chief religions:** Protestant 61%, spiritual cults and other 35%, Roman Catholic 4%.

Geography: Total area: 4,244 sq mi, 10,991 sq km; **Land area:** 4,182 sq mi, 10,831 sq km. **Location:** In West Indies. **Neighbors:** Nearest are Cuba to N, Haiti to E. **Topography:** Four-fifths of Jamaica is covered by mountains. **Capital:** Kingston, 575,000.

Government: Type: Parliamentary democracy. **Head of state:** Queen Elizabeth II, represented by Gov.-Gen. Sir Howard Cooke; b Nov. 13, 1915; in office: Aug. 1, 1991. **Head of gov.:** Prime Min. Percival J. Patterson; b Apr. 10, 1935; in office: Mar. 30, 1992. **Local divisions:** 14 parishes. **Defense budget** (2004): $50 mil. **Active troops:** 2,830.

Economy: Industries: tourism, bauxite, textiles, food proc., light manufactures, rum, cement, metal, paper, chemical products. **Chief crops:** sugarcane, bananas, coffee, citrus, potatoes. **Natural resources:** bauxite, gypsum, limestone. **Arable land:** 14%. **Livestock** (2004): cattle: 430,000; chickens: 12.5 mil; goats: 440,000; pigs: 150,000; sheep: 1,280. **Fish catch** (2003): 11,671 metric tons. **Electricity prod.** (2003): 6.6 bil. kWh. **Labor force** (2003): agriculture 20.1%, industry 16.6%, services 63.4%.

Finance: Monetary unit: Jamaican Dollar (JMD) (Sept. 2005: 62.13 = $1 U.S.). **GDP** (2004 est.): $11.1 bil.; **per capita GDP:** $4,100; **GDP growth:** 1.9%. **Imports** (2004 est.): $3.6 bil.; partners (2004): US 38.3%, Trinidad and Tobago 10.3%, Venezuela 5.6%, France 5.5%, Japan 4.6%. **Exports** (2004 est.): $1.7 bil.; partners (2004): US 17.2%, Canada 14.3%, France 12.6%, China 11.4%, UK 8.6%, Netherlands 7%, Norway 5.8%, Germany 5.6%. **Tourism:** $1,355 mil. **Budget** (2004 est.): $3.2 bil. **Intl. reserves less gold:** $1.19 bil.

Transport: Railroad: Length: 169 mi. **Motor vehicles:** 129,400 pass. cars, 65,200 comm. vehicles. **Civil aviation:** 2.7 bil pass.-mi; 11 airports. **Chief ports:** Kingston, Montego Bay.

Communications: TV sets: 191 per 1,000 pop. **Radios:** 796 per 1,000 pop. **Telephone lines** (2002) 444,400. **Daily newspaper circ.:** 62 per 1,000 pop. **Internet** (2002): 600,000 users.

Health: Life expect.: 71.6 male; 75.1 female. **Births** (per 1,000 pop.): 21.3. **Deaths** (per 1,000 pop.): 6.5. **Natural inc.:** 1.48%. **Infant mortality** (per 1,000 live births): 16.3. **AIDS rate:** 1.2%.

Education: Compulsory: ages 6-11. **Literacy:** 87.9%.

Major Intl. Organizations: UN (FAO, IBRD, ILO, IMF, IMO, WHO, WTrO), Caricom, the Commonwealth, OAS.

Embassy: 1520 New Hampshire Ave. NW 20036; 452-0660.

Website: www.jis.gov.jm

Jamaica was visited by Columbus, 1494, and ruled by Spain (under whom Arawak Indians died out) until seized by Britain, 1655. Jamaica won independence Aug. 6, 1962.

In 1974 Jamaica sought an increase in taxes paid by U.S. and Canadian bauxite mines. The socialist government acquired 50% ownership of the companies' Jamaican interests in 1976, and was reelected that year. Rudimentary welfare state measures were passed. Relations with the U.S. improved in the 1980s when Jamaican politics entered a more conservative phase. Violence between government forces and West Kingston slum residents claimed at least 20 lives July 7-10, 2001. At least 17 died when Hurricane Ivan hit S Jamaica Sept. 10-11, 2004.

Japan

People: Population: 127,417,244. **Age distrib.** (%): <15: 14.3; 65+: 19.5. **Pop. density:** 873 per sq mi, 337 per sq km **Urban:** 52.1%. **Ethnic groups:** Japanese 99%; Korean, Chinese, and other 1%. **Principal languages:** Japanese (official), Ainu, Korean. **Chief religions:** Shinto and Buddhist, observed together by 84%.

Geography: Total area: 145,883 sq mi, 377,835 sq km; **Land area:** 144,689 sq mi, 374,744 sq km. **Location:** Archipelago off E coast of Asia. **Neighbors:** Russia to N, South Korea to W. **Topography:** Japan consists of 4 main islands: Honshu ("mainland"), 87,805 sq. mi.; Hokkaido, 30,144 sq. mi.; Kyushu, 14,114 sq. mi.; and Shikoku, 7,049 sq. mi. The coast, deeply indented, measures 16,654 mi. The northern islands are a continuation of the Sakhalin Mts. The Kunlun range of China continues into southern islands, the ranges meeting in the Japanese Alps. In a vast transverse fissure crossing Honshu E-W rises a group of volcanoes, mostly extinct or inactive, including 12,388 ft. Mt. Fuji (Fujiyama) near Tokyo. **Capital:** Tokyo, 34,997,000. **Cities (urban aggr.)**: Osaka, 11,165,000, (1998 city proper: 2,599,642); Nagoya, 3,122,000; Sapporo, 1,756,000; Kyoto, 1,806,000.

Government: Type: Parliamentary democracy. **Head of state:** Emp. Akihito; b Dec. 23, 1933; in office: Jan. 7, 1989. **Head of gov.:** Prime Min. Junichiro Koizumi; b Jan. 8, 1942; in office: Apr. 26, 2001. **Local divisions:** 47 prefectures. **Defense budget** (2004): $45.1 bil. **Active troops:** 239,900.

Economy: Industries: motor vehicles, electronic equip., machine tools, steel & nonferrous metals, ships, chemicals, textiles, proc. foods. **Chief crops:** rice, sugar beets, vegetables, fruit. **Natural resources:** fish. **Crude oil reserves** (2004): 59 mil bbls. **Arable land:** 11%. **Livestock** (2004): cattle: 4.5 mil; chickens: 286 mil.; goats: 34,000; pigs: 9.7 mil; sheep: 11,000. **Fish catch** (2003): 5,455,828 metric tons. **Electricity prod.** (2003): 1017.5 bil. kWh. **Labor force** (2002 est.): agriculture 5%, industry 25%, services 70%.

Finance: Monetary unit: Yen (JPY) (Sept. 2005: 110.04 = $1 U.S.). **GDP** (2004 est.): $3.7 tril.; **per capita GDP:** $29,400; **GDP growth:** 2.9%. **Imports** (2004 est.): $401.8 bil.; partners (2004): China 20.7%, US 14%, South Korea 4.9%, Australia 4.3%, Indonesia 4.1%, Saudi Arabia 4.1%, UAE 4%. **Exports** (2004 est.): $538.8 bil.; partners (2004): US 22.7%, China 13.1%, South Korea 7.8%, Taiwan 7.4%, Hong Kong 6.3%. **Tourism:** $8,848 mil. **Budget** (2004 est.): $1.7 tril. **Intl. reserves less gold:** $536.95 bil. **Gold:** 24.6 mil. oz t. **Consumer prices:** –0.01%.

Transport: Railroad: Length: 14,395 mi. **Motor vehicles:** 54.5405 mil pass. cars, 17.7163 mil comm. vehicles. **Civil aviation:** 100.8 bil pass.-mi; 141 airports. **Chief ports:** Tokyo, Kobe, Osaka, Nagoya, Chiba, Kawasaki, Hakodate.

Communications: TV sets: 719 per 1,000 pop. **Radios:** 956 per 1,000 pop. **Telephone lines:** 60.2 mil. **Daily newspaper circ.:** 578 per 1,000 pop. **Internet:** 61.6 mil. users.

Health: Life expect.: 77.9 male; 84.6 female. **Births** (per 1,000 pop.): 9.5. **Deaths** (per 1,000 pop.): 9.0. **Natural inc.:** 0.05%. **Infant mortality** (per 1,000 live births): 3.3. **AIDS rate:** <0.1%.

Education: Compulsory: ages 6-15. **Literacy:** 99%.

Major Intl. Organizations: UN and all its specialized agencies, APEC, OECD.

Embassy: 2520 Massachusetts Ave. NW 20008; 238-6700.

Website: www.kantei.go.jp/foreign/index-e.html

According to Japanese legend, the empire was founded by Emperor Jimmu, 660 BC, but earliest records of a unified Japan date from 1,000 years later. Chinese influence was strong in the formation of Japanese civilization. Buddhism was introduced before the 6th century AD.

A feudal system, with locally powerful noble families and their samurai warrior retainers, dominated from 1192. Central power was held by successive families of shoguns (military dictators), 1192-1867, until recovered by Emperor Meiji, 1868. The Portuguese and Dutch had minor trade with Japan in the 16th and 17th centuries; U.S. Commodore Matthew C. Perry opened the country to U.S. trade in a treaty ratified 1854. Industrialization was begun in the late 19th century. Japan fought China, 1894-95, gaining Taiwan. After war with Russia, 1904-5, Russia ceded S half of Sakhalin and gave concessions in China. Japan annexed Korea 1910.

In World War I Japan ousted Germany from Shandong in China and took over German Pacific islands. Japan took Manchuria in 1931 and launched full-scale war in China in 1937. Japan launched war against the U.S. by attacking Pearl Harbor Dec. 7, 1941. The U.S. dropped atomic bombs on Hiroshima, Aug. 6, and Nagasaki, Aug. 9, 1945. Japan surrendered Aug. 14, 1945.

In a new constitution adopted May 3, 1947, Japan renounced the right to wage war; the emperor gave up claims to divinity; the Diet became the sole law-making authority. The U.S. and 48 other non-Communist nations signed a peace treaty and the U.S. a bilateral defense agreement with Japan, in San Francisco Sept. 8, 1951, restoring Japan's sovereignty as of April 28, 1952.

Rebuilding after World War II, Japan emerged as one of the most powerful economies in the world, and as a leader in technology.The U.S. and Western Europe criticized Japan for its restrictive policy on imports, which eventually allowed Japan to accumulate huge trade surpluses.

On June 26, 1968, the U.S. returned to Japanese control the Bonin Isls., Volcano Isls. (including Iwo Jima), and Marcus Isls. On May 15, 1972, Okinawa, the other Ryukyu Isls., and the Daito Isls. were returned by the U.S.; it was agreed the U.S. would continue to maintain military bases on Okinawa.

The Recruit scandal, the nation's worst political scandal since World War II, which involved illegal political donations and stock trading, led to the resignation of Premier Noboru Takeshita in May 1989. Following new political and economic scandals, the ruling Liberal Democratic Party (LDP) was denied a majority in general elections July 18, 1993. On June 29, 1994, Tomiichi Murayama became Japan's first Socialist premier since 1947-48.

An earthquake in the Kobe area in Jan. 1995 claimed more than 5,000 lives, injured nearly 35,000, and caused over $90 billion in property damage. On Mar. 20, a nerve gas attack in the Tokyo subway (blamed on a religious cult) killed 12 and injured thousands. Public anger at the rape of a 12-year-old Okinawa schoolgirl by 3 U.S. servicemen, Sept. 4, led the U.S. to begin reducing its military presence there.

Murayama resigned as prime minister, Jan. 5, 1996, and was replaced by Ryutaro Hashimoto of the LDP. Hashimoto signed a joint security declaration with U.S. Pres. Bill Clinton in Tokyo, Apr. 17, 1996. Nagano hosted the Winter Olympics, Feb. 7-22, 1998.

Murayama resigned as prime minister, Jan. 5, 1996, and was replaced by Ryutaro Hashimoto of the LDP. Nagano hosted the Winter Olympics, Feb. 7-22, 1998.

With the country mired in a lengthy recession, a series of weak LDP governments led Japan. In Apr. 2001 Junichiro Koizumi, a populist reformer, became LDP leader and prime minister. In Sept. 2002, Koizumi became the first Japanese leader to visit N. Korea; during the meeting N. Korean Prem. Kim Jong-Il apologized for abducting Japanese citizens. Five of these abductees returned to Japan in Oct. 2002.

Koizumi's parliamentary coalition retained power in the elections of Nov. 9, 2003. The cabinet Dec. 9 approved deploying more than 500 noncombat troops to aid Iraq reconstruction, the first time since WWII that Japanese troops were sent to a combat zone. A commuter train crash at Amagasaki, W Japan Apr. 25, 2005, killed over 100 people. Voters in legislative elections Sept. 11 gave Koizumi a mandate to restructure the economy.

Jordan

Hashemite Kingdom of Jordan

People: Population: 5,759,732. **Age distrib.** (%): <15: 34.5; 65+: 3.8. **Pop. density:** 162 per sq mi, 62 per sq km. **Urban:** 79.0%. **Ethnic groups:** Arab 98%, Armenian 1%, Circassian 1%. **Principal languages:** Arabic (official), English. **Chief religions:** Muslim (official; mostly Sunni) 92%, Christian 6%.

Geography: Total area: 35,637 sq mi, 92,300 sq km; **Land area:** 35,510 sq mi, 91,971 sq km. **Location:** In Middle East. **Neighbors:** Israel and West Bank on W, Saudi Arabia on S, Iraq on E, Syria on N. **Topography:** About 88% of Jordan is arid. Fertile areas are in W. Only port is on short Aqaba Gulf coast. Country shares Dead Sea (about 1,300 ft. below sea level) with Israel. **Capital:** Amman, 1,237,000.

Government: Type: Constitutional monarchy. **Head of state:** King Abdullah II; b Jan. 30, 1962; in office: Feb. 7, 1999. **Head of gov.:** Prime Min. Adnan Badran; b Dec. 15, 1935; in office: Apr. 7, 2005.**Local divisions:** 12 governorates. **Defense budget** (2004): $877 mil. **Active troops:** 100,500.

Economy: Industries: phosphates, oil refining, cement, potash, light mfg. **Chief crops:** wheat, barley, citrus, tomatoes, melons, olives. **Natural resources:** phosphates, potash, shale oil. **Crude oil reserves** (2004): 1 mil bbls. **Arable land:** 4%. **Livestock** (2004): cattle: 68,000; chickens: 25 mil; goats: 530,000; sheep: 1.5 mil. **Fish catch** (2003): 1,131 metric tons. **Electricity prod.** (2003): 7.5 bil. kWh. **Labor force** (2001 est.): agriculture 5%, industry 12.5%, services 82.5%.

Finance: Monetary unit: Dinar (JOD) (Sept. 2005: 0.71 = $1 U.S.). **GDP** (2004 est.): $25.5 bil.; **per capita GDP:** $4,500; **GDP growth:** 5.1%. **Imports** (2004 est.): $7.6 bil.; partners (2004): Saudi Arabia 19.9%, China 8.4%, Germany 6.8%, US 6.7%. **Exports** (2004 est.): $3.2 bil.; partners (2004): US 25.8%, Iraq 18.4%, India 6.4%, Saudi Arabia 5.2%. **Tourism:** $815 mil. **Budget** (2004 est.): $3.6 bil. **Intl. reserves less gold:** $3.39 bil. **Gold:** 410,000 oz t. **Consumer prices:** 3.37%.

Transport: Railroad: Length: 314 mi. **Motor vehicles:** 346,000 pass. cars, 176,700 comm. vehicles. **Civil aviation:** 2.4 bil pass.-mi; 15 airports. **Chief port:** Al Aqabah.

Communications: TV sets: 83 per 1,000 pop. **Radios:** 271 per 1,000 pop. **Telephone lines:** 622,600. **Daily newspaper circ.:** 75.5 per 1,000 pop. **Internet**: 444,000 users.

Health: Life expect.: 75.8 male; 80.9 female. **Births** (per 1,000 pop.): 21.8. **Deaths** (per 1,000 pop.): 2.6. **Natural inc.:** 1.91%. **Infant mortality** (per 1,000 live births): 17.4. **AIDS rate:** <0.1%.

Education: Compulsory: ages 6-15. **Literacy:** 91.3%.

Major Intl. Organizations: UN (FAO, IBRD, ILO, IMF, IMO, WHO), AL.

Embassy: 3504 International Dr. NW 20008; 966-2664.

Website: www.nic.gov.jo/en/index.html

From ancient times to 1922 the lands to the E of the Jordan River were culturally and politically united with the lands to the W. Arabs conquered the area in the 7th century; the Ottomans took control in the 16th. Britain's 1920 Palestine Mandate covered both sides of the Jordan. In 1921, Abdullah, son of the ruler of Hejaz in Arabia, was installed by Britain as emir of an autonomous Transjordan, covering two-thirds of Palestine. An independent kingdom was proclaimed, 1946.

During the 1948 Arab-Israeli war the West Bank and East Jerusalem were added to the kingdom, which changed its name to Jordan. All these territories were lost to Israel in the 1967 war, which swelled the number of Arab refugees on the East Bank.

Some 700,000 refugees entered Jordan following Iraq's invasion of Kuwait, Aug. 1990. Jordan was viewed as supporting Iraq during the 1990-1991 Persian Gulf crisis.

Jordan and Israel officially agreed, July 25, 1994, to end their state of war; a formal peace treaty was signed Oct. 26. Following a prolonged bout with cancer, King Hussein died Feb. 7, 1999; his eldest son and designated successor immediately assumed the throne as Abdullah II.

Jordanian authorities Apr. 2004 said they had foiled a possible chemical attack against the U.S. embassy and other Amman targets; the plot was traced to Abu Musab al-Zarqawi, a high-ranking Jordanian member of al-Qaeda whom the U.S. accused of leading guerrilla activities in Iraq. Zarqawi was also linked to a rocket attack at Aqaba, Aug. 19, 2005, that narrowly missed a U.S. warship.

Kazakhstan

Republic of Kazakhstan

People: Population: 15,185,844. **Age distrib.** (%): <15: 23.7; 65+: 7.9. **Pop. density:** 14 per sq mi, 6 per sq km. **Urban:** 55.8%. **Ethnic groups:** Kazakh 53%, Russian 30%, Ukrainian 4%, Uzbek 3%, German 2%, Uighur 1%. **Principal languages:** Kazakh, Russian (both official); Ukrainian, German, Uzbek. **Chief religions:** Muslim 47%, Russian Orthodox 44%.

Geography: Total area: 1,049,155 sq mi, 2,717,300 sq km; **Land area:** 1,030,816 sq mi, 2,669,800 sq km. **Location:** In Central Asia. **Neighbors:** Russia on N; China on E; Kyrgyzstan, Uzbekistan, Turkmenistan on S; Caspian Sea on W. **Topography:** Extends from the lower reaches of Volga in Europe to the Altay Mts. on the Chinese border. **Capital:** Astana, 332,000. **Cities (urban aggr.)**: Alma-Ata, 1,130,000.

Government: Type: Republic. **Head of state:** Pres. Nursultan A. Nazarbayev; b July 6, 1940; in office: Apr. 1990. **Head of gov.:** Prime Min. Daniyal Akhmetov; b June 15, 1954; in office: June 13, 2003. **Local divisions:** 14 oblystar, 3 cities. **Defense budget** (2004): $362 mil. **Active troops:** 65,800.

Economy: Industries: mining and oil producer, agric. machinery, electric motors, constr. materials. **Chief crops:** wheat, cotton, wool. **Natural resources:** oil, nat. gas, coal, iron ore, mang., chrome ore, nickel, cobalt, copper, molybd., lead, zinc, bauxite, gold, uranium. **Crude oil reserves** (2004): 9.0 bil. bbls. **Arable land:** 12%. **Livestock** (2004): cattle: 4.9 mil; chickens: 24.7 mil; goats: 1.5 mil; pigs: 1.1 mil; sheep: 10.8 mil. **Fish catch** (2004): 23,885 metric tons. **Electricity prod.** (2003): 60.3 bil. kWh. **Labor force** (2002 est.): agriculture 20%, industry 30%, services 50%.

Finance: Monetary unit: Tenge (KZT) (Sept. 2005: 135.19 = $1 U.S.). **GDP** (2004 est.): $118.4 bil.; **per capita GDP:** $7,800; **GDP growth:** 9.1%. **Imports** (2004 est.): $13.1 bil.; partners (2004): Russia 33.9%, China 13.6%, Germany 9.6%, France 6.8%. **Exports** (2004 est.): $18.5 bil.; partners (2004): Russia 13.5%, Bermuda 13.4%, China 10.4%, Germany 9.2%, Switzerland 9.1%, France 6.7%. **Tourism:** $564 mil. **Budget** (2004 est.): $9.0 bil. **Intl. reserves less gold:** $5.46 bil. **Gold:** 1.83 mil. oz t. **Consumer prices:** 6.88%.

Transport: Railroad: Length: 8,451 mi. **Motor vehicles:** 1.06 mil pass. cars, 280,300 comm. vehicles. **Civil aviation:** 787.9 mil. pass.-mi; 60 airports. **Chief ports:** Aqtau, Atyrau.

Communications: TV sets: 240 per 1,000 pop. **Radios:** 395 per 1,000 pop. **Telephone lines**: 2.2 mil. **Internet** (2002): 250,000 users.

Health: Life expect.: 61.2 male; 72.2 female. **Births** (per 1,000 pop.): 15.8. **Deaths** (per 1,000 pop.): 9.5. **Natural inc.:** 0.63%. **Infant mortality** (per 1,000 live births): 29.2. **AIDS rate:** 0.2%.

Education: Compulsory: ages 7-17. **Literacy:** 98.4%.

Major Intl. Organizations: UN (IBRD, ILO, IMF, IMO, WHO), CIS, OSCE.

Embassy: 1401 16th St. NW 20036; 232-5488.

Website: http://www.president.kz/page.php?lang=2

The region came under the Mongols' rule in the 13th century and gradually came under Russian rule, 1730-1853. It was admitted to the USSR as a constituent republic in 1936.

Kazakhstan declared independence Dec. 16, 1991. It became an independent state when the Soviet Union dissolved Dec. 26, 1991. The party chief, Nursultan Nazarbayev, was elected president unopposed. He boosted the economy by encouraging Western investment in the oil industry. Dissent was suppressed.

Kazakhstan agreed, Feb. 14, 1994, to dismantle nuclear missiles and adhere to the 1968 Nuclear Nonproliferation Treaty. Private land ownership was legalized Dec. 26, 1995. Astana (formerly Akmola) was dedicated as the nation's new capital on June 9, 1998. Reelected in 1999, Pres. Nazarbayev further tightened political controls in anticipation of Dec. 2005 elections.

Kenya

Republic of Kenya

People: Population: 33,829,590. **Age distrib.** (%): <15: 42.5; 65+: 2.3. **Pop. density:** 150 per sq mi, 58 per sq km. **Urban:** 39.4%. **Ethnic groups:** Kikuyu 22%, Luhya 14%, Luo 13%, Kalenjin 12%, Kamba 11%, Kisii 6%, Meru 6%. **Principal languages:** English, Swahili (both official); numerous indigenous languages. **Chief religions:** Protestant 45%, Roman Catholic 33%, indigenous beliefs 10%, Muslim 10%.

Geography: Total area: 224,962 sq mi, 582,650 sq km; **Land area:** 219,789 sq mi, 569,250 sq km. **Location:** E Africa, on coast of Indian O. **Neighbors:** Uganda on W, Tanzania on S, Somalia on E, Ethiopia on N, Sudan on NW. **Topography:** The northern three-fifths of Kenya is arid. To the S, a low coastal area and a plateau varying from 3,000 to 10,000 ft. The Great Rift Valley enters the country N-S, flanked by high mountains. **Capital:** Nairobi, 2,575,000. **Cities (urban aggr.):** Mombasa (1991 est.), 600,000.

Government: Type: Republic. **Head of state and gov.:** Pres. Mwai Kibaki; b Nov. 15, 1931; in office: Dec. 30, 2002. **Local divisions:** 7 provinces and Nairobi area. **Defense budget** (2004): $252 mil. **Active troops:** 24,120.

Economy: Industries: light consumer goods, agric. proc., oil refining, cement, tourism. **Chief crops:** coffee, tea, corn, wheat, sugarcane, fruit. **Natural resources:** gold, limestone, soda ash, salt barites, rubies, fluorspar, garnets, wildlife, hydropower. **Arable land:** 7%. **Livestock** (2004): cattle: 12.0 mil; chickens: 26 mil; goats: 12.0 mil; pigs: 415,000; sheep: 10.0 mil. **Fish catch** (2003): 120,534 metric tons. **Electricity prod.** (2003): 4.3 bil. kWh. **Labor force** (2003 est.): agriculture 75%.

Finance: Monetary unit: Shilling (KES) (Sept. 2005: 75.65 = $1 U.S.). **GDP** (2004 est.): $34.7 bil.; **per capita GDP:** $1,100; **GDP growth:** 2.2% **Imports** (2004 est.): $4.2 bil.; partners (2004): UAE 13.2%, Saudi Arabia 9.6%, South Africa 9.3%, US 8%, UK 7.2%, China 6.7%, Japan 5.4%, India 4.9%. **Exports** (2004 est.): $2.6 bil.; partners (2004): Uganda 12.8%, UK 11.6%, US 10.4%, Netherlands 8.3%, Pakistan 5.1%, Egypt 4.7%, Tanzania 4.3%. **Tourism:** $339 mil. **Budget** (2004 est.): $3.4 bil. **Intl. reserves less gold:** $978 mil. **Consumer prices:** 11.62%.

Transport: Railroad: Length: 1,726 mi. **Motor vehicles:** 255,400 pass. cars, 263,700 comm. vehicles. **Civil aviation:** 2.3 bil pass.-mi ; 19 airports. **Chief ports:** Mombasa, Kisumu, Lamu.

Communications: TV sets: 22 per 1,000 pop. **Radios:** 216 per 1,000 pop. **Telephone lines:** 328,400. **Daily newspaper circ.:** 9.4 per 1,000 pop. **Internet** (2002): 400,000 users.

Health: Life expect.: 48.9 male; 47.1 female. **Births** (per 1,000 pop.): 40.1. **Deaths** (per 1,000 pop.): 14.7. **Natural inc.:** 2.55%. **Infant mortality** (per 1,000 live births): 61.5. **AIDS rate:** 6.7%.

Education: Compulsory: ages 6-13. **Literacy:** 85.1%.

Major Intl. Organizations: UN and all of its specialized agencies, the Commonwealth, AU.

Embassy: 2249 R St. NW 20008; 387-6101.

Website: www.kenyaembassy.com

Arab colonies exported spices and slaves from the Kenya coast as early as the 8th century. Britain obtained control in the 19th century. Kenya won independence Dec. 12, 1963, 4 years after the end of the violent Mau Mau uprising.

Kenya had steady growth in industry and agriculture under a modified private enterprise system, and enjoyed a relatively free political life. But stability was shaken in 1974-75, with opposition charges of corruption and oppression. Jomo Kenyatta, the country's leader since independence, died Aug. 22, 1978. He was succeeded by his vice president, Daniel arap Moi.

During the first half of the 1990s, Kenya suffered widespread unemployment and high inflation. Tribal clashes in the western provinces claimed thousands of lives and left tens of thousands homeless. Pres. Moi won a third term in Dec. 1992 elections, which were marred by violence and fraud. Clashes in the Mombasa region, Aug. 1997, left more than 40 people dead. Pres. Moi was reelected Dec. 29, in an election again plagued by irregularities.

A truck bomb explosion at the U.S. embassy in Nairobi, Aug. 7, 1998, killed more than 200 people and injured about 5,000. The U.S. blamed the attack and a near-simultaneous embassy bombing in Tanzania on al-Qaeda. After a trial in New York City, 4 conspirators were convicted May 29, 2001. In Mombasa, Nov. 28, 2002, terrorists linked with al-Qaeda killed 12 Kenyans and 3 Israeli tourists at an Israeli-owned hotel and narrowly missed shooting down an Israeli-bound jet.

Constitutionally barred from seeking another term, Pres. Moi was succeeded Dec. 30, 2002, by Mwai Kibaki, the candidate of the opposition Democratic Party. Violence triggered by a cattle-rustling raid in N Kenya July 12, 2005, left 65 people dead.

Kiribati

Republic of Kiribati

People: Population: 103,092. **Age distrib.** (%): <15: 38.9; 65+: 3.3. **Pop. density:** 329 per sq mi, 127 per sq km. **Urban:** 47.3%. **Ethnic groups:** Micronesian. **Principal languages:** English (official), I-Kiribati. **Chief religions:** Roman Catholic 52%, Protestant 40%.

Geography: Total area: 313 sq mi, 811 sq km; **Land area:** 313 sq mi, 811 sq km. **Location:** 33 Micronesian islands (the Gilbert, Line, and Phoenix groups) in the mid-Pacific scattered in a 2-mil sq. mi. chain around the point where the International Date Line formerly cut the Equator. In 1997 the Date Line was moved to follow Kiribati's E border. **Neighbors:** Nearest are Nauru to SW, Tuvalu and Tokelau Isls. to S. **Topography:** Except Banaba (Ocean) Isl., all are low-lying, with soil of coral sand and rock fragments, subject to erratic rainfall. **Capital:** South Tarawa, 42,000.

Government: Type: Republic. **Head of state and gov.:** Pres. Anote Tong; b June 11, 1952; in office: July 10, 2003. **Local divisions:** 3 units, 6 districts.

Economy: Industries: fishing, handicrafts. **Chief crops:** copra, taro, breadfruit, sweet potatoes. **Natural resources:** phosphates. **Livestock** (2004): chickens: 460,000; pigs: 12,200. **Fish catch** (2003): 32,043 metric tons. **Electricity prod.** (2003): 0.01 bil. kWh.

Finance: Monetary unit: Australian Dollar (Sept. 2005: 1.31 = $1 U.S.). **GDP** (2001 est.): $79.0 mil; **per capita GDP:** $800; **GDP growth:** 1.5%. **Imports** (2002): $83.0 mil; partners (2004): Australia 36%, Fiji 24.8%, Japan 11%, New Zealand 8.7%, France 4.4%. **Exports** (-2002): $35.0 mil; partners (2004): France 45.1%, Japan 28.9%, US 9%, Thailand 5.4%. **Tourism** (2001): $3 mil. **Budget** (2000 est.): $37.2 mil.

Transport: Civil aviation: 6.84 mil. pass.-mi.; 4 airports. **Chief port:** Tarawa.

Communications: TV sets: 23 per 1,000 pop. **Radios:** 341 per 1,000 pop. **Telephone lines**: 3,600. **Internet:** 2,000 users.

Health: Life expect.: 58.7 male; 64.9 female. **Births** (per 1,000 pop.): 30.9. **Deaths** (per 1,000 pop.): 8.4. **Natural inc.:** 2.25%. **Infant mortality** (per 1,000 live births): 48.5.

Education: Compulsory: ages 6-15. **Literacy:** NA%.

Major Intl. Organizations: UN (IBRD, IMF, WHO), the Commonwealth.

Website: www.state.gov/p/eap/ci/kr

A British protectorate since 1892, the Gilbert and Ellice Islands colony was completed with the inclusion of the Phoenix Islands, 1937. Tarawa Atoll was the scene of some of the bloodiest fighting in the Pacific during World War II.

Self-rule was granted 1971; the Ellice Islands separated from the colony 1975 and became independent Tuvalu, 1978. Kiribati (pronounced *Kiribass)* independence was attained July 12, 1979. Under a treaty of friendship the U.S. relinquished its claims to several Line and Phoenix islands, including Christmas (Kiritimati), Canton, and Enderbury. Kiribati was admitted to the UN Sept. 14, 1999.

Korea, North

Democratic People's Republic of Korea

People: Population: 22,912,177. **Age distrib.** (%): <15: 24.2; 65+: 7.9. **Pop. density:** 492 per sq mi, 190 per sq km. **Urban:** 61.1%. **Ethnic group:** Korean. **Principal languages:** Korean (official). **Chief religions:** Activities almost non-existent; traditionally Buddhist, Confucianist, Chondogyo.

Geography: Total area: 46,541 sq mi, 120,540 sq km; **Land area:** 46,491 sq mi, 120,410 sq km. **Location:** In northern E Asia. **Neighbors:** China and Russia on N, South Korea on S. **Topography:** Mountains and hills cover nearly all the country, with narrow valleys and small plains in between. The N and the E coasts are the most rugged areas. **Capital:** Pyongyang, 3,228,000. **Cities (urban aggr.):** Nampo, 1,022,000.

Government: Type: Communist state. **Leader:** Kim Jong Il; b Feb. 16, 1942; officially assumed post Oct. 8, 1997. **Local divisions:** 9 provinces, 4 special cities. **Defense budget** (2002): $1.8 bil. **Active troops:** 1,106,000.

Economy: Industries: armaments, machine building, electric power, chemicals, mining, metallurgy, textiles. **Chief crops:** rice, corn, potatoes, soybeans. **Natural resources:** coal, lead, tungsten, zinc, graphite, magnesite, iron ore, copper, gold, pyrites, salt, fluorspar, hydropower. **Arable land:** 14%. **Livestock** (2004): cattle: 566,000; chickens: 20.3 mil; goats: 2.7 mil; pigs: 3.2 mil; sheep: 171,000. **Fish catch** (2003): 268,700 metric tons. **Electricity prod.** (2003): 18.7 bil. kWh. **Labor force**: agricultural 36%, nonagricultural 64%.

Finance: Monetary unit: Won (KPW) (Sept. 2005: 2.20 = $1 U.S.). **GDP** (2004 est.): $40.0 bil.; **per capita GDP:** $1,700; **GDP growth:** 1%. **Imports** (2003): $2.1 bil.; partners (2004): China 32.9%, Thailand 10.7%, Japan 4.8%. **Exports** (2003 est.): $1.2 bil.; partners (2004): China 29.9%, South Korea 24.1%, Japan 13.2%. **Tourism** (2002): $150 mil.

Transport: Railroad: Length: 3,240 mi. **Civil Aviation:** 20.5 mil. pass.-mi; 34 airports. **Chief ports:** Chongjin, Hamhung, Nampo.

Communications: TV sets: 55 per 1,000 pop. **Radios:** 146 per 1,000 pop. **Telephone lines** (1998): 23,257,000. **Daily newspaper circ.:** 199 per 1,000 pop.

Health: Life expect.: 68.7 male; 74.2 female. **Births** (per 1,000 pop.): 16.1. **Deaths** (per 1,000 pop.): 7.1. **Natural inc.:** 0.90%. **Infant mortality** (per 1,000 live births): 24.0.

Labor force: agri. 36%, other 64%.

Education: Compulsory: ages 6-15. **Literacy:** 99%.

Major Intl. Organizations: UN (FAO, IMO, WHO).

Permanent UN Representative: 820 Second Ave., 13th Floor, New York, NY 10017; (212) 972-3105.

Website: www.korea-dpr.com/menu.htm

The Democratic People's Republic of Korea was founded May 1, 1948, in the zone occupied by Russian troops after World War II. Its armies tried to conquer the south, 1950. After 3 years of fighting, with Chinese and U.S. intervention, a cease-fire was proclaimed. For the next four decades, a hardline Communist regime headed by Kim Il Sung kept tight control over the nation's political, economic, and cultural life. The nation used its abundant mineral and hydroelectric resources to develop its military strength and heavy industry. By the early 1990s, North Korea was widely believed to be developing nuclear weapons. The U.S. and North Korea signed an agreement, Oct. 21, 1994, providing for phased dismantling of North Korea's nuclear development program in return for U.S. energy aid and improved ties with the U.S.

Kim Il Sung died July 8, 1994. He was succeeded by his son, Kim Jong Il. North Korea suffered from defections by high officials, a deteriorating economy, and severe food shortages in the late 1990s.

On Sept. 17, 1999, the U.S. eased travel and trade restrictions on North Korea after Pyongyang agreed to suspend long-range missile testing. A first-ever summit conference in Pyongyang between North and South Korean leaders, June 13-15, 2000, marked an unexpected improvement in relations between the 2 Koreas, and brought an end to many U.S. sanctions. In Sept. 2002, Japanese Prime Min. Junichiro Koizumi became the 1st Japanese prime minister to visit North Korea; there, in a landmark summit, North Korea agreed to begin normalizing relations and admitted for the 1st time that its agents had helped to kidnap 11 Japanese in the late 1970s.

Pres. George Bush, in a speech Jan. 31, 2002, included North Korea with Iraq and Iran as part of an "axis of evil." In Oct. 2002, N. Korea admitted to pursuing a secret nuclear weapons program, in violation of past agreements, and, in Jan. 2003, withdrew from the Nuclear Non-Proliferation Treaty. The U.S. insisted that North Korea dismantle its nuclear weapons program, while North Korea demanded a nonaggression treaty and economic aid from the U.S. Six-nation talks sponsored by China in 2003 and 2004 failed to result in an agreement.

A huge explosion in the Ryongchon railway station Apr. 22, 2004, killed 161 people, injured more than 1,300, and destroyed at least 8,100 homes.

North Korea declared Feb. 10, 2005, that it had produced nuclear weapons. In a draft accord reached at 6-nation talks Sept. 19, 2005, N. Korea agreed to scrap its nuclear weapons program in exchange for aid. Left unresolved was Pyongyang's continuing demand for international donors to provide light-water nuclear reactors for "peaceful uses."

Korea, South

Republic of Korea

People: Population: 48,640,671. **Age distrib.** (%): <15: 19.4; 65+: 8.6. **Pop. density:** 1,279 per sq mi, 494 per sq km. **Urban:** 80.3%. **Ethnic group:** Korean. **Principal languages:** Korean (official). **Chief religions:** no affliiation 46%, Christian 26%, Buddhist 47%.

Geography: Total area: 38,023 sq mi, 98,480 sq km; **Land area:** 37,911 sq mi, 98,190 sq km. **Location:** In northern E Asia. **Neighbors:** North Korea on N. **Topography:** The country is mountainous, with a rugged east coast. The western and southern coasts are deeply indented, with many islands and harbors. **Capital:** Seoul, 9,714,000. **Cities (urban aggr.)**: Pusan, 3,673,000; Inch'on, 2,464,000: Taegu, 2,478,000.

Government: Type: Republic. **Head of state:** Pres. Roh Moo Hyun; b Aug. 6, 1946; in office: Feb. 25, 2003. **Head of gov.:** Prime Min. Lee Hai Chan; b 1952; in office: June 30, 2004 **Local divisions:** 9 provinces, 7 special cities. **Defense budget** (2004): $16.4 bil. **Active troops:** 687,700.

Economy: Industries: electronics, autos, chemicals, shipbuilding, steel, textiles, clothing, footwear, food proc. **Chief crops:** rice, root crops, barley, vegetables, fruit. **Natural resources:** coal, tungsten, graphite, molybd., lead, hydropower potential. **Arable land:** 19%. **Livestock** (2004): cattle: 2.1 mil; chickens: 97 mil; goats: 430,000; pigs: 9.1 mil; sheep: 1,000. **Fish catch** (2003): 2,035,337 metric tons. **Electricity prod.** (2003): 326.2 bil. kWh. **Labor force** (2004 est.): agriculture 8%, industry 19%, services 73%.

Finance: Monetary unit: Won (KRW) (Sept. 2004: 1,147.30 = $1 U.S.). **GDP** (2004 est.): $925.1 bil.; **per capita GDP:** $19,200; **GDP growth:** 4.6%. **Imports** (2004 est.): $214.2 bil.; partners (2004): Japan 21.6%, US 12.7%, China 12.3%, Saudi Arabia 5.1%. **Exports** (2004 est.): $250.6 bil.; partners (2004): China 22.4%, US 17.8%, Japan 8.3%, Hong Kong 4.8%. **Tourism:** $5,256 mil. **Budget** (2004 est.): $155.8 bil. **Gold** (2003): 450,000 oz t. **Consumer prices** (2003): 3.6%.

Transport: Railroad: Length: 1,942 mi. **Motor vehicles:** 9.74 mil pass. cars, 4.17 mil comm. vehicles. **Civil aviation:** 37.4 bil pass.-mi; 69 airports. **Chief ports:** Pusan, Inchon.

Communications: TV sets: 364 per 1,000 pop. **Radios:** 1,039 per 1,000 pop. **Telephone lines:** 25.8 mil. **Daily newspaper circ.:** 393 per 1,000 pop. **Internet:** 29.2 mil. users.

Health: Life expect.: 73.4 male; 80.6 female. **Births** (per 1,000 pop.): 10.0. **Deaths** (per 1,000 pop.): 5.7. **Natural inc.:** 0.43%. **Infant mortality** (per 1,000 live births): 6.3. **AIDS rate:** <0.1%.

Education: Compulsory: ages 6-14. **Literacy:** 97.9%.

Major Intl. Organizations: UN (FAO, IBRD, ILO, IMF, IMO, WHO, WTrO), APEC, OECD.

Embassy: 2450 Massachusetts Ave. NW 20008; 939-5600.

Website: www.korea.net

Korea, once called the Hermit Kingdom, has a recorded history since the 1st century BC. It was united in a kingdom under the Silla Dynasty, AD 668. It was at times associated with the Chinese empire; the treaty that concluded the Sino-Japanese war of 1894-95 recognized Korea's complete independence. In 1910 Japan forcibly annexed Korea as Chosun.

At the Potsdam conference, July 1945, the 38th parallel was designated as the line dividing the Soviet and the American occupation. Russian troops entered Korea Aug. 10, 1945; U.S. troops entered Sept. 8, 1945.

The South Koreans formed the Republic of Korea in May 1948 with Seoul as the capital. Dr. Syngman Rhee was chosen president. A separate, Communist regime was formed in the N; its army attacked the S in June 1950, initiating the Korean War. UN troops, under U.S. command, supported the S in the war, which ended in an armistice (July 1953) leaving Korea divided by a "no-man's land" along the 38th parallel.

Rhee's authoritarian rule became increasingly unpopular, and a movement spearheaded by college students forced his resignation Apr. 26, 1960. In an army coup May 16, 1961, Gen. Park Chung Hee became chairman of a ruling junta. He was elected president, 1963; a 1972 referendum allowed him to be reelected for an unlimited series of 6-year terms. Park was assassinated by the chief of the Korean CIA, Oct. 26, 1979.

In May 1980, Gen. Chun Doo Hwan, head of military intelligence, ordered the brutal suppression of pro-democracy demonstrations in Kwangju. On July 1, 1987, following weeks of antigovernment protests, some of them violent, Chun agreed to permit election of the next president by direct popular vote and other democratic reforms. In Dec., Roh Tae Woo was elected president. In 1990, the nation's 3 largest political parties merged; some 100,000 students protested the merger as undemocratic.

Pres. Kim Young Sam took office in 1993. Convicted of mutiny, treason, and corruption, Chun was sentenced to death by a Seoul court, Aug. 26, 1996, for his role in the 1979 coup and 1980 Kwangju massacre; Roh received a 22-1/2 year prison sentence. On Dec. 16, Chun's term was reduced to life in prison, and Roh's to 17 years.

The collapse in Jan. 1997 of the Hanbo steel firm triggered a series of corruption scandals. With currency and stock values plummeting, the nation averted default by agreeing, Dec. 4, on a $57 billion bailout from the IMF. Kim Dae Jung, a longtime dissident, won the presidential election Dec. 18. Chun and Roh were released and pardoned Dec. 22, 1997.

At an unprecedented summit meeting in Pyongyang, June 13-15, 2000, Pres. Kim Dae Jung and North Korean leader Kim Jong Il agreed to work for reconciliation and eventual reunification of their 2 countries. On Oct. 13, 2000, Kim Dae Jung was named the winner of the 2000 Nobel Peace Prize. Roh Moo Hyun won a presidential election Dec. 19.

A subway fire in Taegu, Feb. 18, 2003, killed 198 people; the arsonist was given a life term, and 8 subway officials charged with negligence also received prison sentences. Typhoon Maemi battered Pusan and other areas Sept. 12-13, 2003, leaving about 130 people dead and causing at least $4.1 billion in damage.

The National Assembly, Mar. 12, 2004, impeached Pres. Roh Moo Hyun for violating political neutrality and urging voters to support the Uri Party in upcoming legislative elections; voters backed Roh Apr. 15 by electing a Uri majority, and the Constitutional Court May 14 restored Roh to office. In Aug., South Korea began deploying 3,000 troops to N Iraq.

The International Atomic Energy Agency Sept. 2 said South Korea had acknowledged having secretly processed a small amount of uranium to near weapons-grade level in 2000, in violation of the Nuclear Non-Proliferation Treaty and a bilateral agreement with North Korea.

Kuwait

State of Kuwait

People: Population: 2,335,648. **Age distrib.** (%): <15: 27.2; 65+: 2.7. **Pop. density:** 339 per sq mi, 131 per sq km. **Urban:** 96.3%. **Ethnic groups:** Arab 80%, South Asian 9%, Iranian 4%. **Principal languages:** Arabic (official), English. **Chief religion:** Muslim 85% (official; Sunni 70%, Shi'a 30%).

Geography: Total area: 6,880 sq mi, 17,820 sq km; **Land area:** 6,880 sq mi, 17,820 sq km. **Location:** In Middle East, at N end of Persian Gulf. **Neighbors:** Iraq on N, Saudi Arabia on S. **Topography:** The country is flat, very dry, and extremely hot. **Capital:** Kuwait City, 1,222,000.

Government: Type: Constitutional monarchy. **Head of state:** Emir Sheikh Jabir al-Ahmad al-Jabir as-Sabah; b June 29, 1926; in office: Dec. 31, 1977. **Head of gov.:** Prime Min. Sheikh Sabah al-Ahmad as-Sabah; b 1929; in office: July 13, 2003. **Local divisions:** 5 governorates. **Defense budget** (2004): $4 bil. **Active troops:** 15,500.

Economy: Industries: oil, petrochems., desalination, food proc., constr. materials. **Natural resources:** oil, fish, shrimp, nat. gas. **Crude oil reserves** (2004): 101.5 bil. bbls. **Livestock** (2004): cattle: 25,000; chickens: 32 mil; goats: 150,000; sheep: 900,000.

Fish catch (2003): 6,095 metric tons. **Electricity prod.** (2003): 38.2 bil. kWh.

Finance: Monetary unit: Dinar (KWD) (Sept. 2005: 0.29 = $1 U.S.). **GDP** (2004 est.): $48.0 bil.; **per capita GDP:** $21,300; **GDP growth:** 6.8%. **Imports** (2004 est.): $11.1 bil.; partners (2004): US 13.1%, Germany 12.7%, Japan 8.2%, China 5.9%, Italy 5.4%, UK 5.4%, Saudi Arabia 4.7%, France 4.6%. **Exports** (2004 est.): $27.4 bil.; partners (2004): Japan 22.6%, US 13.4%, South Korea 13.4%, Singapore 12.4%, Taiwan 8.4%, Netherlands 4.1%. **Tourism:** $117 mil. **Budget** (2004 est.): $19.5 bil. **Intl. reserves less gold:** $5.31 bil. **Gold:** 2.54 mil. oz t. **Consumer prices:** 1.14%.

Transport: Motor vehicles: 715,000 pass. cars, 226,000 comm. vehicles. **Civil aviation:** 37.4 bil pass.-mi; 3 airports. **Chief port:** Mina al-Ahmadi.

Communications: TV sets: 480 per 1,000 pop. **Radios:** 633 per 1,000 pop. **Telephone lines:** 486,900. **Daily newspaper circ.:** 374 per 1,000 pop. **Internet**: 567,000 users.

Health: Life expect.: 76.0 male; 78.1 female. **Births** (per 1,000 pop.): 21.9. **Deaths** (per 1,000 pop.): 2.4. **Natural inc.:** 1.95%. **Infant mortality** (per 1,000 live births): 10.0.

Education: Compulsory: ages 6-13. **Literacy:** 83.5%.

Major Intl. Organizations: UN (FAO, IBRD, ILO, IMF, IMO, WHO, WTrO), AL, OPEC.

Embassy: 2940 Tilden St. NW 20008; 966-0702.

Website: www.kuwait-info.org

Kuwait is ruled by the Sabah dynasty, founded 1759. Britain ran foreign relations and defense from 1899 until independence in 1961. The majority of the population is non-Kuwaiti, with many Palestinians, and cannot vote.

Oil is the fiscal mainstay, providing most of Kuwait's income. Oil pays for free medical care, education, and social security. There are no taxes, except customs duties.

Kuwait was attacked and overrun by Iraqi forces Aug. 2, 1990. The emir and senior members of the ruling family fled to Saudi Arabia to establish a government in exile. On Aug. 28, Iraq announced that Kuwait was its 19th province. Following several weeks of aerial attacks on Iraq and Iraqi forces in Kuwait, a U.S.-led coalition began a ground attack Feb. 23, 1991. By Feb. 27, Iraqi forces were routed and Kuwait liberated.

Former U.S. Pres. George Bush visited Kuwait, Apr. 14-16, 1993. Kuwaiti authorities arrested 14 Iraqis and Kuwaitis for allegedly plotting to assassinate him during his visit; 13 were convicted and sentenced to prison or death, June 4, 1994. The UN Security Council ruled, Sept. 27, 2000, that Iraq had to pay the Kuwait Petroleum Corp. $15.9 billion for damage to Kuwaiti oil fields during the Persian Gulf War. Iraq recognized Kuwait's territorial integrity Mar. 28, 2002. N Kuwait was used by U.S. and British troops as a staging area prior to the Mar. 2003 invasion of Iraq. Political rights were extended to women, May 16, 2005; the nation's 1st female cabinet member was appointed June 12.

Kyrgyzstan

Kyrgyz Republic

People: Population: 5,146,281. **Age distrib.** (%): <15: 31.6; 65+: 6.2. **Pop. density:** 67 per sq mi, 26 per sq km. **Urban:** 33.9%. **Ethnic groups:** Kyrgyz 52%, Russian 18%, Uzbek 13%, Ukrainian 3%, German 2%. **Principal languages:** Kyrgyz, Russian (both official); Uzbek. **Chief religions:** Muslim 75%, Russian Orthodox 20%.

Geography: Total area: 76,641 sq mi, 198,500 sq km; **Land area:** 73,861 sq mi, 191,300 sq km. **Location:** In Central Asia. **Neighbors:** Kazakhstan on N, China on E, Uzbekistan on W, Tajikistan on S. Topography: Kyrgystan is a landlocked country nearly covered by Tien Shan and Pamir Mts.; avg. elevation 9,020 ft. A large lake, Issyk-Kul, in NE is 1 mi. above sea level. **Capital:** Bishkek, 806,000.

Government: Type: In transition. **Head of state :** Pres. Kurmanbek Bakiyev; b Aug. 1, 1949; in office: Aug. 14, 2005 (acting from Mar. 25). **Head of gov.:** Prime Min. Feliks Kulov; b Oct. 29, 1948; in office: Sept. 1, 2005 (acting from Aug. 15). **Local divisions:** 7 oblasts and Bishkek. **Defense budget** (2004): $31 mil. **Active troops:** 12,500.

Economy: Industries: small machinery, textiles, food proc., cement, shoes, timber, refrigerators, furniture, electric motors. **Chief crops:** tobacco, cotton, potatoes, vegetables, grapes, fruits & berries. **Natural resources:** hydropower, gold, rare earth metals, coal, oil, nat. gas, nepheline, mercury, bismuth, lead, zinc. **Crude oil reserves** (2004): 40 mil bbls. **Arable land:** 7%. **Livestock** (2004): cattle: 1.0 mil; chickens: 3.8 mil; goats: 647,300; pigs: 82,800; sheep: 3.0 mil. **Fish catch** (2003): 26 metric tons. **Electricity prod.** (2003): 13.8 bil. kWh. **Labor force** (2000 est.): agriculture 55%, industry 15%, services 30%.

Finance: Monetary unit: Som (KGS) (Sept. 2005: 40.95 = $1 U.S.). **GDP** (2004 est.): $8.5 bil.; **per capita GDP:** $1,700; **GDP growth:** 6%. **Imports** (2004 est.): $775.1 mil; partners (2004): Russia 23.1%, China 22.9%, Kazakhstan 19.3%, Turkey 7.2%, Germany 4.5%, Uzbekistan 4.4%, US 4.2%. **Exports** (2004 est.): $646.7 mil; partners (2004): UAE 23.8%, Switzerland 16.9%, Russia 16.9%, Kazakhstan 10.1%, China 9.8%. **Tourism:** $48 mil. **Budget** (2004 est.): $445.4 mil. **Gold:** 80,000 oz t. **Consumer prices** (2003): 3.5%.

Transport: Railroad: Length: 261 mi. **Motor vehicles**: 188,700 pass. cars. **Civil aviation:** 225.6 mil. pass.-mi. **Chief port:** Ysyk-Kol.

Communications: TV sets: 49 per 1,000 pop. **Radios:** 113 per 1,000 pop. **Telephone lines**: 396,200. **Daily newspaper circ.:** 11 per 1,000 pop. **Internet:** 200,000 users.

Health: Life expect.: 64.2 male; 72.4 female. **Births** (per 1,000 pop.): 22.5. **Deaths** (per 1,000 pop.): 7.1. **Natural inc.:** 1.54%. **Infant mortality** (per 1,000 live births): 35.6. **AIDS rate:** 0.1%.

Education: Compulsory: ages 7-15. **Literacy:** 97%.

Major Intl. Organizations: UN (FAO, IBRD, ILO, IMF, WHO), CIS, OSCE.

Embassy: 1001 Pennsylvania Avenue, Suite #600, NW Washington, DC 20004 338 5141

Website: www.gov.kg/index.php?newlang=eng

The region was inhabited around the 13th century by the Kyrgyz. It was annexed to Russia 1864. After 1917, it was nominally a Kara-Kyrgyz autonomous area, which was reorganized 1926, and made a constituent republic of the USSR in 1936. Kyrgyzstan declared independence Aug. 31, 1991. It became an independent state when the USSR disbanded Dec. 26, 1991. A constitution was adopted May 5, 1993.

Reelected Dec. 24, 1995, Pres. Askar Akayev gained approval by referendum of a constitutional amendment expanding his presidential powers, Feb. 10, 1996. Amendments restricting the powers of parliament and allowing private ownership of land were ratified by referendum Oct. 17, 1998. Akayev won a 3d 5-year term in the Oct. 29, 2000, election. The U.S. military presence in Kyrgyzstan expanded from Dec. 2001.

Fraud by Akayev loyalists in parliamentary elections Feb.-Mar. 2005 sparked protests. Akayev fled the country, Mar. 24, and formally resigned, Apr. 4. His interim successor, former Prime Min. Kurmanbek Bakiyev, a leader of the "tulip revolution," won by a landslide in the July 10 presidential vote.

Laos

Lao People's Democratic Republic

People: Population: 6,217,141. **Age distrib.** (%): <15: 41.6; 65+: 3.2. **Pop. density:** 68 per sq mi, 26 per sq km. **Urban:** 20.7%. **Ethnic groups:** Lao Loum 68%, Lao Theung 22%, Lao Soung (incl. Hmong and Yao) 9%. **Principal languages:** Lao (official), French, English, and various ethnic languages. **Chief religions:** Buddhist 60%, animist and other 40%.

Geography: Total area: 91,429 sq mi, 236,800 sq km; **Land area:** 89,112 sq mi, 230,800 sq km. **Location:** In Indochina Peninsula in SE Asia. **Neighbors:** Myanmar and China on N, Vietnam on E, Cambodia on S, Thailand on W. **Topography:** Landlocked, dominated by jungle. High mountains along eastern border are the source of the E-W rivers slicing across the country to the Mekong R., which defines most of the western border. **Capital:** Vientiane, 716,000.

Government: Type: Communist. **Head of state:** Pres. Khamtai Siphandon; b Feb. 8, 1924; in office: Feb. 24, 1998. **Head of gov.:** Prime Min. Boungnang Vorachith; b Aug. 15, 1937; in office: Mar. 27, 2001. **Local divisions:** 16 provinces, 1 municipality, 1 special zone. **Defense budget** (2003): $15 mil. **Active troops:** 29,100.

Economy: Industries: mining, timber, electric power, agric. proc., constr., garments, tourism. **Chief crops:** sweet potatoes, vegetables, corn, coffee, sugarcane. **Natural resources:** timber, hydropower, gypsum, tin, gold, gemstones. **Arable land:** 3%. **Livestock** (2004): cattle: 1.2 mil; chickens: 14 mil; goats: 139,400; pigs: 1.7 mil. **Fish catch** (2003): 94,700 metric tons. **Electricity prod.** (2003): 3.8 bil. kWh. **Labor force** (1997 est.): agriculture 80%.

Finance: Monetary unit: Kip (LAK) (Sept. 2005: 10,380.00 = $1 U.S.). **GDP** (2004 est.): $11.3 bil.; **per capita GDP:** $1,900; **GDP growth:** 6%. **Imports** (2004 est.): $579.5 mil; partners (2004): Thailand 60.5%, China 9.2%, Vietnam 8.7%. **Exports** (2004 est.): $365.5 mil; partners (2004): Thailand 19%, Vietnam 16.4%, France 7.9%, Germany 5.6%, UK 4.9%. **Tourism:** $87 mil. **Budget** (2004 est.): $416.5 mil. **Gold:** 120,000 oz t. **Consumer prices:** 10.46%.

Transport: Motor vehicles: 9,000 pass. cars, 9,000 comm. vehicles. **Civil aviation:** 53.4 mil. pass.-mi; 9 airports.

Communications: TV sets: 10 per 1,000 pop. **Radios:** 145 per 1,000 pop. **Telephone lines:** 69,800. **Daily newspaper circ.:** 3.7 per 1,000 pop. **Internet:** 19,000 users.

Health: Life expect.: 53.1 male; 57.2 female. **Births** (per 1,000 pop.): 36.0. **Deaths** (per 1,000 pop.): 11.8. **Natural inc.:** 2.42%. **Infant mortality** (per 1,000 live births): 85.2. **AIDS rate:** 0.1%.

Education: Compulsory: ages 6-10. **Literacy:** 66.4%.

Major Intl. Organizations: UN (FAO, IBRD, ILO, IMF, WHO), ASEAN.

Embassy: 2222 S St. NW 20008; 332-6416.

Website: www.tourismlaos.gov.la

Laos became a French protectorate in 1893, but regained independence as a constitutional monarchy July 19, 1949.

Conflicts among neutralist, Communist, and conservative factions created a chaotic political situation. Armed conflict increased after 1960.

The 3 factions formed a coalition government in June 1962, with neutralist Prince Souvanna Phouma as premier. A 14-nation conference in Geneva signed agreements, 1962, guaranteeing neutrality and independence. By 1964 the Pathet Lao had withdrawn from the coalition, and, with aid from North Vietnamese troops, renewed sporadic attacks. U.S. planes bombed the Ho Chi Minh trail, supply line from North Vietnam to Communist forces in Laos and South Vietnam.

In 1970 the U.S. stepped up air support and military aid. After Pathet Lao military gains, Souvanna Phouma in May 1975 ordered government troops to cease fighting; the Pathet Lao took control. The Lao People's Democratic Republic was proclaimed Dec. 3, 1975.

From the mid-1970s through the 1980s, the Laotian government relied on Vietnam for military and financial aid. Since easing its foreign investment laws in 1988, Laos has attracted more than $5 billion from Thailand, the U.S., and other nations. Laos was admitted to ASEAN on July 23, 1997. The U.S. Congress, Nov. 19, 2004, approved normalization of trade with Laos.

Latvia

Republic of Latvia

People: Population: 2,290,237. **Age distrib.** (%): <15: 14.4; 65+: 16.1. **Pop. density:** 92 per sq mi, 35 per sq km. **Urban:** 66.2%. **Ethnic groups:** Latvian 58%, Russian 30%, Belarusian 4%, Ukrainian 3%, Polish 2%, Lithuanian 1%. **Principal languages:** Latvian (official), Russian, Belorusian, Ukrainian, Polish. **Chief religions:** Lutheran, Roman Catholic, Russian Orthodox.

Geography: Total area: 24,938 sq mi, 64,589 sq km; **Land area:** 24,552 sq mi, 63,589 sq km. **Location:** E Europe, on the Baltic Sea. **Neighbors:** Estonia on N, Lithuania and Belarus on S, Russia on E. Topography: Latvia is a lowland with numerous lakes, marshes and peat bogs. Principal river, W. Dvina (Daugava), rises in Russia. There are glacial hills in E. **Capital:** Riga, 733,000.

Government: Type: Republic. **Head of state:** Pres. Vaira Vike-Freiberga; b Dec. 1, 1937; in office: July 8, 1999. **Head of gov.:** Prime Min. Aigars Kalvitis; b June 27, 1966; in office: Dec. 2, 2004. **Local divisions:** 26 counties, 7 municipalities. **Defense budget** (2004): $226 mil. **Active troops:** 4,880.

Economy: Industries: vehicles, railroad cars, synthetics, agric. machinery, fertilizers, washing machines. **Chief crops:** grain, sugar beets, potatoes, other vegetables. **Natural resources:** peat, limestone, dolomite, hydropower, wood, amber. **Arable land:** 27%. **Livestock** (2004): cattle: 378,600; chickens: 4 mil; goats: 15,000; pigs: 444,400; sheep: 39,200. **Fish catch** (2003): 115,180 metric tons. **Electricity prod.** (2003): 3.6 bil. kWh. **Labor force** (2000 est.): agriculture 15%, industry 25%, services 60%.

Finance: Monetary unit: Lats (LVL) (Sept. 2005: 0.56 = $1 U.S.). **GDP** (2004 est.): $26.5 bil.; **per capita GDP:** $11,500; **GDP growth:** 7.6%. **Imports** (2004 est.): $6.0 bil.; partners (2004): Germany 16.1%, Russia 14.4%, Lithuania 7.6%, Finland 6.5%, Sweden 5.6%, Estonia 5.1%, Italy 4.2%, Poland 4%. **Exports** (2004 est.): $3.6 bil.; partners (2004): UK 22.1%, Germany 9.9%, US 8.2%, Sweden 7.3%, France 6.6%, Lithuania 6.4%, Estonia 5.2%, Denmark 4.2%, Russia 4.1%. **Tourism:** $222 mil. **Budget** (2004 est.): $4.5 bil. **Intl. reserves less gold:** $1.23 bil. **Gold:** 250,000 oz t. **Consumer prices:** 6.19%.

Transport: Railroad: Length: 1,458 mi. **Motor vehicles:** 619,100 pass. cars, 113,900 comm. vehicles. **Civil aviation:** 111.85 mil. pass.-mi; 22 airports. **Chief port:** Riga.

Communications: TV sets: 757 per 1,000 pop. **Radios:** 701 per 1,000 pop. **Telephone lines:** 661,900. **Daily newspaper circ.:** 135.1 per 1,000 pop. **Internet**: 936,000 users.

Health: Life expect.: 65.8 male; 76.6 female. **Births** (per 1,000 pop.): 9.0. **Deaths** (per 1,000 pop.): 13.7. **Natural inc.:** –0.47%. **Infant mortality** (per 1,000 live births): 9.6. **AIDS rate:** 0.6%.

Education: Compulsory: ages 7-15. **Literacy:** 99.8%.

Major Intl. Organizations: UN (FAO, IBRD, ILO, IMF, IMO, WHO), EU, NATO, OSCE.

Embassy: 4325 17th St. NW 20011; 726-8213.

Website: www.president.lv/index.php?pid=210

Prior to 1918, Latvia was occupied by the Russians and Germans. It was an independent republic, 1918-39. The Aug. 1939 Soviet-German agreement assigned Latvia to the Soviet sphere of influence. It was officially accepted as part of the USSR on Aug. 5, 1940. It was overrun by the German army in 1941, but retaken in 1945.

During an abortive Soviet coup, Latvia declared independence, Aug. 21, 1991. The Soviet Union recognized Latvia's independence in Sept. 1991. The last Russian troops in Latvia withdrew by Aug. 31, 1994. Responding to international pressure, Latvian voters on Oct. 3, 1998, eased citizenship laws that had discriminated against some 500,000 ethnic Russians. On June 17, 1999, the legislature elected Vaira Vike-Freiberga as Latvia's 1st woman president. Latvia joined the EU and NATO in 2004. Latvia ratified a proposed EU constitution, June 2, 2005.

Lebanon

Lebanese Republic

People: Population: 3,826,018. **Age distrib.** (%): <15: 26.7; 65+: 6.9. **Pop. density:** 953 per sq mi, 368 per sq km. **Urban:** 87.5%. **Ethnic groups:** Arab 95%, Armenian 4%. **Principal languages:** Arabic (official), French, English, Armenian. **Chief religions:** Muslim 60%, Christian 39%.

Geography: Total area: 4,015 sq mi, 10,400 sq km; **Land area:** 3,950 sq mi, 10,230 sq km. **Location:** In Middle East, on E end of Mediterranean Sea. **Neighbors:** Syria on E, Israel on S. **Topography:** There is a narrow coastal strip, and 2 mountain ranges running N-S enclosing the fertile Beqaa Valley. The Litani R. runs S through the valley, turning W to empty into the Mediterranean. **Capital:** Beirut, 1,792,000.

Government: Type: Republic. **Head of state:** Pres. Emile Lahoud; b Jan. 12, 1936; in office: Nov. 24, 1998. **Head of gov.:** Prime Min. Fouad Siniora; b 1943; in office: July 19, 2005. **Local divisions:** 6 governorates. **Defense budget** (2004): $528 mil. **Active troops:** 72,100.

Economy: Industries: banking, food proc., jewelry, cement, textiles, mineral & chemical products. **Chief crops:** citrus, grapes, tomatoes, apples, vegetables, potatoes, olives, tobacco. **Natural resources:** limestone, iron ore, salt, water. **Arable land:** 21%. **Livestock** (2004): cattle: 90,000; chickens: 35 mil; goats: 430,000; pigs: 20,000; sheep: 350,000. **Fish catch** (2003): 4,688 metric tons. **Electricity prod.** (2003): 10.7 bil. kWh.

Finance: Monetary unit: Pound (LBP) (Sept. 2005: 1,503.00 = $1 U.S.). **GDP** (2004 est.): $18.8 bil.; **per capita GDP:** $5,000; **GDP growth:** 4%. **Imports** (2004 est.): $8.2 bil.; partners (2004): Italy 12.2%, France 11.2%, Germany 8.9%, China 6.3%, US 6%, Syria 5.1%, UK 5%. **Exports** (2004 est.): $1.8 bil.; partners (2004): Switzerland 10%, UAE 9.5%, Turkey 9.3%, Saudi Arabia 7.1%, France 5.1%, US 5.1%. Tourism: $1,016 mil. **Budget** (2004 est.): $6.6 bil. **Intl. reserves less gold:** $7.56 bil. **Gold:** 9.22 mil. oz t.

Transport: Railroad: Length: 249 mi. **Motor vehicles**: 1.37 mil pass. cars, 102,400 comm. vehicles. **Civil aviation:** 1.0 bil pass.-mi; 5 airports. **Chief ports:** Beirut, Tripoli, Sidon.

Communications: TV sets: 355 per 1,000 pop. **Radios:** 907 per 1,000 pop. **Telephone lines**: 700,000. **Newspaper circ.:** 107 per 1,000 pop. **Internet**: 500,000 users.

Health: Life expect.: 70.2 male; 75.2 female. **Births** (per 1,000 pop.): 18.9. **Deaths** (per 1,000 pop.): 6.2. **Natural inc.:** 1.30%. **Infant mortality** (per 1,000 live births): 24.5. **AIDS rate:** 0.1%.

Education: Compulsory: ages 6-14. **Literacy:** 87.4%

Major Intl. Organizations: UN (FAO, IBRD, ILO, IMF, IMO, WHO), AL.

Embassy: 2560 28th St. NW 20008; 939-6300.

Website: www.lebanonembassyus.org

Formed from 5 former Turkish Empire districts, Lebanon became an independent state Sept. 1, 1920, administered under French mandate 1920-41. French troops withdrew in 1946.

Under the 1943 National Covenant, all public positions were divided among the various religious communities, with Christians in the majority. By the 1970s, Muslims became the majority and demanded a larger political and economic role.

U.S. Marines intervened, May-Oct. 1958, during a Syrian-aided revolt. Continued raids against Israeli civilians, 1970-75, brought Israeli retaliation in S Lebanon.

An estimated 60,000 were killed and billions of dollars in damage inflicted in a 1975-76 civil war. Palestinian units and leftist Muslims fought against the Maronite militia, the Phalange, and other Christians. Several Arab countries provided political and arms support to the various factions, while Israel aided Christian forces. Up to 15,000 Syrian troops intervened in 1976 to fight Palestinian groups. A cease-fire was mainly policed by Syria.

Israeli forces invaded Lebanon June 6, 1982, in a coordinated land, sea, and air attack aimed at crushing strongholds of the Palestine Liberation Organization (PLO). Israeli and Syrian forces engaged in the Bekaa Valley. By June 14, Israeli troops had encircled Beirut. On Aug. 21, the PLO evacuated west Beirut after massive Israeli bombings there. Israeli troops entered west Beirut following the Sept. 14 assassination of newly elected Lebanese Pres. Bashir Gemayel. On Sept. 16, Lebanese Christian troops entered 2 refugee camps and massacred hundreds of Palestinian refugees. An agreement May 17, 1983, between Lebanon, Israel, and the U.S. (but not Syria) provided for the withdrawal of Israeli troops; at least 30,000 Syrian troops remained in Lebanon, and Israeli forces continued to occupy a "security zone" in the south.

In 1983, terrorist bombings became a way of life in Beirut as some 50 people were killed in an explosion at the U.S. Embassy, Apr. 18; 241 U.S. servicemen and 58 French soldiers died in separate Muslim suicide attacks, Oct. 23.

Kidnapping of foreign nationals by Islamic militants became common in the 1980s. U.S., British, French, and Soviet citizens were victims. All were released by 1992.

A treaty signed May 22, 1991, between Lebanon and Syria recognized Lebanon as a separate state for the first time since the 2 countries gained independence in 1943.

Israeli forces conducted air raids and artillery strikes against guerrilla bases and villages in S Lebanon, causing over 200,000 to flee their homes July 25-29, 1993. Some 500,000 civilians fled their homes in Apr. 1996 when Israel again struck suspected guerrilla bases in the south. The economy revived in the 1990s, but Syria continued to dominate Lebanon's political affairs. Israel withdrew virtually all its troops from S Lebanon by May 24, 2000, leaving Hezbollah, an Iranian-backed guerrilla group, in control of much of the region.

Rafik al-Hariri, a former prime minister (1992-98, 2000-04), was killed by truck bomb, Feb. 14, 2005. Many Lebanese blamed Syria, which denied involvement. As anti-Syrian protests mounted, Syria pulled nearly all its troops out of Lebanon, although some intelligence agents may have remained. An anti-Syrian bloc won parliamentary elections held in May and June. A new cabinet, installed July 19, was headed by Fouad Siniora, a friend and aide to Hariri, and included a Hezbollah member.

Lesotho
Kingdom of Lesotho

People: Population: 2,031,348. **Age distrib.** (%): <15: 36.9; 65+: 5.5. **Pop. density:** 173 per sq mi, 67 per sq km. **Urban:** 17.9%. **Ethnic groups:** Sotho 99%. **Principal languages:** Sesotho, English (both official), Zulu, Xhosa. **Chief religions:** Christian 80%, indigenous beliefs 20%.

Geography: Total area: 11,720 sq mi, 30,355 sq km; **Land area:** 11,720 sq mi, 30,355 sq km. **Location:** In southern Africa. **Neighbors:** Completely surrounded by Republic of South Africa. **Topography:** Landlocked and mountainous, altitudes from 5,000 to 11,000 ft. **Capital:** Maseru, 170,000.

Government: Type: Modified constitutional monarchy. **Head of state:** King Letsie III; b July 17, 1963; in office: Feb. 7, 1996. **Head of gov.:** Pakalitha Mosisili; b Mar. 14, 1945; in office: May 29, 1998. **Local divisions:** 10 districts. **Defense budget** (2004): $33 mil. **Active troops:** 2,000.

Economy: Industries: food, beverages, textiles, apparel, handicrafts. **Chief crops:** corn, wheat, sorghum, barley. **Natural resources:** water, diamonds, other minerals. **Arable land:** 11%. **Livestock** (2004): cattle: 540,000; chickens: 1.8 mil; goats: 650,000; pigs: 65,000; sheep: 850,000. **Fish catch** (2003): 32 metric tons. **Electricity prod.** (2003): 0.35 bil. kWh. **Labor force**: 86% of resident population engaged in subsistence agriculture; roughly 35% of the active male wage earners work in South Africa.

Finance: Monetary unit: Loti (LSL) (Sept. 2005: 6.29 = $1 U.S.). **GDP** (2004 est.): $5.9 bil.; **per capita GDP:** $3,200; **GDP growth:** 3.3%. **Imports** (2004 est.): $730.9 mil; partners (2004): Hong Kong 34.2%, Taiwan 33.9%, China 11.2%, Germany 9.2%. **Exports** (2004 est.): $484.5 mil; partners (2004): US 96%, Canada 1.5%, Belgium/Luxembourg 1.1%. **Tourism** (2002): $20 mil. **Budget** (2004 est.): $697.6 mil. **Intl. reserves less gold:** $324 mil. **Consumer prices** (2003): 6.7%.

Transport: Railroad: Length: 2 mi. **Motor vehicles:** 5,000 pass. cars, 18,000 comm. vehicles. **Civil aviation:** 4 airports.

Communications: TV sets: 16 per 1,000 pop. **Radios:** 52 per 1,000 pop. **Telephone lines:** 35,100. **Daily newspaper circ.:** 7.6 per 1,000 pop. **Internet**: 30,000 users.

Health: Life expect.: 35.5 male; 33.4 female. **Births** (per 1,000 pop.): 25.1. **Deaths** (per 1,000 pop.): 28.7. **Natural inc.:** –0.36%. **Infant mortality** (per 1,000 live births): 88.8. **AIDS rate:** 28.9%.

Education: Compulsory: ages 6-12. **Literacy:** 84.8%.

Major Intl. Organizations: UN (FOA, IBRD, ILO, IMF, WHO, WTrO), the Commonwealth, AU.

Embassy: 2511 Massachusetts Ave. NW 20008; 797-5533.

Website: www.lesotho.gov.ls

Lesotho (once called Basutoland) became a British protectorate in 1868 when Chief Moshesh sought protection against the Boers. Independence came Oct. 4, 1966. Elections were suspended in 1970. Most of Lesotho's GNP is provided by citizens working in South Africa. Livestock raising is the chief industry; diamonds are the chief export.

South Africa imposed a blockade, Jan. 1, 1986, because Lesotho had given sanctuary to anti-apartheid groups. The blockade sparked a Jan. 20 military coup, and was lifted, Jan. 25, when the new leaders agreed to expel the rebels.

In Mar. 1990, King Moshoeshoe was exiled by the military government. Letsie III became king Nov. 12. In Mar. 1993, Ntsu Mokhehle, a civilian, was elected prime minister, ending 23 years of military rule. After a series of violent disturbances, the king dismissed the Mokhele government Aug. 17, 1994; constitutional rule was restored Sept. 14. Letsie abdicated and Moshoeshoe was reinstated Jan. 25, 1995.

Moshoeshoe died in an automobile accident, Jan. 15, 1996. Letsie was reinstated Feb. 7; his formal coronation was Oct. 31, 1997. South Africa and Botswana sent troops Sept. 22, 1998, to help suppress violent antigovernment protests.

According to UN estimates, about 30% of the adult population has HIV/AIDS.

Liberia
Republic of Liberia

People: Population: 2,900,269. **Age distrib.** (%): <15: 43.6; 65+: 3.7. **Pop. density:** 67 per sq mi, 26 per sq km. **Urban:** 46.7%. **Ethnic groups:** Kpelle, Bassa, Dey, and other tribes 95%; Americo-Liberians 2.5%, Caribbean 2.5%. **Principal languages:** English (official); Mande, West Atlantic, and Kwa languages. **Chief religions:** Indigenous beliefs 40%, Christian 40%, Muslim 20%.

Geography: Total area: 43,000 sq mi, 111,370 sq km; **Land area:** 37,189 sq mi, 96,320 sq km. **Location:** On SW coast of W Africa. **Neighbors:** Sierra Leone on W, Guinea on N, Côte d'Ivoire on E. **Topography:** Marshy Atlantic coastline rises to low mountains and plateaus in the forested interior; 6 major rivers flow in parallel courses to the ocean. **Capital**: Monrovia, 572,000.

Government: Type: In transition. **Head of state and gov.:** Chmn. Charles Gyude Bryant; b Jan. 17, 1949; in office: Oct. 14, 2003 (interim). **Local divisions:** 15 counties. **Defense budget:** NA. **Active troops:** 11,000-15,000.

Economy: Industries: rubber & palm oil proc., timber, diamonds. **Chief crops:** rubber, coffee, cocoa, rice, cassava, palm oil, sugarcane, bananas. **Natural resources:** iron ore, timber, diamonds, gold, hydropower. **Arable land:** 1%. **Livestock** (2004): cattle: 36,000; chickens: 5 mil; goats: 220,000; pigs: 130,000; sheep: 210,000. **Fish catch** (2003): 11,314 metric tons. **Electricity prod.** (2003): 0.51 bil. kWh. **Labor force** (2000 est.): agriculture 70%, industry 8%, services 22%.

Finance: Monetary unit: Liberian Dollar (LRD) (Sept. 2005: 49.00 = $1 U.S.). **GDP** (2004 est.): $2.9 bil.; **per capita GDP:** $900; **GDP growth:** 21.8%. **Imports** (2002 est.): $5.1 bil.; partners (2004): South Korea 38.1%, Japan 21.9%, Singapore 12.6%, Croatia 4.8%. **Exports** (2002 est.): $1.1 bil.; partners (2004): Germany 36.9%, Poland 18.6%, US 11.4%, Greece 10.6%. **Budget** (2000 est.): $90.5 mil. **Intl. reserves less gold:** $12 mil.

Transport: Railroad: Length: 304 mi. **Motor vehicles:** 17,100 pass. cars, 12,800 comm. vehicles; 2 airports. **Chief ports:** Monrovia, Buchanan, Greenville, Harper.

Communications: TV sets: 26 per 1,000 pop. **Radios:** 329 per 1,000 pop. **Telephone lines:** 6,700 main lines. **Daily newspaper circ.:** 17 per 1,000 pop.

Health: Life expect.: 37.0 male; 40.8 female. **Births** (per 1,000 pop.): 45.6. **Deaths** (per 1,000 pop.): 23.9. **Natural inc.:** 2.17%. **Infant mortality** (per 1,000 live births): 162. **AIDS rate:** 5.9%.

Education: Compulsory: ages 6-15. **Literacy:** 57.5%.

Major Intl. Organizations: UN and most of its specialized agencies, AU.

Embassy: 5201 16th St. NW 20011; 723-0437.

Website: www.embassyofliberia.org

Liberia was founded in 1822 by U.S. black freedmen who settled at Monrovia with the aid of colonization societies. It became a republic July 26, 1847, with a constitution modeled on that of the U.S. Descendants of freedmen dominated politics.

Under Pres. William V. S. Tubman, Liberia was a founding member of the UN in 1945. Tubman died in 1971 and was succeeded by his vice-president, William R. Tolbert, Jr. Charging rampant corruption, an Army Redemption Council of enlisted men staged a bloody predawn coup, April 12, 1980, in which Pres. Tolbert was killed and replaced as head of state by Sgt. Samuel Doe. In 1985, Doe was chosen president in a disputed election and survived a subsequent coup.

A civil war began Dec. 1989. In Sept. 1990, Pres. Doe was captured and put to death. Despite the introduction of peacekeeping forces from several countries, factional fighting intensified, and a series of cease-fires failed. Factional fighting devastated Monrovia in Apr. 1996.

On Sept. 3, 1996, Ruth Perry became modern Africa's first female head of state, leading another transitional government. By then, the civil war had claimed more than 150,000 lives and uprooted over half the population.

Former rebel leader Charles Taylor was elected president July 19, 1997, in Liberia's 1st national election in 12 years. The UN imposed sanctions May 4, 2001, to punish Liberia for aiding the Revolutionary United Front (RUF) insurgency in Sierra Leone. Taylor declared a state of emergency Feb. 8, 2002, after Liberian rebels launched raids near Monrovia.

A UN-sponsored war crimes tribunal indicted Taylor June 4, 2003, for his role in Sierra Leone. With rebels again threatening Monrovia, Taylor resigned Aug. 11 and went into exile. The UN authorized a 15,000-member peacekeeping force (UNMIL) Sept. 19 to help stabilize the nation. A businessman, Charles Gyude Bryant, was sworn in Oct. 14 to head a power-sharing interim government. Presidential and legislative elections were scheduled for Oct. 11, 2005.

Libya
Great Socialist People's Libyan Arab Jamahiriya

People: Population: 5,765,563. **Age distrib.** (%): <15: 33.9; 65+: 4.2. **Pop. density:** 8 per sq mi, 3 per sq km. **Urban:** 86.3%. **Ethnic groups:** Arab-Berber 97%. **Principal languages:** Arabic (official), Italian, English. **Chief religion:** Muslim (official; mostly Sunni) 97%.

Geography: Total area: 679,362 sq mi, 1,759,540 sq km; **Land area:** 679,362 sq mi, 1,759,540 sq km. **Location:** On Mediterranean coast of N Africa. **Neighbors:** Tunisia, Algeria on W; Niger, Chad on S; Sudan, Egypt on E. **Topography:** Desert and semidesert regions cover 92% of the land, with low mountains in N, higher mountains in S, and a narrow coastal zone. **Capital**, Tripoli, 2,006,000. **Cities (urban aggr.)**: Benghazi, 912,000.

Government: Type: Islamic Arabic Socialist "Mass-State." **Head of state and gov.:** Col. Muammar al-Qaddafi; b Sept. 1942; in power: Sept. 1969. **Local divisions:** 25 municipalities. **Defense budget:** NA. **Active troops:** 76,000.

Economy: Industries: oil, food proc., textiles, handicrafts, cement. **Chief crops:** wheat, barley, olives, dates, citrus, vegetables, peanuts, soybeans. **Natural resources:** oil, nat. gas, gypsum. **Crude oil reserves** (2004): 39.0 bil. bbls. **Arable land:** 1%. **Livestock** (2004): cattle: 130,000; chickens: 25 mil; goats: 1.3 mil; sheep: 4.5 mil. **Fish catch** (2003): 33,666 metric tons. **Electricity prod.** (2003): 14.4 bil. kWh. **Labor force** (1997 est.): agriculture 17%, industry 29%, services 54%.

Finance: Monetary unit: Dinar (LYD) (Sept. 2005: 1.31 = $1 U.S.). **GDP** (2004 est.): $37.5 bil.; **per capita GDP:** $6,700; **GDP growth:** 4.9%. **Imports** (2004 est.): $7.2 bil.; partners (2004): Italy 28.2%, Germany 11.1%, Tunisia 6%, UK 5.8%, Turkey 5%, France 4.1%. **Exports** (2004 est.): $18.7 bil.; partners (2004): Italy 37.7%, Germany 16.7%, Spain 11.6%, Turkey 7.5%, France

6.5%. **Tourism:** $79 mil. **Budget** (2004 est.): $12.2 bil. **Intl. reserves less gold:** $16.54 bil. **Gold:** 4.62 mil. oz t.

Transport: Motor vehicles: 552,700 pass. cars, 195,500 comm. vehicles. **Civil aviation:** 254.1 mil. pass.-mi; 58 airports. **Chief ports:** Tripoli, Banghazi.

Communications: TV sets: 139 per 1,000 pop. **Radios:** 259 per 1,000 pop. **Telephone lines:** 750,000. **Daily newspaper circ.:** 14 per 1,000 pop. **Internet:** 160,000 users.

Health: Life expect.: 74.3 male; 78.8 female. **Births** (per 1,000 pop.): 26.8. **Deaths** (per 1,000 pop.): 3.5. **Natural inc.:** 2.33%. **Infant mortality** (per 1,000 live births): 24.6. **AIDS rate:** 0.3%.

Education: Compulsory: ages 6-14. **Literacy:** 82.6%.

Major Intl. Organizations: UN (FAO, IBRD, ILO, IMF, IMO, WHO), AL, AU, OPEC.

Permanent UN Representative: 309-315 E. 48th St., New York, NY 10017; (212) 752-5775.

Website: www.libya-un.org

First settled by Berbers, Libya was ruled in succession by Carthage, Rome, the Vandals, and the Ottomans. Italy ruled from 1912, and Britain and France after WW II. Libya became an independent constitutional monarchy Jan. 2, 1952. In 1969 a junta led by Col. Muammar al-Qaddafi seized power.

Libya and Egypt fought several air and land battles along their border in July 1977. Chad charged Libya with military occupation of its uranium-rich northern region in 1977. Libyan troops were driven from their last major stronghold by Chad forces in 1987, leaving over $1 billion in military equipment behind.

Libya reportedly helped arm violent revolutionary groups in Egypt and Sudan and aided terrorists of various nationalities, and was blamed for aiding the attacks on the Rome and Vienna airports in Dec. 1985. The U.S. and Libya clashed, Jan.-Mar. 1986, over access to the Gulf of Sidra, which Libya claimed as territorial waters. The U.S. accused Qaddafi of ordering the Apr. 5, bombing of a West Berlin discotheque, which killed 3, including a U.S. serviceman. In response, the U.S. sent warplanes to attack what it called "terrorist-related targets" in Tripoli and Banghazi, Libya, Apr. 14; the targets included Qaddafi's barracks.

Libyan agents were accused of planting bombs that blew up Pan Am Flight 103 over Lockerbie, Scotland, killing 270 people Dec. 21, 1988; and UTA Flight 772 over Niger, killing 170 people Sept. 19, 1989. The UN imposed sanctions, Apr. 15, 1992, for Libya's failure to cooperate in the Lockerbie and UTA cases.

Libya agreed in 2003 to renounce terrorism and settle compensation cases for the families of the Lockerbie and UTA bombing victims. The UN lifted sanctions, Sept. 12, 2003. Secret talks with the U.S. and UK led to Libya's announcement Dec. 19 that it would stop developing nuclear, chemical, and biological weapons and long-range missiles. The U.S. ended most economic sanctions Apr. 23, 2004, and restored diplomatic relations June 28, but Libya remained on the State Dept. list of nations sponsoring terrorism. Libya pledged Aug. 10 to compensate non-U.S. victims of the 1986 Berlin disco bombing. EU sanctions were lifted Oct. 11, 2004.

Liechtenstein

Principality of Liechtenstein

People: Population: 33,717. **Age distrib.** (%): <15: 17.6; 65+: 12.0. **Pop. density:** 544 per sq mi, 211 per sq km. **Urban:** 21.6%. **Ethnic groups:** Alemannic 86%; Italian, Turkish, and other 14%. **Principal languages:** German (official), Alemannic dialect. **Chief religions:** Roman Catholic 76%, Protestant 7%.

Geography: Total area: 62 sq mi, 160 sq km; **Land area:** 62 sq mi, 160 sq km. **Location:** Central Europe, in the Alps. **Neighbors:** Switzerland on W, Austria on E. **Topography:** The Rhine Valley occupies one-third of the country, the Alps cover the rest. **Capital:** Vaduz, 5,000.

Government: Type: Hereditary constitutional monarchy. **Head of state:** Prince Hans-Adam II; b Feb. 14, 1945; in office: Nov. 13, 1989. **Head of gov.:** Otmar Hasler; b Sept. 28, 1953; in office: Apr. 5, 2001. **Local divisions:** 11 communes.

Economy: Industries: electronics, metallurgy, textiles, ceramics, pharm., food products, precision instruments, tourism. **Chief crops:** wheat, barley, corn, potatoes. **Natural resources:** hydropower. **Arable land:** 24%. **Livestock** (2004): cattle: 6,000; goats: 280; pigs: 3,000; sheep: 2,900. **Labor force** (2001 est.): agriculture 1.3%, industry 47.4%, services 51.3%.

Finance: Monetary unit: Swiss Franc (CHF) (Sept. 2005: 1.23 = $1 U.S.). **GDP** (1999 est.): $825.0 mil; **per capita GDP:** $25,000; **GDP growth:** 11%. **Imports** (1996): $917.3 mil; partners: EU, Switzerland. **Exports** (1996): $2.5 bil.; partners : EU 62.6%, (Germany 24.3%, Austria 9.5%, France 8.9%, Italy 6.6%, UK 4.6%), US 18.9%, Switzerland 15.7%. **Budget** (1998 est.): $414.1 mil.

Transport: Railroad: Length: 11 mi.

Communications: TV sets: 469 per 1,000 pop. **Radios:** 656 per 1,000 pop. **Daily newspaper circ.:** 602 per 1,000 pop.

Health: Life expect.: 76.0 male; 83.2 female. **Births** (per 1,000 pop.): 10.4. **Deaths** (per 1,000 pop.): 7.1. **Natural inc.:** 0.34%. **Infant mortality** (per 1,000 live births): 4.7.

Education: Compulsory: ages 7-16. **Literacy:** 100%.

Major Intl. Organizations: UN (WTrO), EFTA, OSCE.

Permanent UN Representative: 1300 I St NW, Washington, DC 20005 216-0460; (212) 599-0220.

Website: www.liechtenstein.li/en

Liechtenstein became sovereign in 1806. Austria administered Liechtenstein's ports up to 1920; Switzerland has administered its postal services since 1921. Liechtenstein is united with Switzerland by a customs and monetary union. Taxes are low; many international corporations have headquarters there. Foreign workers comprise 2/3 of the labor force. On Aug. 15, 2004, Prince Hans-Adam II assigned day-to-day responsibilities for running the tiny country to his son, Crown Prince Alois.

Lithuania

Republic of Lithuania

People: Population: 3,596,617. **Age distrib.** (%): <15: 16.1; 65+: 15.2. **Pop. density:** 143 per sq mi, 55 per sq km. **Urban:** 66.7%. **Ethnic groups:** Lithuanian 81%, Russian 9%, Polish 7%, Belarusian 2%. **Principal languages:** Lithuanian (official), Belorusian, Russian, Polish. **Chief religion:** Roman Catholic 79%, none 9.5%.

Geography: Total area: 25,174 sq mi, 65,200 sq km. **Land area:** 25,174 sq mi, 65,200 sq km. **Location:** In E Europe, on SE coast of Baltic. **Neighbors:** Latvia on N, Belarus on E, S, Poland and Russia on W. **Topography:** Lithuania is a lowland with hills in W and S; fertile soil; many small lakes and rivers, with marshes espec. in N and W. **Capital:** Vilnius, 549,000. **Cities (urban aggr.):** Kaunas, 412,639.

Government: Type: Republic. **Head of state:** Pres. Valdas Adamkus; b Nov. 3, 1926; in office: July 12, 2004. **Head of gov.:** Prime Min. Algirdas Brazauskas; b Sept. 22, 1932; in office: July 3, 2001. **Local divisions:** 10 provinces. **Defense budget** (2004): $310 mil. **Active troops:** 13,510.

Economy: Industries: machine tools, electric motors, large appliances, oil refining, shipbuilding. **Chief crops:** grain, potatoes, sugar beets, flax, vegetables. **Natural resources:** peat. **Crude oil reserves** (2004): 12 mil bbls. **Arable land:** 35%. **Livestock** (2004): cattle: 812,100; chickens: 7.9 mil; goats: 27,200; pigs: 1.1 mil; sheep: 16,900. **Fish catch** (2003): 159,561 metric tons. **Electricity prod.** (2003): 18.6 bil. kWh. **Labor force** (1997 est.): agriculture 20%, industry 30%, services 50%.

Finance: Monetary unit: Litai (LTL) (Sept. 2005: 2.76 = $1 U.S.). **GDP** (2004 est.): $45.2 bil.; **per capita GDP:** $12,500; **GDP growth:** 6.6%. **Imports** (2004 est.): $11.0 bil.; partners (2004): Russia 23.1%, Germany 18.1%, Poland 4.7%, Italy 4.6%. **Exports** (2004 est.): $8.9 bil.; partners (2004): Switzerland 10.7%, Latvia 10%, Germany 9.5%, Russia 7.9%, France 7.5%, US 5.2%, UK 5.1%, Estonia 4.5%, Denmark 4.3%. **Tourism:** $638 mil. **Budget** (2004 est.): $7.1 bil. **Intl. reserves less gold:** $2.26 bil. **Gold:** 190,000 oz t. **Consumer prices:** 1.2%.

Transport: Railroad: Length: 1,241 mi. **Motor vehicles:** 1.18 mil. pass. cars, 120,900 comm. vehicles. **Civil aviation:** 215.6 mil. pass.-mi; 22 airports. **Chief port:** Klaipeda.

Communications: TV sets: 422 per 1,000 pop. **Radios:** 502 per 1,000 pop. **Telephone lines:** 824,200. **Daily newspaper circ.:** 29.3 per 1,000 pop. **Internet:** 695,700 users.

Health: Life expect.: 68.9 male; 79.3 female. **Births** (per 1,000 pop.): 8.6. **Deaths** (per 1,000 pop.): 10.9. **Natural inc.:** –0.23%. **Infant mortality** (per 1,000 live births): 6.9. **AIDS rate:** 0.1%.

Education: Compulsory: ages 7-15. **Literacy:** 99.6%.

Major Intl. Organizations: UN (FAO, IBRD, ILO, IMF, IMO, WHO), EU, NATO, OSCE.

Embassy: 2622 16th St. NW 20009; 234-5860.

Website: www.president.lt/en

Lithuania was occupied by the German army, 1914-18. It was annexed by the Soviet Russian army, but the Soviets were overthrown, 1919. Lithuania was a democratic republic until 1926, when the regime was ousted by a coup. In 1939 the Soviet-German treaty assigned most of Lithuania to the Soviet sphere of influence. Lithuania was annexed by the USSR Aug. 3, 1940.

Lithuania formally declared its independence from the Soviet Union Mar. 11, 1990. During an abortive Soviet coup in Aug., the Western nations recognized Lithuania's independence, which was ratified by the Soviet Union in Sept. 1991.

The last Russian troops withdrew on Aug. 31, 1993. The conservative Homeland Union defeated the former Communists in parliamentary elections Oct.–Nov. 10, 1996. A Lithuanian-American, Valdas Adamkus, won the presidency in a runoff election Jan. 4, 1998. He lost to Rolandas Paksas in a runoff, Jan. 5, 2003. But after the legislature impeached and removed Paksas from office, Apr. 6, 2004, Adamkus regained the presidency in a runoff vote June 27. Lithuania joined the EU and NATO in 2004.

Luxembourg

Grand Duchy of Luxembourg

People: Population: 468,571. **Age distrib.** (%): <15: 18.9; 65+: 14.6. **Pop. density:** 470 per sq mi, 181 per sq km. **Urban:** 91.9%. **Ethnic groups:** Mixture of French and German. **Principal languages:** Luxembourgish (national); German, French (official). **Chief religion:** Roman Catholic 87%, 13% Protestant, Jewish, and Muslim.

Geography: Total area: 998 sq mi, 2,586 sq km; **Land area:** 998 sq mi, 2,586 sq km. **Location:** In W Europe. **Neighbors:** Belgium on W, France on S, Germany on E. **Topography:** Heavy forests (Ardennes) cover N, S is a low, open plateau. **Capital:** Luxembourg-Ville, 77,000.

Government: Type: Constitutional monarchy. **Head of state:** Grand Duke Henri; b Apr. 16, 1955; in office: Oct. 7, 2000. **Head of**

gov.: Prime Min. Jean-Claude Juncker; b Dec. 9, 1954; in office: Jan. 19, 1995. **Local divisions:** 3 districts. **Defense budget** (2004): $256 mil. **Active troops:** 900.

Economy: Industries: banking, iron & steel, food proc., chemicals, metal products, engineering, tires, glass, aluminum. **Chief crops:** barley, oats, potatoes, wheat, fruits, grapes. **Natural resources:** iron ore. **Arable land:** 24%. **Livestock** (2004): cattle: 185,000; chickens: 80 mil; goats: 2,000; pigs: 76,000; sheep: 7,000. **Electricity prod.** (2003): 2.8 bil. kWh. **Labor force** (2004 est.): agriculture 1%, industry 13%, services 86%.

Finance: Monetary unit: Euro (EUR) (Sept. 2005: 0.80 = $1 U.S.). **GDP** (2004 est.): $27.3 bil.; **per capita GDP:** $58,900; **GDP growth:** 2.3%. **Imports** (2003): $16.3 bil.; partners (2004): Belgium 30%, Germany 21.8%, France 12.5%, China 11.9%, Netherlands 4.5%. **Exports** (2003): $13.4 bil.; partners (2004): Germany 21.8%, France 20.1%, Belgium 10.5%, UK 9.3%, Italy 7.1%, Spain 5.6%, Netherlands 4.3%. **Tourism:** $2,793 mil. **Budget** (2004 est.): $14.5 bil. **Intl. reserves less gold:** $192 mil. **Gold:** 70,000 oz t. **Consumer prices:** 2.23%.

Transport: Railroad: Length: 170 mi. **Motor vehicles:** 280,700 pass. cars, 48,700 comm. vehicles. **Civil aviation:** 364.1 mil. pass.-mi; 1 airport. **Chief port:** Mertert.

Communications: TV sets: 599 per 1,000 pop. **Radios:** 683 per 1,000 pop. **Telephone lines**: 360,100. **Daily newspaper circ.:** 332 per 1,000 pop. **Internet**: 170,000 users.

Health: Life expect.: 75.5 male; 82.2 female. **Births** (per 1,000 pop.): 12.1. **Deaths** (per 1,000 pop.): 8.4. **Natural inc.:** 0.37%. **Infant mortality** (per 1,000 live births): 4.8. **AIDS rate:** 0.2%.

Education: Compulsory: ages 6-15. **Literacy:** 100%.

Major Intl. Organizations: UN (FAO, IBRD, ILO, IMF, IMO, WHO, WTrO), EU, NATO, OECD, OSCE.

Embassy: 2200 Massachusetts Ave. NW 20008; 265-4171.

Website: www.luxembourg-usa.org

Luxembourg, founded about 963, was ruled by Burgundy, Spain, Austria, and France from 1448 to 1815. It left the Germanic Confederation in 1866. Overrun by Germany in 2 world wars, Luxembourg ended its neutrality in 1948, when a customs union with Belgium and Netherlands was adopted.

Luxembourg was one of the 6 founding members (1951) of what became the European Union. Its voters ratified the EU constitution in July 2005.

Macedonia

Former Yugoslav Republic of Macedonia

People: Population: 2,045,262. **Age distrib.** (%): <15: 20.5; 65+: 10.8. **Pop. density:** 209 per sq mi, 81 per sq km. **Urban:** 59.5%. **Ethnic groups:** Macedonian 67%, Albanian 23%, Turkish 4%, Roma 2%, Serb 2%. **Principal languages:** Macedonian (official), Albanian, Turkish, Romani, Serbo-Croatian. **Chief religions:** unspecified 51%, Macedonian Orthodox 32%, Muslim 17%.

Geography: Total area: 9,781 sq mi, 25,333 sq km; **Land area:** 9,597 sq mi, 24,856 sq km. **Location:** In SE Europe. **Neighbors:** Bulgaria on E, Greece on S, Albania on W, Serbia on N. Topography: Macedonia is a landlocked, mostly mountainous country, with deep river valleys, 3 large lakes; country is bisected by Vardar R. **Capital:** Skopje, 447,000.

Government: Type: Republic. **Head of state:** Pres. Branko Crvenkovski; b Oct. 12, 1962; in office: May 12, 2004. **Head of gov.:** Prime Min. Vlado Buckovski; b Dec. 2, 1962; in office: Dec. 17, 2004. **Local divisions:** 123 municipalities. **Defense budget** (2004): $149 mil. **Active troops:** 10,890.

Economy: Industries: mining, textiles, wood products, tobacco, food proc., buses. **Chief crops:** rice, tobacco, wheat, corn, millet, cotton, sesame. **Natural resources:** chromium, lead, zinc, mang., tungsten, nickel, iron ore, asbestos, sulfur, timber. **Arable land:** 24%. **Livestock** (2004): cattle: 255,000; chickens: 2.7 mil; pigs: 158,231; sheep: 1.4 mil. **Fish catch** (2003): 1,648 metric tons. **Electricity prod.** (2003): 5.6 bil. kWh.

Finance: Monetary unit: (MKD) Denar (Sept. 2005: 47.81 = $1 U.S.). **GDP** (2004 est.): $14.4 bil.; **per capita GDP:** $7,100; **GDP growth:** 1.3%. **Imports** (2004 est.): $2.7 bil.; partners (2004): Greece 18%, Germany 14.4%, Serbia and Montenegro 9.3%, Slovenia 8.1%, Bulgaria 7.6%, Turkey 7%. **Exports** (2004 est.): $1.6 bil.; partners (2004): Serbia and Montenegro 30.8%, Germany 20.1%, Greece 9%, Croatia 7%, US 4.8%. **Tourism:** $57 mil. **Budget** (2004 est.): $1.2 bil. **Gold:** 200,000 oz t. **Consumer prices:** –0.37%.

Transport: Railroad: Length: 434 mi. **Motor vehicles:** 307,600 pass. cars, 33,000 comm. vehicles. **Civil aviation:** 234.3 mil. pass.-mi; 10 airports.

Communications: TV sets: 273 per 1,000 pop. **Radios:** 550 per 1,000 pop. **Telephone lines** (2002): 560,000. **Daily newspaper circ.:** 53.3 per 1,000 pop. **Internet** (2002): 100,000 users.

Health: Life expect.: 71.3 male; 76.4 female. **Births** (per 1,000 pop.): 12.0. **Deaths** (per 1,000 pop.): 8.7. **Natural inc.:** 0.33%. **Infant mortality** (per 1,000 live births): 10.1. **AIDS rate:** <0.1%.

Education: Compulsory: ages 7-14. **Literacy:** NA%.

Major Intl. Organizations: UN (FAO, IBRD, ILO, IMF, IMO, WHO, WTro).

Embassy: 1101 30th St., NW, Ste., 302, 20007; 337-3063.

Website: www.vlada.mk/english/index_en.htm

Macedonia, as part of a larger region also called Macedonia, was ruled by Muslim Turks from 1389 to 1912, when native Greeks, Bulgarians, and Slavs won independence. Serbia received the largest part of the territory, the rest going to Greece and Bulgaria. In 1913, the area was incorporated into Serbia, which in 1918 became part of the Kingdom of Serbs, Croats, and Slovenes (later Yugoslavia). In 1946, Macedonia became a constituent republic of Yugoslavia.

Macedonia declared its independence Sept. 8, 1991, and was admitted to the UN under a provisional name in 1993. A UN force, which included several hundred U.S. troops, was deployed there to deter the warring factions in Bosnia from carrying their dispute into other areas of the Balkans.

In Feb. 1994 both Russia and the U.S. recognized Macedonia. Greece, which objected to Macedonia's use of what it considered a Hellenic name and symbols, imposed a trade blockade on the landlocked nation; the 2 countries agreed to normalize relations Sept. 13, 1995. A car bombing, Oct. 3, seriously injured Pres. Kiro Gligorov. Macedonia and Yugoslavia signed a treaty normalizing relations Apr. 8, 1996.

By the end of NATO's air war against Yugoslavia, Mar.-June 1999, Macedonia had a Kosovar refugee population of more than 250,000; over 90% had been repatriated by Sept. 1. Boris Trajkovski, candidate of the ruling center-right coalition, won a presidential runoff vote Nov. 14.

Ethnic Albanian guerrillas launched an offensive Mar. 2001 in NW Macedonia. An accord signed Aug. 13 paved the way for the introduction of a NATO peacekeeping force. A law broadening the rights of ethnic Albanians was enacted Jan. 24, 2002. A 320-member EU force replaced the NATO peacekeepers Mar. 31, 2003. After Trajkovski died in a plane crash Feb. 26, 2004, Prime Min. Branko Crvenkovski won a presidential runoff vote Apr. 28.

Madagascar

Republic of Madagascar

People: Population: 18,040,341. **Age distrib.** (%): <15: 44.8; 65+: 3.0. **Pop. density:** 80 per sq mi, 31 per sq km. **Urban:** 26.5%. **Ethnic groups:** Mainly Malagasy (Indonesian-African); also Cotiers, French, Indian, Chinese. **Principal languages:** Malagasy, French (both official). **Chief religions:** Indigenous beliefs 52%, Christian 41%, Muslim 7%.

Geography: Total area: 226,657 sq mi, 587,040 sq km; **Land area:** 224,534 sq mi, 581,540 sq km. **Location:** In the Indian O., off the SE coast of Africa. **Neighbors:** Comoro Isls. to NW, Mozambique to W. **Topography:** Humid coastal strip in the E, fertile valleys in the mountainous center plateau region, and a wider coastal strip on the W. **Capital:** Antananarivo, 1,678,000.

Government: Type: Republic. **Head of state:** Pres. Marc Ravalomanana; b Dec. 12, 1949; in office: Feb. 22, 2002. **Head of gov.:** Prime Min. Jacques Sylla; b 1946; in office: Feb. 26, 2002. **Local divisions:** 6 provinces. **Defense budget** (2003): $53 mil. **Active troops:** 13,500.

Economy: Industries: meat proc., soap, brewing, hides, sugar, textiles, glassware, cement, autos. **Chief crops:** coffee, vanilla, sugarcane, cloves, cocoa, rice, cassava, beans, bananas, peanuts. **Natural resources:** graphite, chromite, coal, bauxite, salt, quartz, tar sands, gemstones, mica, fish, hydropower. **Arable land:** 4%. **Livestock** (2004): cattle: 10.5 mil; chickens: 24 mil; goats: 1.2 mil; pigs: 1.6 mil; sheep: 650,000. **Fish catch** (2003): 150,345 metric tons. **Electricity prod.** (2003): 0.83 bil. kWh.

Finance: Monetary unit: Ariary (MGA) (Sept. 2005: 1,810.05 = $1 U.S.). **GDP** (2004 est.): $14.6 bil.; **per capita GDP:** $800; **GDP growth:** 5.5%. **Imports** (2004 est.): $1.2 bil.; partners (2004): France 17.6%, China 11.1%, Hong Kong 6.7%, Iran 6.2%, South Africa 5.8%. **Exports** (2004 est.): $868.2 mil; partners (2004): US 35.7%, France 30.7%, Germany 7.1%, Mauritius 4.4%. **Tourism:** $76 mil. **Budget** (2004 est.): $1.1 bil. **Intl. reserves less gold:** $324 mil. **Consumer prices:** 13.81%.

Transport: Railroad: Length: 455 mi. **Motor vehicles** 64,000 pass. cars, 9,100 comm. vehicles. **Civil aviation:** 518.8 mil. pass.-mi; 29 airports. **Chief ports:** Toamasina, Antsiranana, Mahajanga, Toliara, Antsohimbondrona.

Communications: TV sets: 23 per 1,000 pop. **Radios:** 209 per 1,000 pop. **Telephone lines:** 59,600. **Daily newspaper circ.:** 4.6 per 1,000 pop. **Internet:** 70,500 users.

Health: Life expect.: 54.6 male; 59.4 female. **Births** (per 1,000 pop.): 41.7. **Deaths** (per 1,000 pop.): 11.4. **Natural inc.:** 3.03%. **Infant mortality** (per 1,000 live births): 76.8. **AIDS rate:** 1.7%.

Education: Compulsory: ages 6-14. **Literacy:** 68.9%.

Major Intl. Organizations: UN (FAO, IBRD, ILO, IMF, IMO, WHO, WTrO), AU.

Embassy: 2374 Massachusetts Ave. NW 20008; 265-5525.

Website: www.assemblee-nationale.mg/en

Madagascar was settled 2,000 years ago by Malayan-Indonesian people, whose descendants still predominate. A unified kingdom ruled the 18th and 19th centuries. The island became a French protectorate, 1885, and a colony 1896. Independence came June 26, 1960.

Discontent with inflation and French domination led to a coup in 1972. The new regime nationalized French-owned financial interests, closed French bases and a U.S. space-tracking station, and obtained Chinese aid. The government conducted a program of arrests, expulsion of foreigners, and repression of strikes, 1979.

In 1990, Madagascar ended a ban on multiparty politics that had been in place since 1975. Albert Zafy was elected president in 1993, ending the 17-year rule of Adm. Didier Ratsiraka. After Zafy was impeached by the legislature, Madagascar's constitutional court removed him from office, Sept. 5, 1996. Prime Min. Norbert Ratsirahonana then became interim president pending national elections, Nov. 3 and Dec. 29, in which Ratsiraka edged Zafy. A cholera epidemic, exacerbated by cyclones in Feb. and Apr. 2000, claimed at least 1,600 lives.

Marc Ravalomanana won a power struggle with Ratsiraka that followed a disputed presidential election Dec. 16, 2001.

Malawi

Republic of Malawi

People: Population: 12,707,464. **Age distrib.** (%): <15: 46.9; 65+: 2.8. **Pop. density:** 278 per sq mi, 107 per sq km. **Urban:** 16.3%. **Ethnic groups:** Chewa, Nyanja, Tumbuka, Yao, Lomwe, Sena, Tonga, Ngoni, Ngonde. **Principal languages:** Chichewa, English (both official), several African languages. **Chief religions:** Protestant 39%, Roman Catholic 25%, Muslim 15%.

Geography: Total area: 45,745 sq mi, 118,480 sq km; **Land area:** 36,324 sq mi, 94,080 sq km. **Location:** In SE Africa. **Neighbors:** Zambia on W, Mozambique on S and E, Tanzania on N. **Topography:** Malawi stretches 560 mi. N-S along Lake Malawi (Lake Nyasa), most of which belongs to Malawi. High plateaus and mountains line the Rift Valley the length of the nation. **Capital:** Lilongwe, 587,000. **Cities (urban aggr., 1998 est.)**: Blantyre, 2,000,000.

Government: Type: Republic. **Head of state and gov.:** Pres. Bingu wa Mutharika; b Feb. 24, 1934; in office: May 24, 2004. **Local divisions:** 3 regions, 26 districts. **Defense budget** (2004): $11 mil. **Active troops:** 5,300.

Economy: Industries: tobacco, tea, sugar, wood products, cement, consumer goods. **Chief crops:** tobacco, sugarcane, cotton, tea, corn, potatoes, cassava, sorghum. **Natural resources:** limestone, hydropower, uranium, coal, bauxite. **Arable land:** 18%. **Livestock** (2004): cattle: 750,000; chickens: 15.2 mil; goats: 1.7 mil; pigs: 456,300; sheep: 115,000. **Fish catch** (2003): 54,209 metric tons. **Electricity prod.** (2003): 1.3 bil. kWh. **Labor force** (2003 est.): agriculture 90%.

Finance: Monetary unit: Kwacha (MWK) (Sept. 2005: 123.88 = $1 U.S.). **GDP** (2004 est.): $7.4 bil.; **per capita GDP:** $600; **GDP growth:** 4%. **Imports** (2004 est.): $521.1 mil; partners (2004): South Africa 43.5%, India 6.8%, Tanzania 4.1%. **Exports** (2004 est.): $503.4 mil; partners (2004): South Africa 13.8%, US 12.3%, Germany 11.8%, Egypt 8.2%, UK 6.8%. **Tourism:** $33 mil. **Budget** (2004 est.): $635.6 mil. **Intl. reserves less gold:** $86 mil. **Gold:** 10,000 oz t. **Consumer prices:** 11.26%.

Transport: Railroad: Length: 495 mi. **Motor vehicles:** 22,500 pass. cars, 57,600 comm. vehicles. **Civil aviation:** 137.3 mil. pass.-mi; 6 airports.

Communications: TV sets: 3 per 1,000 pop. Radios: 476 per 1,000 pop. **Telephone lines:** 85,000. **Daily newspaper circ.:** 3 per 1,000 pop. **Internet**: 36,000 users.

Health: Life expect.: 41.7 male; 41.2 female. **Births** (per 1,000 pop.): 43.5. **Deaths** (per 1,000 pop.): 19.6. **Natural inc.:** 2.39%. **Infant mortality** (per 1,000 live births): 96.1. **AIDS rate:** 14.2%.

Education: Compulsory: ages 6-13. **Literacy:** 62.7%.

Major Intl. Organizations: UN (FAO, IBRD, ILO, IMF, IMO, WHO, WTrO), the Commonwealth, AU.

Embassy: 2408 Massachusetts Ave. NW 20008; 797-1007.

Website: www.malawi.gov.mw

Bantus came to the land in the 16th century, Arab slavers in the 19th. The area became the British protectorate Nyasaland in 1891. It became independent July 6, 1964, and a republic in 1966. After 3 decades as a one-party state under Pres. Hastings Kamuzu Banda, Malawi adopted a new constitution and, in multiparty elections held May 17, 1994, chose a new leader, Bakili Muluzi. Banda was acquitted, Dec. 23, 1995, of complicity in the deaths of 4 political opponents in 1983; he died Nov. 25, 1997. Bingu wa Mutharika, candidate of the ruling United Democratic Front, won a disputed presidential election May 20, 2004.

Malaysia

People: Population: 23,953,136. **Age distrib.** (%): <15: 33.0; 65+: 4.6. **Pop. density:** 188 per sq mi, 73 per sq km. **Urban:** 63.9%. **Ethnic groups:** Malay and other indigenous 58%, Chinese 24%, Indian 8%. **Principal languages:** Malay (official), English, Chinese dialects, Tamil, Telugu, Malayalam, Panjabi, Thai, Iban, and Kadazan in East. **Chief religions:** Muslim (official) 60%, Buddhist 19%, Christian 9%, Hindu 6%, Confucianist/Taoist 3%.

Geography: Total area: 127,317 sq mi, 329,750 sq km; **Land area:** 126,854 sq mi, 328,550 sq km. **Location:** On the SE tip of Asia, plus the N coast of the island of Borneo. **Neighbors:** Thailand on N, Indonesia on S. **Topography:** Most of W Malaysia is covered by tropical jungle, including the central mountain range that runs N-S through the peninsula. The western coast is marshy, the eastern, sandy. E Malaysia has a wide, swampy coastal plain, with interior jungles and mountains. **Capital:** Kuala Lumpur, 1,352,000.

Government: Type: Constitutional monarchy. **Head of state:** Paramount Ruler Syed Sirajuddin Syed Putra Jamalullail; b May 16, 1943; in office: Dec. 13, 2001. **Head of gov.:** Prime Min. Datuk Seri Abdullah Ahmad Badawi; b Nov. 26, 1939; in office: Oct. 31, 2003. **Local divisions:** 13 states, 3 federal territories. **Defense budget** (2004): $2.2 bil. **Active troops:** 110,000.

Economy: Industries: rubber & palm oil proc., light mfg., electronics, tin, mining, timber, oil. **Chief crops:** rubber, palm oil, cocoa, rice, coconuts, pepper. **Natural resources:** tin, oil, timber, copper, iron ore, nat. gas, bauxite. **Crude oil reserves** (2003): 3.0 bil. bbls. **Arable land:** 3%. **Livestock** (2004): cattle: 750,000; chickens: 180 mil; goats: 227,000; pigs: 2.1 mil; sheep: 120,000. **Fish catch** (2003): 1,454,244 metric tons. **Electricity prod.** (2003): 79.3 bil. kWh. **Labor force** (2000 est.): agriculture 14.5%, industry 36%, services 49.5%.

Finance: Monetary unit: Ringgit (MYR) (Sept. 2005: 3.76 = $1 U.S.). **GDP** (2004 est.): $229.3 bil.; **per capita GDP:** $9,700; **GDP growth:** 7.1%. **Imports** (2004 est.): $99.3 bil.; partners (2004): Japan 16.1%, US 14.6%, Singapore 11.2%, China 9.9%, Thailand 5.6%, Taiwan 5.5%, South Korea 5%, Germany 4.5%, Indonesia 4%. **Exports** (2004 est.): $123.5 bil.; partners (2004): US 18.8%, Singapore 15%, Japan 10.1%, China 6.7%, Hong Kong 6%, Thailand 4.8%. **Tourism:** $5,901 mil. **Budget** (2004 est.): $29.3 bil. **Intl. reserves less gold:** $42.75 bil. **Gold:** 1.17 mil. oz t. **Consumer prices:** 1.45%.

Transport: Railroad: Length: 1,502 mi. **Motor vehicles:** 400,400 pass. cars, 40,100 comm. vehicles. **Civil aviation:** 22.2 bil pass.-mi; 35 airports. **Chief ports:** Kuantan, Kelang, Kota Kinabalu, Kuching.

Communications: TV sets: 174 per 1,000 pop. **Radios:** 434 per 1,000 pop. **Telephone lines:** 4.6 mil. **Daily newspaper circ.:** 158 per 1,000 pop. **Internet**: 8.7 mil. users.

Health: Life expect.: 69.6 male; 75.1 female. **Births** (per 1,000 pop.): 23.1. **Deaths** (per 1,000 pop.): 5.1. **Natural inc.:** 1.80%. **Infant mortality** (per 1,000 live births): 17.7. **AIDS rate:** 0.4%.

Education: Compulsory: ages 6-16. **Literacy:** 88.7%.

Major Intl. Organizations: UN (FAO, IBRD, ILO, IMF, IMO, WHO, WTrO), APEC, ASEAN, the Commonwealth.

Embassy: 3516 International Court NW 20008; 572-9700.

Website: www.gov.my

European traders appeared in the 16th century; Britain established control in 1867. Malaysia was created Sept. 16, 1963. It included Malaya (which had become independent in 1957 after the suppression of Communist rebels), plus the formerly British Singapore, Sabah (N Borneo), and Sarawak (NW Borneo). Singapore was separated in 1965, in order to end tensions between Chinese, the majority in Singapore, and Malays in control of the Malaysian government.

A monarch is elected by a council of hereditary rulers of the Malayan states every 5 years.

Abundant natural resources have bolstered prosperity, and foreign investment has aided industrialization. Work on a new federal capital at Putrajaya, south of Kuala Lumpur, began in 1995. However, sagging stock and currency prices forced the postponement of major development projects in Sept. 1997.

Mahathir bin Mohamad dominated Malaysian politics as prime minister, 1981-2003. His successor, Abdullah Ahmad Badawi, took office Oct. 31, 2003, and led his National Front coalition to a resounding win in parliamentary elections Mar. 21, 2004. The Indian Ocean tsunami of Dec. 26 left at least 68 people dead and 8,000 displaced in Malaysia.

Maldives

Republic of Maldives

People: Population: 349,106. **Age distrib.** (%): <15: 43.9; 65+: 3.1. **Pop. density:** 3,010 per sq mi, 1,164 per sq km. **Urban:** 28.8%. **Ethnic groups:** Dravidian, Sinhalese, Arab. **Principal languages:** Divehi (Sinhala dialect, Arabic script; official), English. **Chief religion:** Muslim (official; mostly Sunni).

Geography: Total area: 116 sq mi, 300 sq km; **Land area:** 116 sq mi, 300 sq km. **Location:** In the Indian O., SW of India. **Neighbors:** Nearest is India on N. **Topography:** 19 atolls with 1,190 islands, 198 inhabited. None of the islands are over 5 sq. mi. in area, and all are nearly flat. **Capital:** Male, 83,000.

Government: Type: Republic. **Head of state and gov.:** Pres. Maumoon Abdul Gayoom; b Dec. 29, 1937; in office: Nov. 11, 1978. **Local divisions:** 19 atolls and Male capital atoll. **Defense budget:** $36 mil. **Active troops:** NA.

Economy: Industries: fish proc., tourism, shipping, boat building, coconut proc., garments. **Chief crops:** coconuts, corn, sweet potatoes. **Natural resources:** fish. **Arable land:** 10%. **Fish catch** (2003): 155,415 metric tons. **Electricity prod.** (2003): 0.14 bil. kWh. **Labor force** (1995): agriculture 22%, industry 18%, services 60%.

Finance: Monetary unit: Rufiyaa (MVR) (Sept. 2005: 12.80 = $1 U.S.). **GDP** (2002 est.): $1.3 bil.; **per capita GDP:** $3,900; **GDP growth:** 2.3% **Imports** (2002 est.): $392.0 mil; partners (2004): Singapore 32.9%, Sri Lanka 11%, India 8.2%, UAE 7.2%, Malaysia 6.4%, Thailand 5.2%. **Exports** (2002 est.): $90.0 mil; partners (2004): US 40.4%, Thailand 14.6%, Sri Lanka 9.5%, Japan 8.6%, UK 8.2%. **Tourism:** $402 mil. **Budget** (2002 est.): $282.0 mil. **Intl. reserves less gold:** $131 mil. **Consumer prices:** 6.41%.

Transport: Motor vehicles: 100 pass. cars, 100 comm. vehicles. **Civil aviation:** 277.8 mil. pass.-mi; 2 airports. **Chief ports:** Male, Gan.

Communications: TV sets: 38 per 1,000 pop. **Radios:** 129 per 1,000 pop. **Telephone lines** (2002): 28,700. **Daily newspaper circ.:** 12 per 1,000 pop. **Internet** (2002): 15,000 users.

Health: Life expect.: 62.8 male; 65.4 female. **Births** (per 1,000 pop.): 35.4. **Deaths** (per 1,000 pop.): 7.2. **Natural inc.:** 2.82%. **Infant mortality** (per 1,000 live births): 56.5.

Education: Compulsory: ages 6-12. **Literacy:** 97.2%.

Major Intl. Organizations: UN (FAO, IBRD, IMF, IMO, WHO, WTrO), the Commonwealth.

Permanent UN Representative: 800 Second Avenue, Suite 400E, New York N.Y. 10017, USA (212) 599 6194.

Website: www.maldivesinfo.gov.mv

The islands had been a British protectorate since 1887. The country became independent July 26, 1965. Long a sultanate, the Maldives became a republic in 1968. Natural resources and tourism are being developed; however, the Maldives remains one of the world's poorest countries. Tourism and fishing are the most important sectors of the economy. Pres. Gayoom has held power since 1978; political parties are suppressed. The Indian Ocean tsunami of Dec. 26, 2004, killed at least 82 people and displaced more than 21,600 in Maldives.

Mali

Republic of Mali

People: Population: 11,415,261. **Age distrib.** (%): <15: 47.1; 65+: 3.0. **Pop. density:** 24 per sq mi, 9 per sq km. **Urban:** 32.3%. **Ethnic groups:** Mande 50% (Bambara, Malinke, Soninke), Peul 17%, Voltaic 12%, Tuareg and Moor 10%, Songhai 6%. **Principal languages:** French (official); Bambara and other African languages. **Chief religions:** Muslim 90%, indigenous beliefs 9%.

Geography: Total area: 478,767 sq mi, 1,240,000 sq km; **Land area:** 471,045 sq mi, 1,220,000 sq km. **Location:** In the interior of W Africa. **Neighbors:** Mauritania, Senegal on W; Guinea, Côte d'Ivoire, Burkina Faso on S; Niger on E; Algeria on N. **Topography:** A landlocked grassy plain in the upper basins of the Senegal and Niger rivers, extending N into the Sahara. **Capital:** Bamako, 1,264,000.

Government: Type: Republic. **Head of state:** Pres. Amadou Toumani Touré; b Nov. 4, 1948; in office: June 8, 2002. **Head of gov.:** Prime Min. Ousmane Issoufi Maïga; b 1946; in office: Apr. 30, 2004. **Local divisions:** 8 regions, 1 capital district. **Defense budget** (2004): $94 mil. **Active troops:** 7,350.

Economy: Industries: food proc., constr., phosphates, gold. **Chief crops:** cotton, millet, rice, corn, vegetables, peanuts. **Natural resources:** gold, phosphates, kaolin, salt, limestone, uranium, hydropower. **Arable land:** 2%. **Livestock** (2004): cattle: 7.5 mil; chickens: 30 mil; goats: 12.0 mil; pigs: 68,000; sheep: 8.4 mil. **Fish catch** (2003): 101,008 metric tons. **Electricity prod.** (2003): 0.82 bil. kWh. **Labor force** (2001 est.): agriculture and fishing 80%.

Finance: Monetary unit: CFA Franc BCEAO (XOF) (Sept. 2005: 525.28 = $1 U.S.). **GDP** (2004 est.): $11.0 bil.; **per capita GDP:** $900; **GDP growth:** 4%. **Imports** (2002 est.): $927.0 mil; partners (2004): France 15.4%, Senegal 7.2%, Côte d'Ivoire 6.6%, Germany 4.1%. **Exports** (2002 est.): $915.0 mil; partners (2004): China 32%, India 10.3%, Italy 7.6%, Bangladesh 6.8%, Thailand 5.9%, Germany 5.2%, Taiwan 4%. **Tourism** (2002): $104 mil. **Budget** (2002 est.): $828.0 mil. **Intl. reserves less gold:** $670 mil. **Consumer prices:** –3.1%.

Transport: Railroad: Length: 453 mi. **Motor vehicles:** 18,900 pass. cars, 31,700 comm. vehicles. **Civil aviation:** 80.8 mil. pass.-mi; 7 airports. **Chief port:** Koulikoro.

Communications: TV sets: 13 per 1,000 pop. **Radios:** 55 per 1,000 pop. **Telephone lines** (2002): 56,600. **Daily newspaper circ.:** 1.2 per 1,000 pop. **Internet** (2002): 25,000 users.

Health: Life expect.: 46.7 male; 50.7 female. **Births** (per 1,000 pop.): 50.0. **Deaths** (per 1,000 pop.): 17.2. **Natural inc.:** 3.28%. **Infant mortality** (per 1,000 live births): 109.5. **AIDS rate:** 1.9%.

Education: Compulsory: ages 7-15. **Literacy:** 46.4%.

Major Intl. Organizations: UN and most of its specialized agencies, AU.

Embassy: 2130 R St. NW 20008; 332-2249.

Website: www.maliembassy.us

Until the 15th century the area was part of the great Mali Empire. Timbuktu (Tombouctou) was a center of Islamic study. French rule was secured, 1898. The Sudanese Rep. and Senegal became independent as the Mali Federation June 20, 1960, but Senegal withdrew, and the Sudanese Rep. was renamed Mali.

Mali signed economic agreements with France and, in 1963, with Senegal. In 1968, a coup ended the socialist regime. Famine struck in 1973-74, killing as many as 100,000 people. Drought conditions returned in the 1980s.

The military, Mar. 26, 1991, overthrew the government of Pres. Moussa Traoré, who had been in power since 1968. Oumar Konare, a coup leader, was elected president, Apr. 26, 1992. A peace accord between the government and a Tuareg rebel group was signed in June 1994. Konare and his party won a series of flawed elections, Apr.-Aug. 1997. Twice condemned to death for crimes committed in office, Traoré had his sentences commuted to life imprisonment in Dec. 1997 and Sept. 1999.

Amadou Toumani Touré, who led the 1991 coup, won a presidential runoff election May 12, 2002.

Malta

Republic of Malta

People: Population: 398,534. **Age distrib.** (%): <15: 17.6; 65+: 13.6. **Pop. density:** 3,267 per sq mi, 1,261 per sq km. **Urban:** 91.7%. **Ethnic group:** Maltese, other Mediterranean. **Principal languages:** Maltese (a Semitic dialect), English (both official). **Chief religion:** Roman Catholic 98% (official).

Geography: Total area: 122 sq mi, 316 sq km; **Land area:** 122 sq mi, 316 sq km. **Location:** In center of Mediterranean Sea. **Neighbors:** Nearest is Italy on N. **Topography:** Island of Malta is 95 sq. mi.; other islands in the group: Gozo, 26 sq. mi.; Comino, 1 sq. mi. The coastline is heavily indented. Low hills cover the interior. **Capital:** Valletta, 83,000.

Government: Type: Parliamentary democracy. **Head of state:** Pres. Edward (Eddie) Fenech-Adami; b Feb. 7, 1934; in office: Apr. 4, 2004. **Head of gov.:** Prime Min. Lawrence Gonzi; b July 1, 1953; in office: Mar. 23, 2004. **Local divisions:** 3 regions comprising 67 local councils. **Defense budget** (2004): $102 mil. **Active troops:** 2,140.

Economy: Industries: tourism, electronics, shipbuilding, food & beverages, textiles. **Chief crops:** potatoes, cauliflower, grapes, wheat, barley, tomatoes, citrus. **Natural resources:** limestone, salt. **Arable land:** 38%. **Livestock** (2004): cattle: 17,900; chickens: 1 mil; goats: 5,400; pigs: 73,100; sheep: 14,900. **Fish catch** (2003): 2,019 metric tons. **Electricity prod.** (2003): 2.1 bil. kWh. **Labor force** (1999 est.): agriculture 5%, industry 24%, services 71%.

Finance: Monetary unit: Lira (MTL) (Sept. 2005: 0.34 = $1 U.S.). **GDP** (2004 est.): $7.2 bil.; **per capita GDP:** $18,200; **GDP growth:** 1%. **Imports** (2004 est.): $3.4 bil.; partners (2004): Italy 18.2%, France 17.9%, UK 9.7%, Germany 9.2%, Singapore 6.9%, China 5.7%. **Exports** (2004 est.): $2.6 bil.; partners (2004): Singapore 15.5%, US 12%, France 10.5%, UK 10.1%, Germany 9%, China 5.8%. **Tourism:** $696 mil. **Budget** (2004 est.): $2.5 bil. **Intl. reserves less gold:** $1.74 bil. **Consumer prices:** 2.79%.

Transport: Motor vehicles: 227,000 pass. cars, 53,300 comm. vehicles. **Civil aviation:** 1.5 bil pass.-mi; 1 airport. **Chief ports:** Valletta, Marsaxlokk.

Communications: TV sets: 549 per 1,000 pop. **Radios:** 669 per 1,000 pop. **Telephone lines:** 208,300. **Daily newspaper circ.:** 133 per 1,000 pop. **Internet** (2002): 120,000 users.

Health: Life expect.: 76.7 male; 81.2 female. **Births** (per 1,000 pop.): 10.2. **Deaths** (per 1,000 pop.): 8.0. **Natural inc.:** 0.22%. **Infant mortality** (per 1,000 live births): 3.9. **AIDS rate:** 0.2%.

Education: Compulsory: ages 5-15. **Literacy:** 92.8%.

Major Intl. Organizations: UN (FAO, IBRD, ILO, IMF, IMO, WHO, WTrO), the Commonwealth, EU,OSCE.

Embassy: 2017 Connecticut Ave. NW 20008; 462-3611.

Website: www.gov.mt/index.asp?l=2

Malta was ruled by Phoenicians, Romans, Arabs, Normans, the Knights of Malta, France, and Britain (since 1814). It became independent Sept. 21, 1964. Malta became a republic in 1974. The withdrawal of the last British sailors, Apr. 1, 1979, ended 179 years of British military presence on the island.

From 1971 to 1987 and again from 1996 to 1998, Malta was governed by the socialist Labour Party; the Nationalist Party, which pressed for Malta's entry into the EU, held office 1987-96 and won the elections of Sept. 5, 1998, and Apr. 12, 2003. Malta became a full member of the EU May 1, 2004.

Marshall Islands

Republic of the Marshall Islands

People: Population: 59,071. **Age distrib.** (%): <15: 38.2; 65+: 2.7. **Pop. density:** 844 per sq mi, 326 per sq km. **Urban:** 66.3%. **Ethnic groups:** Micronesian. **Principal languages:** English, Marshallese (both official); Malay-Polynesian dialects, Japanese. **Chief religion:** Protestant 55%, Assembly of God 26%.

Geography: Total area: 70 sq mi, 181 sq km; **Land area:** 70 sq mi, 181 sq km. **Location:** In N Pacific Ocean; composed of two 800-mi-long parallel chains of coral atolls. **Neighbors:** Nearest are Micronesia to W, Nauru and Kiribati to S. Topography: Marshall Islands are low coral limestone and sand islands. **Capital:** Majuro, 25,000.

Government: Type: Republic. **Head of state and gov.:** Pres. Kessai Note; b 1950; in office: Jan. 10, 2000. **Local divisions:** 33 municipalities.

Economy: Industries: copra, fish, tourism, handicrafts, wood, pearls. **Chief crops:** coconuts, tomatoes, melons, taro, breadfruit, fruits. **Natural resources:** fish, minerals. **Fish catch** (2003): 38,375 metric tons. **Labor force**: agriculture 21.4%, industry 20.9%, services 57.7%.

Finance: Monetary unit: U.S. Dollar. **GDP** (2001 est.): $115.0 mil; **per capita GDP:** $1,600; **GDP growth:** 1.0%. **Imports** (2000): $54.0 mil; partners (2000): US, Japan, Australia, NZ, Singapore, Fiji, China, Philippines. **Exports** (2000): $9.0 mil; partners (2000): US, Japan, Australia, China. **Tourism** (2002): $4 mil. **Budget** (1999): $40.0 mil.

Transport: Civil aviation: 15.5 mil. pass.-mi; 4 airports. **Chief port:** Majuro.

Communications: Telephone lines: 4,500. **Internet**: 1,400 users.

Health: Life expect.: 68.1 male; 72.1 female. **Births** (per 1,000 pop.): 33.5. **Deaths** (per 1,000 pop.): 4.9. **Natural inc.:** 2.86%. **Infant mortality** (per 1,000 live births): 29.5.

Education: Compulsory: ages 6-14. **Literacy:** 93.7%.
Major Intl. Organizations: UN (IBRD, IMF, WHO).
Embassy: 2433 Massachusetts Ave. NW 20008; 234-5414.
Website: www.rmiembassyus.org

The Marshall Islands were a German possession until World War I and were administered by Japan between the World Wars. After WW II, they were administered as part of the UN Trust Territory of the Pacific Islands by the U.S. From 1946-1958, Bikini and Enewetak atolls were used as test sites for the U.S. nuclear weapons program, including the hydrogen bomb.

The Compact of Free Association, ratified by the U.S. on Oct. 21, 1986, gave the islands their independence. In the compact, the U.S. agreed to provide financial aid to the islands, maintain their defense, and compensate victims of nuclear testing; it was renewed Dec. 2003. The Marshall Islands joined the UN Sept. 17, 1991. Amata Kabua, the islands' first and only president since 1979, died Dec. 19, 1996. His cousin Imata Kabua, elected president Jan. 13, 1997, was succeeded by Kessai Note on Jan. 10, 2000; he began a 2nd term Jan. 5, 2004.

Mauritania

Islamic Republic of Mauritania

People: Population: 3,086,859. **Age distrib.** (%): <15: 45.8; 65+: 2.2. **Pop. density:** 8 per sq mi, 3 per sq km. **Urban:** 61.8%. **Ethnic groups:** Mixed Maur/Black 40%, Maur 30%, Black 30%. **Principal languages:** Hassaniya Arabic, Wolof (both official); Fulani, Pulaar, Soninke (all national); French. **Chief religion:** Predominantly Muslim (official).mil bbls

Geography: Total area: 397,956 sq mi, 1,030,700 sq km; **Land area:** 397,840 sq mi, 1,030,400 sq km. **Location:** In NW Africa. **Neighbors:** Morocco on N, Algeria and Mali on E, Senegal on S. **Topography:** The fertile Senegal R. valley in the S gives way to a wide central region of sandy plains and scrub trees. The N is arid and extends into the Sahara. **Capital:** Nouakchott, 600,000.

Government: Type: In transition. **Head of state:** Col. Ely Ould Mohamed Vall; b 1952; in office: Aug. 3, 2005. **Head of gov.:** Prime Min. Sidi Mohamed Ould Boubacar; in office: Aug. 7, 2005. **Local divisions:** 12 regions, 1 capital district. **Defense budget** (2003): $18.7 mil. **Active troops:** 15,750.

Economy: Industries: fish proc., iron ore, gypsum. **Chief crops:** dates, millet, sorghum, rice, corn. **Natural resources:** iron ore, gypsum, copper, phosphate, diamonds, gold, oil, fish. **Livestock** (2004): cattle: 1.6 mil; chickens: 4.2 mil; goats: 5.6 mil; sheep: 8.9 mil. **Fish catch** (2003): 80,000 metric tons. **Electricity prod.** (2003): 0.19 bil. kWh. **Labor force** (2001 est.): agriculture 50%, industry 10%, services 40%.

Finance: Monetary unit: Ouguiya (MRO) (Sept. 2005: 263.54 = $1 U.S.). **GDP** (2004 est.): $5.5 bil.; **per capita GDP:** $1,800; **GDP growth:** 3%. **Imports** (2002): $860.0 mil; partners (2004): France 14.5%, US 7.7%, China 7.4%, Spain 5.9%, Belgium 4.3%, UK 4.3%. **Exports** (2002): $541.0 mil; partners (2004): Japan 13%, France 10.9%, Spain 9.6%, Italy 9.5%, Germany 8.7%, Belgium 7.4%, China 5.8%, Russia 4.8%. **Tourism** (1995): $11 mil. **Budget** (2002 est.): $378.0 mil. **Gold:** 10,000 oz t. **Consumer prices** (2003): 5.2%.

Transport: Railroad: Length: 446 mi. **Motor vehicles:** 12,200 pass. cars, 18,200 comm. vehicles. **Civil aviation:** 108.1 mil. pass.-mi; 10 airports. **Chief ports:** Nouakchott, Nouadhibou.

Communications: TV sets: 95 per 1,000 pop. **Radios:** 146 per 1,000 pop. **Telephone lines:** 38,200. **Daily newspaper circ.:** 0.5 per 1,000 pop. **Internet**: 12,000 users.

Health: Life expect.: 50.5 male; 55.0 female. **Births** (per 1,000 pop.): 41.4. **Deaths** (per 1,000 pop.): 12.4. **Natural inc.:** 2.90%. **Infant mortality** (per 1,000 live births): 70.9. **AIDS rate:** 0.6%.

Education: Compulsory: ages 6-14. **Literacy:** 41.7%.
Major Intl. Organizations: UN (FAO, IBRD, ILO, IMF, IMO, WHO, WTrO), AL, AU.
Embassy: 2129 Leroy Pl. NW 20008; 232-5700.
Website: www.ambarim-dc.org

Mauritania was a French protectorate from 1903. It became independent Nov. 28, 1960 and annexed the south of former Spanish Sahara (now Western Sahara) in 1976. Saharan guerrillas of the Polisario Front stepped up attacks in 1977; 8,000 Moroccan troops and French bomber raids aided the government. Mauritania signed a peace treaty with the Polisario Front, 1979, and renounced sovereignty over its share of Western Sahara.

Maaouiya Ould Sid Ahmed Taya took power in a military coup in 1984. Major oil finds have recently been developed. Taya, a U.S. ally, was toppled in a bloodless military coup, Aug. 3, 2005.

Although slavery has been repeatedly abolished, most recently in 1980, thousands of Mauritanians continued to live under conditions of servitude.

WORLD ALMANAC QUICK QUIZ

Can you rank these countries by population density, from most crowded to least crowded?

(a) United States (b) Australia
(c) United Kingdom (d) Bangladesh

For the answer look in this chapter, or see page 1008.

Mauritius

Republic of Mauritius

People: Population: 1,230,602. **Age distrib.** (%): <15: 24.4; 65+: 6.5. **Pop. density:** 1,562 per sq mi, 603 per sq km. **Urban:** 43.3%. **Ethnic groups:** Indo-Mauritian 68%, Creole 27%, Sino-Mauritian 3%, Franco-Mauritian 2%. **Principal languages:** English (official), Creole, French, Hindi, Urdu, Hakka, Bhojpuri. **Chief religions:** Hindu 48%, Roman Catholic 24%, Muslim 17%.

Geography: Total area: 788 sq mi, 2,040 sq km; **Land area:** 784 sq mi, 2,030 sq km. **Location:** In the Indian O., 500 mi. E of Madagascar. **Neighbors:** Nearest is Madagascar to W. **Topography:** A volcanic island nearly surrounded by coral reefs. A central plateau is encircled by mountain peaks. **Capital:** Port Louis, 143,000.

Government: Type: Republic. **Head of state:** Pres. Anerood Jugnauth; b Mar. 29, 1930; in office: Oct. 7, 2003. **Head of gov.:** Prime Min. Navin Ramgoolam; b July 1947; in office: July 5, 2005. **Local divisions:** 9 districts, 3 dependencies. **Defense budget** (2003): $8.9 mil. **Active troops**: Nil

Economy: Industries: sugar & food proc., textiles, clothing, chemicals. **Chief crops:** sugarcane, tea, corn, potatoes, bananas. **Natural resources:** fish. **Arable land:** 49%. **Livestock** (2004): cattle: 28,000; chickens: 9.8 mil; goats: 93,000; pigs: 12,925; sheep: 11,500. **Fish catch** (2003): 11,169 metric tons. **Electricity prod.** (2003): 1.9 bil. kWh. **Labor force** (1995): agriculture and fishing 14%, construction and industry 36%, transportation and communication 7%, trade, restaurants, hotels 16%, finance 3%, other services 24%.

Finance: Monetary unit: Rupee (MUR) (Sept. 2005: 29.82 = $1 U.S.). **GDP** (2004 est.): $15.7 bil.; **per capita GDP:** $12,800; **GDP growth:** 4.7%. **Imports** (2004 est.): $2.3 bil.; partners (2004): France 13.1%, South Africa 10.8%, India 7.6%, China 5.9%, Germany 4.5%, Singapore 4%. **Exports** (2004 est.): $2.0 bil.; partners (2004): UK 30.6%, France 22.7%, US 13.7%, Madagascar 7.7%. **Tourism:** $697 mil. **Budget** (2004 est.): $1.6 bil. **Intl. reserves less gold:** $1.03 bil. **Gold:** 60,000 oz t. **Consumer prices:** 4.71%.

Transport: Motor vehicles: 98,900 pass. cars, 38,000 comm. vehicles. **Civil aviation:** 3.2 bil pass.-mi; 2 airports. **Chief port:** Port Louis.

Communications: TV sets: 248 per 1,000 pop. **Radios:** 371 per 1,000 pop. **Telephone lines:** 348,200. **Daily newspaper circ.:** 118.8 per 1,000 pop. **Internet**: 150,000 users.

Health: Life expect.: 68.4 male; 76.4 female. **Births** (per 1,000 pop.): 15.6. **Deaths** (per 1,000 pop.): 6.8. **Natural inc.:** 0.88%. **Infant mortality** (per 1,000 live births): 15.0.

Education: Compulsory: ages 6-11. **Literacy:** 85.6%.
Major Intl. Organizations: UN and all of its specialized agencies, the Commonwealth, AU.
Embassy: 4301 Connecticut Ave. NW, Suite 441, 20008; 244-1491.
Website: www.gov.mu

Mauritius was uninhabited when settled in 1638 by the Dutch, who introduced sugarcane. France took over in 1721, bringing African slaves. Britain ruled from 1810 to Mar. 12, 1968, bringing Indian workers for the sugar plantations.

Mauritius formally severed its association with the British crown Mar. 12, 1992.

Mexico

United Mexican States

People: Population: 106,202,903. **Age distrib.** (%): <15: 31.1; 65+: 5.6. **Pop. density:** 139 per sq mi, 54 per sq km. **Urban:** 75.5%. **Ethnic groups:** Mestizo 60%, Amerindian 30%, White 9%. **Principal languages:** Spanish (official), Náhuatl, Maya, Zapotec, Otomi, Mixtec, other indigenous. **Chief religions:** Roman Catholic 89%, Protestant 6%.

Geography: Total area: 761,606 sq mi, 1,972,550 sq km; **Land area:** 742,490 sq mi, 1,923,040 sq km. **Location:** In southern North America. **Neighbors:** U.S. on N, Guatemala and Belize on S. **Topography:** The Sierra Madre Occidental Mts. run NW-SE near the west coast; the Sierra Madre Oriental Mts. run near the Gulf of Mexico. They join S of Mexico City. Between the 2 ranges lies the dry central plateau, 5,000 to 8,000 ft. alt., rising toward the S, with temperate vegetation. Coastal lowlands are tropical. About 45% of land is arid. **Capital:** Mexico City, 18,660,000. **Cities (urban aggr.):** Guadalajara, 3,697,000; Monterrey, 3,267,000; Puebla, 1,888,000.

Government: Type: Federal republic. **Head of state and gov.:** Pres. Vicente Fox Quesada; b July 2, 1942; in office: Dec. 1, 2000. **Local divisions:** 31 states, 1 federal district. **Defense budget** (2004): $2.8 bil. **Active troops:** 192,770.

Economy: Industries: food & beverages, tobacco, chemicals, iron & steel, oil, mining, textiles, clothing, autos, consumer durables, tourism. **Chief crops:** corn, wheat, soybeans, rice, beans, cotton, coffee, fruit, tomatoes. **Natural resources:** oil, silver, copper, gold, lead, zinc, nat. gas, timber. **Crude oil reserves** (2004): 14.6 bil. bbls. **Arable land:** 12%. **Livestock** (2004): cattle: 31.5 mil; chickens: 425 mil; goats: 9 mil; pigs: 14.6 mil; sheep: 6.8 mil. **Fish catch** (2003): 1,523,675 metric tons. **Electricity prod.** (2003): 209.2 bil. kWh. **Labor force** (2003): agriculture 18%, industry 24%, services 58%.

Finance: Monetary unit: Peso (MXN) (Sept. 2005: 10.74 = $1 U.S.). **GDP** (2004 est.): $1.0 tril.; **per capita GDP:** $9,600; **GDP growth:** 4.1%. **Imports** (2004 est.): $190.8 bil.; partners (2004): US 65.8%, Germany 3.8%, China 3.7%. **Exports** (2004 est.): $182.4 bil.; partners (2004): US 81%, Canada 5.9%, Japan 1.1%. **Tourism:** $9,457 mil. **Budget** (2004 est.): $158.0 bil. **Intl. reserves less gold:** $41.30 bil. **Gold:** 140,000 oz t. **Consumer prices:** 4.69%.

Transport: Railroad: Length: 12,123 mi. **Motor vehicles:** 12.97 mil pass. cars, 5.92 mil comm. vehicles. **Civil aviation:** 18.4 bil. pass.-mi; 231 airports. **Chief ports:** Coatzacoalcos, Mazatlan, Tampico, Veracruz.

Communications: TV sets: 272 per 1,000 pop. **Radios:** 329 per 1,000 pop. **Telephone lines**: 16.3 mil. **Daily newspaper circ.:** 93.6 per 1,000 pop. **Internet**: 12.3 mil. users.

Health: Life expect.: 72.4 male; 78.1 female. **Births** (per 1,000 pop.): 21.0. **Deaths** (per 1,000 pop.): 4.7. **Natural inc.:** 1.63%. **Infant mortality** (per 1,000 live births): 20.9. **AIDS rate:** 0.3%.

Education: Compulsory: ages 6-15. **Literacy:** 92.2%.

Major Intl. Organizations: UN (FAO, IBRD, ILO, IMF, IMO, WHO, WTrO), APEC, OAS, OECD.

Embassy: 1911 Pennsylvania Ave. NW 20006; 728-1600.

Website: portal.sre.gob.mx/usa

Mexico was the site of advanced Indian civilizations. The Mayas, an agricultural people, moved up from Yucatan, built immense stone pyramids, invented a calendar. The Toltecs were overcome by the Aztecs, who founded Tenochtitlan AD 1325, now Mexico City. Hernando Cortes, Spanish conquistador, destroyed the Aztec empire, 1519-21.

After 3 centuries of Spanish rule the people rose, under Fr. Miguel Hidalgo y Costilla, 1810, Fr. Morelos y Payon, 1812, and Gen. Agustin Iturbide, who made himself emperor as Agustin I, 1821. A republic was declared in 1823.

Mexican territory extended into the present American Southwest and California until Texas revolted and established a republic in 1836; the Mexican legislature refused recognition but was unable to enforce its authority there. After numerous clashes, the U.S.-Mexican War, 1846-48, resulted in the loss by Mexico of the lands north of the Rio Grande.

French arms supported an Austrian archduke on the throne of Mexico as Maximilian I, 1864-67, but pressure from the U.S. forced France to withdraw. Dictatorial rule by Porfirio Diaz, president 1877-80, 1884-1911, led to a period of rebellion and factional fighting. A new constitution, Feb. 5, 1917, brought social reform.

The Institutional Revolutionary Party (PRI) dominated politics from 1929 until the late 1990s. Radical opposition, including some guerrilla activity, was contained by strong measures. Some gains in agriculture, industry, and social services were achieved, but much of the work force remained jobless or underemployed. Although prospects brightened with the discovery of vast oil reserves, inflation and a drop in world oil prices aggravated Mexico's economic problems in the 1980s.

Mexico reached agreement with the U.S. and Canada on the North American Free Trade Agreement (NAFTA) Aug. 12, 1992; it took effect Jan. 1, 1994.

Guerrillas of the Zapatista National Liberation Army (EZLN) launched an uprising, Jan. 1, 1994, in southern Mexico. A tentative peace accord was reached Mar. 2. The presidential candidate of the governing PRI, Luis Donaldo Colosio Murrieta, was assassinated at a political rally in Tijuana, Mar. 23. The new PRI candidate, Ernesto Zedillo Ponce de León, won election Aug. 21 and was inaugurated Dec. 1, 1994.

An austerity plan and pledges of aid from the U.S. saved Mexico's currency from collapse in early 1995. Popular Revolutionary Army guerrillas launched coordinated attacks on government targets in Aug. 1996. In elections July 6, 1997, the PRI failed to win a congressional majority for the first time since 1929. An armed gang massacred 45 peasants in Chiapas on Dec. 22, 1997.

In the presidential election of July 2, 2000, the PRI lost for the 1st time in over 7 decades; the winner, opposition candidate Vicente Fox Quesada, took office Dec. 1, 2000. Fox's National Action Party suffered a setback in midterm elections, July 6, 2003. A 2005 law allows an estimated 11 million emigrants, mostly in the U.S., to vote by mail-in ballot in the 2006 presidential election.

Micronesia

Federated States of Micronesia

People: Population: 108,105. **Age distrib.** (%): <15: 37.1; 65+: 3.0. **Pop. density:** 399 per sq mi, 154 per sq km. **Urban:** 29.3%. **Ethnic groups:** Nine distinct Micronesian and Polynesian groups. **Principal languages:** English (official), Trukese, Pohnpeian, Yapese, Kosrean, Ulithian, Woleaian, Nukuoro, Kapingamaran. **Chief religions:** Roman Catholic 50%, Protestant 47%.

Geography: Total area: 271 sq mi, 702 sq km; **Land area:** 271 sq mi, 702 sq km. **Location:** Consists of 607 islands in the W Pacific Ocean. **Topography:** The country includes both high mountainous islands and low coral atolls; volcanic outcroppings on Pohnpei, Kosrae, and Truk. Climate is tropical. **Capital:** Palikir, on Pohnpei, 7,000 (1994 island pop.) 33,372.

Government: Type: Republic. **Head of state and gov.:** Pres. Joseph J. Urusemal; b Mar. 19, 1952; in office: May 11, 2003. **Local divisions:** 4 states.

Economy: Industries: tourism, constr., fish proc., handicrafts. **Chief crops:** black pepper, fruits & vegetables, coconuts, cassava, sweet potatoes. **Natural resources:** timber, fish, minerals. **Livestock** (2004): cattle: 13,900; chickens: 185,000; goats: 4,000; pigs: 32,000. **Fish catch** (2003): 32,041 metric tons. **Labor force**: two-thirds are government employees.

Finance: Monetary unit: U.S. Dollar. **GDP** (2004 est.): $277.0 mil; **per capita GDP:** $2,000; **GDP growth:** 1%. **Imports** (2000): $149.0 mil; partners (2000): US, Australia, Japan. **Exports** (2000): $22.0 mil; partners (2000): Japan, US, Guam. **Tourism:** $17 mil. **Budget** (1998 est.): $160.0 mill. **Intl. reserves less gold** (2003): $60 mil.

Transport: 6 airports. **Chief ports:** Colonia (Yap), Kolonia (Pohnpei), Lele, Moen.

Communications: TV sets: 20 per 1,000 pop. **Radios:** 70 per 1,000 pop. **Telephone lines:** 10,100. **Internet:** 5,000 users.

Health: Life expect.: 68.0 male; 71.6 female. **Births** (per 1,000 pop.): 25.1. **Deaths** (per 1,000 pop.): 4.9. **Natural inc.:** 2.02%. **Infant mortality** (per 1,000 live births): 30.2.

Education: Compulsory: ages 6-13. **Literacy**: 89%.

Major Intl. Organizations: UN (IBRD, IMF, WHO).

Embassy: 1725 N St. NW 20036; 223-4383.

Website: www.fsmgov.org

The Federated States of Micronesia, formerly known as the Caroline Islands, was ruled successively by Spain, Germany, Japan, and the U.S. The nation gained independence under a compact of free association with the U.S., Nov. 1986 and was admitted to the UN, Sept. 17, 1991. Tropical Storm Chata'an July 1-2, 2002, left 47 people dead and over 1,000 homeless in Chuuk. Typhoon Sudal battered Yap Apr. 9, 2004, leaving at least 1,500 homeless.

Moldova

Republic of Moldova

People: Population: 4,445,421. **Age distrib.** (%): <15: 20.2 65+:10.3. **Pop. density:** 342 per sq mi, 132 per sq km. **Urban:** 46.0%. **Ethnic groups:** Moldovan/Romanian 65%, Ukrainian 14%, Russian 13%. **Principal languages:** Moldovan (official,), Russian, Gagauz (a Turkish dialect). **Chief religion:** Eastern Orthodox 98%.

Geography: Total area: 13,067 sq mi, 33,843 sq km; **Land area:** 12,885 sq mi, 33,371 sq km. **Location:** In E Europe. **Neighbors:** Romania on W; Ukraine on N, E, and S. Topography: The country is landlocked; mainly hilly plains, with steppelands in S near the Black Sea. **Capital**: Chisinau, 662,000.

Government: Type: Republic. **Head of state:** Pres. Vladimir Voronin; b May 25, 1941; in office: Apr. 7, 2001. **Head of gov.:** Prime Min. Vasile Tarlev; b Oct. 9, 1963; in office: Apr. 19, 2001. **Local divisions:** 9 counties, 1 municipality, 1 autonomous territory. **Defense budget** (2004): $8.9 mil. **Active troops:** 6,809.

Economy: Industries: food proc., agric. machinery, foundry equip. **Chief crops:** vegetables, grapes, grain, sunflower seed, tobacco. **Natural resources:** lignite, phosphorite, gypsum, limestone. **Arable land:** 53%. **Livestock** (2004): cattle: 373,000; chickens: 15.7 mil; goats: 121,000; pigs: 446,000; sheep: 817,000. **Fish catch** (2003): 2,981 metric tons. **Electricity prod.** (2003): 2.9 bil kWh. **Labor force** (1998): agriculture 40%, industry 14%, services 46%.

Finance: Monetary unit: Leu (MDL) (Sept. 2005: 12.49 = $1 U.S.). **GDP** (2004 est.): $8.6 bil.; **per capita GDP:** $1,800; **GDP growth:** 6.3%. **Imports** (2004 est.): $1.8 bil.; partners (2004): Ukraine 16.8%, Russia 14.7%, Germany 12.5%, France 9.9%, Italy 8%, Romania 5.3%. **Exports** (2004 est.): $1.0 bil.; partners (2004): Russia 31.4%, Italy 10.7%, Germany 9.5%, Romania 9.4%, France 6.9%, Ukraine 5.8%, Belarus 4.3%. **Tourism** (2003): $58 mil. **Budget** (2004 est.): $634.8 mil. **Intl. reserves less gold**: $203 mil. **Consumer prices** (2003): 11.7%.

Transport: Railroad: Length: 808 mi. **Motor vehicles:** 268,900 pass. cars, 57,000 comm. vehicles. **Civil aviation:** 90.7 mil. pass.-mi; 8 airport.

Communications: TV sets: 297 per 1,000 pop. **Radios:** 742 per 1,000 pop. **Telephone lines:** 791,100. **Daily newspaper circ.:** 153 per 1,000 pop. **Internet**: 288,000 users.

Health: Life expect.: 61.1 male; 69.4 female. **Births** (per 1,000 pop.): 15.3. **Deaths** (per 1,000 pop.): 12.8. **Natural inc.:** 0.25%. **Infant mortality** (per 1,000 live births): 41.0. **AIDS rate:** 0.2%

Education: Compulsory: ages 6-16. **Literacy:** 99.1%.

Major Intl. Organizations: UN (FAO, IBRD, ILO, IMF, WHO, WTrO), CIS, OSCE.

Embassy: 2101 S St. NW 20008; 667-1130.

Website: www.moldova.org

In 1918, Romania annexed all of Bessarabia that Russia had acquired from Turkey in 1812 by the Treaty of Bucharest. In 1924, the Soviet Union established the Moldavian Autonomous Soviet Socialist Republic on the eastern bank of the Dniester. It was merged with the Romanian-speaking districts of Bessarabia in 1940 to form the Moldavian SSR.

During World War II, Romania, allied with Germany, occupied the area. It was recaptured by the USSR in 1944. Moldova declared independence Aug. 27, 1991. It became an independent state when the USSR disbanded Dec. 26, 1991.

Fighting erupted Mar. 1992 in the Dnestr (Dniester) region between Moldovan security forces and Slavic separatists—ethnic Russians and ethnic Ukrainians—who feared Moldova would merge with neighboring Romania. In a plebiscite on Mar. 6, 1994, voters in Moldova supported independence, without unification with Romania.

Defying the Moldovan government, voters in the breakaway Dnestr region held legislative elections and approved a separatist constitution Dec. 24, 1995. Petru Lucinschi, a former Communist, won a presidential runoff election Dec. 1, 1996. A peace accord with Dnestr separatists was signed in Moscow May 8, 1997. The Communists won the most seats in parliamentary elections Mar. 22, 1998, but a coalition of three center-right parties formed the government. The Communists gained legislative majorities in elections Feb. 25, 2001, and Mar. 6, 2005.

Monaco

Principality of Monaco

People: Population: 32,409. **Age distrib.** (%): <15: 15.5; 65+: 22.4. **Pop. density:** 32,409 per sq mi, 16,205 per sq km. **Urban:** 100.0%. **Ethnic groups:** French 47%, Monegasque 16%, Italian 16%. **Principal languages:** French (official), English, Italian, Monegasque. **Chief religion:** Roman Catholic 90% (official).

Geography: Total area: <1 sq mi, 2 sq km; **Land area:** <1 sq mi, 2 sq km. **Location:** On the NW Mediterranean coast. **Neighbors:** France to W, N, E. **Topography:** Monaco-Ville sits atop a high promontory, the rest of the principality rises from the port up the hillside. **Capital:** Monaco-ville, 34,000.

Government: Type: Constitutional monarchy. **Head of state:** Prince Albert II; b Mar. 14, 1958; in office: Apr. 6, 2005. **Head of gov.:** Min. of State Jean-Paul Proust; b Mar. 3, 1940; in office: June 1, 2005. **Local divisions:** 4 quarters.

Economy: Industries: tourism, constr., light industrial products. **Chief crops:** none. **Natural resources:** none. **Fish catch** (2003): 3 metric tons.

Finance: Monetary unit: Euro (EUR) (Sept. 2005: 0.80 = $1 U.S.). **GDP** (2000 est.): $870.0 mil; **per capita GDP:** $27,000; **GDP growth:** 0.9%. **Budget** (1995): $531.0 mil.

Transport: Railroad: Length: 1 mi. **Motor vehicles:** 17,000 pass. cars, 4,000 comm. vehicles. **Civil aviation:** 1.24 mil. pass.-mi. **Chief port:** Monaco.

Communications: TV sets: 758 per 1,000 pop. **Radios:** 1,030 per 1,000 pop. **Daily newspaper circ.:** 251 per 1,000 pop.

Health: Life expect.: 75.7 male; 83.6 female. **Births** (per 1,000 pop.): 9.3. **Deaths** (per 1,000 pop.): 12.7. **Natural inc.:** –0.35%. **Infant mortality** (per 1,000 live births): 5.4.

Education: Compulsory: ages 6-15 (16). **Literacy:** 99%.

Major Intl. Organizations: UN (IMO, WHO), OSCE.

Consulate General: 565 Fifth Ave., 23rd Fl. New York, NY 10017; (212) 286-0500.

Website: www.gouv.mc/PortGb

An independent principality for over 300 years, Monaco has belonged to the House of Grimaldi since 1297, except during the French Revolution. It was placed under the protectorate of Sardinia in 1815, and under France, 1861. The Prince of Monaco was an absolute ruler until the 1911 constitution. Monaco was admitted to the UN on May 28, 1993.

Monaco is noted for its mild climate, magnificent scenery, and elegant casinos. Prince Rainier III, who ruled Monaco, 1949-2005, and turned it into one of Europe's top tourist spots, died Apr. 6 and was succeeded by his son, Albert II.

Mongolia

People: Population: 2,791,272. **Age distrib.** (%): <15: 28.7; 65+: 3.7. **Pop. density:** 5 per sq mi, 2 per sq km. **Urban:** 56.7%. **Ethnic groups:** Mongol 85%, Turkic 7%, Tungusic 5%. **Principal languages:** Khalkha Mongol, Turkic, Russian. **Chief religion:** Tibetan Buddhist Lamaism 50%, none 40%.

Geography: Total area: 603,909 sq mi, 1,564,116 sq km; **Land area:** 604,250 sq mi, 1,565,000 sq km. **Location:** In E Central Asia. **Neighbors:** Russia on N, China on E, W, and S. **Topography:** Mostly a high plateau with mountains, salt lakes, and vast grasslands. Arid lands in the S are part of the Gobi Desert. **Capital:** Ulaanbaatar, 812,000.

Government: Type: Republic. **Head of state:** Pres. Nambaryn Enkhbayar; b 1958; in office: June 24, 2005. **Head of gov.:** Prime. Min. Tsakhiagiyn Elbegdorj; b Mar. 30, 1963; in office: Aug. 20, 2004. **Local divisions:** 18 provinces, 3 municipalities. **Defense budget** (2003): $26.6 mil. **Active troops:** 8,600.

Economy: Industries: constr. materials, mining, oil, food, beverages. **Chief crops:** wheat, barley, potatoes, forage crops. **Natural resources:** oil, coal, copper, molybd., tungsten, phosphates, tin, nickel, zinc, fluorspar, gold, silver, iron. **Arable land:** 1%. **Livestock** (2004): cattle: 2.2 mil; chickens: 70,000; goats: 9.0 mil; pigs: 14,500; sheep: 12.0 mil. **Fish catch** (2003): 130 metric tons. **Electricity prod.** (2003): 3.0 bil. kWh. **Labor force** (2003): herding/agriculture 42%, mining 4%, manufacturing 6%, trade 14%, services 29%, public sector 5%, other 3.7%.

Finance: Monetary unit: Tugrik (MNT) (Sept. 2005: 1,193.00 = $1 U.S.). **GDP** (2004 est.): $5.3 bil.; **per capita GDP:** $1,900; **GDP growth:** 10.6%. according to official estimate (2004 est.) **Imports** (2004 est.): $1.0 bil.; partners (2004): Russia 31%, China 23.1%, Japan 8.4%, South Korea 6.7%. **Exports** (2004 est.): $853.0 mil; partners (2004): China 50.7%, US 26.3%, Canada 5.3%, UK 4.3%, Russia 4.2%. **Tourism:** $143 mil. **Budget** (2004 est.): $602.0 mil. **Intl. reserves less gold:** $152 mil. **Gold:** 30,000 oz t. **Consumer prices** (change 2000–2001): 8.0%.

Transport: Railroad: Length: 1,128 mi. **Motor vehicles:** 21,000 pass. cars, 27,000 comm. vehicles. **Civil aviation:** 356.7 mil. pass.-mi; 10 airports.

Communications: TV sets: 58 per 1,000 pop. **Radios:** 142 per 1,000 pop. **Telephone lines**: 138,100. **Daily newspaper circ.:** 27 per 1,000 pop. **Internet**: 142,800 users.

Health: Life expect.: 62.3 male; 66.9 female. **Births** (per 1,000 pop.): 21.5. **Deaths** (per 1,000 pop.): 7.0. **Natural inc.:** 1.45%. **Infant mortality** (per 1,000 live births): 53.8. **AIDS rate:** <0.1%.

Education: Compulsory: ages 8-16. **Literacy:** 97.8%.

Major Intl. Organizations: UN (FAO, IBRD, ILO, IMF, IMO, WHO, WTrO).

Embassy: 2833 M St. NW 20007; 333-7117.

Website: www.pmis.gov.mn/indexeng.php

One of the world's oldest countries, Mongolia reached the zenith of its power in the 13th century when Genghis Khan and his successors conquered all of China and extended their influence as far west as Hungary and Poland. In later centuries, the empire dissolved and Mongolia became a province of China.

With the advent of the 1911 Chinese revolution, Mongolia, with Russian backing, declared its independence. A Communist regime was established July 11, 1921.

In 1990, the Mongolian Communist Party yielded its monopoly on power but won election in July. A new constitution took effect Feb. 12, 1992. A democratic alliance won legislative elections, June 30, 1996. Natsagiyn Bagabandi, a former Communist, won the presidential election of May 18, 1997. A protracted political crisis took a violent turn Oct. 2, 1998, with the murder of Sanjaasuregiyn Zorig, a popular cabinet member seeking to become prime minister. The former Communists won 72 of 76 seats in parliamentary elections, July 2, 2000. Pres. Bagabandi was reelected May 20, 2001. Nambaryn Enkhbayar, a former prime minister (2000-04), won the presidential election of May 22, 2005.

Morocco

Kingdom of Morocco

People: Population: 32,725,847. **Age distrib.** (%): <15: 32.1; 65+: 4.9. **Pop. density:** 190 per sq mi, 73 per sq km. **Urban:** 57.5%. **Ethnic groups:** Arab-Berber 99%. **Principal languages:** Arabic (official), Berber dialects, French, Spanish, English. **Chief religion:** Muslim 99% (official).

Geography: Total area: 172,414 sq mi, 446,550 sq km; **Land area:** 172,317 sq mi, 446,300 sq km. **Location:** On NW coast of Africa. **Neighbors:** Western Sahara on S, Algeria on E. **Topography:** Consists of 5 natural regions: mountain ranges (Riff in the N, Middle Atlas, Upper Atlas, and Anti-Atlas); rich plains in the W; alluvial plains in SW; well-cultivated plateaus in the center; a pre-Sahara arid zone extending from SE. **Capital:** Rabat, 1,759,000. **Cities (urban aggr.):** Casablanca, 3,344,000; Fes, 904,000.

Government: Type: Constitutional monarchy. **Head of state:** King Mohammed VI; b Aug. 21, 1963; in office: July 23, 1999. **Head of gov.:** Prime Min. Driss Jettou; b May 24, 1945; in office: Oct. 9, 2002. **Local divisions:** 16 regions. **Defense budget** (2004): $2.0 bil. **Active troops:** 196,300.

Economy: Industries: mining, food proc., leather goods, textiles, constr., tourism. **Chief crops:** barley, wheat, citrus, grapes, vegetables, olives. **Natural resources:** phosphates, iron ore, mang., lead, zinc, fish, salt. **Crude oil reserves** (2004): 2 mil bbls. **Arable land:** 21%. **Livestock** (2004): cattle: 2.7 mil; chickens: 137 mil; goats: 5.4 mil; pigs: 8,000; sheep: 17.0 mil. **Fish catch** (2003): 886,669 metric tons. **Electricity prod.** (2003): 17.3 bil. kWh. **Labor force** (2003 est.): agriculture 40%, industry 15%, services 45%.

Finance: Monetary unit: Dirham (MAD) (Sept. 2005: 8.85 = $1 U.S.). **GDP** (2004 est.): $134.6 bil.; **per capita GDP:** $4,200; **GDP growth:** 4.4%. **Imports** (2004 est.): $15.6 bil.; partners (2004): France 21.2%, Spain 14.9%, Germany 7.3%, Italy 6.9%, Saudi Arabia 4.8%, China 4.8%. **Exports** (2004 est.): $9.8 bil.; partners (2004): France 25.3%, Spain 18.4%, UK 8%, Italy 4.9%, Germany 4.6%, US 4.6%. **Tourism:** $2,856 mil. **Budget** (2004 est.): $15.4 bil. **Intl. reserves less gold:** $10.52 bil. **Gold:** 710,000 oz t. **Consumer prices** (2003): 1.2%.

Transport: Railroad: Length: 1,185 mi. **Motor vehicles** 1.25 mil pass. cars, 431,000 comm. vehicles. **Civil aviation:** 4.4 bil pass.-mi; 26 airports. **Chief ports:** Tangier, Casablanca, Kenitra.

Communications: TV sets: 165 per 1,000 pop. **Radios:** 247 per 1,000 pop. **Telephone lines:** 1.2 mil. **Daily newspaper circ.:** 28.3 per 1,000 pop. **Internet**: 1.0 mil. users.

Health: Life expect.: 68.4 male; 73.1 female. **Births** (per 1,000 pop.): 22.3. **Deaths** (per 1,000 pop.): 5.6. **Natural inc.:** 1.67%. **Infant mortality** (per 1,000 live births): 41.6. **AIDS rate:** 0.1%.

Education: Compulsory: ages 6-14. **Literacy:** 51.7%.

Major Intl. Organizations: UN (FAO, IBRD, ILO, IMF, IMO, WHO, WTrO), AL.

Embassy: 1601 21st St. NW 20009; 462-7979.

Website: www.mincom.gov.ma/english/e_page.html

Berbers were the original inhabitants, followed by Carthaginians and Romans. Arabs conquered in 683. In the 11th and 12th centuries, a Berber empire ruled all NW Africa and most of Spain from Morocco.

Part of Morocco came under Spanish rule in the 19th century; France controlled the rest in the early 20th. Tribal uprisings lasted from 1911 to 1933. The country became independent Mar. 2, 1956. Tangier, an internationalized seaport, was turned over to Morocco, 1956. Ifni, a Spanish enclave, was ceded in 1969. Morocco annexed the disputed territory of Western Sahara during the second half of the 1970s.

King Hassan II assumed the throne in 1961, reigning until his death on July 23, 1999; he was immediately succeeded by his eldest son. Political reforms in the 1990s included the establishment of a bicameral legislature in 1997.

Five terrorist attacks in Casablanca May 16, 2003, left about 40 people dead, including 10 suicide bombers; the government blamed Salafia Jihadia, an extremist group connected with al-Qaeda. An earthquake Feb. 24, 2004, killed at least 629 people in the vicinity of al-Hoceima, N coastal Morocco.

Western Sahara

Western Sahara, formerly the protectorate of Spanish Sahara, is bounded the in N by Morocco, the NE by Algeria, the E and S by Mauritania, and on the W by the Atlantic Ocean. Phosphates are the major resource. Population (2004 est.): 267,405; capital: Laayoune (El Aaiun). Area: 102,600 sq mi.

Spain withdrew from its protectorate in Feb. 1976. On Apr. 14, 1976, Morocco annexed over 70,000 sq. mi, with the remainder annexed by Mauritania. A guerrilla movement, the Polisario Front, which had proclaimed the region independent Feb. 27, launched attacks with Algerian support. After Mauritania signed a treaty with Polisario on Aug. 5, 1979, Morocco occupied Mauritania's portion of Western Sahara.

After years of bitter fighting, Morocco controlled the main urban areas, but Polisario guerrillas moved freely in the vast, sparsely populated deserts. The 2 sides implemented a cease-fire in 1991, when a UN peacekeeping force was deployed. Former U.S. Sec. of State James A. Baker III served as UN envoy, 1997-2004, but was unable to resolve the dispute.

Mozambique

Republic of Mozambique

People: Population: 19,406,703. **Age distrib.** (%): <15: 43.1; 65+: 2.8. **Pop. density:** 63 per sq mi, 24 per sq km. **Urban:** 35.6%. **Ethnic groups:** Shangaan, Chokwe, Manyika, Sena, Makua. **Principal languages:** Portuguese (official) and dialects, English. **Chief religions:** Indigenous beliefs 50%, Christian 38%, Muslim 11%.

Geography: Total area: 309,496 sq mi, 801,590 sq km; **Land area:** 302,739 sq mi, 784,090 sq km. **Location:** On SE coast of Africa. **Neighbors:** Tanzania on N; Malawi, Zambia, Zimbabwe on W; South Africa, Swaziland on S. **Topography:** Coastal lowlands comprise nearly half the country with plateaus rising in steps to the mountains along the western border. **Capital:** Maputo, 1,221,000.

Government: Type: Republic. **Head of state:** Pres. Armando Guebuza; b Jan. 20, 1943; in office: Feb. 2, 2005. **Head of gov.:** Prime Min. Luisa Diogo; b Apr. 11, 1958; in office: Feb. 17, 2004. **Local divisions:** 10 provinces and Maputo municipality. **Defense budget** (2003): $86 mil. **Active troops:** 8,200.

Economy: Industries: food, beverages, chemicals, oil products, textiles, cement. **Chief crops:** cotton, cashews, sugarcane, tea, cassava, corn, coconuts, sisal, trop. fruits. **Natural resources:** coal, titanium, nat. gas, hydropower, tantalum, graphite. **Arable land:** 4%. **Livestock** (2004): cattle: 1.3 mil; chickens: 28 mil; goats: 392,000; pigs: 180,000; sheep: 125,000. **Fish catch** (2003): 89,486 metric tons. **Electricity prod.** (2003): 15.1 bil. kWh. **Labor force** (1997 est.): agriculture 81%, industry 6%, services 13%.

Finance: Monetary unit: Metical (MZM) (Sept. 2005: 24,410.00 = $1 U.S.). **GDP** (2004 est.): $23.4 bil.; **per capita GDP:** $1,200; **GDP growth:** 8.2%. **Imports** (2004 est.): $972.9 mil; partners (2004): South Africa 35.7%, Australia 10.9%, US 3.7%. **Exports** (2004 est.): $689.4 mil; partners (2004): Belgium 32%, Italy 13.9%, Spain 12.6%, Germany 9.8%, Zimbabwe 4.7%. **Tourism:** $98 mil. **Budget** (2004 est.): $1.4 bil. **Intl. reserves less gold:** $728 mil. **Gold:** 60,000 oz t. **Consumer prices:** 11.1%.

Transport: Railroad: Length: 1,941 mi. **Motor vehicles:** 81,600 pass. cars, 76,000 comm. vehicles. **Civil aviation:** 219.3 mil. pass.-mi; 22 airports. **Chief ports:** Maputo, Beira, Nacala, Inhambane.

Communications: TV sets: 5 per 1,000 pop. **Radios:** 40 per 1,000 pop. **Telephone lines** (2002): 83,700. **Daily newspaper circ.:** 2.5 per 1,000 pop. **Internet** (2002): 50,000 users.

Health: Life expect.: 39.9 male; 40.8 female. **Births** (per 1,000 pop.): 35.8. **Deaths** (per 1,000 pop.): 21.0. **Natural inc.:** 1.48%. **Infant mortality** (per 1,000 live births): 130.8. **AIDS rate:** 12.2%.

Education: Compulsory: ages 6-12. **Literacy:** 47.8%.

Major Intl. Organizations: UN (FAO, IBRD, ILO, IMF, IMO, WHO, WTrO), the Commonwealth, AU.

Embassy: 1990 M St. NW, Suite 570, 20036; 293-7146.

Website: www.embamoc-usa.org

The first Portuguese post on the Mozambique coast was established in 1505, on the trade route to the East. Mozambique became independent June 25, 1975, after a ten-year war against Portuguese colonial domination. The 1974 revolution in Portugal had paved the way for the orderly transfer of power to Frelimo (Front for the Liberation of Mozambique). Frelimo took over local administration Sept. 20, 1974.

The new Frelimo government, headed by Pres. Samora Machel, a former guerrilla commander, provided for a gradual transition to a Communist system. Most of the country's whites emigrated. In the 1980s, severe drought and civil war caused famine and heavy loss of life. Pres. Machel was killed in a plane crash just inside the South African border, Oct. 19, 1986. Frelimo formally abandoned Marxist-Leninism in 1989, and a new constitution, effective Nov. 30, 1990, provided for multiparty elections and a free-market economy.

On Oct. 4, 1992, a peace agreement was signed aimed at ending hostilities between the government and the rebel Mozambique National Resistance (MNR). Repatriation of 1.7 million Mozambican refugees officially ended June 1995. In Mar. 1999 the heaviest floods in 4 decades left nearly 200,000 people stranded. Even worse flooding in Feb.-Mar. 2000 claimed more than 600 lives, displaced over 1 million people, and devastated the economy. A train crash May 25, 2002, in S Mozambique killed 196 people. Frelimo retained its hold under Pres. Joaquim Chissano (in office 1986-2005) and his successor, Pres. Armando Guebuza, elected Dec. 1-2, 2004.

Myanmar (*formerly* Burma)

Union of Myanmar

People: Population: 46,996,558. **Age distrib.** (%): <15: 27.2; 65+: 5.0. **Pop. density:** 179 per sq mi, 69 per sq km. **Urban:** 29.4%. **Ethnic groups:** Burman 68%, Shan 9%, Karen 7%, Rakhine 4%, Chinese 3%, Indian 2%, Mon 2%. **Principal languages:** Burmese (official); many ethnic minority languages. **Chief religions:** Buddhist 89%, Christian 4%, Muslim 4%, Animist 1%.

Geography: Total area: 261,970 sq mi, 678,500 sq km; **Land area:** 253,955 sq mi, 657,740 sq km. **Location:** Between S and SE Asia, on Bay of Bengal. **Neighbors:** Bangladesh, India on W; China, Laos, Thailand on E. **Topography:** Mountains surround Myanmar on W, N, and E, and dense forests cover much of the nation. N-S rivers provide habitable valleys and communications, especially the Irrawaddy, navigable for 900 miles. The country has a tropical monsoon climate. **Capital:** Yangon (Rangoon), 3,874,000. **Cities (urban aggr.):** Mandalay, 807,000.

Government: Type: Military. **Head of state:** Gen. Than Shwe; b Feb. 2, 1933; in office: Apr. 23, 1992. **Head of gov.:** Lt. Gen. Soe Win; b 1949; in office: Oct. 19, 2004. **Local divisions:** 7 states, 7 divisions. **Defense budget** (2003): $1.5 bil. **Active troops:** 488,000.

Economy: Industries: agric. proc., apparel, wood & wood products, mining, constr. materials. **Chief crops:** rice, beans, sesame, peanuts, sugarcane. **Natural resources:** oil, timber, tin, antimony, zinc, copper, tungsten, lead, coal, marble, limestone, gemstones, nat. gas, hydropower. **Crude oil reserves** (2004): 50 mil bbls. **Arable land:** 15%. **Livestock** (2004): cattle: 11.9 mil; chickens: 57 mil; goats: 1.8 mil; pigs: 5.2 mil; sheep: 492,000. **Fish catch** (2003): 1,606,252 metric tons. **Electricity prod.** (2003): 7.4 bil. kWh. **Labor force** (2001 est.): agriculture 70%, industry 7%, services 23%.

Finance: Monetary unit: Kyat (MMK) (Sept. 2005: 5.78 = $1 U.S.). **GDP** (2004 est.): $74.3 bil.; **per capita GDP:** $1,700; **GDP growth:** –1.3%. **Imports** (2004 est.): $1.8 bil.; partners (2004): China 28.3%, Singapore 20.6%, Thailand 19.1%, South Korea 6.2%, Malaysia 4.7%. **Exports** (2004 est.): $2.1 bil.; partners (2004): Thailand 37%, India 14%, China 6.2%, Japan 5.1%, UK 4%. **Tourism:** $58 mil. **Budget** (2004 est.): $955.5 mil. **Intl. reserves less gold:** $433 mil. **Gold:** 230,000 oz t. **Consumer prices** (2003): 36.6%.

Transport: Railroad: Length: 2,458 mi. **Motor vehicles** 175,400 pass. cars, 98,900 comm. vehicles. **Civil aviation:** 220.6 mil. pass.-mi; 8 airports. **Chief ports:** Bassein, Moulmein.

Communications: TV sets: 7 per 1,000 pop. **Radios:** 72 per 1,000 pop. **Telephone lines:** 363,000. **Daily newspaper circ.:** 8.6 per 1,000 pop. **Internet:** 28,000 users.

Health: Life expect.: 57.8 male; 63.8 female. **Births** (per 1,000 pop.): 18.1. **Deaths** (per 1,000 pop.): 9.9. **Natural inc.:** 0.83%. **Infant mortality** (per 1,000 live births): 63.6. **AIDS rate:** 1.2%.

Education: Compulsory: ages 5-9. **Literacy:** 85.3%.

Major Intl. Organizations: UN (FAO, IBRD, ILO, IMF, IMO, WHO, WTrO), ASEAN.

Embassy: 2300 S St. NW 20008; 332-3344.

Website: www.myanmar.gov.mm

The Burmese arrived from Tibet before the 9th century, displacing earlier cultures, and a Buddhist monarchy was established by the 11th. Burma was conquered by the Mongol dynasty of China in 1272, then ruled by Shans as a Chinese tributary, until the 16th century. Britain subjugated Burma in 3 wars, 1824-84, and ruled the country as part of India until 1937, when it became self-governing. Independence outside the Commonwealth was achieved Jan. 4, 1948.

Gen. Ne Win dominated politics from 1962 to 1988, first as military ruler, then as constitutional president. His regime drove Indians from the civil service and Chinese from commerce. Economic socialization was advanced, isolation from foreign countries enforced. In 1987 Burma, once the richest nation in SE Asia, was granted less-developed status by the UN.

Ne Win resigned July 1988, following antigovernment riots. In Sept. the military seized power, under Gen. Saw Maung. In 1989 the country's name was changed to Myanmar.

The first free multiparty elections in 30 years took place May 27, 1990, with the main opposition party winning a decisive victory, but the military refused to hand over power. A key opposition leader,

Aung San Suu Kyi, awarded the Nobel Peace Prize in 1991, was held under house arrest, 1989-1995, 2000-02, and again from 2003. Because of the regime's poor human rights record and continued harassment of Aung San Suu Kyi and her supporters, the U.S. has imposed sanctions. The Indian Ocean tsunami of Dec. 26, 2004, killed at least 61 people in Myanmar.

The country was admitted to ASEAN July 23, 1997. Yielding to pressure from critics of the regime, Myanmar announced July 26, 2005, that it would forgo its turn to chair ASEAN in 2006. In Sept. a human rights investigator reported to the UN that Myanmar held more than 1,100 political prisoners, who were subject to torture.

Namibia

Republic of Namibia

People: Population: 2,030,692. **Age distrib.** (%): <15: 38.7; 65+: 3.6. **Pop. density:** 6 per sq mi, 2 per sq km. **Urban:** 32.4%. **Ethnic groups:** Ovambo 50%, Kavangos 9%, Herero 7%, Damara 7% White 6%, mixed 7%. **Principal languages:** English (official), Afrikaans, German, Oshivambo, Herero, Nama. **Chief religions:** Lutheran 50%, other Christian 30%, indigenous beliefs 10-20%.

Geography: Total area: 318,696 sq mi, 825,418 sq km; **Land area:** 318,696 sq mi, 825,418 sq km. **Location:** In S Africa on the coast of the Atlantic Ocean. **Neighbors:** Angola on N, Botswana on E, South Africa on S. **Topography:** Three distinct regions incl. Namib desert along the Atlantic coast, a mountainous central plateau with woodland savanna, and Kalahari desert in E. True forests are found in NE. There are 4 rivers, but little other surface water. **Capital:** Windhoek, 237,000.

Government: Type: Republic. **Head of state:** Pres. Hifikepunye Pohamba; b Aug. 18, 1935; in office: Mar. 21, 2005. **Head of gov.:** Prime Min. Nahas Angula; b Aug. 22, 1943; in office: Mar. 21, 2005. **Local divisions:** 13 regions. **Defense budget** (2003): $131 mil. **Active troops:** 9,000.

Economy: meatpacking, fish proc., dairy products, mining. **Chief crops:** millet, sorghum, peanuts. **Natural resources:** diamonds, copper, uranium, gold, lead, tin, lithium, cadmium, zinc, salt, vanadium, nat. gas, hydropower, fish. **Arable land:** 1%. **Livestock** (2004): cattle: 2.5 mil; chickens: 2.8 mil; goats: 2.1 mil; pigs: 28,000; sheep: 2.9 mil. **Fish catch** (2003): 636,346 metric tons. **Electricity prod.** (2003): 1.5 bil. kWh. **Labor force** (1999 est.): agriculture 47%, industry 20%, services 33%.

Finance: Monetary unit: Namibia Dollar (NAD) (Sept. 2005: 6.30 = $1 U.S.). **GDP** (2004 est.): $14.8 bil.; **per capita GDP:** $7,300; **GDP growth:** 4.8%. **Imports** (2004 est.): $1.5 bil.; partners (2001): US 50%, EU 31%. **Exports** (2004 est.): $1.4 bil.; partners (2001): EU 79%, US 4%. **Tourism:** $333 mil. **Budget** (2004 est.): $2.0 bil. **Intl. reserves less gold:** $222 mil. **Consumer prices:** 3.91%.

Transport: Railroad: Length: 1,480 mi. **Motor vehicles:** 62,500 pass. cars, 66,500 comm. vehicles. **Civil aviation:** 468.5 mil. pass.-mi; 21 airports. **Chief ports:** Luderitz, Walvis Bay.

Communications: TV sets: 38 per 1,000 pop. **Radios:** 143 per 1,000 pop. **Telephone lines:** 127,400 **Daily newspaper circ.:** 19 per 1,000 pop. **Internet:** 65,000 users.

Health: Life expect.: 44.7 male; 43.1 female. **Births** (per 1,000 pop.): 25.2. **Deaths** (per 1,000 pop.): 18.4. **Natural inc.:** 0.68%. **Infant mortality** (per 1,000 live births): 49.0. **AIDS rate:** 21.3%.

Education: Compulsory: ages 6-15. **Literacy:** 84%.

Major Intl. Organizations: UN (FAO, IBRD, ILO, IMF, IMO, WHO, WTrO), the Commonwealth, AU.

Embassy: 1605 New Hampshire Ave. NW 20009; 986-0540.

Website: www.grnnet.gov.na

Namibia was declared a German protectorate in 1890 and officially called South-West Africa. South Africa seized the territory from Germany in 1915 during World War I; the League of Nations gave South Africa a mandate over the territory in 1920. In 1966, the Marxist South-West Africa People's Organization (SWAPO) launched a guerrilla war for independence. The UN General Assembly named the area Namibia in 1968.

After many years of guerrilla warfare, South Africa, Angola, and Cuba signed a U.S.-mediated agreement Dec. 22, 1988, to end South African administration of Namibia and provide for a cease-fire and transition to independence, in accordance with a 1978 UN plan. A separate accord between Cuba and Angola provided for a phased withdrawal of Cuban troops from Namibia. A constitution providing for multiparty government was adopted Feb. 9, 1990, and Namibia gained independence Mar. 21. SWAPO has remained the dominant political group.

Walvis Bay, the principal deepwater port, had been turned over to South African administration in 1922. It remained in South African hands after independence, but South Africa turned control of the port back to Namibia, as of Mar. 1, 1994. Separatist violence flared in the Caprivi Strip in the late 1990s.

Nauru

Republic of Nauru

People: Population: 13,048. **Age distrib.** (%): <15: 37.5; 65+: 1.9. **Pop. density:** 1,631 per sq mi, 621 per sq km. **Urban:** 100.0%. **Ethnic groups:** Nauruan 58%, other Pacific Islander 26%, Chinese 8%, European 8%. **Principal languages:** Nauruan (official), English. **Chief religions:** Protestant 66%, Roman Catholic 33%.

Geography: Total area: 8 sq mi, 21 sq km; **Land area:**8 sq mi, 21 sq km. **Location:** In W Pacific O. just S of the Equator. **Neighbors:** Nearest is Kiribati to E. **Topography:** Mostly a plateau bearing high-grade phosphate deposits, surrounded by a sandy shore and coral reef in concentric rings. **Capital:** Nauru, 13,000.

Government: Type: Republic. **Head of state and gov.:** Pres. Ludwig Scotty; in office June 22, 2004. **Local divisions:** 14 districts.

Economy: Industries: phosphate mining, offshore banking, coconut products. **Chief crops:** coconuts. **Natural resources:** phosphates, fish. **Livestock** (2004): chickens: 5,000; pigs: 2,800. **Fish catch** (2003): 43 metric tons. **Electricity prod.** (2003): 0.02 bil. kWh. **Labor force**: employed in mining phosphates, public administration, education, and transportation.

Finance: Monetary unit: Australian Dollar (AUD) (Sept. 2005: 1.31 = $1 U.S.). **GDP** (2001 est.): $60.0 mil; **per capita GDP:** $5,000; **GDP growth:** NA. **Imports** (2004 est.): $19.8 mil; partners (2004): Australia 59.1%, Indonesia 16.7%, UK 4.3%, Germany 4.1%. **Exports** (2004 est.): $640000.0 ; partners (2004): South Africa 37.6%, India 19.7%, Germany 17.9%, South Korea 10.2%, Japan 6.3%. **Budget** (1996): $64.8 mil.

Transport: Railroad: Length: 3 mi. **Civil aviation:** 178 mil. pass.-mi; 1 airport. **Chief port:** Nauru.

Communications: TV sets: 1 per 1,000 pop. **Radios:** 45 per 1,000 pop.

Health: Life expect.: 59.2 male; 66.5 female. **Births** (per 1,000 pop.): 25.1. **Deaths** (per 1,000 pop.): 6.8. **Natural inc.:** 1.83%. **Infant mortality** (per 1,000 live births): 10.0.

Education: Compulsory: ages 6-16. **Literacy:** NA%.

Major Intl. Organizations: UN (WHO), the Commonwealth.

Permanent UN Representative: 800 Second Avenue, Ste. 400D New York, NY 10017; (212) 937-0074.

Website: www.un.int/nauru

The island was discovered in 1798 by the British but was formally annexed to the German Empire in 1886. After World War I, Nauru became a League of Nations mandate administered by Australia. During World War II the Japanese occupied the island. In 1947 Nauru was made a UN trust territory, administered by Australia. It became an independent republic Jan. 31, 1968, and was admitted to the UN Sept. 14, 1999.

Phosphate exports provided Nauru with per capita revenues that were among the highest in the Third World. Phosphate reserves, however, are nearly depleted, and environmental damage from strip-mining has been severe. Lax banking practices have made Nauru a haven for money laundering; the country has also raised funds by selling passports to noncitizens, possibly to some with terrorist connections. Nauru defaulted on a loan payment for its real estate holdings in Australia and was virtually bankrupt in 2004.

Nepal

Kingdom of Nepal

People: Population: 27,676,547. **Age distrib.** (%): <15: 39.0; 65+: 3.7. **Pop. density:** 509 per sq mi, 197 per sq km. **Urban:** 15.0%. **Ethnic groups:** Newar, Indian, Gurung, Magar, Tamang, Rai, Limbu, Sherpa, Tharu. **Principal languages:** Nepali (official); about 30 dialects and 12 other languages. **Chief religions:** Hinduism 81% (official), Buddhism 11%, Muslim 4%.

Geography: Total area: 54,363 sq mi, 140,800 sq km; **Land area:** 52,819 sq mi, 136,800 sq km. **Location:** Astride the Himalaya Mts. **Neighbors:** China on N, India on S. **Topography:** The Himalayas stretch across the N, the hill country with its fertile valleys extends across the center, while the S border region is part of the flat, subtropical Ganges Plain. **Capital:** Kathmandu, 741,000. **Cities (urban aggr.):** (1995 metro. est.) Lalitpur, 190,000; Biratnagar, 132,000.

Government: Type: In transition. **Head of state and gov.:** King Gyanendra Bir Bikram Shah Dev; b July 7, 1947; in office: June 4, 2001. **Local divisions:** 5 regions subdivided into 14 zones. **Defense budget** (2003): $96 mil. **Active troops:** 63,000.

Economy: Industries: tourism, carpets, textiles, rice, jute, sugar, oilseed. **Chief crops:** rice, corn, wheat, sugarcane. **Natural resources:** quartz, water, timber, hydropower, lignite, copper, cobalt, iron ore. **Arable land:** 17%. **Livestock** (2004): cattle: 7.0 mil; chickens: 23 mil; goats: 7.0 mil; pigs: 935,076; sheep: 824,187. **Fish catch** (2003): 36,568 metric tons. **Electricity prod.** (2003): 2.5 bil. kWh. **Labor force**: agriculture 81%, industry 3%, services 16%.

Finance: Monetary unit: Rupee (NPR) (Sept. 2005: 71.45 = $1 U.S.). **GDP** (2004 est.): $39.5 bil.; **per capita GDP:** $1,500; **GDP growth:** 3%. **Imports** (2002 est.): $1.4 bil.; partners (2004): India 43%, UAE 10%, China 10%, Saudi Arabia 4.4%, Singapore 4%. **Exports** (2002 est.): $568.0 mil; partners (2004): India 48.8%, US 22.3%, Germany 8.5%. **Tourism:** $199 mil. **Budget** (2000): $1.1 bil. **Intl. reserves less gold:** $942 mil. **Gold:** 150,000 oz t. **Consumer prices:** 2.79%.

Transport: Railroad: Length: 37 mi. **Motor vehicles:** 63,500 pass. cars, 72,700 comm. vehicles. **Civil aviation:** 716.4 mil. pass.-mi.; 9 airports.

AP/WIDE WORLD PHOTOS

US ARMY BY SPC. ARTHUR D. HAMILTON

AP/WIDE WORLD PHOTOS

AP/WIDE WORLD PHOTOS

1 2 IRAQ ELECTS A GOVERNMENT
An Iraqi shows her purple finger, a sign that she has just voted in the Jan. 30, 2005 Iraqi elections. An estimated 58% of eligible Iraqis braved threats of insurgent violence to go the polls. Voting produced a government led by (left to right) Prime Min. Ibrahim al-Jaafari (a Shiite), Pres. Jalal Talabani (a Kurd), Vice Pres. Ghazi al-Yawer (a Sunni), and Vice Pres. Adel Abdul-Mahdi (a Shiite).

3 SOLDIERS AT WORK
U.S. soldiers from the Alaskan National Guard assemble a swing set for Iraqi children in Al Hilah, Iraq. Through mid-September, about 1, 900 U.S. soldiers had lost their lives in the Iraq War, which began in Mar. 2003.

4 CANDY BOMBING
Relatives of a 9-year-old grieve after a suicide car bomber attacked an American patrol distributing candy to children in Baghdad July 13. A dozen children were believed among the 27 victims of the attack by insurgents opposing the U.S. presence and seeking to undermine the Iraqi government.

World

AP/WIDE WORLD PHOTOS

AP/WIDE WORLD PHOTOS

AP/WIDE WORLD PHOTOS

AP/WIDE WORLD PHOTOS

1 NO TO THE EU

Voters in France rejected the European Union's proposed constitution May 29, as did Dutch voters three days later. The rejections caused the EU to abandon a planned Nov. 2006 deadline for ratification by its 25 members.

2 NEW IRANIAN PRESIDENT

Mahmoud Ahmadinejad, the hard-line mayor of Tehran, was elected Iranian president in a runoff June 24, defeating former Pres. Ali Akbar Hashemi Rafsanjani. Iran continued to press forward with its nuclear program despite opposition from the West and the International Atomic Energy Agency.

3 SYRIA LEAVES LEBANON

Syria Apr. 26 formally ended its 29-year military presence in Lebanon, when the last Syrian military forces returned home. The pullout followed widespread popular opposition to the Syrian presence, kindled by the assassination Feb. 14 of Rafik al-Hariri, the longtime Lebanese premier who had resigned in Oct. 2004 to protest Syrian political hegemony in his country.

4 ISRAEL LEAVES GAZA

Israel completed its evacuation of settlers from the Gaza Strip Aug. 22, after 38 years of occupation. Here security forces carry off a resisting settler and her daughter.

WHITE HOUSE PHOTO BY TINA HAGER

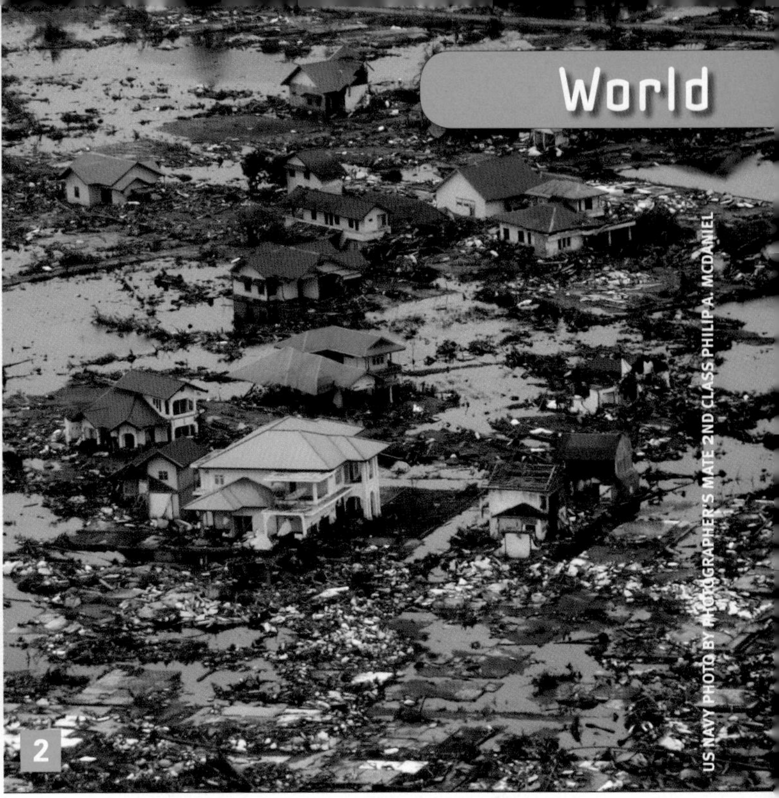

US NAVY PHOTO BY PHOTOGRAPHER'S MATE 2ND CLASS PHILIP A. MCDANIEL

1 2 CATASTROPHIC TSUNAMI

After the Dec. 2004 Asian tsunami, Pres. George W. Bush named former presidents George H. W. Bush and Bill Clinton to head up charitable relief efforts by the United States. At right, a devastated coastal village. The tsunami killed over 200,000 people in Indonesia and 11 other countries bordering the Indian Ocean.

3 4 LONDON BOMBINGS

Four coordinated suicide bombings against London's mass transit system killed 52 victims and the 4 bombers July 7 and injured some 700. The city was rattled again only 2 weeks later, when, again, 4 coordinated attacks were launched, though this time botched. Both operations were attributed to British Muslims. Suspects in the later attacks were arrested.

AP/WIDE WORLD PHOTOS

AP/WIDE WORLD PHOTOS

AP/WIDE WORLD PHOTOS

AP/WIDE WORLD PHOTOS

1 2 3 VATICAN SUCCESSION
Pope John Paul II (pictured at left in 1987) died Apr. 2 at the Vatican, at the age of 84. Some 200 world leaders and 300,000 others attended his funeral, Apr. 8 in St. Peter's Square in Rome (below). The Polish pontiff, who had served for 26 years, was succeeded by German Cardinal Joseph Ratzinger, 78 (above), elected Apr. 19 by the College of Cardinals; he chose the name Benedict XVI.

AP/WIDE WORLD PHOTOS

1 **WORLDCOM RECORD FRAUD**
Bernard Ebbers, former CEO of Worldcom, was convicted Mar. 15 of orchestrating an $11 bil fraud that bankrupted his company—the largest corporate fraud in U.S. history. Shown after the verdict with his wife, Kristie, he was sentenced July 13 to 25 years in prison.

3 **A FINAL CRUSADE?**
Billy Graham, 86, during a crusade in Queens, NY, June 24. The internationally known evangelical preacher had indicated that the crusade, which drew 230,000 people over 3 days, would be his last.

2 **SUPERSTAR ACQUITTED**
Michael Jackson, shown arm in arm with his mother, Katherine, was acquitted of child molestation charges June 13 by a county court jury in Santa Maria, CA.

4 **ROYAL NUPTIALS**
Charles, the Prince of Wales and the heir to Britain's throne, Apr. 9 married Camilla Parker-Bowles, his longtime companion, in a civil service at the Guildhall in the town of Windsor. The bride assumed the title of Her Royal Highness the Duchess of Cornwall.

AP/WIDE WORLD PHOTOS

1 3 OUT OF 4

New England Patriots quarterback Tom Brady led his team to its 3rd title in 4 years with a 24-21 victory over the Philadelphia Eagles in Super Bowl XXXIX in Jacksonville, FL, Feb. 6.

2 NHL SEASON MELTS

The nearly 10-month NHL lockout that led to cancellation of the 2004-2005 season ended July 22 with an agreement between the league and the NHL Players Association.

3 FLYING HIGH

Bode Miller Mar. 12 became the first American skier in 22 years to win the overall World Cup skiing title.

AP/WIDE WORLD PHOTOS

AP/WIDE WORLD PHOTOS

AP/WIDE WORLD PHOTOS

1 WOMAN DRIVER
Rookie Indy racer Danica Patrick finished 4th in the Indy 500 on May 29, the best finish ever for a female driver. The 23-year-old Patrick had led as late as the 194th of 200 laps.

2 3 MAJOR ACCOMPLISHMENTS
Annika Sorenstam of Sweden celebrating after a birdie at the LPGA Championship at Havre de Grace, MD, June 12. She won it, becoming the first woman golfer to win the same major event 3 years in a row.

Tiger Woods, after winning his 2nd British Open at St. Andrews, Scotland, July 27. Woods, who also took the 2005 Masters, became the only golfer besides Jack Nicklaus to have won each Grand Slam title twice. Nicklaus, 65, said the British Open would be his last major tournament.

4 TOUGH QUESTIONS
From right to left, Boston Red Sox player Curt Schilling, Baltimore Oriole Rafael Palmeiro, former St. Louis Cardinal Mark McGwire, and Oriole Sammy Sosa appeared Mar. 17 before a House committee investigating steroid abuse in baseball. On Aug. 1, Palmeiro, who had testified, "I have never used steroids—period," was suspended for 10 days after testing positive for steroids.

AP/WIDE WORLD PHOTOS

AP/WIDE WORLD PHOTOS

AP/WIDE WORLD PHOTOS

1 2 *UN GRAND CHAMPION*

On July 24, American cyclist Lance Armstrong won his 7th straight Tour de France, which he said would be his last. A cancer survivor, Armstrong is also shown in 1997, a few months after being diagnosed with the disease.

3 SO VALUABLE

Tim Duncan led the San Antonio Spurs to an 81-74 win over the Detroit Pistons in Game 7 of the NBA finals on June 23. Duncan, shown shooting over Detroit's Antonio McDyess, was named finals MVP for the 3rd time.

4 CENTER COURT STAR

Roger Federer, 24, of Switzerland, beat Andy Roddick in straight sets to win his 3rd straight men's singles title at Wimbledon, July 3. He went on to defend his U.S. Open title, defeating Andre Agassi in the final on Sept. 11.

Communications: TV sets: 6 per 1,000 pop. **Radios:** 38 per 1,000 pop. **Telephone lines:** 371,800. **Daily newspaper circ.:** 11 per 1,000 pop. **Internet** (2002): 80,000.

Health: Life expect.: 60.1 male; 59.5 female. **Births** (per 1,000 pop.): 31.5. **Deaths** (per 1,000 pop.): 9.5. **Natural inc.:** 2.20%. **Infant mortality** (per 1,000 live births): 67.0. **AIDS rate:** 0.5%.

Education: Compulsory: ages 6-10. **Literacy:** 45.2%.

Major Intl. Organizations: UN (FAO, IBRD, ILO, IMF, IMO, WHO, WTrO).

Embassy: 2131 Leroy Pl. NW 20008; 667-4550.

Website: www.nepalhmg.gov.np/index_eng.php

Nepal was originally a group of petty principalities, the inhabitants of one of which, the Gurkhas, became dominant about 1769. In 1951 King Tribhubana Bir Bikram, member of the Shah family, ended the system of rule by hereditary premiers of the Ranas family, who had kept the kings virtual prisoners, and established a cabinet system of government.

Virtually closed to the outside world for centuries, Nepal is now linked to India and Pakistan by roads and air service and to Tibet by road. Polygamy, child marriage, and the caste system were officially abolished in 1963.

The government announced the legalization of political parties in 1990. Elections on Nov. 15, 1994, led to the installation of Nepal's first Communist government, which held power until a no-confidence vote Sept. 10, 1995.

Nine members of Nepal's royal family, including King Birendra and Queen Aishwarya, died as the result of a massacre on the night of June 1, 2001. An official inquiry blamed the carnage on a 10th family member, Crown Prince Dipendra, who reportedly shot himself that night and died 3 days later, allowing Birendra's brother Gyanendra to assume the throne. A Maoist insurgency has claimed more than 10,000 lives since 1996. A seven-month truce collapsed in Aug. 2003 and violence continued.

Citing the government's failure to stop a Maoist insurgency that had claimed 11,000 lives since 1996, King Gyanendra assumed absolute authority, Feb. 1, 2005. A state of emergency ended Apr. 29, but curbs on civil liberties remained in effect.

Netherlands

Kingdom of the Netherlands

People: Population: 16,407,491. **Age distrib.** (%): <15: 18.1; 65+: 14.1. **Pop. density:** 1,023 per sq mi, 395 per sq km. **Urban:** 65.8%. **Ethnic groups:** Dutch 83%. **Principal languages:** Dutch (official), Frisian, Flemish. **Chief religions:** Roman Catholic 31%, Protestant 21%, Muslim 4%.

Geography: Total area: 16,033 sq mi, 41,526 sq km; **Land area:** 13,082 sq mi, 33,883 sq km. **Location:** In NW Europe on North Sea. **Neighbors:** Germany on E, Belgium on S. **Topography:** The land is flat, an average alt. of 37 ft. above sea level, with much land below sea level reclaimed and protected by some 1,500 miles of dikes. Since 1920 the government has been draining the IJsselmeer, formerly the Zuider Zee. **Capital:** Amsterdam (official), 1,145,000, The Hague (administrative), 705,000. **Cities (urban aggr.):** Rotterdam, 1,094,000.

Government: Type: Parliamentary democracy under a constitutional monarch. **Head of state:** Queen Beatrix; b Jan. 31, 1938; in office: Apr. 30, 1980. **Head of gov.:** Prime Min. Jan Peter Balkenende; b May 7, 1956; in office: July 22, 2002. **Seat of govt.:** The Hague. **Local divisions:** 12 provinces. **Defense budget** (2004): $7.6 bil. **Active troops:** 53,130.

Economy: Industries: agro industries, metal & engineering products, electrical machinery & equip., chemicals, oil, constr., microelectronics, fishing. **Chief crops:** grains, potatoes, sugar beets, fruits, vegetables. **Natural resources:** nat. gas, oil. **Crude oil reserves** (2004): 106 mil bbls. **Livestock** (2004): cattle: 3.8 mil; chickens: 100 mil; goats: 265,000; pigs: 11.1 mil; sheep: 1.2 mil. **Fish catch** (2003): 593,305 metric tons. **Electricity prod.** (2003): 91.0 bil. kWh. **Labor force** (1998 est.): agriculture 4%, industry 23%, services 73%.

Finance: Monetary unit: Euro (EUR) (Sept. 2005: 0.80 = $1 U.S.). **GDP** (2004 est.): $481.1 bil.; **per capita GDP:** $29,500; **GDP growth:** 1.2%. **Imports** (2004 est.): $252.7 bil.; partners (2004): Germany 17.7%, Belgium 10.2%, US 7.8%, China 7.1%, UK 6.6%, France 4.9%. **Exports** (2004 est.): $293.1 bil.; partners (2004): Germany 25%, Belgium 12.6%, UK 10.1%, France 9.8%, Italy 6%, US 4.2%. **Tourism:** $9,249 mil. **Budget** (2004 est.): $274.4 bil. **Intl. reserves less gold:** $6.51 bil. **Gold:** 25 mil. oz t. **Consumer prices:** 1.23%.

Transport: Railroad: Length: 1,745 mi. **Motor vehicles:** 6.12 mil pass. cars, 806,000 comm. vehicles. **Civil aviation:** 42.7 bil. pass.-mi; 21 airports. **Chief ports:** Rotterdam, Amsterdam, Ijmuiden.

Communications: TV sets: 540 per 1,000 pop. **Radios:** 980 per 1,000 pop. **Telephone lines:** 10.0 mil. **Daily newspaper circ.:** 306 per 1,000 pop. **Internet:** 8.5 mil. users.

Health: Life expect.: 76.3 male; 81.5 female. **Births** (per 1,000 pop.): 11.1. **Deaths** (per 1,000 pop.): 8.7. **Natural inc.:** 0.25%. **Infant mortality** (per 1,000 live births): 5.0. **AIDS rate:** 0.2%.

Education: Compulsory: ages 6-18. **Literacy:** 99%.

Major Intl. Organizations: UN and all of its specialized agencies, EU, NATO, OECD, OSCE.

Embassy: 4200 Linnean Ave. NW 20008; 244-5300.

Website: www.government.nl

Julius Caesar conquered the region in 55 BC, when it was inhabited by Celtic and Germanic tribes. After the empire of Charlemagne fell apart, the Netherlands (Holland, Belgium, Flanders) split among counts, dukes, and bishops, passed to Burgundy and thence to Spain. William the Silent, prince of Orange, led a confederation of the northern provinces, called Estates, in the Union of Utrecht, 1579; in 1581 they repudiated allegiance to Spain. The rise of the Dutch republic to naval, economic, and artistic eminence came in the 17th century.

The United Dutch Republic ended 1795 when the French formed the Batavian Republic. Napoleon made his brother Louis king of Holland, 1806; Louis abdicated 1810 when Napoleon annexed Holland. In 1813 the French were expelled. In 1815 the Congress of Vienna formed a kingdom of the Netherlands, including Belgium, under William I. In 1830, the Belgians seceded and formed a separate kingdom.

The constitution, promulgated 1814, and subsequently revised, provides for a hereditary constitutional monarchy.

The Netherlands maintained its neutrality in World War I, but was invaded and brutally occupied by Germany, 1940-45. In 1949, after several years of fighting, the Netherlands granted independence to Indonesia.

The murder May 6, 2002, of right-wing populist leader Pim Fortuyn, 9 days before legislative elections, marked the 1st political assassination in modern Dutch history. The killing of filmmaker Theo van Gogh, Nov. 2, 2004, by an Islamic extremist also shocked many Dutch. Concerns about immigration contributed to the defeat of a proposed EU constitution by 62% to 38% in a referendum, June 1, 2005.

Netherlands Dependencies

The **Netherlands Antilles,** constitutionally on a level of equality with the Netherlands homeland within the kingdom, consist of 2 groups of islands in the West Indies. **Curaçao** and **Bonaire** are near the coast of Venezuela; **St. Eustatius, Saba,** and the southern part of **St. Maarten** are SE of Puerto Rico. The northern two-thirds of St. Maarten belongs to French Guadeloupe; the French call the island St. Martin. Total area of the 2 groups is 370.7 sq. mi., including Bonaire (111), Curaçao (171), St. Eustatius (8), Saba (5), St. Maarten (Dutch part) (13). St. Maarten suffered extensive damage from Hurricane Luis, Sept. 1995. Total pop. of the Netherlands Antilles (2005 est.) was 219,958. Willemstad, on Curaçao, is the capital. The principal industry is the refining of crude oil from Venezuela. Tourism is also an important industry, as is shipbuilding.

Aruba, about 26 mi. W of Curaçao, was separated from the Netherlands Antilles on Jan. 1, 1986; it is an autonomous member of the Netherlands, the same status as the Netherland Antilles. Area 74.5 sq. mi.; pop. (2005 est.) 71,566; capital Oranjestad. Chief industries are oil refining and tourism.

New Zealand

People: Population: 4,035,461. **Age distrib.** (%): <15: 21.4; 65+: 11.7. **Pop. density:** 39 per sq mi, 15 per sq km. **Urban:** 85.9%. **Ethnic groups:** New Zealand European 75%, Maori 10%, other European 5%, Pacific Islander 4%. **Principal languages:** English, Maori (both official). **Chief religions:** none 26%, unspecified 17%, Anglican 15%, Roman Catholic 13%.

Geography: Total area: 103,738 sq mi, 268,680 sq km. **Land area:** 103,484 sq mi, 268,021 sq km. **Location:** In SW Pacific O. **Neighbors:** Nearest are Australia on W, Fiji and Tonga on N. **Topography:** Each of the 2 main islands (North and South Isls.) is mainly hilly and mountainous. The east coasts consist of fertile plains, especially the broad Canterbury Plains on South Isl. A volcanic plateau is in center of North Isl. South Isl. has glaciers and 15 peaks over 10,000 ft. **Capital:** Wellington, 343,000. **Cities (urban aggr.):** Auckland, 1,063,000; Christchurch, 331,443.

Government: Type: Parliamentary democracy. **Head of state:** Queen Elizabeth II, represented by Gov.-Gen. Dame Silvia Cartwright; b Nov. 7, 1943; in office: Apr. 4, 2001. **Head of gov.:** Prime Min. Helen Clark; b Feb. 26, 1950; in office: Dec. 10, 1999. **Local divisions:** 16 regions. **Defense budget** (2004): $1.1 bil. **Active troops:** 8,610.

Economy: Industries: food proc., wood & paper products, textiles, machinery, transp. equip., banking & insurance, tourism, mining. **Chief crops:** wheat, barley, potatoes, fruits, vegetables. **Natural resources:** nat. gas, iron ore, sand, coal, timber, hydropower, gold, limestone. **Crude oil reserves** (2004): 51 mil bbls. **Arable land:** 9%. **Livestock** (2004): cattle: 9.5 mil; chickens: 20 mil; goats: 153,000; pigs: 390,000; sheep: 40.0 mil. **Fish catch** (2003): 633,788 metric tons. **Electricity prod.** (2003): 39.8 bil. kWh. **Labor force** (1995): agriculture 10%, industry 25%, services 65%.

Finance: Monetary unit: New Zealand Dollar (NZD) (Sept. 2005: 1.42 = $1 U.S.). **GDP** (2004 est.): $92.5 bil.; **per capita GDP:** $23,200; **GDP growth:** 4.8%. **Imports** (2004 est.): $19.8 bil.; partners (2004): Australia 28.6%, Japan 10.7%, US 10%, China 6.6%, Germany 4.2%, Singapore 4.1%. **Exports** (2004 est.): $19.9 bil.; partners (2004): Australia 19.6%, US 14.3%, Japan 11.4%, China 6.3%, UK 5.1%. **Tourism:** $3,974 mil. **Budget** (2004 est.): $36.1 bil. **Intl. reserves less gold:** $3.41 bil. **Consumer prices:** 2.29%.

Transport: Railroad: Length: 2,422 mi. **Motor vehicles:** 1.99 mil pass. cars, 443,000 comm. vehicles. **Civil aviation:** 14.3 bil pass.-mi; 46 airports. **Chief ports:** Auckland, Christchurch, Wellington, Dunedin, Tauranga.

Communications: TV sets: 516 per 1,000 pop. **Radios:** 997 per 1,000 pop. **Telephone lines:** 1.8 mil. **Daily newspaper circ.:** 202.5 per 1,000 pop. **Internet:** 2.1 mil. users.

Health: Life expect.: 75.7 male; 81.8 female. **Births** (per 1,000 pop.): 13.9. **Deaths** (per 1,000 pop.): 7.5. **Natural inc.:** 0.64%. **Infant mortality** (per 1,000 live births): 5.9. **AIDS rate:** 0.1%.

Education: Compulsory: ages 5-16. **Literacy:** 99%.

Major Intl. Organizations: UN (FAO, IBRD, ILO, IMF, IMO, WHO, WTrO), APEC, the Commonwealth, OECD.

Embassy: 37 Observatory Cir. NW 20008; 328-4800.

Website: www.govt.nz

The Maoris, a Polynesian group from the eastern Pacific, reached New Zealand before and during the 14th century. The first European to sight New Zealand was Dutch navigator Abel Janszoon Tasman, but Maoris refused to allow him to land. British Capt. James Cook explored the coasts, 1769-1770.

British sovereignty was proclaimed and Maori land rights were recognized in the Treaty of Waitangi, 1840, with organized settlement beginning in the same year. Representative institutions were granted in 1853. Maori Wars ended in 1870 with British victory. The colony became a dominion in 1907 and gained full independence in 1947. It is a member of the Commonwealth.

A progressive tradition in politics dates back to the 19th century, when New Zealand was internationally known for social experimentation; much of the nation's economy has been deregulated in recent years. Jenny Shipley of the National Party became the nation's first female prime minister, Dec. 8, 1997. The Labour Party, led by Helen Clark, won the general elections of Nov. 27, 1999, and July 27, 2002.

The legislature legalized prostitution June 2003. In July, New Zealand contributed troops to the Aus.-led force in the Solomon Islands. A measure establishing a Supreme Court and ending appeals to the UK Privy Council passed Oct. 14.

The native Maoris make up nearly 15% of the population. Six of 120 members of the House of Representatives are elected directly by the Maori people. Prime Min. Clark, May 4, 2004, survived a no-confidence vote on a plan to nationalize New Zealand's coastline. The coastline plan was opposed by some Maoris, who claimed it infringed their land rights under the Waitangi Treaty. Clark moved to form a coalition government after elections Sept. 17 gave the Labour Party a thin plurality.

New Zealand comprises **North Island,** 44,702 sq. mi.; **South Island,** 58,384 sq. mi.; **Stewart Island,** 674 sq. mi.; **Chatham Islands,** 372 sq. mi.; and several groups of smaller islands.

In 1965, the **Cook Islands** (pop.,2004 est., 21,200; area 92.7 sq. mi.), halfway between New Zealand and Hawaii, became self-governing; New Zealand retains responsibility for defense and foreign affairs. **Niue** attained the same status in 1974; it lies 400 mi. to W. (pop., 2004 est., 2,156; area 100 sq. mi.) Cyclone Heta devastated Niue Jan. 6, 2004. **Tokelau** (pop., 2004 est., 1,405; area 4 sq. mi sq. mi.) comprises 3 atolls 300 mi. N of Samoa.

Ross Dependency, administered by New Zealand since 1923, comprises 160,000 sq. mi. of Antarctic territory.

Nicaragua

Republic of Nicaragua

People: Population: 5,465,100. **Age distrib.** (%): <15: 37.2; 65+: 3.1. **Pop. density:** 109 per sq mi, 42 per sq km. **Urban:** 57.3%. **Ethnic groups:** Mestizo 69%, White 17%, Black 9%, Amerindian 5%. **Principal languages:** Spanish (official); indigenous languages, English on Atlantic coast. **Chief religion:** Roman Catholic 73%, Evangelical 15%.

Geography: Total area: 49,998 sq mi, 129,494 sq km; **Land area:** 46,430 sq mi, 120,254 sq km. **Location:** In Central America. **Neighbors:** Honduras on N, Costa Rica on S. **Topography:** Both Caribbean and Pacific coasts are over 200 mi. long. The Cordillera Mts., with many volcanic peaks, run NW-SE through the middle of the country. Between this and a volcanic range to the E lie Lakes Managua and Nicaragua. **Capital:** Managua, 1,098,000.

Government: Type: Republic. **Head of state and gov.:** Pres. Enrique Bolaños Geyer; b May 13, 1928; in office Jan. 10, 2002. **Local divisions:** 15 departments, 2 autonomous regions. **Defense budget** (2004): $32 mil. **Active troops:** 14,000.

Economy: Industries: food proc., chemicals, machinery & metal products, textiles, clothing, oil refining & distribution, beverages, footwear, wood. **Chief crops:** coffee, bananas, sugarcane, cotton, rice, corn, tobacco, sesame, soya. **Natural resources:** gold, silver, copper, tungsten, lead, zinc, timber, fish. **Arable land:** 9%. **Livestock** (2004): cattle: 3.4 mil; chickens: 16.5 mil; goats: 7,000; pigs: 450,000; sheep: 4,400. **Fish catch** (2003): 22,331 metric tons. **Electricity prod.** (2003): 2.5 bil. kWh. **Labor force** (2003 est.): agriculture 30.5%, industry 17.3%, services 52.2%.

Finance: Monetary unit: Cordoba (NIO) (Sept. 2005: 16.36 = $1 U.S.). **GDP** (2004 est.): $12.3 bil.; **per capita GDP:** $2,300; **GDP growth:** 4%. **Imports** (2004 est.): $2.0 bil.; partners (2004): US 26.3%, Venezuela 9.6%, Costa Rica 7.5%, Mexico 7.1%, Guatemala 6.1%, El Salvador 4.1%. **Exports** (2004 est.): $750.0 mil; partners (2004): US 63.5%, El Salvador 9%, Costa Rica 4.2%. **Tourism:** $151 mil. **Budget** (2004 est.): $1.0 bil. **Intl. reserves less gold:** $430 mil. **Consumer prices:** 8.44%.

Transport: Railroad: Length: 4 mi. **Motor vehicles:** 82,200 pass. cars, 107,700 comm. vehicles. **Civil aviation:** 44.7 mil. pass.-mi; 11 airports. **Chief ports:** Corinto, Puerto Sandino, San Juan del Sur.

Communications: TV sets: 69 per 1,000 pop. **Radios:** 270 per 1,000 pop. **Telephone lines:** 205,000. **Daily newspaper circ.:** 30 per 1,000 pop. **Internet** (2002): 90,000 users.

Health: Life expect.: 68.3 male; 72.5 female. **Births** (per 1,000 pop.): 24.9. **Deaths** (per 1,000 pop.): 4.5. **Natural inc.:** 2.04%. **Infant mortality** (per 1,000 live births): 29.1. **AIDS rate:** 0.2%.

Education: Compulsory: ages 7-12. **Literacy:** 67.5%.

Major Intl. Organizations: UN and most of its specialized agencies, OAS.

Embassy: 1627 New Hampshire Ave. NW 20009; 939-6570.

Website: www.consuladodenicaragua.com

Nicaragua, inhabited by various Indian tribes, was conquered by Spain in 1552. After gaining independence from Spain, 1821, Nicaragua was united for a short period with Mexico, then with the United Provinces of Central America, finally becoming an independent republic, 1838. U.S. Marines occupied the country at times in the early 20th century, the last time from 1926 to 1933.

Gen. Anastasio Somoza Debayle was elected president in 1967. He resigned in 1972, but was re-elected president in 1974. Martial law was imposed in Dec. 1974, after officials were kidnapped by the Marxist Sandinista guerrillas. Violent opposition spread to nearly all classes in 1978; nationwide strikes called against the government touched off a civil war, which ended when Somoza fled Nicaragua and the Sandinistas took control of Managua in July 1979. Somoza was assassinated in Paraguay, Sept. 17, 1980.

Relations with the U.S. were strained as a result of Nicaragua's aid to leftist guerrillas in El Salvador and U.S. backing of anti-Sandinista contra guerrilla groups. In 1983 the contras launched a major offensive; the Sandinistas imposed rule by decree. In 1985 the U.S. House rejected Pres. Reagan's request for military aid to the contras. The subsequent diversion of funds to the contras from the proceeds of a secret arms sale to Iran caused a major scandal in the U.S.

In a stunning upset, Violeta Barrios de Chamorro defeated Sandinista leader Daniel Ortega Saavedra in national elections, Feb. 25, 1990. Arnoldo Alemán Lacayo, a conservative former mayor of Managua, defeated Ortega in the presidential election of Oct. 20, 1996. Up to 2,000 people died in W Nicaragua Oct. 30, 1998, in a mudslide caused by rains from Hurricane Mitch.

Drought and a drop in coffee prices plunged Nicaragua into an economic crisis in 2001. Enrique Bolaños Geyer, a conservative businessman, won the presidency that year. The corruption trial of former Pres. Alemán ended with a guilty verdict, Dec. 7, 2003; he was fined $10 million and sentenced to 20 years in prison. After a medical review, Alemán was allowed to serve the sentence under house arrest.

Niger

Republic of Niger

People: Population: 12,162,856. **Age distrib.** (%): <15: 47.3; 65+: 2.1. **Pop. density:** 25 per sq mi, 10 per sq km. **Urban:** 22.2%. **Ethnic groups:** Hausa 56%, Djerma 22%, Fula 9%, Tuareg 8%, Beri Beri (Kanouri) 4%. **Principal languages:** French (official); Hausa, Djerma, Fulani (all national). **Chief religion:** Muslim 80%.

Geography: Total area: 489,192 sq mi, 1,267,000 sq km; **Land area:** 489,076 sq mi, 1,266,700 sq km. **Location:** In the interior of N Africa. **Neighbors:** Libya, Algeria on N; Mali, Burkina Faso on W; Benin, Nigeria on S; Chad on E. **Topography:** Mostly arid desert and mountains. A narrow savanna in the S and the Niger R. basin in the SW contain most of the population. **Capital:** Niamey, 890,000.

Government: Type: Republic. **Head of state:** Pres. Mamadou Tandja; b 1938; in office: Dec. 22, 1999. **Head of gov.:** Prime Min. Hama Amadou; b 1950; in office: Jan. 3, 2000. **Local divisions:** 7 departments, 1 capital district. **Defense budget** (2003): $45 mil. **Active troops:** 5,300.

Economy: Industries: uranium mining, cement, brick, textiles, food proc., chemicals. **Chief crops:** cowpeas, cotton, peanuts, millet, sorghum, cassava, rice. **Natural resources:** uranium, coal, iron ore, tin, phosphates, gold, oil. **Arable land:** 3%. **Livestock** (2004): cattle: 2.3 mil; chickens: 25 mil; goats: 6.9 mil; pigs: 39,500; sheep: 4.5 mil. **Fish catch** (2003): 55,900 metric tons. **Electricity prod.** (2003): 0.23 bil. kWh. **Labor force:** agriculture 90%, industry and commerce 6%, government 4%.

Finance: Monetary unit: CFA Franc BCEAO (XOF) (Sept. 2005: 525.28 = $1 U.S.). **GDP** (2004 est.): $9.7 bil.; **per capita GDP:** $900; **GDP growth:** 3.5%. **Imports** (2002 est.): $400.0 mil; partners (2004): France 17.4%, Côte d'Ivoire 11.3%, Italy 8.4%, Nigeria 7.3%, Germany 6.5%, US 5.5%, China 4.8%. **Exports** (2002 est.): $280.0 mil; partners (2004): France 47.1%, Nigeria 22.7%, Japan 8.6%, US 5.4%. **Tourism** (2002): $28 mil. **Budget** (2002 est.): $320.0 mil. **Intl. reserves less gold:** $44 mil. **Consumer prices:** 0.26%.

Transport: Motor vehicles: 57,800 pass. cars, 41,000 comm. vehicles. **Civil aviation:** 80.8 mil. pass.-mi; 9 airports.

Communications: TV sets: 15 per 1,000 pop. **Radios:** 36 per 1,000 pop. **Telephone lines** (2002): 22,400. **Daily newspaper circ.:** 0.2 per 1,000 pop. **Internet** (2002): 15,000 users.

Health: Life expect.: 43.5 male; 43.5 female. **Births** (per 1,000 pop.): 51.3. **Deaths** (per 1,000 pop.): 21.2. **Natural inc.:** 3.01%. **Infant mortality** (per 1,000 live births): 119.7. **AIDS rate:** 1.2%.

Education: Compulsory: ages 7-12. **Literacy:** 17.6%.

Major Intl. Organizations: UN (FAO, IBRD, ILO, IMF, WHO, WTrO), AU.

Embassy: 2204 R St. NW 20008; 483-4224.

Website: www.nigerembassyusa.org

Niger was part of ancient and medieval African empires. European explorers reached the area in the late 18th century. The French colony of Niger was established 1900-22, after the defeat of Tuareg fighters, who had invaded the area from the N a century before. The country became independent Aug. 3, 1960.

In 1993, Niger held its first free and open elections since independence; an opposition leader, Mahamane Ousmane, won the presidency. A peace accord Apr. 24, 1995, ended a Tuareg rebellion that began in 1990. A coup, Jan. 27, 1996, followed by a disputed presidential election in July, left the military in control of Niger. On Apr. 9, 1999, Gen. Ibrahim Bare Mainassara, Niger's president since 1996, was assassinated, apparently by members of his security team. Elections were held Oct. 17 and Nov. 24, 1999, under a new constitution, approved by referendum July 18, that restored civilian rule. One of the world's poorest countries, Niger was threatened with famine in 2005 after locusts and drought ruined the grain harvest.

Nigeria

Federal Republic of Nigeria

People: Population: 128,765,768. **Age distrib.** (%): <15: 42.3; 65+: 3.1. **Pop. density:** 361 per sq mi, 139 per sq km. **Urban:** 46.7%. **Ethnic groups:** More than 250; Hausa and Fulani 29%, Yoruba 21%, Igbo (Ibo) 18%, Ijaw 10%. **Principal languages:** English (official), Hausa, Yoruba, Igbo (Ibo), Fulani. **Chief religions:** Muslim 50%, Christian 40%, indigenous beliefs 10%.

Geography: Total area: 356,669 sq mi, 923,768 sq km; **Land area:** 351,650 sq mi, 910,768 sq km. **Location:** On the S coast of W Africa. **Neighbors:** Benin on W, Niger on N, Chad and Cameroon on E. **Topography:** 4 E-W regions divide Nigeria: a coastal mangrove swamp 10-60 mi. wide, a tropical rain forest 50-100 mi. wide, a plateau of savanna and open woodland, and semidesert in the N. **Capital:** Abuja, 452,000. **Cities (urban aggr.):** Lagos, 8,665,000; Ibadan, 2,160,000; Ogbomosho, 829,000.

Government: Type: Republic. **Head of state and gov.:** Pres. Olusegun Obasanjo; b Mar. 5, 1937; in office: May 29, 1999. **Local divisions:** 36 states, 1 capital territory. **Defense budget** (2004): $572 mil. **Active troops:** 78,500.

Economy: Industries: crude oil, mining, palm oil, peanuts, cotton, rubber. **Chief crops:** cocoa, peanuts, palm oil, corn, rice, sorghum, millet, cassava, yams, rubber. **Natural resources:** nat. gas, oil, tin, columbite, iron ore, coal, limestone, lead, zinc. **Crude oil reserves** (2004): 35.3 bil. bbls. **Arable land:** 33%. **Livestock** (2004): cattle: 15.2 mil; chickens: 140,000; goats: 28.0 mil; pigs: 6.6 mil; sheep: 23.0 mil. **Fish catch** (2003): 505,839 metric tons. **Electricity prod.** (2003): 15.6 bil. kWh. **Labor force** (1999 est.): agriculture 70%, industry 10%, services 20%.

Finance: Monetary unit: Naira (NGN) (Sept. 2005: 131.94 = $1 U.S.). **GDP** (2004 est.): $125.7 bil.; **per capita GDP:** $1,000; **GDP growth:** 6.2%. **Imports** (2004 est.): $17.1 bil.; partners (2004): US 9.1%, China 8.8%, UK 8.7%, Netherlands 6.3%, France 6.1%, Germany 5.7%, Italy 4.7%. **Exports** (2004 est.): $34.0 bil.; partners (2004): US 48.2%, India 8.1%, Spain 7.4%, Brazil 5.5%, Japan 4.1%. **Tourism** (2002): $263 mil. **Budget** (2004 est.): $11.5 bil. **Intl. reserves less gold:** $10.92 bil. **Gold:** 690,000 oz t. **Consumer prices:** 15%.

Transport: Railroad: Length: 2,210 mi. **Motor vehicles:** 52,300 pass. cars, 13,500 comm. vehicles. **Civil aviation:** 249.8 mil. pass.-mi; 36 airports. **Chief ports:** Port Harcourt, Lagos, Warri, Calabar.

Communications: TV sets: 69 per 1,000 pop. **Radios:** 226 per 1,000 pop. **Telephone lines:** 853,100. **Daily newspaper circ.:** 24 per 1,000 pop. **Internet:** 750,000 users.

Health: Life expect.: 46.2 male; 47.3 female. **Births** (per 1,000 pop.): 40.7. **Deaths** (per 1,000 pop.): 17.2. **Natural inc.:** 2.35%. **Infant mortality** (per 1,000 live births): 98.8. **AIDS rate:** 5.4%.

Education: Compulsory: ages 6-11. **Literacy:** 68%.

Major Intl. Organizations: UN (FAO, IBRD, ILO, IMF, IMO, WHO, WTrO), the Commonwealth, AU, OPEC.

Embassy: 1333 16th St. NW 20036; 986-8400.

Website: www.nigeria.gov.ng

Early cultures in Nigeria date back to at least 700 BC. From the 12th to the 14th centuries, more advanced cultures developed in the Yoruba area, at Ife, and in the north, where Muslim influence prevailed. Portuguese and British slavers appeared from the 15th-16th centuries. Britain seized Lagos, 1861, and gradually extended control inland until 1900. Nigeria became independent Oct. 1, 1960, and a republic Oct. 1, 1963.

On May 30, 1967, the Eastern Region seceded, proclaiming itself the Republic of Biafra, plunging the country into civil war. Casualties in the war were estimated at over 1 million, including many "Biafrans" (mostly Ibos) who died of starvation despite international efforts to provide relief. The secessionists, after steadily losing ground, capitulated Jan. 12, 1970.

Nigeria emerged as one of the world's leading oil exporters in the 1970s, but much of the revenue has been squandered through corruption and mismanagement.

After 13 years of military rule, the nation made a peaceful return to civilian government, Oct. 1979. Military rule resumed, Dec. 31, 1983; a second coup came in 1985.

Headed by Gen. Ibrahim Babangida, the military regime held elections June 12, 1993, but annulled the vote June 23 when it appeared that Moshood Abiola would win. Riots followed and many were killed. Babangida resigned and appointed a civilian to head an interim government, Aug. 26, but that government was ousted Nov. 17 in a coup led by Gen. Sani Abacha. On June 11, 1994, Abiola declared himself president; he was jailed June 23.

Abacha's brutal rule ended June 8, 1998, when he died of an apparent heart attack. Abiola died in prison July 7, as Abacha's successor, Gen. Abdulsalam Abubakar, was reportedly preparing to free him. Abiola's death sparked riots in Lagos and other cities; on July 20, Abubakar promised early elections and a return to civilian rule. Olusegun Obasanjo (a former military ruler) won the presidential vote Feb. 27, 1999, Nigeria's 1st civilian government in 15 years.

An oil fire that exploded from a ruptured pipeline in S. Nigeria, Oct. 17, 1998, killed at least 700 people who were scavenging for fuel. The imposition of strict Islamic law in northern states led to clashes, Jan.-Mar. 2000, in which at least 800 people died. U.S. Pres. Bill Clinton visited Nigeria Aug. 26-27, 2000, the 1st visit there by a U.S. head of state in 22 years. Clashes between Muslims and Christians Sept. 7-12 and Oct. 13-14 claimed an estimated 600 lives; another 200 people died when soldiers went on a rampage in SE Nigeria Oct. 22-24.

At least 1,000 people were killed Jan. 27, 2002, when an army weapons depot in Lagos exploded; many of the victims drowned in a drainage canal while fleeing the blasts.

By 2002, the strict Islamic legal code of sharia had been adopted by about one-third of Nigeria's 36 states. Controversy over Nigeria's plans to host a Miss World pageant sparked sectarian riots in Kaduna, Nov. 20-24, leaving more than 200 people dead and 1,100 injured. Obasanjo won reelection Apr. 19, 2003.

Christian militia members massacred about 630 Muslims at Yelwa, central Nigeria, May 2, 2004. Although the World Court awarded the oil-rich Bakassi peninsula to Cameroon in 2002 and the handover was scheduled for Sept. 2004, Nigeria did not begin pulling troops out of the region until mid-2005.

Norway

Kingdom of Norway

People: Population: 4,593,041. **Age distrib.** (%): <15: 19.5; 65+: 14.8. **Pop. density:** 37 per sq mi, 14 per sq km. **Urban:** 78.6%. **Ethnic groups:** Norwegian, Sami. **Principal languages:** Norwegian (official), Sami, Finnish. **Chief religion:** Evangelical Lutheran 86% (official).

Geography: Total area: 125,182 sq mi, 324,220 sq km; **Land area:** 118,865 sq mi, 307,860 sq km. **Location:** W part of Scandinavian peninsula in NW Europe (extends farther north than any European land). **Neighbors:** Sweden, Finland, Russia on E. **Topography:** A highly indented coast is lined with tens of thousands of islands. Mountains and plateaus cover most of the country, which is only 25% forested. **Capital:** Oslo, 795,000. **Cities (urban aggr.):** Bergen (1996 est.), 223,773.

Government: Type: Hereditary constitutional monarchy. **Head of state:** King Harald V; b Feb. 21, 1937; in office: Jan. 17, 1991. **Head of gov.:** Prime Min. Kjell Magne Bondevik; b Sept. 3, 1947; in office: Oct. 19, 2001. **Local divisions:** 19 provinces. **Defense budget** (2004): $4.2 bil. **Active troops:** 26,600.

Economy: Industries: oil & gas, food proc., shipbuilding, pulp & paper products, metals, chemicals, timber, mining, textiles, fishing. **Chief crops:** barley, wheat, potatoes. **Natural resources:** oil, copper, nat. gas, pyrites, nickel, iron ore, zinc, lead, fish, timber, hydropower. **Crude oil reserves** (2004): 8.5 bil bbls. **Arable land:** 3%. **Livestock** (2004): cattle: 965,000; chickens: 3.3 mil; goats: 64,000; pigs: 459,000; sheep: 2.4 mil. **Fish catch** (2003): 3,132,207 metric tons. **Electricity prod.** (2003): 105.6 bil kWh. **Labor force** (1995): agriculture, forestry, and fishing 4%, industry 22%, services 74%.

Finance: Monetary unit: Kroner (NOK) (Sept. 2005: 6.27 = $1 U.S.). **GDP** (2004 est.): $183.0 bil; **per capita GDP:** $40,000; **GDP growth:** 3.3%. **Imports** (2004 est.): $46.0 bil; partners (2004): Sweden 15.7%, Germany 13.6%, Denmark 7.3%, UK 6.5%, China 5%, US 4.9%, Netherlands 4.4%, France 4.3%, Finland 4.1%. **Exports** (2004 est.): $76.6 bil; partners (2004): UK 22.4%, Germany 12.9%, Netherlands 9.9%, France 9.6%, US 8.4%, Sweden 6.7%. **Tourism:** $2,541 mil. **Budget** (2004 est.): $116.8 bil. **Intl. reserves less gold:** $28.53 bil. **Consumer prices:** 0.47%.

Transport: Railroad: Length: 2,596 mi. **Motor vehicles** 1.90 mil pass. cars, 464,800 comm. vehicles. **Civil aviation:** 6.5 bil pass.-mi; 66 airports. **Chief ports:** Bergen, Stavanger, Oslo, Kristiansand.

Communications: TV sets: 653 per 1,000 pop. **Radios:** 917 per 1,000 pop. **Telephone lines:** 3.3 mil. **Daily newspaper circ.:** 569.5 per 1,000 pop. **Internet:** 1.6 mil users.

Health: Life expect.: 76.8 male; 82.2 female. **Births** (per 1,000 pop.): 11.7. **Deaths** (per 1,000 pop.): 9.5. **Natural inc.:** 0.22%. **Infant mortality** (per 1,000 live births): 3.7. **AIDS rate:** 0.1%.

Education: Compulsory: ages 6-16. **Literacy:** 100%.

Major Intl. Organizations: UN and all of its specialized agencies, EFTA, NATO, OECD, OSCE.

Embassy: 2720 34th St. NW 20008; 333-6000.

Website: www.norway.no

The first ruler of Norway was Harald the Fairhaired, who came to power in AD 872. Between 800 and 1000, Norway's Vikings raided and occupied widely dispersed parts of Europe.

The country was united with Denmark 1381-1814, and with Sweden, 1814-1905. In 1905, the country became independent with Prince Charles of Denmark as king.

Norway remained neutral during World War I. Germany attacked Norway Apr. 9, 1940, and held it until liberation May 8, 1945. The country abandoned its neutrality after the war, and joined NATO. In a referendum Nov. 28, 1994, Norwegian voters rejected European Union membership.

Abundant hydroelectric resources provided the base for industrialization, giving Norway one of the highest living standards in the world. The country is a leading producer and exporter of crude oil, with extensive reserves in the North Sea. Norway's merchant marine is one of the world's largest.

A center-left bloc led by Jens Stoltenberg won parliamentary elections of Sept. 12, 2005, and Prime Min. Kjell Bonderik planned to resign Oct. 14 assuming a new coalition was formed by then.

Svalbard is a group of mountainous islands in the Arctic O., area 23,957.2 sq mi, pop. (2004 est.) 2,756. The largest, Spitsbergen (formerly called West Spitsbergen), 15,060 sq mi, seat of the governor, is about 370 mi. N of Norway. By a treaty signed in Paris, 1920, major European powers recognized the sovereignty of Norway, which incorporated it in 1925.

Jan Mayen, area 144 sq mi, is a volcanic island located about 565 mi WNW of Norway; it was annexed in 1929.

Oman

Sultanate of Oman

People: Population: 3,001,583. **Age distrib.** (%): <15: 42.6; 65+: 2.5. **Pop. density:** 37 per sq mi, 14 per sq km. **Urban:** 77.6%. **Ethnic groups:** Arab, Baluchi, South Asian, African. **Principal languages:** Arabic (official), English, Baluchi, Urdu, Indian dialects. **Chief religion:** Muslim 75% (official; mostly Ibadhi).

Geography: Total area: 82,031 sq mi, 212,460 sq km; **Land area:** 82,031 sq mi, 212,460 sq km. **Location:** On SE coast of Arabian peninsula. **Neighbors:** United Arab Emirates, Saudi Arabia, Yemen on W. **Topography:** Oman has a narrow coastal plain up to 10 mi. wide, a range of barren mountains reaching 9,900 ft., and a wide, stony, mostly waterless plateau, avg. alt. 1,000 ft. Also, an exclave at the tip of the Musandam peninsula controls access to the Persian Gulf. **Capital:** Muscat, 638,000.

Government: Type: Absolute monarchy. **Head of state and gov.:** Sultan Qabus bin Said; b Nov. 18, 1940; in office: July 23, 1970 (also prime min. since Jan. 2, 1972). **Local divisions:** 6 regions and 2 governorates. **Defense budget** (2004): $2.6 bil. **Active troops:** 41,700.

Economy: Industries: oil, gas, constr., cement, copper. **Chief crops:** dates, limes, bananas, alfalfa, vegetables. **Natural resources:** oil, copper, asbestos, marble, limestone, chromium, gypsum, nat. gas. **Crude oil reserves** (2004): 5.5 bil bbls. **Livestock** (2004): cattle: 330,000; chickens: 4 mil; goats: 1.1 mil; sheep: 370,000. **Fish catch** (2003): 138,833 metric tons. **Electricity prod.** (2003): 10.3 bil kWh.

Finance: Monetary unit: Rial (OMR) (Sept. 2005: 0.38 = $1 U.S.). **GDP** (2004 est.): $38.1 bil; **per capita GDP:** $13,100; **GDP growth:** 1.2%. **Imports** (2004 est.): $6.4 bil; partners (2004): UAE 17.5%, Japan 16.6%, UK 8.5%, Italy 6.4%, Germany 5.2%, US 4.7%, India 4.3%. **Exports** (2004 est.): $13.1 bil; partners (2004): China 27.6%, South Korea 17.8%, Japan 12.7%, Thailand 11.7%, UAE 6.6%. **Tourism:** $219 mil. **Budget** (2004 est.): $8.7 bil. **Intl. reserves less gold:** $2.32 bil. **Consumer prices:** 0.36%.

Transport: Motor vehicles: 390,000 pass. cars, 140,200 comm. vehicles. **Civil aviation:** 2.5 bil pass.-mi; 6 airports. **Chief ports:** Matrah, Mina' al Fahl.

Communications: TV sets: 575 per 1,000 pop. **Radios:** 607 per 1,000 pop. **Telephone lines**: 229,700. **Daily newspaper circ.:** 29 per 1,000 pop. **Internet** (2002): 180,000 users.

Health: Life expect.: 70.9 male; 75.5 female. **Births** (per 1,000 pop.): 36.7. **Deaths** (per 1,000 pop.): 3.9. **Natural inc.:** 3.29%. **Infant mortality** (per 1,000 live births): 19.5. **AIDS rate:** 0.1%.

Education: Literacy: 75.8%.

Major Intl. Organizations: UN (FAO, IBRD, ILO, IMF, IMO, WHO), AL.

Embassy: 2535 Belmont Rd. NW 20008; 387-1980.

Website: www.omanet.om/english/home.asp

Oman was originally called Muscat and Oman. A long history of rule by other lands, including Portugal in the 16th century, ended with the ouster of the Persians in 1744. By the early 19th century, Muscat and Oman was one of the most important countries in the region, controlling much of the Persian and Pakistan coasts, and also ruling far-away Zanzibar, which was separated in 1861 under British mediation.

British influence was confirmed in a 1951 treaty, and Britain helped suppress an uprising by traditionally rebellious interior tribes against control by Muscat in the 1950s.

On July 23, 1970, Sultan Said bin Taimur was overthrown by his son, who changed the nation's name to Sultanate of Oman.

Oil is the major source of income.

Oman opened its air bases to Western forces following the Iraqi invasion of Kuwait on Aug. 2, 1990. Oman served as a base for U.S. aircraft in the Afghanistan war, 2001. After a secret trail, 31 suspected Islamists received prison sentences, May 2, 2005, for plotting a coup.

Pakistan

Islamic Republic of Pakistan

People: Population: 162,419,946. **Age distrib.** (%): <15: 39.6; 65+: 4.1. **Pop. density:** 523 per sq mi, 202 per sq km. **Urban:** 34.1%. **Ethnic groups:** Punjabi, Sindhi, Pashtun, Balochi. **Principal languages:** English, Urdu (both official); Punjabi, Sindhi, Siraiki, Pashtu, Balochi, Hindko, Brahui, Burushaski. **Chief religions:** Muslim 97% (official; Sunni 77%, Shi'a 20%).

Geography: Total area: 310,403 sq mi, 803,940 sq km; **Land area:** 300,666 sq mi, 778,720 sq km. **Location:** In W part of South Asia. **Neighbors:** Iran on W, Afghanistan and China on N, India on E. **Topography:** The Indus R. rises in the Hindu Kush and Himalaya Mts. in the N (highest is K2, or Godwin Austen, 28,250 ft., 2nd highest in world), then flows over 1,000 mi. through fertile valley and empties into Arabian Sea. Thar Desert, Eastern Plains flank Indus Valley. **Capital:** Islamabad, 698,000. **Cities (urban aggr.):** Karachi, 10,032,000; Lahore, 5,452,000; Faisalabad, 2,142,000.

Government: Type: Republic with strong military influence. **Head of state:** Pres. Pervez Musharraf; b Aug. 11,1943; in office: Oct. 5, 1999 (as pres. from June 20, 2001). **Head of gov.:** Shaukat Aziz; b Mar. 6, 1949; in office: Aug. 28, 2004. **Local divisions:** 4 provinces and 1 capital territory, plus federally administered tribal areas. **Defense budget** (2004): $3.3 bil. **Active troops:** 619,000.

Economy: Industries: textiles, food proc., beverages, constr. materials, clothing, paper products. **Chief crops:** cotton, wheat, rice, sugarcane, fruits. **Natural resources:** nat. gas, oil, coal, iron ore, copper, salt, limestone. **Crude oil reserves** (2004): 289 mil bbls. **Arable land:** 27%. **Livestock** (2004): cattle: 23.8 mil; chickens: 160.0 mil; goats: 54.7 mil; sheep: 24.7 mil. **Fish catch** (2003): 576,804 metric tons. **Electricity prod.** (2003): 76.9 bil kWh. **Labor force** (2004 est.): agriculture 42%, industry 20%, services 38%.

Finance: Monetary unit: Rupee (PKR) (Sept. 2005: 59.66 = $1 U.S.). **GDP** (2004 est.): $347.3 bil; **per capita GDP:** $2,200; **GDP growth:** 6.1%. **Imports** (2004 est.): $14.0 bil; partners (2004): China 10.8%, US 10.2%, UAE 9.3%, Saudi Arabia 9%, Japan 7%, Kuwait 5.3%, Germany 4.2%. **Exports** (2004 est.): $15.1 bil; partners (2004): US 21.3%, UAE 9.8%, UK 7.1%, Germany 5.2%, Hong Kong 4.2%, Saudi Arabia 4.1%. **Tourism:** $120 mil. **Budget** (2004 est.): $16.5 bil. **Intl. reserves less gold:** $6.31 bil. **Gold:** 2.1 mil oz t. **Consumer prices:** 7.44%.

Transport: Railroad: Length: 5,072 mi. **Motor vehicles** 1.17 mil pass. cars, 488,600 comm. vehicles. **Civil aviation:** 7.2 bil pass.-mi; 87 airports. **Chief port:** Karachi.

Communications: TV sets: 105 per 1,000 pop. **Radios:** 94 per 1,000 pop. **Telephone lines:** 4.0 mil. **Daily newspaper circ.:** 40.4 per 1,000 pop. **Internet** (2002): 1.5 mil users.

Health: Life expect.: 62.0 male; 64.0 female. **Births** (per 1,000 pop.): 30.4. **Deaths** (per 1,000 pop.): 8.5. **Natural inc.:** 2.20%. **Infant mortality** (per 1,000 live births): 72.4. **AIDS rate:** 0.1%.

Education: Compulsory: ages 5-9. **Literacy:** 45.7%.

Major Intl. Organizations: UN (FAO, IBRD, ILO, IMF, IMO, WHO, WTrO), the Commonwealth.

Embassy: 3517 International Ct., NW Washington DC 20008; 243-6500.

Website: www.pakistan.gov.pk

Pakistan shares the 5,000-year history of the India-Pakistan subcontinent. At present-day Harappa and Mohenjo Daro, the Indus Valley Civilization, with large cities and elaborate irrigation systems, flourished c. 4,000-2,500 BC. Aryan invaders from the NW conquered the region around 1,500 BC, forging the Vedic civilization that dominated the region for over a thousand years. Other invaders from the W followed. The first Arab invasion, AD 712, introduced Islam. Present-day Pakistan and India were part of the Mogul empire from 1526 to 1857. Muslim power faded by the end of the 19th cent. as the British gained control of the N and NW areas of the subcontinent.

After World War I, the Muslims of British India began agitation for minority rights in elections. Muhammad Ali Jinnah (1876-1948) was the principal architect of Pakistan. When the British withdrew Aug. 14, 1947, the Islamic majority areas of India acquired self-government as Pakistan, with dominion status in the Commonwealth. Pakistan was divided into 2 sections, West Pakistan and East Pakistan. The 2 areas were nearly 1,000 mi. apart on opposite sides of India.

The Awami League, which had sought regional autonomy for East Pakistan for several years, won a majority in Dec. 1970 elections to a constituent assembly. In Mar. 1971, Pakistan's military-dominated government postponed the assembly. Rioting and strikes broke out in the East. On Mar. 25, 1971, government troops launched attacks in the East. The Easterners, aided by India, proclaimed the independent nation of Bangladesh. In months of widespread fighting, countless thousands were killed. Some 10 million Easterners fled into India. Full-scale war between India and Pakistan had spread to both the East and West fronts by Dec. 3. Pakistan troops in the East surrendered Dec. 16; Pakistan agreed to a cease-fire in the West Dec. 17. On July 3, 1972, Pakistan and India signed a pact agreeing to withdraw troops from their borders and resolve problems peacefully.

Zulfikar Ali Bhutto, leader of the Pakistan People's Party, which had won the most West Pakistan votes in Dec. 1970 elections, became president Dec. 20, 1971. Bhutto was overthrown in a military coup July 1977. Convicted of complicity in a 1974 political murder, he was executed Apr. 4, 1979. Over 3 million Afghan refugees flooded into Pakistan after the USSR invaded Afghanistan Dec. 1979; by 2005, 2.3 million refugees had been repatriated, but more than a million remained.

Pres. Mohammad Zia ul-Haq was killed when his plane exploded in Aug. 1988. Following Nov. elections, Benazir Bhutto, daughter of Zulfikar Ali Bhutto, was named prime minister, becoming the first woman leader of a Muslim nation. She was accused of corruption and dismissed by the president, Aug. 1990. Bhutto returned to power Oct. 1993, but was dismissed again, Nov. 1996, amid further corruption charges.

Responding to nuclear weapons tests by India, Pakistan conducted its own tests, May 28-30, 1998; the U.S. imposed economic sanctions on both countries.

In mid-1999, Muslim infiltrators, apparently including Pakistani troops, seized Indian-held positions in the disputed territory of Kashmir, which witnessed its heaviest fighting in over 2 decades (see). After meeting with Pres. Bill Clinton on July 4, Prime Min. Nawaz Sharif agreed to a Pakistani pullback. Growing conflict between Sharif and the military climaxed in his firing on Oct. 12 of army chief Gen. Pervez Musharraf, whose supporters staged a bloodless coup. Musharraf assumed the presidency June 20, 2001.

Following the Sept. 11, 2001, terrorist attack on the U.S., Pres. Musharraf, Sept. 19, pledged cooperation with the U.S. in fighting Taliban and al-Qaeda militants within its own tribal areas and in neighboring Afghanistan. In return, the U.S. waived its 1998 sanctions and offered Pakistan financial aid and debt relief. Guerrilla violence in Kashmir and Pakistani missile tests May 25-28, 2002, heightened fears of war with India, but the crisis was eased in June with U.S. mediation. A referendum Apr. 30, 2002, extended Musharraf's rule for another 5 years; many observers called the vote rigged.

During 2002-04 there was evidence of growing al-Qaeda and Taliban activity within Pakistan. Militants kidnapped *Wall Street Journal* reporter Daniel Pearl Jan. 23, 2002, and eventually killed him; 4 Islamic extremists were convicted July 15. Several alleged al-Qaeda operatives, including Ramzi bin al-Shibh, believed to have been a close associate of Sept. 11 ringleader Mohamed Atta, were captured in a shootout in Karachi, Sept. 11, 2002. The alleged mastermind of the Sept. 11 attack, Khalid Sheikh Mohammed, was apprehended in Rawalpindi, Mar. 1, 2003. Islamic extremists carried out bombings in Rawalpindi Dec. 14 and 25, in unsuccessful attempts to assassinate Musharraf. A top al-Qaeda figure implicated in those attempts, Amjad Hussain Farooqi, was killed by security forces in late Sept. 2004.

Accused of selling atomic secrets to Iran, Libya, and North Korea, Pakistan's top nuclear scientist, Abdul Qadeer Khan, made a televised apology, Feb. 4, 2004, and said his actions were unauthorized; he received a pardon from Musharraf Feb. 5. A joint U.S.-Pakistani raid July 25 broke up an al-Qaeda cell in Gujrat, revealing possible evidence of planned attacks against U.S. financial institutions. Shaukat Aziz, who survived a suicide bomb attack July 30, was elected prime min. Aug. 27.

On Oct. 1, at least 30 worshippers were killed in the bombing of a Shiite mosque in Sialkot. Earlier bombings and other attacks on Shiite religious targets in Karachi and Quetta had killed more than 100. A car bomb, Oct. 7, at a Sunni religious gathering in Multan left more than 40 people dead. British ties with Pakistan were frayed by reports that 3 of 4 suspects in the London train and bus bombings, July 7, 2005, were of Pakistani ancestry, and that 2 had recently been to Pakistan. Musharraf pledged July 29 to arrest leaders of banned Islamist groups and to expel foreign students from Islamic schools, or *madrassas*.

Palau

Republic of Palau

People: Population: 20,303. **Age distrib.** (%): <15: 26.4; 65+: 4.6. **Pop. density:** 115 per sq mi, 44 per sq km. **Urban:** 68.6%. **Ethnic groups:** Palauan (Micronesian/Malayan/Melanesian mix) 70%, Asian 28%, White 2%. **Principal languages:** English (official); Palauan, Sonsorolese, Tobi, Angaur, Japanese (all official in certain states). **Chief religions:** Roman Catholic 42%, Protestant 23%, Modekngei 9%.

Geography: Total area: 177 sq mi, 458 sq km; **Land area:** 177 sq mi, 458 sq km. **Location:** Archipelago (26 islands, more than 300 islets) in the W Pacific Ocean, about 530 mi SE of the Philippines. **Neighbors:** Micronesia to E, Indonesia to S. **Topography:** Palau is comprised of a mountainous main island and low coral atolls, usually fringed with large barrier reefs. **Capital:** Koror, 14,000. (Note: a new capital is being built in Babelthuap.)

Government: Type: Republic. **Head of state and gov.:** Pres. Tommy Esang Remengesau, Jr.; b Feb. 28, 1956; in office: Jan. 19, 2001. **Local divisions:** 16 states.

Economy: Industries: tourism, handicrafts, constr., garment making. **Chief crops:** coconuts, copra, cassava, sweet potatoes. **Natural resources:** timber, gold & other minerals, fish. **Fish catch** (2003): 1,051 metric tons. **Labor force** (1990): agriculture 20%.

Finance: Monetary unit: U.S. Dollar. **GDP** (2001 est.): $174.0 mil; **per capita GDP:** $9,000; **GDP growth:** 1%. **Imports** (2001 est.): $99.0 mil; partners (2000): US, Guam, Japan, Singapore, South Korea. **Exports** (2001 est.): $18.0 mil; partners (2000): US, Japan, Singapore. **Tourism** (2002): $59 mil. **Budget** (1999): $80.8 mill.

Transport: 1 airport.

Communications: TV sets: 98 per 1,000 pop. **Radios:** 550 per 1,000 pop. **Telephone lines:** NA. **Internet:** NA.

Health: Life expect.: 67.0 male; 73.5 female. **Births** (per 1,000 pop.): 18.4. **Deaths** (per 1,000 pop.): 6.9. **Natural inc.:** 1.15%. **Infant mortality** (per 1,000 live births): 14.8.

Education: Compulsory: ages 6-14. **Literacy:** 92%.

Major Intl. Organizations: UN (WHO).

Embassy: 1700 Pennsylvania Ave 20006 452-6814

Website: www.palaugov.net

Spain acquired the Palau Islands in 1886 and sold them to Germany in 1899. Japan seized them in 1914. American forces occupied the islands in 1944; in 1947, they became part of the U.S.-administered UN Trust Territory of the Pacific Islands. In 1981 Palau became an autonomous republic; in 1993 the republic ratified a compact of free association with the U.S., which provides financial aid in return for U.S. use of Palauan military facilities over 15 years. Palau became an independent nation on Oct. 1, 1994. Vice-Pres. Tommy Remengesau won the presidential election held Nov. 7, 2000, and was reelected Nov. 2, 2004.

Panama

Republic of Panama

People: Population: 3,140,232. **Age distrib.** (%): <15: 29.8; 65+: 6.4. **Pop. density:** 104 per sq mi, 40 per sqq km. **Urban:** 57.1%. **Ethnic groups:** Mestizo 70%, Amerindian-West Indian 14%, White 10%, Amerindian 6%. **Principal languages:** Spanish (official), English. **Chief religions:** Roman Catholic 85%, Protestant 15%.

Geography: Total area: 30,193 sq mi, 78,200 sq km; **Land area:** 29,340 sq mi, 75,990 sq km. **Location:** In Central America. **Neighbors:** Costa Rica on W, Colombia on E. **Topography:** 2 mountain ranges run the length of the isthmus. Tropical rain forests cover the Caribbean coast and eastern Panama. **Capital**: Panama City, 930,000.

Government: Type: Republic. **Head of state and gov.:** Pres. Martin Torrijos Espino; b July 18, 1963; in office: Sept. 1, 2004. **Local divisions:** 9 provinces, 5 territories. **Defense budget:** NA. **Active troops**: Nil. (11,800 paramilitary).

Economy: Industries: constr., oil refining, brewing, constr. materials, sugar milling. **Chief crops:** bananas, rice, corn, coffee, sugarcane. **Natural resources:** copper, mahogany, shrimp, hydropower. **Arable land:** 7%. **Livestock** (2004): cattle: 1.6 mil; chickens: 13.5 mil; goats: 6,200; pigs: 315,000. **Fish catch** (2003): 229,652 metric tons. **Electricity prod.** (2003): 5.4 bil kWh. **Labor force** (1995 est.): agriculture 20.8%, industry 18%, services 61.2%.

Finance: Monetary unit: Balboa (PAB) (Sept. 2005: 1.00 = $1 U.S.). **GDP** (2004 est.): $20.6 bil; **per capita GDP:** $6,900; **GDP growth:** 6%. **Imports** (2004 est.): $7.2 bil; partners (2004): Japan 32.9%, China 10.6%, US 9.8%, South Korea 7.2%, Singapore 7.1%, Italy 4.5%. **Exports** (2004 est.): $5.7 bil; partners (2004): US 12.2%, Nigeria 9.4%, Germany 8.4%, South Korea 8.2%, El Salvador 5.7%, Peru 5.1%, Costa Rica 5.1%, Japan 4.1%. **Tourism:** $585 mil. **Budget** (2004 est.): $3.7 bil. **Intl. reserves less gold:** $406 mil. **Consumer prices:** 0.27%.

Transport: Railroad: Length: 221 mi. **Motor vehicles:** 219,400 pass. cars, 70,300 comm. vehicles. **Civil aviation:** 1.9 bil. pass.-mi; 41 airports. **Chief ports:** Balboa, Cristobal.

Communications: TV sets: 192 per 1,000 pop. **Radios:** 299 per 1,000 pop. **Telephone lines:** 380,200. **Daily newspaper circ.:** 62 per 1,000 pop. **Internet:** 192,100 users.

Health: Life expect.: 72.7 male; 77.9 female. **Births** (per 1,000 pop.): 22.0. **Deaths** (per 1,000 pop.): 5.3. **Natural inc.:** 1.67%. **Infant mortality** (per 1,000 live births): 16.7. **AIDS rate:** 0.9%.

Education: Compulsory: ages 6-11. **Literacy:** 92.6%.

Major Intl. Organizations: UN (FAO, IBRD, ILO, IMF, IMO, WHO), the Commonwealth.

Embassy: 2862 McGill Terrace NW 20008; 483-1407.

Website: www.visitpanama.com

The coast of Panama was sighted by Rodrigo de Bastidas, sailing with Columbus for Spain in 1501, and was visited by Columbus in 1502. Vasco Nunez de Balboa crossed the isthmus and "discovered" the Pacific Ocean, Sept. 13, 1513. Spanish colonies were ravaged by Francis Drake, 1572-95, and Henry Morgan, 1668-71. Morgan destroyed the old city of Panama which had been founded in 1519. Freed from Spain, Panama joined Colombia in 1821.

Panama declared its independence from Colombia Nov. 3, 1903, with U.S. recognition. In support of Panama, U.S. naval forces deterred action by Colombia. Panama granted use, occupation, and control of the Canal Zone to the U.S. by treaty, ratified Feb. 26, 1904. In 1978, a new treaty provided for a gradual takeover by Panama of the canal, and withdrawal of U.S. troops, to be completed before the end of the century. U.S. payments were substantially increased in the interim.

President Delvalle was ousted by the National Assembly, Feb. 26, 1988, after he tried to fire the head of the Panama Defense Forces, Gen. Manuel Antonio Noriega, who was under U.S. federal indictment on drug charges. U.S. troops invaded Panama Dec. 20, 1989, and Noriega surrendered Jan. 3, 1990.

Mireya Moscoso, widow of former Pres. Arnulfo Arias, was elected president May 2, 1999, becoming Panama's first female head of state. The U.S. handed over control of the Panama Canal to Panama Dec. 31, 1999. Martin Torrijos Espino, son of Brig. Gen. Omar Torrijos Herrera (dictator of Panama, 1968-81), won the presidential election of May 2, 2004.

Papua New Guinea

Independent State of Papua New Guinea

People: Population: 5,545,268. **Age distrib.** (%): <15: 38.1; 65+: 3.8. **Pop. density:** 31 per sq mi, 12 per sq km. **Urban:** 13.2%. **Ethnic groups:** Melanesian, Papuan, Negrito, Micronesian, Polynesian. **Principal languages:** English (official), pidgin English, Motu; 715 indigenous languages. **Chief religions:** Indigenous beliefs 34%, Roman Catholic 22%, Protestant 44%.

Geography: Total area: 178,704 sq mi, 462,840 sq km; **Land area:** 174,850 sq mi, 452,860 sq km. **Location:** SE Asia, occupying E half of island of New Guinea and about 600 nearby islands. **Neighbors:** Indonesia (West Irian) on W, Australia on S. **Topography:** Thickly forested mts. cover much of the center of the country, with lowlands along the coasts. Included are some islands of Bismarck and Solomon groups, such as the Admiralty Isls., New Ireland, New Britain, and Bougainville. **Capital:** Port Moresby, 275,000.

Government: Type: Parliamentary democracy. **Head of state:** Queen Elizabeth II, represented by Gov.-Gen. Sir Paulias Matane; b 1931; in office: June 29, 2004. **Head of gov.:** Prime Min. Sir Michael Somare; b Apr. 9, 1936; in office: Aug. 5, 2002. **Local divisions:** 20 provinces. **Defense budget** (2004): $25 mil. **Active troops:** 3,100.

Economy: Industries: copra & palm oil proc., wood products, mining. **Chief crops:** coffee, cocoa, coconuts, palm kernels, tea, rubber, sweet potatoes. **Natural resources:** gold, copper, silver, nat. gas, timber, oil, fish. **Crude oil reserves** (2004): 240 mil; **Livestock** (2004): cattle: 91,000; chickens: 3.9 mil; goats: 2,600; pigs: 1.7 mil; sheep: 7,000. **Fish catch** (2003): 187,915 metric tons. **Electricity prod.** (2003): 1.6 bil kWh.

Finance: Monetary unit: Kina (PGK) (Sept. 2005: 3.01 = $1 U.S.). **GDP** (2004 est.): $12.0 bil; **per capita GDP:** $2,200; **GDP growth:** 0.9%. **Imports** (2004 est.): $1.4 bil; partners (2004): Australia 45.2%, Singapore 21.1%, New Zealand 7.5%, Japan 4.2%, China 4.2%. **Exports** (2004 est.): $2.4 bil; partners (2004): Australia 27.7%, China 5.8%, Japan 5.7%, Germany 5%. **Tourism** (2001): $5 mil. **Budget** (2004 est.): $1.2 bil. **Intl. reserves less gold:** $407 mil. **Gold:** 60,000 oz t. **Consumer prices:** 2.07%.

Transport: Motor vehicles: 24,900 pass. cars, 87,800 comm. vehicles. **Civil aviation:** 689.72 mil pass.-mi; 21 airports. **Chief ports:** Port Moresby, Lae.

Communications: TV sets: 13 per 1,000 pop. **Radios:** 91 per 1,000 pop. **Telephone lines** (2002): 62,000. **Daily newspaper circ.:** 15 per 1,000 pop. **Internet** (2002): 75,000 users.

Health: Life expect.: 62.8 male; 67.2 female. **Births** (per 1,000 pop.): 30.0. **Deaths** (per 1,000 pop.): 7.4. **Natural inc.:** 2.26%. **Infant mortality** (per 1,000 live births): 51.5. **AIDS rate:** 0.6%.

Education: Compulsory: ages 6-14. **Literacy:** 64.6%.

Major Intl. Organizations: UN (FAO, IBRD, ILO, IMF, IMO, WHO, WTrO), the Commonwealth, APEC.

Embassy: 1779 Massachusetts Ave NW, 20036; 745-3680.

Website: www.pngonline.gov.pg

Human remains have been found in the interior of New Guinea dating back at least 10,000 years and possibly much earlier. Successive waves of peoples probably entered the country from Asia through Indonesia. The indigenous population consists of a huge number of tribes, many living in almost complete isolation with mutually unintelligible languages.

Europeans visited in the 15th century, but actual land claims did not begin until the 19th century, when the Dutch took control of the island's western half. The southern half of eastern New Guinea was first claimed by Britain in 1884, and transferred to Australia in 1905. The northern half was claimed by Germany in 1884, but captured in World War I by Australia, which was first granted a League of Nations mandate and then a UN trusteeship over the area. The 2 territories were administered jointly after 1949, given self-government Dec. 1, 1973, and became independent Sept. 16, 1975.

Secessionist rebels clashed with government forces on Bougainville beginning in 1988; a truce signed Oct. 10, 1997, brought a halt to the fighting, which had claimed an estimated 20,000 lives. The country suffered from a severe drought in 1997. A tsunami killed at least 3,000 people July 17, 1998. A Bougainville autonomy agreement was signed Aug. 30, 2001. Army mutinies were suppressed in Mar. 2001 and Mar. 2002.

Paraguay

Republic of Paraguay

People: Population: 6,347,884. **Age distrib.** (%): <15: 37.9; 65+: 4.8. **Pop. density:** 40 per sq mi, 16 per sq km. **Urban:** 57.2%. **Ethnic groups:** Mestizo 95%. **Principal languages:** Spanish, Guaraní (both official). **Chief religions:** Roman Catholic 90%.

Geography: Total area: 157,047 sq mi, 406,750 sq km; **Land area:** 153,398 sq mi, 397,300 sq km. **Location:** Landlocked country in central South America. **Neighbors:** Bolivia on N, Argentina on S, Brazil on E. **Topography:** Paraguay R. bisects the country. To E are fertile plains, wooded slopes, grasslands. To W is the Gran Chaco plain, with marshes and scrub trees. Extreme W is arid. **Capital**: Asunción, 1,639,000.

Government: Type: Republic. **Head of state and gov.:** Pres. Nicanor Duarte Frutos; b Oct. 11, 1956; in office: Aug. 15, 2003. **Local divisions:** 17 departments and capital city. **Defense budget** (2004): $51 mil. **Active troops:** 10,100.

Economy: Industries: sugar, cement, textiles, beverages, wood products. **Chief crops:** cotton, sugarcane, soybeans, corn, wheat, tobacco, cassava. **Natural resources:** hydropower, timber, iron ore, mang., limestone. **Arable land:** 6%. **Livestock** (2004): cattle: 9.6 mil; chickens: 17.0 mil; goats: 159,469; pigs: 1.7 mil; sheep: 524,524. **Fish catch** (2003): 25,000 metric tons. **Electricity prod.** (2003): 51.3 bil kWh. **Labor force**: agriculture 45%.

Finance: Monetary unit: Guarani (PYG) (Sept. 2005: 6,088.30 = $1 U.S.). **GDP** (2004 est.): $29.9 bil; **per capita GDP:** $4,800; **GDP growth:** 2.8%. **Imports** (2004 est.): $3.3 bil; partners (2004): Brazil 24.3%, US 22.3%, Argentina 16.2%, China 9.9%, Hong Kong 5%. **Exports** (2004 est.): $2.9 bil; partners (2004): Brazil 27.8%, Uruguay 15.9%, Italy 7.1%, Switzerland 5.6%, Argentina 4.3%, Netherlands 4.2%. **Tourism:** $64 mil. **Budget** (2004 est.): $1.1 bil. **Intl. reserves less gold:** $752 mil. **Gold** (2003): 30,000 oz t. **Consumer prices** (2003): 14.2%.

Transport: Railroad: Length: 274 mi. **Motor vehicles** 415,800 pass. cars, 56,400 comm. vehicles. **Civil aviation:** 182.7 mil pass.-mi; 11 airports. **Chief port:** Asunción.

Communications: TV sets: 205 per 1,000 pop. **Radios:** 182 per 1,000 pop. **Telephone lines:** 273,200. **Daily newspaper circ.:** 43 per 1,000 pop. **Internet**: 120,000 users.

Health: Life expect.: 72.4 male; 77.6 female. **Births** (per 1,000 pop.): 29.4. **Deaths** (per 1,000 pop.): 4.5. **Natural inc.:** 2.49%. **Infant mortality** (per 1,000 live births): 25.6. **AIDS rate:** 0.5%.

Education: Compulsory: ages 6-14. **Literacy:** 94%.

Major Intl. Organizations: UN (FAO, IBRD, ILO, IMF, IMO, WHO, WTrO), OAS.

Embassy: 2400 Massachusetts Ave. NW, 20008; 483-6960.

Website: www.paraguayconsulatela.com

The Guarani Indians were settled farmers speaking a common language before the arrival of Europeans. Visited by Sebastian Cabot in 1527 and settled as a Spanish possession in 1535, Paraguay gained its independence from Spain in 1811. It lost much of its territory to Brazil, Uruguay, and Argentina in the War of the Triple Alliance, 1865-1870. Large areas were won from Bolivia in the Chaco War, 1932-35.

Gen. Alfredo Stroessner, who had ruled since 1954, was ousted in a military coup led by Gen. Andrés Rodríguez on Feb. 3, 1989. Rodríguez was elected president May 1. Juan Carlos Wasmosy was elected president May 9, 1993, becoming the nation's first civilian head of state in many years.

A prolonged power struggle involving a popular military leader, Gen. Lino César Oviedo, who was accused of insubordination, culminated in his surrender Dec. 12, 1997. He was freed Aug. 18, 1998, following the inauguration of Pres. Raúl Cubas Grau, Oviedo's successor as Colorado Party nominee.

The assassination of Vice Pres. Luis María Argaña, Mar. 23, 1999, by an unidentified gunman, was widely attributed to Cubas and triggered protests and an impeachment vote; Cubas resigned Mar. 28 and was succeeded by Senate leader Luis Angel González Macchi. An attempted military coup was suppressed May 18, 2000.

Mass protests over the depressed economy led to the proclamation of a state of emergency July 15, 2002. Nicanor Duarte Frutos won the presidency, Apr. 27, 2003, maintaining 55 years of uninterrupted Colorado Party rule.

A supermarket fire in Asunción Aug. 1, 2004, killed more than 400 people. Paraguayan authorities blamed a leftist group, Patria Libre, for the Sept. 2004 kidnapping and subsequent murder of Cecilia Cubas, daugher of former Pres. Cubas.

Peru

Republic of Peru

People: Population: 27,925,628. **Age distrib.** (%): <15: 31.5; 65+: 5.2. **Pop. density:** 56 per sq mi, 22 per sq km. **Urban:** 73.9%. **Ethnic groups:** Amerindian 45%, Mestizo 37%, White 15%. **Principal languages:** Spanish, Quechua (both official); Aymara. **Chief religions:** Roman Catholic 81% (official), unspecified, none 16%.

Geography: Total area: 496,226 sq mi, 1,285,220 sq km; **Land area:** 494,211 sq mi, 1,280,000 sq km. **Location:** On the Pacific coast of South America. **Neighbors:** Ecuador, Colombia on N; Brazil, Bolivia on E; Chile on S. **Topography:** An arid coastal strip, 10 to 100 mi. wide, supports much of the population thanks to widespread irrigation. The Andes cover 27% of land area. The uplands are well-watered, as are the eastern slopes reaching the Amazon basin, which covers half the country with its forests and jungles. **Capital:** Lima, 7,899,000. **Cities (urban aggr.):** Arequipa, 710,103; Callao, 424,294.

Government: Type: Republic. **Head of state:** Pres. Alejandro Toledo; b Mar. 28, 1946; in office: July 28, 2001. **Head of gov.:** Prime Min. Pedro-Pablo Kuczynski Godard; b Oct. 1938; in office: Aug. 16, 2005. **Local divisions:** 12 regions, 24 departments, 1 constitutional province. **Defense budget** (2003): $900 mil. **Active troops:** 100,000.

Economy: Industries: mining, oil, fishing, textiles, clothing, food proc. **Chief crops:** coffee, cotton, sugarcane, rice, wheat, potatoes, corn, plantains, coca. **Natural resources:** copper, silver, gold, oil, timber, fish, iron ore, coal, phosphate, potash, hydropower, nat. gas. **Crude oil reserves** (2004): 953 mil; **Arable land:** 3%. **Livestock** (2004): cattle: 5.1 mil; chickens: 93.0 mil; goats: 2.0 mil; pigs: 2.9 mil; sheep: 14.1 mil. **Fish catch** (2003): 6,103,478 metric tons. **Electricity prod.** (2003): 22.7 bil kWh. **Labor force** (2001): agriculture 9%, industry 18%, services 73%.

Finance: Monetary unit: Nuevo Sol (PEN) (Sept. 2005: 3.28 = $1 U.S.). **GDP** (2004 est.): $155.3 bil; **per capita GDP:** $5,600; **GDP growth:** 4.5%. **Imports** (2004 est.): $9.6 bil; partners (2004): US 29.2%, Spain 8.5%, Chile 6.9%, Brazil 5.6%, Colombia 5.2%, China 4%. **Exports** (2004 est.): $12.3 bil; partners (2004): US 29.5%, China 9.8%, UK 8%, Chile 5.3%, Japan 4.7%, Switzerland 4.4%. **Tourism:** $923 mil. **Budget** (2004 est.): $14.6 bil. **Intl. reserves less gold:** $7.84 bil. **Gold:** 1.11 mil oz t. **Consumer prices:** 3.66%.

Transport: Railroad: Length: 1,136 mi. **Motor vehicles:** 834,200 pass. cars, 508,000 comm. vehicles. **Civil aviation:** 1.6 bil pass.-mi; 49 airports. **Chief ports:** Callao, Chimbote, Matarani, Salaverry.

Communications: TV sets: 147 per 1,000 pop. **Radios:** 273 per 1,000 pop. **Telephone lines:** 1.8 mil. **Daily newspaper circ.:** 85 per 1,000 pop. **Internet**: 2.9 mil users.

Health: Life expect.: 67.8 male; 71.4 female. **Births** (per 1,000 pop.): 20.9. **Deaths** (per 1,000 pop.): 6.3. **Natural inc.:** 1.46%. **Infant mortality** (per 1,000 live births): 31.9. **AIDS rate:** 0.5%.

Education: Compulsory: ages 6-16. **Literacy:** 90.9%.

Major Intl. Organizations: UN and all of its specialized agencies, APEC, OAS.

Embassy: 1700 Massachusetts Ave. NW 20036; 833-9860.

Website: www.peru.info/perueng.asp

The powerful Inca empire had its seat at Cuzco in the Andes and covered most of Peru, Bolivia, and Ecuador, as well as parts of Colombia, Chile, and Argentina. Building on the achievements of 800 years of Andean civilization, the Incas had a high level of skill in architecture, engineering, textiles, and social organization.

A civil war had weakened the empire when Francisco Pizarro, Spanish conquistador, began raiding Peru for its wealth, 1532. In 1533 he seized the ruling Inca, Atahualpa, filled a room with gold as a ransom, then executed him and enslaved the natives.

Lima was the seat of Spanish viceroys until the Argentine liberator, José de San Martin, captured it in 1821; Spanish forces were ultimately routed by Simón Bolívar, 1824.

On Oct. 3, 1968, a military coup ousted Pres. Fernando Belaunde Terry. In 1968-74, the military government started socialist programs. Food shortages, escalating foreign debt, and strikes led to another coup, Aug. 29, 1976.

After 12 years of military rule, Peru returned to democratic leadership in 1980 but was plagued by economic problems and by leftist Shining Path (Sendero Luminoso) guerrillas. Conflict between guerrillas and government troops, 1980-2000, killed more than 69,000 people, mostly Andean Indians.

Elected president in June 1990, Alberto Fujimori, the son of Japanese immigrants, dissolved the National Congress, suspended parts of the constitution, and initiated press censorship, Apr. 5, 1992. The leader of Shining Path was captured Sept. 12.

With the economy booming and signs of significant progress in curtailing guerrilla activity, Fujimori won reelection Apr. 9, 1995. Repressive antiterrorism tactics, however, drew international criticism. On Dec. 17, 1996, leftist Tupac Amaru guerrillas infiltrated a reception at the Japanese ambassador's residence in Lima and took hundreds of hostages, most of whom were later released. Peruvian soldiers stormed the embassy Apr. 22, 1997, rescuing 71 of the remaining hostages; 1 hostage, 2 soldiers, and all 14 guerrillas were killed. Fujimori's path to a 3rd term was cleared when his lone remaining challenger withdrew, charging electoral fraud, 6 days before a runoff vote on May 28, 2000. Scandals involving his top aide and intelligence chief, Vladimiro Montesinos, led Fujimori to resign his office Nov. 20, while on a visit to Japan; instead of accepting his resignation, Congress ousted him as "morally unfit."

Alejandro Toledo won a presidential runoff election June 3, 2001. Montesinos was captured in Venezuela June 23 and extradited to Peru and sentenced on abuse of power charges July 1, 2002. Charges were filed Sept. 5 against the exiled Fujimori, alleging his complicity in the killings by a paramilitary death squad of at least 25 people during 1991-92.

Fireworks explosions killed 291 people in a crowded Lima commercial district Dec. 29, 2001. A sagging economy, resurgent rebel activity, and a series of scandals eroded Toledo's popularity during 2003-05.

Philippines
Republic of the Philippines

People: Population: 87,857,473. **Age distrib.** (%): <15: 35.4; 65+: 4.0. **Pop. density:** 758 per sq mi, 293 per sq km. **Urban:** 61.0%. **Ethnic groups:** Christian Malay 91.5%, Muslim Malay 4%, Chinese 1.5%. **Principal languages:** Filipino, English (both official); many dialects. **Chief religions:** Roman Catholic 81%, Muslim 5%.

Geography: Total area: 115,831 sq mi, 300,000 sq km; **Land area:** 115,124 sq mi, 298,170 sq km. **Location:** An archipelago off the SE coast of Asia. **Neighbors:** Nearest are Malaysia and Indonesia on S, Taiwan on N. **Topography:** The country consists of some 7,100 islands stretching 1,100 mi. N-S. About 95% of area and population are on 11 largest islands, which are mountainous, except for the heavily indented coastlines and for the central plain on Luzon. **Capital:** Manila, 10,352,000. **Cities (urban aggr.):** Quezon City, 2,160,000; Davao, 1,152,000.

Government: Type: Republic. **Head of state and gov.:** Pres. Gloria Macapagal Arroyo; b Apr. 5, 1947; in office: Jan. 20, 2001. **Local divisions:** 79 provinces. **Defense budget** (2004): $807 mil. **Active troops:** 106,000.

Economy: Industries: textiles, pharm., chemicals, wood products, food proc., electronics. **Chief crops:** rice, coconuts, corn, sugarcane, bananas, pineapples. **Natural resources:** timber, oil, nickel, cobalt, silver, gold, salt, copper. **Crude oil reserves** (2004): 152 mil. **Arable land:** 19%. **Livestock** (2004): cattle: 2.6 mil; chickens: 122.0 mil; goats: 6.3 mil; pigs: 12.6 mil; sheep: 30,000. **Fish catch** (2003): 2,628,779 metric tons. **Electricity prod.** (2003): 47.8 bil kWh. **Labor force** (2004 est.): agriculture 36%, industry 16%, services 48%

Finance: Monetary unit: Peso (PHP) (Sept. 2005: 56.21 = $1 U.S.). **GDP** (2004 est.): $430.6 bil; **per capita GDP:** $5,000; **GDP growth:** 5.9%. **Imports** (2004 est.): $37.5 bil; partners (2004): Japan 20.6%, US 16%, Singapore 8.4%, China 7.4%, Hong Kong 5.3%, South Korea 5.2%, Taiwan 4.5%, Malaysia 4.4%. **Exports** (2004 est.): $38.6 bil; partners (2004): US 17.5%, Japan 15.8%, China 11.4%, Hong Kong 8.3%, Singapore 7.7%, Taiwan 6.4%, Netherlands 6%, Malaysia 5.5%, Germany 4.2%. **Tourism:** $1,464 mil. **Budget** (2004 est.): $15.8 bil. **Intl. reserves less gold:** $8.45 bil. **Gold:** 7.12 mil oz t. **Consumer prices:** 5.98%.

Transport: Railroad: Length: 557 mi. **Motor vehicles:** 2.4 mil pass. cars, 291,700 comm. vehicles. **Civil aviation:** 8.4 bil pass.-mi; 82 airports. **Chief ports:** Cebu, Manila, Iloilo, Davao.

Communications: TV sets: 110 per 1,000 pop. **Radios:** 161 per 1,000 pop. **Telephone lines:** 3.3 mil. **Daily newspaper circ.:** 79 per 1,000 pop. **Internet** (2002): 3.5 mil users.

Health: Life expect.: 67.0 male; 72.9 female. **Births** (per 1,000 pop.): 25.3. **Deaths** (per 1,000 pop.): 5.5. **Natural inc.:** 1.98%. **Infant mortality** (per 1,000 live births): 23.5. **AIDS rate:** <0.1%.

Education: Compulsory: ages 6-12. **Literacy:** 92.6%.

Major Intl. Organizations: UN (FAO, IBRD, ILO, IMF, IMO, WHO, WTrO), ASEAN.

Embassy: 1600 Massachusetts Ave. NW 20036; 467-9300.

Website: www.gov.ph

Originally inhabited by Malay peoples, the archipelago was visited by Magellan, 1521. The Spanish founded Manila, 1571. The islands, named for King Philip II of Spain, were ceded by Spain to the U.S. for $20 million, 1898, following the Spanish-American War. U.S. troops suppressed a guerrilla uprising in a brutal 6-year war, 1899-1905.

Japan attacked the Philippines Dec. 8, 1941, and occupied the islands during WW II. On July 4, 1946, independence was proclaimed in accordance with an act passed by the U.S. Congress in 1934. A republic was established.

The repressive and corrupt regime of Pres. Ferdinand Marcos and his wife, Imelda, ruled the Philippines 1965-86. The assassination of prominent opposition leader Benigno S. Aquino Jr., Aug. 21, 1983, sparked demonstrations calling for Marcos's resignation. After a bitter presidential campaign, amid allegations of widespread election fraud, Marcos was declared the victor Feb. 16, 1986, over Corazon Aquino, widow of the slain opposition leader. With his support collapsing, Marcos fled the country Feb. 25, and Corazon Aquino became president.

Her government was plagued by a weak economy, widespread poverty, Communist and Muslim insurgencies, and lukewarm military support. Rebel troops seized military bases and TV stations and bombed the presidential palace, Dec. 1, 1989. Government forces, with U.S. air support, defeated the attempted coup. Aquino endorsed Fidel Ramos in the May 1992 presidential election, which he won. The U.S. vacated the Subic Bay Naval Station in late 1992, ending its long military presence in the Philippines. The government signed a cease-fire agreement, Jan. 30, 1994, with Muslim separatist guerrillas, but some rebels refused to abide by the accord. A new treaty providing for expansion and development of an autonomous Muslim region on Mindanao was signed Sept. 2, 1996, formally ending a rebellion that had claimed more than 120,000 lives since 1972.

Running as a populist, Joseph (Erap) Estrada, a former movie actor, won the presidential election of May 11, 1998. Charged with bribery and corruption, he was impeached Nov. 13, 2000. When the Supreme Court ruled the presidency vacant Jan. 20, 2001, Vice-Pres. Gloria Macapagal Arroyo became president.

As part of the war on terrorism, the U.S. assisted Filipino troops in combating Abu Sayyaf, an Islamic guerrilla group; the leader of the extremists, Abu Sabaya, was killed June 21, 2002. A resurgence of terrorism on Mindanao in 2003 included bombings at Davao's airport, Mar. 4, and ferry terminal, Apr. 2. A mutiny by some 300 troops in Manila, July 27, was suppressed.

Pres. Arroyo won reelection May 10, 2004. Arroyo, who sent a small contingent of Filipino troops to support the U.S. in Iraq, removed them July 19, ahead of schedule, in order to win the freedom of a Filipino truck driver held hostage by Iraqi insurgents. Flooding and mudslides from tropical storms, Nov.-Dec. 2004, left at least 1,060 people dead, more than 560 missing, and 880,000 displaced. Arroyo's supporters in the legislature beat back, Sept. 6, 2005, an effort to impeach her based on corruption charges involving her husband and allegations that she had interfered in the 2004 vote counting.

Poland
Republic of Poland

People: Population: 38,557,984. **Age distrib.** (%): <15: 16.7; 65+: 13.0. **Pop. density:** 319 per sq mi, 123 per sq km. **Urban:** 61.9%. **Ethnic groups:** Polish 98%, German 1%. **Principal languages:** Polish (official), Ukrainian, German. **Chief religion:** Roman Catholic 90%, unspecified 8%.

Geography: Total area: 120,728 sq mi, 312,685 sq km; **Land area:** 117,555 sq mi, 304,465 sq km. **Location:** On the Baltic Sea in E central Europe. **Neighbors:** Germany on W; Czech Rep., Slovakia on S; Lithuania, Belarus, Ukraine on E; Russia on N. **Topography:** Mostly lowlands forming part of the Northern European Plain. The Carpathian Mts. along the S border rise to 8,200 ft. **Capital:** Warsaw, 2,200,000. **Cities:** Katowice, 3,069,000; Lodz, 974,000; Krakow, 859,000.

Government: Type: Republic. **Head of state:** Pres. Aleksander Kwasniewski; b Nov. 15, 1954; in office: Dec. 23, 1995. **Head of gov.:** New government pending after Sept. 25, 2005 elections. **Local divisions:** 16 provinces. **Defense budget** (2004): $4.4 bil. **Active troops:** 141,500.

Economy: Industries: machinery, iron & steel, coal, chemicals, shipbuilding, food proc., glass, beverages, textiles. **Chief crops:** potatoes, fruits, vegetables, wheat. **Natural resources:** coal, sulfur, copper, nat. gas, silver, lead, salt. **Crude oil reserves** (2004): 96 mil. **Arable land:** 47%. **Livestock** (2004): cattle: 5.3 mil; chickens: 49.0 mil; pigs: 18.1 mil; sheep: 340,000. **Fish catch** (2003): 214,780 metric tons. **Electricity prod.** (2003): 141.2 bil kWh. **Labor force** (2002): agriculture 16.1%, industry 29%, services 54.9%.

Finance: Monetary unit: Zloty (PLN) (Sept. 2005: 3.19 = $1 U.S.). **GDP** (2004 est.): $463.0 bil; **per capita GDP:** $12,000; **GDP growth:** 5.6%. **Imports** (2004 est.): $81.6 bil; partners (2004): Germany 29.8%, Italy 8%, France 7%, Russia 6.9%, Netherlands 5.3%, Belgium 4.2%. **Exports** (2004 est.): $76.0 bil; partners (2004): Germany 29.8%, Italy 6.3%, France 5.4%, UK 4.7%, Czech Republic 4.4%. **Tourism:** $4,069 mil. **Budget** (2004 est.): $54.9 bil. **Intl. reserves less gold:** $22.75 bil. **Gold:** 3.31 mil oz t. **Consumer prices:** 2.4%.

Transport: Railroad: Length: 14,553 mi. **Motor vehicles:** 10.5 mil pass. cars, 2.06 mil comm. vehicles. **Civil aviation:** 3.1 bil pass.-mi; 88 airports. **Chief ports:** Gdansk, Gdynia, Ustka, Szczecin.

Communications: TV sets: 387 per 1,000 pop. **Radios:** 522 per 1,000 pop. **Telephone lines:** 12.3 mil. **Daily newspaper circ.:** 101.8 per 1,000 pop. **Internet**: 9.0 mil users.

Health: Life expect.: 70.7 male; 79.0 female. **Births** (per 1,000 pop.): 9.7. **Deaths** (per 1,000 pop.): 9.8. **Natural inc.:** -0.01%. **Infant mortality** (per 1,000 live births): 7.4. **AIDS rate:** 0.1%.

Education: Compulsory: ages 7-15. **Literacy:** 99.8%.

Major Intl. Organizations: UN (FAO, IBRD, ILO, IMF, IMO, WHO, WTrO), EU, NATO, OECD, OSCE.

Embassy: 2640 16th St. NW 20009; 234-3800.

Website: www.poland.pl

Slavic tribes in the area were converted to Latin Christianity in the 10th century. Poland was a great power from the 14th to the 17th centuries. In 3 partitions (1772, 1793, 1795) it was apportioned among Prussia, Russia, and Austria. Overrun by the Austro-German armies in World War I, it declared its independence on Nov. 11, 1918, and was recognized as independent by the Treaty of Versailles, June 28, 1919. Large territories to the east were taken in a war with Russia, 1921.

Germany and the USSR invaded Poland Sept. 1-27, 1939, and divided the country. During the war, some 6 million Polish citizens, half of them Jews, were killed by the Nazis. With Germany's defeat, a Polish government-in-exile in London was recognized by the U.S., but the USSR pressed the claims of a rival group. The election of 1947 was completely dominated by the Communists.

In compensation for 69,860 sq. mi. ceded to the USSR, in 1945 Poland received approx. 40,000 sq. mi. of German territory E of the Oder-Neisse line comprising Silesia, Pomerania, West Prussia, and part of East Prussia.

In 12 years of rule by Stalinists, large estates were abolished, industries nationalized, schools secularized, and Roman Catholic prelates jailed. Farm production fell off. Harsh working conditions caused a riot in Poznan, June 28-29, 1956. A new Politburo, committed to a more independent Polish Communism, was named Oct. 1956, with Wladyslaw Gomulka as first secretary of the party. Collectivization of farms was ended. Gomulka agreed to permit religious liberty and religious publications, provided the church kept out of politics.

In Dec. 1970 workers in port cities rioted because of price rises and new incentive wage rules. On Dec. 20 Gomulka resigned as party leader; he was succeeded by Edward Gierek. The rules were dropped and price rises revoked.

After 2 months of labor turmoil had crippled the country, the Polish government, Aug. 30, 1980, met the demands of striking workers at the Lenin Shipyard, Gdansk. Government concessions included the right to form independent trade unions and the right to strike. By 1981, 9.5 mil workers had joined the independent trade union (Solidarity). As Solidarity's demands grew bolder, the government, spurred by fear of Soviet intervention, imposed martial law Dec. 13. Lech Walesa and other Solidarity leaders were arrested.

On Apr. 5, 1989, an accord was reached between the government and opposition factions on political and economic reforms, including free elections. Candidates endorsed by Solidarity swept the parliamentary elections, June 4. Lech Walesa became president Dec. 22, 1990.

A radical economic program designed to transform the economy into a free-market system led to inflation and unemployment. In Sept. 1993, former Communists and other leftists won a majority in the lower house of Parliament. Walesa lost to a former Communist, Aleksander Kwasniewski, in a presidential runoff election, Nov. 19, 1995.

A new constitution was approved by referendum May 25, 1997. Flooding in July caused more than $1 billion in property damage. Solidarity won parliamentary elections held Sept. 21. Poland became a full member of NATO on Mar. 12, 1999. Pres. Kwasniewski was reelected Oct. 8, 2000. The former Communists won a plurality in parliamentary voting Sept. 23, 2001. But on Sept. 25, 2005, the scandal-ridden former communists achieved only 11% of the votes, leaving government to a center-right coalition.

Poland, a close U.S. ally, assumed command Sept. 3, 2003, of a 9,000-member multinational force in south-central Iraq. Poland entered the European Union May 1, 2004.

Portugal
Portuguese Republic

People: Population: 10,566,212. **Age distrib.** (%): <15: 16.6; 65+: 17.1. **Pop. density:** 296 per sq mi, 114 per sq km. **Urban:** 54.6%. **Ethnic groups:** Mainly Portuguese. **Principal languages:** Portuguese (official). **Chief religion:** Roman Catholic 94%.

Geography: Total area: 35,672 sq mi, 92,391 sq km; **Land area:** 35,502 sq mi, 91,951 sq km. **Location:** At SW extreme of Europe. Neighbors: Spain on N, E. **Topography:** Portugal N of Tajus R., which bisects the country NE-SW, is mountainous, cool and rainy. To the S there are drier, rolling plains, and a warm climate. **Capital:** Lisbon, 1,962,000. **Cities (urban agg.):** Porto, 1,254,000.

Government: Type: Republic. **Head of state:** Pres. Jorge Sampaio; b Sept. 18, 1939; in office: Mar. 9, 1996. **Head of gov.:** Prime Min. José Sócrates Carvalho Pinto de Sousa; b Sept. 6, 1957; in office: Mar. 12, 2005. **Local divisions:** 18 districts, 2 autonomous regions. **Defense budget** (2004): $2.1 bil. **Active troops:** 44,900.

Economy: Industries: textiles, footwear, wood and paper products, metalworking, oil refining, chemicals, fish proc, wine, tourism. **Chief crops:** grain, potatoes, olives, grapes. **Natural resources:** fish, cork, tungsten, iron ore, uranium ore, marble, hydropower. **Arable land:** 26%. **Livestock** (2004): cattle: 1.4 mil; chickens: 35.0 mil; goats: 502,000; pigs: 2.2 mil; sheep: 5.5 mil. **Fish catch** (2003): 220,778 metric tons. **Electricity prod.** (2003): 44.3 bil kWh. **Labor force** (1999 est.): agriculture 10%, industry 30%, services 60%.

Finance: Monetary unit: Euro (EUR) (Sept. 2005: 0.80 = $1 U.S.). **GDP** (2004 est.): $188.7 bil; **per capita GDP:** $17,900; **GDP growth:** 1.1%. **Imports** (2004 est.): $52.1 bil; partners (2004): Spain 29.3%, Germany 14.4%, France 9.7%, Italy 6.1%, Netherlands 4.6%, UK 4.5%. **Exports** (2004 est.): $37.7 bil; partners (2004): Spain 24.8%, France 14%, Germany 13.5%, UK 9.6%, US 6%, Italy 4.3%, Belgium 4.1%. **Tourism:** $6,937 mil. **Budget** (2004 est.): $79.9 bil. **Intl. reserves less gold:** $3.33 bil. **Gold:** 14.86 mil oz t. **Consumer prices:** 2.36%.

Transport: Railroad: Length: 1,771 mi. **Motor vehicles:** 5.54 mil pass. cars, 1.83 mil comm. vehicles. **Civil aviation:** 6.9 bil pass.-mi; 40 airports. **Chief ports:** Lisbon, Setubal, Leixoes.

Communications: TV sets: 567 per 1,000 pop. **Radios:** 306 per 1,000 pop. **Telephone lines:** 4.3 mil. **Daily newspaper circ.:** 32 per 1,000 pop. **Internet** (2002): 2.0 mil users.

Health: Life expect.: 74.3 male; 81.0 female. **Births** (per 1,000 pop.): 10.8. **Deaths** (per 1,000 pop.): 10.4. **Natural inc.:** 0.04%. **Infant mortality** (per 1,000 live births): 5.1. **AIDS rate:** 0.4%.

Education: Compulsory: ages 6-14. **Literacy:** 93.3%.

Major Intl. Organizations: UN (FAO, IBRD, ILO, IMF, IMO, WHO, WTrO), EU, NATO, OECD, OSCE.

Embassy: 2125 Kalorama Rd. NW 20008; 328-8610.

Website: www.portugal.gov.pt/Portal/EN/

Portugal, an independent state since the 12th century, was a kingdom until a revolution in 1910 drove out King Manoel II and a republic was proclaimed. From 1932 a strong, repressive government was headed by Premier Antonio de Oliveira Salazar. Illness forced his retirement in Sept. 1968.

On Apr. 25, 1974, the government was seized by a military junta led by Gen. Antonio de Spinola, who became president. The new government reached agreements providing independence for

Guinea-Bissau, Mozambique, Cape Verde Islands, Angola, and São Tomé and Príncipe. Banks, insurance companies, and other industries were nationalized.

Parliament approved, June 1, 1989, a program to denationalize industries. Portugal returned Macao to China on Dec. 20, 1999. With the economy lagging, opposition Socialists won a parliamentary majority in elections Feb. 20, 2005.

Azores Islands, in the Atlantic, 740 mi W of Portugal, have an area of 868 sq mi and a pop. (1993 est.) of 238,000. A 1951 agreement gave the U.S. rights to use defense facilities in the Azores. The **Madeira Islands,** 350 mi off the NW coast of Africa, have an area of 306 sq mi and a pop. (1993 est.) of 437,312. Both groups were offered partial autonomy in 1976.

Qatar

State of Qatar

People: Population: 863,051. **Age distrib.** (%): <15: 23.7; 65+: 3.4. **Pop. density:** 195 per sq mi, 75 per sq km. **Urban:** 92.0%. **Ethnic groups:** Arab 40%, Pakistani 18%, Indian 18%, Iranian 10%. **Principal languages:** Arabic (official), English. **Chief religion:** Muslim 95% (official).

Geography: Total area: 4,416 sq mi, 11,437 sq km; **Land area:** 4,416 sq mi, 11,437 sq km. **Location:** Middle East, occupying peninsula on W coast of Persian Gulf. **Neighbors:** Saudi Arabia on S. **Topography:** Mostly a flat desert, with some limestone ridges; vegetation of any kind is scarce. **Capital:** Doha, 286,000.

Government: Type: Traditional monarchy. **Head of state:** Emir Hamad bin Khalifa ath-Thani; b 1952; in office: June 27, 1995. **Head of gov.:** Prime Min. Abdullah bin Khalifa ath-Thani; b Dec. 25, 1959; in office: Oct. 29, 1996. **Local divisions:** 9 municipalities. **Defense budget** (2004): $2.1 bil. **Active troops:** 12,400.

Economy: Industries: oil prod. & refining, fertilizers, petrochems., constr. materials. **Chief crops:** fruits, vegetables. **Natural resources:** oil, nat. gas, fish. **Crude oil reserves** (2004): 15.2 bil bbls. **Livestock** (2004): cattle: 10,000; chickens: 4.5 mil; goats: 180,000; sheep: 200,000. **Fish catch** (2003): 11,000 metric tons. **Electricity prod.** (2003): 9.7 bil kWh.

Finance: Monetary unit: Riyal (QAR) (Sept. 2005: 3.64 = $1 U.S.). **GDP** (2004 est.): $19.5 bil; **per capita GDP:** $23,200; **GDP growth:** 8.7%. **Imports** (2004 est.): $6.2 bil; partners (2004): France 24.4%, UK 8.9%, Germany 8.8%, Japan 8.7%, US 6.2%, Italy 5.5%, UAE 4.1%. **Exports** (2004 est.): $15.0 bil; partners (2004): Japan 43.8%, South Korea 16.1%, Singapore 10.8%. **Budget** (2004 est.): $7.6 bil. **Intl. reserves less gold:** $2.19 bil. **Gold:** 40,000 oz t. **Consumer prices:** 6.8%

Transport: Motor vehicles: 199,600 pass. cars, 92,900 comm. vehicles. **Civil aviation:** 4.0 bil. pass.-mi; 2 airports. **Chief ports:** Doha, Umm Sáid.

Communications: TV sets: 866 per 1,000 pop. **Radios:** 450 per 1,000 pop. **Telephone lines:** 184,500. **Daily newspaper circ.:** 146 per 1,000 pop. **Internet**: 140,800 users.

Health: Life expect.: 71.2 male; 76.3 female. **Births** (per 1,000 pop.): 15.5. **Deaths** (per 1,000 pop.): 4.6. **Natural inc.:** 1.09%. **Infant mortality** (per 1,000 live births): 18.6.

Education: Compulsory: ages 6-17. **Literacy:** 82.5%.

Major Intl. Organizations: UN (FAO, IBRD, ILO, IMF, IMO, WHO, WTrO), AL, OPEC.

Embassy: 2555 M St NW 20037 274-1603.

Website: english.mofa.gov.qa/

Qatar was under Bahrain's control until the Ottoman Turks took power, 1872 to 1915. In a treaty signed 1916, Qatar gave Great Britain responsibility for its defense and foreign relations. After Britain announced it would remove its military forces from the Persian Gulf area by the end of 1971, Qatar sought a federation with other British-protected states in the area; this failed and Qatar declared itself independent, Sept. 1, 1971. Crown Prince Hamad bin Khalifa ath-Thani ousted his father, Emir Khalifa bin Hamad ath-Thani, June 27, 1995. In municipal elections held Mar. 8, 1999, women participated for the 1st time as candidates and voters.

Oil and natural gas revenues give Qatar a per capita income among the world's highest. Military ties with the U.S. have been expanding; Camp As-Sayliyah, a base near Doha, served as a command center for the U.S.-led invasion of Iraq, Mar. 2003. The influential Arab news network Al-Jazeera is based in Qatar.

Romania

People: Population: 22,329,977. **Age distrib.** (%): <15: 15.9; 65+: 14.6. **Pop. density:** 244 per sq mi, 94 per sq km. **Urban:** 54.5%. **Ethnic groups:** Romanian 90%, Hungarian, Roma, and others 10%. **Principal languages:** Romanian (official), Hungarian, German, Romani. **Chief religions:** Romanian Orthodox 87%, Protestant 8%, Roman Catholic 5%.

Geography: Total area: 91,699 sq mi, 237,500 sq km; **Land area:** 88,935 sq mi, 230,340 sq km. **Location:** SE Europe, on the Black Sea. **Neighbors:** Moldova on E, Ukraine on N, Hungary and Serbia and Montenegro on W, Bulgaria on S. **Topography:** The Carpathian Mts. encase the north-central Transylvanian plateau. There are wide plains S and E of the mountains, through which flow the lower reaches of the rivers of the Danube system. **Capital:** Bucharest ,1,853,000.

Government: Type: Republic. **Head of state:** Pres. Traian Basescu; b Nov. 4, 1951; in office: Dec. 20, 2004. **Head of gov.:** Prime Min. Calin Constantin Anton Popescu-Tariceanu; b Jan. 14, 1952; in office: Dec. 29, 2004. **Local divisions:** 41 counties and Bucharest. **Defense budget** (2002): $1.4 bil. **Active troops:** 97,200.

Economy: Industries: textiles & footwear, light machinery, auto assembly, mining, timber. **Chief crops:** wheat, corn, sugar beets, sunflower seed, potatoes, grapes. **Natural resources:** oil, timber, nat. gas, coal, iron ore, salt, hydropower. **Crude oil reserves** (2004): 956 mil bbls. **Arable land:** 41%. **Livestock** (2004): cattle: 2.9 mil; chickens: 76.6 mil; goats: 678,000; pigs: 5.1 mil; sheep: 7.5 mil. **Fish catch** (2003): 19,092 metric tons. **Electricity prod.** (2003): 51.7 bil kWh. **Labor force** (2004): agriculture 31.6%, industry 30.7%, services 37.7%.

Finance: Monetary unit: Lei (RON) (Sept. 2005: 2.98 = $1 U.S.). **GDP** (2004 est.): $171.5 bil; **per capita GDP:** $7,700; **GDP growth:** 8.1%. **Imports** (2004 est.): $28.4 bil; partners (2004): Italy 18.3%, Germany 17.9%, France 7.2%, Hungary 6.1%, Russia 5.7%, Austria 5.5%, Turkey 4.3%. **Exports** (2004 est.): $23.5 bil; partners (2004): Italy 20.9%, Germany 15.4%, France 7.3%, Turkey 7%, UK 6.1%, Austria 5%. **Tourism:** $449 mil. **Budget** (2004 est.): $23.2 bil. **Intl. reserves less gold:** $9.41 bil. **Gold:** 3.38 mil oz t. **Consumer prices:** 11.88%.

Transport: Railroad: Length: 7,074 mi **Motor vehicles:** 3.23 mil pass. cars, 504,000 comm. vehicles. **Civil aviation:** 1.2 bil pass.-mi; 26 airports. **Chief ports:** Constanta, Braila.

Communications: TV sets: 312 per 1,000 pop. **Radios:** 335 per 1,000 pop. **Telephone lines:** 4.3 mil. **Daily newspaper circ.:** 300 per 1,000 pop. **Internet**: 4.0 mil users.

Health: Life expect.: 67.9 male; 75.1 female. **Births** (per 1,000 pop.): 10.7. **Deaths** (per 1,000 pop.): 11.7. **Natural inc.:** -0.10%. **Infant mortality** (per 1,000 live births): 26.4. **AIDS rate:** <0.1%.

Education: Compulsory: ages 7-14. **Literacy:** 98.4%.

Major Intl. Organizations: UN (FAO, IBRD, ILO, IMF, IMO, WHO, WTrO), NATO, OSCE.

Embassy: 1607 23rd St. NW 20008; 332-4846.

Website: www.guv.ro/engleza/index.php

Romania's earliest known people merged with invading Proto-Thracians, preceding by centuries the Dacians. The Dacian kingdom was occupied by Rome, AD 106-271; people and language were Romanized. The principalities of Wallachia and Moldavia, dominated by Turkey, were united in 1859, became Romania in 1861, and gained recognition as an independent kingdom, 1881.

After World War I, Romania acquired Bessarabia, Bukovina, Transylvania, and Banat. In 1940 it ceded Bessarabia and Northern Bukovina to the USSR, part of southern Dobrudja to Bulgaria, and northern Transylvania to Hungary. In 1941, Prem. Marshal Ion Antonescu led Romania in support of Germany against the USSR. In 1944 he was overthrown, and Romania joined the Allies. After occupation by Soviet troops, a People's Republic was proclaimed, Dec. 30, 1947.

On Aug. 22, 1965, a new constitution proclaimed Romania a Socialist Republic. Pres. Nicolae Ceausescu maintained an independent course in foreign affairs, but his domestic policies were repressive. All industry was state-owned, and state farms and cooperatives owned almost all arable land. Ceasescu's security forces fired on antigovernment demonstrators in Dec. 1989, killing hundreds, but when the army sided with the protesters, his regime fell. Ceausescu and his wife were captured and, following a trial in which they were found guilty of genocide, were executed Dec. 25, 1989.

Former Communists dominated the government in succeeding years. A new constitution providing for a multiparty system took effect Dec. 8, 1991. Many of Romania's state-owned companies were privatized in 1996. The former Communists lost in elections Nov. 3 and 17, 1996, but made a comeback in balloting Nov. 26 and Dec. 10, 2000. Opposition leader Traian Basescu, the mayor of Bucharest, won a presidential runoff vote, Dec. 12, 2004. Romania, a firm US ally, had about 860 troops in Iraq and 700 in Afghanistan in mid-2005.

Floods in Jul.-Aug. 2005 left more than 50 people dead.

Romania became a full NATO member in 2004 and is expected to enter the EU in 2007.

Russia

Russian Federation

People: Population: 143,420,309. **Age distrib.** (%): <15: 14.6; 65+: 14.2. **Pop. density:** 22 per sq mi, 8 per sq km. **Urban:** 73.3%. **Ethnic groups:** Russian 82%, Tatar 4%, Ukrainian 3%, Chuvash 1%, Bashkir 1%, Belarusian 1%, Moldavian 1%. **Principal languages:** Russian (official), many others. **Chief religions:** Russian Orthodox, Muslim.

Geography: Total area: 6,592,772 sq mi, 17,075,200 sq km; **Land area:** 6,562,116 sq mi, 16,995,800 sq km., more than 76% of total area of the former USSR and the largest country in the world. **Location:** Stretches from E Europe across N Asia to the Pacific O. **Neighbors:** Finland, Norway, Estonia, Latvia, Belarus, Ukraine on W; Georgia, Azerbaijan, Kazakhstan, China, Mongolia, North Korea on S; Kaliningrad exclave bordered by Poland on the S, Lithuania on the N and E. **Topography:** Russia contains every type of climate except the distinctly tropical, and has a varied topography. The European portion is a low plain, grassy in S, wooded in N, with Ural Mts. on the E, and Caucasus Mts. on the S. Urals stretch N-S for 2,500 mi The Asiatic portion is also a vast plain, with mountains on the S and in the E; tundra covers extreme N, with forest belt below; plains, marshes are in W, desert in SW. **Capital:** Moscow, 10,469,000. **Cities (urban aggr.):** St. Petersburg, 5,214,000; Nizhniy Novgorod, 1,331,000; Novosibirsk, 1,426,000.

Government: Type: Federal republic. **Head of state:** Vladimir Putin; b Oct. 7, 1952; in office: May 7, 2000. **Head of gov.:** Prime Min. Mikhail Fradkov; b Sep. 1, 1950; in office: Mar. 5, 2004. **Local divisions:** 7 federal districts incl. 49 provinces, 21 autonomous republics, 6 territories, 1 autonomous region, 10 autonomous districts, 2 federal cities. **Defense budget** (2004): $14.2 bil. **Active troops:** 1,212,700.

Economy: Industries: coal, oil, gas, chemicals, metals; light machinery, shipbuilding; transp., communic. equip., agric. machinery, constr. equip., electric power equip., medical & scientific instruments, consumer durables, textiles. **Chief crops:** grain, sugar beets, sunflower seed, vegetables, fruits. **Natural resources:** oil, nat. gas, coal, minerals, timber. **Crude oil reserves** (2004): 60 bil bbls. **Arable land:** 8%. **Livestock** (2004): cattle: 24.9 mil; chickens: 328.5 mil; goats: 2.3 mil; pigs: 16.0 mil; sheep: 14.7 mil. **Fish catch** (2003): 3,389,932 metric tons. **Electricity prod.** (2003): 883.3 bil kWh. **Labor force** (2002 est.): agriculture 12.3%, industry 22.7%, services 65%.

Finance: Monetary unit: Ruble (RUB) (Sept. 2005: 28.42 = $1 U.S. NOTE: On Jan 1, 1998, Russia eliminated 3 digits from the ruble.) **GDP** (2004 est.): $1.4 tril.; **per capita GDP:** $9,800; **GDP growth:** 6.7%. **Imports** (2004 est.): $92.9 bil; partners (2004): Germany 16.7%, China 7.1%, Ukraine 6.7%, Italy 5.9%, Finland 5%, France 4.5%, Japan 4.5%. **Exports** (2004 est.): $162.5 bil; partners (2004): Germany 8.4%, Netherlands 6.7%, China 6.4%, US 5.8%, Ukraine 5.7%, Italy 5.4%, Turkey 4.5%. **Tourism:** $4,502 mil. **Budget** (2004 est.): $93.3 bil. **Intl. reserves less gold:** $77.79 bil. **Gold:** 12.44 mil oz t. **Consumer prices:** 10.88%.

Transport: Railroad: Length: 54,157 mi **Motor vehicles:** 22.34 mil pass. cars, 4.33 mil comm. vehicles. **Civil aviation:** 30.0 bil pass.-mi; 471 airports. **Chief ports:** St. Petersburg, Murmansk, Arkhangelsk.

Communications: TV sets: 421 per 1,000 pop. **Radios:** 417 per 1,000 pop. **Telephone lines**: 37.0 mil. **Daily newspaper circ.:** 105 per 1,000 pop. **Internet** (2002): 6.0 mil users.

Health: Life expect.: 60.6 male; 74.0 female. **Births** (per 1,000 pop.): 9.8. **Deaths** (per 1,000 pop.): 14.5. **Natural inc.:** -0.47%. **Infant mortality** (per 1,000 live births): 15.4. **AIDS rate:** 1.1%.

Education: Compulsory: ages 6-15. **Literacy:** 99.6%.

Major Intl. Organizations: UN (IBRD, ILO, IMF, IMO, WHO), APEC, CIS, OSCE.

Embassy: 2650 Wisconsin Ave. NW 20007; 298-5700.

Website: www.russianembassy.org

History. Slavic tribes began migrating into Russia from the W in the 5th century AD. The first Russian state, founded by Scandinavian chieftains, was established in the 9th century, centering in Novgorod and Kiev. In the 13th century the Mongols overran the country. It recovered under the grand dukes and princes of Muscovy, or Moscow, and by 1480 freed itself from the Mongols. Ivan the Terrible was the first to be formally proclaimed Tsar (1547). Peter the Great (1682-1725) extended the domain and, in 1721, founded the Russian Empire.

Western ideas and the beginnings of modernization spread through the huge Russian empire in the 19th and early 20th centuries. But political evolution failed to keep pace.

Military reverses in the 1905 war with Japan and in World War I led to the breakdown of the Tsarist regime. The 1917 Revolution began in March with a series of sporadic strikes for higher wages by factory workers. A provisional democratic government under Prince Georgi Lvov was established but was quickly followed in May by the second provisional government, led by Alexander Kerensky. The Kerensky government and the freely-elected Constituent Assembly were overthrown in a Communist coup led by Vladimir Ilyich Lenin Nov. 7.

Soviet Union

Lenin's death Jan. 21, 1924, resulted in an internal power struggle from which Joseph Stalin eventually emerged on top. Stalin secured his position at first by exiling opponents, but from the 1930s to 1953, he resorted to a series of "purge" trials, mass executions, and mass exiles to work camps. These measures resulted in millions of deaths, according to most estimates.

Germany and the Soviet Union signed a non-aggression pact Aug. 1939; Germany launched a massive invasion of the Soviet Union, June 1941. A notable heroic episode was the "900 days" siege of Leningrad (now St. Petersburg), lasting to Jan. 1944, and causing a million deaths; the city was never taken. Russian winter counterthrusts, 1941-42 and 1942-43, stopped the German advance. Turning point was the failure of German troops to take and hold Stalingrad (now Volgograd), Sept. 1942 to Feb. 1943. With British and U.S. Lend-Lease aid and sustaining great casualties, the Russians drove the German forces from eastern Europe and the Balkans in the next 2 years.

After Stalin died, Mar. 5, 1953, Nikita Khrushchev was elected first secretary of the Central Committee. In 1956 he condemned Stalin and "de-Stalinization" began.

Under Khrushchev the open antagonism of Poles and Hungarians toward domination by Moscow was brutally suppressed in 1956. He advocated peaceful co-existence with the capitalist countries, but continued arming the Soviet Union with nuclear weapons. He aided the Cuban revolution under Fidel Castro but withdrew Soviet missiles from Cuba during confrontation by U.S. Pres. Kennedy, Sept.-Oct. 1962. Khrushchev was suddenly deposed, Oct. 1964, and replaced by Leonid I. Brezhnev.

In Aug. 1968 Russian, Polish, East German, Hungarian, and Bulgarian military forces invaded Czechoslovakia to put a curb on liberalization policies of the Czech government.

Massive Soviet military aid to North Vietnam in the late 1960s and early 1970s helped assure Communist victories throughout Indo-China. Soviet arms aid and advisers were sent to several African countries in the 1970s.

In Dec. 1979, Soviet forces entered Afghanistan to support that government against rebels. In Apr. 1988, the Soviets agreed to withdraw their troops, ending a futile 8-year war.

Mikhail Gorbachev was chosen gen. secy. of the Communist Party, Mar. 1985. He held 4 summit meetings with U.S. Pres. Ronald Reagan.In 1987 he initiated a program of political and economic reforms, through openness (*glasnost*) and restructuring (*perestroika*). Gorbachev faced economic problems as well as ethnic and nationalist unrest in the republics. An apparent coup by Communist hardliners. Aug. 1991, was foiled with help from the pres. of the Russian Republic, Boris Yeltsin. On Aug. 24, Gorbachev resigned as leader of the Communist Party. Several republics declared their independence, including Russia, Ukraine, and Kazakhstan. On Aug. 29, the Soviet Parliament voted to suspend all activities of the Communist Party.

The Soviet Union officially broke up Dec. 26, 1991. The Soviet hammer and sickle flying over the Kremlin was lowered and replaced by the flag of Russia, ending the domination of the Communist Party over all areas of national life since 1917.

Russian Federation

Led by Pres. Yeltsin, Russia took steps toward privatization; immediate effects were inflation and a severe economic downturn. In June 1992, Yeltsin and U.S. Pres. George H.W. Bush agreed to massive arms reductions. A power struggle between Yeltsin and the Congress of People's Deputies, which was dominated by conservatives and former Communists, reached a climax Oct. 3, 1993, when anti-Yeltsin forces attacked some facilities in Moscow and broke into the Parliament building. Yeltsin ordered the army to seize the building; about 140 people were killed in the fighting.

Yeltsin remained in power, and in a referendum Dec. 12, 1993, a new constitution was approved. In Dec. 1994 the Russian government sent troops into the breakaway republic of Chechnya. Grozny, the Chechen capital, fell in Feb. 1995 after heavy fighting, but Chechen rebels continued to resist.

Despite poor health, Yeltsin won a presidential runoff election over a Communist opponent, July 3, 1996. On Aug. 14, after rebels embarrassed the Russian military by retaking Grozny, Yeltsin gave his security chief, Alexander Lebed, broad powers to negotiate an end to the Chechnya war. Lebed and Chechen leaders signed a peace accord Aug. 31. On Oct. 17, Yeltsin dismissed Lebed for insubordination. Russian troops remaining in Chechnya were pulled out Jan. 1997. On May 27, Yeltsin signed a "founding act" increasing cooperation with NATO and paving the way for NATO to admit Eastern European nations.

Russia's economic crisis deepened in the late 1990s, heightening tensions between Yeltsin and parliament. Russia moved forcibly in Aug. 1999 to suppress Islamic rebels in Dagestan; the conflict soon spread to neighboring Chechnya, where Russia launched a full-scale assault. A series of 5 bombings in Moscow and Dagestan, which the Russian government attributed to Chechen rebels, killed over 300 people.

Yeltsin unexpectedly resigned Dec. 31, 1999, naming Prime Min. Vladimir Putin as his interim successor. Russian troops took control of Grozny in early Feb. 2000. Putin defeated 10 opponents in a presidential election Mar. 26. The Russian parliament ratified 2 nuclear weapons treaties, the START II arms-reduction accord Apr. 14 and the Comprehensive Test Ban Treaty Apr. 21. A reorganization plan announced May 17 sought to reassert Moscow's control over Russia's regional governments. The Russian nuclear submarine *Kursk* sank in the Barents Sea Aug. 12, killing 118 sailors.

Russia and China signed a 20-year friendship and cooperation treaty July 16, 2001. Putin and U.S. Pres. George W. Bush signed May 24, 2002, an agreement calling for a 2/3 reduction in nuclear weapons stockpiles. However, Russia pulled out of the START II treaty Jun. 14 after the U.S. withdrew from the 1972 ABM Treaty June 13 to develop a missile defense program. Russia joined a new partnership agreement with NATO May 28.

As Russian forces continued their campaign against Islamic separatists in Chechnya, some 50 Chechen guerrillas seized more than 800 hostages in a Moscow theater, Oct. 23, 2002; 129 hostages and nearly all the guerrillas were killed Oct. 26 when Russian special forces used knockout gas in retaking the theater. Russia, which supported the U.S.-led war in Afghanistan in 2001, sided with France and Germany in blocking UN Security Council endorsement of the U.S.-led invasion of Iraq, Mar. 2003.

Putin's allies won legislative elections, Dec. 7, 2003, and the president was reelected Mar. 14, 2004, with 71% of the vote; international election monitors cited flaws on both occasions. Putin blamed Chechen terrorists for a blast on a Moscow subway car, Feb. 6, that killed at least 39 people. A bomb in Grozny, May 9, killed Chechnya's pro-Moscow president, Akhmad Kadyrov, and at least 6 others. Putin's choice for the Chechen presidency, Maj. Gen. Alu Alkhanov, was elected Aug. 29.

The Chechnya conflict unleashed a wave of terrorism elsewhere during Aug.-Sept. 2004. After taking off the night of Aug. 24 from Moscow's Domodedovo airport, 2 passenger planes exploded in midair, killing 90 people. A suicide bombing in a Moscow subway station Aug. 31 left 11 dead. Chechen rebels Sept. 1 seized control of a school in Beslan, N Ossetia, taking more than 1,100 hostages; Russian troops stormed the school Sept. 3; in the end more than 330 people died, about half of them children. Putin cited the terrorist threat Sept. 13 in proposing a government overhaul that would tighten his control over parliament and regional officeholders.

On Nov. 5, 2004, Russia ratified the Kyoto Protocol, which aims to curb greenhouse gas emissions and global warming. Russian forces killed Chechen rebel leader Aslan Maskhadov, Mar. 8, 2005. Mikhail Khodorkovsky, an oil tycoon whose political agenda had rivaled Putin's, was convicted of fraud and tax evasion, May 31, and sentenced to 9 years in prison.

Rwanda

Republic of Rwanda

People: Population: 8,440,820. **Age distrib.** (%): <15: 41.9; 65+: 2.6. **Pop. density:** 830 per sq mi, 320 per sq km. **Urban:** 18.3%. **Ethnic groups:** Hutu 84%, Tutsi 15%, Twa (Pygmy) 1%. **Principal languages:** Kinyarwanda, French, English (all official); Swahili. **Chief religions:** Roman Catholic 57%, Protestant 26%, Adventist 11%, Muslim 5%.

Geography: Total area: 10,169 sq mi, 26,338 sq km; **Land area:** 9,632 sq mi, 24,948 sq km. **Location:** In E central Africa. **Neighbors:** Uganda on N, Congo (formerly Zaire) on W, Burundi on S, Tanzania on E. **Topography:** Grassy uplands and hills cover most of the country, with a chain of volcanoes in the NW. The source of the Nile R. has been located in the headwaters of the Kagera (Akagera) R., SW of Kigali. **Capital:** Kigali, 656,000.

Government: Type: Republic. **Head of state:** Pres. Paul Kagame; b Oct. 1957; in office: Apr. 22, 2000 (de facto from Mar. 24). **Head of gov.:** Prime Min. Bernard Makuza; b 1961; in office: Mar. 8, 2000. **Local divisions:** 12 prefectures subdivided into 155 communes. **Defense budget** (2004): $46 mil. **Active troops:** 51,000.

Economy: Industries: cement, agric. products. **Chief crops:** coffee, tea, pyrethrum (insecticide made from chrysanthemums), bananas. **Natural resources:** gold, tin, tungsten, methane, hydropower. **Crude oil reserves** (2002): 48.6 bil bbls. **Arable land:** 35%. **Livestock** (2004): cattle: 1.0 mil; chickens: 1.3 mil; goats: 760,000; pigs: 180,000; sheep: 260,000. **Fish catch** (2003): 8,427 metric tons. **Electricity prod.** (2003): 0.10 bil kWh. **Labor force**: agriculture 90%.

Finance: Monetary unit: Franc (RWF) (Sept. 2005: 542.23 = $1 U.S.). **GDP** (2004 est.): $10.4 bil; **per capita GDP:** $1,300; **GDP growth:** 0.9%. **Imports** (2004 est.): $260.0 mil; partners (2004): Kenya 21.9%, Germany 7.8%, Belgium 7.7%, Uganda 5.9%, France 5.9%. **Exports** (2004 est.): $69.8 mil; partners (2004): Indonesia 35.4%, China 7.1%, Germany 3.4%. **Tourism** (2002): $31 mil. **Budget** (2004 est.): $385.0 mil. **Intl. reserves less gold:** $203 mil. **Consumer prices:** 11.9%.

Transport: Motor vehicles: 10,700 pass. cars, 16,300 comm. vehicles. **Civil aviation:** 1.2 mil pass.-mi; 4 airports. **Chief ports:** Gisenyi, Cyangugu.

Communications: TV sets: .09 per 1,000 pop. **Radios:** 101 per 1,000 pop. **Telephone lines** (2002): 23,200. **Daily newspaper circ.:** 0.1 per 1,000 pop. **Internet** (2002): 25,000 users.

Health: Life expect.: 45.9 male; 48.0 female. **Births** (per 1,000 pop.): 40.6. **Deaths** (per 1,000 pop.): 16.3. **Natural inc.:** 2.43%. **Infant mortality** (per 1,000 live births): 91.2. **AIDS rate:** 5.1%.

Education: Compulsory: ages 7-12. **Literacy:** 70.4%.

Major Intl. Organizations: UN (FAO, IBRD, ILO, IMF, WHO, WTrO), AU.

Embassy: 1714 New Hampshire Ave. NW 20009; 232-2882.

Website: www.gov.rw

For centuries, the Tutsi (an extremely tall people) dominated the Hutu (90% of the population). A civil war broke out in 1959 and Tutsi power was ended. Many Tutsi went into exile. A referendum in 1961 abolished the monarchic system. Rwanda, which had been part of the Belgian UN trusteeship of Rwanda-Urundi, became independent July 1, 1962.

In 1963 Tutsi exiles invaded in an unsuccessful coup; a large-scale massacre of Tutsi followed. Rivalries among Hutu led to a bloodless coup July 1973 in which Juvénal Habyarimana took power. After an invasion and coup attempt by Tutsi exiles in 1990, a multiparty democracy was established.

Renewed ethnic strife led to an Aug. 1993 peace accord between the government and rebels of the Tutsi-led Rwandan Patriotic Front (RPF). But after Habyarimana and the president of Burundi were killed Apr. 6, 1994, in a suspicious plane crash, massive violence broke out. More than 1 million may have died in massacres, mostly of Tutsi by Hutu militias, and in civil warfare as the RPF sought power. About 2 million Tutsi and Hutu fled to camps in Zaire (now Congo) and other countries, where many died of cholera and other natural causes. French troops under a UN mandate moved into SW Rwanda June 23 to establish a so-called safe zone. The RPF claimed victory, installing a government in July led by a moderate Hutu president. French troops pulled out Aug. 22. A UN peacekeeping mission ended Mar. 8, 1996, but the Rwandan government and a UN-sponsored tribunal in Tanzania continued to gather evidence against those responsible for genocide. More than 1 million refugees (mostly Hutu) flooded back to Rwanda from Tanzania and Zaire in Nov. and Dec. 1996.

Firing squads in Rwanda on Apr. 24, 1998, executed 22 people convicted of genocide. Former Prime Min. Jean Kambanda pleaded guilty May 1 before the UN tribunal and received a life sentence Sept. 4, 1998. Maj. Gen. Paul Kagame, leader of the RPF, was sworn in as Rwanda's 1st Tutsi president Apr. 22, 2000. A Belgian court June 8, 2001, convicted 2 Roman Catholic nuns and 2 other Rwandans for their role in the 1994 genocide.

Rwanda and the Congo signed an accord July 30, 2002, in which Rwanda agreed to withdraw troops from the Congo and the Congo agreed to stop harboring Hutu guerrillas. Rwandans in 2003 approved a new constitution, May 26, reelected Pres. Kagame, Aug. 25, and chose a new parliament, Sept. 29-30. Former Pres. Bizimungu was sentenced to 15 yrs. for embezzlement, June 2004. Village tribunals have also begun trying genocide suspects, who may number in the hundreds of thousands.

Saint Kitts and Nevis

Federation of Saint Kitts and Nevis

People: Population: 38,958. **Age distrib.** (%): <15: 28.0; 65+: 8.3. **Pop. density:** 386 per sq mi, 149 per sq km. **Urban:** 32.2%. **Ethnic group:** Black, British, Portuguese, Lebanese. **Principal languages:** English (official). **Chief religions:** Anglican, other Protestant, Roman Catholic.

Geography: Total area: 101 sq mi, 261 sq km; **Land area:** 101 sq mi, 261 sq km. **Location:** In the N part of the Leeward group of the Lesser Antilles in the E Caribbean Sea. **Neighbors:** Antigua and Barbuda to E. Topography: St. Kitts has forested volcanic slopes; Nevis rises from beaches to central peak. Climate is tropical moderated by sea breezes. **Capital:** Basseterre, 13,000.

Government: Type: Constitutional monarchy. **Head of state:** Queen Elizabeth II, represented by Gov-Gen. Sir Cuthbert M. Sebastian; b Oct. 22, 1921; in office: Jan. 1, 1996. **Head of gov.:** Prime Min. Denzil Llewellyn Douglas; b Jan. 14, 1953; in office: July 7, 1995. **Local divisions:** 14 parishes.

Economy: Industries: sugar proc., tourism, cotton, salt, copra, clothing, footwear, beverages. **Chief crops:** sugarcane, rice, yams, vegetables, bananas. **Arable land:** 22%. **Livestock** (2004): cattle: 4,300; chickens: 60,000; goats: 14,400; pigs: 4,000; sheep: 14,000. **Fish catch** (2003): 370 metric tons. **Electricity prod.** (2003): 0.11 bil kWh.

Finance: Monetary unit: East Caribbean Dollar (XCD) (Sept. 2005: 2.67 = $1 U.S.). **GDP** (2002 est.): $339.0 mil; **per capita GDP:** $8,800; **GDP growth:** -1.9%. **Imports** (2002 est.): $195.0 mil; partners (2004): US 33.1%, Italy 19.4%, Trinidad and Tobago 10.5%, UK 9.8%, Denmark 6%. **Exports** (2002 est.): $70.0 mil; partners (2004): US 58%, Canada 9%, Portugal 8.3%, UK 6.9%. **Tourism:** $61 mil. **Budget** (2003 est.): $128.2 mil. **Intl. reserves less gold** (2003): $44 mil. **Consumer prices** (change in 1999): 3.9%.

Transport: Railroad: Length: 31 mi. **Motor vehicles**: 7,700 pass. cars, 3,900 comm. vehicles. **Civil aviation:** 2 airports. **Chief ports:** Basseterre, Charlestown.

Communications: TV sets: 256 per 1,000 pop. **Radios:** 718 per 1,000 pop. **Telephone lines** (2002): 23,500. **Internet** (2002): 10,000 users.

Health: Life expect.: 69.3 male; 75.2 female. **Births** (per 1,000 pop.): 18.1. **Deaths** (per 1,000 pop.): 8.5. **Natural inc.:** 0.97%. **Infant mortality** (per 1,000 live births): 14.5.

Education: Compulsory: ages 5-16. **Literacy:** 97%.

Major Intl. Organizations: UN (FAO, IBRD, ILO, IMF, WHO, WTrO), Caricom, the Commonwealth, OAS, OECS.

Embassy: 3216 New Mexico Ave., NW 20016; 686-2636.

Website: www.stkittsnevis.net

St. Kitts (formerly St. Christopher; known by the natives as Liamuiga) and Nevis were reached (and named) by Columbus in 1493. They were settled by Britain in 1623, but ownership was disputed with France until 1713. They were part of the Leeward Islands Federation, 1871-1956, and the Federation of the West Indies, 1958-62. The colony achieved self-government as an Associated State of the UK in 1967, and became fully independent Sept. 19, 1983. A secession referendum on Nevis, Aug. 10, 1998, fell short of the two-thirds majority required.

Saint Lucia

People: Population: 166,312. **Age distrib.** (%): <15: 30.3; 65+: 5.2. **Pop. density:** 699 per sq mi, 270 per sq km. **Urban:** 30.5%. **Ethnic groups:** Black 90%, mixed 6%, East Indian 3%, White 1%. **Principal languages:** English (official), French patois. **Chief religions:** Roman Catholic 68%, Protestant 8%.

Geography: Total area: 238 sq mi, 616 sq km; **Land area:** 234 sq mi, 606 sq km. **Location:** In E Caribbean, 2d largest of the Windward Isls. **Neighbors:** Martinique to N, St. Vincent to S. **Topography:** Mountainous, volcanic in origin; Soufriere, a volcanic crater, in the S. Wooded mountains run N-S to Mt. Gimie, 3,145 ft., with streams through fertile valleys. **Capital:** Castries, 14,000.

Government: Type: Parliamentary democracy. **Head of state:** Queen Elizabeth II, represented by Gov.-Gen. Dame Calliopa

Pearlette Louisy; b June 8, 1946; in office: Sept. 17, 1997. **Head of gov.:** Prime Min. Kenny Anthony; b Jan. 8, 1951; in office: May 24, 1997. **Local divisions:** 11 quarters.

Economy: Industries: clothing, electronic components, beverages, cardboard, tourism, lime & coconut proc. **Chief crops:** bananas, coconuts, vegetables, citrus, root crops, cocoa. **Natural resources:** timber, pumice, mineral springs, geothermal areas. **Arable land:** 8%. **Livestock** (2004): cattle: 12,400; chickens: 270,000; goats: 9,800; pigs: 14,950; sheep: 12,500. **Fish catch** (2003): 1,464 metric tons. **Electricity prod.** (2003): 0.28 bil kWh. **Labor force** (2002 est.): agriculture 21.7%, industry, commerce, and manufacturing 24.7%, services 53.6%.

Finance: Monetary unit: East Caribbean Dollar (XCD) (Sept. 2005: 2.67 = $1 U.S.). **GDP** (2002 est.): $866.0 mil; **per capita GDP:** $5,400; **GDP growth:** 3.3%. **Imports** (2002 est.): $267.0 mil; partners (2004): US 30%, Trinidad and Tobago 17.5%, UK 8.5%, Venezuela 8.4%. **Exports** (2002 est.): $66.0 mil; partners (2004): UK 49.3%, US 19.9%, Antigua and Barbuda 5.4%, Dominica 5.2%, Trinidad and Tobago 4.4%. **Tourism:** $282 mil. **Budget** (2000 est.): $146.7 mil. **Intl. reserves less gold** (2003): $73 mil. **Consumer prices:** 4.66%.

Transport: Motor vehicles 13,500 pass. cars, 10,800 comm. vehicles. **Civil aviation:** 2 airports. **Chief ports:** Castries, Vieux Fort.

Communications: TV sets: 368 per 1,000 pop. **Radios:** 750 per 1,000 pop. **Telephone lines** (2002): 51,100. **Internet** (2001): 13,000 users.

Health: Life expect.: 70.1 male; 77.4 female. **Births** (per 1,000 pop.): 20.1. **Deaths** (per 1,000 pop.): 5.1. **Natural inc.:** 1.49%. **Infant mortality** (per 1,000 live births): 13.5.

Education: Compulsory: ages 5-16. **Literacy:** 67%.

Major Intl. Organizations: UN (FAO, IBRD, ILO, IMF, IMO, WHO, WTrO), Caricom, the Commonwealth, OAS, OECS.

Embassy: 3216 New Mexico Ave. NW 20016; 364-6792.

Website: www.stlucia.gov.lc

St. Lucia was ceded to Britain by France at the Treaty of Paris, 1814. Self-government was granted with the West Indies Act, 1967. Independence was attained Feb. 22, 1979.

Saint Vincent and the Grenadines

People: Population: 117,534. **Age distrib.** (%): <15: 27.1; 65+: 6.4 **Pop. density:** 784 per sq mi, 302 per sq km. **Urban:** 58.3%. **Ethnic groups:** Black 66%, mixed 19%, East Indian 6%, Carib Amerindian 2%. **Principal languages:** English (official), French patois. **Chief religions:** Anglican 47%, Methodist 28%, Roman Catholic 13%.

Geography: Total area: 150 sq mi, 389 sq km; **Land area:** 150 sq mi, 389 sq km. **Location:** In the E Caribbean, St. Vincent (133 sq mi) and the northern islets of the Grenadines form a part of the Windward chain. **Neighbors:** St. Lucia to N, Barbados to E, Grenada to S. **Topography:** St. Vincent is volcanic, with a ridge of thickly wooded mountains running its length. **Capital:** Kingstown, 29,000.

Government: Constitutional monarchy. **Head of State:** Queen Elizabeth II, represented by Sir Frederick Ballantyne; in office: Sept. 2, 2002. **Head of gov.:** Prime Min. Ralph Gonsalves; b Aug. 8, 1946; in office: Mar. 29, 2001. **Local divisions:** 6 parishes.

Economy: Industries: food proc., cement, furniture, clothing, starch. **Chief crops:** bananas, coconuts, sweet potatoes, spices. **Natural resources:** hydropower. **Arable land:** 10%. **Livestock** (2004): cattle: 5,000; chickens: 125,000; goats: 7,000; pigs: 9,150; sheep: 12,000. **Fish catch** (2003): 4,782 metric tons. **Electricity prod.** (2003): 0.10 bil kWh. **Labor force** (1980 est.): agriculture 26%, industry 17%, services 57%.

Finance: Monetary unit: East Caribbean Dollar (XCD) (Sept. 2005: 2.67 = $1 U.S.). **GDP** (2002 est.): $342.0 mil; **per capita GDP:** $2,900; **GDP growth:** 0.7%. **Imports** (2002 est.): $174.0 mil; partners (2004): France 21%, Italy 12.4%, Singapore 11.2%, US 10.9%, Trinidad and Tobago 9.9%, Japan 7.3%, Spain 4.9%. **Exports** (2002 est.): $38.0 mil; partners (2004): France 30.5%, Spain 19.6%, Italy 17.7%, Greece 11.7%, UK 7.8%. **Tourism:** $85 mil. **Budget** (2000 est.): $85.8 mil. **Intl. reserves less gold** (2003): $34 mil. **Consumer prices:** 2.94%.

Transport: Motor vehicles: 9,900 pass. cars, 4,000 comm. vehicles. **Civil aviation:** 5 airports. **Chief port:** Kingstown.

Communications: TV sets: 230 per 1,000 pop. **Radios:** 688 per 1,000 pop. **Telephone lines:** 32,400. **Daily newspaper circ.:** 9 per 1,000 pop. **Internet** (2002): 7,000 users.

Health: Life expect.: 71.8 male; 75.5 female. **Births** (per 1,000 pop.): 16.3. **Deaths** (per 1,000 pop.): 6.0. **Natural inc.:** 1.03%. **Infant mortality** (per 1,000 live births): 14.8.

Education: Compulsory: ages 5-15. **Literacy:** 96%.

Major Intl. Organizations: UN (FAO, IBRD, ILO, IMF, IMO, WHO, WTrO), Caricom, the Commonwealth, OAS, OECS.

Embassy: 3216 New Mexico Ave. NW 20016; 364-6730.

Website: www.embsvg.com

Columbus landed on St. Vincent on Jan. 22, 1498 (St. Vincent's Day). Britain and France both laid claim to the island in the 17th and 18th centuries; the Treaty of Versailles, 1783, finally ceded it to Britain. Associated State status was granted 1969; independence was attained Oct. 27, 1979.

Samoa (*formerly* Western Samoa)
Independent State of Samoa

People: Population: 177,287. **Age distrib.** (%): <15: 27.2; 65+: 6.4. **Pop. density:** 156 per sq mi, 60 per sq km. **Urban:** 22.3%. **Urban:** 22%. **Ethnic groups:** Samoan 92.5%, Euronesians 7%. **Principal languages:** Samoan, English (both official). **Chief religion:** Christian 99.7%.

Geography: Total area: 1,137 sq mi, 2,944 sq km; **Land area:** 1,133 sq mi, 2,934 sq km. **Location:** In the S Pacific O. **Neighbors:** Nearest are Fiji to SW, Tonga to S. **Topography:** Main islands, Savaii (659 sq mi) and Upolu (432 sq mi), both ruggedly mountainous, and small islands Manono and Apolima. **Capital:** Apia, 40,000.

Government: Type: Constitutional monarchy. **Head of state:** Malietoa Tanumafili II; b Jan. 4, 1913; in office: Jan. 1, 1962. **Head of gov.:** Prime Min. Tuilaepa Sailele Malielegaoi; b Apr. 14, 1945; in office: Nov. 23, 1998. **Local divisions:** 11 districts.

Economy: Industries: food proc., building materials, auto parts. **Chief crops:** coconuts, bananas, taro, yams. **Natural resources:** timber, fish, hydropower. **Arable land:** 19%. **Livestock** (2004): cattle: 29,000; chickens: 450,000; pigs: 201,000. **Fish catch** (2003): 10,267 metric tons. **Electricity prod.** (2003): 0.12 bil kWh.

Finance: Monetary unit: Tala (WST) (Sept. 2005: 2.73 = $1 U.S.). **GDP** (2002 est.): $1.0 bil; **per capita GDP:** $5,600; **GDP growth:** 5%. **Imports** (2002): $113.0 mil; partners (2004): New Zealand 23.1%, Fiji 17.9%, Taiwan 10.7%, Australia 9.6%, Singapore 9.1%, Japan 8.1%, US 5.3%. **Exports** (2002): $14.0 mil; partners (2004): Australia 60.7%, Indonesia 17.1%, US 4.9%. **Tourism:** $53 mil. **Budget** (2001-02): $119.0 mil. **Intl. reserves less gold:** $62 mil. **Consumer prices:** 16.34%.

Transport: Motor vehicles: 6,200 pass. cars, 700 comm. vehicles. **Civil aviation:** 180.8 mil pass.-mi; 3 airports. **Chief ports:** Apia, Asau.

Communications: TV sets: 56 per 1,000 pop. **Radios:** 1,035 per 1,000 pop. **Telephone lines**: 13,300. **Internet** (2002): 4,000 users.

Health: Life expect.: 67.9 male; 73.7 female. **Births** (per 1,000 pop.): 16.0. **Deaths** (per 1,000 pop.): 6.5. **Natural inc.:** 0.94%. **Infant mortality** (per 1,000 live births): 27.7.

Education: Compulsory: ages 5-14. **Literacy:** 99.7%.

Major Intl. Organizations: UN (FAO, IBRD, IMF, IMO, WHO), the Commonwealth.

Embassy: 800 Second Avenue, Ste. 400D, New York, NY 10017; (212) 599-6196.

Website: www.govt.ws

Samoa (formerly known as Western Samoa to distinguish it from American Samoa, a small U.S. territory) was a German colony, 1899 to 1914, when New Zealand landed troops and took over. It became a New Zealand mandate under the League of Nations and, in 1945, a New Zealand UN Trusteeship.

An elected local government took office in Oct. 1959, and the country became fully independent Jan. 1, 1962.

San Marino
Republic of San Marino

People: Population: 28,880. **Age distrib.** (%): <15: 16.7; 65+: 16.9. **Pop. density:** 1,203 per sq mi, 473 per sq km. **Urban:** 88.7%. **Ethnic groups:** Sammarinese, Italian **Principal language:** Italian (official). **Chief religion:** Predominantly Roman Catholic.

Geography: Total area: 24 sq mi, 61 sq km; **Land area:** 24 sq mi, 61 sq km. **Location:** In N central Italy near Adriatic coast. **Neighbors:** Completely surrounded by Italy. **Topography:** The country lies on the slopes of Mt. Titano. **Capital:** San Marino, 5,000.

Government: Type: Republic. **Heads of state and gov.:** Two co-regents appt. every 6 months. **Local divisions:** 9 castelli.

Economy: Industries: tourism, banking, textiles, electronics, ceramics, cement, wine. **Chief crops:** wheat, grapes, corn, olives. **Natural resources:** building stone. **Arable land:** 17%. **Labor force** (2000 est.): agriculture 1%, industry 42%, services 57%

Finance: Monetary unit: Euro (EUR) (Sept. 2005: 0.80 = $1 U.S.). **GDP** (2001 est.): $940.0 mil; **per capita GDP:** $34,600; **GDP growth:** 7.5%. **Budget** (2000 est.): $400.0 mil. **Intl. reserves less gold:** $229 mil.

Transport: Motor vehicles (1997): 24,825 pass. cars, 4,149 comm. vehicles.

Communications: TV sets: 875 per 1,000 pop. **Radios:** 1,346 per 1,000 pop. **Daily newspaper circ.:** 70.4 per 1,000 pop.

Health: Life expect.: 78.1 male; 85.4 female. **Births** (per 1,000 pop.): 10.2. **Deaths** (per 1,000 pop.): 8.1. **Natural inc.:** 0.21%. **Infant mortality** (per 1,000 live births): 5.7.

Education: Compulsory: ages 6-14. **Literacy:** 96%.

Major Intl. Organizations: UN (ILO, IMF, WHO), OSCE.

Website: www.visitsanmarino.com/defaulte.asp

San Marino claims to be the oldest state in Europe and to have been founded in the 4th century. A Communist-led coalition ruled 1947-57; a similar coalition ruled 1978-86. San Marino has had a treaty of friendship with Italy since 1862.

São Tomé and Príncipe

Democratic Republic of São Tomé and Príncipe

People: Population: 187,410. **Age distrib.** (%): <15: 47.6; 65+: 3.9. **Pop. density:** 486 per sq mi, 187 per sq km. **Urban:** 37.8%. **Ethnic groups:** Mestizo, Black, Portuguese. **Principal languages:** Portuguese (official), Creole, Fang. **Chief religions:** Predominantly Roman Catholic.

Geography: Total area: 386 sq mi, 1,001 sq km; **Land area:** 386 sq mi, 1,001 sq km. **Location:** In the Gulf of Guinea about 125 miles off W central Africa. **Neighbors:** Gabon, Equatorial Guinea to E. **Topography:** São Tomé and Príncipe islands, part of an extinct volcano chain, are both covered by lush forests and croplands. **Capital:** São Tomé, 54,000.

Government: Type: Republic. **Head of state:** Pres. Fradique Melo de Menezes; b Mar. 21, 1942; in office: Sept. 3, 2001. **Head of gov.:** Prime Min. Maria do Carmo Silveira; in office: June 8, 2005. **Local divisions:** 2 provinces.

Economy: Industries: light constr., textiles, soap, beer; fish proc. **Chief crops:** cocoa, coconuts, palm kernels, cinnamon, pepper, coffee. **Natural resources:** fish, hydropower. **Arable land:** 2%. **Livestock** (2004): cattle: 4,600; chickens: 350,000; goats: 5,000; pigs: 2,500; sheep: 2,800. **Fish catch** (2003): 3,283 metric tons. **Electricity prod.** (2003): 0.02 bil kWh. **Labor force**: population mainly engaged in subsistence agriculture and fishing.

Finance: Monetary unit: Dobra (STD) (Sept. 2005: 7,967.00 = $1 U.S.). **GDP** (2003 est.): $214.0 mil; **per capita GDP:** $1,200; **GDP growth:** 6%. **Imports** (2004 est.): $41.0 mil; partners (2004): Portugal 50.5%, Germany 10%, US 5.1%, Netherlands 4.5%, South Africa 4.2%. **Exports** (2004 est.): $6.7 mil; partners (2004): Netherlands 39.1%, China 11.8%, Germany 8.6%, Belgium 6.9%, Philippines 6.7%, France 4.5%. **Tourism** (2002): $10 mil. **Budget** (2004 est.): $43.9 mil. **Intl. reserves less gold** (2003): $17 mil.

Transport: Civil aviation: 8.7 mil pass.-mi; 2 airports. **Chief ports:** São Tomé, Santo Antonio.

Communications: TV sets: 229 per 1,000 pop. **Radios:** 319 per 1,000 pop. **Telephone lines:** 7,000. **Internet**: 15,000 users.

Health: Life expect.: 65.4 male; 68.6 female. **Births** (per 1,000 pop.): 40.8. **Deaths** (per 1,000 pop.): 6.7. **Natural inc.:** 3.41%. **Infant mortality** (per 1,000 live births): 43.1.

Education: Compulsory: ages 7-12. **Literacy:** 79.3%.

Major Intl. Organizations: UN (FAO, IBRD, ILO, IMF, IMO, WHO), AU.

Permanent UN Representative: 400 Park Ave., 7th Floor, New York, NY 10022; (212) 317-0580.

Website: www.saotome.org

The islands were discovered in 1471 by the Portuguese, who brought the first settlers—convicts and exiled Jews. Sugar planting was replaced by the slave trade as the chief economic activity until coffee and cocoa were introduced in the 19th century.

Portugal agreed, 1974, to turn the colony over to the Gabon-based Movement for the Liberation of São Tomé and Príncipe, which proclaimed as first president its East German-trained leader, Manuel Pinto da Costa. Independence came July 12, 1975. Democratic reforms were instituted in 1987. In 1991 Miguel Trovoada won the first free presidential election following da Costa's withdrawal. A military coup that ousted Trovoada Aug. 15, 1995, was reversed a week later after Angolan mediation. Trovoada defeated da Costa in a presidential runoff election, July 21, 1996.

Fradique de Menezes, a wealthy cocoa exporter, easily beat da Costa in the presidential election of July 29, 2001. The government was ousted in a military coup July 16, 2003, but restored to power July 23. The country, long one of the world's poorest, is expected to reap billions of dollars from oil development in the Gulf of Guinea.

Saudi Arabia

Kingdom of Saudi Arabia

People: Population: 26,417,599. **Age distrib.** (%): <15: 38.2; 65+: 2.4. **Pop. density:** 35 per sq mi, 13 per sq km. **Urban:** 87.7%. **Ethnic groups:** Arab 90%, Afro-Asian 10% **Principal languages:** Arabic (official). **Chief religion:** Muslim (official).

Geography: Total area: 756,985 sq mi, 1,960,582 sq km; **Land area:** 756,985 sq mi, 1,960,582 sq km. **Location:** Occupies most of Arabian Peninsula in Mid-East. **Neighbors:** Kuwait, Iraq, Jordan on N; Yemen, Oman on S; United Arab Emirates, Qatar on E. **Topography:** Bordered by Red Sea on the W. The highlands on W, up to 9,000 ft., slope as an arid, barren desert to the Persian Gulf on the E. **Capital:** Riyadh, 5,126,000. **Cities (urban aggr.):** Jeddah, 3,171,000; Mecca, 1,326,000.

Government: Type: Monarchy with council of ministers. **Head of state and gov.:** King Abdullah bin Abdul Aziz; b 1924; in office: Aug. 1, 2005. **Local divisions:** 13 provinces. **Defense budget** (2003): $18.4 bil. **Active troops:** 124,500.

Economy: Industries: oil prod. & refining, petrochems., cement, construction, fertilizers, plastics. **Chief crops:** wheat, barley, tomatoes, melons, dates, citrus. **Natural resources:** oil, nat. gas, iron ore, gold, copper. **Crude oil reserves** (2004): 261.9 bil bbls. **Arable land:** 2%. **Livestock** (2004): cattle: 341,958; chickens: 137.0 mil; goats: 2.2 mil; sheep: 7.0 mil. **Fish catch** (2003): 64,753 metric tons. **Electricity prod.** (2003): 145.1 bil kWh. **Labor force** (1999 est.): agriculture 12%, industry 25%, services 63%.

Finance: Monetary unit: Riyal (SAR) (Sept. 2005: 3.75 = $1 U.S.). **GDP** (2004 est.): $310.2 bil; **per capita GDP:** $12,000; **GDP growth:** 5%. **Imports** (2004 est.): $36.2 bil; partners (2004): US 9.3%, Germany 6.8%, Japan 6.7%, UK 5.4%, China 5%. **Exports** (2004 est.): $113.0 bil; partners (2004): US 19.3%, Japan 16.4%, South Korea 8.7%, China 5.8%, Singapore 4.5%. **Tourism** (2002): $3,418 mil. **Budget** (2004 est.): $78.7 bil. **Intl. reserves less gold:** $17.57 bil. **Gold:** 4.6 mil oz t. **Consumer prices:** 0.55%.

Transport: Railroad: Length: 865 mi. **Motor vehicles**: 7.05 mil pass. cars. **Civil aviation:** 12.6 bil pass.-mi; 71 airports. **Chief ports:** Jiddah, Ad Dammam.

Communications: TV sets: 263 per 1,000 pop. **Radios:** 321 per 1,000 pop. **Telephone lines:** 3.5 mil. **Daily newspaper circ.:** 318.1 per 1,000 pop. **Internet**: 1.5 mil users.

Health: Life expect.: 73.5 male; 77.6 female. **Births** (per 1,000 pop.): 29.6. **Deaths** (per 1,000 pop.): 2.6. **Natural inc.:** 2.69%. **Infant mortality** (per 1,000 live births): 13.2.

Education: Compulsory: ages 6-11. **Literacy:** 78.8%.

Major Intl. Organizations: UN (FAO, IBRD, ILO, IMF, IMO, WHO), AL, OPEC.

Embassy: 601 New Hampshire Ave. NW 20037; 342-3800.

Website: www.saudiembassy.net

Before Muhammad, Arabia was divided among numerous warring tribes and small kingdoms. It was united for the first time by Muhammad, in the early 7th century AD. His successors conquered the entire Near East and North Africa, bringing Islam and the Arabic language. But Arabia itself soon returned to its former status.

Nejd, in central Arabia, long an independent state and center of the Wahhabi sect, fell under Turkish rule in the 18th century. In 1913 Ibn Saud, founder of the Saudi dynasty, overthrew the Turks and captured the Turkish province of Hasa in E Arabia; he took the Hejaz region in W Arabia in 1925 and most of Asir, in SW Arabia, by 1926. The discovery of oil in the 1930s transformed the new country.

Ibn Saud reigned until his death, Nov. 1953. Subsequent kings have been sons of Ibn Saud. The king exercises authority together with a Council of Ministers. The Islamic religious code is the law of the land. Alcohol and public entertainments are restricted, and women have an inferior legal status. There is no constitution and no parliament, although a Consultative Council was established by the king in 1993.

Saudi Arabia has often allied itself with the U.S. and other Western nations, and billions of dollars of advanced arms have been purchased from Britain, France, and the U.S.; however, Western support for Israel has often strained relations. Saudi units fought against Israel in the 1948 and 1973 Arab-Israeli wars. Beginning with the 1967 Arab-Israeli war, Saudi Arabia provided large annual financial gifts to Egypt; aid was later extended to Syria, Jordan, and Palestinian groups, as well as to other Islamic countries.

King Faisal played a leading role in the 1973-74 Arab oil embargo against the U.S. and other nations. Crown Prince Khalid was proclaimed king on Mar. 25, 1975, after the assassination of Faisal. Fahd became king on June 13, 1982, following Khalid's death.

The Hejaz contains the holy cities of Islam—Medina, where the Mosque of the Prophet enshrines the tomb of Muhammad, and Mecca, his birthplace. More than 2 million Muslims make pilgrimage to Mecca annually. In 1987, Iranians making a pilgrimage to Mecca clashed with anti-Iranian pilgrims and Saudi police; more than 400 were killed. Some 1,426 Muslim pilgrims died July 2, 1990, in a stampede in a pedestrunnel leading to Mecca. Nearly 300 pilgrims were killed in a stampede in Mecca, May 26, 1994. More than 340 pilgrims died in a tent fire near Mecca, Apr. 15, 1997. A stampede at Mina killed more than 250, Feb. 1, 2004.

Following Iraq's attack on Kuwait, Aug. 2, 1990, Saudi Arabia accepted the Kuwait royal family and more than 400,000 Kuwaiti refugees. King Fahd invited Western and Arab troops to deploy on its soil in support of Saudi defense forces. During the 1991 Persian Gulf War, 28 U.S. soldiers were killed when an Iraqi missile hit their barracks in Dhahran, Feb. 25, 1991. Islamic extremists were blamed for truck bombs that killed 7 (5 from the U.S.) at a military training center in Riyadh, Nov. 13, 1995, and 19 Americans at a base in Dhahran, June 25, 1996.

The presence of 15 Saudis among the 19 al-Qaeda hijackers who took part in the Sept. 11, 2001, attacks on the U.S. raised new tensions between the U.S. and Saudi governments, and some blamed the Saudi government for allowing Muslim extremism to flourish in Saudi Arabia. Policy differences over Iraq and the Israeli-Palestinian dispute were further irritants. The U.S. completed a pullout of its combat forces in Sept. 2003. Alarmed at guerrilla attacks that killed more than 100 people, mostly foreigners, in Saudi Arabia during 2003-04, the Saudi government stepped up antiterrorist activities in cooperation with the U.S. Islamist candidates on a "golden list" circulated by conservative clerics fared well in municipal council elections, Feb.-Apr. 2005; women were barred from voting in the elections, the country's first since 1963.

King Fahd, on the throne since 1982, died Aug. 1, 2005. He was succeeded by his half-brother, Abdullah, who had in effect ruled the Kingdom since Fahd suffered a stroke in Nov. 1995.

Senegal
Republic of Senegal

People: Population: 11,706,498. **Age distrib.** (%): <15: 42.8; 65+: 3.0. **Pop. density:** 155 per sq mi, 60 per sq km. **Urban:** 49.6%. **Ethnic groups:** Wolof 43%, Pular 24%, Serer 15%, Jola 4%, Mandinka 3%, Soninke 1%. **Principal languages:** French (official), Wolof, Pulaar, Jola, Mandinka. **Chief religions:** Muslim 94%, Christian 5%.

Geography: Total area: 75,749 sq mi, 196,190 sq km; **Land area:** 74,132 sq mi, 192,000 sq km. **Location:** At W extreme of Africa. **Neighbors:** Mauritania on N, Mali on E, Guinea and Guinea-Bissau on S; surrounds Gambia on three sides. **Topography:** Low rolling plains cover most of Senegal, rising somewhat in the SE. Swamp and jungles are in SW. **Capital:** Dakar, 2,167,000.

Government: Type: Republic. **Head of state:** Pres. Abdoulaye Wade; b May 29, 1926; in office: Apr. 1, 2000. **Head of gov.:** Prime Min. Macky Sall; b Dec. 11, 1961; in office: Apr. 21, 2004. **Local divisions:** 11 regions. **Defense budget** (2004): $94 mil. **Active troops:** 13,620.

Economy: Industries: food & fish proc., phosphate mining, fertilizer. **Chief crops:** peanuts, millet, corn, sorghum, rice, cotton. **Natural resources:** fish, phosphates, iron ore. **Arable land:** 12%. **Livestock** (2004): cattle: 3.1 mil; chickens: 46.0 mil; goats: 4.0 mil; pigs: 315,000; sheep: 4.7 mil. **Fish catch** (2003): 448,271 metric tons. **Electricity prod.** (2003): 1.3 bil kWh. **Labor force**: agriculture 70%.

Finance: Monetary unit: CFA Franc BCEAO (XOF) (Sept. 2005: 525.28 = $1 U.S.). **GDP** (2004 est.): $18.4 bil; **per capita GDP:** $1,700; **GDP growth:** 3.2%. **Imports** (2004 est.): $2.1 bil; partners (2004): France 26.2%, Nigeria 12.1%, Thailand 5.3%, Belgium 5%, Spain 4.2%. **Exports** (2004 est.): $1.4 bil; partners (2004): India 13.8%, France 10.6%, Mali 10%, Italy 6%, Côte d'Ivoire 5.7%, Spain 4%. **Tourism:** $184 mil. **Budget** (2004 est.): $1.6 bil. **Intl. reserves less gold:** $643 mil. **Consumer prices:** 0.51%.

Transport: Railroad: Length: 563 mi. **Motor vehicles:** 193,000 pass. cars, 79,000 comm. vehicles. **Civil aviation:** 198.2 mil pass.-mi; 9 airports. **Chief ports:** Dakar, Saint-Louis.

Communications: TV sets: 41 per 1,000 pop. **Radios:** 141 per 1,000 pop. **Telephone lines:** 228,800. **Daily newspaper circ.:** 5.3 per 1,000 pop. **Internet**: 225,000 users.

Health: Life expect.: 57.4 male; 60.5 female. **Births** (per 1,000 pop.): 33.4. **Deaths** (per 1,000 pop.): 9.6. **Natural inc.:** 2.38%. **Infant mortality** (per 1,000 live births): 54.1. **AIDS rate:** 0.8%.

Education: Compulsory: ages 7-12. **Literacy:** 40.2%.

Major Intl. Organizations: UN and all of its specialized agencies, AU.

Embassy: 2112 Wyoming Ave. NW 20008; 234-0540.

Website: www.senegal-tourism.com

Portuguese settlers arrived in the 15th century, but French control grew from the 17th century. The last independent Muslim state was subdued in 1893. Senegal became an independent republic Aug. 20, 1960, but French political and economic influence remained strong. Senegambia, a loose confederation of Senegal and The Gambia, was established in 1982 but dissolved 7 years later.

Forty years of Socialist Party rule ended when Abdoulaye Wade, leader of the Senegalese Democratic Party, won a presidential runoff election Mar. 19, 2000. A Senegalese ferry capsized off the coast of The Gambia Sept. 26, 2002, killing at least 1,863 people. A peace accord signed Dec. 30, 2004, with separatists in Cassamance Province, S Senegal, sought to end a 22-year insurgency.

Serbia and Montenegro
(*formerly* Yugoslavia)

People: Population: 10,829,175. **Age distrib.** (%): <15: 18.1; 65+: 15.0. **Pop. density:** 274 per sq mi, 106 per sq km. **Urban:** 52.0%. **Ethnic groups:** Serb 63%, Albanian 17%, Montenegrin 5%, Hungarian 3%. **Principal languages:** Serbian (official), Albanian. **Chief religions:** Orthodox 65%, Muslim 19%, Roman Catholic 4%.

Geography: Total area: 39,518 sq mi, 102,350 sq km; **Land area:** 39,435 sq mi, 102,136 sq km. **Location:** On the Balkan Peninsula in SE Europe. **Neighbors:** Croatia, Bosnia and Herzegovina on W; Hungary on N; Romania, Bulgaria on E; Albania, on S. Topography: Terrain varies widely, with fertile plains drained by the Danube and other rivers in N, limestone basins in E, ancient mountains and hills in SE, and very high coastline in Montenegro along SW. **Capital:** Belgrade, 1,118,000.

Government: Type: Federal republic. **Head of state and gov.:** Pres. Svetozar Marovic; b Mar. 31, 1955; in office: Mar. 7, 2003. **Local divisions:** 2 republics, 2 autonomous provinces. **Defense budget** (2004): $678 mil. **Active troops:** 65,300.

Economy: Industries: aircraft, vehicle, & other machine building; metallurgy, mining, consumer goods, electronics, oil products, chemicals. **Chief crops:** cereals, fruits, vegetables, tobacco, olives. **Natural resources:** oil, gas, coal, antimony, copper, lead, zinc, nickel, gold, pyrite, chrome, hydropower. **Crude oil reserves** (2004): 78 mil bbls. **Livestock** (2004): cattle: 1.3 mil; chickens: 15.0 mil; goats: 195,000; pigs: 3.5 mil; sheep: 1.8 mil. **Fish catch** (2003): 3,662 metric tons. **Electricity prod.** (2003): 36.0 bil kWh.

Finance: Monetary unit: Dinar (CSD) (Sept. 2005: 68.41 = $1 U.S.). **GDP** (2004 est.): $26.3 bil; **per capita GDP:** $2,400; **GDP growth:** 6.5%. **Imports** (2004 est.): $9.5 bil; partners (2004): Germany 20.2%, Italy 18.1%, Austria 9%, Slovenia 6.1%, France 5.1%, Netherlands 4.4%, Bulgaria 4.3%, Greece 4.2%. **Exports** (2004 est.): $3.2 bil; partners (2004): Italy 30.1%, Germany 16.6%, Austria 7.4%, Greece 7.1%, France 5.3%, Slovenia 4.2%, US 4.1%. **Tourism:** $150 mil. **Budget** (2004 est.): $10.5 bil.

Transport: Railroad: Length: 2,522 mi. **Motor vehicles:** 1.48 mil pass. cars, 330,500 comm. vehicles. **Civil aviation:** 557.4 mil pass.-mi; 19 airports. **Chief ports:** Bar, Novi Sad.

Communications: TV sets: 277 per 1,000 pop. **Radios:** 296 per 1,000 pop. **Telephone lines:** 2.6 mil. **Daily newspaper circ.:** 107 per 1,000 pop. **Internet**: 847,000 users.

Health: Life expect.: 72.2 male; 77.5 female. **Births** (per 1,000 pop.): 12.1. **Deaths** (per 1,000 pop.): 10.5. **Natural inc.:** 0.16%. **Infant mortality** (per 1,000 live births): 12.9. **AIDS rate:** 0.2%.

Education: Compulsory: ages 7-14. **Literacy:** 93%.

Major Intl. Organizations: Currently suspended from UN and its agencies.

Embassy: 2134 Kalorama Rd. NW 20008; 332-0333.

Website: www.gov.yu

Serbia, which had since 1389 been a vassal principality of Turkey, was established as an independent kingdom by the Treaty of Berlin, 1878. Montenegro, independent since 1389, also obtained international recognition in 1878. After the Balkan wars, Serbia's boundaries were enlarged by the annexation of Old Serbia and Macedonia, 1913.

When the Austro-Hungarian empire collapsed after World War I, the Kingdom of Serbs, Croats, and Slovenes was formed from the former provinces of Croatia, Dalmatia, Bosnia, Herzegovina, Slovenia, Vojvodina, and the independent state of Montenegro. The name became Yugoslavia in 1929.

Nazi Germany invaded in 1941. Many Yugoslav partisan troops continued to operate. Among these were the Chetniks led by Draja Mikhailovich, who fought other partisans led by Josip Broz, known as Marshal Tito. Tito, backed by the USSR and Britain from 1943, was in control by the time the Germans had been driven from Yugoslavia in 1945. Mikhailovich was executed July 17, 1946, by the Tito regime.

A constituent assembly proclaimed Yugoslavia a republic Nov. 29, 1945. It became a federal republic Jan. 31, 1946, with Tito, a Communist, heading the government. Tito rejected Stalin's policy of dictating to all Communist nations, and he accepted economic and military aid from the West.

Pres. Tito died May 4, 1980. After his death, Yugoslavia was governed by a collective presidency, with a rotating succession. On Jan. 22, 1990, the Communist Party renounced its leading role in society.

Croatia and Slovenia formally declared independence June 25, 1991. In Croatia, fighting began between Croats and ethnic Serbs. Serbia sent arms and medical supplies to the Serb rebels in Croatia. Croatian forces clashed with Yugoslav army units and their Serb supporters.

The republics of Serbia and Montenegro proclaimed a new "Federal Republic of Yugoslavia" Apr. 17, 1992. Serbia, under Pres. Slobodan Milosevic, was the main arms supplier to ethnic Serb fighters in Bosnia and Herzegovina. The UN imposed sanctions May 30 on the newly reconstituted Yugoslavia as a means of ending the bloodshed in Bosnia.

A peace agreement initialed in Dayton, Ohio, Nov. 21, 1995, was signed in Paris, Dec. 14, by Milosevic and leaders of Bosnia and Croatia. In May 1996, a UN tribunal in the Netherlands began trying suspected war criminals from the former Yugoslavia. The UN lifted sanctions against Yugoslavia Oct. 1, 1996, after elections were held in Bosnia. Mass protests erupted when Milosevic refused to accept opposition victories in local elections Nov. 17; non-Communist governments took office in Belgrade and other cities in Feb. 1997. Barred from running for a 3rd term as Serbian president, Milosevic had himself inaugurated as president of Yugoslavia on July 23, 1997.

Fearful that the Serbs were employing "ethnic cleansing" tactics, as they had in Bosnia, the U.S. and its NATO allies sought to pressure the Yugoslav government. When Milosevic refused to comply, NATO launched an air war against Yugoslavia, Mar.-June 1999; the Serbs retaliated by terrorizing the Kosovars and forcing hundreds of thousands to flee, mostly to Albania and Macedonia. A 50,000-member multinational force (KFOR) entered Kosovo in June, and most of the Kosovar refugees had returned by Sept. 1. In the worst fighting there since 1999, Albanians and Serbs clashed in Mar. 2004, killing about 30 people, and injuring 500+, incl. UN/NATO troops. As of 2005, Kosovo was under UN administration (UNMIK), with a NATO-led security force of about 17,000.

Kosovo: A nominally autonomous province in southern Serbia (4,203 sq. mi.), with a population of about 2,000,000, mostly Albanians. The capital is Pristina. Revoking provincial autonomy, Serbia began ruling Kosovo by force in 1989. Albanian secessionists proclaimed an independent Republic of Kosovo in July 1990. Guerrilla attacks by the Kosovo Liberation Army in 1997 brought a ferocious counteroffensive by Serbian authorities.

Fearful that the Serbs were employing "ethnic cleansing" tactics, as they had in Bosnia, the U.S. and its NATO allies sought to pressure the Yugoslav government. When Milosevic refused to comply,

NATO launched an air war against Yugoslavia, Mar.-June 1999; the Serbs retaliated by terrorizing the Kosovars and forcing hundreds of thousands to flee, mostly to Albania and Macedonia. A 50,000-member multinational force (KFOR) entered Kosovo in June, and most of the Kosovar refugees had returned by Sept. 1. In the worst fighting there since 1999, Albanians and Serbs clashed in Mar. 2004, killing about 30 people, and injuring 500+, incl. UN/NATO troops. As of 2005, Kosovo was under UN administration (UNMIK), with a NATO-led security force of more than 17,000.

Vojvodina: A nominally autonomous province in northern Serbia (8,304 sq. mi.), with a population of about 2,000,000, mostly Serbian. The capital is Novi Sad.

Seychelles

Republic of Seychelles

People: Population: 81,188. **Age distrib.** (%): <15: 26.4; 65+: 6.2. **Pop. density:** 461 per sq mi, 178 per sq km. **Urban:** 49.9%. **Ethnic groups:** Mainly Seychellois (mix of French, African, and Asian). **Principal languages:** English, French, Creole (all official). **Chief religions:** Roman Catholic 83%, Anglican 7%.

Geography: Total area: 176 sq mi, 455 sq km; **Land area:** 176 sq mi, 455 sq km. **Location:** In the Indian O. 700 miles NE of Madagascar. **Neighbors:** Nearest are Madagascar on SW, Somalia on NW. **Topography:** A group of 86 islands, about half of them composed of coral, the other half granite, the latter predominantly mountainous. **Capital:** Victoria, 25,000.

Government: Type: Republic. **Head of state and gov.:** Pres. James Michel, b. Aug. 18, 1944; in office: Apr. 14, 2004. **Local divisions:** 23 districts. **Defense budget** (2004): $11 mil. **Active troops:** 450.

Economy: Industries: fishing, tourism, coconut & vanilla proc., rope, boats. **Chief crops:** coconuts, cinnamon, vanilla, sweet potatoes, cassava, bananas. **Natural resources:** fish, copra, cinnamon. **Arable land:** 2%. **Livestock** (2004): cattle: 1,400; chickens: 330,000; goats: 5,150; pigs: 18,500. **Fish catch** (2003): 86,869 metric tons. **Electricity prod.** (2003): 0.24 bil kWh. **Labor force** (1989): agriculture 10%, industry 19%, services 71%.

Finance: Monetary unit: Rupee (SCR) (Sept. 2005: 5.42 = $1 U.S.). **GDP** (2002 est.): $626.0 mil; **per capita GDP:** $7,800; **GDP growth:** 1.5%. **Imports** (2004 est.): $393.4 mil; partners (2004): Saudi Arabia 15.6%, Spain 14.1%, France 11%, Singapore 7.5%, Italy 7.3%, South Africa 7.3%, UK 5%. **Exports** (2004 est.): $256.2 mil; partners (2004): UK 29.1%, France 17.1%, Spain 11.8%, Japan 9.2%, Italy 8.1%, Germany 6.2%, Netherlands 4.3%. **Tourism:** $171 mil. **Budget** (2004 est.): $298.5 mil. **Intl. reserves less gold:** $22 mil. **Consumer prices:** 3.84%.

Transport: Motor vehicles: 6,400 pass. cars, 2,200 comm. vehicles. **Civil aviation:** 574.8 mil pass.-mi.; 7 airports. **Chief port:** Victoria.

Communications: TV sets: 214 per 1,000 pop. **Radios:** 560 per 1,000 pop. **Telephone lines:** 21,200. **Daily newspaper circ.:** 45 per 1,000 pop. **Internet** (2002): 11,700 users.

Health: Life expect.: 66.4 male; 77.4 female. **Births** (per 1,000 pop.): 16.2. **Deaths** (per 1,000 pop.): 6.3. **Natural inc.:** 0.99%. **Infant mortality** (per 1,000 live births): 15.5.

Education: Compulsory: ages 6-15. **Literacy:** 58%.

Major Intl. Organizations: UN (FAO, IBRD, ILO, IMF, IMO, WHO), the Commonwealth, AU.

Embassy: 800 2d Ave., Ste. 400C, New York, NY 10017; 212-972-1785.

Website: www.virtualseychelles.sc

The islands were occupied by France in 1768, and seized by Britain in 1794. Ruled as part of Mauritius from 1814, the Seychelles became a separate colony in 1903. Independence was declared June 29, 1976. The first president was ousted in a coup a year later by a socialist leader, France Albert René. A new constitution, approved June 1993, provided for a multiparty state. After nearly 27 years in power, Pres. René resigned Apr. 14, 2004, and was succeeded by Vice Pres. James Michel.

Sierra Leone

Republic of Sierra Leone

People: Population: 5,867,426. **Age distrib.** (%): <15: 44.7; 65+: 3.3. **Pop. density:** 212 per sq mi, 82 per sq km. **Urban:** 38.8%. **Ethnic groups:** Temne 30%, Mende 30%, other tribes 30%; Creole 10%. **Principal languages:** English (official), Mende in S, Temne in N, Krio (English Creole). **Chief religions:** Muslim 60%, indigenous beliefs 30%, Christian 10%.

Geography: Total area: 27,699 sq mi, 71,740 sq km; **Land area:** 27,653 sq mi, 71,620 sq km. **Location:** On W coast of W Africa. **Neighbors:** Guinea on N and E, Liberia on S. **Topography:** The heavily-indented, 210-mi. coastline has mangrove swamps. Behind are wooded hills, rising to a plateau and mountains in the E. **Capital:** Freetown, 921,000.

Government: Type: Republic. **Head of state and gov.:** Ahmad Tejan Kabbah; b Feb. 16, 1932; in office: Mar. 10, 1998. **Local divisions:** 3 provinces, 1 area. **Defense budget** (2004): $16 mil. **Active troops:** 12,000-13,000.

Economy: Industries: diamonds, light mfg., oil refining. **Chief crops:** rice, coffee, cocoa, palm kernels & oil, peanuts. **Natural resources:** diamonds, titanium ore, bauxite, iron ore, gold, chromite. **Arable land:** 7%. **Livestock** (2004): cattle: 400,000; chickens: 7.5 mil; goats: 220,000; pigs: 52,000; sheep: 375,000. **Fish catch** (2003): 96,926 metric tons. **Electricity prod.** (2003): 0.26 bil kWh.

Finance: Monetary unit: Leone (SLL) (Sept. 2005: 2,401.76 = $1 U.S.). **GDP** (2004 est.): $3.3 bil; **per capita GDP:** $600; **GDP growth:** 6%. **Imports** (2002 est.): $264.0 mil; partners (2004): Germany 17.3%, UK 9.2%, Côte d'Ivoire 8%, US 8%, Ukraine 4.9%, Netherlands 4.7%, China 4.5%, Denmark 4.2%. **Exports** (2002 est.): $49.0 mil; partners (2004): Belgium 63.1%, Germany 11.9%, US 5.8%. **Tourism:** $60 mil. **Budget** (2000 est.): $351.0 mil. **Intl. reserves less gold:** $81 mil. **Consumer prices:** 14.19%.

Transport: Railroad: Length: 52 mi. **Motor vehicles**: 20,100 pass. cars, 15,800 comm. vehicles. **Civil aviation:** 45.4 mil pass.-mi.; 1 airport. **Chief ports:** Freetown, Bonthe.

Communications: TV sets: 13 per 1,000 pop. **Radios:** 274 per 1,000 pop. **Telephone lines** (2002): 24,000. **Daily newspaper circ.:** 4.7 per 1,000 pop. **Internet** (2002): 8,000 users.

Health: Life expect.: 37.7 male; 42.1 female. **Births** (per 1,000 pop.): 46.1. **Deaths** (per 1,000 pop.): 23.4. **Natural inc.:** 2.27%. **Infant mortality** (per 1,000 live births): 162.6.

Education: Literacy : 31.4%.

Major Intl. Organizations: UN (FAO, IBRD, ILO, IMF, IMO, WHO, WTrO), the Commonwealth, AU.

Embassy: 1701 19th St. NW 20009; 939-9261.

Website: www.statehouse-sl.org

Freetown was founded in 1787 by the British government as a haven for freed slaves. Their descendants, known as Creoles, number more than 60,000.

Successive steps toward independence followed the 1951 constitution. Ten years later, full independence arrived Apr. 27, 1961. Sierra Leone declared itself a republic Apr. 19, 1971. A one-party state approved by referendum in 1978 brought political stability, but mismanagement and corruption plagued the economy.

Mutinous soldiers ousted Pres. Joseph Momoh Apr. 30, 1992. Another coup, Jan. 16, 1996, paved the way for multiparty elections and a return to civilian rule. A peace accord, signed Nov. 30 with the Revolutionary United Front (RUF), brought a temporary halt to a civil war that had claimed over 10,000 lives in 5 years.

A coup on May 25, 1997, was met with widespread international opposition. Armed intervention by Nigeria restored Pres. Ahmad Tejan Kabbah to power on Mar. 10, 1998, but RUF rebels mounted a guerrilla counteroffensive, reportedly killing thousands of civilians and mutilating thousands more. The Kabbah government signed a power-sharing agreement with the RUF on July 7, 1999. A UN mission (UNAMSIL) was established in Oct. to help maintain the agreement. The accord collapsed in early May 2000, as RUF guerrillas took more than 500 UN peacekeepers hostage. Rebel leader Foday Sankoh was captured in Freetown May 17. The hostages were freed by the end of May, and 233 more UN personnel behind rebel lines were rescued July 15.

A UN-sponsored disarmament program in 2001 reduced the level of violence. On Jan. 16, 2002, the government and the UN signed an agreement creating the Sierra Leone Special Court to try war crimes that had occurred from Nov. 1996 onwards. Government and rebel leaders declared an official end to the war Jan. 18. Kabbah won the May 14 presidential election.

Sankoh, an indicted war criminal, died in UN custody July 29, 2003. A UN helicopter crashed June 29, 2004, in E Sierra Leone, killing all 24 people on board. UNAMSIL still had about 3200 troops in Sierra Leone in mid-2005.

Singapore

Republic of Singapore

People: Population: 4,425,720. **Age distrib.** (%): <15: 16.0; 65+: 8.1. **Pop. density:** 16,514 per sq mi, 6,386 per sq km. **Urban:** 100.0%. **Ethnic groups:** Chinese 77%, Malay 14%, Indian 8%. **Principal languages:** Chinese, Malay, Tamil, English (all official). **Chief religions:** Buddhist 43%, Muslim 15%, Christian 15%, Taoist 9%.

Geography: Total area: 267 sq mi, 693 sq km; **Land area:** 264 sq mi, 683 sq km. **Location:** Off tip of Malayan Peninsula in SE Asia. **Neighbors:** Nearest are Malaysia on N, Indonesia on S. **Topography:** Singapore is a flat, formerly swampy island. The nation includes 40 nearby islets. **Capital:** Singapore, 4,253,000.

Government: Type: Republic. **Head of state:** Pres. S. R. Nathan; b July 3, 1924; in office: Sept. 1, 1999. **Head of gov.:** Prime Min. Lee Hsien Loong; b Feb. 10, 1952; in office: Aug. 12, 2004. **Defense budget** (2004): $5 bill. **Active troops:** 72,500.

Economy: Industries: electronics, chemicals, financial services, oil drilling equip., oil refining, rubber proc. **Chief crops:** rubber, copra, fruit, orchids, vegetables. **Natural resources:** fish. **Arable land:** 2%. **Livestock** (2004): cattle: 200; chickens: 2.0 mil; goats: 600; pigs: 250,000. **Fish catch** (2003): 7,109 metric tons. **Electricity prod.** (2003): 33.2 bil kWh. **Labor force** (2003): manufacturing 18%, construction 6%, transportation and communication 11%, financial, business, and other services 49%, other 16%.

Finance: Monetary unit: Singapore Dollar (SGD) (Sept. 2005: 1.68 = $1 U.S.). **GDP** (2004 est.): $120.9 bil; **per capita GDP:** $27,800; **GDP growth:** 8.1%. **Imports** (2004 est.): $155.2 bil; partners (2004): Malaysia 15.3%, US 12.7%, Japan 11.7%, China 9.9%, Taiwan 5.7%, South Korea 4.3%, Thailand 4.1%. **Exports** (2004 est.): $174.0 bil; partners (2004): Malaysia 15.2%, US 13%, Hong Kong 9.8%, China 8.6%, Japan 6.4%, Taiwan 4.6%, Thailand 4.3%, South Korea 4.1%. **Tourism:** $3,998 mil. **Budget** (2004 est.): $18.5 bil. **Intl. reserves less gold:** $72.27 bil. **Consumer prices:** 1.66%.

Transport: Railroad: Length: 24 mi. **Motor vehicles:** 425,700 pass. cars, 138,600 comm. vehicles. **Civil aviation:** 43.6 bil pass.-mi; 9 airports. **Chief port:** Singapore.

Communications: TV sets: 341 per 1,000 pop. **Radios:** 744 per 1,000 pop. **Telephone lines** (2002): 1.9 mil. **Daily newspaper circ.:** 324 per 1,000 pop. **Internet** (2002): 2.1 mil users.

Health: Life expect.: 79.1 male; 84.4 female. **Births** (per 1,000 pop.): 9.5. **Deaths** (per 1,000 pop.): 4.2. **Natural inc.:** 0.53%. **Infant mortality** (per 1,000 live births): 2.3. **AIDS rate:** 0.2%

Education: Compulsory: ages 6-16. **Literacy:** 92.5%.

Major Intl. Organizations: UN (IBRD, ILO, IMF, IMO, WHO, WTrO), the Commonwealth, APEC, ASEAN.

Embassy: 3501 International Pl. NW 20008; 537-3100.

Website: www.gov.sg

Founded in 1819 by Sir Thomas Stamford Raffles, Singapore was a British colony until 1959, when it became autonomous within the Commonwealth. On Sept. 16, 1963, it joined with Malaya, Sarawak, and Sabah to form the Federation of Malaysia. Tensions between Malayans, dominant in the federation, and ethnic Chinese, dominant in Singapore, led to an accord under which Singapore became a separate nation, Aug. 9, 1965.

Singapore is one of the world's largest ports and a major center of manufacturing, banking, and commerce. Standards in health, education, and housing are generally high. The government, dominated by a single party, has taken strong actions to keep order and suppress dissent.

In Dec. 2001, the government thwarted an alleged plot to blow up the U.S. Embassy; in Sept. 2002, authorities reported arrests of 21 militants identified as members of Jemaah Islamiah, a radical Muslim group active in Southeast Asia.

Singapore has had only 3 prime ministers: Lee Kuan Yew, who dominated national politics, 1959-90; Goh Chok Tong, 1990-2004; and Lee Kuan Yew's son, Lee Hsien Loong, who took office Aug. 12, 2004. At the White House, July 12, 2005, the prime minister and Pres. George W. Bush signed an agreement tightening U.S.-Singapore defense ties.

Slovakia

Slovak Republic

People: Population: 5,431,363. **Age distrib.** (%): <15: 17.1; 65+: 11.9. **Pop. density:** 288 per sq mi, 111 per sq km. **Urban:** 57.4%. **Ethnic groups:** Slovak 86%, Hungarian 11%, Roma 2%. **Principal languages:** Slovak (official), Hungarian. **Chief religions:** Roman Catholic 69%, Protestant 11%.

Geography: Total area: 18,859 sq mi, 48,845 sq km; **Land area:** 18,842 sq mi, 48,800 sq km. **Location:** In E central Europe. **Neighbors:** Poland on N, Hungary on S, Austria and Czech Rep. on W, Ukraine on E. **Topography:** Mountains (Carpathians) in N, fertile Danube plane in S. **Capital:** Bratislava, 425,000. **Cities (urban aggr.):** Kosice, 242,000.

Government: Type: Republic. **Head of state:** Ivan Gasparovic; b Mar. 27, 1941; in office: June 15, 2004. **Head of gov.:** Prime Min. Mikulás Dzurinda; b Feb. 4, 1955; in office: Oct. 30, 1998. **Local divisions:** 8 departments. **Defense budget** (2004): $717 mil. **Active troops:** 20,195.

Economy: Industries: metals; food & beverages; electricity, gas, coke, oil, nuclear fuels. **Chief crops:** grains, potatoes, sugar beets, hops, fruit. **Natural resources:** coal, lignite, iron ore, copper, mang., salt. **Crude oil reserves** (2004): 9 mil bbls. **Arable land:** 31%. **Livestock** (2004): cattle: 540,146; chickens: 6.3 mil; goats: 39,012; pigs: 1.1 mil; sheep: 321,227. **Fish catch** (2003): 2,527 metric tons. **Electricity prod.** (2003): 29.7 bil kWh. **Labor force** (2003): agriculture 5.8%, industry 29.3%, construction 9%, services 55.9%.

Finance: Monetary unit: Koruna (SKK) (Sept. 2005: 30.86 = $1 U.S.). **GDP** (2004 est.): $78.9 bil; **per capita GDP:** $14,500; **GDP growth:** 5.3%. **Imports** (2004 est.): $29.7 bil; partners (2004): Germany 29.6%, Czech Republic 17.1%, Russia 9.5%, Austria 7.1%, Italy 5.4%, Hungary 4.3%. **Exports** (2004 est.): $29.2 bil; partners (2004): Germany 35.7%, Czech Republic 13.4%, Austria 8.6%, Italy 5.6%, US 4.8%, Poland 4.8%, Hungary 4.3%. **Tourism:** $865 mil. **Budget** (2004 est.): $16.7 bil. **Intl. reserves less gold** (2003): $7.86 bil. **Gold** (2003): 1.13 mil. oz t. **Consumer prices:** 7.55%.

Transport: Railroad: Length: 2,279 mi. **Motor vehicles:** 1.33 mil pass. cars, 174,300 comm. vehicles. **Civil aviation:** 52.8 mil pass.-mi; 20 airports. **Chief ports:** Bratislava, Komarno.

Communications: TV sets: 418 per 1,000 pop. **Radios:** 967 per 1,000 pop. **Telephone lines:** 1.3 mil. **Daily newspaper circ.:** 130.6 per 1,000 pop. **Internet:** 1.4 mil users.

Health: Life expect.: 70.5 male; 78.7 female. **Births** (per 1,000 pop.): 10.6. **Deaths** (per 1,000 pop.): 9.4. **Natural inc.:** 0.12%. **Infant mortality** (per 1,000 live births): 7.4. **AIDS rate:** <0.1%.

Education: Compulsory: ages 6-15. **Literacy:** NA.

Major Intl. Organizations: UN (FAO, IBRD, ILO, IMF, IMO, WHO, WTrO), EU, NATO, OSCE.

Embassy: 3523 International Ct. NW 20008; 237-1054.

Website: www.government.gov.sk/english

Slovakia was originally settled by Illyrian, Celtic, and Germanic tribes and was incorporated into Great Moravia in the 9th century. It became part of Hungary in the 11th century. Overrun by Czech Hussites in the 15th century, it was restored to Hungarian rule in 1526. The Slovaks disassociated themselves from Hungary after World War I and joined the Czechs of Bohemia to form the Republic of Czechoslovakia, Oct. 28, 1918.

Germany invaded Czechoslovakia, 1939, and declared Slovakia independent. Slovakia rejoined Czechoslovakia in 1945.

Czechoslovakia split into 2 separate states—the Czech Republic and Slovakia—on Jan. 1, 1993. A prolonged parliamentary standoff left the country without a president for much of 1998.

Prime Min. Vladimir Meciar, a nationalist, suffered a setback in legislative elections Sept. 25-26, 1998, and was defeated in a presidential runoff vote by Rudolf Schuster, May 29, 1999. A center-right coalition governed Slovakia after parliamentary elections Sept. 20-21, 2002. Meciar lost another bid for the presidency to his former ally, Ivan Gasparovic, Apr. 17, 2004. Slovakia became a full member of the EU and NATO in 2004.

Slovenia

Republic of Slovenia

People: Population: 2,011,070. **Age distrib.** (%): <15: 14.0; 65+: 15.4. **Pop. density:** 257 per sq mi, 99 per sq km. **Urban:** 50.8%. **Ethnic groups:** Slovene 88%, Croat 3%, Serb 2%, Bosniak 1%. **Principal languages:** Slovenian (official), Serbo-Croatian. **Chief religion:** Roman Catholic 58%, other, unspecified 23%.

Geography: Total area: 7,827 sq mi, 20,273 sq km; **Land area:** 7,780 sq mi, 20,151 sq km. **Location:** In SE Europe. **Neighbors:** Italy on W, Austria on N, Hungary on NE, Croatia on SE, S. **Topography:** Mostly hilly; 42% of the land is forested. **Capital:** Ljubljana, 256,000.

Government: Type: Republic. **Head of state:** Pres. Janez Drnovsek; b May 17, 1950; in office: Dec. 22, 2002. **Head of gov.:** Prime Min. Janez Jansa; b Sept. 17, 1958; in office: Nov. 9, 2004. **Local divisions:** 183 municipalities, 11 urban municipalities. **Defense budget** (2004): $458 mil. **Active troops:** 6,550.

Economy: Industries: metallurgy, electronics, trucks, electric power equip., wood products, textiles, chemicals, machine tools. **Chief crops:** potatoes, hops, wheat, sugar beets, corn, grapes. **Natural resources:** lignite, lead, zinc, mercury, uranium, silver, hydropower, timber. **Crude oil reserves:** NA. **Livestock** (2004): cattle: 450,226; chickens: 4.5 mil; goats: 23,031; pigs: 620,506; sheep: 105,660. **Fish catch** (2003): 2,634 metric tons. **Electricity prod.** (2003): 13.2 bil kWh. **Labor force** (2002): agriculture 6%, industry 40%, services 55%.

Finance: Monetary unit: Tolar (SIT) (Sept. 2005: 191.45 = $1 U.S.). **GDP** (2004 est.): $39.4 bil; **per capita GDP:** $19,600; **GDP growth:** 3.9%. **Imports** (2004 est.): $16.1 bil; partners (2004): Germany 20.1%, Italy 17%, Austria 14.1%, France 10.4%. **Exports** (2004 est.): $15.0 bil; partners (2004): Germany 18.4%, Austria 11.4%, Italy 11.1%, Croatia 7.6%, France 7.5%, Bosnia and Herzegovina 4.6%. **Tourism:** $1,342 mil. **Budget** (2004 est.): $14.0 bil. **Intl. reserves less gold:** $5.66 bil. **Gold:** 240,000 oz t. **Consumer prices:** 3.58%.

Transport: Railroad: Length: 746 mi. **Motor vehicles:** 896,700 pass. cars, 54,300 comm. vehicles. **Civil aviation:** 408.2 mil pass.-mi; 6 airports. **Chief ports:** Izola, Koper, Piran.

Communications: TV sets: 362 per 1,000 pop. **Radios:** 404 per 1,000 pop. **Telephone lines:** 812,300. **Daily newspaper circ.:** 168.5 per 1,000 pop. **Internet:** 800,000 users.

Health: Life expect.: 72.4 male; 80.1 female. **Births** (per 1,000 pop.): 9.0. **Deaths** (per 1,000 pop.): 10.2. **Natural inc.:** -0.13%. **Infant mortality** (per 1,000 live births): 4.5. **AIDS rate:** <0.1%.

Education: Compulsory: ages 7-13. **Literacy:** 99.7%.

Major Intl. Organizations: UN (FAO, IBRD, ILO, IMF, IMO, WHO, WTrO), EU, NATO, OSCE.

Embassy: 1525 New Hampshire Ave. NW 20036; 667-5363.

Website: e-uprava.gov.si/e-uprava/en/portal.euprava

The Slovenes settled in their current territory during the period from the 6th to the 8th century. They fell under German domination as early as the 9th century. Modern Slovenian political history began after 1848 when the Slovenes, who were divided among several Austrian provinces, began their struggle for political and national unification. In 1918 a majority of Slovenes became part of the Kingdom of Serbs, Croats, and Slovenes, later renamed Yugoslavia.

Slovenia declared independence June 25, 1991, and joined the UN May 22, 1992. The country attained full membership in the EU and NATO in 2004.

Solomon Islands

People: Population: 538,032. **Age distrib.** (%): <15: 41.9; 65+: 3.2. **Pop. density:** 49 per sq mi, 19 per sq km. **Urban:** 16.5%. **Ethnic groups:** Melanesian 93%, Polynesian 4%, Micronesian, European, and others 3%. **Principal languages:** English (official), Melanesian pidgin, and 120 indigenous languages. **Chief religions:** Protestant 74%, Roman Catholic 11%.

Geography: Total area: 10,985 sq mi, 28,450 sq km; **Land area:** 10,633 sq mi, 27,540 sq km. **Location:** Melanesian Archipelago in the W Pacific O. **Neighbors:** Nearest is Papua New Guinea to W. **Topography:** 10 large volcanic and rugged islands and 4 groups of smaller ones. **Capital:** Honiara, 56,000.

Government: Type: Parliamentary democracy. **Head of state:** Queen Elizabeth II, represented by Gov.-Gen. Sir Nathaniel Waena; in office: July 7, 2004. **Head of gov.:** Prime Min. Sir Allan Kemakeza; b 1951; in office: Dec. 17, 2001. **Local divisions:** 9 provinces and Honiara.

Economy: Industries: tuna, mining, timber. **Chief crops:** cocoa, beans, coconuts, palm kernels, rice, potatoes. **Natural resources:** fish, timber, gold, bauxite, phosphates, lead, zinc, nickel. **Arable land:** 1%. **Crude oil reserves:** NA. **Livestock** (2004): cattle: 13,500; chickens: 230,000; pigs: 69,000. **Fish catch** (2003): 39,849 metric tons. **Electricity prod.** (2003): 0.06 bil kWh. **Labor force** (2000 est.): agriculture 75%, industry 5%, services 20%.

Finance: Monetary unit: Dollar (SBD) (Sept. 2005: 7.27 = $1 U.S.). **GDP** (2002 est.): $800.0 mil; **per capita GDP:** $1,700; **GDP growth:** 5.8%. **Imports** (2003): $67.0 mil; partners (2004): Australia 25.3%, Singapore 23.8%, New Zealand 5.3%, India 4.8%. **Exports** (2003 est.): $74.0 mil; partners (2004): China 28.2%, Thailand 15.7%, South Korea 15.7%, Japan 9.7%, Philippines 5.1%. **Tourism:** $2 mil. **Budget** (2003): $75.1 mil. **Intl. reserves less gold:** $52 mil. **Consumer prices:** 7.12%.

Transport: Civil aviation: 32.3 mil pass.-mi; 2 airports. **Chief port:** Honiara.

Communications: TV sets: 16 per 1,000 pop. **Radios:** 141 per 1,000 pop. **Telephone lines:** 6,200. **Internet:** 2,500 users.

Health: Life expect.: 70.2 male; 75.3 female. **Births** (per 1,000 pop.): 30.7. **Deaths** (per 1,000 pop.): 4.0. **Natural inc.:** 2.68%. **Infant mortality** (per 1,000 live births): 21.3.

Major Intl. Organizations: UN (FAO, IBRD, ILO, IMF, IMO, WHO, WTrO), the Commonwealth.

Embassy: 800 Second Avenue, Suite 8008, New York, NY 10017; 212-599-6192

Website: www.commerce.gov.sb

The Solomon Islands were sighted in 1568 by an expedition from Peru. Britain established a protectorate in the 1890s over most of the group, inhabited by Melanesians. The islands saw major World War II battles. Self-government came Jan. 2, 1976, and independence was formally attained July 7, 1978.

A coup attempt June 5, 2000, sparked factional fighting in Honiara. During the next 3 years, violence, lawlessness, and corruption became widespread. To restore order, a 2,225-member intervention force, led by Australia and authorized by the Pacific Islands Forum, began arriving in Honiara July 24, 2003; nearly all foreign troops had been removed by mid-2005.

Somalia

People: Population: 8,591,629. **Age distrib.** (%): <15: 44.5; 65+: 2.6. **Pop. density:** 35 per sq mi, 13 per sq km. **Urban:** 34.8%. **Ethnic groups:** Somali 85%, Bantu and other 15%. **Principal languages:** Somali, Arabic (both official); Italian, English. **Chief religion:** Sunni Muslim (official).

Geography: Total area: 246,201 sq mi, 637,657 sq km; **Land area:** 242,216 sq mi, 627,337 sq km. **Location:** Occupies the eastern horn of Africa. **Neighbors:** Djibouti, Ethiopia, Kenya on W. **Topography:** The coastline extends for 1,700 mi. Hills cover the N; the center and S are flat. **Capital:** Mogadishu, 1,175,000.

Government: Type: In transition. **Head of state:** Abdullahi Yusuf Ahmed; b Dec. 15, 1934; in office: Oct. 14, 2004. **Head of gov.:** Prime Min. Ali Muhammad Ghedi; b 1952; in office: Nov. 3, 2004. **Local divisions:** 18 regions. **Defense budget:** NA. **Active troops:** Nil.

Economy: Industries: a few light industries, incl. sugar refining, textiles, wireless communication. **Chief crops:** bananas, sorghum, corn, coconuts, rice. **Natural resources:** uranium, iron ore, tin, gypsum, bauxite, copper, salt, nat. gas, oil. **Arable land:** 2%. **Livestock** (2002): cattle: 5.30 mil; chickens: 3.30 mil; goats: 12.50 mil; pigs: 4,000; sheep: 13.20 mil. **Fish catch** (2003): 18,000 metric tons. **Electricity prod.** (2003): 0.24 bil kWh. **Labor force:** agriculture (mostly pastoral nomadism) 71%, industry and services 29%.

Finance: Monetary unit: Shilling (SOS) (Sept. 2005: 2,267.00 = $1 U.S.).**GDP** (2004 est.): $4.6 bil; **per capita GDP:** $600; **GDP growth:** 2.8%. **Imports** (2002 est.): $344.0 mil; partners (2004): Djibouti 28.8%, Kenya 13.1%, India 9.3%, Brazil 5.4%, Oman 5.2%, UAE 5.1%. **Exports** (2002 est.): $79.0 mil; partners (2004): Thailand 31.3%, UAE 22.8%, Yemen 14.9%, India 8.5%, Oman 5.4%, China 4.1%.

Transport: Motor vehicles: 12,000 pass. cars, 12,000 comm. vehicles. **Civil aviation:** 86.9 mil pass.-mi; 6 airports. **Chief ports:** Mogadishu, Berbera.

Communications: TV sets: 14 per 1,000 pop. **Radios:** 53 per 1,000 pop. **Telephone lines:** 15,000 main lines. **Daily newspaper circ.:** 1.2 per 1,000 pop.

Health: Life expect.: 46.4 male; 49.9 female. **Births** (per 1,000 pop.): 45.6. **Deaths** (per 1,000 pop.): 17.0. **Natural inc.:** 2.87%. **Infant mortality** (per 1,000 live births): 116.7.

Education: Compulsory: ages 6-13. **Literacy** (2001 est.): 37.8%.

Major Intl. Organizations: UN (FAO, IBRD, ILO, IMF, IMO, WHO), AL, AU.

Website: www.state.gov/p/af/ci/so/

British Somaliland (present-day N Somalia) was formed in the 19th century, as was Italian Somaliland (now central and S Somalia). Italy lost its African colonies in World War II. British Somaliland gained independence, June 26, 1960, and by prearrangement, merged July 1 with the UN Trust Territory of Somalia to create the independent Somali Republic.

On Oct. 16, 1969, Pres. Abdi Rashid Ali Shirmarke was assassinated. On Oct. 21, a military group led by Maj. Gen. Muhammad Siad Barre seized power. In 1970, Barre declared the country a socialist state—the Somali Democratic Republic.

Somalia has laid claim to Ogaden, the huge eastern region of Ethiopia, peopled mostly by Somalis. Ethiopia battled Somali rebels in 1977. Some 11,000 Cuban troops with Soviet arms defeated Somali army troops and ethnic Somali rebels in Ethiopia, 1978. As many as 1.5 million refugees entered Somalia. Guerrilla fighting in Ogaden continued until 1988, when a peace agreement was reached with Ethiopia.

The civil war intensified again and Barre was forced to flee the capital, Jan. 1991. Fighting between rival factions caused 40,000 casualties in 1991 and 1992, and by mid-1992 the civil war, drought, and banditry combined to produce a famine that threatened some 1.5 million people with starvation.

In Dec. 1992 the UN accepted a U.S. offer of troops to safeguard food delivery to the starving. The UN took control of the multinational relief effort from the U.S. May 4, 1993. While the operation helped alleviate the famine, there were significant U.S. and other casualties; a failed mission Oct. 3-4 left 18 U.S. troops and more than 500 Somalis dead. The U.S. withdrew its peacekeeping forces Mar. 25, 1994.

When the last UN troops pulled out Mar. 3, 1995, Mogadishu had no functioning central government, and armed factions controlled different regions. By 1999 a joint police force was operating in the capital, but much of the country, especially in S Somalia, faced continued violence and food shortages. After political and factional leaders signed a peace deal Jan. 29, 2004, a transitional parliament, Somalia's 1st legislature in 13 yrs, was inaugurated Aug. 22. Meeting in Nairobi, Kenya, the parliament chose Abdullahi Yusuf Ahmed as president; he was sworn in Oct. 14. Because Mogadishu was controlled by his rivals, Pres. Yusuf moved, July 26, 2005, to establish his capital at Jowhar.

The Indian Ocean tsunami of Dec. 26, 2004, killed at least 150 people and displaced about 5,000 in Somalia.

South Africa

Republic of South Africa

People: Population: 44,344,136. **Age distrib.** (%): <15: 30.3; 65+: 5.2. **Pop. density:** 94 per sq mi, 36 per sq km. **Urban:** 56.9%. **Ethnic groups:** Black 75%, White 14%, mixed 8%, Indian 3%. **Principal languages:** Afrikaans, English, Ndebele, Pedi, Sotho, Swazi, Tsonga, Tswana, Venda, Xhosa, Zulu (all official). **Chief religions:** Christian 68%, indigenous beliefs and animist 29%.

Geography: Total area: 471,011 sq mi, 1,219,912 sq km; **Land area:** 471,011 sq mi, 1,219,912 sq km. **Location:** At the southern extreme of Africa. **Neighbors:** Namibia, Botswana, Zimbabwe on N; Mozambique, Swaziland on E; surrounds Lesotho. **Topography:** The large interior plateau reaches close to the country's 1,739-mi. coastline. There are few major rivers or lakes; rainfall is sparse in W, more plentiful in E. **Capitals:** Cape Town (legislative), 2,967,000, Pretoria (administrative), 1,209,000, and Bloemfontein (judicial), 381,000. **Cities (urban aggr.):** Durban, 2,370,000; Johannesburg, 2,732,000.

Government: Type: Republic. **Head of state and gov.:** Pres. Thabo Mvuyelwa Mbeki; b: June 18, 1942; in office: June 16, 1999. **Local divisions:** 9 provinces. **Defense budget** (2004): $3.3 bil. **Active troops:** 55,750.

Economy: Industries: mining (espec. platinum, gold, chromium), auto assembly, metalworking, machinery, textiles, chemicals, fertilizer, foodstuffs. **Chief crops:** corn, wheat, sugarcane, fruits, vegetables. **Natural resources:** gold, chromium, antimony, coal, iron ore, mang., nickel, phosphates, tin, uranium, diamonds, platinum, copper, vanadium, salt, nat. gas. **Crude oil reserves** (2004): 16 mil bbls. **Arable land:** 10%. **Livestock** (2004): cattle: 13.5 mil; chickens: 145.0 mil; goats: 6.4 mil; pigs: 1.7 mil; sheep: 29.1 mil. **Fish catch** (2003): 827,750 metric tons. **Electricity prod.** (2003): 215.9 bil kWh. **Labor force** (1999 est.): agriculture 30%, industry 25%, services 45%.

Finance: Monetary unit: Rand (ZAR) (Sept. 2005: 6.31 = $1 U.S.). **GDP** (2004 est.): $491.4 bil; **per capita GDP:** $11,100; **GDP growth:** 3.5%. **Imports** (2004 est.): $39.4 bil; partners (2004): Germany 14.2%, US 8.5%, China 7.5%, Japan 6.9%, UK 6.9%, France 6%, Saudi Arabia 5.6%, Iran 5%. **Exports** (2004 est.): $42.0 bil; partners (2004): US 10.2%, UK 9.2%, Japan 9%, Germany 7.1%, Netherlands 4%. **Tourism:** $4,270 mil. **Budget** (2004 est.): $52.5 bil. **Intl. reserves less gold:** $8.46 bil. **Gold:** 3.98 mil oz t. **Consumer prices:** 1.39%.

Transport: Railroad: Length: 13,855 mi. **Motor vehicles** : 3.97 mil pass. cars, 2.25 mil comm. vehicles. **Civil aviation:** 13.7 bil pass.-mi. **Chief ports:** Durban, Cape Town, East London, Port Elizabeth.

Communications: TV sets: 138 per 1,000 pop. **Radios:** 355 per 1,000 pop. **Telephone lines** (2002): 4.8 mil. **Daily newspaper circ.:** 32 per 1,000 pop. **Internet** (2002): 3.1 mil users.

Health: Life expect.: 43.5 male; 43.1 female. **Births** (per 1,000 pop.): 18.5. **Deaths** (per 1,000 pop.): 21.3. **Natural inc.:** -0.28%. **Infant mortality** (per 1,000 live births): 61.8. **AIDS rate:** 21.5%.

Education: Compulsory: ages 7-15. **Literacy:** 86.4%.

Major Intl. Organizations: UN (FAO, IBRD, ILO, IMF, IMO, WHO, WTrO), the Commonwealth, AU.

Embassy: 3051 Massachusetts Ave. NW 20008; 232-4400.

Website: www.gov.za

Bushmen and KhoiKhoi were the original inhabitants. Bantus, including Zulu, Xhosa, Swazi, and Sotho, had occupied the area from NE to S South Africa before the 17th century.

The Cape of Good Hope area was settled by Dutch, beginning in the 17th century. Britain seized the Cape in 1806. Many Dutch trekked north and founded 2 republics, Transvaal and Orange Free State. Diamonds were discovered, 1867, and gold, 1886. The Dutch (Boers) resented encroachments by the British and others; the Anglo-Boer War followed, 1899-1902. Britain won and, effective May 31, 1910, created the Union of South Africa, incorporating 2 British colonies (Cape and Natal) with Transvaal and Orange Free State. After a referendum, the Union became the Republic of South Africa, May 31, 1961, and withdrew from the Commonwealth.

With the election victory of Daniel Malan's National Party in 1948, the policy of separate development of the races, or apartheid, already existing unofficially, became official. Under apartheid, blacks were severely restricted to certain occupations, and paid far lower wages than whites for similar work. Only whites could vote or run for public office. Persons of Asian Indian ancestry and those of mixed race (Coloureds) had limited political rights. In 1959 the government passed acts providing for the eventual creation of several Bantu nations, or Bantustans.

Protests against apartheid were brutally suppressed. At Sharpeville on Mar. 21, 1960, 69 black protesters were killed by government troops. At least 600 persons, mostly Bantus, were killed in 1976 riots protesting apartheid. In 1981, South Africa launched military operations in Angola and Mozambique to combat guerrilla groups.

A new constitution was approved by referendum, Nov. 1983, extending the parliamentary franchise to the Coloured and Asian minorities. Laws banning interracial sex and marriage were repealed in 1985.

In 1986, Nobel Peace Prize winner Bishop Desmond Tutu called for Western nations to apply sanctions against South Africa to force an end to apartheid. Pres. P. W. Botha announced in Apr. the end to the nation's system of racial pass laws and offered blacks an advisory role in government. On May 19, South Africa attacked 3 neighboring countries—Zimbabwe, Botswana, Zambia—to strike at guerrilla strongholds of the black nationalist African National Congress (ANC). A nationwide state of emergency was declared June 12, giving almost unlimited power to the security forces.

Some 2 million South African black workers staged a massive strike, June 6-8, 1988. Pres. Botha, head of the government since 1978, resigned Aug. 14, 1989, and was replaced by F. W. de Klerk. In 1990 the government lifted its ban on the ANC. Black nationalist leader Nelson Mandela was freed Feb. 11 after more than 27 years in prison. In Feb. 1991, Pres. de Klerk announced plans to end all apartheid laws.

In 1993 negotiators agreed on basic principles for a new democratic constitution. South Africa's partially self-governing black territories, or "homelands," were dissolved and incorporated into a national system of 9 provinces. In elections Apr. 26-29, 1994, the ANC won 62.7% of the vote, making Mandela president. The National Party won 20.4%. The Inkatha Freedom Party won 10.5% and control of the legislature in a mainly Zulu province. By then, fighting between the ANC and Inkatha (aided, during the apartheid era, by South African defense forces) had killed more than 14,000 people in the Zulu region since the mid-1980s.

In 1995, Mandela appointed a truth commission, led by Desmond Tutu, to document human rights abuses under apartheid. A post-apartheid constitution, modified to meet the objections of the Constitutional Court, became law Dec. 10, 1996, with provisions to take effect over a 3-year period.

The ANC won a landslide victory in elections held June 2, 1999. ANC leader Thabo Mbeki, Mandela's deputy president, thus became South Africa's 2nd popularly elected president. Led by Mbeki, the ANC won almost 70% of the vote in national elections Apr. 14, 2004. In a farewell address before parliament, Nelson Mandela, 85, retired from public life, May 10.

The UN recently estimated that more than 5 million South Africans, including 21.5% of all adults, have HIV/AIDS.

Spain

Kingdom of Spain

People: Population: 40,341,462. **Age distrib.** (%): <15: 14.4; 65+: 17.6. **Pop. density:** 207 per sq mi, 80 per sq km. **Urban:** 76.5%. **Ethnic groups:** Castilian, Catalan, Basque, Galician. **Principal languages:** Castilian Spanish (official), Catalan, Galician, Basque. **Chief religion:** Roman Catholic 94%.

Geography: Total area: 194,897 sq mi, 504,782 sq km; **Land area:** 192,874 sq mi, 499,542 sq km. **Location:** In SW Europe. **Neighbors:** Portugal on W, France on N. **Topography:** The interior is a high, arid plateau broken by mountain ranges and river valleys. The NW is heavily watered, the S has lowlands and a Mediterranean climate. **Capital:** Madrid, 5,103,000. **Cities (urban agg.):** Barcelona, 4,378,000; Valencia, 754,000.

Government: Type: Constitutional monarchy. **Head of state:** King Juan Carlos I de Borbon y Borbon; b Jan. 5, 1938; in office: Nov. 22, 1975. **Head of gov.:** Prime Min. José Luis Rodríguez Zapatero; b Aug. 4, 1960; in office: Apr. 17, 2004. **Local divisions:** 17 automonous communities and two autonomous cities. **Defense budget** (2004): $8 bil. **Active troops:** 150,700.

Economy: Industries: textiles & apparel, food & beverages, metals, chemicals, shipbuilding, autos, machine tools, tourism. **Chief crops:** grain, vegetables, olives, grapes, sugar beets, citrus. **Natural resources:** coal, lignite, iron ore, uranium, mercury, pyrites, fluorspar, gypsum, zinc, lead, tungsten, copper, kaolin, potash, hydropower. **Crude oil reserves** (2004): 158 mil bbls. **Arable land:** 30%. **Livestock** (2004): cattle: 6.5 mil; chickens: 128.0 mil; goats: 3.0 mil; pigs: 24.0 mil; sheep: 24.0 mil. **Fish catch** (2003): 1,209,605 metric tons. **Electricity prod.** (2003): 247.3 bil kWh. **Labor force** (2004 est.): agriculture 5.3%, manufacturing, mining, and construction 30.1%, services 64.6%.

Finance: Monetary unit: Euro (EUR) (Sept. 2005: 0.80 = $1 U.S.) **GDP** (2004 est.): $937.6 bil; **per capita GDP:** $23,300; **GDP growth:** 2.6%. **Imports** (2004 est.): $222.0 bil; partners (2004): Germany 16.5%, France 15.7%, Italy 8.8%, UK 6.3%, Netherlands 4.8%. **Exports** (2004 est.): $172.5 bil; partners (2004): France 19.3%, Germany 11.7%, Portugal 9.6%, UK 9.1%, Italy 9.1%. **Tourism:** $41,770 mil. **Budget** (2004 est.): $386.4 bil. **Intl. reserves less gold:** $7.98 bil. **Gold:** 16.83 mil oz t. **Consumer prices:** 3.03%.

Transport: Railroad: Length: 8,817 mi. **Motor vehicles:** 18.2 mil pass. cars, 4.16 mil. comm. vehicles. **Civil aviation:** 34.4 bil pass.-mi; 93 airports. **Chief ports:** Barcelona, Bilbao, Valencia, Cartagena.

Communications: TV sets: 555 per 1,000 pop. **Radios:** 331 per 1,000 pop. **Telephone lines:** 17.6 mil. **Daily newspaper circ.:** 100.3 per 1,000 pop. **Internet:** 9.8 mil users.

Health: Life expect.: 76.2 male; 83.1 female. **Births** (per 1,000 pop.): 10.1. **Deaths** (per 1,000 pop.): 9.6. **Natural inc.:** 0.05%. **Infant mortality** (per 1,000 live births): 4.4. **AIDS rate:** 0.7%.

Education: Compulsory: ages 6-16. **Literacy:** 97.9%.

Major Intl. Organizations: UN and all of its specialized agencies, EU, NATO, OECD, OSCE.

Embassy: 2375 Pennsylvania Ave. NW 20037; 452-0100.

Website: www.la-moncloa.es/weblngles/asp/inicio.asp

Initially settled by Iberians, Basques, and Celts, Spain was successively ruled (wholly or in part) by Carthage, Rome, and the Visigoths. Muslims invaded Iberia from North Africa in 711. Reconquest of the peninsula by Christians from the N laid the foundations of modern Spain. In 1469 the kingdoms of Aragon and Castile were united by the marriage of Ferdinand II and Isabella I. Moorish rule ended with the fall of the kingdom of Granada, 1492. Spain's large Jewish community was expelled the same year.

Spain obtained a colonial empire with the "discovery" of America by Columbus, 1492, the conquest of Mexico by Cortes, and Peru by Pizarro. It also controlled the Netherlands and parts of Italy and Germany. Spain lost its American colonies in the early 19th century. It lost Cuba, the Philippines, and Puerto Rico during the Spanish-American War, 1898.

Primo de Rivera became dictator in 1923. King Alfonso XIII revoked the dictatorship, 1930, but was forced to leave the country in 1931. A republic was proclaimed, which disestablished the church, curtailed its privileges, and secularized education. During 1936-39 a Popular Front composed of socialists, Communists, republicans, and anarchists governed Spain.

Army officers under Francisco Franco revolted against the government, 1936. In a destructive 3-year war, in which some one million died, Franco received massive help and troops from Italy and Germany, while the USSR, France, and Mexico supported the republic. The war ended Mar. 28, 1939. Franco was named caudillo, leader of the nation. Spain was officially neutral in World War II, but its cordial relations with fascist countries caused its exclusion from the UN until 1955.

In July 1969, Franco and the Cortes (Parliament) designated Prince Juan Carlos as the future king and chief of state. After Franco's death, Nov. 20, 1975, Juan Carlos was sworn in as king. In free elections June 1977, moderates and democratic socialists emerged as the largest parties.

In 1981 a coup attempt by right-wing military officers was thwarted by the king. The Socialist Workers' Party, under Felipe González Márquez, won 4 consecutive general elections, from 1982 to 1993, but lost to a coalition of conservative and regional parties in the election of Mar. 3, 1996.

Catalonia and the Basque country were granted autonomy, Jan. 1980, following overwhelming approval in home-rule referendums. Basque extremists, however, have pushed for independence. Bombings carried out by the militant Basque separatist group ETA have killed about 800 people since 1968. A plan for "free association" with Spain passed the Basque legislature Dec. 30, 2004, but was rejected by the Spanish parliament Feb. 2, 2005.

The Popular Party of conservative Prime Min. José María Aznar won a majority in the parliamentary election of Mar. 12, 2000. Aznar, going against Spanish public opinion, openly supported the U.S.-led invasion of Iraq, Mar. 2003.

Four commuter trains were bombed in central Madrid, Mar. 11, 2004, killing 191 people. Aznar's govt initially blamed the attacks on ETA, but evidence pointed to Islamic extremists angered by Spain's role in Iraq. The opposition Socialist Workers Party won elections 3 days later, and Socialist leader José Luis Rodríguez Zapatero, who became prime min. Apr. 17, fulfilled a campaign pledge to remove the 1,300 Spanish troops stationed in Iraq. Spanish authorities arrested several suspects in the bombing, mainly from Morocco. In April, 4 other suspects, including the leader of the terrorist cell, blew themselves up in their Madrid apt. Same-sex marriage became legal in Spain, July 3, 2005.

The **Balearic Islands** in the W Mediterranean, 1,927 sq. mi., are a province of Spain; they include **Majorca** (Mallorca; capital Palma de Mallorca), **Minorca, Cabrera, Ibiza,** and **Formentera.** The **Canary Islands,** 2,807 sq. mi., in the Atlantic W of Morocco, form 2 provinces, and include the islands of **Tenerife, Palma, Gomera, Hierro, Grand Canary, Fuerteventura,** and **Lanzarote;** Las Palmas and Santa Cruz are thriving ports. **Ceuta** and **Melilla,** small Spanish enclaves on Morocco's Mediterranean coast, gained limited autonomy in Sept. 1994.

Spain has sought the return of Gibraltar, in British hands since 1704.

Sri Lanka

Democratic Socialist Republic of Sri Lanka

People: Population: 20,064,776. **Age distrib.** (%): <15: 24.5; 65+: 7.2. **Pop. density:** 792 per sq mi, 306 per sq km. **Urban:** 21.0%. **Ethnic groups:** Sinhalese 74%, Tamil 18%, Moor 7%. **Principal languages:** Sinhala, Tamil (both official); English. **Chief religions:** Buddhist 77%, Hindu 8%, Christian 7%, Muslim 9%.

Geography: Total area: 25,332 sq mi, 65,610 sq km; **Land area:** 24,996 sq mi, 64,740 sq km. **Location:** In Indian O. off SE coast of India. **Neighbors:** India on NW. **Topography:** The coastal area and the northern half are flat; the S-central area is hilly and mountainous. **Capital:** Colombo, 648,000; Kotte (seat of Parliament), 117,000.

Government: Type: Republic. **Head of state:** Pres. Chandrika Bandaranaike Kumaratunga; b June 29, 1945; in office: Nov. 12, 1994. **Head of gov.:** Prime Min. Mahinda Rajapakse; b Nov. 18, 1945; in office: Apr. 6, 2004. **Local divisions:** 9 provinces with 25 districts. **Defense budget** (2004): $510 mil. **Active troops:** 151,000.

Economy: Industries: rubber proc., tea & coconut prod., clothing, cement, oil refining, textiles, tobacco. **Chief crops:** rice, sugarcane, grains, oilseed, spices, tea, rubber. **Natural resources:** limestone, graphite, mineral sands, gems, phosphates, clay, hydropower. **Arable land:** 14%. **Livestock** (2004): cattle: 1.2 mil; chickens: 9.8 mil; goats: 415,000; pigs: 70,000; sheep: 9,000. **Fish catch** (2003): 289,266 metric tons. **Electricity prod.** (2003): 7.3 bil kWh. **Labor force** (1998 est.): agriculture 38%, industry 17%, services 45%.

Finance: Monetary unit: Rupee (LKR) (Sept. 2005: 101.22 = $1 U.S.). **GDP** (2004 est.): $80.6 bil; **per capita GDP:** $4,000; **GDP growth:** 5.2%. **Imports** (2004 est.): $7.3 bil; partners (2004): India 14%, Singapore 8%, China 7.6%, Hong Kong 5.9%, Malaysia 4.6%, Japan 4.6%. **Exports** (2004 est.): $5.3 bil; partners (2004): US 31%, UK 12.9%, India 5.1%, Belgium 4.9%, Germany 4.9%. **Tourism:** $424 mil. **Budget** (2004 est.): $4.7 bil. **Intl. reserves less gold:** $1.37 bil. **Gold** (2002): 60,000 oz t. **Consumer prices:** 7.58%.

Transport: Railroad: Length: 937 mi. **Motor vehicles:** 386,600 pass. cars, 255,300 comm. vehicles. **Civil aviation:** 4.1 bil pass.-mi; 14 airports. **Chief ports:** Colombo, Trincomalee, Galle.

Communications: TV sets: 102 per 1,000 pop. **Radios:** 211 per 1,000 pop. **Telephone lines**: 939,000. **Daily newspaper circ.:** 29 per 1,000 pop. **Internet**: 250,000 users.

Health: Life expect.: 70.6 male; 75.9 female. **Births** (per 1,000 pop.): 15.6. **Deaths** (per 1,000 pop.): 6.5. **Natural inc.:** 0.91%. **Infant mortality** (per 1,000 live births): 14.4. **AIDS rate:** <0.1%.

Education: Compulsory: ages 5-13. **Literacy:** 92.3%.

Major Intl. Organizations: UN (FAO, IBRD, ILO, IMF, IMO, WHO, WTrO), the Commonwealth.

Embassy: 2148 Wyoming Ave. NW 20008; 483-4025.

Website www.priu.gov.lk

The island was known to the ancient world as Taprobane (Greek for copper-colored) and later as Serendip (from Arabic). Colonists from N India subdued the indigenous Veddahs about 543 BC; their descendants, the Buddhist Sinhalese, still form most of the population. Hindu descendants of Tamil immigrants from S India account for about one-fifth of the population.

Parts were occupied by the Portuguese in 1505 and the Dutch in 1658. The British seized the island in 1796. As Ceylon it became an independent member of the Commonwealth in 1948, and the Republic of Sri Lanka May 22, 1972.

Prime Min. W. R. D. Bandaranaike was assassinated Sept. 25, 1959. His widow, Mrs. Sirimavo Bandaranaike, served as prime minister 1960-65, 1970-77, 1994-2000. In 1971 the nation suffered economic problems and terrorist activities by ultra-leftists, thousands of whom were executed. Massive land reform and nationalization of foreign-owned plantations were undertaken in the mid-1970s.

Tensions between Sinhalese and Tamil separatists erupted into violence in the early 1980s. More than 64,000 died in the civil war, which continued through the late 1990s; another 20,000, mostly young Tamils, "disappeared" after they were taken into custody by government security forces.

Pres. Ranasinghe Premadasa was assassinated May 1, 1993, by a Tamil rebel. Mrs. Bandaranaike's daughter, Chandrika Bandaranaike Kumaratunga, became prime minister after the Aug. 16, 1994, general elections. Elected president Nov. 9, Kumaratunga appointed her mother prime minister. Kumaratunga, who was injured in a suicide bomb attack at a campaign rally Dec. 18, 1999, won a 2nd 6-year term 3 days later. In failing health, Mrs. Bandaranaike resigned Aug. 10 and died Oct. 10, 2000.

Facing a possible no-confidence motion, Pres. Kumaratunga suspended parliament July 10, 2001. Elections Dec. 5 resulted in a victory for the United National Party, headed by Ranil Wickremesinghe. A truce accord intended to bring an end to the 18-year-long civil war was signed Feb. 22, 2002. Severe monsoon flooding in the S and SW, May 2003, killed at least 265 people.

A dispute with Wickremesinghe over how to negotiate with rebel Tamils led Kumaratunga again to suspend parliament, Nov. 4, 2003. Her United People's Freedom Alliance won a plurality in legislative elections Apr. 2, 2004, and formed a coalition govt. Foreign Min. Lakshman Kadirgamar, a Tamil who took a hard line against the rebels, died Aug. 12, 2005, after he was shot by a sniper.

The Indian Ocean tsunami of Dec. 26 left more than 31,100 dead, 4,100 missing, and 519,000 displaced in Sri Lanka.

Sudan

Republic of the Sudan

People: Population: 40,187,486. **Age distrib.** (%): <15: 43.2; 65+: 2.4. **Pop. density:** 42 per sq mi, 16 per sq km. **Urban:** 38.9%. **Ethnic groups:** Black 52%, Arab 39%, Beja 6%. **Principal languages:** Arabic (official), Nubian, Ta Bedawie; Nilotic, Sudanic dialects; English. **Chief religions:** Sunni Muslim 70%, indigenous beliefs 25%, Christian 5%.

Geography: Total area: 967,499 sq mi, 2,505,810 sq km; **Land area:** 917,379 sq mi, 2,376,000 sq km. **Location:** At the E end of Sahara desert zone. **Neighbors:** Egypt on N; Libya, Chad, Central African Republic on W; Congo (formerly Zaire), Uganda, Kenya on S; Ethiopia, Eritrea on E. **Topography:** The N consists of the Libyan Desert in the W, and the mountainous Nubia Desert in E, with narrow Nile valley between. The center contains large, fertile, rainy areas with fields, pasture, and forest. The S has rich soil, heavy rain. **Capital:** Khartoum, 4,286,000. **Cities (urban aggr.):** Omdurman (1993), 1,271,403.

Government: Type: Republic with strong military influence. **Head of state and gov.:** Pres. Gen. Omar Hassan Ahmad Al-Bashir; b Jan. 1, 1944; in office: June 30, 1989. **Local divisions:** 26 states. **Defense budget** (2004): $465 mil. **Active troops:** 104,800.

Economy: Industries: oil, cotton ginning, textiles, cement, edible oils, sugar. **Chief crops:** cotton, peanuts, sorghum, millet, wheat, gum arabic, sugarcane. **Natural resources:** oil, iron ore, copper, chromium ore, zinc, tungsten, mica, silver, gold, hydropower. **Crude oil reserves** (2004): 563 mil bbls. **Arable land:** 5%. **Livestock** (2004): cattle: 38.3 mil; chickens: 37.0 mil; goats: 42.0 mil; sheep: 48.0 mil. **Fish catch** (2003): 59,600 metric tons. **Electricity prod.** (2003): 3.2 bil kWh. **Labor force** (1998 est.): agriculture 80%, industry and commerce 7%, government 13%.

Finance: Monetary unit: Dinar (SDD) (Sept. 2005: 241.68 = $1 U.S.). **GDP** (2004 est.): $76.2 bil; **per capita GDP:** $1,900; **GDP growth:** 6.4%. **Imports** (2004 est.): $3.5 bil; partners (2004): Saudi Arabia 11.7%, China 10.7%, UAE 6.2%, Egypt 5.2%, Germany 4.9%, India 4.6%, Australia 4.1%, UK 4%. **Exports** (2004 est.): $3.4 bil; partners (2004): China 64.3%, Japan 13.8%, Saudi Arabia 3.7%. **Tourism:** $118 mil. **Budget** (2004 est.): $3.0 bil. **Intl. reserves less gold:** $1.05 bil. **Consumer prices:** 8.51%.

Transport: Railroad: Length: 3,715 mi. **Motor vehicles**: 46,000 pass. cars, 60,500 comm. vehicles. **Civil aviation:** 472.9 mil pass.-mi; 12 airports. **Chief port:** Port Sudan.

Communications: TV sets: 173 per 1,000 pop. **Radios:** 480 per 1,000 pop. **Telephone lines:** 900,000. **Daily newspaper circ.:** 27 per 1,000 pop. **Internet**: 300,000 users.

Health: Life expect.: 57.3 male; 59.8 female. **Births** (per 1,000 pop.): 35.2. **Deaths** (per 1,000 pop.): 9.2. **Natural inc.:** 2.60%. **Infant mortality** (per 1,000 live births): 62.5. **AIDS rate:** 2.3%.

Education: Compulsory: ages 6-13. **Literacy:** 61.1%.

Major Intl. Organizations: UN (FAO, IBRD, ILO, IMF, IMO, WHO), AL, AU.

Embassy: 2210 Massachusetts Ave. NW 20008; 338-8565.

Website: www.sudan.gov.sd/english.htm

Northern Sudan, ancient Nubia, was settled by Egyptians in antiquity. The population was converted to Coptic Christianity in the 6th century. Arab conquests brought Islam to the area in the 15th century.

In the 1820s Egypt took over Sudan, defeating the last of earlier empires, including the Fung. In the 1880s a revolution was led by Muhammad Ahmad, who called himself the Mahdi (leader of the faithful), and his followers, the dervishes.

In 1898 an Anglo-Egyptian force crushed the Mahdi's successors. In 1951 the Egyptian Parliament abrogated its 1899 and 1936 treaties with Great Britain and amended its constitution to provide for a separate Sudanese constitution. Sudan voted for complete independence effective Jan. 1, 1956.

In 1969, a Revolutionary Council took power, but a civilian premier and cabinet were appointed; the government announced it would create a socialist state

Economic problems plagued the nation in the 1980s and 1990s, aggravated by civil war and influxes of refugees from neighboring countries. After 16 years in power, Pres. Jaafar al-Nimeiry was overthrown in a bloodless coup, Apr. 6, 1985. Sudan held its first democratic parliamentary elections in 18 years in 1986, but the elected government was overthrown in a bloodless coup June 30, 1989.

In the mid-1980s, rebels in the south (populated largely by black Christians and followers of tribal religions) took up arms against government domination by northern Sudan, mostly Arab-Muslim. War and related famine cost an estimated 2 million lives and displaced millions of southerners. In 1993, Amnesty International accused the Sudanese government of "ethnic cleansing."

A new constitution based on Islamic law took effect June 30, 1998. On Aug. 20, in retaliation for bombings in Kenya and Tanzania, U.S. missiles destroyed a Khartoum pharmaceutical plant the U.S. alleged was associated with terrorist activities; independent inquiries later cast some doubt on the U.S. claim.

During 2003-05, a rebellion in the Darfur region of W Sudan led to a new crisis. Marauding Arab militias, known as the *janjaweed*, retaliated by attacking black African villagers, looting and burning homes and killing inhabitants, reportedly in collusion with Sudanese government troops. By mid-2005, at least 180,000 people in Darfur had been killed and over 2 million had fled to refugee camps. The African Union announced, July 7, 2005, that it would increase its peacekeeping force in Darfur from 3,200 to more than 7,100 by the end of Sept.

An accord to end the rebellion in the south was signed Jan. 9, 2005. Under a power-sharing constitution with autonomy for S Sudan, former rebel leader John Garang became 1st vice pres., July 9. His death 3 weeks later in a helicopter crash sparked riots in Khartoum and other cities, Aug. 1-3, killing at least 130 people. A national unity government was installed Sept. 20.

Suriname

Republic of Suriname

People: Population: 438,144. **Age distrib.** (%): <15: 29.6; 65+: 6.2. **Pop. density:** 7 per sq mi, 3 per sq km. **Urban:** 76.1%. **Ethnic groups:** East Indians 37%, Creole 31%, Javanese 15%, Maroons 10%, Amerindian 2%, Chinese 2%, White 1%. **Principal languages:** Dutch (official), English, Sranang Tongo (an English Creole), Hindustani, Javanese. **Chief religions:** Hindu 27%, Protestant 25%, Roman Catholic 23%, Muslim 20%.

Geography: Total area: 63,039 sq mi, 163,270 sq km; **Land area:** 62,344 sq mi, 161,470 sq km. **Location:** On N shore of South America. **Neighbors:** Guyana on W, Brazil on S, French Guiana on E. **Topography:** A flat Atlantic coast, where dikes permit agriculture. Inland is a forest belt; to the S, largely unexplored hills cover 75% of the country. **Capital:** Paramaribo, 253,000.

Government: Type: Republic. **Head of state and gov.:** Pres. Runaldo Ronald Venetiaan; b June 18, 1936; in office: Aug. 12, 2000. **Local divisions:** 10 districts. **Defense budget:** NA. **Active troops:** 1,840.

Economy: Industries: mining, oil, lumber, food proc., fishing. **Chief crops:** rice, bananas, palm kernels, coconuts, plantains, peanuts. **Natural resources:** timber, hydropower, fish, kaolin, shrimp, bauxite, gold, nickel, copper, platinum, iron ore. **Crude oil reserves** (2004): 111 mil bbls. **Livestock** (2004): cattle: 137,000; chickens: 3.8 mil; goats: 7,100; pigs: 24,500; sheep: 7,700. **Fish catch** (2003): 28,357 metric tons. **Electricity prod.** (2003): 2.0 bil kWh.

Finance: Monetary unit: Dollar (SRD) (Sept. 2005: 2.74 = $1 U.S.). **GDP** (2004 est.): $1.9 bil; **per capita GDP:** $4,300; **GDP growth:** 4.2%. **Imports** (2002): $604.0 mil; partners (2004): US 28.2%, Netherlands 21.1%, Trinidad and Tobago 11.4%, Japan 7.2%, China 4.3%. **Exports** (2002): $495.0 mil; partners (2004): Norway 31.1%, US 16%, Canada 13.2%, Belgium 10.8%, France 8.8%, Iceland 4.6%. **Tourism:** $4 mil. **Budget** (2003): $440.0 mil. **Intl. reserves less gold:** $83 mil. **Gold:** 20,000 oz t. **Consumer prices** (2003): 23.0%.

Transport: Railroad: Length: 103 mi. **Motor vehicles:** 61,400 pass. cars, 23,500 comm. vehicles. **Civil aviation:** 558.0 mil pass.-mi; 5 airports. **Chief ports:** Paramaribo, New Nickerie, Albina.

Communications: TV sets: 241 per 1,000 pop. **Radios:** 728 per 1,000 pop. **Telephone lines:** 79,800. **Daily newspaper circ.:** 67.7 per 1,000 pop. **Internet:** 23,000 users.

Health: Life expect.: 66.8 male; 71.3 female. **Births** (per 1,000 pop.): 18.4. **Deaths** (per 1,000 pop.): 7.2. **Natural inc.:** 1.12%. **Infant mortality** (per 1,000 live births): 23.6. **AIDS rate:** 1.7%.

Education: Compulsory: ages 6-11. **Literacy:** 93%.

Major Intl. Organizations: UN (FAO, IBRD, ILO, IMF, IMO, WHO, WTrO), Caricom, OAS.

Embassy: 4301 Connecticut Ave., Suite 460, NW 20008; 244-7488.

Website: www.surinameembassy.org

The Netherlands acquired Suriname in 1667 from Britain, in exchange for New Netherlands (New York). The 1954 Dutch constitution raised the colony to a level of equality with the Netherlands and the Netherlands Antilles. Independence was granted Nov. 25, 1975, despite objections from East Indians. Some 40% of the population (mostly East Indians) immigrated to the Netherlands in the months before independence.

The National Military Council took control of the government, Feb. 1982. Civilian rule was restored in 1987, but political turmoil continued until 1992, disrupting the nation's economy.

Swaziland

Kingdom of Swaziland

People: Population: 1,138,227. **Age distrib.** (%): <15: 40.6; 65+: 3.8. **Pop. density:** 170 per sq mi, 66 per sq km. **Urban:** 23.5%. **Ethnic groups:** African 97%, European 3% **Principal languages:** English, siSwati (both official). **Chief religions:** Christian 60%, Muslim 10%, indigenous and other 30%.

Geography: Total area: 6,704 sq mi, 17,363 sq km; **Land area:** 6,642 sq mi, 17,203 sq km. **Location:** In southern Africa, near Indian O. coast. **Neighbors:** South Africa on N, W, S; Mozambique on E. **Topography:** The country descends from W-E in broad belts, becoming more arid in the low veld region, then rising to a plateau in the E. **Capitals:** Mbabane (administrative), 70,000; Lobamba (legislative).

Government: Type: Constitutional monarchy. **Head of state:** King Mswati III; b Apr. 19, 1968; in office: Apr. 25, 1986. **Head of gov.:** Prime Min. Absalom Themba Dlamini; b Dec. 1, 1950; in office: Nov. 26, 2003. **Local divisions:** 4 districts.

Economy: Industries: coal mining, pulp, sugar, soft drinks, textiles, apparel. **Chief crops:** sugarcane, cotton, corn, tobacco, rice, citrus. **Natural resources:** asbestos, coal, clay, cassiterite, hydropower, timber, gold, diamonds, quarry stone, talc. **Arable land:** 11%. **Livestock** (2004): cattle: 580,000; chickens: 3.2 mil; goats: 273,576; pigs: 30,000; sheep: 27,000. **Fish catch** (2003): 70 metric tons. **Electricity prod.** (2003): 0.39 bil kWh.

Finance: Monetary unit: Lilangeni (SZL) (Sept. 2005: 6.29 = $1 U.S.). **GDP** (2004 est.): $6.0 bil; **per capita GDP:** $5,100; **GDP growth:** 2.5%. **Imports** (2004 est.): $1.1 bil; partners (2004): South Africa 95.6%, EU 0.9%, Japan 0.9%, Singapore 0.3%. **Exports** (2004 est.): $900.1 mil; partners (2004): South Africa 59.7%, EU 8.8%, US 8.8%, Mozambique 6.2%. **Tourism** (2002): $26 mil. **Budget** (2004 est.): $552.7 mil. **Intl. reserves less gold:** $208 mil. **Consumer prices** (2003): 7.3%.

Transport: Railroad: Length: 187 mi. **Motor vehicles:** 41,500 pass. cars, 51,800 comm. vehicles. **Civil aviation:** 42.3 mil pass.-mi; 1 airport.

Communications: TV sets: 112 per 1,000 pop. **Radios:** 168 per 1,000 pop. **Telephone lines:** 46,200. **Daily newspaper circ.:** 17 per 1,000 pop. **Internet:** 27,000 users.

Health: Life expect.: 32.5 male; 34.0 female. **Births** (per 1,000 pop.): 27.9. **Deaths** (per 1,000 pop.): 28.8. **Natural inc.:** -0.09%. **Infant mortality** (per 1,000 live births): 72.9. **AIDS rate:** 38.8%.

Education: Compulsory: ages 6-12. **Literacy:** 81.6%.

Major Intl. Organizations: UN (FAO, IBRD, ILO, IMF, WHO, WTrO), the Commonwealth, AU.

Embassy: 1712 New Hampshire Avenue 20009 234 5002.

Website: www.gov.sz

The royal house of Swaziland traces back 400 years, and is one of Africa's last ruling dynasties. The Swazis, a Bantu people, were driven to Swaziland from lands to the N by the Zulus in 1820. Their autonomy was later guaranteed by Britain and Transvaal (later part of South Africa), with Britain assuming control after 1903. Independence came Sept. 6, 1968. In 1973 the king repealed the constitution and assumed full powers.

A new constitution banning political parties took effect Oct. 13, 1978. A shrinking economy and the AIDS crisis have fueled student and labor unrest in recent years. The UN has estimated that nearly 40% of the adult population has HIV/AIDS.

Sweden

Kingdom of Sweden

People: Population: 9,001,774. **Age distrib.** (%): <15: 17.1; 65+: 17.4. **Pop. density:** 52 per sq mi, 20 per sq km. **Urban:** 83.4%. **Ethnic groups:** Swedish 89%, Finnish 2%; Sami and others 9%. **Principal languages:** Swedish (official), Sami, Finnish. **Chief religion:** Lutheran 87%.

Geography: Total area: 173,732 sq mi, 449,964 sq km; **Land area:** 158,663 sq mi, 410,934 sq km. **Location:** On Scandinavian Peninsula in N Europe. **Neighbors:** Norway on W, Denmark on S (across Kattegat), Finland on E. **Topography:** Mountains along NW border cover 25% of Sweden, flat or rolling terrain covers the central and southern areas, which include several large lakes. **Capital:** Stockholm,1,697,000. **Cities (urban aggr.):** Göteborg, 792,000.

Government: Type: Constitutional monarchy. **Head of state:** King Carl XVI Gustaf; b Apr. 30, 1946; in office: Sept. 19, 1973. **Head of gov.:** Prime Min. Goran Persson; b June 20, 1949; in office: Mar. 21, 1996. **Local divisions:** 21 counties. **Defense budget** (2004): $5.9 bil. **Active troops:** 27,600.

Economy: Industries: iron & steel, precision equip., wood & paper products, proc. foods, autos. **Chief crops:** barley, wheat, sugar beets. **Natural resources:** zinc, iron ore, lead, copper, silver, timber, uranium, hydropower. **Arable land:** 7%. **Livestock** (2004): cattle: 1.6 mil; chickens: 6.0 mil; pigs: 1.9 mil; sheep: 450,000. **Fish catch** (2003): 293,209 metric tons. **Electricity prod.** (2003): 127.9 bil kWh. **Labor force** (2000 est.): agriculture 2%, industry 24%, services 74%.

Finance: Monetary unit: Krona (SEK) (Sept. 2005: 7.45 = $1 U.S.). **GDP** (2004 est.): $255.4 bil; **per capita GDP:** $28,400; **GDP growth:** 3.6%. **Imports** (2004 est.): $98.0 bil; partners (2004): Germany 20.2%, Denmark 8.2%, UK 7.9%, Netherlands 7.2%, Finland 7%, France 6.1%, Norway 5.9%, Belgium 4.5%. **Exports** (2004 est.): $121.7 bil; partners (2004): US 10.7%, Germany 10.3%, UK 7.2%, Denmark 6.6%, Norway 6.2%, Finland 5.9%, Belgium 5.1%, Netherlands 4.8%, France 4.7%. **Tourism:** $5,304 mil. **Budget** (2004 est.): $199.6 bil. **Intl. reserves less gold:** $14.25 bil. **Gold:** 5.96 mil oz t. **Consumer prices:** 0.38%.

Transport: Railroad: Length: 7,134 mi. **Motor vehicles:** 4.0 mil pass. cars, 769,600 comm. vehicles. **Civil aviation:** 7.0 bil. pass.-mi; 145 airports. **Chief ports:** Göteborg, Stockholm, Malmö.

Communications: TV sets: 551 per 1,000 pop. **Radios:** 932 per 1,000 pop. **Telephone lines** (2002): 6.6 mil. **Daily newspaper circ.:** 410.2 per 1,000 pop. **Internet** (2002): 5.1 mil users.

Health: Life expect.: 78.2 male; 82.7 female. **Births** (per 1,000 pop.): 10.4. **Deaths** (per 1,000 pop.): 10.4. **Natural inc.:** 0%. **Infant mortality** (per 1,000 live births): 2.8. **AIDS rate:** 0.1%.

Education: Compulsory: ages 7-16. **Literacy:** 99%.

Major Intl. Organizations: UN and all of its specialized agencies, EU, OECD, OSCE.

Embassy: 1501 M St. NW 20005; 467-2600.

Website: www.sweden.gov.se

The Swedes have lived in present-day Sweden for at least 5,000 years, longer than nearly any other European people. Gothic tribes from Sweden played a major role in the disintegration of the Roman Empire. Other Swedes helped create the first Russian state in the 9th century.

The Swedes were Christianized from the 11th century, and a strong centralized monarchy developed. A parliament, the Riksdag, was first called in 1435, the earliest parliament on the European continent, with all classes of society represented.

Swedish independence from rule by Danish kings (dating from 1397) was secured by Gustavus I in a revolt, 1521-23; he built up the government and military and established the Lutheran Church. In the 17th century Sweden was a major European power, gaining most of the Baltic seacoast, but its international position subsequently declined. The Napoleonic wars, 1799-1815, in which Sweden acquired Norway (it became independent 1905), were the last in which Sweden participated. Armed neutrality was maintained in both world wars.

More than 4 decades of Social Democratic rule ended in the 1976 parliamentary elections; the party returned to power in the 1982 elections. After Prime Min. Olof Palme was shot to death in Stockholm, Feb. 28, 1986, Ingvar Carlsson took office. Carl Bildt, a non-Socialist, became prime minister Oct. 1991, with a mandate to restore Sweden's economic competitiveness. The Social Democrats returned to power following 1994 elections.

Swedish voters approved membership in the European Union Nov. 13, 1994, and Sweden entered the EU as of Jan. 1, 1995. Carlsson retired and was succeeded by Goran Persson in Mar. 1996. Persson and his Social Democrats led coalition governments after the elections of Sept. 20, 1998, and Sept. 15, 2002. Foreign Min. Anna Lindh died Sept. 11, 2003, after being stabbed in a Stockholm department store. Her killer, Mijailo Mijailovic, was sentenced to life in prison Mar. 2004; an appeals court later deemed him mentally ill and sent him to a psychiatric ward.

Swedish voters Sept. 14, 2003, rejected adoption of the euro currency. In June 2005, the government said it was postponing a parliamentary vote on the EU constitution.

Switzerland

Swiss Confederation

People: Population: 7,489,370. **Age distrib.** (%): <15: 16.6; 65+: 15.4. **Pop. density:** 470 per sq mi, 181 per sq km. **Urban:** 67.5%. **Ethnic groups:** German 65%, French 18%, Italian 10%, Romansch 1%. **Principal languages:** German, French, Italian (all official); Romansch (semi-official). **Chief religions:** Roman Catholic 42%, Protestant 35%.

Geography: Total area: 15,942 sq mi, 41,290 sq km; **Land area:** 15,355 sq mi, 39,770 sq km. **Location:** In the Alps Mts. in central Europe. **Neighbors:** France on W, Italy on S, Austria on E, Germany on N. **Topography:** The Alps cover 60% of the land area; the Jura, near France, 10%. Running between, from NE to SW, are midlands, 30%. **Capitals:** Bern (administrative), 320,000; Lausanne (judicial). **Cities (urban aggr.):** Zurich, 939,000; Basel, 166,700; Geneva, 398,910.

Government: Type: Federal republic. **Head of state and gov.:** The president is elected by the Federal Assembly to a nonrenewable 1-year term. **Local divisions:** 20 full cantons, 6 half cantons. **Defense budget** (2004): $3.8 bil. **Active troops:** 4,400.

Economy: Industries: machinery, chemicals, watches, textiles, precision instruments. **Chief crops:** grains, fruits, vegetables. **Natural resources:** hydropower, timber, salt. **Arable land:** 10%. **Livestock** (2004): cattle: 1.6 mil; chickens: 7.5 mil; goats: 67,500; pigs: 1.5 mil; sheep: 441,000. **Fish catch** (2003): 2,950 metric tons. **Electricity prod.** (2003): 63.4 bil kWh. **Labor force** (1998): agriculture 4.6%, industry 26.3%, services 69.1%

Finance: Monetary unit: Franc (CHF) (Sept. 2005: 1.24 = $1 U.S.). **GDP** (2004 est.): $251.9 bil; **per capita GDP:** $33,800; **GDP growth:** 1.8%. **Imports** (2004 est.): $121.1 bil; partners (2004): Germany 29%, Italy 11.8%, France 11.1%, US 7.6%, Austria 4.5%, UK 4.5%, Netherlands 4.3%. **Exports** (2004 est.): $130.7 bil; partners (2004): Germany 20%, US 9.1%, France 9.1%, Italy 8.8%, UK 4.9%. **Tourism:** $9,325 mil. **Budget** (2004 est.): $140.4 bil. **Intl. reserves less gold:** $35.74 bil. **Gold:** 43.54 mil oz t. **Consumer prices:** 0.82%.

Transport: Railroad: Length: 2,803 mi. **Motor vehicles:** 3.7 mil pass. cars, 332,500 comm. vehicles. **Civil aviation:** 20.8 bil pass.-mi; 41 airports. **Chief port:** Basel.

Communications: TV sets: 457 per 1,000 pop. **Radios:** 979 per 1,000 pop. **Telephone lines:** 5.3 mil. **Daily newspaper circ.:** 373.2 per 1,000 pop. **Internet:** 2.9 mil users.

Health: Life expect.: 77.6 male; 83.4 female. **Births** (per 1,000 pop.): 9.8. **Deaths** (per 1,000 pop.): 8.5. **Natural inc.:** 0.13%. **Infant mortality** (per 1,000 live births): 4.4. **AIDS rate:** 0.4%.

Education: Compulsory: ages 7-15. **Literacy:** 99%.

Major Intl. Organizations: UN and most of its specialized agencies, EFTA, OECD, OSCE.

Embassy: 2900 Cathedral Ave. NW 20008; 745-7900.

Website: www.swissemb.org

Switzerland, the former Roman province of Helvetia, traces its modern history to 1291, when 3 cantons created a defensive league. Other cantons were subsequently admitted to the Swiss Confederation, which obtained its independence from the Holy Roman Empire through the Peace of Westphalia (1648). The cantons were joined under a federal constitution in 1848, with large powers of local control retained by each.

Switzerland has maintained an armed neutrality since 1815, and has not been involved in a foreign war since 1515. It is the seat of many UN and other international agencies but did not become a full member of the UN until Sept. 10, 2002.

Switzerland is a world banking center. Stung by charges that assets seized by the Nazis and deposited in Swiss banks in World War II had not been properly returned, the government announced, March 5, 1997, a $4.7 billion fund to compensate victims of the Holocaust and other catastrophies. Swiss banks agreed Aug. 12, 1998, to pay $1.25 billion in reparations. Abortion was decriminalized by a June 2, 2002 referendum. The rightist Swiss People's Party topped Oct. 2003 parlimentary voting and entered a coalition government.

Syria

Syrian Arab Republic

People: Population: 18,448,752. **Age distrib.** (%): <15: 37.4; 65+: 3.3. **Pop. density:** 258 per sq mi, 100 per sq km. **Urban:** 50.1%. **Ethnic groups:** Arab 90%, Kurds, Armenians, and other 10%. **Principal languages:** Arabic (official); Kurdish, Armenian. **Chief religions:** Sunni Muslim 74%, other Muslims 16%, Christian 10%.

Geography: Total area: 71,498 sq mi, 185,180 sq km; **Land area:** 71,062 sq mi, 184,050 sq km. **Location:** Middle East, at E end of Mediterranean Sea. **Neighbors:** Lebanon and Israel on W, Jordan on S, Iraq on E, Turkey on N. **Topography:** Syria has a short Mediterranean coastline, then stretches E and S with fertile lowlands and plains, alternating with mountains and large desert areas. **Capital:** Damascus, 2,228,000. **Cities (urban aggr.):** Aleppo, 2,188,000; Homs, 797,000.

Government: Type: Republic (under military regime). **Head of state:** Pres. Bashar al-Assad; b Sept. 11, 1965; in office: July 17, 2000. **Head of gov.:** Prime Min. Muhammad Naji al-Otari; b 1944; in office: Sept. 10, 2003. **Local divisions:** 14 provinces. **Defense budget** (2004): $1.6 bil. **Active troops:** 296,800.

Economy: Industries: oil, textiles, food proc., beverages, tobacco, phosphate mining. **Chief crops:** wheat, barley, cotton, lentils, chickpeas, olives, sugar beets. **Natural resources:** oil, phosphates, chrome, mang., asphalt, iron ore, salt, marble, gypsum, hydropower. **Crude oil reserves** (2004): 2.5 bil bbls. **Arable land:** 28%. **Livestock** (2004): cattle: 940,000; chickens: 30.0 mil; goats: 1.0 mil; sheep: 15.3 mil. **Fish catch** (2003): 16,128 metric tons. **Electricity prod.** (2003): 27.2 bil kWh. **Labor force** (2002 est.): agriculture 30%, industry 27%, services 43%.

Finance: Monetary unit: Pound (SYP) (Sept. 2005: 51.92 = $1 U.S.). **GDP** (2004 est.): $60.4 bil; **per capita GDP:** $3,400; **GDP growth:** 2.3%. **Imports** (2004 est.): $5.0 bil; partners (2004): Italy 7.7%, China 7.6%, Germany 7.4%, Turkey 4.5%, France 4.4%. **Exports** (2004 est.): $6.1 bil; partners (2004): Germany 16.5%, Italy 13.5%, UAE 8.6%, Lebanon 7.7%, France 6.3%, Turkey 5.1%. **Tourism:** $1,408 mil. **Budget** (2004 est.): $9.5 bil. **Gold** (2003): 830,000 oz t. **Consumer prices** (changed in 2002): 1.0%.

Transport: Railroad: Length: 1,704 mi. **Motor vehicles:** 193,500 pass. cars, 348,700 comm. vehicles. **Civil aviation:** 910.3 mil pass.-mi; 24 airports. **Chief ports:** Latakia, Tartus.

Communications: TV sets: 68 per 1,000 pop. **Radios:** 278 per 1,000 pop. **Telephone lines** (2002): 2.1 mil. **Daily newspaper circ.:** 20 per 1,000 pop. **Internet:** 610,000 users.

Health: Life expect.: 68.8 male; 71.4 female. **Births** (per 1,000 pop.): 28.3. **Deaths** (per 1,000 pop.): 4.9. **Natural inc.:** 2.34%. **Infant mortality** (per 1,000 live births): 29.5. **AIDS rate:** <0.1%.

Education: Compulsory: ages 6-14. **Literacy:** 76.9%.

Major Intl. Organizations: UN (FAO, IBRD, ILO, IMF, IMO, WHO), AL.

Embassy: 2215 Wyoming Ave. NW 20008; 232-6313.

Website: www.syrianembassy.us

Syria was the center of the Seleucid empire, but later became absorbed in the Roman and Arab empires. Ottoman rule prevailed for 4 centuries, until the end of World War I.

The state of Syria was formed from former Turkish districts, separated by the Treaty of Sevres, 1920, and divided into the states of Syria and Greater Lebanon. Both were administered under a French League of Nations mandate 1920-1941.

Syria was proclaimed a republic by the occupying French Sept. 16, 1941, and exercised full independence Apr. 17, 1946. Syria joined the Arab invasion of Israel in 1948.

Syria joined Egypt Feb. 1958 in the United Arab Republic but seceded Sept. 1961. The Socialist Baath party and military leaders seized power Mar. 1963. The Baath, a pan-Arab organization, became the only legal party. The government has been dominated by the Alawite minority.

In the Arab-Israeli war of June 1967, Israel seized and occupied the Golan Heights, from which Syria had shelled Israeli settlements. On Oct. 6, 1973, Syria joined Egypt in an attack on Israel. Syrian troops entered Lebanon in 1976, during the Lebanese civil war, and remained a strong presence in the country. They fought Palestinian guerrillas and, later, Christian militiamen. Syria sided with Iran during the Iran-Iraq war, 1980-88.

Following Israel's invasion of Lebanon, June 6, 1982, Israeli planes destroyed 17 Syrian antiaircraft missile batteries in the Bekaa Valley, June 9. Some 25 Syrian planes were downed during the engagement. Israel and Syria agreed to a cease-fire June 11. Syria's alleged role in promoting international terrorism led to strained relations with the U.S. and Great Britain.

Syria condemned the Aug. 1990 Iraqi invasion of Kuwait and sent troops to help Allied forces in the Gulf War. In 1991, Syria accepted U.S. proposals for the terms of an Arab-Israeli peace conference. Syria subsequently participated in negotiations with Israel, but progress toward peace was slow.

Former Prime Min. Mahmoud al-Zoubi killed himself May 21, 2000, after being charged with corruption. Hafez al-Assad, president of Syria since 1971, died June 10, 2000, and was succeeded by his son Bashar al-Assad.

Following the invasion of Iraq, Mar. 2003, the U.S. pressured Syria to rein in extremist groups and deny safe haven to fugitive Iraqi leaders. Israeli planes attacked an alleged terrorist camp near Damascus Oct. 4, 2003. Stating that the government. continued to support terrorists and was allowing militants to enter Iraq from its territory, the U.S. imposed limited sanctions on Syria, May 11, 2004. The killing of former Lebanese Prime Min. Rafik al-Hariri by a truck bomb in Beirut, Feb. 14, 2005, was a catalyst for massive anti-Syrian protests in Lebanon. Syria denied responsibility for the blast but pulled nearly all its troops out of Lebanon by Apr. 26; some Syrian intelligence agents may have remained.

Taiwan

Republic of China

People: Population: 22,894,384. **Age distrib.** (%): <15: 19.7; 65+: 9.6. **Pop. density:** 1,648 per sq mi, 636 per sq km. **Ethnic groups:** Taiwanese 84%, mainland Chinese 14%, Aborigine 2%. **Principal languages:** Mandarin Chinese (official), Taiwanese (Min), Hakka dialects. **Chief religions:** Buddhist, Confucian, and Taoist 93%; Christian 5%.

Geography: Total area: 13,892 sq mi, 35,980 sq km; **Land area:** 12,456 sq mi, 32,260 sq km. **Location:** Off SE coast of China, between East and South China seas. **Neighbors:** Nearest is China. **Topography:** A mountain range forms the backbone of the island; the eastern half is very steep and craggy, the western slope is flat, fertile, and well cultivated. **Capital:** Taipei, 2,550,000. **Cities:** Kaohsiung, 1,463,000; Taichung, 950,000.

Government: Type: Democracy. **Head of state:** Pres. Chen Shui-bian; b 1950; in office: May 20, 2000. **Head of gov.:** Prime Min. Frank Chang-ting Hsieh; b May 18, 1946; in office: Feb. 1, 2005. **Local divisions:** 16 counties, 5 municipalities, 2 special municipalities (Taipei, Kaohsiung). **Defense budget** (2003): 6.6 bil. **Active troops:** 290,000.

Economy: Industries: electronics, oil refining, chemicals, textiles, iron & steel, machinery, cement, food proc. **Chief crops:** rice, corn, vegetables, fruit, tea. **Natural resources:** coal, nat. gas, limestone, marble, asbestos. **Crude oil reserves** (2004): 4 mil bbls. **Arable land:** 24%. **Fish catch** (2003): 1,486,291 metric tons. **Electricity prod.** (2003): 166.0 bil kWh. **Labor force** (2001 est.): agriculture 8%, industry 35%, services 57%.

Finance: Monetary unit: Dollar (TWD) (Sept. 2005: 32.71 = $1 U.S.). **GDP** (2004 est.): $576.2 bil; **per capita GDP:** $25,300; **GDP growth:** 6%. **Imports** (2004 est.): $165.4 bil; partners (2004): Japan 26%, US 13%, China, including Hong Kong 11%, South Korea 6.9%. **Exports** (2004 est.): $170.5 bil; partners (2004): China, including Hong Kong 37%, US 16%, Japan 7.7%. **Tourism:** $2,976 mil. **Budget** (2004 est.): $76.7 bil.

Transport: Railroad: Length: 688 mi. **Motor vehicles** (1997): 4.40 mil pass. cars, 833,545 comm. vehicles. **Civil aviation:** 22.8 bil pass.-mi; 37 airports. **Chief ports:** Kaohsiung, Chilung (Keelung), Hualien, Taichung.

Communications: TV sets: 327 per 1,000 pop. **Radios:** 402 per 1,000 pop. **Telephone lines:** 13.4 mil. **Daily newspaper circ.:** 20.2 per 1,000 pop. **Internet:** 8.8 mil users.

Health: Life expect.: 74.5 male; 80.3 female. **Births** (per 1,000 pop.): 12.6. **Deaths** (per 1,000 pop.): 6.4. **Natural inc.:** 0.63%. **Infant mortality** (per 1,000 live births): 6.4.

Education: Free, compulsory: ages 6-15. **Literacy**: 96.1%.

Major Intl. Organizations: APEC.

Embassy: 4201 Wisconsin Ave. NW, 20016; 895-1800.

Website: www.gio.gov.tw

Large-scale Chinese immigration began in the 17th century. The island came under mainland control after an interval of Dutch rule, 1620-62. Taiwan (also called Formosa) was ruled by Japan 1895-1945. The Kuomintang (Chinese nationalist govt) fled to Taiwan in 1949 and established the Republic of China under Chang Kai-shek, who ruled for over 20 years with increasingly broad power. The U.S. provided military aid deterring a Communist invasion. In 1971, the UN expelled Taiwan from its seat and recognized the mainland govt. The U.S. officially recognized the People's Republic, Dec. 15, 1978, and severed ties with Taiwan. However, the U.S. and Taiwan have continued a strong trading relationship, and maintain contact via quasi-official agencies.

Land reform, government planning, U.S. aid and investment, and free universal education brought huge advances in industry, agriculture, and living standards. In 1987 martial law was lifted after 38 years, and in 1991 the 43-year period of emergency rule ended. Taiwan held its first direct presidential election Mar. 23, 1996. An earthquake on Sept. 21, 1999, killed more than 2,300 people and injured thousands more. Five decades of Nationalist Party rule ended with the presidential election of Mar. 18, 2000, won by Chen Shui-bian, leader of the pro-independence Democratic Progressive Party. Chen was wounded in an apparent assassination attempt Mar. 19, 2004, one day before he narrowly won a 2nd term as president; police said Mar, 7, 2005, that Chen's assailant drowned himself 10 days after the shooting.

Since 1949, the People's Republic has considered Taiwan a rebel province of the mainland, while, until 1991, Taiwan claimed to be the sole government of both. Beijing and Taipei increased economic cooperation in the 1990s. In 1999, relations between the 2 soured, when Taiwan redefined its relationship with mainland China as "state to state." China has warned that any Taiwan move toward independence could provoke military action.

Taiwan has one of the world's strongest economies and is among the 10 leading capital exporters.

The **Penghu Isls.** (Pescadores), 49 sq mi, pop. (1996 est.) 90,142, lie between Taiwan and the mainland. **Quemoy** and **Matsu,** pop. (1996 est.) 53,286, lie just off the mainland.

Tajikistan

Republic of Tajikistan

People: Population: 7,163,506. **Age distrib.** (%): <15: 38.5; 65+: 4.8. **Pop. density:** 130 per sq mi, 50 per sq km. **Urban:** 24.7%. **Ethnic groups:** Tajik 65%, Uzbek 25%, Russian 4%. **Principal languages:** Tajik (official), Russian. **Chief religions:** Sunni Muslim 85%, Shi'a Muslim 5%.

Geography: Total area: 55,251 sq mi, 143,100 sq km; **Land area:** 55,097 sq mi, 142,700 sq km. **Location:** Central Asia. **Neighbors:** Uzbekistan on N and W, Kyrgyzstan on N, China on E, Afghanistan on S. **Topography:** Mountainous region that contains the Pamirs, Trans-Alai mountain system. **Capital:** Dushanbe, 554,000.

Government: Type: Republic. **Head of state:** Pres. Imomali Rakhmonov; b Oct. 5, 1952; in office: Nov. 6, 1994. **Head of gov.:** Akil Akilov; b 1944; in office: Dec. 20, 1999. **Local divisions:** 2 viloyats, 1 autonomous viloyat. **Defense budget** (2004): $18 mil. **Active troops:** 7,600.

Economy: Industries: metals, chemicals & fertilizers, cement, vegetable oil, machine tools. **Chief crops:** cotton, grain, fruits, grapes, vegetables. **Natural resources:** hydropower, oil, uranium, mercury, lignite, lead, zinc, antimony, tungsten, silver, gold. **Crude oil reserves** (2004): 12 mil bbls. **Arable land:** 6%. **Livestock** (2004): cattle: 1.1 mil; chickens: 1.5 mil; goats: 850,000; pigs: 500; sheep: 1.6 mil. **Fish catch** (2003): 325 metric tons. **Electricity prod.** (2003): 15.4 bil kWh. **Labor force** (2000 est.): agriculture 67.2%, industry 7.5%, services 25.3%.

Finance: Monetary unit: Somoni (TJS) (Sept. 2005: 2.79 = $1 U.S.). **GDP** (2004 est.): $8.0 bil; **per capita GDP:** $1,100; **GDP growth:** 10.5%. **Imports** (2004 est.): $1.3 bil; partners (2004): Russia 17.8%, Uzbekistan 13.4%, Kazakhstan 9.7%, Ukraine 6.3%, Azerbaijan 6.3%, US 5.8%, Turkey 4.3%. **Exports** (2004 est.): $1.1 bil; partners (2004): Latvia 13.1%, Switzerland 11.5%, Uzbekistan 11.3%, Norway 9.9%, Russia 8.2%, Iran 7.9%, Turkey 7.7%, Italy 6.6%, Hungary 4.4%. **Tourism:** $2 mil. **Budget** (2004 est.): $321.5 mil. **Intl. reserves less gold:** $101 mil. **Gold:** 30,000 oz t.

Transport: Railroad: Length: 300 mi. **Motor vehicles:** 117,100 pass. cars, 16,800 comm. vehicles. **Civil aviation:** 356.0 mil pass.-mi; 13 airport.

Communications: TV sets: 328 per 1,000 pop. **Radios:** 143 per 1,000 pop. **Telephone lines:** 245,200. **Daily newspaper circ.:** 20 per 1,000 pop. **Internet**: 4,100 users.

Health: Life expect.: 61.7 male; 67.6 female. **Births** (per 1,000 pop.): 32.6. **Deaths** (per 1,000 pop.): 8.4. **Natural inc.:** 2.42%. **Infant mortality** (per 1,000 live births): 110.8. **AIDS rate:** <0.1%.

Education: Compulsory: ages 7-15. **Literacy:** 99.4%.

Major International Organizations: UN (FAO, IBRD, ILO, IMF, WHO), CIS, OSCE.

Embassy: 1005 New Hampshire Avenue, 20037 223-6090.

Website: tajikistan.tajnet.com/english/index.html

There were settled societies in the region from about 3000 BC. Invaders have included Iranians (Arabs who converted the population to Islam), Mongols, Uzbeks, Afghans, and Russians. The USSR gained control of the region 1918-25. In 1924, the Tajik ASSR was created within the Uzbek SSR. The Tajik SSR was proclaimed in 1929.

Tajikistan declared independence Sept. 9, 1991. Factional fighting led to the installation of a pro-Communist regime, Jan. 1993. A new constitution establishing a presidential system was approved by referendum Nov. 6, 1994.

Clashes between Muslim rebels, reportedly armed by Afghanistan, and troops loyal to the government and supported by Russia, claimed an estimated 55,000 lives by mid-1997, despite a series of peace accords. Constitutional changes including legalization of Islamic political parties were approved by referendum Sept. 26, 1999. Pres. Imomali Rakhmonov won a Nov. 6 election called "a farce" by human-rights observers. Voters approved, June 22, 2003, constitutional changes giving Rakhmonov the right to serve as president until 2020.

Tanzania

United Republic of Tanzania

People: Population: 36,766,356. **Age distrib.** (%): <15: 44.0; 65+: 2.6. **Pop. density:** 101 per sq mi, 39 per sq km. **Urban:** 35.4%. **Ethnic groups:** Mainland: Bantu 95%; Zanzibar: Arab, African, mixed. **Principal languages:** Swahili, English (both official); Arabic, many local languages. **Chief religions:** Christian 30%, Muslim 35%, indigenous beliefs 35%; Zanzibar is 99% Muslim.

Geography: Total area: 364,900 sq mi, 945,087 sq km; **Land area:** 342,101 sq mi, 886,037 sq km. **Location:** On coast of E Africa. **Neighbors:** Kenya, Uganda on N; Rwanda, Burundi, Congo (formerly Zaire) on W; Zambia, Malawi, Mozambique on S. **Topography:** Hot, arid central plateau, surrounded by the lake region in the W, temperate highlands in N and S, the coastal plains. Mt. Kilimanjaro, 19,340 ft., is highest in Africa. **Capital:** Dodoma, 155,000. **Cities (urban aggr.):** Dar-es-Salaam, 2,347,000.

Government: Type: Republic. **Head of state:** Pres. Benjamin William Mkapa; b Nov. 12, 1938; in office: Nov. 23, 1995. **Head of gov.:** Prime Min. Frederick Tluway Sumaye; b May 29, 1950; in office: Nov. 28, 1995. **Local divisions:** 25 regions. **Defense budget** (2004): $362 mil. **Active troops:** 27,000.

Economy: Industries: agric. proc., diamond & gold mining, oil refining, shoes. **Chief crops:** coffee, sisal, tea, cotton, pyrethrum (insecticide from chrysanthemums), cashews. **Natural resources:** hydropower, tin, phosphates, iron ore, coal, diamonds, gemstones, gold, nat. gas, nickel. **Arable land:** 3%. **Livestock** (2004): cattle: 17.8 mil; chickens: 30.0; goats: 12.6 mil; pigs: 455,000; sheep: 3.5 mil. **Fish catch** (2003): 351,127 metric tons. **Electricity prod.** (2003): 3.2 bil kWh. **Labor force** (2002 est.): agriculture 80%, industry and services 20%.

Finance: Monetary unit: Shilling (TZS) (Sept. 2005: 1,122.00 = $1 U.S.). **GDP** (2004 est.): $23.7 bil; **per capita GDP:** $700; **GDP growth:** 5.8%. **Imports** (2004 est.): $2.0 bil; partners (2004): South Africa 13.1%, China 8.8%, India 6.6%, Zambia 5.4%, UAE 5.4%, US 4.8%, UK 4.8%, Kenya 4.3%. **Exports** (2004 est.): $1.2 bil; partners (2004): India 10.2%, Netherlands 6.8%, Japan 6.1%, UK 5.3%, China 5.2%, Kenya 4.8%, Germany 4.4%. **Tourism:** $450 mil. **Budget** (2004 est.): $2.1 bil. **Intl. reserves less gold:** $1.48 bil. **Consumer prices:** 0.03%.

Transport: Railroad: Length: 2,293 mi. **Motor vehicles:** 35,600 pass. cars, 98,800 comm. vehicles. **Civil aviation:** 112.5 mil pass.-mi; 11 airports. **Chief ports:** Dar-es-Salaam, Mtwara, Tanga.

Communications: TV sets: 21 per 1,000 pop. **Radios:** 280 per 1,000 pop. **Telephone lines:** 149,100. **Daily newspaper circ.:** 3.9 per 1,000 pop. **Internet**: 250,000 users.

Health: Life expect.: 44.6 male; 45.9 female. **Births** (per 1,000 pop.): 38.2. **Deaths** (per 1,000 pop.): 16.7. **Natural inc.:** 2.15%. **Infant mortality** (per 1,000 live births): 98.5. **AIDS rate:** 8.8%.

Education: Compulsory: ages 7-13. **Literacy:** 78.2%.

Major Intl. Organizations: UN and all of its specialized agencies, the Commonwealth, AU.

Embassy: 2139 R St. NW 20008; 939-6125.

Website: www.tanzania.go.tz/index2E.html

The Republic of Tanganyika in E Africa and the island Republic of Zanzibar, off the coast of Tanganyika, both of which had recently gained independence, joined into a single nation, the United Republic of Tanzania, Apr. 26, 1964. Zanzibar retains internal self-government.

Until resigning as president in 1985, Julius K. Nyerere, a former Tanganyikan independence leader, dominated Tanzania's politics, which emphasized government planning and control of the economy, with single-party rule. In 1992 the constitution was amended to establish a multiparty system. Privatization of the economy was undertaken in the 1990s.

At least 500 people died when an overcrowded Tanzanian ferry sank in Lake Victoria, May 21, 1996. About 460,000 Rwandan refugees, mostly Hutu, returned from Tanzania to Rwanda in Dec. 1996. A bomb at the U.S. embassy in Dar-es-Salaam, Aug. 7, 1998, killed 11 people and injured at least 70 others. The U.S. blamed the attack and a near-simultaneous embassy bombing in Kenya on Islamic terrorists associated with Osama bin Laden. After a trial in New York City, 4 conspirators were convicted May 29, 2001.

Former Pres. Nyerere died in London Oct. 14, 1999. President since 1995, Benjamin Mkapa was reelected Oct. 29, 2000. Over 280 people died in a train wreck June 24, 2002, SE of Dodoma.

Tanganyika. Arab colonization and slaving began in the 8th century AD; Portuguese sailors explored the coast by about 1500. Other Europeans followed.

In 1885 Germany established German East Africa of which Tanganyika formed the bulk. It became a League of Nations mandate and, after 1946, a UN trust territory, both under Britain. It became independent Dec. 9, 1961, and a republic within the Commonwealth a year later.

Zanzibar, the Isle of Cloves, lies 23 mi off mainland Tanzania; area 640 sq mi and pop. (2002) 622,459. The island of **Pemba,** 25 mi to the NE, area 380 sq mi and pop. (2002) 362,166 is included in the administration.

Chief industry is cloves and clove oil production, of which Zanzibar and Pemba produce most of the world's supply.

Zanzibar was for centuries the center for Arab slave traders. Portugal ruled the region for 2 centuries until ousted by Arabs around 1700. Zanzibar became a British Protectorate in 1890; independence came Dec. 10, 1963. Revolutionary forces overthrew the Sultan Jan. 12, 1964. The new government ousted Western diplomats and newsmen, slaughtered thousands of Arabs, and nationalized farms. Union with Tanganyika followed.

Thailand

Kingdom of Thailand

People: Population: 64,185,502. **Age distrib.** (%): <15: 23.9; 65+: 7.5. **Pop. density:** 323 per sq mi, 125 per sq km. **Urban:** 31.9%. **Ethnic groups:** Thai 75%, Chinese 14%. **Principal languages:** Thai, Chinese, Malay, Khmer. **Chief religions:** Buddhism 95% (official), Muslim 5%.

Geography: Total area: 198,457 sq mi, 514,000 sq km; **Land area:** 197,596 sq mi, 511,770 sq km. **Location:** On Indochinese and Malayan peninsulas in SE Asia. **Neighbors:** Myanmar on W and N, Laos on N, Cambodia on E, Malaysia on S. **Topography:** A plateau dominates the NE third of Thailand, dropping to the fertile alluvial valley of the Chao Phraya R. in the center. Forested mountains are in the N, with narrow fertile valleys. The S peninsula region is covered by rain forests. **Capital:** Bangkok, 6,486,000.

Government: Type: Constitutional monarchy. **Head of state:** King Bhumibol Adulyadej; b Dec. 5, 1927; in office: June 9, 1946. **Head of gov.:** Prime Min. Thaksin Shinawatra; b July 26, 1949; in office: Feb. 18, 2001. **Local divisions:** 76 provinces. **Defense budget** (2004): $1.9 bil. **Active troops:** 306,600.

Economy: Industries: tourism; textiles & garments, agric. proc., beverages, tobacco, cement, light mfg.; electric appliances & components, computers & parts. **Chief crops:** rice, cassava, rubber, corn, sugarcane, coconuts, soybeans. **Natural resources:** tin, rubber, nat. gas, tungsten, tantalum, timber, lead, fish, gypsum, lignite, fluorite. **Crude oil reserves** (2004): 583.4 mil bbls. **Arable land:** 34%. **Livestock** (2004): cattle: 5.0 mil; chickens: 170.0 mil; goats: 178,000; pigs: 7.2 mil; sheep: 42,000. **Fish catch** (2003): 3,590,452 metric tons. **Electricity prod.** (2003): 114.7 bil kWh. **Labor force** (2000 est.): agriculture 49%, industry 14%, services 37%.

Finance: Monetary unit: Baht (THB) (Sept. 2005: 41.11 = $1 U.S.). **GDP** (2004 est.): $524.8 bil; **per capita GDP:** $8,100; **GDP growth:** 6.1%. **Imports** (2004 est.): $80.8 bil; partners (2004): Japan 23.6%, China 8.6%, US 7.6%, Malaysia 5.8%, Singapore 4.4%, Taiwan 4.1%. **Exports** (2004 est.): $87.9 bil; partners (2004): US 15.9%, Japan 13.9%, China 7.3%, Singapore 7.2%, Malaysia 5.4%, Hong Kong 5.1%. **Tourism:** $7,822 mil. **Budget** (2004 est.): $31.9 bil. **Intl. reserves less gold:** $31.34 bil. **Gold:** 2.7 mil oz t. **Consumer prices:** 2.77%.

Transport: Railroad: Length: 2,530 mi. **Motor vehicles:** 3.26 mil pass. cars, 4.58 mil comm. vehicles. **Civil aviation:** 27.4 bil pass.-mi; 62 airports. **Chief ports:** Bangkok, Sattahip.

Communication: TV sets: 274 per 1,000 pop. **Radios:** 234 per 1,000 pop. **Telephone lines:** 6.6 mil. **Daily newspaper circ.:** 63 per 1,000 pop. **Internet:** 7.0 mil users.

Health: Life expect.: 69.7 male; 74.4 female. **Births** (per 1,000 pop.): 14.0. **Deaths** (per 1,000 pop.): 7.0. **Natural inc.:** 0.70%. **Infant mortality** (per 1,000 live births): 20.2. **AIDS rate:** 1.5%.

Education: Compulsory: ages 6-14. **Literacy:** 92.6%.

Major Intl. Organizations: UN (FAO, IBRD, ILO, IMF, IMO, WHO, WTrO), ASEAN, APEC.

Embassy: 1024 Wisconsin Ave., Suite 401, NW 20007; 944-3600.

Website: www.thaiembdc.org

Thais began migrating from southern China during the 11th century. A unified Thai kingdom was established in 1350. Known as Siam until 1939, Thailand is the only country in SE Asia never taken over by a European power, thanks to King Mongkut and his son King Chulalongkorn. Ruling successively from 1851 to 1910, they modernized the country and signed trade treaties with Britain and France. A bloodless revolution in 1932 limited the monarchy. Thailand was an ally of Japan during World War II and of the U.S. during the postwar period. For decades, the military had a dominant role in governing the country.

A steep downturn in the economy forced Thailand to seek more than $15 billion in emergency international loans in Aug. 1997. A new constitution won legislative approval Sept. 27. By the end of the 1990s, according to UN estimates, more than 750,000 people in Thailand had HIV/AIDS; a nationwide prevention campaign has reduced the number of new infections.

Following elections in Jan. 2001, Thaksin Shinawatra, a wealthy former telecommunications executive, became prime minister. On Feb. 1, 2003, Thaksin launched a nationwide crackdown on methamphetamines; human rights observers criticized police tactics in the drug war, which killed more than 2,200 people by Apr. 30. The Indian Ocean tsunami of Dec. 26, 2004 left about 5,400 people dead and more than 2,800 missing in Thailand.

Elections Feb. 6, 2005, gave Thaksin's party a huge majority in parliament. He assumed emergency powers July 15 to deal with an Islamic insurgency in S Thailand that had claimed more than 800 lives since Jan. 2004.

Timor-Leste

(East Timor)

Democratic Republic of Timor-Leste

People: Population: 1,040,880. **Age distrib.** (%): <15: 37.1; 65+: 3.0. **Pop. density:** 180 per sq mi, 69 per sq km. **Urban:** 7.6%. **Ethnic groups:** Austronesian, Papuan. **Principal languages:** Tetum, Portuguese (both official); Indonesian, English, other native languages. **Chief religions:** Roman Catholic 90%, Muslim 4%, Protestant 3%.

Geography: Total area: 5,794 sq mi, 15,007 sq km. **Land area:** 5,641 sq mi, 14,609 sq km. **Location:** E half of Timor Is. in the SW Pacific O. **Neighbors:** Indonesia (West Timor) on W. **Topography:** Terrain is rugged, rising to 9,721 ft at Mt. Ramelau. **Capital:** Dili, 49,000.

Government: Type: Republic. **Head of state:** Pres. Xanana Gusmão; b June 20, 1946; in office: May 20, 2002. **Head of gov.:** Prime Min. Mari Alkatiri; b Nov. 26, 1949; in office: May 20, 2002. **Local divisions:** 13 districts. **Active troops:** 1,250.

Economy: Industries: printing, soap, handicrafts, clothing. **Chief crops:** coffee, rice, maize, cassava, sweet potatoes. **Natural resources:** gold, oil, nat. gas, mang., marble. **Livestock** (2004): cattle: 170,000; chickens: 2.1 mil; goats: 80,000; pigs: 346,000; sheep: 25,000. **Fish catch** (2003): 350 metric tons.

Finance: Monetary unit: U.S. dollar (Sept. 2005). **GDP** (2004 est.): $370.0 mil; **per capita GDP:** $400; **GDP growth:** 1%. **Imports** (2004 est.): $167.0 mil; partners (: Indonesia, Australia, Singapore, Vietnam, Portugal, Malaysia, China. **Exports** (2004 est.): $8.0 mil; partners : Portugal, Taiwan, Germany, US, Indonesia, Australia. **Budget** (2004 est.): $73.0 mil.

Transport: Civil aviation: 3 airports. **Chief port:** Dili.

Health: Life expect.: 63.6 male; 68.3 female. **Births** (per 1,000 pop.): 27.2. **Deaths** (per 1,000 pop.): 6.3. **Natural inc.:** 2.09%. **Infant mortality** (per 1,000 live births): 47.4.

Education: Compulsory: ages 7-15. **Literacy:** 58.6%.

Major Intl. Organizations: UN.

Embassy: 4201 Conn. Ave., NW, 20008; 202-966-3202

Website: timor-leste.gov.tl

The collapse of Portuguese rule in East Timor led to an outbreak of factional fighting in Aug. 1975 and an invasion by Indonesia in Dec. Indonesia annexed East Timor as a 27th province in 1976, despite international condemnation. In over 2 decades some 200,000 Timorese died as a result of civil war, famine, and persecution by Indonesian authorities. In a referendum held Aug. 30, 1999, under UN auspices, Timorese voted overwhelmingly for independence. Pro-Indonesian militias then went on a rampage, terrorizing the population. Under pressure, the government allowed entrance of an international peacekeeping force, which began arriving in Sept.; a UN interim administration formally took command Oct. 26, 1999.

Pro-independence forces won elections for a constituent assembly Aug. 30, 2001. Xanana Gusmão, a former guerrilla leader, won the presidential election Apr. 14, 2002. As Timor-Leste the territory became independent May 20 and entered the UN Sept. 27. A sovereignty dispute with Australia over the oil-rich Timor Sea was resolved in Aug. 2004.

Togo

Togolese Republic

People: Population: 5,399,991. **Age distrib.** (%): <15: 43.2; 65+: 2.6. **Pop. density:** 246 per sq mi, 95 per sq km. **Urban:** 35.1%. **Ethnic groups:** 37 African tribes; largest are Ewe, Mina, and Kabre. **Principal languages:** French (official); Ewe, Mina in S; Kabye, Dagomba in N. **Chief religions:** Indigenous beliefs 51%, Christian 29%, Muslim 20%.

Geography: Total area: 21,925 sq mi, 56,785 sq km; **Land area:** 20,998 sq mi, 54,385 sq km. **Location:** On S coast of W Africa. **Neighbors:** Ghana on W, Burkina Faso on N, Benin on E. **Topography:** A range of hills running SW-NE splits Togo into 2 savanna plains regions. **Capital:** Lomé, 799,000.

Government: Type: Republic. **Head of state:** Pres. Faure Gnassingbé; b June 6, 1966; in office: May 4, 2005. **Head of gov.:** Prime Min. Edem Kodjo; b. May 23, 1938; in office: June 9, 2005. **Local divisions:** 5 regions. **Defense budget** (2003): $32 mil. **Active troops:** 8,550.

Economy: Industries: phosphates mining, agric. proc., cement, handicrafts. **Chief crops:** coffee, cocoa, cotton, yams, cassava, corn. **Natural resources:** phosphates, limestone, marble. **Arable land:** 38%. **Livestock** (2004): cattle: 279,000; chickens: 9.0 mil; goats: 1.5 mil; pigs: 320,000; sheep: 1.9 mil. **Fish catch** (2003): 28,706 metric tons. **Electricity prod.** (2003): 0.17 bil kWh. **Labor force** (1998 est.): agriculture 65%, industry 5%, services 30%.

Finance: Monetary unit: CFA Franc BCEAO (XOF) (Sept. 2005: 525.28 = $1 U.). **GDP** (2004 est.): $8.7 bil; **per capita GDP:** $1,600; **GDP growth:** 3%. **Imports** (2004 est.): $824.9 mil; partners (2004): China 24.7%, France 16.1%, Malaysia 5.3%, Italy 4.6%, Germany 4.6%, UK 4.3%, Netherlands 4.2%, Thailand 4.2%, Belgium 4.2%. **Exports** (2004 est.): $663.1 mil; partners (2004): Burkina Faso 16%, Ghana 14.7%, Benin 9.2%, China 8.1%, Mali 7.5%, Netherlands 6.6%, Taiwan 4.2%. **Tourism** (2002): $13 mil. **Budget** (2004 est.): $273.3 mil. **Intl. reserves less gold:** $208 mil. **Consumer prices:** 0.39%.

Transport: Railroad: Length: 326 mi. **Motor vehicles:** 51,400 pass. cars, 24,500 comm. vehicles. **Civil aviation:** 80.8 mil pass.-mi; 2 airports. **Chief port:** Lomé.

Communications: TV sets: 22 per 1,000 pop. **Radios:** 244 per 1,000 pop. **Telephone lines:** 60,600. **Daily newspaper circ.:** 2.2 per 1,000 pop. **Internet:** 210,000 users.

Health: Life expect.: 55.0 male; 59.1 female. **Births** (per 1,000 pop.): 37.2. **Deaths** (per 1,000 pop.): 10.0. **Natural inc.:** 2.72%. **Infant mortality** (per 1,000 live births): 62.2. **AIDS rate:** 4.1%.

Education: Compulsory: ages 6-15. **Literacy:** 60.9%.

Major Intl. Organizations: UN (FAO, IBRD, ILO, IMF, IMO, WHO, WTrO), AU.

Embassy: 2208 Massachusetts Ave. NW, 20008; 234-4212.

Website: www.state.gov/p/af/ci/to

Togoland was administered by Germany and then by France and Britain. The French sector became the republic of Togo Apr. 27, 1960. In office since 1967, Pres. Gnassingbé Eyadéma was Africa's longest-serving head of state until his death Feb. 5, 2005. His son, Faure Gnassingbé, was immediately installed as president, but other African leaders pressured Togo to hold an election, which Gnassingbé won Apr. 24. Opposition parties disputed the result, and protests led to violent clashes in Lomé.

Tonga

Kingdom of Tonga

People: Population: 112,422. **Age distrib.** (%): <15: 36.2; 65+: 4.2. **Pop. density:** 389 per sq mi, 150 per sq km. **Urban:** 33.4%. **Ethnic groups:** Polynesian. **Principal languages:** Tongan, English (both official). **Chief religions:** Wesleyan 41%, Roman Catholic 16%, Mormon 14%.

Geography: Total area: 289 sq mi, 748 sq km; **Land area:** 277 sq mi, 718 sq km. **Location:** In western South Pacific O. **Neighbors:** Nearest are Fiji to W, Samoa to NE. **Topography:** Tonga comprises 170 volcanic and coral islands, 36 inhabited. **Capital:** Nuku'alofa, 35,000.

Government: Type: Constitutional monarchy. **Head of state:** King Taufa'ahau Tupou IV; b July 4, 1918; in office: Dec. 16, 1965. **Head of gov.:** Prime Min. Prince Ulukalala Lavaka Ata; b July 12, 1959; in office: Jan. 3, 2000. **Local divisions:** 3 island groups.

Economy: Industries: tourism, fishing. **Chief crops:** squash, coconuts, copra, bananas, vanilla, cocoa. **Natural resources:** fish. **Arable land:** 24%. **Livestock** (2004): cattle: 11,250; chickens: 300,000; goats: 12,500; pigs: 81,000. **Fish catch** (2003): 4,458 metric tons. **Electricity prod.** (2003): 0.03 bil kWh. **Labor force** (1997 est.): agriculture 65%.

Finance: Monetary unit: Pa'anga (TOP) (Sept. 2005: 1.97 = $1 U.S.). **GDP** (2002 est.): $244.0 mil; **per capita GDP:** $2,300; **GDP growth:** 1.5%. **Imports** (2002 est.): $86.0 mil; partners (2004): New Zealand 46.7%, Fiji 21.1%, Australia 10.3%, US 6.7%. **Exports** (2002 est.): $27.0 mil; partners (2004): Japan 51.4%, US 24.9%, India 4.1%. **Tourism** (2002): $6 mil. **Budget** (2000 est.): $52.4 mil. **Intl. reserves less gold:** $38 mil. **Consumer prices:** 10.98%.

Transport: Motor vehicles: 4,800 pass. cars, 4,400 comm. vehicles. **Civil aviation:** 8.08 mil pass.-mi; 1 airport. **Chief port:** Nuku'alofa.

Communications: TV sets: 61 per 1,000 pop. **Radios:** 663 per 1,000 pop. **Telephone lines** (2002): 11,200. **Daily newspaper circ.:** 72 per 1,000 pop. **Internet** (2002): 2,900 users.

Health: Life expect.: 67.1 male; 72.1 female. **Births** (per 1,000 pop.): 25.2. **Deaths** (per 1,000 pop.): 5.4. **Natural inc.:** 1.98%. **Infant mortality** (per 1,000 live births): 12.6.

Education: Compulsory: ages 6-14. **Literacy** (1996 est.): 98.5%.

Major Intl. Organizations: UN (FAO, IBRD, IMF, WHO), the Commonwealth.

Embassy: 250 E. 51st St. New York, NY 10022; (917) 369-1025.

Website: pmo.gov.to

The islands were first visited by the Dutch in the early 17th century. A series of civil wars ended in 1845 with establishment of the Tupou dynasty. In 1900 Tonga became a British protectorate. On June 4, 1970, Tonga became independent and a member of the Commonwealth. It joined the UN on Sept. 14, 1999.

Trinidad and Tobago

Republic of Trinidad and Tobago

People: Population: 1,075,066. **Age distrib.** (%): <15: 20.7; 65+: 8.3. **Pop. density:** 543 per sq mi, 210 per sq km. **Urban:** 75.4%. **Ethnic groups:** Black 40%, East Indian 40%, mixed 18%. **Principal languages:** English (official), Hindi, French, Spanish, Chinese. **Chief religions:** Roman Catholic 26%, Hindu 23%, Protestant 14%, Muslim 6%.

Geography: Total area: 1,980 sq mi, 5,128 sq km; **Land area:** 1,980 sq mi, 5,128 sq km. **Location:** In Caribbean, off E coast of Venezuela. **Neighbors:** Nearest is Venezuela to SW. **Topography:** Three low mountain ranges cross Trinidad E-W, with a well-watered plain between N and central ranges. Parts of E and W coasts are swamps. Tobago, 116 sq. mi., lies 20 mi. NE. **Capital:** Port-of-Spain, 55,000.

Government: Type: Parliamentary democracy. **Head of state:** Pres. George Maxwell Richards; b 1931; in office: Mar. 17, 2003. **Head of gov.:** Prime Min. Patrick Augustus Mervyn Manning; b Aug. 17, 1946; in office: Dec. 24, 2001. **Local divisions:** 8 counties, 3 municipalities, 1 ward. **Defense budget** (2004): $32 mil. **Active troops:** 2,700.

Economy: Industries: oil, chemicals, tourism, food proc. **Chief crops:** cocoa, sugarcane, rice, citrus, coffee, vegetables. **Natural resources:** oil, nat. gas, asphalt. **Crude oil reserves** (2004): 990 mil bbls. **Arable land:** 15%. **Livestock** (2004): cattle: 28,980; chickens: 28.2 mil; goats: 59,000; pigs: 78,000; sheep: 3,400. **Fish catch** (2003): 9,747 metric tons. **Electricity prod.** (2003): 6.1 bil kWh. **Labor force** (1997 est.): agriculture 9.5%, manufacturing, mining, and quarrying 14%, construction and utilities 12.4%, services 64.1%.

Finance: Monetary unit: Tobago Dollar (TTD) (Sept. 2005: 6.19 = $1 U.S.). **GDP** (2004 est.): $11.5 bil; **per capita GDP:** $10,500; **GDP growth:** 5.7%. **Imports** (2004 est.): $4.7 bil; partners (2004): US 24.6%, Venezuela 12%, Germany 10.8%, Spain 7%, Italy 5.5%, Brazil 5%. **Exports** (2004 est.): $6.7 bil; partners (2004): US 66.7%, Jamaica 5.7%, France 3.5%. **Tourism** (2002): $242 mil. **Budget** (2004 est.): $3.2 bil. **Intl. reserves less gold:** $2.04 bil. **Gold:** 60,000 oz t. **Consumer prices:** 3.72%.

Transport: Motor vehicles: 229,400 pass. cars, 53,900 comm. vehicles. **Civil aviation:** 1.7 bil pass.-mi; 3 airports. **Chief ports:** Port-of-Spain, Scarborough.

Communications: TV sets: 337 per 1,000 pop. **Radios:** 532 per 1,000 pop. **Telephone lines:** (2002): 325,100. **Daily newspaper circ.:** 123 per 1,000 pop. **Internet** (2002): 138,000 users.

Health: Life expect.: 65.6 male; 67.9 female. **Births** (per 1,000 pop.): 12.7. **Deaths** (per 1,000 pop.): 10.4. **Natural inc.:** 0.24%. **Infant mortality** (per 1,000 live births): 25.8. **AIDS rate:** 3.2%.

Education: Compulsory: ages 5-11. **Literacy:** 98.6%.

Major Intl. Organizations: UN (FAO, IBRD, ILO, IMF, IMO, WHO, WTrO), Caricom, the Commonwealth, OAS.

Embassy: 1708 Massachusetts Ave. NW 20036; 467-6490.

Website: www.gov.tt

Columbus sighted Trinidad in 1498. A British possession since 1802, Trinidad and Tobago won independence Aug. 31, 1962. It became a republic in 1976.

The nation is one of the most prosperous in the Caribbean. Oil production has increased with offshore finds. Middle Eastern oil is refined and exported, mostly to the U.S.

In July 1990, some 120 Muslim extremists captured the Parliament building and TV station and took about 50 hostages, including Prime Min. Arthur N. R. Robinson, who was beaten, shot in the legs, and tied to explosives. After a 6-day siege, the rebels surrendered.

Basdeo Panday, the country's first prime minister of East Indian ancestry, took office Nov. 9, 1995. Robinson became president on Mar. 19, 1997. Patrick Manning of the People's National Movement became prime minister after elections Dec. 10, 2001. George Maxwell Richards, a former university dean, succeeded Robinson as president, Mar. 17, 2003.

Tunisia

Tunisian Republic

People: Population: 10,074,951. **Age distrib.** (%): <15: 25.3; 65+: 6.6. **Pop. density:** 159 per sq mi, 62 per sq km. **Urban:** 63.7%. **Ethnic groups:** Arab 98%, European 1%, Jewish and other 1%. **Principal languages:** Arabic (official), French prevalent. **Chief religion:** Muslim 98% (official; mostly Sunni).

Geography: Total area: 63,170 sq mi, 163,610 sq km; **Land area:** 59,985 sq mi, 155,360 sq km. **Location:** On N coast of Africa. **Neighbors:** Algeria on W, Libya on E. **Topography:** The N is wooded and fertile. The central coastal plains are given to grazing and orchards. The S is arid, approaching Sahara Desert. **Capital:** Tunis 1,996,000.

Government: Type: Republic. **Head of state:** Pres. Gen. Zine al-Abidine Ben Ali; b Sept. 3, 1936; in office: Nov. 7, 1987. **Head of gov.:** Prime Min. Mohamed Ghannouchi; b Aug. 18, 1941; in office: Nov. 17, 1999. **Local divisions:** 24 governorates. **Defense budget** (2004): $537 mil. **Active troops:** 35,000.

Economy: Industries: oil, mining, tourism, textiles, footwear, agribusiness. **Chief crops:** olives, grain, tomatoes, citrus, sugar beets, dates, almonds. **Natural resources:** oil, phosphates, iron ore, lead, zinc, salt. **Crude oil reserves** (2004): 308 mil bbls. **Arable land:** 19%. **Livestock** (2004): cattle: 760,000; chickens: 62.0 mil; goats: 1.4 mil; pigs: 6,000; sheep: 6.9 mil. **Fish catch** (2003): 92,471 metric tons. **Electricity prod.** (2003): 11.6 bil kWh. **Labor force** (1995 est.): services 55%, industry 23%, agriculture 22%.

Finance: Monetary unit: Dinar (TND) (Sept. 2005: 1.30 = $1 U.S.). **GDP** (2004 est.): $70.9 bil; **per capita GDP:** $7,100; **GDP growth:** 5.1%. **Imports** (2004 est.): $11.5 bil; partners (2004): France 27.5%, Italy 20.8%, Germany 9.2%, Spain 5.7%. **Exports** (2004 est.): $9.9 bil; partners (2004): France 30%, Italy 23.3%, Germany 9.3%, Spain 5.3%, Belgium 4.3%, Libya 4.2%. **Tourism:** $1,583 mil. **Budget** (2004 est.): $7.6 bil. **Intl. reserves less gold:** $2.53 bil. **Gold:** 220,000 oz t. **Consumer prices:** 3.57%.

Transport: Railroad: Length: 1,337 mi. **Motor vehicles:** 552,900 pass. cars, 281,500 comm. vehicles. **Civil aviation:** 1.7 bil pass.-mi; 14 airports. **Chief ports:** Tunis, Sfax, Bizerte.

Communications: TV sets: 190 per 1,000 pop. **Radios:** 158 per 1,000 pop. **Telephone lines:** 1.2 mil. **Daily newspaper circ.:** 19 per 1,000 pop. **Internet**: 630,000 users.

Health: Life expect.: 73.2 male; 76.7 female. **Births** (per 1,000 pop.): 15.5. **Deaths** (per 1,000 pop.): 5.1. **Natural inc.:** 1.04%. **Infant mortality** (per 1,000 live births): 24.8. **AIDS rate:** <0.1%.

Education: Compulsory: ages 6-16. **Literacy:** 74.2%.

Major Intl. Organizations: UN (FAO, IBRD, ILO, IMF, IMO, WHO, WTrO), AL, AU.

Embassy: 1515 Massachusetts Ave. NW 20005; 862-1850.

Website: www.tourismtunisia.com

Site of ancient Carthage and a former Barbary state under the suzerainty of Turkey, Tunisia became a protectorate of France under a treaty signed May 12, 1881. The nation became independent Mar. 20, 1956, and ended the monarchy the following year. Habib Bourguiba, an independence leader, served as president until 1987, when he was deposed by his prime minister, Zine al-Abidine Ben Ali, who then won 4 presidential elections, 1989-2004, all tightly controlled by the ruling party.

Tunisia has actively repressed Islamic fundamentalism. A synagogue blast on Djerba Is., Apr. 11, 2002, apparently set off by al-Qaeda, killed 17 people, including 12 German tourists.

Turkey

Republic of Turkey

People: Population: 69,660,559. **Age distrib.** (%): <15: 26.0; 65+: 6.7. **Pop. density:** 231 per sq mi, 89 per sq km. **Urban:** 66.3%. **Ethnic groups:** Turkish 80%, Kurdish 20%. **Principal languages:** Turkish (official), Kurdish, Arabic, Armenian, Greek. **Chief religion:** Muslim 99.8% (mostly Sunni).

Geography: Total area: 301,384 sq mi, 780,580 sq km; **Land area:** 297,592 sq mi, 770,760 sq km. **Location:** Occupies Asia Minor, stretches into continental Europe; borders on Mediterranean and Black seas. **Neighbors:** Bulgaria, Greece on W; Georgia, Armenia on N; Iran on E; Iraq, Syria on S. **Topography:** Central Turkey has wide plateaus, with hot, dry summers and cold winters. High mountains ring the interior on all but W, with more than 20 peaks over 10,000 ft. Rolling plains are in W; mild, fertile coastal plains are in S, W. **Capital:** Ankara, 3,428,000. **Cities (urban aggr.):** Istanbul, 8,744,000; Izmir, 2,216,000.

Government: Type: Republic. **Head of state:** Pres. Ahmet Necdet Sezer; b Sept. 13, 1941; in office: May 16, 2000. **Head of gov.:** Prime Min. Recep Tayyip Erdogan; b Feb. 26, 1954; in office: Mar. 14, 2003. **Local divisions:** 81 provinces. **Defense budget** (2004): $8.5 bil. **Active troops:** 514,850.

Economy: Industries: textiles, food proc., autos, mining, steel, oil, constr. **Chief crops:** tobacco, cotton, grain, olives, sugar beets, citrus. **Natural resources:** antimony, coal, chromium, mercury, copper, borate, sulfur, iron ore, hydropower. **Crude oil reserves** (2004): 300 mil bbls. **Arable land:** 32%. **Livestock** (2004): cattle: 9.8 mil; chickens: 250.0 mil; goats: 6.7 mil; pigs: 3,000; sheep: 25.0 mil. **Fish catch** (2003): 587,715 metric tons. **Electricity prod.** (2003): 133.6 bil kWh. **Labor force** (3rd qtr, 2004): agriculture 35.9%, industry 22.8%, services 41.2%.

Finance: Monetary unit: Lira (TRL) (Sept. 2005: 1,342,500.03 = $1 U.S.). **GDP** (2004 est.): $508.7 bil; **per capita GDP:** $7,400; **GDP growth:** 8.2%. **Imports** (2004 est.): $94.5 bil; partners (2004): Germany 12.9%, Russia 9.3%, Italy 7.1%, France 6.4%, US 4.8%, China 4.6%, UK 4.4%. **Exports** (2004 est.): $69.5 bil; partners (2004): Germany 13.9%, UK 8.8%, US 7.7%, Italy 7.4%, France 5.8%, Spain 4.2%. **Tourism:** $13,203 mil. **Budget** (2004 est.): $110.9 bil. **Intl. reserves less gold:** $22.97 bil. **Gold:** 3.73 mil oz t. **Consumer prices:** 8.6%.

Transport: Railroad: Length: 5,348 mi. **Motor vehicles:** 4.6 mil pass. cars, 1.68 mil comm. vehicles. **Civil aviation:** 10.0 bil. pass.-mi; 86 airports. **Chief ports:** Istanbul, Izmir, Mersin.

Communications: TV sets: 328 per 1,000 pop. **Radios:** 510 per 1,000 pop. **Telephone lines:** 18.9 mil. **Daily newspaper circ:** 111 per 1,000 pop. **Internet:** 6.0 mil users.

Health: Life expect.: 69.9 male; 74.9 female. **Births** (per 1,000 pop.): 16.8. **Deaths** (per 1,000 pop.): 6.0. **Natural inc.:** 1.09%. **Infant mortality** (per 1,000 live births): 41.0.

Education: Compulsory: ages 6-14. **Literacy:** 86.5%.

Major Intl. Organizations: UN (FAO, IBRD, ILO, IMF, IMO, WHO, WTrO), NATO, OECD, OSCE.

Embassy: 2525 Massachusetts Ave. NW 20008; 612-6700.

Website: www.turkishembassy.org

Ancient inhabitants of Turkey were among the world's first agriculturalists. Such civilizations as the Hittite, Phrygian, and Lydian flourished in Asiatic Turkey (Asia Minor), as did much of Greek civilization. After the fall of Rome in the 5th century, Constantinople (now Istanbul) was the capital of the Byzantine Empire for 1,000 years. It fell in 1453 to Ottoman Turks, who ruled a vast empire for over 400 years.

Just before World War I, Turkey, or the Ottoman Empire, ruled what is now Syria, Lebanon, Iraq, Jordan, Israel, Saudi Arabia, Yemen, and islands in the Aegean Sea. Turkey joined Germany and Austria in World War I, and its defeat resulted in the loss of much territory and the fall of the sultanate. A republic was declared Oct. 29, 1923, with Mustafa Kemal (later Kemal Ataturk) as its first president. Ataturk led Turkey until his death in 1938.

Turkey kept neutral during most of World War II. The country became a full member of NATO in 1952 and remained a Western ally despite domestic political instability. Military coups overthrew civilian governments in 1960 and 1980. Turkey invaded nearby Cyprus July 20, 1974, to prevent that country from being united with Greece; since then, Cyprus has been divided into Greek and Turkish zones.

In recent decades, Turkish governments have contended with Kurdish separatism and the rise of militant Islam. Turkey was a member of the U.S.-led force that ousted Iraq from Kuwait, 1991. In the aftermath of the war, millions of Kurdish refugees fled to Turkey's border to escape Iraqi forces. Turkish offensives against the Kurds caused heavy casualties among guerrillas and civilians. Kurdish militants raided Turkish diplomatic missions in some 25 Western European cities June 24, 1993.

Tansu Ciller officially became Turkey's first woman prime minister July 5, 1993. The Welfare Party, an Islamic group, gained strength in the 1990s but was unable to form a government until June 1996, when it came to power in coalition with Ciller's True Path Party. The pro-Islamic government resigned June 18, 1997, under pressure from the military, which stepped up its campaign against Islamic fundamentalism in 1998.

Kurdish rebel leader Abdullah Öcalan was captured Feb. 15, 1999; convicted of terrorism June 29, he was sentenced to death by a Turkish security court. His organization, the Kurdistan Workers' Party, announced Aug. 5, 1999, that it would abandon its 14-year-old armed insurgency. A major earthquake Aug. 17, 1999, in NW Turkey killed over 17,000 people and injured thousands more. Another quake in the same region Nov. 12 claimed at least 675 lives.

The IMF announced $7.5 billion in emergency loans Dec. 6, 2000, to help Turkey cope with a severe financial crisis. The death penalty was abolished Aug. 3, 2002, and Öcalan's sentence was commuted to life in prison Oct. 3. The Justice and Development Party, an Islamic group headed by Recep Tayyip Erdogan, won a plurality in parliamentary elections Nov. 3.

During the U.S.-led invasion of Iraq, Mar.-Apr. 2003, Turkey, a NATO ally, refused to allow coalition forces to launch attacks on N Iraq from Turkish soil. Suicide bombings by Islamic extremists Nov. 15-20, 2003, killed 58 people and wounded about 750 at 2 synagogues, the British consulate, and the offices of a London-based bank, all in Istanbul.

Turkey has long sought to become a full member of the European Union, but the EU has deferred talks on accession until economic, human rights, and immigration issues are resolved.

Turkmenistan

People: Population: 4,952,081. **Age distrib.** (%): <15: 35.7; 65+: 4.1. **Pop. density:** 26 per sq mi, 10 per sq km. **Urban:** 45.3%. **Ethnic groups:** Turkmen 77%, Uzbek 9%, Russian 7%, Kazakh 2%. **Principal languages:** Turkmen, Russian, Uzbek. **Chief religions:** Muslim 89%, Eastern Orthodox 9%.

Geography: Total area: 188,457 sq mi, 488,100 sq km; **Land area:** 188,457 sq mi, 488,100 sq km. **Neighbors:** Kazakhstan on N, Uzbekistan on N and E, Afghanistan and Iran on S. **Topography:** The Kara Kum Desert occupies 80% of the area. Bordered on W by Caspian Sea. **Capital:** Ashgabat, 574,000.

Government: Type: Republic with authoritarian rule. **Head of state and gov.:** Pres. Saparmurad Niyazov; b Feb. 18, 1940; in office: Oct. 27, 1990. **Local divisions:** 5 regions. **Defense budget** (2003): $173 mil. **Active troops:** 26,000.

Economy: Industries: nat. gas, oil, oil products, textiles, food proc. **Chief crops:** cotton, grain. **Natural resources:** oil, nat. gas, coal, sulfur, salt. **Crude oil reserves** (2004): 546 mil bbls. **Arable land:** 3%. **Livestock** (2004): cattle: 2.0 mil; chickens: 7.0 mil; goats: 750,000; pigs: 30,000; sheep: 13.2 mil. **Fish catch** (2003): 14,567 metric tons. **Electricity prod.** (2003): 10.8 bil kWh. **Labor force** (2003 est.): agriculture 48.2%, industry 13.8%, services 37%.

Finance: Monetary unit: Manat (TMM) (Sept. 2005: 5,200.05 = $1 U.S.). **GDP** (2004 est.): $27.6 bil; **per capita GDP:** $5,700; **GDP growth:** (IMF est.): 7.5%. **Imports** (2004 est.): $2.9 bil; partners (2004): Russia 14%, Ukraine 13.8%, US 11.1%, UAE 8.1%, Turkey 8%, Germany 6.8%, France 4.6%. **Exports** (2004 est.): $4.0 bil; partners (2004): Ukraine 49.8%, Iran 17.2%, Italy 5.3%, Turkey 4.7%. **Tourism** (2002): $292 mil. **Budget** (2004 est.): $3.1 bil.

Transport: Railroad: Length: 1,516 mi. **Civil aviation:** 1.0 bil. pass.-mi; 13 airports. **Chief port:** Turkmenbashi.

Communications: TV sets: 198 per 1,000 pop. **Radios:** 289 per 1,000 pop. **Telephone lines:** 376,100. **Daily newspaper circ.:** 6.7 per 1,000 pop. **Internet** (2001): 8,000 users.

Health: Life expect.: 58.0 male; 64.9 female. **Births** (per 1,000 pop.): 27.7. **Deaths** (per 1,000 pop.): 8.8. **Natural inc.:** 1.89%. **Infant mortality** (per 1,000 live births): 73.1. **AIDS rate:** <0.1%.

Education: Compulsory: ages 7-15. **Literacy:** 98%.

Major Intl. Organizations: UN (FAO, IBRD, ILO, IMF, IMO, WHO), CIS, OSCE.

Embassy: 2207 Massachusetts Ave., NW 20008; 588-1500.

Website: www.turkmenistanembassy.org

The region has been inhabited by Turkic tribes since the 10th century. It became part of Russian Turkestan in 1881, and a constituent republic of the USSR in 1925. Turkmenistan declared independence Oct. 27, 1991, and became an independent state when the USSR disbanded Dec. 26, 1991.

Extensive oil and gas reserves place Turkmenistan in a more favorable economic position than other former Soviet republics. A new rail line linking Iran and Turkmenistan was inaugurated May 13, 1996. Political power centered around the former Communist Party apparatus, and Pres. Saparmurad Niyazov became the object of a personality cult. An alleged coup plot Nov. 25, 2002, triggered a crackdown on Niyazov's political opponents.

Tuvalu

People: Population: 11,636. **Age distrib.** (%): <15: 30.8; 65+: 5.1. **Pop. density:** 1,164 per sq mi, 448 per sq km. **Urban:** 55.2%. **Ethnic group:** Polynesian 96%, Micronesian 4%. **Principal languages:** Tuvaluan, English, Samoan, Kiribati (on the island of Nui). **Chief religions:** Church of Tuvalu (Congregationalist) 97%.

Geography: Total area: 10 sq mi, 26 sq km; **Land area:** 10 sq mi, 26 sq km. **Location:** 9 islands forming a NW-SE chain 360 mi. long in the SW Pacific O. **Neighbors:** Nearest are Kiribati to N, Fiji to S. **Topography:** The islands are all low-lying atolls, nowhere rising more than 15 ft. above sea level, composed of coral reefs. **Capital:** Funafuti, 6,000.

Government: Type: Parliamentary democracy. **Head of state:** Queen Elizabeth II, represented by Gov.-Gen. Filoimea Telito; in office: Apr. 15, 2005. **Head of gov.:** Prime Min. Maatia Toafa; in office: Oct. 11, 2004.

Economy: Industries: fishing, tourism, copra. **Chief crops:** coconuts. **Natural resources:** fish. **Livestock:** (2004): chickens: 45,000; pigs: 13,500. **Fish catch** (2003): 1,505 metric tons. **Electricity prod.** (2003): 0.00 bil kWh. **Labor force**: people make a living mainly through exploitation of the sea, reefs, and atolls and from wages sent home by those abroad (mostly workers in the phosphate industry and sailors).

Finance: Monetary unit: Australian Dollar (AUD and TVD) (Sept. 2005: 1.31 = $1 U.S.). **GDP** (2000 est.): $12.2 mil; **per capita GDP:** $1,100; **GDP growth:** 3%. **Imports** (2002): $79.0 mil; partners (2004): Fiji 43.1%, Japan 20%, Australia 10.6%, Poland 9.9%. **Exports** (2002): $1.0 mil; partners (2004): Germany 34.6%, Poland 25.9%, Philippines 12.5%, Fiji 8.4%, Italy 6.7%, UK 4.7%. **Budget** (2000 est.): $11.2 mil.

Transport: Civil aviation: 1 airport. **Chief port:** Funafuti.

Communications: TV sets: 9 per 1,000 pop. **Radios:** 364 per 1,000 pop.

Health: Life expect.: 65.8 male; 70.3 female. **Births** (per 1,000 pop.): 21.9. **Deaths** (per 1,000 pop.): 7.2. **Natural inc.:** 1.47%. **Infant mortality** (per 1,000 live births): 20.0.

Education: Compulsory: ages 7-14. **Literacy**: NA%.

Major Intl. Organizations: UN, WHO, the Commonwealth.

UN Mission: 800 Second Ave., Ste. 400B, New York, NY 10017; (212) 490-0534.

Website: www.timelesstuvalu.com

The Ellice Islands separated from the British Gilbert and Ellice Islands Colony in 1975 and became Tuvalu; independence came Oct. 1, 1978. In 2000, Tuvalu joined the United Nations.

Uganda

Republic of Uganda

People: Population: 27,269,482. **Age distrib.** (%): <15:50.1; 65+: 2.2. **Pop. density:** 299 per sq mi, 116 per sq km. **Urban:** 12.2%. **Ethnic groups:** Baganda 17%, Ankole 8%, Basoga 8%, Iteso 8%, Bakiga 7%; many other groups. **Principal languages:** English (official), Swahili, Ganda, many Bantu and Nilotic languages, Arabic. **Chief religions:** Roman Catholic 33%, Protestant 33%, Muslim 16%, indigenous beliefs 18%.

Geography: Total area: 91,136 sq mi, 236,040 sq km; **Land area:** 77,108 sq mi, 199,710 sq km. **Location:** In E Central Africa. **Neighbors:** Sudan on N, Congo (formerly Zaire) on W, Rwanda and Tanzania on S, Kenya on E. **Topography:** Most of Uganda is a high plateau 3,000-6,000 ft. high, with high Ruwenzori range in W (Mt. Margherita 16,763 ft.), volcanoes in SW; NE is arid, W and SW rainy. Lakes Victoria, Edward, Albert form much of borders. **Capital:** Kampala, 1,246,000.

Government: Type: Republic. **Head of state:** Pres. Yoweri Kaguta Museveni; Aug. 15, 1944; in office: Jan. 29, 1986. **Head of gov.:** Prime Min. Apolo Nsibambi; b Nov. 27, 1938; in office: Apr. 5, 1999. **Local divisions:** 56 districts. **Defense budget** (2004): $153 mil. **Active troops:** 60,000.

Economy: Industries: sugar, brewing, tobacco, cotton textiles, cement. **Chief crops:** coffee, tea, cotton, tobacco, cassava, potatoes. **Natural resources:** copper, cobalt, hydropower, limestone, salt. **Arable land:** 25%. **Livestock** (2004): cattle: 6.1 mil; chickens:

24.0 mil; goats: 7.7 mil; pigs: 1.3 mil; sheep: 1.6 mil. **Fish catch** (2003): 245,431 metric tons. **Electricity prod.** (2003): 1.7 bil kWh. **Labor force** (1999 est.): agric. 82%, industry 5%, services 13%.

Finance: Monetary unit: Shilling (UGX) (Sept. 2005: 1,802.00 = $1 U.S.). **GDP** (2004 est.): $39.4 bil; **per capita GDP:** $1,500; **GDP growth:** 5%. **Imports** (2004 est.): $1.3 bil; partners (2004): Kenya 27.9%, India 8%, UAE 7.4%, South Africa 6.9%, UK 5.9%, China 5.6%, Japan 5.1%, US 4.6%. **Exports** (2004 est.): $621.7 mil; partners (2004): Kenya 13.6%, Switzerland 11.2%, Netherlands 9.8%, Belgium 8.6%, France 4.2%. **Tourism:** $189 mil. **Budget** (2004 est.): $1.7 bil. **Intl. reserves less gold:** $0.84 mil. **Consumer prices:** 3.33%.

Transport: Railroad: Length: 771 mi. **Motor vehicles:** 54,200 pass. cars, 82,300 comm. vehicles. **Civil aviation:** 146.0 mil pass.-mi; 4 airports. **Chief ports:** Entebbe, Jinja.

Communications: TV sets: 28 per 1,000 pop. **Radios:** 130 per 1,000 pop. **Telephone lines:** 61,000. **Daily newspaper circ.:** 2.1 per 1,000 pop. **Internet:** 125,000 users.

Health: Life expect.: 50.7 male; 52.5 female. **Births** (per 1,000 pop.): 47.4. **Deaths** (per 1,000 pop.): 12.8. **Natural inc.:** 3.46%. **Infant mortality** (per 1,000 live births): 67.8. **AIDS rate:** 4.1%

Education: Literacy: 69.9%.

Major Intl. Organizations: UN (FAO, IBRD, ILO, IMF, WHO, WTrO), the Commonwealth, AU.

Embassy: 5911 16th St. NW 20011; 726-7100.

Websites: www.visituganda.com

Britain obtained a protectorate over Uganda in 1894. The country became independent Oct. 9, 1962, and a republic within the Commonwealth a year later. In 1967, the traditional kingdoms, including the powerful Buganda state, were abolished.

Gen. Idi Amin seized power from Prime Min. Milton Obote in 1971. During his 8 years of dictatorial rule, he was responsible for the deaths of up to 300,000 of his opponents. In 1972 he expelled nearly all of Uganda's 45,000 Asians. Tanzanian troops and Ugandan exiles and rebels ousted Amin, Apr. 11, 1979.

Obote held the presidency from Dec. 1980 until his ouster in a military coup July 27, 1985. Guerrilla war and rampant human rights abuses plagued Uganda under Obote's regime.

Conditions improved after Yoweri Museveni took power in Jan. 1986. In 1993 the government authorized restoration of the Buganda and other monarchies, but only for ceremonial purposes. Under a constitution ratified Oct. 1995, nonparty presidential and legislative elections were held in 1996. Uganda helped Laurent Kabila seize power in the Congo (formerly Zaire) in 1997 but sent troops in 1998 to aid insurgents seeking his ouster. A withdrawal accord was signed Sept. 6, 2002. Pres. Museveni won reelection Mar. 12, 2001.

At least 330 members of the Movement for the Restoration of the Ten Commandments of God died in a church fire in Kanungu, Mar. 17, 2000; in all, over 900 deaths were linked to the cult.

An ongoing insurgency against Museveni in N Uganda has killed more than 100,000 people and forced up to 2 million to flee their homes. The Lord's Resistance Army, a rebel group, has fought the govt since 1986 and has abducted some 30,000 children over the last decade to serve as soldiers and sex slaves.

In a referendum July 28, 2005, Ugandan voters approved a multiparty political system.

Ukraine

People: Population: 46,996,765. **Age distrib.** (%): <15: 15.6; 65+: 15.6. **Pop. density:** 202 per sq mi, 78 per sq km. **Urban:** 67.2%. **Ethnic groups:** Ukrainian 78%, Russian 17%. **Principal languages:** Ukrainian (official), Russian, Romanian, Polish, Hungarian. **Chief religions:** Ukrainian Orthodox (Kiev patriarchate and Russian patriarchate), Autocephalous Orthodox, Ukrainian Greek Catholic.

Geography: Total area: 233,090 sq mi, 603,700 sq km; **Land area:** 233,090 sq mi, 603,700 sq km. **Location:** In E Europe. **Neighbors:** Belarus on N; Russia on NE and E; Moldova and Romania on SW; Hungary, Slovakia, and Poland on W. **Topography:** Part of the E European plain. Mountainous areas include the Carpathians in the SW and Crimean chain in the S. Arable black soil constitutes a large part of the country. **Capital:** Kiev, 2,618,000. **Cities (urban aggr.):** Kharkov, 1,484,000 Dnepropetrovsk, 1,077,000.

Government: Type: Republic. **Head of state:** Pres. Viktor Andriyovych Yushchenko; b Feb. 23, 1954; in office: Jan. 23, 2005. **Head of gov.:** Prime Min. Yuriy Yekhanurov; b Aug. 23, 1948; in office: Sept. 8, 2005 (acting). **Local divisions:** 24 oblasts, 2 municipalities, 1 autonomous republic. **Defense budget** (2003): $843 mil. **Active troops:** 295,500.

Economy: Industries: coal, electric power, metals, machinery & transp. equip., chemicals, sugar. **Chief crops:** grain, sugar beets, sunflower seeds, vegetables. **Natural resources:** iron ore, coal, mang., nat. gas, oil, salt, sulfur, graphite, titanium, magnesium, kaolin, nickel, mercury, timber. **Crude oil reserves** (2004): 395 mil bbls. **Arable land:** 58%. **Livestock** (2004): cattle: 7.7 mil; chickens: 121 mil; goats: 966,000; pigs: 7.3 mil; sheep: 893,000. **Fish catch** (2003): 247,965 metric tons. **Electricity prod.** (2003): 169.9 bil kWh. **Labor force** (1996): agriculture 24%, industry 32%, services 44%.

Finance: Monetary unit: Hryvnia (UAH) (Sept. 2005: 4.98 = $1 U.S.). **GDP** (2004 est.): $299.1 bil; **per capita GDP:** $6,300; **GDP growth:** 12%. **Imports** (2004 est.): $31.5 bil; partners (2004): Russia 31.9%, Germany 11.9%, Turkmenistan 5.8%, Italy 4.5%. **Exports** (2004 est.): $32.9 bil; partners (2004): Russia 17.4%, Turkey 7.1%, Italy 5.7%. **Tourism:** $935 mil. **Budget** (2004 est.): $12.3 bil. **Intl. reserves less gold:** $5.99 bil. **Gold:** 510,000 oz t. **Consumer prices:** 9.04%.

Transport: Railroad: Length: 13,964 mi. **Motor vehicles:** 5.31 mil pass. cars. **Civil aviation:** 881.1 mil pass.-mi; 182 airports. **Chief ports:** Odesa, Kiev, Berdiansk.

Communications: TV sets: 433 per 1,000 pop. **Radios:** 882 per 1,000 pop. **Telephone lines:** 11.1 mil. **Daily newspaper circ.:** 175.2 per 1,000 pop. **Internet** (2002): 900,000 users.

Health: Life expect.: 64.4 male; 75.3 female. **Births** (per 1,000 pop.): 8.7. **Deaths** (per 1,000 pop.): 14.4. **Natural inc.:** -0.58%. **Infant mortality** (per 1,000 live births): 10.1. **AIDS rate:** 1.4%.

Education: Compulsory: ages 6-17. **Literacy:** 99.7%.

Major Intl. Organizations: UN (IBRD, ILO, IMF, IMO, WHO), CIS, OSCE.

Embassy: 3350 M St. NW 20007; 333-0606.

Website: www.kmu.gov.ua/control/en

Ukrainians' Slavic ancestors inhabited modern Ukrainian territory well before the first century AD. In the 9th century, the princes of Kiev established a strong state called Kievan Rus, which included much of present-day Ukraine. At the crossroads of European trade routes, Kievan Rus reached its zenith under Yaroslav the Wise (1019-1054). Internal conflicts led to the disintegration of the Ukrainian state by the 13th century. Mongol rule was supplanted by Poland and Lithuania in the 14th and 15th centuries. The N Black Sea coast and Crimea came under the control of the Turks in 1478. Ukrainian Cossacks, starting in the late 16th century, rebelled against the occupiers of Ukraine: Russia, Poland, and Turkey.

An independent Ukrainian National Republic was proclaimed on Jan. 22, 1918. But in 1921, Ukraine's neighbors occupied and divided Ukrainian territory. In 1922, Ukraine became a constituent republic of the USSR as the Ukrainian SSR. In 1932-33, the Soviet government engineered a famine in eastern Ukraine, resulting in the deaths of 6-7 million Ukrainians. During World War II the Ukrainian nationalist underground fought both Nazi and Soviet forces. Over 5 million Ukrainians died in the war. With the reoccupation of Ukraine by Soviet troops in 1944 came a renewed wave of mass arrests, executions, and deportations.

The world's worst nuclear power plant disaster occurred in Chernobyl, Ukraine, in April 1986; many thousands were killed or disabled as a result of the radiation leak. The plant was finally shut down Dec. 15, 2000.

Ukrainian independence was restored in Dec. 1991 with the dissolution of the Soviet Union. In the post-Soviet period Ukraine was burdened with a deteriorating economy. Following a 1994 accord with Russia and the U.S., Ukraine's large nuclear arsenal was transferred to Russia for destruction. A new constitution legalizing private property and establishing Ukrainian as the sole official language was approved by parliament June 29, 1996. In May 1997, Russia and Ukraine resolved disputes over the Black Sea fleet and the future of Sevastopol and signed a long-delayed treaty of friendship.

President since 1994, Leonid Kuchma attempted to engineer the election in 2004 of his handpicked successor, Prime Min. Viktor Yanukovych, also favored by Russia. The main challenger, Viktor Yushchenko, a former prime min., was poisoned in Sept. with dioxin, but continued to campaign. Official results of a runoff vote Nov. 21 showed a win for Yanukovych. Yushchenko supporters, calling the election fraudulent, staged massive protests (the "orange revolution"), and the vote was annulled. An election rerun Dec. 26 gave the victory to Yushchenko. Inaugurated Jan. 23, 2005, he dismissed his cabinet Sept. 8, amid allegations of infighting and corruption among his top aides. Ukraine, with 1,650 troops in Iraq, said it would pull them out by October.

United Arab Emirates

People: Population: 2,563,212. **Age distrib.** (%): <15: 25.3; 65+: 3.6. **Pop. density:** 80 per sq mi, 31 per sq km. **Urban:** 85.1%. **Ethnic groups:** Arab and Iranian 42%, Indian 50%. **Principal languages:** Arabic (official), Persian, English, Hindi, Urdu. **Chief religion:** Muslim 96% (official; Shi'a 16%).

Geography: Total area: 32,000 sq mi, 82,880 sq km; **Land area:** 32,000 sq mi, 82,880 sq km. **Location:** Middle East, on the S shore of the Persian Gulf. **Neighbors:** Saudi Arabia on W and S, Oman on E. **Topography:** A barren, flat coastal plain gives way to uninhabited sand dunes on the S. Hajar Mts. are on E. **Capital:** Abu Dhabi, 475,000.

Government: Type: Federation of emirates. **Head of state:** Pres. Sheik Khalifa ibn Zaid an-Nahayan; b 1948; in office: Nov. 3, 2004. **Head of gov.:** Prime Min. Sheik Maktum ibn Rashid al-Maktum; b 1946; in office: Nov. 20, 1990. **Local divisions:** 7 autonomous emirates: Abu Dhabi, Ajman, Dubai, Fujaira, Ras al-Khaimah, Sharjah, Umm al-Qaiwain. **Defense budget** (2004): $1.6 bil. **Active troops:** 50,500.

Economy: Industries: oil, fishing, petrochems., constr. materials, boat building, handicrafts, pearling. **Chief crops:** dates, vegetables, watermelons. **Natural resources:** oil, nat. gas. **Crude oil reserves** (2004): 97.8 bil bbls. **Livestock** (2004): cattle: 115,000; chickens: 13 mil; goats: 1.5 mil; sheep: 590,000. **Fish catch** (2003): 97,450 metric tons. **Electricity prod.** (2003): 41.2 bil kWh. **Labor force** (2000 est.): agriculture 7%, industry 15%, services 78%.

Finance: Monetary unit: Dirham (AED) (Sept. 2005: 3.67 = $1 U.S.). **GDP** (2004 est.): $63.7 bil; **per capita GDP:** $25,200; **GDP growth:** 5.7%. **Imports** (2004 est.): $45.7 bil; partners (2004): China 10.4%, India 8.3%, Japan 7.2%, Germany 6.6%, France 6.4%, UK 6.2%, US 6%, Italy 4.1%. **Exports** (2004 est.): $69.5 bil; partners (2004): Japan 28.5%, South Korea 9.5%, Thailand 5.9%. **Tourism:** $1,439 mil. **Budget** (2004 est.): $25.5 bil. **Intl. reserves less gold:** $11.93 bil. **Gold** (2002): 40,000 oz t.

Transport: Motor vehicles: 794,110 pass. cars, 477,910 comm. vehicles. **Civil aviation:** 16.3 bil pass.-mi; 22 airports. **Chief ports:** Ajman, Das Island.

Communications: TV sets: 309 per 1,000 pop. **Radios:** 355 per 1,000 pop. **Telephone lines:** 1.1 mil. **Daily newspaper circ.:** 156 per 1,000 pop. **Internet**: 1.1 mil users.

Health: Life expect.: 72.7 male; 77.9 female. **Births** (per 1,000 pop.): 18.8. **Deaths** (per 1,000 pop.): 4.3. **Natural inc.:** 1.45%. **Infant mortality** (per 1,000 live births): 14.5.

Education: Compulsory: ages 6-15. **Literacy:** 77.9%.

Major Intl. Organizations: UN (FAO, IBRD, ILO, IMF, IMO, WHO, WTrO), AL, OPEC.

Embassy: 3522 International Ct. NW, Suite 400, 20008; 243-2400.

Website: www.government.ae/gov/en/index.jsp

The 7 "Trucial Sheikdoms" gave Britain control of defense and foreign relations in the 19th century. They merged to become an independent state Dec. 2, 1971.

The Abu Dhabi Petroleum Co. was fully nationalized in 1975. Oil revenues have given the UAE one of the highest per capita GDPs in the world. International banking has grown in recent years.

United Kingdom

United Kingdom of Great Britain and Northern Ireland

People: Population: 60,441,457. **Age distrib.** (%): <15: 17.7; 65+: 15.8. **Pop. density:** 639 per sq mi, 247 per sq km. **Urban:** 89.1%. **Ethnic groups:** English 81.5%, Scottish 9.6%, Irish 2.4%, Welsh 1.9%, Ulster 1.9%, West Indian, Indo-Pakistani, and other 2.8%. **Principal languages:** English (official), Welsh and Scottish Gaelic. **Chief religions:** Christian 72%, Muslim 3%, many others.

Geography: Total area: 94,526 sq mi, 244,820 sq km; **Land area:** 93,278 sq mi, 241,590 sq km. **Location:** Off the NW coast of Europe, across English Channel, Strait of Dover, and North Sea. **Neighbors:** Ireland to W, France to SE. **Topography:** England is mostly rolling land, rising to Uplands of southern Scotland; Lowlands are in center of Scotland, granite Highlands are in N. Coast is heavily indented, especially on W. British Isles have milder climate than N Europe due to the Gulf Stream and ample rainfall. Severn, 220 mi., and Thames, 215 mi., are longest rivers. **Capital:** London, 7,619,000. **Cities (urban aggr.):** Birmingham, 2,243,000; Manchester, 2,223,000; Leeds, 1,417,000; Liverpool 924,000.

Government: Type: Constitutional monarchy. **Head of state:** Queen Elizabeth II; b Apr. 21, 1926; in office: Feb. 6, 1952. **Head of gov.:** Prime Min. Tony Blair; b May 6, 1953; in office: May 2, 1997. **Local divisions:** 467 local authorities, including England: 387; Wales: 22; Scotland: 32; Northern Ireland: 26. **Defense budget** (2004): $49 bil. **Active troops:** 207,630.

Economy: Industries: machine tools, electric power equip., automation equip., railroad equip., shipbuilding, aircraft, vehicles, electronics & comm. equip., metals, chemicals, coal, oil. **Chief crops:** cereals, oilseed, potatoes, vegetables. **Natural resources:** coal, oil, nat. gas, tin, limestone, iron ore, salt, clay, chalk, gypsum, lead, silica. **Crude oil reserves** (2004): 4.5 bil bbls. **Arable land:** 25%. **Livestock** (2004): cattle: 10.5 mil; chickens: 170 mil; pigs: 5.0 mil; sheep: 35.5 mil. **Fish catch** (2003): 817,323 metric tons. **Electricity prod.** (2003): 369.9 bil kWh. **Labor force** (2004): agriculture 1.5%, industry 19.1%, services 79.5%.

Finance: Monetary unit: Pound (GBP) (Sept. 2005: 0.68 = $1 U.S.). **GDP** (2004 est.): $1.8 tril.; **per capita GDP:** $29,600; **GDP growth:** 3.2%. **Imports** (2004 est.): $439.4 bil; partners (2004): Germany 13%, US 9.2%, France 7.5%, Netherlands 6.6%, Belgium 5%, Italy 4.3%, China 4.2%. **Exports** (2004 est.): $347.2 bil; partners (2004): US 15%, Germany 10.7%, France 9.2%, Ireland 6.8%, Netherlands 6.1%, Belgium 5.2%, Spain 4.5%, Italy 4.2%. **Tourism:** $22,752 mil. **Budget** (2004 est.): $896.7 bil. **Intl. reserves less gold:** $29.20 bil. **Gold:** 10.04 mil oz t. **Consumer prices:** 2.96%.

Transport: Railroad: Length: 10,497 mi. **Motor vehicles:** 25.8 mil pass. cars, 3.5 mil comm. vehicles. **Civil aviation:** 98.6 bil pass.-mi; 334 airports. **Chief ports:** London, Liverpool, Cardiff, Belfast.

Communications: TV sets: 661 per 1,000 pop. **Radios:** 1,437 per 1,000 pop. **Telephone lines** (2002): 34.9 mil. **Daily newspaper circ.:** 329 per 1,000 pop. **Internet** (2002): 25.0 mil users.

Health: Life expect.: 75.9 male; 81.0 female. **Births** (per 1,000 pop.): 10.8. **Deaths** (per 1,000 pop.): 10.2. **Natural inc.:** 0.06%. **Infant mortality** (per 1,000 live births): 5.2. **AIDS rate:** 0.2%.

Education: Compulsory: ages 5-16. **Literacy:** 99%.

Major Intl. Organizations: UN and all of its specialized agencies, the Commonwealth, EU, NATO, OECD, OSCE.

Embassy: 3100 Massachusetts Ave. NW 20008; 588-6500.

Website: www.direct.gov.uk

The United Kingdom of Great Britain and Northern Ireland comprises England, Wales, Scotland, and Northern Ireland.

Queen and Royal Family. The ruling sovereign is Elizabeth II of the House of Windsor, b Apr. 21, 1926, elder daughter of King George VI. She succeeded to the throne Feb. 6, 1952, and was crowned June 2, 1953. She was married Nov. 20, 1947, to Lt. Philip Mountbatten, b June 10, 1921, former Prince of Greece. He was created Duke of Edinburgh, and given the title H.R.H., Nov. 19, 1947; he was named Prince of the United Kingdom and Northern Ireland Feb. 22, 1957. Prince Charles Philip Arthur George, b Nov. 14, 1948, is the Prince of Wales and heir apparent. His 1st son, William Philip Arthur Louis, b June 21, 1982, is second in line to the throne.

Parliament is the legislative body for the UK, with certain powers over dependent units. It consists of 2 houses: The **House of Commons** has 646 members, elected by direct ballot and divided as follows: England 529; Wales 40; Scotland 59; Northern Ireland 18. Following a drastic reduction in the number of hereditary peerages, the **House of Lords** (July 2005) comprised 92 hereditary peers, 614 life peers, and 1 archbishop and 24 bishops of the Church of England, for a total of 731.

Resources and Industries. Great Britain's major occupations are manufacturing and trade. Metals and metal-using industries contribute more than 50% of exports. Of about 60 million acres of land in England, Wales, and Scotland, 46 million are farmed, of which 17 million are arable, the rest pastures.

Large oil and gas fields have been found in the North Sea. Commercial oil production began in 1975. There are large deposits of coal.

Britain imports all of its cotton, rubber, sulphur, about 80% of its wool, half of its food and iron ore, also certain amounts of paper, tobacco, chemicals. Manufactured goods made from these basic materials have been exported since the industrial age began. Main exports are machinery, chemicals, textiles, clothing, autos and trucks, iron and steel, locomotives, ships, jet aircraft, farm machinery, drugs, radio, TV, radar and navigation equipment, scientific instruments, arms, whisky.

Religion and Education. The Church of England is Protestant Episcopal. The queen is its temporal head, with rights of appointments to archbishoprics, bishoprics, and other offices. There are 2 provinces, Canterbury and York, each headed by an archbishop. The most famous church is Westminster Abbey (1050-1760), site of coronations, tombs of Elizabeth I, Mary, Queen of Scots, kings, poets, and of the Unknown Warrior.

The most celebrated British universities are Oxford and Cambridge, each dating to the 13th century. There are about 70 other universities.

History. Britain was part of the continent of Europe until about 6,000 BC, but migration across the English Channel continued long afterward. Celts arrived 2,500 to 3,000 years ago. Their language survives in Welsh, and Gaelic enclaves.

England was added to the Roman Empire in AD 43. After the withdrawal of Roman legions in 410, waves of Jutes, Angles, and Saxons arrived from German lands. They contended with Danish raiders for control from the 8th through 11th centuries. The last successful invasion was by French speaking Normans in 1066, who united the country with their dominions in France.

Opposition by nobles to royal authority forced King John to agree to the Magna Carta in 1215, a guarantee of rights and the rule of law. In the ensuing decades, the foundations of the parliamentary system were laid.

English dynastic claims to large parts of France led to the Hundred Years War, 1338-1453, and the defeat of England. A long civil war, the War of the Roses, lasted 1455-85, and ended with the establishment of the powerful Tudor monarchy. A distinct English civilization flourished. The economy prospered over long periods of domestic peace unmatched in continental Europe. Religious independence was secured when the Church of England was separated from the authority of the pope in 1534.

Under Queen Elizabeth I, England became a major naval power, leading to the founding of colonies in the new world and the expansion of trade with Europe and the Orient. Scotland was united with England when James VI of Scotland was crowned James I of England in 1603.

A struggle between Parliament and the Stuart kings led to a bloody civil war, 1642-49, and the establishment of a republic under the Puritan Oliver Cromwell. The monarchy was restored in 1660, but the "Glorious Revolution" of 1688 confirmed the sovereignty of Parliament: a Bill of Rights was granted 1689.

In the 18th century, parliamentary rule was strengthened. Technological and entrepreneurial innovations led to the Industrial Revolution. The 13 North American colonies were lost, but replaced by growing empires in Canada and India. Britain's role in the defeat of Napoleon, 1815, strengthened its position as the leading world power.

The extension of the franchise in 1832 and 1867, the formation of trade unions, and the development of universal public education were among the drastic social changes that accompanied the spread of industrialization and urbanization in the 19th century. Large parts of Africa and Asia were added to the empire during the reign of Queen Victoria, 1837-1901.

Though victorious in World War I, Britain suffered huge casualties and economic dislocation. Ireland became independent in 1921, and independence movements became active in India and other colonies. The country suffered major bombing damage in

World War II, but held out against Germany single-handedly for a year after France fell in 1940.

Industrial growth continued in the postwar period, but Britain lost its leadership position to other powers. Labor governments passed socialist programs nationalizing some basic industries and expanding social security. Prime Min. Margaret Thatcher's Conservative government, however, tried to increase the role of private enterprise. In 1987, Thatcher became the first British leader in 160 years to be elected to a 3rd consecutive term as prime minister. Falling on unpopular times, she resigned as prime minister in Nov. 1990. Her successor, John Major, led Conservatives to an upset victory at the polls, Apr. 9, 1992.

The UK supported the UN resolutions against Iraq and sent military forces to the Persian Gulf War. The Channel Tunnel linking Britain to the Continent was inaugurated May 6, 1994. Britain's relations with the European Union, and France especially, were frayed in 1996 when the EU banned British beef because of the threat of "mad cow" disease.

On May 1, 1997, the Labour Party swept into power in a landslide victory, the largest of any party since 1935. Labour Party leader Tony Blair, 43, became Britain's youngest prime minister since 1812. Diana, Princess of Wales, died in a car crash in Paris, Aug. 31. Britain played a leading role in the NATO air war against Yugoslavia, Mar.-June 1999, and contributed 12,000 troops to the multinational security force in Kosovo (KFOR).

Blair led Labour to another landslide election victory June 7, 2001. After the Sept. 11 attack on the U.S., Britain took an important role in the U.S.-led war against terrorism. The U.K. participated in the bombing of Afghanistan that began Oct. 7. Overcoming dissent within his own cabinet, Blair committed British troops to the U.S.-led invasion of Iraq, Mar.-Apr. 2003. Forces from the U.K. (8,500 in mid-2005) remained to occupy S Iraq.

In elections May 5, 2005, Blair became the first Labour prime minister to win 3 consecutive terms, but continued controversy over Iraq reduced his parliamentary majority. Suicide bombings on 3 London underground trains and a bus, July 7, left 56 people dead and hundreds injured; police identified the bombers as 4 British Muslim men (3 of Pakistani origin). Another series of bombs on July 21 misfired, causing minimal damage to London transport. All 4 suspected would-be bombers were arrested. On Aug. 5 Blair unveiled a series of proposed measures to crack down on extremism and terrorism.

Wales

The Principality of Wales in western Britain has an area of 8,019 sq. mi. and a population (2003 est.) of 2,938,200. Cardiff is the capital, pop. (2001 est.; city proper) 305,000.

Less than 20% of Wales residents speak English and Welsh; about 32,000 speak Welsh solely. A 1979 referendum rejected, 4-1, the creation of an elected Welsh assembly; a similar proposal passed by a thin margin on Sept. 18, 1997. Elections for the 60-seat assembly were held May 6, 1999, and May 1, 2003.

Early Anglo-Saxon invaders drove Celtic peoples into the mountains of Wales, terming them Waelise (Welsh, or foreign). There they developed a distinct nationality. Members of the ruling house of Gwynedd in the 13th century fought England but were crushed, 1283. Edward of Caernarvon, son of Edward I of England, was created Prince of Wales, 1301.

Scotland

Scotland, a kingdom now united with England and Wales in Great Britain, occupies the northern 37% of the main British island, and the Hebrides, Orkney, Shetland, and smaller islands. Length 275 mi., breadth approx. 150 mi., area 30,418 sq. mi., population (2003 est) 5,057,400.

The Lowlands, a belt of land approximately 60 mi. wide from the Firth of Clyde to the Firth of Forth, divide the farming region of the Southern Uplands from the granite Highlands of the North; they contain 75% of the population and most of the industry. The Highlands, famous for hunting and fishing, have been opened to industry by many hydroelectric power stations.

Edinburgh, pop. (2001 est., city proper) 449,000, is the capital. Glasgow, pop. (2001 est.; city proper) 579,000, is Britain's greatest industrial center. It is a shipbuilding complex on the Clyde and an ocean port. Aberdeen, pop. (1996 est.) 227,430, NE of Edinburgh, is a major port, center of granite industry, fish-processing, and North Sea oil exploration. Dundee, pop. (1996 est.) 150,250, NE of Edinburgh, is an industrial and fish-processing center. About 90,000 persons speak Gaelic as well as English.

History. Scotland was called Caledonia by the Romans who battled early Celtic tribes and occupied southern areas from the 1st to the 4th centuries. Missionaries from Britain introduced Christianity in the 4th century; St. Columba, an Irish monk, converted most of Scotland in the 6th century.

The Kingdom of Scotland was founded in 1018. William Wallace and Robert Bruce both defeated English armies 1297 and 1314, respectively.

In 1603 James VI of Scotland, son of Mary, Queen of Scots, succeeded to the throne of England as James I, and effected the Union of the Crowns. In 1707 Scotland received representation in the British Parliament, resulting from the union of former separate Parliaments. Its executive in the British cabinet is the Secretary of State for Scotland. The growing Scottish National Party urges independence. A 1979 referendum on the creation of an elected Scottish assembly was defeated, but a proposal to create a regional legislature with limited taxing authority passed by a landslide Sept. 11, 1997. Elections for the 129-seat parliament were held May 6, 1999, and May 1, 2003.

Memorials of Robert Burns, Sir Walter Scott, John Knox, and Mary, Queen of Scots, draw many tourists, as do the beauties of the Trossachs, Loch Katrine, Loch Lomond, and abbey ruins.

Industries. Engineering products are the most important industry, with growing emphasis on office machinery, autos, electronics, and other consumer goods. Oil has been discovered offshore in the North Sea, stimulating on-shore support industries.

Scotland produces fine woolens, worsteds, tweeds, silks, fine linens, and jute. It is known for its special breeds of cattle and sheep. Fisheries have large hauls of herring, cod, whiting. Whisky is the biggest export.

The Hebrides are a group of c. 500 islands, 100 inhabited, off the W coast. The Inner Hebrides include **Skye, Mull,** and **Iona,** the last famous for the arrival of St. Columba, AD 563. The Outer Hebrides include **Lewis** and **Harris.** Industries include sheep raising and weaving. The **Orkney Islands,** c. 90, are to the NE. The capital is Kirkwall, on Pomona Isl. Fish curing, sheep raising, and weaving are occupations. NE of the Orkneys are the 200 **Shetland Islands,** 24 inhabited, home of Shetland ponies. The Orkneys and Shetlands are centers for the North Sea oil industry.

Northern Ireland

Northern Ireland was constituted in 1920 from 6 of the 9 counties of Ulster, the NE corner of Ireland. Area 5,452 sq. mi., pop. (2003 est) 1,702,600. Capital and chief industrial center, Belfast, pop. (2001 est.; city proper) 277,000.

Industries. Shipbuilding, including large tankers, has long been an important industry, centered in Belfast, the largest port. Linen manufacture is also important, along with apparel, rope, and twine. Growing diversification has added engineering products, synthetic fibers, and electronics. There are large numbers of cattle, hogs, and sheep. Potatoes, poultry, and dairy foods are also produced.

Government. An act of the British Parliament, 1920, divided Northern from Southern Ireland, each with a parliament and government. When Ireland became a dominion, 1921, and later a republic, Northern Ireland chose to remain a part of the United Kingdom. It elects 18 members to the House of Commons.

During 1968-69, large demonstrations were conducted by Roman Catholics who charged they were discriminated against in voting rights, housing, and employment. The Catholics, a minority comprising about a third of the population, demanded abolition of property qualifications for voting in local elections. Violence and terrorism intensified, involving branches of the Irish Republican Army (outlawed in the Irish Republic), Protestant groups, police, and British troops.

A succession of Northern Ireland prime ministers pressed reform programs but failed to satisfy extremists on both sides. Between 1969 and 1994 more than 3,000 were killed in sectarian violence, many in England itself. Britain suspended the Northern Ireland parliament Mar. 30, 1972, and imposed direct British rule. A coalition government was formed in 1973 when moderates won election to a new one-house Assembly. But a Protestant general strike overthrew the government in 1974 and direct rule was resumed.

The agony of Northern Ireland was dramatized in 1981 by the deaths of 10 Irish nationalist hunger strikers in Maze Prison near Belfast. In 1985 the Hillsborough agreement gave the Rep. of Ireland a voice in the governing of Northern Ireland; the accord was strongly opposed by Ulster loyalists. On Dec. 12, 1993, Britain and Ireland announced a declaration of principles to resolve the Northern Ireland conflict.

A settlement reached on Good Friday, April 10, 1998, provided for restoration of home rule and election of a 108-member assembly with safeguards for minority rights. Both Ireland and Great Britain agreed to give up their constitutional claims on Northern Ireland. The accord was approved May 22 by voters in Northern Ireland and the Irish Republic, and elections to the assembly were held June 25. IRA dissidents seeking to derail the agreement were responsible for a bomb at Omagh Aug. 15 that killed 29 people and injured over 330.

London transferred authority to a Northern Ireland power-sharing government Dec. 2, 1999. Delays in IRA disarmament led to several suspensions of self-government, most recently from Oct. 15, 2002. The IRA stated July 28, 2005, that it had renounced violence and ordered all units to disarm. In response, the British began reducing their military presence in the region. On Sept. 26, an international monitoring group reported that the IRA had apparently scrapped its entire arsenal.

Education and Religion. Northern Ireland is about 58% Protestant, 42% Roman Catholic. Education is compulsory between the ages of 5 and 16 years.

Channel Islands

The Channel Islands, area 75 sq. mi., pop. (2003 est.) 145,000, off the NW coast of France, the only parts of the one-time Dukedom of Normandy belonging to England, are Jersey, Guernsey and the dependencies of Guernsey—Alderney, Brechou, Great Sark, Little Sark, Herm, Jethou and Lihou. Jersey, pop. (2004 est.) 90,502, and Guernsey, pop. (2004 est.) 65,031, have separate legal existences and lieutenant governors named by the Crown. The islands were the only British soil occupied by German troops in World War II.

Isle of Man

The Isle of Man, area 220.9 sq. mi., pop. (2004 est.) 74,655, is in the Irish Sea, 20 mi. from Scotland, 30 mi. from Cumberland. It is rich in lead and iron. The island has its own laws and a lieutenant governor appointed by the Crown. The Tynwald (legislature) consists of the Legislative Council, partly elected, and House of Keys, elected. Capital: Douglas. Farming, tourism, and fishing (kippers, scallops) are chief occupations. Man is famous for the Manx tailless cat.

Gibraltar

Gibraltar, a dependency on the southern coast of Spain, guards the entrance to the Mediterranean. The Rock of Gibraltar has been in British possession since 1704. The Rock is 2.5 mi. long, 3/4 of a mi. wide and 1,396 ft. in height; a narrow isthmus connects it with the mainland. Pop. (2004 est.) 27,833.

Gibraltar has historically been an object of contention between Britain and Spain. Residents voted with near unanimity to remain under British rule, in a 1967 referendum held in pursuance of a UN resolution on decolonization. A new constitution, May 30, 1969, increased Gibraltarian control of domestic affairs (the UK continues to handle defense and internal security matters). Following a 1984 agreement between Britain and Spain, the border, closed by Spain in 1969, was fully reopened in Feb. 1985. A UN General Assembly resolution requested Britain to end Gibraltar's colonial status by Oct. 1, 1996. A plan for the U.K. and Spain to share sovereignty was rejected by Gibraltar voters, Nov. 7, 2002.

British West Indies

Swinging in a vast arc from the coast of Venezuela NE, then N and NW toward Puerto Rico are the Leeward Islands, forming a coral and volcanic barrier sheltering the Caribbean from the open Atlantic. Many of the islands are self-governing British possessions. Universal suffrage was instituted 1951-54; ministerial systems were set up 1956-1960.

The **Leeward Islands** still associated with the UK are **Montserrat**, area 39.4 sq. mi., pop. (2004 est.) 9,245, capital Plymouth; the **British Virgin Islands,** 59.1 sq. mi., pop. (2004 est.) 22,187, capital Road Town; and **Anguilla**, the most northerly of the Leeward Islands, 39.4 sq. mi., pop. (2004 est.) 13,008, capital The Valley. Montserrat has been devastated by the Soufrière Hills volcano, which began erupting July 18, 1995.

The three **Cayman Islands,** a dependency, lie S of Cuba, NW of Jamaica. Pop. (2004 est.) 43,103, most of it on Grand Cayman. It is a free port; in the 1970s Grand Cayman became a tax-free refuge for foreign funds and branches of many Western banks were opened there. Total area 101.2 sq. mi., capital Georgetown.

The **Turks and Caicos Islands** are a dependency at the SE end of the Bahama Islands. Of about 30 islands, only 6 are inhabited; area 166 sq. mi., pop. (2004 est.) 19,956; capital Grand Turk. Salt, shellfish, and conch shells are the main exports.

Bermuda

Bermuda is a British dependency governed by a royal governor and an assembly, dating from 1620, the oldest legislative body among British dependencies. Capital is Hamilton.

It is a group of about 150 small islands of coral formation, 20 inhabited, comprising 20.6 sq. mi. in the western Atlantic, 580 mi. E of North Carolina. Pop. (2004 est.) 64,935 (about 61% of African descent). Pop. density is high.

The U.S. maintains a NASA tracking facility; a U.S. naval air base was closed in 1995.

Tourism is the major industry; Bermuda boasts many resort hotels. The government raises most revenue from import duties. Exports: petroleum products, medicine. In a referendum Aug. 15, 1995, voters rejected independence by nearly a 3-to-1 majority.

Hurricane Fabian, the most potent storm to reach Bermuda in 50 years, struck Sept. 5, 2003; 4 people were missing and presumed dead, and damage was estimated at over $300 million.

South Atlantic

The **Falkland Islands,** a dependency, lie 300 mi. E of the Strait of Magellan at the southern end of South America.

The Falklands or Islas Malvinas include 2 large islands and about 200 smaller ones, area 4,700 sq. mi., pop. (2004 est.) 2,967, capital Stanley. The licensing of foreign fishing vessels has become the major source of revenue. Sheep-grazing is a main industry; wool is the principal export. There are indications of large oil and gas deposits. The islands are also claimed by Argentina, though 97% of inhabitants are of British origin. Argentina invaded the islands Apr. 2, 1982. The British responded by sending a task force to the area, landing their main force on the Falklands, May 21, and forcing an Argentine surrender at Port Stanley, June 14. A pact resuming commercial air service with Argentina was signed July 14, 1999.

British Antarctic Territory, south of 60° S lat., formerly a dependency of the Falkland Isls., was made a separate colony in 1962 and includes the **South Shetland Islands,** the **South Orkneys**, and the Antarctic Peninsula. A chain of meteorological stations is maintained.

South Georgia and the South Sandwich Islands, formerly administered by the Falklands Isls., became a separate dependency in 1985. South Georgia, 1507 sq mi, with no permanent population, is about 800 mi SE of the Falklands; the South Sandwich Isls., 130 sq mi, are uninhabited, about 470 mi SE of South Georgia.

St. Helena, an island 1,200 mi. off the W. coast of Africa and 1,800 mi. E of South America, 158 sq. mi. and pop. (2004 est.) 7,415. Flax, lace, and rope-making are the chief industries. After Napoleon Bonaparte was defeated at Waterloo the Allies exiled him to St. Helena, where he lived from Oct. 16, 1815, to his death, May 5, 1821. Capital is Jamestown.

Tristan da Cunha is the principal island in a group of islands of volcanic origin, total area 40 sq. mi., halfway between the Cape of Good Hope and South America. A volcanic peak 6,760 ft. high erupted in 1961. The 262 inhabitants were removed to England, but most returned in 1963. The islands are dependencies of St. Helena. Pop. (2002) 284.

Ascension is an island of volcanic origin, 34 sq mi in area, 700 mi. NW of St. Helena, through which it is administered. It is a communications relay center for Britain, and has a U.S. satellite tracking center. Pop. (2002) was 1,050, half of them communications workers. The island is noted for sea turtles.

Hong Kong

(*See* China/Hong Kong)

British Indian Ocean Territory

Formed Nov. 1965, embracing islands formerly dependencies of Mauritius or Seychelles: the Chagos Archipelago (including Diego Garcia), Aldabra, Farquhar, and Des Roches. The latter 3 were transferred to Seychelles, which became independent in 1976. Area 23 sq. mi. No permanent civilian population remains; the U.K. and the U.S. maintain a military presence.

Pacific Ocean

Pitcairn Island is in the Pacific, halfway between South America and Australia. The island was discovered in 1767 by Philip Carteret but was not inhabited until 23 years later when the mutineers of the *Bounty* landed there. The area is 18 sq. mi. and 2004 pop. was 46. It is a British dependency and is administered by a British High Commissioner in New Zealand and a local Council. The uninhabited islands of **Henderson, Ducie,** and **Oeno** are in the Pitcairn group.

United States

United States of America

People: Population: 295,734,134. (incl. 50 states & Dist. of Columbia). (Note: U.S. pop. figures may differ elsewhere in *The World Almanac.*) **Age distrib.** (%): <15: 20.6; 65+: 12.4. **Pop. density:** 80 per sq mi, 31 per sq km. **Urban:** 80.1%. **Ethnic groups:** White 75.1%, Black 12.3%, Asian 3.6%, Amerindian and Alaska native 0.9%. (Hispanics of any race or group 12.5%.) **Principal languages:** English, Spanish. **Chief religions:** Protestant 52%, Roman Catholic 24%, Jewish 1%.

Geography: Total area: 3,718,712 sq mi, 9,631,418 sq km; **Land area:** 3,537,439 sq mi, 9,161,923 sq km. **Topography:** Vast central plain, mountains in west, hills and low mountains in east. **Capital:** Washington, D.C., 4,098,000.

Government: Federal republic, strong democratic tradition. **Head of state and gov.:** Pres. George W. Bush; b July 6, 1946; in office: Jan. 20, 2001. **Local divisions:** 50 states and Dist. of Columbia. **Defense budget** (2004): $460.5 bil. **Active troops:** 1,433,600.

Economy: Industries: oil, steel, motor vehicles, aerospace, telecom., chemicals, electronics, food proc., consumer goods, lumber, mining. **Chief crops:** wheat, corn, fruits, vegetables, cotton. **Natural resources:** coal, copper, lead, molybd., phosphates, uranium, bauxite, gold, iron, mercury, nickel, potash, silver, tungsten, zinc, oil, nat. gas, timber. **Crude oil reserves** (2004): 21.9 bil bbls. **Arable land:** 19%. **Livestock** (2004): cattle: 94.9 mil; chickens: 2.0 mil; goats: 1.2 mil; pigs: 60.4 mil; sheep: 6.1 mil. **Fish catch** (2003): 5,483,285 metric tons. **Electricity prod.** (2003): 3891.7 bil kWh. **Labor force** (2004): farming, forestry, and fishing 0.7%, manuf., extraction, transp., and crafts 22.7%, managerial, prof., and technical 34.9%, sales and office 25.5%, other services 16.3%.

Finance: GDP (2004 est.): $11.8 tril.; **per capita GDP:** $40,100; **GDP growth:** 4.4%. **Imports** (2004 est.): $1.5 tril.; partners (2004): Canada 17.1%, China 13.7%, Mexico 10.4%, Japan 8.8%, Germany 5.2%. **Exports** (2004 est.): $795.0 bil; partners (2004): Canada 23%, Mexico 13.6%, Japan 6.7%, UK 4.4%, China 4.3%. **Tourism:** $64,509 mil. **Budget** (2004 est.): $2.3 tril. **Intl. reserves less gold:** $48.87 bil. **Gold:** 261.59 mil oz t. **Consumer prices:** 2.68%.

Transport: Railroad: Length: 121,000 mi. **Motor vehicles**: 221.82 mil pass. cars, 8.61 mil comm. vehicles. **Civil aviation:** 646.5 bil. pass.-mi; 5,131 airports.

Communications: TV sets: 844 per 1,000 pop. **Radios:** 2,116 per 1,000 pop. **Telephone lines:** 181.4 mil. **Daily newspaper circ.:** 212 per 1,000 pop. **Internet**: 161.6 mil users.

Health: Life expect.: 74.9 male; 80.7 female. **Births** (per 1,000 pop.): 14.1. **Deaths** (per 1,000 pop.): 8.3. **Natural inc.:** 0.59%. **Infant mortality** (per 1,000 live births): 6.5. **AIDS rate:** 0.6%.

Education: Compulsory: ages 6-17. **Literacy:** 97%.

Major Intl. Organizations: UN (FAO, IBRD, ILO, IMF, IMO, WHO, WTrO), APEC, NATO, OAS, OECD, OSCE.

Website: www.firstgov.gov

See also U.S. History chapter; Chronology of the Year's Events.

Uruguay

Oriental Republic of Uruguay

People: Population: 3,415,920. **Age distrib.** (%): <15: 23.2; 65+: 13.2. **Pop. density:** 50 per sq mi, 19 per sq km. **Urban:** 92.6%. **Ethnic groups:** White 88%, Mestizo 8%, Black 4%. **Principal languages:** Spanish (official), Portunol/Brazilero (Portuguese-Spanish). **Chief religion:** Roman Catholic 66%.

Geography: Total area: 68,039 sq mi, 176,220 sq km; **Land area:** 67,035 sq mi, 173,620 sq km. **Location:** In southern South America, on the Atlantic O. **Neighbors:** Argentina on W, Brazil on N. **Topography:** Uruguay is composed of rolling, grassy plains and hills, well watered by rivers flowing W to Uruguay R. **Capital:** Montevideo, 1,341,000.

Government: Type: Republic. **Head of state and gov.:** Pres. Tabaré Ramón Vázquez Rosas; b Jan. 17, 1940; in office: Mar. 1, 2005. **Local divisions:** 19 departments. **Defense budget** (2003): $170 mil. **Active troops:** 24,000.

Economy: Industries: food proc., electrical machinery, transp. equip., oil products, textiles. **Chief crops:** rice, wheat, corn, barley. **Natural resources:** hydropower, minor minerals, fisheries. **Arable land:** 7%. **Livestock** (2004): cattle: 11.7 mil; chickens: 13.3 mil; goats: 16,000; pigs: 240,000; sheep: 9.5 mil. **Fish catch** (2003): 116,935 metric tons. **Electricity prod.** (2003): 8.6 bil kWh. **Labor force**: agriculture 14%, industry 16%, services 70%.

Finance: Monetary unit: Peso (UYU) (Sept. 2005: 24.21 = $1 U.S.). **GDP** (2004 est.): $49.3 bil; **per capita GDP:** $14,500; **GDP growth:** 10.2%. **Imports** (2003): $2.1 bil; partners (2004): Argentina 21.3%, Brazil 17.1%, US 12.3%, China 6.9%, Russia 5.1%. **Exports** (2003 est.): $2.2 bil; partners (2004): Brazil 19.4%, US 18%, Germany 6.6%, Argentina 6.4%. **Tourism:** $345 mil. **Budget** (2004 est.): $3.8 bil. **Intl. reserves less gold:** $1.62 bil. **Gold:** 10,000 oz t. **Consumer prices:** 9.16%.

Transport: Railroad: Length: 1,288 mi. **Motor vehicles:** 652,300 pass. cars, 56,100 comm. vehicles. **Civil aviation:** 361.6 mil pass.-mi; 15 airports. **Chief port:** Montevideo.

Communications: TV sets: 531 per 1,000 pop. **Radios:** 603 per 1,000 pop. **Telephone lines** (2002): 946,500. **Daily newspaper circ.:** 293 per 1,000 pop. **Internet** (2001): 400,000 users.

Health: Life expect.: 72.9 male; 79.5 female. **Births** (per 1,000 pop.): 14.1. **Deaths** (per 1,000 pop.): 9.1. **Natural inc.:** 0.5%. **Infant mortality** (per 1,000 live births): 12.0. **AIDS rate:** 0.3%.

Education: Compulsory: ages 6-15. **Literacy:** 98%.

Major Intl. Organizations: UN (FAO, IBRD, ILO, IMF, IMO, WHO, WTrO), OAS.

Embassy: 1913 I St. NW, 20006; 331-1313.

Website: www.uruwashi.org

Spanish settlers began to supplant the indigenous Charrua Indians in 1624. Portuguese from Brazil arrived later, but Uruguay was attached to the Spanish Viceroyalty of Rio de la Plata in the 18th century. Rebels fought against Spain beginning in 1810. An independent republic was declared Aug. 25, 1825.

Terrorist activities led Pres. Juan María Bordaberry to agree to military control of his administration Feb. 1973. In June he abolished Congress and set up a Council of State in its place. Bordaberry was removed by the military in a 1976 coup. Civilian government was restored in 1985.

Socialist measures were adopted in the early 1900s. The state retains a dominant role in the power, telephone, railroad, cement, oil-refining, and other industries, although some privatization began in the early 2000s. Uruguay's standard of living remains one of the highest in South America, and political and labor conditions among the freest. A leftist, Tabaré Vázquez, was elected president Oct. 31, 2004, and took office Mar. 1, 2005.

Uzbekistan

Republic of Uzbekistan

People: Population: 26,851,195. **Age distrib.** (%): <15: 33.5; 65+: 4.8. **Pop. density:** 155 per sq mi, 60 per sq km. **Urban:** 36.6%. **Ethnic groups:** Uzbek 80%, Russian 6%, Tajik 5%, Kazakh 3%, Karakalpak 3%, Tatar 2%. **Principal languages:** Uzbek (official), Russian, Tajik. **Chief religions:** Muslim 88% (mostly Sunni), Eastern Orthodox 9%.

Geography: Total area: 172,742 sq mi, 447,400 sq km; **Land area:** 164,248 sq mi, 425,400 sq km. **Location:** Central Asia. **Neighbors:** Kazakhstan on N and W, Kyrgyzstan and Tajikistan on E, Afghanistan and Turkmenistan on S. **Topography:** Mostly plains and desert. **Capital:** Tashkent, 2,155,000.

Government: Type: Republic. **Head of state:** Pres. Islam A. Karimov; b Jan. 30, 1938; in office: Mar. 24, 1990. **Head of gov.:** Prime Min. Shavkat Mirziyaev; b 1957; in office: Dec. 11, 2003. **Local divisions:** 12 regions, 1 autonomous republic, 1 city. **Defense budget** (2004): $54 mil. **Active troops:** 50,000–55,000.

Economy: Industries: textiles, food proc., machine building, metallurgy, nat. gas, chemicals. **Chief crops:** cotton, vegetables, fruits, grain. **Natural resources:** nat. gas, oil, coal, gold, uranium, silver, copper, lead, zinc, tungsten, molybd. **Crude oil reserves** (2004): 594 mil bbls. **Arable land:** 9%. **Livestock** (2004): cattle: 5.4 mil; chickens: 15.0 mil; goats: 900,000; pigs: 90,000; sheep: 8.8 mil. **Fish catch** (2003): 7,112 metric tons. **Electricity prod.** (2003): 46.5 bil kWh. **Labor force** (1995): agriculture 44%, industry 20%, services 36%.

Finance: Monetary unit: Som (UZS) (Sept. 2005: 1,109.82 = $1 U.S.). **GDP** (2004 est.): $47.6 bil; **per capita GDP:** $1,800; **GDP growth:** 4.4%. **Imports** (2004 est.): $2.8 bil; partners (2004): Russia 26.4%, South Korea 10.8%, Germany 9.4%, China 8.3%, Kazakhstan 6%, Turkey 6%. **Exports** (2004 est.): $3.7 bil; partners (2004): Russia 21.2%, China 14%, Ukraine 7%, Turkey 6.3%, Tajikistan 5.8%, Bangladesh 4.2%. **Tourism:** $48 mil. **Budget** (2004 est.): $2.5 bil.

Transport: Railroad: Length: 2,454 mi. **Motor vehicles:** 865,000 pass. cars, 14,500 comm. vehicles. **Civil aviation:** 3.3 bil. pass.-mi; 27 airports. **Chief port:** Termiz.

Communications: TV sets: 280 per 1,000 pop. **Radios:** 465 per 1,000 pop. **Telephone lines:** 1.7 mil. **Daily newspaper circ.:** 3.3 per 1,000 pop. **Internet:** 492,000 users.

Health: Life expect.: 60.8 male; 67.7 female. **Births** (per 1,000 pop.): 26.2. **Deaths** (per 1,000 pop.): 8.0. **Natural inc.:** 1.83%. **Infant mortality** (per 1,000 live births): 71.1. **AIDS rate:** 0.1%.

Education: Compulsory: ages 7-16. **Literacy:** 99.3%.

Major Intl. Organizations: UN (IBRD, ILO, IMF, WHO), CIS, OSCE.

Embassy: 1746 Massachusetts Ave. NW 20036; 887-5300.

Website: www.gov.uz

The region was overrun by the Mongols under Genghis Khan in 1220. In the 14th century, Uzbekistan became the center of a native Timurid empire. In later centuries Muslim feudal states emerged. Russian military conquest began in the 19th century. Uzbek SSR became a Soviet republic in 1925.

Uzbekistan declared independence Aug. 29, 1991. It became an independent republic when the Soviet Union disbanded Dec. 26, 1991. Since then, the authoritarian government of Uzbekistan has been led by a former Communist.

Attacks by Islamic militants, Mar.-July 2004, killed more than 50 people. In June 2004, Russia's 2nd largest oil producer, OAO Lukoil, signed a $1 billion agreement with the govt to develop its natural gas fields. Militants bombed the U.S. and Israeli embassies in Tashkent, July 30.

After armed dissidents at Andizhan, E Uzbekistan, attacked government buildings and freed hundreds of prisoners, May 12-13, 2005, Uzbek security forces opened fire on rebels and unarmed demonstrators, killing many. Irritated by U.S. human rights pressures, Karimov ordered the U.S. to vacate by Jan. 2006 an airbase used to support operations in Afghanistan.

Vanuatu

Republic of Vanuatu

People: Population: 205,754. **Age distrib.** (%): <15: 33.3; 65+: 3.6. **Pop. density:** 44 per sq mi, 17 per sq km. **Urban:** 22.8%. **Ethnic groups:** Melanesian 98%, French, Vietnamese, Chinese, other Pacific Islanders. **Principal languages:** Bislama, English, French (all official); more than 100 local languages. **Chief religions:** Presbyterian 37%, Anglican 15%, Roman Catholic 15%, indigenous beliefs 8%, other Christian 10%.

Geography: Total area: 4,710 sq mi, 12,200 sq km; **Land area:** 4,710 sq mi, 12,200 sq km. **Location:** SW Pacific, 1,200 mi. NE of Brisbane, Australia. **Neighbors:** Fiji to E, Solomon Isls. to NW. **Topography:** Dense forest with narrow coastal strips of cultivated land. **Capital:** Port-Vila, 34,000.

Government: Type: Republic. **Head of state:** Pres. Kalkot Mataskelekele; in office: Aug. 16, 2004. **Head of gov.:** Prime Min. Ham Lini; in office: Dec. 11, 2004. **Local divisions:** 6 provinces

Economy: Industries: food & fish freezing, wood proc., meat canning. **Chief crops:** copra, coconuts, cocoa, coffee, taro, yams. **Natural resources:** mang., timber, fish. **Arable land:** 2%. **Livestock** (2004): cattle: 150,000; chickens: 340,000; goats: 12,000; pigs: 62,000. **Fish catch** (2003): 31,329 metric tons. **Electricity prod.** (2003): 0.04 bil kWh. **Labor force** (2000 est.): agriculture 65%, industry 5%, services 30%.

Finance: Monetary unit: Vatu (VUV) (Sept. 2005: 108.95 = $1 U.S.). **GDP** (2003 est.): $580.0 mil; **per capita GDP:** $2,900; **GDP growth:** 1.1%. **Imports** (2002): $138.0 mil; partners (2004): Taiwan 34.6%, Australia 15.5%, Japan 10.7%, Singapore 8%, New Zealand 6%, Fiji 4.6%. **Exports** (2003): $26.6 mil; partners (2004): Thailand 46.3%, Malaysia 18.1%, Japan 7.4%, Belgium 5.3%, Indonesia 5.3%. **Tourism** (2001): $46 mil. **Budget** (2003 est.): $54.3 mil. **Intl. reserves less gold:** $40 mil. **Consumer prices** (changed in 2002): 2.0%.

Transport: Motor vehicles: 2,600 pass. cars, 4,400 comm. vehicles. **Civil aviation:** 131.7 mil pass.-mi; 3 airports. **Chief ports:** Forai, Port-Vila.

Communications: TV sets: 12 per 1,000 pop. **Radios:** 350 per 1,000 pop. **Telephone lines:** 6,500. **Internet:** 7,500 users.

Health: Life expect.: 61.0 male; 64.1 female. **Births** (per 1,000 pop.): 23.1. **Deaths** (per 1,000 pop.): 7.9. **Natural inc.:** 1.52%. **Infant mortality** (per 1,000 live births): 55.2.

Education: Compulsory: ages 6-12. **Literacy:** 53%.

Major Intl. Organizations: UN (FAO, IBRD, IMF, IMO, WHO), the Commonwealth.

Website: www.vanuatugovernment.gov.vu

The Anglo-French condominium of the New Hebrides, administered jointly by France and Great Britain since 1906, became the independent Republic of Vanuatu on July 30, 1980.

Vatican City (The Holy See)

People: Population: 921. **Urban:** 100%. **Ethnic groups:** Italian, Swiss, other. **Principal languages:** Latin (official), Italian, French, Monastic Sign Language, various others. **Chief religion:** Roman Catholic.

Geography: Area: (total): 108.7 acres. **Location:** In Rome, Italy. **Neighbors:** Completely surrounded by Italy. Note: dignitaries, priests, nuns, guards, and 3,000 lay workers live outside the Vatican.

Finance: Euro (EUR) (Sept. 2005: 0.80 = $1 U.S.). **Budget** (2002): $260.4 mil.

Transport: Railroad: Length: 1 mi.

Labor force: essentially services with a small amount of industry.

Apostolic Nunciature in U.S.: 3339 Massachusetts Ave. NW 20008; 333-7121.

Website: www.vatican.va/phome_en.htm

The popes for many centuries, with brief interruptions, held temporal sovereignty over mid-Italy (the so-called Papal States), comprising an area of some 16,000 sq. mi., with a population in the 19th century of more than 3 million. This territory was incorporated in the new Kingdom of Italy (1861), the sovereignty of the pope being confined to the palaces of the Vatican and the Lateran in Rome and the villa of Castel Gandolfo, by an Italian law, May 13, 1871. This law also guaranteed to the pope and his successors a yearly indemnity of over $620,000. The allowance, however, remained unclaimed.

A Treaty of Conciliation, a concordat, and a financial convention were signed Feb. 11, 1929, by Cardinal Gasparri and Premier Mussolini. The documents established the independent state of Vatican City and gave the Roman Catholic church special status in Italy. The treaty (Lateran Agreement) was made part of the Constitution of Italy (Article 7) in 1947. Italy and the Vatican signed an agreement in 1984 on revisions of the concordat; the accord eliminated Roman Catholicism as the state religion and ended required religious education in Italian schools.

Vatican City includes the Basilica of Saint Peter, the Vatican Palace and Museum covering over 13 acres, the Vatican gardens, and neighboring buildings between Viale Vaticano and the church. Thirteen buildings in Rome, outside the boundaries, enjoy extraterritorial rights; these buildings house congregations or officers necessary for the administration of the Holy See.

The legal system is based on the code of canon law, the apostolic constitutions, and laws especially promulgated for the Vatican City by the pope. The Secretariat of State represents the Holy See in its diplomatic relations. By the Treaty of Conciliation the pope is pledged to a perpetual neutrality unless his mediation is specifically requested. This, however, does not prevent the defense of the Church whenever it is persecuted.

The present sovereign of the State of Vatican City is the Supreme Pontiff Benedict XVI, born Joseph Ratzinger in Marktl am Inn, Germany, Apr. 16, 1927, elected Apr. 19, 2005.

The U.S. restored formal relations in 1984 after the U.S. Congress repealed an 1867 ban on diplomatic relations with the Vatican. The Vatican and Israel agreed to establish formal relations Dec. 30, 1993.

Venezuela

Bolivarian Republic of Venezuela

People: Population: 25,375,281. **Age distrib.** (%): <15: 29.9; 65+: 5.1. **Pop. density:** 72 per sq mi, 28 per sq km. **Urban:** 87.7%. **Ethnic groups:** Spanish, Italian, Portuguese, Arab, German, Black, indigenous. **Principal languages:** Spanish (official), numerous indigenous dialects. **Chief religion:** Roman Catholic 96%.

Geography: Total area: 352,145 sq mi, 912,050 sq km; **Land area:** 340,561 sq mi, 882,050 sq km. **Location:** On Caribbean coast of South America. **Neighbors:** Colombia on W, Brazil on S, Guyana on E. **Topography:** Flat coastal plain and Orinoco Delta are bordered by Andes Mts. and hills. Plains, called llanos, extend between mountains and Orinoco. Guiana Highlands and plains are S of Orinoco, which stretches 1,600 mi. and drains 80% of Venezuela. **Capital:** Caracas, 3,226,000. **Cities (urban aggr.):** Maracaibo, 1,901,000; Valencia, 1,893,000.

Government: Type: Federal republic. **Head of state and gov.:** Pres. Hugo Rafael Chávez Frías; b July 28, 1954; in office: Feb. 2, 1999. **Local divisions:** 23 states, 1 federal district (Caracas), 1 federal dependency (72 islands). **Defense budget** (2004): $953 mil. **Active troops:** 82,300.

Economy: Industries: oil, iron, constr. materials, food proc., textiles, steel, aluminum, auto assembly. **Chief crops:** corn, sorghum, sugarcane, rice, bananas, vegetables, coffee. **Natural resources:** oil, nat. gas, iron ore, gold, bauxite, other minerals, hydropower, diamonds. **Crude oil reserves** (2004): 77.2 bil bbls. **Arable land:** 4%. **Livestock** (2004): cattle: 16.2 mil; chickens: 110,000; goats: 1.3 mil; pigs: 3.0 mil; sheep: 530,194. **Fish catch** (2003): 540,161 metric tons. **Electricity prod.** (2003): 87.4 bil kWh. **Labor force** (1997 est.): agriculture 13%, industry 23%, services 64%.

Finance: Monetary unit: Bolivar (VEB) (Sept. 2005: 2,144.60 = $1 U.S.). **GDP** (2004 est.): $145.2 bil; **per capita GDP:** $5,800; **GDP growth:** 16.8%. **Imports** (2004 est.): $15.0 bil; partners (2004): US 33.2%, Colombia 5.7%, Brazil 5%, Germany 4%. **Exports** (2004 est.): $35.8 bil; partners (2004): US 58.7%, Netherlands Antilles 4.1%, Canada 2.5%. **Tourism:** $323 mil. **Budget** (2004 est.): $30.7 bil. **Intl. reserves less gold** (2003): $10.79 bil. **Gold** (2003): 11.47 mil oz t. **Consumer prices:** 21.75%.

Transport: Railroad: Length: 424 mi. **Motor vehicles:** 1.37mil pass. cars, 1.11 mil comm. vehicles. **Civil aviation:** 2.3 bil pass.-mi; 127 airports. **Chief ports:** Maracaibo, La Guaira, Puerto Cabello.

Communications: TV sets: 185 per 1,000 pop. **Radios:** 296 per 1,000 pop. **Telephone lines:** 2.8 mil. **Daily newspaper circ.:** 206 per 1,000 pop. **Internet:** 1.5 mil users.

Health: Life expect.: 71.3 male; 77.6 female. **Births** (per 1,000 pop.): 18.9. **Deaths** (per 1,000 pop.): 4.9. **Natural inc.:** 1.40%. **Infant mortality** (per 1,000 live births): 22.2. **AIDS rate:** 0.7%.

Education: Compulsory: ages 6-15. **Literacy:** 93.4%.

Major Intl. Organizations: UN (FAO, IBRD, ILO, IMF, IMO, WHO, WTrO), OAS, OPEC.

Embassy: 1099 30th St. NW 20007; 342-2214.

Website: www.embavenez-us.org

Columbus first set foot on the South American continent on the peninsula of Paria, Aug. 1498. Alonso de Ojeda, 1499, was the first European to see Lake Maracaibo. He called the land Venezuela, or Little Venice, because the Indians had houses on stilts. Spanish colonialists dominated Venezuela until Simón Bolívar's victory near Carabobo in June 1821. The republic was formed after secession from the Colombian Federation in 1830. Military strongmen ruled Venezuela for much of its history. Since 1959, the country has had democratically elected governments.

Oil accounts for more than 75% of export earnings and about half of government revenues. Venezuela helped found the Organization of Petroleum Exporting Countries (OPEC) in 1960. The government, Jan. 1, 1976, nationalized the oil industry with compensation. The economy suffered a cash crisis in the 1980s and 1990s as a result of depressed oil revenues. Government attempts to reduce dependence on oil have met with limited success.

An attempted coup by midlevel military officers was thwarted by loyalist troops Feb. 4, 1992. A 2nd coup attempt was thwarted in Nov. Pres. Carlos Andrés Pérez was removed from office on corruption charges, May 1993; he was convicted, May 1996, of mismanaging a $17 million secret government fund. A 1992 coup leader, Hugo Chávez, who ran as a populist, was elected president Dec. 6, 1998. Voters on Dec. 15 approved a new constitution greatly increasing his powers. Floods and mudslides in Dec. 1999 killed, by official estimates, at least 30,000.

Popular among the poor, Chávez alienated some middle- and upper-class Venezuelans with his program of economic and political reform, and his foreign policy antagonized the U.S. Gunfire erupted at a mass protest Apr. 11, 2002, in Caracas, killing at least 17 people. Chávez was forced to relinquish power, but when an interim government issued decrees suspending democratic institutions, Chávez loyalists rebelled; the coup fell apart, and the president reclaimed his office Apr. 14. Opponents of Chávez mounted a crippling general strike, Dec. 2002-Feb. 2003, which ended after mediation by the OAS and former U.S. Pres. Jimmy Carter. Several dissidents were killed later that month. The Colombian and Spanish embassies in Caracas were bombed Feb. 25. Chávez and opposition groups pledged, May 29, 2003, to halt political violence.

Opponents presented petitions with over 3 mil. signatures Aug. 20, 2003, demanding a vote to recall Chávez. After prolonged legal wrangling, the recall election was set for Aug. 15, 2004. The referendum was monitored by Carter and the OAS, and Chávez won with 59% of the vote. An MD-82 jet flying from Panama to Martinique crashed in Venezuela, Aug. 16, 2005, killing all 160 people on board.

Vietnam

Socialist Republic of Vietnam

People: Population: 83,535,576. **Age distrib.** (%): <15: 27.9; 65+: 5.8. **Pop. density:** 656 per sq mi, 253 per sq km. **Urban:** 25.7%. **Ethnic groups:** Vietnamese 85%-90%, Chinese, Hmong, Thai, Khmer, Cham. **Principal languages:** Vietnamese (official), French, Chinese, English. **Chief religions:** Buddhist, Taoist, Roman Catholic, indigenous beliefs.

Geography: Total area: 127,244 sq mi, 329,560 sq km; **Land area:** 125,622 sq mi, 325,360 sq km. **Location:** SE Asia, on the E coast of the Indochinese Peninsula. **Neighbors:** China on N, Laos and Cambodia on W. **Topography:** Vietnam is long and narrow, with a 1,400-mi. coast. About 22% of country is readily arable, including the densely settled Red R. valley in the N, narrow coastal plains in center, and the wide, often marshy Mekong R. Delta in the S. The rest consists of semi-arid plateaus and barren mountains, with some stretches of tropical rain forest. **Capital:** Hanoi, 3,977,000. **Cities (urban aggr.):** Ho Chi Minh City, 4,619,000; Hai Phong, 1,676,000.

Government: Type: Communist. **Head of state:** Pres. Tran Duc Luong; b May 1937; in office: Sept. 24, 1997. **Head of gov.:** Prime Min. Phan Van Khai; b Dec. 1933; in office: Sept. 25, 1997. **Local divisions:** 58 provinces, 3 cities, 1 capital region. **Defense budget** (2003): $3.2 bil. **Active troops:** 484,000.

Economy: Industries: food proc., garments, shoes, machinery, mining. **Chief crops:** rice, corn, potatoes, rubber, soybeans, coffee, tea. **Natural resources:** phosphates, coal, mang., bauxite, chromate, oil, nat. gas, timber, hydropower. **Crude oil reserves** (2004): 600 mil bbls. **Arable land:** 17%. **Livestock** (2004): cattle: 4.9 mil; chickens: 159.2 mil; goats: 1.0 mil; pigs: 26.1 mil. **Fish catch** (2003): 2,604,388 metric tons. **Electricity prod.** (2003): 39.7

bil kWh. **Labor force** (2000 est.): agriculture 63%, industry and services 37%.

Finance: Monetary unit: Dong (VND) (Sept. 2005: 15,875.00 = $1 U.S.). **GDP** (2004 est.): $227.2 bil; **per capita GDP:** $2,700; **GDP growth:** 7.7%. **Imports** (2004 est.): $26.3 bil; partners (2004): China 13.6%, Japan 11.5%, Singapore 11.5%, Taiwan 10.2%, South Korea 9.8%, Thailand 6.7%, Hong Kong 4.4%, US 4.1%, Malaysia 4.1%. **Exports** (2004 est.): $23.7 bil; partners (2004): US 19.8%, Japan 13.7%, China 8.4%, Australia 7%, Germany 5.7%, Singapore 4.8%, UK 4.6%. **Tourism** (1990): $85 mil. **Budget** (2004 est.): $13.1 bil. **Intl. reserves less gold** (2003): $4.19 bil. **Consumer prices:** 7.8%.

Transport: Railroad: Length: 1,952 mi. **Motor vehicles:** 69,900 comm. vehicles. **Civil aviation:** 3.5 bil pass.-mi. **Chief ports:** Ho Chi Minh City, Haiphong, Da Nang.

Communications: TV sets: 184 per 1,000 pop. **Radios:** 107 per 1,000 pop. **Telephone lines:** 4.4 mil. **Daily newspaper circ.:** 4 per 1,000 pop. **Internet:** 3.5 mil users.

Health: Life expect.: 67.8 male; 73.6 female. **Births** (per 1,000 pop.): 17.1. **Deaths** (per 1,000 pop.): 6.2. **Natural inc.:** 1.09%. **Infant mortality** (per 1,000 live births): 26.0. **AIDS rate:** 0.4%.

Education: Compulsory: ages 6-14. **Literacy:** 90.3%.

Major Intl. Organizations: UN (FAO, IBRD, ILO, IMF, IMO, WHO), APEC, ASEAN.

Embassy: 1233 20th St. NW, Ste. 400, 20036; 861-0737.

Website: www.na.gov.vn/english/index.html

Vietnam's recorded history began in Tonkin before the Christian era. Settled by Viets from central China, Vietnam was held by China, 111 BC-AD 939, and was a vassal state during subsequent periods. Vietnam defeated the armies of Kublai Khan, 1288. Conquest by France began in 1858 and ended in 1884 with the protectorates of Tonkin and Annam in the N and the colony of Cochin-China in the S.

Japan occupied Vietnam in 1940; nationalist aims gathered force. A number of groups formed the Vietminh (Independence) League, headed by Ho Chi Minh, Communist guerrilla leader. In Aug. 1945 the Vietminh forced out Bao Dai, former emperor of Annam, head of a Japan-sponsored regime. France, seeking to reestablish colonial control, battled Communist and nationalist forces, 1946-54, and was defeated at Dienbienphu, May 8, 1954. Meanwhile, on July 1, 1949, Bao Dai had formed a State of Vietnam, with himself as chief of state, with French approval. China backed Ho Chi Minh.

A cease-fire signed in Geneva July 21, 1954, provided for a buffer zone, withdrawal of French troops from the North, and elections to determine the country's future. Under the agreement the Communists gained control of territory north of the 17th parallel, with its capital at Hanoi and Ho Chi Minh as president. South Vietnam came to comprise the 39 southern provinces. Some 900,000 North Vietnamese fled to South Vietnam. On Oct. 26, 1955, Ngo Dinh Diem proclaimed the Republic of Vietnam and became its president.

Communists in the North sought to take over South Vietnam beginning in 1954. The North provided aid to Vietcong guerrillas in the South; the Soviet Union and China supplied weapons for the Communist cause. The U.S. began sending military advisers to help the anti-Communist South. Northern aid to Vietcong guerrillas was intensified in 1959, and large-scale troop infiltration began in 1964, with Soviet and Chinese arms assistance. Large Northern forces were stationed in border areas of Laos and Cambodia.

During 1963, Buddhists in the South denounced the Diem government's authoritarianism and brutality. This paved the way for a military coup Nov. 1-2, 1963, which overthrew Diem. Several other military coups followed.

In 1964, the U.S. launched air strikes against North Vietnam. Beginning in 1965, the raids were stepped up and U.S. troops became combatants. U.S. troop strength in Vietnam reached a high of 543,400 in Apr. 1969, but the North Vietnamese and Vietcong continued to mount new offensives. In response to a growing antiwar movement in the U.S., Pres. Nixon gradually withdrew U.S. ground troops. U.S. warplanes conducted massive bombing raids on the Northern cities of Hanoi and Haiphong in Dec. 1972.

A cease-fire agreement was signed in Paris Jan. 27, 1973 by the U.S., North and South Vietnam, and the Vietcong. It was never implemented. North Vietnamese forces attacked remaining government outposts in the Central Highlands in the first months of 1975. Government retreats turned into a rout, and the Saigon regime surrendered April 30. North Vietnam assumed control, and began transforming society along Communist lines. The country was officially reunited July 2, 1976. The war's toll included—Combat deaths: U.S. 47,369; South Vietnam more than 200,000; other allied forces 5,225. Total U.S. fatalities numbered more than 58,000. Vietnamese civilian casualties were more than a million. Displaced war refugees in South Vietnam totaled more than 6.5 million.

Conditions in the region remained unstable after the Vietnam War ended. Heavy fighting with Cambodia took place, 1977-80. Relations with China soured as 140,000 ethnic Chinese left Vietnam charging discrimination; China cut off economic aid. Reacting to Vietnam's invasion of Cambodia, China attacked 4 Vietnamese border provinces, Feb. 1979. Vietnam launched an offensive against Cambodian refugee strongholds along the Thai-Cambodian border in 1985; they also engaged Thai troops.

Vietnam announced reforms aimed at reducing central control of the economy in 1987, as many of the old revolutionary followers of Ho Chi Minh were removed from office.

Citing Vietnamese cooperation in returning remains of U.S. soldiers killed in the Vietnam War, the U.S. announced an end, Feb. 3, 1994, to a 19-year-old U.S. embargo on trade with Vietnam. The U.S. extended full diplomatic recognition to Vietnam July 11, 1995. The Communist Party replaced the country's ill and aging leadership in Sept. 1997.

Floods in central Vietnam, Oct.-Nov. 1999, killed some 550 people and left over 600,000 families homeless. U.S. Pres. Bill Clinton made a historic visit to Vietnam Nov. 17-19, 2000. Nong Duc Manh, a moderate, was named to head the Communist Party Apr. 22, 2001. The U.S. has become Vietnam's top export market, with total annual trade over $6 billion.

Western Samoa

See Samoa.

Yemen

Republic of Yemen

People: Population: 20,727,063. **Age distrib.** (%): <15: 46.5; 65+: 2.7. **Pop. density:** 102 per sq mi, 39 per sq km. **Urban:** 25.6%. **Ethnic groups:** Mainly Arab; Afro-Arab, South Asian, European. **Principal languages:** Arabic (official). **Chief religion:** Muslim (official; Sunni 60% and Shi'a 40%).

Geography: Total area: 203,850 sq mi, 527,970 sq km; **Land area:** 203,850 sq mi, 527,970 sq km. **Location:** Middle East, on the S coast of the Arabian Peninsula. **Neighbors:** Saudi Arabia on N, Oman on the E. **Topography:** A sandy coastal strip leads to well-watered fertile mountains in interior. **Capital:** Sana'a, 1,469,000. **Cities (urban aggr.):** Aden (1995 est.), 562,000.

Government: Type: Republic. **Head of state:** Pres. Ali Abdullah Saleh; b. 1942; in office: July 17, 1978. **Head of gov.:** Prime Min. Abd-al-Qadir Bajamal; b 1946; in office: Apr. 4, 2001. **Local divisions:** 19 governorates and capital region. **Defense budget** (2004): $885 mil. **Active troops:** 66,700

Economy: Industries: oil prod. & refining, cotton textiles, leather goods, food proc. **Chief crops:** grain, fruits, vegetables, pulses, coffee, cotton. **Natural resources:** oil, fish, salt, marble, coal, gold, lead, nickel, copper. **Crude oil reserves** (2004): 4.0 bil bbls. **Arable land:** 3%. **Livestock** (2004): cattle: 1.4 mil; chickens: 34.8 mil; goats: 7.3 mil; sheep: 6.6 mil. **Fish catch** (2003): 159,000 metric tons. **Electricity prod.** (2003): 3.8 bil kWh. **Labor force**: most people are employed in agriculture and herding; services, construction, industry, and commerce account for less than one-fourth of the labor force.

Finance: Monetary unit: Rial (YER) (Sept. 2005: 180.78 = $1 U.S.). **GDP** (2004 est.): $16.25 bil; **per capita GDP:** $800; **GDP growth:** 1.9%. **Imports** (2004 est.): $3.7 bil; partners (2004): UAE 12.8%, Saudi Arabia 10.2%, China 9%, France 7.9%, Kuwait 4.4%, US 4.4%, India 4.3%, Turkey 4.1%. **Exports** (2004 est.): $4.5 bil; partners (2004): China 33.5%, Thailand 31.4%, Singapore 7.2%, South Korea 6.1%. **Tourism:** $139 mil. **Budget** (2004 est.): $4.6 bil. **Intl. reserves less gold** (2003): $3.36 bil. **Gold** (2003): 50,000 oz t. **Consumer prices** (2003): 10.8%.

Transport: Motor vehicles: 346,600 pass. cars, 587,900 comm. vehicles. **Civil aviation:** 981.8 mil pass.-mi; 16 airports. **Chief ports:** Al Hudaydah, Al Mukalla, Aden.

Communications: TV sets: 286 per 1,000 pop. **Radios:** 64 per 1,000 pop. **Telephone lines** (2002): 542,200. **Daily newspaper circ.:** 15 per 1,000 pop. **Internet** (2002): 100,000 users.

Health: Life expect.: 59.9 male; 63.7 female. **Births** (per 1,000 pop.): 43.1. **Deaths** (per 1,000 pop.): 8.5. **Natural inc.:** 3.45%. **Infant mortality** (per 1,000 live births): 61.5. **AIDS rate:** 0.1%.

Education: Compulsory: ages 6-14. **Literacy:** 50.2%.

Major Intl. Organizations: UN (FAO, IBRD, ILO, IMF, IMO, WHO), AL.

Embassy: 2319 Wyoming Ave. NW 20008; 965-4760.

Website: www.nic.gov.ye

Yemen's territory once was part of the ancient biblical Kingdom of Sheba, or Saba, a prosperous link in trade between Africa and India. Yemen became independent in 1918, after centuries of Ottoman Turkish rule, but remained politically and economically backward.

Imam Ahmed ruled 1948-1962. Army officers headed by Brig. Gen. Abdullah al-Salal declared the country to be the Yemen Arab Republic, Sept. 1962. Ahmed's heir, the Imam Mohamad al-Badr, fled to the mountains where tribesmen joined royalist forces, aided by the Saudi monarchy. Fighting between royalists and republicans killed about 150,000 people until hostilities ended in 1970.

Meanwhile, South Yemen, formed from the British colony of Aden and the British protectorate of South Arabia, became independent Nov. 1967. A Marxist state and a Soviet ally, it took the name People's Democratic Republic of Yemen in 1970. More than 300,000 Yemenis fled from the South to the North after independence, contributing to 2 decades of hostility between the 2 states that flared into warfare twice in the 1970s.

The 2 countries were formally united May 21, 1990, but regional clan-based rivalries led to full-scale civil war in 1994. Secessionists declared a breakaway state in S Yemen, May 21, 1994, but northern troops captured the former southern capital of Aden in July. A new constitution was approved Sept. 28.

Yemen, the ancestral home of Osama bin Laden, has been caught in a crossfire between the U.S. and Islamic extremists. While on a refueling stop in Aden, Oct. 12, 2000, the destroyer

U.S.S. *Cole* was bombed, leaving 17 Americans dead and more than 3 dozen injured; the U.S. government blamed the attack on terrorists associated with bin Laden. The U.S. sent troops in 2002 to help track down members of al-Qaeda.

A missile fired Nov. 3, 2002, from an unmanned CIA surveillance aircraft killed 6 suspected al-Qaeda members, including an American. Three U.S. missionaries were slain at a Baptist hospital in Jibla, Dec. 30; the gunman, an Islamic militant, received a death sentence May 10, 2003. Clashes beginning in June 2004 between Yemeni government forces and rebels led by an anti-U.S. cleric, Hussein al-Houthi, left more than 200 people dead. The government announced Sept. 10 that Yemeni troops had killed al-Houthi, but the insurgency continued into 2005.

Yugoslavia

See Serbia and Montenegro.

Zaire

See Congo.

Zambia

Republic of Zambia

People: Population: 11,261,795. **Age distrib.** (%): <15: 46.5; 65+: 2.4. **Pop. density:** 39 per sq mi, 15 per sq km. **Urban:** 35.7%. **Ethnic groups:** More than 70 groups; largest are Bemba, Tonga, Ngoni, and Lozi. **Principal languages:** English (official), Bemba, Kaonda, Lozi, Lunda, Luvale, Nyanja, Tonga, 70 others. **Chief religions:** Christian 50%-75%, Muslim and Hindu 24%-49%.

Geography: Total area: 290,586 sq mi, 752,614 sq km; **Land area:** 285,995 sq mi, 740,724 sq km. **Location:** In S central Africa. **Neighbors:** Congo (formerly Zaire) on N; Tanzania, Malawi, Mozambique on E; Zimbabwe, Namibia on S; Angola on W. **Topography:** Zambia is mostly high plateau country covered with thick forests, and drained by several important rivers, including the Zambezi. **Capital:** Lusaka, 1,394,000.

Government: Type: Republic. **Head of state and gov.:** Pres. Levy Patrick Mwanawasa; b Sept. 3, 1948; in office: Jan. 2, 2002. **Local divisions:** 9 provinces. **Defense budget** (2004): $29 mil. **Active troops:** 18,100.

Economy: Industries: copper mining & proc., constr., foodstuffs. **Chief crops:** corn, sorghum, rice, peanuts, sunflower seeds. **Natural resources:** copper, cobalt, zinc, lead, coal, emeralds, gold, silver, uranium, hydropower. **Arable land:** 7%. **Livestock** (2004): cattle: 2.6 mil; chickens: 30.0 mil; goats: 1.3 mil; pigs: 340,000; sheep: 150,000. **Fish catch** (2003): 69,501 metric tons. **Electricity prod.** (2003): 8.3 bil kWh. **Labor force**: agriculture 85%, industry 6%, services 9%.

Finance: Monetary unit: Kwacha (ZMK) (Sept. 2005: 4,302.00 = $1 U.S.). **GDP** (2004 est.): $9.409 bil; **per capita GDP:** $900; **GDP growth:** 4.6%. **Imports** (2004 est.): $1.5 bil; partners (2004): South Africa 50.3%, Zimbabwe 13.2%, UAE 5.3%. **Exports** (2004 est.): $1.5 bil; partners (2004): Tanzania 14.1%, South Africa 13.2%, China 9.1%, Japan 7.9%, Thailand 7.9%, Switzerland 7.3%, Belgium 6.7%, Malaysia 4%. **Tourism:** $149 mil. **Budget** (2004 est.): $1.3 bil. **Intl. reserves less gold:** $217 mil. **Consumer prices:** 17.97%.

Transport: Railroad: Length: 1,350 mi. **Motor vehicles:** 3,700 pass. cars, 3,900 comm. vehicles. **Civil aviation:** 9.94 mil pass.-mi; 11 airports. **Chief port:** Mpulungu.

Communications: TV sets: 145 per 1,000 pop. **Radios:** 160 per 1,000 pop. **Telephone lines:** 88,400. **Daily newspaper circ.:** 21.9 per 1,000 pop. **Internet**: 68,200 users.

Health: Life expect.: 39.4 male; 40.0 female. **Births** (per 1,000 pop.): 41.4. **Deaths** (per 1,000 pop.): 20.2. **Natural inc.:** 2.12%. **Infant mortality** (per 1,000 live births): 88.3. **AIDS rate:** 16.5%.

Education: Compulsory: ages 7-13. **Literacy:** 80.6%.

Major Intl. Organizations: UN (FAO, IBRD, ILO, IMF, WHO, WTrO), the Commonwealth, AU.

Embassy: 2419 Massachusetts Ave. NW 20008; 265-9717.

Website: www.zana.gov.zm

Ruled by the British as Northern Rhodesia, the country became the independent republic of Zambia within the Commonwealth Oct. 24, 1964. Independence leader Kenneth Kaunda governed the country as president, 1964-91. A Zambian government corporation in 1970 took over 51% of 2 foreign-owned copper-mining companies. Privately-held land and other enterprises were nationalized in 1975. In the 1980s and 1990s lowered copper prices hurt the economy and severe drought caused famine.

Food riots erupted in June 1990, as the nation suffered its worst violence since independence. Elections held Oct. 1991 brought an end to Kaunda's one-party rule. The new government sought to sell state enterprises, including the copper industry. Pres. Frederick Chiluba won reelection Nov. 18, 1996, but international observers cited harassment of opposition parties. A coup attempt was suppressed Oct. 28, 1997.

Thwarted in his effort to change the constitution to allow himself to run for a 3rd term, Chiluba endorsed Levy Patrick Mwanawasa, who won a disputed election Dec. 27, 2001. Chiluba was arrested Feb. 24, 2003, on charges that he stole government funds while he was president; his trial began Dec. 9 but was slowed by prosecution delays.

Food shortages threatened more than 2 million Zambians in 2002; the government refused to distribute shipments of U.S. grain because it was genetically modified. According to UN estimates, about one-sixth of the adult population has HIV/AIDS.

Zimbabwe

Republic of Zimbabwe

People: Population: 12,160,782. **Age distrib.** (%): <15: 39.2; 65+: 3.7. **Pop. density:** 81 per sq mi, 31 per sq km. **Urban:** 34.9%. **Ethnic groups:** Shona 82%, Ndebele 14%. **Principal languages:** English (official), Shona, Sindebele, numerous dialects. **Chief religions:** Syncretic (Christian-indigenous mix) 50%, Christian 25%, indigenous beliefs 24%.

Geography: Total area: 150,804 sq mi, 390,580 sq km; **Land area:** 149,294 sq mi, 386,670 sq km. **Location:** In southern Africa. **Neighbors:** Zambia on N, Botswana on W, South Africa on S, Mozambique on E. **Topography:** Zimbabwe is high plateau country, rising to mountains on eastern border, sloping down on the other borders. **Capital:** Harare, 1,469,000. **Cities (urban aggr.):** Bulawayo, 824,000.

Government: Type: Republic. **Head of state and gov.:** Pres. Robert Mugabe; b Feb. 21, 1924; in office: Dec. 31, 1987. **Local divisions:** 8 provinces, 2 cities. **Defense budget** (2004): $237 mil. **Active troops:** 29,000.

Economy: Industries: mining, steel, wood products, cement, chemicals. **Chief crops:** corn, cotton, tobacco, wheat, coffee. **Natural resources:** coal, chromium ore, asbestos, gold, nickel, copper, iron ore, vanadium, lithium, tin, platinum. **Arable land:** 7%. **Livestock** (2004): cattle: 5.4 mil; chickens: 22.0 mil; goats: 3.0 mil; pigs: 62,000; sheep: 610,000. **Fish catch** (2003): 15,600 metric tons. **Electricity prod.** (2003): 8.9 bil kWh. **Labor force** (1996): agriculture 66%, industry 10%, services 24%.

Finance: Monetary unit: Zimbabwe Dollar (ZWD) (Sept. 2005: 24,505.00 = $1 U.S.). **GDP** (2004 est.): $24.37 bil; **per capita GDP:** $1,900; **GDP growth:** -8.2%. **Imports** (2004 est.): $1.6 bil; partners (2004): South Africa 47.2%, Democratic Republic of the Congo 6.2%, China 4.4%. **Exports** (2004 est.): $1.4 bil; partners (2004): South Africa 11.9%, Zambia 6.3%, China 3.4%. **Tourism:** $44 mil. **Budget** (2004 est.): $1.6 bil. **Intl. reserves less gold** (2002): $61 mil. **Gold** (2002): 140,000 oz t. **Consumer prices** (changed in 2002): 140.1%.

Transport: Railroad: Length: 1,912 mi. **Motor vehicles**: 567,300 pass. cars, 83,500 comm. vehicles. **Civil aviation:** 449.3 mil pass.-mi; 17 airports. **Chief ports:** Binga, Kariba.

Communications: TV sets: 35 per 1,000 pop. **Radios:** 389 per 1,000 pop. **Telephone lines:** 300,900. **Daily newspaper circ.:** 19 per 1,000 pop. **Internet** (2002): 500,000 users.

Health: Life expect.: 40.2 male; 38.0 female. **Births** (per 1,000 pop.): 28.2. **Deaths** (per 1,000 pop.): 21.9. **Natural inc.:** 0.63%. **Infant mortality** (per 1,000 live births): 52.3. **AIDS rate:** 24.6%.

Education: Compulsory: ages 6-12. **Literacy:** 90.7%.

Major Intl. Organizations: UN (FAO, IBRD, ILO, IMF, WHO, WTrO), AU.

Embassy: 1608 New Hampshire Ave. NW 20009; 332-7100.

Website: www.zim.gov.zw

Britain took over the area as Southern Rhodesia in 1923 from the British South Africa Co. (which, under Cecil Rhodes, had conquered it by 1897) and granted internal self-government. Under a 1961 constitution, voting was restricted to keep whites in power. On Nov. 11, 1965, Prime Min. Ian D. Smith announced his country's unilateral declaration of independence.

Britain termed the act illegal and demanded that the country (known as Rhodesia until 1980) broaden voting rights to provide for eventual rule by the black African majority. The UN imposed sanctions and, in May 1968, a trade embargo. Intermittent negotiations between the government and various black nationalist groups failed to prevent increasing guerrilla warfare.

In the country's first universal-franchise election, Apr. 21, 1979, Bishop Abel Muzorewa's United African National Council gained a bare majority of the black-dominated Parliament. A cease-fire was accepted by all parties, Dec. 5. Independence as Zimbabwe was finally achieved Apr. 18, 1980.

On Mar. 6, 1992, Pres. Robert Mugabe declared a national disaster because of drought and appealed to foreign donors for food, money, and medicine. An economic adjustment program caused widespread hardship. Mugabe was reelected Mar. 1996 after opposition candidates withdrew. A land redistribution campaign launched by Mugabe triggered violent attacks in Apr. 2000 against some white farmers; whites made up less than 1% of the population but held 70% of the land. Mugabe's opponents gained in legislative elections June 24-25, 2000.

International observers criticized Mugabe for relying on fraud and intimidation to win the presidential election of Mar. 9-11, 2002. The EU, the U.S., and the Commonwealth imposed sanctions on the Mugabe regime. Zimbabwe withdrew from the Commonwealth as of Dec. 7, 2003. In May 2005, Mugabe launched Operation Murambatsvina ("Drive out rubbish"), razing shanty dwellings and illegal street markets in urban areas and leaving some 700,000 people homeless. The UN recently estimated that about 25% of the adult population has HIV/AIDS.

World Population Growth

Although the population of the world in ancient times can only be very roughly estimated, it is believed that there were perhaps 50 million people in the world in 1000 BC. The United Nations Population Division estimates a figure of 300 million for AD 1; this chart shows estimated population growth from that time onward as estimated by the UN.

While other sources may vary, it is clear from all sources that world population began growing more rapidly in the 18th and 19th centuries, and grew much more rapidly in the 20th century. According to UN estimates, world population reached 1 billion in 1804, and went to 2 billion in 123 years, 3 billion in 33 years, 4 billion in 14 years, 5 billion in 13 years, and 6 billion in 12 years. According to UN estimates, the 6 billion figure was reached in 1999. By mid-2005 the total world population was estimated at about 6.45 billion.

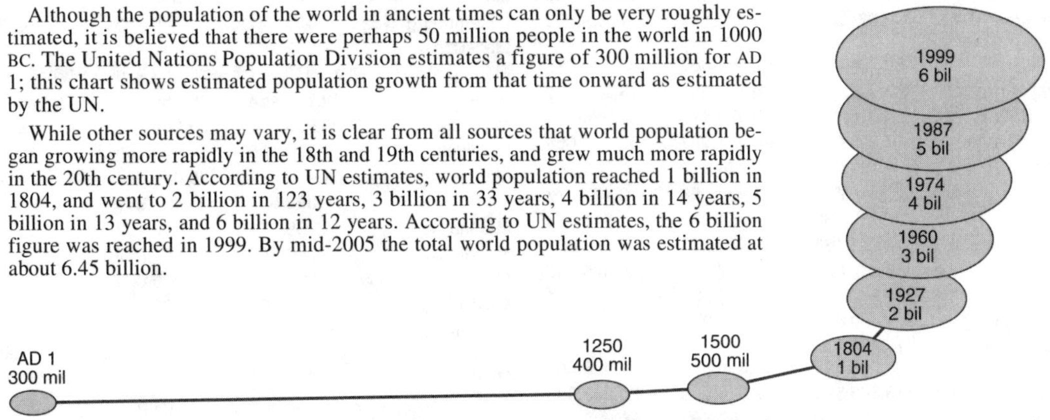

Area and Population of the Continents

Source: International Programs Center, Bureau of the Census, U.S. Dept. of Commerce

Continent or Region	AREA[1] (sq km)	AREA[1] (sq mi)	% of Earth	POPULATION (est., midyear) 2005	% World Total, 2005	1950	1975	2000	2025[2]
Asia	31,027,230	11,979,676	21.4	3,913,842,171	60.7	1,436,893,576	2,415,569,909	3,686,061,532	4,753,366,405
Africa	29,805,048	11,507,789	20.6	891,437,541	13.8	227,332,997	410,827,151	803,234,623	1,327,428,990
Europe	22,825,905	8,813,128	15.7	729,341,014	11.3	546,415,793	677,127,418	729,934,730	711,525,502
N. America	21,393,762	8,260,174	14.8	512,422,558	7.9	220,857,588	346,832,644	487,223,694	618,801,943
S. America	17,522,371	6,765,422	12.1	371,271,037	5.8	111,384,890	215,773,399	348,336,602	447,180,663
Oceania, incl. Australia	8,428,702	3,254,339	5.8	32,744,469	0.5	12,476,128	21,220,574	30,744,658	39,685,917
Antarctica[3]	14,000,000	5,405,428	9.7	—	—	—	—	—	—
WORLD	145,003,018	55,985,955		6,451,058,790		2,555,360,972	4,087,351,095	6,085,527,778	7,897,989,420

Note: (1) Areas are as defined by the U.S. Bureau of the Census. Area for Europe includes all of Russia. Figures may not add to totals because of rounding. (2) Projected. (3) Antarctica has no indigenous inhabitants; researchers stay for various periods of time.

Current Population and Projections for All Countries: 2005, 2025, and 2050

Source: International Programs Center, Bureau of the Census, U.S. Dept. of Commerce

(midyear figures, in thousands)

Country	2005	2025	2050
Afghanistan	29,928,987	50,252,227	81,933,479
Albania	3,563,112	3,944,360	4,016,945
Algeria	32,531,853	40,254,833	43,983,870
Andorra	70,549	77,973	69,129
Angola	11,827,315	17,747,093	25,570,556
Antigua and Barbuda	68,722	75,116	69,259
Argentina	39,537,943	45,757,375	48,740,060
Armenia	2,982,904	3,044,164	2,943,441
Australia	20,090,437	23,022,980	24,175,783
Austria	8,184,691	8,189,560	7,520,950
Azerbaijan	7,911,974	9,452,978	10,664,940
Bahamas, The	301,790	327,317	324,052
Bahrain	688,345	865,890	973,412
Bangladesh	144,319,628	204,538,715	279,955,405
Barbados	278,870	293,744	274,523
Belarus	10,300,483	10,135,057	9,067,076
Belgium	10,364,388	10,453,261	9,882,599
Belize	281,084	410,468	541,734
Benin	7,649,360	11,911,838	16,356,458
Bhutan	2,232,291	3,294,556	4,653,447
Bolivia	8,857,870	11,369,857	13,772,819
Bosnia and Herzegovina	4,430,494	4,535,296	3,891,669
Botswana	1,640,115	1,582,776	1,411,662
Brazil	186,112,794	217,825,222	228,426,737
Brunei	372,361	505,644	600,998
Bulgaria	7,450,349	6,257,716	4,651,477
Burkina Faso	13,491,736	23,995,152	43,656,786
Burundi	7,795,426	13,912,642	22,852,556
Cambodia	13,636,398	19,289,143	25,089,909
Cameroon	16,988,132	24,260,231	32,346,099
Canada	32,805,041	38,164,606	41,429,579
Cape Verde	418,224	451,021	380,614
Central African Republic	4,237,703	5,486,686	6,502,151
Chad	9,657,069	16,979,059	29,547,665
Chile	15,980,912	18,521,153	19,244,843

World Almanac Quick Quiz

Which of these nations joined the UN last?

(a) Belgium (b) Russia/U.S.S.R.
(c) Austria (d) Guatemala

For the answer look in this chapter, or see page 1008.

Country	2005	2025	2050
China	1,306,313,812	1,453,123,817	1,424,161,948
Colombia	42,954,279	55,064,507	64,534,230
Comoros	671,247	1,127,194	1,835,099
Congo, Dem. Rep. of	60,764,490	107,981,867	183,177,415
Congo, Rep. of	3,602,269	6,165,891	9,618,358
Costa Rica	4,016,173	5,074,472	5,696,700
Côte d'Ivoire	17,298,040	24,381,767	32,400,664
Croatia	4,495,904	4,374,007	3,864,201
Cuba	11,346,670	11,668,658	10,477,677
Cyprus	780,133	851,733	841,102
Czech Republic	10,241,138	9,844,275	8,540,221
Denmark	5,432,335	5,697,913	5,575,147
Djibouti	476,703	681,030	993,011
Dominica	69,029	77,936	81,961
Dominican Republic	9,049,595	11,805,878	14,425,863
Ecuador	13,363,593	17,099,305	20,332,088
Egypt	77,505,756	103,352,882	126,920,512
El Salvador	6,704,932	9,107,608	12,039,149
Equatorial Guinea	529,034	768,236	1,063,071
Eritrea	4,669,638	7,244,126	10,164,076
Estonia	1,332,893	1,149,245	861,913
Ethiopia	73,053,286	107,804,235	144,716,331
Fiji	893,354	1,153,122	1,447,573
Finland	5,223,442	5,251,272	4,819,615
France	60,656,178	63,085,101	61,017,122
Gabon	1,394,307	2,059,662	3,221,749
Gambia, The	1,595,086	2,624,964	4,068,861
Georgia	4,677,401	4,341,061	3,784,724
Germany	82,431,390	80,637,451	73,607,121
Ghana	21,946,247	30,718,241	39,135,324
Greece	10,668,354	10,670,697	10,035,935
Greenland	56,375	56,473	56,644
Grenada	89,502	96,253	87,136
Guatemala	12,013,907	17,396,401	22,846,787
Guinea	9,452,670	15,806,084	28,713,509
Guinea-Bissau	1,413,446	2,060,522	2,895,666
Guyana	765,283	755,884	597,806
Haiti	8,121,622	12,628,950	18,403,447
Honduras	7,167,902	10,004,876	12,641,869
Hungary	10,006,835	9,437,569	8,374,619
Iceland	296,737	337,632	350,922
India	1,080,264,388	1,361,625,090	1,601,004,572
Indonesia	241,973,879	300,277,490	336,247,428
Iran	68,017,860	83,186,886	89,691,431
Iraq	26,074,906	40,418,381	56,360,779
Ireland	4,015,676	4,842,255	5,396,215
Israel	6,276,883	7,612,022	8,516,835
Italy	58,103,033	56,234,163	50,389,841
Jamaica	2,735,520	3,128,416	3,499,068
Japan	127,417,244	120,001,048	99,886,568
Jordan	5,759,732	8,651,714	11,772,789
Kazakhstan	15,185,844	16,041,146	15,099,700
Kenya	33,829,590	49,357,449	64,820,325
Kiribati	103,092	158,047	235,342
Korea, North	22,912,177	25,755,007	26,363,688
Korea, South	48,640,671	50,560,956	45,224,224
Kuwait	2,335,648	4,175,172	6,374,800
Kyrgyzstan	5,146,281	6,678,722	8,237,623
Laos	6,217,141	9,450,131	13,176,153
Latvia	2,290,237	1,992,516	1,544,073
Lebanon	3,826,018	4,564,539	4,940,731
Lesotho	2,031,348	1,806,490	1,448,643
Liberia	2,900,269	4,745,521	7,072,402
Libya	5,765,563	8,322,662	10,817,176

Country	2005	2025	2050
Liechtenstein	33,717	37,567	35,776
Lithuania	3,596,617	3,355,985	2,787,516
Luxembourg	468,571	586,296	720,603
Macedonia	2,045,262	2,119,511	1,990,728
Madagascar	18,040,341	32,965,970	65,460,246
Malawi	12,707,464	19,969,185	30,670,779
Malaysia	23,953,136	33,064,523	43,122,397
Maldives	349,106	563,760	815,031
Mali	11,415,261	20,435,694	40,138,869
Malta	398,534	421,239	395,639
Marshall Islands	59,071	83,105	102,761
Mauritania	3,086,859	5,291,845	8,635,801
Mauritius	1,230,602	1,406,809	1,451,156
Mexico	106,202,903	130,198,692	147,907,650
Micronesia, Fed. States of	108,105	98,879	74,296
Moldova	4,455,421	4,780,435	4,795,531
Monaco	32,409	34,590	32,964
Mongolia	2,791,272	3,576,128	4,086,025
Morocco	32,725,847	42,553,182	50,871,553
Mozambique	19,406,703	23,594,600	26,402,616
Myanmar	46,996,558	52,681,969	53,217,981
Namibia	2,030,692	2,061,106	1,795,852
Nauru	13,048	17,887	22,696
Nepal	27,676,547	39,917,760	53,293,874
Netherlands	16,407,491	17,539,636	17,334,090
New Zealand	4,035,461	4,672,537	4,842,397
Nicaragua	5,465,100	7,510,206	9,437,504
Niger	12,162,856	20,951,836	34,419,502
Nigeria	128,765,768	206,165,946	356,523,597
Norway	4,593,041	4,916,787	4,966,385
Oman	3,001,583	5,294,475	8,337,734
Pakistan	162,419,946	228,822,199	294,995,104
Palau	20,303	24,320	26,300
Panama	3,140,232	4,109,552	5,038,122
Papua New Guinea	5,545,268	8,001,357	10,670,394
Paraguay	6,347,884	9,880,421	14,635,743
Peru	27,925,628	34,476,469	38,300,067
Philippines	87,857,473	118,685,776	147,630,852
Poland	38,557,984	37,349,696	32,084,570
Portugal	10,566,212	10,806,202	9,933,334
Qatar	863,051	1,153,966	1,239,216
Romania	22,329,977	21,260,138	18,678,226
Russia	143,420,309	130,534,651	110,763,998
Rwanda	8,440,820	13,140,506	19,935,307
Saint Kitts and Nevis	38,958	46,486	52,348
Saint Lucia	166,312	209,064	235,420
Saint Vincent and the Grenadines	117,534	118,308	92,335
Samoa	177,287	177,452	170,739
San Marino	28,880	34,565	35,335
São Tomé and Príncipe	187,410	328,825	502,489
Saudi Arabia	26,417,599	35,668,686	49,706,851
Senegal	11,706,498	17,080,470	22,543,308
Serbia and Montenegro	10,829,175	10,641,832	9,782,457
Seychelles	81,188	88,071	89,713
Sierra Leone	5,867,426	9,140,077	13,998,936
Singapore	4,425,720	5,100,929	4,635,110
Slovakia	5,431,363	5,458,581	4,943,616
Slovenia	2,011,070	1,907,560	1,596,947
Solomon Islands	538,032	815,582	1,110,514
Somalia	8,591,629	14,861,596	25,499,605
South Africa	44,344,136	39,905,523	33,002,952

Country	2005	2025	2050
Spain	40,341,462	39,578,066	35,564,293
Sri Lanka	20,064,776	22,593,636	23,085,782
Sudan	40,187,486	61,338,891	84,192,309
Suriname	438,144	435,208	357,891
Swaziland	1,138,227	1,008,990	751,328
Sweden	9,001,774	9,315,507	9,084,788
Switzerland	7,489,370	7,774,334	7,296,092
Syria	18,448,752	26,547,725	34,437,235
Taiwan	22,894,384	24,635,783	23,203,650
Tajikistan	7,163,506	11,041,648	16,630,004
Tanzania	36,766,356	53,015,251	71,949,135
Thailand	64,185,502	70,523,958	69,268,817
Timor-Leste	1,040,880	1,493,841	1,942,734
Togo	5,399,991	8,986,546	14,714,623
Tonga	112,422	150,787	188,340
Trinidad and Tobago	1,075,066	881,713	622,011
Tunisia	10,074,951	11,931,451	12,462,798
Turkey	69,660,559	82,204,623	86,473,786
Turkmenistan	4,952,081	7,052,993	9,626,193
Tuvalu	11,636	15,821	20,018
Uganda	27,269,482	56,560,727	132,699,173
Ukraine	46,996,765	41,784,662	34,341,529
United Arab Emirates	2,563,212	3,269,743	3,696,962
United Kingdom	60,441,457	63,818,586	63,977,435
United States	295,734,134	349,666,199	420,080,587
Uruguay	3,415,920	3,675,259	3,728,264
Uzbekistan	26,851,195	36,947,068	48,597,111
Vanuatu	205,754	263,267	310,486
Vatican City	921	(2)	(2)
Venezuela	25,375,281	32,060,880	37,106,394
Vietnam	83,535,576	99,977,731	107,772,641
Yemen	20,727,063	39,643,901	71,119,251
Zambia	11,261,795	16,406,984	22,188,064
Zimbabwe	12,160,782	12,915,433	12,221,257

(1) Excludes Hong Kong, population 6,898,686 and Macao, population 449,198. (2) 2025, 2050 not available.

Population of the World's Largest Cities

Source: United Nations, Dept. for Economic and Social Information and Policy Analysis

Population figures are UN estimates and projections for "urban agglomerations"—i.e., contiguous densely populated urban areas, not demarcated by administrative boundaries, as revised in 2003. Data may differ from figures elsewhere in *The World Almanac*.

Rank[1]	City, Country	Pop. (thousands) 2000	Pop. (thousands) 2015[2]	Annual growth rate (percent) 1995-2000	Pop. (thousands) 1975	Total Growth (percent) 1975-2000	Total Growth (percent) 2000-15[2]	Pop. of city as percentage of nation's 2000 pop.
1.	Tokyo, Japan	34,450	36,214	0.51	26,615	29.4	5.1	27.1
2.	Mexico City, Mexico	18,066	20,647	1.47	10,690	69.0	14.3	18.3
3.	New York City, U.S.	17,846	19,717	1.04	15,880	12.4	10.5	6.3
4.	São Paulo, Brazil	17,099	19,963	1.39	9,614	77.9	16.7	10.0
5.	Mumbai (Bombay), India	16,086	22,645	2.62	7,347	118.9	40.8	1.6
6.	Kolkata (Calcutta), India	13,058	16,798	1.82	7,888	65.5	28.6	1.3
7.	Shanghai, China	12,887	12,666	−0.35	11,443	12.6	−1.7	1.0
8.	Buenos Aires, Argentina	12,583	14,563	1.18	9,143	37.6	15.7	33.9
9.	Delhi, India	12,441	20,946	4.18	4,426	181.1	68.4	1.2
10.	Los Angeles, U.S.	11,814	12,904	0.82	8,926	32.4	9.2	4.1
11.	Osaka, Japan	11,165	11,359	0.20	9,844	13.4	1.7	8.8
12.	Jakarta, Indonesia	11,018	17,498	3.69	4,813	128.9	58.8	5.2
13.	Beijing, China	10,839	11,060	0.02	8,545	26.8	2.0	0.8
14.	Rio de Janeiro, Brazil	10,803	12,364	1.20	7,557	43.0	14.4	6.3
15.	Cairo, Egypt	10,398	13,123	1.38	6,437	61.5	26.2	15.3

(1) Ranked by 2000 population. (2) Projected.

National Rankings by Population, Area, Population Density, 2005

Source: International Programs Center, Bureau of the Census, U.S. Dept. of Commerce

As of mid-2005, according to U.S. Census Bureau projections, the world had an estimated population of 6,451,058,790. China was the most populous nation, with 1/5 of the world total. India, the 2nd-largest, passed the 1-billion mark in 1999. Russia is the largest country in land area.

Largest Populations

Rank	Country	Population
1.	China[1]	1,306,313,812
2.	India	1,080,264,388
3.	United States	295,734,134
4.	Indonesia	241,973,879
5.	Brazil	186,112,794
6.	Pakistan	162,419,946
7.	Bangladesh	144,319,628
8.	Russia	143,420,309
9.	Nigeria	128,765,768
10.	Japan	127,417,244
11.	Mexico	106,202,903
12.	Philippines	87,857,473
13.	Vietnam	83,535,576
14.	Germany	82,431,390
15.	Egypt	77,505,756
16.	Ethiopia	73,053,286
17.	Turkey	69,660,559
18.	Iran	68,017,860
19.	Thailand	64,185,502
20.	Congo, Dem. Rep. of	60,764,490

Smallest Populations

Rank	Country	Population
1.	Vatican City	921
2.	Tuvalu	11,636
3.	Nauru	13,048
4.	Palau	20,303
5.	San Marino	28,880
6.	Monaco	32,409
7.	Liechtenstein	33,717
8.	Saint Kitts and Nevis	38,958
9.	Marshall Islands	59,071
10.	Antigua and Barbuda	68,722

IT'S A FACT: The 3 nations with the highest birthrates (calculated as births per 1,000 people in 2005) are all in Africa: Niger (51.33), Mali (49.9), and Uganda (47.99). The 3 countries with the lowest birthrate are all in Europe: Germany (8.33), Lithuania (8.62), and Ukraine (8.67). The birth rate for the U.S. was 14.14.

Largest Land Areas[2]

Rank	Country	Area (sq km)	Area (sq mi)
1.	Russia	16,995,800	6,562,112
2.	China	9,326,410	3,600,946
3.	United States	9,161,923	3,537,437
4.	Canada	9,093,507	3,511,021
5.	Brazil	8,456,510	3,265,075
6.	Australia	7,617,930	2,941,298
7.	India	2,973,190	1,147,955
8.	Argentina	2,736,690	1,056,641
9.	Kazakhstan	2,669,800	1,030,815
10.	Algeria	2,381,740	919,595

Smallest Land Areas[2]

Rank	Country	Area (sq km)	Area (sq mi)
1.	Vatican City	0.4	0.15
2.	Monaco	1.95	.75
3.	Nauru	21	8
4.	Tuvalu	26	10
5.	San Marino	61	24
6.	Liechtenstein	160	62
7.	Marshall Islands	181	70
8.	Saint Kitts and Nevis	261	101
9.	Maldives	300	116
10.	Malta	316	122

Most Densely Populated[2]

Rank	Country	Persons per sq km	Persons per sq mi
1.	Monaco	16,620.0	43,045.6
2.	Singapore	6,482.7	16,790.0
3.	Vatican City	2,302.5	6,140.0
4.	Malta	1,261.2	3,266.5
5.	Maldives	1,163.7	3,013.9
6.	Bangladesh	1,077.1	2,791.3
7.	Bahrain	1,035.1	2,680.9
8.	Taiwan	709.7	1,838.1
9.	Barbados	647.0	1,675.8
10.	Nauru	621.3	1,609.2

Most Sparsely Populated[3]

Rank	Country	Persons per sq km	Persons per sq mi
1.	Mongolia	1.8	4.6
2.	Namibia	2.5	6.4
3.	Australia	2.6	6.8
4.	Suriname	2.7	7.0
5.	Botswana	2.8	7.3
6.	Iceland	3.0	7.7
7.	Mauritania	3.0	7.8
8.	Libya	3.3	8.5
9.	Canada	3.6	9.3
10.	Guyana	3.9	10.1

(1) Excluding Hong Kong, pop. 6,898,686, and Macao, population 449,198. (2) Note: Land area of a country does not include inland water. Rankings by total area, including inland water, may differ from these. For total area figures, see the Nations chapter. (3) Density is calculated here according to land area.

Countries With Highest & Lowest Gross Domestic Product and Per Capita GDP[1]

Source: Central Intelligence Agency, *The World Factbook 2005*

HIGHEST

GDP, in millions		Per Capita GDP	
1. U.S.	$11,750,000	1. Luxembourg	$58,900
2. China[2]	7,262,000	2. United States	40,100
3. Japan	3,745,000	3. Norway	40,000
4. India	3,319,000	4. San Marino	34,600
5. Germany	2,362,000	5. Switzerland	33,800
6. UK	1,782,000	6. Denmark	32,200
7. France	1,737,000	7. Iceland	31,900
8. Italy	1,609,000	Ireland	31,900
9. Brazil	1,492,000	9. Canada	31,500
10. Russia	1,408,000	10. Austria	31,300
11. Canada	1,023,000	11. Australia	30,700
12. Mexico	1,006,000	12. Belgium	30,600
13. Spain	938,000	13. United Kingdom	29,600
14. South Korea	925,000	14. Netherlands	29,500
15. Indonesia	827,000	15. Japan	29,400
16. Australia	612,000	16. Finland	29,000
17. Taiwan	576,000	17. France	28,700
18. Thailand	525,000	Germany	28,700
19. Iran	517,000	19. Sweden	28,400
20. Turkey	509,000	20. Singapore	27,800

LOWEST

GDP, in millions		Per Capita GDP[7]	
1. Tuvalu	$12[3]	1. Timor-Leste	$363
2. Nauru	60[4]	2. Burundi	532
3. Kiribati	79[4]	3. Somalia	554
4. Marshall Islands	115[4]	4. Sierra Leone	582
5. Palau	174[4]	5. Malawi	597
6. Tonga	244[5]	6. Tanzania	657
7. São Tomé and Príncipe	214[3]	7. Congo, Rep	664
8. Micronesia	277[5]	8. Comoros	718[5]
9. St. Kitts & Nevis	339[5]	9. Congo, Dem	725
10. St. Vincent & Gren.	342[5]	10. Guinea-Bissau	727
11. Timor-Leste	370	11. Ethiopia	769
12. Dominica	384[6]	12. Afghanistan	795[5]
13. Grenada	440[5]	13. Yemen	811
14. Comoros	441[5]	14. Niger	823
15. Vanuatu	580[6]	15. Madagascar	832
16. Cape Verde	600[5]	16. Kiribati	839
17. Djibouti	619[5]	17. Zambia	853
18. Seychelles	626[5]	18. Eritrea	912
19. Antigua & Barbuda	750[5]	19. Mali	989
20. Solomon Islands	800[5]	20. Liberia	1,034

(1) All figures are for 2004, unless otherwise indicated. Data may differ from estimates by the U.S. Bureau of Economic Analysis. International GDP estimates derive from purchasing power parity calculations, which involve the use of intl. dollar price weights applied to quantities of goods and services produced in a given economy. Countries do not include some territories or former territories. (2) Does not include Hong Kong, which had a GDP of $234.5 million and a per capita GDP of $34,200 in 2004, or Macao, which had a GDP of $9.1 billion and a per capita GDP of $19,400 in 2003. (3) 2000 est. (4) 2001 est. (5) 2002 est. (6) 2003 est. (7) Per capita GDP calculated using U.S. census population figures for the year each GDP was available.

Gold Reserves of Central Banks and Governments

Source: International Financial Statistics, IMF; million fine troy ounces

Year end	All countries[1]	United States	Belgium	Canada	France	Germany[2]	Italy	Japan	Nether-lands	Switzer-land	United Kingdom
1975	1,018.71	274.71	42.17	21.95	100.93	117.61	82.48	21.11	54.33	83.20	21.03
1980	952.99	264.32	34.18	20.98	81.85	95.18	66.67	24.23	43.94	83.28	18.84
1985	949.39	262.65	34.18	20.11	81.85	95.18	66.67	24.33	43.94	83.28	19.03
1990	939.01	261.91	30.23	14.76	81.85	95.18	66.67	24.23	43.94	83.28	18.94
1995	908.79	261.70	20.54	3.41	81.85	95.18	66.67	24.23	34.77	83.28	18.43
1996	906.10	261.66	15.32	3.09	81.85	95.18	66.67	24.23	34.77	83.28	18.43
1997	890.57	261.64	15.32	3.09	81.89	95.18	66.67	24.23	27.07	83.28	18.42
1998	966.15	261.61	9.52	2.49	102.37	118.98	83.36	24.23	33.83	83.28	23.00
1999	967.07	261.67	8.30	1.81	97.25	111.52	78.83	24.23	31.57	83.28	20.55
2000	952.09	261.61	8.30	1.18	97.25	111.52	78.83	24.55	29.32	77.79	15.67
2001	942.76	262.00	8.30	1.05	97.25	111.13	78.83	24.60	28.44	70.68	11.42
2002	930.55	262.00	8.29	0.60	97.25	110.79	78.83	24.60	27.38	61.62	10.09
2003	913.10	261.55	8.29	0.11	97.25	110.58	78.83	24.60	25.00	52.51	10.07
2004	900.22	261.59	8.29	0.11	95.98	110.38	78.83	24.60	25.00	43.54	10.04

(1) Covers IMF members with reported gold holdings. For countries not listed above, see International Monetary Fund's *International Financial Statistics Report.* (2) West Germany prior to 1991.

Consumer Price Changes in Selected Countries, 1975-2004

Source: International Monetary Fund

(annual averages)

COUNTRY	1975-1980	1980-1985	1992-1993	1993-1994	1994-1995	1995-1996	1996-1997	1997-1998	1998-1999	1999-2000	2000-2001	2001-2002	2002-2003	2003-2004
Canada	8.7	7.4	1.8	0.2	2.2	1.6	1.6	1.0	1.7	2.7	2.5	2.2	2.8	1.83
France	10.5	9.6	2.1	1.7	1.8	2.0	1.2	0.7	0.5	1.7	1.6	1.9	2.1	2.13
Germany	4.1	3.9	4.1	3.0	1.8	1.5	1.8	1.0	0.6	1.5	2.0	1.4	1.0	1.67
Italy	16.3	13.7	4.5	4.0	5.2	4.0	2.0	2.0	1.7	2.5	2.8	2.5	2.7	2.21
Japan	6.5	2.7	1.3	0.7	–0.1	0.1	1.7	0.6	–0.3	–0.7	–0.7	–0.9	–0.3	–0.1
Spain	18.6	12.2	4.6	4.7	4.7	3.6	2.0	1.8	2.3	3.4	3.6	3.1	3.0	3.03
Sweden	10.5	9.0	4.6	2.2	2.5	0.5	0.5	–0.1	0.5	0.9	2.4	2.2	1.9	.38
Switzerland	2.3	4.3	3.3	0.8	1.8	0.8	0.5	0.1	0.7	1.5	1.0	0.6	0.6	0.82
United Kingdom	14.4	7.2	1.6	2.5	3.4	2.4	3.1	3.4	1.6	2.9	1.8	1.6	2.9	2.96
United States	8.9	5.5	3.0	2.6	2.8	3.0	2.3	1.6	2.2	3.4	2.8	1.6	2.3	2.68

Hourly Compensation Costs[1], by Selected Country, 1975-2003

Source: Bureau of Labor Statistics, U.S. Dept. of Labor

(in U.S. dollars, compensation for production workers in manufacturing)

Country/Territory	1975	1985	1995	2002	2003
Australia	5.62	8.21	15.42	15.5	20.05
Austria	4.5	7.57	25.26	20.69	25.38
Belgium	6.39	8.94	27.53	22.74	27.73
Brazil	—	—	—	2.53	2.67
Denmark	6.24	8.1	25.43	25.62	32.18
Finland	4.63	8.2	24.31	21.78	27.17
France	4.5	7.48	19.26	17.12	21.13
Germany[2]	—	—	30.08	24.34	29.91
Greece	1.69	3.65	8.94	—	—
Hong Kong SA[3]	0.75	1.73	4.8	5.66	5.54
Ireland	3.06	6	13.77	15.31	19.14
Israel	2.03	3.66	9.5	11.01	11.73
Italy	4.64	7.56	15.91	14.97	18.35
Japan	2.97	6.27	23.55	18.49	20.09
South Korea	0.32	1.23	7.26	9	10.28
Luxembourg	6.22	7.48	23.36	18.71	23.11
Mexico	1.47	1.59	1.46	2.6	2.48
New Zealand	3.1	4.3	9.78	8.63	11.13
Norway	6.9	10.47	24.84	27.29	31.55
Portugal	1.52	1.46	5.09	5.07	6.23
Singapore	0.84	2.45	7.23	6.9	7.41
Spain	2.52	4.64	12.7	11.93	14.96
Sri Lanka	0.28	0.28	0.48	0.49	—
Sweden	7.14	9.61	21.46	20.23	25.18
Switzerland	6.03	9.55	28.99	23.84	27.87
Taiwan	0.38	1.5	5.88	5.73	5.84
United Kingdom	3.39	6.23	13.79	17.89	20.37
United States	6.16	12.71	17.02	21.11	21.97

— Data not available. (1) Compensation includes all direct pay (including bonuses, etc.), paid benefits, and for some countries, labor taxes. (2) 1975 and 1985 data are for area covered by the former West Germany. 1995 and 2002 are unified Germany. (3) Part of China since 1997.

Unemployment Rates, by Selected Country, 1970-2004[1]

Source: Bureau of Labor Statistics, U.S. Dept. of Labor; civilian labor force, seasonally adjusted

Year	U.S.	Australia	Canada	France	Germany[2]	Italy	Japan	Sweden	UK
1970	4.9	1.6	5.7	2.5	0.5	3.2	1.2	1.5	3.1
1975	8.5	4.9	6.9	4.2	3.4	3.4	1.9	1.6	4.5
1980	7.1	6.1	7.3	6.5	2.8	4.4	2.0	2.0	6.9
1981	7.6	5.8	7.3	7.6	4.0	4.9	2.2	2.5	9.7
1982	9.7	7.2	10.7	8.3	5.6	5.4	2.4	3.1	10.8
1983	9.6	10.0	11.6	8.6	6.9	5.9	2.7	3.5	11.5
1984	7.5	9.0	10.9	10.0	7.1	5.9	2.8	3.1	11.8
1985	7.2	8.3	10.2	10.5	7.2	6.0	2.7	2.8	11.4
1986	7.0	7.9	9.3	10.6	6.6	7.5	2.8	2.6	11.4
1987	6.2	7.9	8.4	10.8	6.3	7.9	2.9	2.2	10.5
1988	5.5	7.0	7.4	10.3	6.3	7.9	2.5	1.9	8.6
1989	5.3	6.0	7.1	9.6	5.7	7.8	2.3	1.6	7.3
1990	5.6	6.7	7.7	8.6	5.0	7.0	2.1	1.8	7.1
1991	6.8	9.3	9.8	9.1	5.6	6.9	2.1	3.1	8.9
1992	7.5	10.5	10.7	10.0	6.7	7.3	2.2	5.6	10.0
1993	6.9	10.6	10.8	11.3	8.0	9.8	2.5	9.4	10.4
1994	6.1	9.4	9.6	11.9	8.5	10.7	2.9	9.6	8.7
1995	5.6	8.2	8.7	11.3	8.2	11.3	3.2	9.1	8.7
1996	5.4	8.2	8.9	11.8	9.0	11.3	3.4	9.9	8.1
1997	4.9	8.3	8.4	11.7	9.9	11.4	3.4	10.1	7.0
1998	4.5	7.7	7.7	11.2	9.3	11.5	4.1	8.4	6.3
1999	4.2	6.9	7.0	10.5	8.5	11.0	4.7	7.1	6.0
2000	4.0	6.3	6.1	9.1	7.8	10.2	4.8	5.8	5.5
2001	4.7	6.8	6.5	8.4	7.9	9.2	5.1	5.0	5.1
2002	5.8	6.4	7.0	9.0	8.7	8.7	5.4	5.1	5.2
2003	6.0	6.1	6.9	9.6	9.7	8.5	5.3	5.8	5.0
2004	5.5	5.5	6.4	9.8	9.8	8.1	4.8	6.6	4.8

NOTE: For the sake of comparisons, U.S. unemployment rate concepts were applied to unemployment data for other countries.
(1) As a result of revisions in survey methodology, there are breaks in the data series for the U.S. (1994, 1997-2000), France (1992), Germany (1983, 1991), Italy (1986, 1991, 1993), Sweden (1987), and Australia (1986, 2001); data prior to a survey change are not fully comparable to data after a survey change. (2) For former West Germany only, through 1990; from 1991 on figures are for unified Germany and not adjusted by the Bureau of Labor Statistics.

Tax Burden in Selected Countries[1]

Source: Organization for Economic Cooperation and Development, 2004

Country[2]	Income tax	Social Security	Total payment[3]	Country[2]	Income tax	Social Security	Total payment[3]	Country[2]	Income tax	Social Security	Total payment[3]
Denmark	31%	11%	41%	Italy	19%	9%	28%	New Zealand	21%	0%	21%
Belgium	27	14	41	France	13	14	27	Switzerland	10	11	21
Germany	20	21	41	Iceland	26	0	26	Slovakia	8	13	21
Netherlands	9	26	34	Hungary	12	14	26	Spain	12	6	19
Poland	6	25	32	Canada	18	7	25	Portugal	6	11	17
Sweden	24	7	31	Australia	24	0	24	Japan	6	12	17
Finland	24	6	30	**U.S.**	**17**	**8**	**24**	Greece	1	16	17
Turkey	15	15	30	U.K.	16	9	24	Ireland	11	5	16
Norway	21	8	29	Czech Rep.	11	13	24	Korea	2	7	9
Austria	11	18	29	Luxembourg	9	14	23	Mexico	3	2	5

(1) Does not include taxes not listed, such as sales tax or VAT. Rates shown apply to a single person with average earnings. (2) Ranked by total payment %. Ties ranked by income tax % where different. (3) Totals may not add due to rounding.

The World's Refugees, 2004

Source: *World Refugee Survey 2005,* U.S. Committee for Refugees, a nonprofit corp.

These estimates are conservative and have been rounded. Totals include individuals granted asylum and those who had pending asylum claims as of year-end 2004. Figures generally do not include those who have achieved permanent resettlement. Region totals include nations not listed.

(as of Dec. 31, 2004; only countries estimated to host 50,000 or more refugees are listed)

Place of asylum	Origin of Most Refugees	Number
AFRICA		**3,295,900**
Algeria	Morocco, Palestinians	102,000
Angola	Dem. Rep. of Congo	14,900
Burundi	Dem. Rep. of Congo	60,700
Cameroon	Chad, Nigeria, Dem. Rep. of Congo	65,000
Chad	Sudan, Central African Republic	260,000
Dem. Rep. of the Congo	Angola, Sudan, Burundi, Uganda	200,700
Rep. of the Congo	Dem. Rep. of Congo, Rwanda	71,700
Côte d'Ivoire	Liberia	74,200
Egypt	Palestinians, Sudan, Somalia	85,800
Ethiopia	Sudan, Somalia, Eritrea	116,000
Guinea	Liberia, Sierra Leone, Côte d'Ivoire	145,200
Kenya	Somalia, Sudan, Ethiopia	269,300
Sierra Leone	Liberia	65,700
South Africa	Dem. Rep. of the Congo, Somalia, Angola	149,900
Sudan	Eritrea, Ethiopia, Uganda	225,900
Tanzania	Burundi, Dem. Rep. of the Congo, Somalia	602,300
Uganda	Sudan, Rwanda, Dem. Rep. of the Congo	252,300
Zambia	Angola, Dem. Rep. of the Congo, Rwanda	174,000
EUROPE		**612,100**
Germany	Iraq, Turkey, Iran, Serbia and Montenegro (Kosovo), Afghanistan	83,300
Russia	Afghanistan, Georgia	150,000
Serbia and Montenegro	Croatia, Bosnia and Herzegovina	76,500
AMERICAS AND THE CARIBBEAN		**543,800**
Canada	Colombia, Mexico, Pakistan	54,800
United States	Cuba, Colombia, Haiti, China, Somalia	232,800
Venezuela	Colombia	180,100
EAST ASIA AND THE PACIFIC		**1,033,000**
China	Vietnam, North Korea	401,500
Malaysia	Philippines, Myanmar, Indonesia	101,200
Thailand	Myanmar, Laos	460,800
SOUTH AND CENTRAL ASIA		**1,724,800**
Bangladesh	Myanmar	150,000
India	China, Nepal, Sri Lanka, Myanmar, Afghanistan, Bhutan	393,300
Nepal	Bhutan, China	130,600
Pakistan	Afghanistan	968,800
MIDDLE EAST		**4,288,500**
Gaza Strip	Palestinians	952,300
Iran	Afghanistan, Iraq	1,046,100
Iraq	Palestinians, Turkey, Iran	96,600
Jordan	Palestinians, Iraq	168,300
Kuwait	Palestinians	51,800
Lebanon	Palestinians	265,800
Saudi Arabia	Palestinians	243,700
Syria	Palestinians, Iraq	701,700*
West Bank	Palestinians	682,700
Yemen	Somalia, Ethiopia	74,200
TOTAL		**11,498,100**

* Estimates vary widely in number reported. **Approximate number of refugees based on cases reported.

Principal Sources of Refugees, 2004

Sources: *World Refugee Survey 2005,* U.S. Committee for Refugees (as of Dec. 31, 2004)

Former Palestine	2,985,500*	Somalia	324,900	Nepal	101,400
Afghanistan	2,088,200*	Vietnam	310,300	Sri Lanka	88,200
Sudan	703,000	Colombia	263,600	Philippines	66,200
Myanmar	691,800*	Angola	223,300	Rwanda	59,300
Burundi	482,200	Eritrea	204,200	Tajikistan	56,200
Dem. Rep. of the Congo	469,100	China	158,100	Chad	54,200
Iraq	366,100*	Bhutan	120,500	Ethiopia	52,100
Liberia	328,300*	North Korea	101,900*		

*Estimates from different sources may vary significantly.

Estimated HIV Infection and Reported AIDS Cases, Year-end 2004

Source: UNAIDS, Joint United Nations Program on HIV/AIDS

The spread of AIDS (acquired immune deficiency syndrome) has had a major impact on life expectancies in sub-Saharan Africa. Life expectancy at birth has dropped below 40 years in nine African countries—Botswana, Central African Republic, Lesotho, Malawi, Mozambique, Rwanda, Swaziland, Zambia, and Zimbabwe, primarily as a result of AIDS.

At year-end 2004, the number of people living with HIV/AIDS worldwide continued to climb, with about 39.4 million people infected with the virus, up from 37.8 million at year-end 2003. The steepest increases have been in East Asia, Eastern Europe, and Central Asia. In those areas, almost nine times as many people were infected at year-end 2004 as were in 1994. In East Asia, the number of people living with HIV rose by almost 50% between 2002 and 2004, due to China's growing epidemic. Sub-Saharan Africa was still by far the worst-affected region, with about 64% of all people living with HIV.

The Caribbean had an HIV prevalence (the percentage of adults who have the disease) of 2.2%—the second-highest of all regions, after sub-Saharan Africa (7.4%). In the Caribbean, AIDS was the leading cause of death among adults aged 15-44.

Globally, just under half of all people living with HIV are female. However, in many regions the percentage of the HIV infected population that is female is expected to grow, especially in Eastern Europe, Asia, and Africa. In Russia, for example, the proportion of women among people diagnosed with HIV increased to 38% in 2003, compared with 24% in 2001.

In 2004, there were a total of 4.9 million new AIDS cases. Children under age 15 accounted for 2.2 million of those living with HIV. About 3.1 million people living with AIDS died in 2004.

Global funding has almost tripled since 2001. In 2001, about $2.1 bil was given to fund AIDS response (including all spending by affected people, national spending, and international and nonprofit spending), which increased to $6.1 bil in 2004.

Current, New HIV/AIDS Cases and Deaths by Region, Year-end 2004

Region	Current cases[1]	Percent[2]	New Cases 2004	Est. Deaths 2004
Sub-Saharan Africa	25,400,000	64.5	3,100,000	2,300,000
North Africa and Middle East	540,000	1.4	92,000	28,000
South and South-East Asia	7,100,000	18.0	890,000	490,000
East Asia	1,100,000	2.8	290,000	51,000
Oceania	35,000	0.1	5,000	700
Latin America	1,700,000	4.3	240,000	95,000
Caribbean	440,000	1.1	53,000	36,000
Eastern Europe/Central Asia	1,400,000	3.6	210,000	60,000
Western/Central Europe	610,000	1.5	21,000	6,500
North America	1,000,000	2.5	44,000	16,000
WORLD[3]	**39,400,000**	**100.0**	**4,900,000**	**3,100,000**

(1) Adults and children living with HIV/AIDS. (2) Percentage of total number of people worldwide living with HIV. (3) Details do not add to total because of rounding. (—) Dash means less than 1%.

Top 10 Recipients of U.S. Development Aid, 2002-2003

Source: Organization for Economic Cooperation and Development

Country	Millions of U.S. $ (avg. 2002-03)	Country	Millions of U.S. $ (avg. 2002-03)	Country	Millions of U.S. $ (avg. 2002-03)
1. Egypt	831	5. Israel	666	8. Colombia	513
2. Russia	808	6. Pakistan	656	9. Afghanistan	427
3. Iraq	775	7. Jordan	622	10. Ethiopia	374
4. Congo, Dem Rep.	749				

Major Foreign Development Aid Donors, 2003-2004

Source: Organization for Economic Cooperation and Development; ranked by percent of GNI (Gross National Income) in 2004.

In 2004, the U.S. gave the highest total amount of development aid but ranked 21st by percent of GNI.

	ODA[1], as % of GNI		ODA[1] in U.S. dollars (millions)	
Country	2004	2003	2004	2003
1. Norway	0.87	0.92	2,200	2,042
2. Luxembourg	0.85	0.81	241	194
3. Denmark	0.84	0.84	2,025	1,748
4. Sweden	0.77	0.79	2,704	2,400
5. Netherlands	0.74	0.80	4,235	3,981
6. Portugal	0.63	0.22	1,028	320
7. France	0.42	0.41	8,475	7,253
8. Belgium	0.41	0.60	1,452	1,853
9. Ireland	0.39	0.39	586	504
10. Switzerland	0.37	0.39	1,379	1,299
11. United Kingdom	0.36	0.34	7,836	6,282
12. Finland	0.35	0.35	655	558
13. Germany	0.28	0.28	7,497	6,784
14. Canada	0.26	0.24	2,537	2,031
Spain	0.26	0.23	2,547	1,961
16. Australia	0.25	0.25	1,465	1,219
17. Austria	0.24	0.20	691	505
18. New Zealand	0.23	0.23	210	165
Greece	0.23	0.21	464	362
20. Japan	0.19	0.20	8,859	8,880
21. United States	0.16	0.15	18,999	16,320
22. Italy	0.15	0.17	2,484	2,433
23. Poland	0.05	0.01	124	27
24. G7 Nations	0.22	0.21	56,686	49,982

(1) ODA = official development assistance.

IT'S A FACT: People who are displaced within their own country due to persecution or armed conflict are not considered refugees. Instead, they are Internally Displaced Persons (IDPs). There is no legal definition for an IDP, and IDPs are not protected by international law. According to the *World Refugee Survey 2005*, Sudan in 2004 had the most IDPs of any country—between 5.3 and 6.7 million. Colombia had 2.9 million, and Dem. Rep. of Congo had 2.3 million.

Nuclear Powers of the World

As of Sept. 2005, 7 countries were acknowledged nuclear powers: **Britain**, **France**, **China**, **India**, **Pakistan**, **Russia**, and the **United States**. In addition, **Israel** was thought to have a nuclear arsenal of 98 to 172 warheads, and **Iran** and **North Korea** were suspected of developing nuclear weapons, despite strong international pressure for them to desist. More than 40 nations have the knowledge or technology needed to produce nuclear weapons. All have signed the Nuclear Non-Proliferation Treaty (NPT) except for Israel, India, and Pakistan. North Korea withdrew in Jan. 2003. In a draft accord reached at 6-nation talks Sept. 19, 2005, N. Korea agreed to scrap its nuclear weapons program in exchange for aid. Left unresolved was Pyongyang's continuing demand for international donors to provide light-water nuclear reactors for "peaceful uses."

Several countries have abandoned their nuclear ambitions. **South Africa** announced in 1993 that it had built 7 fission weapons, but had dismantled all of them. In the 1980s **Argentina** and **Brazil** had active nuclear weapons programs, but they abandoned them by mutual treaty and signed the NPT. After the Soviet Union dissolved in 1993, **Belarus**, **Kazakhstan**, and **Ukraine** joined the NPT and allowed Russia to remove its nuclear weapons located there.

Estimate Numbers of Nuclear Weapons by Country, 1945-2002

Source: Natural Resources Defense Council; Carnegie Endowment for Int. Peace

End Year	United States	U.S.S.R. Russia	United Kingdom	France	China[3]	India	Pakistan
1945	6	—	—	—	—	—	—
1950	369	5	—	—	—	—	—
1960	20,434	1,605	30	—	—	—	—
1970	26,119	11,643	280	36	75	—	—
1980	23,764	30,062	350	250	280	—	—
1990	21,211	33,417	300	505	430	—	—
1995	10,953	14,978	300	500	400	—	—
2000	10,615	10,201	185	450	400	—	—
2002	10,640[1]	8,600[2]	200	350	400	50-90[4]	50[4]

(1) Number excludes weapons marked for dismantlement. (2) Excludes weapons marked for dismantlement or in reserve status; in 2002 there were an estimated 18,000 intact warheads. (3) Based on estimates of number of tactical warheads that may be up to 50% inaccurate. (4) Estimated number of weapons the nation has enough weapons-grade material to produce; number of assembled weapons is unknown.

Major International Organizations

African Union (AU), inaugurated July 9, 2002, in Durban, South Africa, following disbanding of the Organization of African Unity, and consisting of the same 53 members; i.e., all countries of Africa except Morocco, including the territory of Western Sahara. The new organization was intended to focus achieving greater socio-economic integration, peace, and unity among its member states. The founders provided for a peer review committee to oversee member states' adherence to standards of good government, respect for human rights, and financial transparency. The AU's founding document authorized the organization to intervene to stop genocide, war crimes, or human rights abuses within individual member nations. **Headquarters:** Ethiopia. **Website:** www.africa-union.org

Asia-Pacific Economic Cooperation (APEC), founded Nov. 1989 as a forum to further cooperation on trade and investment between nations of the region and the rest of the world. Members in 2005 were Australia, Brunei, Canada, Chile, China, Hong Kong, Indonesia, Japan, Malaysia, Mexico, New Zealand, Papua New Guinea, Peru, Philippines, Russia, Singapore, South Korea, Taiwan, Thailand, U.S., and Vietnam. **Headquarters:** Singapore. **Website:** www.apecsec.org.sg

Association of Southeast Asian Nations (ASEAN), formed Aug. 8, 1967, to promote economic, social, and cultural cooperation and development among states of the Southeast Asian region. Members in 2005 were Brunei, Cambodia, Indonesia, Laos, Malaysia, Myanmar, Philippines, Singapore, Thailand, and Vietnam. **Headquarters:** Jakarta. **Website:** www.aseansec.org

Caribbean Community and Common Market (CARICOM), established Aug. 1, 1973. Its aim is to increase cooperation in economics, health, education, culture, science and technology, and tax administration, as well as the coordination of foreign policy. Members in 2005 were Antigua and Barbuda, Bahamas (Community only), Barbados, Belize, Dominica, Grenada, Guyana, Haiti, Jamaica, Montserrat, Saint Kitts and Nevis, Saint Lucia, Saint Vincent and the Grenadines, Suriname, and Trinidad and Tobago. Associate members in 2005 were Anguilla, Bermuda, Virgin Islands, Cayman Islands, Turks and Caicos. **Headquarters:** Georgetown, Guyana. **Website:** www.caricom.org

The Commonwealth, originally called the British Commonwealth of Nations, then the Commonwealth of Nations; an association of nations and dependencies that were once parts of the former British Empire. The British monarch is the symbolic head of the Commonwealth.

There are 53 independent nations in the Commonwealth. As of 2005, regular members included the United Kingdom and 15 other nations recognizing the British monarch, represented by a governor-general, as their head of state: Antigua and Barbuda, Australia, Bahamas, Barbados, Belize, Canada, Grenada, Jamaica, New Zealand, Papua New Guinea, Saint Kitts and Nevis, Saint Lucia, Saint Vincent and the Grenadines, the Solomon Islands, and Tuvalu. Also members in good standing were 37 countries with their own heads of state: Bangladesh, Botswana, Brunei, Cameroon, Cyprus, Dominica, Fiji, The Gambia, Ghana, Guyana, India, Kenya, Kiribati, Lesotho, Malawi, Malaysia, Maldives, Malta, Mauritius, Mozambique (the only member never part of the British Empire), Namibia, Nauru, Nigeria, Pakistan, Samoa, Seychelles, Sierra Leone, Singapore, South Africa, Sri Lanka, Swaziland, Tanzania, Tonga, Trinidad and Tobago, Uganda, Vanuatu, and Zambia.

Pakistan was suspended from the councils of the Commonwealth in Oct. 1999, following a military coup, but regained its member status March 22, 2004. Zimbabwe was suspended in Mar. 2002, following election and land redistribution controversies; Zimbabwe withdrew from the Commonwealth, Dec. 7, 2003. The Commonwealth facilitates consultation among members through meetings of ministers and through a permanent Secretariat. **Headquarters:** London. **Website:** www.thecommonwealth.org

Commonwealth of Independent States (CIS), an alliance established in Dec. 1991, made up of former Soviet constituent republics. Members in 2005 were: Armenia, Azerbaijan, Belarus, Georgia, Kazakhstan, Kyrgyzstan, Moldova, Russia, Tajikistan, Turkmenistan, Ukraine, and Uzbekistan. Policy is set through coordinating bodies such as a Council of Heads of State and Council of Heads of Government. **Headquarters:** Minsk, Belarus. **Website:** www.cis.minsk.by

European Free Trade Association (EFTA), created May 3, 1960, to promote expansion of free trade. By Dec. 31, 1966, tariffs and quotas between member nations had been eliminated. Members entered into free trade agreements with the EU in 1972 and 1973. In 1992, EFTA and EU agreed to create a single market—with free flow of goods, services, capital, and labor—among nations of the 2 organizations. Members in 2005 were Iceland, Liechtenstein, Norway, and Switzerland. Many former EFTA members are now EU members. **Headquarters:** Geneva. **Website:** www.efta.int

European Union (EU)—known as the European Community (EC) until 1994; the name covers 3 organizations with common membership: the European Economic Community (Common Market), European Coal and Steel Community, and European Atomic Energy Community (Euratom). A merger of the 3 communities' executives went into effect July 1, 1967. As of Sept. 2005, there were 25 EU members. These included 12 original members (Belgium, Denmark, France, Germany, Greece, Ireland, Italy, Luxembourg, Netherlands, Portugal, Spain, and UK), 3 states that entered Jan. 1, 1995 (Austria, Finland, and Sweden), and 10 members that joined on May 1, 2004 (Cyprus, Czech Republic, Estonia, Hungary, Latvia, Lithuania, Malta, Poland, Slovakia, and Slovenia.). Some 70 nations in Africa, the Caribbean, and the Pacific are affiliated under the Lomé Convention. **Headquarters:** Brussels, Belgium. **Website:** europa.eu.int

The EU aims to integrate the economies, coordinate social developments, and bring about political union of the member states. The Council of the Union, European Commission, European Parliament, and European Courts of Justice and of Auditors comprise the permanent structure. Effective Dec. 31, 1992, there are no restrictions on the movement of goods, services, capital, workers, and tourists within the EU. There are also common agricultural, fisheries, and nuclear research policies.

Leaders of member nations (12 at the time), meeting Dec. 9-11, 1991, in Maastricht, the Netherlands, committed the organization to launching a common currency (the euro) by 1999; sought to establish common foreign policies; laid the groundwork for a common defense policy; gave the organization a leading role in social policy (Britain was not included in this plan); pledged increased aid for poorer member nations; and slightly increased the powers of the 567-member European Parliament. The treaties went into effect Nov. 1, 1993, following ratification by all 12 members.

In June 1998 the European Central Bank was established. In Jan. 1999, 11 of the then-15 EU countries began using the euro for some purposes: Austria, Belgium, Finland, France, Germany, Ireland, Italy, Luxembourg, Netherlands, Portugal, and Spain. By Feb. 2002, national currencies in these 11 countries and Greece were removed from circulation and replaced with the euro as the only currency of legal tender. EU peacekeeping forces replaced NATO troops in Macedonia, Mar. 31, 2003, the first such mission for the organization.

In July 2005, Luxembourg became the 13th EU member to ratify the EU constitution, but the constitution was rejected in May and June by voters in France and the Netherlands and some other EU nations were deferring action on ratifying it. In Sept., Turkey began negotiations to join the EU, despite concerns from some member nations.

Group of Eight (G-8), established Sept. 22, 1985; organization of 7 major industrial democracies (Canada, France, Germany, Italy, Japan, UK, and U.S.) and (later) Russia, meeting periodically to discuss economic and other issues. At its annual economic summit in May 1998, the name was changed to G-8 from G-7. The 7 were still free to meet without Russia on some issues, especially those relating to global finance. The annual G-8 summit was hosted in the U.S. at Sea Island, GA, June 8-10, 2004. The 2005 summit was held July 6-8 in Perthshire, Scotland. It was interrupted by the July 7 bombings in London, but finished as scheduled. The 2006 summit was scheduled to be held in St. Petersburg, Russia.

International Criminal Police Organization (Interpol), created June 13, 1956, to promote mutual assistance among all police authorities within the limits of the law existing in the different countries. There were 182 members (independent nations), plus 14 sub-bureaus (dependencies) in 2005. **Website:** www.interpol.com

League of Arab States (Arab League), created Mar. 22, 1945. The League promotes economic, social, political, and military cooperation, mediates disputes, and represents Arab states in certain international negotiations. Members in 2005 were Algeria, Bahrain, Comoros, Djibouti, Egypt, Iraq, Jordan, Kuwait, Lebanon, Mauritania, Morocco, Oman, Palestine (considered an independent state by the League), Qatar, Saudi Arabia, Somalia, Sudan, Syria, Tunisia, United Arab Emirates, and Yemen. **Headquarters:** Cairo. **Website:** www.arableagueonline.org

North Atlantic Treaty Organization (NATO), created by treaty (signed Apr. 4, 1949; in effect Aug. 24, 1949). Members in 2005 included Belgium, Bulgaria, Canada, Czech Republic, Denmark, Estonia, France, Germany, Greece, Hungary, Iceland, Italy, Latvia, Lithuania, Luxembourg, Netherlands, Norway, Poland, Portugal, Romania, Slovakia, Slovenia, Spain, Turkey, U.K, and U.S. Of these, states—Bulgaria, Estonia, Latvia, Lithuania, Romania, Slovakia, and Slovenia—joined the alliance in 2004. All are former Warsaw Pact nations from Eastern Europe. This marked the fifth time NATO increased its membership, and was the largest expansion at one time.

Members have agreed to settle disputes by peaceful means, to develop their capacity to resist armed attack, to regard an attack on one as an attack on all, and to take necessary action to repel an attack under Article 51 of the UN Charter. **Headquarters:** Brussels. **Website:** www.nato.int

The NATO structure consists of the North Atlantic Council (NAC), the Defense Planning Committee, the Military Committee (realigned in June 2003 and consisting of 2 commands: Allied Command Operations, and Allied Command Transformation), the Nuclear Planning Group, and the Canada-U.S. Regional Planning Group. France detached itself from the military command structure in 1966.

With the end of the cold war in the early 1990s, members put greater stress on political action and on creating a rapid deployment force to react to local crises. By the mid-1990s, 27 nations, including Russia and other former Soviet republics, had joined with NATO in the so-called Partnership for Peace (PfP; drafted Dec. 1993), which provided for limited joint military exercises, peace-keeping missions, and information exchange. NATO has proceeded gradually toward extending full membership to former Eastern bloc nations. On Mar. 12, 1999, 3 former Warsaw Pact members, Hungary, Poland, and the Czech Republic, formally became members. NATO and Russia signed a cooperation pact May 28, 2002, forming NATO-Russia Council, and NATO invited 7 former eastern-bloc nations to join the alliance, Nov. 21.

In Dec. 1995, a NATO-led multinational force (SFOR) was deployed to help keep the peace in Bosnia and Herzegovina; in 1999, another force (KFOR) was deployed in Kosovo.

Following the terrorist attacks on the U.S., the NATO Council agreed, Sept. 12, 2001, to invoke for the first time Article 5 of the treaty, which stipulates mutual defense of alliance members. NATO assumed control of the International Security Assistance Force in Afghanistan (ISAF), Aug. 2003, marking the first time NATO led a mission outside Europe. As of Sept. 2005, the ISAF numbered about 8,000.

Organization of African Unity (OAU), formed May 25, 1963, by 32 African countries. Disbanded July, 2002, and reformed as the African Union (AU). **Website:** www.africa–union.org

Organization of American States (OAS), formed in Bogotá, Colombia, Apr. 30, 1948. It has a Permanent Council, Inter-American Council for Integral Development, Juridical Committee, and Commission on Human Rights. The Permanent Council can call meetings of foreign ministers to deal with urgent security matters. A General Assembly meets annually.

Members in 2005 were Antigua and Barbuda, Argentina, Bahamas, Barbados, Belize, Bolivia, Brazil, Canada, Chile, Colombia, Costa Rica, Cuba, Dominica, Dominican Republic, Ecuador, El Salvador, Grenada, Guatemala, Guyana, Haiti, Honduras, Jamaica, Mexico, Nicaragua, Panama, Paraguay, Peru, Saint Kitts and Nevis, Saint Lucia, Saint Vincent and the Grenadines, Suriname, Trinidad and Tobago, U.S., Uruguay, and Venezuela. In 1962, the OAS suspended Cuba from participation in activities but not from membership. **Headquarters:** Washington, DC. **Website:** www.oas.org

Organization for Economic Cooperation and Development (OECD), established Dec. 14, 1960, to promote the economic and social welfare of all its member countries and to stimulate efforts on behalf of developing nations. The OECD also collects and disseminates economic and environmental information. Members in 2005 were Australia, Austria, Belgium, Canada, Czech Republic, Denmark, Finland, France, Germany, Greece, Hungary,

Iceland, Ireland, Italy, Japan, Luxembourg, Mexico, Netherlands, New Zealand, Norway, Poland, Portugal, Slovakia, South Korea, Spain, Sweden, Switzerland, Turkey, United Kingdom, and the United States. **Headquarters:** Paris. **Website:** www.oecd.org

Organization of Petroleum Exporting Countries (OPEC), created Sept. 14, 1960. This group made up of most—but not all—major petroleum exporting nations, seeks to stabilize the oil market and set world oil prices by controlling production. Members in 2005 were Algeria, Indonesia, Iran, Iraq, Kuwait, Libya, Nigeria, Qatar, Saudi Arabia, United Arab Emirates, and Venezuela. **Headquarters:** Vienna. **Website:** www.opec.org

Organization for Security and Cooperation in Europe (OSCE), established in 1972 as the Conference on Security and Cooperation in Europe; name adopted Jan. 1, 1995. The group, formed by NATO and Warsaw Pact members, seeks improved East-West relations through a commitment to nonaggression and human rights as well as cooperation in economics, science and technology, cultural exchange, and environmental protection. There were 55 member states in 2005. **Headquarters:** Vienna. **Website:** www.osce.org

United Nations

The 60th regular session of United Nations General Assembly opened Sept. 13, 2005, attended by world leaders and other delegates from 191 nations.

UN headquarters is in New York, NY, between First Ave. and Roosevelt Drive and E. 42d St. and E. 48th St.

The 6 main organs of the UN are the General Assembly, Security Council, Economic and Social Council, Trusteeship Council, International Court of Justice, and Secretariat. The UN family is much larger, encompassing 15 agencies and several programs and bodies.

The UN Dept. of Public Information maintains a news service, at www.un.org/news. It also publishes the *UN Chronicle*, available at www.un.org/pubs/chronicle. The UN has a post office originating its own stamps.

Proposals to establish an organization of nations for maintenance of world peace led to convening of the United Nations Conference on International Organization at San Francisco, Apr. 25-June 26, 1945, where the UN charter was drawn up. It was signed June 26 by 50 nations, and by Poland, one of the original 51 members, on Oct. 15, 1945. It came into effect Oct. 24, 1945, upon ratification by the permanent members of the Security Council and a majority of other signatories.

Purposes: To maintain international peace and security; to develop friendly relations among nations; to achieve international cooperation in solving economic, social, cultural, and humanitarian problems and in promoting respect for human rights and basic freedoms; to be a center for harmonizing the actions of nations in attaining these common ends.

Visitors to the UN: Headquarters is open to the public every day except Thanksgiving, Christmas, New Year's holidays, President's Day, Eid al-Adha (Jan. 10, 2006), and Eid al Fitr (Oct 24, 2006). Guided tours are given about every half hour from 9:30 AM to 4:45 PM weekdays; 10 AM to 4:30 PM weekends. The UN is closed weekends in Jan. and Feb.

Groups of 12 or more should write to the Group Programmes Unit, Room GA-56, United Nations, New York, NY 10017, e-mail unitg@un.org, or telephone (212) 963-TOUR. Children under 5 not permitted on tours.

Organization of the United Nations

The United Nations consists of 6 principal organs, 15 agencies, and many programs and other bodies. The 6 principal organs are the General Assembly, the Security Council, the Secretariat, the Economic and Social Council, the Trusteeship Council, and the Intl. Court for Justice.

General Assembly. The General Assembly is composed of representatives of all the member nations. Each nation is entitled to one vote. The General Assembly meets in regular annual sessions and in special session when convoked at the request of the Security Council or a majority of UN members. On important questions a two-thirds majority of members present and voting is required; on other questions a simple majority is sufficient.

The General Assembly must approve the UN budget and apportion expenses among members. A member in arrears can lose its vote if the amount of arrears equals or exceeds the amount of the contributions due for the preceding 2 full years. **Website:** www.un.org/ga

Security Council. The Security Council consists of 15 members, 5 with permanent seats. The remaining 10 are elected for 2-year terms by the General Assembly. **Website:** www.un.org/docs/sc

Permanent members of the Council are: China, France, Russia, United Kingdom, and the United States. Nonpermanent members are (with terms expiring Dec. 31, 2005): Algeria, Benin, Brazil, Philippines, Romania; (with terms expiring Dec. 31, 2006): Argentina, Denmark, Greece, Japan, Tanzania.

The Security Council has the primary responsibility within the UN for maintaining international peace and security. The Council may investigate any dispute that threatens international peace and security.

Any member of the UN at UN headquarters may, if invited by the Council, participate in its discussions, and a nation not a member of the UN may appear if it is a party to a dispute. Decisions on procedural questions are made by an affirmative vote of 9 members. On all other matters the affirmative vote of 9 members must include the concurring votes of all permanent members (giving them veto power). A party to a dispute must refrain from voting.

The Security Council directs the various peacekeeping forces deployed throughout the world.

Secretariat. The Secretariat is an international staff of about 8,900 that carries out the day-to-day operations of the UN and is headed by the secretary general. The secretary general is the chief administrative officer of the UN, and is appointed by the General Assembly, on the recommendation of the Security Council, for a five-year, renewable term. The Secretary General reports to the General Assembly and may bring to the attention of the Security Council any matter that threatens international peace.

Economic and Social Council. The Economic and Social Council consists of 54 members elected by the General Assembly for 3-year terms. The council is responsible for carrying out UN functions with regard to international economic, social, cultural, educational, health, and related matters. It meets once a year. **Website:** www.un.org/esa

Trusteeship Council. The administration of trust territories was under UN supervision; however, all 11 Trust Territories have attained their right to self-determination. The work of the Council was suspended May 1994.

Budget. The General Assembly approved a total budget for the biennium 2004-05 of $3.16 billion.

International Court of Justice (World Court). The International Court of Justice is the principal judicial organ of the UN. All members are ipso facto parties to the statute of the Court. The Court has jurisdiction over cases the parties submit to it and matters especially provided for in the charter or in treaties. It gives advisory opinions and renders judgments. In disputes between nations, the Court's decisions are binding only between parties concerned and in respect to a particular dispute. If any party to a case fails to heed a judgment, the other party may have recourse to the Security Council.

The 15 judges are elected for 9-year terms by the General Assembly and the Security Council. Retiring judges are eligible for reelection. The Court remains permanently in session, except during vacations. All questions are decided by majority. The International Court of Justice sits in The Hague, Netherlands. **Website:** www.icj-cij.org

The text of the **UN Charter** may be obtained from the Public Inquiries Unit, Department of Public Information, United Nations, New York, NY 10017. (212) 963-4475. **Website:** www.un.org/aboutUN/charter/index.html

Roster of the United Nations

The 191 members of the United Nations, with the years in which they became members; as of Feb. 2005.

Member	Year
Afghanistan	1946
Albania	1955
Algeria	1962
Andorra	1993
Angola	1976
Antigua and Barbuda	1981
Argentina	1945
Armenia	1992
Australia	1945
Austria	1955
Azerbaijan	1992
Bahamas	1973
Bahrain	1971
Bangladesh	1974
Barbados	1966
Belarus	1945
Belgium	1945
Belize	1981
Benin	1960
Bhutan	1971
Bolivia	1945
Bosnia & Herzegovina	1992
Botswana	1966
Brazil	1945
Brunei	1984
Bulgaria	1955
Burkina Faso	1960
Burundi	1962
Cambodia	1955
Cameroon	1960
Canada	1945
Cape Verde	1975
Central African Rep.	1960
Chad	1960
Chile	1945
China[1]	1945
Colombia	1945
Comoros	1975
Congo, Democratic Rep. of the (Zaire)	1960
Congo, Republic of the	1960
Costa Rica	1945
Côte d'Ivoire	1960
Croatia	1992
Cuba	1945
Cyprus	1960
Czech Republic[2]	1993
Denmark	1945
Djibouti	1977
Dominica	1978
Dominican Republic	1945
Ecuador	1945
Egypt[3]	1945
El Salvador	1945
Equatorial Guinea	1968
Eritrea	1993
Estonia	1991
Ethiopia	1945
Fiji	1970
Finland	1955
France	1945
Gabon	1960
Gambia, The	1965
Georgia	1992
Germany	1973
Ghana	1957
Greece	1945
Grenada	1974
Guatemala	1945
Guinea	1958
Guinea-Bissau	1974
Guyana	1966
Haiti	1945
Honduras	1945
Hungary	1955
Iceland	1946
India	1945
Indonesia[4]	1950
Iran	1945
Iraq	1945
Ireland	1955
Israel	1949
Italy	1955
Jamaica	1962
Japan	1956
Jordan	1955
Kazakhstan	1992
Kenya	1963
Kiribati	1999
Korea, North	1991
Korea, South	1991
Kuwait	1963
Kyrgyzstan	1992
Laos	1955
Latvia	1991
Lebanon	1945
Lesotho	1966
Liberia	1945
Libya	1955
Liechtenstein	1990
Lithuania	1991
Luxembourg	1945
Macedonia[5]	1993
Madagascar	1960
Malawi	1964
Malaysia[6]	1957
Maldives	1965
Mali	1960
Malta	1964
Marshall Islands	1991
Mauritania	1961
Mauritius	1968
Mexico	1945
Micronesia	1991
Moldova	1992
Monaco	1993
Mongolia	1961
Morocco	1956
Mozambique	1975
Myanmar (Burma)	1948
Namibia	1990
Nauru	1999
Nepal	1955
Netherlands	1945
New Zealand	1945
Nicaragua	1945
Niger	1960
Nigeria	1960
Norway	1945
Oman	1971
Pakistan	1947
Palau	1994
Panama	1945
Papua New Guinea	1975
Paraguay	1945
Peru	1945
Philippines	1945
Poland	1945
Portugal	1955
Qatar	1971
Romania	1955
Russia[7]	1945
Rwanda	1962
Saint Kitts and Nevis	1983
Saint Lucia	1979
Saint Vincent and the Grenadines	1980
Samoa (formerly Western Samoa)	1976
San Marino	1992
São Tomé and Príncipe	1975
Saudi Arabia	1945
Senegal	1960
Serbia and Montenegro[8]	1945
Seychelles	1976
Sierra Leone	1961
Singapore[6]	1965
Slovakia[2]	1993
Slovenia	1992
Solomon Islands	1978
Somalia	1960
South Africa[9]	1945
Spain	1955
Sri Lanka	1955
Sudan	1956
Suriname	1975
Swaziland	1968
Sweden	1946
Switzerland	2002
Syria[3]	1945
Tajikistan	1992
Tanzania[10]	1961
Thailand	1946
Timor-Leste	2002
Togo	1960
Tonga	1999
Trinidad and Tobago	1962
Tunisia	1956
Turkey	1945
Turkmenistan	1992
Tuvalu	2000
Uganda	1962
Ukraine	1945
United Arab Emirates	1971
United Kingdom	1945
United States	1945
Uruguay	1945
Uzbekistan	1992
Vanuatu	1981
Venezuela	1945
Vietnam	1977
Yemen[11]	1947
Zambia	1964
Zimbabwe	1980

(1) The General Assembly voted in 1971 to expel the Chinese government on Taiwan and admit the Beijing government. (2) Czechoslovakia, which split into Czech Republic and Slovakia on Jan. 1, 1993, was a UN member from 1945 to 1992. (3) Egypt and Syria were original members. In 1958, the United Arab Republic was established by a union of Egypt and Syria and continued as one single member of the UN. In 1961, Syria resumed its separate membership. (4) Indonesia withdrew from the UN in 1965 and rejoined in 1966. (5) Admitted under the provisional name of The Former Yugoslav Republic of Macedonia. (6) Malaya joined the UN in 1957. In 1963, its name was changed to Malaysia following the accession of Singapore, Sabah, and Sarawak. Singapore became an independent UN member in 1965. (7) The USSR was an original member from 1945. After the USSR's dissolution in 1991, Russia informed the UN it would be continuing the USSR's membership in the Security Council and all other UN organs with the support of the Commonwealth of Independent States (comprising most of the former Soviet republics). (8) The Socialist Federal Republic of Yugoslavia became a member in 1945. After 4 of its 6 republics (Bosnia and Herzegovina, Croatia, Macedonia, and Slovenia) declared independence in 1991-92, the 2 remaining republics, Montenegro and Serbia, reconstituted themselves as the Federal Republic of Yugoslavia, which assumed Yugoslavia's UN seat Apr. 8, 1992. In Sept. 1992, the General Assembly decided the Federal Republic of Yugoslavia could not automatically take the seat of the former Yugoslavia. Membership was granted in Nov. 2000 by a vote of the General Assembly. In Feb. 2003, Yugoslavia changed its name to Serbia and Montenegro. (9) In 1994, the General Assembly admitted the South African delegation, which had been rejected for 24 years because of apartheid. (10) Tanganyika was a member from 1961 and Zanzibar from 1963. Following the ratification in 1964 of Articles of Union between Tanganyika and Zanzibar, the United Republic of Tanganyika and Zanzibar continued as a single member of the UN, later changing its name to United Republic of Tanzania. (11) The Yemen Arab Republic was admitted in 1947; the People's Republic of Yemen, in 1967. The 2 nations merged in 1990. **NOTE:** Vatican City and China (Taiwan) are not members. Vatican CIty is a permanent observer. Taiwan's bid for UN membership was rejected for the 13th consecutive year on Sept. 14, 2005.

United Nations Secretaries General

Took Office	Secretary, Nation
1946	Trygve Lie, Norway
1953	Dag Hammarskjold, Sweden
1961	U Thant, Burma
1972	Kurt Waldheim, Austria
1982	Javier Perez de Cuellar, Peru
1992	Boutros Boutros-Ghali, Egypt
1997	Kofi Annan, Ghana

U.S. Representatives to the United Nations

The U.S. Representative to the United Nations is the chief of the U.S. Mission to the United Nations in New York and holds the rank and status of Ambassador Extraordinary and Plenipotentiary (A.E.P.). Year given is the year each took office.

Year	Representative	Year	Representative	Year	Representative	Year	Representative
1946	Edward R. Stettinius, Jr.	1968	George W. Ball	1976	William W. Scranton	1992	Edward J. Perkins
1946	Herschel V. Johnson (act.)	1968	James Russell Wiggins	1977	Andrew Young	1993	Madeleine K. Albright
1947	Warren R. Austin	1969	Charles W. Yost	1979	Donald McHenry	1997	Bill Richardson
1953	Henry Cabot Lodge, Jr.	1971	George H. W. Bush	1981	Jeane J. Kirkpatrick	1999	Richard C. Holbrooke
1960	James J. Wadsworth	1973	John A. Scali	1985	Vernon A. Walters	2001	John D. Negroponte
1961	Adlai E. Stevenson	1975	Daniel P. Moynihan	1989	Thomas R. Pickering	2004	John C. Danforth
1965	Arthur J. Goldberg					2005	John R. Bolton

Selected Specialized and Related Agencies

These specialized and related agencies are autonomous, with their own memberships and organs, and at the same time have a functional relationship or working agreement with the UN (headquarters), except for UNICEF and UNHCR, which report directly to the Economic and Social Council and to the General Assembly.

Food and Agriculture Organization (FAO) aims to increase production from farms, forests, and fisheries; improve food distribution and marketing, nutrition, and the living conditions of rural people. (Viale delle Terme di Caracalla, 00100 Rome, Italy.) **Website:** www.fao.org

International Atomic Energy Agency (IAEA) aims to promote the safe, peaceful uses of atomic energy. (Vienna International Centre, P.O. Box 100, Wagramer Strasse 5, A-1400, Vienna, Austria.) **Website:** www.iaea.org

International Civil Aviation Org. (ICAO) promotes international civil aviation standards and regulations. (999 University St., Montreal, Quebec, Canada H3C 5H7.) **Website:** www.icao.int

International Fund for Agricultural Development (IFAD) aims to mobilize funds for agricultural and rural projects in developing countries. (Via del Serafico 107, 00142 Rome, Italy.) **Website:** www.ifad.org

International Labor Org. (ILO) aims to promote employment; improve labor conditions and living standards. (4 route des Morillons, CH-1211 Geneva 22, Switzerland.) **Website:** www.ilo.org

International Maritime Org. (IMO) aims to promote cooperation on technical matters affecting international shipping. (4 Albert Embankment, London SE1 7SR, U.K.) **Website:** www.imo.org

International Monetary Fund (IMF) aims to promote international monetary cooperation and currency stabilization and expansion of international trade. (700 19th St. NW, Washington, DC 20431.) **Website:** www.imf.org

International Telecommunication Union (ITU) establishes regulations for radio, telegraph, telephone, and space radio-communications, and allocates radio frequencies. (Place des Nations, 1211 Geneva 20, Switzerland.) **Website:** www.itu.int

Office of the High Commissioner for Human Rights (OHCHR) seeks to uphold human rights standards by monitoring areas of concern, investigating abuses, and working with gov. institutions to improve conditions. (United Nations office at Geneva, 1211 Geneva 10, Switzerland.) **Website:** www.ohchr.org/english

United Nations Children's Fund (UNICEF) provides financial aid and development assistance to programs for children and mothers in developing countries. (3 United Nations Plaza, New York, NY 10017.) **Website:** www.unicef.org

United Nations Educational, Scientific, and Cultural Org. (UNESCO) aims to promote collaboration among nations through education, science, and culture. After a 19-year boycott, the United States rejoined the organization on Sept. 29, 2003. (7 Place de Fontenoy, 75352 Paris 07 SP, France.) **Website:** www.unesco.org

United Nations High Commissioner for Refugees (UNHCR) provides essential assistance for refugees. (UN High Comm. for Refugees, 2500 CH-1211, Geneva 2, Switzerland.) **Website:** www.unhcr.ch

United Nations Industrial Development Org. (UNIDO) helps developing nations and those in transition pursue sustainable industrial development while promoting economic, environmental, and labor practices. (Vienna Intl. Centre, P.O. Box 300, Wagramer 5, 1400-A Vienna, Austria). **Website:** www.unido.org

Universal Postal Union (UPU) aims to perfect postal services and promote international collaboration. (Case Postale 13, 3000 Berne 15, Switzerland.) **Website:** www.upu.int

World Bank Group encompasses 2 development institutions and 3 affiliates focused on worldwide poverty reduction. **The International Bank for Reconstruction and Development (IBRD)** provides loans and technical assistance for projects in developing member countries; encourages cofinancing for projects from other public and private sources. The **International Development Association (IDA)** provides funds for development projects on concessionary terms to the poorer developing member countries. The **International Finance Corporation (IFC)** promotes the growth of the private sector in developing member countries; encourages the development of local capital markets; stimulates the international flow of private capital. The **Multilateral Investment Guarantee Agency (MIGA)** promotes investment in developing countries; guarantees investments to protect investors from noncommercial risks, such as nationalization; advises governments on attracting private investment. The **International Center for Settlement of Investment Disputes (ICSID)** provides conciliation and arbitration services for disputes between foreign investors and host governments which arise out of an investment. (1818 H St., NW Washington, DC 20433.) **Website:** www.worldbank.org

World Health Org. (WHO) aims to aid the attainment of the highest possible level of health. (Avenue Appia 20, CH-1211 Geneva 27, Switzerland.) **Website:** www.who.int

World Intellectual Property Org. (WIPO) seeks to protect, through international cooperation, literary, industrial, scientific, and artistic works. (34, Chemin des Colombettes, 1211 Geneva 20, Switzerland.) **Website:** www.wipo.int

World Meteorological Org. (WMO) aims to coordinate and improve world meteorological work. (7 bis avenue de la Paix, CP 2300, 1211 Geneva 2, Switzerland.) **Website:** www.wmo.ch

World Tourism Org. (WTO) promotes development of responsible, sustainable, and universally accessible tourism, and provides incentives for environmental and cultural protection. (Capitán Haya 42, 28020 Madrid, Spain.) **Website:** www.world-tourism.org

World Trade Org. (WTrO) replacing the General Agreement on Tariffs and Trade (GATT), administers trade agreements and treaties, examines the trade regimes of members, keeps track of various trade measures and statistics, and attempts to settle trade disputes. (Centre William Rappard, Rue de Lausanne 154, CH-1211 Geneva 21, Switzerland.) **Website:** www.wto.org

Ongoing UN Peacekeeping Missions, 2005

Source: United Nations Cartographic Section, Map No. 4000(E) Rev. 29

(Year given is the year each mission began operation)

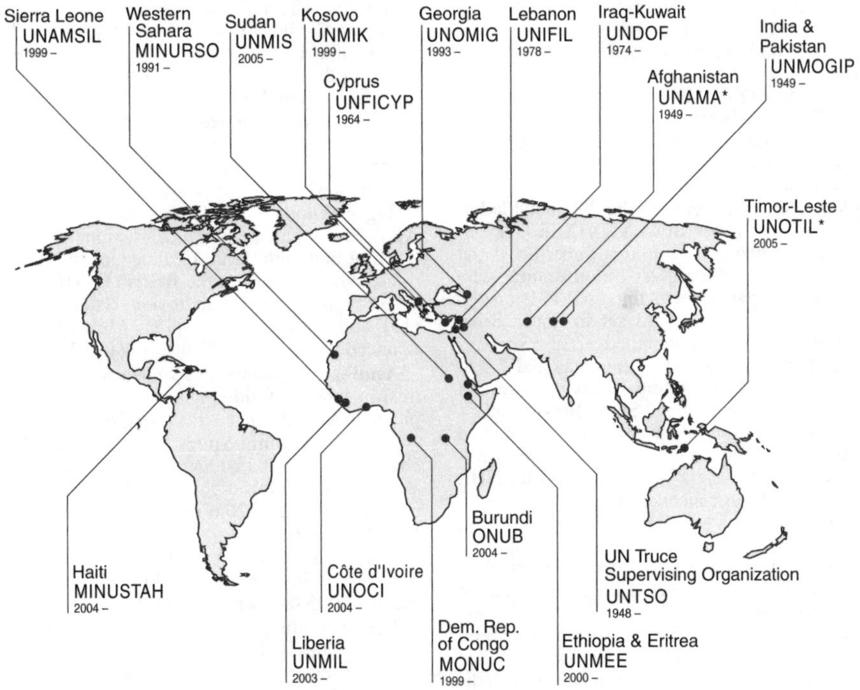

*Political mission directed and supported by the Department of Peacekeeping Operations

Peacekeeping personnel
As of July 31, 2005

Military personnel and civilian police serving in peacekeeping operations	67,392
Countries contributing military personnel and civilian police	106
International civilian personnel	4,504
Local civilian personnel	7,904
Total number of fatalities in peacekeeping operations since 1948	1,997

International Criminal Court (ICC)

The International Criminal Court was created when 120 nations signed the Rome Statute on July 17, 1998. Its mission is to try individuals accused of genocide, war crimes, or other crimes against humanity, as has been undertaken in the past by temporary tribunals. The statute came into force July 1, 2002, 60 days after the 60th nation ratified it. As of May 12, 2005, 99 nations were members of the ICC, although China, Japan, Russia, and the U.S. had not joined. The U.S. expressed opposition to some provisions of the ICC, mainly regarding liability of its military in peace-keeping situations.

The ICC, unlike the World Court, is not an organ of the UN, but an independent international agency with its own budget and administration. It consists of 18 judges elected by member nations. A president and 1st and 2nd vice presidents are elected for 3-year, renewable terms by an absolute majority of the judges. A Registry handles the nonjudicial aspects of administration. The Office of the Prosecutor will review, investigate, and, when necessary, prosecute cases referred to it by a state or by the UN Security Council.

Jurisdiction is limited to member nations, and only when their courts are deemed either inoperable or unfit for fair trial. The court will hear cases in The Hague, Netherlands.
Website: www.icc-cpi.int

See also coverage of genocide in the Crime chapter. In June 2005, the ICC prosecutor opened an investigation into the situation in Darfur, Sudan.

Geneva Conventions

The Geneva Conventions are 4 international treaties governing the protection of civilians in time of war, the treatment of prisoners of war, and the care of the wounded and sick in the armed forces. The first convention, covering the sick and wounded, was concluded in Geneva, Switzerland, in 1864; it was amended and expanded in 1906. A third convention, in 1929, covered prisoners of war. Outrage at the treatment of prisoners and civilians during World War II by some belligerents, notably Germany and Japan, prompted the conclusion, in Aug. 1949, of 4 new conventions. Three of these restated and strengthened the previous conventions, and the fourth codified general principles of international law governing the treatment of civilians in wartime.

The 1949 convention for civilians provided for special safeguards for wounded persons, children under 15 years of age, pregnant women, and the elderly. Discrimination on racial, religious, national, or political grounds was forbidden. Torture, collective punishment, reprisals, unwarranted destruction of property, and forced use of civilians for an occupier's armed forces were also prohibited. Also included was a pledge to treat prisoners humanely, feed them adequately, and deliver relief supplies to them. They were not to be forced to disclose more than minimal information. Two additional protocols were adopted in June 1977 dealing with the protection of war victims, especially civilians, and protection for non-international conflicts.

Most countries have formally accepted all or most of the humanitarian conventions as binding. However, there is no permanent machinery in place to apprehend, try, or punish violators.

SPORTS

SPORTS HIGHLIGHTS OF 2005

On Jan. 4, the **Univ. of Southern California** Trojans won the **NCAA football Division I-A championship title**, trouncing the Univ. of Oklahoma Sooners, 55-19, in the Orange Bowl, in Miami, FL. USC finished the season with a record of 13 wins and no losses to top both the *USA Today*/ESPN coaches' poll and the Associated Press poll of media members. The game was a matchup between 2 Heisman trophy winners, USC quarterback Matt Leinart (2004) and Oklahoma QB Jason White (2003). The win gave USC 22 straight victories, dating back to 2003. They had shared the 2003 title with Louisiana State Univ.

The **New England Patriots** defeated the Philadelphia Eagles, 24-21, Feb. 6 to win **Super Bowl XXXIX** in Jacksonville, FL. New England won its 2nd straight Super Bowl and its 3rd in 4 years. Patriots wide receiver Deion Branch, who caught 11 passes for 133 yards, was named MVP. Branch's 11 receptions tied Jerry Rice's record set in Super Bowl XXIII. Patriots QB Tom Brady completed 23 of 33 passes for 236 yards and 2 touchdowns. The game was tied 7-7 at the half, only the 2nd 1st-half tie in Super Bowl history, and tied at 14 going into the 4th quarter—a Super Bowl first.

The **NHL lockout** that began Sept. 16, 2004, continued into early 2005. After last-minute attempts to resolve differences between owners and players were unsuccessful, NHL Commissioner Gary Bettman cancelled the 2004-05 season Feb. 16. It was the first time a North American professional sports league had cancelled an entire season due to a labor dispute; the Stanley Cup was not awarded for the first time since 1919. An agreement announced July 13 allowed for the 2005-06 season to open Oct. 5.

The NBA imposed new arena security regulations and a code of conduct for fans Feb. 17 in response to the **"Malice at the Palace"** brawl between Detroit Pistons fans and Indiana Pacers players at a Nov. 19, 2004, game at Detroit. Several fans and Pacers players were sentenced to probation and community service.

Six current and former MLB stars, Jose Canseco, Mark McGwire, Rafael Palmeiro, Sammy Sosa, Curt Schilling, and Frank Thomas, were among those who testified Mar. 17 before the House Committtee on Gov. Reform in Wash., DC. The hearing was held mainly in response to the 2004 **BALCO scandal** that implicated several players in ongoing steroid use. Palmeiro, who denied using steroids, later tested positive for steroids and, as part of the league's stricter drug policies, was given a 10-day suspension Aug. 1.

The **Univ. of North Carolina** Tar Heels defeated the Univ. of Illinois Fighting Illini, 75-70, in St. Louis, MO, April 4 to win the **men's NCAA basketball tournament**. The **Baylor Univ.** Lady Bears won the women's NCAA title April 5, beating the Michigan State Spartans, 84-62, in Indianapolis, IN. North Carolina forward Sean May, who had 26 points and 10 rebounds in the final game, was named most outstanding player of the Final Four. Baylor forward Sophia Young, who had 26 points and 9 rebounds in the title game, received the women's honor. Tar Heels coach Roy Williams, who had made 4 Final Four trips with Kansas, won his first title as coach. Baylor coach Kim Mulkey-Robertson became the first woman to win a national title as both a player and head coach.

Tiger Woods won the 69th annual **Masters** tournament April 10, capturing his 4th Masters and 9th major title; this left him tied with Arnold Palmer for the 2nd-most Masters titles. Woods also won the **British Open** July 17, for a total of 10 majors—more than anyone else except Walter Hagen (11) and Jack Nicklaus (18). Meanwhile, Nicklaus announced he was retiring following the British Open.

Annika Sorenstam of Sweden won the **LPGA championship** June 12, following a win at the Kraft Nabisco Championship Mar. 27. The wins gave her 9 major LPGA titles.

The **San Antonio Spurs** June 23 defeated the defending champion Detroit Pistons, 81-74, in San Antonio, TX, to win the **NBA finals** 4 games to 3. Spurs forward Tim Duncan, who averaged 20.6 points per game, was named finals MVP for the 3rd time.

U.S. cyclist **Lance Armstrong** won the **Tour de France** for a record 7th straight year July 24. Armstrong announced that the 2005 race would be his last.

Venus Williams won her 3rd **Wimbledon** title July 2, beating Lindsay Davenport. The 14th seed, Williams became the lowest-seeded woman to win Wimbledon since the Open era began in 1968. **Roger Federer** of Switzerland captured his 3rd straight Wimbledon championship, July 3, when he beat Andy Roddick (U.S.).

The **U.S. men's soccer team** clinched its 5th straight World Cup spot Sept. 3 when it beat Mexico, 2-0, in Columbus, OH.

Legendary NFL receiver **Jerry Rice** announced his retirement Sept. 5 after 20 seasons in the league. He left with 3 Super Bowl rings and 38 receiving records, including most career receptions (1,549), most career yards receiving (22,895), and most career touchdowns receiving (197).

Federer beat Andre Agassi Sept. 11 to defend his men's singles title at the **U.S. Open**, taking his 6th Grand Slam title. **Kim Clijsters** of Belgium had defeated Mary Pierce of France **Sept. 10** to win the women's title.

WORLD ALMANAC EDITORS' PICKS
MOST MEMORABLE WINTER OLYMPIC EVENTS

The editors of *The World Almanac* have ranked the following as the most memorable events in Winter Olympics history.

1. **U.S. Upsets 20-Year Hockey Champ U.S.S.R.** (Lake Placid, 1980)—The 7th-seeded U.S. team thrilled the nation by beating the Soviets 4-3 on its way to winning the final game against Finland.
2. **Jean Claude Killy Sweeps Alpine Skiing** (Grenoble, 1968)—The debonair French star won 3 gold medals, for downhill, slalom, and giant slalom.
3. **Starring on the Slopes: Mrs. Lawrence** (Oslo, 1952)—Andrea Mead Lawrence became the first and only American to win 2 gold medals in Alpine Ski events in the same Olympics, winning both the slalom and giant slalom.
4. **Eric Heiden Sweeps Speed Skating** (Lake Placid, 1980)—Speed skater Eric Heiden of the U.S. became the first and only athlete ever to win 5 gold medals for individual events during the course of a single Olympics, setting records in all speed skating events.
5. **Skating Pairs Judging Scandal** (Salt Lake City, 2002)—In the pairs competition, Yelena Berezhnaya and Anton Sikharulidze of Russia were awarded gold medals, to the surprise of the crowd. But after a French judge who voted for the Russians was suspended by the International Skating Union, Canada's Jamie Salé and David Pelletier were awarded a second set of gold medals.
6. **Dan Jansen Snaps Losing Streak** (Lillehammer, 1994)—Jansen had competed in the 1988 Calgary Olympic Games just after learning his sister had died of leukemia. He failed to win a medal there, or in Albertville in the 1992 games. But he won the 1,000-meter speedskating event in 1994, with a world-record time of 1 minute, 12.43 seconds.
7. **Henie's Thirties Threepeat** (Garmisch, 1936)—Norwegian Sonja Henie, whose acrobatics and style helped revolutionize women's figure skating, won her 3rd straight gold medal, a feat never repeated.
8. **Baiul Overshadows Harding-Kerrigan** (Lillehammer, 1994)—Ukrainian Oksana Baiul's inspired women's figure skating gold medal performance helped offset controversy over the competition between Nancy Kerrigan (the silver medalist) and Tonya Harding, the 8th place finisher who had been cleared to compete despite being implicated in an assault on Kerrigan.
9. **Jamaican Bobsledders** (Calgary, 1988)—The first-time Jamaican team was a crowd favorite, despite crashing during the 4-man race and finishing in last place. Their brave effort inspired a movie, and at the 1994 Olympics, the Jamaican national team placed 14th—one ahead of the U.S.
10. **Björn Dæhlie of Norway Wins Record-Setting 8th Gold** (Nagano, 1998)—Dæhlie won a record 8 gold medals in Nordic events over 3 Olympiads (1992, 1994, 1998).

OLYMPICS

Highlights of the 2004 Summer Olympic Games

Athens, Greece, Aug. 13-29, 2004

The Olympic Games were born in ancient Greece and the first modern Games were held in Athens in 1896. In 2004, 10,500 athletes representing 202 nations gathered in Athens to compete in 301 events in 28 sports at the 28th Olympiad. Women competed for the first time in freestyle wrestling and the sabre event in fencing.

American swimmer Michael Phelps captured 8 medals—6 gold and 2 bronze—in individual and relay events, tying a record for the number of medals won in a single Olympics. American gymnasts Paul Hamm and Carly Patterson claimed gold medals in the individual all-around gymnastics competitions, but controversy erupted when it emerged that judges had erred in scoring Yang Tae Young (S. Kor.), who won the men's bronze medal, on his parallel bar routine. South Korea filed a protest, pointing out that Yang would have won gold if his routine had been scored correctly by the judges. The International Gymnastics Federation admitted that the gold medal had been awarded to Hamm in error, but allowed the results to stand. The U.S. also fared well in women's team sports, with the soccer, softball, and basketball teams all capturing golds. Argentina won the gold medal in men's soccer and basketball; the favored U.S. men's basketball team won the bronze. Windsurfer Gal Fridman became the first Israeli to win an Olympic gold medal when he captured the men's Mistral event.

Many track and field stars were absent because of doping scandals or failure to qualify. A record 24 athletes were expelled for drug violations as of the closing ceremony. Medals in 7 events, including 3 golds, were taken away for doping violations. The Games also featured unprecedented spending on security, more than $1.5 bil, almost entirely by the Greek government.

Final Medal Standings

(top 23 medal-winning nations)

	G	S	B	T
United States	35	39	29	103
Russia	27	27	38	92
China	32	17	14	63
Australia	17	16	16	49
Germany	14	16	18	48
Japan	16	9	12	37
France	11	9	13	33
Italy	10	11	11	32
South Korea	9	12	9	30
Great Britain	9	9	12	30
Cuba	9	7	11	27
Ukraine	9	5	9	23
Netherlands	4	9	9	22
Romania	8	5	6	19
Spain	3	11	5	19
Hungary	8	6	3	17
Greece	6	6	4	16
Belarus	2	6	7	15
Canada	3	6	3	12
Bulgaria	2	1	9	12
Brazil	4	3	3	10
Turkey	3	3	4	10
Poland	3	2	5	10

Summer Olympic Games Champions, 1896-2004

(*indicates Olympic record; w indicates wind-aided)

The 1980 games were boycotted by 62 nations, including the U.S. The 1984 games were boycotted by the USSR and most Eastern bloc nations. E and W Germany competed separately, 1968-88. The 1992 Unified Team consisted of 12 former Soviet republics. The 1992 Independent Olympic Participants (I.O.P.) were from Serbia, Montenegro, and Macedonia.

Track and Field—Men

100-Meter Run

1896	Thomas Burke, United States	12.0s
1900	Francis W. Jarvis, United States	11.0s
1904	Archie Hahn, United States	11.0s
1908	Reginald Walker, South Africa	10.8s
1912	Ralph Craig, United States	10.8s
1920	Charles Paddock, United States	10.8s
1924	Harold Abrahams, Great Britain	10.6s
1928	Percy Williams, Canada	10.8s
1932	Eddie Tolan, United States	10.3s
1936	Jesse Owens, United States	10.3s
1948	Harrison Dillard, United States	10.3s
1952	Lindy Remigino, United States	10.4s
1956	Bobby Morrow, United States	10.5s
1960	Armin Hary, Germany	10.2s
1964	Bob Hayes, United States	10.0s
1968	Jim Hines, United States	9.95s
1972	Valery Borzov, USSR	10.14s
1976	Hasely Crawford, Trinidad	10.06s
1980	Allan Wells, Great Britain	10.25s
1984	Carl Lewis, United States	9.99s
1988	Carl Lewis, United States	9.92s
1992	Linford Christie, Great Britain	9.96s
1996	Donovan Bailey, Canada	9.84s*
2000	Maurice Greene, United States	9.87s
2004	Justin Gatlin, United States	9.85s

200-Meter Run

1900	Walter Tewksbury, United States	22.2s
1904	Archie Hahn, United States	21.6s
1908	Robert Kerr, Canada	22.6s
1912	Ralph Craig, United States	21.7s
1920	Allan Woodring, United States	22.0s
1924	Jackson Scholz, United States	21.6s
1928	Percy Williams, Canada	21.8s
1932	Eddie Tolan, United States	21.2s
1936	Jesse Owens, United States	20.7s
1948	Mel Patton, United States	21.1s
1952	Andrew Stanfield, United States	20.7s
1956	Bobby Morrow, United States	20.6s
1960	Livio Berruti, Italy	20.5s
1964	Henry Carr, United States	20.3s
1968	Tommie Smith, United States	19.83s
1972	Valeri Borzov, USSR	20.00s
1976	Donald Quarrie, Jamaica	20.23s
1980	Pietro Mennea, Italy	20.19s
1984	Carl Lewis, United States	19.80s
1988	Joe DeLoach, United States	19.75s
1992	Mike Marsh, United States	20.01s
1996	Michael Johnson, United States	19.32s*
2000	Konstantinos Kenteris, Greece	20.09s
2004	Shawn Crawford, United States	19.79s

400-Meter Run

1896	Thomas Burke, United States	54.2s
1900	Maxey Long, United States	49.4s
1904	Harry Hillman, United States	49.2s
1908	Wyndham Halswelle, Great Brit., walkover	50.0s
1912	Charles Reidpath, United States	48.2s
1920	Bevil Rudd, South Africa	49.6s
1924	Eric Liddell, Great Britain	47.6s
1928	Ray Barbuti, United States	47.8s
1932	William Carr, United States	46.2s
1936	Archie Williams, United States	46.5s
1948	Arthur Wint, Jamaica	46.2s
1952	George Rhoden, Jamaica	45.9s
1956	Charles Jenkins, United States	46.7s
1960	Otis Davis, United States	44.9s
1964	Michael Larrabee, United States	45.1s
1968	Lee Evans, United States	43.86s
1972	Vincent Matthews, United States	44.66s
1976	Alberto Juantorena, Cuba	44.26s
1980	Viktor Markin, USSR	44.60s
1984	Alonzo Babers, United States	44.27s
1988	Steven Lewis, United States	43.87s
1992	Quincy Watts, United States	43.50s
1996	Michael Johnson, United States	43.49s*
2000	Michael Johnson, United States	43.84s
2004	Jeremy Wariner, United States	44.00s

800-Meter Run

1896	Edwin Flack, Australia	2m. 11s
1900	Alfred Tysoe, Great Britain	2m. 1.2s
1904	James Lightbody, United States	1m. 56s
1908	Mel Sheppard, United States	1m. 52.8s
1912	James Meredith, United States	1m. 51.9s
1920	Albert Hill, Great Britain	1m. 53.4s
1924	Douglas Lowe, Great Britain	1m. 52.4s
1928	Douglas Lowe, Great Britain	1m. 51.8s
1932	Thomas Hampson, Great Britain	1m. 49.8s
1936	John Woodruff, United States	1m. 52.9s
1948	Mal Whitfield, United States	1m. 49.2s

800-Meter Run

1952	Mal Whitfield, United States	1m. 49.2s
1956	Thomas Courtney, United States	1m. 47.7s
1960	Peter Snell, New Zealand	1m. 46.3s
1964	Peter Snell, New Zealand	1m. 45.1s
1968	Ralph Doubell, Australia	1m. 44.3s
1972	Dave Wottle, United States	1m. 45.9s
1976	Alberto Juantorena, Cuba	1m. 43.50s
1980	Steve Ovett, Great Britain	1m. 45.40s
1984	Joaquim Cruz, Brazil	1m. 43.00s
1988	Paul Ereng, Kenya	1m. 43.45s
1992	William Tanui, Kenya	1m. 43.66s
1996	Vebjoern Rodal, Norway	1m. 42.58s*
2000	Nils Schumann, Germany	1m. 45.08s
2004	Yuriy Borzakovskiy, Russia	1m. 44.45s

1,500-Meter Run

1896	Edwin Flack, Australia	4m. 33.2s
1900	Charles Bennett, Great Britain	4m. 6.2s
1904	James Lightbody, United States	4m. 5.4s
1908	Mel Sheppard, United States	4m. 3.4s
1912	Arnold Jackson, Great Britain	3m. 56.8s
1920	Albert Hill, Great Britain	4m. 1.8s
1924	Paavo Nurmi, Finland	3m. 53.6s
1928	Harry Larva, Finland	3m. 53.2s
1932	Luigi Beccali, Italy	3m. 51.2s
1936	Jack Lovelock, New Zealand	3m. 47.8s
1948	Henri Eriksson, Sweden	3m. 49.8s
1952	Joseph Barthel, Luxembourg	3m. 45.2s
1956	Ron Delany, Ireland	3m. 41.2s
1960	Herb Elliott, Australia	3m. 35.6s
1964	Peter Snell, New Zealand	3m. 38.1s
1968	Kipchoge Keino, Kenya	3m. 34.9s
1972	Pekka Vasala, Finland	3m. 36.3s
1976	John Walker, New Zealand	3m. 39.17s
1980	Sebastian Coe, Great Britain	3m. 38.4s
1984	Sebastian Coe, Great Britain	3m. 32.53s
1988	Peter Rono, Kenya	3m. 35.96s
1992	Fermin Cacho Ruiz, Spain	3m. 40.12s
1996	Noureddine Morceli, Algeria	3m. 35.78s
2000	Noah Ngeny, Kenya	3m. 32.07s*
2004	Hicham el-Guerrouj, Morocco	3m. 34.18s

5,000-Meter Run

1912	Hannes Kolehmainen, Finland	14m. 36.6s
1920	Joseph Guillemot, France	14m. 55.6s
1924	Paavo Nurmi, Finlands	14m. 31.2s
1928	Willie Ritola, Finland	14m. 38s
1932	Lauri Lehtinen, Finland	14m. 30s
1936	Gunnar Hockert, Finland	14m. 22.2s
1948	Gaston Reiff, Belgium	14m. 17.6s
1952	Emil Zatopek, Czechoslovakia	14m. 6.6s
1956	Vladimir Kuts, USSR	13m. 39.6s
1960	Murray Halberg, New Zealand	13m. 43.4s
1964	Bob Schul, United States	13m. 48.8s
1968	Mohamed Gammoudi, Tunisia	14m. 05.0s
1972	Lasse Viren, Finland	13m. 26.4s
1976	Lasse Viren, Finland	13m. 24.76s
1980	Miruts Yifter, Ethiopia	13m. 21.0s
1984	Said Aouita, Morocco	13m. 05.59s*
1988	John Ngugi, Kenya	13m. 11.70s
1992	Dieter Baumann, Germany	13m. 12.52s
1996	Venuste Niyongabo, Burundi	13m. 07.96s
2000	Millon Wolde, Ethiopia	13m. 35.49s
2004	Hicham el-Guerrouj, Morocco	13m. 14.39s

10,000-Meter Run

1912	Hannes Kolehmainen, Finland	31m. 20.8s
1920	Paavo Nurmi, Finland	31m. 45.8s
1924	Willie Ritola, Finland	30m. 23.2s
1928	Paavo Nurmi, Finland	30m. 18.8s
1932	Janusz Kusocinski, Poland	30m. 11.4s
1936	Ilmari Salminen, Finland	30m. 15.4s
1948	Emil Zatopek, Czechoslovakia	29m. 59.6s
1952	Emil Zatopek, Czechoslovakia	29m. 17.0s
1956	Vladimir Kuts, USSR	28m. 45.6s
1960	Pyotr Bolotnikov, USSR	28m. 32.2s
1964	Billy Mills, United States	28m. 24.4s
1968	Naftali Temu, Kenya	29m. 27.4s
1972	Lasse Viren, Finland	27m. 38.4s
1976	Lasse Viren, Finland	27m. 40.4s
1980	Miruts Yifter, Ethiopia	27m. 42.7s
1984	Alberto Cova, Italy	27m. 47.54s
1988	Brahim Boutaib, Morocco	27m. 21.46s
1992	Khalid Skah, Morocco	27m. 46.70s
1996	Haile Gebrselassie, Ethiopia	27m. 07.34s
2000	Haile Gebrselassie, Ethiopia	27m. 18.20s
2004	Kenenisa Bekele, Ethiopia	27m. 05.10s*

110-Meter Hurdles

1896	Thomas Curtis, United States	17.6s
1900	Alvin Kraenzlein, United States	15.4s
1904	Frederick Schule, United States	16.0s
1908	Forrest Smithson, United States	15.0s
1912	Frederick Kelly, United States	15.1s
1920	Earl Thomson, Canada	14.8s
1924	Daniel Kinsey, United States	15.0s
1928	Sydney Atkinson, South Africa	14.8s
1932	George Saling, United States	14.6s
1936	Forrest Towns, United States	14.2s
1948	William Porter, United States	13.9s
1952	Harrison Dillard, United States	13.7s
1956	Lee Calhoun, United States	13.5s
1960	Lee Calhoun, United States	13.8s
1964	Hayes Jones, United States	13.6s
1968	Willie Davenport, United States	13.33s
1972	Rod Milburn, United States	13.24s
1976	Guy Drut, France	13.30s
1980	Thomas Munkelt, E. Germany	13.39s
1984	Roger Kingdom, United States	13.20s
1988	Roger Kingdom, United States	12.98s
1992	Mark McCoy, Canada	13.12s
1996	Allen Johnson, United States	12.95s
2000	Anier Garcia, Cuba	13.00s
2004	Liu Xiang, China	12.91s*

400-Meter Hurdles

1900	J.W.B. Tewksbury, United States	57.6s
1904	Harry Hillman, United States	53.0s
1908	Charles Bacon, United States	55.0s
1920	Frank Loomis, United States	54.0s
1924	F. Morgan Taylor, United States	52.6s
1928	Lord Burghley, Great Britain	53.4s
1932	Robert Tisdall, Ireland	51.7s
1936	Glenn Hardin, United States	52.4s
1948	Roy Cochran, United States	51.1s
1952	Charles Moore, United States	50.8s
1956	Glenn Davis, United States	50.1s
1960	Glenn Davis, United States	49.3s
1964	Rex Cawley, United States	49.6s
1968	Dave Hemery, Great Britain	48.12s
1972	John Akii-Bua, Uganda	47.82s
1976	Edwin Moses, United States	47.64s
1980	Volker Beck, E. Germany	48.70s
1984	Edwin Moses, United States	47.75s
1988	Andre Phillips, United States	47.19s
1992	Kevin Young, United States	46.78s*
1996	Derrick Adkins, United States	47.54s
2000	Angelo Taylor, United States	47.50s
2004	Felix Sanchez, Dominican Republic	47.63s

400-Meter Relay

1912	Great Britain	42.4s
1920	United States	42.2s
1924	United States	41.0s
1928	United States	41.0s
1932	United States	40.0s
1936	United States	39.8s
1948	United States	40.6s
1952	United States	40.1s
1956	United States	39.5s
1960	Germany (U.S. disqualified)	39.5s
1964	United States	39.0s
1968	United States	38.24s
1972	United States	38.19s
1976	United States	38.33s
1980	USSR	38.26s
1984	United States	37.83s
1988	USSR (U.S. disqualified)	38.19s
1992	United States	37.40s*
1996	Canada	37.69s
2000	United States	37.61s
2004	Great Britain	38.07s

1,600-Meter Relay

1908	United States	3m. 29.4s
1912	United States	3m. 16.6s
1920	Great Britain	3m. 22.2s
1924	United States	3m. 16s
1928	United States	3m. 14.2s
1932	United States	3m. 8.2s
1936	Great Britain	3m. 9s
1948	United States	3m. 10.4s
1952	Jamaica	3m. 03.9s
1956	United States	3m. 04.8s
1960	United States	3m. 02.2s
1964	United States	3m. 00.7s
1968	United States	2m. 56.16s
1972	Kenya	2m. 59.8s
1976	United States	2m. 58.65s
1980	USSR	3m. 01.1s

1,600-Meter Relay

1984	United States	2m. 57.91s
1988	United States	2m. 56.16s
1992	United States	2m. 55.74s*
1996	United States	2m. 55.99s
2000	United States	2m. 56.35s
2004	United States	2m. 55.91s

3,000-Meter Steeplechase

1920	Percy Hodge, Great Britain	10m. 0.4s
1924	Willie Ritola, Finland	9m. 33.6s
1928	Toivo Loukola, Finland	9m. 21.8s
1932	Volmari Iso-Hollo, Finland (About 3,450 m; extra lap by error.)	10m. 33.4s
1936	Volmari Iso-Hollo, Finland	9m. 3.8s
1948	Thore Sjoestrand, Sweden	9m. 4.6s
1952	Horace Ashenfelter, United States	8m. 45.4s
1956	Chris Brasher, Great Britain	8m. 41.2s
1960	Zdzislaw Krzyszkowiak, Poland	8m. 34.2s
1964	Gaston Roelants, Belgium	8m. 30.8s
1968	Amos Biwott, Kenya	8m. 51s
1972	Kipchoge Keino, Kenya	8m. 23.6s
1976	Anders Garderud, Sweden	8m. 08.2s
1980	Bronislaw Malinowski, Poland	8m. 09.7s
1984	Julius Korir, Kenya	8m. 11.8s
1988	Julius Kariuki, Kenya	8m. 05.51s*
1992	Matthew Birir, Kenya	8m. 08.84s
1996	Joseph Keter, Kenya	8m. 07.12s
2000	Reuben Kosgei, Kenya	8m. 21.43s
2004	Ezekiel Kemboi, Kenya	8m. 05.81s

20-Kilometer Walk

1956	Leonid Spirin, USSR	1h. 31m. 27.4s
1960	Vladimir Golubnichy, USSR	1h. 33m. 7.2s
1964	Kenneth Mathews, Great Britain	1h. 29m. 34.0s
1968	Vladimir Golubnichy, USSR	1h. 33m. 58.4s
1972	Peter Frenkel, E. Germany	1h. 26m. 42.4s
1976	Daniel Bautista, Mexico	1h. 24m. 40.6s
1980	Maurizio Damilano, Italy	1h. 23m. 35.5s
1984	Ernesto Canto, Mexico	1h. 23m. 13.0s
1988	Josef Pribilinec, Czechoslovakia	1h. 19m. 57.0s
1992	Daniel Plaza Montero, Spain	1h. 21m. 45.0s
1996	Jefferson Perez, Ecuador	1h. 20m. 7s
2000	Robert Korzeniowski, Poland	1h. 18m. 59.0s*
2004	Ivano Brugnetti, Italy	1h. 19m. 40s

50-Kilometer Walk

1932	Thomas W. Green, Great Britain	4h. 50m. 10s
1936	Harold Whitlock, Great Britain	4h. 30m. 41.4s
1948	John Ljunggren, Sweden	4h. 41m. 52s
1952	Giuseppe Dordoni, Italy	4h. 28m. 07.8s
1956	Norman Read, New Zealand	4h. 30m. 42.8s
1960	Donald Thompson, Great Britain	4h. 25m. 30s
1964	Abdon Pamich, Italy	4h. 11m. 12.4s
1968	Christoph Hohne, E. Germany	4h. 20m. 13.6s
1972	Bern Kannenberg, W. Germany	3h. 56m. 11.6s
1980	Hartwig Gauter, E. Germany	3h. 49m. 24.0s
1984	Raul Gonzalez, Mexico	3h. 47m. 26.0s
1988	Vyacheslav Ivanenko, USSR	3h. 38m. 29.0s*
1992	Andrei Perlov, Unified Team	3h. 50m. 13.0s
1996	Robert Korzeniowski, Poland	3h. 43m. 30s
2000	Robert Korzeniowski, Poland	3h. 42m. 22s
2004	Robert Korzeniowski, Poland	3h. 38m. 46s

Marathon

1896	Spiridon Loues, Greece	2h. 58m. 50s
1900	Michel Theato, France	2h. 59m. 45s
1904	Thomas Hicks, United States	3h. 28m. 63s
1908	John J. Hayes, United States	2h. 55m. 18.4s
1912	Kenneth McArthur, South Africa	2h. 36m. 54.8s
1920	Hannes Kolehmainen, Finland	2h. 32m. 35.8s
1924	Albin Stenroos, Finland	2h. 41m. 22.6s
1928	A.B. El Ouafi, France	2h. 32m. 57s
1932	Juan Zabala, Argentina	2h. 31m. 36s
1936	Kijung Son, Japan (Korean)	2h. 29m. 19.2s
1948	Delfo Cabrera, Argentina	2h. 34m. 51.6s
1952	Emil Zatopek, Czechoslovakia	2h. 23m. 03.2s
1956	Alain Mimoun, France	2h. 25m.
1960	Abebe Bikila, Ethiopia	2h. 15m. 16.2s
1964	Abebe Bikila, Ethiopia	2h. 12m. 11.2s
1968	Mamo Wolde, Ethiopia	2h. 20m. 26.4s
1972	Frank Shorter, United States	2h. 12m. 19.8s
1976	Waldemar Cierpinski, E. Germany	2h. 09m. 55s
1980	Waldemar Cierpinski, E. Germany	2h. 11m. 03s
1984	Carlos Lopes, Portugal	2h. 09m. 21s*
1988	Gelindo Bordin, Italy	2h. 10m. 32s
1992	Hwang Young-Cho, S. Korea	2h. 13m. 23s
1996	Josia Thugwane, South Africa	2h. 12m. 36s
2000	Gezahgne Abera, Ethiopia	2h. 10m. 11s
2004	Stefano Baldino, Italy	2h. 10m. 55s

High Jump

1896	Ellery Clark, United States	1.81m.	(5'11¼")
1900	Irving Baxter, United States	1.90m.	(6' 2¾")
1904	Samuel Jones, United States	1.80m.	(5' 11")
1908	Harry Porter, United States	1.90m.	(6' 2¾")
1912	Alma Richards, United States	1.93m.	(6' 4")
1920	Richmond Landon, United States	1.93m.	(6' 4")
1924	Harold Osborn, United States	1.98m.	(6' 6")
1928	Robert W. King, United States	1.94m.	(6' 4¼")
1932	Duncan McNaughton, Canada	1.97m.	(6' 5½")
1936	Cornelius Johnson, United States	2.03m.	(6' 8")
1948	John L. Winter, Australia	1.98m.	(6' 6")
1952	Walter Davis, United States	2.04m.	(6' 8¼")
1956	Charles Dumas, United States	2.12m.	(6' 11½")
1960	Robert Shavlakadze, USSR	2.16m.	(7' 1")
1964	Valery Brumel, USSR	2.18m.	(7' 1¾")
1968	Dick Fosbury, United States	2.24m.	(7' 4¼")
1972	Jüri Tarmak, USSR	2.23m.	(7' 3¾")
1976	Jacek Wszola, Poland	2.25m.	(7' 4½")
1980	Gerd Wessig, E. Germany	2.36m.	(7' 8¾")
1984	Dietmar Mögenburg, W. Germany	2.35m.	(7' 8½")
1988	Hennady Avdeyenko, USSR	2.38m.	(7' 9¾")
1992	Javier Sotomayor Sanabria, Cuba	2.34m.	(7' 8")
1996	Charles Austin, United States	2.39m.	(7' 10")*
2000	Sergey Kliugin, Russia	2.35m.	(7' 8½")
2004	Stefen Holm, Sweden	2.63m.	(7' 8¾")

Long Jump

1896	Ellery Clark, United States	6.35m.	(20' 10")
1900	Alvin Kraenzlein, United States	7.18m.	(23' 6¾")
1904	Meyer Prinstein, United States	7.34m.	(24' 1")
1908	Frank Irons, United States	7.48m.	(24' 6½")
1912	Albert Gutterson, United States	7.60m.	(24' 11¼")
1920	William Petterssen, Sweden	7.15m.	(23' 5½")
1924	William DeHart Hubbard, United States	7.44m.	(24' 5")
1928	Edward B. Hamm, United States	7.73m.	(25' 4½")
1932	Edward Gordon, United States	7.64m.	(25' ¾")
1936	Jesse Owens, United States	8.06m.	(26' 5½")
1948	Willie Steele, United States	7.82m.	(25' 8")
1952	Jerome Biffle, United States	7.57m.	(24' 10")
1956	Gregory Bell, United States	7.83m.	(25' 8¼")
1960	Ralph Boston, United States	8.12m.	(26' 7¾")
1964	Lynn Davies, Great Britain	8.07m.	(26' 5¾")
1968	Bob Beamon, United States	8.90m.	(29' 2½")*
1972	Randy Williams, United States	8.24m.	(27' ½")
1976	Arnie Robinson, United States	8.35m.	(27' 4¾")
1980	Lutz Dombrowski, E. Germany	8.54m.	(28' ¼")
1984	Carl Lewis, United States	8.54m.	(28' ¼")
1988	Carl Lewis, United States	8.72m.	(28' 7½")
1992	Carl Lewis, United States	8.67m.	(28' 5½")
1996	Carl Lewis, United States	8.50m.	(27' 10¾")
2000	Ivan Pedroso, Cuba	8.55m.	(28' ¾")
2004	Dwight Phillips, United States	8.59m.	(28' 2¼")

Triple Jump

1896	James Connolly, United States	13.71m.	(44' 11¾")
1900	Meyer Prinstein, United States	14.47m.	(47' 5¾")
1904	Meyer Prinstein, United States	14.35m.	(47' 1")
1908	Timothy Ahearne, G.B.-Ireland	14.92m.	(48' 11½")
1912	Gustaf Lindblom, Sweden	14.76m.	(48' 5")
1920	Vilho Tuulos, Finland	14.50m.	(47' 7")
1924	Anthony Winter, Australia	15.52m.	(50' 11")
1928	Mikio Oda, Japan	15.21m.	(49' 11")
1932	Chuhei Nambu, Japan	15.72m.	(51' 7")
1936	Naoto Tajima, Japan	16.00m.	(52' 6")
1948	Arne Ahman, Sweden	15.40m.	(50' 6¼")
1952	Adhemar Ferreira da Silva, Brazil	16.22m.	(53' 2¾")
1956	Adhemar Ferreira da Silva, Brazil	16.35m.	(53' 7¾")
1960	Jozef Schmidt, Poland	16.81m.	(55' 1½")
1964	Jozef Schmidt, Poland	16.85m.	(55' 3½")
1968	Viktor Saneyev, USSR	17.39m.	(57' ¾")
1972	Viktor Saneyev, USSR	17.35m.	(56' 11¼")
1976	Viktor Saneyev, USSR	17.29m.	(56' 8¾")
1980	Jaak Uudmae, USSR	17.35m.	(56' 11")
1984	Al Joyner, United States	17.26m.	(56' 7½")
1988	Khristo Markov, Bulgaria	17.61m.	(57' 9½")
1992	Mike Conley, United States	18.17m.	(59' 7½")(w)
1996	Kenny Harrison, United States	18.09m.	(59' 4¼")*
2000	Jonathan Edwards, Britain	17.71m.	(58' 1¼")
2004	Christian Olsson, Sweden	17.79m.	(58' 4 ½")

Discus Throw

1896	Robert Garrett, United States	29.15m.	(95' 7")
1900	Rudolf Bauer, Hungary	36.04m.	(118' 3")
1904	Martin Sheridan, United States	39.28m.	(128' 10")
1908	Martin Sheridan, United States	40.89m.	(134' 1")
1912	Armas Taipale, Finland	45.21m.	(148' 3")
1920	Elmer Niklander, Finland	44.68m.	(146' 7")
1924	Clarence Houser, United States	46.15m.	(151' 4")
1928	Clarence Houser, United States	47.32m.	(155' 3")
1932	John Anderson, United States	49.49m.	(162' 4")
1936	Ken Carpenter, United States	50.48m.	(165' 7")

Discus Throw

1948	Adolfo Consolini, Italy	52.78m.	(173' 2")
1952	Sim Iness, United States	55.03m.	(180' 6")
1956	Al Oerter, United States	56.36m.	(184' 11")
1960	Al Oerter, United States	59.18m.	(194' 2")
1964	Al Oerter, United States	61.00m.	(200' 1")
1968	Al Oerter, United States	64.78m.	(212' 6")
1972	Ludvik Danek, Czechoslovakia	64.40m.	(211' 3")
1976	Mac Wilkins, United States	67.50m.	(221' 5")
1980	Viktor Rashchupkin, USSR	66.64m.	(218' 8")
1984	Rolf Dannenberg, W. Germany	66.60m.	(218' 6")
1988	Jurgen Schult, E. Germany	68.82m.	(225' 9")
1992	Romas Ubartas, Lithuania	65.12m.	(213' 8")
1996	Lars Riedel, Germany	69.40m.	(227' 8")
2000	Virgilijus Alekna, Lithuania	69.30m.	(227' 4")
2004	Virgilijus Alekna, Lithuania	69.89m.	(228' 9¾")*

Hammer Throw

1900	John Flanagan, United States	49.73m.	(163' 1")
1904	John Flanagan, United States	51.22m.	(168' 0")
1908	John Flanagan, United States	51.92m.	(170' 4")
1912	Matt McGrath, United States	54.74m.	(179' 7")
1920	Pat Ryan, United States	52.86m.	(173' 5")
1924	Fred Tootell, United States	53.28m.	(174' 10")
1928	Patrick O'Callaghan, Ireland	51.38m.	(168' 7")
1932	Patrick O'Callaghan, Ireland	53.92m.	(176' 11")
1936	Karl Hein, Germany	56.48m.	(185' 4")
1948	Imre Németh, Hungary	56.06m.	(183' 11")
1952	József Csérmák, Hungary	60.34m.	(197' 11")
1956	Harold Connolly, United States	63.18m.	(207' 3")
1960	Vasily Rudenkov, USSR	67.10m.	(202' 0")
1964	Romuald Klim, USSR	69.74m.	(228' 10")
1968	Gyula Zsivótsky, Hungary	73.36m.	(240' 8")
1972	Anatoly Bondarchuk, USSR	75.50m.	(247' 8")
1976	Yuri Syedykh, USSR	77.52m.	(254' 4")
1980	Yuri Syedykh, USSR	81.80m.	(268' 4")
1984	Juha Tiainen, Finland	78.08m.	(256' 2")
1988	Sergei Litvinov, USSR	84.80m.	(278' 2")*
1992	Andrey Abduvaliyev, Unified Team	82.54m.	(270' 9")
1996	Balázs Kiss, Hungary	81.24m.	(266' 6")
2000	Szymon Ziolkowski, Poland	80.02m.	(262' 6")
2004	Koji Murofushi, Japan	82.91m.	(272')

Javelin Throw

1908	Erik Lemming, Sweden	54.82m.	(179' 10")
1912	Erik Lemming, Sweden	60.64m.	(198' 11")
1920	Jonni Myyrä, Finland	64.78m.	(215' 10")
1924	Jonni Myyrä, Finland	62.96m.	(206' 7")
1928	Eric Lundkvist, Sweden	66.60m.	(218' 6")
1932	Matti Järvinen, Finland	72.70m.	(238' 6")
1936	Gerhard Stöck, Germany	71.84m.	(235' 8")
1948	Kai Tapio Rautavaara, Finland	69.76m.	(228' 11")
1952	Cy Young, United States	73.78m.	(242' 1")
1956	Egil Danielsen, Norway	85.70m.	(281' 2")
1960	Viktor Tsibulenko, USSR	84.64m.	(277' 8")
1964	Pauli Nevala, Finland	82.66m.	(271' 2")
1968	Janis Lusis, USSR	90.10m.	(295' 7")
1972	Klaus Wolfermann, W. Germany	90.48m.	(296' 10")
1976	Miklós Németh, Hungary	94.58m.	(310' 4")
1980	Dainis Kula, USSR	91.20m.	(299' 2")
1984	Arto Härkönen, Finland	86.76m.	(284' 8")
1988	Tapio Korjus, Finland	84.28m.	(276' 6")
1992	Jan Zelezny, Czechoslovakia (a)	89.66m.	(294' 2")
1996	Jan Zelezny, Czech Republic	88.16m.	(289' 3")
2000	Jan Zelezny, Czech Republic	90.17m.	(295' 9½")*
2004	Andreas Thorkildsen, Norway	86.50m.	(283' 10")

(a) New records were kept after javelin was modified in 1986.

Pole Vault

1896	William Welles Hoyt, United States	3.30m.	(10' 10")
1900	Irving Baxter, United States	3.30m.	(10' 10")
1904	Charles Dvorak, United States	3.50m.	(11' 6")
1908	A. C. Gilbert, United States Edward Cooke Jr., United States	3.71m.	(12' 2")
1912	Harry Babcock, United States	3.95m.	(12' 11½")
1920	Frank Foss, United States	4.09m.	(13' 5")
1924	Lee Barnes, United States	3.95m.	(12' 11½")
1928	Sabin W. Carr, United States	4.20m.	(13' 9¼")
1932	William Miller, United States	4.31m.	(14' 1¾")
1936	Earle Meadows, United States	4.35m.	(14' 3¼")
1948	Guinn Smith, United States	4.30m.	(14' 1¼")
1952	Robert Richards, United States	4.55m.	(14' 11¼")
1956	Robert Richards, United States	4.56m.	(14' 11½")
1960	Don Bragg, United States	4.70m.	(15' 5")
1964	Fred Hansen, United States	5.10m.	(16' 8¾")
1968	Bob Seagren, United States	5.40m.	(17' 8½")
1972	Wolfgang Nordwig, E. Germany	5.50m.	(18' ½")
1976	Tadeusz Slusarski, Poland	5.50m.	(18' ½")
1980	Wladyslaw Kozakiewicz, Poland	5.78m.	(18' 11½")
1984	Pierre Quinon, France	5.75m.	(18' 10¼")
1988	Sergei Bubka, USSR	5.90m.	(19' 4¼")
1992	Maksim Tarassov, Unified Team	5.80m.	(19' ¼")
1996	Jean Galfione, France	5.92m.	(19' 5")*
2000	Nick Hysong, United States	5.90m.	(19' 4¼")
2004	Timothy Mack, United States	5.95m.	(19' 6¼")

16-lb. Shot Put

1896	Robert Garrett, United States	11.22m.	(36' 9¾")
1900	Richard Sheldon, United States	14.10m.	(46' 3¼")
1904	Ralph Rose, United States	14.81m.	(48' 7")
1908	Ralph Rose, United States	14.21m.	(46' 7½")
1912	Pat McDonald, United States	15.34m.	(50' 4")
1920	Ville Pörhölä, Finland	14.81m.	(48' 7¼")
1924	L. Clarence Houser, United States	14.99m.	(49' 2¼")
1928	John Kuck, United States	15.87m.	(52' ¾")
1932	Leo Sexton, United States	16.00m.	(52' 6")
1936	Hans Woellke, Germany	16.20m.	(53' 1¾")
1948	Wilbur Thompson, United States	17.12m.	(56' 2")
1952	W. Parry O'Brien, United States	17.41m.	(57' 1½")
1956	W. Parry O'Brien, United States	18.57m.	(60' 11¼")
1960	William Nieder, United States	19.68m.	(64' 6¾")
1964	Dallas Long, United States	20.33m.	(66' 8½")
1968	Randy Matson, United States	20.54m.	(67' 4¾")
1972	Wladyslaw Komar, Poland	21.18m.	(69' 6")
1976	Udo Beyer, E. Germany	21.05m.	(69' ¾")
1980	Vladimir Kyselyov, USSR	21.35m.	(70' ½")
1984	Alessandro Andrei, Italy	21.26m.	(69' 9")
1988	Ulf Timmermann, E. Germany	22.47m.	(73' 8¾")*
1992	Michael Stulce, United States	21.70m.	(71' 2½")
1996	Randy Barnes, United States	21.62m.	(70' 11¼")
2000	Arsi Harju, Finland	21.29m.	(69' 10¼")
2004	Yuriy Bilonog, Ukraine	21.16m.	(69' 5¼")

Decathlon (not held 1908)

1904	Thomas Kiely, Ireland	6,036 pts.
1912	Hugo Wieslander, Sweden (a)	7,724.49 pts.
1920	Helge Lovland, Norway	6,804.35 pts.
1924	Harold Osborn, United States	7,710.77 pts.
1928	Paavo Yrjola, Finland	8,053.29 pts.
1932	James Bausch, United States	8,462.23 pts.
1936	Glenn Morris, United States	7,900 pts.
1948	Robert Mathias, United States	7,139 pts.
1952	Robert Mathias, United States	7,887 pts.
1956	Milton Campbell, United States	7,937 pts.
1960	Rafer Johnson, United States	8,392 pts.
1964	Willi Holdorf, Germany (b)	7,887 pts.
1968	Bill Toomey, United States	8,193 pts.
1972	Nikolai Avilov, USSR	8,454 pts.
1976	Bruce Jenner, United States	8,617 pts.
1980	Daley Thompson, Great Britain	8,495 pts.
1984	Daley Thompson, Great Britain (c)	8,798 pts.
1988	Christian Schenk, E. Germany	8,488 pts.
1992	Robert Zmelik, Czechoslovakia	8,611 pts.
1996	Dan O'Brien, United States	8,824 pts.
2000	Erki Nool, Estonia	8,641 pts.
2004	Roman Sebrle, Czech Republic	8,893 pts.*

(a) Jim Thorpe of the U.S. won the 1912 Decathlon with 8,413 pts. but was disqualified and had to return his medals because he had played pro baseball prior to the Olympics. The IOC in 1982 posthumously restored his decathlon and pentathlon golds. (b) Former point systems used prior to 1964. (c) Scoring change effective Apr. 1985; Thompson's readjusted score is 8,847 pts.

Track and Field—Women

100-Meter Run

1928	Elizabeth Robinson, United States	12.2s
1932	Stella Walsh, Poland (a)	11.9s
1936	Helen Stephens, United States	11.5s
1948	Francina Blankers-Koen, Netherlands	11.9s
1952	Marjorie Jackson, Australia	11.5s
1956	Betty Cuthbert, Australia	11.5s
1960	Wilma Rudolph, United States	11.0s
1964	Wyomia Tyus, United States	11.4s
1968	Wyomia Tyus, United States	11.08s
1972	Renate Stecher, E. Germany	11.07s
1976	Annegret Richter, W. Germany	11.08s
1980	Lyudmila Kondratyeva, USSR	11.06s
1984	Evelyn Ashford, United States	10.97s
1988	Florence Griffith-Joyner, United States	10.54s (w)
1992	Gail Devers, United States	10.82s
1996	Gail Devers, United States	10.94s
2000	Marion Jones, United States	10.75s
2004	Yuliya Nesterenko, Belarus	10.93s

(a) A 1980 autopsy determined that Walsh was a man.

200-Meter Run

1948	Francina Blankers-Koen, Netherlands	24.4s
1952	Marjorie Jackson, Australia	23.7s
1956	Betty Cuthbert, Australia	23.4s

200-Meter Run

1960	Wilma Rudolph, United States	24.0s
1964	Edith McGuire, United States	23.0s
1968	Irena Szewinska, Poland	22.5s
1972	Renate Stecher, E. Germany	22.40s
1976	Barbel Eckert, E. Germany	22.37s
1980	Barbel Wockel, E. Germany	22.03s
1984	Valerie Brisco-Hooks, United States	21.81s
1988	Florence Griffith-Joyner, United States	21.34s*
1992	Gwen Torrence, United States	21.81s
1996	Marie-Jose Perec, France	22.12s
2000	Marion Jones, United States	21.84s
2004	Veronica Campbell, Jamaica	22.05s

400-Meter Run

1964	Betty Cuthbert, Australia	52.0s
1968	Colette Besson, France	52.0s
1972	Monika Zehrt, E. Germany	51.08s
1976	Irena Szewinska, Poland	49.29s
1980	Marita Koch, E. Germany	48.88s
1984	Valerie Brisco-Hooks, United States	48.83s
1988	Olga Bryzgina, USSR	48.65s
1992	Marie-Jose Perec, France	48.83s
1996	Marie-Jose Perec, France	48.25s*
2000	Cathy Freeman, Australia	49.11s
2004	Tonique Williams-Darling, Bahamas	49.41s

800-Meter Run

1928	Lina Radke, Germany	2m. 16.8s
1960	Ludmila Shevtsova, USSR	2m. 4.3s
1964	Ann Packer, Great Britain	2m. 1.1s
1968	Madeline Manning, United States	2m. 0.9s
1972	Hildegard Falck, W. Germany	1m. 58.6s
1976	Tatyana Kazankina, USSR	1m. 54.94s
1980	Nadezhda Olizarenko, USSR	1m. 53.43s*
1984	Doina Melinte, Romania	1m. 57.60s
1988	Sigrun Wodars, E. Germany	1m. 56.10s
1992	Ellen Van Langen, Netherlands	1m. 55.54s
1996	Svetlana Masterkova, Russia	1m. 57.73s
2000	Maria Mutola, Mozambique	1m. 56.15s
2004	Kelly Holmes, Great Britain	1m. 56.38s

1,500-Meter Run

1972	Lyudmila Bragina, USSR	4m. 01.4s
1976	Tatyana Kazankina, USSR	4m. 05.48s
1980	Tatyana Kazankina, USSR	3m. 56.6s
1984	Gabriella Dorio, Italy	4m. 03.25s
1988	Paula Ivan, Romania	3m. 53.96s*
1992	Hassiba Boulmerka, Algeria	3m. 55.30s
1996	Svetlana Masterkova, Russia	4m. 00.83s
2000	Nouria Benida Merah, Algeria	4m. 05.10s
2004	Kelly Holmes, Great Britain	3m. 57.90s

3,000-Meter Run

1984	Maricica Puica, Romania	8m. 35.96s
1988	Tatyana Samolenko, USSR	8m. 26.53s*
1992	Elena Romanova, Unified Team	8m. 46.04s

5,000-Meter Run

1996	Wang Junxia, China	14m. 59.88s
2000	Gabriela Szabo, Romania	14m. 40.79s*
2004	Meseret Defar, Ethiopa	14m. 45.65s

10,000-Meter Run

1988	Olga Boldarenko, USSR	31m. 44.69s
1992	Derartu Tulu, Ethiopia	31m. 06.02s
1996	Fernanda Ribeiro, Portugal	31m. 01.63s
2000	Derartu Tulu, Ethiopia	30m. 17.49s*
2004	Xing Huina, China	30m. 24.36s

100-Meter Hurdles

1972	Annelie Ehrhardt, E. Germany	12.59s
1976	Johanna Schaller, E. Germany	12.77s
1980	Vera Komisova, USSR	12.56s
1984	Benita Brown-Fitzgerald, United States	12.84s
1988	Jordanka Donkova, Bulgaria	12.38s
1992	Paraskevi Patoulidou, Greece	12.64s
1996	Ludmila Enquist, Sweden	12.58s
2000	Olga Shishigina, Kazakhstan	12.65s
2004	Joanna Hayes, United States	12.37s*

400-Meter Hurdles

1984	Nawal el Moutawakii, Morocco	54.61s
1988	Debra Flintoff-King, Australia	53.17s
1992	Sally Gunnell, Great Britain	53.23s
1996	Deon Hemmings, Jamaica	52.82s
2000	Irina Privalova, Russia	53.02s
2004	Fani Halkia, Greece	52.82s*

400-Meter Relay

1928	Canada	48.4s
1932	United States	46.9s
1936	United States	46.9s
1948	Netherlands	47.5s
1952	United States	45.9s
1956	Australia	44.5s
1960	United States	44.5s

400-Meter Relay

1964	Poland	43.6s
1968	United States	42.88s
1972	West Germany	42.81s
1976	East Germany	42.55s
1980	East Germany	41.60s*
1984	United States	41.65s
1988	United States	41.98s
1992	United States	42.11s
1996	United States	41.95s
2000	Bahamas	41.95s
2004	Jamaica	41.73s

1,600-Meter Relay

1972	East Germany	3m. 23s
1976	East Germany	3m. 19.23s
1980	USSR	3m. 20.02s
1984	United States	3m. 18.29s
1988	USSR	3m. 15.17s*
1992	Unified Team	3m. 20.20s
1996	United States	3m. 20.91s
2000	United States	3m. 22.62s
2004	United States	3m. 19.01s

10-Kilometer Walk

1992	Chen Yueling, China	44m. 32s
1996	Elena Nikolayeva, Russia	41m. 49s*

20-Kilometer Walk

2000	Wang Liping, China	1m. 29.05s*
2004	Athanasia Tsoumeleka, Greece	1m. 29.12s

Marathon

1984	Joan Benoit, United States	2h. 24m. 52s
1988	Rosa Mota, Portugal	2h. 25m. 40s
1992	Valentina Yegorova, Unified Team	2h. 32m. 41s
1996	Fatuma Roba, Ethiopia	2h. 26m. 05s
2000	Naoko Takahashi, Japan	2h. 23m. 14s*
2004	Mizuki Noguchi, Japan	2h. 26m. 20s

High Jump

1928	Ethel Catherwood, Canada	1.59m. (5' 2½")
1932	Jean Shiley, United States	1.65m. (5' 5")
1936	Ibolya Csák, Hungary	1.60m. (5' 3")
1948	Alice Coachman, U. S.	1.68m. (5' 6")
1952	Esther Brand, South Africa	1.67m. (5' 5¾")
1956	Mildred L. McDaniel, U. S.	1.76m. (5' 9¼")
1960	Iolanda Balas, Romania	1.85m. (6' ¾")
1964	Iolanda Balas, Romania	1.90m. (6' 2¾")
1968	Miloslava Resková, Czech.	1.82m. (5' 11½")
1972	Ulrike Meyfarth, W. Germany	1.92m. (6' 3½")
1976	Rosemarie Ackermann, E. Ger.	1.93m. (6' 4")
1980	Sara Simeoni, Italy	1.97m. (6' 5½")
1984	Ulrike Meyfarth, W. Germany	2.02m. (6' 7½")
1988	Louise Ritter, United States	2.03m. (6' 8")
1992	Heike Henkel, Germany	2.02m. (6' 7½")
1996	Stefka Kostadinova, Bulgaria	2.05m. (6' 8¾")*
2000	Yelena Yelesina, Russia	2.01m. (6' 7")
2004	Yelena Slesarenko, Russia	2.06m. (6' 9")*

Long Jump

1948	Olga Gyarmati, Hungary	5.69m. (18' 8")
1952	Yvette Williams, New Zealand	6.24m. (20' 5¼")
1956	Elzbieta Krzeskinska, Poland	6.35m. (20' 10")
1960	Vira Krepkina, USSR	6.37m. (20' 10¾")
1964	Mary Rand, Great Britain	6.76m. (22' 2¼")
1968	Viorica Viscopoleanu, Romania	6.82m. (22' 4½")
1972	Heidemarie Rosendahl, W. Ger.	6.78m. (22' 3")
1976	Angela Voigt, E. Germany	6.72m. (22' ¾")
1980	Tatyana Kolpakova, USSR	7.06m. (23' 2")
1984	Anisoara Cusmir-Stanciu, Rom.	6.96m. (22' 10")
1988	Jackie Joyner-Kersee, United States	7.40m. (24' 3½")*
1992	Heike Drechsler, Germany	7.14m. (23' 5¼")
1996	Chioma Ajunwa, Nigeria	7.12m. (23' 4½")
2000	Heike Drechsler, Germany	6.99m. (22' 11¼")
2004	Tatyana Lebedeva, Russia	7.07m. (23' 2½")

Triple Jump

1996	Inessa Kravets, Ukraine	15.33m. (50' 3½")*
2000	Tereza Marinova, Bulgaria	15.20m. (49' 10½")
2004	Francoise Mbango Etone, Cameroon	15.30m. (50' 2⅓")

Discus Throw

1928	Halina Konopacka, Poland	39.62m. (130' 0")
1932	Lillian Copeland, United States	40.58m. (133' 2")
1936	Gisela Mauermayer, Germany	47.62m. (156' 3")
1948	Micheline Ostermeyer, France	41.92m. (137' 6")
1952	Nina Ponomareva, USSR	51.42m. (168' 8")
1956	Olga Fikotová, Czech.	53.68m. (176' 1")
1960	Nina Ponomareva, USSR	55.10m. (180' 9")
1964	Tamara Press, USSR	57.26m. (187' 10")
1968	Lia Manoliu, Romania	58.28m. (191' 2")
1972	Faina Melnik, USSR	66.62m. (218' 7")
1976	Evelin Jahl, E. Germany	69.00m. (226' 4")
1980	Evelin Jahl, E. Germany	69.96m. (229' 6")
1984	Ria Stalman, Netherlands	65.36m. (214' 5")

Discus Throw

1988	Martina Hellmann, E. Germany	72.30m. (237' 2")*
1992	Maritza Martén Garcia, Cuba	70.06m. (229' 10")
1996	Ilke Wyludda, Germany	69.66m. (228' 6")
2000	Ellina Zvereva, Belarus	68.40m. (224' 5")
2004	Natalya Sadova, Russia	67.02m. (219' 9")

Hammer Throw

2000	Kamila Skolimowska, Poland	71.16m. (233' 5¾")*
2004	Olga Kuzenkova, Russia	75.02m. (246' 1")

Pole Vault

2000	Stacy Dragila, United States	4.60m. (15' 1")*
2004	Yelena Isinbayeva, Russia	4.91m. (16' 1⅓")

Shot Put (8 lb., 13 oz.)

1948	Micheline Ostermeyer, France	13.75m. (45' 1½")
1952	Galina Zybina, USSR	15.28m. (50' 1½")
1956	Tamara Tyshkyevich, USSR	16.59m. (54' 5¼")
1960	Tamara Press, USSR	17.32m. (56' 10")
1964	Tamara Press, USSR	18.14m. (59' 6¼")
1968	Margitta Gummel, E. Germany	19.61m. (64' 4")
1972	Nadezhda Chizova, USSR	21.03m. (69' 0")
1976	Ivanka Khristova, Bulgaria	21.16m. (69' 5¼")
1980	Ilona Slupianek, E. Germany	22.41m. (73' 6¼")*
1984	Claudia Losch, W. Germany	20.49m. (67' 2¼")
1988	Natalya Lisovskaya, USSR	22.24m. (72' 11¾")
1992	Svetlana Krivelyova, Unified Team	21.06m. (69' 1¼")
1996	Astrid Kumbernuss, Germany	20.56m. (67' 5½")
2000	Yanina Karolchik, Belarus	20.56m. (67' 5½")
2004	Yumileidi Cumba Jay, Cuba	19.59m. (64' 3¼")

Javelin Throw

1932	"Babe" Didrikson, United States	43.68m. (143' 4")
1936	Tilly Fleischer, Germany	45.18m. (148' 3")
1948	Herma Bauma, Austria	45.56m. (149' 6")
1952	Dana Zátopková, Czech.	50.46m. (165' 7")
1956	Inese Jaunzeme, USSR	53.86m. (176' 8")
1960	Elvira Ozolina, USSR	55.98m. (183' 8")
1964	Mihaela Penes, Romania	60.54m. (198' 7")
1968	Angéla Németh, Hungary	60.36m. (198' 0")
1972	Ruth Fuchs, E. Germany	63.88m. (209' 7")
1976	Ruth Fuchs, E. Germany	65.94m. (216' 4")
1980	Maria Colón Ruenes, Cuba	68.40m. (224' 5")
1984	Tessa Sanderson, Great Britain	69.56m. (228' 2")
1988	Petra Felke, E. Germany	74.68m. (245' 0")
1992	Silke Renke, Germany	68.34m. (224' 2")
1996	Heli Rantanen, Finland	67.94m. (222' 11")
2000	Trine Hattestad, Norway (a)	68.91m. (226' 1")
2004	Osleidys Menendez, Cuba	71.53m. (234' 8")*

(a) New records were kept after javelin was modified in 1999.

Heptathlon

1984	Glynis Nunn, Australia	6,390 pts.
1988	Jackie Joyner-Kersee, United States	7,291 pts.*
1992	Jackie Joyner-Kersee, United States	7,044 pts.
1996	Ghada Shouaa, Syria	6,780 pts.
2000	Denise Lewis, Britain	6,584 pts.
2004	Carolina Kluft, Sweden	6,952 pts.

Swimming and Diving—Men

50-Meter Freestyle

1988	Matt Biondi, United States	22.14
1992	Aleksandr Popov, Unified Team	21.91*
1996	Aleksandr Popov, Russia	22.13
2000	Anthony Ervin, United States	21.98
2000	Gary Hall Jr., United States	21.98
2004	Gary Hall Jr., United States	21.93

100-Meter Freestyle

1896	Alfred Hajos, Hungary	1:22.2
1904	Zoltan de Halmay, Hungary (100 yards)	1:02.8
1908	Charles Daniels, United States	1:05.6
1912	Duke P. Kahanamoku, United States	1:03.4
1920	Duke P. Kahanamoku, United States	1:01.4
1924	John Weissmuller, United States	59.0
1928	John Weissmuller, United States	58.6
1932	Yasuji Miyazaki, Japan	58.2
1936	Ferenc Csik, Hungary	57.6
1948	Wally Ris, United States	57.3
1952	Clark Scholes, United States	57.4
1956	Jon Henricks, Australia	55.4
1960	John Devitt, Australia	55.2
1964	Don Schollander, United States	53.4
1968	Mike Wenden, Australia	52.2
1972	Mark Spitz, United States	51.22
1976	Jim Montgomery, United States	49.99
1980	Jorg Woithe, E. Germany	50.40
1984	Rowdy Gaines, United States	49.80
1988	Matt Biondi, United States	48.63
1992	Aleksandr Popov, Unified Team	49.02
1996	Aleksandr Popov, Russia	48.74
2000	Pieter van den Hoogenband, Netherlands	48.30
2004	Pieter van den Hoogenband, Netherlands	48.17

200-Meter Freestyle

1968	Mike Wenden, Australia	1:55.2
1972	Mark Spitz, United States	1:52.78
1976	Bruce Furniss, United States	1:50.29
1980	Sergei Kopliakov, USSR	1:49.81
1984	Michael Gross, W. Germany	1:47.44
1988	Duncan Armstrong, Australia	1:47.25
1992	Yevgeny Sadovyi, Unified Team	1:46.70
1996	Danyon Loader, New Zealand	1:47.63
2000	Pieter van den Hoogenband, Netherlands	1:45.35
2004	Ian Thorpe, Australia	1:44.71*

400-Meter Freestyle

1904	C. M. Daniels, United States (440 yards)	6:16.2
1908	Henry Taylor, Great Britain	5:36.8
1912	George Hodgson, Canada	5:24.4
1920	Norman Ross, United States	5:26.8
1924	John Weissmuller, United States	5:04.2
1928	Albert Zorilla, Argentina	5:01.6
1932	Clarence Crabbe, United States	4:48.4
1936	Jack Medica, United States	4:44.5
1948	William Smith, United States	4:41.0
1952	Jean Boiteux, France	4:30.7
1956	Murray Rose, Australia	4:27.3
1960	Murray Rose, Australia	4:18.3
1964	Don Schollander, United States	4:12.2
1968	Mike Burton, United States	4:09.0
1972	Brad Cooper, Australia	4:00.27
1976	Brian Goodell, United States	3:51.93
1980	Vladimir Salnikov, USSR	3:51.31
1984	George DiCarlo, United States	3:51.23
1988	Ewe Dassler, E. Germany	3:46.95
1992	Yevgeny Sadovyi, Unified Team	3:45.00
1996	Danyon Loader, New Zealand	3:47.97
2000	Ian Thorpe, Australia	3:40.59*
2004	Ian Thorpe, Australia	3:43.10

1,500-Meter Freestyle

1908	Henry Taylor, Great Britain	22:48.4
1912	George Hodgson, Canada	22:00.0
1920	Norman Ross, United States	22:23.2
1924	Andrew Charlton, Australia	20:06.6
1928	Arne Borg, Sweden	19:51.8
1932	Kusuo Kitamura, Japan	19:12.4
1936	Noboru Terada, Japan	19:13.7
1948	James McLane, United States	19:18.5
1952	Ford Konno, United States	18:30.3
1956	Murray Rose, Australia	17:58.9
1960	Jon Konrads, Australia	17:19.6
1964	Robert Windle, Australia	17:01.7
1968	Mike Burton, United States	16:38.9
1972	Mike Burton, United States	15:52.58
1976	Brian Goodell, United States	15:02.40
1980	Vladimir Salnikov, USSR	14:58.27
1984	Michael O'Brien, United States	15:05.20
1988	Vladimir Salnikov, USSR	15:00.40
1992	Kieren Perkins, Australia	14:43.48
1996	Kieren Perkins, Australia	14:56.40
2000	Grant Hackett, Australia	14:48.33
2004	Grant Hackett, Australia	14:43.40*

100-Meter Backstroke

1904	Walter Brack, Germany (100 yds.)	1:16.8
1908	Arno Bieberstein, Germany	1:24.6
1912	Harry Hebner, United States	1:21.2
1920	Warren Kealoha, United States	1:15.2
1924	Warren Kealoha, United States	1:13.2
1928	George Kojac, United States	1:08.2
1932	Masaji Kiyokawa, Japan	1:08.6
1936	Adolph Kiefer, United States	1:05.9
1948	Allen Stack, United States	1:06.4
1952	Yoshi Oyakawa, United States	1:05.4
1956	David Thiele, Australia	1:02.2
1960	David Thiele, Australia	1:01.9
1968	Roland Matthes, E. Germany	58.7
1972	Roland Matthes, E. Germany	56.58
1976	John Naber, United States	55.49
1980	Bengt Baron, Sweden	56.33
1984	Rick Carey, United States	55.79
1988	Daichi Suzuki, Japan	55.05
1992	Mark Tewksbury, Canada	53.98
1996	Jeff Rouse, United States	54.10
2000	Lenny Krayzelburg, United States	53.72
2004	Aaron Peirsol, United States	54.06

200-Meter Backstroke

1964	Jed Graef, United States	2:10.3
1968	Roland Matthes, E. Germany	2:09.6
1972	Roland Matthes, E. Germany	2:02.82
1976	John Naber, United States	1:59.19
1980	Sandor Wladar, Hungary	2:01.93
1984	Rick Carey, United States	2:00.23

200-Meter Backstroke

1988	Igor Polianski, USSR	1:59.37
1992	Martin Lopez-Zubero, Spain	1:58.47
1996	Brad Bridgewater, United States	1:58.54
2000	Lenny Krayzelburg, United States	1:56.76
2004	Aaron Peirsol, United States	1:54.95*

100-Meter Breaststroke

1968	Don McKenzie, United States	1:07.79
1972	Nobutaka Taguchi, Japan	1:04.94
1976	John Hencken, United States	1:03.11
1980	Duncan Goodhew, Great Britain	1:03.44
1984	Steve Lundquist, United States	1:01.65
1988	Adrian Moorhouse, Great Britain	1:02.04
1992	Nelson Diebel, United States	1:01.50
1996	Fred Deburghgraeve, Belgium	1:00.60
2000	Domenico Fioravanti, Italy	1:00.46
2004	Kosuke Kitajima, Japan	1:00.08

200-Meter Breaststroke

1908	Frederick Holman, Great Britain	3:09.2
1912	Walter Bathe, Germany	3:01.8
1920	Haken Malmroth, Sweden	3:04.4
1924	Robert Skelton, United States	2:56.6
1928	Yoshiyuki Tsuruta, Japan	2:48.8
1932	Yoshiyuki Tsuruta, Japan	2:45.4
1936	Tetsuo Hamuro, Japan	2:41.5
1948	Joseph Verdeur, United States	2:39.3
1952	John Davies, Australia	2:34.4
1956	Masura Furukawa, Japan	2:34.7
1960	William Mulliken, United States	2:37.4
1964	Ian O'Brien, Australia	2:27.8
1968	Felipe Munoz, Mexico	2:28.7
1972	John Hencken, United States	2:21.55
1976	David Wilkie, Great Britain	2:15.11
1980	Robertas Zhulpa, USSR	2:15.85
1984	Victor Davis, Canada	2:13.34
1988	Jozsef Szabo, Hungary	2:13.52
1992	Mike Barrowman, United States	2:10.16
1996	Norbert Rozsa, Hungary	2:12.57
2000	Domenico Fioravanti, Italy	2:10.87
2004	Kosuke Kitajima, Japan	2:09.44*

100-Meter Butterfly

1968	Doug Russell, United States	55.9
1972	Mark Spitz, United States	54.27
1976	Matt Vogel, United States	54.35
1980	Par Arvidsson, Sweden	54.92
1984	Michael Gross, W. Germany	53.08
1988	Anthony Nesty, Suriname	53.00
1992	Pablo Morales, United States	53.32
1996	Denis Pankratov, Russia	52.27
2000	Lars Froelander, Sweden	52.00
2004	Michael Phelps, United States	51.25*

200-Meter Butterfly

1956	William Yorzyk, United States	2:19.3
1960	Michael Troy, United States	2:12.8
1964	Kevin J. Berry, Australia	2:06.6
1968	Carl Robie, United States	2:08.7
1972	Mark Spitz, United States	2:00.70
1976	Mike Bruner, United States	1:59.23
1980	Sergei Fesenko, USSR	1:59.76
1984	Jon Sieben, Australia	1:57.04
1988	Michael Gross, W. Germany	1:56.94
1992	Mel Stewart, United States	1:56.26
1996	Denis Pankratov, Russia	1:56.51
2000	Tom Malchow, United States	1:55.35
2004	Michael Phelps, United States	1:54.04*

200-Meter Individual Medley

1968	Charles Hickcox, United States	2:12.0
1972	Gunnar Larsson, Sweden	2:07.17
1984	Alex Baumann, Canada	2:01.42
1988	Tamas Darnyi, Hungary	2:00.17
1992	Tamas Darnyi, Hungary	2:00.76
1996	Attila Czene, Hungary	1:59.91
2000	Massimiliano Rosolino, Italy	1:58.98
2004	Michael Phelps, United States	1:57.14*

400-Meter Individual Medley

1964	Dick Roth, United States	4:45.4
1968	Charles Hickcox, United States	4:48.4
1972	Gunnar Larsson, Sweden	4:31.98
1976	Rod Strachan, United States	4:23.68
1980	Aleksandr Sidorenko, USSR	4:22.89
1984	Alex Baumann, Canada	4:17.41
1988	Tamas Darnyi, Hungary	4:14.75
1992	Tamas Darnyi, Hungary	4:14.23
1996	Tom Dolan, United States	4:14.90
2000	Tom Dolan, United States	4:11.76
2004	Michael Phelps, United States	4:08.26*

400-Meter Freestyle Relay

1964	United States	3:31.2
1968	United States	3:31.7
1972	United States	3:26.42
1984	United States	3:19.03
1988	United States	3:16.53
1992	United States	3:16.74
1996	United States	3:15.41
2000	Australia	3:13.67
2004	South Africa	3:13.17*

800-Meter Freestyle Relay

1908	Great Britain	10:55.6
1912	Australia	10:11.6
1920	United States	10:04.4
1924	United States	9:53.4
1928	United States	9:36.2
1932	Japan	8:58.4
1936	Japan	8:51.5
1948	United States	8:46.0
1952	United States	8:31.1
1956	Australia	8:23.6
1960	United States	8:10.2
1964	United States	7:52.1
1968	United States	7:52.33
1972	United States	7:35.78
1976	United States	7:23.22
1980	USSR	7:23.50
1984	United States	7:15.69
1988	United States	7:12.51
1992	Unified Team	7:11.95
1996	United States	7:14.84
2000	Australia	7:07.05*
2004	United States	7:07.33

400-Meter Medley Relay

1960	United States	4:05.4
1964	United States	3:58.4
1968	United States	3:54.9
1972	United States	3:48.16
1976	United States	3:42.22
1980	Australia	3:45.70
1984	United States	3:39.30
1988	United States	3:36.93
1992	United States	3:36.93
1996	United States	3:34.84
2000	United States	3:33.73
2004	United States	3:30.68*

	Springboard Diving	**Points**
1908	Albert Zurner, Germany	85.50
1912	Paul Guenther, Germany	79.23
1920	Louis Kuehn, U.S	675.40
1924	Albert White, United States	97.46
1928	Pete Desjardins, United States	185.04
1932	Michael Galitzen, United States	161.38
1936	Richard Degener, United States	163.57
1948	Bruce Harlan, United States	163.64
1952	David Browning, United States	205.29
1956	Robert Clotworthy, United States	159.56
1960	Gary Tobian, United States	170.00
1964	Kenneth Sitzberger, United States	159.90
1968	Bernie Wrightson, United States	170.15
1972	Vladimir Vasin, USSR	594.09
1976	Phil Boggs, United States	619.52
1980	Aleksandr Portnov, USSR	905.02
1984	Greg Louganis, United States	754.41
1988	Greg Louganis, United States	730.80
1992	Mark Lenzi, United States	676.53
1996	Xiong Ni, China	701.46
2000	Xiong Ni, China	708.72
2004	Peng Bo, China	787.30

	Platform Diving	**Points**
1904	Dr. G.E. Sheldon, United States	112.75
1908	Hjalmar Johansson, Sweden	183.75
1912	Erik Adlerz, Sweden	73.94
1920	Clarence Pinkston, United States	100.67
1924	Albert White, United States	97.46
1928	Pete Desjardins, United States	98.74
1932	Harold Smith, United States	124.80
1936	Marshall Wayne, United States	113.58
1948	Sammy Lee, United States	130.05
1952	Sammy Lee, United States	156.28
1956	Joaquin Capilla, Mexico	152.44
1960	Robert Webster, United States	165.56
1964	Robert Webster, United States	148.58
1968	Klaus Dibiasi, Italy	164.18
1972	Klaus Dibiasi, Italy	504.12
1976	Klaus Dibiasi, Italy	600.51
1980	Falk Hoffmann, E. Germany	835.65
1984	Greg Louganis, United States	710.91

Platform Diving — Points

1988 Greg Louganis, United States 638.61
1992 Sun Shuwei, China 677.31
1996 Dmitri Sautin, Russia 692.34
2000 Tian Liang, China 724.53
2004 Hu Jia, China 748.08

Synchronized Platform

2004 Tian Liang and Yang Jinghui, China 383.88

Synchronized Springboard

2004 Nikolaos Siranidis and Thomas Bimis, Greece 353.34

Swimming and Diving—Women

50-Meter Freestyle

1988 Kristin Otto, E. Germany 25.49
1992 Yang Wenyi, China 24.76
1996 Amy Van Dyken, United States 24.87
2000 Inge de Bruijn, Netherlands 24.32
2004 Inge de Bruijn, Netherlands 24.58

100-Meter Freestyle

1912 Fanny Durack, Australia 1:22.2
1920 Ethelda Bleibtrey, United States 1:13.6
1924 Ethel Lackie, United States 1:12.4
1928 Albina Osipowich, United States 1:11.0
1932 Helene Madison, United States 1:06.8
1936 Hendrika Mastenbroek, Holland 1:05.9
1948 Greta Andersen, Denmark 1:06.3
1952 Katalin Szoke, Hungary 1:06.8
1956 Dawn Fraser, Australia 1:02.0
1960 Dawn Fraser, Australia 1:01.2
1964 Dawn Fraser, Australia 59.5
1968 Jan Henne, United States 1:00.0
1972 Sandra Neilson, United States 58.59
1976 Kornelia Ender, E. Germany 55.65
1980 Barbara Krause, E. Germany 54.79
1984 (tie) Carrie Steinseifer, United States 55.92
Nancy Hogshead, United States 55.92
1988 Kristin Otto, E. Germany 54.93
1992 Zhuang Yong, China 54.64
1996 Li Jingyi, China 54.50
2000 Inge de Bruijn, Netherlands 53.83
2004 Jodie Henry, Australia 53.84

200-Meter Freestyle

1968 Debbie Meyer, United States 2:10.5
1972 Shane Gould, Australia 2:03.56
1976 Kornelia Ender, E. Germany 1:59.26
1980 Barbara Krause, E. Germany 1:58.33
1984 Mary Wayte, United States 1:59.23
1988 Heike Friedrich, E. Germany 1:57.65*
1992 Nicole Haislett, United States 1:57.90
1996 Claudia Poll, Costa Rica 1:58.16
2000 Susie O'Neill, Australia 1:58.24
2004 Camelia Potec, Romania 1:58.03

400-Meter Freestyle

1924 Martha Norelius, United States 6:02.2
1928 Martha Norelius, United States 5:42.8
1932 Helene Madison, United States 5:28.5
1936 Hendrika Mastenbroek, Netherlands 5:26.4
1948 Ann Curtis, United States 5:17.8
1952 Valerie Gyenge, Hungary 5:12.1
1956 Lorraine Crapp, Australia 4:54.6
1960 Susan Chris von Saltza, United States 4:50.6
1964 Virginia Duenkel, United States 4:43.3
1968 Debbie Meyer, United States 4:31.8
1972 Shane Gould, Australia 4:19.44
1976 Petra Thuemer, E. Germany 4:09.89
1980 Ines Diers, E. Germany 4:08.76
1984 Tiffany Cohen, United States 4:07.10
1988 Janet Evans, United States 4:03.85*
1992 Dagmar Hase, Germany 4:07.18
1996 Michelle Smith, Ireland 4:07.25
2000 Brooke Bennett, United States 4:05.80
2004 Laure Manaudou, France 4:05.34

800-Meter Freestyle

1968 Debbie Meyer, United States 9:24.0
1972 Keena Rothhammer, United States 8:53.68
1976 Petra Thuemer, E. Germany 8:37.14
1980 Michelle Ford, Australia 8:28.90
1984 Tiffany Cohen, United States 8:24.95
1988 Janet Evans, United States 8:20.20
1992 Janet Evans, United States 8:25.52
1996 Brooke Bennett, United States 8:27.89
2000 Brooke Bennett, United States 8:19.67*
2004 Ai Shibata, Japan 8:24.54

100-Meter Backstroke

1924 Sybil Bauer, United States 1:23.2
1928 Marie Braun, Netherlands 1:22.0
1932 Eleanor Holm, United States 1:19.4
1936 Dina Senff, Netherlands 1:18.9
1948 Karen Harup, Denmark 1:14.4
1952 Joan Harrison, South Africa 1:14.3
1956 Judy Grinham, Great Britain 1:12.9
1960 Lynn Burke, United States 1:09.3
1964 Cathy Ferguson, United States 1:07.7
1968 Kaye Hall, United States 1:06.2
1972 Melissa Belote, United States 1:05.78
1976 Ulrike Richter, E. Germany 1:01.83
1980 Rica Reinisch, E. Germany 1:00.86
1984 Theresa Andrews, United States 1:02.55
1988 Kristin Otto, E. Germany 1:00.89
1992 Krisztina Egerszegi, Hungary 1:00.68
1996 Beth Botsford, United States 1:01.19
2000 Diana Mocanu, Romania 1:00.21
2004 Natalie Coughlin, United States 1:00.37

200-Meter Backstroke

1968 Pokey Watson, United States 2:24.8
1972 Melissa Belote, United States 2:19.19
1976 Ulrike Richter, E. Germany 2:13.43
1980 Rica Reinisch, E. Germany 2:11.77
1984 Jolanda De Rover, Netherlands 2:12.38
1988 Krisztina Egerszegi, Hungary 2:09.29
1992 Krisztina Egerszegi, Hungary 2:07.06*
1996 Krisztina Egerszegi, Hungary 2:07.83
2000 Diana Mocanu, Romania 2:08.16
2004 Kirsty Coventry, Zimbabwe 2:09.19

100-Meter Breaststroke

1968 Djurdjica Bjedov, Yugoslavia 1:15.8
1972 Cathy Carr, United States 1:13.58
1976 Hannelore Anke, E. Germany 1:11.16
1980 Ute Geweniger, E. Germany 1:10.22
1984 Petra Van Staveren, Netherlands 1:09.88
1988 Tania Dangalakova, Bulgaria 1:07.95
1992 Elena Roudkovskaia, Unified Team 1:08.00
1996 Penny Heyns, South Africa 1:07.73
2000 Megan Quann, United States 1:07.05
2004 Luo Xuejuan, China 1:06.64*

200-Meter Breaststroke

1924 Lucy Morton, Great Britain 3:33.2
1928 Hilde Schrader, Germany 3:12.6
1932 Clare Dennis, Australia 3:06.3
1936 Hideko Maehata, Japan 3:03.6
1948 Nelly Van Vliet, Netherlands 2:57.2
1952 Eva Szekely, Hungary 2:51.7
1956 Ursula Happe, Germany 2:53.1
1960 Anita Lonsbrough, Great Britain 2:49.5
1964 Galina Prozumenschikova, USSR 2:46.4
1968 Sharon Wichman, United States 2:44.4
1972 Beverly Whitfield, Australia 2:41.71
1976 Marina Koshevaia, USSR 2:33.35
1980 Lina Kachushite, USSR 2:29.54
1984 Anne Ottenbrite, Canada 2:30.38
1988 Silke Hoerner, E. Germany 2:26.71
1992 Kyoko Iwasaki, Japan 2:26.65
1996 Penny Heyns, South Africa 2:25.41
2000 Agnes Kovacs, Hungary 2:24.35
2004 Amanda Beard, United States 2:23.37*

100-Meter Butterfly

1956 Shelley Mann, United States 1:11.0
1960 Carolyn Schuler, United States 1:09.5
1964 Sharon Stouder, United States 1:04.7
1968 Lynn McClements, Australia 1:05.5
1972 Mayumi Aoki, Japan 1:03.34
1976 Kornelia Ender, E. Germany 1:00.13
1980 Caren Metschuck, E. Germany 1:00.42
1984 Mary T. Meagher, United States 59.26
1988 Kristin Otto, E. Germany 59.00
1992 Qian Hong, China 58.62
1996 Amy Van Dyken, United States 59.13
2000 Inge de Bruijn, Netherlands 56.61*
2004 Petria Thomas, Australia 57.72

200-Meter Butterfly

1968 Ada Kok, Netherlands 2:24.7
1972 Karen Moe, United States 2:15.57
1976 Andrea Pollack, E. Germany 2:11.41
1980 Ines Geissler, E. Germany 2:10.44
1984 Mary T. Meagher, United States 2:06.90
1988 Kathleen Nord, E. Germany 2:09.51
1992 Summer Sanders, United States 2:08.67
1996 Susan O'Neill, Australia 2:07.76
2000 Misty Hyman, United States 2:05.88*
2004 Otylia Jedrzejczak, Poland 2:06.05

200-Meter Individual Medley

1968 Claudia Kolb, United States 2:24.7
1972 Shane Gould, Australia 2:23.07
1984 Tracy Caulkins, United States 2:12.64
1988 Daniela Hunger, E. Germany 2:12.59
1992 Lin Li, China 2:11.65

200-Meter Individual Medley

1996 Michelle Smith, Ireland 2:13.93
2000 Yana Klochkova, Ukraine 2:10.68*
2004 Yana Klochkova, Ukraine 2:11.14

400-Meter Individual Medley

1964 Donna de Varona, United States 5:18.7
1968 Claudia Kolb, United States 5:08.5
1972 Gail Neall, Australia 5:02.97
1976 Ulrike Tauber, E. Germany 4:42.77
1980 Petra Schneider, E. Germany 4:36.29
1984 Tracy Caulkins, United States 4:39.24
1988 Janet Evans, United States 4:37.76
1992 Krisztina Egerszegi, Hungary 4:36.54
1996 Michelle Smith, Ireland 4:39.18
2000 Yana Klochkova, Ukraine 4:33.59*
2004 Yana Klochkova, Ukraine 4:34.83

400-Meter Freestyle Relay

1912 Great Britain 5:52.8
1920 United States 5:11.6
1924 United States 4:58.8
1928 United States 4:47.6
1932 United States 4:38.0
1936 Netherlands 4:36.0
1948 United States 4:29.2
1952 Hungary 4:24.4
1956 Australia 4:17.1
1960 United States 4:08.9
1964 United States 4:03.8
1968 United States 4:02.5
1972 United States 3:55.19
1976 United States 3:44.82
1980 East Germany 3:42.71
1984 United States 3:43.43
1988 East Germany 3:40.63
1992 United States 3:39.46
1996 United States 3:39.29
2000 United States 3:36.61
2004 Australia 3:35.94*

800-Meter Freestyle Relay

1996 United States 7:59.87
2000 United States 7:57.80
2004 United States 7:53.42*

400-Meter Medley Relay

1960 United States 4:41.1
1964 United States 4:33.9
1968 United States 4:28.3
1972 United States 4:20.75
1976 East Germany 4:07.95
1980 East Germany 4:06.67
1984 United States 4:08.34
1988 East Germany 4:03.74
1992 United States 4:02.54
1996 United States 4:02.88
2000 United States 3:58.30
2004 Australia 3:57.32*

Springboard Diving — Points

1920 Aileen Riggin, United States 539.90
1924 Elizabeth Becker, United States 474.50
1928 Helen Meany, United States 78.62
1932 Georgia Coleman United States 87.52
1936 Marjorie Gestring, United States 89.27
1948 Victoria M. Draves, United States 108.74
1952 Patricia McCormick, United States 147.30
1956 Patricia McCormick, United States 142.36
1960 Ingrid Kramer, Germany 155.81
1964 Ingrid Engel-Kramer, Germany 145.00
1968 Sue Gossick, United States 150.77
1972 Micki King, United States 450.03
1976 Jenni Chandler, United States 506.19
1980 Irina Kalinina, USSR 725.91
1984 Sylvie Bernier, Canada 530.70
1988 Gao Min, China 580.23
1992 Gao Min, China 572.40
1996 Fu Mingxia, China 547.68
2000 Fu Mingxia, China 609.42
2004 Guo Jingjing, China 633.15

Platform Diving — Points

1912 Greta Johansson, Sweden 39.90
1920 Stefani Fryland-Clausen, Denmark 34.60
1924 Caroline Smith, United States 33.20
1928 Elizabeth B. Pinkston, United States 31.60
1932 Dorothy Poynton, United States 40.26
1936 Dorothy Poynton Hill, United States 33.93
1948 Victoria M. Draves, United States 8.87
1952 Patricia McCormick, United States 79.37
1956 Patricia McCormick, United States 84.85
1960 Ingrid Kramer, Germany 91.28
1964 Lesley Bush, United States 99.80
1968 Milena Duchkova, Czech. 109.59
1972 Ulrika Knape, Sweden 390.00
1976 Elena Vaytsekhouskaya, USSR 406.59
1980 Martina Jaschke, E. Germany 596.25
1984 Zhou Jihong, China 435.51
1988 Xu Yanmei, China 445.20
1992 Fu Mingxia, China 461.43
1996 Fu Mingxia, China 521.58
2000 Laura Wilkinson, United States 543.75
2004 Chantelle Newbery, Australia 590.31

Synchronized Platform

2004 Lao Lishi and Li Ting, China 352.14

Synchronized Springboard

2004 Wu Minxia and Guo Jingjing, China 336.90

BOXING

Lt. Flyweight (48 kg/106 lbs)

1968 Francisco Rodriguez, Venezuela
1972 Gyorgy Gedo, Hungary
1976 Jorge Hernandez, Cuba
1980 Shamil Sabyrov, USSR
1984 Paul Gonzalez, United States
1988 Ivailo Hristov, Bulgaria
1992 Rogelio Marcelo, Cuba
1996 Daniel Petrov, Bulgaria
2000 Brahim Asloum, France
2004 Yan Bhartelemy Varela, Cuba

Flyweight (51 kg/112 lbs)

1904 George Finnegan, United States
1920 William Di Gennara, United States
1924 Fidel LaBarba, United States
1928 Antal Kocsis, Hungary
1932 Istvan Enekes, Hungary
1936 Willi Kaiser, Germany
1948 Pascual Perez, Argentina
1952 Nathan Brooks, United States
1956 Terence Spinks, Great Britain
1960 GyulaTorok, Hungary
1964 Fernando Atzori, Italy
1968 Ricardo Delgado, Mexico
1972 Georgi Kostadinov, Bulgaria
1976 Leo Randolph, United States
1980 Peter Lessov, Bulgaria
1984 Steve McCrory, United States
1988 Kim Kwang Sun, S. Korea
1992 Su Choi Choi, N. Korea
1996 Maikro Romero, Cuba
2000 Wijan Ponlid, Thailand
2004 Yuriorkis Gamboa Toledano, Cuba

Bantamweight (54 kg /119 lbs)

1904 Oliver Kirk, United States
1908 A. Henry Thomas, Great Britain
1920 Clarence Walker, South Africa
1924 William Smith, South Africa
1928 Vittorio Tamagnini, Italy
1932 Horace Gwynne, Canada
1936 Ulderico Sergo, Italy
1948 Tibor Csik, Hungary
1952 Pentti Hamalainen, Finland
1956 Wolfgang Behrendt, E. Germany
1960 Oleg Grigoryev, USSR
1964 Takao Sakurai, Japan
1968 Valery Sokolov, USSR
1972 Orlando Martinez, Cuba
1976 Yong-Jo Gu, N. Korea
1980 Juan Hernandez, Cuba
1984 Maurizio Stecca, Italy
1988 Kennedy McKinney, United States
1992 Joel Casamayor, Cuba
1996 Istvan Kovacs, Hungary
2000 Guillermo Rigondeaux, Cuba
2004 Guillermo Rigondeaux Cuba

Featherweight (57 kg/125 lbs)

1904 Oliver Kirk, United States
1908 Richard Gunn, Great Britain
1920 Paul Fritsch, France
1924 John Fields, United States
1928 Lambertus van Klaveren, Netherlands
1932 Carmelo Robledo, Argentina
1936 Oscar Casanovas, Argentina
1948 Ernesto Formenti, Italy
1952 Jan Zachara, Czechoslovakia
1956 Vladimir Safronov, USSR
1960 Francesco Musso, Italy
1964 Stanislav Stephashkin, USSR
1968 Antonin Roldan, Mexico
1972 Boris Kousnetsov, USSR
1976 Angel Herrera, Cuba
1980 Rudi Fink, E. Germany
1984 Meldrick Taylor, United States
1988 Giovanni Parisi, Italy
1992 Andreas Tews, Germany
1996 Somluck Kamsing, Thailand
2000 Bekzat Sattarkhanov, Kazakhstan
2004 Alexei Tichtchenko, Russia

Lightweight (60 kg/132 lbs)

1904 Harry Spanger, United States
1908 Frederick Grace, Great Britain
1920 Samuel Mosberg, United States
1924 Hans Nielsen, Denmark
1928 Carlo Orlandi, Italy
1932 Lawrence Stevens, South Africa
1936 Imre Harangi, Hungary
1948 Gerald Dreyer, South Africa
1952 Aureliano Bolognesi, Italy
1956 Richard McTaggart, Great Britain
1960 Kazimierz Pazdzior, Poland
1964 Jozef Grudzien, Poland
1968 Ronald Harris, United States
1972 Jan Szczepanski, Poland
1976 Howard Davis, United States
1980 Angel Herrera, Cuba
1984 Pernell Whitaker, United States
1988 Andreas Zuelow, E. Germany
1992 Oscar De La Hoya, United States
1996 Hocine Soltani, Algeria
2000 Mario Kindelan, Cuba
2004 Mario Kindelan, Cuba

Lt. Welterweight (63.5 kg/139 lbs)

1952 Charles Adkins, United States
1956 Vladimir Yengibaryan, USSR
1960 Bohumil Nemecek, Czechoslovazkia
1964 Jerzy Kulej, Poland
1968 Jerzy Kulej, Poland
1972 Ray Seales, United States
1976 Ray Leonard, United States
1980 Patrizio Oliva, Italy
1984 Jerry Page, United States
1988 Viatcheslav Janovski, USSR
1992 Hector Vinent, Cuba
1996 Hector Vinent, Cuba
2000 Mahamadkadyz Abdullaev, Uzbekistan
2004 Manus Boonjumnong, Thailand

Welterweight (67 kg/147 lbs)

1904 Albert Young, United States
1920 Albert Schneider, Canada
1924 Jean Delarge, Belgium
1928 Edward Morgan, New Zealand
1932 Edward Flynn, United States
1936 Sten Suvio, Finland
1948 Julius Torma, Czechoslovakia
1952 Zygmunt Chychia, Poland
1956 Nicolae Linca, Romania
1960 Giovanni Benvenuti, Italy
1964 Marian Kasprzyk, Poland
1968 Manfred Wolke, E. Germany
1972 Emilio Correa, Cuba
1976 Jochen Bachfeld, E. Germany
1980 Andres Aldama, Cuba
1984 Mark Breland, United States
1988 Robert Wangila, Kenya
1992 Michael Carruth, Ireland
1996 Oleg Saitov, Russia
2000 Oleg Saitov, Russia
2004 Artayev Bakhtiyar, Kazakhstan

Lt. Middleweight (71 kg/156 lbs)

1952 Laszlo Papp, Hungary
1956 Laszlo Papp, Hungary
1960 Wilbert McClure, United States
1964 Boris Lagutin, USSR
1968 Boris Lagutin, USSR
1972 Dieter Kottysch, W. Germany
1976 Jerzy Rybicki, Poland
1980 Armando Martinez, Cuba
1984 Frank Tate, United States
1988 Park Si Hun, S. Korea
1992 Juan Lemus, Cuba
1996 David Reid, United States
2000 Yermakhan Ibraimov, Kazakhstan

Middleweight (75 kg/165 lbs)

1904 Charles Mayer, United States
1908 John Douglas, Great Britain
1920 Harry Mallin, Great Britain
1924 Harry Mallin, Great Britain
1928 Piero Toscani, Italy
1932 Carmen Barth, United States
1936 Jean Despeaux, France
1948 Laszlo Papp, Hungary
1952 Floyd Patterson, United States
1956 Gennady Schatkov, USSR
1960 Edward Crook, United States
1964 Valery Popenchenko, USSR
1968 Christopher Finnegan, Great Britain
1972 Vyacheslav Lemechev, USSR
1976 Michael Spinks, United States
1980 Jose Gomez, Cuba
1984 Joon-Sup Shin, S. Korea
1988 Henry Maske, E. Germany
1992 Ariel Hernandez, Cuba
1996 Ariel Hernandez, Cuba
2000 Jorge Gutierrez, Cuba
2004 Gaydarbek Gaydarbekov, Russia

Lt. Heavyweight (81 kg/178 lbs)

1920 Edward Eagan, United States
1924 Harry Mitchell, Great Britain
1928 Victor Avendano, Argentina
1932 David Carstens, South Africa
1936 Roger Michelot, France
1948 George Hunter, South Africa
1952 Norvel Lee, United States
1956 James Boyd, United States
1960 Cassius Clay, United States
1964 Cosimo Pinto, Italy
1968 Dan Poznyak, USSR
1972 Mate Parlov, Yugoslavia
1976 Leon Spinks, United States
1980 Slobodan Kacar, Yugoslavia
1984 Anton Josipovic, Yugoslavia
1988 Andrew Maynard, United States
1992 Torsten May, Germany
1996 Vassili Jirov, Kazakhstan
2000 Alexander Lebziak, Russia
2004 Andre Ward, United States

Heavyweight (91 kg/201 lbs)

1984 Henry Tillman, United States
1988 Ray Mercer, United States
1992 Felix Savon, Cuba
1996 Felix Savon, Cuba
2000 Felix Savon, Cuba
2004 Odlanier Solis Fonte, Cuba

Super Heavyweight (91+ kg/201+ lbs)
(known as heavyweight, 1904-80)

1904 Samuel Berger, United States
1908 Albert Oldham, Great Britain
1920 Ronald Rawson, Great Britain
1924 Otto von Porat, Norway
1928 Arturo Rodriguez Jurado, Argentina
1932 Santiago Lovell, Argentina
1936 Herbert Runge, Germany
1948 Rafael Iglesias, Argentina
1952 H. Edward Sanders, United States
1956 T. Peter Rademacher, United States
1960 Franco De Piccoli, Italy
1964 Joe Frazier, United States
1968 George Foreman, United States
1972 Teofilo Stevenson, Cuba
1976 Teofilo Stevenson, Cuba
1980 Teofilo Stevenson, Cuba
1984 Tyrell Biggs, United States
1988 Lennox Lewis, Canada
1992 Roberto Balado, Cuba
1996 Vladimir Klitchko, Ukraine
2000 Audley Harrison, Britain
2004 Alexander Povetkin, Russia

The 2006 Winter Olympic Games

Turin (Torino), Italy, Feb. 10-26, 2006

The first Winter Olympic Games were held in 1924 in Chamonix, France. In 2006, 2,500 athletes representing 85 nations are expected to compete in 84 medal events in 15 sports at the 20th Winter Olympic Games in Turin, Italy. No new sports were expected to be added to the program. All Winter Games events are contested on a surface of snow or ice. The emblem of the 2006 Games features the silhouette of Mole Antonelliana, a Turin landmark building, recast as a network of ice crystals. Neve and Gliz, the official mascots of the Turin Games, are made from a snowball and an ice cube. For further information, see the official website for the Turin Games: www.torino2006.org or visit the Olympic movement website at www.olympic.org

Winter Olympic Games Champions, 1924-2002

In 1992, the Unified Team represented the former Soviet republics of Russia, Ukraine, Belarus, Kazakhstan, and Uzbekistan.

Alpine Skiing

	Men's Downhill	Time
1948	Henri Oreiller, France	2:55.0
1952	Zeno Colo, Italy	2:30.8
1956	Toni Sailer, Austria	2:52.2
1960	Jean Vuarnet, France	2:06.0
1964	Egon Zimmermann, Austria	2:18.16
1968	Jean-Claude Killy, France	1:59.85
1972	Bernhard Russi, Switzerland	1:51.43
1976	Franz Klammer, Austria	1:45.73
1980	Leonhard Stock, Austria	1:45.50
1984	Bill Johnson, United States	1:45.49
1988	Pirmin Zurbriggen, Switzerland	1:59.63
1992	Patrick Ortlieb, Austria	1:50.37
1994	Tommy Moe, United States	1:45.75
1998	Jean-Luc Cretier, France	1:50.11
2002	Fritz Strobl, Austria	1:39.13

	Men's Super Giant Slalom	Time
1988	Franck Piccard, France	1:39.66
1992	Kjetil-Andre Aamodt, Norway	1:13.04
1994	Markus Wasmeier, Germany	1:32.53
1998	Hermann Maier, Austria	1:34.82
2002	Kjetil Andre Aamodt, Norway	1:21.58

	Men's Giant Slalom	Time
1952	Stein Eriksen, Norway	2:25.0
1956	Toni Sailer, Austria	3:00.1
1960	Roger Staub, Switzerland	1:48.3
1964	Francois Bonlieu, France	1:46.71
1968	Jean-Claude Killy, France	3:29.28
1972	Gustavo Thoeni, Italy	3:09.62
1976	Heini Hemmi, Switzerland	3:26.97
1980	Ingemar Stenmark, Sweden	2:40.74
1984	Max Julen, Switzerland	2:41.18
1988	Alberto Tomba, Italy	2:06.37
1992	Alberto Tomba, Italy	2:06.98
1994	Markus Wasmeier, Germany	2:52.46
1998	Hermann Maier, Austria	2:38.51
2002	Stephan Eberharter, Austria	2:23.28

	Men's Slalom	Time
1948	Edi Reinalter, Switzerland	2:10.3
1952	Othmar Schneider, Austria	2:00.0
1956	Toni Sailer, Austria	3:14.7
1960	Ernst Hinterseer, Austria	2:08.9
1964	Josef Stiegler, Austria	2:11.13
1968	Jean-Claude Killy, France	1:39.73
1972	Francisco Fernandez-Ochoa, Spain	1:49.27
1976	Piero Gros, Italy	2:03.29
1980	Ingemar Stenmark, Sweden	1:44.26
1984	Phil Mahre, United States	1:39.41
1988	Alberto Tomba, Italy	1:39.47
1992	Finn Christian Jagge, Norway	1:44.39
1994	Thomas Stangassinger, Austria	2:02.02
1998	Hans-Petter Buraas, Norway	1:49.31
2002	Jean-Pierre Vidal, France	1:41.06

	Men's Combined	Time
1936	Franz-Pfnuer, Germany	99.25 (pts.)
1948	Henri Oreiller, France	3.27 (pts.)
1988	Hubert Strolz, Austria	36.55 (pts.)
1992	Josef Polig, Italy	14.58 (pts.)
1994	Lasse Kjus, Norway	3:17.53
1998	Mario Reiter, Austria	3:08.06
2002	Kjetil Andre Aamodt, Norway	3:17.56

	Women's Downhill	Time
1948	Hedi Schlunegger, Switzerland	2:28.3
1952	Trude Beiser-Jochum, Austria	1:47.1
1956	Madeleine Berthod, Switzerland	1:40.7
1960	Heidi Biebl, Germany	1:37.6
1964	Christl Haas, Austria	1:55.39
1968	Olga Pall, Austria	1:40.87
1972	Marie-Theres Nadig, Switzerland	1:36.68
1976	Rosi Mittermaier, W. Germany	1:46.16
1980	Annemarie Moser-Proell , Austria	1:37.52
1984	Michela Figini, Switzerland	1:13.36
1988	Marina Kiehl, W. Germany	1:25.86
1992	Kerrin Lee-Gartner, Canada	1:52.55
1994	Katja Seizinger, Germany	1:35.93
1998	Katja Seizinger, Germany	1:28.89
2002	Carole Montillet, France	1:39.56

	Women's Super Giant Slalom	Time
1988	Sigrid Wolf, Austria	1:19.03
1992	Deborah Compagnoni, Italy	1:21.22
1994	Diann Roffe (Steinrotter), United States	1:22.15
1998	Picabo Street, United States	1:18.02
2002	Daniela Ceccarelli, Italy	1:13.59

	Women's Giant Slalom	Time
1952	Andrea Mead Lawrence, United States	2:06.8
1956	Ossi Reichert, Germany	1:56.5
1960	Yvonne Ruegg, Switzerland	1:39.9
1964	Marielle Goitschel, France	1:52.24
1968	Nancy Greene, Canada	1:51.97
1972	Marie-Theres Nadig, Switzerland	1:29.90
1976	Kathy Kreiner, Canada	1:29.13
1980	Hanni Wenzel, Liechtenstein (2 runs)	2:41.66
1984	Debbie Armstrong, United States	2:20.98
1988	Vreni Schneider, Switzerland	2:06.49
1992	Pernilla Wiberg, Sweden	2:12.74
1994	Deborah Compagnoni, Italy	2:30.97
1998	Deborah Compagnoni, Italy	2:50.59
2002	Janica Kostelic, Croatia	2:30.01

	Women's Slalom	Time
1948	Gretchen Fraser, United States	1:57.2
1952	Andrea Mead Lawrence, United States	2:10.6
1956	Renee Colliard, Switzerland	1:52.3
1960	Anne Heggtveit, Canada	1:49.6
1964	Christine Goitschel, France	1:29.86
1968	Marielle Goitschel, France	1:25.86
1972	Barbara Ann Cochran, United States	1:31.24
1976	Rosi Mittermaier, W. Germany	1:30.54
1980	Hanni Wenzel, Liechtenstein	1:25.09
1984	Paoletta Magoni, Italy	1:36.47
1988	Vreni Schneider, Switzerland	1:36.69
1992	Petra Kronberger, Austria	1:32.68
1994	Vreni Schneider, Switzerland	1:56.01
1998	Hilde Gerg, Germany	1:32.40
2002	Janica Kostelic, Croatia	1:46.10

	Women's Combined	Time
1936	Christl Cranz, Germany	97.06 (pts.)
1948	Trude Beiser-Jochum, Austria	6.58 (pts.)
1988	Anita Wachter, Austria	29.25 (pts.)
1992	Petra Kronberger, Austria	2.55 (pts.)
1994	Pernilla Wiberg, Sweden	3:05.16
1998	Katja Seizinger, Germany	2:40.74
2002	Janica Kostelic, Croatia	2:43.28

Biathlon

	Men's 10 Kilometers	Time
1980	Frank Ullrich, E. Germany	32:10.69
1984	Eirik Kvalfoss, Norway	30:53.80
1988	Frank-Peter Roetsch, E. Germany	25:08.10
1992	Mark Kirchner, Germany	26:02.30
1994	Serguei Tchepikov, Russia	28:07.00
1998	Ole Einar Bjoerndalen, Norway	27:16.20
2002	Ole Einar Bjoerndalen, Norway	24:51.30

	Men's 12.5 Kilometers	Time
2002	Ole Einar Bjoerndalen, Norway	32:34.6

	Men's 20 Kilometers	Time
1960	Klas Lestander, Sweden	1:33:21.6
1964	Vladimir Melanin, USSR	1:20:26.8
1968	Magnar Solberg, Norway	1:13:45.9
1972	Magnar Solberg, Norway	1:15:55.50
1976	Nikolai Kruglov, USSR	1:14:12.26
1980	Anatoly Aljabiev, USSR	1:08:16.31
1984	Peter Angerer, W. Germany	1:11:52.7
1988	Frank-Peter Roetsch, E. Germany	0:56:33.33
1992	Yevgeny Redkine, Unified Team	0:57:34.4
1994	Serguei Tarasov, Russia	0:57:25.3
1998	Halvard Hanevold, Norway	0:56:16.4
2002	Ole Einar Bjoerndalen, Norway	0:51:03.03

	Men's 30-Kilometer Relay	Time
1968	USSR, Norway, Sweden (40 km)	2:13:02.4
1972	USSR, Finland, E. Germany (40 km)	1:51:44.92
1976	USSR, Finland, E. Germany (40 km)	1:57:55.64
1980	USSR, E. Germany, W. Germany	1:34:03.27
1984	USSR, Norway, W. Germany	1:38:51.70
1988	USSR, W. Germany, Italy	1:22:30.00
1992	Germany, Unified Team, Sweden	1:24:43.50
1994	Germany, Russia, France	1:30:22.1
1998	Germany, Norway, Russia	1:19:43.3
2002	Norway, Germany, France	1:23:42.3

	Women's 7.5 Kilometers	Time
1992	Anfissa Restsova, Unified Team	24:29.2
1994	Myriam Bedard, Canada	26:08.8
1998	Galina Koukleva, Russia	23:08.0
2002	Kati Wilhelm, Germany	20:41.4

	Women's 10 Kilometers	Time
2002	Olga Pyleva, Russia	31:07.7

	Women's 15 Kilometers	Time
1992	Antje Misersky, Germany	51:47.2
1994	Myriam Bedard, Canada	52:06.6
1998	Ekaterina Dafovska, Bulgaria	54:52.0
2002	Andrea Henkel, Germany	47:30.0

	Women's 22.5-Kilometer Relay	Time
1992	France, Germany, Unified Team	1:15:55.6

	Women's 30-Kilometer Relay	Time
1994	Russia, Germany, France	1:47:19.5
1998	Germany, Russia, Norway	1:40:13.6
2002	Germany, Norway, Russia	1:27:55.0

Bobsledding

(Driver in parentheses)

	4-Man Bob	Time
1924	Switzerland (Eduard Scherrer)	5:45.54
1928	United States (William Fiske) (5-man)	3:20.50
1932	United States (William Fiske)	7:53.68
1936	Switzerland (Pierre Musy)	5:19.85
1948	United States (Francis Tyler)	5:20.10
1952	Germany (Andreas Ostler)	5:07.84
1956	Switzerland (Franz Kapus)	5:10.44
1964	Canada (Victor Emery)	4:14.46
1968	Italy (Eugenio Monti) (2 races)	2:17.39
1972	Switzerland (Jean Wicki)	4:43.07
1976	E. Germany (Meinhard Nehmer)	3:40.43
1980	E. Germany (Meinhard Nehmer)	3:59.92
1984	E. Germany (Wolfgang Hoppe)	3:20.22
1988	Switzerland (Ekkehard Fasser)	3:47.51
1992	Austria (Ingo Appelt)	3:53.90
1994	Germany (Wolfgang Hoppe)	3:27.28
1998	Germany II (Christoph Langen)	2:39.41
2002	Germany II (Andre Lange)	3:07.51

	2-Man Bob	Time
1932	United States (Hubert Stevens)	8:14.74
1936	United States (Ivan Brown)	5:29.29
1948	Switzerland (F. Endrich)	5:29.20
1952	Germany (Andreas Ostler)	5:24.54
1956	Italy (Dalla Costa)	5:30.14
1964	Great Britain (Anthony Nash)	4:21.90
1968	Italy (Eugenio Monti)	4:41.54
1972	W. Germany (Wolfgang Zimmerer)	4:57.07
1976	E. Germany (Meinhard Nehmer)	3:44.42
1980	Switzerland (Erich Schaerer)	4:09.36
1984	E. Germany (Wolfgang Hoppe)	3:25.56
1988	USSR (Janis Kipours)	3:54.19
1992	Switzerland (Gustav Weber)	4:03.26
1994	Switzerland (Gustav Weber)	3:30.81
1998	Canada (Pierre Lueders), Italy (Guenther Huber) (tie)	3:37.24
2002	Germany II (Christoph Langen)	3:10.11

	2-Woman Bob	Time
2002	United States II (Jill Bakken)	1:37.76

Curling

	Men
1998	Switzerland, Canada, Norway
2002	Norway, Canada, Switzerland

Women

1998	Canada, Denmark, Sweden
2002	Britain, Switzerland, Canada

Figure Skating

Men's Singles

1908	Ulrich Salchow, Sweden
1920	Gillis Grafstrom, Sweden
1924	Gillis Grafstrom, Sweden
1928	Gillis Grafstrom, Sweden
1932	Karl Schaefer, Austria
1936	Karl Schaefer, Austria
1948	Richard Button, United States
1952	Richard Button, United States
1956	Hayes Alan Jenkins, United States
1960	David W. Jenkins, United States
1964	Manfred Schnelldorfer, Germany
1968	Wolfgang Schwartz, Austria
1972	Ondrej Nepela, Czechoslovakia
1976	John Curry, Great Britain
1980	Robin Cousins, Great Britain
1984	Scott Hamilton, United States
1988	Brian Boitano, United States
1992	Viktor Petrenko, Unified Team
1994	Aleksei Urmanov, Russia
1998	Ilya Kulik, Russia
2002	Alexei Yagudin, Russia

Women's Singles

1908	Madge Syers, Great Britain
1920	Magda Julin-Mauroy, Sweden
1924	Herma von Szabo-Planck, Austria
1928	Sonja Henie, Norway
1932	Sonja Henie, Norway
1936	Sonja Henie, Norway
1948	Barbara Ann Scott, Canada
1952	Jeanette Altwegg, Great Britan
1956	Tenley Albright, United States
1960	Carol Heiss, United States
1964	Sjoukje Dijkstra, Netherlands
1968	Peggy Fleming, United States
1972	Beatrix Schuba, Austria
1976	Dorothy Hamill, United States
1980	Anett Poetzsch, E. Germany
1984	Katarina Witt, E. Germany
1988	Katarina Witt, E. Germany
1992	Kristi Yamaguchi, United States
1994	Oksana Baiul, Ukraine
1998	Tara Lipinski, United States
2002	Sarah Hughes, United States

Pairs

1908	Anna Hubler & Heinrich Burger, Germany
1920	Ludovika & Walter Jakobsson, Finland
1924	Helene Engelman & Alfred Berger, Austria
1928	Andree Joly & Pierre Brunet, France
1932	Andree Joly & Pierre Brunet, France
1936	Maxi Herber & Ernst Baier, Germany
1948	Micheline Lannoy & Pierre Baugniet, Belgium
1952	Ria and Paul Falk, Germany
1956	Elisabeth Schwartz & Kurt Oppelt, Austria
1964	Ludmila Beloussova & Oleg Protopopov, USSR
1968	Ludmila Beloussova & Oleg Protopopov, USSR
1972	Irina Rodnina & Alexei Ulanov, USSR
1976	Irina Rodnina & Aleksandr Zaitzev, USSR
1980	Irina Rodnina & Aleksandr Zaitzev, USSR
1984	Elena Valova & Oleg Vassiliev, USSR
1988	Ekaterina Gordeeva & Sergei Grinkov, USSR
1992	Natalia Mishkutienok & Artur Dimitriev, Unified Team
1994	Ekaterina Gordeeva & Sergei Grinkov, Russia
1998	Oksana Kazakova & Artur Dmitriev, Russia
2002	Elena Berezhnaya & Anton Sikharulidze, Russia; Jamie Sale & David Pelletier, Canada (tie)

Ice Dancing

1976	Ludmila Pakhomova & Aleksandr Gorschkov, USSR
1980	Natalya Linichuk & Gennadi Karponosov, USSR
1984	Jayne Torvill & Christopher Dean, Great Britain
1988	Natalia Bestemianova & Andrei Bukin, USSR
1992	Marina Klimova & Sergei Ponomarenko, Unified Team
1994	Pasha Grishuk & Evgeny Platov, Russia
1998	Pasha Grishuk & Evgeny Platov, Russia
2002	Marina Anissina & Gwendal Peizerat, France

Freestyle Skiing

	Men's Moguls	Points
1992	Edgar Grospiron, France	25.81
1994	Jean-Luc Brassard, Canada	27.24
1998	Jonny Moseley, United States	26.93
2002	Janne Lahtela, Finland	27.97

	Men's Aerials	Points
1994	Andreas Schoenbaechler, Switzerland	234.67
1998	Eric Bergoust, United States	255.64
2002	Ales Valenta, Czech Republic	257.02

	Women's Moguls	Points
1992	Donna Weinbrecht, United States	23.69
1994	Stine Lise Hattestad, Norway	25.97
1998	Tae Satoya, Japan	25.06
2002	Kari Traa, Norway	25.94

	Women's Aerials	Points
1994	Lina Tcherjazova, Uzbekistan	166.84
1998	Nikki Stone, United States	193.00
2002	Alisa Camplin, Australia	193.47

Ice Hockey

Men

1920	Canada, United States, Czechoslovakia
1924	Canada, United States, Great Britain
1928	Canada, Sweden, Switzerland
1932	Canada, United States, Germany
1936	Great Britain, Canada, United States
1948	Canada, Czechoslovakia, Switzerland
1952	Canada, United States, Sweden
1956	USSR, United States, Canada
1960	United States, Canada, USSR
1964	USSR, Sweden, Czechoslovakia
1968	USSR, Czechoslovakia, Canada
1972	USSR, United States, Czechoslovakia
1976	USSR, Czechoslovakia, W. Germany
1980	United States, USSR, Sweden
1984	USSR, Czechoslovakia, Sweden
1988	USSR, Finland, Sweden
1992	Unified Team, Canada, Czechoslovakia
1994	Sweden, Canada, Finland
1998	Czech Republic, Russia, Finland
2002	Canada, United States, Russia

Women

1998	United States, Canada, Finland
2002	Canada, United States, Sweden

Luge

	Men's Singles	Time
1964	Thomas Keohler, E. Germany	3:27.77
1968	Manfred Schmid, Austria	2:52.48
1972	Wolfgang Scheidel, E. Germany	3:27.58
1976	Detlef Guenther, E. Germany	3:27.688
1980	Bernhard Glass, E. Germany	2:54.796
1984	Paul Hildgartner, Italy	3:04.258
1988	Jens Mueller, E. Germany	3:05.548
1992	Georg Hackl, Germany	3:02.363
1994	Georg Hackl, Germany	3:21.571
1998	Georg Hackl, Germany	3:18.436
2002	Armin Zoeggeler, Italy	2:57.941

	Women's Singles	Time
1964	Ortun Enderlein, Germany	3:24.67
1968	Erica Lechner, Italy	2:28.66
1972	Anna M. Muller, E. Germany	2:59.18
1976	Margit Schumann, E. Germany	2:50.621
1980	Vera Zozulya, USSR	2:36.537
1984	Steffi Martin, E. Germany	2:46.570
1988	Steffi Walter, E. Germany	3:03.973
1992	Doris Neuner, Austria	3:06.696
1994	Gerda Weissensteiner, Italy	3:15.517
1998	Silke Kraushaar, Germany	3:23.779
2002	Sylke Otto, Germany	2:52.464

	Men's Doubles	Time
1964	Austria	1:41.62
1968	E. Germany	1:35.85
1972	Italy, E. Germany (tie)	1:28.35
1976	E. Germany	1:25.604
1980	E. Germany	1:19.331
1984	W. Germany	1:23.620
1988	E. Germany	1:31.940
1992	Germany	1:32.053
1994	Italy	1:36.720
1998	Germany	1:41.105
2002	Germany	1:26.082

Skeleton

	Men	Time
1928	Jennison Heaton, United States	3:01.8
1948	Nino Bibbia, Italy	5:23.2
2002	Jim Shea, United States	1:41.96

	Women	Time
2002	Tristan Gale, United States	1:45.11

Nordic Skiing

Cross-Country Events

	Men's 1.5 Kilometers (0.93 miles)	Time
2002	Tor Arne Hetland, Norway	2:56.9

	Men's 10 Kilometers (6.2 miles)	Time
1992	Vegard Ulvang, Norway	27:36.0
1994	Bjoern Daehlie, Norway	24:20.1
1998	Bjoern Daehlie, Norway	27:24.5
2002	(tie) Thomas Alsgaard, Norway; Frode Estil, Norway (a)	49:48.9

(a) Awarded gold after Johann Muehlegg of Spain was stripped of gold for a drug offense.

	Men's 15 Kilometers (9.3 miles)	Time
1924	Thorleif Haug, Norway	1:14:31
1928	Johan Grottumsbraaten, Norway	1:37:01
1932	Sven Utterstrom, Sweden	1:23:07
1936	Erik-August Larsson, Sweden	1:14:38
1948	Martin Lundstrom, Sweden	1:13:50
1952	Hallgeir Brenden, Norway	1:01:34
1956	Hallgeir Brenden, Norway	0:49:39.0
1960	Haakon Brusveen, Norway	0:51:55.5
1964	Eero Maentyranta, Finland	0:50:54.1
1968	Harald Groenningen, Norway	0:47:54.2
1972	Sven-Ake Lundback, Sweden	0:45:28.24
1976	Nikolai Balukov, USSR	0:43:58.47
1980	Thomas Wassberg, Sweden	0:41:57.63
1984	Gunde Svan, Sweden	0:41:25.6
1988	Mikhail Deviatiarov, USSR	0:41:18.9
1992	Bjoern Daehlie, Norway	0:38:01.9
1994	Bjoern Daehlie, Norway	0:35:48.8
1998	Thomas Alsgaard, Norway	1:07:01.7
2002	Andrus Veerpalu, Estonia	0:37:07.4

(Note: approx. 18-km course 1924-1952)

	Men's 30 Kilometers (18.6 miles)	Time
1956	Veikko Hakulinen, Finland	1:44:06.0
1956	Veikko Hakulinen, Finland	1:44:06.0
1960	Sixten Jernberg, Sweden	1:51:03.9
1964	Eero Maentyranta, Finland	1:30:50.7
1968	Franco Nones, Italy	1:35:39.2
1972	Vyacheslav Vedenine, USSR	1:36:31.15
1976	Sergei Saveliev, USSR	1:30:29.38
1980	Nikolai Zimyatov, USSR	1:27:02.80
1984	Nikolai Zimyatov, USSR	1:28:56.3
1988	Aleksei Prokourorov, USSR	1:24:26.3
1992	Vegard Ulvang, Norway	1:22:27.8
1994	Thomas Alsgaard, Norway	1:12:26.4
1998	Mika Myllylae, Finland	1:33:55.8
2002	Christian Hoffmann, Austria (a)	1:11:31.0

(a) Awarded gold after Johann Muehlegg of Spain was stripped of gold for a drug offense.

	Men's 50 Kilometers (31.2 miles)	Time
1924	Thorleif Haug, Norway	3:44:32.0
1928	Per Erik Hedlund, Sweden	4:52:03.0
1932	Veli Saarinen, Finland	4:28:00.0
1936	Elis Wiklund, Sweden	3:30:11.0
1948	Nils Karlsson, Sweden	3:47:48.0
1952	Veikko Hakulinen, Finland	3:33:33.0
1956	Sixten Jernberg, Sweden	2:50:27.0
1960	Kalevi Hamalainen, Finland	2:59:06.3
1964	Sixten Jernberg, Sweden	2:43:52.6
1968	Ole Ellefsaeter, Norway	2:28:45.8
1972	Paal Tyldum, Norway	2:43:14.75
1976	Ivar Formo, Norway	2:37:30.05
1980	Nikolai Zimyatov, USSR	2:27:24.60
1984	Thomas Wassberg, Sweden	2:15:55.8
1988	Gunde Svan, Sweden	2:04:30.9
1992	Bjoern Daehlie, Norway	2:03:41.5
1994	Vladimir Smirnov, Kazakhstan	2:07:20.3
1998	Bjoern Daehlie, Norway	2:05:08.2
2002	Mikhail Ivanov, Russia	2:06:20.8

	Men's 40-Kilometer Relay	Time
1936	Finland, Norway, Sweden	2:41:33.0
1948	Sweden, Finland, Norway	2:32:08.0
1952	Finland, Norway, Sweden	2:20:16.0
1956	USSR, Finland, Sweden	2:15:30.0
1960	Finland, Norway, USSR	2:18:45.6
1964	Sweden, Finland, USSR	2:18:34.6
1968	Norway, Sweden, Finland	2:08:33.5
1972	USSR, Norway, Switzerland	2:04:47.94
1976	Finland, Norway, USSR	2:07:59.72
1980	USSR, Norway, Finland	1:57:03.46
1984	Sweden, USSR, Finland	1:55:06.30
1988	Sweden, USSR, Czechoslovakia	1:43:58.60
1992	Norway, Italy, Finland	1:39:26.00
1994	Italy, Norway, Finland	1:41:15.00
1998	Norway, Italy, Finland	1:40:55.70
2002	Norway, Italy, Germany	1:32:45.5

	Women's 1.5 Kilometers (0.93 miles)	Time
2002	Julia Tchepalova, Russia	3:10.6

	Women's 5 Kilometers (3.1 miles)	Time
1964	Claudia Boyarskikh, USSR	17:50.5
1968	Toini Gustafsson, Sweden	16:45.2
1972	Galina Koulacova, USSR	17:00.50
1976	Helena Takalo, Finland	15:48.69
1980	Raisa Smetanina, USSR	15:06.92
1984	Marja-Liisa Haemaelainen, Finland	17:04.0
1988	Marjo Matikainen, Finland	15:04.0
1992	Marjut Lukkarinen, Finland	14:13.8
1994	Ljubov Egorova, Russia	14:08.8
1998	Larissa Lazutina, Russia	17:37.9
2002	Beckie Scott, Canada (a)	25:09.9

(a) Awarded gold after Olga Danilova of Russia was stripped of gold and Larissa Lazutina of Russia was stripped of silver for drug offenses.

	Women's 10 Kilometers (6.2 miles)	Time
1952	Lydia Wideman, Finland	41:40.0
1956	Lyubov Kosyreva, USSR	38:11.0
1960	Maria Gusakova, USSR	39:46.6
1964	Claudia Boyarskikh, USSR	40:24.3
1968	Toini Gustafsson, Sweden	36:46.5
1972	Galina Koulacova, USSR	34:17.82
1976	Raisa Smetanina, USSR	30:13.41
1980	Barbara Petzold, E. Germany	30:31.54
1984	Marja-Liisa Haemaelainen, Finland	31:44.2
1988	Vida Ventsene, USSR	30:08.3
1992	Lyubov Egorova, Unified Team	25:53.7
1994	Lyubov Egorova, Russia	27:30.1
1998	Larissa Lazutina, Russia	46.06.9
2002	Bente Skari, Norway	28:05.6

	Women's 15 Kilometers (9.3 miles)	Time
1992	Lyubov Egorova, Unified Team	42:20.8
1994	Manuela Di Centa, Italy	39:44.5
1998	Olga Danilova, Russia	46:55.4
2002	Stefania Belmondo, Italy	39:54.4

	Women's 30 Kilometers (18.6 miles)	Time
1992	Stefania Belmondo, Italy	1:22:30.1
1994	Manuela Di Centa, Italy	1:25:41.6
1998	Julija Tchepalova, Russia	1:22:01.5
2002	Gabriella Paruzzi, Italy	1:30:57.1

	Women's 20-Kilometer Relay	Time
1956	Finland, USSR, Sweden (15 km)	1:09:01.0
1960	Sweden, USSR, Finland (15 km)	1:04:21.4
1964	USSR, Sweden, Finland (15 km)	0:59:20.2
1968	Norway, Sweden, USSR (15 km)	0:57:30.0
1972	USSR, Finland, Norway (15 km)	0:48:46.15
1976	USSR, Finland, E. Germany	1:07:49.75
1980	E. Germany, USSR, Norway	1:02:11.1
1984	Norway, Czechoslovakia, Finland	1:06:49.7
1988	USSR, Norway, Finland	0:59:51.1
1992	United Team, Norway, Italy	0:59:34.8
1994	Russia, Norway, Italy	0:57:12.5
1998	Russia, Norway, Italy	0:55:13.5
2002	Germany, Norway, Switzerland	0:49:30.6

Combined Cross-Country & Jumping (Men)

7.5 Kilometer Nordic Combined

2002 Samppa Lajunen, Finland

15 Kilometer Nordic Combined

1924 Thorleif Haug, Norway
1928 Johan Grottumsbraaten, Norway
1932 Johan Grottumsbraaten, Norway
1936 Oddbjorn Hagen, Norway
1948 Heikki Hasu, Finland
1952 Simon Slattvik, Norway
1956 Sverre Stenersen, Norway
1960 Georg Thoma, W. Germany
1964 Tormod Knutsen, Norway
1968 Franz Keller, W. Germany
1972 Ulrich Wehling, E. Germany
1976 Ulrich Wehling, E. Germany
1980 Ulrich Wehling, E. Germany
1984 Tom Sandberg, Norway
1988 Hippolyt Kempf, Switzerland
1992 Fabrice Guy, France
1994 Fred Barre Lundberg, Norway
1998 Bjarte Engen Vik, Norway
2002 Samppa Lajunen, Finland

Team Nordic Combined

1988	W. Germany, Switzerland, Austria
1992	Japan, Norway, Austria
1994	Japan, Norway, Switzerland
1998	Norway, Finland, France
2002	Finland, Germany, Austria

Ski Jumping (Men)

	Normal Hill	Points
1964	Veikko Kankkonen, Finland	229.9
1968	Jiri Raska, Czechoslovakia	216.5
1972	Yukio Kasaya, Japan	244.2
1976	Hans-Georg Aschenbach, E. Germany	252.0
1980	Toni Innauer, Austria	266.3
1984	Jens Weissflog, E. Germany	215.2
1988	Matti Nykaenen, Finland	230.5
1992	Ernst Vettori, Austria	222.8
1994	Espen Bredesen, Norway	282.0
1998	Jani Soininen, Finland	234.5
2002	Simon Ammann, Switzerland	269.0

	Large Hill	Points
1924	Jacob Tullin Thams, Norway	18.960
1928	Alfred Andersen, Norway	19.208
1932	Birger Ruud, Norway	228.1
1936	Birger Ruud, Norway	232.0
1948	Petter Hugsted, Norway	228.1
1952	Arnfinn Bergmann, Norway	226.0
1956	Antti Hyvarinen, Finland	227.0
1960	Helmut Recknagel, E. Germany	227.2
1964	Toralf Engan, Norway	230.7
1968	Vladimir Beloussov, USSR	231.3
1972	Wojciech Fortuna, Poland	219.9
1976	Karl Schnabl, Austria	234.8
1980	Jouko Tormanen, Finland	271.0
1984	Matti Nykaenen, Finland	231.2
1988	Matti Nykaenen, Finland	224.0
1992	Toni Nieminen, Finland	239.5
1994	Jens Weissflog, Germany	274.5
1998	Kazuyoshi Funaki, Japan	272.3
2002	Simon Ammann, Switzerland	281.4

	Team Large Hill	Points
1988	Finland, Yugoslavia, Norway	634.4
1992	Finland, Austria, Czechoslovakia	644.4
1994	Germany, Japan, Austria	970.1
1998	Japan, Germany, Austria	933.0
2002	Germany, Flnland, Slovenia	974.1

Snowboarding

	Men's Parallel Giant Slalom	Time
1998	Ross Rebagliati, Canada	2:03.96
2002	Philipp Schoch, Switzerland	NA

	Men's Halfpipe	Points
1998	Gian Simmen, Switzerland	85.2
2002	Ross Powers	46.1

	Women's Parallel Giant Slalom	Time
1998	Karine Ruby, France	2:17.34
2002	Isabelle Blanc, France	NA

In 2002, the Giant Slalom became the Parallel Giant Slalom.

	Women's Halfpipe	Points
1998	Nicola Thost, Germany	74.6
2002	Kelly Clark, United States	47.9

Speed Skating

*indicates Olympic record

	Men's 500 Meters	Time[1]
1924	Charles Jewtraw, United States	0:44.0
1928	Thunberg, Finland & Evensen, Norway (tie)	0:43.4
1932	John A. Shea, United States	0:43.4
1936	Ivar Ballangrud, Norway	0:43.4
1948	Finn Helgesen, Norway	0:43.1
1952	Kenneth Henry, United States	0:43.2
1956	Evgeniy Grishin, USSR	0:40.2
1960	Evgeniy Grishin, USSR	0:40.2
1964	Terry McDermott, United States	0:40.1
1968	Erhard Keller, W. Germany	0:40.3
1972	Erhard Keller, W. Germany	0:39.44
1976	Evgeny Kulikov, USSR	0:39.17
1980	Eric Heiden, United States	0:38.03
1984	Sergei Fokichev, USSR	0:38.19
1988	Uwe-Jens Mey, E. Germany	0:36.45
1992	Uwe-Jens Mey, Germany	0:37.14
1994	Aleksandr Golubev, Russia	0:36.33
1998	Hiroyasu Shimizu, Japan	0:35.59
2002	Casey FitzRandolph, United States	0:34.42*

	Men's 1,000 Meters	Time
1976	Peter Mueller, U.S.	1:19.32
1980	Eric Heiden, United States	1:15.18
1984	Gaetan Boucher, Canada	1:15.80
1988	Nikolai Guiliaev, USSR	1:13.03
1992	Olaf Zinke, Germany	1:14.85
1994	Dan Jansen, United States	1:12.43
1998	Ids Postma, Netherlands	1:10.64
2002	Gerard van Velde, Netherlands	1:07.18*

	Men's 1,500 Meters	Time
1924	Clas Thunberg, Finland	2:20.8
1928	Clas Thunberg, Finland	2:21.1
1932	John A. Shea, United States	2:57.5
1936	Charles Mathiesen, Norway	2:19.2
1948	Sverre Farstad, Norway	2:17.6
1952	Hjalmar Andersen, Norway	2:20.4
1956	Grishin, & Mikhailov, both USSR (tie)	2:08.6
1960	Aas, Norway & Grishin, USSR (tie)	2:10.4
1964	Ants Anston, USSR	2:10.3
1968	Cornetis Verkerk, Netherlands	2:03.4
1972	Ard Schenk, Netherlands	2:02.96
1976	Jan Egil Storholt, Norway	1:59.38
1980	Eric Heiden, United States	1:55.44
1984	Gaetan Boucher, Canada	1:58.36
1988	Andre Hoffmann, E. Germany	1:52.06
1992	Johann Koss, Norway	1:54.81
1994	Johann Koss, Norway	1:51.29
1998	Aadne Sondral, Norway	1:47.87
2002	Derek Parra, United States	1:43.95*

	Men's 5,000 Meters	Time
1924	Clas Thunberg, Finland	8:39.0
1928	Ivar Ballangrud, Norway	8:50.5
1932	Irving Jaffee, United States	9:40.8
1936	Ivar Ballangrud, Norway	8:19.6
1948	Reidar Liaklev, Norway	8:29.4
1952	Hjalmar Andersen, Norway	8:10.6
1956	Boris Shilkov, USSR	7:48.7
1960	Viktor Kosichkin, USSR	7:51.3
1964	Knut Johannesen, Norway	7:38.4
1968	F. Anton Maier, Norway	7:22.4
1972	Ard Schenk, Netherlands	7:23.61
1976	Sten Stensen, Norway	7:24.48
1980	Eric Heiden, United States	7:02.29
1984	Sven Tomas Gustafson, Sweden	7:12.28
1988	Tomas Gustafson, Sweden	6:44.63
1992	Geir Karlstad, Norway	6:59.97
1994	Johann Koss, Norway	6:34.96
1998	Gianni Romme, Netherlands	6:22.20
2002	Jochem Uytdehaage, Netherlands	6:14.66*

	Men's 10,000 Meters	Time
1924	Julius Skutnabb, Finland	18:04.8
1928	Event not held because of thawing of ice	
1932	Irving Jaffee, United States	19:13.6
1936	Ivar Ballangrud, Norway	17:24.3
1948	Ake Seyffarth, Sweden	17:26.3
1952	Hjalmar Andersen, Norway	16:45.8
1956	Sigvard Ericsson, Sweden	16:35.9
1960	Knut Johannesen, Norway	15:46.6
1964	Jonny Nilsson, Sweden	15:50.1
1968	Jonny Hoeglin, Sweden	15:23.6
1972	Ard Schenk, Netherlands	15:01.35
1976	Piet Kleine, Netherlands	14:50.59
1980	Eric Heiden, United States	14:28.13
1984	Igor Malkov, USSR	14:39.90
1988	Tomas Gustafson, Sweden	13:48.20
1992	Bart Veldkamp, Netherlands	14:12.12
1994	Johann Koss, Norway	13:30.55
1998	Gianni Romme, Netherlands	13:15.33
2002	Jochem Uytdehaage, Netherlands	12:58.92*

	Women's 500 Meters	Time
1960	Helga Haase, Germany	0:45.9
1964	Lydia Skoblikova, USSR	0:45.0
1968	Ludmila Titova, USSR	0:46.1
1972	Anne Henning, United States	0:43.33
1976	Sheila Young, United States	0:42.76
1980	Karin Enke, E. Germany	0:41.78
1984	Christa Rothenburger, E. Germany	0:41.02
1988	Bonnie Blair, United States	0:39.10
1992	Bonnie Blair, United States	0:40.33
1994	Bonnie Blair, United States	0:39.25
1998	Catriona Le May-Doan, Canada	0:38.21
2002	Catriona Le May Doan, Canada	0:37.30

	Women's 1,000 Meters	Time
1960	Klara Guseva, USSR	1:34.1
1964	Lydia Skoblikova, USSR	1:33.2
1968	Carolina Geijssen, Netherlands	1:32.6
1972	Monika Pflug, W. Germany	1:31.40
1976	Tatiana Averina, USSR	1:28.43
1980	Natalya Petruseva, USSR	1:24.10
1984	Karin Enke, E. Germany	1:21.61
1988	Christa Rothenburger, E. Germany	1:17.65
1992	Bonnie Blair, United States	1:21.90
1994	Bonnie Blair, United States	1:18.74
1998	Marianne Timmer, Netherlands	1:16.51
2002	Chris Witty, United States	1:13.83*

	Women's 1,500 Meters	Time
1960	Lydia Skoblikova, USSR	2:52.2
1964	Lydia Skoblikova, USSR	2:22.6
1968	Kaija Mustonen, Finland	2:22.4
1972	Dianne Holum, United States	2:20.85
1976	Galina Stepanskaya, USSR	2:16.58
1980	Anne Borckink, Netherlands	2:10.95
1984	Karin Enke, E. Germany	2:03.42
1988	Yvonne van Gennip, Netherlands	2:00.68
1992	Jacqueline Boerner, Germany	2:05.87
1994	Emese Hunyady, Austria	2:02.19
1998	Marianne Timmer, Netherlands	1:57.58
2002	Anni Friesinger, Germany	1:54.02*

	Women's 3,000 Meters	Time
1960	Lydia Skoblikova, USSR	5:14.3
1964	Lydia Skoblikova, USSR	5:14.9
1968	Johanna Schut, Netherlands	4:56.2
1972	Christina Baas-Kaiser, Netherlands	4:52.14
1976	Tatiana Averina, USSR	4:45.19
1980	Bjoerg Eva Jensen, Norway	4:32.13
1984	Andrea Schoene, E. Germany	4:24.79
1988	Yvonne van Gennip, Netherlands	4:11.94
1992	Gunda Niemann, Germany	4:19.90
1994	Svetlana Bazhanova, Russia	4:17.43
1998	Gunda Niemann-Stirnemann, Germany	4:07.29
2002	Claudia Pechstein, Germany,	3:57.70*

	Women's 5,000 Meters	Time
1988	Yvonne van Gennip, Netherlands	7:14.13
1992	Gunda Niemann, Germany	7:31.57
1994	Claudia Pechstein, Germany	7:14.37
1998	Claudia Pechstein, Germany	6:59.61
2002	Claudia Pechstein, Germany	6:46.91*

Short-Track Speed Skating

* indicates Olympic record

	Men's 500 Meters	Time
1998	Takafumi Nishitani, Japan	42.862
2002	Marc Gagnon, Canada	41.802*

	Men's 1,000 Meters	Time
1992	Kim Ki-Hoon, S. Korea	1:30.76
1994	Kim Ki-Hoon, S. Korea	1:34.57
1998	Dong-Sung Kim, S. Korea	1:32.375
2002	Steven Bradbury, Australia	1:29.109

	Men's 1,500 Meters	Time
2002	Apolo Anton Ohno, United States	2:18.541

	Men's 5,000-Meter Relay	Time
1992	S. Korea, Canada, Japan	7:14.02
1994	Italy, United States, Australia	7:11.74
1998	Canada, S. Korea, China	7:06.075
2002	Canada, Italy, China	6:51.579

	Women's 500 Meters	Time
1992	Cathy Turner, United States	47.04
1994	Cathy Turner, United States	45.98
1998	Annie Perreault, Canada	46.568
2002	Yang Yang (A)China	44.187

	Women's 1,000 Meters	Time
1998	Chun Lee-Kyung, S. Korea	1:42.776
2002	Yang Yang (A), China	1:36.391

	Women's 1,500 Meters	Time
2002	Gi-Hyun Ko, S. Korea	2:31.581

	Women's 3,000 Meter Relay	Time
1992	Canada, United States, Unified Team	4:36.62
1994	S. Korea, Canada, United States	4:26.64
1998	S. Korea, China, Canada	4:16.26
2002	S. Korea, China, Canada	4:12.793*

Olympic Information

The modern Olympic Games, first held in Athens, Greece, in 1896, were the result of efforts by Baron Pierre de Coubertin, a French educator, to promote interest in education and culture and to foster better international understanding through love of athletics. His inspiration was the ancient Greek Olympic Games, most notable of the 4 Panhellenic celebrations. The games were combined patriotic, religious, and athletic festivals held every 4 years. The first such recorded festival was held in 776 bc, which the Greeks began to keep their calendar by "Olympiads," or 4-year spans between the games.

Baron de Coubertin enlisted 13 nations to send athletes to the first modern Olympics in 1896; now athletes from nearly 200 nations and territories compete in the Summer Olympics. The Winter Olympic Games were started in 1924.

Symbol: Five rings or circles, linked together to represent the sporting friendship of all peoples. They also symbolize 5 geographic areas—Europe, Asia, Africa, Australia, and America. Each ring is a different color—blue, yellow, black, green, or red.

Flag: The symbol of the 5 rings on a plain white background.

Creed: "The most important thing in the Olympic Games is not to win but to take part, just as the most important thing in life is not the triumph but the struggle. The essential thing is not to have conquered but to have fought well."

Motto: "Citius, Altius, Fortius." Latin meaning "swifter, higher, stronger."

Oath: "In the name of all competitors I promise that we will take part in these Olympic Games, respecting and abiding by the rules which govern them, in the true spirit of sportsmanship for the glory of sport and the honor of our teams."

Flame: The modern version of the flame was adopted in 1936. The torch used to kindle it is first lit by the sun's rays at Olympia, Greece, then carried to the site of the Games by relays of runners. Ships and planes are used when necessary.

Sites of Winter Olympic Games

1924 Chamonix, France
1928 St. Moritz, Switzerland
1932 Lake Placid, NY
1936 Garmisch-Partenkirchen, Germany
1948 St. Moritz, Switzerland
1952 Oslo, Norway
1956 Cortina d'Ampezzo, Italy
1960 Squaw Valley, CA
1964 Innsbruck, Austria
1968 Grenoble, France
1972 Sapporo, Japan
1976 Innsbruck, Austria
1980 Lake Placid, NY
1984 Sarajevo, Yugoslavia
1988 Calgary, Canada
1992 Albertville, France
1994 Lillehammer, Norway
1998 Nagano, Japan
2002 Salt Lake City, UT
2006 Turin, Italy
2010 Vancouver, B.C., Canada

Sites of Summer Olympic Games

1896 Athens, Greece
1900 Paris, France
1904 St. Louis, MO
1906 Athens, Greece*
1908 London, England
1912 Stockholm, Sweden
1920 Antwerp, Belgium
1924 Paris, France
1928 Amsterdam, Netherlands
1932 Los Angeles, CA
1936 Berlin, Germany
1948 London, England
1952 Helsinki, Finland
1956 Melbourne, Australia
1960 Rome, Italy
1964 Tokyo, Japan
1968 Mexico City, Mexico
1972 Munich, W. Germany
1976 Montreal, Canada
1980 Moscow, USSR
1984 Los Angeles, CA
1988 Seoul, South Korea
1992 Barcelona, Spain
1996 Atlanta, GA
2000 Sydney, Australia
2004 Athens, Greece
2008 Beijing, China
2012 London, England

*Games not recognized by International Olympic Committee. Games VI (1916), XII (1940), and XIII (1944) were not celebrated.

Paralympics

The first Olympic games for the disabled were held in Rome after the 1960 Summer Olympics; use of the name "paralympic" began with the 1964 games in Tokyo. The Paralympics are held by the Olympic host country in the same year and usually the same city or venue. A goal of the Paralympics is to provide elite competition to athletes with functional disabilities that prevent their involvement in the Olympics. In 1976 the first Winter Paralympics were held, in Ornskoldsvik, Sweden.

The XII Paralympic Summer Games were held Sept. 17-28, 2004, in Athens, Greece. A record 3,969 athletes from a record 136 nations competed in 19 sports. China won the most medals, with 141, and the most golds, with 63. Australia was 2nd, with a total of 100 medals, and Great Britain was 3rd, with 94. Japanese swimmer Mayumi Narita won the most individual medals, with 7 golds and 1 bronze. A total of 304 world and 448 Paralympic records were set in Athens.

The IX Paralympic Winter Games were to be held Mar. 10-19, 2006, in Turin, Italy, where wheelchair curling will be contested for the first time.

Special Olympics

Special Olympics is an international program of year-round sports training and athletic competition for people with intellectual disabilities. All 50 U.S. states, Washington, DC, and Guam have chapter offices. In addition, there are accredited Special Olympics programs in nearly 150 countries. Persons wishing to volunteer or find out more can contact Special Olympics International Headquarters, 1325 G St. NW, Suite 500, Washington, DC 20005, or access the Special Olympics website at www.specialolympics.org

The 11th Special Olympics World Summer Games were held June 21-29, 2003, in Dublin, Ireland. More than 7,000 athletes, 3,000 coaches and delegates, and 28,000 others attended the first Special Olympic World Games outside the U.S. Competition included aquatics, athletics, badminton, bocce, bowling, cycling, equestrian sports, golf, gymnastics (artistic and rhythmic), power lifting, rollerskating, table tennis, and tennis. Scheduled team sports were basketball, handball, sailing, soccer, and volleyball. Kayaking and pitch-and-putt (a form of golf) were included as demonstration sports. The 12th Special Olympics World Summer Games were scheduled to take place in Shanghai, China, Oct. 10-19, 2005.

The 8th Special Olympics World Winter Games were held Feb. 26 through Mar. 5, 2005, in Nagano, Japan's Olympic venues. More than 1,800 athletes from 80 countries competed in alpine skiing, cross-country skiing, floor hockey, figure skating, speed skating, snowshoeing, and snowboarding events.

TRACK AND FIELD

World Track and Field Outdoor Records

As of Oct. 1, 2005

The International Amateur Athletic Federation, the world body of track and field, recognizes only records in metric distances, except for the mile. *Pending ratification.

Men's Records

Running

Event	Record	Holder	Country	Date	Where made
100 meters	**9.77 s.**	Asafa Powell	Jamaica	June 14, 2005	Athens, Greece
200 meters	**19.32 s.**	Michael Johnson	U.S.	Aug. 1, 1996	Atlanta, GA
400 meters	**43.18 s.**	Michael Johnson	U.S.	Aug. 26, 1999	Seville, Spain
800 meters	**1 m., 41.11 s.**	Wilson Kipketer	Denmark	Aug. 24, 1997	Cologne, Germany
1,000 meters	**2 m., 11.96 s.**	Noah Ngeny	Kenya	Sept. 5, 1999	Rieti, Italy
1,500 meters	**3 m., 26.00 s.**	Hicham El Guerrouj	Morocco	July 14, 1998	Rome, Italy
1 mile	**3 m., 43.13 s.**	Hicham El Guerrouj	Morocco	July 7, 1999	Rome, Italy
2,000 meters	**4 m., 44.79 s.**	Hicham El Guerrouj	Morocco	Sept. 7, 1999	Berlin, Germany
3,000 meters	**7 m., 20.67 s.**	Daniel Komen	Kenya	Sept. 1, 1996	Rieti, Italy
5,000 meters	**12 m., 37.35 s.**	Kenenisa Bekele	Ethiopia	May 31, 2004	Hengelo, Netherlands
10,000 meters	**26 m., 17.53 s.***	Kenenisa Bekele	Ethiopia	Aug. 26, 2005	Brussels, Belgium
20,000 meters	**56 m., 55.6 s.**	Arturo Barrios	Mexico	Mar. 30, 1991	La Fléche, France
25,000 meters	**1 hr., 13 m., 55.8 s.**	Toshihiko Seko	Japan	Mar. 22, 1981	Christchurch, NZ
3,000 meter stpl.	**7 m., 53.63 s.**	Saif Saaeed Shaheen	Qatar	Sept. 3, 2004	Brussels, Belgium
Marathon	**2 hr., 4 m., 55 s.**	Paul Tergat	Kenya	Sept. 28, 2003	Berlin, Germany

Hurdles

Event	Record	Holder	Country	Date	Where made
110 meters	**12.91 s.**	Colin Jackson	Gr. Britain	Aug. 20, 1993	Stuttgart, Germany
		Liu Xiang	China	Aug. 27, 2004	Athens, Greece
400 meters	**46.78 s.**	Kevin Young	U.S.	Aug. 6, 1992	Barcelona, Spain

Relay Races

Event	Record	Holder	Country	Date	Where made
400 mtrs. (4x100)	**37.40 s.**	(Marsh, Burrell, Mitchell, Lewis)	U.S.	Aug. 8, 1992	Barcelona, Spain
		(Drummond, Cason, Mitchell, Burrell)	U.S.	Aug. 21, 1993	Stuttgart, Germany
800 mtrs. (4x200)	**1 m., 18.68 s.**	(Marsh, Burrell, Heard, Lewis)	U.S.	Apr. 17, 1994	Walnut, CA
1,600 mtrs. (4x400)	**2 m., 54.20 s.**	(Young, Pettigrew, Washington, Johnson)	U.S.	July 22, 1998	Long Island, NY
3,200 mtrs. (4x800)	**7 m., 03.89 s.**	(Elliott, Cook, Cram, Coe)	Gr. Britain	Aug. 30, 1982	London, England

Field Events

Event	Record	Holder	Country	Date	Where made
High jump	**2.45m** (8' ½")	Javier Sotomayor	Cuba	July 27, 1993	Salamanca, Spain
Long jump	**8.95m** (29' 4½")	Mike Powell	U.S.	Aug. 30, 1991	Tokyo, Japan
Triple jump	**18.29m** (60' ¼")	Jonathan Edwards	Gr. Britain	Aug. 7, 1995	Göteborg, Sweden
Pole vault	**6.14m** (20' 1¾")	Sergei Bubka	Ukraine	July 31, 1994	Sestriere, Italy
16-lb. shot put	**23.12m** (75' 10¼")	Randy Barnes	U.S.	May 20, 1990	Los Angeles, CA
Discus	**74.08m** (243' 0")	Juergen Schult	E. Germany	June 6, 1986	Neubrandenburg, Germany
Javelin	**98.48m** (323' 1")	Jan Zelezny	Czech Rep.	May 25, 1996	Jena, Germany
16-lb. hammer	**86.74m** (284' 7")	Yuri Sedykh	USSR	Aug. 30, 1986	Stuttgart, W. Germany
Decathlon	**9,026 pts.**	Roman Šebrle	Czech Rep.	May 27, 2001	Götzis, Austria

Women's Records

Running

Event	Record	Holder	Country	Date	Where made
100 meters	**10.49 s.**	Florence Griffith-Joyner	U.S.	July 16, 1988	Indianapolis, IN
200 meters	**21.34 s.**	Florence Griffith-Joyner	U.S.	Sept. 29, 1988	Seoul, S. Korea
400 meters	**47.60 s.**	Marita Koch	E. Germany	Oct. 6, 1985	Canberra, Australia
800 meters	**1 m., 53.28 s.**	Jarmila Kratochvilova	Czech Rep.	July 26, 1983	Munich, Germany
1,000 meters	**2 m., 28.98 s.**	Svetlana Masterkova	Russia	Aug. 23, 1996	Brussels, Belgium
1,500 meters	**3 m., 50.46 s.**	Qu Yunxia	China	Sept. 11, 1993	Beijing, China
1 mile	**4 m., 12.56 s.**	Svetlana Masterkova	Russia	Aug. 14, 1996	Zurich, Switzerland
2,000 meters	**5 m., 25.36 s.**	Sonia O'Sullivan	Ireland	July 8, 1994	Edinburgh, Scotland
3,000 meters	**8 m., 06.11 s.**	Wang Junxia	China	Sept. 13, 1993	Beijing, China
3,000 meter stpl.	**9 m., 1.59 s.**	Gulnara Samitova	Russia	July 4, 2004	Iraklio, Greece
5,000 meters	**14 m., 24.68 s.**	Elvan Abeylegesse	Turkey	June 11, 2004	Bergen, Norway
10,000 meters	**29 m., 31.78 s.**	Wang Junxia	China	Sept. 8, 1993	Beijing, China
20,000 meters	**1 h., 05m. 26.6 s.**	Tegla Loroupe	Kenya	Sept. 3, 2000	Borgholzhausen, Germany
30,000 meters	**1 h., 45 m., 50 s.**	Tegla Loroupe	Kenya	June 6, 2003	Warstein, Germany
Marathon	**2 h., 15 m., 25 s.**	Paula Radcliffe	Gr. Britain	April 13, 2003	London, England

Hurdles

Event	Record	Holder	Country	Date	Where made
100 meters	**12.21 s.**	Yordanka Donkova	Bulgaria	Aug. 20, 1988	Stara Zagora, Bulgaria
400 meters	**52.34 s.**	Yuliya Pechonkina	Russia	Aug. 10, 2003	Tula, Russia

Relay Races

Event	Record	Holder	Country	Date	Where made
400 mtrs. (4×100)	**41.37 s.**	(Gladisch, Rieger, Auerswald, Goehr)	E. Germany	Oct. 6, 1985	Canberra, Australia
800 mtrs. (4×200)	**1 m., 27.46 s.**	U.S. "Blue" (Jenkins, Clarke, Richardson, Jamieson)	U.S.	Sept. 28, 2000	Philadelphia, PA
1,600 mtrs. (4×400)	**3 m., 15.17 s.**	(Ledovskaya, Nazarova, Pinigina, Bryzgina)	USSR	Oct. 1, 1988	Seoul, S. Korea
3,200 mtrs. (4×800)	**7 m., 50.17 s.**	(Olizarenko, Gurina, Borisova, Podyalovskaya)	USSR	Aug. 5, 1984	Moscow, USSR

Field Events

Event	Record	Holder	Country	Date	Where made
High jump	**2.09m** (6' 10¼")	Stefka Kostadinova	Bulgaria	Aug. 30, 1987	Rome, Italy
Long jump	**7.52m** (24' 8¼")	Galina Chistyakova	USSR	June 11, 1988	Leningrad
Triple jump	**15.50m** (50' 10¼")	Inessa Kravets	Ukraine	Aug. 10, 1995	Göteborg, Sweden
Pole vault	**5.01m** (16' 5¼)*	Yelena Isinbayeva	Russia	Aug. 12, 2005	Helsinki, Finland
Shot put	**22.63m** (74' 3")	Natalya Lisovskaya	USSR	June 7, 1987	Moscow, Russia
Discus	**76.80m** (252' 0")	Gabriele Reinsch	E. Germany	July 9, 1988	Neubrandenburg, Germany
Hammer	**77.06m** (252' 10")*	Tatyana Lysenko	Russia	July 15, 2005	Moscow, Russia
Javelin	**71.70m** (235' 3")	Osleidys Menéndez	Cuba	Aug. 14, 2005	Helsinki, Finland
Heptathlon	**7,291 pts.**	Jackie Joyner-Kersee	U.S.	Sept. 23-24, 1988	Seoul, S. Korea

World Track and Field Indoor Records

As of Oct. 1, 2005

The International Amateur Athletic Federation first recognized world indoor track and field records on Jan. 1, 1987. World indoor bests set prior to Jan. 1, 1987, were subject to approval as world records providing they met the IAAF world records criteria, including drug testing. Criteria for indoor and outdoor records are the same, except that a track performance cannot be set on an indoor track larger than 200 meters. (a)=altitude.

Men's Records

Event	Record	Holder	Country	Date	Where made
50 meters	**5.56** (a)	Donovan Bailey	Canada	Feb. 9, 1996	Reno, NV
	6.39	Maurice Greene	U.S.	Mar. 3, 2001	Atlanta, GA
60 meters	**6.39**	Maurice Greene	U.S.	Feb. 3, 1998	Madrid, Spain
200 meters	**19.92**	Frankie Fredericks	Namibia	Feb. 18, 1996	Lievin, France
400 meters	**44.57**	Kerron Clement	U.S.	Mar. 12, 2005	Fayetteville, AR
800 meters	**1:42.67**	Wilson Kipketer	Denmark	Mar. 9, 1997	Paris, France
1,000 meters	**2:14.96**	Wilson Kipketer	Denmark	Feb. 20, 2000	Birmingham, England
1,500 meters	**3:31.18**	Hicham El Guerrouj	Morocco	Feb. 2, 1997	Stuttgart, Germany
1 mile	**3:48.45**	Hicham El Guerrouj	Morocco	Feb. 12, 1997	Ghent, Belgium
3,000 meters	**7:24.90**	Daniel Komen	Kenya	Feb. 6, 1998	Budapest, Hungary
5,000 meters	**12:49.60**	Kenenisa Bekele	Ethiopia	Feb. 20, 2004	Birmingham, England
50-meter hurdles	**6.25**	Mark McKoy	Canada	Mar. 5, 1986	Kobe, Japan
60-meter hurdles	**7.30**	Colin Jackson	Gr. Britain	Mar. 6, 1994	Sindelfingen, Germany
High jump	**2.43m** (7' 11½")	Javier Sotomayor	Cuba	Mar. 4, 1989	Budapest, Hungary
Pole vault	**6.15m** (20' 2")	Sergei Bubka	Ukraine	Feb. 21, 1993	Donyetsk, Ukraine
Long jump	**8.79m** (28' 10¼")	Carl Lewis	U.S.	Jan. 27, 1984	New York, NY
Triple jump	**17.83** (58' 6")	Aliecer Urrutia	Cuba	Mar. 1, 1997	Sindelfingen, Germany
		Christian Olsson	Sweden	Mar. 7, 2004	Budapest, Hungary
Shot put	**22.66m** (74' 4¼")	Randy Barnes	U.S.	Jan. 20, 1989	Los Angeles, CA

Women's Records

Event	Record	Holder	Country	Date	Where made
50 meters	**5.96**	Irina Privalova	Russia	Feb. 9, 1995	Madrid, Spain
60 meters	**6.92**	Irina Privalova	Russia	Feb. 9, 1995	Madrid, Spain
		Irina Privalova	Russia	Feb. 11, 1993	Madrid, Spain
200 meters	**21.87**	Merlene Ottey	Jamaica	Feb. 13, 1993	Lievin, France
400 meters	**49.59**	Jarmila Kratochvilova	Czechoslovakia	Mar. 7, 1982	Milan, Italy
800 meters	**1:55.82**	Jolanda Ceplak	Slovenia	Mar. 3, 2002	Vienna, Austria
1,000 meters	**2:30.94**	Maria Mutola	Mozambique	Feb. 25, 1999	Stockholm, Sweden
1,500 meters	**3:59.98**	Regina Jacobs	U.S.	Feb. 1, 2003	Boston, MA
1 mile	**4:17.14**	Doina Melinte	Romania	Feb. 9, 1990	E. Rutherford, NJ
3,000 meters	**8:29.15**	Berhane Adere	Ethiopia	Mar. 3, 2002	Stuttgart, Germany
5,000 meters	**14:32.93**	Tirunesh Dibaba	Ethiopia	Jan. 29, 2005	Boston, MA
50-meter hurdles	**6.58**	Cornelia Oschkenat	E. Germany	Feb. 20, 1988	Berlin, Germany
60-meter hurdles	**7.69**	Ludmila Engquist	USSR	Feb. 4, 1990	Chelyabinsk, USSR
High jump	**2.07m** (6' 9½")	Heike Henkel	Germany	Feb. 8, 1992	Karlsruhe, Germany
Pole vault	**4.90m** (16' 1")	Yelena Isinbayeva	Russia	Mar. 6, 2005	Madrid, Spain
Long jump	**7.37m** (24' 2¼")	Heike Drechsler	E. Germany	Feb. 13, 1988	Vienna, Austria
Triple jump	**15.36m** (50' 4¾")	Tatyana Lebedeva	Russia	Mar. 3, 2004	Budapest, Hungary
Shot put	**22.50m** (73' 10")	Helena Fibingerova	Czechoslovakia	Feb. 19, 1977	Jablonec, Czechoslovakia

IT'S A FACT: Russia's Yelena Isinbayeva—who set 8 world records in the pole vault in 2004, including one at the Olympics—became the first woman ever to clear the 5-meter mark, setting a new world outdoor record at the 10th IAAF World Championships in Athletics, held in Helsinki, Finland, in Aug. 2005.

BASEBALL

Baseball Returns to Washington, DC; Congress Looks Into Steroids; Palmeiro Suspended

The Washington Nationals, formerly the Montreal Expos, played their first MLB game on Apr. 4. Washington, DC, had been without a baseball team since 1971 when the Senators moved to Texas and became the Rangers. Congress began hearings looking into steroid use in baseball, Mar. 17, and called several players including Baltimore first-baseman Rafael Palmeiro to testify. On July 15, Palmeiro got his 3,000th career hit, becoming just the 4th player in history to reach 3,000 hits and 500 home runs (Hank Aaron, Willie Mays, and Eddie Murray were the others). Palmeiro was back in the headlines Aug. 7, after he tested positive for performance-enhancing drugs and was suspended for 10 days. San Diego pitcher Trevor Hoffman recorded his 400th save on May 6. He finished the season with 436 saves, which placed him 2nd on the all-time list behind Lee Smith, who has 478.

Atlanta extended its record for consecutive division titles, winning the NL East for the 14th straight year. St. Louis dominated the NL Central, going 100-62, and posted the best record in the majors for the 2nd year in a row. San Diego in the weak NL West won the division with only a .506 winning percentage. Houston grabbed the NL wild card. In the AL, New York and Boston ended in a tie for the East, but the division title went to the Yankees because they had the better regular season head-to-head record. Boston ended up just barely squeaking by Cleveland to win the wild card. Chicago won the Central with a comfortable 6-game lead over Cleveland. Los Angeles took the West.

The Houston Astros beat the Atlanta Braves on Oct. 9, 7-6, after 18 innings of play to win the divisional series. It was the longest post-season baseball game ever played. St. Louis, Los Angeles, and Chicago also advanced to the league championship series.

Major League Pennant Winners, 1901–1969

National League						American League					
Year	Winner	Won	Lost	Pct	Manager	Year	Winner	Won	Lost	Pct	Manager
1901	Pittsburgh	90	49	.647	Clarke	1901	Chicago	83	53	.610	Griffith
1902	Pittsburgh	103	36	.741	Clarke	1902	Philadelphia	83	53	.610	Mack
1903	Pittsburgh	91	49	.650	Clarke	1903	Boston	91	47	.659	Collins
1904	New York	106	47	.693	McGraw	1904	Boston	95	59	.617	Collins
1905	New York	105	48	.686	McGraw	1905	Philadelphia	92	56	.622	Mack
1906	Chicago	116	36	.763	Chance	1906	Chicago	93	58	.616	Jones
1907	Chicago	107	45	.704	Chance	1907	Detroit	92	58	.613	Jennings
1908	Chicago	99	55	.643	Chance	1908	Detroit	90	63	.588	Jennings
1909	Pittsburgh	110	42	.724	Clarke	1909	Detroit	98	54	.645	Jennings
1910	Chicago	104	50	.675	Chance	1910	Philadelphia	102	48	.680	Mack
1911	New York	99	54	.647	McGraw	1911	Philadelphia	101	50	.669	Mack
1912	New York	103	48	.682	McGraw	1912	Boston	105	47	.691	Stahl
1913	New York	101	51	.664	McGraw	1913	Philadelphia	96	57	.627	Mack
1914	Boston	94	59	.614	Stallings	1914	Philadelphia	99	53	.651	Mack
1915	Philadelphia	90	62	.592	Moran	1915	Boston	101	50	.669	Carrigan
1916	Brooklyn	94	60	.610	Robinson	1916	Boston	91	63	.591	Carrigan
1917	New York	98	56	.636	McGraw	1917	Chicago	100	54	.649	Rowland
1918	Chicago	84	45	.651	Mitchell	1918	Boston	75	51	.595	Barrow
1919	Cincinnati	96	44	.686	Moran	1919	Chicago	88	52	.629	Gleason
1920	Brooklyn	93	60	.604	Robinson	1920	Cleveland	98	56	.636	Speaker
1921	New York	94	56	.614	McGraw	1921	New York	98	55	.641	Huggins
1922	New York	93	61	.604	McGraw	1922	New York	94	60	.610	Huggins
1923	New York	95	58	.621	McGraw	1923	New York	98	54	.645	Huggins
1924	New York	93	60	.608	McGraw	1924	Washington	92	62	.597	Harris
1925	Pittsburgh	95	58	.621	McKechnie	1925	Washington	96	55	.636	Harris
1926	St. Louis	89	65	.578	Hornsby	1926	New York	91	63	.591	Huggins
1927	Pittsburgh	94	60	.610	Bush	1927	New York	110	44	.714	Huggins
1928	St. Louis	95	59	.617	McKechnie	1928	New York	101	53	.656	Huggins
1929	Chicago	98	54	.645	McCarthy	1929	Philadelphia	104	46	.693	Mack
1930	St. Louis	92	62	.597	Street	1930	Philadelphia	102	52	.662	Mack
1931	St. Louis	101	53	.656	Street	1931	Philadelphia	107	45	.704	Mack
1932	Chicago	90	64	.584	Grimm	1932	New York	107	47	.695	McCarthy
1933	New York	91	61	.599	Terry	1933	Washington	99	53	.651	Cronin
1934	St. Louis	95	58	.621	Frisch	1934	Detroit	101	53	.656	Cochrane
1935	Chicago	100	54	.649	Grimm	1935	Detroit	93	58	.616	Cochrane
1936	New York	91	62	.597	Terry	1936	New York	102	51	.667	McCarthy
1937	New York	95	57	.625	Terry	1937	New York	102	52	.662	McCarthy
1938	Chicago	89	63	.586	Hartnett	1938	New York	99	53	.651	McCarthy
1939	Cincinnati	97	57	.630	McKechnie	1939	New York	106	45	.702	McCarthy
1940	Cincinnati	100	53	.654	McKechnie	1940	Detroit	90	64	.584	Baker
1941	Brooklyn	100	54	.649	Durocher	1941	New York	101	53	.656	McCarthy
1942	St. Louis	106	48	.688	Southworth	1942	New York	103	51	.669	McCarthy
1943	St. Louis	105	49	.682	Southworth	1943	New York	98	56	.636	McCarthy
1944	St. Louis	105	49	.682	Southworth	1944	St. Louis	89	65	.578	Sewell
1945	Chicago	98	56	.636	Grimm	1945	Detroit	88	65	.575	O'Neill
1946	St. Louis	98	58	.628	Dyer	1946	Boston	104	50	.675	Cronin
1947	Brooklyn	94	60	.610	Shotton	1947	New York	97	57	.630	Harris
1948	Boston	91	62	.595	Southworth	1948	Cleveland	97	58	.626	Boudreau
1949	Brooklyn	97	57	.630	Shotton	1949	New York	97	57	.630	Stengel
1950	Philadelphia	91	63	.591	Sawyer	1950	New York	98	56	.636	Stengel
1951	New York	98	59	.624	Durocher	1951	New York	98	56	.636	Stengel
1952	Brooklyn	96	57	.627	Dressen	1952	New York	95	59	.617	Stengel
1953	Brooklyn	105	49	.682	Dressen	1953	New York	99	52	.656	Stengel
1954	New York	97	57	.630	Durocher	1954	Cleveland	111	43	.721	Lopez
1955	Brooklyn	98	55	.641	Alston	1955	New York	96	58	.623	Stengel
1956	Brooklyn	93	61	.604	Alston	1956	New York	97	57	.630	Stengel
1957	Milwaukee	95	59	.617	Haney	1957	New York	98	56	.636	Stengel
1958	Milwaukee	92	62	.597	Haney	1958	New York	92	62	.597	Stengel
1959	Los Angeles	88	68	.564	Alston	1959	Chicago	94	60	.610	Lopez
1960	Pittsburgh	95	59	.617	Murtaugh	1960	New York	97	57	.630	Stengel
1961	Cincinnati	93	61	.604	Hutchinson	1961	New York	109	53	.673	Houk

National League

Year	Winner	Won	Lost	Pct	Manager
1962	San Francisco	103	62	.624	Dark
1963	Los Angeles	99	63	.611	Alston
1964	St. Louis	93	69	.574	Keane
1965	Los Angeles	97	65	.599	Alston
1966	Los Angeles	95	67	.586	Alston
1967	St. Louis	101	60	.627	Schoendienst
1968	St. Louis	97	65	.599	Schoendienst
1969	N.Y. Mets	100	62	.617	Hodges

American League

Year	Winner	Won	Lost	Pct	Manager
1962	New York	96	66	.593	Houk
1963	New York	104	57	.646	Houk
1964	New York	99	63	.611	Berra
1965	Minnesota	102	60	.630	Mele
1966	Baltimore	97	63	.606	Bauer
1967	Boston	92	70	.568	Williams
1968	Detroit	103	59	.636	Smith
1969	Baltimore	100	53	.673	Weaver

Major League Pennant Winners, 1970-2004

National League

	East					West					Pennant
Year	Winner	W	L	Pct	Manager	Winner	W	L	Pct	Manager	Winner
1970	Pittsburgh	89	73	.549	Murtaugh	Cincinnati	102	60	.630	Anderson	Cincinnati
1971	Pittsburgh	97	65	.599	Murtaugh	San Francisco	90	72	.556	Fox	Pittsburgh
1972	Pittsburgh	96	59	.619	Virdon	Cincinnati	95	59	.617	Anderson	Cincinnati
1973	N.Y. Mets	82	79	.509	Berra	Cincinnati	99	63	.611	Anderson	New York
1974	Pittsburgh	88	74	.543	Murtaugh	Los Angeles	102	60	.630	Alston	Los Angeles
1975	Pittsburgh	92	69	.571	Murtaugh	Cincinnati	108	54	.667	Anderson	Cincinnati
1976	Philadelphia	101	61	.623	Ozark	Cincinnati	102	60	.630	Anderson	Cincinnati
1977	Philadelphia	101	61	.623	Ozark	Los Angeles	98	64	.605	Lasorda	Los Angeles
1978	Philadelphia	90	72	.556	Ozark	Los Angeles	95	67	.586	Lasorda	Los Angeles
1979	Pittsburgh	98	64	.605	Tanner	Cincinnati	90	71	.559	McNamara	Pittsburgh
1980	Philadelphia	91	71	.562	Green	Houston	93	70	.571	Virdon	Philadelphia
1981(a)	Philadelphia	34	21	.618	Green	Los Angeles	36	21	.632	Lasorda	(c)
1981(b)	Montreal	30	23	.566	Williams, Fanning	Houston	33	20	.623	Virdon	Los Angeles
1982	St. Louis	92	70	.568	Herzog	Atlanta	89	73	.549	Torre	St. Louis
1983	Philadelphia	90	72	.556	Corrales, Owens	Los Angeles	91	71	.562	Lasorda	Philadelphia
1984	Chicago	96	65	.596	Frey	San Diego	92	70	.568	Williams	San Diego
1985	St. Louis	101	61	.623	Herzog	Los Angeles	95	67	.586	Lasorda	St. Louis
1986	N.Y. Mets	108	54	.667	Johnson	Houston	96	66	.593	Lanier	New York
1987	St. Louis	95	67	.586	Herzog	San Francisco	90	72	.556	Craig	St. Louis
1988	N.Y. Mets	100	60	.625	Johnson	Los Angeles	94	67	.584	Lasorda	Los Angeles
1989	Chicago	93	69	.571	Zimmer	San Francisco	92	70	.568	Craig	San Francisco
1990	Pittsburgh	95	67	.586	Leyland	Cincinnati	91	71	.562	Piniella	Cincinnati
1991	Pittsburgh	98	64	.605	Leyland	Atlanta	94	68	.580	Cox	Atlanta
1992	Pittsburgh	96	66	.593	Leyland	Atlanta	98	64	.605	Cox	Atlanta
1993	Philadelphia	97	65	.599	Fregosi	Atlanta	104	58	.642	Cox	Philadelphia

Year	Division	Winner	W	L	Pct	Manager	Playoffs	Pennant Winner
1994(d)	East	Montreal	74	40	.649	Alou	—	—
	Central	Cincinnati	66	48	.579	Johnson		
	West	Los Angeles	58	56	.509	Lasorda		
1995	East	Atlanta	90	54	.625	Cox	Atlanta 3, Colorado* 1	Atlanta
	Central	Cincinnati	85	59	.590	Johnson	Cincinnati 3, Los Angeles 0	
	West	Los Angeles	78	66	.542	Lasorda	Atlanta 4, Cincinnati 0	
1996	East	Atlanta	96	66	.593	Cox	Atlanta 3, Los Angeles* 0	Atlanta
	Central	St. Louis	88	74	.543	La Russa	St. Louis 3, San Diego 0	
	West	San Diego	91	71	.562	Bochy	Atlanta 4, St. Louis 3	
1997	East	Atlanta	101	61	.623	Cox	Atlanta 3, Houston 0	Florida* (e)
	Central	Houston	84	78	.519	Dierker	Florida* 3, San Francisco 0	
	West	San Francisco	90	72	.556	Baker	Florida* 4, Atlanta 2	
1998	East	Atlanta	106	56	.654	Cox	Atlanta 3, Chicago* 0	San Diego
	Central	Houston	102	60	.630	Dierker	San Diego 3, Houston 1	
	West	San Diego	97	64	.602	Bochy	San Diego 4, Atlanta 2	
1999	East	Atlanta	103	59	.636	Cox	Atlanta 3, Houston 1	Atlanta
	Central	Houston	97	65	.599	Dierker	New York* 3, Arizona 1	
	West	Arizona	100	62	.617	Showalter	Atlanta 4, New York 2	
2000	East	Atlanta	95	67	.586	Cox	St. Louis 3, Atlanta 0	New York* (f)
	Central	St. Louis	95	67	.586	La Russa	New York* 3, San Francisco 1	
	West	San Francisco	97	65	.599	Baker	New York* 4, St. Louis 1	
2001	East	Atlanta	88	74	.543	Cox	Atlanta 3, Houston 0	Arizona
	Central	Houston	93	69	.574	Dierker	Arizona 3, St. Louis* 2	
	West	Arizona	92	70	.568	Brenly	Arizona 4, Atlanta 1	
2002	East	Atlanta	101	59	.631	Cox	St. Louis 3, Arizona 0	San Francisco* (g)
	Central	St. Louis	97	65	.599	La Russa	San Francisco* 3, Atlanta 2	
	West	Arizona	98	64	.605	Brenly	San Francisco 4, St. Louis 1	
2003	East	Atlanta	101	61	.623	Cox	Chicago 3, Atlanta 2	Florida*(i)
	Central	Chicago	88	74	.543	Baker	Florida* 3, San Francisco 2	
	West	San Francisco	100	61	.621	Alou	Florida* 4, Chicago 3	
2004	East	Atlanta	96	66	.593	Cox	Houston* 3, Atlanta 2	St. Louis
	Central	St. Louis	105	57	.648	La Russa	St. Louis 3, Dodgers 1	
	West	Los Angeles	93	69	.594	Tracy	St. Louis 4, Houston 3	
2005	East	Atlanta	90	72	.556	Cox	St. Louis 3, San Diego 0	(k)
	Central	St. Louis	100	62	.617	La Russa	Houston* 3, Atlanta 1	
	West	San Diego	82	80	.506	Bochy		

American League

	East					West					Pennant
Year	Winner	W	L	Pct	Manager	Winner	W	L	Pct	Manager	Winner
1970	Baltimore	108	54	.667	Weaver	Minnesota	98	64	.605	Rigney	Baltimore
1971	Baltimore	101	57	.639	Weaver	Oakland	101	60	.627	Williams	Baltimore
1972	Detroit	86	70	.551	Martin	Oakland	93	62	.600	Williams	Oakland
1973	Baltimore	97	65	.599	Weaver	Oakland	94	68	.580	Williams	Oakland
1974	Baltimore	91	71	.562	Weaver	Oakland	90	72	.556	Dark	Oakland
1975	Boston	95	65	.594	Johnson	Oakland	98	64	.605	Dark	Boston
1976	New York	97	62	.610	Martin	Kansas City	90	72	.556	Herzog	New York

Year	East Winner	W	L	Pct	Manager	West Winner	W	L	Pct	Manager	Pennant Winner
1977	New York	100	62	.617	Martin	Kansas City	102	60	.630	Herzog	New York
1978	New York	100	63	.613	Martin, Lemon	Kansas City	92	70	.568	Herzog	New York
1979	Baltimore	102	57	.642	Weaver	California	88	74	.543	Fregosi	Baltimore
1980	New York	103	59	.636	Howser	Kansas City	97	65	.599	Frey	Kansas City
1981(a)	New York	34	22	.607	Michael	Oakland	37	23	.617	Martin	(c)
1981(b)	Milwaukee	31	22	.585	Rodgers	Kansas City	30	23	.566	Frey, Howser	New York
1982	Milwaukee	95	67	.586	Rodgers, Kuenn	California	93	69	.574	Mauch	Milwaukee
1983	Baltimore	98	64	.605	Altobelli	Chicago	99	63	.611	La Russa	Baltimore
1984	Detroit	104	58	.642	Anderson	Kansas City	84	78	.519	Howser	Detroit
1985	Toronto	99	62	.615	Cox	Kansas City	91	71	.562	Howser	Kansas City
1986	Boston	95	66	.590	McNamara	California	92	70	.568	Mauch	Boston
1987	Detroit	98	64	.605	Anderson	Minnesota	85	77	.525	Kelly	Minnesota
1988	Boston	89	73	.549	McNamara, Morgan	Oakland	104	58	.642	La Russa	Oakland
1989	Toronto	89	73	.549	Williams, Gaston	Oakland	99	63	.611	La Russa	Oakland
1990	Boston	88	74	.543	Morgan	Oakland	103	59	.636	La Russa	Oakland
1991	Toronto	91	71	.562	Gaston	Minnesota	95	67	.586	Kelly	Minnesota
1992	Toronto	96	66	.593	Gaston	Oakland	96	66	.593	La Russa	Toronto
1993	Toronto	95	67	.586	Gaston	Chicago	94	68	.580	Lamont	Toronto

Year	Division	Winner	W	L	Pct	Manager	Playoffs	Pennant Winner
1994(d)	East	New York	70	43	.619	Showalter	—	—
	Central	Chicago	67	46	.593	Lamont		
	West	Texas	52	62	.456	Kennedy		
1995	East	Boston	86	58	.597	Kennedy	Cleveland 3, Boston 0	Cleveland
	Central	Cleveland	100	44	.694	Hargrove	Seattle 3, New York* 2	
	West	Seattle	79	66	.545	Piniella	Cleveland 4, Seattle 2	
1996	East	New York	92	70	.568	Torre	Baltimore* 3, Cleveland 1	New York
	Central	Cleveland	99	62	.615	Hargrove	New York 3, Texas 1	
	West	Texas	90	72	.556	Oates	New York 4, Baltimore* 1	
1997	East	Baltimore	98	64	.605	Johnson	Baltimore 3, Seattle 1	Cleveland
	Central	Cleveland	86	75	.534	Hargrove	Cleveland 3, New York* 2	
	West	Seattle	90	72	.556	Piniella	Cleveland 4, Baltimore 2	
1998	East	New York	114	48	.704	Torre	New York 3, Texas 0	New York
	Central	Cleveland	89	73	.549	Hargrove	Cleveland 3, Boston* 1	
	West	Texas	88	74	.543	Oates	New York 4, Cleveland 2	
1999	East	New York	98	64	.605	Torre	New York 3, Texas 0	New York
	Central	Cleveland	97	65	.599	Hargrove	Boston* 3, Cleveland 2	
	West	Texas	95	67	.586	Oates	New York 4, Boston* 1	
2000	East	New York	87	74	.540	Torre	New York 3, Oakland 2	New York
	Central	Chicago	95	67	.586	Manuel	Seattle* 3, Chicago 0	
	West	Oakland	91	70	.565	Howe	New York 4, Seattle* 2	
2001	East	New York	95	65	.594	Torre	Seattle 3, Cleveland 2	New York
	Central	Cleveland	91	71	.562	Manuel	New York 3, Oakland 2	
	West	Seattle	116	46	.716	Piniella	New York 4, Seattle* 1	
2002	East	New York	103	58	.640	Torre	Anaheim* 3, New York 1	Anaheim* (h)
	Central	Minnesota	94	67	.584	Gardenhire	Minnesota 3, Oakland 2	
	West	Oakland	103	59	.636	Howe	Anaheim* 4, Minnesota 1	
2003	East	New York	101	61	.623	Torre	New York 3, Minnesota 1	New York
	Central	Minnesota	90	72	.556	Gardenhire	Boston* 3, Oakland 2	
	West	Oakland	96	66	.593	Macha	New York 4, Boston* 3	
2004	East	New York	101	61	.623	Torre	New York 3, Minnesota 1	Boston (j)
	Central	Minnesota	92	70	.568	Gardenhire	Boston* 3, Anaheim 0	
	West	Anaheim	92	70	.568	Scioscia	Boston 4, New York 3	
2005	East	New York	95	67	.586	Torre	Chicago 3, Boston* 0	(k)
	Central	Chicago	99	63	.611	Guillen	Los Angeles 3, New York 2	
	West	Los Angeles	95	67	.586	Scioscia		

*Wild card team. (a) First half. (b) Second half. (c) Montreal, L.A., N.Y. Yankees, and Oakland won the divisional playoffs. (d) In Aug. 1994, a players' strike began that caused the cancellation of the remainder of the season, the playoffs, and the World Series. Teams listed as division "winners" for 1994 were leading their divisions at the time of the strike. (e) Florida manager: Jim Leyland. (f) New York manager Bobby Valentine. (g) San Francisco manager: Dusty Baker. (h) Anaheim manager: Mike Scioscia. (i) Florida manager: Jack McKeon. (j) Boston manager: Terry Francona. (k) Not decided at press time.

Home Run Leaders, by Season

Note: Asterisk (*) indicates the all-time single-season record for each league.

Year	National League Player, Team	HR	Year	American League Player, Team	HR
1901	Sam Crawford, Cincinnati	16	1901	Napoleon Lajoie, Philadelphia	13
1902	Thomas Leach, Pittsburgh	6	1902	Socks Seybold, Philadelphia	16
1903	James Sheckard, Brooklyn	9	1903	Buck Freeman, Boston	13
1904	Harry Lumley, Brooklyn	9	1904	Harry Davis, Philadelphia	10
1905	Fred Odwell, Cincinnati	9	1905	Harry Davis, Philadelphia	8
1906	Timothy Jordan, Brooklyn	12	1906	Harry Davis, Philadelphia	12
1907	David Brain, Boston	10	1907	Harry Davis, Philadelphia	8
1908	Timothy Jordan, Brooklyn	12	1908	Sam Crawford, Detroit	7
1909	Red Murray, New York	7	1909	Ty Cobb, Detroit	9
1910	Fred Beck, Boston; Frank Schulte, Chicago	10	1910	Jake Stahl, Boston	10
1911	Frank Schulte, Chicago	21	1911	J. Franklin Baker, Philadelphia	9
1912	Henry Zimmerman, Chicago	14	1912	J. Franklin Baker, Philadelphia; Tris Speaker, Boston	10
1913	Gavvy Cravath, Philadelphia	19	1913	J. Franklin Baker, Philadelphia	13
1914	Gavvy Cravath, Philadelphia	19	1914	J. Franklin Baker, Philadelphia	9
1915	Gavvy Cravath, Philadelphia	24	1915	Robert Roth, Chicago-Cleveland	7
1916	Dave Robertson, N.Y.; Fred (Cy) Williams, Chi.	12	1916	Wally Pipp, New York	12
1917	Dave Robertson, N.Y.; Gavvy Cravath, Phi.	12	1917	Wally Pipp, New York	9
1918	Gavvy Cravath, Philadelphia	8	1918	Babe Ruth, Boston; Tilly Walker, Philadelphia	11
1919	Gavvy Cravath, Philadelphia	12	1919	Babe Ruth, Boston	29
1920	Cy Williams, Philadelphia	15	1920	Babe Ruth, New York	54
1921	George Kelly, New York	23	1921	Babe Ruth, New York	59

National League

Year	Player, Team	HR
1922	Rogers Hornsby, St. Louis	42
1923	Cy Williams, Philadelphia	41
1924	Jacques Fournier, Brooklyn	27
1925	Rogers Hornsby, St. Louis	39
1926	Hack Wilson, Chicago	21
1927	Hack Wilson, Chicago; Cy Williams, Philadelphia	30
1928	Hack Wilson, Chicago; Jim Bottomley, St. Louis	31
1929	Chuck Klein, Philadelphia	43
1930	Hack Wilson, Chicago	56
1931	Chuck Klein, Philadelphia	31
1932	Chuck Klein, Philadelphia; Mel Ott, New York	38
1933	Chuck Klein, Philadelphia	28
1934	Rip Collins, St. Louis; Mel Ott, New York	35
1935	Walter Berger, Boston	34
1936	Mel Ott, New York	33
1937	Mel Ott, New York; Joe Medwick, St. Louis	31
1938	Mel Ott, New York	36
1939	John Mize, St. Louis	28
1940	John Mize, St. Louis	43
1941	Dolph Camilli, Brooklyn	34
1942	Mel Ott, New York	30
1943	Bill Nicholson, Chicago	29
1944	Bill Nicholson, Chicago	33
1945	Tommy Holmes, Boston	28
1946	Ralph Kiner, Pittsburgh	23
1947	Ralph Kiner, Pittsburgh; John Mize, New York	51
1948	Ralph Kiner, Pittsburgh; John Mize, New York	40
1949	Ralph Kiner, Pittsburgh	54
1950	Ralph Kiner, Pittsburgh	47
1951	Ralph Kiner, Pittsburgh	42
1952	Ralph Kiner, Pittsburgh; Hank Sauer, Chicago	37
1953	Ed Mathews, Milwaukee	47
1954	Ted Kluszewski, Cincinnati	49
1955	Willie Mays, New York	51
1956	Duke Snider, Brooklyn	43
1957	Hank Aaron, Milwaukee	44
1958	Ernie Banks, Chicago	47
1959	Ed Mathews, Milwaukee	46
1960	Ernie Banks, Chicago	41
1961	Orlando Cepeda, San Francisco	46
1962	Willie Mays, San Francisco	49
1963	Hank Aaron, Milwaukee; Willie McCovey, S.F.	44
1964	Willie Mays, San Francisco	47
1965	Willie Mays, San Francisco	52
1966	Hank Aaron, Atlanta	44
1967	Hank Aaron, Atlanta	39
1968	Willie McCovey, San Francisco	36
1969	Willie McCovey, San Francisco	45
1970	Johnny Bench, Cincinnati	45
1971	Willie Stargell, Pittsburgh	48
1972	Johnny Bench, Cincinnati	40
1973	Willie Stargell, Pittsburgh	44
1974	Mike Schmidt, Philadelphia	36
1975	Mike Schmidt, Philadelphia	38
1976	Mike Schmidt, Philadelphia	38
1977	George Foster, Cincinnati	52
1978	George Foster, Cincinnati	40
1979	Dave Kingman, Chicago	48
1980	Mike Schmidt, Philadelphia	48
1981	Mike Schmidt, Philadelphia	31
1982	Dave Kingman, New York	37
1983	Mike Schmidt, Philadelphia	40
1984	Mike Schmidt, Phi.; Dale Murphy, Atlanta	36
1985	Dale Murphy, Atlanta	37
1986	Mike Schmidt, Philadelphia	37
1987	Andre Dawson, Chicago	49
1988	Darryl Strawberry, New York	39
1989	Kevin Mitchell, San Francisco	47
1990	Ryne Sandberg, Chicago	40
1991	Howard Johnson, New York	38
1992	Fred McGriff, San Diego	35
1993	Barry Bonds, San Francisco	46
1994	Matt Williams, San Francisco	43
1995	Dante Bichette, Colorado	40
1996	Andres Galarraga, Colorado	47
1997[1]	Larry Walker, Colorado	49
1998	Mark McGwire, St. Louis	70
1999	Mark McGwire, St. Louis	65
2000	Sammy Sosa, Chicago	50
2001	Barry Bonds, San Francisco	*73
2002	Sammy Sosa, Chicago	49
2003	Jim Thome, Philadelphia	47
2004	Adrian Beltre, Los Angeles	48
2005	Andruw Jones, Atlanta	51

American League

Year	Player, Team	HR
1922	Ken Williams, St. Louis	39
1923	Babe Ruth, New York	41
1924	Babe Ruth, New York	46
1925	Bob Meusel, New York	33
1926	Babe Ruth, New York	47
1927	Babe Ruth, New York	60
1928	Babe Ruth, New York	54
1929	Babe Ruth, New York	46
1930	Babe Ruth, New York	49
1931	Babe Ruth, Lou Gehrig, both New York	46
1932	Jimmie Foxx, Philadelphia	58
1933	Jimmie Foxx, Philadelphia	48
1934	Lou Gehrig, New York	49
1935	Jimmie Foxx, Philadelphia; Hank Greenberg, Detroit	36
1936	Lou Gehrig, New York	49
1937	Joe DiMaggio, New York	46
1938	Hank Greenberg, Detroit	58
1939	Jimmie Foxx, Boston	35
1940	Hank Greenberg, Detroit	41
1941	Ted Williams, Boston	37
1942	Ted Williams, Boston	36
1943	Rudy York, Detroit	34
1944	Nick Etten, New York	22
1945	Vern Stephens, St. Louis	24
1946	Hank Greenberg, Detroit	44
1947	Ted Williams, Boston	32
1948	Joe DiMaggio, New York	39
1949	Ted Williams, Boston	43
1950	Al Rosen, Cleveland	37
1951	Gus Zernial, Chicago-Philadelphia	33
1952	Larry Doby, Cleveland	32
1953	Al Rosen, Cleveland	43
1954	Larry Doby, Cleveland	32
1955	Mickey Mantle, New York	37
1956	Mickey Mantle, New York	52
1957	Roy Sievers, Washington	42
1958	Mickey Mantle, New York	42
1959	Rocky Colavito, Cleve.; Harmon Killebrew, Wash.	42
1960	Mickey Mantle, New York	40
1961	Roger Maris, New York	*61
1962	Harmon Killebrew, Minnesota	48
1963	Harmon Killebrew, Minnesota	45
1964	Harmon Killebrew, Minnesota	49
1965	Tony Conigliaro, Boston	32
1966	Frank Robinson, Baltimore	49
1967	Carl Yastrzemski, Boston; Harmon Killebrew, Minn.	44
1968	Frank Howard, Washington	44
1969	Harmon Killebrew, Minnesota	49
1970	Frank Howard, Washington	44
1971	Bill Melton, Chicago	33
1972	Dick Allen, Chicago	37
1973	Reggie Jackson, Oakland	32
1974	Dick Allen, Chicago	32
1975	George Scott, Milwaukee; Reggie Jackson, Oakland	36
1976	Graig Nettles, New York	32
1977	Jim Rice, Boston	39
1978	Jim Rice, Boston	46
1979	Gorman Thomas, Milwaukee	45
1980	Reggie Jackson, New York; Ben Oglivie, Milwaukee	41
1981	Bobby Grich, California; Tony Armas, Oakland; Dwight Evans, Boston; Eddie Murray, Baltimore	22
1982	Gorman Thomas, Milwaukee; Reggie Jackson, Cal.	39
1983	Jim Rice, Boston	39
1984	Tony Armas, Boston	43
1985	Darrell Evans, Detroit	40
1986	Jesse Barfield, Toronto	40
1987	Mark McGwire, Oakland	49
1988	Jose Canseco, Oakland	42
1989	Fred McGriff, Toronto	36
1990	Cecil Fielder, Detroit	51
1991	Cecil Fielder, Detroit; Jose Canseco, Oakland	44
1992	Juan Gonzalez, Texas	43
1993	Juan Gonzalez, Texas	46
1994	Ken Griffey Jr., Seattle	40
1995	Albert Belle, Cleveland	50
1996	Mark McGwire, Oakland	52
1997[1]	Ken Griffey Jr., Seattle	56
1998	Ken Griffey Jr., Seattle	56
1999	Ken Griffey Jr., Seattle	48
2000	Troy Glaus, Anaheim	47
2001	Alex Rodriguez, Texas	52
2002	Alex Rodriguez, Texas	57
2003	Alex Rodriguez, Texas	47
2004	Manny Ramirez, Boston	43
2005	Alex Rodriguez, New York	48

(1) In 1997, Mark McGwire hit 58 home runs; 34 with the Oakland Athletics (AL) and 24 with the St. Louis Cardinals (NL).

Runs Batted In Leaders, by Season

Note: Asterisk (*) indicates the all-time single-season record for each league since beginning of "modern" era in 1901.

National League			American League		
Year	**Player, Team**	**RBI**	**Year**	**Player, Team**	**RBI**
1907	Sherwood Magee, Philadelphia	85	1907	Ty Cobb, Detroit	116
1908	Honus Wagner, Pittsburgh	109	1908	Ty Cobb, Detroit	108
1909	Honus Wagner, Pittsburgh	100	1909	Ty Cobb, Detroit	107
1910	Sherwood Magee, Philadelphia	123	1910	Sam Crawford, Detroit	120
1911	Frank Schulte, Chicago	121	1911	Ty Cobb, Detroit	144
1912	Henry Zimmerman, Chicago	103	1912	J. Franklin Baker, Philadelphia	133
1913	Gavvy Cravath, Philadelphia	128	1913	J. Franklin Baker, Philadelphia	126
1914	Sherwood Magee, Philadelphia	103	1914	Sam Crawford, Detroit	104
1915	Gavvy Cravath, Philadelphia	115	1915	Sam Crawford, Detroit; Robert Veach, Detroit	112
1916	Henry Zimmerman, Chicago-NewYork	83	1916	Del Pratt, St. Louis	103
1917	Henry Zimmerman, New York	102	1917	Robert Veach, Detroit	103
1918	Sherwood Magee, Philadelphia	76	1918	Robert Veach, Detroit	78
1919	Hi Myers, Boston	73	1919	Babe Ruth, Boston	114
1920	George Kelly, N.Y.; Rogers Hornsby, St. Louis	94	1920	Babe Ruth, New York	137
1921	Rogers Hornsby, St. Louis	126	1921	Babe Ruth, New York	171
1922	Rogers Hornsby, St. Louis	152	1922	Ken Williams, St. Louis	155
1923	Emil Meusel, New York	125	1923	Babe Ruth, New York	131
1924	George Kelly, New York	136	1924	Goose Goslin, Washington	129
1925	Rogers Hornsby, St. Louis	143	1925	Bob Meusel, New York	138
1926	Jim Bottomley, St. Louis	120	1926	Babe Ruth, New York	145
1927	Paul Waner, Pittsburgh	131	1927	Lou Gehrig, New York	175
1928	Jim Bottomley, St. Louis	136	1928	Babe Ruth, New York; Lou Gehrig, New York	142
1929	Hack Wilson, Chicago	159	1929	Al Simmons, Philadelphia	157
1930	Hack Wilson, Chicago	*191	1930	Lou Gehrig, New York	174
1931	Chuck Klein, Philadelphia	121	1931	Lou Gehrig, New York	*184
1932	Don Hurst, Philadelphia	143	1932	Jimmie Foxx, Philadelphia	169
1933	Chuck Klein, Philadelphia	120	1933	Jimmie Foxx, Philadelphia	163
1934	Mel Ott, New York	135	1934	Lou Gehrig, New York	165
1935	Walter Berger, Boston	130	1935	Hank Greenberg, Detroit	170
1936	Joe Medwick, St. Louis	138	1936	Hal Trosky, Cleveland	162
1937	Joe Medwick, St. Louis	154	1937	Hank Greenberg, Detroit	183
1938	Joe Medwick, St. Louis	122	1938	Jimmie Foxx, Boston	175
1939	Frank McCormick, Cincinnati	128	1939	Ted Williams, Boston	145
1940	John Mize, St. Louis	137	1940	Hank Greenberg, Detroit	150
1941	Adolph Camilli, Brooklyn	120	1941	Joe DiMaggio, New York	125
1942	John Mize, New York	110	1942	Ted Williams, Boston	137
1943	Bill Nicholson, Chicago	128	1943	Rudy York, Detroit	118
1944	Bill Nicholson, Chicago	122	1944	Vern Stephens, St. Louis	109
1945	Dixie Walker, Brooklyn	124	1945	Nick Etten, New York	111
1946	Enos Slaughter, St. Louis	130	1946	Hank Greenberg, Detroit	127
1947	John Mize, New York	138	1947	Ted Williams, Boston	114
1948	Stan Musial, St. Louis	131	1948	Joe DiMaggio, New York	155
1949	Ralph Kiner, Pittsburgh	127	1949	Ted Williams, Bos.; Vern Stephens, Bos.	159
1950	Del Ennis, Philadelphia	126	1950	Walt Dropo, Bos.; Vern Stephens, Bos.	144
1951	Monte Irvin, New York	121	1951	Gus Zernial, Chicago-Philadelphia	129
1952	Hank Sauer, Chicago	121	1952	Al Rosen, Cleveland	105
1953	Roy Campanella, Brooklyn	142	1953	Al Rosen, Cleveland	145
1954	Ted Kluszewski, Cincinnati	141	1954	Larry Doby, Cleveland	126
1955	Duke Snider, Brooklyn	136	1955	Ray Boone, Detroit; Jackie Jensen, Boston	116
1956	Stan Musial, St. Louis	109	1956	Mickey Mantle, New York	130
1957	Hank Aaron, Milwaukee	132	1957	Roy Sievers, Washington	114
1958	Ernie Banks, Chicago	129	1958	Jackie Jensen, Boston	122
1959	Ernie Banks, Chicago	143	1959	Jackie Jensen, Boston	112
1960	Hank Aaron, Milwaukee	126	1960	Roger Maris, New York	112
1961	Orlando Cepeda, San Francisco	142	1961	Roger Maris, New York	142
1962	Tommy Davis, Los Angeles	153	1962	Harmon Killebrew, Minnesota	126
1963	Hank Aaron, Milwaukee	130	1963	Dick Stuart, Boston	118
1964	Ken Boyer, St. Louis	119	1964	Brooks Robinson, Baltimore	118
1965	Deron Johnson, Cincinnati	130	1965	Rocky Colavito, Cleveland	108
1966	Hank Aaron, Atlanta	127	1966	Frank Robinson, Baltimore	122
1967	Orlando Cepeda, St. Louis	111	1967	Carl Yastrzemski, Boston	121
1968	Willie McCovey, San Francisco	105	1968	Ken Harrelson, Boston	109
1969	Willie McCovey, San Francisco	126	1969	Harmon Killebrew, Minnesota	140
1970	Johnny Bench, Cincinnati	148	1970	Frank Howard, Washington	126
1971	Joe Torre, St. Louis	137	1971	Harmon Killebrew, Minnesota	119
1972	Johnny Bench, Cincinnati	125	1972	Dick Allen, Chicago	113
1973	Willie Stargell, Pittsburgh	119	1973	Reggie Jackson, Oakland	117
1974	Johnny Bench, Cincinnati	129	1974	Jeff Burroughs, Texas	118
1975	Greg Luzinski, Philadelphia	120	1975	George Scott, Milwaukee	109
1976	George Foster, Cincinnati	121	1976	Lee May, Baltimore	109
1977	George Foster, Cincinnati	149	1977	Larry Hisle, Minnesota	119
1978	George Foster, Cincinnati	120	1978	Jim Rice, Boston	139
1979	Dave Winfield, San Diego	118	1979	Don Baylor, California	139
1980	Mike Schmidt, Philadelphia	121	1980	Cecil Cooper, Milwaukee	122
1981	Mike Schmidt, Philadelphia	91	1981	Eddie Murray, Baltimore	78
1982	Dale Murphy, Atlanta; Al Oliver, Montreal	109	1982	Hal McRae, Kansas City	133
1983	Dale Murphy, Atlanta	121	1983	Cecil Cooper, Milwaukee; Jim Rice, Boston	126
1984	Gary Carter, Montreal; Mike Schmidt, Phi.	106	1984	Tony Armas, Boston	123
1985	Dave Parker, Cincinnati	125	1985	Don Mattingly, New York	145
1986	Mike Schmidt, Philadelphia	119	1986	Joe Carter, Cleveland	121
1987	Andre Dawson, Chicago	137	1987	George Bell, Toronto	134
1988	Will Clark, San Francisco	109	1988	Jose Canseco, Oakland	124
1989	Kevin Mitchell, San Francisco	125	1989	Ruben Sierra, Texas	119
1990	Matt Williams, San Francisco	122	1990	Cecil Fielder, Detroit	132
1991	Howard Johnson, New York	117	1991	Cecil Fielder, Detroit	133

National League

Year	Player, Team	RBI
1992	Darren Daulton, Philadelphia	109
1993	Barry Bonds, San Francisco	123
1994	Jeff Bagwell, Houston	116
1995	Dante Bichette, Colorado	128
1996	Andres Galarraga, Colorado	150
1997	Andres Galarraga, Colorado	140
1998	Sammy Sosa, Chicago	158
1999	Mark McGwire, St. Louis	147
2000	Todd Helton, Colorado	147
2001	Sammy Sosa, Chicago	160
2002	Lance Berkman, Houston	128
2003	Preston Wilson, Colorado	141
2004	Vinny Castilla, Colorado	131
2005	Andruw Jones, Atlanta	128

American League

Year	Player, Team	RBI
1992	Cecil Fielder, Detroit	124
1993	Albert Belle, Cleveland	129
1994	Kirby Puckett, Minnesota	112
1995	Albert Belle, Cleveland; Mo Vaughn, Boston	126
1996	Albert Belle, Cleveland	148
1997	Ken Griffey Jr., Seattle	147
1998	Juan Gonzalez, Texas	157
1999	Manny Ramirez, Cleveland	165
2000	Edgar Martinez, Seattle	145
2001	Bret Boone, Seattle	141
2002	Alex Rodriguez, Texas	142
2003	Carlos Delgado, Toronto	145
2004	Miguel Tejada, Baltimore	150
2005	David Ortiz, Boston	148

Batting Champions, by Season

Note: Asterisk (*) indicates the all-time single-season record for each league since the beginning of the "modern" era in 1901.

National League

Year	Player	Team	Avg.
1901	Jesse C. Burkett	St. Louis	.382
1902	Clarence Beaumont	Pittsburgh	.357
1903	Honus Wagner	Pittsburgh	.355
1904	Honus Wagner	Pittsburgh	.349
1905	James Seymour	Cincinnati	.377
1906	Honus Wagner	Pittsburgh	.339
1907	Honus Wagner	Pittsburgh	.350
1908	Honus Wagner	Pittsburgh	.354
1909	Honus Wagner	Pittsburgh	.339
1910	Sherwood Magee	Philadelphia	.331
1911	Honus Wagner	Pittsburgh	.334
1912	Henry Zimmerman	Chicago	.372
1913	Jacob Daubert	Brooklyn	.350
1914	Jacob Daubert	Brooklyn	.329
1915	Larry Doyle	New York	.320
1916	Hal Chase	Cincinnati	.339
1917	Edd Roush	Cincinnati	.341
1918	Zach Wheat	Brooklyn	.335
1919	Edd Roush	Cincinnati	.321
1920	Rogers Hornsby	St. Louis	.370
1921	Rogers Hornsby	St. Louis	.397
1922	Rogers Hornsby	St. Louis	.401
1923	Rogers Hornsby	St. Louis	.384
1924	Rogers Hornsby	St. Louis	*.424
1925	Rogers Hornsby	St. Louis	.403
1926	Eugene Hargrave	Cincinnati	.353
1927	Paul Waner	Pittsburgh	.380
1928	Rogers Hornsby	Boston	.387
1929	Lefty O'Doul	Philadelphia	.398
1930	Bill Terry	New York	.401
1931	Chick Hafey	St. Louis	.349
1932	Lefty O'Doul	Brooklyn	.368
1933	Chuck Klein	Philadelphia	.368
1934	Paul Waner	Pittsburgh	.362
1935	Arky Vaughan	Pittsburgh	.385
1936	Paul Waner	Pittsburgh	.373
1937	Joe Medwick	St. Louis	.374
1938	Ernie Lombardi	Cincinnati	.342
1939	John Mize	St. Louis	.349
1940	Debs Garms	Pittsburgh	.355
1941	Pete Reiser	Brooklyn	.343
1942	Ernie Lombardi	Boston	.330
1943	Stan Musial	St. Louis	.357
1944	Dixie Walker	Brooklyn	.357
1945	Phil Cavarretta	Chicago	.355
1946	Stan Musial	St. Louis	.365
1947	Harry Walker	St.L.-Phi.	.363
1948	Stan Musial	St. Louis	.376
1949	Jackie Robinson	Brooklyn	.342
1950	Stan Musial	St. Louis	.346
1951	Stan Musial	St. Louis	.355
1952	Stan Musial	St. Louis	.336
1953	Carl Furillo	Brooklyn	.344
1954	Willie Mays	New York	.345
1955	Richie Ashburn	Philadelphia	.338
1956	Hank Aaron	Milwaukee	.328
1957	Stan Musial	St. Louis	.351
1958	Richie Ashburn	Philadelphia	.350
1959	Hank Aaron	Milwaukee	.355
1960	Dick Groat	Pittsburgh	.325
1961	Roberto Clemente	Pittsburgh	.351
1962	Tommy Davis	Los Angeles	.346
1963	Tommy Davis	Los Angeles	.326
1964	Roberto Clemente	Pittsburgh	.339
1965	Roberto Clemente	Pittsburgh	.329
1966	Matty Alou	Pittsburgh	.342
1967	Roberto Clemente	Pittsburgh	.357
1968	Pete Rose	Cincinnati	.335

American League

Year	Player	Team	Avg.
1901	Napoleon Lajoie	Philadelphia	*.426
1902	Ed Delahanty	Washington	.376
1903	Napoleon Lajoie	Cleveland	.355
1904	Napoleon Lajoie	Cleveland	.381
1905	Elmer Flick	Cleveland	.306
1906	George Stone	St. Louis	.358
1907	Ty Cobb	Detroit	.350
1908	Ty Cobb	Detroit	.324
1909	Ty Cobb	Detroit	.377
1910[1]	Ty Cobb	Detroit	.385
1911	Ty Cobb	Detroit	.420
1912	Ty Cobb	Detroit	.410
1913	Ty Cobb	Detroit	.390
1914	Ty Cobb	Detroit	.368
1915	Ty Cobb	Detroit	.369
1916	Tris Speaker	Cleveland	.386
1917	Ty Cobb	Detroit	.383
1918	Ty Cobb	Detroit	.382
1919	Ty Cobb	Detroit	.384
1920	George Sisler	St. Louis	.407
1921	Harry Heilmann	Detroit	.394
1922	George Sisler	St. Louis	.420
1923	Harry Heilmann	Detroit	.403
1924	Babe Ruth	New York	.378
1925	Harry Heilmann	Detroit	.393
1926	Henry Manush	Detroit	.378
1927	Harry Heilmann	Detroit	.398
1928	Goose Goslin	Washington	.379
1929	Lew Fonseca	Cleveland	.369
1930	Al Simmons	Philadelphia	.381
1931	Al Simmons	Philadelphia	.390
1932	Dale Alexander	Detroit-Boston	.367
1933	Jimmie Foxx	Philadelphia	.356
1934	Lou Gehrig	New York	.363
1935	Buddy Myer	Washington	.349
1936	Luke Appling	Chicago	.388
1937	Charlie Gehringer	Detroit	.371
1938	Jimmie Foxx	Boston	.349
1939	Joe DiMaggio	New York	.381
1940	Joe DiMaggio	New York	.352
1941	Ted Williams	Boston	.406
1942	Ted Williams	Boston	.356
1943	Luke Appling	Chicago	.328
1944	Lou Boudreau	Cleveland	.327
1945	George Stirnweiss	New York	.309
1946	Mickey Vernon	Washington	.353
1947	Ted Williams	Boston	.343
1948	Ted Williams	Boston	.369
1949	George Kell	Detroit	.343
1950	Billy Goodman	Boston	.354
1951	Ferris Fain	Philadelphia	.344
1952	Ferris Fain	Philadelphia	.327
1953	Mickey Vernon	Washington	.337
1954	Roberto Avila	Cleveland	.341
1955	Al Kaline	Detroit	.340
1956	Mickey Mantle	New York	.353
1957	Ted Williams	Boston	.388
1958	Ted Williams	Boston	.328
1959	Harvey Kuenn	Detroit	.353
1960	Pete Runnels	Boston	.320
1961	Norm Cash	Detroit	.361
1962	Pete Runnels	Boston	.326
1963	Carl Yastrzemski	Boston	.321
1964	Tony Oliva	Minnesota	.323
1965	Tony Oliva	Minnesota	.321
1966	Frank Robinson	Baltimore	.316
1967	Carl Yastrzemski	Boston	.326
1968	Carl Yastrzemski	Boston	.301

National League

Year	Player	Team	Avg.
1969	Pete Rose	Cincinnati	.348
1970	Rico Carty	Atlanta	.366
1971	Joe Torre	St. Louis	.363
1972	Billy Williams	Chicago	.333
1973	Pete Rose	Cincinnati	.338
1974	Ralph Garr	Atlanta	.353
1975	Bill Madlock	Chicago	.354
1976	Bill Madlock	Chicago	.339
1977	Dave Parker	Pittsburgh	.338
1978	Dave Parker	Pittsburgh	.334
1979	Keith Hernandez	St. Louis	.344
1980	Bill Buckner	Chicago	.324
1981	Bill Madlock	Pittsburgh	.341
1982	Al Oliver	Montreal	.331
1983	Bill Madlock	Pittsburgh	.323
1984	Tony Gwynn	San Diego	.351
1985	Willie McGee	St. Louis	.353
1986	Tim Raines	Montreal	.334
1987	Tony Gwynn	San Diego	.370
1988	Tony Gwynn	San Diego	.313
1989	Tony Gwynn	San Diego	.336
1990	Willie McGee	St. Louis	.335
1991	Terry Pendleton	Atlanta	.319
1992	Gary Sheffield	San Diego	.330
1993	Andres Galarraga	Colorado	.370
1994	Tony Gwynn	San Diego	.394
1995	Tony Gwynn	San Diego	.368
1996	Tony Gwynn	San Diego	.353
1997	Tony Gwynn	San Diego	.372
1998	Larry Walker	Colorado	.363
1999	Larry Walker	Colorado	.379
2000	Todd Helton	Colorado	.372
2001	Larry Walker	Colorado	.350
2002	Barry Bonds	San Francisco	.370
2003	Albert Pujols	St. Louis	.359
2004	Barry Bonds	San Francisco	.362
2005	Derrek Lee	Chicago	.335

American League

Year	Player	Team	Avg.
1969	Rod Carew	Minnesota	.332
1970	Alex Johnson	California	.329
1971	Tony Oliva	Minnesota	.337
1972	Rod Carew	Minnesota	.318
1973	Rod Carew	Minnesota	.350
1974	Rod Carew	Minnesota	.364
1975	Rod Carew	Minnesota	.359
1976	George Brett	Kansas City	.333
1977	Rod Carew	Minnesota	.388
1978	Rod Carew	Minnesota	.333
1979	Fred Lynn	Boston	.333
1980	George Brett	Kansas City	.390
1981	Carney Lansford	Boston	.336
1982	Willie Wilson	Kansas City	.332
1983	Wade Boggs	Boston	.361
1984	Don Mattingly	New York	.343
1985	Wade Boggs	Boston	.368
1986	Wade Boggs	Boston	.357
1987	Wade Boggs	Boston	.363
1988	Wade Boggs	Boston	.366
1989	Kirby Puckett	Minnesota	.339
1990	George Brett	Kansas City	.329
1991	Julio Franco	Texas	.341
1992	Edgar Martinez	Seattle	.343
1993	John Olerud	Toronto	.363
1994	Paul O'Neill	New York	.359
1995	Edgar Martinez	Seattle	.356
1996	Alex Rodriguez	Seattle	.358
1997	Frank Thomas	Chicago	.347
1998	Bernie Williams	New York	.339
1999	Nomar Garciaparra	Boston	.357
2000	Nomar Garciaparra	Boston	.372
2001	Ichiro Suzuki	Seattle	.350
2002	Manny Ramirez	Boston	.349
2003	Bill Mueller	Boston	.326
2004	Ichiro Suzuki	Seattle	.372
2005	Michael Young	Texas	.331

(1) Some baseball researchers have concluded that Ty Cobb actually hit .382 in 1910 while Napoleon Lajoie, Cleveland, hit .383.

Cy Young Award Winners

Year	Player, Team
1956	Don Newcombe, Dodgers
1957	Warren Spahn, Braves
1958	Bob Turley, Yankees
1959	Early Wynn, White Sox
1960	Vernon Law, Pirates
1961	Whitey Ford, Yankees
1962	Don Drysdale, Dodgers
1963	Sandy Koufax, Dodgers
1964	Dean Chance, Angels
1965	Sandy Koufax, Dodgers
1966	Sandy Koufax, Dodgers
1967	(NL) Mike McCormick, Giants
	(AL) Jim Lonborg, Red Sox
1968	(NL) Bob Gibson, Cardinals
	(AL) Dennis McLain, Tigers
1969	(NL) Tom Seaver, Mets
	(AL) (tie) Dennis McLain, Tigers Mike Cuellar, Orioles
1970	(NL) Bob Gibson, Cardinals
	(AL) Jim Perry, Twins
1971	(NL) Ferguson Jenkins, Cubs
	(AL) Vida Blue, A's
1972	(NL) Steve Carlton, Phillies
	(AL) Gaylord Perry, Indians
1973	(NL) Tom Seaver, Mets
	(AL) Jim Palmer, Orioles
1974	(NL) Mike Marshall, Dodgers
	(AL) Jim (Catfish) Hunter, A's
1975	(NL) Tom Seaver, Mets
	(AL) Jim Palmer, Orioles
1976	(NL) Randy Jones, Padres
	(AL) Jim Palmer, Orioles
1977	(NL) Steve Carlton, Phillies
	(AL) Sparky Lyle, Yankees
1978	(NL) Gaylord Perry, Padres
	(AL) Ron Guidry, Yankees
1979	(NL) Bruce Sutter, Cubs
	(AL) Mike Flanagan, Orioles
1980	(NL) Steve Carlton, Phillies
	(AL) Steve Stone, Orioles
1981	(NL) Fernando Valenzuela, Dodgers
	(AL) Rollie Fingers, Brewers
1982	(NL) Steve Carlton, Phillies
	(AL) Pete Vuckovich, Brewers
1983	(NL) John Denny, Phillies
	(AL) LaMarr Hoyt, White Sox
1984	(NL) Rick Sutcliffe, Cubs
	(AL) Willie Hernandez, Tigers
1985	(NL) Dwight Gooden, Mets
	(AL) Bret Saberhagen, Royals
1986	(NL) Mike Scott, Astros
	(AL) Roger Clemens, Red Sox
1987	(NL) Steve Bedrosian, Phillies
	(AL) Roger Clemens, Red Sox
1988	(NL) Orel Hershiser, Dodgers
	(AL) Frank Viola, Twins
1989	(NL) Mark Davis, Padres
	(AL) Bret Saberhagan, Royals
1990	(NL) Doug Drabek, Pirates
	(AL) Bob Welch, A's
1991	(NL) Tom Glavine, Braves
	(AL) Roger Clemens, Red Sox
1992	(NL) Greg Maddux, Cubs
	(AL) Dennis Eckersley, A's
1993	(NL) Greg Maddux, Braves
	(AL) Jack McDowell, White Sox
1994	(NL) Greg Maddux, Braves
	(AL) David Cone, Royals
1995	(NL) Greg Maddux, Braves
	(AL) Randy Johnson, Mariners
1996	(NL) John Smoltz, Braves
	(AL) Pat Hentgen, Blue Jays
1997	(NL) Pedro Martinez, Expos
	(AL) Roger Clemens, Blue Jays
1998	(NL) Tom Glavine, Braves
	(AL) Roger Clemens, Blue Jays
1999	(NL) Randy Johnson, Diamondbacks
	(AL) Pedro Martinez, Red Sox
2000	(NL) Randy Johnson, Diamondbacks
	(AL) Pedro Martinez, Red Sox
2001	(NL) Randy Johnson, Diamondbacks
	(AL) Roger Clemens, Yankees
2002	(NL) Randy Johnson, Diamondbacks
	(AL) Barry Zito, A's
2003	(NL) Eric Gagne, Dodgers
	(AL) Roy Halladay, Blue Jays
2004	(NL) Roger Clemens, Astros
	(AL) Johan Santana, Twins

Most Valuable Players

(As selected by the Baseball Writers' Assoc. of America. Prior to 1931, MVP honors were named by various sources.)

National League

Year	Player, team
1931	Frank Frisch, St. Louis
1932	Chuck Klein, Philadelphia
1933	Carl Hubbell, New York
1934	Dizzy Dean, St. Louis
1935	Gabby Hartnett, Chicago
1936	Carl Hubbell, N.Y.
1937	Joe Medwick, St. Louis
1938	Ernie Lombardi, Cincinnati
1939	Bucky Walters, Cincinnati
1940	Frank McCormick, Cincinnati
1941	Dolph Camilli, Brooklyn
1942	Mort Cooper, St. Louis
1943	Stan Musial, St. Louis
1944	Martin Marion, St. Louis
1945	Phil Cavarretta, Chicago
1946	Stan Musial, St. Louis
1947	Bob Elliott, Boston
1948	Stan Musial, St. Louis
1949	Jackie Robinson, Brooklyn
1950	Jim Konstanty, Philadelphia
1951	Roy Campanella, Brooklyn
1952	Hank Sauer, Chicago
1953	Roy Campanella, Brooklyn
1954	Willie Mays, N.Y.
1955	Roy Campanella, Brooklyn
1956	Don Newcombe, Brooklyn
1957	Hank Aaron, Milwaukee

Year	Player, team
1958	Ernie Banks, Chicago
1959	Ernie Banks, Chicago
1960	Dick Groat, Pittsburgh
1961	Frank Robinson, Cincinnati
1962	Maury Wills, L.A.
1963	Sandy Koufax, L.A.
1964	Ken Boyer, St. Louis
1965	Willie Mays, San Francisco
1966	Roberto Clemente, Pittsburgh
1967	Orlando Cepeda, St. Louis
1968	Bob Gibson, St. Louis
1969	Willie McCovey, San Francisco
1970	Johnny Bench, Cincinnati
1971	Joe Torre, St. Louis
1972	Johnny Bench, Cincinnati
1973	Pete Rose, Cincinnati
1974	Steve Garvey, L.A.
1975	Joe Morgan, Cincinnati
1976	Joe Morgan, Cincinnati
1977	George Foster, Cincinnati
1978	Dave Parker, Pittsburgh
(tie)	Keith Hernandez, St. Louis
1980	Mike Schmidt, Philadelphia
1981	Mike Schmidt, Philadelphia
1982	Dale Murphy, Atlanta
1983	Dale Murphy, Atlanta
1984	Ryne Sandberg, Chicago
1985	Willie McGee, St. Louis
1986	Mike Schmidt, Philadelphia
1987	Andre Dawson, Chicago
1988	Kirk Gibson, L.A.
1989	Kevin Mitchell, San Francisco
1990	Barry Bonds, Pittsburgh
1991	Terry Pendleton, Atlanta
1992	Barry Bonds, Pittsburgh
1993	Barry Bonds, San Francisco
1994	Jeff Bagwell, Houston
1995	Barry Larkin, Cincinnati
1996	Ken Caminiti, San Diego
1997	Larry Walker, Colorado
1998	Sammy Sosa, Chicago
1999	Chipper Jones, Atlanta
2000	Jeff Kent, San Francisco
2001	Barry Bonds, San Francisco
2002	Barry Bonds, San Francisco
2003	Barry Bonds, San Francisco
2004	Barry Bonds, San Francisco

American League

Year	Player, team
1931	Lefty Grove, Philadelphia
1932	Jimmie Foxx, Philadelphia
1933	Jimmie Foxx, Philadelphia
1934	Mickey Cochrane, Detroit
1935	Hank Greenberg, Detroit
1936	Lou Gehrig, N.Y.
1937	Charley Gehringer, Detroit
1938	Jimmie Foxx, Boston
1939	Joe DiMaggio, N.Y.
1940	Hank Greenberg, Detroit
1941	Joe DiMaggio, N.Y.
1942	Joe Gordon, N.Y.
1943	Spurgeon Chandler, N.Y.
1944	Hal Newhouser, Detroit
1945	Hal Newhouser, Detroit
1946	Ted Williams, Boston
1947	Joe DiMaggio, N.Y.
1948	Lou Boudreau, Cleveland
1949	Ted Williams, Boston
1950	Phil Rizzuto, N.Y.
1951	Yogi Berra, N.Y.
1952	Bobby Shantz, Philadelphia
1953	Al Rosen, Cleveland
1954	Yogi Berra, N.Y.
1955	Yogi Berra, N.Y.
1956	Mickey Mantle, N.Y.
1957	Mickey Mantle, N.Y.
1958	Jackie Jensen, Boston
1959	Nellie Fox, Chicago
1960	Roger Maris, N.Y.
1961	Roger Maris, N.Y.
1962	Mickey Mantle, N.Y.
1963	Elston Howard, N.Y.
1964	Brooks Robinson, Baltimore
1965	Zoilo Versalles, Minnesota
1966	Frank Robinson, Baltimore
1967	Carl Yastrzemski, Boston
1968	Denny McLain, Detroit
1969	Harmon Killebrew, Minnesota
1970	John (Boog) Powell, Baltimore
1971	Vida Blue, Oakland
1972	Dick Allen, Chicago
1973	Reggie Jackson, Oakland
1974	Jeff Burroughs, Texas
1975	Fred Lynn, Boston
1976	Thurman Munson, N.Y.
1977	Rod Carew, Minnesota
1978	Jim Rice, Boston
1979	Don Baylor, California
1980	George Brett, Kansas City
1981	Rollie Fingers, Milwaukee
1982	Robin Yount, Milwaukee
1983	Cal Ripken, Jr., Baltimore
1984	Willie Hernandez, Detroit
1985	Don Mattingly, N.Y.
1986	Roger Clemens, Boston
1987	George Bell, Toronto
1988	Jose Canseco, Oakland
1989	Robin Yount, Milwaukee
1990	Rickey Henderson, Oakland
1991	Cal Ripken, Jr., Baltimore
1992	Dennis Eckersley, Oakland
1993	Frank Thomas, Chicago
1994	Frank Thomas, Chicago
1995	Mo Vaughn, Boston
1996	Juan Gonzalez, Texas
1997	Ken Griffey Jr., Seattle
1998	Juan Gonzalez, Texas
1999	Ivan Rodriguez, Texas
2000	Jason Giambi, Oakland
2001	Ichiro Suzuki, Seattle
2002	Miguel Tejada, Oakland
2003	Alex Rodriguez, Texas
2004	Vladimir Guerrero, L.A.

Rookies of the Year

(As selected by the Baseball Writers' Assoc. of America)

1947—Combined selection—Jackie Robinson, Brooklyn, 1b; 1948—Combined selection—Alvin Dark, Boston, N.L., ss

National League

Year	Player, team
1949	Don Newcombe, Brooklyn, p
1950	Sam Jethroe, Boston, of
1951	Willie Mays, N.Y., of
1952	Joe Black, Brooklyn, p
1953	Jim Gilliam, Brooklyn, 2b
1954	Wally Moon, St. Louis, of
1955	Bill Virdon, St. Louis, of
1956	Frank Robinson, Cincinnati, of
1957	Jack Sanford, Philadelphia, p
1958	Orlando Cepeda, S.F., 1b
1959	Willie McCovey, S.F., 1b
1960	Frank Howard, L.A., of
1961	Billy Williams, Chicago, of
1962	Ken Hubbs, Chicago, 2b
1963	Pete Rose, Cincinnati, 2b
1964	Richie Allen, Philadelphia, 3b
1965	Jim Lefebvre, L.A., 2b
1966	Tommy Helms, Cincinnati, 2b
1967	Tom Seaver, N.Y., p
1968	Johnny Bench, Cincinnati, c
1969	Ted Sizemore, L.A., 2b
1970	Carl Morton, Montreal, p
1971	Earl Williams, Atlanta, c
1972	Jon Matlack, N.Y., p
1973	Gary Matthews, S.F., of
1974	Bake McBride, St. Louis, of
1975	John Montefusco, S.F., p
1976	Butch Metzger, San Diego, p
(tie)	Pat Zachry, Cincinnati, p
1977	Andre Dawson, Montreal, of
1978	Bob Horner, Atlanta, 3b
1979	Rick Sutcliffe, L.A., p
1980	Steve Howe, L.A., p
1981	Fernando Valenzuela, L.A., p
1982	Steve Sax, L.A., 2b
1983	Darryl Strawberry, N.Y., of
1984	Dwight Gooden, N.Y., p
1985	Vince Coleman, St. Louis, of
1986	Todd Worrell, St. Louis, p
1987	Benito Santiago, San Diego, c
1988	Chris Sabo, Cincinnati, 3b
1989	Jerome Walton, Chicago, of
1990	Dave Justice, Atlanta, 1b
1991	Jeff Bagwell, Houston, 1b
1992	Eric Karros, L.A., 1b
1993	Mike Piazza, L.A., c
1994	Raul Mondesi, L.A., of
1995	Hideo Nomo, L.A., p
1996	Todd Hollandsworth, L.A., of
1997	Scott Rolen, Philadelphia, 3b
1998	Kerry Wood, Chicago, p
1999	Scott Williamson, Cincinnati, p
2000	Rafael Furcal, Atlanta, ss
2001	Albert Pujols, St. Louis, of
2002	Jason Jennings, Colorado, p
2003	Dontrelle Willis, Florida, p
2004	Jason Bay, Pittsburgh, of

WORLD ALMANAC EDITORS' PICKS
2005 All-World Baseball Team

The editors of *The World Almanac* have chosen the following as the best players at each position based on 2005 regular season performance.

Position	World Almanac 2005 Best
Catcher	Victor Martinez (Cleveland Indians)
1st base	Derrek Lee (Chicago Cubs)
2nd base	Brian Roberts (Baltimore Orioles)
3rd base	Alex Rodriguez (New York Yankees)
Shortstop	Michael Young (Texas Rangers)
Left field	Miguel Cabrera (Florida Marlins)
Center field	Andruw Jones (Atlanta Braves)
Right Field	Vladimir Guerrero (Los Angeles Angels)
Designated hitter	David Ortiz (Boston Red Sox)
Right-handed starting pitcher	Chris Carpenter (St. Louis Cardinals)
Left-handed starting pitcher	Dontrelle Willis (Florida Marlins)
Right-handed relief pitcher	Mariano Rivera (New York Yankees)
Left-handed relief pitcher	Billy Wagner (Philadelphia Phillies)

Rookies of the Year

American League

Year	Player, team
1949	Roy Sievers, St. Louis, of
1950	Walt Dropo, Boston, 1b
1951	Gil McDougald, N.Y., 3b
1952	Harry Byrd, Philadelphia, p
1953	Harvey Kuenn, Detroit, ss
1954	Bob Grim, N.Y., p
1955	Herb Score, Cleveland, p
1956	Luis Aparicio, Chicago, ss
1957	Tony Kubek, N.Y., if-of
1958	Albie Pearson, Washington, of
1959	Bob Allison, Washington, of
1960	Ron Hansen, Baltimore, ss
1961	Don Schwall, Boston, p
1962	Tom Tresh, N.Y., if-of
1963	Gary Peters, Chicago, p
1964	Tony Oliva, Minnesota, of
1965	Curt Blefary, Baltimore, of
1966	Tommie Agee, Chicago, of
1967	Rod Carew, Minnesota, 2b
1968	Stan Bahnsen, N.Y., p
1969	Lou Piniella, Kansas City, of
1970	Thurman Munson, N.Y., c
1971	Chris Chambliss, Cleveland, 1b
1972	Carlton Fisk, Boston, c
1973	Al Bumbry, Baltimore, of
1974	Mike Hargrove, Texas, 1b
1975	Fred Lynn, Boston, of
1976	Mark Fidrych, Detroit, p
1977	Eddie Murray, Baltimore, dh
1978	Lou Whitaker, Detroit, 2b
1979	John Castino, Minnesota, 3b
(tie)	Alfredo Griffin, Toronto, ss
1980	Joe Charboneau, Cleveland, of
1981	Dave Righetti, N.Y., p
1982	Cal Ripken, Jr., Baltimore, ss
1983	Ron Kittle, Chicago, of
1984	Alvin Davis, Seattle, 1b
1985	Ozzie Guillen, Chicago, ss
1986	Jose Canseco, Oakland, of
1987	Mark McGwire, Oakland, 1b
1988	Walt Weiss, Oakland, ss
1989	Gregg Olson, Baltimore, p
1990	Sandy Alomar, Jr., Cleveland, c
1991	Chuck Knoblauch, Minnesota, 2b
1992	Pat Listach, Milwaukee, ss
1993	Tim Salmon, California, of
1994	Bob Hamelin, Kansas City, dh
1995	Marty Cordova, Minnesota, of
1996	Derek Jeter, N.Y., ss
1997	Nomar Garciaparra, Boston, ss
1998	Ben Grieve, Oakland, of
1999	Carlos Beltran, Kansas City, of
2000	Kazuhiro Sasaki, Seattle, p
2001	Ichiro Suzuki, Seattle, of
2002	Eric Hinske, Toronto, 3b
2003	Angel Berroa, Kansas City, ss
2004	Bobby Crosby, Oakland, ss

Manager of the Year

1983 (NL) Tommy Lasorda, L.A.
(AL) Tony La Russa, Chicago
1984 (NL) Jim Frey, Chicago
(AL) Sparky Anderson, Detroit
1985 (NL) Whitey Herzog, St. Louis
(AL) Bobby Cox, Toronto
1986 (NL) Hal Lanier, Houston
(AL) John McNamara, Boston
1987 (NL) Buck Rodgers, Montreal
(AL) Sparky Anderson, Detroit
1988 (NL) Tommy Lasorda, L.A.
(AL) Tony La Russa, Oakland
1989 (NL) Don Zimmer, Chicago
(AL) Frank Robinson, Baltimore
1990 (NL) Jim Leyland, Pittsburgh
(AL) Jeff Torborg, Chicago
1991 (NL) Bobby Cox, Atlanta
(AL) Tom Kelly, Minnesota
1992 (NL) Jim Leyland, Pittsburgh
(AL) Tony La Russa, Oakland
1993 (NL) Dusty Baker, San Francisco
(AL) Gene Lamont, Chicago
1994 (NL) Felipe Alou, Montreal
(AL) Buck Showalter, N.Y.
1995 (NL) Don Baylor, Colorado
(AL) Lou Piniella, Seattle
1996 (NL) Bruce Bochy, San Diego
(AL) (tie) Joe Torre, N.Y.,
Johnny Oates, Texas
1997 (NL) Dusty Baker, San Francisco
(AL) Davey Johnson, Baltimore
1998 (NL) Larry Dierker, Houston
(AL) Joe Torre, N.Y.
1999 (NL) Jack McKeon, Cincinnati
(AL) Jimy Williams, Boston
2000 (NL) Dusty Baker, San Francisco
(AL) Jerry Manuel, Chicago
2001 (NL) Larry Bowa, Philadelphia
(AL) Lou Piniella, Seattle
2002 (NL) Tony La Russa, St. Louis
(AL) Mike Scioscia, Anaheim
2003 (NL) Jack McKeon, Florida
(AL) Tony Pena, Kansas City
2004 (NL) Bobby Cox, Atlanta
(AL) Buck Showalter, Texas

The Rawlings Gold Glove Awards: 2004 and All-Time Leaders

American League

Kenny Rogers, Texas, P
Ivan Rodriguez, Detroit, C
Darin Erstad, Anaheim, 1B
Bret Boone, Seattle, 2B
Eric Chavez, Oakland, 3B
Derek Jeter, New York, SS
Torii Hunter, Minnesota, OF
Ichiro Suzuki, Seattle, OF
Vernon Wells, Toronto, OF

National League

Greg Maddux, Chicago, P
Mike Matheny, St. Louis, C
Todd Helton, Colorado, 1B
Luis Castillo, Florida, 2B
Scott Rolen, St. Louis, 3B
Cesar Izturis, Los Angeles, SS
Jim Edmonds, St. Louis, OF
Steve Finley, Los Angeles, OF
Andruw Jones, Atlanta, OF

The following are the players at each position who have won the most Gold Gloves since the award was instituted in 1957.

Position	Player	Gold Gloves
Pitcher:	Jim Kaat	16
	Greg Maddux	14
Catcher:	Ivan Rodriguez	11
	Johnny Bench	10
First base:	Keith Hernandez	11
	Don Mattingly	9
Second base:	Roberto Alomar	10
	Ryne Sandberg	9
	Bill Mazeroski	8
	Frank White	8
Third base:	Brooks Robinson	16
	Mike Schmidt	10
Shortstop:	Ozzie Smith	13
	Luis Aparicio	9
Outfield:	Roberto Clemente	12
	Willie Mays	12
	Al Kaline	10
	Ken Griffey Jr.	10

National League Final Standings, 2005

Eastern Division

	W	L	Pct.	GB	Home	Road	vs. East	vs. Central	vs. West	vs. AL
Atlanta	90	72	.556	-	53-28	37-44	42-33	28-14	13-17	7-8
Philadelphia	88	74	.543	2.0	46-35	42-39	38-37	21-20	22-9	7-8
Florida	83	79	.512	7.0	45-36	38-43	34-39	21-22	18-13	10-5
New York	83	79	.512	7.0	48-33	35-46	38-36	20-21	20-12	5-10
Washington DC	81	81	.500	9.0	41-40	40-41	34-41	19-20	16-14	12-6

Central Division

	W	L	Pct.	GB	Home	Road	vs. East	vs. Central	vs. West	vs. AL
St. Louis	100	62	.617	-	50-31	50-31	18-14	51-29	21-14	10-5
Houston*	89	73	.549	11.0	53-28	36-45	20-16	43-36	19-13	7-8
Milwaukee	81	81	.500	19.0	46-35	35-46	18-18	38-41	17-15	8-7
Chicago	79	83	.488	21.0	38-43	41-40	11-23	43-36	19-15	6-9
Cincinnati	73	89	.451	27.0	42-39	31-50	16-19	33-46	17-16	7-8
Pittsburgh	67	95	.414	33.0	34-47	33-48	14-19	30-50	18-19	5-7

Western Division

	W	L	Pct.	GB	Home	Road	vs. East	vs. Central	vs. West	vs. AL
San Diego	82	80	.506	-	46-35	36-45	16-14	20-21	39-34	7-11
Arizona	77	85	.475	5.0	36-45	41-40	11-21	17-22	41-32	8-10
San Francisco	75	87	.463	7.0	37-44	38-43	11-19	20-21	38-35	6-12
Los Angeles	71	91	.438	11.0	40-41	31-50	13-18	20-19	33-41	5-13
Colorado	67	95	.414	15.0	40-41	27-54	14-17	15-28	32-41	6-9

*Wild card team.

National League Statistics, 2005

(Individual Statistics: Batting—at least 150 at-bats; Pitching—at least 70 innings or 10 saves; *changed teams within NL during season; entry includes statistics for more than 1 team; # changed teams to or from AL during season; entry includes only NL stats)

TEAM BATTING

Team	BA	AB	R	H	HR	RBI
Florida	.272	5502	717	1499	128	678
Chicago	.270	5584	703	1506	194	674
St. Louis	.270	5538	805	1494	170	757
Philadelphia	.270	5542	807	1494	167	760
Colorado	.267	5542	740	1477	150	704
Atlanta	.265	5486	769	1453	184	733
Cincinnati	.261	5565	820	1453	222	784
San Francisco	.261	5462	649	1427	128	617
Pittsburgh	.259	5573	680	1445	139	656
Milwaukee	.259	5448	726	1413	175	689
New York	.258	5505	722	1421	175	683
San Diego	.257	5502	684	1416	130	655
Arizona	.256	5550	696	1419	191	670
Houston	.256	5462	693	1400	161	654
Los Angeles	.253	5433	685	1374	149	653
Washington	.252	5426	639	1367	117	615

TEAM PITCHING

Team	ERA	IP	H	SO	BB	SV
St. Louis	3.49	1445.2	1399	974	443	48
Houston	3.51	1443.0	1336	1164	440	45
New York	3.76	1435.2	1390	1012	491	38
Washington	3.87	1458.0	1456	997	539	51
Milwaukee	3.97	1438.0	1382	1173	569	46
Atlanta	3.98	1443.2	1487	929	520	38
San Diego	4.13	1455.1	1452	1133	503	45
Florida	4.16	1442.1	1459	1125	563	42
Chicago	4.19	1440.0	1357	1256	576	39
Philadelphia	4.21	1435.0	1379	1159	487	40
San Francisco	4.33	1444.1	1456	972	592	46
Los Angeles	4.38	1427.1	1434	1004	471	40
Pittsburgh	4.42	1436.0	1456	958	612	35
Arizona	4.84	1456.1	1580	1038	537	45
Colorado	5.13	1418.2	1600	981	604	37
Cincinnati	5.15	1433.0	1657	955	492	31

Arizona Diamondbacks

BATTERS	BA	AB	R	H	HR	RBI	SO	SB
C. Tracy	.308	503	73	155	27	72	78	3
T. Clark	.304	349	47	106	30	87	88	0
S. Green	.286	581	87	166	22	73	95	8
A. Cintron	.273	330	36	90	8	48	33	1
L. Gonzalez	.271	579	90	157	24	79	90	4
R. Clayton	.270	522	59	141	2	44	105	13
T. Glaus	.258	538	78	139	37	97	145	4
C. Counsell	.256	578	85	148	9	42	69	26
Q. McCracken	.237	215	23	51	1	13	35	4
L. Terrero	.230	161	23	37	4	20	40	3
C. Snyder	.202	326	24	66	6	28	87	0

PITCHERS	W-L	ERA	IP	H	BB	SO	SV
J. Valverde	3-4	2.44	66.1	51	20	75	15
B. Webb	14-12	3.54	229.0	229	59	172	0
J. Vazquez	11-15	4.42	215.2	223	46	192	0
B. Halsey	8-12	4.61	160.0	191	39	82	0
S. Estes	7-8	4.80	123.2	132	45	63	0
L. Cormier	7-3	5.11	79.1	86	43	63	0
C. Vargas	9-9	5.24	132.1	146	47	95	0
B. Lyon	0-2	6.44	29.1	44	10	17	14
R. Ortiz	5-11	6.89	115.0	147	65	46	0
B. Bruney	1-3	7.43	46.0	56	35	51	12

Manager-Bob Melvin

Atlanta Braves

BATTERS	BA	AB	R	H	HR	RBI	SO	SB
W. Betemit	.305	246	36	75	4	20	55	1
J. Francoeur	.300	257	41	77	14	45	58	3
P. Orr	.300	150	32	45	1	8	23	7
C. Jones	.296	358	66	106	21	72	56	5
M. Giles	.291	577	104	168	15	63	108	16
R. Furcal	.284	616	100	175	12	58	78	46
B. McCann	.278	180	20	50	5	23	26	1
J. Franco	.275	233	30	64	9	42	57	4
R. Langerhans	.267	326	48	87	8	42	75	0
A. Jones	.263	586	95	154	51	128	112	5
J. Estrada	.261	357	31	93	4	39	38	0
A. LaRoche	.259	451	53	117	20	78	87	0
B. Jordan	.247	231	25	57	3	24	46	2
T. Hollandsworth*	.244	303	26	74	6	36	66	4
K. Johnson	.241	290	46	70	9	40	75	2

PITCHERS	W-L	ERA	IP	H	BB	SO	SV
K. Farnsworth#	0-0	1.98	27.1	15	7	32	10
J. Sosa#	13-3	2.55	134.0	122	64	85	0
J. Smoltz	14-7	3.06	229.2	210	53	169	0
T. Hudson	14-9	3.52	192.0	194	65	115	0
C. Reitsma	3-6	3.93	73.1	79	14	42	15
J. Thomson	4-6	4.47	98.2	111	28	61	0
H. Ramirez	11-9	4.63	202.1	214	67	80	0
K. Davies	7-6	4.93	87.2	98	49	62	0
D. Kolb	3-8	5.93	57.2	78	29	39	11

Manager-Bobby Cox

Chicago Cubs

BATTERS	BA	AB	R	H	HR	RBI	SO	SB
D. Lee	.335	594	120	199	46	107	109	15
T. Walker	.305	397	50	121	12	40	40	1
A. Ramirez	.302	463	72	140	31	92	60	0
N. Garciaparra	.283	230	28	65	9	30	24	0
M. Barrett	.276	424	48	117	16	61	61	0
N. Perez	.274	572	59	157	9	54	47	8
M. Lawton*#	.268	452	61	121	11	49	69	17
J. Hairston	.261	380	51	99	4	30	46	8
J. Burnitz	.258	605	84	156	24	87	109	5
J. Macias	.254	177	15	45	1	13	24	4
H. Blanco	.242	161	16	39	6	25	24	0
C. Patterson	.215	451	47	97	13	34	118	15

PITCHERS	W-L	ERA	IP	H	BB	SO	SV
R. Dempster	5-3	3.13	92.0	83	49	89	33
C. Zambrano	14-6	3.26	223.1	170	86	202	0
M. Prior	11-7	3.67	166.2	143	59	188	0
M. Wuertz	6-2	3.81	75.2	60	40	89	0
G. Maddux	13-15	4.24	225.0	239	36	136	0
J. Williams	6-10	4.26	122.2	119	49	70	0
G. Rusch	9-8	4.52	145.1	175	53	111	0

Manager-Dusty Baker

Cincinnati Reds

BATTERS	BA	AB	R	H	HR	RBI	SO	SB
S. Casey	.312	529	75	165	9	58	48	2
K. Griffey	.301	491	85	148	35	92	93	0
F. Lopez	.291	580	97	169	23	85	111	15
R. Aurilia	.282	426	61	120	14	68	67	2
J. Valentin	.281	221	36	62	14	50	37	0
R. Freel	.271	369	69	100	4	21	59	36
J. LaRue	.260	361	38	94	14	60	101	0
W. Pena	.254	311	42	79	19	51	116	2
A. Dunn	.247	543	107	134	40	101	168	4
A. Kearns	.240	387	62	93	18	67	107	0
E. Encarnacion	.232	211	25	49	9	31	60	3

PITCHERS	W-L	ERA	IP	H	BB	SO	SV
A. Harang	11-13	3.83	211.2	217	51	163	0
D. Weathers	7-4	3.94	77.2	71	29	61	15
B. Claussen	10-11	4.21	166.2	178	57	121	0
M. Belisle	4-8	4.41	85.2	101	26	59	1
R. Ortiz	9-11	5.36	171.1	206	51	96	0
L. Hudson	6-9	6.38	84.2	83	50	53	0
E. Milton	8-15	6.47	186.1	237	52	123	0

Manager-Dave Miley, Jerry Narron

Colorado Rockies

BATTERS	BA	AB	R	H	HR	RBI	SO	SB
T. Helton	.320	509	92	163	20	79	80	3
M. Holliday	.307	479	68	147	19	87	79	14
C. Sullivan	.294	378	64	111	4	30	83	12
L. Gonzalez	.292	404	51	118	9	44	63	3
C. Barmes	.289	350	55	101	10	46	36	6
G. Atkins	.287	519	62	149	13	89	72	0
A. Miles	.281	324	37	91	2	28	38	4
B. Hawpe	.262	305	38	80	9	47	70	2
D. Ardoin	.229	210	28	48	6	22	69	1
D. Relaford	.224	210	24	47	1	16	42	3
J. Closser	.219	237	31	52	7	27	48	1
D. Mohr	.214	266	34	57	17	38	94	1

PITCHERS	W-L	ERA	IP	H	BB	SO	SV
B. Fuentes	2-5	2.91	74.1	59	34	91	31
A. Cook	7-2	3.67	83.1	101	16	24	0
S. Chacon	1-7	4.09	72.2	69	36	39	0
B. Kim	5-12	4.86	148.0	156	71	115	0
S. Kim	6-3	4.90	82.2	97	21	55	0
J. Jennings	6-9	5.02	122.0	130	62	75	0
J. Wright	8-16	5.46	171.1	201	81	101	0
J. Francis	14-12	5.68	183.2	228	70	128	0
J. Kennedy#	4-8	7.04	92.0	128	44	52	0

Manager-Clint Hurdle

Florida Marlins

BATTERS	BA	AB	R	H	HR	RBI	SO	SB
M. Cabrera	.323	613	106	198	33	116	125	1
J. Conine	.304	335	42	102	3	33	58	2
C. Delgado	.301	521	81	157	33	115	121	0
L. Castillo	.301	439	72	132	4	30	32	10
J. Encarnacion	.287	506	59	145	16	76	104	6
P. Lo Duca	.283	445	45	126	6	57	31	4
J. Pierre	.276	656	96	181	2	47	45	57
A. Gonzalez	.264	435	45	115	5	45	81	5

BATTERS	BA	AB	R	H	HR	RBI	SO	SB
D. Easley	.240	267	37	64	9	30	47	4
M. Lowell	.236	500	56	118	8	58	58	4

PITCHERS	W-L	ERA	IP	H	BB	SO	SV
T. Jones	1-5	2.10	73.0	61	14	62	40
D. Willis	22-10	2.63	236.1	213	55	170	0
J. Beckett	15-8	3.37	178.2	153	58	166	0
A. Burnett	12-12	3.44	209.0	184	79	198	0
J. Vargas	5-5	4.03	73.2	71	31	59	0
B. Moehler	6-12	4.55	158.1	198	42	95	0
A. Leiter#	3-7	6.64	80.0	88	60	52	0

Manager-Jack McKeon

Houston Astros

BATTERS	BA	AB	R	H	HR	RBI	SO	SB
L. Berkman	.293	468	76	137	24	82	72	4
W. Taveras	.291	592	82	172	3	29	103	34
O. Palmeiro	.284	204	22	58	3	20	23	3
M. Ensberg	.283	526	86	149	36	101	119	6
J. Lane	.267	517	65	138	26	78	105	6
C. Biggio	.264	590	94	156	26	69	90	11
B. Ausmus	.258	387	35	100	3	47	48	5
A. Everett	.248	549	58	136	11	54	103	21
C. Burke	.248	318	49	79	5	26	62	11
J. Vizcaino	.246	187	15	46	1	23	40	2
M. Lamb	.236	322	41	76	12	53	65	1

PITCHERS	W-L	ERA	IP	H	BB	SO	SV
R. Clemens	13-8	1.87	211.1	151	62	185	0
D. Wheeler	2-3	2.21	73.1	53	19	69	3
B. Lidge	4-4	2.29	70.2	58	23	103	42
A. Pettitte	17-9	2.39	222.1	188	41	171	0
R. Oswalt	20-12	2.94	241.2	243	48	184	0
C. Qualls	6-4	3.28	79.2	73	23	60	0
B. Backe	10-8	4.76	149.1	151	67	97	0
W. Rodriguez	10-10	5.53	128.2	135	53	80	0
E. Astacio	3-6	5.67	81.0	100	25	66	0

Manager-Jimy Williams, Phil Garner

Los Angeles Dodgers

BATTERS	BA	AB	R	H	HR	RBI	SO	SB
A. Perez	.297	259	28	77	3	23	61	11
M. Bradley	.290	283	49	82	13	38	47	6
J. Kent	.289	553	100	160	29	105	85	6
J. Drew	.286	252	48	72	15	36	50	1
R. Ledee	.278	237	31	66	7	39	55	0
D. Navarro	.273	176	21	48	3	14	21	0
O. Robles	.272	364	44	99	5	34	33	0
O. Saenz	.263	319	39	84	15	63	63	0
C. Izturis	.257	444	48	114	2	31	51	8
H. Choi	.253	320	40	81	15	42	80	1
J. Cruz	.251	358	46	90	18	50	97	0
M. Edwards	.247	239	23	59	3	15	34	1
J. Phillips	.238	399	38	95	10	55	50	0
J. Werth	.234	337	46	79	7	43	114	11
J. Repko	.221	276	43	61	8	30	80	5

PITCHERS	W-L	ERA	IP	H	BB	SO	SV
D. Lowe	12-15	3.61	222.0	223	55	146	0
D. Sanchez	4-7	3.73	82.0	75	36	71	8
B. Penny	7-9	3.90	175.1	185	41	122	0
G. Carrara	7-4	3.93	75.2	65	38	56	0
J. Weaver	14-11	4.22	224.0	220	43	157	0
O. Perez	7-8	4.56	108.2	109	28	74	0
D. Houlton	6-9	5.16	129.0	145	52	90	0
Y. Brazoban	4-10	5.33	72.2	70	32	61	21

Manager-Jim Tracy

Milwaukee Brewers

BATTERS	BA	AB	R	H	HR	RBI	SO	SB
B. Clark	.306	599	94	183	13	53	55	10
W. Helms	.298	168	18	50	4	24	30	0
G. Jenkins	.292	538	87	157	25	86	138	0
B. Hall	.291	501	69	146	17	62	103	18
J. Cirillo	.281	185	29	52	4	23	22	4
L. Overbay	.276	537	80	148	19	72	98	1
D. Miller	.273	385	50	105	9	43	94	0
C. Lee	.265	618	85	164	32	114	87	13
R. Branyan	.257	202	23	52	12	31	80	1
J. Hardy	.247	372	46	92	9	50	48	0
R. Weeks	.239	360	56	86	13	42	96	15
C. Moeller	.206	199	23	41	7	23	48	0

PITCHERS	W-L	ERA	IP	H	BB	SO	SV
D. Turnbow	7-1	1.74	67.1	49	24	64	39
B. Sheets	10-9	3.33	156.2	142	25	141	0
D. Davis	11-11	3.84	222.2	196	93	208	0
C. Capuano	18-12	3.99	219.0	212	91	176	0
T. Ohka*	11-9	4.04	180.1	189	55	98	0
V. Santos	4-13	4.57	141.2	153	60	89	0

Manager-Ned Yost

New York Mets

BATTERS	BA	AB	R	H	HR	RBI	SO	SB
D. Wright	.306	575	99	176	27	102	113	17
C. Woodward	.283	173	16	49	3	18	46	0
J. Reyes	.273	696	99	190	7	58	78	60
C. Floyd	.273	550	85	150	34	98	98	12
M. Cameron	.273	308	47	84	12	39	85	13
C. Beltran	.266	582	83	155	16	78	96	17
M. Anderson	.264	235	31	62	7	19	45	6
V. Diaz	.257	280	41	72	12	38	82	6
K. Matsui	.255	267	31	68	3	24	43	6
M. Piazza	.251	398	41	100	19	62	67	0
M. Cairo	.251	327	31	82	2	19	31	13
R. Castro	.244	209	26	51	8	41	58	1
D. Mientkiewicz	.240	275	36	66	11	29	39	0

PITCHERS	W-L	ERA	IP	H	BB	SO	SV
J. Seo	8-2	2.59	90.1	84	16	59	0
P. Martinez	15-8	2.82	217.0	159	47	208	0
A. Heilman	5-3	3.17	108.0	87	37	106	5
T. Glavine	13-13	3.53	211.1	227	61	105	0
B. Looper	4-7	3.94	59.1	65	22	27	28
K. Benson	10-8	4.13	174.1	171	49	95	0
V. Zambrano	7-12	4.17	166.1	170	77	112	0
K. Ishii	3-9	5.14	91.0	87	49	53	0
D. Graves	1-1	6.52	38.2	59	20	20	10

Manager-Willie Randolph

Philadelphia Phillies

BATTERS	BA	AB	R	H	HR	RBI	SO	SB
K. Lofton	.335	367	67	123	2	36	41	22
P. Polanco#	.316	158	26	50	3	20	9	0
J. Michaels	.304	289	54	88	4	31	45	3
C. Utley	.291	543	93	158	28	105	109	16
J. Rollins	.290	677	115	196	12	54	71	41
R. Howard	.288	312	52	90	22	63	100	0
B. Abreu	.286	588	104	168	24	102	134	31
P. Burrell	.281	562	78	158	32	117	160	0
M. Lieberthal	.263	392	48	103	12	47	35	0
T. Pratt	.251	175	17	44	7	23	50	0
D. Bell	.248	557	53	138	10	61	69	0
M. Tucker*	.239	268	35	64	5	36	52	4
T. Perez	.233	159	17	37	0	22	27	1
J. Thome	.207	193	26	40	7	30	59	0

PITCHERS	W-L	ERA	IP	H	BB	SO	SV
B. Wagner	4-3	1.51	77.2	45	20	87	38
A. Fultz	4-0	2.24	72.1	47	23	54	0
R. Tejeda	4-3	3.57	85.2	67	51	72	0
B. Myers	13-8	3.72	215.1	193	68	208	0
R. Madson	6-5	4.14	87.0	84	25	79	0
J. Lieber	17-13	4.20	218.1	223	41	149	0
R. Wolf	6-4	4.39	80.0	87	26	61	0
C. Lidle	13-11	4.53	184.2	210	40	121	0
V. Padilla	9-12	4.71	147.0	146	74	103	0

Manager-Charlie Manuel

Pittsburgh Pirates

BATTERS	BA	AB	R	H	HR	RBI	SO	SB
J. Bay	.306	599	110	183	32	101	142	21
F. Sanchez	.291	453	54	132	5	35	36	2
R. Mackowiak	.272	463	57	126	9	58	100	8
J. Castillo	.268	370	49	99	11	53	59	2
C. Wilson	.264	197	23	52	5	22	69	3
D. Ward	.260	407	46	106	12	63	60	0
T. Wigginton	.258	155	20	40	7	25	30	0
J. Wilson	.257	587	60	151	8	52	58	7
R. Doumit	.255	231	25	59	6	35	48	2
T. Redman	.251	319	33	80	2	26	27	4
H. Cota	.242	297	29	72	7	43	80	0
B. Eldred	.221	190	23	42	12	27	77	1

PITCHERS	W-L	ERA	IP	H	BB	SO	SV
Z. Duke	8-2	1.81	84.2	79	23	58	0
S. Torres	5-5	2.76	94.2	76	36	55	3
R. White	4-7	3.72	75.0	90	29	40	2
D. Williams	10-11	4.41	138.2	137	58	88	0
R. Vogelsong	2-2	4.43	81.1	82	40	52	0
B. Meadows	3-1	4.58	74.2	84	21	44	0
J. Mesa	2-8	4.76	56.2	61	26	37	27
M. Redman	5-15	4.90	178.1	188	56	101	0
J. Fogg	6-11	5.05	169.1	196	53	85	0
K. Wells	8-18	5.09	182.0	186	99	132	0
O. Perez	7-5	5.85	103.0	102	70	97	0

Manager-Lloyd McClendon

St. Louis Cardinals

BATTERS	BA	AB	R	H	HR	RBI	SO	SB
A. Pujols	.330	591	129	195	41	117	65	16
D. Eckstein	.294	630	90	185	8	61	44	11
M. Grudzielanek	.294	528	64	155	8	59	81	8
L. Walker	.289	315	66	91	15	52	64	2
S. Taguchi	.288	396	45	114	8	53	62	11
A. Nunez	.285	421	64	120	5	44	63	0
R. Sanders	.271	295	49	80	21	54	75	14
J. Edmonds	.263	467	88	123	29	89	139	5
Y. Molina	.252	385	36	97	8	49	30	2
J. Mabry	.240	246	26	59	8	32	63	0

BATTERS	BA	AB	R	H	HR	RBI	SO	SB
S. Rolen	.235	196	28	46	5	28	28	1

PITCHERS	W-L	ERA	IP	H	BB	SO	SV
J. Isringhausen	1-2	2.14	59.0	43	27	51	39
C. Carpenter	21-5	2.83	241.2	204	51	213	0
J. Suppan	16-10	3.57	194.1	206	63	114	0
M. Mulder	16-8	3.64	205.0	212	70	111	0
M. Morris	14-10	4.11	192.2	209	37	117	0
J. Marquis	13-14	4.13	207.0	206	69	100	0

Manager-Tony La Russa

San Diego Padres

BATTERS	BA	AB	R	H	HR	RBI	SO	SB
B. Giles	.301	545	92	164	15	83	64	13
M. Sweeney	.294	221	31	65	8	40	58	4
R. Hernandez	.290	369	36	107	12	58	40	1
M. Loretta	.280	404	54	113	3	38	34	8
J. Randa*	.276	555	71	153	17	68	81	0
D. Roberts	.275	411	65	113	8	38	59	23
R. Fick	.265	230	25	61	3	30	33	0
X. Nady	.261	326	40	85	13	43	67	2
P. Nevin#	.256	281	31	72	9	47	67	1
D. Jackson	.255	275	44	70	5	23	45	15
K. Greene	.250	436	51	109	15	70	93	5
S. Burroughs	.250	284	20	71	1	17	41	4
R. Klesko	.248	443	61	110	18	58	80	3
G. Blum#	.241	224	26	54	5	22	28	3

PITCHERS	W-L	ERA	IP	H	BB	SO	SV
S. Linebrink	8-1	1.83	73.2	55	23	70	1
J. Peavy	13-7	2.88	203.0	162	50	216	0
T. Hoffman	1-6	2.97	57.2	52	12	54	43
A. Eaton	11-5	4.27	128.2	140	44	100	0
B. Lawrence	7-15	4.83	195.2	211	57	109	0
W. Williams	9-12	4.85	159.2	174	51	106	0
T. Stauffer	3-6	5.33	81.0	92	29	49	0

Manager-Bruce Bochy

San Francisco Giants

BATTERS	BA	AB	R	H	HR	RBI	SO	SB
R. Winn#	.359	231	39	83	14	26	38	7
M. Alou	.321	427	67	137	19	63	43	5
R. Durham	.290	497	67	144	12	62	59	6
E. Alfonzo	.277	368	36	102	2	43	34	2
J. Snow	.275	367	40	101	4	40	61	1
O. Vizquel	.271	568	66	154	3	45	58	24

BATTERS	BA	AB	R	H	HR	RBI	SO	SB
J. Ellison	.264	352	49	93	4	24	44	14
L. Niekro	.252	278	32	70	12	46	53	0
P. Feliz	.250	569	69	142	20	81	102	0
M. Matheny	.242	443	42	107	13	59	91	0
T. Linden	.216	171	20	37	4	13	54	3

PITCHERS	W-L	ERA	IP	H	BB	SO	SV
N. Lowry	13-13	3.78	204.2	193	76	172	0
J. Fassero	4-7	4.05	91.0	92	31	60	0
T. Walker	6-4	4.23	61.2	68	27	54	23
J. Schmidt	12-7	4.40	172.0	160	85	165	0
B. Tomko	8-15	4.48	190.2	205	57	114	1
A. Benitez	2-3	4.50	30.0	25	16	23	19
B. Hennessey	5-8	4.64	118.1	127	52	64	0
K. Rueter	2-7	5.95	107.1	131	47	25	0

Manager-Felipe Alou

Washington Nationals

BATTERS	BA	AB	R	H	HR	RBI	SO	SB
N. Johnson	.289	453	66	131	15	74	87	3
R. Church	.287	268	41	77	9	42	70	3
J. Guillen	.283	551	81	156	24	76	102	1
J. Vidro	.275	309	38	85	7	32	30	0
B. Schneider	.268	369	38	99	10	44	48	1
M. Byrd	.266	229	20	61	2	26	50	5
D. Cruz*	.265	260	28	69	5	20	34	0
P. Wilson*	.260	520	73	135	25	90	148	6
V. Castilla	.253	494	53	125	12	66	82	4
C. Baerga	.253	158	18	40	2	19	17	0
J. Carroll	.251	303	44	76	0	22	55	3
B. Wilkerson	.248	565	76	140	11	57	147	8
J. Spivey*	.232	259	37	60	7	24	83	9
G. Bennett	.221	199	11	44	1	21	37	0
C. Guzman	.219	456	39	100	4	31	76	7

PITCHERS	W-L	ERA	IP	H	BB	SO	SV
C. Cordero	2-4	1.82	74.1	55	17	61	47
H. Carrasco	5-4	2.04	88.1	59	38	75	2
L. Ayala	8-7	2.66	71.0	75	14	40	1
G. Majewski	4-4	2.93	86.0	80	37	50	1
J. Patterson	9-7	3.13	198.1	172	65	185	0
E. Loaiza	12-10	3.77	217.0	227	55	173	0
L. Hernandez	15-10	3.98	246.1	268	84	147	0
T. Armas	7-7	4.97	101.1	100	54	59	0

Manager-Frank Robinson

American League Final Standings, 2005

Eastern Division

	W	L	Pct.	GB	Home	Road	vs. East	vs. Central	vs. West	vs. NL
New York	95	67	.586	-	53-28	42-39	41-33	18-13	25-14	11-7
Boston*	95	67	.586	-	54-27	41-40	39-35	22-13	22-13	12-6
Toronto	80	82	.494	15.0	43-38	37-44	38-36	15-19	19-17	8-10
Baltimore	74	88	.457	21.0	36-45	38-43	36-37	13-22	17-19	8-10
Tampa Bay	67	95	.414	28.0	40-41	27-54	31-44	15-22	18-14	3-15

Central Division

	W	L	Pct.	GB	Home	Road	vs. East	vs. Central	vs. West	vs. NL
Chicago	99	63	.611	-	47-34	52-29	20-13	52-22	15-22	12-6
Cleveland	93	69	.574	6.0	43-38	50-31	19-17	40-35	19-14	15-3
Minnesota	83	79	.512	16.0	45-36	38-43	18-12	40-35	17-22	8-10
Detroit	71	91	.438	28.0	39-42	32-49	19-19	29-46	14-17	9-9
Kansas City	56	106	.346	43.0	34-47	22-59	13-22	26-49	8-26	9-9

Western Division

	W	L	Pct.	GB	Home	Road	vs. East	vs. Central	vs. West	vs. NL
Los Angeles	95	67	.586	-	49-32	46-35	19-22	30-17	34-22	12-6
Oakland	88	74	.543	7.0	45-36	43-38	21-27	25-15	32-24	10-8
Texas	79	83	.488	16.0	44-37	35-46	20-27	25-15	25-32	9-9
Seattle	69	93	.426	26.0	39-42	30-51	17-25	21-26	21-34	10-8

*Wild card team.

American League Team Statistics, 2005

(Individual Statistics: Batting—at least 150 at-bats; Pitching—at least 70 innings or 10 saves; *changed teams within AL during season, entry includes statistics for more than one team; # changed teams to or from NL during season, entry includes only AL stats)

TEAM BATTING

Team	BA	AB	R	H	HR	RBI
Boston	.281	5626	910	1579	199	863
New York	.276	5624	886	1552	229	847
Tampa Bay	.274	5552	750	1519	157	717
Detroit	.272	5602	723	1521	168	678
Cleveland	.271	5609	790	1522	207	760
Los Angeles	.270	5617	760	1517	147	724
Baltimore	.269	5551	729	1492	189	700
Texas	.267	5716	865	1528	260	834
Toronto	.265	5581	775	1480	136	735
Kansas City	.263	5496	700	1443	126	651
Oakland	.262	5627	772	1476	155	739
Chicago	.262	5529	741	1450	200	713
Minnesota	.259	5564	688	1441	134	644
Seattle	.256	5507	699	1408	130	657

TEAM PITCHING

Team	ERA	IP	H	SO	BB	SV
Cleveland	3.61	1452.2	1363	1050	413	51
Chicago	3.61	1475.2	1392	1040	459	54
Los Angeles	3.68	1464.1	1419	1126	443	54
Oakland	3.69	1450.1	1315	1075	504	38
Minnesota	3.71	1464.1	1458	965	348	44
Toronto	4.06	1447.0	1475	958	444	35
Seattle	4.49	1427.2	1483	892	496	39
Detroit	4.51	1435.2	1504	907	461	37
New York	4.52	1430.2	1495	985	463	46
Baltimore	4.56	1427.2	1458	1052	580	38
Boston	4.74	1429.0	1550	959	440	38
Texas	4.96	1440.0	1589	932	522	46
Tampa Bay	5.39	1421.2	1570	949	615	43
Kansas City	5.49	1413.1	1640	924	580	25

Baltimore Orioles

BATTERS	BA	AB	R	H	HR	RBI	SO	SB
M. Tejada	.304	654	89	199	26	98	83	5
B. Roberts	.314	561	92	176	18	73	83	27
M. Mora	.283	593	86	168	27	88	112	7
L. Matos	.280	389	53	109	4	32	58	17
C. Gomez	.279	219	27	61	1	18	17	2
J. Lopez	.278	395	47	110	15	49	68	0
J. Gibbons	.277	488	72	135	26	79	56	0
R. Palmeiro	.266	369	47	98	18	60	43	2
B. Surhoff	.257	303	30	78	5	34	32	0
S. Fasano	.250	160	25	40	11	20	41	0
L. Bigbie#	.248	206	22	51	5	21	49	3
E. Byrnes#	.231	359	47	83	10	35	60	5
S. Sosa	.221	380	39	84	14	45	84	1
D. Newhan	.202	218	31	44	5	21	45	9

PITCHERS	W-L	ERA	IP	H	BB	SO	SV
B. Ryan	1-4	2.43	70.1	54	26	100	36
T. Williams	5-5	3.30	76.1	72	26	38	1
B. Chen	13-10	3.83	197.1	187	63	133	0
E. Bedard	6-8	4.00	141.2	139	57	125	0
D. Cabrera	10-13	4.52	161.1	144	87	157	0
R. Lopez	15-12	4.90	209.1	232	63	118	0
J. Julio	3-5	5.90	71.2	76	24	58	0
S. Ponson	7-11	6.21	130.1	177	48	68	0

Manager-Lee Mazzill, Sam Perlozzo

Boston Red Sox

BATTERS	BA	AB	R	H	HR	RBI	SO	SB
J. Damon	.316	624	117	197	10	75	69	18
T. Graffanino*	.309	379	68	117	7	38	51	7
D. Ortiz	.300	601	119	180	47	148	124	1
B. Mueller	.295	519	69	153	10	62	74	0
M. Ramirez	.292	554	112	162	45	144	119	1
J. Olerud	.289	173	18	50	7	37	20	0
J. Varitek	.281	470	70	132	22	70	117	2
E. Renteria	.276	623	100	172	8	70	100	9
T. Nixon	.275	408	64	112	13	67	59	2
K. Millar	.272	449	57	122	9	50	74	0
A. Cora*	.232	250	25	58	3	24	30	7

PITCHERS	W-L	ERA	IP	H	BB	SO	SV
M. Timlin	7-3	2.24	80.1	86	20	59	13
T. Wakefield	16-12	4.15	225.1	210	68	151	0
D. Wells	15-7	4.45	184.0	220	21	107	0
B. Arroyo	14-10	4.51	205.1	213	54	100	0
M. Clement	13-6	4.57	191.0	192	68	146	0
W. Miller	4-4	4.95	91.0	96	47	64	0
C. Schilling	8-8	5.69	93.1	121	22	87	9
K. Foulke	5-5	5.91	45.2	53	18	34	15

Manager-Terry Francona

Chicago White Sox

BATTERS	BA	AB	R	H	HR	RBI	SO	SB
S. Podsednik	.290	507	80	147	0	25	75	59
P. Konerko	.283	575	98	163	40	100	109	0
T. Iguchi	.278	511	74	142	15	71	114	15
P. Ozuna	.276	203	27	56	0	11	26	14
J. Dye	.274	529	74	145	31	86	99	11
A. Rowand	.270	578	77	156	13	69	116	16
A. Pierzynski	.257	460	61	118	18	56	68	0
J. Uribe	.252	481	58	121	16	71	77	4
J. Crede	.252	432	54	109	22	62	66	1
C. Everett	.251	490	58	123	23	87	99	4
T. Perez	.218	179	13	39	2	15	25	2

PITCHERS	W-L	ERA	IP	H	BB	SO	SV
D. Hermanson	2-4	2.04	57.1	46	17	33	34
M. Buehrle	16-8	3.12	236.2	240	40	149	0
J. Garland	18-10	3.50	221.0	212	47	115	0
J. Contreras	15-7	3.61	204.2	177	75	154	0
L. Vizcaino	6-5	3.73	70.0	74	29	43	0
F. Garcia	14-8	3.87	228.0	225	60	146	0
O. Hernandez	9-9	5.12	128.1	137	50	91	1

Manager-Ozzie Guillen

Cleveland Indians

BATTERS	BA	AB	R	H	HR	RBI	SO	SB
V. Martinez	.305	547	73	167	20	80	78	0
T. Hafner	.305	486	94	148	33	108	123	0
C. Crisp	.300	594	86	178	16	69	81	15
J. Peralta	.292	504	82	147	24	78	128	0
G. Sizemore	.289	640	111	185	22	81	132	22
R. Belliard	.284	536	71	152	17	78	72	2
B. Broussard	.255	466	59	119	19	68	98	2
A. Boone	.243	511	61	124	16	60	92	9
C. Blake	.241	523	72	126	23	58	116	4
J. Hernandez	.231	234	28	54	6	31	60	1

PITCHERS	W-L	ERA	IP	H	BB	SO	SV
B. Howry	7-4	2.47	73.0	49	16	48	3
B. Wickman	0-4	2.47	62.0	57	21	41	45
K. Millwood	9-11	2.86	192.0	182	52	146	0
D. Riske	3-4	3.10	72.2	55	15	48	1
C. Lee	18-5	3.79	202.0	194	52	143	0
C. Sabathia	15-10	4.03	196.2	185	62	161	0
J. Westbrook	15-15	4.49	210.2	218	56	119	0
S. Elarton	11-9	4.61	181.2	189	48	103	0
S. Douglass	5-5	5.56	87.1	92	33	55	0

Manager-Eric Wedge

Detroit Tigers

BATTERS	BA	AB	R	H	HR	RBI	SO	SB
P. Polanco#	.338	343	58	116	6	36	16	4
C. Guillen	.320	334	48	107	5	23	45	2
R. White	.313	374	49	117	12	53	48	1
M. Ordonez	.302	305	38	92	8	46	35	0
C. Shelton	.299	388	61	116	18	59	87	0
C. Monroe	.277	567	69	157	20	89	95	8
J. McDonald	.277	166	18	46	0	16	24	6
I. Rodriguez	.276	504	71	139	14	50	93	7
C. Granderson	.272	162	18	44	8	20	43	1
D. Young	.271	469	61	127	21	72	100	1
B. Inge	.261	616	75	161	16	72	140	7
N. Logan	.258	322	47	83	1	17	52	23
C. Pena	.235	260	37	61	18	44	95	0
O. Infante	.222	406	36	90	9	43	73	8
V. Wilson	.197	152	18	30	3	19	26	0

PITCHERS	W-L	ERA	IP	H	BB	SO	SV
C. Spurling	3-4	3.44	70.2	58	22	26	0
N. Robertson	7-16	4.48	196.2	202	65	122	0
J. Johnson	8-13	4.54	210.0	233	49	93	0
J. Bonderman	14-13	4.57	189.0	199	57	145	0
M. Maroth	14-14	4.74	209.0	235	51	115	0

Manager-Alan Trammell

Kansas City Royals

BATTERS	BA	AB	R	H	HR	RBI	SO	SB
M. Sweeney	.300	466	63	140	21	83	61	3
D. DeJesus	.293	461	69	135	9	56	76	5
E. Brown	.286	545	75	156	17	86	108	10
T. Long	.279	455	62	127	6	53	56	3
M. Stairs	.275	396	55	109	13	66	69	1
A. Berroa	.270	608	68	164	11	55	108	7
M. Teahen	.246	447	60	110	7	55	107	7
J. Buck	.242	401	40	97	12	47	94	2
J. McEwing	.239	180	16	43	1	6	35	4
R. Gotay	.227	282	32	64	5	29	51	2

PITCHERS	W-L	ERA	IP	H	BB	SO	SV
A. Sisco	2-5	3.11	75.1	68	42	76	0
M. MacDougal	5-6	3.33	70.1	69	24	72	21
M. Wood	5-8	4.46	115.0	129	52	60	2
D. Carrasco	6-8	4.79	114.2	129	51	49	0
R. Hernandez	8-14	5.52	159.2	172	70	88	0
Z. Greinke	5-17	5.80	183.0	233	53	114	0
J. Howell	3-5	6.19	72.2	73	39	54	0
J. Lima	5-16	6.99	168.2	219	61	80	0

Manager-Tony Pena, Buddy Bell

Los Angeles Angels

BATTERS	BA	AB	R	H	HR	RBI	SO	SB
V. Guerrero	.317	520	95	165	32	108	48	13
A. Kennedy	.300	416	49	125	2	37	64	19
B. Molina	.295	410	45	121	15	69	41	0
C. Figgins	.290	642	113	186	8	57	101	62
G. Anderson	.283	575	68	163	17	96	84	1
D. Erstad	.271	605	85	164	7	65	108	10
J. Rivera	.271	350	46	95	15	59	44	1
O. Cabrera	.257	540	70	139	8	57	50	21
M. Izturis	.246	191	18	47	1	15	21	9
D. McPherson	.244	205	29	50	8	26	64	3
J. DaVanon	.231	225	42	52	2	15	44	11
J. Molina	.228	184	14	42	6	25	41	2
S. Finley	.222	406	41	90	12	54	71	8

PITCHERS	W-L	ERA	IP	H	BB	SO	SV
F. Rodriguez	2-5	2.67	67.1	45	32	91	45
S. Shields	10-11	2.75	91.2	66	37	98	7
J. Washburn	8-8	3.20	177.1	184	51	94	0
J. Lackey	14-5	3.44	209.0	208	71	199	0
B. Colon	21-8	3.48	222.2	215	43	157	0
E. Santana	12-8	4.65	133.2	139	47	99	0
P. Byrd	12-11	3.74	204.1	216	28	102	0

Manager-Mike Scioscia

Minnesota Twins

BATTERS	BA	AB	R	H	HR	RBI	SO	SB
J. Mauer	.294	489	61	144	9	55	64	13
S. Stewart	.274	551	69	151	10	56	73	7
T. Hunter	.269	372	63	100	14	56	65	23
L. Rodriguez	.269	175	21	47	2	20	23	2
L. Ford	.264	522	70	138	7	53	85	13
M. Cuddyer	.263	422	55	111	12	42	93	3
M. LeCroy	.260	304	33	79	17	50	85	0
J. Castro	.257	272	27	70	5	33	39	0
J. Jones	.249	523	74	130	23	73	120	13
J. Morneau	.239	490	62	117	22	79	94	0
N. Punto	.239	394	45	94	4	26	86	13
J. Bartlett	.241	224	33	54	3	16	37	4
B. Boone*	.221	326	33	72	7	37	65	4
T. Tiffee	.207	150	9	31	1	15	15	1

PITCHERS	W-L	ERA	IP	H	BB	SO	SV
J. Rincon	6-6	2.45	77.0	63	30	84	0
J. Nathan	7-4	2.70	70.0	46	22	94	43
J. Crain	12-5	2.71	79.2	61	29	25	1
J. Santana	16-7	2.87	231.2	180	45	238	0
M. Guerrier	0-3	3.39	71.2	71	24	46	0
C. Silva	9-8	3.44	188.1	212	9	71	0
B. Radke	9-12	4.04	200.2	214	23	117	0
K. Lohse	9-13	4.18	178.2	211	44	86	0
J. Mays	6-10	5.65	156.0	203	41	59	0

Manager-Ron Gardenhire

New York Yankees

BATTERS	BA	AB	R	H	HR	RBI	SO	SB
A. Rodriguez	.321	605	124	194	48	130	139	21
D. Jeter	.309	654	122	202	19	70	117	14
H. Matsui	.305	629	108	192	23	116	78	2
R. Cano	.297	522	78	155	14	62	68	1
G. Sheffield	.291	584	104	170	34	123	76	10
J. Giambi	.271	417	74	113	32	87	109	0
J. Posada	.262	474	67	124	19	71	94	1
B. Williams	.249	485	53	121	12	64	75	1
T. Womack	.249	329	46	82	0	15	49	27
T. Martinez	.241	303	43	73	17	49	54	2
R. Sierra	.229	170	14	39	4	29	41	0
M. Bellhorn	.210	300	43	63	8	30	112	3

PITCHERS	W-L	ERA	IP	H	BB	SO	SV
M. Rivera	7-4	1.38	78.1	50	18	80	43
T. Gordon	5-4	2.57	80.2	59	29	69	2
S. Chacon#	7-3	2.85	79.0	66	30	40	0
A. Small	10-0	3.20	76.0	71	24	37	0
R. Johnson	17-8	3.79	225.2	207	47	211	0
C. Wang	8-5	4.02	116.1	113	32	47	0
M. Mussina	13-8	4.41	179.2	199	47	142	0
T. Sturtze	5-3	4.73	78.0	76	27	45	1
C. Pavano	4-6	4.77	100.0	129	18	56	0
K. Brown	4-7	6.50	73.1	107	19	50	0
H. Nomo	5-8	7.24	100.2	127	51	59	0

Manager-Joe Torre

Oakland Athletics

BATTERS	BA	AB	R	H	HR	RBI	SO	SB
M. Ellis	.316	434	76	137	13	52	51	1
M. Kotsay	.280	582	75	163	15	82	51	5
B. Crosby	.276	333	66	92	9	38	54	0
D. Johnson	.275	375	54	103	15	58	52	0
J. Kendall	.271	601	70	163	0	53	39	8
E. Chavez	.269	625	92	168	27	101	129	6
J. Payton*	.267	408	62	109	18	63	47	0
B. Kielty	.263	377	55	99	10	57	67	3
S. Hatteberg	.256	464	52	119	7	59	54	0
M. Scutaro	.247	381	48	94	9	37	48	5
E. Durazo	.237	152	15	36	4	16	24	1
N. Swisher	.236	462	66	109	21	74	110	0

PITCHERS	W-L	ERA	IP	H	BB	SO	SV
H. Street	5-1	1.72	78.1	53	26	72	23
J. Duchscherer	7-4	2.21	85.2	67	19	85	5
R. Harden	10-5	2.53	128.0	93	43	121	0
J. Blanton	12-12	3.53	201.1	178	67	116	0
D. Haren	14-12	3.73	217.0	212	53	163	0
B. Zito	14-13	3.86	228.1	185	89	171	0
K. Saarloos	10-9	4.17	159.2	170	54	53	0

Manager-Ken Macha

Seattle Mariners

BATTERS	BA	AB	R	H	HR	RBI	SO	SB
I. Suzuki	.303	679	111	206	15	68	66	33
R. Ibanez	.280	614	92	172	20	89	99	9
M. Morse	.278	230	27	64	3	23	50	3
R. Winn#	.275	386	46	106	6	37	53	12
R. Sexson	.263	558	99	147	39	121	167	1
W. Bloomquist	.257	249	27	64	0	22	38	14
Y. Betancourt	.256	211	24	54	1	15	24	1
A. Beltre	.255	603	69	154	19	87	108	3
J. Reed	.254	488	61	124	3	45	74	12
J. Lopez	.247	190	18	47	2	25	25	4
M. Olivo#	.151	152	14	23	5	18	49	1

PITCHERS	W-L	ERA	IP	H	BB	SO	SV
F. Hernandez	4-4	2.67	84.1	61	23	77	0
E. Guardado	2-3	2.72	56.1	52	15	48	36
J. Mateo#	3-6	3.06	88.1	79	17	52	0
J. Moyer	13-7	4.28	200.0	225	52	102	0
G. Meche	10-8	5.09	143.1	153	72	83	0
R. Franklin	8-15	5.10	190.2	212	62	93	0
J. Pineiro	7-11	5.62	189.0	224	56	107	0

Manager-Mike Hargrove

Tampa Bay Devil Rays

BATTERS	BA	AB	R	H	HR	RBI	SO	SB
C. Crawford	.301	644	101	194	15	81	84	46
J. Lugo	.295	616	89	182	6	57	72	39
T. Hall	.287	432	28	124	5	48	39	0
J. Cantu	.286	598	73	171	28	117	83	1
J. Gomes	.282	348	61	98	21	54	113	9
J. Gathright	.276	203	29	56	0	13	39	20
T. Lee	.272	404	54	110	12	49	66	7
A. Gonzalez	.269	349	47	94	9	38	74	2
J. Phelps	.266	158	21	42	5	26	48	0
A. Huff	.261	575	70	150	22	92	88	8
E. Perez	.255	161	23	41	11	28	30	0
D. Hollins	.249	342	44	85	13	46	63	8
N. Green#	.239	318	53	76	5	29	86	3

PITCHERS	W-L	ERA	IP	H	BB	SO	SV
D. Baez	5-4	2.86	72.1	66	30	51	41
S. Kazmir	10-9	3.77	186.0	172	100	174	0
C. Fossum#	8-12	4.92	162.2	170	60	128	0
D. Waechter	5-12	5.62	157.0	191	38	87	0
M. Hendrickson	11-8	5.90	178.1	227	49	89	0
S. McClung	7-11	6.59	109.1	106	62	92	0
T. Harper	4-6	6.75	73.1	88	24	40	0
D. Brazelton	1-8	7.61	71.0	87	60	43	0

Manager-Lou Piniella

Texas Rangers

BATTERS	BA	AB	R	H	HR	RBI	SO	SB
M. Young	.331	668	114	221	24	91	91	5
M. Teixeira	.301	644	112	194	43	144	124	4
A. Soriano	.268	637	102	171	36	104	125	30
K. Mench	.264	557	71	147	25	73	68	4
H. Blalock	.263	647	80	170	25	92	132	1
G. Matthews	.255	475	72	121	17	55	90	9
R. Barajas	.254	410	53	104	21	60	70	0
D. Dellucci	.251	435	97	109	29	65	121	5
L. Nix	.240	229	28	55	6	32	45	2
A. Gonzalez	.227	150	17	34	6	17	37	0
R. Hidalgo	.221	308	43	68	16	43	74	1

PITCHERS	W-L	ERA	IP	H	BB	SO	SV
F. Cordero	3-1	3.39	69.0	61	30	79	37
K. Loe	9-6	3.42	92.0	89	31	45	1
K. Rogers	14-8	3.46	195.1	205	53	87	0
J. Benoit	4-4	3.72	87.0	69	38	78	0
J. Dominguez	4-6	4.22	70.1	78	25	45	0
C. Young	12-7	4.26	164.2	162	45	137	0
J. Wasdin	3-2	4.28	75.2	77	20	44	4
D. Brocail	5-3	5.52	73.1	90	34	61	1
C. Park#	8-5	5.66	109.2	130	54	80	0
A. Sele	6-12	5.66	116.0	147	41	53	0

Manager-Buck Showalter

Toronto Blue Jays

BATTERS	BA	AB	R	H	HR	RBI	SO	SB
F. Catalanotto	.301	419	56	126	8	59	53	0
S. Hillenbrand	.291	594	91	173	18	82	79	5
A. Hill	.274	361	49	99	3	40	41	2
O. Hudson	.271	461	62	125	10	63	65	7
V. Wells	.269	620	78	167	28	97	86	8
R. Johnson	.269	398	55	107	8	58	82	5
A. Rios	.262	481	71	126	10	59	101	14
E. Hinske	.262	477	79	125	15	68	121	8
R. Adams	.256	481	68	123	8	63	57	11
G. Zaun	.251	434	61	109	11	61	70	2
C. Koskie	.249	354	49	88	11	36	90	4

PITCHERS	W-L	ERA	IP	H	BB	SO	SV
R. Halladay	12-4	2.41	141.2	118	18	108	0
J. Frasor	3-5	3.25	74.2	67	28	62	1
P. Walker	6-6	3.54	84.0	81	33	43	2
J. Towers	13-12	3.71	208.2	237	29	112	0
G. Chacin	13-9	3.72	203.0	213	70	121	0
V. Chulk	0-1	3.88	72.0	68	26	39	0
M. Batista	5-8	4.10	74.2	80	27	54	31
S. Downs	4-3	4.31	94.0	93	34	75	0
D. Bush	5-11	4.49	136.1	142	29	75	0
T. Lilly	10-11	5.56	126.1	135	58	96	0

Manager-John Gibbons

National Baseball Hall of Fame and Museum, Cooperstown, NY[1]

#Aaron, Hank (The Hammer)
Alexander, Grover Cleveland (Old Pete)
Alston, Walt
Anderson, Sparky
Anson, Cap
Aparicio, Luis
Appling, Luke
Ashburn, Richie
Averill, Earl
Baker, Frank (Home Run)
Bancroft, Dave
#Banks, Ernie
Barlick, Al
Barrow, Edward G.
Beckley, Jake
Bell, Cool Papa
#Bench, Johnny
Bender, Chief
Berra, Yogi
*#Boggs, Wade
Bottomley, Jim
Boudreau, Lou
Bresnahan, Roger
#Brett, George
#Brock, Lou
Brouthers, Dan
Brown, Mordecai (Three Finger)
Bulkeley, Morgan C.
Bunning, Jim
Burkett, Jesse C.
Campanella, Roy
#Carew, Rod
Carey, Max
#Carlton, Steve
Carter, Gary
Cartwright, Alexander
Cepeda, Orlando
Chadwick, Henry
Chance, Frank
Chandler, Happy
Charleston, Oscar
Chesbro, John
Chylak, Nestor
Clarke, Fred
Clarkson, John
#Clemente,Roberto
Cobb, Ty[2]
Cochrane, Mickey
Collins, Eddie
Collins, James
Combs, Earle
Comiskey, Charles A.
Conlan, Jocko
Connolly, Thomas H.
Connor, Roger
Coveleski, Stan
Crawford, Sam
Cronin, Joe
Cummings, Candy
Cuyler, Kiki
Dandridge, Ray
Davis, George (Gorgeous)
Day, Leon
Dean, Dizzy
Delahanty, Ed
Dickey, Bill
Dihigo, Martín
DiMaggio, Joe
#Doby, Larry
Doerr, Bobby
Drysdale, Don
Duffy, Hugh
Durocher, Leo
#Eckersly, Dennis
Evans, Billy
Evers, John
Ewing, Buck
Faber, Urban (Red)
#Feller, Bob
Ferrell, Rick
Fingers, Rollie
Fisk, Carlton
Flick, Elmer H.
Ford, Whitey
Foster, Andrew (Rube)
Foster, Bill
Fox, Nellie
Foxx, Jimmie
Frick, Ford
Frisch, Frank
Galvin, Pud
#Gehrig, Lou
Gehringer, Charles
#Gibson, Bob
Gibson, Josh
Giles, Warren
Gomez, Lefty
Goslin, Goose
Greenberg, Hank
Griffith, Clark
Grimes, Burleigh
Grove, Lefty
Hafey, Chick
Haines, Jesee
Hamilton, Bill
Hanlon, Ned
Harridge, Will
Harris, Bucky
Hartnett, Gabby
Heilmann, Harry
Herman, Billy
Hooper, Harry
Hornsby, Rogers
Hoyt, Waite
Hubbard, Cal
Hubbell, Carl
Huggins, Miller
Hulbert, William
Hunter, Catfish
Irvin, Monte
#Jackson, Reggie
Jackson, Travis
Jenkins, Ferguson
Jennings, Hugh
Johnson, Byron (Ban)
Johnson, William (Judy)
Johnson, Walter[2]
Joss, Addie
#Kaline, Al
Keefe, Timothy
Keeler, William
Kell, George
Kelley, Joe
Kelly, George
Kelly, King
Killebrew, Harmon
Kiner, Ralph
Klein, Chuck
Klem, Bill
#Koufax, Sandy
Lajoie, Napoleon
Landis, Kenesaw M.
Lasorda, Tom
Lazzeri, Tony
Lemon, Bob
Leonard, Buck
Lindstrom, Fred
Lloyd, Pop
Lombardi, Ernie
Lopez, Al
Lyons, Ted
Mack, Connie
MacPhail, Larry
MacPhail, Lee
#Mantle, Mickey
Manush, Henry
Maranville, Rabbit
Marichal, Juan
Marquard, Rube
Mathews, Eddie
Mathewson, Christy[2]
#Mays, Willie
Mazeroski, Bill
McCarthy, Joe
McCarthy, Thomas
#McCovey, Willie
McGinnity, Joe
McGowan, Bill
McGraw, John
McKechnie, Bill
McPhee, John (Bid)
Medwick, Joe
Mize, Johnny
#Molitor, Paul
#Morgan, Joe
#Murray, Eddie
#Musial, Stan
Newhouser, Hal
Nichols, Kid
Niekro, Phil
O'Rourke, James
Ott, Mel
Paige, Satchel
#Palmer, Jim
Pennock, Herb
Perez, Tony
Perry, Gaylord
Plank, Ed
#Puckett, Kirby
Radbourn, Charlie
Reese, Pee Wee
Rice, Sam
Rickey, Branch
Rixey, Eppa
Rizzuto, Phil (Scooter)
Roberts, Robin
#Robinson, Brooks
#Robinson, Frank
#Robinson, Jackie
Robinson, Wilbert
Rogan, Joe (Bullet)
Roush, Edd
Ruffing, Red
Rusie, Amos
#Ruth, Babe[2]
#Ryan, Nolan
*Sandberg, Ryne
Schalk, Ray
#Schmidt, Mike
Schoendienst, Red
#Seaver, Tom
Selee, Frank
Sewell, Joe
Simmons, Al
Sisler, George
Slaughter, Enos
Smith, Hilton
#Smith, Ozzie
Snider, Duke
#Spahn, Warren
Spalding, Albert
Speaker, Tris
#Stargell, Willie
Stearnes, Norman (Turkey)
Stengel, Casey
Sutton, Don
Terry, Bill
Thompson, Sam
Tinker, Joe
Traynor, Pie
Vance, Dazzy
Vaughan, Arky
Veeck, Bill
Waddell, Rube
Wagner, Honus[2]
Wallace, Roderick (Bobby)
Walsh, Ed
Waner, Lloyd
Waner, Paul
Ward, John
Weaver, Earl
Weiss, George
Welch, Mickey
Wells, Willie
Wheat, Zach
Wilhelm, Hoyt
Williams, Billy
Williams, Joe (Smokey Joe)
#Willis, Ted
Williams, Vic
Wilson, Hack
#Winfield, Dave
Wright, George
Wright, Harry
Wynn, Early
#Yastrzemski, Carl
Yawkey, Tom
Young, Cy
Youngs, Ross
#Yount, Robin

(1) Player must generally be retired for 5 complete seasons before being eligible for induction. (2) Players inducted in 1936 (the year the Hall of Fame began). # Denotes players chosen in first year of Hall of Fame eligibility or under special circumstances earlier. *Denotes 2005 inductees. **NOTE:** Four players, Babe Ruth (1936), Lou Gehrig (1939), Joe DiMaggio (1955), and Roberto Clemente (1973), were inducted less than 5 years after retirement or, in Clemente's case, death.

Major League Leaders in 2005

American League

Batting: Michael Young, Texas, .331; Alex Rodriguez, New York, .321; Vladimir Guerrero, Los Angeles, .317; Johnny Damon, Boston, .316; Brian Roberts, Baltimore, .314.

Runs: Alex Rodriguez, New York, 124; Derek Jeter, New York, 122; David Ortiz, Boston, 119; Johnny Damon, Boston, 117; Michael Young, Texas, 114.

Runs Batted In: David Ortiz, Boston, 148; Manny Ramirez, Boston, 144; Mark Teixeira, Texas, 144; Alex Rodriguez, New York, 130; Gary Sheffield, New York, 123.

Hits: Michael Young, Texas, 221; Ichiro Suzuki, Seattle, 206; Derek Jeter, New York, 202; Miguel Tejada, Baltimore 199; Johnny Damon, Boston, 197.

Doubles: Miguel Tejada, Baltimore, 50; Hideki Matsui, New York, 45; Brian Roberts, Baltimore, 45; Alfonso Soriano, Texas, 43; Coco Crisp, Cleveland, 42.

Triples: Carl Crawford, Tampa Bay, 15; Ichiro Suzuki, Seattle, 12; Grady Sizemore, Cleveland, 11; Chone Figgins, Los Angeles, 10; Brandon Inge, Detroit, 9.

Home Runs: Alex Rodriguez, New York, 48; David Ortiz, Boston, 47; Manny Ramirez, Boston, 45; Mark Teixeira, Texas, 43; Paul Konerko, Chicago, 40.

Stolen Bases: Chone Figgins, Los Angeles, 62; Scott Podsednik, Chicago, 59; Carl Crawford, Tampa Bay, 46; Julio Lugo, Tampa Bay, 39; Ichiro Suzuki, Seattle, 33.

Pitching Wins: Bartolo Colon, Los Angeles, 21-8; J Garland, Chicago, 18-10; Cliff Lee, Cleveland; 18-5; Randy Johnson, New York, 17-8; Mark Buehrle, Chicago, 16-8.

Earned Run Average: Kevin Millwood, Cleveland, 2.86; Johan Santana, Minnesota, 2.87; Mark Buehrle, Chicago, 3.12; Jarrod Washburn, Los Angeles, 3.20; John Lackey, Los Angeles, 3.44; Carlos Silva, Minnesota, 3.44.

Strikeouts: Johan Santana, Minnesota, 238; Randy Johnson, New York, 211; John Lackey, Los Angeles, 199; Scott Kazmir, Tampa Bay, 174; Barry Zito, Oakland, 171.

Saves: Francisco Rodriguez, Los Angeles, 45; Bob Wickman, Cleveland, 45; Joe Nathan, Minnesota, 43; Mariano Rivera, New York, 43; Danys Baez, Tampa Bay, 41.

National League

Batting: Derrek Lee, Chicago, .335; Albert Pujols, St. Louis, .330; Miguel Cabrera, Florida, .323; Todd Helton, Colorado, .320; Sean Casey, Cincinnati, .312.

Runs: Albert Pujols, St. Louis, 129; Derrek Lee, Chicago, 120; Jimmy Rollins, Philadelphia, 115; Jason Bay, Pittsburgh, 110; Adam Dunn, Cincinnati, 107.

Runs Batted In: Andruw Jones, Atlanta, 128; Pat Burrell, Philadelphia, 117; Albert Pujols, St. Louis, 117; Miguel Cabrera, Florida, 116; Carlos Delgado, Florida, 115.

Hits: Derrek Lee, Chicago, 199; Miguel Cabrera, Florida, 198; Jimmy Rollins, Philadelphia, 196; Albert Pujols, St. Louis, 195; Jose Reyes, New York, 190.

Doubles: Derrek Lee, Chicago, 50; Marcus Giles, Atlanta, 45; Todd Helton, Colorado, 45; Jason Bay, Pittsburgh, 44; Miguel Cabrera, Florida, 43.
Triples: Jose Reyes, New York, 17; Juan Pierre, Florida, 13; Rafael Furcal, Atlanta, 11; Jimmy Rollins, Philadelphia, 11; Dave Roberts, San Diego, 10.
Home Runs: Andruw Jones, Atlanta, 51; Derrek Lee, Chicago, 46; Albert Pujols, St. Louis, 41; Adam Dunn, Cincinnati, 40; Troy Glaus, Arizona, 37.
Stolen Bases: Jose Reyes, New York, 60; Juan Pierre, Florida, 57; Rafael Furcal, Atlanta, 46; Jimmy Rollins, Philadelphia, 41; Ryan Freel, Cincinnati, 36.
Pitching Wins: Dontrelle Willis, Florida, 22-10; Chris Carpenter, St. Louis, 21-5; Roy Oswalt, Houston, 20-12; Chris Capuano, Milwaukee, 18-12; Jon Lieber, Philadelphia, 17-13.
Earned Run Average: Roger Clemens, Houston, 1.87; Andy Pettitte, Houston, 2.39; Dontrelle Willis, Florida, 2.63; Pedro Martinez, New York, 2.82; Chris Carpenter, St. Louis, 2.83.
Strikeouts: Jake Peavy, San Diego, 216; Chris Carpenter, St. Louis, 213; Doug Davis, Milwaukee, 208; Pedro Martinez, New York, 208; Brett Myers, Philadelphia, 208.
Saves: Chad Cordero, Washington, 47; Trevor Hoffman, San Diego, 43; Brad Lidge, Houston, 42; Todd Jones, Florida, 40; Jason Isringhausen, St. Louis, 39; Derrick Turnbow, Milwaukee, 39.

50 Home Run Club

Only Mark McGwire and Barry Bonds have ever hit 70 or more home runs in a season. Five players—including Babe Ruth and Roger Maris—have hit 60 or more, a feat Sammy Sosa accomplished for the 3rd time in 2001. Those 5 are at the pinnacle of a select group of players to have hit 50 or more homers in a season. The following list shows each time a player achieved this mark.

HR	Player, team	Year
73	Barry Bonds, San Francisco Giants	2001
70	Mark McGwire, St. Louis Cardinals	1998
66	Sammy Sosa, Chicago Cubs	1998
65	Mark McGwire, St. Louis Cardinals	1999
64	Sammy Sosa, Chicago Cubs	2001
63	Sammy Sosa, Chicago Cubs	1999
61	Roger Maris, N.Y. Yankees	1961
60	Babe Ruth, N.Y. Yankees	1927
59	Babe Ruth, N.Y. Yankees	1921
58	Jimmie Foxx, Philadelphia Athletics	1932
58	Hank Greenberg, Detroit Tigers	1938
58	Mark McGwire, Oakland A's/St. Louis Cardinals	1997
57	Luis Gonzalez, Arizona Diamondbacks	2001
57	Alex Rodriguez, Texas Rangers	2002
56	Hack Wilson, Chicago Cubs	1930
56	Ken Griffey Jr., Seattle Mariners	1997
56	Ken Griffey Jr., Seattle Mariners	1998
54	Babe Ruth, N.Y. Yankees	1920
54	Babe Ruth, N.Y. Yankees	1928
54	Ralph Kiner, Pittsburgh Pirates	1949
54	Mickey Mantle, N.Y. Yankees	1961
52	Mickey Mantle, N.Y. Yankees	1956
52	Willie Mays, San Francisco Giants	1965
52	George Foster, Cincinnati Reds	1977
52	Mark McGwire, Oakland A's	1996
52	Alex Rodriguez, Texas Rangers	2001
52	Jim Thome, Cleveland Indians	2002
51	Andruw Jones, Atlanta Braves	2005
51	Ralph Kiner, Pittsburgh Pirates	1947
51	Johnny Mize, N.Y. Giants	1947
51	Willie Mays, N.Y. Giants	1955
51	Cecil Fielder, Detroit Tigers	1990
50	Jimmie Foxx, Boston Red Sox	1938
50	Albert Belle, Cleveland Indians	1995
50	Brady Anderson, Baltimore Orioles	1996
50	Greg Vaughn, San Diego Padres	1998
50	Sammy Sosa, Chicago Cubs	2000

Earned Run Average Leaders, by Season

National League					American League				
Year	Player, team	G	IP	ERA	Year	Player, team	G	IP	ERA
1977	John Candelaria, Pittsburgh	33	231	**2.34**	1977	Frank Tanana, California	31	241	**2.54**
1978	Craig Swan, New York	29	207	**2.43**	1978	Ron Guidry, New York	35	274	**1.74**
1979	J. R. Richard, Houston	38	292	**2.71**	1979	Ron Guidry, New York	33	236	**2.78**
1980	Don Sutton, Los Angeles	32	212	**2.21**	1980	Rudy May, New York	41	175	**2.47**
1981	Nolan Ryan, Houston	21	149	**1.69**	1981	Steve McCatty, Oakland	22	186	**2.32**
1982	Steve Rogers, Montreal	35	277	**2.40**	1982	Rick Sutcliffe, Cleveland	34	216	**2.96**
1983	Atlee Hammaker, San Francisco	23	172	**2.25**	1983	Rick Honeycutt, Texas	25	174	**2.42**
1984	Alejandro Pena, Los Angeles	28	199	**2.48**	1984	Mike Boddicker, Baltimore	34	261	**2.79**
1985	Dwight Gooden, New York	35	276	**1.53**	1985	Dave Stieb, Toronto	36	265	**2.48**
1986	Mike Scott, Houston	37	275	**2.22**	1986	Roger Clemens, Boston	33	254	**2.48**
1987	Nolan Ryan, Houston	34	211	**2.76**	1987	Jimmy Key, Toronto	36	261	**2.76**
1988	Joe Magrane, St. Louis	24	165	**2.18**	1988	Allan Anderson, Minnesota	30	202	**2.45**
1989	Scott Garrelts, San Francisco	30	193	**2.28**	1989	Bret Saberhagen, Kansas City	36	262	**2.16**
1990	Danny Darwin, Houston	48	162	**2.21**	1990	Roger Clemens, Boston	31	228	**1.93**
1991	Dennis Martinez, Montreal	31	222	**2.39**	1991	Roger Clemens, Boston	35	271	**2.62**
1992	Bill Swift, San Francisco	30	164	**2.08**	1992	Roger Clemens, Boston	32	246	**2.41**
1993	Greg Maddux, Atlanta	36	267	**2.36**	1993	Kevin Appier, Kansas City	34	238	**2.56**
1994	Greg Maddux, Atlanta	25	202	**1.56**	1994	Steve Ontiveros, Oakland	27	115	**2.65**
1995	Greg Maddux, Atlanta	28	209	**1.63**	1995	Randy Johnson, Seattle	30	214	**2.48**
1996	Kevin Brown, Florida	32	233	**1.89**	1996	Juan Guzman, Toronto	27	187	**2.93**
1997	Pedro Martinez, Montrea	31	241	**1.90**	1997	Roger Clemens, Toronto	34	264	**2.05**
1998	Greg Maddux, Atlanta	34	251	**2.22**	1998	Roger Clemens, Toronto	33	234	**2.65**
1999	Randy Johnson, Arizona	35	271	**2.48**	1999	Pedro Martinez, Boston	31	213	**2.07**
2000	Kevin K. Brown, Los Angeles	33	230	**2.58**	2000	Pedro Martinez, Boston	29	217	**1.74**
2001	Randy Johnson, Arizona	35	249	**2.49**	2001	Freddy Garcia, Seattle	34	238	**3.05**
2002	Randy Johnson, Arizona	35	260	**2.32**	2002	Pedro Martinez, Boston	30	199	**2.26**
2003	Jason Schmidt, San Francisco	29	207	**2.34**	2003	Pedro Martinez, Boston	29	186	**2.22**
2004	Jake Peavy, San Diego	27	166.1	**2.27**	2004	Johan Santana, Minnesota	34	228	**2.61**
2005	Roger Clemens, Houston	32	211.1	**1.87**	2005	Kevin Millwood, Cleveland	30	192	**2.86**

ERA is computed by multiplying earned runs allowed by 9, then dividing by innings pitched.

Strikeout Leaders, by Season

Note: Asterisk (*) indicates the all-time single-season record for each league.

National League			American League		
Year	Pitcher, Team	SO	Year	Pitcher, Team	SO
1901	Noodles Hahn, Cincinnati	239	1901	Cy Young, Boston	158
1902	Vic Willis, Boston	225	1902	Rube Waddell, Philadelphia	210
1903	Christy Mathewson, New York	267	1903	Rube Waddell, Philadelphia	302
1904	Christy Mathewson, New York	212	1904	Rube Waddell, Philadelphia	349
1905	Christy Mathewson, New York	206	1905	Rube Waddell, Philadelphia	287
1906	Fred Beebe, Chicago-St. Louis	171	1906	Rube Waddell, Philadelphia	196
1907	Christy Mathewson, New York	178	1907	Rube Waddell, Philadelphia	232
1908	Christy Mathewson, New York	259	1908	Ed Walsh, Chicago	269
1909	Orval Overall, Chicago	205	1909	Frank Smith, Chicago	177
1910	Earl Moore, Philadelphia	185	1910	Walter Johnson, Washington	313
1911	Rube Marquard, New York	237	1911	Ed Walsh, Chicago	255
1912	Grover Alexander, Philadelphia	195	1912	Walter Johnson, Washington	303

National League

Year	Pitcher, Team	SO
1913	Tom Seaton, Philadelphia	168
1914	Grover Alexander, Philadelphia	214
1915	Grover Alexander, Philadelphia	241
1916	Grover Alexander, Philadelphia	167
1917	Grover Alexander, Philadelphia	201
1918	Hippo Vaughn, Chicago	148
1919	Hippo Vaughn, Chicago	141
1920	Grover Alexander, Chicago	173
1921	Burleigh Grimes, Brooklyn	136
1922	Dazzy Vance, Brooklyn	134
1923	Dazzy Vance, Brooklyn	197
1924	Dazzy Vance, Brooklyn	262
1925	Dazzy Vance, Brooklyn	221
1926	Dazzy Vance, Brooklyn	140
1927	Dazzy Vance, Brooklyn	184
1928	Dazzy Vance, Brooklyn	200
1929	Pat Malone, Chicago	166
1930	Bill Hallahan, St. Louis	177
1931	Bill Hallahan, St. Louis	159
1932	Dizzy Dean, St. Louis	191
1933	Dizzy Dean, St. Louis	199
1934	Dizzy Dean, St. Louis	195
1935	Dizzy Dean, St. Louis	190
1936	Van Lingle Mungo, Brooklyn	238
1937	Carl Hubbell, New York	159
1938	Clay Bryant, Chicago	135
1939	Claude Passeau, Philadelphia-Chicago	137
	Bucky Walters, Cincinnati	
1940	Kirby Higbe, Philadelphia	137
1941	John Vander Meer, Cincinnati	202
1942	John Vander Meer, Cincinnati	186
1943	John Vander Meer, Cincinnati	174
1944	Bill Voiselle, New York	161
1945	Preacher Roe, Pittsburgh	148
1946	Johnny Schmitz, Cincinnati	135
1947	Ewell Blackwell, Cincinnati	193
1948	Harry Brecheen, St. Louis	149
1949	Warren Spahn, Boston	151
1950	Warren Spahn, Boston	191
1951	Warren Spahn, Boston	164
	Don Newcombe, Brooklyn	
1952	Warren Spahn, Boston	183
1953	Robin Roberts, Philadelphia	198
1954	Robin Roberts, Philadelphia	185
1955	Sam Jones, Chicago	198
1956	Sam Jones, Chicago	176
1957	Jack Sanford, Philadelphia	188
1958	Sam Jones, St. Louis	225
1959	Don Drysdale, Los Angeles	242
1960	Don Drysdale, Los Angeles	246
1961	Sandy Koufax, Los Angeles	269
1962	Don Drysdale, Los Angeles	232
1963	Sandy Koufax, Los Angeles	306
1964	Bob Veale, Pittsburgh	250
1965	Sandy Koufax, Los Angeles	382*
1966	Sandy Koufax, Los Angeles	317
1967	Jim Bunning, Philadelphia	253
1968	Bob Gibson, St. Louis	268
1969	Ferguson Jenkins, Chicago	273
1970	Tom Seaver, New York	283
1971	Tom Seaver, New York	289
1972	Steve Carlton, Philadelphia	310
1973	Tom Seaver, New York	251
1974	Steve Carlton, Philadelphia	240
1975	Tom Seaver, New York	243
1976	Tom Seaver, New York	235
1977	Phil Niekro, Atlanta	262
1978	J.R. Richard, Houston	303
1979	J.R. Richard, Houston	313
1980	Steve Carlton, Philadelphia	286
1981	Fernando Valenzuela, Los Angeles	180
1982	Steve Carlton, Philadelphia	286
1983	Steve Carlton, Philadelphia	275
1984	Dwight Gooden, New York	276
1985	Dwight Gooden, New York	268
1986	Mike Scott, Houston	306
1987	Nolan Ryan, Houston	270
1988	Nolan Ryan, Houston	228
1989	Jose DeLeon, St. Louis	201
1990	David Cone, New York	233
1991	David Cone, New York	241
1992	John Smoltz, Atlanta	215
1993	Jose Rijo, Cincinnati	227
1994	Andy Benes, San Diego	189
1995	Hideo Nomo, Los Angeles	236
1996	John Smoltz, Atlanta	276
1997	Curt Schilling, Philadelphia	319

American League

Year	Pitcher, Team	SO
1913	Walter Johnson, Washington	243
1914	Walter Johnson, Washington	225
1915	Walter Johnson, Washington	203
1916	Walter Johnson, Washington	228
1917	Walter Johnson, Washington	188
1918	Walter Johnson, Washington	162
1919	Walter Johnson, Washington	147
1920	Stan Coveleski, Cleveland	133
1921	Walter Johnson, Washington	143
1922	Urban Shocker, St. Louis	149
1923	Walter Johnson, Washington	130
1924	Walter Johnson, Washington	158
1925	Lefty Grove, Philadelphia	116
1926	Lefty Grove, Philadelphia	194
1927	Lefty Grove, Philadelphia	174
1928	Lefty Grove, Philadelphia	183
1929	Lefty Grove, Philadelphia	170
1930	Lefty Grove, Philadelphia	209
1931	Lefty Grove, Philadelphia	175
1932	Red Ruffing, New York	190
1933	Lefty Gomez, New York	163
1934	Lefty Gomez, New York	158
1935	Tommy Bridges, Detroit	163
1936	Tommy Bridges, Detroit	175
1937	Lefty Gomez, New York	194
1938	Bob Feller, Cleveland	240
1939	Bob Feller, Cleveland	246
1940	Bob Feller, Cleveland	261
1941	Bob Feller, Cleveland	260
1942	Tex Hughson, Boston	113
	Bobo Newsom, Washington	
1943	Allie Reynolds, Cleveland	151
1944	Hal Newhouser, Detroit	187
1945	Hal Newhouser, Detroit	212
1946	Bob Feller, Cleveland	348
1947	Bob Feller, Cleveland	196
1948	Bob Feller, Cleveland	164
1949	Virgil Trucks, Detroit	153
1950	Bob Lemon, Cleveland	170
1951	Vic Raschi, New York	164
1952	Allie Reynolds, New York	160
1953	Billy Pierce, Chicago	186
1954	Bob Turley, Baltimore	185
1955	Herb Score, Cleveland	245
1956	Herb Score, Cleveland	263
1957	Early Wynn, Cleveland	184
1958	Early Wynn, Chicago	179
1959	Jim Bunning, Detroit	201
1960	Jim Bunning, Detroit	201
1961	Camilo Pacual, Minnesota	221
1962	Camilo Pacual, Minnesota	206
1963	Camilo Pacual, Minnesota	202
1964	Al Downing, New York	217
1965	Sam McDowell, Cleveland	325
1966	Sam McDowell, Cleveland	225
1967	Jim Lonborg, Boston	246
1968	Sam McDowell, Cleveland	283
1969	Sam McDowell, Cleveland	279
1970	Sam McDowell, Cleveland	304
1971	Mickey Lolich, Detroit	308
1972	Nolan Ryan, California	329
1973	Nolan Ryan, California	383*
1974	Nolan Ryan, California	367
1975	Frank Tanana, California	269
1976	Nolan Ryan, California	327
1977	Nolan Ryan, California	341
1978	Nolan Ryan, California	260
1979	Nolan Ryan, California	223
1980	Len Barker, Cleveland	187
1981	Len Barker, Cleveland	127
1982	Floyd Bannister, Seattle	209
1983	Jack Morris, Detroit	232
1984	Mark Langston, Seattle	204
1985	Bert Blyleven, Cleveland-Minnesota	206
1986	Mark Langston, Seattle	245
1987	Mark Langston, Seattle	262
1988	Roger Clemens, Boston	291
1989	Nolan Ryan, Texas	301
1990	Nolan Ryan, Texas	232
1991	Roger Clemens, Boston	241
1992	Randy Johnson, Seattle	241
1993	Randy Johnson, Seattle	308
1994	Randy Johnson, Seattle	204
1995	Randy Johnson, Seattle	294
1996	Roger Clemens, Boston	257
1997	Roger Clemens, Toronto	292

Year	National League Pitcher, Team	SO	Year	American League Pitcher, Team	SO
1998	Curt Schilling, Philadelphia	300	1998	Roger Clemens, Toronto	271
1999	Randy Johnson, Arizona	364	1999	Pedro Martinez, Boston	313
2000	Randy Johnson, Arizona	347	2000	Pedro Martinez, Boston	284
2001	Randy Johnson, Arizona	372	2001	Hideo Nomo, Boston	220
2002	Randy Johnson, Arizona	334	2002	Pedro Martinez, Boston	239
2003	Kerry Wood, Chicago	266	2003	Esteban Loaiza, Chicago	207
2004	Randy Johnson, Arizona	290	2004	Johan Santana, Minnesota	265
2005	Jake Peavy, San Diego	216	2005	Johan Santana, Minnesota	238

Victory Leaders by Season

Note: Asterisk (*) indicates the all-time single-season record for each league in the "modern" era beginning in 1901.

Year	National League Pitcher, Team	Wins	Year	American League Pitcher, Team	Wins
1901	Bill Donavan, Brooklyn	25	1901	Cy Young, Boston	33
1902	Jack Chesbro, Pittsburgh	28	1902	Cy Young, Boston	32
1903	Joe McGinnity, New York	31	1903	Cy Young, Boston	28
1904	Joe McGinnity, New York	35	1904	Jack Chesbro, New York	41*
1905	Christy Mathewson, New York	31	1905	Rube Waddell, Philadelphia	27
1906	Joe McGinnity, New York	27	1906	Al Orth, New York	27
1907	Christy Mathewson, New York	24	1907	Doc White, Chicago	27
1908	Christy Mathewson, New York	37*	1908	Ed Walsh, Chicago	40
1909	Mordecai Brown, Chicago	27	1909	George Mullin, Detroit	29
1910	Christy Mathewson, New York	27	1910	Jack Coombs, Philadelphia	31
1911	Grover Alexander, Chicago	28	1911	Jack Coombs, Philadelphia	28
1912	Rube Marquard, New York	26	1912	Joe Wood, Boston	34
1913	Tom Seaton, Philadelphia	27	1913	Walter Johnson, Washington	36
1914	Grover Alexander, Philadelphia	27	1914	Walter Johnson, Washington	28
1915	Grover Alexander, Philadelphia	31	1915	Walter Johnson, Washington	27
1916	Grover Alexander, Philadelphia	33	1916	Walter Johnson, Washington	25
1917	Grover Alexander, Philadelphia	30	1917	Eddie Cicotte, Chicago	28
1918	Hippo Vaughn, Chicago	22	1918	Walter Johnson, Washington	23
1919	Jesse Barnes, New York	25	1919	Eddie Cicotte, Chicago	29
1920	Grover Alexander, Philadelphia	27	1920	Jim Bagby, Cleveland	31
1921	Burleigh Grimes, Brooklyn	22	1921	Urban Shocker, St. Louis	27
1922	Eppa Rixey, Cincinnati	25	1922	Eddie Rommel, Philadelphia	27
1923	Dolf Luque, Cincinnati	27	1923	George Uhle, Cleveland	26
1924	Dazzy Vance, Brooklyn	28	1924	Walter Johnson, Washington	23
1925	Dazzy Vance, Brooklyn	22	1925	Eddie Rommel, Philadelphia	21
1926	Flint Rhem, St. Louis	20	1926	George Uhle, Cleveland	27
1927	Charlie Root, Chicago	26	1927	Ted Lyons, Chicago	22
1928	Burleigh Grimes, Pittsburgh	25	1928	George Pipgras, New York	24
1929	Pat Malone, Chicago	22	1929	George Earnshaw, Philadelphia	24
1930	Pat Malone, Chicago	20	1930	Lefty Grove, Philadelphia	28
1931	Heine Meine, Pittsburgh	19	1931	Lefty Grove, Philadelphia	31
1932	Lon Warneke, Chicago	22	1932	Alvin Crowder, Washington	26
1933	Carl Hubbell, New York	23	1933	Lefty Grove, Philadelphia	24
1934	Dizzy Dean, St. Louis	30	1934	Lefty Gomez, New York	26
1935	Dizzy Dean, St. Louis	28	1935	Wes Ferrell, Boston	25
1936	Carl Hubbell, New York	26	1936	Tommy Bridges, Detroit	23
1937	Carl Hubbell, New York	22	1937	Lefty Gomez, New York	21
1938	Bill Lee, Chicago	22	1938	Red Ruffing, New York	21
1939	Bucky Walters, Cincinnati	27	1939	Bob Feller, Cleveland	24
1940	Bucky Walters, Cincinnati	22	1940	Bob Feller, Cleveland	27
1941	Whit Wyatt, Brooklyn	22	1941	Bob Feller, Cleveland	25
1942	Mort Cooper, St. Louis	22	1942	Tex Hughson, Boston	22
1943	Rip Sewell, Pittsburgh	21	1943	Dizzy Trout, Detroit	20
1944	Bucky Walters, Cincinnati	23	1944	Hal Newhouser, Detroit	29
1945	Red Barrett, Boston-St. Louis	23	1945	Hal Newhouser, Detroit	25
1946	Howie Pollet, St. Louis	21	1946	Hal Newhouser, Detroit	26
1947	Ewell Blackwell, Cincinnati	22	1947	Bob Feller, Cleveland	20
1948	Johnny Sain, Boston	24	1948	Hal Newhouser, Detroit	21
1949	Warren Spahn, Boston	21	1949	Mel Parnell, Boston	25
1950	Warren Spahn, Boston	21	1950	Bob Lemon, Cleveland	23
1951	Sal Maglie, New York	23	1951	Bob Feller, Cleveland	22
1952	Robin Roberts, Philadelphia	28	1952	Bobby Shantz, Philadelphia	24
1953	Warren Spahn, Milwaukee	23	1953	Bob Porterfield, Washington	22
1954	Robin Roberts, Philadelphia	23	1954	Early Wynn, Cleveland	23
1955	Robin Roberts, Philadelphia	23	1955	Frank Sullivan, Boston	18
1956	Don Newcombe, Brooklyn	27	1956	Frank Lary, Detroit	21
1957	Warren Spahn, Milwaukee	21	1957	Billy Pierce, Chicago	20
1958	Warren Spahn, Milwaukee	22	1958	Bob Turley, New York	21
1959	Warren Spahn, Milwaukee	21	1959	Early Wynn, Chicago	22
1960	Warren Spahn, Milwaukee	21	1960	Jim Perry, Cleveland	18
1961	Warren Spahn, Milwaukee	21	1961	Whitey Ford, New York	25
1962	Don Drysdale, Los Angeles	25	1962	Ralph Terry, New York	23
1963	Juan Marichal, San Francisco	25	1963	Whitey Ford, New York	24
1964	Larry Jackson, Chicago	24	1964	Gary Peters, Chicago	20
1965	Sandy Koufax, Los Angeles	26	1965	Mudcat (Jim) Grant, Minnesota	21
1966	Sandy Koufax, Los Angeles	27	1966	Jim Kaat, Minnesota	25
1967	Mike McCormick, San Francisco	22	1967	Earl Wilson, Detroit	22
1968	Juan Marichal, San Francisco	26	1968	Denny McLain, Detroit	31
1969	Tom Seaver, New York	25	1969	Denny McLain, Detroit	24
1970	Gaylord Perry, San Francisco	23	1970	Jim Perry, Minnesota	24
1971	Fergie Jenkins, Chicago	24	1971	Mickey Lolich, Detroit	25
1972	Steve Carlton, Philadelphia	27	1972	Wilbur Wood, Chicago	24
1973	Ron Bryant, San Francisco	24	1973	Wilbur Wood, Chicago	24

National League

Year	Pitcher, Team	Wins
1974	Phil Niekro, Atlanta	20
1975	Tom Seaver, New York	22
1976	Randy Jones, San Diego	22
1977	Steve Carlton, Philadelphia	23
1978	Gaylord Perry, San Diego	21
1979	Phil Niekro, Atlanta	21
1980	Steve Carlton, Philadelphia	24
1981	Tom Seaver, Cincinnati	14
1982	Steve Carlton, Philadelphia	23
1983	John Denny, Philadelphia	19
1984	Joaquin Andujar, St. Louis	20
1985	Dwight Gooden, New York	24
1986	Fernando Valenzuela, Los Angeles	21
1987	Rick Sutcliffe, Chicago	18
1988	Danny Jackson, Cincinnati	23
1989	Mike Scott, Houston	20
1990	Doug Drabek, Pittsburgh	22
1991	John Smiley, Pittsburgh	20
1992	Greg Maddux, Chicago	20
1993	Tom Glavine, Atlanta	22
1994	Greg Maddux, Atlanta	16
1995	Greg Maddux, Atlanta	19
1996	John Smoltz, Atlanta	24
1997	Denny Neagle, Atlanta	20
1998	Tom Glavine, Atlanta	20
1999	Mike Hampton, Houston	22
2000	Tom Glavine, Atlanta	21
2001	Matt Morris, St. Louis; Curt Schilling, Arizona	22
2002	Randy Johnson, Arizona	24
2003	Russ Ortiz, Atlanta	21
2004	Roy Oswalt, Houston	20
2005	Dontrelle Willis, Florida	22

American League

Year	Pitcher, Team	Wins
1974	Fergie Jenkins, Texas	25
1975	Jim Palmer, Baltimore	23
1976	Jim Palmer, Baltimore	22
1977	Jim Palmer, Baltimore	20
1978	Ron Guidry, New York	25
1979	Mike Flanagan, Baltimore	23
1980	Steve Stone, Baltimore	25
1981	Pete Vuckovich, Milwaukee	14
1982	La Marr Hoyt, Chicago	19
1983	La Marr Hoyt, Chicago	24
1984	Mike Boddicker, Baltimore	20
1985	Ron Guidry, New York	22
1986	Roger Clemens, Boston	24
1987	Dave Stewart, Oakland; Roger Clemens, Boston	20
1988	Frank Viola, Minnesota	24
1989	Bret Saberhagen, Kansas City	23
1990	Bob Welch, Oakland	27
1991	Bill Gullickson, Detroit	20
1992	Jack Morris, Toronto	21
1993	Jack McDowell, Chicago	22
1994	Jimmy Key, New York	17
1995	Mike Mussina, Baltimore	19
1996	Andy Pettitte, New York	21
1997	Roger Clemens, Toronto	21
1998	Rick Helling, Texas; Roger Clemens, Toronto	20
1999	Pedro Martinez, Boston	23
2000	David Wells, Toronto	20
2001	Mark Mulder, Oakland	21
2002	Barry Zito, Oakland	23
2003	Roy Halladay, Toronto	22
2004	Curt Schilling, Boston	21
2005	Bartolo Colon, Los Angeles	21

All-Time World Series Career Leaders

(Through 2004. * Player active in 2004.)

Batting Leaders

Batter	Hits	AB	Avg.
1. Bobby Brown	18	41	.439
2. Paul Molitor	23	55	.418
3. Pepper Martin	23	55	.418
4. J.T. Snow*	11	27	.407
5. Hal McRae	18	45	.400
6. Lou Brock	34	87	.391
7. Marquis Grissom*	30	77	.390
8. Troy Glaus*	10	26	.385
9. George Brett	19	51	.373
10. Thurman Munson	25	67	.373

Games Played

Yogi Berra	75
Mickey Mantle	65
Elston Howard	54
Hank Bauer	53
Gil McDougald	53
Phil Rizzuto	52
Joe DiMaggio	51
Frankie Frisch	50
Pee Wee Reese	44
Roger Maris	41
Babe Ruth	41

Hits

Yogi Berra	71
Mickey Mantle	59
Frankie Frisch	58
Joe DiMaggio	54
Hank Bauer	46
PeeWee Reese	46
Phil Rizzuto	45
Gil McDougald	45
Lou Gehrig	43
Elston Howard	42
Babe Ruth	42
Eddie Collins	42

Runs

Mickey Mantle	42
Yogi Berra	41
Babe Ruth	37
Lou Gehrig	30
Joe DiMaggio	27
Derek Jeter*	27
Roger Maris	26
Elston Howard	25
Gil McDougald	23
Jackie Robinson	22

Runs Batted In

Mickey Mantle	40
Yogi Berra	39
Lou Gehrig	35
Babe Ruth	33
Joe DiMaggio	30
Bill Skowron	29
Duke Snider	26
Reggie Jackson	24
Hank Bauer	24
Bill Dickey	24
Gil McDougald	24

Home Runs

Mickey Mantle	18
Babe Ruth	15
Yogi Berra	12
Duke Snider	11
Reggie Jackson	10
Lou Gehrig	10
Joe DiMaggio	8
Bill Skowron	8
Frank Robinson	8
Hank Bauer	7
Gil McDougald	7
Goose Goslin	7

Stolen Bases

Lou Brock	14
Eddie Collins	14
Frank Chance	10
Dave Lopes	10
Phil Rizzuto	10
Frank Frisch	9
Honus Wagner	9
Johnny Evers	8
Roberto Alomar*	7
Rickey Henderson	7
Pepper Martin	7
Joe Morgan	7
Joe Tinker	7

Pitching Leaders

Games Pitched

Whitey Ford	22
Mariano Rivera*	20
Rollie Fingers	16
Jeff Nelson*	16
Allie Reynolds	15
Mike Stanton*	15
Bob Turley	15
Clay Carroll	14
Clem Labine	13
Mark Wohlers	13
Waite Hoyt	12
Catfish Hunter	12
Art Nehf	12

Wins

Whitey Ford	10
Bob Gibson	7
Allie Reynolds	7
Red Ruffing	7
Chief Bender	6
Lefty Gomez	6
Waite Hoyt	6
Three Finger Brown	5
Jack Coombs	5
Catfish Hunter	5
Herb Pennock	5
Vic Raschi	5
Christy Mathewson	5

Strikeouts

Whitey Ford	94
Bob Gibson	92
Allie Reynolds	62
Sandy Koufax	61
Red Ruffing	61
Chief Bender	59
George Earnshaw	56
John Smoltz*	52
Waite Hoyt	49
Christy Mathewson	48

Saves

Mariano Rivera*	9
Rollie Fingers	6
Johnny Murphy	4
Allie Reynolds	4
John Wetteland	4
Robb Nen	4

World Series Results, 1903-2004

1903 Boston AL 5, Pittsburgh NL 3
1904 No series
1905 New York NL 4, Philadelphia AL 1
1906 Chicago AL 4, Chicago NL 2
1907 Chicago NL 4, Detroit AL 0, 1 tie
1908 Chicago NL 4, Detroit AL 1
1909 Pittsburgh NL 4, Detroit AL 3
1910 Philadelphia AL 4, Chicago NL 1
1911 Philadelphia AL 4, New York NL 2
1912 Boston AL 4, New York NL 3, 1 tie
1913 Philadelphia AL 4, New York NL 1
1914 Boston NL 4, Philadelphia AL 0
1915 Boston AL 4, Philadelphia NL 1
1916 Boston AL 4, Brooklyn NL 1
1917 Chicago AL 4, New York NL 2
1918 Boston AL 4, Chicago NL 2
1919 Cincinnati NL 5, Chicago AL 3
1920 Cleveland AL 5, Brooklyn NL 2
1921 New York NL 5, New York AL 3
1922 New York NL 4, New York AL 0, 1 tie
1923 New York AL 4, New York NL 2
1924 Washington AL 4, New York NL 3
1925 Pittsburgh NL 4, Washington AL 3
1926 St. Louis NL 4, New York AL 3
1927 New York AL 4, Pittsburgh NL 0
1928 New York AL 4, St. Louis NL 0
1929 Philadelphia AL 4, Chicago NL 1
1930 Philadelphia AL 4, St. Louis NL 2
1931 St. Louis NL 4, Philadelphia AL 3
1932 New York AL 4, Chicago NL 0
1933 New York NL 4, Washington AL 1
1934 St. Louis NL 4, Detroit AL 3
1935 Detroit AL 4, Chicago NL 2
1936 New York AL 4, New York NL 2
1937 New York AL 4, New York NL 1
1938 New York AL 4, Chicago NL 0
1939 New York AL 4, Cincinnati NL 0
1940 Cincinnati NL 4, Detroit AL 3
1941 New York AL 4, Brooklyn NL 1
1942 St. Louis NL 4, New York AL 1
1943 New York AL 4, St. Louis NL 1
1944 St. Louis NL 4, St. Louis AL 2
1945 Detroit AL 4, Chicago NL 3
1946 St. Louis NL 4, Boston AL 3
1947 New York AL 4, Brooklyn NL 3
1948 Cleveland AL 4, Boston NL 2
1949 New York AL 4, Brooklyn NL 1
1950 New York AL 4, Philadelphia NL 0
1951 New York AL 4, New York NL 2
1952 New York AL 4, Brooklyn NL 3
1953 New York AL 4, Brooklyn NL 2
1954 New York NL 4, Cleveland AL 0
1955 Brooklyn NL 4, New York AL 3
1956 New York AL 4, Brooklyn NL 3
1957 Milwaukee NL 4, New York AL 3
1958 New York AL 4, Milwaukee NL 3
1959 Los Angeles NL 4, Chicago AL 2
1960 Pittsburgh NL 4, New York AL 3
1961 New York AL 4, Cincinnati NL 1
1962 New York AL 4, San Francisco NL 3
1963 Los Angeles NL 4, New York AL 0
1964 St. Louis NL 4, New York AL 3
1965 Los Angeles NL 4, Minnesota AL 3
1966 Baltimore AL 4, Los Angeles NL 0
1967 St. Louis NL 4, Boston AL 3
1968 Detroit AL 4, St. Louis NL 3
1969 New York NL 4, Baltimore AL 1
1970 Baltimore AL 4, Cincinnati NL 1
1971 Pittsburgh NL 4, Baltimore AL 3
1972 Oakland AL 4, Cincinnati NL 3
1973 Oakland AL 4, New York NL 3
1974 Oakland AL 4, Los Angeles NL 1
1975 Cincinnati NL 4, Boston AL 3
1976 Cincinnati NL 4, New York AL 0
1977 New York AL 4, Los Angeles NL 2
1978 New York AL 4, Los Angeles NL 2
1979 Pittsburgh NL 4, Baltimore AL 3
1980 Philadelphia NL 4, Kansas City AL 2
1981 Los Angeles NL 4, New York AL 2
1982 St. Louis NL 4, Milwaukee AL 3
1983 Baltimore AL 4, Philadelphia NL 1
1984 Detroit AL 4, San Diego NL 1
1985 Kansas City AL 4, St. Louis NL 3
1986 New York NL 4, Boston AL 3
1987 Minnesota AL 4, St. Louis NL 3
1988 Los Angeles NL 4, Oakland AL 1
1989 Oakland AL 4, San Francisco NL 0
1990 Cincinnati NL 4, Oakland AL 0
1991 Minnesota AL 4, Atlanta NL 3
1992 Toronto AL 4, Atlanta NL 2
1993 Toronto AL 4, Philadelphia NL 2
1994 No series
1995 Atlanta NL 4, Cleveland AL 2
1996 New York AL 4, Atlanta NL 2
1997 Florida NL 4, Cleveland AL 3
1998 New York AL 4, San Diego NL 0
1999 New York AL 4, Atlanta NL 0
2000 New York AL 4, New York NL 1
2001 Arizona NL 4, New York AL 3
2002 Anaheim AL 4, San Francisco NL 3
2003 Florida NL 4, New York AL 2
2004 Boston AL 4, St. Louis NL 0

World Series MVP

Year	Player, Position, Team
1955	Johnny Podres, p, Brooklyn
1956	Don Larsen, p, New York, AL
1957	Lew Burdette, p, Milwaukee, NL
1958	Bob Turley, p, NY AL
1959	Larry Sherry, p, LA
1960[1]	Bobby Richardson, 2b, NY, AL
1961	Whitey Ford, p, NY, AL
1962	Ralph Terry, p, NY, AL
1963	Sandy Koufax, p, Los Angeles, NL
1964	Bob Gibson, p, St. Louis
1965	Sandy Koufax, p, Los Angeles, NL
1966	Frank Robinson, of, Baltimore
1967	Bob Gibson, p, St. Louis
1968	Mickey Lolich, p, Detroit
1969	Donn Clendenon, 1b, NY, NL
1970	Brooks Robinson, 3b, Baltimore
1971	Roberto Clemente, of, Pittsburgh
1972	Gene Tenace, c, Oakland
1973	Reggie Jackson, of, Oakland
1974	Rollie Fingers, p, Oakland
1975	Pete Rose, 3b, Cincinnati
1976	Johnny Bench, c, Cincinnati
1977	Reggie Jackson, of, NY, AL
1978	Bucky Dent, ss, NY, AL
1979	Willie Stargell, 1b, Pittsburgh
1980	Mike Schmidt, 3b, Philadelphia
1981	Ron Cey, 3b, LA
	Pedro Guerrero, of, LA
	Steve Yeager, c, LA
1982	Darrell Porter, c, St. Louis
1983	Rick Dempsey, c, Baltimore
1984	Alan Trammell, ss, Detroit
1985	Bret Saberhagen, p, Kansas City
1986	Ray Knight, 3b, NY, NL
1987	Frank Viola, p, Minnesota
1988	Orel Hershiser, p, LA
1989	Dave Stewart, p, Oakland
1990	Jose Rijo, p, Cincinnati
1991	Jack Morris, p, Minnesota
1992	Pat Borders, c, Toronto
1993	Paul Molitor, dh, Toronto
1994	no series
1995	Tom Glavine, p, Atlanta
1996	John Wetteland, p, NY, AL
1997	Livan Hernandez, p, Florida
1998	Scott Brosius, 3b, NY, AL
1999	Mariano Rivera, p, NY, AL
2000	Derek Jeter, ss, NY, AL
2001	Curt Schilling, p, Arizona
	Randy Johnson, p, Arizona
2002	Troy Glaus, 3b, Anaheim
2003	Josh Beckett, p, Florida
2004	Manny Ramirez, of, Boston

(1) Bobby Richardson won the MVP although Pittsburgh beat New York.

World Series Won-Lost Records, by Franchise[1]

Team	Wins	Losses
New York Yankees	26	13
Philadelphia/Kansas City/Oakland A's	9	5
St. Louis Cardinals	9	7
Boston Red Sox	6	4
Brooklyn/Los Angeles Dodgers	6	12
Pittsburgh Pirates	5	2
Cincinnati Reds	5	4
New York/San Francisco Giants	5	12
Detroit Tigers	4	5
Washington Senators/Minnesota Twins	3	3
St. Louis Browns/Baltimore Orioles	3	4
Boston/Milwaukee/Atlanta Braves	3	6
Florida Marlins	2	0
Toronto Blue Jays	2	0
New York Mets	2	2
Chicago White Sox	2	2
Cleveland Indians	2	3
Chicago Cubs	2	8
LA/California/Anaheim/LA Angels	1	0
Arizona Diamondbacks	1	0
Kansas City Royals	1	1
Philadelphia Phillies	1	4
Seattle Pilots/Milwaukee Brewers	0	1
San Diego Padres	0	2

(1) Through 2004.

All-Time Major League Leaders

(**Source:** www.mlb.com; *player active in 2005 season)

Games		At Bats		Runs Batted In		Runs	
Pete Rose	3,562	Pete Rose	14,053	Hank Aaron	2,297	Rickey Henderson	2,295
Carl Yastrzemski	3,308	Hank Aaron	12,364	Babe Ruth	2,213	Ty Cobb	2,245
Hank Aaron	3,298	Carl Yastrzemski	11,988	Cap Anson	2,076	Hank Aaron	2,174
Rickey Henderson	3,081	Cal Ripken Jr.	11,551	Lou Gehrig	1,995	Babe Ruth	2,174
Ty Cobb	3,035	Ty Cobb	11,429	Stan Musial	1,951	Pete Rose	2,165
Eddie Murray	3,026	Eddie Murray	11,336	Ty Cobb	1,938	Barry Bonds*	2,078
Stan Musial	3,026	Robin Yount	11,008	Jimmie Foxx	1,922	Willie Mays	2,062
Cal Ripken Jr.	3,001	Dave Winfield	11,003	Eddie Murray	1,917	Cap Anson	1,996
Willie Mays	2,992	Stan Musial	10,972	Willie Mays	1,903	Stan Musial	1,949
Dave Winfield	2,973	Rickey Henderson	10,961	Mel Ott	1,860	Lou Gehrig	1,888

Stolen Bases

Rickey Henderson	1,406
Lou Brock	938
Billy Hamilton	912
Ty Cobb	892
Tim Raines	808
Vince Coleman	752
Eddie Collins	745
Max Carey	738
Honus Wagner	722
Joe Morgan	689

Strikeouts

Nolan Ryan	5,714
Roger Clemens*	4,502
Randy Johnson*	4,372
Steve Carlton	4,136
Bert Blyleven	3,701
Tom Seaver	3,640
Don Sutton	3,574
Gaylord Perry	3,534
Walter Johnson	3,508
Phil Niekro	3,342

Triples

Sam Crawford	309
Ty Cobb	297
Honus Wagner	252
Jake Beckley	243
Roger Connor	233
Tris Speaker	222
Fred Clarke	220
Dan Brouthers	205
Joe Kelley	194
Paul Waner	191

Saves

Lee Smith	478
Trevor Hoffman*	436
John Franco*	424
Dennis Eckersley	390
Mariano Rivera*	379
Jeff Reardon	367
Randy Myers	347
Rollie Fingers	341
John Wetteland	330
Roberto Hernandez	324
Troy Percival*	324

Batting Average

Ty Cobb	.367
Rogers Hornsby	.358
Ed Delahanty	.346
Tris Speaker	.345
Billy Hamilton	.344
Ted Williams	.344
Dan Brouthers	.342
Harry Heilmann	.342
Babe Ruth	.342
Willie Keeler	.341
Bill Terry	.341

Shutouts

Walter Johnson	110
Grover Alexander	90
Christy Mathewson	79
Cy Young	76
Eddie Plank	69
Warren Spahn	63
Nolan Ryan	61
Tom Seaver	61
Bert Blyleven	60
Don Sutton	58

Walks

Barry Bonds*	2,311
Rickey Henderson	2,190
Babe Ruth	2,062
Ted Williams	2,019
Joe Morgan	1,865
Carl Yastrzemski	1,845
Mickey Mantle	1,733
Mel Ott	1,708
Eddie Yost	1,614
Darrell Evans	1,605

Losses

Cy Young	316
Jim Galvin	310
Nolan Ryan	292
Walter Johnson	279
Phil Niekro	274
Gaylord Perry	265
Don Sutton	256
Jack Powell	254
Eppa Rixey	251
Bert Blyleven	250

All-Time Home Run Leaders

(**Source:** www.mlb.com; *player active in 2005 season)

Hank Aaron	755
Babe Ruth	714
Barry Bonds*	708
Willie Mays	660
Sammy Sosa*	588
Frank Robinson	586
Mark McGwire	583
Harmon Killebrew	573
Rafael Palmeiro*	569
Reggie Jackson	563
Mike Schmidt	548
Ken Griffey Jr.*	536
Mickey Mantle	536
Jimmie Foxx	534
Willie McCovey	521
Ted Williams	521
Ernie Banks	512
Ed Mathews	512
Mel Ott	511
Eddie Murray	504
Lou Gehrig	493
Fred McGriff*	493
Stan Musial	475
Willie Stargell	475
Dave Winfield	465
Jose Canseco	462
Carl Yastrzemski	452
Jeff Bagwell*	449
Gary Sheffield*	449
Frank Thomas*	448
Dave Kingman	442
Andre Dawson	438
Manny Ramirez*	390
Juan Gonzalez*	434
Cal Ripken Jr.	431
Jim Thome*	430
Alex Rodriguez*	429
Billy Williams	426
Darrell Evans	414
Duke Snider	407
Andres Galarraga	399
Al Kaline	399
Dale Murphy	398
Mike Piazza*	397
Joe Carter	396
Graig Nettles	390
Johnny Bench	389
Dwight Evans	385
Harold Baines	384
Frank Howard	382
Jim Rice	382

Players With 3,000 Major League Hits

(**Source:** www.mlb.com; *player active in 2005 season)

Pete Rose	4,256
Ty Cobb	4,189
Hank Aaron	3,771
Stan Musial	3,630
Tris Speaker	3,514
Carl Yastrzemski	3,419
Cap Anson	3,418
Honus Wagner	3,415
Paul Molitor	3,319
Eddie Collins	3,315
Willie Mays	3,283
Eddie Murray	3,255
Nap Lajoie	3,242
Cal Ripken Jr.	3,184
George Brett	3,154
Paul Waner	3,152
Robin Yount	3,142
Tony Gwynn	3,141
Dave Winfield	3,110
Rickey Henderson	3,055
Rod Carew	3,053
Lou Brock	3,023
Rafael Palmeiro*	3,020
Wade Boggs	3,010
Al Kaline	3,007
Roberto Clemente	3,000

Pitchers With 300 Major League Wins

(**Source:** www.mlb.com; *player active in 2005 season)

Cy Young	511
Walter Johnson	417
Grover Alexander	373
Christy Mathewson	373
Jim Galvin	365
Warren Spahn	363
Kid Nichols	361
Tim Keefe	342
Roger Clemens*	341
Steve Carlton	329
John Clarkson	328
Eddie Plank	326
Nolan Ryan	324
Don Sutton	324
Greg Maddux*	318
Phil Niekro	318
Gaylord Perry	314
Tom Seaver	311
Charley Radbourn	309
Mickey Welch	307
Lefty Grove	300
Early Wynn	300

All-Time Major League Single-Season Leaders

(**Source:** www.mlb.com; *player active in 2005 season; records for "modern" era beginning 1901)

Home Runs

Barry Bonds* (2001)	73
Mark McGwire (1998)	70
Sammy Sosa* (1998)	66
Mark McGwire (1999)	65
Sammy Sosa* (2001)	64

Runs

Babe Ruth (1921)	177
Lou Gehrig (1936)	167
Lou Gehrig (1931)	163
Babe Ruth (1928)	163
Chuck Klein (1930)	158
Babe Ruth (1920, 1927)	158

Hits

Ichiro Suzuki* (2004)	262
George Sisler (1920)	257
Lefty O'Doul (1929)	254
Bill Terry (1930)	254
Al Simmons (1925)	253

Runs Batted In

Hack Wilson (1930)	191
Lou Gehrig (1931)	184
Hank Greenberg (1937)	183
Jimmie Foxx (1938)	175
Lou Gehrig (1927)	175

Batting Average

Nap Lajoie (1901)	.426
Rogers Hornsby (1924)	.424
George Sisler (1922)	.420
Ty Cobb (1911)	.420
Ty Cobb (1912)	.410

Stolen Bases

Rickey Henderson (1982)	130
Lou Brock (1974)	118
Vince Coleman (1985)	110
Vince Coleman (1987)	109
Rickey Henderson (1983)	108

Walks (Batter)

Barry Bonds* (2004)	232
Barry Bonds* (2002)	198
Barry Bonds* (2001)	177
Babe Ruth (1923)	170
Mark McGwire (1998)	162
Ted Williams (1947, 1949)	162

Strikeouts (Batter)

Adam Dunn* (2004)	195
Bobby Bonds (1970)	189
Jose Hernandez* (2002)	188
Bobby Bonds (1969)	187
Preston Wilson* (2000)	187
Rob Deer (1987)	186

Earned Run Average

Dutch Leonard (1914)	0.96
Mordecai Brown (1906)	1.04
Bob Gibson (1968)	1.12
Walter Johnson (1913)	1.14
Christy Mathewson (1909)	1.14

Wins

Jack Chesbro (1904)	41
Ed Walsh (1908)	40
Christy Mathewson (1908)	37
Walter Johnson (1913)	36
Joe McGinnity (1904)	35

Strikeouts

Nolan Ryan (1973)	383
Sandy Koufax (1965)	382
Randy Johnson* (2001)	372
Nolan Ryan (1974)	367
Randy Johnson* (1999)	364

Saves

Bobby Thigpen (1990)	57
Eric Gagne* (2003)	55
John Smoltz* (2002)	55
Trevor Hoffman* (1998)	53
Randy Myers (1993)	53
Mariano Rivera* (2004)	53

Official Major League Perfect Games Since 1900

Date	Pitcher	Teams
5/5/04	Cy Young	Boston 3 vs. Phil. 0 (AL)
10/2/08	Addie Joss	Clev. 1 vs. Chicago 0 (AL)
4/30/22	Charlie Robertson	Chicago 2 at Detroit 0 (AL)
10/8/56	Don Larsen	N.Y. 2 vs. Brooklyn 0 (AL)*
6/21/64	Jim Bunning	Phil. 6 at N.Y. 0 (NL)
9/9/65	Sandy Koufax	L.A. 1 vs. Chicago 0 (NL)
5/8/68	Catfish Hunter	Oakland 4 vs. Minn.0 (AL)
5/15/81	Len Barker	Clev. 3 vs. Toronto 0 (AL)
9/30/84	Mike Witt	Calif.1 at Texas 0 (AL)
9/16/88	Tom Browning	Cincinnati 1 vs. L.A. 0 (NL)
7/28/91	Dennis Martinez	Montreal 2 vs. L.A. 0 (NL)
7/28/94	Kenny Rogers	Texas 4 vs. California 0 (AL)
5/17/98	David Wells	N.Y. 4 vs. Minn. 0 (AL)
7/18/99	David Cone	N.Y. 6 vs. Montreal 0 (AL)
5/18/04	Randy Johnson	Ariz. 2 vs. Atlanta 0 (NL)

*World Series game

Most Career Major League No-Hitters

No.	Pitcher
7	Nolan Ryan
4	Sandy Koufax
3	Larry Corcoran, Bob Feller, Cy Young
2	Jim Bunning, Steve Busby, Carl Erskine, Bob Forsch, Pud Galvin, Ken Holtzman, Randy Johnson, Addie Joss, Dutch Leonard, Jim Maloney, Christy Mathewson, Hideo Nomo, Allie Reynolds, Frank Smith, Warren Spahn, Bill Stoneman, Virgil Trucks, Johnny Vander Meer, Ed Walsh, Don Wilson

All-Star Baseball Games, 1933-2005

Year	Winner, Score	Host team
1933*	American, 4-2	Chicago (AL)
1934*	American, 9-7	New York (NL)
1935*	American, 4-1	Cleveland
1936*	National, 4-3	Boston (NL)
1937*	American, 8-3	Washington
1938*	National, 4-1	Cincinnati
1939*	American, 3-1	New York (AL)
1940*	National, 4-0	St. Louis (NL)
1941*	American, 7-5	Detroit
1942	American, 3-1	New York (NL)
1943	American, 5-3	Philadelphia (AL)
1944	National, 7-1	Pittsburgh
1945	(Not played)	
1946*	American, 12-0	Boston (AL)
1947*	American, 2-1	Chicago (NL)
1948*	American, 5-2	St. Louis (AL)
1949*	American, 11-7	Brooklyn
1950*	National, 4-3[1]	Chicago (AL)
1951*	National, 8-3	Detroit
1952*	National, 3-2	Philadelphia (NL)
1953*	National, 5-1	Cincinnati
1954*	American, 11-9	Cleveland
1955*	National, 6-5[2]	Milwaukee
1956*	National, 7-3	Washington
1957*	American, 6-5	St. Louis
1958*	American, 4-3	Baltimore
1959*	National, 5-4	Pittsburgh
1959*	American, 5-3	Los Angeles
1960*	National, 5-3	Kansas City
1960*	National, 6-0	New York (AL)
1961*	National, 5-4[3]	San Francisco
1961*	Called–rain, 1-1	Boston
1962*	National, 3-1[3]	Washington
1962*	American, 9-4	Chicago (NL)
1963*	National, 5-3	Cleveland
1964*	National, 7-4	New York (NL)
1965*	National, 6-5	Minnesota
1966*	National, 2-1[3]	St. Louis
1967*	National, 2-1[4]	California
1968	National, 1-0	Houston
1969*	National, 9-3	Washington
1970	National, 5-4[2]	Cincinnati
1971	American, 6-4	Detroit
1972	National, 4-3[3]	Atlanta
1973	National, 7-1	Kansas City
1974	National, 7-2	Pittsburgh
1975	National, 6-3	Milwaukee
1976	National, 7-1	Philadelphia
1977	National, 7-5	New York (AL)
1978	National, 7-3	San Diego
1979	National, 7-6	Seattle
1980	National, 4-2	Los Angeles
1981	National, 5-4	Cleveland
1982	National, 4-1	Montreal
1983	American, 13-3	Chicago (AL)
1984	National, 3-1	San Francisco
1985	National, 6-1	Minnesota
1986	American, 3-2	Houston
1987	National, 2-0[5]	Oakland
1988	American, 2-1	Cincinnati
1989	American, 5-3	California
1990	American, 2-0	Chicago (NL)
1991	American, 4-2	Toronto
1992	American, 13-6	San Diego
1993	American, 9-3	Baltimore
1994	National, 8-7[3]	Pittsburgh
1995	National, 3-2	Texas
1996	National, 6-0	Philadelphia
1997	American, 3-1	Cleveland
1998	American, 13-8	Colorado
1999	American, 4-1	Boston
2000	American, 6-3	Atlanta
2001	American, 4-1	Seattle
2002	Tie, 7-7[6]	Milwaukee
2003	American, 7-6[7]	Chicago (AL)
2004	American, 9-4	Houston
2005	American, 7-5	Detroit

*Denotes day game. (1) 14 innings. (2) 12 innings. (3) 10 innings. (4) 15 innings. (5) 13 innings. (6) Commissioner's decision, game called in the 11th inning when both teams ran out of pitchers. (7) Under rule change beginning in 2003, league winning All-Star games earned World Series home-field advantage.

Major League Franchise Shifts and Additions

1953—Boston Braves (NL) became Milwaukee Braves.

1954—St. Louis Browns (AL) became Baltimore Orioles.

1955—Philadelphia Athletics (AL) became Kansas City Athletics.

1958—New York Giants (NL) became San Francisco Giants.

1958—Brooklyn Dodgers (NL) became L.A. Dodgers.

1961—Washington Senators (AL) became Minnesota Twins.

1961—L.A. Angels (renamed California Angels in 1965 and Anaheim Angels in 1997) enfranchised by the American League.

1961—Washington Senators enfranchised by the American League (a new team, replacing the former Washington club, whose franchise was moved to Minneapolis-St. Paul).

1962—Houston Colt .45's (renamed the Houston Astros in 1965) enfranchised by the National League.

1962—New York Mets enfranchised by the National League.

1966—Milwaukee Braves (NL) became Atlanta Braves.

1968—Kansas City Athletics (AL) became Oakland Athletics.

1969—Kansas City Royals and Seattle Pilots enfranchised by the American League; Montreal Expos and San Diego Padres enfranchised by the National League.

1970—Seattle Pilots became Milwaukee Brewers.

1971—Washington Senators became Texas Rangers (Dallas-Fort Worth area).

1977—Toronto Blue Jays and Seattle Mariners enfranchised by the American League.

1993—Colorado Rockies (Denver) and Florida Marlins (Miami) enfranchised by the National League.

1998—Tampa Bay Devil Rays began play in the American League; Arizona Diamondbacks (Phoenix) began play in the National League (both teams enfranchised in 1995). Milwaukee Brewers moved from the AL to the NL.

2005—Montreal Expos (NL) became Washington Nationals; Anaheim Angels became Los Angeles Angels of Anaheim.

Baseball Stadiums[1]

National League

Team	Stadium (year opened)	Surface	Home run distances (ft.) LF	Center	RF	Seating capacity
Arizona Diamondbacks	Chase Field (1998)	Grass	330	407	334	49,033
Atlanta Braves	Turner Field (1997)	Grass	335	401	330	50,096
Chicago Cubs	Wrigley Field (1914)	Grass	355	400	353	38,902
Cincinnati Reds	Great American Ballpark (2003)	Grass	328	404	325	42,059
Colorado Rockies	Coors Field (1995)	Grass	347	415	350	50,445
Florida Marlins	Dolphins Stadium (1987)	Grass	330	434	345	47,662
Houston Astros	Minute Maid Park (2000)	Grass	315	435	326	40,950
Los Angeles Dodgers	Dodger Stadium (1962)	Grass	330	395	330	56,000
Milwaukee Brewers	Miller Park (2001)	Grass	344	400	345	42,400
New York Mets	Shea Stadium (1964)	Grass	338	410	338	55,601

National League

Team	Stadium (year opened)	Surface	Home run distances (ft.) LF	Center	RF	Seating capacity
Philadelphia Phillies	Citizens Bank Park (2004)	Grass	329	401	330	43,500
Pittsburgh Pirates	PNC Park (2001)	Grass	325	399	320	38,365
St. Louis Cardinals	Busch Stadium (1966)	Grass	330	402	330	50,345
San Diego Padres	PETCO Park (2004)	Grass	334	396	322	42,500
San Francisco Giants	SBC Park (2000)	Grass	335	404	307	41,584
Washington Nationals	Robert F. Kennedy Memorial Stadium (1961)	Grass	335	410	335	56,000
American League						
Baltimore Orioles	Oriole Park at Camden Yards (1992)	Grass	333	400	318	48,876
Boston Red Sox	Fenway Park (1912)	Grass	310	420	302	35,095
Chicago White Sox	U.S. Cellular Field (1991)	Grass	330	400	335	47,098
Cleveland Indians	Jacobs Field (1994)	Grass	325	405	325	43,368
Detroit Tigers	Comerica Park (2000)	Grass	345	420	330	40,000
Kansas City Royals	Kauffman Stadium (1973)	Grass	330	410	330	40,793
Los Angeles Angels	Angel Stadium of Anaheim (1966)	Grass	330	406	330	45,050
Minnesota Twins	Hubert H. Humphrey Metrodome (1982)	Artificial	343	408	327	48,678
New York Yankees	Yankee Stadium (1923)	Grass	318	408	314	57,478
Oakland A's	McAfee Coliseum (1968)	Grass	330	400	330	43,662
Seattle Mariners	Safeco Field (1999)	Grass	331	405	327	47,116
Tampa Bay Devil Rays	Tropicana Field (1990)	Artificial	315	404	322	45,000
Texas Rangers	Ameriquest Field in Arlington (1994)	Grass	332	400	325	49,200
Toronto Blue Jays	Rogers Centre (1989)	Artificial	328	400	328	50,516

(1) As of 2005 season.

Little League World Series

The Little League World Series is played annually in Williamsport, PA.

Year	Winning / Losing Team	Score
1947	Williamsport, PA; Lock Haven, PA	16-7
1948	Lock Haven, PA; St. Petersburg, FL	6-5
1949	Hammonton, NJ; Pensacola, FL	5-0
1950	Houston, TX; Bridgeport, CT	2-1
1951	Stamford, CT; Austin, TX	3-0
1952	Norwalk, CT; Monongahela, PA	4-3
1953	Birmingham, AL; Schenectady, NY	1-0
1954	Schenectady, NY; Colton, CA	7-5
1955	Morrisville, PA; Merchantville, NJ	4-3
1956	Roswell, NM; Delaware, NJ	3-1
1957	Mexico; La Mesa, CA	4-0
1958	Mexico; Kankakee, IL	10-1
1959	Hamtramck, MI; Auburn, CA	12-0
1960	Levittown, PA; Ft. Worth, TX	5-0
1961	El Cajon, CA; El Campo, TX	4-2
1962	San Jose, CA; Kankakee, IL	3-0
1963	Granada Hills, CA; Stratford, CT	2-1
1964	Staten Island, NY; Mexico	4-0
1965	Windsor Locks, CT; Ontario, Canada	3-1
1966	Houston, TX; W. New York, NJ	8-2
1967	Tokyo, Japan; Chicago, IL	4-1
1968	Osaka, Japan; Richmond, VA	1-0
1969	Taiwan; Santa Clara, CA	5-0
1970	Wayne, NJ; Campbell, CA	2-0
1971	Taiwan; Gary, IN	12-3
1972	Taiwan; Hammond, IN	6-0
1973	Taiwan; Tucson, AZ	12-0
1974	Taiwan; Red Bluff, CA	12-1
1975	Lakewood, NJ; Tampa, FL	4-3
1976	Tokyo, Japan; Campbell, CA	10-3
1977	Taiwan; El Cajon, CA	7-2
1978	Taiwan; Danville, CA	11-1
1979	Taiwan; Campbell, CA	2-1
1980	Taiwan; Tampa, FL	4-3
1981	Taiwan; Tampa, FL	4-2
1982	Kirkland, WA; Taiwan	6-0
1983	Marietta, GA; Dominican Rep.	3-1
1984	South Korea; Altamonte Springs, FL	6-2
1985	South Korea; Mexico	7-1
1986	Taiwan; Tucson, AZ	12-0
1987	Chinese Taipei; Irvine, CA	21-1
1988	Chinese Taipei; Pearl City, HI	10-0
1989	Trumbull, CT; Chinese Taipei	5-2
1990	Chinese Taipei; Shippensburg, PA	9-0
1991	Chinese Taipei; Danville, CA	11-0
1992	Long Beach, CA; Philippines*	6-0
1993	Long Beach, CA; Panama	3-2
1994	Venezuela; Northridge, CA	4-3
1995	Taiwan; Spring, TX	17-3
1996	Taiwan; Cranston, RI	13-3
1997	Mexico; Mission Viejo, CA	5-4
1998	Toms River, NJ; Japan	12-9
1999	Japan; Phenix City, AL	5-0
2000	Venezuela; Bellaire, TX	3-2
2001	Japan; Apopka, FL	2-1
2002	Louisville, KY; Japan	1-0
2003	Japan; East Boynton Beach, FL	10-1
2004	Curacao; Conejo Valley of Thousand Oaks, CA	5-2
2005	Ewa Beach HI; Curacao	7-6

*Philippines won 15-4, but was disqualified for using ineligible players. Long Beach was awarded title by forfeit 6-0 (1 run per inning).

NCAA Baseball Division I Champions

1947	California
1948	Southern California
1949	Texas
1950	Texas
1951	Oklahoma
1952	Holy Cross
1953	Michigan
1954	Missouri
1955	Wake Forest
1956	Minnesota
1957	California
1958	USC
1959	Oklahoma St.
1960	Minnesota
1961	USC
1962	Michigan
1963	USC
1964	Minnesota
1965	Arizona St.
1966	Ohio St.
1967	Arizona St.
1968	USC
1969	Arizona St.
1970	USC
1971	USC
1972	USC
1973	USC
1974	USC
1975	Texas
1976	Arizona
1977	Arizona St.
1978	USC
1979	Cal. St.-Fullerton
1980	Arizona
1981	Arizona St.
1982	Miami (FL)
1983	Texas
1984	Cal. St.-Fullerton
1985	Miami (FL)
1986	Arizona
1987	Stanford
1988	Stanford
1989	Wichita St.
1990	Georgia
1991	LSU
1992	Pepperdine
1993	LSU
1994	Oklahoma
1995	Cal. St.-Fullerton
1996	LSU
1997	LSU
1998	USC
1999	Miami (FL)
2000	LSU
2001	Miami (FL)
2002	Texas
2003	Rice
2004	Cal. St.-Fullerton
2005	Texas

NCAA Women's Softball Division I Champions

1982	UCLA
1983	Texas A&M
1984	UCLA
1985	UCLA
1986	Cal St. Fullerton
1987	Texas A&M
1988	UCLA
1989	UCLA
1990	UCLA
1991	Arizona
1992	UCLA
1993	Arizona
1994	Arizona
1995	UCLA
1996	Arizona
1997	Arizona
1998	Fresno St.
1999	UCLA
2000	Oklahoma
2001	Arizona
2002	California
2003	UCLA
2004	UCLA
2005	Michigan

NATIONAL BASKETBALL ASSOCIATION

2004-05 Season: Spurs Regain Title, Pistons Fire Brown, Brawl in Detroit, Divisions Realigned

The San Antonio Spurs, June 23, defeated the Detroit Pistons, the defending champions, 4 games to 3, in the 2005 NBA Finals. Spurs guard Tim Duncan was named MVP of the Finals for the 3rd time. The Pistons released coach Larry Brown, replacing him with Flip Saunders. On July 28, 2005, Brown signed on to coach the New York Knicks for $10 mil per season, making him the highest-paid coach in league history. Phoenix Suns guard Steve Nash was named MVP of the 2004-2005 NBA regular season, the first Canadian to win the award, and Philadelphia 76ers guard Allen Iverson led the league in scoring, averaging 30.7 points per game.

A brawl broke out between Indiana Pacers players and Detroit Pistons fans—on the court and in the stands—at a game Nov. 19, 2004, in Auburn Hills, MI. Nine players were banned from playing for more than 130 games in all. Ron Artest received the longest suspension in NBA history—73 games. Pacers Artest, Stephen Jackson, and Jermaine O'Neal also pleaded guilty to assault charges and were sentenced to one year of probation and 60 hours of community service Sept. 23, 2005. The league also issued new arena security rules to all 30 teams. On May 2, Houston Rockets coach Jeff Van Gundy was fined $100,000—the largest fine ever handed out to an NBA coach—for comments he made about NBA officials.

The league instituted a new division realignment with the 2004-05 season. A 3rd division was added to each of the 2 conferences—the Southeast Divison in the Eastern Conference and the Southwest Division in the Western Conference. In the 2005 draft, Andrew Bynum, a high school player from Metuchen, NJ, became the youngest player ever drafted by the NBA (signed by the L.A. Lakers), at 17 years, 8 months.

Final Standings, 2004-05 Season

(playoff seedings in parentheses; in each conference the 3 division winners automatically get the number 1, 2, and 3 seeds)

Eastern Conference

Atlantic Division

	W	L	Pct	GB
Boston (3)	45	37	.549	—
Philadelphia (7)	43	39	.524	2
New Jersey (8)	42	40	.512	3
Toronto (8)	33	49	.402	12
New York	33	49	.402	12

Central Division

	W	L	Pct	GB
Detroit (2)	54	28	.659	—
Chicago (4)	47	35	.573	7
Indiana (6)	44	38	.537	10
Cleveland	42	40	.512	12
Milwaukee	30	52	.366	24

Southeast Division

	W	L	Pct	GB
Miami (1)	59	23	.720	—
Washington (5)	45	37	.549	14
Orlando	36	46	.439	23
Charlotte	18	64	.220	41
Atlanta	13	69	.159	46

Western Conference

Northwest Division

	W	L	Pct	GB
Seattle (3)	52	30	.634	—
Denver (7)	49	33	.598	3
Minnesota	44	38	.537	8
Portland	27	55	.329	25
Utah	26	56	.317	26

Pacific Division

	W	L	Pct	GB
Phoenix (1)	62	20	.756	—
Sacramento (6)	50	32	.610	12
L.A. Clippers	37	45	.451	25
L.A. Lakers	34	48	.415	28
Golden State	34	48	.415	28

Southwest Division

	W	L	Pct	GB
San Antonio (2)	59	23	.720	—
Dallas (4)	58	24	.707	1
Houston (5)	51	31	.622	8
Memphis (8)	45	37	.549	14
New Orleans	18	64	.220	41

NBA Regular Season Individual Highs in 2004-05

Minutes, game: 57, Richard Jefferson, New Jersey v. Chicago, Nov. 10.
Points, game: 60, Allen Iverson, Philadelphia v. Orlando, Feb. 12.
Field goals, game: 20, Damon Stoudamire, Portland v. New Orleans, Jan. 14; Amare Stoudemire, Phoenix v. Portland, Jan. 2.
FG attempts, game: 36, LeBron James, Cleveland v. Toronto, Mar. 20, Allen Iverson, Philadelphia v. Orlando, Feb. 12, Tracy McGrady, Houston v. Dallas, Dec. 2.
3-pointers, game: 12, Donyell Marshall, Toronto v. Philadelphia, Mar. 13.
3-pt. attempts, game: 19, Donyell Marshall, Toronto v. Philadelphia, Mar. 13.
Free throws, game: 24, Allen Iverson, Philadelphia, Mar. 3.
FT attempts, game: 28, Shaquille O'Neal, Miami v. L.A. Clippers, Jan. 14.
Total rebounds, game: 26, Erick Dampier, Dallas v. Philadelphia, Jan. 29.
Assists, game: 20, Brevin Knight, Charlotte v. Cleveland, Jan. 11.
Steals, game: 8, Brevin Knight, Charlotte v. Orlando, Mar. 24, Marquis Daniels, Dallas v. Chicago, Dec. 12, Jamaal Tinsley, Indiana v. Detroit, Nov. 19.
Blocks, game: 10, Josh Smith, Atlanta v. Dallas, Dec. 18.
Minutes, season: 2,982, LeBron James, Cleveland.
Off. rebounds, season: 299, Zydrunas Ilgauskas, Cleveland.
Def. rebounds, season: 861, Kevin Garnett, Minnesota.
Personal fouls, season: 296, Zydrunas Ilgauskas, Cleveland.

2005 NBA Playoff Results

Eastern Conference

Washington defeated Chicago 4 games to 2
Indiana defeated Boston 4 games to 3
Detroit defeated Philadelphia 4 games to 1
Miami defeated New Jersey 4 games to 0
Detroit defeated Indiana 4 games to 2
Miami defeated Washington 4 games to 0
Detroit defeated Miami 4 games to 3

Western Conference

Seattle defeated Sacramento 4 games to 1
Dallas defeated Houston 4 games to 3
San Antonio defeated Denver 4 games to 1
Phoenix defeated Memphis 4 games to 0
San Antonio defeated Seattle 4 games to 2
Phoenix defeated Dallas 4 games to 2
San Antonio defeated Phoenix 4 games to 1

Championship

San Antonio defeated Detroit 4 games to 3 [84-69, 97-76, 79-96, 71-102, 96-95 (OT), 86-95, 81-74].

Spurs Unseat Pistons in 2005 Finals

The San Antonio Spurs won their 3rd NBA championship in 7 seasons, hanging on through 7 games to beat the Detroit Pistons, 81-74, in the deciding game in San Antonio, on June 23. The first 4 games of the series were one-sided victories, with 2 games each going to the home team. A more competitive 5th game went into overtime, won by the Spurs, 96-95. The Pistons won game 6. In the 7th and final game, Spurs guard Tim Duncan blasted out in the 2nd half, scoring 17 of his 25 points in the last 18 minutes. The Spurs, coached by Gregg Popovich, were led by Duncan, who averaged 20.6 points and 14.1 rebounds per game in the series, and Olympic gold medalist Manu Ginobili (Argentina), who averaged 18.6 points per game and gave strong performances in Games 1 and 2, besides getting the assist for the winning basket in overtime in Game 5. Duncan was named MVP of the Finals.

NBA Finals Composite Box Scores

Spurs	FG M-A	FT M-A	Reb O-T	Ast	Avg
Tim Duncan	54-129	36-54	33-99	15	20.6
Manu Ginobili	42-85	35-41	8-41	28	18.7
Tony Parker	44-96	7-16	2-17	24	13.9
Robert Horry	24-54	11-15	13-34	15	10.6
Bruce Bowen	19-50	4-6	1-19	14	7.9
Nazr Mohammed	13-30	8-11	20-42	0	4.9
Brent Barry	11-27	4-5	3-15	11	4.6
Beno Udrih	4-11	2-2	2-5	4	2.4
Devin Brown	3-11	4-7	1-6	3	1.8
Glenn Robinson	1-5	0-0	0-3	0	0.7
Rasho Nesterovic	1-2	0-2	3-8	1	0.5
Tony Massenburg	0-3	0-0	0-3	0	0.0

Detroit	FG M-A	FT M-A	Reb O-T	Ast	Avg
Chauncey Billups	46-106	40-44	9-35	44	20.4
Richard Hamilton	49-127	18-24	9-37	18	16.7
Rasheed Wallace	35-80	1-4	13-39	13	10.9
Ben Wallace	33-58	9-21	27-72	7	10.7
Antonio McDyess	33-65	5-9	18-51	7	10.1
Tayshaun Prince	29-76	12-14	12-34	18	10.1
Lindsey Hunter	16-42	7-8	5-13	19	5.6
Carlos Arroyo	5-10	1-2	0-1	3	2.2
Darko Milicic	1-3	0-0	0-2	0	0.7
Darvin Ham	1-2	0-0	3-3	0	0.4
Elden Campbell	0-0	0-0	0-0	1	0.0
Ronald Dupree	0-2	0-0	0-0	0	0.0

NBA Finals MVP

1969 Jerry West, Los Angeles
1970 Willis Reed, New York
1971 Lew Alcindor (Kareem Abdul-Jabbar), Milwaukee
1972 Wilt Chamberlain, Los Angeles
1973 Willis Reed, New York
1974 John Havlicek, Boston
1975 Rick Barry, Golden State
1976 Jo Jo White, Boston
1977 Bill Walton, Portland
1978 Wes Unseld, Washington
1979 Dennis Johnson, Seattle
1980 Magic Johnson, Los Angeles
1981 Cedric Maxwell, Boston
1982 Magic Johnson, Los Angeles
1983 Moses Malone, Philadelphia
1984 Larry Bird, Boston
1985 Kareem Abdul-Jabbar, L.A. Lakers
1986 Larry Bird, Boston
1987 Magic Johnson, L.A. Lakers
1988 James Worthy, L.A. Lakers
1989 Joe Dumars, Detroit
1990 Isiah Thomas, Detroit
1991 Michael Jordan, Chicago
1992 Michael Jordan, Chicago
1993 Michael Jordan, Chicago
1994 Hakeem Olajuwon, Houston
1995 Hakeem Olajuwon, Houston
1996 Michael Jordan, Chicago
1997 Michael Jordan, Chicago
1998 Michael Jordan, Chicago
1999 Tim Duncan, San Antonio
2000 Shaquille O'Neal, L.A. Lakers
2001 Shaquille O'Neal, L.A. Lakers
2002 Shaquille O'Neal, L.A. Lakers
2003 Tim Duncan, San Antonio
2004 Chauncey Billups, Detroit
2005 Tim Duncan, San Antonio

NBA Finals All-Time Statistical Leaders

(at the end of the 2005 NBA season finals; *denotes active in 2004-05)

Scoring Average (Minimum 10 games)

	G	FG	FT	Pts.	Avg
Rick Barry	10	138	87	363	36.3
Michael Jordan	35	438	258	1,176	33.6
*Shaquille O'Neal	24	306	171	783	32.6
Jerry West	55	612	455	1,679	30.5
Bob Pettit	25	241	227	709	28.4
Hakeem Olajuwon	17	187	91	467	27.5
Elgin Baylor	44	442	277	1,161	26.4
Julius Erving	22	216	128	561	25.5
Joe Fulks	11	84	104	272	24.7
Clyde Drexler	15	126	108	367	24.5

Games Played

Bill Russell	70
Sam Jones	64
Kareem Abdul-Jabbar	56
Jerry West	55
Tom Heinsohn	52

Rebounds

Bill Russell	1,718
Wilt Chamberlain	862
Elgin Baylor	593
Kareem Abdul-Jabbar	507
Tom Heinsohn	473

Assists

Magic Johnson	584
Bob Cousy	400
Bill Russell	315
Jerry West	306
Dennis Johnson	228

NBA Scoring Leaders

Year	Scoring champion	Pts	Avg
1947	Joe Fulks, Philadelphia	1,389	23.2
1948	Max Zaslofsky, Chicago	1,007	21.0
1949	George Mikan, Minneapolis	1,698	28.3
1950	George Mikan, Minneapolis	1,865	27.4
1951	George Mikan, Minneapolis	1,932	28.4
1952	Paul Arizin, Philadelphia	1,674	25.4
1953	Neil Johnston, Philadelphia	1,564	22.3
1954	Neil Johnston, Philadelphia	1,759	24.4
1955	Neil Johnston, Philadelphia	1,631	22.7
1956	Bob Pettit, St. Louis	1,849	25.7
1957	Paul Arizin, Philadelphia	1,817	25.6
1958	George Yardley, Detroit	2,001	27.8
1959	Bob Pettit, St. Louis	2,105	29.2
1960	Wilt Chamberlain, Philadelphia	2,707	37.9
1961	Wilt Chamberlain, Philadelphia	3,033	38.4
1962	Wilt Chamberlain, Philadelphia	4,029	50.4
1963	Wilt Chamberlain, San Francisco	3,586	44.8
1964	Wilt Chamberlain, San Francisco	2,948	36.5
1965	Wilt Chamberlain, San Francisco, Phil.	2,534	34.7
1966	Wilt Chamberlain, Philadelphia	2,649	33.5
1967	Rick Barry, San Francisco	2,775	35.6
1968	Dave Bing, Detroit	2,142	27.1
1969	Elvin Hayes, San Diego	2,327	28.4
1970	Jerry West, Los Angeles	2,309	31.2
1971	Lew Alcindor (Kareem Abdul-Jabbar), Milwaukee	2,596	31.7
1972	Kareem Abdul-Jabbar, Milwaukee	2,822	34.8
1973	Nate Archibald, Kans. City-Omaha	2,719	34.0
1974	Bob McAdoo, Buffalo	2,261	30.6
1975	Bob McAdoo, Buffalo	2,831	34.5
1976	Bob McAdoo, Buffalo	2,427	31.1
1977	Pete Maravich, New Orleans	2,273	31.1
1978	George Gervin, San Antonio	2,232	27.2
1979	George Gervin, San Antonio	2,365	29.6
1980	George Gervin, San Antonio	2,585	33.1
1981	Adrian Dantley, Utah	2,452	30.7
1982	George Gervin, San Antonio	2,551	32.3
1983	Alex English, Denver	2,326	28.4
1984	Adrian Dantley, Utah	2,418	30.6
1985	Bernard King, New York	1,809	32.9
1986	Dominique Wilkins, Atlanta	2,366	30.3
1987	Michael Jordan, Chicago	3,041	37.1
1988	Michael Jordan, Chicago	2,868	35.0
1989	Michael Jordan, Chicago	2,633	32.5
1990	Michael Jordan, Chicago	2,753	33.6
1991	Michael Jordan, Chicago	2,580	31.5
1992	Michael Jordan, Chicago	2,404	30.1
1993	Michael Jordan, Chicago	2,541	32.6
1994	David Robinson, San Antonio	2,383	29.8
1995	Shaquille O'Neal, Orlando	2,315	29.3
1996	Michael Jordan, Chicago	2,465	30.4
1997	Michael Jordan, Chicago	2,431	29.6
1998	Michael Jordan, Chicago	2,357	28.7
1999	Allen Iverson, Philadelphia	1,284	26.8
2000	Shaquille O'Neal, L.A. Lakers	2,344	29.7
2001	Allen Iverson, Philadelphia	2,207	31.1
2002	Allen Iverson, Philadelphia	1,883	31.4
2003	Tracy McGrady, Orlando	2,407	32.1
2004	Tracy McGrady, Orlando	1,878	28.0
2005	Allen Iverson, Philadelphia	2,302	30.7

NBA Most Valuable Player

1956 Bob Pettit, St. Louis
1957 Bob Cousy, Boston
1958 Bill Russell, Boston
1959 Bob Pettit, St. Louis
1960 Wilt Chamberlain, Philadelphia
1961 Bill Russell, Boston
1962 Bill Russell, Boston
1963 Bill Russell, Boston
1964 Oscar Robertson, Cincinnati
1965 Bill Russell, Boston
1966 Wilt Chamberlain, Philadelphia
1967 Wilt Chamberlain, Philadelphia

1968 Wilt Chamberlain, Philadelphia
1969 Wes Unseld, Baltimore
1970 Willis Reed, New York
1971 Lew Alcindor (Kareem Abdul-Jabbar), Milwaukee
1972 Kareem Abdul-Jabbar, Milwaukee
1973 Dave Cowens, Boston
1974 Kareem Abdul-Jabbar, Milwaukee
1975 Bob McAdoo, Buffalo
1976 Kareem Abdul-Jabbar, L.A. Lakers
1977 Kareem Abdul-Jabbar, L.A. Lakers
1978 Bill Walton, Portland
1979 Moses Malone, Houston
1980 Kareem Abdul-Jabbar, L.A. Lakers
1981 Julius Erving, Philadelphia
1982 Moses Malone, Houston
1983 Moses Malone, Philadelphia
1984 Larry Bird, Boston
1985 Larry Bird, Boston
1986 Larry Bird, Boston
1987 Magic Johnson, L.A. Lakers
1988 Michael Jordan, Chicago
1989 Magic Johnson, L.A. Lakers
1990 Magic Johnson, L.A. Lakers
1991 Michael Jordan, Chicago
1992 Michael Jordan, Chicago
1993 Charles Barkley, Phoenix
1994 Hakeem Olajuwon, Houston
1995 David Robinson, San Antonio
1996 Michael Jordan, Chicago
1997 Karl Malone, Utah
1998 Michael Jordan, Chicago
1999 Karl Malone, Utah
2000 Shaquille O'Neal, L.A. Lakers
2001 Allen Iverson, Philadelphia
2002 Tim Duncan, San Antonio
2003 Tim Duncan, San Antonio
2004 Kevin Garnett, Minnesota
2005 Steve Nash, Phoenix

NBA Champions, 1947-2005

	Regular season		Playoffs		
Year	Eastern Conference	Western Conference	Champion	Coach	Runner-up
1947	Washington Capitols	Chicago Stags	Philadelphia	Ed Gottlieb	Chicago
1948	Philadelphia Warriors	St. Louis Bombers	Baltimore	Buddy Jeannette	Philadelphia
1949	Washington Capitols	Rochester	Minneapolis	John Kundla	Washington
1950	Syracuse	Minneapolis	Minneapolis	John Kundla	Syracuse
1951	Philadelphia Warriors	Minneapolis	Rochester	Lester Harrison	New York
1952	Syracuse	Rochester	Minneapolis	John Kundla	New York
1953	New York	Minneapolis	Minneapolis	John Kundla	New York
1954	New York	Minneapolis	Minneapolis	John Kundla	Syracuse
1955	Syracuse	Ft. Wayne	Syracuse	Al Cervi	Ft. Wayne
1956	Philadelphia Warriors	Ft. Wayne	Philadelphia	George Senesky	Ft. Wayne
1957	Boston	St. Louis	Boston	Red Auerbach	St. Louis
1958	Boston	St. Louis	St. Louis	Alex Hannum	Boston
1959	Boston	St. Louis	Boston	Red Auerbach	Minneapolis
1960	Boston	St. Louis	Boston	Red Auerbach	St. Louis
1961	Boston	St. Louis	Boston	Red Auerbach	St. Louis
1962	Boston	Los Angeles	Boston	Red Auerbach	Los Angeles
1963	Boston	Los Angeles	Boston	Red Auerbach	Los Angeles
1964	Boston	San Francisco	Boston	Red Auerbach	San Francisco
1965	Boston	Los Angeles	Boston	Red Auerbach	Los Angeles
1966	Philadelphia	Los Angeles	Boston	Red Auerbach	Los Angeles
1967	Philadelphia	San Francisco	Philadelphia	Alex Hannum	San Francisco
1968	Philadelphia	St. Louis	Boston	Bill Russell	Los Angeles
1969	Baltimore	Los Angeles	Boston	Bill Russell	Los Angeles
1970	New York	Atlanta	New York	Red Holzman	Los Angeles

Year	Atlantic	Central	Midwest	Pacific	Champion	Coach	Runner-up
1971	New York	Baltimore	Milwaukee	Los Angeles	Milwaukee	Larry Costello	Baltimore
1972	Boston	Baltimore	Milwaukee	Los Angeles	Los Angeles	Bill Sharman	New York
1973	Boston	Baltimore	Milwaukee	Los Angeles	New York	Red Holzman	Los Angeles
1974	Boston	Capital	Milwaukee	Los Angeles	Boston	Tom Heinsohn	Milwaukee
1975	Boston	Washington	Chicago	Golden State	Golden State	Al Attles	Washington
1976	Boston	Cleveland	Milwaukee	Golden State	Boston	Tom Heinsohn	Phoenix
1977	Philadelphia	Houston	Denver	Los Angeles	Portland	Jack Ramsay	Philadelphia
1978	Philadelphia	San Antonio	Denver	Portland	Washington	Dick Motta	Seattle
1979	Washington	San Antonio	Kansas City	Seattle	Seattle	Len Wilkens	Washington
1980	Boston	Atlanta	Milwaukee	Los Angeles	Los Angeles	Paul Westhead	Philadelphia
1981	Boston	Milwaukee	San Antonio	Phoenix	Boston	Bill Fitch	Houston
1982	Boston	Milwaukee	San Antonio	Los Angeles	Los Angeles	Pat Riley	Philadelphia
1983	Philadelphia	Milwaukee	San Antonio	Los Angeles	Philadelphia	Billy Cunningham	Los Angeles
1984	Boston	Milwaukee	Utah	Los Angeles	Boston	K.C. Jones	Los Angeles
1985	Boston	Milwaukee	Denver	L.A. Lakers	L.A. Lakers	Pat Riley	Boston
1986	Boston	Milwaukee	Houston	L.A. Lakers	Boston	K.C. Jones	Houston
1987	Boston	Atlanta	Dallas	L.A. Lakers	L.A. Lakers	Pat Riley	Boston
1988	Boston	Detroit	Denver	L.A. Lakers	L.A. Lakers	Pat Riley	Detroit
1989	New York	Detroit	Utah	L.A. Lakers	Detroit	Chuck Daly	L.A. Lakers
1990	Philadelphia	Detroit	San Antonio	L.A. Lakers	Detroit	Chuck Daly	Portland
1991	Boston	Chicago	San Antonio	Portland	Chicago	Phil Jackson	L.A. Lakers
1992	Boston	Chicago	Utah	Portland	Chicago	Phil Jackson	Portland
1993	New York	Chicago	Houston	Phoenix	Chicago	Phil Jackson	Phoenix
1994	New York	Atlanta	Houston	Seattle	Houston	Rudy Tomjanovich	New York
1995	Orlando	Indiana	San Antonio	Phoenix	Houston	Rudy Tomjanovich	Orlando
1996	Orlando	Chicago	San Antonio	Seattle	Chicago	Phil Jackson	Seattle
1997	Miami	Chicago	Utah	Seattle	Chicago	Phil Jackson	Utah
1998	Miami	Chicago	Utah	L.A. Lakers	Chicago	Phil Jackson	Utah
1999	Miami	Indiana	San Antonio	Portland	San Antonio	Gregg Popovich	New York
2000	Miami	Indiana	Utah	L.A. Lakers	L.A. Lakers	Phil Jackson	Indiana
2001	Philadelphia	Milwaukee	San Antonio	L.A. Lakers	L.A. Lakers	Phil Jackson	Philadelphia
2002	New Jersey	Detroit	San Antonio	Sacramento	L.A. Lakers	Phil Jackson	New Jersey
2003	New Jersey	Detroit	San Antonio	Sacramento	San Antonio	Gregg Popovich	New Jersey
2004	New Jersey	Indiana	Minnesota	L.A. Lakers	Detroit	Larry Brown	L.A. Lakers

Year	Atlantic	Central	Southeast	Northwest	Pacific	Southwest	Champion	Coach	Runner-up
2005	Boston	Detroit	Miami	Seattle	Phoenix	San Antonio	San Antonio	Gregg Popovich	Detroit

NBA All-League and All-Defensive Teams, 2004-05

All-League Team			All-Defensive Team	
First team	Second team	Position	First team	Second team
Tim Duncan, San Antonio	LeBron James, Cleveland	Forward	Tim Duncan, San Antonio	Tayshaun Prince, Detroit
Dirk Nowitzki, Dallas	Kevin Garnett, Minnesota	Forward	Kevin Garnett, Minnesota	Andrei Kirilenko, Utah
Shaquille O'Neal, Miami	Amaré Stoudemire, Phoenix	Center	Ben Wallace, Detroit	Marcus Camby, Denver
Allen Iverson, Philadelphia	Dwyane Wade, Miami	Guard	Bruce Bowen, San Antonio	Chauncey Billups, Detroit
Steve Nash, Phoenix	Ray Allen, Seattle	Guard	Larry Hughes, Washington	Jason Kidd, New Jersey
		Guard		Dwyane Wade, Miami

NBA Coach of the Year, 1963-2005

1963 Harry Gallatin, St. Louis Hawks
1964 Alex Hannum, San Francisco Warriors
1965 Red Auerbach, Boston Celtics
1966 Dolph Schayes, Philadelphia 76ers
1967 Johnny Kerr, Chicago Bulls
1968 Richie Guerin, St. Louis Hawks
1969 Gene Shue, Baltimore Bullets
1970 Red Holzman, New York Knicks
1971 Dick Motta, Chicago Bulls
1972 Bill Sharman, Los Angeles Lakers
1973 Tom Heinsohn, Boston Celtics
1974 Ray Scott, Detroit Pistons
1975 Phil Johnson, Kansas City-Omaha Kings
1976 Bill Fitch, Cleveland Cavaliers
1977 Tom Nissalke, Houston Rockets
1978 Hubie Brown, Atlanta Hawks
1979 Cotton Fitzsimmons, Kansas City Kings
1980 Bill Fitch, Boston Celtics
1981 Jack McKinney, Indiana Pacers
1982 Gene Shue, Washington Bullets
1983 Don Nelson, Milwaukee Bucks
1984 Frank Layden, Utah Jazz
1985 Don Nelson, Milwaukee Bucks
1986 Mike Fratello, Atlanta Hawks
1987 Mike Schuler, Portland Trail Blazers
1988 Doug Moe, Denver Nuggets
1989 Cotton Fitzsimmons, Phoenix Suns
1990 Pat Riley, Los Angeles Lakers
1991 Don Chaney, Houston Rockets
1992 Don Nelson, Golden State Warriors
1993 Pat Riley, New York Knicks
1994 Lenny Wilkens, Atlanta Hawks
1995 Del Harris, Los Angeles Lakers
1996 Phil Jackson, Chicago Bulls
1997 Pat Riley, Miami Heat
1998 Larry Bird, Indiana Pacers
1999 Mike Dunleavy, Portland Trail Blazers
2000 Glenn "Doc" Rivers, Orlando Magic
2001 Larry Brown, Philadelphia 76ers
2002 Rick Carlisle, Detroit Pistons
2003 Gregg Popovich, San Antonio
2004 Hubie Brown, Memphis
2005 Mike D'Antoni, Phoenix

NBA Statistical Leaders, 2004-05

Scoring Average
(Minimum 70 games or 1,400 pts)

	G	FG	FT	Pts	Avg
Allen Iverson, Philadelphia	75	771	656	2,302	30.7
Kobe Bryant, Los Angeles	66	573	542	1,819	27.6
LeBron James, Cleveland	80	795	477	2,175	27.2
Dirk Nowitzki, Dallas	78	663	615	2,032	26.1
Amare Stoudemire, Phoenix	80	747	583	2,080	26.0
Tracy McGrady, Houston	78	715	431	2,003	25.7
Gilbert Arenas, Washington	80	656	521	2,038	25.5
Vince Carter, New Jersey	77	696	367	1,886	24.5
Dwyane Wade, Miami	77	630	581	1,854	24.1
Ray Allen, Seattle	78	640	378	1,867	23.9

3-Point Field Goal Percentage
(Minimum 55 3-point field goals made)

	FG	FGA	Pct
Fred Hoiberg, Minnesota	70	145	.483
Joe Johnson, Phoenix	177	370	.478
Cuttino Mobley, Sacramento	150	342	.439
Mike Miller, Memphis	140	323	.433
Damon Jones, Miami	225	521	.432
Steve Nash, Phoenix	94	218	.431
Jon Barry, Houston	71	165	.430
Chauncey Billups, Detroit	165	387	.426
Eric Piatkowski, Chicago	57	134	.425
Jason Terry, Dallas	103	245	.420

Rebounds per Game
(Minimum 70 games or 800 rebounds)

	G	Off	Def	Tot	Avg
Kevin Garnett, Minnesota	82	247	861	1,108	13.5
Ben Wallace, Detroit	74	292	610	902	12.2
Shawn Marion, Phoenix	81	235	680	915	11.3
Emeka Okafor, Charlotte	73	275	520	795	10.9
Troy Murphy, Golden State	70	251	505	756	10.8
Shaquille O'Neal, Miami	73	253	507	760	10.4
Kurt Thomas, New York	80	170	661	831	10.4
Dwight Howard, Orlando	82	287	536	823	10.0
Dirk Nowitzki, Dallas	78	96	661	757	9.7
Tyson Chandler, Chicago	80	261	514	775	9.7

Assists per Game
(Minimum 70 games or 400 assists)

	G	No	Avg
Steve Nash, Phoenix	75	861	11.5
Brevin Knight, Charlotte	66	591	9.0
Jason Kidd, New Jersey	66	545	8.3
Stephon Marbury, New York	82	668	8.1
Allen Iverson, Philadelphia	75	596	7.9
LeBron James, Cleveland	80	577	7.2
Steve Francis, Orlando	78	547	7.0
Andre Miller, Denver	82	569	6.9
Mike Bibby, Sacramento	80	541	6.8
Dwyane Wade, Miami	77	520	6.8

Field Goal Percentage
(Minimum 300 field goals made)

	FGM	FGA	Pct
Shaquille O'Neal, Miami	658	1,095	.601
Amare Stoudemire, Phoenix	747	1,336	.559
Yao Ming, Houston	538	975	.552
Udonis Haslem, Miami	346	641	.540
Eddy Curry, Chicago	393	730	.538
Ruben Patterson, Portland	319	601	.531
Mark Blount, Boston	327	618	.529
Brad Miller, Sacramento	319	609	.524
Carlos Boozer, Utah	361	693	.521
Dwight Howard, Orlando	352	677	.520

Steals per Game
(Minimum 70 games or 125 steals)

	G	No	Avg
Larry Hughes, Washington	61	176	2.89
Allen Iverson, Philadelphia	75	180	2.40
LeBron James, Cleveland	80	177	2.21
Shawn Marion, Phoenix	81	163	2.01
Brevin Knight, Charlotte	66	131	1.98
Gilbert Arenas, Washington	80	139	1.74
Tracy McGrady, Houston	78	135	1.73
Andre Iguodala, Philadelphia	82	138	1.68
Gerald Wallace, Charlotte	70	117	1.67
Paul Pierce, Boston	82	133	1.62

Free Throw Percentage
(Minimum 125 free throws made)

	FTM	FTA	Pct
Reggie Miller, Indiana	250	268	.933
Earl Boykins, Denver	279	303	.921
Peja Stojakovic, Sacramento	253	275	.920
Damon Stoudamire, Portland	182	199	.915
Chauncey Billups, Detroit	343	382	.898
Steve Nash, Phoenix	211	238	.887
Luke Ridnour, Seattle	159	180	.883
Ray Allen, Seattle	378	428	.883
Austin Croshere, Indiana	226	256	.883
Danny Fortson, Seattle	227	258	.880

Blocked Shots per Game
(Minimum 70 games or 100 blocked shots)

	G	Blk	Avg
Andrei Kirilenko, Utah	41	136	3.32
Marcus Camby, Denver	66	199	3.02
Tim Duncan, San Antonio	66	174	2.64
Theo Ratliff, Portland	63	158	2.51
Ben Wallace, Detroit	74	176	2.38
Shaquille O'Neal, Miami	73	171	2.34
Joel Przybilla, Portland	76	163	2.14
Zydrunas Ilgauskas, Cleveland	78	165	2.12
Elton Brand, Los Angeles	81	169	2.09
Adonal Foyle, Golden State	78	159	2.04

NBA Defensive Player of the Year

1983 Sidney Moncrief, Milwaukee
1984 Sidney Moncrief, Milwaukee
1985 Mark Eaton, Utah
1986 Alvin Robertson, San Antonio
1987 Michael Cooper, L.A. Lakers
1988 Michael Jordan, Chicago
1989 Mark Eaton, Utah
1990 Dennis Rodman, Detroit
1991 Dennis Rodman, Detroit
1992 David Robinson, San Antonio
1993 Hakeem Olajuwon, Houston
1994 Hakeem Olajuwon, Houston
1995 Dikembe Mutombo, Denver
1996 Gary Payton, Seattle
1997 Dikembe Mutombo, Atlanta
1998 Dikembe Mutombo, Atlanta
1999 Alonzo Mourning, Miami
2000 Alonzo Mourning, Miami
2001 Dikembe Mutombo, Philadelphia
2002 Ben Wallace, Detroit
2003 Ben Wallace, Detroit
2004 Ron Artest, Indiana
2005 Ben Wallace, Detroit

NBA Rookie of the Year

Year	Player
1953	Don Meineke, Ft. Wayne
1954	Ray Felix, Baltimore
1955	Bob Pettit, Milwaukee
1956	Maurice Stokes, Rochester
1957	Tom Heinsohn, Boston
1958	Woody Sauldsberry, Philadelphia
1959	Elgin Baylor, Minneapolis
1960	Wilt Chamberlain, Philadelphia
1961	Oscar Robertson, Cincinnati
1962	Walt Bellamy, Chicago
1963	Terry Dischinger, Chicago
1964	Jerry Lucas, Cincinnati
1965	Willis Reed, New York
1966	Rick Barry, San Francisco
1967	Dave Bing, Detroit
1968	Earl Monroe, Baltimore
1969	Wes Unseld, Baltimore
1970	Lew Alcindor, Milwaukee
1971	Dave Cowens, Boston; Geoff Petrie, Portland (tie)
1972	Sidney Wicks, Portland
1973	Bob McAdoo, Buffalo
1974	Ernie DiGregorio, Buffalo
1975	Keith Wilkes, Golden State
1976	Alvan Adams, Phoenix
1977	Adrian Dantley, Buffalo
1978	Walter Davis, Phoenix
1979	Phil Ford, Kansas City
1980	Larry Bird, Boston
1981	Darrell Griffith, Utah
1982	Buck Williams, New Jersey
1983	Terry Cummings, San Diego
1984	Ralph Sampson, Houston
1985	Michael Jordan, Chicago
1986	Patrick Ewing, New York
1987	Chuck Person, Indiana
1988	Mark Jackson, New York
1989	Mitch Richmond, Golden State
1990	David Robinson, San Antonio
1991	Derrick Coleman, New Jersey
1992	Larry Johnson, Charlotte
1993	Shaquille O'Neal, Orlando
1994	Chris Webber, Golden State
1995	Grant Hill, Detroit; Jason Kidd, Dallas (tie)
1996	Damon Stoudamire, Toronto
1997	Allen Iverson, Philadelphia
1998	Tim Duncan, San Antonio
1999	Vince Carter, Toronto
2000	Elton Brand, Chicago; Steve Francis, Houston (tie)
2001	Mike Miller, Orlando
2002	Pau Gasol, Memphis
2003	Amaré Stoudemire, Phoenix
2004	LeBron James, Cleveland
2005	Emeka Okafor, Charlotte

NBA Sixth Man Award

1983	Bobby Jones, Philadelphia
1984	Kevin McHale, Boston
1985	Kevin McHale, Boston
1986	Bill Walton, Boston
1987	Ricky Pierce, Milwaukee
1988	Roy Tarpley, Dallas
1989	Eddie Johnson, Phoenix
1990	Ricky Pierce, Milwaukee
1991	Detlef Schrempf, Seattle
1992	Detlef Schrempf, Seattle
1993	Clifford Robinson, Portland
1994	Dell Curry, Charlotte
1995	Anthony Mason, New York
1996	Toni Kukoc, Chicago
1997	John Starks, New York
1998	Danny Manning, Phoenix
1999	Darrell Armstrong, Orlando
2000	Rodney Rogers, Phoenix
2001	Aaron McKie, Philadelphia
2002	Corliss Williamson, Detroit
2003	Bobby Jackson, Sacramento
2004	Antawn Jamison, Dallas
2005	Ben Gordon, Chicago

2005 NBA Player Draft, First-Round Picks

(held June 28, 2005)

	Team	Player, College/Team
1.	Milwaukee	Andrew Bogut, C Utah
2.	Atlanta	Marvin Williams, F North Carolina
3.	Utah[1]	Deron Williams, Illinois
4.	New Orleans	Chris Paul, G Wake Forest
5.	Charlotte	Raymond Felton, G North Carolina
6.	Portland[2]	Martell Webster, G-F Seattle Prep HS
7.	Toronto	Charlie Villanueva, F Connecticut
8.	New York	Channing Frye, C Arizona
9.	Golden State	Ike Diogu, F Arizona State
10.	LA Lakers	Andrew Bynum, C St. Joseph (NJ) HS
11.	Orlando	Fran Vazquez, F-C Spain
12.	LA Clippers	Yaroslav Korolev, F CSKA Moscow
13.	Charlotte[3]	Sean May, F North Carolina
14.	Minnesota	Rashad McCants, G North Carolina
15.	New Jersey	Antoine Wright, G-F Texas A&M
16.	Toronto[4]	Joey Graham, F Oklahoma State
17.	Indiana	Danny Granger, F New Mexico
18.	Boston	Gerald Green, G-F Gulf Shores Acad (TX)
19.	Memphis	Hakim Warrick, F Syracuse
20.	Denver[5]	Julius Hodge, G-F North Carolina State
21.	Phoenix[6]	Nate Robinson[10], G Washington
22.	Denver[7]	Jarrett Jack[11], G Georgia Tech
23.	Sacramento	Francisco Garcia, G-F Louisville
24.	Houston	Luther Head, G Illinois
25.	Seattle	Johan Petro, C France
26.	Detroit	Jason Maxiell, F Cincinnati
27.	Portland[8]	Linas Kleiza[12], F Missouri
28.	San Antonio	Ian Mahinmi, C STB Le Havre (France)
29.	Miami	Wayne Simien, F Kansas
30.	New York[9]	David Lee, F Florida

(1) From Portland. (2) From Utah. (3) From Cleveland via Phoenix. (4) From Philadelphia via Phoenix. (5) From Washington via Orlando. (6) From Chicago. (7) Rights traded to Portland. (8) From Utah via Dallas. (9) From Phoenix via San Antonio. (10) Rights traded to New York. (11) Rights traded to Portland. (12) Rights traded to Denver.

Number-One First-Round NBA Draft Picks, 1966-2005

Year	Team	Player, college
1966	New York	Cazzie Russell, Michigan
1967	Detroit	Jimmy Walker, Providence
1968	Houston	Elvin Hayes, Houston
1969	Milwaukee	Lew Alcindor[1], UCLA
1970	Detroit	Bob Lanier, St. Bonaventure
1971	Cleveland	Austin Carr, Notre Dame
1972	Portland	LaRue Martin, Loyola-Chicago
1973	Philadelphia	Doug Collins, Illinois St.
1974	Portland	Bill Walton, UCLA
1975	Atlanta	David Thompson[2], N.C. State
1976	Houston	John Lucas, Maryland
1977	Milwaukee	Kent Benson, Indiana
1978	Portland	Mychal Thompson, Minnesota
1979	L.A. Lakers	Magic Johnson, Michigan St.
1980	Golden State	Joe Barry Carroll, Purdue
1981	Dallas	Mark Aguirre, DePaul
1982	L.A. Lakers	James Worthy, North Carolina
1983	Houston	Ralph Sampson, Virginia
1984	Houston	Akeem Olajuwon, Houston
1985	New York	Patrick Ewing, Georgetown
1986	Cleveland	Brad Daugherty, North Carolina
1987	San Antonio	David Robinson, Navy
1988	L.A. Clippers	Danny Manning, Kansas
1989	Sacramento	Pervis Ellison, Louisville
1990	New Jersey	Derrick Coleman, Syracuse
1991	Charlotte	Larry Johnson, UNLV
1992	Orlando	Shaquille O'Neal, LSU
1993	Orlando	Chris Webber[3], Michigan
1994	Milwaukee	Glenn Robinson, Purdue
1995	Golden State	Joe Smith, Maryland
1996	Philadelphia	Allen Iverson, Georgetown
1997	San Antonio	Tim Duncan, Wake Forest
1998	L.A. Clippers	Michael Olowokandi, Pacific
1999	Chicago Bulls	Elton Brand, Duke
2000	New Jersey	Kenyon Martin, Cincinnati
2001	Washington	Kwame Brown, Glynn Academy (HS)
2002	Houston	Yao Ming, Shanghai Sharks (China)
2003	Cleveland	LeBron James, St. Vincent-St. Mary (HS)
2004	Orlando	Dwight Howard, Southwest Atlanta Christian Academy (HS)
2005	Milwaukee	Andrew Bogut, Utah

(1) Later Kareem Abdul-Jabbar. (2) Signed with Denver of the ABA. (3) Traded to Golden State.

All-Time NBA Statistical Leaders

(At the end of the 2004-05 season. *Player active in 2004-05 season.)

Scoring Average
(Minimum 400 games or 10,000 points)

	G	Pts.	Avg
Michael Jordan	1,072	32,292	30.1
Wilt Chamberlain	1,045	31,419	30.1
*Allen Iverson	610	16,738	27.4
Elgin Baylor	846	23,149	27.4
Jerry West	932	25,192	27.0
*Shaquille O'Neal	882	23,583	26.7
Jerry West	932	25,192	27.0
Bob Pettit	792	20,880	26.4
George Gervin	791	20,708	26.2
Oscar Robertson	1,040	26,710	25.7

Field Goal Percentage
(Minimum 2,000 field goals made)

	FGA	FGM	Pct.
Artis Gilmore	9,570	5,732	.599
Mark West	4,356	2,528	.580
*Shaquille O'Neal	16,115	9,328	.579
Steve Johnson	4,965	2,841	.572
Darryl Dawkins	6,079	3,477	.572
James Donaldson	5,442	3,105	.571
Jeff Ruland	3,734	2,105	.564
Kareem Abdul-Jabbar	28,307	15,837	.559
Kevin McHale	12,334	6,830	.554
Bobby Jones	6,199	3,412	.550

Free Throw Percentage
(Minimum 1,200 free throws made)

	FTA	FTM	Pct.
Mark Price	2,362	2,135	.904
Rick Barry	4,243	3,818	.900
*Steve Nash	1,647	1,469	.892
Calvin Murphy	3,864	3,445	.892
*Predrag Stojakovic	1,826	1,626	.891
Scott Skiles	1,741	1,548	.889
*Reggie Miller	7,026	6,237	.888
Larry Bird	4,471	3,960	.886
*Ray Allen	2,914	2,577	.884
Bill Sharman	3,559	3,143	.883

3-Point Field Goal Percentage
(Minimum 250 3-point field goals made)

	3-FGA	3-FGM	Pct.
Steve Kerr	1,599	726	.454
Hubert Davis	1,651	728	.441
Drazen Petrovic	583	255	.437
Tim Legler	603	260	.431
B.J. Armstrong	1,026	436	.425
*Wesley Person	2,754	1,150	.418
*Steve Nash	1,836	767	.418
Dana Barros	2,652	1,090	.411
Trent Tucker	1,410	575	.408
*Pat Garrity	1,389	562	.405

Games Played

Robert Parish	1,611
Kareem Abdul-Jabbar	1,560
John Stockton	1,504
Karl Malone	1,476
*Kevin Willis	1,419
*Reggie Miller	1,389
Moses Malone	1,329
Buck Williams	1,307
Elvin Hayes	1,303
Mark Jackson	1,296

Minutes Played

Kareem Abdul-Jabbar	57,446
Karl Malone	54,852
Elvin Hayes	50,000
Wilt Chamberlain	47,859
John Stockton	47,764
*Reggie Miller	47,619
John Havlicek	46,471
Robert Parish	45,704
Moses Malone	45,071
Hakeem Olajuwon	44,222

Personal Fouls

Kareem Abdul-Jabbar	4,657
Karl Malone	4,578
Robert Parish	4,443
Charles Oakley	4,421
Hakeem Olajuwon	4,383
Buck Williams	4,267
Elvin Hayes	4,193
*Kevin Willis	4,161
Otis Thorpe	4,146
James Edwards	4,042

Blocked Shots

Hakeem Olajuwon	3,830
Kareem Abdul-Jabbar	3,189
*Dikembe Mutombo	3,097
Mark Eaton	3,064
David Robinson	2,954
Patrick Ewing	2,894
Tree Rollins	2,542
Robert Parish	2,361
*Shaquille O'Neal	2,273
Manute Bol	2,086

Field Goals Attempted

Kareem Abdul-Jabbar	28,307
Karl Malone	26,210
Michael Jordan	24,537
Elvin Hayes	24,272
John Havlicek	23,930
Wilt Chamberlain	23,497
Dominique Wilkins	21,589
Alex English	21,036
Hakeem Olajuwon	20,991
Elgin Baylor	20,171

Field Goals Made

Kareem Abdul-Jabbar	15,837
Karl Malone	13,528
Wilt Chamberlain	12,681
Michael Jordan	12,192
Elvin Hayes	10,976
Hakeem Olajuwon	10,749
Alex English	10,659
John Havlicek	10,513
Dominique Wilkins	9,963
Patrick Ewing	9,702

3-Point Field Goals Attempted

*Reggie Miller	6,188
Tim Hardaway	4,345
Dale Ellis	4,266
*Nick Van Exel	4,124
Vernon Maxwell	3,931
*Glen Rice	3,896
Mookie Blaylock	3,816
Dan Majerle	3,798
Ray Allen	3,743
John Starks	3,591

3-Point Field Goals Made

*Reggie Miller	2,560
Dale Ellis	1,719
Glen Rice	1,559
Tim Hardaway	1,542
*Ray Allen	1,486
*Nick Van Exel	1,473
Dan Majerle	1,360
Mitch Richmond	1,326
*Allan Houston	1,305
*Eddie Jones	1,301

Points

Kareem Abdul-Jabbar	38,387
Karl Malone	36,928
Michael Jordan	32,292
Wilt Chamberlain	31,419
Moses Malone	27,409
Elvin Hayes	27,313
Hakeem Olajuwon	26,946
Oscar Robertson	26,710
Dominique Wilkins	26,668
John Havlicek	26,395

Rebounds

Wilt Chamberlain	23,924
Bill Russell	21,620
Kareem Abdul-Jabbar	17,440
Elvin Hayes	16,279
Moses Malone	16,212
Karl Malone	14,968
Robert Parish	14,715
Nate Thurmond	14,464
Walt Bellamy	14,241
Wes Unseld	13,769

Assists

John Stockton	15,806
Mark Jackson	10,334
Magic Johnson	10,141
Oscar Robertson	9,887
Isiah Thomas	9,061
*Gary Payton	8,508
*Rod Strickland	7,987
Maurice Cheeks	7,392
Lenny Wilkens	7,211
Terry Porter	7,160

Steals

John Stockton	3,265
Michael Jordan	2,514
*Gary Payton	2,331
Maurice Cheeks	2,310
Scottie Pippen	2,307
Clyde Drexler	2,207
Hakeem Olajuwon	2,162
Alvin Robertson	2,112
Karl Malone	2,085
Mookie Blaylock	2,075

All-Time NBA Coaching Victories

(At the end of the 2004-05 season, ranked by wins. *Active through 2004-05 season.)

Coach	W-L	Pct.
Lenny Wilkens	1,315-1,133	.537
Don Nelson	1,190-880	.575
Pat Riley	1,110-569	.661
Larry Brown*	987-741	.571
Bill Fitch	944-1,106	.460
Jerry Sloan*	943-617	.604
Red Auerbach	938-479	.662
Dick Motta	935-1,017	.479
Jack Ramsay	864-783	.525
Phil Jackson	832-316	.725
Cotton Fitzsimmons	832-775	.518
Gene Shue	784-861	.477
George Karl*	740-507	.587
Rick Adelman*	718-443	.618
John MacLeod	707-657	.518
Red Holzman	696-604	.535
Chuck Daly	638-437	.593
Doug Moe	628-529	.543
Mike Fratello*	612-491	.555
Alvin Attles	557-518	.518

Basketball Hall of Fame, Springfield, MA

(2005 inductees have an asterisk*)

PLAYERS

Abdul-Jabbar, Kareem
Archibald, Nate
Arizin, Paul
Barlow, Thomas
Barry, Rick
Baylor, Elgin
Beckman, John
Bellamy, Walt
Belov, Sergei
Bing, Dave
Bird, Larry
Blazejowski, Carol
Borgmann, Bennie
Bradley, Bill
Brennan, Joseph
Cervi, Al
Chamberlain, Wilt
Cooper, Charles
Cosic, Kresimir
Cousy, Bob
Cowens, Dave
Crawford, Joan
Cunningham, Billy
Curry, Denise
Dalipagic, Drazen
Davies, Bob
DeBernardi, Forrest
DeBusschere, Dave
Denhart, Dutch
Donovan, Anne
Drexler, Clyde
Endacott, Paul
English, Alex
Erving, Julius (Dr. J)
Foster, Bud
Frazier, Walt
Friedman, Max
Fulks, Joe
Gale, Lauren
Gallatin, Harry
Gates, Pop
Gervin, George
Gola, Tom
Goodrich, Gail
Greer, Hal
Gruenig, Ace
Hagan, Cliff
Hanson, Victor
Harris-Stewart, Luisa
Havlicek, John
Hawkins, Connie
Hayes, Elvin
Haynes, Marques
Heinsohn, Tom
Holman, Nat
Houbregs, Bob
Howell, Bailey
Hyatt, Chuck
Issel, Dan
Jeannette, Buddy
Johnson, Earvin "Magic"
Johnson, William
Johnston, Neil
Jones, K.C.
Jones, Sam
Krause, Moose
Kurland, Bob
Lanier, Bob
Lapchick, Joe
Lemon, Meadowlark
Lieberman-Cline, Nancy
Lloyd, Earl
Lovellette, Clyde
Lucas, Jerry
Luisetti, Hank
Macauley, Ed
Malone, Moses
Maravich, Pete
*Marcari, Hortencia
Martin, Slater
McAdoo, Bob
McCracken, Branch
McCracken, Jack
McDermott, Bobby
McGuire, Dick
McHale, Kevin
Meneghin, Dino
Meyers, Ann
Mikan, George
Mikkelsen, Vern
Miller, Cheryl
Monroe, Earl
Murphy, Calvin
Murphy, Stretch
Page, Pat
Parish, Robert
Petrovic, Drazen
Pettit, Bob
Phillip, Andy
Pollard, Jim
Ramsey, Frank
Reed, Willis
Risen, Arnie
Robertson, Oscar
Roosma, John S.
Russell, Bill
Russell, Honey
Schayes, Adolph
Schmidt, Ernest
Schommer, John
Sedran, Barney
Semjonova, Uljana
Sharman, Bill
Steinmetz, Christian
Stokes, Maurice
Thomas, Isiah
Thompson, Cat
Thompson, David
Thurmond, Nate
Twyman, Jack
Unseld, Wes
Vandivier, Fuzzy
Wachter, Edward
Walton, Bill
Wanzer, Bobby
West, Jerry
White, Nera
Wilkens, Lenny
Woodard, Lynette
Wooden, John
Worthy, James
Yardley, George

COACHES

Allen, Forrest (Phog)
Anderson, Harold
Auerbach, Red
Barmore, Leon
Barry, Sam
Blood, Ernest
*Boeheim, Jim
*Brown, Hubie
Brown, Larry
*Calhoun, Jim
Cann, Howard
Carlson, Dr. H. C.
Carnesecca, Lou
Carnevale, Ben
Carril, Pete
Case, Everett
Chaney, John
Conradt, Jody
Crum, Denny
Daly, Chuck
Dean, Everett
Diaz-Miguel, Antonio
Diddle, Edgar
Drake, Bruce
Gaines, Clarence
Gardner, Jack
Gill, Slats
Gomelsky, Aleksandr
*Gunter, Sue
Hannum, Alex
Harshman, Marv
Haskins, Don
Hickey, Edgar
Hobson, Howard
Holzman, Red
Iba, Hank
Julian, Alvin
Keaney, Frank
Keogan, George
Knight, Bob
Krzyzewski, Mike
Kundla, John
Lambert, Ward
Litwack, Harry
Loeffler, Kenneth
Lonborg, Dutch
McCutchan, Arad
McGuire, Al
McGuire, Frank
McLendon, John
Meanwell, Dr. W. E.
Meyer, Ray
Miller, Ralph
Moore, Billie
Newell, Pete
Nikolic, Aleksandar
Olson, Lute
Ramsay, Jack
Rubini, Cesare
Rupp, Adolph
Sachs, Leonard
Sharman, Bill
Shelton, Everett
Smith, Dean
Summitt, Pat
Taylor, Fred
Thompson, John
Wade, Margaret
Watts, Stan
Wilkens, Lenny
Wooden, John
Woolpert, Phil
Wootten, Morgan
Yow, Kay

TEAMS

First Team
Original Celtics
Buffalo Germans
NY Renaissance
Harlem Globetrotters

REFEREES

Enright, James
Hepbron, George
Hoyt, George
Kennedy, Matthew
Leith, Lloyd
Mihalik, Red
Nucatola, John
Quigley, Ernest
Shirley, J. Dallas
Strom, Earl
Tobey, David
Walsh, David

CONTRIBUTORS

Abbott, Senda B.
Bee, Clair
Biasone, Danny
Brown, Walter
Bunn, John
Colangelo, Jerry
Douglas, Bob
Duer, Al O.
Embry, Wayne
Fagan, Cliff
Fisher, Harry
Fleisher, Larry
Gottlieb, Edward
Gulick, Dr. L. H.
Harrison, Lester
Hearn, Francis "Chick"
Hepp, Dr. Ferenc
Hickox, Edward
Hinkle, Tony
Irish, Ned
Jones, R. W.
Kennedy, Walter
Liston, Emil
Mokray, Bill
Morgan, Ralph
Morgenweck, Frank
Naismith, Dr. James
Newton, C. M.
O'Brien, John
O'Brien, Larry
Olsen, Harold
Podoloff, Maurice
Porter, H. V.
Reid, William
Ripley, Elmer
St. John, Lynn
Saperstein, Abe
Schabinger, Arthur
Stagg, Amos Alonzo
Stankovich, Boris
Steitz, Edward
Taylor, Chuck
Teague, Bertha
Tower, Oswald
Trester, Arthur
Wells, Clifford
Wilke, Lou
Zollner, Fred

NBA Home Courts[1]

Team	Name (built)	Capacity
Atlanta	Philips Arena (1999)	20,000
Boston	FleetCenter (1995)	18,624
Charlotte	Charlotte Bobcats Arena (2005)	18,500
Chicago	United Center (1994)	21,500
Cleveland	Quicken Loans Arena (1994)	20,562
Dallas	American Airlines Center (2001)	19,200
Denver	Pepsi Center (1999)	19,099
Detroit	The Palace of Auburn Hills (1988)	22,076
Golden State	Arena in Oakland[2] (1966)	19,596
Houston	Toyota Center (2003)	18,300
Indiana	Conseco Fieldhouse (1999)	18,345
L.A. Clippers	Staples Center (1999)	19,060
L.A. Lakers	Staples Center (1999)	18,997
Memphis	The Pyramid (1991)	20,142
Miami	American Airlines Arena (1999)	19,600
Milwaukee	Bradley Center (1988)	18,600
Minnesota	Target Center (1990)	19,006
New Jersey	Continental Airlines Arena[3] (1981)	20,049
New Orleans[7]	New Orleans Arena (1999)	18,500
New York	Madison Square Garden (1968)	19,763
Orlando	TD Waterhouse Centre[4] (1989)	17,248
Philadelphia	Wachovia Center[5] (1996)	20,444
Phoenix	America West Arena (1992)	19,023
Portland	The Rose Garden (1995)	19,980
Sacramento	ARCO Arena (1988)	17,317
San Antonio	SBC Center (2002)	18,500
Seattle	KeyArena at Seattle Center[6] (1962)	17,072
Toronto	Air Canada Centre (1999)	19,800
Utah	Delta Center (1991)	19,911
Washington	MCI Center (1997)	20,674

(1) At the end of the 2004-05 season. (2) Oakland Coliseum Arena, 1966-96; renovated and renamed in 1997. (3) Brendan Byrne/Meadowlands Arena, 1981-96. (4) Orlando Arena, 1989-2000. (5) CoreStates Center, 1996-98; First Union Center, 1998-2003. (6) Seattle Center Coliseum, 1962-94; renovated, expanded, and renamed in 1995. (7) Due to Hurricane Katrina, the Hornets would play 35 games of the 2005-06 season at the Ford Center in Oklahoma City, OK, and 6 games at LSU in Baton Rouge, LA.

WOMEN'S PROFESSIONAL BASKETBALL

WNBA 2005: Sacramento Monarchs Defeat Connecticut Sun for First Title

The Sacramento Monarchs defeated the Connecticut Sun, 62-59, in Sacramento, CA, on Sept. 20 in the 4th and deciding game of the 2005 WNBA Finals. Sacramento forward Yolanda Griffith had scored 14 points and 23 rebounds in Game 4 to lead the Monarchs to victory. Griffith, who averaged 18.5 points and 9.5 rebounds per game in the Finals, was named the most valuable player of the series. The Monarchs, one of the original 9 WNBA teams, overcame 2 former champion teams, the Los Angeles Sparks and the Houston Comets, on their way to the Finals. The Sun, who had taken both of their regular season matchups against the Monarchs, made their 2nd Finals appearance in as many years, in only their 3rd year of existence as a franchise. They finished the season with the best record in the Eastern Conference and earned a spot in the Finals after defeating the Detroit Shock and the Indiana Fever.

The WNBA finals were expanded from a best-of-3 series to a best-of-5 for the first time in 2005.

WNBA Final Standings, 2005 Season

x-clinched playoff berth; y-clinched top seed

Eastern Conference

	W	L	Pct	GB
y-Connecticut	26	8	0.765	0.0
x-Indiana	21	13	0.618	5.0
x-New York	18	16	0.529	8.0
x-Detroit	16	18	0.471	10.0
Washington	16	18	0.471	10.0
Charlotte	6	28	0.176	20.0

Western Conference

	W	L	Pct	GB
y-Sacramento	25	9	0.735	0.0
x-Seattle	20	14	0.588	5.0
x-Houston	19	15	0.559	6.0
x-Los Angeles	17	17	0.500	8.0
Phoenix	16	18	0.471	9.0
Minnesota	14	20	0.412	11.0
San Antonio	7	27	0.206	18.0

2005 WNBA Playoffs

(Playoff seeding in parentheses; Conference winner automatically gets top seed)

Eastern Conference

Connecticut (1) defeated Detroit (4), 2 games to 0
Indiana (2) defeated New York (3), 2 games to 0
Connecticut (1) defeated Indiana (2), 2 games to 0

Western Conference

Sacramento (1) defeated Los Angeles (4), 2 games to 0
Houston (3) defeated Seattle (2), 2 games to 1
Sacramento (1) defeated Houston (3), 2 games to 0

WNBA Championship (Best of 5)

Sacramento defeated Connecticut, 3 games to 1 [69-65, 70-77 (OT), 66-55, 62-59]

2005 All-WNBA Teams

First Team	Position	Second Team
Sheryl Swoopes, Houston	Forward	Tamika Catchings, Indiana
Lauren Jackson, Seattle	Forward	Taj McWilliams-Franklin, Connecticut
Deanna Nolan, Detroit	Guard	Becky Hammon, New York
Sue Bird, Seattle	Guard	Diana Taurasi, Phoenix
Yolanda Griffith, Sacramento	Center	Lisa Leslie, Los Angeles

WNBA Statistical Leaders and Awards in 2005

Minutes played — 1,225, Sheryl Swoopes, Houston
Total points — 614, Sheryl Swoopes, Houston
Points per game — 18.6, Sheryl Swoopes, Houston
Highest field goal % — .551, Michelle Snow, Houston
Highest 3-pt. field goal % — .467, Laurie Koehn, Washington
Highest free throw % — .901, Becky Hammon, New York
Total rebounds — 322, Cheryl Ford, Detroit
Rebounds per game — 9.8, Cheryl Ford, Detroit
Total assists — 177, Temeka Johnson, Washington
Assists per game — 5.9, Sue Bird, Seattle
Total steals — 90, Tamika Catchings, Indiana
Steals per game — 2.65, Tamika Catchings, Indiana
Total blocked shots — 71, Margo Dydek, Connecticut
Coach of the year — John Whisenant, Sacramento
Defensive player of year — Tamika Catchings, Indiana
Most improved player — Nicole Powell, Sacramento

WNBA Champions

	Regular season		Playoffs		
Year	Eastern Conference	Western Conference	Champion	Coach	Runner-up
1997	Houston Comets	Phoenix Mercury	Houston	Van Chancellor	New York
1998	Cleveland Rockers	Houston Comets	Houston	Van Chancellor	Phoenix
1999	New York Liberty	Houston Comets	Houston	Van Chancellor	New York
2000	New York Liberty	Los Angeles Sparks	Houston	Van Chancellor	New York
2001	Cleveland Rockers	Los Angeles Sparks	Los Angeles	Michael Cooper	Charlotte
2002	New York Liberty	Los Angeles Sparks	Los Angeles	Michael Cooper	New York
2003	Detroit Shock	Los Angeles Sparks	Detroit	Bill Laimbeer	Los Angeles
2004	Connecticut Sun	Los Angeles Sparks	Seattle	Ann Donovan	Connecticut
2005	Connecticut Sun	Sacramento Monarchs	Sacramento	John Whisenant	Connecticut

WNBA Scoring Leaders

Year	Scoring champion	Pts	Avg.
1997	Cynthia Cooper, Houston	621	22.2
1998	Cynthia Cooper, Houston	680	22.7
1999	Cynthia Cooper, Houston	686	22.1
2000	Sheryl Swoopes, Houston	643	20.7
2001	Katie Smith, Minnesota	739	23.1
2002	Chamique Holdsclaw, Washington	397	19.9
2003	Lauren Jackson, Seattle	698	21.2
2004	Lauren Jackson, Seattle	634	20.5
2005	Sheryl Swoopes, Houston	614	18.6

WNBA Finals MVP

1997	Cynthia Cooper, Houston
1998	Cynthia Cooper, Houston
1999	Cynthia Cooper, Houston
2000	Cynthia Cooper, Houston
2001	Lisa Leslie, Los Angeles
2002	Lisa Leslie, Los Angeles
2003	Ruth Riley, Detroit
2004	Betty Lennox, Seattle
2005	Yolanda Griffith, Sacramento

WNBA Most Valuable Player

1997	Cynthia Cooper, Houston
1998	Cynthia Cooper, Houston
1999	Yolanda Griffith, Sacramento
2000	Sheryl Swoopes, Houston
2001	Lisa Leslie, Los Angeles
2002	Sheryl Swoopes, Houston
2003	Lauren Jackson, Seattle
2004	Lisa Leslie, Los Angeles
2005	Sheryl Swoopes, Houston

WNBA Rookie of the Year

1997	no award
1998	Tracy Reid, Charlotte
1999	Chamique Holdsclaw, Washington
2000	Betty Lennox, Minnesota
2001	Jackie Stiles, Portland
2002	Tamika Catchings, Indiana
2003	Cheryl Ford, Detroit
2004	Diana Taurasi, Phoenix
2005	Temeka Johnson, Washington

COLLEGE BASKETBALL

Men's Final NCAA Division I Conference Standings, 2004-2005

(*conference tournament champion)

	Conf. W	Conf. L	All W	All L
America East				
Vermont*	16	2	25	7
Northeastern	15	3	21	10
Boston U.	14	4	20	9
Albany	9	9	13	15
Maine	8	10	14	15
Binghamton	8	10	12	17
Stony Brook	6	12	12	17
MD Baltimore Co.	5	13	11	18
New Hampshire	5	13	9	19
Hartford	4	14	8	20
Atlantic Coast[1]				
North Carolina	14	2	33	4
Wake Forest	13	3	27	6
Duke*	11	5	27	6
Georgia Tech	8	8	20	12
Virginia Tech	8	8	16	14
North Carolina St.	7	9	21	14
Maryland	7	9	19	13
Miami (FL)	7	9	16	13
Clemson	5	11	16	16
Virginia	4	12	14	15
Florida St.	4	12	12	19
Atlantic Sun				
Central Florida*	13	7	24	9
Gardner-Webb	13	7	18	12
Belmont	12	8	14	16
Mercer	11	9	16	12
Lipscomb	11	9	16	12
Jacksonville	11	9	16	13
Georgia St.	11	9	14	15
Troy	10	10	12	18
Florida Atlantic	10	10	10	17
Stetson	8	12	10	17
Campbell	0	20	2	25
Atlantic 10				
East Division				
Saint Joseph's	14	2	24	12
Temple	11	5	16	14
Massachusetts	9	7	16	12
Fordham	8	8	13	16
Rhode Island	4	12	6	22
St. Bonaventure	1	15	2	26
West Division				
George Washington*	11	5	22	8
Dayton	10	6	18	11
Xavier	10	6	17	12
Richmond	8	8	14	15
La Salle	5	11	10	19
Duquesne	5	11	8	22
Big East[1]				
Boston College	13	3	25	5
Connecticut	13	3	23	8
Syracuse*	11	5	27	7
Villanova	11	5	24	8
Pittsburgh	10	6	20	9
Notre Dame	9	7	17	2
West Virginia	8	8	24	11
Georgetown	8	8	19	13
Providence	4	12	14	17
Seton Hall	4	12	12	16
St. John's	3	13	9	18
Rutgers	2	14	10	19
Big Sky				
Portland St.	11	3	19	9
Montana*	9	5	18	13
Montana St.	9	5	14	14
Sacramento St.	8	6	12	16
Weber St.	7	7	14	16
Eastern Wash.	5	9	8	20
Northern Arizona	4	10	11	17
Idaho St.	3	11	9	18
Big South				
Winthrop*	15	1	27	6
Liberty	11	5	13	15
UNC Asheville	8	e	11	17
Birmingham Southern	7	9	16	14
Charleston Southern	7	9	13	17
Radford	7	9	12	16
High Point	7	9	13	18
Coastal Carolina	7	9	10	19
VA Military Institute	3	13	9	18
Big 10				
Illinois*	15	1	37	2
Michigan St.	13	3	26	7
Wisconsin	11	5	25	9
Minnesota	10	6	21	11
Indiana	10	6	15	14
Ohio St.	8	8	20	12
Iowa	7	9	21	12
Northwestern	6	10	15	16
Michigan	4	12	13	18
Purdue	3	13	7	21
Penn St.	1	15	7	23
Big 12				
Kansas	12	4	23	7
Oklahoma	12	4	25	8
Oklahoma St.*	11	5	26	7
Texas Tech	10	6	22	11
Texas	9	7	20	11
Iowa St.	9	7	19	12
Texas A&M	8	8	21	10
Nebraska	7	9	14	14
Missouri	7	9	16	17
Kansas St.	6	10	17	12
Colorado	4	12	14	16
Baylor	1	15	9	19
Big West				
Pacific	18	0	27	4
Utah St.*	13	5	24	8
Cal. St. Fullerton	12	6	21	11
Cal. St. Northridge	12	6	18	13
UC Irvine	8	10	16	13
UC Santa Barbara	7	11	11	18
Long Beach St.	7	11	10	20
Idaho	6	12	8	22
UC Riverside	4	14	9	19
Cal. Poly	3	15	5	22
Colonial Athletic Association				
Old Dominion*	15	3	28	6
UNC Wilmington	13	5	19	10
VA Commonwealth	13	5	19	3
Hofstra	12	6	21	9
Drexel	12	6	17	12
George Mason	10	8	16	13
Delaware	7	11	11	20
William & Mary	3	15	8	21
James Madison	3	15	6	22
Towson	2	16	5	24
Conference USA				
Louisville*	14	2	33	5
Cincinnati	12	4	25	8
Charlotte	12	4	21	8
UAB	10	6	22	11
DePaul	10	6	20	11
Memphis	9	7	22	16
Houston	9	7	18	14
TCU	8	8	21	14
Marquette	7	9	19	12
Saint Louis	6	10	9	21
South Florida	5	11	14	16
Tulane	4	12	10	18
East Carolina	4	12	9	19
Southern Miss.	2	14	11	17
Horizon				
Wisc.-Milwaukee*	14	2	26	6
Wisc.-Green Bay	10	6	17	11
Detroit	9	7	14	16
Illinois-Chicago	8	8	15	14
Wright St.	8	8	15	15
Loyola (Chicago)	8	8	13	17
Butler	7	9	13	15
Cleveland St.	6	10	9	17
Youngstown St.	2	14	5	23
Ivy League[2]				
Penn	13	1	20	9
Cornell	8	6	13	14
Harvard	7	7	12	15
Yale	7	7	11	16
Dartmouth	7	7	10	17
Princeton	6	8	15	13
Brown	5	9	12	16
Columbia	3	11	12	15
Metro Atlantic Athletic				
Niagara*	13	5	20	10
Rider	13	5	19	11
Fairfield	11	7	15	15
St. Peter's	10	8	15	13
Manhattan	9	9	15	14
Iona	9	9	15	16
Marist	8	10	11	17
Canisius	8	10	11	18
Loyola (MD)	5	13	6	22
Siena	4	14	6	24
Mid-American				
East Division				
Miami (OH)	12	6	19	11
Buffalo	11	7	23	10
Ohio*	11	7	21	11
Akron	11	7	19	10
Kent St.	11	7	20	13
Marshall	3	15	6	22
West Division				
Western Mich.	11	7	20	13
Toledo	11	7	16	13
Bowling Green	10	8	18	11
Ball St.	10	8	15	13
Northern Illinois	7	11	11	17
Eastern Mich.	5	13	12	18
Central Mich.	4	14	10	18
Mid-Continent				
Oral Roberts	13	3	25	8
Missouri-KC	12	4	16	12
Valparaiso	10	6	15	16
Indiana-Purdue	9	7	16	13
Oakland*	7	9	13	19
Western Illinois	7	9	11	17
Chicago St.	7	9	9	19
Southern Utah	6	10	13	15
Centenary	1	15	3	24
Mid-Eastern Athletic				
Delaware St.*	14	4	19	14
Hampton	13	5	17	13
Coppin St.	13	5	14	15
South Carolina St.	11	7	19	12
Norfolk St.	11	7	13	14
Morgan St.	11	7	14	16
Florida A&M	10	8	14	15
Bethune-Cookman	8	10	13	17
No. Carolina A&T	5	13	6	24
Howard	2	16	5	23
MD-Eastern Shore	1	17	2	26
Missouri Valley				
Southern Illinois	15	3	27	8
Wichita St.	12	6	22	10
Creighton*	11	7	23	11
Northern Iowa	11	7	21	11
SMS	10	8	19	13
Illinois St.	8	10	17	13
Drake	7	11	13	16
Bradley	6	12	13	15
Evansville	5	13	11	17
Indiana St.	5	13	11	20
Mountain West				
Utah	13	1	29	6
New Mexico*	10	4	26	7
Air Force	9	5	18	12
UNLV	7	7	17	14
Wyoming	7	7	15	13
San Diego St.	4	10	11	18
Colorado St.	3	11	11	17
BYU	3	11	9	21

Team	Conf. W	Conf. L	All W	All L
Northeast				
Monmouth	14	4	16	13
Fairleigh Dickinson*	13	5	20	13
Robert Morris	11	7	14	15
St. Francis (PA)	10	8	15	13
Long Island	10	8	14	15
Wagner	10	8	13	17
St. Francis (NY)	9	9	13	15
Central Conn. St.	8	10	12	16
Quinnipiac	6	12	10	17
Mt. St. Mary's	5	13	7	20
Sacred Heart	3	15	4	23
Ohio Valley				
Tennessee Tech	12	4	18	11
Eastern Kentucky*	11	5	22	9
Murray St.	11	5	17	11
Samford	10	6	15	13
SE Missouri St.	9	7	15	14
Tennessee St.	9	7	14	17
Austin Peay	9	7	13	19
Eastern Illinois	7	9	12	16
Morehead St.	5	11	11	16
Tenn.-Martin	3	13	6	21
Jacksonville St.	2	14	7	22
Pacific-10				
Arizona	15	3	30	7
Washington*	14	4	29	6
UCLA	11	7	18	11
Stanford	11	7	18	13
Oregon St.	8	10	17	15
Arizona St.	7	11	18	14
Washington St.	7	11	12	16
Oregon	6	12	14	13
California	6	12	13	16
USC	5	13	12	17
Patriot				
Holy Cross	13	1	25	7
Bucknell*	10	4	23	10
American	8	6	16	12
Lehigh	7	7	14	15
Colgate	7	7	14	15
Lafayette	5	9	9	19
Navy	5	9	9	19
Army	1	13	3	24
Southeastern				
East Division				
Kentucky	14	2	28	6
Florida*	12	4	24	8
Vanderbilt	8	8	20	14
South Carolina	7	9	20	13
Tennessee	6	10	14	17
Georgia	2	14	8	20
West Division				
Alabama	12	4	24	8
LSU	12	4	20	10
Mississippi St.	9	7	23	11
Arkansas	6	10	18	12
Auburn	4	12	14	17
Ole Miss	4	12	14	17
Southern				
North Division				
Chattanooga*	10	6	20	11
Appalachian St.	9	7	18	12
NC Greensboro	9	7	18	12
Elon	5	11	8	23
E. Tennessee St.	4	12	10	19
Western Carolina	3	13	8	22
South Division				
Davidson	16	0	23	9
Charleston	10	6	18	10
Georgia Southern	10	6	18	13
Furman	9	7	16	13
Wofford	7	9	14	14
Citadel	4	12	12	16
Southland				
SE Louisiana*	13	3	24	9
Northwestern St.	13	3	21	12
Sam Houston St.	11	5	18	12
Texas-San Antonio	10	6	15	13
Lamar	9	7	18	11
Texas St.	8	8	14	14
McNeese St.	8	8	13	15
Texas-Arlington	7	9	13	15
Stephen F. Austin	6	10	12	15
Louisiana-Monroe	2	14	8	19
Nicholls St.	1	15	6	21
Southwestern Athletic				
Alabama A&M*	12	6	18	14
Grambling St.	11	7	14	12
Jackson St.	11	7	16	16
Alabama St.	11	7	15	15
Miss. Valley St.	11	7	13	15
Southern	10	8	14	15
Texas Southern	9	9	11	15
Ark.-Pine Bluff	6	12	8	20
Alcorn St.	6	12	7	22
Prairie View A&M	6	12	6	22
Sun Belt				
East Division				
Ark.-Little Rock	10	4	18	10
Western Kentucky	9	5	22	9
Middle Tenn. St.	7	7	19	12
Arkansas St.	7	7	16	13
Florida Intl.	4	10	13	17
West Division				
Denver	12	3	20	11
La.-Lafayette*	11	4	20	11
New Orleans	7	8	13	17
North Texas	6	9	14	14
South Alabama	6	9	10	18
New Mexico St.	1	14	6	24
West Coast				
Gonzaga*	12	2	26	5
St. Mary's (CA)	11	3	25	9
San Diego	7	7	16	13
Santa Clara	7	7	15	16
Pepperdine	6	8	17	14
San Francisco	6	8	17	14
Portland	4	10	15	15
Loyola Marymount	3	11	11	17
Western Athletic Conference				
Nevada	16	2	25	7
UTEP*	14	4	27	8
Rice	12	6	19	12
Fresno St.	9	9	16	14
SMU	9	9	14	14
Louisiana Tech	9	9	14	15
Hawaii	7	11	16	13
Boise St.	6	12	16	18
Tulsa	5	13	9	20
San Jose St.	3	15	6	23
Independents				
TX A&M-Corp. Christi	—	—	20	8
Utah Valley St.	—	—	16	12
TX Pan American	—	—	12	16
UC Davis	—	—	11	17
Northern Colorado	—	—	8	21
I-P Fort Wayne	—	—	7	22
Longwood	—	—	1	30
Savannah St.	—	—	0	28

(1) In July 2004, Virginia Tech and Miami (FL) joined the ACC from the Big East. (2) Conference does not hold a tournament.

All-Time Winningest Division I College Teams by Percentage

(through 2004-2005 season)

TEAM	Yrs	Won	Lost	Pct.
Kentucky	102	1,904	583	0.766
N. Carolina	95	1,860	681	0.732
UNLV	47	963	390	0.712
Kansas	107	1,848	769	0.706
Duke	100	1,764	787	0.691
UCLA	86	1,548	701	0.688
Syracuse	104	1,657	759	0.686
St. John's-NY	98	1,677	802	0.676
W. Kentucky	86	1,503	745	0.669
Utah	97	1,570	799	0.663
Illinois	100	1,520	805	0.654
Louisville	91	1,484	793	0.652
Arizona	100	1,488	805	0.649
Indiana	105	1,570	853	0.648
Arkansas	82	1,407	770	0.646
Notre Dame	100	1,565	863	0.645
Temple	109	1,639	902	0.645
Pennsylvania	105	1,592	895	0.640
Weber State	43	785	443	0.639
DePaul	82	1,300	737	0.638

Major College Basketball Tournaments

The National Invitation Tournament (NIT), first played in 1938, is the oldest U.S. basketball tournament. The first National Collegiate Athletic Association (NCAA) national championship tournament was played one year later. In Aug. 2005, the NCAA agreed to purchase the NIT from the five New York City area colleges that had run the NIT, and administer its pre- and post-season tournaments.

National Invitation Tournament Champions

Year	Champion
1938	Temple
1939	Long Island Univ.
1940	Colorado
1941	Long Island Univ.
1942	West Virginia
1943	St. John's
1944	St. John's
1945	De Paul
1946	Kentucky
1947	Utah
1948	St. Louis
1949	San Francisco
1950	CCNY
1951	Brigham Young
1952	LaSalle
1953	Seton Hall
1954	Holy Cross
1955	Duquesne
1956	Louisville
1957	Bradley
1958	Xavier (Ohio)
1959	St. John's
1960	Bradley
1961	Providence
1962	Dayton
1963	Providence
1964	Bradley
1965	St. John's
1966	Brigham Young
1967	Southern Illinois
1968	Dayton
1969	Temple
1970	Marquette
1971	North Carolina
1972	Maryland
1973	Virginia Tech
1974	Purdue
1975	Princeton
1976	Kentucky
1977	St. Bonaventure
1978	Texas
1979	Indiana
1980	Virginia
1981	Tulsa
1982	Bradley
1983	Fresno State
1984	Michigan
1985	UCLA
1986	Ohio State
1987	So. Mississippi
1988	Connecticut
1989	St. John's
1990	Vanderbilt
1991	Stanford
1992	Virginia
1993	Minnesota
1994	Villanova
1995	Virginia Tech
1996	Nebraska
1997	Michigan
1998	Minnesota
1999	California
2000	Wake Forest
2001	Tulsa
2002	Memphis
2003	St. John's
2004	Michigan
2005	South Carolina

2005 MEN'S NCAA BASKETBALL TOURNAMENT

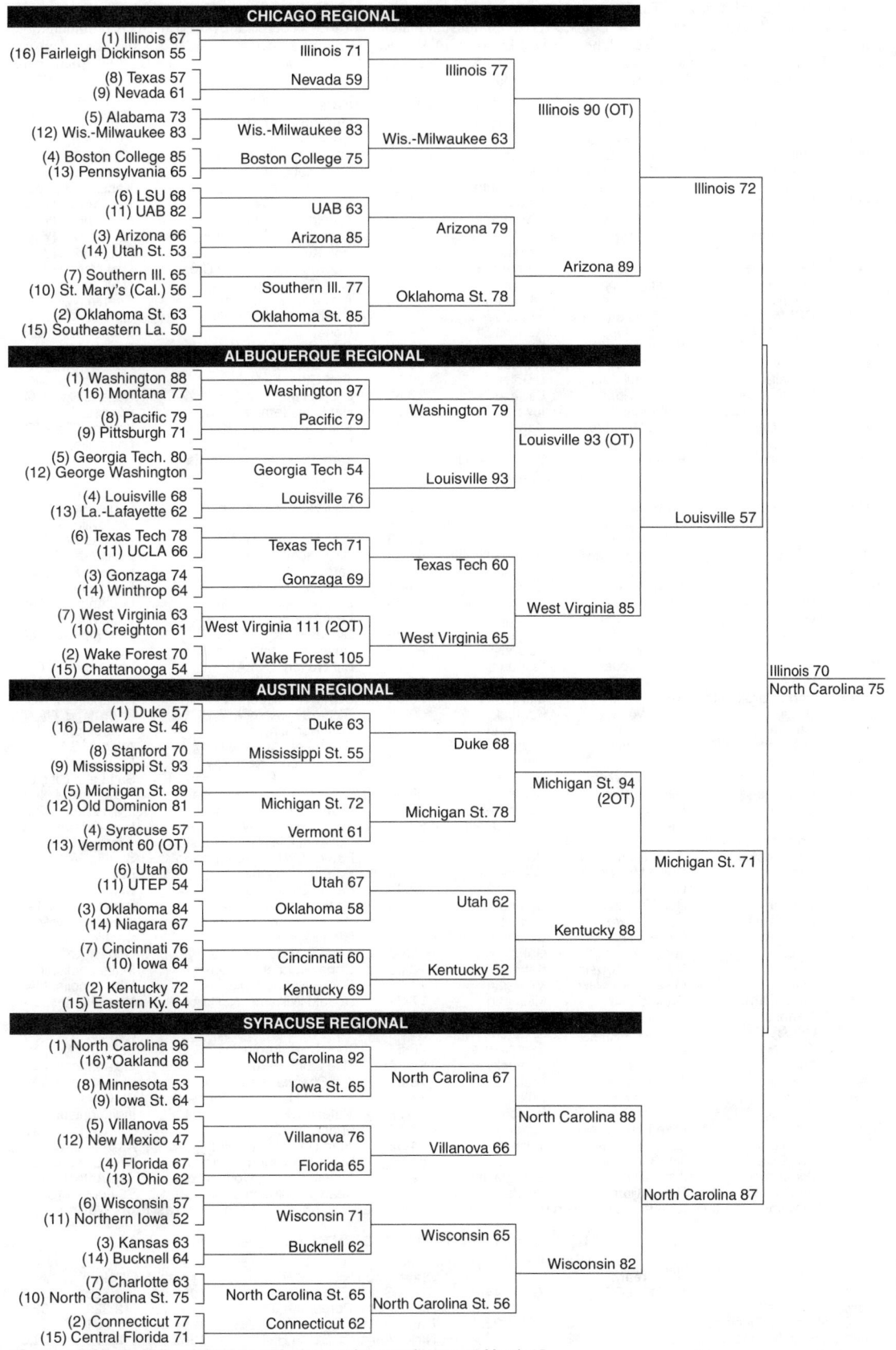

CHICAGO REGIONAL

First round
- (1) Illinois 67, (16) Fairleigh Dickinson 55
- (8) Texas 57, (9) Nevada 61
- (5) Alabama 73, (12) Wis.-Milwaukee 83
- (4) Boston College 85, (13) Pennsylvania 65
- (6) LSU 68, (11) UAB 82
- (3) Arizona 66, (14) Utah St. 53
- (7) Southern Ill. 65, (10) St. Mary's (Cal.) 56
- (2) Oklahoma St. 63, (15) Southeastern La. 50

Second round
- Illinois 71, Nevada 59
- Wis.-Milwaukee 83, Boston College 75
- UAB 63, Arizona 85
- Southern Ill. 77, Oklahoma St. 85

Regional semifinals
- Illinois 77, Wis.-Milwaukee 63
- Arizona 79, Oklahoma St. 78

Regional final
- Illinois 90 (OT), Arizona 89

ALBUQUERQUE REGIONAL

First round
- (1) Washington 88, (16) Montana 77
- (8) Pacific 79, (9) Pittsburgh 71
- (5) Georgia Tech. 80, (12) George Washington
- (4) Louisville 68, (13) La.-Lafayette 62
- (6) Texas Tech 78, (11) UCLA 66
- (3) Gonzaga 74, (14) Winthrop 64
- (7) West Virginia 63, (10) Creighton 61
- (2) Wake Forest 70, (15) Chattanooga 54

Second round
- Washington 97, Pacific 79
- Georgia Tech 54, Louisville 76
- Texas Tech 71, Gonzaga 69
- West Virginia 111 (2OT), Wake Forest 105

Regional semifinals
- Washington 79, Louisville 93
- Texas Tech 60, West Virginia 65

Regional final
- Louisville 93 (OT), West Virginia 85

AUSTIN REGIONAL

First round
- (1) Duke 57, (16) Delaware St. 46
- (8) Stanford 70, (9) Mississippi St. 93
- (5) Michigan St. 89, (12) Old Dominion 81
- (4) Syracuse 57, (13) Vermont 60 (OT)
- (6) Utah 60, (11) UTEP 54
- (3) Oklahoma 84, (14) Niagara 67
- (7) Cincinnati 76, (10) Iowa 64
- (2) Kentucky 72, (15) Eastern Ky. 64

Second round
- Duke 63, Mississippi St. 55
- Michigan St. 72, Vermont 61
- Utah 67, Oklahoma 58
- Cincinnati 60, Kentucky 69

Regional semifinals
- Duke 68, Michigan St. 78
- Utah 62, Kentucky 52

Regional final
- Michigan St. 94 (2OT), Kentucky 88

SYRACUSE REGIONAL

First round
- (1) North Carolina 96, (16)*Oakland 68
- (8) Minnesota 53, (9) Iowa St. 64
- (5) Villanova 55, (12) New Mexico 47
- (4) Florida 67, (13) Ohio 62
- (6) Wisconsin 57, (11) Northern Iowa 52
- (3) Kansas 63, (14) Bucknell 64
- (7) Charlotte 63, (10) North Carolina St. 75
- (2) Connecticut 77, (15) Central Florida 71

Second round
- North Carolina 92, Iowa St. 65
- Villanova 76, Florida 65
- Wisconsin 71, Bucknell 62
- North Carolina St. 65, Connecticut 62

Regional semifinals
- North Carolina 67, Villanova 66
- Wisconsin 65, North Carolina St. 56

Regional final
- North Carolina 88, Wisconsin 82

NATIONAL SEMIFINALS

- Illinois 72, Louisville 57
- Michigan St. 71, North Carolina 87

CHAMPIONSHIP

- Illinois 70
- North Carolina 75

*Oakland defeated Alabama A&M 79-69 in the opening-round game on March 15.

2005 Men's NCAA Tournament: UNC Tar Heels Defeat Illinois Illini for Title

The Univ. of North Carolina Tar Heels (33-4) defeated the Univ. of Illinois Fighting Illini (37-2), 75-70, to win the Division I national title Apr. 4, 2005, in St. Louis, MO. In an unusual matchup of top-seeded teams, the Tar Heels dominated the game from the beginning, and twice led the game by 15 points. Coach Roy Wiliams earned his first NCAA title after 4 unsuccessful Final Four visits heading Kansas. UNC forward Sean May, who had 26 points and 10 rebounds in the final game alone, was named the Final Four's most outstanding player.

NCAA Division I Champions

Year	Champion	Coach	Final opponent	Score	Outstanding player	Site
1939	Oregon	Howard Hobson	Ohio St.	46-33	None	Evanston, IL
1940	Indiana	Branch McCracken	Kansas	60-42	Marvin Huffman, Indiana	Kansas City, MO
1941	Wisconsin	Harold Foster	Washington St.	39-34	John Kotz, Wisconsin	Kansas City, MO
1942	Stanford	Everett Dean	Dartmouth	53-38	Howard Dallmar, Stanford	Kansas City, MO
1943	Wyoming	Everett Shelton	Georgetown	46-34	Ken Sailors, Wyoming	New York, NY
1944	Utah	Vadal Peterson	Dartmouth	42-40[1]	Arnold Ferrin, Utah	New York, NY
1945	Oklahoma St.[2]	Henry Iba	NYU	49-45	Bob Kurland, Oklahoma St.	New York, NY
1946	Oklahoma St. [2]	Henry Iba	North Carolina	43-40	Bob Kurland, Oklahoma St.	New York, NY
1947	Holy Cross	Alvin Julian	Oklahoma	58-47	George Kaftan, Holy Cross	New York, NY
1948	Kentucky	Adolph Rupp	Baylor	58-42	Alex Groza, Kentucky	New York, NY
1949	Kentucky	Adolph Rupp	Oklahoma St.	46-36	Alex Groza, Kentucky	Seattle, WA
1950	CCNY	Nat Holman	Bradley	71-68	Irwin Dambrot, CCNY	New York, NY
1951	Kentucky	Adolph Rupp	Kansas St.	68-58	None	Minneapolis, MN
1952	Kansas	Forrest Allen	St. John's	80-63	Clyde Lovellette, Kansas	Seattle, WA
1953	Indiana	Branch McCracken	Kansas	69-68	B.H. Born, Kansas	Kansas City, MO
1954	La Salle	Kenneth Loeffler	Bradley	92-76	Tom Gola, La Salle	Kansas City, MO
1955	San Francisco	Phil Woolpert	LaSalle	77-63	Bill Russell, San Francisco	Kansas City, MO
1956	San Francisco	Phil Woolpert	Iowa	83-71	Hal Lear, Temple	Evanston, IL
1957	North Carolina	Frank McGuire	Kansas	54-53[1]	Wilt Chamberlain, Kansas	Kansas City, MO
1958	Kentucky	Adolph Rupp	Seattle	84-72	Elgin Baylor, Seattle	Louisville, KY
1959	California	Pete Newell	West Virginia	71-70	Jerry West, West Virginia	Louisville, KY
1960	Ohio St.	Fred Taylor	California	75-55	Jerry Lucas, Ohio St.	San Francisco, CA
1961	Cincinnati	Edwin Jucker	Ohio St.	70-65[1]	Jerry Lucas, Ohio St.	Kansas City, MO
1962	Cincinnati	Edwin Jucker	Ohio St.	71-59	Paul Hogue, Cincinnati	Louisville, KY
1963	Loyola (IL)	George Ireland	Cincinnati	60-58[1]	Art Heyman, Duke	Louisville, KY
1964	UCLA	John Wooden	Duke	98-83	Walt Hazzard, UCLA	Kansas City, MO
1965	UCLA	John Wooden	Michigan	91-80	Bill Bradley, Princeton	Portland, OR
1966	Texas-El Paso[3]	Don Haskins	Kentucky	72-65	Jerry Chambers, Utah	College Park, MD
1967	UCLA	John Wooden	Dayton	79-64	Lew Alcindor, UCLA	Louisville, KY
1968	UCLA	John Wooden	North Carolina	78-55	Lew Alcindor, UCLA	Los Angeles, CA
1969	UCLA	John Wooden	Purdue	92-72	Lew Alcindor, UCLA	Louisville, KY
1970	UCLA	John Wooden	Jacksonville	80-69	Sidney Wicks, UCLA	College Park, MD
1971	UCLA	John Wooden	Villanova*	68-62	Howard Porter, Villanova*	Houston, TX
1972	UCLA	John Wooden	Florida St.	81-76	Bill Walton, UCLA	Los Angeles, CA
1973	UCLA	John Wooden	Memphis St.	87-66	Bill Walton, UCLA	St. Louis, MO
1974	North Carolina St.	Norm Sloan	Marquette	76-64	David Thompson, N.C. St.	Greensboro, NC
1975	UCLA	John Wooden	Kentucky	92-85	Richard Washington, UCLA	San Diego, CA
1976	Indiana	Bob Knight	Michigan	86-68	Kent Benson, Indiana	Philadelphia, PA
1977	Marquette	Al McGuire	North Carolina	67-59	Butch Lee, Marquette	Atlanta, GA
1978	Kentucky	Joe Hall	Duke	94-88	Jack Givens, Kentucky	St. Louis, MO
1979	Michigan St.	Jud Heathcote	Indiana St.	75-64	Magic Johnson, Michigan St.	Salt Lake City, UT
1980	Louisville	Denny Crum	UCLA*	59-54	Darrell Griffith, Louisville	Indianapolis, IN
1981	Indiana	Bob Knight	North Carolina	63-50	Isiah Thomas, Indiana	Philadelphia, PA
1982	North Carolina	Dean Smith	Georgetown	63-62	James Worthy, N. Carolina	New Orleans, LA
1983	North Carolina St.	Jim Valvano	Houston	54-52	Hakeem Olajuwon, Houston	Albuquerque, NM
1984	Georgetown	John Thompson	Houston	84-75	Patrick Ewing, Georgetown	Seattle, WA
1985	Villanova	Rollie Massimino	Georgetown	66-64	Ed Pinckney, Villanova	Lexington, KY
1986	Louisville	Denny Crum	Duke	72-69	Pervis Ellison, Louisville	Dallas, TX
1987	Indiana	Bob Knight	Syracuse	74-73	Keith Smart, Indiana	New Orleans, LA
1988	Kansas	Larry Brown	Oklahoma	83-79	Danny Manning, Kansas	Kansas City, MO
1989	Michigan	Steve Fisher	Seton Hall	80-79[1]	Glen Rice, Michigan	Seattle, WA
1990	UNLV	Jerry Tarkanian	Duke	103-73	Anderson Hunt, UNLV	Denver, CO
1991	Duke	Mike Krzyzewski	Kansas	72-65	Christian Laettner, Duke	Indianapolis, IN
1992	Duke	Mike Krzyzewski	Michigan	71-51	Bobby Hurley, Duke	Minneapolis, MN
1993	North Carolina	Dean Smith	Michigan	77-71	Donald Williams, N. Carolina	New Orleans, LA
1994	Arkansas	Nolan Richardson	Duke	76-72	Corliss Williamson, Arkansas	Charlotte, NC
1995	UCLA	Jim Harrick	Arkansas	89-78	Ed O'Bannon, UCLA	Seattle, WA
1996	Kentucky	Rick Pitino	Syracuse	76-67	Tony Delk, Kentucky	E. Rutherford, NJ
1997	Arizona	Lute Olson	Kentucky	84-79[1]	Miles Simon, Arizona	Indianapolis, IN
1998	Kentucky	Tubby Smith	Utah	78-69	Jeff Sheppard, Kentucky	San Antonio, TX
1999	Connecticut	Jim Calhoun	Duke	77-74	Richard Hamilton, Connecticut	St. Petersburg, FL
2000	Michigan St.	Tom Izzo	Florida	89-76	Mateen Cleaves, Michigan St.	Indianapolis, IN
2001	Duke	Mike Krzyzewski	Arizona	82-72	Shane Battier, Duke	Minneapolis, MN
2002	Maryland	Gary Williams	Indiana	64-52	Juan Dixon, Maryland	Atlanta, GA
2003	Syracuse	Jim Boeheim	Kansas	81-78	Carmelo Anthony, Syracuse	New Orleans, LA
2004	Connecticut	Jim Calhoun	Georgia Tech	82-73	Emeka Okafor, Connecticut	San Antonio, TX
2005	North Carolina	Roy Williams	Illinois	75-70	Sean May, North Carolina	St. Louis, MO

*Declared ineligible after the tournament. (1) Overtime. (2) Then known as Oklahoma A&M. (3) Then known as Texas Western.

Top Division I Career Scorers

(minimum 1,500 points; ranked by average)

Player, school	Years	Points	Avg
Pete Maravich, LSU	1968-70	3,667	44.2
Austin Carr, Notre Dame	1969-71	2,560	34.6
Oscar Robertson, Cincinnati	1958-60	2,973	33.8
Calvin Murphy, Niagara	1968-70	2,548	33.1
Dwight Lamar, SW Louisiana	1972-73	1,862	32.7
Frank Selvy, Furman	1952-54	2,538	32.5
Rick Mount, Purdue	1968-70	2,323	32.3
Darrell Floyd, Furman	1954-56	2,281	32.1
Nick Werkman, Seton Hall	1962-64	2,273	32.0
Willie Humes, Idaho State	1970-71	1,510	31.5

John R. Wooden Award

Awarded to the nation's outstanding college basketball player by the Los Angeles Athletic Club.

1977	Marques Johnson, UCLA
1978	Phil Ford, North Carolina
1979	Larry Bird, Indiana State
1980	Darrell Griffith, Louisville
1981	Danny Ainge, Brigham Young
1982	Ralph Sampson, Virginia
1983	Ralph Sampson, Virginia
1984	Michael Jordan, North Carolina
1985	Chris Mullin, St. John's
1986	Walter Berry, St. John's
1987	David Robinson, Navy
1988	Danny Manning, Kansas
1989	Sean Elliott, Arizona
1990	Lionel Simmons, La Salle
1991	Larry Johnson, UNLV
1992	Christian Laettner, Duke
1993	Calbert Cheaney, Indiana
1994	Glenn Robinson, Purdue
1995	Ed O'Bannon, UCLA
1996	Marcus Camby, Massachusetts
1997	Tim Duncan, Wake Forest
1998	Antawn Jamison, North Carolina
1999	Elton Brand, Duke
2000	Kenyon Martin, Cincinnati
2001	Shane Battier, Duke
2002	Jay Williams, Duke
2003	T.J. Ford, Texas
2004	Jameer Nelson, St. Joseph's
2005	Andrew Bogut, Utah

Most Coaching Victories in the NCAA Tournament Through 2005

(Coaches active in 2004-2005 season in bold)

Coach, School(s), First/Last appearance	Wins	Tournaments	Championships
Mike Krzyzewski, Duke, 1984/2005	66	21	3
Dean Smith, North Carolina, 1967/1997	65	27	2
John Wooden, UCLA, 1950/1975	47	16	10
Bob Knight, Indiana, Texas Tech, 1973/2005	45	27	3
Lute Olson, Iowa, Arizona, 1979/2005	45	25	1
Denny Crum, Louisville, 1972/2000	42	23	2
Jim Boeheim, Syracuse, 1977/2005	40	24	1
Roy Williams, Kansas, N. Carolina, 1990/2005	40	16	1
Eddie Sutton, Creighton, Arkansas, Kentucky, Oklahoma St., 1974/2005	37	25	0
Jim Calhoun, Northeastern, Connecticut, 1981/2005	35	17	2
John Thompson, Georgetown, 1975/1997	34	20	1

WOMEN'S COLLEGE BASKETBALL

2005 Women's NCAA Tournament: Lady Bears Overpower Spartans

The Baylor Univ. Lady Bears beat the top-seeded Michigan State Spartans, 84-62, to win the women's Division I championship Apr. 5 in Indianapolis, IN. Baylor Coach Kim Mulkey-Robertson became the first woman to win national championships as both a player (with Louisiana Tech in 1981-2) and a head coach. Baylor forward Sophia Young, who had played organized basketball for only 6 years, scored 26 points and was named the most outstanding player of the Final Four.

NCAA Division I Women's Champions

Year	Champion	Coach	Final opponent	Score	Outstanding player	Site
1982	Louisiana Tech	Sonja Hogg	Cheyney	76-62	Janice Lawrence, La. Tech	Norfolk, VA
1983	USC	Linda Sharp	Louisiana Tech	69-67	Cheryl Miller, USC	Norfolk, VA
1984	USC	Linda Sharp	Tennessee	72-61	Cheryl Miller, USC	Los Angeles, CA
1985	Old Dominion	Marianne Stanley	Georgia	70-65	Tracy Claxton, Old Dominion	Austin, TX
1986	Texas	Jody Conradt	USC	97-81	Clarissa Davis, Texas	Lexington, KY
1987	Tennessee	Pat Summitt	Louisiana Tech	67-44	Tonya Edwards, Tennessee	Austin, TX
1988	Louisiana Tech	Leon Barmore	Auburn	56-54	Erica Westbrooks, La. Tech	Tacoma, WA
1989	Tennessee	Pat Summitt	Auburn	76-60	Bridgette Gordon, Tennessee	Tacoma, WA
1990	Stanford	Tara VanDerveer	Auburn	88-81	Jennifer Azzi, Stanford	Knoxville, TN
1991	Tennessee	Pat Summitt	Virginia	70-67*	Dawn Staley, Virginia	New Orleans, LA
1992	Stanford	Tara VanDerveer	W. Kentucky	78-62	Molly Goodenbour, Stanford	Los Angeles, CA
1993	Texas Tech	Marsha Sharp	Ohio St.	84-82	Sheryl Swoopes, Texas Tech	Atlanta, GA
1994	North Carolina	Sylvia Hatchell	Louisiana Tech	60-59	Charlotte Smith, North Carolina	Richmond, VA
1995	Connecticut	Geno Auriemma	Tennessee	70-64	Rebecca Lobo, Connecticut	Minneapolis, MN
1996	Tennessee	Pat Summitt	Georgia	83-65	Michelle Marciniak, Tennessee	Charlotte, NC
1997	Tennessee	Pat Summitt	Old Dominion	68-59	Chamique Holdsclaw, Tennessee	Cincinnati, OH
1998	Tennessee	Pat Summitt	Louisiana Tech	93-75	Chamique Holdsclaw, Tennessee	Kansas City, MO
1999	Purdue	Carolyn Peck	Duke	62-45	Ukari Figgs, Purdue	San Jose, CA
2000	Connecticut	Geno Auriemma	Tennessee	71-52	Shea Ralph, Connecticut	Philadelphia, PA
2001	Notre Dame	Muffet McGraw	Purdue	68-66	Ruth Riley, Notre Dame	St. Louis, MO
2002	Connecticut	Geno Auriemma	Oklahoma	82-70	Swin Cash, Connecticut	San Antonio, TX
2003	Connecticut	Geno Auriemma	Tennessee	73-68	Diana Taurasi, Connecticut	Atlanta, GA
2004	Connecticut	Geno Auriemma	Tennessee	70-61	Diana Taurasi, Connecticut	New Orleans, LA
2005	Baylor	Kim Mulkey-Robertson	Michigan State	84-62	Sophia Young, Baylor	Indianapolis, IN

* Overtime.

Wade Trophy

Awarded by National Assn. for Girls and Women in Sport for academics, community service, and player performance.

Year	Player, school
1978	Carol Blazejowski, Montclair St.
1979	Nancy Lieberman, Old Dominion
1980	Nancy Lieberman, Old Dominion
1981	Lynette Woodard, Kansas
1982	Pam Kelly, Louisiana Tech
1983	LaTaunya Pollard, Long Beach St.
1984	Janice Lawrence, Louisiana Tech
1985	Cheryl Miller, USC
1986	Kamie Ethridge, Texas
1987	Shelly Pennefeather, Villanova
1988	Teresa Weatherspoon, Louisiana Tech
1989	Clarissa Davis, Texas
1990	Jennifer Azzi, Stanford
1991	Daedra Charles, Tennessee
1992	Susan Robinson, Penn St.
1993	Karen Jennings, Nebraska
1994	Carol Ann Shudlick, Minnesota
1995	Rebecca Lobo, Connecticut
1996	Jennifer Rizzotti, Connecticut
1997	DeLisha Milton, Florida
1998	Chamique Holdsclaw, Tennessee
1999	Stephanie White-McCarty, Purdue
2000	Edwina Brown, Texas
2001	Jackie Stiles, SW Missouri St.
2002	Sue Bird, Connecticut
2003	Diana Taurasi, Connecticut
2004	Alana Beard, Duke
2005	Seimone Augustus, LSU

Top Division I Women's Career Scorers

(Minimum 1,500 points; ranked by average)

Player, school	Years	Points	Avg
Patricia Hoskins, Miss. Valley St.	1985-89	3,122	28.4
Sandra Hodge, New Orleans	1981-84	2,860	26.7
Jackie Stiles, SW Missouri St.	1997-2001	3,393	26.3
Lorri Bauman, Drake	1981-84	3,115	26.0
Andrea Congreaves, Mercer	1989-93	2,796	25.9
Cindy Blodgett, Maine	1994-98	3,005	25.5
Valorie Whiteside, Appalachian St.	1984-88	2,944	25.4
Joyce Walker, LSU	1981-84	2,906	24.8
Tarcha Hollis, Grambling	1988-91	2,058	24.2
Karen Pelphrey, Marshall	1983-86	2,746	24.1
Korie Hlede, Duquesne	1994-98	2,631	24.1
Erma Jones, Bethune-Cookman	1982-84	2,095	24.1

2005 WOMEN'S NCAA BASKETBALL TOURNAMENT

CHATTANOOGA REGIONAL

(1) LSU 70
(16) Stetson 36
(8) Oklahoma 69
(9) Arizona 72
(5) DePaul 79
(12) Virginia Tech 78
(4) Penn St. 70
(13) Liberty 78
(6) Georgia 75
(11) Rice 49
(3) Texas 64
(14) Oral Roberts 47
(7) Boston College 65
(10) Houston 43
(2) Duke 80
(15) Canisius 48

LSU 76
Arizona 43
DePaul 88
Liberty 79
Georgia 70
Texas 68
Boston College 65
Duke 70

LSU 90
Liberty 48
Georgia 57
Duke 63

LSU 59
Duke 49

LSU 57

TEMPE REGIONAL

(1) North Carolina 97
(16) Coppin St. 82
(8) Mississippi 57
(9) George Washington 60
(5) Arizona St. 87
(12) Eastern Ky. 65
(4) Nortre Dame 61
(13) UC Santa Barb. 51
(6) Virginia 79
(11) Old Dominion 57
(3) Minnesota 64
(14) St. Francis 33
(7) TCU 55
(10) Oregon 58
(2) Baylor 91
(15) Illinois St. 70

North Carolina 71
George Washington 47
Arizona St. 70
Nortre Dame 61
Virginia 58
Minnesota 73
Oregon 46
Baylor 69

North Carolina 79
Arizona St. 72
Minnesota 57
Baylor 64

North Carolina 63
Baylor 72

Baylor 68

KANSAS CITY REGIONAL

(1) Michigan St. 73
(16) Alcorn St. 41
(8) Southern California 65
(9) Louisville 49
(5) Vanderbilt 67
(12) Montana 44
(4) Kansas St. 70
(13) Bowling Green 60
(6) Florida St. 87
(11) Richmond 54
(3) Connecticut 95
(14) Dartmouth 47
(7) Iowa St. 61
(10) Utah 73
(2) Stanford 94
(15) Santa Clara 57

Michigan St. 61
Southern California 59
Vanderbilt 63
Kansas St. 60
Florida St. 52
Connecticut 70
Utah 62
Stanford 88

Michigan St. 76
Vanderbilt 64
Connecticut 59
Stanford 76

Michigan St. 76
Stanford 69

Michigan St. 68

PHILADELPHIA REGIONAL

(1) Tennessee 94
(16) Western Caro. 43
(8) New Mexico 56
(9) Purdue 68
(5) North Carolina St. 58
(12) Middle Tenn. 60
(4) Texas Tech 69
(13) Texas-Arlington 49
(6) Temple 66
(11) Louisiana Tech 61
(3) Rutgers 62
(14) Hartford 37
(7) Maryland 65
(10) Wis.-Green Bay 55
(2) Ohio St. 86
(15) Holy Cross 45

Tennessee 75
Purdue 54
Middle Tenn. 69
Texas Tech 80
Temple 54
Rutgers 61
Maryland 65
Ohio St. 75

Tennessee 75
Texas Tech 59
Rutgers 64
Ohio St. 58

Tennessee 59
Rutgers 49

Tennessee 64

FINAL

Baylor 84
Michigan St. 62

NATIONAL FOOTBALL LEAGUE

NFL 2004-2005: Pats 3rd Super, and Set Consecutive-Wins Record; Manning Breaks TD Pass Record and Earns MVP

The New England Patriots beat the Philadelphia Eagles, 24-21, in Jacksonville, FL, Feb. 6, 2005, in Super Bowl XXXIX, becoming only the 2nd team ever to win 3 Super Bowls in 4 years. Patriots wide receiver Deion Branch tied a Super Bowl record with 11 catches and was named the Super Bowl MVP. New England quarterback Tom Brady improved his playoff record to 9-0. On the Eagles side, wide receiver Terrell Owens, who played despite recent ankle surgery, caught a team-leading 9 passes for 122 yds.

During the regular season the Patriots had set a new consecutive-game-winning record with 21. The streak was broken on Oct. 31, 2004, when they lost to the Pittsburgh Steelers, 34-20. NFL MVP Peyton Manning, quarterback for the Indianapolis Colts, set the NFL record for touchdown passes in a season with 49, breaking Dan Marino's 20-year record of 48. Colts kicker Mike Vanderjagt set a record for consecutive field goals, with 42. Former Miami (Ohio) Univ. standout Ben Roethlisberger won rookie of the year honors as quarterback for the Steelers, whom he led to the playoffs. In other news, NFL commissioner Paul Tagliabue and Players' Assoc. executive director Gene Upshaw testified before Congress in May over the issue of alleged rampant steroid use in professional sports.

Final 2004 Standings

American Football Conference

East Division	W	L	T	Pct.	Pts.	Opp.	Div.
New England	14	2	0	.875	437	260	5-1
*N.Y. Jets	10	6	0	.625	333	261	3-3
Buffalo	9	7	0	.562	395	284	3-3
Miami	4	12	0	.250	275	354	1-5
North Division	**W**	**L**	**T**	**Pct.**	**Pts.**	**Opp.**	**Div.**
Pittsburgh	15	1	0	.938	372	251	5-1
Baltimore	9	7	0	.562	317	268	3-3
Cincinnati	8	8	0	.500	374	372	2-4
Cleveland	4	12	0	.250	276	390	2-4
South Division	**W**	**L**	**T**	**Pct.**	**Pts.**	**Opp.**	**Div.**
Indianapolis	12	4	0	.750	522	351	5-1
Jacksonville	9	7	0	.562	261	280	2-4
Houston	7	9	0	.438	309	339	4-2
Tennessee	5	11	0	.312	344	439	1-5
West Division	**W**	**L**	**T**	**Pct.**	**Pts.**	**Opp.**	**Div.**
San Diego	12	4	0	.750	446	313	5-1
*Denver	10	6	0	.625	381	304	3-3
Kansas City	7	9	0	.438	483	435	3-3
Oakland	5	11	0	.312	320	442	1-5

National Football Conference

East Division	W	L	T	Pct.	Pts.	Opp.	Div.
Philadelphia	13	3	0	.812	386	260	6-0
N.Y. Giants	6	10	0	.375	303	347	3-3
Dallas	6	10	0	.375	293	405	2-4
Washington	6	10	0	.375	240	265	1-5
North Division	**W**	**L**	**T**	**Pct.**	**Pts.**	**Opp.**	**Div.**
Green Bay	10	6	0	.625	424	380	5-1
*Minnesota	8	8	0	.500	405	395	3-3
Detroit	6	10	0	.375	296	350	2-4
Chicago	5	11	0	.312	231	331	2-4
South Division	**W**	**L**	**T**	**Pct.**	**Pts.**	**Opp.**	**Div.**
Atlanta	11	5	0	.688	340	337	4-2
New Orleans	8	8	0	.500	348	405	3-3
Carolina	7	9	0	.438	355	339	3-3
Tampa Bay	5	11	0	.312	301	304	2-4
West Division	**W**	**L**	**T**	**Pct.**	**Pts.**	**Opp.**	**Div.**
Seattle	9	7	0	.562	371	373	3-3
*St. Louis	8	8	0	.500	319	392	5-1
Arizona	6	10	0	.375	284	322	2-4
San Francisco	2	14	0	.125	259	452	2-4

* Wild card team.

AFC Playoffs—N.Y. Jets 20, San Diego 17 (OT); Indianapolis 49, Denver 24; Pittsburgh 20, N.Y. Jets 17 (OT); New England 20, Indianapolis 3; New England 41, Pittsburgh 27.

NFC Playoffs—St. Louis 27, Seattle 20; Minnesota 31, Green Bay 17; Atlanta 47, St. Louis 17; Philadelphia 27, Minnesota 14; Philadelphia 27, Atlanta 10.

Super Bowl—New England 24, Philadelphia 21.

American Football League Champions

Year	Eastern Division	Western Division	Championship
1960	Houston Oilers (10-4-0)	Los Angeles Chargers (10-4-0)	Houston 24, Los Angeles 16
1961	Houston Oilers (10-3-1)	San Diego Chargers (12-2-0)	Houston 10, San Diego 3
1962	Houston Oilers (11-3-0)	Dallas Texans (11-3-0)	Dallas 20, Houston 17 (2 overtimes)
1963	Boston Patriots (7-6-1)(a)	San Diego Chargers (11-3-0)	San Diego 51, Boston 10
1964	Buffalo Bills (12-2-0)	San Diego Chargers (8-5-1)	Buffalo 20, San Diego 7
1965	Buffalo Bills (10-3-1)	San Diego Chargers (9-2-3)	Buffalo 23, San Diego 0
1966	Buffalo Bills (9-4-1)	Kansas City Chiefs (11-2-1)	Kansas City 31, Buffalo 7
1967	Houston Oilers (9-4-1)	Oakland Raiders (13-1-0)	Oakland 40, Houston 7
1968	New York Jets (11-3-0)	Oakland Raiders (12-2-0)(b)	New York 27, Oakland 23
1969	New York Jets (10-4-0)	Oakland Raiders (12-1-1)	Kansas City 17, Oakland 7 (c)

(a) Defeated Buffalo Bills in divisional playoff. (b) Defeated Kansas City Chiefs in divisional playoff. (c) Kansas City Chiefs defeated N.Y. Jets and Oakland Raiders defeated Houston Oilers in divisional playoffs.

National Football League Champions

Year	East Winner (W-L-T)	West Winner (W-L-T)	Playoff
1933	New York Giants (11-3-0)	Chicago Bears (10-2-1)	Chicago Bears 23, New York 21
1934	New York Giants (8-5-0)	Chicago Bears (13-0-0)	New York 30, Chicago Bears 13
1935	New York Giants (9-3-0)	Detroit Lions (7-3-2)	Detroit 26, New York 7
1936	Boston Redskins (7-5-0)	Green Bay Packers (10-1-1)	Green Bay 21, Boston 6
1937	Washington Redskins (8-3-0)	Chicago Bears (9-1-1)	Washington 28, Chicago Bears 21
1938	New York Giants (8-2-1)	Green Bay Packers (8-3-0)	New York 23, Green Bay 17
1939	New York Giants (9-1-1)	Green Bay Packers (9-2-0)	Green Bay 27, New York 0
1940	Washington Redskins (9-2-0)	Chicago Bears (8-3-0)	Chicago Bears 73, Washington 0
1941	New York Giants (8-3-0)	Chicago Bears (10-1-1)(a)	Chicago Bears 37, New York 9
1942	Washington Redskins (10-1-1)	Chicago Bears (11-0-0)	Washington 14, Chicago Bears 6
1943	Washington Redskins (6-3-1)	Chicago Bears (8-1-1)	Chicago Bears, 41, Washington 21
1944	New York Giants (8-1-1)	Green Bay Packers (8-2-0)	Green Bay 14, New York 7
1945	Washington Redskins (8-2-0)	Cleveland Rams (9-1-0)	Cleveland 15, Washington 14
1946	New York Giants (7-3-1)	Chicago Bears (8-2-1)	Chicago Bears 24, New York 14
1947	Philadelphia Eagles (8-4-0)(a)	Chicago Cardinals (9-3-0)	Chicago Cardinals 28, Philadelphia 21
1948	Philadelphia Eagles (9-2-1)	Chicago Cardinals (11-1-0)	Philadelphia 7, Chicago Cardinals 0
1949	Philadelphia Eagles (11-1-0)	Los Angeles Rams (8-2-2)	Philadelphia 14, Los Angeles 0
1950	Cleveland Browns (10-2-0)(a)	Los Angeles Rams (9-3-0)(a)	Cleveland 30, Los Angeles 28
1951	Cleveland Browns (11-1-0)	Los Angeles Rams (8-4-0)	Los Angeles 24, Cleveland 17
1952	Cleveland Browns (8-4-0)	Detroit Lions (9-3-0)(a)	Detroit 17, Cleveland 7
1953	Cleveland Browns (11-1-0)	Detroit Lions (10-2-0)	Detroit 17, Cleveland 16

Year	East Winner (W-L-T)	West Winner (W-L-T)	Playoff
1954	Cleveland Browns (9-3-0)	Detroit Lions (9-2-1)	Cleveland 56, Detroit 10
1955	Cleveland Browns (9-2-1)	Los Angeles Rams (8-3-1)	Cleveland 38, Los Angeles 14
1956	New York Giants (8-3-1)	Chicago Bears (9-2-1)	New York 47, Chicago Bears 7
1957	Cleveland Browns (9-2-1)	Detroit Lions (8-4-0)(a)	Detroit 59, Cleveland 14
1958	New York Giants (9-3-0)(a)	Baltimore Colts (9-3-0)	Baltimore 23, New York 17(b)
1959	New York Giants (10-2-0)	Baltimore Colts (9-3-0)	Baltimore 31, New York 16
1960	Philadelphia Eagles (10-2-0)	Green Bay Packers (8-4-0)	Philadelphia 17, Green Bay 13
1961	New York Giants (10-3-1)	Green Bay Packers (11-3-0)	Green Bay 37, New York 0
1962	New York Giants (12-2-0)	Green Bay Packers (13-1-0)	Green Bay 16, New York 7
1963	New York Giants (11-3-0)	Chicago Bears (11-1-2)	Chicago 14, New York 10
1964	Cleveland Browns (10-3-1)	Baltimore Colts (12-2-0)	Cleveland 27, Baltimore 0
1965	Cleveland Browns (11-3-0)	Green Bay Packers (10-3-1)(a)	Green Bay 23, Cleveland 12
1966	Dallas Cowboys (10-3-1)	Green Bay Packers (12-2-0)	Green Bay 34, Dallas 27
1967	Dallas Cowboys (9-5-0)	Green Bay Packers (9-4-1)	Green Bay 21, Dallas 17
1968	Cleveland Browns (10-4-0)	Baltimore Colts (13-1-0)	Baltimore 34, Cleveland 0
1969	Cleveland Browns (10-3-1)	Minnesota Vikings (12-2-0)	Minnesota 27, Cleveland 7

Year	Conference	Division	Winner (W-L-T)	Playoffs (c)	Year
1970	American	Eastern	Baltimore Colts (11-2-1)	Baltimore 17, Cincinnati 0	1970
		Central	Cincinnati Bengals (8-6-0)	Oakland 21, Miami* 14	
		Western	Oakland Raiders (8-4-2)	Baltimore 27, Oakland 17	
	National	Eastern	Dallas Cowboys (10-4-0)	Dallas 5, Detroit* 0	
		Central	Minnesota Vikings (12-2-0)	San Francisco 17, Minnesota 14	
		Western	San Francisco 49ers (10-3-1)	Dallas 17, San Francisco 10	
1971	American	Eastern	Miami Dolphins (10-3-1)	Miami 27, Kansas City* 24	1971
		Central	Cleveland Browns (9-5-0)	Baltimore 20, Cleveland 3	
		Western	Kansas City Chiefs(10-3-1)	Miami 21, Baltimore 0	
	National	Eastern	Dallas Cowboys (11-3-0)	Dallas 20, Minnesota 12	
		Central	Minnesota Vikings (11-3-0)	San Francisco 24, Washington* 20	
		Western	San Francisco 49ers (9-5-0)	Dallas 14, San Francisco 3	
1972	American	Eastern	Miami Dolphins (14-0-0)	Miami 20, Cleveland* 14	1972
		Central	Pittsburgh Steelers (11-3-0)	Pittsburgh 13, Oakland 7	
		Western	Oakland Raiders (10-3-1)	Miami 21, Pittsburgh 17	
	National	Eastern	Washington Redskins (11-3-0)	Washington 16, Green Bay 3	
		Central	Green Bay Packers (10-4-0)	Dallas* 30, San Francisco 28	
		Western	San Francisco 49ers (8-5-1)	Washington 26, Dallas* 3	
1973	American	Eastern	Miami Dolphins (12-2-0)	Miami 34, Cincinnati 16	1973
		Central	Cincinnati Bengals (10-4-0)	Oakland 33, Pittsburgh* 14	
		Western	Oakland Raiders (9-4-1)	Miami 27, Oakland 10	
	National	Eastern	Dallas Cowboys (10-4-0)	Dallas 27, Los Angeles 16	
		Central	Minnesota Vikings (12-2-0)	Minnesota 27, Washington* 20	
		Western	Los Angeles Rams (12-2-0)	Minnesota 27, Dallas 10	
1974	American	Eastern	Miami Dolphins (11-3-0)	Oakland 28, Miami 26	1974
		Central	Pittsburgh Steelers (10-3-1)	Pittsburgh 32, Buffalo* 14	
		Western	Oakland Raiders (12-2-0)	Pittsburgh 24, Oakland 13	
	National	Eastern	St. Louis Cardinals (10-4-0)	Minnesota 30, St. Louis 14	
		Central	Minnesota Vikings (10-4-0)	Los Angeles 19, Washington* 10	
		Western	Los Angeles Rams (10-4-0)	Minnesota 14, Los Angeles 10	
1975	American	Eastern	Baltimore Colts (10-4-0)	Pittsburgh 28, Baltimore 10	1975
		Central	Pittsburgh Steelers (12-2-0)	Oakland 31, Cincinnati* 28	
		Western	Oakland Raiders (11-3-0)	Pittsburgh 16, Oakland 10	
	National	Eastern	St. Louis Cardinals (11-3-0)	Dallas* 17, Minnesota 14	
		Central	Minnesota Vikings (12-2-0)	Los Angeles 35, St. Louis 23	
		Western	Los Angeles Rams (12-2-0)	Dallas* 37, Los Angeles 7	
1976	American	Eastern	Baltimore Colts (11-3-0)	Pittsburgh 40, Baltimore 14	1976
		Central	Pittsburgh Steelers (10-4-0)	Oakland 24, New England* 21	
		Western	Oakland Raiders (13-1-0)	Oakland 24, Pittsburgh 7	
	National	Eastern	Dallas Cowboys (11-3-0)	Minnesota 35, Washington* 20	
		Central	Minnesota Vikings (11-2-1)	Los Angeles 14, Dallas 12	
		Western	Los Angeles Rams (10-3-1)	Minnesota 24, Los Angeles 13	
1977	American	Eastern	Baltimore Colts (10-4-0)	Oakland* 37, Baltimore 31	1977
		Central	Pittsburgh Steelers (9-5-0)	Denver 34, Pittsburgh 21	
		Western	Denver Broncos (12-2-0)	Denver 20, Oakland* 17	
	National	Eastern	Dallas Cowboys (12-2-0)	Dallas 37, Chicago* 7	
		Central	Minnesota Vikings (9-5-0)	Minnesota 14, Los Angeles 7	
		Western	Los Angeles Rams (10-4-0)	Dallas 23, Minnesota 6	
1978	American	Eastern	New England Patriots (11-5-0)	Pittsburgh 33, Denver 10	1978
		Central	Pittsburgh Steelers (14-2-0)	Houston* 31, New England 14	
		Western	Denver Broncos (10-6-0)	Pittsburgh 34, Houston* 5	
	National	Eastern	Dallas Cowboys (12-4-0)	Dallas 27, Atlanta* 20	
		Central	Minnesota Vikings (8-7-1)	Los Angeles 34, Minnesota 10	
		Western	Los Angeles Rams (12-4-0)	Dallas 28, Los Angeles 0	
1979	American	Eastern	Miami Dolphins (10-6-0)	Houston* 17, San Diego 14	1979
		Central	Pittsburgh Steelers (12-4-0)	Pittsburgh 34, Miami 14	
		Western	San Diego Chargers (12-4-0)	Pittsburgh 27, Houston* 13	
	National	Eastern	Dallas Cowboys (11-5-0)	Tampa Bay 24, Philadelphia* 17	
		Central	Tampa Bay Buccaneers (10-6-0)	Los Angeles 21, Dallas 19	
		Western	Los Angeles Rams (9-7-0)	Los Angeles 9, Tampa Bay 0	
1980	American	Eastern	Buffalo Bills (11-5-0)	San Diego 20, Buffalo 14	1980
		Central	Cleveland Browns (11-5-0)	Oakland* 14, Cleveland 12	
		Western	San Diego Chargers (11-5-0)	Oakland* 34, San Diego 27	
	National	Eastern	Philadelphia Eagles (12-4-0)	Philadelphia 31, Minnesota 16	
		Central	Minnesota Vikings (9-7-0)	Dallas* 30, Atlanta 27	
		Western	Atlanta Falcons (12-4-0)	Philadelphia 20, Dallas* 7	
1981	American	Eastern	Miami Dolphins (11-4-1)	San Diego 41, Miami 38	1981
		Central	Cincinnati Bengals (12-4-0)	Cincinnati 28, Buffalo* 21	
		Western	San Diego Chargers (10-6-0)	Cincinnati 27, San Diego 7	
	National	Eastern	Dallas Cowboys (12-4-0)	Dallas 38, Tampa Bay 0	
		Central	Tampa Bay Buccaneers (9-7-0)	San Francisco 38, N.Y. Giants* 24	
		Western	San Francisco 49ers (13-3-0)	San Francisco 28, Dallas 27	
1982 (d)	American		Los Angeles Raiders (8-1-0)	Strike-shortened season (see playoff results after footnote)	1982 (d)
	National		Washington Redskins (8-1-0)		

Year	Conference	Division	Winner (W-L-T)	Playoffs (c)	Year
1983	American	Eastern	Miami Dolphins (12-4-0)	Seattle* 27, Miami 20	1983
		Central	Pittsburgh Steelers (10-6-0)	L.A. Raiders 38, Pittsburgh 10	
		Western	Los Angeles Raiders (12-4-0)	L.A. Raiders 30, Seattle* 14	
	National	Eastern	Washington Redskins (14-2-0)	Washington 51, L.A. Rams* 7	
		Central	Detroit Lions (9-7-0)	San Francisco 24, Detroit 23	
		Western	San Francisico 49ers (10-6-0)	Washington 24, San Francisco 21	
1984	American	Eastern	Miami Dolphins (14-2-0)	Miami 31, Seattle* 10	1984
		Central	Pittsburgh Steelers (9-7-0)	Pittsburgh 24, Denver 17	
		Western	Denver Broncos (13-3-0)	Miami 45, Pittsburgh 28	
	National	Eastern	Washington Redskins (11-5-0)	Chicago 23, Washington 19	
		Central	Chicago Bears (10-6-0)	San Francisco 21, N.Y. Giants* 10	
		Western	San Francisco 49ers (15-1-0)	San Francisco 23, Chicago 0	
1985	American	Eastern	Miami Dolphins (12-4-0)	New England* 27, L.A. Raiders 20	1985
		Central	Cleveland Browns (8-8-0)	Miami 24, Cleveland 21	
		Western	Los Angeles Raiders (12-4-0)	New England* 31, Miami 14	
	National	Eastern	Dallas Cowboys (10-6-0)	Chicago 21, N.Y. Giants* 0	
		Central	Chicago Bears (15-1-0)	L.A. Rams 20, Dallas 0	
		Western	Los Angeles Rams (11-5-0)	Chicago 24, L.A. Rams 0	
1986	American	Eastern	New England Patriots (11-5-0)	Denver 22, New England 17	1986
		Central	Cleveland Browns (12-4-0)	Cleveland 23, N.Y. Jets* 20	
		Western	Denver Broncos (11-5-0)	Denver 23, Cleveland 20	
	National	Eastern	New York Giants (14-2-0)	N.Y. Giants 49, San Francisco 3	
		Central	Chicago Bears (14-2-0)	Washington* 27, Chicago 13	
		Western	San Francisco 49ers (10-5-1)	N.Y. Giants 17, Washington* 0	
1987	American	Eastern	Indianapolis Colts (9-6-0)	Cleveland 38, Indianapolis 21	1987
		Central	Cleveland Browns (10-5-0)	Denver 34, Houston* 10	
		Western	Denver Broncos (10-4-1)	Denver 38, Cleveland 33	
	National	Eastern	Washington Redskins (11-4-0)	Washington 21, Chicago 17	
		Central	Chicago Bears (11-4-0)	Minnesota* 36, San Francisco 24	
		Western	San Francisco 49ers (13-2-0)	Washington 17, Minnesota* 10	
1988	American	Eastern	Buffalo Bills (12-4-0)	Buffalo 17, Houston* 10	1988
		Central	Cincinnati Bengals (12-4-0)	Cincinnati 21, Seattle 13	
		Western	Seattle Seahawks (9-7-0)	Cincinnati 21, Buffalo 10	
	National	Eastern	Philadelphia Eagles (10-6-0)	Chicago 20, Philadelphia 12	
		Central	Chicago Bears (12-4-0)	San Francisco 34, Minnesota* 9	
		Western	San Francisco 49ers (10-6-0)	San Francisco 28, Chicago 3	
1989	American	Eastern	Buffalo Bills (9-7-0)	Cleveland 34, Buffalo 30	1989
		Central	Cleveland Browns (9-6-1)	Denver 24, Pittsburgh* 23	
		Western	Denver Broncos (11-5-0)	Denver 37, Cleveland 21	
	National	Eastern	New York Giants (12-4-0)	San Francisco 41, Minnesota 13	
		Central	Minnesota Vikings (10-6-0)	L.A. Rams* 19, N.Y. Giants 13	
		Western	San Francisco 49ers (14-2-0)	San Francisco 30, L.A. Rams* 3	
1990	American	Eastern	Buffalo Bills (13-3-0)	L.A. Raiders 20, Cincinnati 10	1990
		Central	Cincinnati Bengals (9-7-0)	Buffalo 44, Miami* 34	
		Western	Los Angeles Raiders (12-4-0)	Buffalo 51, L.A. Raiders 3	
	National	Eastern	New York Giants (13-3-0)	San Francisco 28, Washington* 10	
		Central	Chicago Bears (11-5-0)	N.Y. Giants 31, Chicago 3	
		Western	San Francisco 49ers (14-2-0)	N.Y. Giants 15, San Francisco 13	
1991	American	Eastern	Buffalo Bills (13-3-0)	Denver 26, Houston 24	1991
		Central	Houston Oilers (11-5-0)	Buffalo 37, Kansas City* 14	
		Western	Denver Broncos (12-4-0)	Buffalo 10, Denver 7	
	National	Eastern	Washington Redskins (14-2-0)	Washington 24, Atlanta* 7	
		Central	Detroit Lions (12-4-0)	Detroit 38, Dallas* 6	
		Western	New Orleans Saints (11-5-0)	Washington 41, Detroit 10	
1992	American	Eastern	Miami Dolphins (11-5-0)	Miami 31, San Diego 0	1992
		Central	Pittsburgh Steelers (11-5-0)	Buffalo* 24, Pittsburgh 3	
		Western	San Diego Chargers (11-5-0)	Buffalo* 29, Miami 10	
	National	Eastern	Dallas Cowboys (13-3-0)	Dallas 34, Philadelphia* 10	
		Central	Minnesota Vikings (11-5-0)	San Francisco 20, Washington* 13	
		Western	San Francisco 49ers (14-2-0)	Dallas 30, San Francisco 20	
1993	American	Eastern	Buffalo Bills (12-4-0)	Buffalo 29, L.A. Raiders* 23	1993
		Central	Houston Oilers (12-4-0)	Kansas City 28, Houston 20	
		Western	Kansas City Chiefs (11-5-0)	Buffalo 30, Kansas City 13	
	National	Eastern	Dallas Cowboys (12-4-0)	Dallas 27, Green Bay* 17	
		Central	Detroit Lions (10-6-0)	San Francisco 44, N.Y. Giants* 3	
		Western	San Francisco 49ers (10-6-0)	Dallas 38, San Francisco 21	
1994	American	Eastern	Miami Dolphins (10-6-0)	Pittsburgh 29, Cleveland* 9	1994
		Central	Pittsburgh Steelers (12-4-0)	San Diego 22, Miami 21	
		Western	San Diego Chargers (11-5-0)	San Diego 17, Pittsburgh 13	
	National	Eastern	Dallas Cowboys (12-4-0)	San Francisco 44, Chicago* 15	
		Central	Minnesota Vikings (10-6-0)	Dallas 35, Green Bay* 9	
		Western	San Francisco 49ers (13-3-0)	San Francisco 38, Dallas 28	
1995	American	Eastern	Buffalo Bills (10-6-0)	Indianapolis* 10, Kansas City 7	1995
		Central	Pittsburgh Steelers (11-5-0)	Pittsburgh 40, Buffalo 21	
		Western	Kansas City Chiefs (13-3-0)	Pittsburgh 20, Indianapolis* 16	
	National	Eastern	Dallas Cowboys (12-4-0)	Dallas 30, Philadelphia* 11	
		Central	Green Bay Packers (11-5-0)	Green Bay 27, San Francisco 17	
		Western	San Francisco 49ers (11-5-0)	Dallas 38, Green Bay 27	
1996	American	Eastern	New England Patriots (11-5-0)	Jacksonville* 30, Denver 27	1996
		Central	Pittsburgh Steelers (10-6-0)	New England 28, Pittsburgh 3	
		Western	Denver Broncos (13-3-0)	New England 20, Jacksonville* 6	
	National	Eastern	Dallas Cowboys (10-6-0)	Green Bay 35, San Francisco* 14	
		Central	Green Bay Packers (13-3-0)	Carolina 26, Dallas 17	
		Western	Carolina Panthers (12-4-0)	Green Bay 30, Carolina 13	
1997	American	Eastern	New England Patriots (10-6-0)	Pittsburgh 7, New England 6	1997
		Central	Pittsburgh Steelers (11-5-0)	Denver* 14, Kansas City 10	
		Western	Kansas City Chiefs (13-3-0)	Denver* 24, Pittsburgh 21	
	National	Eastern	New York Giants (10-5-1)	San Francisco 38, Minnesota* 22	
		Central	Green Bay Packers (13-3-0)	Green Bay 21, Tampa Bay* 7	
		Western	San Francisco 49ers (13-3-0)	Green Bay 23, San Francisco 10	

Year	Conference	Division	Winner (W-L-T)	Playoffs (c)	Year
1998	American	Eastern	N.Y. Jets (12-4-0)	Denver 38, Miami* 3	1998
		Central	Jacksonville Jaguars (11-5-0)	N.Y. Jets 34, Jacksonville 24	
		Western	Denver Broncos (14-2-0)	Denver 23, N.Y. Jets 10	
	National	Eastern	Dallas Cowboys (10-6-0)	Atlanta 20, San Francisco* 18	
		Central	Minnesota Vikings (15-1-0)	Minnesota 41, Arizona* 21	
		Western	Atlanta Falcons (14-2-0)	Atlanta 30, Minnesota 27 (OT)	
1999	American	Eastern	Indianapolis Colts (13-3-0)	Jacksonville 62, Miami* 7	1999
		Central	Jacksonville Jaguars (14-2-0)	Tennessee* 19, Indianapolis 16	
		Western	Seattle Seahawks (9-7-0)	Tennessee* 33, Jacksonville 14	
	National	Eastern	Washington Redskins (10-6-0)	Tampa Bay 14, Washington 13	
		Central	Tampa Bay Buccaneers (11-5-0)	St. Louis 49, Minnesota* 37	
		Western	St. Louis Rams (13-3-0)	St. Louis 11, Tampa Bay 6	
2000	American	Eastern	Miami Dolphins (11-5-0)	Oakland 27, Miami 0	2000
		Central	Tennessee Titans (13-3-0)	Baltimore* 24, Tennessee 10	
		Western	Oakland Raiders (12-4-0)	Baltimore* 16, Oakland 3	
	National	Eastern	N.Y. Giants (12-4-0)	Minnesota 34, New Orleans 16	
		Central	Minnesota Vikings (11-5-0)	N.Y. Giants 20, Philadelphia* 10	
		Western	New Orleans Saints (10-6-0)	N.Y. Giants 41, Minnesota 0	
2001	American	Eastern	New England Patriots (11-5-0)	New England 16, Oakland 13	2001
		Central	Pittsburgh Steelers (13-3-0)	Pittsburgh 27, Baltimore* 10	
		Western	Oakland Raiders (10-6-0)	New England 24, Pittsburgh 17	
	National	Eastern	Philadelphia Eagles (11-5-0)	Philadelphia 33, Chicago 19	
		Central	Chicago Bears (13-3-0)	St. Louis 45, Green Bay* 17	
		Western	St. Louis Rams (14-2-0)	St. Louis 29, Philadelphia 24	
2002	American	East	N.Y. Jets (9-7-0)		2002
		North	Pittsburgh Steelers (10-5-1)	Oakland 30, N.Y. Jets 10	
		South	Tennessee Titans (11-5-0)	Tennessee 34, Pittsburgh 31	
		West	Oakland Raiders (11-5-0)	Oakland 41, Tennessee 24	
	National	East	Philadelphia Eagles (12-4-0)		
		North	Green Bay Packers (12-4-0)	Philadelphia 20, Atlanta* 6	
		South	Tampa Bay Buccaneers (12-4-0)	Tampa Bay 31, San Francisco 6	
		West	San Francisco 49ers (10-6-0)	Tampa Bay 27, Philadelphia 10	
2003	American	East	New England Patriots (14-2-0)		2003
		North	Baltimore Ravens (10-6-0)	Indianapolis 38, Kansas City 31	
		South	Indianapolis Colts (12-4-0)	New England 17, Tennessee* 14	
		West	Kansas City Chiefs (13-3-0)	New England 24, Indianapolis 14	
	National	East	Philadelphia Eagles (12-4-0)		
		North	Green Bay Packers (10-6-0)	Carolina 29, St. Louis 23	
		South	Carolina Panthers (11-5-0)	Philadelphia 20, Green Bay 17	
		West	St. Louis Rams (12-4-0)	Carolina 14, Philadelphia 3	
2004	American	East	New England Patriots (14-2-0)		2004
		North	Pittsburgh Steelers(15-1-0)	Pittsburgh 20, N.Y. Jets 17* (OT)	
		South	Indianapolis Colts (12-4-0)	New England 20, Indianapolis 3	
		West	San Diego Chargers (12-4-0)	New England 41, Pittsburgh 27	
	National	East	Philadelphia Eagles (13-3-0)		
		North	Green Bay Packers (10-6-0)	Atlanta 47, St.Louis* 17	
		South	Atlanta Falcons (11-5-0)	Philidelphia 27, Minnesota* 14	
		West	Seattle Seahawks (9-7-0)	Philidelphia 27, Atlanta 10	

*Wild card team. (a) Won divisional playoff. (b) Won at 8:15 of sudden death overtime period. (c) From 1978 on, only the final 2 conference playoff rounds are shown. (d) A strike shortened the 1982 season from 16 to 9 games. The top 8 teams in each conference played in a tournament to determine the conference champion. See below. **AFC playoffs**—Miami 28, New England 13; L.A. Raiders 27, Cleveland 10; N.Y. Jets 44, Cincinnati 17; San Diego 31, Pittsburgh 28; N.Y. Jets 17, L.A. Raiders 14; Miami 34, San Diego 13; Miami 14, N.Y. Jets 0. **NFC playoffs**—Washington 31, Detroit 7; Green Bay 41, St. Louis 16; Dallas 30, Tampa Bay 17; Minnesota 30, Atlanta 24; Washington 21, Minnesota 7; Dallas 37, Green Bay 26; Washington 31, Dallas 17. **AFC Champion**—Miami Dolphins. **NFC Champion**—Washington Redskins.

Super Bowl XXXIX: New England 24, Philadelphia 21

The New England Patriots, on Feb. 6, 2005, defeated the Philadelphia Eagles 24-21, at Alltel Stadium in Jacksonville, FL, to win Super Bowl XXXIX. It was their 2nd straight Super Bowl title, and their 3rd in 4 years. Coach Bill Belichick, who led the Patriots in their previous Super Bowl wins, finished with a career postseason record of 10 wins and 1 loss, surpassing the legendary Vince Lombardi (9-1). Patriots' wide receiver Deion Branch was named Super Bowl MVP. He caught 11 passes, tying a Super Bowl record, for 133 yards. Patriots quarterback Tom Brady completed 23 of 33 passes for 236 yards. Against his doctor's orders, Eagles receiver Terrell Owens started the game. Despite injuries, he caught 9 passes for 122 yards.

Score by Quarters

Team	1	2	3	4	Total
New England	0	7	7	10	24
Philadelphia	0	7	7	7	21

Scoring

Philadelphia—L. Smith 6 yd. pass from D.McNabb (Akers PAT)

New England—D. Givens 4 yd. pass from T. Brady (Vinatieri PAT)

New England—M.Vrabel 2 yd. pass from T. Brady (Vinatieri PAT)

Philadelphia—B. Westbrook 10 yd. pass from D. McNabb (Akers PAT)

New England—C. Dillon 2 yd. run (Vinatieri PAT)

New England—A. Vinatieri 22 yd. field goal

Philadelphia—G. Lewis 30 yd. pass from D. McNabb (Akers kick)

Individual Statistics

Rushing–New England: Dillon 18-75, 1 TD, Faulk 8-38, Pass 1-0 Brady 1-(-1). Philadelphia: Westbrook 15-44, Levens 1-1, McNabb 1-0.

Passing–New England: Brady 33-23, 236 yds, 2 TD, 0 Int. Philadelphia: McNabb, 51-30, 357 yds, 3 TD, 3 Int.

Receiving–New England: Branch 11-133, Dillon 3-31, Givens 3-19, 1 TD, Faulk 2-27, Brown 2-17, Graham 1-7, Vrabel 1-2, 1 TD. Philadelphia: Owens 9-122, Westbrook 7-60, 1 TD, Pinkston 4-82, G. Lewis 4-4-53, 1 TD, L. Smith 4-27, 1 TD, Mitchell 1-11, Parry 1-2.

Team Statistics	NE	PHI
First downs	21	24
Total net yards	331	369
Rushes-yards	28-112	17-45
Passing yards, net	219	324
Punt returns-yards	4-26	3-19
Kickoff returns-yards	4-63	5-114
Interception returns-yards	3-5	0-0
Att.-comp.-int.	33-23-0	51-30-3
Field goals made-attempts	1-1	0-0
Sacked-yards lost	2-17	4-33
Punts-average	7-45.1	5-42.8
Fumbles-lost	1-1	2-1
Penalties-yards	7-47	3-35
Time of possession	31:37	28:23

Attendance—78,125. **Game Length**—3:38.

Super Bowl Results

	Year	Winner	Loser	Winning coach	Site
I	1967	*Green Bay Packers, 35	Kansas City Chiefs, 10	Vince Lombardi	Los Angeles Coliseum, CA
II	1968	Green Bay Packers, 33	*Oakland Raiders, 14	Vince Lombardi	Orange Bowl, Miami, FL
III	1969	*New York Jets, 16	Baltimore Colts, 7	Weeb Ewbank	Orange Bowl, Miami, FL
IV	1970	Kansas City Chiefs, 23	*Minnesota Vikings, 7	Hank Stram	Tulane Stadium, New Orleans, LA
V	1971	Baltimore Colts, 16	*Dallas Cowboys, 13	Don McCafferty	Orange Bowl, Miami, FL
VI	1972	Dallas Cowboys, 24	*Miami Dolphins, 3	Tom Landry	Tulane Stadium, New Orleans, LA
VII	1973	*Miami Dolphins, 14	Washington Redskins, 7	Don Shula	Los Angeles Coliseum, CA
VIII	1974	*Miami Dolphins, 24	Minnesota Vikings, 7	Don Shula	Rice Stadium, Houston, TX
IX	1975	*Pittsburgh Steelers, 16	Minnesota Vikings, 6	Chuck Noll	Tulane Stadium, New Orleans, LA
X	1976	Pittsburgh Steelers, 21	*Dallas Cowboys, 17	Chuck Noll	Orange Bowl, Miami, FL
XI	1977	*Oakland Raiders, 32	Minnesota Vikings, 14	John Madden	Rose Bowl, Pasadena, CA
XII	1978	*Dallas Cowboys, 27	Denver Broncos, 10	Tom Landry	Superdome, New Orleans, LA
XIII	1979	Pittsburgh Steelers, 35	*Dallas Cowboys, 31	Chuck Noll	Orange Bowl, Miami, FL
XIV	1980	Pittsburgh Steelers, 31	*Los Angeles Rams, 19	Chuck Noll	Rose Bowl, Pasadena, CA
XV	1981	Oakland Raiders, 27	*Philadelphia Eagles, 10	Tom Flores	Superdome, New Orleans, LA
XVI	1982	*San Francisco 49ers, 26	Cincinnati Bengals, 21	Bill Walsh	Silverdome, Pontiac, MI
XVII	1983	Washington Redskins, 27	*Miami Dolphins, 17	Joe Gibbs	Rose Bowl, Pasadena, CA
XVIII	1984	*Los Angeles Raiders, 38	Washington Redskins, 9	Tom Flores	Tampa Stadium, FL
XIX	1985	*San Francisco 49ers, 38	Miami Dolphins, 16	Bill Walsh	Stanford Stadium, Palo Alto, CA
XX	1986	*Chicago Bears, 46	New England Patriots, 10	Mike Ditka	Superdome, New Orleans, LA
XXI	1987	New York Giants, 39	*Denver Broncos, 20	Bill Parcells	Rose Bowl, Pasadena, CA
XXII	1988	*Washington Redskins, 42	Denver Broncos, 10	Joe Gibbs	San Diego Stadium, CA
XXIII	1989	*San Francisco 49ers, 20	Cincinnati Bengals, 16	Bill Walsh	Joe Robbie Stadium, Miami, FL
XXIV	1990	San Francisco 49ers, 55	*Denver Broncos, 10	George Seifert	Superdome, New Orleans, LA
XXV	1991	New York Giants, 20	*Buffalo Bills, 19	Bill Parcells	Tampa Stadium, FL
XXVI	1992	*Washington Redskins, 37	Buffalo Bills, 24	Joe Gibbs	Metrodome, Minneapolis, MN
XXVII	1993	Dallas Cowboys, 52	*Buffalo Bills, 17	Jimmy Johnson	Rose Bowl, Pasadena, CA
XXVIII	1994	*Dallas Cowboys, 30	Buffalo Bills, 13	Jimmy Johnson	Georgia Dome, Atlanta, GA
XXIX	1995	*San Francisco 49ers, 49	San Diego Chargers, 26	George Seifert	Joe Robbie Stadium, Miami, FL
XXX	1996	*Dallas Cowboys, 27	Pittsburgh Steelers, 17	Barry Switzer	Sun Devil Stadium, Tempe, AZ
XXXI	1997	Green Bay Packers, 35	*New England Patriots, 21	Mike Holmgren	Superdome, New Orleans, LA
XXXII	1998	Denver Broncos, 31	*Green Bay Packers, 24	Mike Shanahan	Qualcomm Stadium, San Diego, CA
XXXIII	1999	Denver Broncos, 34	*Atlanta Falcons, 19	Mike Shanahan	Pro Player Stadium, Miami, FL
XXXIV	2000	*St. Louis Rams, 23	Tennessee Titans, 16	Dick Vermeil	Georgia Dome, Atlanta, GA
XXXV	2001	Baltimore Ravens, 34	*New York Giants, 7	Brian Billick	Raymond James Stad., Tampa, FL
XXXVI	2002	New England Patriots, 20	*St. Louis Rams, 17	Bill Belichick	Superdome, New Orleans, LA
XXXVII	2003	*Tampa Bay Buccaneers, 48	Oakland Raiders, 21	Jon Gruden	Qualcomm Stadium, San Diego, CA
XXXVIII	2004	New England Patriots, 32	*Carolina Panthers, 29	Bill Belichick	Reliant Stadium, Houston, TX
XXXIX	2005	*New England Patriots, 24	Philadelphia Eagles, 21	Bill Belichick	Alltel Stadium, Jacksonville, FL

*Team that won the coin toss. All teams that won the toss elected to receive.

Super Bowl Single-Game Statistical Leaders

Passing Yards

	Year	Att/Comp	Yds	TDs
Kurt Warner, Rams	2000	45/24	414	2
Kurt Warner, Rams	2002	44/28	365	1
Joe Montana, 49ers	1989	36/23	357	2

Receiving Yards

	Year	Recept.	Yds	TDs
Jerry Rice, 49ers	1989	11	215	1
Ricky Sanders, Redskins	1988	9	193	2
Isaac Bruce, Rams	2000	6	162	1

Rushing Yards

	Year	Attempts	Yds	TDs
Timmy Smith, Redskins	1988	22	204	2
Marcus Allen, Raiders	1984	20	191	2
John Riggins, Redskins	1983	38	166	1

Passing Touchdowns

	Year	Att/Comp	Yds	TDs
Steve Young, 49ers	1995	36/24	325	6
Joe Montana, 49ers	1990	29/22	297	5
Troy Aikman, Cowboys	1993	30/22	273	4
Doug Williams, Redskins	1988	29/18	340	4
Terry Bradshaw, Steelers	1979	30/17	318	4

Scoring

	Year	Points	
Terrell Davis, Broncos	1998	18	3 TDs
Jerry Rice, 49ers	1995	18	3 TDs
Ricky Watters, 49ers	1995	18	3 TDs
Jerry Rice, 49ers	1990	18	3 TDs
Roger Craig, 49ers	1985	18	3 TDs
Don Chandler, Packers	1968	15	4 FG, 3PATs

Super Bowl MVPs

1967 Bart Starr, Green Bay
1968 Bart Starr, Green Bay
1969 Joe Namath, N.Y. Jets
1970 Len Dawson, Kansas City
1971 Chuck Howley, Dallas
1972 Roger Staubach, Dallas
1973 Jake Scott, Miami
1974 Larry Csonka, Miami
1975 Franco Harris, Pittsburgh
1976 Lynn Swann, Pittsburgh
1977 Fred Biletnikoff, Oakland
1978 Randy White, Harvey Martin, Dallas
1979 Terry Bradshaw, Pittsburgh
1980 Terry Bradshaw, Pittsburgh
1981 Jim Plunkett, Oakland
1982 Joe Montana, San Francisco
1983 John Riggins, Washington
1984 Marcus Allen, L.A. Raiders
1985 Joe Montana, San Francisco
1986 Richard Dent, Chicago
1987 Phil Simms, N.Y. Giants
1988 Doug Williams, Washington
1989 Jerry Rice, San Francisco
1990 Joe Montana, San Francisco
1991 Ottis Anderson, N.Y. Giants
1992 Mark Rypien, Washington
1993 Troy Aikman, Dallas
1994 Emmitt Smith, Dallas
1995 Steve Young, San Francisco
1996 Larry Brown, Dallas
1997 Desmond Howard, Green Bay
1998 Terrell Davis, Denver
1999 John Elway, Denver
2000 Kurt Warner, St. Louis
2001 Ray Lewis, Baltimore
2002 Tom Brady, New England
2003 Dexter Jackson, Tampa Bay
2004 Tom Brady, New England
2005 Deion Branch, New England

American Football Conference Leaders

(American Football League, 1960-69)

Passing[1] Player, team	Att	Com	YG	TD	Year	Receiving Player, team	Rec.	YG	TD
Jack Kemp, L.A. Chargers	406	211	3,018	20	**1960**	Lionel Taylor, Denver	92	1,235	12
George Blanda, Houston	362	187	3,330	36	**1961**	Lionel Taylor, Denver	100	1,176	4
Len Dawson, Dallas Texans	310	189	2,759	29	**1962**	Lionel Taylor, Denver	77	908	4
Tobin Rote, San Diego	286	170	2,510	20	**1963**	Lionel Taylor, Denver	78	1,101	10
Len Dawson, Kansas City	354	199	2,879	30	**1964**	Charley Hennigan, Houston	101	1,546	8
John Hadl, San Diego	348	174	2,798	20	**1965**	Lionel Taylor, Denver	85	1,131	6
Len Dawson, Kansas City	284	159	2,527	26	**1966**	Lance Alworth, San Diego	73	1,383	13
Daryle Lamonica, Oakland	425	220	3,228	30	**1967**	George Sauer, N.Y. Jets	75	1,189	6
Len Dawson, Kansas City	224	131	2,109	17	**1968**	Lance Alworth, San Diego	68	1,312	10

Passing[1] Player, team	Att	Com	YG	TD	Year	Receiving Player, team	Rec.	YG	TD
Greg Cook, Cincinnati	197	106	1,854	15	**1969**	Lance Alworth, San Diego	64	1,003	4
Daryle Lamonica, Oakland	356	179	2,516	22	**1970**	Marlin Briscoe, Buffalo	57	1,036	8
Bob Griese, Miami	263	145	2,089	19	**1971**	Fred Biletnikoff, Oakland	61	929	9
Earl Morrall, Miami	150	83	1,360	11	**1972**	Fred Biletnikoff, Oakland	58	802	7
Ken Stabler, Oakland	260	163	1,997	14	**1973**	Fred Willis, Houston	57	371	1
Ken Anderson, Cincinnati	328	213	2,667	18	**1974**	Lydell Mitchell, Baltimore Colts	72	544	2
Ken Anderson, Cincinnati	377	228	3,169	21	**1975**	Reggie Rucker, Cleveland	60	770	3
						Lydell Mitchell, Baltimore Colts	60	554	4
Ken Stabler, Oakland	291	194	2,737	27	**1976**	MacArthur Lane, Kansas City	66	686	1
Bob Griese, Miami	307	180	2,252	22	**1977**	Lydell Mitchell, Baltimore Colts	71	620	4
Terry Bradshaw, Pittsburgh	368	207	2,915	28	**1978**	Steve Largent, Seattle	71	1,168	8
Dan Fouts, San Diego	530	332	4,082	24	**1979**	Joe Washington, Baltimore Colts	82	750	3
Brian Sipe, Cleveland	554	337	4,132	30	**1980**	Kellen Winslow, San Diego	89	1,290	9
Ken Anderson, Cincinnati	479	300	3,754	29	**1981**	Kellen Winslow, San Diego	88	1,075	10
Ken Anderson, Cincinnati	309	218	2,495	12	**1982**	Kellen Winslow, San Diego	54	721	6
Dan Marino, Miami	296	173	2,210	20	**1983**	Todd Christensen, L.A. Raiders	92	1,247	12
Dan Marino, Miami	564	362	5,084	48	**1984**	Ozzie Newsome, Cleveland	89	1,001	5
Ken O'Brien, N.Y. Jets	488	297	3,888	25	**1985**	Lionel James, San Diego	86	1,027	6
Dan Marino, Miami	623	378	4,746	44	**1986**	Todd Christensen, L.A. Raiders	95	1,153	8
Bernie Kosar, Cleveland	389	241	3,033	22	**1987**	Al Toon, N.Y. Jets	68	976	5
Boomer Esiason, Cincinnati	388	223	3,572	28	**1988**	Al Toon, N.Y. Jets	93	1,067	5
Boomer Esiason, Cincinnati	455	258	3,525	28	**1989**	Andre Reed, Buffalo	88	1,312	9
Jim Kelly, Buffalo	346	219	2,829	24	**1990**	Haywood Jeffires, Houston	74	1,048	8
						Drew Hill, Houston	74	1,019	5
Jim Kelly, Buffalo	474	304	3,844	33	**1991**	Haywood Jeffires, Houston	100	1,181	7
Warren Moon, Houston	346	224	2,521	18	**1992**	Haywood Jeffires, Houston	90	913	9
John Elway, Denver	551	348	4,030	25	**1993**	Reggie Langhorne, Indianapolis	85	1,038	3
Dan Marino, Miami	615	385	4,453	30	**1994**	Ben Coates, New England	96	1,174	7
Jim Harbaugh, Indianapolis	314	200	2,575	17	**1995**	Carl Pickens, Cincinnati	99	1,234	17
John Elway, Denver	466	287	3,328	26	**1996**	Carl Pickens, Cincinnati	100	1,180	12
Mark Brunell, Jacksonville	435	264	3,281	18	**1997**	Tim Brown, Oakland	104	1,408	5
Vinny Testaverde, N.Y. Jets	421	259	3,256	29	**1998**	O.J. McDuffie, Miami	90	1,050	7
Peyton Manning, Indianapolis	533	331	4,135	26	**1999**	Jimmy Smith, Jacksonville	116	1,636	6
Brian Griese, Denver	336	216	2,688	19	**2000**	Marvin Harrison, Indianapolis	102	1,413	14
Rich Gannon, Oakland	549	361	3,828	27	**2001**	Marvin Harrison, Indianapolis	109	1,524	15
Chad Pennington, N.Y. Jets	399	275	3,120	22	**2002**	Marvin Harrison, Indianapolis	143	1,722	11
Steve McNair, Tennessee	400	250	3,215	24	**2003**	Chad Johnson, Cincinnati	90	1,355	10
Peyton Manning, Indianapolis	497	336	4,557	49	**2004**	Chad Johnson, Cincinnati	95	1,274	9

Scoring Player, team	TD	PAT	FG	Pts	Year	Rushing Player, team	Yds	Att	TD
Gene Mingo, Denver	6	33	18	123	**1960**	Abner Haynes, Dallas Texans	875	156	9
Gino Cappelletti, Boston	8	48	17	147	**1961**	Billy Cannon, Houston	948	200	6
Gene Mingo, Denver	4	32	27	137	**1962**	Cookie Gilchrest, Buffalo	1,096	214	13
Gino Cappelletti, Boston	2	35	22	113	**1963**	Clem Daniels, Oakland	1,099	215	3
Gino Cappelletti, Boston	7	36	25	155	**1964**	Cookie Gilchrest, Buffalo	981	230	6
Gino Cappelletti, Boston	9	27	17	132	**1965**	Paul Lowe, San Diego	1,121	222	7
Gino Cappelletti, Boston	6	35	16	119	**1966**	Jim Nance, Boston	1,458	299	11
George Blanda, Oakland	0	56	20	116	**1967**	Jim Nance, Boston	1,216	269	7
Jim Turner, N.Y. Jets	0	43	34	145	**1968**	Paul Robinson, Cincinnati	1,023	238	8
Jim Turner, N.Y. Jets	0	33	32	129	**1969**	Dick Post, San Diego	873	182	6
Jan Stenerud, Kansas City	0	26	30	116	**1970**	Floyd Little, Denver	901	209	3
Garo Yepremian, Miami	0	33	28	117	**1971**	Floyd Little, Denver	1,133	284	6
Bobby Howfield, N.Y. Jets	0	40	27	121	**1972**	O.J. Simpson, Buffalo	1,251	292	6
Roy Gerela, Pittsburgh	0	36	29	123	**1973**	O.J. Simpson, Buffalo	2,003	332	12
Roy Gerela, Pittsburgh	0	33	20	93	**1974**	Otis Armstrong, Denver	1,407	263	9
O.J. Simpson, Buffalo	23	0	0	138	**1975**	O.J. Simpson, Buffalo	1,817	329	16
Toni Linhart, Baltimore Colts	0	49	20	109	**1976**	O.J. Simpson, Buffalo	1,503	290	8
Errol Mann, Oakland	0	39	20	99	**1977**	Mark van Eeghen, Oakland	1,273	324	7
Pat Leahy, N.Y. Jets	0	41	22	107	**1978**	Earl Campbell, Houston	1,450	302	13
John Smith, New England	0	46	23	115	**1979**	Earl Campbell, Houston	1,697	368	19
John Smith, New England	0	51	26	129	**1980**	Earl Campbell, Houston	1,934	373	13
Jim Breech, Cincinnati	0	49	22	115	**1981**	Earl Campbell, Houston	1,376	361	10
Nick Lowery, Kansas City	0	37	26	115					
Marcus Allen, L.A. Raiders	14	0	0	84	**1982**	Freeman McNeil, N.Y. Jets	786	151	6
Gary Anderson, Pittsburgh	0	38	27	119	**1983**	Curt Warner, Seattle	1,446	335	13
Gary Anderson, Pittsburgh	0	45	24	117	**1984**	Earnest Jackson, San Diego	1,179	296	8
Gary Anderson, Pittsburgh	0	40	33	139	**1985**	Marcus Allen, L.A. Raiders	1,759	380	11
Tony Franklin, New England	0	44	32	140	**1986**	Curt Warner, Seattle	1,481	319	13
Jim Breech, Cincinnati	0	25	24	97	**1987**	Eric Dickerson, L.A. Rams-Ind.	1,288*	283	6
Scott Norwood, Buffalo	0	33	32	129	**1988**	Eric Dickerson, Indianapolis	1,659	388	14
David Treadwell, Denver	0	39	27	120	**1989**	Christian Okoye, Kansas City	1,480	370	12
Nick Lowery, Kansas City	0	37	34	139	**1990**	Thurman Thomas, Buffalo	1,297	271	11
Pete Stoyanovich, Miami	0	28	31	121	**1991**	Thurman Thomas, Buffalo	1,407	288	7
Pete Stoyanovich, Miami	0	34	30	124	**1992**	Barry Foster, Pittsburgh	1,690	390	11
Jeff Jaeger, L.A. Raiders	0	27	35	132	**1993**	Thurman Thomas, Buffalo	1,315	355	6
John Carney, San Diego	0	33	34	135	**1994**	Chris Warren, Seattle	1,545	333	9
Norm Johnson, Pittsburgh	0	39	34	141	**1995**	Curtis Martin, New England	1,487	368	14
Cary Blanchard, Indianapolis	0	27	36	135	**1996**	Terrell Davis, Denver	1,538	345	13
Mike Hollis, Jacksonville	0	41	31	134	**1997**	Terrell Davis, Denver	1,750	369	15
Steve Christie, Buffalo	0	41	33	140	**1998**	Terrell Davis, Denver	2,008	392	21
Mike Vanderjagt, Indianapolis	0	43	34	145	**1999**	Edgerrin James, Indianapolis	1,553	369	13
Matt Stover, Baltimore	0	30	35	135	**2000**	Edgerrin James, Indianapolis	1,709	387	13
Mike Vanderjagt, Indianapolis	0	41	28	125	**2001**	Priest Holmes, Kansas City	1,555	325	8
Priest Holmes, Kansas City	24	0	0	144	**2002**	Ricky Williams, Miami	1,853	383	16
Priest Holmes, Kansas City	27	0	0	162	**2003**	Jamal Lewis, Baltimore	2,066	387	14
Adam Vinatieri, New England	0	48	31	141	**2004**	Curtis Martin, N.Y. Jets	1,697	371	12

*Includes 277 yards after being traded to NFC; 1,011 yards led AFC. (1) Based on quarterback rating points.

National Football Conference Leaders

(National Football League, 1960-69)

Passing[1] Player, team	Att	Com	YG	TD	Year	Receiving Player, team	Rec.	YG	TD
Milt Plum, Cleveland	250	151	2,297	21	**1960**	Raymond Berry, Baltimore Colts	74	1,298	10
Milt Plum, Cleveland	302	177	2,416	18	**1961**	Jim Phillips, L.A. Rams	78	1,092	5
Bart Starr, Green Bay	285	178	2,438	12	**1962**	Bobby Mitchell, Washington	72	1,384	11
Y.A. Tittle, N.Y. Giants	367	221	3,145	36	**1963**	Bobby Joe Conrad, St. Louis Cardinals	73	967	10
Bart Starr, Green Bay	272	163	2,144	15	**1964**	Johnny Morris, Chicago	93	1,200	10
Rudy Bukich, Chicago	312	176	2,641	20	**1965**	Dave Parks, San Francisco	80	1,344	12
Bart Starr, Green Bay	251	156	2,257	14	**1966**	Charley Taylor, Washington	72	1,119	12
Sonny Jurgensen, Washington	508	288	3,747	31	**1967**	Charley Taylor, Washington	70	990	9
Earl Morrall, Baltimore Colts	317	182	2,909	26	**1968**	Clifton McNeil, San Francisco	71	994	7
Sonny Jurgensen, Washington	442	274	3,102	22	**1969**	Dan Abramowicz, New Orleans	73	1,015	7
John Brodie, San Francisco	378	223	2,941	24	**1970**	Dick Gordon, Chicago	71	1,026	13
Roger Staubach, Dallas	211	126	1,882	15	**1971**	Bob Tucker, N.Y. Giants	59	791	4
Norm Snead, N.Y. Giants	325	196	2,307	17	**1972**	Harold Jackson, Philadelphia	62	1,048	4
Roger Staubach, Dallas	286	179	2,428	23	**1973**	Harold Carmichael, Philadelphia	67	1,116	9
Sonny Jurgensen, Washington	167	107	1,185	11	**1974**	Charles Young, Philadelphia	63	696	3
Fran Tarkenton, Minnesota	425	273	2,994	25	**1975**	Chuck Foreman, Minnesota	73	691	9
James Harris, L.A. Rams	158	91	1,460	8	**1976**	Drew Pearson, Dallas	58	806	6
Roger Staubach, Dallas	361	210	2,620	18	**1977**	Ahmad Rashad, Minnesota	51	681	2
Roger Staubach, Dallas	413	231	3,190	25	**1978**	Rickey Young, Minnesota	88	704	5
Roger Staubach, Dallas	461	267	3,586	27	**1979**	Ahmad Rashad, Minnesota	80	1,156	9
Ron Jaworski, Philadelphia	451	257	3,529	27	**1980**	Earl Cooper, San Francisco	83	567	4
Joe Montana, San Francisco	488	311	3,565	19	**1981**	Dwight Clark, San Francisco	85	1,105	4
Joe Thiesmann, Washington	252	161	2,033	13	**1982**	Dwight Clark, San Francisco	60	913	5
Steve Bartkowski, Atlanta	432	274	3,167	22	**1983**	Roy Green, St. Louis Cardinals	78	1,227	14
						Charlie Brown, Washington	78	1,225	8
						Earnest Gray, N.Y. Giants	78	1,139	5
Joe Montana, San Francisco	432	279	3,630	28	**1984**	Art Monk, Washington	106	1,372	7
Joe Montana, San Francisco	494	303	3,653	27	**1985**	Roger Craig, San Francisco	92	1,016	6
Tommy Kramer, Minnesota	372	208	3,000	24	**1986**	Jerry Rice, San Francisco	86	1,570	15
Joe Montana, San Francisco	398	266	3,054	31	**1987**	J.T. Smith, St. Louis Cardinals	91	1,117	8
Wade Wilson, Minnesota	332	204	2,746	15	**1988**	Henry Ellard, L.A. Rams	86	1,414	10
Joe Montana, San Francisco	386	271	3,521	26	**1989**	Sterling Sharpe, Green Bay	90	1,423	12
Phil Simms, N.Y. Giants	311	184	2,284	15	**1990**	Jerry Rice, San Francisco	100	1,502	13
Steve Young, San Francisco	279	180	2,517	17	**1991**	Michael Irvin, Dallas	93	1,523	8
Steve Young, San Francisco	402	268	3,465	25	**1992**	Sterling Sharpe, Green Bay	108	1,461	13
Steve Young, San Francisco	462	314	4,023	29	**1993**	Sterling Sharpe, Green Bay	112	1,274	11
Steve Young, San Francisco	461	324	3,969	35	**1994**	Cris Carter, Minnesota	122	1,256	7
Brett Favre, Green Bay	570	359	4,413	38	**1995**	Herman Moore, Detroit	123	1,686	14
Steve Young, San Francisco	316	214	2,410	14	**1996**	Jerry Rice, San Francisco	108	1,254	8
Steve Young, San Francisco	356	241	3,029	19	**1997**	Herman Moore, Detroit	104	1,293	8
Randall Cunningham, Minnesota	425	259	3,704	34	**1998**	Frank Sanders, Arizona	89	1,145	3
Kurt Warner, St. Louis	499	325	4,353	41	**1999**	Muhsin Muhammad, Carolina	96	1,253	8
Trent Green, St. Louis	240	145	2,063	16	**2000**	Muhsin Muhammad, Carolina	102	1,183	6
Kurt Warner, St. Louis	546	375	4,830	36	**2001**	David Boston, Arizona	98	1,598	8
Brad Johnson, Tampa Bay	451	281	3,049	22	**2002**	Randy Moss, Minnesota	106	1,347	7
Daunte Culpepper, Minnesota	454	295	3,479	25	**2003**	Torry Holt, St. Louis	117	1,696	12
Daunte Culpepper, Minnesota	548	379	4,717	39	**2004**	Muhsin Muhammad, Carolina	93	1,405	16

Scoring Player, team	TD	PAT	FG	Pts	Year	Rushing Player, team	Yds	Att	TD
Paul Hornung, Green Bay	15	41	15	176	**1960**	Jim Brown, Cleveland	1,257	215	9
Paul Hornung, Green Bay	10	41	15	146	**1961**	Jim Brown, Cleveland	1,408	305	8
Jim Taylor, Green Bay	19	0	0	114	**1962**	Jim Taylor, Green Bay	1,474	272	19
Don Chandler, N.Y. Giants	0	52	18	106	**1963**	Jim Brown, Cleveland	1,863	291	12
Lenny Moore, Baltimore Colts	20	0	0	120	**1964**	Jim Brown, Cleveland	1,446	280	7
Gale Sayers, Chicago	22	0	0	132	**1965**	Jim Brown, Cleveland	1,544	289	17
Bruce Gossett, L.A. Rams	0	29	28	113	**1966**	Gale Sayers, Chicago	1,231	229	8
Jim Bakken, St. Louis Cardinals	0	36	27	117	**1967**	Leroy Kelly, Cleveland	1,205	235	11
Leroy Kelly, Cleveland	20	0	0	120	**1968**	Leroy Kelly, Cleveland	1,239	248	16
Fred Cox, Minnesota	0	43	26	121	**1969**	Gale Sayers, Chicago	1,032	236	8
Fred Cox, Minnesota	0	35	30	125	**1970**	Larry Brown, Washington	1,125	237	5
Curt Knight, Washington	0	27	29	114	**1971**	John Brockington, Green Bay	1,105	216	4
Chester Marcol, Green Bay	0	29	33	128	**1972**	Larry Brown, Washington	1,216	285	8
David Ray, L.A. Rams	0	40	30	130	**1973**	John Brockington, Green Bay	1,144	265	3
Chester Marcol, Green Bay	0	19	25	94	**1974**	Lawrence McCutcheon, L.A. Rams	1,109	236	3
Chuck Foreman, Minnesota	22	0	0	132	**1975**	Jim Otis, St. Louis Cardinals	1,076	269	5
Mark Moseley, Washington	0	31	22	97	**1976**	Walter Payton, Chicago	1,390	311	13
Walter Payton, Chicago	16	0	0	96	**1977**	Walter Payton, Chicago	1,852	339	14
Frank Corral, L.A. Rams	0	31	29	118	**1978**	Walter Payton, Chicago	1,395	333	11
Mark Moseley, Washington	0	39	25	114	**1979**	Walter Payton, Chicago	1,610	369	14
Ed Murray, Detroit	0	35	27	116	**1980**	Walter Payton, Chicago	1,460	317	6
Ed Murray, Detroit	0	46	25	121	**1981**	George Rogers, New Orleans	1,674	378	13
Rafael Septien, Dallas	0	40	27	121					
Wendell Tyler, L.A. Rams	13	0	0	78	**1982**	Tony Dorsett, Dallas	745	177	5
Mark Moseley, Washington	0	62	33	161	**1983**	Eric Dickerson, L.A. Rams	1,808	390	18
Ray Wersching, San Francisco	0	56	25	131	**1984**	Eric Dickerson, L.A. Rams	2,105	379	14
Kevin Butler, Chicago	0	51	31	144	**1985**	Gerald Riggs, Atlanta	1,719	397	10
Kevin Butler, Chicago	0	36	28	120	**1986**	Eric Dickerson, L.A. Rams	1,821	404	11
Jerry Rice, San Francisco	23	0	0	138	**1987**	Charles White, L.A. Rams	1,374	324	11
Mike Cofer, San Francisco	0	40	27	121	**1988**	Herschel Walker, Dallas	1,514	361	5
Mike Cofer, San Francisco	0	49	29	136	**1989**	Barry Sanders, Detroit	1,470	280	14
Chip Lohmiller, Washington	0	41	30	131	**1990**	Barry Sanders, Detroit	1,304	255	13
Chip Lohmiller, Washington	0	56	31	149	**1991**	Emmitt Smith, Dallas	1,563	365	12
Morten Andersen, New Orleans	0	33	29	120	**1992**	Emmitt Smith, Dallas	1,713	373	18
Chip Lohmiller, Washington	0	30	30	120					

Year	Scoring: Player, team	TD	PAT	FG	Pts	Rushing: Player, team	Yds	Att	TD
1993	Jason Hanson, Detroit	0	28	34	130	Emmitt Smith, Dallas	1,486	283	9
1994	Fuad Reveiz, Minnesota	0	30	34	132	Barry Sanders, Detroit	1,883	331	7
	Emmitt Smith, Dallas	22	0	0	132				
1995	Emmitt Smith, Dallas	25	0	0	150	Emmitt Smith, Dallas	1,773	377	25
1996	John Kasay, Carolina	0	34	37	145	Barry Sanders, Detroit	1,553	307	11
1997	Richie Cunningham, Dallas	0	24	34	126	Barry Sanders, Detroit	2,053	335	11
1998	Gary Anderson, Minnesota	0	59	35	164	Jamal Anderson, Atlanta	1,846	410	14
1999	Jeff Wilkins, St. Louis	0	64	20	124	Stephen Davis, Washington	1,405	290	17
2000	Marshall Faulk, St. Louis	26	0	0	156	Robert Smith, Minnesota	1,521	295	7
2001	Marshall Faulk, St. Louis	21	0	0	128	Stephen Davis, Washington	1,432	356	5
2002	Jay Feely, Atlanta	0	42	32	138	Deuce McAllister, New Orleans	1,388	325	13
2003	Jeff Wilkins, St. Louis	0	46	39	163	Ahman Green, Green Bay	1,883	355	15
2004	David Akers, Philadelphia	0	41	27	122	Shaun Alexander, Seattle	1,696	353	16

(1) Based on quarterback rating points.

2004 NFL Individual Leaders

American Football Conference

PASSING	Att	Comp	Pct Comp	Yds	Yds/Att.	Long	TD	Pct TD	Int	Rating Points
Peyton Manning, Indianapolis	497	336	67.6	4,557	9.17	80	49	9.9	10	121.1
Drew Brees, San Diego	400	262	65.5	3,159	7.90	79	27	6.8	7	104.8
Ben Roethlisberger, Pittsburgh	295	196	66.4	2,621	8.89	58	17	5.8	11	98.1
Trent Green, Kansas City	556	369	66.4	4,591	8.26	70	27	4.9	17	95.2
Tom Brady, New England	474	288	60.8	3,692	7.79	50	28	5.9	14	92.6
Chad Pennington, N.Y. Jets	370	242	65.4	2,673	7.22	48	16	4.3	9	91.0
Billy Volek, Tennessee	357	218	61.1	2,486	6.96	48	18	5.0	10	87.1
Jake Plummer, Denver	521	303	58.2	4,089	7.85	85	27	5.2	20	84.5
David Carr, Houston	466	285	61.2	3,531	7.58	69	16	3.4	14	83.5
Byron Leftwich, Jacksonville	441	267	60.5	2,941	6.67	65	15	3.4	10	82.2

RUSHING	Att	Yds	Avg	Long	TD
Curtis Martin, N.Y. Jets	371	1,697	4.6	25	12
Corey Dillon, New England	345	1,635	4.7	44	12
Edgerrin James, Indianapolis	334	1,548	4.6	40	9
Rudi Johnson, Cincinnati	361	1,454	4.0	52	12
LaDainian Tomlinson, San Diego	339	1,335	3.9	42	17
Reuben Droughns, Denver	275	1,240	4.5	51	6
Fred Taylor, Jacksonville	260	1,224	4.7	46	2
Domanick Davis, Houston	302	1,188	3.9	44	13
Willis McGahee, Buffalo	284	1,128	4.0	41	13
Chris Brown, Tennessee	220	1,067	4.9	52	6

RECEIVING	Catches	Yds	Avg	Long	TD
Tony Gonzalez, Kansas City	102	1,258	12.3	32	7
Derrick Mason, Tennessee	96	1,168	12.2	37	7
Chad Johnson, Cincinnati	95	1,274	13.4	53	9
Eric Moulds, Buffalo	88	1,043	11.9	49	5
Marvin Harrison, Indianapolis	86	1,113	12.9	59	15
Antonio Gates, San Diego	81	964	11.9	72	13
Drew Bennett, Tennessee	80	1,247	15.6	48	11
Hines Ward, Pittsburgh	80	1,004	12.6	58	4
Rod Smith, Denver	79	1,144	14.5	85	7

SCORING—KICKERS	PAT	FG	Long	Pts
Adam Vinatieri, New England	48/48	31/33	48	141
Jason Elam, Denver	42/42	29/34	52	129
Jeff Reed, Pittsburgh	40/40	28/33	51	124
Shayne Graham, Cincinnati	41/41	27/31	53	122
Mike Vanderjagt, Indianapolis	59/60	20/25	47	119

SCORING—NON-KICKERS	TD	Rush	Rec.	2 Pt	Pts
LaDainian Tomlinson, San Diego	18	17	1	0	108
Marvin Harrison, Indianapolis	15	0	15	0	90
Priest Holmes, Kansas City	15	14	1	0	90
Curtis Martin, N.Y. Jets	14	12	2	0	84
Domanick Davis, Houston	14	13	1	0	84

INTERCEPTIONS	No.	Yds	Avg	Long	TD
Ed Reed, Baltimore	9	358	39.8	106	1
Tory James, Cincinnati	8	66	8.3	23	0
Dunta Robinson, Houston	6	146	24.3	61	0
Andre Dyson, Tennessee	6	135	22.5	44	0
Nate Clements, Buffalo	6	77	12.8	35	1

KICKOFF RETURNS	No.	Yds	Avg	Long	TD
Terrence McGee, Buffalo	52	1,370	26.3	104	3
Dante Hall, Kansas City	68	1,718	25.3	97	2
Antwaan Randle El, Pittsburgh	21	527	25.1	41	0

PUNT RETURNS	No.	Yds	Avg	Long	TD
Dennis Northcutt, Cleveland	36	432	12.0	44	0
Wesley Welker, Miami/San Diego	43	464	10.8	71	0
B.J. Sams, Baltimore	55	575	10.5	78	2
Rod Smith, Denver	22	223	10.1	30	0
Dante Hall, Kansas City	23	232	10.1	46	0

PUNTING	No.	Yds	Long	Avg
Shane Lechler, Oakland	73	3,409	67	46.7
Hunter Smith, Indianapolis	54	2,443	62	45.2
Brian Moorman, Buffalo	77	3,325	80	43.2
Mike Scifres, San Diego	69	2,974	60	43.1
Chris Gardocki, Pittsburgh	67	2,879	61	43.0

SACKS: Dwight Freeney, Indianapolis, 16.0; Shaun Ellis, N.Y. Jets, 11.0; Terrell Suggs, Baltimore, 10.5; Reggie Hayward, Denver, 10.5; Robert Mathis, Indianapolis, 10.5; Steve Foley, San Diego, 10.0

National Football Conference

PASSING	Att	Comp	Pct Comp	Yds	Yds/Att.	Long	TD	Pct TD	Int	Rating Points
Daunte Culpepper, Minnesota	548	379	69.2	4,717	8.61	82	39	7.1	11	110.9
Donovan McNabb, Philadelphia	469	300	64.0	3,875	8.26	80	31	6.6	8	104.7
Brian Griese, Tampa Bay	336	233	69.3	2,632	7.83	68	20	6.0	12	97.5
Marc Bulger, St. Louis	485	321	66.2	3,964	8.17	56	21	4.3	14	93.7
Brett Favre, Green Bay	540	346	64.1	4,088	7.57	79	30	5.6	17	92.4
Jake Delhomme, Carolina	533	310	58.2	3,886	7.29	63	29	5.4	15	87.3
Kurt Warner, N.Y. Giants	277	174	62.8	2,054	7.42	62	6	2.2	4	86.5
Matt Hasselbeck, Seattle	474	279	58.9	3,382	7.14	60	22	4.6	15	83.1
Aaron Brooks, New Orleans	542	309	57.0	3,810	7.03	57	21	3.9	16	79.5
Tim Rattay, San Francisco	325	198	60.9	2,169	6.67	65	10	3.1	10	78.1

RUSHING	Att	Yds	Avg	Long	TD
Shaun Alexander, Seattle	353	1,696	4.8	44	16
Tiki Barber, N.Y. Giants	322	1,518	4.7	72	13
Clinton Portis, Washington	343	1,315	3.8	64	5
Ahman Green, Green Bay	259	1,163	4.5	90	7
Kevin Jones, Detroit	241	1,133	4.7	74	5
Warrick Dunn, Atlanta	265	1,106	4.2	60	9
Deuce McAllister, New Orleans	269	1,074	4.0	71	9
Thomas Jones, Chicago	240	948	4.0	54	7
Emmitt Smith, Arizona	267	937	3.5	29	9
Michael Pittman, Tampa Bay	219	926	4.2	78	7

RECEIVING	Catches	Yds	Avg	Long	TD
Joe Horn, New Orleans	94	1,399	14.9	57	11
Torry Holt, St. Louis	94	1,372	14.6	75	10
Muhsin Muhammad, Carolina	93	1,405	15.1	51	16
Laveranues Coles, Washington	90	950	10.6	45	1
Javon Walker, Green Bay	89	1,382	15.5	79	12
Isaac Bruce, St. Louis	89	1,292	14.5	56	6
Darrell Jackson, Seattle	87	1,199	13.8	56	7
Jason Witten, Dallas	87	980	11.3	42	6
Donald Driver, Green Bay	84	1,208	14.4	50	9

SCORING—KICKERS	PAT	FG	Long	Pts
David Akers, Philadelphia	41/42	27/32	51	122
Ryan Longwell, Green Bay	48/48	24/28	53	120
Josh Brown, Seattle	40/40	23/25	54	109
John Carney, New Orleans	38/38	22/27	53	104
Jason Hanson, Detroit	28/28	24/28	48	100

SCORING—NON-KICKERS	TD	Rush	Rec.	Ret.	Pts.
Shaun Alexander, Seattle	20	16	4	0	120
Muhsin Muhammad, Carolina	16	0	16	0	96
Tiki Barber, N.Y. Giants	15	13	2	0	90
Terrell Owens, Philadelphia	14	0	14	0	84
Randy Moss, Minnesota	13	0	13	0	78

INTERCEPTIONS	No.	Yds	Avg	Long	TD
Ken Lucas, Seattle	6	46	7.7	25	1
Chris Gamble, Carolina	6	15	2.5	13	0

KICKOFF RETURNS	No.	Yds	Avg	Long	TD
Willie Ponder, N.Y. Giants	36	967	26.9	91	1
Eddie Drummond, Detroit	41	1,092	26.6	99	2
Torrie Cox, Tampa Bay	33	866	26.2	59	0

PUNT RETURNS	No.	Yds	Avg	Long	TD
Eddie Drummond, Detroit	24	316	13.2	83	2
Allen Rossum, Atlanta	37	457	12.4	75	1
Michael Lewis, New Orleans	34	382	11.2	53	0
R. W. McQuarters, Chicago	44	435	9.9	75	1

PUNTING	No.	Yds	Long	Avg
Tom Tupa, Washington	103	4,544	61	44.1
Todd Sauerbrun, Carolina	76	3,351	65	44.1
Mitch Berger, New Orleans	85	3,704	63	43.6
Sean Landeta, St. Louis	40	1,733	63	43.3
Scott Player, Arizona	98	4,230	57	43.2

SACKS: Bertrand Berry, Arizona, 14.5; Kabeer Gbaja-Biamila, Green Bay, 13.5; Patrick Kerney, Atlanta, 13; Kevin Williams, Minnesota, 12.0; Simeon Rice, Tampa Bay, 12.0; James Hall, Detroit, 11.5; Rod Coleman, Atlanta, 11.5; Julius Peppers, Carolina, 11.0; Darren Howard, New Orleans, 11.0; Lance Johnstone, Minnesota, 11.0

First-Round Selections in the 2005 NFL Draft

	Team	Player	Pos	College
1.	San Francisco	Alex D. Smith	QB	Utah
2.	Miami	Ronnie Brown	RB	Auburn
3.	Cleveland	Braylon Edwards	WR	Michigan
4.	Chicago	Cedric Benson	RB	Texas
5.	Tampa Bay	Carnell Williams	RB	Auburn
6.	Tennessee	Adam Jones	CB	West Virginia
7.	Minnesota[1]	Troy Williamson	WR	South Carolina
8.	Arizona	Antrel Rolle	CB	Miami (FL)
9.	Washington	Carlos Rogers	CB	Auburn
10.	Detroit	Mike Williams	WR	USC
11.	Dallas	Demarcus Ware	DE	Troy St.
12.	San Diego[2]	Shawne Merriman	OLB	Maryland
13.	New Orleans[3]	Jammal Brown	OT	Oklahoma
14.	Carolina	Thomas Davis	FS	Georgia
15.	Kansas City	Derrick O. Johnson	OLB	Texas
16.	Houston[4]	Travis Johnson	DT	Florida St.
17.	Cincinnati	David Pollack	DE	Georgia
18.	Minnesota	Erasmus James	DE	Wisconsin
19.	St. Louis	Alex Barron	OT	Florida St.
20.	Dallas[5]	Marcus Spears	DE	Louisiana St.
21.	Jacksonville	Matt Jones	WR	Arkansas
22.	Baltimore	Mark Clayton	WR	Oklahoma
23.	Oakland[6]	Fabian Washington	CB	Nebraska
24.	Green Bay	Aaron Rodgers	QB	California
25.	Washington[7]	ason Campbell	QB	Auburn
26.	Seattle[8]	Chris Spencer	C	Mississippi
27.	Atlanta	Sharod "Roddy" White	WR	Alabama-Birmingham
28.	San Diego	Luis Castillo	DT	Northwestern
29.	Indianapolis	Marlin Jackson	CB	Michigan
30.	Pittsburgh	Heath Miller	TE	Virginia
31.	Philadelphia	Mike Patterson	DT	USC
32.	New England	Logan Mankins	G	Fresno St.

(1) From Oakland. (2) From N.Y. Giants. (3) From Houston. (4) From New Orleans. (5) From Buffalo. (6) From Seattle. (7) From Denver. (8) from N.Y. Jets through Oakland.

Number One NFL Draft Choices, 1936-2005

Year	Team	Player, Pos., College
1936	Philadelphia	Jay Berwanger, HB, Chicago
1937	Philadelphia	Sam Francis, FB, Nebraska
1938	Cleveland Rams	Corbett Davis, FB, Indiana
1939	Chicago Cards	Ki Aldrich, C, TCU
1940	Chicago Cards	George Cafego, HB, Tennessee
1941	Chicago Bears	Tom Harmon, HB, Michigan
1942	Pittsburgh	Bill Dudley, HB, Virginia
1943	Detroit	Frank Sinkwich, HB, Georgia
1944	Boston Yanks	Angelo Bertelli, QB, Notre Dame
1945	Chicago Cards	Charley Trippi, HB, Georgia
1946	Boston Yanks	Frank Dancewicz, QB, Notre Dame
1947	Chicago Bears	Bob Fenimore, HB, Okla. A&M
1948	Washington	Harry Gilmer, QB, Alabama
1949	Philadelphia	Chuck Bednarik, C, Penn
1950	Detroit	Leon Hart, E, Notre Dame
1951	N.Y. Giants	Kyle Rote, HB, SMU
1952	L.A. Rams	Bill Wade, QB, Vanderbilt
1953	San Francisco	Harry Babcock, E, Georgia
1954	Cleveland	Bobby Garrett, QB, Stanford
1955	Baltimore Colts	George Shaw, QB, Oregon
1956	Pittsburgh	Gary Glick, DB, Col. A&M
1957	Green Bay	Paul Hornung, QB, Notre Dame
1958	Chicago Cards	King Hill, QB, Rice
1959	Green Bay	Randy Duncan, QB, Iowa
1960	L.A. Rams	Billy Cannon, HB, LSU
1961	Minnesota	Tommy Mason, HB, Tulane
1962	Washington	Ernie Davis, HB, Syracuse
1963	L.A. Rams	Terry Baker, QB, Oregon St.
1964	San Francisco	Dave Parks, E, Texas Tech
1965	N.Y. Giants	Tucker Frederickson, HB, Auburn
1966	Atlanta	Tommy Nobis, LB, Texas
1967	Baltimore Colts	Bubba Smith, DT, Michigan St.
1968	Minnesota	Ron Yary, T, USC
1969	Buffalo	O.J. Simpson, RB, USC
1970	Pittsburgh	Terry Bradshaw, QB, La.Tech
1971	New England	Jim Plunkett, QB, Stanford
1972	Buffalo	Walt Patulski, DE, Notre Dame
1973	Houston	John Matuszak, DE, Tampa
1974	Dallas	Ed "Too Tall" Jones, DE, Tenn. St.
1975	Atlanta	Steve Bartkowski, QB, Cal.
1976	Tampa Bay	Lee Roy Selmon, DE, Oklahoma
1977	Tampa Bay	Ricky Bell, RB, USC
1978	Houston	Earl Campbell, RB, Texas
1979	Buffalo	Tom Cousineau, LB, Ohio St.
1980	Detroit	Billy Sims, RB, Oklahoma
1981	New Orleans	George Rogers, RB, S.Carolina
1982	New England	Kenneth Sims, DT, Texas
1983	Baltimore Colts	John Elway, QB, Stanford
1984	New England	Irving Fryar, WR, Nebraska
1985	Buffalo	Bruce Smith, DE, Va.Tech
1986	Tampa Bay	Bo Jackson, RB, Auburn
1987	Tampa Bay	Vinny Testaverde, QB, Miami (FL)
1988	Atlanta	Aundray Bruce, LB, Auburn
1989	Dallas	Troy Aikman, QB, UCLA
1990	Indianapolis	Jeff George, QB, Illinois
1991	Dallas	Russell Maryland, DL, Miami (FL)
1992	Indianapolis	Steve Emtman, DL, Washington
1993	New England	Drew Bledsoe, QB, Washington St.
1994	Cincinnati	Dan Wilkinson, DT, Ohio St.
1995	Cincinnati	Ki-Jana Carter, RB, Penn State
1996	N.Y. Jets	Keyshawn Johnson, WR, USC
1997	St. Louis	Orlando Pace, T, Ohio St.
1998	Indianapolis	Peyton Manning, QB, Tennessee
1999	Cleveland	Tim Couch, QB, Kentucky
2000	Cleveland	Courtney Brown, DE, Penn State
2001	Atlanta	Michael Vick, QB, Virginia Tech
2002	Houston	David Carr, QB, Fresno St.
2003	Cincinnati	Carson Palmer, QB, USC
2004	San Diego	Eli Manning, QB, Mississippi
2005	San Francisco	Alex D. Smith, QB, Utah

WORLD ALMANAC QUICK QUIZ

Can you rank these NFL coaches in order of victories (as of end of 2004 season), from most to fewest?

(a) Mike Ditka (c) Tom Landry
(b) Don Shula (d) Bill Parcells

For the answer look in this chapter, or see page 1008.

NFL MVP, Defensive Player of the Year, and Rookie of the Year

The Most Valuable Player and Defensive Player of the Year are two of many awards given out annually by the Associated Press. Rookie of the Year is one of many awards given out annually by *The Sporting News*. Many other organizations give out annual awards honoring the NFL's best players.

Most Valuable Player

1957 Jim Brown, Cleveland
1958 Gino Marchetti, Baltimore Colts
1959 Charley Conerly, N.Y. Giants
1960 Norm Van Brocklin, Philadelphia; Joe Schmidt, Detroit
1961 Paul Hornung, Green Bay
1962 Jim Taylor, Green Bay
1963 Y.A. Tittle, N.Y. Giants
1964 John Unitas, Baltimore Colts
1965 Jim Brown, Cleveland
1966 Bart Starr, Green Bay
1967 John Unitas, Baltimore Colts
1968 Earl Morrall, Baltimore Colts
1969 Roman Gabriel, L.A. Rams
1970 John Brodie, San Francisco
1971 Alan Page, Minnesota
1972 Larry Brown, Washington
1973 O.J. Simpson, Buffalo
1974 Ken Stabler, Oakland
1975 Fran Tarkenton, Minnesota
1976 Bert Jones, Baltimore
1977 Walter Payton, Chicago
1978 Terry Bradshaw, Pittsburgh
1979 Earl Campbell, Houston
1980 Brian Sipe, Cleveland
1981 Ken Anderson, Cincinnati
1982 Mark Moseley, Washington
1983 Joe Theismann, Washington
1984 Dan Marino, Miami
1985 Marcus Allen, L.A. Raiders
1986 Lawrence Taylor, N.Y. Giants
1987 John Elway, Denver
1988 Boomer Esiason, Cincinnati
1989 Joe Montana, San Francisco
1990 Joe Montana, San Francisco
1991 Thurman Thomas, Buffalo
1992 Steve Young, San Francisco
1993 Emmitt Smith, Dallas
1994 Steve Young, San Francisco
1995 Brett Favre, Green Bay
1996 Brett Favre, Green Bay
1997 (tie) Brett Favre, Green Bay; Barry Sanders, Detroit
1998 Terrell Davis, Denver
1999 Kurt Warner, St. Louis
2000 Marshall Faulk, St. Louis
2001 Kurt Warner, St. Louis
2002 Rich Gannon, Oakland
2003 (tie) Peyton Manning, Indianapolis; Steve McNair, Tennessee
2004 Peyton Manning, Indianapolis

Defensive Player of the Year

1966 Larry Wilson, St. Louis
1967 Deacon Jones, Los Angeles
1968 Deacon Jones, Los Angeles
1969 Dick Butkus, Chicago
1970 Dick Butkus, Chicago
1971 Carl Eller, Minnesota
1972 Joe Greene, Pittsburgh
1973 Alan Page, Minnesota
1974 Joe Greene, Pittsburgh
1975 Curley Culp, Houston
1976 Jerry Sherk, Cleveland
1977 Harvey Martin, Dallas
1978 Randy Gradishar, Denver
1979 Lee Roy Selmon, Tampa Bay
1980 Lester Hayes, Oakland
1981 Joe Klecko, N.Y. Jets
1982 Mark Gastineau, N.Y. Jets
1983 Jack Lambert, Pittsburgh
1984 Mike Haynes, L.A. Raiders
1985 Howie Long, L.A. Raiders; Andre Tippett, New England
1986 Lawrence Taylor, N.Y. Giants
1987 Reggie White, Philadelphia
1988 Mike Singletary, Chicago
1989 Tim Harris, Green Bay
1990 Bruce Smith, Buffalo
1991 Pat Swilling, New Orleans
1992 Junior Seau, San Diego
1993 Bruce Smith, Buffalo
1994 Deion Sanders, San Francisco
1995 Bryce Paup, Buffalo
1996 Bruce Smith, Buffalo
1997 Dana Stubblefield, San Francisco
1998 Reggie White, Green Bay
1999 Warren Sapp, Tampa Bay
2000 Ray Lewis, Baltimore
2001 Michael Strahan, NY Giants
2002 Derrick Brooks, Tampa Bay
2003 Ray Lewis, Baltimore
2004 Ed Reed, Baltimore

Rookie of the Year

1964 Charley Taylor, Washington
1965 Gale Sayers, Chicago
1966 Tommy Nobis, Atlanta
1967 Mel Farr, Detroit
1968 Earl McCullouch, Detroit
1969 Calvin Hill, Dallas
1970 NFC: Bruce Taylor, San Francisco; AFC: Dennis Shaw, Buffalo
1971 NFC: John Brockington, Green Bay; AFC: Jim Plunkett, New England
1972 NFC: Chester Marcol, Green Bay; AFC: Franco Harris, Pittsburgh
1973 NFC: Chuck Foreman, Minnesota; AFC: Boobie Clark, Cincinnati
1974 NFC: Wilbur Jackson, San Francisco; AFC: Don Woods, San Diego
1975 NFC: Steve Bartkowski, Atlanta; AFC: Robert Brazile, Houston
1976 NFC: Sammy White, Minnesota; AFC: Mike Haynes, New England
1977 NFC: Tony Dorsett, Dallas; AFC: A. J. Duhe, Miami
1978 NFC: Al Baker, Detroit; AFC: Earl Campbell, Houston
1979 NFC: Ottis Anderson, St. Louis; AFC: Jerry Butler, Buffalo
1980 Billy Sims, Detroit
1981 George Rogers, New Orleans
1982 Marcus Allen, L.A. Raiders
1983 Dan Marino, Miami
1984 Louis Lipps, Pittsburgh
1985 Eddie Brown, Cincinnati
1986 Rueben Mayes, New Orleans
1987 Robert Awalt, St. Louis
1988 Keith Jackson, Philadelphia
1989 Barry Sanders, Detroit
1990 Richmond Webb, Miami
1991 Mike Croel, Denver
1992 Santana Dotson, Tampa Bay
1993 Jerome Bettis, L.A. Rams
1994 Marshall Faulk, Indianapolis
1995 Curtis Martin, New England
1996 Eddie George, Houston
1997 Warrick Dunn, Tampa Bay
1998 Randy Moss, Minnesota
1999 Edgerrin James, Indianapolis
2000 Brian Urlacher, Chicago
2001 Kendrell Bell, Pittsburgh
2002 Clinton Portis, Denver
2003 Anquan Boldin, Arizona
2004 Ben Roethlisberger, Pittsburgh

The Sporting News 2004 NFL All-Pro Team

Offense—Quarterback: Peyton Manning, Indianapolis. Running Backs: Edgerrin James, Indianapolis; Curtis Martin, NY Jets. Wide Receivers: Marvin Harrison, Indianapolis; Terrell Owens, Eagles. Tight End: Antonio Gates, San Diego. Tackles: Walter Jones, Seattle; Orlando Pace, St. Louis. Guards: Alan Faneca, Pittsburgh; Brian Waters, Kansas City. Center: Jeff Hartings, Pittsburgh.

Defense—Linebackers: James Farrior, Pittsburgh; Ray Lewis, Baltimore; Takeo Spikes, Buffalo. Defensive Ends: Dwight Freeney, Indianapolis; Julius Peppers, Carolina. Defensive Tackles: Richard Seymour, New England; Kevin Williams, Minnesota. Cornerbacks: Champ Bailey, Washington; Chris McAlister, Baltimore. Safeties: Brian Dawkings, Philadelphia; Ed Reed, Baltimore.

Special Teams—Kicker: Adam Vinatieri, New England. Punter: Shane Lechler, Oakland. Punt Returner: Eddie Drummond, Detroit. Kick Returner: Terrence McGee, Buffalo.

All-Time NFL Coaching Victories

(at end of 2004 season; ranked by overall career wins; *active in 2004)

			Regular Season				Overall			
Coach	Team	Yrs.	W	L	T	Pct.	W	L	T	Pct.
Don Shula	Colts, Dolphins	33	328	156	6	0.677	347	173	6	0.677
George Halas	Bears	40	318	148	31	0.682	324	151	31	0.682
Tom Landry	Cowboys	29	250	162	6	0.607	270	178	6	0.603
Curly Lambeau	Packers, Cardinals, Redskins	33	226	132	22	0.631	229	134	22	0.631
Paul Brown	Browns, Bengals	25	213	104	9	0.667	222	112	9	0.660
Chuck Noll	Steelers	23	193	148	1	0.566	209	156	1	0.572
Dan Reeves	Broncos, Giants, Falcons	23	190	165	2	0.535	201	174	2	0.536
Chuck Knox	Rams, Bills, Seahawks	22	186	147	1	0.558	193	158	1	0.550
Marty Schottenheimer*	Browns, Chiefs, Redskins, Chargers	19	177	117	1	0.602	182	129	1	0.585
Bud Grant	Vikings	18	158	96	5	0.621	168	108	5	0.608
Bill Parcells*	Giants, Patriots, Jets, Cowboys	17	154	116	1	0.570	165	123	1	0.573
Marv Levy	Chiefs, Bills	17	143	112	0	0.561	154	120	0	0.562

Coach	Team	Yrs.	Regular Season W	L	T	Pct.	Overall W	L	T	Pct.
Steve Owen	Giants	23	151	100	17	0.602	153	108	17	0.586
Joe Gibbs*	Redskins	13	130	70	0	0.650	146	75	0	0.661
Bill Cowher*	Steelers	13	130	77	1	0.627	138	86	1	0.616
Hank Stram	Chiefs, Saints	17	131	97	10	0.574	136	100	10	0.576
Weeb Ewbank*	Colts, Jets	20	130	129	7	0.502	134	130	7	0.508
Mike Holmgren*	Packers, Seahawks	13	125	83	0	0.601	134	91	0	0.596
Mike Ditka	Bears, Saints	14	121	95	0	0.560	127	101	0	0.557
Jim Mora	Saints, Colts	15	125	106	0	0.541	125	112	0	0.527

*active in 2004

All-Time Professional (NFL and AFL) Football Records

Leading Lifetime Scorers

Player	Yrs.	TD	PAT	FG	Total
Gary Anderson*	23	0	820	538	2,434
Morten Anderson*	23	0	798	520	2,358
George Blanda (a)	26	9	943	335	2,002
Norm Johnson	18	0	638	366	1,736
Nick Lowery	18	0	562	383	1,711
Jan Stenerud (a)	19	0	580	373	1,699
Lou Groza (a)	21	1	810	264	1,608
Eddie Murray	19	0	538	352	1,594
Al Del Greco	17	0	543	347	1,584
John Carney*	17	0	442	365	1,537
Matt Stover*	14	0	431	350	1,481
Steve Christie*	15	0	468	336	1,476
Pat Leahy	18	0	558	304	1,470
Jason Elam*	12	0	491	317	1,442
Jim Turner(a)	16	1	521	304	1,439
Matt Bahr	17	0	522	300	1,422
Mark Moseley	16	0	482	300	1,382
Jim Bakken	17	0	534	282	1,380
Fred Cox	15	0	519	282	1,365
Jason Hanson*	13	0	412	308	1,336

*active in 2004. (a) includes AFL statistics.

Leading Lifetime Touchdown Scorers

Player	Yrs.	Rush	Rec.	Ret.	TD
Jerry Rice	20	10	197	1	208
Emmitt Smith	15	164	11	0	175
Marcus Allen	16	123	21	1	145
Marshal Faulk	11	100	35	0	135
Cris Carter	16	0	130	1	131
Jim Brown	9	106	20	0	126
Walter Payton	13	110	15	0	125
John Riggins	14	104	12	0	116
Lenny Moore	12	63	48	2	113
Barry Sanders	10	99	10	0	109
Tim Brown	17	1	100	4	105
Don Hutson	11	3	99	3	105
Steve Largent	14	1	100	0	101
Franco Harris	13	91	9	0	100
Marvin Harrison	9	0	98	0	98
Terrell Owens	9	2	95	0	97
Eric Dickerson	11	90	6	0	96
Curtis Martin	10	85	10	0	95
Jim Taylor	10	83	10	0	93

*active in 2004. (a) includes AFL statistics.

Most Points, Season—176, Paul Hornung, Green Bay Packers, 1960 (15 TDs, 41 PATs, 15 FGs).
Most Points, Game—40, Ernie Nevers, Chicago Cardinals vs. Chicago Bears, Nov. 28, 1929 (6 TDs, 4 PATs).
Most Touchdowns, Season—27, Priest Holmes, Kansas City Chiefs, 2003 (27 rushing, 0 receiving).
Most Touchdowns, Game—6, Ernie Nevers, Chicago Cardinals vs. Chicago Bears, Nov. 28, 1929 (6 rushing); Dub Jones, Cleveland Browns vs. Chicago Bears, Nov. 25, 1951 (4 rushing, 2 pass receptions); Gale Sayers, Chicago Bears vs. San Francisco 49ers, Dec. 12, 1965 (4 rushing, 1 pass reception, 1 punt return).
Most Points After TD, Season—66, Uwe von Schamann, Miami Dolphins, 1984.
Most Consecutive Points After TD—371, Jason Elam, Denver Broncos, 1993-2002.
Most Field Goals, Season—39, Olindo Mare, Miami Dolphins, 1999; Jeff Wilkins, St. Louis Rams, 2003.
Most Field Goals, Game—7, Jim Bakken, St. Louis Cardinals vs. Pittsburgh Steelers, Sept. 24, 1967; Rich Karlis, Minnesota Vikings vs. L.A. Rams, Nov. 5, 1989 (OT); Chris Boniol, Dallas Cowboys vs. Green Bay Packers, Nov. 18, 1996; Billy Cundiff, Dallas Cowboys vs. N.Y. Giants, Sept. 15, 2003 (OT).
Most Field Goals, Career—538, Gary Anderson, Pitts. Steelers-Phil. Eagles-SF 49ers-Minn. Vikings-Tenn. Titans, 1982-2004.
Longest Field Goal—63 yds., Tom Dempsey, New Orleans Saints vs. Detroit Lions, Nov. 8, 1970; Jason Elam, Denver Broncos vs. Jacksonville Jaguars, Oct. 25, 1998.

Defensive Records

(at end of 2004 season)

Most Interceptions, Career— 81, Paul Krause, Washington Redskins-Minnesota Vikings, 1964-79.
Most Interceptions, Season —14, Dick "Night Train" Lane, L. A. Rams, 1952.
Most Touchdowns, Career —12, Rod Woodson, Pittsburgh Steelers-San Francisco 49ers-Baltimore Ravens-Oakland Raiders, 1987-2002.
Most Touchdowns, Season —4, Ken Houston, Houston Oilers, 1971; Jim Kearney, Kansas City Chiefs, 1972; Eric Allen, Philadelphia Eagles, 1993.
Most Sacks, Career (Since 1982)—200, Bruce Smith, Buffalo Bills-Washington Redskins, 1985-2003.
Most Sacks, Season (Since 1982)—22.5, Michael Strahan, N.Y. Giants, 2002.
Most Sacks, Game (Since 1982)—7, Derrick Thomas, Kansas City Chiefs vs. Seattle Seahawks, Nov. 11, 1990.

Leading Lifetime Rushers

(ranked by rushing yards)

Player	Yrs.	Att.	Yards	Avg.	Long	TD
Emmitt Smith*	15	4,409	18,355	4.2	75	164
Walter Payton	13	3,838	16,726	4.4	76	110
Barry Sanders	10	3,062	15,269	5.0	85	99
Curtis Martin*	10	3,298	13,366	4.1	70	85
Jerome Bettis*	12	3,369	13,294	3.9	71	82
Eric Dickerson	11	2,996	13,259	4.4	85	90
Tony Dorsett	12	2,936	12,739	4.3	99	77
Jim Brown	9	2,359	12,312	5.2	80	106
Marcus Allen	16	3,022	12,243	4.1	61	123
Franco Harris	13	2,949	12,120	4.1	75	91
Thurman Thomas	13	2,877	12,074	4.2	80	65
Marshall Faulk*	11	2,771	11,987	4.3	71	100
John Riggins	14	2,916	11,352	3.9	66	104
O.J. Simpson (a)	11	2,404	11,236	4.7	94	61
Ricky Watters	10	2,622	10,643	4.1	57	78
Eddie George*	9	2,865	10,441	3.6	76	68
Otis Anderson	14	2,562	10,273	4.0	76	81
Corey Dillon*	8	2,210	9,696	4.4	96	57
Earl Campbell	8	2,187	9,407	4.3	81	74

*active in 2004. (a) includes AFL statistics.

Most Yards Gained, Season—2,105, Eric Dickerson, L.A. Rams, 1984.
Most Yards Gained, Game—295, Jamal Lewis, Baltimore Ravens vs. Cleveland Browns, Sept. 14, 2003.
Most Touchdowns Rushing, Career—164, Emmitt Smith, Dallas Cowboys-Ariz. Cardinals, 1990-2004.
Most Touchdowns Rushing, Season—27, Priest Holmes, Kansas City Chiefs, 2003.
Most Touchdowns Rushing, Game—6, Ernie Nevers, Chicago Cardinals vs. Chicago Bears, Nov. 28, 1929.
Most Rushing Attempts, Game—45, Jamie Morris, Washington Redskins vs. Cincinnati Bengals, Dec. 17, 1988 (overtime).
Longest Run From Scrimmage—99 yds., Tony Dorsett, Dallas Cowboys vs. Minnesota Vikings, Jan. 3, 1983 (touchdown).

Leading Lifetime Receivers

(ranked by number of receptions)

Player	Yrs.	No.	Yards	Avg.	Long	TD
Jerry Rice*	20	1,549	22,895	14.8	96	197
Cris Carter	16	1,101	13,899	12.6	80	130
Tim Brown*	17	1,094	14,934	13.7	80	100
Andre Reed	16	951	13,198	13.9	83	87
Art Monk	16	940	12,721	13.5	79	68
Irving Fryar	17	851	12,785	15.0	80	84
Marvin Harrison*	9	845	11,185	13.2	79	98
Larry Centers	14	827	6,797	8.2	54	28
Steve Largent	14	819	13,089	16.0	74	100
Shannon Sharpe	14	815	10,060	12.3	82	62
Henry Ellard	16	814	13,777	16.9	81	65
Jimmy Smith	12	792	11,264	14.2	75	61
Isaac Bruce	11	777	11,753	15.1	80	74
James Lofton	16	764	14,004	18.3	80	75
Keenan McCardell*	13	755	9,763	12.9	76	53
Michael Irvin	12	750	11,904	15.9	87	65
Charlie Joiner (a)	18	750	12,146	16.2	80	65
Andre Rison	12	743	10,205	13.7	80	84
Marshall Faulk*	11	723	6,584	9.1	85	35
Rod Smith*	10	712	9,772	13.7	85	59

*active in 2004. (a) includes AFL statistics.

Most Yards Gained, Career—22,895, Jerry Rice, San Francisco 49ers, Oakland Raiders, 1985-2004.
Most Yards Gained, Season—1,848, Jerry Rice, San Francisco 49ers, 1995.
Most Yards Gained, Game—336, Willie "Flipper" Anderson, L. A. Rams vs. New Orleans, Nov. 26, 1989 (overtime).
Most Pass Receptions, Season—143, Marvin Harrison, Indianapolis Colts, 2002.
Most Pass Receptions, Game—20, Terrell Owens, San Francisco 49ers vs. Chicago Bears, Dec. 17, 2000 (283 yards).
Most Touchdown Receptions, Career—194, Jerry Rice, San Francisco 49ers, Oakland Raiders, 1985-2003.
Most Touchdown Receptions, Season—22, Jerry Rice, San Francisco 49ers, 1987.
Most Touchdown Receptions, Game—5, Bob Shaw, Chicago Cardinals vs. Baltimore Colts, Oct. 2, 1950; Kellen Winslow, San Diego Chargers vs. Oakland Raiders, Nov. 22, 1981; Jerry Rice, San Francisco 49ers vs. Atlanta Falcons, Oct. 14, 1990.

Leading Lifetime Passers

(minimum 1,500 attempts; ranked by quarterback rating points)

Player	Yrs.	Att.	Comp.	Yards	TD	Int.	Pts.[1]
Steve Young	15	4,149	2,667	33,124	232	107	96.8
Kurt Warner*	7	1,965	1,295	16,501	108	69	95.7
Daunte Culpepper*	6	2,391	1,539	18,598	129	74	93.2
Peyton Manning*	7	3,880	2,464	29,442	216	120	92.29
Joe Montana	15	5,391	3,409	40,551	273	139	92.26
Trent Green*	7	2,822	1,705	21,607	133	82	87.9
Tom Brady*	5	2,018	1,243	13,925	97	52	87.5
Brett Favre*	14	7,003	4,306	49,734	376	226	87.4
Jeff Garcia*	6	2,612	1,593	18,139	123	65	87.2
Otto Graham (a)	10	2,626	1,464	23,584	174	135	86.6
Dan Marino	17	8,358	4,967	61,361	420	252	86.4
Brian Griese*	7	2,144	1,351	15,208	96	71	85.3
Rich Gannon*	16	4,206	2,533	28,743	180	104	84.7
Jim Kelly	11	4,779	2,874	35,467	237	175	84.4
Brad Johnson*	13	3,504	2,166	23,913	143	98	84.0
Donovan McNabb*	6	2,586	1,507	16,926	118	57	83.94
Mark Brunell*	11	3,880	2,314	26,987	151	92	83.86
Matt Hasselbeck*	6	1,756	1,048	12,466	72	48	83.7
Roger Staubach	11	2,958	1,685	22,700	153	109	83.42
Steve Mcnair*	10	3,395	2,013	23,980	140	92	83.38

*active in 2004. (a) includes AFL statistics. (1) Rating points based on performances in the following categories: Percentage of completions, percentage of touchdown passes, percentage of interceptions, and average gain per pass attempt.

Most Yards Gained, Career—61,361, Dan Marino, Miami Dolphins, 1983-99.
Most Yards Gained, Season—5,084, Dan Marino, Miami Dolphins, 1984.
Most Yards Gained, Game—554, Norm Van Brocklin, L. A. Rams vs. N.Y. Yanks, Sept. 28, 1951 (27 completions in 41 attempts).
Most Touchdowns Passing, Career—420, Dan Marino, Miami Dolphins, 1983-99.
Most Touchdowns Passing, Season—49, Peyton Manning, Indianapolis Colts, 2004.
Most Touchdowns Passing, Game—7, Sid Luckman, Chicago Bears vs. N.Y. Giants, Nov. 14, 1943; Adrian Burk, Phil. Eagles vs. Washington Redskins, Oct. 17, 1954; George Blanda, Houston Oilers vs. N.Y. Titans, Nov. 19, 1961; Y.A. Tittle, N.Y. Giants vs. Washington Redskins, Oct. 28, 1962; Joe Kapp, Minnesota Vikings vs. Baltimore Colts, Sept. 28, 1969.
Most Passes Completed, Career—4,967, Dan Marino, Miami Dolphins, 1983-99.
Most Passes Completed, Season—418, Rich Gannon, Oakland Raiders, 2002.
Most Passes Completed, Game—45, Drew Bledsoe, New England Patriots vs. Minnesota Vikings, Nov. 13, 1994 (OT).

National Football League Franchise Origins

(founding year, league; home stadium location; subsequent history)

Arizona Cardinals—1920, American Professional Football Association (APFA)[1]. Chicago, 1920-59; St. Louis, 1960-87; Tempe, AZ, 1988-present.
Atlanta Falcons—1996, NFL. Atlanta, 1966-present.
Baltimore Ravens—1996, NFL. Baltimore, 1996-present.
Buffalo Bills—1969, American Football League (AFL)[2]. Buffalo, 1960-72; Orchard Park, NY, 1972-present.
Carolina Panthers—1995, NFL. Clemson, SC, 1995; Charlotte, NC, 1996-present.
Chicago Bears—1920 APFA. Decatur, IL, 1920; Chicago, 1921-present.
Cincinnati Bengals—1968, AFL. Cincinnati, 1968-present.
Cleveland Browns—1946, All-America Football Conference (AAFC)[3]. Cleveland, 1946-95; 1999-present.
Dallas Cowboys—1960, NFL. Dallas, 1960-70; Irving, TX, 1971-present.
Denver Broncos—1960, AFL. Denver, 1960-present.
Detroit Lions—1930, NFL. Portsmouth, OH, 1930-33; Detroit, 1934-74; Pontiac, MI, 1975-present.
Green Bay Packers—1921, APFA. Green Bay, WI, 1921-present.
Houston Texans—2002, NFL. Houston 2002-present.
Indianapolis Colts—1953, NFL. Baltimore, 1953-83; Indianapolis, 1984-present.
Jacksonville Jaguars—1995, NFL. Jacksonville, FL, 1995-present.
Kansas City Chiefs—1960, AFL. Dallas, 1960-62; Kansas City, 1963-present.
Miami Dolphins—1966, AFL. Miami, 1966-present.
Minnesota Vikings—1961, NFL. Bloomington, MN, 1961-81; Minneapolis, 1982-present.
New England Patriots—1960, AFL. Boston, 1960-70; Foxboro, MA, 1971-present.
New Orleans Saints—1967, NFL. New Orleans, 1967-2004; Baton Rouge and San Antonio, 2005.
New York Giants—1925, NFL. New York, 1925-73, 1975; New Haven, CT, 1973-74; E. Rutherford, NJ, 1976-present.
New York Jets—1960, AFL. New York, 1960-83; E. Rutherford, NJ, 1984-present.
Oakland Raiders—1960, AFL. Oakland, CA, 1960-81, 1995-present; Los Angeles, 1982-94.
Philadelphia Eagles—1933, NFL. Piladelphia, 1933-present.
Pittsburgh Steelers—1933, NFL. Pittsburgh, 1933-present.
St. Louis Rams—1937, NFL. Cleveland, 1936-45; Los Angeles, 1946-79; Anaheim, 1980-94; St. Louis, 1995-present.
San Diego Chargers—1960, AFL. Los Angeles, 1960; San Diego, 1961-present.
Seattle Seahawks—1976, NFL. Seattle, 1976-present.
San Francisco 49ers—1946, AAFC. San Francisco, 1946-present.
Tampa Bay Buccaneers—1976, NFL. Tampa, 1976-present.
Tennessee Titans—1960, AFL. Houston, 1969-96; Memphis, 1997; Nashville, 1998-present.
Washington Redskins—1932, NFL. Boston, 1932-36, Washington, DC, 1937-96; Landover, MD, 1997-present.

(1) The American Professional Football Association (APFA) was formed in 1920 to standardize the rules of professional football. In 1922, the name was changed to the National Football League. (2) The most successful of 4 separate leagues called the "American Football League" (1926; 1936-37; 1940-41, 1960-69). Congress approved an NFL/AFL merger in 1966. Baltimore, Cleveland, and Pittsburgh agreed to join the 10 incoming AFL teams to form the American Football Conference. The NFL began play in 1970 with 26 teams. (3) The All-America Football Conference, 1946-49. In 1950, 3 of its teams joined the NFL (Baltimore, Cleveland, and San Francisco). The Baltimore franchise failed, but the NFL awarded the city a 2nd one, also called the Colts, in 1953.

Pro Football Hall of Fame, Canton, Ohio

(Asterisks indicate 2005 inductees.)

Herb Adderley
George Allen
Marcus Allen
Lance Alworth
Doug Atkins
Morris "Red" Badgro
Lem Barney
Cliff Battles
Sammy Baugh
Chuck Bednarik
Bert Bell
Bobby Bell
Raymond Berry
Elvin Bethea
Charles Bidwill
Fred Biletnikoff
George Blanda
Mel Blount
Terry Bradshaw
Bob Brown
Jim Brown
Paul Brown
Roosevelt Brown
Willie Brown
Buck Buchanan
Nick Buoniconti
Dick Butkus
Earl Campbell
Tony Canadeo
Joe Carr
Dave Casper
Guy Chamberlin
Jack Christiansen
Earl "Dutch" Clark
George Connor
Jim Conzelman
Lou Creekmur
Larry Csonka
Al Davis
Willie Davis
Len Dawson
Joe DeLamielleure
Eric Dickerson
Dan Dierdorf
Mike Ditka
Art Donovan
Tony Dorsett
John "Paddy" Driscoll
Bill Dudley
Glen "Turk" Edwards
Carl Eller
John Elway
Weeb Ewbank
Tom Fears
Jim Finks
Ray Flaherty
Len Ford
Dr. Daniel Fortmann
Dan Fouts
*Benny Friedman
Frank Gatski
Bill George
Joe Gibbs
Frank Gifford
Sid Gillman
Otto Graham
Red Grange
Bud Grant
Joe Greene
Forrest Gregg
Bob Griese
Lou Groza
Joe Guyon
George Halas
Jack Ham
Dan Hampton
John Hannah
Franco Harris
Mike Haynes
Ed Healey
Mel Hein
Ted Hendricks
Wilbur "Pete" Henry
Arnold Herber
Bill Hewitt
Clarke Hinkle
Elroy "Crazylegs" Hirsch
Paul Hornung
Ken Houston
Cal Hubbard
Sam Huff
Lamar Hunt
Don Hutson
Jimmy Johnson
John Henry Johnson
Charlie Joiner
David "Deacon" Jones
Stan Jones
Henry Jordan
Sonny Jurgensen
Jim Kelly
Leroy Kelly
Walt Kiesling
Frank "Bruiser" Kinard
Paul Krause
Earl "Curly" Lambeau
Jack Lambert
Tom Landry
Dick "Night Train" Lane
Jim Langer
Willie Lanier
Steve Largent
Yale Lary
Dante Lavelli
Bobby Layne
Alphonse "Tuffy" Leemans
Marv Levy
Bob Lilly
Larry Little
James Lofton
Vince Lombardi
Howie Long
Ronnie Lott
Sid Luckman
Roy "Link" Lyman
Tom Mack
John Mackey
Tim Mara
Wellington Mara
Gino Marchetti
*Dan Marino
George Preston Marshall
Ollie Matson
Don Maynard
George McAfee
Mike McCormack
Tommy McDonald
Hugh McElhenny
Johnny "Blood" McNally
Mike Michalske
Wayne Millner
Bobby Mitchell
Ron Mix
Joe Montana
Lenny Moore
Marion Motley
Mike Munchak
Anthony Munoz
George Musso
Bronko Nagurski
Joe Namath
Earle "Greasy" Neale
Ernie Nevers
Ozzie Newsome
Ray Nitschke
Chuck Noll
Leo Nomellini
Merlin Olsen
Jim Otto
Steve Owen
Alan Page
Clarence "Ace" Parker
Jim Parker
Walter Payton
Joe Perry
Pete Pihos
*Fritz Pollard
Hugh "Shorty" Ray
Dan Reeves
Mel Renfro
John Riggins
Jim Ringo
Andy Robustelli
Art Rooney
Dan Rooney
Pete Rozelle
Bob St. Clair
Barry Sanders
Gale Sayers
Joe Schmidt
Tex Schramm
Lee Roy Selmon
Billy Shaw
Art Shell
Don Shula
O.J. Simpson
Mike Singletary
Jackie Slater
Jackie Smith
John Stallworth
Bart Starr
Roger Staubach
Ernie Stautner
Jan Stenerud
Dwight Stephenson
Hank Stram
Ken Strong
Joe Stydahar
Lynn Swann
Fran Tarkenton
Charley Taylor
Jim Taylor
Lawrence "LT" Taylor
Jim Thorpe
Y.A. Tittle
George Trafton
Charley Trippi
Emlen Tunnell
Clyde "Bulldog" Turner
Johnny Unitas
Gene Upshaw
Norm Van Brocklin
Steve Van Buren
Doak Walker
Bill Walsh
Paul Warfield
Bob Waterfield
Mike Webster
Arnie Weinmeister
Randy White
Dave Wilcox
Bill Willis
Larry Wilson
Kellen Winslow
Alex Wojciechowicz
Willie Wood
Ron Yary
*Steve Young
Jack Youngblood

NFL Stadiums[1]

Team—Stadium, Location, Turf (Year Built)	Capacity
Bears—New Soldier Field[2], Chicago, IL, G (1924)	61,500
Bengals—Paul Brown Stad., Cincinnati, OH, G (2000)	65,600
Bills—Ralph Wilson Stad., Orchard Park, NY, A (1973)	73,967
Broncos—Invesco Field at Mile High, Denver, CO, G (2001)	76,125
Browns—Cleveland Browns Stad., Cleveland, OH, G (1999)	73,300
Buccaneers—Raymond James Stad., Tampa, FL, G (1998)	65,657
Cardinals—Sun Devil Stad., Tempe, AZ, G (1958)	73,014
Chargers—Qualcomm Stad.[3], San Diego, CA, G (1967)	71,500
Chiefs—Arrowhead Stad., Kansas City, MO, G (1972)	79,451
Colts—RCA Dome[4], Indianapolis, IN, A (1983)	56,127
Cowboys—Texas Stad., Irving, TX, A (1971)	65,675
Dolphins—Dolphins Stad.[5], Miami, FL, G (1987)	75,192
Eagles—Lincoln Financial Field, Philadelphia, PA, G (2003)	65,352
Falcons—Georgia Dome, Atlanta, GA, A (1992)	71,228
49ers—Monster Park[6], San Francisco, CA, G (1960)	69,734
Giants—Giants Stad., E. Rutherford, NJ, G (1976)	79,469
Jaguars—ALLTEL Stad.[7], Jacksonville, FL, G (1946)	73,000
Jets—Giants Stad., E. Rutherford, NJ, G (1976)	79,466
Lions—Ford Field, Detroit, MI, A (2002)	65,000
Packers—Lambeau Field[8], Green Bay, WI, G (1957)	72,515
Panthers—Bank of America Stad.[9], Charlotte, NC, G (1996)	73,258
Patriots—Gillette Stad., Foxboro, MA, G (2002)	68,000
Raiders—McAfee Coliseum[10], Oakland, CA, G (1966)	63,132
Rams—Edward Jones Dome[11], St. Louis, MO, A (1995)	66,000
Ravens—M & T Bank Stad.[12], Baltimore, MD, SG (1998)	69,354
Redskins—FedEx Field[13], Landover, MD, G (1997)	80,116
Saints—Louisiana Superdome, New Orleans, A (1975)	69,703
Seahawks—Qwest Field[14], Seattle, WA, A (2002)	67,000
Steelers—Heinz Field, Pittsburgh, PA, A (2001)	64,450
Texans—Reliant Stadium, Houston, TX, G (2002)	69,500
Titans—The Coliseum[15], Nashville, TN, G (1999)	67,000
Vikings—Hubert H. Humphrey Metrodome, Minn., MN, A (1982)	64,121

G=Grass. A=Artificial turf. SG=Sport Grass (hybrid of artificial and natural turf). (1) As of the start of the 2005 season. (2) Renovation in 2002 replaced interior of stadium (3) Formerly San Diego Stadium (1967-80), San Diego Jack Murphy Stadium (1981-97). (4) Formerly the Hoosier Dome (1983-94). (5) Formerly Joe Robbie Stadium (1987-96). (6) Formerly Candlestick Park (1960-1994); 3Com Park at Candlestick Point (1995-2004). (7) Formerly Jacksonville Municipal Stadium (1946-97). (8) Formerly City Stadium (1957-65). Renovation completed in 2003, added 11,625 seats. (9) Formerly Ericsson Stadium (1996-2003). (10) Formerly Oakland/Alameda County Coliseum until 1998; Network Associates Coliseum until 2005. (11) Formerly Trans World Dome (1995-2001); full name: Edward Jones Dome at America's Center. (12) Formerly PSINet Stadium (1998-2002); Ravens Stadium (2002-2003). (13) Formerly Jack Kent Cooke Stadium (1997-99). (14) Formerly Seahawks Stadium (2002-04). (15) Formerly Adelphia Col. (1999-2002).

Future Sites of the Super Bowl

(Information subject to change.)

No.	Site	Date
XL	Ford Field, Detroit, MI	Feb. 5, 2006
XLI	Dolphins Stadium, Miami, FL	Feb. 4, 2007
XLII	Cardinals Stadium, Glendale, AZ	Feb. 3, 2008
XLIII	Raymond James Stadium, Tampa, FL	Feb. 1, 2009
XLIV	Dolphins Stadium, Miami, FL	Feb. 2010

COLLEGE FOOTBALL

Undefeated USC Trojans Take Orange Bowl, National Title

The Univ. of Southern California Trojans routed the Univ. of Oklahoma Sooners 55-19 at the Orange Bowl in Miami, FL, to win the 2004 season national championship. The game, Jan. 4, 2005, pitted the 2004 Heisman Trophy recipient, USC quarterback Matt Leinart, against the 2003 Heisman winner, Oklahoma quarterback Jason White. The Sooners scored early in the 1st quarter, but USC's victory was all but assured at halftime, with the Trojans securing 4 unanswered touchdowns in the middle of the 1st half for a 38-10 lead. USC, which had shared the 2003 national title with Louisiana State Univ., finished the season undefeated with 13 wins and held the longest active winning streak in Division I football, at 22 games.

National College Football Champions, 1936-2004

The unofficial champion as selected by the AP poll of writers and USA Today/ESPN (until 1991, UPI; 1991-1996 USA Today/CNN) poll of coaches. Where the polls disagreed, both teams are listed (AP winner first). The AP poll started in 1936; the UPI poll in 1950.

1936	Minnesota
1937	Pittsburgh
1938	Texas Christian
1939	Texas A&M
1940	Minnesota
1941	Minnesota
1942	Ohio St.
1943	Notre Dame
1944	Army
1945	Army
1946	Notre Dame
1947	Notre Dame
1948	Michigan
1949	Notre Dame
1950	Oklahoma
1951	Tennessee
1952	Michigan St.
1953	Maryland
1954	Ohio St., UCLA
1955	Oklahoma
1956	Oklahoma
1957	Auburn, Ohio St.
1958	Louisiana St.
1959	Syracuse
1960	Minnesota
1961	Alabama
1962	USC
1963	Texas
1964	Alabama
1965	Alabama, Mich. St.
1966	Notre Dame
1967	USC
1968	Ohio St.
1969	Texas
1970	Nebraska, Texas
1971	Nebraska
1972	USC
1973	Notre Dame, Alabama
1974	Oklahoma, USC
1975	Oklahoma
1976	Pittsburgh
1977	Notre Dame
1978	Alabama, USC
1979	Alabama
1980	Georgia
1981	Clemson
1982	Penn St.
1983	Miami (FL)
1984	Brigham Young
1985	Oklahoma
1986	Penn St.
1987	Miami (FL)
1988	Notre Dame
1989	Miami (FL)
1990	Colorado, GA Tech
1991	Miami (FL), Washington
1992	Alabama
1993	Florida St.
1994	Nebraska
1995	Nebraska
1996	Florida
1997	Michigan, Nebraska
1998	Tennessee
1999	Florida St.
2000	Oklahoma
2001	Miami (FL)
2002	Ohio State
2003	LSU, USC
2004	USC

2004 Final AP and USA Today/ESPN Rankings

Associated Press Poll

1.	USC	13-0
2.	Auburn	13-0
3.	Oklahoma	12-1
4.	Utah	12-0
5.	Texas	11-1
6.	Louisville	11-1
7.	Georgia	10-2
8.	Iowa	10-2
9.	California	10-2
10.	Virginia Tech	10-3
11.	Miami (FL)	9-3
12.	Boise State	11-1
13.	Tennessee	10-3
14.	Michigan	9-3
15.	Florida State	9-3
16.	LSU	9-3
17.	Wisconsin	9-3
18.	Texas Tech	8-4
19.	Arizona State	9-3
20.	Ohio State	8-4
21.	Boston Coll.	9-3
22.	Fresno State	9-3
23.	Virginia	9-4
24.	Navy	10-2
25.	Pittsburgh	8-4

USA Today/ESPN Coaches' Poll

1.	USC	13-0
2.	Auburn	13-0
3.	Oklahoma	12-1
4.	Texas	11-1
5.	Utah	12-0
6.	Georgia	10-2
7.	Louisville	11-1
8.	Iowa	10-2
9.	California	10-2
10.	Virginia Tech	10-3
11.	Miami (FL)	9-3
12.	Michigan	9-3
13.	Boise State	11-1
14.	Florida State	9-3
15.	Tennessee	10-3
16.	LSU	9-3
17.	Texas Tech	8-4
18.	Wisconsin	9-3
19.	Ohio State	8-4
20.	Arizona State	9-3
21.	Boston Coll.	9-3
22.	Fresno State	9-3
23.	Virginia	8-4
24.	Navy	10-2
25.	Florida	7-5

Note: Team records include bowl games. The American Football Coaches Assn. prohibits coaches from voting for schools on major NCAA probation. The NCAA placed the Univ. of Alabama on 5-year probation Feb. 1, 2002, for recruiting violations.

Annual Results of Major Bowl Games

(Dates indicate year the game was played; bowl games are generally played in late December or early January.)

Rose Bowl, Pasadena, CA

1902	(Jan.) Michigan 49, Stanford 0
1916	Washington St. 14, Brown 0
1917	Oregon 14, Pennsylvania 0
1918-19	Service teams
1920	Harvard 7, Oregon 6
1921	California 28, Ohio St. 0
1922	Wash. & Jeff. 0, California 0
1923	USC 14, Penn St. 3
1924	Navy 14, Washington 14
1925	Notre Dame 27, Stanford 10
1926	Alabama 20, Washington 19
1927	Alabama 7, Stanford 7
1928	Stanford 7, Pittsburgh 6
1929	Georgia Tech 8, California 7
1930	USC 47, Pittsburgh 14
1931	Alabama 24, Wash. St. 0
1932	USC 21, Tulane 12
1933	USC 35, Pittsburgh 0
1934	Columbia 7, Stanford 0
1935	Alabama 29, Stanford 13
1936	Stanford 7, SMU 0
1937	Pittsburgh 21, Washington 0
1938	California 13, Alabama 0
1939	USC 7, Duke 3
1940	USC 14, Tennessee 0
1941	Stanford 21, Nebraska 13
1942*	Oregon St. 20, Duke 16
1943	Georgia 9, UCLA 0
1944	USC 29, Washington 0
1945	USC 25, Tennessee 0
1946	Alabama 34, USC 14
1947	Illinois 45, UCLA 14
1948	Michigan 49, USC 0
1949	Northwestern 20, California 14
1950	Ohio St. 17, California 14
1951	Michigan 14, California 6
1952	Illinois 40, Stanford 7
1953	USC 7, Wisconsin 0
1954	Mich. St. 28, UCLA 20
1955	Ohio St. 20, USC 7
1956	Mich. St. 17, UCLA 14
1957	Iowa 35, Oregon St. 19
1958	Ohio St. 10, Oregon 7
1959	Iowa 38, California 12
1960	Washington 44, Wisconsin 8
1961	Washington 17, Minnesota 7
1962	Minnesota 21, UCLA 3
1963	USC 42, Wisconsin 37
1964	Illinois 17, Washington 7
1965	Michigan 34, Oregon St. 7
1966	UCLA 14, Mich. St. 12
1967	Purdue 14, USC 13
1968	USC 14, Indiana 3
1969	Ohio St. 27, USC 16
1970	USC 10, Michigan 3
1971	Stanford 27, Ohio St. 17
1972	Stanford 13, Michigan 12
1973	USC 42, Ohio St. 17
1974	Ohio St. 42, USC 21
1975	USC 18, Ohio St. 17
1976	UCLA 23, Ohio St. 10
1977	USC 14, Michigan 6
1978	Washington 27, Michigan 20
1979	USC 17, Michigan 10
1980	USC 17, Ohio St. 16
1981	Michigan 23, Washington 6
1982	Washington 28, Iowa 0
1983	UCLA 24, Michigan 14
1984	UCLA 45, Illinois 9
1985	USC 20, Ohio St. 17
1986	UCLA 45, Iowa 28
1987	Arizona St. 22, Michigan 15
1988	Mich. St. 20, USC 17
1989	Michigan 22, USC 14
1990	USC 17, Michigan 10
1991	Washington 46, Iowa 34
1992	Washington 34, Michigan 14
1993	Michigan 38, Washington 31
1994	Wisconsin 21, UCLA 16
1995	Penn St. 38, Oregon 20
1996	USC 41, Northwestern 32
1997	Ohio St. 20, Arizona St. 17
1998	Michigan 21, Wash. St. 16
1999	Wisconsin 38, UCLA 31
2000	Wisconsin 17, Stanford 9
2001	Washington 34, Purdue 24
2002	Miami (FL) 37, Nebraska 14
2003	Oklahoma, 34, Washington St. 14
2004	USC 28, Michigan 14
2005	Texas 38, Michigan 37

*Played at Durham, NC.

Orange Bowl, Miami, FL

1935	(Jan.) Bucknell 26, Miami (FL) 0
1936	Catholic U. 20, Mississippi 19
1937	Duquesne 13, Mississippi St. 12
1938	Auburn 6, Michigan St. 0
1939	Tennessee 17, Oklahoma 0
1940	Georgia Tech 21, Missouri 7
1941	Mississippi St. 14, Georgetown 7
1942	Georgia 40, TCU 26
1943	Alabama 37, Boston Coll. 21
1944	LSU 19, Texas A&M 14
1945	Tulsa 26, Georgia Tech 12
1946	Miami (FL) 13, Holy Cross 6
1947	Rice 8, Tennessee 0
1948	Georgia Tech 20, Kansas 14
1949	Texas 41, Georgia 28
1950	Santa Clara 21, Kentucky 13
1951	Clemson 15, Miami (FL) 14
1952	Georgia Tech 17, Baylor 14

1953 Alabama 61, Syracuse 6
1954 Oklahoma 7, Maryland 0
1955 Duke 34, Nebraska 7
1956 Oklahoma 20, Maryland 6
1957 Colorado 27, Clemson 21
1958 Oklahoma 48, Duke 21
1959 Oklahoma 21, Syracuse 6
1960 Georgia 14, Missouri 0
1961 Missouri 21, Navy 14
1962 LSU 25, Colorado 7
1963 Alabama 17, Oklahoma 0
1964 Nebraska 13, Auburn 7
1965 Texas 21, Alabama 17
1966 Alabama 39, Nebraska 28
1967 Florida 27, Georgia Tech 12
1968 Oklahoma 26, Tennessee 24
1969 Penn St. 15, Kansas 14
1970 Penn St. 10, Missouri 3
1971 Nebraska 17, LSU 12
1972 Nebraska 38, Alabama 6
1973 Nebraska 40, Notre Dame 6
1974 Penn St. 16, LSU 9
1975 Notre Dame 13, Alabama 11
1976 Oklahoma 14, Michigan 6
1977 Ohio St. 27, Colorado 10
1978 Arkansas 31, Oklahoma 6
1979 Oklahoma 31, Nebraska 24
1980 Oklahoma 24, Florida St. 7
1981 Oklahoma 18, Florida St. 17
1982 Clemson 22, Nebraska 15
1983 Nebraska 21, LSU 20
1984 Miami (FL) 31, Nebraska 30
1985 Washington 28, Oklahoma 17
1986 Oklahoma 25, Penn St. 10
1987 Oklahoma 42, Arkansas 8
1988 Miami (FL) 20, Oklahoma 14
1989 Miami (FL) 23, Nebraska 3
1990 Notre Dame 21, Colorado 6
1991 Colorado 10, Notre Dame 9
1992 Miami (FL) 22, Nebraska 0
1993 Florida St. 27, Nebraska 14
1994 Florida St. 18, Nebraska 16
1995 Nebraska 24, Miami (FL) 17
1996 Florida St. 31, Notre Dame 26
1996 (Dec.) Nebraska 41, Virginia Tech 21
1998 (Jan.) Nebraska 42, Tennessee 17
1999 Florida 31, Syracuse 10
2000 Michigan 35, Alabama 34 (OT)
2001 Oklahoma 13, Florida St. 2
2002 Florida 56, Maryland 23
2003 USC 38, Iowa 17
2004 Miami 16, Florida State 14
2005 USC 55, Oklahoma 19

Sugar Bowl, New Orleans, LA

1935 (Jan.) Tulane 20, Temple 14
1936 TCU 3, LSU 2
1937 Santa Clara 21, LSU 14
1938 Santa Clara 6, LSU 0
1939 TCU 15, Carnegie Tech 7
1940 Texas A&M 14, Tulane 13
1941 Boston Col. 19, Tennessee 13
1942 Fordham 2, Missouri 0
1943 Tennessee 14, Tulsa 7
1944 Georgia Tech 20, Tulsa 18
1945 Duke 29, Alabama 26
1946 Oklahoma A&M 33, St. Mary's 13
1947 Georgia 20, N. Carolina 10
1948 Texas 27, Alabama 7
1949 Oklahoma 14, N. Carolina 6
1950 Oklahoma 35, LSU 0
1951 Kentucky 13, Oklahoma 7
1952 Maryland 28, Tennessee 13
1953 Georgia Tech 24, Mississippi 7
1954 Georgia Tech 42, West Virginia 19
1955 Navy 21, Mississippi 0
1956 Georgia Tech 7, Pittsburgh 0
1957 Baylor 13, Tennessee 7
1958 Mississippi 39, Texas 7
1959 LSU 7, Clemson 0
1960 Mississippi 21, LSU 0
1961 Mississippi 14, Rice 6
1962 Alabama 10, Arkansas 3
1963 Mississippi 17, Arkansas 13
1964 Alabama 12, Mississippi 7
1965 LSU 13, Syracuse 10
1966 Missouri 20, Florida 18
1967 Alabama 34, Nebraska 7
1968 LSU 20, Wyoming 13
1969 Arkansas 16, Georgia 2
1970 Mississippi 27, Arkansas 22
1971 Tennessee 34, Air Force 13
1972 Oklahoma 40, Auburn 22
1972 (Dec.) Oklahoma 14, Penn St. 0
1973 Notre Dame 24, Alabama 23
1974 Nebraska 13, Florida 10
1975 Alabama 13, Penn St. 6
1977 (Jan.) Pittsburgh 27, Georgia 3
1978 Alabama 35, Ohio St. 6
1979 Alabama 14, Penn St. 7
1980 Alabama 24, Arkansas 9
1981 Georgia 17, Notre Dame 10
1982 Pittsburgh 24, Georgia 20
1983 Penn St. 27, Georgia 23
1984 Auburn 9, Michigan 7
1985 Nebraska 28, LSU 10
1986 Tennessee 35, Miami (FL) 7
1987 Nebraska 30, LSU 15
1988 Syracuse 16, Auburn 16
1989 Florida St. 13, Auburn 7
1990 Miami (FL) 33, Alabama 25
1991 Tennessee 23, Virginia 22
1992 Notre Dame 39, Florida 28
1993 Alabama 34, Miami (FL) 13
1994 Florida 41, West Virginia 7
1995 Florida St. 23, Florida 17
1995 (Dec.) Virginia Tech 28, Texas 10
1997 (Jan.) Florida 52, Florida St. 20
1998 Florida St. 31, Ohio St. 14
1999 Ohio St. 24, Texas A&M 14
2000 Florida St. 46, Virginia Tech 29
2001 Miami (FL) 37, Florida 20
2002 LSU 47, Illinois 34
2003 Georgia 26, Florida St. 13
2004 LSU 21, Oklahoma 14
2005 Auburn 16, Virginia Tech 13

Cotton Bowl, Dallas, TX

1937 (Jan.) TCU 16, Marquette 6
1938 Rice 28, Colorado 14
1939 St. Mary's 20, Texas Tech 13
1940 Clemson 6, Boston Coll. 3
1941 Texas A&M 13, Fordham 12
1942 Alabama 29, Texas A&M 21
1943 Texas 14, Georgia Tech 7
1944 Randolph Field 7, Texas 7
1945 Oklahoma A&M 34, TCU 0
1946 Texas 40, Missouri 27
1947 Arkansas 0, LSU 0
1948 SMU 13, Penn St. 13
1949 SMU 21, Oregon 13
1950 Rice 27, North Carolina 13
1951 Tennessee 20, Texas 14
1952 Kentucky 20, TCU 7
1953 Texas 16, Tennessee 0
1954 Rice 28, Alabama 6
1955 Georgia Tech 14, Arkansas 6
1956 Mississippi 14, TCU 13
1957 TCU 28, Syracuse 27
1958 Navy 20, Rice 7
1959 TCU 0, Air Force 0
1960 Syracuse 23, Texas 14
1961 Duke 7, Arkansas 6
1962 Texas 12, Mississippi 7
1963 LSU 13, Texas 0
1964 Texas 28, Navy 6
1965 Arkansas 10, Nebraska 7
1966 LSU 14, Arkansas 7
1966 (Dec.) Georgia 24, SMU 9
1968 (Jan.) Texas A&M 20, Alabama 16
1969 Texas 36, Tennessee 13
1970 Texas 21, Notre Dame 17
1971 Notre Dame 24, Texas 11
1972 Penn St. 30, Texas 6
1973 Texas 17, Alabama 13
1974 Nebraska 19, Texas 3
1975 Penn St. 41, Baylor 20
1976 Arkansas 31, Georgia 10
1977 Houston 30, Maryland 21
1978 Notre Dame 38, Texas 10
1979 Notre Dame 35, Houston 34
1980 Houston 17, Nebraska 14
1981 Alabama 30, Baylor 2
1982 Texas 14, Alabama 12
1983 SMU 7, Pittsburgh 3
1984 Georgia 10, Texas 9
1985 Boston Coll. 45, Houston 28
1986 Texas A&M 36, Auburn 16
1987 Ohio St. 28, Texas A&M 12
1988 Texas A&M 35, Notre Dame 10
1989 UCLA 17, Arkansas 3
1990 Tennessee 31, Arkansas 27
1991 Miami (FL) 46, Texas 3
1992 Florida St. 10, Texas A&M 2
1993 Notre Dame 28, Texas A&M 3
1994 Notre Dame 24, Texas A&M 21
1995 USC. 55, Texas Tech 14
1996 Colorado 38, Oregon 6
1997 Brigham Young 19, Kansas St. 15
1998 UCLA 29, Texas A&M 23
1999 Texas 38, Mississippi St. 11
2000 Arkansas 27, Texas 6
2001 Kansas St. 35, Tennessee 21
2002 Oklahoma 10, Arkansas 3
2003 Texas 35, LSU 20
2004 Mississippi 31, Oklahoma St. 28
2005 Tennessee 38, Texas A&M 7

Capital One Bowl, Orlando, FL
(Florida Citrus Bowl 1984-2002, Tangerine Bowl, 1947-1983)

1947 (Jan.) Catawba 31, Maryville 6
1948 Catawba 7, Marshall 0
1949 Murray St. 21, Sul Ross St. 21
1950 St. Vincent 7, Emory & Henry 6
1951 Morris Harvey 35, Emory & Henry 14
1952 Stetson 35, Arkansas St. 20
1953 East Texas St. 33, Tenn. Tech 0
1954 East Texas St. 7, Arkansas St. 7
1955 Neb.-Omaha 7, E. Kentucky 6
1956 Juniata 6, Missouri Valley 6
1957 West Texas St. 20, So. Miss. 13
1958 East Texas St. 10, So. Miss. 9
1958 (Dec.) East Texas St. 26, Missouri Valley 7
1960 (Jan.) Middle Tennessee 21, Presbyterian 12
1960 (Dec.) Citadel 27, Tenn. Tech 0
1961 Lamar 21, Middle Tennessee 14
1962 Houston 49, Miami (OH) 21
1963 Western Ky. 27, Coast Guard 0
1964 E. Carolina 14, Massachusetts 13
1965 E. Carolina 31, Maine 0
1966 Morgan St. 14, West Chester 6
1967 Tenn.-Martin 25, West Chester 8
1968 Richmond 49, Ohio U. 42
1969 Toledo 56, Davidson 33
1970 Toledo 40, William & Mary 12
1971 Toledo 28, Richmond 3
1972 Tampa 21, Kent St. 18
1973 Miami (OH) 16, Florida 7
1974 Miami (OH) 21, Georgia 10
1975 Miami (OH) 20, S. Carolina 7
1976 Okla. St. 49, Brigham Young 21
1977 Florida St. 40, Texas Tech 17
1978 N. Carolina St. 30, Pittsburgh 17
1979 LSU 34, Wake Forest 10
1980 Florida 35, Maryland 20
1981 Missouri 19, So. Mississippi 17
1982 Auburn 33, Boston College 26
1983 Tennessee 30, Maryland 23
1984 Georgia 17, Florida St. 17
1985 Ohio St. 10, Brigham Young 7
1987 (Jan.) Auburn 16, USC 7
1988 Clemson 35, Penn St. 10
1989 Clemson 13, Oklahoma 6
1990 Illinois 31, Virginia 21
1991 Georgia Tech 45, Nebraska 21
1992 California 37, Clemson 13
1993 Georgia 21, Ohio St. 14
1994 Penn St. 31, Tennessee 13
1995 Alabama 24, Ohio St. 17
1996 Tennessee 20, Ohio St. 14
1997 Tennessee 48, Northwestern 28
1998 Florida 21, Penn St. 6
1999 Michigan 45, Arkansas 31
2000 Michigan St. 37, Florida 34
2001 Michigan 31, Auburn 28
2002 Tennessee 45, Michigan 17
2003 Auburn 13, Penn St. 9
2004 Georgia 34, Purdue 27 (OT)
2005 Iowa 30, LSU 25

Fiesta Bowl, Tempe, AZ

1971 (Dec.) Arizona St. 45, Florida St. 38
1972 Arizona St. 49, Missouri 35
1973 Arizona St. 28, Pittsburgh 7
1974 Okla. St. 16, Brigham Young 6
1975 Arizona St. 17, Nebraska 14
1976 Oklahoma 41, Wyoming 7
1977 Penn St. 42, Arizona St. 30
1978 UCLA 10, Arkansas 10
1979 Pittsburgh 16, Arizona 10
1980 Penn St. 31, Ohio St. 19
1982 (Jan.) Penn St. 26, USC 10
1983 Arizona St. 32, Oklahoma 21
1984 Ohio St. 28, Pittsburgh 23
1985 UCLA 39, Miami (FL) 37
1986 Michigan 27, Nebraska 23
1987 Penn St. 14, Miami (FL) 10
1988 Florida St. 31, Nebraska 28
1989 Notre Dame 34, W. Virginia 21
1990 Florida St. 41, Nebraska 17
1991 Louisville 34, Alabama 7
1992 Penn St. 42, Tennessee 17
1993 Syracuse 26, Colorado 22
1994 Arizona 29, Miami (FL) 0
1995 Colorado 41, Notre Dame 24
1996 Nebraska 62, Florida 24
1997 Penn St. 38, Texas 15
1997 (Dec.) Kansas St. 35, Syracuse 18
1999 (Jan.) Tennessee 23, Florida St. 16
2000 Nebraska 31, Tennessee 21
2001 Oregon St. 41, Notre Dame 9
2002 Oregon 38, Colorado 16
2003 Ohio St. 31, Miami 24 (2 OT)
2004 Ohio St. 35, Kansas St. 28
2005 Utah 35, Pittsburgh 7

Gator Bowl, Jacksonville, FL

1946 (Jan.) Wake Forest 26, S. Carolina 14
1947 Oklahoma 34, N. Carolina St. 13
1948 Maryland 20, Georgia 20
1949 Clemson 24, Missouri 23
1950 Maryland 20, Missouri 7
1951 Wyoming 20, Washington & Lee 7
1952 Miami (FL) 14, Clemson 0
1953 Florida 14, Tulsa 13
1954 Texas Tech 35, Auburn 13
1954 (Dec.) Auburn 33, Baylor 13
1955 Vanderbilt 25, Auburn 13
1956 Georgia Tech 21, Pittsburgh 14
1957 Tennessee 3, Texas A&M 0
1958 Mississippi 7, Florida 3
1960 (Jan.) Arkansas 14, Georgia Tech 7
1960 (Dec.) Florida 13, Baylor 12
1961 Penn St. 30, Georgia Tech 15
1962 Florida 17, Penn St. 7
1963 N. Carolina 35, Air Force 0
1965 (Jan.) Florida St. 36, Okla.19
1965 (Dec.) GA Tech 31, Texas Tech 21
1966 Tennessee 18, Syracuse 12
1967 Penn St. 17, Florida St. 17
1968 Missouri 35, Alabama 10
1969 Florida 14, Tennessee 13
1971 (Jan.) Auburn 35, Mississippi 28
1971 (Dec.) Georgia 7, N. Carolina 3
1972 Auburn 24, Colorado 3
1973 Texas Tech 28, Tennessee 19
1974 Auburn 27, Texas 3
1975 Maryland 13, Florida 0
1976 Notre Dame 20, Penn St. 9
1977 Pittsburgh 34, Clemson 3
1978 Clemson 17, Ohio St. 15
1979 N. Carolina 17, Michigan 15
1980 Pittsburgh 37, S. Carolina 9
1981 N. Carolina 31, Arkansas 27
1982 Florida St. 31, West Virginia 12
1983 Florida 14, Iowa 6
1984 Oklahoma St. 21, S. Carolina 14
1985 Florida St. 34, Oklahoma St. 23
1986 Clemson 27, Stanford 21
1987 LSU 30, S. Carolina 13
1989 (Jan.) Georgia 34, Michigan St. 27
1989 (Dec.) Clemson 27, W. Virginia 7
1991 (Jan.) Michigan 35, Mississippi 3
1991 (Dec.) Oklahoma 48, Virginia 14
1992 Florida 27, N. Carolina St. 10
1993 Alabama 24, N. Carolina 10
1994 Tennessee 45, Virginia Tech 23
1996 (Jan.) Syracuse 41, Clemson 0
1997 N. Carolina 20, W. Virginia 13
1998 N. Carolina 42, Virginia Tech 3
1999 Georgia Tech 35, Notre Dame 28
2000 Miami (FL) 28, Georgia Tech 13
2001 Virginia Tech 41, Clemson 20
2002 Florida St. 30, Virginia Tech 17
2003 N. Carolina St. 28, Notre Dame 6
2004 Maryland 41, West Virginia 7
2005 Florida St. 30, West Virginia 18

Liberty Bowl, Memphis, TN

1959 (Dec.) Penn St. 7, Alabama 0
1960 Penn St. 41, Oregon 12
1961 Syracuse 15, Miami (FL) 14
1962 Oregon St. 6, Villanova 0
1963 Mississippi St. 16, N. Carolina St. 12
1964 Utah 32, West Virginia 6
1965 Mississippi 13, Auburn 7
1966 Miami (FL) 14, Virginia Tech 7
1967 N. Carolina St. 14, Georgia 7
1968 Mississippi 34, Virginia Tech 17
1969 Colorado 47, Alabama 33
1970 Tulane 17, Colorado 3
1971 Tennessee 14, Arkansas 13
1972 Georgia Tech 31, Iowa St. 30
1973 N. Carolina St. 31, Kansas 18
1974 Tennessee 7, Maryland 3
1975 USC 20, Texas A&M 0
1976 Alabama 36, UCLA 6
1977 Nebraska 21, N. Carolina 17
1978 Missouri 20, LSU 15
1979 Penn St. 9, Tulane 6
1980 Purdue 28, Missouri 25
1981 Ohio St. 31, Navy 28
1982 Alabama 21, Illinois 15
1983 Notre Dame 19, Boston Coll. 18
1984 Auburn 21, Arkansas 15
1985 Baylor 21, LSU 7
1986 Tennessee 21, Minnesota 14
1987 Georgia 20, Arkansas 17
1988 Indiana 34, S. Carolina 10
1989 Mississippi 42, Air Force 29
1990 Air Force 23, Ohio St. 11
1991 Air Force 38, Mississippi St. 15
1992 Mississippi 13, Air Force 0
1993 Louisville 18, Michigan St. 7
1994 Illinois 30, East Carolina 0
1995 East Carolina 19, Stanford 13
1996 Syracuse 30, Houston 17
1997 So. Mississippi 41, Pittsburgh 7
1998 Tulane 41, Brigham Young 27
1999 So. Mississippi 23, Colorado St. 17
2000 Colorado St. 22, Louisville 17
2001 Louisville 28, BYU 10
2002 TCU 17, Colorado St. 3
2003 Utah 17, So. Mississippi 0
2004 Louisville 44, Boise St. 40

Peach Bowl, Atlanta, GA

1968 (Dec.) LSU 31, Florida St. 27
1969 W. Virginia 14, S. Carolina 3
1970 Arizona St. 48, N. Carolina 26
1971 Mississippi 41, Georgia Tech 18
1972 N. Carolina St. 49, W. Virginia 13
1973 Georgia 17, Maryland 16
1974 Vanderbilt 6, Texas Tech 6
1975 W. Virginia 13, N. Carolina St. 10
1976 Kentucky 21, N. Carolina 0
1977 N. Carolina St. 24, Iowa St. 14
1978 Purdue 41, Georgia Tech. 21
1979 Baylor 24, Clemson 18
1981 (Jan.) Miami (FL) 20, Virginia Tech 10
1981 (Dec.) W. Virginia 26, Florida 6
1982 Iowa 28, Tennessee 22
1983 Florida St. 28, N. Carolina 3
1984 Virginia 27, Purdue 22
1985 Army 31, Illinois 29
1986 Va. Tech 25, N. Carolina St. 24
1988 (Jan.) Tennessee 28, Indiana 22
1988 (Dec.) N. Carolina St. 28, Iowa 23
1989 Syracuse 19, Georgia 18
1990 Auburn 27, Indiana 23
1992 (Jan.) E. Carolina 37, NC St. 34
1993 N. Carolina 21, Mississippi St. 17
1993 (Dec.) Clemson 14, Kentucky 13
1995 (Jan.) N. Carolina St. 28, Miss. St. 24
1995 (Dec.) Virginia 34, Georgia 27
1996 LSU 10, Clemson 7
1998 (Jan.) Auburn 21, Clemson 17
1998 (Dec.) Georgia 35, Virginia 33
1999 Mississippi St. 27, Clemson 7
2000 LSU 28, Georgia Tech 14
2001 North Carolina 16, Auburn 10
2002 Maryland 30, Tennessee 3
2003 Clemson 27, Tennessee 14
2004 Miami (FL) 27, Florida 10

Sun Bowl, El Paso, TX (John Hancock Bowl, 1989-93)

1936 (Jan.) Hardin-Simmons 14, New Mexico St. 14
1937 Hardin-Simmons 34, Texas Mines 6
1938 West Virginia 7, Texas Tech 6
1939 Utah 26, New Mexico 0
1940 Catholic U. 0, Arizona St. 0
1941 Western Reserve 26, Arizona St. 13
1942 Tulsa 6, Texas Tech 0
1943 2d Air Force 13, Hardin-Simmons 7
1944 Southwestern (TX) 7, New Mexico 0
1945 Southwestern (TX) 35, Univ. of Mexico 0
1946 New Mexico 34, Denver 24
1947 Cincinnati 18, Virginia Tech 6
1948 Miami (OH) 13, Texas Tech 12
1949 West Virginia 21, Texas Mines 12
1950 Texas Western 33, Georgetown 20
1951 West Texas St. 14, Cincinnati 13
1952 Texas Tech 25, Pacific (CA) 14
1953 Pacific (CA) 26, S. Mississippi 7
1954 Texas Western 37, S. Miss. 14
1955 Texas Western 47, Florida St. 20
1956 Wyoming 21, Texas Tech 14
1957 Geo. Washington 13, TX Western 0
1958 Louisville 34, Drake 20
1958 (Dec.) Wyoming 14, Hardin-Simmons 6
1959 New Mexico St. 28, N. Texas St. 8
1960 New Mexico St. 20, Utah St. 13
1961 Villanova 17, Wichita 9
1962 West Texas St. 15, Ohio U. 14
1963 Oregon 21, SMU 14
1964 Georgia 7, Texas Tech 0
1965 Texas Western 13, TCU 12
1966 Wyoming 28, Florida St. 20
1967 UTEP 14, Mississippi 7
1968 Auburn 34, Arizona 10
1969 Nebraska 45, Georgia 6
1970 Georgia Tech. 17, Texas Tech 9
1971 LSU 33, Iowa St. 15
1972 North Carolina 32, Texas Tech 28
1973 Missouri 34, Auburn 17
1974 Mississippi St. 26, North Carolina 24
1975 Pittsburgh 33, Kansas 19
1977 (Jan.) Texas A&M 37, Florida 14
1977 (Dec.) Stanford 24, LSU 14
1978 Texas 42, Maryland 0
1979 Washington 14, Texas 7
1980 Nebraska 31, Mississippi St. 17
1981 Oklahoma 40, Houston 14
1982 North Carolina 26, Texas 10
1983 Alabama 28, SMU 7
1984 Maryland 28, Tennessee 27
1985 Georgia 13, Arizona 13
1986 Alabama 28, Washington 6
1987 Oklahoma St. 35, West Virginia 33
1988 Alabama 29, Army 28
1989 Pittsburgh 31, Texas A&M 28
1990 Michigan St. 17, USC 16

1991 UCLA 6, Illinois 3
1992 Baylor 20, Arizona 15
1993 Oklahoma 41, Texas Tech 10
1994 Texas 35, North Carolina 31
1995 Iowa 38, Washington 18
1996 Stanford 38, Michigan St. 0
1997 Arizona St. 17, Iowa 7
1998 TCU 28, USC 19
1999 Oregon 24, Minnesota 20
2000 Wisconsin 21, UCLA 20
2001 Washington St. 33, Purdue 27
2002 Purdue 34, Washington 24
2003 Minnesota 31, Oregon 30
2004 Arizona St. 27, Purdue 23

Other Bowl Results, Late 2004 - Early 2005

Alamo Bowl, San Antonio, TX: Ohio St. 33, Oklahoma St. 7
Champs Sports (formerly Tangerine) Bowl, Orlando, FL: Georgia Tech 51, Syracuse 14
Continental Tire Bowl, Charlotte, NC: Boston Coll. 37, North Carolina 24
Emerald Bowl, San Francisco, CA: Navy 34, New Mexico 19
Fort Worth (Texas) Bowl, Ft. Worth, TX: Cincinnati 32, Marshall 14
GMAC Bowl, Mobile, AL: Bowling Green 52, Memphis 35
Hawaii Bowl, Honolulu, HI: Hawaii 59, UAB 40
Holiday Bowl, San Diego, CA: Texas Tech 45, California 31
Houston Bowl, Houston, TX: Colorado 33, UTEP 28
Independence Bowl, Shreveport, LA: Iowa St. 17, Miami (OH) 13
Insight Bowl, Phoenix, AZ: Oregon St. 38, Notre Dame 21
Las Vegas Bowl, Las Vegas, NV: Wyoming 24, UCLA 21
Motor City Bowl, Pontiac, MI: Connecticut 39, Toledo 10
MPC Computers (formerly Humanitarian) Bowl, Boise, ID: Fresno St. 37, Virginia 34
Music City Bowl, Nashville, TN: Minnesota 20, Alabama 16
New Orleans Bowl, New Orleans, LA: Southern Miss 31, North Texas 10
Outback Bowl, Tampa, FL: Georgia 24, Wisconsin 21
Silicon Valley Classic, San Jose, CA: Northern Illinois 34, Troy 21

All-Time NCAA Division I-A Statistical Leaders

(At end of 2004 season. Prior to 2002, postseason games were not included in NCAA final football statistics or records. Beginning with the 2002 season, all postseason games were included.)

Career Rushing Yards

Player, team	Yrs	Carries	Yds	Avg
Ron Dayne, Wisconsin	1996-99	1,115	6,397	5.74
Ricky Williams, Texas	1995-98	1,011	6,279	6.21
Tony Dorsett, Pittsburgh	1973-76	1,074	6,082	5.66
Charles White, USC	1976-79	1,023	5,598	5.47
Travis Prentice, Miami (OH)	1996-99	1,138	5,596	4.92

Career Rushing Yard/Game (min. 2,500 yds.)

Player, team	Yrs	Carries	Yds	Avg/ Game
Ed Marinaro, Cornell	1969-71	918	4,715	174.6
O.J. Simpson, USC	1967-68	621	3,124	164.4
Herschel Walker, Georgia	1980-82	994	5,259	159.4
LeShon Johnson, N. Illinois	1992-93	592	3,314	150.6
Ron Dayne, Wisconsin	1996-99	1,115	6,397	148.8

Career Passing Yards

Player, team	Yrs	Comp/Att	Yds
Timmy Chang, Hawaii	2000-04	1,388/2,436	17,072
Ty Detmer, BYU	1988-91	958/1,530	15,031
Tim Rattay, Louisiana Tech	1997-99	1,015/1,552	12,746
Chris Redman, Louisville	1996-99	1,031/1,679	12,541
Kliff Kingsbury, Texas Tech	1999-02	1,231/1,883	12,429

Career Receiving Yards

Player, team	Yrs	Rec	Yds	Avg
Trevor Insley, Nevada	1996-99	298	5,005	16.8
Marcus Harris, Wyoming	1993-96	259	4,518	17.4
Ryan Yarborough, Wyoming	1990-93	229	4,357	19.0
Troy Edwards, Louisiana Tech	1996-98	280	4,352	15.5
Aaron Turner, Pacific (CA)	1989-92	266	4,345	16.3

All-Time Team Won-Lost Records*

	Years	Won	Lost	Tied	Pct.	Total
Michigan	125	842	275	36	.746	1,153
Notre Dame	116	802	263	42	.743	1,107
Oklahoma	110	749	285	53	.713	1,087
Texas	112	787	310	33	.711	1,130
Alabama	110	764	299	43	.710	1,106
Ohio St.	115	764	298	53	.709	1,115
Nebraska	115	786	317	40	.705	1,143
Tennessee	108	746	306	53	.699	1,105
USC	112	720	297	54	.697	1,071
Penn St.	118	760	338	41	.685	1,139
Boise St (1996)	37	295	136	2	.684	433
Florida St.	58	428	200	17	.677	645
Georgia	111	683	372	54	.640	1,109
Miami (Ohio)	116	632	348	44	.639	1,024
Miami (Fla)	78	516	288	19	.639	823
LSU	111	658	372	47	.633	1,077
Washington	115	639	363	50	.631	1,052
South Fla. (2000)	8	55	33	0	.625	88
Auburn	112	647	379	47	.625	1,073
Arizona St.	92	516	313	24	.619	853
Florida	98	597	364	40	.616	1,001
Colorado	115	643	396	36	.615	1,075
Central Michigan	104	526	333	36	.608	895
Texas A&M	110	634	409	48	.603	1,091
Syracuse	115	664	434	49	.600	1,147

*As of 2004 season. Includes records as senior college only. Bowl and playoff games are included, and each tie game is computed as half won and half lost. Teams listed with years in parentheses indicates reclassification to Division I-A. The year in parentheses is the first year of Division I-A membership. Tiebreaker rule began with 1996 season.

Heisman Trophy Winners

Awarded annually to the nation's outstanding college football player by the Downtown Athletic Club.

1935 Jay Berwanger, Chicago, HB
1936 Larry Kelley, Yale, E
1937 Clinton Frank, Yale, HB
1938 David O'Brien, Texas Christian, QB
1939 Nile Kinnick, Iowa, HB
1940 Tom Harmon, Michigan, HB
1941 Bruce Smith, Minnesota, HB
1942 Frank Sinkwich, Georgia, HB
1943 Angelo Bertelli, Notre Dame, QB
1944 Leslie Horvath, Ohio St., QB
1945 Felix Blanchard, Army, FB
1946 Glenn Davis, Army, HB
1947 John Lujack, Notre Dame, QB
1948 Doak Walker, SMU, HB
1949 Leon Hart, Notre Dame, E
1950 Vic Janowicz, Ohio St., HB
1951 Richard Kazmaier, Princeton, HB
1952 Billy Vessels, Oklahoma, HB
1953 John Lattner, Notre Dame, HB
1954 Alan Ameche, Wisconsin, FB
1955 Howard Cassady, Ohio St., HB
1956 Paul Hornung, Notre Dame, QB
1957 John Crow, Texas A & M, HB
1958 Pete Dawkins, Army, HB
1959 Billy Cannon, LSU, HB
1960 Joe Bellino, Navy, HB
1961 Ernest Davis, Syracuse, HB
1962 Terry Baker, Oregon St., QB
1963 Roger Staubach, Navy, QB
1964 John Huarte, Notre Dame, QB
1965 Mike Garrett, USC, HB
1966 Steve Spurrier, Florida, QB
1967 Gary Beban, UCLA, QB
1968 O. J. Simpson, USC, RB
1969 Steve Owens, Oklahoma, RB
1970 Jim Plunkett, Stanford, QB
1971 Pat Sullivan, Auburn, QB
1972 Johnny Rodgers, Nebraska, RB-WR
1973 John Cappelletti, Penn St., RB
1974 Archie Griffin, Ohio St., RB
1975 Archie Griffin, Ohio St., RB
1976 Tony Dorsett, Pittsburgh, RB
1977 Earl Campbell, Texas, RB
1978 Billy Sims, Oklahoma, RB
1979 Charles White, USC, RB
1980 George Rogers, S. Carolina, RB
1981 Marcus Allen, USC, RB
1982 Herschel Walker, Georgia, RB
1983 Mike Rozier, Nebraska, RB
1984 Doug Flutie, Boston College, QB
1985 Bo Jackson, Auburn, RB
1986 Vinny Testaverde, Miami, QB
1987 Tim Brown, Notre Dame, WR
1988 Barry Sanders, Oklahoma St., RB
1989 Andre Ware, Houston, QB
1990 Ty Detmer, BYU, QB
1991 Desmond Howard, Michigan, WR
1992 Gino Torretta, Miami, QB
1993 Charlie Ward, Florida St., QB
1994 Rashaan Salaam, Colorado, RB
1995 Eddie George, Ohio St., RB
1996 Danny Wuerffel, Florida, QB
1997 Charles Woodson, Michigan, CB
1998 Ricky Williams, Texas, RB
1999 Ron Dayne, Wisconsin, RB
2000 Chris Weinke, Florida St., QB
2001 Eric Crouch, Nebraska, QB
2002 Carson Palmer, USC, QB
2003 Jason White, Oklahoma, QB
2004 Matt Leinart, USC

All-Time Division I-A Coaching Victories (Including Bowl Games)

#Bobby Bowden	351	Bo Schembechler	234	Dan McGugin	197	Gil Dobie	180
#Joe Paterno	343	Hayden Fry	232	Fielding Yost	196	Jackie Sherrill	180
Paul "Bear" Bryant	323	Jess Neely	207	Howard Jones	194	Carl Snavely	180
Glenn "Pop" Warner	319	Warren Woodson	203	John Cooper	192	Jerry Claiborne	179
Amos Alonzo Stagg	314	Don Nehlen	202	John Vaught	190	Ben Schwartzwalder	178
LaVell Edwards	257	Eddie Anderson	201	George Welsh	189	Frank Kush	176
Tom Osborne	255	Vince Dooley	201	John Heisman	185	Don James	176
#Lou Holtz	249	Jim Sweeney	200	Johnny Majors	185	Ralph Jordan	176
Woody Hayes	238	Dana X. Bible	198	Darrell Royal	184		

#Coaches active in 2004; through 2005 bowl games. John Gagliardi of St. John's Univ. (MN) (Div. III) holds the record for most college football victories, with 421.

College Football Coach of the Year

The Division I-A Coach of the Year has been selected by the American Football Coaches Assn. since 1935 and selected by the Football Writers Assn. of America since 1957. WhenSe, both winners are indicated.

1935 Lynn Waldorf, Northwestern
1936 Dick Harlow, Harvard
1937 Edward Mylin, Lafayette
1938 Bill Kern, Carnegie Tech
1939 Eddie Anderson, Iowa
1940 Clark Shaughnessy, Stanford
1941 Frank Leahy, Notre Dame
1942 Bill Alexander, Georgia Tech
1943 Amos Alonzo Stagg, Pacific
1944 Carroll Widdoes, Ohio St.
1945 Bo McMillin, Indiana
1946 Earl "Red" Blaik, Army
1947 Fritz Crisler, Michigan
1948 Bennie Oosterbaan, Michigan
1949 Bud Wilkinson, Oklahoma
1950 Charlie Caldwell, Princeton
1951 Chuck Taylor, Stanford
1952 Biggie Munn, Michigan St.
1953 Jim Tatum, Maryland
1954 Henry "Red" Sanders, UCLA
1955 Duffy Daugherty, Michigan St.
1956 Bowden Wyatt, Tennessee
1957 Woody Hayes, Ohio St.
1958 Paul Dietzel, LSU
1959 Ben Schwartzwalder, Syracuse
1960 Murray Warmath, Minnesota
1961 Paul "Bear" Bryant, Ala. (AFCA); Darrell Royal, Texas (FWAA)
1962 John McKay, USC
1963 Darrell Royal, Texas
1964 Ara Parseghian, Notre Dame, & Frank Broyles, Arkansas (AFCA); Ara Parseghian (FWAA)
1965 Tommy Prothro, UCLA (AFCA); Duffy Daugherty, Mich. St. (FWAA)
1966 Tom Cahill, Army
1967 John Pont, Indiana
1968 Joe Paterno, Penn St. (AFCA); Woody Hayes, Ohio St. (FWAA)
1969 Bo Schembechler, Michigan
1970 Charles McClendon, LSU, & Darrell Royal, Texas (AFCA); Alex Agase, Northwestern (FWAA)
1971 Paul "Bear" Bryant, Alabama (AFCA); Bob Devaney, Nebraska (FWAA)
1972 John McKay, USC
1973 Paul "Bear" Bryant, Alabama (AFCA); Johnny Majors, Pittsburgh (FWAA)
1974 Grant Teaff, Baylor
1975 Frank Kush, Arizona St. (AFCA); Woody Hayes, Ohio St. (FWAA)
1976 Johnny Majors, Pittsburgh
1977 Don James, Washington (AFCA); Lou Holtz, Arkansas (FWAA)
1978 Joe Paterno, Penn St.
1979 Earle Bruce, Ohio St.
1980 Vince Dooley, Georgia
1981 Danny Ford, Clemson
1982 Joe Paterno, Penn St.
1983 Ken Hatfield, Air Force (AFCA); Howard Schnellenberger, Miami (FL) (FWAA)
1984 LaVell Edwards, Brigham Young
1985 Fisher De Berry, Air Force
1986 Joe Paterno, Penn St.
1987 Dick MacPherson, Syracuse
1988 Don Nehlen, W. Virginia (AFCA); Lou Holtz, Notre Dame (FWAA)
1989 Bill McCartney, Colorado
1990 Bobby Ross, Georgia Tech
1991 Don James, Washington
1992 Gene Stallings, Alabama
1993 Barry Alvarez, Wisconsin (AFCA); Terry Bowden, Auburn (FWAA)
1994 Tom Osborne, Nebraska (AFCA); Rich Brooks, Oregon (FWAA)
1995 Gary Barnett, Northwestern
1996 Bruce Snyder, Arizona St.
1997 Mike Price, Washington St.
1998 Phillip Fulmer, Tennessee
1999 Frank Beamer, Virginia Tech
2000 Bob Stoops, Oklahoma
2001 Larry Coker, Miami (FL) & Ralph Friedgen, Maryland (AFCA); Ralph Friedgen, Maryland (FWAA)
2002 Jim Tressel, Ohio St.
2003 Pete Carroll, USC (AFCA); Nick Saban, LSU (FWAA)
2004 Tommy Tuberville, Auburn (AFCA); Urban Meyer, Utah (FWAA)

NCAA Div. I-A Football Conference Champions (1980-2004)

Atlantic Coast[1]
1980 North Carolina
1981 Clemson
1982 Clemson
1983 Maryland
1984 Maryland
1985 Maryland
1986 Clemson
1987 Clemson
1988 Clemson
1989 Virginia, Duke
1990 Georgia Tech
1991 Clemson
1992 Florida St.
1993 Florida St.
1994 Florida St.
1995 Virginia, Florida St.
1996 Florida St.
1997 Florida St.
1998 Florida St., Georgia Tech
1999 Florida St.
2000 Florida St.
2001 Maryland
2002 Florida St.
2003 Florida St.
2004 Virginia Tech

Big 12[2]
1996 Texas
1997 Nebraska
1998 Texas A&M
1999 Nebraska
2000 Oklahoma
2001 Colorado
2002 Oklahoma
2003 Kansas St.
2004 Oklahoma

Big East
1991 Miami (FL), Syracuse
1992 Miami (FL)
1993 West Virginia
1994 Miami (FL)
1995 Virginia Tech, Miami (FL)
1996 Virginia Tech, Miami (FL), Syracuse
1997 Syracuse
1998 Syracuse
1999 Virginia Tech
2000 Miami (FL)
2001 Miami (FL)
2002 Miami (FL)
2003 Miami (FL)
2004 Pittsburgh, W. Virginia, Boston, Syracuse

Big Ten
1980 Michigan
1981 Iowa, Ohio St.
1982 Michigan
1983 Illinois
1984 Ohio St.
1985 Iowa
1986 Michigan, Ohio St.
1987 Michigan St.
1988 Michigan
1989 Michigan
1990 Iowa, Ill., Mich., Mich. St.
1991 Michigan
1992 Michigan
1993 Ohio St., Wisconsin
1994 Penn St.
1995 Northwestern
1996 Ohio St., Northwestern
1997 Michigan
1998 Ohio St., Wisconsin, Michigan
1999 Wisconsin
2000 Michigan, Northwestern, Purdue
2001 Illinois
2002 Iowa, Ohio St.
2003 Michigan
2004 Iowa, Michigan

Big West[3]
1980 Long Beach St.
1981 San Jose St.
1982 Fresno St.
1983 Cal St.-Fullerton
1984 Cal St.-Fullerton
1985 Fresno St.
1986 San Jose St.
1987 San Jose St.
1988 Fresno St.
1989 Fresno St.
1990 San Jose St.
1991 San Jose St., Fresno St.
1992 Nevada
1993 SW Louisiana, Utah St.
1994 Nevada, SW Louisiana, UNLV
1995 Nevada
1996 Nevada, Utah St.
1997 Nevada, Utah St.
1998 Idaho
1999 Boise St.
2000 Boise St.

Conference USA
1996 So. Mississippi, Houston
1997 So. Mississippi
1998 Tulane
1999 So. Mississippi
2000 Louisville
2001 Louisville
2002 Cincinnati, TCU
2003 So. Mississippi
2004 Louisville

Mid-American Athletic
1980 Central Michigan
1981 Toledo
1982 Bowling Green
1983 Northern Illinois
1984 Toledo
1985 Bowling Green
1986 Miami (OH)
1987 E. Michigan
1988 W. Michigan
1989 Ball St.
1990 Central Michigan
1991 Bowling Green
1992 Bowling Green
1993 Ball St.
1994 Central Michigan
1995 Toledo
1996 Ball St.
1997 Marshall
1998 Marshall
1999 Marshall
2000 Marshall
2001 Toledo
2002 Marshall
2003 Miami (OH)
2004 Toledo

Mountain West[4]
1999 BYU, Colorado St., Utah
2000 Colorado St.
2001 BYU

2002 Colorado St.
2003 Utah
2004 Utah

Pacific Ten
1980 Washington
1981 Washington
1982 UCLA
1983 UCLA
1984 USC
1985 UCLA
1986 Arizona St.
1987 UCLA, USC
1988 USC
1989 USC
1990 Washington
1991 Washington
1992 Washington, Stanford
1993 UCLA, Arizona, USC
1994 Oregon
1995 USC, Washington
1996 Arizona St.
1997 Washington St., UCLA
1998 UCLA
1999 Stanford
2000 Washington, Oregon St., Oregon
2001 Oregon
2002 USC, Washington St.
2003 USC
2004 USC

Southeastern
1980 Georgia
1981 Georgia, Alabama
1982 Georgia
1983 Auburn
1984 Florida (title vacated)
1985 Tennessee
1986 LSU
1987 Auburn
1988 Auburn, LSU
1989 Ala., Tenn., Auburn
1990 Tennessee
1991 Florida
1992 Alabama
1993 Florida
1994 Florida
1995 Florida
1996 Florida
1997 Tennessee
1998 Tennessee
1999 Alabama
2000 Florida
2001 LSU
2002 Georgia
2003 LSU
2004 Auburn

Sun Belt[3]
2001 Middle Tenn. St., North Texas
2002 North Texas
2003 North Texas
2004 North Texas

Western Athletic
1980 Brigham Young (BYU)
1981 Brigham Young
1982 Brigham Young
1983 Brigham Young
1984 Brigham Young
1985 BYU, Air Force
1986 San Diego St.
1987 Wyoming
1988 Wyoming
1989 Brigham Young
1990 Brigham Young
1991 Brigham Young
1992 Hawaii, BYU, Fresno St.
1993 Wyoming, Fresno St., BYU
1994 Colorado St.
1995 Colorado St., Air Force, Utah, BYU
1996 Brigham Young
1997 Colorado St.
1998 Air Force
1999 Fresno St., Hawaii, TCU
2000 Texas Christian, UTEP
2001 Louisiana Tech
2002 Boise St.
2003 Boise St.
2004 Boise St.

(1) In 2004, former Big East teams Miami (FL) and Virginia Tech joined the Atlantic Coast Conf. (2) In 1996 all former Big Eight teams joined with 4 of the 8 Southwest Conf. teams to form the Big 12. (3) In 2001, former Big West teams Ark. St., Idaho, New Mexico St., and N. Texas joined La.-Lafayette, La.-Monroe (Southland), and Middle Tenn. (Ohio Valley) to form the Sun Belt Conf. Boise St. moved to the WAC, and Utah St. became an independent. (4) In 1999, 8 Western Athletic teams formed the Mountain West Conf.

NCAA Div. I-AA Football Conference Champions (1990-2004)

Atlantic 10
1990 Massachusetts
1991 Delaware, Villanova
1992 Delaware
1993 Boston U.
1994 New Hampshire
1995 Delaware
1996 William & Mary
1997 Villanova
1998 Richmond
1999 J. Madison, Mass.
2000 Delaware, Richmond
2001 Hofstra, Maine, Villanova, Will. & Mary
2002 Maine, Northeastern
2003 Delaware, Mass.
2004 Delaware, J. Madison, New Hampshire, William & Mary

Big Sky
1990 Nevada
1991 Nevada
1992 Idaho, Eastern Wash.
1993 Montana
1994 Boise St.
1995 Montana
1996 Montana
1997 Eastern Wash.
1998 Montana
1999 Montana
2000 Montana
2001 Montana
2002 Idaho St., Montana, Montana St.
2003 Montana St., Montana, No. Arizona
2004 Montana, Eastern Wash.

Big South
2002 Gardner-Webb
2003 Gardner-Webb
2004 Coastal Carolina

Gateway
1990 Northern Iowa
1991 Northern Iowa
1992 Northern Iowa
1993 Northern Iowa
1994 Northern Iowa
1995 N. Iowa, Eastern Ill.
1996 Northern Iowa
1997 Western Illinois
1998 Western Illinois
1999 Illinois St.
2000 Western Illinois
2001 Northern Iowa
2002 W. Illinois, W. Kentucky
2003 No. Iowa, So. Illinois
2004 So. Illinois

Great West[1]
2004 Cal. Poly

Ivy League
1990 Cornell, Dartmouth
1991 Dartmouth
1992 Dartmouth, Princeton
1993 Penn
1994 Penn
1995 Princeton
1996 Dartmouth
1997 Harvard
1998 Penn
1999 Brown, Yale
2000 Penn
2001 Harvard
2002 Pennsylvania
2003 Pennsylvania
2004 Harvard

Metro Atlantic
1993 Iona
1994 Marist, St. John's (NY)
1995 Duquesne
1996 Duquesne
1997 Georgetown
1998 Fairfield, Georgetown
1999 Duquesne
2000 Duquesne
2001 Duquesne
2002 Duquesne
2003 Duquesne
2004 Duquesne

Mid-East Athletic
1990 Florida A&M
1991 North Carolina A&T
1992 North Carolina A&T
1993 Howard
1994 South Carolina St.
1995 Florida A&M
1996 Florida A&M
1997 Hampton
1998 Florida A&M, Hampton
1999 North Carolina A&T
2000 Florida A&M
2001 Florida A&M
2002 Bethune-Cookman
2003 North Carolina A&T
2004 Hampton, South Carolina St.

Northeast
1996 R. Morris, Monmouth
1997 Robert Morris
1998 R.Morris, Monmouth
1999 Robert Morris
2000 Robert Morris
2001 Sacred Heart
2002 Albany (NY)
2003 Albany, Monmouth
2004 Central Conn. St., Monmouth

Ohio Valley
1990 E. Ky., Middle Tenn.
1991 Eastern Kentucky
1992 Middle Tennessee
1993 Eastern Kentucky
1994 Eastern Kentucky
1995 Murray St.
1996 Murray St.
1997 Eastern Kentucky
1998 Tennessee St.
1999 Tennessee St.
2000 Western Kentucky
2001 Eastern Illinois
2002 Eastern Illinois
2003 Jacksonville St.
2004 Jacksonville St.

Patriot
1990 Holy Cross
1991 Holy Cross
1992 Lafayette
1993 Lehigh
1994 Lafayette
1995 Lehigh
1996 Bucknell
1997 Colgate
1998 Lehigh
1999 Colgate, Lehigh
2000 Lehigh
2001 Lehigh
2002 Colgate, Fordham
2003 Colgate
2004 Lafayette, Lehigh

Pioneer
1993 Dayton
1994 Dayton, Butler
1995 Drake
1996 Dayton
1997 Dayton
1998 Drake
1999 Dayton
2000 Dayton, Drake, Valparaiso
2001 Dayton
2002 Dayton
2003 Valparaiso
2004 Drake

Southern
1990 Furman
1991 Appalachian St.
1992 Citadel
1993 Georgia Southern
1994 Marshall
1995 Appalachian St.
1996 Marshall
1997 Georgia Southern
1998 Georgia Southern
1999 Appalachian St., GA Southern, Furman
2000 Georgia Southern
2001 Georgia Southern
2002 Georgia Southern
2003 Wofford
2004 Furman, GA Southern

Southland
1990 La.-Monroe
1991 McNeese St.
1992 La.-Monroe
1993 McNeese St.
1994 North Texas
1995 McNeese St.
1996 Troy St.
1997 McNeese St., Northwestern St.
1998 Northwestern St.
1999 Troy St., S. F. Austin
2000 Troy St.
2001 Sam Houston St., McNeese St.
2002 McNeese St.
2003 McNeese St.
2004 Northwestern St., Sam Houston St.

Southwestern Athletic
1990 Jackson St.
1991 Alabama St.
1992 Alcorn St.
1993 Southern U.
1994 Grambling, Alcorn St.
1995 Jackson St.
1996 Jackson St.
1997 Southern U.
1998 Southern U.
1999 Southern U.
2000 Grambling
2001 Grambling
2002 Grambling
2003 Southern U.
2004 Alabama St.

(1) In 2004 six former independent and North Central teams formed the Great West Conference.

Selected College Division I Football Teams in 2004

(W-L records in last column are for 2004 season and include bowl games and Division I-AA playoff games. Conferences and coaches listed are as of July 2005.)

Team	Nickname	Team colors	Conference	Coach	(W-L)
Air Force	Falcons	Blue & silver	Mountain West	Fisher DeBerry	5-6
Akron	Zips	Blue & gold	Mid-American	J.D. Brookhart	6-5
Alabama	Crimson Tide	Crimson & white	Southeastern	Mike Shula	6-6
Arizona	Wildcats	Cardinal & navy	Pacific Ten	Mike Stoops	3-8
Arizona State	Sun Devils	Maroon & gold	Pacific Ten	Dirk Koetter	9-3
Arkansas	Razorbacks	Cardinal & white	Southeastern	Houston Nutt	5-6
Arkansas State	Indians	Scarlet & black	Sun Belt	Steve Roberts	3-8
Army	Cadets, Black Knights	Black, gold, gray	Independent	Bobby Ross	2-9
Auburn	Tigers	Burnt orange & navy	Southeastern	Tommy Tuberville	13-0
Ball State	Cardinals	Cardinal & white	Mid-American	Brady Hoke	2-9
Baylor	Bears	Green & gold	Big Twelve	Guy Morriss	3-8
Boise State	Broncos	Blue & orange	Western Athletic	Dan Hawkins	11-1
Boston College	Eagles	Maroon & gold	Atlantic Coast	Tom O'Brien	9-3
Bowling Green	Falcons	Orange & brown	Mid-American	Gregg Brandon	9-3
Brigham Young (BYU)	Cougars	Royal blue, white, tan	Mountain West	Bronco Mendenhall	5-6
Brown	Bears	Brown, cardinal, white	Ivy League	Phil Estes	6-4
California	Golden Bears	Blue & gold	Pacific Ten	Jeff Tedford	10-2
Central Michigan	Chippewas	Maroon & gold	Mid-American	Brian Kelly	4-7
Cincinnati	Bearcats	Red & black	Big East	Mark Dantonio	7-5
Citadel	Bulldogs	Blue & white	Southern	Kevin Higgens	3-7
Clemson	Tigers	Purple & orange	Atlantic Coast	Tommy Bowden	6-5
Colgate	Red Raiders	Maroon, gray, & white	Patriot League	Dick Biddle	7-4
Colorado	Buffaloes	Silver, gold, & black	Big Twelve	Gary Barnett	8-5
Colorado State	Rams	Green & gold	Mountain West	Sonny Lubick	4-7
Columbia	Lions	Columbia blue & white	Ivy League	Bob Shoop	1-9
Connecticut	Huskies	Blue & white	Independent	Randy Edsall	8-4
Cornell	Big Red	Carnelian & white	Ivy League	Jim Knowles	4-6
Dartmouth	Big Green	Dartmouth green & white	Ivy League	Buddy Teevens	1-9
Delaware	Fightin' Blue Hens	Blue & gold	Atlantic Ten	K.C. Keeler	9-4
Delaware State	Hornets	Red & blue	Mid-Eastern Athletic	Alton Lavan	4-7
Duke	Blue Devils	Royal blue & white	Atlantic Coast	Ted Roof	2-9
East Carolina	Pirates	Purple & gold	Conference USA	Skip Holtz	2-9
Eastern Illinois	Panthers	Blue & gray	Ohio Valley	Bob Spoo	5-6
Eastern Kentucky	Colonels	Maroon & white	Ohio Valley	Danny Hope	6-5
Eastern Michigan	Eagles	Dark green & white	Mid-American	Jeff Genyk	4-7
Eastern Washington	Eagles	Red & white	Big Sky	Paul Wulff	9-4
Florida	Gators	Orange & blue	Southeastern	Urban Meyer	7-5
Florida A&M	Rattlers	Orange & green	Mid-Eastern Athletic	Rubin Carter	3-8
Florida State	Seminoles	Garnet & gold	Atlantic Coast	Bobby Bowden	9-3
Fresno State	Bulldogs	Cardinal & blue	Western Athletic	Pat Hill	9-3
Furman	Paladins	Purple & white	Southern	Bobby Lamb	10-3
Georgia	Bulldogs	Red & black	Southeastern	Mark Richt	10-2
Georgia Southern	Eagles	Blue & white	Southern	Mike Sewak	9-3
Georgia Tech	Yellow Jackets	Old gold & white	Atlantic Coast	Chan Gailey	7-5
Grambling State	Tigers	Black & gold	Southwestern Athletic	Melvin Spears	6-5
Harvard	Crimson	Crimson, black, white	Ivy League	Tim Murphy	10-0
Hawaii	Warriors	Green, black, white, silver	Western Athletic	June Jones	8-5
Holy Cross	Crusaders	Royal purple	Patriot League	Tom Gilmore	3-8
Houston	Cougars	Scarlet & white	Conference USA	Art Briles	3-8
Howard	Bison	Blue, white & red	Mid-Eastern Athletic	Rayford Petty	6-5
Idaho	Vandals	Silver & gold	Sun Belt	Nick Holt	3-9
Idaho State	Bengals	Orange & black	Big Sky	Larry Lewis	3-8
Illinois	Fighting Illini	Orange & blue	Big Ten	Ron Zook	3-8
Illinois State	Redbirds	Red & white	Gateway	Denver Johnson	4-7
Indiana	Hoosiers	Cream & crimson	Big Ten	Terry Hoeppner	3-8
Indiana State	Sycamores	Blue & white	Gateway	Lou West	4-7
Iowa	Hawkeyes	Old gold & black	Big Ten	Kirk Ferentz	10-2
Iowa State	Cyclones	Cardinal & gold	Big Twelve	Dan McCarney	7-5
Jackson State	Tigers	Blue & white	Southwestern Athletic	James Bell	4-7
James Madison	Dukes	Purple & gold	Atlantic Ten	Mickey Matthews	13-2
Kansas	Jayhawks	Crimson & blue	Big Twelve	Mark Mangino	4-7
Kansas State	Wildcats	Purple & white	Big Twelve	Bill Snyder	4-7
Kent State	Golden Flashes	Navy blue & gold	Mid-American	Doug Martin	5-6
Kentucky	Wildcats	Blue & white	Southeastern	Rich Brooks	2-9
Lafayette	Leopards	Maroon & white	Patriot League	Frank Tavani	8-4
Lehigh	Mountain Hawks	Brown & white	Patriot League	Pete Lembo	9-3
Liberty	Flames	Red, white, blue	Big South	Ken Karcher	6-5
Louisiana-Lafayette	Ragin' Cajuns	Vermilion & white	Sun Belt	Rickey Bustle	4-7
Louisiana-Monroe	Indians	Maroon & gold	Sun Belt	Charlie Weatherbie	5-6
Louisiana State (LSU)	Fighting Tigers	Purple & gold	Southeastern	Les Miles	9-3
Louisiana Tech	Bulldogs	Red & blue	Western Athletic	Jack Bicknell	6-6
Louisville	Cardinals	Red, black, white	Big East	Bobby Petrino	11-1
Maine	Black Bears	Blue & white	Atlantic Ten	Jack Cosgrove	5-6
Marshall	Thundering Herd	Green & white	Conference USA	Mark Snyder	6-6
Maryland	Terrapins	Red, white, black, gold	Atlantic Coast	Ralph Friedgen	5-6
Massachusetts	Minutemen	Maroon & white	Atlantic Ten	Don Brown	6-5
McNeese State	Cowboys	Blue & gold	Southland	Tommy Tate	4-7
Memphis	Tigers	Blue & gray	Conference USA	Tommy West	8-4
Miami (Florida)	Hurricanes	Orange, green, white	Big East	Larry Coker	9-3
Miami (Ohio)	RedHawks	Red & white	Mid-American	Shane Montgomery	8-5
Michigan	Wolverines	Maize & blue	Big Ten	Lloyd Carr	9-3
Michigan State	Spartans	Green & white	Big Ten	John L. Smith	5-7
Middle Tennessee State	Blue Raiders	Blue & white	Sun Belt	Andy McCollum	5-6
Minnesota	Golden Gophers	Maroon & gold	Big Ten	Glen Mason	7-5
Mississippi	Rebels	Cardinal red & navy	Southeastern	Ed Orgeron	4-7
Mississippi State	Bulldogs	Maroon & white	Southeastern	Sylvester Croom	3-8
Mississippi Valley State	Delta Devils	Green & white	Southwestern Athletic	Willie Totten	3-8
Missouri	Tigers	Old gold & black	Big Twelve	Gary Pinkel	5-6
Montana	Grizzlies	Copper, silver, gold	Big Sky	Bobby Hauck	12-3

Team	Nickname	Team colors	Conference	Coach	(W-L)
Montana State	Bobcats	Blue & gold	Big Sky	Mike Kramer	6-5
Morehead State	Eagles	Blue & gold	Pioneer	Matt Ballard	6-6
Morgan State	Bears	Blue & orange	Mid-Eastern Athletic	Donald Hill-Eleyl	5-6
Murray State	Racers	Blue & gold	Ohio Valley	Joe Pannunzio	7-4
Navy	Midshipmen	Navy blue & gold	Independent	Paul Johnson	10-2
Nebraska	Cornhuskers	Scarlet & cream	Big Twelve	Bill Callahan	5-6
Nevada	Wolf Pack	Silver & blue	Western Athletic	Chris Ault	5-7
Nev.-Las Vegas (UNLV)	Runnin' Rebels	Scarlet & gray	Mountain West	Mike Sanford	2-9
New Hampshire	Wildcats	Blue & white	Atlantic Ten	Sean McDonnell	10-3
New Mexico	Lobos	Cherry & silver	Mountain West	Rocky Long	7-5
New Mexico State	Aggies	Crimson & white	Sun Belt	Hal Mumme	5-6
Nicholls State	Colonels	Red & gray	Southland	Jay Thomas	5-5
North Carolina	Tar Heels	Carolina blue & white	Atlantic Coast	John Bunting	6-6
North Carolina State	Wolfpack	Red & white	Atlantic Coast	Chuck Amato	5-6
North Texas	Mean Green	Green & white	Sun Belt	Darrell Dickey	7-5
Northeastern	Huskies	Red & black	Atlantic Ten	Rocky Hager	5-6
Northern Arizona	Lumberjacks	Blue & gold	Big Sky	Jerome Souers	4-7
Northern Illinois	Huskies	Cardinal & black	Mid-American	Joe Novak	9-3
Northern Iowa	Panthers	Purple & old gold	Gateway	Mark Farley	7-4
Northwestern	Wildcats	Purple & white	Big Ten	Randy Walker	6-6
Northwestern State	Demons	Purple, white, & orange	Southland	Scott Stoker	8-4
Notre Dame	Fighting Irish	Gold & blue	Independent	Charlie Weis	6-6
Ohio	Bobcats	Hunter green & white	Mid-American	Frank Solich	4-7
Ohio State	Buckeyes	Scarlet & gray	Big Ten	Jim Tressel	8-4
Oklahoma	Sooners	Crimson & cream	Big Twelve	Bob Stoops	12-1
Oklahoma State	Cowboys	Orange & black	Big Twelve	Mike Gundy	7-5
Oregon	Ducks	Green & yellow	Pacific Ten	Mike Bellotti	5-6
Oregon State	Beavers	Orange & black	Pacific Ten	Mike Riley	7-5
Penn State	Nittany Lions	Blue & white	Big Ten	Joe Paterno	4-7
Pennsylvania	Quakers	Red & blue	Ivy League	Al Bagnoli	10-0
Pittsburgh	Panthers	Blue & gold	Big East	Dave Wannstedt	8-4
Princeton	Tigers	Orange & black	Ivy League	Roger Hughes	5-5
Purdue	Boilermakers	Old gold & black	Big Ten	Joe Tiller	7-5
Rhode Island	Rams	Light & dark blue, white	Atlantic Ten	Tim Stowers	4-7
Rice	Owls	Blue & gray	Conference USA	Ken Hatfield	3-8
Richmond	Spiders	Red & white	Atlantic Ten	Dave Clawson	3-8
Rutgers	Scarlet Knights	Scarlet	Big East	Greg Schiano	4-7
Sam Houston State	Bearkats	Orange & white	Southland	Todd Whitten	11-3
Samford	Bulldogs	Crimson & blue	Ohio Valley	Bill Gray	4-7
San Diego State	Aztecs	Scarlet & black	Mountain West	Tom Craft	4-7
San Jose State	Spartans	Gold, white, blue	Western Athletic	Dick Tomey	2-9
South Carolina	Gamecocks	Garnet & black	Southeastern	Steve Spurrier	6-5
South Carolina State	Bulldogs	Garnet & blue	Mid-Eastern Athletic	Oliver Pough	9-2
SE Missouri State	Redhawks	Red & white	Ohio Valley	Tim Billings	3-8
Southern California (USC)	Trojans	Cardinal & gold	Pacific Ten	Pete Carroll	13-0
South Florida	Bulls	Green & gold	Big East	Jim Leavitt	4-7
Southern Illinois	Salukis	Maroon & white	Gateway	Jerry Kill	10-2
Southern Methodist (SMU)	Mustangs	Red & blue	Conference USA	Phil Bennett	3-8
Southern Mississippi	Golden Eagles	Black & gold	Conference USA	Jeff Bower	7-5
SW Missouri State	Bears	Maroon & white	Gateway	Randy Ball	6-5
Stanford	Cardinal	Cardinal & white	Pacific Ten	Walt Harris	4-7
Stephen F. Austin	Lumberjacks	Purple & white	Southland	Robert McFarland	6-5
Syracuse	Orange	Orange	Big East	Greg Robinson	6-6
Temple	Owls	Cherry & white	Independent	Bobby Wallace	2-9
Tennessee	Volunteers	Orange & white	Southeastern	Phillip Fulmer	10-3
Tennessee-Chattanooga	Mocs	Navy blue & gold	Southern	Rodney Allison	2-9
Tennessee-Martin	Skyhawks	Orange, white, blue	Ohio Valley	Matt Griffin	2-9
Tennessee State	Tigers	Royal blue & white	Ohio Valley	James Webster	4-7
Tennessee Tech	Golden Eagles	Purple & gold	Ohio Valley	Mike Hennigan	6-5
Texas	Longhorns	Burnt orange & white	Big Twelve	Mack Brown	11-1
Texas A & M	Aggies	Maroon & white	Big Twelve	Dennis Franchione	7-5
Texas Christian (TCU)	Horned Frogs	Purple & white	Mountain West	Gary Patterson	5-6
Texas Southern	Tigers	Maroon & gray	Southwestern Athletic	Steve Wilson	0-11
Texas State	Bobcats	Maroon & gold	Southland	David Bailiff	5-6
Texas Tech	Red Raiders	Scarlet & black	Big Twelve	Mike Leach	8-4
Toledo	Rockets	Blue & gold	Mid-American	Tom Amstutz	9-4
Troy State	Trojans	Cardinal & black	Independent	Larry Blakeney	7-5
Tulane	Green Wave	Olive green & sky blue	Conference USA	Chris Scelfo	5-6
Tulsa	Golden Hurricane	Blue, gold, crimson	Conference USA	Steve Kragthorpe	4-8
UCLA	Bruins	Blue & gold	Pacific Ten	Karl Dorrell	6-6
Utah	Utes	Crimson & white	Mountain West	Kyle Whittingham	12-0
Utah State	Aggies	Navy blue & white	Sun Belt	Brent Guy	3-8
UTEP (Texas-El Paso)	Miners	Orange, blue, silver	Conference USA	Mike Price	8-4
Vanderbilt	Commodores	Black & gold	Southeastern	Bobby Johnson	2-9
Villanova	Wildcats	Blue & white	Atlantic Ten	Andy Talley	6-5
Virginia	Cavaliers	Burnt orange & blue	Atlantic Coast	Al Groh	8-4
Virginia Military Inst. (VMI)	Keydets	Red, white, yellow	Big South	Cal McCombs	0-11
Virginia Tech	Hokies	Burnt orange & maroon	Big East	Frank Beamer	10-3
Wake Forest	Demon Deacons	Old gold & black	Atlantic Coast	Jim Grobe	4-7
Washington	Huskies	Purple & gold	Pacific Ten	Tyrone Willingham	1-10
Washington State	Cougars	Crimson & gray	Pacific Ten	Bill Doba	5-6
Weber State	Wildcats	Royal purple & white	Big Sky	Ron McBride	1-10
West Virginia	Mountaineers	Old gold & blue	Big East	Rich Rodriquez	8-4
Western Carolina	Catamounts	Purple & gold	Southern	Kent Briggs	4-7
Western Illinois	Leathernecks	Purple & gold	Gateway	Don Patterson	4-7
Western Kentucky	Hilltoppers	Red & white	Gateway	David Elson	9-3
Western Michigan	Broncos	Brown & gold	Mid-American	Bill Cubit	1-10
William & Mary	Tribe	Green, gold, silver	Atlantic Ten	Jimmye Laycock	11-3
Wisconsin	Badgers	Cardinal & white	Big Ten	Barry Alvarez	9-3
Wyoming	Cowboys	Brown & gold	Mountain West	Joe Glenn	7-5
Yale	Bulldogs, Elis	Yale blue & white	Ivy League	Jack Siedlecki	5-5
Youngstown State	Penguins	Red & white	Gateway	Jon Heacock	4-7

NATIONAL HOCKEY LEAGUE

NHL Lockout Ended; Rule Changes

The NHL franchise owners locked out their players on Sept. 16, 2004, a day after the league's collective bargaining agreement had expired. After 10 months of wrangling, and cancellation of the 2004-2005 season, the NHL and the NHL Players' Association on July 22, 2005, finalized a new 6-year collective bargaining agreement, which effectively ended the lockout. It included a team salary cap ($21.5 mi to $39 mil the 1st year), with a limit on total league spending for players (in benefits, bonuses, etc) amounting initially to 54% of the league-wide revenue.

On July 22, 2005, the NHL announced rules changes to prevent ties, enhance play, and reduce fighting, to take effect with the 2005-06 season. Among them were the following:

- If a game is tied at the end of regulation time, a 5-minute overtime period will be played. If there is still a tie, the teams go to a shootout.
- Blue lines are moved 2 feet toward the center to create bigger offensive zones. This will result in a reduced neutral zone, from 54 feet to 50 feet. Goal lines will be 2 feet closer to the end boards than previously.
- The center red line will be ignored for the purposes of the "two line pass." Passes from behind the defensive blue line to the attacking blue line will be considered legal.
- An offensive player who enters the attacking zone before the puck can return to the blue line, touch it, and resume play.
- A team that ices the puck cannot make a line change before the ensuing face-off.
- Linesmen have the authority to wave off icing infractions if they were the result of an attempted pass.
- A player who starts a fight in the final 5 minutes of a game will receive a penalty, and an automatic 1-game suspension, and his coach will be fined $10,000.
- Dimensions of goal-keeper attire, including the leg pads, blocking glove, upper-body protector, pants, and jersey, will be reduced by 11%.
- Goalies may only play the puck behind the goal line in a trapezoid-shaped area behind the goal.

Stanley Cup Champions Since 1927

Year	Champion	Coach	Final opponent
1927	Ottawa	Dave Gill	Boston
1928	N.Y. Rangers	Lester Patrick	Montreal
1929	Boston	Cy Denneny	N.Y. Rangers
1930	Montreal	Cecil Hart	Boston
1931	Montreal	Cecil Hart	Chicago
1932	Toronto	Dick Irvin	N.Y. Rangers
1933	N.Y. Rangers	Lester Patrick	Toronto
1934	Chicago	Tommy Gorman	Detroit
1935	Montreal Maroons	Tommy Gorman	Toronto
1936	Detroit	Jack Adams	Toronto
1937	Detroit	Jack Adams	N.Y. Rangers
1938	Chicago	Bill Stewart	Toronto
1939	Boston	Art Ross	Toronto
1940	N.Y. Rangers	Frank Boucher	Toronto
1941	Boston	Cooney Weiland	Detroit
1942	Toronto	Hap Day	Detroit
1943	Detroit	Jack Adams	Boston
1944	Montreal	Dick Irvin	Chicago
1945	Toronto	Hap Day	Detroit
1946	Montreal	Dick Irvin	Boston
1947	Toronto	Hap Day	Montreal
1948	Toronto	Hap Day	Detroit
1949	Toronto	Hap Day	Detroit
1950	Detroit	Tommy Ivan	N.Y. Rangers
1951	Toronto	Joe Primeau	Montreal
1952	Detroit	Tommy Ivan	Montreal
1953	Montreal	Dick Irvin	Boston
1954	Detroit	Tommy Ivan	Montreal
1955	Detroit	Jimmy Skinner	Montreal
1956	Montreal	Toe Blake	Detroit
1957	Montreal	Toe Blake	Boston
1958	Montreal	Toe Blake	Boston
1959	Montreal	Toe Blake	Toronto
1960	Montreal	Toe Blake	Toronto
1961	Chicago	Rudy Pilous	Detroit
1962	Toronto	Punch Imlach	Chicago
1963	Toronto	Punch Imlach	Detroit
1964	Toronto	Punch Imlach	Detroit
1965	Montreal	Toe Blake	Chicago
1966	Montreal	Toe Blake	Detroit
1967	Toronto	Punch Imlach	Montreal
1968	Montreal	Toe Blake	St. Louis
1969	Montreal	Claude Ruel	St. Louis
1970	Boston	Harry Sinden	St. Louis
1971	Montreal	Al MacNeil	Chicago
1972	Boston	Tom Johnson	N.Y. Rangers
1973	Montreal	Scotty Bowman	Chicago
1974	Philadelphia	Fred Shero	Boston
1975	Philadelphia	Fred Shero	Buffalo
1976	Montreal	Scotty Bowman	Philadelphia
1977	Montreal	Scotty Bowman	Boston
1978	Montreal	Scotty Bowman	Boston
1979	Montreal	Scotty Bowman	N.Y. Rangers
1980	N.Y. Islanders	Al Arbour	Philadelphia
1981	N.Y. Islanders	Al Arbour	Minnesota
1982	N.Y. Islanders	Al Arbour	Vancouver
1983	N.Y. Islanders	Al Arbour	Edmonton
1984	Edmonton	Glen Sather	N.Y. Islanders
1985	Edmonton	Glen Sather	Philadelphia
1986	Montreal	Jean Perron	Calgary
1987	Edmonton	Glen Sather	Philadelphia
1988	Edmonton	Glen Sather	Boston
1989	Calgary	Terry Crisp	Montreal
1990	Edmonton	John Muckler	Boston
1991	Pittsburgh	Bob Johnson	Minnesota
1992	Pittsburgh	Scotty Bowman	Chicago
1993	Montreal	Jacques Demers	Los Angeles
1994	N.Y. Rangers	Mike Keenan	Vancouver
1995	New Jersey	Jacques Lemaire	Detroit
1996	Colorado	Marc Crawford	Florida
1997	Detroit	Scotty Bowman	Philadelphia
1998	Detroit	Scotty Bowman	Washington
1999	Dallas	Ken Hitchcock	Buffalo
2000	New Jersey	Larry Robinson	Dallas
2001	Colorado	Bob Hartley	New Jersey
2002	Detroit	Scotty Bowman	Carolina
2003	New Jersey	Pat Burns	Anaheim
2004	Tampa Bay	John Tortorella	Calgary
2005	No competition		

Most NHL Goals in a Season

Player	Team	Season	Goals
Wayne Gretzky	Edmonton	1981-82	92
Wayne Gretzky	Edmonton	1983-84	87
Brett Hull	St. Louis	1990-91	86
Mario Lemieux	Pittsburgh	1988-89	85
Phil Esposito	Boston	1971-72	76
Alexander Mogilny	Buffalo	1992-93	76
Teemu Selanne	Winnipeg	1992-93	76
Wayne Gretzky	Edmonton	1984-85	73
Brett Hull	St. Louis	1989-90	72
Wayne Gretzky	Edmonton	1982-83	71
Jari Kurri	Edmonton	1984-85	71
Brett Hull	St. Louis	1991-92	70
Mario Lemieux	Pittsburgh	1987-88	70
Bernie Nicholls	Los Angeles	1988-89	70
Mike Bossy	N.Y. Islanders	1978-79	69
Mario Lemieux	Pittsburgh	1992-93	69
Mario Lemieux	Pittsburgh	1995-96	69
Mike Bossy	N.Y. Islanders	1980-81	68
Phil Esposito	Boston	1973-74	68
Jari Kurri	Edmonton	1985-86	68

All-Time Leading Scorers

Player	Goals	Assists	Points
Wayne Gretzky	894	1,963	2,857
Mark Messier*	694	1,193	1,887
Gordie Howe	801	1,049	1,850
Ron Francis*	549	1,249	1,798
Marcel Dionne	731	1,040	1,771
Steve Yzerman*	678	1,043	1,721
Mario Lemieux*	683	1,018	1,701
Phil Esposito	717	873	1,590
Ray Bourque	410	1,169	1,579
Paul Coffey	396	1,135	1,531
Stan Mikita	541	926	1,467
Bryan Trottier	524	901	1,425
Adam Oates*	341	1,079	1,420
Doug Gilmour	450	964	1,414
Dale Hawerchuk	518	891	1,409
Joe Sakic*	542	860	1,402
Jari Kurri	601	797	1,398
Brett Hull*	741	649	1,390
Luc Robitaille*	653	717	1,370
John Bucyk	556	813	1,369

Note: Through end of 2003-2004 season. *Active in the 2003-2004 season.

Hart Memorial Trophy (MVP)

1927 Herb Gardiner, Montreal
1928 Howie Morenz, Montreal
1929 Roy Worters, N.Y. Americans
1930 Nels Stewart, Montreal Maroons
1931 Howie Morenz, Montreal
1932 Howie Morenz, Montreal
1933 Eddie Shore, Boston
1934 Aurel Joliat, Montreal
1935 Eddie Shore, Boston
1936 Eddie Shore, Boston
1937 Babe Siebert, Montreal
1938 Eddie Shore, Boston
1939 Toe Blake, Montreal
1940 Ebbie Goodfellow, Detroit
1941 Bill Cowley, Boston
1942 Tom Anderson, N.Y. Americans
1943 Bill Cowley, Boston
1944 Babe Pratt, Toronto
1945 Elmer Lach, Montreal
1946 Max Bentley, Chicago
1947 Maurice Richard, Montreal
1948 Buddy O'Connor, N.Y. Rangers
1949 Sid Abel, Detroit
1950 Chuck Rayner, N.Y. Rangers
1951 Milt Schmidt, Boston
1952 Gordie Howe, Detroit
1953 Gordie Howe, Detroit
1954 Al Rollins, Chicago
1955 Ted Kennedy, Toronto
1956 Jean Beliveau, Montreal
1957 Gordie Howe, Detroit
1958 Gordie Howe, Detroit
1959 Andy Bathgate, N.Y. Rangers
1960 Gordie Howe, Detroit
1961 Bernie Geoffrion, Montreal
1962 Jacques Plante, Montreal
1963 Gordie Howe, Detroit
1964 Jean Beliveau, Montreal
1965 Bobby Hull, Chicago
1966 Bobby Hull, Chicago
1967 Stan Mikita, Chicago
1968 Stan Mikita, Chicago
1969 Phil Esposito, Boston
1970 Bobby Orr, Boston
1971 Bobby Orr, Boston
1972 Bobby Orr, Boston
1973 Bobby Clarke, Philadelphia
1974 Phil Esposito, Boston
1975 Bobby Clarke, Philadelphia
1976 Bobby Clarke, Philadelphia
1977 Guy Lafleur, Montreal
1978 Guy Lafleur, Montreal
1979 Bryan Trottier, N.Y. Islanders
1980 Wayne Gretzky, Edmonton
1981 Wayne Gretzky, Edmonton
1982 Wayne Gretzky, Edmonton
1983 Wayne Gretzky, Edmonton
1984 Wayne Gretzky, Edmonton
1985 Wayne Gretzky, Edmonton
1986 Wayne Gretzky, Edmonton
1987 Wayne Gretzky, Edmonton
1988 Mario Lemieux, Pittsburgh
1989 Wayne Gretzky, Los Angeles
1990 Mark Messier, Edmonton
1991 Brett Hull, St. Louis
1992 Mark Messier, N.Y. Rangers
1993 Mario Lemieux, Pittsburgh
1994 Sergei Fedorov, Detroit
1995 Eric Lindros, Philadelphia
1996 Mario Lemieux, Pittsburgh
1997 Dominik Hasek, Buffalo
1998 Dominik Hasek, Buffalo
1999 Jaromir Jagr, Pittsburgh
2000 Chris Pronger, St. Louis
2001 Joe Sakic, Colorado
2002 Jose Theodore, Montreal
2003 Peter Forsberg, Colorado
2004 Martin St. Louis, Tampa Bay

Calder Memorial Trophy (Rookie of the Year)

1933 Carl Voss, Detroit
1934 Russ Blinco, Montreal Maroons
1935 Dave Schriner, N.Y. Americans
1936 Mike Karakas, Chicago
1937 Syl Apps, Toronto
1938 Cully Dahlstrom, Chicago
1939 Frank Brimsek, Boston
1940 Kilby Macdonald, N.Y. Rangers
1941 John Quilty, Montreal
1942 Grant Warwick, N.Y. Rangers
1943 Gaye Stewart, Toronto
1944 Gus Bodnar, Toronto
1945 Frank McCool, Toronto
1946 Edgar Laprade, N.Y. Rangers
1947 Howie Meeker, Toronto
1948 Jim McFadden, Detroit
1949 Pentti Lund, N.Y. Rangers
1950 Jack Gelineau, Boston
1951 Terry Sawchuk, Detroit
1952 Bernie Geoffrion, Montreal
1953 Gump Worsley, N.Y. Rangers
1954 Camille Henry, N.Y. Rangers
1955 Ed Litzenberger, Chicago
1956 Glenn Hall, Detroit
1957 Larry Regan, Boston
1958 Frank Mahovlich, Toronto
1959 Ralph Backstrom, Montreal
1960 Bill Hay, Chicago
1961 Dave Keon, Toronto
1962 Bobby Rousseau, Montreal
1963 Kent Douglas, Toronto
1964 Jacques Laperriere, Montreal
1965 Roger Crozier, Detroit
1966 Brit Selby, Toronto
1967 Bobby Orr, Boston
1968 Derek Sanderson, Boston
1969 Danny Grant, Minnesota
1970 Tony Esposito, Chicago
1971 Gilbert Perreault, Buffalo
1972 Ken Dryden, Montreal
1973 Steve Vickers, N.Y. Rangers
1974 Denis Potvin, N.Y. Islanders
1975 Eric Vail, Atlanta
1976 Bryan Trottier, N.Y. Islanders
1977 Willi Plett, Atlanta
1978 Mike Bossy, N.Y. Islanders
1979 Bobby Smith, Minnesota
1980 Ray Bourque, Boston
1981 Peter Stastny, Quebec
1982 Dale Hawerchuk, Winnipeg
1983 Steve Larmer, Chicago
1984 Tom Barrasso, Buffalo
1985 Mario Lemieux, Pittsburgh
1986 Gary Suter, Calgary
1987 Luc Robitaille, Los Angeles
1988 Joe Nieuwendyk, Calgary
1989 Brian Leetch, N.Y. Rangers
1990 Sergei Makarov, Calgary
1991 Ed Belfour, Chicago
1992 Pavel Bure, Vancouver
1993 Teemu Selanne, Winnipeg
1994 Martin Brodeur, New Jersey
1995 Peter Forsberg, Quebec
1996 Daniel Alfredsson, Ottawa
1997 Bryan Berard, N.Y. Islanders
1998 Sergei Samsonov, Boston
1999 Chris Drury, Colorado
2000 Scott Gomez, New Jersey
2001 Evgeni Nabokov, San Jose
2002 Dany Heatley, Atlanta
2003 Barret Jackman, St. Louis
2004 Andrew Raycroft, Boston

Conn Smythe Trophy (MVP in Playoffs)

1965 Jean Beliveau, Montreal
1966 Roger Crozier, Detroit
1967 Dave Keon, Toronto
1968 Glenn Hall, St. Louis
1969 Serge Savard, Montreal
1970 Bobby Orr, Boston
1971 Ken Dryden, Montreal
1972 Bobby Orr, Boston
1973 Yvan Cournoyer, Montreal
1974 Bernie Parent, Philadelphia
1975 Bernie Parent, Philadelphia
1976 Reg Leach, Philadelphia
1977 Guy Lafleur, Montreal
1978 Larry Robinson, Montreal
1979 Bob Gainey, Montreal
1980 Bryan Trottier, N.Y. Islanders
1981 Butch Goring, N.Y. Islanders
1982 Mike Bossy, N.Y. Islanders
1983 Billy Smith, N.Y. Islanders
1984 Mark Messier, Edmonton
1985 Wayne Gretzky, Edmonton
1986 Patrick Roy, Montreal
1987 Ron Hextall, Philadelphia
1988 Wayne Gretzky, Edmonton
1989 Al MacInnis, Calgary
1990 Bill Ranford, Edmonton
1991 Mario Lemieux, Pittsburgh
1992 Mario Lemieux, Pittsburgh
1993 Patrick Roy, Montreal
1994 Brian Leetch, N.Y. Rangers
1995 Claude Lemieux, New Jersey
1996 Joe Sakic, Colorado
1997 Mike Vernon, Detroit
1998 Steve Yzerman, Detroit
1999 Joe Nieuwendyk, Dallas
2000 Scott Stevens, New Jersey
2001 Patrick Roy, Colorado
2002 Nicklas Lidstrom, Detroit
2003 Jean-Sebastien Giguere, Anaheim
2004 Brad Richards, Tampa Bay

Lady Byng Memorial Trophy (Most Gentlemanly Player)

1925 Frank Nighbor, Ottawa
1926 Frank Nighbor, Ottawa
1927 Billy Burch, N.Y. Americans
1928 Frank Boucher, N.Y. Rangers
1929 Frank Boucher, N.Y. Rangers
1930 Frank Boucher, N.Y. Rangers
1931 Frank Boucher, N.Y. Rangers
1932 Joe Primeau, Toronto
1933 Frank Boucher, N.Y. Rangers
1934 Frank Boucher, N.Y. Rangers
1935 Frank Boucher, N.Y. Rangers
1936 Doc Romnes, Chicago
1937 Marty Barry, Detroit
1938 Gordie Drillon, Toronto
1939 Clint Smith, N.Y. Rangers
1940 Bobby Bauer, Boston
1941 Bobby Bauer, Boston
1942 Syl Apps, Toronto
1943 Max Bentley, Chicago
1944 Clint Smith, Chicago
1945 Bill Mosienko, Chicago
1946 Toe Blake, Montreal
1947 Bobby Bauer, Boston
1948 Buddy O'Connor, N.Y. Rangers
1949 Bill Quackenbush, Detroit
1950 Edgar Laprade, N.Y. Rangers
1951 Red Kelly, Detroit
1952 Sid Smith, Toronto
1953 Red Kelly, Detroit
1954 Red Kelly, Detroit
1955 Sid Smith, Toronto
1956 Earl Reibel, Detroit
1957 Andy Hebenton, N.Y. Rangers
1958 Camille Henry, N.Y. Rangers
1959 Alex Delvecchio, Detroit
1960 Don McKenney, Boston
1961 Red Kelly, Toronto
1962 Dave Keon, Toronto
1963 Dave Keon, Toronto
1964 Ken Wharram, Chicago
1965 Bobby Hull, Chicago
1966 Alex Delvecchio, Detroit
1967 Stan Mikita, Chicago
1968 Stan Mikita, Chicago
1969 Alex Delvecchio, Detroit
1970 Phil Goyette, St. Louis
1971 John Bucyk, Boston
1972 Jean Ratelle, N.Y. Rangers
1973 Gil Perreault, Buffalo
1974 John Bucyk, Boston
1975 Marcel Dionne, Detroit
1976 Jean Ratelle, N.Y.R.-Boston
1977 Marcel Dionne, Los Angeles
1978 Butch Goring, Los Angeles
1979 Bob MacMillan, Atlanta
1980 Wayne Gretzky, Edmonton
1981 Rick Kehoe, Pittsburgh
1982 Rick Middleton, Boston
1983 Mike Bossy, N.Y. Islanders
1984 Mike Bossy, N.Y. Islanders
1985 Jari Kurri, Edmonton
1986 Mike Bossy, N.Y. Islanders
1987 Joe Mullen, Calgary
1988 Mats Naslund, Montreal
1989 Joe Mullen, Calgary
1990 Brett Hull, St. Louis

1991 Wayne Gretzky, Los Angeles
1992 Wayne Gretzky, Los Angeles
1993 Pierre Turgeon, N.Y. Islanders
1994 Wayne Gretzky, Los Angeles
1995 Ron Francis, Pittsburgh
1996 Paul Kariya, Anaheim
1997 Paul Kariya, Anaheim
1998 Ron Francis, Pittsburgh
1999 Wayne Gretzky, N.Y. Rangers
2000 Pavol Demitra, St. Louis
2001 Joe Sakic, Colorado
2002 Ron Francis, Carolina
2003 Alexander Mogilny, Toronto
2004 Brad Richards, Tampa Bay

James Norris Memorial Trophy (Outstanding Defenseman)

1954 Red Kelly, Detroit
1955 Doug Harvey, Montreal
1956 Doug Harvey, Montreal
1957 Doug Harvey, Montreal
1958 Doug Harvey, Montreal
1959 Tom Johnson, Montreal
1960 Doug Harvey, Montreal
1961 Doug Harvey, Montreal
1962 Doug Harvey, N.Y. Rangers
1963 Pierre Pilote, Chicago
1964 Pierre Pilote, Chicago
1965 Pierre Pilote, Chicago
1966 Jacques Laperriere, Montreal
1967 Harry Howell, N.Y. Rangers
1968 Bobby Orr, Boston
1969 Bobby Orr, Boston
1970 Bobby Orr, Boston
1971 Bobby Orr, Boston
1972 Bobby Orr, Boston
1973 Bobby Orr, Boston
1974 Bobby Orr, Boston
1975 Bobby Orr, Boston
1976 Denis Potvin, N.Y. Islanders
1977 Larry Robinson, Montreal
1978 Denis Potvin, N.Y. Islanders
1979 Denis Potvin, N.Y. Islanders
1980 Larry Robinson, Montreal
1981 Randy Carlyle, Pittsburgh
1982 Doug Wilson, Chicago
1983 Rod Langway, Washington
1984 Rod Langway, Washington
1985 Paul Coffey, Edmonton
1986 Paul Coffey, Edmonton
1987 Ray Bourque, Boston
1988 Ray Bourque, Boston
1989 Chris Chelios, Montreal
1990 Ray Bourque, Boston
1991 Ray Bourque, Boston
1992 Brian Leetch, N.Y. Rangers
1993 Chris Chelios, Chicago
1994 Ray Bourque, Boston
1995 Paul Coffey, Detroit
1996 Chris Chelios, Chicago
1997 Brian Leetch, N.Y. Rangers
1998 Rob Blake, Los Angeles
1999 Al MacInnis, St. Louis
2000 Chris Pronger, St. Louis
2001 Nicklas Lidstrom, Detroit
2002 Nicklas Lidstrom, Detroit
2003 Nicklas Lidstrom, Detroit
2004 Scott Niedermayer, New Jersey

Art Ross Trophy (Leading Points Scorer)

1927 Bill Cook, N.Y. Rangers
1928 Howie Morenz, Montreal
1929 Ace Bailey, Toronto
1930 Cooney Weiland, Boston
1931 Howie Morenz, Montreal
1932 Harvey Jackson, Toronto
1933 Bill Cook, N.Y. Rangers
1934 Charlie Conacher, Toronto
1935 Charlie Conacher, Toronto
1936 Dave Schriner, N.Y. Americans
1937 Dave Schriner, N.Y. Americans
1938 Gordie Drillon, Toronto
1939 Toe Blake, Montreal
1940 Milt Schmidt, Boston
1941 Bill Cowley, Boston
1942 Bryan Hextall, N.Y. Rangers
1943 Doug Bentley, Chicago
1944 Herbie Cain, Boston
1945 Elmer Lach, Montreal
1946 Max Bentley, Chicago
1947 Max Bentley, Chicago
1948 Elmer Lach, Montreal
1949 Roy Conacher, Chicago
1950 Ted Lindsay, Detroit
1951 Gordie Howe, Detroit
1952 Gordie Howe, Detroit
1953 Gordie Howe, Detroit
1954 Gordie Howe, Detroit
1955 Bernie Geoffrion, Montreal
1956 Jean Beliveau, Montreal
1957 Gordie Howe, Detroit
1958 Dickie Moore, Montreal
1959 Dickie Moore, Montreal
1960 Bobby Hull, Chicago
1961 Bernie Geoffrion, Montreal
1962 Bobby Hull, Chicago
1963 Gordie Howe, Detroit
1964 Stan Mikita, Chicago
1965 Stan Mikita, Chicago
1966 Bobby Hull, Chicago
1967 Stan Mikita, Chicago
1968 Stan Mikita, Chicago
1969 Phil Esposito, Boston
1970 Bobby Orr, Boston
1971 Phil Esposito, Boston
1972 Phil Esposito, Boston
1973 Phil Esposito, Boston
1974 Phil Esposito, Boston
1975 Bobby Orr, Boston
1976 Guy Lafleur, Montreal
1977 Guy Lafleur, Montreal
1978 Guy Lafleur, Montreal
1979 Bryan Trottier, N.Y. Islanders
1980 Marcel Dionne, Los Angeles
1981 Wayne Gretzky, Edmonton
1982 Wayne Gretzky, Edmonton
1983 Wayne Gretzky, Edmonton
1984 Wayne Gretzky, Edmonton
1985 Wayne Gretzky, Edmonton
1986 Wayne Gretzky, Edmonton
1987 Wayne Gretzky, Edmonton
1988 Mario Lemieux, Pittsburgh
1989 Mario Lemieux, Pittsburgh
1990 Wayne Gretzky, Los Angeles
1991 Wayne Gretzky, Los Angeles
1992 Mario Lemieux, Pittsburgh
1993 Mario Lemieux, Pittsburgh
1994 Wayne Gretzky, Los Angeles
1995 Jaromir Jagr, Pittsburgh
1996 Mario Lemieux, Pittsburgh
1997 Mario Lemieux, Pittsburgh
1998 Jaromir Jagr, Pittsburgh
1999 Jaromir Jagr, Pittsburgh
2000 Jaromir Jagr, Pittsburgh
2001 Jaromir Jagr, Pittsburgh
2002 Jarome Iginla, Calgary
2003 Peter Forsberg, Colorado
2004 Martin St. Louis, Tampa Bay

Vezina Trophy (Outstanding Goalie)*

1927 George Hainsworth, Montreal
1928 George Hainsworth, Montreal
1929 George Hainsworth, Montreal
1930 Tiny Thompson, Boston
1931 Roy Worters, N.Y. Americans
1932 Charlie Gardiner, Chicago
1933 Tiny Thompson, Boston
1934 Charlie Gardiner, Chicago
1935 Lorne Chabot, Chicago
1936 Tiny Thompson, Boston
1937 Normie Smith, Detroit
1938 Tiny Thompson, Boston
1939 Frank Brimsek, Boston
1940 Dave Kerr, N.Y. Rangers
1941 Turk Broda, Toronto
1942 Frank Brimsek, Boston
1943 Johnny Mowers, Detroit
1944 Bill Durnan, Montreal
1945 Bill Durnan, Montreal
1946 Bill Durnan, Montreal
1947 Bill Durnan, Montreal
1948 Turk Broda, Toronto
1949 Bill Durnan, Montreal
1950 Bill Durnan, Montreal
1951 Al Rollins, Toronto
1952 Terry Sawchuk, Detroit
1953 Terry Sawchuk, Detroit
1954 Harry Lumley, Toronto
1955 Terry Sawchuk, Detroit
1956 Jacques Plante, Montreal
1957 Jacques Plante, Montreal
1958 Jacques Plante, Montreal
1959 Jacques Plante, Montreal
1960 Jacques Plante, Montreal
1961 John Bower, Toronto
1962 Jacques Plante, Montreal
1963 Glenn Hall, Chicago
1964 Charlie Hodge, Montreal
1965 Sawchuk, Bower, Toronto
1966 Worsley, Hodge, Montreal
1967 Hall, DeJordy, Chicago
1968 Worsley, Vachon, Montreal
1969 Hall, Plante, St. Louis
1970 Tony Esposito, Chicago
1971 Giacomin, Villemure, N.Y. Rangers
1972 Esposito, Smith, Chicago
1973 Ken Dryden, Montreal
1974 Bernie Parent, Philadelphia; Tony Esposito, Chicago
1975 Bernie Parent, Philadelphia
1976 Ken Dryden, Montreal
1977 Dryden, Larocque, Montreal
1978 Dryden, Larocque, Montreal
1979 Dryden, Larocque, Montreal
1980 Sauve, Edwards, Buffalo
1981 Sevigny, Larocque, Herron, Montreal
1982 Bill Smith, N.Y. Islanders
1983 Pete Peeters, Boston
1984 Tom Barrasso, Buffalo
1985 Pelle Lindbergh, Philadelphia
1986 John Vanbiesbrouck, N.Y. Rangers
1987 Ron Hextall, Philadelphia
1988 Grant Fuhr, Edmonton
1989 Patrick Roy, Montreal
1990 Patrick Roy, Montreal
1991 Ed Belfour, Chicago
1992 Patrick Roy, Montreal
1993 Ed Belfour, Chicago
1994 Dominik Hasek, Buffalo
1995 Dominik Hasek, Buffalo
1996 Jim Carey, Washington
1997 Dominik Hasek, Buffalo
1998 Dominik Hasek, Buffalo
1999 Dominik Hasek, Buffalo
2000 Olaf Kolzig, Washington
2001 Dominik Hasek, Buffalo
2002 Jose Theodore, Montreal
2003 Martin Brodeur, New Jersey
2004 Martin Brodeur, New Jersey

*Before 1982, awarded to the goalie or goalies who played a minimum of 25 games for the team that allowed the fewest goals; since 1982, awarded to the outstanding goalie, as determined by a vote of NHL general managers.

National Hockey Hall of Fame, Toronto, Ontario

(2005 inductees have an asterisk*)

PLAYERS
Abel, Sid
Adams, Jack
Apps, Syl
Armstrong, George
Bailey, Ace
Bain, Dan
Baker, Hobey
Barber, Bill
Barry, Marty
Bathgate, Andy
Bauer, Bobby
Beliveau, Jean
Benedict, Clint
Bentley, Doug
Bentley, Max
Blake, Toe
Boivin, Leo
Boon, Dickie
Bossy, Mike
Bouchard, Butch
Boucher, Frank
Boucher, George
Bourque, Ray
Bower, Johnny
Bowie, Dubbie
Brimsek, Frank
Broadbent, Punch
Broda, Turk
Bucyk, John
Burch, Billy
Cameron, Harry
Bucyk, John
Burch, Billy
Cameron, Harry
Cheevers, Gerry
Clancy, King
Clapper, Dit
Clarke, Bobby
Cleghorn, Sprague
Coffey, Paul
Colville, Neil

Conacher, Charlie
Conacher, Lionel
Conacher, Roy
Connell, Alex
Cook, Bill
Cook, Bun
Coulter, Art
Cournoyer, Yvan
Cowley, Bill
Crawford, Rusty
Darragh, Jack
Davidson, Scotty
Day, Hap
Delvecchio, Alex
Denneny, Cy
Dionne, Marcel
Drillon, Gordie
Drinkwater, Graham
Dryden, Ken
Dumart, Woody
Dunderdale, Tommy
Durnan, Bill
Dutton, Red
Dye, Babe
Esposito, Phil
Esposito, Tony
Farrel, Arthur
Federko, Bernie
Fetisov, Viacheslav
Flaman, Fernie
Foyston, Frank
Fredrickson, Frank
Fuhr, Grant
Gadsby, Bill
Gainey, Bob
Gardiner, Chuck
Gardiner, Herb
Gardiner, Jimmy
Gartner, Mike
Geoffrion, Bernie
Gerard, Eddie
Giacomin, Eddie
Gilbert, Rod
Gillies, Clark
Gilmour, Billy
Goheen, Moose
Goodfellow, Ebbie
Goulet, Michel
Grant, Mike
Green, Shorty
Gretzky, Wayne
Griffis, Si
Hainsworth, George
Hall, Glenn
Hall, Joe
Harvey, Doug
Hawerchuk, Dale
Hay, George
Hern, Riley
Hextall, Bryan
Holmes, Hap
Hooper, Tom
Horner, Red
Horton, Tim
Howe, Gordie
Howe, Syd
Howell, Harry
Hull, Bobby
Hutton, Bouse
Hyland, Harry
Irvin, Dick
Jackson, Busher
Johnson, Ching
Johnson, Ernie
Johnson, Tom
Joliat, Aurel
*Kharlamov, Valeri
Keats, Duke
Kelly, Red
Kennedy, Ted
Keon, Dave
Kurri, Jari
Lach, Elmer
Lafleur, Guy
LaFontaine, Pat
Lalonde, Newsy
Langway, Rod
Laperriere, Jacques
Lapointe, Guy
Laprade, Edgar
Laviolette, Jack
LeSueur, Percy
Lehman, Hughie
Lemaire, Jacques
Lemieux, Mario
Lewis, Herbie
Lindsay, Ted
Lumley, Harry
MacKay, Mickey
Mahovlich, Frank
Malone, Joe
Mantha, Sylvio
Marshall, Jack
Maxwell, Fred
McDonald, Lanny
McGee, Frank
McGimsie, Billy
McNamara, George
Mikita, Stan
Moore, Dickie
Moran, Paddy
Morenz, Howie
Mosienko, Bill
Mullen, Joe
Murphy, Larry
*Neely, Cam
Nighbor, Frank
Noble, Reg
O'Connor, Buddy
Oliver, Harry
Olmstead, Bert
Orr, Bobby
Parent, Bernie
Park, Brad
Patrick, Lester
Patrick, Lynn
Perreault, Gilbert
Phillips, Tom
Pilote, Pierre
Pitre, Didier
Plante, Jacques
Potvin, Denis
Pratt, Babe
Primeau, Joe
Pronovost, Marcel
Pulford, Bob
Pulford, Harvey
Quackenbush, Bill
Rankin, Frank
Ratelle, Jean
Rayner, Chuck
Reardon, Kenny
Richard, Henri
Richard, Maurice
Richardson, George
Roberts, Gordie
Robinson, Larry
Ross, Art
Russel, Blair
Russell, Ernie
Ruttan, Jack
Salming, Borje
Savard, Denis
Savard, Serge
Sawchuk, Terry
Scanlan, Fred
Schmidt, Milt
Schriner, Sweeney
Seibert, Earl
Seibert, Oliver
Shore, Eddie
Shutt, Steve
Siebert, Babe
Simpson, Joe
Sittler, Darryl
Smith, Alf
Smith, Billy
Smith, Clint
Smith, Hooley
Smith, Tommy
Stanley, Allan
Stanley, Barney
Stastny, Peter
Stewart, Jack
Stewart, Nels
Stuart, Bruce
Stuart, Hod
Taylor, Cyclone
Thompson, Tiny
Tretiak, Vladislav
Trihey, Harry
Trottier, Bryan
Ullman, Norm
Vezina, Georges
Walker, Jack
Walsh, Marty
Watson, Harry (Moose)
Watson, Harry Percival
Weiland, Cooney
Westwick, Harry
Whitcroft, Fred
Wilson, Phat
Worsley, Gump
Worters, Roy

BUILDERS

Adams, Charles
Adams, Weston
Ahearn, Bunny
Ahearn, Frank
Allan, Sir Montagu
Allen, Keith
Arbour, Al
Ballard, Harold
Bauer, Father David
Bickell, J.P.
Bowman, Scotty
Brown, George
Brown, Walter
Buckland, Frank
Bush, Walter, Jr.
Butterfield, Jack
Calder, Frank
Campbell, Angus
Campbell, Clarence
Cattarinich, Joseph
*Costello, Murray
Dandurand, Leo
Dilio, Frank
Dudley, George
Dunn, James
Fletcher, Cliff
Francis, Emile
Gibson, Jack
Gorman, Tommy
Griffiths, Frank
Hanley, Bill
Hay, Charles
Hendy, Jim
Hewitt, Foster
Hewitt, William
Hume, Fred
Ilitch, Mike
Imlach, Punch
Ivan, Tommy
Jennings, William
Johnson, Bob
Juckes, Gordon
Kilpatrick, John
Kilrea, Brian
Knox, Seymour
LeBel, Robert
Leader, Al
Lockhart, Thomas
Loicq, Paul
Mariucci, John
Mathers, Frank
McLaughlin, Frederic
Milford, Jake
Molson, Sen. Hartland
Morrison, Ian "Scotty"
Murray, Pere Athol
Neilson, Roger
Nelson, Francis
Norris, Bruce
Norris, James
Norris, James Sr.
Northey, William
O'Brien, J. Ambrose
O'Neill, Brian Francis
Page, Frederick
Patrick, Craig
Patrick, Frank
Pickard, Allan
Pilous, Rudy
Poile, Bud
Pollock, Sam
Raymond, Sen. Donat
Robertson, John Ross
Robinson, Claude
Ross, Phillip
Sabetzki, Gunther
Sather, Glen
Selke, Frank
Sinden, Harry
Smith, Frank
Smythe, Conn
Snider, Ed
Stanley, Lord (of Preston)
Sutherland, Capt. James T.
Tarasov, Anatoli
Torrey, Bill
Turner, Lloyd
Tutt, William
Voss, Carl
Waghorne, Fred
Wirtz, Arthur
Wirtz, Bill
Ziegler, John A., Jr.

REFEREES AND LINESMEN

Armstrong, Neil
Ashley, John
Chadwick, Bill
D'Amico, John
Elliott, Chaucer
Hayes, George
Hewiston, Bobby
Ion, Mickey
Pavelich, Matt
Rodden, Mike
Smeaton, Cooper
Storey, Red
Udvari, Frank
Van Hellemond, Andy

NHL Home Ice[1]

Team	Name (built)	Capacity
Anaheim	The Arrowhead Pond of Anaheim (1993)	17,174
Atlanta	Philips Arena (1999)	18,750
Boston	FleetCenter (1995)	17,565
Buffalo	HSBC Arena[2] (1996)	18,690
Calgary	Pengrowth Saddledome (1983)	17,104
Carolina	RBC Center[3] (1999)	18,730
Chicago	United Center (1994)	20,500
Colorado	Pepsi Center (1999)	18,007
Columbus	Nationwide Arena (2000)	18,500
Dallas	American Airlines Center (2001)	18,000
Detroit	Joe Louis Arena (1979)	19,983
Edmonton	Rexall Place[4] (1974)	17,100
Florida	Office Depot Center[5] (1998)	19,250
Los Angeles	Staples Center (1999)	18,118
Minnesota	Xcel Energy Arena (2000)	18,600
Montreal	Le Centre Bell[6] (1996)	21,273
Nashville	Gaylord Entertainment Center[7] (1996)	17,500
New Jersey	Continental Airlines Arena[8] (1981)	19,040
N.Y. Islanders	Nassau Veterans Memorial Col. (1972)	16,297
N.Y. Rangers	Madison Square Garden (1968)	18,200
Ottawa	Corel Centre (1996)	18,500
Philadelphia	Wachovia Center[9] (1996)	19,519
Phoenix	Glendale Arena (2003)	17,500
Pittsburgh	Mellon Arena[10] (1961)	17,537
St. Louis	Savvis Center[11] (1994)	21,000
San Jose	HP Pavilion[12] (1993)	17,483
Tampa Bay	St. Pete Times Forum[13] (1996)	19,758
Toronto	Air Canada Centre (1999)	18,800
Vancouver	GM Place (1995	18,422
Washington	MCI Center (1997)	19,700

(1) At the end of the 2003-04 season. (2) Marine Midland Arena, 1996-2000. (3) Entertainment & Sports Arena, 1996-2002. (4) Northlands Col., 1974-79; Edmonton Col., 1979-98; Skyreach Centre, 1998-2003. (5) National Car Rental Center, 1998-2002. (6) Le Centre Molson, 1996-2002. (7) Nashville Arena, 1997-99. (8) Brendan Byrne/Meadowlands Arena, 1981-96. (9) First Union Center, 1996-2003. (10) Civic Arena, 1961-99. (11) Kiel Center, 1994-2000. (12) San Jose Arena, 1993-2000; Compaq Center, 2001. (13) Ice Palace, 1996-2002.

NCAA HOCKEY CHAMPIONS

1948 Michigan
1949 Boston College
1950 Colorado College
1951 Michigan
1952 Michigan
1953 Michigan
1954 RPI
1955 Michigan
1956 Michigan
1957 Colorado College
1958 Denver
1959 North Dakota
1960 Denver
1961 Denver
1962 Michigan Tech
1963 North Dakota
1964 Michigan
1965 Michigan Tech
1966 Michigan State
1967 Cornell
1968 Denver
1969 Denver
1970 Cornell
1971 Boston Univ.
1972 Boston Univ.
1973 Wisconsin
1974 Minnesota
1975 Michigan Tech
1976 Minnesota
1977 Wisconsin
1978 Boston Univ.
1979 Minnesota
1980 North Dakota
1981 Wisconsin
1982 North Dakota
1983 Wisconsin
1984 Bowling Green
1985 RPI
1986 Michigan State
1987 North Dakota
1988 Lake Superior St.
1989 Harvard
1990 Wisconsin
1991 N. Michigan
1992 Lake Superior St.
1993 Maine
1994 Lake Superior St.
1995 Boston Univ.
1996 Michigan
1997 North Dakota
1998 Michigan
1999 Maine
2000 North Dakota
2001 Boston College
2002 Minnesota
2003 Minnesota
2004 Denver
2005 Denver

SOCCER

UEFA (European) Champions League

The 2004/2005 UEFA Champions League final was won by Liverpool over Milan in the 50th final, held in Istanbul, Turkey May 25, 2005. After battling back from 3-0, Liverpool brought the game to a tie. In penalty kicks, they defeated AC Milan, 3-2. The 2005/2006 UEFA Champions League final will be played at in Paris on May 17, 2006.

UEFA Championship League Winners and Runners-Up, 1956-2005

Year	Winner	Runner Up	Score	Year	Winner	Runner Up	Score
1956	Real Madrid	Reims	4-3	1981	Liverpool	Real Madrid	1-0
1957	Real Madrid	Fiorentina	2-0	1982	Villa	Bayern Munich	1-0
1958	Real Madrid	AC Milan	3-2#	1983	Hamburg	Juventus	1-0
1959	Real Madrid	Reims	2-0	1984	Liverpool	Roma	1-1 (4-2)*
1960	Real Madrid	Eintracht	7-3	1985	Juventus	Liverpool	1-0
1961	Benfica	Barcelona	3-2	1986	Steaua	Barcelona	0-0 (2-0)*
1962	Benfica	Real Madrid	5-3	1987	Porto	Bayern Munich	2-1
1963	AC Milan	Benfica	2-1	1988	PSV	Benfica	0-0 (6-5)*
1964	Inter Milan	Real Madrid	3-1	1989	AC Milan	Steaua	4-0
1965	Inter Milan	Benfica	1-0	1990	AC Milan	Benfica	1-0
1966	Real Madrid	Partizan	2-1	1991	Crvena zvezda	Marseille	0-0 (5-3)*
1967	Celtic	Inter Milan	2-1	1992	Barcelona	Sampdoria	1-0#
1968	Man. United	Benfica	4-1#	1993	Marseille	AC Milan	1-0
1969	AC Milan	Ajax	4-1	1994	AC Milan	Barcelona	4-0
1970	Feyenoord	Celtic	2-1#	1995	Ajax	AC Milan	1-0
1971	Ajax	Panathinaikos	2-0	1996	Juventus	Ajax	1-1 (4-2)*
1972	Ajax	Inter Milan	2-0	1997	Dortmund	Juventus	3-1
1973	Ajax	Juventus	1-0	1998	Real Madrid	Juventus	1-0
1974	Bayern Munich	Atlético	5-1[1]	1999	Man. United	Bayern Munich	2-1
1975	Bayern Munich	Leeds	2-0	2000	Real Madrid	Valencia	3-0
1976	Bayern Munich	St-Etienne	1-0	2001	Bayern Munich	Valencia	1-1 (5-4)*
1977	Liverpool	Mönchen-gladbach	3-1	2002	Real Madrid	Leverkusen	2-1
1978	Liverpool	Club Brugge	1-0	2003	AC Milan	Juventus	0-0 (3-2)*
1979	Notts Forest	Malmö	1-0	2004	Porto	Monaco	3-0
1980	Notts Forest	Hamburg	1-0	2005	Liverpool	AC Milan	3-3 (3-2)*

* Match decided in penalty kicks (shootout score in parentheses). (#) Match decided in extra time. (1) Aggregate score. First game 1-1; 4-0.

European Championships

The final rounds of the 2008 European Championships will be jointly hosted by Austria and Switzerland, and were scheduled to open June 7, 2008, in Basel, Switzerland, with the final match to be played at Ernst Happle Stadium in Vienna, Austria, on June 29, 2008.

European Championships, 1960-2004

Year	Winner	Final opponent	Score	Site
1960	USSR	Yugoslavia	2-1 (extra time)	France
1964	Spain	USSR	2-1	Spain
1968	Italy	Yugoslavia	2-0	Italy
1972	W. Germany	USSR	3-0	Belgium
1976	Czechoslovakia	W. Germany	2-2 (Czech. won 5-3 on pens.)	Yugoslavia
1980	W. Germany	Belgium	2-1	Italy
1984	France	Spain	2-0	France
1988	Netherlands	USSR	2-0	W. Germany
1992	Denmark	Germany	2-0	Sweden
1996	Germany	Czech Rep.	2-1 (extra time)	England
2000	France	Italy	2-1 (extra time)	Belgium/Neth.
2004	Greece	Portugal	1-0	Portugal

Men's World Cup

Soccer superpower Brazil won 7 straight matches, including a 2-0 win over Germany on June 30, 2002, to claim a record 5th World Cup. Favorites France, Argentina, and Portugal failed to advance to the 2nd round, while the U.S. had an unexpectedly strong showing, defeating Mexico, 2-0, before losing 1-0 to Germany in the quarterfinals. Brazilian forward Ronaldo won the Golden Boot for most goals, 8, including 2 in the final. Germany's Oliver Kahn became the 1st goalkeeper to win the Golden Ball as the tournament's best player.

The next World Cup was scheduled to be held in 12 German cities, June 9-July 9, 2006, with Berlin scheduled to host the finals. South Africa was awarded the 2010 World Cup on May 15, 2004, becoming the 1st African nation to win the rights to host the tournament.

Men's World Cup, 1930-2002

Year	Winner	Final opponent	Score	Site
1930	Uruguay	Argentina	4-2	Uruguay
1934	Italy	Czechoslovakia	2-1 (extra time)	Italy
1938	Italy	Hungary	4-2	France
1950	Uruguay	Brazil	2-1	Brazil
1954	W. Germany	Hungary	3-2	Switzerland
1958	Brazil	Sweden	5-2	Sweden
1962	Brazil	Czechoslovakia	3-1	Chile
1966	England	W. Germany	4-2 (extra time)	England
1970	Brazil	Italy	4-1	Mexico
1974	W. Germany	Netherlands	2-1	W. Germany
1978	Argentina	Netherlands	3-1 (extra time)	Argentina
1982	Italy	W. Germany	3-1	Spain
1986	Argentina	W. Germany	3-2	Mexico

Year	Winner	Final opponent	Score	Site
1990	W. Germany	Argentina	1-0	Italy
1994	Brazil	Italy	0-0 (Braz. won 3-2 on pens.)	U.S.
1998	France	Brazil	3-0	France
2002	Brazil	Germany	2-0	Japan/S. Korea

FIFA Men's National Team Rankings

(As of Sept. 2005)

Rank	Team	Rank	Team	Rank	Team	Rank	Team	Rank	Team
1.	Brazil	3.	Argentina	5.	Mexico	7.	U.S.	9.	Portugal
2.	Netherlands	4.	Czech Republic	6.	France	8.	Spain	10.	Sweden

Women's World Cup

Germany defeated Sweden, 2-1, in extra time, in the final of the Women's World Cup Oct. 12, 2003, at the Home Depot Center in Carson, CA. The U.S. defeated Canada, 3-1, in the 3rd-place game Oct. 11. The next Women's World Cup was scheduled to be held in 2007 in China.

Women's World Cup, 1991-2003

Year	Winner	Final Opponent	Score	Site	Third Place
1991	U.S.	Norway	2-1	China	Germany
1995	Norway	Germany	2-0	Sweden	U.S.
1999	U.S.	China	0-0*	Pasadena, CA	Brazil
2003	Germany	Sweden	2-1 (extra time)	Carson, CA	U.S.

* U.S. 5-4, penalty kicks

Major League Soccer

D.C. United won the Major League Soccer (MLS) championship on Nov. 14, 2004, with a 3-2 victory over the Kansas City Wizards in Carson, CA. Striker and U.S. national team star Landon Donovan signed with the L.A. Galaxy Mar. 31, 2005 following a 2½-month stint with German club Bayer Leverkusen. On Apr. 14, MLS players ratified the first collective bargaining agreement in league history.

With the addition of 2 teams in the Western Conference—Real Salt Lake and Club Deportivo (CD) Chivas USA, which plays out of Carson, CA—MLS began season play Apr. 2, 2005. There were 12 teams for the first time since 2002, when 2 unprofitable Florida franchises were eliminated. Defending champs D.C. United defeated Chivas USA, 2-0, in the team's MLS debut on opening day. The league's expansion was seen in part as a move to attract a broader, more international audience. Jorge Vergara, co-owner of Chivas USA, is also an owner of Mexico's popular CD Guadalajara club, known familiarly as Chivas. Real (pronounced RAY-al, Spanish for "royal") Salt Lake and the former Dallas Burn, which changed its name to FC (Football Club) Dallas for the 2005 season, joined D.C. United in adopting names that evoked popular world soccer clubs Real Madrid, FC Barcelona, and Manchester United.

Major League Soccer (MLS) Cup Champions, 1996-2004

Year	Winner	Final opponent	Score	Site	MVP
1996	D.C. United	Los Angeles Galaxy	3-2 (OT)	Foxboro, MA	Marco Etcheverry
1997	D.C. United	Colorado Rapids	2-1	Washington, DC	Jaime Moreno
1998	Chicago Fire	D.C. United	2-0	Pasadena, CA	Peter Nowak
1999	D.C. United	Los Angeles Galaxy	2-0	Foxboro, MA	Ben Olsen
2000	Kansas City Wizards	Chicago Fire	1-0	Washington, DC	Tony Meola
2001	San Jose Earthquakes	Los Angeles Galaxy	2-1 (OT)	Columbus, OH	Dwayne DeRosario
2002	Los Angeles Galaxy	New England Revolution	1-0 (OT)	Foxboro, MA	Carlos Ruiz
2003	San Jose Earthquakes	Chicago Fire	4-2	Carson, CA	Landon Donovan
2004	D.C. United	Kansas City Wizards	3-2	Carson, CA	Alecko Eskandarian

NCAA Soccer Champions, 1982-2004

Year[1]	Men	Women
1982	Indiana	North Carolina
1983	Indiana	North Carolina
1984	Clemson	North Carolina
1985	UCLA	George Mason
1986	Duke	North Carolina
1987	Clemson	North Carolina
1988	Indiana	North Carolina
1989	Santa Clara (tie, 2 OT) Virginia	North Carolina
1990	UCLA	North Carolina
1991	Virginia	North Carolina
1992	Virginia	North Carolina
1993	Virginia	North Carolina
1994	Virginia	North Carolina
1995	Wisconsin	Notre Dame
1996	St. John's (NY)	North Carolina
1997	UCLA	North Carolina
1998	Indiana	Florida
1999	Indiana	North Carolina
2000	Connecticut	North Carolina
2001	North Carolina	Santa Clara
2002	UCLA	Portland
2003	Indiana	North Carolina
2004	Indiana	Notre Dame

(1) NCAA Championships began in 1959 for men, in 1982 for women.

RUGBY

2003 Rugby World Cup

England defeated defending champion Australia, 20-17, in extra time on Nov. 22, 2003, to win the Rugby World Cup, rugby union's premier tournament, before a crowd of 82,957 at Telstra Stadium in Sydney, Australia. England won the final in the last 30 seconds of the 20-minute extra-time period, when star fly-half Jonny Wilkinson slotted a drop goal from just outside the 22-meter line. Wilkinson, 24, tallied 113 points in the tournament, the most of any player. England became the 1st team from the Northern Hemisphere to win the quadrennial Rugby World Cup, which had first been played in 1987.

The 2007 Rugby World Cup was scheduled to be held Sept. 7-Oct. 20, 2007, in France (with some matches played in Wales and Scotland).

Rugby World Cup, 1987-2003

Year	Winner	Final Opponent	Score	Site
1987	New Zealand	France	29-9	Australia/New Zealand
1991	Australia	England	12-6	G. Britain/Ireland/France
1995	South Africa	New Zealand	15-12 (extra time)	South Africa
1999	Australia	France	35-12	G. Britain/Ireland/France
2003	England	Australia	20-17 (extra time)	Australia

GOLF

Men's All-Time Major Professional Championship Leaders

(Through the 2004 season; *active PGA player; (a)=amateur.)

Player	Masters	U.S. Open	British Open	PGA	Total
Jack Nicklaus	1963, '65-66, '72, '75, '86	1962, '67, '72, '80	1966, '70, '78	1963, '71, '73, '75, '80	18
Walter Hagen	—	1914, '19	1922, '24, '28-29	1921, '24-27	11
Tiger Woods*	1997, 2001, 2002, 2005	2000, 2002	2000, 2005	1999, 2000	10
Ben Hogan	1951, '53	1948, '50-51, '53	1953	1946, '48	9
Gary Player	1961, '74, '78	1965	1959, '68, '74	1962, '72	9
Tom Watson*	1977, '81	1982	1975, '77, '80, '82-83	—	8
Bobby Jones (a)	—	1923, '26, '29-30	1926-27, '30	—	7
Arnold Palmer	1958, '60, '62, '64	1960	1961-62	—	7
Gene Sarazen	1935	1922, '32	1932	1922-23, '33	7
Sam Snead	1949, '52, '54	—	1946	1942, '49, '51	7
Harry Vardon	—	1900	1896, '98-99, 1903, '11, '14	—	7
Nick Faldo*	1989-90, '96	—	1987, '90, '92	—	6
Lee Trevino	—	1968, '71	1971-72	1974, '84	6

Professional Golfers' Association Leading Money Winners, by Year

Year	Player	Earnings
1946	Ben Hogan	$42,556
1947	Jimmy Demaret	27,936
1948	Ben Hogan	36,812
1949	Sam Snead	31,593
1950	Sam Snead	35,758
1951	Lloyd Mangrum	26,088
1952	Julius Boros	37,032
1953	Lew Worsham	34,002
1954	Bob Toski	65,819
1955	Julius Boros	65,121
1956	Ted Kroll	72,835
1957	Dick Mayer	65,835
1958	Arnold Palmer	42,407
1959	Art Wall, Jr.	53,167
1960	Arnold Palmer	75,262
1961	Gary Player	64,540
1962	Arnold Palmer	81,448
1963	Arnold Palmer	128,230
1964	Jack Nicklaus	113,284
1965	Jack Nicklaus	140,752
1966	Billy Casper	$121,944
1967	Jack Nicklaus	188,988
1968	Billy Casper	205,168
1969	Frank Beard	175,223
1970	Lee Trevino	157,037
1971	Jack Nicklaus	244,490
1972	Jack Nicklaus	320,542
1973	Jack Nicklaus	308,362
1974	Johnny Miller	353,201
1975	Jack Nicklaus	323,149
1976	Jack Nicklaus	266,438
1977	Tom Watson	310,653
1978	Tom Watson	362,429
1979	Tom Watson	462,636
1980	Tom Watson	530,808
1981	Tom Kite	375,699
1982	Craig Stadler	446,462
1983	Hal Sutton	426,668
1984	Tom Watson	476,260
1985	Curtis Strange	$542,321
1986	Greg Norman	653,296
1987	Curtis Strange	925,941
1988	Curtis Strange	1,147,644
1989	Tom Kite	1,395,278
1990	Greg Norman	1,165,477
1991	Corey Pavin	979,430
1992	Fred Couples	1,344,188
1993	Nick Price	1,478,557
1994	Nick Price	1,499,927
1995	Greg Norman	1,654,959
1996	Tom Lehman	1,780,159
1997	Tiger Woods	2,066,833
1998	David Duval	2,591,031
1999	Tiger Woods	6,616,585
2000	Tiger Woods	9,188,321
2001	Tiger Woods	5,687,777
2002	Tiger Woods	6,912,625
2003	Vijay Singh	7,573,907
2004	Vijay Singh	10,905,166

Masters Golf Tournament Winners

Year	Winner
1934	Horton Smith
1935	Gene Sarazen
1936	Horton Smith
1937	Byron Nelson
1938	Henry Picard
1939	Ralph Guldahl
1940	Jimmy Demaret
1941	Craig Wood
1942	Byron Nelson
1943-45	not played
1946	Herman Keiser
1947	Jimmy Demaret
1948	Claude Harmon
1949	Sam Snead
1950	Jimmy Demaret
1951	Ben Hogan
1952	Sam Snead
1953	Ben Hogan
1954	Sam Snead
1955	Cary Middlecoff
1956	Jack Burke
1957	Doug Ford
1958	Arnold Palmer
1959	Art Wall Jr.
1960	Arnold Palmer
1961	Gary Player
1962	Arnold Palmer
1963	Jack Nicklaus
1964	Arnold Palmer
1965	Jack Nicklaus
1966	Jack Nicklaus
1967	Gay Brewer, Jr.
1968	Bob Goalby
1969	George Archer
1970	Billy Casper
1971	Charles Coody
1972	Jack Nicklaus
1973	Tommy Aaron
1974	Gary Player
1975	Jack Nicklaus
1976	Ray Floyd
1977	Tom Watson
1978	Gary Player
1979	Fuzzy Zoeller
1980	Seve Ballesteros
1981	Tom Watson
1982	Craig Stadler
1983	Seve Ballesteros
1984	Ben Crenshaw
1985	Bernhard Langer
1986	Jack Nicklaus
1987	Larry Mize
1988	Sandy Lyle
1989	Nick Faldo
1990	Nick Faldo
1991	Ian Woosnam
1992	Fred Couples
1993	Bernhard Langer
1994	Jose Maria Olazabal
1995	Ben Crenshaw
1996	Nick Faldo
1997	Tiger Woods
1998	Mark O'Meara
1999	Jose Maria Olazabal
2000	Vijay Singh
2001	Tiger Woods
2002	Tiger Woods
2003	Mike Weir
2004	Phil Mickelson
2005	Tiger Woods

United States Open Winners

(First contested in 1895)

Year	Winner
1934	Olin Dutra
1935	Sam Parks, Jr.
1936	Tony Manero
1937	Ralph Guldahl
1938	Ralph Guldahl
1939	Byron Nelson
1940	Lawson Little
1941	Craig Wood
1942-45	not played
1946	Lloyd Mangrum
1947	L. Worsham
1948	Ben Hogan
1949	Cary Middlecoff
1950	Ben Hogan
1951	Ben Hogan
1952	Julius Boros
1953	Ben Hogan
1954	Ed Furgol
1955	Jack Fleck
1956	Cary Middlecoff
1957	Dick Mayer
1958	Tommy Bolt
1959	Billy Casper
1960	Arnold Palmer
1961	Gene Littler
1962	Jack Nicklaus
1963	Julius Boros
1964	Ken Venturi
1965	Gary Player
1966	Billy Casper
1967	Jack Nicklaus
1968	Lee Trevino
1969	Orville Moody
1970	Tony Jacklin
1971	Lee Trevino
1972	Jack Nicklaus
1973	Johnny Miller
1974	Hale Irwin
1975	Lou Graham
1976	Jerry Pate
1977	Hubert Green
1978	Andy North
1979	Hale Irwin
1980	Jack Nicklaus
1981	David Graham
1982	Tom Watson
1983	Larry Nelson
1984	Fuzzy Zoeller
1985	Andy North
1986	Ray Floyd
1987	Scott Simpson
1988	Curtis Strange
1989	Curtis Strange
1990	Hale Irwin
1991	Payne Stewart
1992	Tom Kite
1993	Lee Janzen
1994	Ernie Els
1995	Corey Pavin
1996	Steve Jones
1997	Ernie Els
1998	Lee Janzen
1999	Payne Stewart
2000	Tiger Woods
2001	Retief Goosen
2002	Tiger Woods
2003	Jim Furyk
2004	Retief Goosen
2005	Michael Campbell

IT'S A FACT: Before his victory in the Masters on Apr. 10, 2005, Tiger Woods had not won a major professional golf tournament in almost 3 years, since his U.S. Open win in June 2002.

British Open Winners

(First contested in 1860)

Year	Winner	Year	Winner	Year	Winner	Year	Winner
1934	Henry Cotton	1956	Peter Thomson	1973	Tom Weiskopf	1990	Nick Faldo
1935	Alf Perry	1957	Bobby Locke	1974	Gary Player	1991	Ian Baker-Finch
1936	Alf Padgham	1958	Peter Thomson	1975	Tom Watson	1992	Nick Faldo
1937	T.H. Cotton	1959	Gary Player	1976	Johnny Miller	1993	Greg Norman
1938	R.A. Whitcombe	1960	Kel Nagle	1977	Tom Watson	1994	Nick Price
1939	Richard Burton	1961	Arnold Palmer	1978	Jack Nicklaus	1995	John Daly
1940-45	not played	1962	Arnold Palmer	1979	Seve Ballesteros	1996	Tom Lehman
1946	Sam Snead	1963	Bob Charles	1980	Tom Watson	1997	Justin Leonard
1947	Fred Daly	1964	Tony Lema	1981	Bill Rogers	1998	Mark O'Meara
1948	Henry Cotton	1965	Peter Thomson	1982	Tom Watson	1999	Paul Lawrie
1949	Bobby Locke	1966	Jack Nicklaus	1983	Tom Watson	2000	Tiger Woods
1950	Bobby Locke	1967	Roberto de Vicenzo	1984	Seve Ballesteros	2001	David Duval
1951	Max Faulkner	1968	Gary Player	1985	Sandy Lyle	2002	Ernie Els
1952	Bobby Locke	1969	Tony Jacklin	1986	Greg Norman	2003	Ben Curtis
1953	Ben Hogan	1970	Jack Nicklaus	1987	Nick Faldo	2004	Todd Hamilton
1954	Peter Thomson	1971	Lee Trevino	1988	Seve Ballesteros	2005	Tiger Woods
1955	Peter Thomson	1972	Lee Trevino	1989	Mark Calcavecchia		

PGA Championship Winners

(First contested in 1916)

Year	Winner	Year	Winner	Year	Winner	Year	Winner
1934	Paul Runyan	1952	James Turnesa	1970	Dave Stockton	1988	Jeff Sluman
1935	Johnny Revolta	1953	Walter Burkemo	1971	Jack Nicklaus	1989	Payne Stewart
1936	Denny Shute	1954	Melvin Harbert	1972	Gary Player	1990	Wayne Grady
1937	Denny Shute	1955	Doug Ford	1973	Jack Nicklaus	1991	John Daly
1938	Paul Runyan	1956	Jack Burke	1974	Lee Trevino	1992	Nick Price
1939	Henry Picard	1957	Lionel Hebert	1975	Jack Nicklaus	1993	Paul Azinger
1940	Byron Nelson	1958	Dow Finsterwald	1976	Dave Stockton	1994	Nick Price
1941	Victor Ghezzi	1959	Bob Rosburg	1977	Lanny Wadkins	1995	Steve Elkington
1942	Sam Snead	1960	Jay Hebert	1978	John Mahaffey	1996	Mark Brooks
1943	not played	1961	Jerry Barber	1979	David Graham	1997	Davis Love III
1944	Bob Hamilton	1962	Gary Player	1980	Jack Nicklaus	1998	Vijay Singh
1945	Byron Nelson	1963	Jack Nicklaus	1981	Larry Nelson	1999	Tiger Woods
1946	Ben Hogan	1964	Bob Nichols	1982	Ray Floyd	2000	Tiger Woods
1947	Jim Ferrier	1965	Dave Marr	1983	Hal Sutton	2001	David Toms
1948	Ben Hogan	1966	Al Geiberger	1984	Lee Trevino	2002	Rich Beem
1949	Sam Snead	1967	Don January	1985	Hubert Green	2003	Shaun Micheel
1950	Chandler Harper	1968	Julius Boros	1986	Bob Tway	2004	Vijay Singh
1951	Sam Snead	1969	Ray Floyd	1987	Larry Nelson	2005	Phil Mickelson

Women's All-Time Major Professional Championship Leaders

(Through the 2005 season; *active in 2005 LPGA season.)

Player	Nabisco[1]	LPGA	U.S. Women's Open	du Maurier/ British Open[2]	Titleholders[3]	Western Open[4]	Total
Patty Berg	—	—	1946	—	1937-39, '48, '53, '55, '57	1941, '43, '48, '51, '55, '57-58	15
Mickey Wright	—	1958, '60-61, '63	1958-59, '61, '64	—	1961-62	1962-63, '66	13
Louise Suggs	—	1957	1949, '52	—	1946, '54, '56, '59	1946-47, '49, '53	11
Babe Zaharias	—	—	1948, '50, '54	—	1947, '50, '52	1940, '44-45, '50	10
Annika Sorenstam*	2001-02, '05	2003-05	1995-96	2003	—	—	9
Betsy Rawls	—	1959, '69	1951, '53, '57, '60	—	—	1952, '59	8
Juli Inkster*	1984, '89	1999, 2000	1999, 2002	1984	—	—	7
Pat Bradley	1986	1986	1981	1980, '85-86	—	—	6
Betsy King*	1987, '90, '97	1992	1989-90	—	—	—	6
Patty Sheehan	1996	1983-84, '93	1992, '94	—	—	—	6
Kathy Whitworth	—	1967, '71, '75	—	—	1965-66	1967	6
Karrie Webb*	2000	2001	2000-01	1999, 2002	—	—	6

(1) Nabisco Championship, formerly Nabisco Dinah Shore (1982-99), designated major in 1983. (2) In 2001, the British Open replaced the du Maurier Classic as the LPGA's 4th major. (3) Title holders Championship was a major from 1930 to 1972. (4) Western Open was a major from 1937 to 1967.

Ladies Professional Golf Association Leading Money Winners

Year	Player	Earnings	Year	Player	Earnings	Year	Player	Earnings
1954	Patty Berg	$16,011	1971	Kathy Whitworth	$41,181	1988	Sherri Turner	$347,255
1955	Patty Berg	16,492	1972	Kathy Whitworth	65,063	1989	Betsy King	654,132
1956	Marlene Hagge	20,235	1973	Kathy Whitworth	82,854	1990	Beth Daniel	863,578
1957	Patty Berg	16,272	1974	JoAnne Carner	87,094	1991	Pat Bradley	763,118
1958	Beverly Hanson	12,629	1975	Sandra Palmer	94,805	1992	Dottie Mochrie	693,335
1959	Betsy Rawls	26,774	1976	Judy Rankin	150,734	1993	Betsy King	595,992
1960	Louise Suggs	16,892	1977	Judy Rankin	122,890	1994	Laura Davies	687,201
1961	Mickey Wright	22,236	1978	Nancy Lopez	189,813	1995	Annika Sorenstam	666,533
1962	Mickey Wright	21,641	1979	Nancy Lopez	215,987	1996	Karrie Webb	1,002,000
1963	Mickey Wright	31,269	1980	Beth Daniel	231,000	1997	Annika Sorenstam	1,236,789
1964	Mickey Wright	29,800	1981	Beth Daniel	206,977	1998	Annika Sorenstam	1,092,748
1965	Kathy Whitworth	28,658	1982	JoAnne Carner	310,399	1999	Karrie Webb	1,591,959
1966	Kathy Whitworth	33,517	1983	JoAnne Carner	291,404	2000	Karrie Webb	1,876,853
1967	Kathy Whitworth	32,937	1984	Betsy King	266,771	2001	Annika Sorenstam	2,105,868
1968	Kathy Whitworth	48,379	1985	Nancy Lopez	416,472	2002	Annika Sorenstam	2,863,904
1969	Carol Mann	49,152	1986	Pat Bradley	492,021	2003	Annika Sorenstam	2,029,506
1970	Kathy Whitworth	30,235	1987	Ayako Okamoto	466,034	2004	Annika Sorenstam	2,544,707

Nabisco Championship Winners[1]

Year	Winner	Year	Winner	Year	Winner	Year	Winner
1983	Amy Alcott	1989	Juli Inkster	1995	Nanci Bowen	2000	Karrie Webb
1984	Juli Inkster	1990	Betsy King	1996	Patty Sheehan	2001	Annika Sorenstam
1985	Alice Miller	1991	Amy Alcott	1997	Betsy King	2002	Annika Sorenstam
1986	Pat Bradley	1992	Dottie Pepper	1998	Pat Hurst	2003	Patricia Meunier-Lebouc
1987	Betsy King	1993	Helen Alfredsson	1999	Dottie Pepper	2004	Grace Park
1988	Amy Alcott	1994	Donna Andrews			2005	Annika Sorenstam

(1) Formerly the Colgate Dinah Shore (1972-81), the Nabisco Dinah Shore (1982-99). Designated as a major championship in 1983.

LPGA Championship Winners

Year	Winner	Year	Winner	Year	Winner	Year	Winner
1955	Beverly Hanson	1968	Sandra Post	1981	Donna Caponi	1993	Patty Sheehan
1956	Marlene Hagge	1969	Betsy Rawls	1982	Jan Stephenson	1994	Laura Davies
1957	Louise Suggs	1970	Shirley Englehorn	1983	Patty Sheehan	1995	Kelly Robbins
1958	Mickey Wright	1971	Kathy Whitworth	1984	Patty Sheehan	1996	Laura Davies
1959	Betsy Rawls	1972	Kathy Ahern	1985	Nancy Lopez	1997	Chris Johnson
1960	Mickey Wright	1973	Mary Mills	1986	Pat Bradley	1998	Se Ri Pak
1961	Mickey Wright	1974	Sandra Haynie	1987	Jane Geddes	1999	Juli Inkster
1962	Judy Kimball	1975	Kathy Whitworth	1988	Sherri Turner	2000	Juli Inkster
1963	Mickey Wright	1976	Betty Burfeindt	1989	Nancy Lopez	2001	Karrie Webb
1964	Mary Mills	1977	Chako Higuchi	1990	Beth Daniel	2002	Se Ri Pak
1965	Sandra Haynie	1978	Nancy Lopez	1991	Meg Mallon	2003	Annika Sorenstam
1966	Gloria Ehret	1979	Donna Caponi	1992	Betsy King	2004	Annika Sorenstam
1967	Kathy Whitworth	1980	Sally Little			2005	Annika Sorenstam

U.S. Women's Open Winners

Year	Winner	Year	Winner	Year	Winner	Year	Winner
1946	Patty Berg	1961	Mickey Wright	1975	Sandra Palmer	1990	Betsy King
1947	Betty Jameson	1962	Murle Lindstrom	1976	JoAnne Carner	1991	Meg Mallon
1948	Babe Zaharias	1963	Mary Mills	1977	Hollis Stacy	1992	Patty Sheehan
1949	Louise Suggs	1964	Mickey Wright	1978	Hollis Stacy	1993	Lauri Merten
1950	Babe Zaharias	1965	Carol Mann	1979	Jerilyn Britz	1994	Patty Sheehan
1951	Betsy Rawls	1966	Sandra Spuzich	1980	Amy Alcott	1995	Annika Sorenstam
1952	Louise Suggs	1967	Catherine Lacoste (amateur)	1981	Pat Bradley	1996	Annika Sorenstam
1953	Betsy Rawls	1968	Susie Maxwell Berning	1982	Janet Alex	1997	Alison Nicholas
1954	Babe Zaharias	1969	Donna Caponi	1983	Jan Stephenson	1998	Se Ri Pak
1955	Fay Crocker	1970	Donna Caponi	1984	Hollis Stacy	1999	Juli Inkster
1956	Mrs. K. Cornelius	1971	JoAnne Carner	1985	Kathy Baker	2000	Karrie Webb
1957	Betsy Rawls	1972	Susie Maxwell Berning	1986	Jane Geddes	2001	Karrie Webb
1958	Mickey Wright	1973	Susie Maxwell Berning	1987	Laura Davies	2002	Juli Inkster
1959	Mickey Wright	1974	Sandra Haynie	1988	Liselotte Neumann	2003	Hilary Lunke
1960	Betsy Rawls			1989	Betsy King	2004	Meg Mallon
						2005	Birdie Kim

Women's British Open Winners[1]

Year	Winner	Year	Winner	Year	Winner	Year	Winner
2001	Se Ri Pak	2003	Annika Sorenstam	2004	Karen Stupples	2005	Jeong Jang
2002	Karrie Webb						

(1) First held as the Ladies' British Open in 1976; became the LPGA's 4th major championship in 2001, replacing the du Maurier Classic.

du Maurier Classic Winners[1]

Year	Winner	Year	Winner	Year	Winner	Year	Winner
1979	Amy Alcott	1985	Pat Bradley	1991	Nancy Scranton	1996	Laura Davies
1980	Pat Bradley	1986	Pat Bradley	1992	Sherri Steinhauer	1997	Colleen Walker
1981	Jan Stephenson	1987	Jody Rosenthal	1993	Brandie Burton	1998	Brandie Burton
1982	Sandra Haynie	1988	Sally Little	1994	Martha Nause	1999	Karrie Webb
1983	Hollis Stacy	1989	Tammie Green	1995	Jenny Lidback	2000	Meg Mallon
1984	Juli Inkster	1990	Cathy Johnston				

(1) Formerly the Peter Jackson Classic (1974-82). Designated a major championship, 1979-2000.

International Golf

Ryder Cup

Began as a biennial team competition between pro golfers from the U.S. and Great Britain. The British team was expanded in 1973 to include players from Ireland and in 1979 from the rest of Europe. Europe routed the Americans in the 2004 Ryder Cup, held Sept. 17-19 at Oakland Hills CC, Bloomfield Township, MI. The 2006 Ryder Cup was scheduled to be held Sept. 22-24 at K Club in Straffan, Ireland.

Year	Winner	Year	Winner	Year	Winner	Year	Winner
1927	U.S., 9½-2½	1951	U.S., 9½-2½	1969	Draw, 16-16	1987	Europe, 15-13
1929	Britain-Ireland, 7-5	1953	U.S., 6½-5½	1971	U.S., 18½-13½	1989	Draw, 14-14
1931	U.S., 9-3	1955	U.S., 8-4	1973	U.S., 19-13	1991	U.S., 14½-13½
1933	Britain, 6½-5½	1957	Britain-Ireland, 7½-4½	1975	U.S., 21-11	1993	U.S., 15-13
1935	U.S., 9-3	1959	U.S., 8½-3½	1977	U.S., 12½-7½	1995	Europe, 14½-13½
1937	U.S., 8-4	1961	U.S., 14½-9½	1979	U.S., 17-11	1997	Europe, 14½-13½
1939-45	Not played	1963	U.S., 23-9	1981	U.S., 18½-9½	1999	U.S., 14½-13½
1947	U.S., 11-1	1965	U.S., 19½-12½	1983	U.S., 14½-13½	2002	Europe, 15½-12½
1949	U.S., 7-5	1967	U.S., 23½-8½	1985	Europe, 16½-11½	2004	Europe, 18½-9½

Solheim Cup

Began in 1990 as a biennial team competition between pro women golfers from Europe and the U.S. Competition moved to odd years in 2003 to alternate with the Ryder Cup, which was postponed and moved to even years after the Sept. 2001 terrorist attacks. In 2005 the U.S. team defeated Europe at the Crooked Stick Golf Club in Carmel, IN, in the Sept. 11 final, after the first 2 days of competition ended with an 8-8 tie. Paula Creamer, at 19 the youngest Solheim competitor ever, won the first singles match over Laura Davies, and the U.S. won 6 additional matches to take the cup. The next Solheim Cup was scheduled for Sept. 14-16, 2007, at Halmstad Golfklubb in Sweden.

Year	Winner	Year	Winner	Year	Winner	Year	Winner
1990	U.S., 11½-4½	1996	U.S., 17-11	2000	Europe, 14½-11½	2003	Europe, 17½-10½
1992	Europe, 11½-6½	1998	U.S., 16-12	2002	U.S., 15½-12½	2005	U.S., 15-12
1994	U.S., 13-7						

TENNIS

Australian Open Singles Champions, 1969-2005

(First contested 1905 for men, 1922 for women. Became an Open Championship in 1969.)

*2 tournaments held in 1977 (Jan. & Dec.). **In 1986 tournament moved to Jan. 1987; no championship in 1986.

Men's Singles

Year	Champion	Final Opponent
1969	Rod Laver	Andres Gimeno
1970	Arthur Ashe	Dick Crealy
1971	Ken Rosewall	Arthur Ashe
1972	Ken Rosewall	Mal Anderson
1973	John Newcombe	Onny Parun
1974	Jimmy Connors	Phil Dent
1975	John Newcombe	Jimmy Connors
1976	Mark Edmondson	John Newcombe
1977*	Roscoe Tanner	Guillermo Vilas
	Vitas Gerulaitis	John Lloyd
1978	Guillermo Vilas	John Marks
1979	Guillermo Vilas	John Sadri
1980	Brian Teacher	Kim Warwick
1981	Johan Kriek	Steve Denton
1982	Johan Kriek	Steve Denton
1983	Mats Wilander	Ivan Lendl
1984	Mats Wilander	Kevin Curren
1985**	Stefan Edberg	Mats Wilander
1987	Stefan Edberg	Pat Cash
1988	Mats Wilander	Pat Cash
1989	Ivan Lendl	Miloslav Mecir
1990	Ivan Lendl	Stefan Edberg
1991	Boris Becker	Ivan Lendl
1992	Jim Courier	Stefan Edberg
1993	Jim Courier	Stefan Edberg
1994	Pete Sampras	Todd Martin
1995	Andre Agassi	Pete Sampras
1996	Boris Becker	Michael Chang
1997	Pete Sampras	Carlos Moya
1998	Petr Korda	Marcelo Rios
1999	Yevgeny Kafelnikov	Thomas Enqvist
2000	Andre Agassi	Yevgeny Kafelnikov
2001	Andre Agassi	Arnaud Clement
2002	Thomas Johansson	Marat Safin
2003	Andre Agassi	Rainer Schuettler
2004	Roger Federer	Marat Safin
2005	Marat Safin	Lleyton Hewitt

Women's Singles

Year	Champion	Final Opponent
1969	Margaret Smith Court	Billie Jean King
1970	Margaret Smith Court	Kerry Melville Reid
1971	Margaret Smith Court	Evonne Goolagong
1972	Virginia Wade	Evonne Goolagong
1973	Margaret Smith Court	Evonne Goolagong
1974	Evonne Goolagong	Chris Evert
1975	Evonne Goolagong	Martina Navratilova
1976	Evonne Goolagong	Renata Tomanova
1977*	Kerry Reid	Dianne Balestrat
	Evonne Goolagong	Helen Gourlay
1978	Chris O'Neill	Betsy Nagelsen
1979	Barbara Jordan	Sharon Walsh
1980	Hana Mandlikova	Wendy Turnbull
1981	Martina Navratilova	Chris Evert Lloyd
1982	Chris Evert Lloyd	Martina Navratilova
1983	Martina Navratilova	Kathy Jordan
1984	Chris Evert Lloyd	Helena Sukova
1985**	Martina Navratilova	Chris Evert Lloyd
1987	Hana Mandlikova	Martina Navratilova
1988	Steffi Graf	Chris Evert
1989	Steffi Graf	Helena Sukova
1990	Steffi Graf	Mary Joe Fernandez
1991	Monica Seles	Jana Novotna
1992	Monica Seles	Mary Joe Fernandez
1993	Monica Seles	Steffi Graf
1994	Steffi Graf	Arantxa Sánchez Vicario
1995	Mary Pierce	Arantxa Sánchez Vicario
1996	Monica Seles	Anke Huber
1997	Martina Hingis	Mary Pierce
1998	Martina Hingis	Conchita Martínez
1999	Martina Hingis	Amelie Mauresmo
2000	Lindsay Davenport	Martina Hingis
2001	Jennifer Capriati	Martina Hingis
2002	Jennifer Capriati	Martina Hingis
2003	Serena Williams	Venus Williams
2004	Justine Henin-Hardenne	Kim Clijsters
2005	Serena Williams	Lindsay Davenport

French Open Singles Champions, 1968-2005

(First contested 1891 for men, 1897 for women. Became an Open Championship in 1968.)

Men's Singles

Year	Champion	Final Opponent
1968	Ken Rosewall	Rod Laver
1969	Rod Laver	Ken Rosewall
1970	Jan Kodes	Zeljko Franulovic
1971	Jan Kodes	Ilie Nastase
1972	Andres Gimeno	Patrick Proisy
1973	Ilie Nastase	Nikki Pilic
1974	Bjorn Borg	Manuel Orantes
1975	Bjorn Borg	Guillermo Vilas
1976	Adriano Panatta	Harold Solomon
1977	Guillermo Vilas	Brian Gottfried
1978	Bjorn Borg	Guillermo Vilas
1979	Bjorn Borg	Victor Pecci
1980	Bjorn Borg	Vitas Gerulaitis
1981	Bjorn Borg	Ivan Lendl
1982	Mats Wilander	Guillermo Vilas
1983	Yannick Noah	Mats Wilander
1984	Ivan Lendl	John McEnroe
1985	Mats Wilander	Ivan Lendl
1986	Ivan Lendl	Mikael Pernfors
1987	Ivan Lendl	Mats Wilander
1988	Mats Wilander	Henri Leconte
1989	Michael Chang	Stefan Edberg
1990	Andres Gomez	Andre Agassi
1991	Jim Courier	Andre Agassi
1992	Jim Courier	Petr Korda
1993	Sergi Bruguera	Jim Courier
1994	Sergi Bruguera	Alberto Berasategui
1995	Thomas Muster	Michael Chang
1996	Yevgeny Kafelnikov	Michael Stich
1997	Gustavo Kuerten	Sergei Bruguera
1998	Carlos Moya	Alex Corretja
1999	Andre Agassi	Andrei Medvedev
2000	Gustavo Kuerten	Magnus Norman
2001	Gustavo Kuerten	Alex Corretja
2002	Albert Costa	Juan Carlos Ferrero
2003	Juan Carlos Ferrero	Martin Verkerk
2004	Gaston Gaudio	Guillermo Coria
2005	Rafael Nadal	Mariano Puerta

Women's Singles

Year	Champion	Final Opponent
1968	Nancy Richey	Ann Jones
1969	Margaret Smith Court	Ann Jones
1970	Margaret Smith Court	Helga Niessen
1971	Evonne Goolagong	Helen Gourlay
1972	Billie Jean King	Evonne Goolagong
1973	Margaret Smith Court	Chris Evert
1974	Chris Evert	Olga Morozova
1975	Chris Evert	Martina Navratilova
1976	Sue Barker	Renata Tomanova
1977	Mima Jausovec	Florenza Mihai
1978	Virginia Ruzici	Mima Jausovec
1979	Chris Evert Lloyd	Wendy Turnbull
1980	Chris Evert Lloyd	Virginia Ruzici
1981	Hana Mandlikova	Sylvia Hanika
1982	Martina Navratilova	Andrea Jaeger
1983	Chris Evert Lloyd	Mima Jausovec
1984	Martina Navratilova	Chris Evert Lloyd
1985	Chris Evert Lloyd	Martina Navratilova
1986	Chris Evert Lloyd	Martina Navratilova
1987	Steffi Graf	Martina Navratilova
1988	Steffi Graf	Natalia Zvereva
1989	Arantxa Sánchez Vicario	Steffi Graf
1990	Monica Seles	Steffi Graf
1991	Monica Seles	Arantxa Sánchez Vicario
1992	Monica Seles	Steffi Graf
1993	Steffi Graf	Mary Joe Fernandez
1994	Arantxa Sánchez Vicario	Mary Pierce
1995	Steffi Graf	Arantxa Sánchez Vicario
1996	Steffi Graf	Arantxa Sánchez Vicario
1997	Iva Majoli	Martina Hingis
1998	Arantxa Sánchez Vicario	Monica Seles
1999	Steffi Graf	Martina Hingis
2000	Mary Pierce	Conchita Martinez
2001	Jennifer Capriati	Kim Clijsters
2002	Serena Williams	Venus Williams
2003	Justine Henin-Hardenne	Kim Clijsters
2004	Anastasia Myskina	Elena Dementieva
2005	Justine Henin-Hardenne	Mary Pierce

U.S. Open Champions, 1925-2005

(Became an Open Championship in 1970.)

Men's Singles

(First contested 1881)

Year	Champion	Final Opponent
1925	Bill Tilden	William Johnston
1926	Rene Lacoste	Jean Borotra
1927	Rene Lacoste	Bill Tilden
1928	Henri Cochet	Francis Hunter
1929	Bill Tilden	Francis Hunter
1930	John Doeg	Francis Shields
1931	H. Ellsworth Vines	George Lott
1932	H. Ellsworth Vines	Henri Cochet
1933	Fred Perry	John Crawford
1934	Fred Perry	Wilmer Allison
1935	Wilmer Allison	Sidney Wood
1936	Fred Perry	Don Budge
1937	Don Budge	Baron G. von Cramm
1938	Don Budge	C. Gene Mako
1939	Robert Riggs	S. Welby Van Horn
1940	Don McNeill	Robert Riggs
1941	Robert Riggs	F. L. Kovacs
1942	F. R. Schroeder Jr.	Frank Parker
1943	Joseph Hunt	Jack Kramer
1944	Frank Parker	William Talbert
1945	Frank Parker	William Talbert
1946	Jack Kramer	Thomas Brown Jr.
1947	Jack Kramer	Frank Parker
1948	Pancho Gonzales	Eric Sturgess
1949	Pancho Gonzales	F. R. Schroeder Jr.
1950	Arthur Larsen	Herbert Flam
1951	Frank Sedgman	E. Victor Seixas Jr.
1952	Frank Sedgman	Gardnar Mulloy
1953	Tony Trabert	E. Victor Seixas Jr.
1954	E. Victor Seixas Jr.	Rex Hartwig
1955	Tony Trabert	Ken Rosewall
1956	Ken Rosewall	Lewis Hoad
1957	Malcolm Anderson	Ashley Cooper
1958	Ashley Cooper	Malcolm Anderson
1959	Neale A. Fraser	Alejandro Olmedo
1960	Neale A. Fraser	Rod Laver
1961	Roy Emerson	Rod Laver
1962	Rod Laver	Roy Emerson
1963	Rafael Osuna	F. A. Froehling 3rd
1964	Roy Emerson	Fred Stolle
1965	Manuel Santana	Cliff Drysdale
1966	Fred Stolle	John Newcombe
1967	John Newcombe	Clark Graebner
1968	Arthur Ashe	Tom Okker
1969	Rod Laver	Tony Roche
1970	Ken Rosewall	Tony Roche
1971	Stan Smith	Jan Kodes
1972	Ilie Nastase	Arthur Ashe
1973	John Newcombe	Jan Kodes
1974	Jimmy Connors	Ken Rosewall
1975	Manuel Orantes	Jimmy Connors
1976	Jimmy Connors	Bjorn Borg
1977	Guillermo Vilas	Jimmy Connors
1978	Jimmy Connors	Bjorn Borg
1979	John McEnroe	Vitas Gerulaitis
1980	John McEnroe	Bjorn Borg
1981	John McEnroe	Bjorn Borg
1982	Jimmy Connors	Ivan Lendl
1983	Jimmy Connors	Ivan Lendl
1984	John McEnroe	Ivan Lendl
1985	Ivan Lendl	John McEnroe
1986	Ivan Lendl	Miloslav Mecir
1987	Ivan Lendl	Mats Wilander
1988	Mats Wilander	Ivan Lendl
1989	Boris Becker	Ivan Lendl
1990	Pete Sampras	Andre Agassi
1991	Stefan Edberg	Jim Courier
1992	Stefan Edberg	Pete Sampras
1993	Pete Sampras	Cedric Pioline
1994	Andre Agassi	Michael Stich
1995	Pete Sampras	Andre Agassi
1996	Pete Sampras	Michael Chang
1997	Patrick Rafter	Greg Rusedski
1998	Patrick Rafter	Mark Philippoussis
1999	Andre Agassi	Todd Martin
2000	Marat Safin	Pete Sampras
2001	Lleyton Hewitt	Pete Sampras
2002	Pete Sampras	Andre Agassi
2003	Andy Roddick	Juan Carlos Ferrero
2004	Roger Federer	Lleyton Hewitt
2005	Roger Federer	Andre Agassi

Women's Singles

(First contested 1887)

Year	Champion	Final Opponent
1925	Helen Willis	Kathleen McKane
1926	Molla B. Mallory	Elizabeth Ryan
1927	Helen Wills	Betty Nuthall
1928	Helen Wills	Helen Jacobs
1929	Helen Wills	M. Watson
1930	Betty Nuthall	L. A. Harper
1931	Helen Wills Moody	E. B. Whittingstall
1932	Helen Jacobs	Carolin A. Babcock
1933	Helen Jacobs	Helen Wills Moody
1934	Helen Jacobs	Sarah H. Palfrey
1935	Helen Jacobs	Sarah Palfrey Fabyan
1936	Alice Marble	Helen Jacobs
1937	Anita Lizana	Jadwiga Jedrzejowska
1938	Alice Marble	Nancye Wynne
1939	Alice Marble	Helen Jacobs
1940	Alice Marble	Helen Jacobs
1941	Sarah Palfrey Cooke	Pauline Betz
1942	Pauline Betz	Louise Brough
1943	Pauline Betz	Louise Brough
1944	Pauline Betz	Margaret Osborne
1945	Sarah Palfrey Cooke	Pauline Betz
1946	Pauline Betz	Doris Hart
1947	Louise Brough	Margaret Osborne
1948	Margaret Osborne duPont	Louise Brough
1949	Margaret Osborne duPont	Doris Hart
1950	Margaret Osborne duPont	Doris Hart
1951	Maureen Connolly	Shirley Fry
1952	Maureen Connolly	Doris Hart
1953	Maureen Connolly	Doris Hart
1954	Doris Hart	Louise Brough
1955	Doris Hart	Patricia Ward
1956	Shirley Fry	Althea Gibson
1957	Althea Gibson	Louise Brough
1958	Althea Gibson	Darlene Hard
1959	Maria Bueno	Christine Truman
1960	Darlene Hard	Maria Bueno
1961	Darlene Hard	Ann Haydon
1962	Margaret Smith	Darlene Hard
1963	Maria Bueno	Margaret Smith
1964	Maria Bueno	Carole Graebner
1965	Margaret Smith	Billie Jean Moffitt
1966	Maria Bueno	Nancy Richey
1967	Billie Jean King	Ann Haydon Jones
1968	Virginia Wade	Billie Jean King
1969	Margaret Smith Court	Nancy Richey
1970	Margaret Smith Court	Rosemary Casals
1971	Billie Jean King	Rosemary Casals
1972	Billie Jean King	Kerry Melville
1973	Margaret Smith Court	Evonne Goolagong
1974	Billie Jean King	Evonne Goolagong
1975	Chris Evert	Evonne Goolagong
1976	Chris Evert	Evonne Goolagong
1977	Chris Evert	Wendy Turnbull
1978	Chris Evert	Pam Shriver
1979	Tracy Austin	Chris Evert Lloyd
1980	Chris Evert Lloyd	Hana Mandlikova
1981	Tracy Austin	Martina Navratilova
1982	Chris Evert Lloyd	Hana Mandlikova
1983	Martina Navratilova	Chris Evert Lloyd
1984	Martina Navratilova	Chris Evert Lloyd
1985	Hana Mandlikova	Martina Navratilova
1986	Martina Navratilova	Helena Sukova
1987	Martina Navratilova	Steffi Graf
1988	Steffi Graf	Gabriela Sabatini
1989	Steffi Graf	Martina Navratilova
1990	Gabriela Sabatini	Steffi Graf
1991	Monica Seles	Martina Navratilova
1992	Monica Seles	Arantxa Sanchez Vicario
1993	Steffi Graf	Helena Sukova
1994	Arantxa Sanchez Vicario	Steffi Graf
1995	Steffi Graf	Monica Seles
1996	Steffi Graf	Monica Seles
1997	Martina Hingis	Venus Williams
1998	Lindsay Davenport	Martina Hingis
1999	Serena Williams	Martina Hingis
2000	Venus Williams	Lindsay Davenport
2001	Venus Williams	Serena Williams
2002	Serena Williams	Venus Williams
2003	Justine Henin-Hardenne	Kim Clijsters
2004	Svetlana Kuznetsova	Elena Dementieva
2005	Kim Clijsters	Mary Pierce

All-England Champions, Wimbledon, 1925-2005

(First contested 1877 for men, 1884 for women. Became an Open Championship in 1968. Not held 1940-45)

Men's Singles

Year	Champion	Final Opponent
1925	Rene Lacoste	Jean Borotra
1926	Jean Borotra	Howard Kinsey
1927	Henri Cochet	Jean Borotra
1928	Rene Lacoste	Henri Cochet
1929	Henri Cochet	Jean Borotra
1930	Bill Tilden	Wilmer Allison
1931	Sidney B. Wood	Francis X. Shields
1932	Ellsworth Vines	Henry Austin
1933	Jack Crawford	Ellsworth Vines
1934	Fred Perry	Jack Crawford
1935	Fred Perry	Gottfried von Cramm
1936	Fred Perry	Gottfried von Cramm
1937	Donald Budge	Gottfried von Cramm
1938	Donald Budge	Henry Austin
1939	Bobby Riggs	Elwood Cooke
1946	Yvon Petra	Geoff E. Brown
1947	Jack Kramer	Tom P. Brown
1948	Bob Falkenburg	John Bromwich
1949	Ted Schroeder	Jaroslav Drobny
1950	Budge Patty	Frank Sedgman
1951	Dick Savitt	Ken McGregor
1952	Frank Sedgman	Jaroslav Drobny
1953	Vic Seixas	Kurt Nielsen
1954	Jaroslav Drobny	Ken Rosewall
1955	Tony Trabert	Kurt Nielsen
1956	Lew Hoad	Ken Rosewall
1957	Lew Hoad	Ashley Cooper
1958	Ashley Cooper	Neale Fraser
1959	Alex Olmedo	Rod Laver
1960	Neale Fraser	Rod Laver
1961	Rod Laver	Chuck McKinley
1962	Rod Laver	Martin Mulligan
1963	Chuck McKinley	Fred Stolle
1964	Roy Emerson	Fred Stolle
1965	Roy Emerson	Fred Stolle
1966	Manuel Santana	Dennis Ralston
1967	John Newcombe	Wilhelm Bungert
1968	Rod Laver	Tony Roche
1969	Rod Laver	John Newcombe
1970	John Newcombe	Ken Rosewall
1971	John Newcombe	Stan Smith
1972	Stan Smith	Ilie Nastase
1973	Jan Kodes	Alex Metreveli
1974	Jimmy Connors	Ken Rosewall
1975	Arthur Ashe	Jimmy Connors
1976	Bjorn Borg	Ilie Nastase
1977	Bjorn Borg	Jimmy Connors
1978	Bjorn Borg	Jimmy Connors
1979	Bjorn Borg	Roscoe Tanner
1980	Bjorn Borg	John McEnroe
1981	John McEnroe	Bjorn Borg
1982	Jimmy Connors	John McEnroe
1983	John McEnroe	Chris Lewis
1984	John McEnroe	Jimmy Connors
1985	Boris Becker	Kevin Curren
1986	Boris Becker	Ivan Lendl
1987	Pat Cash	Ivan Lendl
1988	Stefan Edberg	Boris Becker
1989	Boris Becker	Stefan Edberg
1990	Stefan Edberg	Boris Becker
1991	Michael Stich	Boris Becker
1992	Andre Agassi	Goran Ivanisevic
1993	Pete Sampras	Jim Courier
1994	Pete Sampras	Goran Ivanisevic
1995	Pete Sampras	Boris Becker
1996	Richard Krajicek	MaliVai Washington
1997	Pete Sampras	Cedric Pioline
1998	Pete Sampras	Goran Ivanisevic
1999	Pete Sampras	Andre Agassi
2000	Pete Sampras	Patrick Rafter
2001	Goran Ivanisevic	Patrick Rafter
2002	Lleyton Hewitt	David Nalbandian
2003	Roger Federer	Mark Philippoussis
2004	Roger Federer	Andy Roddick
2005	Roger Federer	Andy Roddick

Women's Singles

Year	Champion	Final Opponent
1925	Suzanne Lenglen	Joan Fry
1926	Kathleen McKane Godfree	Lili de Alvarez
1927	Helen Wills	Lili de Alvarez
1928	Helen Wills	Lili de Alvarez
1929	Helen Wills	Helen Jacobs
1930	Helen Wills Moody	Elizabeth Ryan
1931	Cilly Aussem	Hilde Kranwinkel
1932	Helen Wills Moody	Helen Jacobs
1933	Helen Wills Moody	Dorothy Round
1934	Dorothy Round	Helen Jacobs
1935	Helen Wills Moody	Helen Jacobs
1936	Helen Jacobs	Hilde Kranwinkel Sperling
1937	Dorothy Round	Jadwiga Jedrzejowska
1938	Helen Wills Moody	Helen Jacobs
1939	Alice Marble	Kay Stammers
1946	Pauline Betz	Louise Brough
1947	Margaret Osborne	Doris Hart
1948	Louise Brough	Doris Hart
1949	Louise Brough	Margaret Osborne duPont
1950	Louise Brough	Margaret Osborne duPont
1951	Doris Hart	Shirley Fry
1952	Maureen Connolly	Louise Brough
1953	Maureen Connolly	Doris Hart
1954	Maureen Connolly	Louise Brough
1955	Louise Brough	Beverly Fleitz
1956	Shirley Fry	Angela Buxton
1957	Althea Gibson	Darlene Hard
1958	Althea Gibson	Angela Mortimer
1959	Maria Bueno	Darlene Hard
1960	Maria Bueno	Sandra Reynolds
1961	Angela Mortimer	Christine Truman
1962	Karen Hantze-Susman	Vera Sukova
1963	Margaret Smith	Billie Jean Moffitt
1964	Maria Bueno	Margaret Smith
1965	Margaret Smith	Maria Bueno
1966	Billie Jean King	Maria Bueno
1967	Billie Jean King	Ann Haydon Jones
1968	Billie Jean King	Judy Tegart
1969	Ann Haydon-Jones	Billie Jean King
1970	Margaret Smith Court	Billie Jean King
1971	Evonne Goolagong	Margaret Smith Court
1972	Billie Jean King	Evonne Goolagong
1973	Billie Jean King	Chris Evert
1974	Chris Evert	Olga Morozova
1975	Billie Jean King	Evonne Goolagong Cawley
1976	Chris Evert	Evonne Goolagong Cawley
1977	Virginia Wade	Betty Stove
1978	Martina Navratilova	Chris Evert
1979	Martina Navratilova	Chris Evert Lloyd
1980	Evonne Goolagong	Chris Evert Lloyd
1981	Chris Evert Lloyd	Hana Mandlikova
1982	Martina Navratilova	Chris Evert Lloyd
1983	Martina Navratilova	Andrea Jaeger
1984	Martina Navratilova	Chris Evert Lloyd
1985	Martina Navratilova	Chris Evert Lloyd
1986	Martina Navratilova	Hana Mandlikova
1987	Martina Navratilova	Steffi Graf
1988	Steffi Graf	Martina Navratilova
1989	Steffi Graf	Martina Navratilova
1990	Martina Navratilova	Zina Garrison
1991	Steffi Graf	Gabriela Sabatini
1992	Steffi Graf	Monica Seles
1993	Steffi Graf	Jana Novotna
1994	Conchita Martinez	Martina Navratilova
1995	Steffi Graf	Arantxa Sánchez Vicario
1996	Steffi Graf	Arantxa Sánchez Vicario
1997	Martina Hingis	Jana Novotna
1998	Jana Novotna	Nathalie Tauziat
1999	Lindsay Davenport	Steffi Graf
2000	Venus Williams	Lindsay Davenport
2001	Venus Williams	Justine Henin
2002	Serena Williams	Venus Williams
2003	Serena Williams	Venus Williams
2004	Maria Sharapova	Serena Williams
2005	Venus Williams	Lindsay Davenport

WORLD ALMANAC QUICK QUIZ

Can you rank these tennis champions by the number of career grand slam singles titles each one achieved (from most to fewest)?

(a) Martina Navratilova (b) Pete Sampras (c) Ivan Lendl (d) Bjorn Borg

For the answer look in this chapter, or see page 1008.

Davis Cup, 1900-2004*

Year	Result	Year	Result	Year	Result
1900	United States 3, British Isles 0	1936	Great Britain 3, Australia 2	1973	Australia 5, United States 0
1901	Not held	1937	United States 4, Great Britain 1	1974	South Africa (default by India)
1902	United States 3, British Isles 2	1938	United States 3, Australia 2	1975	Sweden 3, Czechoslovakia 2
1903	British Isles 4, United States 1	1939	Australia 3, United States 2	1976	Italy 4, Chile 1
1904	British Isles 5, Belgium 0	1940-45	Not held	1977	Australia 3, Italy 1
1905	British Isles 5, United States 0	1946	United States 5, Australia 0	1978	United States 4, Great Britain 1
1906	British Isles 5, United States 0	1947	United States 4, Australia 1	1979	United States 5, Italy 0
1907	Australia 3, British Isles 2	1948	United States 5, Australia 0	1980	Czechoslovakia 4, Italy 1
1908	Australasia 3, United States 2	1949	United States 4, Australia 1	1981	United States 3, Argentina 1
1909	Australasia 5, United States 0	1950	Australia 4, United States 1	1982	United States 4, France, 1
1910	Not held	1951	Australia 3, United States 2	1983	Australia 3, Sweden 2
1911	Australasia 5, United States 0	1952	Australia 4, United States 1	1984	Sweden 4, United States 1
1912	British Isles 3, Australasia 2	1953	Australia 3, United States 2	1985	Sweden 3, W. Germany 2
1913	United States 3, British Isles 2	1954	United States 3, Australia 2	1986	Australia 3, Sweden 2
1914	Australasia 3, United States 2	1955	Australia 5, United States 0	1987	Sweden 5, India 0
1915-18	Not held	1956	Australia 5, United States 0	1988	W. Germany 4, Sweden 1
1919	Australasia 4, British Isles 1	1957	Australia 3, United States 2	1989	W. Germany 3, Sweden 2
1920	United States 5, Australasia 0	1958	United States 3, Australia 2	1990	United States 3, Australia 2
1921	United States 5, Japan 0	1959	Australia 3, United States 2	1991	France 3, United States 1
1922	United States 4, Australasia 1	1960	Australia 4, Italy 1	1992	United States 3, Switzerland 1
1923	United States 4, Australasia 1	1961	Australia 5, Italy 0	1993	Germany 4, Australia 1
1924	United States 5, Australasia 0	1962	Australia 5, Mexico 0	1994	Sweden 4, Russia 1
1925	United States 5, France 0	1963	United States 3, Australia 2	1995	United States 3, Russia 2
1926	United States 4, France 1	1964	Australia 3, United States 2	1996	France 3, Sweden 2
1927	France 3, United States 2	1965	Australia 4, Spain 1	1997	Sweden 5, United States 0
1928	France 4, United States 1	1966	Australia 4, India 1	1998	Sweden 4, Italy 1
1929	France 3, United States 2	1967	Australia 4, Spain 1	1999	Australia 3, France 2
1930	France 4, United States 1	1968	United States 4, Australia	2000	Spain 3, Australia 1
1931	France 3, Great Britain 2	1969	United States 5, Romania 0	2001	France 3, Australia 2
1932	France 3, United States 2	1970	United States 5, W. Germany 0	2002	Russia 3, France 2
1933	Great Britain 3, France 2	1971	United States 3, Romania 2	2003	Australia 3, Spain 1
1934	Great Britain 4, United States 1	1972	United States 3, Romania 2	2004	Spain 3, U.S. 2
1935	Great Britain 5, United States 0				

*The challenge round format, which guaranteed the previous year's winner a spot in the finals at home, was eliminated in 1972.

All-Time Grand Slam Singles Titles Leaders

Men	Australian Open	French Open[2]	Wimbledon	U.S. Open	Total
Pete Sampras	1994, '97	—	1993-95, 1997-2000	1990, '93, '95-96, 2002	14
Roy Emerson	1961, '63-67	1963, '67	1964-65	1961, '64	12
Bjorn Borg	—	1974-75, 1978-81	1976-80	—	11
Rod Laver	1960, '62, '69	1962, '69	1961-62, '68-69	1962, '69	11
Bill Tilden	—	—	1920-21, '30	1920-25, '29	10
Andre Agassi[1]	1995, 2000, '01, '03	1999	1992	1994, '99	8
Jimmy Connors	1974	—	1974, '82	1974, '76, '78, '82-83	8
Ivan Lendl	1989-90	1984, '86-87	—	1985-87	8
Fred Perry	1934	1935	1934-36	1933-34, '36	8
Ken Rosewall	1953, '55, '71-72	1953, '68	—	1956, '70	8
Women					
Margaret Smith Court	1960-66, '69-71, '73	1962, '64, '69-70, '73	1963, '65, '70	1962, '65, '69-70, '73	24
Steffi Graf	1988-90, '94	1987-88, '93, '95-96, '99	1988-89, '91-93, '95-96	1988-89, '93, '95-96	22
Helen Wills Moody	—	1928-30, '32	1927-30, '32-33, '35, '38	1923-25, '27-29, '31	19
Chris Evert Lloyd	1982, '84	1974-75, '79-80, '83, '85-86	1974, '76, '81	1975-78, '80, '82	18
Martina Navratilova	1981, '83, '85	1982, '84	1978-79, '82-87, '90	1983-84, '86-87	18
Billie Jean King	1968	1972	1966-68, '72-73, '75	1967, '71-72, '74	12
Suzanne Lenglen	—	1920-23, '25-26	1919-23, '25	—	12
Maureen Connolly	1953	1953-54	1952-54	1951-53	9
Monica Seles[1]	1991-93, '96	1990-92	—	1991-92	9

(1) Active player in 2004. (2) Prior to 1925, French Open entry was limited to members of French clubs.

RIFLE AND PISTOL INDIVIDUAL CHAMPIONSHIPS

Source: National Rifle Association

NRA Bianchi Cup National Action Pistol Championships in 2005

Action Pistol—Doug Koenig, Albertus, PA, 1920-185x
Woman Action Pistol—Vera Koo, Menlo Park, CA, 1894-149x
Junior Action Pistol—Jordan Dick, Hutchinson, KS, 1888-136x

National Outdoor Rifle and Pistol Championships in 2005

Pistol—Gunnery Sgt. Brian H. Zins, USMC, King George, VA, 2645-111x
Civilian Pistol—Kimberly L. Hobart, New Philadelphia, OH, 2562-79x
Woman Pistol—Kimberly L. Hobart, New Philadelphia, OH, 2562-79x
Smallbore Rifle Prone—SFC Thomas A. Tamas, USA, Pittsview, AL, 6395-559x
Civilian Smallbore Rifle Prone—Jamie L. Beyerle, Lebanon, PA, 6394-513x
Woman Smallbore Rifle Prone—Jamie L. Beyerle, Lebanon, PA, 6394-513x
Smallbore Rifle NRA 3-Position—SGT Shane M. Barnhart, USA, Phenix City, AL, 2282-88x
Civilian Smallbore Rifle NRA 3-Position—Vincent P. Pestilli, Lebanon, PA, 2276-78x
Woman Smallbore Rifle NRA 3-Position—Jamie L. Beyerle, Lebanon, PA, 2266-75x
High Power Rifle—Dennis W. Demille, Oceanside, CA, 2385-119x
Civilian High Power Rifle—Dennis W. Demille, Oceanside, CA, 2385–119x
Woman High Power Rifle—GYSG Julia L. Watson, Albuquerque, NM, 2366-93x
High Power Rifle Long Range—Norman F. Crawford, Fayetteville, NC, 1444-68x
Woman High Power Rifle Long Range—Nancy H. Tompkins-Gallagher, Prescott, AZ, 1440-91x

National Indoor Rifle and Pistol Championships in 2005

Smallbore Rifle 4-Position—Jason Parker, Fortson, GA, 800-76x
Woman Smallbore Rifle 4-Position—Michelle Bohren, Taylor, MI, 794-68x
Smallbore Rifle NRA 3-Position—Jamie Beyerle, Lebanon, PA, 1188-86x
Woman Smallbore Rifle NRA 3-Position—Jamie Beyerle, Lebanon, PA, 1188-86x
International Smallbore Rifle—Jamie Beyerle, Lebanon, PA, 1189-80x
Woman International Smallbore Rifle—Jamie Beyerle, Lebanon, PA, 1189-80x
Air Rifle—Jason Parker, Fortson, GA, 597-50x
Woman Air Rifle—Jamie Beyerle, Lebanon, PA, 590-20x
Conventional Pistol—Christopher Johnson, Libertyville, IL, 885-35x
Woman Conventional Pistol—Kathy Chatterton, Glen Rock, NJ, 862-21x
International Free Pistol—John Zurek, Phoenix, AZ, 557-50x
Woman International Free Pistol—Leslie Nelson, Salt Lake City, UT, 501-20x
International Standard Pistol—Eric Weeldreyer, Kalamazoo, MI, 568-50x
Woman International Standard Pistol—Frances Spear, Harpursville, NY, 543-20x
Air Pistol—John Zurek, Phoenix, AZ, 581-50x
Woman Air Pistol—Vladimira Borisora, Schiller Park, IL 563-20x

AUTO RACING

Indianapolis 500 Winners, 1911-2005

(At Indianapolis Motor Speedway in Indianapolis, IN)

Year	Winner, Car (Chassis-Engine)	MPH[1]
1911	Ray Harroun, Marmon	74.602
1912	Joe Dawson, National	78.719
1913	Jules Goux, Peugeot	75.933
1914	Rene Thomas, Delage	82.474
1915	Ralph DePalma, Mercedes	89.840
1916	Dario Resta, Peugeot	84.001
1917-18	Not held	
1919	Howdy Wilcox, Peugeot	88.050
1920	Gaston Chevrolet, Frontenac	88.618
1921	Tommy Milton, Frontenac	89.621
1922	Jimmy Murphy, Duesenberg-Miller	94.484
1923	Tommy Milton, Miller	90.954
1924	L.L. Corum-Joe Boyer, Duesenberg	98.234
1925	Peter DePaolo, Duesenberg	101.127
1926	Frank Lockhart, Miller	95.904
1927	George Souders, Duesenberg	97.545
1928	Louie Meyer, Miller	99.482
1929	Ray Keech, Miller	97.585
1930	Billy Arnold, Summers-Miller	100.448
1931	Louis Schneider, Stevens-Miller	96.629
1932	Fred Frame, Wetteroth-Miller	104.144
1933	Louie Meyer, Miller	104.162
1934	Bill Cummings, Miller	104.863
1935	Kelly Petillo, Wetteroth-Offy	106.240
1936	Louie Meyer, Stevens-Miller	109.069
1937	Wilbur Shaw, Shaw-Offy	113.580
1938	Floyd Roberts, Wetteroth-Miller	117.200
1939	Wilbur Shaw, Maserati	115.035
1940	Wilbur Shaw, Maserati	114.277
1941	Floyd Davis-Mauri Rose, Wetteroth-Offy	115.117
1942-45	Not held	
1946	George Robson, Adams-Sparks	114.820
1947	Mauri Rose, Deidt-Offy	116.338
1948	Mauri Rose, Deidt-Offy	119.814
1949	Bill Holland, Deidt-Offy	121.327
1950	Johnnie Parsons, Kurtis-Offy	124.002
1951	Lee Wallard, Kurtis-Offy	126.244
1952	Troy Ruttman, Kuzma-Offy	128.922
1953	Bill Vukovich, KK500A-Offy	128.740
1954	Bill Vukovich, KK500A-Offy	130.840
1955	Bob Sweikert, KK500C-Offy	128.213
1956	Pat Flaherty, Watson-Offy	128.490
1957	Sam Hanks, Salih-Offy	135.601
1958	Jimmy Bryan, Salih-Offy	133.791
1959	Rodger Ward, Watson-Offy	135.857
1960	Jim Rathmann, Watson-Offy	138.767
1961	A.J. Foyt Jr., Trevis-Offy	139.130
1962	Rodger Ward, Watson-Offy	140.293
1963	Parnelli Jones, Watson-Offy	143.137
1964	A.J. Foyt Jr., Watson-Offy	147.350
1965	Jim Clark, Lotus-Ford	150.686
1966	Graham Hill, Lola-Ford	144.317
1967	A.J. Foyt Jr., Coyote-Ford	151.207
1968	Bobby Unser, Eagle-Offy	152.882
1969	Mario Andretti, Hawk-Ford	156.867
1970	Al Unser, P.J. Colt-Ford	155.749
1971	Al Unser, P.J. Colt-Ford	157.735
1972	Mark Donohue, McLaren-Offy	162.962
1973	Gordon Johncock, Eagle-Offy	159.036
1974	Johnny Rutherford, McLaren-Offy	158.589
1975	Bobby Unser, Eagle-Offy	149.213
1976	Johnny Rutherford, McLaren-Offy	148.725
1977	A.J. Foyt Jr., Coyote-Foyt	161.331
1978	Al Unser, Lola-Cosworth	161.363
1979	Rick Mears, Penske-Cosworth	158.899
1980	Johnny Rutherford, Chaparral-Cosworth	142.862
1981	Bobby Unser, Penske-Cosworth	139.084
1982	Gordon Johncock, Wildcat-Cosworth	162.029
1983	Tom Sneva, March-Cosworth	162.117
1984	Rick Mears, March-Cosworth	163.612
1985	Danny Sullivan, March-Cosworth	152.982
1986	Bobby Rahal, March-Cosworth	170.722
1987	Al Unser, March-Cosworth	162.175
1988	Rick Mears, Penske-Chevy Indy V8	144.809
1989	Emerson Fittipaldi, Penske-Chevy Indy V8	167.581
1990	Arie Luyendyk, Lola-Chevy Indy V8	185.981*
1991	Rick Mears, Penske-Chevy Indy V8	176.457
1992	Al Unser Jr., Galmer-Chevy Indy V8A	134.477
1993	Emerson Fittipaldi, Penske-Chevy Indy V8C	157.207
1994	Al Unser Jr., Penske-Mercedes Benz	160.872
1995	Jacques Villeneuve, Reynard-Ford Cosworth XB	153.616
1996	Buddy Lazier, Reynard-Ford Cosworth	147.956
1997	Arie Luyendyk, G Force-Aurora	145.827
1998	Eddie Cheever, Dallara-Aurora	145.155
1999	Kenny Brack, Dallara-Aurora	153.176
2000	Juan Montoya, G Force-Aurora	167.607
2001	Helio Castroneves, Reynard-Honda	131.294
2002	Helio Castroneves, Reynard-Honda	166.499
2003	Gil de Ferran, G Force-Toyota	156.291
2004	Buddy Rice, G Force-Honda	138.518
2005	Dan Wheldon, Dallara-Honda	157.603

(1) Average speed. *Race record. **Note:** The race was less than 500 mi in the following years: 1916 (300 mi), 1926 (400 mi), 1950 (345 mi), 1973 (332.5 mi), 1975 (435 mi), 1976 (255 mi), 2004 (450 mi).

Champ Car World Series Vanderbilt Cup Winners, 1959-2004

(U.S. Auto Club Champions prior to 1979; Championship Auto Racing Teams [CART] Champions, 1979-2003; Champ Car World Series Champion, 2004-present. The Vanderbilt Cup became the series' championship trophy in 2000.)

Year	Driver
1959	Roger Ward
1960	A. J. Foyt
1961	A. J. Foyt
1962	Rodger Ward
1963	A. J. Foyt
1964	A. J. Foyt
1965	Mario Andretti
1966	Mario Andretti
1967	A. J. Foyt
1968	Bobby Unser
1969	Mario Andretti
1970	Al Unser
1971	Joe Leonard
1972	Joe Leonard
1973	Roger McCluskey
1974	Bobby Unser
1975	A. J. Foyt
1976	Gordon Johncock
1977	Tom Sneva
1978	Tom Sneva
1979	Rick Mears
1980	Johnny Rutherford
1981	Rick Mears
1982	Rick Mears
1983	Al Unser
1984	Mario Andretti
1985	Al Unser
1986	Bobby Rahal
1987	Bobby Rahal
1988	Danny Sullivan
1989	Emerson Fittipaldi
1990	Al Unser Jr.
1991	Michael Andretti
1992	Bobby Rahal
1993	Nigel Mansell
1994	Al Unser Jr.
1995	Jacques Villeneuve
1996	Jimmy Vasser
1997	Alex Zanardi
1998	Alex Zanardi
1999	Juan Montoya
2000	Gil de Ferran
2001	Gil de Ferran
2002	Cristiano da Matta
2003	Paul Tracy
2004	Sebastien Bourdais

Indy Racing League (IRL) Winners, 1996-2004

(The Indy Racing League was begun in 1994 by a break-away group of CART drivers; its first championship was awarded in 1996)

Year	Driver
1996	(tie) Scott Sharp, Buzz Calkins
1997	Tony Stewart
1998	Kenny Brack
1999	Greg Ray
2000	Buddy Lazier
2001	Sam Hornish, Jr.
2002	Sam Hornish, Jr.
2003	Scott Dixon
2004	Tony Kanaan

NASCAR Racing

Nextel Cup Champions, 1949-2004

(Strictly Stock, 1949; Grand National, 1950-1970; Winston Cup 1971-2003)

Year	Driver
1949	Red Byron
1950	Bill Rexford
1951	Herb Thomas
1952	Tim Flock
1953	Herb Thomas
1954	Lee Petty
1955	Tim Flock
1956	Buck Baker
1957	Buck Baker
1958	Lee Petty
1959	Lee Petty
1960	Rex White
1961	Ned Jarrett
1962	Joe Weatherly
1963	Joe Weatherly
1964	Richard Petty
1965	Ned Jarrett
1966	David Pearson
1967	Richard Petty
1968	David Pearson
1969	David Pearson
1970	Bobby Isaac
1971	Richard Petty
1972	Richard Petty
1973	Benny Parsons
1974	Richard Petty
1975	Richard Petty
1976	Cale Yarborough
1977	Cale Yarborough
1978	Cale Yarborough
1979	Richard Petty
1980	Dale Earnhardt
1981	Darrell Waltrip
1982	Darrell Waltrip
1983	Bobby Allison
1984	Terry Labonte
1985	Darrell Waltrip
1986	Dale Earnhardt
1987	Dale Earnhardt
1988	Bill Elliott
1989	Rusty Wallace
1990	Dale Earnhardt
1991	Dale Earnhardt
1992	Alan Kulwicki
1993	Dale Earnhardt
1994	Dale Earnhardt
1995	Jeff Gordon
1996	Terry Labonte
1997	Jeff Gordon
1998	Jeff Gordon
1999	Dale Jarrett
2000	Bobby Labonte
2001	Jeff Gordon
2002	Tony Stewart
2003	Matt Kenseth
2004	Kurt Busch

NASCAR Rookie of the Year, 1958-2004

Year	Driver
1958	Shorty Rollins
1959	Richard Petty
1960	David Pearson
1961	Woodie Wilson
1962	Tom Cox
1963	Billy Wade
1964	Doug Cooper
1965	Sam McQuagg
1966	James Hylton
1967	Donnie Allison
1968	Pete Hamilton
1969	Dick Brooks
1970	Bill Dennis
1971	Walter Ballard
1972	Larry Smith
1973	Lennie Pond
1974	Earl Ross
1975	Bruce Hill
1976	Skip Manning
1977	Ricky Rudd
1978	Ronnie Thomas
1979	Dale Earnhardt
1980	Jody Riley
1981	Ron Bouchard
1982	Geoff Bodine
1983	Sterling Marlin
1984	Rusty Wallace
1985	Ken Schrader
1986	Alan Kulwicki
1987	Davey Allison
1988	Ken Bouchard
1989	Dick Trickle
1990	Rob Moroso
1991	Bobby Hamilton
1992	Jimmy Hensley
1993	Jeff Gordon
1994	Jeff Burton
1995	Ricky Craven
1996	Johnny Benson
1997	Mike Skinner
1998	Kenny Irwin
1999	Tony Stewart
2000	Matt Kenseth
2001	Kevin Harvick
2002	Ryan Newman
2003	Jamie McMurray
2004	Kasey Kahne

Daytona 500 Winners, 1959-2005

(At Daytona International Speedway in Daytona Beach, FL)

Year	Driver, car	Avg. MPH
1959	Lee Petty, Oldsmobile	135.521
1960	Junior Johnson, Chevrolet	124.740
1961	Marvin Panch, Pontiac	149.601
1962	Fireball Roberts, Pontiac	152.529
1963	Tiny Lund, Ford	151.566
1964	Richard Petty, Plymouth	154.334
1965	Fred Lorenzen, Ford (a)	141.539
1966	Richard Petty, Plymouth (b)	160.627
1967	Mario Andretti, Ford	146.926
1968	Cale Yarborough, Mercury	143.251
1969	LeeRoy Yarbrough, Ford	160.875
1970	Pete Hamilton, Plymouth	149.601
1971	Richard Petty, Plymouth	144.456
1972	A. J. Foyt, Mercury	161.550
1973	Richard Petty, Dodge	157.205
1974	Richard Petty, Dodge (c)	140.894
1975	Benny Parsons, Chevrolet	153.649
1976	David Pearson, Mercury	152.181
1977	Cale Yarborough, Chevrolet	153.218
1978	Bobby Allison, Ford	159.730
1979	Richard Petty, Oldsmobile	143.977
1980	Buddy Baker, Oldsmobile	177.602
1981	Richard Petty, Buick	169.651
1982	Bobby Allison, Buick	153.991
1983	Cale Yarborough, Pontiac	155.979
1984	Cale Yarborough, Chevrolet	150.994
1985	Bill Elliott, Ford	172.265
1986	Geoff Bodine, Chevrolet	148.124
1987	Bill Elliott, Ford	176.263
1988	Bobby Allison, Buick	137.531
1989	Darrell Waltrip, Chevrolet	148.466
1990	Derrike Cope, Chevrolet	165.761
1991	Ernie Irvan, Chevrolet	148.148
1992	Davey Allison, Ford	160.256
1993	Dale Jarrett, Chevrolet	154.972
1994	Sterling Marlin, Chevrolet	156.931
1995	Sterling Marlin, Chevrolet	141.710
1996	Dale Jarrett, Ford	154.308
1997	Jeff Gordon, Chevrolet	148.295
1998	Dale Earnhardt, Chevrolet	172.712
1999	Jeff Gordon, Chevrolet	161.551
2000	Dale Jarrett, Ford	155.669
2001	Michael Waltrip, Chevrolet	161.783
2002	Ward Burton, Dodge	142.971
2003	Michael Waltrip, Chevrolet (d)	133.870
2004	Dale Earnhardt Jr., Chevrolet	156.345
2005	Jeff Gordon	135.173

(a) 322.5 mi. (b) 495 mi. (c) 450 mi. (d) 272.5 mi.

Coca-Cola 600 Winners, 1960-2005

(At Lowe's Motor Speedway in Concord, NC. Known as World 600, 1960-85. *=rain-shortened.)

Year	Driver, car	Avg. MPH
1960	Joe Lee Johnson, Chevrolet	107.735
1961	David Pearson, Pontiac	111.633
1962	Nelson Stacy, Ford	125.552
1963	Fred Lorenzen, Ford	132.418
1964	Jim Paschal, Plymouth	125.772
1965	Fred Lorenzen, Ford	121.772
1966	Marvin Panch, Plymouth	135.042
1967	Jim Paschal, Plymouth	135.832
1968	Buddy Baker, Dodge*	104.207
1969	LeeRoy Yarborough, Mercury	134.361
1970	Donnie Allison, Ford	129.680
1971	Bobby Allison, Mercury	140.422
1972	Buddy Baker, Dodge	142.255
1973	Buddy Baker, Dodge	134.890
1974	David Pearson, Mercury	135.720
1975	Richard Petty, Dodge	145.327
1976	David Pearson, Mercury	137.352
1977	Richard Petty, Dodge	137.676
1978	Darrell Waltrip, Chevrolet	138.355
1979	Darrell Waltrip, Chevrolet	136.674
1980	Benny Parsons, Chevrolet	119.265
1981	Bobby Allison, Buick	129.326
1982	Neil Bonnett, Ford	130.058
1983	Neil Bonnett, Chevrolet	140.707
1984	Bobby Allison, Buick	129.233
1985	Darrell Waltrip, Chevrolet	141.807
1986	Dale Earnhardt, Chevrolet	140.406
1987	Kyle Petty, Ford	131.483
1988	Darrell Waltrip, Chevrolet	124.460
1989	Darrell Waltrip, Chevrolet	144.077
1990	Rusty Wallace, Pontiac	137.650
1991	Davey Allison, Ford	138.951
1992	Dale Earnhardt, Chevrolet	132.980
1993	Dale Earnhardt, Chevrolet	145.504
1994	Jeff Gordon, Chevrolet	139.445
1995	Bobby Labonte, Chevrolet	151.952
1996	Dale Jarrett, Ford	147.581
1997	Jeff Gordon, Chevrolet*	136.745
1998	Jeff Gordon, Chevrolet	136.424
1999	Jeff Burton, Ford	151.367
2000	Matt Kenseth, Ford	142.640
2001	Jeff Burton, Ford	138.107
2002	Mark Martin, Ford	137.729
2003	Jimmie Johnson, Chevrolet*	126.198
2004	Jimmie Johnson, Chevrolet	142.763
2005	Jimmie Johnson, Chevrolet	114.698

Brickyard 400 Winners, 1994-2005

(At Indianapolis Motor Speedway in Indianapolis, IN)

Year	Driver, car	Avg. MPH
1994	Jeff Gordon, Chevrolet	131.977
1995	Dale Earnhardt, Chevrolet	155.206
1996	Dale Jarrett, Ford	139.508
1997	Ricky Rudd, Ford	130.814
1998	Jeff Gordon, Chevrolet	126.772
1999	Dale Jarrett, Ford	148.194
2000	Bobby Labonte, Pontiac	155.912
2001	Jeff Gordon, Chevrolet	130.790
2002	Bill Elliott, Dodge	125.033
2003	Kevin Harvick, Chevrolet	134.554
2004	Jeff Gordon, Chevrolet	115.037
2005	Tony Stewart, Chevrolet	118.782

Southern 500 Winners, 1950-2004

(At Darlington International Raceway in Darlington, SC. *=rain-shortened.)

Year	Driver, car	Avg. MPH
1950	Johnny Mantz, Plymouth	76.260
1951	Herb Thomas, Hudson	76.900
1952	Fonty Flock, Oldsmobile	74.510
1953	Buck Baker, Oldsmobile	92.780
1954	Herb Thomas, Hudson	94.930
1955	Herb Thomas, Chevrolet	93.281
1956	Curtis Turner, Ford	95.067
1957	Speedy Thompson, Chevrolet	100.094
1958	Fireball Roberts, Chevrolet	102.590
1959	Jim Reed, Chevrolet	111.840
1960	Buck Baker, Pontiac	105.901
1961	Nelson Stacy, Ford	117.787
1962	Larry Frank, Ford	117.965
1963	Fireball Roberts, Ford	129.784
1964	Buck Baker, Dodge	117.757
1965	Ned Jarrett, Ford	115.924
1966	Darel Dieringer, Mercury	114.830
1967	Richard Petty, Plymouth	130.423
1968	Cale Yarborough, Mercury	126.132
1969	LeeRoy Yarbrough, Ford*	105.612
1970	Buddy Baker, Dodge	128.817
1971	Bobby Allison, Mercury	131.398
1972	Bobby Allison, Chevrolet	128.124
1973	Cale Yarborough, Oldsmobile	134.033
1974	Cale Yarborough, Chevrolet	111.075
1975	Bobby Allison, Matador	116.825
1976	David Pearson, Mercury	120.534
1977	David Pearson, Mercury	106.797
1978	Cale Yarborough, Oldsmobile	116.828
1979	David Pearson, Chevrolet	126.259
1980	Terry Labonte, Chevrolet	115.210
1981	Neil Bonnett, Ford	126.410
1982	Cale Yarborough, Buick	115.224
1983	Bobby Allison, Buick	123.343
1984	Harry Gant, Chevrolet	128.270
1985	Bill Elliott, Ford	121.254
1986	Tim Richmond, Chevrolet	121.068
1987	Dale Earnhardt, Chevrolet*	115.520
1988	Bill Elliott, Ford	128.297
1989	Dale Earnhardt, Chevrolet	135.462
1990	Dale Earnhardt, Chevrolet	123.141
1991	Harry Gant, Oldsmobile	133.508
1992	Darrell Waltrip, Chevrolet*	129.114
1993	Mark Martin, Ford*	137.932
1994	Bill Elliott, Ford	127.952
1995	Jeff Gordon, Chevrolet	121.231
1996	Jeff Gordon, Chevrolet	135.757
1997	Jeff Gordon, Chevrolet*	121.149
1998	Jeff Gordon, Chevrolet	139.031
1999	Jeff Burton, Ford*	107.816
2000	Bobby Labonte, Pontiac*	108.273
2001	Ward Burton, Dodge	122.773
2002	Jeff Gordon, Chevrolet	118.617
2003	Terry Labonte, Chevrolet	120.744
2004	Jimmie Johnson, Chevrolet	125.044

Formula One Racing

World Grand Prix Champions, 1950-2005

Year	Driver
1950	Nino Farini, Italy
1951	Juan Manuel Fangio, Argentina
1952	Alberto Ascari, Italy
1953	Alberto Ascari, Italy
1954	Juan Manuel Fangio, Argentina
1955	Juan Manuel Fangio, Argentina
1956	Juan Manuel Fangio, Argentina
1957	Juan Manuel Fangio, Argentina
1958	Mike Hawthorne, England
1959	Jack Brabham, Australia
1960	Jack Brabham, Australia
1961	Phil Hill, United States
1962	Graham Hill, England
1963	Jim Clark, Scotland
1964	John Surtees, England
1965	Jim Clark, Scotland
1966	Jack Brabham, Australia
1967	Denis Hulme, New Zealand
1968	Graham Hill, England
1969	Jackie Stewart, Scotland
1970	Jochen Rindt, Austria
1971	Jackie Stewart, Scotland
1972	Emerson Fittipaldi, Brazil
1973	Jackie Stewart, Scotland
1974	Emerson Fittipaldi, Brazil
1975	Niki Lauda, Austria
1976	James Hunt, England
1977	Niki Lauda, Austria
1978	Mario Andretti, United States
1979	Jody Scheckter, South Africa
1980	Alan Jones, Australia
1981	Nelson Piquet, Brazil
1982	Keke Rosberg, Finland
1983	Nelson Piquet, Brazil
1984	Niki Lauda, Austria
1985	Alain Prost, France
1986	Alain Prost, France
1987	Nelson Piquet, Brazil
1988	Ayrton Senna, Brazil
1989	Alain Prost, France
1990	Ayrton Senna, Brazil
1991	Ayrton Senna, Brazil
1992	Nigel Mansell, Britain
1993	Alain Prost, France
1994	Michael Schumacher, Germany
1995	Michael Schumacher, Germany
1996	Damon Hill, England
1997	Jacques Villeneuve, Canada
1998	Mika Hakkinen, Finland
1999	Mika Hakkinen, Finland
2000	Michael Schumacher, Germany
2001	Michael Schumacher, Germany
2002	Michael Schumacher, Germany
2003	Michael Schumacher, Germany
2004	Michael Schumacher, Germany
2005	Fernando Alonso, Spain

2005 Le Mans 24 Hours Race

Danish driver Tom Kristensen was part of a 3-man team, driving the Champion Racing Audi R8, that won the "24 Hours of Le Mans" race held June 19, 2005. It was the 7th career victory for Kristensen, setting a new record for most wins in the race's history; the previous record of 6 was held by Jacky Ickx. Kristensen also became the 1st driver to win the race 6 straight years. Kristensen, Marco Werner (Germany), and J.J. Lehto (Finland) completed 370 laps, with a best lap speed of 3:39.781.

Notable One-Mile Land Speed Records

Andy Green, a Royal Air Force pilot, broke the sound barrier and set the first supersonic world speed record on land, Oct. 15, 1997, in Black Rock Desert, NV. Green, driving a car built by Richard Noble, had 2 runs at an average speed of 763.035 mph, as calculated under the rules of the Fédération Internationale de l'Automobile (FIA). This record and speed exceeded the speed of sound, calculated at 751.251 mph for that place and time.

Date	Driver	Car	MPH
1/26/06	Marriott	Stanley (Steam)	127.659
3/16/10	Oldfield	Benz	131.724
4/23/11	Burman	Benz	141.732
2/12/19	DePalma	Packard	149.875
4/27/20	Milton	Dusenberg	155.046
4/28/26	Parry-Thomas	Thomas Spl.	170.624
3/29/27	Seagrave	Sunbeam	203.790
4/22/28	Keech	White Triplex	207.552
3/11/29	Seagrave	Irving-Napier	231.446
2/05/31	Campbell	Napier-Campbell	246.086
2/24/32	Campbell	Napier-Campbell	253.96
2/22/33	Campbell	Napier-Campbell	272.109
9/03/35	Campbell	Bluebird Special	301.13
11/19/37	Eyston	Thunderbolt 1	311.42
9/16/38	Eyston	Thunderbolt 1	357.5
8/23/39	Cobb	Railton	368.9
9/16/47	Cobb	Railton-Mobil	394.2
8/05/63	Breedlove	Spirit of America	407.45
10/27/64	Arfons	Green Monster	536.71
11/15/65	Breedlove	Spirit of America	600.601
10/23/70	Gabelich	Blue Flame	622.407
10/09/79	Barrett	Budweiser Rocket	638.637*
10/04/83	Noble	Thrust 2	633.468
9/25/97	Green	Thrust SSC	714.144
10/15/97	Green	Thrust SSC	763.035

*Not recognized as official by sanctioning bodies.

BOXING

There are many boxing governing bodies, including the World Boxing Council, World Boxing Assn., International Boxing Fed., World Boxing Org., U.S. Boxing Assn., N. American Boxing Fed., and European Boxing Union. All have their own champions and divisions.

Champions by Classes*

Class (weight limit)	WBA	WBC	IBF
Heavyweight	John Ruiz, U.S.	Vitali Klitschko, Ukraine	Chris Byrd, U.S.
Cruiserweight (200 lb)	Jean-Marc Mormeck, France	Jean-Marc Mormeck, France	O'Neil Bell, U.S.
Light Heavyweight (175 lb)	Fabrice Tiozzo, France	Tomasz Adamek, Poland	Clinton Woods, England
Super Middleweight (168 lb)	Mikkel Kessler, Denmark	Markus Beyer, Germany	Jeff Lacy, U.S.
Middleweight (160 lb)	Jermain Taylor, U.S.[1]	Jermain Taylor, U.S.	Jermain Taylor, U.S.
Jr. Middleweight (154 lb)	Alejandro Garcia, Mexico	Ricardo Mayorga, Nicaragua	Roman Karmazin, Russia
Welterweight (147 lb)	Zab Judah, U.S.[2]	Zab Judah, U.S.	Zab Judah, U.S.
Jr. Welterweight (140 lb)	Carlos Maussa, Colombia	Floyd Mayweather, U.S.	Ricky Hatton, England
Lightweight (135 lb)	Juan Diaz, U.S.	Diego Corrales, U.S.	Jesus Chavez, U.S.
Jr. Lightweight (130 lb)	Vicente Mosquera, Panama	Marco Antonio Barrera, Mexico	Marco Antonio Barrera, Mexico
Featherweight (126 lb)	Juan Manuel Marquez, Mexico[3]	In-Jin Chi, South Korea	Juan Manuel Marquez, Mexico
Jr. Featherweight (122 lb)	Mahyar Monshipour, France	Oscar Larios, Mexico	Israel Vazquez, Mexico
Bantamweight (118 lb)	Wladimir Sidorenko, Ukraine	Hozumi Hasegawa, Japan	Rafael Marquez, Mexico
Jr. Bantamweight (115 lb)	Martin Castillo, Mexico	Masamori Tokuyama, Japan	Luis Perez, Nicaragua
Flyweight (112 lb)	Lorenzo Parra, Venezuela	Pongsaklek Wonjongkam, Thailand	Vic Darchinyan, Australia
Jr. Flyweight (108 lb)	Roberto Vasques, Panama	Brian Viloria, U.S.	Will Grigsby, U.S.
Strawweight (105 lb)	Yukata Niida, Japan	Eagle Kyowa, Japan	Muhammad Rachman, Indo.

*As of Oct. 10, 2005. **Note:** Interim champions not listed. The WBA and WBC designate certain title holders as "Super World Champs" (listed above), and permit concurrent "World" champions in those classes. Following are the "World" champions: (1) Maselino Masoe, New Zed., middleweight. (2) Luis Collazo, U.S., welterweight. (3) Chris John, Indo., featherweight.

Ring Champions by Years

(*abandoned the title or was stripped of it; IBF champions listed only for heavyweight division)

Heavyweights

1882-1892	John L. Sullivan (a)
1892-1897	James J. Corbett (b)
1897-1899	Robert Fitzsimmons
1899-1905	James J. Jeffries* (c)
1905-1906	Marvin Hart
1906-1908	Tommy Burns
1908-1915	Jack Johnson
1915-1919	Jess Willard
1919-1926	Jack Dempsey
1926-1928	Gene Tunney*
1928-1930	Vacant
1930-1932	Max Schmeling
1932-1933	Jack Sharkey
1933-1934	Primo Carnera
1934-1935	Max Baer
1935-1937	James J. Braddock
1937-1949	Joe Louis*
1949-1951	Ezzard Charles
1951-1952	Joe Walcott
1952-1956	Rocky Marciano*
1956-1959	Floyd Patterson
1959-1960	Ingemar Johansson
1960-1962	Floyd Patterson
1962-1964	Sonny Liston
1964-1967	Cassius Clay (Muhammad Ali) (d)
1970-1973	Joe Frazier
1973-1974	George Foreman
1974-1978	Muhammad Ali
1978-1979	Muhammad Ali* (WBA)
1978	Leon Spinks (WBC*, WBA) (e); Ken Norton (WBC)
1978-1983	Larry Holmes* (WBC) (f)
1979-1980	John Tate (WBA)
1980-1982	Mike Weaver (WBA)
1982-1983	Michael Dokes (WBA)
1983-1984	Gerrie Coetzee (WBA)
1983-1985	Larry Holmes (IBF) (f)
1984	Tim Witherspoon (WBC)
1984-1985	Greg Page (WBA)
1984-1986	Pinklon Thomas (WBC)
1985-1986	Tony Tubbs (WBA)
1985-1987	Michael Spinks* (IBF)
1986	Tim Witherspoon (WBA); Trevor Berbick (WBC)
1986-1987	Mike Tyson (WBC); James "Bonecrusher" Smith (WBA)
1987	Tony Tucker (IBF)
1987-1990	Mike Tyson (WBC, WBA, IBF)
1990	"Buster" Douglas (WBA, WBC, IBF)
1990-1992	Evander Holyfield (WBA, WBC, IBF)
1992-1993	Riddick Bowe (WBA, IBF,WBC*)
1992-1994	Lennox Lewis (WBC)
1993-1994	Evander Holyfield (WBA, IBF)
1994	Michael Moorer (WBA, IBF)
1994-1995	Oliver McCall (WBC); George Foreman (WBA*, IBF*)
1995	Frans Botha* (IBF)
1995-1996	Bruce Seldon (WBA); Frank Bruno (WBC)
1996	Mike Tyson (WBC*, WBA)
1996-1997	Michael Moorer (IBF)
1996-1999	Evander Holyfield (WBA, IBF)
1997-2001	Lennox Lewis (WBC)
1999-2001	Lennox Lewis (WBA*, WBC, IBF)
2000-2001	Evander Holyfield (WBA)
2001-2004	John Ruiz (WBA)
2001	Hasim Rahman (WBC, IBF)
2001-2002	Lennox Lewis (IBF*)
2001-2004	Lennox Lewis (WBC)(g)
2002-2005	Chris Byrd (IBF)
2003	Roy Jones Jr. (WBA)
2004-2005	Vitali Klitschko (WBC)
2005	James Toney (WBA)(h)*; John Ruiz (WBA); Chris Byrd (IBF)

(a) London Prize Ring (bare knuckle champion). (b) First Marquis of Queensberry champion. (c) Jeffries vacated title (1905), designated Marvin Hart and Jack Root as logical contenders. Hart defeated Root in 12 rounds (1905), in turn was defeated by Tommy Burns (1906), who claimed the title. Jack Johnson def. Burns (1908) and was recognized as champ. Johnson won the title by defeating Jeffries in the latter's attempted comeback (1910). (d) Title declared vacant by the WBA and others in 1967 after Ali refused military induction. Joe Frazier recognized as champ by 6 states, Mexico, and S. America. Jimmy Ellis declared champ by the WBA. Frazier KOd Ellis, Feb. 16, 1970. (e) After Spinks defeated Ali, the WBC recognized Ken Norton as champ. Ali defeated Spinks in 1978 rematch for WBA title, retired in 1979. (f) Holmes relinquished WBC title in Dec. 1983, to fight as champ of the new IBF. (g) Lewis retired in Feb. 2004. (h) Toney defeated Ruiz to claim the title, but it was rescinded when Toney tested positive for steroids.

Light Heavyweights

1903	Jack Root, George Gardner
1903-1905	Bob Fitzsimmons
1905-1912	Philadelphia Jack O'Brien*
1912-1916	Jack Dillon
1916-1920	Battling Levinsky
1920-1922	George Carpentier
1922-1923	Battling Siki
1923-1925	Mike McTigue
1925-1926	Paul Berlenbach
1926-1927	Jack Delaney*
1927-1929	Tommy Loughran*
1930-1934	Maxey Rosenbloom
1934-1935	Bob Olin
1935-1939	John Henry Lewis*
1939	Melio Bettina
1939-1941	Billy Conn*
1941	Anton Christoforidis (won NBA title)
1941-1948	Gus Lesnevich, Freddie Mills
1948-1950	Freddie Mills
1950-1952	Joey Maxim
1952-1962	Archie Moore
1962-1963	Harold Johnson
1963-1965	Willie Pastrano
1965-1966	Jose Torres
1966-1968	Dick Tiger
1968-1974	Bob Foster*
1974-1977	John Conteh (WBC)
1974-1978	Victor Galindez (WBA)
1977-1978	Miguel Cuello (WBC)
1978	Mate Parlov (WBC)
1978-1979	Mike Rossman (WBA); Marvin Johnson (WBC)
1979-1981	Matthew Saad Muhammad (WBC)
1979-1980	Marvin Johnson (WBA)
1980-1981	Eddie Mustafa Muhammad (WBA)
1981-1983	Michael Spinks (WBA); Dwight Braxton (WBC)
1983-1985	Michael Spinks*
1985-1986	J. B. Williamson (WBC)
1986-1987	Marvin Johnson (WBA); Dennis Andries (WBC)
1987	Leslie Stewart (WBA)
1987-1991	Virgil Hill (WBA)
1987	Thomas Hearns* (WBC)
1987-1988	Don Lalonde (WBC)
1988	Sugar Ray Leonard* (WBC)
1989	Dennis Andries (WBC)
1989-1990	Jeff Harding (WBC)
1990-1991	Dennis Andries (WBC)
1991-1994	Jeff Harding (WBC)
1991-1992	Thomas Hearns (WBA)
1992	Iran Barkley* (WBA)
1992-1997	Virgil Hill (WBA)
1994-1995	Mike McCallum (WBC)
1995-1996	Fabrice Tiozzo* (WBC)
1996-1997	Roy Jones Jr. (WBC)
1997	Montell Griffin (WBC); Roy Jones Jr. (WBC); Darius Michalczewski* (WBA)
1997-1998	Lou Del Valle (WBA)
1998-2003	Roy Jones Jr. (WBA*, WBC*)
2003	Mehdi Sahnoune (WBA)
2003-2004	Antonio Tarver (WBC)
2004-2005	Fabrice Tiozzo (WBA)
2005	Tomasz Adamek (WBC)

Middleweights

1884-1891	Jack "Nonpareil" Dempsey
1891-1897	Bob Fitzsimmons*
1897-1907	Tommy Ryan*
1907-1908	Stanley Ketchel; Billy Papke
1908-1910	Stanley Ketchel
1911-1913	vacant
1913	Frank Klaus; George Chip
1914-1917	Al McCoy
1917-1920	Mike O'Dowd
1920-1923	Johnny Wilson
1923-1926	Harry Greb
1926-1931	Tiger Flowers; Mickey Walker
1931-1932	Gorilla Jones (NBA)
1932-1937	Marcel Thil
1938	Al Hostak (NBA); Solly Krieger (NBA)
1939-1940	Al Hostak (NBA)
1941-1947	Tony Zale
1947-1948	Rocky Graziano
1948	Tony Zale; Marcel Cerdan
1949-1951	Jake LaMotta
1951	Ray Robinson; Randy Turpin; Ray Robinson*
1953-1955	Carl (Bobo) Olson
1955-1957	Ray Robinson
1957	Gene Fullmer; Ray Robinson
1957-1958	Carmen Basilio
1958	Ray Robinson
1959	Gene Fullmer (NBA); Ray Robinson (NY)
1960	Gene Fullmer (NBA); Paul Pender (NY and MA)
1961	Gene Fullmer (NBA); Terry Downes (NY, MA, Europe)
1962	Gene Fullmer; Dick Tiger (NBA); Paul Pender (NY and MA)*
1963	Dick Tiger (universal)
1963-1965	Joey Giardello
1965-1966	Dick Tiger
1966-1967	Emile Griffith
1967	Nino Benvenuti
1967-1968	Emile Griffith
1968-1970	Nino Benvenuti
1970-1977	Carlos Monzon*
1977-1978	Rodrigo Valdez
1978-1979	Hugo Corro
1979-1980	Vito Antuofermo
1980	Alan Minter
1980-1987	Marvin Hagler
1987	Sugar Ray Leonard* (WBC)
1987-1989	Sumbu Kalambay (WBA)
1987-1988	Thomas Hearns (WBC)
1988-1989	Iran Barkley (WBC)
1989-1990	Roberto Duran* (WBC)
1989-1991	Mike McCallum (WBA)
1990-1993	Julian Jackson (WBC)
1992-1993	Reggie Johnson (WBA)
1993-1995	Gerald McClellan* (WBC)
1993-1994	John David Jackson (WBA)
1994-1997	Jorge Castro (WBA)
1995	Julian Jackson (WBC)
1995-1996	Quincy Taylor (WBC); Shinji Takehara (WBA)
1996-1998	Keith Holmes (WBC)
1996-1997	William Joppy (WBA)
1997	Julio Cesar Green (WBA)
1998-2001	William Joppy (WBA)
1998-1999	Hassine Cherifi (WBC)
1999-2001	Keith Holmes (WBC)
2001	Felix Trinidad (WBA)
2001-2004	Bernard Hopkins (WBC, WBA)
2005	Jermain Taylor (WBC, WBA)

Welterweights

1892-1894	Mysterious Billy Smith
1894-1896	Tommy Ryan
1896	Kid McCoy*
1900	Rube Ferns; Matty Matthews
1901	Rube Ferns
1901-1904	Joe Walcott
1904-1906	Dixie Kid; Joe Walcott; Honey Mellody
1907-1911	Mike Sullivan
1911-1915	Vacant
1915-1919	Ted Lewis
1919-1922	Jack Britton
1922-1926	Mickey Walker
1926	Pete Latzo
1927-1929	Joe Dundee
1929	Jackie Fields
1930	Jack Thompson; Tommy Freeman
1931	Tommy Freeman; Jack Thompson; Lou Brouillard
1932	Jackie Fields
1933	Young Corbett; Jimmy McLarnin
1934	Barney Ross; Jimmy McLarnin
1935-1938	Barney Ross
1938-1940	Henry Armstrong
1940-1941	Fritzie Zivic
1941-1946	Fred Cochrane
1946	Marty Servo*
1946-1951	Ray Robinson* (a)
1951	Johnny Bratton (NBA)
1951-1954	Kid Gavilan
1954-1955	Johnny Saxton
1955	Tony De Marco
1955-1956	Carmen Basilio
1956	Johnny Saxton
1956-1957	Carmen Basilio*
1958	Virgil Akins
1958-1960	Don Jordan
1960-1961	Benny Paret
1961	Emile Griffith
1961-1962	Benny Paret
1962-1963	Emile Griffith
1963	Luis Rodriguez
1963-1966	Emile Griffith*
1966-1969	Curtis Cokes
1969-1970	Jose Napoles
1970-1971	Billy Backus
1971-1975	Jose Napoles
1975-1976	John Stracey (WBC); Angel Espada (WBA)
1976-1979	Carlos Palomino (WBC)
1976-1980	Jose Cuevas (WBA)
1979	Wilfredo Benitez (WBC)
1979-1980	Sugar Ray Leonard (WBC)
1980	Roberto Duran (WBC)
1980-1981	Thomas Hearns (WBA)
1980-1982	Sugar Ray Leonard*
1983-1985	Donald Curry (WBA); Milton McCrory (WBC)
1985-1986	Donald Curry
1986-1987	Lloyd Honeyghan (WBC)
1987	Mark Breland (WBA)
1987-1988	Marlon Starling (WBA); Jorge Vaca (WBC)
1988-1989	Tomas Molinares (WBA); Lloyd Honeyghan (WBC)
1989-1990	Marlon Starling (WBC); Mark Breland (WBA)
1990-1991	Maurice Blocker (WBC); Aaron Davis (WBA)
1991	Simon Brown (WBC)
1991-1992	Meldrick Taylor (WBA)
1991-1993	Buddy McGirt (WBC)
1992-1994	Crisanto Espana (WBA)
1993-1997	Pernell Whitaker (WBC)
1994-1998	Ike Quartey (WBA*)
1997-1999	Oscar De La Hoya (WBC*)
1998	James Page (WBA*)
1999-2000	Felix Trinidad (WBC*)
2000	Oscar De La Hoya (WBC*)
2000-2002	Shane Mosley (WBC)
2001-2002	Andrew Lewis (WBA)
2002	Ricardo Mayorga (WBA)
2002-2003	Vernon Forrest (WBC)
2003	Ricardo Mayorga (WBA, WBC)
2004	Cory Spinks (WBA, WBC)
2005	Zab Judah (WBA, WBC)

(a) Robinson gained the title by defeating Tommy Bell in an elimination agreed to by the New York Commission and the National Boxing Association. Both claimed Robinson waived his title when he won the middleweight crown from LaMotta in 1951.

Lightweights

1896-1899	Kid Lavigne
1899-1902	Frank Erne
1902-1908	Joe Gans
1908-1910	Battling Nelson
1910-1912	Ad Wolgast
1912-1914	Willie Ritchie
1914-1917	Freddie Welsh
1917-1925	Benny Leonard*
1925	Jimmy Goodrich; Rocky Kansas
1926-1930	Sammy Mandell
1930	Al Singer; Tony Canzoneri
1930-1933	Tony Canzoneri
1933-1935	Barney Ross*
1935-1936	Tony Canzoneri
1936-1938	Lou Ambers
1938	Henry Armstrong
1939	Lou Ambers
1940	Lew Jenkins
1941-1943	Sammy Angott
1944	S. Angott (NBA); J. Zurita (NBA)
1945-1951	Ike Williams (NBA: later universal)
1951-1952	James Carter
1952	Lauro Salas; James Carter
1953-1954	James Carter
1954	Paddy De Marco; James Carter
1955	James Carter; Bud Smith
1956	Bud Smith; Joe Brown
1956-1962	Joe Brown
1962-1965	Carlos Ortiz
1965	Ismael Laguna
1965-1968	Carlos Ortiz
1968-1969	Teo Cruz
1969-1970	Mando Ramos
1970	Ismael Laguna
1970-1972	Ken Buchanan (WBA)
1971-1972	Pedro Carrasco (WBC)
1972-1979	Roberto Duran* (WBA)
1972	Mando Ramos (WBC); Chango Carmona (WBC)
1972-1974	Rodolfo Gonzalez (WBC)
1974-1976	Ishimatsu Suzuki (WBC)
1976-1978	Esteban De Jesus (WBC)
1979-1981	Jim Watt (WBC)
1979-1980	Ernesto Espana (WBA)
1980-1981	Hilmer Kenty (WBA)
1981	Sean O'Grady (WBA); Claude Noel (WBA)
1981-1983	Alexis Arguello* (WBC)
1981-1982	Arturo Frias (WBA)
1982-1984	Ray Mancini (WBA)
1983-1984	Edwin Rosario (WBC)
1984-1986	Livingstone Bramble (WBA)
1984-1985	Jose Luis Ramirez (WBC)
1985-1986	Hector (Macho) Camacho (WBC)
1986-1987	Edwin Rosario (WBA)
1987-1988	Julio Cesar Chavez (WBA); Jose Luis Ramirez (WBC)
1988-1989	Julio Cesar Chavez (WBA, WBC)
1989-1990	Edwin Rosario (WBA); Pernell Whitaker (WBC)
1990	Juan Nazario (WBA)
1990-1992	Pernell Whitaker*
1992	Joey Gamache (WBA)
1992-1996	Miguel Angel Gonzalez* (WBC)
1992-1993	Tony Lopez (WBA)
1993	Dingaan Thobela (WBA)
1993-1998	Orzubek Nazarov (WBA)
1996-1997	Jean-Baptiste Mendy (WBC)
1997-1998	Steve Johnston (WBC)
1998-1999	Jean-Baptiste Mendy (WBA);Cesar Bazan (WBC)
1999	Julian Lorcy (WBA); Stefano Zoff (WBA)
1999-2000	Gilberto Serrano (WBA); Steve Johnston (WBC)
2000-2001	Takanori Hatakeyama (WBA);
2000-2002	Jose Luis Castillo (WBC)
2001	Julien Lorcy (WBA)
2001-2002	Raul Balbi (WBA)
2002-2003	Leonard Dorin (WBA)
2002-2004	Floyd Mayweather (WBC)
2004-2005	Juan Diaz (WBA)
2005	Diego Corrales (WBC)

Featherweights

1892-1900	George Dixon (disputed)	1968	Paul Rojas (WBA)	1985-1986	Barry McGuigan (WBA)
1900-1901	Terry McGovern; Young Corbett*	1968-1969	Jose Legra (WBC)	1986-1987	Steve Cruz (WBA)
1901-1912	Abe Attell	1968-1971	Shozo Saijyo (WBA)	1987-1991	Antonio Esparragoza (WBA)
1912-1923	Johnny Kilbane	1969-1970	Johnny Famechon (WBC)	1988-1990	Jeff Fenech* (WBC)
1923	Eugene Criqui; Johnny Dundee	1970	Vicente Salvidar (WBC)	1990-1991	Marcos Villasana (WBC)
1923-1925	Johnny Dundee*	1970-1972	Kuniaki Shibata (WBC)	1991-1993	Park Yung Kyun (WBA); Paul Hodkinson (WBC)
1925-1927	Kid Kaplan*	1971-1972	Antonio Gomez (WBA)	1993	Goyo Vargas (WBC)
1927-1928	Benny Bass; Tony Canzoneri	1972	Clemente Sanchez* (WBC)	1993-1995	Kevin Kelley (WBC)
1928-1929	Andre Routis	1972-1974	Ernesto Marcel* (WBA)	1993-1996	Eloy Rojas (WBA)
1929-1932	Battling Battalino*	1972-1973	Jose Legra (WBC)	1995	Alejandro Gonzalez (WBC)
1932-1934	Tommy Paul (NBA)	1973-1974	Eder Jofre* (WBC)	1995-1996	Manuel Medina (WBC)
1933-1936	Freddie Miller	1974	Ruben Olivares (WBA)	1995-1999	Luisito Espinosa (WBC)
1936-1937	Petey Sarron	1974-1975	Bobby Chacon (WBC)	1996-1997	Wilfredo Vasquez* (WBA)
1937-1938	Henry Armstrong*	1974-1976	Alexis Arguello* (WBA)	1998	Freddie Norwood (WBA)
1938-1940	Joey Archibald (a)	1975	Ruben Olivares (WBC)	1998-1999	Antonio Ceremeno (WBA)
1940-1941	Harry Jeffra	1975-1976	David Kotey (WBC)	1999	Cesar Soto (WBC); Naseem Hamed* (WBC); Freddie Norwood (WBA)
1942-1948	Willie Pep	1976-1980	Danny Lopez (WBC)	2000-2001	Guty Espadas (WBC)
1948-1949	Sandy Saddler	1977	Rafael Ortega (WBA)	2000-2003	Derrick Gainer (WBA)
1949-1950	Willie Pep	1977-1978	Cecilio Lastra (WBA)	2001-2004	Erik Morales (WBC)(b)
1950-1957	Sandy Saddler*	1978-1985	Eusebio Pedrosa (WBA)	2003-2005	Juan Manuel Marquez (WBA)
1957-1959	Hogan (Kid) Bassey	1980-1982	Salvador Sanchez (WBC)	2004-2005	In-jin Chi (WBC)
1959-1963	Davey Moore	1982-1984	Juan LaPorte (WBC)		
1963-1964	Sugar Ramos	1984	Wilfredo Gomez (WBC)		
1964-1967	Vicente Saldivar*	1984-1988	Azumah Nelson (WBC)		

(a) After Petey Scalzo knocked out Archibald in an overweight match and was refused a title bout, the NBA named Scalzo champion. NBA title succession: Scalzo, 1938-41; Richard Lemos, 1941; Jackie Wilson, 1941-43; Jackie Callura, 1943; Phil Terranova, 1943-44; Sal Bartolo, 1944-46. (b) Marco Antonio Barrera won unan. decision over Morales, June 22, 2002, but refused WBC title. Morales regained WBC title with unan. decision over Paulie Ayala, Nov. 16, 2002. Morales moved up to Junior Lightweight div. in 2004.

History of Heavyweight Championship Bouts

(bouts in which title changed hands)

1889: July 8, John L. Sullivan def. Jake Kilrain, 75, Richburg, MS.

1892: Sept. 7, James J. Corbett def. John L. Sullivan, 21, New Orleans.

1897: Bob Fitzsimmons def. James J. Corbett, 14, Carson City, NV.

1899: June 9, James J. Jeffries def. Bob Fitzsimmons, 11, Coney Island, NY. (Jeffries retired as champion in 1905.)

1905: July 3, Marvin Hart KOd Jack Root, 12, Reno, NV. (Jeffries refereed, gave title to Hart. Jack O'Brien also claimed the title.)

1906: Feb. 23, Tommy Burns def. Marvin Hart, 20, Los Angeles.

1908: Dec. 26, Jack Johnson KOd Tommy Burns, 14, Sydney, Australia. (Police halted contest.)

1915: April 5, Jess Willard KOd Jack Johnson, 26, Havana.

1919: July 4, Jack Dempsey KOd Jess Willard, Toledo, OH. (Willard failed to answer bell for 4th round.)

1926: Sept. 23, Gene Tunney def. Jack Dempsey, 10, Philadelphia. (Tunney retired as champion in 1928.)

1930: June 12, Max Schmeling def. Jack Sharkey, 4, NY. (Resulted in the election of a successor to Tunney.)

1932: June 21, Jack Sharkey def. Max Schmeling, 15, NY.

1933: June 29, Primo Carnera KOd Jack Sharkey, 6, NY.

1934: June 14, Max Baer KOd Primo Carnera, 11, NY.

1935: June 13, James J. Braddock def. Max Baer, 15, NY.

1937: June 22, Joe Louis KOd James J. Braddock, 8, Chicago. (Louis retired as champion in 1949.)

1949: June 22, Ezzard Charles def. Joe Walcott, 15, Chicago; NBA recognition only.

1951: July 18, Joe Walcott KOd Ezzard Charles, 7, Pittsburgh.

1952: Sept. 23, Rocky Marciano KOd Joe Walcott, 13, Philadelphia. (Marciano retired as champion in 1956.)

1956: Nov. 30, Floyd Patterson KOd Archie Moore, 5, Chicago.

1959: June 26, Ingemar Johansson KOd Floyd Patterson, 3, NY.

1960: June 20, Floyd Patterson KOd Ingemar Johansson, 5, NY.

1962: Sept. 25, Sonny Liston KOd Floyd Patterson, 1, Chicago.

1964: Feb. 25, Cassius Clay (Muhammad Ali) KOd Sonny Liston, 7, Miami Beach, FL. (In 1967, Ali was stripped of his title by the WBA and others for refusing military service.)

1970: Feb. 16, Joe Frazier KOd Jimmy Ellis, 5, NY. (Frazier def. Ali in 15 rounds, Mar. 8, 1971, in NY.)

1973: Jan. 22, George Foreman KOd Joe Frazier, 2, Jamaica.

1974: Oct. 30, Muhammad Ali KOd George Foreman, 8, Kinshasa, Zaire.

1978: Feb. 15, Leon Spinks def. Muhammad Ali, 15, Las Vegas. (WBC recognized Ken Norton as champion after Spinks refused to fight him before his rematch with Ali.); June 9, (WBC) Larry Holmes def. Ken Norton, 15, Las Vegas. (Holmes gave up title in Dec. 1983.); Sept. 15, (WBA) Muhammad Ali def. Leon Spinks, 15, New Orleans. (Ali retired as champion in 1979.)

1979: Oct. 20, (WBA) John Tate def. Gerrie Coetzee, 15, Pretoria, South Africa.

1980: Mar. 31, (WBA) Mike Weaver KOd John Tate, 15, Knoxville.

1982: Dec. 10, (WBA) Michael Dokes KOd Mike Weaver, 1, Las Vegas.

1983: Sept. 23, (WBA) Gerrie Coetzee KOd Michael Dokes, 10, Richfield, OH; in Dec., Larry Holmes relinquished the WBC title and was named champion of the newly formed IBF.

1984: Mar. 9, (WBC) Tim Witherspoon def. Greg Page, 12, Las Vegas; Aug. 31, (WBC) Pinklon Thomas def. Tim Witherspoon, 12, Las Vegas; Dec. 2, (WBA) Greg Page KOd Gerrie Coetzee, 8, Sun City, Bophuthatswana.

1985: Apr. 29, (WBA) Tony Tubbs def. Greg Page, 15, Buffalo, NY; Sept. 21, (IBF) Michael Spinks def. Larry Holmes, 15, Las Vegas. (Spinks relinquished title in Feb. 1987.)

1986: Jan. 17, (WBA) Tim Witherspoon def. Tony Tubbs, 15, Atlanta, GA; Mar. 23, (WBC) Trevor Berbick def. Pinklon Thomas, 12, Miami; Nov. 22, (WBC) Mike Tyson KOd Trevor Berbick, 2, Las Vegas; Dec. 12, (WBA) James "Bonecrusher" Smith KOd Tim Witherspoon, 1, NY.

1987: Mar. 7, (WBA, WBC) Mike Tyson def. James "Bonecrusher" Smith, 12, Las Vegas; May 30, (IBF) Tony Tucker KO'd James "Buster" Douglas, 10, Las Vegas; Aug. 1, (WBA, WBC, IBF) Mike Tyson def. Tony Tucker, 12, Las Vegas. (Tyson became undisputed champion.)

1990: Feb. 11, (WBA, WBC, IBF) James "Buster" Douglas KOd Mike Tyson, 10, Tokyo; Oct. 25, (WBA, WBC, IBF) Evander Holyfield KOd James "Buster" Douglas, 3, Las Vegas.

1992: Nov. 13, (WBA, WBC, IBF) Riddick Bowe def. Evander Holyfield, 12, Las Vegas. (Lennox Lewis was later named WBC champion when Bowe refused to fight him.)

1993: Nov. 6, (WBA, IBF) Evander Holyfield def. Riddick Bowe, 12, Las Vegas.

1994: Apr. 22, (WBA, IBF) Michael Moorer def. Evander Holyfield, 12, Las Vegas; Sept. 24, (WBC) Oliver McCall KOd Lennox Lewis, 2, London; Nov. 5, (WBA, IBF) George Foreman KOd Michael Moorer, 10, Las Vegas. (In Mar. 1995, Foreman was stripped of the WBA title; he relinquished the IBF title in June.)

1995: Sept. 2, (WBC) Frank Bruno def. Oliver McCall, 12, London; Dec. 9, (IBF) Frans Botha def. Axel Schulz, 12, Las Vegas. (Botha was subsequently stripped of title.)

1996: Mar. 16, (WBC) Mike Tyson KOd Frank Bruno, 3, Las Vegas; June 22, (IBF) Michael Moorer def. Axel Schulz, 12, Dortmund, Germany; Sept. 7, (WBA, WBC) Mike Tyson KOd Bruce Seldon, 1, Las Vegas. (Tyson was subsequently stripped of WBC title.); Nov. 9, (WBA) Evander Holyfield KOd Mike Tyson, 11, Las Vegas.

1997: Feb. 7, (WBC) Lennox Lewis KOd Oliver McCall, 5, Las Vegas; Nov. 8, (IBF) Evander Holyfield def. Michael Moorer, 8, Las Vegas.

1999: Nov. 13, (WBA, WBC, IBF) Lennox Lewis def. Evander Holyfield, 12, Las Vegas. (Lewis became undisputed champion. In April 2000, Lewis was stripped of his WBA title.)

2000: Aug. 12, (WBA) Evander Holyfield def. John Ruiz, 12, Las Vegas.

2001: Mar. 3, (WBA) John Ruiz def. Evander Holyfield, 12, Las Vegas; Apr. 21, (WBC, IBF) Hasim Rahman KOd Lennox Lewis, 5, Brakpan, South Africa; Nov. 17, (WBC, IBF) Lennox Lewis KOd Hasim Rahman, 4, Las Vegas.

2002: Dec. 14, (IBF) Chris Byrd def. Evander Holyfield, 12, Atl. Cty.

2003: Mar. 1, (WBA) Roy Jones Jr. def. John Ruiz, 12, Las Vegas. Dec. 13, (WBA) John Ruiz def. Hasim Rahman, 12, Atlantic City, NJ, to take "interim" title. (Ruiz gained full title when Jones Jr. relinquished it Feb. 20, 2004.)

2004: Apr. 24, (WBC) Vitali Klitschko TKOd Corrie Sanders, 8, Los Angeles, CA, to win title vacated when champ Lennox Lewis retired in Feb.

2005: Apr. 30, (WBA) James Toney def. John Ruiz, 12, NYC (Toney tested positive for steroids; title returned to Ruiz; Aug. 13, (WBC) Hasim Rahman def. Monte Barrett, 12, Chicago, to take "interim" title. Rahman No. 1 contender to face Klitschko for "undisputed" belt.

THOROUGHBRED RACING

Triple Crown Winners

Since 1920, colts have carried 126 lb. in triple crown events; fillies, 121 lb.

(Kentucky Derby, Preakness, and Belmont Stakes)

Year	Horse	Jockey	Trainer
1919	Sir Barton	J. Loftus	H. G. Bedwell
1930	Gallant Fox	E. Sande	J. Fitzsimmons
1935	Omaha	W. Sanders	J. Fitzsimmons
1937	War Admiral	C. Kurtsinger	G. Conway
1941	Whirlaway	E. Arcaro	B. A. Jones
1943	Count Fleet	J. Longden	G. D. Cameron
1946	Assault	W. Mehrtens	M. Hirsch
1948	Citation	E. Arcaro	H. A. Jones
1973	Secretariat	R. Turcotte	L. Laurin
1977	Seattle Slew	J. Cruguet	W. H. Turner Jr.
1978	Affirmed	S. Cauthen	L. S. Barrera

Kentucky Derby

Churchill Downs, Louisville, KY; inaug. 1875; distance 1-1/4 mi; 1-1/2 mi until 1896. 3-year-olds.
Best time: 1:59 2/5, by Secretariat, 1973; 2005 time: 2:02.75.

Year	Winner	Jockey
1875	Aristides	O. Lewis
1876	Vagrant	R. Swim
1877	Baden Baden	W. Walker
1878	Day Star	Carter
1879	Lord Murphy	C. Schauer
1880	Fonso	G. Lewis
1881	Hindoo	J. McLaughlin
1882	Apollo	B. Hurd
1883	Leonatus	W. Donohue
1884	Buchanan	I. Murphy
1885	Joe Cotton	E. Henderson
1886	Ben Ali	P. Duffy
1887	Montrose	I. Lewis
1888	Macbeth II.	G. Covington
1889	Spokane	T. Kiley
1890	Riley	I. Murphy
1891	Kingman	I. Murphy
1892	Azra	A. Clayton
1893	Lookout	E. Kunze
1894	Chant	F. Goodale
1895	Halma	J. Perkins
1896	Ben Brush	W. Simms
1897	Typhoon II.	F. Garner
1898	Plaudit	W. Simms
1899	Manuel	F. Taral
1900	Lieut. Gibson	J. Boland
1901	His Eminence	J. Winkfield
1902	Alan-a-Dale	J. Winkfield
1903	Judge Himes	H. Booker
1904	Elwood	F. Prior
1905	Agile	J. Martin
1906	Sir Huon	R. Troxler
1907	Pink Star	A. Minder
1908	Stone Street	A. Pickens
1909	Wintergreen	V. Powers
1910	Donau	F. Herbert
1911	Meridian	G. Archibald
1912	Worth	C.H. Shilling
1913	Donerail	R. Goose
1914	Old Rosebud	J. McCabe
1915	Regret*	J. Notter
1916	George Smith	J. Loftus
1917	Omar Khayyam	C. Borel
1918	Exterminator	W. Knapp
1919	Sir Barton	J. Loftus
1920	Paul Jones	T. Rice
1921	Behave Yourself	C. Thompson
1922	Morvich	A. Johnson
1923	Zev	E. Sande
1924	Black Gold	J. D. Mooney
1925	Flying Ebony	E. Sande
1926	Bubbling Over	A. Johnson
1927	Whiskery	L. McAtee
1928	Reigh Count	C. Lang
1929	Clyde Van Dusen	L. McAtee
1930	Gallant Fox	E. Sande
1931	Twenty Grand	C. Kurtsinger
1932	Burgoo King	E. James
1933	Brokers Tip	D. Meade
1934	Cavalcade	M. Garner
1935	Omaha	W. Saunders
1936	Bold Venture	I. Hanford
1937	War Admiral	C. Kurtsinger
1938	Lawrin	E. Arcaro
1939	Johnstown	J. Stout
1940	Gallahadion	C. Bierman
1941	Whirlaway	E. Arcaro
1942	Shut Out	W. D. Wright
1943	Count Fleet	J. Longden
1944	Pensive	C. McCreary
1945	Hoop, Jr.	E. Arcaro
1946	Assault	W. Mehrtens
1947	Jet Pilot	E. Guerin
1948	Citation	E. Arcaro
1949	Ponder	S. Brooks
1950	Middleground	W. Boland
1951	Count Turf	C. McCreary
1952	Hill Gail	E. Arcaro
1953	Dark Star	H. Moreno
1954	Determine	R. York
1955	Swaps	W. Shoemaker
1956	Needles	D. Erb
1957	Iron Liege	W. Hartack
1958	Tim Tam	I. Valenzuela
1959	Tomy Lee	W. Shoemaker
1960	Venetian Way	W. Hartack
1961	Carry Back	J. Sellers
1962	Decidedly	W. Hartack
1963	Chateaugay	B. Baeza
1964	Northern Dancer	W. Hartack
1965	Lucky Debonair	W. Shoemaker
1966	Kauai King	D. Brumfield
1967	Proud Clarion	R. Ussery
1968	Dancer's Image#	R. Ussery
1969	Majestic Prince	W. Hartack
1970	Dust Commander	M. Manganello
1971	Canonero II	G. Avila
1972	Riva Ridge	R. Turcotte
1973	Secretariat	R. Turcotte
1974	Cannonade	A. Cordero
1975	Foolish Pleasure	J. Vasquez
1976	Bold Forbes	A. Cordero
1977	Seattle Slew	J. Cruguet
1978	Affirmed	S. Cauthen
1979	Spectacular Bid	R. Franklin
1980	Genuine Risk*	J. Vasquez
1981	Pleasant Colony	J. Velasquez
1982	Gato del Sol	E. Delahoussaye
1983	Sunny's Halo	E. Delahoussaye
1984	Swale	L. Pincay
1985	Spend a Buck	A. Cordero
1986	Ferdinand	W. Shoemaker
1987	Alysheba	C. McCarron
1988	Winning Colors*	G. Stevens
1989	Sunday Silence	P. Valenzuela
1990	Unbridled	C. Perret
1991	Strike the Gold	C. Antley
1992	Lil E. Tee	P. Day
1993	Sea Hero	J. Bailey
1994	Go for Gin	C. McCarron
1995	Thunder Gulch	G. Stevens
1996	Grindstone	J. Bailey
1997	Silver Charm	G. Stevens
1998	Real Quiet	K. Desormeaux
1999	Charismatic	C. Antley
2000	Fusaichi Pegasus	K. Desormeaux
2001	Monarchos	J. Chavez
2002	War Emblem	V. Espinoza
2003	Funny Cide	J. Santos
2004	Smarty Jones	S. Elliot
2005	Giacomo	M. Smith

*Regret, Genuine Risk, and Winning Colors are the only fillies to have won the Derby. # Dancer's Image was disqualified from purse money after tests disclosed that he had run with a pain-killing drug, phenylbutazone, in his system. All wagers were paid on Dancer's Image. Forward Pass was awarded first place money. The Kentucky Derby has been won 5 times by 2 jockeys: Eddie Arcaro, 1938, 1941, 1945, 1948, and 1952; and Bill Hartack, 1957, 1960, 1962, 1964, and 1969. It was won 4 times by Willie Shoemaker, 1955, 1959, 1965, and 1986; and 3 times by each of 4 jockeys: Isaac Murphy, 1884, 1890, and 1891; Earle Sande, 1923, 1925, and 1930; Angel Cordero, 1974, 1976, and 1985; and Gary Stevens, 1988, 1995, and 1997.

Top 10 Fastest Winning Times for the Kentucky Derby

(Official Kentucky Derby times measured in fifths of a second.)

Time	Horse	Jockey	Year
1m. 59 2/5 s.	Secretariat	Ron Turcotte	1973
1m. 59 4/5 s.	Monarchos	Jorge Chavez	2001
2m.	Northern Dancer	Bill Hartack	1964
2m. 1/5 s.	Spend a Buck	Angel Cordero Jr.	1985
2m. 2/5 s.	Decidedly	Bill Hartack	1962
2m. 3/5 s.	Proud Clarion	Robert Ussery	1967
2m. 1 s.	Funny Cide	Jose Santos	2003
	War Emblem	Victor Espinoza	2002
	Fusaichi Pegasus	Kent Desormeaux	2000
	Grindstone	Jerry Bailey	1996
2m. 1 1/5 s.	Thunder Gulch	Gary Stevens	1995
	Affirmed	Steve Cauthen	1978
	Lucky Debonair	Bill Shoemaker	1965
2m. 1 2/5 s.	Whirlaway	Eddie Arcaro	1941
2m. 1 3/5 s.	Bold Forbes	Angel Cordero Jr.	1976
	Hill Gail	Eddie Arcaro	1952
	Middleground	William Boland	1950

Preakness Stakes

Pimlico Race Course, Baltimore, MD; inaug. 1873; distance 1-3/16 mi. 3-year-olds.
Best time: 1:53 2/5, by Tank's Prospect (1985) and Louis Quatorze (1996); 2005 time: 1:55.04.

Year	Winner	Jockey
1873	Survivor	G. Barbee
1874	Culpepper	M. Donohue
1875	Tom Ochiltree	L. Hughes
1876	Shirley	G. Barbee
1877	Cloverbrook	C. Holloway
1878	Duke of Magenta	C. Holloway
1879	Harold	L. Hughes
1880	Grenada	L. Hughes
1881	Saunterer	W. Costello
1882	Vanguard	W. Costello
1883	Jacobus	G. Barbee
1884	Knight of Ellerslie	S. H. Fisher
1885	Tecumseh	J. McLaughlin
1886	The Bard	S. H. Fisher
1887	Dunboyne	W. Donohue
1888	Refund	F. Littlefield
1889	Buddhist	G. Anderson
1890	Montague	W. Martin
1894	Assignee	F. Taral
1895	Belmar	F. Taral
1896	Margrave	H. Griffin
1897	Paul Kauvar	C. Thorpe
1898	Sly Fox	W. Simms
1899	Half Time	R. Clawson
1900	Hindus	H. Spencer
1901	The Parader	F. Landry
1902	Old England	L. Jackson
1903	Flocarline	W. Gannon
1904	Bryn Mawr	E. Hildebrand
1905	Cairngorm	W. Davis
1906	Whimsical	W. Miller
1907	Don Enrique	G. Mountain
1908	Royal Tourist	E. Dugan
1909	Effendi	W. Doyle
1910	Layminster	R. Estep
1911	Watervale	E. Dugan
1912	Colonel Holloway	C. Turner
1913	Buskin	J. Butwell
1914	Holiday	A. Schuttinger
1915	Rhine Maiden	D. Hoffman
1916	Damrosch	L. McAtee
1917	Kalitan	E. Haynes
1918*	War Cloud	J. Loftus
	Jack Hare Jr.	C. Peak
1919	Sir Barton	J. Loftus
1920	Man o' War	C. Kummer
1921	Broomspun	F. Coltiletti
1922	Pillory	L. Morris
1923	Vigil	B. Marinelli
1924	Nellie Morse	J. Merimee
1925	Coventry	C. Kummer
1926	Display	J. Malben
1927	Bostonian	A. Abel
1928	Victorian	R. Workman
1929	Dr. Freeland	L. Schaefer
1930	Gallant Fox	E. Sande
1931	Mate	G. Ellis
1932	Burgoo King	E. James
1933	Head Play	C. Kurtsinger
1934	High Quest	R. Jones
1935	Omaha	W. Saunders
1936	Bold Venture	G. Woolf
1937	War Admiral	C. Kurtsinger
1938	Dauber	M. Peters
1939	Challedon	G. Seabo
1940	Bimelech	F.A. Smith
1941	Whirlaway	E. Arcaro
1942	Alsab	B. James
1943	Count Fleet	J. Longden
1944	Pensive	C. McCreary
1945	Polynesian	W.D. Wright
1946	Assault	W. Mehrtens
1947	Faultless	D. Dodson
1948	Citation	E. Arcaro
1949	Capot	T. Atkinson
1950	Hill Prince	E. Arcaro
1951	Bold	E. Arcaro
1952	Blue Man	C. McCreary
1953	Native Dancer	E. Guerin
1954	Hasty Road	J. Adams
1955	Nashua	E. Arcaro
1956	Fabius	W. Hartack
1957	Bold Ruler	E. Arcaro
1958	Tim Tam	I. Valenzuela
1959	Royal Orbit	W. Harmatz
1960	Bally Ache	R. Ussery
1961	Carry Back	J. Sellers
1962	Greek Money	J.L. Rotz
1963	Candy Spots	W. Shoemaker
1964	Northern Dancer	W. Hartack
1965	Tom Rolfe	R. Turcotte
1966	Kauai King	D. Brumfield
1967	Damascus	W. Shoemaker
1968	Forward Pass	I. Valenzuela
1969	Majestic Prince	W. Hartack
1970	Personality	E. Belmonte
1971	Canonero II	G. Avila
1972	Bee Bee Bee	E. Nelson
1973	Secretariat	R. Turcotte
1974	Little Current	M. Rivera
1975	Master Derby	D. McHargue
1976	Elocutionist	J. Lively
1977	Seattle Slew	J. Cruguet
1978	Affirmed	S. Cauthen
1979	Spectacular Bid	R. Franklin
1980	Codex	A. Cordero
1981	Pleasant Colony	J. Velasquez
1982	Aloma's Ruler	J. Kaenel
1983	Deputed Testamony	D. Miller
1984	Gate Dancer	A. Cordero
1985	Tank's Prospect	P. Day
1986	Snow Chief	A. Solis
1987	Alysheba	C. McCarron
1988	Risen Star	E. Delahoussaye
1989	Sunday Silence	P. Valenzuela
1990	Summer Squall	P. Day
1991	Hansel	J. Bailey
1992	Pine Bluff	C. McCarron
1993	Prairie Bayou	M. Smith
1994	Tabasco Cat	P. Day
1995	Timber Country	P. Day
1996	Louis Quatorze	P. Day
1997	Silver Charm	G. Stevens
1998	Real Quiet	K. Desormeaux
1999	Charismatic	C. Antley
2000	Red Bullet	J. Bailey
2001	Point Given	G. Stevens
2002	War Emblem	V. Espinoza
2003	Funny Cide	J. Santos
2004	Smarty Jones	S. Elliot
2005	Afleet Alex	J. Rose

*Horses ran in 2 divisions.

Belmont Stakes

Belmont Park, Elmont, NY; inaug. 1867; distance 1-1/2 mi. 3-year-olds. Best time: 2:24, Secretariat, 1973; 2005 time: 2:28.60.

Year	Winner	Jockey
1867	Ruthless	J. Gilpatrick
1868	General Duke	R. Swim
1869	Fenian	C. Miller
1870	Kingfisher	W. Dick
1871	Harry Bassett	W. Miller
1872	Joe Daniels	J. Rowe
1873	Springbok	J. Rowe
1874	Saxon	G. Barbee
1875	Calvin	R. Swim
1876	Algerine	W. Donohue
1877	Cloverbrook	C. Holloway
1878	Duke of Magenta	L. Hughes
1879	Spendthrift	S. Evans
1880	Grenada	L. Hughes
1881	Saunterer	T. Costello
1882	Forester	J. McLaughlin
1883	George Kinney	J. McLaughlin
1884	Panique	J. McLaughlin
1885	Tyrant	P. Duffy
1886	Inspector	B.J. McLaughlin
1887	Hanover	J. McLaughlin
1888	Sir Dixon	J. McLaughlin
1889	Eric	W. Hayward
1890	Burlington	S. Barnes
1891	Foxford	E. Garrison
1892	Patron	W. Hayward
1893	Comanche	W. Simms
1894	Henry of Navarre	W. Simms
1895	Belmar	F. Taral
1896	Hastings	H. Griffin
1897	Scottish Chieftain	J. Scherrer
1898	Bowling Brook	F. Littlefield
1899	Jean Bereaud	R. R. Clawson
1900	Ildrim	N. Turner
1901	Commando	H. Spencer
1902	Masterman	J. Bullman
1903	Africander	J. Bullman
1904	Delhi	G. Odom
1905	Tanya	E. Hildebrand
1906	Burgomaster	L. Lyne
1907	Peter Pan	G. Mountain
1908	Colin	J. Notter
1909	Joe Madden	E. Dugan
1910	Sweep	J. Butwell
1913	Prince Eugene	R. Troxler
1914	Luke McLuke	M. Buxton
1915	The Finn	G. Byrne
1916	Friar Rock	E. Haynes
1917	Hourless	J. Butwell
1918	Johren	F. Robinson
1919	Sir Barton	J. Loftus
1920	Man o' War	C. Kummer
1921	Grey Lag	E. Sande
1922	Pillory	C. H. Miller
1923	Zev	E. Sande
1924	Mad Play	E. Sande
1925	American Flag	A. Johnson
1926	Crusader	A. Johnson
1927	Chance Shot	E. Sande
1928	Vito	C. Kummer
1929	Blue Larkspur	M. Garner
1930	Gallant Fox	E. Sande
1931	Twenty Grand	C. Kurtsinger
1932	Faireno	T. Malley
1933	Hurryoff	M. Garner
1934	Peace Chance	W. D. Wright
1935	Omaha	W. Saunders
1936	Granville	J. Stout
1937	War Admiral	C. Kurtsinger
1938	Pasteurized	J. Stout
1939	Johnstown	J. Stout
1940	Bimelech	F. A. Smith
1941	Whirlaway	E. Arcaro
1942	Shut Out	E. Arcaro
1943	Count Fleet	J. Longden
1944	Bounding Home	G. L. Smith
1945	Pavot	E. Arcaro
1946	Assault	W. Mehrtens
1947	Phalanx	R. Donoso
1948	Citation	E. Arcaro
1949	Capot	T. Atkinson
1950	Middleground	W. Boland
1951	Counterpoint	D. Gorman
1952	One Count	E. Arcaro
1953	Native Dancer	E. Guerin
1954	High Gun	E. Guerin
1955	Nashua	E. Arcaro
1956	Needles	D. Erb
1957	Gallant Man	W. Shoemaker
1958	Cavan	P. Anderson
1959	Sword Dancer	W. Shoemaker
1960	Celtic Ash	W. Hartack
1961	Sherluck	B. Baeza
1962	Jaipur	W. Shoemaker
1963	Chateaugay	B. Baeza
1964	Quadrangle	M. Ycaza
1965	Hail to All	J. Sellers
1966	Amberoid	W. Boland
1967	Damascus	W. Shoemaker
1968	Stage Door Johnny	H. Gustines
1969	Arts and Letters	B. Baeza
1970	High Echelon	J. L. Rotz
1971	Pass Catcher	W. Blum
1972	Riva Ridge	R. Turcotte
1973	Secretariat	R. Turcotte
1974	Little Current	M. Rivera
1975	Avatar	W. Shoemaker
1976	Bold Forbes	A. Cordero
1977	Seattle Slew	J. Cruguet
1978	Affirmed	S. Cauthen
1979	Coastal	R. Hernandez

Year	Winner	Jockey
1980	Temperence Hill	E. Maple
1981	Summing	G. Martens
1982	Conquistador Cielo	L. Pincay
1983	Caveat	L. Pincay
1984	Swale	L. Pincay
1985	Creme Fraiche	E. Maple
1986	Danzig Connection	C. McCarron
1987	Bet Twice	C. Perret
1988	Risen Star	E. Delahoussaye
1989	Easy Goer	P. Day
1990	Go and Go	M. Kinane
1991	Hansel	J. Bailey
1992	A.P. Indy	E. Delahoussaye
1993	Colonial Affair	J. Krone
1994	Tabasco Cat	P. Day
1995	Thunder Gulch	G. Stevens
1996	Editor's Note	R. Douglas
1997	Touch Gold	C. McCarron
1998	Victory Gallop	G. Stevens
1999	Lemon Drop Kid	J. Santos
2000	Commendable	P. Day
2001	Point Given	G. Stevens
2002	Sarava	E. Prado
2003	Empire Maker	J. Bailey
2004	Birdstone	E. Prado
2005	Afleet Alex	J. Rose

Annual Leading Jockey — Money Won[1]

Year	Jockey	Earnings
1957	Bill Hartack	$3,060,501
1958	Willie Shoemaker	2,961,693
1959	Willie Shoemaker	2,843,133
1960	Willie Shoemaker	2,123,961
1961	Willie Shoemaker	2,690,819
1962	Willie Shoemaker	2,916,844
1963	Willie Shoemaker	2,526,925
1964	Willie Shoemaker	2,649,553
1965	Braulio Baeza	2,582,702
1966	Braulio Baeza	2,951,022
1967	Braulio Baeza	3,088,888
1968	Braulio Baeza	2,835,108
1969	Jorge Velasquez	2,542,315
1970	Laffit Pincay, Jr.	2,626,526
1971	Laffit Pincay, Jr.	3,784,377
1972	Laffit Pincay, Jr.	3,225,827
1973	Laffit Pincay, Jr.	$4,093,492
1974	Laffit Pincay, Jr.	4,251,060
1975	Braulio Baeza	3,695,198
1976	Angel Cordero, Jr.	4,709,500
1977	Steve Cauthen	6,151,750
1978	Darrel McHargue	6,029,885
1979	Laffit Pincay, Jr.	8,193,535
1980	Chris McCarron	7,663,300
1981	Chris McCarron	8,397,604
1982	Angel Cordero, Jr.	9,483,590
1983	Angel Cordero, Jr.	10,116,697
1984	Chris McCarron	12,045,813
1985	Laffit Pincay, Jr.	13,353,299
1986	Jose Santos	11,329,297
1987	Jose Santos	12,375,433
1988	Jose Santos	14,877,298
1989	Jose Santos	$13,838,389
1990	Gary Stevens	13,881,198
1991	Chris McCarron	14,441,083
1992	Kent Desormeaux	14,193,006
1993	Mike Smith	14,024,815
1994	Mike Smith	15,979,820
1995	Jerry Bailey	16,311,876
1996	Jerry Bailey	19,465,376
1997	Jerry Bailey	18,320,743
1998	Gary Stevens	19,622,855
1999	Pat Day	18,092,845
2000	Pat Day	17,479,838
2001	Jerry Bailey	22,597,720
2002	Jerry Bailey	22,871,814
2003	Jerry Bailey	22,829,570
2004	John R. Velazquez	22,248,661

(1) Total earnings for all horses that jockey raced in year listed; does not reflect jockey's earnings.

Breeders' Cup World Thoroughbred Championships

The Breeders' Cup was inaugurated in 1984 and consists of 7 races at one track on one day late in the year to determine Thoroughbred racing's champion contenders. It has been held at the following locations:

1984	Hollywood Park, CA
1985	Aqueduct Racetrack, NY
1986	Santa Anita Park, CA
1987	Hollywood Park, CA
1988	Churchill Downs, KY
1989	Gulfstream Park, FL
1990	Belmont Park, NY
1991	Churchill Downs, KY
1992	Gulfstream Park, FL
1993	Santa Anita Park, CA
1994	Churchill Downs, KY
1995	Belmont Park, NY
1996	Woodbine Racetrack, Ontario
1997	Hollywood Park, CA
1998	Churchill Downs, KY
1999	Gulfstream Park, FL
2000	Churchill Downs, KY
2001	Belmont Park, NY
2002	Arlington Park, IL
2003	Santa Anita Park, CA
2004	Lone Star Park, TX

Juvenile

Distances: 1 mi 1984-85, 1987; 1-1/16 mi 1986 and since 1988

Year	Winner	Jockey
1984	Chief's Crown	D. MacBeth
1985	Tasso	L. Pincay, Jr.
1986	Capote	L. Pincay, Jr.
1987	Success Express	J. Santos
1988	Is It True	L. Pincay, Jr.
1989	Rhythm	C. Perret
1990	Fly So Free	J. Santos
1991	Arazi	P. Valenzuela
1992	Gilded Time	C. McCarron
1993	Brocco	G. Stevens
1994	Timber Country	P. Day
1995	Unbridled's Song	M. Smith
1996	Boston Harbor	J. Bailey
1997	Favorite Trick	P. Day
1998	Answer Lively	J. Bailey
1999	Anees	G. Stevens
2000	Macho Uno	J. Bailey
2001	Johannesburg	M. Kinane
2002	Vindication	M. Smith
2003	Action This Day	D. Flores
2004	Wilko	F. Dettori

Juvenile Fillies

Distances: 1 mi 1984-85, 1987; 1-1/16 mi 1986 and since 1988

Year	Winner	Jockey
1984	*Outstandingly	W. Guerra
1985	Twilight Ridge	J. Velasquez
1986	Brave Raj	P. Valenzuela
1987	Epitome	P. Day
1988	Open Mind	A. Cordero, Jr.
1989	Go for Wand	R. Romero
1990	Meadow Star	J. Santos
1991	Pleasant Stage	E. Delahoussaye
1992	Eliza	P. Valenzuela
1993	Phone Chatter	L. Pincay, Jr.
1994	Flanders	P. Day
1995	My Flag	J. Bailey
1996	Storm Song	C. Perret
1997	Countess Diana	S. Sellers
1998	Silverbulletday	G. Stevens
1999	Cash Run	J. Bailey
2000	Caressing	J. Velazquez
2001	Tempera	D. Flores
2002	Storm Flag Flying	J. Velazquez
2003	Halfbridled	J. Krone
2004	Sweet Catomine	C. Nakatani

*By disqualification.

Sprint

Distance: 6 furlongs

Year	Winner	Jockey
1984	Eillo	C. Perret
1985	Precisionist	C. McCarron
1986	Smile	J. Vasquez
1987	Very Subtle	P. Valenzuela
1988	Gulch	A. Cordero, Jr.
1989	Dancing Spree	A. Cordero, Jr.
1990	Safely Kept	C. Perret
1991	Sheikh Albadou	P. Eddery
1992	Thirty Slews	E. Delahoussaye
1993	Cardmania	E. Delahoussaye
1994	Cherokee Run	M. Smith
1995	Desert Stormer	K. Desormeaux
1996	Lit De Justice	C. Nakatani
1997	Elmhurst	C. Nakatani
1998	Reraise	C. Nakatani
1999	Artax	J. Chaves
2000	Kona Gold	A. Solis
2001	Squirtle Squirt	J. Bailey
2002	Orientate	J. Bailey
2003	Cajun Beat	C. Velasquez
2004	Speightstown	J. Velazquez

Mile

Year	Winner	Jockey
1984	Royal Heroine	F. Toro
1985	Cozzene	W. Guerra
1986	Last Tycoon	Y. St.-Martin
1987	Miesque	F. Head
1988	Miesque	F. Head
1989	Steinlen	J. Santos
1990	Royal Academy	L. Piggott
1991	Opening Verse	P. Valenzuela
1992	Lure	M. Smith
1993	Lure	M. Smith
1994	Barathea	L. Dettori
1995	Ridgewood Pearl	J. Murtagh
1996	Da Hoss	G. Stevens
1997	Spinning World	C. Asmussan
1998	Da Hoss	J. Velazquez
1999	Silic	C. Nakatani
2000	War Chant	G. Stevens
2001	Val Royal	J. Valdivia Jr.
2002	Domedriver	T. Thulliez
2003	Six Perfections	J. Bailey
2004	Singletary	D. Flores

Filly & Mare Turf

Distances: 1-3/8 mi 1999-2000, 1-1/4 mi 2002

Year	Winner	Jockey
1999	Soaring Softly	J. Bailey
2000	Perfect Sting	J. Bailey
2001	Banks Hill	O. Peslier
2002	Starine	J. Velazquez
2003	Islington	K. Fallon
2004	Ouija Board	K. Fallon

Distaff

Distances: 1-1/4 mi 1984-87; 1-1/8 mi since 1988

Year		Jockey	Year		Jockey	Year		Jockey
1984	Princess Rooney	E. Delahoussaye	1991	Dance Smartly	P. Day	1998	Escena	G. Stevens
1985	Life's Magic	A. Cordero, Jr.	1992	Paseana	C. McCarron	1999	Beautiful Pleasure	J. Chaves
1986	Lady's Secret	P. Day	1993	Hollywood Wildcat	E. Delahoussaye	2000	Spain	V. Espinoza
1987	Sacahuista	R. Romero	1994	One Dreamer	G. Stevens	2001	Unbridled Elaine	P. Day
1988	Personal Ensign	R. Romero	1995	Inside Information	M. Smith	2002	Azeri	M. Smith
1989	Bayakoa	L. Pincay, Jr.	1996	Jewel Princess	C. Nakatani	2003	Adoration	P. Valenzuela
1990	Bayakoa	L. Pincay, Jr.	1997	Ajina	M. Smith	2004	Ashado	J. Velazquez

Turf

Distance: 1-1/2 mi

Year		Jockey	Year		Jockey	Year		Jockey
1984	Lashkari	Y. St.-Martin	1991	Miss Alleged	E. Legrix	1999	Daylami	L. Dettori
1985	Pebbles	P. Eddery	1992	Fraise	P. Valenzuela	2000	Kalanisi	J. Murtagh
1986	Manila	J. Santos	1993	Kotashaan	K. Desormeaux	2001	Fantastic Light	L. Dettori
1987	Theatrical	P. Day	1994	Tikkanen	M. Smith	2002	High Chaparral	M. Kinane
1988	Great Communicator	R. Sibille	1995	Northern Spur	C. McCarron	2003	tie-High Chaparral	M. Kinane
			1996	Pilsudski	W. Swinburn		Johar	A. Solis
1989	Prized	E. Delahoussaye	1997	Chief Bearhart	J. Santos	2004	Better Talk Now	R. Dominguez
1990	In The Wings	G. Stevens	1998	Buck's Boy	S. Sellers			

Classic

Distance: 1-1/4 mi

Year		Jockey	Year		Jockey	Year		Jockey
1984	Wild Again	P. Day	1991	Black Tie Affair	J. Bailey	1998	Awesome Again	P. Day
1985	Proud Truth	J. Velasquez	1992	A.P. Indy	E. Delahoussaye	1999	Cat Thief	P. Day
1986	Skywalker	L. Pincay, Jr.	1993	Arcangues	J. Bailey	2000	Tiznow	C. McCarron
1987	Ferdinand	W. Shoemaker	1994	Concern	J. Bailey	2001	Tiznow	C. McCarron
1988	Alysheba	C. McCarron	1995	Cigar	J. Bailey	2002	Volponi	P. Johnson
1989	Sunday Silence	C. McCarron	1996	Alphabet Soup	C. McCarron	2003	Pleasantly Perfect	A. Solis
1990	Unbridled	P. Day	1997	Skip Away	M. Smith	2004	Ghostzapper	J. Castellano

Eclipse Awards

The Eclipse Awards, honoring the Horse of the Year and other champions of the sport, began in 1971 and are sponsored by the *Daily Racing Form,* the National Thoroughbred Racing Association, and the National Turf Writers Assn. Prior to 1971, the *DRF* (1936-70) and the TRA (1950-70) issued separate selections for Horse of the Year.

Eclipse Awards for 2004

Horse of the Year—Ghostzapper
2-year-old colt or gelding—Declan's Moon
2-year-old filly—Sweet Catomine
3-year-old colt or gelding—Smarty Jones
3-year-old filly—Ashado
Older male (4-year-olds & up)—Ghostzapper
Older female (4-year-olds & up)—Azeri
Male turf horse—Kitten's Joy
Turf filly or mare—Ouija Board (Britain)
Sprinter—Speightstown
Steeplechase horse—Hirapour (Ireland)
Trainer—Todd Pletcher
Jockey—John R. Velazquez
Apprentice jockey—Brian Hernandez Jr.
Breeder—Adena Springs
Owner—Kenneth and Sarah Ramsey

Horse of the Year

1936	Granville	1954	Native Dancer	1970	Fort Marcy (DRF) Personality (TRA)	1987	Ferdinand
1937	War Admiral	1955	Nashua	1971	Ack Ack	1988	Alysheba
1938	Seabiscuit	1956	Swaps	1972	Secretariat	1989	Sunday Silence
1939	Challedon	1957	Bold Ruler (DRF) Dedicate (TRA)	1973	Secretariat	1990	Criminal Type
1940	Challedon	1958	Round Table	1974	Forego	1991	Black Tie Affair
1941	Whirlaway	1959	Sword Dancer	1975	Forego	1992	A.P. Indy
1942	Whirlaway	1960	Kelso	1976	Forego	1993	Kotashaan
1943	Count Fleet	1961	Kelso	1977	Seattle Slew	1994	Holy Bull
1944	Twilight Tear	1962	Kelso	1978	Affirmed	1995	Cigar
1945	Busher	1963	Kelso	1979	Affirmed	1996	Cigar
1946	Assault	1964	Kelso	1980	Spectacular Bid	1997	Favorite Trick
1947	Armed	1965	Roman Brother (DRF) Moccasin (TRA)	1981	John Henry	1998	Skip Away
1948	Citation	1966	Buckpasser	1982	Conquistador Cielo	1999	Charismatic
1949	Capot	1967	Damascus	1983	All Along	2000	Tiznow
1950	Hill Prince	1968	Dr. Fager	1984	John Henry	2001	Point Given
1951	Counterpoint	1969	Arts and Letters	1985	Spend A Buck	2002	Azeri
1952	One Count (DRF) Native Dancer (TRA)			1986	Lady's Secret	2003	Mineshaft
1953	Tom Fool					2004	Ghostzapper

HARNESS RACING

Harness Horse of the Year

(Chosen by the U.S. Trotting Assn. and the U.S. Harness Writers Assn.)

1947	Victory Song	1962	Su Mac Lad	1977	Green Speed	1991	Precious Bunny
1948	Rodney	1963	Speedy Scot	1978	Abercrombie	1992	Artsplace
1949	Good Time	1964	Bret Hanover	1979	Niatross	1993	Staying Together
1950	Proximity	1965	Bret Hanover	1980	Niatross	1994	Cam's Card Shark
1951	Pronto Don	1966	Bret Hanover	1981	Fan Hanover	1995	CR Kay Suzie
1952	Good Time	1967	Nevele Pride	1982	Cam Fella	1996	Continentalvictory
1953	Hi Lo's Forbes	1968	Nevele Pride	1983	Cam Fella	1997	Malabar Man
1954	Stenographer	1969	Nevele Pride	1984	Fancy Crown	1998	Moni Maker
1955	Scott Frost	1970	Fresh Yankee	1985	Nihilator	1999	Moni Maker
1956	Scott Frost	1971	Albatross	1986	Forrest Skipper	2000	Gallo Blue Chip
1957	Torpid	1972	Albatross	1987	Mack Lobell	2001	Bunny Lake
1958	Emily's Pride	1973	Sir Dalrae	1988	Mack Lobell	2002	Real Desire
1959	Bye Bye Byrd	1974	Delmonica Hanover	1989	Matt's Scooter	2003	No Pan Intended
1960	Adios Butler	1975	Savoir	1990	Beach Towel	2004	Rainbow Blue
1961	Adios Butler	1976	Keystone Ore				

The Hambletonian (3-year-old trotters)

Year	Winner	Driver
1965	Egyptian Candor	Del Cameron
1966	Kerry Way	Frank Ervin
1967	Speedy Streak	Del Cameron
1968	Nevele Pride	Stanley Dancer
1969	Lindy's Pride	Howard Beissinger
1970	Timothy T	John Simpson, Sr.
1971	Speedy Crown	Howard Beissinger
1972	Super Bowl	Stanley Dancer
1973	Flirth	Ralph Baldwin
1974	Christopher T	Bill Haughton
1975	Bonefish	Stanley Dancer
1976	Steve Lobell	Bill Haughton
1977	Green Speed	Bill Haughton
1978	Speedy Somolli	Howard Beissinger
1979	Legend Hanover	George Sholty
1980	Burgomeister	Bill Haughton
1981	Shiaway St. Pat	Ray Remmen
1982	Speed Bowl	Tommy Haughton
1983	Duenna	Stanley Dancer
1984	Historic Freight	Ben Webster
1985	Prakas	Bill O'Donnell
1986	Nuclear Kosmos	Ulf Thoresen
1987	Mack Lobell	John Campbell
1988	Armbro Goal	John Campbell
1989	Park Avenue Joe	Ron Waples
1990	Harmonious	John Campbell
1991	Giant Victory	Jack Moiseyev
1992	Alf Palema	Mickey McNicholl
1993	American Winner	Ron Pierce
1994	Victory Dream	Michel Lachance
1995	Tagliabue	John Campbell
1996	Continental-victory	Michel Lachance
1997	Malabar Man	Malvern Burroughs
1998	Muscles Yankee	John Campbell
1999	Self Possessed	Mike Lachance
2000	Yankee Paco	Trevor Ritchie
2001	Scarlet Knight	Stefan Melander
2002	Chip Chip Hooray	Eric Ledford
2003	Amigo Hall	Mike Lachance
2004	Windsong's Legacy	Trond Smedshammer
2005	Vivid Photo	Roger Hammer

NCAA WRESTLING CHAMPIONS

Year	Champion
1964	Oklahoma State
1965	Iowa State
1966	Oklahoma State
1967	Michigan State
1968	Oklahoma State
1969	Iowa State
1970	Iowa State
1971	Oklahoma State
1972	Iowa State
1973	Iowa State
1974	Oklahoma
1975	Iowa
1976	Iowa
1977	Iowa State
1978	Iowa
1979	Iowa
1980	Iowa
1981	Iowa
1982	Iowa
1983	Iowa
1984	Iowa
1985	Iowa
1986	Iowa
1987	Iowa State
1988	Arizona State
1989	Oklahoma State
1990	Oklahoma State
1991	Iowa
1992	Iowa
1993	Iowa
1994	Oklahoma State
1995	Iowa
1996	Iowa
1997	Iowa
1998	Iowa
1999	Iowa
2000	Iowa
2001	Minnesota
2002	Minnesota
2003	Oklahoma State
2004	Oklahoma State
2005	Oklahoma State

CHESS

World Chess Champions

Sources: U.S. Chess Federation; International Chess Federation (FIDE)

Official world champions since the title was first used are as follows:

1866-1894	Wilhelm Steinitz, Austria
1894-1921	Emanuel Lasker, Germany
1921-1927	Jose R. Capablanca, Cuba
1927-1935	Alexander A. Alekhine, France
1935-1937	Max Euwe, Netherlands
1937-1946	Alexander A. Alekhine, France (a)
1948-1957	Mikhail Botvinnik, USSR
1957-1958	Vassily Smyslov, USSR
1958-1959	Mikhail Botvinnik, USSR
1960-1961	Mikhail Tal, USSR
1961-1963	Mikhail Botvinnik, USSR
1963-1969	Tigran Petrosian, USSR
1969-1972	Boris Spassky, USSR
1972-1975	Bobby Fischer, U.S. (b)
1975-1985	Anatoly Karpov, USSR
1985-1993	Garry Kasparov, USSR/Russia (c)
1993-1995	Garry Kasparov, Russia (PCA) (d)
1993-1999	Anatoly Karpov, Russia (FIDE)
1999	Aleksandr Khalifman, Russia (FIDE)
2000-2002	Viswanathan Anand, India (FIDE) (e)
2002-2004	Ruslan Ponomariov, Ukraine (FIDE)
2004-	Rustam Kasimdzhanov, Uzbekistan (FIDE)

(a) After Alekhine died in 1946, the title was vacant until 1948, when Botvinnik won the 1st championship match sanctioned by the International Chess Federation (FIDE). (b) Defaulted championship after refusal to accept FIDE rules for a championship match, Apr. 1975. (c) Kasparov broke with FIDE, Feb. 26, 1993. FIDE stripped Kasparov of his title Mar. 23. Kasparov defeated Nigel Short of Great Britain in a world championship match played Sept.-Oct. 1993 under the auspices of a new organization the two had founded, the Professional Chess Association (PCA). FIDE held a championship match between Anatoly Karpov (Russia) and Jan Timman (the Netherlands), which Karpov won in Nov. 1993. (d) The PCA folded in 1995. (e) In Nov. 2000, Vladimir Kramnik (Russia) defeated Garry Kasparov (Russia), widely recognized as the unofficial world champion, 8½-6½, at the Braingames World Chess Championships in London. **Recent developments:** FIDE announced in Oct. 2004 that Kasimdzhanov would play Garry Kasparov (Russia), the world's top-ranked player, in Jan. 2005, but the match was canceled for lack of funds, and Kasparov announced his retirement from competitive chess in Mar. 2005. The 2005 World Championship Tournament was to be held Sept. 27-Oct. 16, 2005, in San Luis, Argentina. **Further information:** More information on chess and chess champions may be accessed on FIDE's Internet site, www.fide.com; or www.worldchesschampionship.com

BOWLING

Professional Bowlers Association

Hall of Fame

PERFORMANCE

Bill Allen
Glenn Allison
Earl Anthony
Mike Aulby
Joe Berardi
Ray Bluth
Parker Bohn III
Roy Buckley
Nelson Burton Jr.
Don Carter
Pat Colwell
Steve Cook
Dave Davis
Gary Dickinson
Mike Durbin
Buzz Fazio
Dave Ferraro
Jim Godman
Billy Hardwick
Marshall Hollman
Tommy Hudson
Dave Husted
Don Johnson
Joe Joseph
Larry Laub
Amleto Monacelli
David Ozio
George Pappas
Johnny Petraglia
Dick Ritger
Mark Roth
Carmen Salvino
Ernie Schlegel
Harry Smith
Dave Soutar
Jim Stefanich
Brian Voss
Wayne Webb
Dick Weber
Pete Weber
Billy Welu
Mark Williams
Walter Ray Williams Jr.
Wayne Zahn

MERITORIOUS SERVICE

Glenn Allison
Joe Antenora
John Archibald
Barry Asher
Tom Baker
Chuck Clemens
Eddie Elias
Frank Esposito
Dick Evans
Matt Fiorito
Raymond Firestone
E. A. "Bud" Fisher
Jim Fitzgerald
Skee Foremsky
Lou Frantz
Harry Golden
John Guenther
Ted Hoffman Jr.
Joe Joseph
John Jowdy
Joe Kelley
Larry Lichstein
Mike Limongello
Mort Luby Jr.
Andy Marzich
Don McCune
Mike McGrath
Steve Nagy
Keijiro Nakano
Chuck Pezzano
Jack Reichert
Joe Richards
Jim St. John
Chris Schenkel
Ernie Schlegel
Teata Semiz
Lorraine Stilzlein
Bob Strampe
Al Thompson
Roger Zeller

PBA Tournament of Champions, 1965-2005[1]

Year	Winner	Year	Winner	Year	Winner	Year	Winner
1965	Billy Hardwick	1975	Dave Davis	1985	Mark Williams	1994	Norm Duke
1966	Wayne Zahn	1976	Marshall Holman	1986	Marshall Holman	1996	Dave D'Entremont
1967	Jim Stefanich	1977	Mike Berlin	1987	Pete Weber	1997	John Gant
1968	Dave Davis	1978	Earl Anthony	1988	Mark Williams	1998	Bryan Goebel
1969	Jim Godman	1979	George Pappas	1989	Del Ballard, Jr.	1999	Jason Couch
1970	Don Johnson	1980	Wayne Webb	1990	Dave Ferraro	2000	Jason Couch
1971	Johnny Petraglia	1981	Steve Cook	1991	David Ozio	2002	Jason Couch
1972	Mike Durbin	1982	Mike Durbin	1992	Marc McDowell	2003	Patrick Healey Jr
1973	Jim Godman	1983	Joe Berardi	1993	George Branham, 3rd	2005	Steve Jaros
1974	Earl Anthony	1984	Mike Durbin				

(1) No tournament held in 2001 because of schedule changes; in the 2004-2005 season, the tournament was held in Apr. 2005, at the end of the PBA season (previously held in Dec.).

PBA Leading Money Winners

Total winnings are from PBA, ABC Masters, and BPAA All-Star tournaments only and do not include numerous other tournaments or earnings from special television shows and matches. In 2001, the PBA began an Oct.-Apr. season schedule. After 2000, year shown is year the season ended.

Year	Bowler	Amount	Year	Bowler	Amount	Year	Bowler	Amount
1962	Don Carter	$49,972	1977	Mark Roth	$105,583	1991	David Ozio	$225,585
1963	Dick Weber	46,333	1978	Mark Roth	134,500	1992	Marc McDowell	174,215
1964	Bob Strampe	33,592	1979	Mark Roth	124,517	1993	Walter Ray Williams Jr.	296,370
1965	Dick Weber	47,674	1980	Wayne Webb	116,700	1994	Norm Duke	273,753
1966	Wayne Zahn	54,720	1981	Earl Anthony	164,735	1995	Mike Aulby	219,792
1967	Dave Davis	54,165	1982	Earl Anthony	134,760	1996	Walter Ray Williams Jr.	241,330
1968	Jim Stefanich	67,377	1983	Earl Anthony	135,605	1997	Walter Ray Williams Jr.	240,544
1969	Billy Hardwick	64,160	1984	Mark Roth	158,712	1998	Walter Ray Williams Jr.	238,225
1970	Mike McGrath	52,049	1985	Mike Aulby	201,200	1999	Parker Bohn III	240,912
1971	Johnny Petraglia	85,065	1986	Walter Ray Williams Jr.	145,550	2000	Norm Duke	143,325
1972	Don Johnson	56,648	1987	Pete Weber	175,491	2002	Parker Bohn III	245,200
1973	Don McCune	69,000	1988	Brian Voss	225,485	2003	Walter Ray Williams Jr.	419,700
1974	Earl Anthony	99,585	1989	Mike Aulby	298,237	2004	Mika Koivuniemi	238,590
1975	Earl Anthony	107,585	1990	Amleto Monacelli	204,775	2005	Patrick Allen	350,740
1976	Earl Anthony	110,833						

Leading PBA Averages by Year

Year	Bowler	Average	Year	Bowler	Average	Year	Bowler	Average
1962	Don Carter	212.84	1977	Mark Roth	218.17	1991	Norm Duke	218.20
1963	Billy Hardwick	210.34	1978	Mark Roth	219.83	1992	Dave Ferraro	219.70
1964	Ray Bluth	210.51	1979	Mark Roth	221.66	1993	Walter Ray Williams Jr.	222.98
1965	Dick Weber	211.89	1980	Earl Anthony	218.53	1994	Norm Duke	222.83
1966	Wayne Zahn	208.66	1981	Mark Roth	216.69	1995	Mike Aulby	225.49
1967	Wayne Zahn	212.34	1982	Marshall Holman	212.84	1996	Walter Ray Williams Jr.	225.37
1968	Jim Stefanich	211.89	1983	Earl Anthony	216.64	1997	Walter Ray Williams Jr.	222.00
1969	Bill Hardwick	212.95	1984	Marshall Holman	213.91	1998	Walter Ray Williams Jr.	226.13
1970	Nelson Burton Jr.	214.90	1985	Mark Baker	213.71	1999	Parker Bohn III	228.04
1971	Don Johnson	213.97	1986	John Gant	214.37	2000	Chris Barnes	220.93
1972	Don Johnson	215.29	1987	Marshall Holman	216.80	2002	Parker Bohn III	221.54
1973	Earl Anthony	215.79	1988	Mark Roth	218.03	2003	Walter Ray Williams Jr.	224.94
1974	Earl Anthony	219.39	1989	Pete Weber	215.43	2004	Mika Koivuniemi	222.73
1975	Earl Anthony	219.06	1990	Amleto Monacelli	218.15	2005	Walter Ray Williams Jr.	227.07
1976	Mark Roth	215.97						

American Bowling Congress

Most Sanctioned 300 Games

Bowler	Games	Bowler	Games	Bowler	Games
Jeff Carter, Springfield, IL	83	John Delp III, West Lawn, PA	65	Gordon Childers, Benton, AR	60
Joe Jimenez, Saginaw, MI	75	Randy Choat, Granite City, IL	63	Bob Buckery, McAdoo, PA	57
Chris Hayward, Toledo, OH	71	Robert Faragon, Albany, NY	61	Jim Hosier, Wayne, NJ	57
Jeff Ripic, Endicott, NY	71	Jeff Jensen, Wichita, KS	60	Dale Strike, Saginaw, MI	56
Dean Wolf, Reading, PA	71	Bob Learn Jr., Erie, PA	60	John Wilcox Jr., Lewisburg, PA	55
Jerry Kessler, Dayton, OH	70	Jim Tomek Jr., Camp Hill, PA	60	David Bingham, Brainard, NY	55
Frank Massengale Jr., Hixon, TN	70	John Chacko Jr., Larksville, PA	60		

ABC Masters Tournament Champions

Year	Winner	Year	Winner	Year	Winner
1980	Neil Burton, St. Louis, MO	1989	Mike Aulby, Indianapolis, IN	1998	Mike Aulby, Indianapolis, IN
1981	Randy Lightfoot, St. Charles, MO	1990	Chris Warren, Dallas, TX	1999	Brian Boghosian, Middletown, CT
1982	Joe Berardi, Brooklyn, NY	1991	Doug Kent, Canandaigua, NY	2000	MIka Koivuniemi, Finland
1983	Mike Lastowski, Havre de Grace, MD	1992	Ken Johnson, N. Richmond Hills, TX	2001	Parker Bohn III, Jackson, NJ
1984	Earl Anthony, Dublin, CA	1993	Norm Duke, Oklahoma City, OK	2002	Brett Wolfe, Reno, NV
1985	Steve Wunderlich, St. Louis, MO	1994	Steve Fehr, Cincinnati, OH	2003	Bryon Smith, Roseburg, OR
1986	Mark Fahy, Chicago, IL	1995	Mike Aulby, Indianapolis, IN	2004	Walter Ray Williams Jr., FL
1987	Rick Steelsmith, Wichita, KS	1996	Ernie Schlegel, Vancouver, WA	2005	Walter Ray Williams Jr., FL (Jan.) Danny Wiseman, MD (Oct.)
1988	Del Ballard, Jr., Richardson, TX	1997	Jason Queen, Decatur, IL		

Champions in 2005

Regular Singles: David Adam, Maryland Heights, MO
Regular Doubles: Jeff Richgels, Oregon, WI, & Steve Richter, Sheboygan Falls, WI
Regular All-Events: Scott Craddock, Wichita Falls, TX
Regular Team: KR Strikeforce, Decatur, IL
Classic Singles: Wesley Turner, Columbus, OH
Classic Doubles: Dustin & Chris Rhodes, Wichita Falls, TX
Classic All-Events: Michael Hal, Knoxville, TN
Classic Team: Flirtin With Disaster 1, Tallahassee, FL

Women's International Bowling Congress

Champions in 2005

Queens Tournament: Tennelle Milligan, Costa Mesa, CA
Classic Singles: Leanne Barrette, Elk Grove, CA
Classic Doubles: Brenda Norman, Stroudsburg, PA, & Karen Stroud, Victoria, TX
Classic All Events: Leanne Barrette, Elk Grove, CA
Classic Team: Shootin' Nines, Stroudsburg, PA
Div. I Singles: Lil Martindale, Longmont, CO
Div. I Doubles: Belinda Brown, Macon, GA, & Renee Serfass, Stroudsburg, PA
Div. I All Events: Cindy Mattingly, Puyallup, WA
Div. I Team: New Beginnings, Austin, TX

Most Sanctioned 300 Games

Tish Johnson, Panorama City, CA 35
Jodi Musto, Schenectady, NY 35
Altramese Webb, Detroit, MI 34
Dede Davidson, Woodland Hills, CA . . 29
Aleta Sill, Dearborn, MI 27
Debbie McMullen, Denver, CO 26
Leanne Barrette, Yukon, OK 26
Marianne DiRupo, Succasunna, NJ . . . 26
Anne-Marie Duggan, Edmond, OK . . . 25
Jeanne Naccarato, Tacoma, WA 23
Vicki Fischel, Wheat Ridge, CO 23
Shannon Duplantis, New Orleans, LA 23
Cheryl Daniels, Detroit, MI 22
Jodi Hughes, Greenville, SC 21
Carolyn Dorin-Ballard, N. Richland Hills, TX 21
Kim Terrell, San Francisco, CA 21
Jeanette Menacho, Sacramento, CA 20
Mandy Wilson, Dayton, OH 19
Kim Adler, Palm City, FL 18
Cindy Coburn-Carroll, Tonawanda, NY 18
Tammy Jones, Decatur, IL 18

FIGURE SKATING

U.S. and World Individual Champions, 1952-2005

U.S. Champions			World Champions	
MEN	**WOMEN**	**YEAR**	**MEN**	**WOMEN**
Dick Button	Tenley Albright	**1952**	Dick Button, U.S.	Jacqueline du Bief, France
Hayes Jenkins	Tenley Albright	**1953**	Hayes Jenkins, U.S.	Tenley Albright, U.S.
Hayes Jenkins	Tenley Albright	**1954**	Hayes Jenkins, U.S.	Gundi Busch, W. Germany
Hayes Jenkins	Tenley Albright	**1955**	Hayes Jenkins, U.S.	Tenley Albright, U.S.
Hayes Jenkins	Tenley Albright	**1956**	Hayes Jenkins, U.S.	Carol Heiss, U.S.
Dave Jenkins	Carol Heiss	**1957**	Dave Jenkins, U.S.	Carol Heiss, U.S.
Dave Jenkins	Carol Heiss	**1958**	Dave Jenkins, U.S.	Carol Heiss, U.S.
Dave Jenkins	Carol Heiss	**1959**	Dave Jenkins, U.S.	Carol Heiss, U.S.
Dave Jenkins	Carol Heiss	**1960**	Alain Giletti, France	Carol Heiss, U.S.
Bradley Lord	Laurence Owen	**1961**	none	none
Monty Hoyt	Barbara Roles Pursley	**1962**	Don Jackson, Canada	Sjoukje Dijkstra, Netherlands
Tommy Litz	Lorraine Hanlon	**1963**	Don McPherson, Canada	Sjoukje Dijkstra, Netherlands
Scott Allen	Peggy Fleming	**1964**	Manfred Schnelldorfer, W. Germany	Sjoukje Dijkstra, Netherlands
Gary Visconti	Peggy Fleming	**1965**	Alain Calmat, France	Petra Burka, Canada
Scott Allen	Peggy Fleming	**1966**	Emmerich Danzer, Austria	Peggy Fleming, U.S.
Gary Visconti	Peggy Fleming	**1967**	Emmerich Danzer, Austria	Peggy Fleming, U.S.
Tim Wood	Peggy Fleming	**1968**	Emmerich Danzer, Austria	Peggy Fleming, U.S.
Tim Wood	Janet Lynn	**1969**	Tim Wood, U.S.	Gabriele Seyfert, E. Germany
Tim Wood	Janet Lynn	**1970**	Tim Wood, U.S.	Gabriele Seyfert, E. Germany
John Misha Petkevich	Janet Lynn	**1971**	Ondrej Nepela, Czechoslovakia	Beatrix Schuba, Austria
Ken Shelley	Janet Lynn	**1972**	Ondrej Nepela, Czechoslovakia	Beatrix Schuba, Austria
Gordon McKellen, Jr.	Janet Lynn	**1973**	Ondrej Nepela, Czechoslovakia	Karen Magnussen, Canada
Gordon McKellen, Jr.	Dorothy Hamill	**1974**	Jan Hoffmann, E. Germany	Christine Errath, E. Germany
Gordon McKellen, Jr.	Dorothy Hamill	**1975**	Sergei Volkov, USSR	Dianne de Leeuw, Neth.-U.S.
Terry Kubicka	Dorothy Hamill	**1976**	John Curry, Gr. Britain	Dorothy Hamill, U.S.
Charles Tickner	Linda Fratianne	**1977**	Vladimir Kovalev, USSR	Linda Fratianne, U.S.
Charles Tickner	Linda Fratianne	**1978**	Charles Tickner, U.S.	Anett Poetzsch, E. Germany
Charles Tickner	Linda Fratianne	**1979**	Vladimir Kovalev, USSR	Linda Fratianne, U.S.
Charles Tickner	Linda Fratianne	**1980**	Jan Hoffmann, E. Germany	Anett Poetzsch, E. Germany
Scott Hamilton	Elaine Zayak	**1981**	Scott Hamilton, U.S.	Denise Biellmann, Switzerland
Scott Hamilton	Rosalynn Sumners	**1982**	Scott Hamilton, U.S.	Elaine Zayak, U.S.
Scott Hamilton	Rosalynn Sumners	**1983**	Scott Hamilton, U.S.	Rosalynn Sumners, U.S.
Scott Hamilton	Rosalynn Sumners	**1984**	Scott Hamilton, U.S.	Katarina Witt, E. Germany
Brian Boitano	Tiffany Chin	**1985**	Aleksandr Fadeev, USSR	Katarina Witt, E. Germany
Brian Boitano	Debi Thomas	**1986**	Brian Boitano, U.S.	Debi Thomas, U.S.
Brian Boitano	Jill Trenary	**1987**	Brian Orser, Canada	Katarina Witt, E. Germany
Brian Boitano	Debi Thomas	**1988**	Brian Boitano, U.S.	Katarina Witt, E. Germany
Christopher Bowman	Jill Trenary	**1989**	Kurt Browning, Canada	Midori Ito, Japan
Todd Eldredge	Jill Trenary	**1990**	Kurt Browning, Canada	Jill Trenary, U.S.
Todd Eldredge	Tonya Harding	**1991**	Kurt Browning, Canada	Kristi Yamaguchi, U.S.
Christopher Bowman	Kristi Yamaguchi	**1992**	Viktor Petrenko, Ukraine	Kristi Yamaguchi, U.S.
Scott Davis	Nancy Kerrigan	**1993**	Kurt Browning, Canada	Oksana Baiul, Ukraine
Scott Davis	vacant[1]	**1994**	Elvis Stojko, Canada	Yuka Sato, Japan
Todd Eldredge	Nicole Bobek	**1995**	Elvis Stojko, Canada	Chen Lu, China
Rudy Galindo	Michelle Kwan	**1996**	Todd Eldredge, U.S.	Michelle Kwan, U.S.
Todd Eldredge	Tara Lipinski	**1997**	Elvis Stojko, Canada	Tara Lipinski, U.S.
Todd Eldredge	Michelle Kwan	**1998**	Alexei Yagudin, Russia	Michelle Kwan, U.S.
Michael Weiss	Michelle Kwan	**1999**	Alexei Yagudin, Russia	Maria Butyrskaya, Russia
Michael Weiss	Michelle Kwan	**2000**	Alexei Yagudin, Russia	Michelle Kwan, U.S.
Timothy Goebel	Michelle Kwan	**2001**	Yevgeny Plushchenko, Russia	Michelle Kwan, U.S.
Todd Eldredge	Michelle Kwan	**2002**	Alexei Yagudin, Russia	Irina Slutskaya, Russia
Michael Weiss	Michelle Kwan	**2003**	Yevgeny Plushchenko, Russia	Michelle Kwan, U.S.
Johnny Weir	Michelle Kwan	**2004**	Yevgeny Plushchenko, Russia	Shizuka Arakawa, Japan
Johnny Weir	Michelle Kwan	**2005**	Stephane Lambiel, Switzerland	Irina Slutskaya, Russia

(1) Tonya Harding was stripped of title.

SKIING

World Cup Alpine Champions, 1967-2005

Men

1967 Jean Claude Killy, France
1968 Jean Claude Killy, France
1969 Karl Schranz, Austria
1970 Karl Schranz, Austria
1971 Gustavo Thoeni, Italy
1972 Gustavo Thoeni, Italy
1973 Gustavo Thoeni, Italy
1974 Piero Gros, Italy
1975 Gustavo Thoeni, Italy
1976 Ingemar Stenmark, Sweden
1977 Ingemar Stenmark, Sweden
1978 Ingemar Stenmark, Sweden
1979 Peter Luescher, Switzerland
1980 Andreas Wenzel, Liechtenstein
1981 Phil Mahre, U.S.
1982 Phil Mahre, U.S.
1983 Phil Mahre, U.S.
1984 Pirmin Zurbriggen, Switzerland
1985 Marc Girardelli, Luxembourg
1986 Marc Girardelli, Luxembourg
1987 Pirmin Zurbriggen, Switzerland
1988 Pirmin Zurbriggen, Switzerland
1989 Marc Girardelli, Luxembourg
1990 Pirmin Zurbriggen, Switzerland
1991 Marc Girardelli, Luxembourg
1992 Paul Accola, Switzerland
1993 Marc Girardelli, Luxembourg
1994 Kjetil Andre Aamodt, Norway
1995 Alberto Tomba, Italy
1996 Lasse Kjus, Norway
1997 Luc Alphand, France
1998 Hermann Maier, Austria
1999 Lasse Kjus, Norway
2000 Hermann Maier, Austria
2001 Hermann Maier, Austria
2002 Stephan Eberharter, Austria
2003 Stephan Eberharter, Austria
2004 Hermann Maier, Austria
2005 Bode Miller, U.S.

Women

1967 Nancy Greene, Canada
1968 Nancy Greene, Canada
1969 Gertrud Gabl, Austria
1970 Michele Jacot, France
1971 Annemarie Proell, Austria
1972 Annemarie Proell, Austria
1973 Annemarie Proell, Austria
1974 Annemarie Proell, Austria
1975 Annemarie Proell, Austria
1976 Rose Mittermaier, W. Germany
1977 Lise-Marie Morerod, Switzerland
1978 Hanni Wenzel, Liechtenstein
1979 Annemarie Proell Moser, Austria
1980 Hanni Wenzel, Liechtenstein
1981 Marie-Theres Nadig, Switzerland
1982 Erika Hess, Switzerland
1983 Tamara McKinney, U.S.
1984 Erika Hess, Switzerland
1985 Michela Figini, Switzerland
1986 Maria Walliser, Switzerland
1987 Maria Walliser, Switzerland
1988 Michela Figini, Switzerland
1989 Vreni Schneider, Switzerland
1990 Petra Kronberger, Austria
1991 Petra Kronberger, Austria
1992 Petra Kronberger, Austria
1993 Anita Wachter, Austria
1994 Vreni Schneider, Switzerland
1995 Vreni Schneider, Switzerland
1996 Katja Seizinger, Germany
1997 Pernilla Wiberg, Sweden
1998 Katja Seizinger, Germany
1999 Alexandra Meissnitzer, Austria
2000 Renate Goetschl, Austria
2001 Janica Kostelic, Croatia
2002 Michaela Dorfmeister, Austria
2003 Janica Kostelic, Croatia
2004 Anja Paerson, Sweden
2005 Anja Paerson, Sweden

LACROSSE

Lacrosse Champions in 2005

Major League Lacrosse—Boston, MA, Aug. 22: Philadelphia Barrage 13, Boston Cannons 11.
U.S. Club Lacrosse Association Championship—Baltimore, MD, June 12: Team Source 16, MAB Philly Paints 8.
National Lacrosse League Championship—Toronto, ON, May 14: Toronto Rock 19, Arizona Sting 13.
NCAA Men's Division I Championship—Philadelphia, PA, May 30: Johns Hopkins 9, Duke 8.
NCAA Women's Division I Championship—Annapolis, MD, May 22: Northwestern 13, Virginia 10.

2005 Men's NCAA Division I All-America Team

Attack: Matt Danowski, Duke; Jed Prossner, North Carolina; John Walker, Army.
Midfield: Graham Gill, Navy; Kyle Harrison, Johns Hopkins; Bill McGlone, Maryland; Matt Zash, Duke.
Defense: Mitch Hendler, Navy; Tom Garvey, Johns Hopkins; Brodie Merrill, Georgetown.
Goal: Aaron Fenton, Duke.

2005 Women's NCAA Division I All-America Team

Attack: Amy Appelt, Virginia; Lindsay Biles, Princeton; Katie Chrest, Duke; Lindsey Munday, Northwestern; Coco Stanwick, Georgetown.
Midfield: Katieanne Christian, Dartmouth; Kristen Kjellman, Northwestern; Nikki Lieb, Virginia; Elizabeth Pillion, Princeton; Alyssa Trudel, Boston Univ.; Acacia Walker, Maryland.
Defense: Bridget Eder, Hofstra; Courtney Koester, Norwestern; Caline McHenry, Duke.
Goal: Megan Huether, Duke; Anne Sheridan, Boston Univ.

NCAA Division I Lacrosse Champions 1982-2005

Year[1]	Men	Women
1982	North Carolina	Massachusetts
1983	Syracuse	Delaware
1984	Johns Hopkins	Temple
1985	Johns Hopkins	New Hampshire
1986	North Carolina	Maryland
1987	Johns Hopkins	Penn St.
1988	Syracuse	Temple
1989	Syracuse	Penn St.
1990	vacated	Harvard
1991	North Carolina	Virginia
1992	Princeton	Maryland
1993	Syracuse	Virginia
1994	Princeton	Princeton
1995	Syracuse	Maryland
1996	Princeton	Maryland
1997	Princeton	Maryland
1998	Princeton	Maryland
1999	Virginia	Maryland
2000	Syracuse	Maryland
2001	Princeton	Maryland
2002	Syracuse	Princeton
2003	Virginia	Princeton
2004	Syracuse	Virginia
2005	Johns Hopkins	Northwestern

(1) NCAA Championships began in 1971 for men, in 1982 for women.

SWIMMING

World Swimming Records

(Long course, as of Oct. 2005)

Men's Records

Freestyle

Distance	Time	Holder	Country	Where made	Date
50 meters	**0:21.64**	Alexander Popov	Russia	Moscow, Russia	June 16, 2000
100 meters	**0:47.84**	Pieter van den Hoogenband	Netherlands	Sydney, Australia	Sept. 19, 2000
200 meters	**1:44.06**	Ian Thorpe	Australia	Fukuoka, Japan	July 25, 2001
400 meters	**3:40.08**	Ian Thorpe	Australia	Manchester, England	July 30, 2002
800 meters	**7:38.65**	Grant Hackett	Australia	Montreal, Canada	July 27, 2005
1,500 meters	**14:34.56**	Grant Hackett	Australia	Fukuoka, Japan	July 29, 2001

Breaststroke

Distance	Time	Holder	Country	Where made	Date
50 meters	**0:27.18**	Oleg Lisogor	Ukraine	Berlin, Germany	Aug. 2, 2002
100 meters	**0:59.30**	Brendan Hansen	U.S.	Long Beach, CA	July 8, 2004
200 meters	**2:09.04**	Brendan Hansen	U.S.	Long Beach, CA	July 11, 2004

Butterfly					
50 meters	**0:22.96**	Roland Schoeman	Russia	Montreal, Canada	July 25, 2005
100 meters	**0:50.40**	Ian Crocker	U.S.	Montreal, Canada	July 30, 2005
200 meters	**1:53.93**	Michael Phelps	U.S.	Barcelona, Spain	July 22, 2003
Backstroke					
50 meters	**0:24.80**	Thomas Rupprath	Germany	Barcelona, Spain	July 27, 2003
100 meters	**0:53.17**	Aaron Peirsol	U.S.	Indianapolis, IN	Apr. 2, 2005
200 meters	**1:54.66**	Aaron Peirsol	U.S.	Montreal, Canada	July 29, 2005
Individual Medley					
200 meters	**1:55.94**	Michael Phelps	U.S.	College Park, MD	Aug. 9, 2003
400 meters	**4:08.26**	Michael Phelps	U.S.	Athens, Greece	Aug. 14, 2004
Medley Relay					
400 m. (4×100)	**3:30.68**	(Peirsol, Hansen, Crocker, Lezak)	U.S.	Athens, Greece	Aug. 21, 2004
Freestyle Relays					
400 m. (4×100)	**3:13.17**	(Schoeman, Ferns, Townsend, Neethling)	South Africa	Athens, Greece	Aug. 15, 2004
800 m. (4×200)	**7:04.66**	(Hackett, Klim, Kirby, Thorpe)	Australia	Fukuoka, Japan	July 27, 2001

Women's Records

Distance	Time	Holder	Country	Where made	Date
Freestyle					
50 meters	**0:24.13**	Inge de Bruijn	Netherlands	Sydney, Australia	Sept. 22, 2000
100 meters	**0:53.52**	Jodie Henry	Australia	Athens, Greece	Aug. 18, 2004
200 meters	**1:56.64**	Franziska Van Almsick	Germany	Berlin, Germany	Aug. 3, 2002
400 meters	**4:03.85**	Janet Evans	U.S.	Seoul, South Korea	Sept. 22, 1988
800 meters	**8:16.22**	Janet Evans	U.S.	Tokyo, Japan	Aug. 20, 1989
1,500 meters	**15:52.10**	Janet Evans	U.S.	Orlando, FL	Mar. 26, 1988
Breaststroke					
50 meters	**0:30.45**	Jade Edmistone	Australia	Montreal, Canada	July 31, 2005
100 meters	**1:06.20**	Jessica Hardy	U.S.	Montreal, Canada	July 25, 2005
200 meters	**2:21.72**	Leisel Jones	Australia	Montreal, Canada	July 29, 2005
Butterfly					
50 meters	**0:25.57**	Anna-Karin Kammerling	Sweden	Berlin, Germany	July 30, 2000
100 meters	**0:56.61**	Inge de Bruijn	Netherlands	Sydney, Australia	Sept. 17, 2000
200 meters	**2:05.61**	Otylia Jedrejczak	Poland	Montreal, Canada	July 28, 2005
Backstroke					
50 meters	**0:28.19**	Janine Pietsch	Germany	Berlin, Germany	May 25, 2005
100 meters	**0:59.58**	Natalie Coughlin	U.S.	Ft. Lauderdale, FL	Aug. 13, 2002
200 meters	**2:06.62**	Kristina Egerszegi	Hungary	Athens, Greece	Aug. 25, 1991
Individual Medley					
200 meters	**2:09.72**	Yanyan Wu	China	Shanghai, China	Oct. 17, 1997
400 meters	**4:33.59**	Yana Klochkova	Ukraine	Sydney, Australia	Sept. 16, 2000
Freestyle Relays					
400 m. (4×100)	**3:35.94**	(Mills, Lenton, Thomas, Henry)	Australia	Athens, Greece	Aug. 14, 2004
800 m. (4×200)	**7:53.42**	(Coughlin, Piper, Vollmer, Sandeno)	U.S.	Athens, Greece	Aug. 18, 2004
Medley Relay					
400 m. (4×100)	**3:57.32**	(Rooney, Jones, Thomas, Henry)	Australia	Athens, Greece	Aug. 21, 2004

CYCLING

2005 Tour de France

On July 24, 2005, America's Lance Armstrong won the 102nd Tour de France, cycling's premier event, for a record 7th straight year. The 2,233-mi Tour began July 2, in Fromentine, France, and ended 21 stages later in Paris. Armstrong, riding for the Discovery Channel team, finished the race in 86 hours, 15 minutes, and 2 seconds. Italy's Ivan Basso came in 2nd, 4:40 behind Armstrong, and Germany's Jan Ullrich was 3rd, 6:21 behind the winner. Armstrong, 33, retired from competitive cycling after the 2005 Tour, as he had announced beforehand.

Tour de France Winners, 1980-2005

Year	Winner
1980	Zoop Zoetemelk, The Netherlands
1981	Bernard Hinault, France
1982	Bernard Hinault, France
1983	Laurent Fignon, France
1984	Laurent Fignon, France
1985	Bernard Hinault, France
1986	Greg LeMond, U.S.
1987	Stephen Roche, Ireland
1988	Pedro Delgado, Spain
1989	Greg LeMond, U.S.
1990	Greg LeMond, U.S.
1991	Miguel Indurain, Spain
1992	Miguel Indurain, Spain
1993	Miguel Indurain, Spain
1994	Miguel Indurain, Spain
1995	Miguel Indurain, Spain
1996	Bjarne Riis, Denmark
1997	Jan Ullrich, Germany
1998	Marco Pantani, Italy
1999	Lance Armstrong, U.S.
2000	Lance Armstrong, U.S.
2001	Lance Armstrong, U.S.
2002	Lance Armstrong, U.S.
2003	Lance Armstrong, U.S.
2004	Lance Armstrong, U.S.
2005	Lance Armstrong, U.S.

RODEO

Pro Rodeo Cowboy All-Around Champions, 1977-2004

Year	Winner	Money won
1977	Tom Ferguson, Miami, OK	$76,730
1978	Tom Ferguson, Miami, OK	103,734
1979	Tom Ferguson, Miami, OK	96,272
1980	Paul Tierney, Rapid City, SD	105,568
1981	Jimmie Cooper, Monument, NM	105,862
1982	Chris Lybbert, Coyote, CA	123,709
1983	Roy Cooper, Durant, OK	153,391
1984	Dee Pickett, Caldwell, ID	122,618
1985	Lewis Feild, Elk Ridge, UT	130,347
1986	Lewis Feild, Elk Ridge, UT	166,042
1987	Lewis Feild, Elk Ridge, UT	144,335
1988	Dave Appleton, Arlington, TX	121,546
1989	Ty Murray, Odessa, TX	134,806
1990	Ty Murray, Stephenville, TX	213,772
1991	Ty Murray, Stephenville, TX	$244,230
1992	Ty Murray, Stephenville, TX	225,992
1993	Ty Murray, Stephenville, TX	297,896
1994	Ty Murray, Stephenville, TX	246,170
1995	Joe Beaver, Huntsville, TX	141,753
1996	Joe Beaver, Huntsville, TX	166,103
1997	Dan Mortensen, Manhattan, MT	184,559
1998	Ty Murray, Stephenville, TX	264,673
1999	Fred Whitfield, Hockley, TX	217,819
2000	Joe Beaver, Huntsville, TX	225,396
2001	Cody Ohl, Stephensville, TX	296,419
2002	Trevor Brazile, Anson, TX	273,997
2003	Trevor Brazile, Anson, TX	294,839
2004	Trevor Brazile, Decatur, TX	253,170

MARATHONS

Boston Marathon, 2005

Catherine Ndereba (aka "Catherine the Great") of Kenya won the women's race in the 109th Boston Marathon Apr. 18 for the 4th time in her career, finishing in 2 hours, 25 minutes, and 13 seconds. Elfenesh Alemu of Ethiopia placed 2nd, followed by Italy's Bruna Genovese. In the men's race, Hailu Negussie of Ethiopia won with a time of 2:11:45; Kenya's Wilson Onsare and Benson Cherono placed 2nd and 3rd, respectively.

Boston Marathon Winners, 1972-2005

All times in hour:minute:second format. *Course records

Men's Winner	Time	Year	Women's Winner	Time
Olavi Suomalainen, Finland	2:15:39	**1972**	Nina Kuscsik, U.S.	3:10:26
Jon Anderson, U.S.	2:16:03	**1973**	Jacqueline Hansen, U.S.	3:05:59
Neil Cusack, Ireland	2:13:39	**1974**	Michiko Gorman, U.S.	2:47:11
Bill Rodgers, U.S.	2:09:55	**1975**	Liane Winter, West Germany	2:42:24
Jack Fultz, U.S.	2:20:19	**1976**	Kim Merritt, U.S.	2:47:10
Jerome Drayton, Canada	2:14:46	**1977**	Michiko Gorman, U.S.	2:48:33
Bill Rodgers, U.S.	2:10:13	**1978**	Gayle S. Barron, U.S.	2:44:52
Bill Rodgers, U.S.	2:09:27	**1979**	Joan Benoit, U.S.	2:35:15
Bill Rodgers, U.S.	2:12:11	**1980**	Jacqueline Gareau, Canada	2:34:28
Toshihiko Seko, Japan	2:09:26	**1981**	Allison Roe, N. Zealand	2:26:46
Alberto Salazar, U.S.	2:08:52	**1982**	Charlotte Teske, West Germany	2:29:33
Greg Meyer, U.S.	2:09:00	**1983**	Joan Benoit, U.S.	2:22:43
Geoff Smith, Great Britain	2:10:34	**1984**	Lorraine Moller, New Zealand	2:29:28
Geoff Smith, Great Britain	2:14:05	**1985**	Lisa Larsen Weidenbach, U.S.	2:34:06
Robert de Castella, Australia	2:07:51	**1986**	Ingrid Kristiansen, Norway	2:24:55
Toshihiko Seko, Japan	2:11:50	**1987**	Rosa Mota, Portugal	2:25:21
Ibrahim Hussein, Kenya	2:08:43	**1988**	Rosa Mota, Portugal	2:24:30
Abebe Mekonnen, Ethiopia	2:09:06	**1989**	Ingrid Kristiansen, Norway	2:24:33
Gelindo Bordin, Italy	2:08:19	**1990**	Rosa Mota, Portugal	2:25:24
Ibrahim Hussein, Kenya	2:11:06	**1991**	Wanda Panfil, Poland	2:24:18
Ibrahim Hussein, Kenya	2:08:14	**1992**	Olga Markova, Russia	2:23:43
Cosmas Ndeti, Kenya	2:09:33	**1993**	Olga Markova, Russia	2:25:27
Cosmas Ndeti, Kenya	2:07:15*	**1994**	Uta Pippig, Germany	2:21:45*
Cosmas Ndeti, Kenya	2:09:22	**1995**	Uta Pippig, Germany	2:25:11
Moses Tanui, Kenya	2:09:15	**1996**	Uta Pippig, Germany	2:27:12
Lameck Aguta, Kenya	2:10:34	**1997**	Fatuma Roba, Ethiopia	2:26:23
Moses Tanui, Kenya	2:07:34	**1998**	Fatuma Roba, Ethiopia	2:23:21
Joseh Chebet, Kenya	2:09:52	**1999**	Fatuma Roba, Ethiopia	2:23:25
Elijah Lagat, Kenya	2:09:47	**2000**	Catherine Ndereba, Kenya	2:26:11
Lee Bong-ju, S. Korea	2:09:43	**2001**	Catherine Ndereba, Kenya	2:23:53
Rodgers Rop, Kenya	2:09:02	**2002**	Margaret Okayo, Kenya	2:20:43
Robert K. Cheruiyot, Kenya	2:10:11	**2003**	Svetlana Zakharova, Russia	2:25:20
Timothy Cherigat, Kenya	2:10:37	**2004**	Catherine Ndereba, Kenya	2:24:27
Hailu Negussie, Ethiopia	2:11:45	**2005**	Catherine Ndereba, Kenya	2:25:13

Boston Marathon Winners, 1897-1971

The 1st Boston Marathon was held in 1897. Women were officially accepted into the race in 1972.

Year	Winner	Time
1897	John J. McDermott, New York	2:55:10
1898	Ronald J. MacDonald, Canada	2:42:00
1899	Lawrence Brignolia, Massachusetts	2:54:38
1900	John Caffery, Canada	2:39:44
1901	John Caffery, Canada	2:29:23
1902	Sammy Mellor, New York	2:43:12
1903	John Lorden , Massachusetts	2:41:29
1904	Michael Spring, New York	2:38:04
1905	Frederick Lorz, New York	2:38:25
1906	Tim Ford, Massachusetts	2:45:45
1907	Thomas Longboat, Canada	2:24:24
1908	Thomas Morrissey, New York	2:25:43
1909	Henri Renaud, New Hampshire	2:53:36
1910	Fred Cameron, Canada	2:28:52
1911	Clarence DeMar, Massachusetts	2:21:39
1912	Michael Ryan, New York	2:21:18
1913	Fritz Carlson, Minnesota	2:25:14
1914	James Duffy, Canada	2:25:14
1915	Edouard Fabre, Canada	2:31:41
1916	Arthur Roth, Massachusetts	2:27:16
1917	Bill Kennedy, New York	2:28:37
1918	Military Relay, Camp Devens	2:29:53
1919	Carl Linder, Massachusetts	2:29:13
1920	Peter Trivoulides, New York	2:29:31
1921	Frank Zuna, New York	2:18:57
1922	Clarence DeMar, Massachusetts	2:18:10
1923	Clarence DeMar, Massachusetts	2:23:47
1924	Clarence DeMar, Massachusetts	2:29:40
1925	Charles Mellor, Illinois	2:33:00
1926	John C. Miles, Canada	2:25:40
1927	Clarence DeMar, Massachusetts	2:40:22
1928	Clarence DeMar, Massachusetts	2:37:07
1929	John C. Miles, Canada	2:33:08
1930	Clarence DeMar, Massachusetts	2:34:48
1931	James P. Henigan, Massachusetts	2:46:45
1932	Paul DeBruyn, Germany	2:33:36
1933	Leslie S. Pawson, Rhode Island	2:31:01
1934	Dave Komonen, Canada	2:32:53
1935	John A. Kelley, Massachusetts	2:32:07
1936	Ellison M. Brown, Rhode Island	2:33:40
1937	Walter Young, Canada	2:33:20
1938	Leslie S. Pawson, Rhode Island	2:35:34
1939	Ellison M. Brown, Rhode Island	2:28:51
1940	Gerard Cote, Canada	2:28:28
1941	Leslie S. Pawson, Rhode Island	2:30:38
1942	Joe Smith, Massachusetts	2:26:51
1943	Gerard Cote, Canada	2:28:25
1944	Gerard Cote, Canada	2:31:50
1945	John A. Kelley, Massachusetts	2:30:40
1946	Stylianos Kyriakides, Greece	2:29:27
1947	Yun Bok Suh, Korea	2:25:39
1948	Gerard Cote, Canada	2:31:02
1949	Karl Leandersson, Sweden	2:31:50
1950	Kee Yong Ham, Korea	2:32:39
1951	Shigeki Tanaka, Japan	2:27:45
1952	Doroteo Flores, Guatamela	2:31:53
1953	Keizo Yamada, Japan	2:18:51
1954	Veikko Karvonen, Finland	2:20:39
1955	Hideo Hamamura, Japan	2:18:22
1956	Antti Viskari, Finland	2:14:14
1957	John J. Kelley, Connecticut	2:20:05
1958	Franjo Mihalic, Yugoslavia	2:25:54
1959	Eino Oksanen, Finland	2:22:42
1960	Paavo Kotila, Finland	2:20:54
1961	Eino Oksanen, Finland	2:23:39
1962	Eino Oksanen, Finland	2:23:48
1963	Aurele Vandendriessche, Belgium	2:18:58
1964	Aurele Vandendriessche, Belgium	2:19:59
1965	Morio Shigematsu, Japan	2:16:33
1966	Kenji Kemihara, Japan	2:17:11
1967	David McKenzie, New Zealand	2:15:45
1968	Amby Burfoot, Connecticut	2:22:17
1969	Yoshiaki Unetani, Japan	2:13:49
1970	Ron Hill, Great Britain	2:10:30
1971	Alvaro Mejia, Colombia	2:18:45

New York City Marathon Winners, 1970-2004

All time in hour:minute:second format; *Course record.

Men's Winner	Time	Year	Women's Winner	Time
Gary Muhrcke, U.S.	2:31:38	**1970**	no finisher	—
Norman Higgins, U.S.	2:22:54	**1971**	Beth Bonner, U.S.	2:55:22
Sheldon Karlin, U.S.	2:27:52	**1972**	Nina Kuscsik, U.S.	3:08:41
Tom Fleming, U.S.	2:19:25	**1973**	Nina Kuscsik, U.S.	2:57:07
Norbert Sander, U.S.	2:26:30	**1974**	Katherine Switzer, U.S.	3:07:29
Tom Fleming, U.S.	2:19:27	**1975**	Kim Merritt, U.S.	2:46:14
Bill Rodgers, U.S.	2:10:10	**1976**	Miki Gorman, U.S.	2:39:11
Bill Rodgers, U.S.	2:11:28	**1977**	Miki Gorman, U.S.	2:43:10
Bill Rodgers, U.S.	2:12:12	**1978**	Grete Waitz, Norway	2:32:30
Bill Rodgers, U.S.	2:11:42	**1979**	Grete Waitz, Norway	2:27:33
Alberto Salazar, U.S.	2:09:41	**1980**	Grete Waitz, Norway	2:25:42
Alberto Salazar, U.S.	2:08:13	**1981**	Allison Roe, New Zealand	2:25:29
Alberto Salazar, U.S.	2:09:29	**1982**	Grete Waitz, Norway	2:27:14
Rod Dixon, New Zealand	2:08:59	**1983**	Grete Waitz, Norway	2:27:00
Orlando Pizzolato, Italy	2:14:53	**1984**	Grete Waitz, Norway	2:29:30
Orlando Pizzolato, Italy	2:11:34	**1985**	Grete Waitz, Norway	2:28:34
Gianni Poli, Italy	2:11:06	**1986**	Grete Waitz, Norway	2:28:06
Ibrahim Hussein, Kenya	2:11:01	**1987**	Priscilla Welch,England	2:30:17
Steve Jones, Great Britain	2:08:20	**1988**	Grete Waitz, Norway	2:28:07
Juma Ikangaa, Tanzania	2:08:01	**1989**	Ingrid Kristiansen, Norway	2:25:30
Douglas Wakiihuri, Kenya	2:12:39	**1990**	Wanda Panfil, Poland	2:30:45
Salvador Garcia, Mexico	2:09:28	**1991**	Liz McColgan, Great Britain	2:27:32
Willie Mtolo, South Africa	2:09:29	**1992**	Lisa Ondieki, Australia	2:24:40*
Andres Espinosa, Mexico	2:10:04	**1993**	Uta Pippig, Germany	2:26:24
German Silva, Mexico	2:11:21	**1994**	Tegla Loroupe, Kenya	2:27:37
German Silva, Mexico	2:11:00	**1995**	Tegla Loroupe, Kenya	2:28:06
Giacomo Leone, Italy	2:09:54	**1996**	Anuta Catuna, Romania	2:28:43
John Kagwe, Kenya	2:08:12	**1997**	F. Rochat-Moser, Switzerland	2:28:43
John Kagwe, Kenya	2:08:45	**1998**	Franca Fiacconi, Italy	2:25:17
Joseph Chebet, Kenya	2:09:14	**1999**	Adriana Fernandez, Mexico	2:25:06
Abdelkhader El Mouaziz, Morocco	2:10:09	**2000**	Ludmila Petrova, Russia	2:25:45
Tesfaye Jifar, Ethiopia	2:07:43*	**2001**	Margaret Okayo, Kenya	2:24:21
Rodgers Rop, Kenya	2:08:07	**2002**	Joyce Chepchumba, Kenya	2:25:56
Martin Lel, Kenya	2:10:30	**2003**	Margaret Okayo, Kenya	2:22:31*
Hendrik Ramaala, South Africa	2:09:28	**2004**	Paula Radcliffe, England	2:23:10

Other Marathon Results in 2005

Los Angeles Marathon—Mar. 6. *Men:* Mark Saina, Kenya, 2:09:35. *Women:* Lyubov Denisova, Russia, 2:26:11.
Paris Marathon—Apr. 10. *Men:* Salim Kipsang, Kenya, 2:08:04. *Women:* Lydiya Grigoryeva, Russia, 2:27:01.
Rotterdam Marathon—Apr. 10. *Men:* Jimmy Muindi, Kenya, 2:07:50. *Women:* Lornah Kiplagat, Kenya, 2:27:36.
London Marathon—Apr. 17. *Men*: Martin Lel, Kenya, 2:07:26. *Women:* Paula Radcliffe, England, 2:17:42.
Berlin Marathon—Sept. 25. *Men:* Philip Manyim, Kenya, 2:07:41. *Women:* Mizuki Noguchi, Japan, 2:19:12.
Chicago Marathon—Oct. 9. *Men:* Felix Limo, Kenya, 2:07:02. *Women:* Deena Kastor, U.S.,2:21:25.

Ironman Triathlon World Championships

The Ironman Triathlon World Championships—a 2.4-mile ocean swim, 112-mile bike ride, and 26.2-mile run—are held annually at Kailua-Kona, Hawaii. On Oct. 16, 2004, the men's race was won by Germany's Normann Stadler in 8:33:29. Switzerland's Natascha Badmann won the women's race in 9:50:04. Victory in the women's race initially went to Germany's Nina Kraft, who had a better time by 17 min., but she was disqualified Nov. 15, 2004, after she admitted using a performance enhancing drug.

All times in hour:minute:second format. *Course records.

Men's Winner	Time	Year	Women's Winner	Time
Gordon Haller, U.S.	11:46:58	**1978**	no finisher	—
Tom Warren, U.S.	11:15:56	**1979**	Lyn Lemaire, U.S.	12:55:00
Dave Scott, U.S.	9:24:33	**1980**	Robin Beck, U.S.	11:21:24
John Howard, U.S.	9:38:29	**1981**	Linda Sweeney, U.S.	12:00:32
Dave Scott, U.S.	9:08:23	**1982**	Julie Leach, U.S.	10:54:08
Dave Scott, U.S.	9:05:57	**1983**	Sylviane Puntous, Canada	10:43:36
Dave Scott, U.S	8:54:20	**1984**	Sylvanie Puntous, Canada	10:25:13
ScottTinley, U.S.	8:50:54	**1985**	Joanne Ernst, U.S.	10:25:22
Dave Scott, U.S.	8:28:37	**1986**	Paula Newby-Fraser, Zimbabwe	9:49:14
Dave Scott, U.S.	8:34:13	**1987**	Erin Baker, New Zealand	9:35:25
Scott Molina, U.S.	8:31:00	**1988**	Paula Newby-Fraser, Zimbabwe	9:01:01
Mark Allen, U.S.	8:09:15	**1989**	Paula Newby-Fraser, Zimbabwe	9:00:56
Mark Allen, U.S.	8:28:17	**1990**	Erin Baker, New Zealand	9:13:42
Mark Allen, U.S.	8:18:32	**1991**	Paula Newby-Fraser, Zimbabwe	9:07:52
Mark Allen, U.S.	8:09:08	**1992**	Paula Newby-Fraser, Zimbabwe	8:55:28*
Mark Allen, U.S.	8:07:45	**1993**	Paula Newby-Fraser, Zimbabwe	8:58:23
Greg Welch, Australia	8:20:27	**1994**	Paula Newby-Fraser, Zimbabwe	9:20:14
Mark Allen, U.S.	8:20:34	**1995**	Karen Smyers, U.S.	9:16:46
Luc Van Lierde, Belgium	8:04:08*	**1996**	Paula Newby-Fraser, Zimbabwe	9:06:49
Thomas Hellriegel, Germany	8:33:01	**1997**	Heather Fuhr, Canada	9:31:43
Peter Reid, Canada	8:24:20	**1998**	Natascha Badmann, Switz.	9:24:16
Luc Van Lierde, Belgium	8:17:17	**1999**	Lori Bowden, U.S.	9:13:02
Peter Reid, Canada	8:21:01	**2000**	Natascha Badmann, Switz.	9:26:16
Timothy Deboom, U.S.	8:31:18	**2001**	Natascha Badmann, Switz.	9:28:37
Timothy Deboom, U.S.	8:29:56	**2002**	Natascha Badmann, Switz.	9:07:54
Peter Reid, Canada	8:22:35	**2003**	Lori Bowden, Canada	9:11:55
Norman Stadler, Germany	8:33:29	**2004**	Natascha Badmann, Switz.	9:50:04

POWER BOATING

American Power Boat Assn. Gold Cup Champions, 1978-2005

Year	Boat	Driver
1978	Atlas Van Lines	Bill Muncey
1979	Atlas Van Lines	Bill Muncey
1980	Miss Budweiser	Dean Chenoweth
1981	Miss Budweiser	Dean Chenoweth
1982	Atlas Van Lines	Chip Hanauer
1983	Atlas Van Lines	Chip Hanauer
1984	Atlas Van Lines	Chip Hanauer
1985	Miller American	Chip Hanauer
1986	Miller American	Chip Hanauer
1987	Miller American	Chip Hanauer
1988	Circus Circus	Chip Hanauer
1989	Miss Budweiser	Tom D'Eath
1990	Miss Budweiser	Tom D'Eath
1991	Winston Eagle	Mark Tate
1992	Miss Budweiser	Chip Hanauer
1993	Miss Budweiser	Chip Hanauer
1994	Smokin' Joe's	Mark Tate
1995	Miss Budweiser	Chip Hanauer
1996	Pico American Dream	Dave Villwock
1997	Miss Budweiser	Dave Villwock
1998	Miss Budweiser	Dave Villwock
1999	Miss PICO	Chip Hanauer
2000	Miss Budweiser	Dave Villwock
2001	Miss Tubby's Subs	Mike Hanson
2002	Miss Budweiser	Dave Villwock
2003	Miss Fox Hills	Mitch Evans
2004	Miss Detroit Yacht Club	Nate Brown
2005	Miss Al Deeby Dodge	Terry Troxell

YACHTING

The America's Cup

In the 31st America's Cup, the Swiss boat *Alinghi* swept 2-time defending champion *Team New Zealand,* 5-0, in the best-of-nine series, held in the Hauraki Gulf off the coast of Auckland, New Zealand in Feb. and Mar. 2003. *Alinghi* was skippered by New Zealander Russell Coutts, who had helped guide New Zealand to victory in 1995 and 2000. For the 1st time in its 152-year history, the Cup resides on the European continent, in landlocked Switzerland.

The *Alinghi* team announced on Nov. 26, 2003, that the next America's Cup would be held in Valencia, on Spain's Mediterranean coast, in 2007. However, Coutts was unlikely to be involved in *Alinghi*'s title defense—he was fired on July 26, 2004, after reportedly clashing with syndicate owner Ernesto Bertarelli.

Competition for the America's Cup grew out of the first contest to establish a world yachting championship, one of the carnival features of the London Exposition of 1851. The race covered a 60-mile course around the Isle of Wight; the prize was a cup worth about $500, donated by the Royal Yacht Squadron of England, known as the "America's Cup" because it was first won by the U.S. yacht *America.* It was held by American yachts until 1983.

Winners of the America's Cup

1851 America
1870 Magic defeated Cambria, England, (1-0)
1871 Columbia (first three races) and Sappho (last two races) defeated Livonia, England, (4-1)
1876 Madeline defeated Countess of Dufferin, Canada, (2-0)
1881 Mischief defeated Atalanta, Canada, (2-0)
1885 Puritan defeated Genesta, England, (2-0)
1886 Mayflower defeated Galatea, England, (2-0)
1887 Volunteer defeated Thistle, Scotland, (2-0)
1893 Vigilant defeated Valkyrie II, England, (3-0)
1895 Defender defeated Valkyrie III, England, (3-0)
1899 Columbia defeated Shamrock, England, (3-0)
1901 Columbia defeated Shamrock II, England, (3-0)
1903 Reliance defeated Shamrock III, England, (3-0)
1920 Resolute defeated Shamrock IV, England, (3-2)
1930 Enterprise defeated Shamrock V, England, (4-0)
1934 Rainbow defeated Endeavour, England, (4-2)
1937 Ranger defeated Endeavour II, England, (4-0)
1958 Columbia defeated Sceptre, England, (4-0)
1962 Weatherly defeated Gretel, Australia, (4-1)
1964 Constellation defeated Sovereign, England, (4-0)
1967 Intrepid defeated Dame Pattie, Australia, (4-0)
1970 Intrepid defeated Gretel II, Australia, (4-1)
1974 Courageous defeated Southern Cross, Australia, (4-0)
1977 Courageous defeated Australia, Australia, (4-0)
1980 Freedom defeated Australia, Australia, (4-1)
1983 Australia II, Australia, defeated Liberty, (4-3)
1987 Stars & Stripes defeated Kookaburra III, Australia, (4-0)
1988 Stars & Stripes defeated New Zealand, New Zealand, (2-0)
1992 America^3 defeated Il Moro di Venezia, Italy, (4-1)
1995 Black Magic 1, New Zealand, defeated Young America, (5-0)
2000 New Zealand, NZ, defeated Luna Rossa, Italy, (5-0)
2003 Alinghi, Switzerland, defeated Team New Zealand, NZ, (5-0)

DOGS

Westminster Kennel Club, 1989-2005

Year	Best-in-show	Breed	Owner(s)
1989	Ch. Royal Tudor's Wild As The Wind	Doberman	Sue & Art Kemp, Richard & Carolyn Vida, Beth Wilhite
1990	Ch. Wendessa Crown Prince	Pekingese	Ed Jenner
1991	Ch. Whisperwind on a Carousel	Poodle	Joan & Frederick Hartsock
1992	Ch. Registry's Lonesome Dove	Fox Terrier	Marion & Sam Lawrence
1993	Ch. Salilyn's Condor	English Springer Spaniel	Donna & Roger Herzig
1994	Ch. Chidley Willum	Norwich Terrier	Ruth Cooper & Patricia Lussier
1995	Ch. Gaelforce Post Script	Scottish Terrier	Dr. Vandra Huber & Dr. Joe Kinnarney
1996	Ch. Clussexx Country Sunrise	Clumber Spaniel	Judith & Richard Zaleski
1997	Ch. Parsifal Di Casa Netzer	Standard Schnauzer	Rita Holloway & Gabrio Del Torre
1998	Ch. Fairewood Frolic	Norwich Terrier	Sandina Kennels
1999	Ch. Loteki Supernatural Being	Papillon	John Oulton
2000	Ch. Salilyn 'N Erin's Shameless	English Springer Spaniel	Carl Blain, Fran Sunseri, & Julia Gasow
2001	Ch. Special Times Just Right	Bichons Frises	Cecilia Ruggles, E. McDonald, & F. Werneck
2002	Ch. Surrey Spice Girl	Poodle (Miniature)	Ron L. & Barbara Scott
2003	Ch. Torum's Scarf Michael	Kerry Blue Terrier	Marilu Hanson
2004	Ch. Darbydale's All Rise Pouchcove	Newfoundland	Peggy Helming & Carol A. Bernard Bergmann
2005	Ch. Kan-Point's VJK Autumn Roses	German Shorthaired Pointer	Linda & Richard Stark, Carol Cronk, Valerie Nunes-Atkinson

2005 Iditarod Trail Sled Dog Race

Robert Sørlie won the 33rd annual Iditarod Trail Sled Dog Race from Anchorage to Nome, Alaska, on Mar. 16, 2005. Sørlie, a 47-year-old native of Norway, finished the 1,131-mile course along the southern Iditarod route in 9 days, 18 hours, 39 minutes, and 31 seconds. In all, 63 mushers completed the race to Nome and shared a $750,000 purse. The 2006 race was scheduled to begin Mar. 4 in Anchorage and follow the 1,112-mile northern route to Nome.

SULLIVAN AWARD

James E. Sullivan Memorial Trophy Winners

The James E. Sullivan Memorial Trophy, named after the former president of the Amateur Athletic Union (AAU) and inaugurated in 1930, is awarded annually by the AAU to the athlete who "by his or her performance, example and influence as an amateur, has done the most during the year to advance the cause of sportsmanship."

Year	Winner	Sport
1930	Bobby Jones	Golf
1931	Barney Berlinger	Track
1932	Jim Bausch	Track
1933	Glenn Cunningham	Track
1934	Bill Bonthron	Track
1935	Lawson Little	Golf
1936	Glenn Morris	Track
1937	Don Budge	Tennis
1938	Don Lash	Track
1939	Joe Burk	Rowing
1940	Greg Rice	Track
1941	Leslie MacMitchell	Track
1942	Cornelius Warmerdam	Track
1943	Gilbert Dodds	Track
1944	Ann Curtis	Swimming
1945	Doc Blanchard	Football
1946	Arnold Tucker	Football
1947	John Kelly, Jr.	Rowing
1948	Robert Mathias	Track
1949	Dick Button	Skating
1950	Fred Wilt	Track
1951	Rev. Robert Richards	Track
1952	Horace Ashenfelter	Track
1953	Dr. Sammy Lee	Diving
1954	Mal Whitfield	Track
1955	Harrison Dillard	Track
1956	Patricia McCormick	Diving
1957	Bobby Joe Morrow	Track
1958	Glenn Davis	Track
1959	Parry O'Brien	Track
1960	Rafer Johnson	Track
1961	Wilma Rudolph Ward	Track
1962	James Beatty	Track
1963	John Pennel	Track
1964	Don Schollander	Swimming
1965	Bill Bradley	Basketball
1966	Jim Ryun	Track
1967	Randy Matson	Track
1968	Debbie Meyer	Swimming
1969	Bill Toomey	Track
1970	John Kinsella	Swimming
1971	Mark Spitz	Swimming
1972	Frank Shorter	Track
1973	Bill Walton	Basketball
1974	Rick Wohlhutter	Track
1975	Tim Shaw	Swimming
1976	Bruce Jenner	Track
1977	John Naber	Swimming
1978	Tracy Caulkins	Swimming
1979	Kurt Thomas	Gymnastics
1980	Eric Heiden	Speed Skating
1981	Carl Lewis	Track
1982	Mary Decker	Track
1983	Edwin Moses	Track
1984	Greg Louganis	Diving
1985	Joan Benoit Samuelson	Marathon
1986	Jackie Joyner-Kersee	Track
1987	Jim Abbott	Baseball
1988	Florence Griffith Joyner	Track
1989	Janet Evans	Swimming
1990	John Smith	Wrestling
1991	Mike Powell	Track
1992	Bonnie Blair	Speed Skating
1993	Charlie Ward	Football, Basketball
1994	Dan Jansen	Speed Skating
1995	Bruce Baumgartner	Wrestling
1996	Michael Johnson	Track
1997	Peyton Manning	Football
1998	Chamique Holdsclaw	Basketball
1999	Coco Miller and Kelly Miller	Basketball
2000	Rulon Gardner	Wrestling
2001	Michelle Kwan	Figure Skating
2002	Sarah Hughes	Figure Skating
2003	Michael Phelps	Swimming
2004	Paul Hamm	Gymnastics

FISHING

Selected IGFA Saltwater & Freshwater All-Tackle World Records

Source: International Game Fish Association; based on latest records released

Saltwater Fish Records

Species	Weight	Where caught	Date	Angler
Albacore	88 lbs. 2 oz.	Canary Islands, Spain	Nov. 19, 1977	Siegfried Dickemann
Amberjack, greater	155 lbs. 12 oz.	Bermuda	Aug. 16, 1992	Larry Trott
Barracuda, great	85 lbs.	Christmas Island, Kiribati	Apr. 11, 1992	John W. Helfrich
Barracuda, Mexican	21 lbs.	Phantom Isle, Costa Rica	Mar. 27, 1987	E. Greg Kent
Barracuda, Pacific	26 lbs. 8 oz.	Playa Matapalo, Costa Rica	Jan. 3, 1999	Doug Hettinger
Bass, barred sand	13 lbs. 3 oz.	Huntington Beach, CA	Aug. 29, 1988	Robert Halal
Bass, black sea	10 lbs. 4 oz.	Virginia Beach, VA	Jan. 1, 2000	Allan P. Paschall
Bass, giant sea	563 lbs. 8 oz.	Anacapa Island, CA	Aug. 20, 1968	James D. McAdam Jr.
Bass, striped	78 lbs. 8 oz.	Atlantic City, NJ	Sept. 21, 1982	Albert R. McReynolds
Bluefish	31 lbs. 12 oz.	Hatteras Inlet, NC	Jan. 30, 1972	James M. Hussey
Bonefish	19 lbs.	Zululand, South Africa	May 26, 1962	Brian W. Batchelor
Bonito, Atlantic	18 lbs. 4 oz.	Faial Island, Azores	July 8, 1953	D. Gama Higgs
Bonito, Pacific	21 lbs. 3 oz.	Malibu, CA	July 30, 1978	Gino M. Picciolo
Cabezon	23 lbs.	Juan De Fuca Strait, WA	Aug. 4, 1990	Wesley S. Hunter
Cobia	135 lbs. 9 oz.	Shark Bay, Australia	July 9, 1985	Peter W. Goulding
Cod, Atlantic	98 lbs. 12 oz.	Isle of Shoals, NH	June 8, 1969	Alphonse J. Bielevich
Cod, Pacific	35 lbs.	Unalaska Bay, AK	June 16, 1999	Jim Johnson
Conger	133 lbs. 4 oz.	Berry Head, S. Devon, England	June 5, 1995	Vic Evans
Dolphin	88 lbs.	Exuma, Bahamas	May 5, 1998	Richard D. Evans
Drum, black	113 lbs. 1 oz.	Lewes, DE	Sept. 15, 1975	Gerald M. Townsend
Drum, red	94 lbs. 2 oz.	Avon, NC	Nov. 7, 1984	David G. Deuel
Eel, American	9 lbs. 4 oz.	Cape May, NJ	Nov. 9, 1995	Jeff Pennick
Eel, marbled	36 lbs. 1 oz.	Hazelmere Dam, South Africa	June 10, 1984	Ferdie Van Nooten
Flounder, southern	20 lbs. 9 oz.	Nassau Sound, FL	Dec. 23, 1983	Larenza W. Mungin
Flounder, summer	22 lbs. 7 oz.	Montauk, NY	Sept. 15, 1975	Charles Nappi
Grouper, Goliath	680 lbs.	Fernandina Beach, FL	May 20, 1961	Lynn Joyner
Grouper, Warsaw	436 lbs. 12 oz.	Gulf of Mexico, Destin, FL	Dec. 22, 1985	Steve Haeusler
Halibut, Atlantic	355 lbs. 6 oz.	Valevag, Norway	Oct. 20, 1997	Odd Arve Gunderstad
Halibut, California	58 lbs. 9 oz.	Santa Rosa Island, CA	June 26, 1999	Roger W. Borrell
Halibut, Pacific	459 lbs.	Dutch Harbor, AK	June 11, 1996	Jack Tragis
Jack, crevalle	58 lbs. 6 oz.	Barra do Kwanza, Angola	Dec. 10, 2000	Nuno Abohbot Po da Silva
Jack, horse-eye	29 lbs. 8 oz.	Ascencion Island, South Atlantic	May 28, 1993	Mike Hanson
Jack, Pacific crevalle	39 lbs.	Playa Zancudo, Costa Rica	Mar. 3, 1997	Ingrid Callaghan
Kawakawa	29 lbs.	Clarion Island, Mexico	Dec. 17, 1986	Ronald Nakamura
Lingcod	76 lbs. 9 oz.	Gulf of Alaska, AK	Aug. 11, 2001	Antwan D. Tinsley
Mackerel, cero	17 lbs. 2 oz.	Islamorada, FL	Apr. 5, 1986	G. Michael Mills
Mackerel, king	93 lbs.	San Juan, PR	Apr. 18, 1999	Steve Perez Graulau
Mackerel, Spanish	13 lbs.	Ocracoke Inlet, NC	Nov. 4, 1987	Robert Cranton
Marlin, Atlantic blue	1,402 lbs. 2 oz.	Vitoria, Brazil	Feb. 29, 1992	Paulo Roberto A. Amorim
Marlin, black	1,560 lbs.	Cabo Blanco, Peru	Aug. 4, 1953	Alfred C. Glassell Jr.
Marlin, Pacific blue	1,376 lbs.	Kaaiwi Pt., Kona, HI	May 31, 1982	Jay W. deBeaubien
Marlin, striped	494 lbs.	Tutukaka, New Zealand	Jan. 16, 1986	Bill Boniface
Marlin, white	181 lbs. 14 oz.	Vitoria, Brazil	Dec. 8, 1979	Evandro Luiz Coser
Permit	60 lbs. 0 oz.	Ilha do Mel, Paranagua, Brazil	Dec. 14, 2002	Renato P. Fiedler
Pollack, European	27 lbs. 6 oz.	Salcombe, Devon, England	Jan. 16, 1986	Robert Samuel Milkins
Pollock	50 lbs.	Salstraumen, Norway	Nov. 30, 1995	Thor-Magnus Lekang
Pompano, African	50 lbs. 8 oz.	Daytona Beach, FL	Apr. 21, 1990	Tom Sargent

Species	Weight	Where caught	Date	Angler
Roosterfish	114 lbs.	La Paz, Baja Cal., Mexico	June 1, 1960	Abe Sackheim
Runner, blue	11 lbs. 2 oz.	Dauphin Isl., AL	June 28, 1997	Stacey Michelle Moiren
Runner, rainbow	37 lbs. 9 oz.	Clarion Island, Mexico	Nov. 21, 1991	Tom Pfleger
Sailfish, Atlantic	141 lbs. 1 oz.	Luanda, Angola	Feb. 19, 1994	Alfredo de Sousa Neves
Sailfish, Pacific	221 lbs.	Santa Cruz Island, Ecuador	Feb. 12, 1947	C. W. Stewart
Seabass, white	83 lbs. 12 oz.	San Felipe, Mexico	Mar. 31, 1953	L. C. Baumgardner
Seatrout, spotted	17 lbs. 7 oz.	Ft. Pierce, FL	May 11, 1995	Craig F. Carson
Shark, bigeye thresher	802 lbs.	Tutukaka, New Zealand	Feb. 8, 1981	Dianne North
Shark, bignose	369 lbs. 14 oz.	Markham R., Papua New Guinea	Oct. 23, 1993	Lester J. Rohrlach
Shark, blue	528 lbs.	Montauk Point, NY	Aug. 9, 2001	Joe Seidel
Shark, great hammerhead	991 lbs.	Sarasota, FL	May 30, 1982	Allen Ogle
Shark, Greenland	1,708 lbs. 9 oz.	Trondheimsfjord, Norway	Oct. 18, 1987	Terje Nordtvedt
Shark, porbeagle	507 lbs.	Caithness, Scotland	Mar. 9, 1993	Christopher Bennett
Shark, shortfin mako	1,221 lbs.	Chatham, MA	July 21, 2001	Luke Sweeney
Shark, tiger	1,780 lbs.	Cherry Grove, SC	June 14, 1964	Walter Maxwell
Shark, white	2,664 lbs.	Ceduna, S.A., Australia	Apr. 21, 1959	Alfred Dean
Sheepshead	21 lbs. 4 oz.	New Orleans, LA	Apr. 16, 1982	Wayne Desselle
Skipjack, black	26 lbs.	Thetis Bank, Baja Cal., Mexico	Oct. 23, 1991	Clifford Hamaishi
Snapper, cubera	121 lbs. 8 oz.	Cameron, LA	July 5, 1982	Mike Hebert
Snapper, red	50 lbs. 4 oz.	Gulf of Mexico, LA	June 23, 1996	Capt. Doc Kennedy
Snook, common	53 lbs. 10 oz.	Parismina Ranch, Costa Rica	Oct. 18, 1978	Gilbert Ponzi
Spearfish, Mediterranean	90 lbs. 13 oz.	Madeira Island, Portugal	June 2, 1980	Joseph Larkin
Swordfish	1,182 lbs.	Iquique, Chile	May 7, 1953	L. B. Marron
Tarpon	286 lbs. 9 oz.	Rubane, Guinea-Bissau	Mar. 20, 2003	Max Domecq
Tautog	25 lbs.	Ocean City, NJ	Jan. 20, 1998	Anthony R. Monica
Trevally, bigeye	31 lbs. 8 oz.	Poivre Isl., Seychelles	Apr. 23, 1997	Les Sampson
Trevally, giant	145 lbs. 8 oz.	Makena, Maui, HI	Mar. 28, 1991	Russell Mori
Tuna, Atlantic bigeye	392 lbs. 6 oz.	Canary Islands, Spain	July 25, 1996	Dieter Vogel
Tuna, blackfin	45 lbs. 8 oz.	Key West, FL	May 4, 1996	Sam J. Burnett
Tuna, bluefin	1,496 lbs.	Aulds Cove, Nova Scotia	Oct. 26, 1979	Ken Fraser
Tuna, longtail	79 lbs. 2 oz.	Montague Isl., N.S.W., Australia	Apr. 12, 1982	Tim Simpson
Tuna, Pacific bigeye	435 lbs.	Cabo Blanco, Peru	Apr. 17, 1957	Dr. Russel V. A. Lee
Tuna, skipjack	45 lbs. 4 oz.	Flathead Bank, Baja Cal., Mexico	Nov. 16, 1996	Brian Evans
Tuna, southern bluefin	348 lbs. 5 oz.	Whakatane, New Zealand	Jan. 16, 1981	Rex Wood
Tuna, yellowfin	388 lbs. 12 oz.	San Benedicto Island, Mexico	Apr. 1, 1977	Curt Wiesenhutter
Tunny, little	35 lbs. 2 oz.	Cap de Garde, Algeria	Dec. 14, 1988	Jean Yves Chatard
Wahoo	158 lbs. 8 oz.	Loreto, Baja Cal., Mexico	June 10, 1996	Keith Winter
Weakfish	19 lbs. 2 oz.	Jones Beach Inlet, NY	Oct. 11, 1984	Dennis Roger Rooney
		Delaware Bay, DE	May 20, 1989	William E. Thomas
Yellowtail, California	88 lbs. 3 oz.	Alijos Rocks, Baja Cal., Mexico	June 21, 2000	Ronald Tadashi Fujii
Yellowtail, southern	114 lbs. 10 oz.	Tauranga, New Zealand	Feb. 5, 1984	Mike Godfrey
		White Island, New Zealand	Jan. 9, 1987	David Lugton

Freshwater Fish Records

Species	Weight	Where caught	Date	Angler
Barramundi	83 lbs. 7 oz.	Lake Tinaroo, N. Queensland, Australia	Sept. 23, 1999	David Powell
Bass, largemouth	22 lbs. 4 oz.	Montgomery Lake, GA	June 2, 1932	George W. Perry
Bass, rock	3 lbs.	York River, Ontario	Aug. 1, 1974	Peter Gulgin
	3 lbs.	Lake Erie, PA	June 18, 1998	Herbert G. Ratner, Jr.
Bass, shoal	8 lbs. 12 oz.	Apalachicola River, FL	Jan. 28, 1995	Carl W. Davis
Bass, smallmouth	10 lbs. 14 oz.	Dale Hollow Lake, TN	Apr. 24, 1969	John T. Gorman
Bass, white	6 lbs. 13 oz.	Lake Orange, VA	July 31, 1989	Ronald L. Sprouse
Bass, whiterock	27 lbs. 5 oz.	Greers Ferry Lake, AR	April 24, 1997	Jerald C. Shaum
Bass, yellow	2 lbs. 9 oz.	Waverly, TN	Feb. 27, 1998	John T. Chappell
Bluegill	4 lbs. 12 oz.	Ketona Lake, AL	Apr. 9, 1950	T. S. Hudson
Bowfin	21 lbs. 8 oz.	Florence, SC	Jan. 29, 1980	Robert L. Harmon
Bream	13 lbs. 3 oz.	Hagbyan Creek, Sweden	May 11, 1984	Luis Kilian Rasmussen
Buffalo, bigmouth	70 lbs. 5 oz.	Bastrop, LA	Apr. 21, 1980	Delbert Sisk
Buffalo, black	63 lbs. 6 oz.	Mississippi River, IA	Aug. 14, 1999	Jim Winters
Buffalo, smallmouth	82 lbs. 3 oz.	Athens Lake, AR	June 6, 1993	Randy Collins
Bullhead, brown	6 lbs. 5 oz.	Lake Mahopac, NY	Sept. 8, 2002	Ray Lawrence
Bullhead, yellow	4 lbs. 4 oz.	Mormon Lake, AZ	May 11, 1984	Emily Williams
Burbot	18 lbs. 11 oz.	Angenmanalren, Sweden	Oct. 22, 1996	Margit Agren
Carp, common	75 lbs. 11 oz.	Lac de St. Cassien, France	May 21, 1987	Leo van der Gugten
Catfish, blue	116 lbs. 12 oz.	Mississippi R., AR	Aug 3, 2001	Charles Ashley Jr.
Catfish, channel	58 lbs.	Santee-Cooper Res., SC	July 7, 1964	W. B. Whaley
Catfish, flathead	123 lbs. 9 oz.	Independence, KS	May 14, 1998	Ken Paulie
Catfish, white	21 lbs. 8 oz.	Gorton Pond, CT	Apr. 22, 2001	Thomas Urguhart
Char, Arctic	32 lbs. 9 oz.	Tree River, Canada	July 30, 1981	Jeffrey L. Ward
Crappie, white	5 lbs. 3 oz.	Enid Dam, MS	July 31, 1957	Fred L. Bright
Dolly Varden	20 lbs. 14oz.	Wulik R., AK	July 7, 2001	Raz Reid
Dorado	51 lbs. 5 oz.	Toledo (Corrientes), Argentina	Sept. 27, 1984	Armando Giudice
Drum, freshwater	54 lbs. 8 oz.	Nickajack Lake, TN	Apr. 20, 1972	Benny E. Hull
Gar, alligator	279 lbs.	Rio Grande, TX	Dec. 2, 1951	Bill Valverde
Gar, Florida	10 lbs.	Everglades, FL	Jan. 28, 2002	Herbert G. Ratner Jr.
Gar, longnose	50 lbs. 5 oz.	Trinity River, TX	July 30, 1954	Townsend Miller
Gar, shortnose	5 lbs. 12 oz.	Ren Lake, IL	July 16, 1995	Donna K. Willmert
Gar, spotted	9 lbs. 12 oz.	Lake Mexia, TX	Apr. 7, 1994	Rick Rivard
Grayling, Arctic	5 lbs. 15 oz.	Katseyedie River, N.W.T.	Aug. 16, 1967	Jeanne P. Branson
Inconnu	53 lbs.	Pah River, AK	Aug. 20, 1986	Lawrence E. Hudnall
Kokanee	9 lbs. 6 oz.	Okanagan Lake, Vernon, B.C.	June 18, 1988	Norm Kuhn
Muskellunge	67 lbs. 8 oz.	Lake Court Oreilles, WI	July 24, 1949	Cal Johnson
Muskellunge, tiger	51 lbs. 3 oz.	Lac Vieux-Desert, MI	July 16, 1919	John Knobla
Perch, Nile	230 lbs.	Lake Nasser, Egypt	Dec. 20, 2000	William Toth
Perch, white	3 lbs. 1 oz.	Forest Hill Park, NJ	May 6, 1989	Edward Tango
Perch, yellow	4 lbs. 3 oz.	Bordentown, NJ	May, 1865	Dr. C. C. Abbot
Pickerel, chain	9 lbs. 6 oz.	Homerville, GA	Feb. 17, 1961	Baxley McQuaig Jr.
Pike, northern	55 lbs. 1 oz.	Lake of Grefeern, W. Germany	Oct. 16, 1986	Lothar Louis
Redhorse, greater	9 lbs. 3 oz.	Salmon River, Pulaski, NY	May 11, 1985	Jason Wilson
Redhorse, silver	11 lbs. 7 oz.	Plum Creek, WI	May 29, 1985	Neal Long

Species	Weight	Where caught	Date	Angler
Salmon, Atlantic	79 lbs. 2 oz.	Tana River, Norway	1928	Henrik Henriksen
Salmon, chinook	97 lbs. 4 oz.	Kenai River, AK	May 17, 1985	Les Anderson
Salmon, chum	35 lbs.	Edye Pass, BC	July 11, 1995	Todd A. Johansson
Salmon, coho	33 lbs. 4 oz.	Salmon River, Pulaski, NY	Sept. 27, 1989	Jerry Lifton
Salmon, pink	14 lbs. 13 oz.	Monroe, WA	Sept. 30, 2001	Alexander Minerich
Salmon, sockeye	15 lbs. 3 oz.	Kenai River, AK	Aug. 9, 1987	Stan Roach
Sauger	8 lbs. 12 oz.	Lake Sakakawea, ND	Oct. 6, 1971	Mike Fischer
Shad, American	11 lbs. 4 oz.	Connecticut River, MA	May 19, 1986	Bob Thibodo
Sturgeon, beluga	224 lbs. 13 oz.	Guryev, Kazakhstan	May 3, 1993	Merete Lehne
Sturgeon, white	468 lbs.	Benicia, CA	July 9, 1983	Joey Pallotta III
Sunfish, green	2 lbs. 2 oz.	Stockton Lake, MO	June 18, 1971	Paul M. Dilley
Sunfish, redbreast	1 lb. 12 oz.	Suwannee River, FL	May 29, 1984	Alvin Buchanan
Sunfish, redear	5 lbs. 7oz.	Diverson Canal, SC	Nov. 6, 1998	Amos M. Gay
Tigerfish, giant	97 lbs.	Zaire River, Kinshasa, Zaire	July 9, 1988	Raymond Houtmans
Tilapia, Nile	13 lbs. 3 oz.	Antelope Isl., Karibe, Zimbabwe	July 5, 2002	Sorel van Rooyen
Trout, Apache	5 lb. 3 oz.	Apache Res., AZ	May 29, 1991	John Baldwin
Trout, brook	14 lbs. 8 oz.	Nipigon River, Ontario	July, 1916	Dr. W. J. Cook
Trout, bull	32 lbs.	Lake Pend Oreille, ID	Oct. 27, 1949	N. L. Higgins
Trout, cutthroat	41 lbs.	Pyramid Lake, NV	Dec., 1925	John Skimmerhorn
Trout, golden	11 lbs.	Cooks Lake, WY	Aug. 5, 1948	Charles S. Reed
Trout, lake	72 lbs.	Great Bear Lake, N.W.T.	Aug. 19, 1995	Lloyd E. Bull
Trout, rainbow	42 lbs. 2 oz.	Bell Island, AK	June 22, 1970	David Robert White
Trout, tiger	20 lbs. 13 oz.	Lake Michigan, WI	Aug. 12, 1978	Pete M. Friedland
Walleye	25 lbs.	Old Hickory Lake, TN	Aug. 2, 1960	Mabry Harper
Warmouth	2 lbs. 7 oz.	Yellow River, Holt, FL	Oct. 19, 1985	Tony D. Dempsey
Whitefish, lake	14 lbs. 6 oz.	Meaford, Ontario	May 21, 1984	Dennis M. Laycock
Whitefish, mountain	5 lbs. 8 oz.	Elbow River, Calgary, AB	Aug. 1, 1995	Randy G. Woo
Whitefish, round	6 lbs.	Putahow R., Manitoba, Can.	June 14, 1984	Allan J. Ristori
Zander	25 lbs. 2 oz.	Trosa, Sweden	June 12, 1986	Harry Lee Tennison

DIRECTORY OF SPORTS ORGANIZATIONS

Major League Baseball

Office of the Commissioner, 245 Park Ave., 31st Fl., New York, NY 10167. **Website:** www.mlb.com

American League

Baltimore Orioles
333 W. Camden St.
Baltimore, MD 21201

Boston Red Sox
4 Yawkey Way
Boston, MA 02215

Chicago White Sox
333 W. 35th St.
Chicago, IL 60616

Cleveland Indians
2401 Ontario St.
Cleveland, OH 44115-4003

Detroit Tigers
2100 Woodward Ave.
Detroit, MI 48201

Kansas City Royals
One Royal Way
Kansas City, MO 64129

Los Angles Angels of Anaheim
2000 Gene Autry Way
Anaheim, CA 92806

Minnesota Twins
34 Kirby Puckett Place
Minneapolis, MN 55415

New York Yankees
161st St. and River Ave.
Bronx, NY 10452

Oakland Athletics
7000 Coliseum Way
Oakland, CA 94621

Seattle Mariners
83 King St.
Seattle, WA 98104

Tampa Bay Devil Rays
One Tropicana Dr.
St. Petersburg, FL 33705

Texas Rangers
1000 Ballpark Way
Arlington, TX 76011

Toronto Blue Jays
One Blue Jays Way
Toronto, ON M5V 1J1

National League

Arizona Diamondbacks
401 E. Jefferson St.
Phoenix, AZ 85004

Atlanta Braves
755 Hank Aaron Drive
Atlanta, GA 30315

Chicago Cubs
1060 W. Addison St.
Chicago, IL 60613

Cincinnati Reds
100 Main St.
Cincinnati, OH 45202

Colorado Rockies
2001 Blake St.
Denver, CO 80205

Florida Marlins
2267 Dan Marino Blvd.
Miami, FL 33056

Houston Astros
501 Crawford St.
Houston, TX 77002

Los Angeles Dodgers
1000 Elysian Park Ave.
Los Angeles, CA 90012

Milwaukee Brewers
One Brewers Way
Milwaukee, WI 53214

New York Mets
123-01 Roosevelt Ave.
Flushing, NY 11368

Philadelphia Phillies
One Citizens Bank Way
Philadelphia, PA 19148

Pittsburgh Pirates
115 Federal St.
Pittsburgh, PA 15212

St. Louis Cardinals
250 Stadium Plaza
St. Louis, MO 63102

San Diego Padres
100 Park Blvd.
San Diego, CA 92101

San Francisco Giants
24 Willie Mays Plaza
San Francisco, CA 94101

Washington Nationals
2400 E. Capitol St. SE
Washington, DC 20003

National Basketball Association

League Office, Olympic Tower, 645 5th Ave., New York, NY 10022. **Website:** www.nba.com

Atlanta Hawks
101 Marietta St. SW, Ste. 1900
Atlanta, GA 30303

Boston Celtics
226 Causeway St.
Boston, MA 02114

Charlotte Bobcats
333 E. Trade St.
Charlotte, NC 28202

Chicago Bulls
1901 W. Madison St.
Chicago, IL 60612

Cleveland Cavaliers
One Center Court
Cleveland, OH 44115

Dallas Mavericks
2909 Taylor St.
Dallas, TX 75226

Denver Nuggets
1000 Chopper Circle
Denver, CO 80204

Detroit Pistons
Four Championship Dr.
Auburn Hills, MI 48326

Golden State Warriors
1011 Broadway
Oakland, CA 94607

Houston Rockets
1510 Polk St.
Houston, TX 77002

Indiana Pacers
125 S. Pennsylvania St
Indianapolis, IN 46204

Los Angeles Clippers
1111 S. Figueroa St.,
Ste. 1100
Los Angeles, CA 9061

Los Angeles Lakers
555 N. Nash St.
El Segundo, CA 90245

Memphis Grizzlies
191 Beale St.
Memphis, TN 38103

Miami Heat
601 Biscayne Blvd.
Miami, FL 33132

Milwaukee Bucks
1001 N. 4th St.
Milwaukee, WI 53203

Minnesota Timberwolves
600 1st Ave. North
Minneapolis, MN 55403

New Jersey Nets
390 Murray Hill Parkway
E. Rutherford, NJ 07073

New Orleans Hornets[1]
1501 Girod St.
New Orleans, LA 70113

New York Knickerbockers
Two Pennsylvania Plaza
New York, NY 10121

Orlando Magic
8701 Maitland Summit Blvd.
Orlando, FL 32810

Philadelphia 76ers
3601 S. Broad St.
Philadelphia, PA 19148

Phoenix Suns
201 E. Jefferson
Phoenix, AZ 85004

Portland Trail Blazers
One Center Ct.
Portland, OR 97227

Sacramento Kings
One Sports Parkway
Sacramento, CA 95834

San Antonio Spurs
One SBC Center
San Antonio, TX 78219

Seattle SuperSonics
305 Harrison St.
Seattle, WA 98109

Toronto Raptors
40 Bay St., Ste. 400
Toronto, ON M5J 2X2

Utah Jazz
301 W. South Temple
Salt Lake City, UT 84101

Washington Wizards
601 F St. NW
Washington, DC 20004

(1) Most of the New Orleans Hornets' home games in 2005-06 were to be played at the Ford Center in Oklahoma City.

National Hockey League

League Headquarters, 1251 Ave. of the Americas, 47th Fl., New York, NY 10020. **Website:** www.nhl.com

Mighty Ducks of Anaheim
2695 E. Katella Ave.
Anaheim, CA 92806

Atlanta Thrashers
Centennial Tower
101 Marietta St. NW
Atlanta, GA 30303

Boston Bruins
One TD Banknorth Garden
Boston, MA 02114

Buffalo Sabres
One Seymour H. Knox III Plaza
Buffalo, NY 14203

Calgary Flames
PO Box 1540, Station M
Calgary, AB T2P 3B9

Carolina Hurricanes
1400 Edwards Mill Rd.
Raleigh, NC 27607

Chicago Blackhawks
1901 W. Madison St.
Chicago, IL 60612

Colorado Avalanche
1000 Chopper Circle
Denver, CO 80204

Columbus Blue Jackets
200 W. Nationwide Blvd.
Columbus, OH 43215

Dallas Stars
2601 Avenue of the Stars
Frisco, TX 75034

Detroit Red Wings
600 Civic Center Dr.
Detroit, MI 48226

Edmonton Oilers
11230 110 St.
Edmonton, AB T5G 3H7

Florida Panthers
One Panther Parkway
Sunrise, FL 33323

Los Angeles Kings
1111 S. Figueroa St.
Los Angeles, CA 90015

Minnesota Wild
317 Washington St.
St. Paul, MN 55102

Montreal Canadiens
1275 St. Antonie St. W
Montreal, QC H3C 5L2

Nashville Predators
501 Broadway
Nashville, TN 37203

New Jersey Devils
P.O. Box 504
E. Rutherford, NJ 07073

New York Islanders
Nassau Veterans Memorial Coliseum
1255 Hempstead Tpke.
Uniondale, NY 11553

New York Rangers
Two Pennsylvania Plaza
New York, NY 10121

Ottawa Senators
1000 Palladium Dr.
Kanata, ON K2V 1A5

Philadelphia Flyers
3601 South Broad St.
Philadelphia, PA 19148

Phoenix Coyotes
5800 W. Glenn Dr., Ste. 350
Glendale, AZ 85301

Pittsburgh Penguins
66 Mario Lemieux Place
Pittsburgh, PA 15219

St. Louis Blues
1401 Clark Ave.
St. Louis, MO 63103

San Jose Sharks
525 W. Santa Clara St.
San Jose, CA 95113

Tampa Bay Lightning
401 Channelside Dr.
Tampa, FL 33602

Toronto Maple Leafs
40 Bay St., Ste. 400
Toronto, ON M5J 2X2

Vancouver Canucks
800 Griffiths Way
Vancouver, BC V6B 6G1

Washington Capitals
401 9th St. NW, Ste. 750
Washington, DC 20004

National Football League

League Office, 280 Park Ave., New York, NY 10017 **Website:** www.nfl.com

Arizona Cardinals
P.O. Box 888
Phoenix AZ 85001

Atlanta Falcons
4400 Falcon Parkway
Flowery Branch, GA 30542

Baltimore Ravens
1101 Russel St.
Baltimore, MD 21230

Buffalo Bills
One Bills Drive
Orchard Park, NY 14127

Carolina Panthers
800 S. Mint St.
Charlotte, NC 28202

Chicago Bears
1000 Football Dr.
Lake Forest, IL 60045

Cincinnati Bengals
One Paul Brown Stadium
Cincinnati, OH 45202

Cleveland Browns
76 Lou Groza Blvd.
Berea, OH 44017

Dallas Cowboys
2401 E. Airport Fwy.
Irving, TX 75062

Denver Broncos
13655 Broncos Pkwy.
Englewood, CO 80112

Detroit Lions
222 Republic Dr.
Allen Park, MI 48101

Green Bay Packers
1265 Lombardi Ave.
Green Bay, WI 54304

Houston Texans
Two Reliant Park
Houston, TX 77054

Indianapolis Colts
7001 W. 56th St.
Indianapolis, IN 46254

Jacksonville Jaguars
One Alltell Stadium Place
Jacksonville, FL 32202

Kansas City Chiefs
One Arrowhead Drive
Kansas City, MO 64129

Miami Dolphins
7500 SW 30th St.
Davie, FL 33329

Minnesota Vikings
9520 Viking Dr.
Eden Prairie, MN 55344

New England Patriots
60 Washington St.
Foxboro, MA 02035

New Orleans Saints[1]
5800 Airline Dr.
Metairie, LA 70003

New York Giants
Giants Stadium
E. Rutherford, NJ 07073

New York Jets
1000 Fulton Ave.
Hempstead, NY 11550

Oakland Raiders
1220 Harbor Bay Pkwy.
Alameda, CA 94502

Philadelphia Eagles
3501 S. Broad St.
Philadelphia, PA 19148

Pittsburgh Steelers
100 Art Rooney Ave.
Pittsburgh, PA 15212

St. Louis Rams
One Rams Way
St. Louis, MO 63045

San Diego Chargers
4020 Murphy Rd.
PO Box 609609
San Diego, CA 92160

San Francisco 49ers
4949 Centennial Blvd.
Santa Clara, CA 95054

Seattle Seahawks
11220 NE 53rd St.
Kirkland, WA 98033

Tampa Bay Buccaneers
One Buccaneer Place
Tampa, FL 33607

Tennessee Titans
460 Great Circle Rd.
Nashville, TN 37228

Washington Redskins
21300 Redskin Park Dr.
Ashburn, VA 20147

(1) New Orleans Saints 2005 homegames were to be played at San Antonio's Alamodome and at (LSU) Tiger Stadium in Baton Rouge.

Other North American Sports Organizations

Amateur Athletic Union,
PO Box 22409,
Lake Buena Vista, FL 32830
www.aausports.org

Amateur Softball Assn.
2801 NE 50th St.
Oklahoma City, OK 73111
www.softball.org

American Kennel Club
260 Madison Ave.
New York, NY 10016
www.akc.org

Canadian Football League
50 Wellington St. E., 3rd Fl.
Toronto, Ont. M5E 1C8
www.cfl.ca

CART (Championship Auto Racing Teams)
5350 Lakeview Pkwy. S. Dr.
Indianapolis, IN 46268
www.champcarworldseries.com

Intl. Game Fish Assn.
300 Gulf Stream Way
Dania Beach, FL 33004
www.igfa.org

LPGA
100 International Golf Dr.
Daytona Beach, FL 32124
www.lpga.com

Little League Baseball
PO Box 3485
Williamsport, PA 17701
www.littleleague.org

Major League Soccer
420 5th Ave.
New York, NY 10018
www.mlsnet.com

NASCAR
P.O. Box 2875
Daytona Beach, FL 32120
www.nascar.com

NCAA
700 W. Washington St.
P.O. Box 6222
Indianapolis, IN 46206
www.ncaa.org

National Rifle Assn.
11250 Waples Mill Rd.
Fairfax, VA 22030
www.nra.org

Pro Bowlers Assn.
719 2nd Ave., Ste. 701
Seattle, WA 98104
www.pbatour.com

PGA
112 PGA Tour Blvd.
Ponte Vedra Beach, FL 32082
www.pga.com

Pro Rodeo Cowboys Assn.
101 Pro Rodeo Dr.
Colorado Springs, CO 80919
www.prorodeo.org

Special Olympics
1133 19th St. NW
Washington, DC 20036
www.specialolympics.org

Thoroughbred Racing Assn.
420 Fair Hill Dr.
Elkton, MD 21921
www.tra-online.com

US Equestrian Federation
4047 Iron Works Pkwy.
Lexington, KY 40511
www.usef.org

USA Rugby
1033 Walnut St., Suite 200
Boulder, CO 80302
www.usarugby.org

USA Swimming
One Olympic Plaza
Colorado Springs, CO 80909
www.usa-swimming.org

USA Track & Field
One RCA Dome, Ste. 140
Indianapolis, IN 46225
www.usatf.org

U.S. Auto Club
4910 W. 16th St.
Speedway, IN 46224
www.usacracing.com

U.S. Figure Skating Assn.
20 First St.
Colorado Springs, CO 80906
www.usfigureskating.org

U.S. Olympic Committee
One Olympic Plaza
Colorado Springs, CO 80909
www.usoc.org

U.S. Ski and Snowboard Assn.
1500 Kearns Blvd.
P.O. Box 100
Park City, UT 84060
www.ussa.org

U.S. Soccer Federation
1801 S. Prairie Ave.
Chicago, IL 60616
www.ussoccer.com

U.S. Tennis Assn.
70 W. Red Oak Lane
White Plains, NY 10604
www.usta.com

U.S. Trotting Assn.
750 Michigan Ave.
Columbus, OH 43215
www.ustrotting.com

WNBA
Olympic Tower
645 5th Ave.
New York, NY 10022
www.wnba.com

NOTABLE SPORTS PERSONALITIES

Henry (Hank) Aaron, b. 1934: Milwaukee-Atlanta outfielder; hit record 755 home runs, led NL 4 times; record 2,297 RBI.

Kareem Abdul-Jabbar, b. 1947: Milwaukee, L.A. Lakers center; MVP 6 times; all-time leading NBA scorer, 38,387 points.

Andre Agassi, b. 1970: won: Wimbledon, '92; U.S. Open, '94, '99, '99; Aust. Open, '95, 2000-01, 2003; French Open, '99.

Troy Aikman, b. 1966: quarterback; led Dallas Cowboys to Super Bowl wins in 1993-94, 1996; Super Bowl MVP, 1993.

Amy Alcott, b. 1956: golfer; 29 career wins (5 majors), inducted into World Golf Hall of Fame in 1999.

Grover Cleveland "Pete" Alexander (1887-1950): pitcher; won 373 NL games; pitched 16 shutouts, 1916.

Muhammad Ali, b. 1942: 3-time heavyweight champion.

Gary Anderson, b. 1959: kicker; NFL's career points leader, with 2,434 through the end of the 2003 season.

Sparky Anderson, b. 1934: only manager to win World Series in the NL (Cincinnati, 1975-76) and the AL (Detroit, 1984).

Mario Andretti, b. 1940: race-car driver; won Daytona 500 (1967), Indy 500 (1969); Formula 1 world title (1978).

Earl Anthony (1938-2001): bowler; won record 6 PBA Championships (1973-75, 1981-83), 41 career PBA tournaments.

Eddie Arcaro (1916-97): only jockey to win racing's Triple Crown twice, 1941,1948; rode to 4,779 wins in his career.

Lance Armstrong, b. 1971: cyclist; record 7-time winner of the Tour de France (1999-2005).

Arthur Ashe (1943-93): tennis player; won U.S. Open (1968); Wimbledon (1975); died of AIDS.

Evelyn Ashford, b. 1957: sprinter; won 100m gold (1984) and silver (1988); member of 5 U.S. Olympic teams (1976-1992).

Red Auerbach, b. 1917: coached Boston to 9 NBA titles.

Tracy Austin, b. 1962: youngest player to win U.S. Open tennis title (age 16 in 1979), 2-time AP Female Athlete of the Year.

Ernie Banks, b. 1931: Chicago Cubs slugger; hit 512 NL homers; twice MVP; never played in World Series.

Roger Bannister, b. 1929: British physician; ran first sub 4-minute mile, May 6, 1954 (3 min. 59.4 sec.).

Charles Barkely, b. 1963: NBA MVP, 1993; 4th player ever to surpass 20,000 pts, 10,000 rebounds, and 4,000 assists.

Rick Barry, b. 1944: NBA scoring leader, 1967; ABA, 1969.

Sammy Baugh, b. 1914: Washington Redskins quarterback; held numerous records upon retirement after 16 seasons.

Elgin Baylor, b. 1934: L.A. Lakers forward; 10-time all-star.

Bob Beamon, b. 1946: Olympic long jump gold medalist in 1968; world record jump of 29' 2½" stood until 1991.

Boris Becker, b. 1967: German tennis star; won U.S. Open 1989; Wimbledon champ 3 times.

David Beckham, b. 1975: English soccer star; captain of 2002 World Cup team.

Bill Belichick, b. 1952: NFL coach; led New England Patriots to Super Bowl wins in 2001, 2003, 2004; best all-time post-season coaching record.

Jean Beliveau, b. 1931: Montreal Canadiens center; scored 507 goals; twice MVP.

Johnny Bench, b. 1947: Cincinnati Reds catcher; MVP twice; led league in home runs twice, RBIs 3 times.

Patty Berg, b. 1918: won more than 80 golf tournaments; AP Woman Athlete of the Year 3 times.

Yogi Berra, b. 1925: Yankee catcher (1946-63); 3-time MVP.

Abebe Bikila (1932-73): Ethiopian runner; won consecutive Olympic marathon gold medals in 1960 (barefoot), 1964.

Matt Biondi, b. 1965: swimmer; won 5 golds, 1988 Olympics.

Larry Bird, b. 1956: Boston Celtics forward; NBA MVP, 1984-86; 1998 coach of the year with Indiana Pacers.

Bonnie Blair, b. 1964: speed skater; won 5 individual gold medals in 3 Olympics (1988, '92, '94).

George Blanda, b. 1927: quarterback, kicker; 26 years as active player, scored 2,002 career points.

Fanny Blankers-Koen (1918-2004): track; won 4 golds in 1948 Olympics.

Wade Boggs, b. 1958: AL batting champ, 1983, 1985-88; reached 3,000 career hits, 1999 (3,010).

Barry Bonds, b. 1964: outfielder; hit record 73 homers in 2001; NL MVP 1990, 1992-93, 2001-04; 3rd all-time in HRs (708).

Bjorn Borg, b. 1956: led Sweden to first Davis Cup, 1975; Wimbledon champion 5 times.

Ray Bourque, b. 1960: Boston defenseman,1979-2000; 5-time Norris Trophy winner; won Stanley Cup with Colorado, 2001.

Bill Bradley, b. 1943: All-America at Princeton; led N.Y. Knicks to 2 NBA titles (1970, '73); U.S. senator, 1979-97.

Donald Bradman (1908-2001): Australian widely regarded as the greatest cricketer ever; set several batting records.

Terry Bradshaw, b. 1948: quarterback; led Pittsburgh to 4 Super Bowl wins (1975-76, 1979-80); NFL MVP, 1978.

George Brett, b. 1953: Kansas City Royals infielder; led AL in batting, 1976, 1980, 1990; MVP, 1980.

Lou Brock, b. 1939: St. Louis Cardinals outfielder; stole NL record 118 bases, 1974; led NL 8 times.

Jim Brown, b. 1936: Clev. fullback; 12,312 career yds.; 2-time Associated Press MVP.

Paul Brown (1908-91): football owner, coach; led eponymous Cleveland Browns to 3 NFL championships.

Kobe Bryant, b. 1978: guard; won 3 straight titles with Lakers (2000-02).

Paul "Bear" Bryant (1913-83): college football coach with 323 wins; led Alabama to 5 national titles (1961, '64, '65, '78, '79).

Sergei Bubka, b. 1963: Ukrainian pole vaulter; first to clear 20 feet; gold medal, 1988 Olympics.

Don Budge (1915-2000): won numerous amateur and pro tennis titles; Grand Slam, 1938.

Dick Butkus, b. 1942: Chicago Bears linebacker; twice chosen NFL defensive player of the year.

Dick Button, b. 1929: figure skater; won 1948, 1952 Olympic gold medals; world titlist, 1948-52.

Walter Camp (1859-1925): Yale football player, coach, athletic director; established many rules for modern football.

Roy Campanella (1921-93): Hall of Fame catcher for the Brooklyn Dodgers (1948-57); 3-time NL MVP.

Earl Campbell, b. 1955: NFL running back; MVP 1978-79.

Jennifer Capriati, b. 1976: won Aust. (2001-02) and French Opens (2001), at 14 in 1990 was youngest top-10 player.

Rod Carew, b. 1945: AL infielder; 7 batting titles, 1977 MVP.

Steve Carlton, b. 1944: NL pitcher; won 20 games 6 times, Cy Young award 4 times; 4,136 career strikeouts.

Pete Carroll, b. 1951: college football coach; coached the USC Trojans to 2 championships (2003-4).

Billy Casper, b. 1931: PGA Player of the Year 3 times; U.S. Open champ twice.

Wilt Chamberlain (1936-99): center; was NBA leading scorer 7 times, MVP 4 times; scored 100 pts. in a game, 1962.

Bobby Clarke, b. 1949: Philadelphia Flyers center; led team to 2 Stanley Cup championships; MVP 3 times.

Roger Clemens, b. 1962: pitcher; 1986 AL MVP; only 7-time Cy Young winner (1986-87, '91, '97-98, 2001, '04); twice recorded record 20 Ks in a game; 341 wins, 4,502 Ks (2nd all-time).

Roberto Clemente (1934-72): Pittsburgh Pirates outfielder; won 4 batting titles; MVP, 1966; killed in plane crash.

Ty Cobb (1886-1961): Detroit Tigers outfielder; had record .367 lifetime batting average, 12 batting titles.

Sebastian Coe, b. 1956: British runner; won Olympic 1,500m gold medal and 800m silver medal in 1980 and 1984.

Nadia Comaneci, b. 1961: Romanian gymnast; won 3 gold medals, achieved 7 perfect scores, 1976 Olympics.

Maureen Connolly (1934-69): won tennis Grand Slam, 1953; AP Woman-Athlete-of-the-Year 3 times.

Jimmy Connors, b. 1952: tennis; 5 U.S. titles, 2 Wimbledon.

Cynthia Cooper, b. 1963: basketball; 4-time MVP of the WNBA finals and 2-time league MVP for the Houston Comets.

James J. Corbett (1866-1933): heavyweight champion, 1892-97; credited with being the first "scientific" boxer.

Angel Cordero Jr., b. 1942: jockey; leading money winner, 1976, 1982-83; rode 3 Kentucky Derby winners.

Margaret Smith Court, b. 1942: Australian tennis great; won 24 Grand Slam events.

Bob Cousy, b. 1928: Boston guard; 6 NBA titles; 1957 MVP.

Bjoern Daehlie, b. 1967: Norwegian cross-country skier; won record 8 Winter Olympic gold medals.

Lindsay Davenport, b. 1976: tennis; won Olympic gold (1996), U.S. Open (1998), Wimbledon (1999), Aust. Open (2000).

Dizzy Dean (1910-74): pitcher; St. Louis Cardinals' "Gashouse Gang" in the 30s.

Mary Decker Slaney, b. 1958: runner; has held 7 separate American records from the 800m to 10,000m.

Oscar De La Hoya, b. 1972: won IBF lightweight (1995); WBC super lightweight (1996) and welterweight (1997, 2000) titles.

Donna de Varona, b. 1947: 2 Olympic swimming golds,1964; 1st female sportscaster at a major network (ABC), 1965.

Jack Dempsey (1895-1983): heavyweight champ, 1919-26.

Gail Devers, b. 1966: Olympic 100m gold medalist, 1992, '96.

Eric Dickerson, b. 1960: NFL record 2,105 rushing yds.,1984.

Joe DiMaggio (1914-99): N.Y. Yankees outfielder; hit safely in record 56 consecutive games, 1941; AL MVP 3 times.

Tony Dorsett, b. 1954: Heisman winner who led the Dallas Cowboys to an NFL title in his rookie year (1977).

Tim Duncan, b. 1976: San Antonio center; 3-time NBA Finals MVP (1999, 2003, 2005); NBA MVP, 2002-03.

Roberto Duran, b. 1951: Panamanian boxer, held titles at 3 weights; lost 1980 "no mas" fight to Sugar Ray Leonard.

Leo Durocher (1905-91): manager; won 3 NL pennants (Brooklyn-1941, N.Y. Giants-1951, '54) and 1954 World Series.

Dale Earnhardt (1951-2001): 7-time NASCAR Winston Cup champ; died in a last-lap crash at 2001 Daytona 500.

Stefan Edberg, b. 1966: Swedish tennis player; U.S. Open champ, 1991, 1992; Wimbledon champ, 1988, 1990.

Gertrude Ederle (1906-2003): first woman to swim English Channel, broke existing men's record, 1926.

Teresa Edwards, b. 1964: basketball; 5-time Olympian; gold medalist in 1984, '88, '96, 2000 and bronze medal in 1992.
Hicham El Guerrouj, b. 1974: Moroccan runner; holds world records in mile (3:43.13) and 1,500m (3:26); won gold medals in 1,500m and 5,000m in 2004 Olympics.
John Elway, b. 1960: quarterback; led Denver Broncos to 2 Super Bowl wins, 1998, 1999; regular-season MVP, 1987.
Julius "Dr. J" Erving, b. 1950: 3-time ABA MVP, 1981 NBA MVP.
Phil Esposito, b. 1942: NHL scoring leader 5 times.
Janet Evans, b. 1971: 4 Olympic swimming golds, 1988-92.
Lee Evans, b. 1947: Olympic 400m gold medalist in 1968 with a 43.86 sec. world record not broken until 1988.
Chris Evert, b. 1954: U.S. Open tennis champ 6 times, Wimbledon champ 3 times.
Ray Ewry (1873-1937): track-and-field star; won 8 gold medals, 1900, 1904, and 1908 Olympics.
Nick Faldo, b. 1957: British golfer; won Masters, British Open 3 times each.
Juan Manuel Fangio (1911-95): Argentinian; 5-time World Grand Prix driving champ (1951, 1954-57).
Marshall Faulk, b. 1973: 2000 NFL MVP; scored then-record 26 TDs in 2001; 3-time Off. Player of the Year (1999-2001).
Brett Favre, b. 1969: quarterback; led Green Bay to Super Bowl win, 1997; NFL MVP, 1995, 1996; co-MVP, 1997.
Roger Federer, b. 1981: Swiss winner of 6 Grand Slam tennis tournaments.
Bob Feller, b. 1918: Cleveland Indians pitcher; won 266 games; pitched 3 no-hitters, 12 one-hitters.
Rollie Fingers, b. 1946: pitcher; 341 career saves; AL MVP, Cy Young Award, 1981; World Series MVP, 1974.
Peggy Fleming, b. 1948: world figure skating champion, 1966-68; gold medalist, 1968 Olympics.
Whitey Ford, b. 1928: N.Y. Yankees pitcher; won record 10 World Series games.
George Foreman, b. 1949: heavyweight champion, 1973-74, 1994-95; at 45, the oldest to win a heavyweight title.
Dick Fosbury, b. 1947: high jumper; won 1968 Olympic gold medal; developed the "Fosbury Flop."
Jimmie Foxx (1907-67): Red Sox, Athletics slugger; MVP 3 times; triple crown, 1933.
A.J. Foyt, b. 1935: won Indy 500 4 times; U.S. Auto Club champ 7 times.
Joe Frazier, b. 1944: heavyweight champion, 1970-73.
Walt Frazier, b. 1945: Hall of Fame guard for N.Y. Knicks' NBA championship teams (1970, '73).
Lou Gehrig (1903-41): N.Y. Yankees 1st baseman; MVP, 1927, 1936; triple crown, 1934; AL record 184 RBIs, 1931; played in 2,130 straight games (1925-39), a record that stood untl 1995.
Althea Gibson (1927-2003): 2-time U.S. and Wimbledon champ.
Bob Gibson, b. 1935: St. Louis Cardinals pitcher; won Cy Young award twice; struck out 3,117 batters.
Josh Gibson (1911-47): Hall of Fame catcher; known as "Babe Ruth of the Negro Leagues"; credited with as many as 84 homers in 1 season and about 800 in his career.
Marc Girardelli, b. 1963: skier (Lux.); won 5 World Cup titles.
Jeff Gordon, b. 1971: race car driver; youngest to win NASCAR title 4 times (1995, 1997-98, 2001).
Steffi Graf, b. 1969: German; won tennis Grand Slam, 1988; U.S. champ 5 times; Wimbledon champ 7 times.
Otto Graham, b. (1921-2003): Cleveland quarterback; 4-time all-pro.
Red Grange (1903-91): All-American at Univ. of Illinois, 1923-25; played for Chicago Bears, 1925-35.
"Mean" Joe Greene, b. 1946: Pittsburgh Steelers lineman; twice NFL outstanding defensive player.
Wayne Gretzky, b. 1961: top scorer in NHL history with record 894 goals, 1,963 assists, 2,857 points; MVP, 1980-87, 1989.
Bob Griese, b. 1945: All-Pro quarterback; led Miami Dolphins to 17-0 season (1972) and 2 Super Bowl titles (1973-74).
Ken Griffey Jr., b. 1969: outfielder; led AL in homers 1994, 1997-1999; 1997 AL MVP; 10 gold gloves.
Archie Griffin, b. 1954: Ohio State running back; only 2-time winner of the Heisman Trophy (1974-75).
Florence Griffith Joyner (1959-98): sprinter; won 3 gold medals at 1988 Olympics; world and Olympic record for 100m.
Lefty Grove (1900-75): pitcher; won 300 AL games.
Janet Guthrie, b. 1938: 1st woman driver in Indy 500 (1977).
Tony Gwynn, b. 1960: 8-time NL batting champ, 1984, 1987-89, 1994-97; 3,141 career hits.
Walter Hagen (1892-1969): golfer; 5 PGA, 4 British Open titles.
George Halas (1895-1983): founder-coach of Chicago Bears; won 5 NFL championships.
Dorothy Hamill, b. 1956: figure skater; gold medalist at the Olympics and World championships in 1976.
Scott Hamilton, b. 1958: U.S. and world figure skating champion, 1981-84; Olympic gold medalist, 1984.
Mia Hamm, b. 1972: led U.S. to World Cup (1991, '99) and Olympic ('96, 2004) titles; most career internat. goals (144).
Franco Harris, b. 1950: running back; 4 Super Bowls with Steelers (1975-76, 1979-80); 1,000+ yds. in a season 8 times.
Bill Hartack, b. 1932: jockey; rode 5 Kentucky Derby winners.
Dominik Hasek, b. 1965: NHL goaltender; won Vezina Trophy, 1994-95, 1997-99, 2001; NHL MVP, 1997-98.
John Havlicek, b. 1940: Boston Celtics forward; scored 26,395 career pts.
Eric Heiden, b. 1958: speed skater; won 5 Olympic golds, 1980.
Rickey Henderson, b. 1958; outfielder; 1990 AL MVP; record 130 stolen bases, 1982; all-time leader in steals, runs.
Sonja Henie (1912-69): Norwegian world champion figure skater, 1927-36; Olympic gold medalist, 1928, 1932, 1936.
Martina Hingis, b. 1980: Swiss; won Aust. and U.S. Opens, Wimbledon; youngest No. 1 player (16 yrs., 6 m.), 1997.
Ben Hogan (1912-97): golfer; won 4 U.S. Open titles, 2 PGA Championships, 2 Masters.
Chamique Holdsclaw, b. 1977: L.A. Sparks forward.
Evander Holyfield, b. 1962: 4-time heavyweight champion.
Rogers Hornsby (1896-1963): NL 2nd baseman; batted record .424 in 1924; twice won triple crown.
Paul Hornung, b. 1935: Green Bay Packers runner, placekicker; scored record 176 points, 1960.
Gordie Howe, b. 1928: hockey forward; NHL MVP 6 times; scored 801 goals in 26 NHL seasons.
Carl Hubbell (1903-88): N.Y. Giants pitcher; 20-game winner 5 consecutive years, 1933-37.
Bobby Hull, b. 1939: NHL all-star 10 times; MVP, 1965-66.
Brett Hull, b. 1964: St. Louis Blues forward; led NHL in goals, 1990-92; MVP, 1991.
Catfish Hunter (1946-99): pitched perfect game, 1968; 20-game winner 5 times.
Don Hutson (1913-97): Packers receiver; caught 99 TD passes; 2-time NFL MVP.
Juli Inkster, b. 1960: Hall of Fame golfer; 2nd to win all 4 of LPGA's modern majors; won 7 career major titles.
Phil Jackson, b. 1945: won 9 NBA titles as coach of Bulls and Lakers; 1973 title as a player with N.Y Knicks.
Reggie Jackson, b. 1946: slugger; led AL in home runs 4 times; MVP, 1973; hit 5 World Series home runs, 1977.
"Shoeless" Joe Jackson (1889-1951): outfielder; 3rd highest career batting average (.356); one of the "Black Sox" banned for allegedly throwing 1919 World Series.
Jaromir Jagr, b. 1972: Czech hockey player; NHL MVP in 1999; Art Ross Trophy (leading scorer) 1995, 1998-2001.
Bruce Jenner, b. 1949: Olympic decathlon gold medalist, 1976.
Lynn Jennings, b. 1960: runner; 3-time World and 9-time U.S. cross country champ; bronze at 1992 Olympics (10,000m).
Earvin "Magic" Johnson, b. 1959: NBA MVP, 1987, 1989, 1990; Playoff MVP, 1980, 1982, 1987; 2nd in career assists.
Jack Johnson (1878-1946): heavyweight champion, 1908-15.
Michael Johnson, b. 1967: 5-time Olympic gold medalist (1996, 2000); world and Olympic record, 200m and 400m.
Randy Johnson, b. 1963: 5-time Cy Young winner; strikeout leader: 1992-95, 1999-2004; 4,372 strikeouts (3rd all-time); pitched perfect game, 2004.
Walter Johnson (1887-1946): Washington Senators pitcher; won 416 games; record 110 shutouts.
Bobby Jones (1902-71): won golf's Grand Slam, 1930; U.S. Amateur champ 5 times, U.S. Open champ 4 times.
David "Deacon" Jones, b. 1938: 5-time All-Pro with L.A. Rams (1965-69); "sack" specialist credited with inventing the term.
Marion Jones, b. 1975: 2000 Olympic 100m, 200m, 1,600m relay gold medalist, bronze in long jump and 400m relay.
Roy Jones Jr., b. 1969: light heavyweight champ, 1999-2004.
Michael Jordan, b. 1963: guard; leading NBA scorer, 1987-93, 1996-98; MVP, 1988, 1991-92, '96, '98; playoff MVP, 1991-93, 1996-98; ESPN Athlete of the Century.
Dorothy Kamenshek, b. 1925: led Rockford (IL) Peaches to 4 All-American Girls Baseball League titles in the 1940s.
Jackie Joyner-Kersee, b. 1962: Olympic gold medalist in heptathlon (1988,'92) and long jump (1988).
Harmon Killebrew, b. 1936: Minnesota Twins slugger; led AL in home runs 6 times; 573 lifetime.
Jean Claude Killy, b. 1943: French skier; 3 Olympic golds, 1968.
Ralph Kiner, b. 1922: Pittsburgh Pirates slugger; led NL in home runs 7 consecutive years, 1946-52.
Billie Jean King, b. 1943: U.S. singles champ 4 times; Wimbledon champ 6 times; beat Bobby Riggs, 1973.
Bob Knight, b. 1940: basketball coach; led Indiana U. to NCAA title in 1976, '81, '87.
Olga Korbut, b. 1955: Soviet gymnast; 3 1972 Olympic golds.
Sandy Koufax, b. 1935: 3-time Cy Young winner; lowest ERA in NL, 1962-66; pitched 4 no-hitters, one a perfect game.
Ingrid Kristiansen, b. 1956: Norwegian; only runner to have held world records in 5,000m, 10,000m, and marathon.
Julie Krone, b. 1963: winningest female jockey; only woman to ride a winner in a Triple Crown race (Belmont, 1993).
Michelle Kwan, b.1980: figure skater; 9 U.S. and 5 World titles; silver medalist at 1998 Olympics, bronze in 2002.
Guy Lafleur, b. 1951: 3-time NHL scoring leader; 1977-78 MVP.

Kennesaw Mountain Landis (1866-1944): 1st commissioner of baseball (1920-44); banned the 8 "Black Sox" involved in fixing 1919 World Series.
Tom Landry (1924-2000): Dallas Cowboys head coach, 1960-88; won 2 Super Bowls (1972, '78); 3rd in career wins (270).
Dick "Night Train" Lane (1928-2002): Hall of Fame defensive back, intercepted an NFL season record 14 passes (1952).
Don Larsen, b. 1929: As N.Y. Yankee, pitched only World Series perfect game, Oct. 8, 1956—a 2-0 win over Brooklyn.
Rod Laver, b. 1938: Australian; won tennis Grand Slam twice, 1962, 1969; Wimbledon champ 4 times.
Mario Lemieux, b. 1965: 6-time NHL leading scorer; MVP, 1988, 1993, 1996; playoff MVP, 1991-92.
Greg Lemond, b. 1961: cyclist; 3-time Tour de France winner (1986, '89-90); first American to win the event.
Ivan Lendl, b. 1960: Czech; U.S. Open tennis champ, 1985-87.
Sugar Ray Leonard, b. 1956: boxer; held titles in 5 different weight classes.
Carl Lewis, b. 1961: track-and-field star; won 9 Olympic gold medals in sprinting and the long jump.
Lennox Lewis, b. 1965: Brit.; heavyweight champ, 1997-2004.
Tara Lipinski, b. 1982: youngest figure skater to win U.S. and world championships, 1997, and Winter Olympic gold, 1998.
Vince Lombardi (1913-70): Green Bay Packers coach; led team to 5 NFL championships and 2 Super Bowl victories.
Nancy Lopez, b. 1957: Hall of Fame golfer; 4-time LPGA Player of the Year, 3-time winner of the LPGA Championship.
Greg Louganis, b. 1960: won Olympic gold medals in both springboard and platform diving, 1984, 1988.
Joe Louis (1914-81): heavyweight champion, 1937-49.
Sid Luckman (1916-98): Chicago Bears quarterback; led team to 4 NFL championships; MVP, 1943.
Connie Mack (1862-1956): Philadelphia Athletics manager, 1901-50; won 9 pennants, 5 championships.
John Madden, b. 1936: won Super Bowl as coach of the Oakland Raiders (1977); NFL TV analyst since 1982.
Greg Maddux, b. 1966: NL pitcher, won 4 consecutive Cy Young awards, 1992-95; 318 career wins.
Karl Malone, b. 1963: Utah Jazz, L.A. Laker forward; MVP, 1997, 1999; 14-time All-Star; 36,928 career points (2nd all-time).
Moses Malone, b. 1955: NBA center; MVP, 1979, 1982-83.
Mickey Mantle (1931-95): N.Y. Yankees outfielder; triple crown, 1956; 18 World Series home runs; MVP 3 times.
Diego Maradona, b. 1960: soccer player; led Argentina to World Cup in 1986.
"Pistol" Pete Maravich (1948-88): guard; scored NCAA record 44.2 ppg during collegiate career; led NBA in scoring, 1977.
Rocky Marciano (1923-69): heavyweight champion, 1952-56; retired undefeated.
Dan Marino, b. 1961: Miami quarterback; NFL record 5,084 yds passing and 48 TDs, 1984; career leader, TDs, yds passing.
Roger Maris (1934-85): N.Y. Yankees outfielder; hit AL record 61 home runs, 1961; MVP, 1960 and 1961.
Eddie Mathews (1931-2000): Milwaukee-Atlanta 3rd baseman; hit 512 career home runs.
Christy Mathewson (1880-1925): pitcher; won 373 games.
Bob Mathias, b. 1930: decathlon gold, 1948, 1952 Olympics.
Willie Mays, b. 1931: N.Y.-S.F. Giants center fielder; hit 660 home runs, led NL 4 times; had 3,283 hits; twice MVP.
Willie McCovey, b. 1938: S.F. Giants slugger; hit 521 home runs; led NL 3 times; MVP, 1969.
John McEnroe, b. 1959: U.S. Open tennis champ, 1979-81, 1984; Wimbledon champ, 1981, 1983-84.
John McGraw (1873-1934): N.Y. Giants manager; led team to 10 pennants, 3 championships.
Mark McGwire, b. 1963: hit then-record 70 home runs in 1998; 583 career home runs (6th).
Tamara McKinney, b. 1962: 1st U.S. skier to win overall Alpine World Cup championship (1983).
Andrea Mead Lawrence, b. 1932: hall of fame skier; only woman to win 2 gold medals in alpine skiing at one Olympics (1952).
Mark Messier, b. 1961: center; NHL MVP, 1990, 1992; Conn Smythe Trophy, 1984.
Debbie Meyer, b. 1952: 1st swimmer to win 3 individual Olympic golds (1968).
George Mikan, b. 1924: Minn. Lakers center; considered the best basketball player of the first half of the 20th century.
Stan Mikita, b. 1940: Chicago Blackhawks center; led NHL in scoring 4 times; MVP twice.
Billy Mills, b. 1938: runner; upset winner of the 1964 Olympic 10,000m; only American man ever to win the event.
Joe Montana, b. 1956: S.F. 49ers quarterback; Super Bowl MVP, 1982, 1985, 1990.
Archie Moore (1913-98): light-heavyweight champ, 1952-62.
Howie Morenz (1902-37): Montreal Canadiens forward; considered best hockey player of first half of the 20th century.
Edwin Moses, b. 1955: undefeated in 122 consecutive 400m hurdles races, 1977-87; Olympic gold medalist, 1976, '84.
Shirley Muldowney, b. 1940: 1st woman to race National Hot Rod Assoc. Top Fuel dragsters; 3-time NHRA points champ.
Eddie Murray, b. 1956: durable slugger; 3rd player to combine 3,000+ hits with 500+ home runs.
Stan Musial, b. 1920: St. Louis Cardinals star; won 7 NL batting titles; MVP 3 times.
Bronko Nagurski (1908-90): Chicago Bears fullback and tackle; gained more than 4,000 yds. rushing.
Joe Namath, b. 1943: Jets quarterback; 1969 Super Bowl MVP.
Martina Navratilova, b. 1956: Wimbledon champ 9 times, U.S. Open champ 1983-84, 1986-87.
Byron Nelson, b. 1912: won 11 consecutive golf tournaments in 1945; twice Masters and PGA titlist.
Ernie Nevers (1903-76): Stanford football star; selected as best college fullback to play between 1919-69.
Paula Newby-Fraser, b. 1972: 8-time Ironman Triathlon World Champ; holds women's course record.
John Newcombe, b. 1943: Australian; twice U.S. Open tennis champ; Wimbledon titlist 3 times.
Jack Nicklaus, b. 1940: PGA Player of the Year, 1967, 1972; leading money winner 8 times; won 18 majors (6 Masters).
Chuck Noll, b. 1931: Pittsburgh coach; won 4 Super Bowls.
Paavo Nurmi (1897-1973): Finnish distance runner; won 6 Olympic gold medals, 1920, 1924, 1928.
Al Oerter, b. 1936: discus thrower; won gold medal at 4 consecutive Olympics, 1956-68.
Hakeem Olajuwon, b. 1963: Houston center; NBA MVP, 1994, playoffs MVP, 1994-95; career blocked shots leader.
Barney Oldfield (1878-1946): pioneer auto racer; was first to drive a car 60 mph (1903).
Shaquille O'Neal, b. 1972: center; led L.A. Lakers to NBA titles, 2000-2002; 2000, 2002 Finals MVP; 2000 NBA MVP.
Bobby Orr, b. 1948: Boston Bruins defenseman; 8-time Norris Trophy winner; led NHL in scoring twice, assists 5 times.
Mel Ott (1909-1958): N.Y. Giants outfielder; hit 511 home runs; led NL 6 times.
Jesse Owens (1913-80): track and field; 4 1936 Olympic golds.
Satchel Paige (1906-82): pitcher; starred in Negro leagues, 1924-48; entered major leagues at age 42.
Arnold Palmer, b. 1929: golf's first $1 million winner; won 4 Masters, 2 British Opens.
Jim Palmer, b. 1945: Baltimore Orioles pitcher; won Cy Young award 3 times; 20-game winner 8 times.
Joe Paterno, b. 1926: football coach; 2nd-most wins in NCAA Div. I-A (343 through 2004); led Penn St. to titles, 1982, 1986.
Danica Patrick, b. 1982: racecar driver; 4th woman to race at Indy 500, and 1st to lead (2005).
Floyd Patterson, b. 1935: 2-time heavyweight champion.
Walter Payton (1954-1999): Chicago Bears running back; most rushing yards in NFL history; top NFC rusher, 1976-80.
Pelé (Edson Arantes do Nascimento), b. 1940: soccer; led Brazil to 3 World Cups (1958, '62, '70); scored 1,281 goals.
Bob Pettit, b. 1932: first NBA player to score 20,000 points; twice NBA scoring leader.
Richard Petty, b. 1937: NASCAR national champ 7 times; 7-time Daytona 500 winner.
Michael Phelps, b. 1985: swimmer; won 8 medals (6 gold, 2 bronze) at 2004 Olympics; set numerous world records.
Laffit Pincay Jr., b. 1946: jockey; leading money-winner, 1970-74, 1979, 1985.
Jacques Plante (1929-86): NHL goaltender; 7 Vezina trophies; first goalie to wear a mask in a game.
Gary Player, b. 1936: South African golfer; won 3 Masters, 3 British Opens, 2 PGA Championships, and the U.S. Open.
Steve Prefontaine (1951-75): runner; 1st to win 4 NCAA titles in same event (5,000m, 1970-73); died in auto accident.
Paula Radcliffe, b. 1973: British runner; set marathon world record of 2:15:25 in London, 2003.
Willis Reed, b. 1942: N.Y. Knicks center; MVP, 1970; playoff MVP, 1970, 1973.
Mary Lou Retton, b. 1968: gymnast; won all-around gold medal at 1984 Olympics; also won 2 silvers and 2 bronzes.
Jerry Rice, b. 1962: receiver; 1989 Super Bowl MVP; NFL record for career touchdowns (208) and receptions (1,549).
Maurice Richard (1921-2000): Montreal Canadiens forward; scored 544 regular season goals, 82 playoff goals.
Branch Rickey (1881-1965): MLB executive; helped break baseball's color barrier, 1947; initiated farm system, 1919.
Cal Ripken Jr., b. 1960: Baltimore shortstop; AL MVP 1983, 1991; most consecutive games played (2,632).
Oscar Robertson, b. 1938: NBA guard; averaged career 25.7 points per game; 4th in career assists (9,887); MVP, 1964.
Brooks Robinson, b. 1937: Baltimore Orioles 3rd baseman; played in 4 World Series; MVP, 1964; 16 gold gloves.
Frank Robinson, b. 1935: MVP in both NL and AL; triple crown, 1966; 586 career home runs; first black manager in majors.
Jackie Robinson (1919-72): broke baseball's color barrier with Brooklyn Dodgers, 1947; MVP, 1949.
Sugar Ray Robinson (1920-89): boxer; middleweight champion 5 times, welterweight champion.
Knute Rockne (1888-1931): Notre Dame football coach, 1918-31; revolutionized game by stressing forward pass.

Bill Rodgers, b. 1947: runner; won Boston and New York City marathons 4 time each, 1975-80.

Juan "Chi Chi" Rodriguez, b. 1935: champion golfer; 8 PGA tour wins and 22 Champions tour wins.

Ronaldo (Ronaldo Luiz Nazario de Lima), b. 1976: soccer player; led Brazil to 2002 World Cup; 3-time FIFA world player of the year (1996-97, 2002).

Art Rooney, (1901-88): famous NFL owner, bought Pittsburgh Pirates in 1933, renamed Steelers, in 1940.

Pete Rose, b. 1941: won 3 NL batting titles; hit in 44 consecutive games, 1978; most career hits, 4,256; banned for gambling, 1989; admitted betting on his team, 2004.

Ken Rosewall, b. 1934: Australian tennis player; 2-time U.S. champ, 8 Grand Slam singles titles.

Patrick Roy, b. 1965: Montreal-Colorado goalie; only 3-time NHL Playoffs MVP (Conn Smythe Trophy), 1986, '93, 2001.

Wilma Rudolph (1940-94): sprinter; won 3 1960 Olympic golds.

Adolph Rupp (1901-77): NCAA basketball coach; led Kentucky to 4 national titles, 1948-49, 1951, 1958.

Bill Russell, b. 1934: Boston Celtics center; led team to 11 NBA titles; MVP 5 times; first black coach of major pro sports team.

Babe Ruth (1895-1948): N.Y. Yankees outfielder; hit 60 home runs, 1927; 714 lifetime (2nd all-time); led AL 12 times.

Johnny Rutherford, b. 1938: auto racer; won 3 Indy 500s.

Nolan Ryan, b. 1947: pitcher; holds season (383), career (5,714) strikeout records; won 324 games (7 no-hitters).

Pete Sampras, b. 1971: tennis star; 1st man in Open era to win 7 Wimbledons; most career Grand Slam wins (14).

Joan Benoit Samuelson, b. 1968: won 1st Olympic women's marathon (1984), Boston Marathon (1979, '83).

Barry Sanders, b. 1968: rushed for 2,053 yards in 1997; led NFL in rushing, 1990, 1994, 1996, 1997.

Gale Sayers, b. 1943: Chicago back; twice led NFL in rushing.

Mike Schmidt, b. 1949: Phillies 3rd baseman; led NL in home runs 8 times; 548 lifetime; NL MVP, 1980, 1981, 1986.

Michael Schumacher, b. 1969: German race-car driver; 7-time Formula 1 world champ (1994-95, 2000-2004).

Tom Seaver, b. 1944: pitcher; won NL Cy Young award 3 times; won 311 major league games.

Monica Seles, b. 1973: tennis; won U.S. ('91-92), Aust. ('91-93, '96), French ('90-92) Opens; stabbed on court by fan, 1993.

Patty Sheehan, b. 1956: Hall of Fame golfer; 3 LPGA Championships (1983-84, '93).

Willie Shoemaker (1931-2003): jockey; rode 4 Kentucky Derby and 5 Belmont Stakes winners; leading career money winner.

Frank Shorter, b. 1947: runner, only American to win men's Olympic marathon (1972) since 1908; silver medalist in 1976.

Don Shula, b. 1930: all-time winningest NFL coach (347 games).

Al Simmons (1902-56): AL outfielder; lifetime .334 batting avg.

O.J. Simpson, b. 1947: running back; rushed for 2,003 yds., 1973; AFC leading rusher 4 times; acquitted of murder, 1995.

George Sisler (1893-1973): St. Louis Browns 1st baseman; had then-record 257 hits, 1920; batted .340 lifetime.

Dean Smith, b. 1931: basketball coach; most career Division I wins (879); led North Carolina to 2 NCAA titles (1982, '93).

Emmitt Smith, b. 1969: running back; NFL and Super Bowl MVP, 1993.

Lee Smith, b. 1957: relief pitcher; all-time saves leader (478).

Conn Smythe (1895-1980): won 7 Stanley Cups as Toronto GM (1929-1961); playoff MVP award named in his honor.

Sam Snead (1912-2002): PGA and Masters champ 3 times each, record 82 PGA tournament victories.

Annika Sorenstam, b. 1970: Swedish golfer; set LPGA 18-hole record of 59 (–13) and 72-hole record of 27-under-par, 2001; won 9 LPGA majors, including career Grand Slam.

Sammy Sosa, b. 1968: Cubs outfielder; 66 homers, NL MVP, 1998; 1st to hit 60+ homers 3 times (1998, 1999, 2001).

Warren Spahn, (1921-2003): pitcher; won 363 NL games; 20-game winner 13 times; Cy Young award, 1957.

Tris Speaker (1885-1958): AL outfielder; batted .345 over 22 seasons; hit record 792 career doubles.

Mark Spitz, b. 1950: swimmer; won 7 golds at 1972 Olympics.

Amos Alonzo Stagg (1862-1965): football innovator; Univ. of Chicago football coach for 41 years, 5 undefeated seasons.

Bart Starr, b. 1934: Green Bay Packers quarterback; led team to 5 NFL titles and 2 Super Bowl victories.

Roger Staubach, b. 1942: Dallas Cowboys quarterback; leading NFC passer 5 times.

Casey Stengel (1890-1975): managed Yankees to 10 pennants, 7 championships, 1949-60.

Jackie Stewart, b. 1939: Scot auto racer; 27 Grand Prix wins.

John Stockton b. 1962: Utah Jazz guard; NBA career leader in assists, steals; NBA assists leader, 1988-96.

Picabo Street, b. 1971: skier; 2-time World Cup downhill champion (1995-96); Olympic super G gold medalist, 1998.

Louise Suggs, b. 1923: golfer; U.S. Women's Open champ., 1949, '52; 11 major victories, ranks 3rd all-time.

John L. Sullivan (1858-1918): last bareknuckle heavyweight champion, 1882-1892.

Pat Summit, b. 1952: women's basketball coach; led Tennessee Lady Vols to 6 NCAA titles (1987, '89, '91, '96-98).

Fran Tarkenton, b. 1940: Minnesota, N.Y. Giants quarterback; 3rd in career TD passes (342); 1975 Player of the Year.

Lawrence Taylor, b. 1959; linebacker; led N.Y. Giants to 2 Super Bowl titles; played in 10 Pro Bowls.

Jenny Thompson, b. 1973: swimmer; most decorated U.S. female Olympian; 12 medals (8 gold) in 1992, '96, 2000, '04.

Daley Thompson, b. 1958: British decathlete; Olympic gold medalist in 1980, '84.

Jim Thorpe (1888-1953): football All-America, 1911, 1912; won pentathlon and decathlon, 1912 Olympics.

Bill Tilden (1893-1953): won 7 U.S. tennis titles, 3 Wimbledon.

Y. A. Tittle, b. 1926: N.Y. Giants quarterback; MVP, 1961, 1963.

Alberto Tomba, b. 1966: Italian skier; 5 Olympic alpine medals (3 golds, 2 silver) in 1988, 1992.

Lee Trevino, b. 1939: golfer; won U.S., British Open twice.

Bryan Trottier, b. 1956: Islanders, Penguins center for 6 Stanley Cup champs.

Gene Tunney, (1897-1978): heavyweight champion, 1926-28.

Mike Tyson, b. 1966: undisputed heavyweight champ, 1987-1990; at 19, youngest to win a heavyweight title (WBC, 1986).

Wyomia Tyus, b. 1945: Olympic 100m gold medalist, 1964, '68.

Johnny Unitas, (1933-2002): Baltimore Colts quarterback; passed for more than 40,000 yds; MVP, 1957, 1967.

Al Unser, b. 1939: Indy 500 winner 4 times.

Bobby Unser, b. 1934: Indy 500 winner 3 times.

Norm Van Brocklin (1926-83): quarterback; passed for game record 554 yds., 1951; MVP, 1960.

Amy Van Dyken, b. 1973: swimmer, first American woman to win 4 gold medals in one Olympics (1996).

Lasse Viren, b. 1949: Finnish runner; Olympic 5,000m and 10,000m gold medalist in 1972 and 1976.

Honus Wagner (1874-1955): Pirates shortstop; 8 NL batting titles.

Grete Waitz, b. 1953: Norwegian; 9-time winner of the New York City Marathon (1978-80, 1982-86, '88).

"Jersey" Joe Walcott (1914-94): boxer; became heavyweight champion at age 37, 1951-52.

Bill Walton, b. 1952: center; led Portland Trail Blazers to 1977 NBA title; MVP, 1978; NBA TV commentator.

Kurt Warner, b. 1971: Rams, Giants, Cardinals quarterback; NFL MVP 1999, 2001; Super Bowl MVP, 2000.

Tom Watson, b. 1949: golfer; 6-time PGA Player of the Year, won 5 British Opens, 2 Masters, U.S. Open.

Karrie Webb, b. 1974: Australian golfer; youngest woman (26 yrs. 6 mos.) to win career Grand Slam, 1999-2001.

Johnny Weissmuller (1903-84): swimmer; won 52 national championships, 5 Olympic gold medals; set 67 world records.

Jerry West, b. 1938: L.A. Lakers guard; had career average 27 points per game; first team all-star 10 times.

Byron "Whizzer" White (1917-2002): running back; led NCAA in scoring and rushing at Colorado (1937); led NFL in rushing twice (1938, '40); Supreme Court justice, 1962-93.

Kathy Whitworth, b. 1939: 7-time LPGA Player of the Year (1966-69, 1971-73); 88 tour wins most on LPGA or PGA tour.

Michelle Wie, b. 1989: golfer; in 2002 became youngest-ever qualifier for an LPGA event; turned pro at age 15.

Lenny Wilkens, b. 1937: winningest coach in NBA history; in Hall of Fame as player and coach.

Serena Williams, b. 1981: tennis; Wimbledon (2002, 2003), U.S. Open champ; Australian Open (2003, 2005); French Open (2002).

Ted Williams (1918-2002): Boston Red Sox outfielder; won 6 batting titles, 2 triple crowns; hit .406 in 1941.

Venus Williams, b. 1980: champ at Wimbledon (2000, 2001, 2005) Australian Open (2003), French Open (2002).

Helen Wills Moody (1905-98): tennis star; won U.S. Open 7 times, Wimbledon 8 times.

Katarina Witt, b. 1965: German figure skater; won Olympic gold medal, 1984, 1988; world champ, 1984-84, 1987-88.

John Wooden, b. 1910: UCLA basketball coach; 10 NCAA titles.

Tiger Woods, b. 1975: golfer; youngest to win career Grand Slam, at age 24 (1997-2000); 10 major titles.

Mickey Wright, b. 1935: golfer; won LPGA and U.S. Open championship 4 times; 82 career wins, including 13 majors.

Kristi Yamaguchi, b. 1971: figure skater; won national, world, and Olympic titles in 1992.

Carl Yastrzemski, b. 1939: Boston Red Sox slugger; won 3 batting titles; triple crown, 1967.

Cy Young (1867-1955): pitcher; won record 511 games.

Steve Young, b. 1961: 49ers quarterback; led NFL in passing, 1991-94, 1996, 1997; Super Bowl MVP, 1995.

Babe Didrikson Zaharias (1911-56): all-around athlete; 3 track & field medals (2 golds), 1932 Olympics; won 10 golf majors; also played baseball; 6-time AP Female Athlete of the Year.

Emil Zátopek (1922-2000): Czech runner; won 3 gold medals at 1952 Olympics (5,000m, 10,000m, and marathon).

Zinedine Zidane, b. 1972: soccer; led France to 1998 World Cup (named top player); 3-time FIFA world player.

GENERAL INDEX

Note: Page numbers in **boldface** indicate key reference. Page numbers in *italics* indicate photos.

S

CROSSWORD PUZZLE ANSWERS

ACROSS: 1 Peale, 6 Teas, 10 Agr., 13 Axial, 14 Zebra, 15 Dre, 16 Singin' in Bahrain, 19 Otto, 20 EOE, 21 Aimee, 22 Oman the Range, 26 Atonal, 29 Et al., 30 Matsu, 31 Alan, 33 Semi, 37 Ali, 38 I am Iraq, 41 Liv, 42 NASA, 44 Bout, 45 Utica, 47 Sabu, 49 Airmen, 50 Help me Rwanda, 55 Albee, 56 Ect., 57 Ital., 61 Teen Niger in Love, 65 CNA, 66 Drake, 67 Begin, 68 Han, 69 SARS, 70 Cross

DOWN: 1 Paso, 2 Exit, 3 Ain't, 4 Lagoons, 5 Eli, 6 Tenet, 7 Ebb, 8 Ara, 9 Sahara, 10 A damn, 11 Grieg, 12 Renee, 14 Zion, 17 Neal, 18 Rials, 23 Maui, 24 Heart, 25 Etna, 26 A man, 27 Tala, 28 Otis, 31 Amour, 32 Liu, 34 Elim, 35 Mice, 36 Ivan, 39 Abbe, 40 Quid, 43 Aspen, 46 Trailer, 48 Amends, 49 Anti, 50 Hatch, 51 Elena, 52 L. Bean, 53 Weeks, 54 Acre, 58 Togo, 59 Avis, 60 Lens, 62 IRA, 63 Gar, 64 NBC

SPORTS QUICK REFERENCE INDEX

FOR COMPLETE INDEX, SEE PAGES 979-1007.

WORLD ALMANAC QUICK QUIZ ANSWERS

142–c, a, d, b; **220**–a; **273**–c; **279**–b; **291**–d; **310**–a; **312**–b, a, c, d; **313**–b; **360**–b; **366**–c; **372**–d; **389**–c; **410**–d; **419**–c; **422**–a; **424**–b; **439**–d; **452**–b; **482**–a; **485**–c; **490**–a; **546**–a; **568**–1-b, 2-d, 3-a, 4-c; **574**–1-b, 2-c, 3-d, 4-a; **575**–d; **604**–c; **641**–b, d, c, a; **690**–b; **692**–c; **699**–d; **702**–a; **707**–d; **709**–c; **716**–a; **728**–c; **732**–1-c, 2-a, 3-b, 4-d; **742**–c; **774**–b, d, c, a; **804**–d, c, a, b; **851**–c; **927**–b, c, d, a; **951**–a, b, d, c